2012 Standard Catalog of®

WORLD COINS

2001 to Date

6th Edition

George S. Cuhaj, Editor • **Thomas Michael**, Market Analyst • **Harry Miller**, U.S. Market Analyst
Deborah McCue, Database Specialist • **Kay Sanders**, Editorial Assistant

---

Special Contributors

Melvyn Kassenoff
Egon Conti Rossini
Gerhard Schön
Erik J. VanLoon

Bullion Value (BV) Market Valuations

Valuations for all platinum, gold, palladium and silver coins of the more common, basically bullion types, or those possessing only modest numismatic premiums are presented in this edition based on the market ranges of:

$1,750 - $1,850 per ounce for **platinum**
$1,350 - $1,450 per ounce for **gold**
$785 - $850 per ounce for **palladium**
$30.00 - $35.00 per ounce for **silver**

Published by

Krause Publications, a division of F+W Media, Inc.
700 East State Street • Iola, WI 54990-0001
715-445-2214 • 888-457-2873
www.krausebooks.com

To order books or other products call toll-free 1-800-258-0929
or visit us online at www.shopnumismaster.com

ISSN 1935-4339
ISBN-13: 978-1-4402-1575-9
ISBN-10: 1-4402-1575-8

Cover Design by Jana Tappa
Designed by Sandi Carpenter
Edited by George Cuhaj

Printed in The United States of America

ACKNOWLEDGMENTS

Many individuals have contributed countless changes, which have been incorporated into the current edition. While all may not be acknowledged, special appreciation is extended to the following who have exhibited a special enthusiasm for this edition.

David Addey
Esko Ahlroth
James T. Anderson
Dylan Arthur
Antonio Alessandrini
Paul Baker
Oksana Bandrivska
Yuri Barshay
Albert Beck
Anton Belcev
Jan Bendix
Richard Benson
Peter N. Berger
Allen G. Berman
Sharon Blocker
Joseph E. Boling
Richard Borek jun.
Al Boulanger
Maruta Brûkle
Mahdi Bseiso
Chris Budesa
John T. Bucek
Doru Calin
Michael Hans Lun Chou
Fred Colombo
Luis V. Costa
Raymond E. Czahor
Howard A. Daniel III
Joanne Davison
Konstantinos Dellios
Yossi Dotan
James R. Douglas
Dr. Jan M. Dyroff
Stephen Eccles
Andrzej Fischer
Thomas Fitzgerald
Dagmar Flachén
Eugene Freeman
Peter Frei
Arthur Friedburg
Carmen Fuhiniu
Lorraine Gallagher
Tom Galway
David R. Gotkin
Andrew Greatorex
Marcel Häberling
J. Halfpenny
Flemming Lyngbeck Hansen
David Harrison
Martin Rodney Hayter
Emanuel Henry
Jennifer Hird
Teréz Horváth
Serge Huard
Nelva G. Icaza
Ton Jacobs
A.K. Jain
Hector Carlos Janson
Yun-Su Ji
Alex Kaglyan
Melvyn Kassenoff
Craig Keplinger
Rodolphe Krempp
Rob Looy
Aditya Kulkarni
Michel Labourdette
Alex Lazarovici
Ma Tak Wo
Miguel Angel Pratt Mayans
Bernhard H. Mayer
Bill McKay
Juozas Minikevicius
Andy Mirski
Robert Mish
Ing. Benjamin M. Mizrachi R.
Dr. Richard Montrey
Edward Moschetti
Arkady Nakhimovsky
Michael G. Nielsen
Bill Nichols
Janusz Parchimowicz
Dick Parker
Frank Passic
Martin Peeters
Marc Pelletier
Kirsten F. Petersen
Tay Hwee Ping
Andreas Pitsillides
Gastone Polacco
Jordi Puigdemasa
Martin Purdy
Luis R. Ponte Puigbo
Kitty Quan
Yahya Qureshi
Mircea Raicopol
Dr. Dennis G. Rainey
Ivan Rakitin
Marta Reig
Ilan Rinetzky
William M. Rosenblum
Egon Conti Rossini
Pabitra K. Saha
Remy Said
Leon Saryan
Erwin Schäffer
Jacco Scheper
Dr. Andreas Schikora
Gerhard Schön
George Schumacher
Dr. Wolfgang Schuster
Alexander Shapiro
Ladislav Sin
Ole Sjoelund
Mira Spijker
Heimo Steriti
Benjamin Swagerty
Peter Swanston
Steven Tan
Mehmet Tolga Taner
Rivka Toledano
Amelia Travaglini
Anthony Tumonis
Erik J. Van Loon
Natanya van Niekerk
Neil Vance
Carmen Viciedo
Mel Wacks
Wakim Wakim
Paul Welz
Stewart Westdal
J. Brix Westergaard
J. Hugh Witherow
Ishagh Yousefzadeh
Joseph Zaffern

AUCTION HOUSES

Dix-Noonan-Webb
Heritage World Coin Auctions
Hess-Divo Ltd.
Gerhard Hirsch
Thomas Høiland Møntauktion
Fritz Rudolf Künker
Leu Numismatik AG
MPO Auctions
Münzenhandlung Harald Möller, GmbH
Noble Numismatics, Pty. Ltd.
Ponterio & Associates
Stack's
UBS, AG
World Wide Coins of California

WORLD MINTS, CENTRAL BANKS AND DISTRIBUTORS

Austrian Mint
Banco de Mexico
Banque Centrale Du Luxembourg
Black Mountain Coins
Casa de la Moneda de Cuba
Central Bank of D.P.R. Korea - Kumbyol Trading Corp.
Central Bank of the Russian Federation
CIT
Czech National Bank
Educational Coin Company
Faude & Huguenin
Global Coins & Medals Ltd. - Official Sales Company of the Bulgarian Mint
Imprensa Nacional - Casa da Moeda, S.A.
Israel Coins & Medals Corp.
Istituto Poligrafico e Zecca dello Stato I.p.A.
Jablonex Group - Division of Czech Mint
Japan Mint
Kazakhstan Mint
KOMSCO - South Korea
Latvijas Banka
Lietuvos Bankas
Lithuanian Mint
Magyar Penzvero Zrt.
Mayer's Mint GmbH
MDM
Mennica Polska
Mincovna Kremnica
Mint of Finland, Ltd.
Mint of Norway
Monnaie de Paris
Moscow Mint
National Bank of the Republic of Belarus
National Bank of Ukraine
New Zealand Mint
Numiscom
Numistrade Gmbh & Co. kg.
Omni Trading B.V.
PandaAmerica
Perth Mint
Pobjoy Mint
Real Casa de la Moneda - Spain
Royal Mint
Royal Australian Mint
Royal Belgian Mint
Royal Canadian Mint
Royal Dutch Mint
Royal Thai Mint
SamlerHuset Group B.V.
Servei D'Emissions Principat D'Andorra
Singapore Mint
SoftSky, Inc.
South African Mint
Staatliche Munze Berlin
Staatliche Munze Baden-Wurttemberg
Talisman Coins
Thailand Treasury Department
Ufficio Filatelico e Numismatico - Vatican
United States Mint

COUNTRY INDEX

FOREIGN EXCHANGE TABLE

The latest foreign exchange rates below apply to trade with banks in the country of origin. The left column shows the number of units per U.S. dollar at the official rate. The right column shows the number of units per dollar at the free market rate.

COUNTRY	Official #/$	Market #/$
Afghanistan (New Afghani)	45	–
Albania (Lek)	100	–
Algeria (Dinar)	72	–
Andorra uses Euro	.715	–
Angola (Readjust Kwanza)	93	–
Anguilla uses E.C. Dollar	2.7	–
Antigua uses E.C. Dollar	2.7	–
Argentina (Peso)	4.0	–
Armenia (Dram)	368	–
Aruba (Florin)	1.79	–
Australia (Dollar)	.986	–
Austria (Euro)	.715	–
Azerbaijan (New Manat)	.795	–
Bahamas (Dollar)	1.0	–
Bahrain Is. (Dinar)	.377	–
Bangladesh (Taka)	71	–
Barbados (Dollar)	2.0	–
Belarus (Ruble)	3,016	–
Belgium (Euro)	.715	–
Belize (Dollar)	1.95	–
Benin uses CFA Franc West	471	–
Bermuda (Dollar)	1.0	–
Bhutan (Ngultrum)	45	–
Bolivia (Boliviano)	7.0	–
Bosnia-Herzegovina (Conv. marka)	1.40	–
Botswana (Pula)	6.59	–
British Virgin Islands uses U.S. Dollar	1.0	–
Brazil (Real)	1.65	–
Brunei (Dollar)	1.27	–
Bulgaria (Lev)	1.40	–
Burkina Faso uses CFA Franc West	471	–
Burma (Kyat)	6.42	1,250
Burundi (Franc)	1,236	–
Cambodia (Riel)	4,039	–
Cameroon uses CFA Franc Central	470	–
Canada (Dollar)	.973	–
Cape Verde (Escudo)	79	–
Cayman Islands (Dollar)	0.82	–
Central African Rep.	471	–
CFA Franc Central	471	–
CFA Franc West	471	–
CFP Franc	85	–
Chad uses CFA Franc Central	470	–
Chile (Peso)	474	–
China, P.R. (Renminbi Yuan)	6.6	–
Colombia (Peso)	1,894	–
Comoros (Franc)	352	–
Congo uses CFA Franc Central	470	–
Congo-Dem.Rep. (Congolese Franc)	923	–
Cook Islands (Dollar)	1.36	–
Costa Rica (Colon)	502	–
Croatia (Kuna)	5.29	–
Cuba (Peso)	1.00	27.00
Cyprus (Euro)	.403	–
Czech Republic (Koruna)	17.4	–
Denmark (Danish Krone)	5.3	–
Djibouti (Franc)	178	–
Dominica uses E.C. Dollar	2.7	–
Dominican Republic (Peso)	38	–
East Caribbean (Dollar)	2.7	–
Ecuador (U.S. Dollar)	1.00	–
Egypt (Pound)	5.9	–
El Salvador (U.S. Dollar)	1.00	–
Equatorial Guinea uses CFA Franc Central	470	–
Eritrea (Nafka)	15.0	–
Estonia (Kroon)	11.2	–
Ethiopia (Birr)	16.7	–
Euro	.715	–
Falkland Is. (Pound)	.615	–
Faroe Islands (Krona)	5.3	–
Fiji Islands (Dollar)	1.83	–
Finland (Euro)	.715	–
France (Euro)	.715	–
French Polynesia uses CFP Franc	85	–
Gabon (CFA Franc)	470	–
Gambia (Dalasi)	29	–
Georgia (Lari)	1.72	–
Germany (Euro)	.715	–
Ghana (New Cedi)	1.52	–
Gibraltar (Pound)	.615	–
Greece (Euro)	.715	–
Greenland uses Danish Krone	5.33	–
Grenada uses E.C. Dollar	2.7	–
Guatemala (Quetzal)	7.76	–
Guernsey uses Sterling Pound	.615	–
Guinea Bissau (CFA Franc)	471	–
Guinea Conakry (Franc)	7,650	–
Guyana (Dollar)	205	–
Haiti (Gourde)	40	–
Honduras (Lempira)	19	–
Hong Kong (Dollar)	7.79	–
Hungary (Forint)	194	–
Iceland (Krona)	115	–
India (Rupee)	45	–
Indonesia (Rupiah)	8,792	–
Iran (Rial)	10,325	–
Iraq (Dinar)	1,169	–
Ireland (Euro)	.715	–
Isle of Man uses Sterling Pound	.615	–
Israel (New Sheqalim)	3.62	–
Italy (Euro)	.715	–
Ivory Coast uses CFA Franc West	471	–
Jamaica (Dollar)	86	–
Japan (Yen)	82	–
Jersey uses Sterling Pound	.615	–
Jordan (Dinar)	.707	–
Kazakhstan (Tenge)	146	–
Kenya (Shilling)	83	–
Kiribati uses Australian Dollar	.986	–
Korea-PDR (Won)	135	–
Korea-Rep. (Won)	1,115	–
Kuwait (Dinar)	.278	–
Kyrgyzstan (Som)	47	–
Laos (Kip)	8,050	–
Latvia (Lats)	.505	–
Lebanon (Pound)	1,502	–
Lesotho (Maloti)	6.88	–
Liberia (Dollar)	73	–
Libya (Dinar)	1.22	–
Liechtenstein uses Swiss Franc	.925	–
Lithuania (Litas)	2.47	–
Luxembourg (Euro)	.715	–
Macao (Pataca)	8.0	–
Macedonia (New Denar)	44	–
Madagascar (Franc)	1,998	–
Malawi (Kwacha)	152	–
Malaysia (Ringgit)	3.03	–
Maldives (Rufiya)	12.8	–
Mali uses CFA Franc West	471	–
Malta (Euro)	.715	–
Marshall Islands uses U.S.Dollar	1.00	–
Mauritania (Ouguiya)	283	–
Mauritius (Rupee)	29	–
Mexico (Peso)	12.0	–
Moldova (Leu)	12.0	–
Monaco uses Euro	.715	–
Mongolia (Tugrik)	1,248	–
Montenegro uses Euro	.715	–
Montserrat uses E.C. Dollar	2.7	–
Morocco (Dirham)	8.0	–
Mozambique (New Metical)	31	–
Namibia (Rand)	6.88	–
Nauru uses Australian Dollar	.986	–
Nepal (Rupee)	72	–
Netherlands (Euro)	.715	–
Netherlands Antilles (Gulden)	1.79	–
New Caledonia uses CFP Franc	85	–
New Zealand (Dollar)	1.35	–
Nicaragua (Cordoba Oro)	22	–
Niger uses CFA Franc West	471	–
Nigeria (Naira)	154	–
Northern Ireland uses Sterling Pound	.615	–
Norway (Krone)	5.6	–
Oman (Rial)	.385	–
Pakistan (Rupee)	85	–
Palau uses U.S.Dollar	1.00	–
Panama (Balboa) uses U.S.Dollar	1.00	–
Papua New Guinea (Kina)	2.57	–
Paraguay (Guarani)	4,465	–
Peru (Nuevo Sol)	2.77	–
Philippines (Peso)	43	–
Poland (Zloty)	2.84	–
Portugal (Euro)	.715	–
Qatar (Riyal)	3.64	–
Romania (New Leu)	3.01	–
Russia (Ruble)	28	–
Rwanda (Franc)	600	–
St. Helena (Pound)	.615	–
St. Kitts uses E.C. Dollar	2.7	–
St. Lucia uses E.C. Dollar	2.7	–
St. Vincent uses E.C. Dollar	2.7	–
San Marino uses Euro	.715	–
Sao Tome e Principe (Dobra)	17,907	–
Saudi Arabia (Riyal)	3.75	–
Scotland uses Sterling Pound	.615	–
Senegal uses CFA Franc West	471	–
Serbia (Dinar)	74	–
Seychelles (Rupee)	12.2	–
Sierra Leone (Leone)	4,292	–
Singapore (Dollar)	1.27	–
Slovakia (Sk. Koruna)	22	–
Slovenia (Euro)	.715	–
Solomon Islands (Dollar)	7.79	–
Somalia (Shilling)	1,600	–
Somaliland (Somali Shilling)	1,600	4,000
South Africa (Rand)	6.88	–
Spain (Euro)	.715	–
Sri Lanka (Rupee)	110	–
Sudan (Pound)	2.55	–
Surinam (Dollar)	3.3	–
Swaziland (Lilangeni)	6.88	–
Sweden (Krona)	6.35	–
Switzerland (Franc)	.925	–
Syria (Pound)	47	–
Taiwan (NT Dollar)	29	–
Tajikistan (Somoni)	4.43	–
Tanzania (Shilling)	1,519	–
Thailand (Baht)	30	–
Togo uses CFA Franc West	471	–
Tonga (Pa'anga)	1.81	–
Transdniestra (Ruble)	12.0	–
Trinidad & Tobago (Dollar)	6.35	–
Tunisia (Dinar)	1.40	–
Turkey (New Lira)	1.60	–
Turkmenistan (Manat)	14,250	–
Turks & Caicos uses U.S. Dollar	1.00	–
Tuvalu uses Australian Dollar	.986	–
Uganda (Shilling)	2,384	–
Ukraine (Hryvnia)	7.94	–
United Arab Emirates (Dirham)	3.67	–
United Kingdom (Sterling Pound)	.615	–
Uruguay (Peso Uruguayo)	19	–
Uzbekistan (Sum)	1,667	–
Vanuatu (Vatu)	95	–
Vatican City uses Euro	.715	–
Venezuela (New Bolivar)	4.29	8.1
Vietnam (Dong)	20,835	–
Western Samoa (Tala)	2.38	–
Yemen (Rial)	214	–
Zambia (Kwacha)	4,730	–
Zimbabwe (Dollar)	–	–

HOW TO USE THIS CATALOG

This catalog is designed to serve the needs of both the novice and advanced collectors. It is generally arranged so that persons with no more than a basic knowledge of world history and a casual acquaintance with coin collecting can consult it with confidence and ease. The following explanations summarize the general practices used in preparing this catalog's listings.

ARRANGEMENT

Countries are arranged alphabetically. Political changes within a country are arranged chronologically. In countries where Rulers are the single most significant political entity, a chronological arrangement by Ruler has been employed. Distinctive sub-geographic regions are listed alphabetically following the country's main listings.

Diverse coinage types relating to fabrication methods, revaluations, denomination systems, non-circulating categories and such have been identified, separated and arranged in logical fashion. Chronological arrangement is employed for most circulating coinage. Monetary reforms will flow in order of their institution. Non-circulating types such as Essais, Piefort, Patterns, Trial Strikes, Mint and Proof sets will follow the main listings.

Within a coinage type coins will be listed by denomination, from smallest to largest. Numbered types within a denomination will be ordered by their first date of issue.

IDENTIFICATION

The most important step in the identification of a coin is the determination of the nation of origin. This is generally easily accomplished where English-speaking lands are concerned, however, use of the country index is sometimes required.

The coins of many countries beyond the English-language realm, such as those of French, Italian or Spanish heritage, are also quite easy to identify through reference to their legends, which appear in the national languages based on Western alphabets. In many instances the name is spelled exactly the same in English as in the national language, such as France; while in other cases it varies only slightly, like Italia for Italy, Belgique or Belgie for Belgium, Brasil for Brazil and Danmark for Denmark.

This is not always the case, however, as in Norge for Norway, Espana for Spain, Sverige for Sweden and Helvetia for Switzerland. Coins bearing Cyrillic lettering are attributable to Bulgaria, Russia, the Slavic states and Mongolia; the Greek script peculiar to Greece, Crete and the Ionian Islands; the Amharic characters of Ethiopia; or Hebrew in the case of Israel.

The toughra monogram, occurs on some of the coins of Afghanistan, Egypt, Sudan, Pakistan, and Turkey. A predominant design feature on the coins of Nepal is the trident; while neighboring Tibet features a lotus blossom or lion on many of their issues.

DATING

Coin dating is the final basic attribution consideration. Here, the problem can be more difficult because the reading of a coin date is subject not only to the vagaries of numeric styling, but to calendar variations caused by the observance of various religious eras or regal periods from country to country, or even within a country. Here again, with the exception of the sphere from North Africa through the Orient, it will be found that most countries rely on Western date numerals and Christian (AD) era reckoning, although in a few instances, coin dating has been tied to the year of a reign or government. The Vatican, for example dates its coinage according to the year of reign of the current pope, in addition to the Christian-era date.

Countries in the Arabic sphere generally date their coins to the Muslim era (AH).

The following table indicates the year dating for the various eras, which correspond to 2009 in Christian calendar reckoning, but it must be remembered that there are overlaps between the eras in some instances.

Christian era (AD)	-2010
Muslim era (AH)	-AH1431
Solar year (SH)	-SH1388
Monarchic Solar era (MS)	-MS2569
Vikrama Samvat (VS)	-VS2067
Saka era (SE)	-SE1932
Buddhist era (BE)	-BE2553
Bangkok era (RS)	-RS229
Chula-Sakarat era (CS)	-CS1372
Ethiopian era (EE)	-EE2003
Korean era	-4343
Javanese Aji Saka era (AS)	-AS1943
Fasli era (FE)	-FE1420
Jewish era (JE)	-JE5770

More detailed guides to less prevalent coin dating systems, which are strictly local in nature, are presented with the appropriate listings.

AH Hejira	AD Christian Date	AH Hejira	AD Christian Date
1420	1999, April 17	1436	2014, October 25
1421	2000, April 6*	1437	2015, October 15*
1422	2001, March 26	1438	2016, October 3
1423	2002, March 15	1439	2017, September 22
1424	2003, March 5	1440	2018, September 12
1425	2004, February 22*	1441	2019, September 11*
1426	2005, February 10	1442	2020, August 20
1427	2006, January 31	1443	2021, August 10
1428	2007, January 20	1444	2022, July 30
1429	2008, January 10*	1445	2023, July 19*
1430	2008, December 29	1446	2024, July 8
1431	2009, December 18	1447	2025, June 27
1432	2010, December 8	1448	2026, June 17
1433	2011, November 27*	1449	2027, June 6*
1434	2012, November 15	1450	2028, May25
1435	2013, November 5		

Some coins carry dates according to both locally observed and Christian eras. This is particularly true in the Arabic world, where the Hejira date may be indicated in Arabic numerals and the Christian date in Western numerals, or both dates in either form.

HEJIRA DATE CONVERSION CHART

HEJIRA (Hijira, Hegira), the name of the Muslim era (A.H. = Anno Hegirae) dates back to the Christian year 622 when Mohammed "fled" from Mecca, escaping to Medina to avoid persecution from the Koreish tribemen. Based on a lunar year the Muslim year is 11 days shorter.

*=Leap Year (Christian Calendar)

The date actually carried on a given coin is generally cataloged here in the first column (Date) to the right of the catalog number. If this date is by a non-Christian dating system, such as 'AH' (Muslim), the Christian equivalent date will appear in parentheses(), for example AH1336(1917). Dates listed alone in the date column which do not actually appear on a given coin, or dates which are known, but do not appear on the coin, are generally enclosed by parentheses with 'ND' at the left, for example ND(2001).

Timing differentials between some era of reckoning, particularly the 354-day Mohammedan and 365-day Christian years, cause situations whereby coins which carry dates for both eras exist bearing two year dates from one calendar combined with a single date from another.

Countermarked Coinage is presented with both 'Countermark Date' and 'Host Coin' date for each type. Actual date representation follows the rules outlined above.

DENOMINATIONS

The second basic consideration to be met in the attribution of a coin is the determination of denomination. Since denominations are usually expressed in numeric rather than word form on a coin, this is usually quite easily accomplished on coins from nations which use Western numerals, except in those instances where issues are devoid of any mention of face value, and denomination must be attributed by size, metallic composition or weight. Coins listed in this volume are generally illustrated in actual size.

The sphere of countries stretching from North Africa through the Orient, on which numeric symbols generally unfamiliar to Westerners are employed, often provide the collector with a much greater challenge. This is particularly true on nearly all pre-20th Century issues. On some of the more modern issues and increasingly so as the years progress, Western-style numerals usually presented in combination with the local numeric system are becoming more commonplace on these coins.

The included table of Standard International Numeral Systems presents charts of the basic numeric designations found on coins of non-Western origin. Although denomination numerals are generally prominently displayed on coins, it must be remembered that these are general representations of characters, which individual coin engravers may have rendered in widely varying styles. Where numeric or script denominations designation forms peculiar to a given coin or country apply, such as the script used on some Persian (Iranian) issues. They are so indicated or illustrated in conjunction with the appropriate listings.

MINTAGES

Quantities minted of each date are indicated where that information is available, generally stated in millions or rounded off to the nearest 10,000 pieces when more exact figures are not available. On quantities of a few thousand or less, actual mintages are generally indicated. For combined mintage figures the abbreviation "Inc. Above" means Included Above, while "Inc. Below" means Included Below. "Est." beside a mintage figure indicates the number given is an estimate or mintage limit.

METALS

Each numbered type listing will contain a description of the coins metallic content. The traditional coinage metals and their symbolic chemical abbreviations sometimes used in this catalog are:

Platinum - (PT)	Copper - (Cu)
Gold - (Au)	Brass -
Silver - (Ag)	Copper-nickel- (CN)
Billion -	Lead - (Pb)
Nickel - (Ni)	Steel -
Zinc - (Zn)	Tin - (Sn)
Bronze - (Ae)	Aluminum - (Al)

Modern commemorative coins have employed still more unusual methods such as bimetallic coins, color applications and precious metal or gem inlays.

PRECIOUS METAL WEIGHTS

Listings of weight, fineness and actual silver (ASW), gold (AGW), platinum or palladium (APW) content of most machine-struck silver, gold, platinum and palladium coins are provided in this edition. This information will be found incorporated in each separate type listing, along with other data related to the coin.

The ASW, AGW or APW figure can be multiplied by the spot price of each precious metal to determine the current intrinsic value of any coin accompanied by these designations.

As the silver and gold bullion markets have advanced and declined sharply over the years, the fineness and total precious metal content of coins has become especially significant where bullion coins - issues which trade on the basis of their intrinsic metallic content rather than numismatic value - are concerned. In many instances, such issues have become worth more in bullion form than their nominal collector values or denominations indicate.

BULLION VALUE

The simplest method for determining the bullion value of a precious metal coin is to multiply the actual precious metal weight by the current spot price for that metal. A silver coin with a .6822 actual silver weight (ASW) would have an intrinsic value of

$8.70 when the spot price of silver is $12.75. If the spot price of silver rose to $17.95 that same coins intrinsic value would rise to $12.25.

PHOTOGRAPHS

To assist the reader in coin identification, every effort has been made to present actual size photographs of every coinage type listed. Obverse and reverse are illustrated, except when a change in design is restricted to one side, and the coin has a diameter of 39mm or larger, in which case only the side required for identification of the type is generally illustrated. All coins up to 60mm are illustrated actual size, to the nearest 1/2mm up to 25mm, and to the nearest 1mm thereafter. Coins larger than 60mm diameter are illustrated in reduced size, with the actual size noted in the descriptive text block. Where slight change in size is important to coin type identification, actual millimeter measurements are stated.

VALUATIONS

Values quoted in this catalog represent the current market and are compiled from recommendations provided and verified through various source documents and specialized consultants. It should be stressed, however, that this book is intended to serve only as an aid for evaluating coins, actual market conditions are constantly changing and additional influences, such as particularly strong local demand for certain coin series, fluctuation of international exchange rates, changes in spot price of precious metals and worldwide collection patterns must also be considered. Publication of this catalog is not intended as a solicitation by the publisher, editors or contributors to buy or sell the coins listed at the prices indicated.

All valuations are stated in U.S. dollars, based on careful assessment of the varied international collector market. Valuations for coins priced below $100.00 are generally stated in full amounts - i.e. 37.50 or 95.00 - while valuations at or above that figure are rounded off in even dollars - i.e. $125.00 is expressed 125. A comma is added to indicate thousands of dollars in value.

For the convenience of overseas collectors and for U.S. collectors doing business with overseas dealers, the base exchange rate for the national currencies of approximately 180 countries are presented in the Foreign Exchange Table.

It should be noted that when particularly select uncirculated or proof-like examples of uncirculated coins become available they can be expected to command proportionately high premiums. Such examples in reference to choice Germanic Thalers are referred to as "erst schlage" or first strikes.

NEW ISSUES

All newly released coins dated up to the year 2006 that have been physically observed by our staff or identified by reliable sources and have been confirmed by press time have been incorporated in this edition. Exceptions exist in some countries where current date coin production lags far behind or information on current issues is less accessible.

SETS

Listings in this catalog for specimen, proof and mint sets are for official, government-produced sets. In many instances privately packaged sets also exist.

Mint Sets/Fleur de Coin Sets: Specially prepared by worldwide mints to provide banks, collectors and government dignitaries with examples of current coinage. Usually subjected to rigorous inspection to insure that top quality specimens of selected business strikes are provided.

Coin Alignment **Medal Alignment**

COIN vs MEDAL ALIGNMENT

Some coins are struck with obverse and reverse aligned at a rotation of 180 degrees from each other. When a coin is held for vertical viewing with the obverse design aligned upright and the index finger and thumb at the top and bottom, upon rotation from left to right for viewing the reverse, the latter will be upside down. Such alignment is called "coin rotation." Other coins are struck with the obverse and reverse designs mated on an alignment of zero or 360 degrees. If such an example is held and rotated as described, the reverse will appear upright. This is the alignment, which is generally observed in the striking of medals, and for that reason coins produced in this manner are considered struck in "medal rotation". In some instances, often through error, certain coin issues have been struck to both alignment standards, creating interesting collectible varieties, which will be found noted in some listings. In addition, some countries are now producing coins with other designated obverse to reverse alignments which are considered standard for this type.

Specimen Sets: Forerunners of today's proof sets. In most cases the coins were specially struck, perhaps even double struck, to produce a very soft or matte finish on the effigies and fields, along with high, sharp, "wire" rims. The finish is rather dull to the naked eye.

The original purpose of these sets was to provide VIPs, monarchs and mintmasters around the world with samples of the highest quality workmanship of a particular mint. These were usually housed in elaborate velvet-lined leather and metal cases.

Proof-like Sets are relatively new to the field of numismatics. During the mid 1950s the Royal Canadian Mint furnished the hobby with specially selected early business strike coins that exhibited some qualities similar to proof coinage. However, the "proof-like" fields are generally flawed and the edges are rounded. These pieces are not double struck. These are commonly encountered in cardboard holders, later in soft plastic or pliofilm packaging. Of late, the Royal Canadian Mint packages such sets in rigid plastic cases.

Many worldwide officially issued proof sets would in reality fall into this category upon careful examination of the quality of the coin's finish.

Another term encountered in this category is "Special Select," used to describe the crowns of the Union of South Africa and 100-schilling coins produced for collectors in the late 1970s by the Austrian Mint.

Proof Sets: This is undoubtedly among the most misused terms in the hobby, not only by collectors and dealers, but also by many of the world mints.

A true proof set must be at least double-struck on specially prepared polished planchets and struck using dies (often themselves polished) of the highest quality.

Modern-day proof quality consists of frosted effigies surrounded by absolute mirror-like fields.

Listings for proof sets in this catalog are for officially issued proof sets so designated by the issuing authority, and may or may not possess what are considered modern proof quality standards.

It is necessary for collectors to acquire the knowledge to allow them to differentiate true proof sets from would-be proof sets and proof-like sets which may be encountered.

CONDITIONS/GRADING

Wherever possible, coin valuations are given in four or five grades of preservation. For modern commemoratives, which do not circulate, only uncirculated values are usually sufficient. Proof issues are indicated by the word "Proof" next to the date, with valuation proceeded by the word "value" following the mintage. For very recent circulating coins and coins of limited value, one, two or three grade values are presented.

There are almost no grading guides for world coins. What follows is an attempt to help bridge that gap until a detailed, illustrated guide becomes available.

In grading world coins, there are two elements to look for: 1) Overall wear, and 2) loss of design details, such as strands of hair, feathers on eagles, designs on coats of arms, etc.

The age, rarity or type of a coin should not be a consideration in grading.

Grade each coin by the weaker of the two sides. This method appears to give results most nearly consistent with conservative American Numismatic Association standards for U.S. coins. Split grades, i.e., F/VF for obverse and reverse, respectively, are normally no more than one grade apart. If the two sides are more than one grade apart, the series of coins probably wears differently on each side and should then be graded by the weaker side alone.

Grade by the amount of overall wear and loss of design detail evident on each side of the coin. On coins with a moderately small design element, which is prone to early wear, grade by that design alone. For example, the 5-ore (KM#554) of Sweden has a crown above the monogram on which the beads on the arches show wear most clearly. So, grade by the crown alone.

For **Brilliant Uncirculated** (BU) grades there will be no visible signs of wear or handling, even under a 30-power microscope. Full mint luster will be present. Ideally no bags marks will be evident.

For **Uncirculated** (Unc. or MS-60) grades there will be no visible signs of wear or handling, even under a 30-power microscope. Bag marks may be present.

For **Almost Uncirculated** (AU or AU-50), all detail will be visible. There will be wear only on the highest point of the coin. There will often be half or more of the original mint luster present.

On the **Extremely Fine** (EF or XF or XF-40) coin, there will be about 95% of the original detail visible. Or, on a coin with a design with no inner detail to wear down, there will be a light wear over nearly all the coin. If a small design is used as the grading area, about 90% of the original detail will be visible. This latter rule stems from the logic that a smaller amount of detail needs to be present because a small area is being used to grade the whole coin.

The **Very Fine** (VF or VF-20) coin will have about 75% of the original detail visible. Or, on a coin with no inner detail, there will be moderate wear over the entire coin. Corners of letters and numbers may be weak. A small grading area will have about 66% of the original detail.

For **Fine** (F or F-12), there will be about 50% of the original detail visible. Or, on a coin with no inner detail, there will be fairly heavy wear over all of the coin. Sides of letters will be weak. A typically uncleaned coin will often appear as dirty or dull. A small grading area will have just under 50% of the original detail.

On the **Very Good** (VG or VG-8) coin, there will be about 25% of the original detail visible. There will be heavy wear on all of the coin.

The **Good** (G or G-4) coin's design will be clearly outlined but with substantial wear. Some of the larger detail may be visible. The rim may have a few weak spots of wear.

On the **About Good** (AG) coin, there will typically be only a silhouette of a large design. The rim will be worn down into the letters if any.

Strong or weak strikes, partially weak strikes, damage, corrosion, attractive or unattractive toning, dipping or cleaning should be described along with the above grades. These factors affect the quality of the coin just as do wear and loss of detail, but are easier to describe.

SILVER BULLION VALUE CHART

Oz.	15.00	15.50	16.00	16.50	17.00	17.50	18.00	18.50	19.00	19.50	20.00	20.50	21.00	21.50	22.00	Oz.
0.001	0.015	0.016	0.016	0.017	0.017	0.018	0.018	0.019	0.019	0.020	0.020	0.021	0.021	0.022	0.022	**0.001**
0.002	0.030	0.031	0.032	0.033	0.034	0.035	0.036	0.037	0.038	0.039	0.040	0.041	0.042	0.043	0.044	**0.002**
0.003	0.045	0.047	0.048	0.050	0.051	0.053	0.054	0.056	0.057	0.059	0.060	0.062	0.063	0.065	0.066	**0.003**
0.004	0.060	0.062	0.064	0.066	0.068	0.070	0.072	0.074	0.076	0.078	0.080	0.082	0.084	0.086	0.088	**0.004**
0.005	0.075	0.078	0.080	0.083	0.085	0.088	0.090	0.093	0.095	0.098	0.100	0.103	0.105	0.108	0.110	**0.005**
0.006	0.090	0.093	0.096	0.099	0.102	0.105	0.108	0.111	0.114	0.117	0.120	0.123	0.126	0.129	0.132	**0.006**
0.007	0.105	0.109	0.112	0.116	0.119	0.123	0.126	0.130	0.133	0.137	0.140	0.144	0.147	0.151	0.154	**0.007**
0.008	0.120	0.124	0.128	0.132	0.136	0.140	0.144	0.148	0.152	0.156	0.160	0.164	0.168	0.172	0.176	**0.008**
0.009	0.135	0.140	0.144	0.149	0.153	0.158	0.162	0.167	0.171	0.176	0.180	0.185	0.189	0.194	0.198	**0.009**
0.010	0.150	0.155	0.160	0.165	0.170	0.175	0.180	0.185	0.190	0.195	0.200	0.205	0.210	0.215	0.220	**0.010**
0.020	0.300	0.310	0.320	0.330	0.340	0.350	0.360	0.370	0.380	0.390	0.400	0.410	0.420	0.430	0.440	**0.020**
0.030	0.450	0.465	0.480	0.495	0.510	0.525	0.540	0.555	0.570	0.585	0.600	0.615	0.630	0.645	0.660	**0.030**
0.040	0.600	0.620	0.640	0.660	0.680	0.700	0.720	0.740	0.760	0.780	0.800	0.820	0.840	0.860	0.880	**0.040**
0.050	0.750	0.775	0.800	0.825	0.850	0.875	0.900	0.925	0.950	0.975	1.000	1.025	1.050	1.075	1.100	**0.050**
0.060	0.900	0.930	0.960	0.990	1.020	1.050	1.080	1.110	1.140	1.170	1.200	1.230	1.260	1.290	1.320	**0.060**
0.070	1.050	1.085	1.120	1.155	1.190	1.225	1.260	1.295	1.330	1.365	1.400	1.435	1.470	1.505	1.540	**0.070**
0.080	1.200	1.240	1.280	1.320	1.360	1.400	1.440	1.480	1.520	1.560	1.600	1.640	1.680	1.720	1.760	**0.080**
0.090	1.350	1.395	1.440	1.485	1.530	1.575	1.620	1.665	1.710	1.755	1.800	1.845	1.890	1.935	1.980	**0.090**
0.100	1.500	1.550	1.600	1.650	1.700	1.750	1.800	1.850	1.900	1.950	2.000	2.050	2.100	2.150	2.200	**0.100**
0.110	1.650	1.705	1.760	1.815	1.870	1.925	1.980	2.035	2.090	2.145	2.200	2.255	2.310	2.365	2.420	**0.110**
0.120	1.800	1.860	1.920	1.980	2.040	2.100	2.160	2.220	2.280	2.340	2.400	2.460	2.520	2.580	2.640	**0.120**
0.130	1.950	2.015	2.080	2.145	2.210	2.275	2.340	2.405	2.470	2.535	2.600	2.665	2.730	2.795	2.860	**0.130**
0.140	2.100	2.170	2.240	2.310	2.380	2.450	2.520	2.590	2.660	2.730	2.800	2.870	2.940	3.010	3.080	**0.140**
0.150	2.250	2.325	2.400	2.475	2.550	2.625	2.700	2.775	2.850	2.925	3.000	3.075	3.150	3.225	3.300	**0.150**
0.160	2.400	2.480	2.560	2.640	2.720	2.800	2.880	2.960	3.040	3.120	3.200	3.280	3.360	3.440	3.520	**0.160**
0.170	2.550	2.635	2.720	2.805	2.890	2.975	3.060	3.145	3.230	3.315	3.400	3.485	3.570	3.655	3.740	**0.170**
0.180	2.700	2.790	2.880	2.970	3.060	3.150	3.240	3.330	3.420	3.510	3.600	3.690	3.780	3.870	3.960	**0.180**
0.190	2.850	2.945	3.040	3.135	3.230	3.325	3.420	3.515	3.610	3.705	3.800	3.895	3.990	4.085	4.180	**0.190**
0.200	3.000	3.100	3.200	3.300	3.400	3.500	3.600	3.700	3.800	3.900	4.000	4.100	4.200	4.300	4.400	**0.200**
0.210	3.150	3.255	3.360	3.465	3.570	3.675	3.780	3.885	3.990	4.095	4.200	4.305	4.410	4.515	4.620	**0.210**
0.220	3.300	3.410	3.520	3.630	3.740	3.850	3.960	4.070	4.180	4.290	4.400	4.510	4.620	4.730	4.840	**0.220**
0.230	3.450	3.565	3.680	3.795	3.910	4.025	4.140	4.255	4.370	4.485	4.600	4.715	4.830	4.945	5.060	**0.230**
0.240	3.600	3.720	3.840	3.960	4.080	4.200	4.320	4.440	4.560	4.680	4.800	4.920	5.040	5.160	5.280	**0.240**
0.250	3.750	3.875	4.000	4.125	4.250	4.375	4.500	4.625	4.750	4.875	5.000	5.125	5.250	5.375	5.500	**0.250**
0.260	3.900	4.030	4.160	4.290	4.420	4.550	4.680	4.810	4.940	5.070	5.200	5.330	5.460	5.590	5.720	**0.260**
0.270	4.050	4.185	4.320	4.455	4.590	4.725	4.860	4.995	5.130	5.265	5.400	5.535	5.670	5.805	5.940	**0.270**
0.280	4.200	4.340	4.480	4.620	4.760	4.900	5.040	5.180	5.320	5.460	5.600	5.740	5.880	6.020	6.160	**0.280**
0.290	4.350	4.495	4.640	4.785	4.930	5.075	5.220	5.365	5.510	5.655	5.800	5.945	6.090	6.235	6.380	**0.290**
0.300	4.500	4.650	4.800	4.950	5.100	5.250	5.400	5.550	5.700	5.850	6.000	6.150	6.300	6.450	6.600	**0.300**
0.310	4.650	4.805	4.960	5.115	5.270	5.425	5.580	5.735	5.890	6.045	6.200	6.355	6.510	6.665	6.820	**0.310**
0.320	4.800	4.960	5.120	5.280	5.440	5.600	5.760	5.920	6.080	6.240	6.400	6.560	6.720	6.880	7.040	**0.320**
0.330	4.950	5.115	5.280	5.445	5.610	5.775	5.940	6.105	6.270	6.435	6.600	6.765	6.930	7.095	7.260	**0.330**
0.340	5.100	5.270	5.440	5.610	5.780	5.950	6.120	6.290	6.460	6.630	6.800	6.970	7.140	7.310	7.480	**0.340**
0.350	5.250	5.425	5.600	5.775	5.950	6.125	6.300	6.475	6.650	6.825	7.000	7.175	7.350	7.525	7.700	**0.350**
0.360	5.400	5.580	5.760	5.940	6.120	6.300	6.480	6.660	6.840	7.020	7.200	7.380	7.560	7.740	7.920	**0.360**
0.370	5.550	5.735	5.920	6.105	6.290	6.475	6.660	6.845	7.030	7.215	7.400	7.585	7.770	7.955	8.140	**0.370**
0.380	5.700	5.890	6.080	6.270	6.460	6.650	6.840	7.030	7.220	7.410	7.600	7.790	7.980	8.170	8.360	**0.380**
0.390	5.850	6.045	6.240	6.435	6.630	6.825	7.020	7.215	7.410	7.605	7.800	7.995	8.190	8.385	8.580	**0.390**
0.400	6.000	6.200	6.400	6.600	6.800	7.000	7.200	7.400	7.600	7.800	8.000	8.200	8.400	8.600	8.800	**0.400**
0.410	6.150	6.355	6.560	6.765	6.970	7.175	7.380	7.585	7.790	7.995	8.200	8.405	8.610	8.815	9.020	**0.410**
0.420	6.300	6.510	6.720	6.930	7.140	7.350	7.560	7.770	7.980	8.190	8.400	8.610	8.820	9.030	9.240	**0.420**
0.430	6.450	6.665	6.880	7.095	7.310	7.525	7.740	7.955	8.170	8.385	8.600	8.815	9.030	9.245	9.460	**0.430**
0.440	6.600	6.820	7.040	7.260	7.480	7.700	7.920	8.140	8.360	8.580	8.800	9.020	9.240	9.460	9.680	**0.440**
0.450	6.750	6.975	7.200	7.425	7.650	7.875	8.100	8.325	8.550	8.775	9.000	9.225	9.450	9.675	9.900	**0.450**
0.460	6.900	7.130	7.360	7.590	7.820	8.050	8.280	8.510	8.740	8.970	9.200	9.430	9.660	9.890	10.120	**0.460**
0.470	7.050	7.285	7.520	7.755	7.990	8.225	8.460	8.695	8.930	9.165	9.400	9.635	9.870	10.105	10.340	**0.470**
0.480	7.200	7.440	7.680	7.920	8.160	8.400	8.640	8.880	9.120	9.360	9.600	9.840	10.080	10.320	10.560	**0.480**

SILVER BULLION VALUE CHART

Oz.	15.00	15.50	16.00	16.50	17.00	17.50	18.00	18.50	19.00	19.50	20.00	20.50	21.00	21.50	22.00	Oz.
0.490	7.350	7.595	7.840	8.085	8.330	8.575	8.820	9.065	9.310	9.555	9.800	10.045	10.290	10.535	10.780	**0.490**
0.500	7.500	7.750	8.000	8.250	8.500	8.750	9.000	9.250	9.500	9.750	10.000	10.250	10.500	10.750	11.000	**0.500**
0.510	7.650	7.905	8.160	8.415	8.670	8.925	9.180	9.435	9.690	9.945	10.200	10.455	10.710	10.965	11.220	**0.510**
0.520	7.800	8.060	8.320	8.580	8.840	9.100	9.360	9.620	9.880	10.140	10.400	10.660	10.920	11.180	11.440	**0.520**
0.530	7.950	8.215	8.480	8.745	9.010	9.275	9.540	9.805	10.070	10.335	10.600	10.865	11.130	11.395	11.660	**0.530**
0.540	8.100	8.370	8.640	8.910	9.180	9.450	9.720	9.990	10.260	10.530	10.800	11.070	11.340	11.610	11.880	**0.540**
0.550	8.250	8.525	8.800	9.075	9.350	9.625	9.900	10.175	10.450	10.725	11.000	11.275	11.550	11.825	12.100	**0.550**
0.560	8.400	8.680	8.960	9.240	9.520	9.800	10.080	10.360	10.640	10.920	11.200	11.480	11.760	12.040	12.320	**0.560**
0.570	8.550	8.835	9.120	9.405	9.690	9.975	10.260	10.545	10.830	11.115	11.400	11.685	11.970	12.255	12.540	**0.570**
0.580	8.700	8.990	9.280	9.570	9.860	10.150	10.440	10.730	11.020	11.310	11.600	11.890	12.180	12.470	12.760	**0.580**
0.590	8.850	9.145	9.440	9.735	10.030	10.325	10.620	10.915	11.210	11.505	11.800	12.095	12.390	12.685	12.980	**0.590**
0.600	9.000	9.300	9.600	9.900	10.200	10.500	10.800	11.100	11.400	11.700	12.000	12.300	12.600	12.900	13.200	**0.600**
0.610	9.150	9.455	9.760	10.065	10.370	10.675	10.980	11.285	11.590	11.895	12.200	12.505	12.810	13.115	13.420	**0.610**
0.620	9.300	9.610	9.920	10.230	10.540	10.850	11.160	11.470	11.780	12.090	12.400	12.710	13.020	13.330	13.640	**0.620**
0.630	9.450	9.765	10.080	10.395	10.710	11.025	11.340	11.655	11.970	12.285	12.600	12.915	13.230	13.545	13.860	**0.630**
0.640	9.600	9.920	10.240	10.560	10.880	11.200	11.520	11.840	12.160	12.480	12.800	13.120	13.440	13.760	14.080	**0.640**
0.650	9.750	10.075	10.400	10.725	11.050	11.375	11.700	12.025	12.350	12.675	13.000	13.325	13.650	13.975	14.300	**0.650**
0.660	9.900	10.230	10.560	10.890	11.220	11.550	11.880	12.210	12.540	12.870	13.200	13.530	13.860	14.190	14.520	**0.660**
0.670	10.050	10.385	10.720	11.055	11.390	11.725	12.060	12.395	12.730	13.065	13.400	13.735	14.070	14.405	14.740	**0.670**
0.680	10.200	10.540	10.880	11.220	11.560	11.900	12.240	12.580	12.920	13.260	13.600	13.940	14.280	14.620	14.960	**0.680**
0.690	10.350	10.695	11.040	11.385	11.730	12.075	12.420	12.765	13.110	13.455	13.800	14.145	14.490	14.835	15.180	**0.690**
0.700	10.500	10.850	11.200	11.550	11.900	12.250	12.600	12.950	13.300	13.650	14.000	14.350	14.700	15.050	15.400	**0.700**
0.710	10.650	11.005	11.360	11.715	12.070	12.425	12.780	13.135	13.490	13.845	14.200	14.555	14.910	15.265	15.620	**0.710**
0.720	10.800	11.160	11.520	11.880	12.240	12.600	12.960	13.320	13.680	14.040	14.400	14.760	15.120	15.480	15.840	**0.720**
0.730	10.950	11.315	11.680	12.045	12.410	12.775	13.140	13.505	13.870	14.235	14.600	14.965	15.330	15.695	16.060	**0.730**
0.740	11.100	11.470	11.840	12.210	12.580	12.950	13.320	13.690	14.060	14.430	14.800	15.170	15.540	15.910	16.280	**0.740**
0.750	11.250	11.625	12.000	12.375	12.750	13.125	13.500	13.875	14.250	14.625	15.000	15.375	15.750	16.125	16.500	**0.750**
0.760	11.400	11.780	12.160	12.540	12.920	13.300	13.680	14.060	14.440	14.820	15.200	15.580	15.960	16.340	16.720	**0.760**
0.770	11.550	11.935	12.320	12.705	13.090	13.475	13.860	14.245	14.630	15.015	15.400	15.785	16.170	16.555	16.940	**0.770**
0.780	11.700	12.090	12.480	12.870	13.260	13.650	14.040	14.430	14.820	15.210	15.600	15.990	16.380	16.770	17.160	**0.780**
0.790	11.850	12.245	12.640	13.035	13.430	13.825	14.220	14.615	15.010	15.405	15.800	16.195	16.590	16.985	17.380	**0.790**
0.800	12.000	12.400	12.800	13.200	13.600	14.000	14.400	14.800	15.200	15.600	16.000	16.400	16.800	17.200	17.600	**0.800**
0.810	12.150	12.555	12.960	13.365	13.770	14.175	14.580	14.985	15.390	15.795	16.200	16.605	17.010	17.415	17.820	**0.810**
0.820	12.300	12.710	13.120	13.530	13.940	14.350	14.760	15.170	15.580	15.990	16.400	16.810	17.220	17.630	18.040	**0.820**
0.830	12.450	12.865	13.280	13.695	14.110	14.525	14.940	15.355	15.770	16.185	16.600	17.015	17.430	17.845	18.260	**0.830**
0.840	12.600	13.020	13.440	13.860	14.280	14.700	15.120	15.540	15.960	16.380	16.800	17.220	17.640	18.060	18.480	**0.840**
0.850	12.750	13.175	13.600	14.025	14.450	14.875	15.300	15.725	16.150	16.575	17.000	17.425	17.850	18.275	18.700	**0.850**
0.860	12.900	13.330	13.760	14.190	14.620	15.050	15.480	15.910	16.340	16.770	17.200	17.630	18.060	18.490	18.920	**0.860**
0.870	13.050	13.485	13.920	14.355	14.790	15.225	15.660	16.095	16.530	16.965	17.400	17.835	18.270	18.705	19.140	**0.870**
0.880	13.200	13.640	14.080	14.520	14.960	15.400	15.840	16.280	16.720	17.160	17.600	18.040	18.480	18.920	19.360	**0.880**
0.890	13.350	13.795	14.240	14.685	15.130	15.575	16.020	16.465	16.910	17.355	17.800	18.245	18.690	19.135	19.580	**0.890**
0.900	13.500	13.950	14.400	14.850	15.300	15.750	16.200	16.650	17.100	17.550	18.000	18.450	18.900	19.350	19.800	**0.900**
0.910	13.650	14.105	14.560	15.015	15.470	15.925	16.380	16.835	17.290	17.745	18.200	18.655	19.110	19.565	20.020	**0.910**
0.920	13.800	14.260	14.720	15.180	15.640	16.100	16.560	17.020	17.480	17.940	18.400	18.860	19.320	19.780	20.240	**0.920**
0.930	13.950	14.415	14.880	15.345	15.810	16.275	16.740	17.205	17.670	18.135	18.600	19.065	19.530	19.995	20.460	**0.930**
0.940	14.100	14.570	15.040	15.510	15.980	16.450	16.920	17.390	17.860	18.330	18.800	19.270	19.740	20.210	20.680	**0.940**
0.950	14.250	14.725	15.200	15.675	16.150	16.625	17.100	17.575	18.050	18.525	19.000	19.475	19.950	20.425	20.900	**0.950**
0.960	14.400	14.880	15.360	15.840	16.320	16.800	17.280	17.760	18.240	18.720	19.200	19.680	20.160	20.640	21.120	**0.960**
0.970	14.550	15.035	15.520	16.005	16.490	16.975	17.460	17.945	18.430	18.915	19.400	19.885	20.370	20.855	21.340	**0.970**
0.980	14.700	15.190	15.680	16.170	16.660	17.150	17.640	18.130	18.620	19.110	19.600	20.090	20.580	21.070	21.560	**0.980**
0.990	14.850	15.345	15.840	16.335	16.830	17.325	17.820	18.315	18.810	19.305	19.800	20.295	20.790	21.285	21.780	**0.990**
1.000	15.000	15.500	16.000	16.500	17.000	17.500	18.000	18.500	19.000	19.500	20.000	20.500	21.000	21.500	22.000	**1.000**

GOLD BULLION VALUE CHART

Oz.	1200.00	1210.00	1220.00	1230.00	1240.00	1250.00	1260.00	1270.00	1280.00	1290.00	1300.00	1310.00	1320.00	1330.00	1340.00	1350.00	1360.00	1370.00	1380.00	1390.00	1400.00
0.001	1.20	1.21	1.22	1.23	1.24	1.25	1.26	1.27	1.28	1.29	1.30	1.31	1.32	1.33	1.34	1.35	1.36	1.37	1.38	1.39	1.40
0.002	2.40	2.42	2.44	2.46	2.48	2.50	2.52	2.54	2.56	2.58	2.60	2.62	2.64	2.66	2.68	2.70	2.72	2.74	2.76	2.78	2.80
0.003	3.60	3.63	3.66	3.69	3.72	3.75	3.78	3.81	3.84	3.87	3.90	3.93	3.96	3.99	4.02	4.05	4.08	4.11	4.14	4.17	4.20
0.004	4.80	4.84	4.88	4.92	4.96	5.00	5.04	5.08	5.12	5.16	5.20	5.24	5.28	5.32	5.36	5.40	5.44	5.48	5.52	5.56	5.60
0.005	6.00	6.05	6.10	6.15	6.20	6.25	6.30	6.35	6.40	6.45	6.50	6.55	6.60	6.65	6.70	6.75	6.80	6.85	6.90	6.95	7.00
0.006	7.20	7.26	7.32	7.38	7.44	7.50	7.56	7.62	7.68	7.74	7.80	7.86	7.92	7.98	8.04	8.10	8.16	8.22	8.28	8.34	8.40
0.007	8.40	8.47	8.54	8.61	8.68	8.75	8.82	8.89	8.96	9.03	9.10	9.17	9.24	9.31	9.38	9.45	9.52	9.59	9.66	9.73	9.80
0.008	9.60	9.68	9.76	9.84	9.92	10.00	10.08	10.16	10.24	10.32	10.40	10.48	10.56	10.64	10.72	10.80	10.88	10.96	11.04	11.12	11.20
0.009	10.80	10.89	10.98	11.07	11.16	11.25	11.34	11.43	11.52	11.61	11.70	11.79	11.88	11.97	12.06	12.15	12.24	12.33	12.42	12.51	12.60
0.010	12.00	12.10	12.20	12.30	12.40	12.50	12.60	12.70	12.80	12.90	13.00	13.10	13.20	13.30	13.40	13.50	13.60	13.70	13.80	13.90	14.00
0.020	24.00	24.20	24.40	24.60	24.80	25.00	25.20	25.40	25.60	25.80	26.00	26.20	26.40	26.60	26.80	27.00	27.20	27.40	27.60	27.80	28.00
0.030	36.00	36.30	36.60	36.90	37.20	37.50	37.80	38.10	38.40	38.70	39.00	39.30	39.60	39.90	40.20	40.50	40.80	41.10	41.40	41.70	42.00
0.040	48.00	48.40	48.80	49.20	49.60	50.00	50.40	50.80	51.20	51.60	52.00	52.40	52.80	53.20	53.60	54.00	54.40	54.80	55.20	55.60	56.00
0.050	60.00	60.50	61.00	61.50	62.00	62.50	63.00	63.50	64.00	64.50	65.00	65.50	66.00	66.50	67.00	67.50	68.00	68.50	69.00	69.50	70.00
0.060	72.00	72.60	73.20	73.80	74.40	75.00	75.60	76.20	76.80	77.40	78.00	78.60	79.20	79.80	80.40	81.00	81.60	82.20	82.80	83.40	84.00
0.070	84.00	84.70	85.40	86.10	86.80	87.50	88.20	88.90	89.60	90.30	91.00	91.70	92.40	93.10	93.80	94.50	95.20	95.90	96.60	97.30	98.00
0.080	96.00	96.80	97.60	98.40	99.20	100.00	100.80	101.60	102.40	103.20	104.00	104.80	105.60	106.40	107.20	108.00	108.80	109.60	110.40	111.20	112.00
0.090	108.00	108.90	109.80	110.70	111.60	112.50	113.40	114.30	115.20	116.10	117.00	117.90	118.80	119.70	120.60	121.50	122.40	123.30	124.20	125.10	126.00
0.100	120.00	121.00	122.00	123.00	124.00	125.00	126.00	127.00	128.00	129.00	130.00	131.00	132.00	133.00	134.00	135.00	136.00	137.00	138.00	139.00	140.00
0.110	132.00	133.10	134.20	135.30	136.40	137.50	138.60	139.70	140.80	141.90	143.00	144.10	145.20	146.30	147.40	148.50	149.60	150.70	151.80	152.90	154.00
0.120	144.00	145.20	146.40	147.60	148.80	150.00	151.20	152.40	153.60	154.80	156.00	157.20	158.40	159.60	160.80	162.00	163.20	164.40	165.60	166.80	168.00
0.130	156.00	157.30	158.60	159.90	161.20	162.50	163.80	165.10	166.40	167.70	169.00	170.30	171.60	172.90	174.20	175.50	176.80	178.10	179.40	180.70	182.00
0.140	168.00	169.40	170.80	172.20	173.60	175.00	176.40	177.80	179.20	180.60	182.00	183.40	184.80	186.20	187.60	189.00	190.40	191.80	193.20	194.60	196.00
0.150	180.00	181.50	183.00	184.50	186.00	187.50	189.00	190.50	192.00	193.50	195.00	196.50	198.00	199.50	201.00	202.50	204.00	205.50	207.00	208.50	210.00
0.160	192.00	193.60	195.20	196.80	198.40	200.00	201.60	203.20	204.80	206.40	208.00	209.60	211.20	212.80	214.40	216.00	217.60	219.20	220.80	222.40	224.00
0.170	204.00	205.70	207.40	209.10	210.80	212.50	214.20	215.90	217.60	219.30	221.00	222.70	224.40	226.10	227.80	229.50	231.20	232.90	234.60	236.30	238.00
0.180	216.00	217.80	219.60	221.40	223.20	225.00	226.80	228.60	230.40	232.20	234.00	235.80	237.60	239.40	241.20	243.00	244.80	246.60	248.40	250.20	252.00
0.190	228.00	229.90	231.80	233.70	235.60	237.50	239.40	241.30	243.20	245.10	247.00	248.90	250.80	252.70	254.60	256.50	258.40	260.30	262.20	264.10	266.00
0.200	240.00	242.00	244.00	246.00	248.00	250.00	252.00	254.00	256.00	258.00	260.00	262.00	264.00	266.00	268.00	270.00	272.00	274.00	276.00	278.00	280.00
0.210	252.00	254.10	256.20	258.30	260.40	262.50	264.60	266.70	268.80	270.90	273.00	275.10	277.20	279.30	281.40	283.50	285.60	287.70	289.80	291.90	294.00
0.220	264.00	266.20	268.40	270.60	272.80	275.00	277.20	279.40	281.60	283.80	286.00	288.20	290.40	292.60	294.80	297.00	299.20	301.40	303.60	305.80	308.00
0.230	276.00	278.30	280.60	282.90	285.20	287.50	289.80	292.10	294.40	296.70	299.00	301.30	303.60	305.90	308.20	310.50	312.80	315.10	317.40	319.70	322.00
0.240	288.00	290.40	292.80	295.20	297.60	300.00	302.40	304.80	307.20	309.60	312.00	314.40	316.80	319.20	321.60	324.00	326.40	328.80	331.20	333.60	336.00
0.250	300.00	302.50	305.00	307.50	310.00	312.50	315.00	317.50	320.00	322.50	325.00	327.50	330.00	332.50	335.00	337.50	340.00	342.50	345.00	347.50	350.00
0.260	312.00	314.60	317.20	319.80	322.40	325.00	327.60	330.20	332.80	335.40	338.00	340.60	343.20	345.80	348.40	351.00	353.60	356.20	358.80	361.40	364.00
0.270	324.00	326.70	329.40	332.10	334.80	337.50	340.20	342.90	345.60	348.30	351.00	353.70	356.40	359.10	361.80	364.50	367.20	369.90	372.60	375.30	378.00
0.280	336.00	338.80	341.60	344.40	347.20	350.00	352.80	355.60	358.40	361.20	364.00	366.80	369.60	372.40	375.20	378.00	380.80	383.60	386.40	389.20	392.00
0.290	348.00	350.90	353.80	356.70	359.60	362.50	365.40	368.30	371.20	374.10	377.00	379.90	382.80	385.70	388.60	391.50	394.40	397.30	400.20	403.10	406.00
0.300	360.00	363.00	366.00	369.00	372.00	375.00	378.00	381.00	384.00	387.00	390.00	393.00	396.00	399.00	402.00	405.00	408.00	411.00	414.00	417.00	420.00
0.310	372.00	375.10	378.20	381.30	384.40	387.50	390.60	393.70	396.80	399.90	403.00	406.10	409.20	412.30	415.40	418.50	421.60	424.70	427.80	430.90	434.00
0.320	384.00	387.20	390.40	393.60	396.80	400.00	403.20	406.40	409.60	412.80	416.00	419.20	422.40	425.60	428.80	432.00	435.20	438.40	441.60	444.80	448.00
0.330	396.00	399.30	402.60	405.90	409.20	412.50	415.80	419.10	422.40	425.70	429.00	432.30	435.60	438.90	442.20	445.50	448.80	452.10	455.40	458.70	462.00
0.340	408.00	411.40	414.80	418.20	421.60	425.00	428.40	431.80	435.20	438.60	442.00	445.40	448.80	452.20	455.60	459.00	462.40	465.80	469.20	472.60	476.00
0.350	420.00	423.50	427.00	430.50	434.00	437.50	441.00	444.50	448.00	451.50	455.00	458.50	462.00	465.50	469.00	472.50	476.00	479.50	483.00	486.50	490.00
0.360	432.00	435.60	439.20	442.80	446.40	450.00	453.60	457.20	460.80	464.40	468.00	471.60	475.20	478.80	482.40	486.00	489.60	493.20	496.80	500.40	504.00
0.370	444.00	447.70	451.40	455.10	458.80	462.50	466.20	469.90	473.60	477.30	481.00	484.70	488.40	492.10	495.80	499.50	503.20	506.90	510.60	514.30	518.00
0.380	456.00	459.80	463.60	467.40	471.20	475.00	478.80	482.60	486.40	490.20	494.00	497.80	501.60	505.40	509.20	513.00	516.80	520.60	524.40	528.20	532.00
0.390	468.00	471.90	475.80	479.70	483.60	487.50	491.40	495.30	499.20	503.10	507.00	510.90	514.80	518.70	522.60	526.50	530.40	534.30	538.20	542.10	546.00
0.400	480.00	484.00	488.00	492.00	496.00	500.00	504.00	508.00	512.00	516.00	520.00	524.00	528.00	532.00	536.00	540.00	544.00	548.00	552.00	556.00	560.00
0.410	492.00	496.10	500.20	504.30	508.40	512.50	516.60	520.70	524.80	528.90	533.00	537.10	541.20	545.30	549.40	553.50	557.60	561.70	565.80	569.90	574.00
0.420	504.00	508.20	512.40	516.60	520.80	525.00	529.20	533.40	537.60	541.80	546.00	550.20	554.40	558.60	562.80	567.00	571.20	575.40	579.60	583.80	588.00
0.430	516.00	520.30	524.60	528.90	533.20	537.50	541.80	546.10	550.40	554.70	559.00	563.30	567.60	571.90	576.20	580.50	584.80	589.10	593.40	597.70	602.00
0.440	528.00	532.40	536.80	541.20	545.60	550.00	554.40	558.80	563.20	567.60	572.00	576.40	580.80	585.20	589.60	594.00	598.40	602.80	607.20	611.60	616.00
0.450	540.00	544.50	549.00	553.50	558.00	562.50	567.00	571.50	576.00	580.50	585.00	589.50	594.00	598.50	603.00	607.50	612.00	616.50	621.00	625.50	630.00
0.460	552.00	556.60	561.20	565.80	570.40	575.00	579.60	584.20	588.80	593.40	598.00	602.60	607.20	611.80	616.40	621.00	625.60	630.20	634.80	639.40	644.00

GOLD BULLION VALUE CHART

Oz.	1200.00	1210.00	1220.00	1230.00	1240.00	1250.00	1260.00	1270.00	1280.00	1290.00	1300.00	1310.00	1320.00	1330.00	1340.00	1350.00	1360.00	1370.00	1380.00	1390.00	1400.00
0.470	564.00	568.70	573.40	578.10	582.80	587.50	592.20	596.90	601.60	606.30	611.00	615.70	620.40	625.10	629.80	634.50	639.20	643.90	648.60	653.30	658.00
0.480	576.00	580.80	585.60	590.40	595.20	600.00	604.80	609.60	614.40	619.20	624.00	628.80	633.60	638.40	643.20	648.00	652.80	657.60	662.40	667.20	672.00
0.490	588.00	592.90	597.80	602.70	607.60	612.50	617.40	622.30	627.20	632.10	637.00	641.90	646.80	651.70	656.60	661.50	666.40	671.30	676.20	681.10	686.00
0.500	600.00	605.00	610.00	615.00	620.00	625.00	630.00	635.00	640.00	645.00	650.00	655.00	660.00	665.00	670.00	675.00	680.00	685.00	690.00	695.00	700.00
0.510	612.00	617.10	622.20	627.30	632.40	637.50	642.60	647.70	652.80	657.90	663.00	668.10	673.20	678.30	683.40	688.50	693.60	698.70	703.80	708.90	714.00
0.520	624.00	629.20	634.40	639.60	644.80	650.00	655.20	660.40	665.60	670.80	676.00	681.20	686.40	691.60	696.80	702.00	707.20	712.40	717.60	722.80	728.00
0.530	636.00	641.30	646.60	651.90	657.20	662.50	667.80	673.10	678.40	683.70	689.00	694.30	699.60	704.90	710.20	715.50	720.80	726.10	731.40	736.70	742.00
0.540	648.00	653.40	658.80	664.20	669.60	675.00	680.40	685.80	691.20	696.60	702.00	707.40	712.80	718.20	723.60	729.00	734.40	739.80	745.20	750.60	756.00
0.550	660.00	665.50	671.00	676.50	682.00	687.50	693.00	698.50	704.00	709.50	715.00	720.50	726.00	731.50	737.00	742.50	748.00	753.50	759.00	764.50	770.00
0.560	672.00	677.60	683.20	688.80	694.40	700.00	705.60	711.20	716.80	722.40	728.00	733.60	739.20	744.80	750.40	756.00	761.60	767.20	772.80	778.40	784.00
0.570	684.00	689.70	695.40	701.10	706.80	712.50	718.20	723.90	729.60	735.30	741.00	746.70	752.40	758.10	763.80	769.50	775.20	780.90	786.60	792.30	798.00
0.580	696.00	701.80	707.60	713.40	719.20	725.00	730.80	736.60	742.40	748.20	754.00	759.80	765.60	771.40	777.20	783.00	788.80	794.60	800.40	806.20	812.00
0.590	708.00	713.90	719.80	725.70	731.60	737.50	743.40	749.30	755.20	761.10	767.00	772.90	778.80	784.70	790.60	796.50	802.40	808.30	814.20	820.10	826.00
0.600	720.00	726.00	732.00	738.00	744.00	750.00	756.00	762.00	768.00	774.00	780.00	786.00	792.00	798.00	804.00	810.00	816.00	822.00	828.00	834.00	840.00
0.610	732.00	738.10	744.20	750.30	756.40	762.50	768.60	774.70	780.80	786.90	793.00	799.10	805.20	811.30	817.40	823.50	829.60	835.70	841.80	847.90	854.00
0.620	744.00	750.20	756.40	762.60	768.80	775.00	781.20	787.40	793.60	799.80	806.00	812.20	818.40	824.60	830.80	837.00	843.20	849.40	855.60	861.80	868.00
0.630	756.00	762.30	768.60	774.90	781.20	787.50	793.80	800.10	806.40	812.70	819.00	825.30	831.60	837.90	844.20	850.50	856.80	863.10	869.40	875.70	882.00
0.640	768.00	774.40	780.80	787.20	793.60	800.00	806.40	812.80	819.20	825.60	832.00	838.40	844.80	851.20	857.60	864.00	870.40	876.80	883.20	889.60	896.00
0.650	780.00	786.50	793.00	799.50	806.00	812.50	819.00	825.50	832.00	838.50	845.00	851.50	858.00	864.50	871.00	877.50	884.00	890.50	897.00	903.50	910.00
0.660	792.00	798.60	805.20	811.80	818.40	825.00	831.60	838.20	844.80	851.40	858.00	864.60	871.20	877.80	884.40	891.00	897.60	904.20	910.80	917.40	924.00
0.670	804.00	810.70	817.40	824.10	830.80	837.50	844.20	850.90	857.60	864.30	871.00	877.70	884.40	891.10	897.80	904.50	911.20	917.90	924.60	931.30	938.00
0.680	816.00	822.80	829.60	836.40	843.20	850.00	856.80	863.60	870.40	877.20	884.00	890.80	897.60	904.40	911.20	918.00	924.80	931.60	938.40	945.20	952.00
0.690	828.00	834.90	841.80	848.70	855.60	862.50	869.40	876.30	883.20	890.10	897.00	903.90	910.80	917.70	924.60	931.50	938.40	945.30	952.20	959.10	966.00
0.700	840.00	847.00	854.00	861.00	868.00	875.00	882.00	889.00	896.00	903.00	910.00	917.00	924.00	931.00	938.00	945.00	952.00	959.00	966.00	973.00	980.00
0.710	852.00	859.10	866.20	873.30	880.40	887.50	894.60	901.70	908.80	915.90	923.00	930.10	937.20	944.30	951.40	958.50	965.60	972.70	979.80	986.90	994.00
0.720	864.00	871.20	878.40	885.60	892.80	900.00	907.20	914.40	921.60	928.80	936.00	943.20	950.40	957.60	964.80	972.00	979.20	986.40	993.60	1000.80	1008.00
0.730	876.00	883.30	890.60	897.90	905.20	912.50	919.80	927.10	934.40	941.70	949.00	956.30	963.60	970.90	978.20	985.50	992.80	1000.10	1007.40	1014.70	1022.00
0.740	888.00	895.40	902.80	910.20	917.60	925.00	932.40	939.80	947.20	954.60	962.00	969.40	976.80	984.20	991.60	999.00	1006.40	1013.80	1021.20	1028.60	1036.00
0.750	900.00	907.50	915.00	922.50	930.00	937.50	945.00	952.50	960.00	967.50	975.00	982.50	990.00	997.50	1005.00	1012.50	1020.00	1027.50	1035.00	1042.50	1050.00
0.760	912.00	919.60	927.20	934.80	942.40	950.00	957.60	965.20	972.80	980.40	988.00	995.60	1003.20	1010.80	1018.40	1026.00	1033.60	1041.20	1048.80	1056.40	1064.00
0.770	924.00	931.70	939.40	947.10	954.80	962.50	970.20	977.90	985.60	993.30	1001.00	1008.70	1016.40	1024.10	1031.80	1039.50	1047.20	1054.90	1062.60	1070.30	1078.00
0.780	936.00	943.80	951.60	959.40	967.20	975.00	982.80	990.60	998.40	1006.20	1014.00	1021.80	1029.60	1037.40	1045.20	1053.00	1060.80	1068.60	1076.40	1084.20	1092.00
0.790	948.00	955.90	963.80	971.70	979.60	987.50	995.40	1003.30	1011.20	1019.10	1027.00	1034.90	1042.80	1050.70	1058.60	1066.50	1074.40	1082.30	1090.20	1098.10	1106.00
0.800	960.00	968.00	976.00	984.00	992.00	1000.00	1008.00	1016.00	1024.00	1032.00	1040.00	1048.00	1056.00	1064.00	1072.00	1080.00	1088.00	1096.00	1104.00	1112.00	1120.00
0.810	972.00	980.10	988.20	996.30	1004.40	1012.50	1020.60	1028.70	1036.80	1044.90	1053.00	1061.10	1069.20	1077.30	1085.40	1093.50	1101.60	1109.70	1117.80	1125.90	1134.00
0.820	984.00	992.20	1000.40	1008.60	1016.80	1025.00	1033.20	1041.40	1049.60	1057.80	1066.00	1074.20	1082.40	1090.60	1098.80	1107.00	1115.20	1123.40	1131.60	1139.80	1148.00
0.830	996.00	1004.30	1012.60	1020.90	1029.20	1037.50	1045.80	1054.10	1062.40	1070.70	1079.00	1087.30	1095.60	1103.90	1112.20	1120.50	1128.80	1137.10	1145.40	1153.70	1162.00
0.840	1008.00	1016.40	1024.80	1033.20	1041.60	1050.00	1058.40	1066.80	1075.20	1083.60	1092.00	1100.40	1108.80	1117.20	1125.60	1134.00	1142.40	1150.80	1159.20	1167.60	1176.00
0.850	1020.00	1028.50	1037.00	1045.50	1054.00	1062.50	1071.00	1079.50	1088.00	1096.50	1105.00	1113.50	1122.00	1130.50	1139.00	1147.50	1156.00	1164.50	1173.00	1181.50	1190.00
0.860	1032.00	1040.60	1049.20	1057.80	1066.40	1075.00	1083.60	1092.20	1100.80	1109.40	1118.00	1126.60	1135.20	1143.80	1152.40	1161.00	1169.60	1178.20	1186.80	1195.40	1204.00
0.870	1044.00	1052.70	1061.40	1070.10	1078.80	1087.50	1096.20	1104.90	1113.60	1122.30	1131.00	1139.70	1148.40	1157.10	1165.80	1174.50	1183.20	1191.90	1200.60	1209.30	1218.00
0.880	1056.00	1064.80	1073.60	1082.40	1091.20	1100.00	1108.80	1117.60	1126.40	1135.20	1144.00	1152.80	1161.60	1170.40	1179.20	1188.00	1196.80	1205.60	1214.40	1223.20	1232.00
0.890	1068.00	1076.90	1085.80	1094.70	1103.60	1112.50	1121.40	1130.30	1139.20	1148.10	1157.00	1165.90	1174.80	1183.70	1192.60	1201.50	1210.40	1219.30	1228.20	1237.10	1246.00
0.900	1080.00	1089.00	1098.00	1107.00	1116.00	1125.00	1134.00	1143.00	1152.00	1161.00	1170.00	1179.00	1188.00	1197.00	1206.00	1215.00	1224.00	1233.00	1242.00	1251.00	1260.00
0.910	1092.00	1101.10	1110.20	1119.30	1128.40	1137.50	1146.60	1155.70	1164.80	1173.90	1183.00	1192.10	1201.20	1210.30	1219.40	1228.50	1237.60	1246.70	1255.80	1264.90	1274.00
0.920	1104.00	1113.20	1122.40	1131.60	1140.80	1150.00	1159.20	1168.40	1177.60	1186.80	1196.00	1205.20	1214.40	1223.60	1232.80	1242.00	1251.20	1260.40	1269.60	1278.80	1288.00
0.930	1116.00	1125.30	1134.60	1143.90	1153.20	1162.50	1171.80	1181.10	1190.40	1199.70	1209.00	1218.30	1227.60	1236.90	1246.20	1255.50	1264.80	1274.10	1283.40	1292.70	1302.00
0.940	1128.00	1137.40	1146.80	1156.20	1165.60	1175.00	1184.40	1193.80	1203.20	1212.60	1222.00	1231.40	1240.80	1250.20	1259.60	1269.00	1278.40	1287.80	1297.20	1306.60	1316.00
0.950	1140.00	1149.50	1159.00	1168.50	1178.00	1187.50	1197.00	1206.50	1216.00	1225.50	1235.00	1244.50	1254.00	1263.50	1273.00	1282.50	1292.00	1301.50	1311.00	1320.50	1330.00
0.960	1152.00	1161.60	1171.20	1180.80	1190.40	1200.00	1209.60	1219.20	1228.80	1238.40	1248.00	1257.60	1267.20	1276.80	1286.40	1296.00	1305.60	1315.20	1324.80	1334.40	1344.00
0.970	1164.00	1173.70	1183.40	1193.10	1202.80	1212.50	1222.20	1231.90	1241.60	1251.30	1261.00	1270.70	1280.40	1290.10	1299.80	1309.50	1319.20	1328.90	1338.60	1348.30	1358.00
0.980	1176.00	1185.80	1195.60	1205.40	1215.20	1225.00	1234.80	1244.60	1254.40	1264.20	1274.00	1283.80	1293.60	1303.40	1313.20	1323.00	1332.80	1342.60	1352.40	1362.20	1372.00
0.990	1188.00	1197.90	1207.80	1217.70	1227.60	1237.50	1247.40	1257.30	1267.20	1277.10	1287.00	1296.90	1306.80	1316.70	1326.60	1336.50	1346.40	1356.30	1366.20	1376.10	1386.00
1.000	1200.00	1210.00	1220.00	1230.00	1240.00	1250.00	1260.00	1270.00	1280.00	1290.00	1300.00	1310.00	1320.00	1330.00	1340.00	1350.00	1360.00	1370.00	1380.00	1390.00	1400.00

HEJIRA DATE CONVERSION CHART

HEJIRA (Hijira, Hegira), the name of the Muslim era (A.H. = Anno Hegirae) dates back to the Christian year 622 when Mohammed "fled" from Mecca, escaping to Medina to avoid persecution from the Koreish tribemen. Based on a lunar year the Muslim year is 11 days shorter.

*=Leap Year (Christian Calendar)

AH Hejira	AD Christian Date
1010	1601, July 2
1011	1602, June 21
1012	1603, June 11
1013	1604, May 30
1014	1605, May 19
1015	1606, May 9
1016	1607, April 28
1017	1608, April 17
1018	1609, April 6
1017	1608, April 28
1018	1609, April 6
1019	1610, March 26
1020	1611, March 16
1021	1612, March 4
1022	1613, February 21
1023	1614, February 11
1024	1615, January 31
1025	1616, January 20
1026	1617, January 9
1027	1617, December 29
1028	1618, December 19
1029	1619, December 8
1030	1620, November 26
1031	1621, November 16
1032	1622, November 5
1033	1623, October 25
1034	1624, October 14
1035	1625, October 3
1036	1626, September 22
1037	1627, September 12
1038	1628, August 31
1039	1629, August 21
1040	1630, August 10
1041	1631, July 30
1042	1632, July 19
1043	1633, July 8
1044	1634, June 27
1045	1635, June 17
1046	1636, June 5
1047	1637, May 26
1048	1638, May 15
1049	1639, May 4
1050	1640, April 23
1051	1641, April 12
1052	1642, April 1
1053	1643, March 22
1054	1644, March 10
1055	1645, February 27
1056	1646, February 17
1057	1647, February 6
1058	1648, January 27
1059	1649, January 15
1060	1650, January 4
1061	1650, December 25
1062	1651, December 14
1063	1652, December 2
1064	1653, November 22
1065	1654, November 11
1066	1655, October 31
1067	1656, October 20
1068	1657, October 9
1069	1658, September 29
1070	1659, September 18
1071	1660, September 6
1072	1661, August 27
1073	1662, August 16
1074	1663, August 5
1075	1664, July 25
1076	1665, July 14
1077	1666, July 4
1078	1667, June 23
1079	1668, June 11
1080	1669, June 1
1081	1670, May 21
1082	1671, May 10
1083	1672, April 29
1084	1673, April 18
1085	1674, April 7

AH Hejira	AD Christian Date
1086	1675, March 28
1087	1676, March 16*
1088	1677, March 6
1089	1678, February 23
1090	1679, February 12
1091	1680, February 2*
1092	1681, January 21
1093	1682, January 10
1094	1682, December 31
1095	1683, December 20
1096	1684, December 8*
1097	1685, November 28
1098	1686, November 17
1099	1687, November 7
1100	1688, October 26*
1101	1689, October 15
1102	1690, October 5
1103	1691, September 24
1104	1692, September 12*
1105	1693, September 2
1106	1694, August 22
1107	1695, August 12
1108	1696, July 31*
1109	1697, July 20
1110	1698, July 10
1111	1699, June 29
1112	1700, June 18
1113	1701, June 8
1114	1702, May 28
1115	1703, May 17
1116	1704, May 6*
1117	1705, April 25
1118	1706, April 15
1119	1707, April 4
1120	1708, March 23*
1121	1709, March 13
1122	1710, March 2
1123	1711, February 19
1124	1712, February 9*
1125	1713, January 28
1126	1714, January 17
1127	1715, January 7
1128	1715, December 27
1129	1716, December 16*
1130	1717, December 5
1131	1718, November 24
1132	1719, November 14
1133	1720, November 2*
1134	1721, October 22
1135	1722, October 12
1136	1723, October 1
1137	1724, September 19
1138	1725, September 9
1139	1726, August 29
1140	1727, August 19
1141	1728, August 7*
1142	1729, July 27
1143	1730, July 17
1144	1731, July 6
1145	1732, June 24*
1146	1733, June 14
1147	1734, June 3
1148	1735, May 24
1149	1736, May 12*
1150	1737, May 1
1151	1738, April 21
1152	1739, April 10
1153	1740, March 29*
1154	1741, March 19
1155	1742, March 8
1156	1743, February 25
1157	1744, February 15*
1158	1745, February 3
1159	1746, January 24
1160	1747, January 13
1161	1748, January 2
1162	1748, December 22*
1163	1749, December 11
1164	1750, November 30
1165	1751, November 20
1166	1752, November 8*
1167	1753, October 29
1168	1754, October 18
1169	1755, October 7
1170	1756, September 26*
1171	1757, September 15
1172	1758, September 4
1173	1759, August 25
1174	1760, August 13*
1175	1761, August 2
1176	1762, July 23

AH Hejira	AD Christian Date
1177	1763, July 12
1178	1764, July 1*
1179	1765, June 20
1180	1766, June 9
1181	1767, May 30
1182	1768, May 18*
1183	1769, May 7
1184	1770, April 27
1185	1771, April 16
1186	1772, April 4*
1187	1773, March 25
1188	1774, March 14
1189	1775, March 4
1190	1776, February 21*
1191	1777, February 1
1192	1778, January 30
1193	1779, January 19
1194	1780, January 8*
1195	1780, December 28*
1196	1781, December 17
1197	1782, December 7
1198	1783, November 26
1199	1784, November 14*
1200	1785, November 4
1201	1786, October 24
1202	1787, October 13
1203	1788, October 2*
1204	1789, September 21
1205	1790, September 10
1206	1791, August 31
1207	1792, August 19*
1208	1793, August 9
1209	1794, July 29
1210	1795, July 18
1211	1796, July 7*
1212	1797, June 26
1213	1798, June 15
1214	1799, June 5
1215	1800, May 25
1216	1801, May 14
1217	1802, May 4
1218	1803, April 23
1219	1804, April 12*
1220	1805, April 1
1221	1806, March 21
1222	1807, March 11
1223	1808, February 28*
1224	1809, February 16
1225	1810, February 6
1226	1811, January 26
1227	1812, January 16*
1228	1813, January 6
1229	1813, December 24
1230	1814, December 14
1231	1815, December 3
1232	1816, November 21*
1233	1817, November 11
1234	1818, October 31
1235	1819, October 20
1236	1820, October 9*
1237	1821, September 28
1238	1822, September 18
1239	1823, September 8
1240	1824, August 26*
1241	1825, August 16
1242	1826, August 5
1243	1827, July 25
1244	1828, July 14*
1245	1829, July 3
1246	1830, June 22
1247	1831, June 12
1248	1832, May 31*
1249	1833, May 21
1250	1834, May 10
1251	1835, April 29
1252	1836, April 18*
1253	1837, April 7
1254	1838, March 27
1255	1839, March 17
1256	1840, March 5*
1257	1841, February 23
1258	1842, February 12
1259	1843, February 1
1260	1844, January 22*
1261	1845, January 10
1262	1845, December 30
1263	1846, December 20
1264	1847, December 9
1265	1848, November 27*
1266	1849, November 17
1267	1850, November 6

AH Hejira	AD Christian Date
1268	1851, October 27
1269	1852, October 15*
1270	1853, October 4
1271	1854, September 24
1272	1855, September 13
1273	1856, September 1*
1274	1857, August 22
1275	1858, August 11
1276	1859, July 31
1277	1860, July 20*
1278	1861, July 9
1279	1862, June 29
1280	1863, June 18
1281	1864, June 6*
1282	1865, May 27
1283	1866, May 16
1284	1867, May 5
1285	1868, April 24*
1286	1869, April 13
1287	1870, April 3
1288	1871, March 23
1289	1872, March 11*
1290	1873, March 1
1291	1874, February 18
1292	1875, February 7
1293	1876, January 28*
1294	1877, January 16
1295	1878, January 5
1296	1878, December 26
1297	1879, December 15
1298	1880, December 4*
1299	1881, November 23
1300	1882, November 12
1301	1883, November 2
1302	1884, October 21*
1303	1885, October 10
1304	1886, September 30
1305	1887, September 19
1306	1888, September 7*
1307	1889, August 28
1308	1890, August 17
1309	1891, August 7
1310	1892, July 26*
1311	1893, July 15
1312	1894, July 5
1313	1895, June 24
1314	1896, June 12*
1315	1897, June 2
1316	1898, May 22
1317	1899, May 12
1318	1900, May 1
1319	1901, April 20
1320	1902, April 10
1321	1903, March 30
1322	1904, March 18*
1323	1905, March 8
1324	1906, February 25
1325	1907, February 14
1326	1908, February 4*
1327	1909, January 23
1328	1910, January 13
1329	1911, January 2
1330	1911, December 22
1332	1913, November 30
1333	1914, November 19
1334	1915, November 9
1335	1916, October 28*
1336	1917, October 17
1337	1918, October 7
1338	1919, September 26
1339	1920, September 15*
1340	1921, September 4
1341	1922, August 24
1342	1923, August 14
1343	1924, August 2*
1344	1925, July 22
1345	1926, July 12
1346	1927, July 1
1347	1928, June 20*
1348	1929, June 9
1349	1930, May 29
1350	1931, May 19
1351	1932, May 7*
1352	1933, April 26
1353	1934, April 16
1354	1935, April 5
1355	1936, March 24*
1356	1937, March 14
1357	1938, March 3
1358	1939, February 21
1359	1940, February 10*

AH Hejira	AD Christian Date
1360	1941, January 29
1361	1942, January 19
1362	1943, January 8
1363	1943, December 28
1364	1944, December 17*
1365	1945, December 6
1366	1946, November 25
1367	1947, November 15
1368	1948, November 3*
1369	1949, October 24
1370	1950, October 13
1371	1951, October 2
1372	1952, September 21*
1373	1953, September 10
1374	1954, August 30
1375	1955, August 20
1376	1956, August 8*
1377	1957, July 29
1378	1958, July 18
1379	1959, July 7
1380	1960, June 25*
1381	1961, June 14
1382	1962, June 4
1383	1963, May 25
1384	1964, May 13*
1385	1965, May 2
1386	1966, April 22
1387	1967, April 11
1388	1968, March 31*
1389	1969, March 20
1390	1970, March 9
1391	1971, February 27
1392	1972, February 16*
1393	1973, February 4
1394	1974, January 25
1395	1975, January 14
1396	1976, January 3*
1397	1976, December 23*
1398	1977, December 12
1399	1978, December 2
1400	1979, November 21
1401	1980, November 9*
1402	1981, October 30
1403	1982, October 19
1404	1984, October 8
1405	1984, September 27*
1406	1985, September 16
1407	1986, September 6
1409	1987, August 26
1409	1988, August 14*
1410	1989, August 3
1411	1990, July 24
1412	1991, July 13
1413	1992, July 2*
1414	1993, June 21
1415	1994, June 10
1416	1995, May 31
1417	1996, May 19*
1418	1997, May 9
1419	1998, April 28
1420	1999, April 17
1421	2000, April 6*
1422	2001, March 26
1423	2002, March 15
1424	2003, March 5
1425	2004, February 22*
1426	2005, February 10
1427	2006, January 31
1428	2007, January 20
1429	2008, January 10*
1430	2008, December 29
1431	2009, December 18
1432	2010, December 8
1433	2011, November 27*
1434	2012, November 15
1435	2013, November 5
1436	2014, October 25
1437	2015, October 15*
1438	2016, October 3
1439	2017, September 22
1440	2018, September 12
1441	2019, September 1*
1442	2020, August 20
1443	2021, August 10
1444	2022, July 30
1445	2023, July 19*
1446	2024, July 8
1447	2025, June 27
1448	2026, June 17
1449	2027, June 6*
1450	2028, May25

AFGHANISTAN

The Islamic State of Afghanistan, which occupies a mountainous region of Southwest Asia, has an area of 251,825 sq. mi. (652,090 sq. km.) and a population of 25.59 million. Presently, about a fifth of the total population lives in exile as refugees, (mostly in Pakistan). Capital: Kabul. It is bordered by Iran, Pakistan, Turkmenistan, Uzbekistan, Tajikistan, and China's Sinkiang Province. Agriculture and herding are the principal industries; textile mills and cement factories add to the industrial sector. Cotton, wool, fruits, nuts, oil, sheepskin coats and hand-woven carpets are normally exported but foreign trade has been interrupted since 1979.

On September 11, 2001, a terrorist attack on the United States, supported by the Taliban, led to retaliatory strikes by the U.S. Military in coalition with Afghans of a Northern Alliance. The Taliban regime was deposed. During a UN-sponsored conference on Afghanistan that was held in Bonn, Germany, in early November 2001, an agreement was reached for an Interim Authority, under the leadership of Hamid Karzai, to be installed in Afghanistan on December 22, 2001 and to hold power for the following four to six months. A "loya jirga" (Grand Council) then established a Transitional Authority with Hamid Karzai as president to prepare for general elections and a new constitution.

The national symbol on most coins of the kingdom is a stylized mosque, within which is seen the *mihrab*, a niche indicating the direction of Mecca, and the *minbar*, the pulpit, with a flight of steps leading up to it. Inscriptions in Pashtu were first used under the rebel Habibullah, but did not become standard until 1950.

ISLAMIC STATE

SH1373-1381 / 1994-2002AD

STANDARD COINAGE

KM# 1043 500 AFGHANIS

19.8700 g., 0.9990 Silver 0.6382 oz. ASW, 37.9 mm. **Subject:** World Championship of Soccer - 2006 - Germany **Obv:** State Emblem **Rev:** Soccer ball on German map **Edge:** Reeded

Date	Mintage	F	VF	XF	Unc	BU
2001 Proof	—	Value: 50.00				

KM# 1048 500 AFGHANIS

15.0000 g., Silver, 35.08 mm. **Subject:** 100th Anniversary Death of Giuseppe Verdi **Obv:** National arms **Rev:** Bust of Verdi 3/4 left, music score below **Edge:** Plain

Date	Mintage	F	VF	XF	Unc	BU
SH1380(2001) Proof	—	Value: 35.00				

REPUBLIC

SH1381- / 2002- AD

DECIMAL COINAGE

100 Pul = 1 Afghani; 20 Afghani = 1 Amani

KM# 1044 AFGHANI

3.2800 g., Copper Plated Steel, 20 mm. **Obv:** Value, legend above, legend and date below **Rev:** Mosque with flags in wreath

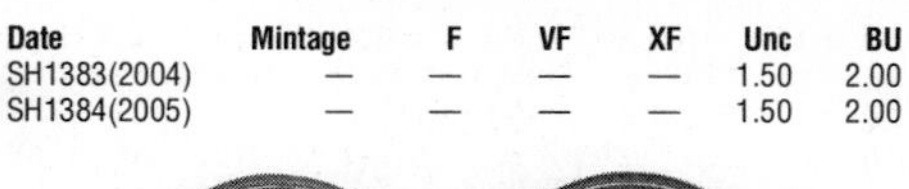

Date	Mintage	F	VF	XF	Unc	BU
SH1383(2004)	—	—	—	—	1.50	2.00
SH1384(2005)	—	—	—	—	1.50	2.00

KM# 1045 2 AFGHANIS

4.1000 g., Stainless Steel, 22 mm. **Obv:** Value, legend above, legend and date below **Rev:** Mosque with flags in wreath

Date	Mintage	F	VF	XF	Unc	BU
SH1383(2004)	—	—	—	—	2.00	2.50
SH1384(2005)	—	—	—	—	2.00	2.50

KM# 1046 5 AFGHANIS

5.0800 g., Brass, 24 mm. **Obv:** Value, legend above, legend and date below **Rev:** Mosque with flags in wreath

Date	Mintage	F	VF	XF	Unc	BU
SH1383(2004)	—	—	—	—	2.50	3.00
SH1384(2005)	—	—	—	—	2.50	3.00

ALBANIA

REPUBLIC

STANDARD COINAGE

KM# 93 10 LEKE

3.5400 g., Aluminum-Nickel-Bronze, 21.34 mm. **Subject:** 85th Anniversary Tirana as capital **Obv:** Archaic tomb **Obv. Legend:** SHQIPERI • ALBANIA **Rev:** Outlined bird above value **Edge:** Reeded

Date	Mintage	F	VF	XF	Unc	BU
2005	—	—	—	—	2.00	3.00

KM# 94 10 LEKE

3.6600 g., Aluminum-Nickel-Bronze, 21.40 mm. **Subject:** Culture **Obv:** Ornate vest **Obv. Legend:** SHQIPERI • ALBANIA **Rev:** Ornate value **Rev. Legend:** OBJEKTE TE TRASHEGIMISE KULTURORE **Edge:** Reeded

Date	Mintage	F	VF	XF	Unc	BU
2005	—	—	—	—	2.00	3.00

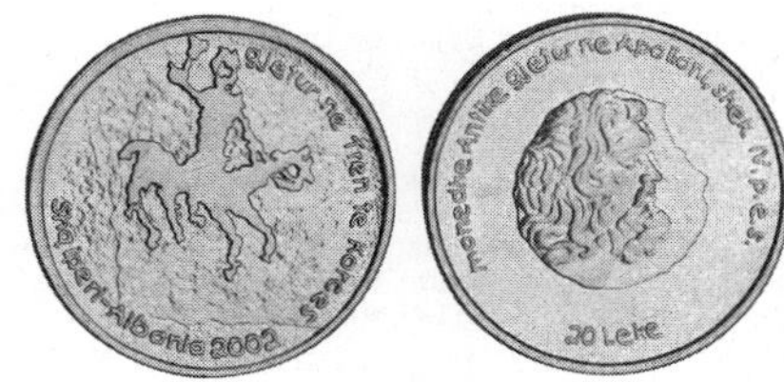

KM# 87 20 LEKE

8.5400 g., Brass, 26.1 mm. **Subject:** Prehistoric art **Obv:** Horseman **Rev:** Ancient coin design with Apollo portrait **Edge:** Reeded

Date	Mintage	F	VF	XF	Unc	BU
2002	—	—	—	—	3.00	4.00

KM# 81 50 LEKE

7.5000 g., Copper-Nickel, 28 mm. **Subject:** Michaelangelo's "David" **Obv:** Towered building **Rev:** Statue's head and denomination **Edge:** Plain

Date	Mintage	F	VF	XF	Unc	BU
2001	1,000	—	—	—	6.50	8.00

KM# 88 50 LEKE

11.9200 g., Brass, 28.1 mm. **Obv:** Value within circle **Rev:** Bust facing, dates below **Edge:** Reeded

Date	Mintage	F	VF	XF	Unc	BU
2002	—	—	—	—	3.00	4.00

KM# 89 50 LEKE

11.8400 g., Brass, 28 mm. **Obv:** Bust 3/4 facing, dates below, circle surrounds **Rev:** Value within box within circle **Edge:** Plain

Date	Mintage	F	VF	XF	Unc	BU
2003	—	—	—	—	3.00	4.00

KM# 86 50 LEKE

5.5000 g., Copper-Nickel, 24.25 mm. **Obv:** Value and legend **Rev:** Ancient Illyrian helmet **Edge:** Reeded

Date	Mintage	F	VF	XF	Unc	BU
2003 (2004)	200,000	—	—	—	6.00	7.50

KM# 90 50 LEKE

5.5000 g., Copper-Nickel, 24.25 mm. **Obv:** Wheel design **Rev:** Ancient bust above value within circle **Edge:** Reeded

Date	Mintage	F	VF	XF	Unc	BU
2004	—	—	—	—	3.00	4.00

KM# 91 50 LEKE

5.5000 g., Copper-Nickel, 24.25 mm. **Obv:** Soldier within circle **Rev:** Value within circle **Edge:** Reeded

Date	Mintage	F	VF	XF	Unc	BU
2004	—	—	—	—	3.00	4.00

KM# 82 100 LEKE

15.7000 g., 0.9250 Silver 0.4669 oz. ASW, 32.65 mm. **Subject:** Michaelangelo's "David" **Obv:** Arch of Triumph **Rev:** Statue's upper half and denomination **Edge:** Plain

Date	Mintage	F	VF	XF	Unc	BU
2001	1,000	—	—	—	32.00	35.00

KM# 84 100 LEKE

15.0000 g., 0.9250 Silver 0.4461 oz. ASW, 32 mm. **Subject:** Albanian-European Integration **Obv:** Dove in flight, stars encircle **Rev:** European and Albanian maps, stars encircle **Edge:** Plain

Date	Mintage	F	VF	XF	Unc	BU
2001	1,000	—	—	—	30.00	32.50

KM# 92 100 LEKE

15.7000 g., 0.9250 Silver 0.4669 oz. ASW **Subject:** 90th Anniversary - Ismail Qemali as President of National Assembly **Obv:** Crossed rifle and pistol on manuscript, quill pen **Obv. Legend:** SHQIPERI - ALBANIA **Rev:** Bust of Qemali 3/4 right

Date	Mintage	F	VF	XF	Unc	BU
2002 Proof	—	Value: 50.00				

KM# 83 200 LEKE

7.6500 g., 0.9000 Gold 0.2213 oz. AGW, 25.45 mm. **Subject:** Michaelangelo's "David" **Obv:** City plaza **Rev:** Statue of "David" and denomination **Edge:** Plain

Date	Mintage	F	VF	XF	Unc	BU
2001	500	—	—	—	325	350

KM# 85 200 LEKE
15.0000 g., 0.9250 Silver 0.4461 oz. ASW, 32 mm. **Subject:** Albanian-European Integration **Obv:** Dove in flight within inner circle, stars encircle **Rev:** Adult and infant hand within inner circle, stars encircle **Edge:** Plain

Date	Mintage	F	VF	XF	Unc	BU
2001	1,000	—	—	—	37.50	40.00

MINT SETS

KM#	Date	Mintage	Identification	Issue Price	Mkt Val
MS3	2002-03 (4)	—	KM86, 89 (2003), 87, 88 (2002)	—	22.50

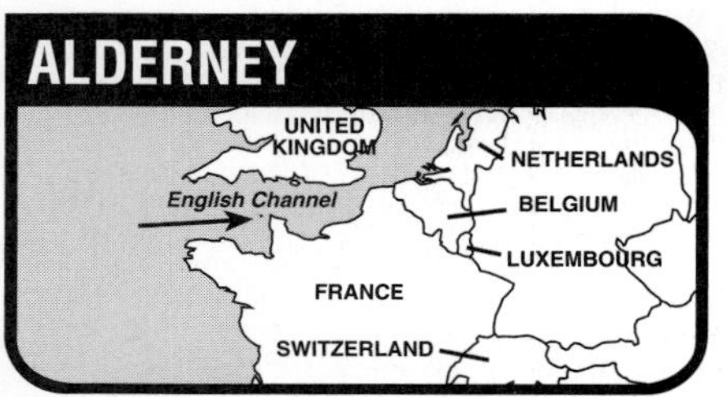

Alderney, the northernmost and third largest of the Channel Islands, separated from the coast of France by the dangerous 8-mile-wide tidal channel, has an area of 3 sq. mi. (8 km.) and a population of 1,686. It is a dependency of the British island of Guernsey, to the southwest. Capital: St. Anne. Principal industries are agriculture and raising cattle.

The Channel Islands have never been subject to the British Parliament and are self-governing units under the direct rule of the Crown acting through the Privy Council. Alderney is one of the nine Channel Islands, the only part of the Duchy of Normandy still belonging to the British Crown, and has been a British possession since the Norman Conquest of 1066. Legislation was only recently introduced for the issue of its own coinage, a right it now shares with Jersey and Guernsey.

RULER
British

MONETARY SYSTEM
100 Pence = 1 Pound Sterling

DEPENDENCY

STANDARD COINAGE

KM# 75 50 PENCE
8.0000 g., 0.9250 Silver 0.2379 oz. ASW **Ruler:** Elizabeth II **Subject:** 50th Anniversary of Coronation **Obv:** Crowned head right **Rev:** Royal coach **Edge:** Plain **Shape:** 7-sided

Date	Mintage	F	VF	XF	Unc	BU
2003 Proof	—	Value: 20.00				

KM# 76 50 PENCE
8.0000 g., 0.9250 Silver 0.2379 oz. ASW **Ruler:** Elizabeth II **Subject:** 50th Anniversary of Coronation **Obv:** Crowned head right **Rev:** St. Edward's crown **Edge:** Plain **Shape:** 7-sided

Date	Mintage	F	VF	XF	Unc	BU
2003 Proof	—	Value: 20.00				

KM# 77 50 PENCE
8.0000 g., 0.9250 Silver 0.2379 oz. ASW **Ruler:** Elizabeth II **Subject:** 50th Anniversay of Coronation **Obv:** Crowned head right **Rev:** Elizabeth II horseback **Edge:** Plain **Shape:** 7-sided

Date	Mintage	F	VF	XF	Unc	BU
2003 Proof	—	Value: 20.00				

KM# 78 50 PENCE
8.0000 g., 0.9250 Silver 0.2379 oz. ASW **Ruler:** Elizabeth II **Subject:** 50th Anniversary of Coronation **Obv:** Crowned head right **Rev:** Elizabeth II seated on throne **Edge:** Plain **Shape:** 7-sided

Date	Mintage	F	VF	XF	Unc	BU
2003 Proof	—	Value: 20.00				

KM# 73 POUND
9.5000 g., 0.9250 Silver 0.2825 oz. ASW **Ruler:** Elizabeth II **Subject:** Queen's 75th Birthday **Obv:** Crowned head right

Date	Mintage	F	VF	XF	Unc	BU
2001 Proof	—	Value: 20.00				

KM# 91 POUND
1.2400 g., 0.9990 Gold 0.0398 oz. AGW, 13.92 mm. **Ruler:** Elizabeth II **Rev:** State arms

Date	Mintage	F	VF	XF	Unc	BU
2002 Proof	Est. 50,000	Value: 65.00				

KM# 119 POUND
1.2400 g., 0.9990 Gold 0.0398 oz. AGW **Ruler:** Elizabeth II **Subject:** Trafalgar - Horatio Nelson

Date	Mintage	F	VF	XF	Unc	BU
2005 Proof	Est. 20,000	Value: 70.00				

KM# 122 POUND
1.2400 g., 0.9990 Gold 0.0398 oz. AGW, 13.92 mm. **Ruler:** Elizabeth II **Rev:** Queen Elizabeth I

Date	Mintage	F	VF	XF	Unc	BU
2006 Proof	Est. 20,000	Value: 70.00				

KM# 123 POUND
1.2400 g., 0.9990 Gold 0.0398 oz. AGW, 13.92 mm. **Ruler:** Elizabeth II **Rev:** Sir Isaac Newton

Date	Mintage	F	VF	XF	Unc	BU
2006 Proof	Est. 20,000	Value: 70.00				

KM# 124 POUND
1.2400 g., 0.9990 Gold 0.0398 oz. AGW, 13.92 mm. **Ruler:** Elizabeth II **Rev:** William Shakespeare

Date	Mintage	F	VF	XF	Unc	BU
2006 Proof	20,000	Value: 70.00				

KM# 125 POUND
1.2400 g., 0.9990 Gold 0.0398 oz. AGW, 13.92 mm. **Ruler:** Elizabeth II **Rev:** Charles Dickens

Date	Mintage	F	VF	XF	Unc	BU
2006 Proof	Est. 20,000	Value: 70.00				

KM# 130 POUND
1.2400 g., 0.9990 Gold 0.0398 oz. AGW, 13.92 mm. **Ruler:** Elizabeth II **Rev:** Sir Winston Churchill

Date	Mintage	F	VF	XF	Unc	BU
2006 Proof	Est. 20,000	Value: 70.00				

KM# 131 POUND
1.2400 g., 0.9990 Gold 0.0398 oz. AGW, 13.92 mm. **Ruler:** Elizabeth II **Rev:** Elizabeth II corronation

Date	Mintage	F	VF	XF	Unc	BU
2006 Proof	—	Value: 70.00				

KM# 154 POUND
1.2400 g., 0.9990 Gold 0.0398 oz. AGW, 13.92 mm. **Ruler:** Elizabeth II **Rev:** Capt. James Cook

Date	Mintage	F	VF	XF	Unc	BU
2007 Proof	Est. 20,000	Value: 70.00				

KM# 155 POUND
1.2400 g., 0.9990 Gold 0.0398 oz. AGW, 13.92 mm. **Ruler:** Elizabeth II **Rev:** Sir Edward Elgar

Date	Mintage	F	VF	XF	Unc	BU
2007 Proof	Est. 20,000	Value: 70.00				

KM# 156 POUND
1.2400 g., 0.9990 Gold 0.0398 oz. AGW, 13.92 mm. **Ruler:** Elizabeth II **Rev:** Sir Francis Drake

Date	Mintage	F	VF	XF	Unc	BU
2007 Proof	20,000	Value: 70.00				

KM# 157 POUND
1.2400 g., 0.9990 Gold 0.0398 oz. AGW, 13.92 mm. **Ruler:** Elizabeth II **Rev:** John Constable

Date	Mintage	F	VF	XF	Unc	BU
2007 Proof	Est. 20,000	Value: 70.00				

KM# 174 POUND
1.2400 g., 0.9990 Gold 0.0398 oz. AGW, 13.92 mm. **Ruler:** Elizabeth II **Subject:** Princess Diana, 10th Anniversary of Death **Rev:** Bust 3/4 facing left

Date	Mintage	F	VF	XF	Unc	BU
2007 Proof	Est. 20,000	Value: 70.00				

KM# 175a POUND
28.2800 g., 0.9250 Silver 0.8410 oz. ASW, 38.61 mm. **Ruler:** Elizabeth II **Rev. Designer:** Princess Diana, 10th Anniversary of Death

Date	Mintage	F	VF	XF	Unc	BU
2007 Proof	Est. 10,000	Value: 55.00				

KM# 175b POUND
39.9400 g., 0.9160 Gold 1.1762 oz. AGW, 38.61 mm. **Ruler:** Elizabeth II **Subject:** Princess Diana, 10th Anniversary of Death

Date	Mintage	F	VF	XF	Unc	BU
2007 Proof	—	Value: 1,750				

KM# 189 POUND
1.2400 g., 0.9990 Gold 0.0398 oz. AGW, 13.92 mm. **Ruler:** Elizabeth II **Rev:** Concord

Date	Mintage	F	VF	XF	Unc	BU
2008 Proof	Est. 1,000	Value: 70.00				

KM# 84 POUND
1.2400 g., 0.9990 Gold 0.0398 oz. AGW, 13.92 mm. **Ruler:** Elizabeth II **Subject:** Mini Cooper 50th Anniversary **Rev:** Mini Cooper on tiled floor **Rev. Designer:** David Cornell

Date	Mintage	F	VF	XF	Unc	BU
2009 Proof	5,000	Value: 100				

KM# 59 5 POUNDS
28.2800 g., 0.9250 Silver 0.8410 oz. ASW, 38.6 mm. **Ruler:** Elizabeth II **Subject:** Queen's 75th Birthday **Obv:** Queen's portrait right **Obv. Designer:** Raphael Maklouf **Rev:** Queen in casual dress surrounded by rose, thistle, daffodil and pimper nickel **Rev. Designer:** David Cornell

Date	Mintage	F	VF	XF	Unc	BU
2001 Proof	—	Value: 50.00				

KM# 60 5 POUNDS
28.2800 g., Copper-Nickel, 38.6 mm. **Ruler:** Elizabeth II **Subject:** Queen's 75th Birrthday **Obv:** Queen's portrait right **Obv. Designer:** Raphael Maklouf **Rev:** Queen in casual dress surrounded by rose, thistle, daffodil and primper nickel **Rev. Designer:** David Cornell

Date	Mintage	F	VF	XF	Unc	BU
2001	—	—	—	—	13.50	15.00

KM# 24 5 POUNDS
28.2800 g., 0.9250 Copper-Nickel 0.8410 oz., 38.6 mm. **Ruler:** Elizabeth II **Subject:** Queen Elizabeth II - 50 Years of Reigh **Obv:** Queen's head right **Rev:** Sword hilt and denomination with royal arms background **Rev. Designer:** Marcel Canioni **Edge:** Reeded

Date	Mintage	F	VF	XF	Unc	BU
2002 Proof	15,000	Value: 15.00				

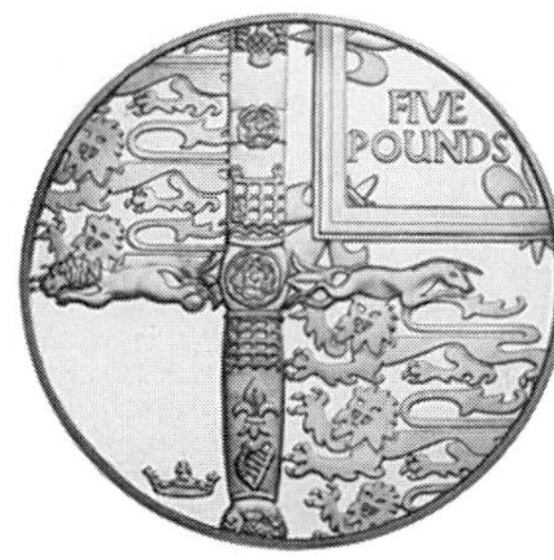

KM# 24a 5 POUNDS
28.2800 g., 0.9250 Silver 0.8410 oz. ASW, 38.6 mm. **Ruler:** Elizabeth II **Subject:** Queen Elizabeth II - 50 Years of Reign **Obv:** Queen's head right **Rev:** Sword hilt and denomination with royal arms background **Rev. Designer:** Marcel Canioni **Edge:** Reeded

Date	Mintage	F	VF	XF	Unc	BU
2002 Proof	15,000	Value: 45.00				

KM# 25 5 POUNDS
28.2800 g., 0.9250 Silver 0.8410 oz. ASW, 38.6 mm. **Ruler:** Elizabeth II **Subject:** Queen's Golden Jubilee **Obv:** Queen's portrait **Rev:** Honor guard and trumpets **Rev. Designer:** Robert Lowe **Edge:** Reeded

Date	Mintage	F	VF	XF	Unc	BU
2002 Proof	15,000	Value: 45.00				

KM# 27 5 POUNDS
28.2800 g., Copper-Nickel, 38.6 mm. **Ruler:** Elizabeth II **Subject:** 5th Anniversary Death of Princess Diana **Obv:** Crowned head right **Rev:** Diana accepting flowers from girl **Edge:** Reeded

Date	Mintage	F	VF	XF	Unc	BU
2002	—	—	—	—	13.50	15.00

KM# 27a 5 POUNDS
28.2800 g., 0.9250 Silver 0.8410 oz. ASW, 38.6 mm. **Ruler:** Elizabeth II **Subject:** 5th Anniversary Death of Princess Diana **Obv:** Crowned head right **Rev:** Diana accepting flowers from girl **Edge:** Reeded

Date	Mintage	F	VF	XF	Unc	BU
2002 Proof	20,000	Value: 45.00				

KM# 27b 5 POUNDS
39.9400 g., 0.9167 Gold 1.1771 oz. AGW, 38.6 mm. **Ruler:** Elizabeth II **Subject:** 5th Anniversary Death of Princess Diana **Obv:** Crowned head right **Rev:** Diana accepting flowers from girl **Edge:** Reeded

Date	Mintage	F	VF	XF	Unc	BU
2002 Proof	100	Value: 1,850				

KM# 29 5 POUNDS
28.2800 g., Copper-Nickel, 38.6 mm. **Ruler:** Elizabeth II **Subject:** 150th Anniversary Death of the Duke of Wellington **Obv:** Queen's portrait **Rev:** Coat of arms, castle and portrait **Rev. Designer:** Willem Vis **Edge:** Reeded

Date	Mintage	F	VF	XF	Unc	BU
2002	—	—	—	—	13.50	15.00

KM# 29a 5 POUNDS
28.2800 g., 0.9250 Silver 0.8410 oz. ASW, 38.6 mm. **Ruler:** Elizabeth II **Subject:** 150th Anniversary Death of the Duke of Wellington **Obv:** Queen's portrait **Rev:** Multicolor coat of arms, portrait and castle **Rev. Designer:** Willem Vis **Edge:** Reeded

Date	Mintage	VG	F	VF	XF	Unc
2002 Proof	15,000	Value: 55.00				

KM# 29b 5 POUNDS
39.9400 g., 0.9167 Gold 1.1771 oz. AGW, 38.6 mm. **Ruler:** Elizabeth II **Subject:** 150th Anniversary Death of the Duke of Wellington **Obv:** Queen's portrait **Rev:** Coat of arms, castle and portrait **Rev. Designer:** Willem Vis **Edge:** Reeded

Date	Mintage	VG	F	VF	XF	Unc
2002 Proof	200	Value: 1,800				

KM# 31 5 POUNDS
28.2800 g., Copper-Nickel, 38.6 mm. **Ruler:** Elizabeth II **Subject:** Prince William **Obv:** Queen's portrait **Obv. Designer:** Raphael Maklouf **Rev:** Portrait with open shirt collar **Edge:** Reeded

Date	Mintage	F	VF	XF	Unc	BU
2003	—	—	—	—	16.50	18.00

KM# 44 5 POUNDS
28.2800 g., Copper-Nickel, 38.6 mm. **Ruler:** Elizabeth II **Obv:** Queen's portrait **Rev:** HMS Mary Rose **Rev. Designer:** Willem Vis **Edge:** Reeded

Date	Mintage	F	VF	XF	Unc	BU
2003	—	—	—	—	12.00	13.50

KM# 44a 5 POUNDS
28.2800 g., 0.9250 Silver 0.8410 oz. ASW, 38.6 mm. **Ruler:** Elizabeth II **Obv:** Queen's portrait **Rev:** HMS Mary Rose below multicolor flag **Rev. Designer:** Willem Vis **Edge:** Reeded

Date	Mintage	F	VF	XF	Unc	BU
2003 Proof	15,000	Value: 60.00				

KM# 45 5 POUNDS
28.2800 g., Copper-Nickel, 38.6 mm. **Ruler:** Elizabeth II **Obv:** Queen's portrait **Rev:** Alfred the Great on ship **Rev. Designer:** Willem Vis **Edge:** Reeded

Date	Mintage	F	VF	XF	Unc	BU
2003	—	—	—	—	12.00	13.50

KM# 45a 5 POUNDS
28.2800 g., 0.9250 Silver 0.8410 oz. ASW, 38.6 mm. **Ruler:** Elizabeth II **Obv:** Queen's portrait **Rev:** Alfred the Great on ship below multicolor flag **Rev. Designer:** Willem Vis **Edge:** Reeded

Date	Mintage	F	VF	XF	Unc	BU
2003 Proof	15,000	Value: 60.00				

KM# 45b 5 POUNDS
39.9400 g., 0.9167 Gold 1.1771 oz. AGW, 38.6 mm. **Ruler:** Elizabeth II **Obv:** Queen's portrait **Rev:** Alfred the Great on ship **Rev. Designer:** Willem Vis **Edge:** Reeded

Date	Mintage	F	VF	XF	Unc	BU
2003 Proof	500	Value: 1,750				

KM# 31a 5 POUNDS
28.2800 g., 0.9250 Silver 0.8410 oz. ASW, 38.6 mm. **Ruler:** Elizabeth II **Subject:** Prince William **Obv:** Queen's portrait **Obv. Designer:** Raphael Maklouf **Rev:** Portrait with open shirt collar **Edge:** Reeded

Date	Mintage	F	VF	XF	Unc	BU
2003 Proof	—	Value: 47.50				

KM# 31b 5 POUNDS
39.9400 g., 0.9166 Gold 1.1770 oz. AGW, 38.6 mm. **Ruler:** Elizabeth II **Subject:** Prince Willliam **Obv:** Queen's portrait **Obv. Designer:** Raphael Maklouf **Rev:** Portrait with open shirt collar **Edge:** Reeded

Date	Mintage	F	VF	XF	Unc	BU
2003 Proof	200	Value: 1,800				

KM# 35a 5 POUNDS
28.5500 g., 0.9250 Silver 0.8490 oz. ASW, 38.61 mm. **Ruler:** Elizabeth II **Subject:** Last Flight of the Concorde, October 24, 2003 **Obv:** Crowned bust right **Obv. Legend:** ELIZABETH II - ALDERNEY **Obv. Designer:** Raphael Maklouf **Rev:** Concorde in flight **Rev. Legend:** CONCORDE 1969 - 2003 **Rev. Designer:** Emma Noble **Edge:** Reeded

Date	Mintage	F	VF	XF	Unc	BU
2003 Proof	5,000	Value: 50.00				

KM# 35 5 POUNDS
28.2800 g., Copper-Nickel, 38.61 mm. **Ruler:** Elizabeth II **Subject:** Last Flight of the Concorde, October 24, 2003 **Obv:** Crowned bust right **Obv. Legend:** ELIZABETH II - ALDERNEY **Obv. Designer:** Raphael Maklouf **Rev:** Concorde in flight **Rev. Legend:** CONCORDE 1969 - 2003 **Rev. Designer:** Emma Noble **Edge:** Reeded

Date	Mintage	F	VF	XF	Unc	BU
2003	5,000	—	—	—	12.00	15.50

KM# 35b 5 POUNDS
39.9400 g., 0.9166 Gold 1.1770 oz. AGW, 38.6 mm. **Ruler:** Elizabeth II **Obv:** Queen's portrait **Rev:** Concorde in flight, October 24, 2003 **Rev. Designer:** Emma Noble **Edge:** Reeded

Date	Mintage	F	VF	XF	Unc	BU
2003 Proof	500	Value: 1,750				

KM# 38 5 POUNDS
28.2800 g., Copper-Nickel, 38.6 mm. **Ruler:** Elizabeth II **Obv:** Queen's portrait **Rev:** Battleship and transports, HMS Belfast **Rev. Designer:** Mike Guilfoyle **Edge:** Reeded **Note:** D-Day

Date	Mintage	F	VF	XF	Unc	BU
2004	—	—	—	—	15.00	17.50

KM# 38a 5 POUNDS
28.2800 g., 0.9250 Silver 0.8410 oz. ASW, 38.6 mm. **Ruler:** Elizabeth II **Obv:** Queen's portrait **Rev:** Battleship and transports **Rev. Designer:** Mike Guilfoyle

Date	Mintage	F	VF	XF	Unc	BU
2004 Proof	10,000	Value: 85.00				

KM# 38b 5 POUNDS
39.9400 g., 0.9167 Gold 1.1771 oz. AGW, 38.6 mm. **Ruler:** Elizabeth II **Obv:** Queen's portrait **Rev:** Battleship and transports **Rev. Designer:** Mike Guilfoyle

Date	Mintage	F	VF	XF	Unc	BU
2004 Proof	500	Value: 1,750				

KM# 42 5 POUNDS
28.2800 g., Copper-Nickel, 38.6 mm. **Ruler:** Elizabeth II **Obv:** Crowned head right **Rev:** Florence Nightingale **Edge:** Reeded

Date	Mintage	F	VF	XF	Unc	BU
2004	—	—	—	—	18.00	20.00

KM# 42a 5 POUNDS
28.2800 g., 0.9250 Silver 0.8410 oz. ASW, 38.6 mm. **Ruler:** Elizabeth II **Obv:** Queen's portrait **Rev:** Florence Nightingale **Edge:** Reeded

Date	Mintage	F	VF	XF	Unc	BU
2004 Proof	25,000	Value: 70.00				

KM# 43 5 POUNDS
28.2800 g., Copper-Nickel, 38.6 mm. **Ruler:** Elizabeth II **Subject:** 150th Anniversary of the Crimean War **Obv:** Crowned head right **Rev:** Florence Nightingale head above the Battle of Inkerman scene with one multicolor soldier **Edge:** Reeded

Date	Mintage	F	VF	XF	Unc	BU
2004 plain	—	—	—	—	25.00	27.50
2004 partial color	—	—	—	—	25.00	27.50

KM# 43a 5 POUNDS
28.2800 g., 0.9250 Silver 0.8410 oz. ASW, 38.6 mm. **Ruler:** Elizabeth II **Subject:** 150th Anniversary Crimean War **Obv:** Crowned head right **Rev:** Florence Nightingale head above Battle of Inkerman scene with one multicolor soldier **Edge:** Reeded

Date	Mintage	F	VF	XF	Unc	BU
2004 Proof	10,000	Value: 85.00				

KM# 43b 5 POUNDS
39.9400 g., 0.9166 Gold 1.1770 oz. AGW, 38.6 mm. **Ruler:** Elizabeth II **Subject:** 150th Anniversary Crimean War **Obv:** Crowned head right **Rev:** Florence Nightingale head above Battle of Inkerman scene with one multicolor soldier **Edge:** Reeded

Date	Mintage	F	VF	XF	Unc	BU
2004 Proof	500	Value: 1,750				

KM# 94 5 POUNDS
28.2800 g., 0.9250 Silver 0.8410 oz. ASW, 38.61 mm. **Ruler:** Elizabeth II **Subject:** David Beckham **Rev:** Soccer player and ball as background

Date	Mintage	F	VF	XF	Unc	BU
2004 Proof	—	Value: 45.00				

KM# 95 5 POUNDS
28.2800 g., 0.9250 Silver 0.8410 oz. ASW, 38.61 mm. **Ruler:** Elizabeth II **Subject:** Michael Owen **Rev:** Soccer player and ball as background

Date	Mintage	F	VF	XF	Unc	BU
2004 Proof	—	Value: 45.00				

KM# 47 5 POUNDS
28.2800 g., Copper-Nickel, 38.6 mm. **Ruler:** Elizabeth II **Obv:** Queen's portrait **Rev:** Locomotive, The Rocket **Rev. Designer:** Robert Lowe **Edge:** Reeded

Date	Mintage	F	VF	XF	Unc	BU
2004	—	—	—	—	16.00	18.50

KM# 47a 5 POUNDS
28.2800 g., 0.9250 Silver 0.8410 oz. ASW, 38.6 mm. **Ruler:** Elizabeth II **Obv:** Queen's portrait **Rev:** Locomotive, The Rocket **Rev. Designer:** Robert Lowe **Edge:** Reeded

Date	Mintage	F	VF	XF	Unc	BU
2004 Proof	20,000	Value: 60.00				

KM# 47b 5 POUNDS
39.9400 g., 0.9167 Gold 1.1771 oz. AGW, 38.6 mm. **Ruler:** Elizabeth II **Obv:** Queen's portrait **Rev:** Locomotive, The Rocket **Rev. Designer:** Robert Lowe **Edge:** Reeded

Date	Mintage	F	VF	XF	Unc	BU
2004 Proof	500	Value: 1,750				

KM# 48 5 POUNDS
28.2800 g., Copper-Nickel, 38.6 mm. **Ruler:** Elizabeth II **Obv:** Queen's portrait **Rev:** Locomotive, The Royal Scot **Rev. Designer:** Robert Lowe **Edge:** Reeded

Date	Mintage	F	VF	XF	Unc	BU
2004	—	—	—	—	16.00	18.50

KM# 48a 5 POUNDS
28.2800 g., 0.9250 Silver 0.8410 oz. ASW, 38.6 mm. **Ruler:** Elizabeth II **Obv:** Queen's portrait **Rev:** Locomotive, The Royal Scot **Rev. Designer:** Robert Lowe **Edge:** Reeded

Date	Mintage	F	VF	XF	Unc	BU
2004 Proof	10,000	Value: 60.00				

KM# 49 5 POUNDS
28.2800 g., Copper-Nickel, 38.6 mm. **Ruler:** Elizabeth II **Obv:** Queen's portrait **Rev:** Locomotive, The Merchant Navy 21C1 **Edge:** Reeded

Date	Mintage	F	VF	XF	Unc	BU
2004	—	—	—	—	16.00	18.50

KM# 49a 5 POUNDS
28.2800 g., 0.9250 Silver 0.8410 oz. ASW, 38.6 mm. **Ruler:** Elizabeth II **Obv:** Queen's portrait **Rev:** Locomotive, The Merchant Navy 21C1 **Rev. Designer:** Robert Lowe **Edge:** Reeded

Date	Mintage	F	VF	XF	Unc	BU
2004 Proof	10,000	Value: 60.00				

KM# 53a 5 POUNDS
28.2800 g., 0.9250 Silver 0.8410 oz. ASW, 38.6 mm. **Ruler:** Elizabeth II **Subject:** End of WWII **Obv:** Elizabeth II by Maklouf **Rev:** Flag waving crowd **Edge:** Reeded

Date	Mintage	F	VF	XF	Unc	BU
2005 Proof	5,000	Value: 85.00				

KM# 79 5 POUNDS
Copper-Nickel **Ruler:** Elizabeth II **Subject:** 200th Anniversary Battle of Trafalgar **Obv:** Crowned head right

Date	Mintage	F	VF	XF	Unc	BU
2005	—	—	—	—	16.00	18.50

KM# 96 5 POUNDS
28.2800 g., 0.9250 Silver 0.8410 oz. ASW **Ruler:** Elizabeth II **Subject:** Locomotives, 200th Anniversary **Rev:** Train station on a branch line

Date	Mintage	F	VF	XF	Unc	BU
2005 Proof	Est. 10,000	Value: 60.00				
2006 Proof	Est. 25,000	Value: 55.00				

KM# 97 5 POUNDS

28.2800 g., 0.9250 Silver 0.8410 oz. ASW **Ruler:** Elizabeth II **Subject:** Locomotives, 200th Anniversary **Rev:** Locomotive Shop

Date	Mintage	F	VF	XF	Unc	BU
2005 Proof	Est. 10,000	Value: 60.00				
2006 proof	Est. 25,000	Value: 55.00				

KM# 98 5 POUNDS

28.2800 g., 0.9250 Silver 0.8410 oz. ASW **Ruler:** Elizabeth II **Subject:** Locomotives, 200th Anniversary **Rev:** Viaduct

Date	Mintage	F	VF	XF	Unc	BU
2005 Proof	Est. 10,000	Value: 60.00				
2006 Proof	Est. 25,000	Value: 55.00				

KM# 79a 5 POUNDS

28.2800 g., 0.9250 Silver 0.8410 oz. ASW **Ruler:** Elizabeth II **Subject:** 200th Anniversary Battle of Trafalgar **Obv:** Crowned head right

Date	Mintage	F	VF	XF	Unc	BU
2005 Proof	—	Value: 60.00				

KM# 53b 5 POUNDS

39.9400 g., 0.9167 Gold 1.1771 oz. AGW, 38.6 mm. **Ruler:** Elizabeth II **Subject:** 60th Anniversary - End of WWII **Obv:** Elizabeth II by Maklouf **Rev:** Flag waving crowd **Edge:** Reeded

Date	Mintage	F	VF	XF	Unc	BU
2005 Proof	150	Value: 1,800				

KM# 54b 5 POUNDS

39.9400 g., 0.9167 Gold 1.1771 oz. AGW, 38.6 mm. **Ruler:** Elizabeth II **Subject:** WWII Liberation **Obv:** Elizabeth II by Maklouf **Rev:** Churchill flashing the "V" sign **Edge:** Reeded

Date	Mintage	F	VF	XF	Unc	BU
2005 Proof	150	Value: 1,800				

KM# 66 5 POUNDS

28.2800 g., Copper-Nickel, 38.6 mm. **Ruler:** Elizabeth II **Subject:** Viscount Samuel Hood on his flagship after the Battle of Saints Passage in 1782 **Obv:** Queen's portrait **Rev. Designer:** Willem Vis

Date	Mintage	F	VF	XF	Unc	BU
2005	—	—	—	—	13.50	15.00

KM# 53 5 POUNDS

Copper-Nickel, 38.61 mm. **Ruler:** Elizabeth II **Subject:** End of World War II, 60th Anniversary

Date	Mintage	F	VF	XF	Unc	BU
2005	—	—	—	—	—	15.00

KM# 54 5 POUNDS

Copper-Nickel **Ruler:** Elizabeth II **Subject:** Winston Churchill

Date	Mintage	F	VF	XF	Unc	BU
2005	Est. 5,000	—	—	—	—	15.00

KM# 54a 5 POUNDS

39.9400 g., 0.9160 Silver 1.1762 oz. ASW, 38.61 mm. **Ruler:** Elizabeth II **Subject:** Sir Winston Churchill

Date	Mintage	F	VF	XF	Unc	BU
2005 Proof	—	Value: 65.00				

KM# 66a 5 POUNDS

28.2800 g., 0.9250 Silver 0.8410 oz. ASW, 38.6 mm. **Ruler:** Elizabeth II **Subject:** Viscount Samuel Hood on his flagship after the Battle of Saints Passage in 1782 **Obv:** Queen's portrait **Rev. Designer:** Willem Vis **Note:** Ensign is colored.

Date	Mintage	F	VF	XF	Unc	BU
2005 Proof	—	Value: 50.00				

KM# 68 5 POUNDS

28.2800 g., Copper-Nickel, 38.6 mm. **Ruler:** Elizabeth II **Obv:** Crowned head right **Rev:** HMS Revenge fighting at Azores, 1591 **Rev. Designer:** Willem Vis

Date	Mintage	F	VF	XF	Unc	BU
2005	—	—	—	—	12.00	14.00

KM# 83 5 POUNDS

Copper-Nickel, 38.61 mm. **Ruler:** Elizabeth II **Subject:** Royal Navy - Admiral Sir John Foster Woodward

Date	Mintage	F	VF	XF	Unc	BU
2005	—	—	—	—	—	15.00

KM# 83a 5 POUNDS

28.4300 g., Silver, 38 mm. **Ruler:** Elizabeth II **Subject:** History of the Royal Navy **Obv:** Heraldic shield **Rev:** Admiral John Woodward, partially colored

Date	Mintage	F	VF	XF	Unc	BU
2005 Proof	—	Value: 45.00				

KM# 68a 5 POUNDS

28.2800 g., 0.9250 Silver 0.8410 oz. ASW, 38.6 mm. **Ruler:** Elizabeth II **Obv:** Crowned head right **Rev:** HMS Revenge fighting at Azores, 1591 **Rev. Designer:** Willem Vis **Note:** Ensign is colorized.

Date	Mintage	F	VF	XF	Unc	BU
2005 Proof	—	Value: 60.00				

KM# 99 5 POUNDS

28.2800 g., 0.9250 Silver 0.8410 oz. ASW, 38.61 mm. **Ruler:** Elizabeth II **Subject:** Wayne Rooney **Obv:** Shield **Rev:** Soccer player and ball design

Date	Mintage	F	VF	XF	Unc	BU
2005 Proof	—	Value: 45.00				

KM# 100 5 POUNDS

28.2800 g., 0.9250 Silver 0.8410 oz. ASW, 38.61 mm. **Ruler:** Elizabeth II **Subject:** Frank Lampard **Obv:** Shield **Rev:** Soccer player and ball design

Date	Mintage	F	VF	XF	Unc	BU
2005 Proof	—	Value: 45.00				

KM# 101 5 POUNDS

28.2800 g., 0.9250 Silver 0.8410 oz. ASW, 38.61 mm. **Ruler:** Elizabeth II **Obv:** Shield **Rev:** Soccer player and ball design

Date	Mintage	F	VF	XF	Unc	BU
2005 Proof	—	Value: 45.00				

KM# 102 5 POUNDS

28.2800 g., 0.9250 Silver 0.8410 oz. ASW, 38.61 mm. **Ruler:** Elizabeth II **Subject:** Steven Gerrard **Obv:** Shield **Rev:** Soccer player and ball design

Date	Mintage	F	VF	XF	Unc	BU
2005 Proof	—	Value: 45.00				

KM# 103 5 POUNDS

28.2800 g., 0.9250 Silver 0.8410 oz. ASW, 38.61 mm. **Ruler:** Elizabeth II **Obv:** Shield **Rev:** Soccer player and ball design

Date	Mintage	F	VF	XF	Unc	BU
2005 Proof	—	Value: 45.00				

KM# 104 5 POUNDS

28.2800 g., 0.9250 Silver 0.8410 oz. ASW, 38.61 mm. **Ruler:** Elizabeth II **Obv:** Shield **Rev:** Soccer player and ball design

Date	Mintage	F	VF	XF	Unc	BU
2005 Proof	—	Value: 45.00				

KM# 105 5 POUNDS

28.2800 g., 0.9250 Silver 0.8410 oz. ASW, 38.61 mm. **Ruler:** Elizabeth II **Obv:** Shield **Rev:** Soccer player and ball design

Date	Mintage	F	VF	XF	Unc	BU
2005 Proof	—	Value: 45.00				

KM# 106 5 POUNDS

28.2800 g., 0.9250 Silver 0.8410 oz. ASW, 38.61 mm. **Ruler:** Elizabeth II **Obv:** Shield **Rev:** Soccer player and ball design

Date	Mintage	F	VF	XF	Unc	BU
2005 Proof	—	Value: 45.00				

KM# 107 5 POUNDS

28.2800 g., 0.9250 Silver 0.8410 oz. ASW, 38.61 mm. **Ruler:** Elizabeth II **Obv:** Shield **Rev:** Soccer player and ball design

Date	Mintage	F	VF	XF	Unc	BU
2005 Proof	—	Value: 45.00				

KM# 108 5 POUNDS

28.2500 g., 0.9250 Silver 0.8401 oz. ASW, 38.61 mm. **Ruler:** Elizabeth II **Obv:** Shield **Rev:** Soccer player and ball design

Date	Mintage	F	VF	XF	Unc	BU
2005 Proof	—	Value: 45.00				

KM# 113 5 POUNDS

Copper-Nickel, 38.61 mm. **Ruler:** Elizabeth II **Rev. Designer:** Prince William, 21st Birthday

Date	Mintage	F	VF	XF	Unc	BU
2005	—	—	—	—	—	15.00

KM# 113a 5 POUNDS

28.2800 g., 0.9250 Silver 0.8410 oz. ASW, 38.61 mm. **Ruler:** Elizabeth II **Subject:** Prince William, 21st Birthday

Date	Mintage	F	VF	XF	Unc	BU
2005 Proof	Est. 2,500	Value: 60.00				

KM# 113b 5 POUNDS

39.9400 g., 0.9160 Gold 1.1762 oz. AGW, 38.61 mm. **Ruler:** Elizabeth II **Subject:** Prince William, 21st Birthday

Date	Mintage	F	VF	XF	Unc	BU
2005 Proof	Est. 150	Value: 1,800				

KM# 116 5 POUNDS

Copper-Nickel, 38.61 mm. **Ruler:** Elizabeth II **Subject:** Royal Navy - H.M.S. Warspite

Date	Mintage	F	VF	XF	Unc	BU
2005	—	—	—	—	—	15.00

KM# 116a 5 POUNDS

28.2800 g., 0.9250 Silver 0.8410 oz. ASW, 38.61 mm. **Ruler:** Elizabeth II **Subject:** British Navy - H.M.S. Warspite **Rev:** Multicolor flag

Date	Mintage	F	VF	XF	Unc	BU
2005 Proof	Est. 15,000	Value: 55.00				

KM# 70 5 POUNDS

28.2800 g., 0.9250 Silver 0.8410 oz. ASW, 38.6 mm. **Ruler:** Elizabeth II **Subject:** Queen's 80th Birthday **Obv:** Crowned bust right - gilt **Obv. Legend:** ELIZABETH II - ALDERNARY **Rev:** 1/2 length figures of Queen mother and daughter hugging, facing

Date	Mintage	F	VF	XF	Unc	BU
2006 Proof	—	Value: 45.00				

KM# 126 5 POUNDS

Copper-Nickel, 38.61 mm. **Ruler:** Elizabeth II **Rev:** Elizabeth I

Date	Mintage	F	VF	XF	Unc	BU
2006	—	—	—	—	—	12.00

KM# 126a 5 POUNDS

28.2800 g., 0.9250 Silver 0.8410 oz. ASW, 38.61 mm. **Ruler:** Elizabeth II **Rev:** Queen Elizabeth I

Date	Mintage	F	VF	XF	Unc	BU
2006 Proof	Est. 25,000	Value: 55.00				

KM# 126b 5 POUNDS

39.9400 g., 0.9160 Gold 1.1762 oz. AGW, 38.61 mm. **Ruler:** Elizabeth II **Rev:** Queen Elizabeth I

Date	Mintage	F	VF	XF	Unc	BU
2006 Proof	—	Value: 1,850				

KM# 127 5 POUNDS

Copper-Nickel, 38.61 mm. **Ruler:** Elizabeth II **Rev:** Sir Isaac Newton

Date	Mintage	F	VF	XF	Unc	BU
2006	—	—	—	—	—	15.00

KM# 127a 5 POUNDS

28.2800 g., 0.9250 Silver 0.8410 oz. ASW, 38.61 mm. **Ruler:** Elizabeth II **Rev:** Sir Isaac Newton

Date	Mintage	F	VF	XF	Unc	BU
2006 Proof	—	Value: 55.00				

KM# 127b 5 POUNDS

39.9400 g., 0.9160 Gold 1.1762 oz. AGW, 38.61 mm. **Ruler:** Elizabeth II **Rev:** Sir Isaac Newton

Date	Mintage	F	VF	XF	Unc	BU
2006 Proof	—	Value: 1,850				

KM# 128 5 POUNDS

Copper-Nickel, 38.61 mm. **Ruler:** Elizabeth II **Rev:** William Shapespeare

Date	Mintage	F	VF	XF	Unc	BU
2006	—	—	—	—	—	15.00

KM# 128a 5 POUNDS

28.2800 g., 0.9250 Silver 0.8410 oz. ASW, 38.61 mm. **Ruler:** Elizabeth II **Rev:** William Shakespeare

Date	Mintage	F	VF	XF	Unc	BU
2006 Proof	—	Value: 55.00				

KM# 128b 5 POUNDS

39.9400 g., 0.9160 Gold 1.1762 oz. AGW, 38.61 mm. **Ruler:** Elizabeth II **Rev:** William Shakespeare

Date	Mintage	F	VF	XF	Unc	BU
2006 Proof	—	Value: 1,850				

KM# 129 5 POUNDS

Copper-Nickel, 38.61 mm. **Ruler:** Elizabeth II **Rev:** Charles Dickens

Date	Mintage	F	VF	XF	Unc	BU
2006	—	—	—	—	—	15.00

KM# 129a 5 POUNDS

28.2800 g., 0.9250 Silver 0.8410 oz. ASW, 38.61 mm. **Ruler:** Elizabeth II **Rev:** Charles Dickens

Date	Mintage	F	VF	XF	Unc	BU
2006 Proof	—	Value: 55.00				

KM# 129b 5 POUNDS
39.9400 g., 0.9160 Gold 1.1762 oz. AGW, 38.61 mm. **Ruler:** Elizabeth II **Rev:** Charles Dickens

Date	Mintage	F	VF	XF	Unc	BU
2006 Proof	—	Value: 1,850				

KM# 132 5 POUNDS
Copper-Nickel, 38.61 mm. **Ruler:** Elizabeth II **Rev:** Elizabeth II Corronation

Date	Mintage	F	VF	XF	Unc	BU
2006	—	—	—	—	—	15.00

KM# 132a 5 POUNDS
28.2800 g., 0.9250 Silver 0.8410 oz. ASW, 38.61 mm. **Ruler:** Elizabeth II **Rev:** Elizabeth II Corronation

Date	Mintage	F	VF	XF	Unc	BU
2006 Proof	Est. 25,000	Value: 55.00				

KM# 133 5 POUNDS
28.2800 g., Copper-Nickel, 38.61 mm. **Ruler:** Elizabeth II **Obv:** Head in tiara right **Obv. Designer:** Ian Rank-Broadley **Rev:** Bust in tiara right **Rev. Designer:** Raphael Maklouf

Date	Mintage	F	VF	XF	Unc	BU
2006	—	—	—	—	—	15.00

KM# 133a 5 POUNDS
28.2800 g., 0.9250 Silver 0.8410 oz. ASW, 38.61 mm. **Ruler:** Elizabeth II **Obv:** Head in tiara right **Obv. Designer:** Ian Rank-Broadley **Rev:** Bust in tiara right **Rev. Designer:** Raphael Maklouf

Date	Mintage	F	VF	XF	Unc	BU
2006 Proof	—	Value: 55.00				

KM# 133b 5 POUNDS
39.9400 g., 0.9160 Gold 1.1762 oz. AGW, 38.61 mm. **Ruler:** Elizabeth II **Obv:** Head in tiara right **Obv. Designer:** Ian Rank-Broadley **Rev:** Bust in tiara right **Rev. Designer:** Raphael Maklouf

Date	Mintage	F	VF	XF	Unc	BU
2006 Proof	—	Value: 1,850				

KM# 133b.1 5 POUNDS
38.9400 g., 0.9160 Gold with diamonds 1.1467 oz. AGW, 38.61 mm. **Ruler:** Elizabeth II **Obv:** Head in tiara right **Obv. Designer:** Ira Rank-Broadley **Rev:** Bust in tiara right **Rev. Designer:** Raphael Maklouf

Date	Mintage	F	VF	XF	Unc	BU
2006 Proof	—	Value: 2,000				

KM# 138 5 POUNDS
28.2800 g., 0.9250 Silver 0.8410 oz. ASW, 38.61 mm. **Ruler:** Elizabeth II **Obv:** Shield **Rev:** Soccer player

Date	Mintage	F	VF	XF	Unc	BU
2006 Proof	—	Value: 55.00				

KM# 139 5 POUNDS
28.2800 g., 0.9250 Silver 0.8410 oz. ASW, 38.61 mm. **Ruler:** Elizabeth II **Obv:** Shield **Rev:** Soccer player

Date	Mintage	F	VF	XF	Unc	BU
2006 Proof	—	Value: 55.00				

KM# 140 5 POUNDS
28.2800 g., 0.9250 Silver 0.8410 oz. ASW, 38.61 mm. **Ruler:** Elizabeth II **Obv:** Shield **Rev:** Soccer player

Date	Mintage	F	VF	XF	Unc	BU
2006 Proof	—	Value: 55.00				

KM# 141 5 POUNDS
28.2800 g., 0.9250 Silver 0.8410 oz. ASW, 38.61 mm. **Ruler:** Elizabeth II **Obv:** Shield **Rev:** Soccer player

Date	Mintage	F	VF	XF	Unc	BU
2006 Proof	—	Value: 55.00				

KM# 142 5 POUNDS
28.2800 g., 0.9250 Silver 0.8410 oz. ASW, 38.61 mm. **Ruler:** Elizabeth II **Obv:** Shield **Rev:** Soccer player

Date	Mintage	F	VF	XF	Unc	BU
2006 Proof	—	Value: 55.00				

KM# 143 5 POUNDS
28.2800 g., 0.9250 Silver 0.8410 oz. ASW, 38.61 mm. **Ruler:** Elizabeth II **Obv:** Shield **Rev:** Soccer player

Date	Mintage	F	VF	XF	Unc	BU
2006 Proof	—	Value: 55.00				

KM# 144 5 POUNDS
28.2800 g., 0.9250 Silver 0.8410 oz. ASW, 38.61 mm. **Ruler:** Elizabeth II **Obv:** Shield **Rev:** Soccer player

Date	Mintage	F	VF	XF	Unc	BU
2006 Proof	—	Value: 55.00				

KM# 145 5 POUNDS
28.2800 g., 0.9250 Silver 0.8410 oz. ASW, 38.61 mm. **Ruler:** Elizabeth II **Obv:** Shield **Rev:** Soccer player

Date	Mintage	F	VF	XF	Unc	BU
2006 Proof	—	Value: 55.00				

KM# 146 5 POUNDS
28.2800 g., 0.9250 Silver 0.8410 oz. ASW, 38.61 mm. **Ruler:** Elizabeth II **Obv:** Shield **Rev:** Soccer player

Date	Mintage	F	VF	XF	Unc	BU
2006 Proof	—	Value: 55.00				

KM# 147 5 POUNDS
28.2800 g., 0.9250 Silver 0.8410 oz. ASW, 38.61 mm. **Ruler:** Elizabeth II **Obv:** Shield **Rev:** Soccer player

Date	Mintage	F	VF	XF	Unc	BU
2006 Proof	—	Value: 55.00				

KM# 148 5 POUNDS
Copper-Nickel, 38.61 mm. **Ruler:** Elizabeth II **Subject:** Victoria Cross, 150th Anniversary **Rev:** Henry Ramage and Victoria Cross medal

Date	Mintage	F	VF	XF	Unc	BU
2006	—	—	—	—	—	15.00

KM# 148a 5 POUNDS
28.2800 g., 0.9250 Silver 0.8410 oz. ASW, 38.61 mm. **Ruler:** Elizabeth II **Subject:** Victoria Cross, 150th Anniversary **Rev:** Henry Ramage and Victoria Cross medal

Date	Mintage	F	VF	XF	Unc	BU
2006 Proof	Est. 30,000	Value: 55.00				

KM# 149 5 POUNDS
28.2800 g., 0.9250 Silver 0.8410 oz. ASW, 38.61 mm. **Ruler:** Elizabeth II **Subject:** Victoria Cross, 150th Anniversary **Rev:** Charles Lucas, Victoria Cross medal

Date	Mintage	F	VF	XF	Unc	BU
2006 Proof	Est. 30,000	Value: 55.00				

KM# 150 5 POUNDS
28.2800 g., 0.9250 Silver 0.8410 oz. ASW, 38.61 mm. **Ruler:** Elizabeth II **Subject:** Victoria Cross, 150th Anniversary **Rev:** Ernest Smith, Victoria Cross medal

Date	Mintage	F	VF	XF	Unc	BU
2006 Proof	Est. 30,000	Value: 55.00				

KM# 151 5 POUNDS
28.2800 g., 0.9250 Silver 0.8410 oz. ASW, 38.61 mm. **Ruler:** Elizabeth II **Subject:** Victoria Cross, 150th Anniversary **Rev:** Stanley Hollis, Victoria Cross medal

Date	Mintage	F	VF	XF	Unc	BU
2006 Proof	Est. 30,000	Value: 55.00				

KM# 152 5 POUNDS
28.2800 g., 0.9250 Silver 0.8410 oz. ASW, 38.61 mm. **Ruler:** Elizabeth II **Subject:** Victoria Cross, 150th Anniversary **Rev:** Geoffrey Keyes, Victoria Cross medal

Date	Mintage	F	VF	XF	Unc	BU
2006 Proof	Est. 30,000	Value: 55.00				

KM# 153 5 POUNDS
28.2800 g., 0.9250 Silver 0.8410 oz. ASW, 38.61 mm. **Ruler:** Elizabeth II **Subject:** Victoria Cross, 150th Anniversary **Rev:** Daniel Laidlow, Victoria Cross medal

Date	Mintage	F	VF	XF	Unc	BU
2006 Proof	Est. 30,000	Value: 55.00				

KM# 158 5 POUNDS
Copper-Nickel, 38.61 mm. **Ruler:** Elizabeth II **Rev:** Capt. James Cook

Date	Mintage	F	VF	XF	Unc	BU
2007	—	—	—	—	—	15.00

KM# 158a 5 POUNDS
28.2800 g., 0.9250 Silver 0.8410 oz. ASW, 38.61 mm. **Ruler:** Elizabeth II **Rev:** Capt. Jmes Cook

Date	Mintage	F	VF	XF	Unc	BU
2007 Proof	Est. 25,000	Value: 55.00				

KM# 158b 5 POUNDS
39.9400 g., 0.9160 Gold 1.1762 oz. AGW, 38.61 mm. **Ruler:** Elizabeth II **Rev:** Capt. James Cook

Date	Mintage	F	VF	XF	Unc	BU
2007 Proof	—	Value: 1,850				

KM# 159 5 POUNDS
Copper-Nickel, 38.61 mm. **Ruler:** Elizabeth II **Rev:** Sir Edward Elgar

Date	Mintage	F	VF	XF	Unc	BU
2007	—	—	—	—	—	15.00

KM# 159a 5 POUNDS
28.2800 g., 0.9250 Silver 0.8410 oz. ASW, 38.61 mm. **Ruler:** Elizabeth II **Rev:** Sir Edward Elgar

Date	Mintage	F	VF	XF	Unc	BU
2007 Proof	Est. 25,000	Value: 55.00				

KM# 159b 5 POUNDS
0.9160 g., 39.9400 Gold 1.1762 oz. AGW, 38.61 mm. **Ruler:** Elizabeth II **Rev:** Sir Edward Elgar

Date	Mintage	F	VF	XF	Unc	BU
2007 Proof	—	Value: 1,850				

KM# 160 5 POUNDS
Copper-Nickel, 38.61 mm. **Ruler:** Elizabeth II **Rev:** Sir Francis Drake

Date	Mintage	F	VF	XF	Unc	BU
2007	—	Value: 15.00				

KM# 160a 5 POUNDS
28.2800 g., 0.9250 Silver 0.8410 oz. ASW, 38.61 mm. **Ruler:** Elizabeth II **Rev:** Sir Francis Drake

Date	Mintage	F	VF	XF	Unc	BU
2007 Proof	Est. 25,000	Value: 55.00				

KM# 160b 5 POUNDS
39.9400 g., 0.9160 Gold 1.1762 oz. AGW, 38.61 mm. **Ruler:** Elizabeth II **Rev:** Sir Francis Drake

Date	Mintage	F	VF	XF	Unc	BU
2007 Proof	—	Value: 1,850				

KM# 161 5 POUNDS
Copper-Nickel, 38.61 mm. **Ruler:** Elizabeth II **Rev:** John Constable

Date	Mintage	F	VF	XF	Unc	BU
2007	—	—	—	—	—	15.00

KM# 161a 5 POUNDS
28.2800 g., 0.9260 Silver 0.8419 oz. ASW, 38.61 mm. **Ruler:** Elizabeth II **Rev:** John Constable

Date	Mintage	F	VF	XF	Unc	BU
2007 Proof	Est. 25,000	Value: 55.00				

KM# 162 5 POUNDS
28.2800 g., 0.9250 Silver partially gilt 0.8410 oz. ASW, 38.61 mm. **Ruler:** Elizabeth II **Rev:** Henry VII

Date	Mintage	F	VF	XF	Unc	BU
2007 Proof	Est. 37,500	Value: 55.00				

KM# 161b 5 POUNDS
39.9400 g., 0.9160 Gold 1.1762 oz. AGW, 39.94 mm. **Ruler:** Elizabeth II **Rev:** John Constable

Date	Mintage	F	VF	XF	Unc	BU
2007 Proof	—	Value: 1,850				

KM# 163 5 POUNDS
28.2800 g., 0.9250 Silver partially gilt 0.8410 oz. ASW, 38.61 mm. **Ruler:** Elizabeth II **Rev:** Henry VIII

Date	Mintage	F	VF	XF	Unc	BU
2007 Proof	Est. 37,500	Value: 55.00				

KM# 164 5 POUNDS
28.2800 g., 0.9250 Silver partially gilt 0.8410 oz. ASW, 38.61 mm. **Ruler:** Elizabeth II **Rev:** Edward VI

Date	Mintage	F	VF	XF	Unc	BU
2007 Proof	Est. 37,500	Value: 55.00				

KM# 165 5 POUNDS
28.2800 g., 0.9250 Silver partially gilt 0.8410 oz. ASW, 38.61 mm. **Ruler:** Elizabeth II **Rev:** Mary I

Date	Mintage	F	VF	XF	Unc	BU
2007 Proof	Est. 37,500	Value: 55.00				

KM# 166 5 POUNDS
28.2800 g., 0.9250 Silver 0.8410 oz. ASW, 38.61 mm. **Ruler:** Elizabeth II **Rev:** Elizabeth I

Date	Mintage	F	VF	XF	Unc	BU
2007 Proof	Est. 37,500	Value: 55.00				

KM# 167 5 POUNDS
28.2800 g., 0.9250 Silver partially gilt 0.8410 oz. ASW, 38.61 mm. **Ruler:** Elizabeth II **Rev:** James I

Date	Mintage	F	VF	XF	Unc	BU
2007 Proof	Est. 37,500	Value: 55.00				

KM# 168 5 POUNDS
28.2800 g., 0.9250 Silver 0.8410 oz. ASW, 38.61 mm. **Ruler:** Elizabeth II **Rev:** Charles I

Date	Mintage	F	VF	XF	Unc	BU
2007 Proof	Est. 37,500	Value: 55.00				

KM# 169 5 POUNDS
28.2800 g., 0.9250 Silver partially gilt 0.8410 oz. ASW, 38.61 mm. **Ruler:** Elizabeth II **Rev:** Charles II

Date	Mintage	F	VF	XF	Unc	BU
2007 Proof	Est. 37,500	Value: 55.00				

KM# 170 5 POUNDS
28.2800 g., 0.9160 Silver partially gilt 0.8328 oz. ASW, 38.61 mm. **Ruler:** Elizabeth II **Rev:** James II

Date	Mintage	F	VF	XF	Unc	BU
2007 Proof	Est. 37,500	Value: 55.00				

KM# 171 5 POUNDS
28.2800 g., 0.9250 Silver partially gilt 0.8410 oz. ASW, 38.61 mm. **Ruler:** Elizabeth II **Rev:** William and Mary

Date	Mintage	F	VF	XF	Unc	BU
2007 Proof	Est. 37,500	Value: 55.00				

KM# 172 5 POUNDS
28.2800 g., 0.9250 Silver partially gilt 0.8410 oz. ASW, 38.61 mm. **Ruler:** Elizabeth II **Rev:** William III

Date	Mintage	F	VF	XF	Unc	BU
2007 Proof	37,500	Value: 55.00				

KM# 173 5 POUNDS
28.2800 g., 0.9250 Silver 0.8410 oz. ASW, 38.61 mm. **Ruler:** Elizabeth II **Rev:** Anne

Date	Mintage	F	VF	XF	Unc	BU
2007 Proof	Est. 37,500	Value: 55.00				

KM# 175 5 POUNDS
28.2800 g., 0.9250 Copper-Nickel 0.8410 oz., 38.61 mm. **Ruler:** Elizabeth II **Subject:** Princess Diana, 10th Anniversary of Death

Date	Mintage	F	VF	XF	Unc	BU
2007	—	—	—	—	—	15.00

KM# 177 5 POUNDS
Copper-Nickel, 38.61 mm. **Ruler:** Elizabeth II **Subject:** Elizabeth II & Prince Philip, 60th Wedding Anniversary **Rev:** 1947 Wedding Portrait

Date	Mintage	F	VF	XF	Unc	BU
2007	—	—	—	—	—	15.00

KM# 177a 5 POUNDS
28.2800 g., 0.9250 Silver 0.8410 oz. ASW, 38.61 mm. **Ruler:** Elizabeth II **Subject:** Elizabeth II and Prince Philip, 60th Wedding Anniversary **Rev:** 1947 Wedding Portrait

Date	Mintage	F	VF	XF	Unc	BU
2007 Proof	—	Value: 55.00				

KM# 178 5 POUNDS
Copper-Nickel, 38.61 mm. **Ruler:** Elizabeth II **Subject:** Elizabeth II and Prince Philip, 60th Wedding Anniversary **Rev:** State Carriage

Date	Mintage	F	VF	XF	Unc	BU
2007	—	—	—	—	—	15.00

KM# 178a 5 POUNDS
28.2800 g., 0.9250 Silver 0.8410 oz. ASW, 38.61 mm. **Ruler:** Elizabeth II **Subject:** Elizabeth II and Prince Philip, 60th Wedding Anniversary **Rev:** State Carriage

Date	Mintage	F	VF	XF	Unc	BU
2007 Proof	—	Value: 55.00				

KM# 179 5 POUNDS
Copper-Nickel, 38.61 mm. **Ruler:** Elizabeth II **Subject:** Elizabeth II and Prince Philip, 60th Wedding Anniversary **Rev:** Honeymoon departure

Date	Mintage	F	VF	XF	Unc	BU
2007	—	—	—	—	—	15.00

KM# 179a 5 POUNDS

28.2800 g., 0.9250 Silver 0.8410 oz. ASW, 38.61 mm. **Ruler:** Elizabeth II **Subject:** Elizabeth II and Prince Philip, 60th Wedding Anniversary **Rev:** Honeymoon departure

Date	Mintage	F	VF	XF	Unc	BU
2007 Proof	—	Value: 55.00				

KM# 180 5 POUNDS

Copper-Nickel, 38.61 mm. **Ruler:** Elizabeth II **Subject:** Elizabeth II and Prince Philip, 60th Wedding Anniversary **Rev:** Portraits

Date	Mintage	F	VF	XF	Unc	BU
2007	—	—	—	—	—	15.00

KM# 180a 5 POUNDS

28.2800 g., 0.9250 Silver 0.8410 oz. ASW, 38.61 mm. **Ruler:** Elizabeth II **Subject:** Elizabeth II and Prince Philip, 60th Wedding Anniversary **Rev:** Elizabeth II and Philip portraits

Date	Mintage	F	VF	XF	Unc	BU
2007 Proof	—	Value: 55.00				

KM# 181 5 POUNDS

28.2800 g., 0.9250 Silver 0.8410 oz. ASW, 38.61 mm. **Ruler:** Elizabeth II **Subject:** Elizabeth II and Prince Philip, 60th Wedding Anniversary **Rev:** Bridal couple outside Westminster Abbey

Date	Mintage	F	VF	XF	Unc	BU
2007 Proof	Est. 30,000	Value: 55.00				

KM# 182 5 POUNDS

28.2800 g., 0.9250 Silver 0.8410 oz. ASW, 38.61 mm. **Ruler:** Elizabeth II **Subject:** Elizabeth II and Prince Philip, 60th Wedding Anniversary **Rev:** Birth of Prince Charles

Date	Mintage	F	VF	XF	Unc	BU
2007 Proof	Est. 30,000	Value: 55.00				

KM# 183 5 POUNDS

28.2800 g., 0.9250 Silver 0.8410 oz. ASW, 38.61 mm. **Ruler:** Elizabeth II **Subject:** Elizabeth II and Prince Philip, 60th Wedding Anniversary **Rev:** Modern portrait of Elizabeth and Philip

Date	Mintage	F	VF	XF	Unc	BU
2007 Proof	Est. 30,000	Value: 55.00				

KM# 184 5 POUNDS

28.2800 g., 0.9250 Silver 0.8410 oz. ASW, 38.61 mm. **Ruler:** Elizabeth II **Subject:** End of World War I, 90th Anniversary **Rev:** Soldiers and workers, flag in background

Date	Mintage	F	VF	XF	Unc	BU
2008 Proof	Est. 15,000	Value: 55.00				

KM# 184a 5 POUNDS

39.9400 g., 0.9160 Gold 1.1762 oz. AGW, 38.61 mm. **Ruler:** Elizabeth II **Subject:** End of World War I, 90th Anniversary **Rev:** Soldiers and workers, flag in background

Date	Mintage	F	VF	XF	Unc	BU
2008 Proof	Est. 250	Value: 1,800				

KM# 185 5 POUNDS

28.2800 g., 0.9250 Silver 0.8410 oz. ASW, 38.61 mm. **Ruler:** Elizabeth II **Subject:** End of World War I, 90th Anniversary **Rev:** Tank and soldier

Date	Mintage	F	VF	XF	Unc	BU
2008 Proof	Est. 15,000	Value: 55.00				

KM# 185a 5 POUNDS

39.9400 g., 0.9160 Gold 1.1762 oz. AGW, 38.61 mm. **Ruler:** Elizabeth II **Subject:** End of World War I, 90th Anniversary **Rev:** Tank and soldier

Date	Mintage	F	VF	XF	Unc	BU
2008 Proof	Est. 250	Value: 1,800				

KM# 186 5 POUNDS

28.2800 g., 0.9250 Silver 0.8410 oz. ASW, 38.61 mm. **Ruler:** Elizabeth II **Subject:** End of World War I, 90th Anniversary **Rev:** Soldiers and gravesites

Date	Mintage	F	VF	XF	Unc	BU
2008 Proof	Est. 15,000	Value: 55.00				

KM# 186a 5 POUNDS

39.9400 g., 0.9160 Gold 1.1762 oz. AGW, 38.61 mm. **Ruler:** Elizabeth II **Subject:** End of World War I, 90th Anniversary **Rev:** Soldiers and gravesites

Date	Mintage	F	VF	XF	Unc	BU
2008 Proof	Est. 250	Value: 1,800				

KM# 187 5 POUNDS

28.2800 g., 0.9250 Silver 0.8410 oz. ASW, 38.61 mm. **Ruler:** Elizabeth II **Subject:** End of World War I, 90th Anniversary **Rev:** Propaganda

Date	Mintage	F	VF	XF	Unc	BU
2008 Proof	Est. 250	Value: 1,800				

KM# 190 5 POUNDS

Copper-Nickel, 38.61 mm. **Ruler:** Elizabeth II **Rev:** Concorde

Date	Mintage	F	VF	XF	Unc	BU
2008	—	—	—	—	—	15.00

KM# 190a 5 POUNDS

28.2800 g., 0.9250 Silver 0.8410 oz. ASW, 38.61 mm. **Ruler:** Elizabeth II **Rev:** Concorde

Date	Mintage	F	VF	XF	Unc	BU
2008 Proof	—	Value: 55.00				

KM# 190b 5 POUNDS

1090.8600 g., 0.9160 Gold 32.124 oz. AGW, 38.61 mm. **Ruler:** Elizabeth II **Rev:** Concorde

Date	Mintage	F	VF	XF	Unc	BU
2008 Proof	Est. 250	Value: 1,800				

KM# 85 5 POUNDS

28.2800 g., Copper-Nickel, 38.61 mm. **Ruler:** Elizabeth II **Subject:** Mini Cooper 50th Anniversary **Rev:** 1959 Mini Cooper on tiled floor **Rev. Designer:** David Cornell

Date	Mintage	F	VF	XF	Unc	BU
2009	50,000	—	—	—	—	17.50

KM# 86 5 POUNDS

28.2800 g., 0.9250 Silver 0.8410 oz. ASW, 38.61 mm. **Ruler:** Elizabeth II **Subject:** Mini Cooper, 50th Anniversary **Rev:** 1959 Mini Cooper multicolor British flag on roof **Rev. Designer:** David Cornell

Date	Mintage	F	VF	XF	Unc	BU
2009 Proof	—	Value: 75.00				

KM# 87 5 POUNDS

28.2800 g., 0.9250 Silver 0.8410 oz. ASW, 38.61 mm. **Ruler:** Elizabeth II **Subject:** Mini Cooper, 50th Anniversary **Rev:** Mini Cooper, red and pink flowers **Rev. Designer:** David Cornell

Date	Mintage	F	VF	XF	Unc	BU
2009 Proof	2,000	Value: 75.00				

KM# 88 5 POUNDS

28.2800 g., 0.9250 Silver 0.8410 oz. ASW, 38.61 mm. **Ruler:** Elizabeth II **Subject:** Mini Cooper, 50th Anniversary **Rev:** Mini Cooper, 4 views **Rev. Designer:** Kerry Jones

Date	Mintage	F	VF	XF	Unc	BU
2009 Proof	2,000	Value: 75.00				

KM# 89 5 POUNDS

28.2800 g., 0.9250 Silver 0.8410 oz. ASW, 38.61 mm. **Ruler:** Elizabeth II **Subject:** Mini Cooper, 50th Anniversary **Rev:** Rally Minis **Rev. Designer:** Kerry Jones and David Cornell

Date	Mintage	F	VF	XF	Unc	BU
2009 Proof	2,000	Value: 75.00				

KM# 193 5 POUNDS

28.2800 g., 0.9250 Silver 0.8410 oz. ASW, 38.61 mm. **Ruler:** Elizabeth II **Subject:** British Automobiles **Rev:** Morris Minor

Date	Mintage	F	VF	XF	Unc	BU
2009 Proof	20,000	Value: 55.00				

KM# 194 5 POUNDS

28.2800 g., 0.9250 Silver 0.8410 oz. ASW, 38.61 mm. **Ruler:** Elizabeth II **Subject:** British Automobiles **Rev:** Land Rover series 1

Date	Mintage	F	VF	XF	Unc	BU
2009 Proof	Est. 20,000	Value: 55.00				

KM# 195 5 POUNDS

28.2800 g., 0.9250 Silver 0.8410 oz. ASW, 38.61 mm. **Ruler:** Elizabeth II **Subject:** British Automobiles **Rev:** Jaguar E type series 1

Date	Mintage	F	VF	XF	Unc	BU
2009 Proof	Est. 20,000	Value: 55.00				

KM# 196 5 POUNDS

28.2800 g., 0.9250 Silver 0.8410 oz. ASW, 38.61 mm. **Ruler:** Elizabeth II **Subject:** British Automobiles **Rev:** Rolls Royce Silver Ghost

Date	Mintage	F	VF	XF	Unc	BU
2009 Proof	Est. 20,000	Value: 55.00				

KM# 197 5 POUNDS

28.2800 g., 0.9250 Silver 0.8410 oz. ASW, 38.61 mm. **Ruler:** Elizabeth II **Subject:** British Automobiles **Rev:** Austrin Seven "Baby Austin"

Date	Mintage	F	VF	XF	Unc	BU
2009 Proof	Est. 20,000	Value: 55.00				

KM# 198 5 POUNDS

28.2800 g., 0.9250 Silver 0.8410 oz. ASW, 38.61 mm. **Ruler:** Elizabeth II **Subject:** British Automobiles **Rev:** Triumph Herald

Date	Mintage	F	VF	XF	Unc	BU
2009 Proof	Est. 20,000	Value: 55.00				

KM# 199 5 POUNDS

28.2800 g., 0.9250 Silver 0.8410 oz. ASW **Ruler:** Elizabeth II **Subject:** British Automobiles **Rev:** Bentley R type Contiental

Date	Mintage	F	VF	XF	Unc	BU
2009 Proof	Est. 20,000	Value: 55.00				

KM# 200 5 POUNDS

28.2800 g., 0.9250 Silver 0.8410 oz. ASW, 38.61 mm. **Ruler:** Elizabeth II **Subject:** British Automobiles **Rev:** Lotus Elite (1957)

Date	Mintage	F	VF	XF	Unc	BU
2009 Proof	Est. 20,000	Value: 55.00				

KM# 202 5 POUNDS

28.2800 g., 0.9250 Silver 0.8410 oz. ASW, 38.61 mm. **Ruler:** Elizabeth II **Subject:** British Automobiles **Rev:** Austin healey Sprint MK 1

Date	Mintage	F	VF	XF	Unc	BU
2009 Proof	Est. 20,000	Value: 55.00				

KM# 203 5 POUNDS

28.2800 g., 0.9250 Silver 0.8410 oz. ASW, 38.61 mm. **Ruler:** Elizabeth II **Subject:** British Automobiles **Rev:** Bentley 4-1/2 Litre

Date	Mintage	F	VF	XF	Unc	BU
2009 Proof	Est. 20,000	Value: 55.00				

KM# 204 5 POUNDS

28.2800 g., 0.9250 Silver 0.8410 oz. ASW, 38.61 mm. **Ruler:** Elizabeth II **Subject:** British Automobiles **Rev:** Hillman Imp

Date	Mintage	F	VF	XF	Unc	BU
2009 Proof	Est. 20,000	Value: 55.00				

KM# 205 5 POUNDS

28.2800 g., 0.9250 Silver 0.8410 oz. ASW, 38.61 mm. **Ruler:** Elizabeth II **Subject:** British Automobiles **Rev:** MGB Roadster MK 1

Date	Mintage	F	VF	XF	Unc	BU
2009 Proof	Est. 20,000	Value: 55.00				

KM# 206 5 POUNDS

28.2800 g., 0.9250 Silver 0.8410 oz. ASW, 38.61 mm. **Ruler:** Elizabeth II **Subject:** British Automobiles **Rev:** MG TC Midget

Date	Mintage	F	VF	XF	Unc	BU
2009 Proof	Est. 20,000	Value: 55.00				

KM# 207 5 POUNDS

28.2800 g., 0.9250 Silver 0.8410 oz. ASW, 38.61 mm. **Ruler:** Elizabeth II **Subject:** British Automobiles **Rev:** BMC Mini

Date	Mintage	F	VF	XF	Unc	BU
2009 Proof	Est. 20,000	Value: 55.00				

KM# 208 5 POUNDS

28.2800 g., 0.9250 Silver 0.8410 oz. ASW, 38.61 mm. **Ruler:** Elizabeth II **Subject:** British Automobiles **Rev:** Morgan Plus Four

Date	Mintage	F	VF	XF	Unc	BU
2009 Proof	Est. 20,000	Value: 55.00				

KM# 209 5 POUNDS

28.2800 g., 0.9250 Silver 0.8410 oz. ASW, 38.61 mm. **Ruler:** Elizabeth II **Subject:** British Automobiles **Rev:** Rover P5B

Date	Mintage	F	VF	XF	Unc	BU
2009 Proof	Est. 20,000	Value: 55.00				

KM# 210 5 POUNDS

28.2800 g., 0.9250 Silver 0.8410 oz. ASW, 38.61 mm. **Ruler:** Elizabeth II **Subject:** British Automobiles **Rev:** Vauhall - Prince Henry

Date	Mintage	F	VF	XF	Unc	BU
2009 Proof	Est. 20,000	Value: 55.00				

KM# 201 5 POUNDS

28.2800 g., 0.9250 Silver 0.8410 oz. ASW, 38.61 mm. **Ruler:** Elizabeth II **Subject:** British Automobiles **Rev:** Aston Martin DB 5 (1963)

Date	Mintage	F	VF	XF	Unc	BU
2009 Proof	Est. 20,000	Value: 55.00				

KM# 36 10 POUNDS

155.5170 g., 0.9250 Silver 4.6248 oz. ASW, 65.06 mm. **Ruler:** Elizabeth II **Subject:** Last Flight of the Concorde **Obv:** Crowned bust right **Obv. Legend:** ELIIZABETH II - ALDERNEY **Obv. Designer:** Raphael Maklouf **Rev:** Concorde in flight **Rev. Legend:** CONCORDE 1969 - 2003 **Rev. Designer:** Emma Noble **Edge:** Reeded **Note:** Illustration reduced.

Date	Mintage	F	VF	XF	Unc	BU
2003 Proof	1,969	Value: 200				

KM# 55 10 POUNDS

155.5100 g., 0.9250 Silver 4.6246 oz. ASW, 65 mm. **Ruler:** Elizabeth II **Subject:** WWII Liberation **Obv:** Elizabeth II by Maklouf sign **Rev:** Churchill flashing the "V" **Edge:** Reeded

Date	Mintage	F	VF	XF	Unc	BU
2005 Proof	1,945	Value: 350				

KM# 120 10 POUNDS

155.5000 g., 0.9250 Silver 4.6243 oz. ASW, 65 mm. **Ruler:** Elizabeth II **Subject:** Trafalgar - England espects that every man will do his duty

Date	Mintage	F	VF	XF	Unc	BU
2005 Proof	—	Value: 275				

KM# 82 10 POUNDS

155.5170 g., Silver, 65.03 mm. **Ruler:** Elizabeth II **Obv:** Crowned bust right **Obv. Legend:** ELIZABETH II - ALDERNEY **Obv. Designer:** Raphael Maklouf **Rev:** Four small gilt coinage busts in ornate quadralobe **Rev. Legend:** + HER MAJESTY QUEEN ELIZABETH II + EIGHTIETH BIRTHDAY + **Rev. Designer:** Michael Guilfoyle **Edge:** Reeded, gilt

Date	Mintage	F	VF	XF	Unc	BU
2006 Proof	1,926	Value: 200				

KM# 135 10 POUNDS

155.5000 g., 0.9250 Silver with diamonds 4.6243 oz. ASW, 65 mm. **Ruler:** Elizabeth II **Obv:** Head in tiara right **Rev:** Bust in tiara right

Date	Mintage	F	VF	XF	Unc	BU
2006 Proof	Est. 1,000	Value: 250				

KM# 176 10 POUNDS

155.5000 g., 0.9250 Silver 4.6243 oz. ASW, 65 mm. **Ruler:** Elizabeth II **Subject:** Princess Diana, 10th Anniversary of Death

Date	Mintage	F	VF	XF	Unc	BU
2007 Proof	Est. 1,500	Value: 275				

KM# 188 10 POUNDS

155.5000 g., 0.9250 Silver 4.6243 oz. ASW, 65 mm. **Ruler:** Elizabeth II **Subject:** End of World War I, 90th Anniversary

Date	Mintage	F	VF	XF	Unc	BU
2008 Proof	Est. 150	Value: 350				

KM# 191 10 POUNDS

155.5000 g., 0.9250 Silver 4.6243 oz. ASW, 65 mm. **Ruler:** Elizabeth II **Rev:** Corcorde

Date	Mintage	F	VF	XF	Unc	BU
2008 Proof	Est. 750	Value: 275				

KM# 61 25 POUNDS

7.9800 g., 0.9167 Gold 0.2352 oz. AGW, 22 mm. **Ruler:** Elizabeth II **Subject:** Queen's 75th Birthday **Obv:** Queen's portrait right **Obv. Designer:** Raphael Maklouf **Rev:** Queen in casual dress surrounded by rose, thistle, daffodil and pimpernel **Rev. Designer:** David Cornell

Date	Mintage	F	VF	XF	Unc	BU
2001 Proof	—	Value: 375				

KM# 74 25 POUNDS

7.9800 g., 0.9166 Gold 0.2352 oz. AGW **Ruler:** Elizabeth II **Subject:** Queen Elizabet II - Golden Jubilee of Reign **Obv:** Crowned head right **Rev:** Honor guard and trumpets

Date	Mintage	F	VF	XF	Unc	BU
2002 Proof	—	Value: 375				

KM# 28 25 POUNDS

7.9800 g., 0.9167 Gold 0.2352 oz. AGW, 22.05 mm. **Ruler:** Elizabeth II **Subject:** 5th Anniversary Death of Princess Diana **Obv:** Queen's portrait **Rev:** Diana's cameo portrait above denomination **Rev. Designer:** Avril Vaughan **Edge:** Reeded

Date	Mintage	VG	F	VF	XF	Unc
2002 Proof	2,500	Value: 350				

KM# 30 25 POUNDS
7.9800 g., 0.9166 Gold 0.2352 oz. AGW, 22 mm. **Ruler:** Elizabeth II **Subject:** 150th Anniversary Death of the Duke of Wellington **Obv:** Queen's portrait **Rev:** Coat of arms, castle and portrait **Rev. Designer:** Willem Vis **Edge:** Reeded

Date	Mintage	VG	F	VF	XF	Unc
2002 Proof	2,500	Value: 350				

KM# 58 25 POUNDS
7.9800 g., 0.9166 Gold 0.2352 oz. AGW, 22 mm. **Ruler:** Elizabeth II **Subject:** Queen Elizabeth II - Golden Jubilee of Reign **Obv:** Crowned head right **Rev:** Sword hilt and denomination with royal arms in background

Date	Mintage	F	VF	XF	Unc	BU
2002 Proof	2,500	Value: 350				

KM# 32 25 POUNDS
7.9800 g., 0.9166 Gold 0.2352 oz. AGW, 22 mm. **Ruler:** Elizabeth II **Subject:** Prince William **Obv:** Queen's portrait **Rev:** Portrait with open shirt collar **Edge:** Reeded

Date	Mintage	F	VF	XF	Unc	BU
2003 Proof	1,500	Value: 385				

KM# 46 25 POUNDS
7.9800 g., 0.9167 Gold 0.2352 oz. AGW, 22 mm. **Ruler:** Elizabeth II **Obv:** Queen's portrait **Rev:** HMS Mary Rose **Rev. Designer:** Willem Vis **Edge:** Reeded

Date	Mintage	F	VF	XF	Unc	BU
2003 Proof	2,500	Value: 400				

KM# 93 25 POUNDS
7.9800 g., 0.9160 Gold 0.2350 oz. AGW **Ruler:** Elizabeth II **Subject:** Royal navy - Alfred the Great

Date	Mintage	F	VF	XF	Unc	BU
2003 Proof	Est. 1,000	Value: 425				

KM# 39 25 POUNDS
7.9800 g., 0.9167 Gold 0.2352 oz. AGW, 22 mm. **Ruler:** Elizabeth II **Subject:** D-Day **Obv:** Queen's portrait **Rev:** Battleship and transports **Edge:** Reeded

Date	Mintage	F	VF	XF	Unc	BU
2004 Proof	500	Value: 385				

KM# 50 25 POUNDS
7.9800 g., 0.9167 Gold 0.2352 oz. AGW, 22 mm. **Ruler:** Elizabeth II **Obv:** Queen's portrait **Rev:** Locomotive, The Rocket **Rev. Designer:** Robert Lowe **Edge:** Reeded

Date	Mintage	F	VF	XF	Unc	BU
2004 Proof	2,500	Value: 400				

KM# 51 25 POUNDS
7.9800 g., 0.9167 Gold 0.2352 oz. AGW, 22 mm. **Ruler:** Elizabeth II **Obv:** Queen's portrait **Rev:** Locomotive, The Merchant Navy 21C1 **Rev. Designer:** Robert Lowe **Edge:** Reeded

Date	Mintage	F	VF	XF	Unc	BU
2004 Proof	1,500	Value: 400				

KM# 67 25 POUNDS
7.9800 g., 0.9167 Gold 0.2352 oz. AGW, 22 mm. **Ruler:** Elizabeth II **Subject:** Viscount Samuel Hood on his flagship after the Battle of Saints Passage in 1782 **Obv:** Queen's portrait **Rev. Designer:** Willem Vis

Date	Mintage	F	VF	XF	Unc	BU
2005 Proof	—	Value: 350				

KM# 69 25 POUNDS
7.9800 g., 0.9167 Gold 0.2352 oz. AGW, 22 mm. **Ruler:** Elizabeth II **Obv:** Queen's portrait right **Rev:** HMS Revenge fighting at Azores, 1591 **Rev. Designer:** Willem Vis

Date	Mintage	F	VF	XF	Unc	BU
2005 Proof	—	Value: 400				

KM# 109 25 POUNDS
7.9800 g., 0.9160 Gold 0.2350 oz. AGW **Ruler:** Elizabeth II **Subject:** David Beckham **Obv:** Shield **Rev:** Soccer player and ball design

Date	Mintage	F	VF	XF	Unc	BU
2005 Proof	Est. 5,000	Value: 425				

KM# 110 25 POUNDS
7.9800 g., 0.9160 Gold 0.2350 oz. AGW **Ruler:** Elizabeth II **Subject:** Michael Owen **Obv:** Shield **Rev:** Soccer player and ball design

Date	Mintage	F	VF	XF	Unc	BU
2005 Proof	Est. 5,000	Value: 425				

KM# 111 25 POUNDS
7.9800 g., 0.9160 Gold 0.2350 oz. AGW **Ruler:** Elizabeth II **Subject:** Lrank Lampard **Obv:** Shield **Rev:** Soccer player and ball design

Date	Mintage	F	VF	XF	Unc	BU
2005 Proof	Est. 5,000	Value: 425				

KM# 112 25 POUNDS
7.9800 g., 0.9160 Gold 0.2350 oz. AGW **Ruler:** Elizabeth II **Subject:** Jeremiah Campbell **Obv:** Shield **Rev:** Soccer player and ball design.

Date	Mintage	F	VF	XF	Unc	BU
2005 Proof	Est. 5,000	Value: 425				

KM# 117 25 POUNDS
7.9800 g., 0.9160 Gold 0.2350 oz. AGW **Ruler:** Elizabeth II **Subject:** Royal Navy - H.M.S. Warspite

Date	Mintage	F	VF	XF	Unc	BU
2005 Proof	Est. 1,500	Value: 425				

KM# 118 25 POUNDS
7.9800 g., 0.9160 Gold 0.2350 oz. AGW **Ruler:** Elizabeth II **Subject:** Royal Navy - Admiral Sir John Foster Woodward

Date	Mintage	F	VF	XF	Unc	BU
2005 Proof	Est. 1,500	Value: 425				

KM# 121 25 POUNDS
7.9800 g., 0.9160 Gold 0.2350 oz. AGW **Ruler:** Elizabeth II **Series:** Trafalgar - England expects that every man will do his duty

Date	Mintage	F	VF	XF	Unc	BU
2005 Proof	—	Value: 425				

KM# 92 50 POUNDS
1000.0000 g., 0.9250 Silver 29.738 oz. ASW, 100 mm. **Ruler:** Elizabeth II **Rev:** Coronation at Westminster

Date	Mintage	F	VF	XF	Unc	BU
2002	Est. 2,002	Value: 1,100				

KM# 62 50 POUNDS
1000.0000 g., 0.9250 Silver 29.738 oz. ASW, 100 mm. **Ruler:** Elizabeth II **Subject:** 50th Anniversary of Coronation **Obv:** Queen's portrait right **Rev:** State coach in which the Queen travelled to and from her coronation

Date	Mintage	F	VF	XF	Unc	BU
2003 Proof	—	Value: 1,150				

KM# 33 50 POUNDS
1000.0000 g., 0.9250 Silver 29.738 oz. ASW, 100 mm. **Ruler:** Elizabeth II **Subject:** Prince William **Obv:** Queen's portrait **Rev:** Portrait with open shirt collar **Edge:** Reeded

Date	Mintage	F	VF	XF	Unc	BU
2003 Proof	500	Value: 1,200				

KM# 63 50 POUNDS
1000.0000 g., 0.9250 Silver 29.738 oz. ASW, 100 mm. **Ruler:** Elizabeth II **Subject:** 50th Anniversary of Coronation **Obv:** Queen's portrait right **Rev:** St. Edward's crown, royal scepter, orb of England

Date	Mintage	F	VF	XF	Unc	BU
2003 Proof	—	Value: 1,150				

KM# 64 50 POUNDS
1000.0000 g., 0.9250 Silver 29.738 oz. ASW, 100 mm. **Ruler:** Elizabeth II **Subject:** 50th Anniversary of Coronation **Obv:** Queen's portrait right **Rev:** Queen on horseback dressed in the ceremonial uniform of the Colonel in Chief of the Household Brigade

Date	Mintage	F	VF	XF	Unc	BU
2003 Proof	—	Value: 1,150				

KM# 65 50 POUNDS
1000.0000 g., 0.9250 Silver 29.738 oz. ASW, 100 mm. **Ruler:** Elizabeth II **Subject:** 50th Anniversary of Coronation **Obv:** Queen's portrait right **Rev:** The Queen crowned, seated, holding the orb and scepter

Date	Mintage	F	VF	XF	Unc	BU
2003 Proof	—	Value: 1,150				

KM# 40 50 POUNDS
1000.0000 g., 0.9250 Silver 29.738 oz. ASW, 100 mm. **Ruler:** Elizabeth II **Subject:** D-Day **Obv:** Queen's portrait **Rev:** US and British troops wading ashore **Rev. Designer:** Matthew Bonaccorsi **Edge:** Reeded

Date	Mintage	F	VF	XF	Unc	BU
2004 Proof	600	Value: 1,200				

KM# 80 50 POUNDS
1000.0000 g., 0.9250 Silver 29.738 oz. ASW **Ruler:** Elizabeth II **Subject:** 200th Anniversary Battle of Trafalgar **Obv:** Crowned head right

Date	Mintage	F	VF	XF	Unc	BU
2005 Proof	—	Value: 1,200				

KM# 114 50 POUNDS
1000.0000 g., 0.9250 Silver 29.738 oz. ASW, 100 mm. **Ruler:** Elizabeth II **Subject:** Prince William, 21st Birthday

Date	Mintage	F	VF	XF	Unc	BU
2005 Proof	Est. 100	Value: 1,200				

KM# 136 50 POUNDS
1000.0000 g., 0.9250 Silver partially gilt 29.738 oz. ASW, 100 mm. **Ruler:** Elizabeth II **Rev:** Portraits of Elizabeth II and cross of 8 floral emblems

Date	Mintage	F	VF	XF	Unc	BU
2006 Proof	Est. 250	Value: 1,150				

KM# 34 100 POUNDS
1000.0000 g., 0.9166 Gold 29.468 oz. AGW, 100 mm. **Ruler:** Elizabeth II **Subject:** Prince William **Obv:** Queen's portrait **Rev:** Portrait with open shirt collar **Edge:** Reeded

Date	Mintage	F	VF	XF	Unc	BU
2003 Proof	—	Value: 43,500				

KM# 81 100 POUNDS
1000.0000 g., 0.9166 Gold 29.468 oz. AGW **Ruler:** Elizabeth II **Subject:** 200th Anniversary Battle of Trafalgar **Obv:** Crowned head right

Date	Mintage	F	VF	XF	Unc	BU
2005 Proof	—	Value: 43,500				

KM# 37 1000 POUNDS
1090.8600 g., 0.9166 Gold 32.145 oz. AGW, 100 mm. **Ruler:** Elizabeth II **Subject:** Last Flight of the Concorde **Obv:** Queen's portrait **Rev:** Concorde in flight **Edge:** Reeded

Date	Mintage	F	VF	XF	Unc	BU
2003 Proof	34	Value: 47,500				

KM# 41 1000 POUNDS
1000.0000 g., 0.9167 Gold 29.471 oz. AGW, 100 mm. **Ruler:** Elizabeth II **Subject:** D-Day **Obv:** Queen's portrait **Rev:** US and British troops wading ashore **Rev. Designer:** Matthew Bonaccorsi **Edge:** Reeded

Date	Mintage	F	VF	XF	Unc	BU
2004 Proof	60	Value: 43,500				

KM# 115 1000 POUNDS
1098.8600 g., 0.9160 Gold 32.360 oz. AGW, 38.61 mm. **Ruler:** Elizabeth II **Subject:** Prince William, 21st Birthday

Date	Mintage	F	VF	XF	Unc	BU
2005 Proof	Est. 21	Value: 47,500				

KM# 137 1000 POUNDS
1090.8600 g., 0.9160 Gold 32.124 oz. AGW, 100 mm. **Ruler:** Elizabeth II **Rev:** Portraits of Elizabeth II and cross of 8 floral emblems

Date	Mintage	F	VF	XF	Unc	BU
2006 Proof	—	Value: 47,500				

KM# 192 1000 POUNDS
1090.8600 g., 0.9160 Gold 32.124 oz. AGW, 100 mm. **Ruler:** Elizabeth II **Subject:** Prince Charles, 60th Birthday

Date	Mintage	F	VF	XF	Unc	BU
2008 Proof	Est. 30	Value: 47,500				

MINT SETS

KM#	Date	Mintage	Identification	Issue Price	Mkt Val
MS1	2004 (1)	—	Alderney KM#43, Guernsey KM#155, Jersey KM#126, 150th Anniversary of the Crimean War	—	95.00

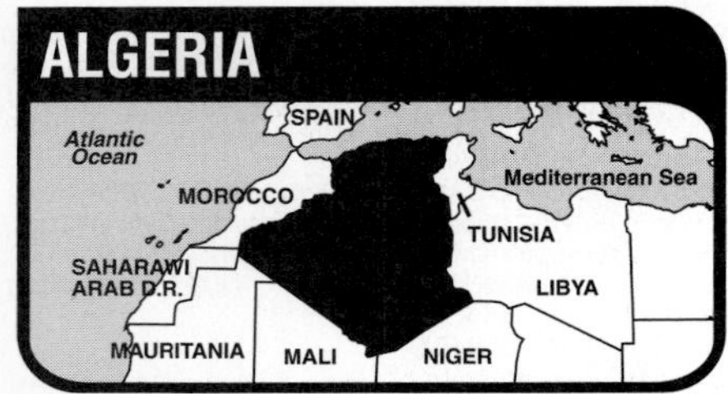

The Democratic and Popular Republic of Algeria, a North African country fronting on the Mediterranean Sea between Tunisia and Morocco, has an area of 919,595 sq. mi. (2,381,740 sq. km.) and a population of 31.6 million. Capital: Algiers (Alger). Most of the country's working population is engaged in agriculture although a recent industrial diversification, financed by oil revenues, is making steady progress. Wines, fruits, iron and zinc ores, phosphates, tobacco products, liquified natural gas, and petroleum are exported.

MONETARY SYSTEMS

100 Centimes = 1 Franc

REPUBLIC

STANDARD COINAGE

KM# 127 1/4 DINAR

1.1400 g., Aluminum, 16.53 mm. **Subject:** Fennec Fox **Obv:** Value in small circle **Rev:** Head facing

Date	Mintage	F	VF	XF	Unc	BU
2003-AH1423	—	—	1.50	3.00	4.50	5.50

KM# 129 DINAR

4.2400 g., Steel, 20.6 mm. **Obv:** Value on silhouette of country, within circle **Rev:** African buffalo's head 3/4 left, ancient drawings above **Edge:** Plain

Date	Mintage	F	VF	XF	Unc	BU
AH1422-2002	—	—	1.00	2.00	3.50	5.50
AH1423-2002	—	—	1.00	2.00	3.50	5.50
AH1423-2003	—	—	1.00	2.00	3.50	5.50
AH1424-2003	—	—	1.00	2.00	3.50	5.50
AH1424-2004	—	—	1.00	2.00	3.50	5.50
AH1426-2005	—	—	1.00	2.00	3.50	5.50
AH1427-2006	—	—	1.00	2.00	3.50	5.50
AH1428-2007	—	—	1.00	2.00	3.50	5.50
AH1430-2009	—	—	1.00	2.00	3.50	5.50

KM# 130 2 DINARS

5.1300 g., Steel, 22.5 mm. **Obv:** Value on silhouette of country **Rev:** Dromedary camel's head right **Edge:** Plain

Date	Mintage	F	VF	XF	Unc	BU
AH1422-2002	—	—	1.00	2.00	4.00	6.00
AH1423-2002	—	—	1.00	2.00	4.00	6.00
AH1424-2003	—	—	1.00	2.00	4.00	6.00
AH1424-2004	—	—	1.00	2.00	4.00	6.00
AH1426-2005	—	—	1.00	2.00	4.00	6.00
AH1427-2006	—	—	1.00	2.00	4.00	6.00
AH1428-2007	—	—	1.00	2.00	4.00	6.00

KM# 123 5 DINARS

6.2000 g., Steel, 24.5 mm. **Obv:** Denomination within circle **Rev:** Forepart of African elephant right **Edge:** Plain

Date	Mintage	F	VF	XF	Unc	BU
AH1422-2003	—	—	1.50	3.50	6.50	9.50
AH1423-2003	—	—	1.50	3.50	6.50	9.50
AH1424-2003	—	—	1.00	3.00	5.50	8.00
AH1424-2004	—	—	1.50	3.50	6.50	9.50
AH1426-2005	—	—	1.00	3.00	5.50	8.00
AH1426-2006	—	—	1.00	3.50	6.50	9.50
AH1427-2006	—	—	1.00	3.00	5.50	8.00
AH1428-2007	—	—	1.00	3.00	5.50	8.00
AH1430-2009	—	—	1.00	3.00	5.50	8.00

KM# 124 10 DINARS

4.9500 g., Bi-Metallic Aluminum center in Steel ring, 26.5 mm. **Obv:** Denomination **Rev:** Barbary falcon's head right **Edge:** Plain

Date	Mintage	F	VF	XF	Unc	BU
AH1422-2002	—	—	1.75	4.00	9.00	—
AH1423-2002	—	—	1.75	4.00	9.00	—
AH1424-2003	—	—	1.75	4.00	9.00	—
AH1425-2004	—	—	1.75	4.00	9.00	—
AH1427-2006	—	—	1.75	4.00	9.00	—
AH1428-2007	—	—	1.75	4.00	9.00	—
AH1429-2008	—	—	1.75	4.00	9.00	—

KM# 125 20 DINARS

8.5200 g., Bi-Metallic Aluminum-Bronze center in Stainless Steel ring, 27.5 mm. **Subject:** Lion **Obv:** Denomination **Rev:** Head left

Date	Mintage	F	VF	XF	Unc	BU
AH1424-2004	—	—	3.00	6.00	12.00	—
AH1426-2005	—	—	3.00	6.00	12.00	—
AH1428-2007	—	—	3.00	6.00	12.00	—
AH1430-2009	—	—	3.00	6.00	12.00	—

KM# 126 50 DINARS

9.2700 g., Bi-Metallic Stainless Steel center in Aluminum-Brass ring, 28.5 mm. **Obv:** Denomination **Rev:** Dama gazelle with head left

Date	Mintage	F	VF	XF	Unc	BU
AH1424-2003	—	—	4.00	8.00	16.50	—
AH1425-2004	—	—	4.00	8.00	16.50	—
AH1428-2007	—	—	4.00	8.00	16.50	—
AH1429-2008	—	—	4.00	8.00	16.50	—

KM# 138 50 DINARS

9.2700 g., Bi-Metallic Stainless Steel center in Aluminum-Bronze ring, 28.5 mm. **Subject:** 50th Anniversary of Liberation **Obv:** Large value **Rev:** Stylized flag and two Moudjahid (revolutionaries)

Date	Mintage	F	VF	XF	Unc	BU
AH1425-2004	3,000,000	—	—	5.00	12.50	15.00
AH1429-2008	—	—	—	5.00	12.50	15.00

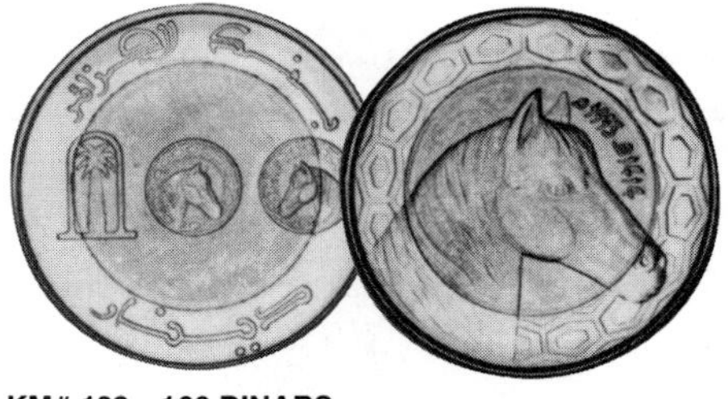

KM# 132 100 DINARS

11.0000 g., Bi-Metallic Copper-Nickel center in Stainless Steel ring, 29.5 mm. **Obv:** Denomination stylized with reverse design **Rev:** Horse head right

Date	Mintage	F	VF	XF	Unc	BU
AH1422-2002	—	—	5.00	10.00	20.00	24.00
AH1423-2002	—	—	5.00	10.00	20.00	24.00
AH1423-2003	—	—	5.00	10.00	20.00	24.00
AH1425-2004	—	—	5.00	10.00	20.00	24.00
AH1428-2007	—	—	5.00	10.00	20.00	24.00

KM# 137 100 DINARS

11.0000 g., Bi-Metallic Brass center in Stainless Steel ring, 29.5 mm. **Subject:** 40th Anniversary of Independence **Obv:** Stylized value using palm tree in doorway and two coins depicting horses' heads **Rev:** Number 40 and stylized face **Edge:** Reeded

Date	Mintage	F	VF	XF	Unc	BU
AH1422-2002	—	—	—	—	25.00	28.00

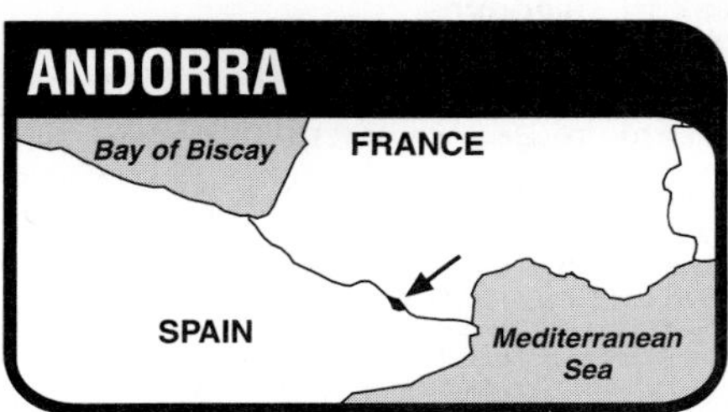

Principality of Andorra (Principat d'Andorra), situated on the southern slopes of the Pyrenees Mountains between France and Spain, has an area of 181 sq. mi. (453 sq. km.) and a population of 80,000. Capital: Andorra la Vella. Tourism is the chief source of income. Timber, cattle and derivatives, and furniture are exported.

RULER

Joan D.M. Bisbe D'Urgell I

MONETARY SYSTEM

100 Centims = 1 Diner

NOTE: The Diners have been struck for collectors while the Euro is used in everyday commerce.

MINT MARK

Crowned M = Madrid

PRINCIPALITY

DECIMAL COINAGE

KM# 176 CENTIM

2.1000 g., Aluminum, 27 mm. **Subject:** Charlemagne **Obv:** National arms, date below **Rev:** Crowned head facing, denomination below **Edge:** Plain

Date	Mintage	F	VF	XF	Unc	BU
2002	—	—	—	—	1.50	2.00

KM# 177 CENTIM

2.1300 g., Aluminum, 27 mm. **Subject:** Isard **Obv:** National arms, date below **Rev:** Chamois left facing, denomination at right **Edge:** Plain

Date	Mintage	F	VF	XF	Unc	BU
2002	—	—	—	—	1.50	2.00

KM# 178 CENTIM

2.1400 g., Aluminum, 27 mm. **Subject:** Agnus Dei **Obv:** National arms **Rev:** Lamb of God **Edge:** Plain

Date	Mintage	F	VF	XF	Unc	BU
2002	—	—	—	—	1.00	1.50

KM# 198 CENTIM

Aluminum-Magnesium, 27 mm. **Obv:** National arms **Rev:** A piece of the wall paintings belonging to the 12th century Romanesque church of St. Marti de la Cortinado

Date	Mintage	F	VF	XF	Unc	BU
2003	—	—	—	—	1.25	1.75

KM# 200 CENTIM

Aluminum-Magnesium, 27 mm. **Obv:** National arms **Rev:** Image of the 12th century Romanesque church of St. Miquel d'Engolasters with its bell tower, the Romanesque apse, the small portico and the large Lombard windows

Date	Mintage	F	VF	XF	Unc	BU
2003	—	—	—	—	1.25	1.75

KM# 199 CENTIM

Aluminum-Magnesium, 27 mm. **Obv:** National arms **Rev:** Pont de la Margineda, reproduction of the bridge

Date	Mintage	F	VF	XF	Unc	BU
2003	—	—	—	—	1.25	1.75

KM# 229 CENTIM

Aluminum **Obv:** Crowned arms **Rev:** Santa Coloma

Date	Mintage	F	VF	XF	Unc	BU
2004	—	—	—	—	0.90	1.20

KM# 230 CENTIM

Aluminum **Obv:** Crowned arms **Rev:** Sant Martí de la Cortinada

Date	Mintage	F	VF	XF	Unc	BU
2004	—	—	—	—	0.90	1.20

KM# 231 CENTIM
Aluminum **Obv:** Crowned arms **Rev:** Altar at Santa Coloma

Date	Mintage	F	VF	XF	Unc	BU
2004	—	—	—	—	0.90	1.20

KM# 236 CENTIM
2.8000 g., Brass, 18 mm. **Subject:** Death of Pope John Paul II **Obv:** National arms **Rev:** Karol Wojtyla as priest **Edge:** Reeded

Date	Mintage	F	VF	XF	Unc	BU
2005	15,000	—	—	0.30	0.80	1.20

KM# 245 CENTIM
2.8000 g., Brass, 18 mm. **Obv:** National arms **Rev:** Findern flower - Poet's Daffodil

Date	Mintage	F	VF	XF	Unc	BU
2005	15,000	—	—	—	0.80	1.20
2006	10,000	—	—	—	0.80	1.20
2007	10,000	—	—	—	0.80	1.20
2008	5,000	—	—	—	0.80	1.20

KM# 290 CENTIM
2.8000 g., Brass, 18 mm. **Obv:** National Arms **Rev:** Portrait of Joseph Ratzinger as priest **Edge:** Reeded

Date	Mintage	F	VF	XF	Unc	BU
2006	15,000	—	—	—	—	1.20

KM# 306 CENTIM
2.8000 g., Brass, 18 mm. **Subject:** Popes of the 20th Century **Obv:** National arms **Rev:** Pope Leo XIII **Edge:** Reeded

Date	Mintage	F	VF	XF	Unc	BU
2007	5,000	—	—	—	—	1.20

KM# 179 2 CENTIMS
Brass, 18 mm. **Subject:** Grandalla **Obv:** National arms **Rev:** Edelweiss flower **Edge:** Plain

Date	Mintage	F	VF	XF	Unc	BU
2002	—	—	—	—	1.50	2.00

KM# 201 2 CENTIMS
Copper-Nickel-Zinc, 18.15 mm. **Obv:** National arms **Rev:** Clavell Deltoide, a flower found in Andorra

Date	Mintage	F	VF	XF	Unc	BU
2003	—	—	—	—	1.75	2.50

KM# 232 2 CENTIMS
Brass **Obv:** Crowned arms **Rev:** West Gothic robe

Date	Mintage	F	VF	XF	Unc	BU
2004	—	—	—	—	1.20	1.60

KM# 237 2 CENTIMS
4.0000 g., Brass, 21.3 mm. **Subject:** Death of Pope John-Paul II **Obv:** National arms **Rev:** Karol Wojtyla as priest

Date	Mintage	F	VF	XF	Unc	BU
2005	15,000	—	—	0.50	1.20	1.60

KM# 246 2 CENTIMS
4.0000 g., Brass, 21.3 mm. **Obv:** National arms **Rev:** Pyrenean Chamois **Edge:** Reeded

Date	Mintage	F	VF	XF	Unc	BU
2005	15,000	—	—	—	1.20	1.60
2006	10,000	—	—	—	1.20	1.60
2007	10,000	—	—	—	1.20	1.60
2008	5,000	—	—	—	1.20	1.60

KM# 291 2 CENTIMS
4.0000 g., Brass, 21.3 mm. **Obv:** National Arms **Rev:** Portrait of Joseph Ratzinger as priest

Date	Mintage	F	VF	XF	Unc	BU
2006	15,000	—	—	—	—	1.60

KM# 307 2 CENTIMS
4.0000 g., Brass, 21.3 mm. **Subject:** Popes of the 20th Century **Obv:** National Arms **Rev:** Pope Pius X

Date	Mintage	F	VF	XF	Unc	BU
2007	5,000	—	—	—	—	1.60

KM# 282 2 CENTIMS
0.7300 g., 0.9990 Gold 0.0234 oz. AGW, 11 mm. **Subject:** Berlin Wall, 20th anniversary **Obv:** Shield **Rev:** Brandenburg Gate and brick wall **Edge:** Reeded

Date	Mintage	F	VF	XF	Unc	BU
2009 Proof	5,000	Value: 75.00				

KM# 180 5 CENTIMS
Brass, 21.8 mm. **Subject:** Squirrel **Obv:** National arms **Rev:** Red Squirrel on tree stump **Edge:** Plain

Date	Mintage	F	VF	XF	Unc	BU
2002	—	—	—	—	2.00	2.50

KM# 181 5 CENTIMS
Brass, 21.8 mm. **Subject:** Gall Fer **Obv:** National arms **Rev:** Male Eurasian Capercaillie (grouse) displaying plumage **Edge:** Plain

Date	Mintage	F	VF	XF	Unc	BU
2002	—	—	—	—	2.00	2.50

KM# 203 5 CENTIMS
Brass, 21.8 mm. **Obv:** National arms **Rev:** Wall painting from the 11th century church of Sant Serni de Nagol showing an eagle

Date	Mintage	F	VF	XF	Unc	BU
2003	—	—	—	—	2.25	2.75

KM# 202 5 CENTIMS
Brass, 21.8 mm. **Obv:** National arms **Rev:** The cross of Seven Arms, traditional Gothic cross

Date	Mintage	F	VF	XF	Unc	BU
2003	—	—	—	—	2.25	2.75

KM# 233 5 CENTIMS
Brass **Obv:** Crowned arms **Rev:** Gothic cross

Date	Mintage	F	VF	XF	Unc	BU
2004	—	—	—	—	1.80	2.40

KM# 234 5 CENTIMS
Brass **Obv:** Crowned arms **Rev:** Lady of Canolic

Date	Mintage	F	VF	XF	Unc	BU
2004	—	—	—	—	1.80	2.40

KM# 238 5 CENTIMS
5.5000 g., Brass, 24.5 mm. **Subject:** Death of Pope John-Paul II **Obv:** National arms **Rev:** Karol Wojtyla as bishop **Edge:** Reeded

Date	Mintage	F	VF	XF	Unc	BU
2005	15,000	—	—	0.70	1.80	2.40

KM# 247 5 CENTIMS
5.5000 g., Brass, 24.5 mm. **Obv:** National arms **Rev:** Wall painting from Santa Coloma church **Edge:** Reeded

Date	Mintage	F	VF	XF	Unc	BU
2005	15,000	—	—	—	1.80	2.40
2006	10,000	—	—	—	1.80	2.40
2007	10,000	—	—	—	1.80	2.40
2008	5,000	—	—	—	1.80	2.40

KM# 292 5 CENTIMS
5.5000 g., Brass, 24.5 mm. **Obv:** National Arms **Rev:** Portrait of Joseph Ratzinger as archbishop

Date	Mintage	F	VF	XF	Unc	BU
2006	15,000	—	—	—	—	2.50

KM# 308 5 CENTIMS
5.5000 g., Brass, 24.5 mm. **Subject:** Popes of the 20th Century **Obv:** National Arms **Rev:** Pope Benedict XV

Date	Mintage	F	VF	XF	Unc	BU
2007	5,000	—	—	—	—	2.40

KM# 182 10 CENTIMS
Brass **Subject:** St. Joan de Caselles **Obv:** National arms **Rev:** Tower and building **Edge:** Plain

Date	Mintage	F	VF	XF	Unc	BU
2002	—	—	—	—	3.00	4.00

KM# 204 10 CENTIMS
Nickel Plated Steel, 27.8 mm. **Obv:** National arms **Rev:** 12th century wood carving image from Our Lady of Meritxell

Date	Mintage	F	VF	XF	Unc	BU
2003	—	—	—	—	3.50	4.50

KM# 235 10 CENTIMS
Nickel Plated Steel **Obv:** Crowned arms **Rev:** Casa de la Vall

Date	Mintage	F	VF	XF	Unc	BU
2004	—	—	—	—	3.00	4.00

KM# 239 10 CENTIMS
6.5000 g., Copper-Nickel, 22.2 mm. **Subject:** Death of Pope John-Paul II **Obv:** National arms **Rev:** Karol Wojtyla as archbishop **Edge:** Reeded

Date	Mintage	F	VF	XF	Unc	BU
2005	15,000	—	—	1.00	2.40	3.20

KM# 248 10 CENTIMS
6.5000 g., Copper-Nickel, 22.2 mm. **Obv:** National arms **Rev:** Saint Vicenç d'Enclar church

Date	Mintage	F	VF	XF	Unc	BU
2005	15,000	—	—	—	2.40	3.20
2006	10,000	—	—	—	2.40	3.20
2007	10,000	—	—	—	2.40	3.20
2008	5,000	—	—	—	2.40	3.20

KM# 293 10 CENTIMS
6.5000 g., Copper-Nickel, 22.2 mm. **Obv:** National Arms **Rev:** Portrait of Joseph Ratzinger as archbishop

Date	Mintage	F	VF	XF	Unc	BU
2006	15,000	—	—	—	—	4.00

KM# 309 10 CENTIMS
6.5000 g., Copper-Nickel, 22.2 mm. **Subject:** Popes of the 20th Century **Obv:** National Arms **Rev:** Pope Pius XI

Date	Mintage	F	VF	XF	Unc	BU
2007	5,000	—	—	—	—	3.40

KM# 240 25 CENTIMS
7.7500 g., Copper-Nickel, 24.2 mm. **Subject:** Death of Pope John-Paul II **Obv:** National arms **Rev:** Karol Wojtyla as cardinal

Date	Mintage	F	VF	XF	Unc	BU
2005	15,000	—	—	1.20	3.00	4.00

KM# 249 25 CENTIMS
7.7500 g., Copper-Nickel, 24.2 mm. **Obv:** National arms **Rev:** Our Lady of Meritxell sanctuary

Date	Mintage	F	VF	XF	Unc	BU
2005	15,000	—	—	—	3.00	4.00
2006	10,000	—	—	—	3.00	4.00
2007	10,000	—	—	—	3.00	4.00
2008	5,000	—	—	—	3.00	4.00

KM# 294 25 CENTIMS
7.7500 g., Copper-Nickel, 24.2 mm. **Obv:** National Arms **Rev:** Portrait of Joseph Ratzinger as cardinal

Date	Mintage	F	VF	XF	Unc	BU
2006	15,000	—	—	—	—	4.00

KM# 310 25 CENTIMS
7.7500 g., Copper-Nickel, 24.2 mm. **Subject:** Popes of the 20th Century **Obv:** National Arms **Rev:** Pope Pius XII

Date	Mintage	F	VF	XF	Unc	BU
2007	5,000	—	—	—	—	4.00

KM# 241 50 CENTIMS
9.0000 g., Copper-Nickel, 25.9 mm. **Subject:** Death of Pope John-Paul II **Obv:** National arms **Rev:** Karol Wojtyla as cardinal

Date	Mintage	F	VF	XF	Unc	BU
2005	15,000	—	—	2.70	3.60	4.80

KM# 250 50 CENTIMS
9.0000 g., Copper-Nickel, 25.9 mm. **Obv:** National arms **Rev:** Map of Andorra, 7 towns highlighted

Date	Mintage	F	VF	XF	Unc	BU
2005	15,000	—	—	—	4.00	5.00
2006	10,000	—	—	—	4.00	5.00
2007	10,000	—	—	—	4.00	5.00
2008	5,000	—	—	—	4.00	5.00

KM# 295 50 CENTIMS
9.0000 g., Copper-Nickel, 25.9 mm. **Obv:** National Arms **Rev:** Portrait of Joseph Ratzinger as cardinal

Date	Mintage	F	VF	XF	Unc	BU
2006	15,000	—	—	—	—	4.80

KM# 311 50 CENTIMS
9.0000 g., Copper-Nickel, 25.9 mm. **Subject:** Popes of the 20th Century **Obv:** National Arms **Rev:** Pope John XXIII

Date	Mintage	F	VF	XF	Unc	BU
2007	5,000	—	—	—	—	6.00

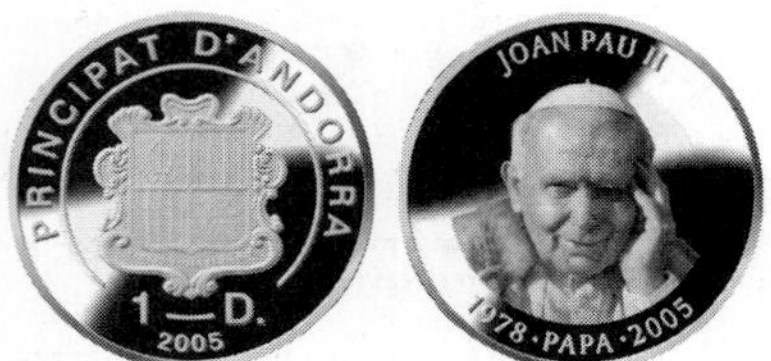

KM# 242 DINER
8.5000 g., Bi-Metallic Brass center in Copper-Nickel ring, 24.5 mm. **Subject:** Death of Pope John-Paul II **Obv:** National arms **Rev:** Karol Wojtyla as pope **Edge:** Reeded

Date	Mintage	F	VF	XF	Unc	BU
2005	15,000	—	—	1.60	4.00	6.00

KM# 251 DINER
8.5000 g., Bi-Metallic Brass center in Copper-Nickel ring, 24.5 mm. **Obv:** National arms **Rev:** Our Lady of Meritxell **Edge:** Reeded

Date	Mintage	F	VF	XF	Unc	BU
2005	15,000	—	—	—	4.50	6.00
2006	10,000	—	—	—	4.50	6.00
2007	10,000	—	—	—	4.50	6.00
2008	5,000	—	—	—	4.50	6.00

KM# 262 DINER
Bi-Metallic Brass center in Copper-Nickel ring **Subject:** Pope John Paul II

Date	Mintage	F	VF	XF	Unc	BU
2005	15,000	—	—	1.60	4.00	6.00

KM# 263 DINER
Bi-Metallic Brass center in Copper-Nickel ring **Subject:** Andorra Virgin

Date	Mintage	F	VF	XF	Unc	BU
2005	15,000	—	—	1.60	4.00	6.00

KM# 264 DINER
Bi-Metallic Brass center in Copper-Nickel ring **Series:** Pope Benedict XVI

Date	Mintage	F	VF	XF	Unc	BU
2006	15,000	—	—	1.60	4.00	6.00

KM# 296 DINER
8.5000 g., Bi-Metallic Brss center in Copper-Nickel ring, 24.5 mm. **Obv:** National Arms **Rev:** Portrait of Joseph Ratzinger as Pope Benedict XVI

Date	Mintage	F	VF	XF	Unc	BU
2006	15,000	—	—	—	—	6.00

KM# 299 DINER
11.0000 g., Nickel, 25x25 mm. **Subject:** Chess Set **Obv:** National Arms **Rev:** Pawn **Shape:** Square

Date	Mintage	F	VF	XF	Unc	BU
2006	40,000	—	—	—	—	6.00

KM# 299a DINER
11.0000 g., Brass Gilt, 25x25 mm. **Subject:** Chess Set **Obv:** National Arms **Rev:** Pawn **Shape:** Square

Date	Mintage	F	VF	XF	Unc	BU
2006	40,000	—	—	—	—	6.00

KM# 300 DINER
11.0000 g., Nickel, 25x25 mm. **Subject:** Chess Set **Obv:** National arms **Rev:** Rook **Shape:** Square

Date	Mintage	F	VF	XF	Unc	BU
2006	10,000	—	—	—	—	12.00

KM# 300a DINER
11.0000 g., Brass Gilt, 25x25 mm. **Subject:** Chess Set **Obv:** National Arms **Rev:** Rook **Shape:** Square

Date	Mintage	F	VF	XF	Unc	BU
2006	10,000	—	—	—	—	12.00

KM# 301 DINER
11.0000 g., Nickel, 25x25 mm. **Subject:** Chess Set **Obv:** National Arms **Rev:** Knight **Shape:** Square

Date	Mintage	F	VF	XF	Unc	BU
2006	10,000	—	—	—	—	12.00

KM# 301a DINER
11.0000 g., Brass Gilt, 25x25 mm. **Subject:** Chess Set **Obv:** National Arms **Rev:** Knight **Shape:** Square

Date	Mintage	F	VF	XF	Unc	BU
2006	10,000	—	—	—	—	12.00

KM# 302 DINER
11.0000 g., Nickel, 25x25 mm. **Subject:** Chess Set **Obv:** National Arms **Rev:** Bishop **Shape:** Square

Date	Mintage	F	VF	XF	Unc	BU
2006	10,000	—	—	—	—	12.00

KM# 302a DINER
11.0000 g., Brass Gilt, 25x25 mm. **Subject:** Chess Set **Obv:** National Arms **Rev:** Bishop **Shape:** Square

Date	Mintage	F	VF	XF	Unc	BU
2006	10,000	—	—	—	—	12.00

KM# 303 DINER
11.0000 g., Nickel, 25x25 mm. **Subject:** Chess Set **Obv:** National Arms **Rev:** Queen **Shape:** Square

Date	Mintage	F	VF	XF	Unc	BU
2006	5,000	—	—	—	—	18.00

KM# 303a DINER
11.0000 g., Brass Gilt, 25x25 mm. **Subject:** Chess Set **Obv:** National Arms **Rev:** Queen **Shape:** Square

Date	Mintage	F	VF	XF	Unc	BU
2006	5,000	—	—	—	—	18.00

KM# 304 DINER
11.0000 g., Nickel, 25x25 mm. **Subject:** Chess Set **Obv:** National Arms **Rev:** King **Shape:** Square

Date	Mintage	F	VF	XF	Unc	BU
2006	5,000	—	—	—	—	18.00

KM# 304a DINER
11.0000 g., Brass Gilt, 25x25 mm. **Subject:** Chess Set **Obv:** National Arms **Rev:** King **Shape:** Square

Date	Mintage	F	VF	XF	Unc	BU
2006	5,000	—	—	—	—	18.00

KM# 312 DINER
8.5000 g., Bi-Metallic Brass center in Copper-Nickel ring, 24.5 mm. **Subject:** Popes of the 20th Century **Obv:** National Arms **Rev:** Pope Paul VI

Date	Mintage	F	VF	XF	Unc	BU
2007	5,000	—	—	—	—	8.00

KM# 268 DINER
31.1050 g., 0.9990 Silver 0.9990 oz. ASW, 38.6 mm. **Obv:** National arms **Rev:** Eagle with wings outstretched

Date	Mintage	F	VF	XF	Unc	BU
2008	—	—	—	—	—	37.50

KM# 253 DINER
31.1050 g., 0.9990 Silver 0.9990 oz. ASW **Obv:** Arms **Rev:** Eagle in nest

Date	Mintage	F	VF	XF	Unc	BU
2010	—	—	—	—	—	37.50

KM# 243 2 DINERS
11.2500 g., Bi-Metallic Copper-Nickel center in Brass ring, 28.4 mm. **Subject:** Death of Pope John-Paul II **Obv:** National arms **Rev:** Karol Wojtyla as pope **Edge:** Reeded

Date	Mintage	F	VF	XF	Unc	BU
2005	15,000	—	—	2.40	6.00	8.00

KM# 252 2 DINERS
11.2500 g., Bi-Metallic Copper-Nickel center in Brass ring, 28.4 mm. **Obv:** National arms **Rev:** Signing of the Umpirage between the Bishop of Urgell and Count of Foix **Edge:** Reeded

Date	Mintage	F	VF	XF	Unc	BU
2005	15,000	—	—	—	6.00	8.00
2006	10,000	—	—	—	6.00	8.00
2007	10,000	—	—	—	6.00	8.00
2008	5,000	—	—	—	6.00	8.00

KM# 265 2 DINERS
Bi-Metallic Copper-Nickel center in Brass ring **Subject:** Pope John Paul II

Date	Mintage	F	VF	XF	Unc	BU
2005	15,000	—	—	—	6.00	8.00

KM# 266 2 DINERS
Bi-Metallic Copper-Nickel center in Brass ring **Subject:** Wall

Date	Mintage	F	VF	XF	Unc	BU
2005	15,000	—	—	—	6.00	8.00

KM# 267 2 DINERS
Bi-Metallic Copper-Nickel center in Brass ring **Subject:** Pope Benedict XVI

Date	Mintage	F	VF	XF	Unc	BU
2006	15,000	—	—	—	6.00	8.00

KM# 297 2 DINERS
11.2500 g., Bi-Metallic Copper-Nickel center in Brass ring, 28.4 mm. **Obv:** National Arms **Rev:** Portrait of Joseph Ratzinger as Pope Benedict XVI

Date	Mintage	F	VF	XF	Unc	BU
2006	15,000	—	—	—	—	8.00

KM# 313 2 DINERS
6.0000 g., Bi-Metallic Copper-Nickel center in Brass ring, 28.4 mm. **Subject:** Popes of the 20th Century **Obv:** National Arms **Rev:** Pope John Paul I

Date	Mintage	F	VF	XF	Unc	BU
2007	5,000	—	—	—	—	10.00

KM# 269 2 DINERS
0.7300 g., 0.9990 Gold 0.0234 oz. AGW, 11 mm. **Subject:** von Beethoven **Obv:** National arms **Rev:** Beethoven seated at desk

Date	Mintage	F	VF	XF	Unc	BU
2008 Proof	5,000	Value: 75.00				

KM# 281 2 DINERS
0.7300 g., 0.9990 Gold 0.0234 oz. AGW, 11 mm. **Obv:** Shield **Rev:** Charlemagne **Edge:** Reeded

Date	Mintage	F	VF	XF	Unc	BU
2009 Proof	5,000	Value: 75.00				

KM# 193 5 DINERS
1.2400 g., 0.9990 Gold 0.0398 oz. AGW, 13.92 mm. **Obv:** National arms **Rev:** The Escorial Palace in Madrid **Edge:** Reeded

Date	Mintage	F	VF	XF	Unc	BU
2004 Proof	3,000	Value: 70.00				

KM# 194 5 DINERS
1.2400 g., 0.9990 Gold 0.0398 oz. AGW, 13.92 mm. **Obv:** National arms **Rev:** Eiffel Tower **Edge:** Reeded

Date	Mintage	F	VF	XF	Unc	BU
2004 Proof	3,000	Value: 70.00				

KM# 195 5 DINERS
1.2400 g., 0.9990 Gold 0.0398 oz. AGW, 13.92 mm. **Obv:** National arms **Rev:** Atomic model monument **Edge:** Reeded

Date	Mintage	F	VF	XF	Unc	BU
2004 Proof	3,000	Value: 70.00				

KM# 196 5 DINERS
1.2400 g., 0.9990 Gold 0.0398 oz. AGW, 13.92 mm. **Subject:** Andorran membership in the United Nations **Obv:** National arms **Rev:** Seated woman, world globe and UN logo **Edge:** Reeded

Date	Mintage	F	VF	XF	Unc	BU
2004 Proof	3,000	Value: 75.00				

KM# 257 5 DINERS
1.5500 g., 0.9990 Gold 0.0498 oz. AGW, 13.92 mm. **Obv:** Arms **Rev:** Eagle in nest

Date	Mintage	F	VF	XF	Unc	BU
2010	—	—	—	—	—	85.00

KM# 172 10 DINERS
31.4700 g., 0.9250 Silver 0.9359 oz. ASW, 38.6 mm. **Subject:** Europa **Obv:** National arms **Rev:** Europa in chariot **Edge:** Reeded

Date	Mintage	F	VF	XF	Unc	BU
2001 Proof	15,000	Value: 45.00				

KM# 173 10 DINERS
31.4700 g., 0.9250 Silver 0.9359 oz. ASW, 38.6 mm. **Subject:** Concordia Europea **Obv:** National arms **Rev:** Two crowned women holding hands **Edge:** Reeded

Date	Mintage	F	VF	XF	Unc	BU
2001 Proof	15,000	Value: 45.00				

KM# 175 10 DINERS
31.4700 g., 0.9250 Silver 0.9359 oz. ASW, 38.6 mm. **Subject:** Olympics **Obv:** National arms **Rev:** Snowboarder **Edge:** Reeded

Date	Mintage	F	VF	XF	Unc	BU
2002 Proof	15,000	Value: 45.00				

KM# 183 10 DINERS
31.4700 g., 0.9250 Silver 0.9359 oz. ASW, 38.6 mm. **Subject:** Mouflon **Obv:** National arms **Rev:** Mouflon ram **Edge:** Reeded

Date	Mintage	F	VF	XF	Unc	BU
2002 Proof	15,000	Value: 50.00				

KM# 289 10 DINERS
31.4700 g., 0.9250 Silver 0.9359 oz. ASW, 38.61 mm. **Subject:** FIFA World Cup **Obv:** National Arms **Rev:** Soccer ball, names and years of previous World Cup host countries **Edge:** Reeded

Date	Mintage	F	VF	XF	Unc	BU
2003 Proof	50,000	Value: 85.00				

KM# 188 10 DINERS
31.1035 g., 0.9250 Silver 0.9250 oz. ASW, 38.6 mm. **Obv:** National arms **Rev:** Pope with doves **Edge:** Reeded

Date	Mintage	F	VF	XF	Unc	BU
2004 Proof	9,999	Value: 70.00				

KM# 189 10 DINERS
31.1035 g., 0.9250 Silver 0.9250 oz. ASW, 38.6 mm. **Obv:** National arms **Rev:** Pope holding staff with 2 hands **Edge:** Reeded

Date	Mintage	F	VF	XF	Unc	BU
2004 Proof	9,999	Value: 70.00				

KM# 190 10 DINERS
31.1035 g., 0.9250 Silver 0.9250 oz. ASW, 38.6 mm. **Obv:** National arms **Rev:** Pope raising a chalice **Edge:** Reeded

Date	Mintage	F	VF	XF	Unc	BU
2004 Proof	9,999	Value: 70.00				

KM# 191 10 DINERS
31.1035 g., 0.9250 Silver 0.9250 oz. ASW, 38.6 mm. **Obv:** National arms **Rev:** Pope with hammer **Edge:** Reeded

Date	Mintage	F	VF	XF	Unc	BU
2004 Proof	9,999	Value: 70.00				

KM# 192 10 DINERS
31.1035 g., 0.9250 Silver 0.9250 oz. ASW, 38.6 mm. **Obv:** National arms **Rev:** Gold-plated Pope writing **Edge:** Reeded

Date	Mintage	F	VF	XF	Unc	BU
2004 Proof	9,999	Value: 70.00				

KM# 205 10 DINERS
31.1000 g., 0.9250 Silver 0.9249 oz. ASW, 38.6 mm. **Obv. Designer:** National arms **Rev:** Gold plated Pope John Paul II wearing mitre and holding crucifix staff **Edge:** Reeded

Date	Mintage	F	VF	XF	Unc	BU
2005 Proof	9,999	Value: 70.00				

KM# 206 10 DINERS
31.1000 g., 0.9250 Silver 0.9249 oz. ASW, 38.6 mm. **Obv:** National arms **Rev:** Pope John Paul II with the Holy Virgin in background **Edge:** Reeded

Date	Mintage	F	VF	XF	Unc	BU
2005 Proof	9,999	Value: 70.00				

KM# 207 10 DINERS
31.1000 g., 0.9250 Silver 0.9249 oz. ASW, 38.6 mm. **Obv:** National arms **Rev:** Pope John Paul II in prayer with crucifix at right **Edge:** Reeded

Date	Mintage	F	VF	XF	Unc	BU
2005 Proof	9,999	Value: 70.00				

KM# 208 10 DINERS
31.1000 g., 0.9250 Silver 0.9249 oz. ASW, 38.6 mm. **Obv:** National arms **Rev:** Pope John Paul II blessing Vatican crowd **Edge:** Reeded

Date	Mintage	F	VF	XF	Unc	BU
2005 Proof	9,999	Value: 70.00				

KM# 209 10 DINERS
31.1000 g., 0.9250 Silver 0.9249 oz. ASW, 38.6 mm. **Obv:** National arms **Rev:** Pope John Paul II and Mother Teresa **Edge:** Reeded

Date	Mintage	F	VF	XF	Unc	BU
2005 Proof	9,999	Value: 70.00				

KM# 210 10 DINERS
31.1000 g., 0.9250 Silver 0.9249 oz. ASW, 38.6 mm. **Obv:** National arms **Rev:** Bearded man above Vatican City **Edge:** Reeded

Date	Mintage	F	VF	XF	Unc	BU
2005 Proof	9,999	Value: 60.00				

KM# 211 10 DINERS
31.1000 g., 0.9250 Silver 0.9249 oz. ASW, 38.6 mm. **Obv:** National arms **Rev:** Sad woman above Fatima **Edge:** Reeded

Date	Mintage	F	VF	XF	Unc	BU
2005 Proof	9,999	Value: 60.00				

KM# 212 10 DINERS
31.1000 g., 0.9250 Silver 0.9249 oz. ASW, 38.6 mm. **Obv:** National arms **Rev:** Radiant woman above Guadalupe Cathedral **Edge:** Reeded

Date	Mintage	F	VF	XF	Unc	BU
2005 Proof	9,999	Value: 60.00				

KM# 213 10 DINERS
31.1000 g., 0.9250 Silver 0.9249 oz. ASW, 38.6 mm. **Obv:** National arms **Rev:** Sea shell above Santiago De Compostel-la Cathedral **Edge:** Reeded

Date	Mintage	F	VF	XF	Unc	BU
2005 Proof	9,999	Value: 60.00				

KM# 214 10 DINERS
31.1000 g., 0.9250 Silver 0.9249 oz. ASW, 38.6 mm. **Obv:** National arms **Rev:** Dead man's face with Church of the Holy Sepulchure in the background **Edge:** Reeded

Date	Mintage	F	VF	XF	Unc	BU
2005 Proof	9,999	Value: 60.00				

KM# 215 10 DINERS
28.8000 g., 0.9250 Silver 0.8565 oz. ASW, 38.61 mm. **Obv:** National arms **Rev:** 2006 Olympics freestyle skier **Edge:** Reeded

Date	Mintage	F	VF	XF	Unc	BU
2005 Proof	15,000	Value: 50.00				

KM# 217 10 DINERS
3.1100 g., 0.9999 Gold 0.1000 oz. AGW, 20 mm. **Obv:** National arms **Rev:** Jesus carrying the cross **Edge:** Reeded

Date	Mintage	F	VF	XF	Unc	BU
2006 Proof	9,999	Value: 165				

KM# 218 10 DINERS
31.1035 g., 0.9250 Silver 0.9250 oz. ASW, 38.6 mm. **Obv:** National arms **Rev:** Birth of Jesus **Edge:** Reeded

Date	Mintage	F	VF	XF	Unc	BU
2006 Proof	9,999	Value: 60.00				

KM# 219 10 DINERS
31.1035 g., 0.9250 Silver 0.9250 oz. ASW, 38.6 mm. **Obv:** National arms **Rev:** The Last Supper **Edge:** Reeded

Date	Mintage	F	VF	XF	Unc	BU
2006 Proof	9,999	Value: 60.00				

KM# 276 10 DINERS
28.2800 g., 0.9250 Silver 0.8410 oz. ASW, 38.6 mm. **Subject:** Extreme Sports - Mountain Bike **Obv:** Arms **Rev:** Multicolor biker

Date	Mintage	F	VF	XF	Unc	BU
2007 Proof	5,000	Value: 65.00				

KM# 277 10 DINERS
28.2800 g., 0.9250 Silver 0.8410 oz. ASW, 38.6 mm. **Subject:** Extreme Sports - Snowboarding **Obv:** Arms **Rev:** Multicolor snowboarder

Date	Mintage	F	VF	XF	Unc	BU
2007 Proof	5,000	Value: 65.00				

KM# 278 10 DINERS
28.2800 g., 0.9250 Silver 0.8410 oz. ASW, 38.6 mm. **Subject:** Extreme Sports - Heliskiing **Obv:** Arms **Rev:** Multicolor heliskier

Date	Mintage	F	VF	XF	Unc	BU
2007 Proof	5,000	Value: 65.00				

KM# 244 10 DINERS
28.2800 g., 0.9250 Silver 0.8410 oz. ASW, 28x40 mm. **Subject:** Great Painters of the World **Obv:** Mona lisa, national arms at left, multicolor **Rev:** Head of Leonardo daVinci at lower left, study of man in background, multicolor **Edge:** Plain **Shape:** Vertical rectangular

Date	Mintage	F	VF	XF	Unc	BU
2008	15,000	—	—	—	—	60.00

KM# 270 10 DINERS
28.2800 g., 0.9250 Silver 0.8410 oz. ASW, 40x28 mm. **Obv:** Arms and multicolor **Rev:** DaVinci multicolor **Shape:** Vertical rectangle

Date	Mintage	F	VF	XF	Unc	BU
2008	15,000	—	—	—	—	60.00

KM# 272 10 DINERS
33.0000 g., 0.9250 Silver parially gilt 0.9814 oz. ASW, 38.6 mm. **Subject:** Vikings

Date	Mintage	F	VF	XF	Unc	BU
2008	15,000	—	—	—	—	50.00

KM# 273 10 DINERS
28.2800 g., 0.9250 Silver 0.8410 oz. ASW, 38.6 mm. **Subject:** Cross-country Skiing

Date	Mintage	F	VF	XF	Unc	BU
2008 Proof	10,000	Value: 45.00				

KM# 280 10 DINERS
28.2800 g., 0.9250 Silver 0.8410 oz. ASW, 38.61 mm. **Subject:** World Cup Football, 2010 **Obv:** Shield **Rev:** Linear and shaded player skicking ball **Edge:** Reeded

Date	Mintage	F	VF	XF	Unc	BU
2009 Proof	10,000	Value: 50.00				

KM# 258 10 DINERS
3.1100 g., 0.9990 Gold 0.0999 oz. AGW, 16.46 mm. **Obv:** Arms **Rev:** Eagle in nest

Date	Mintage	F	VF	XF	Unc	BU
2010	—	—	—	—	—	165

KM# 283 10 DINERS
28.2800 g., 0.9250 Silver 0.8410 oz. ASW, 40x28 mm. **Subject:** Albrecht Durer **Obv:** Adama dn even engraving and shield **Rev:** Durer's Adoration of the Holy Trinity

Date	Mintage	F	VF	XF	Unc	BU
2010 Proof	15,000	Value: 50.00				

KM# 284 10 DINERS
28.2800 g., 0.9250 Silver 0.8410 oz. ASW, 38.61 mm. **Obv:** Shield **Rev:** St. Christopher

Date	Mintage	F	VF	XF	Unc	BU
2010 Proof	5,000	Value: 65.00				

KM# 285 10 DINERS
28.2800 g., 0.9990 Silver 0.9083 oz. ASW, 38.61 mm. **Obv:** Shield **Rev:** St. George **Edge:** Reeded

Date	Mintage	F	VF	XF	Unc	BU
2010 Proof	5,000	Value: 65.00				

KM# 286 10 DINERS
28.2800 g., 0.9990 Silver 0.9083 oz. ASW, 38.61 mm. **Obv:** Shield **Rev:** St. Catherine **Edge:** Reeded

Date	Mintage	F	VF	XF	Unc	BU
2010 Proof	5,000	Value: 65.00				

KM# 287 10 DINERS
28.2800 g., 0.9990 Silver 0.9083 oz. ASW, 38.61 mm. **Obv:** Shield **Rev:** St. Barbara **Edge:** Reeded

Date	Mintage	F	VF	XF	Unc	BU
2010 Proof	5,000	Value: 65.00				

KM# 174 25 DINERS
12.4414 g., 0.9990 Gold 0.3996 oz. AGW, 26 mm. **Subject:** Christmas **Obv:** National arms **Rev:** Nativity scene **Edge:** Reeded

Date	Mintage	F	VF	XF	Unc	BU
2001 Proof	3,000	Value: 625				

KM# 184 25 DINERS
10.0000 g., 0.9999 Gold 0.3215 oz. AGW, 26 mm. **Subject:** Christmas **Obv:** National arms **Rev:** Standing Christ child **Edge:** Reeded

Date	Mintage	F	VF	XF	Unc	BU
2002 Proof	2,000	Value: 550				

KM# 185 25 DINERS
7.7759 g., 0.9990 Gold 0.2497 oz. AGW, 26 mm. **Subject:** Christmas **Obv:** National arms **Rev:** Madonna-like mother and child **Edge:** Reeded

Date	Mintage	F	VF	XF	Unc	BU
2003 Proof	3,000	Value: 400				

KM# 197 25 DINERS
8.0000 g., 0.9990 Gold 0.2569 oz. AGW, 26 mm. **Subject:** Christmas **Obv:** National arms **Rev:** Nativity scene **Edge:** Reeded

Date	Mintage	F	VF	XF	Unc	BU
2004 Proof	5,000	Value: 400				

KM# 216 25 DINERS
6.0000 g., 0.9999 Gold 0.1929 oz. AGW, 26 mm. **Obv:** National arms **Rev:** St. Joseph holding infant Jesus **Edge:** Reeded

Date	Mintage	F	VF	XF	Unc	BU
2005 Proof	9,999	Value: 325				

KM# 305 25 DINERS
6.0000 g., 0.9990 Gold 0.1927 oz. AGW, 26 mm. **Subject:** Christmas - the Holy Family **Obv:** National Arms **Rev:** St. Joseph, Mary and Jesus

Date	Mintage	F	VF	XF	Unc	BU
2006 Proof	5,000	Value: 500				

KM# 314 25 DINERS
6.0000 g., 0.9990 Gold 0.1927 oz. AGW, 26 mm. **Subject:** Christmas **Obv:** National Arms **Rev:** Angels playing musical instruments

Date	Mintage	F	VF	XF	Unc	BU
2007 Proof	2,000	Value: 500				

KM# 274 25 DINERS
6.0000 g., 0.9990 Gold 0.1927 oz. AGW, 26 mm. **Subject:** Constitution

Date	Mintage	F	VF	XF	Unc	BU
2008 Proof	2,000	Value: 325				

KM# 275 25 DINERS
6.0000 g., 0.9990 Gold 0.1927 oz. AGW, 26 mm. **Subject:** Three Kings **Rev:** Magi following star

Date	Mintage	F	VF	XF	Unc	BU
2008 Proof	2,000	Value: 325				

KM# 279 25 DINERS
6.0000 g., 0.9990 Gold 0.1927 oz. AGW, 26 mm. **Obv:** Shield **Rev:** Madonna and child, star of Bethlehem in backgorund **Edge:** Reeded

Date	Mintage	F	VF	XF	Unc	BU
2009 Proof	1,200	Value: 325				

KM# 259 25 DINERS
7.7700 g., 0.9990 Gold 0.2496 oz. AGW, 22.5 mm. **Obv:** Arms **Rev:** Eagle in nest

Date	Mintage	F	VF	XF	Unc	BU
2010	—	—	—	—	—	400

KM# 288 25 DINERS
6.0000 g., 0.9990 Gold 0.1927 oz. AGW, 26 mm. **Subject:** Christmas **Obv:** Shield **Rev:** Archangel Gabriel telling the good news to Mary

Date	Mintage	F	VF	XF	Unc	BU
2010 Proof	1,200	Value: 325				

KM# 186 50 DINERS
159.5000 g., 0.9990 Bi-Metallic .999 Silver 155.5g coin with .999 Gold 4g, 20x50mm insert 5.1227 oz., 65 mm. **Subject:** 10th Anniversary of Constitution **Obv:** National arms **Rev:** Seated allegorical woman holding scrolled constitution **Edge:** Reeded **Note:** Illustration reduced.

Date	Mintage	F	VF	XF	Unc	BU
2003	3,000	—	—	—	300	350

KM# 260 50 DINERS
15.5500 g., 0.9990 Gold 0.4994 oz. AGW, 26 mm. **Obv:** Arms **Rev:** Eagle in nest

Date	Mintage	F	VF	XF	Unc	BU
2010	—	—	—	—	—	800

KM# 254 50 DINERS
1000.0000 g., 0.9990 Silver 32.117 oz. ASW, 100 mm. **Obv:** Arms **Rev:** Eagle in nest

Date	Mintage	F	VF	XF	Unc	BU
2010	—	—	—	—	—	1,200

KM# 298 100 DINERS
31.1035 g., 0.9990 Gold 0.9990 oz. AGW, 35 mm. **Obv:** Details of National Arms **Rev:** Eagle with open wings **Edge:** Reeded

Date	Mintage	F	VF	XF	Unc	BU
2006	1,500	—	—	—	—	1,750

KM# 255 100 DINERS
3110.5000 g., 0.9990 Silver 99.900 oz. ASW, 120 mm. **Obv:** Arms **Rev:** Eagle in nest **Note:** 29mm thick.

Date	Mintage	F	VF	XF	Unc	BU
2010	—	—	—	—	—	22,000

KM# 261 100 DINERS
31.1050 g., 0.9990 Gold 0.9990 oz. AGW, 33 mm. **Obv:** Arms **Rev:** Eagle in nest

Date	Mintage	F	VF	XF	Unc	BU
2010	—	—	—	—	—	1,550

KM# 256 200 DINERS
6221.0000 g., 0.9990 Silver 199.80 oz. ASW, 140 mm. **Obv:** Arms **Rev:** Eagle in nest **Note:** 42mm thick

Date	Mintage	F	VF	XF	Unc	BU
2010	—	—	—	—	—	44,000

The Argentine Republic, located in southern South America, has an area of 1,073,518 sq. mi. (3,761,274 sq. km.) and an estimated population of 37.03 million. Capital: Buenos Aires. Its varied topography ranges from the subtropical lowlands of the north to the towering Andean Mountains in the west and the wind-swept Patagonian steppe in the south. The rolling, fertile pampas of central Argentina are ideal for agriculture and grazing, and support most of the republic's population. Meatpacking, flour milling, textiles, sugar refining and dairy products are the principal industries. Oil is found in Patagonia, but most mineral requirements must be imported.

Internal conflict through the first half century of Argentine independence resulted in a provisional national coinage, chiefly of crown-sized silver. Provincial issues mainly of minor denominations supplemented this.

REPUBLIC

REFORM COINAGE

1992; 100 Centavos = 1 Peso

KM# 109 5 CENTAVOS
2.0200 g., Aluminum-Bronze, 17.2 mm. **Obv:** Radiant sunface **Rev:** Large value, date below **Edge:** Reeded **Note:** Prev. KM#84.

Date	Mintage	F	VF	XF	Unc	BU
2004	30,000,000	—	—	—	0.45	0.60
2005	76,000,000	—	—	—	0.45	0.60

KM# 109b 5 CENTAVOS
2.0000 g., Brass Plated Steel, 17.2 mm. **Obv:** Radiant Sunface **Rev:** Large value, date below **Edge:** Plain

Date	Mintage	F	VF	XF	Unc	BU
2006	23,800,000	—	—	—	0.45	0.60
2007	183,000,000	—	—	—	0.45	0.60
2008	114,000,000	—	—	—	0.45	0.60
2009	—	—	—	—	0.45	0.60

KM# 107 10 CENTAVOS
2.2500 g., Aluminum-Bronze, 18.2 mm. **Obv:** Argentine arms **Rev:** Value, date below **Edge:** Reeded **Note:** Prev. KM#82.

Date	Mintage	F	VF	XF	Unc	BU
2004	190,000,000	—	—	—	0.65	0.85
2005	114,400,000	—	—	—	0.65	0.85

KM# 107a 10 CENTAVOS
2.2000 g., Brass Plated Steel, 18.2 mm. **Obv:** Argentine arms **Rev:** Large value, date below **Edge:** Plain

Date	Mintage	F	VF	XF	Unc	BU
2006	99,600,000	—	—	—	0.65	0.85
2007	204,000,000	—	—	—	0.65	0.85
2008	317,000,000	—	—	—	0.65	0.85
2009	—	—	—	—	0.65	0.85

KM# 110.1 25 CENTAVOS
5.4000 g., Aluminum-Bronze, 24.2 mm. **Obv:** Buenos Aires City Hall, fine lettering **Rev:** Large value, date below **Edge:** Reeded **Note:** Prev. KM#85.1.

Date	Mintage	F	VF	XF	Unc	BU
2009	—	—	—	—	1.25	1.50
2010	—	—	—	—	1.25	1.50

KM# 111.1 50 CENTAVOS

5.8000 g., Aluminum-Bronze, 25.2 mm. **Obv:** Tucuman Province Capital Building; fine lettering **Rev:** Large value, date below **Note:** Prev. KM#86.1.

Date	Mintage	F	VF	XF	Unc	BU
2009	—	—	—	—	1.75	2.00
2010	—	—	—	—	1.75	2.00

KM# 111.2 50 CENTAVOS

5.8400 g., Aluminum-Bronze, 25.2 mm. **Obv:** Tucuman Province Capital Building; bold lettering **Rev:** Large value, date below **Note:** Prev. KM#86.2.

Date	Mintage	F	VF	XF	Unc	BU
2009	—	—	—	—	1.75	2.00

KM# 132.1 PESO

6.3500 g., Bi-Metallic Aluninum-Bronze center in Copper-Nickel ring, 23 mm. **Subject:** General Urquiza **Obv:** Stylized portrait facing **Rev:** Church tower and denomination **Edge:** Reeded

Date	Mintage	F	VF	XF	Unc	BU
2001	995,000	—	—	—	3.75	4.50

KM# 132.2 PESO

6.3500 g., Bi-Metallic Aluminum-Bronze center in Copper-Nickel ring, 23 mm. **Subject:** General Urquiza **Obv:** Stylized portrait facing **Rev:** Church tower and denomination **Edge:** Plain

Date	Mintage	F	VF	XF	Unc	BU
2001	5,000	—	—	—	7.50	8.00

KM# 141 PESO

25.0000 g., 0.9000 Silver 0.7234 oz. ASW, 37 mm. **Obv:** Maria Eva Duarte de Peron **Rev:** "EVITA" audience **Edge:** Reeded

Date	Mintage	F	VF	XF	Unc	BU
ND (2004) Proof	5,000	Value: 45.00				

KM# 140 PESO

25.0000 g., 0.9000 Silver 0.7234 oz. ASW, 37 mm. **Subject:** 70th Anniversary of Central Bank **Obv:** Bank building **Rev:** Liberty head in wreath **Edge:** Reeded

Date	Mintage	F	VF	XF	Unc	BU
2005 Proof	2,000	Value: 50.00				

KM# 155 PESO

25.0000 g., 0.9000 Silver 0.7234 oz. ASW, 37 mm. **Subject:** Jorge Luis Borges **Obv:** Stylized bust facing **Rev:** Man walking at street corner

Date	Mintage	F	VF	XF	Unc	BU
2006A	—	—	—	—	—	42.50

KM# 112.1 PESO

6.3500 g., Bi-Metallic Aluminum-Bronze center in Copper-Nickel ring, 23 mm. **Obv:** Argentine arms in circle **Rev:** Design of first Argentine coin in center **Edge:** Plain **Note:** Prev. KM#87.1.

Date	Mintage	F	VF	XF	Unc	BU
2006	30,000,000	—	—	0.50	1.20	1.60
2007	33,000,000	—	—	0.50	1.20	1.60
2008	89,600,000	—	—	0.50	1.20	1.60
2009 D	—	—	—	0.50	1.20	1.60
2010 E	—	—	—	0.50	1.20	1.60

KM# 153 PESO

25.0000 g., 0.9000 Silver 0.7234 oz. ASW, 37 mm. **Subject:** 25th Anniversary Malvinas Islands Occupation - Heroes **Obv:** Soldier's bust facing **Obv. Legend:** REPUBLICA ARGENTINA - 1982 - 2007 - LA NACIÓN A SUS HÉROES **Rev:** Outlined map of islands **Rev. Legend:** MALVINAS ARGENTINAS **Rev. Inscription:** 2 DE APRIL / 1982 **Edge:** Reeded

Date	Mintage	F	VF	XF	Unc	BU
2007 Proof	3,000	Value: 75.00				

KM# 156 PESO

6.3500 g., Bi-Metallic Aluminum-Bronze center in Copper-Nickel ring, 23 mm. **Subject:** Bicentennial - El Palmar **Obv:** Stylized radiant sun **Rev:** Palm trees

Date	Mintage	F	VF	XF	Unc	BU
2010	—	—	—	—	1.20	1.60

KM# 157 PESO

6.3500 g., Bi-Metallic Aluminum-Bronze center in Copper-Nickel ring, 23 mm. **Subject:** Bicentennial - Aconcagua **Obv:** Stylized radiant run **Rev:** Mountains

Date	Mintage	F	VF	XF	Unc	BU
2010	—	—	—	—	1.20	1.60

KM# 158 PESO

6.3500 g., Bi-Metallic Aluminum-Bronze center in Copper-Nickel ring, 23 mm. **Subject:** Bicentennial - Mar del Plata **Obv:** Stylized radiant sun **Rev:** Elephant seal and fishing boat

Date	Mintage	F	VF	XF	Unc	BU
2010	—	—	—	—	1.20	1.60

KM# 159 PESO

6.3500 g., Bi-Metallic Aluminum-Bronze center in Copper-Nickel ring, 23 mm. **Subject:** Bicentennial - Pucara de Tilcara **Obv:** Stylized radiant sun **Rev:** Cactus and mountains

Date	Mintage	F	VF	XF	Unc	BU
2010	—	—	—	—	1.20	1.60

KM# 160 PESO

6.3500 g., Bi-Metallic Aluminum-Bronze center in Copper-Nickel ring, 23 mm. **Subject:** Bicentennial - Glaciar Perito Moreno **Obv:** Stylized radiant sun **Rev:** Glaciar ice bridge and sea

Date	Mintage	F	VF	XF	Unc	BU
2010	—	—	—	—	1.20	1.60

KM# 135.1 2 PESOS

10.4000 g., Copper-Nickel, 30 mm. **Subject:** Eva Peron **Obv:** Head left **Rev:** Stylized crowd scene, value **Rev. Inscription:** EVITA **Edge:** Reeded

Date	Mintage	F	VF	XF	Unc	BU
2002	1,995,000	—	—	0.85	1.85	2.50

KM# 135.2 2 PESOS

10.4000 g., Copper-Nickel, 30 mm. **Subject:** Eva Peron **Obv:** Head left **Rev:** Stylized crowd scene, value **Rev. Inscription:** EVITA **Edge:** Plain

Date	Mintage	F	VF	XF	Unc	BU
2002	5,000	—	—	—	6.00	8.00

KM# 161 2 PESOS

10.4700 g., Copper-Nickel, 30.35 mm. **Subject:** Declaration of Human Rights **Obv:** Legend **Rev:** Female's scarf

Date	Mintage	F	VF	XF	Unc	BU
2006	—	—	—	—	1.85	2.50

KM# 144.1 2 PESOS

10.4000 g., Copper-Nickel, 30 mm. **Subject:** Malvinas Islands War, 25th Anniversary **Obv:** Soldier's bust facing **Obv. Legend:** REPUBLICA ARGENTINA - 1982 - 2007 - LA NACIÓN A SUS HÉROES **Rev:** Outlined map of islands **Rev. Legend:** MALVINAS ARGENTINAS **Rev. Inscription:** 2 DE APRIL / 1982 **Edge:** Reeded

Date	Mintage	F	VF	XF	Unc	BU
2007	1,995,000	—	—	0.85	1.85	2.50

KM# 144.2 2 PESOS

10.4000 g., Copper-Nickel, 30 mm. **Subject:** Malvinas Islands War, 25th Anniversary **Obv:** Soldier's bust facing **Obv. Legend:** REPUBLICA ARGENTINA - 1982 - 2007 - LA NACIÓN A SUS HÉROES **Rev:** Outlined map of islands **Rev. Legend:** MALVINAS ARGENTINAS **Rev. Inscription:** 2 DE APRIL / 1982 **Edge:** Plain

Date	Mintage	F	VF	XF	Unc	BU
2007	5,000	—	—	—	—	9.00

KM# 145 2 PESOS

Copper-Nickel, 30.35 mm. **Subject:** 100th Anniversary First Oil Well **Obv:** Oil well **Obv. Legend:** REPÚBLICA ARGENTINA - DESCUBRIMIENTO DEL PETRÓLEO **Rev:** Modern pump **Rev. Inscription:** CHUBUT **Edge:** Reeded

Date	Mintage	F	VF	XF	Unc	BU
2007	995,000	—	—	—	6.00	8.00

KM# 162 2 PESOS

10.4700 g., Copper-Nickel, 30.35 mm. **Subject:** Central Bank, 75th Anniversary **Obv:** Head at right, facing left **Rev:** Bank's main doors

Date	Mintage	F	VF	XF	Unc	BU
2010	—	—	—	—	1.85	2.50

KM# 133 5 PESOS

8.0640 g., 0.9000 Gold 0.2333 oz. AGW, 22 mm. **Subject:** Gral. Justo Jose de Urquiza **Obv:** Stylized portrait facing **Rev:** Church tower and denomination **Edge:** Reeded

Date	Mintage	F	VF	XF	Unc	BU
2001 Proof	1,000	Value: 350				

KM# 149 5 PESOS
8.0640 g., 0.9000 Gold 0.2333 oz. AGW **Subject:** 100th Anniversary City of Comodoro Rivadavia

Date	Mintage	F	VF	XF	Unc	BU
2001 Proof	750	Value: 375				

KM# 143 5 PESOS
27.0000 g., 0.9250 Silver 0.8029 oz. ASW, 40 mm. **Subject:** FIFA - XVIII World Championship Football - Germany 2006 **Obv:** Football at right on grass, chaff in background **Obv. Legend:** REPÚBLICA ARGENTINA **Rev:** Logo **Rev. Legend:** COPA MUNDIAL DE LA FIFA **Rev. Inscription:** ALEMANIA **Edge:** Reeded

Date	Mintage	F	VF	XF	Unc	BU
2003 Proof	50,000	Value: 55.00				

KM# 146 5 PESOS
27.0000 g., 0.9250 Silver 0.8029 oz. ASW **Subject:** FIFA - XVIII World Football Championship - Germany 2006 **Obv. Legend:** REPÚBLICA ARGENTINA **Rev:** Logo **Edge:** Reeded

Date	Mintage	F	VF	XF	Unc	BU
2004 Proof	50,000	Value: 55.00				

KM# 142 5 PESOS
8.0640 g., 0.9000 Gold 0.2333 oz. AGW, 22 mm. **Obv:** Maria Eva Duarte de Peron **Rev:** "EVITA" and audience

Date	Mintage	F	VF	XF	Unc	BU
ND (2004) Proof	1,000	Value: 350				

KM# 150 5 PESOS
27.0000 g., 0.9250 Silver 0.8029 oz. ASW **Subject:** FIFA - XVIII World Championship Football - Germany 2006 **Obv:** Forward player **Rev:** Logo

Date	Mintage	F	VF	XF	Unc	BU
2005 Proof	—	Value: 65.00				

KM# 154 5 PESOS
8.0640 g., 0.9000 Gold 0.2333 oz. AGW, 22 mm. **Subject:** 25th Anniversary Malvinas Islands Occupation - Heroes **Obv:** Soldier's bust facing **Obv. Legend:** REPUBLICA ARGENTINA - 1982 - 2007 - LA NACIÓN A SUS HÉROES **Rev:** Outlined map of islands **Rev. Legend:** MALVINAS ISLANDS **Rev. Inscription:** 2 DE APRIL / 1982 **Edge:** Reeded

Date	Mintage	F	VF	XF	Unc	BU
2007 Proof	1,000	Value: 400				

KM# 147 10 PESOS
6.7500 g., 0.9990 Gold 0.2168 oz. AGW **Subject:** FIFA - XVIII World Football Championship - Germany 2006 **Obv. Legend:** REPÚBLICA ARGENTINA **Edge:** Reeded

Date	Mintage	F	VF	XF	Unc	BU
2004 Proof	25,000	Value: 350				

KM# 151 10 PESOS
6.7500 g., 0.9990 Gold 0.2168 oz. AGW **Subject:** FIFA - XVIII World Championship Football - Germany 2006 **Obv:** Forward player **Rev:** Logo

Date	Mintage	F	VF	XF	Unc	BU
2005 Proof	—	Value: 350				

KM# 138 25 PESOS
27.0000 g., 0.9250 Silver 0.8029 oz. ASW, 40 mm. **Subject:** IBERO-AMERICA Series **Obv:** Coats of arms **Rev:** Tall ship "Presidente Sarmiento" **Edge:** Reeded

Date	Mintage	F	VF	XF	Unc	BU
2002 Proof	—	Value: 60.00				

KM# 139 25 PESOS
27.0000 g., 0.9250 Silver 0.8029 oz. ASW, 40 mm. **Subject:** Ibero-America **Obv:** National arms in circle of arms **Rev:** Colon Theater building **Edge:** Reeded

Date	Mintage	F	VF	XF	Unc	BU
2005 Proof	15,500	Value: 55.00				

PROOF SETS

KM#	Date	Mintage	Identification	Issue Price	Mkt Val
PS6	2007 (2)	300	KM#153, 154	475	485

ARMENIA

The Republic of Armenia, formerly Armenian S.S.R., is bordered to the north by Georgia, the east by Azerbaijan and the south and west by Turkey and Iran. It has an area of 11,506 sq. mi. (29,800 sq. km) and an estimated population of 3.66 million. Capital: Yerevan. Agriculture including cotton, vineyards and orchards, hydroelectricity, chemicals - primarily synthetic rubber and fertilizers, vast mineral deposits of copper, zinc and aluminum, and production of steel and paper are major industries.

Fighting between Christians in Armenia and Muslim forces of Azerbaijan escalated in 1992 and continued through early 1994. Each country claimed the Nagorno-Karabakh, an Armenian ethnic enclave, in Azerbaijan. A temporary cease-fire was announced in May 1994.

MONETARY SYSTEM
100 Luma = 1 Dram

MINT NAME
Revan, (Erevan, now Yerevan)

REPUBLIC

STANDARD COINAGE

KM# 112 10 DRAM
1.3000 g., Aluminum, 20 mm. **Obv:** National arms **Rev:** Value **Edge:** Reeded

Date	Mintage	F	VF	XF	Unc	BU
2004	—	—	—	—	1.00	1.50

KM# 93 20 DRAM
2.8000 g., Copper Plated Steel, 20.5 mm. **Obv:** National arms **Rev:** Denomination **Edge:** Plain

Date	Mintage	F	VF	XF	Unc	BU
2003	—	—	—	—	1.00	1.50

KM# 94 50 DRAM
3.4500 g., Brass Plated Steel, 21.5 mm. **Obv:** National arms **Rev:** Value **Edge:** Reeded

Date	Mintage	F	VF	XF	Unc	BU
2003	—	—	—	—	1.25	1.50

KM# 86 100 DRAM
31.1000 g., 0.9990 Silver 0.9988 oz. ASW, 38 mm. **Obv:** National arms **Rev:** Bust of General Garegin Nzhdeh facing at right **Edge:** Plain **Edge Lettering:** Serial number

Date	Mintage	F	VF	XF	Unc	BU
2001 Proof	170	Value: 1,000				

KM# 86a 100 DRAM
31.1000 g., 0.9990 Silver Gilt 0.9988 oz. ASW, 38 mm. **Obv:** National arms **Obv. Inscription:** Bust of General Garegin Nzhdeh facing at right **Edge:** Plain **Edge Lettering:** Serial number

Date	Mintage	F	VF	XF	Unc	BU
2001 Proof	30	Value: 3,000				

KM# 87 100 DRAM
31.0400 g., 0.9990 Silver 0.9969 oz. ASW, 38 mm. **Subject:** Armenian Membership in the Council of Europe joined January 1, 2001 **Obv:** National arms **Rev:** Spiral design with star circle **Edge:** Plain **Edge Lettering:** Serial number

Date	Mintage	F	VF	XF	Unc	BU
2001 Proof	200	Value: 300				

KM# 98 100 DRAM
31.1000 g., 0.9250 Silver 0.9249 oz. ASW, 40 mm. **Obv:** National arms **Rev:** Aram Khachatryan, Birth Centennial **Edge:** Reeded

Date	Mintage	F	VF	XF	Unc	BU
2002	300	—	—	—	65.00	100

KM# 99 100 DRAM
31.1000 g., 0.9250 Silver 0.9249 oz. ASW, 40 mm. **Obv:** The Book of Sadness **Rev:** Saint Grigor Narekatsi with book and quill millennium of his poem "The Book of Sadness" **Edge:** Reeded

Date	Mintage	F	VF	XF	Unc	BU
2002 Proof	500	Value: 100				

KM# 110 100 DRAM
33.9200 g., 0.9250 Silver 1.0087 oz. ASW, 39 mm. **Subject:** 110th Anniversary of State Banking in Armenia and 10th Year of National Currency October 7 1893 - November 22, 1993 **Obv:** Building above value **Rev:** State Bank emblem **Edge:** Reeded

Date	Mintage	F	VF	XF	Unc	BU
2003 Proof	300	Value: 200				

KM# 95 100 DRAM
4.0000 g., Nickel Plated Steel, 22.5 mm. **Obv:** National arms **Rev:** Value **Edge:** Reeded

Date	Mintage	F	VF	XF	Unc	BU
2003	—	—	—	—	1.50	2.00

KM# 111 100 DRAM
28.2800 g., 0.9250 Silver 0.8410 oz. ASW, 38.6 mm. **Subject:** FIFA World Cup Soccer Games - Germany **Obv:** National arms **Rev:** Three soccer players

Date	Mintage	F	VF	XF	Unc	BU
2004 Proof	300	Value: 150				

KM# 113 100 DRAM
31.1000 g., 0.9990 Silver 0.9988 oz. ASW, 38 mm. **Subject:** Gandzasar Monastery **Obv:** Monastery **Rev:** Folk art crucifix and denomination

Date	Mintage	F	VF	XF	Unc	BU
2004 Proof	500	Value: 100				

KM# 115 100 DRAM
31.1000 g., 0.9250 Silver 0.9249 oz. ASW, 40 mm. **Subject:** Anania Shirakatsi 1400 Anniversary, Scientist **Obv:** Profile of Shirakatsi, deep in thought **Rev:** Planets and stars, denomination

Date	Mintage	F	VF	XF	Unc	BU
2005 Proof	500	Value: 100				

KM# 123 100 DRAM
31.1000 g., 0.9250 Silver 0.9249 oz. ASW, 40.00 mm. **Subject:** Creation of the Armenian alphabet **Obv:** National arms **Rev:** King Vramshapuh standing at left, alphabet at right

Date	Mintage	F	VF	XF	Unc	BU
2005 Proof	500	Value: 150				

KM# 124 100 DRAM
31.1000 g., 0.9250 Silver 0.9249 oz. ASW, 40.00 mm. **Subject:** Creation of the Armenian alphabet **Obv:** National arms **Rev:** Sahak Partev standing at left, alphabet at right

Date	Mintage	F	VF	XF	Unc	BU
2005 Proof	500	Value: 150				

KM# 125 100 DRAM
31.1000 g., 0.9250 Silver 0.9249 oz. ASW, 40.00 mm. **Subject:** 100th Anniversary - Birth of Artem Mikoyan - Inventor of MIG Jet **Obv:** Three jet airplanes **Rev:** Bust of Mikoyan 3/4 left

Date	Mintage	F	VF	XF	Unc	BU
2005 Proof	500	Value: 125				

KM# 127 100 DRAM
28.2800 g., 0.9250 Silver 0.8410 oz. ASW, 38.61 mm. **Subject:** International Polar Year **Obv:** National arms **Obv. Legend:** REPUBLIC OF ARMENIA **Rev:** Bust of Fridtjof Nansen right at left, ship stuck in ice at lower right, multicolor emblem above

Date	Mintage	F	VF	XF	Unc	BU
2006 Proof	10,000	Value: 100				

KM# 129 100 DRAM
28.2800 g., 0.9250 Silver 0.8410 oz. ASW **Subject:** Hovhannes Aivazovsky **Obv:** National arms at lower left, sailing ship listing at center right multicolor **Rev:** Bust of Aivazovsky 3/4 left at lower left, sailing ships at center right **Shape:** Rectangular, 40 x 28 mm

Date	Mintage	F	VF	XF	Unc	BU
2006 Proof	5,000	Value: 700				

KM# 119 100 DRAM
28.3500 g., 0.9250 Silver 0.8431 oz. ASW, 38.5 mm. **Obv:** National arms **Rev:** Brown bear and two red lines **Edge:** Plain

Date	Mintage	F	VF	XF	Unc	BU
2006 Proof	3,000	Value: 185				

KM# 120 100 DRAM
28.3500 g., 0.9250 Silver 0.8431 oz. ASW, 38.5 mm. **Obv:** National arms **Rev:** Long-eared Hedgehog and two red lines **Edge:** Plain

Date	Mintage	F	VF	XF	Unc	BU
2006 Proof	3,000	Value: 185				

KM# 121 100 DRAM
28.2800 g., 0.9250 Silver 0.8410 oz. ASW, 38.6 mm. **Obv:** National arms, date and value **Rev:** Caucasian Forest Cat **Edge:** Plain

Date	Mintage	F	VF	XF	Unc	BU
2006 Proof	3,000	Value: 100				

KM# 122 100 DRAM
28.2800 g., 0.9250 Silver 0.8410 oz. ASW, 38.6 mm. **Obv:** National arms, date and value **Rev:** Armenian Tortoise **Edge:** Plain

Date	Mintage	F	VF	XF	Unc	BU
2006 Proof	3,000	Value: 135				

KM# 135 100 DRAM
28.2400 g., 0.9250 Silver 0.8398 oz. ASW, 38.53 mm. **Subject:** Caucasion Leopard **Obv:** National arms **Obv. Legend:** REPUBLIC OF ARMENIA **Rev:** Leopard walking left **Edge:** Plain

Date	Mintage	F	VF	XF	Unc	BU
2007 Proof	3,000	Value: 110				

KM# 136 100 DRAM
28.2400 g., 0.9250 Silver 0.8398 oz. ASW, 38.5 mm. **Subject:** Northern Shoveler duck **Obv:** National arms **Obv. Legend:** REPUBLIC OF ARMENIA **Rev:** Duck standing left **Edge:** Plain

Date	Mintage	F	VF	XF	Unc	BU
2007 Proof	3,000	Value: 85.00				

KM# 141 100 DRAM
28.2800 g., 0.9250 Silver Zircon crystal attached. 0.8410 oz. ASW, 38.5 mm. **Series:** Signs of the Zodiac **Obv:** National arms within ring of signs of the Zodiac **Obv. Legend:** REPUBLIC OF ARMENIA **Obv. Designer:** Ursula Valenazh **Rev:** Capricorn with jeweled star at left, multicolor **Edge:** Plain

Date	Mintage	F	VF	XF	Unc	BU
2007 Proof	12,000	Value: 85.00				

KM# 153 100 DRAM
28.2800 g., 0.9250 Silver 0.8410 oz. ASW, 38.6 mm. **Obv:** National arms **Obv. Legend:** REPUBLIC OF ARMENIA **Rev:** Lake Sevan Salmon

Date	Mintage	F	VF	XF	Unc	BU
2007 Proof	3,000	Value: 100				

KM# 154 100 DRAM
28.2800 g., 0.9250 Silver 0.8410 oz. ASW, 38.6 mm. **Obv:** National arms **Obv. Legend:** REPUBLIC OF ARMENIA **Rev:** Armenian viper

Date	Mintage	F	VF	XF	Unc	BU
2007 Proof	3,000	Value: 85.00				

KM# 157 100 DRAM
28.2800 g., 0.9250 Silver 0.8410 oz. ASW, 38.6 mm. **Subject:** Aquarius

Date	Mintage	F	VF	XF	Unc	BU
2007 Proof	—	Value: 100				

KM# 158 100 DRAM
28.2800 g., 0.9250 Silver 0.8410 oz. ASW, 38.6 mm. **Subject:** Pisces

Date	Mintage	F	VF	XF	Unc	BU
2007 Proof	—	Value: 100				

KM# 155 100 DRAM
28.2800 g., 0.9250 Silver 0.8410 oz. ASW, 39 mm. **Subject:** National Arms **Obv:** Roussana and Andrzej Nowakowscy **Rev:** Caucasian owl on branch, (Aegolius Funereus Caucasious) red arcs at top and bottom

Date	Mintage	F	VF	XF	Unc	BU
2008 Proof	3,000	Value: 75.00				

KM# 159 100 DRAM
28.2800 g., 0.9250 Silver 0.8410 oz. ASW, 38.6 mm. **Subject:** Aries

Date	Mintage	F	VF	XF	Unc	BU
2008 Proof	—	Value: 100				

KM# 160 100 DRAM
28.2800 g., 0.9250 Silver 0.8410 oz. ASW, 38.6 mm. **Subject:** Taurus

Date	Mintage	F	VF	XF	Unc	BU
2008 Proof	—	Value: 100				

KM# 161 100 DRAM
28.2800 g., 0.9250 Silver 0.8410 oz. ASW, 38.6 mm. **Subject:** Gemini

Date	Mintage	F	VF	XF	Unc	BU
2008 Proof	—	Value: 100				

KM# 162 100 DRAM
28.2800 g., 0.9250 Silver 0.8410 oz. ASW **Subject:** Cancer

Date	Mintage	F	VF	XF	Unc	BU
2008 Proof	—	Value: 100				

KM# 163 100 DRAM
28.2800 g., 0.9250 Silver 0.8410 oz. ASW, 38.6 mm. **Subject:** Leo

Date	Mintage	F	VF	XF	Unc	BU
2008 Proof	—	Value: 100				

KM# 164 100 DRAM
28.2800 g., 0.9250 Silver 0.8410 oz. ASW, 38.6 mm. **Subject:** Virgo

Date	Mintage	F	VF	XF	Unc	BU
2008 Proof	—	Value: 100				

KM# 165 100 DRAM
28.2800 g., 0.9250 Silver 0.8410 oz. ASW, 38.6 mm. **Subject:** Libra

Date	Mintage	F	VF	XF	Unc	BU
2008 Proof	—	Value: 100				

KM# 167 100 DRAM
28.2800 g., 0.9250 Silver 0.8410 oz. ASW, 38.6 mm. **Subject:** Bezoar

Date	Mintage	F	VF	XF	Unc	BU
2008 Proof	—	Value: 100				

KM# 172 100 DRAM
28.2800 g., 0.9250 Silver 0.8410 oz. ASW, 38.6 mm. **Subject:** Scorpio

Date	Mintage	F	VF	XF	Unc	BU
2008 Proof	—	Value: 100				

KM# 174 100 DRAM
28.2800 g., 0.9250 Silver 0.8410 oz. ASW, 38.6 mm. **Subject:** Sagittarius

Date	Mintage	F	VF	XF	Unc	BU
2008 Proof	—	Value: 100				

KM# 177 100 DRAM
28.2800 g., 0.9250 Silver 0.8410 oz. ASW, 38.6 mm. **Subject:** Armenian Moufflon

Date	Mintage	F	VF	XF	Unc	BU
2008 Proof	—	Value: 75.00				

KM# 178 100 DRAM
28.2800 g., 0.9250 Silver 0.8410 oz. ASW, 38.6 mm. **Subject:** Toad Agama

Date	Mintage	F	VF	XF	Unc	BU
2008 Proof	—	Value: 75.00				

KM# 182 100 DRAM
28.2800 g., 0.9250 Silver 0.8410 oz. ASW, 38.6 mm. **Subject:** Pele

Date	Mintage	F	VF	XF	Unc	BU
2008 Proof	—	Value: 60.00				

KM# 183 100 DRAM
28.2800 g., 0.9250 Silver 0.8410 oz. ASW, 38.6 mm. **Subject:** Eusebio

Date	Mintage	F	VF	XF	Unc	BU
2008 Proof	—	Value: 60.00				

KM# 184 100 DRAM
28.2800 g., 0.9250 Silver 0.8410 oz. ASW, 38.6 mm. **Subject:** Lev Jashin

Date	Mintage	F	VF	XF	Unc	BU
2008 Proof	—	Value: 60.00				

KM# 187 100 DRAM
28.2800 g., 0.9250 Silver 0.8410 oz. ASW, 38.6 mm. **Subject:** Franz Beckenbauer

Date	Mintage	F	VF	XF	Unc	BU
2008 Proof	—	Value: 60.00				

KM# 156 100 DRAM
28.2800 g., 0.9250 Silver 0.8410 oz. ASW, 38.6 mm. **Subject:** Zbigniew Boniek **Rev:** Portrait facing, multicolor flag

Date	Mintage	F	VF	XF	Unc	BU
2009 Proof	50,000	Value: 85.00				

KM# 96 200 DRAM
4.5000 g., Brass, 24 mm. **Obv:** National arms **Rev:** Value **Edge:** Reeded

Date	Mintage	F	VF	XF	Unc	BU
2003	—	—	—	—	3.00	4.00

KM# 106 500 DRAM
155.5000 g., 0.9250 Silver 4.6243 oz. ASW, 63 mm. **Subject:** 10th Anniversary of Independence **Obv:** National arms **Rev:** Tower with flag, logo at right 9-21-91

Date	Mintage	F	VF	XF	Unc	BU
2001 Proof	200	Value: 400				

KM# 97 500 DRAM
5.0000 g., Bi-Metallic Copper-Nickel center in a Brass ring, 22 mm. **Obv:** National arms **Rev:** Value **Edge:** Segmented reeding

Date	Mintage	F	VF	XF	Unc	BU
2003	—	—	—	—	6.00	8.00

KM# 109 1000 DRAM
15.5500 g., 0.5850 Gold 0.2925 oz. AGW, 26 mm. **Obv:** National arms on ancient coin design **Rev:** Tigran the Great ancient coin portrait

Date	Mintage	F	VF	XF	Unc	BU
2003	500	—	—	—	785	1,200

KM# 128 1000 DRAM
33.6000 g., 0.9250 Silver 0.9992 oz. ASW, 38 mm. **Subject:** 100th Anniversary Birth of Marshal Babajanian **Obv:** National arms **Rev:** Bust of Babajanian 3/4 right

Date	Mintage	F	VF	XF	Unc	BU
2006 Proof	500	Value: 150				

KM# 133 1000 DRAM
33.6000 g., 0.9250 Silver 0.9992 oz. ASW, 40 mm. **Series:** Armenian grapes **Obv:** National arms **Rev:** Large bunch of grapes at left

Date	Mintage	F	VF	XF	Unc	BU
2007 Proof	5,000	Value: 150				

KM# 169 1000 DRAM
33.6000 g., 0.9250 Silver 0.9992 oz. ASW, 40 mm. **Subject:** Viktor Ambartsumian, 100th Anniversary of Birth

Date	Mintage	F	VF	XF	Unc	BU
2008 Proof	—	Value: 100				

KM# 171 1000 DRAM
33.6000 g., 0.9250 Silver 0.9992 oz. ASW, 40 mm. **Subject:** A. Spendiaryan Theater of Ballet and Opera, 75th Anniversary

Date	Mintage	F	VF	XF	Unc	BU
2008 Proof	—	Value: 100				

KM# 192 1000 DRAM
33.6000 g., 0.9250 Silver 0.9992 oz. ASW, 40 mm. **Subject:** Mkhitar Gosh - The Codex

Date	Mintage	F	VF	XF	Unc	BU
2009 Proof	—	Value: 55.00				

KM# 193 1000 DRAM
31.1000 g., 0.9990 Silver 0.9988 oz. ASW, 38 mm. **Subject:** Gladzor University, 750th Anniversary

Date	Mintage	F	VF	XF	Unc	BU
2009 Proof	—	Value: 55.00				

KM# 134 1957 DRAM
33.6000 g., 0.9250 Silver 0.9992 oz. ASW, 40 mm. **Subject:** 50th Anniversay of Matenadaran **Obv:** Small national arms at center surrounded by intricate pattern **Rev:** Building at left center

Date	Mintage	F	VF	XF	Unc	BU
2007 Proof	500	Value: 125				

KM# 117 5000 DRAM
31.1000 g., 0.9250 Silver 0.9249 oz. ASW, 38 mm. **Subject:** Armenian Armed Forces **Obv:** Order of the Combat Cross of the Second Degree and the Emblem of the Ministry of Defense of the Republic of Armenia **Obv. Designer:** H. Samuelian **Rev:** Arms, date and denomination **Shape:** Octagonal

Date	Mintage	F	VF	XF	Unc	BU
2005 Proof	500	Value: 130				

KM# 126 5000 DRAM
168.1000 g., 0.9250 Silver 4.9990 oz. ASW, 63 mm. **Subject:** 15th Anniversary of Independence **Obv:** National arms **Rev:** Building at center left, multicolor emblem above, mountains in background

Date	Mintage	F	VF	XF	Unc	BU
2006 Proof	300	Value: 400				

KM# 139 5000 DRAM
4.3000 g., 0.9000 Gold 0.1244 oz. AGW, 18 mm. **Subject:** Haik Nahapet **Obv:** Small national arms at upper left, Orion constellation at right **Rev:** 3/4 length classical Archer right

Date	Mintage	F	VF	XF	Unc	BU
2007 Proof	3,000	Value: 400				

KM# 179 5000 DRAM
168.1000 g., 0.9250 Silver partially gold plated 4.9990 oz. ASW, 63 mm. **Subject:** National Currency, 15th Anniversary

Date	Mintage	F	VF	XF	Unc	BU
2008 Proof	—	Value: 150				

KM# 195 5000 DRAM
4.3000 g., 0.9000 Gold 0.1244 oz. AGW, 18 mm. **Subject:** St. Sargis the Commander

Date	Mintage	F	VF	XF	Unc	BU
2009 Proof	—	Value: 225				

KM# 107 10000 DRAM
8.6000 g., 0.9990 Gold 0.2762 oz. AGW, 22 mm. **Obv:** Mesrop Mashtots, creator of the Armenian alphabet **Rev:** Armenian alphabet

Date	Mintage	F	VF	XF	Unc	BU
2002 Proof	1,000	Value: 450				

KM# 108 10000 DRAM
8.6000 g., 0.9990 Gold 0.2762 oz. AGW, 22 mm. **Obv:** Building above value **Rev:** Aram Khachatryan left birth centennial

Date	Mintage	F	VF	XF	Unc	BU
2002 Proof	500	Value: 475				

KM# 114 10000 DRAM
8.6000 g., 0.9990 Gold 0.2762 oz. AGW, 22 mm. **Subject:** Arshile Gorky birth April 15, 1904 **Obv:** Bust of Gorky **Rev:** Denomination

Date	Mintage	F	VF	XF	Unc	BU
2004 Proof	1,000	Value: 450				

KM# 116 10000 DRAM
8.6000 g., 0.9990 Gold 0.2762 oz. AGW, 22 mm. **Subject:** Martiros Saryan 125th Anniversary of Birth **Obv:** Bust of Saryan **Rev:** Landscape, denomination

Date	Mintage	F	VF	XF	Unc	BU
2005 Proof	1,000	Value: 450				

KM# 130 10000 DRAM
8.6000 g., 0.9990 Gold 0.2762 oz. AGW, 22 mm. **Subject:** Komitas Vardapet **Obv:** Musical notations and score **Rev:** Bust of Vardapet 3/4 right

Date	Mintage	F	VF	XF	Unc	BU
2006 Proof	1,000	Value: 500				

KM# 131 10000 DRAM
8.6000 g., 0.9000 Gold 0.2488 oz. AGW, 22 mm. **Subject:** 37th Chess Olympiad **Obv:** Chess piece at right **Rev:** National arms within 6 chess pieces in circle

Date	Mintage	F	VF	XF	Unc	BU
2006 Proof	1,000	Value: 450				

KM# 132 10000 DRAM
8.6000 g., 0.9000 Gold 0.2488 oz. AGW, 22 mm. **Subject:** Hakob Gurjian **Obv:** Seated female sculpture **Rev:** Head 3/4 right

Date	Mintage	F	VF	XF	Unc	BU
2006 Proof	1,000	Value: 500				

KM# 137 10000 DRAM
8.6000 g., 0.9000 Gold 0.2488 oz. AGW, 22 mm. **Subject:** Jean Carzou **Obv:** National arms with stylized view of shopping bourse **Rev:** Bust of Carzou 3/4 right at laft center

Date	Mintage	F	VF	XF	Unc	BU
2007 Proof	1,000	Value: 500				

KM# 138 10000 DRAM
8.6000 g., 0.9000 Gold 0.2488 oz. AGW, 22 mm. **Subject:** 15th Anniversary of Armenian Army **Obv:** National arms **Rev:** Military badge

Date	Mintage	F	VF	XF	Unc	BU
2007 Proof	1,000	Value: 500				

KM# 140 10000 DRAM
8.6000 g., 0.9000 Gold 0.2488 oz. AGW, 22 mm. **Subject:** 15th Anniversary Liberation of Shusi **Obv:** Bird with wings outspread above two shields **Rev:** Swirl in background

Date	Mintage	F	VF	XF	Unc	BU
2007 Proof	1,000	Value: 500				

KM# 175 10000 DRAM
8.6000 g., 0.9000 Gold 0.2488 oz. AGW, 22 mm. **Subject:** Sagittarius

Date	Mintage	F	VF	XF	Unc	BU
2008 Proof	—	Value: 425				

KM# 166 10000 DRAM
8.6000 g., 0.9000 Gold 0.2488 oz. AGW, 22 mm. **Subject:** Libra

Date	Mintage	F	VF	XF	Unc	BU
2008 Proof	—	Value: 425				

KM# 168 10000 DRAM
8.6000 g., 0.9000 Gold 0.2488 oz. AGW, 22 mm. **Subject:** Court, 10th Anniversary

Date	Mintage	F	VF	XF	Unc	BU
2008 Proof	—	Value: 425				

KM# 170 10000 DRAM
8.6000 g., 0.9000 Gold 0.2488 oz. AGW, 22 mm. **Subject:** William Saroyan, 100th Anniversary of Birth

Date	Mintage	F	VF	XF	Unc	BU
2008 Proof	—	Value: 425				

KM# 173 10000 DRAM
8.6000 g., 0.9000 Gold 0.2488 oz. AGW, 22 mm. **Subject:** Scorpio

Date	Mintage	F	VF	XF	Unc	BU
2008 Proof	—	Value: 425				

KM# 176 10000 DRAM
8.6000 g., 0.9000 Gold 0.2488 oz. AGW, 22 mm. **Subject:** Capricorn

Date	Mintage	F	VF	XF	Unc	BU
2008 Proof	—	Value: 425				

KM# 180 10000 DRAM
8.6000 g., 0.9000 Gold 0.2488 oz. AGW, 22 mm. **Subject:** Aquarius

Date	Mintage	F	VF	XF	Unc	BU
2008 Proof	—	Value: 425				

KM# 181 10000 DRAM
8.6000 g., 0.9000 Gold 0.2488 oz. AGW, 22 mm. **Subject:** Pisces

Date	Mintage	F	VF	XF	Unc	BU
2008 Proof	—	Value: 425				

KM# 185 10000 DRAM
8.6000 g., 0.9000 Gold 0.2488 oz. AGW, 22 mm. **Subject:** Aries

Date	Mintage	F	VF	XF	Unc	BU
2008 Proof	—	Value: 425				

KM# 186 10000 DRAM
8.6000 g., 0.9000 Gold 0.2488 oz. AGW, 22 mm. **Subject:** Taurus

Date	Mintage	F	VF	XF	Unc	BU
2008 Proof	—	Value: 425				

KM# 188 10000 DRAM
8.6000 g., 0.9000 Gold 0.2488 oz. AGW, 22 mm. **Subject:** Gemini

Date	Mintage	F	VF	XF	Unc	BU
2008 Proof	—	Value: 425				

KM# 189 10000 DRAM
8.6000 g., 0.9000 Gold 0.2488 oz. AGW, 22 mm. **Subject:** Cancer

Date	Mintage	F	VF	XF	Unc	BU
2008 Proof	—	Value: 425				

KM# 190 10000 DRAM
8.6000 g., 0.9000 Gold 0.2488 oz. AGW, 22 mm. **Subject:** Leo

Date	Mintage	F	VF	XF	Unc	BU
2008 Proof	—	Value: 425				

KM# 191 10000 DRAM
8.6000 g., 0.9000 Gold 0.2488 oz. AGW, 22 mm. **Subject:** Virgo

Date	Mintage	F	VF	XF	Unc	BU
2009 Proof	—	Value: 425				

KM# 194 10000 DRAM
8.6000 g., 0.9000 Gold 0.2488 oz. AGW, 22 mm. **Subject:** Khachatour Aboryan, 200th Anniversary of Birth

Date	Mintage	F	VF	XF	Unc	BU
2009 Proof	—	Value: 425				

KM# 118 50000 DRAM
8.6000 g., 0.9990 Gold 0.2762 oz. AGW, 22 mm. **Subject:** Armenian Armed Forces **Obv:** Order of the Combat Cross of the Second Degree and the Emblem of the Ministry of Defense of the Republic of Armenia **Obv. Designer:** H. Samuelian **Rev:** Arms, date and denomination

Date	Mintage	F	VF	XF	Unc	BU
2005 Proof	1,000	Value: 450				

ARUBA

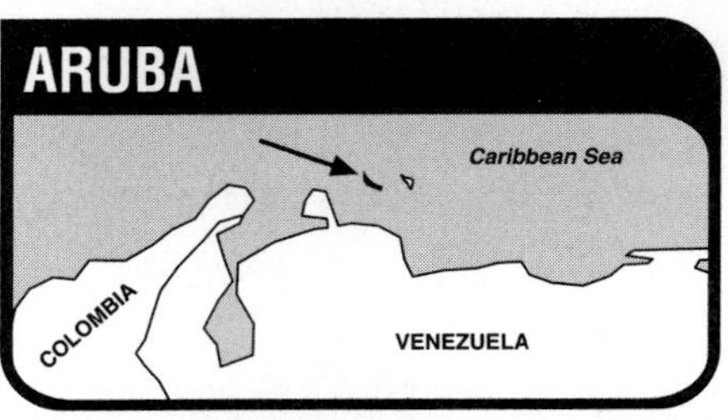

The second largest island of the Netherlands Antilles, Aruba is situated near the Venezuelan coast. The island has an area of 74-1/2 sq. mi. (193 sq. km.) and a population of 65,974. Capital: Oranjestad, named after the Dutch royal family. Aruba was important in the processing and transportation of petroleum products in the first part of the twentieth century, but today the chief industry is tourism.

For earlier issues see Curacao and the Netherlands Antilles.

RULER
Dutch

MINT MARKS
(u) Utrecht - Privy marks only
Wine tendril with grapes, 2001-
Wine tendril with grapes plus star, 2002-
Sails of a clipper, 2003-

MONETARY SYSTEM
100 Cents = 1 Florin

DUTCH STATE
"Status Aparte"

DECIMAL COINAGE

KM# 1 5 CENTS
2.0000 g., Nickel Bonded Steel, 16 mm. **Ruler:** Beatrix **Obv:** National arms **Rev:** Geometric design with value **Edge:** Plain

Date	Mintage	F	VF	XF	Unc	BU
2001(u)	946,900	—	—	—	0.30	0.60
2002(u)	1,006,000	—	—	—	0.20	0.50
2003(u)	1,104,100	—	—	—	0.20	0.50
2004(u)	502,500	—	—	0.20	0.50	1.00
2005(u)	602,500	—	—	—	0.20	0.50
2006(u)	602,000	—	—	—	0.20	0.50
2007(u)	1,152,000	—	—	—	0.20	0.50
2008(u)	1,152,000	—	—	—	0.20	0.50
2009(u)	—	—	—	—	0.20	0.50
2010(u)	—	—	—	—	0.20	0.50
2011(u)	—	—	—	—	0.20	0.50

KM# 2 10 CENTS
3.0000 g., Nickel Bonded Steel, 17.95 mm. **Ruler:** Beatrix **Obv:** National arms **Rev:** Geometric design with value **Edge:** Reeded

Date	Mintage	F	VF	XF	Unc	BU
2001(u)	1,006,900	—	—	—	0.30	0.60
2002(u)	1,006,000	—	—	—	0.30	0.60
2003(u)	1,004,000	—	—	—	0.30	0.60
2004(u)	402,500	—	0.20	0.35	0.60	0.90
2005(u)	402,500	—	—	—	0.30	0.60
2006(u)	452,500	—	—	—	0.30	0.60
2007(u)	1,102,000	—	—	—	0.30	0.60
2008(u)	1,442,000	—	—	—	0.30	0.60
2009(u)	—	—	—	—	0.30	0.60
2009(u)	—	—	—	—	0.30	0.60
2010(u)	—	—	—	—	0.30	0.60
2011	—	—	—	—	0.30	0.60

KM# 3 25 CENTS
3.5000 g., Nickel Bonded Steel, 20 mm. **Ruler:** Beatrix **Obv:** National arms **Rev:** Geometric design with value **Edge:** Plain

Date	Mintage	F	VF	XF	Unc	BU
2001(u)	716,900	—	—	—	0.35	0.80
2002(u)	806,000	—	—	—	0.35	0.80
2003(u)	804,000	—	—	—	0.35	0.80
2004(u)	362,500	—	—	—	0.40	0.80
2005(u)	302,500	—	—	—	0.40	0.80
2006(u)	302,000	—	—	—	0.40	0.80
2007(u)	202,000	—	—	—	0.50	1.00
2008(u)	202,000	—	—	—	0.50	1.00
2009(u)	—	—	—	—	0.50	1.00
2010(u)	—	—	—	—	0.50	1.00
2011(u)	—	—	—	—	0.50	1.00

KM# 4 50 CENTS
5.0000 g., Nickel Bonded Steel, 20 mm. **Ruler:** Beatrix **Obv:** National arms **Rev:** Geometric design with value **Edge:** Plain **Shape:** 4-sided

Date	Mintage	F	VF	XF	Unc	BU
2001(u)	506,900	—	—	0.30	0.65	0.80
2002(u)	306,000	—	—	0.30	0.65	0.80
2003(u)	279,000	—	—	0.40	0.80	1.00
2004(u)	402,500	—	—	0.50	0.85	1.10
2005(u)	102,500	—	—	0.35	0.65	0.85
2006(u)	102,500	—	—	0.35	0.65	0.85
2007(u)	32,000	—	—	0.60	1.50	2.50
2008(u)	302,000	—	—	0.60	1.50	2.50
2009(u)	—	—	—	0.60	1.50	2.50
2010(u)	—	—	—	0.60	1.50	2.50
2011(u)	—	—	—	0.60	1.50	2.50

KM# 5 FLORIN
8.5000 g., Nickel Bonded Steel, 26 mm. **Ruler:** Beatrix **Obv:** Head left **Rev:** National arms **Edge:** Lettered **Edge Lettering:** GOD * ZEiJ * MET * ONS

Date	Mintage	F	VF	XF	Unc	BU
2001(u)	406,900	—	—	0.65	1.25	2.25
2002(u)	206,000	—	—	0.75	1.30	2.50
2003(u)	179,000	—	—	0.80	1.50	3.00
2004(u)	410,000	—	—	0.70	1.35	2.35
2005(u)	352,500	—	—	0.70	1.35	2.35
2006(u)	402,000	—	—	0.70	1.35	2.35
2007(u)	502,000	—	—	0.70	1.35	2.35
2008(u)	289,000	—	—	0.70	1.35	2.35
2009(u)	—	—	—	0.70	1.35	2.35
2010(u)	—	—	—	0.70	1.35	2.35
2011(u)	—	—	—	0.70	1.35	2.35

KM# 6 2-1/2 FLORIN
10.3000 g., Nickel Bonded Steel, 30 mm. **Ruler:** Beatrix **Obv:** Head left **Rev:** National arms **Edge:** Lettered **Edge Lettering:** GOD * ZEiJ * MET * ONS

Date	Mintage	F	VF	XF	Unc	BU
2001(u) In sets only	6,900	—	—	—	3.50	5.00
2002(u) In sets only	6,000	—	—	—	3.50	5.00
2003(u) In sets only	4,000	—	—	—	3.50	5.00
2004(u) In sets only	2,500	—	—	—	3.50	5.00
2005(u) In sets only	2,500	—	—	—	3.50	5.00
2006(u) In sets only	2,000	—	—	—	3.50	5.00
2007(u) In sets only	2,000	—	—	—	3.50	5.00
2008(u) In sets only	2,000	—	—	—	3.50	5.00
2009(u) In sets only	2,000	—	—	—	3.50	5.00
2010(u) In sets only	—	—	—	—	3.50	5.00
2011(u)	—	—	—	—	3.50	5.00

KM# 12 5 FLORIN

8.6400 g., Nickel Bonded Steel, 26 mm. **Ruler:** Beatrix **Obv:** Head left **Rev:** National arms **Edge:** Plain **Shape:** Square

Date	Mintage	F	VF	XF	Unc	BU
2001(u) In sets only	6,900	—	—	—	6.00	8.50
2002(u) In sets only	6,000	—	—	—	6.00	8.50
2003(u) In sets only	4,000	—	—	—	6.00	8.50
2004(u) In sets only	2,500	—	—	—	7.00	8.50
2005(u) In sets only	2,500	—	—	—	7.00	8.50

KM# 25 5 FLORIN

11.9000 g., 0.9250 Silver 0.3539 oz. ASW, 29 mm. **Ruler:** Beatrix **Subject:** 50th Anniversary Charter for the Kingdom of the Netherlands including Netherlands Antilles **Obv:** Head left **Rev:** Royal seal **Rev. Designer:** E. Fingal **Edge Lettering:** GOD ZIJ MET ONS

Date	Mintage	F	VF	XF	Unc	BU
2004(u) Proof	4,000	Value: 38.00				

KM# 34 5 FLORIN

11.9000 g., 0.9250 Silver 0.3539 oz. ASW, 29 mm. **Ruler:** Beatrix **Subject:** Queen's Silver Jubilee **Obv:** Head left **Rev:** Flag **Rev. Designer:** F.L. Croes **Edge:** Lettered **Edge Lettering:** GOD Z'J MET ONS

Date	Mintage	F	VF	XF	Unc	BU
2005(u) Proof	3,100	Value: 32.50				

KM# 38 5 FLORIN

8.4000 g., Aluminum-Bronze, 22.5 mm. **Ruler:** Beatrix **Obv:** Queen with a half crown on face **Rev:** Value and arms **Edge:** Reeded and lettered **Edge Lettering:** GOD Z'J MET ONS **Shape:** Round

Date	Mintage	F	VF	XF	Unc	BU
2005(u)	827,500	—	—	—	5.50	7.00
2006(u)	102,000	—	—	—	5.50	10.00
2007(u)	52,000	—	—	—	5.50	10.00
2008(u)	22,000	—	—	—	5.50	10.00
2009(u)	—	—	—	—	5.50	10.00
2010(u)	—	—	—	—	5.50	10.00
2011(u)	—	—	—	—	5.50	10.00

KM# 41 5 FLORIN

11.9000 g., 0.9250 Silver 0.3539 oz. ASW, 29 mm. **Ruler:** Beatrix **Subject:** Year of the dolphin **Obv:** Head left **Rev:** Two dolphins bounding out of the water **Edge Lettering:** GOD * ZIJ * MET * ONS *

Date	Mintage	F	VF	XF	Unc	BU
2007 Proof	1,250	Value: 35.00				

KM# 38a 5 FLORIN

8.2800 g., Aluminum-Bronze, 23.5 mm. **Ruler:** Beatrix **Obv:** Queen **Rev:** Value and arms **Shape:** Round

Date	Mintage	F	VF	XF	Unc	BU
2008(u)	—	—	—	—	5.50	7.00

KM# 42 5 FLORIN

11.9000 g., 0.9250 Silver 0.3539 oz. ASW, 29 mm. **Ruler:** Beatrix **Subject:** Fiesta de San Juan **Rev:** Phoenix rising from flames and dancers **Edge Lettering:** GOD * ZIJ * MET * ONS

Date	Mintage	F	VF	XF	Unc	BU
2008 Proof	1,250	Value: 40.00				

KM# 43 5 FLORIN

11.9000 g., 0.9250 Silver 0.3539 oz. ASW, 29 mm. **Ruler:** Beatrix **Subject:** Dante at New Year's **Obv:** Head left **Rev:** Dance at New Year's, Hand dropping coins into hat **Edge Lettering:** GOD * ZIJ * MET * ONS

Date	Mintage	F	VF	XF	Unc	BU
2009(u) Proof	1,250	Value: 40.00				

KM# 45 5 FLORIN

11.9000 g., 0.9250 Silver 0.3539 oz. ASW, 29 mm. **Ruler:** Beatrix **Series:** Olympic Games 2012 **Obv:** Queen Beatrix **Rev:** Two judoka fight men in action **Edge Lettering:** GOD * ZIJ * MET * ONS *

Date	Mintage	F	VF	XF	Unc	BU
2010 Proof	5,000	Value: 32.00				

KM# 20 10 FLORIN

25.0000 g., 0.9250 Silver 0.7435 oz. ASW, 38 mm. **Ruler:** Beatrix **Subject:** Green Sea Turtles **Obv:** Head left **Rev:** Seven sea turtles **Edge:** Plain **Designer:** E. Fingal

Date	Mintage	F	VF	XF	Unc	BU
2001(u) Prooflike	2,000	—	—	—	—	60.00

KM# 24 10 FLORIN

17.8000 g., 0.9250 Silver 0.5293 oz. ASW, 33 mm. **Ruler:** Beatrix **Subject:** Crown Prince's Wedding **Obv:** Head left **Rev:** Conjoined busts of prince and princess Maxima, right **Edge Lettering:** GOD ZIJ MET ONS **Designer:** G. Colley

Date	Mintage	F	VF	XF	Unc	BU
ND(2002)(u) Prooflike	5,000	—	—	—	—	40.00

KM# 27 10 FLORIN

25.0000 g., 0.9250 Silver 0.7435 oz. ASW, 38 mm. **Ruler:** Beatrix **Obv:** Head left **Obv. Designer:** E. Fingal **Rev:** Sea shell **Edge:** Plain

Date	Mintage	F	VF	XF	Unc	BU
2003(u) Proof	2,000	Value: 50.00				

KM# 28 10 FLORIN

25.0000 g., 0.9250 Silver 0.7435 oz. ASW, 38 mm. **Ruler:** Beatrix **Obv:** Head left **Obv. Designer:** E. Fingal **Rev:** Snake **Edge:** Plain

Date	Mintage	F	VF	XF	Unc	BU
2003(u) Proof	2,000	Value: 50.00				

KM# 29 10 FLORIN

25.0000 g., 0.9250 Silver 0.7435 oz. ASW, 38 mm. **Ruler:** Beatrix **Obv:** Head left **Obv. Designer:** E. Fingal **Rev:** Owl **Edge:** Plain

Date	Mintage	F	VF	XF	Unc	BU
2003(u) Proof	1,000	Value: 65.00				

KM# 30 10 FLORIN

25.0000 g., 0.9250 Silver 0.7435 oz. ASW, 38 mm. **Ruler:** Beatrix **Obv:** Head left **Obv. Designer:** E. Fingal **Rev:** Tree Frog **Edge:** Plain

Date	Mintage	F	VF	XF	Unc	BU
2004(u) Proof	1,000	Value: 65.00				

KM# 31 10 FLORIN

25.0000 g., 0.9250 Silver 0.7435 oz. ASW, 38 mm. **Ruler:** Beatrix **Obv:** Head left **Obv. Designer:** E. Fingal **Rev:** Fish right **Edge:** Plain

Date	Mintage	F	VF	XF	Unc	BU
2004(u) Proof	1,000	Value: 65.00				

KM# 26 10 FLORIN

6.7200 g., 0.9000 Gold 0.1944 oz. AGW, 22.5 mm. **Ruler:** Beatrix **Subject:** 20th Anniversary of Autonomy **Obv:** Head left **Rev:** Royal seal **Edge:** Reeded **Designer:** E. Fingal

Date	Mintage	F	VF	XF	Unc	BU
2004(u) Proof	1,000	Value: 275				

KM# 33 10 FLORIN
1.2442 g., 0.9990 Gold 0.0400 oz. AGW, 13.9 mm. **Ruler:** Beatrix **Subject:** Death of Juliana **Obv:** Head left **Obv. Designer:** E. Fingal **Rev:** Juliana in center **Edge:** Reeded

Date	Mintage	F	VF	XF	Unc	BU
ND (2005)(u) Proof	10,000	Value: 65.00				

KM# 35 10 FLORIN
6.7200 g., 0.9000 Gold 0.1944 oz. AGW, 22.5 mm. **Ruler:** Beatrix **Subject:** Queen's Silver Jubilee **Obv:** Head left **Rev:** Flag **Edge:** Reeded **Designer:** F.L. Croes

Date	Mintage	F	VF	XF	Unc	BU
2005(u) Proof	750	Value: 250				

KM# 36 10 FLORIN
25.0000 g., 0.9250 Silver 0.7435 oz. ASW, 38 mm. **Ruler:** Beatrix **Subject:** Status Aparte 20th Anniversary - Flag 30th Anniversary **Obv:** Queen's portrait **Rev:** Queen standing next to value and country name **Edge Lettering:** DIOS TA CU NOS

Date	Mintage	F	VF	XF	Unc	BU
2006(u) Proof	1,250	Value: 40.00				

KM# 37 10 FLORIN
6.7200 g., 0.9000 Gold 0.1944 oz. AGW, 22.5 mm. **Ruler:** Beatrix **Obv:** Queen's portrait **Rev:** Queen standing next to value and country name **Edge:** Reeded **Note:** Status Aparte

Date	Mintage	F	VF	XF	Unc	BU
2006(u) Proof	1,000	Value: 300				

KM# 44 10 FLORIN
6.7200 g., 1.2442 Gold 0.2688 oz. AGW, 13.9 mm. **Ruler:** Beatrix **Subject:** Carnival **Obv:** Head left **Rev:** Carnival feathered facemask

Date	Mintage	F	VF	XF	Unc	BU
2009 Proof	5,000	Value: 400				

KM# 22 25 FLORIN
25.0000 g., 0.9250 Silver 0.7435 oz. ASW, 38 mm. **Ruler:** Beatrix **Subject:** 15th Anniversary of Autonomy **Obv:** Head left **Rev:** National arms and inscription **Edge:** Plain

Date	Mintage	F	VF	XF	Unc	BU
2001(u) Proof	3,000	Value: 45.00				

KM# 23 100 FLORIN
6.7200 g., Gold, 22.5 mm. **Ruler:** Beatrix **Subject:** Independence **Obv:** Arms, treaty name, dates **Rev:** Head left **Edge:** Grained

Date	Mintage	F	VF	XF	Unc	BU
2001(u) Proof	1,000	Value: 400				

MINT SETS

KM#	Date	Mintage	Identification	Issue Price	Mkt Val
MS18	2001 (7)	—	KM#1-6, 12, with medal	15.00	20.00
MS19	2001 (7)	6,900	KM#1-6, 12	13.25	20.00
MS20	2002 (6)	6,000	KM# 1-6, 12	15.00	20.00
MS21	2003 (7)	4,000	KM# 1-6, 12	15.00	20.00
MS22	2004 (7)	2,500	KM# 1-6, 12	15.00	22.50
MS23	2005 (7)	2,500	KM# 1-6, 12	15.00	22.50
MS24	2006 (7)	2,000	KM# 1-6, 38	15.00	22.50
MS25	2007 (7)	2,500	KM#1-6, 38	20.00	22.50
MS26	2008 (7)	2,000	KM#1-6, 38	26.00	22.50
MS27	2009 (7)	2,000	KM#1-6, 38	26.00	22.50

ASCENSION ISLAND

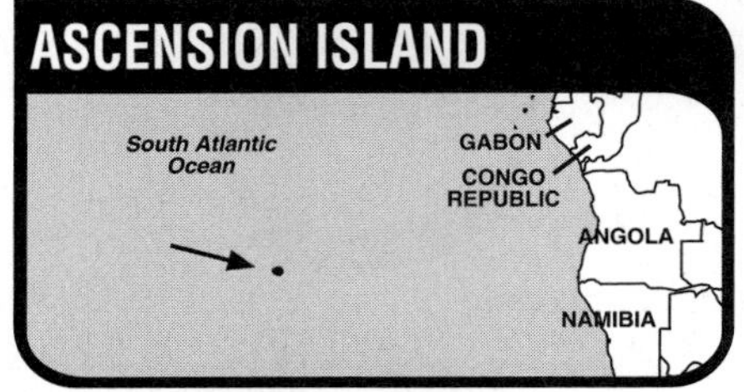

An island of volcanic origin, Ascension Island lies in the South Atlantic, 700 miles (1,100 km.) northwest of St. Helena. It has an area of 34 sq. mi. (88 sq. km.) on an island 9 miles (14 km.) long and 6 miles (10 km.) wide. Approximate population: 1,146. Although having little vegetation and scant rainfall, the island has a very healthy climate. The island is the nesting place for a large number of sea turtles and sooty terns. Phosphates and guano are the chief natural sources of income. Ascension is a dependency of the British Colony of St. Helena.

RULER
British

MINT MARKS
PM - Pobjoy Mint

BRITISH ADMINISTRATION

STANDARD COINAGE

KM# 13 50 PENCE
28.6300 g., Copper-Nickel, 38.6 mm. **Subject:** 75th Birthday of Queen Elizabeth **Obv:** Crowned bust right, denomination below **Obv. Designer:** Raphael Maklouf **Rev:** Crowned monogram above flowers within circle, date below **Edge:** Reeded

Date	Mintage	F	VF	XF	Unc	BU
2001	—	—	—	—	8.00	9.50

KM# 13a 50 PENCE
28.2800 g., 0.9250 Silver 0.8410 oz. ASW, 38.6 mm. **Subject:** Queen Elizabeth II's 75th Birthday **Obv:** Crowned bust right, denomination below **Obv. Designer:** Raphael Maklouf **Rev:** Crowned monogram above roses within circle, date below **Edge:** Reeded

Date	Mintage	F	VF	XF	Unc	BU
2001 Proof	10,000	Value: 45.00				

KM# 13b 50 PENCE
47.5400 g., 0.9166 Gold 1.4009 oz. AGW, 38.6 mm. **Subject:** Queen Elizabeth II's 75th Birthday **Obv:** Crowned bust right, denomination below **Obv. Designer:** Raphael Maklouf **Rev:** Crowned monogram above roses within circle, date below **Edge:** Reeded

Date	Mintage	F	VF	XF	Unc	BU
2001 Proof	75	Value: 2,150				

KM# 14 50 PENCE
28.6300 g., Copper-Nickel, 38.6 mm. **Subject:** Centennial - Queen Victoria's Death **Obv:** Crowned bust right, denomination below **Obv. Designer:** Raphael Maklouf **Rev:** Crowned bust left, three dates **Edge:** Reeded

Date	Mintage	F	VF	XF	Unc	BU
2001	—	—	—	—	8.00	9.50

KM# 14a 50 PENCE
28.2800 g., 0.9250 Silver 0.8410 oz. ASW, 38.6 mm. **Subject:** Centennial of Queen Victoria's Death **Obv:** Crowned bust right, denomination below **Obv. Designer:** Raphael Maklouf **Rev:** Crowned bust left, three dates **Edge:** Reeded

Date	Mintage	F	VF	XF	Unc	BU
2001 Proof	10,000	Value: 45.00				

KM# 14b 50 PENCE
47.5400 g., 0.9166 Gold 1.4009 oz. AGW, 38.6 mm. **Subject:** Centennial of Queen Victoria's Death **Obv:** Crowned bust right, denomination below **Obv. Designer:** Raphael Maklouf **Rev:** Crowned bust left, three dates **Edge:** Reeded

Date	Mintage	F	VF	XF	Unc	BU
2001 Proof	100	Value: 2,150				

KM# 15 50 PENCE
28.3500 g., Copper-Nickel, 38.6 mm. **Subject:** Queen's Golden Jubilee **Obv:** Crowned bust right, denomination below **Obv. Designer:** Raphael Maklouf **Rev:** Westminster Abby, monogram at left, circle surrounds, two dates below **Edge:** Reeded

Date	Mintage	F	VF	XF	Unc	BU
ND(2002)	—	—	—	—	8.00	9.50

KM# 15a 50 PENCE
28.2800 g., 0.9250 Silver 0.8410 oz. ASW, 38.6 mm. **Subject:** Queen Elizabeth II's Golden Jubilee **Obv:** Gold-plated crowned bust right, denomination below **Obv. Designer:** Raphael Maklouf **Rev:** Monogram and Westminster Abbey within circle, dates below **Edge:** Reeded

Date	Mintage	F	VF	XF	Unc	BU
ND(2002) Proof	10,000	Value: 45.00				

KM# 18 50 PENCE
28.2800 g., Copper-Nickel, 38.6 mm. **Subject:** Death of Queen Mother **Obv:** Crowned bust right, denomination below **Obv. Designer:** Raphael Maklouf **Rev:** Queen Mother bust right, between her life dates **Edge:** Reeded

Date	Mintage	F	VF	XF	Unc	BU
ND(2002)	—	—	—	—	10.00	12.00

KM# 18a 50 PENCE
28.2800 g., 0.9250 Silver 0.8410 oz. ASW, 38.6 mm. **Subject:** Death of Queen Mother **Obv:** Crowned bust right, denomination below **Rev:** Queen Mother bust right, between her life dates **Edge:** Reeded

Date	Mintage	F	VF	XF	Unc	BU
ND(2002) Proof	10,000	Value: 45.00				

KM# 16 50 PENCE
28.3600 g., Copper-Nickel, 38.6 mm. **Subject:** Coronation Jubilee **Obv:** Crowned bust right, denomination below **Obv. Designer:** Raphael Maklouf **Rev:** Crown, two scepters and the ampula **Edge:** Reeded

Date	Mintage	F	VF	XF	Unc	BU
ND (2003) Prooflike	—	—	—	—	10.00	12.00

KM# 16a 50 PENCE
28.2800 g., 0.9250 Silver 0.8410 oz. ASW, 38.6 mm. **Subject:** Queen Elizabeth II's - 50th Anniversary of Coronation **Obv:** Crowned bust right, denomination below **Obv. Designer:** Raphael Maklouf **Rev:** Crown, two scepters and the ampula **Edge:** Reeded

Date	Mintage	F	VF	XF	Unc	BU
ND(2003) Proof	5,000	Value: 50.00				

KM# 16b 50 PENCE
39.9400 g., 0.9166 Gold 1.1770 oz. AGW, 38.6 mm. **Subject:** Queen Elizabeth II's - 50th Anniversary of Coronation **Obv:** Crowned bust right, denomination below **Obv. Designer:** Raphael Maklouf **Rev:** Crown, two scepters and the ampula **Edge:** Reeded

Date	Mintage	F	VF	XF	Unc	BU
ND(2003) Proof	50	Value: 1,850				

KM# 17 50 PENCE
28.2800 g., Copper-Nickel, 38.6 mm. **Subject:** Queen Elizabeth II's- 50th Anniversary of Coronation **Obv:** Crowned head right, denomination below **Obv. Designer:** Raphael Maklouf **Rev:** Crowned monogram **Edge:** Reeded

Date	Mintage	F	VF	XF	Unc	BU
ND(2003)	—	—	—	—	10.00	12.00

KM# 17a 50 PENCE
28.2800 g., 0.9250 Silver 0.8410 oz. ASW, 38.6 mm. **Subject:** Queen Elizabeth II's- 50th Anniversary of Coronation **Obv:** Crowned head right, denomination below **Obv. Designer:** Raphael Maklouf **Rev:** Crowned monogram **Edge:** Reeded

Date	Mintage	F	VF	XF	Unc	BU
ND(2003) Proof	5,000	Value: 50.00				

KM# 17b 50 PENCE
39.9400 g., 0.9166 Gold 1.1770 oz. AGW, 38.6 mm. **Subject:** Queen Elizabeth II's - 50th Anniversary of Coronation **Obv:** Crowned bust right, denomination below **Obv. Designer:** Raphael Maklouf **Rev:** Crowned monogram **Edge:** Reeded

Date	Mintage	F	VF	XF	Unc	BU
ND(2003) Proof	50	Value: 1,850				

The Commonwealth of Australia, the smallest continent in the world, is located south of Indonesia between the Indian and Pacific oceans. It has an area of 2,967,893 sq. mi. (7,686,850 sq. km.) and an estimated population of 18.84 million. Capital: Canberra. Due to its early and sustained isolation, Australia is the habitat of such curious and unique fauna as the kangaroo, koala, platypus, wombat, echidna and frilled-necked lizard. The continent possesses extensive mineral deposits, the most important of which are iron ore, coal, gold, silver, nickel, uranium, lead and zinc. Raising livestock, mining and manufacturing are the principal industries. Chief exports are wool, meat, wheat, iron ore, coal and nonferrous metals.

Australia is a founding member of the Commonwealth of Nations. Elizabeth II is the Head of State as Queen of Australia; the Prime Minister is Head of Government.

NOTE: Home market grading of Australian coinage is generally stricter than USA practiced standards. The pricing in this catalog reflects strict home market grading standard.

RULER
British until 1942

MONETARY SYSTEM

Decimal Coinage (Commencing 1966)
100 Cents = 1 Dollar

COMMONWEALTH OF AUSTRALIA

DECIMAL COINAGE

KM# 767 CENT
2.6000 g., Bronze, 17.53 mm. **Ruler:** Elizabeth II **Obv:** Head with tiara right **Obv. Designer:** Ian Rank-Broadley **Rev:** Feather-tailed glider and value **Rev. Designer:** Stuart Devlin **Edge:** Plain

Date	Mintage	F	VF	XF	Unc	BU
2006B In sets only	—	—	—	—	—	15.00
2006B Proof	—	Value: 18.00				

KM# 62a CENT
2.6000 g., 0.9990 Silver 0.0835 oz. ASW, 17.53 mm. **Ruler:** Elizabeth II **Obv:** Young bust right **Rev:** Feather-tailed glider and value **Rev. Designer:** Stuart Devlin **Edge:** Plain

Date	Mintage	F	VF	XF	Unc	BU
2006 Proof	6,500	Value: 15.00				

KM# 767b CENT
5.6100 g., 0.9990 Gold 0.1802 oz. AGW, 17.53 mm. **Ruler:** Elizabeth II **Obv:** Head with tiara right **Obv. Designer:** Ian Rank-Broadley **Rev:** Feather-tailed glider **Rev. Designer:** Stuart Devlin **Edge:** Plain

Date	Mintage	F	VF	XF	Unc	BU
2006 Proof	300	Value: 600				

KM# 1249 CENT
2.4300 g., 0.9990 Silver 0.0780 oz. ASW, 17.6 mm. **Ruler:** Elizabeth II **Subject:** 1966 Decimal Pattern **Obv:** Head right **Obv. Designer:** Ian Rank-Broadley **Rev:** Waratah, flower of New South Wales **Rev. Designer:** Andor Meszaros

Date	Mintage	F	VF	XF	Unc	BU
2009P Proof	7,500	Value: 15.00				

KM# 768 2 CENTS

5.1800 g., Bronze, 21.59 mm. **Ruler:** Elizabeth II **Obv:** Head with tiara right **Obv. Designer:** Ian Rank-Broadley **Rev:** Frill-necked lizard and value

Date	Mintage	F	VF	XF	Unc	BU
2006B	—	—	—	—	15.00	—
2006B Proof	—	Value: 5.00				

KM# 63a 2 CENTS

5.1800 g., 0.9990 Silver 0.1664 oz. ASW, 21.6 mm. **Ruler:** Elizabeth II **Obv:** Young bust right **Obv. Designer:** Arnold Machin **Rev:** Frill-necked lizard and value **Rev. Designer:** Stuart Devlin **Edge:** Plain

Date	Mintage	F	VF	XF	Unc	BU
2006 Proof	6,500	Value: 15.00				

KM# 768b 2 CENTS

11.3100 g., 0.9990 Gold 0.3632 oz. AGW, 21.6 mm. **Ruler:** Elizabeth II **Obv:** Head with tiara right **Obv. Designer:** Ian Rank-Broadley **Rev:** Frill-necked Lizard and value **Rev. Designer:** Stuart Devlin **Edge:** Plain

Date	Mintage	F	VF	XF	Unc	BU
2006 Proof	300	Value: 650				

KM# 1250 2 CENTS

5.5300 g., 0.9990 Silver 0.1776 oz. ASW, 21.6 mm. **Ruler:** Elizabeth II **Subject:** 1966 Decimal Pattern **Obv:** Head right **Obv. Designer:** Ian Rank-Broadley **Rev:** Wattle, national flower **Rev. Designer:** Andor Meszaros

Date	Mintage	F	VF	XF	Unc	BU
2009P Proof	7,500	Value: 20.00				

KM# 401 5 CENTS

2.8300 g., Copper-Nickel, 19.41 mm. **Ruler:** Elizabeth II **Obv:** Head with tiara right **Obv. Designer:** Ian Rank-Broadley **Rev:** Echidna and value **Rev. Designer:** Stuart Devlin **Edge:** Reeded

Date	Mintage	F	VF	XF	Unc	BU
2001	174,579,000	—	—	—	2.00	3.00
Note: Large obverse head, IRB spaced						
2001	Inc. above	—	—	—	2.00	3.00
Note: Smaller obverse head, RB joined						
2001 Proof	59,569	Value: 15.00				
2002	148,812,000	—	—	—	2.00	3.00
2002 Proof	39,514	Value: 15.00				
2003	115,470,000	—	—	—	2.00	3.00
2003 Proof	39,090	Value: 5.00				
2004	147,658,000	—	—	—	2.00	3.00
Note: Normal sized SD						
2004	Inc. above	—	—	—	2.00	3.00
Note: Smaller SD						
2004 Proof	50,000	Value: 5.00				
2005	194,300,000	—	—	—	2.00	3.00
Note: Normal sized SD						
2005	Inc. above	—	—	—	2.00	3.00
Note: Smaller SD						
2005 Proof	33,520	Value: 5.00				
2006	—	—	—	—	2.00	3.00
2006 Proof	—	Value: 5.00				
2007	—	—	—	—	2.00	3.00
2007 Proof	—	Value: 5.00				
2008	—	—	—	—	2.00	3.00
2008 Proof	—	Value: 5.00				
2009	—	—	—	—	2.00	3.00
2009 Proof	—	Value: 5.00				
2010	—	—	—	—	2.00	3.00
2010 Proof	—	Value: 5.00				

KM# 401a 5 CENTS

6.0300 g., 0.9990 Gold 0.1937 oz. AGW, 19.41 mm. **Ruler:** Elizabeth II **Subject:** Federation Centennial **Obv:** Head with tiara right **Obv. Designer:** Ian Rank-Broadley **Rev:** Echidna **Rev. Designer:** Stuart Devlin

Date	Mintage	F	VF	XF	Unc	BU
2001B Proof	650	Value: 600				
2005B Proof	650	Value: 400				
2006B Proof	300	Value: 650				

KM# 401b 5 CENTS

3.2400 g., 0.9999 Silver 0.1042 oz. ASW, 19.41 mm. **Ruler:** Elizabeth II **Obv:** Head with tiara right **Obv. Designer:** Ian Rank-Broadley **Rev:** Echidna **Rev. Designer:** Stuart Devlin **Edge:** Reeded

Date	Mintage	F	VF	XF	Unc	BU
2003B Proof	6,500	Value: 30.00				
2004B Proof	6,500	Value: 20.00				
2005B Proof	6,500	Value: 20.00				
2006B Proof	—	Value: 20.00				
2007B Proof	—	Value: 20.00				
2008B Proof	—	Value: 20.00				
2009B Proof	—	Value: 20.00				

KM# 64a 5 CENTS

3.2400 g., 0.9990 Silver 0.1041 oz. ASW, 19.41 mm. **Ruler:** Elizabeth II **Obv:** Young bust right **Obv. Designer:** Arnold Machin **Rev:** Echidna **Rev. Designer:** Stuart Devlin **Edge:** Reeded

Date	Mintage	F	VF	XF	Unc	BU
2006 Proof	6,500	Value: 20.00				

KM# 1251 5 CENTS

2.7400 g., 0.9990 Silver 0.0880 oz. ASW, 19.6 mm. **Ruler:** Elizabeth II **Subject:** 1966 Decimal Pattern **Obv:** Head right **Obv. Designer:** Ian Rank-Broadley **Rev:** Platypus and yabbie **Rev. Designer:** Andor Meszaros

Date	Mintage	F	VF	XF	Unc	BU
2009P Proof	7,500	Value: 35.00				

KM# 402 10 CENTS

5.6600 g., Copper-Nickel, 23.6 mm. **Ruler:** Elizabeth II **Obv:** Head with tiara right **Obv. Designer:** Ian Rank-Broadley **Rev:** Lyrebird and value **Rev. Designer:** Stuart Devlin **Edge:** Reeded

Date	Mintage	F	VF	XF	Unc	BU
2001	109,357,000	—	—	—	3.00	4.00
Note: Large obverse head, IRB spaced						
2001	Inc. above	—	—	—	3.00	4.00
Note: Smaller obverse head, RB joined						
2001 Proof	59,569	Value: 15.00				
2002	70,329,000	—	—	—	3.00	4.00
2002 Proof	39,514	Value: 5.00				
2003	53,635,000	—	—	—	2.00	3.00
2003 Proof	39,090	Value: 5.00				
2004	89,000,000	—	—	—	3.00	4.00
2004 Proof	50,000	Value: 5.00				
2005	116,700,000	—	—	—	2.00	3.00
2005 Proof	33,520	Value: 5.00				
2006	157,087,000	—	—	—	2.00	3.00
2006 Proof	—	Value: 5.00				
2007	61,096,000	—	—	—	3.00	4.00
2007 Proof	—	Value: 4.00				
2008	82,860,000	—	—	—	3.00	4.00
2008 Proof	—	Value: 5.00				
2009	—	—	—	—	3.00	4.00
2009 Proof	—	Value: 5.00				
2010	—	—	—	—	3.00	4.00
2010 Proof	—	Value: 5.00				

KM# 402a 10 CENTS

12.1400 g., 0.9999 Gold 0.3903 oz. AGW, 23.6 mm. **Ruler:** Elizabeth II **Subject:** Federation Centennial **Obv:** Head with tiara right **Obv. Designer:** Ian Rank-Broadley **Rev:** Lyrebird **Rev. Designer:** Stuart Devlin **Edge:** Reeded

Date	Mintage	F	VF	XF	Unc	BU
2001B Proof	650	Value: 650				
2005B Proof	650	Value: 600				
2006B Proof	300	Value: 750				

KM# 402b 10 CENTS

6.5700 g., 0.9999 Silver 0.2112 oz. ASW, 23.6 mm. **Ruler:** Elizabeth II **Obv:** Head with tiara right **Obv. Designer:** Ian Rank-Broadley **Rev:** Lyrebird **Rev. Designer:** Stuart Devlin **Edge:** Reeded

Date	Mintage	F	VF	XF	Unc	BU
2003B Proof	6,500	Value: 20.00				
2004B Proof	6,500	Value: 15.00				
2005B Proof	6,500	Value: 15.00				
2006B Proof	—	Value: 15.00				
2007B Proof	—	Value: 15.00				
2008B Proof	—	Value: 15.00				
2009B Proof	—	Value: 15.00				

KM# 65a 10 CENTS

6.5700 g., 0.9990 Silver 0.2110 oz. ASW, 23.6 mm. **Ruler:** Elizabeth II **Obv:** Young bust right **Obv. Designer:** Arnold Machin **Rev:** Superb Lyrebird **Rev. Designer:** Stuart Devlin **Edge:** Reeded

Date	Mintage	F	VF	XF	Unc	BU
2006 Proof	6,500	Value: 15.00				

KM# 1252 10 CENTS

6.0700 g., 0.9990 Silver 0.1950 oz. ASW, 23.6 mm. **Ruler:** Elizabeth II **Subject:** 1966 Decimal Pattern **Obv:** Head right **Obv. Designer:** Ian Rank-Broadley **Rev:** Kookabura eating snake **Rev. Designer:** Andor Meszaros

Date	Mintage	F	VF	XF	Unc	BU
2009P Proof	7,500	Value: 45.00				

KM# 403 20 CENTS

11.3000 g., Copper-Nickel, 28.5 mm. **Ruler:** Elizabeth II **Obv:** Head with tiara right **Obv. Designer:** Ian Rank-Broadley **Rev:** Duckbill Platypus **Rev. Designer:** Stuart Devlin **Edge:** Reeded

Date	Mintage	F	VF	XF	Unc	BU
2001	81,967,000	—	—	—	3.00	4.00
Note: IRB spaced						
2001	Inc. above	—	—	—	3.00	4.00
Note: RB joined						
2001	Inc. above	—	—	—	3.00	4.00
Note: IRB joined						
2001 Proof	59,569	Value: 25.00				
2002	27,244,000	—	—	—	3.00	4.00
2002 Proof	39,514	Value: 2.00				
2004	74,609,000	—	—	—	3.00	4.00
Note: Small obverse head, flat top A						
2004	Est. 400,000	—	—	—	15.00	20.00
Note: Large obverse head, pointed A						
2004 Proof	50,000	Value: 10.00				
Note: Large obverse head, pointed top A						
2004 Proof	Inc. above	Value: 10.00				
Note: Small obverse head, flat top A						
2005	58,600,000	—	—	—	9.00	10.00
2005 Proof	—	Value: 25.00				
2006	102,462,000	—	—	—	3.00	4.00
2006 Proof	—	Value: 6.00				
2007	42,712,000	—	—	—	3.00	4.00
2007 Proof	—	Value: 25.00				
2008	106,220,000	—	—	—	1.00	2.00
2008 Proof	—	Value: 12.00				
2009	—	—	—	—	1.00	2.00
2009 Proof	—	Value: 12.00				
2010	—	—	—	—	1.00	2.00
2010 Proof	—	Value: 12.00				

KM# 532 20 CENTS

11.3100 g., Copper-Nickel, 28.52 mm. **Ruler:** Elizabeth II **Subject:** Centenary of Federation - Norfolk Island **Obv:** Head with tiara right **Obv. Designer:** Ian Rank-Broadley **Rev:** Norfolk Pine over map of island **Rev. Designer:** Megan Cummings **Edge:** Reeded

Date	Mintage	F	VF	XF	Unc	BU
2001B	2,000,000	—	—	—	3.50	5.00
2001B Proof	—	Value: 10.00				

KM# 550 20 CENTS
11.3000 g., Copper-Nickel, 28.5 mm. **Ruler:** Elizabeth II **Series:** Centenary of Federation - New South Wales **Obv:** Head with tiara right **Obv. Designer:** Ian Rank-Broadley **Rev:** Waratah on state map **Rev. Designer:** Joseph Neve **Edge:** Reeded

Date	Mintage	F	VF	XF	Unc	BU
2001	2,000,000	—	—	—	3.50	5.00
2001 Proof	—	Value: 10.00				

KM# 552 20 CENTS
11.3000 g., Copper-Nickel, 28.5 mm. **Ruler:** Elizabeth II **Series:** Centenary of Federation - Australian Capital Territory **Obv:** Head with tiara right **Obv. Designer:** Ian Rank-Broadley **Rev:** Parliament House, map, flowers **Rev. Designer:** Stacy Jo-Ann Paine **Edge:** Reeded **Note:** Prev. KM#551.

Date	Mintage	F	VF	XF	Unc	BU
2001	2,000,000	—	—	—	5.00	6.00
2001 Proof	—	Value: 20.00				

KM# 554 20 CENTS
11.3000 g., Copper-Nickel, 28.5 mm. **Ruler:** Elizabeth II **Series:** Centenary of Federation - Queensland **Obv:** Head with tiara right **Obv. Designer:** Ian Rank-Broadley **Rev:** Jennifer Gray **Edge:** Reeded

Date	Mintage	F	VF	XF	Unc	BU
2001	2,320,000	—	—	—	6.00	8.00
2001 Proof	—	Value: 20.00				

KM# 556 20 CENTS
11.3000 g., Copper-Nickel, 28.5 mm. **Ruler:** Elizabeth II **Series:** Centenary of Federation - Victoria **Obv:** Head with tiara right **Obv. Designer:** Ian Rank-Broadley **Rev:** Capital building **Rev. Designer:** Ryan Ladd & Mark Kennedy **Edge:** Reeded

Date	Mintage	F	VF	XF	Unc	BU
2001	2,000,000	—	—	—	6.00	8.00
2001 Proof	—	Value: 20.00				

KM# 558 20 CENTS
11.3000 g., Copper-Nickel, 28.5 mm. **Ruler:** Elizabeth II **Series:** Centenary of Federation - Northern Territory **Obv:** Head with tiara right **Obv. Designer:** Ian Rank-Broadley **Rev:** Two brolga cranes in ritual dance **Rev. Designer:** Lisa Brett **Edge:** Reeded

Date	Mintage	F	VF	XF	Unc	BU
2001	2,100,000	—	—	—	6.00	9.00
2001 Proof	—	Value: 20.00				

KM# 560 20 CENTS
11.3000 g., Copper-Nickel, 28.5 mm. **Ruler:** Elizabeth II **Series:** Centenary of Federation - South Australia **Obv:** Head with tiara right **Obv. Designer:** Ian Rank-Broadley **Rev:** Sturt's Desert Pea, landscape and southern cross **Rev. Designer:** Lisa Murphy **Edge:** Reeded

Date	Mintage	F	VF	XF	Unc	BU
2001	2,320,000	—	—	—	6.00	8.00
2001 Proof	—	Value: 20.00				

KM# 562 20 CENTS
11.3000 g., Copper-Nickel, 28.5 mm. **Ruler:** Elizabeth II **Series:** Centenary of Federation - Western Australia **Obv:** Head with tiara right **Obv. Designer:** Ian Rank-Broadley **Rev:** Rabbit-eared Bandicoot (bilby), plant and map **Rev. Designer:** Janice Ng **Edge:** Reeded

Date	Mintage	F	VF	XF	Unc	BU
2001	2,000,000	—	—	—	6.00	10.00
2001 Proof	—	Value: 20.00				

KM# 564 20 CENTS
11.3000 g., Copper-Nickel, 28.5 mm. **Ruler:** Elizabeth II **Series:** Centenary of Federation - Tasmania **Obv:** Head with tiara right **Obv. Designer:** Ian Rank-Broadley **Rev:** Tasmanian Tiger on map **Rev. Designer:** Abbey MacDonald **Edge:** Reeded

Date	Mintage	F	VF	XF	Unc	BU
2001	2,000,000	—	—	—	6.00	10.00
2001 Proof	—	Value: 20.00				

KM# 589 20 CENTS
11.3000 g., Copper-Nickel, 28.5 mm. **Ruler:** Elizabeth II **Subject:** Sir Donald Bradman **Obv:** Head with tiara right **Obv. Designer:** Ian Rank-Broadley **Rev:** Sir Donald Bradman **Rev. Designer:** Vladimir Gottwald **Edge:** Reeded

Date	Mintage	F	VF	XF	Unc	BU
2001B	10,000,000	—	—	—	35.00	40.00

KM# 819 20 CENTS
24.3600 g., 0.9990 Gold 0.7824 oz. AGW, 28.52 mm. **Ruler:** Elizabeth II **Obv:** Head with tiara right **Obv. Designer:** Ian Rank-Broadley **Rev:** Platypus with Federation Star **Rev. Designer:** Stuart Devlin **Edge:** Reeded

Date	Mintage	F	VF	XF	Unc	BU
2001 Proof	650	Value: 1,250				

KM# 403a 20 CENTS
13.3600 g., 0.9999 Silver 0.4295 oz. ASW, 28.52 mm. **Ruler:** Elizabeth II **Obv:** Head with tiara right **Obv. Designer:** Ian Rank-Broadley **Rev:** Platypus **Rev. Designer:** Stuart Devlin **Edge:** Reeded

Date	Mintage	F	VF	XF	Unc	BU
2003B Proof	6,500	Value: 30.00				
2004B Proof	6,500	Value: 25.00				
2006B Proof	6,500	Value: 25.00				
2007B Proof	—	Value: 25.00				
2008B Proof	—	Value: 25.00				
2009B Proof	—	Value: 25.00				

KM# 688 20 CENTS
11.3000 g., Copper-Nickel, 28.52 mm. **Ruler:** Elizabeth II **Obv:** Head with tiara right **Obv. Designer:** Ian Rank-Broadley **Rev:** Group of Australian Volunteers **Rev. Designer:** Sir Vladimir Gottwald **Edge:** Reeded

Date	Mintage	F	VF	XF	Unc	BU
2003B	7,600,000	—	—	—	3.00	4.00
2003B Proof	—	Value: 15.00				

KM# 688a 20 CENTS
11.3000 g., 0.9990 Silver 0.3629 oz. ASW, 28.52 mm. **Ruler:** Elizabeth II **Obv:** Head right **Rev:** Group of Australian Volunteers **Edge:** Reeded

Date	Mintage	F	VF	XF	Unc	BU
2003B Proof	6,500	Value: 35.00				

KM# 688b 20 CENTS
24.3600 g., 0.9990 Gold 0.7824 oz. AGW, 28.52 mm. **Ruler:** Elizabeth II **Obv:** Head with tiara right **Obv. Designer:** Ian Rank-Broadley **Rev:** Group of Australian Volunteers **Rev. Designer:** Vladimir Gottwald **Edge:** Reeded

Date	Mintage	F	VF	XF	Unc	BU
2003B Proof	650	Value: 1,250				

KM# 745 20 CENTS
11.3000 g., Copper-Nickel, 28.52 mm. **Ruler:** Elizabeth II **Subject:** 60th Anniversary - End of WWII **Obv:** Head right **Obv. Designer:** Ian Rank-Broadley **Rev:** Soldier with wife and child **Rev. Designer:** Vladimir Gottwald **Edge:** Reeded

Date	Mintage	F	VF	XF	Unc	BU
2005B	33,500,000	—	—	—	2.00	3.00
2005B Proof	—	Value: 10.00				

KM# 745a 20 CENTS
13.3600 g., 0.9990 Silver 0.4291 oz. ASW, 28.52 mm. **Ruler:** Elizabeth II **Obv:** Head right **Rev:** Soldier with wife and child **Edge:** Reeded

Date	Mintage	F	VF	XF	Unc	BU
2005B Proof	6,500	Value: 35.00				

KM# 745b 20 CENTS
24.3600 g., 0.9999 Gold 0.7831 oz. AGW, 28.52 mm. **Ruler:** Elizabeth II **Obv:** Head right **Rev:** Soldier with wife and child **Edge:** Reeded

Date	Mintage	F	VF	XF	Unc	BU
2005B Proof	650	Value: 1,250				

KM# 66a 20 CENTS
13.3600 g., 0.9990 Silver 0.4291 oz. ASW, 28.52 mm. **Ruler:**

Elizabeth II **Obv:** Young bust right **Obv. Designer:** Arnold Machin **Rev:** Platypus **Rev. Designer:** Stuart Devlin **Edge:** Reeded

Date	Mintage	F	VF	XF	Unc	BU
2006 Proof	6,500	Value: 28.00				

KM# 403b 20 CENTS

24.5600 g., 0.9999 Gold 0.7895 oz. AGW, 28.52 mm. **Ruler:** Elizabeth II **Subject:** Federation Centennial **Obv:** Head with tiara right **Obv. Designer:** Ian Rank-Broadley **Rev:** Duckbill Platyus **Rev. Designer:** Stuart Devlin **Edge:** Reeded

Date	Mintage	F	VF	XF	Unc	BU
2006B Proof	300	Value: 1,350				

KM# 820 20 CENTS

11.3100 g., Copper-Nickel, 28.52 mm. **Ruler:** Elizabeth II **Subject:** Year of the Surf Lifesaver **Obv:** Head with tiara right **Obv. Designer:** Ian Rank-Broadley **Rev:** Female lifesaver working line **Rev. Designer:** Vladimir Gottwald **Edge:** Reeded

Date	Mintage	F	VF	XF	Unc	BU
2007	—	—	—	—	10.00	7.00
2007 Proof	—	Value: 20.00				

KM# 820a 20 CENTS

13.3600 g., 0.9990 Silver 0.4291 oz. ASW, 28.52 mm. **Ruler:** Elizabeth II **Subject:** Year of the Surfer Lifesaver **Rev:** Female with rope line

Date	Mintage	F	VF	XF	Unc	BU
2007B Proof	—	Value: 25.00				

KM# 1058 20 CENTS

11.3000 g., Copper-Nickel, 30 mm. **Ruler:** Elizabeth II **Subject:** Planet earth **Rev:** Map of Australia with water and rocks around **Rev. Designer:** V. Gottwald

Date	Mintage	F	VF	XF	Unc	BU
2008	—	—	—	—	12.00	10.00
2008 Proof	—	Value: 12.00				

KM# 1075 20 CENTS

15.5500 g., Copper-Nickel, 28.52 mm. **Ruler:** Elizabeth II **Subject:** Year of Astronomy **Rev:** Star gazers

Date	Mintage	F	VF	XF	Unc	BU
2009 Unc	—	—	—	—	10.00	12.00
2009 Proof	—	Value: 25.00				

KM# 1088 20 CENTS

15.5500 g., Copper-Nickel, 28.52 mm. **Ruler:** Elizabeth II **Rev:** Poppy

Date	Mintage	F	VF	XF	Unc	BU
2009	—	—	—	—	10.00	12.00

KM# 1253 20 CENTS

12.8600 g., 0.9990 Silver 0.4130 oz. ASW, 28.6 mm. **Ruler:** Elizabeth II **Subject:** 1966 Decimal Pattern **Obv:** Head right **Obv. Designer:** Ian Rank-Broadley **Rev:** Black swan in flight **Rev. Designer:** Andor Meszaros

Date	Mintage	F	VF	XF	Unc	BU
2009P Proof	10,000	Value: 200				

KM# 1433 20 CENTS

11.3000 g., Copper-Nickel, 28.5 mm. **Ruler:** Elizabeth II **Subject:** Nurses **Obv:** Nurse looking over serviceman **Rev. Designer:** W. Pietranik

Date	Mintage	F	VF	XF	Unc	BU
2009C	—	—	—	—	5.00	7.00

KM# 1430 20 CENTS

Copper-Nickel **Ruler:** Elizabeth II **Subject:** Burke & Wills, 150th Anniversary **Rev:** Burke and Wills on camels

Date	Mintage	F	VF	XF	Unc	BU
2010C	—	—	—	—	5.00	7.00
2010C Proof	—	Value: 10.00				

KM# 1502 20 CENTS

11.3000 g., Copper-Nickel, 28.52 mm. **Ruler:** Elizabeth II **Subject:** Wool Industry **Rev:** Wheel with sheep industry design in spoke wedges

Date	Mintage	F	VF	XF	Unc	BU
2010	—	—	—	—	2.00	4.00

KM# 1513 20 CENTS

11.3000 g., Copper-Nickel, 28.52 mm. **Ruler:** Elizabeth II **Subject:** Taxation office, 100th Anniversary

Date	Mintage	F	VF	XF	Unc	BU
2010	—	—	—	—	1.50	2.50

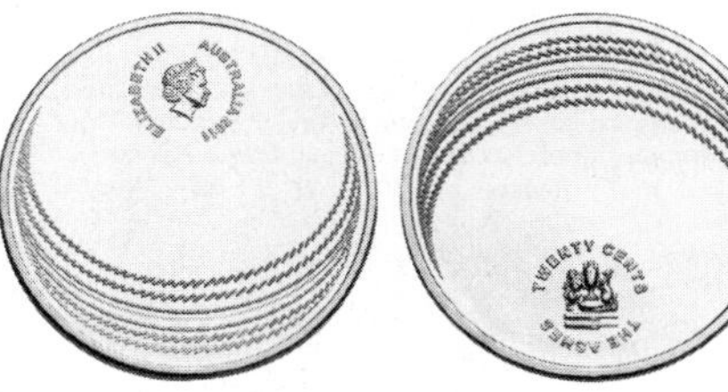

KM# 1517 20 CENTS

11.3000 g., Copper-Nickel, 28.52 mm. **Ruler:** Elizabeth II **Subject:** Ashes Cricket tournament

Date	Mintage	F	VF	XF	Unc	BU
2010	—	—	—	—	1.50	2.50

KM# 1518 20 CENTS

11.3000 g., Copper-Nickel, 28.52 mm. **Ruler:** Elizabeth II **Subject:** Lost soldiersof Promelles **Rev:** Soldier carries another on his shoulder

Date	Mintage	F	VF	XF	Unc	BU
2010	—	—	—	—	1.50	2.50

KM# 599 25 CENTS

7.7750 g., 0.9990 Silver 0.2497 oz. ASW, 24.8 mm. **Ruler:** Elizabeth II **Obv:** Head with tiara right **Obv. Designer:** Ian Rank-Broadley **Rev:** Parliament House **Edge:** Plain **Shape:** 7-pointed star **Note:** "The Dump" portion of the "Holey Dollar" KM#598.

Date	Mintage	F	VF	XF	Unc	BU
2001 Prooflike	30,000	—	—	—	—	28.00

KM# 491.1 50 CENTS

15.7000 g., Copper-Nickel, 32 mm. **Ruler:** Elizabeth II **Subject:** Centenary of Federation, 1901-2001 **Obv:** Head with tiara right **Obv. Designer:** Ian Rank-Broadley **Rev:** Commonwealth coat of arms **Edge:** Plain **Shape:** 12-sided **Note:** Prev. KM#491.

Date	Mintage	F	VF	XF	Unc	BU
2001B	43,149,600	—	—	—	5.00	6.00
2001B Proof	—	Value: 40.00				

KM# 491.1a 50 CENTS

33.8800 g., 0.9999 Gold 1.0891 oz. AGW, 31.51 mm. **Ruler:** Elizabeth II **Subject:** Federation Centennial **Obv:** Elizabeth II **Obv. Designer:** Ian Rank-Broadley **Rev:** Commonwealth arms above value

Date	Mintage	F	VF	XF	Unc	BU
2001B Proof	650	Value: 1,700				

KM# 491.2 50 CENTS

15.5500 g., Copper-Nickel, 31.51 mm. **Ruler:** Elizabeth II **Subject:** Federation Centennial **Obv:** Elizabeth II right **Obv. Designer:** Ian Rank-Broadley **Rev:** Multicolor arms above value **Edge:** Plain **Shape:** 12-sided

Date	Mintage	F	VF	XF	Unc	BU
2001B Proof	60,000	Value: 50.00				

KM# 491.2a 50 CENTS

Copper-Nickel, 31.5 mm. **Ruler:** Elizabeth II **Subject:** Centenary of Federation, 1901-2001 **Obv:** Head with tiara right **Obv. Designer:** Ian Rank-Broadley **Rev:** Multicolored Commonwealth coat of arms **Edge:** Plain **Shape:** 12-sided **Note:** Prev. KM#491a.

Date	Mintage	F	VF	XF	Unc	BU
2001B Proof	—	Value: 50.00				

KM# 533 50 CENTS

15.6000 g., Copper-Nickel, 31.51 mm. **Ruler:** Elizabeth II **Subject:** Centennial - Norfolk Island Federation **Obv:** Head with tiara right **Obv. Designer:** Ian Rank-Broadley **Rev:** Norfolk Island coat of arms **Edge:** Plain **Shape:** 12-sided

Date	Mintage	F	VF	XF	Unc	BU
2001B	2,000,000	—	—	—	6.00	15.00
2001B Proof	—	Value: 70.00				

KM# 535 50 CENTS
16.8860 g., 0.9990 Silver 0.5423 oz. ASW, 32.1 mm. **Ruler:** Elizabeth II **Subject:** Year of the Snake **Obv:** Head right **Obv. Designer:** Ian Rank-Broadley **Rev:** Snake with eggs **Edge:** Plain

Date	Mintage	F	VF	XF	Unc	BU
2001	500,000	—	—	—	—	20.00
2001P Proof	5,000	Value: 65.00				

KM# 551 50 CENTS
15.5500 g., Copper-Nickel, 31.5 mm. **Ruler:** Elizabeth II **Series:** Centenary of Federation - New South Wales **Obv:** Head with tiara right **Obv. Designer:** Ian Rank-Broadley **Rev:** New South Wales state arms **Edge:** Plain **Shape:** 12-sided

Date	Mintage	F	VF	XF	Unc	BU
2001	3,000,000	—	—	—	6.00	7.00
2001 Proof	—	Value: 40.00				

KM# 553 50 CENTS
15.5500 g., Copper-Nickel, 31.5 mm. **Ruler:** Elizabeth II **Series:** Centenary of Federation - Australian Capital Territory **Obv:** Head right **Obv. Designer:** Ian Rank-Broadley **Rev:** Australian Capital Territory arms **Edge:** Plain **Shape:** 12-sided

Date	Mintage	F	VF	XF	Unc	BU
2001	2,000,000	—	—	—	6.00	9.00
2001 Proof	—	Value: 40.00				

KM# 555 50 CENTS
15.5500 g., Copper-Nickel, 31.5 mm. **Ruler:** Elizabeth II **Series:** Centenary of Federation - Queensland **Obv:** Head with tiara right **Obv. Designer:** Ian Rank-Broadley **Rev:** Queensland state arms **Edge:** Plain **Shape:** 12-sided

Date	Mintage	F	VF	XF	Unc	BU
2001	2,300,000	—	—	—	6.00	9.00
2001 Proof	—	Value: 40.00				

KM# 557 50 CENTS
15.5500 g., Copper-Nickel, 31.5 mm. **Ruler:** Elizabeth II **Series:** Centenary of Federation - Victoria **Obv:** Head with tiara right **Obv. Designer:** Ian Rank-Broadley **Rev:** Victoria state arms **Edge:** Plain **Shape:** 12-sided

Date	Mintage	F	VF	XF	Unc	BU
2001	2,800,000	—	—	—	6.00	8.00
2001 Proof	—	Value: 40.00				

KM# 559 50 CENTS
15.5500 g., Copper-Nickel, 31.5 mm. **Ruler:** Elizabeth II **Series:** Centenary of Federation - Northern Territory **Obv:** Head with tiara right **Obv. Designer:** Ian Rank-Broadley **Rev:** Northern Territory state arms **Edge:** Plain **Shape:** 12-sided

Date	Mintage	F	VF	XF	Unc	BU
2001	2,100,000	—	—	—	6.00	10.00
2001 Proof	—	Value: 50.00				

KM# 561 50 CENTS
15.5500 g., Copper-Nickel, 31.5 mm. **Ruler:** Elizabeth II **Series:** Centenary of Federation - South Australia **Obv:** Head with tiara right **Obv. Designer:** Ian Rank-Broadley **Rev:** South Australia state arms **Edge:** Plain **Shape:** 12-sided

Date	Mintage	F	VF	XF	Unc	BU
2001	2,400,000	—	—	—	6.00	20.00
2001 Proof	—	Value: 60.00				

KM# 563 50 CENTS
15.5500 g., Copper-Nickel, 31.5 mm. **Ruler:** Elizabeth II **Series:** Centenary of Federation - Western Australia **Obv:** Head with tiara right **Obv. Designer:** Ian Rank-Broadley **Rev:** Western Australia state arms **Edge:** Plain **Shape:** 12-sided

Date	Mintage	F	VF	XF	Unc	BU
2001	2,400,000	—	—	—	6.00	15.00
2001 Proof	—	Value: 50.00				

KM# 565 50 CENTS
15.5500 g., Copper-Nickel, 31.5 mm. **Ruler:** Elizabeth II **Series:** Centenary of Federation - Tasmania **Obv:** Head with tiara right **Obv. Designer:** Ian Rank-Broadley **Rev:** Tasmania state arms **Edge:** Plain **Shape:** 12-sided

Date	Mintage	F	VF	XF	Unc	BU
2001	2,200,000	—	—	—	6.00	10.00
2001 Proof	—	Value: 50.00				

KM# 694 50 CENTS
15.7200 g., Copper-Nickel, 32 mm. **Ruler:** Elizabeth II **Obv:** Head with tiara right **Obv. Designer:** Ian Rank-Broadley **Rev:** Koala, Lorikeet (bird) and Wombat **Rev. Designer:** John Serranno & Vladimir Gottwald **Edge:** Plain **Shape:** 12-sided

Date	Mintage	F	VF	XF	Unc	BU
2001 Proof	—	Value: 9.00				
2004B	10,577,000	—	—	—	3.00	5.00

KM# 602 50 CENTS
15.5500 g., Copper-Nickel, 31.5 mm. **Ruler:** Elizabeth II **Subject:** The Outback Region **Obv:** Head right **Obv. Designer:** Ian Rank-Broadley **Rev:** Windmill **Rev. Designer:** Wojciech Pietranik **Edge:** Plain **Shape:** 12-sided

Date	Mintage	F	VF	XF	Unc	BU
2002B	11,507,000	—	—	—	6.00	7.00
2002B Proof	39,000	Value: 25.00				

KM# 645 50 CENTS
15.5500 g., Copper-Nickel, 31.51 mm. **Ruler:** Elizabeth II **Subject:** Queen's 50th Anniversary of Accession **Obv:** Head right **Rev:** Crown and star **Rev. Designer:** Peter Soobik & Wojciech Pietranik **Shape:** 12-sided

Date	Mintage	F	VF	XF	Unc	BU
2002B	32,102	—	—	—	30.00	60.00

Note: Issued only in PNC cover

KM# 645a 50 CENTS
18.2400 g., 0.9990 Silver 0.5858 oz. ASW, 31.51 mm. **Ruler:** Elizabeth II **Subject:** Queen's 50th Anniversary of Accession **Obv:** Head right **Rev:** Crown and star **Rev. Designer:** Peter Soobik & Wojciech Pietranik **Shape:** 12-sided

Date	Mintage	F	VF	XF	Unc	BU
2002B Proof	13,500	Value: 60.00				

KM# 404a 50 CENTS
18.2400 g., 0.9999 Silver 0.5863 oz. ASW, 31.51 mm. **Ruler:** Elizabeth II **Obv:** Head with tiara right **Obv. Designer:** Ian Rank-Broadley **Rev:** Arms **Rev. Designer:** Stuart Devlin **Edge:** Plain **Shape:** 12-sided

Date	Mintage	F	VF	XF	Unc	BU
2003B Proof	—	Value: 35.00				
2004B Proof	6,500	Value: 35.00				
2005B Proof	—	Value: 35.00				
2006B Proof	—	Value: 35.00				
2007B Proof	—	Value: 35.00				
2008B Proof	—	Value: 35.00				
2009B Proof	—	Value: 35.00				

KM# 689 50 CENTS

15.5500 g., Copper-Nickel, 31.5 mm. **Ruler:** Elizabeth II **Obv:** Head right **Obv. Designer:** Ian Rank-Broadley **Rev:** Value within circle of volunteer activities **Rev. Designer:** Vladimir Gottwald **Edge:** Plain **Shape:** 12-sided

Date	Mintage	F	VF	XF	Unc	BU
2003B	13,927,000	—	—	—	4.50	5.00
2003B Proof	—	Value: 20.00				

KM# 689a 50 CENTS

15.5500 g., 0.9990 Silver 0.4994 oz. ASW, 31.5 mm. **Ruler:** Elizabeth II **Obv:** Head right **Rev:** Value within circle of volunteer activities

Date	Mintage	F	VF	XF	Unc	BU
2003B Proof	6,500	Value: 45.00				

KM# 799 50 CENTS

14.0900 g., Aluminum-Bronze, 31.51 mm. **Ruler:** Elizabeth II **Subject:** 50th Anniversary of the Coronation of Elizabeth II **Obv:** Head with tiara right **Obv. Designer:** Ian Rank-Broadley **Rev:** Crown, Federation star, dates **Rev. Designer:** Peter Soobik & Wojciech Pietranik **Edge:** Plain **Shape:** 12-sided

Date	Mintage	F	VF	XF	Unc	BU
2003	65,003	—	—	—	35.00	40.00

KM# 799a 50 CENTS

18.2400 g., 0.9990 Silver 0.5858 oz. ASW, 31.51 mm. **Ruler:** Elizabeth II **Subject:** 50th Anniversary of the Coronation of Elizabeth II **Obv:** Head with tiara right **Obv. Designer:** Ian Rank-Broadley **Rev:** Crown, Federation star, dates **Rev. Designer:** Peter Soobik & Wojciech Pietranik **Edge:** Plain **Shape:** 12-sided

Date	Mintage	F	VF	XF	Unc	BU
2003 Proof	6,967	Value: 60.00				

KM# 404 50 CENTS

15.6000 g., Copper-Nickel, 32 mm. **Ruler:** Elizabeth II **Obv:** Head with tiara right **Obv. Designer:** Ian Rank-Broadley **Rev:** Australian coat of arms with kangaroo and emu supporters **Rev. Designer:** Stuart Devlin **Edge:** Plain **Shape:** 12-sided

Date	Mintage	F	VF	XF	Unc	BU
2004	17,918,000	—	—	—	9.00	10.00
2004 Proof	—	Value: 25.00				
2005	30,000	—	—	—	25.00	40.00
Note: Issued as part of a PNC only						
2005 Proof	—	Value: 10.00				
2006	—	—	—	—	9.00	10.00
2006 Proof	—	Value: 25.00				
2007	—	—	—	—	1.00	1.50
2007 Proof	—	Value: 10.00				
2008	—	—	—	—	7.00	8.00
2008 Proof	—	Value: 10.00				
2009	—	—	—	—	7.00	8.00
2009 Proof	—	Value: 10.00				
2010	—	—	—	—	7.00	8.00
2010 Proof	—	Value: 10.00				

KM# 694a 50 CENTS

18.2400 g., 0.9990 Silver 0.5858 oz. ASW, 31.5 mm. **Ruler:** Elizabeth II **Obv:** Head with tiara right **Rev:** Wombat, lorikeet and koala **Rev. Designer:** John Serranno & Vladimir Gottwald **Edge:** Plain **Shape:** 12-sided

Date	Mintage	F	VF	XF	Unc	BU
2004B Proof	8,203	Value: 75.00				

KM# 746 50 CENTS

15.5500 g., Copper-Nickel, 31.51 mm. **Ruler:** Elizabeth II **Obv:** Head with tiara right **Obv. Designer:** Ian Rank-Broadley **Rev:** Military cemetery scene **Rev. Designer:** Wojciech Pietranik **Edge:** Plain **Shape:** 12-sided

Date	Mintage	F	VF	XF	Unc	BU
2005B	11,033,000	—	—	—	3.00	4.00
2005B Proof	—	Value: 20.00				

KM# 746a 50 CENTS

18.2400 g., 0.9990 Silver 0.5858 oz. ASW, 31.51 mm. **Ruler:** Elizabeth II **Obv:** Head with tiara right **Obv. Designer:** Ian Rank-Broadley **Rev:** Military cemetery scene **Rev. Designer:** Wojciech Pietranik **Edge:** Plain **Shape:** 12-sided

Date	Mintage	F	VF	XF	Unc	BU
2005B Proof	6,500	Value: 38.00				

KM# 746b 50 CENTS

33.6300 g., 0.9999 Gold 1.0811 oz. AGW, 31.51 mm. **Ruler:** Elizabeth II **Obv:** Head with tiara right **Obv. Designer:** Ian Rank-Broadley **Rev:** Military cemetery scene **Rev. Designer:** Wojciech Pietranik **Edge:** Plain **Shape:** 12-sided

Date	Mintage	F	VF	XF	Unc	BU
2005B Proof	650	Value: 1,650				

KM# 769 50 CENTS

15.6000 g., Copper-Nickel, 31.6 mm. **Ruler:** Elizabeth II **Subject:** Commonweath Games, Secondary School Design Competition **Obv:** Head with tiara right **Obv. Designer:** Ian Rank-Broadley **Rev:** Athletes **Rev. Designer:** Kelly Just

Date	Mintage	F	VF	XF	Unc	BU
2005	20,500,000	—	—	—	2.50	3.50
2005 Proof	5,402	Value: 65.00				

KM# 774 50 CENTS

15.5500 g., Copper-Nickel, 31.50 mm. **Ruler:** Elizabeth II **Subject:** Gymnastics **Obv:** Head with tiara right **Obv. Legend:** ELIZABETH II - AUSTRALIA **Obv. Designer:** Ian Rank-Broadley **Rev:** Gymnast standing with right leg up, Melbourne 2006 logo at left **Rev. Legend:** XVIII COMMONWEALTH GAMES **Rev. Designer:** Wojciech Pietranik **Edge:** Plain **Shape:** 12-sided

Date	Mintage	F	VF	XF	Unc	BU
2006	3,000	—	—	—	8.50	10.00

KM# 67a 50 CENTS

18.2400 g., 0.9990 Silver 0.5858 oz. ASW, 31.51 mm. **Ruler:** Elizabeth II **Obv:** Young bust right **Obv. Designer:** Arnold Machin **Rev:** Australian coat of arms **Rev. Designer:** Stuart Devlin **Edge:** Reeded

Date	Mintage	F	VF	XF	Unc	BU
2006 Proof	6,500	Value: 65.00				

KM# 770 50 CENTS

15.5500 g., Copper-Nickel, 31.50 mm. **Ruler:** Elizabeth II **Subject:** Basketball **Obv:** Head with tiara right **Obv. Legend:** ELIZABETH II - AUSTRALIA **Obv. Designer:** Ian Rank-Broadley **Rev:** Basketball player shooting basket, Melbourne 2006 logo at left **Rev. Legend:** XVIII COMMONWEALTH GAMES **Rev. Designer:** Wojciech Pietranik **Shape:** 12-sided

Date	Mintage	F	VF	XF	Unc	BU
2006	5,002	—	—	—	8.50	10.00

KM# 771 50 CENTS

15.5500 g., Copper-Nickel, 31.50 mm. **Ruler:** Elizabeth II **Subject:** Hockey **Obv:** Head with tiara right **Obv. Legend:** ELIZABETH II - AUSTRALIA **Obv. Designer:** Ian Rank-Broadley **Rev:** Hockey player hitting puck, Melboune 2006 logo at upper left **Rev. Legend:** XVIII COMMONWEALTH GAMES **Rev. Designer:** Wojciech Pietranik **Shape:** 12-sided

Date	Mintage	F	VF	XF	Unc	BU
2006	4,082	—	—	—	8.50	10.00

KM# 772 50 CENTS

15.5500 g., Copper-Nickel, 31.50 mm. **Ruler:** Elizabeth II **Subject:** Shooting **Obv:** Head with tiara right **Obv. Legend:** ELIZABETH II - AUSTRALIA **Obv. Designer:** Ian Rank-Broadley **Rev:** Shooter, Melbourne 2006 logo at upper right **Rev. Legend:** XVIII COMMONWEALTH GAMES **Rev. Designer:** Wojciech Pietranik **Shape:** 12-sided

Date	Mintage	F	VF	XF	Unc	BU
2006	21,070	—	—	—	8.50	10.00

KM# 773 50 CENTS

15.5500 g., Copper-Nickel, 31.50 mm. **Ruler:** Elizabeth II **Subject:** Weightlifting **Obv:** Head with tiara right **Obv. Legend:** ELIZABETH II - AUSTRALIA **Obv. Designer:** Ian Rank-Broadley **Rev:** Weightlifter holding barbells above head, Melbourne 2006 logo at left **Rev. Legend:** XVIII COMMONWEALTH GAMES **Rev. Designer:** Wojciech Pietranik **Shape:** 12-sided

Date	Mintage	F	VF	XF	Unc	BU
2006	22,332	—	—	—	8.50	10.00

KM# 775 50 CENTS

15.5500 g., Copper-Nickel, 31.50 mm. **Ruler:** Elizabeth II **Subject:** Rugby 7's **Obv:** Head with tiara right **Obv. Legend:** ELIZABETH II - AUSTRALIA **Obv. Designer:** Ian Rank-Broadley **Rev:** Rugby player running right, Melbourne 2006 logo at upper left **Rev. Legend:** XVIII COMMONWEALTH GAMES **Rev. Designer:** Wojciech Pietranik **Shape:** 12-sided

Date	Mintage	F	VF	XF	Unc	BU
2006	24,427	—	—	—	8.50	10.00

KM# 776 50 CENTS

15.5500 g., Copper-Nickel, 31.50 mm. **Ruler:** Elizabeth II **Subject:** Cycling **Obv:** Head with tiara right **Obv. Legend:** ELIZABETH II - AUSTRALIA **Obv. Designer:** Ian Rank-Broadley **Rev:** Cyclist heading right, Melbourne 2006 logo at upper right **Rev. Legend:** XVIII COMMONWEALTH GAMES **Rev. Designer:** Wojciech Pietranik **Shape:** 12-sided

Date	Mintage	F	VF	XF	Unc	BU
2006	22,861	—	—	—	8.50	10.00

KM# 777 50 CENTS

15.5500 g., Copper-Nickel, 31.50 mm. **Ruler:** Elizabeth II **Subject:** Athletics **Obv:** Head with tiara right **Obv. Legend:** ELIZABETH II - AUSTRALIA **Obv. Designer:** Ian Rank-Broadley **Rev:** Runner right, Melbourne 2006 logo at lower right **Rev. Legend:** XVIII COMMONWEALTH GAMES **Rev. Designer:** Wojciech Pietranik **Shape:** 12-sided

Date	Mintage	F	VF	XF	Unc	BU
2006	22,475	—	—	—	8.50	10.00

KM# 778 50 CENTS

15.5500 g., Copper-Nickel, 31.50 mm. **Ruler:** Elizabeth II **Subject:** Triathlon **Obv:** Head with tiara right **Obv. Legend:** ELIZABETH II - AUSRALIA **Obv. Designer:** Ian Rank-Broadley **Rev:** Bicycle, runner, Melbourne 2006 logo below **Rev. Legend:** XVIII COMMONWEALTH GAMES **Rev. Designer:** Wojciech Pietranik **Shape:** 12-sided

Date	Mintage	F	VF	XF	Unc	BU
2006	22,302	—	—	—	8.50	10.00

KM# 779 50 CENTS

15.5500 g., Copper-Nickel, 31.50 mm. **Ruler:** Elizabeth II **Subject:** Netball **Obv:** Head with tiara right **Obv. Legend:** ELIZABETH II - AUSTRALIA **Obv. Designer:** Ian Rank-Broadley **Rev:** Player shooting basket, Melbourne 2006 logo at upper left **Rev. Legend:** XVIII COMMONWEALTH GAMES **Rev. Designer:** Wojciech Pietranik **Shape:** 12-sided

Date	Mintage	F	VF	XF	Unc	BU
2006	22,432	—	—	—	8.50	10.00

KM# 780 50 CENTS

15.5500 g., Copper-Nickel, 31.50 mm. **Ruler:** Elizabeth II **Subject:** Table tennis **Obv:** Head with tiara right **Obv. Legend:** ELIZABETH II - AUSTRALIA **Obv. Designer:** Ian Rank-Broadley **Rev:** Player hitting ball, Melbourne 2006 logo below **Rev. Legend:** XVIII COMMONWEALTH GAMES **Rev. Designer:** Wojciech Pietranik **Shape:** 12-sided

Date	Mintage	F	VF	XF	Unc	BU
2006	22,070	—	—	—	8.50	10.00

KM# 781 50 CENTS

15.5500 g., Copper-Nickel, 31.50 mm. **Ruler:** Elizabeth II **Subject:** Aquatics **Obv:** Head with tiara right **Obv. Legend:** ELIZABETH II - AUSTRALIA **Obv. Designer:** Ian Rank-Broadley **Rev:** Swimmer, Melbourne 2006 logo **Rev. Legend:** XVIII COMMONWEALTH GAMES **Rev. Designer:** Wojciech Pietranik **Shape:** 12-sided

Date	Mintage	F	VF	XF	Unc	BU
2006	31,702	—	—	—	8.50	10.00

KM# 801 50 CENTS
15.5500 g., Copper-Nickel, 31.51 mm. **Ruler:** Elizabeth II **Subject:** 80th Birthday of Queen Elizabeth II **Obv:** Head with tiara right **Obv. Designer:** Ian Rank-Broadley **Rev:** Royal Cipher **Rev. Designer:** Stuart Devlin **Shape:** 12-sided

Date	Mintage	F	VF	XF	Unc	BU
2006	28,191	—	—	—	45.00	60.00

KM# 801a 50 CENTS
18.2400 g., 0.9990 Silver partially gilt 0.5858 oz. ASW, 31.51 mm. **Ruler:** Elizabeth II **Subject:** 80th Birthday of Queen Elizabeth II **Obv:** Head with tiara right **Obv. Designer:** Ian Rank-Broadley **Rev:** Crowned Royal Cipher on large 80, border of alternating British and Australian flags **Rev. Designer:** Stuart Devlin **Shape:** 12-sided

Date	Mintage	F	VF	XF	Unc	BU
2006 Proof	7,500	Value: 85.00				

KM# 802 50 CENTS
15.5500 g., Copper-Nickel, 31.51 mm. **Ruler:** Elizabeth II **Subject:** Visit of Queen Elizabeth II **Obv:** Head with tiara right **Obv. Designer:** Ian Rank-Broadley **Rev:** Australian map and world globe **Rev. Designer:** Stuart Devlin **Shape:** 12-sided

Date	Mintage	F	VF	XF	Unc	BU
2006	—	—	—	—	30.00	45.00

KM# 802a 50 CENTS
18.2400 g., 0.9990 Silver partially gilt 0.5858 oz. ASW, 31.51 mm. **Ruler:** Elizabeth II **Subject:** Visit of Queen Elizabeth II **Obv:** Head with tiara right **Obv. Designer:** Ian Rank-Broadley **Rev:** Australian map and world globe **Rev. Designer:** Stuart Devlin **Shape:** 12-sided

Date	Mintage	F	VF	XF	Unc	BU
2006 Proof	7,500	Value: 90.00				

KM# 821 50 CENTS
13.2800 g., 0.8000 Silver 0.3416 oz. ASW, 31.51 mm. **Ruler:** Elizabeth II **Obv:** Head with tiara right **Obv. Designer:** Ian Rank-Broadley **Rev:** Australian coat of arms **Rev. Designer:** Stuart Devlin **Edge:** Reeded

Date	Mintage	F	VF	XF	Unc	BU
2006 Proof	—	Value: 70.00				

KM# 821a 50 CENTS
25.3000 g., 0.9990 Gold 0.8126 oz. AGW, 31.51 mm. **Ruler:** Elizabeth II **Obv:** Head with tiara right **Obv. Designer:** Ian Rank-Broadley **Rev:** Australian coat of arms **Rev. Designer:** Stuart Devlin **Edge:** Reeded

Date	Mintage	F	VF	XF	Unc	BU
2006 Proof	300	Value: 1,300				

KM# 1001 50 CENTS
15.5500 g., Copper-Nickel, 31.50 mm. **Ruler:** Elizabeth II **Subject:** XVIII COMMONWEALTH GAMES **Obv:** Head with tiara right **Obv. Legend:** ELIZABETH II - AUSTRALIA **Obv. Designer:** Ian Rank-Broadley **Rev:** Squash player, Melbourne 2006 logo **Rev. Designer:** Wojciech Pietranik **Edge:** Plain **Shape:** 12-sided

Date	Mintage	F	VF	XF	Unc	BU
2006	—	—	—	—	12.50	15.00

KM# 1002 50 CENTS
15.5500 g., Copper-Nickel, 31.50 mm. **Ruler:** Elizabeth II **Subject:** XVIII COMMONWEALTH GAMES **Obv:** Head with tiara right **Obv. Legend:** ELIZABETH II - AUSTRALIA **Obv. Designer:** Ian Rank-Broadley **Rev:** Lawn bowler, Melbourne 2006 logo **Rev. Designer:** Wojciech Pietranik **Edge:** Plain **Shape:** 12-sided

Date	Mintage	F	VF	XF	Unc	BU
2006	22,602	—	—	—	12.50	15.00

KM# 1003 50 CENTS
15.5500 g., Copper-Nickel, 31.50 mm. **Ruler:** Elizabeth II **Subject:** XVIII COMMONWEALTH GAMES **Obv:** Head with tiara right **Obv. Legend:** ELIZABETH II - AUSTRALIA **Obv. Designer:** Ian Rank-Broadley **Rev:** Boxer, Melbourne 2006 logo **Rev. Designer:** Wojciech Pietranik **Edge:** Plain **Shape:** 12-sided

Date	Mintage	F	VF	XF	Unc	BU
2006	—	—	—	—	12.50	15.00

KM# 1004 50 CENTS
Aluminum-Bronze, 30 mm. **Ruler:** Elizabeth II **Obv:** Head with tiara right **Obv. Legend:** ELIZABETH II - AUSTRALIA **Obv. Designer:** Ian Rank-Broadley **Rev:** Everage head facing, multicolor **Rev. Legend:** DAME EDNA EVERAGE - 50TH ANNIVERSARY

Date	Mintage	F	VF	XF	Unc	BU
ND(2006)P	—	—	—	—	20.00	25.00

KM# 1041 50 CENTS
15.5500 g., Copper-Nickel, 31.5 mm. **Ruler:** Elizabeth II **Subject:** Elizabeth and Philip Wedding Anniversary **Rev:** Profile portraits and diamond at center of circle of trumpets **Rev. Designer:** Stuart Devlin

Date	Mintage	F	VF	XF	Unc	BU
2007B	60,030	—	—	—	15.00	18.00

KM# 1049 50 CENTS
15.5500 g., Copper-Nickel, 31.51 mm. **Ruler:** Elizabeth II **Subject:** Scouting Centennial in Australia **Rev:** Australian Scout Emblem **Rev. Designer:** C. Goodall

Date	Mintage	F	VF	XF	Unc	BU
2008	49,517	—	—	—	10.00	12.00

KM# 1062 50 CENTS
15.5500 g., Copper-Nickel, 31.5 mm. **Ruler:** Elizabeth II **Subject:** 25th Anniversary Australia's Win of the America's Cup **Rev:** Yacht Australia II

Date	Mintage	F	VF	XF	Unc	BU
2008	32,916	—	—	—	15.00	18.00

KM# 1100 50 CENTS
15.5500 g., 0.9990 Silver 0.4994 oz. ASW, 36.6 mm. **Ruler:** Elizabeth II **Subject:** Great Barrier Reef **Obv:** Head right **Obv. Designer:** Ian rank-Broadley **Rev:** Lion fish, multicolor **Edge:** reeded

Date	Mintage	F	VF	XF	Unc	BU
2009(p) Proof	Est. 10,000	Value: 60.00				

KM# 1101 50 CENTS
15.5500 g., 0.9990 Silver 0.4994 oz. ASW, 36.6 mm. **Ruler:** Elizabeth II **Subject:** Great Barrier Reef **Obv:** Head right **Obv. Designer:** Ian Rank-Broadley **Rev:** Leafy Sea Dragon, multicolor **Edge:** Reeded

Date	Mintage	F	VF	XF	Unc	BU
2009(p) Proof	Est. 10,000	Value: 60.00				

KM# 1432 50 CENTS
15.5500 g., Copper-Nickel, 31.5 mm. **Ruler:** Elizabeth II **Subject:** Moon Landing 40th Anniversary **Rev:** Earth, moon and orbiter **Rev. Designer:** C. Goodall

Date	Mintage	F	VF	XF	Unc	BU
2009C	—	—	—	—	—	10.00

KM# 1328 50 CENTS
15.5500 g., 0.9990 Silver 0.4994 oz. ASW, 36.6 mm. **Ruler:** Elizabeth II **Subject:** Great Barrier Reef **Obv:** Head right **Obv. Designer:** Ian Rank Broadley **Rev:** Clownfish, multicolor

Date	Mintage	F	VF	XF	Unc	BU
2010P Proof	—	Value: 60.00				

KM# 1329 50 CENTS

15.5730 g., 0.9990 Silver 0.5002 oz. ASW, 36.6 mm. **Ruler:** Elizabeth II **Subject:** Great Barrier Reef **Rev:** Big belly sea horse in multicolor

Date	Mintage	F	VF	XF	Unc	BU
2010P Proof	—	Value: 30.00				

KM# 1389 50 CENTS

15.5500 g., 0.9990 Silver 0.4994 oz. ASW, 36.6 mm. **Ruler:** Elizabeth II **Subject:** Great Barrier Reef - Morey Eel **Obv:** Hear right **Rev:** Tessellate Moray Eel, multicolor

Date	Mintage	F	VF	XF	Unc	BU
2010(p) Proof	—	Value: 45.00				

KM# 1450 50 CENTS

15.5600 g., 0.9990 Silver 0.4997 oz. ASW **Ruler:** Elizabeth II **Rev:** Australian Sugar Glider, multicolor

Date	Mintage	F	VF	XF	Unc	BU
2010P	—	Value: 30.00				

KM# 1456 50 CENTS

15.5600 g., 0.9990 Silver 0.4997 oz. ASW **Ruler:** Elizabeth II **Rev:** Australian kangaroo, multicolor

Date	Mintage	F	VF	XF	Unc	BU
2010P Proof	—	Value: 25.00				

KM# 1493 50 CENTS

15.5000 g., 0.9990 Silver 0.4978 oz. ASW, 36.6 mm. **Ruler:** Elizabeth II **Rev:** Dingo

Date	Mintage	F	VF	XF	Unc	BU
2010 Proof	—	Value: 50.00				

KM# 1500 50 CENTS

15.5500 g., Copper-Nickel, 31.5 mm. **Ruler:** Elizabeth II **Subject:** Australia Day **Shape:** 12-sided

Date	Mintage	F	VF	XF	Unc	BU
2010	—	—	—	—	2.50	4.50

KM# 1501 50 CENTS

153.5500 g., Copper-Nickel, 31.5 mm. **Ruler:** Elizabeth II **Subject:** Melbourne Cup **Rev:** Horses racing **Shape:** 12-sided

Date	Mintage	F	VF	XF	Unc	BU
2010	—	—	—	—	2.50	4.50

KM# 1519 50 CENTS

18.2400 g., 0.9990 Silver 0.5858 oz. ASW, 31.5 mm. **Ruler:** Elizabeth II **Subject:** Melbourne Cup, 150th race **Rev:** Trophy, partially gilt **Shape:** 12-sided

Date	Mintage	F	VF	XF	Unc	BU
2010 Proof	—	Value: 80.00				

KM# 1520 50 CENTS

18.2400 g., 0.9990 Silver 0.5858 oz. ASW, 31.5 mm. **Ruler:** Elizabeth II **Subject:** Melbourne Cup **Rev:** Horse and rider, partially gilt **Shape:** 12-sided

Date	Mintage	F	VF	XF	Unc	BU
2010 Proof	—	Value: 80.00				

KM# 1521 50 CENTS

15.5500 g., Copper-Nickel, 31.5 mm. **Ruler:** Elizabeth II **Subject:** National Service, 60th Anniversary **Shape:** 12-sided

Date	Mintage	F	VF	XF	Unc	BU
2010	—	—	—	—	4.00	5.00

KM# 1524 50 CENTS

15.5500 g., Copper-Nickel, 31.5 mm. **Ruler:** Elizabeth II **Subject:** Melbourne Cup, 150th race **Rev:** Horses right racing **Shape:** 12-sided

Date	Mintage	F	VF	XF	Unc	BU
2011	—	—	—	—	3.00	5.00

KM# 1525 50 CENTS

15.5500 g., Copper-Nickel, 31.5 mm. **Ruler:** Elizabeth II **Subject:** Australia Day **Rev:** Circle of people clasping hands

Date	Mintage	F	VF	XF	Unc	BU
2011	—	—	—	—	4.00	5.00

KM# 1525a 50 CENTS

18.2400 g., Silver, 31.5 mm. **Ruler:** Elizabeth II **Subject:** Australia day **Rev:** Circle of people clasping hands, partially gilt

Date	Mintage	F	VF	XF	Unc	BU
2011 Proof	—	Value: 40.00				

KM# 1254 55 CENTS

15.5500 g., 0.9990 Silver 0.4994 oz. ASW, 26x38 mm. **Ruler:** Elizabeth II **Subject:** Postal Service, 200th Anniversary **Obv:** Head right **Obv. Designer:** Ian Rank-Broadley **Rev:** Early post box **Edge:** Irregular as with a stamp **Shape:** Vertical rectangle

Date	Mintage	F	VF	XF	Unc	BU
2009P Proof	8,700	Value: 90.00				

KM# 1255 55 CENTS

15.5500 g., 0.9990 Silver 0.4994 oz. ASW, 26x38 mm. **Ruler:** Elizabeth II **Subject:** Postal Service, 200th Anniversary **Obv:** Head right **Obv. Designer:** Ian Rank-Broadley **Rev:** Home delivery **Edge:** Irregular as with a stamp **Shape:** Vertical rectangle

Date	Mintage	F	VF	XF	Unc	BU
2009P Proof	8,700	Value: 90.00				

KM# 489 DOLLAR

9.0000 g., Aluminum-Bronze, 25 mm. **Ruler:** Elizabeth II **Obv:** Head with tiara right **Obv. Designer:** Ian Rank-Broadley **Rev:** Circle of 5 kangaroos **Rev. Designer:** Stuart Devlin **Edge:** Segmented reeding

Date	Mintage	F	VF	XF	Unc	BU
2001B Proof	1,001,000	Value: 55.00				
2004B	8,800,000	—	—	—	6.00	7.00
2004B Proof	50,000	Value: 75.00				
2005B	5,792,000	—	—	—	6.00	7.00
2005B Proof	33,520	Value: 85.00				
2006B	38,691,000	—	—	—	4.00	5.00
2006B Proof	—	Value: 45.00				
2006B Special Proof	—	Value: 3,500				
Note: Mintage of 25-35 pieces						
2007B	—	—	—	—	20.00	25.00
2007B Proof	—	Value: 45.00				
2008B	30,106,000	—	—	—	3.00	5.00
2008B Proof	—	Value: 45.00				
2009B	4,682,000	—	—	—	4.00	6.00
2009B Proof	—	Value: 45.00				
2010B	—	—	—	—	—	5.00
2010B Proof	—	Value: 45.00				

KM# 588 DOLLAR

9.0000 g., Aluminum-Bronze, 25 mm. **Ruler:** Elizabeth II **Subject:** 90th Anniversary Royal Australian Navy **Obv:** Head with tiara right **Obv. Designer:** Ian Rank-Broadley **Rev:** Navy crest **Rev. Designer:** Vladimir Gottwald **Edge:** Segmented reeding

Date	Mintage	F	VF	XF	Unc	BU
2001	62,429	—	—	—	60.00	65.00

KM# 530 DOLLAR

9.0000 g., Aluminum-Bronze, 25 mm. **Ruler:** Elizabeth II **Subject:** Army Centennial **Obv:** Head with tiara right **Obv. Designer:** Ian Rank-Broadley **Rev:** Army crest **Rev. Designer:** Vladimir Gottwald **Edge:** Segmented reeding

Date	Mintage	F	VF	XF	Unc	BU
2001C	125,186	—	—	—	18.00	20.00
Note: Large head, IRB spaced						
2001C	Inc. above	—	—	—	18.00	20.00
Note: Small head, IRB joined						
2001S	38,095	—	—	—	25.00	30.00

KM# 530a DOLLAR

11.6600 g., 0.9990 Silver 0.3745 oz. ASW, 24.9 mm. **Ruler:** Elizabeth II **Subject:** Army Centennial **Obv:** Head with tiara right **Obv. Designer:** Ian Rank-Broadley **Rev:** Army crest **Rev. Designer:** Vladimir Gottwald **Edge:** Segmented reeding

Date	Mintage	F	VF	XF	Unc	BU
2001 Proof	17,839	Value: 50.00				

KM# 531 DOLLAR

9.0000 g., Aluminum-Bronze, 25 mm. **Ruler:** Elizabeth II **Subject:** 80th Anniversary Royal Australian Air Force **Obv:** Head with tiara right **Obv. Designer:** Ian Rank-Broadley **Rev:** Air Force crest **Rev. Designer:** Vladimir Gottwald **Edge:** Segmented reeding

Date	Mintage	F	VF	XF	Unc	BU
2001B	99,281	—	—	—	18.00	20.00
Note: IRB spaced						
2001B	Inc. above	—	—	—	25.00	30.00
Note: IRB joined						

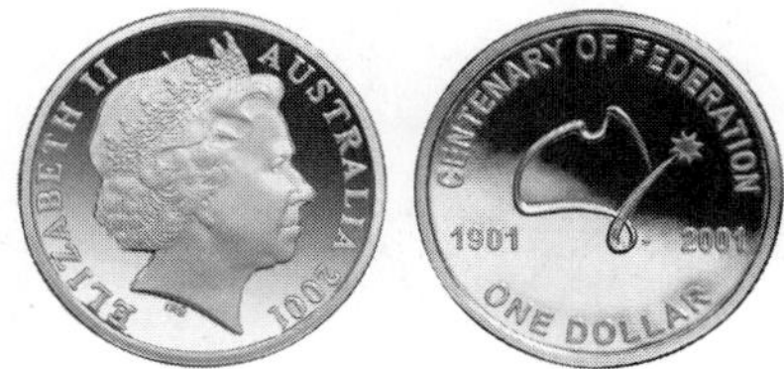

KM# 534.1 DOLLAR

9.0000 g., Aluminum-Bronze, 25 mm. **Ruler:** Elizabeth II **Subject:** Australian Centenary of Federation - Norfolk Island **Obv:** Head with tiara right **Obv. Designer:** Ian Rank-Broadley **Rev:** Stylized ribbon map of Australia with star **Rev. Designer:** Wojciech Pietranik **Edge:** Segmented reeding **Note:** Reverse design raised above field. Prev. KM#534.

Date	Mintage	F	VF	XF	Unc	BU
2001B	6,781,200	—	—	—	50.00	55.00
Note: IRB joined						
2001B	Inc. above	—	—	—	50.00	55.00
Note: IRB spaced						
2001B Proof	—	Value: 5.00				

KM# 534.1a DOLLAR

21.7000 g., 0.9999 Gold 0.6976 oz. AGW, 25 mm. **Ruler:** Elizabeth II **Subject:** Federation Centennial **Obv:** Elizabeth II **Rev:** Federation logo

Date	Mintage	F	VF	XF	Unc	BU
2001B Proof	650	Value: 1,150				

KM# 534.2 DOLLAR

9.0000 g., Aluminum-Bronze, 25 mm. **Ruler:** Elizabeth II **Subject:** Australian Centenary of Federation - Norfolk Island **Obv:** Head with tiara right **Obv. Designer:** Ian Rank-Broadley **Rev:** Multicolor ribbon design of Australia with star, printed on the surface. **Rev. Designer:** Wojciech Pietranik **Edge:** Segmented reeding

Date	Mintage	F	VF	XF	Unc	BU
2001 Proof	—	Value: 12.50				
2001	27,905,000	—	—	—	5.00	—

KM# 594 DOLLAR

31.1035 g., 0.9990 Silver partially gilt 0.9990 oz. ASW, 40 mm. **Ruler:** Elizabeth II **Subject:** Millennium **Obv:** Head with tiara right **Obv. Designer:** Ian Rank-Broadley **Rev:** Gold inset sun on multicolor earth above Egyptian obelisk **Edge:** Reeded

Date	Mintage	F	VF	XF	Unc	BU
2001 Prooflike	30,000	—	—	—	35.00	40.00

KM# 598 DOLLAR

31.1000 g., 0.9990 Silver 0.9988 oz. ASW, 40.4 mm. **Ruler:** Elizabeth II **Subject:** Centenary of Federation "Holey Dollar" **Obv:** Legend around star-shaped center hole **Rev:** Seven coats of arms around star-shaped hole **Edge:** Reeded

Date	Mintage	F	VF	XF	Unc	BU
ND(2001) Prooflike	30,000	—	—	—	28.00	32.00

KM# 682 DOLLAR

9.0000 g., Aluminum-Bronze, 25 mm. **Ruler:** Elizabeth II **Subject:** International Year of Volunteers **Obv. Designer:** Ian Rank-Broadley **Rev:** Volunteers in wreath **Rev. Designer:** Wojciech Pietranik **Edge:** Segmented reeding

Date	Mintage	F	VF	XF	Unc	BU
2001B	6,000,000	—	—	—	12.00	15.00

KM# 632 DOLLAR

31.1035 g., 0.9990 Silver 0.9990 oz. ASW, 40 mm. **Ruler:** Elizabeth II **Subject:** Queen's Golden Jubilee **Obv:** Head right **Rev:** Queen on horse with multicolor flag background **Edge:** Reeded

Date	Mintage	F	VF	XF	Unc	BU
2002	34,074,000	—	—	—	—	50.00
2002P Proof	40,000	Value: 65.00				

KM# 600.1 DOLLAR

9.0000 g., Aluminum-Bronze, 25 mm. **Ruler:** Elizabeth II **Subject:** Year of the Outback **Obv:** Head with tiara right **Obv. Designer:** Ian Rank-Broadley **Rev:** Stylized map of Australia **Rev. Designer:** Wojciech Pietranik **Edge:** Segmented reeding **Note:** Prev. KM#600.

Date	Mintage	F	VF	XF	Unc	BU
2002	34,074,000	—	—	—	5.00	7.00
2002 Proof	—	Value: 10.00				
2002C	68,447	—	—	—	7.00	9.00
2002B	32,698	—	—	—	7.00	9.00
2002M	31,694	—	—	—	7.00	9.00
2002S	36,931	—	—	—	7.00	9.00

KM# 600.1a DOLLAR

11.6600 g., 0.9900 Silver 0.3711 oz. ASW, 25 mm. **Ruler:** Elizabeth II **Subject:** Year of the Outback **Obv:** Head with tiara right **Obv. Designer:** Ian Rank-Broadley **Rev:** Stylized map of Australia **Rev. Designer:** Elizabeth Robinson and Wojciech Pietranik **Edge:** Segmented reeding

Date	Mintage	F	VF	XF	Unc	BU
2002B Proof	12,500	Value: 65.00				

KM# 600.2 DOLLAR

9.0000 g., Aluminum-Bronze, 25 mm. **Ruler:** Elizabeth II **Subject:** Year of the Outback **Obv:** Head with tiara right **Obv. Designer:** Ian Rank-Broadley **Rev:** Multicolor stylized map of Australia **Rev. Designer:** Wojciech Pietranik **Edge:** Segmented reeding

Date	Mintage	F	VF	XF	Unc	BU
2002B Proof	39,514	Value: 15.00				

KM# 660 DOLLAR

31.1035 g., 0.9990 Silver partially gilt 0.9990 oz. ASW, 40 mm. **Ruler:** Elizabeth II **Subject:** Melbourne Mint **Obv:** Head with tiara right **Obv. Designer:** Ian Rank-Broadley **Rev:** Mint entrance between two gold foil inserts replicating gold sovereign reverse designs **Edge:** Reeded

Date	Mintage	F	VF	XF	Unc	BU
2002B Proof	13,328	Value: 55.00				

KM# 489a DOLLAR

11.6600 g., 0.9990 Silver 0.3745 oz. ASW, 25 mm. **Ruler:** Elizabeth II **Obv:** Head with tiara right **Obv. Designer:** Ian Rank-Broadley **Rev:** Kangaroos **Rev. Designer:** Stuart Devlin **Edge:** Segmented reeding

Date	Mintage	F	VF	XF	Unc	BU
2003B Proof	—	Value: 40.00				
2004B Proof	6,500	Value: 40.00				
2005B Proof	—	Value: 40.00				
2006B Proof	—	Value: 40.00				
2007B Proof	—	Value: 40.00				
2008B Proof	—	Value: 40.00				
2009B Proof	—	Value: 40.00				

KM# 823 DOLLAR

31.1035 g., 0.9990 Silver 0.9990 oz. ASW, 40 mm. **Ruler:** Elizabeth II **Subject:** 50th Anniversary - Coronation Elizabeth II **Obv:** Head with tiara right **Obv. Designer:** Ian Rank-Broadley **Rev:** Crown in lettered garland **Note:** Colored design.

Date	Mintage	F	VF	XF	Unc	BU
2003P Proof	40,400	Value: 40.00				

KM# 663 DOLLAR

9.0000 g., Aluminum-Bronze, 25 mm. **Ruler:** Elizabeth II **Subject:** 50th Anniversary - End of Korean War **Obv:** Head with tiara right **Obv. Designer:** Ian Rank-Broadley **Rev:** Dove of Peace **Rev. Designer:** Vladimir Gottwald **Edge:** Segmented reeding

Date	Mintage	F	VF	XF	Unc	BU
2003B	34,949	—	—	—	6.00	8.00
2003C	93,572	—	—	—	6.00	8.00
2003M	36,142	—	—	—	6.00	8.00
2003S	36,091	—	—	—	6.00	8.00

KM# 663a DOLLAR

11.6600 g., 0.9990 Silver 0.3745 oz. ASW, 25 mm. **Ruler:** Elizabeth II **Subject:** Korean War **Obv:** Queens head right **Obv. Designer:** Ian Rank-Broadley **Rev:** Dove of Peace **Rev. Designer:** Vladimir Gottwald **Edge:** Segmented reeding

Date	Mintage	F	VF	XF	Unc	BU
2003B	15,000	Value: 55.00				

KM# 685 DOLLAR

31.1035 g., 0.9990 Silver 0.9990 oz. ASW, 40.6 mm. **Ruler:** Elizabeth II **Subject:** 21st Birthday of William **Obv:** Head right **Rev:** Multicolor Prince William **Edge:** Segmented reeding

Date	Mintage	F	VF	XF	Unc	BU
ND(2003)P Proof	12,500	Value: 40.00				

KM# 690 DOLLAR

9.0000 g., Aluminum-Bronze, 25 mm. **Ruler:** Elizabeth II **Obv:** Queens head right **Rev:** Australia Volunteers logo **Edge:** Segmented reeding

Date	Mintage	F	VF	XF	Unc	BU
2003B	4,149,000	—	—	—	15.00	17.00

KM# 690a DOLLAR

9.0000 g., 0.9990 Silver 0.2891 oz. ASW, 25 mm. **Ruler:** Elizabeth II **Obv:** Queens head right **Rev:** Australia Volunteers logo

Date	Mintage	F	VF	XF	Unc	BU
2003B Proof	6,500	Value: 30.00				

KM# 690.1 DOLLAR

9.0000 g., Aluminum-Bronze, 25 mm. **Ruler:** Elizabeth II **Subject:** Australia's Volunteers **Obv:** Elizabeth II **Rev:** Multicolor Australia's Volunteers logo **Edge:** Segmented reeding

Date	Mintage	F	VF	XF	Unc	BU
2003B Proof	39,090	Value: 15.00				

KM# 754 DOLLAR

9.0000 g., Aluminum-Bronze, 25 mm. **Ruler:** Elizabeth II **Subject:** Womens Suffrage **Obv:** Queens head right **Obv. Designer:** Ian Rank-Broadley **Rev:** Suffragette talking to Britannia **Rev. Designer:** Vladimir Gottwald **Edge:** Segmented reeding

Date	Mintage	F	VF	XF	Unc	BU
2003B	10,007,000	—	—	—	5.00	7.00

KM# 763 DOLLAR

13.3600 g., 0.9990 Silver 0.4291 oz. ASW, 28.5 mm. **Ruler:** Elizabeth II **Series:** Masterpieces in Silver - Port Phillip Patterns **Obv:** 1/4 Ounce design **Rev:** Kangaroo design **Edge:** Reeded

Date	Mintage	F	VF	XF	Unc	BU
2003B Proof	10,000	Value: 80.00				

KM# 803 DOLLAR

9.0000 g., Aluminum-Bronze, 25 mm. **Ruler:** Elizabeth II **Subject:** Vietnam War Veterans 1962-1973 **Obv:** Head with tiara right **Obv. Designer:** Ian Rank-Broadley **Rev:** Australian Vietnam Forces National Memorial **Rev. Designer:** Wojciech Pietranik

Date	Mintage	F	VF	XF	Unc	BU
2003	57,000	—	—	—	45.00	50.00

KM# 822 DOLLAR

54.3000 g., 0.9990 Silver 1.7440 oz. ASW, 50 mm. **Ruler:** Elizabeth II **Obv:** Superimposed head above replica of Holey Dollar **Obv. Designer:** Ian Rank-Broadley **Rev:** Replica of Holey Dollar **Edge:** Reeded **Note:** Holey Dollar replica is embedded in silver collar and comes with replica Dump also in 0.999 silver.

Date	Mintage	F	VF	XF	Unc	BU
2003 Proof	11,000	Value: 85.00				

KM# 824 DOLLAR

31.1035 g., 0.9990 Silver 0.9990 oz. ASW, 40 mm. **Ruler:** Elizabeth II **Subject:** Golden Pipeline **Obv:** Head with tiara right **Obv. Designer:** Ian Rank-Broadley **Rev:** Charles Yelverton O'Connor, innovative engineer, multicolor

Date	Mintage	F	VF	XF	Unc	BU
2003P Proof	5,000	Value: 125				

KM# 725 DOLLAR

56.2300 g., 0.9990 Bi-Metallic Copper center in Silver ring 1.8060 oz., 50 mm. **Ruler:** Elizabeth II **Subject:** The Last Penny **Obv:** 1964 dated penny obverse **Rev:** 1964 date penny reverse **Edge:** Reeded

Date	Mintage	F	VF	XF	Unc	BU
2004B Proof	16,437	Value: 80.00				

KM# 726 DOLLAR

9.0000 g., Aluminum-Bronze, 25 mm. **Ruler:** Elizabeth II **Subject:** Eureka Stockade 1854-2004 **Obv:** Head with tiara right **Obv. Designer:** Ian Rank-Broadley **Rev:** Stockade and stylized soldiers **Rev. Designer:** Wojciech Pietranik **Edge:** Segmented reeding

Date	Mintage	F	VF	XF	Unc	BU
2004	—	—	—	—	8.00	10.00
2004B	33,835	—	—	—	5.00	6.00
2004C	70,913	—	—	—	5.00	6.00
2004 E	95,948	—	—	—	5.00	6.00
2004S	45,098	—	—	—	5.00	6.00
2004M	37,526	—	—	—	5.00	6.00
2004 3 known	—	—	—	—	—	1,000

KM# 726a DOLLAR

11.6600 g., 0.9990 Silver 0.3745 oz. ASW, 25 mm. **Ruler:** Elizabeth II **Subject:** Eureka Stockade **Obv:** Head with tiara right **Obv. Designer:** Ian Rank-Broadley **Rev:** Stockade and stylized soldiers **Rev. Designer:** Wojciech Pietranik **Edge:** Segmented reeding

Date	Mintage	F	VF	XF	Unc	BU
2004B Proof	17,697	Value: 38.00				

KM# 733 DOLLAR

9.0000 g., Aluminum-Bronze, 25 mm. **Ruler:** Elizabeth II **Obv:** Head with tiara right **Obv. Designer:** Ian Rank-Broadley **Rev:** Multicolor holographic five kangaroos design **Rev. Designer:** Stuart Devlin **Edge:** Segmented reeding

Date	Mintage	F	VF	XF	Unc	BU
2004B Proof	—	Value: 25.00				

KM# 733.1 DOLLAR

9.0000 g., Aluminum-Bronze, 25 mm. **Ruler:** Elizabeth II **Rev:** Five kangaroos **Edge:** Segmented reeding

Date	Mintage	F	VF	XF	Unc	BU
2004B	—	—	—	—	—	4.50

KM# 733.1a DOLLAR

11.6600 g., 0.9999 Silver 0.3748 oz. ASW, 25 mm. **Ruler:** Elizabeth II **Rev:** Five Kangaroos

Date	Mintage	F	VF	XF	Unc	BU
2004B Proof	6,500	Value: 35.00				

KM# 734 DOLLAR

31.1035 g., 0.9990 Silver 0.9990 oz. ASW, 40 mm. **Ruler:** Elizabeth II **Subject:** First Moon Walk **Obv:** Head with tiara right **Rev:** Multicolor rocket in flight **Edge:** Reeded

Date	Mintage	F	VF	XF	Unc	BU
2004P Proof	40,000	Value: 100				

KM# 735 DOLLAR

31.1035 g., 0.9990 Silver 0.9990 oz. ASW, 40 mm. **Ruler:** Elizabeth II **Subject:** First Moon Walk **Obv:** Head with tiara right **Rev:** Multicolor scene of astronauts planting flag on moon **Edge:** Reeded

Date	Mintage	F	VF	XF	Unc	BU
2004P Proof	40,000	Value: 110				

KM# 736 DOLLAR

31.1035 g., 0.9990 Silver 0.9990 oz. ASW, 40 mm. **Ruler:** Elizabeth II **Subject:** First Moon Walk **Obv:** Head with tiara right **Rev:** Multicolor close up of astronaut on moon **Edge:** Reeded

Date	Mintage	F	VF	XF	Unc	BU
2004P Proof	40,000	Value: 95.00				

KM# 737 DOLLAR

31.1035 g., 0.9990 Silver 0.9990 oz. ASW, 40 mm. **Ruler:** Elizabeth II **Obv:** Head with tiara right **Rev:** Multicolor Antarctic view of Mawson Station and penguins **Edge:** Reeded

Date	Mintage	F	VF	XF	Unc	BU
2004P Proof	7,500	Value: 45.00				

KM# 738 DOLLAR

31.1035 g., 0.9990 Silver partially gilt 0.9990 oz. ASW, 40 mm. **Ruler:** Elizabeth II **Subject:** 50th Anniversary of Royal Visit **Obv:** Queens head right **Rev:** Gilt lion and kangaroo **Rev. Designer:** Leslie Bowles **Edge:** Reeded

Date	Mintage	F	VF	XF	Unc	BU
ND (2004) Proof	12,500	Value: 85.00				

KM# 740 DOLLAR

24.3750 g., 0.9990 Silver Encapsulated gold nuggets in center 0.7829 oz. ASW, 40.6 mm. **Ruler:** Elizabeth II **Obv:** Crowned head right **Obv. Designer:** Ian Rank-Broadley **Rev:** Eureka Stockade leader, miners and flag **Rev. Designer:** Wojciech Pietranik **Edge:** Reeded

Date	Mintage	F	VF	XF	Unc	BU
2004 Proof	12,500	Value: 135				

KM# 747 DOLLAR

9.0000 g., Aluminum-Bronze, 25 mm. **Ruler:** Elizabeth II **Subject:** 60th Anniversary World War II **Obv:** Head with tiara right **Obv. Designer:** Ian Rank-Broadley **Rev:** Rejoicing serviceman **Rev. Designer:** Wojciech Pietranik **Edge:** Segmented reeding

Date	Mintage	F	VF	XF	Unc	BU
2005B	31,788,000	—	—	—	3.00	4.00
2005B Proof	—	Value: 35.00				

KM# 747a DOLLAR

11.6600 g., 0.9990 Silver 0.3745 oz. ASW, 25 mm. **Ruler:** Elizabeth II **Obv:** Queen's head right **Rev:** Rejoicing servicemen **Edge:** Segmented reeding

Date	Mintage	F	VF	XF	Unc	BU
2005B Proof	6,500	Value: 45.00				

KM# 747b DOLLAR

21.5200 g., 0.9999 Gold 0.6918 oz. AGW, 25 mm. **Ruler:** Elizabeth II **Obv:** Queen's head right **Rev:** Rejoicing servicemen **Edge:** Segmented reeding

Date	Mintage	F	VF	XF	Unc	BU
2005B Proof	629	Value: 1,100				

KM# 748 DOLLAR

9.0000 g., Aluminum-Bronze, 25 mm. **Ruler:** Elizabeth II **Subject:** 90th Anniversary Gallipoli Landing 1915-2005 **Obv:** Head with tiara right **Obv. Designer:** Ian Rank-Broadley **Rev:** Bugler silhouette **Rev. Designer:** Vladimir Gottwald **Edge:** Segmented reeding

Date	Mintage	F	VF	XF	Unc	BU
2005	15,000	—	—	—	25.00	30.00
2005B	36,108	—	—	—	5.00	6.00
2005C	76,173	—	—	—	5.00	6.00
2005G	35,452	—	—	—	35.00	40.00
2005M	38,727	—	—	—	5.00	6.00
2005S	39,569	—	—	—	6.00	7.00

KM# 748a DOLLAR

11.6600 g., 0.9990 Silver 0.3745 oz. ASW, 25 mm. **Ruler:** Elizabeth II **Subject:** Gallipoli **Obv:** Queen's head right **Rev:** Bugler silhouette **Edge:** Segmented reeding

Date	Mintage	F	VF	XF	Unc	BU
2005B Proof	17,749	Value: 45.00				
2005B Proof, 2 known	—	Value: 1,500				

KM# 825 DOLLAR

56.4500 g., 0.9990 Silver partially gilt 1.8130 oz. ASW, 50 mm. **Ruler:** Elizabeth II **Obv:** Small head with tiara right superimposed above replica of Sydney Mint Sovereign **Obv. Designer:** Ian Rank-Broadley **Rev:** Replica of Sydney Mint Sovereign **Edge:** Reeded

Date	Mintage	F	VF	XF	Unc	BU
2005 Proof	11,845	Value: 85.00				

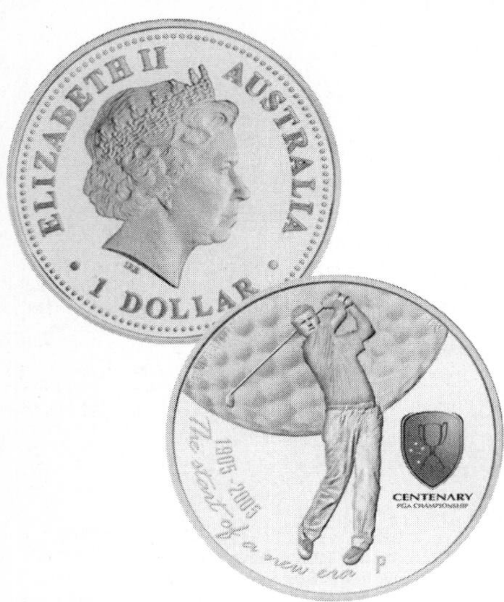

KM# 830 DOLLAR

31.6000 g., 0.9990 Silver 1.0149 oz. ASW, 40 mm. **Ruler:** Elizabeth II **Subject:** Centenary Australian Tennis Open 1905-2005 **Obv:** Head with tiara right **Obv. Designer:** Ian Rank-Broadley **Rev:** Tennis players

Date	Mintage	F	VF	XF	Unc	BU
2005 Proof	10,000	Value: 45.00				

KM# 831 DOLLAR

31.6000 g., 0.9990 Silver 1.0149 oz. ASW, 40 mm. **Ruler:** Elizabeth II **Subject:** Centenary Australian PGA Gold Open 1905-2005 **Obv:** Head with tiara right **Obv. Designer:** Ian Rank-Broadley **Rev:** Golfer

Date	Mintage	F	VF	XF	Unc	BU
2005 Proof	7,500	Value: 85.00				

KM# 832 DOLLAR

31.6000 g., 0.9990 Silver 1.0149 oz. ASW, 40 mm. **Ruler:** Elizabeth II **Subject:** Centenary Rotary 1905-2005 **Obv:** Head with tiara right **Obv. Designer:** Ian Rank-Broadley **Rev:** Rotary International Logo

Date	Mintage	F	VF	XF	Unc	BU
2005 Proof	10,000	Value: 90.00				

KM# 833 DOLLAR

31.1035 g., 0.9990 Silver 0.9990 oz. ASW, 40 mm. **Ruler:** Elizabeth II **Subject:** 90th Anniversary Gallipoli Landings **Obv:** Head with tiara right **Obv. Designer:** Ian Rank-Broadley **Rev:** Multicolor Australian and New Zealand soldiers beneath Australian flag

Date	Mintage	F	VF	XF	Unc	BU
2005 Proof	15,000	Value: 185				

KM# 835 DOLLAR

Aluminum-Bronze, 38.74 mm. **Ruler:** Elizabeth II **Subject:** Living Icons of Australia and New Zealand **Obv:** Head with tiara right **Obv. Designer:** Ian Rank-Broadley **Rev:** Indigenous image of kangaroo **Rev. Designer:** Charmaine Cole

Date	Mintage	F	VF	XF	Unc	BU
2005	20,000	—	—	—	15.00	20.00

KM# 836 DOLLAR

31.1035 g., 0.9990 Silver 0.9990 oz. ASW, 40 mm. **Ruler:** Elizabeth II **Subject:** 21st Birthday Prince Harry of Wales **Obv:** Head with tiara right **Obv. Designer:** Ian Rank-Broadley **Rev:** Prince Harry

Date	Mintage	F	VF	XF	Unc	BU
2005 Proof	12,500	Value: 75.00				

KM# 1015 DOLLAR

31.6000 g., 0.9990 Silver 1.0149 oz. ASW, 40.5 mm. **Ruler:** Elizabeth II **Subject:** 50th Anniversary Australian Territory **Obv:** Head with tiara right **Obv. Legend:** ELIZABETH II • AUSTRALIA **Obv. Designer:** Ian Rank-Broadley **Rev:** Red-footed Booby perched on a branch, multicolor **Rev. Legend:** COCOS (KEELING) ISLANDS **Edge:** Reeded

Date	Mintage	F	VF	XF	Unc	BU
2005P Proof	7,500	Value: 65.00				

KM# 1018 DOLLAR

31.7500 g., 0.9990 Silver 1.0197 oz. ASW, 40.5 mm. **Ruler:** Elizabeth II **Obv:** Head with tiara right **Obv. Legend:** ELIZABETH II - AUSTRALIA **Obv. Designer:** Ian Rank-Broadley **Rev:** Leopard seal with pup on ice, multicolor **Rev. Legend:** Australian Antarctic Territory **Edge:** Reeded

Date	Mintage	F	VF	XF	Unc	BU
2005P Proof	7,500	Value: 55.00				

KM# 77a DOLLAR

11.6600 g., 0.9990 Silver 0.3745 oz. ASW, 25 mm. **Ruler:** Elizabeth II **Obv:** Young bust right **Obv. Designer:** Arnold Machin **Rev:** Kangaroos **Rev. Designer:** Stuart Devlin **Edge:** Segmented reeding

Date	Mintage	F	VF	XF	Unc	BU
2006 Proof	6,500	Value: 40.00				

KM# 489b DOLLAR

21.5200 g., 0.9990 Gold 0.6912 oz. AGW, 25 mm. **Ruler:** Elizabeth II **Obv:** Head with tiara right **Obv. Designer:** Ian Rank-Broadley **Rev:** Kangaroos **Rev. Designer:** Stuart Devlin **Edge:** Segmented reeding

Date	Mintage	F	VF	XF	Unc	BU
2006 Proof	300	Value: 1,100				

KM# 804 DOLLAR

9.0000 g., Aluminum-Bronze, 25 mm. **Ruler:** Elizabeth II **Subject:** XVIII Commonwealth Games **Obv:** Head with tiara right

Date	Mintage	F	VF	XF	Unc	BU
2006	—	—	—	—	3.50	5.00

KM# 805 DOLLAR

9.0000 g., Aluminum-Bronze, 25 mm. **Ruler:** Elizabeth II **Subject:** 50 Years of Television **Obv:** Head with tiara right **Obv. Designer:** Ian Rank-Broadley **Rev:** TV mast and camera **Rev. Designer:** Vladimir Gottwald **Edge:** Segmented reeding

Date	Mintage	F	VF	XF	Unc	BU
2006C	135,221	—	—	—	5.00	6.00
2006 TV	46,370	—	—	—	15.00	17.00
2006S	48,490	—	—	—	5.00	6.00
2006B	47,228	—	—	—	5.00	6.00
2006M	39,600	—	—	—	5.00	6.00
2006 4 known	—	—	—	—	—	1,000

KM# 805a DOLLAR

11.6600 g., 0.9990 Silver 0.3745 oz. ASW, 25 mm. **Ruler:** Elizabeth II **Subject:** 50 Years of Television **Obv:** Head with tiara right **Obv. Designer:** Ian Rank-Broadley **Rev:** TV mast and camera **Rev. Designer:** Vladimir Gottwald **Edge:** Segmented reeding

Date	Mintage	F	VF	XF	Unc	BU
2006 Proof	10,790	Value: 45.00				
2006A Proof	3,859	Value: 60.00				

KM# 806 DOLLAR

9.0000 g., Aluminum-Bronze Issued in folder., 25 mm. **Ruler:** Elizabeth II **Series:** Colored Oceans **Obv:** Head with tiara right **Obv. Designer:** Ian Rank-Broadley **Rev:** Multicolor jumping Bottlenose dolphins **Rev. Designer:** T. Dean **Edge:** Segmented reeding

Date	Mintage	F	VF	XF	Unc	BU
2006	29,310	—	—	—	—	35.00

KM# 807 DOLLAR

9.0000 g., Aluminum-Bronze, 25 mm. **Ruler:** Elizabeth II **Series:** Colored Oceans **Obv:** Head with tiara right **Obv. Designer:** Ian Rank-Broadley **Rev:** Multicolor clown fish **Rev. Designer:** T. Dean **Edge:** Segmented reeding **Note:** Issued in folder.

Date	Mintage	F	VF	XF	Unc	BU
2006	29,310	—	—	—	25.00	30.00

KM# 826 DOLLAR

60.5000 g., 0.9990 Silver 1.9431 oz. ASW, 50 mm. **Ruler:**

Elizabeth II **Obv:** Replica of 1758 Mexico City Mint 8 Reales **Obv. Legend:** ELIZABETH II (small head right) AUSTRALIA **Rev:** Replica of 1758 Mexico City Mint 8 Reales **Rev. Legend:** PILLAR DOLLAR **Edge:** Reeded

Date	Mintage	F	VF	XF	Unc	BU
2006	9,846	—	—	—	100	—

KM# 841 DOLLAR
31.1035 g., 0.9990 Silver Colorized lenticular display. 0.9990 oz. ASW **Ruler:** Elizabeth II **Subject:** 50 Years of Television in Australia 1956-2006 **Obv:** Head with tiara right **Obv. Designer:** Ian Rank-Broadley **Rev:** SIx different historic TV show images **Shape:** Square with rounded corners

Date	Mintage	F	VF	XF	Unc	BU
2006 Proof	12,500	Value: 95.00				

KM# 842 DOLLAR
31.1035 g., 0.9990 Silver 0.9990 oz. ASW, 40 mm. **Ruler:** Elizabeth II **Subject:** 40th Anniversary of Demise of Pre-Decimal Coins **Obv:** Head with tiara right above transparent locket containing small replicas of pre-decimal currency **Obv. Designer:** Ian Rank-Broadley **Rev:** Rim legend about locket

Date	Mintage	F	VF	XF	Unc	BU
2006P Proof	7,500	Value: 150				

KM# 843 DOLLAR
31.1035 g., 0.9990 Silver 0.9990 oz. ASW, 40 mm. **Ruler:** Elizabeth II **Subject:** 80th Birthday of Queen Elizabeth II **Obv:** Head with tiara right **Obv. Designer:** Ian Rank-Broadley **Rev:** Queen Elizabeth II

Date	Mintage	F	VF	XF	Unc	BU
2006P Proof	12,500	Value: 80.00				

KM# 844 DOLLAR
31.1035 g., 0.9990 Silver 0.9990 oz. ASW, 40 mm. **Ruler:** Elizabeth II **Subject:** Figures of Note **Obv:** Head with tiara right **Obv. Designer:** Ian Rank-Broadley **Rev:** Queen Elizabeth as portrayed on Australia 1 dollar banknote

Date	Mintage	F	VF	XF	Unc	BU
2006P Proof	1,000	Value: 175				

KM# 845 DOLLAR
31.1035 g., 0.9990 Silver 0.9990 oz. ASW, 40 mm. **Ruler:** Elizabeth II **Subject:** Figures of Note **Obv:** Head with tiara right **Obv. Designer:** Ian Rank-Broadley **Rev:** MacArthur and Farrer as portrayed on Australia 2 dollar banknote

Date	Mintage	F	VF	XF	Unc	BU
2006P Proof	1,000	Value: 95.00				

KM# 846 DOLLAR
31.1035 g., 0.9990 Silver 0.9990 oz. ASW, 40 mm. **Ruler:** Elizabeth II **Subject:** Figures of Note **Obv:** Head with tiara right **Obv. Designer:** Ian Rank-Broadley **Rev:** Banks and Chisholm as portrayed on Australia 5 dollar banknote

Date	Mintage	F	VF	XF	Unc	BU
2006P Proof	1,000	Value: 95.00				

KM# 847 DOLLAR
31.1035 g., 0.9990 Silver 0.9990 oz. ASW, 40 mm. **Ruler:** Elizabeth II **Subject:** Figures of Note **Obv:** Head with tiara right **Obv. Designer:** Ian Rank-Broadley **Rev:** Greenway and Lawson as portrayed on Australia 10 dollar banknote

Date	Mintage	F	VF	XF	Unc	BU
2006P Proof	1,000	Value: 95.00				

KM# 848 DOLLAR
31.1035 g., 0.9990 Silver 0.9990 oz. ASW, 40 mm. **Ruler:** Elizabeth II **Subject:** Figures of Note **Obv:** Head with tiara right **Obv. Designer:** Ian Rank-Broadley **Rev:** Kingsford-Smith and Hargrave as portrayed on Australia 20 dollar banknote

Date	Mintage	F	VF	XF	Unc	BU
2006P Proof	1,000	Value: 95.00				

KM# 849 DOLLAR
31.1035 g., 0.9990 Silver 0.9990 oz. ASW, 40 mm. **Ruler:** Elizabeth II **Subject:** 50th Anniversary of Dame Edna Everage **Obv:** Head with tiara right **Obv. Designer:** Ian Rank-Broadley **Rev:** Dame Edna

Date	Mintage	F	VF	XF	Unc	BU
2006P Proof	6,500	Value: 85.00				

KM# 1005 DOLLAR
31.1030 g., 0.9990 Silver 0.9989 oz. ASW, 40 mm. **Ruler:** Elizabeth II **Obv:** Head with tiara right **Obv. Legend:** ELIZABETH II - AUSTRALIA **Obv. Designer:** Ian Rank-Broadley **Rev:** Everage head facing, multicolor **Rev. Legend:** DAME EDNA EVERAGE - 50TH ANNIVERSARY

Date	Mintage	F	VF	XF	Unc	BU
ND(2006)P Proof	6,500	Value: 55.00				

KM# 1019 DOLLAR
31.3000 g., 0.9990 Silver 1.0053 oz. ASW, 40.5 mm. **Ruler:** Elizabeth II **Subject:** 20th Anniversary of base **Obv:** Head with tiara right **Obv. Legend:** ELIZABETH II - AUSTRALIA **Obv. Designer:** Ian Rank-Broadley **Rev:** Plane above Albatross and chick on ice, multicolor **Rev. Legend:** Australian Antarctic Territory - EDGEWORTH DAVID BASE **Edge:** Reeded

Date	Mintage	F	VF	XF	Unc	BU
2006P Proof	7,500	Value: 55.00				

KM# 808 DOLLAR
9.0000 g., Aluminum-Bronze, 25 mm. **Ruler:** Elizabeth II **Subject:** Ashes Cricket Series 1882-2007 **Obv:** Head with tiara right **Obv. Designer:** Ian Rank-Broadley **Rev:** Urn with supporters **Rev. Designer:** Vladimir Gottwald **Edge:** Segmented reeding

Date	Mintage	F	VF	XF	Unc	BU
2007	—	—	—	—	3.00	4.00

KM# 828 DOLLAR
9.0000 g., Aluminum-Bronze, 25 mm. **Ruler:** Elizabeth II **Subject:** Year of the Surf Lifesaver **Obv:** Head with tiara right **Obv. Designer:** Ian Rank-Broadley **Rev:** Three lifesavers carrying rescued person **Rev. Designer:** Vladimir Gottwald **Edge:** Segmented reeding

Date	Mintage	F	VF	XF	Unc	BU
2007 Proof	34,500	Value: 20.00				

KM# 829 DOLLAR
9.0000 g., Aluminum-Bronze, 25 mm. **Ruler:** Elizabeth II **Subject:** Norman Lindsay and his Magic Pudding **Obv:** Head with tiara right **Obv. Designer:** Ian Rank-Broadley **Rev:** Lindsay and Pudding characters **Rev. Designer:** Vladimir Gottwald **Edge:** Segmented reeding

Date	Mintage	F	VF	XF	Unc	BU
2007	33,690	—	—	—	65.00	—

KM# 850 DOLLAR
27.2200 g., Copper-Nickel, 38.74 mm. **Ruler:** Elizabeth II **Obv:** Head with tiara right **Obv. Designer:** Ian Rank-Broadley **Rev:** Kangaroo mother and joey **Rev. Designer:** Rolf Harris **Edge:** Reeded

Date	Mintage	F	VF	XF	Unc	BU
2007	5,000	—	—	—	275	300

KM# 1009 DOLLAR
31.1030 g., 0.9990 Silver 0.9989 oz. ASW, 40 mm. **Ruler:** Elizabeth II **Subject:** 75th Anniversary Death of Phar Lap **Obv:** Head with tiara right **Obv. Legend:** ELIZABETH II - AUSTRALIA **Rev:** Horse and rider racing right

Date	Mintage	F	VF	XF	Unc	BU
ND(2007)P Proof	7,500	Value: 95.00				

KM# 1012 DOLLAR
31.1030 g., 0.9990 Silver 0.9989 oz. ASW, 40 mm. **Ruler:** Elizabeth II **Obv:** Bust with tiara right **Obv. Legend:** ELIZABETH II - AUSTRALIA **Obv. Designer:** Ian Rank-Broadley **Rev:** Bridge, multicolor fireworks above **Rev. Legend:** 75th ANNIVERSARY - SYDNEY HARBOUR BRIDGE **Rev. Designer:** Vladimir Gottwald

Date	Mintage	F	VF	XF	Unc	BU
ND(2007)P Proof	10,000	Value: 85.00				

KM# 1016 DOLLAR
11.6600 g., 0.9990 Silver 0.3745 oz. ASW, 25 mm. **Ruler:** Elizabeth II **Subject:** 75th Anniversary - Sydney Harbor Bridge **Obv:** Head with tiara right **Obv. Legend:** ELIZABETH II _ AUSTRALIA **Obv. Designer:** Ian Rank-Broadley **Rev:** Three men standing at bridge joint **Edge:** Segmented reeding

Date	Mintage	F	VF	XF	Unc	BU
2007B Proof	12,500	Value: 35.00				

KM# 1020 DOLLAR
31.4800 g., 0.9990 Silver 1.0111 oz. ASW, 40.5 mm. **Ruler:** Elizabeth II **Subject:** 50th Anniversary of Station **Obv:** Head with tiara right **Obv. Legend:** ELIZABETH II - AUSTRALIA **Obv. Designer:** Ian Rank-Broadley **Rev:** Ship "Kista Dan", multicolor **Rev. Legend:** Australian Antarctic Territory - DAVIS STATION **Edge:** Reeded

Date	Mintage	F	VF	XF	Unc	BU
2007P Proof	7,500	Value: 55.00				

KM# 1024 DOLLAR
9.0000 g., Aluminum-Bronze, 25 mm. **Ruler:** Elizabeth II **Series:** Colored Oceans **Obv:** Head with tiara right **Obv. Designer:** Ian Rank-Broadley **Rev:** Biscuit Star, multicolor **Rev. Designer:** T. Dean **Edge:** Segmented reeding **Note:** Issued in folder.

Date	Mintage	F	VF	XF	Unc	BU
2007	—	—	—	—	—	20.00

KM# 1025 DOLLAR
9.0000 g., Aluminum-Bronze, 25 mm. **Ruler:** Elizabeth II **Series:** Colored Oceans **Obv:** Head with tiara right **Obv. Designer:** Ian Rank-Broadley **Rev:** Longfin Banner fish, multicolor **Rev. Designer:** T. Dean **Edge:** Segmented reeding

Date	Mintage	F	VF	XF	Unc	BU
2007	25,930	—	—	—	—	20.00

KM# 1026 DOLLAR
9.0000 g., Aluminum-Bronze, 25 mm. **Ruler:** Elizabeth II **Series:** Colored Oceans **Obv:** Head with tiara right **Obv. Designer:** Ian Rank-Broadley **Rev:** White Shark, multicolor **Rev. Designer:** T. Dean **Edge:** Segmented reeding **Note:** Issued in folder.

Date	Mintage	F	VF	XF	Unc	BU
2007	30,416	—	—	—	—	20.00

KM# 1027 DOLLAR
9.0000 g., Aluminum-Bronze, 25 mm. **Ruler:** Elizabeth II **Series:** Colored Oceans **Obv:** Head with tiara right **Obv. Designer:** Ian Rank-Broadley **Rev:** Big Belly seahorse **Edge:** Segmented reeding

Date	Mintage	F	VF	XF	Unc	BU
2007	—	—	—	—	—	20.00

KM# 1040 DOLLAR
9.0000 g., Aluminum-Bronze, 25 mm. **Ruler:** Elizabeth II **Subject:** APEC **Rev:** Multiple stars

Date	Mintage	F	VF	XF	Unc	BU
2007B	20,108,000	—	—	—	3.00	4.00

KM# 1042 DOLLAR
9.0000 g., Aluminum-Brass, 25 mm. **Ruler:** Elizabeth II **Subject:** 60th Anniversary - Peacekeepers **Rev:** Hand holding globe within wreath, dove above

Date	Mintage	F	VF	XF	Unc	BU
2007B	31,028	—	—	—	—	15.00

KM# 1044a DOLLAR
11.6600 g., 0.9990 Silver 0.3745 oz. ASW, 25 mm. **Ruler:** Elizabeth II **Subject:** Year of the Surfer Lifesaver **Rev:** Three men saving fourth

Date	Mintage	F	VF	XF	Unc	BU
2007B	—	Value: 40.00				

KM# 1437 DOLLAR
Silver gilt **Ruler:** Elizabeth II **Subject:** Lunar dollar

Date	Mintage	F	VF	XF	Unc	BU
2007 Proof	—	—	—	—	—	—

KM# 1438 DOLLAR
Silver gilt **Ruler:** Elizabeth II **Subject:** One Johanna

Date	Mintage	F	VF	XF	Unc	BU
2007 Proof	—	—	—	—	—	—

KM# 1047 DOLLAR
9.0000 g., Aluminum-Brass, 25 mm. **Ruler:** Elizabeth II **Rev:** First coat of arms

Date	Mintage	F	VF	XF	Unc	BU
2008B	32,500	—	—	—	5.00	6.00
2008M	25,202	—	—	—	5.00	6.00
2008C	104,689	—	—	—	15.00	17.00
2008S	32,500	—	—	—	5.00	6.00

KM# 1047a DOLLAR
11.6000 g., 0.9990 Silver 0.3726 oz. ASW, 25 mm. **Ruler:** Elizabeth II **Rev:** First coat of arms

Date	Mintage	F	VF	XF	Unc	BU
2008C Proof	12,500	Value: 45.00				

KM# 1063 DOLLAR
9.0000 g., Aluminum-Brass, 25 mm. **Ruler:** Elizabeth II **Subject:** Saint Sister Mary Mackillop **Rev:** Nun and three children, world map in background **Rev. Designer:** V. Gottwald

Date	Mintage	F	VF	XF	Unc	BU
2008	29,800	—	—	—	15.00	17.00

KM# 1039 DOLLAR
9.0000 g., Aluminum-Bronze, 25 mm. **Ruler:** Elizabeth II **Subject:** Boy Scouts, 100th Anniversary

Date	Mintage	F	VF	XF	Unc	BU
2008	—	—	—	—	6.00	7.00

KM# 1052 DOLLAR
9.0000 g., Aluminum-Brass, 25 mm. **Ruler:** Elizabeth II **Subject:** Rugby League Centennial **Rev:** Rugby anniversary logo **Rev. Designer:** V. Gottwald

Date	Mintage	F	VF	XF	Unc	BU
2008	60,400	—	—	—	15.00	17.00

KM# 1059 DOLLAR
9.0000 g., Aluminum-Bronze, 25 mm. **Ruler:** Elizabeth II **Subject:** Planet Earth **Rev:** Four hands and elements **Rev. Designer:** V. Gottwald

Date	Mintage	F	VF	XF	Unc	BU
2008	28,399	—	—	—	20.00	22.00
2008 Proof	—	Value: 25.00				

KM# 1061 DOLLAR
27.2200 g., Copper-Nickel, 38.74 mm. **Ruler:** Elizabeth II **Rev:** Kangaroo holding football **Rev. Designer:** Reg Mombassa

Date	Mintage	F	VF	XF	Unc	BU
2008	9,234	—	—	—	—	25.00

KM# 1061a DOLLAR
31.1050 g., 0.9990 Silver 0.9990 oz. ASW, 40 mm. **Ruler:** Elizabeth II **Rev:** Kangaroo holding football **Rev. Designer:** Reg Mombassa

Date	Mintage	F	VF	XF	Unc	BU
2008	7,500	—	—	—	—	65.00
2008 Proof	10,000	Value: 50.00				

KM# 1061b DOLLAR
31.1050 g., 0.9990 Silver 0.9990 oz. ASW, 40 mm. **Ruler:** Elizabeth II **Rev:** Kangaroo holding football **Rev. Designer:** Reg Mombassa

Date	Mintage	F	VF	XF	Unc	BU
2008 Proof	12,500	Value: 95.00				

KM# 1064 DOLLAR
9.0000 g., Aluminum-Brass, 25 mm. **Ruler:** Elizabeth II **Subject:** Centennial of Quarantine **Rev:** Beagle and suitcase like map of Australia **Rev. Designer:** W. Pietranik

Date	Mintage	F	VF	XF	Unc	BU
2008	30,094	—	—	—	15.00	17.00

KM# 1068 DOLLAR
9.0000 g., Aluminum-Brass, 25 mm. **Ruler:** Elizabeth II **Rev:** Multicolor Echidna **Rev. Designer:** S. Foster

Date	Mintage	F	VF	XF	Unc	BU
2008	20,589	—	—	—	18.00	20.00

KM# 1069 DOLLAR
9.0000 g., Aluminum-Brass, 25 mm. **Ruler:** Elizabeth II **Rev:** Multicolor Rock Wallaby **Rev. Designer:** S. Foster

Date	Mintage	F	VF	XF	Unc	BU
2008	24,863	—	—	—	18.00	20.00

KM# 1070 DOLLAR
9.0000 g., Aluminum-Brass, 25 mm. **Ruler:** Elizabeth II **Rev:** Multicolor koala **Rev. Designer:** S. Foster

Date	Mintage	F	VF	XF	Unc	BU
2008	27,045	—	—	—	18.00	20.00

KM# 1071 DOLLAR
9.0000 g., Aluminum-Brass, 25 mm. **Ruler:** Elizabeth II **Rev:** Multicolor wombat **Rev. Designer:** S. Foster

Date	Mintage	F	VF	XF	Unc	BU
2008	22,295	—	—	—	18.00	20.00

KM# 1087 DOLLAR
9.0000 g., Aluminum-Brass, 25 mm. **Ruler:** Elizabeth II **Subject:** 60th Anniversary - Citizenship **Obv:** Head right **Rev:** Portraits around globe

Date	Mintage	F	VF	XF	Unc	BU
2008C Proof	—	Value: 28.00				

KM# 1087a DOLLAR
11.9000 g., 0.9990 Silver 0.3822 oz. ASW, 25 mm. **Ruler:** Elizabeth II **Subject:** 60th Anniversary - Citizenship **Rev:** Portraits around globe

Date	Mintage	F	VF	XF	Unc	BU
2008C Proof	—	Value: 40.00				

KM# 1090 DOLLAR
13.5000 g., Aluminum-Bronze, 29.5 mm. **Ruler:** Elizabeth II **Subject:** Ghost Bat **Obv:** Head right **Rev:** Ghost bat against night sky **Edge:** Reeded

Date	Mintage	F	VF	XF	Unc	BU
2008	—	—	—	—	—	12.00

KM# 1091 DOLLAR
31.1350 g., 0.9990 Silver 100000 oz. ASW, 40.6 mm. **Ruler:** Elizabeth II **Subject:** UNESCO Heritage site - Kakadu National Park **Rev:** Saltwater crocodile and multicolor swamp

Date	Mintage	F	VF	XF	Unc	BU
2008P Proof	7,500	Value: 75.00				

KM# 1168 DOLLAR
13.5000 g., Aluminum-Bronze, 29.5 mm. **Ruler:** Elizabeth II **Obv:** Head right **Obv. Designer:** Ian Rank-Broadley **Rev:** Common wombat

Date	Mintage	F	VF	XF	Unc	BU
2008P	—	—	—	—	—	12.00

KM# 1169 DOLLAR
13.5000 g., Aluminum-Bronze, 29.5 mm. **Ruler:** Elizabeth II **Obv:** Head right **Obv. Designer:** Ian Rank-Broadley **Rev:** Echidna

Date	Mintage	F	VF	XF	Unc	BU
2008P	—	—	—	—	—	12.00

KM# 1170 DOLLAR
13.5000 g., Aluminum-Bronze, 29.5 mm. **Ruler:** Elizabeth II **Obv:** Head right **Obv. Designer:** Ian Rank-Broadley **Rev:** Frilled-neck lizard

Date	Mintage	F	VF	XF	Unc	BU
2008P	—	—	—	—	—	12.00

KM# 1171 DOLLAR
13.5000 g., Aluminum-Bronze, 29.5 mm. **Ruler:** Elizabeth II **Obv:** Head right **Obv. Designer:** Ian Rank-Broadley **Rev:** Grey kangaroo

Date	Mintage	F	VF	XF	Unc	BU
2008P	—	—	—	—	—	12.00

KM# 1172 DOLLAR
13.5000 g., Aluminum-Bronze, 29.5 mm. **Ruler:** Elizabeth II **Obv:** Head right **Obv. Designer:** Ian Rank-Broadley **Rev:** Splendid wren

Date	Mintage	F	VF	XF	Unc	BU
2008P	—	—	—	—	—	12.00

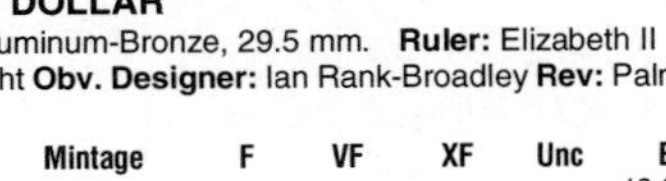

KM# 1173 DOLLAR
13.5000 g., Aluminum-Bronze, 29.5 mm. **Ruler:** Elizabeth II **Obv:** Head right **Obv. Designer:** Ian Rank-Broadley **Rev:** Palm cockatoo

Date	Mintage	F	VF	XF	Unc	BU
2008P	—	—	—	—	—	12.00

KM# 1174 DOLLAR
13.5000 g., Aluminum-Bronze, 29.5 mm. **Ruler:** Elizabeth II **Obv:** Head right **Obv. Designer:** Ian Rank-Broadley **Rev:** Wedge-tailed eagle

Date	Mintage	F	VF	XF	Unc	BU
2008P	—	—	—	—	—	12.00

KM# 1175 DOLLAR
13.5000 g., Aluminum-Bronze, 29.5 mm. **Ruler:** Elizabeth II **Obv:** Head right **Obv. Designer:** Ian Rank-Broadley **Rev:** Whale shark

Date	Mintage	F	VF	XF	Unc	BU
2008P	—	—	—	—	—	12.00

KM# 1176 DOLLAR
13.5000 g., Aluminum-Bronze, 29.5 mm. **Ruler:** Elizabeth II **Obv:** Head right **Obv. Designer:** Ian Rank-Broadley **Rev:** Green sea turtle

Date	Mintage	F	VF	XF	Unc	BU
2008P	—	—	—	—	—	12.00

KM# 1177 DOLLAR
13.5000 g., Aluminum-Bronze, 29.5 mm. **Ruler:** Elizabeth II **Obv:** Head right **Obv. Designer:** Ian Rank-Broadley **Rev:** Platypus

Date	Mintage	F	VF	XF	Unc	BU
2008P	—	—	—	—	—	12.00

KM# 1178 DOLLAR
13.5000 g., Aluminum-Bronze, 29.5 mm. **Ruler:** Elizabeth II **Obv:** Head right **Obv. Designer:** Ian Rank-Broadley **Rev:** Australian sea lion

Date	Mintage	F	VF	XF	Unc	BU
2008P	—	—	—	—	—	12.00

KM# 1179 DOLLAR

31.1050 g., 0.9990 Silver 0.9990 oz. ASW, 40.6 mm. **Ruler:** Elizabeth II **Subject:** 90th Anniversary - End of WWI **Obv:** Head right **Obv. Designer:** Ian Rank-Broadley **Rev:** Silhouette of bugler, multicolor poppies below

Date	Mintage	F	VF	XF	Unc	BU
2008P Proof	12,500	Value: 90.00				

KM# 1428 DOLLAR

13.8000 g., Aluminum-Bronze, 30.6 mm. **Ruler:** Elizabeth II **Subject:** Citizenship **Obv:** Head in tiara right **Rev:** National arms

Date	Mintage	F	VF	XF	Unc	BU
2009(p)	—	—	—	—	—	14.00
2010(p)	—	—	—	—	—	14.00

KM# 1429 DOLLAR

9.0000 g., Aluminum-Bronze, 25 mm. **Ruler:** Elizabeth II **Subject:** Steve Irwin **Rev:** Steve Irwin and animal montage

Date	Mintage	F	VF	XF	Unc	BU
2009(p)	—	—	—	—	—	12.00

KM# 1076 DOLLAR

9.0000 g., Aluminum-Brass, 25 mm. **Ruler:** Elizabeth II **Subject:** Year of Astronomy **Rev:** Parkes Telescope **Rev. Designer:** Caitlin Goodall

Date	Mintage	F	VF	XF	Unc	BU
2009	—	—	—	—	12.00	14.00
2009 Proof	—	Value: 25.00				

KM# 1077 DOLLAR

9.0000 g., Aluminum-Brass, 25 mm. **Ruler:** Elizabeth II **Subject:** Dorothy Wall **Rev:** Portrait and four characters to right **Rev. Designer:** C. Goodall

Date	Mintage	F	VF	XF	Unc	BU
2009	—	—	—	—	—	12.00

KM# 1082 DOLLAR

27.2200 g., Copper-Nickel, 38.74 mm. **Ruler:** Elizabeth II **Rev:** Kangaroo **Rev. Designer:** K. Done

Date	Mintage	F	VF	XF	Unc	BU
2009	—	—	—	—	—	25.00

KM# 1089 DOLLAR

Aluminum-Bronze **Ruler:** Elizabeth II **Subject:** Postal Service, 200th Anniversary **Obv:** Head with tiara right **Rev:** Isaac Nichols, first postman

Date	Mintage	F	VF	XF	Unc	BU
2009	—	—	—	—	—	13.00

KM# 1092 DOLLAR

13.3000 g., Aluminum-Bronze, 30.6 mm. **Ruler:** Elizabeth II **Subject:** Celebrate Australia - Western Australia **Rev:** Kangaroo and multicolor Perth city view

Date	Mintage	F	VF	XF	Unc	BU
2009	—	—	—	—	—	13.00

KM# 1093 DOLLAR

13.3000 g., Aluminum-Bronze, 30.6 mm. **Ruler:** Elizabeth II **Series:** Celebrate Australia - Victoria **Rev:** Little Penguin and multicolor Melbourne city view

Date	Mintage	F	VF	XF	Unc	BU
2009	—	—	—	—	—	13.00

KM# 1094 DOLLAR

13.3000 g., Aluminum-Bronze, 30.6 mm. **Ruler:** Elizabeth II **Subject:** Celebrate Australia - Tasmania **Rev:** Tasmanian Devil and multicolor Cradle Mountain National Park

Date	Mintage	F	VF	XF	Unc	BU
2009P	—	—	—	—	—	13.00

KM# 1095 DOLLAR

13.3000 g., Aluminum-Bronze, 30.6 mm. **Ruler:** Elizabeth II **Subject:** Celebrate Australia - South Australia **Rev:** Wombat and multicolor cathedral

Date	Mintage	F	VF	XF	Unc	BU
2009P	—	—	—	—	—	13.00

KM# 1096 DOLLAR

13.3000 g., Aluminum-Bronze, 30.6 mm. **Ruler:** Elizabeth II **Subject:** Celebrate Australia - Queensland **Rev:** Sea Turtle with multicolor skyline of Brisbane

Date	Mintage	F	VF	XF	Unc	BU
2009P	—	—	—	—	—	13.00

KM# 1097 DOLLAR

13.3000 g., Aluminum-Bronze, 30.6 mm. **Ruler:** Elizabeth II **Subject:** Celebrate Australia - Northern Territoty **Rev:** Saltwater crocodile and multicolor Kakadu National Park

Date	Mintage	F	VF	XF	Unc	BU
2009P	—	—	—	—	—	13.00

KM# 1098 DOLLAR

13.3000 g., Aluminum-Bronze, 30.6 mm. **Ruler:** Elizabeth II **Subject:** Celebrate Australia - New South Wales **Rev:** Koala, multicolor Sydney Opera House and Harbor Bridge

Date	Mintage	F	VF	XF	Unc	BU
2009P	—	—	—	—	—	13.00

KM# 1099 DOLLAR

13.3000 g., Aluminum-Bronze, 30.6 mm. **Ruler:** Elizabeth II **Subject:** Celebrate Australia - Capital Territory, Canberra **Rev:** Cockatoo and multicolor design

Date	Mintage	F	VF	XF	Unc	BU
2009P	—	—	—	—	—	13.00

KM# 1102 DOLLAR

31.1050 g., 0.9990 Silver 0.9990 oz. ASW **Ruler:** Elizabeth II **Subject:** Great Barrier Reef **Rev:** Sea turtle, multicolor

Date	Mintage	F	VF	XF	Unc	BU
2009 Proof	—	Value: 70.00				

KM# 1211 DOLLAR

31.1050 g., 0.9990 Silver 0.9990 oz. ASW, 40.6 mm. **Ruler:** Elizabeth II **Subject:** Antarctic Territory **Obv:** Head right **Obv. Designer:** Ian Rank-Broadley **Rev:** Douglas Mawson, one of two men standing on magnetic South Pole

Date	Mintage	F	VF	XF	Unc	BU
2009P Proof	7,500	Value: 85.00				

KM# 1245 DOLLAR

31.1050 g., 0.9990 Silver 0.9990 oz. ASW **Ruler:** Elizabeth II **Subject:** 2010 FIFA World Cup, South Africa **Obv:** Head right **Obv. Designer:** Ian Rank-Broadley **Rev:** Soccer player and kangaroo in background

Date	Mintage	F	VF	XF	Unc	BU
2009P Proof	15,000	Value: 100				

KM# 1248 DOLLAR

31.1050 g., 0.9990 Silver 0.9990 oz. ASW, 40.6 mm. **Ruler:** Elizabeth II **Subject:** World Masters Games **Obv:** Head right **Obv. Designer:** Ian Rank-Broadley **Rev:** Sydney Harbor Bridge, multicolor

Date	Mintage	F	VF	XF	Unc	BU
2009P Proof	5,000	Value: 100				

KM# 1256 DOLLAR

Aluminum-Bronze, 31 mm. **Ruler:** Elizabeth II **Subject:** Space Topics - Astronomers **Obv:** Head right **Obv. Designer:** Ian Rank-Broadley **Rev:** Galileo Galilei and telescope

Date	Mintage	F	VF	XF	Unc	BU
2009P	—	—	—	—	—	12.00

KM# 1257 DOLLAR

Aluminum-Bronze, 31 mm. **Ruler:** Elizabeth II **Subject:** Space Topics - Craters **Obv:** Head right **Obv. Designer:** Ian Rank-Broadley **Rev:** Moon crater Daedalus

Date	Mintage	F	VF	XF	Unc	BU
2009P	—	—	—	—	—	12.00

KM# 1258 DOLLAR

Aluminum-Bronze, 31 mm. **Ruler:** Elizabeth II **Subject:** Space Topics - Moons **Obv:** Head right **Obv. Designer:** Ian Rank-Broadley **Rev:** Apollo astronaut on moon walk

Date	Mintage	F	VF	XF	Unc	BU
2009P	—	—	—	—	—	12.00

KM# 1259 DOLLAR

Aluminum-Bronze, 31 mm. **Ruler:** Elizabeth II **Subject:** Space Topics - Observatories **Obv:** Head right **Obv. Designer:** Ian Rank-Broadley **Rev:** Parkes Observatory, New South Wales

Date	Mintage	F	VF	XF	Unc	BU
2009P	—	—	—	—	—	12.00

KM# 1260 DOLLAR

Aluminum-Bronze, 31 mm. **Ruler:** Elizabeth II **Subject:** Space Topics - Rockets **Obv:** Head right **Obv. Designer:** Ian Rank-Broadley **Rev:** Saturn V rocket on launch pad

Date	Mintage	F	VF	XF	Unc	BU
2009P	—	—	—	—	—	12.00

KM# 1261 DOLLAR

Aluminum-Bronze, 31 mm. **Ruler:** Elizabeth II **Subject:** Space Topics - Rovers **Obv:** Head right **Obv. Designer:** Ian Rank-Broadley **Rev:** Mars rover - Spirit and Opportunity

Date	Mintage	F	VF	XF	Unc	BU
2009P	—	—	—	—	—	12.00

KM# 1262 DOLLAR

Aluminum-Bronze, 31 mm. **Ruler:** Elizabeth II **Subject:** Space Topics - Space Shuttles **Obv:** Head right **Obv. Designer:** Ian Rank-Broadley **Rev:** Shuttle Discovery and Space Exploration

Date	Mintage	F	VF	XF	Unc	BU
2009P	—	—	—	—	—	12.00

KM# 1263 DOLLAR

Aluminum-Bronze, 31 mm. **Ruler:** Elizabeth II **Subject:** Space

Topics - Probes **Obv:** Head right **Obv. Designer:** Ian Rank-Broadley **Rev:** Deep Space Probes - Pioneer 11 and 11

Date	Mintage	F	VF	XF	Unc	BU
2009P	—	—	—	—	—	12.00

KM# 1264 DOLLAR
Aluminum-Bronze, 31 mm. **Ruler:** Elizabeth II **Subject:** Space Topics - Space Telescope **Obv:** Head right **Obv. Designer:** Ian Rank-Broadley **Rev:** Hubble Space Telescope

Date	Mintage	F	VF	XF	Unc	BU
2009P	—	—	—	—	—	12.00

KM# 1265 DOLLAR
31.1050 g., 0.9990 Silver 0.9990 oz. ASW, 27x48 mm. **Ruler:** Elizabeth II **Subject:** Chinese Mythological Character - Wealth **Obv:** Head right **Obv. Designer:** Ian Rank-Broadley **Rev:** Man standing, multicolor **Shape:** Vertical rectangle

Date	Mintage	F	VF	XF	Unc	BU
2009P	—	—	—	—	—	65.00

KM# 1266 DOLLAR
31.1050 g., 0.9990 Silver 0.9990 oz. ASW, 27x48 mm. **Ruler:** Elizabeth II **Subject:** Chinese Mythological Character - Longevity **Obv:** Head right **Obv. Designer:** Ian Rank-Broadley **Rev:** Man standing with staff, multicolor **Edge Lettering:** Vertical rectangle

Date	Mintage	F	VF	XF	Unc	BU
2009P	—	—	—	—	—	65.00

KM# 1267 DOLLAR
31.1050 g., 0.9990 Silver 0.9990 oz. ASW, 27x48 mm. **Ruler:** Elizabeth II **Subject:** Chinese Mythological Character - Success **Obv:** Head right **Obv. Designer:** Ian Rank-Broadley **Rev:** Man standing with deer, multicolor **Shape:** Vertical rectangle

Date	Mintage	F	VF	XF	Unc	BU
2009P	—	—	—	—	—	65.00

KM# 1268 DOLLAR
31.1050 g., 0.9990 Silver 0.9990 oz. ASW, 27x48 mm. **Ruler:** Elizabeth II **Subject:** Chinese Mythological Character - Fortune **Obv:** Head right **Obv. Designer:** Ian Rank-Broadley **Rev:** Man standing with scroll, multicolor **Shape:** Vertical rectangle

Date	Mintage	F	VF	XF	Unc	BU
2009P	—	—	—	—	—	65.00

KM# 1357 DOLLAR
31.1350 g., 0.9990 Silver 100000 oz. ASW, 40.6 mm. **Ruler:** Elizabeth II **Subject:** International Year of Astronomy **Obv:** Head right **Rev:** Youth looking through telescope, pointing at universe

Date	Mintage	F	VF	XF	Unc	BU
2009(p)	7,500	Value: 60.00				

KM# 1358 DOLLAR
30.6000 g., Copper-Nickel, 30.6 mm. **Ruler:** Elizabeth II **Subject:** Swimming **Obv:** Head light **Rev:** Swimmer

Date	Mintage	F	VF	XF	Unc	BU
2009(p) Proof	7,500	Value: 10.00				

KM# 1359 DOLLAR
32.1350 g., 0.9990 Silver 1.0321 oz. ASW, 40 mm. **Ruler:** Elizabeth II **Subject:** Swimming **Obv:** Head right **Rev:** Swimmer with hologram effect added

Date	Mintage	F	VF	XF	Unc	BU
2009(p) Proof	7,500	Value: 65.00				

KM# 1497 DOLLAR
9.0000 g., Aluminum-Bronze, 25 mm. **Ruler:** Elizabeth II **Subject:** ANZAC

Date	Mintage	F	VF	XF	Unc	BU
2009	—	—	—	—	7.50	10.00

KM# 1498 DOLLAR
9.0000 g., Aluminum-Bronze, 25 mm. **Ruler:** Elizabeth II **Subject:** Pensions

Date	Mintage	F	VF	XF	Unc	BU
2009	—	—	—	—	7.50	10.00

KM# 1499 DOLLAR
9.0000 g., Aluminum-Bronze, 25 mm. **Ruler:** Elizabeth II **Subject:** Girl Guides, 100th Anniversary

Date	Mintage	F	VF	XF	Unc	BU
2009	—	—	—	—	7.50	10.00

KM# 1324 DOLLAR
31.1050 g., 0.9990 Silver 0.9990 oz. ASW, 41 mm. **Ruler:** Elizabeth II **Subject:** Lachen Macquarie, Governor of New South Wales **Obv:** Head right **Obv. Designer:** Ian Rank-Broadley **Rev:** Macquarie, Sydney's "Rum" Hospital, Holey Dollar

Date	Mintage	F	VF	XF	Unc	BU
2010P Proof	7,500	Value: 90.00				

KM# 1325 DOLLAR
31.1050 g., 0.9990 Silver 0.9990 oz. ASW, 41 mm. **Ruler:** Elizabeth II **Subject:** 2010 Australian Olympic Team **Obv:** Head right **Obv. Designer:** Ian Rank-Broadley **Rev:** Downhill skier, multicolor Australian flag

Date	Mintage	F	VF	XF	Unc	BU
2010P Proof	5,000	Value: 100				

KM# 1326 DOLLAR
31.1050 g., 0.9990 Silver 0.9990 oz. ASW, 41 mm. **Ruler:** Elizabeth II **Subject:** Century of Flight in Australia **Obv:** Head right **Obv. Designer:** Ian Rank-Broadley **Rev:** Bi-plane, multicolor

Date	Mintage	F	VF	XF	Unc	BU
2010P Proof	7,500	Value: 90.00				

KM# 1380 DOLLAR
9.0000 g., Aluminum-Bronze, 25 mm. **Ruler:** Elizabeth II **Subject:** Anzac Navy **Obv:** Head right **Rev:** Naval crew member and ship

Date	Mintage	F	VF	XF	Unc	BU
2010(p)	—	—	—	—	—	12.00

KM# 1381 DOLLAR
31.1030 g., 0.9990 Silver 0.9989 oz. ASW, 40.5 mm. **Ruler:** Elizabeth II **Subject:** Antarctic - Huskey **Obv:** Head right **Rev:** Huskey in multicolor

Date	Mintage	F	VF	XF	Unc	BU
2010(p) Proof	7,500	Value: 55.00				

KM# 1382 DOLLAR
9.0000 g., Aluminum-Bronze, 25 mm. **Ruler:** Elizabeth II **Subject:** Flight Centennial **Obv:** Head right **Rev:** Bi-plane

Date	Mintage	F	VF	XF	Unc	BU
2010(p)	—	—	—	—	—	13.00

KM# 1383 DOLLAR
31.1035 g., 0.9990 Silver 0.9990 oz. ASW, 40 mm. **Ruler:** Elizabeth II **Subject:** Edward VII Coinage **Obv:** Head right **Rev:** Coin designs and Edward VII in multicolor

Date	Mintage	F	VF	XF	Unc	BU
2010(p)	—	—	—	—	—	50.00

KM# 1384 DOLLAR
9.0000 g., Aluminum-Bronze, 25 mm. **Ruler:** Elizabeth II **Subject:** Celebrate Australia - Barrier Reef **Obv:** Head right

Date	Mintage	F	VF	XF	Unc	BU
2010(p)	—	—	—	—	—	15.00

KM# 1386 DOLLAR
9.0000 g., Aluminum-Bronze, 25 mm. **Ruler:** Elizabeth II **Subject:** Celebrate Australia - Heard Island **Obv:** Head right

Date	Mintage	F	VF	XF	Unc	BU
2010(p)	—	—	—	—	—	15.00

KM# 1387 DOLLAR
9.0000 g., Aluminum-Bronze, 25 mm. **Ruler:** Elizabeth II **Subject:** Celebrate Australia - Shark Bay **Obv:** Head right

Date	Mintage	F	VF	XF	Unc	BU
2010(p)	—	—	—	—	—	15.00

KM# 1385 DOLLAR
9.0000 g., Aluminum-Bronze, 25 mm. **Ruler:** Elizabeth II **Subject:** Celebrate Australia - Blue Mountain **Obv:** Head right

Date	Mintage	F	VF	XF	Unc	BU
2010(p)	—	—	—	—	—	15.00

KM# 1388 DOLLAR
9.0000 g., Aluminum-Bronze, 25 mm. **Ruler:** Elizabeth II **Subject:** Celebrate Australia - Tasmanian Wilderness **Obv:** Head right

Date	Mintage	F	VF	XF	Unc	BU
2010(p)	—	—	—	—	—	15.00

KM# 1391 DOLLAR
31.1050 g., 0.9990 Silver 0.9990 oz. ASW **Ruler:** Elizabeth II **Obv:** Head right **Rev:** Panda and koala

Date	Mintage	F	VF	XF	Unc	BU
2010(p)	—	—	—	—	—	45.00

KM# 1392 DOLLAR
31.1050 g., 0.9990 Silver 0.9990 oz. ASW **Ruler:** Elizabeth II **Subject:** World Expo **Obv:** Head right **Rev:** Austrlian Panham

Date	Mintage	F	VF	XF	Unc	BU
2010(p)	—	—	—	—	—	50.00

KM# 1393 DOLLAR
31.1050 g., 0.9990 Silver 0.9990 oz. ASW **Ruler:** Elizabeth II **Obv:** Head right **Rev:** Kookaburra mascot

Date	Mintage	F	VF	XF	Unc	BU
2010(p)	—	—	—	—	—	45.00

KM# 1394 DOLLAR
31.1050 g., 0.9990 Silver 0.9990 oz. ASW **Ruler:** Elizabeth II **Obv:** Head right **Rev:** City scape

Date	Mintage	F	VF	XF	Unc	BU
2010(p)	—	—	—	—	—	45.00

KM# 1395 DOLLAR
Silver, 40x60 mm. **Ruler:** Elizabeth II **Series:** World Expo **Obv:** Head right **Shape:** Australian outline

Date	Mintage	F	VF	XF	Unc	BU
2010(p)	—	—	—	—	—	60.00

KM# 1396 DOLLAR
9.0000 g., Aluminum-Bronze, 25 mm. **Ruler:** Elizabeth II **Subject:** World Expo **Obv:** Head right

Date	Mintage	F	VF	XF	Unc	BU
2010(p)	—	—	—	—	—	15.00

KM# 1431 DOLLAR
Aureate Bronze **Ruler:** Elizabeth II **Subject:** Burke and Wills 150th Anniversary **Rev:** King seated under dig tree

Date	Mintage	F	VF	XF	Unc	BU
2010C	—	—	—	—	—	12.50
2010C Proof	—	Value: 17.50				

KM# 1434 DOLLAR
31.1350 g., 0.9990 Silver 100000 oz. ASW **Ruler:** Elizabeth II **Subject:** Burke & Wills expedition **Rev:** Multicolor scene of explorers

Date	Mintage	F	VF	XF	Unc	BU
2010P Proof	7,500	Value: 80.00				

KM# 1435 DOLLAR
31.1350 g., 0.9990 Silver 100000 oz. ASW, 40.6 mm. **Ruler:** Elizabeth II **Subject:** Treasures of Australia - Gold **Rev:** Three gold nuggets within insert

Date	Mintage	F	VF	XF	Unc	BU
2010P Proof	—	Value: 135				

KM# 1440 DOLLAR
13.3000 g., Aluminum-Bronze, 30.6 mm. **Ruler:** Elizabeth II **Rev:** Blowfly

Date	Mintage	F	VF	XF	Unc	BU
2010P	—	—	—	—	—	12.00

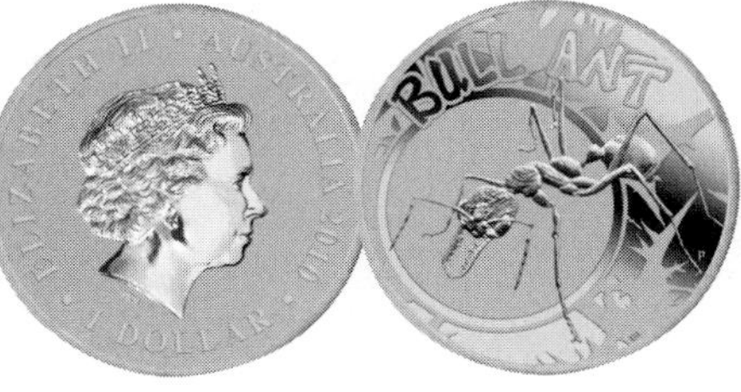

KM# 1441 DOLLAR
13.3000 g., Aluminum-Bronze, 30.6 mm. **Ruler:** Elizabeth II **Rev:** Bull Ant

Date	Mintage	F	VF	XF	Unc	BU
2010P	—	—	—	—	—	12.00

KM# 1442 DOLLAR
13.3000 g., Aluminum-Bronze, 30.6 mm. **Ruler:** Elizabeth II **Rev:** Burlwing Buttlerfly

Date	Mintage	F	VF	XF	Unc	BU
2010P	—	—	—	—	—	12.00

KM# 1443 DOLLAR
13.3000 g., Aluminum-Bronze, 30.6 mm. **Ruler:** Elizabeth II **Rev:** Cicada

Date	Mintage	F	VF	XF	Unc	BU
2010P	—	—	—	—	—	12.00

KM# 1444 DOLLAR
13.3000 g., Aluminum-Bronze, 30.6 mm. **Ruler:** Elizabeth II **Rev:** Dragonfly

Date	Mintage	F	VF	XF	Unc	BU
2010P	—	—	—	—	—	12.00

KM# 1445 DOLLAR
13.3000 g., Aluminum-Bronze, 30.6 mm. **Ruler:** Elizabeth II **Rev:** Grasshopper

Date	Mintage	F	VF	XF	Unc	BU
2010P	—	—	—	—	—	12.00

KM# 1446 DOLLAR
13.3000 g., Aluminum-Bronze, 30.6 mm. **Ruler:** Elizabeth II **Rev:** Ladybug

Date	Mintage	F	VF	XF	Unc	BU
2010P	—	—	—	—	—	12.00

KM# 1447 DOLLAR
13.3000 g., Aluminum-Bronze, 30.6 mm. **Ruler:** Elizabeth II **Rev:** Praying mantis

Date	Mintage	F	VF	XF	Unc	BU
2010P	—	—	—	—	—	12.00

KM# 1448 DOLLAR
13.3000 g., Aluminum-Bronze, 30.6 mm. **Ruler:** Elizabeth II **Rev:** Red-backed spider

Date	Mintage	F	VF	XF	Unc	BU
2010P	—	—	—	—	—	12.00

KM# 1451 DOLLAR
31.1050 g., 0.9990 Silver 0.9990 oz. ASW **Ruler:** Elizabeth II **Subject:** Sidney Coin Show **Rev:** Koala and multicolor opera house and harbor bridge views

Date	Mintage	F	VF	XF	Unc	BU
2010P Proof	—	Value: 45.00				

KM# 1452 DOLLAR
31.1050 g., 0.9990 Silver 0.9990 oz. ASW **Ruler:** Elizabeth II **Subject:** Melbourne Coin Show **Rev:** Penguin and multicolor tram and building

Date	Mintage	F	VF	XF	Unc	BU
2010P Proof	—	Value: 45.00				

KM# 1490 DOLLAR
13.3000 g., Aluminum-Bronze, 30.6 mm. **Ruler:** Elizabeth II **Rev:** Burke & Willis statue

Date	Mintage	F	VF	XF	Unc	BU
2010P	—	—	—	—	—	12.00

KM# 1491 DOLLAR
31.1050 g., 0.9990 Silver 0.9990 oz. ASW, 40.6 mm. **Ruler:** Elizabeth II **Obv:** Head with tiara right **Rev:** Saint Mary Mackillop in color

Date	Mintage	F	VF	XF	Unc	BU
2010 Proof	—	Value: 60.00				

KM# 1494 DOLLAR
31.1050 g., 0.9990 Silver 0.9990 oz. ASW **Ruler:** Elizabeth II **Subject:** New South Wales

Date	Mintage	F	VF	XF	Unc	BU
2010 Proof	—	Value: 50.00				

KM# 1495 DOLLAR
9.0000 g., Aluminum-Bronze, 25 mm. **Ruler:** Elizabeth II **Subject:** Australian coinage, 100th Anniversary **Rev:** Four coinage portraits

Date	Mintage	F	VF	XF	Unc	BU
2010B	—	—	—	—	4.00	5.00
2010C	—	—	—	—	4.00	5.00
2010M	—	—	—	—	4.00	5.00
2010S	—	—	—	—	4.00	5.00

KM# 1495a DOLLAR
11.6600 g., 0.9990 Silver 0.3745 oz. ASW, 25 mm. **Ruler:** Elizabeth II **Subject:** Centennial of Commonwealth Coins **Obv:** Head in tiara right **Rev:** Four portraits

Date	Mintage	F	VF	XF	Unc	BU
2010 Proof	12,500	Value: 50.00				

KM# 1496 DOLLAR
9.0000 g., Aluminum-Bronze, 25 mm. **Ruler:** Elizabeth II **Subject:** Fred Hollows - Inspirational Australians

Date	Mintage	F	VF	XF	Unc	BU
2010	—	—	—	—	3.50	5.00

KM# 1503 DOLLAR
9.0000 g., Aluminum-Bronze, 25 mm. **Ruler:** Elizabeth II **Subject:** Wool Industry **Rev:** Sheep sheering and map of Australia

Date	Mintage	F	VF	XF	Unc	BU
2010	—	—	—	—	5.00	6.00

KM# 1504 DOLLAR
9.0000 g., Aluminum-Bronze, 25 mm. **Ruler:** Elizabeth II **Rev:** Sheep head

Date	Mintage	F	VF	XF	Unc	BU
2010	—	—	—	—	5.00	6.00

KM# 1505 DOLLAR
31.1050 g., 0.9990 Silver 0.9990 oz. ASW, 40.6 mm. **Ruler:** Elizabeth II **Subject:** Perth-ANDA Bridge **Rev:** City view

Date	Mintage	F	VF	XF	Unc	BU
2010 Proof	—	Value: 60.00				

KM# 1515 DOLLAR
31.1050 g., 0.9990 Silver 0.9990 oz. ASW, 40 mm. **Ruler:** Elizabeth II **Rev:** Kangaroo in color

Date	Mintage	F	VF	XF	Unc	BU
2010 Proof	—	Value: 60.00				

KM# 1526 DOLLAR
13.8000 g., Aluminum-Bronze, 30.6 mm. **Ruler:** Elizabeth II **Subject:** 2010 Shanghai World Expo **Obv:** Head with tiara right **Obv. Designer:** Ian Rank-Broadley **Rev:** Artistic tiger seen from above, advancing forward **Rev. Designer:** Wade Robinson

Date	Mintage	F	VF	XF	Unc	BU
2010P	—	—	—	—	—	14.00

KM# 1523 DOLLAR
31.1035 g., 0.9990 Silver 0.9990 oz. ASW, 40.6 mm. **Ruler:** Elizabeth II **Subject:** Australia's Bronze Coinagae, 100th Anniversary **Obv:** Head with tiara right **Rev:** George V and coins, in color

Date	Mintage	F	VF	XF	Unc	BU
2011 Proof	—	Value: 75.00				

KM# 406 2 DOLLARS
6.6000 g., Aluminum-Bronze, 20.5 mm. **Ruler:** Elizabeth II **Obv:** Head with tiara right **Obv. Designer:** Ian Rank-Broadley **Rev:** Aboriginal elder at left, stars above at right **Rev. Designer:** Horst Hahne **Edge:** Segmented reeding

Date	Mintage	F	VF	XF	Unc	BU
2001	35,650,000	—	—	—	5.00	6.00
Note: Large obverse head, IRB spaced						
2001	Inc. above	—	—	—	—	—
Note: Smaller obverse head, IRB joined						
2001 Proof	59,569	Value: 8.00				
2002	29,689,000	—	—	—	4.00	6.00
2002 Proof	39,514	Value: 8.00				
2003	13,656,000	—	—	—	4.00	6.00
2003 Proof	39,090	Value: 8.00				
2004	20,084,000	—	—	—	3.50	5.00
2004 Proof	50,000	Value: 7.00				
2005	—	—	—	—	3.50	5.00
2005 Proof	33,520	Value: 7.00				
2006	—	—	—	—	3.50	5.00
2006 Proof	—	Value: 7.00				
2007	—	—	—	—	3.00	4.50
2007 Proof	—	Value: 6.00				
2008	—	—	—	—	3.00	4.50
2008 Proof	—	Value: 6.00				
2009	—	—	—	—	3.00	4.50
2009 Proof	—	Value: 6.00				
2010	—	—	—	—	3.00	4.50
2010 Proof	—	Value: 6.00				

KM# 406a 2 DOLLARS
15.8800 g., 0.9999 Gold 0.5105 oz. AGW, 20.5 mm. **Ruler:** Elizabeth II **Subject:** Federation Centennial **Obv:** Head with tiara right **Obv. Designer:** Ian Rank-Broadley **Rev:** Aboriginal elder **Rev. Designer:** Horst Hahne **Edge:** Segmented reeding

Date	Mintage	F	VF	XF	Unc	BU
2001B Proof	350	Value: 775				
2005B Proof	650	Value: 750				
2006B Proof	300	Value: 800				

KM# 406b 2 DOLLARS
8.5500 g., 0.9999 Silver 0.2748 oz. ASW, 20.5 mm. **Ruler:** Elizabeth II **Obv:** Head with tiara right **Obv. Designer:** Ian Rank-Broadley **Rev:** Aboriginal elder **Rev. Designer:** Horst Hahne **Edge:** Segmented reeding

Date	Mintage	F	VF	XF	Unc	BU
2003B Proof	6,500	Value: 20.00				
2004B Proof	6,500	Value: 20.00				
2005B Proof	6,500	Value: 20.00				

KM# 764 2 DOLLARS
18.2200 g., 0.9990 Silver 0.5852 oz. ASW, 32.5 mm. **Ruler:** Elizabeth II **Series:** Masterpieces in Silver - Port Phillip Patterns **Obv:** 1/2 ounce design **Rev:** Kangaroo design **Edge:** Reeded

Date	Mintage	F	VF	XF	Unc	BU
2003B Proof	10,000	Value: 35.00				

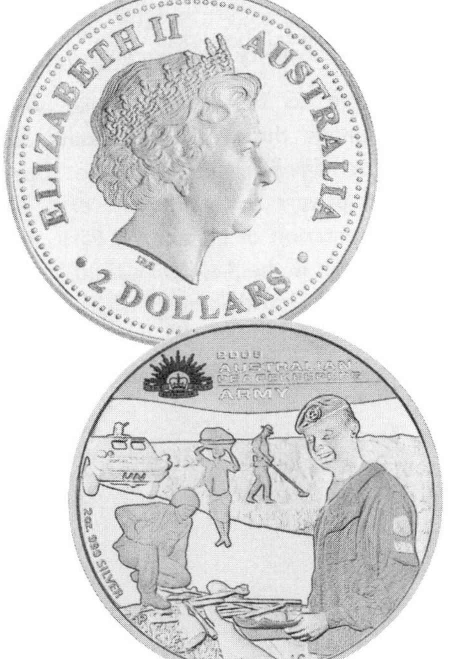

KM# 755 2 DOLLARS
62.2700 g., 0.9990 Silver 1.9999 oz. ASW, 50 mm. **Ruler:** Elizabeth II **Series:** Australian Peacekeepers **Obv:** Queen's head right **Rev:** Australian army and color insignia **Edge:** Reeded

Date	Mintage	F	VF	XF	Unc	BU
2005P Proof	2,500	Value: 85.00				

KM# 756 2 DOLLARS
62.2700 g., 0.9990 Silver 1.9999 oz. ASW, 50.3 mm. **Ruler:** Elizabeth II **Series:** Australian Peacekeepers **Obv:** Queen's head right **Rev:** Australian navy and color insignia **Edge:** Reeded

Date	Mintage	F	VF	XF	Unc	BU
2005P Proof	2,500	Value: 85.00				

KM# 757 2 DOLLARS
62.2700 g., 0.9990 Silver 1.9999 oz. ASW, 50.3 mm. **Ruler:** Elizabeth II **Subject:** Australian Peacekeepers Set **Obv:** Queen's head right **Rev:** Australian airforce and color insignia **Edge:** Reeded

Date	Mintage	F	VF	XF	Unc	BU
2005P Proof	2,500	Value: 85.00				

KM# 758 2 DOLLARS
62.2700 g., 0.9990 Silver 1.9999 oz. ASW, 50.3 mm. **Ruler:** Elizabeth II **Series:** Australian Peacekeepers **Obv:** Queen's head right **Rev:** Australian federal police and color insignia **Edge:** Reeded

Date	Mintage	F	VF	XF	Unc	BU
2005P Proof	2,500	Value: 85.00				

KM# 759 2 DOLLARS
62.2700 g., 0.9990 Silver 1.9999 oz. ASW, 50.3 mm. **Ruler:** Elizabeth II **Series:** Australian Peacekeepers **Obv:** Queen's head right **Rev:** Australian Agency for International Development and color insignia **Edge:** Reeded

Date	Mintage	F	VF	XF	Unc	BU
2005P Proof	2,500	Value: 85.00				

KM# 852 2 DOLLARS
8.8500 g., 0.9990 Silver 0.2842 oz. ASW, 20.5 mm. **Ruler:** Elizabeth II **Obv:** Young bust right **Obv. Designer:** Arnold Machin **Rev:** Aboriginal elder **Rev. Designer:** Horst Hahn **Edge:** Segmented reeding

Date	Mintage	F	VF	XF	Unc	BU
2006 Proof	6,500	Value: 20.00				

KM# 853 2 DOLLARS
1.2441 g., 0.9990 Gold 0.0400 oz. AGW **Ruler:** Elizabeth II **Obv:** Head with tiara right **Obv. Designer:** Ian Rank-Broadley **Rev:** FIFA World Cup

Date	Mintage	F	VF	XF	Unc	BU
2006P Proof	50,000	Value: 65.00				

KM# 1246 2 DOLLARS
0.5000 g., 0.9990 Gold 0.0161 oz. AGW, 12 mm. **Ruler:** Elizabeth II **Subject:** 2010 FIFA World Cup, South Africa **Obv:** Head right **Obv. Designer:** Ian Rank-Broadley **Rev:** Dream kangaroo and soccer ball

Date	Mintage	F	VF	XF	Unc	BU
2009P Proof	7,500	Value: 80.00				

KM# 591 5 DOLLARS
36.3100 g., 0.9990 Silver 1.1662 oz. ASW, 38.74 mm. **Ruler:** Elizabeth II **Subject:** Centennial of Federation Series Finale **Obv:** Queen's head right **Rev:** Multicolor dual hologram: map and rotunda **Edge:** Reeded

Date	Mintage	F	VF	XF	Unc	BU
2001B Proof	—	Value: 55.00				

KM# 592 5 DOLLARS
36.3100 g., 0.9990 Silver 1.1662 oz. ASW, 38.74 mm. **Ruler:** Elizabeth II **Subject:** Barton and Reid **Obv:** Queen's head right **Rev:** Portraits of Dame Flora Reid and Lady Jean Barton **Edge:** Reeded

Date	Mintage	F	VF	XF	Unc	BU
2001B Proof	5,000	Value: 60.00				

KM# 637 5 DOLLARS
36.3100 g., 0.9990 Silver 1.1662 oz. ASW, 38.74 mm. **Ruler:** Elizabeth II **Subject:** Kingston, Barton and Deakin **Obv:** Queen's head right **Rev:** Three rectangular portraits and value **Edge:** Reeded

Date	Mintage	F	VF	XF	Unc	BU
2001B Proof	5,000	Value: 60.00				

KM# 638 5 DOLLARS
36.3100 g., 0.9990 Silver 1.1662 oz. ASW, 38.74 mm. **Ruler:** Elizabeth II **Subject:** Clark, Parkes and Griffith **Obv:** Queen's head right **Rev:** Three rectangular portraits and value **Edge:** Reeded

Date	Mintage	F	VF	XF	Unc	BU
2001B Proof	5,000	Value: 60.00				

KM# 639 5 DOLLARS
36.3100 g., 0.9990 Silver 1.1662 oz. ASW, 38.74 mm. **Ruler:** Elizabeth II **Subject:** Spence, Nicholls and Anderson **Obv:** Queen's head right **Rev:** Three circular portraits and value **Edge:** Reeded

Date	Mintage	F	VF	XF	Unc	BU
2001B Proof	5,000	Value: 60.00				

KM# 640 5 DOLLARS
36.3100 g., 0.9990 Silver 1.1662 oz. ASW, 38.74 mm. **Ruler:** Elizabeth II **Subject:** Reid, Forrest and Quick **Obv:** Queen's head right **Rev:** Three rectangular portraits and value **Edge:** Reeded

Date	Mintage	F	VF	XF	Unc	BU
2001B Proof	5,000	Value: 60.00				

KM# 641 5 DOLLARS
36.3100 g., 0.9990 Silver 1.1662 oz. ASW, 38.74 mm. **Ruler:** Elizabeth II **Subject:** Bathurst Ladies Organizing Committee **Obv:** Queen's head right **Rev:** Circular design with names above value **Edge:** Reeded

Date	Mintage	F	VF	XF	Unc	BU
2001B Proof	5,000	Value: 60.00				

KM# 662 5 DOLLARS
36.3100 g., 0.9990 Silver 1.1662 oz. ASW, 38.74 mm. **Ruler:** Elizabeth II **Subject:** Year of the Outback **Obv:** Queen's head right **Rev:** Multicolor holographic landscape **Edge:** Reeded

Date	Mintage	F	VF	XF	Unc	BU
2002B Proof	15,000	Value: 100				

KM# 761 5 DOLLARS
36.3100 g., 0.9990 Silver 1.1662 oz. ASW **Ruler:** Elizabeth II **Obv:** Queen's head right **Rev:** Sir Donald Bradman

Date	Mintage	F	VF	XF	Unc	BU
2001 Proof	—	Value: 55.00				

KM# 762 5 DOLLARS
20.0000 g., Aluminum-Bronze, 38.74 mm. **Ruler:** Elizabeth II **Obv:** Queen's head right **Rev:** Sir Donald Bradman

Date	Mintage	F	VF	XF	Unc	BU
2001	—	—	—	—	8.50	9.50

KM# 601 5 DOLLARS
10.5200 g., Bi-Metallic Aluminumn-Bronze center in Stainless Steel ring, 27.8 mm. **Ruler:** Elizabeth II **Subject:** Battle of Sunda Strait **Obv:** Head with tiara right **Obv. Designer:** Ian Rank-Broadley **Rev:** Ships bell from the "USS Houston", denomination below **Rev. Designer:** Vladimir Gottwald **Shape:** 24-sided **Note:** Demagnetized.

Date	Mintage	F	VF	XF	Unc	BU
2002B	—	—	—	—	7.50	9.50

KM# 647 5 DOLLARS
28.0000 g., Aluminum-Bronze, 38.74 mm. **Ruler:** Elizabeth II **Subject:** Battle of Sunda Strait **Obv:** Queen's head right **Rev:** Two ships; USS Houston and HMS Perth **Edge:** Reeded

Date	Mintage	F	VF	XF	Unc	BU
2002B Proof	15,000	Value: 25.00				

KM# 649 5 DOLLARS
20.0000 g., Aluminum-Bronze, 38.74 mm. **Ruler:** Elizabeth II **Subject:** Commonwealth Games **Obv:** Head with tiara right, denomination below **Obv. Designer:** Ian Rank-Broadley **Rev:** Eight arms, each represents an event of the games **Edge:** Reeded

Date	Mintage	F	VF	XF	Unc	BU
2002B	11,145	—	—	—	8.50	9.50

KM# 650 5 DOLLARS
20.0000 g., Aluminum-Bronze, 38.74 mm. **Ruler:** Elizabeth II **Subject:** Commonwealth Games **Obv:** Head with tiara right, denomination below **Obv. Designer:** Ian Rank-Broadley **Rev:** Eight arms, each represents an event at the games **Edge:** Reeded

Date	Mintage	F	VF	XF	Unc	BU
2002B	11,145	—	—	—	8.50	9.50

KM# 651 5 DOLLARS
20.0000 g., Aluminum-Bronze, 38.74 mm. **Ruler:** Elizabeth II **Subject:** Commonwealth Games **Obv:** Head with tiara right, denomination below **Rev:** Blue games logo; star above tail of stylized kangaroo and torch **Edge:** Reeded

Date	Mintage	F	VF	XF	Unc	BU
2002B	11,145	—	—	—	8.50	9.50

KM# 652 5 DOLLARS
36.3100 g., 0.9990 Silver 1.1662 oz. ASW, 38.74 mm. **Ruler:** Elizabeth II **Subject:** Commonwealth Games **Obv:** Head with tiara right, denomination below **Obv. Designer:** Ian Rank-Broadley **Rev:** Victorious athletes **Edge:** Reeded

Date	Mintage	F	VF	XF	Unc	BU
2002B Proof	7,581	Value: 40.00				

KM# 653 5 DOLLARS
36.3100 g., 0.9990 Silver 1.1662 oz. ASW, 38.74 mm. **Ruler:** Elizabeth II **Obv:** Queen's head right **Rev:** Dutch sailing ship, The Duyfken **Edge:** Reeded

Date	Mintage	F	VF	XF	Unc	BU
2002B Proof	9,096	Value: 37.50				

KM# 654 5 DOLLARS
36.3100 g., 0.9990 Silver 1.1662 oz. ASW, 38.74 mm. **Ruler:** Elizabeth II **Obv:** Queen's head right **Rev:** HMS Endeavour sailing ship **Edge:** Reeded

Date	Mintage	F	VF	XF	Unc	BU
2002B Proof	9,096	Value: 37.50				

KM# 655 5 DOLLARS
36.3100 g., 0.9990 Silver 1.1662 oz. ASW, 38.74 mm. **Ruler:** Elizabeth II **Obv:** Queen's head right **Rev:** HMS Sirius sailing ship **Edge:** Reeded

Date	Mintage	F	VF	XF	Unc	BU
2002B Proof	9,096	Value: 37.50				

KM# 656 5 DOLLARS
36.3100 g., 0.9990 Silver 1.1662 oz. ASW, 38.74 mm. **Ruler:** Elizabeth II **Obv:** Queen's head right **Rev:** HMS Investigator sailing ship **Edge:** Reeded

Date	Mintage	F	VF	XF	Unc	BU
2002B Proof	9,096	Value: 37.50				

KM# 659 5 DOLLARS
31.1035 g., 0.9990 Silver 0.9990 oz. ASW, 40 mm. **Ruler:** Elizabeth II **Subject:** Queen Mother **Obv:** Queen's head right **Rev:** Queen Mother circa 1927 within wreath of roses **Rev. Designer:** Stuart Devlin **Edge:** Reeded

Date	Mintage	F	VF	XF	Unc	BU
2002B Proof	30,000	Value: 32.50				

KM# 765 5 DOLLARS
36.3100 g., 0.9990 Silver 1.1662 oz. ASW, 38.7 mm. **Ruler:** Elizabeth II **Series:** Masterpieces in Silver - Port Phillip Patterns **Obv:** One ounce design **Rev:** Kangaroo design **Edge:** Reeded

Date	Mintage	F	VF	XF	Unc	BU
2003B Proof	10,000	Value: 40.00				

KM# 810 5 DOLLARS
36.3100 g., 0.9950 Silver partially gilt 1.1615 oz. ASW, 40 mm. **Ruler:** Elizabeth II **Subject:** Rugby World Cup **Obv:** Head with tiara right **Obv. Designer:** Ian Rank-Broadley **Rev:** Rugby World Cup and official logos **Edge:** Reeded

Date	Mintage	F	VF	XF	Unc	BU
2003 Proof	20,501	Value: 85.00				

KM# 854 5 DOLLARS
20.0000 g., Aluminum-Bronze, 38.74 mm. **Ruler:** Elizabeth II **Subject:** Rugby World Cup **Obv:** Head with tiara right **Obv. Designer:** Ian Rank-Broadley **Rev:** Player kicking ball at posts, official logo **Edge:** Reeded

Date	Mintage	F	VF	XF	Unc	BU
2003	43,802	—	—	—	15.00	16.50

KM# 1017 5 DOLLARS
36.2100 g., 0.9990 Silver 1.1630 oz. ASW, 38.7 mm. **Ruler:** Elizabeth II **Obv:** Head with tiara right **Obv. Legend:** ELIZABETH II - AUSTRALIA **Rev:** Faces in oval hologram in ornate frame **Rev. Legend:** AUSTRALIA'S VOLUNTEERS - MAKING A DIFFERENCE **Edge:** Reeded

Date	Mintage	F	VF	XF	Unc	BU
2003B Proof	15,000	Value: 45.00				

KM# 727 5 DOLLARS
36.3100 g., 0.9990 Silver 1.1662 oz. ASW, 38.74 mm. **Ruler:** Elizabeth II **Subject:** Olympics **Obv:** Queen's head right **Rev:** Parthenon, Sydney Opera House and shield with multicolor flag and rings **Edge:** Reeded

Date	Mintage	F	VF	XF	Unc	BU
2004B Proof	17,500	Value: 37.50				

KM# 728 5 DOLLARS
36.3100 g., 0.9990 Silver 1.1662 oz. ASW, 38.74 mm. **Ruler:** Elizabeth II **Subject:** Tasmania **Obv:** Queen's head right **Rev:** Ship on island map **Edge:** Reeded

Date	Mintage	F	VF	XF	Unc	BU
2004B Proof	7,500	Value: 37.50				

KM# 728a 5 DOLLARS
20.0000 g., Aluminum-Bronze, 38.74 mm. **Ruler:** Elizabeth II **Subject:** Tasmanian Bicentennial **Obv:** Head with tiara right **Obv. Designer:** Ian Rank-Broadley **Rev:** Ship, map, state flower **Edge:** Reeded

Date	Mintage	F	VF	XF	Unc	BU
2004	18,561	—	—	—	12.00	14.00
2004H	2,841	—	—	—	17.50	20.00

KM# 729 5 DOLLARS
31.1035 g., 0.9990 Silver 0.9990 oz. ASW, 40 mm. **Ruler:** Elizabeth II **Subject:** Adelaide to Darwin Railroad **Obv:** Queen's head right **Rev:** Train, tracks and outline map **Edge:** Reeded

Date	Mintage	F	VF	XF	Unc	BU
2004B Proof	12,500	Value: 35.00				

KM# 730 5 DOLLARS
31.1035 g., 0.9990 Silver 0.9990 oz. ASW, 40 mm. **Ruler:** Elizabeth II **Subject:** 150 Years of Australian Steam Railways **Obv:** Queen's head right **Rev:** Old steam train **Edge:** Reeded

Date	Mintage	F	VF	XF	Unc	BU
2004B Proof	15,000	Value: 35.00				

KM# 811 5 DOLLARS
20.0000 g., Aluminum-Bronze, 38.74 mm. **Ruler:** Elizabeth II **Subject:** Bicentenary of Tasmania **Obv:** Head with tiara right **Rev. Designer:** Vladimir Gottwald

Date	Mintage	F	VF	XF	Unc	BU
2004H	—	—	—	—	12.00	14.00

KM# 812 5 DOLLARS
Aluminum-Bronze, 38.74 mm. **Ruler:** Elizabeth II **Subject:** Olympic Games 2000-2004 **Obv:** Head with tiara right

Date	Mintage	F	VF	XF	Unc	BU
2004	—	—	—	—	15.00	16.50

KM# 855 5 DOLLARS
27.2500 g., Copper-Nickel partially gilt, 38.74 mm. **Ruler:** Elizabeth II **Subject:** Australia's Own Game **Obv:** Head with tiara right **Obv. Designer:** Ian Rank-Broadley **Rev:** Cup and logos **Edge:** Reeded

Date	Mintage	F	VF	XF	Unc	BU
2004 Proof	16,163	Value: 45.00				

KM# 856 5 DOLLARS
20.0000 g., Aluminum-Bronze, 38.74 mm. **Ruler:** Elizabeth II **Subject:** Olympic Games - Sydney To Athens **Obv:** Head with tiara right **Obv. Designer:** Ian Rank-Broadley **Rev:** Silhouettes ancient Greek athlete and Aboriginal **Edge:** Reeded

Date	Mintage	F	VF	XF	Unc	BU
2004	24,376	—	—	—	15.00	16.50

KM# 750 5 DOLLARS
20.0000 g., Aluminum-Brass, 38.74 mm. **Ruler:** Elizabeth II **Obv:** Queen's head right **Rev:** Tennis player **Edge:** Reeded

Date	Mintage	F	VF	XF	Unc	BU
2005B	—	—	—	—	7.50	8.50

KM# 859 5 DOLLARS
36.3100 g., 0.9990 Silver 1.1662 oz. ASW, 38.74 mm. **Ruler:** Elizabeth II **Subject:** 150 Year of State Government **Obv:** Head with tiara right **Obv. Designer:** Ian Rank-Broadley **Rev:** Outline map of State of Victoria **Rev. Designer:** Wojciech Pietranik **Edge:** Reeded

Date	Mintage	F	VF	XF	Unc	BU
2006 Proof	12,500	Value: 85.00				

KM# 782 5 DOLLARS
36.3100 g., 0.9999 Silver 1.1672 oz. ASW, 38.74 mm. **Ruler:** Elizabeth II **Subject:** XVIII Commonwealth Games City of Sport **Obv:** Head with tiara right, denomination below **Obv. Designer:** Ian Rank-Broadley **Rev:** City skyline alongside river

Date	Mintage	F	VF	XF	Unc	BU
2006 Proof	10,000	Value: 55.00				

KM# 783 5 DOLLARS
20.0000 g., Aluminum-Bronze, 38.74 mm. **Ruler:** Elizabeth II **Subject:** XVIII Commonwealth Games in Melbourne **Obv:** Head with tiara right, denomination below **Obv. Designer:** Ian Rank-Broadley **Rev:** Games logo and crown surrounded by stylized athletes **Rev. Designer:** Wojciech Pietranik **Edge:** Reeded

Date	Mintage	F	VF	XF	Unc	BU
2006	—	—	—	—	15.00	16.50

KM# 786 5 DOLLARS
20.0000 g., Aluminum-Bronze, 38.74 mm. **Ruler:** Elizabeth II **Subject:** XVIII Commonwealth Games Queen's Baton Relay **Obv:** Head with tiara right **Obv. Designer:** Ian Rank-Broadley **Rev:** Stylized baton runner **Rev. Designer:** Peter Soobik **Edge:** Reeded

Date	Mintage	F	VF	XF	Unc	BU
2006	20,488	—	—	—	15.00	16.50

KM# 786a 5 DOLLARS
36.3100 g., 0.9990 Silver 1.1662 oz. ASW, 38.74 mm. **Ruler:** Elizabeth II **Subject:** XVIII Commonwealth Games Queen's Baton Relay **Obv:** Head with tiara right **Obv. Designer:** Ian Rank-Broadley **Rev:** Stylized baton runner **Rev. Designer:** Peter Soobik **Edge:** Reeded

Date	Mintage	F	VF	XF	Unc	BU
2006 Proof	9,100	Value: 75.00				

KM# 787 5 DOLLARS
36.3100 g., 0.9990 Silver 1.1662 oz. ASW, 38.74 mm. **Ruler:** Elizabeth II **Subject:** Masterpieces in Silver: Australia's Artists **Obv:** Head with tiara right **Obv. Designer:** Ian Rank-Broadley **Rev:** Sidney Nolan: Burke & Wills **Rev. Designer:** Vladimir Gottwald

Date	Mintage	F	VF	XF	Unc	BU
2006 Proof	10,000	Value: 60.00				

KM# 788 5 DOLLARS
36.3100 g., 0.9990 Silver 1.1662 oz. ASW, 38.74 mm. **Ruler:** Elizabeth II **Subject:** Masters in Art - Siding

Date	Mintage	F	VF	XF	Unc	BU
2006 Proof	10,000	Value: 55.00				

KM# 789 5 DOLLARS
36.3100 g., 0.9990 Silver 1.1662 oz. ASW, 38.74 mm. **Ruler:** Elizabeth II **Subject:** Masterpieces in Silver: Australia's Artists **Obv:** Head with tiara right **Obv. Designer:** Ian Rank-Broadley **Rev:** Brett Whitley: Self Portrait in the Studio **Rev. Designer:** Vladimir Gottwald

Date	Mintage	F	VF	XF	Unc	BU
2006 Proof	10,000	Value: 60.00				

KM# 790 5 DOLLARS
36.3100 g., 0.9990 Silver 1.1662 oz. ASW, 38.74 mm. **Ruler:** Elizabeth II **Subject:** Masterpieces in Silver: Australia's Artists **Obv:** Head with tiara right **Obv. Designer:** Ian Rank-Broadley **Rev:** Russell Drysdale: The Drover's Wife **Rev. Designer:** Vladimir Gottwald

Date	Mintage	F	VF	XF	Unc	BU
2006 Proof	10,000	Value: 60.00				

KM# 813 5 DOLLARS
20.0000 g., Aluminum-Bronze, 38.74 mm. **Ruler:** Elizabeth II **Subject:** Voyage of Discovery 1606 **Obv:** Head with tiara right **Obv. Designer:** Ian Rank-Broadley **Rev:** Dutch yacht Duyfken **Rev. Designer:** Wojciech Pietranik **Edge:** Reeded **Note:** Mint mark: G.

Date	Mintage	F	VF	XF	Unc	BU
2006	—	—	—	—	15.00	16.50

KM# 813a 5 DOLLARS
36.3100 g., 0.9990 Silver 1.1662 oz. ASW, 38.74 mm. **Ruler:** Elizabeth II **Subject:** Voyage of Discovery 1606 **Obv:** Head with tiara right **Obv. Designer:** Ian Rank-Broadley **Rev:** Dutch yacht Duyfken **Rev. Designer:** Wojciech Pietranik **Edge:** Reeded **Note:** Mint mark: Tulip.

Date	Mintage	F	VF	XF	Unc	BU
2006P Proof	8,500	Value: 125				

KM# 857 5 DOLLARS
36.3100 g., 0.9999 Silver 1.1672 oz. ASW, 38.74 mm. **Ruler:** Elizabeth II **Subject:** 150 Year of State Government **Obv:** Head with tiara right **Obv. Designer:** Ian Rank-Broadley **Rev:** Outline map of State of New South Wales **Rev. Designer:** Wojciech Pietranik **Edge:** Reeded

Date	Mintage	F	VF	XF	Unc	BU
2006 Proof	12,500	Value: 85.00				

KM# 858 5 DOLLARS
36.3100 g., 0.9990 Silver 1.1662 oz. ASW, 38.74 mm. **Ruler:** Elizabeth II **Subject:** 150 Year of State Government **Obv:** Head with tiara right **Obv. Designer:** Ian Rank-Broadley **Rev:** Outline map of State of Tasmania **Rev. Designer:** Wojciech Pietranik **Edge:** Reeded

Date	Mintage	F	VF	XF	Unc	BU
2006 Proof	12,500	Value: 85.00				

KM# 860 5 DOLLARS
36.3100 g., 0.9990 Silver 1.1662 oz. ASW, 38.74 mm. **Ruler:** Elizabeth II **Subject:** Masterpieces in Silver: Australia's Artists **Obv:** Ian Rank-Broadley **Rev:** Jeffrey Smart: Keswick Siding **Rev. Designer:** Vladimir Gottwald

Date	Mintage	F	VF	XF	Unc	BU
2006 Proof	10,000	Value: 60.00				

KM# 1014 5 DOLLARS
1.2441 g., 0.9999 Gold 0.0400 oz. AGW, 19 mm. **Ruler:** Elizabeth II **Obv:** Bust with tiara right **Obv. Legend:** ELIZABETH II - AUSTRALIA **Obv. Designer:** Ian Rank-Broadley **Rev:** Sydney Opera House

Date	Mintage	F	VF	XF	Unc	BU
2006P Proof	100,000	Value: 65.00				

KM# 861 5 DOLLARS
36.3100 g., 0.9990 Silver 1.1662 oz. ASW, 8.74 mm. **Ruler:** Elizabeth II **Subject:** Masterpieces in Silver: Australia's Artists **Obv:** Head with tiara right **Obv. Designer:** Ian Rank-Broadley **Rev:** Grace Cossington-Smith: Curve of the Bridge **Rev. Designer:** Vladimir Gottwald

Date	Mintage	F	VF	XF	Unc	BU
2007 Proof	10,000	Value: 50.00				

KM# 862 5 DOLLARS
36.3100 g., 0.9990 Silver 1.1662 oz. ASW, 38.74 mm. **Ruler:** Elizabeth II **Subject:** Masterpieces in Silver: Australia's Artists **Obv:** Head with tiara right **Obv. Designer:** Ian Rank-Broadley **Rev:** Clifford Possum Tjpaltjarri: Yuelamu Honey Ant Dreaming **Rev. Designer:** Vladimir Gottwald

Date	Mintage	F	VF	XF	Unc	BU
2007 Proof	10,000	Value: 50.00				

KM# 863 5 DOLLARS
36.3100 g., 0.9990 Silver 1.1662 oz. ASW, 38.74 mm. **Ruler:** Elizabeth II **Subject:** Masterpieces in Silver: Australia's Artists **Obv:** Head with tiara right **Obv. Designer:** Ian Rank-Broadley **Rev:** William Dobell: Margaret Olley **Rev. Designer:** Vladimir Gottwald

Date	Mintage	F	VF	XF	Unc	BU
2007 Proof	10,000	Value: 50.00				

KM# 864 5 DOLLARS
36.3100 g., 0.9990 Silver 1.1662 oz. ASW, 38.74 mm. **Ruler:** Elizabeth II **Subject:** Masterpieces in Silver: Australia's Artists **Obv:** Ian Rank-Broadley **Rev:** Margaret Preston: Implement Blue **Rev. Designer:** Vladimir Gottwald

Date	Mintage	F	VF	XF	Unc	BU
2007 Proof	10,000	Value: 50.00				

KM# 865 5 DOLLARS
36.3100 g., 0.9990 Silver 1.1662 oz. ASW, 38.74 mm. **Ruler:** Elizabeth II **Subject:** Ashes Cricket Series 1882-2007 **Obv:** Head with tiara right **Obv. Designer:** Ian Rank-Broadley **Rev:** Urn with supporters **Rev. Designer:** Vladimir Gottwald **Edge:** Reeded

Date	Mintage	F	VF	XF	Unc	BU
2007 Proof	12,500	Value: 45.00				

KM# 1013 5 DOLLARS
36.3100 g., 0.9990 Silver 1.1662 oz. ASW, 38.74 mm. **Ruler:** Elizabeth II **Subject:** Sydney Harbour Bridge, 75th Anniversary **Obv:** Bust with tiara right **Obv. Legend:** ELIZABETH II - AUSTRALIA **Obv. Designer:** Ian Rank-Broadley **Rev:** Bridge **Rev. Inscription:** SYDNEY / HARBOUR / BRIDGE

Date	Mintage	F	VF	XF	Unc	BU
2007 Proof	12,500	Value: 50.00				

KM# 1045 5 DOLLARS
36.3100 g., 0.9990 Silver 1.1662 oz. ASW, 38.74 mm. **Ruler:** Elizabeth II **Subject:** Year of the surfer lifesaver **Rev:** Rowboat in rough seas

Date	Mintage	F	VF	XF	Unc	BU
2007B Proof	12,500	Value: 65.00				

KM# 1046 5 DOLLARS
36.3100 g., 0.9990 Silver 1.1662 oz. ASW, 38.74 mm. **Ruler:** Elizabeth II **Subject:** South Australia State Government **Rev:** Australia map and state enlarged **Rev. Designer:** W. Pietranik

Date	Mintage	F	VF	XF	Unc	BU
2007B Proof	12,500	Value: 65.00				

KM# 1117 5 DOLLARS
1.2400 g., 0.9990 Gold 0.0398 oz. AGW, 14 mm. **Ruler:** Elizabeth II **Subject:** Sydney Harbor Bridge **Obv:** Head right **Obv. Designer:** Ian Rank-Broadley **Rev:** Bridge view

Date	Mintage	F	VF	XF	Unc	BU
2007P Proof	100,000	Value: 100				

KM# 1050 5 DOLLARS
31.1050 g., 0.9990 Silver 0.9990 oz. ASW, 38.74 mm. **Ruler:** Elizabeth II **Subject:** Scouting Centennial in Australia **Rev:** Scout sign and map **Rev. Designer:** C. Goodall

Date	Mintage	F	VF	XF	Unc	BU
2008 Proof	5,000	Value: 65.00				

KM# 1053 5 DOLLARS
36.3100 g., 0.9990 Silver 1.1662 oz. ASW, 38.74 mm. **Ruler:** Elizabeth II **Subject:** Rugby League **Rev:** Two players

Date	Mintage	F	VF	XF	Unc	BU
2008 Proof	10,000	Value: 65.00				

KM# 1055 5 DOLLARS
3.1050 g., 0.9990 Silver 0.0997 oz. ASW, 38.74 mm. **Ruler:** Elizabeth II **Rev:** Antarctic skua in flight over map

Date	Mintage	F	VF	XF	Unc	BU
2008 Proof	12,500	Value: 65.00				

KM# 1065 5 DOLLARS
36.3100 g., 0.9990 Silver 1.1662 oz. ASW, 38.74 mm. **Ruler:** Elizabeth II **Subject:** 30th Anniversary - Northern Territorial Government **Rev:** Territory map and Australia map **Rev. Designer:** W. Pietranik

Date	Mintage	F	VF	XF	Unc	BU
2008 Proof	12,500	Value: 65.00				

KM# 1066 5 DOLLARS
1.1500 g., 0.9990 Gold 0.0369 oz. AGW, 14 mm. **Ruler:** Elizabeth II **Rev:** Kisp Koala

Date	Mintage	F	VF	XF	Unc	BU
2008 Proof	10,000	Value: 100				

KM# 1067 5 DOLLARS
1.1500 g., 0.9990 Gold 0.0369 oz. AGW, 14 mm. **Ruler:** Elizabeth II **Rev:** Binny Bilby

Date	Mintage	F	VF	XF	Unc	BU
2008 Proof	10,000	Value: 100				

KM# 1072 5 DOLLARS
36.3100 g., 0.9990 Silver 1.1662 oz. ASW, 38.74 mm. **Ruler:** Elizabeth II **Rev:** Avro 504K airplane

Date	Mintage	F	VF	XF	Unc	BU
2008 Proof	10,000	Value: 65.00				

KM# 1073 5 DOLLARS
36.3100 g., 0.9990 Silver 1.1662 oz. ASW, 38.74 mm. **Ruler:** Elizabeth II **Rev:** Airbus A380 airplane

Date	Mintage	F	VF	XF	Unc	BU
2008 Proof	10,000	Value: 65.00				

KM# 1084 5 DOLLARS
38.7400 g., Aluminum-Brass, 38.74 mm. **Ruler:** Elizabeth II **Subject:** Sir Donald Bradman 100th Anniversary of Birth **Rev:** Player with cricket bat **Rev. Designer:** V. Gottwald

Date	Mintage	F	VF	XF	Unc	BU
2008	—	—	—	—	—	10.00

KM# 1080 5 DOLLARS
36.3100 g., 0.9990 Silver 1.1662 oz. ASW, 38.74 mm. **Ruler:** Elizabeth II **Rev:** Three arctic explorers on map **Rev. Designer:** W. Pietranik

Date	Mintage	F	VF	XF	Unc	BU
2009 Proof	12,500	Value: 65.00				

KM# 1081 5 DOLLARS
36.3100 g., 0.9990 Silver 1.1662 oz. ASW, 38.74 mm. **Ruler:** Elizabeth II **Subject:** Aurora Australis **Obv:** Head right **Rev:** Sailing ship in Antartic ice in hologram **Rev. Designer:** W. Pietranik

Date	Mintage	F	VF	XF	Unc	BU
2009 Proof	12,500	Value: 50.00				

KM# 1085 5 DOLLARS
1.2000 g., 0.9990 Gold 0.0385 oz. AGW, 14 mm. **Ruler:** Elizabeth II **Obv:** Head right **Rev:** Lilly Pilly full-neck lizard

Date	Mintage	F	VF	XF	Unc	BU
2009 Proof	10,000	Value: 65.00				

KM# 1086 5 DOLLARS
1.2000 g., 0.9990 Gold 0.0385 oz. AGW, 14 mm. **Ruler:** Elizabeth II **Obv:** Head right **Rev:** Petey Platypus

Date	Mintage	F	VF	XF	Unc	BU
2009 Proof	10,000	Value: 65.00				

KM# 1509 5 DOLLARS
36.3100 g., 0.9990 Silver 1.1662 oz. ASW, 38.74 mm. **Ruler:** Elizabeth II **Subject:** Aviation - Constellation L749

Date	Mintage	F	VF	XF	Unc	BU
2010 Proof	—	Value: 60.00				

KM# 1510 5 DOLLARS
36.3100 g., 0.9990 Silver 1.1662 oz. ASW, 37.84 mm. **Ruler:** Elizabeth II **Subject:** Aviation - De Havilland DH 86

Date	Mintage	F	VF	XF	Unc	BU
2010 Proof	—	Value: 60.00				

KM# 1511 5 DOLLARS
36.3100 g., 0.9990 Silver 1.1662 oz. ASW, 38.74 mm. **Ruler:** Elizabeth II **Subject:** Aviation - S.25 Sandringham

Date	Mintage	F	VF	XF	Unc	BU
2010 Proof	—	Value: 60.00				

KM# 1512 5 DOLLARS
36.3100 g., 0.9990 Silver 1.1662 oz. ASW, 38.74 mm. **Ruler:** Elizabeth II **Subject:** Aviation - Boeing 747

Date	Mintage	F	VF	XF	Unc	BU
2010 Proof	—	Value: 60.00				

KM# 1269 8 DOLLARS
5.0000 g., 0.9990 Gold 0.1606 oz. AGW, 14x23 mm. **Ruler:** Elizabeth II **Subject:** Chinese Mythological Character **Obv:** Head right **Obv. Designer:** Ian Rank-Broadley **Rev:** Man standing, multicolor **Shape:** Vertical rectangle

Date	Mintage	F	VF	XF	Unc	BU
2009P	—	—	—	—	—	430

KM# 1270 8 DOLLARS
5.0000 g., 0.9990 Gold 0.1606 oz. AGW, 14x23 mm. **Ruler:** Elizabeth II **Subject:** Chinese Mythological Character - Longevity **Obv:** Head right **Obv. Designer:** Ian Rank-Broadley **Rev:** Nam standing with staff, multicolor **Shape:** Vertical rectangle

Date	Mintage	F	VF	XF	Unc	BU
2009P	—	—	—	—	—	430

KM# 1271 8 DOLLARS
5.0000 g., 0.9990 Gold 0.1606 oz. AGW, 14x23 mm. **Ruler:**

Elizabeth II **Subject:** Chinese Mythological Character - Success **Obv:** Hand right **Obv. Designer:** Ian Rank-Broadley **Rev:** Man standing with deer, multicolor **Shape:** Vertical rectangle

Date	Mintage	F	VF	XF	Unc	BU
2009P	—	—	—	—	—	430

KM# 1272 8 DOLLARS

5.0000 g., 0.9990 Gold 0.1606 oz. AGW, 14x23 mm. **Ruler:** Elizabeth II **Subject:** Mythological Chinese Character - Fortune **Obv:** Head right **Obv. Designer:** Ian Rank-Broadley **Rev:** Man standing with scroll, multicolor **Shape:** Vertical rectangle

Date	Mintage	F	VF	XF	Unc	BU
2009P	—	—	—	—	—	430

KM# 1273 8 DOLLARS

10.0000 g., 0.9990 Gold 0.3212 oz. AGW, 15x25 mm. **Ruler:** Elizabeth II **Subject:** Mythological Chinese Character - Wealth **Obv:** Head right **Obv. Designer:** Ian Rank-Broadley **Rev:** Man standing **Shape:** Vertical rectangle

Date	Mintage	F	VF	XF	Unc	BU
2009P	—	—	—	—	—	800

KM# 593 10 DOLLARS

33.1500 g., Bi-Metallic Gold plated .999 Silver center in Copper ring, 38.74 mm. **Ruler:** Elizabeth II **Subject:** "The Future" **Obv:** Queen's portrait **Rev:** Tree, map and denomination **Rev. Designer:** Peter Soobik and Wojciech Pietraink **Edge:** Reeded

Date	Mintage	F	VF	XF	Unc	BU
2001B Proof	20,000	Value: 50.00				

KM# 596 10 DOLLARS

311.0350 g., 0.9990 Silver 9.9896 oz. ASW, 75.5 mm. **Ruler:** Elizabeth II **Subject:** Calendar Evolution **Obv:** Head with tiara right, denomination below **Obv. Designer:** Ian Rank-Broadley **Rev:** Multicolor solar system in center, zodiac symbols in outer circle **Edge:** Segmented reeding **Note:** Illustration reduced.

Date	Mintage	F	VF	XF	Unc	BU
ND(2001) Proof	15,000	Value: 350				

KM# 633 10 DOLLARS

311.0350 g., 0.9990 Silver 9.9896 oz. ASW, 75.5 mm. **Ruler:** Elizabeth II **Subject:** Evolution of Time **Obv:** Queen's portrait right **Rev:** Various time keeping devices **Edge:** Segmented reeding

Date	Mintage	F	VF	XF	Unc	BU
2002P Proof	1,500	Value: 375				

KM# 661 10 DOLLARS

60.5000 g., 0.9990 Silver 1.9431 oz. ASW, 50 mm. **Ruler:** Elizabeth II **Subject:** The Adelaide Pound **Obv:** Queen's portrait above gold-plated coin design **Rev:** Legend around gold-plated coin design **Edge:** Reeded

Date	Mintage	F	VF	XF	Unc	BU
2002B Proof	10,000	Value: 85.00				

KM# 686 10 DOLLARS

311.0000 g., 0.9990 Silver 9.9885 oz. ASW, 75.5 mm. **Ruler:** Elizabeth II **Obv:** Queen's head right **Rev:** Alphabet evolution design **Edge:** Reeded

Date	Mintage	F	VF	XF	Unc	BU
2003P Proof	1,500	Value: 385				

KM# 751 10 DOLLARS

60.5000 g., 0.9990 Silver Partially gilt 1.9431 oz. ASW, 50 mm. **Ruler:** Elizabeth II **Subject:** 150th Anniversary - Sydney Mint **Obv:** Head with tiara right above gilt 1853 Sovereign Pattern of Queen Victoria facing left **Obv. Designer:** Ian Rank-Broadley **Rev:** Gilt reverse of Sovereign Pattern **Rev. Designer:** Vladimir Gottwald **Edge:** Reeded

Date	Mintage	F	VF	XF	Unc	BU
2003B Proof	10,000	Value: 95.00				
ND(2005)B Proof	10,000	Value: 75.00				

KM# 766 10 DOLLARS

36.3100 g., 0.9990 Silver 1.1662 oz. ASW, 38.7 mm. **Ruler:** Elizabeth II **Series:** Masterpieces in Silver - Port Phillip Patterns **Obv:** Queen's head right **Rev:** Kangaroo design **Edge:** Reeded

Date	Mintage	F	VF	XF	Unc	BU
2003B Proof	10,000	Value: 90.00				

KM# 1439 10 DOLLARS

Silver gilt **Ruler:** Elizabeth II **Subject:** Sydney Mint, 100th Anniversary

Date	Mintage	F	VF	XF	Unc	BU
2003 Proof	10,000	Value: 85.00				

KM# 739 10 DOLLARS

311.0350 g., 0.9990 Silver 9.9896 oz. ASW, 75.5 mm. **Ruler:** Elizabeth II **Subject:** Evolution of Numbers **Obv:** Queen's head right **Rev:** Numbers, symbols, abacus and calculator **Edge:** Reeded

Date	Mintage	F	VF	XF	Unc	BU
2004 Proof	1,500	Value: 375				

KM# 744 10 DOLLARS
311.3460 g., 0.9990 Silver 9.9996 oz. ASW, 75.5 mm. **Ruler:** Elizabeth II **Obv:** Queen's head right **Rev:** Multicolor symbolic design **Edge:** Reeded

Date	Mintage	F	VF	XF	Unc	BU
2005 Proof	1,500	Value: 275				

KM# 866 10 DOLLARS
7.7508 g., 0.9990 Gold 0.2489 oz. AGW, 17.53 mm. **Ruler:** Elizabeth II **Subject:** 90th Anniversary Gallipoli Landings **Obv:** Head with tiara right **Obv. Designer:** Ian Rank-Broadley **Rev:** Australian slouch hat on inverted rifle before memorial

Date	Mintage	F	VF	XF	Unc	BU
2005 Proof	1,000	Value: 750				

KM# 869 10 DOLLARS
7.7759 g., 0.9990 Gold 0.2497 oz. AGW, 17.53 mm. **Ruler:** Elizabeth II **Subject:** FIFA World Cup **Obv:** Head with tiara right **Obv. Designer:** Ian Rank-Broadley **Rev:** Kangaroo and players on football

Date	Mintage	F	VF	XF	Unc	BU
2006P Proof	25,000	Value: 375				

KM# 867 10 DOLLARS
3.1103 g., 0.9990 Gold 0.0999 oz. AGW **Ruler:** Elizabeth II **Subject:** Ashes Cricket Series 1882-2007 **Obv:** Head with tiara right **Obv. Designer:** Ian Rank-Broadley **Rev:** Urn and supporters **Rev. Designer:** Vladimir Gottwald **Edge:** Reeded

Date	Mintage	F	VF	XF	Unc	BU
2007 Proof	—	Value: 165				

KM# 1000 10 DOLLARS
3.1103 g., 0.9990 Gold 0.0999 oz. AGW, 17.53 mm. **Ruler:** Elizabeth II **Subject:** Year of the Pig **Obv:** Head with tiara right **Obv. Designer:** Ian Rank-Broadley **Rev:** Mother kangaroo with joey **Rev. Designer:** Rolf Harris **Edge:** Reeded

Date	Mintage	F	VF	XF	Unc	BU
2007 Proof	—	Value: 175				

KM# 1051 10 DOLLARS
3.1000 g., 0.9990 Gold 0.0996 oz. AGW, 17.5 mm. **Ruler:** Elizabeth II **Subject:** Scouting Centennial in Australia **Rev:** Shadow linear portrait of Baden-Powell **Rev. Designer:** C. Goodall

Date	Mintage	F	VF	XF	Unc	BU
2008 Proof	1,500	Value: 325				

KM# 1054 10 DOLLARS
3.1100 g., 0.9990 Gold 0.0999 oz. AGW, 17.53 mm. **Ruler:** Elizabeth II **Subject:** Rugby League

Date	Mintage	F	VF	XF	Unc	BU
2008 Proof	3,000	Value: 225				

KM# 1492 15 DOLLARS
3.1100 g., 0.9990 Gold 0.0999 oz. AGW, 17.53 mm. **Ruler:** Elizabeth II **Obv:** Head with tiara right **Rev:** Saint Mary Mackillup in color

Date	Mintage	F	VF	XF	Unc	BU
2010 Proof	2,010	Value: 200				

KM# 595 20 DOLLARS
14.0300 g., Bi-Metallic .999 4.5287 Silver center in .9999 9.499 Gold ring, 32.1 mm. **Ruler:** Elizabeth II **Subject:** Gregorian Millennium **Obv:** Head with tiara right **Obv. Designer:** Ian Rank-Broadley **Rev:** Chronograph watch face with observatory in center and three depictions of the earth's rotation **Edge:** Reeded

Date	Mintage	F	VF	XF	Unc	BU
2001 Prooflike	7,500	—	—	—	—	450

KM# 597 20 DOLLARS
19.6300 g., Bi-Metallic .9999 8.8645 Gold center in .9999 10.7618 Silver ring, 32.1 mm. **Ruler:** Elizabeth II **Subject:** Centenary of Federation **Obv:** Head with tiara right within star design **Obv. Designer:** Ian Rank-Broadley **Rev:** National arms on a flowery background **Edge:** Reeded

Date	Mintage	F	VF	XF	Unc	BU
ND(2001) Prooflike	7,500	—	—	—	—	450

KM# 760 20 DOLLARS
Bi-Metallic Gold center in Silver ring **Ruler:** Elizabeth II **Rev:** Sir Donald Bradman portrait

Date	Mintage	F	VF	XF	Unc	BU
2001 Proof	—	Value: 475				

KM# 634 20 DOLLARS
18.3510 g., Bi-Metallic .999 Silver, 4.6655g, breast star shaped center in a .9999 Gold ,13.6855g outer ring, 32.1 mm. **Ruler:** Elizabeth II **Subject:** Queen's Golden Jubilee **Obv:** Queen's head right **Rev:** Queen before Buckingham Palace **Edge:** Reeded

Date	Mintage	F	VF	XF	Unc	BU
2002P Proof	7,500	Value: 650				

KM# 687 20 DOLLARS
13.4056 g., Bi-Metallic .999 Gold 8.3979g Center in a .999 Silver 5.0077g Ring, 32 mm. **Ruler:** Elizabeth II **Subject:** Golden Jubilee of Coronation **Obv:** Head with tiara right **Obv. Designer:** Ian Rank-Broadley **Rev:** Four different coinage portraits of Queen Elizabeth II **Rev. Designer:** Mary Gillick, Arnold Machin, Raphael Maklouf and Ian Rank-Broadley **Edge:** Reeded

Date	Mintage	F	VF	XF	Unc	BU
2003P Proof	7,500	Value: 600				

KM# 868 25 DOLLARS
7.9881 g., 0.9167 Gold 0.2354 oz. AGW **Ruler:** Elizabeth II **Subject:** 150th Anniversary First Australian Sovereign **Obv:** Head with tiara right **Obv. Designer:** Ian Rank-Broadley

Date	Mintage	F	VF	XF	Unc	BU
2005 Proof	7,500	Value: 350				

KM# 1180 25 DOLLARS
7.7700 g., 0.9990 Gold 0.2496 oz. AGW, 20 mm. **Ruler:** Elizabeth II **Subject:** End of WWI, 90th Anniversary **Obv:** Head right **Rev:** Field cross, multicolor poppies **Rev. Legend:** Ian Rank-Broadley **Edge:** Reeded

Date	Mintage	F	VF	XF	Unc	BU
2008P Proof	1,918	Value: 650				

KM# 1110 25 DOLLARS
10.0000 g., 0.9999 Gold 0.3215 oz. AGW, 15.4x25.4 mm. **Ruler:** Elizabeth II **Rev:** Kangaroo dreaming **Rev. Designer:** Darryl Bellotti **Shape:** Vertical rectangle

Date	Mintage	F	VF	XF	Unc	BU
2009 Proof	—	Value: 600				

KM# 1244 25 DOLLARS
0.9170 Gold **Ruler:** Elizabeth II **Subject:** Sovereign **Obv:** Head right **Obv. Designer:** Ian Rank-Broadley **Rev:** National arms

Date	Mintage	F	VF	XF	Unc	BU
2009 Proof	2,500	Value: 650				

KM# 1247 25 DOLLARS
7.7700 g., 0.9990 Gold 0.2496 oz. AGW, 21 mm. **Ruler:** Elizabeth II **Subject:** 2010 FIFA World Cup, South Africa **Obv:** Head right **Obv. Designer:** Ian Rank-Broadley **Rev:** Soccer player and kangaroo

Date	Mintage	F	VF	XF	Unc	BU
2009P Proof	7,500	Value: 750				

KM# 1274 25 DOLLARS
10.0000 g., 0.9990 Gold 0.3212 oz. AGW, 15x25 mm. **Ruler:** Elizabeth II **Subject:** Mythological Chinese Character - Longivity **Obv:** Head right **Obv. Designer:** Ian rank-Broadley **Rev:** Man standing with staff **Shape:** Vertical rectangle

Date	Mintage	F	VF	XF	Unc	BU
2009P	—	—	—	—	—	800

KM# 1275 25 DOLLARS
10.0000 g., 0.9990 Gold 0.3212 oz. AGW, 15x25 mm. **Ruler:** Elizabeth II **Subject:** Mythological Chinese Character - Success **Obv:** Head right **Obv. Designer:** Ian Rank-Broadley **Rev:** Man standing with deer **Shape:** Vertical rectangle

Date	Mintage	F	VF	XF	Unc	BU
2009P	—	—	—	—	—	800

KM# 1276 25 DOLLARS
10.0000 g., 0.9990 Gold 0.3212 oz. AGW, 15x25 mm. **Ruler:** Elizabeth II **Subject:** Mythological Chinese Character - Fortune **Obv:** Head right **Obv. Designer:** Ian Rank-Broadley **Rev:** Man standing with scroll **Shape:** Vertical rectangle

Date	Mintage	F	VF	XF	Unc	BU
2009P	—	—	—	—	—	800

KM# 1397 25 DOLLARS
0.9990 Gold **Ruler:** Elizabeth II **Obv:** Head right **Rev:** Arms

Date	Mintage	F	VF	XF	Unc	BU
2010(p)	—	—	—	—	—	800

KM# 784 30 DOLLARS
1000.0000 g., 0.9990 Silver 32.117 oz. ASW **Ruler:** Elizabeth II **Subject:** Commonwealth Games **Obv:** Head with tiara right **Rev:** Two figures within circle of all the sports

Date	Mintage	F	VF	XF	Unc	BU
2006 Proof	500	Value: 1,150				

KM# 648 50 DOLLARS
36.5100 g., Tri-Metallic .9999 Gold 7.8g, 13.1 mm center in .999 Silver 13.39g, 26.85mm inner ring within a copper 15.32g, 3, 38.74 mm. **Ruler:** Elizabeth II **Subject:** Commonwealth Games **Obv:** Head with tiara right **Obv. Designer:** Ian Rank-Broadley **Rev:** Victorious athletes within inscriptions and runners **Edge:** Reeded

Date	Mintage	F	VF	XF	Unc	BU
2002B Proof	5,000	Value: 550				

KM# 724 50 DOLLARS
36.5100 g., Tri-Metallic .999 Gold 7.8g center in .999 Silver 13.39g ring within .999 Copper 15.32g outer ring, 38.74 mm. **Ruler:** Elizabeth II **Subject:** Olympics - Sydney to Athens **Obv:** Head with tiara right, denomination below **Obv. Designer:** Ian Rank-Broadley **Rev:** Crossed olive and wattle branches about Australian flag and Olympic ring logo **Rev. Designer:** Wojciech Pietranik **Edge:** Reeded

Date	Mintage	F	VF	XF	Unc	BU
2004B Proof	2,500	Value: 575				

KM# 785 50 DOLLARS
Tri-Metallic Gold center within Silver ring within Copper outer ring, 38.74 mm. **Ruler:** Elizabeth II **Subject:** Melbourne Commonwealth Games **Obv:** Head with tiara right, denomination below **Obv. Designer:** Ian Rank-Broadley **Rev:** Two stylized athletes on central plug surrounded by Games legend and circle of athletes **Rev. Designer:** Wojciech Pietranik

Date	Mintage	F	VF	XF	Unc	BU
2006 Proof	5,000	Value: 500				

KM# 1422 50 DOLLARS
15.5000 g., 0.9990 Platinum 0.4978 oz. APW, 26 mm. **Ruler:** Elizabeth II **Obv:** Head right **Obv. Designer:** Ian Rank-Broadley **Rev:** Multicolor wombat

Date	Mintage	F	VF	XF	Unc	BU
2010(p) Proof	1,000	Value: 1,000				

KM# 643 100 DOLLARS
10.3678 g., 0.9999 Gold 0.3333 oz. AGW, 25 mm. **Ruler:** Elizabeth II **Subject:** Golden Wattle Flower **Obv:** Queen's head right **Rev:** Flower and denomination **Edge:** Reeded

Date	Mintage	F	VF	XF	Unc	BU
2001B	3,000	—	—	—	500	525
2001B Proof	2,500	Value: 550				

KM# 635 100 DOLLARS
31.1035 g., 0.9999 Gold 0.9999 oz. AGW, 32.1 mm. **Ruler:** Elizabeth II **Subject:** Gold Panning **Obv:** Queen's head right **Rev:** Two prospectors dry panning for gold with color highlighted pans and dust **Edge:** Reeded

Date	Mintage	F	VF	XF	Unc	BU
2002P Proof	1,500	Value: 1,500				

KM# 636 100 DOLLARS
31.1035 g., 0.9995 Platinum 0.9995 oz. APW, 32.1 mm. **Ruler:** Elizabeth II **Subject:** Multiculturalism **Obv:** Head with tiara right **Obv. Designer:** Ian Rank-Broadley **Rev:** Six racially diverse portraits against a blue background **Edge:** Reeded

Date	Mintage	F	VF	XF	Unc	BU
2002 Proof	1,000	Value: 1,850				

KM# 646 100 DOLLARS
31.4000 g., 0.9999 Gold 1.0094 oz. AGW, 34.1 mm. **Ruler:** Elizabeth II **Subject:** Queen's 50th Anniversary of Accession **Obv:** Queen's head right **Rev:** Silhouette of George VI, queen's portrait and denomination **Rev. Designer:** Peter Soobik **Edge:** Reeded

Date	Mintage	F	VF	XF	Unc	BU
2002B Proof	2,002	Value: 1,500				

KM# 657 100 DOLLARS
10.3678 g., 0.9999 Gold 0.3333 oz. AGW, 25 mm. **Ruler:** Elizabeth II **Obv:** Queen's head right **Rev:** Sturt's Desert Rose **Rev. Designer:** Horst Hahne **Edge:** Reeded

Date	Mintage	F	VF	XF	Unc	BU
2002B	3,000	—	—	—	500	520
2002B Proof	2,500	Value: 550				

KM# 800 100 DOLLARS
31.1036 g., 0.9990 Gold 0.9990 oz. AGW, 34 mm. **Ruler:** Elizabeth II **Subject:** 50th Anniversary of the Coronation of Elizabeth II **Obv:** Head with tiara right **Rev:** Young portrait of Queen Elizabeth facing left, royal cipher, crown **Rev. Designer:** Peter Soobik **Edge:** Plain

Date	Mintage	F	VF	XF	Unc	BU
2003 Proof	660	Value: 1,500				

KM# 870 100 DOLLARS
10.3670 g., 0.9990 Gold 0.3330 oz. AGW, 25 mm. **Ruler:** Elizabeth II **Subject:** State Floral Emblems **Obv:** Head with tiara right **Obv. Designer:** Ian Rank-Broadley **Rev:** Royal Blue Bell flowers **Rev. Designer:** Horst Hahne **Edge:** Reeded

Date	Mintage	F	VF	XF	Unc	BU
2003 Proof	1,383	Value: 550				

KM# 797 100 DOLLARS
31.1070 g., 0.9990 Gold 0.9991 oz. AGW, 25.1 mm. **Ruler:** Elizabeth II **Subject:** 60th Anniversary of end of World War II **Obv:** Head with tiara right **Obv. Designer:** Ian Rank-Broadley **Rev:** Latent news real photographic images of a dancing man celebrating the end of WWII

Date	Mintage	F	VF	XF	Unc	BU
2005P Proof	750	Value: 1,500				

KM# 1243 100 DOLLARS
31.1050 g., 0.9990 Gold 0.9990 oz. AGW, 36 mm. **Ruler:** Elizabeth II **Subject:** Treasures of Australia **Obv:** Head right **Obv. Designer:** Ian Rank-Broadley **Rev:** Mountains **Note:** Insert container with 1 carat of diamonds.

Date	Mintage	F	VF	XF	Unc	BU
2009P Proof	1,000	Value: 2,100				

KM# 1436 100 DOLLARS
Gold **Ruler:** Elizabeth II

Date	Mintage	F	VF	XF	Unc	BU
2010 Proof	—	Value: 1,500				

KM# 644 150 DOLLARS
15.5517 g., 0.9999 Gold 0.4999 oz. AGW, 30 mm. **Ruler:** Elizabeth II **Obv:** Queen's head right **Rev:** Golden Wattle flower, value **Edge:** Reeded

Date	Mintage	F	VF	XF	Unc	BU
2001B Proof	1,500	Value: 750				

KM# 658 150 DOLLARS
15.5517 g., 0.9999 Gold 0.4999 oz. AGW, 30 mm. **Ruler:** Elizabeth II **Subject:** State Floral Emblems **Obv:** Queen's head right **Rev:** Sturt's Desert Rose **Rev. Designer:** Horst Hahne **Edge:** Reeded

Date	Mintage	F	VF	XF	Unc	BU
2002B Proof	1,500	Value: 750				

KM# 872 150 DOLLARS
15.5510 g., 0.9990 Gold 0.4995 oz. AGW, 30 mm. **Ruler:** Elizabeth II **Subject:** State Floral Emblems **Obv:** Head with tiara right **Obv. Designer:** Ian Rank-Broadley **Rev:** Royal Blue Bell flowers **Rev. Designer:** Horst Hahne **Edge:** Reeded

Date	Mintage	F	VF	XF	Unc	BU
2003	1,105	Value: 750				

KM# 874 150 DOLLARS
15.5510 g., 0.9990 Gold 0.4995 oz. AGW, 30 mm. **Ruler:** Elizabeth II **Subject:** Rare Australian Birds **Obv:** Head with tiara right **Obv. Designer:** Ian Rank-Broadley **Rev:** Red-tailed black cockatoo **Rev. Designer:** Wojciech Pietranik **Edge:** Reeded

Date	Mintage	F	VF	XF	Unc	BU
2003 Proof	2,500	Value: 750				

KM# 731 150 DOLLARS
10.3678 g., 0.9990 Gold 0.3330 oz. AGW, 25 mm. **Ruler:** Elizabeth II **Obv:** Queen's head right **Rev:** Cassowary bird **Edge:** Reeded

Date	Mintage	F	VF	XF	Unc	BU
2004B Proof	2,500	Value: 550				

KM# 752 150 DOLLARS
10.3678 g., 0.9999 Gold 0.3333 oz. AGW, 25 mm. **Ruler:** Elizabeth II **Obv:** Queen's head right **Rev:** Malleefowl bird **Edge:** Reeded

Date	Mintage	F	VF	XF	Unc	BU
2005B Proof	2,500	Value: 550				

KM# 873 150 DOLLARS
10.3670 g., 0.9990 Gold 0.3330 oz. AGW, 25 mm. **Ruler:**

Elizabeth II **Subject:** Rare Australian Birds **Obv:** Head with tiara right **Obv. Designer:** Ian Rank-Broadley **Rev:** Red-tailed black cockatoo **Rev. Designer:** Wojciech Pietranik **Edge:** Reeded

Date	Mintage	F	VF	XF	Unc	BU
2006	2,500	Value: 575				

KM# 732 200 DOLLARS

15.5518 g., 0.9990 Gold 0.4995 oz. AGW, 30 mm. **Ruler:** Elizabeth II **Obv:** Queen's head right **Rev:** Cassowary bird **Edge:** Reeded

Date	Mintage	F	VF	XF	Unc	BU
2004B Proof	2,500	Value: 750				

KM# 753 200 DOLLARS

15.5518 g., 0.9999 Gold 0.4999 oz. AGW, 30 mm. **Ruler:** Elizabeth II **Obv:** Queen's head right **Rev:** Malleefowl bird **Edge:** Reeded

Date	Mintage	F	VF	XF	Unc	BU
2005B Proof	2,500	Value: 750				

BULLION - KANGAROO

KM# 590 DOLLAR

31.1035 g., 0.9990 Silver 0.9990 oz. ASW, 40 mm. **Ruler:** Elizabeth II **Obv:** Queen's portrait **Rev:** Aboriginal-kangaroo design with dots **Rev. Designer:** Jeanette Timbery **Edge:** Reeded

Date	Mintage	F	VF	XF	Unc	BU
2001B Frosted Unc	—	—	—	—	—	30.00
2001B Proof	—	Value: 35.00				

KM# 642 DOLLAR

31.1035 g., 0.9990 Silver 0.9990 oz. ASW, 40 mm. **Ruler:** Elizabeth II **Obv:** Head with tiara right, denomination below **Rev:** Aboriginal-style kangaroo with wavy line background **Edge:** Reeded

Date	Mintage	F	VF	XF	Unc	BU
2002B	—	—	—	—	32.00	35.00
2002B Proof	—	Value: 40.00				

KM# 798 DOLLAR

31.1035 g., 0.9990 Silver 0.9990 oz. ASW, 40 mm. **Ruler:** Elizabeth II **Obv:** Head with tiara right **Obv. Designer:** Ian Rank-Broadley **Rev:** Aboriginal-style kangaroo design **Rev. Designer:** Wojcieck Pietranik **Edge:** Reeded

Date	Mintage	F	VF	XF	Unc	BU
2003	35,230	—	—	—	—	35.00
2003 Proof	20,400	Value: 40.00				

KM# 798a DOLLAR

31.1035 g., 0.9990 Silver partially gilt 0.9990 oz. ASW, 40 mm. **Ruler:** Elizabeth II **Obv:** Head with tiara right **Obv. Designer:** Ian Rank-Broadley **Rev:** Aboriginal-style kangaroo design **Rev. Designer:** Wojcieck Pietranik **Edge:** Reeded

Date	Mintage	F	VF	XF	Unc	BU
2003	7,450	—	—	—	—	125

KM# 723 DOLLAR

31.1035 g., 0.9990 Silver 0.9990 oz. ASW, 40 mm. **Ruler:** Elizabeth II **Obv:** Head with tiara right, denomination below **Rev:** Kangaroo with semi-circle background **Edge:** Reeded

Date	Mintage	F	VF	XF	Unc	BU
2004B Frosted Unc	—	—	—	—	—	32.00
2004B Proof	12,500	Value: 40.00				

KM# 723a DOLLAR

31.1035 g., 0.9990 Silver partially gilt 0.9990 oz. ASW, 40 mm. **Ruler:** Elizabeth II **Obv:** Head with tiara right, denomination below **Rev:** Kangaroo with semi-circle background **Edge:** Reeded

Date	Mintage	F	VF	XF	Unc	BU
2004B Frosted Unc	—	—	—	—	—	60.00

KM# 749 DOLLAR

31.6000 g., 0.9990 Silver 1.0149 oz. ASW, 40 mm. **Ruler:** Elizabeth II **Obv:** Head with tiara right **Obv. Designer:** Ian Rank-Broadley **Rev:** Kangaroo bounding under Southern Cross and above Federation Star **Rev. Designer:** Wojcieck Pietranik **Edge:** Reeded

Date	Mintage	F	VF	XF	Unc	BU
2005	—	—	—	—	32.00	45.00
2005 Proof	12,500	Value: 45.00				

KM# 749a DOLLAR

31.1035 g., 0.9990 Silver Partially Gold Plated 0.9990 oz. ASW, 40 mm. **Ruler:** Elizabeth II **Obv:** Head with tiara right **Obv. Designer:** Ian Rank-Broadley **Rev:** Kangaroo bounding under Southern Cross and above Federation Star **Rev. Designer:** Wojcieck Pietranik **Edge:** Reeded

Date	Mintage	F	VF	XF	Unc	BU
2005 Proof	12,500	Value: 50.00				

KM# 838 DOLLAR

31.1035 g., 0.9990 Silver 0.9990 oz. ASW, 40 mm. **Ruler:** Elizabeth II **Subject:** Australain-Japan Year of Exchange **Obv:** Head with tiara right **Obv. Designer:** Ian Rank-Broadley **Rev:** Kangaroo leaping with kangaroo rim decoration

Date	Mintage	F	VF	XF	Unc	BU
2006 Proof	5,000	Value: 35.00				

KM# 837 DOLLAR

31.6000 g., 0.9990 Silver 1.0149 oz. ASW, 40 mm. **Ruler:** Elizabeth II **Obv:** Head with tiara right **Obv. Designer:** Ian Rank-Broadley **Rev:** Kangaroo bounding under Australian sun **Rev. Designer:** Wojcieck Pietranik **Edge:** Reeded

Date	Mintage	F	VF	XF	Unc	BU
2006	—	—	—	—	—	32.00
2006 Proof	12,500	Value: 40.00				

KM# 837a DOLLAR

31.6000 g., 0.9990 Silver partially gilt 1.0149 oz. ASW, 40 mm. **Ruler:** Elizabeth II **Obv:** Head with tiara right **Obv. Designer:** Ian Rank-Broadley **Rev:** Kangaroo bounding under Australian sun **Rev. Designer:** Wojcieck Pietranik **Edge:** Reeded

Date	Mintage	F	VF	XF	Unc	BU
2006	7,500	—	—	—	—	55.00

KM# 851 DOLLAR

31.6000 g., 0.9990 Silver 1.0149 oz. ASW, 40 mm. **Ruler:** Elizabeth II **Obv:** Head with tiara right **Obv. Designer:** Ian Rank-Broadley **Rev:** Kangaroo mother and joey **Rev. Designer:** Rolf Harris **Edge:** Reeded

Date	Mintage	F	VF	XF	Unc	BU
2007	15,000	—	—	—	—	40.00
2007 Proof	12,500	Value: 45.00				

KM# 1083 DOLLAR

31.1050 g., 0.9990 Silver 0.9990 oz. ASW, 40 mm. **Ruler:** Elizabeth II **Rev:** Kangaroo **Rev. Designer:** K. Done

Date	Mintage	F	VF	XF	Unc	BU
2009	20,000	—	—	—	—	50.00
2009 Proof	20,000	Value: 65.00				

KM# 1457 DOLLAR

31.1050 g., 0.9990 Silver 0.9990 oz. ASW, 40 mm. **Ruler:** Elizabeth II **Rev:** Two kangaroos playing

Date	Mintage	F	VF	XF	Unc	BU
2010P Proof	—	Value: 40.00				

KM# 1458 15 DOLLARS

1.2400 g., 0.9990 Gold 0.0398 oz. AGW, 14 mm. **Ruler:** Elizabeth II **Rev:** Two kangaroos playing

Date	Mintage	F	VF	XF	Unc	BU
2010P	—	—	—	—	—	125

KM# 1514 DOLLAR

31.1050 g., 0.9990 Silver 0.9990 oz. ASW, 40. mm. **Ruler:** Elizabeth II **Rev:** Kangaroo in color

Date	Mintage	F	VF	XF	Unc	BU
2010 Proof	—	Value: 60.00				

KM# 1516 DOLLAR

31.1050 g., 0.9990 Silver 0.9990 oz. ASW, 40 mm. **Ruler:** Elizabeth II **Rev:** Kangaroo in color

Date	Mintage	F	VF	XF	Unc	BU
2010 Proof	—	Value: 60.00				

KM# 1390 2 DOLLARS

0.5000 g., 0.9990 Gold 0.0161 oz. AGW **Ruler:** Elizabeth II **Obv:** Head right **Rev:** Kangaroo

Date	Mintage	F	VF	XF	Unc	BU
2010(p)	—	—	—	—	30.00	35.00

KM# 1527 2 DOLLARS

0.5000 g., 0.9990 Gold 0.0161 oz. AGW, 11.6 mm. **Ruler:** Elizabeth II **Obv:** Head in tiara right **Obv. Designer:** Ian Rank-Broadley **Rev:** Kangaroo bounding left **Rev. Designer:** Wase Robinson

Date	Mintage	F	VF	XF	Unc	BU
2010P	—	—	—	—	—	50.00

KM# 893 5 DOLLARS

1.5710 g., 0.9990 Gold 0.0505 oz. AGW **Ruler:** Elizabeth II **Obv:** Head with tiara right **Obv. Designer:** Ian Rank-Broadley **Rev:** Two kangaroos on map of Australia

Date	Mintage	F	VF	XF	Unc	BU
2001	10,000	—	—	—	75.00	80.00

KM# 1522 10 DOLLARS

3.1100 g., 0.9990 Gold 0.0999 oz. AGW, 17.53 mm. **Ruler:** Elizabeth II **Rev:** Two kangaroos

Date	Mintage	F	VF	XF	Unc	BU
2011 Proof	1,500	Value: 265				

KM# 894 15 DOLLARS

3.1101 g., 0.9990 Gold 0.0999 oz. AGW **Ruler:** Elizabeth II **Obv:** Head with tiara right **Obv. Designer:** Ian Rank-Broadley **Rev:** Two kangaroos on map of Australia

Date	Mintage	F	VF	XF	Unc	BU
2001	800	—	—	—	—	155

KM# 897 15 DOLLARS

3.1101 g., 0.9990 Gold 0.0999 oz. AGW **Ruler:** Elizabeth II **Obv:** Head with tiara right **Obv. Designer:** Ian Rank-Broadley **Rev:** Kangaroo browsing

Date	Mintage	F	VF	XF	Unc	BU
2002	800	—	—	—	—	155

KM# 902 15 DOLLARS

3.1101 g., 0.9990 Gold 0.0999 oz. AGW **Ruler:** Elizabeth II **Obv:** Head with tiara right **Obv. Designer:** Ian Rank-Broadley **Rev:** Two kangaroos hopping

Date	Mintage	F	VF	XF	Unc	BU
2003	500	—	—	—	—	165

KM# 907 15 DOLLARS

3.1101 g., 0.9990 Gold 0.0999 oz. AGW **Ruler:** Elizabeth II **Obv:** Head with tiara right **Obv. Designer:** Ian Rank-Broadley **Rev:** Crouching kangaroos facing left, Grass tree plant at right

Date	Mintage	F	VF	XF	Unc	BU
2004	500	—	—	—	—	165

KM# 911 15 DOLLARS

3.1101 g., 0.9990 Gold 0.0999 oz. AGW **Ruler:** Elizabeth II **Obv:** Head with tiara right **Obv. Designer:** Ian Rank-Broadley **Rev:** Kangaroo in bush

Date	Mintage	F	VF	XF	Unc	BU
2005	500	—	—	—	—	165

KM# 1362 15 DOLLARS

3.1100 g., 0.9990 Gold 0.0999 oz. AGW **Ruler:** Elizabeth II **Obv:** Head right **Rev:** Kangaroo

Date	Mintage	F	VF	XF	Unc	BU
2010(p)	—	—	—	—	—	165

KM# 895 25 DOLLARS

7.7508 g., 0.9990 Gold 0.2489 oz. AGW **Ruler:** Elizabeth II **Obv:** Head with tiara right **Obv. Designer:** Ian Rank-Broadley **Rev:** Two kangaroos on map of Australia

Date	Mintage	F	VF	XF	Unc	BU
2001	500	—	—	—	—	375

KM# 898 25 DOLLARS

7.7508 g., 0.9990 Gold 0.2489 oz. AGW **Ruler:** Elizabeth II **Obv:** Head with tiara right **Obv. Designer:** Ian Rank-Broadley **Rev:** Kangaroo browsing

Date	Mintage	F	VF	XF	Unc	BU
2002	500	—	—	—	—	375

KM# 903 25 DOLLARS

7.7508 g., 0.9990 Gold 0.2489 oz. AGW **Ruler:** Elizabeth II **Obv:** Head with tiara right **Obv. Designer:** Ian Rank-Broadley **Rev:** Two kangaroos hopping

Date	Mintage	F	VF	XF	Unc	BU
2003	250	—	—	—	—	375

KM# 908 25 DOLLARS

7.7508 g., 0.9990 Gold 0.2489 oz. AGW **Ruler:** Elizabeth II **Obv:** Head with tiara right **Obv. Designer:** Ian Rank-Broadley **Rev:** Crouching kangaroos facing left, Grass tree plant at right

Date	Mintage	F	VF	XF	Unc	BU
2004	250	—	—	—	—	375

KM# 912 25 DOLLARS

7.7508 g., 0.9990 Gold 0.2489 oz. AGW **Ruler:** Elizabeth II **Obv:** Head with tiara right **Obv. Designer:** Ian Rank-Broadley **Rev:** Kangaroo in bush

Date	Mintage	F	VF	XF	Unc	BU
2005	250	—	—	—	—	375

KM# 1363 25 DOLLARS

7.7500 g., 0.9990 Gold 0.2489 oz. AGW **Ruler:** Elizabeth II **Rev:** Two kangaroos playing

Date	Mintage	F	VF	XF	Unc	BU
2010P	—	—	—	—	—	375

KM# 1506 25 DOLLARS

6.2200 g., 0.9990 Gold 0.1998 oz. AGW, 21.69 mm. **Ruler:** Elizabeth II **Obv:** Head with tiara right **Rev:** Kangaroo in outback, windmill at right

Date	Mintage	F	VF	XF	Unc	BU
2010 Proof	1,000	Value: 825				

KM# 1507 25 DOLLARS

6.2200 g., 0.9990 Gold 0.1998 oz. AGW, 21.69 mm. **Ruler:** Elizabeth II **Obv:** Head in tiara right **Rev:** Kangaroo in outback, windmill at center

Date	Mintage	F	VF	XF	Unc	BU
2010 Proof	1,000	Value: 825				

KM# 1508 25 DOLLARS

6.2200 g., 0.9990 Gold 0.1998 oz. AGW, 21.69 mm. **Ruler:** Elizabeth II **Obv:** Head in tiara right **Rev:** Kangaroo in outback, windmill at left

Date	Mintage	F	VF	XF	Unc	BU
2010 Proof	1,000	Value: 825				

KM# 692 50 DOLLARS

15.5017 g., 0.9999 Gold 0.4983 oz. AGW, 25.1 mm. **Ruler:** Elizabeth II **Subject:** Tribute to Liberty **Obv:** Head with tiara right, denomination below **Obv. Designer:** Ian Rank-Broadley **Rev:** Two kangaroos on map above silver Liberty Bell insert **Edge:** Reeded

Date	Mintage	F	VF	XF	Unc	BU
2001	650	—	—	—	750	—
2002	1,498	—	—	—	750	—
2002 Proof	—	Value: 775				

KM# 899 50 DOLLARS

15.5017 g., 0.9990 Gold 0.4979 oz. AGW **Ruler:** Elizabeth II **Obv:** Head with tiara right **Obv. Designer:** Ian Rank-Broadley **Rev:** Kangaroo browsing

Date	Mintage	F	VF	XF	Unc	BU
2002	650	—	—	—	760	—

KM# 904 50 DOLLARS

15.5017 g., 0.9990 Gold 0.4979 oz. AGW **Ruler:** Elizabeth II **Obv:** Head with tiara right **Obv. Designer:** Ian Rank-Broadley **Rev:** Two kangaroos hopping

Date	Mintage	F	VF	XF	Unc	BU
2003	500	—	—	—	760	—

KM# 909 50 DOLLARS

15.5017 g., 0.9990 Gold 0.4979 oz. AGW **Ruler:** Elizabeth II **Obv:** Head with tiara right **Obv. Designer:** Ian Rank-Broadley **Rev:** Crouching kangaroos facing left, Grass tree plant at right

Date	Mintage	F	VF	XF	Unc	BU
2004	500	—	—	—	760	—

Note: In sets only

KM# 913 50 DOLLARS

15.5017 g., 0.9990 Gold 0.4979 oz. AGW **Ruler:** Elizabeth II **Obv:** Head with tiara right **Obv. Designer:** Ian Rank-Broadley **Rev:** Kangaroo in bush

Date	Mintage	F	VF	XF	Unc	BU
2005	500	—	—	—	765	—

KM# 1364 50 DOLLARS

15.5600 g., 0.9990 Gold 0.4997 oz. AGW, 25 mm. **Ruler:** Elizabeth II **Obv:** Head right **Rev:** Two kangaroos playing

Date	Mintage	F	VF	XF	Unc	BU
2010(p)	—	—	—	—	—	765

KM# 693 100 DOLLARS

31.1035 g., 0.9999 Gold 0.9999 oz. AGW, 32.1 mm. **Ruler:** Elizabeth II **Subject:** Tribute to Liberty **Obv:** Head with tiara right, denomination below **Obv. Designer:** Ian Rank-Broadley **Rev:** Two kangaroos on map above silver Liberty Bell insert, colored image **Edge:** Reeded

Date	Mintage	F	VF	XF	Unc	BU
2001	1,498	—	—	—	1,475	—
2002	—	—	—	—	—	1,475

KM# 900 100 DOLLARS

31.1035 g., 0.9999 Gold 0.9999 oz. AGW, 32 mm. **Ruler:** Elizabeth II **Obv:** Head with tiara right **Obv. Designer:** Ian Rank-Broadley **Rev:** Prospectors dry-blowing gold dust, colored image

Date	Mintage	F	VF	XF	Unc	BU
2002	1,500	—	—	—	1,475	—

KM# 906 100 DOLLARS

31.1035 g., 0.9990 Gold 0.9990 oz. AGW, 32 mm. **Ruler:**

Elizabeth II **Obv:** Head with tiara right **Obv. Designer:** Ian Rank-Broadley **Rev:** Prospectors camp, colored image

Date	Mintage	F	VF	XF	Unc	BU
2003	1,500	—	—	—	1,475	—

KM# 915 100 DOLLARS
31.1035 g., 0.9990 Gold 0.9990 oz. AGW, 32 mm. **Ruler:** Elizabeth II **Subject:** Welcome Stranger Nugget **Obv:** Head with tiara right **Obv. Designer:** Ian Rank-Broadley **Rev:** Welcome Stranger Nugget surrounded by Outback setting, colored image

Date	Mintage	F	VF	XF	Unc	BU
2005	1,500	—	—	—	1,475	—

KM# 1365 100 DOLLARS
31.1035 g., 0.9990 Gold 0.9990 oz. AGW, 32 mm. **Ruler:** Elizabeth II **Obv:** Head right **Rev:** Kangaroo

Date	Mintage	F	VF	XF	Unc	BU
2010(p)	—	—	—	—	—	1,475

KM# 896 200 DOLLARS
62.2140 g., 0.9990 Gold 1.9981 oz. AGW **Ruler:** Elizabeth II **Obv:** Head with tiara right **Obv. Designer:** Ian Rank-Broadley **Rev:** Two kangaroos on map of Australia

Date	Mintage	F	VF	XF	Unc	BU
2001	300	—	—	—	3,000	—

KM# 901 200 DOLLARS
62.2140 g., 0.9990 Gold 1.9981 oz. AGW **Ruler:** Elizabeth II **Obv:** Head with tiara right **Obv. Designer:** Ian Rank-Broadley **Rev:** Kangaroo browsing

Date	Mintage	F	VF	XF	Unc	BU
2002	300	—	—	—	3,000	—

KM# 905 200 DOLLARS
62.2140 g., 0.9990 Gold 1.9981 oz. AGW **Ruler:** Elizabeth II **Obv:** Head with tiara right **Obv. Designer:** Ian Rank-Broadley **Rev:** Two kangaroos hopping

Date	Mintage	F	VF	XF	Unc	BU
2003	200	—	—	—	3,000	—

KM# 910 200 DOLLARS
62.2140 g., 0.9990 Gold 1.9981 oz. AGW **Ruler:** Elizabeth II **Obv:** Head with tiara right **Obv. Designer:** Ian Rank-Broadley **Rev:** Crouching kangaroos facing left, Grass tree plant at right

Date	Mintage	F	VF	XF	Unc	BU
2004	200	—	—	—	3,000	—

KM# 914 200 DOLLARS
62.2140 g., 0.9990 Gold 1.9981 oz. AGW, 41 mm. **Ruler:** Elizabeth II **Obv:** Head with tiara right **Obv. Designer:** Ian Rank-Broadley **Rev:** Kangaroo in multicolor bush

Date	Mintage	F	VF	XF	Unc	BU
2005	200	—	—	—	3,000	—

BULLION - KOOKABURRA

KM# 875 50 CENTS
15.5500 g., 0.9990 Silver 0.4994 oz. ASW, 38.74 mm. **Ruler:** Elizabeth II **Obv:** Head with tiara right **Obv. Designer:** Ian Rank-Broadley **Rev:** Kookaburra on branch, tail above, two leaves **Edge:** Reeded **Shape:** Square **Note:** Lenticular technology makes kookaburra appear to move.

Date	Mintage	F	VF	XF	Unc	BU
2002P Proof	75,350	Value: 35.00				

KM# 684 50 CENTS
15.5500 g., 0.9990 Silver 0.4994 oz. ASW, 32.1 mm. **Ruler:** Elizabeth II **Obv:** Head with tiara right, denomination below **Obv. Designer:** Ian Rank-Broadley **Rev:** Two kookaburras, one in flight **Edge:** Reeded **Shape:** Square

Date	Mintage	F	VF	XF	Unc	BU
2003P Proof	75,350	Value: 32.00				

KM# 876 50 CENTS
15.5500 g., 0.9990 Silver 0.4994 oz. ASW, 38.74 mm. **Ruler:** Elizabeth II **Obv:** Head with tiara right **Obv. Designer:** Ian Rank-Broadley **Rev:** Kookaburra perched on branch, tail below, four leaves **Edge:** Reeded **Shape:** Square with rounded corners

Date	Mintage	F	VF	XF	Unc	BU
2004P Proof	30,350	Value: 32.00				

KM# 877 50 CENTS
15.5500 g., 0.9990 Silver 0.4994 oz. ASW, 25x25 mm. **Ruler:** Elizabeth II **Obv:** Head with tiara right **Obv. Designer:** Ian Rank-Broadley **Rev:** Two kookaburras on branch, one laughing **Edge:** Reeded **Shape:** Square

Date	Mintage	F	VF	XF	Unc	BU
2005P Proof	30,350	Value: 32.00				

KM# 691.1 DOLLAR
31.1035 g., 0.9990 Silver 0.9990 oz. ASW, 40 mm. **Ruler:** Elizabeth II **Obv:** Head with tiara right, denomination below **Obv. Designer:** Ian Rank-Broadley **Rev:** Kookaburra flying over map of Australia **Edge:** Reeded

Date	Mintage	F	VF	XF	Unc	BU
2001P Proof	5,000	Value: 40.00				
2002	—	—	—	—	32.50	35.00

KM# 479 DOLLAR
31.9700 g., 0.9990 Silver 1.0268 oz. ASW **Ruler:** Elizabeth II **Obv:** Head with tiara right, denomination below **Obv. Designer:** Ian Rank-Broadley **Rev:** Two kookaburras back-to-back on branch

Date	Mintage	F	VF	XF	Unc	BU
2001	—	—	—	—	30.00	—
2001	10,000	—	—	—	45.00	—
Note: Federation star privy mark						
2001	50,000	—	—	—	35.00	—
Note: Santa Claus privy mark						
2001	1,000	—	—	—	125	—
Note: Love token personal message						
2001	75,000	—	—	—	42.00	—
Note: New York State Quarter privy mark						
2001	75,000	—	—	—	42.00	—
Note: North Carolina State Quarter privy mark						
2001	75,000	—	—	—	42.00	—
Note: Rhode Island State Quarter privy mark						
2001	75,000	—	—	—	42.00	—
Note: Vermont State Quarter privy mark						
2001	75,000	—	—	—	42.00	—
Note: Kentucky State Quarter privy mark						

KM# 625 DOLLAR
31.1035 g., 0.9990 Silver 0.9990 oz. ASW, 40.4 mm. **Ruler:** Elizabeth II **Subject:** U.S. State Quarter

Date	Mintage	F	VF	XF	Unc	BU
2002	75,000	—	—	—	42.00	—
Note: Tennessee State Quarter privy mark						
2002	75,000	—	—	—	42.00	—
Note: Ohio State Quarter privy mark						
2002	75,000	—	—	—	42.00	—
Note: Louisiana State Quarter privy mark						
2002	75,000	—	—	—	42.00	—
Note: Indiana State Quarter privy mark						
2002	75,000	—	—	—	42.00	—
Note: Mississippi State Quarter privy mark						

KM# 666 DOLLAR
31.6200 g., 0.9990 Silver 1.0155 oz. ASW, 40.3 mm. **Ruler:** Elizabeth II **Obv:** Head with tiara right, denomination below **Obv. Designer:** Ian Rank-Broadley **Rev:** Kookaburra perched on branch **Edge:** Reeded

Date	Mintage	F	VF	XF	Unc	BU
2002	5,000	Value: 35.00				

KM# 691.2 DOLLAR

31.6200 g., 0.9990 Silver 1.0155 oz. ASW, 40.5 mm. **Ruler:** Elizabeth II **Obv:** Head with tiara right, denomination below **Obv. Designer:** Ian Rank-Broadley **Rev:** Multicolor US flag above a kookaburra in flight over Australian map **Edge:** Reeded

Date	Mintage	F	VF	XF	Unc	BU
2002	18,500	—	—	—	35.00	40.00

KM# 683 DOLLAR

31.1035 g., 0.9990 Silver 0.9990 oz. ASW, 40 mm. **Ruler:** Elizabeth II **Obv:** Head with tiara right, denomination below **Obv. Designer:** Ian Rank-Broadley **Rev:** Two kookaburras, one in flight **Edge:** Reeded **Note:** Gilded.

Date	Mintage	F	VF	XF	Unc	BU
2003P Proof	5,000	Value: 35.00				
2004	10,000	—	—	—	—	35.00
2004 Proof	15,000	Value: 45.00				

KM# 883 DOLLAR

31.1050 g., 0.9990 Silver 0.9990 oz. ASW, 40.5 mm. **Ruler:** Elizabeth II **Obv:** Head with tiara right **Obv. Designer:** Ian Rank-Broadley **Rev:** Kookaburra perched on branch with four leaves **Edge:** Reeded

Date	Mintage	F	VF	XF	Unc	BU
2004P Proof	5,000	Value: 25.00				
2005	5,000	—	—	—	42.00	—
Note: Gemini privy mark						
2005	5,000	—	—	—	42.00	—
Note: Aquarius privy mark						
2005	5,000	—	—	—	42.00	—
Note: Pisces privy mark						
2005	5,000	—	—	—	42.00	—
Note: Aries privy mark						
2005	5,000	—	—	—	42.00	—
Note: Taurus privy mark						
2005	5,000	—	—	—	42.00	—
Note: Cancer privy mark						
2005	5,000	—	—	—	42.00	—
Note: Leo privy mark						
2005	5,000	—	—	—	42.00	—
Note: Virgo privy mark						
2005	5,000	—	—	—	42.00	—
Note: Libra privy mark						
2005	5,000	—	—	—	42.00	—
Note: Scorpio privy mark						
2005	5,000	—	—	—	42.00	—
Note: Sagittarius privy mark						
2005	5,000	—	—	—	42.00	—
Note: Capricorn privy mark						

KM# 883a DOLLAR

31.1035 g., 0.9990 Silver 0.9990 oz. ASW, 40 mm. **Ruler:** Elizabeth II **Obv:** Head with tiara right **Obv. Designer:** Ian Rank-Broadley **Rev:** Kookaburra perched on branch with four leaves **Note:** Gilded.

Date	Mintage	F	VF	XF	Unc	BU
2004	10,000	—	—	—	55.00	—

KM# 720 DOLLAR

1.0350 g., 0.9990 Silver partially gilt 0.0332 oz. ASW, 40 mm. **Ruler:** Elizabeth II **Obv:** Head with tiara right, denomination below **Rev:** Kookabarra, partially gilt **Edge:** Reeded

Date	Mintage	F	VF	XF	Unc	BU
2005 Proof	—	Value: 65.00				

KM# 886 DOLLAR

31.5600 g., 0.9990 Silver 1.0136 oz. ASW, 40.5 mm. **Ruler:** Elizabeth II **Obv:** Head with tiara right **Obv. Designer:** Ian Rank-Broadley **Rev:** Two kookaburras on branch, one laughing **Edge:** Reeded

Date	Mintage	F	VF	XF	Unc	BU
2005P Proof	5,000	Value: 40.00				

KM# 889 DOLLAR

31.5600 g., 0.9990 Silver 1.0136 oz. ASW, 40.5 mm. **Ruler:** Elizabeth II **Obv:** Head with tiara right **Obv. Designer:** Ian Rank-Broadley **Rev:** Kookaburras on branch, no leaves

Date	Mintage	F	VF	XF	Unc	BU
2007	300,000	—	—	—	35.00	38.00

KM# 1277 DOLLAR

31.1050 g., 0.9990 Silver 0.9990 oz. ASW, 40 mm. **Ruler:** Elizabeth II **Subject:** Kookaburra 20th Anniversary **Obv:** Head right **Obv. Designer:** Ian Rank-Broadley **Rev:** Kookaburra standing right

Date	Mintage	F	VF	XF	Unc	BU
2009 P20 Proof	10,000	Value: 47.00				

KM# 1278 DOLLAR

31.1050 g., 0.9990 Silver 0.9990 oz. ASW, 40 mm. **Ruler:** Elizabeth II **Subject:** Kookaburra 20th Anniversary **Obv:** Head right **Obv. Designer:** Ian Rank-Broadley **Rev:** Kookaburra on branch, head right

Date	Mintage	F	VF	XF	Unc	BU
2009 P20 Proof	10,000	Value: 47.00				

KM# 1279 DOLLAR

31.1050 g., 0.9990 Silver 0.9990 oz. ASW, 40 mm. **Ruler:** Elizabeth II **Subject:** Kookaburra 20th Anniversary **Obv:** Head right **Obv. Designer:** Ian Rank-Broadley **Rev:** Kookaburra on branch left, head upwards

Date	Mintage	F	VF	XF	Unc	BU
2009 P20 Proof	10,000	Value: 47.00				

KM# 1280 DOLLAR

31.1050 g., 0.9990 Silver 0.9990 oz. ASW, 40 mm. **Ruler:** Elizabeth II **Subject:** Kookaburra 20th Anniversary **Obv:** Head right **Obv. Designer:** Ian Rank-Broadley **Rev:** Kookaburra feeding young in nest at right

Date	Mintage	F	VF	XF	Unc	BU
2009 P20 Proof	10,000	Value: 47.00				

KM# 1281 DOLLAR

31.1050 g., 0.9990 Silver 0.9990 oz. ASW, 40 mm. **Ruler:** Elizabeth II **Subject:** Kookaburra 20th Anniversary **Obv:** Head right **Obv. Designer:** Ian Rank-Broadley **Rev:** Kookaburra pair on branch

Date	Mintage	F	VF	XF	Unc	BU
2009 P20 Proof	10,000	Value: 47.00				

KM# 1282 DOLLAR

31.1050 g., 0.9990 Silver 0.9990 oz. ASW, 40 mm. **Ruler:** Elizabeth II **Obv:** Head right **Obv. Designer:** Ian Rank-Broadley **Rev:** Kookaburra on branch, head left

Date	Mintage	F	VF	XF	Unc	BU
2009 P20 Proof	10,000	Value: 47.00				

KM# 1283 DOLLAR

31.1050 g., 0.9990 Silver 0.9990 oz. ASW, 40 mm. **Ruler:** Elizabeth II **Subject:** Kookaburra 20th Anniversary **Obv:** Head right **Obv. Designer:** Ian rank-Broadley **Rev:** Kookaburra in flight right

Date	Mintage	F	VF	XF	Unc	BU
2009 P20 Proof	10,000	Value: 47.00				

KM# 1284 DOLLAR

31.1050 g., 0.9990 Silver 0.9990 oz. ASW, 40 mm. **Ruler:** Elizabeth II **Subject:** Kookaburra 20th Anniversary **Obv:** Head right **Obv. Designer:** Ian Rank-Broadley **Rev:** Kookaburra by nest at left

Date	Mintage	F	VF	XF	Unc	BU
2009 P20 Proof	10,000	Value: 47.00				

KM# 1285 DOLLAR

31.1050 g., 0.9990 Silver 0.9990 oz. ASW, 40 mm. **Ruler:** Elizabeth II **Subject:** Kookaburra 20th Anniversary **Obv:** Head right **Obv. Designer:** Ian Rank-BroadleyR **Rev:** Kookaburra on fence post

Date	Mintage	F	VF	XF	Unc	BU
2009 P20 Proof	10,000	Value: 47.00				

KM# 1286 DOLLAR

31.1050 g., 0.9990 Silver 0.9990 oz. ASW, 40 mm. **Ruler:** Elizabeth II **Subject:** Kookaburra 20th Anniversary **Obv:** Head right **Obv. Designer:** Ian Rank-Broadleyr **Rev:** Kookaburra pair on branch left

Date	Mintage	F	VF	XF	Unc	BU
2009 P20 Proof	10,000	Value: 47.00				

KM# 1287 DOLLAR

31.1050 g., 0.9990 Silver 0.9990 oz. ASW, 40 mm. **Ruler:** Elizabeth II **Subject:** Kookaburra 20th Anniversary **Obv:** Head right **Obv. Designer:** Ian Rank-Broadley **Rev:** Kookaburra on leafy branch left

Date	Mintage	F	VF	XF	Unc	BU
2009 P20 Proof	10,000	Value: 47.00				

KM# 1288 DOLLAR

31.1050 g., 0.9990 Silver 0.9990 oz. ASW, 40 mm. **Ruler:** Elizabeth II **Subject:** Kookaburra 20th Anniversary **Obv:** Head right **Obv. Designer:** Ian Rank-Broadley **Rev:** Kookaburra pair on branch, beaks upward

Date	Mintage	F	VF	XF	Unc	BU
2009 P20 Proof	10,000	Value: 47.00				

KM# 1289 DOLLAR

31.1050 g., 0.9990 Silver 0.9990 oz. ASW, 40 mm. **Ruler:** Elizabeth II **Subject:** Kookaburra 20th Anniversary **Obv:** Head right **Obv. Designer:** Ian rank-Broadley **Rev:** Kookaburra in flight on map of Australia

Date	Mintage	F	VF	XF	Unc	BU
2009 P20 Proof	10,000	Value: 47.00				

KM# 1290 DOLLAR

31.1050 g., 0.9990 Silver 0.9990 oz. ASW, 40 mm. **Ruler:** Elizabeth II **Subject:** Kookaburra 20th Anniversary **Obv:** Head right **Obv. Designer:** Ian Rank-Broadley **Rev:** Kookaburra on branch right

Date	Mintage	F	VF	XF	Unc	BU
2009 P20 Proof	10,000	Value: 47.00				

KM# 1291 DOLLAR

31.1050 g., 0.9990 Silver 0.9990 oz. ASW, 40 mm. **Ruler:** Elizabeth II **Subject:** Kookaburra 20th Anniversary **Obv:** Head right **Obv. Designer:** Ian Rank-Broadley **Rev:** Two kookaburras, one in flight, one on branch

Date	Mintage	F	VF	XF	Unc	BU
2009 P20 Proof	10,000	Value: 47.00				

KM# 1292 DOLLAR

31.1050 g., 0.9990 Silver 0.9990 oz. ASW, 40 mm. **Ruler:** Elizabeth II **Subject:** Kookaburra 20th Anniversary **Obv:** Head right **Obv. Designer:** Ian Rank-Broadley **Rev:** Kookaburra on branch, head right

Date	Mintage	F	VF	XF	Unc	BU
2009 P20 Proof	10,000	Value: 47.00				

KM# 1293 DOLLAR

31.1050 g., 0.9990 Silver 0.9990 oz. ASW, 40 mm. **Ruler:** Elizabeth II **Subject:** Kookaburra 20th Anniversary **Obv:** Head right **Obv. Designer:** Ian Rank-Broadley **Rev:** Kookaburra pair on branch left

Date	Mintage	F	VF	XF	Unc	BU
2009 P20 Proof	10,000	Value: 47.00				

KM# 1294 DOLLAR

31.1050 g., 0.9990 Silver 0.9990 oz. ASW, 40 mm. **Ruler:** Elizabeth II **Subject:** Kookaburra 20th Anniversary **Obv:** Head right **Obv. Designer:** Ian Rank-Broadley **Rev:** Kookaburra on branch left

Date	Mintage	F	VF	XF	Unc	BU
2009 P20 Proof	10,000	Value: 47.00				

KM# 1295 DOLLAR

31.1050 g., 0.9990 Silver 0.9990 oz. ASW, 40 mm. **Ruler:** Elizabeth II **Subject:** Kookaburra 20th Anniversary **Obv:** Head right **Obv. Designer:** Ian Rank-Broadley **Rev:** Kookaburra admiring spider web

Date	Mintage	F	VF	XF	Unc	BU
2009 P20 Proof	10,000	Value: 47.00				

KM# 1296 DOLLAR

31.1050 g., 0.9990 Silver 0.9990 oz. ASW, 40 mm. **Ruler:** Elizabeth II **Subject:** Kookaburra 20th Anniversary **Obv:** Head right **Obv. Designer:** Ian Rank-Broadley **Rev:** Kookaburra on branch, sunburst in background

Date	Mintage	F	VF	XF	Unc	BU
2009 P20 Proof	10,000	Value: 47.00				

KM# 1471 DOLLAR

31.1050 g., 0.9990 Silver 0.9990 oz. ASW, 40 mm. **Ruler:** Elizabeth II **Rev:** Kookabburra on branch

Date	Mintage	F	VF	XF	Unc	BU
2010P	—	—	—	—	—	45.00

KM# 678 2 DOLLARS

62.2070 g., 0.9990 Silver 1.9979 oz. ASW, 40 mm. **Ruler:** Elizabeth II **Obv:** Head with tiara right, denomination below **Obv. Designer:** Ian Rank-Broadley **Rev:** Kookaburra flying over Australian map **Edge:** Reeded

Date	Mintage	F	VF	XF	Unc	BU
2001P Proof	5,000	Value: 80.00				
2002	1,500	—	—	—	75.00	—
Note: 1661 Spanish cob privy mark						
2002	1,500	—	—	—	75.00	—
Note: 1771 Spanish pillar dollar privy mark						
2002	1,500	—	—	—	75.00	—
Note: 1881 Gold sovereign privy mark						
2002	1,500	—	—	—	75.00	—
Note: 1991 Gold Australian nugget privy mark						

KM# 623.1 2 DOLLARS

62.8500 g., 0.9990 Silver 2.0186 oz. ASW, 50 mm. **Ruler:** Elizabeth II **Obv:** Head with tiara right, denomination below **Rev:** Two kookaburras back to back **Edge:** Reeded

Date	Mintage	F	VF	XF	Unc	BU
2001	—	—	—	—	70.00	75.00

KM# 623.2 2 DOLLARS

62.2070 g., 0.9990 Silver 1.9979 oz. ASW **Ruler:** Elizabeth II **Subject:** USA State Quarters - 2001 **Obv:** Head with tiara right, denomination below **Rev:** Two kookaburras on branch with five state quarter designs added **Edge:** Reeded and plain sections **Note:** Prev. KM#623

Date	Mintage	F	VF	XF	Unc	BU
2001	10,000	—	—	—	145	160

KM# 879 2 DOLLARS

62.8500 g., 0.9990 Silver 2.0186 oz. ASW, 40 mm. **Ruler:** Elizabeth II **Obv:** Head with tiara right **Obv. Designer:** Ian Rank-Broadley **Rev:** Kookaburra on branch plus two leaves **Edge:** Reeded

Date	Mintage	F	VF	XF	Unc	BU
2002P Proof	5,000	Value: 80.00				
2003	1,000	—	—	—	110	—
Note: Boer War privy mark						
2003	1,000	—	—	—	110	—
Note: World War I privy mark						
2003	1,000	—	—	—	110	—
Note: World War II privy mark						
2003	1,000	—	—	—	110	—
Note: Korean War privy mark						
2003	1,000	—	—	—	110	—
Note: Vietnam War privy mark						

KM# 881 2 DOLLARS

62.2070 g., 0.9990 Silver 1.9979 oz. ASW, 50 mm. **Ruler:** Elizabeth II **Obv:** Head with tiara right **Obv. Designer:** Ian Rank-Broadley **Rev:** Two kookaburras, one in flight **Edge:** Reeded

Date	Mintage	F	VF	XF	Unc	BU
2003P Proof	800	Value: 80.00				

KM# 884 2 DOLLARS

62.2070 g., 0.9990 Silver 1.9979 oz. ASW, 50 mm. **Ruler:** Elizabeth II **Obv:** Head with tiara right **Obv. Designer:** Ian Rank-Broadley **Rev:** Kookaburra perched on branch with four leaves **Edge:** Reeded

Date	Mintage	F	VF	XF	Unc	BU
2004P Proof	800	Value: 80.00				

KM# 887 2 DOLLARS

62.2070 g., 0.9990 Silver 1.9979 oz. ASW, 50 mm. **Ruler:** Elizabeth II **Obv:** Head with tiara right **Obv. Designer:** Ian Rank-Broadley **Rev:** Two kookaburras on branch, one laughing **Edge:** Reeded

Date	Mintage	F	VF	XF	Unc	BU
2005P Proof	800	Value: 80.00				

KM# 890 2 DOLLARS

62.2070 g., 0.9990 Silver 1.9979 oz. ASW, 50 mm. **Ruler:** Elizabeth II **Obv:** Head with tiara right **Obv. Designer:** Ian Rank-Broadley **Rev:** Kookaburra on branch, no leaves

Date	Mintage	F	VF	XF	Unc	BU
2007	—	—	—	—	75.00	—

KM# 1297 5 DOLLARS

1.5500 g., 0.9990 Gold 0.0498 oz. AGW, 14 mm. **Ruler:** Elizabeth II **Subject:** Kookaburra 20th Anniversary **Obv:** Head right **Obv. Designer:** Ian Rank-Broadley **Rev:** Kookaburra standing on stump right

Date	Mintage	F	VF	XF	Unc	BU
2009 P20 Proof	2,009	Value: 125				

KM# 1298 5 DOLLARS

1.5500 g., 0.9990 Gold 0.0498 oz. AGW, 14 mm. **Ruler:** Elizabeth II **Subject:** Kookaburra 20th Anniversary **Obv:** Head right **Obv. Designer:** Ian Rank-Broadley **Rev:** Kookaburra on branch, head right

Date	Mintage	F	VF	XF	Unc	BU
2009 P20 Proof	2,009	Value: 125				

KM# 1299 5 DOLLARS

1.5500 g., 0.9990 Gold 0.0498 oz. AGW, 14 mm. **Ruler:** Elizabeth II **Subject:** Kookaburra 20th Anniversary **Obv:** Head right **Obv. Designer:** Ian Rank-Broadley **Rev:** Kookaburra on branch left

Date	Mintage	F	VF	XF	Unc	BU
2009 P20 Proof	2,009	Value: 125				

KM# 1300 5 DOLLARS

1.5500 g., 0.9990 Gold 0.0498 oz. AGW, 14 mm. **Ruler:** Elizabeth II **Subject:** Kookaburra 20th Anniversary **Obv:** Head right **Obv. Designer:** Ian Rank-Broadley **Rev:** Kookaburra on branch feeding young at right

Date	Mintage	F	VF	XF	Unc	BU
2009 P20 Proof	2,009	Value: 125				

KM# 1301 5 DOLLARS

1.5500 g., 0.9990 Gold 0.0498 oz. AGW, 14 mm. **Ruler:** Elizabeth II **Subject:** Kookaburra 20th Anniversary **Obv:** Head right **Obv. Designer:** Ian Rank-Broadley **Rev:** Kookaburra pair on branch, heads opposite

Date	Mintage	F	VF	XF	Unc	BU
2009 P20 Proof	2,009	Value: 125				

KM# 1302 5 DOLLARS

1.5500 g., 0.9990 Gold 0.0498 oz. AGW, 14 mm. **Ruler:** Elizabeth II **Subject:** Kookaburra 20th Anniversary **Obv:** Head right **Obv. Designer:** Ian Rank-Broadley **Rev:** Kookaburra on branch, head left

Date	Mintage	F	VF	XF	Unc	BU
2009 P20 Proof	2,009	Value: 125				

KM# 1303 5 DOLLARS

1.5500 g., 0.9990 Gold 0.0498 oz. AGW, 14 mm. **Ruler:** Elizabeth II **Subject:** Kookaburra 20th Anniversary **Obv:** Head right **Obv. Designer:** Ian Rank-Broadley **Rev:** Kookaburra in flight right

Date	Mintage	F	VF	XF	Unc	BU
2009 P20 Proof	2,009	Value: 125				

KM# 1304 5 DOLLARS

1.5500 g., 0.9990 Gold 0.0498 oz. AGW, 14 mm. **Ruler:** Elizabeth II **Subject:** Kookaburra 20th Anniversary **Obv:** Head right **Obv. Designer:** Ian Rank-Broadley **Rev:** Kookaburra at nest left, head right

Date	Mintage	F	VF	XF	Unc	BU
2009 P20 Proof	2,009	Value: 125				

KM# 1305 5 DOLLARS

1.5500 g., 0.9990 Gold 0.0498 oz. AGW, 14 mm. **Ruler:** Elizabeth II **Subject:** Kookaburra 20th Anniversary **Obv:** Head right **Obv. Designer:** Ian Rank-Broadley **Rev:** Kookaburra on fence post

Date	Mintage	F	VF	XF	Unc	BU
2009 P20 Proof	2,009	Value: 125				

KM# 1306 5 DOLLARS

1.5500 g., 0.9990 Gold 0.0498 oz. AGW, 14 mm. **Ruler:** Elizabeth II **Subject:** Kookaburra 20th Anniversary **Obv:** Head right **Obv. Designer:** Ian Rank-Broadley **Rev:** Kookaburra pair left

Date	Mintage	F	VF	XF	Unc	BU
2009 P20 Proof	2,009	Value: 125				

KM# 1307 5 DOLLARS

1.5500 g., 0.9990 Gold 0.0498 oz. AGW, 14 mm. **Ruler:** Elizabeth II **Subject:** Kookaburra 20th Anniversary **Obv:** Head right **Obv. Designer:** Ian Rank-Broadley **Rev:** Kookaburra left on leafy branch

Date	Mintage	F	VF	XF	Unc	BU
2009 P20 Proof	2,009	Value: 125				

KM# 1308 5 DOLLARS

1.5500 g., 0.9990 Gold 0.0498 oz. AGW, 14 mm. **Ruler:** Elizabeth II **Subject:** Kookaburra 20th Anniversary **Obv:** Head right **Obv. Designer:** Ian Rank-Broadley **Rev:** Kookaburra pair facing opposite

Date	Mintage	F	VF	XF	Unc	BU
2009 P20 Proof	2,009	Value: 125				

KM# 1309 5 DOLLARS

1.5500 g., 0.9990 Gold 0.0498 oz. AGW, 14 mm. **Ruler:** Elizabeth II **Subject:** Kookaburra 20th Anniversary **Obv:** Head right **Obv. Designer:** Ian Rank-Broadley **Rev:** Kookaburra in flight on map of Australia

Date	Mintage	F	VF	XF	Unc	BU
2009 P20 Proof	2,009	Value: 125				

KM# 1310 5 DOLLARS

1.5500 g., 0.9990 Gold 0.0498 oz. AGW, 14 mm. **Ruler:** Elizabeth II **Subject:** Kookaburra 20th Anniversary **Obv:** Head right **Obv. Designer:** Ian Rank-Broadley **Rev:** Kookaburra on branch right

Date	Mintage	F	VF	XF	Unc	BU
2009 P20 Proof	2,009	Value: 125				

KM# 1311 5 DOLLARS

1.5500 g., 0.9990 Gold 0.0498 oz. AGW, 14 mm. **Ruler:** Elizabeth II **Subject:** Kookaburra 20th Anniversary **Obv:** Head right **Obv. Designer:** Ian Rank-Broadley **Rev:** Kookaburras, one in flight, one on branch

Date	Mintage	F	VF	XF	Unc	BU
2009 P20 Proof	2,009	Value: 125				

KM# 1312 5 DOLLARS

1.5500 g., 0.9990 Gold 0.0498 oz. AGW, 14 mm. **Ruler:** Elizabeth II **Subject:** Kookaburra 20th Anniversary **Obv:** Head right **Obv. Designer:** Ian Rank-Broadley **Rev:** Kookaburra on branch, head right

Date	Mintage	F	VF	XF	Unc	BU
2009 P20 Proof	2,009	Value: 125				

KM# 1313 5 DOLLARS

1.5500 g., 0.9990 Gold 0.0498 oz. AGW, 14 mm. **Ruler:** Elizabeth II **Subject:** Kookaburra 20th Anniversary **Obv:** Head right **Obv. Designer:** Ian Rank-Broadley **Rev:** Kookaburra pair on branch, one with head upward

Date	Mintage	F	VF	XF	Unc	BU
2009 P20 Proof	2,009	Value: 125				

KM# 1314 5 DOLLARS

1.5500 g., 0.9990 Gold 0.0498 oz. AGW, 14 mm. **Ruler:** Elizabeth II **Subject:** Kookaburra 20th Anniversary **Obv:** Head right **Obv. Designer:** Ian Rank-Broadley **Rev:** Kookaburra on branch left

Date	Mintage	F	VF	XF	Unc	BU
2009 P20 Proof	2,009	Value: 125				

KM# 1315 5 DOLLARS

1.5500 g., 0.9990 Gold 0.0498 oz. AGW, 14 mm. **Ruler:** Elizabeth II **Subject:** Kookaburra 20th Anniversary **Obv:** Head right **Obv. Designer:** Ian Rank-Broadley **Rev:** Kookaburra on branch admiring spider web

Date	Mintage	F	VF	XF	Unc	BU
2009 P20 Proof	2,009	Value: 125				

KM# 1316 5 DOLLARS

1.5500 g., 0.9990 Gold 0.0498 oz. AGW, 14 mm. **Ruler:** Elizabeth II **Subject:** Kookaburra 20th Anniversary **Obv:** Head right **Obv. Designer:** Ian Rank-Broadley **Rev:** Kookaburra on branch, sunburst in background

Date	Mintage	F	VF	XF	Unc	BU
2009 P20 Proof	2,009	Value: 125				

KM# 603 10 DOLLARS

311.0350 g., 0.9990 Silver 9.9896 oz. ASW, 74.9 mm. **Ruler:** Elizabeth II **Subject:** Kookaburra **Obv:** Head with tiara right, denomination below **Obv. Designer:** Ian Rank-Broadley **Rev:** Flying bird over map **Edge:** Reeded

Date	Mintage	F	VF	XF	Unc	BU
2002 Proof	—	Value: 350				

KM# 891 10 DOLLARS

311.0350 g., 0.9990 Silver 9.9896 oz. ASW, 74.9 mm. **Ruler:** Elizabeth II **Obv:** Head with tiara right **Obv. Designer:** Ian Rank-Broadley **Rev:** Kookaburra on branch, no leaves

Date	Mintage	F	VF	XF	Unc	BU
2007	—	—	—	—	350	—

KM# 1360 10 DOLLARS
311.0350 g., 0.9990 Silver 9.9896 oz. ASW, 75.5 mm. **Ruler:** Elizabeth II **Obv:** Head right **Rev:** Kookaburra **Note:** Illustration reduced.

Date	Mintage	F	VF	XF	Unc	BU
2010(p) Proof	—	Value: 375				

KM# 630 20 DOLLARS
62.2070 g., 0.9990 Silver 1.9979 oz. ASW **Ruler:** Elizabeth II **Subject:** USA State Quarters - 2002 **Obv:** Head with tiara right, denomination below **Rev:** Kookaburra on branch with five state quarter designs added below **Edge:** Reeded and plain sections

Date	Mintage	F	VF	XF	Unc	BU
2002	10,000	—	—	—	72.00	75.00

KM# 680 30 DOLLARS
1002.5020 g., 0.9990 Silver 32.197 oz. ASW, 101 mm. **Ruler:** Elizabeth II **Obv:** Head with tiara right, denomination below **Obv. Designer:** Ian Rank-Broadley **Rev:** Kookaburra in flight above Australian map **Edge:** Segmented reeding

Date	Mintage	F	VF	XF	Unc	BU
2001P Proof	350	Value: 1,150				
2002	—	—	—	—	—	1,200

KM# 624 30 DOLLARS
1002.5020 g., 0.9990 Silver 32.197 oz. ASW, 101 mm. **Ruler:** Elizabeth II **Subject:** USA State Quarters - 2001 **Obv:** Head with tiara right, denomination below **Rev:** Two kookaburras on branch with five state quarter designs added below **Edge:** Reeded and plain sections **Note:** Illustration reduced.

Date	Mintage	F	VF	XF	Unc	BU
2001	1,000	—	—	—	—	1,150

KM# 631 30 DOLLARS
1002.5020 g., 0.9990 Silver 32.197 oz. ASW, 101 mm. **Ruler:** Elizabeth II **Subject:** USA State Quarters - 2002 **Obv:** Head with tiara right, denomination below **Rev:** Kookaburra on branch with five state quarter designs added in gold **Edge:** Reeded and plain sections

Date	Mintage	F	VF	XF	Unc	BU
2002	1,000	—	—	—	—	1,150

KM# 880 30 DOLLARS
1002.5020 g., 0.9990 Silver 32.197 oz. ASW, 101 mm. **Ruler:** Elizabeth II **Obv:** Head with tiara right **Obv. Designer:** Ian Rank-Broadley **Rev:** Kookaburra standing on branch **Edge:** Reeded

Date	Mintage	F	VF	XF	Unc	BU
2002P Proof	350	Value: 1,200				

KM# 882 30 DOLLARS
1002.5020 g., 0.9990 Silver 32.197 oz. ASW, 101 mm. **Ruler:** Elizabeth II **Obv:** Head with tiara right **Obv. Designer:** Ian Rank-Broadley **Rev:** Two kookaburras, one in flight **Edge:** Reeded

Date	Mintage	F	VF	XF	Unc	BU
2003P Proof	350	Value: 1,200				

KM# 885 30 DOLLARS
1002.5020 g., 0.9990 Silver 32.197 oz. ASW, 101 mm. **Ruler:** Elizabeth II **Obv:** Head with tiara right **Obv. Designer:** Ian Rank-Broadley **Rev:** Kookaburra perched on branch with four leaves **Edge:** Reeded

Date	Mintage	F	VF	XF	Unc	BU
2004P Proof	350	Value: 1,200				

KM# 888 30 DOLLARS
1002.5020 g., 0.9990 Silver 32.197 oz. ASW, 101 mm. **Ruler:** Elizabeth II **Obv:** Head with tiara right **Obv. Designer:** Ian Rank-Broadley **Rev:** Two kookaburras on branch, one laughing **Edge:** Reeded

Date	Mintage	F	VF	XF	Unc	BU
2005P Proof	800	Value: 1,200				

KM# 892 30 DOLLARS
1002.5020 g., 0.9990 Silver 32.197 oz. ASW, 101 mm. **Ruler:** Elizabeth II **Obv:** Head with tiara right **Obv. Designer:** Ian Rank-Broadley **Rev:** Kookaburras on branch, no leaves

Date	Mintage	F	VF	XF	Unc	BU
2007	—	—	—	—	1,150	—

KM# 1115 30 DOLLARS
1000.0000 g., 0.9990 Silver 32.117 oz. ASW, 101 mm. **Ruler:** Elizabeth II **Rev:** Kookaburra on branch, sunburst background **Rev. Designer:** Darryl Bettolli

Date	Mintage	F	VF	XF	Unc	BU
2009P Proof	—	Value: 1,250				

KM# 1361 30 DOLLARS
1000.0000 g., 0.9990 Silver 32.117 oz. ASW, 100 mm. **Ruler:** Elizabeth II **Obv:** Head right **Rev:** Kookaburra **Note:** Illustration reduced.

Date	Mintage	F	VF	XF	Unc	BU
2010(p)	—	—	—	—	—	1,150

KM# 878 200 DOLLARS
31.6000 g., 0.9990 Silver 1.0149 oz. ASW, 40 mm. **Ruler:** Elizabeth II **Obv:** Head with tiara right with denomination **Obv. Designer:** Ian Rank-Broadley **Rev:** Kookaburra in flight over map of Australia **Note:** Mule.

Date	Mintage	F	VF	XF	Unc	BU
ND(2001) Proof	Est. 20	Value: 2,500				

BULLION - NUGGET

KM# 741 100 DOLLARS
31.1035 g., 0.9999 Gold 0.9999 oz. AGW, 32 mm. **Ruler:** Elizabeth II **Subject:** Eureka Stockade **Obv:** Head with tiara right, denomination below **Obv. Designer:** Ian Rank-Broadley **Rev:** Eureka Stockade leader Peter Lalor and blue flag, colored image **Edge:** Reeded

Date	Mintage	F	VF	XF	Unc	BU
2004	1,500	—	—	—	1,450	—
2004P Proof	1,500	Value: 1,500				

KM# 1462 300 DOLLARS
1000.0000 g., 0.9990 Gold 32.117 oz. AGW **Ruler:** Elizabeth II **Obv:** Gold nugget **Rev:** Two kangaroos playing

Date	Mintage	F	VF	XF	Unc	BU
2010P	—	—	—	—	—	47,500

BULLION - KOALA

KM# 1366 50 CENTS
15.5500 g., 0.9990 Silver 0.4994 oz. ASW **Ruler:** Elizabeth II **Obv:** Head right **Rev:** Koala

Date	Mintage	F	VF	XF	Unc	BU
2010(p)	—	—	—	—	—	27.50

KM# 1111 DOLLAR
31.1050 g., 0.9990 Silver 0.9990 oz. ASW, 40.6 mm. **Ruler:** Elizabeth II **Rev:** Koala seated left on branch, shimmer background **Rev. Designer:** Darryl Bellotti

Date	Mintage	F	VF	XF	Unc	BU
2009P	—	—	—	—	—	40.00

KM# 1111a DOLLAR
31.1050 g., 0.9999 Silver partially gilt 0.9999 oz. ASW, 40.6 mm. **Ruler:** Elizabeth II **Rev:** Koala seated left on branch **Rev. Designer:** Darryl Bellotti

Date	Mintage	F	VF	XF	Unc	BU
2009P Proof	10,000	Value: 60.00				

KM# 1464 DOLLAR
31.1050 g., 0.9990 Silver 0.9990 oz. ASW, 40 mm. **Ruler:** Elizabeth II **Rev:** Koala on branch

Date	Mintage	F	VF	XF	Unc	BU
2010P	—	—	—	—	—	40.00

KM# 916 5 DOLLARS
1.5710 g., 0.9990 Platinum 0.0505 oz. APW **Ruler:** Elizabeth II **Obv:** Head with tiara right **Obv. Designer:** Ian Rank-Broadley **Rev:** Two koalas on branch

Date	Mintage	F	VF	XF	Unc	BU
2001 Proof	5,000	Value: 100				

KM# 1113 5 DOLLARS
1.2440 g., 0.9999 Gold 0.0400 oz. AGW, 14.1 mm. **Ruler:** Elizabeth II **Rev:** Koala seated left on branch **Rev. Designer:** Darryl Bellotti

Date	Mintage	F	VF	XF	Unc	BU
2009P Proof	15,000	Value: 90.00				

KM# 1467 5 DOLLARS
1.2400 g., 0.9990 Gold 0.0398 oz. AGW **Ruler:** Elizabeth II **Rev:** Koala on branch

Date	Mintage	F	VF	XF	Unc	BU
2010P	—	—	—	—	—	80.00

KM# 1368 10 DOLLARS
311.3500 g., 0.9990 Silver 9.9997 oz. ASW **Ruler:** Elizabeth II **Obv:** Head right **Rev:** Koala **Note:** Illustration reduced.

Date	Mintage	F	VF	XF	Unc	BU
2010(p)	—	—	—	—	—	375

KM# 917 15 DOLLARS
3.1101 g., 0.9990 Platinum 0.0999 oz. APW **Ruler:** Elizabeth II **Obv:** Head with tiara right **Obv. Designer:** Ian Rank-Broadley **Rev:** Two koalas on a branch

Date	Mintage	F	VF	XF	Unc	BU
2001 Proof	650	Value: 200				

KM# 922 15 DOLLARS
3.1101 g., 0.9990 Platinum 0.0999 oz. APW **Ruler:** Elizabeth II **Obv:** Head with tiara right **Obv. Designer:** Ian Rank-Broadley **Rev:** Koala up a gum tree

Date	Mintage	F	VF	XF	Unc	BU
2002 Proof	650	Value: 200				

KM# 926 15 DOLLARS
3.1101 g., 0.9990 Platinum 0.0999 oz. APW **Ruler:** Elizabeth II **Obv:** Head with tiara right **Obv. Designer:** Ian Rank-Broadley **Rev:** Mother and baby koala

Date	Mintage	F	VF	XF	Unc	BU
2003 Proof	500	Value: 200				

KM# 931 15 DOLLARS
3.1101 g., 0.9990 Platinum 0.0999 oz. APW **Ruler:** Elizabeth II **Obv:** Head with tiara right **Obv. Designer:** Ian Rank-Broadley **Rev:** Single koala on branch

Date	Mintage	F	VF	XF	Unc	BU
2004 Proof	500	Value: 200				

KM# 935 15 DOLLARS
3.1101 g., 0.9990 Platinum 0.0999 oz. APW **Ruler:** Elizabeth II **Obv:** Head with tiara right **Obv. Designer:** Ian Rank-Broadley **Rev:** Single koala with gum leaves

Date	Mintage	F	VF	XF	Unc	BU
2005 Proof	500	Value: 200				

KM# 1114 15 DOLLARS
3.1080 g., 0.9999 Gold 0.0999 oz. AGW, 16.1 mm. **Ruler:** Elizabeth II **Rev:** Koala seated left on tree branch **Rev. Designer:** Darryl Bellotti

Date	Mintage	F	VF	XF	Unc	BU
2009P Proof	5,000	Value: 175				

KM# 1468 15 DOLLARS
3.1100 g., 0.9990 Gold 0.0999 oz. AGW **Ruler:** Elizabeth II **Rev:** Koala on branch

Date	Mintage	F	VF	XF	Unc	BU
2010P	—	—	—	—	—	175

KM# 918 25 DOLLARS
7.7508 g., 0.9990 Platinum 0.2489 oz. APW **Ruler:** Elizabeth II **Obv:** Head with tiara right **Obv. Designer:** Ian Rank-Broadley **Rev:** Two koalas on a branch

Date	Mintage	F	VF	XF	Unc	BU
2001 Proof	275	Value: 475				

KM# 923 25 DOLLARS
7.7508 g., 0.9990 Platinum 0.2489 oz. APW **Ruler:** Elizabeth II **Obv:** Head with tiara right **Obv. Designer:** Ian Rank-Broadley **Rev:** Koala up a gum tree

Date	Mintage	F	VF	XF	Unc	BU
2002 Proof	275	Value: 475				

KM# 927 25 DOLLARS
7.7508 g., 0.9990 Platinum 0.2489 oz. APW **Ruler:** Elizabeth II **Obv:** Head with tiara right **Obv. Designer:** Ian Rank-Broadley **Rev:** Mother and baby koala

Date	Mintage	F	VF	XF	Unc	BU
2003 Proof	200	Value: 475				

KM# 932 25 DOLLARS
7.7508 g., 0.9990 Platinum 0.2489 oz. APW **Ruler:** Elizabeth II **Obv:** Head with tiara right **Obv. Designer:** Ian Rank-Broadley **Rev:** Single koala on branch

Date	Mintage	F	VF	XF	Unc	BU
2004 Proof	200	Value: 475				

KM# 936 25 DOLLARS
7.7508 g., 0.9990 Platinum 0.2489 oz. APW **Ruler:** Elizabeth II **Obv:** Head with tiara right **Obv. Designer:** Ian Rank-Broadley **Rev:** Single koala with gum leaves

Date	Mintage	F	VF	XF	Unc	BU
2005 Proof	200	Value: 475				

KM# 1112 30 DOLLARS
1000.0000 g., 0.9999 Silver 32.146 oz. ASW, 101 mm. **Ruler:** Elizabeth II **Rev:** Kola seated left on branch **Rev. Designer:** Darryl Bellotti

Date	Mintage	F	VF	XF	Unc	BU
2009P Prooflike	—	—	—	—	—	1,150

KM# 1369 30 DOLLARS
1000.0000 g., 0.9990 Silver 32.117 oz. ASW **Ruler:** Elizabeth II **Obv:** Head light **Rev:** Koala

Date	Mintage	F	VF	XF	Unc	BU
2010(p)	—	—	—	—	—	1,150

KM# 1466 30 DOLLARS
1000.0000 g., 0.9990 Silver 32.117 oz. ASW **Ruler:** Elizabeth II **Rev:** Koala on branch

Date	Mintage	F	VF	XF	Unc	BU
2010P	—	—	—	—	—	1,200

KM# 919 50 DOLLARS
15.5017 g., 0.9990 Platinum 0.4979 oz. APW **Ruler:** Elizabeth II **Obv:** Head with tiara right **Obv. Designer:** Ian Rank-Broadley **Rev:** Two koalas on a branch

Date	Mintage	F	VF	XF	Unc	BU
2001 Proof	350	Value: 950				

KM# 924 50 DOLLARS
15.5017 g., 0.9990 Platinum 0.4979 oz. APW **Ruler:** Elizabeth II **Obv:** Head with tiara right **Obv. Designer:** Ian Rank-Broadley **Rev:** Koala up a gum tree

Date	Mintage	F	VF	XF	Unc	BU
2002 Proof	350	Value: 950				

KM# 928 50 DOLLARS
15.5017 g., 0.9990 Platinum 0.4979 oz. APW **Ruler:** Elizabeth II **Obv:** Head with tiara right **Obv. Designer:** Ian Rank-Broadley **Rev:** Mother and baby koala

Date	Mintage	F	VF	XF	Unc	BU
2003 Proof	350	Value: 950				

KM# 933 50 DOLLARS
15.5017 g., 0.9990 Platinum 0.4979 oz. APW **Ruler:** Elizabeth II **Obv:** Head with tiara right **Obv. Designer:** Ian Rank-Broadley **Rev:** Single koala on branch

Date	Mintage	F	VF	XF	Unc	BU
2004 Proof	350	Value: 950				

KM# 937 50 DOLLARS
15.5017 g., 0.9990 Platinum 0.4979 oz. APW **Ruler:** Elizabeth II **Obv:** Head with tiara right **Obv. Designer:** Ian Rank-Broadley **Rev:** Single koala with gum leaves

Date	Mintage	F	VF	XF	Unc	BU
2005 Proof	350	Value: 950				

KM# 921 100 DOLLARS
31.1035 g., 0.9990 Platinum 0.9990 oz. APW **Ruler:** Elizabeth II **Obv:** Head with tiara right **Obv. Designer:** Ian Rank-Broadley **Rev:** Federation: Sir Henry Parkes, flag, parliament house, colored image

Date	Mintage	F	VF	XF	Unc	BU
2001 Proof	1,000	Value: 1,875				

KM# 930 100 DOLLARS
31.1035 g., 0.9990 Platinum 0.9990 oz. APW **Ruler:** Elizabeth II **Obv:** Head with tiara right **Obv. Designer:** Ian Rank-Broadley **Rev:** The Arts: Dancers, paint brushes, opera house, colored image

Date	Mintage	F	VF	XF	Unc	BU
2003 Proof	1,000	Value: 1,875				

KM# 742 100 DOLLARS
31.1035 g., 0.9995 Platinum 0.9995 oz. APW, 32.1 mm. **Ruler:** Elizabeth II **Obv:** Head with tiara right, denomination below **Obv. Designer:** Ian Rank-Broadley **Rev:** Sports: Australian sportsmen and women, colored image **Edge:** Reeded

Date	Mintage	F	VF	XF	Unc	BU
2004P Proof	1,000	Value: 1,875				

KM# 939 100 DOLLARS
31.1035 g., 0.9990 Platinum 0.9990 oz. APW **Ruler:** Elizabeth II **Obv:** Head with tiara right **Obv. Designer:** Ian Rank-Broadley **Rev:** Two workers and machine, colored image

Date	Mintage	F	VF	XF	Unc	BU
2005 Proof	1,000	Value: 1,875				

KM# 1469 100 DOLLARS
31.1050 g., 0.9990 Gold 0.9990 oz. AGW, 32.1 mm. **Ruler:** Elizabeth II **Rev:** Koala on branch

Date	Mintage	F	VF	XF	Unc	BU
2010P	—	—	—	—	—	1,500

KM# 920 200 DOLLARS
62.2140 g., 0.9990 Platinum 1.9981 oz. APW **Ruler:** Elizabeth II **Obv:** Head with tiara right **Obv. Designer:** Ian Rank-Broadley **Rev:** Two koalas sitting on branch

Date	Mintage	F	VF	XF	Unc	BU
2001	250	Value: 3,750				

KM# 925 200 DOLLARS
62.2140 g., 0.9990 Platinum 1.9981 oz. APW **Ruler:** Elizabeth II **Obv:** Head with tiara right **Obv. Designer:** Ian Rank-Broadley **Rev:** Koala up a gum tree

Date	Mintage	F	VF	XF	Unc	BU
2002 Proof	250	Value: 3,750				

KM# 929 200 DOLLARS
62.2140 g., 0.9990 Platinum 1.9981 oz. APW **Ruler:** Elizabeth II **Obv:** Head with tiara right **Obv. Designer:** Ian Rank-Broadley **Rev:** Mother and baby koala

Date	Mintage	F	VF	XF	Unc	BU
2003 Proof	200	Value: 3,750				

KM# 934 200 DOLLARS
62.2140 g., 0.9990 Platinum 1.9981 oz. APW **Ruler:** Elizabeth II **Obv:** Head with tiara right **Obv. Designer:** Ian Rank-Broadley **Rev:** Single koala on branch

Date	Mintage	F	VF	XF	Unc	BU
2004 Proof	200	Value: 3,750				

KM# 938 200 DOLLARS
62.2140 g., 0.9990 Platinum 1.9981 oz. APW **Ruler:** Elizabeth II **Obv:** Head with tiara right **Obv. Designer:** Ian Rank-Broadley **Rev:** Single koala with multicolor gum leaves

Date	Mintage	F	VF	XF	Unc	BU
2005 Proof	200	Value: 1,875				

KM# 1470 200 DOLLARS
62.2400 g., 0.9990 Gold 1.9990 oz. AGW **Ruler:** Elizabeth II **Rev:** Koala on branch

Date	Mintage	F	VF	XF	Unc	BU
2010P	—	—	—	—	—	2,950

BULLION - DISCOVER AUSTRALIA

KM# 940 DOLLAR
31.1035 g., 0.9990 Silver 0.9990 oz. ASW **Ruler:** Elizabeth II **Subject:** Australian Landmarks **Obv:** Head with tiara right **Obv. Designer:** Ian Rank-Broadley **Rev:** Melbourne

Date	Mintage	F	VF	XF	Unc	BU
2006 Proof	7,500	Value: 40.00				

KM# 941 DOLLAR
31.1035 g., 0.9990 Silver 0.9990 oz. ASW **Ruler:** Elizabeth II **Subject:** Australian Landmarks **Obv:** Head with tiara right **Obv. Designer:** Ian Rank-Broadley **Rev:** Uluru

Date	Mintage	F	VF	XF	Unc	BU
2006 Proof	7,500	Value: 40.00				

KM# 942 DOLLAR
31.1035 g., 0.9990 Silver 0.9990 oz. ASW **Ruler:** Elizabeth II **Subject:** Australian Landmarks **Obv:** Head with tiara right **Obv. Designer:** Ian Rank-Broadley **Rev:** Canberra

Date	Mintage	F	VF	XF	Unc	BU
2006 Proof	7,500	Value: 40.00				

KM# 943 DOLLAR
31.1035 g., 0.9990 Silver 0.9990 oz. ASW **Ruler:** Elizabeth II **Subject:** Australian Landmarks **Obv:** Head with tiara right **Obv. Designer:** Ian Rank-Broadley **Rev:** Perth

Date	Mintage	F	VF	XF	Unc	BU
2006 Proof	7,500	Value: 40.00				

KM# 944 DOLLAR
31.1035 g., 0.9990 Silver 0.9990 oz. ASW **Ruler:** Elizabeth II **Subject:** Australian Landmarks **Obv:** Head with tiara right **Obv. Designer:** Ian Rank-Broadley **Rev:** Great Barrier Reef

Date	Mintage	F	VF	XF	Unc	BU
2006 Proof	7,500	Value: 40.00				

KM# 1008 DOLLAR
31.1030 g., 0.9990 Silver 0.9989 oz. ASW, 40.5 mm. **Ruler:** Elizabeth II **Subject:** Quadricentennial **Obv:** Head with tiara right **Obv. Legend:** ELIZABETH II - AUSTRALIA **Obv. Designer:** Ian Rank-Broadley **Rev:** Sailing ship at left, early map at right **Rev. Legend:** Australia on the Map

Date	Mintage	F	VF	XF	Unc	BU
2006	—	—	—	—	—	40.00

KM# 949 DOLLAR
31.1035 g., 0.9990 Silver 0.9990 oz. ASW **Ruler:** Elizabeth II **Subject:** Australian Landmarks **Obv:** Head with tiara right **Obv. Designer:** Ian Rank-Broadley **Rev:** Sydney

Date	Mintage	F	VF	XF	Unc	BU
2007	7,500	Value: 60.00				

KM# 945 DOLLAR
31.1035 g., 0.9990 Silver 0.9990 oz. ASW **Ruler:** Elizabeth II **Subject:** Australian Landmarks **Obv:** Head with tiara right **Obv. Designer:** Ian Rank-Broadley **Rev:** Gold Coast

Date	Mintage	F	VF	XF	Unc	BU
2007 Proof	7,500	Value: 60.00				

KM# 946 DOLLAR
31.1035 g., 0.9990 Silver 0.9990 oz. ASW **Ruler:** Elizabeth II **Subject:** Australian Landmarks **Obv:** Head with tiara right **Obv. Designer:** Ian Rank-Broadley **Rev:** Phillip Island

Date	Mintage	F	VF	XF	Unc	BU
2007 Proof	7,500	Value: 60.00				

KM# 947 DOLLAR
31.1035 g., 0.9990 Silver 0.9990 oz. ASW **Ruler:** Elizabeth II **Subject:** Australian Landmarks **Obv:** Head with tiara right **Obv. Designer:** Ian Rank-Broadley **Rev:** Port Arthur

Date	Mintage	F	VF	XF	Unc	BU
2007 Proof	7,500	Value: 60.00				

KM# 948 DOLLAR
31.1035 g., 0.9990 Silver 0.9990 oz. ASW **Ruler:** Elizabeth II

Subject: Australian Landmarks **Obv:** Head with tiara right **Obv. Designer:** Ian Rank-Broadley **Rev:** Adelaide

Date	Mintage	F	VF	XF	Unc	BU
2007 Proof	7,500	Value: 60.00				

KM# 1021 DOLLAR

31.1050 g., 0.9990 Silver 0.9990 oz. ASW, 40 mm. **Ruler:** Elizabeth II **Subject:** Hobart **Rev:** Buildings and harbor **Rev. Legend:** DISCOVER AUSTRALIA

Date	Mintage	F	VF	XF	Unc	BU
2008P Proof	7,500	Value: 80.00				

KM# 1181 DOLLAR

31.1050 g., 0.9990 Silver 0.9990 oz. ASW, 40 mm. **Ruler:** Elizabeth II **Subject:** Darwin **Obv:** Head right **Obv. Designer:** Ian Rank-Broadley **Rev:** Harbor, multicolor **Rev. Legend:** DISCOVER AUSTRALIA

Date	Mintage	F	VF	XF	Unc	BU
2008P Proof	7,500	Value: 80.00				

KM# 1182 DOLLAR

31.1050 g., 0.9990 Silver 0.9990 oz. ASW, 40 mm. **Ruler:** Elizabeth II **Subject:** Kakadu **Obv:** Head right **Obv. Designer:** Ian Rank-Broadley **Rev:** Crocodile and multicolor **Rev. Legend:** DISCOVER AUSTRALIA

Date	Mintage	F	VF	XF	Unc	BU
2008P Proof	7,500	Value: 80.00				

KM# 1183 DOLLAR

31.1050 g., 0.9990 Silver 0.9990 oz. ASW **Ruler:** Elizabeth II **Subject:** Brisbane **Obv:** Head right **Obv. Designer:** Ian Rank-Broadley **Rev:** Bridge and view **Rev. Legend:** DISCOVER AUSTRALIA

Date	Mintage	F	VF	XF	Unc	BU
2008P Proof	7,500	Value: 80.00				

KM# 1184 DOLLAR

31.1050 g., 0.9990 Silver 0.9990 oz. ASW **Ruler:** Elizabeth II **Subject:** Broome **Obv:** Head right **Obv. Designer:** Ian Rank-Broadley **Rev:** Seascape, pearls and multicolor **Rev. Legend:** DISCOVER AUSTRALIA

Date	Mintage	F	VF	XF	Unc	BU
2008P Proof	7,500	Value: 80.00				

KM# 1185 DOLLAR

31.1050 g., 0.9990 Silver 0.9990 oz. ASW **Ruler:** Elizabeth II **Subject:** Sydney **Obv:** Head right **Obv. Designer:** Ian Rank-Broadley **Rev:** Opera House, Harbor Bridge and multicolor **Rev. Legend:** DISCOVER AUSTRALIA

Date	Mintage	F	VF	XF	Unc	BU
2008P Proof	7,500	Value: 80.00				

KM# 1188 DOLLAR

1.2400 g., 0.9990 Gold 0.0398 oz. AGW, 14 mm. **Ruler:** Elizabeth II **Obv:** Head right **Obv. Designer:** Ian Rank-Broadley **Rev:** Brolga **Rev. Legend:** DISCOVER AUSTRALIA

Date	Mintage	F	VF	XF	Unc	BU
2008P Proof	25,000	Value: 100				

KM# 1103 DOLLAR

31.1050 g., 0.9990 Silver 0.9990 oz. ASW, 27x47 mm. **Ruler:** Elizabeth II **Rev:** Turtle Dreaming **Rev. Designer:** Darryl Bellotti **Shape:** Rectangle

Date	Mintage	F	VF	XF	Unc	BU
2009 Proof	—	Value: 75.00				

KM# 1107 DOLLAR

31.1050 g., 0.9999 Silver 0.9999 oz. ASW, 27x47 mm. **Ruler:** Elizabeth II **Rev:** Kangaroo dreaming **Rev. Designer:** Darryl Bellotti **Shape:** Vertical rectangle

Date	Mintage	F	VF	XF	Unc	BU
2009 Proof	—	Value: 75.00				

KM# 1212 DOLLAR

31.1050 g., 0.9990 Silver 0.9990 oz. ASW, 40.6 mm. **Ruler:** Elizabeth II **Obv:** Head right **Obv. Designer:** Ian Rank-Broadley **Rev:** Dreaming kangaroo, multicolor **Rev. Legend:** DISCOVER AUSTRALIA **Rev. Designer:** Darryl Bellotti

Date	Mintage	F	VF	XF	Unc	BU
2009P Proof	10,000	Value: 90.00				

KM# 1213 DOLLAR

31.1050 g., 0.9990 Silver 0.9990 oz. ASW **Ruler:** Elizabeth II **Obv:** Head right **Obv. Designer:** Ian Rank-Broadley **Rev:** Dreaming dolphin, multicolor **Rev. Legend:** DISCOVER AUSTRALIA **Rev. Designer:** Darryl Bellotti **Shape:** 40.6

Date	Mintage	F	VF	XF	Unc	BU
2009P Proof	10,000	Value: 90.00				

KM# 1214 DOLLAR

31.1050 g., 0.9990 Silver 0.9990 oz. ASW, 40.6 mm. **Ruler:** Elizabeth II **Obv:** Head right **Obv. Designer:** Ian Rank-Broadley **Rev:** Dreaming king brown snake, multicolor **Rev. Legend:** DISCOVER AUSTRALIA **Rev. Designer:** Darryl Bellotti

Date	Mintage	F	VF	XF	Unc	BU
2009P Proof	10,000	Value: 90.00				

KM# 1215 DOLLAR

31.1050 g., 0.9990 Silver 0.9990 oz. ASW, 40.6 mm. **Ruler:** Elizabeth II **Obv:** Head right **Obv. Designer:** Ian Rank-Broadley **Rev:** Dreaming brolga, multicolor **Rev. Designer:** Darryl Berllotti

Date	Mintage	F	VF	XF	Unc	BU
2009P Proof	10,000	Value: 90.00				

KM# 1216 DOLLAR

31.1050 g., 0.9990 Silver 0.9990 oz. ASW, 40.6 mm. **Ruler:** Elizabeth II **Obv:** Head right **Obv. Designer:** Ian Rank-Broadley **Rev:** Dreaming echidna, multicolor **Rev. Designer:** Darryl Berllotti

Date	Mintage	F	VF	XF	Unc	BU
2009P Proof	10,000	Value: 90.00				

KM# 1218 DOLLAR

1.2500 g., 0.9990 Gold 0.0401 oz. AGW, 14 mm. **Ruler:** Elizabeth II **Obv:** Head right **Obv. Designer:** Ian Rank-Broadley **Rev:** Dreaming dolphin **Rev. Designer:** Darryl Berttolli

Date	Mintage	F	VF	XF	Unc	BU
2009P Proof	25,000	Value: 125				

KM# 1222 DOLLAR

3.1100 g., 0.9990 Gold 0.0999 oz. AGW, 16 mm. **Ruler:** Elizabeth II **Obv:** Head right **Obv. Designer:** Ian Rank-Broadley **Rev:** Dreaming kangaroo **Rev. Designer:** Darryl Berttolli

Date	Mintage	F	VF	XF	Unc	BU
2009P Proof	2,500	Value: 175				

KM# 1242 DOLLAR

31.1050 g., 0.9990 Silver 0.9990 oz. ASW, 40.6 mm. **Ruler:** Elizabeth II **Subject:** Treasures of Australia **Obv:** Head right **Obv. Designer:** Ian Rank-Broadley **Rev:** Mountains **Note:** Insert container with 1 carat of diamonds.

Date	Mintage	F	VF	XF	Unc	BU
2009P Proof	7,500	Value: 110				

KM# 1403 DOLLAR

31.1050 g., 0.9990 Silver 0.9990 oz. ASW, 40.6 mm. **Ruler:** Elizabeth II **Obv:** Head right **Rev:** Frill-neck lizard, multicolor

Date	Mintage	F	VF	XF	Unc	BU
2010(p) Proof	—	Value: 90.00				

KM# 1409 DOLLAR

31.1050 g., 0.9990 Silver 0.9990 oz. ASW, 40.6 mm. **Ruler:** Elizabeth II **Obv:** Head right **Obv. Designer:** Ian Rank Broadley **Rev:** Koala and multicolor

Date	Mintage	F	VF	XF	Unc	BU
2010(p) Proof	—	Value: 90.00				

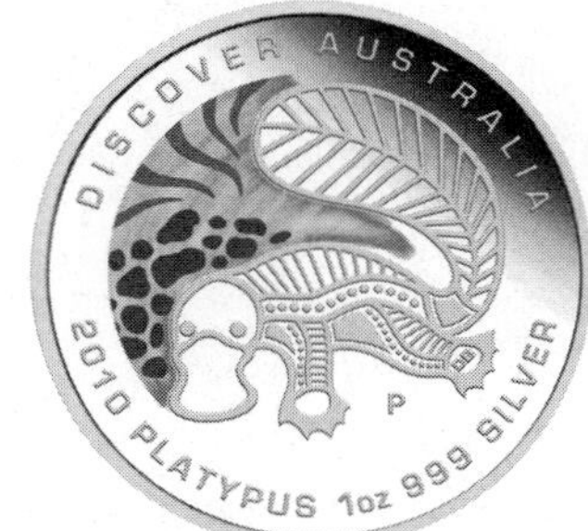

KM# 1415 DOLLAR

31.1050 g., 0.9990 Silver 0.9990 oz. ASW, 40.6 mm. **Ruler:** Elizabeth II **Obv:** Head right **Obv. Designer:** Ian Rank Broadley **Rev:** Multicolor platypus

Date	Mintage	F	VF	XF	Unc	BU
2010(p) Proof	—	Value: 90.00				

KM# 1421 DOLLAR

31.1050 g., 0.9990 Silver 0.9990 oz. ASW, 40.6 mm. **Ruler:** Elizabeth II **Obv:** Head right **Obv. Designer:** Ian Rank Broadley **Rev:** Multicolor saltwater crocodile

Date	Mintage	F	VF	XF	Unc	BU
2010(p) Proof	—	Value: 90.00				

KM# 1427 DOLLAR

31.1050 g., 0.9990 Silver 0.9990 oz. ASW, 40.6 mm. **Ruler:** Elizabeth II **Obv:** Head right **Obv. Designer:** Ian Rank Broadley **Rev:** Multicolor wombat

Date	Mintage	F	VF	XF	Unc	BU
2010(p) Proof	—	Value: 90.00				

KM# 1453 DOLLAR

31.1050 g., 0.9990 Silver 0.9990 oz. ASW, 27x47 mm. **Ruler:** Elizabeth II **Rev:** Dreaming dolphin **Shape:** Vertical rectangle

Date	Mintage	F	VF	XF	Unc	BU
2010P Proof	—	—	—	—	—	80.00

KM# 950 5 DOLLARS

1.2441 g., 0.9990 Gold 0.0400 oz. AGW **Ruler:** Elizabeth II **Subject:** Australian Fauna **Obv:** Head with tiara right **Obv. Designer:** Ian Rank-Broadley **Rev:** Saltwater crocodile

Date	Mintage	F	VF	XF	Unc	BU
2006 Proof	25,000	Value: 95.00				

KM# 953 5 DOLLARS

1.2441 g., 0.9990 Gold 0.0400 oz. AGW **Ruler:** Elizabeth II **Subject:** Australian Fauna **Obv:** Head with tiara right **Obv. Designer:** Ian Rank-Broadley **Rev:** Grey kangaroo

Date	Mintage	F	VF	XF	Unc	BU
2006 Proof	25,000	Value: 95.00				

KM# 956 5 DOLLARS

1.2441 g., 0.9990 Gold 0.0400 oz. AGW **Ruler:** Elizabeth II **Subject:** Australian Fauna **Obv:** Head with tiara right **Obv. Designer:** Ian Rank-Broadley **Rev:** Emu

Date	Mintage	F	VF	XF	Unc	BU
2006 Proof	25,000	Value: 75.00				

KM# 959 5 DOLLARS

1.2441 g., 0.9990 Gold 0.0400 oz. AGW **Ruler:** Elizabeth II **Subject:** Australian Fauna **Obv:** Head with tiara right **Obv. Designer:** Ian Rank-Broadley **Rev:** Koala

Date	Mintage	F	VF	XF	Unc	BU
2006 Proof	25,000	Value: 95.00				

KM# 962 5 DOLLARS

1.2441 g., 0.9990 Gold 0.0400 oz. AGW **Ruler:** Elizabeth II **Subject:** Australian Fauna **Obv:** Head with tiara right **Obv. Designer:** Ian Rank-Broadley **Rev:** Kookaburra

Date	Mintage	F	VF	XF	Unc	BU
2006 Proof	25,000	Value: 95.00				

KM# 965 5 DOLLARS

1.2441 g., 0.9990 Gold 0.0400 oz. AGW **Ruler:** Elizabeth II **Subject:** Australian Fauna **Obv:** Head with tiara right **Obv. Designer:** Ian Rank-Broadley **Rev:** Echidna

Date	Mintage	F	VF	XF	Unc	BU
2007 Proof	25,000	Value: 95.00				

KM# 968 5 DOLLARS

1.2441 g., 0.9990 Gold 0.0400 oz. AGW **Ruler:** Elizabeth II **Subject:** Australian Fauna **Obv:** Head with tiara right **Obv. Designer:** Ian Rank-Broadley **Rev:** Common wombat

Date	Mintage	F	VF	XF	Unc	BU
2007 Proof	25,000	Value: 95.00				

KM# 971 5 DOLLARS

1.2441 g., 0.9990 Gold 0.0400 oz. AGW **Ruler:** Elizabeth II **Subject:** Australian Fauna **Obv:** Head with tiara right **Obv. Designer:** Ian Rank-Broadley **Rev:** Tasmanian devil

Date	Mintage	F	VF	XF	Unc	BU
2007 Proof	25,000	Value: 95.00				

KM# 974 5 DOLLARS

1.2441 g., 0.9990 Gold 0.0400 oz. AGW **Ruler:** Elizabeth II **Subject:** Australian Fauna **Obv:** Head with tiara right **Obv. Designer:** Ian Rank-Broadley **Rev:** Great white shark

Date	Mintage	F	VF	XF	Unc	BU
2007 Proof	25,000	Value: 95.00				

KM# 977 5 DOLLARS

1.2441 g., 0.9990 Gold 0.0400 oz. AGW **Ruler:** Elizabeth II **Subject:** Australian Fauna **Obv:** Head with tiara right **Obv. Designer:** Ian Rank-Broadley **Rev:** Platypus

Date	Mintage	F	VF	XF	Unc	BU
2007 Proof	25,000	Value: 95.00				

KM# 1217 5 DOLLARS

1.2500 g., 0.9990 Gold 0.0401 oz. AGW, 14 mm. **Ruler:** Elizabeth II **Obv:** Head right **Obv. Designer:** Ian Rank-Broadley **Rev:** Dreaming kangaroo **Rev. Designer:** Darryl Berllotti

Date	Mintage	F	VF	XF	Unc	BU
2009P Proof	25,000	Value: 125				

KM# 1219 5 DOLLARS

1.2500 g., 0.9990 Gold 0.0401 oz. AGW, 14 mm. **Ruler:** Elizabeth II **Obv:** Head right **Obv. Designer:** Ian Rank-Broadley **Rev:** Dreaming king brown snake **Rev. Designer:** Darryl Berttolli

Date	Mintage	F	VF	XF	Unc	BU
2009P Proof	25,000	Value: 125				

KM# 1220 5 DOLLARS

1.2500 g., 0.9990 Gold 0.0401 oz. AGW, 14 mm. **Ruler:** Elizabeth II **Obv:** Head right **Obv. Designer:** Ian Rank-Broadley **Rev:** Dreaming brolga **Rev. Designer:** Darryl Berttolli

Date	Mintage	F	VF	XF	Unc	BU
2009P Proof	25,000	Value: 125				

KM# 1221 5 DOLLARS

1.2500 g., 0.9990 Gold 0.0401 oz. AGW, 14 mm. **Ruler:** Elizabeth II **Obv:** Head right **Obv. Designer:** Ian Rank-Broadley **Rev:** Dreaming echidna **Rev. Designer:** Darryl Berttolli

Date	Mintage	F	VF	XF	Unc	BU
2009P Proof	25,000	Value: 125				

KM# 1224 5 DOLLARS

3.1100 g., 0.9990 Gold 0.0999 oz. AGW, 14 mm. **Ruler:** Elizabeth II **Obv:** Head right **Obv. Designer:** Ian Rank-Broadley **Rev:** Dreaming brown snake **Rev. Designer:** Darryl Berttolli

Date	Mintage	F	VF	XF	Unc	BU
2009P Proof	2,500	Value: 175				

KM# 1402 5 DOLLARS

1.2400 g., 0.9990 Gold 0.0398 oz. AGW, 14 mm. **Ruler:** Elizabeth II **Obv:** Head right **Obv. Designer:** Ian Rank Broadley **Rev:** Frill-neck lizard

Date	Mintage	F	VF	XF	Unc	BU
2010(p) Proof	25,000	Value: 130				

KM# 1408 5 DOLLARS

1.2400 g., 0.9990 Gold 0.0398 oz. AGW, 14 mm. **Ruler:** Elizabeth II **Obv:** Head right **Obv. Designer:** Ian Rank Broadley **Rev:** Koala

Date	Mintage	F	VF	XF	Unc	BU
2010(p) Proof	25,000	Value: 130				

KM# 1414 5 DOLLARS

1.2400 g., 0.9990 Gold 0.0398 oz. AGW, 14 mm. **Ruler:** Elizabeth II **Obv:** Head right **Obv. Designer:** Ian Rank Broadley **Rev:** Platypus

Date	Mintage	F	VF	XF	Unc	BU
2010(p) Proof	25,000	Value: 130				

KM# 1420 5 DOLLARS

1.2400 g., 0.9990 Gold 0.0398 oz. AGW, 14 mm. **Ruler:** Elizabeth II **Obv:** Head right **Obv. Designer:** Ian Rank Broadley **Rev:** Saltwater crocodile

Date	Mintage	F	VF	XF	Unc	BU
2010(p) Proof	25,000	Value: 130				

KM# 1426 5 DOLLARS

1.2400 g., 0.9990 Gold 0.0398 oz. AGW, 14 mm. **Ruler:** Elizabeth II **Obv:** Head right **Obv. Designer:** Ian Rank Broadley **Rev:** Wombat

Date	Mintage	F	VF	XF	Unc	BU
2010(p) Proof	25,000	Value: 130				

KM# 1118 10 DOLLARS

1.2400 g., 0.9990 Gold 0.0398 oz. AGW, 14 mm. **Ruler:** Elizabeth II **Obv:** Bust right **Obv. Designer:** Ian Rank-Broadley **Rev:** Saltwater crocodile **Rev. Legend:** DISCOVER AUSTRALIA

Date	Mintage	F	VF	XF	Unc	BU
2006P Proof	25,000	Value: 100				

KM# 1119 10 DOLLARS

1.2400 g., 0.9990 Gold 0.0398 oz. AGW, 14 mm. **Ruler:** Elizabeth II **Obv:** Head right **Obv. Designer:** Ian Rank-Broadley **Rev:** Grey kangaroo **Rev. Legend:** DISCOVER AUSTRALIA

Date	Mintage	F	VF	XF	Unc	BU
2006P Proof	25,000	Value: 100				

KM# 1120 10 DOLLARS

1.2400 g., 0.9990 Gold 0.0398 oz. AGW, 14 mm. **Ruler:** Elizabeth II **Obv:** Head right **Obv. Designer:** Ian Rank-Broadley **Rev:** Emu **Rev. Legend:** DISCOVER AUSTRALIA

Date	Mintage	F	VF	XF	Unc	BU
2006P Proof	25,000	Value: 100				

KM# 1121 10 DOLLARS

1.2400 g., 0.9990 Gold 0.0398 oz. AGW, 14 mm. **Ruler:** Elizabeth II **Obv:** Head right **Obv. Designer:** Ian Rank-Broadley **Rev:** Koala **Rev. Legend:** DISCOVER AUSTRALIA

Date	Mintage	F	VF	XF	Unc	BU
2006P Proof	25,000	Value: 100				

KM# 1122 10 DOLLARS

1.2400 g., 0.9990 Gold 0.0398 oz. AGW, 14 mm. **Ruler:** Elizabeth II **Obv:** Head right **Obv. Designer:** Ian Rank-Broadley **Rev:** Kookaburra **Rev. Legend:** DISCOVER AUSTRALIA

Date	Mintage	F	VF	XF	Unc	BU
2006P Proof	25,000	Value: 100				

KM# 1133 10 DOLLARS

3.1000 g., 0.9990 Platinum 0.0996 oz. APW, 16 mm. **Ruler:** Elizabeth II **Obv:** Head right **Obv. Designer:** Ian rank-Broadley **Rev:** Cooktown orchid, multicolor **Rev. Legend:** DISCOVER AUSTRALIA

Date	Mintage	F	VF	XF	Unc	BU
2006P Proof	2,500	Value: 325				

KM# 1134 10 DOLLARS

3.1000 g., 0.9990 Platinum 0.0996 oz. APW, 16 mm. **Ruler:** Elizabeth II **Obv:** Head right **Obv. Designer:** Ian Rank-Broadley **Rev:** Sturt's desert rose, multicolor **Rev. Legend:** DISCOVER AUSTRALIA

Date	Mintage	F	VF	XF	Unc	BU
2006P Proof	2,500	Value: 325				

KM# 1135 10 DOLLARS

3.1000 g., 0.9990 Platinum 0.0996 oz. APW, 16 mm. **Ruler:** Elizabeth II **Obv:** Head right **Obv. Designer:** Ian Rank-Broadley **Rev:** Royal Bluebell, multicolor **Rev. Legend:** DISCOVER AUSTRALIA

Date	Mintage	F	VF	XF	Unc	BU
2006P Proof	2,500	Value: 325				

KM# 1136 10 DOLLARS

3.1000 g., 0.9990 Platinum 0.0996 oz. APW, 16 mm. **Ruler:** Elizabeth II **Obv:** Head right **Obv. Designer:** Ian Rank-Broadley **Rev:** Red and green kangaroo paw, multicolor **Rev. Legend:** DISCOVER AUSTRALIA

Date	Mintage	F	VF	XF	Unc	BU
2006P Proof	2,500	Value: 325				

KM# 1137 10 DOLLARS

3.1000 g., 0.9990 Platinum 0.0996 oz. APW, 16 mm. **Ruler:** Elizabeth II **Obv:** Head right **Obv. Designer:** Ian Rank-Broadley **Rev:** Common pink heath, multicolor **Rev. Legend:** DISCOVER AUSTRALIA

Date	Mintage	F	VF	XF	Unc	BU
2006P Proof	2,500	Value: 325				

KM# 1143 10 DOLLARS

1.2400 g., 0.9990 Gold 0.0398 oz. AGW, 14 mm. **Ruler:** Elizabeth II **Obv:** Head right **Obv. Designer:** Ian Rank-Broadley **Rev:** Echidna **Rev. Legend:** DISCOVER AUSTRALIA

Date	Mintage	F	VF	XF	Unc	BU
2007P Proof	25,000	Value: 100				

KM# 1144 10 DOLLARS

1.2400 g., 0.9990 Gold 0.0398 oz. AGW, 14 mm. **Ruler:**

Elizabeth II **Obv:** Head right **Obv. Designer:** Ian rank-Broadley **Rev:** Common wombat **Rev. Legend:** DISCOVER AUSTRALIA

Date	Mintage	F	VF	XF	Unc	BU
2007P Proof	25,000	Value: 100				

KM# 1145 10 DOLLARS

1.2400 g., 0.9990 Gold 0.0398 oz. AGW, 14 mm. **Ruler:** Elizabeth II **Obv:** Head right **Obv. Designer:** Ian Rank-Broadley **Rev:** Tasmanian devil **Rev. Legend:** DISCOVER AUSTRALIA

Date	Mintage	F	VF	XF	Unc	BU
2007P Proof	25,000	Value: 100				

KM# 1146 10 DOLLARS

1.2400 g., 0.9990 Gold 0.0398 oz. AGW, 14 mm. **Ruler:** Elizabeth II **Obv:** Head right **Obv. Designer:** Ian Rank-Broadley **Rev:** Great white shark **Rev. Legend:** DISCOVER AUSTRALIA

Date	Mintage	F	VF	XF	Unc	BU
2007P Proof	25,000	Value: 100				

KM# 1147 10 DOLLARS

1.2400 g., 0.9990 Gold 0.0398 oz. AGW, 14 mm. **Ruler:** Elizabeth II **Obv:** Head right **Obv. Designer:** Ian Rank-Broadley **Rev:** Platypus **Rev. Legend:** DISCOVER AUSTRALIA

Date	Mintage	F	VF	XF	Unc	BU
2007P Proof	25,000	Value: 100				

KM# 1159 10 DOLLARS

3.1000 g., 0.9990 Platinum 0.0996 oz. APW, 16 mm. **Ruler:** Elizabeth II **Obv:** Head right **Obv. Designer:** Ian Rank-Broadley **Rev:** Sturt's desert pea, multicolor **Rev. Legend:** DISCOVER AUSTRALIA

Date	Mintage	F	VF	XF	Unc	BU
2007P Proof	2,500	Value: 325				

KM# 1160 10 DOLLARS

3.1000 g., 0.9990 Platinum 0.0996 oz. APW, 16 mm. **Ruler:** Elizabeth II **Obv:** Head right **Obv. Designer:** Ian rank-Broadley **Rev:** Tasmanian bluegum, multicolor **Rev. Legend:** DISCOVER AUSTRALIA

Date	Mintage	F	VF	XF	Unc	BU
2007P Proof	2,500	Value: 325				

KM# 1161 10 DOLLARS

3.1000 g., 0.9990 Platinum 0.0996 oz. APW, 16 mm. **Ruler:** Elizabeth II **Obv:** Head right **Obv. Designer:** Ian Rank-Broadley **Rev:** Waratah, multicolor **Rev. Legend:** DISCOVER AUSTRALIA

Date	Mintage	F	VF	XF	Unc	BU
2007P Proof	2,500	Value: 325				

KM# 1162 10 DOLLARS

3.1000 g., 0.9990 Platinum 0.0996 oz. APW, 16 mm. **Ruler:** Elizabeth II **Obv:** Head right **Obv. Designer:** Ian Rank-Broadley **Rev:** Golden wattle, multicolor **Rev. Legend:** DISCOVER AUSTRALIA

Date	Mintage	F	VF	XF	Unc	BU
2007P Proof	2,500	Value: 325				

KM# 1186 10 DOLLARS

1.2400 g., 0.9990 Gold 0.0398 oz. AGW, 14 mm. **Ruler:** Elizabeth II **Obv:** Head right **Obv. Designer:** Ian Rank-Broadley **Rev:** Dolphin **Rev. Legend:** DISCOVER AUSTRALIA

Date	Mintage	F	VF	XF	Unc	BU
2008P Proof	25,000	Value: 100				

KM# 1187 10 DOLLARS

1.2400 g., 0.9990 Gold 0.0398 oz. AGW, 14 mm. **Ruler:** Elizabeth II **Obv:** Head right **Obv. Designer:** Ian Rank-Broadley **Rev:** King brown snake **Rev. Legend:** DISCOVER AUSTRALIA

Date	Mintage	F	VF	XF	Unc	BU
2008P Proof	25,000	Value: 100				

KM# 1189 10 DOLLARS

1.2400 g., 0.9990 Gold 0.0398 oz. AGW, 14 mm. **Ruler:** Elizabeth II **Obv:** Head right **Obv. Designer:** Ian Rank-Broadley **Rev:** Dingo **Rev. Legend:** DISCOVER AUSTRALIA

Date	Mintage	F	VF	XF	Unc	BU
2008P Proof	25,000	Value: 100				

KM# 1190 10 DOLLARS

1.2400 g., 0.9990 Gold 0.0398 oz. AGW, 14 mm. **Ruler:** Elizabeth II **Obv:** Head right **Obv. Designer:** Ian Rank-Broadley **Rev:** Frill-neck lizard **Rev. Legend:** DISCOVER AUSTRALIA

Date	Mintage	F	VF	XF	Unc	BU
2008P Proof	25,000	Value: 100				

KM# 1201 10 DOLLARS

3.1000 g., 0.9990 Platinum 0.0996 oz. APW, 16 mm. **Ruler:** Elizabeth II **Obv:** Head right **Obv. Designer:** Ian Rank-Broadley **Rev:** Black anther fax lilly, multicolor **Rev. Legend:** DISCOVER AUSTRALIA

Date	Mintage	F	VF	XF	Unc	BU
2008P Proof	2,500	Value: 325				

KM# 1202 10 DOLLARS

3.1000 g., 0.9990 Platinum 0.0996 oz. APW, 16 mm. **Ruler:** Elizabeth II **Obv:** Head right **Obv. Designer:** Ian Rank-Broadley **Rev:** Native frangipani, multicolor **Rev. Legend:** DISCOVER AUSTRALIA

Date	Mintage	F	VF	XF	Unc	BU
2008P Proof	2,500	Value: 325				

KM# 1203 10 DOLLARS

3.1000 g., 0.9990 Platinum 0.0996 oz. APW, 16 mm. **Ruler:** Elizabeth II **Obv:** Head right **Obv. Designer:** DISCOVER AUSTRALIA **Rev:** Geraldton wax, multicolor **Rev. Designer:** Ian Rank-Broadley

Date	Mintage	F	VF	XF	Unc	BU
2008P Proof	2,500	Value: 325				

KM# 1204 10 DOLLARS

3.1000 g., 0.9990 Platinum 0.0996 oz. APW, 16 mm. **Ruler:** Elizabeth II **Obv:** Head right **Obv. Designer:** Ian Rank-Broadley **Rev:** Red-flowered kurrajong, multicolor **Rev. Legend:** DISCOVER AUSTRALIA

Date	Mintage	F	VF	XF	Unc	BU
2008P Proof	2,500	Value: 325				

KM# 1205 10 DOLLARS

3.1000 g., 0.9990 Platinum 0.0996 oz. APW, 16 mm. **Ruler:** Elizabeth II **Obv:** Head right **Obv. Designer:** Ian Rank-Broadley **Rev:** Small-leaf lilly pilly, multicolor **Rev. Legend:** DISCOVER AUSTRALIA

Date	Mintage	F	VF	XF	Unc	BU
2008P Proof	2,500	Value: 325				

KM# 1206 10 DOLLARS

15.5500 g., 0.9990 Gold 0.4994 oz. AGW, 26 mm. **Ruler:** Elizabeth II **Obv:** Head right **Obv. Designer:** Ian Rank-Broadley **Rev:** Black anther flax lilly, multicolor **Rev. Legend:** DISCOVER AUSTRALIA

Date	Mintage	F	VF	XF	Unc	BU
2008P Proof	1,000	Value: 1,500				

KM# 980 15 DOLLARS

3.1101 g., 0.9990 Platinum 0.0999 oz. APW **Ruler:** Elizabeth II **Subject:** Australian Flora **Obv:** Head with tiara right **Obv. Designer:** Ian Rank-Broadley **Rev:** Cooktown orchid

Date	Mintage	F	VF	XF	Unc	BU
2006 Proof	2,500	Value: 220				

KM# 982 15 DOLLARS

3.1101 g., 0.9990 Platinum 0.0999 oz. APW **Ruler:** Elizabeth II **Subject:** Australian Flora **Obv:** Head with tiara right **Obv. Designer:** Ian Rank-Broadley **Rev:** Sturt's desert rose

Date	Mintage	F	VF	XF	Unc	BU
2006 Proof	2,500	Value: 220				

KM# 984 15 DOLLARS

3.1101 g., 0.9990 Platinum 0.0999 oz. APW **Ruler:** Elizabeth II **Subject:** Australian Flora **Obv:** Head with tiara right **Obv. Designer:** Ian Rank-Broadley **Rev:** Royal bluebell

Date	Mintage	F	VF	XF	Unc	BU
2006 Proof	2,500	Value: 220				

KM# 986 15 DOLLARS

3.1101 g., 0.9990 Platinum 0.0999 oz. APW **Ruler:** Elizabeth II **Subject:** Australian Flora **Obv:** Head with tiara right **Obv. Designer:** Ian Rank-Broadley **Rev:** Kangaroo paw

Date	Mintage	F	VF	XF	Unc	BU
2006 Proof	2,500	Value: 220				

KM# 988 15 DOLLARS

3.1101 g., 0.9990 Platinum 0.0999 oz. APW **Ruler:** Elizabeth II **Subject:** Australian Flora **Obv:** Head with tiara right **Obv. Designer:** Ian Rank-Broadley **Rev:** Common pink heath

Date	Mintage	F	VF	XF	Unc	BU
2006 Proof	2,500	Value: 220				

KM# 951 15 DOLLARS

3.1101 g., 0.9990 Gold 0.0999 oz. AGW **Ruler:** Elizabeth II **Subject:** Australian Fauna **Obv:** Head with tiara right **Obv. Designer:** Ian Rank-Broadley **Rev:** Saltwater crocodile

Date	Mintage	F	VF	XF	Unc	BU
2006 Proof	2,500	Value: 175				

KM# 954 15 DOLLARS

3.1101 g., 0.9990 Gold 0.0999 oz. AGW **Ruler:** Elizabeth II **Subject:** Australian Fauna **Obv:** Head with tiara right **Obv. Designer:** Ian Rank-Broadley **Rev:** Grey kangaroo

Date	Mintage	F	VF	XF	Unc	BU
2006 Proof	2,500	Value: 175				

KM# 957 15 DOLLARS

3.1101 g., 0.9990 Gold 0.0999 oz. AGW **Ruler:** Elizabeth II **Subject:** Australian Fauna **Obv:** Head with tiara right **Obv. Designer:** Ian Rank-Broadley **Rev:** Emu

Date	Mintage	F	VF	XF	Unc	BU
2006 Proof	2,500	Value: 175				

KM# 960 15 DOLLARS

3.1101 g., 0.9990 Gold 0.0999 oz. AGW **Ruler:** Elizabeth II **Subject:** Australian Fauna **Obv:** Head with tiara right **Obv. Designer:** Ian Rank-Broadley **Rev:** Koala

Date	Mintage	F	VF	XF	Unc	BU
2006 Proof	2,500	Value: 175				

KM# 963 15 DOLLARS

3.1101 g., 0.9990 Gold 0.0999 oz. AGW **Ruler:** Elizabeth II **Subject:** Australian Fauna **Obv:** Head with tiara right **Obv. Designer:** Ian Rank-Broadley **Rev:** Kookaburra

Date	Mintage	F	VF	XF	Unc	BU
2006 Proof	2,500	Value: 175				

KM# 966 15 DOLLARS

3.1101 g., 0.9990 Gold 0.0999 oz. AGW **Ruler:** Elizabeth II **Subject:** Australian Fauna **Obv:** Head with tiara right **Obv. Designer:** Ian Rank-Broadley **Rev:** Echidna

Date	Mintage	F	VF	XF	Unc	BU
2007 Proof	2,500	Value: 175				

KM# 969 15 DOLLARS

3.1101 g., 0.9990 Gold 0.0999 oz. AGW **Ruler:** Elizabeth II **Subject:** Australian Fauna **Obv:** Head with tiara right **Obv. Designer:** Ian Rank-Broadley **Rev:** Common wombat

Date	Mintage	F	VF	XF	Unc	BU
2007 Proof	2,500	Value: 175				

KM# 972 15 DOLLARS

3.1101 g., 0.9990 Gold 0.0999 oz. AGW **Ruler:** Elizabeth II **Subject:** Australian Fauna **Obv:** Head with tiara right **Obv. Designer:** Ian Rank-Broadley **Rev:** Tasmanian devil

Date	Mintage	F	VF	XF	Unc	BU
2007 Proof	2,500	Value: 175				

KM# 975 15 DOLLARS

3.1101 g., 0.9990 Gold 0.0999 oz. AGW **Ruler:** Elizabeth II **Subject:** Australian Fauna **Obv:** Head with tiara right **Obv. Designer:** Ian Rank-Broadley **Rev:** Great white shark

Date	Mintage	F	VF	XF	Unc	BU
2007 Proof	2,500	Value: 175				

KM# 978 15 DOLLARS

3.1101 g., 0.9990 Gold 0.0999 oz. AGW **Ruler:** Elizabeth II **Subject:** Australian Fauna **Obv:** Head with tiara right **Obv. Designer:** Ian Rank-Broadley **Rev:** Platypus

Date	Mintage	F	VF	XF	Unc	BU
2007 Proof	2,500	Value: 175				

KM# 990 15 DOLLARS

3.1101 g., 0.9990 Platinum 0.0999 oz. APW **Ruler:** Elizabeth II **Subject:** Australian Flora **Obv:** Head with tiara right **Obv. Designer:** Ian Rank-Broadley **Rev:** Anemone buttercup

Date	Mintage	F	VF	XF	Unc	BU
2007 Proof	2,500	Value: 220				

KM# 992 15 DOLLARS

3.1101 g., 0.9990 Platinum 0.0999 oz. APW **Ruler:** Elizabeth II **Subject:** Australian Flora **Obv:** Head with tiara right **Obv. Designer:** Ian Rank-Broadley **Rev:** Sturt's desert pea

Date	Mintage	F	VF	XF	Unc	BU
2007 Proof	2,500	Value: 220				

KM# 994 15 DOLLARS

3.1101 g., 0.9990 Platinum 0.0999 oz. APW **Ruler:** Elizabeth II **Subject:** Australian Flora **Obv:** Head with tiara right **Obv. Designer:** Ian Rank-Broadley **Rev:** Tasmanian bluegum

Date	Mintage	F	VF	XF	Unc	BU
2007 Proof	2,500	Value: 220				

KM# 996 15 DOLLARS

3.1101 g., 0.9990 Platinum 0.0999 oz. APW **Ruler:** Elizabeth II **Subject:** Australian Flora **Obv:** Head with tiara right **Obv. Designer:** Ian Rank-Broadley **Rev:** Waratah

Date	Mintage	F	VF	XF	Unc	BU
2007 Proof	2,500	Value: 220				

KM# 998 15 DOLLARS

3.1101 g., 0.9990 Platinum 0.0999 oz. APW **Ruler:** Elizabeth II **Subject:** Australian Flora **Obv:** Head with tiara right **Obv. Designer:** Ian Rank-Broadley **Rev:** Golden wattle

Date	Mintage	F	VF	XF	Unc	BU
2007 Proof	2,500	Value: 220				

KM# 1104 15 DOLLARS

2.5000 g., 0.9999 Gold 0.0804 oz. AGW, 13x22 mm. **Ruler:** Elizabeth II **Rev:** Turtle Dreaming **Rev. Designer:** Darryl Bellotti **Shape:** Rectangle

Date	Mintage	F	VF	XF	Unc	BU
2009 Proof	—	Value: 175				

KM# 1108 15 DOLLARS

2.5000 g., 0.9999 Gold 0.0804 oz. AGW, 13x22 mm. **Ruler:** Elizabeth II **Rev:** Kangaroo Dreaming **Rev. Designer:** Darryl Bellotti **Shape:** Vertical rectangle

Date	Mintage	Good	VG	F	VF	XF
2009 Proof	—	Value: 175				

KM# 1223 15 DOLLARS

3.1100 g., 0.9990 Gold 0.0999 oz. AGW, 16 mm. **Ruler:** Elizabeth II **Obv:** Head right **Obv. Designer:** Ian Rank-Broadley **Rev:** Dreaming dolphin **Rev. Designer:** Darryl Berttolli

Date	Mintage	F	VF	XF	Unc	BU
2009P Proof	2,500	Value: 175				

KM# 1225 15 DOLLARS

3.1100 g., 0.9990 Gold 0.0999 oz. AGW, 16 mm. **Ruler:** Elizabeth II **Obv:** Head right **Obv. Designer:** Ian Rank-Broadley **Rev:** Dreaming brolga **Rev. Designer:** Darryl Berttolli

Date	Mintage	F	VF	XF	Unc	BU
2009P Proof	2,500	Value: 175				

KM# 1226 15 DOLLARS

3.1100 g., 0.9990 Gold 0.0999 oz. AGW, 16 mm. **Ruler:** Elizabeth II **Obv:** Head right **Obv. Designer:** Ian Rank-Broadley **Rev:** Dreaming echidna **Rev. Designer:** Darryl Berttolli

Date	Mintage	F	VF	XF	Unc	BU
2009P Proof	2,500	Value: 175				

KM# 1228 15 DOLLARS

15.5500 g., 0.9990 Gold 0.4994 oz. AGW, 25 mm. **Ruler:** Elizabeth II **Obv:** Head right **Obv. Designer:** Ian Rank-Broadley **Rev:** Dreaming dolphin **Rev. Designer:** Darryl Berttolli

Date	Mintage	F	VF	XF	Unc	BU
2009P Proof	1,000	Value: 1,100				

KM# 1232 15 DOLLARS

3.1100 g., 0.9990 Platinum 0.0999 oz. APW, 16 mm. **Ruler:** Elizabeth II **Obv:** Head right **Obv. Designer:** Ian Rank-Broadley **Rev:** Dreaming kangaroo, multicolor **Rev. Designer:** Darryl Berttolli

Date	Mintage	F	VF	XF	Unc	BU
2009P Proof	2,500	Value: 400				

KM# 1233 15 DOLLARS

3.1100 g., 0.9990 Platinum 0.0999 oz. APW, 16 mm. **Ruler:** Elizabeth II **Obv:** Head right **Obv. Designer:** Ian Rank-Broadley **Rev:** Dreaming dolphin, multicolor **Rev. Designer:** Darryl Berttolli

Date	Mintage	F	VF	XF	Unc	BU
2009P Proof	2,500	Value: 400				

KM# 1234 15 DOLLARS

3.1100 g., 0.9990 Platinum 0.0999 oz. APW, 16 mm. **Ruler:** Elizabeth II **Obv:** Head right **Obv. Designer:** Ian Rank-Broadley **Rev:** Dreaming king brown snake, multicolor **Rev. Designer:** Darryl Berttolli

Date	Mintage	F	VF	XF	Unc	BU
2009P Proof	2,500	Value: 400				

KM# 1235 15 DOLLARS

3.1100 g., 0.9990 Platinum 0.0999 oz. APW, 16 mm. **Ruler:** Elizabeth II **Obv:** Head right **Obv. Designer:** Ian Rank-Broadley **Rev:** Dreaming brolga **Rev. Designer:** Darryl Berttolli

Date	Mintage	F	VF	XF	Unc	BU
2009P Proof	2,500	Value: 400				

KM# 1236 15 DOLLARS

3.1100 g., 0.9990 Platinum 0.0999 oz. APW, 16 mm. **Ruler:** Elizabeth II **Obv:** Head right **Obv. Designer:** Ian Rank-Broadley **Rev:** Dreaming echidna, multicolor **Rev. Designer:** Darryl Berttolli

Date	Mintage	F	VF	XF	Unc	BU
2009P Proof	2,500	Value: 400				

KM# 1399 15 DOLLARS

3.1100 g., 0.9990 Platinum 0.0999 oz. APW, 17 mm. **Ruler:** Elizabeth II **Obv:** Head right **Obv. Designer:** Ian Rank-Broadley **Rev:** Multicolor frill-neck lizard

Date	Mintage	F	VF	XF	Unc	BU
2010(p)	2,500	Value: 335				

KM# 1401 15 DOLLARS

3.1100 g., 0.9990 Gold 0.0999 oz. AGW, 17 mm. **Ruler:** Elizabeth II **Obv:** Head right **Obv. Designer:** Ian Rank-Broadley **Rev:** Frill-neck lizard

Date	Mintage	F	VF	XF	Unc	BU
2010(p) Proof	2,500	Value: 260				

KM# 1405 15 DOLLARS

3.1100 g., 0.9990 Platinum 0.0999 oz. APW, 17 mm. **Ruler:** Elizabeth II **Obv:** Head right **Obv. Designer:** Ian Rank-Broadley **Rev:** Multicolor koala

Date	Mintage	F	VF	XF	Unc	BU
2010(p) Proof	2,500	Value: 335				

KM# 1407 15 DOLLARS

3.1100 g., 0.9990 Gold 0.0999 oz. AGW, 16 mm. **Ruler:** Elizabeth II **Obv:** Head right **Obv. Designer:** Ian Rank-Broadley **Rev:** Koala

Date	Mintage	F	VF	XF	Unc	BU
2010(p) Proof	2,500	Value: 260				

KM# 1411 15 DOLLARS

3.1100 g., 0.9990 Platinum 0.0999 oz. APW, 17 mm. **Ruler:** Elizabeth II **Obv:** Head right **Obv. Designer:** Ian Rank-Broadley **Rev:** Multicolor platypus

Date	Mintage	F	VF	XF	Unc	BU
2010(p) Proof	2,500	Value: 335				

KM# 1413 15 DOLLARS

0.9990 Gold, 16 mm. **Ruler:** Elizabeth II **Obv:** Head right **Obv. Designer:** Ian Rank-Broadley **Rev:** Platypus

Date	Mintage	F	VF	XF	Unc	BU
2010(p) Proof	2,500	Value: 260				

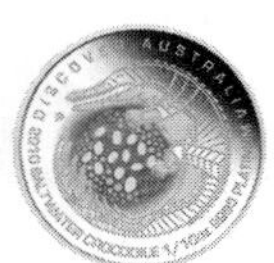

KM# 1417 15 DOLLARS

0.9990 Platinum APW, 17 mm. **Ruler:** Elizabeth II **Obv:** Head right **Obv. Designer:** Ian Rank-Broadley **Rev:** Muticolor saltwater crocodile

Date	Mintage	F	VF	XF	Unc	BU
2010(p) Proof	2,500	Value: 335				

KM# 1419 15 DOLLARS

3.1100 g., 0.9990 Gold 0.0999 oz. AGW, 16 mm. **Ruler:** Elizabeth II **Obv:** Head right **Obv. Designer:** Ian Rank-Broadley **Rev:** Saltwater crocodile

Date	Mintage	F	VF	XF	Unc	BU
2010(p) Proof	2,500	Value: 260				

KM# 1423 15 DOLLARS

3.1100 g., 0.9990 Platinum 0.0999 oz. APW, 17 mm. **Ruler:** Elizabeth II **Obv:** Head right **Obv. Designer:** Ian Rank-Broadley **Rev:** Multicolor wombat

Date	Mintage	F	VF	XF	Unc	BU
2010(p) Proof	2,500	Value: 335				

KM# 1425 15 DOLLARS

0.9990 Gold, 16 mm. **Ruler:** Elizabeth II **Obv:** Head right **Obv. Designer:** Ian Rank-Broadley **Rev:** Wombat

Date	Mintage	F	VF	XF	Unc	BU
2010(p) Proof	2,500	Value: 260				

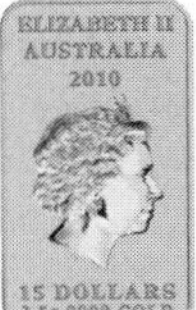

KM# 1454 15 DOLLARS

2.5000 g., 0.9990 Gold 0.0803 oz. AGW, 13x22 mm. **Ruler:** Elizabeth II **Rev:** Dolphin dreaming **Shape:** Vertical rectangle

Date	Mintage	F	VF	XF	Unc	BU
2010P Proof	—	Value: 150				

KM# 1105 20 DOLLARS

5.0000 g., 0.9999 Gold 0.1607 oz. AGW, 14x23.2 mm. **Ruler:** Elizabeth II **Rev:** Turtle Dreaming **Rev. Designer:** Darryl Bellotti **Shape:** Rectangle

Date	Mintage	F	VF	XF	Unc	BU
2009 Proof	—	Value: 325				

KM# 1109 20 DOLLARS

5.0000 g., 0.9999 Gold 0.1607 oz. AGW, 14x23.2 mm. **Ruler:** Elizabeth II **Rev:** Kangaroo dreaming **Rev. Designer:** Darryl Bellotti **Shape:** Vertical rectangle

Date	Mintage	F	VF	XF	Unc	BU
2009 Proof	—	Value: 325				

KM# 1127 25 DOLLARS

3.1000 g., 0.9990 Gold 0.0996 oz. AGW, 15.5 mm. **Ruler:** Elizabeth II **Obv:** Head right **Obv. Designer:** Ian Rank-Broadley **Rev:** Kookaburra **Rev. Legend:** DISCOVER AUSTRALIA

Date	Mintage	F	VF	XF	Unc	BU
2006P Proof	2,500	Value: 185				

KM# 1123 25 DOLLARS

3.1000 g., 0.9990 Gold 0.0996 oz. AGW, 15.5 mm. **Ruler:** Elizabeth II **Obv:** Head right **Obv. Designer:** Ian Rank-Broadley **Rev:** Saltwater crocodile **Rev. Legend:** DISCOVER AUSTRALIA

Date	Mintage	F	VF	XF	Unc	BU
2006P Proof	2,500	Value: 185				

KM# 1124 25 DOLLARS

3.1000 g., 0.9990 Gold 0.0996 oz. AGW, 15.5 mm. **Ruler:** Elizabeth II **Obv:** Head right **Obv. Designer:** Ian Rank-Broadley **Rev:** Grey kangaroo **Rev. Legend:** DISCOVER AUSTRALIA

Date	Mintage	F	VF	XF	Unc	BU
2006P Proof	2,500	Value: 185				

KM# 1125 25 DOLLARS

3.1000 g., 0.9990 Gold 0.0996 oz. AGW, 15.5 mm. **Ruler:** Elizabeth II **Obv:** Head right **Obv. Designer:** Ian Rank-Broadley **Rev:** Emu **Rev. Legend:** DISCOVER AUSTRALIA

Date	Mintage	F	VF	XF	Unc	BU
2006P Proof	2,500	Value: 185				

KM# 1126 25 DOLLARS

3.1000 g., 0.9990 Gold 0.0996 oz. AGW, 15.5 mm. **Ruler:** Elizabeth II **Obv:** Head right **Obv. Designer:** Ian Rank-Broadley **Rev:** Koala **Rev. Legend:** DISCOVER AUSTRALIA

Date	Mintage	F	VF	XF	Unc	BU
2006P Proof	2,500	Value: 185				

KM# 1148 25 DOLLARS

3.1000 g., 0.9990 Gold 0.0996 oz. AGW, 15.5 mm. **Ruler:** Elizabeth II **Obv:** Head right **Obv. Designer:** Ian Rank-Broadley **Rev:** Echinda **Rev. Legend:** DISCOVER AUSTRALIA

Date	Mintage	F	VF	XF	Unc	BU
2007P Proof	2,500	Value: 185				

KM# 1149 25 DOLLARS

3.1000 g., 0.9990 Gold 0.0996 oz. AGW, 15.5 mm. **Ruler:** Elizabeth II **Obv:** Head right **Obv. Designer:** Ian Rank-Broadley **Rev:** Common wombat **Rev. Legend:** DISCOVER AUSTRALIA

Date	Mintage	F	VF	XF	Unc	BU
2007P Proof	2,500	Value: 185				

KM# 1150 25 DOLLARS

3.1000 g., 0.9990 Gold 0.0996 oz. AGW, 15.5 mm. **Ruler:** Elizabeth II **Obv:** Head right **Obv. Designer:** Ian Rank-Braodley **Rev:** Tasmanian devil **Rev. Legend:** DISCOVER AUSTRALIA

Date	Mintage	F	VF	XF	Unc	BU
2007P Proof	2,500	Value: 185				

KM# 1151 25 DOLLARS

3.1000 g., 0.9990 Gold 0.0996 oz. AGW, 15.5 mm. **Ruler:** Elizabeth II **Obv:** Head right **Obv. Designer:** Ian Rank-Broadley **Rev:** Great white shark **Rev. Legend:** DISCOVER AUSTRALIA

Date	Mintage	F	VF	XF	Unc	BU
2007P Proof	2,500	Value: 185				

KM# 1152 25 DOLLARS

3.1000 g., 0.9990 Gold 0.0996 oz. AGW, 15.5 mm. **Ruler:** Elizabeth II **Obv:** Head right **Obv. Designer:** Ian Rank-Broadley **Rev:** Platypus **Rev. Legend:** DISCOVER AUSTRALIA

Date	Mintage	F	VF	XF	Unc	BU
2007P Proof	2,500	Value: 185				

KM# 1158 25 DOLLARS

3.1000 g., 0.9990 Platinum 0.0996 oz. APW, 16 mm. **Ruler:** Elizabeth II **Obv:** Head right **Obv. Designer:** Ian Rank-Broadley **Rev:** Anemone buttercup, multicolor **Rev. Legend:** DISCOVER AUSTRALIA

Date	Mintage	F	VF	XF	Unc	BU
2007P Proof	2,500	Value: 325				

KM# 1191 25 DOLLARS
3.1000 g., 0.9990 Gold 0.0996 oz. AGW, 15.5 mm. **Ruler:** Elizabeth II **Obv:** Head right **Obv. Designer:** Ian Rank-Broadley **Rev:** Dolphin **Rev. Legend:** DISCOVER AUSTRALIA

Date	Mintage	F	VF	XF	Unc	BU
2008P Proof	2,500	Value: 185				

KM# 1192 25 DOLLARS
3.1000 g., 0.9990 Gold 0.0996 oz. AGW, 15.5 mm. **Ruler:** Elizabeth II **Obv:** Head right **Obv. Designer:** Ian Rank-Broadley **Rev:** King brown snake **Rev. Legend:** DISCOVER AUSTRALIA

Date	Mintage	F	VF	XF	Unc	BU
2008P Proof	2,500	Value: 185				

KM# 1193 25 DOLLARS
3.1000 g., 0.9990 Gold 0.0996 oz. AGW, 15.5 mm. **Ruler:** Elizabeth II **Obv:** Head right **Obv. Designer:** Ian Rank-Broadley **Rev:** Brolga **Rev. Legend:** DISCOVER AUSTRALIA

Date	Mintage	F	VF	XF	Unc	BU
2008P Proof	2,500	Value: 185				

KM# 1194 25 DOLLARS
3.1000 g., 0.9990 Gold 0.0996 oz. AGW, 15.5 mm. **Ruler:** Elizabeth II **Obv:** Head right **Obv. Designer:** Ian Rank-Broadley **Rev:** Dingo **Rev. Legend:** DISCOVER AUSTRALIA

Date	Mintage	F	VF	XF	Unc	BU
2008P Proof	2,500	Value: 185				

KM# 1195 25 DOLLARS
3.1000 g., 0.9990 Gold 0.0996 oz. AGW, 15.5 mm. **Ruler:** Elizabeth II **Obv:** Head right **Obv. Designer:** Ian Rank-Broadley **Rev:** Frill-neck lizard **Rev. Legend:** DISCOVER AUSTRALIA

Date	Mintage	F	VF	XF	Unc	BU
2008P Proof	2,500	Value: 185				

KM# 1106 25 DOLLARS
10.0000 g., 0.9999 Gold 0.3215 oz. AGW, 15.4x25.4 mm. **Ruler:** Elizabeth II **Rev:** Turtle dreaming **Rev. Designer:** Darryk Bellotti **Shape:** Verticle rectangle

Date	Mintage	F	VF	XF	Unc	BU
2009 Proof	—	Value: 600				

KM# 1455 25 DOLLARS
10.0000 g., 0.9990 Gold 0.3212 oz. AGW, 15.4x25.4 mm. **Ruler:** Elizabeth II **Rev:** Dolphin dreaming **Shape:** Vertical rectangle

Date	Mintage	F	VF	XF	Unc	BU
2010P Proof	—	Value: 550				

KM# 952 50 DOLLARS
15.5017 g., 0.9990 Gold 0.4979 oz. AGW, 25 mm. **Ruler:** Elizabeth II **Subject:** Australian Fauna **Obv:** Head with tiara right **Obv. Designer:** Ian Rank-Broadley **Rev:** Saltwater crocodile

Date	Mintage	F	VF	XF	Unc	BU
2006 Proof	1,000	Value: 750				

KM# 955 50 DOLLARS
15.5017 g., 0.9990 Gold 0.4979 oz. AGW, 25 mm. **Ruler:** Elizabeth II **Subject:** Australian Fauna **Obv:** Head with tiara right **Obv. Designer:** Ian Rank-Broadley **Rev:** Grey kangaroo

Date	Mintage	F	VF	XF	Unc	BU
2006 Proof	1,000	Value: 750				

KM# 958 50 DOLLARS
15.5017 g., 0.9990 Gold 0.4979 oz. AGW, 25 mm. **Ruler:** Elizabeth II **Subject:** Australian Fauna **Obv:** Head with tiara right **Obv. Designer:** Ian Rank-Broadley **Rev:** Emu

Date	Mintage	F	VF	XF	Unc	BU
2006 Proof	1,000	Value: 750				

KM# 961 50 DOLLARS
15.5017 g., 0.9990 Gold 0.4979 oz. AGW, 25 mm. **Ruler:** Elizabeth II **Subject:** Australian Fauna **Obv:** Head with tiara right **Obv. Designer:** Ian Rank-Broadley **Rev:** Koala

Date	Mintage	F	VF	XF	Unc	BU
2006 Proof	1,000	Value: 750				

KM# 964 50 DOLLARS
15.5017 g., 0.9990 Gold 0.4979 oz. AGW, 25 mm. **Ruler:** Elizabeth II **Subject:** Australian Fauna **Obv:** Head with tiara right **Obv. Designer:** Ian Rank-Broadley **Rev:** Kookaburra

Date	Mintage	F	VF	XF	Unc	BU
2006 Proof	1,000	Value: 750				

KM# 981 50 DOLLARS
15.5017 g., 0.9990 Platinum 0.4979 oz. APW **Ruler:** Elizabeth II **Subject:** Australian Flora **Obv:** Head with tiara right **Obv. Designer:** Ian Rank-Broadley **Rev:** Cooktown orchid

Date	Mintage	F	VF	XF	Unc	BU
2006 Proof	1,000	Value: 975				

KM# 983 50 DOLLARS
15.5017 g., 0.9990 Platinum 0.4979 oz. APW **Ruler:** Elizabeth II **Subject:** Australian Flora **Obv:** Head with tiara right **Obv. Designer:** Ian Rank-Broadley **Rev:** Sturt's desert rose

Date	Mintage	F	VF	XF	Unc	BU
2006 Proof	1,000	Value: 975				

KM# 985 50 DOLLARS
15.5017 g., 0.9990 Platinum 0.4979 oz. APW **Ruler:** Elizabeth II **Subject:** Australian Flora **Obv:** Head with tiara right **Obv. Designer:** Ian Rank-Broadley **Rev:** Royal bluebell

Date	Mintage	F	VF	XF	Unc	BU
2006 Proof	1,000	Value: 975				

KM# 987 50 DOLLARS
15.5017 g., 0.9990 Platinum 0.4979 oz. APW **Ruler:** Elizabeth II **Subject:** Australian Flora **Obv:** Head with tiara right **Obv. Designer:** Ian Rank-Broadley **Rev:** Kangaroo paw

Date	Mintage	F	VF	XF	Unc	BU
2006 Proof	1,000	Value: 975				

KM# 989 50 DOLLARS
15.5017 g., 0.9990 Platinum 0.4979 oz. APW **Ruler:** Elizabeth II **Subject:** Australian Flora **Obv:** Head with tiara right **Obv. Designer:** Ian Rank-Broadley **Rev:** Common pink heath

Date	Mintage	F	VF	XF	Unc	BU
2006 Proof	1,000	Value: 975				

KM# 967 50 DOLLARS
15.5017 g., 0.9990 Gold 0.4979 oz. AGW, 25 mm. **Ruler:** Elizabeth II **Subject:** Australian Fauna **Obv:** Head with tiara right **Obv. Designer:** Ian Rank-Broadley **Rev:** Echidna

Date	Mintage	F	VF	XF	Unc	BU
2007 Proof	1,000	Value: 750				

KM# 970 50 DOLLARS
15.5017 g., 0.9990 Gold 0.4979 oz. AGW, 25 mm. **Ruler:** Elizabeth II **Subject:** Australian Fauna **Obv:** Head with tiara right **Obv. Designer:** Ian Rank-Broadley **Rev:** Common wombat

Date	Mintage	F	VF	XF	Unc	BU
2007 Proof	1,000	Value: 750				

KM# 973 50 DOLLARS
15.5017 g., 0.9990 Gold 0.4979 oz. AGW, 25 mm. **Ruler:** Elizabeth II **Subject:** Australian Fauna **Obv:** Head with tiara right **Obv. Designer:** Ian Rank-Broadley **Rev:** Tasmanian devil

Date	Mintage	F	VF	XF	Unc	BU
2007 Proof	1,000	Value: 750				

KM# 976 50 DOLLARS
15.5017 g., 0.9990 Gold 0.4979 oz. AGW, 25 mm. **Ruler:** Elizabeth II **Subject:** Australian Fauna **Obv:** Head with tiara right **Obv. Designer:** Ian Rank-Broadley **Rev:** Great white shark

Date	Mintage	F	VF	XF	Unc	BU
2007 Proof	1,000	Value: 750				

KM# 979 50 DOLLARS

15.5017 g., 0.9990 Gold 0.4979 oz. AGW, 25 mm. **Ruler:** Elizabeth II **Subject:** Australian Fauna **Obv:** Head with tiara right **Obv. Designer:** Ian Rank-Broadley **Rev:** Platypus

Date	Mintage	F	VF	XF	Unc	BU
2007 Proof	1,000	Value: 750				

KM# 991 50 DOLLARS

15.5017 g., 0.9990 Platinum 0.4979 oz. APW, 24 mm. **Ruler:** Elizabeth II **Subject:** Australian Flora **Obv:** Head with tiara right **Obv. Designer:** Ian Rank-Broadley **Rev:** Anemone buttercup

Date	Mintage	F	VF	XF	Unc	BU
2007 Proof	1,000	Value: 975				

KM# 993 50 DOLLARS

15.5017 g., 0.9990 Platinum 0.4979 oz. APW **Ruler:** Elizabeth II **Subject:** Australian Flora **Obv:** Head with tiara right **Obv. Designer:** Ian Rank-Broadley **Rev:** Sturt's desert pea

Date	Mintage	F	VF	XF	Unc	BU
2007 Proof	1,000	Value: 975				

KM# 995 50 DOLLARS

15.5017 g., 0.9990 Platinum 0.4979 oz. APW, 24 mm. **Ruler:** Elizabeth II **Subject:** Australian Flora **Obv:** Head with tiara right **Obv. Designer:** Ian Rank-Broadley **Rev:** Tasmanian Bluegum

Date	Mintage	F	VF	XF	Unc	BU
2007 Proof	1,000	Value: 975				

KM# 997 50 DOLLARS

15.5017 g., 0.9990 Platinum 0.4979 oz. APW **Ruler:** Elizabeth II **Subject:** Australian Flora **Obv:** Head with tiara right **Obv. Designer:** Ian Rank-Broadley **Rev:** Waratah

Date	Mintage	F	VF	XF	Unc	BU
2007 Proof	1,000	Value: 975				

KM# 999 50 DOLLARS

15.5017 g., 0.9990 Platinum 0.4979 oz. APW **Ruler:** Elizabeth II **Subject:** Australian Flora **Obv:** Head with tiara right **Obv. Designer:** Ian Rank-Broadley **Rev:** Golden wattle

Date	Mintage	F	VF	XF	Unc	BU
2007 Proof	1,000	Value: 975				

KM# 1167 50 DOLLARS

15.5500 g., 0.9990 Platinum 0.4994 oz. APW, 25 mm. **Ruler:** Elizabeth II **Subject:** Australian Flora **Rev:** Black-anther flax lily **Rev. Legend:** DISCOVER AUSTRALIA

Date	Mintage	F	VF	XF	Unc	BU
2008 Proof	—	Value: 975				

KM# 1196 50 DOLLARS

15.5500 g., 0.9990 Gold 0.4994 oz. AGW, 25 mm. **Ruler:** Elizabeth II **Obv:** Head right **Obv. Designer:** Ian Rank-Broadley **Rev:** Dolphin **Rev. Legend:** DISCOVER AUSTRALIA

Date	Mintage	F	VF	XF	Unc	BU
2008P Proof	1,000	Value: 850				

KM# 1197 50 DOLLARS

15.5500 g., 0.9990 Gold 0.4994 oz. AGW, 25 mm. **Ruler:** Elizabeth II **Obv:** Head right **Obv. Designer:** Ian Rank-Broadley **Rev:** King brown snake **Rev. Legend:** DISCOVER AUSTRALIA

Date	Mintage	F	VF	XF	Unc	BU
2008P Proof	1,000	Value: 850				

KM# 1198 50 DOLLARS

15.5500 g., 0.9990 Gold 0.4994 oz. AGW, 25 mm. **Ruler:** Elizabeth II **Obv:** Head right **Obv. Designer:** Ian Rank-Broadley **Rev:** Brogla **Rev. Legend:** DISCOVER AUSTRALIA

Date	Mintage	F	VF	XF	Unc	BU
2008P Proof	1,000	Value: 850				

KM# 1199 50 DOLLARS

15.5500 g., 0.9990 Gold 0.4994 oz. AGW, 25 mm. **Ruler:** Elizabeth II **Obv:** Head right **Obv. Designer:** Ian Rank-Broadley **Rev:** Dingo **Rev. Legend:** DISCOVER AUSTRALIA

Date	Mintage	F	VF	XF	Unc	BU
2008P Proof	1,000	Value: 850				

KM# 1200 50 DOLLARS

15.5500 g., 0.9990 Gold 0.4994 oz. AGW, 25 mm. **Ruler:** Elizabeth II **Obv:** Head right **Obv. Designer:** Ian Rank-Broadley **Rev:** Frill-neck lizard **Rev. Legend:** DISCOVER AUSTRALIA

Date	Mintage	F	VF	XF	Unc	BU
2008P Proof	1,000	Value: 850				

KM# 1207 50 DOLLARS

15.5500 g., 0.9990 Platinum 0.4994 oz. APW, 26 mm. **Ruler:** Elizabeth II **Obv:** Head right **Obv. Designer:** Ian Rank-Broadley **Rev:** Native fragipan, multicolor **Rev. Legend:** DISCOVER AUSTRALIA

Date	Mintage	F	VF	XF	Unc	BU
2008P Proof	1,000	Value: 1,500				

KM# 1208 50 DOLLARS

15.5500 g., 0.9990 Platinum 0.4994 oz. APW, 26 mm. **Ruler:** Elizabeth II **Obv:** Head right **Obv. Designer:** Ian Rank-Broadley **Rev:** Geraldton wax, multicolor **Rev. Legend:** DISCOVER AUSTRALIA

Date	Mintage	F	VF	XF	Unc	BU
2008P Proof	1,000	Value: 1,500				

KM# 1209 50 DOLLARS

15.5500 g., 0.9990 Platinum 0.4994 oz. APW, 26 mm. **Ruler:** Elizabeth II **Obv:** Head right **Obv. Designer:** Ian Rank-Broadley **Rev:** Red-flowered kurrajong, multicolor **Rev. Legend:** DISCOVER AUSTRALIA

Date	Mintage	F	VF	XF	Unc	BU
2008P Proof	1,000	Value: 1,500				

KM# 1210 50 DOLLARS

15.5500 g., 0.9990 Platinum 0.4994 oz. APW **Ruler:** Elizabeth II **Obv:** Head right **Obv. Designer:** Ian Rank-Broadley **Rev:** Small-leaf lilly pilly, multicolor **Rev. Legend:** DISCOVER AUSTRALIA

Date	Mintage	F	VF	XF	Unc	BU
2008P Proof	1,500	Value: 1,500				

KM# 1229 50 DOLLARS

15.5500 g., 0.9990 Gold 0.4994 oz. AGW, 25 mm. **Ruler:** Elizabeth II **Obv:** Head right **Obv. Designer:** Ian Rank-Broadley **Rev:** Dreaming king brown snake **Rev. Designer:** Darryl Berttolli

Date	Mintage	F	VF	XF	Unc	BU
2009P Proof	1,000	Value: 1,100				

KM# 1227 50 DOLLARS

15.5500 g., 0.9990 Gold 0.4994 oz. AGW, 25 mm. **Ruler:** Elizabeth II **Obv:** Head right **Obv. Designer:** Ian Rank-Broadley **Rev:** Dreaming kangaroo **Rev. Designer:** Darryl Berttolli

Date	Mintage	F	VF	XF	Unc	BU
2009P Proof	1,000	Value: 1,100				

KM# 1230 50 DOLLARS

15.5500 g., 0.9990 Gold 0.4994 oz. AGW, 25 mm. **Ruler:** Elizabeth II **Obv:** Head right **Obv. Designer:** Ian Rank-Broadley **Rev:** Dreaming brolga **Rev. Designer:** Darryl Berttolli

Date	Mintage	F	VF	XF	Unc	BU
2009P Proof	1,000	Value: 1,100				

KM# 1231 50 DOLLARS

15.5500 g., 0.9990 Gold 0.4994 oz. AGW, 25 mm. **Ruler:** Elizabeth II **Obv:** Head right **Obv. Designer:** Ian Rank-Broadley **Rev:** Dreaming echidna **Rev. Designer:** Darryl Berttolli

Date	Mintage	F	VF	XF	Unc	BU
2009P Proof	1,000	Value: 1,100				

KM# 1237 50 DOLLARS

15.5500 g., 0.9990 Platinum 0.4994 oz. APW, 25 mm. **Ruler:** Elizabeth II **Obv:** Head right **Obv. Designer:** Ian Rank-Broadley **Rev:** Dreaming kangaroo, multicolor **Rev. Designer:** Darryl Berttolli

Date	Mintage	F	VF	XF	Unc	BU
2009P Proof	1,000	Value: 1,500				

KM# 1238 50 DOLLARS
15.5500 g., 0.9990 Platinum 0.4994 oz. APW, 25 mm. **Ruler:** Elizabeth II **Obv:** Head right **Obv. Designer:** Ian Rank-Broadley **Rev:** Dreaming dolphin, multicolor **Rev. Designer:** Darryl Berttolli

Date	Mintage	F	VF	XF	Unc	BU
2009P Proof	1,000	Value: 1,500				

KM# 1239 50 DOLLARS
15.5500 g., 0.9990 Platinum 0.4994 oz. APW, 25 mm. **Ruler:** Elizabeth II **Obv:** Head right **Obv. Designer:** Ian Rank-Broadley **Rev:** Dreaming king brown snake, multicolor **Rev. Designer:** Darryl Berttolli

Date	Mintage	F	VF	XF	Unc	BU
2009P Proof	1,000	Value: 1,500				

KM# 1240 50 DOLLARS
15.5500 g., 0.9990 Platinum 0.4994 oz. APW, 25 mm. **Ruler:** Elizabeth II **Obv:** Head right **Obv. Designer:** Ian Rank-Broadley **Rev:** Dreaming brolga, multicolor **Rev. Designer:** Darryl Berttolli

Date	Mintage	F	VF	XF	Unc	BU
2009P Proof	1,000	Value: 1,500				

KM# 1241 50 DOLLARS
15.5500 g., 0.9990 Platinum 0.4994 oz. APW, 25 mm. **Ruler:** Elizabeth II **Obv:** Head right **Obv. Designer:** Ian Rank-Broadley **Rev:** Dreaming echidna, multicolor **Rev. Designer:** Darryl Berttolli

Date	Mintage	F	VF	XF	Unc	BU
2009P Proof	1,000	Value: 1,500				

KM# 1398 50 DOLLARS
15.5000 g., 0.9990 Platinum 0.4978 oz. APW, 26 mm. **Ruler:** Elizabeth II **Obv:** Head right **Obv. Designer:** Ian Rank-Broadley **Rev:** Multicolor frill-neck lizard **Rev. Designer:** Darryl Bellotti

Date	Mintage	F	VF	XF	Unc	BU
2010(p) Proof	1,000	Value: 1,550				

KM# 1400 50 DOLLARS
15.5000 g., 0.9990 Gold 0.4978 oz. AGW, 26 mm. **Ruler:** Elizabeth II **Obv:** Head right **Obv. Designer:** Ian Rank-Broadley **Rev:** Frill-neck lizard

Date	Mintage	F	VF	XF	Unc	BU
2010(p) Proof	1,000	Value: 1,250				

KM# 1404 50 DOLLARS
15.5000 g., 0.9990 Platinum 0.4978 oz. APW, 26 mm. **Ruler:** Elizabeth II **Obv:** Head right **Rev:** Multicolor koala

Date	Mintage	F	VF	XF	Unc	BU
2010(p) Proof	1,000	Value: 1,550				

KM# 1406 50 DOLLARS
15.5000 g., 0.9990 Gold 0.4978 oz. AGW, 26 mm. **Ruler:** Elizabeth II **Obv:** Head right **Obv. Designer:** Ian Rank-Broadley **Rev:** Koala

Date	Mintage	F	VF	XF	Unc	BU
2010(p) Proof	1,000	Value: 1,250				

KM# 1410 50 DOLLARS
15.5000 g., 0.9990 Platinum 0.4978 oz. APW, 26 mm. **Ruler:** Elizabeth II **Obv:** Head right **Obv. Designer:** Ian Rank-Broadley **Rev:** Multicolor platypus

Date	Mintage	F	VF	XF	Unc	BU
2010(p) Proof	1,000	Value: 1,550				

KM# 1412 50 DOLLARS
15.5000 g., 0.9990 Gold 0.4978 oz. AGW **Ruler:** Elizabeth II **Obv:** Head right **Obv. Designer:** Ian Rank-Broadley **Rev:** Platypus

Date	Mintage	F	VF	XF	Unc	BU
2010(p) Proof	1,000	Value: 1,250				

KM# 1416 50 DOLLARS
15.5000 g., 0.9990 Platinum 0.4978 oz. APW, 26 mm. **Ruler:** Elizabeth II **Obv:** Head right **Obv. Designer:** Ian Rank-Broadley **Rev:** Multicolor saltwater crocodile

Date	Mintage	F	VF	XF	Unc	BU
2010(p) Proof	1,000	Value: 1,550				

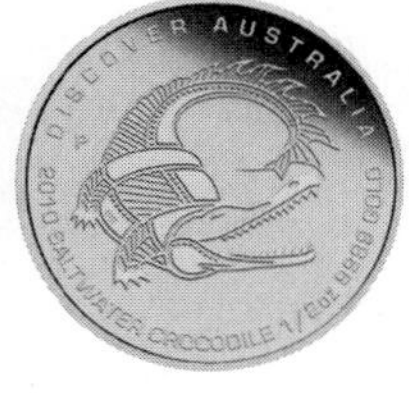

KM# 1418 50 DOLLARS
15.5000 g., 0.9990 Gold 0.4978 oz. AGW, 26 mm. **Ruler:** Elizabeth II **Obv:** Head right **Obv. Designer:** Ian Rank-Broadley **Rev:** Saltwater crocodile

Date	Mintage	F	VF	XF	Unc	BU
2010(p) Proof	1,000	Value: 1,250				

KM# 1424 50 DOLLARS
15.5000 g., 0.9990 Gold 0.4978 oz. AGW, 26 mm. **Ruler:** Elizabeth II **Obv:** Head right **Obv. Designer:** Ian Rank-Broadley **Rev:** Wombat

Date	Mintage	F	VF	XF	Unc	BU
2010(p) Proof	2,500	Value: 1,250				

BULLION - LUNAR YEAR

KM# 1010 25 CENTS
0.9990 Silver Gilt, 17.8 mm. **Ruler:** Elizabeth II **Obv:** Bust with tiara right **Obv. Legend:** ELIZABETH II - AUSTRALIA **Obv. Designer:** Ian Rank-Broadley **Rev:** 4 Chinese characters **Rev. Legend:** LUNAR NEW YEAR - GOOD FORTUNE & PROSPERITY

Date	Mintage	F	VF	XF	Unc	BU
2007 Proof	8,888	Value: 45.00				

KM# 579 50 CENTS
15.5518 g., 0.9990 Silver 0.4995 oz. ASW, 32.1 mm. **Ruler:** Elizabeth II **Subject:** Year of the Horse **Obv:** Head with tiara right, denomination below **Obv. Designer:** Ian Rank-Broadley **Rev:** Horse running left **Edge:** Reeded

Date	Mintage	F	VF	XF	Unc	BU
2002P Proof	5,000	Value: 35.00				

KM# 664 50 CENTS
16.4000 g., 0.9990 Silver 0.5267 oz. ASW, 31.9 mm. **Ruler:** Elizabeth II **Subject:** Year of the Goat **Obv:** Head with tiara right, denomination below **Obv. Designer:** Ian Rank-Broadley **Rev:** Two goats **Edge:** Reeded

Date	Mintage	F	VF	XF	Unc	BU
2003	—	—	—	—	20.00	25.00
2003 Proof	—	Value: 35.00				

KM# 673 50 CENTS
15.5518 g., 0.9990 Silver 0.4995 oz. ASW, 32.1 mm. **Ruler:** Elizabeth II **Subject:** Year of the Monkey **Obv:** Head with tiara right, denomination below **Rev:** Monkey sitting on branch **Edge:** Reeded

Date	Mintage	F	VF	XF	Unc	BU
2004 Proof	11,000	Value: 35.00				

KM# 791 50 CENTS
15.5680 g., 0.9990 Silver 0.5000 oz. ASW, 32.1 mm. **Ruler:** Elizabeth II **Subject:** Year of the Rooster **Obv:** Elizabeth II **Rev:** Standing Rooster looking backwards **Edge:** Reeded

Date	Mintage	F	VF	XF	Unc	BU
2005P Proof	6,000	Value: 50.00				

KM# 814 50 CENTS
15.5500 g., 0.9990 Silver 0.4994 oz. ASW **Ruler:** Elizabeth II **Subject:** Bullion Lunar Year - Rooster **Obv:** Head with tiara right

Date	Mintage	F	VF	XF	Unc	BU
2005	—	—	—	—	—	20.00

KM# 1370 50 CENTS

15.5500 g., 0.9900 Silver 0.4949 oz. ASW, 32 mm. **Ruler:** Elizabeth II **Subject:** Year of the Tiger **Obv:** Head right **Rev:** Tiger at rest left

Date	Mintage	F	VF	XF	Unc	BU
2010(p)	—	—	—	—	—	20.00

KM# 1474 50 CENTS

15.5600 g., 0.9990 Silver 0.4997 oz. ASW **Ruler:** Elizabeth II **Subject:** Year of the Rabbit **Rev:** Mother and baby rabbit nose to nose

Date	Mintage	F	VF	XF	Unc	BU
2011P Proof	—	Value: 30.00				

KM# 536 DOLLAR

31.1035 g., 0.9990 Silver 0.9990 oz. ASW, 40.6 mm. **Ruler:** Elizabeth II **Subject:** Year of the Snake **Obv:** Head with tiara right, denomination below **Obv. Designer:** Ian Rank-Broadley **Rev:** Snake with eggs **Edge:** Reeded

Date	Mintage	F	VF	XF	Unc	BU
2001	300,000	—	—	—	35.00	40.00
2001P Proof	2,500	Value: 50.00				

KM# 536a DOLLAR

31.6350 g., 0.9990 Silver partially gilt 1.0160 oz. ASW, 40.6 mm. **Ruler:** Elizabeth II **Subject:** Year of the Snake **Obv:** Head with tiara right, denomination below **Rev:** Gold-plated snake **Edge:** Reeded

Date	Mintage	F	VF	XF	Unc	BU
2001	50,000	—	—	—	45.00	50.00

KM# 580 DOLLAR

31.1035 g., 0.9990 Silver 0.9990 oz. ASW, 40.6 mm. **Ruler:** Elizabeth II **Subject:** Year of the Horse **Obv:** Head with tiara right, denomination below **Obv. Designer:** Ian Rank-Broadley **Rev:** Horse running left **Edge:** Reeded

Date	Mintage	F	VF	XF	Unc	BU
2002P	—	—	—	—	35.00	40.00
2002P Proof	2,500	Value: 50.00				

KM# 580a DOLLAR

31.6350 g., 0.9990 Silver partially gilt 1.0160 oz. ASW, 40.6 mm. **Ruler:** Elizabeth II **Obv:** Head with tiara right **Rev:** Gold-plated horse **Edge:** Reeded

Date	Mintage	F	VF	XF	Unc	BU
2002	50,000	—	—	—	35.00	40.00

KM# 665 DOLLAR

31.6200 g., 0.9990 Silver 1.0155 oz. ASW, 40.3 mm. **Ruler:** Elizabeth II **Subject:** Year of the Goat **Obv:** Head with tiara right, denomination below **Obv. Designer:** Ian Rank-Broadley **Rev:** Two goats **Edge:** Reeded

Date	Mintage	F	VF	XF	Unc	BU
2003	—	—	—	—	35.00	40.00
2003 Proof	—	Value: 50.00				

KM# 665a DOLLAR

31.6350 g., 0.9990 Silver partially gilt 1.0160 oz. ASW, 40.6 mm. **Ruler:** Elizabeth II **Subject:** Year of the Goat **Obv:** Head with tiara right, denomination below **Rev:** Gold-plated goat **Edge:** Reeded

Date	Mintage	F	VF	XF	Unc	BU
2003	50,000	—	—	—	50.00	55.00

KM# 674a DOLLAR

31.6350 g., 0.9990 Silver partially gilt 1.0160 oz. ASW, 40.6 mm. **Ruler:** Elizabeth II **Subject:** Year of the Monkey **Obv:** Head with tiara right, denomination below **Rev:** Gold-plated monkey **Edge:** Reeded

Date	Mintage	F	VF	XF	Unc	BU
2004	50,000	—	—	—	50.00	55.00

KM# 674 DOLLAR

31.1035 g., 0.9990 Silver 0.9990 oz. ASW, 40.6 mm. **Ruler:** Elizabeth II **Subject:** Year of the Monkey **Obv:** Head with tiara right, denomination below **Rev:** Monkey sitting on branch **Edge:** Reeded

Date	Mintage	F	VF	XF	Unc	BU
2004	—	—	—	—	35.00	40.00
2004 Proof	8,500	Value: 50.00				

KM# 695 DOLLAR

31.1050 g., 0.9990 Silver 0.9990 oz. ASW, 40.5 mm. **Ruler:** Elizabeth II **Subject:** Year of the Rooster **Obv:** Head with tiara right, denomination below **Rev:** Rooster **Edge:** Reeded

Date	Mintage	F	VF	XF	Unc	BU
2005P Proof	—	Value: 70.00				

KM# 695a DOLLAR

31.6350 g., 0.9990 Silver 1.0160 oz. ASW, 40.5 mm. **Ruler:** Elizabeth II **Subject:** Year of the Rooster **Obv:** Head with tiara right, denomination below **Rev:** Gold-plated rooster **Edge:** Reeded

Date	Mintage	F	VF	XF	Unc	BU
2005 Polished fields	47,200	—	—	—	45.00	50.00
2005 Matte fields	2,800	—	—	—	175	185

KM# 792 DOLLAR

31.1035 g., 0.9990 Silver 0.9990 oz. ASW, 40.6 mm. **Ruler:** Elizabeth II **Subject:** Year of the Rooster **Obv:** Elizabeth II **Rev:** Standing rooster looking backwards **Edge:** Reeded

Date	Mintage	F	VF	XF	Unc	BU
2005P Proof	3,500	Value: 45.00				

KM# 792a DOLLAR

31.1035 g., 0.9990 Silver partially gold plated 0.9990 oz. ASW, 40 mm. **Ruler:** Elizabeth II **Subject:** Year of the Rooster **Obv:** Head right **Rev:** Rooster, partially gilt

Date	Mintage	F	VF	XF	Unc	BU
2005P Proof	—	Value: 50.00				

KM# 809 DOLLAR

9.0000 g., Aluminum-Bronze, 25 mm. **Ruler:** Elizabeth II **Subject:** Year of the Pig **Obv:** Head with tiara right **Obv. Designer:** Ian Rank-Broadley **Rev:** Pig **Rev. Designer:** Vladimir Gottwald **Edge:** Segmented reeding

Date	Mintage	F	VF	XF	Unc	BU
2007	7,500	—	—	—	95.00	—

KM# 809a DOLLAR

11.6600 g., 0.9990 Silver 0.3745 oz. ASW, 25 mm. **Ruler:** Elizabeth II **Subject:** Year of the Pig **Obv:** Head with tiara right **Obv. Designer:** Ian Rank-Broadley **Rev:** Pig **Rev. Designer:** Vladimir Gottwald **Edge:** Segmented reeding

Date	Mintage	F	VF	XF	Unc	BU
2007 Proof	—	Value: 25.00				

KM# 1011 DOLLAR

31.1050 g., 0.9990 Silver 0.9990 oz. ASW, 40 mm. **Ruler:** Elizabeth II **Obv:** Crowned bust right at top **Obv. Legend:** ELIZABETH II - AUSTRALIA **Rev:** 12 Lunar figures

Date	Mintage	F	VF	XF	Unc	BU
2007 Proof	8,888	Value: 110				

KM# 1056 DOLLAR

9.0000 g., Aluminum-Brass, 25 mm. **Ruler:** Elizabeth II **Subject:** Year of the Rat **Rev. Designer:** V. Gottwald

Date	Mintage	F	VF	XF	Unc	BU
2008	—	—	—	—	13.00	15.00

KM# 1056a DOLLAR

11.6600 g., 0.9990 Silver 0.3745 oz. ASW, 25 mm. **Ruler:** Elizabeth II **Subject:** Year of the Rat

Date	Mintage	F	VF	XF	Unc	BU
2008 Proof	10,000	Value: 45.00				

KM# 1078 DOLLAR

9.0000 g., Aluminum-Brass, 25 mm. **Ruler:** Elizabeth II **Subject:** Year of the Ox **Rev:** V. Gottwald

Date	Mintage	F	VF	XF	Unc	BU
2009	—	—	—	—	12.00	13.00

KM# 1078a DOLLAR

11.6600 g., 0.9990 Silver 0.3745 oz. ASW, 25 mm. **Ruler:** Elizabeth II **Subject:** Year of the Ox **Rev. Designer:** V. Gottwald

Date	Mintage	F	VF	XF	Unc	BU
2009 Proof	10,000	Value: 45.00				

KM# 1083a DOLLAR

31.1050 g., 0.9990 Silver Partially gilt 0.9990 oz. ASW, 40 mm. **Ruler:** Elizabeth II **Rev:** Kangaroo **Rev. Designer:** K. Done

Date	Mintage	F	VF	XF	Unc	BU
2009	—	—	—	—	—	90.00

KM# 1317 DOLLAR

31.1050 g., 0.9990 Silver 0.9990 oz. ASW, 46 mm. **Ruler:** Elizabeth II **Subject:** Year of the Tiger **Obv:** Head right **Obv. Designer:** Ian Rank-Broadley **Rev:** Tiger at rest left

Date	Mintage	F	VF	XF	Unc	BU
2010P	—	—	—	—	—	45.00
2010P Proof	1,000	Value: 75.00				

KM# 1317a DOLLAR

31.1050 g., 0.9990 Silver 0.9990 oz. ASW, 46 mm. **Ruler:** Elizabeth II **Subject:** Year of the Tiger **Obv:** Head right **Obv. Designer:** Ian Rank-Broadley **Rev:** Tiger at rest left, partially gilt

Date	Mintage	F	VF	XF	Unc	BU
2010P Proof	50,000	Value: 80.00				

KM# 1318 DOLLAR

31.1050 g., 0.9990 Silver 0.9990 oz. ASW, 46 mm. **Ruler:** Elizabeth II **Subject:** Year of the Tiger **Obv:** Head right **Obv. Designer:** Ian Rank-Broadley **Rev:** Multicolor tiger at rest left

Date	Mintage	F	VF	XF	Unc	BU
2010P Proof	170,000	Value: 75.00				

KM# 1475 DOLLAR

31.1050 g., 0.9990 Silver 0.9990 oz. ASW, 40 mm. **Ruler:** Elizabeth II **Subject:** Year of the Rabbit **Rev:** Mother and baby rabbit nose to nose

Date	Mintage	F	VF	XF	Unc	BU
2011P Proof	—	Value: 45.00				

KM# 537 2 DOLLARS

62.2070 g., 0.9990 Silver 1.9979 oz. ASW, 50.3 mm. **Ruler:** Elizabeth II **Subject:** Year of the Snake **Obv:** Head with tiara right, denomination below **Rev:** Snake with eggs **Edge:** Segmented reeding

Date	Mintage	F	VF	XF	Unc	BU
2001	—	—	—	—	75.00	80.00
2001P Proof	1,000	Value: 110				

KM# 581 2 DOLLARS

62.2070 g., 0.9990 Silver 1.9979 oz. ASW, 50 mm. **Ruler:** Elizabeth II **Subject:** Year of the Horse **Obv:** Head with tiara right, denomination below **Rev:** Horse running left **Edge:** Reeded

Date	Mintage	F	VF	XF	Unc	BU
2002	—	—	—	—	75.00	80.00
2002P Proof	1,000	Value: 110				

KM# 679 2 DOLLARS

62.8500 g., 0.9990 Silver 2.0186 oz. ASW, 50 mm. **Ruler:** Elizabeth II **Subject:** Year of the Goat **Obv:** Head with tiara right, denomination below **Rev:** Two goats **Edge:** Reeded

Date	Mintage	F	VF	XF	Unc	BU
2003	—	—	—	—	75.00	80.00

KM# 675 2 DOLLARS

62.2070 g., 0.9990 Silver 1.9979 oz. ASW, 50 mm. **Ruler:** Elizabeth II **Subject:** Year of the Monkey **Obv:** Head with tiara right, denomination below **Rev:** Monkey sitting on branch **Edge:** Reeded

Date	Mintage	F	VF	XF	Unc	BU
2004	—	—	—	—	75.00	80.00
2004 Proof	7,000	Value: 100				

KM# 793 2 DOLLARS

62.2700 g., 0.9990 Silver 1.9999 oz. ASW, 50.3 mm. **Ruler:** Elizabeth II **Subject:** Year of the Rooster **Obv:** Elizabeth II **Rev:** Standing Rooster looking backwards **Edge:** Reeded

Date	Mintage	F	VF	XF	Unc	BU
2005P Proof	2,000	Value: 140				

KM# 1320 2 DOLLARS

62.2100 g., 0.9990 Silver 1.9980 oz. ASW, 46 mm. **Ruler:** Elizabeth II **Subject:** Year of the Tiger **Obv:** Head right **Obv. Designer:** Ian Rank-Broadley **Rev:** Tiger seated left

Date	Mintage	F	VF	XF	Unc	BU
2010P Proof	1,000	Value: 150				

KM# 1476 2 DOLLARS

62.2000 g., 0.9990 Silver 1.9977 oz. ASW **Ruler:** Elizabeth II **Subject:** Year of the Rabbit **Rev:** Mother and baby rabbit nose to nose

Date	Mintage	F	VF	XF	Unc	BU
2011P Proof	—	Value: 100				

KM# 538 5 DOLLARS

1.5710 g., 0.9990 Gold 0.0505 oz. AGW, 14.1 mm. **Ruler:** Elizabeth II **Subject:** Year of the Snake **Obv:** Head with tiara right, denomination below **Rev:** Snake in tree **Edge:** Reeded

Date	Mintage	F	VF	XF	Unc	BU
2001	100,000	—	—	—	—	85.00
2001P Proof	100,000	Value: 95.00				

KM# 582 5 DOLLARS

1.5552 g., 0.9990 Gold 0.0499 oz. AGW, 14.1 mm. **Ruler:** Elizabeth II **Subject:** Year of the Horse **Obv:** Head with tiara right, denomination below **Rev:** Horse galloping left **Edge:** Reeded

Date	Mintage	F	VF	XF	Unc	BU
2002P	100,000	—	—	—	—	85.00

KM# 668 5 DOLLARS

1.5710 g., 0.9999 Gold 0.0505 oz. AGW, 14.1 mm. **Ruler:** Elizabeth II **Subject:** Year of the Monkey **Obv:** Head with tiara right, denomination below **Obv. Designer:** Ian Rank-Broadley **Rev:** Monkey **Edge:** Reeded

Date	Mintage	F	VF	XF	Unc	BU
2004P Proof	100,000	Value: 90.00				

KM# 1022.1 5 DOLLARS

1.5700 g., 0.9999 Gold 0.0505 oz. AGW, 13.93 mm. **Ruler:** Elizabeth II **Obv:** Head with tiara right **Rev:** Rooster standing right **Edge:** Reeded **Note:** Polished images with matte fields.

Date	Mintage	F	VF	XF	Unc	BU
2005 Proof	28,000	Value: 95.00				

KM# 1022.2 5 DOLLARS

1.5700 g., 0.9999 Gold 0.0505 oz. AGW, 13.93 mm. **Ruler:** Elizabeth II **Subject:** Year of the Rooster **Obv:** Head with tiara right **Rev:** Rooster standing right, multicolor **Edge:** Reeded

Date	Mintage	F	VF	XF	Unc	BU
2005 Proof	1,000	Value: 100				

KM# 743 8 DOLLARS
155.5175 g., 0.9990 Silver 4.9948 oz. ASW, 65 mm. **Ruler:** Elizabeth II **Subject:** Year of the Monkey **Obv:** Head with tiara right, denomination below **Rev:** Gold-plated seated monkey and multicolored ornamentation **Edge:** Reeded

Date	Mintage	F	VF	XF	Unc	BU
2004	6,000	—	—	—	—	220

KM# 1023 8 DOLLARS
155.5150 g., 0.9990 Silver Gilt 4.9947 oz. ASW, 65 mm. **Ruler:** Elizabeth II **Subject:** Year of the Rooster **Obv:** Head with tiara right **Rev:** Rooster standing left, multicolor **Edge:** Reeded

Date	Mintage	F	VF	XF	Unc	BU
2005 Proof	10,000	Value: 300				

KM# 1371 8 DOLLARS
155.5175 g., 0.9990 Silver 4.9948 oz. ASW, 65 mm. **Ruler:** Elizabeth II **Subject:** Year of the Tiger **Obv:** Head right **Rev:** Tiger at rest left

Date	Mintage	F	VF	XF	Unc	BU
2010(p)	—	—	—	—	—	225

KM# 539 10 DOLLARS
311.0350 g., 0.9990 Silver 9.9896 oz. ASW, 75.5 mm. **Ruler:** Elizabeth II **Subject:** Year of the Snake **Obv:** Head with tiara right, denomination below **Rev:** Snake with eggs **Edge:** Segmented reeding

Date	Mintage	F	VF	XF	Unc	BU
2001	—	—	—	—	350	375
2001P Proof	250	Value: 450				

KM# 583 10 DOLLARS
311.0350 g., 0.9990 Silver 9.9896 oz. ASW, 75.5 mm. **Ruler:** Elizabeth II **Subject:** Year of the Horse **Obv:** Head with tiara right, denomination below **Rev:** Horse running left **Edge:** Segmented reeding

Date	Mintage	F	VF	XF	Unc	BU
2002	—	—	—	—	350	375
2002P Proof	500	Value: 425				

KM# 710 10 DOLLARS
311.0350 g., 0.9990 Silver 9.9896 oz. ASW, 75.5 mm. **Ruler:** Elizabeth II **Subject:** Year of the Goat **Obv:** Head with tiara right, denomination below **Rev:** Goat

Date	Mintage	F	VF	XF	Unc	BU
2003	—	—	—	—	350	375
2003 Proof	—	Value: 425				

KM# 1339 10 DOLLARS
311.0350 g., 0.9990 Silver 9.9896 oz. ASW, 75.5 mm. **Ruler:** Elizabeth II **Subject:** Year of the Goat **Obv:** Head right

Date	Mintage	F	VF	XF	Unc	BU
2003P	—	—	—	—	375	350
2003P Proof	—	Value: 425				

KM# 676 10 DOLLARS
311.0350 g., 0.9990 Silver 9.9896 oz. ASW, 75.5 mm. **Ruler:** Elizabeth II **Subject:** Year of the Monkey **Obv:** Head with tiara right, denomination below **Rev:** Monkey sitting on branch **Edge:** Segmented reeding

Date	Mintage	F	VF	XF	Unc	BU
2004	—	—	—	—	350	375
2004 Proof	5,000	Value: 425				

KM# 696 10 DOLLARS
311.0350 g., 0.9990 Silver 9.9896 oz. ASW, 75.5 mm. **Ruler:** Elizabeth II **Subject:** Year of the Rooster **Obv:** Head with tiara right, denomination below **Rev:** Rooster

Date	Mintage	F	VF	XF	Unc	BU
2005	—	—	—	—	350	375
2005 Proof	—	Value: 425				

KM# 1057 10 DOLLARS
3.1100 g., 0.9990 Gold 0.0999 oz. AGW, 17.53 mm. **Ruler:** Elizabeth II **Subject:** Year of the Rat

Date	Mintage	F	VF	XF	Unc	BU
2008 Proof	2,500	Value: 200				

KM# 1079 10 DOLLARS
3.1100 g., 0.9990 Gold 0.0999 oz. AGW, 17.53 mm. **Ruler:** Elizabeth II **Subject:** Year of the Ox

Date	Mintage	F	VF	XF	Unc	BU
2009 Proof	2,500	Value: 245				

KM# 1321 10 DOLLARS
3.1100 g., 0.9990 Gold 0.0999 oz. AGW, 19 mm. **Ruler:** Elizabeth II **Subject:** Year of the Tiger **Obv:** Head right **Obv. Designer:** Ian Rank-Broadley **Rev:** Tiger head facing

Date	Mintage	F	VF	XF	Unc	BU
2010P Proof	8,000	Value: 260				

KM# 1372 10 DOLLARS
311.0350 g., 0.9990 Silver 9.9896 oz. ASW, 75.5 mm. **Ruler:** Elizabeth II **Subject:** Year of the Tiger **Obv:** Head right **Rev:** Tiger at rest left **Note:** Illustration reduced.

Date	Mintage	F	VF	XF	Unc	BU
2010(p)	—	—	—	—	—	375

KM# 540 15 DOLLARS
3.1103 g., 0.9990 Gold 0.0999 oz. AGW, 16.1 mm. **Ruler:** Elizabeth II **Subject:** Year of the Snake **Obv:** Head with tiara right, denomination below **Rev:** Snake in tree **Edge:** Reeded

Date	Mintage	F	VF	XF	Unc	BU
2001	80,000	—	—	—	—	150
2001P Proof	7,000	Value: 180				

KM# 584 15 DOLLARS
3.1103 g., 0.9990 Gold 0.0999 oz. AGW, 16.1 mm. **Ruler:** Elizabeth II **Subject:** Year of the Horse **Obv:** Head with tiara right, denomination below **Rev:** Horse galloping half left **Edge:** Reeded

Date	Mintage	F	VF	XF	Unc	BU
2002P	—	—	—	—	—	150
2002P Proof	7,000	Value: 180				

KM# 711 15 DOLLARS
3.1100 g., 0.9999 Gold 0.1000 oz. AGW, 16.1 mm. **Ruler:** Elizabeth II **Subject:** Year of the Goat **Obv:** Head with tiara right, denomination below **Rev:** Goat

Date	Mintage	F	VF	XF	Unc	BU
2003	—	—	—	—	—	150
2003 Proof	—	Value: 180				

KM# 1340 15 DOLLARS
3.1100 g., 0.9990 Gold 0.0999 oz. AGW, 16.1 mm. **Ruler:** Elizabeth II **Subject:** Year of the Goat **Obv:** Head right

Date	Mintage	F	VF	XF	Unc	BU
2003P	—	—	—	—	—	160
2003P Proof	—	Value: 190				

KM# 669 15 DOLLARS
3.1103 g., 0.9999 Gold 0.1000 oz. AGW, 16.1 mm. **Ruler:** Elizabeth II **Subject:** Year of the Monkey **Obv:** Head with tiara right, denomination below **Rev:** Monkey **Edge:** Reeded

Date	Mintage	F	VF	XF	Unc	BU
2004P	—	—	—	—	—	150
2004P Proof	80,000	Value: 180				

KM# 794 15 DOLLARS
3.1103 g., 0.9999 Gold 0.1000 oz. AGW, 16.1 mm. **Ruler:** Elizabeth II **Subject:** Year of the Rooster **Obv:** Elizabeth II **Rev:** Standing rooster right **Edge:** Reeded

Date	Mintage	F	VF	XF	Unc	BU
2005P Proof	7,000	Value: 180				

KM# 794a 15 DOLLARS

31.1030 g., 0.7500 Gold 0.7500 oz. AGW **Ruler:** Elizabeth II **Subject:** Year of the Rooster **Obv:** Head with tiara right **Rev:** Rooster standing right **Edge:** Reeded

Date	Mintage	F	VF	XF	Unc	BU
2005P Proof	15,000	Value: 1,150				

KM# 1373 15 DOLLARS

500.0000 g., 0.9990 Silver 16.058 oz. ASW **Ruler:** Elizabeth II **Subject:** Year of the Tiger **Obv:** Head right **Rev:** Tiger at rest left

Date	Mintage	F	VF	XF	Unc	BU
2010(p)	—	—	—	—	—	650

KM# 1375 15 DOLLARS

3.1100 g., 0.9990 Gold 0.0999 oz. AGW, 16.1 mm. **Ruler:** Elizabeth II **Subject:** Year of the Tiger **Obv:** Head right

Date	Mintage	F	VF	XF	Unc	BU
2010(p)	—	—	—	—	—	150

KM# 1482 15 DOLLARS

3.1000 g., 0.9990 Gold 0.0996 oz. AGW, 16.1 mm. **Ruler:** Elizabeth II **Subject:** Year of the Rabbit **Rev:** Rabbit left

Date	Mintage	F	VF	XF	Unc	BU
2011P Proof	—	Value: 180				

KM# 541 25 DOLLARS

7.7508 g., 0.9990 Gold 0.2489 oz. AGW, 20.1 mm. **Ruler:** Elizabeth II **Subject:** Year of the Snake **Obv:** Head with tiara right, denomination below **Rev:** Snake in tree **Edge:** Reeded

Date	Mintage	F	VF	XF	Unc	BU
2001	60,000	—	—	—	—	375
2001P Proof	7,000	Value: 400				

KM# 585 25 DOLLARS

7.7759 g., 0.9990 Gold 0.2497 oz. AGW, 20.1 mm. **Ruler:** Elizabeth II **Subject:** Year of the Horse **Obv:** Head with tiara right, denomination below **Rev:** Horse galloping half left **Edge:** Reeded

Date	Mintage	F	VF	XF	Unc	BU
2002P	—	—	—	—	—	375
2002P Proof	7,000	Value: 400				

KM# 712 25 DOLLARS

7.7500 g., 0.9999 Gold 0.2491 oz. AGW **Ruler:** Elizabeth II **Subject:** Year of the Goat **Obv:** Head with tiara right, denomination below **Rev:** Goat

Date	Mintage	F	VF	XF	Unc	BU
2003	—	—	—	—	—	375
2003 Proof	—	Value: 400				

KM# 1341 25 DOLLARS

7.7600 g., 0.9990 Gold 0.2492 oz. AGW, 20 mm. **Ruler:** Elizabeth II **Subject:** Year of the Goat **Obv:** Head right

Date	Mintage	F	VF	XF	Unc	BU
2003P	—	—	—	—	—	385
2003P Proof	—	Value: 425				

KM# 670 25 DOLLARS

7.7508 g., 0.9999 Gold 0.2492 oz. AGW, 20.1 mm. **Ruler:** Elizabeth II **Subject:** Year of the Monkey **Obv:** Head with tiara right, denomination below **Rev:** Monkey **Edge:** Reeded

Date	Mintage	F	VF	XF	Unc	BU
2004P	—	—	—	—	—	375
2004P Proof	60,000	Value: 400				

KM# 795 25 DOLLARS

7.7759 g., 0.9999 Gold 0.2500 oz. AGW, 20.1 mm. **Ruler:** Elizabeth II **Subject:** Year of the Rooster **Obv:** Elizabeth II **Rev:** Standing rooster right **Edge:** Reeded

Date	Mintage	F	VF	XF	Unc	BU
2005P Proof	7,000	Value: 400				

KM# 1322 25 DOLLARS

7.7700 g., 0.9990 Gold 0.2496 oz. AGW, 22 mm. **Ruler:** Elizabeth II **Subject:** Year of the Tiger **Obv:** Head right **Obv. Designer:** Ian Rank-Broadley **Rev:** Tiger head facing

Date	Mintage	F	VF	XF	Unc	BU
2010P Proof	8,000	Value: 650				

KM# 1483 25 DOLLARS

7.7700 g., 0.9990 Gold 0.2496 oz. AGW **Ruler:** Elizabeth II **Subject:** Year of the Rabbit **Rev:** Rabbit left

Date	Mintage	F	VF	XF	Unc	BU
2011P Proof	—	Value: 400				

KM# 542 30 DOLLARS

1002.5020 g., 0.9990 Silver 32.197 oz. ASW, 101 mm. **Ruler:** Elizabeth II **Subject:** Year of the Snake **Obv:** Head with tiara right, denomination below **Rev:** Snake with eggs **Edge:** Segmented reeding

Date	Mintage	F	VF	XF	Unc	BU
2001	—	—	—	—	—	1,150
2001P Proof	250	Value: 1,200				

KM# 586 30 DOLLARS

1002.5020 g., 0.9990 Silver 32.197 oz. ASW, 101 mm. **Ruler:** Elizabeth II **Subject:** Year of the Horse **Obv:** Head with tiara right, denomination below **Rev:** Horse running left **Edge:** Segmented reeding **Note:** Illustration reduced.

Date	Mintage	F	VF	XF	Unc	BU
2002	—	—	—	—	—	1,150
2002P Proof	250	Value: 1,200				

KM# 681 30 DOLLARS

1000.0000 g., 0.9990 Silver 32.117 oz. ASW, 101 mm. **Ruler:** Elizabeth II **Subject:** Year of the Goat **Obv:** Head with tiara right, denomination below **Rev:** Nanny goat and kid **Edge:** Segmented reeding

Date	Mintage	F	VF	XF	Unc	BU
2003	—	—	—	—	—	1,150
2003P Proof	—	Value: 1,200				

KM# 677.1 30 DOLLARS

1000.0000 g., 0.9990 Silver 32.117 oz. ASW, 101 mm. **Ruler:** Elizabeth II **Subject:** Year of the Monkey **Obv:** Head with tiara right, denomination below **Rev:** Monkey sitting on branch **Edge:** Segmented reeding

Date	Mintage	F	VF	XF	Unc	BU
2004	—	—	—	—	—	1,150
2004 Proof	5,250	Value: 1,200				

KM# 677.2 30 DOLLARS

1000.0000 g., 0.9990 Silver 32.117 oz. ASW, 101 mm. **Ruler:** Elizabeth II **Subject:** Year of the Monkey **Obv:** Head with tiara right, denomination below **Obv. Designer:** Ian Rank-Broadley **Rev:** Multicolor ornamentation and monkey with diamond chip eyes sitting on branch **Edge:** Segmented reeding **Note:** Illustration reduced.

Date	Mintage	F	VF	XF	Unc	BU
2004 Proof	5,000	Value: 1,250				

KM# 697 30 DOLLARS

1000.0000 g., 0.9990 Silver 32.117 oz. ASW, 101 mm. **Ruler:** Elizabeth II **Subject:** Year of the Rooster **Obv:** Head with tiara right, denomination below **Rev:** Rooster, partially gilt and colored **Note:** Illustration reduced.

Date	Mintage	F	VF	XF	Unc	BU
2005 Proof	—	Value: 1,200				

KM# 1374 30 DOLLARS

1000.0000 g., 0.9990 Silver 32.117 oz. ASW **Ruler:** Elizabeth II **Subject:** Year of the Tiger **Obv:** Head right

Date	Mintage	F	VF	XF	Unc	BU
2010(p)	—	—	—	—	—	1,150

KM# 1319 30 DOLLARS
1000.0000 g., 0.9990 Silver 32.117 oz. ASW, 100.6 mm. **Ruler:** Elizabeth II **Subject:** Year of the Tiger **Obv:** Head right **Obv. Designer:** Ian Rank-Broadley **Rev:** Tiger at rest left **Note:** Illustration reduced.

Date	Mintage	F	VF	XF	Unc	BU
2010P Proof	5,000	Value: 1,600				

KM# 1479 30 DOLLARS
1000.0000 g., 0.9990 Silver 32.117 oz. ASW **Ruler:** Elizabeth II **Subject:** Year of the Rabbit **Rev:** Mother and baby rabbit nose to nose **Note:** Illustration reduced.

Date	Mintage	F	VF	XF	Unc	BU
2010P Proof	—	Value: 1,250				

KM# 671 50 DOLLARS
15.5940 g., 0.9999 Gold 0.5013 oz. AGW, 25.1 mm. **Ruler:** Elizabeth II **Subject:** Year of the Monkey **Obv:** Head with tiara right, denomination below **Rev:** Monkey **Edge:** Reeded

Date	Mintage	F	VF	XF	Unc	BU
2004P Proof	40,000	Value: 750				

KM# 1376 50 DOLLARS
15.5940 g., 0.9990 Gold 0.5008 oz. AGW, 25 mm. **Ruler:** Elizabeth II **Subject:** Year of the Tiger **Obv:** Head right

Date	Mintage	F	VF	XF	Unc	BU
2010(p) Proof	—	Value: 750				

KM# 543 100 DOLLARS
31.1035 g., 0.9990 Gold 0.9990 oz. AGW, 32.1 mm. **Ruler:** Elizabeth II **Subject:** Year of the Snake **Obv:** Head with tiara right, denomination below **Obv. Designer:** Ian Rank-Broadley **Rev:** Snake in tree **Edge:** Reeded

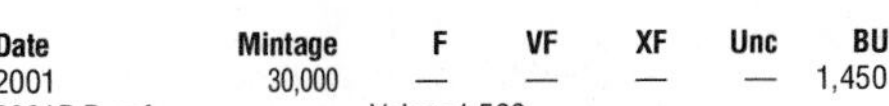

Date	Mintage	F	VF	XF	Unc	BU
2001	30,000	—	—	—	—	1,450
2001P Proof	—	Value: 1,500				

KM# 587 100 DOLLARS
31.1035 g., 0.9990 Gold 0.9990 oz. AGW, 32.1 mm. **Ruler:** Elizabeth II **Subject:** Year of the Horse **Obv:** Head with tiara right, denomination below **Rev:** Horse running left **Edge:** Reeded

Date	Mintage	F	VF	XF	Unc	BU
2002	—	—	—	—	—	1,250
2002P Proof	—	Value: 1,300				

KM# 713 100 DOLLARS
31.1035 g., 0.9999 Gold 0.9999 oz. AGW, 32.1 mm. **Ruler:** Elizabeth II **Subject:** Year of the Goat **Obv:** Head with tiara right, denomination below **Rev:** Goat

Date	Mintage	F	VF	XF	Unc	BU
2003	—	—	—	—	—	1,450
2003 Proof	—	Value: 1,500				

KM# 672 100 DOLLARS
31.1035 g., 0.9999 Gold 0.9999 oz. AGW, 32.1 mm. **Ruler:** Elizabeth II **Subject:** Year of the Monkey **Obv:** Head with tiara right, denomination below **Rev:** Monkey walking left on branch **Edge:** Reeded

Date	Mintage	F	VF	XF	Unc	BU
2004	30,000	—	—	—	—	1,450
2004P Proof	—	Value: 1,500				

KM# 796 100 DOLLARS
31.1035 g., 0.9999 Gold 0.9999 oz. AGW, 32.1 mm. **Ruler:** Elizabeth II **Subject:** Year of the Rooster **Obv:** Elizabeth II **Rev:** Standing rooster right **Edge:** Reeded

Date	Mintage	F	VF	XF	Unc	BU
2005P Proof	3,000	Value: 1,500				

KM# 1323 100 DOLLARS
31.1050 g., 0.9990 Gold 0.9990 oz. AGW, 40 mm. **Ruler:** Elizabeth II **Subject:** Year of the Tiger **Obv:** Head right **Obv. Designer:** Ian Rank-Broadley **Rev:** Tiger head facing

Date	Mintage	F	VF	XF	Unc	BU
2010P Proof	6,000	Value: 2,430				

KM# 1485 100 DOLLARS
31.1050 g., 0.9990 Gold 0.9990 oz. AGW, 32.1 mm. **Ruler:** Elizabeth II **Subject:** Year of the Rabbit **Rev:** Rabbit seated left

Date	Mintage	F	VF	XF	Unc	BU
2011P Proof	—	Value: 1,500				

KM# 704 200 DOLLARS
62.2140 g., 0.9999 Gold 1.9999 oz. AGW **Ruler:** Elizabeth II **Subject:** Year of the Snake **Obv:** Head with tiara right, denomination below **Rev:** Snake

Date	Mintage	F	VF	XF	Unc	BU
2001 Proof	—	Value: 2,950				

KM# 1333 200 DOLLARS
62.2100 g., 0.9990 Gold 1.9980 oz. AGW **Ruler:** Elizabeth II **Subject:** Year of the Snake **Obv:** Head right

Date	Mintage	F	VF	XF	Unc	BU
2001P Proof	—	Value: 2,950				

KM# 707 200 DOLLARS
62.2140 g., 0.9999 Gold 1.9999 oz. AGW **Ruler:** Elizabeth II **Subject:** Year of the Horse **Rev:** Horse

Date	Mintage	F	VF	XF	Unc	BU
2002 Proof	—	Value: 2,950				

KM# 1336 200 DOLLARS
62.2100 g., 0.9990 Gold 1.9980 oz. AGW **Ruler:** Elizabeth II **Subject:** Year of the Horse

Date	Mintage	F	VF	XF	Unc	BU
2002P Proof	—	Value: 2,750				

KM# 714 200 DOLLARS
62.2140 g., 0.9999 Gold 1.9999 oz. AGW **Ruler:** Elizabeth II **Subject:** Year of the Goat **Obv:** Head with tiara right **Rev:** Goat

Date	Mintage	F	VF	XF	Unc	BU
2003 Proof	—	Value: 2,950				

KM# 717 200 DOLLARS
62.2100 g., 0.9999 Gold 1.9998 oz. AGW **Ruler:** Elizabeth II **Subject:** Year of the Monkey **Obv:** Head with tiara right **Rev:** Monkey

Date	Mintage	F	VF	XF	Unc	BU
2004 Proof	—	Value: 2,950				

KM# 698 200 DOLLARS
62.2100 g., 0.9999 Gold 1.9998 oz. AGW **Ruler:** Elizabeth II **Subject:** Year of the Rooster **Obv:** Head with tiara right **Rev:** Rooster

Date	Mintage	F	VF	XF	Unc	BU
2005 Proof	—	Value: 2,950				

KM# 1377 200 DOLLARS
62.2100 g., 0.9990 Gold 1.9980 oz. AGW **Ruler:** Elizabeth II **Obv:** Year of the Tiger **Rev:** Tiger head facing

Date	Mintage	F	VF	XF	Unc	BU
2010(p)	—	—	—	—	—	2,950

KM# 1006 300 DOLLARS
10000.0000 g., 0.9990 Silver 321.17 oz. ASW **Ruler:** Elizabeth II **Series:** Lunar year **Subject:** Year of the Dog **Obv:** Head with tiara right **Obv. Legend:** ELIZABETH II - AUSTRALIA **Obv. Designer:** Ian Rank-Broadley **Rev:** Dog sitting, facing right

Date	Mintage	F	VF	XF	Unc	BU
2006	—	—	—	—	—	11,500

KM# 705 1000 DOLLARS
311.0480 g., 0.9999 Gold 9.9990 oz. AGW **Ruler:** Elizabeth II **Subject:** Year of the Snake **Obv:** Head with tiara right, denomination below **Rev:** Snake

Date	Mintage	F	VF	XF	Unc	BU
2001	—	—	—	—	—	15,000

KM# 1334 1000 DOLLARS
311.0480 g., 0.9990 Gold 9.9900 oz. AGW **Ruler:** Elizabeth II **Subject:** Year of the Snake **Obv:** Head right

Date	Mintage	F	VF	XF	Unc	BU
2001P	—	—	—	—	—	15,000

KM# 708 1000 DOLLARS

311.0480 g., 0.9999 Gold 9.9990 oz. AGW **Ruler:** Elizabeth II **Subject:** Year of the Horse **Obv:** Head with tiara right, denomination below **Rev:** Horse

Date	Mintage	F	VF	XF	Unc	BU
2002	—	—	—	—	—	15,000

KM# 1337 1000 DOLLARS

311.0480 g., 0.9990 Gold 9.9900 oz. AGW **Ruler:** Elizabeth II **Subject:** Year of the Horse **Obv:** Head right

Date	Mintage	F	VF	XF	Unc	BU
2002P	—	—	—	—	—	15,000

KM# 715 1000 DOLLARS

311.0480 g., 0.9999 Gold 9.9990 oz. AGW **Ruler:** Elizabeth II **Subject:** Year of the Goat **Obv:** Head with tiara right, denomination below **Rev:** Goat

Date	Mintage	F	VF	XF	Unc	BU
2003	—	—	—	—	—	15,000

KM# 718 1000 DOLLARS

311.0480 g., 0.9999 Gold 9.9990 oz. AGW **Ruler:** Elizabeth II **Subject:** Year of the Monkey **Obv:** Head with tiara right, denomination below **Rev:** Monkey

Date	Mintage	F	VF	XF	Unc	BU
2004	—	—	—	—	—	15,000

KM# 699 1000 DOLLARS

311.0480 g., 0.9999 Gold 9.9990 oz. AGW **Ruler:** Elizabeth II **Subject:** Year of the Rooster **Obv:** Head with tiara right, denomination below **Rev:** Rooster

Date	Mintage	F	VF	XF	Unc	BU
2005	—	—	—	—	—	15,000

KM# 1378 1000 DOLLARS

311.0480 g., 0.9990 Gold 9.9900 oz. AGW **Ruler:** Elizabeth II **Subject:** Year of the Tiger **Obv:** Head right

Date	Mintage	F	VF	XF	Unc	BU
2010(p)	—	—	—	—	—	15,000

KM# 706 3000 DOLLARS

1000.0000 g., 0.9999 Gold 32.146 oz. AGW **Ruler:** Elizabeth II **Subject:** Year of the Snake **Obv:** Head with tiara right, denomination below **Rev:** Snake

Date	Mintage	F	VF	XF	Unc	BU
2001	—	—	—	—	—	BV+3%

KM# 1335 3000 DOLLARS

1000.0000 g., 0.9990 Gold 32.117 oz. AGW **Ruler:** Elizabeth II **Subject:** Year of the Snake **Obv:** Head right

Date	Mintage	F	VF	XF	Unc	BU
2001P	—	—	—	—	—	BV+3%

KM# 709 3000 DOLLARS

1000.0000 g., 0.9999 Gold 32.146 oz. AGW **Ruler:** Elizabeth II **Subject:** Year of the Horse **Obv:** Head with tiara right, denomination below **Rev:** Horse

Date	Mintage	F	VF	XF	Unc	BU
2002	—	—	—	—	—	BV+3%

KM# 1338 3000 DOLLARS

1000.0000 g., 0.9990 Gold 32.117 oz. AGW **Ruler:** Elizabeth II **Subject:** Year of the Horse **Obv:** Head right

Date	Mintage	F	VF	XF	Unc	BU
2002P	—	—	—	—	—	BV+3%

KM# 716 3000 DOLLARS

1000.0000 g., 0.9999 Gold 32.146 oz. AGW **Ruler:** Elizabeth II **Subject:** Year of the Goat **Obv:** Head with tiara right, denomination below **Rev:** Goat

Date	Mintage	F	VF	XF	Unc	BU
2003	—	—	—	—	—	BV+3%

KM# 719 3000 DOLLARS

1000.0000 g., 0.9999 Gold 32.146 oz. AGW **Ruler:** Elizabeth II **Subject:** Year of the Monkey **Obv:** Head with tiara right, denomination below **Rev:** Monkey

Date	Mintage	F	VF	XF	Unc	BU
2004	—	—	—	—	—	BV+3%

KM# 700 3000 DOLLARS

1000.0000 g., 0.9999 Gold 32.146 oz. AGW **Ruler:** Elizabeth II **Subject:** Year of the Rooster **Obv:** Head with tiara right, denomination below **Rev:** Rooster

Date	Mintage	F	VF	XF	Unc	BU
2005	—	—	—	—	—	BV+3%

KM# 1379 3000 DOLLARS

1000.0000 g., 0.9990 Gold 32.117 oz. AGW **Ruler:** Elizabeth II **Subject:** Year of the Tiger **Obv:** Head right

Date	Mintage	F	VF	XF	Unc	BU
2010(p)	—	—	—	—	—	BV+3%

KM# 1007 30000 DOLLARS

10000.0000 g., 0.9999 Gold 321.46 oz. AGW, 40.5 mm. **Ruler:** Elizabeth II **Series:** Lunar year **Subject:** Year of the Dog **Obv:** Head with tiara right **Obv. Legend:** ELIZABETH II - AUSTRALIA **Obv. Designer:** Ian Rank-Broadley **Rev:** Dog standing left

Date	Mintage	F	VF	XF	Unc	BU
2006	—	—	—	—	—	BV+2%

BABY MINT SETS

KM#	Date	Mintage	Identification	Issue Price	Mkt Val
BMS9	2001 (6)	32,494	KM#401-403, 406, 491.1, 534.1 plus bronze medal	—	110
BMS10	2002 (6)	32,479	KM#401-403, 406, 600.1, 602 plus bronze medal	—	47.50
BMS11	2003 (6)	37,748	KM#401-402, 406, 688-690 plus bronze medal	—	40.00
BMS12	2004 (6)	31,000	KM#401-404, 406, 733.1 plus bronze medal	—	40.00
BMS13	2005 (6)	34,748	KM#401-402, 406, 745-747 plus bronze medal	24.00	27.50
BMS14	2006 (6)	—	KM#401-404, 406, 489 plus bronze medal	24.00	35.00

BABY PROOF SETS

KM#	Date	Mintage	Identification	Issue Price	Mkt Val
BPS7	2001 (6)	15,011	KM#401-403, 406, 491.1, 534.1 plus silver medal	—	165
BPS8	2002 (6)	13,996	KM#401, 403, 406, 600.2, 602 plus silver medal	—	153
BPS9	2003 (6)	14,799	KM#401-402, 406, 688-689, 690.1 plus silver medal	—	125
BPS10	2004 (6)	13,996	KM#401-404, 406, 733 plus silver medal	—	110
BPS11	2005 (6)	—	KM#401-402, 406, 745-747 plus silver medal	—	100
BPS12	2006 (6)	—	KM#401-404, 406, 489 plus silver medal	—	120

MINT SETS

KM#	Date	Mintage	Identification	Issue Price	Mkt Val
MS49	2001 (6)	—	KM#401-403, 406, 491.1, 534.1	—	80.00
MS39	2001 (3)	—	KM532, 533, 534.1	7.80	75.00
MS48	2001 (20)	—	KM532-533, 534.1, 491.1, 550-565	43.68	235
MS40	2001 (3)	—	KM534.1, 550, 551	7.80	70.00
MS41	2001 (3)	—	KM534.1, 552, 553	7.80	70.00
MS42	2001 (3)	—	KM534.1, 554, 555	7.80	75.00
MS43	2001 (3)	—	KM534.1, 556, 557	7.80	72.50
MS44	2001 (3)	—	KM534.1, 558, 559	7.80	75.00
MS45	2001 (3)	—	KM534.1, 560, 561	7.80	85.00
MS46	2001 (3)	—	KM534.1, 562, 563	7.80	80.00
MS47	2001 (3)	—	KM534.1, 564, 565	7.80	75.00
MS51	2002 (3)	—	KM#691.2, 692, 693	—	2,300
MS50	2002 (6)	—	KM#401-403, 406, 600.1, 602	—	65.00
MS52	2003 (5)	—	KM401, 402, 406, 689, 690	—	35.00
MS53	2004 (6)	—	KM401-404, 406, 733.1	—	32.50
MS54	2005 (6)	—	KM#401, 402, 406, 745-747	—	25.00
MS55	2006 (8)	—	KM#401-404, 406, 489, 767-768 40 Years of Decimal Currency	18.50	55.00
MS56	2006 (15)	—	KM#770-781, 1001-1003	80.00	165

PROOF SETS

KM#	Date	Mintage	Identification	Issue Price	Mkt Val
PS107	2001 (3)	—	KM532, 533, 534.2	21.00	95.00
PS108	2001 (3)	—	KM534.2, 550, 551	21.00	65.00
PS109	2001 (3)	—	KM534.2, 552, 553	21.00	75.00
PS110	2001 (3)	—	KM534.2, 554, 555	21.00	75.00
PS111	2001 (3)	—	KM534.2, 556, 557	21.00	75.00
PS112	2001 (3)	—	KM534.2, 558, 559	21.00	85.00
PS113	2001 (3)	—	KM534.2, 560, 561	21.00	95.00
PS114	2001 (3)	—	KM534.2, 562, 563	21.00	85.00
PS115	2001 (3)	—	KM534.2, 564, 565	21.00	85.00
PS116	2001 (20)	—	KM491.2, 532-533, 534.2, 549.2, 550-565	120	665
PS117	2001 (6)	—	KM#401-403, 406, 491.1, 534.1	—	145
PS118	2001 (1)	650	Federation Centennial Set	—	6,000
PS119	2002 (6)	39,513	KM#401-403, 406, 600.2, 602	—	95.00
PS120	2006 (6)	39,090	KM#401-402, 406, 688-689, 690.1	—	70.00
PS121	2003 (6)	6,500	KM#401b, 402b, 406b, 688a, 689a, 690a	—	180
PS122	2003 (4)	10,000	KM763-766	118	250
PS123	2004 (6)	50,000	KM#401-404, 406, 733	—	80.00
PS124	2004 (6)	6,500	KM#401b, 402b, 403b, 404a, 406b, 733.1a	—	150
PS125	2005 (6)	—	KM#401, 402, 406, 745-747	—	85.00
PS126	2005 (6)	6,500	KM#401b, 402b, 406b, 745a, 746a, 747a	—	175
PS127	2005 (6)	650	KM#401a, 402a, 406a, 745b, 746b, 747b	—	5,850
PS128	2006 (8)	—	KM#401-404, 406, 489, 767-768	62.50	120
PS129	2006 (8)	6,500	KM#62a, 63a, 64a, 65a, 66a, 77a, 852	180	220

WEDDING SPECIMEN SETS

KM#	Date	Mintage	Identification	Issue Price	Mkt Val
WSS1	2002 (6)	3,322	KM#401-403, 406, 600.1, 602 Plaque	—	97.50
WSS2	2003 (6)	3,249	KM#401-402, 406, 688-690 Plaque	—	55.00
WSS3	2004 (6)	4,000	KM#401-404, 406, 733.1 Plaque	—	58.50
WSS4	2005 (6)	—	KM#401-402, 406, 745-747 Plaque	60.00	60.00
WSS5	2006 (8)	—	KM#401-404, 406, 489, 767-768 Plaque	60.00	60.00

AUSTRIA

The Republic of Austria, a parliamentary democracy located in mountainous central Europe, has an area of 32,374 sq. mi. (83,850 sq. km.) and a population of 8.08 million. Capital: Wien (Vienna). Austria is primarily an industrial country. Machinery, iron, steel, textiles, yarns and timber are exported.

REPUBLIC

POST WWII DECIMAL COINAGE

100 Groschen - 1 Schilling

KM# 2878 10 GROSCHEN

1.1000 g., Aluminum, 20 mm. **Obv:** Small Imperial Eagle with Austrian shield on breast, at top between numbers, scalloped rim, stylized inscription below **Rev:** Large value above date, scalloped rim **Edge:** Plain **Designer:** Hans Köttenstorfer

Date	Mintage	F	VF	XF	Unc	BU
2001 Special Unc	75,000	—	—	—	—	5.00

KM# 2885 50 GROSCHEN
3.0000 g., Aluminum-Bronze, 19.5 mm. **Obv:** Austrian shield **Obv. Designer:** Hans Köttenstorfer **Rev:** Large value above date **Rev. Designer:** Ferdinand Welz **Edge:** Reeded

Date	Mintage	F	VF	XF	Unc	BU
2001 Special Unc	75,000	—	—	—	—	5.00

KM# 2886 SCHILLING
4.2000 g., Aluminum-Bronze, 22.5 mm. **Obv:** Large value above date **Obv. Designer:** Edwin Grienauer **Rev:** Edelweiss flower **Rev. Designer:** Ferdinand Welz **Edge:** Plain

Date	Mintage	F	VF	XF	Unc	BU
2001 Special Unc	75,000	—	—	—	—	5.00

KM# 2889a 5 SCHILLING
4.8000 g., Copper-Nickel, 23.5 mm. **Obv:** Lippizaner stallion with rider, rearing left **Obv. Designer:** Hans Köttenstorfer **Rev:** Austrian shield divides date, value above, sprays below **Rev. Designer:** Josef Köblinger **Edge:** Plain

Date	Mintage	F	VF	XF	Unc	BU
2001 Special Unc	75,000	—	—	—	—	5.50

KM# 2918 10 SCHILLING
6.2000 g., Copper-Nickel Plated Nickel, 26 mm. **Obv:** Imperial Eagle with Austrian shield on breast, holding hammer and sickle **Obv. Designer:** Kurt Bodlak **Rev:** Woman of Wachau left, value and date right of hat **Rev. Designer:** Ferdinand Welz **Edge:** Reeded

Date	Mintage	F	VF	XF	Unc	BU
2001 Special Unc	75,000	—	—	—	—	6.00

KM# 3075 20 SCHILLING
8.0000 g., Copper-Aluminum-Nickel, 27.7 mm. **Subject:** Johann Nepomuk Nestroy **Obv:** Denomination within square **Rev:** Bust half left **Edge:** 19 incuse dots **Designer:** Herbert Wähner

Date	Mintage	F	VF	XF	Unc	BU
2001	225,000	—	—	—	4.50	—
2001 Special Unc	75,000	—	—	—	—	10.00

KM# 3076 50 SCHILLING
8.1500 g., Bi-Metallic Copper-Nickel clad Nickel center in Aluminumn-Bronze ring, 26.5 mm. **Subject:** The Schilling Era **Obv:** Denomination and shields **Rev:** Four old coin designs **Edge:** Plain

Date	Mintage	F	VF	XF	Unc	BU
2001	600,000	—	—	—	7.50	—
2001 Special Unc.	100,000	—	—	—	—	9.50

KM# 3073 100 SCHILLING
13.7000 g., Bi-Metallic Titanium center in 9.95g .900 silver ring., 34 mm. **Subject:** Transportation **Obv:** Automobile engine **Obv. Designer:** Thomas Pesendorfer **Rev:** Car, train, truck, and plane **Rev. Designer:** Andreas Zanaschka **Edge:** Plain

Date	Mintage	F	VF	XF	Unc	BU
2001 Proof	50,000	Value: 40.00				

KM# 3077 100 SCHILLING
20.0000 g., 0.9000 Silver 0.5787 oz. ASW, 34 mm. **Subject:** Charlemagne **Obv:** Holy Roman Emperor's crown above denomination **Obv. Designer:** Thomas Pesendorfer **Rev:** Bust 3/4 facing with scepter, two shields at right **Rev. Designer:** Herbert Wähner **Edge:** Reeded

Date	Mintage	F	VF	XF	Unc	BU
2001 Proof	50,000	Value: 40.00				

KM# 3079 100 SCHILLING
20.0000 g., 0.9000 Silver 0.5787 oz. ASW, 34 mm. **Subject:** Duke Rudolf IV **Obv:** University teaching scene **Obv. Designer:** Thomas Pesendorfer **Rev:** Bust on right looking left, St. Stephen's Cathedral at left **Rev. Designer:** Herbert Wähner **Edge:** Reeded

Date	Mintage	F	VF	XF	Unc	BU
2001 Proof	50,000	Value: 40.00				

KM# 3074 500 SCHILLING
10.1400 g., 0.9860 Gold 0.3214 oz. AGW, 22 mm. **Subject:** 2000 Years of Christianity - Bible **Obv:** Bible and symbols of the saints: Matthew, Luke, Mark, and John **Rev:** St. Paul reading from a scroll to two listeners **Designer:** Thomas Pesendorfer

Date	Mintage	F	VF	XF	Unc	BU
2001 Proof	50,000	Value: 475				

KM# 3078 500 SCHILLING
24.0000 g., 0.9250 Silver 0.7137 oz. ASW, 37 mm. **Subject:** Kufstein Castle **Obv:** Castle view above denomination **Rev:** Emperor Maximilian being shown one of his new cannons **Edge:** Plain with engraved lettering **Designer:** Thomas Pesendorfer

Date	Mintage	F	VF	XF	Unc	BU
2001	50,000	—	—	—	45.00	—
2001 Special Unc.	15,000	—	—	—	—	50.00
2001 Proof	30,000	Value: 60.00				

KM# 3080 500 SCHILLING
24.0000 g., 0.9250 Silver 0.7137 oz. ASW, 37 mm. **Subject:** Schattenburg Castle **Obv:** Castle view **Obv. Designer:** Thomas Pesendorfer **Rev:** Two medieval armourers at work **Rev. Designer:** Helmut Andexlinger **Edge:** Plain with engraved lettering

Date	Mintage	F	VF	XF	Unc	BU
2001	37,000	—	—	—	42.00	—
2001 Special Unc	15,000	—	—	—	—	50.00
2001 Proof	43,000	Value: 60.00				

KM# 3081 1000 SCHILLING
16.2200 g., 0.9860 Gold 0.5142 oz. AGW, 30 mm. **Subject:** Austrian National Library **Obv:** Archduke Maximilian as a student **Obv. Designer:** Thomas Pesendorfer **Rev:** Library interior view **Rev. Designer:** Herbert Wähner **Edge:** Reeded

Date	Mintage	F	VF	XF	Unc	BU
2001 Proof	30,000	Value: 760				

BULLION COINAGE

Philharmonic Issues

KM# 3004 200 SCHILLING
3.1210 g., 0.9999 Gold 0.1003 oz. AGW, 16 mm. **Series:** Vienna Philharmonic Orchestra **Obv:** The Golden Hall organ **Rev:** Wind and string instruments **Designer:** Thomas Pesendorfer

Date	Mintage	F	VF	XF	Unc	BU
2001	26,400	—	—	—	BV+13%	—

KM# 2989 500 SCHILLING
7.7760 g., 0.9999 Gold 0.2500 oz. AGW, 22 mm. **Series:** Vienna Philharmonic Orchestra **Obv:** The Golden Hall organ **Rev:** Wind and string instruments **Edge:** Reeded **Designer:** Thomas Pesendorfer

Date	Mintage	F	VF	XF	Unc	BU
2001	25,800	—	—	—	BV+10%	—

KM# 3031 1000 SCHILLING

15.5520 g., 0.9999 Gold 0.4999 oz. AGW, 28 mm. **Series:** Vienna Philharmonic Orchestra **Obv:** The Golden Hall organ **Rev:** Wind and string instruments **Edge:** Reeded **Designer:** Thomas Pesendorfer

Date	Mintage	F	VF	XF	Unc	BU
2001	26,800	—	—	—	BV+8%	—

KM# 2990 2000 SCHILLING

31.1035 g., 0.9999 Gold 0.9999 oz. AGW, 37 mm. **Series:** Vienna Philharmonic Orchestra **Obv:** The Golden Hall organ **Rev:** Wind and string instruments **Edge:** Reeded **Designer:** Thomas Pesendorfer

Date	Mintage	F	VF	XF	Unc	BU
2001	54,700	—	—	—	BV+4%	—

EURO COINAGE

European Union Issues

KM# 3082 EURO CENT

2.3000 g., Copper Plated Steel, 16.25 mm. **Obv:** Gentian flower **Obv. Legend:** EIN EURO CENT **Obv. Designer:** Josef Kaiser **Rev:** Denomination and globe **Rev. Designer:** Luc Luycx **Edge:** Plain

Date	Mintage	F	VF	XF	Unc	BU
2002	378,400,000	—	—	—	0.35	—
2002 Special Unc	100,000	—	—	—	—	0.50
2002 Proof	10,000	Value: 15.00				
2003	10,800,000	—	—	—	0.35	—
2003 Special Unc	125,000	—	—	—	—	0.50
2003 Proof	25,000	Value: 3.00				
2004	115,000,000	—	—	—	0.35	—
2004 Special Unc	100,000	—	—	—	—	0.50
2004 Proof	20,000	Value: 3.00				
2005	122,900,000	—	—	—	0.35	—
2005 Special Unc	100,000	—	—	—	—	0.50
2005 Proof	20,000	Value: 4.00				
2006	48,300,000	—	—	—	0.35	—
2006 Special Unc	100,000	—	—	—	—	0.50
2006 Proof	20,000	Value: 4.00				
2007	111,900,000	—	—	—	0.35	—
2007 Special Unc	75,000	—	—	—	—	0.50
2007 Proof	20,000	Value: 4.00				
2008	50,900,000	—	—	—	0.35	—
2008 Special Unc	50,000	—	—	—	—	0.50
2008 Proof	15,000	Value: 4.00				
2009	158,900,000	—	—	—	0.35	—
2009 Special Unc	75,000	—	—	—	—	0.50
2009 Proof	15,000	Value: 4.00				
2010	—	—	—	—	0.35	—
2010 Special Unc	50,000	—	—	—	—	0.50
2010 Proof	15,000	Value: 4.00				
2011	—	—	—	—	0.35	—
2011 Special Unc	—	—	—	—	—	0.50
2011 Proof	—	Value: 4.00				

KM# 3083 2 EURO CENT

3.0600 g., Copper Plated Steel, 18.75 mm. **Obv:** Edelweiss flower in inner circle, stars in outer circle **Obv. Legend:** ZWEI EURO CENT **Obv. Designer:** Josef Kaiser **Rev:** Denomination and globe **Rev. Designer:** Luc Luycx **Edge:** Grooved

Date	Mintage	F	VF	XF	Unc	BU
2002	326,400,000	—	—	—	0.50	—
2002 Special Unc	100,000	—	—	—	—	0.65
2002 Proof	10,000	Value: 20.00				
2003	118,500,000	—	—	—	0.50	—
2003 Special Unc	125,000	—	—	—	—	0.65
2003 Proof	25,000	Value: 5.00				
2004	156,400,000	—	—	—	0.50	—
2004 Special Unc	100,000	—	—	—	—	0.65
2004 Proof	20,000	Value: 5.00				
2005	113,000,000	—	—	—	0.50	—
2005 Special Unc	100,000	—	—	—	—	0.65
2005 Proof	20,000	Value: 6.00				
2006	39,800,000	—	—	—	0.35	—
2006 Special Unc	100,000	—	—	—	—	0.65
2006 Proof	20,000	Value: 6.00				
2007	72,200,000	—	—	—	0.35	—
2007 Special Unc	75,000	—	—	—	—	0.65
2007 Proof	20,000	Value: 6.00				
2008	125,100,000	—	—	—	0.35	—
2008 Special Unc	50,000	—	—	—	—	0.65
2008 Proof	15,000	Value: 6.00				
2009	120,400,000	—	—	—	0.35	—
2009 Special Unc	75,000	—	—	—	—	0.65
2009 Proof	15,000	Value: 6.00				
2010	—	—	—	—	0.35	—
2010 Special Unc	50,000	—	—	—	—	0.65
2010 Proof	15,000	Value: 6.00				
2011	—	—	—	—	0.35	—
2011 Special Unc	—	—	—	—	—	0.65
2011 Proof	—	Value: 6.00				

KM# 3084 5 EURO CENT

3.9200 g., Copper Plated Steel, 21.25 mm. **Obv:** Alpine prim rose flower in inner ring, stars in outer ring **Obv. Legend:** FUNF EURO CENT **Obv. Designer:** Josef Kaiser **Rev:** Denomination and globe **Rev. Designer:** Luc Luycx **Edge:** Plain

Date	Mintage	F	VF	XF	Unc	BU
2002	217,000,000	—	—	—	0.75	—
2002 Special Unc	100,000	—	—	—	—	1.00
2002 Proof	10,000	Value: 30.00				
2003	108,500,000	—	—	—	0.75	—
2003 Special Unc	125,000	—	—	—	—	1.00
2003 Proof	25,000	Value: 8.50				
2004	89,300,000	—	—	—	0.75	—
2004 Special Unc	100,000	—	—	—	—	1.00
2004 Proof	20,000	Value: 9.00				
2005	66,100,000	—	—	—	0.75	—
2005 Special Unc	100,000	—	—	—	—	1.00
2005 Proof	20,000	Value: 10.00				
2006	5,600,000	—	—	—	0.75	—
2006 Special Unc	100,000	—	—	—	—	1.00
2006 Proof	20,000	Value: 10.00				
2007	52,700,000	—	—	—	0.75	—
2007 Special Unc	75,000	—	—	—	—	1.00
2007 Proof	20,000	Value: 10.00				
2008	96,700,000	—	—	—	0.75	—
2008 Special Unc	50,000	—	—	—	—	1.00
2008 Proof	15,000	Value: 10.00				
2009	5,800,000	—	—	—	0.75	—
2009 Special Unc	75,000	—	—	—	—	1.00
2009 Proof	15,000	Value: 10.00				
2010	—	—	—	—	0.75	—
2010 Special Unc	50,000	—	—	—	—	1.00
2010 Proof	15,000	Value: 10.00				
2011	—	—	—	—	0.75	—
2011 Special Unc	—	—	—	—	—	1.00
2011 Proof	—	Value: 10.00				

KM# 3085 10 EURO CENT

4.1000 g., Brass, 19.75 mm. **Obv:** St. Stephen's Cathedral spires **Obv. Designer:** Josef Kaiser **Rev:** Relief map of European Union at left, denomination at center right **Rev. Designer:** Luc Luycx **Edge:** Reeded

Date	Mintage	F	VF	XF	Unc	BU
2002	441,600,000	—	—	—	0.75	—
2002 Special Unc	100,000	—	—	—	—	1.00
2002 Proof	10,000	Value: 45.00				
2003 Special Unc	125,000	—	—	—	—	4.00
2003 Proof	25,000	Value: 8.50				
2004	5,200,000	—	—	—	0.80	—
2004 Special Unc	100,000	—	—	—	—	1.00
2004 Proof	20,000	Value: 9.00				
2005	5,200,000	—	—	—	0.80	—
2005 Special Unc	100,000	—	—	—	—	1.00
2005 Proof	20,000	Value: 10.00				
2006	40,000,000	—	—	—	0.75	—
2006 Special Unc	100,000	—	—	—	—	1.00
2006 Proof	20,000	Value: 10.00				
2007	81,300,000	—	—	—	0.75	—
2007 Special Unc	75,000	—	—	—	—	1.00
2007 Proof	20,000	Value: 10.00				

KM# 3139 10 EURO CENT

4.1000 g., Brass, 19.75 mm. **Obv:** St. Stephen's Cathedral spires **Obv. Designer:** Josef Kaiser **Rev:** Relief Map of Western Europe, stars, lines and value **Rev. Designer:** Luc Luycx **Edge:** Reeded

Date	Mintage	F	VF	XF	Unc	BU
2008	70,200,000	—	—	—	0.75	—
2008 Special Unc	50,000	—	—	—	—	1.00
2008 Proof	15,000	Value: 10.00				
2009	15,900,000	—	—	—	0.75	—
2009 Special Unc	75,000	—	—	—	—	1.00
2009 Proof	—	Value: 10.00				
2010 Special Unc	50,000	—	—	—	—	1.00
2010 Proof	15,000	Value: 10.00				
2011 Special Unc	—	—	—	—	—	1.00
2011 Proof	—	Value: 10.00				

KM# 3086 20 EURO CENT

5.7400 g., Brass, 22.25 mm. **Obv:** Belvedere Palace gate **Obv. Designer:** Josef Kaiser **Rev:** Relief map of European Union at left, denomination at center right **Rev. Designer:** Luc Luycx **Edge:** Notched

Date	Mintage	F	VF	XF	Unc	BU
2002	203,400,000	—	—	—	1.00	—
2002 Special Unc	100,000	—	—	—	—	1.25
2002 Proof	10,000	Value: 60.00				
2003	50,900,000	—	—	—	1.00	—
2003 Special Unc	125,000	—	—	—	—	1.25
2003 Proof	25,000	Value: 10.00				
2004	54,800,000	—	—	—	1.00	—
2004 Special Unc	100,000	—	—	—	—	1.25
2004 Proof	20,000	Value: 11.50				
2005	4,100,000	—	—	—	1.10	—
2005 Special Unc	100,000	—	—	—	—	1.25
2005 Proof	20,000	Value: 12.50				
2006	8,200,000	—	—	—	1.00	—
2006 Special Unc	100,000	—	—	—	—	1.25
2006 Proof	20,000	Value: 12.50				
2007	45,000,000	—	—	—	1.00	—
2007 Special Unc	75,000	—	—	—	—	1.25
2007 Proof	20,000	Value: 12.50				

KM# 3140 20 EURO CENT

5.7400 g., Brass, 22.25 mm. **Obv:** Belvedere Palace gate **Obv. Designer:** Josef Kaiser **Rev:** Expanded relief map of European Union at left, denomination at center right **Rev. Designer:** Luc Luycx **Edge:** Notched

Date	Mintage	F	VF	XF	Unc	BU
2008	45,300,000	—	—	—	1.00	—
2008 Special Unc.	50,000	—	—	—	—	1.50
2008 Proof	15,000	Value: 12.50				
2009	49,800,000	—	—	—	1.00	—
2009 Special Unc.	75,000	—	—	—	—	1.50
2009 Proof	15,000	Value: 12.50				
2010 Special Unc.	50,000	—	—	—	—	1.50
2010 Proof	15,000	Value: 12.50				
2011 Proof	—	Value: 12.50				
2011 Special Unc.	—	—	—	—	—	1.50

KM# 3087 50 EURO CENT

7.8000 g., Brass, 24.25 mm. **Obv:** Secession building in Vienna **Obv. Designer:** Josef Kaiser **Rev:** Relief map of European Union at left, denomination at center right **Rev. Designer:** Luc Luycx **Edge:** Reeded

Date	Mintage	F	VF	XF	Unc	BU
2002	16,100,000	—	—	—	1.25	—
2002 Special Unc	100,000	—	—	—	—	1.50
2002 Proof	10,000	Value: 75.00				
2003	9,100,000	—	—	—	1.25	—
2003 Special Unc	125,000	—	—	—	—	1.50
2003 Proof	25,000	Value: 12.50				
2004	3,100,000	—	—	—	1.25	—
2004 Special Unc	100,000	—	—	—	—	1.50
2004 Proof	20,000	Value: 13.50				
2005	3,100,000	—	—	—	1.25	—
2005 Special Unc	100,000	—	—	—	—	1.50
2005 Proof	20,000	Value: 15.00				
2006	3,200,000	—	—	—	1.25	—
2006 Special Unc	100,000	—	—	—	—	1.50
2006 Proof	20,000	Value: 15.00				
2007	3,000,000	—	—	—	1.25	—
2007 Special Unc	75,000	—	—	—	—	1.50
2007 Proof	20,000	Value: 15.00				

KM# 3141 50 EURO CENT

7.8000 g., Brass, 24.25 mm. **Obv:** Secession building in Vienna **Obv. Designer:** Josef Kaiser **Rev:** Expanded relief map of European Union at left, denomination at right **Rev. Designer:** Luc Luycx **Edge:** Reeded

Date	Mintage	F	VF	XF	Unc	BU
2008	3,000,000	—	—	—	1.25	—
2008 Special Unc	50,000	—	—	—	—	1.50
2008 Proof	15,000	Value: 15.00				
2009	14,700,000	—	—	—	1.25	—
2009 Special Unc	75,000	—	—	—	—	1.50
2009 Proof	15,000	Value: 15.00				
2010	—	—	—	—	1.25	—
2010 Special Unc	50,000	—	—	—	—	1.50
2010 Proof	15,000	Value: 15.00				
2011 Special Unc	—	—	—	—	—	1.50
2011 Proof	—	Value: 15.00				

KM# 3088 EURO

7.5000 g., Bi-Metallic Copper-Nickel center in Brass ring, 23.25 mm. **Obv:** Bust of Mozart right within inner circle, stars in outer circle **Obv. Designer:** Josef Kaiser **Rev:** Value at left, relief map of European Union at right **Rev. Designer:** Luc Luycx **Edge:** Reeded and plain sections

Date	Mintage	F	VF	XF	Unc	BU
2002	223,500,000	—	—	—	2.50	—
2002 Special Unc	100,000	—	—	—	—	2.75
2002 Proof	10,000	Value: 100				
2003 Special Unc	125,000	—	—	—	—	5.00
2003 Proof	25,000	Value: 16.50				
2004	2,600,000	—	—	—	2.50	—
2004 Special Unc	100,000	—	—	—	—	2.75
2004 Proof	20,000	Value: 17.50				
2005	2,600,000	—	—	—	2.50	—
2005 Special Unc	100,000	—	—	—	—	2.75
2005 Proof	20,000	Value: 18.50				
2006	7,700,000	—	—	—	2.50	—
2006 Special Unc	100,000	—	—	—	—	2.75
2006 Proof	20,000	Value: 18.50				
2007	41,100,000	—	—	—	2.50	—
2007 Special Unc	75,000	—	—	—	—	2.75
2007 Proof	20,000	Value: 18.50				

KM# 3142 EURO

7.5000 g., Bi-Metallic Copper-Nickel center in Brass ring, 23.2 mm. **Obv:** Bust of Mozart right within inner circle, stars in outer circle **Obv. Designer:** Josef Kaiser **Rev:** Value at left, expanded relief map of European Union at right **Rev. Designer:** Luc Luycx **Edge:** Reeded and plain sections

Date	Mintage	F	VF	XF	Unc	BU
2008	65,500,000	—	—	—	2.00	—
2008 Special Unc	50,000	—	—	—	—	2.75
2008 Proof	15,000	Value: 15.00				
2009	40,300,000	—	—	—	2.00	—
2009 Special Unc	75,000	—	—	—	—	2.75
2009 Proof	15,000	Value: 15.00				
2010	—	—	—	—	2.00	—
2010 Special Unc	50,000	—	—	—	—	2.75
2010 Proof	150,000	Value: 15.00				
2011 Special Unc	—	—	—	—	—	2.75
2011 Proof	—	Value: 15.00				

KM# 3089 2 EURO

8.5000 g., Bi-Metallic Nickel-Brass center in Copper-Nickel ring, 25.75 mm. **Obv:** Bust of Bertha von Suttner, Novelist and winner of 1905 Peace Prize, facing left within inner circle, stars in outer circle **Obv. Designer:** Joaef Kaiser **Rev:** Value at left, relief map of European Union at right **Rev. Designer:** Luc Luycx **Edge Lettering:** 2 EURO (star) (star) (star) (star)

Date	Mintage	F	VF	XF	Unc	BU
2002	196,400,000	—	—	—	3.75	—
2002 Special Unc	100,000	—	—	—	—	4.00
2002 Proof	10,000	Value: 125				
2003	4,700,000	—	—	—	3.75	—
2003 Special Unc	125,000	—	—	—	—	4.00
2003 Proof	25,000	Value: 25.00				
2004	2,500,000	—	—	—	3.75	—
2004 Special Unc	100,000	—	—	—	—	4.00
2004 Proof	20,000	Value: 27.50				
2006	2,300,000	—	—	—	3.75	—
2006 Special Unc	100,000	—	—	—	—	4.00
2006 Proof	20,000	Value: 27.50				

KM# 3124 2 EURO

8.5000 g., Bi-Metallic Nickel-Brass center in Copper-Nickel ring, 25.75 mm. **Subject:** 50th Anniversary of the State Treaty **Obv:** Treaty seals and signatures **Rev:** Denomination and map **Edge:** Reeding over lettering **Edge Lettering:** "2 EURO" and 3 stars repeated four times

Date	Mintage	F	VF	XF	Unc	BU
2005	6,880,000	—	—	—	5.00	—
2005 Special Unc	100,000	—	—	—	—	6.00
2005 Proof	20,000	Value: 27.50				

KM# 3150 2 EURO

8.5000 g., Bi-Metallic Nickel-Brass center in Copper-Nickel ring, 25.75 mm. **Subject:** 50th Anniversary - Treaty of Rome **Edge:** Reeded and lettered

Date	Mintage	F	VF	XF	Unc	BU
2007	8,905,000	—	—	—	4.00	—
2007 Special Unc	75,000	—	—	—	—	5.00
2007 Proof	20,000	Value: 27.50				

KM# 3143 2 EURO

8.5000 g., Bi-Metallic Nickel-Brass center in Copper-Nickel ring, 25.75 mm. **Obv:** Bust of Bertha von Suttner, Novelist and winner of 1905 Peace Prize, at right facing left in inner circle, stars in outer circle **Obv. Designer:** Josef Kaiser **Rev:** Value at left, expanded relief map of European Union at right **Rev. Designer:** Luc Luycx **Edge Lettering:** 2 EURO ★ ★ ★

Date	Mintage	F	VF	XF	Unc	BU
2008	2,600,000	—	—	—	5.00	—
2008 Special Unc	50,000	—	—	—	—	6.00
2008 Proof	15,000	Value: 25.00				
2009	4,900,000	—	—	—	5.00	—
2009 Special Unc	75,000	—	—	—	—	6.00
2009 Proof	15,000	Value: 25.00				
2010	—	—	—	—	5.00	—
2010 Special Unc	50,000	—	—	—	—	6.00
2010 Proof	15,000	Value: 25.00				
2011 Special Unc	—	—	—	—	—	6.00
2011 Proof	—	Value: 25.00				

KM# 3175 2 EURO

8.5000 g., Bi-Metallic Nickel-Brass center in Copper-Nickel ring, 25.75 mm. **Subject:** 10th Anniversary - European Monetary Union **Edge:** Reeded and lettered

Date	Mintage	F	VF	XF	Unc	BU
2009	4,910,000	—	—	—	7.50	—

KM# 3091 5 EURO

10.0000 g., 0.8000 Silver 0.2572 oz. ASW, 28.5 mm. **Subject:** Schoenbrunn Zoo **Obv:** Denomination within sun design at center, provincial arms surround **Rev:** Building and animals **Edge:** Plain **Shape:** 9-sided

Date	Mintage	F	VF	XF	Unc	BU
ND(2002)	500,000	—	—	—	12.50	—
ND(2002) Special Unc	100,000	—	—	—	—	22.50

KM# 3105 5 EURO

10.0000 g., 0.8000 Silver 0.2572 oz. ASW, 28.5 mm. **Subject:** Water Power **Obv:** Denomination within sun design at center, provincial arms surround **Rev:** Dam with turbine, electric power plant and fish **Edge:** Plain **Shape:** 9-sided

Date	Mintage	F	VF	XF	Unc	BU
2003	500,000	—	—	—	11.50	—
2003 Special Unc	100,000	—	—	—	—	15.00

KM# 3122 5 EURO
10.0000 g., 0.8000 Silver 0.2572 oz. ASW, 28.5 mm. **Subject:** Enlargement of the European Union **Obv:** Denomination within sun design at center, provincial arms surround **Rev:** Map of Europe above country names **Edge:** Plain **Shape:** 9-sided

Date	Mintage	F	VF	XF	Unc	BU
2004	275,000	—	—	—	10.00	—
2004 Special Unc	125,000	—	—	—	—	12.50

KM# 3113 5 EURO
10.0000 g., 0.8000 Silver 0.2572 oz. ASW, 28.5 mm. **Obv:** Denomination within sun design at center, provincial arms surround **Rev:** Soccer player scoring a goal **Edge:** Plain **Shape:** 9-sided **Note:** Centennial of Austrian Soccer

Date	Mintage	F	VF	XF	Unc	BU
2004	600,000	—	—	—	10.00	—
2004 Special Unc	100,000	—	—	—	—	12.50

KM# 3117 5 EURO
10.0000 g., 0.8000 Silver 0.2572 oz. ASW, 28.5 mm. **Subject:** Centennial of Sport Skiing **Obv:** Denomination within sun design at center, provincial arms surround **Rev:** Skier within snowflake design **Edge:** Plain **Shape:** 9-sided

Date	Mintage	F	VF	XF	Unc	BU
2005	500,000	—	—	—	10.00	—
2005 Special Unc	100,000	—	—	—	—	14.50

KM# 3120 5 EURO
10.0000 g., 0.8000 Silver 0.2572 oz. ASW, 28.5 mm. **Subject:** 10th Anniversary of Austrian E U Membership **Obv:** Denomination within sun design at center, provincial arms surround **Rev:** Carinthian Gate Theater and Beethoven cameo portrait **Edge:** Plain **Shape:** 9-sided

Date	Mintage	F	VF	XF	Unc	BU
2005	275,000	—	—	—	12.50	—
2005 Special Unc	125,000	—	—	—	—	14.50

KM# 3131 5 EURO
10.0000 g., 0.8000 Silver 0.2572 oz. ASW, 28.5 mm. **Subject:** Mozart **Obv:** Denomination within sun design at center, provincial arms surround **Rev:** Mozart and the Salzburg Cathedral **Edge:** Plain **Shape:** Nine sided

Date	Mintage	F	VF	XF	Unc	BU
2006	375,000	—	—	—	15.00	—
2006 Special Unc	125,000	—	—	—	—	17.50

KM# 3132 5 EURO
10.0000 g., 0.8000 Silver 0.2572 oz. ASW, 28.5 mm. **Subject:** Austrian Presidency of the EU **Obv:** Value in circle of arms **Rev:** Vienna Hofburg and Josefsplatz view **Edge:** Plain **Shape:** Nine sided

Date	Mintage	F	VF	XF	Unc	BU
2006	250,000	—	—	—	12.50	—
2006 Special Unc	100,000	—	—	—	—	14.50

KM# 3144 5 EURO
10.0000 g., 0.8000 Silver 0.2572 oz. ASW, 28.5 mm. **Subject:** Universal Male Suffrage Centennial **Obv:** Value in circle of shields **Rev:** Cameo portraits of Franz Joseph and von Beck on Reichsrat scene **Edge:** Plain **Shape:** 9-sided

Date	Mintage	F	VF	XF	Unc	BU
2007	150,000	—	—	—	13.00	—
2007 Special Unc	100,000	—	—	—	—	15.00

KM# 3145 5 EURO
10.0000 g., 0.8000 Silver 0.2572 oz. ASW, 28.5 mm. **Obv:** Value in circle of shields **Rev:** Mariazell church **Edge:** Plain **Shape:** 9-sided

Date	Mintage	F	VF	XF	Unc	BU
2007	450,000	—	—	—	12.50	—
2007 Special Unc	100,000	—	—	—	—	15.00

KM# 3156 5 EURO
10.0000 g., 0.8000 Silver 0.2572 oz. ASW, 28.5 mm. **Subject:** Herbert Von Karajan, 100th Birth Anniversary **Obv:** Value and nine provincial shields **Rev:** Bust and notes of Beethoven's Ninth Symphony **Shape:** 9-sided

Date	Mintage	F	VF	XF	Unc	BU
2008	150,000	—	—	—	17.00	—
2008 Special Unc	100,000	—	—	—	—	17.50

KM# 3163 5 EURO
10.0000 g., 0.8000 Silver 0.2572 oz. ASW, 28.5 mm. **Obv:** Value within center of nine shields **Rev:** Two soccer players **Shape:** 9-sided

Date	Mintage	F	VF	XF	Unc	BU
2008	225,000	—	—	—	10.00	—
2008 Special Unc	100,000	—	—	—	—	12.50

KM# 3164 5 EURO
10.0000 g., 0.8000 Silver 0.2572 oz. ASW, 28.5 mm. **Obv:** Value within center of nine shields **Rev:** One soccer player **Shape:** 9-sided

Date	Mintage	F	VF	XF	Unc	BU
2008	225,000	—	—	—	11.50	—
2008 Special Unc	100,000	—	—	—	—	15.00

KM# 3170 5 EURO
10.0000 g., 0.8000 Silver 0.2572 oz. ASW, 28.5 mm. **Subject:** Joseph Haydn, 200th Anniversary of Death **Obv:** Value at center of nine shields **Rev:** Bust facing right at left, pair of violins at right **Shape:** 9-sided

Date	Mintage	F	VF	XF	Unc	BU
2009	450,000	—	—	—	15.00	—
2009 Special Unc	100,000	—	—	—	—	20.00

KM# 3177 5 EURO
10.0000 g., 0.8000 Silver 0.2572 oz. ASW, 28.5 mm. **Subject:** Tyrolean Resistance Fighters, 1809 **Shape:** 9-sided

Date	Mintage	F	VF	XF	Unc	BU
2009	250,000	—	—	—	20.00	—
2009 Special Unc	100,000	—	—	—	—	30.00

KM# 3183 5 EURO
10.0000 g., 0.8000 Silver 0.2572 oz. ASW, 28.5 mm. **Subject:** Vancouver Olympics **Shape:** 9-sided

Date	Mintage	F	VF	XF	Unc	BU
2010	—	—	—	—	—	20.00

KM# 3184 5 EURO
10.0000 g., 0.8000 Silver 0.2572 oz. ASW, 28.5 mm. **Subject:** Grossglockner - High Alpine Road **Shape:** 9-sided

Date	Mintage	F	VF	XF	Unc	BU
2010	250,000	—	—	—	15.00	—
2010 Special Unc	100,000	—	—	—	—	20.00

KM# 3192 5 EURO
10.0000 g., 0.8000 Silver 0.2572 oz. ASW, 28.5 mm. **Subject:** Winter sports **Obv:** Nine provincial shields **Rev:** Snowboarding **Rev. Designer:** Helmut Andexlinger **Shape:** 9-sided

Date	Mintage	F	VF	XF	Unc	BU
2010	225,000	—	—	—	15.00	—
2010 Special Unc	50,000	—	—	—	—	20.00

KM# 3193 5 EURO
10.0000 g., 0.8000 Silver 0.2572 oz. ASW, 28.5 mm. **Subject:** Winter Sports **Obv:** Nine provincial shields **Rev:** Ski jumper **Shape:** 9-sided

Date	Mintage	F	VF	XF	Unc	BU
2010	225,000	—	—	—	15.00	—
2010 Special Unc	50,000	—	—	—	—	20.00

KM# 3195 5 EURO
10.0000 g., 0.8000 Silver 0.2572 oz. ASW, 28.5 mm. **Subject:** Pummerin, 1711-2011 **Obv:** Value within circle of shields **Rev:** Large bell **Shape:** 9-sided

Date	Mintage	F	VF	XF	Unc	BU
2011	—	—	—	—	9.50	—
2011 Special Unc.	—	—	—	—	—	12.50

KM# 3196 5 EURO
10.0000 g., 0.8000 Silver 0.2572 oz. ASW, 28.5 mm. **Subject:** Land of Forests **Shape:** 9-sided

Date	Mintage	F	VF	XF	Unc	BU
2011	—	—	—	—	9.50	—
2011 Special Unc.	—	—	—	—	—	12.50

KM# 3096 10 EURO
17.3000 g., 0.9250 Silver 0.5145 oz. ASW, 32 mm. **Subject:** Ambras Palace **Obv:** Palace, denomination below **Rev:** Three strolling musicians **Edge:** Reeded

Date	Mintage	F	VF	XF	Unc	BU
2002	130,000	—	—	—	20.00	—
2002 Special Unc	20,000	—	—	—	—	30.00
2002 Proof	50,000	Value: 40.00				

KM# 3099 10 EURO
17.3000 g., 0.9250 Silver 0.5145 oz. ASW, 32 mm. **Subject:** Eggenberg Palace and Johannes Kepler **Obv:** Palace, denomination below **Rev:** Half figure seated with tools **Edge:** Reeded

Date	Mintage	F	VF	XF	Unc	BU
2002	130,000	—	—	—	20.00	—
2002 Special Unc	20,000	—	—	—	—	30.00
2002 Proof	50,000	Value: 32.50				

KM# 3103 10 EURO
17.3000 g., 0.9250 Silver 0.5145 oz. ASW, 32 mm. **Subject:** Castle of Schloss Hof **Obv:** Baroque fountain and palace, denomination below **Rev:** Two gardeners at work

Date	Mintage	F	VF	XF	Unc	BU
2003	130,000	—	—	—	20.00	—
2003 Special Unc	20,000	—	—	—	—	30.00
2003 Proof	50,000	Value: 32.50				

KM# 3106 10 EURO
17.3000 g., 0.9250 Silver 0.5145 oz. ASW, 32 mm. **Subject:** Schoenbrunn Palace **Obv:** Fountain with palace background, denomination below **Rev:** Palmenhaus greenhouse

Date	Mintage	F	VF	XF	Unc	BU
2003	100,000	—	—	—	20.00	—
2003 Special Unc	40,000	—	—	—	—	27.50
2003 Proof	60,000	Value: 30.00				

KM# 3111 10 EURO
17.3000 g., 0.9250 Silver 0.5145 oz. ASW, 32 mm. **Obv:** Hellbrunn Castle, denomination below **Rev:** Archbishop Marcus Sitticus and Hellbrunn's "Roman Theatre" **Edge:** Reeded

Date	Mintage	F	VF	XF	Unc	BU
2004	130,000	—	—	—	20.00	—
2004 Special Unc	40,000	—	—	—	—	25.00
2004 Proof	60,000	Value: 30.00				

KM# 3115 10 EURO
17.3000 g., 0.9250 Silver 0.5145 oz. ASW, 32 mm. **Obv:** Artstetten Castle, denomination below **Rev:** Crypt entrance behind portraits of Franz Ferdinand and Sophie

Date	Mintage	F	VF	XF	Unc	BU
2004	130,000	—	—	—	20.00	—
2004 Special Unc	40,000	—	—	—	—	25.00
2004 Proof	60,000	Value: 30.00				

KM# 3121 10 EURO
17.3000 g., 0.9250 Silver 0.5145 oz. ASW, 32 mm. **Subject:** 60th Anniversary of the Second Republic **Obv:** Statue of Athena, nine provincial shields and denomination at right **Rev:** Parliament building above broken chain, crowd below

Date	Mintage	F	VF	XF	Unc	BU
2005	130,000	—	—	—	20.00	—
2005 Special Unc	40,000	—	—	—	—	25.00
2005 Proof	60,000	Value: 35.00				

KM# 3125 10 EURO
17.3000 g., 0.9250 Silver 0.5145 oz. ASW, 32 mm. **Subject:** Reopening of the Burg Theater and Opera **Obv:** Two large buildings, denomination at left **Rev:** Comedy and Tragedy Masks

Date	Mintage	F	VF	XF	Unc	BU
2005	130,000	—	—	—	20.00	—
2005 Special Unc	40,000	—	—	—	—	25.00
2005 Proof	60,000	Value: 35.00				

KM# 3129 10 EURO
17.3000 g., 0.9250 Silver 0.5145 oz. ASW, 32 mm. **Subject:** Nonnenberg Abbey **Obv:** Abbey view, denomination below **Rev:** Statue of St. Erentrudis **Edge:** Reeded

Date	Mintage	F	VF	XF	Unc	BU
2006	130,000	—	—	—	20.00	—
2006 Special Unc	40,000	—	—	—	—	25.00
2006 Proof	60,000	Value: 35.00				

KM# 3137 10 EURO
17.3000 g., 0.9250 Silver 0.5145 oz. ASW, 32 mm. **Obv:** Gottweig Abby above value **Rev:** Charles VI and staircase

Date	Mintage	F	VF	XF	Unc	BU
2006	130,000	—	—	—	20.00	—
2006 Special Unc	40,000	—	—	—	—	30.00
2006 Proof	60,000	Value: 40.00				

KM# 3146 10 EURO
17.3000 g., 0.9250 Silver 0.5145 oz. ASW, 32 mm. **Obv:** Melk Abbey view **Rev:** Inner view of the Melk Abbey dome

Date	Mintage	F	VF	XF	Unc	BU
2007	130,000	—	—	—	20.00	—
2007 Special Unc	40,000	—	—	—	—	25.00
2007 Proof	60,000	Value: 35.00				

KM# 3148 10 EURO
17.3000 g., 0.9250 Silver 0.5145 oz. ASW, 32 mm. **Obv:** St. Paul's Abbey complex **Obv. Legend:** ST. PAUL IM LAVANTTAL **Obv. Inscription:** REPUBLIK / ÖSTERREICH **Rev:** Entrance facade

Date	Mintage	F	VF	XF	Unc	BU
2007	130,000	—	—	—	20.00	—
2007 Special Unc	60,000	—	—	—	—	25.00
2007 Proof	40,000	Value: 35.00				

KM# 3157 10 EURO
17.3000 g., 0.9250 Silver 0.5145 oz. ASW, 32 mm. **Subject:** Abby of Klosterneuburg **Obv:** Aerial exterior view of church complex **Rev:** Cloister

Date	Mintage	F	VF	XF	Unc	BU
2008	130,000	—	—	—	20.00	—
2008 Special Unc	40,000	—	—	—	—	25.00
2008 Proof	60,000	Value: 45.00				

KM# 3162 10 EURO
17.3000 g., 0.9250 Silver 0.5145 oz. ASW, 32 mm. **Subject:** Seckau Benediction Abbey **Obv:** Exterior of abby, value, date and inscriptions "BENEDIKTINERABTEI SECKAU" and "REPUBLIK OESTERREICH" **Rev:** Interior of abbey

Date	Mintage	F	VF	XF	Unc	BU
2008	130,000	—	—	—	20.00	—
2008 Special Unc	40,000	—	—	—	—	25.00
2008 Proof	60,000	Value: 45.00				

KM# 3176 10 EURO
17.3000 g., 0.9250 Silver 0.5145 oz. ASW, 32 mm. **Series:** Tales and Legends **Subject:** Basilisk of Vienna

Date	Mintage	F	VF	XF	Unc	BU
2009	130,000	—	—	—	20.00	—
2009 Special Unc	30,000	—	—	—	—	25.00
2009 Proof	40,000	Value: 40.00				

KM# 3180 10 EURO
17.3000 g., 0.9250 Silver 0.5145 oz. ASW, 32 mm. **Series:** Tales and Legends **Subject:** Richard the Lionheart in Dürnstein

Date	Mintage	F	VF	XF	Unc	BU
2009	130,000	—	—	—	20.00	—
2009 Special Unc	30,000	—	—	—	—	25.00
2009 Proof	40,000	Value: 45.00				

KM# 3185 10 EURO
17.3000 g., 0.9250 Silver 0.5145 oz. ASW, 32 mm. **Subject:** Erzberg in Styria **Obv:** Iron Mine **Rev:** Two mermen with cloak

Date	Mintage	F	VF	XF	Unc	BU
2010	130,000	—	—	—	25.00	—
2010 Special Unc	30,000	—	—	—	—	28.00
2010 Proof	40,000	Value: 40.00				

KM# 3186 10 EURO
17.3000 g., 0.9250 Silver 0.5145 oz. ASW, 32 mm. **Subject:** Charlemagne in the Undersberg

Date	Mintage	F	VF	XF	Unc	BU
2010(h)	130,000	—	—	—	25.00	—
2010(h) Special Unc	30,000	—	—	—	—	28.00
2010(h) Proof	40,000	Value: 40.00				

KM# 3197 10 EURO
17.3000 g., 0.9250 Silver 0.5145 oz. ASW **Subject:** The Lindworm in Klagenfurt

Date	Mintage	F	VF	XF	Unc	BU
2011	—	—	—	—	17.00	—
2011 Special Unc.	—	—	—	—	—	25.00
2011 Proof	—	Value: 40.00				

KM# 3198 10 EURO
17.3000 g., 0.9250 Silver 0.5145 oz. ASW **Subject:** My dear old Augustin

Date	Mintage	F	VF	XF	Unc	BU
2011	—	—	—	—	17.00	—
2011 Special Unc.	—	—	—	—	—	25.00
2011 Proof	—	Value: 40.00				

KM# 3097 20 EURO
20.0000 g., 0.9000 Silver 0.5787 oz. ASW, 34 mm. **Subject:** Ferdinand I - Renaissance **Obv:** Hofburg Palace "Swiss Gate" with two guards, denomination below **Rev:** Bust looking left, coat of arms at left, dates at right **Edge:** Reeded

Date	Mintage	F	VF	XF	Unc	BU
2002 Proof	50,000	Value: 37.50				

KM# 3098 20 EURO
20.0000 g., 0.9000 Silver 0.5787 oz. ASW, 34 mm. **Subject:** Prince Eugen - Baroque Period **Obv:** Baroque staircase with statues, denomination below **Rev:** Uniformed bust 1/4 left and dates at right, flags above cannons at left **Edge:** Reeded

Date	Mintage	F	VF	XF	Unc	BU
2002 Proof	50,000	Value: 42.00				

KM# 3104 20 EURO
20.0000 g., 0.9000 Silver 0.5787 oz. ASW, 34 mm. **Subject:** Prince Metternich **Obv:** Early steam locomotive, denomination below **Rev:** Portrait with map background **Edge:** Reeded

Date	Mintage	F	VF	XF	Unc	BU
2003 Proof	50,000	Value: 45.00				

KM# 3107 20 EURO
20.0000 g., 0.9000 Silver 0.5787 oz. ASW, 34 mm. **Obv:** Republic of Austria arms, denomination below **Rev:** Four men in a jeep **Edge:** Reeded **Note:** Post War Austrian Reconstruction

Date	Mintage	F	VF	XF	Unc	BU
2003 Proof	50,000	Value: 50.00				

KM# 3112 20 EURO
20.0000 g., 0.9000 Silver 0.5787 oz. ASW, 34 mm. **Obv:** S.M.S Novara under sail in Chinese waters, denomination below **Rev:** Standing figures behind table with globe and microscope **Edge:** Reeded **Note:** First Global Circumnavigation by an Austrian ship.

Date	Mintage	F	VF	XF	Unc	BU
2004 Proof	50,000	Value: 50.00				

KM# 3114 20 EURO
20.0000 g., 0.9000 Silver 0.5787 oz. ASW, 34 mm. **Obv:** SMS Erzherzog Ferdinand Max sailing to the Battle of Lissa, denomination below **Rev:** Sailors at the wheel with Admiral Tegetthof in background **Edge:** Reeded

Date	Mintage	F	VF	XF	Unc	BU
2004 Proof	50,000	Value: 52.50				

KM# 3126 20 EURO
20.0000 g., 0.9000 Silver 0.5787 oz. ASW, 34 mm. **Obv:** Ship, "Admiral Tegetthoff" in arctic waters, denomination below **Rev:** Expedition leaders, von Payer and Weyprecht with their icebound ship behind them **Edge:** Reeded

Date	Mintage	F	VF	XF	Unc	BU
2005 Proof	50,000	Value: 50.00				

KM# 3127 20 EURO
20.0000 g., 0.9000 Silver 0.5787 oz. ASW, 34 mm. **Obv:** SMS St. George sailing past the Statue of Liberty, denomination below **Rev:** Shipyard at Pola, boat on water **Edge:** Reeded

Date	Mintage	F	VF	XF	Unc	BU
2005 Proof	50,000	Value: 50.00				

KM# 3133 20 EURO
20.0000 g., 0.9000 Silver 0.5787 oz. ASW, 34 mm. **Subject:** Austrian Merchant Marine **Obv:** Two passing steam ships **Rev:** 19th Century Triest harbor view **Edge:** Reeded

Date	Mintage	F	VF	XF	Unc	BU
2006 Proof	50,000	Value: 50.00				

KM# 3134 20 EURO
20.0000 g., 0.9000 Silver 0.5787 oz. ASW, 34 mm. **Obv:** SMS Viribus Unitis, flag ship of the Austrian fleet, and other ships steaming left **Rev:** SMS Viribus Unitis, submarine conning tower and seaplane **Edge:** Reeded

Date	Mintage	F	VF	XF	Unc	BU
2006 Proof	50,000	Value: 50.00				

KM# 3149 20 EURO
20.0000 g., 0.9000 Silver 0.5787 oz. ASW, 34 mm. **Series:** Austrian Railways **Obv:** Steam locomotive 1837 with passenger wagons **Obv. Legend:** REPUBLIK ÖSTERREICH **Obv. Inscription:** DAMPFLOKOMOTIVE / AUSTRIA / 1837 **Rev:** People waving at passenger train crossing a trestle **Rev. Legend:** KAISER - FERDINANDS - NORDBAHN **Edge:** Reeded

Date	Mintage	F	VF	XF	Unc	BU
2007 Proof	50,000	Value: 50.00				

KM# 3151 20 EURO
20.0000 g., 0.9000 Silver 0.5787 oz. ASW, 34 mm. **Series:** Austrian Railways **Obv:** Steam locomotive 1848 standing still, viaduct in background **Obv. Legend:** REPUBLIK ÖSTERREICH **Obv. Inscription:** DAMPF-/ LOKOMOTIVE / STEINBRØCK / 1848 **Rev:** Steam train traveling right through city **Rev. Legend:** K.K. SÜDBAHN WIEN - TRIEST **Edge:** Reeded

Date	Mintage	F	VF	XF	Unc	BU
2007 Proof	50,000	Value: 50.00				

KM# 3154 20 EURO
20.0000 g., 0.9000 Silver 0.5787 oz. ASW, 34 mm. **Subject:** Southern Railways **Obv:** Steam Locomotive on iron railway bridge **Obv. Inscription:** KOK kkStB 306 **Rev:** Statue of Empress Elizabeth and train platform in Vienna's West Railway station **Rev. Inscription:** KAISERIN-/ ELIZABETH-/ WESTBAHN **Edge:** Reeded

Date	Mintage	F	VF	XF	Unc	BU
2008 Proof	50,000	Value: 70.00				

KM# 3161 20 EURO
20.0000 g., 0.9000 Silver 0.5787 oz. ASW, 34 mm. **Subject:** Imperial - Royal State Railway **Obv:** Locomotive steaming left **Obv. Legend:** Nordbahnhof/Wein **Rev:** Female on platform

Date	Mintage	F	VF	XF	Unc	BU
2008 Proof	50,000	Value: 70.00				

KM# 3178 20 EURO
20.0000 g., 0.9000 Silver 0.5787 oz. ASW, 34 mm. **Subject:** The Electric Railway **Obv:** Locomotive model 1189, the Crocodile **Obv. Designer:** Thomas Pesendorfer **Rev:** Train on the Trisanna Bridge, Wiesburg Castle in background **Rev. Designer:** Herbert Wahner

Date	Mintage	F	VF	XF	Unc	BU
2009 Proof	50,000	Value: 50.00				

KM# 3179 20 EURO
20.0000 g., 0.9000 Silver 0.5787 oz. ASW, 34 mm. **Subject:** Railways of the Future **Obv:** Railjet highspeed OBB train **Obv. Designer:** Helmut Andexlinger **Rev:** Electric locomotive of the 1063 class in freight yard **Rev. Designer:** Thomas Pesendorfer **Edge:** Reeded

Date	Mintage	F	VF	XF	Unc	BU
2009 Proof	50,000	Value: 50.00				

KM# 3187 20 EURO
20.0000 g., 0.9000 Silver 0.5787 oz. ASW, 34 mm. **Subject:** Rome on the Danube - Virunum **Obv:** Emperor Claudium, 2-horse wagon, gravestone **Obv. Designer:** Helmut Andexlinger **Rev:** Street scene, wagon and temple facade **Rev. Designer:** Herbert Waehner **Edge:** Reeded

Date	Mintage	F	VF	XF	Unc	BU
2010 Proof	50,000	Value: 75.00				

KM# 3188 20 EURO
20.0000 g., 0.9000 Silver 0.5787 oz. ASW, 34 mm. **Subject:** Rome on the Danube - Vindovona **Edge:** Reeded

Date	Mintage	F	VF	XF	Unc	BU
2010 Proof	50,000	Value: 75.00				

KM# 3199 20 EURO
20.0000 g., 0.9250 Silver 0.5948 oz. ASW, 34 mm. **Subject:** Rome on the Danube - Carnuntum

Date	Mintage	F	VF	XF	Unc	BU
2011 Proof	—	Value: 70.00				

KM# 3200 20 EURO
20.0000 g., 0.9000 Silver 0.5787 oz. ASW, 34 mm. **Subject:** Rome on the Danube - Aguntum

Date	Mintage	F	VF	XF	Unc	BU
2011 Proof	—	Value: 70.00				

KM# 3201 20 EURO
20.0000 g., 0.9000 Silver 0.5787 oz. ASW, 34 mm. **Subject:** Nikolaus Joseph von Jacquin **Obv:** Bust at left, flower at right **Rev:** Karibuk Expedition, Jacquin taking notes of plants in book

Date	Mintage	F	VF	XF	Unc	BU
2011 Proof	—	Value: 70.00				

KM# 3101 25 EURO
17.1500 g., Bi-Metallic 7.15g pure Niobium (Columbium) blue color center in a 10 g., 0.900 Silver ring, 34 mm. **Subject:** City of Hall in Tyrol **Obv:** Satellite mapping the city from outer space **Rev:** Depiction of the die face used to strike the 1486 guldiner coin **Edge:** Plain

Date	Mintage	F	VF	XF	Unc	BU
2003 Special Unc	50,000	—	—	—	—	125

KM# 3109 25 EURO
17.1500 g., Bi-Metallic 7.15g Niobium center (7.15) in 0.900 Silver 10g, ring, 34 mm. **Subject:** Semmering Alpine Railway **Obv:** Modern and antique locomotives **Rev:** Steam train **Edge:** Plain

Date	Mintage	F	VF	XF	Unc	BU
2004 Special Unc	50,000	—	—	—	—	100

KM# 3119 25 EURO
17.1500 g., Bi-Metallic Purple color pure Niobium 7.15g center in 0.900 Silver 10g, ring, 34 mm. **Subject:** 50 Years Austrian Television **Obv:** The original test pattern of the 1950's **Rev:** World globe behind "rabbit ear" antenna; television developmental milestones from 7-1 o'clock **Edge:** Plain

Date	Mintage	F	VF	XF	Unc	BU
2005 Special Unc	65,000	—	—	—	—	65.00

KM# 3135 25 EURO
17.1500 g., Bi-Metallic Niobium 7.15g center in 0.900 Silver 10g ring, 34 mm. **Subject:** European Satellite Navigation **Obv:** Austrian Mint's global location inscribed on a compass face **Rev:** Satellites in orbit around the world globe **Edge:** Plain

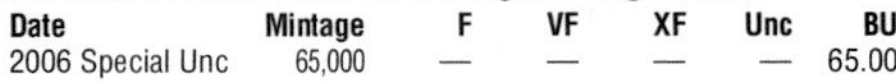

Date	Mintage	F	VF	XF	Unc	BU
2006 Special Unc	65,000	—	—	—	—	65.00

KM# 3147 25 EURO
16.5000 g., Bi-Metallic 6.5g Niobium center in 0.900 Silver 10g ring, 34 mm. **Subject:** Austrian Aviation **Obv:** Interior view of modern cockpit **Rev:** Taube airplane flying above glider and pilot **Edge:** Plain

Date	Mintage	F	VF	XF	Unc	BU
2007 Special Unc	65,000	—	—	—	—	65.00

KM# 3158 25 EURO
16.5000 g., Bi-Metallic 6.5g Niobium center in 0.900 silver 10g ring, 34 mm. **Subject:** 150th Anniversary of Birth - Carl Baron Auer von Welsbach, **Obv:** Lighting gas lamp before Vienna City Wall **Obv. Designer:** Herbert Waehner **Rev:** Head of Welsbach, development of light bulbs

Date	Mintage	F	VF	XF	Unc	BU
2008 Special Unc	65,000	—	—	—	—	75.00

KM# 3174 25 EURO
16.5000 g., Bi-Metallic 6.5g Niobium center in 0.900 silver 10g ring, 34 mm. **Subject:** Year of Astronomy **Obv:** Galileo head and instruments **Rev:** Space exploration satellite

Date	Mintage	F	VF	XF	Unc	BU
2009 Special Unc	65,000	—	—	—	—	75.00

KM# 3189 25 EURO
16.5000 g., Bi-Metallic 6.5g Niobium center in 0.900 Silver 10g ring, 34 mm. **Obv:** Tree and four elements of earth, wind, water, and fire **Rev:** Solar panels, hydroelectric turbine, global thermal energy and wind turbine **Designer:** Helmut Andexlinger

Date	Mintage	F	VF	XF	Unc	BU
2010 Special Unc	65,000	—	—	—	—	75.00

KM# 3204 25 EURO
16.5000 g., Bi-Metallic 6.5g Niobium center in 0.900 Silver 10g ring, 34 mm. **Subject:** Robotics **Rev:** Mars rover

Date	Mintage	F	VF	XF	Unc	BU
2011 Special Unc.	65,000	—	—	—	—	75.00

KM# 3090 50 EURO
10.1400 g., 0.9860 Gold 0.3214 oz. AGW, 22 mm. **Subject:** Saints Benedict and Scholastica **Obv:** St. Benedict and his sister St. Scholastica **Rev:** Monk copying a manuscript **Edge:** Reeded

Date	Mintage	F	VF	XF	Unc	BU
2002 Proof	50,000	Value: 500				

KM# 3102 50 EURO
10.1400 g., 0.9860 Gold 0.3214 oz. AGW, 22 mm. **Subject:** Christian Charity **Obv:** Nursing Sister with hospital patient **Rev:** The Good Samaritan **Edge:** Reeded

Date	Mintage	F	VF	XF	Unc	BU
2003 Proof	50,000	Value: 500				

KM# 3110 50 EURO
10.1400 g., 0.9860 Gold 0.3214 oz. AGW, 22 mm. **Subject:** Great Composers - Joseph Haydn (1732-1809) **Obv:** Esterhazy Palace **Rev:** Bust 3/4 right

Date	Mintage	F	VF	XF	Unc	BU
2004 Proof	50,000	Value: 500				

KM# 3118 50 EURO
10.1400 g., 0.9860 Gold 0.3214 oz. AGW, 22 mm. **Subject:** Great Composers - Ludwig Van Beethoven (1770-1827) **Obv:** Lobkowitz Palace above value and document **Rev:** Bust 3/4 facing, dates at left

Date	Mintage	F	VF	XF	Unc	BU
2005 Proof	50,000	Value: 500				

KM# 3130 50 EURO
10.1400 g., 0.9860 Gold 0.3214 oz. AGW, 22 mm. **Subject:** Great Composers - Mozart **Obv:** Mozart's birthplace, denomination below **Rev:** Leopold and Wolfgang Mozart

Date	Mintage	F	VF	XF	Unc	BU
2006 Proof	50,000	Value: 500				

KM# 3138 50 EURO
10.1400 g., 0.9860 Gold 0.3214 oz. AGW, 22 mm. **Obv:** Gerard Van Swieten holding book and facing left **Rev:** Akademie der Wissenschaften building

Date	Mintage	F	VF	XF	Unc	BU
2007 Proof	50,000	Value: 500				

KM# 3153 50 EURO
10.1400 g., 0.9860 Gold 0.3214 oz. AGW, 22 mm. **Subject:** Ignaz Philipp Sammelweis - Personal Hygiene **Obv:** Bust of Sammelweis 3/4 right, staff of Aesculapius at lower right **Obv. Legend:** REPUBLIK ÖSTERREICH **Rev:** Vienna General Hospital, Sammelweis helping patient wash at lower right **Rev. Legend:** ALLGEMEINES KRANKENHAUS WEIN

Date	Mintage	F	VF	XF	Unc	BU
2008 Proof	50,000	Value: 500				

KM# 3171 50 EURO
10.1400 g., 0.9860 Gold 0.3214 oz. AGW, 22 mm. **Subject:** Theodor Billroth **Obv:** Bust and Aesculapius staff **Rev:** Operation scene

Date	Mintage	F	VF	XF	Unc	BU
2009 Proof	50,000	Value: 500				

KM# 3190 50 EURO
10.1400 g., 0.9860 Gold 0.3214 oz. AGW, 22 mm. **Subject:** Karl Landsteiner

Date	Mintage	F	VF	XF	Unc	BU
2010 Proof	—	Value: 500				

KM# 3194 50 EURO
10.1400 g., 0.9860 Gold 0.3214 oz. AGW, 22 mm. **Subject:** Baron Clemens von Pirquet **Obv:** Portrait of von Pirquet **Obv. Designer:** Helmut Andexlinger **Rev:** Facade of Children's Clinic of Vienna

Date	Mintage	F	VF	XF	Unc	BU
2010 Proof	50,000	Value: 500				

KM# 3202 50 EURO
10.1400 g., 0.9860 Gold 0.3214 oz. AGW, 22 mm. **Subject:** Joanneum Museum **Obv:** Exterior of Art Museum **Rev:** Armor display

Date	Mintage	F	VF	XF	Unc	BU
2011 Proof	—	Value: 675				

KM# 3100 100 EURO
16.2272 g., 0.9860 Gold 0.5144 oz. AGW, 30 mm. **Subject:** Raphael Donner **Obv:** Portrait in front of building **Rev:** Providentia Fountain **Edge:** Reeded

Date	Mintage	F	VF	XF	Unc	BU
2002 Proof	30,000	Value: 760				

KM# 3108 100 EURO
16.2270 g., 0.9860 Gold 0.5144 oz. AGW, 30 mm. **Obv:** Gustav Klimt standing **Rev:** Klimt's painting "The Kiss" **Edge:** Reeded

Date	Mintage	F	VF	XF	Unc	BU
2003 Proof	30,000	Value: 760				

KM# 3116 100 EURO
16.2270 g., 0.9860 Gold 0.5144 oz. AGW, 30 mm. **Obv:** Secession Exhibit Hall in Vienna **Rev:** Knight in armor, "strength" with two women, "ambition and sympathy"

Date	Mintage	F	VF	XF	Unc	BU
2004 Proof	30,000	Value: 760				

KM# 3128 100 EURO
16.2270 g., 0.9860 Gold 0.5144 oz. AGW, 30 mm. **Subject:** St. Leopold's Church at Steinhof **Obv:** Domed church building, denomination below **Rev:** Two angels flank stained glass portrait

Date	Mintage	F	VF	XF	Unc	BU
2005 Proof	30,000	Value: 760				

KM# 3136 100 EURO
16.2270 g., 0.9860 Gold 0.5144 oz. AGW, 30 mm. **Subject:** Vienna's River Gate Park **Obv:** Bridge over river scene **Rev:** One of two "sculpted ladies" flanking the park entrance

Date	Mintage	F	VF	XF	Unc	BU
2006 Proof	30,000	Value: 760				

KM# 3155 100 EURO
16.2270 g., 0.9860 Gold 0.5144 oz. AGW, 30 mm. **Obv:** Building at Linke Wienzeile Nr 38 by architect Otto Koloman Wagner **Rev:** Ornate elevator and stairwell

Date	Mintage	F	VF	XF	Unc	BU
2007 Proof	30,000	Value: 750				

KM# 3160 100 EURO
16.2270 g., 0.9860 Gold 0.5144 oz. AGW, 30 mm. **Series:** Crowns of the Habsburgs **Obv:** Crown of the Holy Roman Emperor set upon coronation robe **Rev:** Otto I seated facing and old St. Peter's Bastilica, Rome

Date	Mintage	F	VF	XF	Unc	BU
2008 Proof	30,000	Value: 760				

KM# 3181 100 EURO
16.2270 g., 0.9860 Gold 0.5144 oz. AGW, 30 mm. **Series:** Crowns of the Habsburgs **Subject:** Archducal crown of Austria **Obv:** Crown resting on pillow **Rev:** Procession of the crown, orb and sceptre, Plague memorial column in background

Date	Mintage	F	VF	XF	Unc	BU
2009 Proof	30,000	Value: 760				

KM# 3191 100 EURO
16.2270 g., 0.9860 Gold 0.5144 oz. AGW, 30 mm. **Series:** Crowns of the Habsburgs **Subject:** St. Stephen's Hungarian Crown **Obv:** Crown of St. Stephen **Rev:** Naria Theresa on horseback

Date	Mintage	F	VF	XF	Unc	BU
2010 Proof	30,000	Value: 800				

KM# 3203 100 EURO
16.2272 g., 0.9860 Gold 0.5144 oz. AGW, 30 mm. **Subject:** King Wenceslas

Date	Mintage	F	VF	XF	Unc	BU
2011 Proof	—	Value: 750				

EURO BULLION COINAGE

Philharmonic Issues

KM# 3159 1-1/2 EURO

31.1030 g., 0.9990 Silver 0.9989 oz. ASW, 37 mm. **Obv:** Golden Concert Hall **Rev:** Bouquet of Instruments **Edge:** Plain

Date	Mintage	F	VF	XF	Unc	BU
2008	7,800,000	—	—	—	BV	37.50
2009	900,000	—	—	—	BV	37.50
2010	—	—	—	—	BV	37.50
2011	—	—	—	—	BV	37.50

KM# 3092 10 EURO

3.1210 g., 0.9999 Gold 0.1003 oz. AGW, 16 mm. **Subject:** Vienna Philharmonic **Obv:** The Golden Hall organ **Rev:** Musical instruments **Edge:** Segmented reeding

Date	Mintage	F	VF	XF	Unc	BU
2002	75,789	—	—	—	—	BV+13%
2003	59,654	—	—	—	—	BV+13%
2004	67,994	—	—	—	—	BV+13%
2005	62,071	—	—	—	—	BV+13%
2006	39,892	—	—	—	—	BV+13%
2007	76,325	—	—	—	—	BV+13%
2008	176,700	—	—	—	—	BV+13%
2009	437,700	—	—	—	—	BV+13%
2010	—	—	—	—	—	BV+13%
2011	—	—	—	—	—	BV+13%

KM# 3093 25 EURO

7.7760 g., 0.9999 Gold 0.2500 oz. AGW, 22 mm. **Subject:** Vienna Philharmonic **Obv:** The Golden Hall organ **Rev:** Musical instruments **Edge:** Segmented reeding

Date	Mintage	F	VF	XF	Unc	BU
2002	40,807	—	—	—	—	BV+10%
2003	34,019	—	—	—	—	BV+10%
2004	32,449	—	—	—	—	BV+10%
2005	32,817	—	—	—	—	BV+10%
2006	29,609	—	—	—	—	BV+10%
2007	34,631	—	—	—	—	BV+10%
2008	97,100	—	—	—	—	BV+10%
2009	172,000	—	—	—	—	BV+10%
2010	—	—	—	—	—	BV+10%
2011	—	—	—	—	—	BV+10%

KM# 3094 50 EURO

15.5520 g., 0.9999 Gold 0.4999 oz. AGW, 28 mm. **Subject:** Vienna Philharmonic **Obv:** The Golden Hall organ **Rev:** Musical instruments **Edge:** Segmented reeding

Date	Mintage	F	VF	XF	Unc	BU
2002	40,922	—	—	—	—	BV+8%
2003	26,848	—	—	—	—	BV+8%
2004	24,269	—	—	—	—	BV+8%
2005	21,049	—	—	—	—	BV+8%
2006	20,085	—	—	—	—	BV+8%
2007	25,091	—	—	—	—	BV+8%
2008	73,800	—	—	—	—	BV+8%
2009	92,300	—	—	—	—	BV+8%
2010	—	—	—	—	—	BV+8%
2011	—	—	—	—	—	BV+8%

KM# 3095 100 EURO

31.1035 g., 0.9999 Gold 0.9999 oz. AGW, 37 mm. **Subject:** Vienna Philharmonic **Obv:** The Golden Hall organ **Rev:** Musical instruments **Edge:** Segmented reeding

Date	Mintage	F	VF	XF	Unc	BU
2002	164,105	—	—	—	—	BV+4%
2003	179,881	—	—	—	—	BV+4%
2004	176,319	—	—	—	—	BV+4%
2005	158,564	—	—	—	—	BV+4%
2006	82,174	—	—	—	—	BV+4%
2007	108,675	—	—	—	—	BV+4%
2008	715,800	—	—	—	—	BV+4%
2009	835,700	—	—	—	—	BV+4%
2010	—	—	—	—	—	BV+4%
2011	—	—	—	—	—	BV+4%

KM# 3182 2000 EURO

622.1000 g., 0.9999 Gold 19.998 oz. AGW, 74 mm. **Subject:** Vienna Philharmonic **Obv:** The Golden Hall Organ **Rev:** Musical instruments

Date	Mintage	F	VF	XF	Unc	BU
2009	6,027	—	—	—	—	BV+5%

KM# 3123 100000 EURO

31103.5000 g., 0.9999 Gold 999.85 oz. AGW, 370 mm. **Obv:** The Golden Hall organ **Rev:** Musical instruments **Edge:** Reeded

Date	Mintage	F	VF	XF	Unc	BU
2004	15	BV+5%				

MINT SETS

KM#	Date	Mintage	Identification	Issue Price	Mkt Val
MS10	2001 (6)	75,000	KM#2878, 2885, 2886, 2889a, 2918, 3075	25.00	40.00
MS11	2002 (8)	100,000	KM#3082-3089, Euro	22.50	25.00
MS12	2003 (8)	125,000	KM#3082-3089, Mozart	22.50	25.00
MS13	2004 (8)	100,000	KM#3082-3089, von Suttner	—	25.00
MS14	2005 (8)	100,000	KM#3082-3088, 3124, State treaty	—	25.00
MS15	2006 (8)	100,000	KM#3082-3089, St. Stephan's Cathedral	—	35.00
MS16	2007 (8)	75,000	KM#3082-3088, 3150, Treaty of Rome	—	25.00
MS17	2008 (8)	50,000	KM#3082-3084, 3139-3143, European Map	—	35.00
MS18	2009 (8)	75,000	KM#3082-3084, 3139-3143	—	25.00
MS19	2010 (8)	—	KM#3082-3084, 3139-3143	—	35.00

PROOF SETS

KM#	Date	Mintage	Identification	Issue Price	Mkt Val
PS53	2002 (8)	10,000	KM#3082-3089	85.00	485
PS54	2003 (8)	25,000	KM#3082-3089	85.00	95.00
PS55	2004 (8)	20,000	KM#3082-3089	—	105
PS56	2005 (8)	20,000	KM#3082-3088, 3124	—	110
PS57	2006 (8)	20,000	KM#3082-3089	—	110
PS58	2007 (8)	20,000	KM#3082-3088, 3150	—	110
PS59	2008 (8)	15,000	KM#3082-3084, 3139-3143	—	120
PS60	2009 (8)	15,000	3KM#3082-3084, 3139-3143	—	120
PS61	2010 (8)	15,000	KM#3082-3084, 3139-3143	—	100

AZERBAIJAN

The Republic of Azerbaijan (formerly Azerbaijan S.S.R.) includes the Nakhichevan Autonomous Republic. Situated in the eastern area of Transcaucasia, it is bordered in the west by Armenia, in the north by Georgia and Dagestan, to the east by the Caspian Sea and to the south by Iran. It has an area of 33,430 sq. mi. (86,600 sq. km.) and a population of 7.8 million. Capital: Baku. The area is rich in mineral deposits of aluminum, copper, iron, lead, salt and zinc, with oil as its leading industry. Agriculture and livestock follow in importance.

MONETARY SYSTEM

100 Qapik = 1 Manat

REPUBLIC

DECIMAL COINAGE

KM# 39 QAPIK

2.7000 g., Copper Plated Steel, 16.2 mm. **Obv:** Map above value **Rev:** Value and musical instruments **Edge:** Plain **Designer:** Robert Kalina

Date	Mintage	F	VF	XF	Unc	BU
ND (2006)	—	—	—	—	—	2.00

KM# 40 3 QAPIK

3.4000 g., Copper Plated Steel, 18 mm. **Obv:** Map above value **Rev:** Value above books **Edge:** Grooved **Designer:** Robert Kalina

Date	Mintage	F	VF	XF	Unc	BU
ND (2006)	—	—	—	—	—	2.50

KM# 41 5 QAPIK

4.7200 g., Copper Plated Steel, 19.8 mm. **Obv:** Map above value **Rev:** The Maiden Tower, Baku, above value **Edge:** Reeded **Designer:** Robert Kalina

Date	Mintage	F	VF	XF	Unc	BU
ND (2006)	—	—	—	—	—	2.75

KM# 42 10 QAPIK

5.1000 g., Brass Plated Steel, 22.2 mm. **Obv:** Map above value **Rev:** Value and Military Helmet, Symbolic of desire to regain Nagorno-Karabakh **Edge:** Notched **Designer:** Robert Kalina

Date	Mintage	F	VF	XF	Unc	BU
ND (2006)	—	—	—	—	—	3.00

KM# 43 20 QAPIK

6.5000 g., Brass Plated Steel, 24.3 mm. **Obv:** Map above value **Rev:** Value and spiral staircase **Edge:** Segmented reeding **Designer:** Robert Kalina

Date	Mintage	F	VF	XF	Unc	BU
ND (2006)	—	—	—	—	—	4.00

KM# 44 50 QAPIK

7.4200 g., Bi-Metallic Brass plated Steel center in Stainless Steel ring, 25.4 mm. **Obv:** Map above value **Rev:** Two oil wells **Edge:** Reeding over lettering **Designer:** Robert Kalina

Date	Mintage	F	VF	XF	Unc	BU
ND (2006)	—	—	—	—	—	5.00

KM# 37 50 MANAT

28.3400 g., 0.9250 Silver 0.8428 oz. ASW, 38.6 mm. **Subject:** Heydar Aliyev **Obv:** National map **Rev:** Bust 3/4 right **Edge:** Reeded

Date	Mintage	F	VF	XF	Unc	BU
2004 Proof	2,000	Value: 75.00				

KM# 46 100 MANAT

39.9400 g., 0.9167 Gold 1.1771 oz. AGW **Subject:** Heydar Aliyev **Obv:** National map **Rev:** Bust 3/4 right **Edge:** Reeded

Date	Mintage	F	VF	XF	Unc	BU
2004 Proof	1,000	Value: 1,850				

KM# 47 500 MANAT

50.0000 g., 0.9990 Platinum 1.6059 oz. APW **Subject:** Heydar Aliyev **Obv:** National map **Rev:** Bust 3/4 right **Edge:** Reeded

Date	Mintage	F	VF	XF	Unc	BU
2004 Proof	100	Value: 3,500				

MINT SETS

KM#	Date	Mintage	Identification	Issue Price	Mkt Val
MS1	2006 (6)	—	KM#39-44.	—	150

BAHAMAS

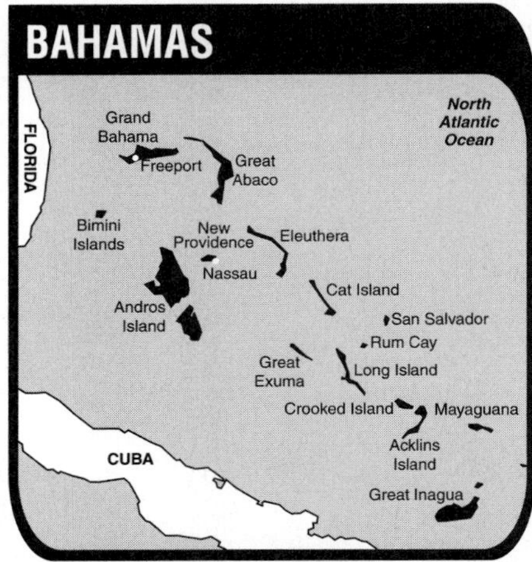

The Commonwealth of the Bahamas is an archipelago of about 3,000 islands, cays and rocks located in the Atlantic Ocean east of Florida and north of Cuba. The total land area of the 800 mile (1,287 km.) long chain of islands is 5,382 sq. mi. (13,935 sq. km.). They have a population of 302,000. Capital: Nassau. The Bahamas import most of their food and manufactured products and export cement, refined oil, pulpwood and lobsters. Tourism is the principal industry. The Bahamas is a member of the Commonwealth of Nations. Elizabeth II is Head of State as Queen of The Bahamas.

The coinage of Great Britain was legal tender in the Bahamas from 1825 to the issuing of a definitive coinage in 1966.

RULER
British

COMMONWEALTH

DECIMAL COINAGE

100 Cents = 1 Dollar

KM# 59a CENT

2.5000 g., Copper Plated Zinc, 19 mm. **Ruler:** Elizabeth II **Obv:** National arms above date **Obv. Legend:** COMMONWEALTH OF THE BAHAMAS **Rev:** Starfish, value at top **Edge:** Plain

Date	Mintage	F	VF	XF	Unc	BU
2000	—	—	—	0.10	0.25	0.75
2001	—	—	—	0.10	0.25	0.75
2004	—	—	—	0.10	0.25	0.75

KM# 218 CENT

2.5000 g., Copper Plated Zinc, 17 mm. **Ruler:** Elizabeth II **Obv:** National arms above date **Rev:** Three starfish

Date	Mintage	F	VF	XF	Unc	BU
2006	—	—	—	—	0.25	0.75
2007	—	—	—	—	0.25	0.75
2009	—	—	—	—	0.25	0.75

KM# 60 5 CENTS

3.9400 g., Copper-Nickel, 21 mm. **Ruler:** Elizabeth II **Obv:** National arms above date **Obv. Legend:** COMMONWEALTH OF THE BAHAMAS **Rev:** Pineapple above garland divides value at top **Rev. Designer:** Arnold Machin **Edge:** Smooth

Date	Mintage	F	VF	XF	Unc	BU
2004	—	—	—	0.10	0.25	0.75
2005	—	—	—	0.10	0.25	0.75

KM# 61 10 CENTS

5.5400 g., Copper-Nickel, 23.5 mm. **Ruler:** Elizabeth II **Obv:** National arms, date below, within beaded circle **Rev:** Two bonefish above denomination **Rev. Designer:** Arnold Machin **Edge:** Plain **Shape:** Scalloped

Date	Mintage	F	VF	XF	Unc	BU
2005	—	—	—	0.25	0.60	0.80

KM# 219 10 CENTS

5.5400 g., Copper-Nickel, 23 mm. **Ruler:** Elizabeth II **Obv:** National arms, date below **Rev:** Two fish, value above **Shape:** Scalloped

Date	Mintage	F	VF	XF	Unc	BU
2007	—	—	—	0.25	0.60	0.80

KM# 63.2 25 CENTS

5.7500 g., Copper-Nickel, 24.26 mm. **Ruler:** Elizabeth II **Obv:** National arms, date below **Rev:** Bahamian Sloop, value above **Edge:** Reeded

Date	Mintage	F	VF	XF	Unc	BU
2005	—	—	—	0.30	0.50	1.50

KM# 217 DOLLAR

Silver and gold plated ring **Ruler:** Elizabeth II **Subject:** Queen Mother's 100th Birthday

Date	Mintage	F	VF	XF	Unc	BU
2002 Proof	—	Value: 50.00				

BAHRAIN

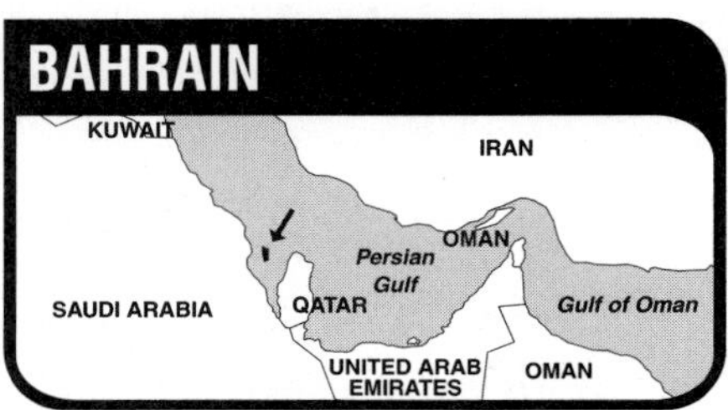

The Kingdom of Bahrain, a group of islands in the Persian Gulf off Saudi Arabia, has an area of 268 sq. mi. (622 sq. km.) and a population of 618,000. Capital: Manama. Prior to the depression of the 1930's, the economy was based on pearl fishing. Petroleum and aluminum industries and transit trade are the vital factors in the economy today.

The coinage of the Kingdom of Bahrain was struck at the Royal Mint, London, England.

RULERS

Al Khalifa Dynasty
Hamed Bin Isa, 1999-

TITLES

دولة البحرين

State of Bahrain

مملكة البحرين

Kingdom of Bahrain

KINGDOM

STANDARD COINAGE

KM# 30 5 FILS

2.5000 g., Brass, 19 mm. **Ruler:** Hamed Bin Isa **Obv:** Palm tree **Obv. Legend:** KINGDOM OF BAHRAIN **Rev:** Denomination in chain link border **Edge:** Plain

Date	Mintage	F	VF	XF	Unc	BU
AH1426-2005	—	—	—	—	0.50	0.75
AH1428-2007	—	—	—	—	0.50	0.75

KM# 30a 5 FILS

0.9250 Silver **Ruler:** Hamed Bin Isa

Date	Mintage	F	VF	XF	Unc	BU
AH1431-2010 Proof	500	Value: 15.00				

KM# 28 10 FILS
3.3500 g., Brass, 21 mm. **Ruler:** Hamed Bin Isa **Obv:** Palm tree **Obv. Legend:** KINGDOM OF BAHRAIN **Rev:** Denomination in chain link border **Edge:** Plain

Date	Mintage	F	VF	XF	Unc	BU
AH1423-2002	—	—	—	0.30	0.75	1.00
AH1424-2004	—	—	—	0.30	0.75	1.00
AH1426-2005	—	—	—	0.30	0.75	1.00
AH1428-2007	—	—	—	0.30	0.75	1.00

KM# 28a 10 FILS
0.9250 Silver **Ruler:** Hamed Bin Isa

Date	Mintage	F	VF	XF	Unc	BU
AH1431-2010 Proof	500	Value: 25.00				

KM# 24 25 FILS
3.5000 g., Copper-Nickel, 20 mm. **Ruler:** Hamed Bin Isa **Obv:** Ancient painting **Obv. Legend:** KINGDOM OF BAHRAIN **Rev:** Denomination in chain link border **Edge:** Reeded

Date	Mintage	F	VF	XF	Unc	BU
AH1423-2002	—	—	—	0.45	1.10	1.50
AH1426-2005	—	—	—	0.45	1.10	1.50
AH1428-2007	—	—	—	0.45	1.10	1.50
AH1429-2008	—	—	—	0.45	1.10	1.50

KM# 24a 25 FILS
0.9250 Silver **Ruler:** Hamed Bin Isa

Date	Mintage	F	VF	XF	Unc	BU
AH1431-2010 Proof	500	Value: 25.00				

KM# 25 50 FILS
4.5000 g., Copper-Nickel, 22 mm. **Ruler:** Hamed Bin Isa **Subject:** Kingdom **Obv:** Stylized sailboats **Obv. Legend:** KINGDOM OF BAHRAIN **Rev:** Denomination in chain link border **Edge:** Reeded

Date	Mintage	F	VF	XF	Unc	BU
AH1423-2002	—	—	—	0.60	1.50	2.00
AH1426-2005	—	—	—	0.60	1.50	2.00
AH1428-2007	—	—	—	0.60	1.50	2.00
AH1429-2008	—	—	—	0.60	1.50	2.00
AH1431-2010	—	—	—	0.60	1.50	2.00

KM# 25a 50 FILS
0.9250 Silver **Ruler:** Hamed Bin Isa

Date	Mintage	F	VF	XF	Unc	BU
AH1431-2010 Proof	500	Value: 25.00				

KM# 20 100 FILS
6.0000 g., Bi-Metallic Copper-Nickel center in Brass ring, 24 mm. **Obv:** Coat of arms within circle, dates at either side **Obv. Legend:** STATE OF BAHRAIN **Rev:** Numeric denomination back of boxed denomination within circle, chain surrounds **Edge:** Reeded

Date	Mintage	F	VF	XF	Unc	BU
AH1422-2001	—	—	—	—	3.50	4.00

KM# 26 100 FILS
6.0000 g., Bi-Metallic Copper-Nickel center in Brass ring, 24 mm. **Ruler:** Hamed Bin Isa **Subject:** Kingdom **Obv:** National arms **Obv. Legend:** KINGDOM OF BAHRAIN **Rev:** Denomination in chain link border **Edge:** Reeded

Date	Mintage	F	VF	XF	Unc	BU
AH1423-2002	—	—	—	0.90	2.25	3.00
AH1426-2005	—	—	—	0.90	2.25	3.00
AH1427-2006	—	—	—	0.90	2.25	3.00
AH1428-2007	—	—	—	0.90	2.25	3.00
AH1429-2008	—	—	—	0.90	2.25	3.00
AH1430-2009	—	—	—	0.90	2.25	3.00

KM# 26a 100 FILS
0.9250 Silver **Ruler:** Hamed Bin Isa

Date	Mintage	F	VF	XF	Unc	BU
AH1431-2010 Proof	500	Value: 30.00				

KM# 29 100 FILS
6.0000 g., Bi-Metallic Copper-Nickel center in Brass ring, 24 mm. **Subject:** 1st Bahrain Grand Prix **Obv:** Maze design within circle **Rev:** Numeric denomination back of boxed denomination within circle, chain surrounds **Edge:** Reeded

Date	Mintage	F	VF	XF	Unc	BU
AH1425-2004	30,000	—	—	—	30.00	35.00

KM# 22 500 FILS
9.0000 g., Bi-Metallic Brass center in Copper-Nickel ring, 27 mm. **Ruler:** Hamed Bin Isa **Obv:** Monument and inscription **Obv. Inscription:** STATE OF BAHRAIN **Rev:** Denomination **Edge:** Reeded

Date	Mintage	F	VF	XF	Unc	BU
2001	—	—	—	—	6.00	7.50

KM# 27 500 FILS
9.0000 g., Bi-Metallic Brass center Copper-Nickel ring, 27 mm. **Subject:** Kingdom **Obv:** Monument and inscription **Obv. Legend:** KINGDOM OF BAHRAIN **Rev:** Denomination **Edge:** Reeded

Date	Mintage	F	VF	XF	Unc	BU
2002	—	—	—	—	6.50	8.00

KM# 27a 500 FILS
0.9250 Silver **Ruler:** Hamed Bin Isa

Date	Mintage	F	VF	XF	Unc	BU
AH1431-2010 Proof	500	Value: 40.00				

PROOF SETS

KM#	Date	Mintage	Identification	Issue Price	Mkt Val
PS4	2010 (6)	500	KM#30a, 28a, 24a, 25a, 26a, 27a	160	160

BANGLADESH

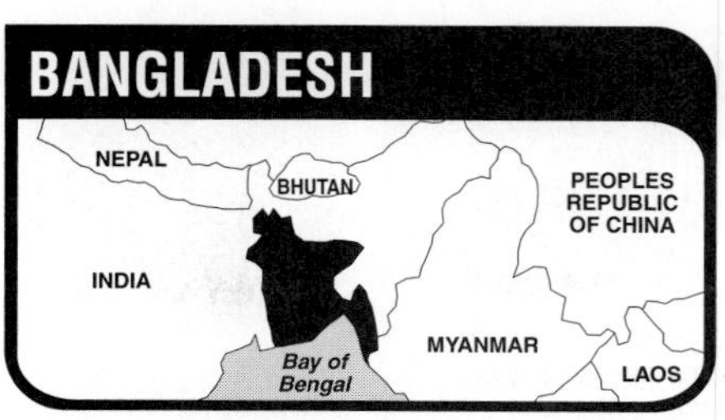

The Peoples Republic of Bangladesh (formerly East Pakistan), a parliamentary democracy located on the Bay of Bengal bordered by India and Burma, has an area of 55,598 sq. mi. (143,998 sq. km.) and a population of 128.1 million. Capital: Dhaka. The economy is predominantly agricultural. Jute products, jute and tea are exported.

Bangladesh is a member of the Commonwealth of Nations. The president is the Head of State and the Government.

MONETARY SYSTEM
100 Poisha = 1 Taka

DATING
Christian era using Bengali numerals.

PEOPLES REPUBLIC

STANDARD COINAGE

KM# 24 50 POISHA
2.6000 g., Stainless Steel, 19.3 mm. **Obv:** National emblem, Shapla (water lily) within wreath above water **Rev:** Fish, chicken and produce within inner circle **Edge:** Plain **Shape:** Octagonal

Date	Mintage	F	VF	XF	Unc	BU
2001	—	—	—	—	1.50	2.50

KM# 9c TAKA
4.2500 g., Stainless Steel, 24.91 mm. **Obv:** National emblem, Shapla (water lily) within wreath above water in octagonal frame **Rev:** Stylized family, value at right within octagonal frame **Edge:** Reeded **Note:** Prev. KM # 9.5.

Date	Mintage	F	VF	XF	Unc	BU
2001	—	—	—	0.80	2.00	3.00
2002	—	—	—	0.80	2.00	3.00
2003	—	—	—	0.80	2.00	3.00
2007	—	—	—	0.80	2.00	3.00

KM# 9b TAKA
4.0000 g., Brass, 25 mm. **Obv:** National emblem, Shapla (water lily) **Rev:** Stylized family, value at right **Edge:** Reeded **Note:** Prev. KM # 9.3.

Date	Mintage	F	VF	XF	Unc	BU
2003	—	—	0.20	0.55	1.20	1.60

KM# 25 2 TAKA
7.0000 g., Stainless Steel, 26.03 mm. **Obv:** State emblem and "TWO 2 TAKA" within beaded border **Rev:** Two children reading, legend within beaded border **Edge:** Plain

Date	Mintage	F	VF	XF	Unc	BU
2004	—	—	—	1.20	3.00	4.00

KM# 26 5 TAKA
8.1700 g., Steel, 26.8 mm. **Obv:** National emblem, Shapla (water lily) within wreath above water **Rev:** Bridge, date and denomination below **Note:** Prev. KM#18.3.

Date	Mintage	F	VF	XF	Unc	BU
2006	—	—	—	1.00	2.50	3.50

BARBADOS

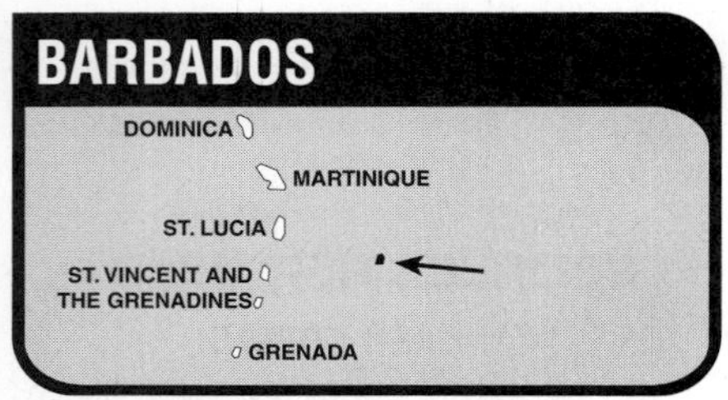

Barbados, a Constitutional Monarchy within the Commonwealth of Nations, is located in the Windward Islands of the West Indies east of St. Vincent. The coral island has an area of 166 sq. mi. (430 sq. km.) and a population of 269,000. Capital: Bridgetown. The economy is based on sugar and tourism. Sugar, petroleum products, molasses, and rum are exported.

MONETARY SYSTEM
100 Cents = 1 Dollar

COMMONWEALTH

DECIMAL COINAGE

KM# 10a CENT
2.5000 g., Copper Plated Zinc, 19 mm. **Obv:** National arms **Rev:** Trident above value **Rev. Designer:** Philip Nathan **Edge:** Plain

Date	Mintage	F	VF	XF	Unc	BU
2001	—	—	—	0.10	0.25	0.75
2002	—	—	—	—	0.25	0.75
2003	—	—	—	—	0.25	0.75
2004	—	—	—	—	0.25	0.75
2005	—	—	—	—	0.25	0.75
2006	—	—	—	—	0.25	0.75
2007	—	—	—	—	0.25	0.75

KM# 10b CENT
2.7800 g., Copper Plated Steel, 18.86 mm. **Obv:** National arms **Rev:** Trident above value

Date	Mintage	F	VF	XF	Unc	BU
2008	—	—	—	—	0.25	0.75
2009	—	—	—	—	0.25	0.75
2010	—	—	—	—	0.25	0.75

KM# 11 5 CENTS
3.7500 g., Brass, 21 mm. **Obv:** National arms **Rev:** South Point Lighthouse, value below **Rev. Designer:** Philip Nathan **Edge:** Plain

Date	Mintage	F	VF	XF	Unc	BU
2001	—	—	—	—	0.25	0.75
2002	—	—	—	—	0.25	0.75
2004	—	—	—	—	0.25	0.75
2005	—	—	—	—	0.25	0.75
2006	—	—	—	—	0.25	0.75
2007	—	—	—	—	0.25	0.75

KM# 11a 5 CENTS
3.4600 g., Brass Plated Steel, 21 mm. **Obv:** National arms **Rev:** South Point Lighthouse, value below

Date	Mintage	F	VF	XF	Unc	BU
2008	—	—	—	—	—	—
2009	—	—	—	—	—	—
2010	—	—	—	—	—	—

KM# 12 10 CENTS
2.2900 g., Copper-Nickel, 17.77 mm. **Obv:** National arms **Rev:** Tern flying left, value below **Rev. Designer:** Philip Nathan **Edge:** Reeded

Date	Mintage	F	VF	XF	Unc	BU
2001	—	—	—	0.15	0.50	1.50
2003	—	—	—	0.15	0.50	1.50
2004	—	—	—	0.15	0.50	1.50
2005	—	—	—	0.15	0.50	1.50
2007	—	—	—	0.15	0.50	1.50

KM# 12a 10 CENTS
2.0900 g., Nickel Plated Steel, 17.77 mm. **Obv:** National arms **Rev:** Tern flying left, value below **Edge:** Reeded

Date	Mintage	F	VF	XF	Unc	BU
2008	—	—	—	—	0.50	1.50

KM# 13 25 CENTS
5.6500 g., Copper-Nickel, 23.66 mm. **Obv:** National arms **Rev:** Morgan Lewis Windmill, value above **Edge:** Reeded **Designer:** Philip Nathan

Date	Mintage	F	VF	XF	Unc	BU
2001	—	—	—	0.30	0.60	1.60
2003	—	—	—	0.30	0.60	1.60
2004	—	—	—	0.30	0.60	1.60
2005	—	—	—	0.30	0.60	1.60
2006	—	—	—	0.30	0.60	1.60
2007	—	—	—	0.30	0.60	1.60

KM# 13a 25 CENTS
5.1000 g., Nickel Plated Steel, 23.66 mm. **Obv:** National arms **Rev:** Morgan Lewis Windmill, value above **Edge:** Reeded

Date	Mintage	F	VF	XF	Unc	BU
2008	—	—	—	0.30	0.60	1.60
2009	—	—	—	0.30	0.60	1.60

KM# 14.2 DOLLAR
5.9500 g., Copper-Nickel, 25.85 mm. **Obv:** National arms **Rev:** Flying fish left, value below **Shape:** 7-sided **Note:** Thinner planchet.

Date	Mintage	F	VF	XF	Unc	BU
2004	—	—	—	0.75	2.25	3.00
2007	—	—	—	0.75	2.25	3.00

KM# 14.2a DOLLAR
5.9500 g., Nickel Plated Steel, 25.85 mm. **Obv:** National arms **Rev:** Flying fish left, value below

Date	Mintage	F	VF	XF	Unc	BU
2008	—	—	—	0.75	2.25	3.00

KM# 69 5 DOLLARS
28.2800 g., 0.9250 Silver 0.8410 oz. ASW, 38.6 mm. **Subject:** UNICEF **Obv:** National arms divide date, denomination below **Rev:** Three boys playing cricket **Edge:** Reeded

Date	Mintage	F	VF	XF	Unc	BU
2001 Proof	—	Value: 45.00				

BELARUS

Belarus (Byelorussia, Belorussia, or White Russia- formerly the Belorussian S.S.R.) is situated along the western Dvina and Dnieper Rivers, bounded in the west by Poland, to the north by Latvia and Lithuania, to the east by Russia and the south by the Ukraine. It has an area of 80,154 sq. mi. (207,600 sq. km.) and a population of 4.8 million. Capital: Minsk. Chief products: peat, salt, and agricultural products including flax, fodder and grasses for cattle breeding and dairy products.

MONETARY SYSTEM
100 Kapeek = 1 Rouble

REPUBLIC

STANDARD COINAGE

KM# 110 ROUBLE
Copper-Nickel, 32 mm. **Subject:** 900th Anniversary of Euphrasinta **Obv:** National arms **Rev:** Euphrasinta of Polatsk **Designer:** S.P. Zaskevitch

Date	Mintage	F	VF	XF	Unc	BU
2001	Est. 2,000	—	—	—	50.00	—

KM# 112 ROUBLE
Copper-Nickel, 32 mm. **Subject:** Tower of Kamyantes **Obv:** National arms **Rev:** Kamyanets Tower, seal **Designer:** S.P. Zaskevich

Date	Mintage	F	VF	XF	Unc	BU
2001	2,000	—	—	—	40.00	—

KM# 47 ROUBLE
13.1400 g., Copper-Nickel, 31.9 mm. **Obv:** National arms **Rev:** European Bison **Edge:** Reeded **Designer:** S.P. Zaskevich

Date	Mintage	F	VF	XF	Unc	BU
2001 Proof	5,000	Value: 40.00				

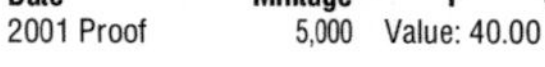

KM# 50 ROUBLE
13.1500 g., Copper-Nickel, 28.7 mm. **Subject:** 2002 Winter Olympics **Obv:** National arms **Rev:** Two freestyle skiers **Edge:** Reeded **Designer:** S.P. Zaskevich

Date	Mintage	F	VF	XF	Unc	BU
2001 Prooflike	2,000	—	—	—	—	35.00

KM# 114 ROUBLE
Copper-Nickel, 32 mm. **Subject:** 200th Birthday of Ignatius Dameika **Obv:** National arms **Rev:** Ignatius Dameika, hammer **Rev. Designer:** S.P. Zaskevich

Date	Mintage	F	VF	XF	Unc	BU
2002 Prooflike	2,000	—	—	—	—	40.00

KM# 116 ROUBLE
33.0000 Copper-Nickel, 33 mm. **Subject:** 120th Birthday of Yanka Kupala **Obv:** National arms **Rev:** Yanka Kupala, 1882-1942 **Rev. Designer:** S.P. Zaskevich

Date	Mintage	F	VF	XF	Unc	BU
2002 Prooflike	2,000	—	—	—	—	40.00

KM# 118 ROUBLE
Copper-Nickel, 33 mm. **Subject:** 120th Birthday of Yakub Kolas **Obv:** National arms **Rev:** Yukab Kolas, 1882-1956 **Rev. Designer:** S.P. Zaskevich

Date	Mintage	F	VF	XF	Unc	BU
2002	2,000	—	—	—	40.00	—

KM# 69 ROUBLE
Copper-Nickel, 33 mm. **Subject:** 80th Anniversary of the Savings Bank **Obv:** Folk art design **Obv. Designer:** S.P. Zaskevich **Rev. Designer:** V. Titor

Date	Mintage	F	VF	XF	Unc	BU
2002 Prooflike	10,000	—	—	—	15.00	—

KM# 105 ROUBLE
Copper-Nickel, 31.9 mm. **Subject:** Pointer Yanka Kupala 1881-1942

Date	Mintage	F	VF	XF	Unc	BU
2002 Proof	2,000	Value: 35.00				

KM# 106 ROUBLE
Copper-Nickel, 31.9 mm. **Subject:** Jakub Kalas 1881-1956

Date	Mintage	F	VF	XF	Unc	BU
2002 Proof	2,000	Value: 35.00				

KM# 44 ROUBLE
13.1400 g., Copper-Nickel, 31.9 mm. **Obv:** National arms **Rev:** Eurasian Beaver and young **Edge:** Reeded **Designer:** S.P. Zaskevich

Date	Mintage	F	VF	XF	Unc	BU
2002 Proof	5,000	Value: 25.00				

KM# 61 ROUBLE
12.5000 g., Copper-Nickel, 32 mm. **Obv:** National arms **Rev:** Wrestlers **Edge:** Reeded **Designer:** S.P. Zaskevich

Date	Mintage	F	VF	XF	Unc	BU
2003 Proof	5,000	Value: 10.00				

KM# 54 ROUBLE
13.1200 g., Copper-Nickel, 31.9 mm. **Obv:** National arms **Rev:** Mute swans on water with reflections **Edge:** Reeded **Designer:** S.P. Zaskevich

Date	Mintage	F	VF	XF	Unc	BU
2003 Proof	5,000	Value: 30.00				

KM# 55 ROUBLE
13.1000 g., Copper-Nickel, 31.9 mm. **Obv:** State arms **Rev:** Herring gull in flight **Edge:** Reeded **Designer:** S.P. Zaskevich

Date	Mintage	F	VF	XF	Unc	BU
2003 Proof	5,000	Value: 25.00				

KM# 56 ROUBLE
13.1000 g., Copper-Nickel, 32 mm. **Obv:** National arms **Rev:** Church of the Savior and Transfiguration **Edge:** Reeded **Designer:** S.P. Zaskevich

Date	Mintage	F	VF	XF	Unc	BU
2003	2,000	—	—	—	35.00	—

KM# 60 ROUBLE
13.1000 g., Copper-Nickel, 31.9 mm. **Obv:** National arms **Rev:** Two common cranes **Edge:** Reeded **Designer:** S.P. Zaskevich

Date	Mintage	F	VF	XF	Unc	BU
2004 Proof	5,000	Value: 25.00				

KM# 75 ROUBLE
15.9200 g., Copper-Nickel Antiqued Finish, 33 mm. **Subject:** "Kupalle" **Obv:** Folk art cross design **Rev:** Flower above ferns **Edge:** Reeded **Designer:** S.P. Zaskevich

Date	Mintage	F	VF	XF	Unc	BU
2004	5,000	—	—	—	40.00	—

KM# 76 ROUBLE
15.9200 g., Copper-Nickel, 33 mm. **Subject:** "Kalyady" **Obv:** Folk art cross design **Rev:** Stylized sunflower **Edge:** Reeded **Designer:** S.P. Zaskevich

Date	Mintage	F	VF	XF	Unc	BU
2004	5,000	—	—	—	35.00	—

KM# 78 ROUBLE
15.9000 g., Copper-Nickel, 33 mm. **Obv:** National arms **Rev:** Radziwill's Castle in Neswizh **Edge:** Reeded **Designer:** S.P. Zaskevich

Date	Mintage	F	VF	XF	Unc	BU
2004 Prooflike	2,000	—	—	—	—	35.00

KM# 80 ROUBLE
15.9000 g., Copper-Nickel, 33 mm. **Subject:** Defenders of Brest **Obv:** Soviet Patriotic War Order **Rev:** "Courage" monument **Edge:** Reeded **Designer:** S.P. Zaskevich

Date	Mintage	F	VF	XF	Unc	BU
2004	5,000	—	—	—	25.00	—

KM# 85 ROUBLE
Copper-Nickel, 33 mm. **Subject:** Soviet Warriors - Liberators **Obv:** Order of the Patriotric War **Obv. Designer:** S.P. Zaskevich **Rev:** Partisans with blown up railway track **Rev. Designer:** E.N. Vishnyakova

Date	Mintage	F	VF	XF	Unc	BU
2004	3,000	—	—	—	25.00	—

KM# 83 ROUBLE
Copper-Nickel, 33 mm. **Subject:** Memory of Facist Victims **Obv:** National arms **Obv. Designer:** S.P. Zaskevich **Rev:** Man holding dead **Rev. Designer:** E.N. Vishnyakova

Date	Mintage	F	VF	XF	Unc	BU
2004	3,000	—	—	—	25.00	—

KM# 62 ROUBLE
Copper-Nickel, 31.9 mm. **Subject:** Sculling **Obv:** National arms **Obv. Designer:** S.P. Zaskevich **Rev:** Two rowers against a background of stylized oars **Rev. Designer:** S.V. Nekrasova

Date	Mintage	F	VF	XF	Unc	BU
2004	3,000	—	—	—	15.00	—

KM# 81 ROUBLE
Copper-Nickel, 33 mm. **Subject:** 60th Anniversary of Victory **Obv:** Order of the Victory **Rev:** Star and arrows **Rev. Designer:** S.V. Necrasova

Date	Mintage	F	VF	XF	Unc	BU
2005	2,000	—	—	—	25.00	—

KM# 127 ROUBLE
Copper-Nickel, 32 mm. **Subject:** 1000th Anniversary of Vaukavysk **Obv:** National arms **Rev:** National arms of Vaukavysk **Rev. Designer:** S.P. Zaskevitch

Date	Mintage	F	VF	XF	Unc	BU
2005	2,000	—	—	—	40.00	—

KM# 130 ROUBLE
Copper-Nickel, 32 mm. **Subject:** Jesnit Roman Catholic Church **Obv:** National arms **Rev:** Jesnit Roman Catholic Church in Neswizh **Designer:** S.P. Zaskevich

Date	Mintage	F	VF	XF	Unc	BU
2005	2,000	—	—	—	40.00	—

KM# 104 ROUBLE
Copper-Nickel, 33 mm. **Subject:** Christmas Egg **Obv:** National arms and folk art cross design **Rev:** Easter egg **Designer:** S.P. Zaskevich

Date	Mintage	F	VF	XF	Unc	BU
2005	5,000	—	—	—	35.00	—

KM# 107 ROUBLE
Copper-Nickel, 31.9 mm. **Subject:** Bagach - Candle in Basket **Obv:** National arms and solar symbol **Rev:** Basket of grain, candle, ear, table, tablecloth

Date	Mintage	F	VF	XF	Unc	BU
2005	5,000	—	—	—	35.00	—

KM# 132 ROUBLE
Copper-Nickel, 33 mm. **Subject:** Usyaslau of Polatsk **Obv:** Cathedral of St. Sophia **Rev:** Usyaslav of Polatsk, wolf on a solar disk

Date	Mintage	F	VF	XF	Unc	BU
2005 Proof	5,000	Value: 15.00				

KM# 134 ROUBLE
Copper-Nickel, 33 mm. **Subject:** Tennis **Obv:** National arms **Rev:** Tennis player against racket background **Rev. Designer:** S.V. Nekrasova

Date	Mintage	F	VF	XF	Unc	BU
2005	5,000	—	—	—	12.00	—

KM# 97 ROUBLE
14.5000 g., Copper-Nickel, 33 mm. **Subject:** Almany Bogs **Obv:** Blooming plant on frosted design **Rev:** Great Grey Owl **Edge:** Lettered **Designer:** S.V. Nekrasova

Date	Mintage	F	VF	XF	Unc	BU
2005 Proof	5,000	Value: 25.00				

KM# 135 ROUBLE
Copper-Nickel, 32 mm. **Subject:** Vtaselle Wedding **Obv:** National arms, birds, shamrock **Rev:** Loaf of bread, wedding rings, diadem of flowers, background of honeycomb

Date	Mintage	F	VF	XF	Unc	BU
2006	5,000	—	—	—	12.00	—

KM# 138 ROUBLE
Copper-Nickel, 33 mm. **Subject:** Sophia of Galshany 600th Anniversary **Obv:** Castle of Galshany **Rev:** National arms and Sophia of Galshany **Designer:** S.P. Zaskevich

Date	Mintage	F	VF	XF	Unc	BU
2006	5,000	—	—	—	20.00	—

KM# 140 ROUBLE
Copper-Nickel, 33 mm. **Subject:** Syomukha **Obv:** National arms, solar symbol **Rev:** Chalice, Chaplet of birch, maple, rowan sweet flag leaves **Designer:** S.P. Zaskevich

Date	Mintage	F	VF	XF	Unc	BU
2006	5,000	—	—	—	25.00	—

KM# 146 ROUBLE
Copper-Nickel, 33 mm. **Subject:** Chyrvomy Bar **Obv:** National arms, blooming plant **Rev:** European Mink **Designer:** S.V. Nekrasova

Date	Mintage	F	VF	XF	Unc	BU
2006 Proof	5,000	Value: 17.50				

KM# 150 ROUBLE
16.0000 g., Copper-Nickel, 33 mm. **Subject:** Holidays and Ceremonies **Obv:** Small arms above quilted star design **Rev:** Food, bowl with spoon - Maslenica

Date	Mintage	F	VF	XF	Unc	BU
2007 Antique	5,000	—	—	—	35.00	—

KM# 151 ROUBLE
13.2400 g., Copper-Nickel, 31.86 mm. **Obv:** Thrush Nightingale in hands in oval **Obv. Legend:** РЭСПУБЛІКА БЕЛАРУСЬ **Rev:** Thrush Nightingale perched on branch in oval **Edge:** Reeded

Date	Mintage	F	VF	XF	Unc	BU
2007 Proof	5,000	Value: 17.50				

KM# 217 ROUBLE
14.3500 g., Copper-Nickel, 33 mm. **Rev:** Sturgeon

Date	Mintage	F	VF	XF	Unc	BU
2007 Proof	5,000	Value: 15.00				

KM# 215 ROUBLE
Copper-Nickel, 33 mm. **Obv:** Sea chart and compose rose **Rev:** Sailing ship Sedov

Date	Mintage	F	VF	XF	Unc	BU
2008 Proof	—	Value: 50.00				

KM# 218 ROUBLE
13.1600 g., Copper-Nickel, 32 mm. **Subject:** Belavezhskaya Pushcha

Date	Mintage	F	VF	XF	Unc	BU
2009 Proof	5,000	Value: 15.00				

KM# 219 ROUBLE
13.1600 g., Copper-Nickel, 32 mm. **Subject:** Greyleg goose

Date	Mintage	F	VF	XF	Unc	BU
2009 Proof	5,000	Value: 13.00				

KM# 220 ROUBLE
14.3500 g., Copper-Nickel, 32 mm. **Subject:** Pakatigaroshak **Rev:** Man clubbing dragon

Date	Mintage	F	VF	XF	Unc	BU
2009 Proof	3,500	Value: 13.00				

KM# 221 ROUBLE
15.5000 g., Copper-Nickel, 33 mm. **Subject:** Legend of the Skylark

Date	Mintage	F	VF	XF	Unc	BU
2009 Proof	5,000	Value: 13.00				

KM# 222 ROUBLE
15.5000 g., Copper-Nickel, 33 mm. **Subject:** Folk Art - Straw Weaving **Rev:** Horse

Date	Mintage	F	VF	XF	Unc	BU
2009 Proof	5,000	Value: 13.00				

KM# 223 ROUBLE
14.3500 g., Copper-Nickel, 33 mm. **Subject:** EURASEC, 10th Anniversary **Obv:** Folk embrodery pattern **Rev:** Six flags around globe

Date	Mintage	F	VF	XF	Unc	BU
2010 Proof	3,500	Value: 13.00				

KM# 226 ROUBLE
13.1600 g., Copper-Nickel, 33 mm. **Subject:** 1st Belarus Front **Rev:** Gen. Konstantin Rokossovsky

Date	Mintage	F	VF	XF	Unc	BU
2010 Proof	3,000	Value: 13.00				

KM# 227 ROUBLE
13.1600 g., Copper-Nickel, 33 mm. **Subject:** 2nd Belarus Front **Rev:** Col. Gen. G.F. Zaharov

Date	Mintage	F	VF	XF	Unc	BU
2010 Proof	3,000	Value: 13.00				

KM# 228 ROUBLE
13.1600 g., Copper-Nickel, 33 mm. **Subject:** 3rd Belarus Front **Rev:** Col. Gen. Ivan Chernyakhovsky

Date	Mintage	F	VF	XF	Unc	BU
2010 Proof	3,000	Value: 13.00				

KM# 229 ROUBLE
13.1600 g., Copper-Nickel, 33 mm. **Subject:** 1st Baltic Forces **Rev:** Gen. Hovhannes Bagramayn

Date	Mintage	F	VF	XF	Unc	BU
2010 Proof	3,000	Value: 13.00				

KM# 236 ROUBLE
15.5000 g., Copper-Nickel, 33 mm. **Subject:** Legend of the tortoise

Date	Mintage	F	VF	XF	Unc	BU
2010 Proof	3,000	Value: 13.00				

KM# 240 ROUBLE
Copper-Nickel, 32 mm. **Subject:** Age of Majority **Rev:** Flowers and folk patterns

Date	Mintage	F	VF	XF	Unc	BU
2010 Proof	4,000	Value: 13.00				

KM# 234 ROUBLE
13.1600 g., Copper-Nickel, 32 mm. **Rev:** U.S. Frigate Constitution

Date	Mintage	F	VF	XF	Unc	BU
2010 Proof	3,000	Value: 13.00				

KM# 64 10 ROUBLES
16.8200 g., 0.9250 Silver 0.5002 oz. ASW, 32.9 mm. **Obv:** National arms **Rev:** Jakub Kolas (1882-1956) **Edge:** Reeded **Designer:** S.P. Zaskevich

Date	Mintage	F	VF	XF	Unc	BU
2002 Proof	1,000	Value: 150				

KM# 117 10 ROUBLES
15.5500 g., 0.9250 Silver 0.4624 oz. ASW, 33 mm. **Subject:** 120th Birthday of Yanka Kupala **Obv:** National arms **Rev:** Yanka Kupala, 1882-1942 **Rev. Designer:** S.P. Zaskevich

Date	Mintage	F	VF	XF	Unc	BU
2002 Proof	1,000	Value: 150				

KM# 129 10 ROUBLES
1.2400 g., 0.9990 Gold 0.0398 oz. AGW, 13.92 mm. **Subject:** Belarussian Ballet **Obv:** National arms **Obv. Designer:** S.P. Zaskevich **Rev:** Dancing ballerina **Rev. Designer:** Michael Schulze

Date	Mintage	F	VF	XF	Unc	BU
2005	25,000	—	—	—	70.00	80.00

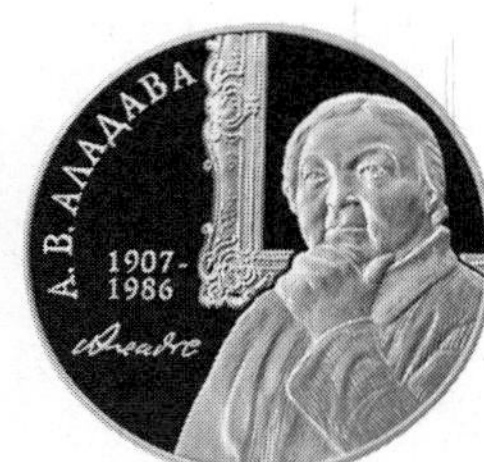

KM# 156 10 ROUBLES
16.8100 g., 0.9250 Silver 0.4999 oz. ASW, 32 mm. **Subject:** Alena Aladana **Rev:** Half-length figure facing, picture in background

Date	Mintage	F	VF	XF	Unc	BU
2007 Proof	4,000	Value: 35.00				

KM# 157 10 ROUBLES
16.8100 g., 0.9250 Silver 0.4999 oz. ASW, 32 mm. **Subject:** Thrush Nightingale **Rev:** Bird standing right on branch

Date	Mintage	F	VF	XF	Unc	BU
2007 Proof	5,000	Value: 40.00				

KM# 172 10 ROUBLES
16.8100 g., 0.9250 Silver 0.4999 oz. ASW, 32 mm. **Subject:** Zair Azgur **Rev:** Profile right

Date	Mintage	F	VF	XF	Unc	BU
2008 Proof	3,000	Value: 40.00				

KM# 173 10 ROUBLES
16.8100 g., 0.9250 Silver 0.4999 oz. ASW, 32 mm. **Subject:** Great White Egret **Rev:** Bird standing left

Date	Mintage	F	VF	XF	Unc	BU
2008 Proof	5,000	Value: 45.00				

KM# 174 10 ROUBLES
16.8100 g., 0.9250 Silver 0.4999 oz. ASW, 32 mm. **Subject:** Vincent Dunin **Rev:** Bust facing

Date	Mintage	F	VF	XF	Unc	BU
2008 Proof	3,000	Value: 35.00				

KM# 175 10 ROUBLES
16.8100 g., 0.9250 Silver 0.4999 oz. ASW, 32 mm. **Subject:** St. Euphrosyne of Polotsk **Rev:** Half-length figure facing within frame

Date	Mintage	F	VF	XF	Unc	BU
2008 Proof	5,000	Value: 40.00				

KM# 176 10 ROUBLES
16.8100 g., 0.9250 Silver 0.4999 oz. ASW, 32 mm. **Subject:** St. Steraphin of Sarov **Rev:** Half-length figure standing within frame

Date	Mintage	F	VF	XF	Unc	BU
2008 Proof	5,000	Value: 40.00				

KM# 177 10 ROUBLES
16.8100 g., 0.9250 Silver 0.4999 oz. ASW, 32 mm. **Subject:** St. Sergii of Radonezh **Rev:** Half-length figure standing within frame

Date	Mintage	F	VF	XF	Unc	BU
2008 Proof	5,000	Value: 40.00				

KM# 178 10 ROUBLES
16.8100 g., 0.9250 Silver 0.4999 oz. ASW, 32 mm. **Subject:** St. Nicholas **Rev:** Half-length figure standing within frame

Date	Mintage	F	VF	XF	Unc	BU
2008 Proof	5,000	Value: 40.00				

KM# 179 10 ROUBLES
16.8100 g., 0.9250 Silver 0.4999 oz. ASW, 32 mm. **Subject:** St. Panteleimon **Rev:** Half-length figure standing within frame

Date	Mintage	F	VF	XF	Unc	BU
2008 Proof	5,000	Value: 40.00				

KM# 194 10 ROUBLES
16.8100 g., 0.9250 Silver 0.4999 oz. ASW, 32 mm. **Subject:** Academy of Science, 80th Anniversary **Rev:** Building

Date	Mintage	F	VF	XF	Unc	BU
2009 Proof	3,000	Value: 40.00				

KM# 195 10 ROUBLES
16.8100 g., 0.9250 Silver 0.4999 oz. ASW, 32 mm. **Subject:** Greylag goose **Rev:** Goose swimming left

Date	Mintage	F	VF	XF	Unc	BU
2009 Proof	5,000	Value: 32.00				

KM# 230 10 ROUBLES
16.8100 g., 0.9250 Silver 0.4999 oz. ASW, 33 mm. **Subject:** 1st Belarus Front **Rev:** Gen. Konstantin Rokosovsky

Date	Mintage	F	VF	XF	Unc	BU
2010 Proof	2,500	Value: 25.00				

KM# 231 10 ROUBLES
16.8100 g., 0.9250 Silver 0.4999 oz. ASW, 33 mm. **Subject:** 2nd Belarus Front **Rev:** Col. Gen. G.F. Zakharov

Date	Mintage	F	VF	XF	Unc	BU
2010 Proof	2,500	Value: 25.00				

KM# 232 10 ROUBLES
16.5500 g., 0.9250 Silver 0.4922 oz. ASW, 33 mm. **Subject:** 3rd Belarus front **Rev:** Col. Gen. Ivan Chernyakovsky

Date	Mintage	F	VF	XF	Unc	BU
2010 Proof	2,500	Value: 25.00				

KM# 233 10 ROUBLES
16.5500 g., 0.9250 Silver 0.4922 oz. ASW, 33 mm. **Subject:** 1st Baltic Front **Rev:** Gen. Hovhannes Bagramgan

Date	Mintage	F	VF	XF	Unc	BU
2010 Proof	2,500	Value: 25.00				

KM# 111 20 ROUBLES
31.1000 g., 0.9250 Silver 0.9249 oz. ASW, 38.61 mm. **Subject:** 900th Anniversary of Euphrasinta **Obv:** National arms **Rev:** Euphrasinta of Polatsk, gold cross **Designer:** S.P. Zaskevitch

Date	Mintage	F	VF	XF	Unc	BU
2001 Proof	Est. 2,000	Value: 350				

KM# 113 20 ROUBLES
31.1000 g., 0.9250 Silver 0.9249 oz. ASW, 38.61 mm. **Subject:** Tower of Kamyantes **Obv:** National arms **Rev:** Kamyanets Tower, seal **Designer:** S.P. Zaskevich

Date	Mintage	F	VF	XF	Unc	BU
2001 Proof	2,000	Value: 100				

KM# 46 20 ROUBLES
33.7300 g., 0.9250 Silver 1.0031 oz. ASW, 38.6 mm. **Subject:** Wildlife **Obv:** National arms **Rev:** European Bison **Edge:** Reeded **Designer:** S.P. Zaskevich

Date	Mintage	F	VF	XF	Unc	BU
2001 Proof	2,000	Value: 650				

KM# 49 20 ROUBLES
28.3200 g., 0.9250 Silver 0.8422 oz. ASW, 38.6 mm. **Subject:** 2002 Winter Olympics **Obv:** National arms **Rev:** Marksman aiming at bullseye **Edge:** Reeded **Designer:** S.P. Zaskevich

Date	Mintage	F	VF	XF	Unc	BU
2001 Proof	15,000	Value: 45.00				

KM# 51 20 ROUBLES
33.6500 g., 0.9250 Silver 1.0007 oz. ASW, 38.6 mm. **Subject:** 2002 Winter Olympics **Obv:** National arms **Rev:** Two freestyle skiers **Edge:** Reeded **Designer:** S.P. Zaskevich

Date	Mintage	F	VF	XF	Unc	BU
2001 Proof	2,000	Value: 60.00				

KM# 45 20 ROUBLES
33.7300 g., 0.9250 Silver 1.0031 oz. ASW, 38.8 mm. **Obv:** National arms **Rev:** European beaver and young **Edge:** Reeded **Designer:** S.P. Zaskevich

Date	Mintage	F	VF	XF	Unc	BU
2002 Proof	2,000	Value: 200				

KM# 115 20 ROUBLES
31.1000 g., 0.9250 Silver 0.9249 oz. ASW, 38.61 mm. **Subject:** 200th Birthday of Ignatius Dameika **Obv:** National arms **Rev:** Ignatius Dameika, hammer and inset with a dameikit stone **Rev. Designer:** S.P. Zaskevich

Date	Mintage	F	VF	XF	Unc	BU
2002 Proof	1,000	Value: 350				

KM# 119 20 ROUBLES
31.1000 g., 0.9250 Silver 0.9249 oz. ASW, 38.61 mm. **Subject:** 2006 World Cup Football **Obv:** National arms **Rev:** Stylized 2006, football **Designer:** S.P. Zaskevich

Date	Mintage	F	VF	XF	Unc	BU
2002 Proof	Est. 25,000	Value: 45.00				

KM# 59 20 ROUBLES
28.6300 g., 0.9250 Silver 0.8514 oz. ASW, 38.6 mm. **Obv:** National arms **Obv. Designer:** S.P. Zaskevich **Rev:** Brown bear with two cubs **Rev. Designer:** Waldemar Vronski **Edge:** Reeded

Date	Mintage	F	VF	XF	Unc	BU
2002 Proof	5,000	Value: 120				

KM# 70 20 ROUBLES
33.8500 g., 0.9250 Silver 1.0066 oz. ASW, 38.61 mm. **Obv:** National arms **Obv. Designer:** S.P. Zaskevich **Rev:** 80th Anniversary - National Savings Bank **Rev. Designer:** V. Titov **Edge:** Reeded

Date	Mintage	F	VF	XF	Unc	BU
2002 Proof	1,000	Value: 225				

KM# 120 20 ROUBLES
31.1000 g., 0.9250 Silver 0.9249 oz. ASW, 38.61 mm. **Subject:** Freestyle Wrestling **Obv:** National arms **Rev:** Two wrestlers **Designer:** S.P. Zaskevich

Date	Mintage	F	VF	XF	Unc	BU
2003 Proof	3,000	Value: 50.00				

KM# 122 20 ROUBLES
31.1000 g., 0.9250 Silver 0.9249 oz. ASW, 38.61 mm. **Obv:** National arms **Rev:** Herring gull in flight **Designer:** S.P. Zaskevitch

Date	Mintage	F	VF	XF	Unc	BU
2003 Proof	2,000	Value: 150				

KM# 53 20 ROUBLES
33.8400 g., 0.9250 Silver 1.0063 oz. ASW, 38.5 mm. **Obv:** State arms **Rev:** Two Mute swans on water with reflections **Edge:** Reeded **Designer:** S.P. Zaskevich

Date	Mintage	F	VF	XF	Unc	BU
2003 Proof	2,000	Value: 200				

KM# 57 20 ROUBLES
31.1000 g., 0.9250 Silver 0.9249 oz. ASW, 38.6 mm. **Obv:** National arms **Rev:** Church of the Savior and Transfiguration **Edge:** Reeded **Designer:** S.P. Zaskevich

Date	Mintage	F	VF	XF	Unc	BU
2003 Proof	2,000	Value: 100				

KM# 149 20 ROUBLES
26.1600 g., 0.9250 Silver 0.7780 oz. ASW, 38.61 mm. **Subject:** 2004 Olympic Games **Obv:** National arms **Rev:** Female shot-putter **Designer:** S.P. Zaskevich

Date	Mintage	F	VF	XF	Unc	BU
2003 Proof	25,000	Value: 32.00				

KM# 91 20 ROUBLES

31.1000 g., 0.9250 Silver 0.9249 oz. ASW, 38.61 mm. **Subject:** Trade Union Movement Centennial **Obv:** National arms **Obv. Designer:** S.P. Zaskevich **Rev. Designer:** G.A. Maximor

Date	Mintage	F	VF	XF	Unc	BU
2004 Proof	1,500	Value: 200				

KM# 86 20 ROUBLES

31.1000 g., 0.9250 Silver 0.9249 oz. ASW, 38.61 mm. **Subject:** Soviet Warriors - Liberators **Obv:** Multicolored Order of the Patriotic War **Obv. Designer:** S.P. Zaskevich **Rev:** Partisans with blown up railway track **Rev. Designer:** E.N. Vishnyakova

Date	Mintage	F	VF	XF	Unc	BU
2004	2,000	—	—	—	100	—

KM# 84 20 ROUBLES

31.1000 g., 0.9250 Silver 0.9249 oz. ASW, 38.61 mm. **Subject:** Memory of Facist Victims **Obv:** Multicolored Order of the Patriotic War **Obv. Designer:** S.P. Zaskevich **Rev:** Man holding dead **Rev. Designer:** E.N. Vishnyakova

Date	Mintage	F	VF	XF	Unc	BU
2004	2,000	—	—	—	100	—

KM# 124 20 ROUBLES

31.1000 g., 0.9250 Silver 0.9249 oz. ASW, 38.61 mm. **Subject:** Sculling **Obv:** National arms **Obv. Designer:** S.P. Zaskevich **Rev:** Two rowers against a background of stylized oars **Rev. Designer:** S.V. Nekrasova

Date	Mintage	F	VF	XF	Unc	BU
2004	3,000	—	—	—	50.00	—

KM# 71 20 ROUBLES

31.1000 g., 0.9250 Silver 0.9249 oz. ASW, 38.6 mm. **Subject:** "Kupalle" **Obv:** Folk art design **Rev:** Fern flower with inset red synthetic crystal **Edge:** Reeded **Designer:** S.P. Zaskevich

Date	Mintage	F	VF	XF	Unc	BU
2004 Antique finish	3,000	—	—	—	600	—

KM# 72 20 ROUBLES

31.1000 g., 0.9250 Silver 0.9249 oz. ASW, 38.6 mm. **Subject:** Defense of Brest **Obv:** Multicolor Soviet Order of the Patriotic War **Rev:** "Courage" monument **Edge:** Reeded **Designer:** S.P. Zaskevich

Date	Mintage	F	VF	XF	Unc	BU
2004 Proof	3,000	Value: 100				

KM# 73 20 ROUBLES

31.1000 g., 0.9250 Silver 0.9249 oz. ASW, 38.6 mm. **Obv:** National arms **Rev:** Two common cranes **Edge:** Reeded

Date	Mintage	F	VF	XF	Unc	BU
2004 Proof	2,000	Value: 150				

KM# 77 20 ROUBLES

31.1000 g., 0.9250 Silver 0.9249 oz. ASW, 38.6 mm. **Subject:** "Kalyady" **Obv:** Folk art cross design **Rev:** Stylized sunflower with inset blue synthetic crystal **Edge:** Reeded **Designer:** S.P. Zaskevich

Date	Mintage	F	VF	XF	Unc	BU
2004 Antique finish	5,000	—	—	—	350	—

KM# 79 20 ROUBLES

31.1000 g., 0.9250 Silver 0.9249 oz. ASW, 38.6 mm. **Obv:** National arms **Rev:** Radziwill's Castle in Neswizh **Edge:** Reeded **Designer:** S.P. Zaskevich

Date	Mintage	F	VF	XF	Unc	BU
2004 Proof	2,000	Value: 100				

KM# 82 20 ROUBLES

28.7200 g., 0.9250 Silver 0.8541 oz. ASW, 38.6 mm. **Subject:** WW II Victory **Obv:** Multicolor Soviet Order of Victory **Rev:** Soviet soldiers raising their flag in the Reichstag in Berlin **Rev. Designer:** S.V. Necrasova **Edge:** Reeded

Date	Mintage	F	VF	XF	Unc	BU
2005 Proof	12,000	Value: 60.00				

KM# 92 20 ROUBLES

28.6300 g., 0.9250 Silver 0.8514 oz. ASW, 38.6 mm. **Obv:** Two children sitting on crescent moon **Rev:** Symon the Musician and inset orange color glass crystal **Edge:** Plain **Designer:** S.V. Necrasova

Date	Mintage	F	VF	XF	Unc	BU
2005 Antique finish	20,000	—	—	—	60.00	—

KM# 93 20 ROUBLES

28.6300 g., 0.9250 Silver 0.8514 oz. ASW, 38.6 mm. **Subject:** Kalyady's star **Obv:** Two children sitting on a crescent moon **Rev:** Snow Queen, blue glass crystal inset on forehead, flower **Edge:** Plain **Designer:** S.V. Necrasova

Date	Mintage	F	VF	XF	Unc	BU
2005 Antique finish	20,000	—	—	—	60.00	—

KM# 94 20 ROUBLES

28.6300 g., 0.9250 Silver 0.8514 oz. ASW, 38.6 mm. **Obv:** Two children sitting on a crescent moon **Rev:** White glass crystal inset above landscape with fox, the Little Prince **Edge:** Plain **Designer:** S.V. Necrasova

Date	Mintage	F	VF	XF	Unc	BU
2005 Antique finish	20,000	—	—	—	60.00	—

KM# 95 20 ROUBLES

28.6300 g., 0.9250 Silver 0.8514 oz. ASW, 38.61 mm. **Obv:** Two children sitting on a crescent moon **Rev:** The Stone Flower, Yellow glass crystal inset in flower design, heads flank **Edge:** Plain **Designer:** S.V. Necrasova

Date	Mintage	F	VF	XF	Unc	BU
2005 Antique finish	20,000	—	—	—	60.00	—

KM# 96 20 ROUBLES

33.6600 g., 0.9250 Silver 1.0010 oz. ASW, 38.6 mm. **Obv:** Small national arms above quilted star design **Rev:** Yellow glass crystal inset in candle flame above basket **Edge:** Reeded **Designer:** S.P. Zaskevich

Date	Mintage	F	VF	XF	Unc	BU
2005 Antique finish	5,000	—	—	—	170	—

KM# 98 20 ROUBLES

33.6300 g., 0.9250 Silver 1.0000 oz. ASW, 38.6 mm. **Subject:** Almany Bogs **Obv:** Blooming plant on frosted design **Rev:** Great grey owl in flight **Edge:** Reeded **Designer:** S.V. Nekrasova

Date	Mintage	F	VF	XF	Unc	BU
2005 Proof	5,000	Value: 60.00				

KM# 99 20 ROUBLES

31.1000 g., 0.9250 Silver 0.9249 oz. ASW, 38.6 mm. **Series:** Easter Egg **Obv:** Quilted cross design **Rev:** Decorated Easter egg with inset pink glass crystal

Date	Mintage	F	VF	XF	Unc	BU
2005 Antique finish	5,000	—	—	—	250	—

KM# 100 20 ROUBLES

33.6200 g., 0.9250 Silver 0.9998 oz. ASW, 38.6 mm. **Obv:** Large church **Rev:** Usyaslau of Polatsk

Date	Mintage	F	VF	XF	Unc	BU
2005 Proof	5,000	Value: 60.00				

KM# 102 20 ROUBLES

33.9400 g., 0.9250 Silver 1.0093 oz. ASW, 39 mm. **Obv:** National arms **Rev:** Female tennis player

Date	Mintage	F	VF	XF	Unc	BU
2005 Proof	7,000	Value: 60.00				

KM# 128 20 ROUBLES

31.1000 g., 0.9250 Silver 0.9249 oz. ASW, 38.61 mm. **Subject:** 1000th Anniversary of Vaukavysk **Obv:** National arms **Rev:** National arms of Vaukavysk **Rev. Designer:** S.P. Zaskevitch

Date	Mintage	F	VF	XF	Unc	BU
2005 Proof	2,000	Value: 100				

KM# 131 20 ROUBLES

31.1000 g., 0.9250 Silver 0.9249 oz. ASW, 38.61 mm. **Subject:** Jesnit Roman Catholic Church **Obv:** National arms **Rev:** Jesnit Roman Catholic Church in Niasvizh **Designer:** S.P. Zaskevich

Date	Mintage	F	VF	XF	Unc	BU
2005 Proof	2,000	Value: 100				

KM# 133 20 ROUBLES

26.1600 g., 0.9250 Silver 0.7780 oz. ASW, 38.61 mm. **Subject:** 2006 Olympic Games **Obv:** National arms **Obv. Designer:** S.P. Zaskevich **Rev:** Two hockey players **Rev. Designer:** S.V. Necrasova and Ruth Oswald Koppers

Date	Mintage	F	VF	XF	Unc	BU
2005	15,000	—	—	—	30.00	—

KM# 101 20 ROUBLES

25.0000 g., 0.9250 Silver 0.7435 oz. ASW, 38.6 mm. **Subject:** 2006 FIFA World Cup Germany **Obv:** National arms **Rev:** Multicolor Europe, Asia and African maps on soccer ball **Rev. Designer:** S.V. Nekrasova **Note:** 2006 World Cup Soccer

Date	Mintage	F	VF	XF	Unc	BU
2005 Proof	50,000	Value: 50.00				

KM# 148 20 ROUBLES

28.2800 g., 0.9250 Silver 0.8410 oz. ASW, 38.5 mm. **Subject:** Twelve Months **Obv:** Two children sitting on a crescent moon **Rev:** Campfire with inset amber in a circle of produce **Edge:** Plain **Note:** Antiqued finish. Prev. duplicate of KM #137.

Date	Mintage	F	VF	XF	Unc	BU
2006	20,000	—	—	—	60.00	—

KM# 136 20 ROUBLES

33.6300 g., 0.9250 Silver 1.0000 oz. ASW, 38.61 mm. **Subject:** Vtaselle Wedding **Obv:** National arms, birds, shamrock **Rev:** Loaf of bread, golden wedding rings, diadem of flowers, background of honeycomb

Date	Mintage	F	VF	XF	Unc	BU
2006	25,000	—	—	—	70.00	—

KM# 139 20 ROUBLES

33.6200 g., 0.9250 Silver 0.9998 oz. ASW, 38.61 mm. **Subject:** Sophia of Galshany 600th Anniversary **Obv:** Castle of Galshany **Rev:** National arms and Sophia of Galshany **Designer:** S.P. Zaskevich

Date	Mintage	F	VF	XF	Unc	BU
2006 Proof	5,000	Value: 60.00				

KM# 141 20 ROUBLES

33.6200 g., 0.9250 Silver 0.9998 oz. ASW, 38.61 mm. **Subject:** Syomukha **Obv:** National arms, solar symbol **Rev:** Chalice, Chaplet of birch, maple, rowan, sweet flag leaves inserted in green crystal **Designer:** S.P. Zaskevich

Date	Mintage	F	VF	XF	Unc	BU
2006	5,000	—	—	—	150	—

KM# 147 20 ROUBLES

33.6300 g., 0.9250 Silver 1.0000 oz. ASW, 38.61 mm. **Subject:** Chyrvomy Bar **Obv:** National arms, blooming plant **Rev:** European mink **Designer:** S.V. Nekrasova

Date	Mintage	F	VF	XF	Unc	BU
2006 Proof	5,000	Value: 60.00				

KM# 155 20 ROUBLES

33.6200 g., 0.9250 Silver 0.9998 oz. ASW, 36x36 mm. **Subject:** Struve Geodetic Arc **Rev:** Map of Eastern Europe **Shape:** Square

Date	Mintage	F	VF	XF	Unc	BU
2006 Proof	5,000	Value: 55.00				

KM# 166 20 ROUBLES

33.6200 g., 0.9250 Silver 0.9998 oz. ASW, 38.61 mm. **Subject:** Legend of the Stork **Obv:** Woven basket design **Rev:** Stylized bird

Date	Mintage	F	VF	XF	Unc	BU
2007 Proof	5,000	Value: 60.00				

KM# 158 20 ROUBLES

33.6200 g., 0.9250 Silver 0.9998 oz. ASW, 38.61 mm. **Subject:** Belarus - China diplomatic relations **Rev:** Double arches with country scene

Date	Mintage	F	VF	XF	Unc	BU
2007 Proof	2,000	Value: 100				

KM# 159 20 ROUBLES

33.6200 g., 0.9250 Silver 0.9998 oz. ASW, 38.61 mm. **Subject:** Maslenitsea **Rev:** Pancake and syrup

Date	Mintage	F	VF	XF	Unc	BU
2007 Matte Proof	5,000	Value: 130				

KM# 160 20 ROUBLES
33.6300 g., 0.9250 Silver 1.0000 oz. ASW, 38.61 mm. **Subject:** Napoleon Orda **Rev:** Bust facing, record and musical notes in background

Date	Mintage	F	VF	XF	Unc	BU
2007 Proof	5,000	Value: 45.00				

KM# 161 20 ROUBLES
28.2800 g., 0.9250 Silver 0.8410 oz. ASW, 38.61 mm. **Subject:** Alice in Wonderland **Obv:** Two children sitting on crescent moon reading book **Rev:** Alice and the March Hare

Date	Mintage	F	VF	XF	Unc	BU
2007 Matte Proof	20,000	Value: 50.00				

KM# 162 20 ROUBLES
28.2800 g., 0.9250 Silver 0.8410 oz. ASW, 38.61 mm. **Subject:** Alice Through the Looking Glass **Obv:** Two children sitting on crescent moon reading book **Rev:** Alice and chess board

Date	Mintage	F	VF	XF	Unc	BU
2007 Matte Proof	20,000	Value: 50.00				

KM# 163 20 ROUBLES
31.1050 g., 0.9990 Silver 0.9990 oz. ASW, 40 mm. **Subject:** Belarusian Ballet **Rev:** Ballerina and mirror view

Date	Mintage	F	VF	XF	Unc	BU
2007 Proof	10,000	Value: 50.00				

KM# 164 20 ROUBLES
31.1000 g., 0.9250 Silver 0.9249 oz. ASW, 38.61 mm. **Subject:** International Polar Year **Obv:** IPY logo **Rev:** Antartic map behind two penguins

Date	Mintage	F	VF	XF	Unc	BU
2007 Proof	10,000	Value: 45.00				

KM# 165 20 ROUBLES
33.6200 g., 0.9250 Silver 0.9998 oz. ASW, 38.61 mm. **Subject:** Prince Gleb of Mensk **Obv:** Wood log building **Rev:** Knight seated left

Date	Mintage	F	VF	XF	Unc	BU
2007 Proof	5,000	Value: 60.00				

KM# 167 20 ROUBLES
31.1050 g., 0.9990 Silver 0.9990 oz. ASW, 38.61 mm. **Subject:** Wolf - Canis Lupus **Rev:** Wolf head facing

Date	Mintage	F	VF	XF	Unc	BU
2007 Proof	7,000	Value: 60.00				

KM# 168 20 ROUBLES
31.1050 g., 0.9990 Silver 0.9990 oz. ASW, 38.61 mm. **Subject:** Wolf - Canis Lupis **Rev:** Wolf standing on rock ledge behind second wolf's head facing

Date	Mintage	F	VF	XF	Unc	BU
2007 Proof	7,000	Value: 60.00				

KM# 169 20 ROUBLES
33.6300 g., 0.9250 Silver 1.0000 oz. ASW, 38.61 mm. **Subject:** Dniepra - Sozhsky **Rev:** Sturgeon fish

Date	Mintage	F	VF	XF	Unc	BU
2007 Proof	5,000	Value: 60.00				

KM# 180 20 ROUBLES
33.6300 g., 0.9250 Silver 1.0000 oz. ASW, 38.61 mm. **Subject:** Minsk **Rev:** Old and new city views

Date	Mintage	F	VF	XF	Unc	BU
2008 Proof	7,000	Value: 50.00				

KM# 181 20 ROUBLES
33.6300 g., 0.9250 Silver 1.0000 oz. ASW, 38.61 mm. **Subject:** Financial System, 90th Anniversary **Rev:** Shield

Date	Mintage	F	VF	XF	Unc	BU
2008 Proof	3,000	Value: 60.00				

KM# 182 20 ROUBLES
33.6300 g., 0.9250 Silver 1.0000 oz. ASW, 38.61 mm. **Subject:** Lipichanskaya Pushcha **Rev:** Kingfisher seated on branch

Date	Mintage	F	VF	XF	Unc	BU
2008 Proof	5,000	Value: 65.00				

KM# 183 20 ROUBLES
33.6200 g., 0.9250 Silver 0.9998 oz. ASW, 38.61 mm. **Subject:** Dzyady **Rev:** Two angels above table

Date	Mintage	F	VF	XF	Unc	BU
2008 Antique	—	—	—	—	90.00	—

KM# 184 20 ROUBLES
33.6200 g., 0.9250 Silver 0.9998 oz. ASW, 38.61 mm. **Subject:** David of Garadzen **Rev:** Half-length figure of knight

Date	Mintage	F	VF	XF	Unc	BU
2008 Proof	5,000	Value: 60.00				

KM# 185 20 ROUBLES
31.1050 g., 0.9990 Silver 0.9990 oz. ASW, 40 mm. **Rev:** Figure skater

Date	Mintage	F	VF	XF	Unc	BU
2008 Proof	10,000	Value: 50.00				

KM# 186 20 ROUBLES
31.1050 g., 0.9990 Silver 0.9990 oz. ASW, 38.61 mm. **Subject:** Lynx **Rev:** Lynx head facing

Date	Mintage	F	VF	XF	Unc	BU
2008 Proof	8,000	Value: 95.00				

KM# 187 20 ROUBLES
31.1050 g., 0.9990 Silver 0.9990 oz. ASW, 38.61 mm. **Subject:** Lynx **Rev:** Adult lynx with cub

Date	Mintage	F	VF	XF	Unc	BU
2008 Proof	8,000	Value: 85.00				

KM# 188 20 ROUBLES
33.6200 g., 0.9250 Silver 0.9998 oz. ASW, 38.61 mm. **Subject:** Cuckoo Legend **Rev:** Stylized cuckoo

Date	Mintage	F	VF	XF	Unc	BU
2008 Proof	5,000	Value: 55.00				

KM# 189 20 ROUBLES
28.2800 g., 0.9250 Silver 0.8410 oz. ASW, 38.61 mm. **Subject:** Turandot **Rev:** Female opera character

Date	Mintage	F	VF	XF	Unc	BU
2008 Antique	—	—	—	—	60.00	—

KM# 190 20 ROUBLES
38.6100 g., 0.9250 Silver 1.1482 oz. ASW, 38.61 mm. **Subject:** House Warming **Obv:** Cat **Rev:** Plated key within house facade

Date	Mintage	F	VF	XF	Unc	BU
2008 Proof	25,000	Value: 50.00				

KM# 191 20 ROUBLES
28.2800 g., 0.9250 Silver 0.8410 oz. ASW, 38.61 mm. **Subject:** Sedov **Obv:** Compass star, multicolor **Rev:** Sailing ship

Date	Mintage	F	VF	XF	Unc	BU
2008 Proof	25,000	Value: 65.00				

KM# 196 20 ROUBLES
33.6300 g., 0.9250 Silver 1.0000 oz. ASW, 38.61 mm. **Subject:** 65th Anniversary of Liberation **Rev:** Child looking upward to freeded birds

Date	Mintage	F	VF	XF	Unc	BU
2009 Proof	4,000	Value: 60.00				

KM# 197 20 ROUBLES
28.2800 g., 0.9250 Silver 0.8410 oz. ASW, 40x28 mm. **Subject:** Llya Repin **Rev:** Bust and house, artist's palet in corner **Shape:** Rectangle

Date	Mintage	F	VF	XF	Unc	BU
2009 Proof	1,500	Value: 60.00				

KM# 198 20 ROUBLES
28.2800 g., 0.9250 Silver 0.8410 oz. ASW, 38.61 mm. **Subject:** Sapsy **Rev:** Bee honey comb, apple tree, grain

Date	Mintage	F	VF	XF	Unc	BU
2009 Proof	5,000	Value: 80.00				

KM# 199 20 ROUBLES
33.6300 g., 0.9990 Silver 1.0801 oz. ASW, 38.61 mm. **Subject:** Christening **Rev:** Child in christening gown

Date	Mintage	F	VF	XF	Unc	BU
2009 Proof	5,000	Value: 80.00				

KM# 200 20 ROUBLES
28.2800 g., 0.9250 Silver 0.8410 oz. ASW, 38.61 mm. **Subject:** Dar Pomorza **Rev:** Sail training vessel

Date	Mintage	F	VF	XF	Unc	BU
2009 Proof	25,000	Value: 60.00				

KM# 201 20 ROUBLES
33.6300 g., 0.9250 Silver 1.0000 oz. ASW, 38.61 mm. **Subject:** White stork **Rev:** Bird and nest

Date	Mintage	F	VF	XF	Unc	BU
2009 Proof	7,000	Value: 65.00				

KM# 202 20 ROUBLES
33.6300 g., 0.9250 Silver 1.0000 oz. ASW, 38.61 mm. **Subject:** Belavezhskaya Pushcha **Rev:** Range animals

Date	Mintage	F	VF	XF	Unc	BU
2009 Proof	8,000	Value: 60.00				

KM# 203 20 ROUBLES
28.2800 g., 0.9250 Silver 0.8410 oz. ASW, 38.61 mm. **Series:** Zodiac - Pisces **Rev:** Two fish

Date	Mintage	F	VF	XF	Unc	BU
2009 Matte Proof	25,000	Value: 55.00				

KM# 204 20 ROUBLES
28.2800 g., 0.9250 Silver 0.8410 oz. ASW, 38.61 mm. **Subject:** Zodiac - Aries **Rev:** Ram

Date	Mintage	F	VF	XF	Unc	BU
2009 Matte Proof	25,000	Value: 55.00				

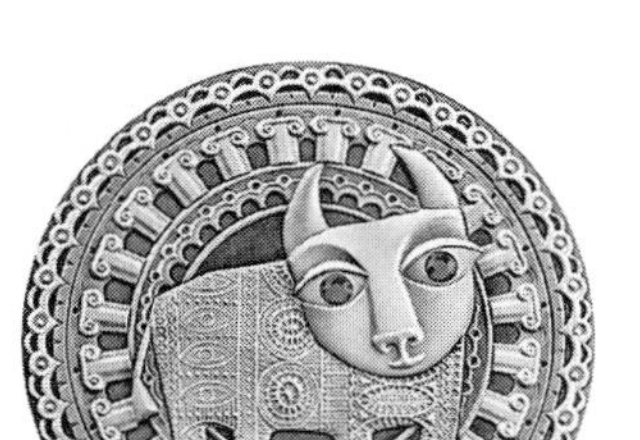

KM# 205 20 ROUBLES
28.2800 g., 0.9250 Silver 0.8410 oz. ASW, 38.61 mm. **Subject:** Zodiac - Taurus **Rev:** Bull

Date	Mintage	F	VF	XF	Unc	BU
2009 Matte Proof	25,000	Value: 55.00				

KM# 206 20 ROUBLES
28.2800 g., 0.9250 Silver 0.8410 oz. ASW, 38.61 mm. **Subject:** Zodiac - Gemini **Rev:** Twins

Date	Mintage	F	VF	XF	Unc	BU
2009 Matte Proof	25,000	Value: 55.00				

KM# 207 20 ROUBLES
28.2800 g., 0.9250 Silver 0.8410 oz. ASW, 38.61 mm. **Subject:** Zodiac - Cancer **Rev:** Crab

Date	Mintage	F	VF	XF	Unc	BU
2009 Matte Proof	25,000	Value: 55.00				

KM# 208 20 ROUBLES
28.2800 g., 0.9250 Silver 0.8410 oz. ASW, 38.61 mm. **Subject:** Zodiac - Leo **Rev:** Lion

Date	Mintage	F	VF	XF	Unc	BU
2009 Matte Proof	25,000	Value: 55.00				

KM# 209 20 ROUBLES
28.2800 g., 0.9250 Silver 0.8410 oz. ASW, 38.61 mm. **Subject:** Zodiac - Virgo **Rev:** Little girl

Date	Mintage	F	VF	XF	Unc	BU
2009 Matte Proof	25,000	Value: 55.00				

KM# 210 20 ROUBLES
28.2800 g., 0.9250 Silver 0.8410 oz. ASW, 38.61 mm. **Subject:** Zodiac - Libra **Rev:** Balance scales

Date	Mintage	F	VF	XF	Unc	BU
2009 Matte Proof	25,000	Value: 55.00				

KM# 211 20 ROUBLES
28.2800 g., 0.9250 Silver 0.8410 oz. ASW, 38.61 mm. **Obv. Designer:** Zodiac - Scorpio **Rev:** Scorpion

Date	Mintage	F	VF	XF	Unc	BU
2009 Matte Proof	25,000	Value: 55.00				

KM# 254 20 ROUBLES
28.2800 g., 0.9250 Silver 0.8410 oz. ASW, 45.3x35.3 mm. **Subject:** Pushkin's stories **Rev:** Tale of Tsar Saltan **Shape:** Vertical oval

Date	Mintage	F	VF	XF	Unc	BU
2010 Proof	7,000	Value: 85.00				

KM# 224 20 ROUBLES
33.6300 g., 0.9250 Silver 1.0000 oz. ASW, 38.61 mm. **Subject:** EURASEC, 10th Anniversary **Obv:** Folk embrodery pattern **Rev:** Six flags around multicolor golbe

Date	Mintage	F	VF	XF	Unc	BU
2010 Proof	3,000	Value: 60.00				

KM# 225 20 ROUBLES
33.6300 g., 0.9250 Silver 1.0000 oz. ASW, 38.6 mm. **Subject:** Syarednіaya Pripyat Reserve **Obv:** Eight ferns forming double cross **Rev:** Marsh turtle

Date	Mintage	F	VF	XF	Unc	BU
2010 Proof	3,000	Value: 60.00				

KM# 235 20 ROUBLES
28.2800 g., 0.9250 Silver 0.8410 oz. ASW, 38.61 mm. **Rev:** U.S. Frigate Constitution

Date	Mintage	F	VF	XF	Unc	BU
2010 Proof	7,000	Value: 75.00				

KM# 237 20 ROUBLES
33.6200 g., 0.9250 Silver 0.9998 oz. ASW, 38.61 mm. **Subject:** Legend of the tortoise

Date	Mintage	F	VF	XF	Unc	BU
2010 Proof	3,000	Value: 55.00				

KM# 239 20 ROUBLES
28.2800 g., 0.9250 Silver 0.8410 oz. ASW, 38.6 mm. **Subject:** Battle of Grunwald **Obv:** Figure with outstretched arms **Rev:** Legend within Fingerprint

Date	Mintage	F	VF	XF	Unc	BU
2010 Proof	2,500	Value: 60.00				

KM# 241 20 ROUBLES
33.6300 g., 0.9250 Silver 1.0000 oz. ASW, 38.61 mm. **Subject:** Age of Majority **Rev:** Multicolor flowers within folk patterns

Date	Mintage	F	VF	XF	Unc	BU
2010 Proof	—	Value: 55.00				

KM# 242 20 ROUBLES
28.2800 g., 0.9250 Silver 0.8410 oz. ASW, 38.61 mm. **Subject:** 3 Musketeers **Rev:** D'Artagnan, with red stone insert

Date	Mintage	F	VF	XF	Unc	BU
2010 Proof	5,000	Value: 85.00				

KM# 243 20 ROUBLES
28.2800 g., 0.9250 Silver 0.8410 oz. ASW, 38.61 mm. **Subject:** The Three Musketeers **Rev:** Aramis, light blue stone insert

Date	Mintage	F	VF	XF	Unc	BU
2010 Proof	5,000	Value: 85.00				

KM# 244 20 ROUBLES
28.2800 g., 0.9250 Silver 0.8410 oz. ASW, 38.61 mm. **Subject:** The Three Musketeers **Rev:** Athos, blue stone insert

Date	Mintage	F	VF	XF	Unc	BU
2010 Proof	5,000	Value: 85.00				

KM# 245 20 ROUBLES
28.2800 g., 0.9250 Silver 0.8410 oz. ASW, 38.61 mm. **Subject:** The Three Musketeers **Rev:** Pathos, red stone insert

Date	Mintage	F	VF	XF	Unc	BU
2010 Proof	5,000	Value: 85.00				

KM# 246 20 ROUBLES
28.2800 g., 0.9250 Silver 0.8410 oz. ASW, 38.61 mm. **Subject:** Orthodox Churches **Rev:** Cathedral of the Assumption

Date	Mintage	F	VF	XF	Unc	BU
2010 Proof	3,000	Value: 75.00				

KM# 247 20 ROUBLES
28.2800 g., 0.9250 Silver 0.8410 oz. ASW, 38.61 mm. **Subject:** Orthodox Churches **Rev:** Cathedral of SS Peter and Paul

Date	Mintage	F	VF	XF	Unc	BU
2010 Proof	3,000	Value: 75.00				

KM# 248 20 ROUBLES
28.2800 g., 0.9250 Silver 0.8410 oz. ASW, 38.61 mm. **Subject:** Orthodox Churches **Rev:** Cathedral of Alexander Nevsky

Date	Mintage	F	VF	XF	Unc	BU
2010 Proof	3,000	Value: 75.00				

KM# 249 20 ROUBLES
28.2800 g., 0.9250 Silver 0.8410 oz. ASW, 38.61 mm. **Subject:** Orthodox Churches **Rev:** Cathedral of St. Nicholas

Date	Mintage	F	VF	XF	Unc	BU
2010 Proof	3,000	Value: 75.00				

KM# 250 20 ROUBLES
28.2800 g., 0.9250 Silver 0.8410 oz. ASW, 45.3x35.3 mm. **Subject:** Pushkin's stories **Rev:** Tale of the Golden Cockerel in multicolor **Shape:** Vertical oval

Date	Mintage	F	VF	XF	Unc	BU
2010 Proof	7,000	Value: 85.00				

KM# 251 20 ROUBLES
28.2800 g., 0.9250 Silver 0.8410 oz. ASW, 45.3x35.3 mm. **Subject:** Pushkin's stories **Rev:** Tale of the fisherman and the fish **Shape:** Vertical oval

Date	Mintage	F	VF	XF	Unc	BU
2010 Proof	7,000	Value: 85.00				

KM# 252 20 ROUBLES
28.2800 g., 0.9250 Silver 0.8410 oz. ASW, 45.3x35.3 mm. **Subject:** Pushkin's stories **Rev:** Tale of one Dead Princess and Seven Knights **Shape:** Vertical oval

Date	Mintage	F	VF	XF	Unc	BU
2010 Proof	7,000	Value: 85.00				

KM# 253 20 ROUBLES
28.2800 g., 0.9250 Silver 0.8410 oz. ASW, 45.3x35.3 mm. **Subject:** Pushkin's stories **Rev:** Ruslan and Ludmila **Shape:** Vertical oval

Date	Mintage	F	VF	XF	Unc	BU
2010 Proof	7,000	Value: 85.00				

KM# 255 20 ROUBLES
28.2800 g., 0.9250 Silver 0.8410 oz. ASW, 38.61 mm. **Subject:** My Love **Rev:** Two cats, red heart shaped crystal insert at top

Date	Mintage	F	VF	XF	Unc	BU
2011 Proof	15,000	Value: 100				

KM# 121 50 ROUBLES
4.4500 g., 0.9990 Gold 0.1429 oz. AGW, 25 mm. **Subject:** Fox **Obv:** National arms **Obv. Designer:** S.P. Zaskevich **Rev:** Red fox with inset diamond eyes **Rev. Designer:** Waldemar Wronski

Date	Mintage	F	VF	XF	Unc	BU
2002	Est. 2,000	—	—	—	1,000	—

KM# 126 50 ROUBLES
62.2000 g., 0.9250 Silver 1.8497 oz. ASW, 50 mm. **Subject:** 60th Anniversary of Victory **Obv:** Order of the Victory, multicolored **Rev:** Stars and arrows **Rev. Designer:** S.V. Necrasova

Date	Mintage	F	VF	XF	Unc	BU
2005	2,000	—	—	—	—	—
2005 Proof	—	Value: 220				

KM# 142 50 ROUBLES
7.7800 g., 0.9990 Gold 0.2499 oz. AGW, 25 mm. **Subject:** Peregrine Falcon **Obv:** National arms **Obv. Designer:** S.P. Zaskevich **Rev:** Peregrine falcon with inset diamond eye **Rev. Designer:** S.V. Nekrasova

Date	Mintage	F	VF	XF	Unc	BU
2006	2,000	—	—	750	1,000	—

KM# 143 50 ROUBLES
7.2000 g., 0.9000 Gold 0.2083 oz. AGW, 21 mm. **Subject:** Bison **Obv:** National arms **Rev:** European bison **Designer:** S.P. Zaskevich

Date	Mintage	F	VF	XF	Unc	BU
2006	3,000	—	—	—	400	—

KM# 144 50 ROUBLES
7.2000 g., 0.9000 Gold 0.2083 oz. AGW, 21 mm. **Subject:** Beaver **Obv:** National arms **Rev:** Family of Eurasian beavers **Designer:** S.P. Zaskovich

Date	Mintage	F	VF	XF	Unc	BU
2006	3,000	—	—	—	370	—

KM# 145 50 ROUBLES
7.2000 g., 0.9000 Gold 0.2083 oz. AGW, 21 mm. **Subject:** Mute Swan **Obv:** National arms **Rev:** Pair of mute swans **Designer:** S.P. Zaskevich

Date	Mintage	F	VF	XF	Unc	BU
2006	3,000	—	—	—	370	—

KM# 123 50 ROUBLES
7.2000 g., 0.9000 Gold 0.2083 oz. AGW, 21 mm. **Obv:** National arms **Rev:** Herring gull in flight **Designer:** S.P. Zaskevitch

Date	Mintage	F	VF	XF	Unc	BU
2006	3,000	—	—	—	350	—

KM# 125 50 ROUBLES
7.2000 g., 0.9000 Gold 0.2083 oz. AGW, 21 mm. **Obv:** National arms **Rev:** Pair of common cranes **Designer:** S.P. Zaskevich

Date	Mintage	F	VF	XF	Unc	BU
2006	3,000	—	—	—	350	—

KM# 58 100 ROUBLES
155.5000 g., 0.9250 Silver 4.6243 oz. ASW, 64 mm. **Obv:** Theater building **Rev:** Two ballet dancers **Edge:** Reeded **Designer:** S.P. Zaskevich **Note:** Illustration reduced.

Date	Mintage	F	VF	XF	Unc	BU
2003 Proof	1,000	Value: 750				

KM# 216 100 ROUBLES
17.2800 g., 0.9000 Gold 0.5000 oz. AGW, 32 mm. **Subject:** China - Belarus relations, 15th Anniversary **Obv:** National arms **Rev:** Two archways, forest in left, Great Wall on right

Date	Mintage	F	VF	XF	Unc	BU
2007 Proof	1,000	Value: 800				

KM# 192 100 ROUBLES
155.5000 g., 0.9990 Silver 4.9942 oz. ASW, 65 mm. **Subject:** Figure skating **Rev:** Pair of skates and snowflakes **Note:** Illustration reduced.

Date	Mintage	F	VF	XF	Unc	BU
2008 Proof	500	Value: 450				

KM# 193 100 ROUBLES
155.5000 g., 0.9990 Silver 4.9942 oz. ASW, 65 mm. **Subject:** White Stork Legend **Rev:** Stylized stork

Date	Mintage	F	VF	XF	Unc	BU
2008 Proof	500	Value: 350				

KM# 103 200 ROUBLES
31.1000 g., 0.9990 Gold 0.9988 oz. AGW, 40 mm. **Obv:** National arms **Obv. Designer:** S.P. Zaskevich **Rev:** Belarussian ballerina **Rev. Designer:** Michael Schulze

Date	Mintage	F	VF	XF	Unc	BU
2005 Proof	1,500	Value: 1,650				

KM# 74 1000 ROUBLES
1000.0000 g., 0.9990 Silver 32.117 oz. ASW, 100 mm. **Subject:** 2004 Olympics **Obv:** National arms **Rev:** Ancient charioteer **Rev. Designer:** Waldemar Wronski **Note:** Illustration reduced.

Date	Mintage	F	VF	XF	Unc	BU
2004 Proof	650	Value: 1,500				

KM# 170 1000 ROUBLES
1000.0000 g., 0.9250 Silver 29.738 oz. ASW, 100 mm. **Subject:** Belarusian Ballet **Rev:** Ballerina and mirror image **Note:** Illustration reduced.

Date	Mintage	F	VF	XF	Unc	BU
2007 Proof	300	Value: 1,150				

KM# 171 1000 ROUBLES
1083.8000 g., 0.9250 Silver partially gilt 32.230 oz. ASW, 100 mm. **Subject:** Cross of St. Euphrosyne of Polotsk **Obv:** Church facade **Rev:** Gold-plated pectorial cross **Note:** Illustration reduced.

Date	Mintage	F	VF	XF	Unc	BU
2007 Proof	2,000	Value: 1,100				

BELGIUM

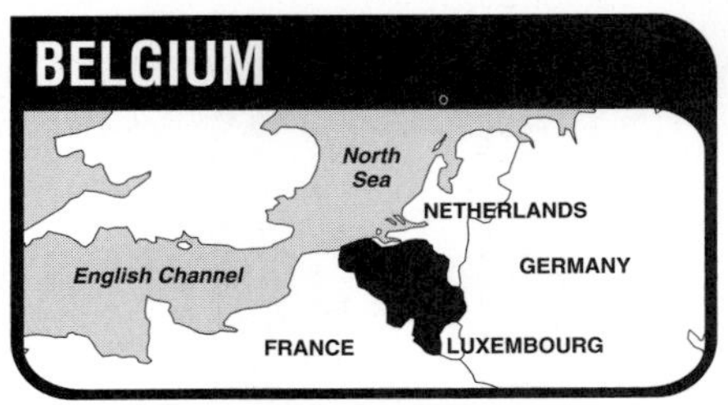

The Kingdom of Belgium, a constitutional monarchy in northwest Europe, has an area of 11,780 sq. mi. (30,519 sq. km.) and a population of 10.1 million, chiefly Dutch-speaking Flemish and French-speaking Walloons. Capital: Brussels. Agriculture, dairy farming, and the processing of raw materials for re-export are the principal industries. Beurs voor Diamant in Antwerp is the world's largest diamond trading center. Iron and steel, machinery motor vehicles, chemicals, textile yarns and fabrics comprise the principal exports.

RULER
Albert II, 1993-

MINT MARK
Angel head - Brussels

MINTMASTERS' INITIALS & PRIVY MARKS
(b) - bird - Vogelier
Lamb head – Lambret
Goose Feather – Serge Lesens (2010)

NOTE: Beginning in 1987, the letters "qp" appear on the coins - (quality proof)

MONETARY SYSTEM
100 Centimes = 1 Franc
1 Euro = 100 Cents

LEGENDS
Belgian coins are usually inscribed either in Dutch, French or both. However some modern coins are being inscribed in Latin or German. The language used is best told by noting the spelling of the name of the country.
(Fr) French: BELGIQUE or BELGES
(Du) Dutch: BELGIE or BELGEN
(La) Latin: BELGICA
(Ge) German: BELGIEN

KINGDOM

DECIMAL COINAGE

KM# 148.1 50 CENTIMES
2.7000 g., Bronze, 19 mm. **Ruler:** Baudouin I **Obv:** Crowned denomination divides date, legend in French **Obv. Legend:** BELGIQUE **Rev:** Helmeted mine worker left, miner's lamp at right, large head, tip of neck 1/2 mm from rim **Edge:** Plain **Designer:** Rau

Date	Mintage	F	VF	XF	Unc	BU
2001 In sets only	60,000	—	—	—	2.00	—
2001 Proof	5,000	Value: 25.00				

Note: Medal alignment

KM# 149.1 50 CENTIMES
2.7500 g., Bronze, 19 mm. **Ruler:** Baudouin I **Obv:** Crowned denomination divides date, legend in Dutch **Obv. Legend:** BELGIE **Rev:** Helmeted mine worker left, miner's lamp at right, large head **Edge:** Plain **Designer:** Rau

Date	Mintage	F	VF	XF	Unc	BU
2001 In sets only	60,000	—	—	—	3.00	—
2001 Proof	5,000	Value: 25.00				
Note: Medal alignment						
2007 In sets only	60,000	—	—	—	2.00	—

KM# 148.2 50 CENTIMES
2.7500 g., Bronze, 19 mm. **Ruler:** Baudouin I **Obv:** Crowned denomination divides date, legend in French **Obv. Legend:** BELGIQUE **Rev:** Helmeted mine worker left, miner's lamp at right, large head, tip of neck 1/2 mm from rim **Edge:** Plain **Designer:** Rau **Note:** Medal alignment.

Date	Mintage	F	VF	XF	Unc	BU
2001 Proof	—	Value: 30.00				

KM# 149.2 50 CENTIMES

2.7500 g., Bronze, 19 mm. **Ruler:** Baudouin I **Obv:** Crowned denomination divides date, legend in French **Obv. Legend:** BELGIQUE **Rev:** Helmeted mine worker left, miner's lamp at right, large head, tip of neck 1/2 mm from rim **Edge:** Plain **Designer:** Rau **Note:** Medal alignment.

Date	Mintage	F	VF	XF	Unc	BU
2001 Proof	—	Value: 30.00				

KM# 188 FRANC

2.7500 g., Nickel Plated Iron, 18 mm. **Ruler:** Albert II **Obv:** Head left, outline around back of head **Rev:** Vertical line divides date and large denomination, legend in Dutch **Rev. Legend:** BELGIE **Edge:** Plain

Date	Mintage	F	VF	XF	Unc	BU
2001 In sets only	60,000	—	—	—	3.00	—
2001 Proof	5,000	Value: 25.00				

Note: Medal alignment

KM# 187 FRANC

2.7500 g., Nickel Plated Iron, 18 mm. **Ruler:** Albert II **Obv:** Head left, outline around back of head **Rev:** Vertical line divides date and large denomination, legend in French **Rev. Legend:** BELGIQUE **Note:** Mint mark: angel head. Unknown mintmaster's privy mark: scales.

Date	Mintage	F	VF	XF	Unc	BU
2001 In sets only	60,000	—	—	—	3.00	—
2001 Proof	5,000	Value: 25.00				

Note: Medal alignment

KM# 189 5 FRANCS (5 Frank)

5.5000 g., Aluminum-Bronze, 24 mm. **Ruler:** Albert II **Obv:** Head left, outline around back of head **Rev:** Vertical line divides date and denomination, legend in French **Rev. Legend:** BELGIQUE **Note:** Mint mark: angel head. Mintmaster R. Coenen's privy mark: scale.

Date	Mintage	F	VF	XF	Unc	BU
2001 In sets only	60,000	—	—	—	4.00	—
2001 Proof	5,000	Value: 25.00				

Note: Medal alignment

KM# 190 5 FRANCS (5 Frank)

5.5000 g., Aluminum-Bronze, 24 mm. **Ruler:** Albert II **Obv:** Head left, outline around back of head **Rev:** Vertical line divides date and large denomination, legend in Dutch **Rev. Legend:** BELGIE **Note:** Mint mark: angel head. Mintmaster R. Coenen's privy mark: scale.

Date	Mintage	F	VF	XF	Unc	BU
2001 In sets only	60,000	—	—	—	4.00	—
2001 Proof	5,000	Value: 25.00				

Note: Medal alignment

KM# 191 20 FRANCS (20 Frank)

8.5000 g., Nickel-Bronze, 25.65 mm. **Ruler:** Albert II **Obv:** Head left, outline around back of head **Rev:** Vertical line divides date and large denomination, legend in French **Rev. Legend:** BELGIQUE **Note:** Mint mark: angel head. Mintmaster R. Coenen's privy mark: scale.

Date	Mintage	F	VF	XF	Unc	BU
2001 In sets only	60,000	—	—	—	4.00	—
2001 Proof	5,000	Value: 25.00				

Note: Medal alignment

KM# 192 20 FRANCS (20 Frank)

8.5000 g., Nickel-Bronze, 25.7 mm. **Ruler:** Albert II **Obv:** Head left, outline around back of head **Rev:** Vertical line divides date and large denomination, legend in Dutch **Rev. Legend:** BELGIE **Note:** Mint mark: angel head. Mintmaster R. Coenen's privy mark: scale.

Date	Mintage	F	VF	XF	Unc	BU
2001 In sets only	60,000	—	—	—	5.00	—
2001 Proof	5,000	Value: 25.00				

Note: Medal alignment

KM# 193 50 FRANCS (50 Frank)

7.0000 g., Nickel, 22.7 mm. **Ruler:** Albert II **Obv:** Head left, outline around back of head **Rev:** Vertical line divides large denomination and date, legend in French **Rev. Legend:** BELGIQUE **Note:** Mint mark: angel head. Mintmaster R. Coenen's privy mark: scale.

Date	Mintage	F	VF	XF	Unc	BU
2001 In sets only	60,000	—	—	—	8.00	—
2001 Proof	5,000	Value: 25.00				

Note: Medal alignment

KM# 194 50 FRANCS (50 Frank)

7.0000 g., Nickel, 22.75 mm. **Ruler:** Albert II **Obv:** Head left, outline around back of head **Rev:** Vertical line divides large denomination and date, legend in Dutch **Rev. Legend:** BELGIE **Note:** Mint mark: angel head. Mintmaster R. Coenen's privy mark: scale.

Date	Mintage	F	VF	XF	Unc	BU
2001 In sets only	60,000	—	—	—	8.00	—
2001 Proof	5,000	Value: 25.00				

Note: Medal alignment

KM# 222 500 FRANCS (500 Frank)

22.8500 g., 0.9250 Silver 0.6795 oz. ASW, 37 mm. **Ruler:** Albert II **Subject:** Europe: Europa and the Bull **Obv:** Map and denomination **Rev:** Europa sitting on a bull **Edge:** Plain

Date	Mintage	F	VF	XF	Unc	BU
2001 (qp) Proof	40,000	Value: 50.00				

KM# 223 5000 FRANCS

15.5500 g., 0.9990 Gold 0.4994 oz. AGW, 29 mm. **Ruler:** Albert II **Subject:** Europe: Europa and the Bull **Obv:** Map and denomination **Rev:** Europa sitting on a bull **Edge:** Plain

Date	Mintage	F	VF	XF	Unc
2001 (qp) Proof	2,000	Value: 775			

EURO COINAGE

European Union Issues

KM# 307 100 ECU

15.5500 g., 0.9990 Gold 0.4994 oz. AGW, 29 mm. **Ruler:** Albert II **Subject:** Prince Philippe, 50th Birthday

Date	Mintage	F	VF	XF	Unc	BU
2010 Proof	—	Value: 750				

KM# 224 EURO CENT

2.2700 g., Copper Plated Steel, 16.2 mm. **Ruler:** Albert II **Obv:** Head left within inner circle, stars 3/4 surround, date below **Obv. Designer:** Jan Alfons Keustermans **Rev:** Denomination and globe **Rev. Designer:** Luc Luycx **Edge:** Plain

Date	Mintage	F	VF	XF	Unc	BU
2001	99,840,000	—	—	0.30	0.75	1.00
2001 Proof	15,000	Value: 12.00				
2002 In sets only	140,000	—	—	—	18.50	25.00
2002 Proof	15,000	Value: 15.00				
2003	10,135,000	—	—	0.25	0.60	0.80
2003 Proof	15,000	Value: 12.00				
2004	180,000,000	—	—	0.25	0.60	0.80
2004 Proof	—	Value: 12.00				
2005 In sets only	—	—	—	—	—	18.50
2005 Proof	3,000	Value: 12.00				
2006	15,000,000	—	—	0.25	0.60	0.80
2006 Proof	—	Value: 12.00				
2007	60,000,000	—	—	0.25	0.60	0.80
2007 Proof	—	Value: 12.00				

KM# 274 EURO CENT

2.2700 g., Copper Plated Steel, 16.2 mm. **Ruler:** Albert II **Obv:** Head of Albert II left, crowned monogram at right, date below

Date	Mintage	F	VF	XF	Unc	BU
2008 (os)	50,000,000	—	—	—	0.35	0.75
2008 (os) Proof	—	Value: 12.00				

KM# 295 EURO CENT

2.2700 g., Copper Plated Steel, 16.2 mm. **Ruler:** Albert II **Obv:** Redesigned head of Albert II left

Date	Mintage	F	VF	XF	Unc	BU
2009	—	—	—	—	0.35	0.75
2009 Proof	—	Value: 12.00				
2010	—	—	—	—	0.35	0.75
2010 Proof	—	Value: 12.00				

KM# 225 2 EURO CENT

3.0300 g., Copper Plated Steel, 18.7 mm. **Ruler:** Albert II **Obv:** Head left within circle, stars 3/4 surround, date below **Obv. Designer:** Jan Alfons Keustermans **Rev:** Denomination and globe **Rev. Designer:** Luc Luycx **Edge:** Grooved

Date	Mintage	F	VF	XF	Unc	BU
2001 In sets only	40,000	—	—	—	—	9.00

Note: Only available in sets at present, circulation strikes not yet released

Date	Mintage	F	VF	XF	Unc	BU
2001 Proof	15,000	Value: 15.00				
2002 In sets only	140,000	—	—	—	—	6.50
2002 Proof	15,000	Value: 12.00				
2003	40,135,000	—	—	0.30	0.75	1.00
2003 Proof	15,000	Value: 12.00				
2004	140,000,000	—	—	0.30	0.75	1.00
2004 Proof	15,000	Value: 12.00				
2005 In sets only	—	—	—	—	—	1.00
2005 Proof	—	Value: 12.00				
2006	30,000,000	—	—	0.30	0.75	1.00
2006 Proof	—	Value: 12.00				
2007	70,000,000	—	—	0.30	0.75	1.00
2007 Proof	—	Value: 12.00				

KM# 275 2 EURO CENT

3.0300 g., Copper Plated Steel, 18.7 mm. **Ruler:** Albert II **Obv:** Head of Albert II left, crowned monogram at right, date below

Date	Mintage	F	VF	XF	Unc	BU
2008 (os)	40,000,000	—	—	0.25	0.65	1.00
2008 (os) Proof	—	Value: 12.00				

KM# 296 2 EURO CENT

3.0300 g., Copper Plated Steel, 18.7 mm. **Ruler:** Albert II **Obv:** Redesigned head of Albert II left

Date	Mintage	F	VF	XF	Unc	BU
2009	—	—	—	—	0.75	1.00
2009 Proof	—	Value: 12.00				
2010	—	—	—	—	0.75	1.00
2010 Proof	—	Value: 12.00				

KM# 226 5 EURO CENT

3.8600 g., Copper Plated Steel, 21.2 mm. **Ruler:** Albert II **Obv:** Head left within circle, stars 3/4 surround, date below **Obv. Designer:** Jan Alfons Keustermans **Rev:** Denomination and globe **Rev. Designer:** Luc Luycx **Edge:** Plain

Date	Mintage	F	VF	XF	Unc	BU
2001 In sets only	40,000	—	—	—	—	12.50
2001 Proof	15,000	Value: 15.00				
2002 In sets only	140,000	—	—	—	—	8.00
2002 Proof	15,000	Value: 15.00				
2003	30,135,000	—	—	0.30	0.80	1.20
2003 Proof	15,000	Value: 12.00				
2004	75,000,000	—	—	0.30	0.80	1.20
2004 Proof	—	Value: 12.00				
2005	110,000,000	—	—	0.30	0.80	1.20
2005 Proof	3,000	Value: 12.00				
2006	35,000,000	—	—	0.30	0.80	1.20
2006 Proof	—	Value: 12.00				
2007 In sets only	—	—	—	—	—	8.00
2007 Proof	—	Value: 12.00				

KM# 276 5 EURO CENT

3.8600 g., Copper Plated Steel, 21.2 mm. **Ruler:** Albert II **Obv:** Head of Albert II left, crowned monogram right, date below

Date	Mintage	F	VF	XF	Unc	BU
2008 (os)	—	—	—	—	—	6.50
2008 (os) Proof	—	Value: 12.00				

KM# 297 5 EURO CENT

3.8600 g., Copper Plated Steel, 21.2 mm. **Ruler:** Albert II **Obv:** Redesigned head of Albert II left

Date	Mintage	F	VF	XF	Unc	BU
2009	—	—	—	—	0.80	1.20
2009 Proof	—	Value: 12.00				
2010	—	—	—	—	0.80	1.20
2010 Proof	—	Value: 12.00				

KM# 227 10 EURO CENT
4.0700 g., Brass, 19.7 mm. **Ruler:** Albert II **Obv:** Head left within inner circle, stars 3/4 surround, date below **Obv. Designer:** Jan Alfons Keustermans **Rev:** Denomination and map **Rev. Designer:** Luc Luycx **Edge:** Reeded

Date	Mintage	F	VF	XF	Unc	BU
2001	145,790,000	—	—	—	0.75	1.25
2001 Proof	15,000	Value: 12.00				
2002 In sets only	140,000	—	—	—	6.00	8.00
2002 Proof	15,000	Value: 15.00				
2003 In sets only	135,000	—	—	—	6.00	8.00
2003 Proof	15,000	Value: 15.00				
2004	20,000,000	—	—	—	1.00	1.50
2004 Proof	—	Value: 12.00				
2005	10,000,000	—	—	—	1.00	1.50
2005 Proof	3,000	Value: 12.00				
2006 In sets only	—	—	—	—	1.00	1.50
2006 Proof	—	Value: 12.00				

KM# 242 10 EURO CENT
4.0700 g., Brass, 19.7 mm. **Ruler:** Albert II **Obv:** King's portrait **Obv. Designer:** Jan Alfons Keustermans **Rev:** Relief map of Western Europe, stars, lines and value **Rev. Designer:** Luc Luycx **Edge:** Reeded

Date	Mintage	F	VF	XF	Unc	BU
2007	—	—	—	—	1.00	1.50
2007 Proof	—	Value: 12.00				

KM# 277 10 EURO CENT
4.0700 g., Brass, 19.7 mm. **Ruler:** Albert II **Obv:** Head of Albert II left, crowned monogram right, date below

Date	Mintage	F	VF	XF	Unc	BU
2008 (os)	—	—	—	—	—	12.50
2008 (os) Proof	—	Value: 12.00				

KM# 298 10 EURO CENT
4.0700 g., Brass, 19.7 mm. **Ruler:** Albert II **Obv:** Redesigned head of Albert II left

Date	Mintage	F	VF	XF	Unc	BU
2009	—	—	—	—	1.00	1.50
2009 Proof	—	Value: 12.00				
2010	—	—	—	—	1.00	1.50
2010 Proof	—	Value: 12.00				

KM# 228 20 EURO CENT
5.7300 g., Brass, 22.2 mm. **Ruler:** Albert II **Obv:** Head left within circle, stars 3/4 surround, date below **Obv. Designer:** Jan Alfons Keustermans **Rev:** Denomination and map **Rev. Designer:** Luc Luycx **Edge:** Notched

Date	Mintage	F	VF	XF	Unc	BU
2001 In sets only	40,000	—	—	—	10.00	12.50
Note: Only available in sets at present, circulation strikes not yet released						
2001 Proof	15,000	Value: 15.00				
2002	104,140,000	—	—	—	1.00	1.50
2002 Proof	15,000	Value: 12.00				
2003	30,135,000	—	—	—	1.25	1.75
2003 Proof	15,000	Value: 12.00				
2004	109,550,000	—	—	—	1.25	1.75
2004 Proof	—	Value: 12.00				
2005	10,000,000	—	—	—	1.25	1.75
2005 Proof	3,000	Value: 12.00				
2006	40,000,000	—	—	—	1.25	1.75
2006 Proof	—	Value: 12.00				

KM# 243 20 EURO CENT
5.7300 g., Brass, 22.1 mm. **Ruler:** Albert II **Obv:** King's portrait **Obv. Designer:** Jan Alfons Keustermans **Rev:** Relief map of Western Europe, stars, lines and value **Rev. Designer:** Luc Luycx **Edge:** Notched

Date	Mintage	F	VF	XF	Unc	BU
2007	—	—	—	—	1.25	1.75
2007 Proof	—	Value: 12.00				

KM# 278 20 EURO CENT
5.7300 g., Brass, 22.1 mm. **Ruler:** Albert II **Obv:** Head of Albert II left, crowned monogram right, date below

Date	Mintage	F	VF	XF	Unc	BU
2008 (os)	—	—	—	—	—	12.50
2008 (os) Proof	—	Value: 12.00				

KM# 299 20 EURO CENT
5.7300 g., Brass, 22.1 mm. **Ruler:** Albert II **Obv:** Redesigned ehad of Albert II left

Date	Mintage	F	VF	XF	Unc	BU
2009	—	—	—	—	1.25	1.75
2009 Proof	—	Value: 12.00				
2010	—	—	—	—	1.25	1.75
2010 Proof	—	Value: 12.00				

KM# 229 50 EURO CENT
7.8100 g., Brass, 24.2 mm. **Ruler:** Albert II **Obv:** Head left within circle, stars 3/4 surround, date below **Obv. Designer:** Jan Alfons Keustermans **Rev:** Denomination and map **Rev. Designer:** Luc Luycx **Edge:** Reeded

Date	Mintage	F	VF	XF	Unc	BU
2001 In sets only	40,000	—	—	—	10.00	12.50
2001 Proof	15,000	Value: 15.00				
2002	50,040,000	—	—	—	1.00	1.50
2002 Proof	15,000	Value: 12.00				
2003 In sets only	135,000	—	—	—	—	12.50
2003 Proof	15,000	Value: 12.00				
2004	8,000,000	—	—	—	1.25	1.75
2004 Proof	—	Value: 12.00				
2005 In sets only	—	—	—	—	—	12.50
2005 Proof	3,000	Value: 12.00				
2006 In sets only	—	—	—	—	—	12.50
2006 Proof	—	Value: 12.00				

KM# 244 50 EURO CENT
7.8100 g., Brass, 24.2 mm. **Ruler:** Albert II **Obv:** King's portrait **Obv. Designer:** Jan Alfons Keustermans **Rev:** Relief map of Western Europe, stars, lines and value **Rev. Designer:** Luc Luycx **Edge:** Reeded

Date	Mintage	F	VF	XF	Unc	BU
2007	—	—	—	—	1.25	1.75
2007 Proof	—	Value: 12.00				

KM# 279 50 EURO CENT
7.8100 g., Brass, 24.2 mm. **Ruler:** Albert II **Obv:** Head of Albert II left, crowned monogram right, date below

Date	Mintage	F	VF	XF	Unc	BU
2008 (os)	—	—	—	—	—	12.00
2008 (os) Proof	—	Value: 12.00				

KM# 300 50 EURO CENT
7.8100 g., Brass, 24.2 mm. **Ruler:** Albert II **Obv:** Redesigned head of Albert II left

Date	Mintage	F	VF	XF	Unc	BU
2009	—	—	—	—	2.00	3.00
2009 Proof	—	Value: 12.00				
2010	—	—	—	—	2.00	3.00
2010 Proof	—	Value: 12.00				

KM# 230 EURO
7.5700 g., Bi-Metallic Copper-Nickel center in Brass ring, 23.2 mm. **Ruler:** Albert II **Obv:** Head left within circle, stars 3/4 surround, date below **Obv. Designer:** Jan Alfons Keustermans **Rev:** Denomination and map **Rev. Designer:** Luc Luycx **Edge:** Reeded and plain sections

Date	Mintage	F	VF	XF	Unc	BU
2001 In sets only	40,000	—	—	—	—	15.00
Note: Only available in sets at present, circulation strikes not yet released						
2001 Proof	15,000	Value: 18.00				
2002	90,640,000	—	—	—	3.00	5.00
Note: Only a fraction of the mintage released at present						
2002 Proof	15,000	Value: 15.00				
2003	6,000,000	—	—	—	3.00	5.00
2003 Proof	15,000	Value: 15.00				
2004	15,000,000	—	—	—	3.00	5.00
2004 Proof	—	Value: 15.00				
2005 In sets only	—	—	—	—	—	15.00
2005 Proof	3,000	Value: 15.00				
2006 In sets only	—	—	—	—	—	15.00
2006 Proof	—	Value: 15.00				

KM# 245 EURO
7.5000 g., Bi-Metallic Copper-Nickel center in Brass ring, 23.2 mm. **Ruler:** Albert II **Obv:** King's portrait **Obv. Designer:** Jan Alfons Keustermans **Rev:** Relief map of Western Europe, stars, lines and value **Rev. Designer:** Luc Luycx **Edge:** Reeded and plain sections

Date	Mintage	F	VF	XF	Unc	BU
2007	—	—	—	—	3.00	5.00
2007 Proof	—	Value: 15.00				

KM# 280 EURO
7.5000 g., Bi-Metallic Copper-nickel center in brass ring, 23.2 mm. **Ruler:** Albert II **Obv:** Head of Albert II right

Date	Mintage	F	VF	XF	Unc	BU
2008 (os)	—	—	—	—	—	12.50
2008 (os) Proof	—	Value: 12.50				

KM# 301 EURO
7.5700 g., Bi-Metallic Copper-Nickel center in Brass ring., 23.2 mm. **Ruler:** Albert II **Obv:** Redesigned head of Albert II left

Date	Mintage	F	VF	XF	Unc	BU
2009	—	—	—	—	3.00	5.00
2009 Proof	—	—	—	—	—	—
2010	—	—	—	—	3.00	5.00
2010 Proof	—	—	—	—	—	—

KM# 231 2 EURO
8.5200 g., Bi-Metallic Brass center in Copper-Nickel ring, 25.7 mm. **Ruler:** Albert II **Obv:** Head left within circle, stars 3/4 surround, date below **Obv. Designer:** Jan Alfons Keustermans **Rev:** Denomination and map **Rev. Designer:** Luc Luycx **Edge:** Reeded with 2's and stars

Date	Mintage	F	VF	XF	Unc	BU
2001 In sets only	40,000	—	—	—	12.50	15.00

Note: Only available in sets at present, circulation strikes not yet released

Date	Mintage	F	VF	XF	Unc	BU
2001 Proof	15,000	Value: 20.00				
2002	50,140,000	—	—	—	3.75	6.00
2002 Proof	15,000	Value: 18.00				
2003	30,135,000	—	—	—	3.75	6.00
2003 Proof	15,000	Value: 18.00				
2004	65,500,000	—	—	—	3.75	6.00
2004 Proof	—	Value: 18.00				
2005	10,500,000	—	—	—	3.75	6.00
2005 Proof	3,000	Value: 18.00				
2006	20,000,000	—	—	—	3.75	6.00
2006 Proof	—	Value: 18.00				

KM# 240 2 EURO

8.5200 g., Bi-Metallic Brass center in Copper-Nickel ring, 25.7 mm. **Ruler:** Albert II **Subject:** Schengen Agreement **Obv:** Albert II of Belgium and Henri of Luxembourg **Rev:** Value and map **Edge:** Reeding over stars

Date	Mintage	F	VF	XF	Unc	BU
2005	5,977,000	—	—	—	5.00	7.50
2005 Prooflike	20,000	—	—	—	—	20.00
2005 Proof	3,000	Value: 25.00				

KM# 241 2 EURO

8.5200 g., Bi-Metallic Brass center in Copper-Nickel ring, 25.7 mm. **Ruler:** Albert II **Obv:** Atomic model **Rev:** Value and map **Edge:** Reeding over stars and 2's

Date	Mintage	F	VF	XF	Unc	BU
2006	4,977,000	—	—	—	4.00	6.00
2006 Prooflike	20,000	—	—	—	—	25.00
2006 Proof	3,000	Value: 100				

KM# 246 2 EURO

8.5200 g., Bi-Metallic Brass center in Copper-Nickel ring, 25.7 mm. **Ruler:** Albert II **Obv:** King's portrait **Obv. Designer:** Jan Alfons Keustermans **Rev:** Relief map of Western Europe, stars, lines and value **Rev. Designer:** Luc Luycx **Edge:** Reeded with 2's and stars

Date	Mintage	F	VF	XF	Unc	BU
2007	—	—	—	—	3.75	6.00
2007 Proof	—	Value: 25.00				

KM# 247 2 EURO

8.4500 g., Bi-Metallic Brass center in Copper-Nickel ring, 25.7 mm. **Ruler:** Albert II **Subject:** 50th Anniversary Treaty of Rome **Obv:** Open treaty book **Rev:** Large value at left, modified outline of Europe at right **Edge:** Reeded with stars and 2's

Date	Mintage	F	VF	XF	Unc	BU
2007	4,960,000	—	—	—	—	9.00
2007 Prooflike	35,000	—	—	—	—	25.00
2007 Proof	10,000	Value: 75.00				

KM# 248 2 EURO

8.5200 g., Bi-Metallic Nickel-Brass center in Copper-Nickel ring, 25.7 mm. **Ruler:** Albert II **Subject:** Universal Declaration of Human Rights **Obv:** Book in bow **Rev:** Large value "2" at left, modified map of Europe at right **Edge:** Reeded with incuse stars

Date	Mintage	F	VF	XF	Unc	BU
2008	—	—	—	—	—	6.00

KM# 281 2 EURO

8.5000 g., Bi-Metallic Brass center in Copper-Nickel ring, 25.7 mm. **Ruler:** Albert II **Obv:** Head of Albert II left, crowned monogram right, date below

Date	Mintage	F	VF	XF	Unc	BU
2008 (os)	—	—	—	—	—	12.50
2008 (os) Proof	—	Value: 12.50				

KM# 302 2 EURO

8.4500 g., Bi-Metallic Brass center in Copper-Nickel ring., 25.7 mm. **Ruler:** Albert II **Obv:** Redesigned head of Albert II left

Date	Mintage	F	VF	XF	Unc	BU
2009	—	—	—	—	4.00	6.00
2009 Proof	—	Value: 18.00				
2010	—	—	—	—	4.00	6.00
2010 Proof	—	Value: 18.00				

KM# 282 2 EURO

8.5000 g., Bi-Metallic Brass center in copper-nickel ring, 25.7 mm. **Ruler:** Albert II **Subject:** 10th Anniversary of EMU **Obv:** Stick figure and E symbol

Date	Mintage	F	VF	XF	Unc	BU
2009	5,000,000	—	—	—	15.00	—
2009 Prooflike	—	—	—	—	—	20.00
2009 Proof	—	Value: 70.00				

KM# 288 2 EURO

8.4500 g., Bi-Metallic Brass center in Copper-Nickel ring., 25.7 mm. **Ruler:** Albert II **Subject:** Louis Braille, 200th Anniversary of birth **Obv:** Bust right with braile text

Date	Mintage	F	VF	XF	Unc	BU
2009	5,000,000	—	—	—	—	5.00

KM# 289 2 EURO

Bi-Metallic Brass center in copper-nickel ring, 25.7 mm. **Ruler:** Albert II **Subject:** EU Council Presidency **Rev:** eu in script

Date	Mintage	F	VF	XF	Unc	BU
2010	—	—	—	—	3.00	7.50

KM# 270 5 EURO

14.6000 g., 0.9250 Silver 0.4342 oz. ASW, 30 mm. **Ruler:** Albert II **Subject:** Smurfs - 50th Anniversary **Obv:** Map of Western Europe **Rev:** Smurf

Date	Mintage	F	VF	XF	Unc	BU
2008 Proof	25,000	Value: 50.00				

KM# 270a 5 EURO

14.6000 g., 0.9250 Silver 0.4342 oz. ASW, 30 mm. **Ruler:** Albert II **Subject:** Smurf - 50th Anniversary **Obv:** Map of Western Europe **Rev:** Multicolor 50 and Smurf

Date	Mintage	F	VF	XF	Unc	BU
2008 Proof	—	Value: 75.00				

KM# 303 5 EURO

14.6000 g., 0.9250 Silver 0.4342 oz. ASW, 30 mm. **Ruler:** Albert II **Subject:** Belgian Railways, 175th Anniversary

Date	Mintage	F	VF	XF	Unc	BU
2010 Proof	—	Value: 50.00				

KM# 233 10 EURO

18.9300 g., 0.9250 Silver 0.5629 oz. ASW, 32.9 mm. **Ruler:** Albert II **Subject:** Belgian Railway System **Obv:** Value, head at right transposed on map **Rev:** Train exiting tunnel **Edge:** Reeded

Date	Mintage	F	VF	XF	Unc	BU
ND (2002) Proof	50,000	Value: 50.00				

KM# 235 10 EURO

18.9300 g., 0.9250 Silver 0.5629 oz. ASW, 32.9 mm. **Ruler:** Albert II **Subject:** "Simenon" **Edge:** Reeded

Date	Mintage	F	VF	XF	Unc	BU
2003 Proof	50,000	Value: 40.00				

KM# 236 10 EURO

18.9300 g., 0.9250 Silver 0.5629 oz. ASW, 32.9 mm. **Ruler:** Albert II **Subject:** "Tintin" **Edge:** Reeded

Date	Mintage	F	VF	XF	Unc	BU
2004 Proof	50,000	Value: 85.00				

KM# 234 10 EURO

18.7500 g., 0.9250 Silver 0.5576 oz. ASW, 33 mm. **Ruler:** Albert II **Obv:** Value **Rev:** Western Europe map and Goddess Europa riding a bull **Edge:** Reeded

Date	Mintage	F	VF	XF	Unc	BU
2004 Proof	50,000	Value: 40.00				

KM# 252 10 EURO

18.7500 g., 0.9250 Silver 0.5576 oz. ASW, 33 mm. **Ruler:** Albert II **Subject:** 60th Anniversary of Liberation **Obv:** Map of Western Europe and stars **Rev:** Phoenix

Date	Mintage	F	VF	XF	Unc	BU
2005 Proof	50,000	Value: 50.00				

KM# 251 10 EURO

18.7500 g., 0.9250 Silver 0.5576 oz. ASW, 33 mm. **Ruler:** Albert II **Subject:** Netherland-Belgium Soccer, 75th Anniversary **Obv:** Map of Western Europe and stars **Rev:** Soccer Player

Date	Mintage	F	VF	XF	Unc	BU
2005 Proof	50,000	Value: 45.00				

KM# 255 10 EURO

18.7500 g., 0.9250 Silver 0.5576 oz. ASW, 33 mm. **Ruler:** Albert II **Subject:** Justus Lipsius, 400th Anniversary of Death **Obv:** Map of Western Europe and stars **Rev:** Half-length figure of Justus Lipsius

Date	Mintage	F	VF	XF	Unc	BU
2006 Proof	50,000	Value: 45.00				

KM# 257 10 EURO

18.7500 g., 0.9250 Silver 0.5576 oz. ASW, 33 mm. **Ruler:** Albert II **Subject:** 50th Anniversary - Mine Accident in Marcinelle **Obv:** Map of Western Europe and stars **Rev:** Male head and industrial mine scene

Date	Mintage	F	VF	XF	Unc	BU
2006 Proof	50,000	Value: 45.00				

KM# 257a 10 EURO

18.7500 g., 0.9250 Silver 0.5576 oz. ASW, 33 mm. **Ruler:** Albert II **Subject:** 50th Anniversary, Mine Accident in Marcinelle **Obv:** Map of Western Europe and stars **Rev:** Multicolor male head and industrial mine scene

Date	Mintage	F	VF	XF	Unc	BU
2006 Proof	2,000	Value: 75.00				

KM# 260 10 EURO

18.7500 g., 0.9250 Silver 0.5576 oz. ASW, 33 mm. **Ruler:** Albert II **Subject:** Treaty of Rome, 50th Anniversary **Obv:** Map of Western Europe **Rev:** Document and feather pen

Date	Mintage	F	VF	XF	Unc	BU
2007 Proof	40,000	Value: 45.00				

KM# 263 10 EURO

18.7500 g., 0.9250 Silver 0.5576 oz. ASW, 33 mm. **Ruler:** Albert II **Subject:** International Polar Year **Obv:** Map of Western Europe **Rev:** Wind farm and polar station

Date	Mintage	F	VF	XF	Unc	BU
2007 Proof	40,000	Value: 50.00				

KM# 266 10 EURO

18.7500 g., 0.9250 Silver 0.5576 oz. ASW, 33 mm. **Ruler:** Albert II **Subject:** 100th Anniversary Maurice Maeterlinck **Obv:** Map of Western Europe **Rev:** Gateway and dome in blue

Date	Mintage	F	VF	XF	Unc	BU
2008 Proof	20,000	Value: 75.00				

KM# 268 10 EURO

18.7500 g., 0.9250 Silver 0.5576 oz. ASW, 33 mm. **Ruler:** Albert II **Subject:** Beijing Olympics **Obv:** Map of Western Europe **Rev:** Sport events, logo and torch

Date	Mintage	F	VF	XF	Unc	BU
2008 Proof	20,000	Value: 50.00				

KM# 284 10 EURO

10.9300 g., 0.9250 Silver 0.3250 oz. ASW **Ruler:** Albert II **Subject:** 75th Birthday of the King **Obv:** Head at left, laurel sprigs

Date	Mintage	F	VF	XF	Unc	BU
2009	—	—	—	—	—	50.00

KM# 285 10 EURO

18.9300 g., 0.9250 Silver 0.5629 oz. ASW **Ruler:** Albert II **Subject:** Erasmus

Date	Mintage	F	VF	XF	Unc	BU
2009	—	—	—	—	—	50.00

KM# 290 10 EURO

18.7500 g., 0.9250 Silver 0.5576 oz. ASW, 33 mm. **Ruler:** Albert II **Subject:** Royal Museum for Central Asia 100th Anniversary

Date	Mintage	F	VF	XF	Unc	BU
2010	—	—	—	—	—	45.00

KM# 291 10 EURO

18.7500 g., 0.9250 Silver 0.5576 oz. ASW, 33 mm. **Ruler:** Albert II **Subject:** Jean Django' Reinhart Birth Centennial

Date	Mintage	F	VF	XF	Unc	BU
2010 Proof	—	Value: 45.00				

KM# 304 10 EURO

18.7500 g., 0.9250 Silver 0.5576 oz. ASW, 33 mm. **Ruler:** Albert II **Subject:** Jean "Django" Reinhardt, 100th Anniversary of Birth

Date	Mintage	F	VF	XF	Unc	BU
2010 Proof	—	Value: 50.00				

KM# 259 12 1/2 EURO

1.2500 g., 0.9990 Gold 0.0401 oz. AGW, 13.92 mm. **Ruler:** Albert II **Subject:** Saxe-Coburg-Gotha, 175th Anniversary **Obv:** Lion and tablet with constitution **Rev:** Head of Leopold I left

Date	Mintage	F	VF	XF	Unc	BU
2006 Proof	15,000	Value: 75.00				

KM# 265 12 1/2 EURO

1.2500 g., 0.9990 Gold 0.0401 oz. AGW, 13.92 mm. **Subject:** 175th Anniversary Saxe-Coburg-Gotha **Obv:** Lion and tablet **Rev:** Leopold II head left

Date	Mintage	F	VF	XF	Unc	BU
2007 Proof	15,000	Value: 75.00				

KM# 271 12 1/2 EURO

1.2500 g., 0.9990 Gold 0.0401 oz. AGW, 13.92 mm. **Ruler:** Albert II **Subject:** 175th Anniversary - Saxe-Coburg-Gotha **Obv:** Lion and tablet **Rev:** Albert I bust right

Date	Mintage	F	VF	XF	Unc	BU
2008 Proof	15,000	Value: 75.00				

KM# 292 12 1/2 EURO

1.2440 g., 0.9990 Gold 0.0400 oz. AGW, 14 mm. **Ruler:** Albert II **Subject:** Leopold III

Date	Mintage	F	VF	XF	Unc	BU
2009 Proof	—	Value: 85.00				

KM# 293 12 1/2 EURO

0.9990 Gold, 14 mm. **Ruler:** Albert II

Date	Mintage	F	VF	XF	Unc	BU
2010 Proof	—	Value: 85.00				

KM# 254 20 EURO

22.8500 g., 0.9990 Silver 0.7339 oz. ASW, 37 mm. **Ruler:** Albert II **Subject:** FIFA World Cup in Germany **Obv:** Albert II head left **Rev:** Soccer player with ball

Date	Mintage	F	VF	XF	Unc	BU
2005 Proof	25,000	Value: 65.00				

KM# 262 20 EURO

22.8500 g., 0.9250 Silver 0.6795 oz. ASW, 37 mm. **Ruler:** Albert II **Subject:** Georges Remi, 100th Anniversary of Birth **Obv:** Map of Western Europe and stars **Rev:** Profile of Georges Renir and his character Tin Tin right

Date	Mintage	F	VF	XF	Unc	BU
2007 Proof	50,000	Value: 75.00				

KM# 287 20 EURO

22.8500 g., 0.9500 Silver 0.6979 oz. ASW, 37 mm. **Ruler:** Albert II **Obv:** Value and map of euro countries **Rev:** Fr. Damien and churches in Tremblo and Molokai, date of canionization below

Date	Mintage	F	VF	XF	Unc	BU
2009 Proof	15,000	Value: 75.00				

KM# 305 20 EURO

22.8500 g., 0.9250 Silver 0.6795 oz. ASW, 37 mm. **Ruler:** Albert II **Subject:** A Dog of Flanders

Date	Mintage	F	VF	XF	Unc	BU
2010 Proof	—	Value: 75.00				

KM# 269 25 EURO

3.1100 g., 0.9990 Gold 0.0999 oz. AGW, 18 mm. **Ruler:** Albert II **Subject:** Beijing Olympics **Obv:** Map of Western Europe **Rev:** Sport events, logo, torch

Date	Mintage	F	VF	XF	Unc	BU
2008 Proof	5,000	Value: 200				

KM# 250 50 EURO

6.2200 g., 0.9990 Gold 0.1998 oz. AGW, 21 mm. **Ruler:** Albert II **Subject:** Albert II, 70th Birthday **Obv:** Map of Western Europe and stars **Rev:** Portrait of Albert II

Date	Mintage	F	VF	XF	Unc	BU
2004 Proof	10,000	Value: 325				

KM# 256 50 EURO

6.2200 g., 0.9990 Gold 0.1998 oz. AGW, 21 mm. **Ruler:** Albert II **Subject:** Justus Lipsius, 400th Anniversary of Death **Obv:** Map of Western Europe and stars **Rev:** Half-length figure of Justus Lipius right

Date	Mintage	F	VF	XF	Unc	BU
2006 Proof	2,500	Value: 350				

KM# 261 50 EURO

6.2200 g., 0.9990 Gold 0.1998 oz. AGW, 21 mm. **Ruler:** Albert II **Subject:** Treaty of Rome, 50th Anniversary **Obv:** Map of Western Europe **Rev:** Document and feather pen

Date	Mintage	F	VF	XF	Unc	BU
2007 Proof	2,500	Value: 350				

KM# 267 50 EURO

6.2200 g., 0.9990 Gold 0.1998 oz. AGW, 21 mm. **Ruler:** Albert II **Subject:** 100th Anniversary Maurice Maeterlinck **Obv:** Map of Western Europe **Rev:** Gate and dove

Date	Mintage	F	VF	XF	Unc	BU
2008 Proof	2,500	Value: 400				

KM# 286 50 EURO

8.4500 g., 0.9990 Gold 0.2714 oz. AGW **Ruler:** Albert II **Subject:** Erasmus

Date	Mintage	F	VF	XF	Unc	BU
2009	—	—	—	—	—	425

KM# 306 50 EURO

6.2200 g., 0.9990 Gold 0.1998 oz. AGW, 22 mm. **Ruler:** Albert II **Subject:** Royal Museum for Central Africa

Date	Mintage	F	VF	XF	Unc	BU
2010 Proof	—	Value: 400				

KM# 237 100 EURO

15.5500 g., 0.9990 Gold 0.4994 oz. AGW, 29 mm. **Ruler:** Albert II **Subject:** Founding Fathers

Date	Mintage	F	VF	XF	Unc	BU
2002 Proof	5,000	Value: 775				

KM# 238 100 EURO

15.5500 g., 0.9990 Gold 0.4994 oz. AGW, 29 mm. **Ruler:** Albert II **Subject:** 10th Anniversary of Reign

Date	Mintage	F	VF	XF	Unc	BU
2003 Proof	5,000	Value: 775				

KM# 239 100 EURO

15.5500 g., 0.9990 Gold 0.4994 oz. AGW, 29 mm. **Ruler:** Albert II **Subject:** Franc Germinal

Date	Mintage	F	VF	XF	Unc	BU
2004 Proof	5,000	Value: 775				

KM# 253 100 EURO

15.5500 g., 0.9990 Gold 0.4994 oz. AGW, 29 mm. **Ruler:** Albert II **Subject:** 175th Anniversary of Liberty **Obv:** Albert II head left **Rev:** Scene of the 1830 Revolution

Date	Mintage	F	VF	XF	Unc	BU
2005 Proof	5,000	Value: 775				

KM# 258 100 EURO

15.5500 g., 0.9990 Gold 0.4994 oz. AGW, 29 mm. **Ruler:** Albert II **Subject:** Saxe-Coburg-Gotha, 175th Anniversary **Obv:** Map of Western Europe and stars **Rev:** Church in Laeken, Kings monogram around

Date	Mintage	F	VF	XF	Unc	BU
2006 Proof	5,000	Value: 775				

KM# 264 100 EURO

15.5500 g., 0.9990 Gold 0.4994 oz. AGW, 29 mm. **Ruler:** Albert II **Subject:** Belgian Coins 175th Anniversary **Obv:** Map of Western Europe **Rev:** Screw press, coin designs

Date	Mintage	F	VF	XF	Unc	BU
2007 Proof	5,000	Value: 775				

KM# 272 100 EURO

15.5500 g., 0.9990 Gold 0.4994 oz. AGW, 29 mm. **Ruler:** Albert II **Subject:** 50th Anniversary: Brussels Exposition **Obv:** Map of Western Europe

Date	Mintage	F	VF	XF	Unc	BU
2008 Proof	5,000	Value: 775				

KM# 283 100 EURO

15.5500 g., 0.9990 Gold 0.4994 oz. AGW **Ruler:** Albert II **Subject:** Royal Wedding Anniversary **Obv:** Conjoined leads at right

Date	Mintage	F	VF	XF	Unc	BU
2009 Proof	—	Value: 775				

MINT SETS

KM#	Date	Mintage	Identification	Issue Price	Mkt Val
MS14	2001 (10)	60,000	KM#148.1, 149.1, 187-194	15.00	45.00
MS15	1999/2000/ 2001 (24)	40,000	Euro Intro	—	250
MS16	2002 (8)	100,000	KM#224-231, 700th Anniversary	—	62.50
MS17	2002 (8)	20,000	KM#224-231, Cycling	—	62.50
MS18	2002 (8)	20,000	KM#224-231, Euros plus waffle francs	—	62.50
MS19	2003 (8)	100,000	KM#224-231, Television 50th	—	37.50
MS20	2003 (8)	15,000	KM#224-231, Ford Production in Belgium Centennial	—	37.50
MS21	2003 (8)	10,000	KM#224-231, Rose	—	37.50
MS22	2003 (8)	10,000	KM#224-231, Baby	—	37.50
MS23.1	2004 (9)	60,000	KM#224-231, Belgian Red Cross, plain medal	—	25.00
MS23.2	2004 (9)	2,000	KM#224-231, Belgian Red Cross, enameled medal	—	175
MS24	2004 (9)	5,000	KM#224-231, Love, medal for engraving	—	37.50
MS25	2004 (9)	5,000	KM#224-231, Baby, medal for engraving	—	37.50
MS26.1	2005 (9)	38,000	KM#224-231, Grand Palace, UNESCO site, plain medal	—	60.00
MS26.2	2005 (9)	2,000	KM#224-231, Grand Palace, UNESCO site, gilt medal	—	85.00
MS27.1	2006 (9)	38,000	KM#224-231, Flemish Houses, UNESCO site, plain medal	—	40.00
MS27.2	2006 (9)	2,000	KM#224-231, Flemish Houses, UNESCO site, colored medal	—	75.00
MS28.1	2007 (9)	38,000	KM#224-226, 242-246, Canal. UNESCO site, plain medal	—	27.50
MS28.2	2007 (9)	2,000	KM#224-226, 242-246, Canal, UNESCO site, colored medal	—	70.00
MS29.1	2008 (9)	25,000	KM#274-281, Belltower, UNESCO site, plain medal	—	75.00
MS29.2	2008 (9)	2,000	KM#274-281, Belltower, UNESCO site, colored medal	—	85.00

PROOF SETS

KM#	Date	Mintage	Identification	Issue Price	Mkt Val
PS10	2001 (8)	15,000	KM#224-231	80.00	125
PS11	2002 (8)	3,240	KM#224-231	80.00	115
PS12	2003 (8)	3,241	KM#224-231	80.00	110
PS13	2004 (8)	3,006	KM#224-231	80.00	105
PS14	2005 (8)	3,006	KM#224-231	—	110
PS15	2006 (8)	3,006	KM#224-231	—	115
PS17	2007 (8)	3,000	KM#224-226, 242-247	—	175
PS18	2008 (8)	2,500	KM#224-227, 276-278, 280-281	—	100

BELIZE

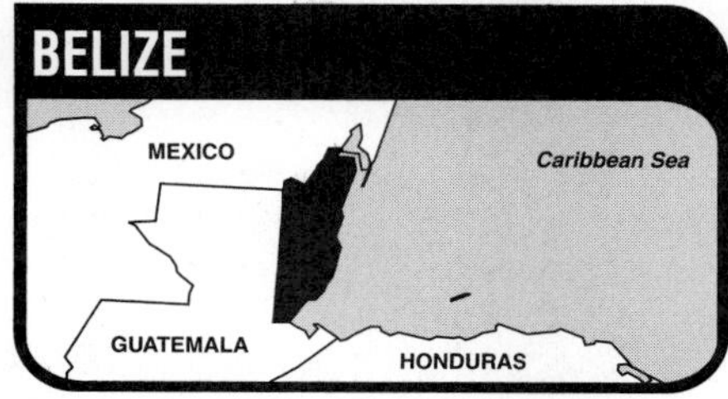

Belize, formerly British Honduras, but now a Constitutional Monarchy within the Commonwealth of Nations, is situated in Central America south of Mexico and east and north of Guatemala, with an area of 8,867 sq. mi. (22,960 sq. km.) and a population of *242,000. Capital: Belmopan. Tourism now augments Belize's economy, in addition to sugar, citrus fruits, chicle and hardwoods, which are exported.

MONETARY SYSTEM

Commencing 1864
100 Cents = 1 Dollar

COMMONWEALTH

DECIMAL COINAGE

KM# 33a CENT
0.8000 g., Aluminum, 19.5 mm. **Obv:** Bust of Queen Elizabeth right **Rev:** Denomination within circle **Edge:** Smooth, scalloped

Date	Mintage	F	VF	XF	Unc	BU
2002	—	—	—	0.10	0.15	0.45
2005	—	—	—	0.10	0.15	0.45
2007	—	—	—	0.10	0.15	0.45

KM# 34a 5 CENTS
1.0400 g., Aluminum, 20.2 mm. **Obv:** Bust of Queen Elizabeth II right **Obv. Designer:** Cecil Thomas **Rev:** Denomination within circle **Edge:** Plain

Date	Mintage	F	VF	XF	Unc	BU
2002	—	—	—	0.10	0.20	0.45
2003	—	—	—	0.10	0.20	0.45
2005	—	—	—	0.10	0.20	0.45
2006	—	—	—	0.10	0.20	0.45

KM# 115 5 CENTS
1.0500 g., Aluminum, 20.2 mm.

Date	Mintage	F	VF	XF	Unc	BU
2002	—	—	—	0.10	0.20	0.40

KM# 36 25 CENTS
5.7200 g., Copper-Nickel, 23.6 mm. **Obv:** Crowned bust of Queen Elizabeth II right **Obv. Designer:** Cecil Thomas **Rev:** Denomination within circle, date below **Edge:** Reeded

Date	Mintage	F	VF	XF	Unc	BU
2003	—	—	0.20	0.35	0.75	1.50
2007	—	—	0.20	0.35	0.75	1.50

KM# 134 DOLLAR
30.9400 g., 0.9990 Silver 0.9937 oz. ASW, 39.9 mm. **Subject:** Mayan King **Obv:** National arms **Rev:** Mayan portrait in ornate headdress **Edge:** Reeded

Date	Mintage	F	VF	XF	Unc	BU
2002	—	—	—	—	37.50	40.00

KM# 99 DOLLAR
8.9000 g., Nickel-Brass, 27 mm. **Obv:** Crowned bust of Queen Elizabeth II right **Obv. Designer:** Raphael Maklouf **Rev:** Columbus' three ships, denomination above, date below **Rev. Designer:** Robert Elderton **Edge:** Alternating reeded and plain **Shape:** 10-sided

Date	Mintage	F	VF	XF	Unc	BU
2003	—	—	—	—	2.25	3.00
2007	—	—	—	—	2.25	3.00

BENIN

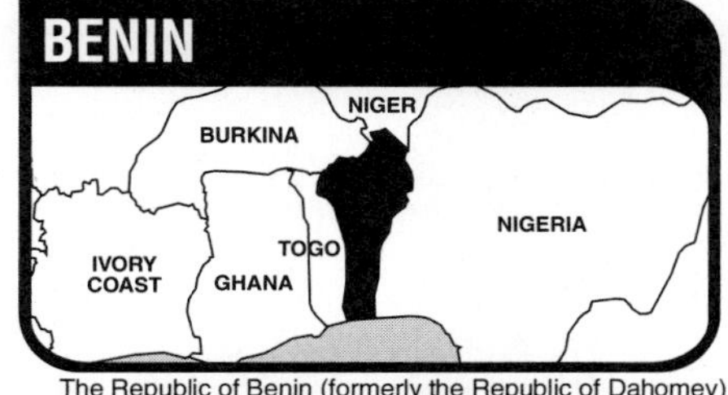

The Republic of Benin (formerly the Republic of Dahomey), located on the south side of the African bulge between Togo and Nigeria, has an area of 43,500 sq. mi. (112,620 sq. km.) and a population of 5.5 million. Capital: Porto-Novo. The principal industry of Benin, one of the poorest countries of West Africa, is the processing of palm oil products. Palm kernel oil, peanuts, cotton, and coffee are exported.

PEOPLES REPUBLIC

STANDARD COINAGE

KM# 53 100 CFA FRANCS
27.0000 g., Copper-Nickel Silver plated, 38.61 mm. **Rev:** Multicolor Cannabis Sativa, Aeromatic

Date	Mintage	F	VF	XF	Unc	BU
2010 Proof	2,500	Value: 75.00				

KM# 54 1000 FRANCS
20.0000 g., 0.9990 Silver 0.6423 oz. ASW, 36 mm. **Rev:** Multicolor Lockheed Orion

Date	Mintage	F	VF	XF	Unc	BU
2002 Proof	—	Value: 35.00				

KM# 55 1000 FRANCS
20.0000 g., 0.9990 Silver 0.6423 oz. ASW, 36 mm. **Rev:** Multicolor Convair 990 Coronado over mountains

Date	Mintage	F	VF	XF	Unc	BU
2002 Proof	—	Value: 35.00				

KM# 60 1000 FRANCS
Silver **Subject:** Sir Francis Drake and the Golden Hind

Date	Mintage	F	VF	XF	Unc	BU
2003 Proof	—	Value: 37.50				

KM# 62 1000 FRANCS
Silver **Rev:** Klaus Stortebeker and ship

Date	Mintage	F	VF	XF	Unc	BU
2003 Proof	—	Value: 37.50				

KM# 56 1000 FRANCS
20.0000 g., 0.9990 Silver 0.6423 oz. ASW, 36 mm. **Rev:** Multicolor Douglas DC-8 at airport

Date	Mintage	F	VF	XF	Unc	BU
2003 Proof	—	Value: 35.00				

KM# 57 1000 FRANCS
20.0000 g., 0.9990 Silver 0.6423 oz. ASW, 36 mm. **Rev:** Multicolor Fokker 100 left

Date	Mintage	F	VF	XF	Unc	BU
2003 Proof	—	Value: 35.00				

KM# 58 1000 FRANCS
20.0000 g., 0.9990 Silver 0.6423 oz. ASW, 36 mm. **Rev:** Multicolor Douglas DC-4 right

Date	Mintage	F	VF	XF	Unc	BU
2004 Proof	—	Value: 35.00				

KM# 59 1000 FRANCS
20.0000 g., 0.9990 Silver 0.6423 oz. ASW, 36 mm. **Rev:** Multicolor General Aviation GA-43 against blue sky

Date	Mintage	F	VF	XF	Unc	BU
2004 Proof	—	Value: 45.00				

BERMUDA

The Parliamentary British Colony of Bermuda, situated in the western Atlantic Ocean 660 miles (1,062 km.) east of North Carolina, has an area of 20.6 sq. mi. (53 sq. km.) and a population of 61,600. Capital: Hamilton. Concentrated essences, beauty preparations, and cut flowers are exported. Most Bermudians derive their livelihood from tourism. The British monarch is the head of state and is represented by a governor. U.S. Currency circulates in common with the Eastern Caribbean Dollar.

RULER
British

BRITISH COLONY

DECIMAL COINAGE

100 Cents = 1 Dollar

KM# 107 CENT
2.5000 g., Copper Plated Zinc, 19 mm. **Ruler:** Elizabeth II **Obv:** Head with tiara right **Obv. Designer:** Ian Rank-Broadley **Rev:** Wild boar left **Rev. Designer:** Michael Rizzello **Edge:** Plain

Date	Mintage	F	VF	XF	Unc	BU
2001	1,600,000	—	—	—	0.50	0.75
2002	1,120,000	—	—	—	0.50	0.75
2003	800,000	—	—	—	0.50	0.75
2004	1,600,000	—	—	—	0.25	0.50
2005	3,200,000	—	—	—	0.25	0.50
2006	800,000	—	—	—	0.25	0.50

KM# 107a CENT
2.5000 g., Copper Plated Steel **Ruler:** Elizabeth II

Date	Mintage	F	VF	XF	Unc	BU
2008	2,400,000	—	—	—	0.25	0.50
2009	4,000,000	—	—	—	0.25	0.50

KM# 108 5 CENTS
5.0600 g., Copper-Nickel, 21 mm. **Ruler:** Elizabeth II **Obv:** Head with tiara right **Obv. Designer:** Ian Rank-Broadley **Rev:** Queen angel fish left **Rev. Designer:** Michael Rizzello **Edge:** Plain

Date	Mintage	F	VF	XF	Unc	BU
2001	1,000,000	—	—	—	0.75	1.00
2002	700,000	—	—	—	0.75	1.00
2003	700,000	—	—	—	0.75	1.00
2004	700,000	—	—	—	0.75	1.00
2005	600,000	—	—	—	0.75	1.00
2008	500,000	—	—	—	0.75	1.00
2009	1,500,000	—	—	—	0.50	0.75

KM# 109 10 CENTS
2.5000 g., Copper-Nickel, 17.8 mm. **Ruler:** Elizabeth II **Obv:** Head with tiara right **Obv. Designer:** Ian Rank-Broadley **Rev:** Bermuda lily **Rev. Designer:** Michael Rizzello **Edge:** Reeded

Date	Mintage	F	VF	XF	Unc	BU
2001	1,400,000	—	—	—	0.85	1.00
2002	800,000	—	—	—	0.85	1.00
2003	600,000	—	—	—	0.85	1.00
2004	800,000	—	—	—	0.85	1.00
2005	800,000	—	—	—	0.85	1.00
2008	2,000,000	—	—	—	0.50	0.75
2009	2,000,000	—	—	—	0.50	0.75

KM# 110 25 CENTS
Copper-Nickel, 24 mm. **Ruler:** Elizabeth II **Obv:** Head with tiara right **Obv. Designer:** Ian Rank-Broadley **Rev:** Yellow-billed tropical bird right **Rev. Designer:** Michael Rizzello **Edge:** Reeded

Date	Mintage	F	VF	XF	Unc	BU
2001	800,000	—	—	—	1.50	2.00
2002	800,000	—	—	—	1.50	2.00
2003	800,000	—	—	—	1.50	2.00
2004	800,000	—	—	—	1.50	2.00
2005	1,440,000	—	—	—	1.50	2.00
2006	320,000	—	—	—	1.50	2.00
2008	1,200,000	—	—	—	1.00	1.50
2009	2,000,000	—	—	—	1.00	1.50

KM# 111 DOLLAR
Nickel-Brass, 26 mm. **Ruler:** Elizabeth II **Obv:** Head with tiara right **Obv. Designer:** Rank-Broadley **Rev:** Sailboat **Rev. Designer:** Eldron Trimingham III

Date	Mintage	F	VF	XF	Unc	BU
2001	12,000	—	—	—	3.00	3.50
2002	12,000	—	—	—	3.00	3.50
2003	12,000	—	—	—	3.00	3.50
2004	12,000	—	—	—	3.00	3.50
2005	240,000	—	—	—	2.00	3.00
2008	300,000	—	—	—	2.00	3.00
2009	600,000	—	—	—	2.00	3.00

KM# 139 DOLLAR
28.2800 g., Copper-Nickel, 38.6 mm. **Obv:** Head with tiara right **Obv. Designer:** Ian Rank-Broadley **Rev:** 4 Gombey dancers **Rev. Designer:** Robert Elderton **Edge:** Reeded

Date	Mintage	F	VF	XF	Unc	BU
2001	—	—	—	—	12.00	14.00

KM# 124 DOLLAR
28.4100 g., Copper-Nickel, 38.5 mm. **Ruler:** Elizabeth II **Subject:** Queen's Golden Jubilee **Obv:** Head with tiara right **Obv.**

Designer: Ian Rank-Broadley **Rev:** Stylized trumpeters above monogram and date **Edge:** Reeded

Date	Mintage	F	VF	XF	Unc	BU
2002	—	—	—	—	10.00	12.00

KM# 380 2 DOLLARS

31.6040 g., 0.9990 Silver 1.0150 oz. ASW, 38.61 mm. **Ruler:** Elizabeth II **Subject:** Bermuda Hawksbill Turtle **Obv:** Bust right **Rev:** Turtle **Rev. Legend:** BERMUDA HAWKSBILL TURTLE / TWO DOLLARS

Date	Mintage	F	VF	XF	Unc	BU
2008 Proof	2,500	Value: 50.00				

KM# 157 3 DOLLARS

33.6300 g., 0.9250 Silver 1.0000 oz. ASW, 35 mm. **Subject:** Shipwrecks Series **Obv:** Elizabeth II **Rev:** Gold-plated image of the Hunter Galley **Edge:** Plain

Date	Mintage	F	VF	XF	Unc	BU
2006 Proof	15,000	Value: 90.00				

KM# 158 3 DOLLARS

33.6300 g., 0.9250 Silver 1.0000 oz. ASW, 35 mm. **Subject:** Shipwrecks Series **Obv:** Elizabeth II **Rev:** Gold-plated image of the North Carolina **Edge:** Plain

Date	Mintage	F	VF	XF	Unc	BU
2006 Proof	15,000	Value: 90.00				

KM# 159 3 DOLLARS

33.6300 g., 0.9250 Silver 1.0000 oz. ASW, 35 mm. **Subject:** Shipwrecks Series **Obv:** Elizabeth II **Rev:** Gold-plated image of the Pollockshields **Edge:** Plain

Date	Mintage	F	VF	XF	Unc	BU
2006 Proof	15,000	Value: 90.00				

KM# 140 3 DOLLARS

33.6300 g., 0.9250 Silver 1.0000 oz. ASW, 35 mm. **Subject:** Shipwreck Series **Obv:** Elizabeth II **Rev:** The Mary Celestia gold-plated image **Edge:** Plain **Shape:** Triangular

Date	Mintage	F	VF	XF	Unc	BU
2006 Proof	15,000	Value: 90.00				

KM# 141 3 DOLLARS

1.5550 g., 0.9990 Gold 0.0499 oz. AGW, 15 mm. **Subject:** Shipwreck Series **Obv:** Elizabeth II **Rev:** The Mary Celestia **Edge:** Plain **Shape:** Triangular

Date	Mintage	F	VF	XF	Unc	BU
2006 Proof	15,000	Value: 100				

KM# 148 3 DOLLARS

33.6300 g., 0.9250 Silver 1.0000 oz. ASW, 35 mm. **Subject:** Shipwreck Series **Obv:** Elizabeth II **Rev:** The Constellation in gold-plated image **Edge:** Plain **Shape:** Triangular

Date	Mintage	F	VF	XF	Unc	BU
2006 Proof	15,000	Value: 90.00				

KM# 149 3 DOLLARS

1.5550 g., 0.9990 Gold 0.0499 oz. AGW, 15 mm. **Subject:** Shipwreck Series **Obv:** Elizabeth II **Rev:** The Constellation **Edge:** Plain **Shape:** Triangular

Date	Mintage	F	VF	XF	Unc	BU
2006 Proof	15,000	Value: 100				

KM# 156 3 DOLLARS

33.6300 g., 0.9250 Silver 1.0000 oz. ASW, 35 mm. **Subject:** Shipwrecks Series **Obv:** Elizabeth II **Rev:** Gold-plated image of the Sea Venture **Edge:** Plain

Date	Mintage	F	VF	XF	Unc	BU
2007 Proof	15,000	Value: 90.00				

KM# 164 3 DOLLARS

33.6300 g., 0.9250 Silver 1.0000 oz. ASW, 35 mm. **Ruler:** Elizabeth II **Series:** Bermuda Shipwrecks **Obv:** Head with tiara right, gilt **Obv. Designer:** Ian Rank-Broadley **Rev:** Dutchman sailing ship "Manilla", gilt, 1739 **Edge:** Plain, gilt **Shape:** Triangular

Date	Mintage	F	VF	XF	Unc	BU
2007 Proof	15,000	Value: 85.00				

KM# 165 3 DOLLARS

33.6300 g., 0.9250 Silver 1.0000 oz. ASW, 35 mm. **Ruler:** Elizabeth II **Series:** Bermuda Shipwrecks **Obv:** Head with tiara right, gilt **Obv. Designer:** Ian Rank-Broadley **Rev:** 16th century Spanish sailing ship "Santa Lucia", gilt, 1584 **Edge:** Plain, gilt **Shape:** Triangular

Date	Mintage	F	VF	XF	Unc	BU
2007 Proof	15,000	Value: 85.00				

KM# 166 3 DOLLARS

33.6300 g., 0.9250 Silver 1.0000 oz. ASW **Ruler:** Elizabeth II **Series:** Bermuda Shipwrecks **Obv:** Head with tiara right, gilt **Obv. Designer:** Ian Rank-Broadley **Rev:** Spanish luxury steamship "Cristobal Colon", gilt, 1936 **Edge:** Plain

Date	Mintage	F	VF	XF	Unc	BU
2007 Proof	15,000	Value: 85.00				

KM# 167 3 DOLLARS

33.6300 g., 0.9250 Silver 1.0000 oz. ASW, 35 mm. **Ruler:** Elizabeth II **Series:** Bermuda Shipwrecks **Obv:** Head with tiara right, gilt **Obv. Designer:** Ian Rank-Broadley **Rev:** English iron-hulled steamer with sails "Kate", gilt, 1878 **Edge:** Plain **Shape:** Triangular

Date	Mintage	F	VF	XF	Unc	BU
2007 Proof	15,000	Value: 85.00				

KM# 168 3 DOLLARS

33.6300 g., 0.9250 Silver 1.0000 oz. ASW, 35 mm. **Ruler:** Elizabeth II **Series:** Bermuda Shipwrecks **Obv:** Head with tiara right, gilt **Obv. Designer:** Ian Rank-Broadley **Rev:** 16th century Spanish sailing ship "San Pedro", gilt, 1596 **Edge:** Plain, gilt **Shape:** Triangular

Date	Mintage	F	VF	XF	Unc	BU
2007 Proof	15,000	Value: 85.00				

KM# 169 3 DOLLARS

33.6300 g., 0.9250 Silver 1.0000 oz. ASW, 35 mm. **Ruler:** Elizabeth II **Series:** Bermuda Shipwrecks **Obv:** Head with tiara right, gilt **Obv. Designer:** Ian Rank-Broadley **Rev:** American luxury yacht "Col. William G. Ball", gilt, 1943 **Edge:** Plain, gilt **Shape:** Triangular

Date	Mintage	F	VF	XF	Unc	BU
2007 Proof	15,000	Value: 85.00				

KM# 381 4 DOLLARS

34.0000 g., 0.9250 Silver 1.0111 oz. ASW, 40 mm. **Ruler:** Elizabeth II **Obv:** Bust right **Obv. Legend:** Elizabeth II, Value, BERMUDA **Rev:** Sea venture sailing ship **Rev. Legend:** 1609-2009 400th ANNIVERSARY OF THE SETTLEMENT OF BERMUDA **Shape:** Square

Date	Mintage	F	VF	XF	Unc	BU
ND(2009) Proof	2,000	Value: 55.00				

KM# 120 5 DOLLARS
28.2800 g., 0.9250 Silver 0.8410 oz. ASW, 38.6 mm. **Subject:** Gombey Dancers **Obv:** Head with tiara right **Obv. Designer:** Ian Rank-Broadley **Rev:** Multicolor costumed dancers **Edge:** Reeded

Date	Mintage	F	VF	XF	Unc	BU
2001 Proof	3,500	Value: 60.00				

KM# 161 5 DOLLARS
28.2800 g., 0.9250 Silver 0.8410 oz. ASW, 38.6 mm. **Ruler:** Elizabeth II **Obv:** Bust with tiara right **Rev:** Statehouse facade, St. George's **Edge:** Reeded

Date	Mintage	F	VF	XF	Unc	BU
2001 Proof	3,500	Value: 45.00				

KM# 129 5 DOLLARS
28.2800 g., 0.9250 Silver 0.8410 oz. ASW, 38.6 mm. **Subject:** Queen's Jubilee **Obv:** Gold-plated head with tiara right, denomination below **Rev:** Trumpeters, monogram and date below **Edge:** Reeded

Date	Mintage	F	VF	XF	Unc	BU
2002 Proof	20,000	Value: 42.00				

KM# 162 5 DOLLARS
28.2800 g., 0.9250 Silver 0.8410 oz. ASW, 38.6 mm. **Ruler:** Elizabeth II **Subject:** 100th Anniversary Cup Match - Cricket **Obv:** Head with tiara right **Rev:** Two players with caps and teams shields below, multicolor **Edge:** Reeded

Date	Mintage	F	VF	XF	Unc	BU
2002 Proof	3,500	Value: 45.00				

KM# 171 5 DOLLARS
28.2800 g., 0.9250 Silver 0.8410 oz. ASW, 38.6 mm. **Ruler:** Elizabeth II **Subject:** Queen's Golden Jubilee **Obv:** Head with tiara right **Obv. Designer:** Ian Rank-Broadley **Rev:** Stylized trumpeters above monogram and date **Edge:** Reeded

Date	Mintage	F	VF	XF	Unc	BU
2002 Proof	3,500	Value: 50.00				

KM# 170 5 DOLLARS
28.2800 g., 0.9250 Silver 0.8410 oz. ASW, 38.6 mm. **Ruler:** Elizabeth II **Subject:** 100th Anniversary Fitted Dinghy Racing **Obv:** Head with tiara right **Rev:** Two dinghies, multicolor sails **Edge:** Reeded

Date	Mintage	F	VF	XF	Unc	BU
ND(2003) Proof	3,500	Value: 50.00				

KM# 128 5 DOLLARS
28.2800 g., 0.9250 Silver 0.8410 oz. ASW, 38.6 mm. **Obv:** Head with tiara right **Rev:** 2 fitted racing dinghies with multicolor sails **Edge:** Reeded

Date	Mintage	F	VF	XF	Unc	BU
ND (2003) Proof	3,500	Value: 60.00				

KM# 130 5 DOLLARS
28.2800 g., 0.9250 Silver 0.8410 oz. ASW, 38.6 mm. **Subject:** Queen's Jubilee **Obv:** Gold-plated head with tiara right **Rev:** Royal visit scene **Edge:** Reeded

Date	Mintage	F	VF	XF	Unc	BU
2003 Proof	20,000	Value: 42.00				

KM# 131 5 DOLLARS
28.2800 g., 0.9250 Silver 0.8410 oz. ASW, 38.6 mm. **Obv:** Head with tiara right **Rev:** Bermudan stone quarry scene **Edge:** Reeded

Date	Mintage	F	VF	XF	Unc	BU
2004 Proof	3,500	Value: 60.00				

KM# 160 5 DOLLARS
14.5000 g., 0.9250 Silver partially gilt 0.4312 oz. ASW, 30.9 mm. **Ruler:** Elizabeth II **Subject:** Bermuda Quincentennial **Obv:** Head with tiara right, partially gold-plated **Rev:** Caravel sailing ship partially gold-plated compass face **Edge:** Plain **Shape:** Pentagonal

Date	Mintage	F	VF	XF	Unc	BU
2005 Proof	2,500	Value: 45.00				

KM# 142 9 DOLLARS
155.5200 g., 0.9990 Silver 4.9949 oz. ASW, 65 mm. **Subject:** Shipwreck Series **Obv:** Elizabeth II **Rev:** The Mary Celestia **Edge:** Plain **Shape:** Triangular

Date	Mintage	F	VF	XF	Unc	BU
2007 Proof	1,000	Value: 200				

KM# 150 9 DOLLARS
155.5200 g., 0.9990 Silver 4.9949 oz. ASW, 65 mm. **Subject:** Shipwreck Series **Obv:** Elizabeth II **Rev:** The Constellation **Edge:** Plain **Shape:** Triangular

Date	Mintage	F	VF	XF	Unc	BU
2007 Proof	1,000	Value: 200				

KM# 143 30 DOLLARS
31.4890 g., 0.9990 Gold 1.0113 oz. AGW, 35 mm. **Subject:** Shipwreck Series **Obv:** Elizabeth II **Rev:** The Mary Celestia **Edge:** Plain **Shape:** Triangular

Date	Mintage	F	VF	XF	Unc	BU
2006 Proof	750	Value: 1,500				

KM# 151 30 DOLLARS
31.4890 g., 0.9990 Gold 1.0113 oz. AGW, 35 mm. **Subject:** Shipwreck Series **Obv:** Elizabeth II **Rev:** The Constellation **Edge:** Plain **Shape:** Triangular

Date	Mintage	F	VF	XF	Unc	BU
2006 Proof	750	Value: 1,500				

KM# 144 60 DOLLARS
1000.0000 g., 0.9990 Silver 32.117 oz. ASW, 100 mm. **Subject:** Shipwreck Series **Obv:** Elizabeth II **Rev:** The Mary Celestia **Edge:** Plain

Date	Mintage	F	VF	XF	Unc	BU
2007 Proof	300	Value: 1,200				

KM# 152 60 DOLLARS
1000.0000 g., 0.9990 Silver 32.117 oz. ASW, 100 mm. **Subject:** Shipwreck Series **Obv:** Elizabeth II **Rev:** The Constellation **Edge:** Plain **Shape:** Triangular

Date	Mintage	F	VF	XF	Unc	BU
2007 Proof	300	Value: 1,200				

KM# 145 90 DOLLARS
155.5200 g., 0.9990 Gold 4.9949 oz. AGW, 65 mm. **Subject:** Shipwreck Series **Obv:** Elizabeth II **Rev:** The Mary Celestia **Edge:** Plain **Shape:** Triangular

Date	Mintage	F	VF	XF	Unc	BU
2006 Proof	90	Value: 7,500				

KM# 153 90 DOLLARS
155.5200 g., 0.9990 Gold 4.9949 oz. AGW, 65 mm. **Subject:** Shipwreck Series **Obv:** Elizabeth II **Rev:** The Constellation **Edge:** Plain **Shape:** Triangular

Date	Mintage	F	VF	XF	Unc	BU
2006 Proof	90	Value: 7,500				

KM# 173 100 DOLLARS
1000.0000 g., 0.9250 Silver selective gold plating 29.738 oz. ASW, 100 mm. **Ruler:** Elizabeth II **Subject:** 500th Anniversary of Discovery **Obv:** Head right **Rev:** Caraval within compass **Shape:** 5-sided

Date	Mintage	F	VF	XF	Unc	BU
2005 Proof	250	Value: 1,150				

KM# 146 300 DOLLARS
155.5200 g., 0.9995 Platinum 4.9974 oz. APW, 65 mm. **Subject:** Shipwrecks Series **Obv:** Elizabeth II **Rev:** The Mary Celestia **Edge:** Plain **Shape:** Triangular

Date	Mintage	F	VF	XF	Unc	BU
2006 Proof	60	Value: 9,500				

KM# 154 300 DOLLARS
155.5200 g., 0.9995 Platinum 4.9974 oz. APW, 65 mm. **Subject:** Shipwreck Series **Obv:** Elizabeth II **Rev:** The Constellation **Edge:** Plain **Shape:** Triangular

Date	Mintage	F	VF	XF	Unc	BU
2006 Proof	60	Value: 9,500				

KM# 172 500 DOLLARS
31.1050 g., 0.9990 Gold with selective silver plating 0.9990 oz. AGW, 30.89 mm. **Ruler:** Elizabeth II **Obv:** Queen Elizabeth II **Rev:** Caravel sailing ship in compass face **Edge:** Plain **Shape:** 5-sided **Note:** Bermuda Quincentennial. Prev. KM#160a.

Date	Mintage	F	VF	XF	Unc	BU
2005 Proof	—	Value: 1,500				

KM# 147 600 DOLLARS
1096.0000 g., 0.9180 Gold 32.346 oz. AGW, 100 mm. **Subject:** Shipwreck Series **Obv:** Elizabeth II **Rev:** The Mary Celestia **Edge:** Plain **Shape:** Triangular

Date	Mintage	F	VF	XF	Unc	BU
2007 Proof	300	Value: 47,500				

KM# 155 600 DOLLARS
1096.0000 g., 0.9180 Gold 32.346 oz. AGW, 100 mm. **Subject:** Shipwreck Series **Obv:** Elizabeth II **Rev:** The Constellation **Edge:** Plain **Shape:** Triangular

Date	Mintage	F	VF	XF	Unc	BU
2007 Proof	300	Value: 47,500				

PIEFORTS

KM#	Date	Mintage	Identification	Mkt Val
P3	2005	250	5 Dollars. 0.9250 Silver. 29.0000 g. 30.89 mm. Gold plated bust and rim. Caravel type sailing ship in partially gold plated compass face and rim. Plain, gold plated edge.	—

MINT SETS

KM#	Date	Mintage	Identification	Issue Price	Mkt Val
MS8	2004 (5)	2,300	KM#107-111.	—	10.00

BHUTAN

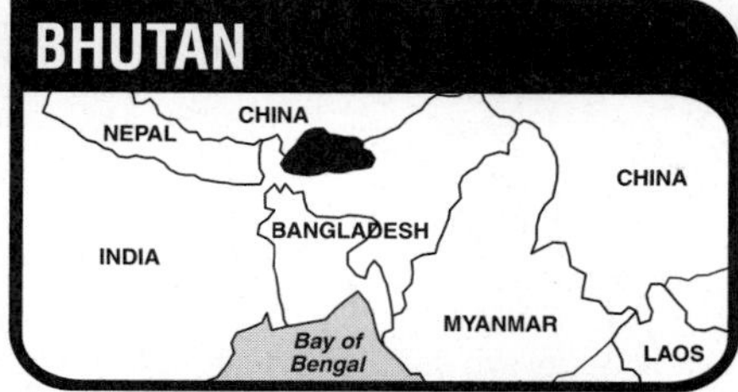

The Kingdom of Bhutan, a landlocked Himalayan country bordered by Tibet and India, has an area of 18,150 sq. mi. (47,000 sq. km.) and a population of *2.03 million. Capital: Thimphu. Virtually the entire population is engaged in agricultural and pastoral activities. Rice, wheat, barley, and yak butter are produced in sufficient quantity to make the country self-sufficient in food. The economy of Bhutan is primitive and many transactions are conducted on a barter basis.

RULER
Jigme Singye Wangchuck, 1972-2006
King Jigme Khesar Namgyel Wangchuck, 2006-

KINGDOM

REFORM COINAGE

Commencing 1974; 100 Chetrums (Paisa) = 1 Ngultrum (Rupee); 100 Ngultrums = 1 Sertum

KM# 105 5 CHETRUMS
3.8600 g., Brass, 21.9 mm. **Obv:** Monkey right, date below **Rev:** Effigy of the old "Ma-tam", value below **Edge:** Plain

Date	Mintage	F	VF	XF	Unc	BU
2003	—	—	—	—	0.25	0.50

KM# 116 NGULTRUM
8.1000 g., Nickel Plated Steel **Ruler:** Jigme Khesar Namgyel Wangchuck

Date	Mintage	F	VF	XF	Unc	BU
2008	—	—	—	—	3.00	4.00

KM# 115 100 NGULTRUMS
20.2000 g., Silver, 38 mm. **Ruler:** Jigme Khesar Namgyel Wangchuck **Subject:** Coronation **Obv:** Portrait left **Rev:** Seal

Date	Mintage	F	VF	XF	Unc	BU
2008 Proof	—	Value: 60.00				

BOLIVIA

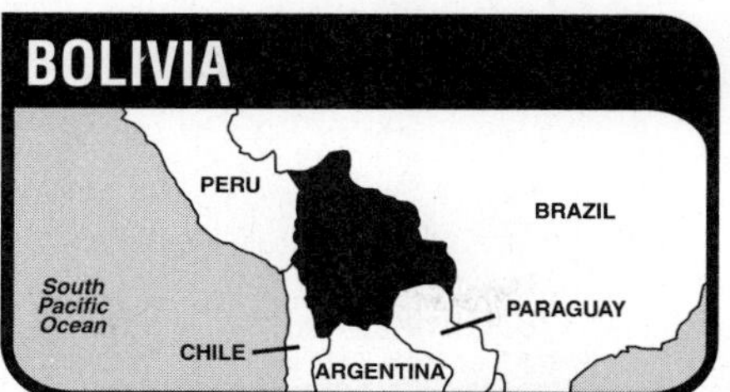

The Republic of Bolivia, a landlocked country in west central South America, has an area of 424,165 sq. mi. (1,098,580 sq. km.) and a population of *8.33 million. Its capitals are: La Paz (administrative) and Sucre (constitutional). Principal exports are tin, zinc, antimony, tungsten, petroleum, natural gas, cotton and coffee.

MINT MARKS
A - Paris
(a) - Paris, privy marks only
CHI - Valcambia
H - Heaton
KN - Kings' Norton

REPUBLIC

REFORM COINAGE

1987-; 1,000,000 Peso Bolivianos = 1 Boliviano;
100 Centavos = 1 Boliviano

KM# 213 10 CENTAVOS
Copper Clad Steel

Date	Mintage	F	VF	XF	Unc	BU
2001	—	—	—	—	0.50	1.00

KM# 202 10 CENTAVOS
1.8500 g., Stainless Steel, 19 mm. **Obv:** National arms, star below **Rev:** Denomination within circle, date below

Date	Mintage	F	VF	XF	Unc	BU
2006	—	—	—	0.20	0.50	0.70

KM# 202a 10 CENTAVOS
1.8500 g., Copper Clad Steel, 19 mm. **Obv:** National arms **Obv. Legend:** REPUBLICA DE BOLIVIA **Rev:** Denomination **Rev. Legend:** LA UNION ES LA FUERZA **Edge:** Plain

Date	Mintage	F	VF	XF	Unc	BU
2006	—	—	—	0.20	0.50	0.65
2008	—	—	—	0.20	0.50	0.65

KM# 203 20 CENTAVOS
3.2500 g., Stainless Steel, 22 mm. **Obv:** National arms, star below **Obv. Legend:** REPUBLICA DE BOLIVIA **Rev:** Denomination within circle, date below **Rev. Legend:** LA UNION ES LA FUERZA **Edge:** Plain

Date	Mintage	F	VF	XF	Unc	BU
2001	—	—	—	0.25	0.60	0.80
2006	—	—	—	0.25	0.60	0.80
2008	—	—	—	0.25	0.60	0.80

KM# 204 50 CENTAVOS
3.7500 g., Stainless Steel, 24 mm. **Obv:** National arms, star below **Obv. Legend:** REPUBLICA DE BOLIVIA **Rev:** Denomination within circle, date below **Rev. Legend:** LA UNION ES LA FUERZA **Edge:** Plain

Date	Mintage	F	VF	XF	Unc	BU
2001	—	—	—	0.30	0.75	1.00
2006	—	—	—	0.30	0.75	1.00
2008	—	—	—	0.30	0.75	1.00
2010	—	—	—	0.30	0.75	1.00

KM# 205 BOLIVIANO
5.0000 g., Stainless Steel, 27 mm. **Obv:** National arms, star below **Obv. Legend:** REPUBLICA DE BOLIVIA **Rev:** Denomination within circle, date below sprays **Rev. Legend:** LA UNION ES LA FUERZA **Edge:** Plain

Date	Mintage	F	VF	XF	Unc	BU
2001	—	—	—	0.35	0.90	1.20
2004	—	—	—	0.35	0.90	1.20
2008	—	—	—	0.35	0.90	1.20
2010	—	—	—	0.35	0.90	1.20

KM# 206.2 2 BOLIVIANOS
6.2500 g., Stainless Steel, 27 mm. **Obv:** National arms, star below **Rev:** Denomination within circle, date below **Shape:** 11-sided **Note:** Increased size.

Date	Mintage	F	VF	XF	Unc	BU
2008	—	—	—	—	2.00	3.00

KM# 212 5 BOLIVIANOS
5.0000 g., Bi-Metallic Bronze clad Steel center in Stainless Steel ring., 23 mm. **Obv:** National arms **Obv. Legend:** REPUBLICA DE BOLIVIA **Rev:** Denomination **Rev. Legend:** LA UNION ES LA FUERZA **Edge:** Reeded

Date	Mintage	F	VF	XF	Unc	BU
2001	—	—	—	0.90	2.25	3.00
2004	—	—	—	0.90	2.25	3.00
2010	—	—	—	0.90	2.25	3.00

BOSNIA - HERZEGOVINA

The Republic of Bosnia and Herzegovina borders Croatia to the north and west, Serbia to the east and Montenegro in the southeast with only 12.4 mi. of coastline. The total land area is 19,735 sq. mi. (51,129 sq. km.). They have a population of *4.34 million. Capital: Sarajevo. Electricity, mining and agriculture are leading industries.

MONETARY SYSTEM

1 Convertible Marka = 100 Convertible Feniga =
1 Deutschemark 1998-

NOTE: German Euros circulate freely.

REPUBLIC

REFORM COINAGE

1998-

KM# 121 5 FENINGA

2.6600 g., Nickel Plated Steel, 18 mm. **Obv:** Denomination on map **Rev:** Triangle and stars **Edge:** Reeded

Date	Mintage	F	VF	XF	Unc	BU
2005	—	—	—	—	1.00	1.25

KM# 115 10 FENINGA

3.9000 g., Copper Plated Steel, 20 mm. **Obv:** Denomination on map within circle **Rev:** Triangle and stars, date at left within circle **Edge:** Plain

Date	Mintage	F	VF	XF	Unc	BU
2004	—	—	—	—	0.50	0.75

KM# 116 20 FENINGA

4.5000 g., Copper Plated Steel, 22 mm. **Obv:** Denomination on map within circle **Rev:** Triangle and stars, date at left within circle

Date	Mintage	F	VF	XF	Unc	BU
2004	—	—	—	—	1.00	1.25
2007	—	—	—	—	1.00	1.25

KM# 117 50 FENINGA

5.1500 g., Copper Plated Steel, 24 mm. **Obv:** Denomination on map within circle **Rev:** Triangle and stars, date at left within circle

Date	Mintage	F	VF	XF	Unc	BU
2007	—	—	—	—	—	3.00

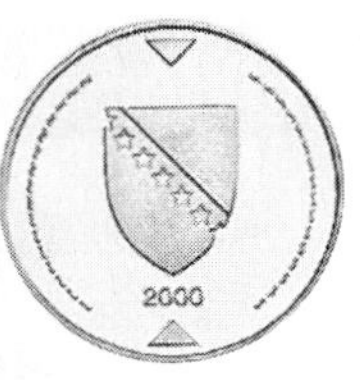

KM# 118 KONVERTIBLE MARKA

4.9500 g., Nickel Plated Steel, 23.25 mm. **Obv:** Denomination **Rev:** Coat of arms above date **Edge:** Segmented reeding

Date	Mintage	F	VF	XF	Unc	BU
2002	—	—	—	—	5.50	6.00
2003	—	—	—	—	5.50	6.00
2006	—	—	—	—	4.00	5.00
2009	—	—	—	—	4.00	5.00

KM# 119 2 KONVERTIBLE MARKA

6.9000 g., Bi-Metallic Copper-Nickel center in Nickel-Brass ring, 25.75 mm. **Obv:** Denomination within circle **Rev:** Dove of Peace, date at right within circle **Edge:** Segmented reeding

Date	Mintage	F	VF	XF	Unc	BU
2002	—	—	—	—	13.50	15.00
2003	—	—	—	—	13.50	15.00
2008	—	—	—	—	13.50	15.00

KM# 120 5 KONVERTIBLE MARKA

10.3500 g., Bi-Metallic Nickel-Brass center in Copper-Nickel ring, 30 mm. **Obv:** Denomination within circle **Rev:** Dove of Peace in flight **Edge:** Reeded

Date	Mintage	F	VF	XF	Unc	BU
2005	—	—	—	—	17.50	20.00
2009	—	—	—	—	17.50	20.00

BOTSWANA

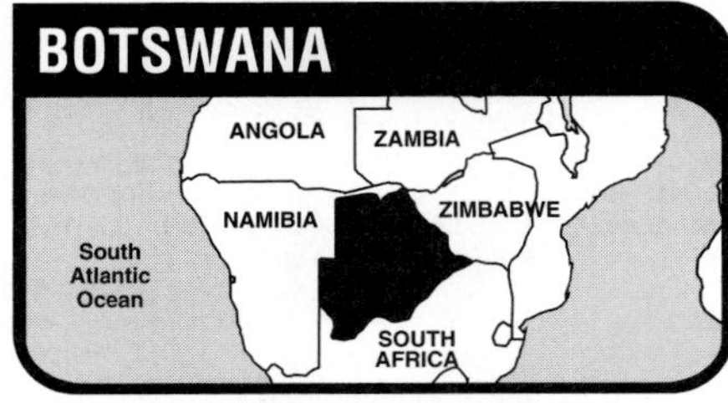

The Republic of Botswana (formerly Bechuanaland), located in south central Africa between Namibia and Zimbabwe, has an area of 224,607 sq. mi. (600,370 sq. km.) and a population of *1.62 million. Capital: Gaborone. Botswana is a member of a Customs Union with South Africa, Lesotho, and Swaziland. The economy is primarily pastoral with a rapidly developing mining industry, of which diamonds, copper and nickel are the chief elements. Meat products and diamonds comprise 85 percent of the exports.

Botswana is a member of the Commonwealth of Nations. The president is Chief of State and Head of government.

MINT MARK

B - Berne

MONETARY SYSTEM

100 Cents = 1 Thebe

REPUBLIC

REFORM COINAGE

100 Thebe = 1 Pula

KM# 26 5 THEBE

2.4100 g., Bronze Clad Steel, 16.9 mm. **Obv:** National arms above date **Rev:** Toko bird left, value above **Rev. Designer:** Mike Hibbit **Edge:** Plain **Shape:** 7-sided

Date	Mintage	F	VF	XF	Unc	BU
2002	—	—	—	0.25	0.50	1.00
2007	—	—	—	0.25	0.50	1.00

KM# 27 10 THEBE

2.8000 g., Nickel Plated Steel, 18 mm. **Obv:** National arms above date **Rev:** South African Oryx right, value above **Rev. Designer:** Mike Hibbit

Date	Mintage	F	VF	XF	Unc	BU
2002	—	—	—	0.30	0.75	1.25
2008	—	—	—	0.30	0.75	1.25

KM# 28 25 THEBE

3.5000 g., Nickel Plated Steel, 21 mm. **Obv:** National arms, date below **Rev:** Zebu left, value above **Rev. Designer:** Mike Hibbit **Shape:** 7-sided

Date	Mintage	F	VF	XF	Unc	BU
2007	—	—	0.30	0.60	1.50	2.00

KM# 29 50 THEBE

4.8200 g., Nickel Plated Steel, 21.5 mm. **Obv:** National arms, date below **Rev:** African Fish Eagle left, value above **Rev. Designer:** Mike Hibbit

Date	Mintage	F	VF	XF	Unc	BU
2001	—	—	0.50	1.00	2.00	2.50

KM# 24 PULA

8.7000 g., Nickel-Brass, 23.5 mm. **Obv:** National arms, date below **Rev:** Zebra left, denomination above **Rev. Designer:** Mike Hibbit **Shape:** 7-sided

Date	Mintage	F	VF	XF	Unc	BU
2007	—	—	1.00	1.75	3.50	6.00

KM# 25a 2 PULA

Brass **Subject:** Wildlife **Obv:** National arms, date below **Rev:** Rhinoceros left, denomination above **Shape:** 7-sided

Date	Mintage	F	VF	XF	Unc	BU
2004	—	—	—	—	2.75	3.50

KM# 30 5 PULA

6.2000 g., Bi-Metallic Copper-Nickel center in Brass ring, 23.4 mm. **Obv:** National arms, date below **Rev:** Mophane worm on a mophane leaf, denomination below within circle **Edge:** Reeded

Date	Mintage	F	VF	XF	Unc	BU
2007	—	—	—	—	6.50	10.00

The Federative Republic of Brazil, which comprises half the continent of South America and is the only Latin American country deriving its culture and language from Portugal, has an area of 3,286,488 sq. mi. (8,511,965 sq. km.) and a population of *169.2 million. Capital: Brasilia. The economy of Brazil is as varied and complex as any in the developing world. Agriculture is a mainstay of the economy, while only 4 percent of the area is under cultivation. Known mineral resources are almost unlimited in variety and size of reserves. A large, relatively sophisticated industry ranges from basic steel and chemical production to finished consumer goods. Coffee, cotton, iron ore and cocoa are the chief exports.

MINT MARKS

(a) - Paris, privy marks only
B - Bahia

REPUBLIC

REFORM COINAGE

1994-present

2750 Cruzeiros Reais = 1 Real; 100 Centavos = 1 Real

KM# 647 CENTAVO

2.4300 g., Copper Plated Steel, 17 mm. **Obv:** Cabral bust at right **Rev:** Denomination on linear design at left, 3/4 globe with sash on right, date below **Edge:** Plain

Date	Mintage	F	VF	XF	Unc	BU
2001	242,924,000	—	—	—	0.10	0.20
2002	161,824,000	—	—	—	0.10	0.20
2003	250,000,000	—	—	—	0.10	0.20
2004	167,232,000	—	—	—	0.10	0.20

KM# 648 5 CENTAVOS

4.1000 g., Copper Plated Steel, 22 mm. **Obv:** Tiradente bust at right, dove at left **Rev:** Denomination on linear design at left, 3/4 globe with sash on right, date below **Edge:** Plain

Date	Mintage	F	VF	XF	Unc	BU
2001	175,940,000	—	—	—	0.45	0.65
2002	153,088,000	—	—	—	0.45	0.65
2003	260,000,000	—	—	—	0.45	0.65
2004	262,656,000	—	—	—	0.45	0.65
2005	230,144,000	—	—	—	0.45	0.65
2006	255,488,000	—	—	—	0.45	0.65
2007	403,968,000	—	—	—	0.45	0.65
2008	28,672,000	—	—	—	0.45	0.65
2009	—	—	—	—	0.45	0.65

KM# 649.2 10 CENTAVOS

4.8000 g., Bronze Plated Steel, 20 mm. **Obv:** Bust of Pedro at right, horseman with sword in right hand at left **Rev:** Denomination on linear design at left, 3/4 globe with sash on right, date below **Edge:** Reeded

Date	Mintage	F	VF	XF	Unc	BU
2001	134,701,000	—	—	—	0.60	0.80
2002	172,032,000	—	—	—	0.60	0.80
2003	252,666,000	—	—	—	0.60	0.80
2004	348,480,000	—	—	—	0.60	0.80
2005	362,112,000	—	—	—	0.60	0.80
2006	265,728,000	—	—	—	0.60	0.80
2007	316,800,000	—	—	—	0.60	0.80
2008	270,144,000	—	—	—	0.50	0.75
2009	—	—	—	—	0.50	0.75

KM# 650 25 CENTAVOS

7.5500 g., Brass Plated Steel, 25 mm. **Obv:** Deodoro bust at right, national arms at left **Rev:** Denomination on linear design at left, 3/4 globe with sash on right, date below **Edge:** Reeded

Date	Mintage	F	VF	XF	Unc	BU
2001	92,642,000	—	—	—	0.75	1.00
2002	100,096,000	—	—	—	0.75	1.00
2003	147,200,000	—	—	—	0.75	1.00
2004	160,000,000	—	—	—	0.75	1.00
2005	100,096,000	—	—	—	0.75	1.00
2006	110,720,000	—	—	—	0.75	1.00
2007	118,784,000	—	—	—	0.75	1.00
2008	150,016,000	—	—	—	0.75	1.00
2009	—	—	—	—	0.60	0.75

KM# 651 50 CENTAVOS

9.2500 g., Copper-Nickel, 23 mm. **Obv:** Rio Branco bust at right, map at left **Rev:** Denomination on linear design at left, 3/4 globe with sash on right, date below **Edge Lettering:** BRASIL ORDEM E PROGRESSO

Date	Mintage	F	VF	XF	Unc	BU
2001	14,735,000	—	—	—	1.50	1.75

KM# 651a 50 CENTAVOS

7.9000 g., Stainless Steel, 23 mm. **Obv:** Rio Branco bust at right, map at left **Rev:** Denomination on linear design at left, 3/4 globe with sash on right, date below **Edge Lettering:** BRASIL ORDEM E PROGRESSO

Date	Mintage	F	VF	XF	Unc	BU
2002	189,952,000	—	—	—	1.25	1.50
2003	143,696,000	—	—	—	1.25	1.50
2005	122,416,000	—	—	—	1.25	1.50
2006	39,948,000	—	—	—	1.25	1.50
2007	130,032,000	—	—	—	1.25	1.50
2008	290,080,000	—	—	—	1.25	1.50
2009	—	—	—	—	1.25	1.50

KM# 652a REAL

7.0000 g., Bi-Metallic Stainless Steel center in Brass Plated Steel ring, 27 mm. **Obv:** Allegorical portrait **Rev:** Denomination on linear design at left, 3/4 globe with sash on right, date below **Edge:** Segmented reeding

Date	Mintage	F	VF	XF	Unc	BU
2002	54,192,000	—	—	—	3.50	4.50
2003	100,000,000	—	—	—	3.50	4.50
2004	150,016,000	—	—	—	3.50	4.50
2005	43,776,000	—	—	—	3.50	4.50
2006	179,968,000	—	—	—	3.50	4.50
2007	275,712,000	—	—	—	3.50	4.50
2008	400,000,000	—	—	—	3.50	4.50
2009	—	—	—	—	2.50	3.00

KM# 656 REAL

7.0000 g., Bi-Metallic Stainless Steel center in Brass Plated Steel ring, 27 mm. **Subject:** Centennial of Juscelino Kubitschek, president **Obv:** Head left **Obv. Designer:** Alzira Duim **Rev:** Denomination on linear design at left, 3/4 globe with sash on right, date below **Edge:** Segmented reeding

Date	Mintage	F	VF	XF	Unc	BU
2002	50,000,000	—	—	—	3.50	4.50

KM# 668 REAL

7.0000 g., Bi-Metallic Stainless Steel center in Brass plated Stainless Steel ring, 27 mm. **Subject:** 40th Anniversary of Central Bank **Obv:** Monument **Rev:** Value on flag **Edge:** Segmented reeding

Date	Mintage	F	VF	XF	Unc	BU
2005	40,000,000	—	—	—	5.00	6.50

KM# 657 2 REAIS

28.0000 g., 0.9990 Silver 0.8993 oz. ASW, 40 mm. **Subject:** Centennial - Carlos Drummond de Andrade **Obv:** Denomination and writer **Rev:** Stylized portrait **Edge:** Reeded

Date	Mintage	F	VF	XF	Unc	BU
ND(2002) Proof	6,999	Value: 60.00				

KM# 658 2 REAIS

28.0000 g., 0.9990 Silver 0.8993 oz. ASW, 40 mm. **Subject:** Centennial - Juscelino Kubitschek **Obv:** Bust facing in upper right, initials at left **Rev:** Denomination **Edge:** Reeded

Date	Mintage	F	VF	XF	Unc	BU
2002 Proof	12,999	Value: 55.00				

KM# 663 2 REAIS

27.0000 g., 0.9250 Silver 0.8029 oz. ASW, 40 mm. **Obv:** Value and piano player **Rev:** Ary Barroso singing **Edge:** Reeded

Date	Mintage	F	VF	XF	Unc	BU
2003 Proof	7,000	Value: 60.00				

KM# 665 2 REAIS

27.0000 g., 0.9250 Silver 0.8029 oz. ASW, 40 mm. **Subject:** Centennial - Cándido Con Portinari **Obv:** Starving family scene, value and country name **Rev:** Portinari's portrait, stars in squares design **Edge:** Reeded

Date	Mintage	F	VF	XF	Unc	BU
ND(2003) Proof	2,000	Value: 75.00				

KM# 666 2 REAIS

27.0000 g., 0.9250 Silver 0.8029 oz. ASW, 40 mm. **Subject:** FIFA Centennial **Obv:** Soccer ball and value **Rev:** Center part of a Brazilian flag and stars **Edge:** Reeded

Date	Mintage	F	VF	XF	Unc	BU
2004 Proof	12,166	Value: 75.00				

KM# 671 2 REAIS

27.0000 g., 0.9250 Silver 0.8029 oz. ASW, 40 mm. **Subject:** Centennial of Flight 14 bis **Obv:** Image of 14 Bis **Obv. Legend:** "Centenario Do Voo Do 14 Bis Brasil 1906-2006" **Rev:** Image and signature of Santos Dumont and value **Edge:** Reeded

Date	Mintage	F	VF	XF	Unc	BU
2006 Proof	4,000	Value: 65.00				

KM# 672 2 REAIS

10.1700 g., Copper-Nickel, 30 mm. **Subject:** Pan-American Games XV **Obv:** Official logo of Pan-American Games XV **Rev:** Image of running athlete, XV Jogos Pan-Americanos, value, Brasil and date. **Edge:** Reeded

Date	Mintage	F	VF	XF	Unc	BU
2007	10,000	—	—	—	—	12.00

KM# 675 2 REAIS

10.1700 g., Copper-Nickel, 30 mm. **Subject:** Japanese immigration to Brazil, 100th Anniversary **Obv:** Farmer and persimmon crop **Rev:** Ship "Kasato Maru"

Date	Mintage	F	VF	XF	Unc	BU
2008	10,000	—	—	—	—	16.00

KM# 661 5 REAIS

28.0000 g., 0.9990 Silver 0.8993 oz. ASW, 40 mm. **Subject:** World Cup 2000 **Obv:** Soccer player and Brazilian flag **Rev:** Soccer ball and value **Edge:** Reeded

Date	Mintage	F	VF	XF	Unc	BU
2002 Proof	10,149	Value: 60.00				

KM# 673 5 REAIS

27.0000 g., 0.9250 Silver 0.8029 oz. ASW, 40 mm. **Subject:** Pan-American Games XV **Obv:** Official logo of Pan-American Games XV **Rev:** Sugar Loaf, lines of Copacabana sidewalk, "XV Jogos Pan-Americanos", value, Brasil and date. **Edge:** Reeded

Date	Mintage	F	VF	XF	Unc	BU
2007 Proof	4,000	Value: 65.00				

KM# 674 5 REAIS

27.0000 g., 0.9250 Silver 0.8029 oz. ASW, 40 mm. **Subject:** Royal Family's arrival in Brazil, 200th Anniversary **Obv:** Ship "Martim de Freitas" **Rev:** Names and dates of institutions created by Dom John **Edge:** Reeded

Date	Mintage	F	VF	XF	Unc	BU
2008 Proof	2,000	Value: 75.00				

KM# 676 5 REAIS

27.0000 g., 0.9250 Silver 0.8029 oz. ASW, 40 mm. **Subject:** World Heritage Sites, Brasilia, 50th Anniversary **Obv:** Schematic city plan **Rev:** Brasilia's architecture montage: Congress, Cathedral, Presidential palace and Warriors sculpture **Edge:** Reeded

Date	Mintage	F	VF	XF	Unc	BU
2010 Proof	Est. 6,000	Value: 65.00				

KM# 677 5 REAIS

27.0000 g., 0.9250 Silver 0.8029 oz. ASW, 40 mm. **Subject:** 2010 World Cup, South Africa **Obv:** Two players with scoccer ball **Rev:** African savannah, soccer player **Edge:** Reeded

Date	Mintage	F	VF	XF	Unc	BU
2010 Proof	12,000	Value: 65.00				

KM# 659 20 REAIS

8.0000 g., 0.9000 Gold 0.2315 oz. AGW, 22 mm. **Obv:** Juscelino Kubitschek de Oliveira's portrait **Rev:** Value **Edge:** Reeded

Date	Mintage	F	VF	XF	Unc	BU
2002 Proof	2,499	Value: 375				

KM# 660 20 REAIS

8.0000 g., 0.9000 Gold 0.2315 oz. AGW, 22 mm. **Obv:** Carlos Drummond de Andrade portrait and value **Rev:** Andrade caricature, name and dates **Edge:** Reeded

Date	Mintage	F	VF	XF	Unc	BU
ND(2002) Proof	2,499	Value: 375				

KM# 662 20 REAIS

8.0000 g., 0.9000 Gold 0.2315 oz. AGW, 22 mm. **Subject:** World Cup 2002 **Obv:** Soccer player **Rev:** Value, inscription and shooting stars **Edge:** Reeded

Date	Mintage	F	VF	XF	Unc	BU
2002	2,499	Value: 375				

KM# 664 20 REAIS

8.0000 g., 0.9000 Gold 0.2315 oz. AGW, 22 mm. **Subject:** Centennial - Ary Barroso **Obv:** Piano keyboard and musical notes above value **Rev:** Caricature of Ary Barroso **Edge:** Reeded

Date	Mintage	F	VF	XF	Unc	BU
2003 Proof	2,500	Value: 375				

KM# 670 20 REAIS

8.0000 g., 0.9000 Gold 0.2315 oz. AGW, 22 mm. **Subject:** FIFA Centennial **Obv:** Soccer ball, value, date **Obv. Legend:** BRAZIL **Rev:** Christ Redeemer, sugar loaf **Rev. Legend:** FUTBUL MONDIAL CENTENARIO DA FIFA

Date	Mintage	F	VF	XF	Unc	BU
2004 Proof	4,060	Value: 375				

BRITISH ANTARCTIC TERRITORY

BRITISH TERRITORY

DECIMAL COINAGE

KM# 1 2 POUNDS

Copper-Nickel, 38.6 mm. **Ruler:** Elizabeth II **Subject:** 200th Anniversary of the Granting of Letters Patent **Obv:** Elizabeth II bust facing right **Rev:** Arms with denomination below **Rev. Legend:** 1908 . CENTENARY OF GRANTING OF LETTERS PATENT . 2008

Date	Mintage	F	VF	XF	Unc	BU
2008	—	—	—	—	17.50	20.00

KM# 5 2 POUNDS

28.2800 g., Copper-Nickel **Ruler:** Elizabeth II **Subject:** Antartic treaty **Obv:** Bust right **Rev:** Whale and other Antarctic wildlife **Shape:** 38.6

Date	Mintage	F	VF	XF	Unc	BU
2009	50,000	—	—	—	15.00	18.00

KM# 5a 2 POUNDS

28.2800 g., 0.9250 Silver 0.8410 oz. ASW, 38.6 mm. **Ruler:** Elizabeth II **Obv:** Bust right **Rev:** Whale and other Antarctic wildlife

Date	Mintage	F	VF	XF	Unc	BU
2009 Proof	10,000	Value: 45.00				

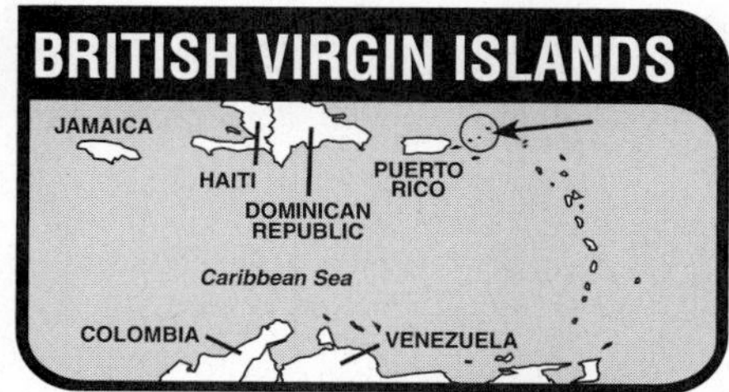

The Colony of the Virgin Islands, a British colony situated in the Caribbean Sea northeast of Puerto Rico and west of the Leeward Islands, has an area of 59 sq. mi. (155 sq. km.) and a population of 13,000. Capital: Road Town. The principal islands of the 36-island group are Tortola, Virgin Gorda, Anegada, and Jost Van Dyke. The chief industries are fishing and stock raising. Fish, livestock and bananas are exported. U.S. currency and Sterling circulate in common with the East Caribbean Dollar.

BRITISH COLONY

STANDARD COINAGE

KM# 196 DOLLAR

28.2800 g., Copper-Nickel, 38.6 mm. **Subject:** Queen's Golden Jubilee **Obv:** Queen's bust right **Obv. Designer:** Ian Rank-Broadley **Rev:** Carnival dancers **Edge:** Reeded

Date	Mintage	F	VF	XF	Unc	BU
2002	—	—	—	—	7.50	9.50

KM# 180 DOLLAR

28.2800 g., Copper-Nickel, 25.7 mm. **Subject:** Sir Francis Drake **Obv:** Queen's bust right **Obv. Designer:** Ian Rank-Broadley **Rev:** Ship, portrait and map **Edge:** Reeded

Date	Mintage	F	VF	XF	Unc	BU
2002	—	—	—	—	7.50	9.50

KM# 183 DOLLAR

28.2800 g., Copper-Nickel, 38.6 mm. **Subject:** Sir Walter Raleigh **Obv:** Queen's bust right **Obv. Designer:** Ian Rank-Broadley **Rev:** Ship, portrait and map **Edge:** Reeded

Date	Mintage	F	VF	XF	Unc	BU
2002	—	—	—	—	7.50	9.50

KM# 187 DOLLAR

28.2800 g., Copper-Nickel, 38.6 mm. **Subject:** Queen's Golden Jubilee **Obv:** Queen's bust right **Obv. Designer:** Ian Rank-Broadley **Rev:** Queen on horse **Edge:** Reeded

Date	Mintage	F	VF	XF	Unc	BU
2002	—	—	—	—	7.50	9.50

KM# 190 DOLLAR

28.2800 g., Copper-Nickel, 38.6 mm. **Subject:** Queen's Golden Jubilee **Obv:** Queen's bust right **Obv. Designer:** Ian Rank-Broadley **Rev:** Queen on throne **Edge:** Reeded

Date	Mintage	F	VF	XF	Unc	BU
2002	—	—	—	—	7.50	9.50

KM# 193 DOLLAR

28.2800 g., Copper-Nickel, 38.6 mm. **Subject:** Queen's Golden Jubilee **Obv:** Queen's bust right **Obv. Designer:** Ian Rank-Broadley **Rev:** Queen with President Ronald Reagan and First Lady Nancy Reagan **Edge:** Reeded

Date	Mintage	F	VF	XF	Unc	BU
2002	—	—	—	—	7.50	9.50

KM# 199 DOLLAR

28.2800 g., Copper-Nickel, 38.6 mm. **Subject:** Teddy Bear Centennial **Obv:** Queen's bust right **Obv. Designer:** Ian Rank-Broadley **Rev:** Teddy bear **Edge:** Reeded

Date	Mintage	F	VF	XF	Unc	BU
2002	—	—	—	—	8.50	15.00

KM# 204 DOLLAR

28.2800 g., Copper-Nickel, 38.6 mm. **Subject:** Princess Diana **Obv:** Queen's bust right **Obv. Designer:** Ian Rank-Broadley **Rev:** Diana's portrait **Edge:** Reeded

Date	Mintage	F	VF	XF	Unc	BU
2002	—	—	—	—	7.50	9.50

KM# 207 DOLLAR

28.2800 g., Copper-Nickel, 38.6 mm. **Subject:** September 11, 2001 **Obv:** Queen's bust right **Obv. Designer:** Ian Rank-Broadley **Rev:** World Trade Center twin towers **Edge:** Reeded

Date	Mintage	F	VF	XF	Unc	BU
2002	—	—	—	—	12.00	13.50

KM# 210 DOLLAR

28.2800 g., Copper-Nickel, 38.6 mm. **Subject:** September 11, 2001 **Obv:** Queen's bust right **Obv. Designer:** Ian Rank-Broadley **Rev:** Statue of Liberty **Edge:** Reeded

Date	Mintage	F	VF	XF	Unc	BU
2002	—	—	—	—	12.00	13.50

KM# 213 DOLLAR

28.2800 g., Copper-Nickel, 38.6 mm. **Subject:** Queen Mother **Obv:** Queen's bust right **Obv. Designer:** Ian Rank-Broadley **Rev:** Queen Mother and a young Prince Charles **Edge:** Reeded

Date	Mintage	F	VF	XF	Unc	BU
2002PM	—	—	—	—	10.00	12.00

KM# 216 DOLLAR

28.2800 g., Copper-Nickel, 38.6 mm. **Subject:** Queen Mother **Obv:** Queen's bust right **Obv. Designer:** Ian Rank-Broadley **Rev:** Queen Mother with four grandchildren **Edge:** Reeded

Date	Mintage	F	VF	XF	Unc	BU
2002PM	—	—	—	—	10.00	12.00

KM# 219 DOLLAR

28.2800 g., Copper-Nickel, 38.6 mm. **Subject:** Queen Mother Series **Obv:** Queen's bust right **Obv. Designer:** Ian Rank-Broadley **Rev:** Queen Mother with uniformed Prince Charles **Edge:** Reeded

Date	Mintage	F	VF	XF	Unc	BU
2002PM	—	—	—	—	10.00	12.00

KM# 222 DOLLAR

28.2800 g., Copper-Nickel, 38.6 mm. **Subject:** Queen Mother Series **Obv:** Queen's bust right **Obv. Designer:** Ian Rank-Broadley **Rev:** Queen Mother's coffin **Edge:** Reeded

Date	Mintage	F	VF	XF	Unc	BU
2002PM	—	—	—	—	10.00	12.00

KM# 225 DOLLAR

28.4400 g., Copper-Nickel, 38.6 mm. **Subject:** Kennedy Assassination **Obv:** Queen's bust right **Obv. Designer:** Ian Rank-Broadley **Rev:** President Kennedy's portrait left **Edge:** Reeded

Date	Mintage	F	VF	XF	Unc	BU
2003	—	—	—	—	10.00	12.00

KM# 229 DOLLAR

28.2800 g., Copper-Nickel, 38.6 mm. **Subject:** Powered Flight Centennial **Obv:** Queen's bust right **Obv. Designer:** Ian Rank-Broadley **Rev:** Three historic airplanes and rocket **Edge:** Reeded

Date	Mintage	F	VF	XF	Unc	BU
2003	—	—	—	—	10.00	12.00

KM# 232 DOLLAR

28.2800 g., Copper-Nickel, 38.6 mm. **Obv:** Queen's bust right **Obv. Designer:** Ian Rank-Broadley **Rev:** Henry VIII and Elizabeth I **Edge:** Reeded

Date	Mintage	F	VF	XF	Unc	BU
2003	—	—	—	—	10.00	12.00

KM# 235 DOLLAR

28.2800 g., Copper-Nickel, 38.6 mm. **Obv:** Queen's bust right **Obv. Designer:** Ian Rank-Broadley **Rev:** Matthew Parker, Archbishop of Canterbury **Edge:** Reeded

Date	Mintage	F	VF	XF	Unc	BU
2003	—	—	—	—	10.00	12.00

KM# 238 DOLLAR

28.2800 g., Copper-Nickel, 38.6 mm. **Obv:** Queen's bust right **Obv. Designer:** Ian Rank-Broadley **Rev:** Sir Francis Drake and ships **Edge:** Reeded

Date	Mintage	F	VF	XF	Unc	BU
2003	—	—	—	—	10.00	12.00

KM# 241 DOLLAR

28.2800 g., Copper-Nickel, 38.6 mm. **Obv:** Queen's bust right **Obv. Designer:** Ian Rank-Broadley **Rev:** Sir Walter Raleigh **Edge:** Reeded

Date	Mintage	F	VF	XF	Unc	BU
2003	—	—	—	—	10.00	12.00

KM# 244 DOLLAR

28.2800 g., Copper-Nickel, 38.6 mm. **Obv:** Queen's bust right **Obv. Designer:** Ian Rank-Broadley **Rev:** Sir William Shakespeare **Edge:** Reeded

Date	Mintage	F	VF	XF	Unc	BU
2003	—	—	—	—	10.00	12.00

KM# 247 DOLLAR

28.2800 g., Copper-Nickel, 38.6 mm. **Obv:** Queen's bust right **Obv. Designer:** Ian Rank-Broadley **Rev:** Elizabeth I above her funeral procession **Edge:** Reeded

Date	Mintage	F	VF	XF	Unc	BU
2003	—	—	—	—	10.00	12.00

KM# 250 DOLLAR

28.2800 g., Copper-Nickel, 38.6 mm. **Subject:** Olympics **Obv:** Queen's bust right **Obv. Designer:** Ian Rank-Broadley **Rev:** Ancient bust, runners and coin **Edge:** Reeded

Date	Mintage	F	VF	XF	Unc	BU
2003	—	—	—	—	10.00	12.00

KM# 253 DOLLAR

28.2800 g., Copper-Nickel, 38.6 mm. **Subject:** Olympics **Obv:** Queen's bust right **Obv. Designer:** Ian Rank-Broadley **Rev:** Ancient bust, charioteer and coin **Edge:** Reeded

Date	Mintage	F	VF	XF	Unc	BU
2003	—	—	—	—	10.00	12.00

KM# 303 DOLLAR

28.2800 g., Copper-Nickel, 38.6 mm. **Subject:** 2004 Athens Olympics **Obv:** Queen's bust right **Obv. Designer:** Ian Rank-Broadley **Rev:** Ancient athlete's bust right, runners at lower right, ancient coin with owl at upper right **Edge:** Reeded

Date	Mintage	F	VF	XF	Unc	BU
2003	—	—	—	—	10.00	12.00

KM# 306 DOLLAR

28.2800 g., Copper-Nickel, 38.6 mm. **Subject:** 2004 Athens Olympics **Obv:** Queen's bust right **Obv. Designer:** Ian Rank-Broadley **Rev:** Ancient athlete bust left, chariot race at lower left, ancient coin at upper left **Edge:** Reeded

Date	Mintage	F	VF	XF	Unc	BU
2003	—	—	—	—	10.00	12.00

KM# 310 DOLLAR

28.2800 g., Copper-Nickel, 38.6 mm. **Subject:** Queen Elizabeth's Golden Coronation Jubilee **Obv:** Elizabeth II **Rev:** Cameo portraits above the ship "Gothic" **Edge:** Reeded

Date	Mintage	F	VF	XF	Unc	BU
2003	—	—	—	—	7.50	9.50

KM# 319 DOLLAR

28.2800 g., Copper-Nickel **Subject:** 50th Anniversary of Coronation **Rev:** Queen riding in automobile

Date	Mintage	F	VF	XF	Unc	BU
2003	—	—	—	—	12.00	15.00

KM# 320 DOLLAR

28.2800 g., Copper-Nickel **Subject:** Golden Jubilee of Coronation **Rev:** Sir. Edmond Hillary on Mt. Everest, Queen II above mountain climbers

Date	Mintage	F	VF	XF	Unc	BU
2003	—	—	—	—	12.00	15.00

KM# 321 DOLLAR

28.2800 g., Copper-Nickel **Rev:** Queen presenting Ascot Horse Racing prize

Date	Mintage	F	VF	XF	Unc	BU
2003	—	—	—	—	10.00	12.00

KM# 265 DOLLAR

28.2800 g., Copper-Nickel, 38.6 mm. **Obv:** Queen's bust right **Obv. Designer:** Ian Rank-Broadley **Rev:** Sir Francis Drake, ship and map **Edge:** Reeded

Date	Mintage	F	VF	XF	Unc	BU
2004	—	—	—	—	10.00	12.00

KM# 267.1 DOLLAR

28.2800 g., Copper-Nickel, 38.6 mm. **Obv:** Queen's bust right **Obv. Designer:** Ian Rank-Broadley **Rev:** Peter Rabbit **Edge:** Reeded

Date	Mintage	F	VF	XF	Unc	BU
2004	—	—	—	—	15.00	17.00

KM# 267.2 DOLLAR

28.2800 g., Copper-Nickel, 38.6 mm. **Obv:** Queen's bust right **Obv. Designer:** Ian Rank-Broadley **Rev:** Multicolor Peter Rabbit **Edge:** Reeded

Date	Mintage	F	VF	XF	Unc	BU
2004	—	—	—	—	20.00	22.00

KM# 268 DOLLAR

3.1100 g., 0.9990 Silver 0.0999 oz. ASW, 18 mm. **Obv:** Queen's bust right **Obv. Designer:** Ian Rank-Broadley **Rev:** Peter Rabbit **Edge:** Reeded

Date	Mintage	F	VF	XF	Unc	BU
2004 Proof	10,000	Value: 25.00				

KM# 281 DOLLAR

28.2800 g., Copper-Nickel, 38.6 mm. **Obv:** Queen's bust right **Obv. Designer:** Ian Rank-Broadley **Rev:** Sailor above two D-Day landing craft **Edge:** Reeded

Date	Mintage	F	VF	XF	Unc	BU
2004	—	—	—	—	10.00	12.00

KM# 286 DOLLAR

28.2800 g., Copper-Nickel, 38.6 mm. **Obv:** Queen's bust right **Obv. Designer:** Ian Rank-Broadley **Rev:** Dolphin **Edge:** Reeded

Date	Mintage	F	VF	XF	Unc	BU
2004	—	—	—	—	12.00	14.00

KM# 297 DOLLAR

28.2800 g., Copper-Nickel, 38.6 mm. **Obv:** Queen's bust right **Obv. Designer:** Ian Rank-Broadley **Rev:** Soldier above tank and jeeps **Edge:** Reeded

Date	Mintage	F	VF	XF	Unc	BU
2004	—	—	—	—	10.00	12.00

KM# 300 DOLLAR

28.2800 g., Copper-Nickel, 38.6 mm. **Obv:** Queen's bust right **Obv. Designer:** Ian Rank-Broadley **Rev:** Pilot and planes above D-Day landing **Edge:** Reeded

Date	Mintage	F	VF	XF	Unc	BU
2004	—	—	—	—	10.00	12.00

KM# 330 DOLLAR

Copper-Nickel **Ruler:** Elizabeth II **Rev:** Battle of Britain

Date	Mintage	F	VF	XF	Unc	BU
2005	—	—	—	—	15.00	17.00

KM# 331 DOLLAR

Copper-Nickel **Ruler:** Elizabeth II **Rev:** Battle of Berlin

Date	Mintage	F	VF	XF	Unc	BU
2005	—	—	—	—	15.00	17.00

KM# 312 DOLLAR

28.2800 g., Copper-Nickel, 38.6 mm. **Obv:** Bust of Queen Elizabeth II right **Rev:** Mother and baby dolphins **Edge:** Reeded

Date	Mintage	F	VF	XF	Unc	BU
2005	—	—	—	—	12.00	14.00

KM# 322 DOLLAR

28.2800 g., Copper-Nickel **Rev:** VJ Day, McArthur and U.S.S. Missiouri Battleship

Date	Mintage	F	VF	XF	Unc	BU
2005	—	—	—	—	10.00	12.00

KM# 323 DOLLAR
28.2800 g., Copper-Nickel **Rev:** Warships near Atlantic coast, West Indies islands

Date	Mintage	F	VF	XF	Unc	BU
2005	—	—	—	—	10.00	12.00

KM# 324 DOLLAR
28.2800 g., Copper-Nickel **Rev:** Death of Nelson

Date	Mintage	F	VF	XF	Unc	BU
2005	—	—	—	—	10.00	12.00

KM# 325 DOLLAR
28.2800 g., Copper-Nickel **Rev:** Nelson and Order Star above ships

Date	Mintage	F	VF	XF	Unc	BU
2005	—	—	—	—	10.00	12.00

KM# 326 DOLLAR
28.2800 g., Copper-Nickel **Rev:** Nelson and Napoleon

Date	Mintage	F	VF	XF	Unc	BU
2005	—	—	—	—	10.00	12.00

KM# 327 DOLLAR
28.2800 g., Copper-Nickel **Rev:** Nelson's Column, statue and ships

Date	Mintage	F	VF	XF	Unc	BU
2005	—	—	—	—	10.00	12.00

KM# 328 DOLLAR
28.2800 g., Copper-Nickel **Rev:** V.E. Day, Montgomery and Eisenhower

Date	Mintage	F	VF	XF	Unc	BU
2005	—	—	—	—	10.00	12.00

KM# 329 DOLLAR
Copper-Nickel **Rev:** Two dolphins

Date	Mintage	F	VF	XF	Unc	BU
2006	—	—	—	—	10.00	12.00

KM# 349 DOLLAR
28.2800 g., Copper-Nickel, 38.60 mm. **Ruler:** Elizabeth II **Subject:** 5th Anniversary Attack on Twin Towers, New York City **Obv:** Crowned bust right **Obv. Legend:** BRITISH VIRGIN ISLANDS - QUEEN ELIZABETH II **Rev:** Twin Towers in sprays, remembrance ribbon privy mark at upper right **Rev. Inscription:** LEST WE FORGET **Edge:** Reeded

Date	Mintage	F	VF	XF	Unc	BU
2006	—	—	—	—	15.00	17.00

KM# 332 DOLLAR
28.2800 g., Copper-Nickel, 38.60 mm. **Ruler:** Elizabeth II **Subject:** 400th Anniversary Founding of Jamestown **Obv:** Bust with tiara right **Obv. Legend:** BRITISH VIRGIN ISLANDS - QUEEN ELIZABETH II **Rev:** British lion laying, American eagle perched on sprays **Rev. Legend:** UNITED IN FRIENDSHIP **Edge:** Reeded

Date	Mintage	F	VF	XF	Unc	BU
2007	—	—	—	—	16.50	18.50

KM# 370 DOLLAR
28.2800 g., Copper-Nickel, 38.6 mm. **Ruler:** Elizabeth II **Obv:** Bust right **Rev:** Two soccer players and leopard

Date	Mintage	F	VF	XF	Unc	BU
2009	—	—	—	—	12.00	15.00

KM# 373 DOLLAR
28.2800 g., Copper-Nickel, 38.6 mm. **Ruler:** Elizabeth II **Obv:** Bust right **Rev:** Queen Elizabeth I aboard ship

Date	Mintage	F	VF	XF	Unc	BU
2009	—	—	—	—	12.00	15.00

KM# 375 DOLLAR
28.2800 g., Copper-Nickel, 38.6 mm. **Ruler:** Elizabeth II **Obv:** Bust right **Rev:** Elizabeth I between two columns

Date	Mintage	F	VF	XF	Unc	BU
2009	—	—	—	—	12.00	15.00

KM# 393 DOLLAR
28.2800 g., Copper-Nickel, 38.6 mm. **Ruler:** Elizabeth II **Subject:** Peanuts 60th Anniversary **Rev:** Snoopy sleeping atop doghouse

Date	Mintage	F	VF	XF	Unc	BU
2010PM	—	—	—	—	—	25.00

KM# 396 DOLLAR
28.2800 g., Bronze with antique patina, 38.6 mm. **Ruler:** Elizabeth II **Subject:** Elgin Marbles **Rev:** Two horsemen

Date	Mintage	F	VF	XF	Unc	BU
2010PM	—	—	—	—	25.00	—

KM# 402 DOLLAR
28.2800 g., Copper-Nickel, 38.61 mm. **Ruler:** Elizabeth II **Subject:** Birth of Venus

Date	Mintage	F	VF	XF	Unc	BU
2010PM	—	—	—	—	—	15.00

KM# 278 2 DOLLARS
58.0000 g., Bronze, 50 mm. **Obv:** Queen's bust right **Obv. Designer:** Ian Rank-Broadley **Rev:** 1896 Olympic medal design **Edge:** Reeded

Date	Mintage	F	VF	XF	Unc	BU
2004 Proof	3,500	Value: 20.00				

KM# 380 2 DOLLARS
Bronze with patina, 50 mm. **Ruler:** Elizabeth II **Rev:** Turtle

Date	Mintage	F	VF	XF	Unc	BU
2008PM	—	—	—	—	—	20.00

KM# 269.1 2.50 DOLLARS
7.7758 g., 0.9990 Silver 0.2497 oz. ASW, 26 mm. **Obv:** Queen's bust right **Obv. Designer:** Ian Rank-Broadley **Rev:** Peter Rabbit **Edge:** Reeded

Date	Mintage	F	VF	XF	Unc	BU
2004 Proof	—	Value: 18.00				

KM# 269.2 2.50 DOLLARS
7.7758 g., 0.9990 Silver 0.2497 oz, ASW, 26 mm. **Obv:** Queen's bust right **Obv. Designer:** Ian Rank-Broadley **Rev:** Multicolor Peter Rabbit **Edge:** Reeded

Date	Mintage	F	VF	XF	Unc	BU
2004 Proof	7,500	Value: 25.00				

KM# 381 4 DOLLARS
Silver **Ruler:** Elizabeth II **Subject:** 400th Anniversary of Settlement

Date	Mintage	F	VF	XF	Unc	BU
2009PM	—	—	—	—	—	35.00

KM# 284 5 DOLLARS
10.0000 g., 0.9900 Titanium 0.3183 oz., 36.1 mm. **Obv:** Queen's bust right **Obv. Designer:** Ian Rank-Broadley **Rev:** British Guiana stamp design **Edge:** Reeded

Date	Mintage	F	VF	XF	Unc	BU
2004 Proof	7,500	Value: 90.00				

KM# 340 5 DOLLARS
0.9999 Bi-Metallic Silver center in Gold ring. **Ruler:** Elizabeth II **Obv:** Conjoined busts with Philip right, within gold ring **Obv. Legend:** BRITISH VIRGIN ISLANDS — QUEEN ELIZABETH II **Rev:** Conjoined busts of Princess Elizabeth and Prince Philip right within gold ring **Rev. Legend:** WITH THIS RING, I THEE WED **Edge:** Reeded

Date	Mintage	F	VF	XF	Unc	BU
2007 Proof	—	Value: 450				

KM# 383 5 DOLLARS
Titanium **Ruler:** Elizabeth II **Subject:** Bejing Olympics - Tennis

Date	Mintage	F	VF	XF	Unc	BU
2009PM Proof	—	Value: 35.00				

KM# 384 5 DOLLARS
Titanium **Ruler:** Elizabeth II **Subject:** Bejing Olympics - Swimming

Date	Mintage	F	VF	XF	Unc	BU
2009PM Proof	—	Value: 35.00				

KM# 385 5 DOLLARS
Titanium **Ruler:** Elizabeth II **Subject:** Bejing Olympics

Date	Mintage	F	VF	XF	Unc	BU
2009PM Proof	—	Value: 35.00				

KM# 386 5 DOLLARS
Titanium **Ruler:** Elizabeth II **Subject:** Bejing Olympics

Date	Mintage	F	VF	XF	Unc	BU
2009PM Proof	—	Value: 35.00				

KM# 387 5 DOLLARS
Titanium **Ruler:** Elizabeth II **Subject:** Bejing Olympics

Date	Mintage	F	VF	XF	Unc	BU
2009PM Proof	—	Value: 35.00				

KM# 399 5 DOLLARS
7.0000 g., Bi-Metallic Gold and Titanium, 38.6 mm. **Ruler:** Elizabeth II **Subject:** 200th Anniversary of Publication of Hans Christian Anderson's first book **Rev:** Scene from the Little Mermaid

Date	Mintage	F	VF	XF	Unc	BU
2010PM Proof	Est. 5,000	Value: 100				

KM# 400 5 DOLLARS
10.0000 g., Tri-Metallic Silver, Gold and Titanium, 38.6 mm. **Ruler:** Elizabeth II **Subject:** 200th Anniversary of Publication of Hans Christian Andersen's first book **Rev:** Scene from the Little Mermaid

Date	Mintage	F	VF	XF	Unc	BU
2010PM Proof	Est. 7,500	Value: 100				

KM# 181 10 DOLLARS
28.2800 g., 0.9250 Silver 0.8410 oz. ASW, 38.6 mm. **Subject:** Sir Francis Drake **Obv:** Queen's bust right **Obv. Designer:** Ian Rank-Broadley **Rev:** Ship, portrait and map **Edge:** Reeded

Date	Mintage	F	VF	XF	Unc	BU
2002 Proof	—	Value: 42.00				

KM# 184 10 DOLLARS
28.2800 g., 0.9250 Silver 0.8410 oz. ASW, 38.6 mm. **Subject:** Sir Walter Raleigh **Obv:** Queen's bust right **Obv. Designer:** Ian Rank-Broadley **Rev:** Ship, portrait and map **Edge:** Reeded

Date	Mintage	F	VF	XF	Unc	BU
2002 Proof	—	Value: 42.00				

KM# 188 10 DOLLARS
28.2800 g., 0.9250 Gold Clad Silver 0.8410 oz., 38.6 mm. **Subject:** Queen's Golden Jubilee **Obv:** Queen's bust right **Obv. Designer:** Ian Rank-Broadley **Rev:** Queen on horse trotting left **Edge:** Reeded

Date	Mintage	F	VF	XF	Unc	BU
2002 Proof	10,000	Value: 42.50				

KM# 191 10 DOLLARS
28.2800 g., 0.9250 Gold Clad Silver 0.8410 oz., 38.6 mm. **Subject:** Queen's Golden Jubilee **Obv:** Queen's bust right **Obv. Designer:** Ian Rank-Broadley **Rev:** 3/4-length Queen seated on throne **Edge:** Reeded

Date	Mintage	F	VF	XF	Unc	BU
2002 Proof	10,000	Value: 45.00				

KM# 194 10 DOLLARS
28.2800 g., 0.9250 Gold Clad Silver 0.8410 oz., 38.6 mm. **Subject:** Queen's Golden Jubilee **Obv:** Queen's bust right **Obv. Designer:** Ian Rank-Broadley **Rev:** Queen with President Ronald Reagan and First Lady Nancy Reagan **Edge:** Reeded

Date	Mintage	F	VF	XF	Unc	BU
2002 Proof	10,000	Value: 45.00				

KM# 197 10 DOLLARS
28.2800 g., 0.9250 Gold Clad Silver 0.8410 oz., 38.6 mm. **Subject:** Queen's Golden Jubilee **Obv:** Queen's bust right **Obv. Designer:** Ian Rank-Broadley **Rev:** Carnival dancers **Edge:** Reeded

Date	Mintage	F	VF	XF	Unc	BU
2002 Proof	10,000	Value: 45.00				

KM# 200 10 DOLLARS
28.2800 g., 0.9250 Silver 0.8410 oz. ASW, 38.6 mm. **Subject:** Teddy Bear Centennial **Obv:** Queen's bust right **Obv. Designer:** Ian Rank-Broadley **Rev:** Teddy bear **Edge:** Reeded

Date	Mintage	F	VF	XF	Unc	BU
2002 Proof	10,000	Value: 40.00				

KM# 205 10 DOLLARS
28.2800 g., 0.9250 Silver 0.8410 oz. ASW, 38.6 mm. **Subject:** Princess Diana **Obv:** Queen's bust right **Obv. Designer:** Ian Rank-Broadley **Rev:** Diana's portrait **Edge:** Reeded

Date	Mintage	F	VF	XF	Unc	BU
2002 Proof	10,000	Value: 40.00				

KM# 208.1 10 DOLLARS

28.2800 g., 0.9250 Silver 0.8410 oz. ASW, 38.6 mm. **Subject:** September 11, 2001 **Obv:** Queen's bust right **Obv. Designer:** Ian Rank-Broadley **Rev:** World Trade Center twin towers **Edge:** Reeded

Date	Mintage	F	VF	XF	Unc	BU
2002 Proof	10,000	Value: 50.00				

KM# 208.2 10 DOLLARS

28.2800 g., 0.9250 Silver 0.8410 oz. ASW, 38.6 mm. **Subject:** September 11, 2001 **Obv:** Queen's bust right **Obv. Designer:** Ian Rank-Broadley **Rev:** Holographic multicolor World Trade Center twin towers **Edge:** Reeded

Date	Mintage	F	VF	XF	Unc	BU
2002 Proof	10,000	Value: 45.00				

KM# 211 10 DOLLARS

28.2800 g., 0.9250 Silver 0.8410 oz. ASW, 38.6 mm. **Subject:** September 11, 2001 **Obv:** Queen's bust right **Obv. Designer:** Ian Rank-Broadley **Rev:** Statue of Liberty **Edge:** Reeded

Date	Mintage	F	VF	XF	Unc	BU
2002 Proof	10,000	Value: 40.00				

KM# 214 10 DOLLARS

28.2800 g., 0.9250 Silver 0.8410 oz. ASW, 38.6 mm. **Subject:** Queen Mother **Obv:** Queen's bust right **Obv. Designer:** Ian Rank-Broadley **Rev:** Queen Mother with young Prince Charles **Edge:** Reeded

Date	Mintage	F	VF	XF	Unc	BU
2002PM Proof	10,000	Value: 40.00				

KM# 217 10 DOLLARS

28.2800 g., 0.9250 Silver 0.8410 oz. ASW, 38.6 mm. **Subject:** Queen Mother Series **Obv:** Queen's bust right **Obv. Designer:** Ian Rank-Broadley **Rev:** Queen Mother with four grandchildren **Edge:** Reeded

Date	Mintage	F	VF	XF	Unc	BU
2002PM Proof	10,000	Value: 40.00				

KM# 220 10 DOLLARS

28.2800 g., 0.9250 Silver 0.8410 oz. ASW, 38.6 mm. **Subject:** Queen Mother Series **Obv:** Queen's bust right **Obv. Designer:** Ian Rank-Broadley **Rev:** Queen Mother with uniformed Prince Charles **Edge:** Reeded

Date	Mintage	F	VF	XF	Unc	BU
2002PM Proof	10,000	Value: 40.00				

KM# 223 10 DOLLARS

28.2800 g., 0.9250 Silver 0.8410 oz. ASW, 38.6 mm. **Subject:** Queen Mother Series **Obv:** Queen's bust right **Obv. Designer:** Ian Rank-Broadley **Rev:** Queen Mother's coffin **Edge:** Reeded

Date	Mintage	F	VF	XF	Unc	BU
2002PM Proof	10,000	Value: 40.00				

KM# 226 10 DOLLARS

28.2800 g., 0.9250 Silver 0.8410 oz. ASW, 38.6 mm. **Subject:** Kennedy Assassination **Obv:** Queen's bust right **Obv. Designer:** Ian Rank-Broadley **Rev:** President Kennedy's head left **Edge:** Reeded

Date	Mintage	F	VF	XF	Unc	BU
2003 Proof	10,000	Value: 50.00				

KM# 230 10 DOLLARS

28.2800 g., 0.9250 Silver 0.8410 oz. ASW, 38.6 mm. **Subject:** Powered Flight Centennial **Obv:** Queen's bust right **Obv. Designer:** Ian Rank-Broadley **Rev:** Three historic airplanes and rocket **Edge:** Reeded

Date	Mintage	F	VF	XF	Unc	BU
2003 Proof	10,000	Value: 45.00				

KM# 233 10 DOLLARS

28.2800 g., 0.9250 Silver 0.8410 oz. ASW, 38.6 mm. **Obv:** Queen's bust right **Obv. Designer:** Ian Rank-Broadley **Rev:** Henry VIII and Elizabeth I **Edge:** Reeded

Date	Mintage	F	VF	XF	Unc	BU
2003 Proof	10,000	Value: 42.00				

KM# 236 10 DOLLARS

28.2800 g., 0.9250 Silver 0.8410 oz. ASW, 38.6 mm. **Obv:** Queen's bust right **Obv. Designer:** Ian Rank-Broadley **Rev:** Matthew Parker, Archbishop of Canterbury **Edge:** Reeded

Date	Mintage	F	VF	XF	Unc	BU
2003 Proof	10,000	Value: 42.00				

KM# 239 10 DOLLARS

28.2800 g., 0.9250 Silver 0.8410 oz. ASW, 38.6 mm. **Obv:** Queen's bust right **Obv. Designer:** Ian Rank-Broadley **Rev:** Sir Francis Drake and ships **Edge:** Reeded

Date	Mintage	F	VF	XF	Unc	BU
2003 Proof	10,000	Value: 42.00				

KM# 242 10 DOLLARS

28.2800 g., 0.9250 Silver 0.8410 oz. ASW, 38.6 mm. **Obv:** Queen's bust right **Obv. Designer:** Ian Rank-Broadley **Rev:** Sir Walter Raleigh **Edge:** Reeded

Date	Mintage	F	VF	XF	Unc	BU
2003 Proof	10,000	Value: 42.00				

KM# 245 10 DOLLARS
28.2800 g., 0.9250 Silver 0.8410 oz. ASW, 38.6 mm. **Obv:** Queen's bust right **Obv. Designer:** Ian Rank-Broadley **Rev:** Sir William Shakespeare **Edge:** Reeded

Date	Mintage	F	VF	XF	Unc	BU
2003 Proof	10,000	Value: 42.00				

KM# 248 10 DOLLARS
28.2800 g., 0.9250 Silver 0.8410 oz. ASW, 38.6 mm. **Obv:** Queen's bust right **Obv. Designer:** Ian Rank-Broadley **Rev:** Elizabeth I above her funeral procession **Edge:** Reeded

Date	Mintage	F	VF	XF	Unc	BU
2003 Proof	10,000	Value: 42.00				

KM# 251 10 DOLLARS
28.2800 g., 0.9250 Silver 0.8410 oz. ASW, 38.6 mm. **Subject:** Olympics **Obv:** Queen's bust right **Obv. Designer:** Ian Rank-Broadley **Rev:** Ancient bust, runners and coin **Edge:** Reeded

Date	Mintage	F	VF	XF	Unc	BU
2003 Proof	10,000	Value: 42.00				

KM# 254 10 DOLLARS
28.2800 g., 0.9250 Silver 0.8410 oz. ASW, 38.6 mm. **Subject:** Olympics **Obv:** Queen's bust right **Obv. Designer:** Ian Rank-Broadley **Rev:** Ancient bust, charioteer and coin **Edge:** Reeded

Date	Mintage	F	VF	XF	Unc	BU
2003 Proof	10,000	Value: 42.00				

KM# 311 10 DOLLARS
28.3000 g., 0.9250 Gold Clad Silver 0.8416 oz., 38.6 mm. **Subject:** Queen Elizabeth's Golden Coronation Jubilee **Obv:** Elizabeth II **Rev:** Cameo portrait above ship "Gothic" **Edge:** Reeded

Date	Mintage	F	VF	XF	Unc	BU
2003 Proof	—	Value: 50.00				

KM# 266 10 DOLLARS
28.2800 g., 0.9250 Silver 0.8410 oz. ASW, 38.6 mm. **Obv:** Queen's bust right **Obv. Designer:** Ian Rank-Broadley **Rev:** Sir Francis Drake, ship and map **Edge:** Reeded

Date	Mintage	F	VF	XF	Unc	BU
2004 Proof	10,000	Value: 45.00				

KM# 270.1 10 DOLLARS
28.2800 g., 0.9250 Silver 0.8410 oz. ASW, 38.6 mm. **Obv:** Queen's bust right **Obv. Designer:** Ian Rank-Broadley **Rev:** Peter Rabbit **Edge:** Reeded

Date	Mintage	F	VF	XF	Unc	BU
2004 Proof	5,000	Value: 47.50				

KM# 270.2 10 DOLLARS
28.2800 g., 0.9250 Silver 0.8410 oz. ASW, 38.6 mm. **Obv:** Queen's bust right **Obv. Designer:** Ian Rank-Broadley **Rev:** Multicolor Peter Rabbit **Edge:** Reeded

Date	Mintage	F	VF	XF	Unc	BU
2004 Proof	—	Value: 65.00				

KM# 274 10 DOLLARS
1.2440 g., 0.9999 Gold 0.0400 oz. AGW, 14 mm. **Obv:** Queen's bust right **Obv. Designer:** Ian Rank-Broadley **Rev:** Hernando Pizarro **Edge:** Reeded

Date	Mintage	F	VF	XF	Unc	BU
2004 Proof	350	Value: 80.00				

KM# 282 10 DOLLARS
28.2800 g., 0.9250 Silver 0.8410 oz. ASW, 38.6 mm. **Obv:** Queen's bust right **Obv. Designer:** Ian Rank-Broadley **Rev:** Sailor above two D-Day landing craft **Edge:** Reeded

Date	Mintage	F	VF	XF	Unc	BU
2004 Proof	10,000	Value: 50.00				

KM# 287 10 DOLLARS
31.1035 g., 0.9990 Silver 0.9990 oz. ASW, 38.6 mm. **Obv:** Queen's bust right **Obv. Designer:** Ian Rank-Broadley **Rev:** Dolphin **Edge:** Reeded

Date	Mintage	F	VF	XF	Unc	BU
2004 Proof	10,000	Value: 55.00				

KM# 288 10 DOLLARS
1.2440 g., 0.9999 Gold 0.0400 oz. AGW, 14 mm. **Obv:** Queen's bust right **Obv. Designer:** Ian Rank-Broadley **Rev:** Dolphin **Edge:** Reeded

Date	Mintage	F	VF	XF	Unc	BU
2004 Proof	10,000	Value: 70.00				

KM# 298 10 DOLLARS
28.2800 g., 0.9250 Silver 0.8410 oz. ASW, 38.6 mm. **Obv:** Queen's bust right **Obv. Designer:** Ian Rank-Broadley **Rev:** Soldier above tank and jeeps **Edge:** Reeded

Date	Mintage	F	VF	XF	Unc	BU
2004 Proof	10,000	Value: 50.00				

KM# 301 10 DOLLARS
28.2800 g., 0.9250 Silver 0.8410 oz. ASW, 38.6 mm. **Obv:** Queen's bust right **Obv. Designer:** Ian Rank-Broadley **Rev:** Pilot and planes above D-Day landing **Edge:** Reeded

Date	Mintage	F	VF	XF	Unc	BU
2004 Proof	10,000	Value: 50.00				

KM# 304 10 DOLLARS
28.2800 g., 0.9250 Silver 0.8410 oz. ASW, 38.6 mm. **Obv:** Queen's bust right **Obv. Designer:** Ian Rank-Broadley **Rev:** Ancient Olympic bust, runners and owl coin **Edge:** Reeded

Date	Mintage	F	VF	XF	Unc	BU
2004 Proof	10,000	Value: 50.00				

KM# 307 10 DOLLARS
28.2800 g., 0.9250 Silver 0.8410 oz. ASW, 38.6 mm. **Obv:** Queen's bust right **Obv. Designer:** Ian Rank-Broadley **Rev:** Ancient Olympic bust, charioteer and Zeus coin **Edge:** Reeded

Date	Mintage	F	VF	XF	Unc	BU
2004 Proof	10,000	Value: 50.00				

KM# 313 10 DOLLARS
31.1030 g., 0.9990 Silver 0.9989 oz. ASW, 38.6 mm. **Obv:** Bust of Queen Elizabeth II right **Rev:** Mother and baby dolphin **Edge:** Reeded

Date	Mintage	F	VF	XF	Unc	BU
2005 Proof	10,000	Value: 55.00				

KM# 314 10 DOLLARS
1.2440 g., 0.9999 Gold 0.0400 oz. AGW, 13.92 mm. **Obv:** Bust of Queen Elizabeth II right **Rev:** Mother and baby dolphin **Edge:** Reeded

Date	Mintage	F	VF	XF	Unc	BU
2005 Proof	10,000	Value: 65.00				

KM# 350 10 DOLLARS
28.2800 g., 0.9250 Silver 0.8410 oz. ASW, 38.60 mm. **Ruler:** Elizabeth II **Subject:** 5th Anniversary - Attack on Twin Towers, New York City **Obv:** Crowned bust right **Obv. Legend:** BRITISH VIRGIN ISLANDS — QUEEN ELIZABETH II **Rev:** Twin Towers in sprays, remembrance ribbon privy mark at upper right **Rev. Inscription:** LEST WE FORGET **Edge:** Reeded

Date	Mintage	F	VF	XF	Unc	BU
2006 Proof	10,000	Value: 77.50				

KM# 333 10 DOLLARS
28.2800 g., 0.9167 Silver 0.8334 oz. ASW, 38.60 mm. **Ruler:** Elizabeth II **Subject:** 400th Anniversary Founding of Jamestown **Obv:** Bust with tiara right **Obv. Legend:** BRITISH VIRGIN ISLANDS — QUEEN ELIZABETH II **Rev:** British lion laying, American eagle perched on sprays **Rev. Legend:** UNITED IN FRIENDSHIP **Edge:** Reeded

Date	Mintage	F	VF	XF	Unc	BU
2007 Proof	25,000	Value: 75.00				

KM# 334 10 DOLLARS
1.2444 g., 0.9999 Gold 0.0400 oz. AGW, 13.92 mm. **Ruler:** Elizabeth II **Subject:** 400th Anniversary Founding of Jamestown **Obv:** Bust with tiara right **Obv. Legend:** BRITISH VIRGIN ISLANDS — QUEEN ELIZABETH II **Rev:** British lion laying, American eagle perched on sprays **Rev. Legend:** UNITED IN FRIENDSHIP **Edge:** Reeded

Date	Mintage	F	VF	XF	Unc	BU
2007 Proof	20,000	Value: 75.00				

KM# 339 10 DOLLARS
28.2800 g., Copper-Nickel **Ruler:** Elizabeth II **Subject:** 10th Anniversary Death of Princess Diana **Obv:** Bust with tiara right **Obv. Legend:** BRITISH VIRGIN ISLANDS — QUEEN ELIZABETH II **Rev:** Mother Teresa at left, Princess Diana at right **Rev. Legend:** MOTHER TERESA • IN LOVING MEMORY • PRINCESS DIANA **Edge:** Reeded

Date	Mintage	F	VF	XF	Unc	BU
2007	—	—	—	—	18.50	—

KM# 339a 10 DOLLARS
0.9167 Silver **Ruler:** Elizabeth II **Subject:** 10th Anniversary - Death of Princess Diana **Obv:** Bust with tiara right **Obv. Legend:** BRITISH VIRGIN ISLANDS — QUEEN ELIZABETH II **Rev:** Mother Teresa at left, Princess Diana at right **Rev. Legend:** MOTHER TERESA • IN LOVING MEMORY • PRINCESS DIANA **Edge:** Reeded

Date	Mintage	F	VF	XF	Unc	BU
2007 Proof	—	Value: 75.00				

KM# 341 10 DOLLARS
28.2800 g., Copper-Nickel **Ruler:** Elizabeth II **Subject:** Diamond Wedding Anniversary **Obv:** Conjoined busts with Philip right **Obv. Legend:** BRITISH VIRGIN ISLANDS — QUEEN ELIZABETH II **Rev:** Bride to be and King George VI standing facing **Rev. Legend:** Diamond Wedding of H.M. Queen Elizabeth II & H.R.H. Prince Philip **Rev. Inscription:** THE GIVING AWAY **Edge:** Reeded

Date	Mintage	F	VF	XF	Unc	BU
2007	—	—	—	—	16.50	18.50

KM# 341a 10 DOLLARS
28.2800 g., 0.9250 Silver 0.8410 oz. ASW **Ruler:** Elizabeth II **Subject:** Diamond Wedding Anniversary **Obv:** Conjoined busts with Philip right **Obv. Legend:** BRITISH VIRGIN ISLANDS — QUEEN ELIZABETH II **Rev:** Bride to be and King George VI standing facing **Rev. Legend:** Diamond Wedding of H.M. Queen Elizabeth II & H.R.H. Prince Philip **Rev. Inscription:** THE GIVING AWAY **Edge:** Reeded

Date	Mintage	F	VF	XF	Unc	BU
2007 Proof	—	Value: 75.00				

KM# 342 10 DOLLARS
28.2800 g., Copper-Nickel **Ruler:** Elizabeth II **Subject:** Diamond Wedding Anniversary **Obv:** Conjoined busts with Philip right **Obv. Legend:** BRITISH VIRGIN ISLANDS — QUEEN ELIZABETH II **Rev. Legend:** Diamond Wedding of H.M. Queen Elizabeth II & H.R.H. Prince Philip **Rev. Inscription:** THE GLASS COACH **Edge:** Reeded

Date	Mintage	F	VF	XF	Unc	BU
2007	—	—	—	—	16.50	18.50

KM# 342a 10 DOLLARS
28.2800 g., 0.9250 Silver 0.8410 oz. ASW **Ruler:** Elizabeth II **Subject:** Diamond Wedding Anniversary **Obv:** Conjoined busts with Philip right **Obv. Legend:** BRITISH VIRGIN ISLANDS — QUEEN ELIZABETH II **Rev. Legend:** Diamond Wedding of H.M. Queen Elizabeth II & H.R.H. Prince Philip **Rev. Inscription:** THE GLASS COACH **Edge:** Reeded

Date	Mintage	F	VF	XF	Unc	BU
2007 Proof	—	Value: 75.00				

KM# 343 10 DOLLARS
28.2800 g., Copper-Nickel **Ruler:** Elizabeth II **Subject:** Diamond Wedding Anniversary **Obv:** Conjoined busts with Philip right **Obv. Legend:** BRITISH VIRGIN ISLANDS — QUEEN ELIZABETH II **Rev. Legend:** Diamond Wedding of H.M. Queen Elizabeth II & H.R.H. Prince Philip **Rev. Inscription:** THE HONEYMOON **Edge:** Reeded

Date	Mintage	F	VF	XF	Unc	BU
2007	—	—	—	—	16.50	18.50

KM# 343a 10 DOLLARS
28.2800 g., 0.9250 Silver 0.8410 oz. ASW **Ruler:** Elizabeth II **Subject:** Diamond Wedding Anniversary **Obv:** Conjoined busts with Philip right **Obv. Legend:** BRITISH VIRGIN ISLANDS — QUEEN ELIZABETH II **Rev. Legend:** Diamond Wedding of H.M. Queen Elizabeth II & H.R.H. Prince Philip **Rev. Inscription:** THE HONEYMOON **Edge:** Reeded

Date	Mintage	F	VF	XF	Unc	BU
2007 Proof	—	Value: 75.00				

KM# 344 10 DOLLARS
28.2800 g., Copper-Nickel **Ruler:** Elizabeth II **Subject:** Diamond Wedding Anniversary **Obv:** Conjoined busts with Philip right **Obv. Legend:** BRITISH VIRGIN ISLANDS — QUEEN ELIZABETH II **Rev. Legend:** Diamond Wedding of H.M. Queen Elizabeth II & H.R.H. Prince Philip **Rev. Inscription:** THE WEDDING PROGRAM **Edge:** Reeded

Date	Mintage	F	VF	XF	Unc	BU
2007	—	—	—	—	16.50	18.50

KM# 344a 10 DOLLARS
28.2800 g., 0.9250 Silver 0.8410 oz. ASW **Ruler:** Elizabeth II **Subject:** Diamond Wedding Anniversary **Obv:** Conjoined busts with Philip right **Obv. Legend:** BRITISH VIRGIN ISLANDS — QUEEN ELIZABETH II **Rev. Legend:** Diamond Wedding of H.M. Queen Elizabeth II & H.R.H. Prince Philip **Rev. Inscription:** THE WEDDING PROGRAM **Edge:** Reeded

Date	Mintage	F	VF	XF	Unc	BU
2007 Proof	—	Value: 75.00				

KM# 371 10 DOLLARS
28.2800 g., 0.9250 Silver 0.8410 oz. ASW, 38.6 mm. **Ruler:** Elizabeth II **Obv:** Bust right **Rev:** Two soccer players and leopard

Date	Mintage	F	VF	XF	Unc	BU
2009 Proof	10,000	Value: 40.00				

KM# 372 10 DOLLARS
1.2400 g., 0.9990 Gold 0.0398 oz. AGW, 13.92 mm. **Ruler:** Elizabeth II **Obv:** Bust right **Rev:** Henry VIII facing

Date	Mintage	F	VF	XF	Unc	BU
2009PM Proof	5,000	Value: 80.00				

KM# 374 10 DOLLARS
28.2800 g., 0.9250 Silver 0.8410 oz. ASW, 38.6 mm. **Ruler:** Elizabeth II **Obv:** Bust right **Rev:** Elizabeth I aboard ship

Date	Mintage	F	VF	XF	Unc	BU
2009 Proof	10,000	Value: 40.00				

KM# 376 10 DOLLARS
28.2800 g., 0.9250 Silver 0.8410 oz. ASW, 38.6 mm. **Ruler:** Elizabeth II **Obv:** Bust right **Rev:** Elizabeth I between two columns

Date	Mintage	F	VF	XF	Unc	BU
2009 Proof	10,000	Value: 40.00				

KM# 382 10 DOLLARS
28.2800 g., Copper-Nickel, 38.6 mm. **Ruler:** Elizabeth II **Subject:** Centennial of Naval Aviation **Rev:** 1936 Fairey Swordfish returning to carrier HMS Fencer

Date	Mintage	F	VF	XF	Unc	BU
2009	—	—	—	—	—	7.50

KM# 382a 10 DOLLARS
28.2800 g., Silver, 38.6 mm. **Ruler:** Elizabeth II **Subject:** Centennial of Naval Aviation **Rev:** 1936 Fairey Swordfish returing to carrier HMS Fencer

Date	Mintage	F	VF	XF	Unc	BU
2009 Proof	10,000	Value: 40.00				

KM# 394 10 DOLLARS
28.2800 g., 0.9250 Silver 0.8410 oz. ASW, 38.6 mm. **Ruler:** Elizabeth II **Subject:** Peanuts 60th Anniversary **Rev:** Multicolor Snoopy asleep atop doghouse

Date	Mintage	F	VF	XF	Unc	BU
2010PM Proof	10,000	Value: 40.00				

KM# 395 10 DOLLARS
1.2400 g., 0.9990 Gold 0.0398 oz. AGW, 13.92 mm. **Ruler:** Elizabeth II **Series:** Peanuts 60th Anniversary **Rev:** Snoopy asleep atop doghouse

Date	Mintage	F	VF	XF	Unc	BU
2010PM Proof	10,000	Value: 100				

KM# 397 10 DOLLARS
31.1060 g., 0.9990 Silver 0.9990 oz. ASW, 38.6 mm. **Ruler:** Elizabeth II **Subject:** Elgin Marbles **Rev:** Two horsemen

Date	Mintage	F	VF	XF	Unc	BU
2010PM Proof	10,000	Value: 45.00				

KM# 398 10 DOLLARS
1.2200 g., 0.9990 Gold 0.0392 oz. AGW, 13.92 mm. **Ruler:** Elizabeth II **Subject:** Birth of Venus

Date	Mintage	F	VF	XF	Unc	BU
2010PM Proof	Est. 10,000	Value: 100				

KM# 401 10 DOLLARS
28.2800 g., 0.9250 Silver 0.8410 oz. ASW, 38.6 mm. **Ruler:** Elizabeth II **Subject:** Birth of Venus

Date	Mintage	F	VF	XF	Unc	BU
2010 Proof	Est. 10,000	Value: 50.00				

KM# 201 20 DOLLARS
1.2441 g., 0.9999 Gold 0.0400 oz. AGW, 13.92 mm. **Subject:** Teddy Bear Centennial **Obv:** Queen's bust right **Obv. Designer:** Ian Rank-Broadley **Rev:** Teddy bear **Edge:** Reeded

Date	Mintage	F	VF	XF	Unc	BU
2002 Proof	10,000	Value: 65.00				

KM# 227 20 DOLLARS
1.2400 g., 0.9999 Gold 0.0399 oz. AGW, 13.92 mm. **Subject:** Kennedy Assassination **Obv:** Queen's bust right **Obv. Designer:** Ian Rank-Broadley **Rev:** President Kennedy's portrait **Edge:** Reeded

Date	Mintage	F	VF	XF	Unc	BU
2003 Proof	10,000	Value: 65.00				

KM# 279a 20 DOLLARS
63.5900 g., 0.9990 Silver Gilt 2.0423 oz. ASW, 49.93 mm. **Ruler:** Elizabeth II **Subject:** XXVII Olympic Games **Obv:** Bust with tiara right **Rev:** 1896 Olympic medal design **Edge:** Reeded

Date	Mintage	F	VF	XF	Unc	BU
2004PM Proof	—	Value: 100				

KM# 271 20 DOLLARS
1.2440 g., 0.9999 Gold 0.0400 oz. AGW, 14 mm. **Obv:** Queen's bust right **Obv. Designer:** Ian Rank-Broadley **Rev:** Peter Rabbit **Edge:** Reeded

Date	Mintage	F	VF	XF	Unc	BU
2004 Proof	5,000	Value: 75.00				

KM# 279 20 DOLLARS
58.0000 g., 0.9990 Silver 1.8628 oz. ASW, 50 mm. **Subject:** XXVIII Olympic Games **Obv:** Bust with tiara right **Obv. Designer:** Ian Rank-Broadley **Rev:** 1896 Olympic medal design **Edge:** Reeded

Date	Mintage	F	VF	XF	Unc	BU
2004PM Proof	2,004	Value: 85.00				

KM# 345 20 DOLLARS
3.9600 g., 0.7500 Gold 0.0955 oz. AGW, 21.78 mm. **Ruler:** Elizabeth II **Subject:** 500th Anniversary - Death of Columbus **Obv:** Crowned bust right **Obv. Legend:** BRITISH VIRGIN ISLANDS - QUEEN ELIZABETH II **Rev:** Bust of Columbus facing 3/4 left at right, outlined map of the Americas at left **Rev. Legend:** 1451 - CHRISTOPHER COLUMBUS - 1506 **Edge:** Reeded **Note:** Struck in white gold.

Date	Mintage	F	VF	XF	Unc	BU
2006 Proof	1,506	Value: 150				

KM# 346 20 DOLLARS
4.0200 g., 0.7500 Gold 0.0969 oz. AGW, 21.78 mm. **Ruler:** Elizabeth II **Subject:** 500th Anniversary - Death of Columbus **Obv:** Crowned bust right **Obv. Legend:** BRITISH VIRGIN ISLANDS - QUEEN ELIZABETH II **Rev:** Sailing ship "Santa Maria" **Rev. Legend:** 1451 - CHRISTOPHER COLUMBUS - 1506 **Edge:** Reeded **Note:** Struck in rose gold.

Date	Mintage	F	VF	XF	Unc	BU
2006 Proof	1,506	Value: 150				

KM# 347 20 DOLLARS
3.9900 g., 0.7500 Gold 0.0962 oz. AGW, 21.78 mm. **Ruler:** Elizabeth II **Subject:** 500th Anniversary - Death of Columbus **Obv:** Crowned bust right **Obv. Legend:** BRITISH VIRGIN ISLANDS - QUEEN ELIZABETH II **Rev:** Sailing ships "Niña" and "Pinta" **Rev. Legend:** 1451 - CHRISTOPHER COLUMBUS - 1506 **Edge:** Reeded **Note:** Struck in yellow gold.

Date	Mintage	F	VF	XF	Unc	BU
2006 Proof	1,506	Value: 150				

KM# 379 30 DOLLARS
155.5000 g., 0.9990 Silver 4.9942 oz. ASW **Ruler:** Elizabeth II **Subject:** Nelson's Victory at Trafalgar **Rev:** Two ships

Date	Mintage	F	VF	XF	Unc	BU
2008 Proof	—	Value: 250				

KM# 275 25 DOLLARS
3.1100 g., 0.9999 Gold 0.1000 oz. AGW, 18 mm. **Obv:** Queen's bust right **Obv. Designer:** Ian Rank-Broadley **Rev:** Hernando Pizarro portrait and life events pictorial **Edge:** Reeded

Date	Mintage	F	VF	XF	Unc	BU
2004 Proof	350	Value: 175				

KM# 289 25 DOLLARS
3.1100 g., 0.9999 Gold 0.1000 oz. AGW, 18 mm. **Obv:** Queen's bust right **Obv. Designer:** Ian Rank-Broadley **Rev:** Dolphin **Edge:** Reeded

Date	Mintage	F	VF	XF	Unc	BU
2004 Proof	6,000	Value: 160				

KM# 315 25 DOLLARS
3.1100 g., 0.9999 Gold 0.1000 oz. AGW, 18 mm. **Obv:** Bust of Queen Elizabeth II right **Rev:** Mother and baby dolphins **Edge:** Reeded

Date	Mintage	F	VF	XF	Unc	BU
2005 Proof	6,000	Value: 160				

KM# 335 25 DOLLARS
3.1120 g., 0.9999 Gold AGW 0.1004 0.1000 oz. AGW, 17.95 mm. **Ruler:** Elizabeth II **Subject:** 400th Anniversary Founding of Jamestown **Obv:** Bust with tiara right **Obv. Legend:** BRITISH VIRGIN ISLANDS - QUEEN ELIZABETH II **Rev:** British lion laying, American eagle perched on sprays **Rev. Legend:** UNITED IN FRIENDSHIP **Edge:** Reeded

Date	Mintage	VG	F	VF	XF	Unc
2007 Proof	7,500	Value: 160				

KM# 202 50 DOLLARS
3.1104 g., 0.9999 Gold 0.1000 oz. AGW, 17.95 mm. **Subject:** Teddy Bear Centennial **Obv:** Queen's bust right **Obv. Designer:** Ian Rank-Broadley **Rev:** Teddy bear **Edge:** Reeded

Date	Mintage	F	VF	XF	Unc	BU
2002 Proof	7,000	Value: 160				

KM# 272 50 DOLLARS
3.1100 g., 0.9999 Gold 0.1000 oz. AGW, 18 mm. **Obv:** Queen's bust right **Obv. Designer:** Ian Rank-Broadley **Rev:** Peter Rabbit **Edge:** Reeded

Date	Mintage	F	VF	XF	Unc	BU
2004 Proof	3,000	Value: 165				

KM# 276 50 DOLLARS
6.2200 g., 0.9999 Gold 0.1999 oz. AGW, 22 mm. **Obv:** Queen's bust right **Obv. Designer:** Ian Rank-Broadley **Rev:** Treasure ship with blue color sail **Edge:** Reeded

Date	Mintage	F	VF	XF	Unc	BU
2004 Proof	350	Value: 350				

KM# 290 50 DOLLARS
6.2200 g., 0.9999 Gold 0.1999 oz. AGW, 22 mm. **Obv:** Queen's bust right **Obv. Designer:** Ian Rank-Broadley **Rev:** Dolphin **Edge:** Reeded

Date	Mintage	F	VF	XF	Unc	BU
2004 Proof	3,500	Value: 325				

KM# 316 50 DOLLARS
6.2200 g., 0.9999 Gold 0.1999 oz. AGW, 22 mm. **Obv:** Bust of Queen Elizabeth II right **Rev:** Mother and baby dolphins **Edge:** Reeded

Date	Mintage	F	VF	XF	Unc	BU
2005	3,500	Value: 325				

KM# 351 50 DOLLARS
6.2200 g., 0.9999 Gold 0.1999 oz. AGW, 22.00 mm. **Ruler:** Elizabeth II **Subject:** 5th Anniversary - Attack on Twin Towers, New York City **Obv:** Crowned bust right **Obv. Legend:** BRISH VIRGIN ISLANDS - QUEEN ELIZABETH II **Rev:** Twin Towers in sprays, remembrance ribbon privy mark at upper right **Rev. Inscription:** LEST WE FORGET **Edge:** Reeded

Date	Mintage	F	VF	XF	Unc	BU
2006 Proof	2,000	Value: 335				

KM# 336 50 DOLLARS
6.2230 g., 0.9999 Gold AGW 0.1999 0.2000 oz. AGW, 22.00 mm. **Ruler:** Elizabeth II **Subject:** 400th Anniversary Founding of Jamestown **Obv:** Bust with tiara right **Obv. Legend:** BRITISH VIRGIN ISLANDS - QUEEN ELIZABETH II **Rev:** British lion laying, American eagle perched on sprays **Rev. Legend:** UNITED IN FRIENDSHIP **Edge:** Reeded

Date	Mintage	F	VF	XF	Unc	BU
2007 Proof	5,000	Value: 300				

KM# 377 50 DOLLARS
6.2200 g., 0.9990 Gold 0.1998 oz. AGW, 22 mm. **Ruler:** Elizabeth II **Obv:** Bust right **Rev:** Elizabeth II aboard ship with 1mm pearl

Date	Mintage	F	VF	XF	Unc	BU
2009 Proof	750	Value: 350				

KM# 378 50 DOLLARS
6.2200 g., 0.9990 Gold 0.1998 oz. AGW, 22 mm. **Ruler:** Elizabeth II **Obv:** Bust right **Rev:** Elizabeth II between two columns, .01ct ruby insert

Date	Mintage	F	VF	XF	Unc	BU
2009 Proof	750	Value: 350				

KM# 285 75 DOLLARS
11.0000 g., Bi-Metallic .990 Titanium 2g center in .9999 Gold 9g ring, 36.5 mm. **Obv:** Queen's bust right **Obv. Designer:** Ian Rank-Broadley **Rev:** British Guiana stamp design **Edge:** Reeded

Date	Mintage	F	VF	XF	Unc	BU
2004 Proof	2,500	Value: 400				

KM# 389 75 DOLLARS
Bi-Metallic Titanium and gold **Ruler:** Elizabeth II **Subject:** Mozart

Date	Mintage	F	VF	XF	Unc	BU
2006PM Proof	—	Value: 400				

KM# 388 75 DOLLARS
Titanium **Ruler:** Elizabeth II **Subject:** Bejing Olympics

Date	Mintage	F	VF	XF	Unc	BU
2009PM Proof	—	Value: 35.00				

KM# 182 100 DOLLARS
6.2200 g., 0.9990 Gold 0.1998 oz. AGW, 22 mm. **Subject:** Sir Francis Drake **Obv:** Queen's bust right **Obv. Designer:** Ian Rank-Broadley **Rev:** Ship, portrait and map **Edge:** Reeded

Date	Mintage	F	VF	XF	Unc	BU
2002 Proof	5,000	Value: 300				

KM# 185 100 DOLLARS
6.2200 g., 0.9990 Gold 0.1998 oz. AGW, 22 mm. **Subject:** Sir Walter Raleigh **Obv:** Queen's bust right **Obv. Designer:** Ian Rank-Broadley **Rev:** Ship, portrait and map **Edge:** Reeded

Date	Mintage	F	VF	XF	Unc	BU
2002 Proof	5,000	Value: 300				

KM# 189 100 DOLLARS
6.2208 g., 0.9999 Gold 0.2000 oz. AGW, 22 mm. **Subject:** Queen's Golden Jubilee **Obv:** Queen's bust right **Obv. Designer:** Ian Rank-Broadley **Rev:** Queen on horse **Edge:** Reeded

Date	Mintage	F	VF	XF	Unc	BU
2002 Proof	2,002	Value: 335				

KM# 192 100 DOLLARS
6.2208 g., 0.9999 Gold 0.2000 oz. AGW, 22 mm. **Subject:** Queen's Golden Jubilee **Obv:** Queen's bust right **Obv. Designer:** Ian Rank-Broadley **Rev:** Queen on throne **Edge:** Reeded

Date	Mintage	F	VF	XF	Unc	BU
2002 Proof	2,002	Value: 335				

KM# 195 100 DOLLARS
6.2208 g., 0.9999 Gold 0.2000 oz. AGW, 22 mm. **Subject:** Queen's Golden Jubilee **Obv:** Queen's bust right **Obv. Designer:** Ian Rank-Broadley **Rev:** Queen with President Ronald Reagan and Mrs. Nancy Reagan **Edge:** Reeded

Date	Mintage	F	VF	XF	Unc	BU
2002 Proof	2,002	Value: 335				

KM# 198 100 DOLLARS
6.2208 g., 0.9999 Gold 0.2000 oz. AGW, 22 mm. **Subject:** Queen's Golden Jubilee **Obv:** Queen's bust right **Obv. Designer:** Ian Rank-Broadley **Rev:** Carnival dancers **Edge:** Reeded

Date	Mintage	F	VF	XF	Unc	BU
2002 Proof	2,002	Value: 335				

KM# 203 100 DOLLARS
6.2200 g., 0.9999 Gold 0.1999 oz. AGW, 22 mm. **Subject:** Teddy Bear Centennial **Obv:** Queen's bust right **Obv. Designer:** Ian Rank-Broadley **Rev:** Teddy bear **Edge:** Reeded

Date	Mintage	F	VF	XF	Unc	BU
2002 Proof	5,000	Value: 300				

KM# 206 100 DOLLARS
6.2200 g., 0.9999 Gold 0.1999 oz. AGW, 22 mm. **Subject:** Princess Diana **Obv:** Queen's bust right **Obv. Designer:** Ian Rank-Broadley **Rev:** Diana's portrait **Edge:** Reeded

Date	Mintage	F	VF	XF	Unc	BU
2002 Proof	5,000	Value: 300				

KM# 209.1 100 DOLLARS
6.2200 g., 0.9999 Gold 0.1999 oz. AGW, 22 mm. **Subject:** September 11, 2001 **Obv:** Queen's bust right **Obv. Designer:** Ian Rank-Broadley **Rev:** World Trade Center twin towers **Edge:** Reeded

Date	Mintage	F	VF	XF	Unc	BU
2002 Proof	5,000	Value: 300				

KM# 209.2 100 DOLLARS
6.2200 g., 0.9999 Gold 0.1999 oz. AGW, 22 mm. **Subject:** September 11, 2001 **Obv:** Queen's bust right **Obv. Designer:** Ian Rank-Broadley **Rev:** Holographic multicolor World Trade Center twin towers **Edge:** Reeded

Date	Mintage	F	VF	XF	Unc	BU
2002 Proof	5,000	Value: 300				

KM# 212 100 DOLLARS
6.2200 g., 0.9999 Gold 0.1999 oz. AGW, 22 mm. **Subject:** September 11, 2001 **Obv:** Queen's bust right **Obv. Designer:** Ian Rank-Broadley **Rev:** Statue of Liberty **Edge:** Reeded

Date	Mintage	F	VF	XF	Unc	BU
2002 Proof	5,000	Value: 300				

KM# 215 100 DOLLARS
6.2200 g., 0.9999 Gold 0.1999 oz. AGW, 22 mm. **Subject:** Queen Mother Series **Obv:** Queen's bust right **Obv. Designer:** Ian Rank-Broadley **Rev:** Queen Mother with young Prince Charles **Edge:** Reeded

Date	Mintage	F	VF	XF	Unc	BU
2002PM Proof	5,000	Value: 300				

KM# 218 100 DOLLARS
6.2200 g., 0.9999 Gold 0.1999 oz. AGW, 22 mm. **Subject:** Queen Mother Series **Obv:** Queen's bust right **Obv. Designer:** Ian Rank-Broadley **Rev:** Queen Mother with four grandchildren **Edge:** Reeded

Date	Mintage	F	VF	XF	Unc	BU
2002PM Proof	5,000	Value: 275				

KM# 221 100 DOLLARS
6.2200 g., 0.9999 Gold 0.1999 oz. AGW, 22 mm. **Subject:** Queen Mother Series **Obv:** Queen's bust right **Obv. Designer:** Ian Rank-Broadley **Rev:** Queen Mother with uniformed Prince Charles **Edge:** Reeded

Date	Mintage	F	VF	XF	Unc	BU
2002PM Proof	5,000	Value: 300				

KM# 224 100 DOLLARS
6.2200 g., 0.9999 Gold 0.1999 oz. AGW, 22 mm. **Subject:** Queen Mother Series **Obv:** Queen's bust right **Obv. Designer:** Ian Rank-Broadley **Rev:** Queen Mother's coffin **Edge:** Reeded

Date	Mintage	F	VF	XF	Unc	BU
2002PM Proof	5,000	Value: 300				

KM# 228 100 DOLLARS
6.2200 g., 0.9999 Gold 0.1999 oz. AGW, 22 mm. **Subject:** Kennedy Assassination **Obv:** Queen's bust right **Obv. Designer:** Ian Rank-Broadley **Rev:** President Kennedy's portrait **Edge:** Reeded

Date	Mintage	F	VF	XF	Unc	BU
2003 Proof	5,000	Value: 300				

KM# 231 100 DOLLARS
15.5500 g., 0.9999 Gold 0.4999 oz. AGW, 30 mm. **Subject:** Powered Flight Centennial **Obv:** Queen's bust right **Obv. Designer:** Ian Rank-Broadley **Rev:** Three historic airplanes and rocket **Edge:** Reeded

Date	Mintage	F	VF	XF	Unc	BU
2003 Proof	—	Value: 750				

KM# 234 100 DOLLARS
6.2200 g., 0.9999 Gold 0.1999 oz. AGW, 22 mm. **Obv:** Queen's bust right **Obv. Designer:** Ian Rank-Broadley **Rev:** Henry VIII and Elizabeth I **Edge:** Reeded

Date	Mintage	F	VF	XF	Unc	BU
2003 Proof	5,000	Value: 300				

KM# 237 100 DOLLARS
6.2200 g., 0.9999 Gold 0.1999 oz. AGW, 22 mm. **Obv:** Queen's bust right **Obv. Designer:** Ian Rank-Broadley **Rev:** Matthew Parker, Archbishop of Canterbury **Edge:** Reeded

Date	Mintage	F	VF	XF	Unc	BU
2003 Proof	5,000	Value: 300				

KM# 240 100 DOLLARS
6.2200 g., 0.9999 Gold 0.1999 oz. AGW, 22 mm. **Obv:** Queen's bust right **Obv. Designer:** Ian Rank-Broadley **Rev:** Sir Francis Drake and ships **Edge:** Reeded

Date	Mintage	F	VF	XF	Unc	BU
2003 Proof	5,000	Value: 275				

KM# 243 100 DOLLARS
6.2200 g., 0.9999 Gold 0.1999 oz. AGW, 22 mm. **Obv:** Queen's bust right **Obv. Designer:** Ian Rank-Broadley **Rev:** Sir Walter Raleigh **Edge:** Reeded

Date	Mintage	F	VF	XF	Unc	BU
2003 Proof	5,000	Value: 300				

KM# 246 100 DOLLARS
6.2200 g., 0.9999 Gold 0.1999 oz. AGW, 22 mm. **Obv:** Queen's bust right **Obv. Designer:** Ian Rank-Broadley **Rev:** Sir William Shakespeare **Edge:** Reeded

Date	Mintage	F	VF	XF	Unc	BU
2003 Proof	5,000	Value: 300				

KM# 249 100 DOLLARS
6.2200 g., 0.9999 Gold 0.1999 oz. AGW, 22 mm. **Obv:** Queen's bust right **Obv. Designer:** Ian Rank-Broadley **Rev:** Elizabeth I above her funeral procession **Edge:** Reeded

Date	Mintage	F	VF	XF	Unc	BU
2003 Proof	5,000	Value: 300				

KM# 252 100 DOLLARS
6.2200 g., 0.9999 Gold 0.1999 oz. AGW, 22 mm. **Subject:** Olympics **Obv:** Queen's bust right **Obv. Designer:** Ian Rank-Broadley **Rev:** Ancient Olympic bust, runners in background and coin upper right **Edge:** Reeded

Date	Mintage	F	VF	XF	Unc	BU
2003 Proof	5,000	Value: 300				

KM# 255 100 DOLLARS
6.2200 g., 0.9999 Gold 0.1999 oz. AGW, 22 mm. **Subject:** Olympics **Obv:** Queen's bust right **Obv. Designer:** Ian Rank-Broadley **Rev:** Ancient bust, charioteer and coin **Edge:** Reeded

Date	Mintage	F	VF	XF	Unc	BU
2003 Proof	5,000	Value: 300				

KM# 273.1 100 DOLLARS
6.2200 g., 0.9999 Gold 0.1999 oz. AGW, 22 mm. **Obv:** Queen's bust right **Obv. Designer:** Ian Rank-Broadley **Rev:** Peter Rabbit **Edge:** Reeded

Date	Mintage	F	VF	XF	Unc	BU
2004 Proof	2,000	Value: 335				

KM# 273.2 100 DOLLARS
6.2200 g., 0.9999 Gold 0.1999 oz. AGW, 22 mm. **Obv:** Queen's bust right **Obv. Designer:** Ian Rank-Broadley **Rev:** Multicolor Peter Rabbit **Edge:** Reeded

Date	Mintage	F	VF	XF	Unc	BU
2004 Proof	—	Value: 335				

KM# 283 100 DOLLARS
6.2200 g., 0.9999 Gold 0.1999 oz. AGW, 22 mm. **Obv:** Queen's bust right **Obv. Designer:** Ian Rank-Broadley **Rev:** Sailor above two D-Day landing craft **Edge:** Reeded

Date	Mintage	F	VF	XF	Unc	BU
2004 Proof	5,000	Value: 300				

KM# 299 100 DOLLARS
6.2200 g., 0.9999 Gold 0.1999 oz. AGW, 22 mm. **Obv:** Queen's bust right **Obv. Designer:** Ian Rank-Broadley **Rev:** Soldier above tank and jeeps **Edge:** Reeded

Date	Mintage	F	VF	XF	Unc	BU
2004 Proof	5,000	Value: 300				

KM# 302 100 DOLLARS
6.2200 g., 0.9999 Gold 0.1999 oz. AGW, 22 mm. **Obv:** Queen's bust right **Obv. Designer:** Ian Rank-Broadley **Rev:** Pilot and planes above D-Day landing **Edge:** Reeded

Date	Mintage	F	VF	XF	Unc	BU
2004 Proof	5,000	Value: 300				

KM# 305 100 DOLLARS
6.2200 g., 0.9999 Gold 0.1999 oz. AGW, 22 mm. **Obv:** Queen's bust right **Obv. Designer:** Ian Rank-Broadley **Rev:** Ancient Olympic bust, runners and owl coin **Edge:** Reeded

Date	Mintage	F	VF	XF	Unc	BU
2004 Proof	5,000	Value: 300				

KM# 308 100 DOLLARS
6.2200 g., 0.9999 Gold 0.1999 oz. AGW, 22 mm. **Obv:** Queen's bust right **Obv. Designer:** Ian Rank-Broadley **Rev:** Ancient Olympic bust, charioteer and Zeus coin **Edge:** Reeded

Date	Mintage	F	VF	XF	Unc	BU
2004 Proof	5,000	Value: 300				

KM# 317 125 DOLLARS
15.5510 g., 0.9999 Gold 0.4999 oz. AGW, 30 mm. **Obv:** Bust of Queen Elizabeth II right **Rev:** Mother and baby dolphin **Edge:** Reeded

Date	Mintage	F	VF	XF	Unc	BU
2005	1,500	Value: 775				

KM# 337 125 DOLLARS
15.5590 g., 0.9999 Gold AGW 0.5000 0.5002 oz. AGW, 30.00 mm. **Ruler:** Elizabeth II **Subject:** 400th Anniversary Founding of Jamestown **Obv:** Bust with tiara right **Obv. Legend:** BRITISH VIRGIN ISLANDS - QUEEN ELIZABETH II **Rev:** British lion laying, American eagle perched on sprays **Rev. Legend:** UNITED IN FRIENDSHIP **Edge:** Reeded

Date	Mintage	F	VF	XF	Unc	BU
2007 Proof	3,000	Value: 750				

KM# 309 250 DOLLARS
15.5517 g., 0.9990 Gold 0.4995 oz. AGW, 30 mm. **Obv:** Queen's bust right **Obv. Designer:** Ian Rank-Broadley **Rev:** Statue of Liberty and the date "11 Sept. 2001" **Edge:** Reeded

Date	Mintage	F	VF	XF	Unc	BU
2002	250	Value: 850				

KM# 280 250 DOLLARS
58.0000 g., 0.5000 Gold 0.9323 oz. AGW, 50 mm. **Obv:** Queen's bust right **Obv. Designer:** Ian Rank-Broadley **Rev:** 1896 Olympic medal design **Edge:** Reeded

Date	Mintage	F	VF	XF	Unc	BU
2004 Proof	1,000	Value: 1,450				

KM# 318 250 DOLLARS
31.1030 g., 0.9999 Gold 0.9998 oz. AGW, 32.7 mm. **Obv:** Bust of Queen Elizabeth II right **Rev:** Mother and baby dolphin **Edge:** Reeded

Date	Mintage	F	VF	XF	Unc	BU
2005 Proof	750	Value: 1,500				

KM# 390 250 DOLLARS
Gold **Ruler:** Elizabeth II **Subject:** Mozart

Date	Mintage	F	VF	XF	Unc	BU
2006PM Proof	—	Value: 1,500				

KM# 338 250 DOLLARS
31.1030 g., 0.9999 Gold AGW 0.9999 0.9998 oz. AGW, 32.70 mm. **Ruler:** Elizabeth II **Subject:** 400th Anniversary Founding of Jamestown **Obv:** Bust with tiara right **Obv. Legend:** BRITISH VIRGIN ISLANDS - QUEEN ELIZABETH II **Rev:** British lion laying, American eagle perched on sprays **Rev. Legend:** UNITED IN FRIENDSHIP **Edge:** Reeded

Date	Mintage	F	VF	XF	Unc	BU
2007 Proof	1,000	Value: 1,500				

KM# 277 500 DOLLARS
160.7562 g., 0.9990 Gold 5.1630 oz. AGW, 150 mm. **Obv:** Queen's bust right **Obv. Designer:** Ian Rank-Broadley **Rev:** Gold-plated portrait of Hernando Pizarro, small inset emerald above Pizarro's life events pictoral **Edge:** Reeded **Note:** Photo reduced.

Date	Mintage	F	VF	XF	Unc	BU
2004 Proof	500	Value: 8,000				

KM# 348 500 DOLLARS
160.7562 g., 0.9990 Gold 5.1630 oz. AGW, 150.00 mm. **Ruler:** Elizabeth II **Subject:** 500th Anniversary - Death of Columbus **Obv:** Crowned bust right **Obv. Legend:** BRITISH VIRGIN ISLANDS - QUEEN ELIZABETH II **Rev:** Ship in background at left, Columbus standing at right with right arm outstreched looking right, compass below. **Rev. Legend:** 1451 - DISCOVERER OF AMERICA - CHRISTOPHER COLUMBUS - 1506 **Edge:** Reeded

Date	Mintage	F	VF	XF	Unc	BU
2006 Proof	1,506	Value: 7,750				

KM# 392 500 DOLLARS
160.7560 g., 0.9990 Silver 5.1630 oz. ASW, 150 mm. **Ruler:** Elizabeth II **Subject:** Battle of Trafalgar **Rev:** Two naval ships in battle

Date	Mintage	F	VF	XF	Unc	BU
2008PM Proof	—	Value: 2,500				

MINT SETS

KM#	Date	Mintage	Identification	Issue Price	Mkt Val
MS12	2007 (4)	—	KM# 341 - 344	65.00	80.00

PROOF SETS

KM#	Date	Mintage	Identification	Issue Price	Mkt Val
PS20	2007 (4)	—	KM# 341a - 344a	300	300

BRUNEI

South China Sea
PHILIPPINES
MALAYSIA
MALAYSIA
SINGAPORE
Indian Ocean
INDONESIA

Negara Brunei Darussalam (State of Brunei), an independent sultanate on the northwest coast of the island of Borneo, has an area of 2,226 sq. mi. (5,765 sq. km.) and a population of *326,000. Capital: Bandar Seri Begawan. Crude oil and rubber are exported.

TITLES

نكري بروني

Negri Brunei

RULERS
Sultan Hassanal Bolkiah I, 1967-

SULTANATE

DECIMAL COINAGE

100 Sen = 1 Dollar (Ringgit)

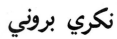

KM# 34 SEN
1.7500 g., Copper Clad Steel, 17.74 mm. **Ruler:** Sultan Hassanal Bolkiah **Obv:** Uniformed bust facing **Rev:** Native design, denomination below, date at right **Edge:** Plain

Date	Mintage	F	VF	XF	Unc	BU
2001	576,000	—	—	0.15	0.40	0.50
2002	804,900	—	—	0.15	0.40	0.50
2004	—	—	—	0.15	0.40	0.50
2005	—	—	—	0.15	0.40	0.50

KM# 35 5 SEN
1.4100 g., Copper-Nickel, 16.26 mm. **Ruler:** Sultan Hassanal Bolkiah **Obv:** Uniformed bust facing **Rev:** Native design, denomination below, date at right **Edge:** Reeded

Date	Mintage	F	VF	XF	Unc	BU
2001	808,000	—	—	0.20	0.50	0.75
2002	1,418,178	—	—	0.20	0.50	0.75
2004	—	—	—	0.20	0.50	0.75
2005	—	—	—	0.20	0.50	0.75
2006	—	—	—	0.20	0.50	0.75
2008	—	—	—	0.20	0.50	0.75

KM# 36 10 SEN
2.8200 g., Copper-Nickel, 19.4 mm. **Ruler:** Sultan Hassanal Bolkiah **Obv:** Uniformed bust facing **Rev:** Native design, denomination below, date at right **Edge:** Reeded

Date	Mintage	F	VF	XF	Unc	BU
2001	164,000	—	—	0.30	0.75	1.00
2002	476,452	—	—	0.30	0.75	1.00
2005	—	—	—	0.30	0.75	1.00
2006	—	—	—	0.30	0.75	1.00

KM# 37 20 SEN
5.6500 g., Copper-Nickel, 23.5 mm. **Ruler:** Sultan Hassanal Bolkiah **Obv:** Uniformed bust facing **Rev:** Native design, denomination below, date at right **Edge:** Reeded

Date	Mintage	F	VF	XF	Unc	BU
2001	270,647	—	—	0.45	1.10	1.50
2002	597,272	—	—	0.45	1.10	1.50
2004	—	—	—	0.45	1.10	1.50
2005	—	—	—	0.45	1.10	1.50
2008	—	—	—	0.45	1.10	1.50

KM# 38 50 SEN
9.3300 g., Copper-Nickel, 27.7 mm. **Ruler:** Sultan Hassanal Bolkiah **Obv:** Uniformed bust facing **Rev:** National arms within circle, denomination below, date at right **Edge:** Security

Date	Mintage	F	VF	XF	Unc	BU
2001	50,000	—	—	1.00	2.50	3.00
2002	1,325	—	—	1.40	3.50	5.00
2005	—	—	—	0.75	1.80	2.50
2006	—	—	—	0.75	1.80	2.50

KM# 80 2 DOLLARS
31.1000 g., Copper-Nickel, 40.7 mm. **Ruler:** Sultan Hassanal Bolkiah **Subject:** 20th Anniversary of Independence **Obv:** Bust 3/4 left, facing **Obv. Legend:** SULTAN HAJI HASSANAL BOLKIAH **Rev:** National arms **Rev. Legend:** NEGARI BRUNEI DARUSSALAM

Date	Mintage	F	VF	XF	Unc	BU
2004 Proof	4,000	Value: 65.00				

KM# 86 2 DOLLARS
31.1000 g., Copper-Nickel, 40.7 mm. **Ruler:** Sultan Hassanal Bolkiah **Subject:** 60th Birthday **Obv:** Bust 3/4 left, facing **Obv. Legend:** SULTAN HAJI HASSANAL BOLKIAH **Rev:** Multicolor 1/2-length figure in civilian clothes, facing

Date	Mintage	F	VF	XF	Unc	BU
2006 Proof	200	Value: 120				

KM# 77 3 DOLLARS
24.0000 g., Copper-Nickel, 40 mm. **Ruler:** Sultan Hassanal Bolkiah **Obv:** Uniformed bust facing **Obv. Legend:** SULTAN HAJI HASSANAL BOLKIAH **Rev:** Logo at center **Rev. Legend:** COMMONWEALTH FINANCE MINISTERS MEETING **Edge:** Reeded

Date	Mintage	F	VF	XF	Unc	BU
2003 Proof	4,000	Value: 40.00				

KM# 83 3 DOLLARS
31.1000 g., Copper-Nickel, 40.7 mm. **Ruler:** Sultan Hassanal Bolkiah **Subject:** Royal Wedding **Obv:** Multicolor portraits of Royal couple

Date	Mintage	F	VF	XF	Unc	BU
2004 Proof	5,000	Value: 50.00				

KM# 81 20 DOLLARS
31.1000 g., 0.9990 Silver 0.9988 oz. ASW, 40.7 mm. **Ruler:** Sultan Hassanal Bolkiah **Subject:** 20th Anniversary of Independence **Obv:** Bust 3/4 left, facing **Obv. Legend:** SULTAN HAJI HASSANAL BOLKIAH **Rev:** National arms **Rev. Legend:** NEGARI BRUNEI DARUSSALAM

Date	Mintage	F	VF	XF	Unc	BU
2004 Proof	1,000	Value: 120				

KM# 87 20 DOLLARS
31.1000 g., 0.9990 Silver 0.9988 oz. ASW, 40.7 mm. **Ruler:** Sultan Hassanal Bolkiah **Subject:** 60th Birthday **Obv:** Bust 3/4 left, facing **Obv. Legend:** SULTAN HAJI HASSANAL BOLKIAH **Rev:** Multicolor 1/2-length figure in civilian clothes, facing

Date	Mintage	F	VF	XF	Unc	BU
2006 Proof	200	Value: 275				

KM# 78 30 DOLLARS
62.2000 g., 0.9990 Silver 1.9977 oz. ASW **Ruler:** Sultan Hassanal Bolkiah **Subject:** Commonwealth Finance Ministers' Meeting **Obv:** Logo at upper left, multicolor bust of Sultan 3/4 left, facing at right **Obv. Legend:** SULTAN HAJI HASSANAL BOLIAH **Rev:** World map at left - center, national arms at upper right **Shape:** Rectangular, 65 x 31 mm

Date	Mintage	F	VF	XF	Unc	BU
2003 Proof	1,000	Value: 210				

KM# 84 30 DOLLARS
31.1000 g., 0.9990 Silver 0.9988 oz. ASW, 40.7 mm. **Ruler:** Sultan Hassanal Bolkiah **Subject:** Royal Wedding **Obv:** Multicolor portraits of Royal couple

Date	Mintage	F	VF	XF	Unc	BU
2004 Proof	1,000	Value: 180				

KM# 82 200 DOLLARS
31.1000 g., 0.9999 Gold 0.9997 oz. AGW, 32.1 mm. **Ruler:** Sultan Hassanal Bolkiah **Subject:** 20th Anniversary of Independence **Obv:** Bust 3/4 left, facing **Obv. Legend:** SULTAN HAJI HASSANAL BOLKIAH **Rev:** National arms **Rev. Legend:** NEGARI BRUNEI DARUSSALAM

Date	Mintage	F	VF	XF	Unc	BU
2004 Proof	200	Value: 1,600				

KM# 85 200 DOLLARS
31.1000 g., 0.9999 Gold 0.9997 oz. AGW, 32 mm. **Ruler:** Sultan Hassanal Bolkiah **Subject:** Royal Wedding **Obv:** Multicolor portraits of Royal couple

Date	Mintage	F	VF	XF	Unc	BU
2004 Proof	200	Value: 1,600				

KM# 88 200 DOLLARS
31.1000 g., 0.9999 Gold 0.9997 oz. AGW, 32.1 mm. **Ruler:** Sultan Hassanal Bolkiah **Subject:** 60th Birthday **Obv:** Bust 3/4 left, facing **Obv. Legend:** SULTAN HAJI HASSANAL BOLKIAH **Rev:** Multicolor 1/2-length figure in civilian clothes, facing

Date	Mintage	F	VF	XF	Unc	BU
2006 Proof	200	Value: 1,800				

PROOF SETS

KM#	Date	Mintage	Identification	Issue Price	Mkt Val
PS20	2003 (2)	500	KM#77-78	—	250
PS21	2004 (3)	200	KM80-82	—	1,800
PS22	2004 (3)	200	KM83-85	—	1,850
PS23	2006 (3)	200	KM86-88	—	2,200

BULGARIA

The Republic of Bulgaria, formerly the Peoples Republic of Bulgaria, a Balkan country on the Black Sea in southeastern Europe, has an area of 42,855 sq. mi. (110,910 sq. km.) and a population of *8.31 million. Capital: Sofia. Agriculture remains a key component of the economy but industrialization, particularly heavy industry, has been emphasized since the late 1940s. Machinery, tobacco and cigarettes, wines and spirits, clothing and metals are the chief exports. Bulgaria joined the European Union in January 2007.

MONETARY SYSTEM
100 Stotinki = 1 Lev

REPUBLIC

REFORM COINAGE

KM# 237 STOTINKA
1.8000 g., Aluminum-Bronze, 16 mm. **Obv:** Madara horseman right, animal below **Rev:** Denomination above date **Edge:** Plain

Date	Mintage	F	VF	XF	Unc	BU
2002 Proof	10,000	Value: 1.00				

KM# 237a STOTINKA
1.8000 g., Brass Plated Steel, 16 mm. **Obv:** Madara horseman right **Rev:** Denomination above date

Date	Mintage	F	VF	XF	Unc	BU
2002 Proof	10,000	Value: 1.00				

KM# 238a 2 STOTINKI
2.5000 g., Brass Plated Steel, 18 mm. **Obv:** Madara horseman right **Rev:** Denomination above date

Date	Mintage	F	VF	XF	Unc	BU
2002 Proof	10,000	Value: 1.50				

KM# 238 2 STOTINKI
2.5000 g., Aluminum-Bronze, 18 mm. **Obv:** Madara horseman right, animal below **Rev:** Denomination above date **Edge:** Plain

Date	Mintage	F	VF	XF	Unc	BU
2002 Proof	10,000	Value: 1.50				

KM# 239a 5 STOTINKI
3.5000 g., Brass Plated Steel, 20 mm. **Obv:** Madara horseman right **Rev:** Denomination above date

Date	Mintage	F	VF	XF	Unc	BU
2002 Proof	10,000	Value: 2.00				

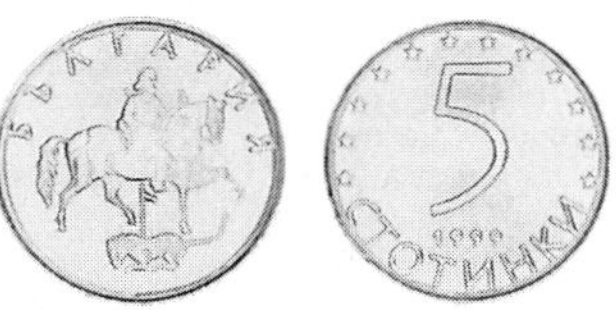

KM# 239 5 STOTINKI
3.5000 g., Aluminum-Bronze, 20 mm. **Obv:** Madara horseman right, animal below **Rev:** Denomination above date **Edge:** Plain **Note:** Prev. KM#A239.

Date	Mintage	F	VF	XF	Unc	BU
2002 Proof	10,000	Value: 2.00				

KM# 240 10 STOTINKI
3.0000 g., Copper-Nickel-Zinc, 18.5 mm. **Obv:** Madara horseman right, animal below **Rev:** Denomination above date **Edge:** Reeded

Date	Mintage	F	VF	XF	Unc	BU
2002 Proof	10,000	Value: 2.50				

KM# 241 20 STOTINKI
4.0000 g., Copper-Nickel-Zinc, 20.5 mm. **Obv:** Madara horseman right, animal below **Rev:** Denomination above date **Edge:** Reeded

Date	Mintage	F	VF	XF	Unc	BU
2002 Proof	10,000	Value: 3.00				

KM# 242 50 STOTINKI
5.0000 g., Copper-Nickel-Zinc, 22.5 mm. **Obv:** Madara horseman right, animal below **Rev:** Denomination above date **Edge:** Reeded

Date	Mintage	F	VF	XF	Unc	BU
2002 Proof	10,000	Value: 5.00				

KM# 272 50 STOTINKI
5.0000 g., Copper-Nickel-Zinc, 22.5 mm. **Obv:** Stylized Bulgarian arms, lion left, NATO - 2004 under lion **Rev:** Denomination above date **Edge:** Reeded

Date	Mintage	F	VF	XF	Unc	BU
2004	—	—	—	—	2.00	3.00

KM# 282 50 STOTINKI
5.0000 g., Copper-Nickel-Zinc, 22.5 mm. **Obv:** European Union seated woman allegory **Rev:** Value above date **Edge:** Reeded **Note:** Prev. KM#274.

Date	Mintage	F	VF	XF	Unc	BU
2005	—	—	—	—	1.25	1.75

KM# 291 50 STOTINKI
5.0000 g., Copper-Nickel-Zinc, 22.5 mm. **Obv:** Value **Rev:** Pillar behind open book **Edge:** Reeded **Note:** Prev. KM#276.

Date	Mintage	F	VF	XF	Unc	BU
2007	500,000	—	—	—	—	1.50

KM# 254 LEV
7.0000 g., Bi-Metallic Copper-Nickel center in Brass ring, 24.5 mm. **Obv:** St. Ivan of Rila **Rev:** Denomination **Edge:** Segmented reeding

Date	Mintage	F	VF	XF	Unc	BU
2002	24,842,000	—	—	—	3.00	4.00
2002 Proof	10,000	Value: 10.00				

KM# 257 LEV
15.5500 g., 0.9990 Gold 0.4994 oz. AGW **Obv:** St. Ivan of Rila **Rev:** Large number one **Edge:** Plain

Date	Mintage	F	VF	XF	Unc	BU
2002 Proof	2,000	Value: 750				

KM# 290 1.95583 LEVA
20.0000 g., 0.9990 Silver Partially gold plated 0.6423 oz. ASW, 40 mm. **Subject:** Bulgaria in the EU **Obv:** National Arms **Rev:** Column and open window design **Rev. Designer:** Bogomil Nikolov and Elena Dimitrova

Date	Mintage	F	VF	XF	Unc	BU
2007 Proof	14,000	Value: 45.00				

KM# 304 2 LEVA
16.4000 g., 0.9990 Copper 0.5267 oz., 34.2 mm. **Subject:** Dechko, Uzunov 110th Anniversary of Birth **Obv:** National arms **Rev:** Petar Stoikov

Date	Mintage	F	VF	XF	Unc	BU
2009 Proof	8,000	Value: 15.00				

KM# 258 5 LEVA
1.2400 g., 0.9990 Gold 0.0398 oz. AGW **Obv:** Denomination **Rev:** Olympic archer **Edge:** Plain

Date	Mintage	F	VF	XF	Unc	BU
2002 Proof	12,000	Value: 65.00				

KM# 259 5 LEVA
1.2400 g., 0.9990 Gold 0.0398 oz. AGW **Obv:** Denomination **Rev:** Olympic cyclist **Edge:** Plain

Date	Mintage	F	VF	XF	Unc	BU
2002 Proof	12,000	Value: 65.00				

KM# 260 5 LEVA
1.2400 g., 0.9990 Gold 0.0398 oz. AGW **Obv:** Denomination **Rev:** Olympic fencing **Edge:** Plain

Date	Mintage	F	VF	XF	Unc	BU
2002 Proof	12,000	Value: 65.00				

KM# 261 5 LEVA
1.2400 g., 0.9990 Gold 0.0398 oz. AGW **Obv:** Denomination **Rev:** Olympic wrestling **Edge:** Plain

Date	Mintage	F	VF	XF	Unc	BU
2002 Proof	12,000	Value: 65.00				

KM# 262 5 LEVA
1.2400 g., 0.9990 Gold 0.0398 oz. AGW, 14 mm. **Obv:** Denomination **Rev:** Olympic gymnastics **Edge:** Plain

Date	Mintage	F	VF	XF	Unc	BU
2002 Proof	12,000	Value: 65.00				

KM# 263 5 LEVA
1.2400 g., 0.9990 Gold 0.0398 oz. AGW, 14 mm. **Obv:** Denomination **Rev:** Olympics founder Pierre du Coubertin **Edge:** Plain

Date	Mintage	F	VF	XF	Unc	BU
2002 Proof	17,000	Value: 65.00				

KM# 264 5 LEVA
1.2400 g., 0.9990 Gold 0.0398 oz. AGW, 14 mm. **Obv:** Denomination **Rev:** Olympic running **Edge:** Plain

Date	Mintage	F	VF	XF	Unc	BU
2002 Proof	12,000	Value: 65.00				

KM# 265 5 LEVA
1.2400 g., 0.9990 Gold 0.0398 oz. AGW, 14 mm. **Obv:** Denomination **Rev:** Olympic swimming **Edge:** Plain

Date	Mintage	F	VF	XF	Unc	BU
2002 Proof	12,000	Value: 65.00				

KM# 266 5 LEVA
1.2400 g., 0.9990 Gold 0.0398 oz. AGW, 14 mm. **Obv:** Denomination **Rev:** Olympic tennis **Edge:** Plain

Date	Mintage	F	VF	XF	Unc	BU
2002 Proof	12,000	Value: 65.00				

KM# 267 5 LEVA
1.2400 g., 0.9990 Gold 0.0398 oz. AGW, 14 mm. **Obv:** Denomination **Rev:** Olympic weight lifting **Edge:** Plain

Date	Mintage	F	VF	XF	Unc	BU
2002 Proof	12,000	Value: 65.00				

KM# 274 5 LEVA
15.0000 g., Copper-Nickel, 34.2 mm. **Subject:** Sourvakari **Obv:** National arms **Rev:** Multicolor children in winter clothes **Rev. Designer:** Stephan Nenov

Date	Mintage	F	VF	XF	Unc	BU
2002 Proof	5,000	Value: 15.00				

KM# 276 5 LEVA
15.0000 g., Copper-Nickel, 34.2 mm. **Obv:** National arms, date and denomination below **Rev:** Multicolor child on rocking horse **Edge:** Plain **Note:** Prev. KM#275.

Date	Mintage	F	VF	XF	Unc	BU
2003 Proof	10,000	Value: 35.00				

KM# 268 5 LEVA
28.2800 g., 0.9250 Silver 0.8410 oz. ASW, 38.5 mm. **Obv:** Denomination **Rev:** FIFA Soccer trophy cup **Edge:** reeded

Date	Mintage	F	VF	XF	Unc	BU
2003 Proof	50,000	Value: 40.00				

KM# 277 5 LEVA
15.0000 g., Copper-Nickel, 34.2 mm. **Subject:** Palm Sunday **Obv:** National Arms **Rev:** Bogomil Nikolov and Elena Dimitrova

Date	Mintage	F	VF	XF	Unc	BU
2004 Proof	10,000	Value: 15.00				

KM# 279 5 LEVA
15.0000 g., Copper-Nickel, 34.2 mm. **Subject:** Baba Marta **Obv:** National Arms **Rev:** Multicolor flora and butterfly **Rev. Designer:** Vanya Dimitrova

Date	Mintage	F	VF	XF	Unc	BU
2005 Proof	10,000	Value: 15.00				

KM# 284 5 LEVA
23.3000 g., 0.5000 Silver 0.3745 oz. ASW, 38.6 mm. **Subject:** Bulgaria Crafts - winemaking **Obv:** National Arms **Rev:** Multicolor grapes - wine caraffe **Rev. Designer:** Ivan Todorov and Plamen Dzhermanov

Date	Mintage	F	VF	XF	Unc	BU
2006 Proof	10,000	Value: 30.00				

KM# 296 5 LEVA
23.3000 g., 0.5000 Silver 0.3745 oz. ASW, 38.6 mm. **Subject:** Bulgarian Crafts - Carpet Weaving **Obv:** National Arms **Rev:** Ivan Todorov and Plamen Dzhermanov

Date	Mintage	F	VF	XF	Unc	BU
2007 Proof	7,000	Value: 30.00				

KM# 305 5 LEVA
23.3000 g., 0.9990 Silver 0.7483 oz. ASW, 38.6 mm. **Subject:** Bulgarian National Bank, 130th Anniversary **Obv:** Bank emblem **Obv. Designer:** Razvigor Kolev and Borislav Kyossev **Rev:** Multicolor lion mozaic, fragment of stained glass

Date	Mintage	F	VF	XF	Unc	BU
2009 Proof	4,000	Value: 45.00				

KM# 306 5 LEVA
0.5000 Silver **Subject:** Traditional Bulgarian Crafts - Pottery **Rev:** Color pot and design

Date	Mintage	F	VF	XF	Unc	BU
2009	—	—	—	—	—	35.00

KM# 247 10 LEVA
23.3300 g., 0.9250 Silver 0.6938 oz. ASW, 38.5 mm. **Subject:** Olympics **Obv:** National arms, date and denomination below **Rev:** Ski jumper **Edge:** Plain with serial number

Date	Mintage	F	VF	XF	Unc	BU
2001 Proof	25,000	Value: 45.00				

KM# 246 10 LEVA
23.6000 g., 0.9250 Silver 0.7018 oz. ASW, 38.5 mm. **Subject:** Higher Education **Obv:** National arms, date and denomination below **Rev:** Graduate before building **Edge:** Plain

Date	Mintage	F	VF	XF	Unc	BU
2001 Proof	10,000	Value: 45.00				

KM# 275 10 LEVA
23.3000 g., 0.9250 Silver 0.6929 oz. ASW, 38.6 mm. **Obv:** National arms **Rev:** Head and Star of David **Rev. Designer:** Peter Stoikov

Date	Mintage	F	VF	XF	Unc	BU
2003 Proof	2,000	Value: 40.00				

KM# 270 10 LEVA
23.3300 g., 0.9990 Silver 0.7493 oz. ASW, 38.6 mm. **Subject:** National Theater Centennial **Edge:** Plain

Date	Mintage	F	VF	XF	Unc	BU
2004 Proof	5,000	Value: 50.00				

KM# 273 10 LEVA
23.2000 g., 0.9250 Silver 0.6899 oz. ASW, 38.5 mm. **Obv:** National arms, date and denomination below **Rev:** St. Nikolay Mirlikiisky Chudofvorez with gold-plated crosses and halo **Edge:** Plain

Date	Mintage	F	VF	XF	Unc	BU
2004 Proof	10,000	Value: 45.00				

KM# 280 10 LEVA
23.3000 g., 0.9250 Silver 0.6929 oz. ASW, 38.6 mm. **Subject:** XX Olympic Games - Turino, Italy **Obv:** National arms **Rev:** Short track speed skater **Rev. Designer:** Plamen Chernev

Date	Mintage	F	VF	XF	Unc	BU
2005 Proof	4,000	Value: 40.00				

KM# 283 10 LEVA
20.0000 g., 0.9990 Silver Partially gold plated 0.6423 oz. ASW, 40 mm. **Obv:** National arms **Rev:** Ancient sculpture

Date	Mintage	F	VF	XF	Unc	BU
2005 Proof	10,000	Value: 45.00				

KM# 285 10 LEVA
23.3000 g., 0.9250 Silver 0.6929 oz. ASW, 38.6 mm. **Subject:** National Parks - Black Sea Coast **Obv:** National arms **Rev:** Map and three circular motifs **Rev. Designer:** Eugenia Isankoa and Plamen Chernev

Date	Mintage	F	VF	XF	Unc	BU
2006 Proof	7,000	Value: 40.00				

KM# 286 10 LEVA
20.0000 g., 0.9990 Silver 0.6423 oz. ASW, 40 mm. **Subject:** Treasures of Bulgaria - Letnitsa **Obv:** National arms **Rev:** Horseman statue **Rev. Designer:** Eugenie Evtimov

Date	Mintage	F	VF	XF	Unc	BU
2006 Proof	10,000	Value: 40.00				

KM# 295 10 LEVA
23.3000 g., 0.9250 Silver 0.6929 oz. ASW, 38.6 mm. **Subject:** National Parks - Pirin Mountain **Obv:** National arms **Rev:** Vanya Dimitrova

Date	Mintage	F	VF	XF	Unc	BU
2007 Proof	6,000	Value: 40.00				

KM# 297 10 LEVA
20.0000 g., 0.9990 Silver Partially gold plated 0.6423 oz. ASW, 40 mm. **Subject:** Treasures of Bulgaria - Pegasus from Vayovo **Obv:** National arms **Rev:** Pegasus forepart **Rev. Designer:** Razvigor Klov, Borislav Kyossev and Krassimis Angelov

Date	Mintage	F	VF	XF	Unc	BU
2007 Proof	10,000	Value: 45.00				

KM# 292 10 LEVA
31.1000 g., 0.9990 Silver 0.9988 oz. ASW, 40 mm. **Subject:** Boris Christov **Obv:** National arms **Obv. Legend:** БЪЛГАРСКА НАРОДНА БАНКА **Rev:** Early regal 1/2-length male figure facing holding orb **Rev. Legend:** ИМЕНИТИ БЪГАРСКИ ГЛАСОВЕ **Note:** Prev. KM#277.

Date	Mintage	F	VF	XF	Unc	BU
2007 Proof	10,000	Value: 50.00				

KM# 298 10 LEVA
23.3000 g., 0.9250 Silver 0.6929 oz. ASW, 38.6 mm. **Subject:** 130th Anniversary Bulgarian Liberation **Obv:** National arms **Rev:** Two figures in 19th century coats

Date	Mintage	F	VF	XF	Unc	BU
2008 Proof	10,000	Value: 40.00				

KM# 299 10 LEVA
23.3000 g., 0.9250 Silver 0.6929 oz. ASW, 38.6 mm. **Subject:** Shooting sports **Obv:** National Arms **Rev:** Target, bowhunter, rifleman **Rev. Designer:** Todor Todorov and Yana Vassileva

Date	Mintage	F	VF	XF	Unc	BU
2008 Proof	5,000	Value: 40.00				

KM# 300 10 LEVA
20.0000 g., 0.9990 Silver Partially gold plated 0.6423 oz. ASW, 40 mm. **Subject:** Treasures of Bulgaria - Sevt III **Obv:** Statue head of King Sevt III **Rev:** Elena Todorova and Todor Todorav

Date	Mintage	F	VF	XF	Unc	BU
2008 Proof	8,000	Value: 45.00				

KM# 301 10 LEVA
23.3000 g., 0.9250 Silver 0.6929 oz. ASW, 38.6 mm. **Subject:** Bulgarian Independence - 100th Anniversary **Rev:** Crowned shield **Rev. Designer:** Ivan Todorov

Date	Mintage	F	VF	XF	Unc	BU
2008 Proof	5,000	Value: 40.00				

KM# 302 10 LEVA
31.1000 g., 0.9990 Silver Partially gold plated 0.9988 oz. ASW, 40 mm. **Subject:** Great Bulgarian Voices: Nikolay Gyaurov **Obv:** National arms **Rev:** Elena Todorov and Todor Todorov

Date	Mintage	F	VF	XF	Unc	BU
2008 Proof	6,000	Value: 50.00				

KM# 269 20 LEVA
1.5500 g., 0.9990 Gold 0.0498 oz. AGW, 16 mm. **Obv:** Denomination **Rev:** Mother of God **Edge:** Plain

Date	Mintage	F	VF	XF	Unc	BU
2003 Proof	20,000	Value: 80.00				

KM# 287 20 LEVA
1.5500 g., 0.9990 Gold 0.0498 oz. AGW, 13.9 mm. **Subject:** Iconography St John the Baptist **Obv:** National arms **Rev:** Saint facing **Rev. Designer:** Rada Dimitroua

Date	Mintage	F	VF	XF	Unc	BU
2006 Proof	12,000	Value: 80.00				

KM# 294 20 LEVA
1.5500 g., 0.9990 Gold 0.0498 oz. AGW, 13.9 mm. **Subject:** Iconography - St. George the Victorious **Rev:** St. George slaying dragon **Rev. Designer:** Plamen Chernev

Date	Mintage	F	VF	XF	Unc	BU
2007 Proof	8,000	Value: 80.00				

KM# 303 20 LEVA
1.5500 g., 0.9990 Gold 0.0498 oz. AGW, 13.9 mm. **Subject:** Tsar Boris I, the Baptist **Obv:** Half-length figure facing **Rev:** Krassimir Angelov, Borislav Kyossev, Razvigov Kolev

Date	Mintage	F	VF	XF	Unc	BU
2008 Proof	8,000	Value: 80.00				

KM# 293 100 LEVA
8.6400 g., 0.9990 Gold 0.2775 oz. AGW **Subject:** Iconography - St. George the Victorious **Obv:** National arms **Rev:** Plamen Chernev

Date	Mintage	F	VF	XF	Unc	BU
2007 Proof	1,500	Value: 450				

KM# 307 100 LEVA
7.7700 g., 0.9990 Gold 0.2496 oz. AGW, 22 mm. **Subject:** Bulgarian Iconography - St. Dimitar the Wonder Worker

Date	Mintage	F	VF	XF	Unc	BU
2009 Proof	—	Value: 375				

KM# 271 125 LEVA
7.7800 g., 0.9990 Gold 0.2499 oz. AGW, 21 mm. **Subject:** Bulgarian National Bank 125th Anniversary

Date	Mintage	F	VF	XF	Unc	BU
2004 Proof	3,000	Value: 375				

PIEFORTS

KM#	Date	Mintage	Identification	Mkt Val
P4	2004	5,000	10 Leva. 0.9990 Silver. 46.6600 g. 100 Years - National Theatre, 38.61mm.	75.00

PROOF SETS

KM#	Date	Mintage	Identification	Issue Price	Mkt Val
PS8	2002 (7)	10,000	KM#237-242, 254	—	25.00

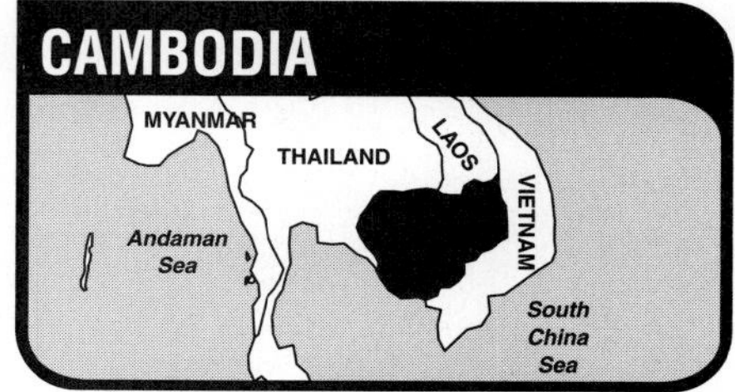

The State of Cambodia, formerly Democratic Kampuchea and the Khmer Republic, a land of paddy fields and forest-clad hills located on the Indo-Chinese peninsula, fronting on the Gulf of Thailand, has an area of 70,238 sq. mi. (181,040 sq. km.) and a population of *11.21 million. Capital: Phnom Penh. Agriculture is the basis of the economy, with rice the chief crop. Native industries include cattle breeding, weaving and rice milling. Rubber, cattle, corn, and timber are exported.

RULERS

Kings of Cambodia

Norodom Sihanouk, 1991-1993

Chairman, Supreme National Council

King, 1993-

KINGDOM
1993 -

DECIMAL COINAGE

KM# 98 500 RIELS

19.9200 g., Brass, 38.7 mm. **Subject:** Angkor Wat **Obv:** Armless statue of Jayavarman VII **Rev:** View of Angkor Wat in center **Edge:** Reeded

Date	Mintage	F	VF	XF	Unc	BU
2001	28,000	—	—	—	7.50	10.00

KM# 99 3000 RIELS

1.2441 g., 0.9999 Gold 0.0400 oz. AGW, 13.92 mm. **Subject:** Angkor Wat **Obv:** Armless statue of Jayavarman VII **Rev:** View of Angkor Wat in center **Edge:** Reeded

Date	Mintage	F	VF	XF	Unc	BU
2001	28,000	—	—	—	70.00	80.00

KM# 100 3000 RIELS

20.0000 g., 0.9250 Silver 0.5948 oz. ASW, 38.7 mm. **Subject:** Buddha **Obv:** Armless statue of Jayavarman VII **Rev:** Radiant Buddha next to a carved Buddha face **Edge:** Reeded

Date	Mintage	F	VF	XF	Unc	BU
2001 Proof	10,000	Value: 55.00				

KM# 101 3000 RIELS

20.0000 g., 0.9250 Silver 0.5948 oz. ASW, 38.7 mm. **Subject:** Apsara Dance **Obv:** Armless statue of Jayavarman VII **Rev:** Dancer next to multicolor carpet pattern **Edge:** Reeded

Date	Mintage	F	VF	XF	Unc	BU
2001 Proof	10,000	Value: 60.00				

KM# 103 3000 RIELS

20.0000 g., 0.9990 Silver 0.6423 oz. ASW, 38.7 mm. **Obv:** King Jayavarman VII (1162-1201) **Rev:** Multicolor Tutankhamen's mask **Edge:** Reeded

Date	Mintage	F	VF	XF	Unc	BU
2004 Proof	9,100	Value: 65.00				

KM# 104 3000 RIELS

1.2440 g., 0.9990 Gold 0.0400 oz. AGW, 13.92 mm. **Obv:** King Jayavarman VII (1162-1201) **Rev:** Sphinx and pyramid **Edge:** Reeded

Date	Mintage	F	VF	XF	Unc	BU
2004 Proof	27,900	Value: 95.00				

KM# 124 3000 RIELS

1.2400 g., 0.9990 Gold 0.0398 oz. AGW, 13.92 mm. **Rev:** Pyramids

Date	Mintage	F	VF	XF	Unc	BU
2004	—	—	—	—	70.00	80.00

KM# 126 3000 RIELS

1.2200 g., 0.9990 Gold 0.0392 oz. AGW, 13.92 mm. **Rev:** Taj Mahal

Date	Mintage	F	VF	XF	Unc	BU
2005	—	—	—	—	70.00	80.00

KM# 127 3000 RIELS

31.1050 g., Silver, 38.7 mm. **Rev:** Indian Dancer, multicolor

Date	Mintage	F	VF	XF	Unc	BU
2005	—	Value: 65.00				

KM# 129 3000 RIELS

1.2200 g., 0.9990 Gold 0.0392 oz. AGW, 13.92 mm. **Rev:** Colosseum in Rome

Date	Mintage	F	VF	XF	Unc	BU
2006	—	—	—	—	70.00	80.00

KM# 130 3000 RIELS

Silver, 38.7 mm. **Rev:** Multicolor Roman soldier

Date	Mintage	F	VF	XF	Unc	BU
2006 Proof	—	Value: 80.00				

KM# 110 3000 RIELS

31.1050 g., 0.9990 Silver 0.9990 oz. ASW, 40.7 mm. **Subject:** Year of the Dog **Rev:** Multicolor St. Bernard

Date	Mintage	F	VF	XF	Unc	BU
2006 Prooflike	4,000	—	—	—	—	80.00

KM# 111 3000 RIELS

31.1050 g., 0.9990 Silver 0.9990 oz. ASW, 40.7 mm. **Subject:** Year of the Dog **Rev:** Multicolor Bloodhound

Date	Mintage	F	VF	XF	Unc	BU
2006 Prooflike	4,000	—	—	—	—	80.00

KM# 112 3000 RIELS

31.1050 g., 0.9990 Silver 0.9990 oz. ASW, 40.7 mm. **Subject:** Year of the Dog **Rev:** Multicolor Siberian Husky

Date	Mintage	F	VF	XF	Unc	BU
2006 Prooflike	4,000	—	—	—	—	80.00

KM# 113 3000 RIELS

31.1050 g., 0.9990 Silver 0.9990 oz. ASW, 40.7 mm. **Subject:** Year of the Dog **Rev:** Multicolor Shar Pei

Date	Mintage	F	VF	XF	Unc	BU
2006 Prooflike	4,000	—	—	—	—	80.00

KM# 114 3000 RIELS

31.1050 g., 0.9990 Silver 0.9990 oz. ASW, 40.7 mm. **Subject:** Year of the Dog **Rev:** Multicolor Borzaya

Date	Mintage	F	VF	XF	Unc	BU
2006 Prooflike	51,000	—	—	—	—	80.00

KM# 115 3000 RIELS

31.1050 g., 0.9990 Silver 0.9990 oz. ASW, 40.7 mm. **Subject:** Year of the Dog **Rev:** Multicolor Labrador

Date	Mintage	F	VF	XF	Unc	BU
2006 Prooflike	51,000	—	—	—	—	80.00

KM# 116 3000 RIELS

31.1050 g., 0.9990 Silver 0.9990 oz. ASW, 40.7 mm. **Subject:** Year of the Dog **Rev:** Multicolor Russian Spaniel

Date	Mintage	F	VF	XF	Unc	BU
2006 Prooflike	51,000	—	—	—	—	80.00

KM# 117 3000 RIELS

31.1050 g., 0.9990 Silver 0.9990 oz. ASW, 40.7 mm. **Subject:** Year of the Dog **Rev:** Multiocolor Newfoundland

Date	Mintage	F	VF	XF	Unc	BU
2006 Prooflike	51,000	—	—	—	—	80.00

KM# 132 3000 RIELS

1.2200 g., 0.9990 Gold 0.0392 oz. AGW, 13.92 mm. **Rev:** Borobudur Temple, Indonesia

Date	Mintage	F	VF	XF	Unc	BU
2007	28,000	—	—	—	70.00	80.00

KM# 133 3000 RIELS

31.1050 g., 0.9990 Silver 0.9990 oz. ASW, 38.7 mm. **Rev:** Legomo dancer, multicolor

Date	Mintage	F	VF	XF	Unc	BU
2007 Proof	10,000	Value: 80.00				

KM# 118 3000 RIELS

31.1050 g., 0.9990 Silver 0.9990 oz. ASW, 40.7 mm. **Subject:** Year of the Pig **Rev:** Multicolor pig

Date	Mintage	F	VF	XF	Unc	BU
2007 Prooflike	—	—	—	—	—	80.00

KM# 121 3000 RIELS
1.2400 g., 0.9990 Gold 0.0398 oz. AGW, 13.9 mm. **Subject:** Statue torso **Rev:** Shwe Dragon Pagoda, Mynamar

Date	Mintage	F	VF	XF	Unc	BU
2008 Proof	—	Value: 75.00				

KM# 123 3000 RIELS
31.1035 g., 0.9990 Silver 0.9990 oz. ASW, 40.7 mm. **Obv:** Statue torso **Rev:** Multicolor Padaung

Date	Mintage	F	VF	XF	Unc	BU
2009 Proof	—	Value: 75.00				

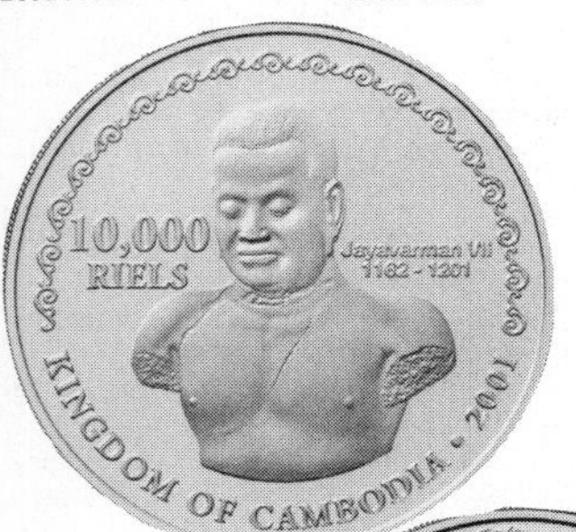

KM# 102 10000 RIELS
31.1035 g., 0.9990 Bi-Metallic Gold center in silver ring. 0.9990 oz., 40.7 mm. **Subject:** Angkor Wat **Obv:** Armless statue of Jayavarman **Rev:** Multicolor holographic view of Angkor Wat in center **Edge:** Reeded

Date	Mintage	F	VF	XF	Unc	BU
2001 Proof	3,000	Value: 325				

KM# 125 10000 RIELS
31.1050 g., 0.9990 Silver 0.9990 oz. ASW, 40.7 mm. **Rev:** Great Wall of China, holographic insert

Date	Mintage	F	VF	XF	Unc	BU
2003 Proof	—	Value: 300				

KM# 105 10000 RIELS
31.1035 g., 0.9990 Silver 0.9990 oz. ASW, 40.7 mm. **Obv:** King Jayavarman VII (1162-1201) **Rev:** Sphinx and pyramid on holographic gold insert **Edge:** Reeded

Date	Mintage	F	VF	XF	Unc	BU
2004 Proof	2,100	Value: 300				

KM# 119 10000 RIELS
31.1050 g., 0.9990 Silver 0.9990 oz. ASW, 38.7 mm. **Subject:** Zheng He 600th Anniversary **Rev:** Sailing ship with latent image

Date	Mintage	F	VF	XF	Unc	BU
2005 Proof	200	Value: 150				

KM# 120 10000 RIELS
31.1050 g., 0.9990 Silver 0.9990 oz. ASW, 38.7 mm. **Subject:** Zheng He 600th Anniversary **Rev:** Multicolor figure standing

Date	Mintage	F	VF	XF	Unc	BU
2005 Proof	200	Value: 150				

KM# 128 10000 RIELS
31.1050 g., 0.9990 Silver 0.9990 oz. ASW, 40.7 mm. **Rev:** Taj Mahal in multicolor hologram at center

Date	Mintage	F	VF	XF	Unc	BU
2005 Proof	—	Value: 300				

KM# 131 10000 RIELS
31.1050 g., 0.9990 Silver 0.9990 oz. ASW, 40.7 mm. **Rev:** Colosseum in multicolor hologram

Date	Mintage	F	VF	XF	Unc	BU
2006 Proof	—	Value: 300				

KM# 134 10000 RIELS
31.1050 g., 0.9990 Silver 0.9990 oz. ASW, 40.7 mm. **Rev:** Boraburdur temple, Indonesia

Date	Mintage	F	VF	XF	Unc	BU
2007 Proof	300	Value: 300				

KM# 122 10000 RIELS
31.1035 g., 0.9990 Silver 0.9990 oz. ASW, 40.7 mm. **Obv:** Statue torso **Rev:** Hologram of Shwe Dragon Pagoda, Mynamar

Date	Mintage	F	VF	XF	Unc	BU
2009 Proof	—	Value: 150				

CAMEROON

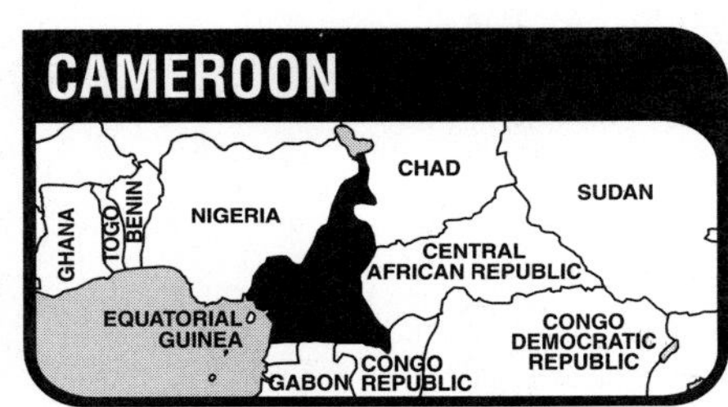

The Republic of Cameroon, located in west-central Africa on the Gulf of Guinea, has an area of 183,569 sq. mi. (475,445 sq. km.) and a population of *15.13 million. Capital: Yaounde. About 90 percent of the labor force is employed on the land; cash crops account for 80 percent of the country's export revenue. Cocoa, coffee, aluminum, cotton, rubber, and timber are exported. Cameroon is a member of the Commonwealth of Nations. The President is the Head of State; the Prime Minister is the Head of Government.

MINT MARKS
(a) - Paris, privy marks only
SA - Pretoria, 1943

MONETARY SYSTEM
100 Centimes = 1 Franc

REPUBLIC

STANDARD COINAGE

KM# 34 1000 FRANCS
25.0000 g., Copper-Nickel, 39 mm. **Obv:** Arms **Rev:** Papillons D'Amour butterfly **Edge:** Reeded

Date	Mintage	F	VF	XF	Unc	BU
2010 Proof	—	Value: 65.00				

CANADA

Canada is located to the north of the United States, and spans the full breadth of the northern portion of North America from Atlantic to Pacific oceans, except for the State of Alaska. It has a total area of 3,850,000 sq. mi. (9,971,550 sq. km.) and a population of 30.29 million. Capital: Ottawa.

Canada is a member of the Commonwealth of Nations. Elizabeth II is Head of State as Queen of Canada.

RULER
British 1763-

MONETARY SYSTEM
1 Dollar = 100 Cents

CONFEDERATION

CIRCULATION COINAGE

KM# 289 CENT

2.2500 g., Copper Plated Steel, 19.05 mm. **Ruler:** Elizabeth II **Obv:** Crowned head right **Obv. Designer:** Dora dePédery-Hunt **Rev:** Maple twig design **Rev. Designer:** George E. Kruger-Gray **Edge:** Round and plain

Date	Mintage	MS-63	Proof
2001	919,358,000	0.30	—
2001P Proof	—	—	5.00
2003	92,219,775	0.30	—
2003P Proof	—	—	5.00
2003P	235,936,799	1.50	—

KM# 445 CENT

2.2500 g., Copper Plated Steel, 19.1 mm. **Ruler:** Elizabeth II **Subject:** Elizabeth II Golden Jubilee **Obv:** Crowned head right, Jubilee commemorative dates 1952-2002 **Obv. Designer:** Dora dePédery-Hunt **Rev:** Denomination above maple leaves **Rev. Designer:** George E. Kruger-Gray **Edge:** Plain

Date	Mintage	MS-63	Proof
ND(2002)	716,366,000	0.75	—
ND(2002)P	114,212,000	1.00	—
ND(2002)P Proof	32,642	—	5.00

KM# 445a CENT

0.9250 Silver **Ruler:** Elizabeth II **Subject:** Elizabeth II Golden Jubilee **Obv:** Crowned head right, Jubilee commemorative dates 1952-2002 **Obv. Designer:** Dora dePédery-Hunt **Rev:** Denomination above maple leaves **Rev. Designer:** George E. Kruger-Gray

Date	Mintage	MS-63	Proof
ND(2002)	21,537	—	3.00

KM# 490 CENT

2.2500 g., Copper Plated Zinc, 19.05 mm. **Ruler:** Elizabeth II **Obv:** New effigy of Queen Elizabeth II right **Obv. Designer:** Susanna Blunt **Rev:** Two maple leaves **Edge:** Plain

Date	Mintage	MS-63	Proof
2003	56,877,144	0.25	—
2004	653,317,000	0.25	—
2004 Proof	—	—	2.50
2005	759,658,000	0.25	—
2005 Proof	—	—	2.50
2006	886,275,000	0.25	—
2006 Proof	—	—	2.50

KM# 490a CENT

2.2500 g., Copper Plated Steel, 19.05 mm. **Ruler:** Elizabeth II **Obv:** Bust right **Obv. Designer:** Susanna Blunt **Rev:** Two maple leaves **Rev. Designer:** G. E. Kruger-Gray

Date	Mintage	MS-63	Proof
2003P	591,257,000	0.25	—
2003 WP	Inc. above	0.25	—
2004P	134,906,000	0.25	—
2005P	30,525,000	0.25	—
2006P	137,733,000	0.25	—
2006(ml)	Inc. above	0.25	—
2007(ml)	938,270,000	0.25	—
2007(ml) Proof	—	—	2.50
2008(ml)	787,625,000	0.25	—
2008(ml) Proof	—	—	2.50
2009(ml)	455,680,000	0.25	—
2009(ml) Proof	—	—	2.50
2010(ml)	—	0.25	—
2010(ml) Proof	—	—	2.50
2011(ml)	—	0.25	—
2011(ml) Proof	—	—	2.50

KM# 468 CENT

2.5000 g., Copper **Ruler:** Elizabeth II **Subject:** 50th Anniversary of the Coronation of Elizabeth II **Obv:** 1953 Effigy of the Queen, Jubilee commemorative dates 1952-2002 **Obv. Designer:** Mary Gillick

Date	Mintage	MS-63	Proof
ND(2002) Proof	—	—	2.50

KM# 490b CENT

2.2500 g., Copper Plated Zinc **Ruler:** Elizabeth II **Obv:** Head right **Rev:** Maple leaf, selectively gold plated **Note:** Bound into Annual Report.

Date	Mintage	MS-63	Proof
2003 Proof	7,746	—	35.00

KM# 1023 CENT

Copper, 19.1 mm. **Ruler:** Elizabeth II **Obv:** George V bust left **Rev:** Value within wreath, dual dates below

Date	Mintage	MS-63	Proof
1935-2010 Proof	—	—	10.00

KM# 410 3 CENTS

3.1100 g., 0.9250 Silver Gilt 0.0925 oz. ASW, 21.3 mm. **Ruler:** Elizabeth II **Subject:** 1st Canadian Postage Stamp **Obv:** Crowned head right **Obv. Designer:** Dora dePédery-Hunt **Rev:** Partial stamp design **Rev. Designer:** Sandford Fleming **Edge:** Plain

Date	Mintage	MS-63	Proof
2001 Proof	59,573	—	12.50

KM# 182 5 CENTS

4.6000 g., Copper-Nickel, 19.55 mm. **Ruler:** Elizabeth II **Obv:** Crowned head right **Obv. Designer:** Dora dePedery-Hunt **Rev:** Beaver on rock divides dates and denomination **Rev. Designer:** George E. Kruger-Gray **Edge:** Plain

Date	Mintage	MS-63	Proof
2001	30,035,000	12.50	—
2001P Proof	—	—	10.00
2003	—	0.30	—

KM# 182b 5 CENTS

3.9000 g., Nickel Plated Steel, 21.2 mm. **Ruler:** Elizabeth II **Obv:** Crowned head right **Obv. Designer:** Dora dePedery-Hunt **Rev:** Beaver on rock divides date and denomination **Rev. Designer:** George E. Kruger-Gray **Edge:** Plain

Date	Mintage	MS-63	Proof
2001 P	136,650,000	0.35	—
2003 P	32,986,921	0.35	—

KM# 182a 5 CENTS

5.3500 g., 0.9250 Silver 0.1591 oz. ASW, 21.2 mm. **Ruler:** Elizabeth II **Obv:** Crowned head right **Obv. Designer:** Dora dePedery-Hunt **Rev:** Beaver on rock divides date and denomination **Rev. Designer:** George E. Kruger-Gray

Date	Mintage	MS-63	Proof
2001 Proof	—	—	5.00
2003 Proof	—	—	5.00

KM# 413 5 CENTS

5.3500 g., 0.9250 Silver 0.1591 oz. ASW, 21.2 mm. **Ruler:** Elizabeth II **Subject:** Royal Military College **Obv:** Crowned head right **Rev:** Marching cadets and arch **Rev. Designer:** Gerald T. Locklin **Edge:** Plain

Date	Mintage	MS-63	Proof
2001 Proof	25,834	—	7.00

KM# 446 5 CENTS

3.9000 g., Nickel Plated Steel, 21.2 mm. **Ruler:** Elizabeth II **Subject:** Elizabeth II Golden Jubilee **Obv:** Crowned head right, Jubilee commemorative dates 1952-2002 **Obv. Designer:** Dora dePedery-Hunt **Rev. Designer:** George E. Kruger-Gray **Note:** Magnetic.

Date	Mintage	MS-63	Proof
ND(2002)P	135,960,000	0.45	—
ND(2002)P Proof	32,642	—	10.00

KM# 446a 5 CENTS

5.3500 g., 0.9250 Silver 0.1591 oz. ASW, 21.2 mm. **Ruler:** Elizabeth II **Subject:** Elizabeth II Golden Jubilee **Obv:** Queen, Jubilee commemorative dates 1952-2002

Date	Mintage	MS-63	Proof
ND(2002) Proof	21,573	—	11.50

KM# 453 5 CENTS

5.3500 g., 0.9250 Silver 0.1591 oz. ASW, 21.2 mm. **Ruler:** Elizabeth II **Subject:** Vimy Ridge - WWI **Obv:** Crowned head right **Rev:** Vimy Ridge Memorial, allegorical figure and dates 1917-2002 **Rev. Designer:** S. A. Allward

Date	Mintage	MS-63	Proof
ND(2002) Proof	22,646	—	11.50

KM# 491 5 CENTS

3.9000 g., Nickel Plated Steel, 21.2 mm. **Ruler:** Elizabeth II **Obv:** Bare head right **Obv. Designer:** Susanna Blunt **Rev:** Beaver divides date and denomination **Rev. Designer:** George E. Kruger-Gray **Note:** Magnetic.

Date	Mintage	MS-63	Proof
2003P	61,392,180	0.45	—
2004P	132,097,000	0.45	—
2004P Proof	—	—	2.50
2005P	89,664,000	0.45	—
2005P Proof	—	—	2.50
2006P	139,308,000	0.50	—
2006P Proof	—	—	2.50
2006(ml)	184,874,000	0.45	—
2006(ml) Proof	—	—	2.50
2007(ml)	221,472,000	0.45	—
2007(ml) Proof	—	—	2.50
2008(ml)	278,530,000	0.45	—
2008(ml) Proof	—	—	2.50
2009(ml)	266,488,000	0.45	—
2009(ml) Proof	—	—	2.50
2010(ml)	—	0.45	—
2010(ml) Proof	—	—	2.50
2011(ml)	—	0.45	—
2011(ml) Proof	—	—	2.50

KM# 469 5 CENTS

5.3500 g., 0.9250 Silver 0.1591 oz. ASW, 21.2 mm. **Ruler:** Elizabeth II **Subject:** 50th Anniversary of the Coronation of Elizabeth II **Obv:** Crowned head right, Jubilee commemorative dates 1953-2003 **Obv. Designer:** Mary Gillick

Date	Mintage	MS-63	Proof
ND(2003) Proof	21,573	—	11.50

KM# 491a 5 CENTS

5.3500 g., 0.9250 Silver 0.1591 oz. ASW, 21.1 mm. **Ruler:** Elizabeth II **Obv:** Crowned head right **Obv. Designer:** Susanna Blunt **Rev:** Beaver divides date and denomination **Edge:** Plain

Date	Mintage	MS-63	Proof
2004 Proof	—	—	3.50

KM# 506 5 CENTS

5.3500 g., 0.9250 Silver 0.1591 oz. ASW, 21.3 mm. **Ruler:** Elizabeth II **Obv:** Bare head right **Rev:** "Victory " design of the KM-40 reverse **Edge:** Plain **Shape:** 12-sided

Date	Mintage	MS-63	Proof
ND(2004) Proof	20,019	—	15.00

KM# 627 5 CENTS

3.9000 g., Nickel, 21.18 mm. **Ruler:** Elizabeth II **Subject:** 60th

Anniversary, Victory in Europe 1945-2005 **Obv:** Head right **Rev:** Large V **Edge:** Plain

Date	Mintage	MS-63	Proof
ND2005P	59,269,192	4.50	—

KM# 758 5 CENTS

5.3000 g., 0.9250 Silver 0.1576 oz. ASW **Ruler:** Elizabeth II **Obv:** George VI head left **Rev:** Torch and large V

Date	Mintage	MS-63	Proof
ND(1945-2005) Proof	42,792	—	35.00

KM# 758a 5 CENTS

5.3000 g., 0.9250 Silver selectively gold plated 0.1576 oz. ASW **Ruler:** Elizabeth II **Obv:** George VI head left **Rev:** Torch and large V **Note:** Bound into Annual Report.

Date	Mintage	MS-63	Proof
ND(1945-2005) Proof	6,065	—	40.00

KM# 491b 5 CENTS

4.6000 g., Copper-Nickel **Ruler:** Elizabeth II **Obv:** Bust right **Rev:** Beaver

Date	Mintage	MS-63	Proof
2006	43,008,000	5.00	—

KM# 1024 5 CENTS

Nickel, 21.2 mm. **Ruler:** Elizabeth II **Obv:** George V bust left **Rev:** Value within wreath, dual dates below

Date	Mintage	MS-63	Proof
1935-2010 Proof	—	—	15.00

KM# 412a 10 CENTS

2.4000 g., 0.9250 Silver 0.0714 oz. ASW, 18 mm. **Ruler:** Elizabeth II **Subject:** Year of the Volunteer **Obv:** Crowned head right **Rev:** Three portraits left above banner, radiant sun below **Edge:** Reeded

Date	Mintage	MS-63	Proof
2001P Proof	40,634	—	9.00

KM# 183b 10 CENTS

1.7700 g., Nickel Plated Steel, 18.03 mm. **Ruler:** Elizabeth II **Obv:** Crowned head right **Obv. Designer:** Dora dePedery-Hunt **Rev:** Bluenose sailing left, date at right, denomination below **Rev. Designer:** Emanuel Hahn **Edge:** Reeded

Date	Mintage	MS-63	Proof
2001 P	266,000,000	0.45	—
2003 P	162,398,000	0.20	—

KM# 183a 10 CENTS

2.4000 g., 0.9250 Silver 0.0714 oz. ASW, 18.03 mm. **Ruler:** Elizabeth II **Obv:** Crowned head right **Rev:** Bluenose sailing left, date at right, denomination below

Date	Mintage	MS-63	Proof
2001 Proof	—	—	5.00
2002 Proof	—	—	7.50
2003 Proof	—	—	7.50

KM# 412 10 CENTS

1.7700 g., Nickel Plated Steel, 18 mm. **Ruler:** Elizabeth II **Subject:** Year of the Volunteer **Obv:** Crowned head right **Rev:** Three portraits left and radiant sun **Edge:** Reeded

Date	Mintage	MS-63	Proof
2001P	224,714,000	4.50	—

KM# 447 10 CENTS

1.7700 g., Nickel Plated Steel, 18 mm. **Ruler:** Elizabeth II **Subject:** Elizabeth II Golden Jubilee **Obv:** Crowned head right, Jubilee commemorative dates 1952-2002

Date	Mintage	MS-63	Proof
ND(2002)P	252,563,000	1.00	—
ND(2002) Proof	32,642	—	2.50

KM# 447a 10 CENTS

2.3200 g., 0.9250 Silver 0.0690 oz. ASW, 18 mm. **Ruler:** Elizabeth II **Subject:** Elizabeth II Golden Jubilee **Obv:** Crowned head right, Jubilee commemorative dates 1952-2002

Date	Mintage	MS-63	Proof
ND(2002) Proof	21,537	—	12.50

KM# 492 10 CENTS

1.7700 g., Nickel Plated Steel, 18 mm. **Ruler:** Elizabeth II **Obv:** Head right **Obv. Designer:** Susanna Blunt **Rev:** Bluenose sailing left

Date	Mintage	MS-63	Proof
2003P	—	1.25	—
2004P	211,924,000	0.60	—
2004P Proof	—	—	2.50
2005P	212,175,000	0.60	—
2005P Proof	—	—	2.50
2006P	312,122,000	0.60	—
2006P Proof	—	—	2.50
2007(ml) Straight 7	304,110,000	0.60	—
2007(ml) Curved 7	Inc. above	0.60	—
2007(ml) Proof	—	—	2.50
2008(ml)	467,495,000	0.60	—
2008(ml) Proof	—	—	2.50
2009(ml)	370,700,000	0.60	—
2009(ml) Proof	—	—	2.50
2010(ml)	—	0.60	—
2010(ml) Proof	—	—	2.50
2011(ml)	—	0.60	—
2011(ml) Proof	—	—	2.50

KM# 470 10 CENTS

2.3200 g., 0.9250 Silver 0.0690 oz. ASW **Ruler:** Elizabeth II **Subject:** 50th Anniversary of the Coronation of Elizabeth II **Obv:** Head right **Rev:** Bluenose sailing left

Date	Mintage	MS-63	Proof
ND(2003) Proof	21,537	—	12.00

KM# 492a 10 CENTS

2.4000 g., 0.9250 Silver 0.0714 oz. ASW, 18 mm. **Ruler:** Elizabeth II **Obv:** Bare head right **Obv. Designer:** Susanna Blunt **Rev:** Sailboat **Edge:** Reeded

Date	Mintage	MS-63	Proof
2004 Proof	—	—	5.00

KM# 524 10 CENTS

2.4000 g., 0.9250 Silver 0.0714 oz. ASW, 18 mm. **Ruler:** Elizabeth II **Subject:** Golf, Championship of Canada, Centennial. **Obv:** Head right

Date	Mintage	MS-63	Proof
2004	39,486	12.50	—

KM# 1025 10 CENTS

Silver, 18.03 mm. **Ruler:** Elizabeth II **Obv:** George V bust left **Rev:** Value within wreath, dual dates below

Date	Mintage	MS-63	Proof
1935-2010 Proof	—	—	20.00

KM# 184 25 CENTS

5.0700 g., Nickel, 23.88 mm. **Ruler:** Elizabeth II **Obv:** Crowned head right **Obv. Designer:** Dora dePedery-Hunt **Rev:** Caribou left, denomination above, date at right **Rev. Designer:** Emanuel Hahn

Date	Mintage	MS-63	Proof
2001	8,415,000	5.00	—
2001 Proof	—	—	7.50

KM# 184b 25 CENTS

4.4000 g., Nickel Plated Steel, 23.88 mm. **Ruler:** Elizabeth II **Obv:** Crowned head right **Rev:** Caribou left, denomination above, date at right

Date	Mintage	MS-63	Proof
2001 P	55,773,000	0.95	—
2001 P Proof	—	—	5.00
2002 P	156,105,000	2.50	—
2002 P Proof	—	—	5.00
2003 P	87,647,000	2.50	—
2003 P Proof	—	—	5.00

KM# 184a 25 CENTS

5.9000 g., 0.9250 Silver 0.1755 oz. ASW, 23.88 mm. **Ruler:** Elizabeth II **Obv:** Crowned head right **Rev:** Caribou left, denomination above, date at right

Date	Mintage	MS-63	Proof
2001 Proof	—	—	9.50
2003 Proof	—	—	9.50

KM# 419 25 CENTS

4.4000 g., Nickel Plated Steel, 23.9 mm. **Ruler:** Elizabeth II **Subject:** Canada Day **Obv:** Crowned head right **Rev:** Maple leaf at center, children holding hands below **Rev. Designer:** Silke Ware **Edge:** Reeded

Date	Mintage	MS-63	Proof
2001	96,352	7.00	—

KM# 448 25 CENTS

4.4000 g., Nickel Plated Steel, 23.9 mm. **Ruler:** Elizabeth II **Subject:** Elizabeth II Golden Jubilee **Obv:** Crowned head right **Rev:** Caribou left

Date	Mintage	MS-63	Proof
ND(2002)P	152,485,000	2.00	—
ND(2002)P Proof	32,642	—	6.00

KM# 448a 25 CENTS

5.9000 g., 0.9250 Silver 0.1755 oz. ASW, 23.9 mm. **Ruler:** Elizabeth II **Subject:** Elizabeth II Golden Jubilee **Obv:** Crowned head right, Jubilee commemorative dates 1952-2002

Date	Mintage	MS-63	Proof
ND(2002) Proof	100,000	—	12.50

KM# 451 25 CENTS

4.4000 g., Nickel Plated Steel, 23.9 mm. **Ruler:** Elizabeth II **Rev:** Small human figures supporting large maple leaf

Date	Mintage	MS-63	Proof
ND(1952-2002)P	30,627,000	5.00	—

KM# 451a 25 CENTS

4.4000 g., Nickel Plated Steel, 23.9 mm. **Ruler:** Elizabeth II **Subject:** Canada Day **Obv:** Crowned head right **Rev:** Human figures supporting large red maple leaf **Edge:** Reeded

Date	Mintage	MS-63	Proof
ND(1952-2002)P	49,903	6.00	—

KM# 471 25 CENTS

5.9000 g., 0.9250 Silver 0.1755 oz. ASW, 23.9 mm. **Ruler:** Elizabeth II **Subject:** 50th Anniversary of the Coronation of Elizabeth II **Obv:** 1953 Effigy of the Queen, Jubilee commemorative dates 1952-2002 **Obv. Designer:** Mary Gillick

Date	Mintage	MS-63	Proof
ND(2002) Proof	21,537	—	12.50

KM# 493 25 CENTS

4.4000 g., Nickel Plated Steel, 23.9 mm. **Ruler:** Elizabeth II **Obv:** Bare head right **Obv. Designer:** Susanna Blunt **Rev:** Caribou left, denomination above, date at right

Date	Mintage	MS-63	Proof
2003P	66,861,633	2.00	—
2003P W	—	—	—
2004P	177,466,000	2.50	—
2004P Proof	—	—	5.00
2005P	206,346,000	2.50	—
2005P Proof	—	—	5.00
2006P	423,189,000	2.50	—
2006P Proof	—	—	5.00
2007(ml)	386,763,000	2.50	—
2007(ml) Proof	—	—	5.00
2008(ml)	387,222,000	2.50	—
2008(ml) Proof	—	—	5.00
2009(ml)	266,766,000	2.50	—
2009(ml) Proof	—	—	5.00
2010(ml)	—	2.50	—
2010(ml) Proof	—	—	5.00
2011(ml)	—	2.50	—
2011(ml) Proof	—	—	5.00

KM# 474 25 CENTS

4.4000 g., 0.9250 Silver 0.1308 oz. ASW, 23.9 mm. **Ruler:** Elizabeth II **Subject:** Canada Day **Obv:** Queen's head right **Rev:** Polar bear and red colored maple leaves

Date	Mintage	MS-63	Proof
2003 Proof	—	—	12.00

KM# 493a 25 CENTS

5.9000 g., 0.9250 Silver 0.1755 oz. ASW, 23.9 mm. **Ruler:** Elizabeth II **Obv:** Bare head right **Obv. Designer:** Suanne Blunt **Rev:** Caribou **Edge:** Reeded

Date	Mintage	MS-63	Proof
2004 Proof	—	—	6.50

KM# 510 25 CENTS

4.4000 g., Nickel Plated Steel, 23.9 mm. **Ruler:** Elizabeth II **Obv:** Bare head right **Rev:** Red poppy in center of maple leaf **Edge:** Reeded

Date	Mintage	MS-63	Proof
2004	28,500,000	5.00	—

KM# 510a 25 CENTS

5.9000 g., 0.9250 Silver 0.1755 oz. ASW, 23.9 mm. **Ruler:** Elizabeth II **Obv:** Bare head right **Rev:** Poppy at center of maple leaf, selectively gold plated **Edge:** Reeded **Note:** Housed in Annual Report.

Date	Mintage	MS-63	Proof
2004 Proof	12,677	—	20.00

KM# 525 25 CENTS

4.4000 g., Nickel Plated Steel, 23.9 mm. **Ruler:** Elizabeth II **Obv:** Bare head right **Rev:** Maple leaf, colorized

Date	Mintage	MS-63	Proof
2004	16,028	8.00	—

KM# 628 25 CENTS

4.4000 g., Nickel Plated Steel, 23.9 mm. **Ruler:** Elizabeth II **Subject:** First Settlement, Ile Ste Croix 1604-2004 **Obv:** Bare head right **Rev:** Sailing ship Bonne-Renommee

Date	Mintage	MS-63	Proof
ND2004P	15,400,000	5.00	—

KM# 698 25 CENTS

4.4000 g., Nickel Plated Steel **Ruler:** Elizabeth II **Rev:** Santa, colorized

Date	Mintage	MS-63	Proof
2004	62,777	5.00	—

KM# 699 25 CENTS

4.4000 g., Nickel Plated Steel, 23.9 mm. **Ruler:** Elizabeth II **Series:** Canada Day **Rev:** Moose head, humorous

Date	Mintage	MS-63	Proof
2004	44,752	5.00	—

KM# 529 25 CENTS

4.4000 g., Nickel Plated Steel, 23.9 mm. **Ruler:** Elizabeth II **Subject:** WWII, 60th Anniversary **Obv:** Head right **Rev:** Three soldiers and flag

Date	Mintage	MS-63	Proof
2005	3,500	20.00	—

KM# 530 25 CENTS

4.4000 g., Nickel Plated Steel, 23.9 mm. **Ruler:** Elizabeth II **Subject:** Alberta **Obv:** Head right

Date	Mintage	MS-63	Proof
2005P	20,640,000	7.00	—

KM# 531 25 CENTS

4.4000 g., Nickel Plated Steel, 23.9 mm. **Ruler:** Elizabeth II **Subject:** Canada Day **Obv:** Head right **Rev:** Beaver, colorized

Date	Mintage	MS-63	Proof
2005P	58,370	8.50	—

KM# 532 25 CENTS

4.4000 g., Nickel Plated Steel, 23.9 mm. **Ruler:** Elizabeth II **Subject:** Saskatchewan **Obv:** Head right

Date	Mintage	MS-63	Proof
2005P	19,290,000	7.00	—

KM# 533 25 CENTS

4.4000 g., Nickel Plated Steel, 23.9 mm. **Ruler:** Elizabeth II **Obv:** Head right **Rev:** Stuffed bear in Christmas stocking, colorized

Date	Mintage	MS-63	Proof
2005P	72,831	10.00	—

KM# 535 25 CENTS

4.4000 g., Nickel Plated Steel, 23.9 mm. **Ruler:** Elizabeth II **Subject:** Year of the Veteran **Obv:** Head right **Rev:** Conjoined busts of young and veteran left **Edge:** Reeded

Date	Mintage	MS-63	Proof
2005P	29,390,000	7.00	—

KM# 576 25 CENTS

4.4000 g., Nickel Plated Steel, 23.9 mm. **Ruler:** Elizabeth II **Subject:** Quebec Winter Carnival **Obv:** Head right **Rev:** Snowman, colorized

Date	Mintage	MS-63	Proof
2006	8,200	10.00	—

KM# 534 25 CENTS

4.4000 g., Nickel Plated Steel, 23.9 mm. **Ruler:** Elizabeth II **Subject:** Toronto Maple Leafs **Obv:** Head right **Rev:** Colorized team logo

Date	Mintage	MS-63	Proof
2006P	—	12.50	—

KM# 575 25 CENTS

4.4000 g., Nickel Plated Steel, 23.9 mm. **Ruler:** Elizabeth II **Subject:** Montreal Canadiens **Obv:** Head right **Rev:** Colorized logo

Date	Mintage	MS-63	Proof
2006P	—	12.50	—

KM# 629 25 CENTS

4.4000 g., Nickel Plated Steel, 23.9 mm. **Ruler:** Elizabeth II **Obv:** Head right **Rev:** Medal of Bravery **Edge:** Reeded

Date	Mintage	MS-63	Proof
2006(ml)	20,040,000	2.50	—

KM# 632 25 CENTS

12.6100 g., Nickel Plated Steel, 35 mm. **Ruler:** Elizabeth II **Subject:** Queen Elizabeth II 80th Birthday **Rev:** Crown, colorized

Date	Mintage	MS-63	Proof
2006 Specimen	24,977	—	25.00

KM# 633 25 CENTS

4.4300 g., Nickel Plated Steel, 23.9 mm. **Ruler:** Elizabeth II **Subject:** Canada Day **Obv:** Crowned head right **Rev:** Boy marching with flag, colorized

Date	Mintage	MS-63	Proof
2006P	29,760	6.00	—

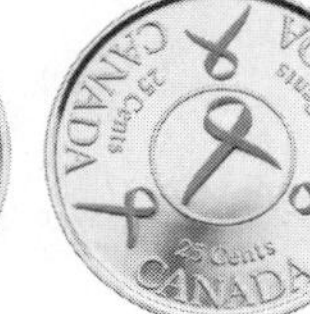

KM# 634 25 CENTS

4.4300 g., Nickel Plated Steel **Ruler:** Elizabeth II **Subject:** Breast Cancer **Rev:** Four ribbons, all colorized **Note:** Sold housed in a bookmark.

Date	Mintage	MS-63	Proof
2006P	40,911	10.00	—

KM# 635 25 CENTS

4.4300 g., Nickel Plated Steel **Ruler:** Elizabeth II **Subject:** Breast Cancer **Rev:** Colorized pink ribbon applique in center.

Date	Mintage	MS-63	Proof
2006P	29,798,000	1.50	—

KM# 636 25 CENTS

4.4000 g., Nickel Plated Steel **Ruler:** Elizabeth II **Obv:** Head right **Obv. Designer:** Susana Blunt **Rev:** Medal of Bravery design (maple leaf within wreath)

Date	Mintage	MS-63	Proof
2006	20,045,111	7.00	—

KM# 637 25 CENTS

4.4300 g., Nickel Plated Steel **Ruler:** Elizabeth II **Subject:** Wedding **Rev:** Colorized bouquet of flowers

Date	Mintage	MS-63	Proof
2007(ml)	10,318	5.00	—

KM# 642 25 CENTS

4.4300 g., Nickel Plated Steel **Ruler:** Elizabeth II **Subject:** Ottawa Senators **Obv:** Head right **Rev:** Logo

Date	Mintage	MS-63	Proof
2006P	—	12.50	—

KM# 644 25 CENTS

4.4300 g., Nickel Plated Steel **Ruler:** Elizabeth II **Subject:** Calgary Flames **Obv:** Head right **Rev:** Logo

Date	Mintage	MS-63	Proof
2007(ml)	832	12.50	—

KM# 645 25 CENTS

4.4300 g., Nickel Plated Steel **Ruler:** Elizabeth II **Subject:** Edmonton Oilers **Obv:** Head right **Rev:** Logo

Date	Mintage	MS-63	Proof
2007(ml)	2,213	12.50	—

KM# 647 25 CENTS

4.4300 g., Nickel Plated Steel **Ruler:** Elizabeth II **Subject:** Santa and Rudolph **Rev:** Colorized Santa in sled lead by Rudolph

Date	Mintage	MS-63	Proof
2006P	99,258	5.00	—

KM# 711 25 CENTS

12.6100 g., Nickel Plated Steel, 35 mm. **Ruler:** Elizabeth II **Subject:** 60th Wedding Anniversary **Obv:** Bust right **Rev:** Carriage, multicolor

Date	Mintage	MS-63	Proof
ND(2007)	16,264	19.50	—

KM# 682 25 CENTS

4.4300 g., Nickel Plated Steel **Ruler:** Elizabeth II **Subject:** Curling **Obv:** Head right

Date	Mintage	MS-63	Proof
2007	22,400,000	7.50	—
2008 Mule	—	—	—

KM# 683 25 CENTS

4.4300 g., Nickel Plated Steel **Ruler:** Elizabeth II **Subject:** Ice Hockey **Obv:** Head right

Date	Mintage	MS-63	Proof
2007	22,400,000	7.50	—
2008 Mule	—	—	—

KM# 684 25 CENTS
4.4300 g., Nickel Plated Steel, 23.8 mm. **Ruler:** Elizabeth II **Subject:** Paraolympic Winter Games **Obv:** Head right **Rev:** Wheelchair curling

Date	Mintage	MS-63	Proof
2007	22,400,000	7.50	—
2008 Mule	—	—	—

KM# 685 25 CENTS
4.4300 g., Nickel Plated Steel **Ruler:** Elizabeth II **Subject:** Biathlon **Obv:** Head right

Date	Mintage	MS-63	Proof
2007	22,400,000	7.50	—
2008 Mule	—	—	—

KM# 638 25 CENTS
4.4300 g., Nickel Plated Steel **Ruler:** Elizabeth II **Subject:** Birthday **Rev:** Colorized baloons

Date	Mintage	MS-63	Proof
2007(ml)	24,531	5.00	—

KM# 639 25 CENTS
4.4300 g., Nickel Plated Steel **Ruler:** Elizabeth II **Subject:** Baby birth **Rev:** Colorized baby rattle **Edge:** Reeded

Date	Mintage	MS-63	Proof
2007(ml)	29,964	5.00	—

KM# 640 25 CENTS
4.4300 g., Nickel Plated Steel **Ruler:** Elizabeth II **Subject:** Oh Canada **Obv:** Head right **Rev:** Maple leaf, colorized

Date	Mintage	MS-63	Proof
2006(ml)	23,582	8.50	—

KM# 641 25 CENTS
4.4300 g., Nickel Plated Steel **Ruler:** Elizabeth II **Subject:** Congratulations **Obv:** Head right **Rev:** Fireworks, colorized

Date	Mintage	MS-63	Proof
2006(ml)	8,910	8.00	—

KM# 643 25 CENTS
4.4300 g., Nickel Plated Steel **Ruler:** Elizabeth II **Subject:** Vancouver Canucks **Obv:** Head right **Rev:** Logo

Date	Mintage	MS-63	Proof
2007(ml)	1,264	12.50	—

KM# 686 25 CENTS
4.4300 g., Nickel Plated Steel, 23.8 mm. **Ruler:** Elizabeth II **Subject:** Alpine Skiing **Obv:** Head right

Date	Mintage	MS-63	Proof
2007	22,400,000	7.50	—
2008 Mule	—	—	—

KM# 701 25 CENTS
4.4300 g., Nickel Plated Steel **Ruler:** Elizabeth II **Subject:** Birthday **Rev:** Party hat, multicolor

Date	Mintage	MS-63	Proof
2007	—	8.00	—

KM# 702 25 CENTS
4.4300 g., Nickel Plated Steel **Ruler:** Elizabeth II **Subject:** Congratulations **Rev:** Trophy, multicolor

Date	Mintage	MS-63	Proof
2007	—	8.00	—

KM# 703 25 CENTS
4.4300 g., Nickel Plated Steel **Ruler:** Elizabeth II **Subject:** Wedding **Rev:** Cake, multicolor

Date	Mintage	MS-63	Proof
2007	—	8.00	—

KM# 704 25 CENTS
4.4300 g., Nickel Plated Steel **Ruler:** Elizabeth II **Subject:** Canada Day **Rev:** Mountie, colorized

Date	Mintage	MS-63	Proof
2007(ml)	27,743	8.00	—

KM# 705 25 CENTS
4.4300 g., Nickel Plated Steel **Ruler:** Elizabeth II **Subject:** Christmas **Rev:** Multicolor tree

Date	Mintage	MS-63	Proof
2007	—	8.00	—

KM# 706 25 CENTS
12.6100 g., Nickel Plated Steel, 35.0 mm. **Ruler:** Elizabeth II **Subject:** Red-breasted Nuthatch **Obv:** Head right **Obv. Legend:** ELIZABETH II - D • G • REGINA **Obv. Designer:** Susanna Blunt **Rev:** Nuthatch perched on pine branch multicolor **Rev. Legend:** CANADA **Rev. Designer:** Arnold Nogy **Edge:** Plain

Date	Mintage	MS-63	Proof
2007(ml) Specimen	10,581	25.00	—

KM# 707 25 CENTS
12.6100 g., Nickel Plated Steel, 35 mm. **Ruler:** Elizabeth II **Obv:** Elizabeth II **Rev:** Multicolor ruby-throated hummingbird and flower **Edge:** Plain

Date	Mintage	MS-63	Proof
2007 Specimen	16,256	—	25.00

KM# 708 25 CENTS
5.9000 g., 0.9250 Silver 0.1755 oz. ASW **Ruler:** Elizabeth II **Subject:** Queen's 60th Wedding Anniversary **Rev:** Royal carriage

Date	Mintage	MS-63	Proof
2007 Specimen	16,264	—	24.00

KM# 713 25 CENTS
4.4000 g., Nickel Plated Steel **Ruler:** Elizabeth II **Rev:** Toronto Maple Leaf logo, colorized

Date	Mintage	MS-63	Proof
2007(ml)	3,527	5.00	—

KM# 714 25 CENTS
4.4000 g., Nickel Plated Steel **Ruler:** Elizabeth II **Rev:** Ottawa Senators logo, colorized

Date	Mintage	MS-63	Proof
2007(ml)	1,634	5.00	—

KM# 723 25 CENTS
4.4000 g., Nickel Plated Steel **Ruler:** Elizabeth II **Rev:** Montreal Canadiens logo, colorized

Date	Mintage	MS-63	Proof
2007(ml)	2,952	5.00	—

KM# 1039 25 CENTS
4.4300 g., Nickel Plated Steel, 23.9 mm. **Ruler:** Elizabeth II **Subject:** Canada Day **Rev:** Colorized moose head

Date	Mintage	MS-63	Proof
2008	—	12.50	—

KM# 760 25 CENTS
4.4300 g., Nickel Plated Steel **Ruler:** Elizabeth II **Subject:** Baby **Rev:** Multicolor blue teddy bear

Date	Mintage	MS-63	Proof
2008	—	8.00	—

KM# 761 25 CENTS
4.4300 g., Nickel Plated Steel **Ruler:** Elizabeth II **Subject:** Birthday **Rev:** Multicolor party hat

Date	Mintage	MS-63	Proof
2008	—	8.00	—

KM# 762 25 CENTS
4.4300 g., Nickel Plated Steel **Ruler:** Elizabeth II **Subject:** Congratulations **Rev:** Multicolor trophy

Date	Mintage	MS-63	Proof
2008	—	8.00	—

KM# 763 25 CENTS
4.4300 g., Nickel Plated Steel **Ruler:** Elizabeth II **Subject:** Wedding **Rev:** Multicolor wedding cake

Date	Mintage	MS-63	Proof
2008	—	8.00	—

KM# 764 25 CENTS
4.4300 g., Nickel Plated Steel **Ruler:** Elizabeth II **Subject:** Santa Claus **Rev:** Multicolor Santa

Date	Mintage	MS-63	Proof
2008	—	8.00	—

KM# 765 25 CENTS
4.4300 g., Nickel Plated Steel, 23.9 mm. **Ruler:** Elizabeth II **Subject:** Vancouver Olympics **Rev:** Freestyle skiing

Date	Mintage	MS-63	Proof
2008	—	2.00	—

KM# 766 25 CENTS
4.4300 g., Nickel Plated Steel, 23.8 mm. **Ruler:** Elizabeth II **Subject:** Vancouver Olympics **Rev:** Figure skating

Date	Mintage	MS-63	Proof
2008	—	2.00	—

KM# 768 25 CENTS

4.4300 g., Nickel Plated Steel **Ruler:** Elizabeth II **Subject:** Vancouver Olympics **Rev:** Snow boarding

Date	Mintage	MS-63	Proof
2008	—	2.00	—

KM# 769 25 CENTS

4.4300 g., Nickel Plated Steel **Ruler:** Elizabeth II **Subject:** Vancouver Olympics **Rev:** Olympic mascott - Miga

Date	Mintage	MS-63	Proof
2008	—	3.00	—

KM# 770 25 CENTS

4.4300 g., Nickel Plated Steel **Ruler:** Elizabeth II **Subject:** Vancouver Olympics **Rev:** Olympic mascott - Quatchi

Date	Mintage	MS-63	Proof
2008	—	3.00	—

KM# 771 25 CENTS

4.4300 g., Nickel Plated Steel **Ruler:** Elizabeth II **Subject:** Vancouver Olympics **Rev:** Olympic mascott - Sumi

Date	Mintage	MS-63	Proof
2008	—	3.00	—

KM# 772 25 CENTS

4.4300 g., Nickel Plated Steel **Ruler:** Elizabeth II **Subject:** Oh Canada **Rev:** Multicolor red flag

Date	Mintage	MS-63	Proof
2008	—	8.00	—

KM# 773 25 CENTS

12.6100 g., Nickel Plated Steel, 35 mm. **Ruler:** Elizabeth II **Obv:** Bust right **Obv. Designer:** Susanna Blunt **Rev:** Downy woodpecker in tree, multicolor **Rev. Designer:** Arnold Nogy **Edge:** Plain **Note:** Prev. KM#717.

Date	Mintage	MS-63	Proof
2008(ml)	25,000	24.00	—

KM# 774 25 CENTS

12.6100 g., Nickel Plated Steel, 35 mm. **Ruler:** Elizabeth II **Obv:** Bust right **Obv. Designer:** Susanna Blunt **Rev:** Northern cardinal perched on branch - multicolor **Rev. Designer:** Arnold Nogy **Edge:** Plain **Note:** Prev. KM#718.

Date	Mintage	MS-63	Proof
2008(ml)	25,000	25.00	—

KM# 775 25 CENTS

4.4300 g., Nickel Plated Steel, 23.8 mm. **Ruler:** Elizabeth II **Subject:** End of WWI, 90th Anniversary **Rev:** Multicolor poppy

Date	Mintage	MS-63	Proof
2008	—	8.00	—

KM# 776 25 CENTS

12.6100 g., Nickel Plated Steel, 35 mm. **Ruler:** Elizabeth II **Subject:** Anne of Green Gables **Rev:** Image of young girl, multicolor **Rev. Designer:** Ben Stahl

Date	Mintage	MS-63	Proof
2008	25,000	20.00	—

KM# 841 25 CENTS

4.4300 g., Nickel Plated Steel **Ruler:** Elizabeth II **Subject:** Vancouver Olympics **Rev:** Bobsleigh **Shape:** 23.8

Date	Mintage	MS-63	Proof
2008	—	3.00	—

KM# 1041 25 CENTS

4.4300 g., Nickel Plated Steel **Ruler:** Elizabeth II **Subject:** WWI **Rev:** Three military men standing over tomb

Date	Mintage	MS-63	Proof
2008(ml)	—	12.50	—

KM# 840 25 CENTS

4.4300 g., Nickel Plated Steel, 23.8 mm. **Ruler:** Elizabeth II **Subject:** Valcouver 2010 Olympics **Rev:** Cross-country skiing

Date	Mintage	MS-63	Proof
2009	—	3.00	—

KM# 842 25 CENTS

4.4300 g., Nickel Plated Steel, 23.9 mm. **Ruler:** Elizabeth II **Subject:** Edmonton Olympics **Rev:** Speed skating

Date	Mintage	MS-63	Proof
2009	—	3.00	—

KM# 885 25 CENTS

4.4000 g., Nickel Plated Steel, 35 mm. **Ruler:** Elizabeth II **Subject:** Canada Day **Rev:** Animals in boat with flag **Rev. Legend:** Canada 25 cents

Date	Mintage	MS-63	Proof
2009	—	5.00	—

KM# 886 25 CENTS

12.6100 g., Nickel Plated Steel, 35 mm. **Ruler:** Elizabeth II **Subject:** Notre-Dame-Du-Saguenay **Obv:** Bust right **Obv. Legend:** Elizabeth II DG Regina **Obv. Designer:** Susanna Blunt **Rev:** Color photo of fjord and statue **Rev. Legend:** Canada 25 cents

Date	Mintage	MS-63	Proof
2009 Specimen	—	—	25.00

KM# 915 25 CENTS

4.4300 g., Nickel Plated Steel, 23.9 mm. **Ruler:** Elizabeth II **Subject:** Surprise Birthday **Obv:** Bust right **Obv. Designer:** Susanna Blunt **Rev:** Colorized

Date	Mintage	MS-63	Proof
2009	—	12.50	—

KM# 916 25 CENTS

4.4300 g., Nickel Plated Steel, 23.9 mm. **Ruler:** Elizabeth II **Subject:** Share the Excitement **Obv:** Bust right **Obv. Designer:** Susanna Blunt **Rev:** Colorized

Date	Mintage	MS-63	Proof
2009	—	12.50	—

KM# 917 25 CENTS

4.4300 g., Nickel Plated Steel, 23.9 mm. **Ruler:** Elizabeth II **Subject:** Share the Love **Obv:** Bust right **Obv. Designer:** Susanna Blunt **Rev:** Colorized

Date	Mintage	MS-63	Proof
2009	—	12.50	—

KM# 918 25 CENTS

4.4300 g., Nickel Plated Steel, 23.9 mm. **Ruler:** Elizabeth II **Subject:** Thank You **Obv:** Bust right **Obv. Designer:** Susanna Blunt **Rev:** Colorized

Date	Mintage	MS-63	Proof
2009	—	12.50	—

KM# 932 25 CENTS

4.4000 g., Nickel Plated Steel, 23.9 mm. **Ruler:** Elizabeth II **Rev:** Yellow maple leaves

Date	Mintage	MS-63	Proof
2009	—	16.50	—

KM# 933 25 CENTS
4.4000 g., Nickel Plated Steel, 23.9 mm. **Ruler:** Elizabeth II **Rev:** Santa Claus, multicolor

Date	Mintage	MS-63	Proof
2009 In sets only	—	16.50	—

KM# 934 25 CENTS
4.4000 g., Nickel Plated Steel, 23.9 mm. **Ruler:** Elizabeth II **Rev:** Multicolor teddy bear, crescent moon

Date	Mintage	MS-63	Proof
2009	—	16.50	—

KM# 935 25 CENTS
4.4000 g., Nickel Plated Steel, 23.9 mm. **Ruler:** Elizabeth II **Subject:** Oh Canada **Rev:** Maple leaves, yellow color

Date	Mintage	MS-63	Proof
2009 In sets only	—	16.50	—

KM# 952 25 CENTS
4.4000 g., Nickel Plated Steel, 23.9 mm. **Ruler:** Elizabeth II **Rev:** Sledge hockey

Date	Mintage	MS-63	Proof
2009	—	3.00	—

KM# 1063 25 CENTS
Nickel Plated Steel **Ruler:** Elizabeth II **Subject:** Men's Hockey **Rev:** Hockey player and maple leaf outline

Date	Mintage	MS-63	Proof
2009	—	2.50	—

KM# 1063a 25 CENTS
Nickel Plated Steel **Ruler:** Elizabeth II **Subject:** Men's Hockey **Rev:** Hockey player and maple leaf outline in red

Date	Mintage	MS-63	Proof
2009	—	7.50	—

KM# 1064 25 CENTS
Nickel Plated Steel **Ruler:** Elizabeth II **Subject:** Women's Hockey **Rev:** Hockey player and maple leaf outline

Date	Mintage	MS-63	Proof
2009	—	2.50	—

KM# 1064a 25 CENTS
Nickel Plated Steel **Ruler:** Elizabeth II **Subject:** Women's Hockey **Rev:** Hockey player and male leaf outline in red

Date	Mintage	MS-63	Proof
2009	—	7.50	—

KM# 1065 25 CENTS
Nickel Plated Steel **Ruler:** Elizabeth II **Subject:** Klassen - Female hockey player **Rev:** Skater and maple leaf outline

Date	Mintage	MS-63	Proof
2009	—	2.50	—

KM# 1065a 25 CENTS
Nickel Plated Steel **Ruler:** Elizabeth II **Subject:** Klassen - female skater **Rev:** Skater and maple leaf outline in red

Date	Mintage	MS-63	Proof
2009	—	7.50	—

KM# 880 25 CENTS
4.4000 g., Nickel Plated Steel, 23.88 mm. **Ruler:** Elizabeth II **Subject:** Miga Mascot Vancouver Olympics **Rev:** Mica Mascot - color **Rev. Legend:** Vancouver 2010 25 cents

Date	Mintage	MS-63	Proof
2010	—	3.00	—

KM# 881 25 CENTS
4.4000 g., Nickel Plated Steel, 23.88 mm. **Ruler:** Elizabeth II **Subject:** Quatchi Mascot - Vancouver Olympics **Obv:** Bust right **Rev:** Quatchi Mascot color **Rev. Legend:** Vancouver 2010 25 cents

Date	Mintage	MS-63	Proof
2010	—	3.00	—

KM# 882 25 CENTS
4.4000 g., Nickel Plated Steel, 23.88 mm. **Ruler:** Elizabeth II **Subject:** Sumi Mascot **Rev:** Sumi Mascot color **Rev. Legend:** Vancouver 2010 25 cents

Date	Mintage	MS-63	Proof
2010	—	3.00	—

KM# 953 25 CENTS
4.4000 g., Nickel Plated Steel, 23.9 mm. **Ruler:** Elizabeth II **Rev:** Ice hockey

Date	Mintage	MS-63	Proof
2010	—	3.00	—

KM# 953a 25 CENTS
4.4000 g., Nickel Plated Steel, 23.9 mm. **Ruler:** Elizabeth II **Rev:** Ice Hockey - red enamel

Date	Mintage	MS-63	Proof
2010	—	8.00	—

KM# 954 25 CENTS
4.4000 g., Nickel Plated Steel, 23.9 mm. **Ruler:** Elizabeth II **Rev:** Curling

Date	Mintage	MS-63	Proof
2010	—	3.00	—

KM# 954a 25 CENTS
4.4000 g., Nickel Plated Steel, 23.9 mm. **Ruler:** Elizabeth II **Rev:** Curling red enamel

Date	Mintage	MS-63	Proof
2010	—	8.00	—

KM# 955 25 CENTS
4.4000 g., Nickel Plated Steel, 23.9 mm. **Ruler:** Elizabeth II **Rev:** Wheelchair curling

Date	Mintage	MS-63	Proof
2010	—	3.00	—

KM# 955a 25 CENTS
4.4000 g., Nickel Plated Steel, 23.9 mm. **Ruler:** Elizabeth II **Rev:** Wheelchair curling - red enamel

Date	Mintage	MS-63	Proof
2010	—	8.00	—

KM# 956 25 CENTS
4.4000 g., Nickel Plated Steel, 23.9 mm. **Ruler:** Elizabeth II **Rev:** Biathlon

Date	Mintage	MS-63	Proof
2010	—	3.00	—

KM# 956a 25 CENTS
4.4000 g., Nickel Plated Steel, 23.9 mm. **Ruler:** Elizabeth II **Rev:** Biathlon - red enamel

Date	Mintage	MS-63	Proof
2010	—	8.00	—

KM# 957 25 CENTS
4.4000 g., Nickel Plated Steel, 23.9 mm. **Ruler:** Elizabeth II **Rev:** Alpine skiing

Date	Mintage	MS-63	Proof
2010	—	3.00	—

KM# 957a 25 CENTS
4.4000 g., Nickel Plated Steel, 23.9 mm. **Ruler:** Elizabeth II **Rev:** Alpine skiing - red enamel

Date	Mintage	MS-63	Proof
2010	—	8.00	—

KM# 958 25 CENTS
4.4000 g., Nickel Plated Steel, 23.9 mm. **Ruler:** Elizabeth II **Rev:** Snowboarding

Date	Mintage	MS-63	Proof
2010	—	3.00	—

KM# 958a 25 CENTS
4.4000 g., Nickel Plated Steel, 23.9 mm. **Ruler:** Elizabeth II **Rev:** Snowboarding - red enamel

Date	Mintage	MS-63	Proof
2010	—	8.00	—

KM# 959 25 CENTS
23.9000 g., Nickel Plated Steel, 23.9 mm. **Ruler:** Elizabeth II **Rev:** Free-style skiing

Date	Mintage	MS-63	Proof
2010	—	3.00	—

KM# 959a 25 CENTS
4.4000 g., Nickel Plated Steel, 23.9 mm. **Ruler:** Elizabeth II **Rev:** Free-style skiing - red enamel

Date	Mintage	MS-63	Proof
2010	—	8.00	—

KM# 960 25 CENTS
4.4000 g., Nickel Plated Steel, 23.9 mm. **Ruler:** Elizabeth II **Rev:** Alpine skiing

Date	Mintage	MS-63	Proof
2010	—	3.00	—

KM# 960a 25 CENTS
4.4000 g., Nickel Plated Steel, 23.9 mm. **Ruler:** Elizabeth II **Rev:** Alpine skiing - red enamel

Date	Mintage	MS-63	Proof
2010	—	8.00	—

KM# 988 25 CENTS
4.4000 g., Multi-Ply Plated Steel, 23.88 mm. **Ruler:** Elizabeth II **Rev:** Blue baby carriage

Date	Mintage	MS-63	Proof
2010	—	10.00	—

KM# 989 25 CENTS
4.4000 g., Nickel Plated Steel, 23.9 mm. **Ruler:** Elizabeth II **Rev:** Purple gift box

Date	Mintage	MS-63	Proof
2010	—	10.00	—

KM# 990 25 CENTS
4.4000 g., Nickel Plated Steel, 23.9 mm. **Ruler:** Elizabeth II **Rev:** Four stars

Date	Mintage	MS-63	Proof
2010	—	10.00	—

KM# 991 25 CENTS
4.4000 g., Nickel Plated Steel, 23.9 mm. **Ruler:** Elizabeth II **Rev:** Three maple leaves

Date	Mintage	MS-63	Proof
2010	—	12.50	—

KM# 992 25 CENTS
4.4000 g., Nickel Plated Steel, 23.9 mm. **Ruler:** Elizabeth II **Rev:** Three zinnias

Date	Mintage	MS-63	Proof
2010	—	12.50	—

KM# 993 25 CENTS
23.9000 g., Nickel Plated Steel, 23.9 mm. **Ruler:** Elizabeth II **Rev:** Pink hearts and roses

Date	Mintage	MS-63	Proof
2010	—	10.00	—

KM# 994 25 CENTS
12.6100 g., Nickel Plated Steel, 35 mm. **Ruler:** Elizabeth II **Rev:** Goldfinch, multicolor **Rev. Designer:** Arnold Nogy

Date	Mintage	MS-63	Proof
2010 Proof	Est. 14,000	—	25.00

KM# 1001 25 CENTS

12.6100 g., Nickel Plated Steel, 35 mm. **Ruler:** Elizabeth II **Subject:** Blue Jay **Rev:** Multicolor blue jay on yellow maple leaves

Date	Mintage	MS-63	Proof
2010 Specimen	—	—	25.00

KM# 1006 25 CENTS

0.5000 g., 0.9990 Gold 0.0161 oz. AGW, 11 mm. **Ruler:** Elizabeth II **Rev:** Caribou head left

Date	Mintage	MS-63	Proof
2010 Proof	15,000	—	80.00

KM# 1021 25 CENTS

Nickel Plated Steel, 23.9 mm. **Ruler:** Elizabeth II **Rev:** Santa Claus in color

Date	Mintage	MS-63	Proof
2010	—	15.00	—

KM# 1026 25 CENTS

Silver, 23.8 mm. **Ruler:** Elizabeth II **Obv:** George V bust left **Rev:** Value within wreath, dual dates below

Date	Mintage	MS-63	Proof
1935-2010 Proof	—	—	25.00

KM# 1079 25 CENTS

12.6100 g., Nickel Plated Steel, 35 mm. **Ruler:** Elizabeth II **Rev:** Barn Swallow in color **Rev. Designer:** Arnold Nagy

Date	Mintage	MS-63	Proof
2011	14,000	—	25.00

KM# 1080 25 CENTS

4.4300 g., Nickel Plated Steel, 23.88 mm. **Ruler:** Elizabeth II **Subject:** Oh Canada! **Rev:** Maple leaf and circular legend

Date	Mintage	MS-63	Proof
2011	—	2.50	—

KM# 1081 25 CENTS

4.4300 g., Nickel Plated Steel, 23.88 mm. **Ruler:** Elizabeth II **Subject:** Wedding **Rev:** Two rings

Date	Mintage	MS-63	Proof
2011	—	2.50	—

KM# 1082 25 CENTS

4.4300 g., Nickel Plated Steel, 23.88 mm. **Ruler:** Elizabeth II **Subject:** Birthday **Rev:** Three baloons

Date	Mintage	MS-63	Proof
2011	—	2.50	—

KM# 1083 25 CENTS

4.4300 g., Nickel Plated Steel, 23.88 mm. **Ruler:** Elizabeth II **Subject:** New Baby! **Rev:** Baby's feet

Date	Mintage	MS-63	Proof
2011	—	2.50	—

KM# 1084 25 CENTS

4.4300 g., Nickel Plated Steel, 23.88 mm. **Ruler:** Elizabeth II **Rev:** Tooth Fairy

Date	Mintage	MS-63	Proof
2011	—	2.50	—

KM# 290 50 CENTS

6.9000 g., Nickel, 27.13 mm. **Ruler:** Elizabeth II **Obv:** Crowned head right **Obv. Designer:** Dora dePedery-Hunt **Rev:** Redesigned arms **Rev. Designer:** Cathy Bursey-Sabourin

Date	Mintage	MS-63	Proof
2001P	—	1.50	—
2001P Proof	—	—	5.00
2003P	—	1.50	—
2003P Proof	—	—	5.00

KM# 290b 50 CENTS

6.9000 g., Nickel Plated Steel, 27.13 mm. **Ruler:** Elizabeth II **Obv:** Crowned head right **Obv. Designer:** Dora dePedery-Hunt **Rev:** Redesigned arms **Rev. Designer:** Cathy Bursey-Sabourin

Date	Mintage	MS-63	Proof
2001 P	389,000	1.50	—
2003 P	—	5.00	—

KM# 290a 50 CENTS

11.6380 g., 0.9250 Silver 0.3461 oz. ASW, 27.13 mm. **Ruler:** Elizabeth II **Obv:** Crowned head right **Obv. Designer:** Dora dePedery-Hunt **Rev:** Redesigned arms **Rev. Designer:** Cathy Bursey-Sabourin

Date	Mintage	MS-63	Proof
2001 Proof	—	—	12.00
2003 Proof	—	—	12.00

KM# 420 50 CENTS

9.3000 g., 0.9250 Silver 0.2766 oz. ASW, 27.13 mm. **Ruler:** Elizabeth II **Series:** Festivals - Quebec **Obv:** Crowned head right **Rev:** Snowman and Chateau Frontenac **Rev. Designer:** Sylvie Daigneault **Edge:** Reeded

Date	Mintage	MS-63	Proof
2001 Proof	58,123	—	8.50

KM# 421 50 CENTS

9.3000 g., 0.9250 Silver 0.2766 oz. ASW, 27.13 mm. **Ruler:** Elizabeth II **Series:** Festivals - Nunavut **Obv:** Crowned head right **Rev:** Dancer, dog sled and snowmobiles **Rev. Designer:** John Mardon **Edge:** Reeded

Date	Mintage	MS-63	Proof
2001 Proof	58,123	—	8.50

KM# 422 50 CENTS

9.3000 g., 0.9250 Silver 0.2766 oz. ASW, 27.13 mm. **Ruler:** Elizabeth II **Series:** Festivals - Newfoundland **Obv:** Crowned head right **Rev:** Sailor and musical people **Rev. Designer:** David Craig **Edge:** Reeded

Date	Mintage	MS-63	Proof
2001 Proof	58,123	—	8.50

KM# 423 50 CENTS

9.3000 g., 0.9250 Silver 0.2766 oz. ASW, 27.13 mm. **Ruler:** Elizabeth II **Series:** Festivals - Prince Edward Island **Obv:** Crowned head right **Rev:** Family, juggler and building **Rev. Designer:** Brenda Whiteway **Edge:** Reeded

Date	Mintage	MS-63	Proof
2001 Proof	58,123	—	8.50

KM# 424 50 CENTS

9.3000 g., 0.9250 Silver 0.2766 oz. ASW, 27.13 mm. **Ruler:** Elizabeth II **Series:** Folklore - The Sled **Obv:** Crowned head right **Rev:** Family scene **Rev. Designer:** Valentina Hotz-Entin **Edge:** Reeded

Date	Mintage	MS-63	Proof
2001 Proof	28,979	—	9.00

KM# 425 50 CENTS

9.3000 g., 0.9250 Silver 0.2766 oz. ASW, 27.13 mm. **Ruler:** Elizabeth II **Series:** Folklore - The Maiden's Cave **Obv:** Crowned head right **Rev:** Woman shouting **Rev. Designer:** Peter Kiss **Edge:** Reeded

Date	Mintage	MS-63	Proof
2001 Proof	28,979	—	9.00

KM# 426 50 CENTS

9.3000 g., 0.9250 Silver 0.2766 oz. ASW, 27.13 mm. **Ruler:** Elizabeth II **Series:** Folklore - The Small Jumpers **Obv:** Crowned head right **Rev:** Jumping children on seashore **Rev. Designer:** Miynki Tanobe **Edge:** Reeded

Date	Mintage	MS-63	Proof
2001 Proof	28,979	—	9.00

KM# 509 50 CENTS

6.9000 g., Nickel Plated Steel, 27.13 mm. **Ruler:** Elizabeth II **Obv:** Crowned head right **Rev:** National arms **Edge:** Reeded

Date	Mintage	MS-63	Proof
ND(2001) P	—	1.50	—

KM# 444 50 CENTS

6.9000 g., Nickel Plated Steel, 27.13 mm. **Ruler:** Elizabeth II **Subject:** Queen's Golden Jubilee **Obv:** Coronation crowned head right and monogram **Rev:** Canadian arms **Rev. Designer:** Bursey Sabourin **Edge:** Reeded

Date	Mintage	MS-63	Proof
ND(2002)P	14,440,000	2.50	—

KM# 444a 50 CENTS

9.3000 g., 0.9250 Silver 0.2766 oz. ASW, 27.13 mm. **Ruler:** Elizabeth II **Subject:** Elizabeth II Golden Jubilee **Obv:** Crowned head right, Jubilee commemorative dates 1952-2002

Date	Mintage	MS-63	Proof
ND(2002) Proof	100,000	—	17.50

KM# 444b 50 CENTS

9.3000 g., 0.9250 Silver Gilt 0.2766 oz. ASW, 27.13 mm. **Ruler:** Elizabeth II **Subject:** Queen's Golden Jubilee **Obv:** Crowned head right and monogram **Rev:** Canadian arms **Edge:** Reeded **Note:** Special 24 karat gold-plated issue of KM#444.

Date	Mintage	MS-63	Proof
ND(2002) Proof	32,642	—	35.00

KM# 454 50 CENTS

9.3000 g., 0.9250 Silver 0.2766 oz. ASW, 27.13 mm. **Ruler:** Elizabeth II **Subject:** Nova Scotia Annapolis Valley Apple Blossom Festival **Obv:** Crowned head right **Rev. Designer:** Bonnie Ross

Date	Mintage	MS-63	Proof
2002 Proof	59,998	—	8.50

KM# 455 50 CENTS

9.3000 g., 0.9250 Silver 0.2766 oz. ASW, 27.13 mm. **Ruler:** Elizabeth II **Subject:** Stratford Festival **Obv:** Crowned head right **Rev:** Couple with building in background **Rev. Designer:** Laurie McGaw

Date	Mintage	MS-63	Proof
2002 Proof	59,998	—	8.50

KM# 456 50 CENTS

9.3000 g., 0.9250 Silver 0.2766 oz. ASW, 27.13 mm. **Ruler:** Elizabeth II **Subject:** Folklorama **Obv:** Crowned head right **Rev. Designer:** William Woodruff

Date	Mintage	MS-63	Proof
2002 Proof	59,998	—	8.50

KM# 457 50 CENTS

9.3000 g., 0.9250 Silver 0.2766 oz. ASW, 27.13 mm. **Ruler:** Elizabeth II **Subject:** Calgary Stampede **Obv:** Crowned head right **Rev. Designer:** Stan Witten

Date	Mintage	MS-63	Proof
2002 Proof	59,998	—	8.50

KM# 458 50 CENTS

9.3000 g., 0.9250 Silver 0.2766 oz. ASW, 27.13 mm. **Ruler:** Elizabeth II **Subject:** Squamish Days Logger Sports **Obv:** Crowned head right **Rev. Designer:** Jose Osio

Date	Mintage	MS-63	Proof
2002 Proof	59,998	—	8.50

KM# 459 50 CENTS

9.3000 g., 0.9250 Silver 0.2766 oz. ASW, 27.13 mm. **Ruler:** Elizabeth II **Series:** Folklore and Legends **Obv:** Crowned head right **Rev:** The Shoemaker in Heaven **Rev. Designer:** Francine Gravel

Date	Mintage	MS-63	Proof
2002 Proof	19,267	—	9.50

KM# 460 50 CENTS

9.3000 g., 0.9250 Silver 0.2766 oz. ASW, 27.13 mm. **Ruler:** Elizabeth II **Series:** Folklore and Legends **Subject:** The Ghost Ship **Obv:** Crowned head right **Rev. Designer:** Colette Boivin

Date	Mintage	MS-63	Proof
2002 Proof	19,267	—	9.50

KM# 461 50 CENTS

9.3000 g., 0.9250 Silver 0.2766 oz. ASW, 27.13 mm. **Ruler:** Elizabeth II **Series:** Folklore and Legends **Subject:** The Pig That Wouldn't Get Over the Stile **Obv:** Crowned head right **Rev. Designer:** Laura Jolicoeur

Date	Mintage	MS-63	Proof
2002 Proof	19,267	—	9.50

KM# 494 50 CENTS

6.9000 g., Nickel Plated Steel, 27.13 mm. **Ruler:** Elizabeth II **Obv:** Crowned head right **Obv. Designer:** Susanna Blunt **Rev. Designer:** Cathy Bursey-Sabourin

Date	Mintage	MS-63	Proof
2003P W	—	5.00	—
2003P W Proof	—	—	7.50
2004P	—	5.00	—
2004P Proof	—	—	7.50
2005P	200,000	1.50	—
2005P Proof	—	—	5.00
2006P	98,000	1.50	—
2006P Proof	—	—	5.00
2007(ml)	250,000	1.50	—
2007(ml) Proof	—	—	5.00
2008(ml)	211,000	1.50	—
2008(ml) Proof	—	—	5.00
2009(ml)	150,000	1.50	—
2009(ml) Proof	—	—	5.00
2010(ml)	—	1.50	—
2010(ml) Proof	—	—	5.00
2011(ml)	—	1.50	—
2011(ml) Proof	—	—	5.00

KM# 472 50 CENTS

11.6200 g., 0.9250 Silver 0.3456 oz. ASW, 27.13 mm. **Ruler:** Elizabeth II **Subject:** 50th Anniversary of the Coronation of Elizabeth II **Obv:** Crowned head right, Jubilee commemorative dates 1952-2002 **Obv. Designer:** Mary Gillick

Date	Mintage	MS-63	Proof
ND(2003) Proof	30,000	—	15.00

KM# 475 50 CENTS

9.3000 g., 0.9250 Silver 0.2766 oz. ASW, 27.13 mm. **Ruler:** Elizabeth II **Obv:** Crowned head right **Obv. Designer:** Dora dePédery-Hunt **Rev:** Golden daffodil **Rev. Designer:** Christie Paquet, Stan Witten

Date	Mintage	MS-63	Proof
2003 Proof	36,293	—	25.00

KM# 476 50 CENTS

9.3000 g., 0.9250 Silver 0.2766 oz. ASW, 27.13 mm. **Ruler:** Elizabeth II **Subject:** Yukon International Storytelling Festival **Obv:** Crowned head right **Obv. Designer:** Dora dePédery-Hunt **Rev. Designer:** Ken Anderson, Jose Oslo

Date	Mintage	MS-63	Proof
2003 Proof	—	—	11.00

KM# 477 50 CENTS

9.3000 g., 0.9250 Silver 0.2766 oz. ASW, 27.13 mm. **Ruler:** Elizabeth II **Subject:** Festival Acadien de Caraquet **Obv:** Crowned head right **Obv. Designer:** Dora dePédery-Hunt **Rev:** Sailboat and couple **Rev. Designer:** Susan Taylor, Hudson Design Group

Date	Mintage	MS-63	Proof
2003 Proof	—	—	11.00

KM# 478 50 CENTS

9.3000 g., 0.9250 Silver 0.2766 oz. ASW, 27.13 mm. **Ruler:** Elizabeth II **Subject:** Back to Batoche **Obv:** Crowned head right **Obv. Designer:** Dora dePédery-Hunt **Rev. Designer:** David Hannan, Stan Witten

Date	Mintage	MS-63	Proof
2003 Proof	—	—	11.00

KM# 479 50 CENTS

9.3000 g., 0.9250 Silver 0.2766 oz. ASW, 27.13 mm. **Ruler:** Elizabeth II **Subject:** Great Northern Arts Festival **Obv:** Crowned head right **Obv. Designer:** Dora dePédery-Hunt **Rev. Designer:** Dawn Oman, Susan Taylor

Date	Mintage	MS-63	Proof
2003 Proof	—	—	11.00

KM# 494a 50 CENTS

9.3000 g., 0.9250 Silver 0.2766 oz. ASW, 27.13 mm. **Ruler:** Elizabeth II **Obv:** Crowned head right **Obv. Designer:** Susanna Blunt **Rev:** Canadian coat of arms **Edge:** Reeded

Date	Mintage	MS-63	Proof
2004 Proof	—	—	7.50

KM# 526 50 CENTS

1.2700 g., 0.9999 Gold 0.0408 oz. AGW, 14 mm. **Ruler:** Elizabeth II **Subject:** Moose **Obv:** Head right **Rev:** Moose head facing right

Date	Mintage	MS-63	Proof
2004 Proof	—	—	85.00

KM# 606 50 CENTS

9.3000 g., 0.9250 Silver 0.2766 oz. ASW, 27.13 mm. **Ruler:** Elizabeth II **Obv:** Head right **Obv. Designer:** Susanna Blunt **Rev:** Clouded Sulphur Butterfly, hologram **Rev. Designer:** Susan Taylor

Date	Mintage	MS-63	Proof
2004 Proof	15,281	—	30.00

KM# 712 50 CENTS

9.3000 g., 0.9250 Silver 0.2766 oz. ASW, 27.13 mm. **Ruler:** Elizabeth II **Rev:** Hologram of Tiger Swallowtail butterfly

Date	Mintage	MS-63	Proof
2004 Proof	20,462	—	30.00

KM# 536 50 CENTS

9.3000 g., 0.9250 Silver with partial gold plating 0.2766 oz. ASW, 27.13 mm. **Ruler:** Elizabeth II **Subject:** Golden rose **Obv:** Head right **Obv. Designer:** Susanna Blunt **Rev. Designer:** Christie Paquet

Date	Mintage	MS-63	Proof
2005 Proof	17,418	—	19.00

KM# 537 50 CENTS

9.3000 g., 0.9250 Silver 0.2766 oz. ASW, 27.13 mm. **Ruler:** Elizabeth II **Obv:** Head right **Obv. Designer:** Susanna Blunt **Rev:** Great Spangled Fritillary butterfly, hologram **Rev. Designer:** Jianping Yan

Date	Mintage	MS-63	Proof
2005 Proof	20,000	—	35.00

KM# 538 50 CENTS

9.3000 g., 0.9250 Silver 0.2766 oz. ASW, 27.13 mm. **Ruler:** Elizabeth II **Subject:** Toronto Maple Leafs **Obv:** Head right **Obv. Designer:** Susanna Blunt **Rev:** Darryl Sittler

Date	Mintage	MS-63	Proof
2005 Specimen	25,000	—	16.00

KM# 539 50 CENTS

9.3000 g., 0.9250 Silver 0.2766 oz. ASW, 27.13 mm. **Ruler:** Elizabeth II **Subject:** Toronto Maple Leafs **Obv:** Head right **Obv. Designer:** Susanna Blunt **Rev:** Dave Keon

Date	Mintage	MS-63	Proof
2005 Specimen	25,000	—	16.00

KM# 540 50 CENTS

9.3000 g., 0.9250 Silver 0.2766 oz. ASW, 27.13 mm. **Ruler:** Elizabeth II **Subject:** Toronto Maple Leafs **Obv:** Head right **Obv. Designer:** Susanna Blunt **Rev:** Jonny Bover

Date	Mintage	MS-63	Proof
2005 Specimen	25,000	—	16.00

KM# 541 50 CENTS

9.3000 g., 0.9250 Silver 0.2766 oz. ASW, 27.13 mm. **Ruler:** Elizabeth II **Subject:** Toronto Maple Leafs **Obv:** Head right **Obv. Designer:** Susanna Blunt **Rev:** Tim Horton

Date	Mintage	MS-63	Proof
2005 Specimen	25,000	—	16.00

KM# 542 50 CENTS

1.2700 g., 0.9999 Gold 0.0408 oz. AGW **Ruler:** Elizabeth II **Subject:** Voyageurs **Obv:** Head right

Date	Mintage	MS-63	Proof
2005 Proof	—	—	65.00

KM# 543 50 CENTS

9.3000 g., 0.9250 Silver 0.2766 oz. ASW **Ruler:** Elizabeth II **Subject:** WWII - Battle of Britain **Obv:** Head right **Rev:** Fighter plane in sky

Date	Mintage	MS-63	Proof
2005 Specimen	20,000	—	22.50

KM# 544 50 CENTS

9.3000 g., 0.9250 Silver 0.2766 oz. ASW, 27.13 mm. **Ruler:** Elizabeth II **Subject:** WWII - Battle of Scheldt **Obv:** Head right **Obv. Designer:** Susanna Blunt **Rev:** Four soldiers walking down road **Rev. Designer:** Peter Mossman

Date	Mintage	MS-63	Proof
2005 Specimen	20,000	—	19.00

KM# 545 50 CENTS

9.3000 g., 0.9250 Silver 0.2766 oz. ASW, 27.13 mm. **Ruler:** Elizabeth II **Subject:** WWII - Battle of the Atlantic **Obv:** Head right **Obv. Designer:** Susanna Blunt **Rev:** Merchant ship sinking **Rev. Designer:** Peter Mossman

Date	Mintage	MS-63	Proof
2005 Specimen	20,000	—	19.00

KM# 546 50 CENTS

9.3000 g., 0.9250 Silver 0.2766 oz. ASW, 27.13 mm. **Ruler:** Elizabeth II **Subject:** WWII - Conquest of Sicily **Obv:** Head right **Obv. Designer:** Susanna Blunt **Rev:** Tank among town ruins **Rev. Designer:** Peter Mossman

Date	Mintage	MS-63	Proof
2005 Specimen	20,000	—	19.00

KM# 547 50 CENTS

9.3000 g., 0.9250 Silver 0.2766 oz. ASW, 27.13 mm. **Ruler:** Elizabeth II **Subject:** WWII - Liberation of the Netherlands **Obv:** Head right **Obv. Designer:** Susanna Blunt **Rev:** Soldiers in parade, one holding flag **Rev. Designer:** Peter Mossman

Date	Mintage	MS-63	Proof
2005 Specimen	20,000	—	19.00

KM# 548 50 CENTS

9.3000 g., 0.9250 Silver 0.2766 oz. ASW, 27.13 mm. **Ruler:** Elizabeth II **Subject:** WWII - Raid of Dieppe **Obv:** Head right **Obv. Designer:** Susanna Blunt **Rev:** Three soldiers exiting landing craft **Rev. Designer:** Peter Mossman

Date	Mintage	MS-63	Proof
2005 Specimen	20,000	—	19.00

KM# 577 50 CENTS

9.3000 g., 0.9250 Silver 0.2766 oz. ASW, 27.13 mm. **Ruler:** Elizabeth II **Subject:** Montreal Canadiens **Obv:** Head right **Obv. Designer:** Susanna Blunt **Rev:** Guy LaFleur

Date	Mintage	MS-63	Proof
2005 Specimen	25,000	—	17.50

KM# 578 50 CENTS

9.3000 g., 0.9250 Silver 0.2766 oz. ASW, 27.13 mm. **Ruler:** Elizabeth II **Subject:** Montreal Canadiens **Obv:** Head right **Obv. Designer:** Susanna Blunt **Rev:** Jaque Plante

Date	Mintage	MS-63	Proof
2005 Specimen	25,000	—	17.50

KM# 579 50 CENTS

9.3000 g., 0.9250 Silver 0.2766 oz. ASW, 27.13 mm. **Ruler:** Elizabeth II **Subject:** Montreal Canadiens **Obv:** Head right **Obv. Designer:** Susanna Blunt **Rev:** Jean Beliveau

Date	Mintage	MS-63	Proof
2005 Specimen	25,000	—	17.50

KM# 580 50 CENTS

9.3000 g., 0.9250 Silver 0.2766 oz. ASW, 27.13 mm. **Ruler:** Elizabeth II **Subject:** Montreal Canadiens **Obv:** Head right **Obv. Designer:** Susanna Blunt **Rev:** Maurice Richard

Date	Mintage	MS-63	Proof
2005 Specimen	25,000	—	17.50

KM# 599 50 CENTS

9.3000 g., 0.9250 Silver 0.2766 oz. ASW, 27.13 mm. **Ruler:** Elizabeth II **Subject:** Monarch butterfly, colorized **Obv:** Head right **Obv. Designer:** Susanna Blunt **Rev. Designer:** Susan Taylor

Date	Mintage	MS-63	Proof
2005 Proof	20,000	—	35.00

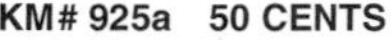

KM# 925a 50 CENTS

1.2700 g., 0.9990 Gold 0.0408 oz. AGW, 13.92 mm. **Ruler:** Elizabeth II **Rev:** Voyagers with northern lights above **Rev. Designer:** Emanuel Hahn

Date	Mintage	MS-63	Proof
2005 Proof	Est. 25,000	—	100

KM# 648 50 CENTS

9.3000 g., 0.9250 Silver With Partial Gold Plating 0.2766 oz. ASW **Ruler:** Elizabeth II **Subject:** Golden Daisy **Obv:** Head right

Date	Mintage	MS-63	Proof
2006	18,190	22.00	—

KM# 649 50 CENTS

9.3000 g., 0.9250 Silver 0.2766 oz. ASW **Ruler:** Elizabeth II **Subject:** Short-tailed swallowtail **Obv:** Head right **Rev:** Colorized butterfly

Date	Mintage	MS-63	Proof
2006	20,000	25.00	—

KM# 650 50 CENTS

9.3000 g., 0.9250 Silver 0.2766 oz. ASW **Ruler:** Elizabeth II **Obv:** Head right **Rev:** Silvery blue hologram

Date	Mintage	MS-63	Proof
2006	16,000	25.00	—

KM# 651 50 CENTS

9.3000 g., 0.9250 Silver 0.2766 oz. ASW **Ruler:** Elizabeth II **Subject:** Cowboy **Obv:** Head right

Date	Mintage	MS-63	Proof
2006	—	17.50	—

KM# 716 50 CENTS

9.3000 g., 0.9250 Silver 0.2766 oz. ASW **Ruler:** Elizabeth II **Rev:** Multicolor holiday ornaments

Date	Mintage	MS-63	Proof
2006	16,989	17.50	—

KM# 717 50 CENTS

1.2400 g., 0.9990 Gold 0.0398 oz. AGW, 13.9 mm. **Ruler:** Elizabeth II **Rev:** Wolf

Date	Mintage	MS-63	Proof
2006 Proof	—	—	100

KM# 926 50 CENTS

1.2400 g., 0.9990 Gold 0.0398 oz. AGW, 13.9 mm. **Ruler:** Elizabeth II **Rev:** Cowboy and bronco rider

Date	Mintage	MS-63	Proof
2006 Proof	—	—	100

KM# 715 50 CENTS

9.3000 g., 0.9250 Silver with partial gold plating 0.2766 oz. ASW, 27.12 mm. **Ruler:** Elizabeth II **Rev:** Forget-me-not flower

Date	Mintage	MS-63	Proof
2007 Proof	22,882	—	29.00

KM# 927 50 CENTS

1.2400 g., 0.9990 Gold 0.0398 oz. AGW, 13.9 mm. **Ruler:** Elizabeth II **Subject:** Gold Louis

Date	Mintage	MS-63	Proof
2007 Proof	—	—	100

KM# 777 50 CENTS

1.2400 g., 0.9990 Gold 0.0398 oz. AGW, 13.9 mm. **Ruler:** Elizabeth II **Subject:** DeHavilland beaver

Date	Mintage	MS-63	Proof
2008 Proof	20,000	—	100

KM# 778 50 CENTS

20.0000 g., 0.9250 Silver colorized green 0.5948 oz. ASW, 34.06 mm. **Ruler:** Elizabeth II **Subject:** Milk delivery **Obv:** Bust right **Rev:** Cow head and milk can **Shape:** Triangle

Date	Mintage	MS-63	Proof
2008 Proof	25,000	—	35.00

KM# 779 50 CENTS

9.3000 g., 0.9250 Silver 0.2766 oz. ASW **Ruler:** Elizabeth II **Rev:** Multicolor snowman

Date	Mintage	MS-63	Proof
2008	—	17.50	—

KM# 780 50 CENTS

9.3000 g., 0.9250 Silver 0.2766 oz. ASW **Ruler:** Elizabeth II **Subject:** Ottawa Mint Centennial 1908-2008

Date	Mintage	MS-63	Proof
2008	—	20.00	—

KM# 845 50 CENTS

9.3000 g., 0.9250 Silver 0.2766 oz. ASW, 27.13 mm. **Ruler:** Elizabeth II **Rev:** Calgary Flames lenticular design, old and new logos

Date	Mintage	MS-63	Proof
2009	—	15.00	—

KM# 846 50 CENTS

9.3000 g., 0.9250 Silver 0.2766 oz. ASW, 27.13 mm. **Ruler:** Elizabeth II **Rev:** Edmonton Oiler's lenticular design, old and new logos

Date	Mintage	MS-63	Proof
2009	—	15.00	—

KM# 847 50 CENTS

9.3000 g., 0.9250 Silver 0.2766 oz. ASW, 27.13 mm. **Ruler:** Elizabeth II **Rev:** Montreal Canadiens lenticular design, old and new logos

Date	Mintage	MS-63	Proof
2009	—	15.00	—

KM# 848 50 CENTS

9.3000 g., 0.9250 Silver 0.2766 oz. ASW, 27.13 mm. **Ruler:** Elizabeth II **Rev:** Ottawa Senators lenticular design, old and new logos

Date	Mintage	MS-63	Proof
2009	—	15.00	—

KM# 849 50 CENTS

9.3000 g., 0.9250 Silver 0.2766 oz. ASW, 27.13 mm. **Ruler:** Elizabeth II **Rev:** Toronto Maple Leafs lenticular design, old and new logos

Date	Mintage	MS-63	Proof
2009	—	15.00	—

KM# 850 50 CENTS

9.3000 g., 0.9250 Silver 0.2766 oz. ASW, 27.13 mm. **Ruler:** Elizabeth II **Rev:** Vancouver Canucks lenticular design, old and new logos

Date	Mintage	MS-63	Proof
2009	—	15.00	—

KM# 857 50 CENTS

6.9000 g., Nickel Plated Steel, 35 mm. **Ruler:** Elizabeth II **Rev:** Calgary Flames lenticular old and new logos

Date	Mintage	MS-63	Proof
2009	—	25.00	—

KM# 858 50 CENTS

6.9000 g., Nickel Plated Steel, 35 mm. **Ruler:** Elizabeth II **Rev:** Edmonton Oilers lenticular old and new logos

Date	Mintage	MS-63	Proof
2009	—	25.00	—

KM# 859 50 CENTS

35.0000 g., Nickel Plated Steel, 35 mm. **Ruler:** Elizabeth II **Rev:** Montreal Canadians lenticular old and new logo

Date	Mintage	MS-63	Proof
2009	—	25.00	—

KM# 860 50 CENTS

6.9000 g., Nickel Plated Steel, 35 mm. **Ruler:** Elizabeth II **Rev:** Ottawa Senators lenticular old and new logos

Date	Mintage	MS-63	Proof
2009	—	25.00	—

KM# 861 50 CENTS

6.9000 g., Nickel Plated Steel, 35 mm. **Ruler:** Elizabeth II **Rev:** Toronto Maple Leafs lenticular old and new logos

Date	Mintage	MS-63	Proof
2009	—	25.00	—

KM# 862 50 CENTS

6.9000 g., Nickel Plated Steel, 35 mm. **Ruler:** Elizabeth II **Rev:** Vancouver Canucks lenticular old and new logos

Date	Mintage	MS-63	Proof
2009	—	25.00	—

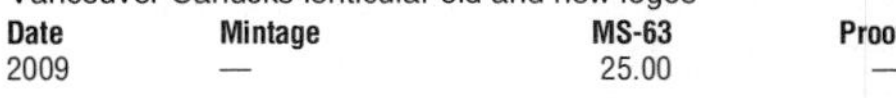

KM# 887 50 CENTS
19.1000 g., Copper-Nickel, 34.06 mm. **Ruler:** Elizabeth II **Subject:** Six-string national guitar **Obv:** Bust right **Obv. Legend:** Elizabeth II DG Regina **Obv. Designer:** Susanna Blunt **Rev:** Hologram with 6 "strings" **Rev. Legend:** 50 cents Canada **Shape:** Triangle

Date	Mintage	MS-63	Proof
2009 Proof	30,000	—	50.00

KM# 936 50 CENTS
9.3000 g., Nickel **Ruler:** Elizabeth II **Rev:** Vancouver Canucks goalie jersey

Date	Mintage	MS-63	Proof
2009	—	15.00	—

KM# 937 50 CENTS
6.9000 g., Nickel Plated Steel, 35 mm. **Ruler:** Elizabeth II **Rev:** Calgary Flames player - colorized

Date	Mintage	MS-63	Proof
2009	—	15.00	—

KM# 938 50 CENTS
6.9000 g., Nickel Plated Steel, 35 mm. **Ruler:** Elizabeth II **Rev:** Edmonton Oilers player

Date	Mintage	MS-63	Proof
2009	—	15.00	—

KM# 939 50 CENTS
6.9000 g., Nickel Plated Steel, 35 mm. **Ruler:** Elizabeth II **Rev:** Toronto Maple Leafs player

Date	Mintage	MS-63	Proof
2009	—	15.00	—

KM# 940 50 CENTS
6.9000 g., Nickel Plated Steel, 35 mm. **Ruler:** Elizabeth II **Rev:** Montreal Canadiens player

Date	Mintage	MS-63	Proof
2009	—	15.00	—

KM# 941 50 CENTS
6.9000 g., Nickel Plated Steel, 35 mm. **Ruler:** Elizabeth II **Rev:** Ottawa Senators player

Date	Mintage	MS-63	Proof
2009	—	15.00	—

KM# 1035 50 CENTS
Brass Plated Steel **Ruler:** Elizabeth II **Subject:** Christmas toy train **Rev:** movement from far to close

Date	Mintage	MS-63	Proof
2009	—	17.50	—

KM# 961 50 CENTS
6.9000 g., Nickel Plated Steel, 35 mm. **Ruler:** Elizabeth II **Rev:** Bob sleigh

Date	Mintage	MS-63	Proof
2010	—	15.00	—

KM# 961a 50 CENTS
6.9000 g., Nickel Plated Steel, 35 mm. **Ruler:** Elizabeth II **Rev:** Bob sleigh - red enamel

Date	Mintage	MS-63	Proof
2010	—	15.00	—

KM# 962 50 CENTS
6.9000 g., Nickel Plated Steel, 35 mm. **Ruler:** Elizabeth II **Rev:** Speed skating

Date	Mintage	MS-63	Proof
2010	—	15.00	—

KM# 962a 50 CENTS
6.9000 g., Nickel Plated Steel, 35 mm. **Ruler:** Elizabeth II **Rev:** Speed skating - red enamel

Date	Mintage	MS-63	Proof
2010	—	15.00	—

KM# 963 50 CENTS
6.9000 g., Nickel Plated Steel, 35 mm. **Ruler:** Elizabeth II **Rev:** Miga in bob sleigh

Date	Mintage	MS-63	Proof
2010	—	15.00	—

KM# 964 50 CENTS
6.9000 g., Nickel Plated Steel, 35 mm. **Ruler:** Elizabeth II **Rev:** Miga in hockey

Date	Mintage	MS-63	Proof
2010	—	15.00	—

KM# 965 50 CENTS
6.9000 g., Nickel Plated Steel, 35 mm. **Ruler:** Elizabeth II **Rev:** Quatchi in ice hockey

Date	Mintage	MS-63	Proof
2010	—	15.00	—

KM# 966 50 CENTS
6.9000 g., Nickel Plated Steel, 35 mm. **Ruler:** Elizabeth II **Rev:** Sumi Para Sledge

Date	Mintage	MS-63	Proof
2010	—	15.00	—

KM# 967 50 CENTS
6.9000 g., Nickel Plated Zinc, 35 mm. **Ruler:** Elizabeth II **Rev:** Figure-skating mascot

Date	Mintage	MS-63	Proof
2010	—	15.00	—

KM# 968 50 CENTS
6.9000 g., Nickel Plated Steel, 35 mm. **Ruler:** Elizabeth II **Rev:** Free-style mascot

Date	Mintage	MS-63	Proof
2010	—	15.00	—

KM# 969 50 CENTS
6.9000 g., Nickel Plated Steel, 35 mm. **Ruler:** Elizabeth II **Rev:** Skeleton mascot

Date	Mintage	MS-63	Proof
2010	—	15.00	—

KM# 970 50 CENTS
6.9000 g., Nickel Plated Steel, 35 mm. **Ruler:** Elizabeth II **Rev:** Parallel giant slalom mascot

Date	Mintage	MS-63	Proof
2010	—	15.00	—

KM# 971 50 CENTS
6.9000 g., Nickel Plated Steel, 35 mm. **Ruler:** Elizabeth II **Rev:** Alpine skiing mascot

Date	Mintage	MS-63	Proof
2010	—	15.00	—

KM# 972 50 CENTS
6.9000 g., Nickel Plated Steel, 35 mm. **Ruler:** Elizabeth II **Rev:** Para Olympic alpine skiing mascott

Date	Mintage	MS-63	Proof
2010	—	15.00	—

KM# 973 50 CENTS
6.9000 g., Nickel Plated Steel, 35 mm. **Ruler:** Elizabeth II **Rev:** Snowboard mascot

Date	Mintage	MS-63	Proof
2010	—	15.00	—

KM# 974 50 CENTS
6.9000 g., Nickel Plated Steel, 35 mm. **Ruler:** Elizabeth II **Rev:** Speed-skating mascott

Date	Mintage	MS-63	Proof
2010	—	15.00	—

KM# 985 50 CENTS
1.2400 g., 0.9990 Gold 0.0398 oz. AGW, 13.92 mm. **Ruler:** Elizabeth II **Subject:** RCMP **Rev:** Mountie on horseback **Rev. Designer:** Janet Griffin-Scott

Date	Mintage	MS-63	Proof
2010 Proof	Est. 14,000	—	100

KM# 986 50 CENTS
12.6100 g., Brass Plated Steel **Ruler:** Elizabeth II **Rev:** Dasplerosaurus Torosus - 3-D lenticular movement

Date	Mintage	MS-63	Proof
2010 Specimen	—	—	40.00

KM# 1015 50 CENTS
12.6100 g., Brass Plated Steel, 35 mm. **Ruler:** Elizabeth II **Rev:** Sinosauropteryx

Date	Mintage	MS-63	Proof
2010	—	25.00	—

KM# 1016 50 CENTS
12.6100 g., Brass Plated Steel, 35 mm. **Ruler:** Elizabeth II **Rev:** Albertosaurus

Date	Mintage	MS-63	Proof
2010	—	25.00	—

KM# 1043 50 CENTS
Nickel Plated Steel **Ruler:** Elizabeth II **Rev:** Santa Claus transforms into Rudolf the red-nosed reindeer

Date	Mintage	MS-63	Proof
2010	—	17.50	—

KM# 186 DOLLAR
7.0000 g., Aureate-Bronze Plated Nickel, 26.5 mm. **Ruler:** Elizabeth II **Obv:** Crowned head right **Obv. Designer:** Dora dePedery-Hunt **Rev:** Loon right, date and denomination **Rev. Designer:** Robert R. Carmichael **Shape:** 11-sided

Date	Mintage	MS-63	Proof
2001	—	2.50	—
2001 Proof	74,194	—	8.00
2002	—	4.50	—
2002 Proof	65,315	—	7.50
2003	—	5.50	—
Note: Mintage of 5,101,000 includes both KM186 and KM495 examples.			
2003 Proof	—	—	12.00

KM# 414 DOLLAR
25.1750 g., 0.9250 Silver 0.7487 oz. ASW, 36 mm. **Ruler:** Elizabeth II **Subject:** National Ballet **Obv:** Crowned head right **Rev:** Ballet dancers **Rev. Designer:** Scott McKowen **Edge:** Reeded

Date	Mintage	MS-63	Proof
2001	65,000	27.50	—
2001 Proof	225,000	—	35.00

KM# 434 DOLLAR

25.1750 g., 0.9250 Silver 0.7487 oz. ASW, 36 mm. **Ruler:** Elizabeth II **Obv:** Crowned head right **Rev:** Recycled 1911 pattern dollar design: denomination, country name and dates in crowned wreath **Edge:** Reeded

Date	Mintage	MS-63	Proof
ND(2001) Proof	24,996	—	55.00

KM# 186a DOLLAR

Gilt Aureate-Bronze Plated Nickel, 26.5 mm. **Ruler:** Elizabeth II **Subject:** Olympic Win

Date	Mintage	MS-63	Proof
2002 Proof	—	—	40.00

KM# 443 DOLLAR

25.1750 g., 0.9250 Silver 0.7487 oz. ASW, 36 mm. **Ruler:** Elizabeth II **Subject:** Queen's Golden Jubilee **Obv:** Crowned head right, with anniversary date at left **Obv. Designer:** Dora dePédery-Hunt **Rev:** Queen in her coach and a view of the coach, denomination below **Edge:** Reeded

Date	Mintage	MS-63	Proof
ND(2002)	65,140	28.50	—
ND(2002) Proof	29,688	—	40.00

KM# 443a DOLLAR

25.1800 g., 0.9250 Silver Gilt 0.7488 oz. ASW, 36 mm. **Ruler:** Elizabeth II **Subject:** Queen's Golden Jubilee **Obv:** Crowned head right with anniversary date **Rev:** Queen in her coach and a view of the coach **Edge:** Reeded **Note:** Special 24 karat gold plated issue of KM#443.

Date	Mintage	MS-63	Proof
ND(2002) Proof	32,642	—	45.00

KM# 462 DOLLAR

7.0000 g., Aureate-Bronze Plated Nickel **Ruler:** Elizabeth II **Obv:** Commemorative dates 1952-2002 **Obv. Designer:** Dora dePédery-Hunt **Rev:** Family of Loons

Date	Mintage	MS-63	Proof
ND(2002) Specimen	67,672	—	35.00

KM# 467 DOLLAR

7.0000 g., Aureate-Bronze Plated Nickel **Ruler:** Elizabeth II **Subject:** Elizabeth II Golden Jubilee **Obv:** Crowned head right, Jubilee commemorative dates 1952-2002 **Obv. Designer:** Dora dePédery-Hunt

Date	Mintage	MS-63	Proof
ND(2002)	2,302,000	2.50	—
ND(2002) Proof	—	—	8.00

KM# 467a DOLLAR

Gold **Ruler:** Elizabeth II **Subject:** 50th Anniversary, Accession to the Throne **Obv:** Crowned head right **Note:** Sold on the internet.

Date	Mintage	MS-63	Proof
ND(2002)	1	—	55,500

KM# 503 DOLLAR

25.1750 g., 0.9250 Silver 0.7487 oz. ASW, 36 mm. **Ruler:** Elizabeth II **Subject:** Queen Mother **Obv:** Crowned head right **Obv. Designer:** Dora de Pedery-Hunt **Rev:** Queen Mother facing

Date	Mintage	MS-63	Proof
2002 Proof	9,994	—	250

KM# 450 DOLLAR

25.1750 g., 0.9999 Silver 0.8093 oz. ASW, 36 mm. **Ruler:** Elizabeth II **Subject:** Cobalt Mining Centennial **Obv:** Queens portrait right **Obv. Designer:** Dora dePédery-Hunt **Rev:** Mine tower and fox **Edge:** Reeded

Date	Mintage	MS-63	Proof
ND(2003)	51,130	30.00	—
ND(2003) Proof	88,536	—	45.00

KM# 495 DOLLAR

7.0000 g., Aureate-Bronze Plated Nickel, 26.5 mm. **Ruler:** Elizabeth II **Obv:** Bare head right **Obv. Designer:** Susanna Blunt **Rev:** Loon right **Rev. Designer:** Robert R. Carmichael **Shape:** 11-sided

Date	Mintage	MS-63	Proof
2003	5,102,000	5.50	—
Note: Mintage of 5,101,000 includes both KM 186 and 495 examples.			
2003W Prooflike	—	—	—
2003 Proof	62,507	—	7.50
2004	10,894,000	1.75	—
2004 Proof	—	—	12.00
2005	44,375,000	3.00	—
2005 Proof	—	—	7.50
2006	49,111,000	3.00	—
2006 Proof	—	—	7.50
2006(ml)	49,111,000	3.00	—
2006(ml) Proof	—	—	7.50
2007(ml)	38,045,000	3.00	—
2007(ml) Proof	—	—	7.50
2008(ml)	29,561,000	3.00	—
2008(ml) Proof	—	—	7.50
2009(ml)	39,601,000	3.00	—
2009(ml) Proof	—	—	7.50
2010(ml)	—	3.00	—
2010(ml) Proof	—	—	7.50
2011(ml)	—	3.00	—
2011(ml) Proof	—	—	7.50

KM# 473 DOLLAR

25.1750 g., 0.9999 Silver 0.8093 oz. ASW **Ruler:** Elizabeth II **Subject:** 50th Anniversary of the Coronation of Elizabeth II **Obv:** 1953 effigy of the Queen, Jubilee dates 1953-2003 **Obv. Designer:** Mary Gillick **Rev:** Voyageur, date and denomination below

Date	Mintage	MS-63	Proof
ND(2003) Proof	29,586	—	45.00

KM# 473a DOLLAR

Gold **Ruler:** Elizabeth II **Subject:** 50th Anniversary of Coronation **Obv. Designer:** Mary Gilick **Rev:** Voyageur **Note:** Sold on the internet.

Date	Mintage	MS-63	Proof
2003	1	—	62,750

KM# 480 DOLLAR

25.1750 g., 0.9999 Silver 0.8093 oz. ASW **Ruler:** Elizabeth II **Subject:** Coronation of Queen Elizabeth II **Obv:** Head right **Rev:** Voyaguers **Rev. Designer:** Emanuel Hahn

Date	Mintage	MS-63	Proof
ND2003 Proof	21,400	—	50.00

KM# 507 DOLLAR

7.0000 g., Aureate-Bronze Plated Nickel, 26.5 mm. **Ruler:** Elizabeth II **Obv:** Bare head right, date below **Obv. Designer:** Susanna Blunt **Rev:** Loon **Edge:** Plain **Shape:** 11-sided

Date	Mintage	MS-63	Proof
2004 Proof	12,550	—	75.00

KM# 511 DOLLAR

25.1750 g., 0.9999 Silver 0.8093 oz. ASW, 36 mm. **Ruler:** Elizabeth II **Obv:** Elizabeth II **Rev:** Poppy on maple leaf **Edge:** Reeded

Date	Mintage	MS-63	Proof
2004 Proof	25,000	—	50.00

KM# 512 DOLLAR

25.1750 g., 0.9999 Silver 0.8093 oz. ASW, 36 mm. **Ruler:** Elizabeth II **Subject:** First French Settlement in America **Obv:** Crowned head right **Rev:** Sailing ship **Edge:** Reeded

Date	Mintage	MS-63	Proof
2004	42,582	30.00	—
2004 Fleur-dis-lis	8,315	60.00	—
2004 Proof	106,974	—	50.00

KM# 513 DOLLAR

7.0000 g., Aureate-Bronze Plated Nickel, 26.5 mm. **Ruler:** Elizabeth II **Subject:** Olympics **Obv:** Bare head right **Rev:** Maple leaf, Olympic flame and rings above loon **Edge:** Plain **Shape:** 11-sided

Date	Mintage	MS-63	Proof
2004	6,526,000	8.00	—

KM# 513a DOLLAR

9.3100 g., 0.9250 Silver 0.2769 oz. ASW, 26.5 mm. **Ruler:** Elizabeth II **Subject:** Olympics **Obv:** Bare head right **Rev:** Multicolor maple leaf, Olympic flame and rings above loon **Edge:** Plain **Shape:** 11-sided

Date	Mintage	MS-63	Proof
2004 Proof	19,994	—	50.00

KM# 549 DOLLAR

25.1750 g., 0.9250 Silver 0.7487 oz. ASW **Ruler:** Elizabeth II **Subject:** 40th Anniversary of National Flag **Obv:** Head right **Obv. Designer:** Susanna Blunt **Rev. Designer:** William Woodruff

Date	Mintage	MS-63	Proof
2005	50,948	27.50	—
2005 Proof	95,431	—	40.00

KM# 549a DOLLAR

25.1750 g., 0.9250 Silver partially gilt 0.7487 oz. ASW, 36.07 mm. **Ruler:** Elizabeth II **Subject:** 40th Anniversary of National Flag **Obv:** Head right

Date	Mintage	MS-63	Proof
2005	62,483	75.00	—

KM# 549b DOLLAR

25.1800 g., 0.9250 Silver 0.7488 oz. ASW, 36.07 mm. **Ruler:** Elizabeth II **Subject:** 40th Anniversary National Flag **Rev:** National flag, colorized

Date	Mintage	MS-63	Proof
ND(1965-2005) Proof	4,898	—	350

KM# 552 DOLLAR

7.0000 g., Aureate-Bronze Plated Nickel **Ruler:** Elizabeth II **Subject:** Terry Fox **Obv:** Head right

Date	Mintage	MS-63	Proof
2005	1,290,900	3.50	—

KM# 553 DOLLAR

7.0000 g., Aureate-Bronze Plated Nickel **Ruler:** Elizabeth II **Subject:** Tuffed Puffin **Obv:** Head right **Obv. Designer:** Susanna Blunt

Date	Mintage	MS-63	Proof
2005 Specimen	40,000	—	30.00

KM# 581 DOLLAR

9.3100 g., 0.9250 Silver 0.2769 oz. ASW **Ruler:** Elizabeth II **Subject:** Lullabies Loonie **Obv:** Head right **Obv. Designer:** Susanna Blunt **Rev:** Loon and moon, teddy bear in stars

Date	Mintage	MS-63	Proof
2006	18,103	4.50	—

KM# 582 DOLLAR

7.0000 g., Aureate-Bronze Plated Nickel **Ruler:** Elizabeth II **Subject:** Snowy owl **Obv:** Head right **Obv. Designer:** Susanna Blunt **Rev:** Snowy owl with year above

Date	Mintage	MS-63	Proof
2006 Specimen	40,000	—	30.00

KM# 583 DOLLAR

25.1750 g., 0.9250 Silver 0.7487 oz. ASW **Ruler:** Elizabeth II **Subject:** Victoria Cross **Obv:** Head right

Date	Mintage	MS-63	Proof
2006	27,254	25.00	—
2006 Proof	59,599	—	45.00

KM# 583a DOLLAR

25.1750 g., 0.9250 Silver with partial gold plating 0.7487 oz. ASW **Ruler:** Elizabeth II **Subject:** Victoria Cross **Obv:** Head right

Date	Mintage	MS-63	Proof
2006 Proof	—	—	75.00

KM# 630 DOLLAR

9.3100 g., 0.9250 Silver with enamel 0.2769 oz. ASW **Ruler:** Elizabeth II **Subject:** Olympic Games **Obv:** Crowned head right **Rev:** Loon in flight, colored olympic logo above

Date	Mintage	MS-63	Proof
2006	19,956	30.00	—

KM# 653 DOLLAR

25.1750 g., 0.9250 Silver 0.7487 oz. ASW, 36.07 mm. **Ruler:** Elizabeth II **Subject:** Thayendanegea **Obv:** Head right **Rev:** Bust

Date	Mintage	MS-63	Proof
2006(ml)	16,378	30.00	—
2006(ml) Proof	65,000	—	40.00

KM# 653a DOLLAR

25.1750 g., 0.9250 Silver 0.7487 oz. ASW, 36.07 mm. **Ruler:** Elizabeth II **Subject:** Thayendanega **Obv:** Bust right **Rev:** Bust, partially gilt

Date	Mintage	MS-63	Proof
2006	60,000	—	125

KM# 654 DOLLAR

7.0000 g., 0.9250 Silver 0.2082 oz. ASW **Ruler:** Elizabeth II **Obv:** Head right **Rev:** Snowflake, colorized **Note:** Sold in a CD package.

Date	Mintage	MS-63	Proof
2006(ml)	34,014	35.00	—

KM# 655 DOLLAR

7.0000 g., 0.9250 Silver 0.2082 oz. ASW **Ruler:** Elizabeth II **Subject:** Baby Rattle **Obv:** Head right **Rev:** Baby rattle

Date	Mintage	MS-63	Proof
2006	3,207	20.00	—

KM# 656 DOLLAR

28.1750 g., 0.9250 Silver 0.8379 oz. ASW **Ruler:** Elizabeth II **Subject:** Medal of Bravery **Obv:** Head right

Date	Mintage	MS-63	Proof
2006 Proof	8,343	—	50.00

KM# 656a DOLLAR

28.1750 g., 0.9250 Silver with multicolor enamel 0.8379 oz. ASW **Ruler:** Elizabeth II **Subject:** Medal of Bravery **Obv:** Head right **Rev:** Maple leaf within wreath. Colorized.

Date	Mintage	MS-63	Proof
2006 Proof	4,999	—	150

KM# 688 DOLLAR

7.0000 g., Aureate Bronze, 26.5 mm. **Ruler:** Elizabeth II **Obv:** Head right **Rev:** Trumpeter Swan

Date	Mintage	MS-63	Proof
2007(ml)	40,000	20.00	—

KM# 720 DOLLAR

25.1800 g., 0.9250 Silver 0.7488 oz. ASW, 36.07 mm. **Ruler:** Elizabeth II **Obv:** Bust right **Rev:** Thayendanega multicolor

Date	Mintage	MS-63	Proof
2007 Proof	4,760	—	120

KM# 720a DOLLAR

2.0000 g., 0.9250 Silver 0.0595 oz. ASW, 36.07 mm. **Ruler:** Elizabeth II **Subject:** Thayendanega **Rev:** Partially gold plated

Date	Mintage	MS-63	Proof
2007 Proof	60,000	—	125

KM# 655a DOLLAR

7.0000 g., 0.9250 Silver 0.2082 oz. ASW **Ruler:** Elizabeth II **Obv:** Bust right **Rev:** Baby Rattle, partially gilt

Date	Mintage	MS-63	Proof
2007	1,911	15.00	—

KM# 700 DOLLAR

7.0000 g., 0.9250 Silver 0.2082 oz. ASW **Ruler:** Elizabeth II **Rev:** Alphabet Letter Blocks

Date	Mintage	MS-63	Proof
2007	3,229	—	25.00

KM# 719 DOLLAR

25.1800 g., 0.9250 Silver 0.7488 oz. ASW, 36.07 mm. **Ruler:** Elizabeth II **Subject:** Celebration of the Arts **Rev:** Book, TV set, musical instruments, film montage **Rev. Designer:** Friedrich Peter **Edge:** Reeded

Date	Mintage	MS-63	Proof
2007	6,466	—	55.00

KM# A727 DOLLAR

7.0000 g., Aureate Bronze, 26.5 mm. **Ruler:** Elizabeth II **Subject:** Vancouver Olympic Games **Rev:** Loon splashing in water, Olympics logo at right

Date	Mintage	MS-63	Proof
2007(ml)	30,000	3.00	—

KM# 721 DOLLAR

7.0000 g., Nickel-Bronze, 26.5 mm. **Ruler:** Elizabeth II **Obv:** Bust right **Rev:** Calgary flames, multicolor in circle

Date	Mintage	MS-63	Proof
2008	—	25.00	—

KM# 722 DOLLAR

7.0000 g., Nickel-Bronze, 26.5 mm. **Ruler:** Elizabeth II **Obv:** Bust **Rev:** Edmonton Oilers logo, multicolor in logo

Date	Mintage	MS-63	Proof
2008	—	25.00	—

KM# 723A DOLLAR

7.0000 g., Nickel-Bronze, 26.5 mm. **Ruler:** Elizabeth II **Obv:** Bust right **Rev:** Montreal Canadians, multicolor logo in circle

Date	Mintage	MS-63	Proof
2008	—	25.00	—

KM# 724 DOLLAR

7.0000 g., Nickel, 26.5 mm. **Ruler:** Elizabeth II **Rev:** Ottowa Senators, multicolor logo in circle

Date	Mintage	MS-63	Proof
2008	—	25.00	—

KM# 725 DOLLAR

7.0000 g., Nickel-Bronze, 26.5 mm. **Ruler:** Elizabeth II **Obv:** Bust right **Rev:** Toronto Maple Leafs, multicolor logo in circle

Date	Mintage	MS-63	Proof
2008	—	25.00	—

KM# 726 DOLLAR

7.0000 g., Nickel-Bronze, 26.5 mm. **Ruler:** Elizabeth II **Obv:** Bust left **Rev:** Vancouver Canucks, logo in center

Date	Mintage	MS-63	Proof
2008	—	25.00	—

KM# 781 DOLLAR

25.1800 g., 0.9250 Silver 0.7488 oz. ASW, 36.07 mm. **Ruler:** Elizabeth II **Subject:** Ottawa Mint Centennial 1908-2008 **Rev:** Maple leaf transforming into a common loon **Rev. Designer:** Jason Bowman

Date	Mintage	MS-63	Proof
2008 Proof	25,000	—	65.00

KM# 784 DOLLAR

7.0000 g., Nickel-Bronze, 26.5 mm. **Ruler:** Elizabeth II **Rev:** Common elder

Date	Mintage	MS-63	Proof
2008 Specimen	40,000	—	50.00

KM# 785 DOLLAR

25.1800 g., 0.9250 Silver 0.7488 oz. ASW, 36.07 mm. **Ruler:** Elizabeth II **Subject:** Founding of Quebec 400th Anniversary **Rev:** Samuel de Champlain, ship and town view **Rev. Designer:** Susanne Duranceau

Date	Mintage	MS-63	Proof
2008 Proof	65,000	—	40.00

KM# 785a DOLLAR

25.1800 g., 0.9250 Silver 0.7488 oz. ASW, 36.07 mm. **Ruler:** Elizabeth II **Subject:** Founding of Quebec 400th Anniversary **Rev:** Samuel de Champlain selectively gold plated, ship, town view **Rev. Designer:** Susanne Duranceau

Date	Mintage	MS-63	Proof
2008 Proof	—	—	75.00

KM# 787 DOLLAR
7.0000 g., Nickel-Brass, 26.5 mm. **Ruler:** Elizabeth II **Subject:** Lucky Loonie **Rev:** Loon splashing and Olympic logo at right **Rev. Designer:** Steve Hepurn

Date	Mintage	MS-63	Proof
2008	—	20.00	—

KM# 787a DOLLAR
9.3100 g., 0.9250 Silver 0.2769 oz. ASW, 26.5 mm. **Ruler:** Elizabeth II **Rev:** Loon splashing with Olympic logo and maple leaf in color above **Rev. Designer:** Steve Hepurn

Date	Mintage	MS-63	Proof
2008 Proof	30,000	—	25.00

KM# 790 DOLLAR
6.5000 g., Nickel, 26.5 mm. **Ruler:** Elizabeth II **Rev:** Calgary Flames

Date	Mintage	MS-63	Proof
2008	—	25.00	—

KM# 791 DOLLAR
6.5000 g., Nickel, 26.5 mm. **Ruler:** Elizabeth II **Rev:** Edmonton Oilers

Date	Mintage	MS-63	Proof
2008	—	25.00	—

KM# 792 DOLLAR
6.5000 g., Nickel, 26.5 mm. **Ruler:** Elizabeth II **Rev:** Montreal Canadiens

Date	Mintage	MS-63	Proof
2008	—	25.00	—

KM# 793 DOLLAR
6.5000 g., Nickel, 26.5 mm. **Ruler:** Elizabeth II **Rev:** Ottawa Senators

Date	Mintage	MS-63	Proof
2008	—	25.00	—

KM# 794 DOLLAR
6.5000 g., Nickel, 26.5 mm. **Ruler:** Elizabeth II **Rev:** Toronto Maple Leafs

Date	Mintage	MS-63	Proof
2008	—	25.00	—

KM# 795 DOLLAR
6.5000 g., Nickel, 26.5 mm. **Ruler:** Elizabeth II **Rev:** Vancouver Canucks

Date	Mintage	MS-63	Proof
2008	—	25.00	—

KM# 889 DOLLAR
25.1800 g., 0.9250 Silver 0.7488 oz. ASW, 36.07 mm. **Ruler:** Elizabeth II **Subject:** 100th Anniversary of flight in Canada **Obv:** Bust right **Obv. Legend:** Elizabeth II DG Regina **Obv. Designer:** Susanna Blunt **Rev:** Silhouette with arms spread, 3 planes, plane cutout **Rev. Legend:** Canada Dollar 1909-2009 **Rev. Designer:** Jason Bouwman

Date	Mintage	MS-63	Proof
2009	50,000	35.00	—
2009 Proof	50,000	—	55.00

KM# 914 DOLLAR
7.0000 g., Aureate-Bronze Plated Nickel, 26.5 mm. **Ruler:** Elizabeth II **Obv:** Bust right **Obv. Designer:** Susanna Blunt **Rev:** Blue heron in flight

Date	Mintage	MS-63	Proof
2009 Specimen	40,000	50.00	—

KM# 921 DOLLAR
25.1700 g., 0.9250 Silver 0.7485 oz. ASW, 36.07 mm. **Ruler:** Elizabeth II **Subject:** Montreal Canadiens 100th Anniversary **Obv:** Bust right **Obv. Designer:** Susanna Blunt **Rev:** Montreal Canadiens logo partially gilt

Date	Mintage	MS-63	Proof
2009 Proof in black case	15,000	—	75.00
2009 Proof in acrillic stand	5,000	—	150

KM# 851 DOLLAR
33.6500 g., Nickel, 26.5 mm. **Ruler:** Elizabeth II **Rev:** Calgary Flames Jersey

Date	Mintage	MS-63	Proof
2009	—	25.00	—

KM# 852 DOLLAR
33.6500 g., 0.9990 Nickel 1.0807 oz., 26.5 mm. **Ruler:** Elizabeth II **Rev:** Edmonton Oilers Jersey

Date	Mintage	MS-63	Proof
2009	—	25.00	—

KM# 853 DOLLAR
33.6500 g., Nickel, 26.5 mm. **Ruler:** Elizabeth II **Rev:** Montreal Canadians Jersey

Date	Mintage	MS-63	Proof
2009	—	25.00	—

KM# 854 DOLLAR
33.6500 g., Nickel, 26.5 mm. **Ruler:** Elizabeth II **Rev:** Ottawa Senators Jersey

Date	Mintage	MS-63	Proof
2009	—	25.00	—

KM# 855 DOLLAR
33.6500 g., Nickel, 26.5 mm. **Ruler:** Elizabeth II **Rev:** Toronto Maple Leafs Jersey

Date	Mintage	MS-63	Proof
2009	—	25.00	—

KM# 856 DOLLAR
33.6500 g., Nickel, 26.5 mm. **Ruler:** Elizabeth II **Rev:** Vancouver Canucks Jersey

Date	Mintage	MS-63	Proof
2009	—	25.00	—

KM# 889a DOLLAR
25.1800 g., 0.9250 Silver partially gilt. 0.7488 oz. ASW, 36.07 mm. **Ruler:** Elizabeth II **Obv:** Bust right **Rev:** Silouette with arms spread, 3 planes, plane shadow partially gilt

Date	Mintage	MS-63	Proof
2009(ml) Proof	—	—	50.00

KM# 883 DOLLAR
7.0000 g., Aureate-Bronze Plated Nickel, 26.5 mm. **Ruler:** Elizabeth II **Subject:** Lucky Loonie **Obv:** Bust right **Obv. Legend:** Elizabeth II DG Regina **Rev:** Canadian Olympic logo **Rev. Legend:** Canada Dollar

Date	Mintage	MS-63	Proof
2010	12,000	20.00	—

KM# 883a DOLLAR
9.3100 g., 0.9250 Silver 0.2769 oz. ASW, 26.5 mm. **Ruler:** Elizabeth II **Subject:** Lucky Loonie **Obv:** Bust right **Obv. Legend:** Elizabeth II DG Regina **Rev:** Canadian Olympic logo in color **Rev. Legend:** Vancouver 2010 Canada Dollar **Shape:** 11-sided

Date	Mintage	MS-63	Proof
2010 Proof	40,000	—	55.00

KM# 1046 DOLLAR
Aureate Bronze, 26.5 mm. **Ruler:** Elizabeth II **Subject:** Roughriders **Rev:** S logo **Shape:** 11-sided

Date	Mintage	MS-63	Proof
2010(ml)	—	7.50	—

KM# 975 DOLLAR
0.9250 Silver, 36 mm. **Ruler:** Elizabeth II **Rev:** Sun mask **Rev. Designer:** Xwa lack Tun

Date	Mintage	MS-63	Proof
2010 Proof	5,000	—	200

KM# 996 DOLLAR
7.0000 g., Aureate Bronze, 26.5 mm. **Ruler:** Elizabeth II **Rev:** Northern Harrier Hawk

Date	Mintage	MS-63	Proof
2010	—	30.00	—

KM# 1017 DOLLAR
Aureate Bronze **Ruler:** Elizabeth II **Rev:** Male and female sailors saluting, HMCS Halifax and anchor above

Date	Mintage	MS-63	Proof
2010	—	5.00	—

KM# 1027 DOLLAR
25.1800 g., 0.9250 Silver 0.7488 oz. ASW, 36.07 mm. **Ruler:** Elizabeth II **Obv:** George V bust left **Rev:** Voyaguers, dual dates below

Date	Mintage	MS-63	Proof
1935-2010 Proof	7,500	—	70.00

KM# 1050 DOLLAR
25.1800 g., 0.9250 Silver 0.7488 oz. ASW, 36.07 mm. **Ruler:** Elizabeth II **Rev:** Red poppy in large field of poppies **Edge:** Reeded

Date	Mintage	MS-63	Proof
2010 Proof	—	—	55.00

KM# 1087a DOLLAR
25.1800 g., 0.9250 Silver 0.7488 oz. ASW, 36.07 mm. **Ruler:** Elizabeth II **Subject:** Parks Canada, 100th Anniversary **Rev:** Female head looking down onhands holding nature scene, partially gilt **Rev. Designer:** Luc Normandin

Date	Mintage	MS-63	Proof
2010 Proof	45,000	—	75.00

KM# 1086 DOLLAR
7.0000 g., Bronze Plated Nickel, 26.5 mm. **Ruler:** Elizabeth II **Rev:** Great Grey Owl **Rev. Designer:** Arnold Nagy

Date	Mintage	MS-63	Proof
2011	35,000	13.50	—

KM# 1087 DOLLAR
25.1800 g., 0.9250 Silver 0.7488 oz. ASW, 36.07 mm. **Ruler:** Elizabeth II **Subject:** Parks Canada, 100th Anniversary **Rev:** Female head looking downward into hands holding nature scene **Rev. Designer:** Luc Normandin

Date	Mintage	MS-63	Proof
2011	25,000	50.00	—
2011 Proof	—	—	60.00

KM# 652 DOLLAR (Louis)
1.5000 g., 0.9990 Gold 0.0482 oz. AGW, 14.1 mm. **Ruler:** Elizabeth II **Subject:** Gold Louis **Obv:** Bust right **Obv. Designer:** Susanna Blunt **Rev:** Crowned double L monogram within wreath

Date	Mintage	MS-63	Proof
2006 Proof	5,648	—	100

KM# 756 DOLLAR (Louis)
1.5550 g., 0.9990 Gold 0.0499 oz. AGW, 14.1 mm. **Ruler:** Elizabeth II **Obv:** Bust right **Obv. Designer:** Susanna Blunt **Rev:** Crown above two oval shields

Date	Mintage	MS-63	Proof
2007 Proof	3,457	—	100

KM# 834 DOLLAR (Louis)
1.5550 g., 0.9990 Gold 0.0499 oz. AGW, 14.1 mm. **Ruler:** Elizabeth II **Obv:** Bust right **Obv. Designer:** Susanna Blunt

Date	Mintage	MS-63	Proof
2008 Proof	—	—	125

KM# 270c 2 DOLLARS
8.8300 g., 0.9250 Silver gold plated center 0.2626 oz. ASW, 28 mm. **Ruler:** Elizabeth II **Obv:** Crowned head right within circle, date below **Rev:** Polar bear right within circle, denomination below **Note:** 1.9mm thick.

Date	Mintage	MS-63	Proof
2001 Proof	—	—	12.00

KM# 270 2 DOLLARS
7.3000 g., Bi-Metallic Aluminum-Bronze center in Nickel ring, 28 mm. **Ruler:** Elizabeth II **Obv:** Crowned head right within circle, date below **Obv. Designer:** Dora dePedery-Hunt **Rev:** Polar bear right within circle, denomination below **Rev. Designer:** Brent Townsend **Edge:** Segmented reeding

Date	Mintage	MS-63	Proof
2001	27,008,000	5.00	—
2001 Proof	74,944	—	12.50
2002	11,910,000	5.00	—
2002 Proof	65,315	—	12.50
2003	7,123,697	5.00	—
2003 Proof	62,007	—	12.50

KM# 449 2 DOLLARS
7.3000 g., Bi-Metallic Aluminum-Bronze center in Nickel ring, 28 mm. **Ruler:** Elizabeth II **Subject:** Elizabeth II Golden Jubilee **Obv:** Crowned head right, jubilee commemorative dates 1952-2002 **Edge:** Segmented reeding

Date	Mintage	MS-63	Proof
ND(2002)	27,020,000	4.00	—

KM# 449a 2 DOLLARS
8.8300 g., 0.9250 Silver gold plated center 0.2626 oz. ASW **Ruler:** Elizabeth II **Subject:** Elizabeth II Golden Jubilee **Obv:** Crowned head right, jubilee commemorative dates 1952-2002

Date	Mintage	MS-63	Proof
ND(2002) Proof	100,000	—	14.00

KM# 496 2 DOLLARS
7.3000 g., Bi-Metallic Aluminum-Bronze center in Nickel ring, 28 mm. **Ruler:** Elizabeth II **Obv:** Head right **Obv. Designer:** Susanna Blunt **Rev:** Polar bear advancing right **Rev. Designer:** Brent Townsend **Edge:** Segmented reeding

Date	Mintage	MS-63	Proof
2003	11,244,000	5.00	—
2003W	71,142	25.00	—
2004	12,908,000	5.00	—
2004 Proof	—	—	12.50
2005	38,317,000	5.00	—
2005 Proof	—	—	12.50
2006(ml)	35,319,000	5.00	—
2006(ml) Proof	—	—	12.50
2007(ml)	38,957,000	5.00	—
2007(ml) Proof	—	—	12.50
2008(ml)	18,400,000	5.00	—
2008(ml) Proof	—	—	12.50
2009(ml)	38,430,000	5.00	—
2009(ml) Proof	—	—	12.50
2010(ml)	—	5.00	—
2010(ml) Proof	—	—	12.50
2011(ml)	—	5.00	—
2011(ml) Proof	—	—	12.50

KM# 270d 2 DOLLARS
8.8300 g., 0.9250 Silver gold plated center 0.2626 oz. ASW **Ruler:** Elizabeth II **Subject:** 100th Anniversary of the Cobalt Silver Strike **Obv:** Crowned head right, within circle, date below **Rev:** Polar bear right, within circle, denomination below

Date	Mintage	MS-63	Proof
2003 Proof	100,000	—	25.00

KM# 835 2 DOLLARS
8.8000 g., 0.9250 Silver 0.2617 oz. ASW, 27.95 mm. **Ruler:** Elizabeth II **Rev:** Proud Polar Bear advancing right

Date	Mintage	MS-63	Proof
2004 Proof	12,607	—	40.00

KM# 496a 2 DOLLARS
10.8414 g., 0.9250 Bi-Metallic Gold plated Silver center in Silver ring 0.3224 oz., 28 mm. **Ruler:** Elizabeth II **Obv:** Head right **Obv. Designer:** Susanna Blunt **Rev:** Polar Bear **Edge:** Segmented reeding

Date	Mintage	MS-63	Proof
2004 Proof	—	—	25.00

KM# 836 2 DOLLARS
7.3000 g., Bi-Metallic Aluminum-Bronze center in Nickel ring, 28 mm. **Ruler:** Elizabeth II **Subject:** $2 coin, 10th Anniversary **Rev:** "Churchill" Polar Bear, northern lights **Edge:** Segmented reeding

Date	Mintage	MS-63	Proof
ND(1996-2006)(ml)	—	7.50	—

KM# 837 2 DOLLARS
7.3000 g., Bi-Metallic Aluminum-Bronze center in Nickel ring **Ruler:** Elizabeth II **Obv:** Bust left, date at top **Rev:** Polar Bear advancing right

Date	Mintage	MS-63	Proof
2006(ml)	—	7.50	—
2007(ml)	38,957,000	7.50	—

KM# 631 2 DOLLARS
7.3000 g., Bi-Metallic Aluminum-Bronze center in Nickel ring, 28 mm. **Ruler:** Elizabeth II **Subject:** 10th Anniversary of $2 coin **Obv:** Crowned head right **Edge:** Segmented reeding

Date	Mintage	MS-63	Proof
ND(2006)(ml)	5,005,000	25.00	—
ND(2006)(ml) Proof	—	—	40.00

KM# 631a 2 DOLLARS
Bi-Metallic 22 Kt Gold ring around 4.1 Kt. Gold core **Ruler:** Elizabeth II **Subject:** 10th Anniversary of $2 coin **Obv:** Crowned head right **Rev:** Polar bear

Date	Mintage	MS-63	Proof
ND(2006) Proof	2,068	—	400

KM# 796 2 DOLLARS
8.8300 g., 0.9250 Silver 0.2626 oz. ASW, 28.07 mm. **Ruler:** Elizabeth II **Rev:** Bear, gold plated center

Date	Mintage	MS-63	Proof
2008	—	25.00	—

KM# 1040 2 DOLLARS
7.3000 g., Bi-Metallic Aluminumn-Bronze center in Nickel ring, 27.95 mm. **Ruler:** Elizabeth II **Subject:** Quebec 400th Anniversary **Rev:** Lis and small sailing ship

Date	Mintage	MS-63	Proof
2008	—	7.50	—

KM# 1020 2 DOLLARS
7.3000 g., Bi-Metallic Aluminum-Bronze center in Nickel ring, 28 mm. **Ruler:** Elizabeth II **Rev:** Two lynx cubs **Rev. Designer:** Christie Paquet **Edge:** Segmented reeding

Date	Mintage	MS-63	Proof
2010 Specimen	15,000	—	40.00

KM# 1088 2 DOLLARS
7.3000 g., Bi-Metallic Copper-Nickel center in Nickel ring, 28.03 mm. **Ruler:** Elizabeth II **Rev:** Elk Calf **Rev. Designer:** Christine Paquet

Date	Mintage	MS-63	Proof
2011	—	7.50	—

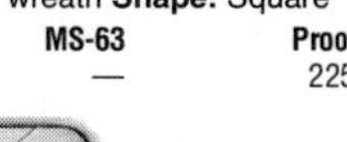

KM# 657 3 DOLLARS
11.7200 g., 0.9250 Silver gilt 0.3485 oz. ASW, 27x27 mm. **Ruler:** Elizabeth II **Rev:** Beaver within wreath **Shape:** Square

Date	Mintage	MS-63	Proof
2006 Proof	19,963	—	225

KM# 1051 3 DOLLARS
0.9250 Silver gilt, 27x27 mm. **Ruler:** Elizabeth II **Subject:** Wildlife conservation **Rev:** Stylized polar bear and northern lights **Shape:** square

Date	Mintage	MS-63	Proof
2010 Specimen	15,000	55.00	—

KM# 978 3 DOLLARS
7.9600 g., Silver Partially Gilt, 27 mm. **Ruler:** Elizabeth II **Rev:** Return of the Tyee (giant salmon)

Date	Mintage	MS-63	Proof
2010 Proof	15,000	—	50.00

KM# 1011 3 DOLLARS
11.6000 g., 0.9250 Silver gilt 0.3450 oz. ASW, 27x27 mm. **Ruler:** Elizabeth II **Rev:** Barn Owl **Rev. Designer:** Jason Bouwman **Shape:** Square

Date	Mintage	MS-63	Proof
2010 Proof	15,000	—	65.00

KM# 1089 3 DOLLARS
11.8000 g., 0.9250 Silver plated Gold 0.3509 oz. ASW, 27x27 mm. **Ruler:** Elizabeth II **Rev:** Orca Whale **Rev. Designer:** Jason Bouwman **Shape:** Square

Date	Mintage	MS-63	Proof
2011 Proof	15,000	—	65.00

KM# 1090 3 DOLLARS
7.9600 g., 0.9990 Silver with red and yellow partial gilding 0.2557 oz. ASW, 27 mm. **Ruler:** Elizabeth II **Rev:** Eskimo mother kneeling, child on back **Rev. Designer:** Andrew Oappik

Date	Mintage	MS-63	Proof
2011 Proof	10,000	—	65.00

KM# 728 4 DOLLARS
15.8700 g., 0.9250 Silver 0.4719 oz. ASW, 34 mm. **Ruler:** Elizabeth II **Subject:** Dinosaur fossil **Obv:** Bust right **Rev:** Parasaurolophus, selective enameling

Date	Mintage	MS-63	Proof
2007 Proof	13,010	—	200

KM# 797 4 DOLLARS
15.8700 g., 0.9990 Silver 0.5097 oz. ASW, 34 mm. **Ruler:** Elizabeth II **Subject:** Dinosaur fossil **Obv:** Bust right **Rev:** Triceratops, enameled **Rev. Designer:** Kerri Burnett

Date	Mintage	MS-63	Proof
2008 Proof	20,000	—	75.00

KM# 890 4 DOLLARS
15.8700 g., 0.9990 Silver 0.5097 oz. ASW, 34 mm. **Ruler:** Elizabeth II **Subject:** Tyrannosaurus Rex **Obv:** Bust right **Obv. Legend:** Elizabeth II DG Regina **Obv. Designer:** Susanna Blunt **Rev:** T-Rex skeleton in selective aging **Rev. Legend:** Canada 4 Dollars **Rev. Designer:** Kerri Burnette

Date	Mintage	MS-63	Proof
2009 Proof	20,000	—	55.00

KM# 942 4 DOLLARS
15.8700 g., Silver, 34 mm. **Ruler:** Elizabeth II **Rev:** Kids hanging stocking on fireplace, Christmas tree on right

Date	Mintage	MS-63	Proof
2009 Proof	Est. 15,000	—	45.00

KM# 1014 4 DOLLARS
15.8700 g., 0.9990 Silver selectively plated 0.5097 oz. ASW **Ruler:** Elizabeth II **Rev:** Euoplocephalus **Rev. Designer:** Kerri Burnett

Date	Mintage	MS-63	Proof
2010 Proof	13,000	—	55.00

KM# 1022 4 DOLLARS
Silver selectively plating **Ruler:** Elizabeth II **Rev:** Dromaeosaurus

Date	Mintage	MS-63	Proof
2010 Proof	13,000	—	55.00

KM# 435 5 DOLLARS
16.8600 g., 0.9250 Silver 0.5014 oz. ASW, 28.4 mm. **Ruler:**

Elizabeth II **Subject:** Guglielmo Marconi **Obv:** Crowned head right **Rev:** Gold-plated cameo portrait of Marconi **Rev. Designer:** Cosme Saffioti **Edge:** Reeded **Note:** Only issued in two coin set with British 2 pounds KM#1014a.

Date	Mintage	MS-63	Proof
ND(2001) Proof	15,011	—	30.00

KM# 519 5 DOLLARS

8.3600 g., 0.9000 Gold 0.2419 oz. AGW, 21.6 mm. **Ruler:** Elizabeth II **Obv:** Crowned head right **Rev:** National arms **Edge:** Reeded

Date	Mintage	MS-63	Proof
ND (2002) Proof	2,002	—	375

KM# 518 5 DOLLARS

31.1200 g., 0.9999 Silver 1.0004 oz. ASW, 38 mm. **Ruler:** Elizabeth II **Subject:** F.I.F.A. World Cup Soccer, Germany 2006 **Obv:** Crowned head right, denomination **Rev:** Goalie on knees **Edge:** Reeded

Date	Mintage	MS-63	Proof
2003 Proof	21,542	—	40.00

KM# 514 5 DOLLARS

31.1200 g., 0.9999 Silver 1.0004 oz. ASW, 38 mm. **Ruler:** Elizabeth II **Obv:** Crowned head right **Rev:** Moose **Edge:** Reeded

Date	Mintage	MS-63	Proof
2004 Proof	12,822	—	175

KM# 527 5 DOLLARS

31.1200 g., 0.9999 Silver 1.0004 oz. ASW **Ruler:** Elizabeth II **Subject:** Golf, Championship of Canada, Centennial **Obv:** Head right

Date	Mintage	MS-63	Proof
2004 Proof	18,750	—	30.00

KM# 554 5 DOLLARS

31.1200 g., 0.9999 Silver 1.0004 oz. ASW **Ruler:** Elizabeth II **Subject:** Alberta **Obv. Designer:** Head right **Rev. Designer:** Michelle Grant

Date	Mintage	MS-63	Proof
2005 Proof	20,000	—	35.00

KM# 555 5 DOLLARS

31.1200 g., 0.9999 Silver 1.0004 oz. ASW **Ruler:** Elizabeth II **Subject:** Saskatchewan **Obv:** Head right **Obv. Designer:** Susanna Blunt **Rev. Designer:** Paulett Sapergia

Date	Mintage	MS-63	Proof
2005 Proof	20,000	—	35.00

KM# 556.1 5 DOLLARS

31.1200 g., 0.9990 Silver 0.9995 oz. ASW, 38.02 mm. **Ruler:** Elizabeth II **Subject:** 60th Anniversay Victory WWII - Veterans **Obv:** Bust right **Rev:** Large V and heads of sailor, soldier and aviator on large maple leaf **Edge:** Reeded

Date	Mintage	MS-63	Proof
2005	25,000	32.00	—

KM# 556.2 5 DOLLARS

31.1200 g., 0.9999 Silver 1.0004 oz. ASW, 38.02 mm. **Ruler:** Elizabeth II **Subject:** 60th Anniversary Victory WW II - Veterans **Obv:** Bust right **Rev:** Large V and heads of sailor, soldier and aviator on maple leaf with small maple leaf added at left and right **Edge:** Reeded

Date	Mintage	MS-63	Proof
2005	10,000	125	—

KM# 557 5 DOLLARS

31.1200 g., 0.9999 Silver 1.0004 oz. ASW, 36 mm. **Ruler:** Elizabeth II **Subject:** Walrus and calf **Obv:** Head right **Obv. Designer:** Susanna Blunt **Rev:** Two walrusus and calf **Rev. Designer:** Pierre Leduc

Date	Mintage	MS-63	Proof
2005 Proof	5,519	—	40.00

KM# 558 5 DOLLARS

31.1200 g., 0.9999 Silver 1.0004 oz. ASW, 36 mm. **Ruler:** Elizabeth II **Subject:** White tailed deer **Obv:** Head right **Obv. Designer:** Susanna Blunt **Rev:** Two deer standing **Rev. Designer:** Xerxes Irani

Date	Mintage	MS-63	Proof
2005 Proof	6,439	—	40.00

KM# 585 5 DOLLARS

31.1200 g., 0.9999 Silver 1.0004 oz. ASW, 36 mm. **Ruler:** Elizabeth II **Obv:** Head right **Obv. Designer:** Susanna Blunt **Rev:** Peregrine Falcon feeding young ones **Rev. Designer:** Dwayne Harty

Date	Mintage	MS-63	Proof
2006 Proof	6,145	—	45.00

KM# 586 5 DOLLARS

31.1200 g., 0.9999 Silver 1.0004 oz. ASW, 36 mm. **Ruler:** Elizabeth II **Subject:** Sable Island horses **Obv:** Head right **Obv. Designer:** Susanna Blunt **Rev:** Horse and foal standing **Rev. Designer:** Christie Paquet

Date	Mintage	MS-63	Proof
2006 Proof	7,589	—	45.00

KM# 658 5 DOLLARS

31.1200 g., 0.9999 Silver 1.0004 oz. ASW, 36.07 mm. **Ruler:** Elizabeth II **Subject:** Breast Cancer Awareness **Rev:** Colorized pink ribbon

Date	Mintage	MS-63	Proof
2006 Proof	11,048	—	50.00

KM# 659 5 DOLLARS

31.1200 g., 0.9999 Silver 1.0004 oz. ASW **Ruler:** Elizabeth II **Subject:** C.A.F. Snowbirds Acrobatic Jet Flying Team **Rev:** Image of fighter jets and piolt

Date	Mintage	MS-63	Proof
2006 Proof	7,896	—	50.00

KM# A799 5 DOLLARS

25.1750 g., 0.9959 Silver 0.8060 oz. ASW, 36.07 mm. **Ruler:** Elizabeth II **Subject:** Breast Cancer Awareness **Rev:** Pink ribbon and groups of people

Date	Mintage	MS-63	Proof
2006 Proof	11,048	—	60.00

KM# 799 5 DOLLARS

31.1050 g., 0.9990 Silver 0.9990 oz. ASW, 38 mm. **Ruler:** Elizabeth II **Subject:** Breast Cancer Awareness **Rev:** Multicolor, green maple leaf and pink ribbon

Date	Mintage	MS-63	Proof
2008	11,048	85.00	—

KM# 1036 5 DOLLARS

31.1200 g., 0.9990 Silver 0.9995 oz. ASW **Ruler:** Elizabeth II **Subject:** 80th Anniversary **Rev:** Two deer standing, one eating branch

Date	Mintage	MS-63	Proof
2009 Proof	—	—	70.00

KM# 1060 5 DOLLARS

31.1050 g., 0.9999 Silver 0.9999 oz. ASW, 38 mm. **Ruler:** Elizabeth II **Rev:** Maple leaf in color, yellow ribbon honoring servicemen

Date	Mintage	MS-63	Proof
2009	—	70.00	—

KM# 995 5 DOLLARS

25.1700 g., 0.9250 Silver 0.7485 oz. ASW, 36.07 mm. **Ruler:** Elizabeth II **Rev:** HMCS Sackville **Rev. Designer:** Yves Berube

Date	Mintage	MS-63	Proof
2010 Proof	Est. 50,000	—	50.00

KM# 995a 5 DOLLARS

25.1700 g., 0.9250 Silver 0.7485 oz. ASW, 36.07 mm. **Ruler:** Elizabeth II **Subject:** Navy Centennial **Rev:** HMCS Sackville, partially gilt

Date	Mintage	MS-63	Proof
2010	—	—	110

KM# 1077 5 DOLLARS

31.3900 g., 0.9990 Silver 1.0082 oz. ASW, 34 mm. **Ruler:** Elizabeth II **Rev:** Maple leaf on 45 degree angle left

Date	Mintage	MS-63	Proof
2010 Proof	9,000	—	80.00

KM# 515 8 DOLLARS
28.8000 g., 0.9250 Silver 0.8565 oz. ASW, 39 mm. **Ruler:** Elizabeth II **Obv:** Head right **Obv. Designer:** Susanna Blunt **Rev:** Grizzly bear walking left **Edge:** Reeded

Date	Mintage	MS-63	Proof
2004 Proof	12,942	—	85.00

KM# 597 8 DOLLARS
32.1500 g., 0.9999 Silver 1.0335 oz. ASW **Ruler:** Elizabeth II **Subject:** Canadian Pacific Railway, 120th Anniversary **Obv:** Head right **Obv. Designer:** Susanna Blunt **Rev:** Railway bridge

Date	Mintage	MS-63	Proof
2005 Proof	9,892	—	65.00

KM# 598 8 DOLLARS
32.1500 g., 0.9999 Silver 1.0335 oz. ASW **Ruler:** Elizabeth II **Subject:** Canadian Pacific Railway, 120th Anniversary **Obv:** Head right **Rev:** Railway memorial to the Chinese workers

Date	Mintage	MS-63	Proof
2005 Proof	9,892	—	65.00

KM# 730 8 DOLLARS
25.1800 g., 0.9999 Silver 0.8094 oz. ASW, 36.07 mm. **Ruler:** Elizabeth II **Obv:** Queens's head at top in circle, three Chinese characters **Rev:** Dragon and other creatures

Date	Mintage	MS-63	Proof
2007 Proof	19,954	—	55.00

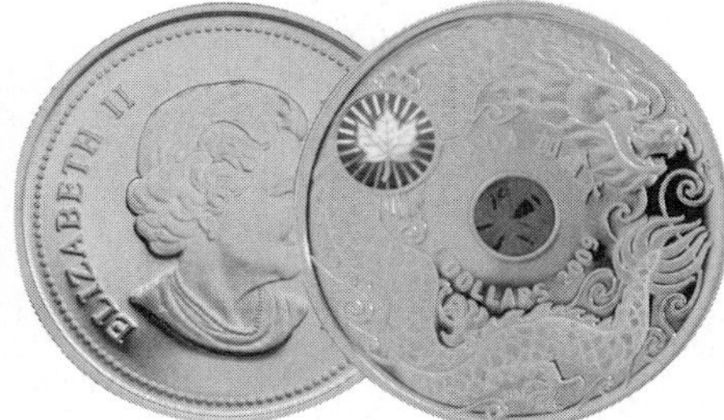

KM# 943 8 DOLLARS
25.1800 g., Silver, 36.1 mm. **Ruler:** Elizabeth II **Rev:** Hollgram maple of wisdom - crystal

Date	Mintage	MS-63	Proof
2009 Proof	11,624	—	90.00

KM# 1012 8 DOLLARS
25.3000 g., 0.9250 Silver 0.7524 oz. ASW, 36.07 mm. **Ruler:** Elizabeth II **Rev:** Horses around central maple leaf hologram **Rev. Designer:** Simon Ng

Date	Mintage	MS-63	Proof
2010 Proof	8,888	—	100

KM# 520 10 DOLLARS
16.7200 g., 0.9000 Gold 0.4838 oz. AGW, 26.92 mm. **Ruler:** Elizabeth II **Obv:** Crowned head right **Rev:** National arms **Edge:** Reeded

Date	Mintage	MS-63	Proof
ND (2002) Proof	2,002	—	750

KM# 559 10 DOLLARS
25.1750 g., 0.9999 Silver 0.8093 oz. ASW **Ruler:** Elizabeth II **Subject:** Pope John Paul II **Obv:** Head right

Date	Mintage	MS-63	Proof
2005 Proof	24,716	—	45.00

KM# 757 10 DOLLARS
25.1750 g., 0.9999 Silver 0.8093 oz. ASW **Ruler:** Elizabeth II **Subject:** Year of the Veteran **Rev:** Profile left of young and old veteran

Date	Mintage	MS-63	Proof
2005 Proof	6,549	—	55.00

KM# 661 10 DOLLARS
25.1750 g., 0.9999 Silver 0.8093 oz. ASW **Ruler:** Elizabeth II **Subject:** National Historic Sites **Obv:** Head right **Rev:** Fortress of Louisbourg

Date	Mintage	MS-63	Proof
2006 Proof	5,544	—	40.00

KM# 1010 10 DOLLARS
0.9990 Silver **Ruler:** Elizabeth II **Subject:** 75th Anniversary Canadian Bank Notes **Rev:** Female seated

Date	Mintage	MS-63	Proof
2010 Proof	—	—	45.00

KM# 1096 10 DOLLARS
27.7800 g., 0.9250 Silver 0.8261 oz. ASW, 40 mm. **Ruler:** Elizabeth II **Rev:** Blue whale diving

Date	Mintage	MS-63	Proof
2010 Proof	10,000	—	85.00

KM# 415 15 DOLLARS
33.6300 g., 0.9250 Silver with gold insert 1.0000 oz. ASW, 40 mm. **Ruler:** Elizabeth II **Subject:** Year of the Snake **Obv:** Crowned head right **Rev:** Snake within circle of lunar calendar signs **Rev. Designer:** Harvey Chain **Edge:** Reeded

Date	Mintage	MS-63	Proof
2001 Proof	60,754	—	85.00

KM# 463 15 DOLLARS
33.6300 g., 0.9250 Silver with gold insert 1.0000 oz. ASW **Ruler:** Elizabeth II **Subject:** Year of the Horse **Obv:** Crowned head right **Obv. Designer:** Dora dePédery-Hunt **Rev:** Horse in center with Chinese Lunar calendar around **Rev. Designer:** Harvey Chain

Date	Mintage	MS-63	Proof
2002 Proof	59,395	—	85.00

KM# 481 15 DOLLARS
33.6300 g., 0.9250 Silver with gold insert 1.0000 oz. ASW, 40 mm. **Ruler:** Elizabeth II **Subject:** Year of the Sheep **Obv:** Crowned head right **Rev:** Sheep in center with Chinese Lunar calendar around **Rev. Designer:** Harvey Chain

Date	Mintage	MS-63	Proof
2003 Proof	53,714	—	85.00

KM# 610 15 DOLLARS
33.6300 g., 0.9250 Silver Gold octagon applique in center 1.0000 oz. ASW **Ruler:** Elizabeth II **Subject:** Year of the Monkey **Obv:** Crowned head right **Rev:** Monkey in center with Chinese Lunar calendar around

Date	Mintage	MS-63	Proof
2004 Proof	46,175	—	150

KM# 560 15 DOLLARS
33.6300 g., 0.9250 Silver with gold insert 1.0000 oz. ASW **Ruler:** Elizabeth II **Subject:** Year of the Rooster **Obv:** Crowned head right **Rev:** Rooster in center with Chinese Lunar calendar around

Date	Mintage	MS-63	Proof
2005 Proof	44,690	—	125

KM# 587 15 DOLLARS
33.6300 g., 0.9250 Silver with gold insert 1.0000 oz. ASW **Ruler:** Elizabeth II **Subject:** Year of the Dog **Obv:** Crowned head left **Rev:** Dog in center with Chinese Lunar calendar around

Date	Mintage	MS-63	Proof
2006 Proof	41,617	—	100

KM# 732 15 DOLLARS
33.6300 g., 0.9250 Silver with gold insert 1.0000 oz. ASW, 40 mm. **Ruler:** Elizabeth II **Subject:** Year of the Pig **Rev:** Pig at center of lunar characters

Date	Mintage	MS-63	Proof
2007 Proof	48,888	—	100

KM# 801 15 DOLLARS
33.6300 g., 0.9250 Silver with gold insert 1.0000 oz. ASW, 40 mm. **Ruler:** Elizabeth II **Subject:** Year of the Rat **Rev:** Rat, gold octagonal insert at center

Date	Mintage	MS-63	Proof
2008 Proof	48,888	—	90.00

KM# 803 15 DOLLARS
30.0000 g., 0.9250 Silver 0.8921 oz. ASW, 36.15 mm. **Ruler:** Elizabeth II **Rev:** Queen Victoria's coinage portrait

Date	Mintage	MS-63	Proof
2008	10,000	100	—

KM# 804 15 DOLLARS
30.0000 g., 0.9250 Silver 0.8921 oz. ASW, 36.15 mm. **Ruler:** Elizabeth II **Rev:** Edward VII coinage portrait **Rev. Designer:** G. W. DeSaulles

Date	Mintage	MS-63	Proof
2008	10,000	100	—

KM# 805 15 DOLLARS
20.0000 g., 0.9250 Silver 0.5948 oz. ASW, 36.15 mm. **Ruler:** Elizabeth II **Rev:** George V coinage portrait

Date	Mintage	MS-63	Proof
2008	10,000	100	—

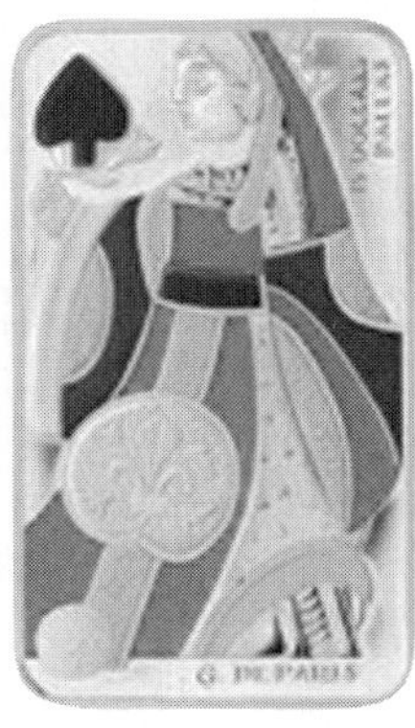

KM# 806 15 DOLLARS

31.5600 g., 0.9250 Silver 0.9385 oz. ASW, 49.8 x 28.6 mm. **Ruler:** Elizabeth II **Rev:** Queen of Spades, multicolor playing card

Date	Mintage	MS-63	Proof
2008 Proof	25,000	—	90.00

KM# 807 15 DOLLARS

31.5600 g., 0.9250 Silver 0.9385 oz. ASW, 49.8 x 28.6 mm. **Ruler:** Elizabeth II **Rev:** Jack of Hearts, multicolor playing card

Date	Mintage	MS-63	Proof
2008 Proof	25,000	—	90.00

KM# 1038 15 DOLLARS

Silver, 38 mm. **Ruler:** Elizabeth II **Subject:** Year of the tiger **Rev:** Tiger in forest **Shape:** scalloped

Date	Mintage	MS-63	Proof
2009 Proof	—	—	85.00

KM# 919 15 DOLLARS

31.5600 g., 0.9250 Silver 0.9385 oz. ASW, 49.8 x 28.6 mm. **Ruler:** Elizabeth II **Obv:** Bust right **Obv. Designer:** Susanna Blunt **Rev:** Ten of spades, multicolor **Shape:** rectangle

Date	Mintage	MS-63	Proof
2009 Proof	25,000	—	90.00

KM# 920 15 DOLLARS

31.5600 g., 0.9250 Silver 0.9385 oz. ASW, 49.8 x 28.6 mm. **Ruler:** Elizabeth II **Obv:** Bust right **Obv. Designer:** Susanna Blunt **Rev:** King of hearts, multicolor **Shape:** Rectangle

Date	Mintage	MS-63	Proof
2009 Proof	25,000	—	90.00

KM# 866 15 DOLLARS

33.6300 g., 0.9250 Silver with gold insert 1.0000 oz. ASW, 40 mm. **Ruler:** Elizabeth II **Subject:** Year of the Ox **Rev:** Ox, octagon gold insert

Date	Mintage	MS-63	Proof
2009 Proof	48,888	—	90.00

KM# 922 15 DOLLARS

30.0000 g., 0.9250 Silver 0.8921 oz. ASW, 36.15 mm. **Ruler:** Elizabeth II **Obv:** Bust right **Obv. Designer:** Susanna Blunt **Rev:** Pages portrait of George VI

Date	Mintage	MS-63	Proof
2009(ml) Prooflike	10,000	100	—

KM# 923 15 DOLLARS

30.0000 g., 0.9250 Silver 0.8921 oz. ASW, 36.15 mm. **Ruler:** Elizabeth II **Obv:** Bust right **Obv. Designer:** Susanna Blunt **Rev:** Gillick portrait of Queen Elizabeth II

Date	Mintage	MS-63	Proof
2009(ml) Prooflike	10,000	100	—

KM# 980 15 DOLLARS

34.0000 g., 0.9250 Silver 1.0111 oz. ASW, 40 mm. **Ruler:** Elizabeth II **Rev:** Tiger in gold insert

Date	Mintage	MS-63	Proof
2010 Proof	48,888	—	100

KM# 1032 15 DOLLARS

0.9990 Silver **Ruler:** Elizabeth II **Subject:** Year of the tiger **Rev:** Tiger walking tiger

Date	Mintage	MS-63	Proof
2010 Proof	—	—	—

KM# 1055 15 DOLLARS

31.1050 g., 0.9990 Silver 0.9990 oz. ASW, 38 mm. **Ruler:** Elizabeth II **Rev:** Rabbit sitting, head turned left **Shape:** scalloped

Date	Mintage	MS-63	Proof
2011 Proof	—	—	85.00

KM# 1091 15 DOLLARS

25.1100 g., 0.9250 Silver 0.7467 oz. ASW, 36.15 mm. **Ruler:** Elizabeth II **Rev:** Prince Charles bust **Rev. Designer:** Laurie McGaw

Date	Mintage	MS-63	Proof
2011 Prooflike	10,000	100	—

KM# 1092 15 DOLLARS

25.1100 g., 0.9250 Silver 0.7467 oz. ASW, 36.15 mm. **Ruler:** Elizabeth II **Rev:** Prince William **Rev. Designer:** Laurie McGaw

Date	Mintage	MS-63	Proof
2011 Prooflike	10,000	100	—

KM# 1093 15 DOLLARS

25.1800 g., 0.9250 Silver 0.7488 oz. ASW, 36.15 mm. **Ruler:** Elizabeth II **Rev:** Prince Harry bust 1/4 right **Rev. Designer:** Laurie McGaw

Date	Mintage	MS-63	Proof
2011 Prooflike	10,000	100	—

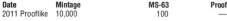

KM# 1094 15 DOLLARS
31.3900 g., 0.9990 Silver 1.0082 oz. ASW, 38 mm. **Ruler:** Elizabeth II **Rev:** Rabbit bounding left **Rev. Designer:** Aries Cheung

Date	Mintage	MS-63	Proof
2011 Proof	9,999	—	100

KM# 411 20 DOLLARS
31.1035 g., 0.9250 Silver 0.9250 oz. ASW, 38 mm. **Ruler:** Elizabeth II **Subject:** Transportation - Steam Locomotive **Obv:** Crowned head right **Obv. Designer:** Dora dePédery-Hunt **Rev:** First Canadian Steel Steam Locomotive and cameo hologram **Rev. Designer:** Don Curely **Edge:** Reeded and plain sections

Date	Mintage	MS-63	Proof
2001 Proof	15,000	—	45.00

KM# 427 20 DOLLARS
31.1030 g., 0.9250 Silver 0.9249 oz. ASW, 38 mm. **Ruler:** Elizabeth II **Series:** Transportation - The Marco Polo **Obv:** Crowned head right **Rev:** Sailship with hologram cameo **Rev. Designer:** J. Franklin Wright **Edge:** Reeded and plain sections

Date	Mintage	MS-63	Proof
2001 Proof	15,000	—	45.00

KM# 428 20 DOLLARS
31.1030 g., 0.9250 Silver 0.9249 oz. ASW, 38 mm. **Ruler:** Elizabeth II **Series:** Transportation - Russell Touring Car **Obv:** Crowned head right **Rev:** Russell touring car with hologram cameo **Rev. Designer:** John Mardon **Edge:** Reeded and plain sections

Date	Mintage	MS-63	Proof
2001 Proof	15,000	—	45.00

KM# 464 20 DOLLARS
31.1030 g., 0.9250 Silver 0.9249 oz. ASW **Ruler:** Elizabeth II **Obv:** Crowned head right **Obv. Designer:** Dora dePédery-Hunt **Rev:** Gray-Dort Model 25-SM with cameo hologram **Rev. Designer:** John Mardon

Date	Mintage	MS-63	Proof
2002 Proof	15,000	—	45.00

KM# 465 20 DOLLARS
31.1030 g., 0.9250 Silver 0.9249 oz. ASW **Ruler:** Elizabeth II **Obv:** Crowned head right **Obv. Designer:** Dora dePédery-Hunt **Rev:** Sailing ship William D. Lawrence **Rev. Designer:** Bonnie Ross

Date	Mintage	MS-63	Proof
2002 Proof	15,000	—	45.00

KM# 523 20 DOLLARS
31.3900 g., 0.9990 Silver 1.0082 oz. ASW **Ruler:** Elizabeth II **Subject:** Canadian Rockies, colorized **Obv:** Crowned head right **Obv. Designer:** Dora dePédery-Hunt **Rev:** Canadian Rockies

Date	Mintage	MS-63	Proof
2003 Proof	29,967	—	50.00

KM# 483 20 DOLLARS
31.1030 g., 0.9250 Silver with selective gold plating 0.9249 oz. ASW **Ruler:** Elizabeth II **Subject:** The HMCS Bras d'or (FHE-400) **Obv:** Crowned head right **Obv. Designer:** Dora dePédery-Hunt **Rev:** Ship in water **Rev. Designer:** Donald Curley, Stan Witten

Date	Mintage	MS-63	Proof
2003 Proof	15,000	—	45.00

KM# 482 20 DOLLARS
31.3900 g., 0.9999 Silver 1.0091 oz. ASW **Ruler:** Elizabeth II **Obv:** Crowned head right **Obv. Designer:** Dora dePédery-Hunt **Rev:** Niagara Falls hologram **Rev. Designer:** Gary Corcoran

Date	Mintage	MS-63	Proof
2003 Proof	29,967	—	75.00

KM# 484 20 DOLLARS
31.1030 g., 0.9250 Silver with selective gold plating 0.9249 oz. ASW **Ruler:** Elizabeth II **Subject:** Canadian National FA-1 diesel-electric locomotive **Obv:** Crowned head right **Obv. Designer:** Dora dePédery-Hunt **Rev. Designer:** John Mardon, William Woodruff

Date	Mintage	MS-63	Proof
2003 Proof	15,000	—	45.00

KM# 485 20 DOLLARS
31.1030 g., 0.9250 Silver with selective gold plating 0.9249 oz. ASW **Ruler:** Elizabeth II **Obv:** Crowned head right **Obv. Designer:** Dora dePédery-Hunt **Rev:** The Bricklin SV-1 **Rev. Designer:** Brian Hughes, José Oslo

Date	Mintage	MS-63	Proof
2003 Proof	15,000	—	45.00

KM# 611 20 DOLLARS
31.3900 g., 0.9999 Silver 1.0091 oz. ASW **Ruler:** Elizabeth II **Obv:** Head right **Obv. Designer:** Susanna Blunt **Rev:** Iceberg, hologram

Date	Mintage	MS-63	Proof
2004 Proof	24,879	—	45.00

KM# 838 20 DOLLARS
31.3900 g., 0.9999 Silver selectively gold plated 1.0091 oz. ASW **Ruler:** Elizabeth II **Rev:** Hopewell Rocks

Date	Mintage	MS-63	Proof
2004 Proof	16,918	—	45.00

KM# 561 20 DOLLARS
31.3900 g., 0.9999 Silver 1.0091 oz. ASW **Ruler:** Elizabeth II **Subject:** Three-masted sailing ship, hologram **Obv:** Head right **Obv. Designer:** Susanna Blunt **Rev. Designer:** Bonnie Ross

Date	Mintage	MS-63	Proof
2005 Proof	18,276	—	55.00

KM# 562 20 DOLLARS
31.3900 g., 0.9999 Silver 1.0091 oz. ASW, 38 mm. **Ruler:** Elizabeth II **Subject:** Northwest Territories Diamonds **Obv:** Head right **Obv. Designer:** Susanna Blunt **Rev:** Multicolor diamond hologram on landscape **Rev. Designer:** José Oslo **Edge:** Reeded

Date	Mintage	MS-63	Proof
2005 Proof	35,000	—	45.00

KM# 563 20 DOLLARS
31.3900 g., 0.9999 Silver 1.0091 oz. ASW **Ruler:** Elizabeth II **Subject:** Mingan Archepelago **Obv:** Head right **Obv. Designer:** Susanna Blunt **Rev:** Cliffs with whale tail out of water **Rev. Designer:** Pierre Leduc

Date	Mintage	MS-63	Proof
2005 Proof	—	—	45.00

KM# 564 20 DOLLARS
31.3900 g., 0.9999 Silver 1.0091 oz. ASW **Ruler:** Elizabeth II **Subject:** Rainforests of the Pacific Northwest **Obv:** Head right **Rev:** Open winged bird **Designer:** Susanna Blunt

Date	Mintage	MS-63	Proof
2005 Proof	—	—	45.00

KM# 565 20 DOLLARS
31.3900 g., 0.9999 Silver 1.0091 oz. ASW **Ruler:** Elizabeth II **Subject:** Toronto Island National Park **Obv:** Head right **Rev:** Toronto Island Lighthouse

Date	Mintage	MS-63	Proof
2005 Proof	—	—	45.00

KM# 588 20 DOLLARS
31.3900 g., 0.9999 Silver 1.0091 oz. ASW **Ruler:** Elizabeth II **Subject:** Georgian Bay National Park **Obv:** Head right **Rev:** Canoe and small trees on island

Date	Mintage	MS-63	Proof
2006 Proof	—	—	60.00

KM# 589 20 DOLLARS
31.1000 g., 0.9999 Silver 0.9997 oz. ASW **Ruler:** Elizabeth II **Subject:** Notre Dame Basilica, Montreal, as a hologram **Obv:** Head right

Date	Mintage	MS-63	Proof
2006 Proof	15,000	—	50.00

KM# 663 20 DOLLARS
31.3900 g., 0.9999 Silver 1.0091 oz. ASW **Ruler:** Elizabeth II **Subject:** Nahanni National Park **Obv:** Head right **Rev:** Bear walking along sream, cliff in background

Date	Mintage	MS-63	Proof
2006 Proof	—	—	60.00

KM# 664 20 DOLLARS
31.3900 g., 0.9999 Silver 1.0091 oz. ASW **Ruler:** Elizabeth II **Subject:** Jasper National Park **Obv:** Head right **Rev:** Cowboy on horseback in majestic scene

Date	Mintage	MS-63	Proof
2006 Proof	—	—	60.00

KM# 665 20 DOLLARS
31.1000 g., 0.9999 Silver 0.9997 oz. ASW **Ruler:** Elizabeth II **Subject:** CN Tower, Toronto **Obv:** Head right **Rev:** Holographic rendering of CN Tower

Date	Mintage	MS-63	Proof
2006 Proof	15,000	—	60.00

KM# 666 20 DOLLARS
31.1000 g., 0.9999 Silver 0.9997 oz. ASW **Ruler:** Elizabeth II **Subject:** Pengrowth (Calgary Saddledome) **Obv:** Head right **Rev:** Holographic view of Saddledome

Date	Mintage	MS-63	Proof
2006 Proof	15,000	—	55.00

KM# 667 20 DOLLARS
31.3900 g., 0.9999 Silver 1.0091 oz. ASW **Ruler:** Elizabeth II **Subject:** Tall Ship **Obv:** Head right **Rev:** Ketch and holographic image

Date	Mintage	MS-63	Proof
2006 Proof	10,299	—	60.00

KM# 734 20 DOLLARS
31.1000 g., 0.9990 Silver 0.9988 oz. ASW, 38 mm. **Ruler:** Elizabeth II **Rev:** Holiday sleigh ride

Date	Mintage	MS-63	Proof
2007 Proof	6,041	—	70.00

KM# 735 20 DOLLARS

31.1000 g., 0.9990 Silver 0.9988 oz. ASW, 38 mm. **Ruler:** Elizabeth II **Rev:** Snowflake, blue crystal

Date	Mintage	MS-63	Proof
2007 Proof	1,433	—	175

KM# 737 20 DOLLARS

31.1000 g., 0.9990 Silver 0.9988 oz. ASW, 38 mm. **Ruler:** Elizabeth II **Subject:** International Polar Year

Date	Mintage	MS-63	Proof
2007 Proof	8,352	—	65.00

KM# 737a 20 DOLLARS

31.1000 g., 0.9990 Silver 0.9988 oz. ASW, 38 mm. **Ruler:** Elizabeth II **Subject:** International Polar Year **Rev:** Blue plasma coating

Date	Mintage	MS-63	Proof
2007 Proof	3,005	—	250

KM# 738 20 DOLLARS

31.3900 g., 0.9999 Silver 1.0091 oz. ASW, 38 mm. **Ruler:** Elizabeth II **Subject:** Tall ships **Rev:** Brigantine in harbor, hologram

Date	Mintage	MS-63	Proof
2007 Proof	16,000	—	60.00

KM# 839 20 DOLLARS

31.3900 g., 0.9999 Silver 1.0091 oz. ASW **Ruler:** Elizabeth II **Rev:** Northern lights in hologram

Date	Mintage	MS-63	Proof
2007	—	35.00	—

KM# 808 20 DOLLARS

31.5000 g., 0.9250 Silver 0.9368 oz. ASW, 40 mm. **Ruler:** Elizabeth II **Subject:** Agriculture trade

Date	Mintage	MS-63	Proof
2008 Proof	10,000	—	70.00

KM# 809 20 DOLLARS

31.1050 g., 0.9990 Silver 0.9990 oz. ASW, 38 mm. **Ruler:** Elizabeth II **Rev:** Royal Hudson Steam locomotive

Date	Mintage	MS-63	Proof
2008 Proof	10,000	—	70.00

KM# 810 20 DOLLARS

31.3900 g., 0.9990 Silver 1.0082 oz. ASW, 38 mm. **Ruler:** Elizabeth II **Rev:** Green leaf and crystal raindrop **Rev. Designer:** Stanley Witten

Date	Mintage	MS-63	Proof
2008 Proof	15,000	—	110

KM# 811 20 DOLLARS

31.1050 g., 0.9990 Silver 0.9990 oz. ASW **Ruler:** Elizabeth II **Rev:** Snowflake, amethyst crystal

Date	Mintage	MS-63	Proof
2008 Proof	15,000	—	90.00

KM# 813 20 DOLLARS

31.1050 g., 0.9990 Silver 0.9990 oz. ASW, 38 mm. **Ruler:** Elizabeth II **Rev:** Carolers around tree

Date	Mintage	MS-63	Proof
2008 Proof	10,000	—	70.00

KM# 872 20 DOLLARS

31.1050 g., 0.9990 Silver 0.9990 oz. ASW, 38 mm. **Ruler:** Elizabeth II **Rev:** Snowflake, sapphire crystal

Date	Mintage	MS-63	Proof
2008 Proof	15,000	—	85.00

KM# 893 20 DOLLARS

31.3900 g., 0.9990 Silver 1.0082 oz. ASW, 38 mm. **Ruler:** Elizabeth II **Subject:** Coal mining trade **Obv:** Bust right **Obv. Legend:** Elizabeth II DG Regina **Obv. Designer:** Susanna Blunt **Rev:** Miner pushing cart with coal **Rev. Legend:** Canada 20 Dollars **Rev. Designer:** John Marder

Date	Mintage	MS-63	Proof
2009 Proof	10,000	—	75.00

KM# 891 20 DOLLARS

31.3900 g., 0.9990 Silver 1.0082 oz. ASW, 38 mm. **Ruler:** Elizabeth II **Subject:** Great Canadian Locomotives - Jubilee **Obv:** Bust right **Obv. Legend:** Elizabeth II DG Regina **Obv. Designer:** Susanna Blunt **Rev:** Jubilee locomotive side view **Rev. Legend:** Canada 20 Dollars **Edge Lettering:** Jubilee

Date	Mintage	MS-63	Proof
2009 Proof	10,000	—	70.00

KM# 892 20 DOLLARS

31.3900 g., 0.9990 Silver 1.0082 oz. ASW, 38 mm. **Ruler:** Elizabeth II **Subject:** Crystal raindrop **Obv:** Bust right **Obv. Legend:** Elizabeth II DG Regina **Obv. Designer:** Susanna Blunt **Rev:** Colored maple leaves with crystal raindrop **Rev. Legend:** Canada 20 Dollars **Rev. Designer:** Celia Godkin

Date	Mintage	MS-63	Proof
2009 Proof	10,000	—	95.00

KM# 870 20 DOLLARS

27.7800 g., 0.9250 Silver 0.8261 oz. ASW, 40 mm. **Ruler:** Elizabeth II **Rev:** Calgary Flames goalie mask multicolor on goal net

Date	Mintage	MS-63	Proof
2009 Proof	10,000	—	70.00

KM# 871 20 DOLLARS
27.7800 g., 0.9250 Silver 0.8261 oz. ASW, 40 mm. **Ruler:** Elizabeth II **Rev:** Edmonton Oilers goalie mask, multicolor on goal net

Date	Mintage	MS-63	Proof
2009 Proof	10,000	—	70.00

KM# 872A 20 DOLLARS
27.7800 g., 0.9250 Silver 0.8261 oz. ASW, 40 mm. **Ruler:** Elizabeth II **Rev:** Montreal Canadians goalie mask multicolor

Date	Mintage	MS-63	Proof
2009 Proof	10,000	—	70.00

KM# 873 20 DOLLARS
27.7800 g., 0.9250 Silver 0.8261 oz. ASW, 40 mm. **Ruler:** Elizabeth II **Rev:** Ottawa Senators goalie mask on goal net

Date	Mintage	MS-63	Proof
2009 Proof	10,000	—	70.00

KM# 874 20 DOLLARS
27.7800 g., 0.9250 Silver 0.8261 oz. ASW, 40 mm. **Ruler:** Elizabeth II **Rev:** Toronto Maple Leafs goalie mask, multicolor on goal net

Date	Mintage	MS-63	Proof
2009 Proof	10,000	—	70.00

KM# 875 20 DOLLARS
27.7800 g., 0.9250 Silver 0.8261 oz. ASW, 40 mm. **Ruler:** Elizabeth II **Rev:** Vancouver Canucks goalie mask, multicolor on goal net

Date	Mintage	MS-63	Proof
2009 Proof	10,000	—	70.00

KM# 876 20 DOLLARS
31.5000 g., 0.9250 Silver 0.9368 oz. ASW, 40 mm. **Ruler:** Elizabeth II **Rev:** Summer moon mask

Date	Mintage	MS-63	Proof
2009 Proof	10,000	—	75.00

KM# 944 20 DOLLARS
31.1050 g., 0.9990 Silver 0.9990 oz. ASW, 38 mm. **Ruler:** Elizabeth II **Rev:** Snowflake - light blue crystal

Date	Mintage	MS-63	Proof
2009 Proof	15,000	—	95.00

KM# 945 20 DOLLARS
31.1050 g., 0.9990 Silver 0.9990 oz. ASW, 38 mm. **Ruler:** Elizabeth II **Rev:** Snowflake - light red crystal

Date	Mintage	MS-63	Proof
2009 Proof	15,000	—	95.00

KM# 946 20 DOLLARS
31.3900 g., 0.9990 Silver 1.0082 oz. ASW, 38 mm. **Ruler:** Elizabeth II **Rev:** Maple leaf and rain drop - fall colors

Date	Mintage	MS-63	Proof
2009 Proof	10,000	—	75.00

KM# 987 20 DOLLARS
31.3900 g., 0.9999 Silver 1.0091 oz. ASW, 31.39 mm. **Ruler:** Elizabeth II **Rev:** Lotus Water Lilly in multicolor and crystal **Rev. Designer:** Cladio D'Angelo

Date	Mintage	MS-63	Proof
2010 Proof	10,000	—	100

KM# 1009 20 DOLLARS
31.3900 g., 0.9990 Silver 1.0082 oz. ASW **Ruler:** Elizabeth II **Subject:** 75th Anniversary of Canadian Bank Notes **Rev:** Female and farmer seated

Date	Mintage	MS-63	Proof
2010 Proof	—	—	70.00

KM# 1013 20 DOLLARS
31.3900 g., 0.9990 Silver 1.0082 oz. ASW, 38 mm. **Ruler:** Elizabeth II **Rev:** Maple leaf and crystal **Rev. Designer:** Celia Godkin

Date	Mintage	MS-63	Proof
2010 Proof	10,000	—	95.00

KM# 1018 20 DOLLARS
31.3900 g., 0.9990 Silver 1.0082 oz. ASW, 38 mm. **Ruler:** Elizabeth II **Rev:** Steam Locomotive Selkirk

Date	Mintage	MS-63	Proof
2010 Proof	10,000	—	70.00

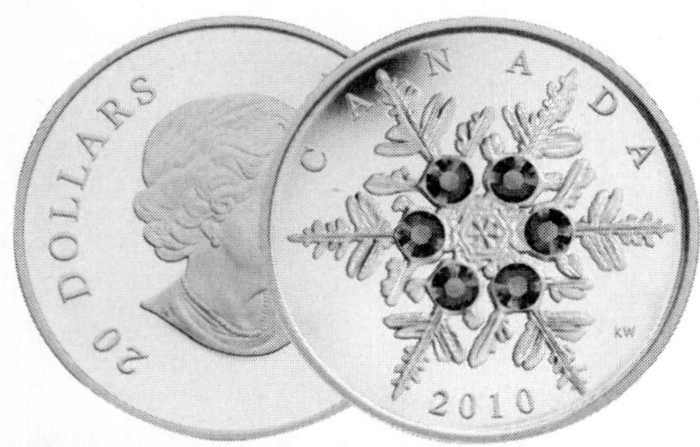

KM# 1048 20 DOLLARS
31.1050 g., 0.9999 Silver 0.9999 oz. ASW, 38 mm. **Ruler:** Elizabeth II **Rev:** Snowflake, blue crystals

Date	Mintage	MS-63	Proof
2010 Proof	—	—	85.00

KM# 1049 20 DOLLARS
31.1050 g., 0.9999 Silver 0.9999 oz. ASW, 38 mm. **Ruler:** Elizabeth II **Rev:** Snowflake, tanzanite crystals

Date	Mintage	MS-63	Proof
2010 Proof	—	—	85.00

KM# 1066 20 DOLLARS
31.9900 g., 0.9990 Silver 1.0274 oz. ASW, 38 mm. **Ruler:** Elizabeth II **Rev:** Pinecone with red crystals **Rev. Designer:** Susan Taylor

Date	Mintage	MS-63	Proof
2010 Proof	5,000	—	120

KM# 1067 20 DOLLARS
31.9900 g., 0.9990 Silver 1.0274 oz. ASW, 38 mm. **Ruler:** Elizabeth II **Rev:** Pinecone with blue crystals **Rev. Designer:** Susan Taylor

Date	Mintage	MS-63	Proof
2010 Proof	5,000	—	120

KM# 1075 20 DOLLARS
27.7800 g., 0.9250 Silver 0.8261 oz. ASW, 40 mm. **Ruler:** Elizabeth II **Subject:** Winter Scene **Rev:** Horse pulling cut Christmas Tree **Rev. Designer:** Rene Clark

Date	Mintage	MS-63	Proof
2011 Proof	8,000	—	70.00

KM# 742 25 DOLLARS
27.7800 g., 0.9250 Silver 0.8261 oz. ASW, 40 mm. **Ruler:** Elizabeth II **Subject:** Vancouver Olympics **Rev:** Alpine skiing, hologram

Date	Mintage	MS-63	Proof
2007 Proof	45,000	—	65.00

KM# 743 25 DOLLARS
27.7800 g., 0.9250 Silver 0.8261 oz. ASW, 40 mm. **Ruler:** Elizabeth II **Subject:** Vancouver Olympics **Rev:** Athletics pride hologram

Date	Mintage	MS-63	Proof
2007 Proof	45,000	—	65.00

KM# 744 25 DOLLARS
27.7500 g., 0.9250 Silver 0.8252 oz. ASW, 40 mm. **Ruler:** Elizabeth II **Subject:** Vancouver Olympics **Rev:** Biathleon hologram

Date	Mintage	MS-63	Proof
2007 Proof	54,000	—	65.00

KM# 745 25 DOLLARS
27.7800 g., 0.9250 Silver 0.8261 oz. ASW, 40 mm. **Ruler:** Elizabeth II **Subject:** Vancouver Olympics **Rev:** Curling hologram

Date	Mintage	MS-63	Proof
2007 Proof	—	—	65.00

KM# 746 25 DOLLARS
27.7800 g., 0.9250 Silver 0.8261 oz. ASW, 40 mm. **Ruler:** Elizabeth II **Subject:** Vancouver Olympics **Rev:** Hockey, hologram

Date	Mintage	MS-63	Proof
2007 Proof	45,000	—	65.00

KM# 814 25 DOLLARS
27.7800 g., 0.9250 Silver 0.8261 oz. ASW, 40 mm. **Ruler:** Elizabeth II **Subject:** Vancouver Olympics **Rev:** Bobsleigh, hologram

Date	Mintage	MS-63	Proof
2008 Proof	45,000	—	65.00

KM# 815 25 DOLLARS
27.7800 g., 0.9250 Silver 0.8261 oz. ASW, 40 mm. **Ruler:** Elizabeth II **Subject:** Vancouver Olympics **Rev:** Figure skating, hologram

Date	Mintage	MS-63	Proof
2008 Proof	45,000	—	65.00

KM# 816 25 DOLLARS
27.7800 g., 0.9250 Silver 0.8261 oz. ASW, 40 mm. **Ruler:** Elizabeth II **Subject:** Vancouver Olympics **Rev:** Freestyle skating, hologram

Date	Mintage	MS-63	Proof
2008 Proof	45,000	—	65.00

KM# 817 25 DOLLARS
27.7800 g., 0.9250 Silver 0.8261 oz. ASW, 40 mm. **Ruler:** Elizabeth II **Subject:** Vancouver Olympics **Rev:** Snowboarding, hologram

Date	Mintage	MS-63	Proof
2008 Proof	45,000	—	65.00

KM# 818 25 DOLLARS
27.7800 g., 0.9250 Silver 0.8261 oz. ASW, 40 mm. **Ruler:** Elizabeth II **Subject:** Vancouver Olympics **Rev:** Home of the 2010 Olympics

Date	Mintage	MS-63	Proof
2008 Proof	45,000	—	65.00

KM# 903 25 DOLLARS
27.7800 g., 0.9250 Silver 0.8261 oz. ASW, 40 mm. **Ruler:** Elizabeth II **Subject:** 2010 Vancouver Olympics **Obv:** Bust right **Obv. Designer:** Susanna Blunt **Rev:** Cross Country Skiing and hologram at left

Date	Mintage	MS-63	Proof
2009 Proof	45,000	—	65.00

KM# 904 25 DOLLARS
27.7800 g., 0.9250 Silver 0.8261 oz. ASW, 40 mm. **Ruler:** Elizabeth II **Subject:** 2010 Vancouver Olympics **Obv:** Bust right **Obv. Designer:** Susanna Blunt **Rev:** Olympians holding torch, hologram at left

Date	Mintage	MS-63	Proof
2009 Proof	45,000	—	65.00

KM# 905 25 DOLLARS
27.7800 g., 0.9250 Silver 0.8261 oz. ASW, 40 mm. **Ruler:** Elizabeth II **Subject:** 2010 Vancouver Olympics **Obv:** Bust right **Obv. Designer:** Susanna Blunt **Rev:** Sled, hologram at left

Date	Mintage	MS-63	Proof
2009 Proof	45,000	—	65.00

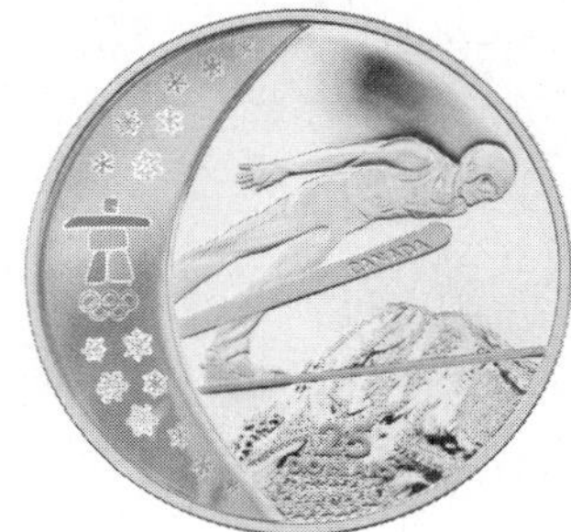

KM# 906 25 DOLLARS
27.7800 g., 0.9250 Silver 0.8261 oz. ASW, 40 mm. **Ruler:** Elizabeth II **Subject:** 2010 Vancouver Olympics **Obv:** Bust right **Obv. Designer:** Susanna Blunt **Rev:** Ski Jumper, hologram at left

Date	Mintage	MS-63	Proof
2009 Proof	45,000	—	65.00

KM# 907 25 DOLLARS
27.7800 g., 0.9250 Silver 0.8261 oz. ASW, 40 mm. **Ruler:** Elizabeth II **Subject:** 2010 Vancouver Olympics **Obv:** Bust right **Obv. Designer:** Susanna Blunt **Rev:** Speed Skaters, hologram at left

Date	Mintage	MS-63	Proof
2009 Proof	45,000	—	65.00

KM# 590 30 DOLLARS
31.5000 g., 0.9250 Silver 0.9368 oz. ASW **Ruler:** Elizabeth II **Subject:** Pacific Northwest Wood Carvings **Obv:** Head right **Rev:** Welcome figure totem pole

Date	Mintage	MS-63	Proof
2006 Proof	9,904	—	75.00

KM# 668 30 DOLLARS
31.5000 g., 0.9250 Silver 0.9368 oz. ASW **Ruler:** Elizabeth II **Subject:** Canadarm and Col. C. Hadfield **Obv:** Head right **Rev:** Hologram of Canadarm

Date	Mintage	MS-63	Proof
2006 Proof	9,357	—	90.00

KM# 669 30 DOLLARS
31.5000 g., 0.9250 Silver 0.9368 oz. ASW **Ruler:** Elizabeth II **Subject:** National War Memorial **Obv:** Head right **Rev:** Statue of three soldiers

Date	Mintage	MS-63	Proof
2006 Proof	8,876	—	85.00

KM# 670 30 DOLLARS
31.5000 g., 0.9250 Silver 0.9368 oz. ASW **Ruler:** Elizabeth II **Subject:** Beaumont Hamel Newfoundland **Obv:** Head right **Rev:** Caribou statue on rock outcrop

Date	Mintage	MS-63	Proof
2006 Proof	15,325	—	95.00

KM# 671 30 DOLLARS
31.5000 g., 0.9250 Silver 0.9368 oz. ASW **Ruler:** Elizabeth II **Subject:** Dog Sled Team **Obv:** Head right **Rev:** Colorized

Date	Mintage	MS-63	Proof
2006 Proof	7,384	—	85.00

KM# 739 30 DOLLARS
31.5000 g., 0.9250 Silver 0.9368 oz. ASW, 40 mm. **Ruler:** Elizabeth II **Rev:** Niagra Falls panoramic hologram

Date	Mintage	MS-63	Proof
2007 Proof	5,181	—	85.00

KM# 741 30 DOLLARS
31.5000 g., 0.9250 Silver 0.9368 oz. ASW, 40 mm. **Ruler:** Elizabeth II **Rev:** War Memorial, Vimy Ridge

Date	Mintage	MS-63	Proof
2007 Proof	5,190	—	85.00

KM# 819 30 DOLLARS
31.5000 g., 0.9250 Silver 0.9368 oz. ASW, 40 mm. **Ruler:** Elizabeth II **Rev:** IMAX

Date	Mintage	MS-63	Proof
2008 Proof	15,000	—	75.00

KM# 895 30 DOLLARS
33.7500 g., 0.9250 Silver 1.0037 oz. ASW, 40 mm. **Ruler:** Elizabeth II **Subject:** International year of astronomy **Obv:** Bust right **Obv. Legend:** Elizabeth II 30 Dollars DG Regina **Obv. Designer:** Susanna Blunt **Rev:** Observatory with planets and colored sky **Rev. Legend:** Canada **Rev. Designer:** Colin Mayne

Date	Mintage	MS-63	Proof
2009 Proof	10,000	—	90.00

KM# 566 50 DOLLARS
12.0000 g., 0.5833 Gold 0.2250 oz. AGW, 27 mm. **Ruler:** Elizabeth II **Subject:** WWII **Obv:** Head right **Rev:** Large V and three portraits

Date	Mintage	MS-63	Proof
2005 Specimen	4,000	—	375

KM# 672 50 DOLLARS
31.1600 g., 0.9995 Palladium 1.0013 oz. **Ruler:** Elizabeth II **Subject:** Constellation in Spring sky position **Rev:** Large Bear at top

Date	Mintage	MS-63	Proof
2006 Proof	297	—	1,200

KM# 673 50 DOLLARS
31.1600 g., 0.9995 Palladium 1.0013 oz. **Ruler:** Elizabeth II

Subject: Constellation in Summer sky position **Rev:** Large Bear at left

Date	Mintage	MS-63	Proof
2006 Proof	296	—	1,200

KM# 674 50 DOLLARS

31.1600 g., 0.9995 Palladium 1.0013 oz. **Ruler:** Elizabeth II **Subject:** Constellation in Autumn sky position **Rev:** Large Bear towards bottom

Date	Mintage	MS-63	Proof
2006 Proof	296	—	1,200

KM# 675 50 DOLLARS

31.1600 g., 0.9995 Palladium 1.0013 oz. **Ruler:** Elizabeth II **Subject:** Constellation in Winter sky position **Rev:** Large Bear towards right

Date	Mintage	MS-63	Proof
2006 Proof	293	—	1,200

KM# 709 50 DOLLARS

155.5000 g., 0.9999 Silver 4.9987 oz. ASW **Ruler:** Elizabeth II **Subject:** Queen's 60th Wedding Anniversary **Rev:** Coat of Arms and Mascots of Elizabeth and Philip

Date	Mintage	MS-63	Proof
2007 Proof	4,000	—	350

KM# 783 50 DOLLARS

156.7700 g., 0.9990 Silver 5.0350 oz. ASW, 65 mm. **Ruler:** Elizabeth II **Subject:** Ottawa Mint Centennial 1908-2008 **Rev:** Mint building facade **Note:** Photo reduced.

Date	Mintage	MS-63	Proof
2008 Proof	4,000	—	400

KM# 1042 50 DOLLARS

31.1050 g., 0.9990 Gold 0.9990 oz. AGW, 30 mm. **Ruler:** Elizabeth II **Rev:** Vancouver logo and maple leaf **Edge:** Reeded

Date	Mintage	MS-63	Proof
2008P	—	1,500	—

KM# 896 50 DOLLARS

156.7700 g., 0.9990 Silver 5.0350 oz. ASW, 65.25 mm. **Ruler:** Elizabeth II **Subject:** 150 Anniversary of the start of construction of the parliament buildings **Obv:** Bust right **Obv. Legend:** Elizabeth II Canada DG Regina **Obv. Designer:** Susanna Blunt **Rev:** Incomplete west block, original architecture **Rev. Legend:** 50 Dollars 1859-2009

Date	Mintage	MS-63	Proof
2009 Proof	2,000	—	450

KM# 1008 50 DOLLARS

157.6000 g., 0.9990 Silver 5.0617 oz. ASW, 65.25 mm. **Ruler:** Elizabeth II **Subject:** 75th Anniverary of Canadian Bank Notes **Rev:** Female seated speaking into microphone **Note:** Photo reduced.

Date	Mintage	MS-63	Proof
2010 Proof	2,000	—	450

KM# 567 75 DOLLARS

31.4400 g., 0.4166 Gold 0.4211 oz. AGW **Ruler:** Elizabeth II **Subject:** Pope John Paul II **Obv:** Head right **Rev:** Pope giving blessing

Date	Mintage	MS-63	Proof
2005 Proof	1,870	—	650

KM# 747 75 DOLLARS

12.0000 g., 0.5830 Gold 0.2249 oz. AGW, 27 mm. **Ruler:** Elizabeth II **Subject:** Vancouver Olympics **Rev:** Athletics Pride, multicolor flag

Date	Mintage	MS-63	Proof
2007 Proof	8,000	—	350

KM# 748 75 DOLLARS

12.0000 g., 0.5830 Gold 0.2249 oz. AGW, 27 mm. **Ruler:** Elizabeth II **Obv:** Bust right **Obv. Designer:** Susanna Blunt **Rev:** Canada geese in flight left, multicolor

Date	Mintage	MS-63	Proof
2007 Proof	8,000	—	350

KM# 749 75 DOLLARS

12.0000 g., 0.5830 Gold 0.2249 oz. AGW, 27 mm. **Ruler:** Elizabeth II **Rev:** Mountie, multicolor

Date	Mintage	MS-63	Proof
2007 Proof	8,000	—	350

KM# 821 75 DOLLARS

12.0000 g., 0.5830 Gold 0.2249 oz. AGW, 27 mm. **Ruler:** Elizabeth II **Subject:** Host Nations of the 2010 Olympics **Obv:** Bust right **Rev:** Four masks

Date	Mintage	MS-63	Proof
2008 Proof	8,000	—	350

KM# 821a 75 DOLLARS

12.0000 g., 0.5830 Gold 0.2249 oz. AGW, 27 mm. **Ruler:** Elizabeth II **Rev:** Four Host Nations emblem, colored **Rev. Designer:** Jody Broomfield

Date	Mintage	MS-63	Proof
2008 Proof	8,000	—	350

KM# 908 75 DOLLARS

12.0000 g., 0.5830 Gold 0.2249 oz. AGW, 27 mm. **Ruler:** Elizabeth II **Subject:** 2010 Vancouver Olympics **Obv:** Bust right **Obv. Designer:** Susana Blunt **Rev:** Multicolor moose

Date	Mintage	MS-63	Proof
2009 Proof	8,000	—	400

KM# 909 75 DOLLARS
12.0000 g., 0.5830 Gold 0.2249 oz. AGW, 27 mm. **Ruler:** Elizabeth II **Subject:** 2010 Vancouver Olympics **Obv:** Bust right **Obv. Designer:** Susanna Blunt **Rev:** Multicolor athletics and torch

Date	Mintage	MS-63	Proof
2009 Proof	8,000	—	375

KM# 910 75 DOLLARS
12.0000 g., 0.5830 Gold 0.2249 oz. AGW, 27 mm. **Ruler:** Elizabeth II **Subject:** 2010 Vancouver Olympics **Obv:** Bust right **Obv. Designer:** Susanna Blunt **Rev:** Wolf, multicolor

Date	Mintage	MS-63	Proof
2009 Proof	8,000	—	400

KM# 947 75 DOLLARS
12.0000 g., 0.5830 Gold 0.2249 oz. AGW, 27 mm. **Ruler:** Elizabeth II **Subject:** Vancouver Olympics **Rev:** Tent building at Olympic

Date	Mintage	MS-63	Proof
2009 Proof	8,000	—	375

KM# 1002 75 DOLLARS
12.0000 g., 0.5830 Gold 0.2249 oz. AGW, 27 mm. **Ruler:** Elizabeth II **Rev:** Spring color maple leaves

Date	Mintage	MS-63	Proof
2010 Proof	1,000	—	600

KM# 1003 75 DOLLARS
12.0000 g., 0.5830 Gold 0.2249 oz. AGW, 27 mm. **Ruler:** Elizabeth II **Rev:** Summer color maple leaves

Date	Mintage	MS-63	Proof
2010 Proof	1,000	—	600

KM# 1004 75 DOLLARS
12.0000 g., 0.5830 Gold 0.2249 oz. AGW, 27 mm. **Ruler:** Elizabeth II **Rev:** Fall color maple leaves

Date	Mintage	MS-63	Proof
2010 Proof	1,000	—	600

KM# 1005 75 DOLLARS
12.0000 g., 0.5830 Gold 0.2249 oz. AGW, 27 mm. **Ruler:** Elizabeth II **Rev:** Winter color maple leaves

Date	Mintage	MS-63	Proof
2010 Proof	1,000	—	600

KM# 416 100 DOLLARS
13.3375 g., 0.5830 Gold alloyed with 5.5579 g of .999 Silver, .1787 oz ASW 0.2500 oz. AGW, 27 mm. **Ruler:** Elizabeth II **Subject:** Library of Parliament **Obv:** Crowned head right **Obv. Designer:** Dora dePedery-Hunt **Rev:** Statue in domed building **Rev. Designer:** Robert R. Carmichael **Edge:** Reeded

Date	Mintage	MS-63	Proof
2001 Proof	8,080	—	375

KM# 452 100 DOLLARS
13.3375 g., 0.5830 Gold 0.2500 oz. AGW, 27 mm. **Ruler:** Elizabeth II **Subject:** Discovery of Oil in Alberta **Obv:** Crowned head right **Rev:** Oil well with black oil spill on ground **Rev. Designer:** John Marden **Edge:** Reeded

Date	Mintage	MS-63	Proof
2002 Proof	9,994	—	425

KM# 486 100 DOLLARS
13.3375 g., 0.5830 Gold 0.2500 oz. AGW **Ruler:** Elizabeth II **Subject:** 100th Anniversary of the Discovery of Marquis Wheat **Obv:** Head right

Date	Mintage	MS-63	Proof
2003 Proof	9,993	—	375

KM# 528 100 DOLLARS
12.0000 g., 0.5830 Gold 0.2249 oz. AGW **Ruler:** Elizabeth II **Subject:** St. Lawrence Seaway, 50th Anniversary **Obv:** Head right

Date	Mintage	MS-63	Proof
2004 Proof	7,454	—	350

KM# 593 100 DOLLARS
12.0000 g., 0.5833 Gold 0.2250 oz. AGW **Ruler:** Elizabeth II **Subject:** 130th Anniversary, Supreme Court **Obv:** Head right

Date	Mintage	MS-63	Proof
2005 Proof	5,092	—	420

KM# 591 100 DOLLARS
12.0000 g., 0.5833 Gold 0.2250 oz. AGW **Ruler:** Elizabeth II **Subject:** 75th Anniversary, Hockey Classic between Royal Military College and U.S. Military Academy **Obv:** Head right

Date	Mintage	MS-63	Proof
2006 Proof	5,439	—	350

KM# 689 100 DOLLARS
12.0000 g., 0.5833 Gold 0.2250 oz. AGW, 27 mm. **Ruler:** Elizabeth II **Subject:** 140th Anniversary Dominion **Obv:** Head right

Date	Mintage	MS-63	Proof
2007 Proof	4,453	—	420

KM# 823 100 DOLLARS
12.0000 g., 0.5830 Gold 0.2249 oz. AGW, 27 mm. **Ruler:** Elizabeth II **Rev:** Fraser River

Date	Mintage	MS-63	Proof
2008 Proof	5,000	—	375

KM# 898 100 DOLLARS
12.0000 g., 0.5830 Gold 0.2249 oz. AGW, 27 mm. **Ruler:** Elizabeth II **Subject:** 10th Anniversary of Nunavut **Obv:** Bust right **Obv. Legend:** Elizabeth II DG Regina **Obv. Designer:** Susanna Blunt **Rev:** Inuit dancer with 3 faces behind **Rev. Legend:** Canada 100 Dollars 1999-2009

Date	Mintage	MS-63	Proof
2009 Proof	5,000	—	500

KM# 997 100 DOLLARS
12.0000 g., 0.5830 Gold 0.2249 oz. AGW, 27 mm. **Ruler:** Elizabeth II **Rev:** Henry Hudson, Map of Hudson's Bay **Rev. Designer:** John Mantha

Date	Mintage	MS-63	Proof
2010 Proof	Est. 5,000	—	550

KM# 1073 100 DOLLARS
12.0000 g., 0.5830 Gold 0.2249 oz. AGW, 27 mm. **Ruler:** Elizabeth II **Subject:** Canadian Railroads, 175th Anniversary **Rev:** Early steam locomotive

Date	Mintage	MS-63	Proof
2011	3,000	—	640

KM# 417 150 DOLLARS

13.6100 g., 0.7500 Gold 0.3282 oz. AGW, 28 mm. **Ruler:** Elizabeth II **Subject:** Year of the Snake **Obv:** Crowned head right **Obv. Designer:** Dora dePedery-Hunt **Rev:** Multicolor snake hologram **Edge:** Reeded

Date	Mintage	MS-63	Proof
2001 Proof	6,571	—	475

KM# 604 150 DOLLARS

13.6100 g., 0.7500 Gold 0.3282 oz. AGW **Ruler:** Elizabeth II **Obv:** Head right **Rev:** Stylized horse left

Date	Mintage	MS-63	Proof
2002 Proof	6,843	—	475

KM# 487 150 DOLLARS

13.6100 g., 0.7500 Gold 0.3282 oz. AGW **Ruler:** Elizabeth II **Subject:** Year of the Ram **Obv:** Crowned head right **Rev:** Stylized ram left, hologram **Rev. Designer:** Harvey Chan

Date	Mintage	MS-63	Proof
2003 Proof	3,927	—	475

KM# 614 150 DOLLARS

13.6100 g., 0.7500 Gold 0.3282 oz. AGW **Ruler:** Elizabeth II **Obv:** Head right **Rev:** Year of the Monkey, hologram

Date	Mintage	MS-63	Proof
2004 Proof	3,392	—	475

KM# 568 150 DOLLARS

13.6100 g., 0.7500 Gold 0.3282 oz. AGW **Ruler:** Elizabeth II **Subject:** Year of the Rooster **Obv:** Head right **Rev:** Rooster left, hologram

Date	Mintage	MS-63	Proof
2005 Proof	3,731	—	475

KM# 592 150 DOLLARS

13.6100 g., 0.7500 Gold 0.3282 oz. AGW **Ruler:** Elizabeth II **Subject:** Year of the Dog, hologram **Obv:** Head right **Rev:** Stylized dog left

Date	Mintage	MS-63	Proof
2006 Proof	2,604	—	500

KM# 733 150 DOLLARS

11.8400 g., 0.7500 Gold 0.2855 oz. AGW, 28 mm. **Ruler:** Elizabeth II **Subject:** Year of the Pig **Obv:** Head right **Rev:** Pig in center with Chinese lunar calendar around, hologram

Date	Mintage	MS-63	Proof
2007 Proof	4,888	—	525

KM# 802 150 DOLLARS

11.8400 g., 0.7500 Gold 0.2855 oz. AGW, 28 mm. **Ruler:** Elizabeth II **Subject:** Year of the Rat **Rev:** Rat, hologram

Date	Mintage	MS-63	Proof
2008 Proof	4,888	—	525

KM# 899 150 DOLLARS

10.4000 g., 0.9990 Gold 0.3340 oz. AGW, 22.5 mm. **Ruler:** Elizabeth II **Subject:** Blessings of wealth **Obv:** Bust right **Obv. Legend:** Elizabeth II, DG Regina, Fine Gold 99999 or PUR **Obv. Designer:** Susanna Blunt **Rev:** Three goldfish surround peony, clouds **Rev. Legend:** Canada 150 Dollars (Chinese symbols of good fortune) **Rev. Designer:** Harvey Chan **Edge:** Scalloped

Date	Mintage	MS-63	Proof
2009 Proof	50,000	—	750

KM# 867 150 DOLLARS

11.8400 g., 0.7500 Gold 0.2855 oz. AGW, 28 mm. **Ruler:** Elizabeth II **Subject:** Year of the Ox **Rev:** Ox, hologram

Date	Mintage	MS-63	Proof
2009 Proof	4,888	—	525

KM# 979 150 DOLLARS

11.8400 g., 0.7500 Gold 0.2855 oz. AGW, 28 mm. **Ruler:** Elizabeth II **Subject:** Year of the Tiger **Rev:** Tiger in hologram

Date	Mintage	MS-63	Proof
2010 Proof	48,888	—	550

KM# 1030 150 DOLLARS

0.9999 Gold **Ruler:** Elizabeth II **Subject:** Blessing of Wealth **Shape:** Scalloped

Date	Mintage	MS-63	Proof
2010 Proof	—	—	650

KM# 1031 150 DOLLARS

Gold **Ruler:** Elizabeth II **Subject:** Year of the Tiger **Rev:** Tiger walking

Date	Mintage	MS-63	Proof
2010 Proof	—	—	550

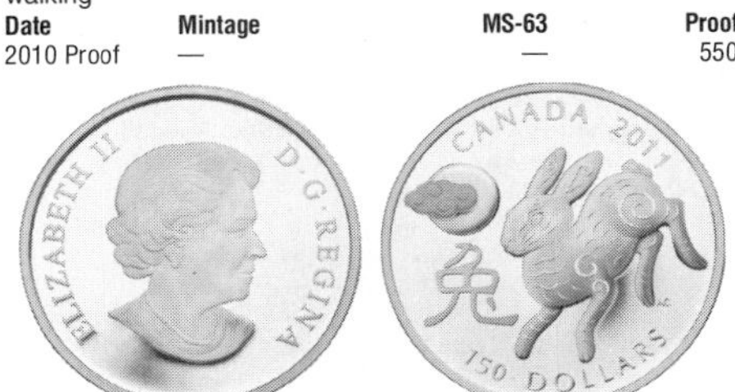

KM# 1054 150 DOLLARS

Gold **Ruler:** Elizabeth II **Subject:** Year of the rabbit **Rev:** Rabit hopping left, character at left

Date	Mintage	MS-63	Proof
2011 Proof	—	—	550

KM# 1053 150 DOLLARS

13.6100 g., 0.7500 Gold 0.3282 oz. AGW, 28 mm. **Ruler:** Elizabeth II **Subject:** Year of the rabbit **Rev:** Rabbit hologram

Date	Mintage	MS-63	Proof
2011 Proof	—	—	525

KM# 418 200 DOLLARS

17.1350 g., 0.9166 Gold 0.5049 oz. AGW, 29 mm. **Ruler:** Elizabeth II **Subject:** Cornelius D. Krieghoff's "The Habitant farm" **Obv:** Queens head right **Edge:** Reeded

Date	Mintage	MS-63	Proof
2001 Proof	5,406	—	750

KM# 466 200 DOLLARS

17.1350 g., 0.9166 Gold 0.5049 oz. AGW, 29 mm. **Ruler:** Elizabeth II **Subject:** Thomas Thompson "The Jack Pine" (1916-17) **Obv:** Crowned head right

Date	Mintage	MS-63	Proof
2002 Proof	5,264	—	750

KM# 488 200 DOLLARS

17.1350 g., 0.9166 Gold 0.5049 oz. AGW **Ruler:** Elizabeth II **Subject:** Fitzgerald's "Houses" (1929) **Obv:** Crowned head right **Rev:** House with trees

Date	Mintage	MS-63	Proof
2003 Proof	4,118	—	750

KM# 516 200 DOLLARS

16.0000 g., 0.9166 Gold 0.4715 oz. AGW, 29 mm. **Ruler:** Elizabeth II **Subject:** "Fragments" **Obv:** Crowned head right **Rev:** Fragmented face **Edge:** Reeded

Date	Mintage	MS-63	Proof
2004 Proof	3,917	—	725

KM# 569 200 DOLLARS

16.0000 g., 0.9166 Gold 0.4715 oz. AGW **Ruler:** Elizabeth II **Subject:** Fur traders **Obv:** Head right **Rev:** Men in canoe riding wave

Date	Mintage	MS-63	Proof
2005 Proof	3,669	—	725

KM# 594 200 DOLLARS

16.0000 g., 0.9166 Gold 0.4715 oz. AGW **Ruler:** Elizabeth II **Subject:** Timber trade **Obv:** Head right **Rev:** Lumberjacks felling tree

Date	Mintage	MS-63	Proof
2006 Proof	3,185	—	725

KM# 691 200 DOLLARS

16.0000 g., 0.9166 Gold 0.4715 oz. AGW, 29 mm. **Ruler:** Elizabeth II **Subject:** Fishing Trade **Obv:** Head right **Rev:** Two fishermen hauling net

Date	Mintage	MS-63	Proof
2007 Proof	4,000	—	725

KM# 824 200 DOLLARS

16.0000 g., 0.9170 Gold 0.4717 oz. AGW, 29 mm. **Ruler:** Elizabeth II **Subject:** Commerce **Rev:** Horse drawn plow

Date	Mintage	MS-63	Proof
2008 Proof	4,000	—	725

KM# 894 200 DOLLARS
16.0000 g., 0.9160 Gold 0.4712 oz. AGW, 29 mm. **Ruler:** Elizabeth II **Subject:** Coal mining trade **Obv:** Bust right **Obv. Legend:** Elizabeth II DG Regina **Obv. Designer:** Susanna Blunt **Rev:** Miner pushing cart with black coal **Rev. Legend:** Canada 200 Dollars **Rev. Designer:** John Marder

Date	Mintage	MS-63	Proof
2009 Proof	4,000	—	800

KM# 1000 200 DOLLARS
16.0000 g., 0.9160 Gold 0.4712 oz. AGW, 29 mm. **Ruler:** Elizabeth II **Subject:** Petroleum and Oil Trade **Rev:** Oil railcar and well head

Date	Mintage	MS-63	Proof
2010 Proof	4,000	—	1,000

KM# 1074 200 DOLLARS
16.0000 g., 0.9167 Gold 0.4715 oz. AGW, 29 mm. **Ruler:** Elizabeth II **Rev:** SS Beaver - Seam Sail ship **Rev. Designer:** John Mardon

Date	Mintage	MS-63	Proof
2011 Proof	2,800	—	1,100

KM# 677 250 DOLLARS
45.0000 g., 0.5833 Gold 0.8439 oz. AGW **Ruler:** Elizabeth II **Subject:** Dog Sled Team

Date	Mintage	MS-63	Proof
2006 Proof	953	—	1,250

KM# 751 250 DOLLARS
1000.0000 g., 0.9999 Silver 32.146 oz. ASW, 101.6 mm. **Ruler:** Elizabeth II **Subject:** Vancouver Olympics, 2010 **Rev:** Early Canada motif **Note:** Illustration reduced.

Date	Mintage	MS-63	Proof
2007 Proof	2,500	—	1,250

KM# 833 250 DOLLARS
1000.0000 g., 0.9990 Silver 32.117 oz. ASW, 101.6 mm. **Ruler:** Elizabeth II **Subject:** Vancouver Olympics 2010 **Rev:** Towards confederation **Note:** Illustration reduced.

Date	Mintage	MS-63	Proof
2008 Proof	2,500	—	1,600

KM# 913 250 DOLLARS
1000.0000 g., 0.9999 Silver 32.146 oz. ASW, 101.5 mm. **Ruler:** Elizabeth II **Obv:** Bust right **Obv. Designer:** Susanna Blunt **Rev:** Mask with fish - Surviving the flood **Note:** Illustration reduced.

Date	Mintage	MS-63	Proof
2009 Proof	—	—	2,000

KM# 949 250 DOLLARS
1000.0000 g., 0.9990 Silver 32.117 oz. ASW, 101.6 mm. **Ruler:** Elizabeth II **Rev:** Modern Canada

Date	Mintage	MS-63	Proof
2009 Proof	—	—	1,600

KM# 981 250 DOLLARS
1000.0000 g., 0.9990 Silver 32.117 oz. ASW, 101.6 mm. **Ruler:** Elizabeth II **Rev:** Eagle head

Date	Mintage	MS-63	Proof
2010 Antique Patina	1,500	1,650	—
2010 Proof	—	—	1,750

KM# 981a 250 DOLLARS
1000.0000 g., 0.9990 Silver 32.117 oz. ASW, 101.6 mm. **Ruler:** Elizabeth II **Rev:** Eagle head, blue enamel

Date	Mintage	MS-63	Proof
2010 Proof	—	—	1,750

KM# 1044 250 DOLLARS
1000.0000 g., 0.9990 Silver 32.117 oz. ASW, 101.6 mm. **Ruler:** Elizabeth II **Subject:** Baniff, 125th Anniversary of resort founding **Rev:** Features of Baniff

Date	Mintage	MS-63	Proof
2010 Proof	—	—	1,650

KM# 501 300 DOLLARS

60.0000 g., 0.5833 Gold 1.1252 oz. AGW, 50 mm. **Ruler:** Elizabeth II **Obv:** Triple cameo portraits of Queen Elizabeth II by Gillick, Machin and de Pedery-Hunt, each in 14K gold, rose in center **Rev:** Dates "1952-2002" and denomination in legend, rose in center **Note:** Housed in anodized gold-colored aluminum box with cherrywood stained siding

Date	Mintage	MS-63	Proof
ND(2002) Proof	999	—	1,750

KM# 517 300 DOLLARS

60.0000 g., 0.5833 Gold 1.1252 oz. AGW, 50 mm. **Ruler:** Elizabeth II **Obv:** Four coinage portraits of Elizabeth II **Rev:** Canadian arms above value **Edge:** Plain

Date	Mintage	MS-63	Proof
2004 Proof	998	—	1,750

KM# 570.1 300 DOLLARS

60.0000 g., 0.5833 Gold 1.1252 oz. AGW **Ruler:** Elizabeth II **Subject:** Standard Time - 4 AM Pacific **Obv:** Head right **Rev:** Roman numeral clock with world inside

Date	Mintage	MS-63	Proof
2005 Proof	200	—	1,650

KM# 596 300 DOLLARS

60.0000 g., 0.5833 Gold 1.1252 oz. AGW **Ruler:** Elizabeth II **Subject:** Shinplaster **Obv:** Head right **Rev:** Britannia bust, spear over shoulder

Date	Mintage	MS-63	Proof
2005 Proof	994	—	1,700

KM# 600 300 DOLLARS

60.0000 g., 0.5833 Gold 1.1252 oz. AGW **Ruler:** Elizabeth II **Subject:** Welcome Figure Totem Pole **Obv:** Head right **Rev:** Men with totem pole

Date	Mintage	MS-63	Proof
2005 Proof	947	—	1,650

KM# 570.2 300 DOLLARS

60.0000 g., 0.5830 Gold 1.1246 oz. AGW **Ruler:** Elizabeth II **Subject:** Standard Time - Mountian 5 AM **Obv:** Head right **Rev:** Roman numeral clock with world inside.

Date	Mintage	MS-63	Proof
2005 Proof	200	—	1,650

KM# 570.3 300 DOLLARS

60.0000 g., 0.5830 Gold 1.1246 oz. AGW **Ruler:** Elizabeth II **Subject:** Standard Time - Central 6 PM **Obv:** Head right **Rev:** Roman numeral clock with world inside

Date	Mintage	MS-63	Proof
2005 Proof	200	—	1,650

KM# 570.4 300 DOLLARS

60.0000 g., 0.5830 Gold 1.1246 oz. AGW **Ruler:** Elizabeth II **Subject:** Standard Time - Eastern 7 AM **Obv:** Head right **Rev:** Roman numeral clock with world inside

Date	Mintage	MS-63	Proof
2005 Proof	200	—	1,650

KM# 570.5 300 DOLLARS

60.0000 g., 0.5830 Gold 1.1246 oz. AGW **Ruler:** Elizabeth II **Subject:** Standard Time - Atlantic 8 AM **Obv:** Head right **Rev:** Roman numeral clock with world inside

Date	Mintage	MS-63	Proof
2005 Proof	200	—	1,650

KM# 570.6 300 DOLLARS

60.0000 g., 0.5830 Gold 1.1246 oz. AGW **Ruler:** Elizabeth II **Subject:** Standard Time - Newfoundland 8:30 **Obv:** Head right **Rev:** Roman numeral clock with world inside

Date	Mintage	MS-63	Proof
2005 Proof	200	—	1,650

KM# 595 300 DOLLARS

60.0000 g., 0.5833 Gold 1.1252 oz. AGW **Ruler:** Elizabeth II **Subject:** Shinplaster **Obv:** Head right **Rev:** Seated Britannia with shield

Date	Mintage	MS-63	Proof
2006 Proof	940	—	1,700

KM# 678 300 DOLLARS

45.0000 g., 0.5833 Gold 0.8439 oz. AGW **Ruler:** Elizabeth II **Subject:** Canadam and Col. C. Hadfield **Rev:** Hologram of Canadarm

Date	Mintage	MS-63	Proof
2006 Proof	581	—	1,250

KM# 679 300 DOLLARS

60.0000 g., 0.5833 Gold 1.1252 oz. AGW **Ruler:** Elizabeth II **Subject:** Queen Elizabeth's 80th Birthday **Rev:** State Crown, colorized

Date	Mintage	MS-63	Proof
2006 Proof	996	—	1,250

KM# 680 300 DOLLARS

60.0000 g., 0.5833 Gold 1.1252 oz. AGW **Ruler:** Elizabeth II **Subject:** Crystal Snowflake

Date	Mintage	MS-63	Proof
2006 Proof	998	—	1,850

KM# 692 300 DOLLARS

60.0000 g., 0.5833 Gold 1.1252 oz. AGW **Ruler:** Elizabeth II **Subject:** Shinplaster **Rev:** 1923 25 cent bank note

Date	Mintage	MS-63	Proof
2007 Proof	778	—	1,700

KM# 740 300 DOLLARS

45.0000 g., 0.5830 Gold 0.8434 oz. AGW, 40 mm. **Ruler:** Elizabeth II **Rev:** Canadian Rockies panoramic hologram

Date	Mintage	MS-63	Proof
2007 Proof	511	—	1,250

KM# 752 300 DOLLARS

60.0000 g., 0.5830 Gold 1.1246 oz. AGW, 50 mm. **Ruler:** Elizabeth II **Subject:** Vancouver Olympics **Rev:** Olympic ideals, classic figures and torch

Date	Mintage	MS-63	Proof
2007 Proof	2,500	—	1,700

KM# 753 300 DOLLARS

31.1050 g., 0.9999 Platinum 0.9999 oz. APW, 50 mm. **Ruler:** Elizabeth II **Rev:** Wooly mammoth

Date	Mintage	MS-63	Proof
2007 Proof	400	—	3,200

KM# 825 300 DOLLARS

45.0000 g., 0.5830 Gold 0.8434 oz. AGW, 40 mm. **Ruler:** Elizabeth II **Rev:** Alberta Coat of Arms

Date	Mintage	MS-63	Proof
2008 Proof	—	—	1,250

KM# 826 300 DOLLARS

45.0000 g., 0.5830 Gold 0.8434 oz. AGW, 40 mm. **Ruler:** Elizabeth II **Rev:** Newfoundland and Labrador Coat of Arms

Date	Mintage	MS-63	Proof
2008 Proof	1,000	—	1,350

KM# 827 300 DOLLARS

45.0000 g., 0.5830 Gold 0.8434 oz. AGW, 40 mm. **Ruler:** Elizabeth II **Subject:** Canadian achievements **Rev:** IMAX

Date	Mintage	MS-63	Proof
2008 Proof	—	—	1,250

KM# 828 300 DOLLARS

45.0000 g., 0.5830 Gold 0.8434 oz. AGW, 40 mm. **Ruler:** Elizabeth II **Rev:** Four seasons moon mask

Date	Mintage	MS-63	Proof
2008 Proof	1,200	—	1,500

KM# 830 300 DOLLARS

60.0000 g., 0.5830 Gold 1.1246 oz. AGW, 50 mm. **Ruler:** Elizabeth II **Subject:** Vancouver Olympics **Rev:** Olympic competition, athletics and torch

Date	Mintage	MS-63	Proof
2008 Proof	—	—	1,700

KM# 831 300 DOLLARS

31.1050 g., 0.9990 Platinum 0.9990 oz. APW **Ruler:** Elizabeth II **Rev:** Saber Tooth Scimitar cat

Date	Mintage	MS-63	Proof
2008 Proof	200	—	3,500

KM# 900 300 DOLLARS
60.0000 g., 0.5830 Gold 1.1246 oz. AGW, 50 mm. **Ruler:** Elizabeth II **Subject:** Yukon Coat of Arms **Obv:** Bust right **Obv. Legend:** Elizabeth II DG Regina **Obv. Designer:** Susanna Blunt **Rev:** Yukon Coat of Arms **Rev. Legend:** Canada 300 Dollars

Date	Mintage	MS-63	Proof
2009 Proof	1,000	—	1,850

KM# 877 300 DOLLARS
45.0000 g., 0.5830 Gold 0.8434 oz. AGW, 40 mm. **Ruler:** Elizabeth II **Rev:** Summer moon mask, enameled

Date	Mintage	MS-63	Proof
2009 Proof	—	—	1,700

KM# 911 300 DOLLARS
60.0000 g., 0.5830 Gold 1.1246 oz. AGW, 50 mm. **Ruler:** Elizabeth II **Subject:** 2010 Vancouver Olympics **Obv:** Bust right **Obv. Designer:** Susanna Blunt **Rev:** Athletics with torch - Olympic firendship

Date	Mintage	MS-63	Proof
2009 Proof	—	—	1,700

KM# 999 300 DOLLARS
54.0000 g., 0.5830 Gold 1.0121 oz. AGW, 40 mm. **Ruler:** Elizabeth II **Rev:** British Columbia Arms

Date	Mintage	MS-63	Proof
2010 Proof	500	—	1,750

KM# 1047 300 DOLLARS
60.0000 g., 0.5830 Gold 1.1246 oz. AGW, 50 mm. **Ruler:** Elizabeth II **Rev:** Snowflake, white crystals

Date	Mintage	MS-63	Proof
2010 Proof	—	—	1,850

KM# 1078 300 DOLLARS
60.0000 g., 0.5830 Gold 1.1246 oz. AGW, 50 mm. **Ruler:** Elizabeth II **Rev:** New Brunswick Coat of arms

Date	Mintage	MS-63	Proof
2010 Proof	500	—	2,450

KM# 1095 300 DOLLARS
60.0000 g., 0.9167 Gold 1.7683 oz. AGW, 50 mm. **Ruler:** Elizabeth II **Rev:** Manitoba Coat of arms

Date	Mintage	MS-63	Proof
2011 Proof	500	—	2,450

KM# 433 350 DOLLARS
38.0500 g., 0.9999 Gold 1.2232 oz. AGW, 34 mm. **Ruler:** Elizabeth II **Subject:** The Mayflower Flower **Obv:** Crowned head right **Rev:** Two flowers **Rev. Designer:** Bonnie Ross **Edge:** Reeded

Date	Mintage	MS-63	Proof
2001 Proof	1,988	—	1,850

KM# 502 350 DOLLARS
38.0500 g., 0.9999 Gold 1.2232 oz. AGW, 34 mm. **Ruler:** Elizabeth II **Subject:** The Wild Rose **Obv:** Crowned head right **Obv. Designer:** Dora de Pedery-Hunt **Rev:** Wild rose plant **Rev. Designer:** Dr. Andreas Kare Hellum

Date	Mintage	MS-63	Proof
2002 Proof	2,001	—	1,850

KM# 504 350 DOLLARS
38.0500 g., 0.9999 Gold 1.2232 oz. AGW, 34 mm. **Ruler:** Elizabeth II **Subject:** The White Trillium **Obv:** Crowned head right **Obv. Designer:** Dora de Pedery-Hunt **Rev:** White Trillium

Date	Mintage	MS-63	Proof
2003 Proof	1,865	—	1,850

KM# 601 350 DOLLARS
38.0500 g., 0.9999 Gold 1.2232 oz. AGW **Ruler:** Elizabeth II **Subject:** Western Red Lilly **Obv:** Head right **Rev:** Western Red Lilies

Date	Mintage	MS-63	Proof
2005 Proof	1,634	—	1,850

KM# 626 350 DOLLARS
38.0500 g., 0.9999 Gold 1.2232 oz. AGW, 34 mm. **Ruler:** Elizabeth II **Subject:** Iris Vericolor **Obv:** Crowned head right **Rev:** Iris

Date	Mintage	MS-63	Proof
2006 Proof	1,995	—	1,850

KM# 754 350 DOLLARS
35.0000 g., 0.9999 Gold 1.1251 oz. AGW, 34 mm. **Ruler:** Elizabeth II **Rev:** Purple violet

Date	Mintage	MS-63	Proof
2007 Proof	1,171	—	1,850

KM# 832 350 DOLLARS
35.0000 g., 0.9999 Gold 1.1251 oz. AGW, 34 mm. **Ruler:** Elizabeth II **Rev:** Purple saxifrage

Date	Mintage	MS-63	Proof
2008 Proof	1,400	—	1,850

KM# 901 350 DOLLARS
35.0000 g., 0.9990 Gold 1.1241 oz. AGW, 34 mm. **Ruler:** Elizabeth II **Subject:** Pitcher plant **Obv:** Bust right **Obv. Legend:** Elizabeth II Canada DG Regina Fine Gold 350 Dollars or PUR 99999 **Obv. Designer:** Susana Blunt **Rev:** Cluster of pitcher flowers **Rev. Legend:** Julie Wilson

Date	Mintage	MS-63	Proof
2009 Proof	1,400	—	2,000

KM# 1019 350 DOLLARS
35.0000 g., 0.9990 Gold 1.1241 oz. AGW, 34 mm. **Ruler:** Elizabeth II **Rev:** Praire Crocus **Rev. Designer:** Celia Godkin

Date	Mintage	MS-63	Proof
2010 Proof	1,400	—	2,600

KM# 710 500 DOLLARS
155.5000 g., 0.9999 Gold 4.9987 oz. AGW, 60 mm. **Ruler:** Elizabeth II **Subject:** Queen's 60th Wedding **Rev:** Coat of Arms and Mascots of Elizabeth and Philip

Date	Mintage	MS-63	Proof
2007	198	8,500	—

KM# 782 500 DOLLARS
155.7600 g., 0.9990 Gold 5.0026 oz. AGW, 60 mm. **Ruler:** Elizabeth II **Subject:** Ottawa Mint Centennial 1908-2008 **Rev:** Mint building facade **Note:** Illustration reduced.

Date	Mintage	MS-63	Proof
2008	250	8,500	—

KM# 897 500 DOLLARS
156.0500 g., 0.9990 Gold 5.0119 oz. AGW, 60.15 mm. **Ruler:** Elizabeth II **Subject:** 150th Anniversary of the start of construction of the Parliament Buildings **Obv:** Bust right **Rev:** Incomplete west block, original architecture **Rev. Legend:** 500 Dollars 1859-2009

Date	Mintage	MS-63	Proof
2009 Proof	200	—	9,500

KM# 1007 500 DOLLARS
156.5000 g., 0.9990 Gold 5.0263 oz. AGW, 60.15 mm. **Ruler:** Elizabeth II **Subject:** 75th Anniversary of Canadian Bank Notes **Rev:** Abundance seated under tree

Date	Mintage	MS-63	Proof
2010 Proof	300	—	10,000

KM# 681 2500 DOLLARS
1000.0000 g., 0.9999 Gold 32.146 oz. AGW, 101.6 mm. **Ruler:** Elizabeth II **Subject:** Kilo **Rev:** Common Characters, Early Canada **Note:** Illustration reduced.

Date	Mintage	MS-63	Proof
2007	20	47,500	—

KM# 902 2500 DOLLARS
1000.0000 g., 0.9990 Silver 32.117 oz. ASW, 101.6 mm. **Ruler:** Elizabeth II **Series:** History and Culture Collection **Subject:** Modern Canada **Obv:** Bust right **Obv. Legend:** Vancouver 2010, 2500 Dollars, Elizabeth II **Obv. Designer:** Susanna Blunt **Rev:** Canadian landscape with modern elements **Note:** Illustration reduced.

Date	Mintage	MS-63	Proof
2009 Proof	2,500	—	1,200

KM# 902a 2500 DOLLARS
1000.0000 g., 0.9990 Gold 32.117 oz. AGW, 101.6 mm. **Ruler:** Elizabeth II **Series:** History and Culture Collection **Subject:** Modern Canada **Obv:** Bust right **Obv. Legend:** Vancouver 2010, 2500 Dollars, Elizabeth II **Obv. Designer:** Susana Blunt **Rev:** Canadian landscape with modern elements

Date	Mintage	MS-63	Proof
2009 Proof	50	—	55,000

KM# 912 2500 DOLLARS
1000.0000 g., 0.9999 Gold 32.146 oz. AGW, 101 mm. **Ruler:** Elizabeth II **Obv:** Bust right **Obv. Designer:** Susanna Blunt **Rev:** Mask with fish - Surviving the flood **Note:** Illustration reduced.

Date	Mintage	MS-63	Proof
2009 Proof	—	—	50,000

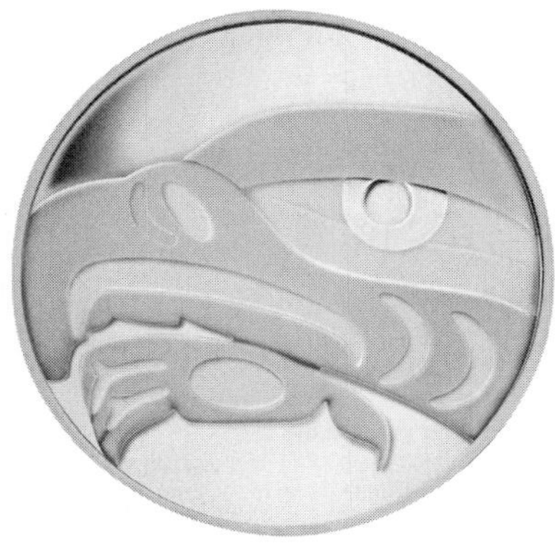

KM# 984 2500 DOLLARS
1000.0000 g., 0.9990 Gold 32.117 oz. AGW, 101 mm. **Ruler:** Elizabeth II **Note:** Illustration reduced.

Date	Mintage	MS-63	Proof
2010 Proof	20	—	50,000

KM# 1045 2500 DOLLARS
1000.0000 g., 0.9999 Gold 32.146 oz. AGW, 101 mm. **Ruler:**

Elizabeth II **Subject:** Baniff, 125th Anniversary **Rev:** Highlights of Baniff **Note:** Illustration reduced.

Date	Mintage	MS-63	Proof
2010	—	—	50,000

SILVER BULLION COINAGE

KM# 617 DOLLAR

1.5550 g., 0.9999 Silver 0.0500 oz. ASW, 16 mm. **Ruler:** Elizabeth II **Obv:** Crowned head right **Rev:** Holographic Maple leaf **Edge:** Reeded

Date	Mintage	MS-63	Proof
2003 Proof	—	—	4.50

KM# 621 DOLLAR

1.5550 g., 0.9999 Silver 0.0500 oz. ASW, 17 mm. **Ruler:** Elizabeth II **Obv:** Crowned head right **Rev:** Maple leaf **Edge:** Reeded

Date	Mintage	MS-63	Proof
2004 Mint logo privy mark Proof	13,859	—	4.50

KM# 718 DOLLAR

15.5500 g., 0.9990 Silver 0.4994 oz. ASW, 32 mm. **Ruler:** Elizabeth II **Obv:** Bust right **Rev:** Grey Wolf standing with moon in background **Rev. Designer:** William Woodruff **Edge:** Reeded

Date	Mintage	MS-63	Proof
2005	106,800	40.00	—
2006 WW	—	40.00	—
2007	—	40.00	—

KM# 618 2 DOLLARS

3.1100 g., 0.9999 Silver 0.1000 oz. ASW, 20.1 mm. **Ruler:** Elizabeth II **Obv:** Crowned head right **Rev:** Holographic Maple leaf **Edge:** Reeded

Date	Mintage	MS-63	Proof
2003 Proof	—	—	7.50

KM# 622 2 DOLLARS

3.1100 g., 0.9999 Silver 0.1000 oz. ASW, 21 mm. **Ruler:** Elizabeth II **Obv:** Crowned head right **Rev:** Maple leaf **Edge:** Reeded

Date	Mintage	MS-63	Proof
2004 Mint logo privy mark Proof	13,859	—	7.50

KM# 571 2 DOLLARS

3.1050 g., 0.9999 Silver 0.0998 oz. ASW **Ruler:** Elizabeth II **Obv:** Head right **Rev:** Lynx

Date	Mintage	MS-63	Proof
2005 Proof	—	—	7.50

KM# 619 3 DOLLARS

7.7760 g., 0.9999 Silver 0.2500 oz. ASW, 26.9 mm. **Ruler:** Elizabeth II **Obv:** Crowned head right **Rev:** Holographic Maple leaf **Edge:** Reeded

Date	Mintage	MS-63	Proof
2003 Proof	—	—	17.50

KM# 623 3 DOLLARS

7.7760 g., 0.9999 Silver 0.2500 oz. ASW, 27 mm. **Ruler:** Elizabeth II **Obv:** Crowned head right **Rev:** Maple leaf **Edge:** Reeded

Date	Mintage	MS-63	Proof
2004 Mint logo privy mark Proof	13,859	—	16.00

KM# 572 3 DOLLARS

7.7760 g., 0.9999 Silver 0.2500 oz. ASW **Ruler:** Elizabeth II **Obv:** Head right **Rev:** Lynx

Date	Mintage	MS-63	Proof
2005 Proof	—	—	12.50

KM# 620 4 DOLLARS

15.5500 g., 0.9999 Silver 0.4999 oz. ASW, 33.9 mm. **Ruler:** Elizabeth II **Obv:** Crowned head right **Rev:** Holographic Maple leaf **Edge:** Reeded

Date	Mintage	MS-63	Proof
2003 Proof	—	—	32.00

KM# 624 4 DOLLARS

15.5500 g., 0.9999 Silver 0.4999 oz. ASW, 34 mm. **Ruler:** Elizabeth II **Obv:** Crowned head right **Rev:** Maple leaf **Edge:** Reeded

Date	Mintage	MS-63	Proof
2004 Mint logo privy mark Proof	13,859	—	28.00

KM# 573 4 DOLLARS

15.5500 g., 0.9999 Silver 0.4999 oz. ASW **Ruler:** Elizabeth II **Obv:** Head right **Rev:** Lynx

Date	Mintage	MS-63	Proof
2005 Proof	—	—	25.00

KM# 437 5 DOLLARS

31.1035 g., 0.9999 Silver 0.9999 oz. ASW, 38 mm. **Ruler:** Elizabeth II **Obv:** Crowned head right, date and denomination below **Rev:** Radiant maple leaf hologram **Edge:** Reeded

Date	Mintage	MS-63	Proof
2001 Good fortune privy mark	29,906	75.00	—

KM# 187 5 DOLLARS

31.1000 g., 0.9999 Silver 0.9997 oz. ASW **Ruler:** Elizabeth II **Obv:** Crowned head right, date and denomination below **Obv. Designer:** Dora de Pedery-Hunt **Rev:** Maple leaf flanked by 9999

Date	Mintage	MS-63	Proof
2001	398,563	35.00	—
2001 Reverse proof, Snake privy mark	25,000	—	45.00
2002	576,196	35.00	—
2002 Reverse proof, Horse privy mark	25,000	—	45.00
2003	—	35.00	—
2003 Reverse proof, sheep privy mark	25,000	—	45.00

KM# 436 5 DOLLARS

31.1035 g., 0.9999 Silver 0.9999 oz. ASW, 38 mm. **Ruler:** Elizabeth II **Obv:** Crowned head right, date and denomination below **Rev:** Three maple leaves in autumn colors, 9999 flanks **Rev. Designer:** Debbie Adams **Edge:** Reeded

Date	Mintage	MS-63	Proof
2001 Proof	49,709	—	40.00

KM# 505 5 DOLLARS

31.1035 g., 0.9999 Silver 0.9999 oz. ASW, 38 mm. **Ruler:** Elizabeth II **Obv:** Crowned head right, date and denomination below **Rev:** Two maple leaves in spring color (green) **Edge:** Reeded

Date	Mintage	MS-63	Proof
2002	29,509	37.50	—

KM# 603 5 DOLLARS

31.1050 g., 0.9999 Silver 0.9999 oz. ASW **Ruler:** Elizabeth II **Obv:** Head right **Rev:** Loon splashing in the water, hologram

Date	Mintage	MS-63	Proof
2002 Satin Proof	30,000	—	45.00

KM# 521 5 DOLLARS

31.1035 g., 0.9999 Silver 0.9999 oz. ASW **Ruler:** Elizabeth II **Obv:** Head right **Rev:** Maple leaf, summer colors **Rev. Designer:** Stan Witten

Date	Mintage	MS-63	Proof
2003	29,416	37.50	—

KM# 607 5 DOLLARS

31.1200 g., 0.9999 Silver 1.0004 oz. ASW **Ruler:** Elizabeth II **Obv:** Head right **Rev:** Maple leaf, winter colors

Date	Mintage	MS-63	Proof
2004	—	37.50	—

KM# 625 5 DOLLARS

31.1035 g., 0.9999 Silver 0.9999 oz. ASW, 38 mm. **Ruler:** Elizabeth II **Obv:** Bust right **Obv. Designer:** Susanna Blunt **Rev:** Maple leaf **Edge:** Reeded

Date	Mintage	MS-63	Proof
2004 Mint logo privy mark Specimen	13,859	—	37.50
2004 Monkey privy mark Specimen	25,000	—	37.50
2004 D-Day privy mark Specimen	11,698	—	37.50
2004 Desjardins privy mark	15,000	37.50	—
2004 Capricorn privy Mark Reverse proof	5,000	—	37.50
2004 Aquarius privy mark Reverse proof	5,000	—	37.50
2004 Pisces privy mark Reverse proof	5,000	—	37.50
2004 Aries privy mark Reverse proof	5,000	—	37.50
2004 Taurus privy mark Reverse proof	5,000	—	37.50

Date	Mintage	MS-63	Proof
2004 Gemini privy mark Reverse proof	5,000	—	37.50
2004 Cancer privy mark Reverse proof	5,000	—	37.50
2004 Leo privy mark Reverse proof	5,000	—	37.50
2004 Virgo privy mark Reverse proof	5,000	—	37.50
2004 Libra privy mark Reverse proof	5,000	—	37.50
2004 Scorpio privy mark Reverse proof	5,000	—	37.50
2004 Sagittarius privy mark Reverse proof	5,000	—	37.50
2005	—	35.00	—
2005 Tulip privy mark Reverse proof	3,500	—	40.00
2005 Tank privy mark Reverse proof	7,000	—	60.00
2005 USS Missouri privy mark Reverse proof	7,000	—	60.00
2005 Rooster privy mark Reverse proof	15,000	—	50.00
2006	—	35.00	—
2006 Dog privy mark Reverse proof	—	—	50.00
2007	—	35.00	—
2007 F12 privy mark Reverse proof	—	—	130
2007 Pig privy mark Reverse proof	—	—	40.00
2008	—	35.00	—
2008 F12 privy mark Reverse proof	—	—	130
2008 Rat privy mark Reverse proof	—	—	40.00
2009	—	35.00	—
2009 Brandenberg Gate privy mark Reverse proof	—	—	50.00
2009 Tower Bridge privy mark Reverse proof	—	—	40.00
2009 Ox Privy mark Reverse proof	—	—	37.50
2010	—	35.00	—
2011	—	35.00	—

KM# 508 5 DOLLARS

31.1035 g., 0.9999 Silver 0.9999 oz. ASW, 38 mm. **Ruler:** Elizabeth II **Obv:** Crowned head right, date and denomination below **Obv. Designer:** Dora de Pedery-Hunt **Rev:** Holographic Maple leaf flanked by 9999 **Edge:** Reeded

Date	Mintage	MS-63	Proof
2003 Proof	—	—	37.50

KM# 522 5 DOLLARS

31.1050 g., 0.9999 Silver 0.9999 oz. ASW **Ruler:** Elizabeth II **Obv:** Head right **Rev:** Maple leaf, winter color **Rev. Designer:** Stan Witten

Date	Mintage	MS-63	Proof
2004	26,763	35.00	—

KM# 574 5 DOLLARS

31.1035 g., 0.9999 Silver 0.9999 oz. ASW **Ruler:** Elizabeth II **Obv:** Head right **Rev:** Lynx

Date	Mintage	MS-63	Proof
2005 Proof	—	—	37.50

KM# 924 5 DOLLARS

31.1050 g., 0.9999 Silver 0.9999 oz. ASW **Ruler:** Elizabeth II **Rev:** Maple Leaf, laser engraved **Rev. Designer:** Joan Nguyen

Date	Mintage	MS-63	Proof
2005 Proof	25,000	—	60.00

KM# 550 5 DOLLARS

31.1035 g., 0.9999 Silver 0.9999 oz. ASW **Ruler:** Elizabeth II **Obv:** Head right **Rev:** Big Leaf Maple, colorized **Rev. Designer:** Stan Witten

Date	Mintage	MS-63	Proof
2005	21,233	35.00	—

KM# 660 5 DOLLARS

31.1035 g., 0.9990 Silver 0.9990 oz. ASW **Ruler:** Elizabeth II **Obv:** Bust right **Obv. Designer:** Susanna Blunt **Rev:** Silver maple, colorized **Rev. Designer:** Stan Witten

Date	Mintage	MS-63	Proof
2006	14,157	37.50	—

KM# 625a 5 DOLLARS

31.1050 g., 0.9999 Silver 0.9999 oz. ASW, 38 mm. **Ruler:** Elizabeth II **Rev:** Maple leaf, gilt

Date	Mintage	MS-63	Proof
2007	—	—	—
2008	—	—	—
2009	—	—	—
2009 Tower Bridge Privy Mark	—	—	—
2010	—	—	—

KM# 729 5 DOLLARS

31.1050 g., 0.9990 Silver 0.9990 oz. ASW, 38 mm. **Ruler:** Elizabeth II **Obv:** Bust right **Rev:** Maple leaf orange multicolor

Date	Mintage	MS-63	Proof
2007 Proof	—	—	45.00

KM# 925 5 DOLLARS

31.1050 g., 0.9990 Silver 0.9990 oz. ASW **Ruler:** Elizabeth II **Obv:** Bust right **Obv. Designer:** Susanna Blunt **Rev:** Sugar maple, colorized **Rev. Designer:** Stan Witten

Date	Mintage	MS-63	Proof
2007	11,495	37.50	—

KM# 928 5 DOLLARS

31.3900 g., 0.9990 Silver 1.0082 oz. ASW, 38 mm. **Ruler:** Elizabeth II **Rev:** Orange sugar maple leaf **Rev. Designer:** Stan Witten

Date	Mintage	MS-63	Proof
2007 Specimen	20,000	—	100

KM# 800 5 DOLLARS

31.1050 g., 0.9990 Silver 0.9990 oz. ASW, 38 mm. **Ruler:** Elizabeth II **Subject:** Vancouver Olympics **Obv:** Bust right **Obv. Designer:** Susanna Blunt **Rev:** Maple leaf, Olympic logo at left, turtle

Date	Mintage	MS-63	Proof
2008	—	37.50	—
2009	—	37.50	—
2010	—	37.50	—

KM# 798 5 DOLLARS

31.1050 g., 0.9990 Silver 0.9990 oz. ASW, 38 mm. **Ruler:** Elizabeth II **Subject:** Maple Leaf 20th Anniversary **Rev:** Maple Leaf, selective gold plating

Date	Mintage	MS-63	Proof
2008 Proof	10,000	—	110

KM# 931 5 DOLLARS

31.1050 g., 0.9990 Silver Part gilt 0.9990 oz. ASW **Ruler:** Elizabeth II **Obv:** Maple leaf, partially gilt

Date	Mintage	MS-63	Proof
2008	—	50.00	—

KM# 1056 5 DOLLARS

31.1050 g., 0.9999 Silver 0.9999 oz. ASW, 38 mm. **Ruler:** Elizabeth II **Rev:** Maple leaf in color, card diamond

Date	Mintage	MS-63	Proof
2008	—	60.00	—

KM# 1057 5 DOLLARS

31.1050 g., 0.9999 Silver 0.9999 oz. ASW, 38 mm. **Ruler:** Elizabeth II **Rev:** Maple Leaf in color, card heart

Date	Mintage	MS-63	Proof
2008	—	60.00	—

KM# 1058 5 DOLLARS

31.1050 g., 0.9999 Silver 0.9999 oz. ASW, 38 mm. **Ruler:** Elizabeth II **Rev:** Maple leaf in color, card club

Date	Mintage	MS-63	Proof
2008	—	60.00	—

KM# 1059 5 DOLLARS

31.1050 g., 0.9999 Silver 0.9999 oz. ASW, 38 mm. **Ruler:** Elizabeth II **Rev:** Maple Leaf in color, card spade

Date	Mintage	MS-63	Proof
2008	—	60.00	—

KM# 863 5 DOLLARS

31.3900 g., 0.9990 Silver 1.0082 oz. ASW, 38 mm. **Ruler:** Elizabeth II **Subject:** Edmonton Olympics **Rev:** Thunderbird Totem **Rev. Designer:** Rick Harry

Date	Mintage	MS-63	Proof
2009	—	50.00	—

KM# 1061 5 DOLLARS

31.1050 g., 0.9999 Silver 0.9999 oz. ASW, 38 mm. **Ruler:** Elizabeth II **Rev:** Maple leaf in color, pink ribbon for breast cancer awareness

Date	Mintage	MS-63	Proof
2009	—	70.00	—

KM# 998 5 DOLLARS

31.1200 g., 0.9990 Silver 0.9995 oz. ASW, 38 mm. **Ruler:** Elizabeth II **Rev:** Olympic Hockey

Date	Mintage	MS-63	Proof
2010 Proof	—	—	42.50

KM# 1052 5 DOLLARS

31.1050 g., 0.9999 Silver 0.9999 oz. ASW, 38 mm. **Ruler:** Elizabeth II **Rev:** Wolf standing with moonlight in background

Date	Mintage	MS-63	Proof
2011	—	40.00	—

KM# 731 8 DOLLARS
0.9990 Silver **Ruler:** Elizabeth II **Rev:** Maple leaf, long life hologram

Date	Mintage	MS-63	Proof
2007	15,000	—	60.00

KM# 1062 20 DOLLARS
7.9600 g., Silver, 27 mm. **Ruler:** Elizabeth II **Rev:** Five Maple leaves at left **Note:** Thick planchet

Date	Mintage	MS-63	Proof
2011	200,000	—	25.00

KM# 676 250 DOLLARS
1000.0000 g., 0.9999 Silver 32.146 oz. ASW **Ruler:** Elizabeth II **Subject:** Kilo

Date	Mintage	MS-63	Proof
2006	—	1,200	—

GOLD BULLION COINAGE

KM# 888 50 CENTS
1.2700 g., 0.9990 Gold 0.0408 oz. AGW, 13.92 mm. **Ruler:** Elizabeth II **Subject:** Red maple **Obv:** Bust right **Obv. Legend:** Elizabeth II 50 cents **Obv. Designer:** Susanna Blunt **Rev:** Two maple leaves **Rev. Legend:** Canada, Fine gold 1/25 oz or PUR 9999

Date	Mintage	MS-63	Proof
2009 Proof	150,000	—	65.00

KM# 1085 50 CENTS
1.2700 g., 0.9990 Gold 0.0408 oz. AGW, 13.92 mm. **Ruler:** Elizabeth II **Rev:** Geese in flight left **Rev. Designer:** Emily Damstra

Date	Mintage	MS-63	Proof
2011 Proof	10,000	—	110

KM# 438 DOLLAR
1.5810 g., 0.9990 Gold 0.0508 oz. AGW, 14.1 mm. **Ruler:** Elizabeth II **Subject:** Holographic Maple Leaves **Obv:** Crowned head right **Rev:** Three maple leaves multicolor hologram **Edge:** Reeded.

Date	Mintage	MS-63	Proof
2001 in sets only	600	85.00	—

KM# 439 5 DOLLARS
3.1310 g., 0.9999 Gold 0.1006 oz. AGW, 16 mm. **Ruler:** Elizabeth II **Subject:** Holographic Maple Leaves **Obv:** Crowned head right **Rev:** Three maple leaves multicolor hologram **Edge:** Reeded

Date	Mintage	MS-63	Proof
2001	600	160	—

KM# 929 5 DOLLARS
3.1300 g., 0.9990 Gold 0.1005 oz. AGW, 16 mm. **Ruler:** Elizabeth II **Obv. Designer:** Susan Blunt **Rev:** Maple leaf **Rev. Designer:** Walter Ott

Date	Mintage	MS-63	Proof
2007	—	—	170
2008	—	—	170
2009	—	—	170

KM# 440 10 DOLLARS
7.7970 g., 0.9999 Gold 0.2506 oz. AGW, 20 mm. **Ruler:** Elizabeth II **Subject:** Holographic Maples Leaves **Obv:** Crowned head right **Rev:** Three maple leaves multicolor hologram **Edge:** Reeded

Date	Mintage	MS-63	Proof
2001	15,000	375	—

KM# 441 20 DOLLARS
15.5840 g., 0.9999 Gold 0.5010 oz. AGW, 25 mm. **Ruler:** Elizabeth II **Subject:** Holographic Maples Leaves **Obv:** Crowned head right **Rev:** Three maple leaves multicolor hologram **Edge:** Reeded

Date	Mintage	MS-63	Proof
2001	600	775	—

KM# 442 50 DOLLARS
31.1500 g., 0.9999 Gold 1.0014 oz. AGW, 30 mm. **Ruler:** Elizabeth II **Subject:** Holographic Maples Leaves **Obv:** Crowned head right **Rev:** Three maple leaves multicolor hologram **Edge:** Reeded

Date	Mintage	MS-63	Proof
2001	600	1,550	—

KM# 1037 50 DOLLARS
31.1050 g., 0.9999 Gold 0.9999 oz. AGW, 30 mm. **Ruler:** Elizabeth II **Rev:** Native eagle **Edge:** Reeded

Date	Mintage	MS-63	Proof
2009	—	1,500	—

KM# 1029 50 DOLLARS
31.1050 g., 0.9999 Gold 0.9999 oz. AGW, 31 mm. **Ruler:** Elizabeth II **Rev:** Hockey player

Date	Mintage	MS-63	Proof
2010	—	—	—

KM# 750 200 DOLLARS
31.1500 g., 1.0000 Gold 1.0014 oz. AGW, 30 mm. **Ruler:** Elizabeth II **Rev:** Three maple leaves

Date	Mintage	MS-63	Proof
2007 Proof	500	—	1,550

KM# 755 1000000 DOLLARS
100000.0000 g., 0.9999 Gold 3214.6 oz. AGW **Ruler:** Elizabeth II **Rev:** Maple leaf **Note:** Cast

Date	Mintage	MS-63	Proof
2007	10	4,750,000	—

PLATINUM BULLION COINAGE

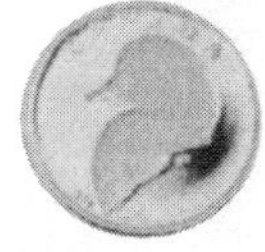

KM# 429 30 DOLLARS
3.1100 g., 0.9995 Platinum 0.0999 oz. APW, 16 mm. **Ruler:** Elizabeth II **Obv:** Crowned head right **Rev:** Harlequin duck's head **Rev. Designer:** Cosme Saffioti and Susan Taylor **Edge:** Reeded

Date	Mintage	MS-63	Proof
2001 Proof	448	—	200

KM# 1097 30 DOLLARS
3.1100 g., 0.9995 Platinum 0.0999 oz. APW, 16 mm. **Ruler:** Elizabeth II **Rev:** Great Blue Heron

Date	Mintage	MS-63	Proof
2002 Proof	344	—	200

KM# 1101 30 DOLLARS
3.1100 g., 0.9995 Platinum 0.0999 oz. APW, 16 mm. **Ruler:** Elizabeth II **Rev:** Atlantic Walrus

Date	Mintage	MS-63	Proof
2003	365	—	250

KM# 1105 30 DOLLARS
3.1100 g., 0.9995 Platinum 0.0999 oz. APW, 16 mm. **Ruler:** Elizabeth II **Rev:** Grizzly Bear

Date	Mintage	MS-63	Proof
2004 Proof	380	—	250

KM# 430 75 DOLLARS
7.7760 g., 0.9995 Platinum 0.2499 oz. APW, 20 mm. **Ruler:** Elizabeth II **Obv:** Crowned head right **Rev:** Harlequin duck in flight **Rev. Designer:** Cosme Saffioti and Susan Taylor **Edge:** Reeded

Date	Mintage	MS-63	Proof
2001 Proof	448	—	500

KM# 1098 75 DOLLARS
7.7700 g., 0.9995 Platinum 0.2497 oz. APW, 20 mm. **Ruler:** Elizabeth II **Rev:** Great Blue Heron

Date	Mintage	MS-63	Proof
2002 Proof	344	—	525

KM# 1102 75 DOLLARS
7.7700 g., 0.9995 Platinum 0.2497 oz. APW, 20 mm. **Ruler:** Elizabeth II **Rev:** Atlantic Walrus

Date	Mintage	MS-63	Proof
2003 Proof	365	—	550

KM# 1106 75 DOLLARS
7.7700 g., 0.9995 Platinum 0.2497 oz. APW, 20 mm. **Ruler:** Elizabeth II **Rev:** Grizzly Bear

Date	Mintage	MS-63	Proof
2004 Proof	380	—	550

KM# 431 150 DOLLARS
15.5500 g., 0.9995 Platinum 0.4997 oz. APW, 25 mm. **Ruler:** Elizabeth II **Obv:** Crowned head right **Rev:** Two harlequin ducks **Rev. Designer:** Cosme Saffioti and Susan Taylor **Edge:** Reeded

Date	Mintage	MS-63	Proof
2001 Proof	448	—	1,000

KM# 1099 150 DOLLARS
15.5500 g., 0.9995 Platinum 0.4997 oz. APW, 25 mm. **Ruler:** Elizabeth II **Rev:** Great Blue Heron

Date	Mintage	MS-63	Proof
2002 Proof	344	—	1,000

KM# 1103 150 DOLLARS
15.5500 g., 0.9995 Platinum 0.4997 oz. APW, 25 mm. **Ruler:** Elizabeth II **Rev:** Atlantic Walrus

Date	Mintage	MS-63	Proof
2003 Proof	365	—	1,000

KM# 1107 150 DOLLARS
15.5500 g., 0.9995 Platinum 0.4997 oz. APW, 25 mm. **Ruler:** Elizabeth II **Rev:** Grizzly Bear

Date	Mintage	MS-63	Proof
2004 Proof	380	—	1,000

KM# 432 300 DOLLARS
31.1035 g., 0.9995 Platinum 0.9995 oz. APW, 30 mm. **Ruler:** Elizabeth II **Obv:** Crowned head right **Rev:** Two standing harlequin ducks **Rev. Designer:** Cosme Saffioti and Susan Taylor **Edge:** Reeded

Date	Mintage	MS-63	Proof
2001 Proof	448	—	1,900

KM# 1100 300 DOLLARS
31.1050 g., 0.9995 Platinum 0.9995 oz. APW, 30 mm. **Ruler:** Elizabeth II **Rev:** Great Blue Heron

Date	Mintage	MS-63	Proof
2002 Proof	344	—	1,950

KM# 1104 300 DOLLARS
31.1050 g., 0.9995 Platinum 0.9995 oz. APW, 30 mm. **Ruler:** Elizabeth II **Rev:** Atlantic Walrus

Date	Mintage	MS-63	Proof
2003 Proof	365	—	1,950

KM# 1108 300 DOLLARS
31.1050 g., 0.9995 Platinum 0.9995 oz. APW, 30 mm. **Ruler:** Elizabeth II **Rev:** Grizzly Bear

Date	Mintage	MS-63	Proof
2004 Proof	380	—	1,950

KM# 951 300 DOLLARS
31.1600 g., 0.9990 Platinum 1.0008 oz. APW, 30 mm. **Ruler:** Elizabeth II **Rev:** Steppe Bison

Date	Mintage	MS-63	Proof
2009 Proof	200	—	3,500

MINT SETS

KM#	Date	Mintage	Identification	Issue Price	Mkt Val
MS8	2001 (5)	600	KM438-442	1,996	2,950
MS9	2002 (7)	135,000	Double-dated 1952-2002, KM#444-449, 467 Elizabeth II Golden Jubilee	11.75	16.00
MS10	2002 (7)	—	KM#444-449, 467, Oh! Canada! 135th Birthday Gift set.	17.00	16.00
MS11	2002 (7)	—	KM#444-449, 467, Tiny Treasures Uncirculated Gift Set	17.00	16.00
MS12	2003 (7)	135,000	KM#289, 182b, 183b, 184b, 290, 186, 270	12.00	16.00
MS13	2003 (7)	75,000	KM490-496	13.25	20.00
MS14	2003 (7)	—	KM289, 182-184, 290, 186, 270, Oh! Canada!	17.75	16.00
MS15	2003 (7)	—	KM289, 182-184, 290, 186, 270, Tiny Treasures Uncirculated Gift Set	17.75	16.00

PROOF SETS

KM#	Date	Mintage	Identification	Issue Price	Mkt Val
PS51	2001 (4)	—	KM429, 430, 431, 432	—	3,600
PS52	2002 (8)	100,000	KM#443, 444a,445,446a-449a, 467 Elizabeth II Golden Jubilee	60.00	125
PS53	2002 (3)	—	KM#459-461 Canadian Folklore and Legends Collection	57.50	35.00
PS54	2002 (2)	—	KM#519, 520	750	1,125
PS55	2003 (8)	100,000	KM#182a,183a,184a, 186, 270d, 289, 290a, 450 100th Anniversary of the Cobalt Silver Strike	62.50	125
PS56	2003 (6)	30,000	KM#468-473 50th Anniversary of the Coronation of Elizabeth II	75.00	100
PS57	2004 (8)	—	KM#490, 491a-494a, 495, 496a, 512	—	115
PS58	2004 (5)	25,000	KM#621-625	—	100

SPECIMEN SETS (SS)

KM#	Date	Mintage	Identification	Issue Price	Mkt Val
SS90	2002 (7)	75,000	KM#444-449,462 Elizabeth II Golden Jubilee	30.00	65.00
SS91	2003 (3)	75,000	KM#(uncertain), 270, 289, 290	30.00	50.00

CAPE VERDE

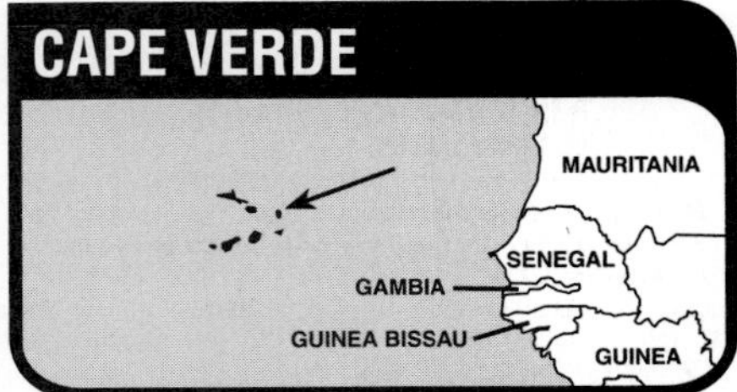

The Republic of Cape Verde, Africa's smallest republic, is located in the Atlantic Ocean, about 370 miles (595 km.) west of Dakar, Senegal, off the coast of Africa. The 14-island republic has an area of 1,557 sq. mi. (4,033 sq. km.) and a population of 435,983. Capital: Praia. The refueling of ships and aircraft is the chief economic function of the country. Fishing is important and agriculture is widely practiced, but the Cape Verdes are not self-sufficient in food. Fish products, salt, bananas, and shellfish are exported.

After 500 years of Portuguese rule, the Cape Verdes became independent on July 5, 1975. At the first general election, all seats of the new national assembly were won by the Party for the Independence of Guinea-Bissau and Cape Verde (PAIGC). The PAIGC linked the two former colonies into one state. Antonio Mascarenhas Monteiro won the first free presidential election in 1991.

RULER
Portuguese, until 1975

MONETARY SYSTEM
100 Centavos = 1 Escudo

REPUBLIC

DECIMAL COINAGE

KM# 46 25 ESCUDOS
15.5517 g., 0.9990 Silver 0.4995 oz. ASW, 30.4 mm. **Obv:** Value above national arms **Rev:** Jesus **Edge:** Plain

Date	Mintage	F	VF	XF	Unc	BU
2006 Proof	—	Value: 40.00				

KM# 47 50 ESCUDOS
1.5550 g., 0.9990 Gold 0.0499 oz. AGW, 16 mm. **Obv:** Value above national arms **Rev:** Jesus **Edge:** Plain

Date	Mintage	F	VF	XF	Unc	BU
2006 Proof	—	Value: 85.00				

KM# 48 50 ESCUDOS
25.1600 g., 0.9250 Silver 0.7482 oz. ASW, 38.8 mm. **Subject:** 500th Anniversary Death of Christopher Columbus **Obv:** National arms **Obv. Legend:** CABO VERDE **Rev:** Sailing ship *Santa Maria* **Rev. Legend:** A SANTA MARIA DE CHRIST?V?O COLOMBO **Edge:** Reeded

Date	Mintage	F	VF	XF	Unc	BU
2006 Proof	—	Value: 55.00				

KM# 49 50 ESCUDOS
25.0000 g., 0.9250 Silver 0.7435 oz. ASW, 38.6 mm. **Subject:** Appearance in Grotto **Obv:** National arms **Obv. Legend:** CABO VERDE **Rev:** Maria standing facing 3/4 left at right **Rev. Legend:** AVE MARIA - LOURDES **Edge:** Reeded

Date	Mintage	F	VF	XF	Unc	BU
2006 Proof	—	Value: 65.00				

KM# 50 50 ESCUDOS
25.2000 g., 0.9250 Silver 0.7494 oz. ASW **Obv:** National arms **Rev:** Red Kite bird

Date	Mintage	F	VF	XF	Unc	BU
2006 Proof	—	Value: 65.00				

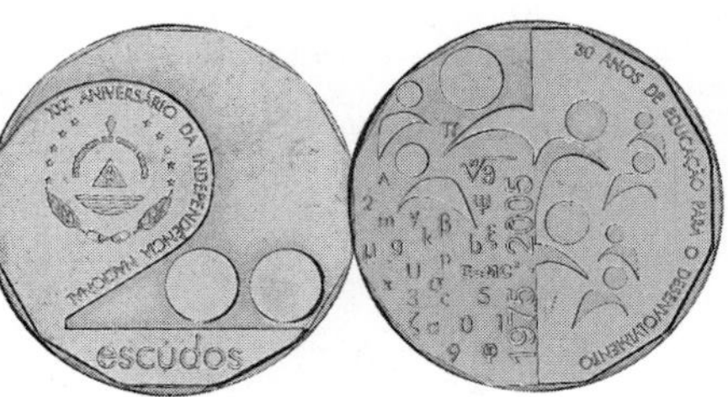

KM# 45 200 ESCUDOS
7.8000 g., Copper-Nickel, 29.5 mm. **Subject:** 30th Anniversary of Independence **Obv:** National arms in number 2 of 200 **Rev:** Symbolic education design **Edge:** Reeded **Shape:** Round

Date	Mintage	F	VF	XF	Unc	BU
2005	—	—	—	—	8.50	10.00

KM# 45a 200 ESCUDOS
18.2800 g., 0.9250 Silver 0.5436 oz. ASW **Subject:** 30th Anniversary of Independence **Obv:** National arms in number 2 of 200 **Rev:** Symbolic education design **Edge:** Reeded **Shape:** Round

Date	Mintage	F	VF	XF	Unc	BU
2005 Proof	—	Value: 70.00				

CAYMAN ISLANDS

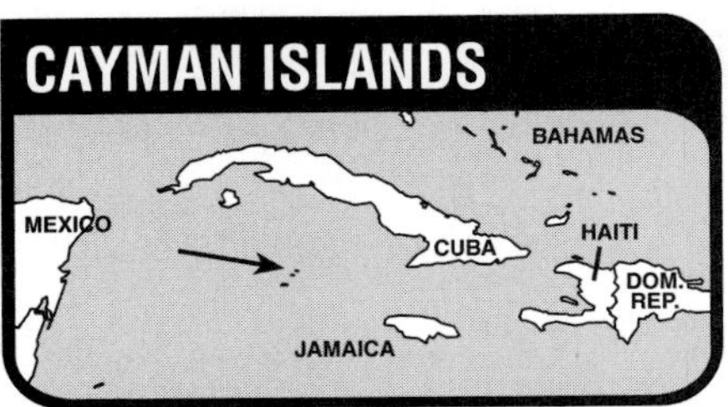

The Cayman Islands are a British Crown Colony situated about 180 miles (280 km) northwest of Jamaica. It consists of three islands: Grand Cayman, Little Cayman, and Cayman Brac. The islands have an area of 102 sq. mi. (259 sq. km.) and a population of 33,200. Capital: George Town. Seafaring, commerce, banking, and tourism are the principal industries. Rope, turtle shells, and sharkskins are exported.

RULER
British

MINT MARKS
CHI - Valcambi

MONETARY SYSTEM
100 Cents = 1 Dollar

BRITISH COLONY

DECIMAL COINAGE

KM# 131 CENT
2.5500 g., Copper Plated Steel, 17 mm. **Ruler:** Elizabeth II **Obv:** Crowned head right **Rev:** Grand Caiman thrush **Rev. Designer:** Stuart Devlin **Edge:** Plain

Date	Mintage	F	VF	XF	Unc	BU
2002	—	—	—	0.20	0.50	1.00
2005	—	—	—	0.20	0.50	1.00
2008	—	—	—	0.20	0.50	1.00

KM# 132 5 CENTS
2.0000 g., Nickel Plated Steel, 18 mm. **Ruler:** Elizabeth II **Obv:** Crowned head right **Rev:** Pink-spotted shrimp **Rev. Designer:** Stuart Devlin **Edge:** Plain

Date	Mintage	F	VF	XF	Unc	BU
2002	—	—	—	0.20	0.50	1.00
2005	—	—	—	0.20	0.50	1.00

KM# 133 10 CENTS
3.4500 g., Nickel Plated Steel, 21 mm. **Ruler:** Elizabeth II **Obv:** Head with tiara right **Rev:** Green turtle surfacing **Rev. Designer:** Stuart Devlin **Edge:** Reeded

Date	Mintage	F	VF	XF	Unc	BU
2002	—	—	0.25	0.40	1.00	1.25
2005	—	—	0.25	0.40	1.00	1.25

KM# 134 25 CENTS
5.1000 g., Nickel Plated Steel, 24.2 mm. **Ruler:** Elizabeth II **Obv:** Head with tiara right **Rev:** Schooner sailing right **Rev. Designer:** Stuart Devlin **Edge:** Reeded

Date	Mintage	F	VF	XF	Unc	BU
2002	—	—	—	0.75	1.50	1.75
2005	—	—	—	0.75	1.50	1.75

KM# 136 2 DOLLARS
28.3400 g., 0.9250 Silver 0.8428 oz. ASW, 38.6 mm. **Ruler:** Elizabeth II **Obv:** Gold plated Queen Elizabeth II **Rev:** British crown and value **Edge:** Reeded

Date	Mintage	F	VF	XF	Unc	BU
2002 Proof	—	Value: 45.00				

KM# 135 2 DOLLARS
28.2800 g., 0.9250 Silver 0.8410 oz. ASW, 38.6 mm. **Ruler:** Elizabeth II **Subject:** 500th Anniversary - Christopher Columbus First Recorded Sighting of the Cayman Islands **Obv:** Crowned head right **Rev:** Quincentennial Celebrations Logo in color

Date	Mintage	F	VF	XF	Unc	BU
2003 Proof	1,500	Value: 75.00				

KM# 138 2 DOLLARS
28.2800 g., 0.9250 Silver 0.8410 oz. ASW, 38.61 mm. **Ruler:** Elizabeth II **Subject:** Royal Horticulture Society **Obv:** Head right, gilt portrait **Rev:** RHS Tent adn flowers

Date	Mintage	F	VF	XF	Unc	BU
2003 Proof	—	Value: 45.00				

KM# 137 5 DOLLARS
28.2800 g., 0.9250 Silver 0.8410 oz. ASW **Ruler:** Elizabeth II **Subject:** Elizabeth II's 80th Birthday **Obv:** Crowned head right - gilt **Obv. Legend:** CAYMAN ISLANDS - ELIZABETH II **Obv. Designer:** Ian Rank-Broadley **Rev:** Queen crowning Charles as Prince of Wales

Date	Mintage	F	VF	XF	Unc	BU
2006 Proof	—	Value: 50.00				

KM# 141 5 DOLLARS
28.2800 g., 0.9250 Silver 0.8410 oz. ASW, 38.6 mm. **Ruler:** Elizabeth II **Subject:** Constitutional Government, 50th Anniversary **Obv:** Bust right **Rev:** Coat of arms

Date	Mintage	F	VF	XF	Unc	BU
2009 Proof	300	Value: 75.00				

KM# 139 10 DOLLARS
28.2800 g., 0.9250 Silver 0.8410 oz. ASW, 38.61 mm. **Ruler:** Elizabeth II **Subject:** Cayman Islands Monetary Authority, 10th Anniversary **Obv:** Bust right **Rev:** Island's coat of arms

Date	Mintage	F	VF	XF	Unc	BU
2007 Proof	200	Value: 110				

KM# 140 10 DOLLARS
7.9800 g., 0.9167 Gold 0.2352 oz. AGW **Ruler:** Elizabeth II **Subject:** Cayman Islands Monetary Authority, 10th Anniversary **Obv:** Bust right **Rev:** Island's coat of arms

Date	Mintage	F	VF	XF	Unc	BU
2007 Proof	75	Value: 450				

KM# 142 10 DOLLARS
7.0000 g., 0.9167 Gold 0.2063 oz. AGW **Ruler:** Elizabeth II **Subject:** Constitutional Government, 50th Anniversary **Obv:** Bust right **Rev:** Coat of Arms

Date	Mintage	F	VF	XF	Unc	BU
2009 Proof	125	Value: 400				

CENTRAL AFRICAN STATES

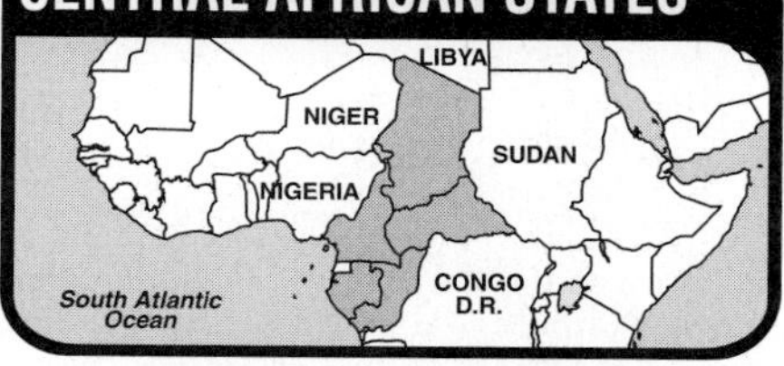

The Central African States, a monetary union comprised of Equatorial Guinea (a former Spanish possession), the former French possessions and now independent states of the Republic of Congo (Brazzaville), Gabon, Central African Republic, Chad and Cameroon, issues a common currency for the member states from a common central bank. The monetary unit, the African Financial Community franc, is tied to and supported by the French franc.

In 1960, an attempt was made to form a union of the newly independent republics of Chad, Congo, Central Africa and Gabon. The proposal was discarded when Chad refused to become a constituent member. The four countries then linked into an Equatorial Customs Unit, to which Cameroon became an associate member in 1961. A more extensive cooperation of the five republics, identified as the Central African Customs and Economic Union, was entered into force at the beginning of 1966.

In 1974 the Central Bank of the Equatorial African States, which had issued coins and paper currency in its own name and with the names of the constituent member nations, changed its name to the Bank of the Central African States. Equatorial Guinea converted to the CFA currency system issuing its first 100 Franc in 1985.

For earlier coinage see French Equatorial Africa.

Country Code Letters

To observe the movement of coinage throughout the states, the country of origin in which the coin is intended to circulate is designated by the following additional code letters:
A = Chad
B = Central African Republic
C = Congo
D = Gabon
E = Cameroon

By 1992 this practice was discontinued as the strategy had proved to be inconclusive.

MONETARY UNION

STANDARD COINAGE

KM# 8 FRANC
1.3000 g., Aluminum, 23 mm. **Obv:** Three giant eland left, date below **Obv. Designer:** G.B.L. Bazor **Rev:** Denomination within wreath

Date	Mintage	F	VF	XF	Unc	BU
2003	—	0.20	0.40	0.80	2.00	—

KM# 16 FRANC
1.6100 g., Stainless Steel, 14.9 mm. **Obv:** Value **Rev:** Value above produce **Edge:** Plain

Date	Mintage	F	VF	XF	Unc	BU
2006(a)	—	—	—	—	0.15	0.25

KM# 17 2 FRANCS
2.4300 g., Stainless Steel, 17.9 mm. **Obv:** Value **Rev:** Value above produce **Edge:** Plain

Date	Mintage	F	VF	XF	Unc	BU
2006(a)	—	—	—	—	0.25	0.35

KM# 7 5 FRANCS
3.0000 g., Aluminum-Bronze, 20 mm. **Obv:** Three giant eland left, date below **Obv. Designer:** G.B.L. Bazor **Rev:** Denomination within wreath

Date	Mintage	F	VF	XF	Unc	BU
2003	—	0.15	0.30	0.60	1.25	—

KM# 18 5 FRANCS
2.4100 g., Brass, 15.9 mm. **Obv:** Value **Rev:** Value above produce **Edge:** Reeded

Date	Mintage	F	VF	XF	Unc	BU
2006(a)	—	—	—	—	0.50	0.65

KM# 9 10 FRANCS
4.0000 g., Aluminum-Bronze, 23 mm. **Obv:** Three giant eland left, date below **Obv. Designer:** G.B.L. Bazor **Rev:** Denomination within wreath

Date	Mintage	F	VF	XF	Unc	BU
2003(a)	—	0.20	0.35	0.75	1.50	—

KM# 19 10 FRANCS
3.0000 g., Brass, 17.9 mm. **Obv:** Value **Rev:** Value above produce **Edge:** Reeded

Date	Mintage	F	VF	XF	Unc	BU
2006(a)	—	—	—	—	0.75	1.00

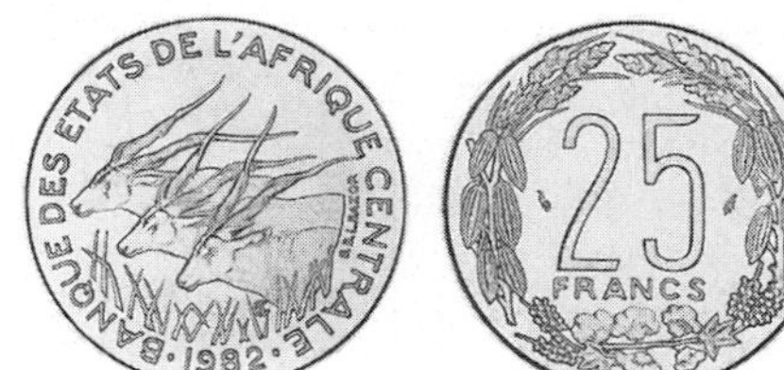

KM# 10 25 FRANCS
8.0000 g., Aluminum-Bronze, 27.2 mm. **Obv:** Three giant eland left, date below **Obv. Designer:** G.B.L. Bazor **Rev:** Denomination within wreath

Date	Mintage	F	VF	XF	Unc	BU
2003(a)	—	0.25	0.50	1.00	2.00	—

KM# 20 25 FRANCS
4.2000 g., Brass, 22.7 mm. **Obv:** Value **Rev:** Value above produce **Edge:** Reeded

Date	Mintage	F	VF	XF	Unc	BU
2006(a)	—	—	—	—	1.00	1.25

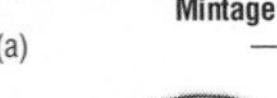

KM# 11 50 FRANCS
4.7000 g., Nickel, 21.5 mm. **Obv:** Three giant eland left, date below **Obv. Designer:** G.B.L. Bazor **Rev:** Denomination within flower design **Edge:** Reeded **Note:** Starting in 1996 an extra flora item was added where the mintmark was formerly located.

Date	Mintage	F	VF	XF	Unc	BU
2003(a)	—	0.75	1.50	3.50	6.00	—

KM# 21 50 FRANCS
4.9000 g., Stainless Steel, 22 mm. **Obv:** Value **Rev:** Value above produce **Edge:** Reeded

Date	Mintage	F	VF	XF	Unc	BU
2006(a)	—	—	—	—	1.25	1.50

KM# 13 100 FRANCS
7.0500 g., Nickel, 25.5 mm. **Obv:** Three giant eland **Rev:** Denomination

Date	Mintage	F	VF	XF	Unc	BU
2003	—	—	—	—	4.50	6.00

KM# 15 100 FRANCS
6.0000 g., Bi-Metallic Stainless Steel center in Brass ring, 23.9 mm. **Obv:** Denomination above initials within beaded circle **Rev:** Value above produce **Edge:** Reeded

Date	Mintage	F	VF	XF	Unc	BU
2006(a)	—	—	—	—	5.00	6.50

KM# 22 500 FRANCS
8.1000 g., Copper-Nickel, 26 mm. **Obv:** Value above produce **Rev:** Value **Edge:** Segmented reeding and lettering

Date	Mintage	F	VF	XF	Unc	BU
2006(a)	—	—	—	—	8.00	10.00

CHAD

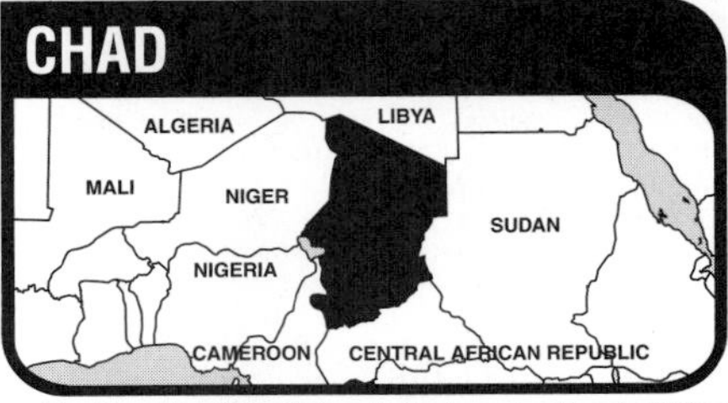

The Republic of Chad, a landlocked country of central Africa, is the largest country of former French Equatorial Africa. It has an area of 495,755 sq. mi. (1,284,000 sq. km.) and a population of *7.27 million. Capital: N'Djamena. An expanding livestock industry produces camels, cattle and sheep. Cotton (the chief product), ivory and palm oil are important exports.

NOTE: For earlier and related coinage see French Equatorial Africa and the Equatorial African States. For later coinage see Central African States.

MINT MARKS
(a) - Paris, privy marks only
(b) = Brussels
NI - Numismatic Italiana, Arezzo, Italy

REPUBLIC

DECIMAL COINAGE

KM# 30 500 FRANCS
Silver, 31 mm. **Obv:** Native portrait within circle **Rev:** Rhino mom and baby

Date	Mintage	F	VF	XF	Unc	BU
2001 Proof	—	Value: 30.00				

KM# 20 1000 FRANCS
15.0000 g., 0.9990 Silver 0.4818 oz. ASW, 35 mm. **Obv:** Native portrait within circle, denomination below **Rev:** Ancient Arabic war ship **Edge:** Plain

Date	Mintage	F	VF	XF	Unc	BU
2001 Proof	—	Value: 40.00				

KM# 21 1000 FRANCS
25.1000 g., 0.9990 Silver 0.8061 oz. ASW, 40 mm. **Obv:** Native portrait within circle, denomination below **Rev:** Soccer player and stadium **Edge:** Reeded

Date	Mintage	F	VF	XF	Unc	BU
2001 Proof	—	Value: 50.00				

KM# 29 1000 FRANCS
15.0000 g., 0.9990 Silver 0.4818 oz. ASW, 36 mm. **Obv:** Native portrait within circle **Rev:** Multicolor orang-outan

Date	Mintage	F	VF	XF	Unc	BU
2001 Proof	—	Value: 35.00				

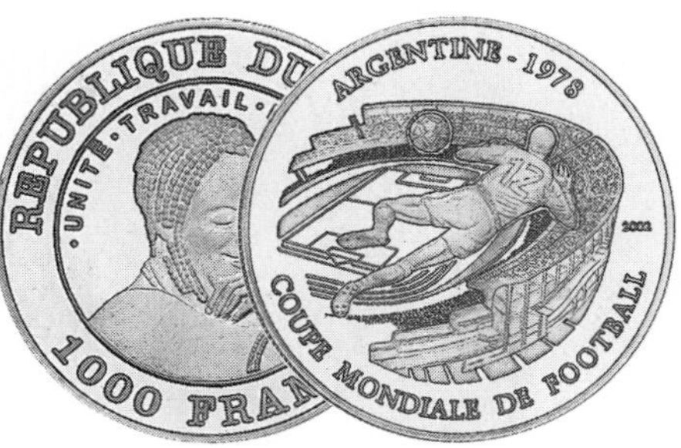

KM# 22 1000 FRANCS
20.0000 g., 0.9990 Silver 0.6423 oz. ASW, 40 mm. **Obv:** Native portrait within circle, denomination below **Rev:** Horizontal soccer player above stadium **Edge:** Reeded

Date	Mintage	F	VF	XF	Unc	BU
2002 Proof	5,000	Value: 45.00				

KM# 23 1000 FRANCS
20.1500 g., 0.9990 Silver 0.6472 oz. ASW, 40 mm. **Obv:** Native portrait within circle, denomination below **Rev:** Soccer player and Arch of Triumph **Edge:** Reeded

Date	Mintage	F	VF	XF	Unc	BU
2002 Proof	—	Value: 40.00				

KM# 31 1000 FRANCS
15.0000 g., 0.9850 Silver 0.4750 oz. ASW, 34 mm. **Rev:** Multicolor McDonnell-Douglass DC-10 landing left

Date	Mintage	F	VF	XF	Unc	BU
2002 Proof	—	Value: 35.00				

KM# 32 1000 FRANCS
15.0000 g., 0.9850 Silver 0.4750 oz. ASW, 34 mm. **Rev:** Multicolor Boeing 747 taking-off right

Date	Mintage	F	VF	XF	Unc	BU
2002 Proof	—	Value: 35.00				

KM# 33 1000 FRANCS
15.0000 g., 0.9850 Silver 0.4750 oz. ASW, 34 mm. **Rev:** Multicolor McDonnell-Douglass DC-9 over mountains

Date	Mintage	F	VF	XF	Unc	BU
2003 Proof	—	Value: 35.00				

KM# 34 1000 FRANCS
15.0000 g., 0.9850 Silver 0.4750 oz. ASW, 34 mm. **Rev:** Multicolor Fokker F-7a top wing

Date	Mintage	F	VF	XF	Unc	BU
2003 Proof	—	Value: 35.00				

The Republic of Chile, a ribbon-like country on the Pacific coast of southern South America, has an area of 292,135 sq. mi. (756,950 sq. km.) and a population of *15.21 million. Capital: Santiago. Historically, the economic base of Chile has been the rich mineral deposits of its northern provinces. Copper has accounted for more than 75 percent of Chile's export earnings in recent years. Other important mineral exports are iron ore, iodine and nitrate of soda. Fresh fruits and vegetables, as well as wine are increasingly significant in inter-hemispheric trade.

MINT MARK
So – Santiago
(ml) – Maple leaf – Royal Canadian Mint (RCM)

REPUBLIC

REFORM COINAGE

100 Centavos = 1 Peso; 1000 Old Escudos = 1 Peso

KM# 219.3 50 CENTAVOS
7.0500 g., Aluminum-Bronze, 25.4 mm. **Obv:** Bust of Gen. Bernardo O'Higgins right **Obv. Legend:** REPUBLICA DE CIIILE **Rev:** Denomination above date within sprays **Note:** Error spelling in legend of CHILE.

Date	Mintage	F	VF	XF	Unc	BU
2009	—	—	—	—	1.50	2.50

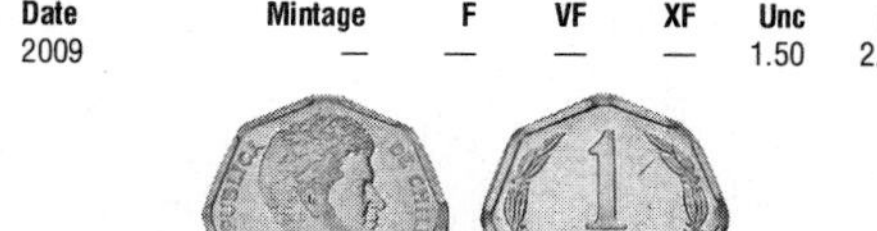

KM# 231 PESO
0.7000 g., Aluminum, 16.3 mm. **Obv:** Gen. Bernardo O'Higgins bust right **Obv. Legend:** REPUBLICA - DE CHILE **Rev:** Denomination above date within wreath **Edge:** Plain **Shape:** 8-sided **Note:** Varieties exist.

Date	Mintage	F	VF	XF	Unc	BU
2001So Narrow date	—	—	—	—	0.10	0.20
2002So Narrow date	—	—	—	—	0.10	0.20
2003So Narrow date	—	—	—	—	0.10	0.20
2004So Narrow date	—	—	—	—	0.10	0.20
2005So Narrow date	—	—	—	—	0.10	0.20
2006So Narrow date	—	—	—	—	0.10	0.20

KM# 232 5 PESOS
2.1600 g., Aluminum-Bronze, 16.4 mm. **Obv:** Gen. Bernardo O'Higgins bust right **Obv. Legend:** REPUBLICA - DE CHILE **Rev:** Denomination above date within wreath **Edge:** Plain **Shape:** 8-sided **Note:** Varieties exist.

Date	Mintage	F	VF	XF	Unc	BU
2001So Narrow date	—	—	—	0.10	0.35	0.60
2001So (sa) Wide date	—	—	—	0.15	0.50	0.75
Note: Without name of sculptor						
2002So Narrow date	—	—	—	0.15	0.50	0.75
2002So Wide date	—	—	—	0.10	0.35	0.60
2003So	—	—	—	0.10	0.35	0.60
2004So	—	—	—	0.10	0.35	0.60
2005So	—	—	—	0.10	0.35	0.60
2006So	—	—	—	0.10	0.35	0.60

KM# 228.2 10 PESOS
3.5000 g., Aluminum-Bronze, 21 mm. **Obv:** Bust of Gen. Bernardo O'Higgins right **Obv. Legend:** REPUBLICA - DE CHILE **Rev:** Denomination above date within sprays **Edge:** Reeded **Note:** All 9's are curl tail 9's except for the 1999 date, these are straight tail 9's. Normal rim.

Date	Mintage	F	VF	XF	Unc	BU
2001So	—	—	0.10	0.20	0.50	0.65
2002So	—	—	0.10	0.20	0.50	0.65
2003So	—	—	0.10	0.20	0.50	0.65
2004So	—	—	0.10	0.20	0.50	0.65
2005So	—	—	0.10	0.20	0.50	0.65
2006So	—	—	0.10	0.20	0.50	0.65
2007	—	—	0.10	0.20	0.50	0.65
Note: Struck in Canada						
2008So	—	—	0.10	0.20	0.50	0.65

KM# 240 20 PESOS
Aluminum-Brass **Subject:** Chile - 200th Anniversary

Date	Mintage	F	VF	XF	Unc	BU
2010	—	—	—	—	0.75	1.00

KM# 219.2 50 PESOS
7.0000 g., Aluminum-Bronze, 25.40 mm. **Obv:** Bust of Gen. Bernardo O'Higgins right **Obv. Legend:** REPUBLICA - DE CHILE **Rev:** Denomination above date within sprays **Edge:** Ornamented **Shape:** 10-sided **Note:** Narrow date.

Date	Mintage	F	VF	XF	Unc	BU
2001So	—	—	0.25	0.50	1.25	1.50
2002So	—	—	0.25	0.50	1.25	1.50
2005So	—	—	0.25	0.50	1.00	1.25
2006So	—	—	0.25	0.50	1.00	1.25
2007	—	—	0.25	0.50	1.00	1.25
Note: Struck in Canada						

KM# 236 100 PESOS
7.5800 g., Bi-Metallic Copper-nickel center in Brass ring, 23.43 mm. **Subject:** Native people **Obv:** Bust of native Mapuche girl facing **Obv. Legend:** REPUBLICA DE CHILE - PUEBLOS ORIGINARIOS **Rev:** National arms above denomination **Edge:** Segmented reeding, 3 reeded & 3 plain regmenti

Date	Mintage	F	VF	XF	Unc	BU
2001So	—	—	0.35	0.90	2.25	3.00
2003So	—	—	0.35	0.90	2.25	3.00
2004So	—	—	0.35	0.90	2.25	3.00
2005So	—	—	0.35	0.90	2.25	3.00
2006So	—	—	0.35	0.90	2.25	3.00
2008So	—	—	0.35	0.90	2.25	3.00

KM# 241 200 PESOS
Aluminum-Bronze **Subject:** Chile - 200th Anniversary

Date	Mintage	F	VF	XF	Unc	BU
2010	—	—	—	—	1.50	2.00

KM# 235 500 PESOS
6.6000 g., Bi-Metallic Aluminum-Bronze center in Copper-Nickel ring, 26 mm. **Subject:** Cardinal Raul Silva Henriquez **Obv:** Bust of cardinal within inner ring facing left **Rev:** Denomination above date within wreath **Edge:** Reeded

Date	Mintage	F	VF	XF	Unc	BU
2001So	—	—	—	—	6.00	6.50
2002So 4.1mm date	—	—	—	—	6.00	6.50
2002So 5.2mm date	—	—	—	—	6.00	6.50
2003So	—	—	—	—	6.00	6.50
2008So	—	—	—	—	6.00	6.50

The Peoples Republic of China, located in eastern Asia, has an area of 3,696,100 sq. mi. (9,596,960 sq. km.) (including Manchuria and Tibet) and a population of *1.20 billion. Capital: Peking (Beijing). The economy is based on agriculture, mining, and manufacturing. Textiles, clothing, metal ores, tea and rice are exported.

MONETARY SYSTEM

After 1949

10 Fen (Cents) = 1 Jiao
10 Jiao = 1 Renminbi Yuan

MINT MARKS
(b) - Beijing (Peking)
(s) - Shanghai
(y) - Shenyang (Mukden)

OBVERSE LEGENDS

ZHONGHUA RENMIN GONGHEGUO (Peoples Republic of China)

ZHONGGUO RENMIN YINHANG (Peoples Bank of China

PEOPLES REPUBLIC

STANDARD COINAGE

KM# 1 FEN
0.7000 g., Aluminum, 18 mm. **Obv:** National emblem **Rev:** Value in wreath, date below **Edge:** Reeded **Note:** Prev. Y#1.

Date	Mintage	F	VF	XF	Unc	BU
2005	—	—	—	0.10	0.15	0.25
2006	—	—	—	0.10	0.15	0.25
2007	—	—	—	0.10	0.15	0.25

KM# 1210 JIAO
1.1200 g., Aluminum, 19 mm. **Obv:** Denomination, date below **Rev:** Orchid **Rev. Legend:** ZHONGGUA RENMIN YINHANG **Edge:** Plain **Note:** Prev. Y#1068.

Date	Mintage	F	VF	XF	Unc	BU
2001	—	—	—	—	0.50	0.75
2002	—	—	—	—	0.50	0.75
2003	—	—	—	—	0.50	0.75

KM# 1210a JIAO
Copper-Nickel, 19 mm. **Obv:** Denomination, date below **Note:** Prev. Y#1068a.

Date	Mintage	F	VF	XF	Unc	BU
2005	—	—	—	—	0.50	0.75

KM# 1210b JIAO
3.2200 g., Steel, 19.03 mm. **Obv:** Value, date below **Rev:** Orchid **Rev. Legend:** ZHONGGUA RENMIN YINHANG **Edge:** Plain **Note:** Prev. Y#1068b.

Date	Mintage	F	VF	XF	Unc	BU
2005	—	—	—	—	—	0.25
2006	—	—	—	—	—	0.25
2007	—	—	—	—	—	0.25
2008	—	—	—	—	—	0.25
2009	—	—	—	—	—	0.25

KM# 336 5 JIAO
3.8000 g., Brass, 20.5 mm. **Obv:** National emblem, date below **Rev:** Denomination above flowers **Edge:** Segmented reeding **Note:** Prev. Y#329.

Date	Mintage	F	VF	XF	Unc	BU
2001	—	—	—	—	1.00	1.25

KM# 1411 5 JIAO
3.8000 g., Brass, 20.5 mm. **Obv:** Denomination **Rev:** Flower **Rev. Legend:** ZHONGGUA RENMIN YINHANG **Edge:** Reeded and plain sections **Note:** Prev. Y#1106.

Date	Mintage	F	VF	XF	Unc	BU
2002	—	—	—	—	1.50	1.75
2003	—	—	—	—	1.50	1.75
2004	—	—	—	—	1.50	1.75
2005	—	—	—	—	1.50	1.75
2006	—	—	—	—	1.50	1.75
2007	—	—	—	—	1.50	1.75
2008	—	—	—	—	1.50	1.75

KM# 1212 YUAN
6.1000 g., Nickel Plated Steel, 24.9 mm. **Obv:** Denomination, date below **Rev:** Chrysanthemum **Rev. Legend:** ZHONGGUA RENMIN YINHANG **Edge:** "RMB" three times **Note:** Prev. Y#1069.

Date	Mintage	F	VF	XF	Unc	BU
2001	—	—	—	—	2.00	2.50
2002	—	—	—	—	2.00	2.50
2003	—	—	—	—	2.00	2.50
2004	—	—	—	—	2.00	2.50
2005	—	—	—	—	2.00	2.50
2006	—	—	—	—	2.00	2.50
2007	—	—	—	—	2.00	2.50
2008	—	—	—	—	2.00	2.50
2009	—	—	—	—	2.00	2.50

KM# 1465 YUAN
6.8500 g., Brass, 25 mm. **Obv:** Value **Rev:** Celebrating child and ram **Edge:** Lettered **Edge Lettering:** "RMB" three times **Note:** Prev. Y#1125.

Date	Mintage	F	VF	XF	Unc	BU
2003	—	—	—	—	5.00	6.00

KM# 1521 YUAN
Brass **Obv:** Denomination **Rev:** Celebrating Child **Note:** Prev. Y#1247.

Date	Mintage	F	VF	XF	Unc	BU
2004	—	—	—	—	2.50	3.00

KM# 1522 YUAN
Nickel Clad Steel **Obv:** Palace **Rev:** Deng Xiao Ping 1904-2004 **Note:** Prev. Y#1248.

Date	Mintage	F	VF	XF	Unc	BU
2004	—	—	—	—	3.50	4.00

KM# 1523 YUAN
Nickel Clad Steel **Subject:** 50th Year of Peoples Congress **Obv:** Congress building **Note:** Prev. Y#1249.

Date	Mintage	F	VF	XF	Unc	BU
2004	—	—	—	—	3.50	4.00

KM# 1574 YUAN
5.9600 g., Nickel Clad Steel, 25 mm. **Obv:** Building **Rev:** Bust of Chenyun **Edge:** Lettered **Note:** Prev. Y#1208.

Date	Mintage	F	VF	XF	Unc	BU
2005	—	—	—	—	3.50	4.00

KM# 1575 YUAN
Brass **Subject:** Year of the Rooster **Obv:** Denomination **Rev:** Celebrating Child **Note:** Prev. Y#1250.

Date	Mintage	F	VF	XF	Unc	BU
2005	—	—	—	—	3.00	3.50

KM# 1650 YUAN
Brass **Subject:** Year of the Dog **Obv:** Denomination **Rev:** Celebrating Child **Note:** Prev. Y#1251.

Date	Mintage	F	VF	XF	Unc	BU
2006	—	—	—	—	7.00	8.00

KM# 1775 YUAN
6.7500 g., Brass, 25 mm. **Subject:** 29th Olympics **Obv:** Stylized Olympics logo **Rev:** Cartoon swimmer **Edge:** Reeded **Note:** Prev. Y#1256.

Date	Mintage	F	VF	XF	Unc	BU
2008 (2006)(y)	—	—	—	—	5.00	6.00

KM# 1776 YUAN
6.7500 g., Brass, 25 mm. **Subject:** 29th Olympics **Obv:** Stylized Olympics logo **Rev:** Cartoon Weight Lifter **Edge:** Reeded **Note:** Prev. Y#1257.

Date	Mintage	F	VF	XF	Unc	BU
2008 (2006)	—	—	—	—	5.00	6.00

KM# 1810 YUAN
Brass, 25 mm. **Obv:** Beijing Olympic logo **Rev:** Character playing ping-pong

Date	Mintage	F	VF	XF	Unc	BU
2008	—	—	—	—	2.50	3.00

KM# 1811 YUAN
Brass, 25 mm. **Obv:** Beijing Olympic logo **Rev:** Character fencingwith bow and arrow

Date	Mintage	F	VF	XF	Unc	BU
2008	—	—	—	—	2.50	3.00

KM# 1812 YUAN
Brass, 25 mm. **Obv:** Beijing Olympic logo **Rev:** Character on horseback

Date	Mintage	F	VF	XF	Unc	BU
2008	—	—	—	—	2.50	3.00

KM# 1813 YUAN
Brass, 25 mm. **Obv:** Large value **Rev:** Boy with rat pattern chinese knot & cluster of fireworks

Date	Mintage	F	VF	XF	Unc	BU
2008	10,000,000	—	—	—	2.50	3.00

KM# 1363 5 YUAN
12.8000 g., Brass, 30 mm. **Subject:** 50th Anniversary - Chinese Occupation of Tibet **Obv:** National emblem **Rev:** Potala Palace, value and two dancers **Edge:** Reeded **Note:** Prev. Y#1126.

Date	Mintage	F	VF	XF	Unc	BU
2001(y)	10,000,000	—	—	—	8.00	—

KM# 1364 5 YUAN
12.8000 g., Brass, 30 mm. **Subject:** Revolution: 90th Anniversary **Obv:** National emblem **Rev:** Battle scene **Edge:** Reeded **Note:** Prev. Y#1109.

Date	Mintage	F	VF	XF	Unc	BU
2001	—	—	—	—	7.50	8.50

KM# 1412 5 YUAN
12.8000 g., Brass, 30 mm. **Subject:** The Great Wall **Obv:** State arms, icroscopic inscription repeated four times on the inner raised rim **Obv. Inscription:** SHI JIE WEN HUA YI CHAN **Rev:** Two views of the Great Wall **Edge:** Reeded **Note:** Prev. Y#1107.

Date	Mintage	F	VF	XF	Unc	BU
2002	—	—	—	—	7.00	8.00

KM# 1413 5 YUAN
12.8000 g., Brass, 30 mm. **Subject:** Terra Cotta Army **Obv:**

State arms and the microscopic inscription repeated four times on the raised inner rim. **Obv. Inscription:** SHI JIE WEN HUA YI CHAN **Rev:** Terra Cotta Soldier close-up with many more in background **Edge:** Reeded **Note:** Prev. Y#1108.

Date	Mintage	F	VF	XF	Unc	BU
2002	—	—	—	—	7.00	8.00

KM# 1461 5 YUAN

12.8000 g., Brass, 30 mm. **Obv:** National emblem **Rev:** Chaotian Temple in Beigang Taiwan **Edge:** Reeded **Note:** Prev. Y#1127.

Date	Mintage	F	VF	XF	Unc	BU
2003	10,000,000	—	—	—	7.00	8.00

KM# 1462 5 YUAN

12.8000 g., Brass, 30 mm. **Obv:** National emblem **Rev:** Chikan Tower on Treasure Island Taiwan **Edge:** Reeded **Note:** Prev. Y#1128.

Date	Mintage	F	VF	XF	Unc	BU
2003(y)	10,000,000	—	—	—	7.00	8.00

KM# 1463 5 YUAN

12.8000 g., Brass, 30 mm. **Subject:** Chaotian Temple in Beijing **Obv:** State emblem **Rev:** Buildings **Edge:** Reeded **Note:** Prev. Y#1230.

Date	Mintage	F	VF	XF	Unc	BU
2003	10,000,000	—	—	—	7.00	8.00

KM# 1464 5 YUAN

Brass, 30 mm. **Obv:** National emblem **Rev:** Imperial Palace **Note:** Prev. Y#1252.

Date	Mintage	F	VF	XF	Unc	BU
2003	—	—	—	—	7.00	8.00

KM# 1524 5 YUAN

Brass, 30 mm. **Obv:** National emblem **Rev:** Island scene **Note:** Prev. Y#1253.

Date	Mintage	F	VF	XF	Unc	BU
2004	—	—	—	—	6.00	7.00

KM# 1525 5 YUAN

Brass, 30 mm. **Obv:** National emblem **Rev:** Lighthouse **Note:** Prev. Y#1254.

Date	Mintage	F	VF	XF	Unc	BU
2004	—	—	—	—	6.00	7.00

KM# 1526 5 YUAN

12.7000 g., Brass, 30 mm. **Obv:** National emblem **Rev:** Peking Man bust and discovery site view **Edge:** Reeded **Note:** Prev. Y#1201.

Date	Mintage	F	VF	XF	Unc	BU
2004	6,000,000	—	—	—	6.00	7.00

KM# 1527 5 YUAN

12.7000 g., Brass, 30 mm. **Obv:** National emblem **Rev:** Pavillion and bridge **Edge:** Reeded **Note:** Prev. Y#1202.

Date	Mintage	F	VF	XF	Unc	BU
2004	6,000,000	—	—	—	6.00	7.00

KM# 1068 5 YUAN

22.0000 g., 0.9000 Silver 0.6366 oz. ASW, 36 mm. **Obv:** Great Wall **Rev:** Gymnast, denomination at right **Edge:** Reeded **Note:** Prev. Y#1189.

Date	Mintage	F	VF	XF	Unc	BU
2005(y)	—	—	—	—	75.00	85.00

KM# 1576 5 YUAN

12.9200 g., Brass, 30 mm. **Obv:** National emblem **Rev:** Lijiang building **Edge:** Reeded **Note:** Prev. Y#1209.

Date	Mintage	F	VF	XF	Unc	BU
2005	—	—	—	—	6.00	7.00

KM# 1577 5 YUAN

12.8000 g., Brass, 30 mm. **Subject:** "Taiwan" **Obv:** State emblem **Rev:** Tower and terrace **Edge:** Reeded **Note:** Prev. Y#1231.

Date	Mintage	F	VF	XF	Unc	BU
2005	—	—	—	—	6.00	7.00

KM# 1578 5 YUAN

12.9200 g., Brass, 30 mm. **Obv:** National emblem **Rev:** Green City Hall **Edge:** Reeded **Note:** Prev. Y#1210.

Date	Mintage	F	VF	XF	Unc	BU
2005	—	—	—	—	6.00	7.00

KM# 1731 5 YUAN

Brass, 30 mm. **Obv:** State emblem **Rev:** Large statue head

Date	Mintage	F	VF	XF	Unc	BU
2006 Proof	10,000,000	Value: 3.00				

KM# 1395 10 YUAN

31.1035 g., 0.9990 Silver 0.9990 oz. ASW, 40 mm. **Subject:** 2008 Olympics Beijing bid **Obv:** Gold-plated "V" design **Rev:** Radiant Temple of Heaven **Edge:** Reeded **Note:** Prev. Y#1103.

Date	Mintage	F	VF	XF	Unc	BU
2001 Proof	60,000	Value: 50.00				

KM# 1384 10 YUAN

31.1035 g., 0.9990 Silver 0.9990 oz. ASW **Series:** Folk Fairy Tales **Rev:** Heroic figure putting ax to mountains

Date	Mintage	F	VF	XF	Unc	BU
2001 Proof	30,000	Value: 120				

KM# 1385 10 YUAN

31.1035 g., 0.9990 Silver 0.9990 oz. ASW, 40 mm. **Series:** Folk Fairy Tales **Rev:** Multicolor angelic figure

Date	Mintage	F	VF	XF	Unc	BU
2001 Proof	30,000	Value: 120				

KM# 1396 10 YUAN

31.1035 g., 0.9990 Silver 0.9990 oz. ASW, 40 mm. **Series:** Folk customs - Mid Autumn Festival **Rev:** Flora and sun

Date	Mintage	F	VF	XF	Unc	BU
2001 Proof	40,000	Value: 180				

KM# 1397 10 YUAN

31.1035 g., 0.9990 Silver 0.9990 oz. ASW, 32 mm. **Subject:** Bejing International Coin Expo **Obv:** Globe hemisphere view **Rev:** Bejing city view

Date	Mintage	F	VF	XF	Unc	BU
2001 Proof	40,000	Value: 125				

KM# 1398 10 YUAN

31.1035 g., 0.9990 Silver 0.9990 oz. ASW, 40 mm. **Subject:** Bejing opera **Rev:** Two multicolor actors, one with hankie

Date	Mintage	F	VF	XF	Unc	BU
2001 Proof	38,000	Value: 100				

KM# 1399 10 YUAN

31.1035 g., 0.9990 Silver 0.9990 oz. ASW, 40 mm. **Subject:** Bejing opera **Rev:** Two actors, one with blue ribbon

Date	Mintage	F	VF	XF	Unc	BU
2001 Proof	38,000	Value: 120				

KM# 1400 10 YUAN

31.1035 g., 0.9990 Silver 0.9990 oz. ASW, 40 mm. **Subject:** Bejing opera **Rev:** Two multicolor actors, one with tassles

Date	Mintage	F	VF	XF	Unc	BU
2001 Proof	38,000	Value: 60.00				

KM# 1401 10 YUAN

31.1035 g., 0.9990 Silver 0.9990 oz. ASW, 40 mm. **Subject:** Bejing opera **Rev:** Two multicolor actors, white or black beard

Date	Mintage	F	VF	XF	Unc	BU
2001 Proof	38,000	Value: 120				

KM# 1428 10 YUAN

31.1035 g., 0.9990 Silver 0.9990 oz. ASW, 40 mm. **Series:** Folk Fairy Tales **Rev:** Multicolor male figure seated

Date	Mintage	F	VF	XF	Unc	BU
2002 Proof	30,000	Value: 120				

KM# 1429 10 YUAN

31.1035 g., 0.9990 Silver Colorized 0.9990 oz. ASW, 40 mm. **Series:** Folk fairy tails **Rev:** Male figure brandishing sword

Date	Mintage	F	VF	XF	Unc	BU
2002 Proof	30,000	Value: 120				

KM# 1438 10 YUAN

31.1035 g., 0.9990 Silver 0.9990 oz. ASW, 40 mm. **Series:** Folk customs **Rev:** Dragon boat

Date	Mintage	F	VF	XF	Unc	BU
2002 Proof	40,000	Value: 120				

KM# 1441 10 YUAN

31.1035 g., 0.9990 Silver Colorized 0.9990 oz. ASW, 40 mm. **Series:** Classic literature **Rev:** Black and red dressed women seated **Shape:** Octagon

Date	Mintage	F	VF	XF	Unc	BU
2002 Proof	38,000	Value: 100				

KM# 1442 10 YUAN

31.1035 g., 0.9990 Silver 0.9990 oz. ASW, 40 mm. **Series:** Classic literature **Rev:** Multicolor white dressed woman standing **Shape:** Octagon

Date	Mintage	F	VF	XF	Unc	BU
2002 Proof	38,000	Value: 100				

KM# 1443 10 YUAN

31.1035 g., 0.9990 Silver 0.9990 oz. ASW, 40 mm. **Series:** Classic literature **Rev:** Multicolor yellow dressed woman walking left **Shape:** Octagon

Date	Mintage	F	VF	XF	Unc	BU
2002 Proof	38,000	Value: 100				

KM# 1444 10 YUAN

31.1035 g., 0.9990 Silver 0.9990 oz. ASW, 40 mm. **Series:** Classic literature **Obv:** Multicolor purple dressed woman **Shape:** Octagon

Date	Mintage	F	VF	XF	Unc	BU
2002 Proof	38,000	Value: 100				

KM# 1447 10 YUAN

31.1035 g., 0.9990 Silver 0.9990 oz. ASW, 40 mm. **Subject:** Bejing Coin and Stamp Fair **Obv:** Hemisphere map **Rev:** Highway design

Date	Mintage	F	VF	XF	Unc	BU
2002 Proof	40,000	Value: 95.00				

KM# 1448 10 YUAN

31.1035 g., 0.9990 Silver 0.9990 oz. ASW, 40 mm. **Subject:** Table tennis, 50th anniversary **Rev:** Trophies, flag

Date	Mintage	F	VF	XF	Unc	BU
2002 Proof	50,000	Value: 100				

KM# 1449 10 YUAN
31.1035 g., 0.9990 Silver 0.9990 oz. ASW **Series:** Bejing opera **Rev:** Two multicolor characters, one seated **Shape:** 40

Date	Mintage	F	VF	XF	Unc	BU
2002 Proof	38,000	Value: 50.00				

KM# 1450 10 YUAN
31.1035 g., 0.9990 Silver 0.9990 oz. ASW, 40 mm. **Series:** Bejing opera **Rev:** Two multicolor characters, white and green

Date	Mintage	F	VF	XF	Unc	BU
2002 Proof	38,000	Value: 125				

KM# 1451 10 YUAN
31.1035 g., 0.9990 Silver 0.9990 oz. ASW, 40 mm. **Series:** Bejing opera **Rev:** Bearded character, black

Date	Mintage	F	VF	XF	Unc	BU
2002 Proof	38,000	Value: 125				

KM# 1452 10 YUAN
31.1035 g., 0.9990 Silver 0.9990 oz. ASW, 40 mm. **Series:** Bejing opera **Rev:** Multicolor bearded character, red

Date	Mintage	F	VF	XF	Unc	BU
2002 Proof	38,000	Value: 125				

KM# A1455 10 YUAN
31.1035 g., 0.9990 Silver 0.9990 oz. ASW, 40 mm. **Subject:** World Expo 2010 **Rev:** Tower

Date	Mintage	F	VF	XF	Unc	BU
2002 Proof	50,000	Value: 100				

KM# 1455 10 YUAN
31.1035 g., 0.9990 Silver 0.9990 oz. ASW, 40 mm. **Subject:** Shanghai World Expo of 2010 **Obv:** Flower design with inset pearl **Rev:** 2010 Logo incorporating a tower **Edge:** Reeded **Note:** Prev. Y#1233.

Date	Mintage	F	VF	XF	Unc	BU
2002 Proof	50,000	Value: 125				

KM# 1507 10 YUAN
31.1035 g., 0.9990 Silver 0.9990 oz. ASW, 40 mm. **Obv:** Stylized forest **Rev:** Cyclists in forest **Edge:** Reeded **Note:** Prev. Y#1132.

Date	Mintage	F	VF	XF	Unc	BU
2003 Proof	30,000	Value: 125				

KM# 1508 10 YUAN
31.1035 g., 0.9990 Silver 0.9990 oz. ASW, 40 mm. **Obv:** Stylized forest **Rev:** Birds flying over forest **Edge:** Reeded **Note:** Prev. Y#1133.

Date	Mintage	F	VF	XF	Unc	BU
2003(y) Proof	30,000	Value: 125				

KM# 1510 10 YUAN
31.1035 g., 0.9990 Silver 0.9990 oz. ASW, 40 mm. **Obv:** Solar system design **Rev:** Multicolor Chinese Astronaut **Edge:** Reeded **Note:** Prev. Y#1134.

Date	Mintage	F	VF	XF	Unc	BU
2003(y) Proof	60,000	Value: 90.00				

KM# 1487 10 YUAN
31.1035 g., 0.9990 Silver 0.9990 oz. ASW, 40 mm. **Rev:** Two Koi

Date	Mintage	F	VF	XF	Unc	BU
2003 Proof	100,000	Value: 90.00				

KM# 1489 10 YUAN
31.1035 g., 0.9990 Silver 0.9990 oz. ASW, 40 mm. **Subject:** Arbor Day **Rev:** Trees with bike riders

Date	Mintage	F	VF	XF	Unc	BU
2003 Proof	30,000	Value: 90.00				

KM# 1490 10 YUAN
31.1035 g., 0.9990 Silver 0.9990 oz. ASW, 40 mm. **Subject:** Arbor Day **Rev:** Close-up of leaves, birds in flight

Date	Mintage	F	VF	XF	Unc	BU
2003 Proof	30,000	Value: 120				

KM# 1491 10 YUAN
31.1035 g., 0.9990 Silver 0.9990 oz. ASW, 40 mm. **Series:** Fairy tails **Rev:** Multicolor blue female

Date	Mintage	F	VF	XF	Unc	BU
2003 Proof	30,000	Value: 120				

KM# 1492 10 YUAN
31.1035 g., 0.9990 Silver 0.9990 oz. ASW, 40 mm. **Subject:** Fairy tails **Rev:** Multicolor red bloused girl

Date	Mintage	F	VF	XF	Unc	BU
2003 Proof	30,000	Value: 120				

KM# 1496 10 YUAN
31.1035 g., 0.9990 Silver 0.9990 oz. ASW, 40 mm. **Series:** Class literature **Rev:** Multicolor purple cloaked man and monkey

Date	Mintage	F	VF	XF	Unc	BU
2003 Proof	38,000	Value: 120				

KM# 1497 10 YUAN
31.1035 g., 0.9990 Silver 0.9990 oz. ASW, 40 mm. **Series:** Classic literature **Rev:** Two multicolor men fighting in clouds

Date	Mintage	F	VF	XF	Unc	BU
2003 Proof	38,000	Value: 120				

KM# 1498 10 YUAN
31.1035 g., 0.9990 Silver 0.9990 oz. ASW, 40 mm. **Rev:** Multicolor female standing, black dress **Shape:** Octagon

Date	Mintage	F	VF	XF	Unc	BU
2003 Proof	38,000	Value: 120				

KM# 1499 10 YUAN
31.1035 g., 0.9990 Silver 0.9990 oz. ASW, 40 mm. **Series:** Classic Literature **Rev:** Multicolor female kneeling **Shape:** Octagon

Date	Mintage	F	VF	XF	Unc	BU
2003 Proof	38,000	Value: 120				

KM# 1500 10 YUAN
31.1035 g., 0.9990 Silver 0.9990 oz. ASW, 40 mm. **Series:** Classic literature **Rev:** Multicolor female walking, rose dress **Shape:** Octagon

Date	Mintage	F	VF	XF	Unc	BU
2003 Proof	—	Value: 120				

KM# 1501 10 YUAN
31.1035 g., 0.9990 Silver 0.9990 oz. ASW, 40 mm. **Series:** Classic literature **Rev:** Multicolor female kneeling, red dress **Shape:** Octagon

Date	Mintage	F	VF	XF	Unc	BU
2003 Proof	—	Value: 120				

KM# 1559 10 YUAN
31.1035 g., 0.9990 Silver 0.9990 oz. ASW, 40 mm. **Obv:** Monkey King leading the Master over bridge **Rev:** Multicolor Monkey King fighting the "Ox Fiend" **Edge:** Reeded **Note:** Prev. Y#1214.

Date	Mintage	F	VF	XF	Unc	BU
2004 Proof	38,000	Value: 110				

KM# 1558 10 YUAN
31.1035 g., 0.9990 Silver 0.9990 oz. ASW, 40 mm. **Obv:** Monkey King leading the Master over bridge **Rev:** Multicolor Pig carrying Monkey King piggy-back style **Edge:** Reeded **Note:** Prev. Y#1215.

Date	Mintage	F	VF	XF	Unc	BU
2004 Proof	38,000	Value: 110				

KM# 1566 10 YUAN
31.1035 g., 0.9990 Silver 0.9990 oz. ASW, 40 mm. **Obv:** Guangan Exposition Hall **Rev:** Deng Xiaoping and value **Edge:** Reeded **Note:** Prev. Y#1240. Photo reduced.

Date	Mintage	F	VF	XF	Unc	BU
2004 Proof	80,000	Value: 90.00				

KM# 1570 10 YUAN
31.1035 g., 0.9990 Silver 0.9990 oz. ASW, 40 mm. **Obv:** National arms above People's Congress Hall and ornamental column **Rev:** Multicolor hologram depicting the hall's overhead lighting **Edge:** Reeded **Note:** Prev. KM#1212.

Date	Mintage	F	VF	XF	Unc	BU
2004 Proof	50,000	Value: 100				

KM# 1539 10 YUAN
31.1035 g., 0.9990 Silver 0.9990 oz. ASW, 40 mm. **Subject:** 20th Anniversary / Bank of China Industrial and Commercial **Rev:** Panda walking with cub

Date	Mintage	F	VF	XF	Unc	BU
2004 Proof	120,000	Value: 90.00				

KM# 1541 10 YUAN
31.1035 g., 0.9990 Silver 0.9990 oz. ASW, 40 mm. **Subject:** 50th Anniversary China Construction Bank **Rev:** Panda walking with cub

Date	Mintage	F	VF	XF	Unc	BU
2004 Proof	170,000	Value: 90.00				

KM# 1543 10 YUAN
31.1035 g., 0.9990 Silver 0.9990 oz. ASW, 40 mm. **Subject:** Bejing International Coin Expo **Rev:** Panda walking with cub, gold plated center

Date	Mintage	F	VF	XF	Unc	BU
2004 Proof	30,000	Value: 120				

KM# 1557 10 YUAN
31.1035 g., 0.9990 Silver 0.9990 oz. ASW, 40 mm. **Series:** Folk customs **Subject:** Lantern Festival **Rev:** Boy holding lantern **Note:** Colorized

Date	Mintage	F	VF	XF	Unc	BU
2004 Proof	60,000	Value: 100				

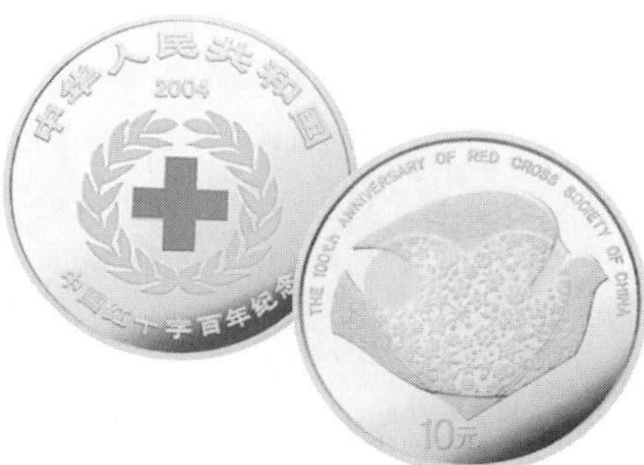

KM# 1555 10 YUAN
31.1035 g., 0.9990 Silver 0.9990 oz. ASW, 40 mm. **Subject:** 100th Anniversary Red Cross **Obv:** Red Cross within wreath **Rev:** Dove **Note:** Colorized

Date	Mintage	F	VF	XF	Unc	BU
2004 Proof	60,000	Value: 85.00				

KM# 1580 10 YUAN
31.1035 g., 0.9990 Silver 0.9990 oz. ASW, 40 mm. **Subject:** 600th Anniversary of Zheng He's voyage **Obv:** Multicolor stylized sailboat on water **Rev:** Ancient Chinese navigational instruments **Edge:** Reeded **Note:** Prev. Y#1239.

Date	Mintage	F	VF	XF	Unc	BU
2005(y) Proof	—	Value: 100				

KM# 1592 10 YUAN
31.1050 g., 0.9990 Silver gilt rim 0.9990 oz. ASW, 40 mm. **Obv:** Temple of Heaven **Rev:** Panda cub and mom seated in bamboo **Note:** Gilt rim

Date	Mintage	F	VF	XF	Unc	BU
2005 Proof	30,000	Value: 85.00				

KM# 1601 10 YUAN
31.1050 g., 0.9990 Silver 0.9990 oz. ASW, 40 mm. **Subject:** Foundation of Industrial & Commercial Bank **Obv:** Temple of Heaven, gilt rim **Rev:** Panda cub and mom seated in bamboo

Date	Mintage	F	VF	XF	Unc	BU
2005 Proof	100,000	Value: 70.00				

KM# 1603 10 YUAN
31.1050 g., 0.9990 Silver 0.9990 oz. ASW, 40 mm. **Subject:** 100th Anniversary of Bank of Shanghai **Obv:** Temple of Heaven **Rev:** Panda cub and mom seated in bamboo

Date	Mintage	F	VF	XF	Unc	BU
2005 Proof	50,000	Value: 80.00				

KM# 1618 10 YUAN
31.1050 g., 0.9990 Silver 0.9990 oz. ASW, 40 mm. **Subject:** 2006 World Cup - Germany **Obv:** Multicolor logo **Rev:** Classical soccer player and goal net **Note:** Prev - Y1255, KM1670

Date	Mintage	F	VF	XF	Unc	BU
2005 Proof	50,000	Value: 90.00				

KM# 1626 10 YUAN
31.1050 g., 0.9990 Silver 0.9990 oz. ASW, 40 mm. **Subject:** 600th Anniversary - Zheng He's Voyages **Obv:** Multicolor logo **Rev:** Nautical invention

Date	Mintage	F	VF	XF	Unc	BU
2005 Proof	60,000	Value: 85.00				

KM# 1628 10 YUAN
31.1050 g., 0.9990 Silver 0.9990 oz. ASW, 40 mm. **Subject:** Chen Yun Birth Centennial **Obv:** House **Rev:** Half-length figure facing

Date	Mintage	F	VF	XF	Unc	BU
2005 Proof	15,000	Value: 140				

KM# 1629 10 YUAN
31.1050 g., 0.9990 Silver 0.9990 oz. ASW, 40 mm. **Subject:** Chen Yun Birth Centennial **Obv:** House **Rev:** Figure seated in chair, arm outstretched

Date	Mintage	F	VF	XF	Unc	BU
2005 Proof	15,000	Value: 140				

KM# 1631 10 YUAN
31.1050 g., 0.9990 Silver 0.9990 oz. ASW, 40 mm. **Subject:** 60th Anniversary of Victory - War of Resistance **Obv:** Monument **Rev:** People celebrating

Date	Mintage	F	VF	XF	Unc	BU
2005 Proof	30,000	Value: 140				

KM# 1636 10 YUAN
31.1050 g., 0.9990 Silver 0.9990 oz. ASW, 40 mm. **Series:** Classical Literature **Obv:** Horseman on arch bridge **Rev:** Multicolor monkey and female

Date	Mintage	F	VF	XF	Unc	BU
2005 Proof	38,000	Value: 130				

KM# 1637 10 YUAN
31.1050 g., 0.9990 Silver 0.9990 oz. ASW, 40 mm. **Series:** Classical Literature **Obv:** Horseman on arch bridge **Rev:** Multicolor man slaying spider on web

Date	Mintage	F	VF	XF	Unc	BU
2005 Proof	38,000	Value: 130				

KM# 1639 10 YUAN
31.1050 g., 0.9990 Silver 0.9990 oz. ASW, 40 mm. **Subject:** Chinese Movie Centennial **Obv:** Winged column **Rev:** Old time movie camera

Date	Mintage	F	VF	XF	Unc	BU
2005 Proof	60,000	Value: 85.00				

KM# 1670 10 YUAN
31.1035 g., 0.9990 Silver 0.9990 oz. ASW **Subject:** World Cup Soccer **Obv:** Colorized logo **Rev:** Classically dressed athlete scoring goal **Note:** Prev. Y#1255.

Date	Mintage	F	VF	XF	Unc	BU
2006 Proof	—	Value: 100				

KM# 1666 10 YUAN
31.1050 g., 0.9990 Silver 0.9990 oz. ASW, 40 mm. **Obv:** Temple of Heaven **Rev:** Two pandas seated with bamboo

Date	Mintage	F	VF	XF	Unc	BU
2006 Proof	50,000	Value: 75.00				

KM# 1668 10 YUAN
31.1050 g., 0.9990 Silver 0.9990 oz. ASW, 40 mm. **Subject:** 10th Anniversary of China Minsheng Banking Corp **Obv:** Temple of Heaven **Rev:** Two pandas seated with bamboo

Date	Mintage	F	VF	XF	Unc	BU
2006 Proof	70,000	Value: 85.00				

KM# A1670 10 YUAN
31.1050 g., 0.9990 Silver 0.9990 oz. ASW, 40 mm. **Subject:** Shengang Horticultural Expo **Obv:** Temple of Heaven **Rev:** Two pandas seated with bamboo

Date	Mintage	F	VF	XF	Unc	BU
2006 Proof	30,000	Value: 85.00				

KM# 1675 10 YUAN
31.1050 g., 0.9990 Silver 0.9990 oz. ASW, 40 mm. **Subject:** 10th Anniversary Jinan City Commercial Bank **Obv:** Temple of Heaven **Rev:** Two pandas seated with bamboo

Date	Mintage	F	VF	XF	Unc	BU
2006 Proof	20,000	Value: 85.00				

KM# 1676 10 YUAN
31.1050 g., 0.9990 Silver Gold plated outer ring 0.9990 oz. ASW, 40 mm. **Subject:** Beijing International Stamp and Coin Expo **Obv:** Temple of Heaven **Rev:** Two pandas seated with bamboo

Date	Mintage	F	VF	XF	Unc	BU
2006 Proof	20,000	Value: 100				

KM# 1690 10 YUAN
31.1050 g., 0.9990 Silver 0.9990 oz. ASW, 40 mm. **Subject:** Yvelv Academy **Obv:** Front door of Academy **Rev:** Exterior view

Date	Mintage	F	VF	XF	Unc	BU
2006 Proof	40,000	Value: 85.00				

KM# 1691 10 YUAN
31.1050 g., 0.9990 Silver 0.9990 oz. ASW, 40 mm. **Subject:** Qinghai - Tibet Railway Opening **Obv:** Lhasa Railway Station with mountains in background **Rev:** Yvante Bridge over the Yangtze River and tibetan antelope and yak

Date	Mintage	F	VF	XF	Unc	BU
2006 Proof	36,000	Value: 150				

KM# 1693 10 YUAN
31.1050 g., 0.9990 Silver 0.9990 oz. ASW, 40 mm. **Obv:** Map of marches and hammer and sickle **Rev:** Group of marchers in snow

Date	Mintage	F	VF	XF	Unc	BU
2006 Proof	25,000	Value: 110				

KM# 1729 10 YUAN
31.1050 g., 0.9990 Silver 0.9990 oz. ASW, 40 mm. **Subject:** 60th Anniversary - Foundry of Mongolia Autonomous Region **Obv:** Wheel of Mongolian Lele Cart **Rev:** Grassland view of Mongolia, huts and horsemen

Date	Mintage	F	VF	XF	Unc	BU
2007 Proof	20,000	Value: 110				

KM# 1702 10 YUAN
31.1050 g., 0.9990 Silver 0.9990 oz. ASW **Subject:** 2007 Summer Olympics **Obv:** Beijing Olympic logo **Rev:** Child with kite, multicolor design **Shape:** 40 **Note:** Issued in 2006

Date	Mintage	F	VF	XF	Unc	BU
2008 Proof	160,000	Value: 45.00				

KM# 1703 10 YUAN
31.1050 g., 0.9990 Silver 0.9990 oz. ASW, 40 mm. **Subject:** 2007 Summer Olympics **Obv:** Beijing Olympics logo **Rev:** Two children playing leapfrog, multicolor **Note:** Issued in 2006

Date	Mintage	F	VF	XF	Unc	BU
2008 Proof	16,000	Value: 65.00				

KM# 1704 10 YUAN
31.1050 g., 0.9990 Silver 0.9990 oz. ASW, 40 mm. **Subject:** 2007 Summer Olympics **Obv:** Beijing Olympics logo **Rev:** Child rolling ring with stick, multicolor **Note:** Issued in 2006

Date	Mintage	F	VF	XF	Unc	BU
2008 Proof	160,000	Value: 55.00				

KM# 1705 10 YUAN
31.1050 g., 0.9990 Silver 0.9990 oz. ASW, 40 mm. **Subject:** 2007 Summer Olympics **Obv:** Beijing Olympic's logo **Rev:** Young girl dancing, multicolor **Note:** Issued in 2006

Date	Mintage	F	VF	XF	Unc	BU
2008 Proof	160,000	Value: 55.00				

KM# 1825 10 YUAN
31.1050 g., 0.9990 Silver 0.9990 oz. ASW, 40 mm. **Subject:** Bank of Communications, Centennial

Date	Mintage	F	VF	XF	Unc	BU
2008 Proof	—	Value: 85.00				

KM# 1843 10 YUAN
31.1050 g., 0.9990 Silver 0.9990 oz. ASW, 40 mm. **Subject:** Beijing Olympics **Rev:** Multicolor mask, stall tea scene

Date	Mintage	F	VF	XF	Unc	BU
2008 Proof	160,000	Value: 55.00				

KM# 1844 10 YUAN
31.1050 g., 0.9990 Silver 0.9990 oz. ASW, 40 mm. **Subject:** Beijing Olympics **Rev:** Multicolor mask, lion dancer

Date	Mintage	F	VF	XF	Unc	BU
2008 Proof	160,000	Value: 55.00				

KM# 1845 10 YUAN
31.1050 g., 0.9990 Silver 0.9990 oz. ASW, 40 mm. **Subject:** Beijing Olympics **Rev:** Multicolor mask, Yangtze dancer

Date	Mintage	F	VF	XF	Unc	BU
2008 Proof	160,000	Value: 55.00				

KM# 1846 10 YUAN
31.1050 g., 0.9990 Silver 0.9990 oz. ASW, 40 mm. **Subject:** Beijing Olympics **Rev:** Multicolor mask, Beijing Opera

Date	Mintage	F	VF	XF	Unc	BU
2008 Proof	160,000	Value: 45.00				

KM# 1852 10 YUAN
31.1050 g., 0.9990 Silver 0.9990 oz. ASW, 40 mm. **Subject:** Hainan Special Economic Zone

Date	Mintage	F	VF	XF	Unc	BU
2008 Proof	20,000	Value: 90.00				

KM# 1854 10 YUAN
31.1050 g., 0.9990 Silver 0.9990 oz. ASW, 40 mm. **Subject:** Para Olympics

Date	Mintage	F	VF	XF	Unc	BU
2008 Proof	30,000	Value: 100				

KM# 1856 10 YUAN
31.1050 g., 0.9990 Silver 0.9990 oz. ASW, 40 mm. **Subject:** Ningxia Hui Autonomous Region

Date	Mintage	F	VF	XF	Unc	BU
2008 Proof	20,000	Value: 105				

KM# 1858 10 YUAN
31.1050 g., 0.9990 Silver 0.9990 oz. ASW, 40 mm. **Subject:** Beijing Coin and Stamp Expo

Date	Mintage	F	VF	XF	Unc	BU
2008 Proof	30,000	Value: 75.00				

KM# 1859 10 YUAN
31.1050 g., 0.9990 Silver 0.9990 oz. ASW, 40 mm. **Subject:** Guangxi Zhuang Autonomous Region

Date	Mintage	F	VF	XF	Unc	BU
2008 Proof	20,000	Value: 90.00				

KM# 1907 10 YUAN
31.1050 g., 0.9990 Silver 0.9990 oz. ASW, 40 mm. **Subject:** Shanghai Expo

Date	Mintage	F	VF	XF	Unc	BU
2009 Proof	—	Value: 60.00				

KM# 1891 10 YUAN
31.1050 g., 0.9990 Silver 0.9990 oz. ASW, 40 mm. **Subject:** Precious Metal Commemoratives, 30th Anniversary

Date	Mintage	F	VF	XF	Unc	BU
2009	300,000	—	—	—	—	40.00

KM# 1892 10 YUAN
31.1050 g., 0.9990 Silver 0.9990 oz. ASW, 40 mm. **Subject:** Beijing International Coin & Stamp Show

Date	Mintage	F	VF	XF	Unc	BU
2009	30,000	—	—	—	—	60.00

KM# 1896 10 YUAN
31.1050 g., 0.9990 Silver 0.9990 oz. ASW, 40 mm. **Subject:** P.R.C. 60th Anniversary

Date	Mintage	F	VF	XF	Unc	BU
2009 Proof	100,000	Value: 50.00				

KM# 1898 10 YUAN
31.1050 g., 0.9990 Silver 0.9990 oz. ASW, 40 mm. **Subject:** P.R.C. 60th Anniversary **Rev:** Multicolor

Date	Mintage	F	VF	XF	Unc	BU
2009 Proof	100,000	Value: 55.00				

KM# 1902 10 YUAN
31.1050 g., 0.9990 Silver 0.9990 oz. ASW, 40 mm. **Subject:** Outlaws of the Marsh, series 1 **Rev:** Multicolor

Date	Mintage	F	VF	XF	Unc	BU
2009 Proof	60,000	Value: 60.00				

KM# 1903 10 YUAN
31.1050 g., 0.9990 Silver 0.9990 oz. ASW, 40 mm. **Subject:** Outlaws of the Marsh, series 1 **Rev:** Multicolor

Date	Mintage	F	VF	XF	Unc	BU
2009 Proof	60,000	Value: 60.00				

KM# 1905 10 YUAN
31.1050 g., 0.9990 Silver 0.9990 oz. ASW, 40 mm. **Subject:** 16th Asian Games

Date	Mintage	F	VF	XF	Unc	BU
2009 Proof	60,000	Value: 48.00				

KM# 1908 10 YUAN
31.1050 g., 0.9990 Silver 0.9990 oz. ASW, 40 mm. **Subject:** Shanghai Expo

Date	Mintage	F	VF	XF	Unc	BU
2009 Proof	—	Value: 48.00				

KM# 1910 10 YUAN
31.1050 g., 0.9990 Silver 0.9990 oz. ASW, 40 mm. **Subject:** China Agricultural Bank

Date	Mintage	F	VF	XF	Unc	BU
2009	100,000	—	—	—	—	40.00

KM# 1939 10 YUAN
31.1050 g., 0.9990 Silver 0.9990 oz. ASW, 40 mm. **Series:** Outlaws of the Marsh, series 2 **Rev:** Multicolor

Date	Mintage	F	VF	XF	Unc	BU
2010 Proof	70,000	Value: 60.00				

KM# 1940 10 YUAN
31.1050 g., 0.9990 Silver 0.9990 oz. ASW, 40 mm. **Series:** Outlaws of the Marsh, series 2 **Rev:** Multicolor

Date	Mintage	F	VF	XF	Unc	BU
2010 Proof	70,000	Value: 60.00				

KM# 1942 10 YUAN
10.3600 g., 0.9990 Gold 0.3327 oz. AGW **Subject:** Shanghai World Expo, 2010

Date	Mintage	F	VF	XF	Unc	BU
2010 Proof	60,000	Value: 550				

KM# 1943 10 YUAN
31.1050 g., 0.9990 Silver 0.9990 oz. ASW, 40 mm. **Subject:** Shanghai World Expo, 2010

Date	Mintage	F	VF	XF	Unc	BU
2010 Proof	80,000	Value: 60.00				

KM# 1944 10 YUAN
31.1050 g., 0.9990 Silver 0.9990 oz. ASW, 40 mm. **Subject:** Shanghai World Expo, 2010

Date	Mintage	F	VF	XF	Unc	BU
2010 Proof	80,000	Value: 60.00				

KM# 1946 10 YUAN
31.1050 g., 0.9990 Silver 0.9990 oz. ASW, 40 mm. **Subject:** Wudang Mountain

Date	Mintage	F	VF	XF	Unc	BU
2010 Proof	60,000	Value: 60.00				

KM# 1953 10 YUAN
31.1050 g., 0.9990 Silver 0.9990 oz. ASW **Subject:** Shenzhen Economic Zone

Date	Mintage	F	VF	XF	Unc	BU
2010 Proof	30,000	Value: 60.00				

KM# 1955 10 YUAN
31.1050 g., 0.9990 Silver 0.9990 oz. ASW, 40 mm. **Subject:** 16th Asian Games

Date	Mintage	F	VF	XF	Unc	BU
2010 Proof	60,000	Value: 60.00				

KM# 1957 10 YUAN
31.1050 g., 0.9990 Silver 0.9990 oz. ASW, 40 mm. **Subject:** Bejing Opera, series 1 **Rev:** Multicolor face mask

Date	Mintage	F	VF	XF	Unc	BU
2010 Proof	50,000	Value: 60.00				

KM# 1958 10 YUAN
31.1050 g., 0.9990 Silver 0.9990 oz. ASW, 40 mm. **Subject:** Bejing Opera, series 1 **Rev:** Multicolor face mask

Date	Mintage	F	VF	XF	Unc	BU
2010 Proof	50,000	Value: 60.00				

KM# 1959 10 YUAN
31.1050 g., 0.9990 Silver 0.9990 oz. ASW, 40 mm. **Subject:** Bejing Stamp & Coin Expo

Date	Mintage	F	VF	XF	Unc	BU
2010 Proof	30,000	Value: 60.00				

KM# 1388 20 YUAN
62.2070 g., 0.9990 Silver 1.9979 oz. ASW, 40 mm. **Subject:** Mogao Grottos **Obv:** 8-story building **Rev:** Buddha-like statue **Edge:** Reeded **Note:** Prev. Y#1082.

Date	Mintage	F	VF	XF	Unc	BU
2001 Proof	30,000	Value: 150				

KM# 1432 20 YUAN
62.2070 g., 0.9990 Silver 1.9979 oz. ASW, 40 mm. **Rev:** Buddha-like statue

Date	Mintage	F	VF	XF	Unc	BU
2002 Proof	30,000	Value: 150				

KM# 1563 20 YUAN
31.1035 g., 0.9990 Silver 0.9990 oz. ASW, 40 mm. **Series:** Maijishan grotto art **Rev:** Two figures standing

Date	Mintage	F	VF	XF	Unc	BU
2004 Proof	20,000	Value: 90.00				

KM# 1390 50 YUAN
155.5175 g., 0.9990 Silver 4.9948 oz. ASW, 70 mm. **Subject:** Mogao Grottoes **Obv:** Eight story building **Rev:** Four musicians **Edge:** Reeded. **Note:** Prev. Y#1083.

Date	Mintage	F	VF	XF	Unc	BU
2001 Proof	8,000	Value: 300				

KM# 1389 50 YUAN
3.1104 g., 0.9990 Gold 0.0999 oz. AGW **Subject:** Mogao Grottoes **Obv:** Eight story building **Rev:** Buddha-like statue **Edge:** Reeded. **Note:** Prev. Y#1084.

Date	Mintage	F	VF	XF	Unc	BU
2001 Proof	50,000	Value: 250				

KM# 1394 50 YUAN
155.5175 g., 0.9990 Silver 4.9948 oz. ASW, 90 x 40 mm. **Subject:** Han Xizai's Dinner Party **Obv:** Tang Dynasty buildings **Rev:** Multicolor "Five Dynasties" painting **Edge:** Plain **Shape:** Rectangular **Note:** Prev. Y#1104.

Date	Mintage	F	VF	XF	Unc	BU
2001 Proof	18,800	Value: 275				

KM# 1386 50 YUAN
155.5175 g., 0.9990 Silver 4.9948 oz. ASW, 90x40 mm. **Series:** Folk fairy tails **Rev:** Seven multicolor figures on beach **Shape:** Rectangle

Date	Mintage	F	VF	XF	Unc	BU
2001 Proof	10,000	Value: 300				

KM# 1402 50 YUAN
155.5190 g., 0.9990 Silver 4.9948 oz. ASW, 90 x 50 mm. **Subject:** Bejing opera **Rev:** Four multicolor actors **Shape:** Rectangle

Date	Mintage	F	VF	XF	Unc	BU
2001 Proof	11,800	Value: 300				

KM# 1433 50 YUAN
155.5190 g., 0.9990 Silver 4.9948 oz. ASW, 70 mm. **Series:** Long men grottoes **Rev:** Two figures

Date	Mintage	F	VF	XF	Unc	BU
2002 Proof	8,000	Value: 300				

KM# 1445 50 YUAN
155.5190 g., 0.9990 Silver 4.9948 oz. ASW, 65x26 mm. **Series:** Classic literature **Rev:** Multicolor crowd of women **Shape:** Fan-like

Date	Mintage	F	VF	XF	Unc	BU
2002 Proof	11,800	Value: 200				

KM# 1430 50 YUAN
155.7900 g., 0.9990 Silver 5.0035 oz. ASW, 90x40 mm. **Series:** Folk fairy tails **Rev:** Multicolor female with red ribbon **Shape:** Rectangle

Date	Mintage	F	VF	XF	Unc	BU
2002 Proof	—	Value: 375				

KM# 1437 50 YUAN
3.1100 g., 0.9990 Gold 0.0999 oz. AGW, 18 mm. **Subject:** Kuan yin **Rev. Designer:** Female holding child, hologram

Date	Mintage	F	VF	XF	Unc	BU
2002 Proof	33,000	Value: 225				

KM# 1453 50 YUAN
155.5190 g., 0.9990 Silver 4.9948 oz. ASW, 90x40 mm. **Series:** Bejing opera **Rev:** Three multicolor characters one with spikes in costume **Shape:** Rectangle

Date	Mintage	F	VF	XF	Unc	BU
2002 Proof	11,800	Value: 300				

KM# 1493 50 YUAN
155.3500 g., 0.9990 Silver 4.9894 oz. ASW, 90x40 mm. **Series:** Fairy tails **Rev:** Multicolor man with two boys in buckets, jenole in flight at left **Shape:** Rectangle

Date	Mintage	F	VF	XF	Unc	BU
2003 Proof	10,000	Value: 350				

KM# 1512 50 YUAN
3.1104 g., 0.9990 Gold 0.0999 oz. AGW, 18 mm. **Obv:** Putuo Mountain Pilgrimage Gate **Rev:** Seated Kuanyin with holographic background **Edge:** Reeded **Note:** Prev. Y#1234.

Date	Mintage	F	VF	XF	Unc	BU
2003 Proof	33,000	Value: 225				

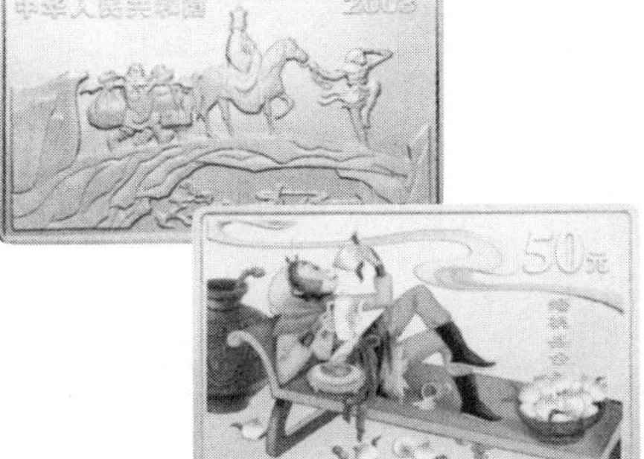

KM# 1502 50 YUAN
155.5000 g., 0.9990 Silver 4.9942 oz. ASW, 80x50 mm. **Series:** Class literature **Rev:** Multicolor man lying on couch **Shape:** Rectangle

Date	Mintage	F	VF	XF	Unc	BU
2003 Proof	10,000	Value: 350				

KM# 1503 50 YUAN
155.1500 g., 0.9990 Silver 4.9830 oz. ASW, 65 x 125 mm. **Series:** Class literature **Rev:** Six people **Shape:** Arc **Note:** Colorized

Date	Mintage	F	VF	XF	Unc	BU
2003 Proof	11,800	Value: 350				

KM# 1572 50 YUAN
3.1100 g., 0.9990 Gold 0.0999 oz. AGW, 18 mm. **Obv:** Putuo Mountain Pilgrimage Gate **Rev:** Kuanyin and value **Edge:** Reeded **Note:** Prev. Y#1237.

Date	Mintage	F	VF	XF	Unc	BU
2004 Proof	33,000	Value: 225				

KM# 1560 50 YUAN
155.5175 g., 0.9990 Silver 4.9948 oz. ASW, 80x50 mm. **Obv:** Monkey King leading the Master over bridge **Rev:** Multicolor Monkey King fighting the Pig Demon of Bones **Edge:** Plain **Shape:** Rectangle **Note:** Prev. Y#1216.

Date	Mintage	F	VF	XF	Unc	BU
2004 Proof	10,000	Value: 375				

KM# 1635 50 YUAN
155.0000 g., 0.9990 Silver 4.9782 oz. ASW, 80 x 50 mm. **Series:** Classical Literature **Obv:** Horseman on arch bridge **Rev:** Multicolor female and lion **Shape:** Rectangle **Note:** Illustration reduced.

Date	Mintage	F	VF	XF	Unc	BU
2005 Proof	10,000	Value: 350				

KM# 1901 50 YUAN
155.5000 g., 0.9990 Silver 4.9942 oz. ASW, 80x50 mm. **Subject:** Outlaws of the Marsh, series 1 **Rev:** Multicolor **Shape:** Rectangle

Date	Mintage	F	VF	XF	Unc	BU
2009 Proof	10,000	Value: 250				

KM# 1938 50 YUAN
155.5000 g., 0.9990 Silver 4.9942 oz. ASW **Subject:** Outlaws of the Marsh, series 2 **Rev:** Multicolor **Shape:** Regtangle

Date	Mintage	F	VF	XF	Unc	BU
2010 Proof	12,000	Value: 225				

KM# 1951 50 YUAN
62.1000 g., 0.9990 Silver 1.9945 oz. ASW **Subject:** Yungang Grotto Art

Date	Mintage	F	VF	XF	Unc	BU
2010 Proof	20,000	Value: 120				

KM# 1514 100 YUAN
3.1013 g., 0.9990 Platinum 0.0996 oz. APW, 18 mm. **Series:** Guan Yi

Date	Mintage	F	VF	XF	Unc	BU
2003 Proof	33,000	Value: 225				

KM# 1534 100 YUAN
15.5500 g., 0.9990 Palladium 0.4994 oz., 27 mm. **Obv:** Temple of Heaven **Rev:** Panda mother and cub, "kissing pandas" **Edge:** Reeded **Note:** Prev. Y#1211.

Date	Mintage	F	VF	XF	Unc	BU
2004 Proof	8,000	Value: 550				

KM# 1573 100 YUAN
3.1100 g., 0.9995 Platinum 0.0999 oz. APW, 18 mm. **Obv:** Putuo Mountain Pilgrimage Gate **Rev:** Kuanyin and value **Edge:** Reeded **Note:** Prev. Y#1238.

Date	Mintage	F	VF	XF	Unc	BU
2004 Proof	33,000	Value: 225				

KM# 1540 100 YUAN
7.8500 g., 0.9990 Gold 0.2521 oz. AGW, 22 mm. **Subject:** 20th Anniversary / Bank of China Industrial and Commercial **Rev:** Panda walking with cub

Date	Mintage	F	VF	XF	Unc	BU
2004 Proof	50,000	Value: 425				

KM# 1542 100 YUAN
7.8400 g., 0.9990 Gold 0.2518 oz. AGW, 22 mm. **Subject:** 50th Anniversary China Construction Bank **Rev:** Panda walking with cub

Date	Mintage	F	VF	XF	Unc	BU
2004 Proof	60,000	Value: 400				

KM# 1600 100 YUAN
7.7700 g., 0.9990 Gold 0.2496 oz. AGW, 22 mm. **Subject:** Foundation of Industrial & Commercial Bank **Obv:** Temple of Heaven **Rev:** Panda cub and mom seated in bamboo

Date	Mintage	F	VF	XF	Unc	BU
2005 Proof	40,000	Value: 500				

KM# 1602 100 YUAN
7.7700 g., 0.9990 Gold 0.2496 oz. AGW, 22 mm. **Subject:** 100th Anniversary of Bank of Shanghai **Obv:** Temple of Heaven **Rev:** Panda cub and mom seated in bamboo

Date	Mintage	F	VF	XF	Unc	BU
2005 Proof	40,000	Value: 500				

KM# 1616 100 YUAN
7.7000 g., 0.9990 Gold 0.2473 oz. AGW, 22 mm. **Subject:** 2006 World Cup - Germany **Obv:** Multicolor logo **Rev:** Temple of Heaven and soccer ball

Date	Mintage	F	VF	XF	Unc	BU
2005 Proof	10,000	Value: 550				

KM# A979 100 YUAN
8.5000 g., 0.9990 Gold 0.2730 oz. AGW, 22 mm. **Subject:** 10th Anniversary Bank of Beijing **Obv:** Temple of Heaven **Rev:** Two pandas

Date	Mintage	F	VF	XF	Unc	BU
2006	100	—	—	—	—	800

KM# A980 100 YUAN
8.5000 g., 0.9990 Gold 0.2730 oz. AGW, 22 mm. **Subject:** 10th Anniversary China Minsheng Banking Corp. **Obv:** Temple of Heaven **Rev:** Two Pandas munching on bamboo

Date	Mintage	F	VF	XF	Unc	BU
2006	100	—	—	—	—	800

KM# 1665 100 YUAN
7.7700 g., 0.9990 Gold 0.2496 oz. AGW, 22 mm. **Subject:** 10th Anniversary Bank of Beijing **Obv:** Temple of Heaven **Rev:** Two pandas seated with bamboo

Date	Mintage	F	VF	XF	Unc	BU
2006 Proof	150,000	Value: 375				

KM# 1667 100 YUAN
7.7700 g., 0.9990 Silver 0.2496 oz. ASW, 22 mm. **Subject:** 10th Anniversary - China Minsheng Banking Corp **Obv:** Temple of Heaven **Rev:** Two pandas seated with bamboo

Date	Mintage	F	VF	XF	Unc	BU
2006 Proof	20,000	Value: 550				

KM# 1669 100 YUAN
7.7700 g., 0.9990 Gold 0.2496 oz. AGW, 22 mm. **Subject:** Shenyang Horticultural Expo **Obv:** Temple of Heaven **Rev:** Two pandas seated with bamboo

Date	Mintage	F	VF	XF	Unc	BU
2006 Proof	10,000	Value: 550				

KM# 1694 100 YUAN
7.7700 g., 0.9990 Gold 0.2496 oz. AGW, 22 mm. **Subject:** Qinghai - Tibet Railway Opening **Obv:** Map of railway route and track layer **Rev:** Kun Lun Tunnel Portal

Date	Mintage	F	VF	XF	Unc	BU
2006 Proof	16,000	Value: 550				

KM# 1730 100 YUAN
7.7700 g., 0.9990 Gold 0.2496 oz. AGW, 22 mm. **Subject:** 60th Anniversary - Foundry of Mongolia Autonomous Region **Obv:** Wheel of Mongolian Lele Cart **Rev:** Female Mongolian in posture of welcome

Date	Mintage	F	VF	XF	Unc	BU
2007 Proof	10,000	Value: 550				

KM# 1824 100 YUAN
7.7700 g., 0.9990 Gold 0.2496 oz. AGW, 23 mm. **Subject:** Bank of Communications, Centennial **Rev:** Panda

Date	Mintage	F	VF	XF	Unc	BU
2008 Proof	10,000	Value: 550				

KM# 1853 100 YUAN
7.7700 g., 0.9990 Gold 0.2496 oz. AGW **Subject:** Hainan Special Economic Zone

Date	Mintage	F	VF	XF	Unc	BU
2008 Proof	10,000	Value: 550				

KM# 1857 100 YUAN
7.7700 g., 0.9990 Gold 0.2496 oz. AGW **Subject:** Ningxia Hui Autonomous Region

Date	Mintage	F	VF	XF	Unc	BU
2008 Proof	10,000	Value: 550				

KM# 1860 100 YUAN
7.7700 g., 0.9990 Gold 0.2496 oz. AGW **Subject:** Guangzi Zhuang Autonomous Region

Date	Mintage	F	VF	XF	Unc	BU
2008 Proof	10,000	Value: 550				

KM# 1890 100 YUAN
7.7700 g., 0.9990 Gold 0.2496 oz. AGW **Subject:** Precious Metal Commemoratives, 30th Anniversary

Date	Mintage	F	VF	XF	Unc	BU
2009	10,000	—	—	—	—	550

KM# 1895 100 YUAN
7.7700 g., 0.9990 Gold 0.2496 oz. AGW, 22 mm. **Subject:** P.R.C. 60th Anniversary

Date	Mintage	F	VF	XF	Unc	BU
2009 Proof	100,000	Value: 400				

KM# 1904 100 YUAN
7.7700 g., 0.9990 Gold 0.2496 oz. AGW, 22 mm. **Subject:** 16th Asian Games

Date	Mintage	F	VF	XF	Unc	BU
2009 Proof	30,000	Value: 500				

KM# 1909 100 YUAN
7.7700 g., 0.9990 Gold 0.2496 oz. AGW, 22 mm. **Subject:** China Agricultural Bank

Date	Mintage	F	VF	XF	Unc	BU
2009	100,000	—	—	—	—	400

KM# 1945 100 YUAN
7.7700 g., 0.9990 Gold 0.2496 oz. AGW **Subject:** Wudang Mountain

Date	Mintage	F	VF	XF	Unc	BU
2010 Proof	30,000	Value: 500				

KM# 1952 100 YUAN
7.7700 g., 0.9990 Gold 0.2496 oz. AGW **Subject:** Shenzhen Economic Zone

Date	Mintage	F	VF	XF	Unc	BU
2010 Proof	20,000	Value: 500				

KM# 1954 100 YUAN
7.7700 g., 0.9990 Gold 0.2496 oz. AGW **Subject:** 16th Asian Games

Date	Mintage	F	VF	XF	Unc	BU
2010 Proof	30,000	Value: 500				

KM# 1956 100 YUAN
7.7700 g., 0.9990 Gold 0.2496 oz. AGW **Subject:** Bejing Opera, series 1 **Rev:** Multicolor

Date	Mintage	F	VF	XF	Unc	BU
2010 Proof	30,000	Value: 500				

KM# 1488 150 YUAN
10.0500 g., 0.9990 Gold 0.3228 oz. AGW, 23 mm. **Subject:** Spring festival **Obv:** Tree with berries **Rev:** Two Koi in ribbon sea

Date	Mintage	F	VF	XF	Unc	BU
2003 Proof	50,000	Value: 600				

KM# 1511 150 YUAN
10.1300 g., 0.9990 Gold 0.3253 oz. AGW, 23 mm. **Subject:** Space flight **Rev:** Multicolor astronaut and ship

Date	Mintage	F	VF	XF	Unc	BU
2003 Proof	30,000	Value: 625				

KM# 1556 150 YUAN
10.5000 g., 0.9990 Gold 0.3372 oz. AGW, 23 mm. **Series:** Folk customs **Subject:** Lantern Festival **Rev:** Boy holding lantern **Note:** Colorized

Date	Mintage	F	VF	XF	Unc	BU
2004 Proof	20,000	Value: 650				

KM# 1638 150 YUAN
10.0500 g., 0.9990 Gold 0.3228 oz. AGW, 23 mm. **Subject:** Chinese Movie Centennial **Obv:** Winged column **Rev:** Movie clipboard

Date	Mintage	F	VF	XF	Unc	BU
2005 Proof	20,000	Value: 650				

KM# 1848 150 YUAN
10.1000 g., 0.9990 Gold 0.3244 oz. AGW, 23 mm. **Subject:** Beijing Olympics **Obv:** Beijing Olympics **Rev:** Classical soccer player

Date	Mintage	F	VF	XF	Unc	BU
2008 Proof	60,000	Value: 600				

KM# 1847 150 YUAN
10.1000 g., 0.9990 Gold 0.3244 oz. AGW, 23 mm. **Subject:** Beijing Olympics **Rev:** Classical wrestlers

Date	Mintage	F	VF	XF	Unc	BU
2008 Proof	60,000	Value: 600				

KM# 1700 150 YUAN
10.0500 g., 0.9990 Gold 0.3228 oz. AGW, 23 mm. **Subject:** 29th Summer Olympics **Obv:** Beijing Olympic logo **Rev:** Ancient horsemaid and new logo **Note:** Issued in 2006

Date	Mintage	F	VF	XF	Unc	BU
2008 Proof	60,000	Value: 600				

KM# 1701 150 YUAN
10.0500 g., 0.9990 Gold 0.3228 oz. AGW, 23 mm. **Subject:** 29th Summer Olympics **Obv:** Beijing Olympic logo **Rev:** Ancient archer and new logo **Note:** Issued in 2006

Date	Mintage	F	VF	XF	Unc	BU
2008 Proof	60,000	Value: 600				

KM# 1855 150 YUAN
10.1000 g., 0.9990 Gold 0.3244 oz. AGW **Subject:** Para Olympics

Date	Mintage	F	VF	XF	Unc	BU
2008 Proof	15,000	Value: 700				

KM# 1900 150 YUAN
10.3600 g., 0.9990 Gold 0.3327 oz. AGW, 23 mm. **Subject:** Outlaws of the Marsh, series 1 **Rev:** Multicolor

Date	Mintage	F	VF	XF	Unc	BU
2009 Proof	30,000	Value: 650				

KM# 1906 150 YUAN
10.3500 g., 0.9990 Gold 0.3324 oz. AGW **Subject:** Shanghai Expo

Date	Mintage	F	VF	XF	Unc	BU
2009 Proof	—	Value: 650				

KM# 1937 150 YUAN
10.3500 g., 0.9990 Gold 0.3324 oz. AGW **Subject:** Outlaws of the Marsh, series 2 **Rev:** Multicolor

Date	Mintage	F	VF	XF	Unc	BU
2010 Proof	35,000	Value: 650				

KM# 1941 150 YUAN
155.5500 g., 0.9990 Gold 4.9958 oz. AGW **Subject:** Shanghai World Expo, 2010

Date	Mintage	F	VF	XF	Unc	BU
2010 Proof	1,000	Value: 8,500				

KM# 1387 200 YUAN
15.5519 g., 0.9990 Gold 0.4995 oz. AGW, 27 mm. **Series:** Folk fairy tails **Rev:** Multicolor heroic figure putting ax to clouds

Date	Mintage	F	VF	XF	Unc	BU
2001 Proof	8,800	Value: 1,050				

KM# 1391 200 YUAN
15.5518 g., 0.9990 Gold 0.4995 oz. AGW, 27 mm. **Subject:** Mogao Grottoes **Obv:** Eight story building **Rev:** Dancing drummer **Edge:** Reeded. **Note:** Prev. Y#1085.

Date	Mintage	F	VF	XF	Unc	BU
2001 Proof	8,800	Value: 1,050				

KM# 1393 200 YUAN
15.5518 g., 0.9990 Gold 0.4995 oz. AGW, 27 mm. **Subject:** 50th Anniversary Chinese Occupation of Tibet **Obv:** Five stars **Rev:** Denomination in flower **Edge:** Reeded **Note:** Prev. Y#1087.

Date	Mintage	F	VF	XF	Unc	BU
2001 Proof	15,000	Value: 950				

KM# 1403 200 YUAN
15.5520 g., 0.9990 Gold 0.4995 oz. AGW, 27 mm. **Subject:** Bejing opera **Rev:** Multicolor ribbon dancer

Date	Mintage	F	VF	XF	Unc	BU
2001 Proof	8,000	Value: 1,100				

KM# 1431 200 YUAN
15.5000 g., 0.9990 Gold 0.4978 oz. AGW **Subject:** Art **Rev:** Multicolor male with snake and staff **Note:** Prev. Y#1148.

Date	Mintage	F	VF	XF	Unc	BU
2002 Proof	8,800	Value: 1,050				

KM# 1434 200 YUAN
15.5500 g., 0.9990 Gold 0.4994 oz. AGW, 27 mm. **Subject:** Buddha **Note:** Prev. Y#1145.

Date	Mintage	F	VF	XF	Unc	BU
2002 Proof	8,800	Value: 1,050				

KM# 1439 200 YUAN
15.5190 g., 0.9990 Gold 0.4984 oz. AGW, 27 mm. **Subject:** Sichuan Sanxingdui relics **Obv:** Museum building **Rev:** Face mask

Date	Mintage	F	VF	XF	Unc	BU
2002 Proof	8,800	Value: 1,050				

KM# 1440 200 YUAN
15.5000 g., 0.9990 Gold 0.4978 oz. AGW **Subject:** Ceremonial Mask **Note:** Prev. Y#1149.

Date	Mintage	F	VF	XF	Unc	BU
2002 Proof	5,000	Value: 1,100				

KM# 1446 200 YUAN
15.5000 g., 0.9990 Gold 0.4978 oz. AGW **Subject:** Dream of the Red Mansion **Shape:** Octagon **Note:** Prev. Y#1147.

Date	Mintage	F	VF	XF	Unc	BU
2002 Proof	8,000	Value: 1,100				

KM# 1454 200 YUAN
15.5000 g., 0.9990 Gold 0.4978 oz. AGW **Subject:** Peking Opera **Note:** Prev. Y#1146.

Date	Mintage	F	VF	XF	Unc	BU
2002 Proof	8,000	Value: 1,050				

KM# 1456 200 YUAN
15.5190 g., 0.9990 Gold 0.4984 oz. AGW, 27 mm. **Subject:** World Expo 2010 **Rev:** Skyline

Date	Mintage	F	VF	XF	Unc	BU
2002 Proof	5,000	Value: 1,100				

KM# 1494 200 YUAN
15.5519 g., 0.9999 Gold 0.4999 oz. AGW **Subject:** Chinese Mythical Folk Tales **Note:** Prev. Y#1160.

Date	Mintage	F	VF	XF	Unc	BU
2003 Proof	8,800	Value: 1,050				

KM# 1495 200 YUAN
15.5150 g., 0.9990 Gold 0.4983 oz. AGW, 27 mm. **Subject:** Finger Sarira of Sakyanmunt **Obv:** Tall tower **Rev:** Flora design

Date	Mintage	F	VF	XF	Unc	BU
2003 Proof	12,000	Value: 950				

KM# 1504 200 YUAN
15.5519 g., 0.9999 Gold 0.4999 oz. AGW **Subject:** Pilgrimage to the West **Note:** Prev. Y#1159.

Date	Mintage	F	VF	XF	Unc	BU
2003 Proof	11,800	Value: 950				

KM# 1506 200 YUAN
15.5130 g., 0.9990 Gold 0.4982 oz. AGW, 40 mm. **Series:** Classical literature **Rev:** Multicolor blue seated female **Shape:** Hexagon

Date	Mintage	F	VF	XF	Unc	BU
2003 Proof	8,000	Value: 1,050				

KM# 1509 200 YUAN
15.5150 g., 0.9990 Gold 0.4983 oz. AGW, 27 mm. **Series:** Wulingyan Scenic Resort

Date	Mintage	F	VF	XF	Unc	BU
2003 Proof	8,000	Value: 950				

KM# 1561 200 YUAN

15.5500 g., 0.9990 Gold 0.4994 oz. AGW, 27 mm. **Obv:** Monkey King leading the Master over bridge **Rev:** Multicolor Monkey King on one knee meeting the Master **Edge:** Reeded **Note:** Prev. Y#1217.

Date	Mintage	F	VF	XF	Unc	BU
2004 Proof	11,800	Value: 950				

KM# 1564 200 YUAN

15.5600 g., 0.9990 Gold 0.4997 oz. AGW, 27 mm. **Series:** Maijishan grotto art **Rev:** Buddha statue

Date	Mintage	F	VF	XF	Unc	BU
2004 Proof	8,800	Value: 1,050				

KM# 1567 200 YUAN

15.5518 g., 0.9990 Gold 0.4995 oz. AGW, 27 mm. **Obv:** Guangan Exposition Hall **Rev:** Deng Xiaoping and value **Edge:** Reeded **Note:** Prev. Y#1241.

Date	Mintage	F	VF	XF	Unc	BU
2004 Proof	10,000	Value: 950				

KM# 1571 200 YUAN

15.5500 g., 0.9990 Gold 0.4994 oz. AGW, 27 mm. **Obv:** National arms above People's Congress Hall and ornamental column **Rev:** Multicolor hologram depicting the hall's overhead lighting **Edge:** Reeded **Note:** Prev. Y#1213.

Date	Mintage	F	VF	XF	Unc	BU
2004 Proof	5,000	Value: 1,050				

KM# 1625 200 YUAN

15.5500 g., 0.9990 Gold 0.4994 oz. AGW, 27 mm. **Subject:** 600th Anniversary of Zheng He's Voyages **Obv:** Multicolor logo **Rev:** Zheng He portrait in linear form

Date	Mintage	F	VF	XF	Unc	BU
2005 Proof	6,000	Value: 950				

KM# 1627 200 YUAN

15.5500 g., 0.9990 Gold 0.4994 oz. AGW, 27 mm. **Subject:** Chen Yun Birth Centennial **Obv:** House **Rev:** Head 3/4 right

Date	Mintage	F	VF	XF	Unc	BU
2005 Proof	5,000	Value: 1,100				

KM# 1630 200 YUAN

15.5500 g., 0.9990 Gold 0.4994 oz. AGW, 27 mm. **Subject:** 60th Anniverasary of Victory - War of Resistance **Obv:** Monument **Rev:** Mob of Peoples Army

Date	Mintage	F	VF	XF	Unc	BU
2005 Proof	5,000	Value: 1,100				

KM# 1633 200 YUAN

15.5500 g., 0.9990 Gold 0.4994 oz. AGW, 27 mm. **Series:** Classical Literature **Obv:** Horseman on arch bridge **Rev:** Two multicolor women, one with monkey, other with rabbit

Date	Mintage	F	VF	XF	Unc	BU
2005 Proof	11,800	Value: 950				

KM# 1689 200 YUAN

15.5500 g., 0.9990 Gold 0.4994 oz. AGW, 27 mm. **Subject:** Yvelv Academy **Obv:** Front door of Academy **Rev:** Interior room

Date	Mintage	F	VF	XF	Unc	BU
2006 Proof	7,000	Value: 950				

KM# 1692 200 YUAN

15.5500 g., 0.9990 Gold 0.4994 oz. AGW, 27 mm. **Subject:** 70th Anniversary of Long March **Obv:** Route of the marches, hammer and sickle symbol **Rev:** Group of marchers advancing with rifles

Date	Mintage	F	VF	XF	Unc	BU
2006 Proof	10,000	Value: 950				

KM# 1949 200 YUAN

15.5500 g., 0.9990 Gold 0.4994 oz. AGW **Subject:** Yungang Grotto Art

Date	Mintage	F	VF	XF	Unc	BU
2010 Proof	10,000	Value: 975				

KM# 1435 300 YUAN

1000.0000 g., 0.9990 Silver 32.117 oz. ASW, 100 mm. **Series:** Long men grottoes **Rev:** Large female statue

Date	Mintage	F	VF	XF	Unc	BU
2002 Proof	8,000	Value: 1,750				

KM# 1513 300 YUAN

1000.0000 g., 0.9990 Silver 32.117 oz. ASW, 100 mm. **Series:** Guan Yi

Date	Mintage	F	VF	XF	Unc	BU
2003 Proof	3,800	Value: 3,500				

KM# 1568 300 YUAN

1000.0000 g., 0.9990 Silver 32.117 oz. ASW, 100 mm. **Obv:** Guangan Exposition Hall **Rev:** Deng Xiaoping and value **Edge:** Reeded **Note:** Prev. Y#1242.

Date	Mintage	F	VF	XF	Unc	BU
2004 Proof	5,000	Value: 1,850				

KM# 1579 300 YUAN

1000.0000 g., 0.9990 Silver 32.117 oz. ASW, 100 mm. **Series:** Kuan Yin **Rev:** Female seated holding flower

Date	Mintage	F	VF	XF	Unc	BU
2004 Proof	3,800	Value: 2,000				

KM# 1617 300 YUAN

1000.0000 g., 0.9990 Silver 32.117 oz. ASW, 100 mm. **Subject:** 2006 World Cup - Germany **Obv:** Multicolor logo **Rev:** World Cup Trophy

Date	Mintage	F	VF	XF	Unc	BU
2005 Proof	3,000	Value: 2,250				

KM# 1634 300 YUAN

1000.0000 g., 0.9990 Silver 32.117 oz. ASW, 100 mm. **Series:** Classical Literature **Obv:** Horseman on arch bridge **Rev:** Multicolor heavenly buddha

Date	Mintage	F	VF	XF	Unc	BU
2005 Proof	5,000	Value: 2,250				

KM# 1849 300 YUAN
1000.0000 g., 0.9990 Silver 32.117 oz. ASW, 100 mm. **Subject:** Beijing Olympics **Obv:** Multicolor logo **Rev:** Classical tug of war **Note:** Photo reduced.

Date	Mintage	F	VF	XF	Unc	BU
2008 Proof	20,008	Value: 2,250				

KM# 1897 300 YUAN
1000.0000 g., 0.9990 Silver 32.117 oz. ASW, 100 mm. **Subject:** P.R.C. 60th Anniversary

Date	Mintage	F	VF	XF	Unc	BU
2009 Proof	6,000	Value: 2,100				

KM# 1950 300 YUAN
1000.0000 g., 0.9990 Silver 32.117 oz. ASW **Subject:** Yungang Grotto Art

Date	Mintage	F	VF	XF	Unc	BU
2010 Proof	3,800	Value: 2,100				

KM# 1392 2000 YUAN
155.5175 g., 0.9990 Gold 4.9948 oz. AGW, 60 mm. **Subject:** Mogao Grottoes **Obv:** Eight story building **Rev:** Two dancers **Edge:** Reeded **Note:** Prev. #Y1086.

Date	Mintage	F	VF	XF	Unc	BU
2001 Proof	288	Value: 13,500				

KM# 1436 2000 YUAN
155.5175 g., 0.9990 Gold 4.9948 oz. AGW, 60 mm. **Subject:** Chinese grottos art - Longmen **Note:** Prev. #Y1151.

Date	Mintage	F	VF	XF	Unc	BU
2002	288	Value: 13,500				

KM# 1505 2000 YUAN
155.5000 g., 0.9990 Gold 4.9942 oz. AGW, 64 x 40 mm. **Series:** Class literature **Rev:** Two multicolor monkey kings **Shape:** Rectangle **Note:** Illustration reduced.

Date	Mintage	F	VF	XF	Unc	BU
2003 Proof	500	Value: 11,500				

KM# 1562 2000 YUAN
155.5175 g., 0.9990 Gold 4.9948 oz. AGW, 64x40 mm. **Obv:** Monkey King leading Master over bridge **Rev:** Multicolor Monkey King fighting the Pig "Demon of Bones" **Edge:** Plain **Shape:** Ingot **Note:** Prev. #Y1218. Illustration reduced.

Date	Mintage	F	VF	XF	Unc	BU
2004 Proof	500	Value: 11,500				

KM# 1565 2000 YUAN
155.5175 g., 0.9990 Gold 4.9948 oz. AGW, 60 mm. **Subject:** Maijishan Grottos **Obv:** Grotto view **Rev:** Buddha portrait within halo of flying devatas **Edge:** Reeded **Note:** Prev. #Y1206.

Date	Mintage	F	VF	XF	Unc	BU
2004(y) Proof	288	Value: 14,500				

KM# 1569 2000 YUAN
155.5175 g., 0.9990 Gold 4.9948 oz. AGW, 60 mm. **Obv:** Guangan Exposition Hall **Rev:** Deng Xiaoping and value **Edge:** Reeded **Note:** Prev. #Y1243.

Date	Mintage	F	VF	XF	Unc	BU
2004 Proof	600	Value: 13,500				

KM# 1632 2000 YUAN
155.0000 g., 0.9990 Gold 4.9782 oz. AGW, 64 x 40 mm. **Series:** Classic Literature Pilgrimage To The West **Obv:** Horseback rider on arch bridge **Rev:** Multicolor court scene **Shape:** Rectangle

Date	Mintage	F	VF	XF	Unc	BU
2005 Proof	500	Value: 13,500				

KM# 1850 2000 YUAN
155.5500 g., 0.9990 Gold 4.9958 oz. AGW, 60 mm. **Subject:** Beijing Olympics **Obv:** Multicolor logo **Rev:** Four sports

Date	Mintage	F	VF	XF	Unc	BU
2008 Proof	—	Value: 16,500				

KM# 1894 2000 YUAN
155.5000 g., 0.9990 Gold 4.9942 oz. AGW, 60 mm. **Subject:** P.R.C. 60th Anniversary

Date	Mintage	F	VF	XF	Unc	BU
2009 Proof	600	Value: 12,000				

KM# 1899 2000 YUAN
155.5000 g., 0.9990 Gold 4.9942 oz. AGW, 64c40 mm. **Subject:** Outlaws of the Marsh, series 1 **Rev:** Multicolor **Shape:** Rectangle

Date	Mintage	F	VF	XF	Unc	BU
2009 Proof	800	Value: 12,000				

KM# 1936 2000 YUAN
155.5500 g., 0.9990 Gold 4.9958 oz. AGW **Series:** Outlaws of the Marsh, series 2 **Rev:** Multicolor **Shape:** Rectangle

Date	Mintage	F	VF	XF	Unc	BU
2010 Proof	900	Value: 12,000				

KM# 1948 2000 YUAN
155.5000 g., 0.9990 Gold 4.9942 oz. AGW **Subject:** Yungang Grotto Art

Date	Mintage	F	VF	XF	Unc	BU
2010 Proof	800	Value: 12,000				

KM# 1893 10000 YUAN
1000.0000 g., 0.9990 Gold 32.117 oz. AGW, 90 mm. **Subject:** P.R.C. 60th Anniversary

Date	Mintage	F	VF	XF	Unc	BU
2009 Proof	100	Value: 50,000				

KM# 1947 10000 YUAN
1000.0000 g., 0.9990 Gold 32.117 oz. AGW **Subject:** Yungang Grotto Art

Date	Mintage	F	VF	XF	Unc	BU
2010 Proof	100	Value: 50,000				

KM# 1851 100000 YUAN
10000.0000 g., 0.9990 Gold 321.17 oz. AGW, 180 mm. **Subject:** Beijing Olympics **Obv:** Multicolor logo **Rev:** Sports montage, Temple of Heaven

Date	Mintage	F	VF	XF	Unc	BU
2008 Proof	29	Value: 650,000				

SILVER BULLION COINAGE

Lunar Series

KM# 1379 10 YUAN
30.8400 g., 0.9990 Silver 0.9905 oz. ASW, 39.9 mm. **Subject:** Year of the Snake **Obv:** Traditional style building **Rev:** Snake **Shape:** Scalloped **Note:** Prev. Y#1041.

Date	Mintage	F	VF	XF	Unc	BU
2001 Proof	6,800	Value: 165				

KM# 1382 10 YUAN
31.1035 g., 0.9990 Silver 0.9990 oz. ASW **Subject:** Year of the Snake **Shape:** Fan-like **Note:** Prev. Y#1042.

Date	Mintage	F	VF	XF	Unc	BU
2001	66,000	—	—	—	100	115

KM# 1375 10 YUAN
31.1035 g., 0.9990 Silver 0.9990 oz. ASW, 40 mm. **Subject:** Year of the Snake **Rev:** Multicolor

Date	Mintage	F	VF	XF	Unc	BU
2001 Proof	6,800	Value: 150				

KM# 1418 10 YUAN
31.1035 g., 0.9990 Silver 0.9990 oz. ASW, 40 mm. **Subject:** Year of the Horse **Obv:** Da Zheng Hall **Rev:** Stylized horse head **Edge:** Reeded **Note:** Prev. Y#1232.

Date	Mintage	F	VF	XF	Unc	BU
2002	50,000	—	—	—	—	140

KM# 1414 10 YUAN
31.1035 g., 0.9990 Silver 0.9990 oz. ASW, 40 mm. **Subject:** Year of the Horse **Rev:** Multicolor horse prancing right

Date	Mintage	F	VF	XF	Unc	BU
2002 Proof	10,000	Value: 150				

KM# 1423 10 YUAN
31.1035 g., 0.9990 Silver 0.9990 oz. ASW, 40 mm. **Subject:** Year of the Horse **Shape:** Fan-like

Date	Mintage	F	VF	XF	Unc	BU
2002 Proof	50,000	Value: 175				

KM# 1425 10 YUAN
31.1035 g., 0.9990 Silver 0.9990 oz. ASW, 40 mm. **Subject:** Year of the Horse **Shape:** Scalloped

Date	Mintage	F	VF	XF	Unc	BU
2002 Proof	6,800	Value: 190				

KM# A1477 10 YUAN
31.1035 g., 0.9990 Silver 0.9990 oz. ASW, 40 mm. **Subject:** Year of the Sheep

Date	Mintage	F	VF	XF	Unc	BU
2003 Proof	66,000	Value: 150				

KM# 1477 10 YUAN
31.1035 g., 0.9990 Silver 0.9990 oz. ASW, 40 mm. **Subject:** Year of the Sheep **Rev:** Multicolor

Date	Mintage	F	VF	XF	Unc	BU
2003 Proof	6,800	Value: 150				

KM# 1485 10 YUAN
31.1035 g., 0.9990 Silver 0.9990 oz. ASW, 30 x 85 mm. **Subject:** Year of the Sheep **Shape:** Fan-like

Date	Mintage	F	VF	XF	Unc	BU
2003 Proof	66,000	Value: 175				

KM# A1545 10 YUAN
31.1035 g., 0.9990 Silver 0.9990 oz. ASW, 40 mm. **Series:** Lunar New Year **Subject:** Year of the Monkey **Rev:** Multicolor monkey

Date	Mintage	F	VF	XF	Unc	BU
2004 Proof	—	Value: 150				

KM# 1545 10 YUAN
31.1035 g., 0.9990 Silver 0.9990 oz. ASW, 40 mm. **Series:** Lunar New Year **Subject:** Year of the Monkey

Date	Mintage	F	VF	XF	Unc	BU
2004 Proof	80,000	Value: 150				

KM# 1548 10 YUAN
31.1035 g., 0.9990 Silver 0.9990 oz. ASW, 40 mm. **Subject:** Lunar New Year **Rev:** Monkey **Shape:** Scalloped

Date	Mintage	F	VF	XF	Unc	BU
2004 Proof	6,800	Value: 190				

KM# 1553 10 YUAN
31.1035 g., 0.9990 Silver 0.9990 oz. ASW, 30 x 85 mm. **Series:** Lunar New Year **Subject:** Year of the Monkey **Rev:** Monkey **Shape:** Fan-like

Date	Mintage	F	VF	XF	Unc	BU
2004 Proof	66,000	Value: 175				

KM# 1612 10 YUAN
31.1050 g., 0.9990 Silver 0.9990 oz. ASW, 40 mm. **Subject:** Year of the rooster **Obv:** Classical rooster **Rev:** Multicolor rooster

Date	Mintage	F	VF	XF	Unc	BU
2005 Proof	100,000	Value: 190				

KM# 1613 10 YUAN
31.1050 g., 0.9990 Silver 0.9990 oz. ASW, 40 mm. **Subject:** Year of the rooster **Obv:** Classical rooster **Rev:** Rooster, hen and chicks **Shape:** Scallop

Date	Mintage	F	VF	XF	Unc	BU
2005 Proof	60,000	Value: 125				

KM# 1614 10 YUAN
31.1050 g., 0.9990 Silver 0.9990 oz. ASW, 40 mm. **Subject:** Year of the rooster **Obv:** Classical rooster **Rev:** Rooster, hen and chicks

Date	Mintage	F	VF	XF	Unc	BU
2005 Proof	8,000	Value: 150				

KM# 1615 10 YUAN
31.1050 g., 0.9990 Silver 0.9990 oz. ASW, 30 x 85 mm. **Subject:** Year of the rooster **Obv:** Temple **Rev:** Rooster, hen and chicks **Shape:** Fan-like **Note:** Photo reduced.

Date	Mintage	F	VF	XF	Unc	BU
2005 Proof	66,000	Value: 190				

KM# 1684 10 YUAN
31.1035 g., 0.9990 Silver 0.9990 oz. ASW, 40 mm. **Obv:** Dog-shaped belt-hook from ancient Chinese bronze ware, decorative design of dog tail-shaped plant leaves **Rev:** 2 smart dogs **Note:** Prev. Y#1225; 1657.

Date	Mintage	F	VF	XF	Unc	BU
2006	80,000	—	—	—	—	125

KM# 1685 10 YUAN
31.1035 g., 0.9990 Silver 0.9990 oz. ASW, 40 mm. **Obv:** Dog-shaped belt-hook depicted from ancient Chinese bronze ware and a decorative design of dog tail-shaped plant leaves **Rev:** 2 smart dogs **Shape:** Scalloped **Note:** Prev. Y#1223; KM#1655.

Date	Mintage	F	VF	XF	Unc	BU
2006 Proof	60,000	Value: 140				

KM# 1686 10 YUAN
31.1035 g., 0.9990 Silver 0.9990 oz. ASW **Obv:** Qing Yuan Gate of the China Great Wall **Rev:** 2 dogs at play **Shape:** Fan-like **Note:** Prev. Y#1219; KM#1651. Photo reduced.

Date	Mintage	F	VF	XF	Unc	BU
2006 Proof	66,000	Value: 165				

KM# 1687 10 YUAN
31.1035 g., 0.9990 Silver 0.9990 oz. ASW, 40 mm. **Obv:** Belt-hook in dog shape from Chinese ancient bronze ware and a decorative design of dog tail-shaped plant leaves **Rev:** 2 dogs at play **Note:** Prev. Y#1221; KM#1653.

Date	Mintage	F	VF	XF	Unc	BU
2006 Proof	100,000	Value: 125				

KM# 1716 10 YUAN
31.1050 g., 0.9990 Silver 0.9990 oz. ASW, 40 mm. **Subject:** Year of the Pig **Obv:** Classical pig **Rev:** Pig walking right

Date	Mintage	F	VF	XF	Unc	BU
2007 Proof	80,000	Value: 140				

KM# 1717 10 YUAN
31.1050 g., 0.9990 Silver 0.9990 oz. ASW, 40 mm. **Subject:** Year of the Pig **Obv:** Classical pig **Rev:** Multicolor sow and four piglets sucking

Date	Mintage	F	VF	XF	Unc	BU
2007 Proof	100,000	Value: 125				

KM# 1718 10 YUAN
31.1050 g., 0.9990 Silver 0.9990 oz. ASW, 85 x 60 mm. **Subject:** Year of the Pig **Obv:** Temple **Rev:** Sow and four pigletts **Shape:** Fan-like

Date	Mintage	F	VF	XF	Unc	BU
2007 Proof	66,000	Value: 190				

KM# 1719 10 YUAN
31.1050 g., 0.9990 Silver 0.9990 oz. ASW, 40 mm. **Subject:** Year of the Pig **Obv:** Classical pig **Rev:** Pig walking right **Shape:** Scalloped

Date	Mintage	F	VF	XF	Unc	BU
2007 Proof	60,000	Value: 140				

KM# 1830 10 YUAN
31.1050 g., 0.9990 Silver 0.9990 oz. ASW, 40 mm. **Rev:** Multicolor

Date	Mintage	F	VF	XF	Unc	BU
2008 Proof	—	Value: 55.00				

KM# 1831 10 YUAN
31.1050 g., 0.9990 Silver 0.9990 oz. ASW, 40 mm. **Subject:** Year of the Rat

Date	Mintage	F	VF	XF	Unc	BU
2008 Proof	—	Value: 140				

KM# 1832 10 YUAN
31.1050 g., 0.9990 Silver 0.9990 oz. ASW, 40 mm. **Subject:** Year of the Rat **Shape:** Scallop

Date	Mintage	F	VF	XF	Unc	BU
2008 Proof	—	Value: 140				

KM# 1833 10 YUAN
31.1050 g., 0.9990 Silver 0.9990 oz. ASW, 85 x 60 mm. **Subject:** Year of the Rat **Shape:** Fan-like

Date	Mintage	F	VF	XF	Unc	BU
2008 Proof	—	Value: 190				

KM# 1875 10 YUAN
31.1050 g., 0.9990 Silver 0.9990 oz. ASW, 40 mm. **Rev:** Multicolor

Date	Mintage	F	VF	XF	Unc	BU
2009 Proof	—	Value: 125				

KM# 1876 10 YUAN
31.1050 g., 0.9990 Silver 0.9990 oz. ASW, 40 mm. **Subject:** Year of the Ox

Date	Mintage	F	VF	XF	Unc	BU
2009 Proof	100,000	Value: 125				

KM# 1877 10 YUAN
31.1050 g., 0.9990 Silver 0.9990 oz. ASW **Subject:** Year of the Ox

Date	Mintage	F	VF	XF	Unc	BU
2009 Proof	66,000	Value: 140				

KM# 1878 10 YUAN
31.1050 g., 0.9990 Silver 0.9990 oz. ASW **Shape:** Fan-like

Date	Mintage	F	VF	XF	Unc	BU
2009 Proof	66,000	Value: 190				

KM# 1922 10 YUAN
31.1050 g., 0.9990 Silver 0.9990 oz. ASW **Subject:** Year of the Tiger **Shape:** Arc

Date	Mintage	F	VF	XF	Unc	BU
2010	66,000	—	—	—	—	100

KM# 1923 10 YUAN
31.1050 g., 0.9990 Silver 0.9990 oz. ASW **Subject:** Year of the Tiger **Shape:** Scalloped

Date	Mintage	F	VF	XF	Unc	BU
2010 Proof	60,000	Value: 100				

KM# 1924 10 YUAN
31.1050 g., 0.9990 Silver 0.9990 oz. ASW **Subject:** Year of the Tiger

Date	Mintage	F	VF	XF	Unc	BU
2010 Proof	100,000	Value: 100				

KM# 1925 10 YUAN
31.1050 g., 0.9990 Silver 0.9990 oz. ASW **Subject:** Year of the Tiger **Rev:** Multicolor

Date	Mintage	F	VF	XF	Unc	BU
2010 Proof	100,000	Value: 125				

KM# 1971 10 YUAN
31.1050 g., 0.9990 Silver 0.9990 oz. ASW **Subject:** Year of the Rabbit **Shape:** Arc

Date	Mintage	F	VF	XF	Unc	BU
2011	66,000	—	—	—	—	100

KM# 1972 10 YUAN
31.1050 g., 0.9990 Silver 0.9990 oz. ASW **Subject:** Year of the Rabbit **Shape:** Scalloped

Date	Mintage	F	VF	XF	Unc	BU
2011 Proof	60,000	Value: 100				

KM# 1973 10 YUAN
31.1050 g., 0.9990 Silver 0.9990 oz. ASW, 40 mm. **Subject:** Year of the Rabbit

Date	Mintage	F	VF	XF	Unc	BU
2011 Proof	100,000	Value: 100				

KM# 1974 10 YUAN
31.1050 g., 0.9990 Silver 0.9990 oz. ASW **Subject:** Year of the Rabbit **Rev:** Multicolor

Date	Mintage	F	VF	XF	Unc	BU
2011 Proof	100,000	Value: 100				

KM# 1377 50 YUAN
155.4400 g., 0.9990 Silver 4.9923 oz. ASW, 80.6 x 50.5 mm.

Subject: Year of the Snake **Obv:** Traditional style building **Rev:** Snake **Edge:** Plain **Shape:** Rectangle **Note:** Illustration reduced. Prev. Y#1040.

Date	Mintage	F	VF	XF	Unc	BU
2001 Proof	1,888	Value: 1,250				

KM# 1421 50 YUAN

155.5190 g., 0.9990 Silver 4.9948 oz. ASW, 80 x 50 mm. **Subject:** Year of the Horse **Rev:** Three horses running left **Shape:** Rectangle

Date	Mintage	F	VF	XF	Unc	BU
2002 Proof	1,888	Value: 1,250				

KM# 1484 50 YUAN

155.5000 g., 0.9990 Silver 4.9942 oz. ASW, 80 x 50 mm. **Subject:** Year of the Sheep **Shape:** Rectangle

Date	Mintage	F	VF	XF	Unc	BU
2003 Proof	1,888	Value: 1,250				

KM# 1551 50 YUAN

155.5000 g., 0.9990 Silver 4.9942 oz. ASW, 80 x 50 mm. **Series:** Lunar New Year **Subject:** Year of the Monkey **Rev:** Monkey **Shape:** Rectangle **Note:** Photo reduced.

Date	Mintage	F	VF	XF	Unc	BU
2004 Proof	1,888	Value: 1,250				

KM# 1611 50 YUAN

155.0000 g., 0.9990 Silver 4.9782 oz. ASW, 80 x 50 mm. **Subject:** Year of the Rooster **Obv:** Classical rooster **Rev:** Rooster, hen and chicks **Shape:** Rectangle **Note:** Photo reduced.

Date	Mintage	F	VF	XF	Unc	BU
2005 Proof	1,888	Value: 1,250				

KM# 1683 50 YUAN

155.4400 g., 0.9990 Silver 4.9923 oz. ASW, 60 x 50 mm. **Subject:** Year of the Dog **Obv:** Classical dog **Rev:** Two dogs **Shape:** Rectangle **Note:** Photo reduced.

Date	Mintage	F	VF	XF	Unc	BU
2006 Proof	1,888	Value: 1,250				

KM# 1720 50 YUAN

155.5500 g., 0.9990 Silver 4.9958 oz. ASW, 80 x 50 mm. **Subject:** Year of the Pig **Obv:** Classical pig **Rev:** Sow and four piglets **Shape:** Rectangle

Date	Mintage	F	VF	XF	Unc	BU
2007 Proof	1,888	Value: 1,250				

KM# 1834 50 YUAN

155.5000 g., 0.9990 Silver 4.9942 oz. ASW, 80 x 50 mm. **Subject:** Year of the Rat **Shape:** Rectangle

Date	Mintage	F	VF	XF	Unc	BU
2008 Proof	—	Value: 1,250				

KM# 1879 50 YUAN

Silver **Subject:** Year of the Ox

Date	Mintage	F	VF	XF	Unc	BU
2009 Proof	1,888	Value: 1,250				

KM# 1920 50 YUAN

155.5000 g., 0.9990 Silver 4.9942 oz. ASW **Subject:** Year of the Tiger **Shape:** Rectangle

Date	Mintage	F	VF	XF	Unc	BU
2010 Proof	1,888	Value: 1,250				

KM# 1921 50 YUAN

155.5000 g., 0.9990 Silver 4.9942 oz. ASW **Subject:** Year of the Tiger

Date	Mintage	F	VF	XF	Unc	BU
2010 Proof	8,800	Value: 850				

KM# 1969 50 YUAN

155.5000 g., 0.9990 Silver 4.9942 oz. ASW, 80x50 mm. **Subject:** Year of the Rabbit **Shape:** Rectangle **Note:** Photo reduced.

Date	Mintage	F	VF	XF	Unc	BU
2011 Proof	1,888	Value: 1,250				

KM# 1970 50 YUAN

155.5000 g., 0.9990 Silver 4.9942 oz. ASW **Subject:** Year of the Rabbit **Rev:** Multicolor

Date	Mintage	F	VF	XF	Unc	BU
2011 Proof	8,800	Value: 750				

KM# 1420 300 YUAN

1000.0000 g., 0.9990 Silver 32.117 oz. ASW, 100 mm. **Series:** Lunar **Subject:** Year of the Horse

Date	Mintage	F	VF	XF	Unc	BU
2002 Proof	3,800	Value: 6,500				

KM# 1479 300 YUAN

1000.0000 g., 0.9990 Silver 32.117 oz. ASW, 100 mm. **Subject:** Year of the Sheep

Date	Mintage	F	VF	XF	Unc	BU
2003 Proof	3,800	Value: 7,500				

KM# 1547 300 YUAN

1000.0000 g., 0.9990 Silver 32.117 oz. ASW, 100 mm. **Series:** Lunar New Year **Subject:** Year of the Monkey **Rev:** Monkey

Date	Mintage	F	VF	XF	Unc	BU
2004 Proof	3,800	Value: 9,000				

KM# 1610 300 YUAN

1000.0000 g., 0.9990 Silver 32.117 oz. ASW, 100 mm. **Subject:** Year of the Rooster **Obv:** Classical rooster **Rev:** Rooster strutting **Note:** Photo reduced.

Date	Mintage	F	VF	XF	Unc	BU
2005 Proof	3,800	Value: 5,000				

KM# 1682 300 YUAN

1000.0000 g., 0.9990 Silver 32.117 oz. ASW, 100 mm. **Obv:** Dog-shaped belt-hook from ancient Chinese bronze ware, decorative design of dog tail-shaped plant leaves **Rev:** 2 dogs **Note:** Prev. Y#1227; KM#1659. Photo reduced.

Date	Mintage	F	VF	XF	Unc	BU
2006 Proof	3,800	Value: 4,500				

KM# 1725 300 YUAN
1000.0000 g., 0.9990 Silver 32.117 oz. ASW, 100 mm. **Subject:** Year of the Pig **Obv:** Classical pig **Rev:** Three pigs

Date	Mintage	F	VF	XF	Unc	BU
2007 Proof	3,800	Value: 5,000				

KM# 1839 300 YUAN
1000.0000 g., 0.9990 Silver 32.117 oz. ASW, 100 mm. **Subject:** Year of the Rat

Date	Mintage	F	VF	XF	Unc	BU
2008 Proof	—	Value: 5,000				

KM# 1884 300 YUAN
1000.0000 g., 0.9990 Silver 32.117 oz. ASW **Subject:** Year of the Ox

Date	Mintage	F	VF	XF	Unc	BU
2009 Proof	3,800	Value: 5,000				

KM# 1919 300 YUAN
1000.0000 g., 0.9990 Silver 32.117 oz. ASW **Subject:** Year of the Tiger

Date	Mintage	F	VF	XF	Unc	BU
2010 Proof	3,800	Value: 4,500				

KM# 1968 300 YUAN
1000.0000 g., 0.9990 Silver 32.117 oz. ASW, 100 mm. **Subject:** Year of the Rabbit **Note:** Photo reduced.

Date	Mintage	F	VF	XF	Unc	BU
2011 Proof	1,888	Value: 1,250				

SILVER BULLION COINAGE

Panda Series

KM# 1772 3 YUAN
7.7700 g., 0.9990 Silver 0.2496 oz. ASW, 25 mm. **Obv:** Temple of Heaven **Rev:** Panda seated on rock

Date	Mintage	F	VF	XF	Unc	BU
2007 Proof	30,000	Value: 30.00				

KM# 1780 3 YUAN
7.7700 g., 0.9990 Silver 0.2496 oz. ASW, 25 mm. **Obv:** Temple of Heaven **Rev:** Panda looking forward

Date	Mintage	F	VF	XF	Unc	BU
2007 Proof	30,000	Value: 30.00				

KM# 1740 3 YUAN
7.7700 g., 0.9990 Silver 0.2496 oz. ASW, 25 mm. **Obv:** Temple of Heaven **Rev:** Panda seated with branch

Date	Mintage	F	VF	XF	Unc	BU
2007 Proof	30,000	Value: 30.00				

KM# 1742 3 YUAN
7.7700 g., 0.9990 Silver 0.2496 oz. ASW, 25 mm. **Obv:** Temple of Heaven **Rev:** Panda walking right

Date	Mintage	F	VF	XF	Unc	BU
2007 Proof	30,000	Value: 30.00				

KM# 1744 3 YUAN
7.7700 g., 0.9990 Silver 0.2496 oz. ASW, 25 mm. **Obv:** Temple of Heaven **Rev:** Panda seated with bamboo branch

Date	Mintage	F	VF	XF	Unc	BU
2007 Proof	30,000	Value: 30.00				

KM# 1746 3 YUAN
7.7700 g., 0.9990 Silver 0.2496 oz. ASW **Obv:** Temple of Heaven **Rev:** Panda hanging from branch

Date	Mintage	F	VF	XF	Unc	BU
2007 Proof	30,000	Value: 30.00				

KM# 1748 3 YUAN
7.7700 g., 0.9990 Silver 0.2496 oz. ASW, 25 mm. **Obv:** Temple of Heaven **Rev:** Panda walking forward

Date	Mintage	F	VF	XF	Unc	BU
2007 Proof	30,000	Value: 30.00				

KM# 1750 3 YUAN
7.7700 g., 0.9990 Silver 0.2496 oz. ASW, 25 mm. **Obv:** Temple of Heaven **Rev:** Panda drinking water

Date	Mintage	F	VF	XF	Unc	BU
2007 Proof	30,000	Value: 30.00				

KM# 1752 3 YUAN
7.7700 g., 0.9990 Silver 0.2496 oz. ASW, 25 mm. **Obv:** Tample of Heaven **Rev:** Panda seated in oval with branch

Date	Mintage	F	VF	XF	Unc	BU
2007 Proof	30,000	Value: 30.00				

KM# 1754 3 YUAN
7.7700 g., 0.9990 Silver 0.2496 oz. ASW, 25 mm. **Obv:** Temple of Heaven **Rev:** Panda seated on geometric background

Date	Mintage	F	VF	XF	Unc	BU
2007 Proof	30,000	Value: 30.00				

KM# 1756 3 YUAN
7.7700 g., 0.9990 Silver 0.2496 oz. ASW, 10 mm. **Obv:** Temple of Heaven **Rev:** Panda on rock

Date	Mintage	F	VF	XF	Unc	BU
2007 Proof	30,000	Value: 30.00				

KM# 1758 3 YUAN
7.7700 g., 0.9990 Silver 0.2496 oz. ASW, 25 mm. **Obv:** Temple of Heaven **Rev:** Panda seated on river bank

Date	Mintage	F	VF	XF	Unc	BU
2007 Proof	30,000	Value: 30.00				

KM# 1760 3 YUAN
7.7700 g., 0.9990 Silver 0.2496 oz. ASW, 25 mm. **Obv:** Temple of Heaven **Rev:** Panda on tree branch

Date	Mintage	F	VF	XF	Unc	BU
2007 Proof	30,000	Value: 30.00				

KM# 1762 3 YUAN
7.7700 g., 0.9990 Silver 0.2496 oz. ASW, 25 mm. **Obv:** Temple of Heaven **Rev:** Panda on rock ledge

Date	Mintage	F	VF	XF	Unc	BU
2007 Proof	30,000	Value: 30.00				

KM# 1764 3 YUAN
7.7700 g., 0.9990 Silver 0.2496 oz. ASW, 25 mm. **Obv:** Temple of Heaven **Rev:** Panda seated munching bamboo

Date	Mintage	F	VF	XF	Unc	BU
2007 Proof	30,000	Value: 30.00				

KM# 1766 3 YUAN
7.7700 g., 0.9990 Silver 0.2496 oz. ASW, 25 mm. **Obv:** Temple of Heaven **Rev:** Panda pulling bamboo

Date	Mintage	F	VF	XF	Unc	BU
2007 Proof	30,000	Value: 30.00				

KM# 1768 3 YUAN
7.7700 g., 0.9990 Silver 0.2496 oz. ASW, 25 mm. **Obv:** Temple of Heaven **Rev:** Panda in tree

Date	Mintage	F	VF	XF	Unc	BU
2007 Proof	30,000	Value: 30.00				

KM# 1770 3 YUAN
7.7700 g., 0.9990 Silver 0.2496 oz. ASW, 25 mm. **Obv:** Temple of Heaven **Rev:** Panda looking over branch

Date	Mintage	F	VF	XF	Unc	BU
2007 Proof	30,000	Value: 30.00				

KM# 1774 3 YUAN
7.7700 g., 0.9990 Silver 0.2496 oz. ASW, 25 mm. **Obv:** Temple of Heaven **Rev:** Panda looking out over rock

Date	Mintage	F	VF	XF	Unc	BU
2007 Proof	30,000	Value: 30.00				

KM# A1776 3 YUAN
7.7700 g., 0.9990 Silver 0.2496 oz. ASW, 25 mm. **Obv:** Temple of Heaven **Rev:** Panda seated on frosted background

Date	Mintage	F	VF	XF	Unc	BU
2007 Proof	30,000	Value: 30.00				

KM# 1778 3 YUAN
7.7700 g., 0.9990 Silver 0.2496 oz. ASW, 25 mm. **Obv:** Temple of Heaven **Rev:** Panda walking amongst bamboo

Date	Mintage	F	VF	XF	Unc	BU
2007 Proof	30,000	Value: 30.00				

KM# 1782 3 YUAN
7.7700 g., 0.9990 Silver 0.2496 oz. ASW, 25 mm. **Obv:** Temple of Heaven **Rev:** Panda and cub walking right

Date	Mintage	F	VF	XF	Unc	BU
2007 Proof	30,000	Value: 30.00				

KM# 1784 3 YUAN
7.7700 g., 0.9990 Silver 0.2496 oz. ASW, 25 mm. **Obv:** Temple of Heaven **Rev:** Panda seated with cub on left

Date	Mintage	F	VF	XF	Unc	BU
2007 Proof	30,000	Value: 30.00				

KM# 1786 3 YUAN
7.7700 g., 0.9990 Silver 0.2496 oz. ASW, 25 mm. **Obv:** Temple of Heaven **Rev:** Panda seated with cub on right

Date	Mintage	F	VF	XF	Unc	BU
2007 Proof	30,000	Value: 30.00				

KM# 1788 3 YUAN
7.7700 g., 0.9990 Silver 0.2496 oz. ASW, 25 mm. **Obv:** Temple of Heaven **Rev:** Panda seated with cub, both munching bamboo

Date	Mintage	F	VF	XF	Unc	BU
2007 Proof	30,000	Value: 30.00				

KM# 1365 10 YUAN
31.1035 g., 0.9990 Silver 0.9990 oz. ASW, 40.1 mm. **Obv:** Temple of Heaven with incuse legend **Rev:** Panda walking left through bamboo **Edge:** Oblique reeding **Note:** Large and small date varieties exist. Prev. Y#1111.

Date	Mintage	F	VF	XF	Unc	BU
2001	250,000	—	—	—	41.25	48.75
2001 D Proof	—	Value: 75.00				
2002 Proof	—	Value: 75.00				

KM# A1365 10 YUAN
31.2300 g., 0.9990 Silver 1.0030 oz. ASW, 40 mm. **Obv:** Temple of Heaven, incuse legend **Rev:** Multicolor panda walking in bamboo **Edge:** Slanted reeding **Note:** Large and small date varieties exist.

Date	Mintage	F	VF	XF	Unc	BU
2002 Proof	—	Value: 90.00				

Note: Privately colored

KM# 1466 10 YUAN
31.1035 g., 0.9990 Silver 0.9990 oz. ASW, 40 mm. **Obv:** Temple of Heaven **Rev:** Panda eating bamboo in a frosted circle **Edge:** Slant reeded **Note:** Prev. Y#1244.

Date	Mintage	F	VF	XF	Unc	BU
2003 Proof	—	Value: 90.00				

KM# 1528 10 YUAN
31.1035 g., 0.9990 Silver 0.9990 oz. ASW, 40 mm. **Obv:** Temple of Heaven **Rev:** Panda nuzzling her cub **Edge:** Slant reeded **Note:** Prev. Y#1245.

Date	Mintage	F	VF	XF	Unc	BU
2004 Proof	—	Value: 90.00				

KM# 1589 10 YUAN
31.1050 g., 0.9990 Silver 0.9990 oz. ASW, 40 mm. **Obv:** Temple of Heaven **Rev:** Panda cub and mom seated in bamboo

Date	Mintage	F	VF	XF	Unc	BU
2005 Proof	60,000	Value: 90.00				

KM# 1664 10 YUAN
31.1050 g., 0.9990 Silver 0.9990 oz. ASW, 40 mm. **Obv:** Temple of Heaven **Rev:** Two pandas seated with bamboo

Date	Mintage	F	VF	XF	Unc	BU
2006 Proof	600,000	Value: 75.00				

KM# 1706 10 YUAN
31.1050 g., 0.9990 Silver 0.9990 oz. ASW, 40 mm. **Obv:** Temple of Heaven **Rev:** Two pandas, one walking, one seated

Date	Mintage	F	VF	XF	Unc	BU
2007 Proof	600,000	Value: 75.00				

KM# 1865 10 YUAN
31.1050 g., 0.9990 Silver 0.9990 oz. ASW, 40 mm. **Obv:** Temple of Heaven **Rev:** Adult panda at left, facing left, cub on right facing left, cub seated

Date	Mintage	F	VF	XF	Unc	BU
2008 Proof	—	Value: 60.00				

KM# 1814 10 YUAN
31.1050 g., 0.9990 Silver 0.9990 oz. ASW, 40 mm. **Rev:** Panda cub pawing mom

Date	Mintage	F	VF	XF	Unc	BU
2008 Proof	—	Value: 60.00				

KM# 1931 10 YUAN
31.1050 g., 0.9990 Silver 0.9990 oz. ASW **Obv:** Temple of Heaven **Rev:** Two pandas, one lying on back

Date	Mintage	F	VF	XF	Unc	BU
2010	800,000	—	—	—	—	60.00

KM# 1468 50 YUAN
151.5000 g., 0.9990 Silver 4.8658 oz. ASW, 80 x 50 mm. **Rev. Designer:** Panda and bamboo **Shape:** Rectangle

Date	Mintage	F	VF	XF	Unc	BU
2003 Proof	1,888	Value: 1,150				

KM# 1530 50 YUAN
155.5000 g., 0.9990 Silver 4.9942 oz. ASW, 70 mm. **Rev:** Panda walking with cub **Note:** Illustration reduced.

Date	Mintage	F	VF	XF	Unc	BU
2004 Proof	10,000	Value: 600				

KM# 1588 50 YUAN
155.0000 g., 0.9990 Silver 4.9782 oz. ASW, 70 mm. **Obv:** Temple of Heaven **Rev:** Panda cub and mom seated in bamboo

Date	Mintage	F	VF	XF	Unc	BU
2005 Proof	10,000	Value: 550				

KM# 1663 50 YUAN
155.5500 g., 0.9990 Silver 4.9958 oz. ASW, 70 mm. **Obv:** Temple of Heaven **Rev:** Two pandas seated with bamboo

Date	Mintage	F	VF	XF	Unc	BU
2006 Proof	10,000	Value: 550				

KM# 1708 50 YUAN
155.5500 g., 0.9990 Silver 4.9958 oz. ASW, 70 mm. **Obv:** Temple of Heaven **Rev:** Two pandas, one walking, one seated

Date	Mintage	F	VF	XF	Unc	BU
2007 Proof	10,000	Value: 550				

KM# 1867 50 YUAN
155.5000 g., 0.9990 Silver 4.9942 oz. ASW

Date	Mintage	F	VF	XF	Unc	BU
2008 Proof	—	Value: 550				

KM# 1816 50 YUAN
155.5000 g., Silver, 70 mm. **Rev:** Panda cub pawing mom

Date	Mintage	F	VF	XF	Unc	BU
2008 Proof	—	Value: 550				

KM# 1935 50 YUAN
155.5500 g., 0.9990 Silver 4.9958 oz. ASW **Obv:** Temple of Heaven **Rev:** Two pandas, one lying on back

Date	Mintage	F	VF	XF	Unc	BU
2010 Proof	10,000	Value: 650				

KM# 1370 300 YUAN
1000.0000 g., 0.9990 Silver 32.117 oz. ASW, 100 mm. **Rev:** Panda walking thru bamboo

Date	Mintage	F	VF	XF	Unc	BU
2001 D Proof	2,000	Value: 2,500				

KM# 1416 300 YUAN
1000.0000 g., 0.9990 Silver 32.117 oz. ASW, 100 mm. **Subject:** Panda Coinage 20th Anniversary **Obv:** Temple of Heaven **Rev:** Two gold inserts with the 1982 and 2002 panda designs on bamboo leaves **Edge:** Plain **Note:** Large and small date varieties exist. Prev. Y#1116.

Date	Mintage	F	VF	XF	Unc	BU
2002 Proof	6,000	Value: 2,000				

KM# 1473 300 YUAN
1000.0000 g., 0.9990 Silver 32.117 oz. ASW **Rev:** Panda and bamboo **Shape:** 100

Date	Mintage	F	VF	XF	Unc	BU
2003 Proof	7,500	Value: 7,500				

KM# 1536 300 YUAN
1000.0000 g., 0.9990 Silver 32.117 oz. ASW, 100 mm. **Rev:** Panda walking with cub

Date	Mintage	F	VF	XF	Unc	BU
2004 Proof	4,000	Value: 9,000				

KM# 1587 300 YUAN
1000.0000 g., 0.9990 Silver 32.117 oz. ASW, 100 mm. **Obv:**

Temple of Heaven **Rev:** Panda cub and mom seated in bamboo **Note:** Photo reduced.

Date	Mintage	F	VF	XF	Unc	BU
2005 Proof	4,000	Value: 2,250				

KM# 1662 300 YUAN
1000.0000 g., 0.9990 Silver 32.117 oz. ASW, 100 mm. **Obv:** Temple of Heaven **Rev:** Two pandas seated with bamboo **Note:** Photo reduced.

Date	Mintage	F	VF	XF	Unc	BU
2006 Proof	4,000	Value: 2,250				

KM# 1712 300 YUAN
1000.0000 g., 0.9990 Silver 32.117 oz. ASW, 100 mm. **Obv:** Temple of Heaven **Rev:** Two pandas, one walking, one seated

Date	Mintage	F	VF	XF	Unc	BU
2007 Proof	4,000	Value: 2,250				

KM# 1820 300 YUAN
1000.0000 g., 0.9990 Silver 32.117 oz. ASW, 100 mm. **Rev:** Panda cub pawing mom

Date	Mintage	F	VF	XF	Unc	BU
2008 Proof	—	Value: 4,000				

KM# 1871 300 YUAN
1000.0000 g., 0.9990 Silver 32.117 oz. ASW

Date	Mintage	F	VF	XF	Unc	BU
2008 Proof	—	Value: 4,000				

KM# 1934 300 YUAN
1000.0000 g., 0.9990 Silver 32.117 oz. ASW **Obv:** Temple of Heaven **Rev:** Two pandas, one lying on back

Date	Mintage	F	VF	XF	Unc	BU
2010 Proof	4,000	Value: 1,500				

GOLD BULLION COINAGE

Panda Series

KM# 1779 15 YUAN
1.2400 g., 0.9990 Gold 0.0398 oz. AGW, 12 mm. **Obv:** Temple of Heaven **Rev:** Panda walking amongst bamboo

Date	Mintage	F	VF	XF	Unc	BU
2007 Proof	18,000	Value: 95.00				

KM# 1741 15 YUAN
1.2400 g., 0.9990 Gold 0.0398 oz. AGW, 12 mm. **Obv:** Temple of Heaven **Rev:** Panda seated with branch

Date	Mintage	F	VF	XF	Unc	BU
2007 Proof	18,000	Value: 95.00				

KM# 1743 15 YUAN
1.2400 g., 0.9990 Gold 0.0398 oz. AGW, 12 mm. **Obv:** Temple of heaven **Rev:** Panda walking right

Date	Mintage	F	VF	XF	Unc	BU
2007 Proof	18,000	Value: 95.00				

KM# 1745 15 YUAN
1.2400 g., 0.9990 Gold 0.0398 oz. AGW, 12 mm. **Obv:** Temple of heaven **Rev:** Panda seated with bamboo branch

Date	Mintage	F	VF	XF	Unc	BU
2007 Proof	18,000	Value: 95.00				

KM# 1747 15 YUAN
1.2400 g., 0.9990 Gold 0.0398 oz. AGW, 12 mm. **Obv:** Temple of Heaven **Rev:** Panda hanging from branch

Date	Mintage	F	VF	XF	Unc	BU
2007 Proof	18,000	Value: 95.00				

KM# 1749 15 YUAN
1.2400 g., 0.9990 Gold 0.0398 oz. AGW, 12 mm. **Obv:** Temple of Heaven **Rev:** Panda walking forward

Date	Mintage	F	VF	XF	Unc	BU
2007 Proof	18,000	Value: 95.00				

KM# 1751 15 YUAN
1.2400 g., 0.9990 Gold 0.0398 oz. AGW, 12 mm. **Obv:** Temple of Heaven **Rev:** Panda drinking water

Date	Mintage	F	VF	XF	Unc	BU
2007 Proof	18,000	Value: 95.00				

KM# 1753 15 YUAN
1.2400 g., 0.9990 Gold 0.0398 oz. AGW, 12 mm. **Obv:** Temple of Heaven **Rev:** Panda seated in oval with branch

Date	Mintage	F	VF	XF	Unc	BU
2007 Proof	18,000	Value: 95.00				

KM# 1755 15 YUAN
1.2400 g., 0.9990 Gold 0.0398 oz. AGW, 12 mm. **Rev:** Panda seated on geometric background

Date	Mintage	F	VF	XF	Unc	BU
2007 Proof	18,000	Value: 95.00				

KM# 1757 15 YUAN
1.2400 g., 0.9990 Gold 0.0398 oz. AGW, 12 mm. **Obv:** Temple of Heaven **Rev:** Panda on rock

Date	Mintage	F	VF	XF	Unc	BU
2007 Proof	18,000	Value: 95.00				

KM# 1759 15 YUAN
1.2400 g., 0.9990 Gold 0.0398 oz. AGW, 12 mm. **Obv:** Temple of Heaven **Rev:** Panda seated on river bank

Date	Mintage	F	VF	XF	Unc	BU
2007 Proof	18,000	Value: 95.00				

KM# 1761 15 YUAN
1.2400 g., 0.9990 Gold 0.0398 oz. AGW, 12 mm. **Obv:** Temple of Heaven **Rev:** Panda on tree branch

Date	Mintage	F	VF	XF	Unc	BU
2007 Proof	18,000	Value: 95.00				

KM# 1763 15 YUAN
1.2400 g., 0.9990 Gold 0.0398 oz. AGW, 12 mm. **Obv:** Temple of Heaven **Rev:** Panda on rock ledge

Date	Mintage	F	VF	XF	Unc	BU
2007 Proof	18,000	Value: 95.00				

KM# 1765 15 YUAN
1.2400 g., 0.9990 Gold 0.0398 oz. AGW, 12 mm. **Obv:** Temple of Heaven **Rev:** Panda seated munching bamboo

Date	Mintage	F	VF	XF	Unc	BU
2007 Proof	18,000	Value: 95.00				

KM# 1767 15 YUAN
1.2400 g., 0.9990 Gold 0.0398 oz. AGW **Obv:** Temple of Heaven **Rev:** Panda pulling bamboo **Shape:** 12

Date	Mintage	F	VF	XF	Unc	BU
2007 Proof	1,800	Value: 95.00				

KM# 1769 15 YUAN
1.2400 g., 0.9990 Gold 0.0398 oz. AGW, 12 mm. **Obv:** Temple of Heaven **Rev:** Panda in tree

Date	Mintage	F	VF	XF	Unc	BU
2007 Proof	18,000	Value: 95.00				

KM# 1771 15 YUAN
1.2400 g., 0.9990 Gold 0.0398 oz. AGW **Obv:** Temple of Heaven **Rev:** Panda looking over branch

Date	Mintage	F	VF	XF	Unc	BU
2007 Proof	18,000	Value: 95.00				

KM# 1773 15 YUAN
1.2400 g., 0.9990 Gold 0.0398 oz. AGW, 12 mm. **Obv:** Temple of Heaven **Rev:** Panda seated on rock

Date	Mintage	F	VF	XF	Unc	BU
2007 Proof	18,000	Value: 95.00				

KM# A1775 15 YUAN
1.2400 g., 0.9990 Gold 0.0398 oz. AGW, 12 mm. **Obv:** Temple of Heaven **Rev:** Panda looking out from rock

Date	Mintage	F	VF	XF	Unc	BU
2007 Proof	18,000	Value: 95.00				

KM# 1777 15 YUAN
1.2400 g., 0.9990 Gold 0.0398 oz. AGW, 12 mm. **Obv:** Temple of Heaven **Rev:** Panda seated on frosted background

Date	Mintage	F	VF	XF	Unc	BU
2007 Proof	18,000	Value: 95.00				

KM# 1781 15 YUAN
1.2400 g., 0.9990 Gold 0.0398 oz. AGW, 12 mm. **Obv:** Temple of Heaven **Rev:** Panda looking forward

Date	Mintage	F	VF	XF	Unc	BU
2007 Proof	18,000	Value: 95.00				

KM# 1783 15 YUAN
1.2400 g., 0.9990 Gold 0.0398 oz. AGW, 12 mm. **Obv:** Temple of Heaven **Rev:** Panda and cub walking right

Date	Mintage	F	VF	XF	Unc	BU
2007 Proof	18,000	Value: 95.00				

KM# 1785 15 YUAN
1.2400 g., 0.9990 Gold 0.0398 oz. AGW, 12 mm. **Obv:** Temple of Heaven **Rev:** Panda seated with cub on left

Date	Mintage	F	VF	XF	Unc	BU
2007 Proof	18,000	Value: 95.00				

KM# 1787 15 YUAN
1.2400 g., 0.9990 Gold 0.0398 oz. AGW, 12 mm. **Obv:** Temple of Heaven **Rev:** Panda seated with cub on right

Date	Mintage	F	VF	XF	Unc	BU
2007 Proof	18,000	Value: 95.00				

KM# 1789 15 YUAN
1.2400 g., 0.9990 Gold 0.0398 oz. AGW, 12 mm. **Obv:** Temple of Heaven **Rev:** Panda seated with cub, both munching bamboo

Date	Mintage	F	VF	XF	Unc	BU
2007 Proof	18,000	Value: 95.00				

KM# 1366 20 YUAN
1.5600 g., 0.9990 Gold 0.0501 oz. AGW, 14 mm. **Obv:** Temple of Heaven **Rev:** Panda walking left through bamboo **Edge:** Reeded **Note:** Large and small date varieties exist. Prev. Y#1112.

Date	Mintage	F	VF	XF	Unc	BU
2001	200,000	—	—	—	95.00	115
2001 D	Inc. above	—	—	—	95.00	115
2002	74,601	—	—	—	95.00	115

KM# 1467 20 YUAN
1.5552 g., 0.9999 Gold 0.0500 oz. AGW, 14.5 mm. **Subject:** Panda **Obv:** Temple of Heaven **Rev:** Panda facing, walking through bamboo **Edge:** Reeded **Note:** Large and small date varieties exist. Prev. Y#1154.

Date	Mintage	F	VF	XF	Unc	BU
2003	117,000	—	—	—	—	110

KM# 1529 20 YUAN
1.5552 g., 0.9999 Gold 0.0500 oz. AGW, 14 mm. **Rev:** Panda walking with cub **Note:** Large and small date varieties exist. Prev. Y#1172.

Date	Mintage	F	VF	XF	Unc	BU
2004	101,000	—	—	—	—	120

KM# 1586 20 YUAN
1.5500 g., 0.9990 Gold 0.0498 oz. AGW, 14 mm. **Obv:** Temple of Heaven **Rev:** Panda cub and mom seated in bamboo

Date	Mintage	F	VF	XF	Unc	BU
2005 Proof	89,500	Value: 125				

KM# 1661 20 YUAN
1.5552 g., 0.9990 Gold 0.0499 oz. AGW, 14 mm. **Obv:** Temple of Heaven **Rev:** Two pandas seated with bamboo

Date	Mintage	F	VF	XF	Unc	BU
2006 Proof	62,000	Value: 145				

KM# 1707 20 YUAN
1.5552 g., 0.9990 Gold 0.0499 oz. AGW, 14 mm. **Obv:** Temple of Heaven **Rev:** Two pandas, one walking, one seated

Date	Mintage	F	VF	XF	Unc	BU
2007 Proof	200,000	Value: 95.00				

KM# 1815 20 YUAN
1.5552 g., 0.9990 Gold 0.0499 oz. AGW, 14 mm. **Rev:** Panda cut pawing mom

Date	Mintage	F	VF	XF	Unc	BU
2008 Proof	—	Value: 95.00				

KM# 1866 20 YUAN
1.5552 g., 0.9990 Gold 0.0499 oz. AGW

Date	Mintage	F	VF	XF	Unc	BU
2008 Proof	—	Value: 95.00				

KM# 1930 20 YUAN
1.5500 g., 0.9990 Gold 0.0498 oz. AGW **Obv:** Temple of Heaven **Rev:** Two pandas, one lying on back

Date	Mintage	F	VF	XF	Unc	BU
2010	120,000	—	—	—	—	100

KM# 1817 30 YUAN
3.1100 g., 0.9990 Gold 0.0999 oz. AGW, 18 mm. **Rev:** Panda cub pawing mom

Date	Mintage	F	VF	XF	Unc	BU
2008 Proof	—	Value: 215				

KM# 1367 50 YUAN
3.1103 g., 0.9990 Gold 0.0999 oz. AGW, 18 mm. **Obv:** Temple of Heaven **Rev:** Panda walking left through bamboo **Edge:** Reeded **Note:** Large and small date varieties exist. Prev. Y#1113.

Date	Mintage	F	VF	XF	Unc	BU
2001	50,000	—	—	—	—	200
2001 D	150,000	—	—	—	—	175

KM# 1457 50 YUAN
3.1103 g., 0.9999 Gold 0.1000 oz. AGW **Subject:** Temple of Heaven **Rev:** Panda walking

Date	Mintage	F	VF	XF	Unc	BU
2002	36,092	—	—	—	—	225

KM# 1469 50 YUAN
3.1103 g., 0.9999 Gold 0.1000 oz. AGW **Subject:** Panda **Note:** Large and small date varieties exist. Prev. Y#1157.

Date	Mintage	F	VF	XF	Unc	BU
2003	47,500	—	—	—	—	215

KM# 1531 50 YUAN
3.1103 g., 0.9999 Gold 0.1000 oz. AGW **Subject:** Panda **Note:** Large and small date varieties exist. Prev. Y#1173.

Date	Mintage	F	VF	XF	Unc	BU
2004	—	—	—	—	—	200

KM# 1585 50 YUAN
3.1100 g., 0.9990 Gold 0.0999 oz. AGW, 18 mm. **Obv:** Temple of Heaven **Rev:** Panda cub and mom seated in bamboo

Date	Mintage	F	VF	XF	Unc	BU
2005	150,000	—	—	—	—	200

KM# 1660 50 YUAN
3.1100 g., 0.9990 Gold 0.0999 oz. AGW, 18 mm. **Obv:** Temple of Heaven **Rev:** Two pandas seated with bamboo

Date	Mintage	F	VF	XF	Unc	BU
2006	150,000	—	—	—	—	200

KM# 1709 50 YUAN
3.1100 g., 0.9990 Gold 0.0999 oz. AGW, 18 mm. **Obv:** Temple of Heaven **Rev:** Two pandas, one walking, one seated

Date	Mintage	F	VF	XF	Unc	BU
2007	150,000	—	—	—	—	200

KM# 1868 50 YUAN
3.1000 g., 0.9990 Gold 0.0996 oz. AGW, 18 mm. **Rev:** Panda cub pawing mom

Date	Mintage	F	VF	XF	Unc	BU
2008	—	—	—	—	—	200

KM# 1929 50 YUAN
3.1100 g., 0.9990 Gold 0.0999 oz. AGW **Obv:** Temple of Heaven **Rev:** Two pandas, one lying on back

Date	Mintage	F	VF	XF	Unc	BU
2010	120,000	—	—	—	—	200

KM# 1368 100 YUAN
7.7759 g., 0.9999 Gold 0.2497 oz. AGW, 22 mm. **Obv:** Temple of Heaven **Rev:** Panda walking left through bamboo **Edge:** Reeded **Note:** Large and small date varieties exist. Prev. Y#1114.

Date	Mintage	F	VF	XF	Unc	BU
2001	85,010	—	—	—	—	425
2001 D	Inc. above	—	—	—	—	425

KM# 1458 100 YUAN
7.7759 g., 0.9999 Gold 0.2500 oz. AGW **Obv:** Temple of Heaven **Rev:** Panda walking

Date	Mintage	F	VF	XF	Unc	BU
2002	19,205	—	—	—	—	450

KM# 1471 100 YUAN
7.7759 g., 0.9999 Gold 0.2500 oz. AGW **Subject:** Panda **Note:** Large and small date varieties exist. Prev. Y#1158.

Date	Mintage	F	VF	XF	Unc	BU
2003	28,000	—	—	—	—	425

KM# 1533 100 YUAN
7.7759 g., 0.9999 Gold 0.2500 oz. AGW **Subject:** Panda **Note:** Large and small date varieties exist. Prev. Y#1174. Photo reduced.

Date	Mintage	F	VF	XF	Unc	BU
2004	41,000	—	—	—	—	425

KM# 1584 100 YUAN
7.7700 g., 0.9990 Gold 0.2496 oz. AGW, 22 mm. **Obv:** Temple of Heaven **Rev:** Panda cub and mom seated in bamboo

Date	Mintage	F	VF	XF	Unc	BU
2005	40,000	—	—	—	—	425

KM# 1659 100 YUAN
7.7700 g., 0.9990 Gold 0.2496 oz. AGW, 22 mm. **Obv:** Temple of Heaven **Rev:** Two pandas seated with bamboo

Date	Mintage	F	VF	XF	Unc	BU
2006	28,500	—	—	—	—	450

KM# 1710 100 YUAN
7.7700 g., 0.9990 Gold 0.2496 oz. AGW, 22 mm. **Obv:** Temple of Heaven **Rev:** Two pandas, one walking, one seated

Date	Mintage	F	VF	XF	Unc	BU
2007	60,000	—	—	—	—	425

KM# 1818 100 YUAN
7.7700 g., 0.9990 Gold 0.2496 oz. AGW, 22 mm. **Rev:** Panda cub pawing mom

Date	Mintage	F	VF	XF	Unc	BU
2008	—	—	—	—	—	425

KM# 1928 100 YUAN
7.7700 g., 0.9990 Gold 0.2496 oz. AGW **Obv:** Temple of Heaven **Rev:** Two panda, one lying on back

Date	Mintage	F	VF	XF	Unc	BU
2010	120,000	—	—	—	—	450

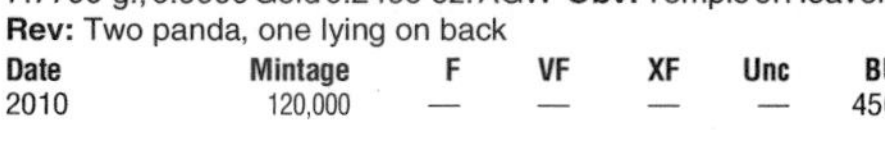

KM# 1369 200 YUAN
15.5518 g., 0.9990 Gold 0.4995 oz. AGW, 27 mm. **Obv:** Temple of Heaven **Rev:** Panda in bamboo forest **Edge:** Slanted reeding **Note:** Illustration reduced. Large and small date varieties exist. Prev. Y#1105.

Date	Mintage	F	VF	XF	Unc	BU
2001	33,215	—	—	—	—	875
2001 D	100,000	—	—	—	—	850

KM# 1459 200 YUAN
15.5518 g., 0.9999 Gold 0.4999 oz. AGW **Rev:** Panda

Date	Mintage	F	VF	XF	Unc	BU
2002	28,514	—	—	—	—	875

KM# 1472 200 YUAN
15.5519 g., 0.9999 Gold 0.4999 oz. AGW **Subject:** Panda **Note:** Large and small date varieties exist. Prev. Y#1162.

Date	Mintage	F	VF	XF	Unc	BU
2003	25,000	—	—	—	—	875

KM# 1535 200 YUAN
15.5519 g., 0.9990 Gold 0.4995 oz. AGW **Subject:** Panda **Note:** Large and small date varieties exist. Prev. Y#1175.

Date	Mintage	F	VF	XF	Unc	BU
2004	42,000	—	—	—	—	850

KM# 1583 200 YUAN
15.5518 g., 0.9990 Gold 0.4995 oz. AGW, 27 mm. **Obv:** Temple of Heaven **Rev:** Panda cub and mom seated in bamboo

Date	Mintage	F	VF	XF	Unc	BU
2005	36,410	—	—	—	—	850

KM# 1658 200 YUAN
15.5500 g., 0.9990 Gold 0.4994 oz. AGW, 27 mm. **Obv:** Temple of Heaven **Rev:** Two pandas seated with bamboo

Date	Mintage	F	VF	XF	Unc	BU
2006	25,600	—	—	—	—	875

KM# 1711 200 YUAN
15.5500 g., 0.9990 Gold 0.4994 oz. AGW **Obv:** Temple of Heaven **Rev:** Two pandas, one walking, one seated

Date	Mintage	F	VF	XF	Unc	BU
2007	60,000	—	—	—	—	850

KM# 1870 200 YUAN
15.5000 g., 0.9990 Gold 0.4978 oz. AGW

Date	Mintage	F	VF	XF	Unc	BU
2009	—	—	—	—	—	850

KM# 1927 200 YUAN
15.5500 g., 0.9990 Gold 0.4994 oz. AGW **Obv:** Temple of Heaven **Rev:** Two pandas, one lying on back

Date	Mintage	F	VF	XF	Unc	BU
2010	120,000	—	—	—	—	900

KM# 1371 500 YUAN
31.1035 g., 0.9990 Gold 0.9990 oz. AGW, 32 mm. **Obv:** Temple of Heaven **Rev:** Panda walking through bamboo **Edge:** Reeded **Note:** Prev. Y#1088.

Date	Mintage	F	VF	XF	Unc	BU
2001	—	—	—	—	—	BV+15%
2001 D	150,000	—	—	—	—	BV+15%

KM# 1405 500 YUAN
31.1050 g., 0.9999 Gold 0.9999 oz. AGW **Rev:** Panda

Date	Mintage	F	VF	XF	Unc	BU
2001	41,411	—	—	—	—	BV+15%

KM# 1460 500 YUAN
31.1050 g., 0.9999 Gold 0.9999 oz. AGW **Rev:** Panda

Date	Mintage	F	VF	XF	Unc	BU
2002	28,345	—	—	—	—	BV+20%

KM# 1474 500 YUAN
31.1320 g., 0.9999 Gold 1.0008 oz. AGW **Subject:** Panda **Note:** Large and small date varieties exist. Prev. Y#1164.

Date	Mintage	F	VF	XF	Unc	BU
2003	36,300	—	—	—	—	BV+15%

KM# 1537 500 YUAN
31.1035 g., 0.9999 Gold 0.9999 oz. AGW **Subject:** Panda **Note:** Large and small date varieties exist. Prev. Y#1176.

Date	Mintage	F	VF	XF	Unc	BU
2004	55,000	—	—	—	—	BV+10%

KM# 1582 500 YUAN
31.1050 g., 0.9990 Gold 0.9990 oz. AGW, 32 mm. **Obv:** Temple of Heaven **Rev:** Panda cub and mom seated in bamboo

Date	Mintage	F	VF	XF	Unc	BU
2005	50,300	BV+10%				

KM# 1657 500 YUAN
31.1050 g., 0.9990 Gold 0.9990 oz. AGW, 32 mm. **Obv:** Temple of Heaven **Rev:** Two panda's seated with bamboo

Date	Mintage	F	VF	XF	Unc	BU
2006	115,600	BV+10%				

KM# 1713 500 YUAN
31.1050 g., 0.9990 Gold 0.9990 oz. AGW, 32 mm. **Obv:** Temple of Heaven **Rev:** Two pandas, one walking, one seated

Date	Mintage	F	VF	XF	Unc	BU
2007	150,000	BV+10%				

KM# 1821 500 YUAN
31.1050 g., 0.9990 Gold 0.9990 oz. AGW, 32 mm. **Rev:** Panda cub pawing mom

Date	Mintage	F	VF	XF	Unc	BU
2008	—	BV+10%				

KM# 1872 500 YUAN
31.1050 g., 0.9990 Gold 0.9990 oz. AGW

Date	Mintage	F	VF	XF	Unc	BU
2009	—	BV+10%				

KM# 1926 500 YUAN
31.1050 g., 0.9990 Gold 0.9990 oz. AGW **Obv:** Temple of Heaven **Rev:** Two pandas, one lying on back

Date	Mintage	F	VF	XF	Unc	BU
2010	300,000	—	—	—	—	1,550

KM# 1581 2000 YUAN
155.0000 g., 0.9990 Gold 4.9782 oz. AGW, 60 mm. **Obv:** Temple of Heaven **Rev:** Panda cub and mom seated in bamboo **Note:** Photo reduced.

Date	Mintage	F	VF	XF	Unc	BU
2005 Proof	1,000	BV+25%				

KM# 1656 2000 YUAN
155.5500 g., 0.9990 Gold 4.9958 oz. AGW, 60 mm. **Obv:** Temple of Heaven **Rev:** Two pandas seated with bamboo **Note:** Photo reduced.

Date	Mintage	F	VF	XF	Unc	BU
2006 Proof	1,000	BV+25%				

KM# 1714 2000 YUAN
155.5500 g., 0.9990 Gold 4.9958 oz. AGW, 60 mm. **Obv:** Temple of Heaven **Rev:** Two pandas, one walking, one seated

Date	Mintage	F	VF	XF	Unc	BU
2007 Proof	1,000	BV+25%				

KM# 1822 2000 YUAN
155.5000 g., 0.9990 Gold 4.9942 oz. AGW, 60 mm. **Rev:** Panda cub pawing mom

Date	Mintage	F	VF	XF	Unc	BU
2008 Proof	1,000	BV+25%				

KM# 1873 2000 YUAN
155.5000 g., 0.9990 Gold 4.9942 oz. AGW

Date	Mintage	F	VF	XF	Unc	BU
2009 Proof	1,000	BV+25%				

KM# 1914 2000 YUAN
155.5000 g., 0.9990 Gold 4.9942 oz. AGW **Subject:** Year of the Tiger **Rev:** Multicolor

Date	Mintage	F	VF	XF	Unc	BU
2010 Proof	1,800	Value: 8,500				

KM# 1933 2000 YUAN
155.5000 g., 0.9990 Gold 4.9942 oz. AGW **Obv:** Temple of Heaven **Rev:** Two pandas, one lying on back

Date	Mintage	F	VF	XF	Unc	BU
2010 Proof	1,000	Value: 8,750				

KM# 1372 10000 YUAN
1000.0000 g., 0.9990 Gold 32.117 oz. AGW **Subject:** Panda **Note:** Large and small date varieties exist. Prev. #Y1138.

Date	Mintage	F	VF	XF	Unc	BU
2001	68	—	—	—	—	BV+35%

KM# A1475 10000 YUAN
1000.0000 g., 0.9999 Gold 32.146 oz. AGW **Subject:** Panda **Note:** Large and small date varieties exist. Prev. #Y1165.

Date	Mintage	F	VF	XF	Unc	BU
2002	68	—	—	—	—	BV+35%

KM# 1475 10000 YUAN
1000.0000 g., 0.9990 Gold 32.117 oz. AGW, 100 mm. **Rev:** Panda and bamboo

Date	Mintage	F	VF	XF	Unc	BU
2003 Proof	68	BV+35%				

KM# 1538 10000 YUAN
1000.0000 g., 0.9999 Gold 32.146 oz. AGW **Subject:** Panda **Note:** Large and small date varieties exist. Prev. #Y1177.

Date	Mintage	F	VF	XF	Unc	BU
2004	68	—	—	—	—	BV+35%

KM# A1580 10000 YUAN
1000.0000 g., 0.9990 Gold 32.117 oz. AGW, 90 mm. **Obv:** Temple of Heaven **Rev:** Panda cub and mom seated in bamboo **Note:** Photo reduced.

Date	Mintage	F	VF	XF	Unc	BU
2005 Proof	100	BV+25%				

KM# 1655 10000 YUAN
1000.0000 g., 0.9990 Gold 32.117 oz. AGW, 90 mm. **Obv:** Temple of Heaven **Rev:** Two pandas seated with bamboo **Note:** Photo reduced.

Date	Mintage	F	VF	XF	Unc	BU
2006 Proof	200	BV+20%				

KM# 1715 10000 YUAN
1000.0000 g., 0.9990 Gold 32.117 oz. AGW **Obv:** Temple of Heaven **Rev:** Two pandas, one walking, one seated

Date	Mintage	F	VF	XF	Unc	BU
2007 Proof	200	BV+20%				

KM# 1823 10000 YUAN
1000.0000 g., 0.9990 Gold 32.117 oz. AGW, 90 mm. **Rev:** Panda cub pawing mom

Date	Mintage	F	VF	XF	Unc	BU
2008 Proof	200	BV+20%				

KM# 1874 10000 YUAN
1000.0000 g., 0.9990 Gold 32.117 oz. AGW

Date	Mintage	F	VF	XF	Unc	BU
2009 Proof	200	BV+20%				

KM# 1932 10000 YUAN
1000.0000 g., 0.9990 Gold 32.117 oz. AGW **Obv:** Temple of Heaven **Rev:** Two pandas, one lying on back

Date	Mintage	F	VF	XF	Unc	BU
2010 Proof	200	Value: 47,500				

GOLD BULLION COINAGE

Lunar Series

KM# 1967 20 YUAN
3.1100 g., 0.9990 Gold 0.0999 oz. AGW, 18 mm. **Subject:** Year of the Rabbit **Rev:** Multicolor

Date	Mintage	F	VF	XF	Unc	BU
2011 Proof	80,000	Value: 225				

KM# 1374 50 YUAN
3.1103 g., 0.9990 Gold 0.0999 oz. AGW, 18 mm. **Subject:** Year of the Snake **Note:** Prev. Y#1141.1; 1043.

Date	Mintage	F	VF	XF	Unc	BU
2001	48,000	—	—	—	—	265

KM# 1376 50 YUAN
3.1105 g., 0.9999 Gold 0.1000 oz. AGW **Subject:** Year of the Snake **Rev:** Multicolor. **Note:** Prev. Y#1141.2.

Date	Mintage	F	VF	XF	Unc	BU
2001	30,000	—	—	—	—	350

KM# 1419 50 YUAN
3.1050 g., 0.9999 Gold 0.0998 oz. AGW **Subject:** Year of the Horse **Rev:** Dramatic horse profile right **Note:** Prev. Y#1143.1.

Date	Mintage	F	VF	XF	Unc	BU
2002	48,000	—	—	—	—	240

KM# 1417 50 YUAN
3.1050 g., 0.9999 Gold 0.0998 oz. AGW **Subject:** Year of the Horse **Rev:** Multicolor horse prancing forward **Note:** Prev. Y#1143.2.

Date	Mintage	F	VF	XF	Unc	BU
2002	30,000	—	—	—	—	425

KM# 1478 50 YUAN
3.1103 g., 0.9999 Gold 0.1000 oz. AGW **Subject:** Year of the Goat **Note:** Prev. Y#1155.1.

Date	Mintage	F	VF	XF	Unc	BU
2003	48,000	—	—	—	—	275

KM# A1478 50 YUAN
3.1105 g., 0.9999 Gold 0.1000 oz. AGW **Subject:** Year of the Goat **Rev:** Multicolor. **Note:** Prev. Y#1155.2

Date	Mintage	F	VF	XF	Unc	BU
2003	30,000	—	—	—	—	400

KM# 1544 50 YUAN
3.1103 g., 0.9999 Gold 0.1000 oz. AGW, 18 mm. **Subject:** Year of the Monkey **Note:** Prev. Y#1167.1.

Date	Mintage	F	VF	XF	Unc	BU
2004	48,000	—	—	—	—	275

KM# 1546 50 YUAN
3.1103 g., 0.9999 Gold 0.1000 oz. AGW **Subject:** Year of the Monkey **Rev:** Multicolor monkey and baby **Note:** Prev. Y#1167.2

Date	Mintage	F	VF	XF	Unc	BU
2004	30,000	—	—	—	—	425

KM# 1608 50 YUAN
3.1100 g., 0.9990 Gold 0.0999 oz. AGW, 18 mm. **Subject:** Year of the Rooster **Obv:** Classical rooster **Rev:** Multicolor rooster

Date	Mintage	F	VF	XF	Unc	BU
2005 Proof	30,000	Value: 375				

KM# 1609 50 YUAN
3.1100 g., 0.9990 Gold 0.0999 oz. AGW, 18 mm. **Subject:** Year of the Rooster **Obv:** Classical rooster **Rev:** Rooster, hen and chicks

Date	Mintage	F	VF	XF	Unc	BU
2005 Proof	60,000	Value: 300				

KM# 1680 50 YUAN
3.1103 g., 0.9990 Gold 0.0999 oz. AGW, 18 mm. **Obv:** Dog-shaped belt-hook from ancient Chinese bronze ware, decorative design of dog tail-shaped plant leaves **Rev:** 2 smart dogs **Note:** Prev. Y#1226; KM#1658.

Date	Mintage	F	VF	XF	Unc	BU
2006	60,000	—	—	—	—	225

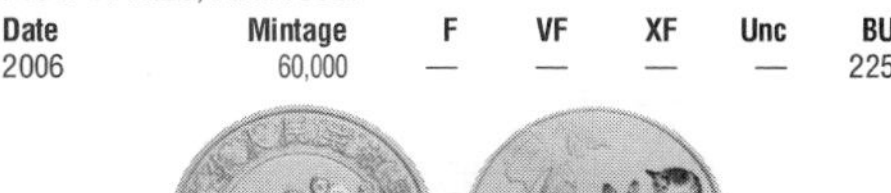

KM# 1681 50 YUAN
3.1103 g., 0.9990 Gold 0.0999 oz. AGW, 18 mm. **Obv:** Dog-shaped belt-hook , an ancient Chinese bronze ware, decorative disign of dog tail-shaped plant leaves **Rev:** 2 dogs at play **Note:** Prev. Y#1222; KM#1654.

Date	Mintage	F	VF	XF	Unc	BU
2006 Proof	30,000	Value: 220				

KM# 1721 50 YUAN
3.1000 g., 0.9990 Gold 0.0996 oz. AGW, 18 mm. **Subject:** Year of the Pig **Obv:** Classical pig **Rev:** Pig walking right

Date	Mintage	F	VF	XF	Unc	BU
2007 Proof	—	Value: 225				

KM# 1722 50 YUAN
3.1000 g., 0.9990 Gold 0.0996 oz. AGW, 18 mm. **Subject:** Year of the Pig **Obv:** Classical pig **Rev:** Multicolor sow and piglets sucking

Date	Mintage	F	VF	XF	Unc	BU
2007 Proof	30,000	Value: 550				

KM# 1835 50 YUAN
3.1100 g., 0.9990 Gold 0.0999 oz. AGW **Subject:** Year of the Rat **Rev:** Multicolor **Shape:** 18

Date	Mintage	F	VF	XF	Unc	BU
2008 Proof	30,000	Value: 350				

KM# 1836 50 YUAN
3.1100 g., 0.9990 Gold 0.0999 oz. AGW, 18 mm. **Subject:** Year of the Rat

Date	Mintage	F	VF	XF	Unc	BU
2008 Proof	60,000	Value: 225				

KM# 1880 50 YUAN
3.1100 g., 0.9990 Gold 0.0999 oz. AGW **Subject:** Year of the Ox colorized

Date	Mintage	F	VF	XF	Unc	BU
2009 Proof	30,000	Value: 400				

KM# 1881 50 YUAN
3.1100 g., 0.9990 Gold 0.0999 oz. AGW **Subject:** Year of the Ox

Date	Mintage	F	VF	XF	Unc	BU
2009 Proof	80,000	Value: 180				

KM# 1917 50 YUAN
3.1100 g., 0.9990 Gold 0.0999 oz. AGW **Subject:** Year of the Tiger

Date	Mintage	F	VF	XF	Unc	BU
2010 Proof	80,000	Value: 225				

KM# 1918 50 YUAN
3.1100 g., 0.9990 Gold 0.0999 oz. AGW **Subject:** Year of the Tiger **Rev:** Multicolor

Date	Mintage	F	VF	XF	Unc	BU
2010 Proof	80,000	Value: 225				

KM# 1966 50 YUAN
3.1100 g., 0.9990 Gold 0.0999 oz. AGW, 18 mm. **Subject:** Year of the Rabbit

Date	Mintage	F	VF	XF	Unc	BU
2011 Proof	80,000	Value: 225				

KM# 1380 200 YUAN
15.5518 g., 0.9990 Gold 0.4995 oz. AGW **Subject:** Year of the Snake **Shape:** Flower **Note:** Prev. Y#1045.

Date	Mintage	F	VF	XF	Unc	BU
2001 Proof	2,300	Value: 1,250				

KM# 1383 200 YUAN
15.5518 g., 0.9990 Gold 0.4995 oz. AGW **Subject:** Year of the Snake **Rev:** Fan **Note:** Prev. Y#1044.

Date	Mintage	F	VF	XF	Unc	BU
2001	6,600	—	—	—	—	950

KM# 1424 200 YUAN
15.5500 g., 0.9990 Gold 0.4994 oz. AGW **Subject:** Year of the Horse **Shape:** Fan

Date	Mintage	F	VF	XF	Unc	BU
2002	6,600	—	—	—	—	1,000

KM# 1426 200 YUAN
15.5000 g., 0.9990 Gold 0.4978 oz. AGW **Subject:** Year of the Horse **Shape:** Flower **Note:** Prev. Y#1150.

Date	Mintage	F	VF	XF	Unc	BU
2002	2,300	—	—	—	—	1,350

KM# 1475.1 200 YUAN
15.5517 g., 0.9999 Gold 0.4999 oz. AGW **Subject:** Year of the Goat **Shape:** Fan

Date	Mintage	F	VF	XF	Unc	BU
2003	6,600	—	—	—	—	900

KM# 1481 200 YUAN
15.5519 g., 0.9999 Gold 0.4999 oz. AGW **Subject:** Year of the Goat **Shape:** Flower **Note:** Prev. Y#1161.

Date	Mintage	F	VF	XF	Unc	BU
2003	2,300	—	—	—	—	1,350

KM# 1486 200 YUAN
15.5130 g., 0.9990 Gold 0.4982 oz. AGW, 58 x 30 mm. **Subject:** Year of the Sheep **Shape:** Fan

Date	Mintage	F	VF	XF	Unc	BU
2003 Proof	6,600	Value: 1,100				

KM# 1549 200 YUAN
15.5519 g., 0.9999 Gold 0.4999 oz. AGW **Subject:** Year of the Monkey **Shape:** Flower **Note:** Prev. Y#1169.

Date	Mintage	F	VF	XF	Unc	BU
2004	2,300	—	—	—	—	1,350

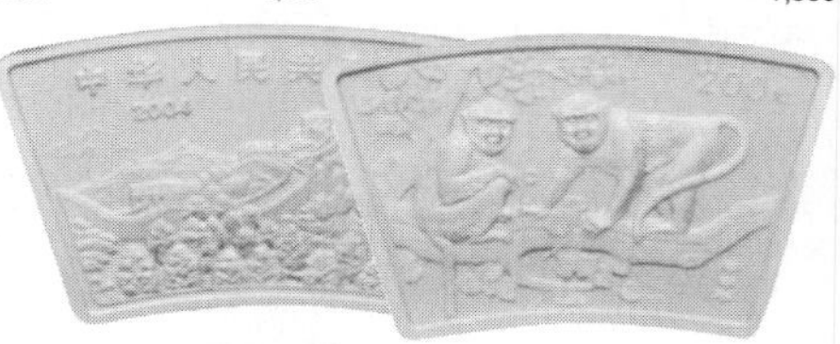

KM# 1554 200 YUAN
15.5519 g., 0.9999 Gold 0.4999 oz. AGW **Subject:** Year of the Monkey **Shape:** Fan **Note:** Prev. Y#1168.

Date	Mintage	F	VF	XF	Unc	BU
2004	6,600	—	—	—	—	1,100

KM# 1606 200 YUAN
15.5500 g., 0.9990 Gold 0.4994 oz. AGW, 27 mm. **Series:** Classical rooster **Subject:** Year of the Rooster **Obv:** Rooster, hen and chicks **Shape:** Scallops

Date	Mintage	F	VF	XF	Unc	BU
2005 Proof	8,000	Value: 925				

KM# 1607 200 YUAN
15.5500 g., 0.9990 Gold 0.4994 oz. AGW, 58 x 30 mm. **Subject:** Year of the Rooster **Obv:** Temple **Rev:** Rooster, hen and chicks **Shape:** Fan

Date	Mintage	F	VF	XF	Unc	BU
2005 Proof	6,600	Value: 950				

KM# 1677 200 YUAN
15.6300 g., 0.9990 Gold 0.5020 oz. AGW, 27 mm. **Subject:** Year of the Dog **Obv:** Dog-shaped belt-hook from ancient Chinese bronze ware, decorative design of dog tail-shaped plant leaves **Rev:** 2 smart dogs **Shape:** Scalloped **Note:** Prev. Y#1224; KM#1656.

Date	Mintage	F	VF	XF	Unc	BU
2006 Proof	8,000	Value: 1,350				

KM# 1679 200 YUAN
15.6300 g., 0.9990 Gold 0.5020 oz. AGW **Subject:** Year of the Dog **Obv:** Qing Yuan Gate of the China Great Wall **Rev:** 2 dogs at play **Shape:** 30° Fan **Note:** Prev. Y#1220; KM#1652.

Date	Mintage	F	VF	XF	Unc	BU
2006 Proof	6,600	Value: 1,100				

KM# 1723 200 YUAN
15.5000 g., 0.9990 Gold 0.4978 oz. AGW, 58 x 39 mm. **Subject:** Year of the Pig **Obv:** Temple **Rev:** Sow and four pigletts **Shape:** Fan

Date	Mintage	F	VF	XF	Unc	BU
2007 Proof	6,600	Value: 1,150				

KM# 1724 200 YUAN
15.5500 g., 0.9990 Gold 0.4994 oz. AGW, 27 mm. **Subject:** Year of the Pig **Obv:** Classical pig **Rev:** Pig walking right **Shape:** Flower

Date	Mintage	F	VF	XF	Unc	BU
2007 Proof	8,000	Value: 950				

KM# 1837 200 YUAN

15.5000 g., 0.9990 Gold 0.4978 oz. AGW, 27 mm. **Subject:** Year of the Rat **Shape:** Flower

Date	Mintage	F	VF	XF	Unc	BU
2008 Proof	8,000	Value: 950				

KM# 1838 200 YUAN

15.5000 g., 0.9990 Gold 0.4978 oz. AGW, 58 x 39 mm. **Subject:** Year of the Rat **Shape:** Fan

Date	Mintage	F	VF	XF	Unc	BU
2008 Proof	6,600	Value: 1,000				

KM# 1883 200 YUAN

15.5000 g., 0.9990 Gold 0.4978 oz. AGW **Subject:** Year of the Ox **Shape:** Fan

Date	Mintage	F	VF	XF	Unc	BU
2009 Proof	6,600	Value: 1,000				

KM# 1882 200 YUAN

15.5000 g., 0.9990 Gold 0.4978 oz. AGW **Subject:** Year of the Ox **Shape:** Flower

Date	Mintage	F	VF	XF	Unc	BU
2009 Proof	8,000	Value: 950				

KM# 1915 200 YUAN

15.5500 g., 0.9990 Gold 0.4994 oz. AGW **Subject:** Year of the Tiger **Shape:** Arc

Date	Mintage	F	VF	XF	Unc	BU
2010	6,600	—	—	—	—	900

KM# 1916 200 YUAN

15.5500 g., 0.9990 Gold 0.4994 oz. AGW **Subject:** Year of the Tiger **Shape:** Scalloped

Date	Mintage	F	VF	XF	Unc	BU
2010 Proof	8,000	Value: 900				

KM# 1964 200 YUAN

15.5000 g., 0.9990 Gold 0.4978 oz. AGW **Subject:** Year of the Rabbit **Shape:** Arc **Note:** Photo reduced.

Date	Mintage	F	VF	XF	Unc	BU
2011	6,600	—	—	—	—	950

KM# 1965 200 YUAN

15.5500 g., 0.9990 Gold 0.4994 oz. AGW, 27 mm. **Subject:** Year of the Rabbit **Shape:** Scallop

Date	Mintage	F	VF	XF	Unc	BU
2011 Proof	8,000	Value: 900				

KM# 1378 2000 YUAN

155.5175 g., 0.9990 Gold 4.9948 oz. AGW, 80 x 50 mm. **Subject:** Year of the Snake **Shape:** Rectangle **Note:** Prev. #Y1046.

Date	Mintage	F	VF	XF	Unc	BU
2001 Proof	118	Value: 22,500				

KM# 1422 2000 YUAN

155.5175 g., 0.9999 Gold 4.9993 oz. AGW **Subject:** Year of the Horse **Shape:** Rectangle **Note:** Prev. #Y1152.

Date	Mintage	F	VF	XF	Unc	BU
2002 Proof	118	Value: 22,500				

KM# 1483 2000 YUAN

155.5190 g., 0.9999 Gold 4.9993 oz. AGW **Subject:** Year of the Goat **Note:** Prev. #Y1163.

Date	Mintage	F	VF	XF	Unc	BU
2003 Proof	118	Value: 22,500				

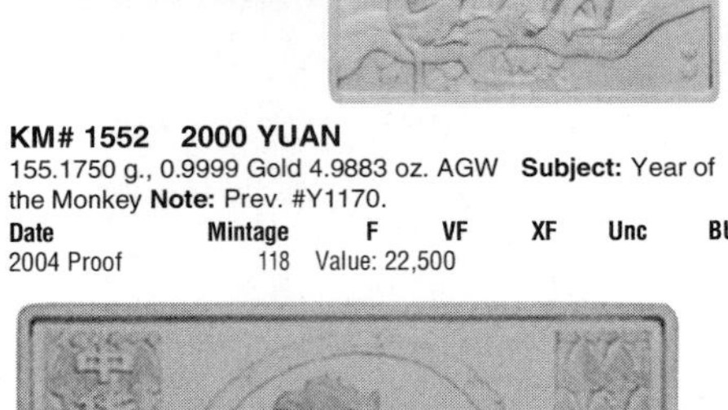

KM# 1552 2000 YUAN

155.1750 g., 0.9999 Gold 4.9883 oz. AGW **Subject:** Year of the Monkey **Note:** Prev. #Y1170.

Date	Mintage	F	VF	XF	Unc	BU
2004 Proof	118	Value: 22,500				

KM# 1605 2000 YUAN

155.5500 g., 0.9990 Gold 4.9958 oz. AGW, 64 x 40 mm. **Subject:** Year of the Rooster **Obv:** Classical rooster **Rev:** Rooster, hen and chicks **Shape:** Rectangle **Note:** Photo reduced.

Date	Mintage	F	VF	XF	Unc	BU
2005 Proof	118	Value: 22,500				

KM# 1678 2000 YUAN

155.5500 g., 0.9990 Gold 4.9958 oz. AGW, 64 x 40 mm. **Subject:** Year of the Dog **Obv:** Classical dog **Rev:** Two dogs **Note:** Photo reduced.

Date	Mintage	F	VF	XF	Unc	BU
2006 Proof	118	Value: 22,500				

KM# 1726 2000 YUAN

155.5500 g., 0.9990 Gold 4.9958 oz. AGW, 64 x 40 mm. **Subject:** Year of the Pig **Obv:** Classical pig **Rev:** Sow and four pigletts **Shape:** Rectangle

Date	Mintage	F	VF	XF	Unc	BU
2007 Proof	118	Value: 22,500				

KM# 1840 2000 YUAN

155.0000 g., 0.9990 Gold 4.9782 oz. AGW, 64 x 40 mm. **Subject:** Year of the Rat **Shape:** Rectangle

Date	Mintage	F	VF	XF	Unc	BU
2008 Proof	118	Value: 22,500				

KM# 1885 2000 YUAN

155.5000 g., 0.9990 Gold 4.9942 oz. AGW, 64x40 mm. **Subject:** Year of the Ox **Shape:** Rectangle

Date	Mintage	F	VF	XF	Unc	BU
2009 Proof	118	Value: 22,500				

KM# 1913 2000 YUAN

155.2000 g., 0.9990 Gold 4.9846 oz. AGW, 64x40 mm. **Subject:** Year of the Tiger **Shape:** Rectangle

Date	Mintage	F	VF	XF	Unc	BU
2010 Proof	118	Value: 20,000				

KM# 1962 2000 YUAN

155.5000 g., 0.9990 Gold 4.9942 oz. AGW, 64x40 mm. **Subject:** Year of the Rabbit **Shape:** Rectangle **Note:** Photo reduced.

Date	Mintage	F	VF	XF	Unc	BU
2011 Proof	118	Value: 20,000				

KM# 1963 2000 YUAN

155.5000 g., 0.9990 Gold 4.9942 oz. AGW **Subject:** Year of the Rabbit **Rev:** Multicolor **Note:** Photo reduced.

Date	Mintage	F	VF	XF	Unc	BU
2011 Proof	1,800	Value: 9,500				

KM# 1381 10000 YUAN

1000.0000 g., 0.9990 Gold 32.117 oz. AGW **Subject:** Year of the Snake **Shape:** Scalloped **Note:** Prev. #Y1047.

Date	Mintage	F	VF	XF	Unc	BU
2001 Proof	15	Value: 125,000				

KM# 1427 10000 YUAN

1000.0000 g., 0.9999 Gold 32.146 oz. AGW **Subject:** Year of the Horse **Shape:** Scalloped **Note:** Prev. #Y1153.

Date	Mintage	F	VF	XF	Unc	BU
2002 Proof	15	Value: 90,000				

KM# 1482 10000 YUAN

1000.0000 g., 0.9999 Gold 32.146 oz. AGW, 100 mm. **Subject:** Year of the Goat **Shape:** Scalloped **Note:** Prev. #Y1166.

Date	Mintage	F	VF	XF	Unc	BU
2003 Proof	15	Value: 75,000				

KM# 1550 10000 YUAN
1000.0000 g., 0.9999 Gold 32.146 oz. AGW, 100 mm. **Subject:** Year of the Monkey **Shape:** Scalloped **Note:** Prev. #Y1171.

Date	Mintage	F	VF	XF	Unc	BU
2004 Proof	15	Value: 90,000				

KM# 1604 10000 YUAN
1000.0000 g., 0.9990 Gold 32.117 oz. AGW, 100 mm. **Obv:** Classical rooster **Rev:** Rooster strutting **Edge:** Scalloped **Note:** Photo reduced.

Date	Mintage	F	VF	XF	Unc	BU
2005 Proof	15	Value: 75,000				

KM# 1727 10000 YUAN
1000.0000 g., 0.9990 Gold 32.117 oz. AGW, 100 mm. **Subject:** Year of the Pig **Obv:** Classical pig **Rev:** Three pigs **Shape:** Scalloped

Date	Mintage	F	VF	XF	Unc	BU
2007 Proof	118	Value: 70,000				

KM# 1841 10000 YUAN
1000.0000 g., 0.9990 Gold 32.117 oz. AGW, 100 mm. **Subject:** Year of the Rat **Shape:** Scalloped

Date	Mintage	F	VF	XF	Unc	BU
2008 Proof	118	Value: 70,000				

KM# 1912 10000 YUAN
1000.0000 g., 0.9990 Gold 32.117 oz. AGW, 100 mm. **Subject:** Year of the Tiger **Shape:** Scalloped

Date	Mintage	F	VF	XF	Unc	BU
2010 Proof	118	Value: 65,000				

KM# 1961 10000 YUAN
1000.0000 g., 0.9990 Gold 32.117 oz. AGW, 100 mm. **Subject:** Year of the Rabbit **Shape:** Scalloped **Note:** Photo reduced.

Date	Mintage	F	VF	XF	Unc	BU
2011 Proof	118	Value: 65,000				

KM# 1728 100000 YUAN
10000.0000 g., 0.9990 Gold 321.17 oz. AGW, 180 mm. **Subject:** Year of the Pig **Obv:** Classical pig **Rev:** Sow with four piglets sucking

Date	Mintage	F	VF	XF	Unc	BU
2007 Proof	18	Value: 500,000				

KM# 1842 100000 YUAN
10000.0000 g., 0.9990 Gold 321.17 oz. AGW, 180 mm.

Date	Mintage	F	VF	XF	Unc	BU
2008 Proof	18	Value: 500,000				

KM# 1886 100000 YUAN
10000.0000 g., 0.9990 Gold 32.117 oz. AGW, 180 mm. **Subject:** Year of the Ox

Date	Mintage	F	VF	XF	Unc	BU
2009 Proof	118	Value: 70,000				

KM# 1887 100000 YUAN
10000.0000 g., 0.9990 Gold 321.17 oz. AGW, 180 mm. **Subject:** Year of the Ox

Date	Mintage	F	VF	XF	Unc	BU
2009 Proof	—	Value: 700,000				

KM# 1911 100000 YUAN
10000.0000 g., 0.9990 Gold 321.17 oz. AGW, 180 mm. **Subject:** Year of the Tiger

Date	Mintage	F	VF	XF	Unc	BU
2010 Proof	18	Value: 700,000				

KM# 1960 100000 YUAN
10000.0000 g., 0.9990 Gold 321.17 oz. AGW, 180 mm. **Subject:** Year of the Rabbit **Note:** Photo reduced.

Date	Mintage	F	VF	XF	Unc	BU
2011 Proof	18	Value: 700,000				

PALLADIUM BULLION COINAGE
Panda Series

KM# A1531 100 YUAN
15.5590 g., 0.9990 Palladium 0.4997 oz., 14 mm. **Rev:** Panda walking with cub

Date	Mintage	F	VF	XF	Unc	BU
2004 Proof	8,000	Value: 475				

KM# 1590 100 YUAN
15.5500 g., 0.9990 Palladium 0.4994 oz., 30 mm. **Obv:** Temple of Heaven **Rev:** Panda cub and mom seated in bamboo

Date	Mintage	F	VF	XF	Unc	BU
2005 Proof	8,000	Value: 450				

PLATINUM BULLION COINAGE
Panda Series

KM# 1470 50 YUAN
1.5500 g., 0.9995 Platinum 0.0498 oz. APW, 14.03 mm. **Obv:** Temple of Heaven, incuse legend **Rev:** Panda standing facing eating bamboo **Edge:** Reeded

Date	Mintage	F	VF	XF	Unc	BU
2003 Proof	50,000	Value: 135				

KM# 1532 50 YUAN
1.4500 g., 0.9995 Platinum 0.0466 oz. APW, 14 mm. **Obv:** Temple of Heaven, incuse legend **Rev:** Panda standing facing with cub **Edge:** Reeded

Date	Mintage	F	VF	XF	Unc	BU
2004 Proof	50,000	Value: 135				

KM# 1415 100 YUAN
3.1103 g., 0.9995 Platinum 0.0999 oz. APW, 18 mm. **Subject:** Panda Coinage 20th Anniversary **Obv:** Seated panda design of 1982 **Rev:** Walking panda design of 2002 **Edge:** Reeded **Note:** Prev. Y#1115.

Date	Mintage	F	VF	XF	Unc	BU
2002 Proof	20,000	Value: 250				

KM# 1591 100 YUAN
3.1100 g., 0.9990 Platinum 0.0999 oz. APW, 18 mm. **Obv:** Temple of Heaven **Rev:** Panda cub and mom seated in bamboo

Date	Mintage	F	VF	XF	Unc	BU
2005 Proof	30,000	Value: 200				

CHINA, REPUBLIC OF

TAIWAN

Chinese migration to Taiwan began as early as the sixth century. The Dutch established a base on the island in 1624 and held it until 1661, when they were driven out by supporters of the Ming dynasty who used it as a base for their unsuccessful attempt to displace the ruling Manchu dynasty of mainland China. After being occupied by Manchu forces in 1683, Taiwan remained under the suzerainty of China until its cession to Japan in 1895. The island was part of the province of Fukien (Fujian) until established as a separate province in the period 1885-1895. (It took 10 years to complete the conversion to a full-fledged province.)

REPUBLIC

STANDARD COINAGE

Y# 550 1/2 YUAN

3.0000 g., Bronze, 18 mm. **Obv:** Orchid **Rev:** Value and Chinese symbols **Edge:** Plain

Date	Mintage	F	VF	XF	Unc	BU
90(2001) Proof	—	Value: 10.00				
92(2003)	—	—	0.15	0.30	1.00	1.25
92(2003) Proof	—	Value: 10.00				

Y# 551 YUAN

3.8000 g., Aluminum-Bronze, 20 mm. **Obv:** Bust of Chiang Kai-shek left **Rev:** Chinese value in center, 1 below **Edge:** Reeded

Date	Mintage	F	VF	XF	Unc	BU
90(2001) Proof	—	Value: 12.50				
92(2003)	—	—	—	0.15	0.30	0.45
92(2003) Proof	—	Value: 12.50				
95(2006)	—	—	—	0.15	0.30	0.45

Y# 552 5 YUAN

4.4000 g., Copper-Nickel, 22 mm. **Obv:** Bust of Chiang Kai-shek left **Rev:** Chinese value in center, 5 below **Edge:** Reeded

Date	Mintage	F	VF	XF	Unc	BU
90(2001) Proof	—	Value: 12.50				
92(2003)	—	—	0.15	0.25	0.50	0.75
92(2003) Proof	—	Value: 12.50				

Y# 553 10 YUAN

7.5000 g., Copper-Nickel, 26 mm. **Obv:** Bust of Chiang Kai-shek left **Rev:** Chinese value in center, 10 below **Edge:** Reeded

Date	Mintage	F	VF	XF	Unc	BU
90(2001) Proof	—	Value: 15.00				
92(2003)	—	—	0.25	0.45	0.75	1.00
92(2003) Proof	—	Value: 15.00				
93(2004)	—	—	0.25	0.45	0.75	1.00
95(2006)	—	—	0.25	0.45	0.75	1.00
96(2007)	—	—	0.25	0.45	0.75	1.00
96(2007) Proof	—	Value: 15.00				

Y# 567 10 YUAN

7.4300 g., Copper-Nickel, 26 mm. **Subject:** 90th Anniversary of the Republic **Obv:** Bust of Sun Yat-sen facing **Rev:** Holographic design and denomination **Edge:** Reeded

Date	Mintage	F	VF	XF	Unc	BU
90 (2001)	30,000,000	—	—	—	2.50	3.00

Y# 572 10 YUAN

7.5000 g., Copper-Nickel, 26 mm. **Subject:** Chiang Ching-kuo, president **Obv:** Portriat facing **Rev:** Two legends in latent format, large value below

Date	Mintage	F	VF	XF	Unc	BU
2010	—	—	—	—	2.00	3.00

Y# 573 10 YUAN

7.5000 g., Copper-Nickel, 26 mm. **Subject:** Chiang Wei-shui **Obv:** Portrait facing **Rev:** Two legends as latent images, large value below

Date	Mintage	F	VF	XF	Unc	BU
2010	—	—	—	—	2.00	3.00

Y# 574 10 YUAN

7.5000 g., Copper-Nickel, 26 mm. **Subject:** Dr. Sun Yat-sen **Obv:** Bust facing **Rev:** Two legends as latent images, large value below

Date	Mintage	F	VF	XF	Unc	BU
2010	—	—	—	—	2.00	3.00

Y# 565 20 YUAN

8.5000 g., Bi-Metallic Copper-Nickel center in Aluminum-Bronze ring., 26.85 mm. **Subject:** Mona Rudao, Sediq chieftain **Obv:** Male portrait **Rev:** Three boats **Edge:** Reeded

Date	Mintage	F	VF	XF	Unc	BU
90(2001)	—	—	—	—	3.50	4.50
90(2001) Proof	—	Value: 18.00				
92(2003)	—	—	—	—	3.50	4.50
92(2003) Proof	—	Value: 18.00				

Y# 568 50 YUAN

10.0000 g., Aluminum-Bronze, 28 mm. **Obv:** Bust **Rev:** Denomination above latent image denomination **Edge:** Reeding and denomination

Date	Mintage	F	VF	XF	Unc	BU
90-2001 Proof	—	Value: 20.00				
91-2002	—	—	—	—	7.50	10.00
92-2003	—	—	—	—	7.50	10.00
92-2003 Proof	—	Value: 20.00				
93-2004	—	—	—	—	7.50	10.00
95-2006	—	—	—	—	7.50	10.00

Y# 570 50 YUAN

15.5680 g., 0.9990 Silver 0.5000 oz. ASW, 33 mm. **Subject:** World Cup Baseball **Obv:** Player at bat with ball background **Rev:** Mount Jade above denomination **Edge:** Reeded

Date	Mintage	F	VF	XF	Unc	BU
90(2001)	130,000	—	—	—	25.00	27.50

Y# 569 50 YUAN

15.5680 g., 0.9990 Silver 0.5000 oz. ASW, 33 mm. **Subject:** 90th Anniversary of the Republic **Obv:** Portrait of Sun Yat-sen **Rev:** Latent image above denomination **Edge:** Reeded

Date	Mintage	F	VF	XF	Unc	BU
90(2001)	230,000	—	—	—	25.00	27.50

Y# 571 50 YUAN

31.1035 g., 0.9990 Silver 0.9990 oz. ASW, 38 mm. **Subject:** Third National Expressway **Obv:** Multicolor island map **Rev:** Kao Ping Hsi bridge **Edge:** Reeded

Date	Mintage	F	VF	XF	Unc	BU
93-2004	20,000	—	—	—	45.00	50.00

MINT SETS

KM#	Date	Mintage	Identification	Issue Price	Mkt Val
MS9	92(2003) (6)	—	Y550-553, 565, 568 plus C-N Year of the Goat medal	—	20.00

PROOF SETS

KM#	Date	Mintage	Identification	Issue Price	Mkt Val
PS10	90(2001) (6)	210,000	Y#550-553, 565, 568 plus medal	29.40	90.00
PS12	92(2003) (6)	—	Y550-553, 565, 568 plus silver Year of the Goat Medal	—	100

COLOMBIA

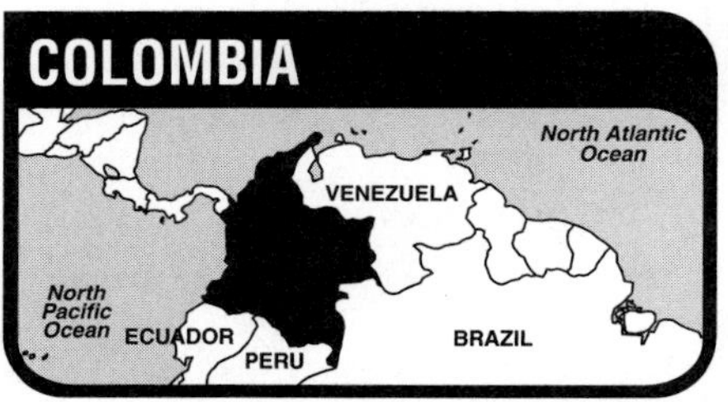

The Republic of Colombia, in the northwestern corner of South America, has an area of 440,831 sq. mi. (1,138,910 sq. km.) and a population of*42.3 million. Capital: Bogota. The economy is primarily agricultural with a mild, rich coffee being the chief crop. Colombia has the world's largest platinum deposits and important reserves of coal, iron ore, petroleum and limestone; other precious metals and emeralds are also mined. Coffee, crude oil, bananas, sugar and emeralds are exported.

MINT MARKS

A, M – Medellin (capital), Antioquia (state)
B - BOGOTA
(D) Denver, USA
H – Birmingham (Heaton & Sons)
(m) - Medellin, w/o mint mark
(Mo) - Mexico City
NI - Numismatica Italiana, Arezzo, Italy mint marks stylized in wreath
(P) - Philadelphia
(S) - San Francisco, USA.
(W) - Waterbury, CT (USA, Scoville mint)

REPUBLIC

DECIMAL COINAGE

100 Centavos = 1 Peso

KM# 282.2 20 PESOS

3.6000 g., Aluminum-Bronze, 20.25 mm. **Obv:** Flagged arms, 68 beads circle around the rim **Rev:** Denomination within wreath

Date	Mintage	F	VF	XF	Unc	BU
2003	15,900,000	—	—	—	0.50	0.75

KM# 294 20 PESOS
2.0000 g., Brass, 17.2 mm. **Obv:** Head of Simon Bolivar left **Rev:** Value **Edge:** Reeded

Date	Mintage	F	VF	XF	Unc	BU
2004	22,700,000	—	—	—	0.15	0.25
2005	56,100,000	—	—	—	0.15	0.25
2006	63,012,500	—	—	—	0.15	0.25
2007	87,300,000	—	—	—	0.15	0.25
2008	5,850,000	—	—	—	0.20	0.30

KM# 283.2 50 PESOS
4.6000 g., Copper-Nickel-Zinc, 21.8 mm. **Obv:** National arms, date below **Rev:** Denomination within wreath, 72 beads circle around rim **Edge:** Reeded

Date	Mintage	F	VF	XF	Unc	BU
2003	59,842,620	—	—	0.30	0.80	1.20
2004	51,700,000	—	—	0.30	0.80	1.20
2005	47,200,000	—	—	0.30	0.80	1.20
2006	22,000,000	—	—	0.30	0.80	1.20
2007	29,324,000	—	—	0.30	0.80	1.20
2008	67,500,000	—	—	0.30	0.80	1.20
2009	3,000,000	—	—	0.40	1.00	1.25
2010	55,100,000	—	—	0.25	0.75	1.00

KM# 283.2a 50 PESOS
Stainless Steel, 21.8 mm. **Obv:** National Arms **Rev:** Denomination within wreath, 72 beads circle around rim **Edge:** Reeded

Date	Mintage	F	VF	XF	Unc	BU
2007	—	—	—	—	0.80	1.20
2008	—	—	—	—	0.80	1.20
2009	—	—	—	—	0.80	1.20
2010	—	—	—	—	0.80	1.20

KM# 285.2 100 PESOS
5.3100 g., Aluminum-Bronze, 23 mm. **Obv:** Flagged arms above date **Rev:** Denomination within wreath, numerals 6mm tall **Edge:** Lettered and reeded **Edge Lettering:** CIEN PESOS (twice) **Note:** Edge varieties exist.

Date	Mintage	F	VF	XF	Unc	BU
2006	59,000,000	—	—	0.60	1.50	2.00
2007	55,000,000	—	—	0.60	1.50	2.00
2008	120,200,000	—	—	0.60	1.50	2.00
2009	41,800,000	—	—	0.60	1.50	2.00
2010	85,400,000	—	—	0.50	1.25	1.50

KM# 287 200 PESOS
7.0800 g., Copper-Nickel-Zinc, 24.4 mm. **Obv:** Denomination within lined circle, date below **Rev:** Quimbaya artwork **Edge Lettering:** MOTIVO QUIMBAYA - 200 PESOS

Date	Mintage	F	VF	XF	Unc	BU
2004	31,200,000	—	—	0.60	1.50	2.00
2005	49,700,000	—	—	0.60	1.50	2.00
2006	75,462,500	—	—	0.60	1.50	2.00
2007	85,000,000	—	—	0.60	1.50	2.00
2008	110,400,000	—	—	0.60	1.50	2.00
2009	42,200,000	—	—	0.60	1.50	2.00
2010	85,600,000	—	—	0.60	1.50	2.00

KM# 286 500 PESOS
7.1400 g., Bi-Metallic Aluminum-Bronze center in Copper-Zinc-Nickel ring, 23.7 mm. **Obv:** Guacari tree within circle **Rev:** Denomination within circle, date below **Edge:** Segmented reeding

Date	Mintage	F	VF	XF	Unc	BU
2002	38,800,000	—	—	1.20	3.00	4.00
2003	26,410,000	—	—	1.20	3.00	4.00
2004	90,454,000	—	—	1.20	3.00	4.00
2005	97,664,000	—	—	1.20	3.00	4.00
2006	70,700,000	—	—	1.20	3.00	4.00
2007	109,624,000	—	—	1.20	3.00	4.00
2008	132,400,000	—	—	1.20	3.00	4.00
2009	39,700,000	—	—	1.20	3.00	4.00
2010	35,800,000	—	—	1.00	2.00	3.00

COMOROS

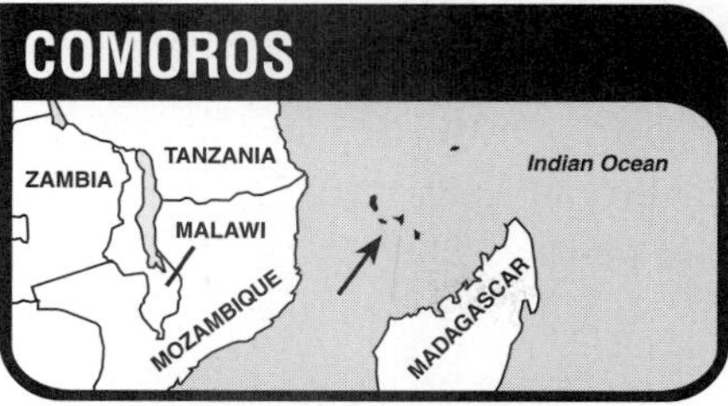

The Federal Islamic Republic of the Comoros, a volcanic archipelago located in the Mozambique Channel of the Indian Ocean 300 miles (483 km.) northwest of Madagascar, has an area of 719 sq. mi. (2,171 sq. km.) and a population of *714,000. Capital: Moroni. The economy of the islands is based on agriculture. There are practically no mineral resources. Vanilla, essence for perfumes, copra, and sisal are exported.

Ancient Phoenician traders were probably the first visitors to the Comoro Islands, but the first detailed knowledge of the area was gathered by Arab sailors. Arab dominion and culture were firmly established when the Portuguese, Dutch, and French arrived in the 16th century. In 1843 a Malagasy ruler ceded the island of Mayotte to France; the other three principal islands of the archipelago-Anjouan, Moheli, and Grand Comore came under French protection in 1886. The islands were joined administratively with Madagascar in 1912. The Comoros became partially autonomous, with the status of a French overseas territory, in 1946, and achieved complete internal autonomy in 1961. On Dec. 31, 1975, after 133 years of French association, the Comoro Islands became the independent Republic of the Comoros.

Mayotte retained the option of determining its future ties and in 1976 voted to remain French. Its present status is that of a French Territorial Collectivity. French currency now circulates there.

MINT MARKS
(a) - Paris, privy marks only
A - Paris

MONETARY SYSTEM
100 Centimes = 1 Franc

FEDERAL ISLAMIC REPUBLIC

BANQUE CENTRAL COINAGE

KM# 14a 25 FRANCS
3.9700 g., Steel, 20 mm. **Series:** F.A.O. **Obv:** Chickens **Rev:** Denomination above date

Date	Mintage	F	VF	XF	Unc	BU
2001(a) Horseshoe	—	0.20	0.40	0.80	2.00	—

KM# 16 50 FRANCS
5.6000 g., Nickel, 23.93 mm. **Obv:** Crescent and stars above denomination, date below **Rev:** Building with tall tower **Edge:** Reeded

Date	Mintage	F	VF	XF	Unc	BU
2001(a) horseshoe	—	—	—	—	2.50	3.50

KM# 16a 50 FRANCS
Nickel Plated Steel, 23.9 mm. **Obv:** Crescent and stars above denomination, date below **Rev:** Building with tall tower **Edge:** Reeded

Date	Mintage	F	VF	XF	Unc	BU
2001(a)	—	0.25	0.50	1.00	2.50	3.50

KM# 18a 100 FRANCS
10.2000 g., Copper-Nickel, 28 mm. **Obv:** Crescent and stars above denomination, date below **Rev:** Boat and fish

Date	Mintage	F	VF	XF	Unc	BU
2003(a)	—	—	—	—	3.50	5.00

CONGO REPUBLIC

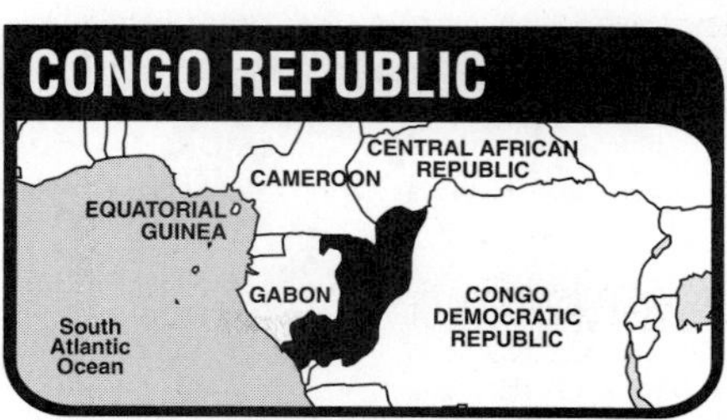

The Republic of the Congo (formerly the Peoples Republic of the Congo), located on the equator in west-central Africa, has an area of 132,047 sq. mi. (342,000 sq. km.) and a population of *2.98 million. Capital: Brazzaville. Agriculture forestry, mining, and food processing are the principal industries. Timber, industrial diamonds, potash, peanuts, and cocoa beans are exported.

NOTE: For earlier and related coinage see French Equatorial Africa and the Equatorial African States. For later coinage see Central African States.

RULER
French until 1960

MINT MARK
(a) - Paris, privy marks only

MONETARY SYSTEM
100 Centimes = 1 Franc

REPUBLIC
Republique du Congo
DECIMAL COINAGE

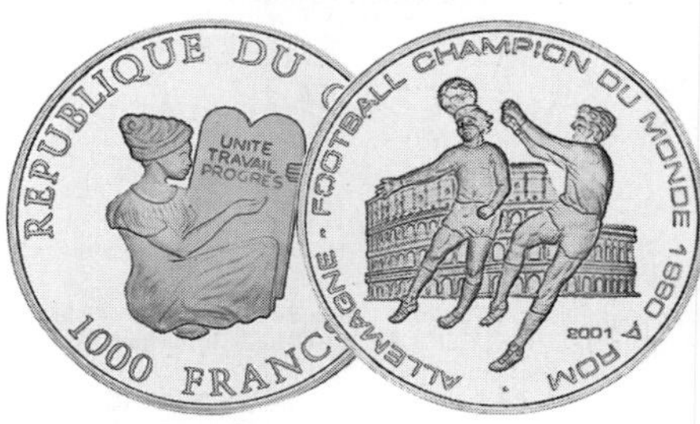

KM# 47 1000 FRANCS
15.0000 g., 0.9990 Silver 0.4818 oz. ASW, 35 mm. **Obv:** Seated woman with tablet **Rev:** Two soccer players and colosseum **Edge:** Plain

Date	Mintage	F	VF	XF	Unc	BU
2001 Proof	—	Value: 40.00				

KM# 48 1000 FRANCS
20.0000 g., 0.9990 Silver 0.6423 oz. ASW, 38 mm. **Obv:** Seated woman with tablet **Rev:** Two soccer players and Mexican pyramid **Edge:** Reeded

Date	Mintage	F	VF	XF	Unc	BU
2001 Proof	—	Value: 45.00				

KM# 109 1000 FRANCS
20.0000 g., 0.9990 Silver 0.6423 oz. ASW, 38.6 mm. **Obv:** Seated woman with tablets **Rev:** Portuguese merchant ship

Date	Mintage	F	VF	XF	Unc	BU
2002 Proof	—	Value: 45.00				

KM# 108 1000 FRANCS
20.0000 g., 0.9990 Silver 0.6423 oz. ASW, 38.6 mm. **Obv:** Seated woman with two tablets **Rev:** James Cook and the Endeavour

Date	Mintage	F	VF	XF	Unc	BU
2003 Proof	—	Value: 45.00				

KM# 50 1000 FRANCS
20.2000 g., Silver, 40 mm. **Series:** Endangered Wildlife **Obv:** Seated woman with tablet **Obv. Legend:** REPUBLIQUE DU CONGO **Rev:** Gorilla seated with infant **Rev. Legend:** - LE MONDE ANIMAL EN PERIL **Edge:** Reeded

Date	Mintage	F	VF	XF	Unc	BU
2003 Proof	—	Value: 50.00				

KM# 51 1000 FRANCS
15.5000 g., Silver, 35.02 mm. **Obv:** Seated woman with tablet **Obv. Legend:** REPUBLIQUE DU CONGO **Rev:** Head of Michelangelo 3/4 right **Edge:** Plain

Date	Mintage	F	VF	XF	Unc	BU
2005 Proof	—	Value: 37.50				

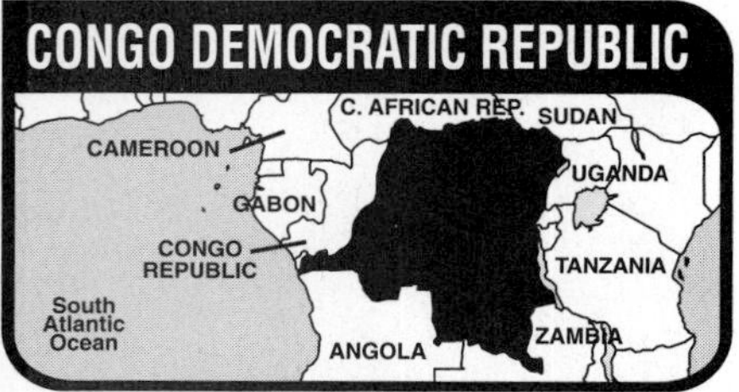

The Democratic Republic of the Congo (formerly the Republic of Zaire, and earlier the Belgian Congo), located in the south-central part of Africa, has an area of 905,568 sq. mi. (2,345,410 sq. km.) and a population of *47.4 million. Capital: Kinshasa. The mineral-rich country produces copper, tin, diamonds, gold, zinc, cobalt and uranium.

DEMOCRATIC REPUBLIC

1998 -

REFORM COINAGE

Congo Francs replace Zaire; July 1998

KM# 76 25 CENTIMES
0.8800 g., Aluminum, 19.90 mm. **Obv:** Lion left **Rev:** Mongoose **Edge:** Plain

Date	Mintage	F	VF	XF	Unc	BU
2002	—	—	—	—	0.75	1.00

KM# 77 25 CENTIMES
0.8500 g., Aluminum, 20 mm. **Obv:** Lion left **Rev:** Ram right, looking left **Edge:** Plain

Date	Mintage	F	VF	XF	Unc	BU
2002	—	—	—	—	0.75	1.00

KM# 83 25 CENTIMES
1.3000 g., Aluminum, 20 mm. **Obv:** Lion left **Rev:** Wild leaping dog right **Edge:** Plain

Date	Mintage	F	VF	XF	Unc	BU
2002	—	—	—	—	0.75	1.00

KM# 75 50 CENTIMES
2.2000 g., Aluminum, 26.97 mm. **Obv:** Lion left **Rev:** Soccer player right, bumping ball with head **Edge:** Plain

Date	Mintage	F	VF	XF	Unc	BU
2002	—	—	—	—	1.25	1.50

KM# 78 50 CENTIMES
2.1600 g., Aluminum, 27 mm. **Obv:** Lion left **Rev:** Giraffe right, looking left **Edge:** Plain

Date	Mintage	F	VF	XF	Unc	BU
2002	—	—	—	—	1.25	1.50

KM# 79 50 CENTIMES
2.2000 g., Aluminum, 26.92 mm. **Obv:** Lion left **Rev:** Gorilla facing, looking left **Edge:** Plain

Date	Mintage	F	VF	XF	Unc	BU
2002	—	—	—	—	1.00	1.25

KM# 80 50 CENTIMES
2.1600 g., Aluminum, 27 mm. **Obv:** Lion left **Rev:** Butterfly **Edge:** Plain

Date	Mintage	F	VF	XF	Unc	BU
2002	—	—	—	—	1.50	1.75

KM# 123 50 CENTIMES
3.9200 g., Stainless Steel, 22.3 mm. **Obv:** Lion left above denomination **Rev:** Verney L. Camereon **Edge:** Plain

Date	Mintage	F	VF	XF	Unc	BU
2002	—	—	—	—	1.00	1.25

KM# 81 FRANC
4.5700 g., Brass, 20.31 mm. **Obv:** Lion left **Rev:** Turtle **Edge:** Plain

Date	Mintage	F	VF	XF	Unc	BU
2002	—	—	—	—	1.25	1.50

KM# 82 FRANC
4.5200 g., Brass, 20.32 mm. **Obv:** Lion left **Rev:** Chicken **Edge:** Plain

Date	Mintage	F	VF	XF	Unc	BU
2002	—	—	—	—	1.50	1.75

KM# 156 FRANC
5.0000 g., Nickel Clad Steel, 24.8 mm. **Subject:** 25th Anniversary - Pope John Paul II's Visit **Obv:** Lion left **Rev:** Pope John Paul II as a priest in 1946 **Edge:** Plain

Date	Mintage	F	VF	XF	Unc	BU
2004	—	—	—	—	2.00	2.50

KM# 157 FRANC
5.0000 g., Nickel Clad Steel, 24.8 mm. **Subject:** 25th Anniversary - Pope John Paul II's Visit **Obv:** Lion left **Rev:** Pope John Paul II as a Cardinal in 1967 **Edge:** Plain

Date	Mintage	F	VF	XF	Unc	BU
2004	—	—	—	—	2.00	2.50

KM# 158 FRANC
5.0000 g., Nickel Clad Steel, 24.8 mm. **Subject:** 25th Anniversary - Pope John Paul II's Visit **Obv:** Lion left **Rev:** Pope John Paul II as newly elected pope in 1978 **Edge:** Plain

Date	Mintage	F	VF	XF	Unc	BU
2004	—	—	—	—	2.00	2.50

KM# 159 FRANC
5.0000 g., Nickel Clad Steel, 24.8 mm. **Subject:** 25th Anniversary - Pope John Paul II's Visit **Obv:** Lion left **Rev:** Pope John Paul II wearing a mitre **Edge:** Plain

Date	Mintage	F	VF	XF	Unc	BU
2004	—	—	—	—	2.00	2.50

KM# 174 FRANC
6.0000 g., Copper-Nickel, 21 mm. **Obv:** Lion left **Rev:** African Golden Cat right **Edge:** Plain

Date	Mintage	F	VF	XF	Unc	BU
2004	5,000	—	—	—	7.25	9.00

KM# 174a FRANC
8.0000 g., 0.9990 Silver 0.2569 oz. ASW, 21 mm. **Obv:** Lion left **Rev:** African Golden Cat right **Edge:** Plain

Date	Mintage	F	VF	XF	Unc	BU
2004	25	—	—	—	270	300

KM# 56 5 FRANCS
22.4000 g., Copper-Nickel, 39.8 mm. **Series:** Wild Life Protection **Obv:** Lion left **Rev:** Multicolor swallowtail butterfly hologram **Edge:** Reeded **Note:** Prev. KM#79.

Date	Mintage	F	VF	XF	Unc	BU
2002(2001)	20,000	—	—	—	35.00	40.00

KM# 57 5 FRANCS
22.4000 g., Copper-Nickel, 39.8 mm. **Series:** Wild Life Protection **Obv:** Lion left **Rev:** Multicolor dark greenish butterfly hologram **Edge:** Reeded **Note:** Prev. KM#80.

Date	Mintage	F	VF	XF	Unc	BU
2002(2001)	20,000	—	—	—	35.00	40.00

KM# 58 5 FRANCS
22.4000 g., Copper-Nickel, 39.8 mm. **Series:** Wild Life Protection **Obv:** Lion left **Rev:** Multicolor red and black butterfly hologram **Edge:** Reeded **Note:** Prev. KM#81.

Date	Mintage	F	VF	XF	Unc	BU
2002(2001)	20,000	—	—	—	35.00	40.00

KM# 170 5 FRANCS
24.3000 g., Copper-Nickel, 38.5 mm. **Obv:** Lion left **Rev:** Multicolor German 1 mark coin dated 2001 **Edge:** Reeded

Date	Mintage	F	VF	XF	Unc	BU
2002	—	—	—	—	15.00	20.00

KM# 146 5 FRANCS
27.0000 g., Copper-Nickel, 38.6 mm. **Obv:** Lion left **Rev:** Multicolor Quetzal bird **Edge:** Reeded

Date	Mintage	F	VF	XF	Unc	BU
2004 Proof	5,000	Value: 45.00				

KM# 147 5 FRANCS
27.0000 g., Copper-Nickel, 38.6 mm. **Obv:** Lion left **Rev:** Multicolor Bird of Paradise **Edge:** Reeded

Date	Mintage	F	VF	XF	Unc	BU
2004 Proof	5,000	Value: 45.00				

KM# 148 5 FRANCS
27.0000 g., Copper-Nickel, 38.6 mm. **Obv:** Lion left **Rev:** Multicolor Kingfisher bird **Edge:** Reeded

Date	Mintage	F	VF	XF	Unc	BU
2004 Proof	5,000	Value: 45.00				

KM# 164 5 FRANCS
25.4000 g., Copper-Nickel, 38.8 mm. **Subject:** Papal Visit **Obv:** Lion left **Rev:** Pope John Paul II with staff and mitre **Edge:** Reeded

Date	Mintage	F	VF	XF	Unc	BU
ND (2004) Proof	—	Value: 25.00				

KM# 165 5 FRANCS
49.5000 g., Copper-Nickel, 45.1 mm. **Obv:** Lion left **Rev:** Rotating 50 year calender **Edge:** Reeded

Date	Mintage	F	VF	XF	Unc	BU
ND(2004) Matte	—	—	—	—	75.00	—

KM# 128 5 FRANCS
8.0000 g., Iron, 27.26x14.13 mm. **Obv:** Country name, lion and date in the bowl part of the spoon; value on the handle part **Edge:** Reeded **Note:** This is the Spoon part of the Compass and Spoon set. (The spoon is the compass needle.)

Date	Mintage	F	VF	XF	Unc	BU
2004	5,000	—	—	—	15.00	—

KM# 181 5 FRANCS
25.9200 g., Copper-Nickel, 38.58 mm. **Series:** Wildlife Protection **Obv:** Lion standing laft **Obv. Legend:** REPUBLIQUE DEMOCRATIQUE DU CONGO **Rev:** Red Perch, multicolor **Edge:** Reeded

Date	Mintage	F	VF	XF	Unc	BU
2005	5,000	—	—	—	—	20.00

KM# 182 5 FRANCS
Copper-Nickel Gilt **Obv:** Lion standing left **Rev:** Two cupids embracing, roses - multicolor **Rev. Legend:** *Endless Love* **Edge:** Reeded **Shape:** Heart

Date	Mintage	F	VF	XF	Unc	BU
2005 Proof	5,000	Value: 35.00				

KM# 166 5 FRANCS
2.1600 g., Wood Maple wood, 39.4 mm. **Obv:** Lion, brown ink **Rev:** Gorilla, brown ink **Edge:** Plain

Date	Mintage	F	VF	XF	Unc	BU
2005	2,000	—	—	—	20.00	—

KM# 179 5 FRANCS
25.9200 g., Copper-Nickel, 38.58 mm. **Series:** Wildlife Protection **Obv:** Lion standing left **Obv. Legend:** REPUBLIQUE DEMOCRATIQUE DU CONGO **Rev:** Butterfly Fish, multicolor **Edge:** Reeded

Date	Mintage	F	VF	XF	Unc	BU
2005	5,000	—	—	—	—	20.00

KM# 180 5 FRANCS
25.9200 g., Copper-Nickel, 38.58 mm. **Series:** Wildlife Protection **Obv:** Lion standing left **Obv. Legend:** REPUBLIQUE DEMOCRATIQYE DU CONGO **Rev:** African Moony Fish, multicolor **Edge:** Reeded

Date	Mintage	F	VF	XF	Unc	BU
2005	5,000	—	—	—	—	20.00

KM# 178 5 FRANCS
26.3000 g., Silver Plated Bronze, 38.6 mm. **Obv:** Lion **Rev:** Multicolor Pope John Paul II wearing a mitre **Edge:** Reeded

Date	Mintage	F	VF	XF	Unc	BU
2007 Proof	—	Value: 40.00				

KM# 72 10 FRANCS
20.0000 g., 0.9250 Silver 0.5948 oz. ASW, 40.1 mm. **Series:** Airplanes **Obv:** Lion left **Rev:** Mikoyan-Gurevich Mig 21 fighter flying left **Edge:** Reeded

Date	Mintage	F	VF	XF	Unc	BU
2001 Proof	—	Value: 40.00				

KM# 74 10 FRANCS
31.1035 g., 0.9990 Silver 0.9990 oz. ASW, 40 mm. **Subject:** 2004 Olympics **Obv:** Lion left **Rev:** Convex chariot **Edge:** Reeded

Date	Mintage	F	VF	XF	Unc	BU
2001 Antique Finish	15,000	—	—	—	45.00	—

KM# 167 10 FRANCS
20.0000 g., 0.9250 Silver 0.5948 oz. ASW, 40.1 mm. **Obv:** Lion left **Rev:** SS Bremen ship at sea **Edge:** Reeded

Date	Mintage	F	VF	XF	Unc	BU
2001 Proof	—	Value: 35.00				

KM# 168 10 FRANCS
20.0000 g., 0.9250 Silver 0.5948 oz. ASW, 40.1 mm. **Obv:** Lion left **Rev:** RMS Queen Elizabeth 2 at sea **Edge:** Reeded

Date	Mintage	F	VF	XF	Unc	BU
2001 Proof	—	Value: 35.00				

KM# 169 10 FRANCS
20.0000 g., 0.9250 Silver 0.5948 oz. ASW, 30 mm. **Obv:** Lion left **Rev:** Sail Ship America **Edge:** Reeded

Date	Mintage	F	VF	XF	Unc	BU
2001 Proof	—	Value: 35.00				

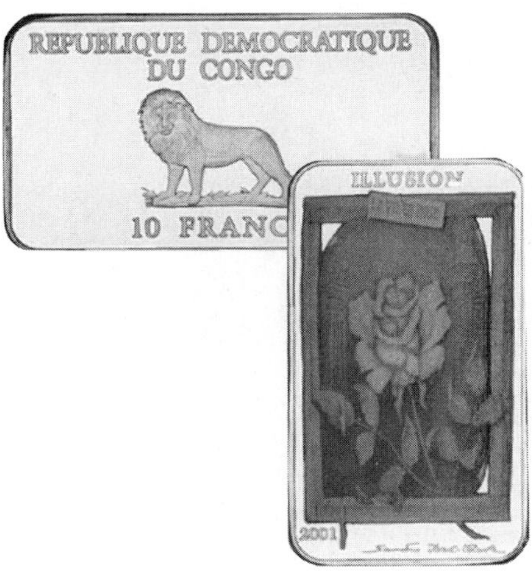

KM# 38 10 FRANCS
31.3000 g., 0.9250 Silver 0.9308 oz. ASW, 27 x 47.1 mm. **Subject:** Illusion **Obv:** Lion left **Rev:** Multicolor couple in flower picture **Edge:** Plain **Shape:** Rectangular **Note:** Prev. KM#61.

Date	Mintage	F	VF	XF	Unc	BU
2001 Proof	—	Value: 50.00				

KM# 59 10 FRANCS
25.9500 g., 0.9250 Silver 0.7717 oz. ASW, 39.9 mm. **Series:** Wild Life Protection **Obv:** Lion left **Rev:** Multicolor swallowtail butterfly hologram **Edge:** Reeded **Note:** Prev. KM#82.

Date	Mintage	F	VF	XF	Unc	BU
2002 (2001) Proof	15,000	Value: 65.00				

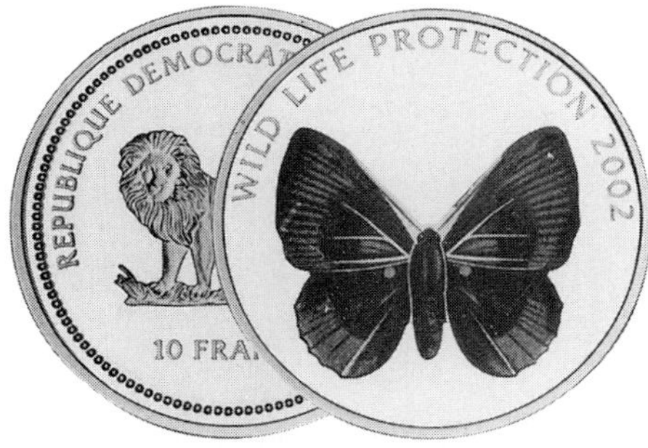

KM# 60 10 FRANCS
25.9500 g., 0.9250 Silver 0.7717 oz. ASW, 39.9 mm. **Series:** Wild Life Protection **Obv:** Lion left **Rev:** Multicolor dark greenish butterfly hologram **Edge:** Reeded **Note:** Prev. KM#83.

Date	Mintage	F	VF	XF	Unc	BU
2002 (2001) Proof	15,000	Value: 65.00				

KM# 61 10 FRANCS
25.9500 g., 0.9250 Silver 0.7717 oz. ASW, 39.9 mm. **Series:** Wild Life Protection **Obv:** Lion left **Rev:** Multicolor red and black butterfly hologram **Edge:** Reeded **Note:** Prev. KM#84.

Date	Mintage	F	VF	XF	Unc	BU
2002 (2001) Proof	15,000	Value: 65.00				

KM# 65 10 FRANCS
20.0000 g., 0.9250 Silver 0.5948 oz. ASW, 40.1 mm. **Series:** Airplanes **Obv:** Lion left **Rev:** Vickers Vimy twin engine biplane flying left **Edge:** Reeded **Note:** Prev. KM#88.

Date	Mintage	F	VF	XF	Unc	BU
2001 Proof	—	Value: 40.00				

KM# 66 10 FRANCS
20.0000 g., 0.9250 Silver 0.5948 oz. ASW, 40.1 mm. **Series:** Airplanes **Obv:** Lion left **Rev:** Fokker DR1 triplane flying left **Edge:** Reeded **Note:** Prev. KM#89.

Date	Mintage	F	VF	XF	Unc	BU
2001 Proof	—	Value: 40.00				

KM# 67 10 FRANCS
20.0000 g., 0.9250 Silver 0.5948 oz. ASW, 40.1 mm. **Series:** Airplanes **Obv:** Lion left **Rev:** Lockheed Vega flying left **Edge:** Reeded **Note:** Prev. KM#90.

Date	Mintage	F	VF	XF	Unc	BU
2001 Proof	—	Value: 40.00				

KM# 68 10 FRANCS
20.0000 g., 0.9250 Silver 0.5948 oz. ASW, 40.1 mm. **Series:** Airplanes **Obv:** Lion left **Rev:** Boeing 314 Clipper flying left **Edge:** Reeded **Note:** Prev. KM#91.

Date	Mintage	F	VF	XF	Unc	BU
2001 Proof	—	Value: 40.00				

KM# 69 10 FRANCS

20.0000 g., 0.9250 Silver 0.5948 oz. ASW, 40.1 mm. **Series:** Airplanes **Obv:** Lion left **Rev:** Junkers JU-87 Stuka in a dive **Edge:** Reeded **Note:** Prev. KM#92.

Date	Mintage	F	VF	XF	Unc	BU
2001 Proof	—	Value: 40.00				

KM# 70 10 FRANCS

20.0000 g., 0.9250 Silver 0.5948 oz. ASW, 40.1 mm. **Series:** Airplanes **Obv:** Lion left **Rev:** B-29 Enola Gay flying left **Edge:** Reeded **Note:** Prev. KM#93.

Date	Mintage	F	VF	XF	Unc	BU
2001 Proof	—	Value: 45.00				

KM# 71 10 FRANCS

20.0000 g., 0.9250 Silver 0.5948 oz. ASW, 40.1 mm. **Series:** Airplanes **Obv:** Lion left **Rev:** Bell X-1 rocket plane flying left **Edge:** Reeded **Note:** Prev. KM#94.

Date	Mintage	F	VF	XF	Unc	BU
2001 Proof	—	Value: 40.00				

KM# 175 10 FRANCS

25.8300 g., Silver, 40 mm. **Obv:** Lion left **Rev:** 3 players **Edge:** Reeded

Date	Mintage	F	VF	XF	Unc	BU
2001	—	—	—	—	—	50.00

KM# 91 10 FRANCS

31.1000 g., 0.9990 Silver 0.9988 oz. ASW, 40 mm. **Subject:** Olympics **Obv:** Lion left **Rev:** Ancient athlete incuse design **Edge:** Plain **Note:** Design hubs with the design of the 500 sika coin KM-42 of Ghana

Date	Mintage	F	VF	XF	Unc	BU
2002 Antiqued finish	—	—	—	—	40.00	—

KM# 124 10 FRANCS

26.0000 g., 0.9250 Silver 0.7732 oz. ASW, 40 mm. **Subject:** Field Marshal Erwin Rommel **Obv:** Lion left above value **Rev:** Rommel, tank and map **Edge:** Reeded

Date	Mintage	F	VF	XF	Unc	BU
2002 Proof	15,000	Value: 42.50				

KM# 125 10 FRANCS

26.0000 g., 0.9250 Silver 0.7732 oz. ASW, 40 mm. **Subject:** George S. Patton **Obv:** Lion left above value **Rev:** Patton, tank and map **Edge:** Reeded

Date	Mintage	F	VF	XF	Unc	BU
2002 Proof	15,000	Value: 42.50				

KM# 162 10 FRANCS

20.2000 g., 0.9990 Silver 0.6488 oz. ASW, 40 mm. **Obv:** Lion left **Rev:** Space shuttle and five astronauts **Edge:** Reeded

Date	Mintage	F	VF	XF	Unc	BU
2002 Proof	—	Value: 40.00				

KM# 189 10 FRANCS

26.1500 g., Copper-Nickel, 40.3 mm. **Series:** Automobiles **Obv:** Lion standing left **Rev:** Rolls Royce **Edge:** Reeded

Date	Mintage	F	VF	XF	Unc	BU
2002 Proof	—	Value: 18.00				

KM# 190 10 FRANCS

26.1500 g., Copper-Nickel, 40.3 mm. **Series:** Automobiles **Obv:** Lion standing left **Rev:** Peujeot

Date	Mintage	F	VF	XF	Unc	BU
2002 Proof	—	Value: 18.00				

KM# 191 10 FRANCS

26.1500 g., Copper-Nickel, 40.3 mm. **Series:** Automobiles **Obv:** Lion standing left **Rev:** Opel **Edge:** Reeded

Date	Mintage	F	VF	XF	Unc	BU
2002 Proof	—	Value: 18.00				

KM# 192 10 FRANCS

26.1500 g., Copper-Nickel, 40.3 mm. **Series:** Automobiles **Obv:** Lion standing left **Rev:** Cadillac

Date	Mintage	F	VF	XF	Unc	BU
2002 Proof	—	Value: 18.00				

KM# 93 10 FRANCS

31.2300 g., 0.9990 Silver 1.0030 oz. ASW, 38.7 mm. **Obv:** Lion left **Rev:** Bearded portrait of Verney L. Camereon **Edge:** Reeded

Date	Mintage	F	VF	XF	Unc	BU
2002	—	—	—	—	45.00	50.00

KM# 94 10 FRANCS

26.1500 g., Copper-Nickel, 40.3 mm. **Subject:** Historic Automobiles **Obv:** Lion left **Rev:** 1908 Berliet car **Edge:** Reeded

Date	Mintage	F	VF	XF	Unc	BU
2002 Proof	—	Value: 18.00				

KM# 95 10 FRANCS

26.1500 g., Copper-Nickel, 40.3 mm. **Subject:** Historic Automobiles **Obv:** Lion left **Rev:** 1919 Hispano Suiza H6 car right **Edge:** Reeded

Date	Mintage	F	VF	XF	Unc	BU
2002 Proof	—	Value: 18.00				

KM# 96 10 FRANCS

32.0000 g., Silver Plated Copper, 40 mm. **Subject:** World Cup Soccer **Obv:** Lion left **Rev:** Soccer player and multicolor American flag **Edge:** Reeded

Date	Mintage	F	VF	XF	Unc	BU
2002 Proof	20,000	Value: 50.00				

KM# 97 10 FRANCS

32.0000 g., Silver Plated Copper, 40 mm. **Subject:** World Cup Soccer **Obv:** Lion left **Rev:** Two soccer players and multicolor flag of Ecuador **Edge:** Reeded

Date	Mintage	F	VF	XF	Unc	BU
2002 Proof	20,000	Value: 50.00				

KM# 103 10 FRANCS

19.0000 g., 0.9990 Silver 0.6102 oz. ASW, 40 mm. **Series:** Airplanes **Obv:** Lion left **Rev:** WWI German Gotha Ursinus G bomber flying left at 8 o'clock **Edge:** Reeded

Date	Mintage	F	VF	XF	Unc	BU
2002 Proof	—	Value: 40.00				

KM# 104 10 FRANCS

19.0000 g., 0.9990 Silver 0.6102 oz. ASW, 40 mm. **Series:** Airplanes **Obv:** Lion left **Rev:** WWII ME 109 German fighter plane flying left **Edge:** Reeded

Date	Mintage	F	VF	XF	Unc	BU
2002 Proof	—	Value: 40.00				

KM# 105 10 FRANCS

19.0000 g., 0.9990 Silver 0.6102 oz. ASW, 40 mm. **Series:** Airplanes **Obv:** Lion left **Rev:** Savoia-Marchetti S 55 seaplane flying left **Edge:** Reeded

Date	Mintage	F	VF	XF	Unc	BU
2002 Proof	—	Value: 40.00				

KM# 106 10 FRANCS

19.0000 g., 0.9990 Silver 0.6102 oz. ASW, 40 mm. **Series:** Airplanes **Obv:** Lion left **Rev:** B-58 Hustler Delta wing bomber flying left at 8 o'clock **Edge:** Reeded

Date	Mintage	F	VF	XF	Unc	BU
2002 Proof	—	Value: 40.00				

KM# 107 10 FRANCS

19.0000 g., 0.9990 Silver 0.6102 oz. ASW, 40 mm. **Series:** Airplanes **Obv:** Lion left **Rev:** CF-105 Arrow jet fighter plane flying right, nose up **Edge:** Reeded

Date	Mintage	F	VF	XF	Unc	BU
2002 Proof	—	Value: 40.00				

KM# 108 10 FRANCS

19.0000 g., 0.9990 Silver 0.6102 oz. ASW, 40 mm. **Series:** Airplanes **Obv:** Lion left **Rev:** XB-70 Valkyrie experimental jet bomber flying right **Edge:** Reeded

Date	Mintage	F	VF	XF	Unc	BU
2002 Proof	—	Value: 40.00				

KM# 187 10 FRANCS

26.1500 g., Copper-Nickel, 40.3 mm. **Series:** Automobiles **Obv:** Lion standing left **Rev:** Buick **Edge:** Reeded

Date	Mintage	F	VF	XF	Unc	BU
2002 Proof	—	Value: 18.00				

KM# 188 10 FRANCS

26.1500 g., Copper-Nickel, 40.3 mm. **Series:** Automobiles **Obv:** Lion standing left **Rev:** Land Rover **Edge:** Reeded

Date	Mintage	F	VF	XF	Unc	BU
2002 Proof	—	Value: 18.00				

KM# 193 10 FRANCS

26.1500 g., Copper-Nickel, 40.3 mm. **Series:** Automobiles **Obv:** Lion standing left **Rev:** Benz **Shape:** Reeded

Date	Mintage	F	VF	XF	Unc	BU
2002 Proof	—	Value: 18.00				

KM# 194 10 FRANCS

26.1500 g., Copper-Nickel, 40.3 mm. **Series:** Automobiles **Obv:** Lion standing left **Rev:** Audi **Edge:** Reeded

Date	Mintage	F	VF	XF	Unc	BU
2002 Proof	—	Value: 18.00				

KM# 195 10 FRANCS

26.1500 g., Copper-Nickel, 40.3 mm. **Series:** Automobiles **Obv:** Lion standing left **Rev:** Alfa Romero

Date	Mintage	F	VF	XF	Unc	BU
2002 Proof	—	Value: 18.00				

KM# 196 10 FRANCS

26.1500 g., Copper-Nickel, 40.3 mm. **Series:** Automobiles **Obv:** Lion standing left **Rev:** Ford Model 'T' **Edge:** Reeded

Date	Mintage	F	VF	XF	Unc	BU
2002 Proof	—	Value: 18.00				

KM# 163 10 FRANCS

39.1000 g., Acrylic, 49.9 mm. **Obv:** Old World Swallowtail butterfly above lion and value **Rev:** Rear view of the obverse **Edge:** Plain

Date	Mintage	F	VF	XF	Unc	BU
2003	—	—	—	—	75.00	—

KM# 171 10 FRANCS

39.1000 g., Acrylic, 49.9 mm. **Obv:** Gorch Fock sail ship above lion and value **Rev:** Rear view of the obverse design **Edge:** Plain

Date	Mintage	F	VF	XF	Unc	BU
2003	1,000	—	—	—	75.00	—

KM# 109 10 FRANCS

19.0000 g., 0.9990 Silver 0.6102 oz. ASW, 40 mm. **Obv:** Lion left **Rev:** 14 BIS early aircraft in flight **Edge:** Reeded

Date	Mintage	F	VF	XF	Unc	BU
2003 Proof	—	Value: 40.00				

KM# 110 10 FRANCS
19.0000 g., 0.9990 Silver 0.6102 oz. ASW, 40 mm. **Obv:** Lion left **Rev:** WWI Sopwith Camel fighter plane flying right **Edge:** Reeded

Date	Mintage	F	VF	XF	Unc	BU
2003 Proof	—	Value: 40.00				

KM# 111 10 FRANCS
19.0000 g., 0.9990 Silver 0.6102 oz. ASW, 40 mm. **Obv:** Lion left **Rev:** Curtiss NC-4 early seaplane flying left **Edge:** Reeded

Date	Mintage	F	VF	XF	Unc	BU
2003 Proof	—	Value: 40.00				

KM# 112 10 FRANCS
19.0000 g., 0.9990 Silver 0.6102 oz. ASW, 40 mm. **Obv:** Lion left **Rev:** Macchi-Castoldi MC-72 seaplane flying left at 8 o'clock **Edge:** Reeded

Date	Mintage	F	VF	XF	Unc	BU
2003 Proof	—	Value: 40.00				

KM# 113 10 FRANCS
19.0000 g., 0.9990 Silver 0.6102 oz. ASW, 40 mm. **Obv:** Lion left **Rev:** WWII CA-12 Boomerang fighter plane flying above map at 10 o'clock **Edge:** Reeded

Date	Mintage	F	VF	XF	Unc	BU
2003 Proof	—	Value: 40.00				

KM# 114 10 FRANCS
19.0000 g., 0.9990 Silver 0.6102 oz. ASW, 40 mm. **Obv:** Lion left **Rev:** B-50A Superfortress bomber flying left **Edge:** Reeded

Date	Mintage	F	VF	XF	Unc	BU
2003 Proof	—	Value: 40.00				

KM# 115 10 FRANCS
19.0000 g., 0.9990 Silver 0.6102 oz. ASW, 40 mm. **Obv:** Lion left **Rev:** WWII Heinkel-178 German jet plane flying left **Edge:** Reeded

Date	Mintage	F	VF	XF	Unc	BU
2003 Proof	—	Value: 40.00				

KM# 116 10 FRANCS
19.0000 g., 0.9990 Silver 0.6102 oz. ASW, 40 mm. **Obv:** Lion left **Rev:** Early De Havilland Comet jet liner flying left **Edge:** Reeded

Date	Mintage	F	VF	XF	Unc	BU
2003 Proof	—	Value: 40.00				

KM# 117 10 FRANCS
19.0000 g., 0.9990 Silver 0.6102 oz. ASW, 40 mm. **Obv:** Lion left **Rev:** Panavia Tornado jet fighter-bomber flying left **Edge:** Reeded

Date	Mintage	F	VF	XF	Unc	BU
2003 Proof	—	Value: 40.00				

KM# 118 10 FRANCS
19.0000 g., 0.9990 Silver 0.6102 oz. ASW, 40 mm. **Obv:** Lion left **Rev:** Hindustan HF24 jet fighter flying left **Edge:** Reeded

Date	Mintage	F	VF	XF	Unc	BU
2003 Proof	—	Value: 40.00				

KM# 119 10 FRANCS
19.0000 g., 0.9990 Silver 0.6102 oz. ASW, 40 mm. **Obv:** Lion left **Rev:** Lockheed F-117 Stealth fighter flying left **Edge:** Reeded

Date	Mintage	F	VF	XF	Unc	BU
2003 Proof	—	Value: 40.00				

KM# 120 10 FRANCS
19.0000 g., 0.9990 Silver 0.6102 oz. ASW, 40 mm. **Obv:** Lion left **Rev:** North American X-15 experimental rocket plane flying right at 1 o'clock **Edge:** Reeded

Date	Mintage	F	VF	XF	Unc	BU
2003 Proof	—	Value: 40.00				

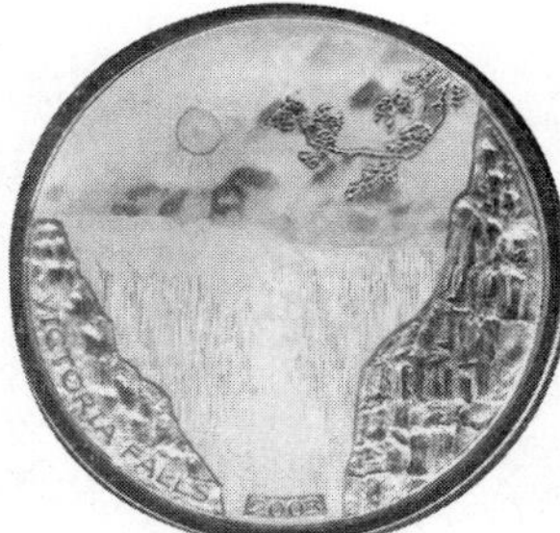

KM# 122 10 FRANCS
25.0000 g., 0.9250 Silver 0.7435 oz. ASW, 38.6 mm. **Obv:** Lion left **Rev:** Multicolor 3D hologram view of Victoria Falls **Edge:** Reeded

Date	Mintage	F	VF	XF	Unc	BU
2003 Proof	5,000	Value: 50.00				

KM# 99.1 10 FRANCS
24.9100 g., 0.9250 Silver 0.7408 oz. ASW, 38.6 mm. **Obv:** Lion left **Rev:** Chameleon **Edge:** Reeded

Date	Mintage	F	VF	XF	Unc	BU
2003 Proof	—	Value: 45.00				

KM# 99.2 10 FRANCS
24.9100 g., 0.9250 Silver 0.7408 oz. ASW, 38.6 mm. **Obv:** Lion left **Rev:** Multicolor chameleon **Edge:** Reeded

Date	Mintage	F	VF	XF	Unc	BU
2003 Proof	—	Value: 50.00				

KM# 100 10 FRANCS
24.9100 g., 0.9250 Silver 0.7408 oz. ASW, 38.6 mm. **Obv:** Lion left **Rev:** Striped skunk **Edge:** Reeded

Date	Mintage	F	VF	XF	Unc	BU
2003 Proof	—	Value: 45.00				

KM# 101 10 FRANCS
24.9100 g., 0.9250 Silver 0.7408 oz. ASW, 38.6 mm. **Obv:** Lion left **Rev:** Porcupine on rock, right **Edge:** Reeded

Date	Mintage	F	VF	XF	Unc	BU
2003 Proof	—	Value: 47.50				

KM# 102 10 FRANCS
24.9100 g., 0.9250 Silver 0.7408 oz. ASW, 38.6 mm. **Obv:** Lion left **Rev:** Giant Pangolin on rock right **Edge:** Reeded

Date	Mintage	F	VF	XF	Unc	BU
2003 Proof	—	Value: 45.00				

KM# 132 10 FRANCS
25.0000 g., 0.9000 Silver 0.7234 oz. ASW, 40 mm. **Obv:** Lion left **Rev:** Multicolor dolphin leaping left **Edge:** Reeded

Date	Mintage	F	VF	XF	Unc	BU
2003 Proof	5,000	Value: 50.00				

KM# 133 10 FRANCS
25.0000 g., 0.9000 Silver 0.7234 oz. ASW, 40 mm. **Obv:** Lion left **Rev:** Multicolor sea turtle left **Edge:** Reeded

Date	Mintage	F	VF	XF	Unc	BU
2003 Proof	5,000	Value: 50.00				

KM# 134 10 FRANCS
25.0000 g., 0.9000 Silver 0.7234 oz. ASW, 40 mm. **Obv:** Lion left **Rev:** Multicolor killer whale jumping right **Edge:** Reeded

Date	Mintage	F	VF	XF	Unc	BU
2003 Proof	5,000	Value: 50.00				

KM# 135 10 FRANCS
26.0000 g., 0.9990 Silver 0.8350 oz. ASW, 40 mm. **Obv:** Lion left **Rev:** Pope John Paul II with staff and mitre, waving **Edge:** Reeded

Date	Mintage	F	VF	XF	Unc	BU
2003 Proof	—	Value: 55.00				

KM# 141 10 FRANCS
25.0000 g., 0.9250 Silver 0.7435 oz. ASW, 38.6 mm. **Obv:** Lion left **Rev:** Multicolor Emperor fish swimming left **Edge:** Reeded

Date	Mintage	F	VF	XF	Unc	BU
2004 Proof	5,000	Value: 55.00				

KM# 142 10 FRANCS
25.0000 g., 0.9250 Silver 0.7435 oz. ASW, 38.6 mm. **Obv:** Lion left **Rev:** Multicolor octopus facing **Edge:** Reeded

Date	Mintage	F	VF	XF	Unc	BU
2004 Proof	5,000	Value: 75.00				

KM# 143 10 FRANCS
25.0000 g., 0.9250 Silver 0.7435 oz. ASW, 38.6 mm. **Obv:** Lion left **Rev:** Formula 1 and GT race cars **Edge:** Reeded

Date	Mintage	F	VF	XF	Unc	BU
2004 Proof	5,000	Value: 45.00				

KM# 145 10 FRANCS
25.0000 g., 0.9250 Silver 0.7435 oz. ASW, 27x47 mm. **Obv:** Lion left **Rev:** Pope with crucifix **Edge:** Plain **Shape:** Rectangular

Date	Mintage	F	VF	XF	Unc	BU
2004 Proof	5,000	Value: 50.00				

KM# 149 10 FRANCS
25.0000 g., 0.9250 Silver 0.7435 oz. ASW, 38.6 mm. **Obv:** Lion left **Rev:** Multicolor Quetzal bird **Edge:** Reeded

Date	Mintage	F	VF	XF	Unc	BU
2004 Proof	5,000	Value: 50.00				

KM# 150 10 FRANCS
25.0000 g., 0.9250 Silver 0.7435 oz. ASW, 38.6 mm. **Obv:** Lion left **Rev:** Multicolor Bird of Paradise on branch left **Edge:** Reeded

Date	Mintage	F	VF	XF	Unc	BU
2004 Proof	5,000	Value: 55.00				

KM# 151 10 FRANCS
25.0000 g., 0.9250 Silver 0.7435 oz. ASW, 38.6 mm. **Obv:** Lion left **Rev:** Multicolor Kingfisher bird left **Edge:** Reeded

Date	Mintage	F	VF	XF	Unc	BU
2004 Proof	5,000	Value: 55.00				

KM# 155 10 FRANCS
Acrylic Clear, 50 mm. **Obv:** Etched nine-masted sailing junk above lion, value and country name **Edge:** Plain

Date	Mintage	F	VF	XF	Unc	BU
2004	2,000	—	—	—	55.00	—

KM# 126 10 FRANCS
25.0000 g., 0.9250 Silver 0.7435 oz. ASW, 38.6 mm. **Obv:** Lion left above value **Rev:** Sundial face with collapsible gnomon **Edge:** Reeded

Date	Mintage	F	VF	XF	Unc	BU
2004 Proof	5,000	Value: 50.00				

KM# 127 10 FRANCS
25.0000 g., 0.9250 Silver 0.7435 oz. ASW, 38.6 mm. **Obv:** Lion left above value **Rev:** Compass face **Edge:** Reeded **Note:** Compass part of the Compass and Spoon set

Date	Mintage	F	VF	XF	Unc	BU
2004 Proof	5,000	Value: 50.00				

KM# 172 10 FRANCS
25.0000 g., Silver, 38.6 mm. **Obv:** Lion left **Rev:** Pope waving half facing at left, cross at upper right, Vatican at lower right

Date	Mintage	F	VF	XF	Unc	BU
2005 Proof	3,000	Value: 50.00				

KM# 179a 10 FRANCS
25.0000 g., 0.9250 Silver 0.7435 oz. ASW, 38.58 mm. **Series:** Wildlife Protection **Obv:** Lion standing left **Obv. Legend:** REPUBLIQUE DEMOCRATIQUE DU CONGO **Rev:** Butterfly Fish, multicolor **Edge:** Reeded

Date	Mintage	F	VF	XF	Unc	BU
2005 Proof	5,000	Value: 45.00				

KM# 180a 10 FRANCS
25.0000 g., 0.9250 Silver 0.7435 oz. ASW, 38.58 mm. **Series:** Wildlife Protection **Obv:** Lion standing left **Obv. Legend:** REPUBLIQUE DEMOCRATIQUE DU CONGO **Rev:** African Moony Fish, multicolor **Edge:** Reeded

Date	Mintage	F	VF	XF	Unc	BU
2005 Proof	5,000	Value: 45.00				

KM# 181a 10 FRANCS
25.0000 g., 0.9250 Silver 0.7435 oz. ASW, 38.58 mm. **Series:** Wildlife Protection **Obv:** Lion standing left **Obv. Legend:** REPUBLIQUE DEMOCRATIQUE DU CONGO **Rev:** Red Perch, multicolor **Edge:** Reeded

Date	Mintage	F	VF	XF	Unc	BU
2005 Proof	5,000	Value: 45.00				

KM# 176 10 FRANCS
32.0000 g., 0.9990 Silver 1.0278 oz. ASW, 40 mm. **Obv:** Lion standing left **Obv. Legend:** REPUBLIQUE DEMOCRATIQUE DU CONGO **Rev:** World Trade Center Twin Towers as they were before 9-11 **Edge:** Reeded

Date	Mintage	F	VF	XF	Unc	BU
2006 Proof	—	Value: 50.00				

KM# 136 20 FRANCS
1.2440 g., 0.9999 Gold 0.0400 oz. AGW, 13.92 mm. **Obv:** Lion left **Rev:** Pope John Paul II with staff and mitre, waving **Edge:** Plain

Date	Mintage	F	VF	XF	Unc	BU
2003 Proof	—	Value: 65.00				

KM# 137 20 FRANCS
1.2440 g., 0.9999 Gold 0.0400 oz. AGW, 13.92 mm. **Obv:** Lion left **Rev:** Skunk **Edge:** Plain

Date	Mintage	F	VF	XF	Unc	BU
2003 Proof	25,000	Value: 65.00				

KM# 138 20 FRANCS
1.2440 g., 0.9999 Gold 0.0400 oz. AGW, 13.92 mm. **Obv:** Lion left **Rev:** Giant anteater right **Edge:** Plain

Date	Mintage	F	VF	XF	Unc	BU
2003 Proof	25,000	Value: 65.00				

KM# 139 20 FRANCS
1.2440 g., 0.9999 Gold 0.0400 oz. AGW, 13.92 mm. **Obv:** Lion left **Rev:** Porcupine right **Edge:** Plain

Date	Mintage	F	VF	XF	Unc	BU
2003 Proof	25,000	Value: 65.00				

KM# 140 20 FRANCS
1.2440 g., 0.9999 Gold 0.0400 oz. AGW, 13.92 mm. **Obv:** Lion left **Rev:** Chameleon **Edge:** Plain

Date	Mintage	F	VF	XF	Unc	BU
2003 Proof	25,000	Value: 65.00				

KM# 184 20 FRANCS
1.2200 g., 0.9999 Gold 0.0392 oz. AGW, 13.74 mm. **Subject:** XXVIII Summer Olympics - Athens **Obv:** Lion standing right **Rev:** Athenian tetradrachm featuring owl perched **Edge:** Reeded

Date	Mintage	F	VF	XF	Unc	BU
2003 Proof	25,000	Value: 65.00				

KM# 186 20 FRANCS
1.2441 g., 0.9999 Gold 0.0400 oz. AGW, 13.92 mm. **Subject:** Christmas **Obv:** Lion standing left **Rev:** Jesus lying in manger

Date	Mintage	F	VF	XF	Unc	BU
ND(2004) Proof	25,000	Value: 65.00				

KM# 144 20 FRANCS
1.2440 g., 0.9999 Gold 0.0400 oz. AGW, 13.92 mm. **Obv:** Lion left **Rev:** Ferrari coat of arms **Edge:** Plain

Date	Mintage	F	VF	XF	Unc	BU
2004 Proof	5,000	Value: 70.00				

KM# 173 20 FRANCS
1.5300 g., 0.9990 Gold 0.0491 oz. AGW, 13.9 mm. **Obv:** Lion left **Rev:** Pope waving at left, cross at upper right, Vatican at lower right

Date	Mintage	F	VF	XF	Unc	BU
2005 Proof	25,000	Value: 80.00				

KM# 185 75 FRANCS
15.5500 g., 0.9999 Gold 0.4999 oz. AGW **Subject:** XXVIII Summer Olympics - Athens **Obv:** Lion standing right **Rev:** Athenian tetradrachm featuring owl perched **Edge:** Reeded

Date	Mintage	F	VF	XF	Unc	BU
2003 Proof	500	Value: 775				

KM# 129 100 FRANCS
31.1000 g., 0.9999 Gold 0.9997 oz. AGW, 40 mm. **Series:** Wild Life Protection **Obv:** Lion left **Rev:** Reflective multicolor swallowtail butterfly **Edge:** Reeded

Date	Mintage	F	VF	XF	Unc	BU
2002 Proof	50	Value: 1,550				

KM# 130 100 FRANCS

31.1000 g., 0.9999 Gold 0.9997 oz. AGW, 40 mm. **Series:** Wild Life Protection **Obv:** Lion left **Rev:** Reflective multicolor dark greenish butterfly **Edge:** Reeded

Date	Mintage	F	VF	XF	Unc	BU
2002 Proof	50	Value: 1,550				

KM# 131 100 FRANCS

31.1000 g., 0.9999 Gold 0.9997 oz. AGW, 40 mm. **Series:** Wild Life Protection **Obv:** Lion left **Rev:** Reflective multicolor red and black butterfly **Edge:** Reeded

Date	Mintage	F	VF	XF	Unc	BU
2002 Proof	50	Value: 1,550				

KM# 152 100 FRANCS

31.1035 g., 0.9999 Gold 0.9999 oz. AGW, 38.6 mm. **Obv:** Lion left **Rev:** Multicolor Quetzal bird **Edge:** Reeded

Date	Mintage	F	VF	XF	Unc	BU
2004 Proof	25	Value: 1,650				

KM# 153 100 FRANCS

31.1035 g., 0.9999 Gold 0.9999 oz. AGW, 38.6 mm. **Obv:** Lion left **Rev:** Multicolor Bird of Paradise left **Edge:** Reeded

Date	Mintage	F	VF	XF	Unc	BU
2004 Proof	25	Value: 1,650				

KM# 154 100 FRANCS

31.1035 g., 0.9999 Gold 0.9999 oz. AGW, 38.6 mm. **Obv:** Lion left **Rev:** Multicolor Kingfisher bird **Edge:** Reeded

Date	Mintage	F	VF	XF	Unc	BU
2004 Proof	25	Value: 1,650				

KM# 179b 100 FRANCS

31.1000 g., 0.9990 Gold 0.9988 oz. AGW, 38.58 mm. **Series:** Wildlife Protection **Obv:** Lion standing left **Obv. Legend:** REPUBLIQUE DEMOCRATIQUE DU CONGO **Rev:** Butterfly Fish, multicolor **Edge:** Reeded

Date	Mintage	F	VF	XF	Unc	BU
2005 Proof	25	Value: 1,650				

KM# 180b 100 FRANCS

31.1000 g., 0.9990 Gold 0.9988 oz. AGW, 38.58 mm. **Series:** Wildlife Protection **Obv:** Lion standing left **Obv. Legend:** REPUBLIQUE DEMOCRATIQUE DU CONGO **Rev:** African Mooney Fish, muticolor **Edge:** Reeded

Date	Mintage	F	VF	XF	Unc	BU
2005 Proof	25	Value: 1,650				

KM# 181b 100 FRANCS

31.1000 g., 0.9990 Gold 0.9988 oz. AGW, 38.58 mm. **Series:** Wildlife Protection **Obv:** Lion standing left **Obv. Legend:** REPUBLIQUE DEMOCRATIQUE DU CONGO **Rev:** Red Perch, multicolor **Edge:** Reeded

Date	Mintage	F	VF	XF	Unc	BU
2005 Proof	25	Value: 1,650				

MINT SETS

KM#	Date	Mintage	Identification	Issue Price	Mkt Val
MS2	2004 (4)	—	KM#156-159	—	12.50

COOK ISLANDS

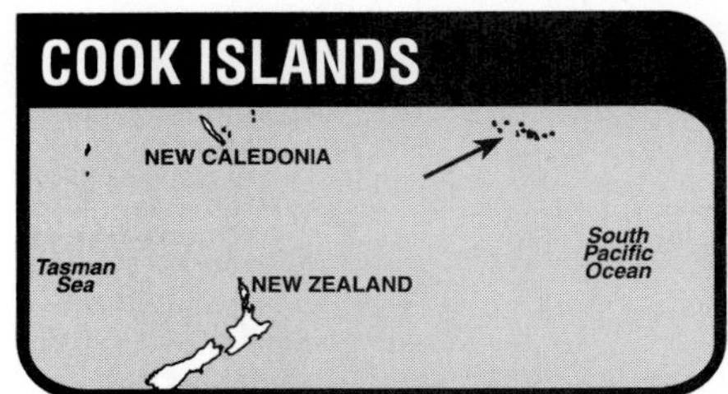

Cook Islands, a self-governing dependency of New Zealand consisting of 15 islands, is located in the South Pacific Ocean about 2,000 miles (3,218 km.) northeast of New Zealand. It has an area of 93 sq. mi. (234 sq. km.) and a population of 17,185. Capital: Avarua. The United States claims the islands of Danger, Manahiki, Penrhyn, and Rakahanga atolls. Citrus and canned fruits and juices, copra, clothing, jewelry, and mother-of-pearl shell are exported.

RULER

British

MINT MARK

PM - Pobjoy Mint

MONETARY SYSTEM

100 Cents = 1 Dollar

DEPENDENCY OF NEW ZEALAND

DECIMAL COINAGE

KM# 419 CENT

1.4400 g., Aluminum, 21.9 mm. **Ruler:** Elizabeth II **Obv:** Crowned head right, date below **Rev:** Bust of Capt. James Cook right, denomination below **Edge:** Plain

Date	Mintage	F	VF	XF	Unc	BU
2003	—	—	—	—	1.25	1.50

KM# 420 CENT

1.4400 g., Aluminum, 21.9 mm. **Ruler:** Elizabeth II **Obv:** Crowned head right, date below **Rev:** Collie dog right, denomination below **Edge:** Plain

Date	Mintage	F	VF	XF	Unc	BU
2003	—	—	—	—	0.75	1.00

KM# 421 CENT

1.4400 g., Aluminum, 21.9 mm. **Ruler:** Elizabeth II **Obv:** Crowned head right, date below **Rev:** Pointer dog right, denomination above **Edge:** Plain

Date	Mintage	F	VF	XF	Unc	BU
2003	—	—	—	—	0.75	1.00

KM# 422 CENT

1.4400 g., Aluminum, 21.9 mm. **Ruler:** Elizabeth II **Obv:** Crowned head right, date below **Rev:** Rooster right, denomination above **Edge:** Plain

Date	Mintage	F	VF	XF	Unc	BU
2003	—	—	—	—	0.75	1.00

KM# 423 CENT

1.4400 g., Aluminum, 22 mm. **Ruler:** Elizabeth II **Obv:** Crowned head right, date below **Rev:** Monkey on branch, denomination at left **Edge:** Plain

Date	Mintage	F	VF	XF	Unc	BU
2003	—	—	—	—	0.75	1.00

KM# 756 CENT

3.6400 g., Brass Plated Steel, 11.8 mm. **Ruler:** Elizabeth II **Obv:** Bust right **Rev:** Female Hula dancer

Date	Mintage	F	VF	XF	Unc	BU
2010	—	—	—	—	0.75	1.00

KM# 757 2 CENTS

5.1000 g., Brass Plated Steel, 19.8 mm. **Ruler:** Elizabeth II **Obv:** Bust right **Rev:** The Endeavor

Date	Mintage	F	VF	XF	Unc	BU
2010	—	—	—	—	0.75	1.00

KM# 758 5 CENTS

6.1500 g., Brass Plated Steel, 21.7 mm. **Ruler:** Elizabeth II **Obv:** Bust right **Rev:** Tiare Maori flower

Date	Mintage	F	VF	XF	Unc	BU
2010	—	—	—	—	1.00	1.50

KM# 759 10 CENTS

11.5000 g., Nickel Plated Steel, 20.5 mm. **Ruler:** Elizabeth II **Obv:** Bust right **Rev:** Yellowfin tuna

Date	Mintage	F	VF	XF	Unc	BU
2010	—	—	—	—	1.00	1.50

KM# 760 20 CENTS

14.1300 g., Nickel Plated Steel, 21.75 mm. **Ruler:** Elizabeth II **Obv:** Bust right **Rev:** Bird

Date	Mintage	F	VF	XF	Unc	BU
2010	—	—	—	—	1.50	2.00

KM# 1116 50 CENTS

28.2800 g., Copper-Nickel, 38.61 mm. **Ruler:** Elizabeth II **Subject:** Elizabeth II Corronation, 50th Anniversary

Date	Mintage	F	VF	XF	Unc	BU
2002	—	—	—	—	—	20.00

KM# 1144 50 CENTS

Copper-Nickel **Ruler:** Elizabeth II **Rev:** Edward "Ned" Kelley in color

Date	Mintage	F	VF	XF	Unc	BU
2004 Proof	Est. 10,000	Value: 15.00				

KM# 761 50 CENTS

Nickel Plated Steel, 24.75 mm. **Ruler:** Elizabeth II **Obv:** Bust right **Rev:** The Endeavor

Date	Mintage	F	VF	XF	Unc	BU
2010	—	—	—	—	2.00	2.50

KM# 1114 DOLLAR

32.0000 g., Copper-Nickel, 40 mm. **Ruler:** Elizabeth II **Subject:** 2002 Winter Olympics, Salt Lake City

Date	Mintage	F	VF	XF	Unc	BU
2001	Est. 20,000	—	—	—	—	15.00

KM# 1115 DOLLAR

9.5000 g., 0.9990 Silver 0.3051 oz. ASW, 22.5 mm. **Ruler:** Elizabeth II **Series:** 2002 Commonwealth Games, Manchester **Rev:** Track field and medals on ribbons

Date	Mintage	F	VF	XF	Unc	BU
2001 Proof	Est. 5,000	Value: 20.00				

KM# 396 DOLLAR
24.8828 g., 0.9990 Silver with Acrylic capsule center containing tiny rubies, sapphires and cubic zirconias 0.7992 oz. ASW, 40.6 mm. **Ruler:** Elizabeth II **Subject:** Crown Jewels **Obv:** Crowned head right, legend **Rev:** Crowns and royal regalia **Edge:** Reeded

Date	Mintage	F	VF	XF	Unc	BU
2002 Proof	50,000	Value: 32.50				

KM# 1117 DOLLAR
0.9990 Silver **Ruler:** Elizabeth II **Subject:** 2002 Winter Olumpics, Salt Lake City **Rev:** Figure skating

Date	Mintage	F	VF	XF	Unc	BU
2002 Proof	—	Value: 35.00				

KM# 1118 DOLLAR
Copper-Nickel **Ruler:** Elizabeth II **Subject:** XVII World Cup, Korea and Japan **Rev:** Soccer player and ball

Date	Mintage	F	VF	XF	Unc	BU
2002 Proof	—	Value: 15.00				

KM# 416 DOLLAR
10.7500 g., Copper-Nickel, 28.5 mm. **Ruler:** Elizabeth II **Obv:** Queen's new portrait **Rev:** Tangaroa statue and value **Edge:** Scalloped

Date	Mintage	F	VF	XF	Unc	BU
2003	—	—	—	—	2.50	3.00

KM# 455 DOLLAR
23.9000 g., Copper-Nickel, 38.5 mm. **Ruler:** Elizabeth II **Obv:** Queen Elizabeth II **Rev:** 50th Anniversary - Playboy magazine logo **Edge:** Reeded

Date	Mintage	F	VF	XF	Unc	BU
2003	—	—	—	—	7.00	9.00

KM# 455a DOLLAR
25.2700 g., Copper-Nickel Gilt, 38.3 mm. **Ruler:** Elizabeth II **Obv:** Elizabeth II **Rev:** Playboy magazine's 50th Anniversary logo **Edge:** Reeded

Date	Mintage	F	VF	XF	Unc	BU
2003 Proof	50,000	Value: 20.00				

KM# 455b DOLLAR
25.2700 g., 0.9990 Silver 0.8116 oz. ASW, 38.3 mm. **Ruler:** Elizabeth II **Obv:** Elizabeth II **Rev:** Playboy magazine's 50th Anniversary logo **Edge:** Reeded

Date	Mintage	F	VF	XF	Unc	BU
2003 Proof	—	Value: 40.00				

KM# 455c DOLLAR
25.2700 g., 0.9990 Silver Gilt 0.8116 oz. ASW, 38.3 mm. **Ruler:** Elizabeth II **Obv:** Elizabeth II **Rev:** Playboy magazine's 50th Anniversary logo **Edge:** Reeded

Date	Mintage	F	VF	XF	Unc	BU
2003 Proof	—	Value: 50.00				

KM# 462 DOLLAR
Copper-Nickel, 41 mm. **Ruler:** Elizabeth II **Rev:** Face of 5 Euro Banknote

Date	Mintage	F	VF	XF	Unc	BU
2003	—	—	—	—	7.00	9.00

KM# 463 DOLLAR
Copper-Nickel, 41 mm. **Ruler:** Elizabeth II **Rev:** Face of 10 Euro Banknote

Date	Mintage	F	VF	XF	Unc	BU
2003	—	—	—	—	7.00	9.00

KM# 464 DOLLAR
Copper-Nickel, 41 mm. **Ruler:** Elizabeth II **Rev:** Face of 20 Euro Banknote

Date	Mintage	F	VF	XF	Unc	BU
2003	—	—	—	—	7.00	9.00

KM# 465 DOLLAR
Copper-Nickel, 41 mm. **Ruler:** Elizabeth II **Rev:** Face of 50 Euro Banknote

Date	Mintage	F	VF	XF	Unc	BU
2003	—	—	—	—	7.00	9.00

KM# 466 DOLLAR
Copper-Nickel, 41 mm. **Ruler:** Elizabeth II **Rev:** Face of 100 Euro Banknote

Date	Mintage	F	VF	XF	Unc	BU
2003	—	—	—	—	7.00	9.00

KM# 467 DOLLAR
Copper-Nickel, 41 mm. **Ruler:** Elizabeth II **Rev:** Face of 500 Euro Banknote

Date	Mintage	F	VF	XF	Unc	BU
2003	—	—	—	—	7.00	9.00

KM# 424 DOLLAR
8.5000 g., 0.9990 Silver 0.2730 oz. ASW, 25.1 mm. **Ruler:** Elizabeth II **Subject:** Zodiac Gemstones - Cancer **Obv:** Crowned head above ornamental center **Rev:** Encapsulated emeralds above Crab (Cancer) **Edge:** Reeded

Date	Mintage	F	VF	XF	Unc	BU
ND(2003) Proof	10,000	Value: 25.00				

KM# 424a DOLLAR
8.5000 g., 0.9990 Silver Gilt 0.2730 oz. ASW, 25.1 mm. **Ruler:** Elizabeth II **Obv:** Crowned head above ornamental center **Rev:** Encapsulated emeralds above Crab (cancer)

Date	Mintage	F	VF	XF	Unc	BU
ND(2003) Proof	10,000	Value: 60.00				

KM# 425 DOLLAR
8.5000 g., 0.9990 Silver 0.2730 oz. ASW, 25.1 mm. **Ruler:** Elizabeth II **Subject:** Zodiac Gemstones - Aquarius **Obv:** Crowned head above ornamental center **Rev:** Encapsulated garnets with Aquarius in background **Edge:** Reeded

Date	Mintage	F	VF	XF	Unc	BU
ND(2004) Proof	10,000	Value: 25.00				

KM# 425a DOLLAR
8.5000 g., 0.9990 Silver Gilt 0.2730 oz. ASW, 25.1 mm. **Ruler:** Elizabeth II **Obv:** Crowned head above ornamental center **Rev:** Encapsulated garnets with Aquarius in background

Date	Mintage	F	VF	XF	Unc	BU
ND(2003) Proof	10,000	Value: 60.00				

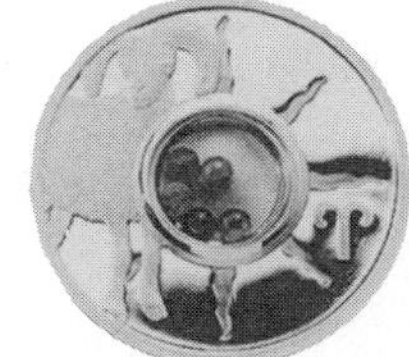

KM# 426 DOLLAR
8.5000 g., 0.9990 Silver 0.2730 oz. ASW, 25.1 mm. **Ruler:** Elizabeth II **Subject:** Zodiac Gemstones - Aries **Obv:** Crowned head above ornamental center **Rev:** Encapsulated Bloodstones in center with ram at left **Edge:** Reeded

Date	Mintage	F	VF	XF	Unc	BU
ND(2003) Proof	10,000	Value: 25.00				

KM# 426a DOLLAR
8.5000 g., 0.9990 Silver Gilt 0.2730 oz. ASW, 25.1 mm. **Ruler:** Elizabeth II **Obv:** Crowned head above ornamental center **Rev:** Encapsulated Bloodstones in center with ram at left

Date	Mintage	F	VF	XF	Unc	BU
ND(2003) Proof	10,000	Value: 60.00				

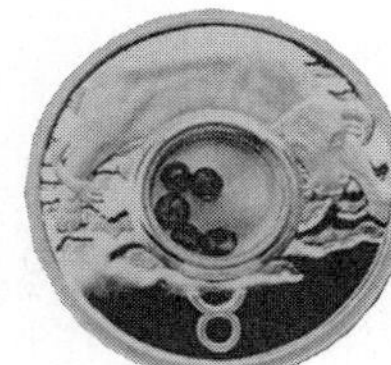

KM# 427 DOLLAR
8.5000 g., 0.9990 Silver 0.2730 oz. ASW, 25.1 mm. **Ruler:** Elizabeth II **Subject:** Zodiac Gemstones - Taurus **Obv:** Crowned head above ornamental center **Rev:** Encapsulated Sapphires with bull in background **Edge:** Reeded

Date	Mintage	F	VF	XF	Unc	BU
ND(2003) Proof	10,000	Value: 25.00				

KM# 427a DOLLAR
8.5000 g., 0.9990 Silver Gilt 0.2730 oz. ASW, 25.1 mm. **Ruler:** Elizabeth II **Subject:** Zodiac Gemstones - Taurus **Obv:** Crowned head above ornamental center **Rev:** Encapsulated Sapphires with bull in background **Edge:** Reeded

Date	Mintage	F	VF	XF	Unc	BU
ND(2003) Proof	10,000	Value: 60.00				

KM# 428 DOLLAR
8.5000 g., 0.9990 Silver 0.2730 oz. ASW, 25.1 mm. **Ruler:** Elizabeth II **Obv:** Crowned head above ornamental center **Rev:** Encapsulated Agates between twins **Edge:** Reeded

Date	Mintage	F	VF	XF	Unc	BU
ND(2003) Proof	10,000	Value: 25.00				

KM# 428a DOLLAR
8.5000 g., 0.9990 Silver Gilt 0.2730 oz. ASW, 25.1 mm. **Ruler:** Elizabeth II **Obv:** Crowned head above ornamental center **Rev:** Encapsulated Agates between twins **Edge:** Reeded

Date	Mintage	F	VF	XF	Unc	BU
ND(2003) Proof	10,000	Value: 60.00				

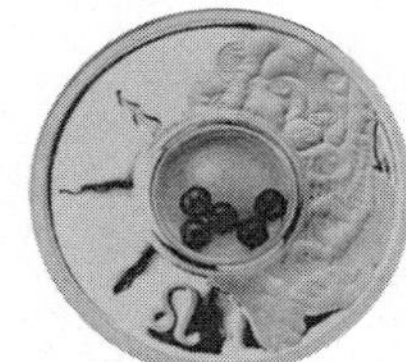

KM# 429 DOLLAR
8.5000 g., 0.9990 Silver 0.2730 oz. ASW, 25.1 mm. **Ruler:** Elizabeth II **Obv:** Crowned head above ornamental center **Rev:** Encapsulated Onyx stones with lion at right **Edge:** Reeded

Date	Mintage	F	VF	XF	Unc	BU
ND(2003) Proof	10,000	Value: 25.00				

KM# 429a DOLLAR
8.5000 g., 0.9990 Silver Gilt 0.2730 oz. ASW, 25.1 mm. **Ruler:** Elizabeth II **Obv:** Crowned head above ornamental center **Rev:** Encapsulated Onyx stones with lion at right **Edge:** Reeded

Date	Mintage	F	VF	XF	Unc	BU
ND(2003) Proof	10,000	Value: 60.00				

KM# 430 DOLLAR
8.5000 g., 0.9990 Silver 0.2730 oz. ASW, 25.1 mm. **Ruler:** Elizabeth II **Subject:** Zodiac Gemstones - Virgo **Obv:** Crowned head above ornamented center **Rev:** Encapsulated Carnelian stones with woman at right **Edge:** Reeded

Date	Mintage	F	VF	XF	Unc	BU
ND(2003) Proof	10,000	Value: 25.00				

KM# 430a DOLLAR
8.5000 g., 0.9990 Silver Gilt 0.2730 oz. ASW, 25.1 mm. **Ruler:** Elizabeth II **Subject:** Zodiac Gemstones - Virgo **Obv:** Crowned head above ornamented center **Rev:** Encapsulated Carnelian stones with Virgo at right **Edge:** Reeded

Date	Mintage	F	VF	XF	Unc	BU
ND(2003) Proof	10,000	Value: 60.00				

KM# 431 DOLLAR

8.5000 g., 0.9990 Silver 0.2730 oz. ASW, 25.1 mm. **Ruler:** Elizabeth II **Subject:** Zodiac Gemstones - Libra **Obv:** Crowned head above ornamented center **Rev:** Encapsulated Peridot stones with balance scale **Edge:** Reeded

Date	Mintage	F	VF	XF	Unc	BU
ND(2003) Proof	10,000	Value: 25.00				

KM# 431a DOLLAR

8.5000 g., 0.9990 Silver Gilt 0.2730 oz. ASW, 25.1 mm. **Ruler:** Elizabeth II **Subject:** Zodiac Gemstones - Libra **Obv:** Crowned head above ornamented center **Rev:** Encapsulated Peridot stones with balance scale **Edge:** Reeded

Date	Mintage	F	VF	XF	Unc	BU
ND(2003) Proof	10,000	Value: 60.00				

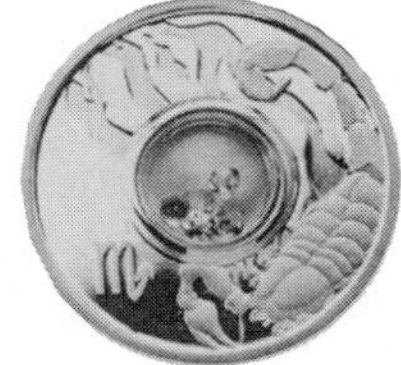

KM# 432 DOLLAR

8.5000 g., 0.9990 Silver 0.2730 oz. ASW, 25.1 mm. **Ruler:** Elizabeth II **Subject:** Zodiac Gemstones - Scorpio **Obv:** Crowned head above ornamented center **Rev:** Encapsulated Aquamarine stones with scorpion at lower right **Edge:** Reeded

Date	Mintage	F	VF	XF	Unc	BU
ND(2003) Proof	10,000	Value: 25.00				

KM# 432a DOLLAR

8.5000 g., 0.9990 Silver Gilt 0.2730 oz. ASW, 25.1 mm. **Ruler:** Elizabeth II **Subject:** Zodiac Gemstones - Scorpio **Obv:** Crowned head above ornamented center **Rev:** Encapsulated Aquamarine stones with scorpion at lower right **Edge:** Reeded

Date	Mintage	F	VF	XF	Unc	BU
ND(2003) Proof	10,000	Value: 60.00				

KM# 433 DOLLAR

8.5000 g., 0.9990 Silver 0.2730 oz. ASW, 25.1 mm. **Ruler:** Elizabeth II **Subject:** Zodiac Gemstones - Sagittarius **Obv:** Crowned head above ornamented center **Rev:** Encapsulated Topaz stones with centaur at right **Edge:** Reeded

Date	Mintage	F	VF	XF	Unc	BU
ND(2003) Proof	10,000	Value: 25.00				

KM# 433a DOLLAR

8.5000 g., 0.9990 Silver Gilt 0.2730 oz. ASW, 25.1 mm. **Ruler:** Elizabeth II **Subject:** Zodiac Gemstones - Sagittarius **Obv:** Crowned head above ornamented center **Rev:** Encapsulated Topaz stones with centaur at right **Edge:** Reeded

Date	Mintage	F	VF	XF	Unc	BU
ND(2003) Proof	10,000	Value: 60.00				

KM# 434 DOLLAR

8.5000 g., 0.9990 Silver 0.2730 oz. ASW, 25.1 mm. **Ruler:** Elizabeth II **Subject:** Zodiac Gemstones - Capricorn **Obv:** Crowned head above ornamental center **Rev:** Encapsulated rubies with goat at right **Edge:** Reeded

Date	Mintage	F	VF	XF	Unc	BU
ND(2003) Proof	10,000	Value: 25.00				

KM# 434a DOLLAR

8.5000 g., 0.9990 Silver Gilt 0.2730 oz. ASW, 25.1 mm. **Ruler:** Elizabeth II **Subject:** Zodiac Gemstones - Capricorn **Obv:** Crowned head above ornamented center **Rev:** Encapsulated Rubies with goat at right **Edge:** Reeded

Date	Mintage	F	VF	XF	Unc	BU
ND(2003) Proof	10,000	Value: 60.00				

KM# 435 DOLLAR

8.5000 g., 0.9990 Silver 0.2730 oz. ASW, 25.1 mm. **Ruler:** Elizabeth II **Subject:** Zodiac Gemstones - Pices **Obv:** Crowned head above ornamented center **Rev:** Encapsulated Amethyst stones and two fish **Edge:** Reeded

Date	Mintage	F	VF	XF	Unc	BU
ND(2003) Proof	10,000	Value: 25.00				

KM# 435a DOLLAR

8.5000 g., 0.9990 Silver Gilt 0.2730 oz. ASW, 25.1 mm. **Ruler:** Elizabeth II **Subject:** Zodiac Gemstones - Pices **Obv:** Crowned head above ornamented center **Rev:** Encapsulated Amethyst stones and 2 fish **Edge:** Reeded

Date	Mintage	F	VF	XF	Unc	BU
ND(2003) Proof	10,000	Value: 60.00				

KM# 746 DOLLAR

24.9000 g., Copper-Nickel **Ruler:** Elizabeth II **Subject:** Historic ships - Espusi **Shape:** 38

Date	Mintage	F	VF	XF	Unc	BU
2003	—	—	—	—	15.00	20.00

KM# 747 DOLLAR

24.9000 g., Copper-Nickel, 38 mm. **Ruler:** Elizabeth II **Subject:** Historic ships - Gorch Foch

Date	Mintage	F	VF	XF	Unc	BU
2003	—	—	—	—	15.00	20.00

KM# 748 DOLLAR

24.9000 g., Copper-Nickel, 38 mm. **Ruler:** Elizabeth II **Subject:** Historic ships - Constitution

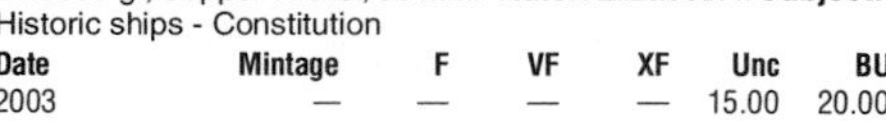

Date	Mintage	F	VF	XF	Unc	BU
2003	—	—	—	—	15.00	20.00

KM# 749 DOLLAR

24.9000 g., Copper-Nickel, 38 mm. **Ruler:** Elizabeth II **Subject:** Historic ships - Beagle

Date	Mintage	F	VF	XF	Unc	BU
2003	—	—	—	—	15.00	20.00

KM# 750 DOLLAR

24.9000 g., Copper-Nickel, 38 mm. **Ruler:** Elizabeth II **Subject:** Historic ship - Endeavour

Date	Mintage	F	VF	XF	Unc	BU
2003	—	—	—	—	15.00	20.00

KM# 751 DOLLAR

24.9000 g., Copper-Nickel, 38 mm. **Ruler:** Elizabeth II **Subject:** Historic Ship - Vasa

Date	Mintage	F	VF	XF	Unc	BU
2003	—	—	—	—	15.00	20.00

KM# 1127 DOLLAR

31.6350 g., 0.9990 Silver 1.0160 oz. ASW, 40.5 mm. **Ruler:** Elizabeth II **Rev:** James Cook and siling ship

Date	Mintage	F	VF	XF	Unc	BU
2003 Proof	Est. 4,999	Value: 50.00				

KM# 1130 DOLLAR

31.1050 g., 0.9990 Silver 0.9990 oz. ASW, 38.6 mm. **Ruler:** Elizabeth II **Subject:** Full Gospel Business Men's Fellowship, 50th Anniversary

Date	Mintage	F	VF	XF	Unc	BU
2003 Proof	Est. 4,999	Value: 55.00				

KM# 1143 DOLLAR

28.2800 g., 0.9250 Silver partially gilt 0.8410 oz. ASW, 38.61 mm. **Ruler:** Elizabeth II **Series:** Elizabeth II, 50th Anniversary of Corronation

Date	Mintage	F	VF	XF	Unc	BU
2003 Proof	Est. 20,000	—	—	—	—	45.00

KM# 438 DOLLAR
31.1035 g., 0.9990 Silver 0.9990 oz. ASW, 40.5 mm. **Ruler:** Elizabeth II **Obv:** Crowned head right **Rev:** Multicolor Deng Xiaoping on Chinese map **Edge:** Plain **Shape:** As a map

Date	Mintage	F	VF	XF	Unc	BU
2004	20,000	—	—	—	45.00	50.00

KM# 454 DOLLAR
27.5300 g., 0.9990 Silver Clad Copper-Nickel 0.8842 oz. ASW, 38.6 mm. **Ruler:** Elizabeth II **Subject:** 60th Anniversary - D-Day Invasion **Obv:** Crowned bust right, new portrait **Rev:** Invasion scene of soldiers storming the beaches (Sword, Gold, Juno, Omaha, and Utah) of Normandy

Date	Mintage	F	VF	XF	Unc	BU
2004	—	—	—	—	15.00	18.00

KM# 1146 DOLLAR
31.6350 g., 0.9990 Silver 1.0160 oz. ASW **Ruler:** Elizabeth II **Subject:** Cobb & Co. 150th Anniversary **Rev:** Hackney Cab in color

Date	Mintage	F	VF	XF	Unc	BU
2004 Proof	Est. 5,000	Value: 55.00				

KM# 1147 DOLLAR
31.6350 g., 0.9990 Silver 1.0160 oz. ASW **Ruler:** Elizabeth II **Subject:** 90th Anniversary, Battle of the Emden and Sydney I

Date	Mintage	F	VF	XF	Unc	BU
2004 Proof	Est. 5,000	Value: 55.00				

KM# 1148 DOLLAR
10.7500 g., Copper-Nickel, 28.28 mm. **Ruler:** Elizabeth II **Rev:** Elvis Presley

Date	Mintage	F	VF	XF	Unc	BU
2004	—	—	—	—	—	15.00

KM# 1150 DOLLAR
31.1050 g., 0.9990 Silver 0.9990 oz. ASW, 45 mm. **Ruler:** Elizabeth II **Subject:** XXVIII Summer Olympics, Athens **Rev:** Cyclist in color

Date	Mintage	F	VF	XF	Unc	BU
2004	Est. 5,000	—	—	—	—	45.00

KM# 1151 DOLLAR
31.1050 g., 0.9990 Silver 0.9990 oz. ASW, 45 mm. **Ruler:** Elizabeth II **Rev:** Gymnast **Rev. Designer:** XXVIII Summer Olympics, Athens

Date	Mintage	F	VF	XF	Unc	BU
2004	Est. 5,000	—	—	—	—	45.00

KM# 1152 DOLLAR
31.1050 g., 0.9990 Silver 0.9990 oz. ASW, 45 mm. **Ruler:** Elizabeth II **Subject:** XXVIII Summer Olympics, Athens **Rev:** Two basketball players in color

Date	Mintage	F	VF	XF	Unc	BU
2004	Est. 5,000	—	—	—	—	45.00

KM# 1153 DOLLAR
31.1050 g., 0.9990 Silver 0.9990 oz. ASW, 45 mm. **Ruler:** Elizabeth II **Subject:** XVIII Summer Olympics, Athens **Rev:** Sprinter in color

Date	Mintage	F	VF	XF	Unc	BU
2004	Est. 5,000	—	—	—	—	45.00

KM# 1154 DOLLAR
31.1050 g., 0.9990 Silver 0.9990 oz. ASW, 45 mm. **Ruler:** Elizabeth II **Subject:** XXVIII Summer Olympics, Athens **Rev:** Archer in color

Date	Mintage	F	VF	XF	Unc	BU
2004	Est. 5,000	—	—	—	—	45.00

KM# 1155 DOLLAR
31.1050 g., 0.9990 Silver 0.9990 oz. ASW, 45 mm. **Ruler:** Elizabeth II **Subject:** XXVIII Summer Olympics, Athens **Rev:** Weightlifter in color

Date	Mintage	F	VF	XF	Unc	BU
2004 Proof	Est. 5,000	—	—	—	—	45.00

KM# 1156 DOLLAR
24.0000 g., Copper-Nickel, 38 mm. **Ruler:** Elizabeth II **Rev:** Mohandas Ghandhi

Date	Mintage	F	VF	XF	Unc	BU
2004	—	—	—	—	—	15.00

KM# 443 DOLLAR
23.9000 g., Copper-Nickel, 38.5 mm. **Ruler:** Elizabeth II **Subject:** Battle of Trafalgar **Obv:** Crowned bust right, new portrait **Rev:** HMS Victory and color portrait of Nelson **Edge:** Reeded

Date	Mintage	F	VF	XF	Unc	BU
2005	—	—	—	—	12.00	14.00

KM# 470 DOLLAR
31.1600 g., 0.9990 Silver 1.0008 oz. ASW, 39.02 mm. **Ruler:** Elizabeth II **Obv:** Twin Towers and Statue of Liberty, Queens Head below **Obv. Legend:** COOK ISLANDS / WE WILL NEVER FORGET **Rev:** Freedoom Tower and Statue of Liberty **Rev. Inscription:** LET / FREEDOM / RING - FREEDOM TOWER **Edge:** Reeded and plain with lettering **Edge Lettering:** 1 TROY OZ. .999 FINE SILVER

Date	Mintage	F	VF	XF	Unc	BU
2005 Proof	—	Value: 45.00				
2006 Proof	—	Value: 40.00				

KM# 1107 DOLLAR
31.1050 g., 0.9990 Silver partially gilt 0.9990 oz. ASW, 40 mm. **Ruler:** Elizabeth II **Rev:** Pope Benedict XVI partially gilt

Date	Mintage	F	VF	XF	Unc	BU
2005 Proof	—	Value: 45.00				

KM# 1133 DOLLAR
Copper-Nickel, 38.6 mm. **Ruler:** Elizabeth II **Subject:** Star Wars, 30th Anniversary

Date	Mintage	F	VF	XF	Unc	BU
2005 Proof	Est. 9,999	Value: 30.00				

KM# 1157 DOLLAR
31.6350 g., 0.9990 Silver 1.0160 oz. ASW **Ruler:** Elizabeth II **Subject:** Australian Automobiles

Date	Mintage	F	VF	XF	Unc	BU
2005 Proof	Est. 1,500	Value: 55.00				

KM# 1158 DOLLAR
31.6350 g., 0.9990 Silver 1.0160 oz. ASW **Ruler:** Elizabeth II **Subject:** Australian Automobiles

Date	Mintage	F	VF	XF	Unc	BU
2005 Proof	Est. 1,500	Value: 55.00				

KM# 1159 DOLLAR
31.6350 g., 0.9990 Silver 1.0160 oz. ASW **Ruler:** Elizabeth II **Subject:** Australian Automobiles

Date	Mintage	F	VF	XF	Unc	BU
2005 Proof	Est. 1,500	Value: 55.00				

KM# 1160 DOLLAR
31.6350 g., 0.9990 Silver 1.0160 oz. ASW **Ruler:** Elizabeth II **Subject:** Australian Automobiles

Date	Mintage	F	VF	XF	Unc	BU
2005 Proof	Est. 1,500	Value: 55.00				

KM# 1161 DOLLAR
31.6350 g., 0.9990 Silver 1.0160 oz. ASW **Ruler:** Elizabeth II **Subject:** Australian Automobiles

Date	Mintage	F	VF	XF	Unc	BU
2005 Proof	Est. 1,500	Value: 55.00				

KM# 1162 DOLLAR
31.6350 g., 0.9990 Silver 1.0160 oz. ASW **Ruler:** Elizabeth II **Subject:** Australian Automobiles

Date	Mintage	F	VF	XF	Unc	BU
2005 Proof	Est. 1,500	Value: 55.00				

KM# 1163 DOLLAR
31.6350 g., 0.9990 Silver 1.0160 oz. ASW **Ruler:** Elizabeth II **Subject:** Australian Automobiles

Date	Mintage	F	VF	XF	Unc	BU
2005 Proof	Est. 1,500	Value: 55.00				

KM# 1164 DOLLAR
31.6350 g., 0.9990 Silver 1.0160 oz. ASW **Ruler:** Elizabeth II **Subject:** Australian Automobiles

Date	Mintage	F	VF	XF	Unc	BU
2005 Proof	Est. 1,500	Value: 55.00				

KM# 1165 DOLLAR
31.6350 g., 0.9990 Silver 1.0160 oz. ASW **Ruler:** Elizabeth II **Subject:** Australian Automobiles

Date	Mintage	F	VF	XF	Unc	BU
2005 Proof	Est. 1,500	Value: 55.00				

KM# 1166 DOLLAR
31.6350 g., 0.9990 Silver 1.0160 oz. ASW **Ruler:** Elizabeth II **Subject:** Australian Automobiles

Date	Mintage	F	VF	XF	Unc	BU
2005 Proof	1,500	Value: 55.00				

KM# 1167 DOLLAR
31.6350 g., 0.9990 Silver 1.0160 oz. ASW **Ruler:** Elizabeth II **Subject:** Australian Automobiles

Date	Mintage	F	VF	XF	Unc	BU
2005 Proof	Est. 1,500	Value: 55.00				

KM# 1168 DOLLAR
31.6350 g., 0.9990 Silver 1.0160 oz. ASW **Ruler:** Elizabeth II **Subject:** Australian Automobiles

Date	Mintage	F	VF	XF	Unc	BU
2005 Proof	Est. 1,500	Value: 55.00				

KM# 1173 DOLLAR
32.0000 g., Copper-Nickel, 40 mm. **Ruler:** Elizabeth II **Rev:** Snowflake, building tower hockey play and figure skater **Rev. Designer:** Winter Olumpics, Turin

Date	Mintage	F	VF	XF	Unc	BU
2005	20,000	—	—	—	—	15.00

KM# 1174 DOLLAR
Copper-Nickel **Ruler:** Elizabeth II **Subject:** Marriage of Prince Charles and Camilla Parker-Bowles

Date	Mintage	F	VF	XF	Unc	BU
2005	Est. 5,000	—	—	—	—	15.00

KM# 1177 DOLLAR
31.6350 g., 0.9990 Silver 1.0160 oz. ASW **Ruler:** Elizabeth II **Rev:** Pope John Paul II in color

Date	Mintage	F	VF	XF	Unc	BU
2005 Proof	5,000	Value: 125				

KM# 479 DOLLAR
Copper-Nickel, 38.6 mm. **Ruler:** Elizabeth II **Subject:** Gun ships of the world **Rev:** HMS Redoutable

Date	Mintage	F	VF	XF	Unc	BU
2006	—	—	—	—	—	25.00

KM# 480 DOLLAR
24.9000 g., Copper-Nickel, 38 mm. **Ruler:** Elizabeth II **Subject:** Gunships of the world **Obv:** Crowned bust right **Rev:** Ark Royal in color **Edge:** Reeded

Date	Mintage	F	VF	XF	Unc	BU
2006	—	—	—	—	—	25.00

KM# 752 DOLLAR
24.9000 g., Copper-Nickel, 38 mm. **Ruler:** Elizabeth II **Subject:** Gun ships - Chesapeak **Rev:** Multicolor naval ship

Date	Mintage	F	VF	XF	Unc	BU
2006	—	—	—	—	15.00	20.00

KM# 753 DOLLAR
24.9000 g., Copper-Nickel, 38 mm. **Ruler:** Elizabeth II **Subject:** Gun ships - Syvende **Rev:** Multicolor naval ship

Date	Mintage	F	VF	XF	Unc	BU
2006	—	—	—	—	15.00	20.00

KM# 754 DOLLAR
24.9000 g., Copper-Nickel, 38 mm. **Ruler:** Elizabeth II **Rev:** Multicolor Naval ship **Rev. Designer:** Gun ships - Vasa

Date	Mintage	F	VF	XF	Unc	BU
2006	—	—	—	—	15.00	20.00

KM# 755 DOLLAR
24.9000 g., Copper-Nickel, 38 mm. **Ruler:** Elizabeth II **Subject:** Gun Ships - Mary Rose **Rev:** Multicolor Naval ship

Date	Mintage	F	VF	XF	Unc	BU
2006	—	—	—	—	15.00	20.00

KM# 1137 DOLLAR
31.6350 g., 0.9990 Silver 1.0160 oz. ASW **Ruler:** Elizabeth II **Subject:** 1923 New South Wales Garford Fire

Date	Mintage	F	VF	XF	Unc	BU
2006 Proof	Est. 5,000	Value: 55.00				

KM# 1169 DOLLAR
0.5000 g., 0.9990 Gold 0.0161 oz. AGW **Ruler:** Elizabeth II **Rev:** Pope Benedict XVI

Date	Mintage	F	VF	XF	Unc	BU
2006 Proof	—	Value: 45.00				

KM# 1179 DOLLAR
Silver **Ruler:** Elizabeth II **Subject:** David Livingstone

Date	Mintage	F	VF	XF	Unc	BU
2006 Proof	—	Value: 45.00				

KM# 1180 DOLLAR
Silver **Ruler:** Elizabeth II **Subject:** Ferdinanad Magellan

Date	Mintage	F	VF	XF	Unc	BU
2006 Proof	—	Value: 45.00				

KM# 1181 DOLLAR
Silver **Ruler:** Elizabeth II **Subject:** Roald Amundsen

Date	Mintage	F	VF	XF	Unc	BU
2006 Proof	—	Value: 45.00				

KM# 1182 DOLLAR
Silver **Ruler:** Elizabeth II **Subject:** Christopher Columbus

Date	Mintage	F	VF	XF	Unc	BU
2006 Proof	—	Value: 45.00				

KM# 1183 DOLLAR
Silver **Ruler:** Elizabeth II **Subject:** Juan Sebastian de Elcano

Date	Mintage	F	VF	XF	Unc	BU
2006 Proof	—	Value: 45.00				

KM# 733 DOLLAR
25.0900 g., Copper-Nickel, 38.8 mm. **Ruler:** Elizabeth II **Rev:** HMS Victory **Rev. Legend:** England expects that every man will do his duty

Date	Mintage	F	VF	XF	Unc	BU
2007	—	—	—	—	—	15.00

KM# 734 DOLLAR
25.0900 g., Copper-Nickel, 38.8 mm. **Ruler:** Elizabeth II **Rev:** Admiral Nelson and two naval vessels **Rev. Legend:** England expects that every man will do his duty

Date	Mintage	F	VF	XF	Unc	BU
2007	—	—	—	—	—	15.00

KM# 735 DOLLAR
0.5000 g., 0.9990 Gold 0.0161 oz. AGW, 11 mm. **Ruler:** Elizabeth II **Rev:** Treaty of Rome - Slovenia

Date	Mintage	F	VF	XF	Unc	BU
2007 Proof	—	Value: 40.00				

KM# 736 DOLLAR
0.5000 g., 0.9990 Gold 0.0161 oz. AGW **Ruler:** Elizabeth II **Rev:** Benedict XVI's 2 Euro Coin

Date	Mintage	F	VF	XF	Unc	BU
2007 Proof	—	Value: 40.00				

KM# 471 DOLLAR
35.8000 g., 0.9990 Silver 1.1498 oz. ASW **Ruler:** Elizabeth II **Subject:** Sputnik 50th Anniversary - 1957-2007 **Obv:** Small bust divides legend above, center globe with color applique **Rev:** Satellite orbiting Earth with color applique **Rev. Legend:** SPUTNIK 50th ANNIVERSARY 1957 - 2007 **Edge:** Plain **Note:** Center piece rotates freely

Date	Mintage	F	VF	XF	Unc	BU
ND2007 Proof	—	Value: 85.00				

KM# 490 DOLLAR
31.1030 g., 0.9990 Silver 0.9989 oz. ASW, 40.6 mm. **Ruler:** Elizabeth II **Subject:** Historical Australian Coins **Obv:** Head with tiara right **Rev:** 1757 New South Wales Holey Dollar **Edge:** Reeded

Date	Mintage	F	VF	XF	Unc	BU
2007 Proof	1,500	Value: 125				

KM# 491 DOLLAR
31.1030 g., 0.9990 Silver 0.9989 oz. ASW, 40.6 mm. **Ruler:** Elizabeth II **Subject:** Historical Australian Coins **Obv:** Head with tiara right **Rev:** Gilt 1857 Sydney Mint Sovereign **Edge:** Reeded

Date	Mintage	F	VF	XF	Unc	BU
2007 Proof	1,500	Value: 125				

KM# 492 DOLLAR
31.1030 g., 0.9990 Silver Selective copper plating 0.9989 oz. ASW, 40.6 mm. **Ruler:** Elizabeth II **Subject:** Historical Australian Coins **Obv:** Head with tiarra right **Rev:** Copper 1937 pattern penny **Edge:** Reeded

Date	Mintage	F	VF	XF	Unc	BU
2007 Proof	1,500	Value: 125				

KM# 1138 DOLLAR
0.5000 g., 0.9990 Gold 0.0161 oz. AGW, 11 mm. **Ruler:** Elizabeth II **Subject:** Treaty of Rome, 50th Anniversary **Rev:** San Marino

Date	Mintage	F	VF	XF	Unc	BU
2007 Proof	Est. 5,000	Value: 50.00				

KM# 1196 DOLLAR
25.0000 g., Copper-Nickel, 38.6 mm. **Ruler:** Elizabeth II **Rev:** Elizabeth II and Prince Philip in color

Date	Mintage	F	VF	XF	Unc	BU
2007 Proof	Est. 50,000	Value: 17.50				

KM# 1197 DOLLAR
25.0000 g., Copper-Nickel, 38.6 mm. **Ruler:** Elizabeth II **Rev:** Elizabeth II and Prince Philip in color

Date	Mintage	F	VF	XF	Unc	BU
2007 Proof	Est. 50,000	Value: 17.50				

KM# 1198 DOLLAR
25.0000 g., Copper-Nickel, 38.6 mm. **Ruler:** Elizabeth II **Rev:** Elizabeth II and Prince Philip in color

Date	Mintage	F	VF	XF	Unc	BU
2007 Proof	Est. 50,000	Value: 17.50				

KM# 1199 DOLLAR
25.0000 g., Copper-Nickel, 38.6 mm. **Ruler:** Elizabeth II **Rev:** Elizabeth II and Prince Philip in color

Date	Mintage	F	VF	XF	Unc	BU
2007 Proof	Est. 50,000	Value: 17.50				

KM# 1200 DOLLAR
25.0000 g., Copper-Nickel, 38.6 mm. **Ruler:** Elizabeth II **Rev:** Elizabth and Prince Philip in color

Date	Mintage	F	VF	XF	Unc	BU
2007 Proof	Est. 50,000	Value: 17.50				

KM# 493 DOLLAR
31.1030 g., 0.9990 Silver 0.9989 oz. ASW, 40.6 mm. **Ruler:** Elizabeth II **Subject:** Historical Australian Coins **Obv:** Head with tiara right **Rev:** 1823 MacIntosh and Degraves Shilling **Edge:** Reeded

Date	Mintage	F	VF	XF	Unc	BU
2008 Proof	1,500	Value: 125				

KM# 494 DOLLAR
31.1030 g., 0.9990 Silver Selective gold plating 0.9989 oz. ASW, 40.6 mm. **Ruler:** Elizabeth II **Subject:** Historic Australian Coins **Obv:** Head with tiara right **Rev:** Gilt 1788 George III Spade Guinea **Edge:** Reeded

Date	Mintage	F	VF	XF	Unc	BU
2008 Proof	1,500	Value: 125				

KM# 495 DOLLAR
31.1030 g., 0.9990 Silver 0.9989 oz. ASW, 40.6 mm. **Ruler:** Elizabeth II **Subject:** Historic Australian Coins **Obv:** Head with tiara right **Rev:** Australian 1910 Florin **Edge:** Reeded

Date	Mintage	F	VF	XF	Unc	BU
2008 Proof	1,500	Value: 125				

KM# 496 DOLLAR
31.1030 g., 0.9990 Silver Selective gold plating 0.9989 oz. ASW, 40.6 mm. **Ruler:** Elizabeth II **Subject:** Historic Australian Coins **Obv:** Head with tiara right **Rev:** Gilt 1808-1815 Gold Pagoda **Edge:** Reeded

Date	Mintage	F	VF	XF	Unc	BU
2008 Proof	1,500	Value: 125				

KM# 497 DOLLAR
31.1030 g., 0.9990 Silver 0.9989 oz. ASW, 40.6 mm. **Ruler:** Elizabeth II **Subject:** Historic Australian Coins **Obv:** Head with tiara right **Rev:** 1850's Taylor's sixpence pattern **Edge:** Reeded

Date	Mintage	F	VF	XF	Unc	BU
2008 Proof	1,500	Value: 125				

KM# 498 DOLLAR
31.1050 g., 0.9990 Silver Selective copper plating 0.9990 oz. ASW, 40.6 mm. **Ruler:** Elizabeth II **Subject:** Historic Australian Coins **Obv:** Head with tiara right **Rev:** Copper Australian WWII Interment Camp Token **Edge:** Reeded

Date	Mintage	F	VF	XF	Unc	BU
2008 Proof	1,500	Value: 125				

KM# 499 DOLLAR
31.1030 g., 0.9990 Silver 0.9989 oz. ASW, 40.6 mm. **Ruler:** Elizabeth II **Subject:** Historic Australian Coins **Obv:** Head with tiara right **Rev:** Australian 1946 Perth Mint Shilling **Edge:** Reeded

Date	Mintage	F	VF	XF	Unc	BU
2008 Proof	1,500	Value: 125				

KM# 500 DOLLAR
31.1030 g., 0.9990 Silver 0.9989 oz. ASW, 40.6 mm. **Ruler:** Elizabeth II **Subject:** Historic Australian Coins **Obv:** Head with tiara right **Rev:** Australian 1938 Crown **Edge:** Reeded

Date	Mintage	F	VF	XF	Unc	BU
2008 Proof	1,500	Value: 125				

KM# 501 DOLLAR
31.1030 g., 0.9990 Silver 0.9989 oz. ASW, 40.6 mm. **Ruler:** Elizabeth II **Subject:** Historic Australian Coins **Obv:** Head with tiara right **Rev:** Copper Australian 1930 Penny **Edge:** Reeded

Date	Mintage	F	VF	XF	Unc	BU
2008 Proof	1,500	Value: 125				

KM# 502 DOLLAR
31.1030 g., 0.9990 Silver 0.9989 oz. ASW, 40.6 mm. **Ruler:** Elizabeth II **Subject:** World War I **Obv:** Head with tiara right **Rev:** Multicolor image of Australian WWI soldier in Europe **Edge:** Reeded

Date	Mintage	F	VF	XF	Unc	BU
2008 Proof	1,918	Value: 85.00				

KM# 504 DOLLAR
31.1030 g., 0.9990 Silver 0.9989 oz. ASW, 40.6 mm. **Ruler:** Elizabeth II **Subject:** WWI **Obv:** Head with tiara right **Rev:** Multicolor image of Australian WWI soldier in Mid-East scene **Edge:** Reeded

Date	Mintage	F	VF	XF	Unc	BU
2008 Proof	1,918	Value: 85.00				

KM# 506 DOLLAR
31.1030 g., 0.9990 Silver 0.9989 oz. ASW, 40.6 mm. **Ruler:** Elizabeth II **Subject:** Captain Cook **Obv:** Head with tiara right **Rev:** Multicolor image of James Cook within letter C **Edge:** Reeded

Date	Mintage	F	VF	XF	Unc	BU
2008 Proof	1,779	Value: 100				

KM# 507 DOLLAR
31.1030 g., 0.9990 Silver 0.9989 oz. ASW, 40.6 mm. **Ruler:** Elizabeth II **Subject:** Captain Cook **Obv:** Head with tiara right **Rev:** Multicolor image of James Cook, Bottany Bay all within letter O **Edge:** Reeded

Date	Mintage	F	VF	XF	Unc	BU
2008 Proof	1,779	Value: 100				

KM# 508 DOLLAR
31.1030 g., 0.9990 Silver 0.9989 oz. ASW, 40.6 mm. **Ruler:** Elizabeth II **Subject:** Captain Cook **Obv:** Head with tiara right **Rev:** Multicolor image of James Cook, a new world all within letter O **Edge:** Reeded

Date	Mintage	F	VF	XF	Unc	BU
2008 Proof	1,779	Value: 100				

KM# 509 DOLLAR
31.1030 g., 0.9990 Silver 0.9989 oz. ASW, 40.6 mm. **Ruler:** Elizabeth II **Subject:** Captain Cook **Obv:** Head with tiara right **Rev:** Multicolor image of James Cook, striking the reef, large letter K in background **Edge:** Reeded

Date	Mintage	F	VF	XF	Unc	BU
2008 Proof	1,779	Value: 100				

KM# 765 DOLLAR
35.8000 g., 0.9990 Silver 1.1498 oz. ASW, 40 mm. **Ruler:** Elizabeth II **Subject:** 1961 First man in Space

Date	Mintage	F	VF	XF	Unc	BU
2008 Proof	—	Value: 110				

KM# 766 DOLLAR
31.1050 g., 0.9990 Silver 0.9990 oz. ASW, 40 mm. **Ruler:** Elizabeth II **Subject:** First man on the Moon **Rev:** Moon and rock fragment

Date	Mintage	F	VF	XF	Unc	BU
2008 Proof	—	Value: 120				

KM# 801 DOLLAR
31.1050 g., 0.9990 Silver 0.9990 oz. ASW, 40 mm. **Ruler:** Elizabeth II **Rev:** An-2, partially gilt

Date	Mintage	F	VF	XF	Unc	BU
2008 Proof	—	Value: 50.00				

KM# 802 DOLLAR
31.1050 g., 0.9990 Silver 0.9990 oz. ASW, 40 mm. **Ruler:** Elizabeth II **Rev:** An-74, partially gilt

Date	Mintage	F	VF	XF	Unc	BU
2008 Proof	—	Value: 50.00				

KM# 803 DOLLAR
31.1050 g., 0.9990 Silver 0.9990 oz. ASW, 40 mm. **Ruler:** Elizabeth II **Rev:** An-124, partially gilt

Date	Mintage	F	VF	XF	Unc	BU
2008 Proof	—	Value: 50.00				

KM# 804 DOLLAR
31.1050 g., 0.9990 Silver 0.9990 oz. ASW, 40 mm. **Ruler:** Elizabeth II **Rev:** An-148, partially gilt

Date	Mintage	F	VF	XF	Unc	BU
2008 Proof	—	Value: 50.00				

KM# 805 DOLLAR
31.1050 g., 0.9990 Silver 0.9990 oz. ASW, 40 mm. **Ruler:** Elizabeth II **Rev:** An-225, partially gilt

Date	Mintage	F	VF	XF	Unc	BU
2008 Proof	—	Value: 50.00				

KM# 1208 DOLLAR
0.5000 g., 0.9990 Gold 0.0161 oz. AGW, 11 mm. **Ruler:** Elizabeth II **Subject:** British Monarchs - Henry V

Date	Mintage	F	VF	XF	Unc	BU
2008 Proof	Est. 14,500	Value: 35.00				

KM# 1209 DOLLAR
0.5000 g., 0.9990 Gold 0.0161 oz. AGW, 11 mm. **Ruler:** Elizabeth II **Subject:** British Monarchs - Henry VIII

Date	Mintage	F	VF	XF	Unc	BU
2008 Proof	Est. 50,000	Value: 35.00				

KM# 1209a DOLLAR
0.5000 g., 0.9990 Platinum 0.0161 oz. APW, 11 mm. **Ruler:** Elizabeth II **Subject:** British Monarchs - Henry VIII

Date	Mintage	F	VF	XF	Unc	BU
2008 Proof	Est. 50,000	Value: 50.00				

KM# 1210 DOLLAR
0.5000 g., 0.9990 Gold 0.0161 oz. AGW, 11 mm. **Ruler:** Elizabeth II **Subject:** British Monarchs - Elizabeth II

Date	Mintage	F	VF	XF	Unc	BU
2008 Proof	Est. 50,000	Value: 35.00				

KM# 701 DOLLAR
31.1050 g., 0.9990 Silver 0.9990 oz. ASW, 39 mm. **Ruler:** Elizabeth II **Subject:** First Man on the Moon, 40th Anniversary **Obv:** Head right at top, multicolor moon in center **Rev:** Rocket, orbiter, moon walk. moon in multicolor at center

Date	Mintage	F	VF	XF	Unc	BU
2009 Proof	25,000	Value: 110				

KM# 702 DOLLAR
31.1050 g., 0.9990 Silver 0.9990 oz. ASW, 33x33 mm. **Ruler:** Elizabeth II **Subject:** Cook's Cottage, 75th Anniversary of

relocation **Obv:** Head right **Rev:** Cottage and multicolor Captain Cook image **Shape:** Square

Date	Mintage	F	VF	XF	Unc	BU
2009 Proof	5,000	Value: 95.00				

KM# 706 DOLLAR
0.5000 g., 0.9990 Gold 0.0161 oz. AGW, 11 mm. **Ruler:** Elizabeth II **Subject:** Pope Benedict XVI visits the Holy Land **Rev:** Dome of the Rock

Date	Mintage	F	VF	XF	Unc	BU
2009 Proof	25,000	Value: 35.00				

KM# 708 DOLLAR
1.0000 g., 0.9990 Gold 0.0321 oz. AGW, 13.9 mm. **Ruler:** Elizabeth II **Rev:** Bridge

Date	Mintage	F	VF	XF	Unc	BU
2009 Proof	250	Value: 65.00				

KM# 709 DOLLAR
1.0000 g., 0.9990 Gold 0.0321 oz. AGW, 13.9 mm. **Ruler:** Elizabeth II **Rev:** Statue and gardens

Date	Mintage	F	VF	XF	Unc	BU
2009 Proof	250	Value: 65.00				

KM# 710 DOLLAR
1.0000 g., 0.9990 Gold 0.0321 oz. AGW, 13.9 mm. **Ruler:** Elizabeth II **Rev:** City Gate tower

Date	Mintage	F	VF	XF	Unc	BU
2009 Proof	250	Value: 65.00				

KM# 711 DOLLAR
1.0000 g., 0.9990 Gold 0.0321 oz. AGW, 13.9 mm. **Ruler:** Elizabeth II **Rev:** Virgin Mary statue and church in background

Date	Mintage	F	VF	XF	Unc	BU
2009 Proof	250	Value: 65.00				

KM# 712 DOLLAR
1.0000 g., 0.9990 Gold 0.0321 oz. AGW, 13.9 mm. **Ruler:** Elizabeth II **Rev:** Multiple church spires

Date	Mintage	F	VF	XF	Unc	BU
2009 Proof	250	Value: 65.00				

KM# 713 DOLLAR
1.0000 g., 0.9990 Gold 0.0321 oz. AGW, 13.9 mm. **Ruler:** Elizabeth II **Rev:** National Theater

Date	Mintage	F	VF	XF	Unc	BU
2009 Proof	250	Value: 65.00				

KM# 714 DOLLAR
1.0000 g., 0.9990 Gold 0.0321 oz. AGW, 13.9 mm. **Ruler:** Elizabeth II **Rev:** Castle

Date	Mintage	F	VF	XF	Unc	BU
2009 Proof	250	Value: 65.00				

KM# 715 DOLLAR
1.0000 g., 0.9990 Gold 0.0321 oz. AGW, 13.9 mm. **Ruler:** Elizabeth II **Rev:** Castle on a hill

Date	Mintage	F	VF	XF	Unc	BU
2009 Proof	250	Value: 65.00				

KM# 716 DOLLAR
1.0000 g., 0.9990 Gold 0.0321 oz. AGW, 13.9 mm. **Ruler:** Elizabeth II **Rev:** Castle

Date	Mintage	F	VF	XF	Unc	BU
2009 Proof	250	Value: 65.00				

KM# 717 DOLLAR
1.0000 g., 0.9990 Gold 0.0321 oz. AGW, 13.9 mm. **Ruler:** Elizabeth II **Rev:** Castle

Date	Mintage	F	VF	XF	Unc	BU
2009 Proof	250	Value: 65.00				

KM# 718 DOLLAR
1.0000 g., 0.9990 Gold 0.0321 oz. AGW, 13.9 mm. **Ruler:** Elizabeth II **Rev:** Church

Date	Mintage	F	VF	XF	Unc	BU
2009 Proof	250	Value: 65.00				

KM# 719 DOLLAR
1.0000 g., 0.9990 Gold 0.0321 oz. AGW, 13.9 mm. **Ruler:** Elizabeth II **Rev:** Ancient ruins

Date	Mintage	F	VF	XF	Unc	BU
2009 Proof	250	Value: 65.00				

KM# 772 DOLLAR
27.0000 g., Copper silver plated, 40 mm. **Ruler:** Elizabeth II **Subject:** Year of Astronomy **Rev:** Sun, multicolor

Date	Mintage	F	VF	XF	Unc	BU
2009	—	—	—	—	—	20.00

KM# 773 DOLLAR
27.0000 g., Copper silver plated, 40 mm. **Ruler:** Elizabeth II **Subject:** Year of Astronomy **Rev:** Mercury, multicolor

Date	Mintage	F	VF	XF	Unc	BU
2009	—	—	—	—	—	20.00

KM# 774 DOLLAR
27.0000 g., Copper silver plated, 40 mm. **Ruler:** Elizabeth II **Subject:** Year of Astronomy **Rev:** Venus, multicolor

Date	Mintage	F	VF	XF	Unc	BU
2009	—	—	—	—	—	20.00

KM# 775 DOLLAR
27.0000 g., Copper silver plated, 40 mm. **Ruler:** Elizabeth II **Subject:** Year of Astronomy **Rev:** Earth, multicolor

Date	Mintage	F	VF	XF	Unc	BU
2009	—	—	—	—	—	20.00

KM# 776 DOLLAR
27.0000 g., Copper silver plated, 40 mm. **Ruler:** Elizabeth II **Subject:** Year of Astronomy **Rev:** Mars, multicolor

Date	Mintage	F	VF	XF	Unc	BU
2009	—	—	—	—	—	20.00

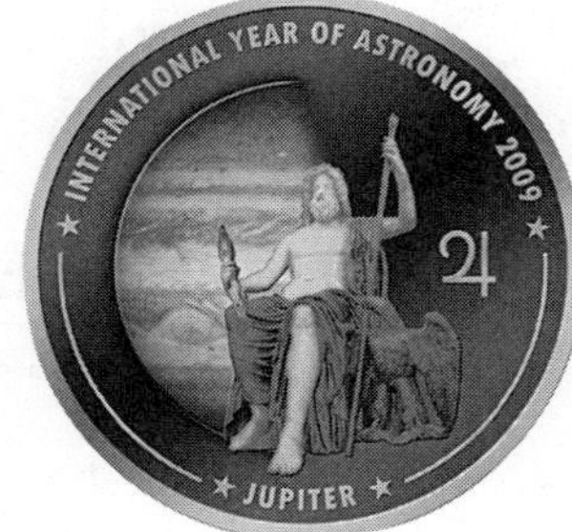

KM# 777 DOLLAR
27.0000 g., Copper silver plated, 40 mm. **Ruler:** Elizabeth II **Subject:** Year of Astronomy **Rev:** Jupiter, multicolor

Date	Mintage	F	VF	XF	Unc	BU
2009	—	—	—	—	—	20.00

KM# 778 DOLLAR

27.0000 g., Copper silver plated, 40 mm. **Ruler:** Elizabeth II **Subject:** Year of Astronomy **Rev:** Saturn, multicolor

Date	Mintage	F	VF	XF	Unc	BU
2009	—	—	—	—	—	20.00

KM# 779 DOLLAR

27.0000 g., Copper silver plated, 40 mm. **Ruler:** Elizabeth II **Subject:** Year of Astronomy **Rev:** Uranus, multicolor

Date	Mintage	F	VF	XF	Unc	BU
2009	—	—	—	—	—	20.00

KM# 780 DOLLAR

27.0000 g., Copper silver plated, 40 mm. **Ruler:** Elizabeth II **Subject:** Year of Astronomy **Rev:** Neptune, multicolor

Date	Mintage	F	VF	XF	Unc	BU
2009	—	—	—	—	—	20.00

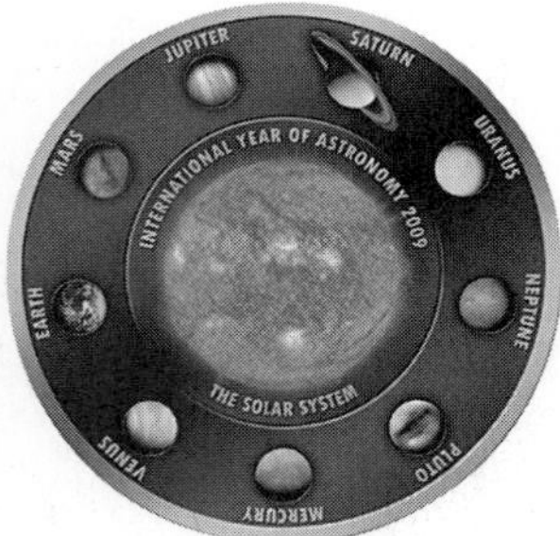

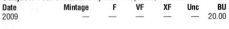

KM# 781 DOLLAR

27.0000 g., Copper silver plated, 40 mm. **Ruler:** Elizabeth II **Subject:** Year of Astronomy **Rev:** Solar System, multicolor

Date	Mintage	F	VF	XF	Unc	BU
2009	—	—	—	—	—	20.00

KM# 794 DOLLAR

Copper-Nickel silver plated, 40 mm. **Ruler:** Elizabeth II **Rev:** Nessie, multicolor

Date	Mintage	F	VF	XF	Unc	BU
2009	—	—	—	—	—	20.00

KM# 795 DOLLAR

Copper-Nickel silver plated, 40 mm. **Ruler:** Elizabeth II **Rev:** Bigfoot, multicolor

Date	Mintage	F	VF	XF	Unc	BU
2009	—	—	—	—	—	20.00

KM# 796 DOLLAR

Copper-Nickel, 40 mm. **Ruler:** Elizabeth II **Rev:** Medussa, multicolor

Date	Mintage	F	VF	XF	Unc	BU
2009	—	—	—	—	—	20.00

KM# 797 DOLLAR

Copper-Nickel, 40 mm. **Ruler:** Elizabeth II **Rev:** Pegasus, multicolor

Date	Mintage	F	VF	XF	Unc	BU
2009	—	—	—	—	—	20.00

KM# 798 DOLLAR

Silver, 40 mm. **Ruler:** Elizabeth II **Rev:** Baba Yaga, multicolor

Date	Mintage	F	VF	XF	Unc	BU
2009	—	—	—	—	—	20.00

KM# 799 DOLLAR

Copper-Nickel, 40 mm. **Ruler:** Elizabeth II **Rev:** Phoenix, multicolor

Date	Mintage	F	VF	XF	Unc	BU
2009	—	—	—	—	—	20.00

KM# 1172 DOLLAR

27.0000 g., Copper-Nickel, 38.6 mm. **Ruler:** Elizabeth II **Subject:** Moon Landing, 40th Anniversary **Rev:** Landing module Eagle and moon in color

Date	Mintage	F	VF	XF	Unc	BU
2009	—	—	—	—	—	17.50

KM# 1231 DOLLAR

25.0000 g., Copper-Nickel partially gilt, 38.6 mm. **Ruler:** Elizabeth II **Subject:** British Monarchs - Henry VIII

Date	Mintage	F	VF	XF	Unc	BU
2009	Est. 50,000	—	—	—	—	17.50

KM# 1241 DOLLAR

31.1350 g., 0.9990 Silver 100000 oz. ASW **Ruler:** Elizabeth II **Subject:** Battle of Gettysburg and General Meade

Date	Mintage	F	VF	XF	Unc	BU
2009 Proof	—	Value: 75.00				

KM# 762 DOLLAR

10.9300 g., Bi-Metallic Brass center in copper-nickel ring. **Ruler:** Elizabeth II **Obv:** Bust right **Rev:** Carved Maori figure (Tangaroa)

Date	Mintage	F	VF	XF	Unc	BU
2010	—	—	—	—	4.00	5.00

KM# 720 DOLLAR

0.1200 g., 0.9990 Silver 0.0039 oz. ASW, 4 mm. **Ruler:** Elizabeth II **Rev:** Fisherman's God statue

Date	Mintage	F	VF	XF	Unc	BU
2010 Prooflike	5,000	—	—	—	—	7.00

KM# 739 DOLLAR

Silver **Ruler:** Elizabeth II **Subject:** Niko & the way to the stars **Rev:** Multicolor deer **Shape:** 7-sided

Date	Mintage	F	VF	XF	Unc	BU
2010 Proof	—	Value: 45.00				

KM# 740 DOLLAR

Silver **Ruler:** Elizabeth II **Subject:** Niko & the way to the stars **Rev:** Multicolor wolf **Shape:** 7-sided

Date	Mintage	F	VF	XF	Unc	BU
2010 Proof	—	Value: 45.00				

KM# 741 DOLLAR

Silver **Ruler:** Elizabeth II **Subject:** Niko & the way to the stars **Rev:** Multicolor flying squirrel **Shape:** 7-sided

Date	Mintage	F	VF	XF	Unc	BU
2010 Proof	—	Value: 45.00				

KM# 742 DOLLAR

Silver **Ruler:** Elizabeth II **Subject:** Niko and the way to the stars **Rev:** Multicolor Ermine **Shape:** 7-sided

Date	Mintage	F	VF	XF	Unc	BU
2010 Proof	—	Value: 45.00				

KM# 743 DOLLAR

Silver **Ruler:** Elizabeth II **Subject:** Niko and the way to the stars **Rev:** Multicolor deer, flying squirrel and ermine **Shape:** 7-sided

Date	Mintage	F	VF	XF	Unc	BU
2010 Proof	—	Value: 45.00				

KM# 744 DOLLAR

Silver **Ruler:** Elizabeth II **Subject:** Battle of Trafalgar, 1805 **Rev:** Multicolor battle scene, HMS Victory

Date	Mintage	F	VF	XF	Unc	BU
2010 Proof	—	Value: 80.00				

KM# 770 DOLLAR

31.1050 g., 0.9990 Silver 0.9990 oz. ASW, 40 mm. **Ruler:** Elizabeth II **Subject:** Battle of Hampton Roads, Va. **Rev:** Monitor, multicolor background

Date	Mintage	F	VF	XF	Unc	BU
2010 Proof	5,000	Value: 80.00				

KM# 1243 DOLLAR

31.1350 g., 0.9990 Silver 100000 oz. ASW, 40.6 mm. **Ruler:** Elizabeth II **Subject:** Battle of Midway **Rev:** Aircraft carrier

Date	Mintage	F	VF	XF	Unc	BU
2010 Proof	5,000	Value: 100				

KM# 1256 DOLLAR

31.1350 g., 0.9990 Silver 100000 oz. ASW, 40.6 mm. **Ruler:** Elizabeth II **Subject:** Battle of Grunwald

Date	Mintage	F	VF	XF	Unc	BU
2010 Proof	—	Value: 50.00				

KM# 1257 DOLLAR

31.1050 g., 0.9990 Silver 0.9990 oz. ASW, 40.6 mm. **Ruler:** Elizabeth II **Subject:** Trafalgar **Rev:** H.M.S. Victory and Battle scene in color

Date	Mintage	F	VF	XF	Unc	BU
2010 Proof	5,000	Value: 80.00				

KM# 1235 DOLLAR

31.1350 g., 0.9990 Silver 100000 oz. ASW, 40.6 mm. **Ruler:** Elizabeth II **Subject:** Battle of Jutland, 1916 **Rev:** Multicolor battleship **Rev. Designer:** Barryl Bellotti

Date	Mintage	F	VF	XF	Unc	BU
2011 Proof	5,000	Value: 85.00				

KM# 1260 DOLLAR

31.1350 g., 0.9990 Silver 100000 oz. ASW, 40.6 mm. **Ruler:** Elizabeth II **Subject:** Battle of Salanis

Date	Mintage	F	VF	XF	Unc	BU
2011 Proof	—	Value: 70.00				

KM# 1269 DOLLAR

31.1350 g., 999.0000 Silver 999.97 oz. ASW, 47.6x27.6 mm. **Ruler:** Elizabeth II **Subject:** Year of the Rabbit **Rev:** Two brown rabbits **Shape:** Rectangle

Date	Mintage	F	VF	XF	Unc	BU
2011 Proof	3,000	Value: 100				

KM# 1270 DOLLAR

31.1350 g., 0.9990 Silver 100000 oz. ASW, 47.6x27.6 mm. **Ruler:** Elizabeth II **Subject:** Year of the Rabbit **Rev:** Two white rabbits **Shape:** Rectangle

Date	Mintage	F	VF	XF	Unc	BU
2011 Proof	3,000	Value: 100				

KM# 1271 DOLLAR

31.1350 g., 0.9990 Silver 100000 oz. ASW, 47.6x27.6 mm. **Ruler:** Elizabeth II **Subject:** Year of the Rabbit **Rev:** One black rabbit **Shape:** Rectangle

Date	Mintage	F	VF	XF	Unc	BU
2011 Proof	3,000	Value: 100				

KM# 1272 DOLLAR

31.1350 g., 0.9990 Silver 100000 oz. ASW, 47.6x27.6 mm. **Ruler:** Elizabeth II **Subject:** Year of the Rabbit **Rev:** One black rabbit **Shape:** Rectangle

Date	Mintage	F	VF	XF	Unc	BU
2011 Proof	3,000	Value: 100				

KM# 554 2 DOLLARS

31.1050 g., 0.9990 Silver 0.9990 oz. ASW, 40.5 mm. **Ruler:** Elizabeth II **Subject:** Asian wildlife **Rev:** Multicolored pheasant-tailed Jacana

Date	Mintage	F	VF	XF	Unc	BU
2001 Proof	3,000	Value: 85.00				

KM# 551 2 DOLLARS

31.1050 g., 0.9990 Silver 0.9990 oz. ASW, 40.5 mm. **Ruler:** Elizabeth II **Subject:** Asian wildlife **Rev:** Multicolor Mikado Pheasant

Date	Mintage	F	VF	XF	Unc	BU
2001 Proof	5,000	Value: 85.00				

KM# 552 2 DOLLARS

31.1050 g., 0.9990 Silver 0.9990 oz. ASW, 40.5 mm. **Ruler:** Elizabeth II **Subject:** Asian wildlife **Rev:** Multicolor black-faced spoonbill

Date	Mintage	F	VF	XF	Unc	BU
2001 Proof	5,000	Value: 85.00				

KM# 553 2 DOLLARS

31.1050 g., 0.9990 Silver 0.9990 oz. ASW, 40.5 mm. **Ruler:** Elizabeth II **Subject:** Asian wildlife **Rev:** Multicolor Indian Pitta

Date	Mintage	F	VF	XF	Unc	BU
2001 Proof	3,000	Value: 85.00				

KM# 468 2 DOLLARS

Copper-Nickel **Ruler:** Elizabeth II **Rev:** Football championship

Date	Mintage	F	VF	XF	Unc	BU
2002	—	—	—	—	5.00	7.00

KM# 1119 2 DOLLARS

Copper-Nickel, 30 mm. **Ruler:** Elizabeth II **Subject:** XXVIII Summer Olympics, Athens **Rev:** Discus thrower

Date	Mintage	F	VF	XF	Unc	BU
2002 Proof	—	Value: 15.00				

KM# 1120 2 DOLLARS

Silver **Ruler:** Elizabeth II **Subject:** Endangered Wildlife **Rev:** Lion family

Date	Mintage	F	VF	XF	Unc	BU
2002 Proof	—	Value: 25.00				

KM# 1282 2 DOLLARS

31.1350 g., 0.9990 Silver 100000 oz. ASW, 40.6 mm. **Ruler:** Elizabeth II **Subject:** Taiwan New Koala Family **Obv:** Head crowned right **Rev:** Multicolor Koala seated with leaves

Date	Mintage	F	VF	XF	Unc	BU
2002 Proof	—	Value: 135				

KM# 417 2 DOLLARS

7.5500 g., Copper-Nickel, 26 mm. **Ruler:** Elizabeth II **Obv:** Crowned bust right, new portrait **Rev:** Mortar and pestle from Atiu Island **Edge:** Triangular

Date	Mintage	F	VF	XF	Unc	BU
2003	—	—	—	—	3.00	3.50

KM# 1123 2 DOLLARS

62.7700 g., 0.9990 Silver 2.0160 oz. ASW, 50 mm. **Ruler:** Elizabeth II **Rev:** Edward "Ned" Kelly in color

Date	Mintage	F	VF	XF	Unc	BU
2003 Proof	Est. 2,500	Value: 100				

KM# 1124 2 DOLLARS

62.7700 g., 0.9990 Silver 2.0160 oz. ASW, 50 mm. **Ruler:** Elizabeth II **Rev:** Daniel Morgan in color

Date	Mintage	F	VF	XF	Unc	BU
2003 Proof	Est. 2,500	Value: 100				

KM# 1125 2 DOLLARS

62.7700 g., 0.9990 Silver 2.0160 oz. ASW **Ruler:** Elizabeth II **Rev:** Ben Hall in color

Date	Mintage	F	VF	XF	Unc	BU
2003 Proof	Est. 2,500	Value: 100				

KM# 1126 2 DOLLARS

62.7700 g., 0.9990 Silver 2.0160 oz. ASW, 50 mm. **Ruler:** Elizabeth II **Rev:** Fred Ward "Captain Thunderbolt" in color

Date	Mintage	F	VF	XF	Unc	BU
2003 Proof	Est. 2,500	Value: 100				

KM# 1139 2 DOLLARS

0.9990 Silver, 30 mm. **Ruler:** Elizabeth II **Subject:** John F. Kennedy, 40th Anniversary of Death

Date	Mintage	F	VF	XF	Unc	BU
2003 Proof	—	Value: 45.00				

KM# 1141 2 DOLLARS

Gold **Ruler:** Elizabeth II **Rev:** Bird in color

Date	Mintage	F	VF	XF	Unc	BU
2003 Proof	Est. 5,000	Value: 85.00				

KM# 1142 2 DOLLARS

Gold **Ruler:** Elizabeth II **Subject:** Love swing **Rev:** Bird in color

Date	Mintage	F	VF	XF	Unc	BU
2003 Proof	Est. 5,000	Value: 85.00				

KM# 536 2 DOLLARS

31.1050 g., 0.9990 Silver 0.9990 oz. ASW, 40.7 mm. **Ruler:** Elizabeth II **Subject:** Birds of New Zealand **Rev:** Multicolor tui

Date	Mintage	F	VF	XF	Unc	BU
2005 Prooflike	8,000	—	—	—	—	90.00

KM# 537 2 DOLLARS

31.1050 g., 0.9990 Silver 0.9990 oz. ASW, 40.7 mm. **Ruler:** Elizabeth II **Subject:** Birds of New Zealand **Rev:** Multicolor bell bird

Date	Mintage	F	VF	XF	Unc	BU
2005 Prooflike	8,000	—	—	—	—	90.00

KM# 538 2 DOLLARS

31.1050 g., 0.9990 Silver 0.9990 oz. ASW, 40.7 mm. **Ruler:** Elizabeth II **Subject:** Birds of New Zealand **Rev:** Multicolor New Zealand Pigeon

Date	Mintage	F	VF	XF	Unc	BU
2005 Prooflike	8,000	—	—	—	—	90.00

KM# 539 2 DOLLARS

31.1050 g., 0.9990 Silver 0.9990 oz. ASW, 40.7 mm. **Ruler:** Elizabeth II **Subject:** Birds of New Zealand **Rev:** Multicolor yellow crowned parakeet

Date	Mintage	F	VF	XF	Unc	BU
2005 Prooflike	8,000	—	—	—	—	90.00

KM# 524 2 DOLLARS

31.1050 g., 0.9990 Silver 0.9990 oz. ASW, 40.7 mm. **Ruler:** Elizabeth II **Subject:** Classic Speedsters from the 1930's **Rev:** Multicolor 1935 Auburn 851 Speedster

Date	Mintage	F	VF	XF	Unc	BU
2006 Prooflike	6,000	—	—	—	—	80.00

KM# 525 2 DOLLARS

31.1050 g., 0.9990 Silver 0.9990 oz. ASW, 40.7 mm. **Ruler:** Elizabeth II **Subject:** Classic Speedsters from the 1930's **Rev:** Multicolor 1935 Bugatti Type 57SC Atlantic Speedster

Date	Mintage	F	VF	XF	Unc	BU
2006 Prooflike	6,000	—	—	—	—	80.00

KM# 526 2 DOLLARS

31.1050 g., 0.9990 Silver 0.9990 oz. ASW, 40.7 mm. **Ruler:** Elizabeth II **Subject:** Speedsters from the 1930's **Rev:** Multicolor 1936 Duesenberg SSJ Speedster

Date	Mintage	F	VF	XF	Unc	BU
2006 Prooflike	—	—	—	—	—	80.00

KM# 527 2 DOLLARS

31.1050 g., 0.9990 Silver 0.9990 oz. ASW, 40.7 mm. **Ruler:** Elizabeth II **Subject:** Speedsters from the 1930's **Rev:** Multicolor 1930 Packard 734 Boattail Speedster

Date	Mintage	F	VF	XF	Unc	BU
2006 Prooflike	6,000	—	—	—	—	80.00

KM# 1170 2 DOLLARS

10.0000 g., 0.9250 Silver 0.2974 oz. ASW, 30 mm. **Ruler:** Elizabeth II **Rev:** Motion Pictures, 100th Anniversary

Date	Mintage	F	VF	XF	Unc	BU
2006	Est. 2,500	—	—	—	—	35.00

KM# 514 2 DOLLARS

31.1050 g., 0.9990 Silver 0.9990 oz. ASW, 40.7 mm. **Ruler:** Elizabeth II **Subject:** Great Motorcycles from the 1930's **Rev:** Multicolor 1930 BSA Sloper

Date	Mintage	F	VF	XF	Unc	BU
2007 Prooflike	6,000	—	—	—	—	70.00

KM# 515 2 DOLLARS

31.1050 g., 0.9990 Silver 0.9990 oz. ASW, 40.7 mm. **Ruler:** Elizabeth II **Subject:** Great motorcycles from the 1930's **Rev:** Multicolor 1937 Ariel 1000 Squarefour

Date	Mintage	F	VF	XF	Unc	BU
2007 Prooflike	6,000	—	—	—	—	70.00

KM# 516 2 DOLLARS

31.1050 g., 0.9990 Silver 0.9990 oz. ASW, 40.7 mm. **Ruler:** Elizabeth II **Subject:** Great motorcycles from the 1930's **Rev:** Multicolor 1938 12H 8

Date	Mintage	F	VF	XF	Unc	BU
2007 Prooflike	6,000	—	—	—	—	70.00

KM# 517 2 DOLLARS

31.1050 g., 0.9990 Silver 0.9990 oz. ASW, 40.7 mm. **Ruler:** Elizabeth II **Subject:** Great motorcycles from the 1930's **Rev:** Multicolor 1931 Matchless Silver Hawk

Date	Mintage	F	VF	XF	Unc	BU
2007 Prooflike	6,000	—	—	—	—	70.00

KM# 518 2 DOLLARS

31.1050 g., 0.9990 Silver 0.9990 oz. ASW, 40.7 mm. **Ruler:** Elizabeth II **Subject:** Great motocycles from the 1930's **Rev:** Multicolor 1932 Brough Superior SS100

Date	Mintage	F	VF	XF	Unc	BU
2007 Prooflike	6,000	—	—	—	—	70.00

KM# 529 2 DOLLARS

31.1050 g., 0.9990 Silver 0.9990 oz. ASW, 40.7 mm. **Ruler:** Elizabeth II **Subject:** International Women's Day **Rev:** Multicolor tulips, large 8

Date	Mintage	F	VF	XF	Unc	BU
2007 Prooflike	4,000	—	—	—	—	65.00

KM# 532 2 DOLLARS

31.1050 g., 0.9990 Silver 0.9990 oz. ASW, 40.7 mm. **Ruler:** Elizabeth II **Subject:** Sherlock Holmes **Rev:** Multicolor portrait

Date	Mintage	F	VF	XF	Unc	BU
2007 Prooflike	8,000	—	—	—	—	100

KM# 1184 2 DOLLARS

31.1050 g., 0.9990 Silver 0.9990 oz. ASW, 40.7 mm. **Ruler:** Elizabeth II **Subject:** Birds of Fiji **Rev:** Island Thrush in color

Date	Mintage	F	VF	XF	Unc	BU
2007	Est. 4,000	—	—	—	—	45.00

KM# 1185 2 DOLLARS

31.1050 g., 0.9990 Silver 0.9990 oz. ASW, 40.7 mm. **Ruler:** Elizabeth II **Subject:** Birds of Fiji **Rev:** Vampire Bat in color

Date	Mintage	F	VF	XF	Unc	BU
2007	Est. 4,000	—	—	—	—	45.00

KM# 1186 2 DOLLARS

31.1050 g., 0.9990 Silver 0.9990 oz. ASW, 40.7 mm. **Ruler:** Elizabeth II **Subject:** Birds of Fiji **Rev:** Kingfisher in color

Date	Mintage	F	VF	XF	Unc	BU
2007	4,000	—	—	—	—	45.00

KM# 1187 2 DOLLARS

31.1050 g., 0.9990 Silver 0.9990 oz. ASW, 40.7 mm. **Ruler:** Elizabeth II **Subject:** Birds of Fiji **Rev:** Lori in color

Date	Mintage	F	VF	XF	Unc	BU
2007	4,000	—	—	—	—	45.00

KM# 510 2 DOLLARS

31.1050 g., 0.9990 Silver 0.9990 oz. ASW, 40.7 mm. **Ruler:** Elizabeth II **Subject:** Year of the Rat **Rev:** Multicolor scene of little girl from Russian animated cartoon

Date	Mintage	F	VF	XF	Unc	BU
2008 Prooflike	10,000	—	—	—	—	80.00

KM# 511 2 DOLLARS

31.1050 g., 0.9990 Silver 0.9990 oz. ASW, 40.7 mm. **Ruler:** Elizabeth II **Subject:** Year of the Rat **Rev:** Multicolor scene of nutcracker from Russian animated cartoon

Date	Mintage	F	VF	XF	Unc	BU
2008 Prooflike	10,000	—	—	—	—	80.00

KM# 512 2 DOLLARS

39.1050 g., 0.9990 Silver 1.2559 oz. ASW, 40.7 mm. **Ruler:** Elizabeth II **Rev:** Multicolor scene of Adventure of Cat Leopold Russian animated cartoon

Date	Mintage	F	VF	XF	Unc	BU
2008 Prooflike	10,000	—	—	—	—	80.00

KM# 513 2 DOLLARS

31.1050 g., 0.9990 Silver 0.9990 oz. ASW, 40.7 mm. **Ruler:** Elizabeth II **Subject:** Year of the Rat **Rev:** Multicolor scene of tough toy soldier from Russian animated cartoon

Date	Mintage	F	VF	XF	Unc	BU
2008 Prooflike	10,000	—	—	—	—	80.00

KM# 519 2 DOLLARS

31.1050 g., 0.9990 Silver 0.9990 oz. ASW, 40.7 mm. **Ruler:** Elizabeth II **Subject:** Racers from the 1930's **Rev:** Multicolor Gee Bee

Date	Mintage	F	VF	XF	Unc	BU
2008 Prooflike	6,000	—	—	—	—	70.00

KM# 520 2 DOLLARS

31.1050 g., 0.9990 Silver 0.9990 oz. ASW, 40.7 mm. **Ruler:** Elizabeth II **Subject:** Racers from the 1930's **Rev:** Multicolor, Hughes H-1 Racer

Date	Mintage	F	VF	XF	Unc	BU
2008 Prooflike	6,000	—	—	—	—	70.00

KM# 521 2 DOLLARS

31.1050 g., 0.9990 Silver 0.9990 oz. ASW, 40.7 mm. **Ruler:** Elizabeth II **Subject:** Racers from the 1930's **Rev:** Multicolor Laird Turner LTR-14 Meteor

Date	Mintage	F	VF	XF	Unc	BU
2008 Prooflike	6,000	—	—	—	—	70.00

KM# 522 2 DOLLARS

31.1050 g., 0.9990 Silver 0.9990 oz. ASW, 40.7 mm. **Ruler:** Elizabeth II **Subject:** Racers from the 1930's **Rev:** Multicolor Spuermarine S.6B Floatplane

Date	Mintage	F	VF	XF	Unc	BU
2008 Prooflike	6,000	—	—	—	—	70.00

KM# 523 2 DOLLARS

31.1050 g., 0.9990 Silver 0.9990 oz. ASW, 40.7 mm. **Ruler:** Elizabeth II **Subject:** Racers from the 1930's **Rev:** Multicolor Polikarpov I-16

Date	Mintage	F	VF	XF	Unc	BU
2008 Prooflike	6,000	—	—	—	—	70.00

KM# 528 2 DOLLARS

31.1050 g., 0.9990 Silver 0.9990 oz. ASW, 40.7 mm. **Ruler:** Elizabeth II **Subject:** Valentines (Love) **Rev:** Multicolor pair of swans **Rev. Legend:** Love is precious

Date	Mintage	F	VF	XF	Unc	BU
2008 Prooflike	16,000	—	—	—	—	90.00

KM# 530 2 DOLLARS
31.1050 g., 0.9990 Silver 0.9990 oz. ASW, 40.7 mm. **Ruler:** Elizabeth II **Subject:** Mikhail Kalasknikov **Rev:** Multicolor portrait in uniform with siver gun

Date	Mintage	F	VF	XF	Unc	BU
2008 Prooflike	20,000	—	—	—	—	100

KM# 531 2 DOLLARS
31.1050 g., 0.9990 Silver 0.9990 oz. ASW, 40.7 mm. **Ruler:** Elizabeth II **Subject:** Mikhail Kalashnikov **Rev:** Multicolor red star, soldier and gun

Date	Mintage	F	VF	XF	Unc	BU
2008 Prooflike	20,000	—	—	—	—	100

KM# 533 2 DOLLARS
31.1050 g., 0.9990 Silver 0.9990 oz. ASW, 40.7 mm. **Ruler:** Elizabeth II **Subject:** Sherlock Holmes **Rev:** Multicolor scene from Hound of the Baskervilles

Date	Mintage	F	VF	XF	Unc	BU
2008 Prooflike	8,000	—	—	—	—	100

KM# 534 2 DOLLARS
31.1050 g., 0.9990 Silver 0.9990 oz. ASW, 40.7 mm. **Ruler:** Elizabeth II **Subject:** Sherlock Holmes **Rev:** Multicolor scehe from the Final Problem

Date	Mintage	F	VF	XF	Unc	BU
2008 Prooflike	8,000	—	—	—	—	100

KM# 535 2 DOLLARS
31.1050 g., 0.9990 Silver 0.9990 oz. ASW, 40.7 mm. **Ruler:** Elizabeth II **Subject:** Sherlock Holmes **Rev:** Multicolor scene from the Sign of the Four

Date	Mintage	F	VF	XF	Unc	BU
2008 Prooflike	8,000	—	—	—	—	100

KM# 540 2 DOLLARS
31.1050 g., 0.9990 Silver 0.9990 oz. ASW, 40.7 mm. **Ruler:** Elizabeth II **Subject:** Ballet dancers **Rev:** Multicolor Vasley Nijinnsky

Date	Mintage	F	VF	XF	Unc	BU
2008 Prooflike	8,000	—	—	—	—	85.00

KM# 541 2 DOLLARS
31.1050 g., 0.9990 Silver 0.9990 oz. ASW, 40.7 mm. **Ruler:** Elizabeth II **Subject:** Ballet Dancers **Rev:** Multicolor Matuilda Kshesinskaya

Date	Mintage	F	VF	XF	Unc	BU
2008 Prooflike	8,000	—	—	—	—	85.00

KM# 542 2 DOLLARS
31.1050 g., 0.9990 Silver 0.9990 oz. ASW, 40.7 mm. **Ruler:** Elizabeth II **Subject:** Ballet dancers **Rev:** Multicolor Sergey Lifar

Date	Mintage	F	VF	XF	Unc	BU
2008 Prooflike	8,000	—	—	—	—	85.00

KM# 543 2 DOLLARS
31.1050 g., 0.9990 Silver 0.9990 oz. ASW, 40.7 mm. **Ruler:** Elizabeth II **Subject:** Ballet dancers **Rev:** Multicolor Anna Pavlova

Date	Mintage	F	VF	XF	Unc	BU
2008 Prooflike	—	—	—	—	—	85.00

KM# 544 2 DOLLARS
31.1050 g., 0.9990 Silver 0.9990 oz. ASW, 40.7 mm. **Ruler:** Elizabeth II **Subject:** White Army **Rev:** Multicolor Anton Denkin

Date	Mintage	F	VF	XF	Unc	BU
2008 Prooflike	6,000	—	—	—	—	85.00

KM# 545 2 DOLLARS
31.1050 g., 0.9990 Silver 0.9990 oz. ASW, 40.7 mm. **Ruler:** Elizabeth II **Subject:** White Army **Rev:** Multicolor Pytor Vrangel

Date	Mintage	F	VF	XF	Unc	BU
2008 Prooflike	6,000	—	—	—	—	85.00

KM# 546 2 DOLLARS
31.1050 g., 0.9990 Silver 0.9990 oz. ASW, 40.7 mm. **Ruler:** Elizabeth II **Subject:** White Army **Rev:** Multicolor Alexander Kutepov

Date	Mintage	F	VF	XF	Unc	BU
2008 Prooflike	6,000	—	—	—	—	85.00

KM# 547 2 DOLLARS
31.1050 g., 0.9990 Silver 0.9990 oz. ASW, 40.7 mm. **Ruler:** Elizabeth II **Subject:** White Army **Rev:** Multicolor Alexander Kolchak

Date	Mintage	F	VF	XF	Unc	BU
2008 Prooflike	6,000	—	—	—	—	85.00

KM# 721 2 DOLLARS
0.1200 g., 0.9990 Gold 0.0039 oz. AGW, 4 mm. **Ruler:** Elizabeth II **Rev:** Lady Penrhyn sailing ship

Date	Mintage	F	VF	XF	Unc	BU
2010 Prooflike	5,000	—	—	—	—	12.00

KM# 722 2 DOLLARS
0.1200 g., 0.9950 Platinum 0.0038 oz. APW, 4 mm. **Ruler:** Elizabeth II **Rev:** Humpback whale

Date	Mintage	F	VF	XF	Unc	BU
2010 Prooflike	5,000	—	—	—	—	15.00

KM# 1121 5 DOLLARS
Silver **Ruler:** Elizabeth II **Rev:** Sir Francis Drake

Date	Mintage	F	VF	XF	Unc	BU
2002 Proof	—	Value: 30.00				

KM# 1122 5 DOLLARS
Silver **Ruler:** Elizabeth II **Rev:** Kon Tiki and Thor Heyerdahl

Date	Mintage	F	VF	XF	Unc	BU
2002 Proof	—	Value: 40.00				

KM# 418 5 DOLLARS
14.0000 g., Aluminum-Bronze, 31.5 mm. **Ruler:** Elizabeth II **Obv:** Crowned bust right, new portrait **Rev:** Conch shell and value **Shape:** 12-sided

Date	Mintage	F	VF	XF	Unc	BU
2003	—	—	—	—	6.00	8.00

KM# 1140 5 DOLLARS
20.0000 g., 0.9990 Silver 0.6423 oz. ASW **Ruler:** Elizabeth II **Subject:** Vincent van Gogh, 150th Anniversary of Birth

Date	Mintage	F	VF	XF	Unc	BU
2003 Proof	Est. 5,000	Value: 35.00				

KM# 469 5 DOLLARS
Copper-Nickel, 40 mm. **Ruler:** Elizabeth II **Obv:** USPS logo, Queens head above **Rev:** 5 cent 1847 Benjamin Franklin stamp

Date	Mintage	F	VF	XF	Unc	BU
2004	—	—	—	—	10.00	12.00

KM# 469a 5 DOLLARS
Silver, 40 mm. **Ruler:** Elizabeth II **Obv:** USPS logo, Queens head above **Rev:** 5 cent 1847 Benjamin Franklin stamp **Edge:** Reeded

Date	Mintage	F	VF	XF	Unc	BU
2004 Proof	—	Value: 25.00				

KM# 1149 5 DOLLARS
31.6350 g., 0.9990 Silver 1.0160 oz. ASW **Ruler:** Elizabeth II **Subject:** Apollo Moon Landing, 35th Anniversary **Rev:** Astronaut in Solar System

Date	Mintage	F	VF	XF	Unc	BU
2004 Proof	Est. 10,000	Value: 55.00				

KM# 1108 5 DOLLARS
25.0000 g., 0.9250 Silver 0.7435 oz. ASW **Ruler:** Elizabeth II **Subject:** Ferrari F2

Date	Mintage	F	VF	XF	Unc	BU
2005 Proof	Est. 8,000	Value: 45.00				

KM# 1109 5 DOLLARS
25.0000 g., 0.9250 Silver 0.7435 oz. ASW **Ruler:** Elizabeth II **Rev:** Ferrari F 2004 in color

Date	Mintage	F	VF	XF	Unc	BU
2005 Proof	Est. 8,000	Value: 45.00				

KM# 1134 5 DOLLARS
31.1050 g., 0.9990 Silver 0.9990 oz. ASW, 38.6 mm. **Ruler:** Elizabeth II **Subject:** Star Wars, 30th Anniversary

Date	Mintage	F	VF	XF	Unc	BU
2005 Proof	Est. 9,999	Value: 45.00				

KM# 1135 5 DOLLARS
31.1050 g., 0.9990 Silver 0.9990 oz. ASW, 38.6 mm. **Ruler:** Elizabeth II **Subject:** Star Wars, 30th Anniversary

Date	Mintage	F	VF	XF	Unc	BU
2005 Proof	Est. 9,999	Value: 45.00				

KM# 1175 5 DOLLARS
25.0000 g., 0.9250 Silver 0.7435 oz. ASW **Ruler:** Elizabeth II **Subject:** Marriage of Prince Charles and Camilla Parker-Bowles

Date	Mintage	F	VF	XF	Unc	BU
2005 Proof	Est. 5,000	Value: 45.00				

KM# 478 5 DOLLARS
Silver Gilt **Ruler:** Elizabeth II **Subject:** Pope Benedict XVI's visit to Valencia, Spain **Obv:** Bust right **Rev:** Valencia Cathedral **Shape:** Cathedral outline **Note:** Jeweled cathedral.

Date	Mintage	F	VF	XF	Unc	BU
2006 Proof	2,500	Value: 100				

KM# 560 5 DOLLARS
25.0000 g., 0.9250 Silver partially gilt 0.7435 oz. ASW, 35x31 mm. **Ruler:** Elizabeth II **Subject:** Benedict XVI Annus Secundus **Rev:** Cross in crystals and gilt Papal Arms **Shape:** 6-sided

Date	Mintage	F	VF	XF	Unc	BU
2006 Proof	5,000	Value: 95.00				

KM# 561 5 DOLLARS
25.0000 g., 0.9990 Silver partially gilt 0.8029 oz. ASW, 42x49 mm. **Ruler:** Elizabeth II **Subject:** Benedict XVI visits Germany **Rev:** Cathedral gilt, crystal inserts **Shape:** oval

Date	Mintage	F	VF	XF	Unc	BU
2006 Proof	5,000	Value: 95.00				

KM# 562 5 DOLLARS
25.0000 g., 0.9990 Silver 0.8029 oz. ASW, 35x35 mm. **Ruler:** Elizabeth II **Subject:** Benedict XVI **Rev:** Profile at left, cross in crystal inserts **Shape:** Square

Date	Mintage	F	VF	XF	Unc	BU
2006 Proof	5,000	Value: 95.00				

KM# 563 5 DOLLARS
25.0000 g., 0.9990 Silver partially gilt 0.8029 oz. ASW, 35x38 mm. **Ruler:** Elizabeth II **Subject:** Christmas in St. Peter's Square **Rev:** St. Peter's partially gilt, star crystal insert **Shape:** Triange

Date	Mintage	F	VF	XF	Unc	BU
2006 Proof	5,000	Value: 95.00				

KM# 564 5 DOLLARS
25.0000 g., 0.9990 Silver 0.8029 oz. ASW, 20x44 mm. **Ruler:** Elizabeth II **Subject:** benedict XVI visits Poland **Rev:** Polish icon, partially gilt, crystal insert **Shape:** Candle

Date	Mintage	F	VF	XF	Unc	BU
2006 Proof	564	Value: 95.00				

KM# 565 5 DOLLARS
25.0000 g., 0.9990 Silver partially gilt 0.8029 oz. ASW, 38.6 mm. **Ruler:** Elizabeth II **Rev:** St. Peter's Basilica, partially gilt, crystals as stars

Date	Mintage	F	VF	XF	Unc	BU
2006 Proof	5,000	Value: 95.00				

KM# 566 5 DOLLARS
25.0000 g., 0.9990 Silver partially gilt 0.8029 oz. ASW, 35x35 mm. **Ruler:** Elizabeth II **Subject:** Swiss Guards, 500th Anniversary **Rev:** Four Swiss guards, partially gilt, crystal insert **Shape:** Diamond

Date	Mintage	F	VF	XF	Unc	BU
2006 Proof	5,000	Value: 95.00				

KM# 567 5 DOLLARS
25.0000 g., 0.9990 Silver 0.8029 oz. ASW, 40x25 mm. **Ruler:** Elizabeth II **Subject:** Benedict XVI visits Turkey **Rev:** Pope and Patrarch, partially gilt, crystal insert **Shape:** Rectangle

Date	Mintage	F	VF	XF	Unc	BU
2006 Proof	5,000	Value: 95.00				

KM# 568 5 DOLLARS
25.0000 g., 0.9990 Silver 0.8029 oz. ASW, 40x25 mm. **Ruler:** Elizabeth II **Subject:** Urbi et Orbi message **Rev:** Benedict XVI giving blessing, partially gilt, crystal insert **Shape:** Rectangle

Date	Mintage	F	VF	XF	Unc	BU
2006 Proof	5,000	Value: 95.00				

KM# 569 5 DOLLARS
0.2500 g., 0.9990 Silver partially gilt 0.0080 oz. ASW, 29x42 mm. **Ruler:** Elizabeth II **Subject:** Benedict XVI visits Vallencia **Rev:** Valencia cathedral facade, partially gilt, crystal inserts **Shape:** Irregular

Date	Mintage	F	VF	XF	Unc	BU
2006 Proof	5,000	Value: 85.00				

KM# 570 5 DOLLARS

31.1000 g., 0.9990 Silver 0.9988 oz. ASW, 38.6 mm. **Ruler:** Elizabeth II **Rev:** Statue of Liberty gilt pop-up

Date	Mintage	F	VF	XF	Unc	BU
2006 Proof	5,000	Value: 100				

KM# 571 5 DOLLARS

31.1000 g., 0.9990 Silver 0.9988 oz. ASW, 38.6 mm. **Ruler:** Elizabeth II **Rev:** Ludwig's castle gilt pop-up

Date	Mintage	F	VF	XF	Unc	BU
2006 Proof	5,000	Value: 100				

KM# 572 5 DOLLARS

25.0000 g., 0.9990 Silver partially gilt 0.8029 oz. ASW, 35x35 mm. **Ruler:** Elizabeth II **Subject:** Benedict XVI visits Marianzell **Rev:** Our Lady or Marianzell, partially gilt, crystal inserts **Shape:** Tablet

Date	Mintage	F	VF	XF	Unc	BU
2007 Proof	5,000	Value: 95.00				

KM# 573 5 DOLLARS

25.0000 g., 0.9990 Silver 0.8029 oz. ASW, 35x35 mm. **Ruler:** Elizabeth II **Rev:** St. Francis, tau cross, partially gilt, crystal insert **Shape:** Dove

Date	Mintage	F	VF	XF	Unc	BU
2007 Proof	5,000	Value: 95.00				

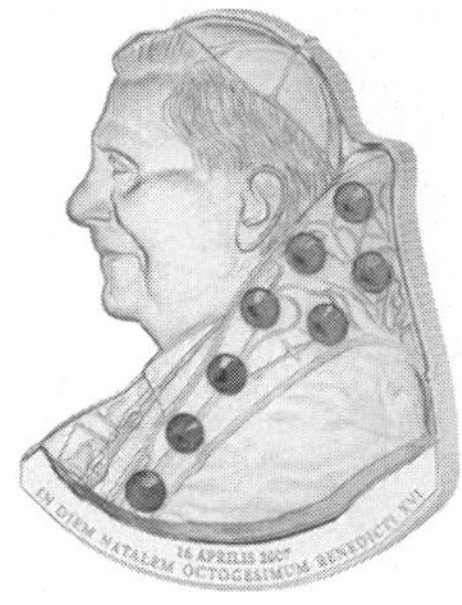

KM# 574 5 DOLLARS

25.0000 g., 0.9990 Silver 0.8029 oz. ASW, 31x40 mm. **Ruler:** Elizabeth II **Rev:** Benedict XVI bust left, partially gilt, crystal insert **Shape:** Irregular

Date	Mintage	F	VF	XF	Unc	BU
2007 Proof	5,000	Value: 95.00				

KM# 575 5 DOLLARS

25.0000 g., 0.9990 Silver 0.8029 oz. ASW, 35x45 mm. **Ruler:** Elizabeth II **Subject:** Benedict XVI visits Brazil **Rev:** Christ statue in Rio, partially gilt, crystal insert **Shape:** Diamond

Date	Mintage	F	VF	XF	Unc	BU
2007 Proof	5,000	Value: 95.00				

KM# 576 5 DOLLARS

25.0000 g., 0.9990 Silver 0.8029 oz. ASW, 37 mm. **Ruler:** Elizabeth II **Subject:** Princess Diana, 10th Anniversary of death **Rev:** Bust at left, multicolored rose **Shape:** Heart

Date	Mintage	F	VF	XF	Unc	BU
2007 Proof	1,997	Value: 75.00				

KM# 577 5 DOLLARS

25.0000 g., 0.9990 Silver partially gilt 0.8029 oz. ASW, 39x24 mm. **Ruler:** Elizabeth II **Subject:** Docrine of the Immaculate Conception **Rev:** Virgin Mary and cathedral, partially gilt, crystal insert **Shape:** Rectangle

Date	Mintage	F	VF	XF	Unc	BU
2007 Proof	5,000	Value: 95.00				

KM# 578 5 DOLLARS

25.0000 g., 0.9990 Silver 0.8029 oz. ASW, 31x35 mm. **Ruler:** Elizabeth II **Subject:** Benedict XVI visits Loredo **Rev:** Pope blessing crowd, cathedral, partially gilt, crystal insert **Shape:** 6-sided

Date	Mintage	F	VF	XF	Unc	BU
2007 Proof	5,000	Value: 95.00				

KM# 579 5 DOLLARS

25.0000 g., 0.9990 Silver 0.8029 oz. ASW, 35x35 mm. **Ruler:** Elizabeth II **Subject:** Santo Subito **Rev:** Pope John Paul II, partially gilt, crystal insert **Shape:** Cross

Date	Mintage	F	VF	XF	Unc	BU
2007 Proof	5,000	Value: 100				

KM# 580 5 DOLLARS

25.0000 g., 0.9990 Silver 0.8029 oz. ASW, 30x45 mm. **Ruler:** Elizabeth II **Subject:** Way of the Cross **Rev:** Benedict XVI holdign cross, collesum in background, partially gilt, crystal insert **Shape:** Vertical oval

Date	Mintage	F	VF	XF	Unc	BU
2007 Proof	5,000	Value: 95.00				

KM# 581 5 DOLLARS

31.1000 g., 0.9990 Silver 0.9988 oz. ASW, 38.6 mm. **Ruler:** Elizabeth II **Rev:** Parthenon gilt pop-up

Date	Mintage	F	VF	XF	Unc	BU
2007 Proof	5,000	Value: 100				

KM# 583 5 DOLLARS

31.1000 g., 0.9990 Silver 0.9988 oz. ASW, 38.6 mm. **Ruler:** Elizabeth II **Rev:** Rio's Christ statue gilt pop-up

Date	Mintage	F	VF	XF	Unc	BU
2007 Proof	5,000	Value: 100				

KM# 584 5 DOLLARS

31.1000 g., 0.9990 Silver 0.9988 oz. ASW, 38.6 mm. **Ruler:** Elizabeth II **Rev:** Collesum gilt pop-up

Date	Mintage	F	VF	XF	Unc	BU
2007 Proof	5,000	Value: 100				

KM# 586 5 DOLLARS

31.1000 g., 0.9990 Silver 0.9988 oz. ASW, 38.6 mm. **Ruler:** Elizabeth II **Rev:** Eifle Tower gilt pop-up

Date	Mintage	F	VF	XF	Unc	BU
2007 Proof	5,000	Value: 100				

KM# 763 5 DOLLARS

Silver **Ruler:** Elizabeth II **Subject:** Brenham Meteor

Date	Mintage	F	VF	XF	Unc	BU
2007 Proof	—	Value: 100				

KM# 1188 5 DOLLARS

20.0000 g., 0.9250 Silver 0.5948 oz. ASW, 38.61 mm. **Ruler:** Elizabeth II **Subject:** Elvis Presley, 30th Anniversary of death

Date	Mintage	F	VF	XF	Unc	BU
2007 Proof	Est. 50,000	Value: 70.00				

KM# 1189 5 DOLLARS

20.0000 g., 0.9250 Silver 0.5948 oz. ASW, 38.61 mm. **Ruler:** Elizabeth II **Subject:** Elvis Presely, 30th Anniversary of Death **Rev:** Love me Tender, 1956

Date	Mintage	F	VF	XF	Unc	BU
2007 Proof	Est. 50,000	Value: 70.00				

KM# 1201 5 DOLLARS

25.0000 g., Copper-Nickel partially gilt, 38.6 mm. **Ruler:** Elizabeth II **Subject:** Lady Diana, 10th Anniversary of Death **Rev:** Diana partially gilt

Date	Mintage	F	VF	XF	Unc	BU
2007 Proof	Est. 50,000	Value: 22.50				

KM# 1202 5 DOLLARS

25.0000 g., Copper-Nickel partially gilt, 38.6 mm. **Ruler:** Elizabeth II **Subject:** Princess Diana, 10th Anniversary of Death **Rev:** Diana in wedding dress, partially gilt

Date	Mintage	F	VF	XF	Unc	BU
2007 Proof	Est. 14,500	Value: 22.50				

KM# 1203 5 DOLLARS

155.5000 g., Copper-Nickel partially gilt, 65 mm. **Ruler:** Elizabeth II **Subject:** Princess Diana, 10th Anniversary of Death **Rev:** Lady Diana, partially gilt

Date	Mintage	F	VF	XF	Unc	BU
2007 Proof	Est. 1,961	Value: 85.00				

KM# 594 5 DOLLARS

25.0000 g., 0.9990 Silver 0.8029 oz. ASW, 35x35 mm. **Ruler:** Elizabeth II **Subject:** Pope John Paul II Election 30th Anniversary **Rev:** John Paul II coat-of-arms, aprtially gilt, crystal insert **Shape:** Diamond

Date	Mintage	F	VF	XF	Unc	BU
2008 Proof	5,000	Value: 120				

KM# 595 5 DOLLARS
25.0000 g., 0.9990 Silver 0.8029 oz. ASW, 30x45 mm. **Ruler:** Elizabeth II **Subject:** Lourdes, 150th Anniversary **Rev:** Statue of Our Lady of Lourdes, partially gilt, crystal insert **Shape:** Vertical oval

Date	Mintage	F	VF	XF	Unc	BU
2008 Proof	5,000	Value: 110				

KM# 596 5 DOLLARS
25.0000 g., 0.9990 Silver 0.8029 oz. ASW, 30x45 mm. **Ruler:** Elizabeth II **Subject:** Lourdes, 150th Anniversary **Rev:** Our Lady of Lourdes, holigram, partially gilt, crystal insert **Shape:** Vertical oval

Date	Mintage	F	VF	XF	Unc	BU
2008 Proof	5,000	Value: 120				

KM# 597 5 DOLLARS
25.0000 g., 0.9990 Silver 0.8029 oz. ASW, 40x25 mm. **Ruler:** Elizabeth II **Subject:** Benedict XVI Annus Novas **Rev:** Benedict XVI and dove **Shape:** Oval

Date	Mintage	F	VF	XF	Unc	BU
2008 Proof	5,000	Value: 100				

KM# 598 5 DOLLARS
25.0000 g., 0.9990 Silver 0.8029 oz. ASW, 32x41 mm. **Ruler:** Elizabeth II **Rev:** St. Peter's Square, cresch and christmas tree, partially gilt, crystal insert **Shape:** Triangle

Date	Mintage	F	VF	XF	Unc	BU
2008 Proof	5,000	Value: 100				

KM# 599 5 DOLLARS
25.0000 g., 0.9990 Silver 0.8029 oz. ASW, 35x35 mm. **Ruler:** Elizabeth II **Subject:** Crufifixio Domini **Rev:** Benedict XVI before cross, partially gilt, crystal inserts **Shape:** Cross

Date	Mintage	F	VF	XF	Unc	BU
2008 Proof	5,000	Value: 100				

KM# 600 5 DOLLARS
25.0000 g., 0.9990 Silver 0.8029 oz. ASW, 29x42 mm. **Ruler:** Elizabeth II **Subject:** Paulus year **Rev:** Benedict XVI in Basicilica, partially gilt, crystal insert **Shape:** Vertical rectangle

Date	Mintage	F	VF	XF	Unc	BU
2008 Proof	5,000	Value: 100				

KM# 601 5 DOLLARS
25.0000 g., 0.9990 Silver 0.8029 oz. ASW, 40x25 mm. **Ruler:** Elizabeth II **Subject:** Sistine Chapel, 500th Anniversary **Rev:** Adam and god, Sistine Chapel ceiling, partially gilt, crystal insert **Shape:** Rectangle

Date	Mintage	F	VF	XF	Unc	BU
2008 Proof	5,000	Value: 120				

KM# 602 5 DOLLARS
25.0000 g., 0.9990 Silver 0.8029 oz. ASW, 40x42 mm. **Ruler:** Elizabeth II **Rev:** St Martin on horseback, partially gilt, crystal insert **Shape:** 8-sided

Date	Mintage	F	VF	XF	Unc	BU
2008 Proof	5,000	Value: 100				

KM# 603 5 DOLLARS
25.0000 g., 0.9990 Silver 0.8029 oz. ASW, 45x34 mm. **Ruler:** Elizabeth II **Subject:** Benedict XVI visits Sydney **Rev:** Sydney Harbor Bridge and Sydney Opera House, partially gilt, crystal insert **Shape:** Irregular oval

Date	Mintage	F	VF	XF	Unc	BU
2008 Proof	5,000	Value: 100				

KM# 604 5 DOLLARS
25.0000 g., 0.9990 Silver 0.8029 oz. ASW, 35x35 mm. **Ruler:** Elizabeth II **Subject:** Tu Es Peterus **Rev:** Cross Keys, Christ handing keys to kneeling St. Peter. Partially gilt, crystal insert. **Shape:** Square

Date	Mintage	F	VF	XF	Unc	BU
2008 Proof	5,000	Value: 120				

KM# 605 5 DOLLARS
25.0000 g., 0.9990 Silver 0.8029 oz. ASW, 38.6 mm. **Ruler:** Elizabeth II **Rev:** Pope blessing crowd, partially gilt, crystal inserts

Date	Mintage	F	VF	XF	Unc	BU
2008 Proof	5,000	Value: 100				

KM# 606 5 DOLLARS
25.0000 g., 0.9990 Silver 0.8029 oz. ASW, 42x29 mm. **Ruler:** Elizabeth II **Subject:** Benedict XVI visits the United States **Rev:** Benedict XVI, the White House, Statue of Liberty, UN Building, partially gilt, crystal inserts **Shape:** Irregular US Map shape

Date	Mintage	F	VF	XF	Unc	BU
2008 Proof	5,000	Value: 100				

KM# 607 5 DOLLARS
25.0000 g., 0.9990 Silver 0.8029 oz. ASW, 40x42 mm. **Ruler:** Elizabeth II **Rev:** St. George slaying dragon, partially gilt, crystal insert **Shape:** 8-sided

Date	Mintage	F	VF	XF	Unc	BU
2008 Proof	5,000	Value: 100				

KM# 608 5 DOLLARS
31.1050 g., 0.9990 Silver 0.9990 oz. ASW, 38.6 mm. **Ruler:** Elizabeth II **Subject:** Conversion of Russia, 1000th Anniversary **Rev:** Baptism scene **Note:** Exclusive to the Russian Market.

Date	Mintage	F	VF	XF	Unc	BU
2008 Proof	500	Value: 120				

KM# 609 5 DOLLARS
31.1050 g., 0.9990 Silver 0.9990 oz. ASW, 47x27 mm. **Ruler:** Elizabeth II **Subject:** Orthodox Communication **Rev:** Patriarch's meeting **Shape:** Rectangle **Note:** Exclusive to the Russian Market.

Date	Mintage	F	VF	XF	Unc	BU
2008 Proof	500	Value: 120				

KM# 610 5 DOLLARS
25.0000 g., 0.9990 Silver 0.8029 oz. ASW, 30x38 mm. **Ruler:** Elizabeth II **Rev:** Icon - Theotokos of Vladimir, wood insert **Shape:** Rectangle **Note:** Exclusive to the Russian Market.

Date	Mintage	F	VF	XF	Unc	BU
2008 Proof	2,500	Value: 120				

KM# 611 5 DOLLARS
31.1050 g., 0.9990 Silver 0.9990 oz. ASW, 38.6 mm. **Ruler:** Elizabeth II **Subject:** Kiev Churches **Rev:** Church of All Saints **Note:** Exclusive to the Russian Market.

Date	Mintage	F	VF	XF	Unc	BU
2008 Proof	500	Value: 120				

KM# 612 5 DOLLARS
31.1050 g., 0.9990 Silver 0.9990 oz. ASW, 38.6 mm. **Ruler:** Elizabeth II **Subject:** Kiev Churches **Rev:** Dormotion of Theotokos **Note:** Exclusive to the Russian Market.

Date	Mintage	F	VF	XF	Unc	BU
2008 Proof	500	Value: 120				

KM# 613 5 DOLLARS
31.1050 g., 0.9990 Silver 0.9990 oz. ASW **Ruler:** Elizabeth II **Subject:** Kiev Churches **Rev:** Refractory of Pechersky **Shape:** 38.6 **Note:** Exclusive to the Russian Market.

Date	Mintage	F	VF	XF	Unc	BU
2008 Proof	500	Value: 120				

KM# 614 5 DOLLARS
31.1050 g., 0.9990 Silver 0.9990 oz. ASW, 38.6 mm. **Ruler:** Elizabeth II **Subject:** Kiev Churches **Rev:** Troitskaya Barbican **Note:** Exclusive to the Russian Market.

Date	Mintage	F	VF	XF	Unc	BU
2008 Proof	500	Value: 120				

KM# 615 5 DOLLARS
25.0000 g., 0.9250 Silver 0.7435 oz. ASW, 37 mm. **Ruler:** Elizabeth II **Rev:** Cupid and roses **Rev. Legend:** My Everlasting Love **Shape:** Heart

Date	Mintage	F	VF	XF	Unc	BU
2008 Proof	2,500	Value: 70.00				

KM# 616 5 DOLLARS
25.0000 g., 0.9250 Silver 0.7435 oz. ASW, 38.6 mm. **Ruler:** Elizabeth II **Subject:** Endangered Wildlife - Arctic **Rev:** Polar bear and cubs, crystal inserts

Date	Mintage	F	VF	XF	Unc	BU
2008 Proof	2,500	Value: 70.00				

KM# 617 5 DOLLARS
25.0000 g., 0.9250 Silver 0.7435 oz. ASW, 38.6 mm. **Ruler:** Elizabeth II **Subject:** Engangered wildlife - Antarctic **Rev:** Penguin, crystal insert

Date	Mintage	F	VF	XF	Unc	BU
2008 Proof	2,500	Value: 70.00				

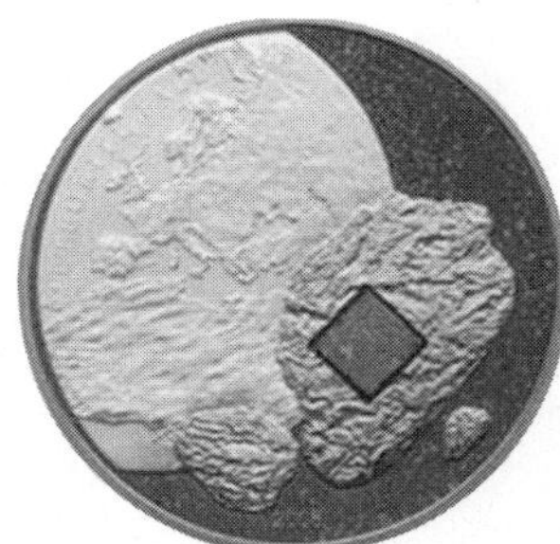

KM# 618 5 DOLLARS
25.0000 g., 0.9250 Silver 0.7435 oz. ASW, 38.6 mm. **Ruler:** Elizabeth II **Subject:** Pultusk Meteorite **Rev:** Earth and Meteorite fragment insert

Date	Mintage	F	VF	XF	Unc	BU
2008 Proof	2,500	Value: 85.00				

KM# 670 5 DOLLARS
141.4000 g., 0.9990 Silver 4.5414 oz. ASW, 65 mm. **Ruler:** Elizabeth II **Subject:** Tall Ships **Rev:** Norway's Christian Raddish

Date	Mintage	F	VF	XF	Unc	BU
2008 Proof	—	Value: 285				

KM# 764 5 DOLLARS
Silver, 25x40 mm. **Ruler:** Elizabeth II **Subject:** Ferrari, the Legend **Rev:** Car and enameled shield **Shape:** Vertical rectangle

Date	Mintage	F	VF	XF	Unc	BU
2008 Proof	—	Value: 125				

KM# 1207 5 DOLLARS
0.5000 g., 0.9990 Gold 0.0161 oz. AGW, 11 mm. **Ruler:** Elizabeth II **Rev:** American Bison

Date	Mintage	F	VF	XF	Unc	BU
2008 Proof	Est. 5,000	Value: 35.00				

KM# 1211 5 DOLLARS
155.5000 g., Copper-Nickel partially gilt, 65 mm. **Ruler:** Elizabeth II **Subject:** British Monarchs - Elizabeth I

Date	Mintage	F	VF	XF	Unc	BU
2008 Proof	Est. 450	Value: 85.00				

KM# 640 5 DOLLARS
25.0000 g., 0.9990 Silver 0.8029 oz. ASW, 38.6 mm. **Ruler:** Elizabeth II **Rev:** Papal Tiara above crossed keys, partially gilt, crystal inserts

Date	Mintage	F	VF	XF	Unc	BU
2009 Proof	5,000	Value: 120				

KM# 641 5 DOLLARS
25.0000 g., 0.9990 Silver 0.8029 oz. ASW **Ruler:** Elizabeth II **Subject:** Benedict XVI visits Israel **Rev:** Benedict XVI and "Dome of the Rock", partially gilt, crystal inserts **Shape:** Diamond

Date	Mintage	F	VF	XF	Unc	BU
2009 Proof	5,000	Value: 110				

KM# 642 5 DOLLARS
25.0000 g., 0.9990 Silver 0.8029 oz. ASW **Ruler:** Elizabeth II **Subject:** Benedict XVI visits Africa **Rev:** Bust at left, partially gilt, crystal inserts **Shape:** Irregular, Africa shape

Date	Mintage	F	VF	XF	Unc	BU
2009 Proof	5,000	Value: 110				

KM# 643 5 DOLLARS
25.0000 g., 0.9990 Silver 0.8029 oz. ASW **Ruler:** Elizabeth II **Subject:** Easter 2009 **Rev:** Statue of the risen Christ, partially gilt, crystal inserts **Shape:** Fish

Date	Mintage	F	VF	XF	Unc	BU
2009 Proof	5,000	Value: 110				

KM# 644 5 DOLLARS
25.0000 g., 0.9990 Silver 0.8029 oz. ASW, 35 mm. **Ruler:** Elizabeth II **Rev:** Star of the Magi, partially gilt, crystal inserts **Shape:** Star

Date	Mintage	F	VF	XF	Unc	BU
2009 Proof	5,000	Value: 110				

KM# 645 5 DOLLARS
25.0000 g., 0.9990 Silver 0.8029 oz. ASW, 35x35 mm. **Ruler:** Elizabeth II **Rev:** Cathedral of Santiago de Composetla, partially gilt, crystal inserts

Date	Mintage	F	VF	XF	Unc	BU
2009 Proof	5,000	Value: 120				

KM# 646 5 DOLLARS
25.0000 g., 0.9990 Silver 0.8029 oz. ASW, 25x35 mm. **Ruler:** Elizabeth II **Rev:** Michangelo's Pieta, partially gilt, crystal inserts **Shape:** Rectangle

Date	Mintage	F	VF	XF	Unc	BU
2009 Proof	5,000	Value: 110				

KM# 647 5 DOLLARS
25.0000 g., 0.9990 Silver 0.8029 oz. ASW, 30x34 mm. **Ruler:** Elizabeth II **Rev:** St. Christopher, partially gilt, crystal inserts **Shape:** Oval

Date	Mintage	F	VF	XF	Unc	BU
2009 Proof	5,000	Value: 110				

KM# 648 5 DOLLARS
25.0000 g., 0.9990 Silver 0.8029 oz. ASW, 40x25 mm. **Ruler:** Elizabeth II **Subject:** Benedict XVI visits the Czech Republic **Rev:** Benedict XVI in Wenceleses square, partially gilt, crystal inserts **Shape:** Rectangle

Date	Mintage	F	VF	XF	Unc	BU
2009 Proof	5,000	Value: 110				

KM# 649 5 DOLLARS
25.0000 g., 0.9990 Silver 0.8029 oz. ASW **Ruler:** Elizabeth II **Rev:** Christmas, village scene, partially gilt, crystal inserts **Shape:** Diamond

Date	Mintage	F	VF	XF	Unc	BU
2009 Proof	5,000	Value: 110				

KM# 650 5 DOLLARS
31.1050 g., 0.9990 Silver 0.9990 oz. ASW, 38.6 mm. **Ruler:** Elizabeth II **Subject:** Kiev Churches **Rev:** Andreevskaya Church **Note:** Exclusive to the Russian Market.

Date	Mintage	F	VF	XF	Unc	BU
2009 Proof	500	Value: 125				

KM# 651 5 DOLLARS
31.1050 g., 0.9990 Silver 0.9990 oz. ASW, 38.6 mm. **Ruler:** Elizabeth II **Subject:** Kiev Churches **Rev:** Kirillovskaya Church **Note:** Exclusive to the Russian Market.

Date	Mintage	F	VF	XF	Unc	BU
2009 Proof	500	Value: 125				

KM# 652 5 DOLLARS
31.1050 g., 0.9990 Silver 0.9990 oz. ASW, 38.6 mm. **Ruler:** Elizabeth II **Subject:** Kiev Chruches **Rev:** Mikailovsky Monastery **Note:** Exclusive to the Russian Market.

Date	Mintage	F	VF	XF	Unc	BU
2009 Proof	500	Value: 125				

KM# 653 5 DOLLARS
31.1050 g., 0.9990 Silver 0.9990 oz. ASW, 38.6 mm. **Ruler:** Elizabeth II **Subject:** Kiev Churches **Rev:** Cathedral of St. Sophia **Note:** Exclusive to the Russian Market.

Date	Mintage	F	VF	XF	Unc	BU
2009 Proof	500	Value: 125				

KM# 654 5 DOLLARS
31.1050 g., 0.9990 Silver 0.9990 oz. ASW, 38.61 mm. **Ruler:** Elizabeth II **Subject:** Ukraine Landmarks - Bendrological park, Sofiyivka **Rev:** Statue and gardens **Note:** Exclusive to the Russian Market.

Date	Mintage	F	VF	XF	Unc	BU
2009 Proof	500	Value: 120				

KM# 655 5 DOLLARS
31.1050 g., 0.9990 Silver 0.9990 oz. ASW, 38.61 mm. **Ruler:** Elizabeth II **Subject:** Ukraine Landmarks - Holy Dormition Kiev Pechersk Lavra **Rev:** Churches **Note:** Exclusive to the Russian Market.

Date	Mintage	F	VF	XF	Unc	BU
2009 Proof	500	Value: 120				

KM# 656 5 DOLLARS
31.1050 g., 0.9990 Silver 0.9990 oz. ASW, 38.61 mm. **Ruler:** Elizabeth II **Subject:** Ukraine Landmarks - Holy Dormition Pochayiv Lavra **Rev:** Buildings **Note:** Exclusive to the Russian Market.

Date	Mintage	F	VF	XF	Unc	BU
2009 Proof	500	Value: 120				

KM# 657 5 DOLLARS
31.1050 g., 0.9990 Silver 0.9990 oz. ASW, 38.61 mm. **Ruler:** Elizabeth II **Subject:** Ukraine Landmarks - Holy Dormition Sviatohirsk Lavra **Rev:** Virgin Mary and Church **Note:** Exclusive to the Russian Market.

Date	Mintage	F	VF	XF	Unc	BU
2009 Proof	500	Value: 120				

KM# 658 5 DOLLARS
31.1050 g., 0.9990 Silver 0.9990 oz. ASW, 38.61 mm. **Ruler:** Elizabeth II **Subject:** Ukraine Landmarks - Kamyanets National Reserve **Rev:** Fortress **Note:** Exclusive to the Russian Market.

Date	Mintage	F	VF	XF	Unc	BU
2009 Proof	500	Value: 120				

KM# 659 5 DOLLARS
31.1050 g., 0.9990 Silver 0.9990 oz. ASW, 38.6 mm. **Ruler:** Elizabeth II **Subject:** Ukraine Landmarks - Khersones Tavrijsky National Reserve **Rev:** Roman ruins **Note:** Exclusive to the Russian Market.

Date	Mintage	F	VF	XF	Unc	BU
2009 Proof	500	Value: 120				

KM# 660 5 DOLLARS
31.1050 g., 0.9990 Silver 0.9990 oz. ASW, 38.6 mm. **Ruler:** Elizabeth II **Subject:** Ukraine Landmarks - Khortytsia National Reserve **Rev:** Stone carvings and bridge **Note:** Exclusive to the Russian Market.

Date	Mintage	F	VF	XF	Unc	BU
2009 Proof	500	Value: 120				

KM# 661 5 DOLLARS
31.1050 g., 0.9990 Silver 0.9990 oz. ASW, 38.6 mm. **Ruler:** Elizabeth II **Subject:** Ukraine Landmarks - National Theatre of Odessa **Rev:** Opera House **Note:** Exclusive to the Russian Market.

Date	Mintage	F	VF	XF	Unc	BU
2009 Proof	500	Value: 120				

KM# 662 5 DOLLARS
31.1050 g., 0.9990 Silver 0.9990 oz. ASW, 38.6 mm. **Ruler:** Elizabeth II **Subject:** Ukraine Landmarks - Olesko Castle **Rev:** Hillside dwelling **Note:** Exclusive to the Russian Market.

Date	Mintage	F	VF	XF	Unc	BU
2009 Proof	500	Value: 120				

KM# 663 5 DOLLARS
31.1050 g., 0.9990 Silver 0.9990 oz. ASW, 38.6 mm. **Ruler:** Elizabeth II **Subject:** Ukraine Landmarks - Palanok Castle in Mukachevo **Rev:** Hilltop fortress **Note:** Exclusive to the Russian Market.

Date	Mintage	F	VF	XF	Unc	BU
2009 Proof	500	Value: 120				

KM# 664 5 DOLLARS
31.1050 g., 0.9990 Silver 0.9990 oz. ASW, 38.6 mm. **Ruler:** Elizabeth II **Subject:** Ukraine Landmarks - Khotyn Fortress Reserve **Rev:** Road to castle **Note:** Exclusive to the Russian Market.

Date	Mintage	F	VF	XF	Unc	BU
2009 Proof	500	Value: 120				

KM# 665 5 DOLLARS
31.1050 g., 0.9990 Silver 0.9990 oz. ASW, 38.6 mm. **Ruler:** Elizabeth II **Subject:** Ukraine Landmarks - Upper Castle of Lutsk **Rev:** Tower **Note:** Exclusive to the Russian Market.

Date	Mintage	F	VF	XF	Unc	BU
2009 Proof	500	Value: 120				

KM# 666 5 DOLLARS
141.4000 g., 0.9990 Silver 4.5414 oz. ASW, 65 mm. **Ruler:** Elizabeth II **Subject:** Tall ships **Obv:** Bust right **Rev:** Germany's Preussen, 5-masted square rigger

Date	Mintage	F	VF	XF	Unc	BU
2009 Proof	—	Value: 285				

KM# 667 5 DOLLARS
141.4000 g., 0.9990 Silver 4.5414 oz. ASW, 65 mm. **Ruler:** Elizabeth II **Subject:** Tall ships **Rev:** France's France II

Date	Mintage	F	VF	XF	Unc	BU
2009 Proof	—	Value: 285				

KM# 668 5 DOLLARS
141.4000 g., 0.9990 Silver 4.5414 oz. ASW, 65 mm. **Ruler:** Elizabeth II **Subject:** Tall Ships **Rev:** America's Thomas W. Lawson, 7-masted schooner

Date	Mintage	F	VF	XF	Unc	BU
2009 Proof	—	Value: 285				

KM# 669 5 DOLLARS
141.4000 g., 0.9990 Silver 4.5414 oz. ASW, 65 mm. **Ruler:** Elizabeth II **Subject:** Tall Ships **Rev:** Russia's Sedov, 4-masted barque

Date	Mintage	F	VF	XF	Unc	BU
2009 Proof	—	Value: 285				

KM# 671 5 DOLLARS
141.4000 g., 0.9990 Silver 4.5414 oz. ASW, 65 mm. **Ruler:** Elizabeth II **Subject:** Tall Ships **Rev:** Russian 4-masted barque Kruzenshtern

Date	Mintage	F	VF	XF	Unc	BU
2009 Proof	—	Value: 285				

KM# 672 5 DOLLARS
25.0000 g., 0.9250 Silver 0.7435 oz. ASW, 38.6 mm. **Ruler:** Elizabeth II **Rev:** HMS Endeavour and James Cook portrait

Date	Mintage	F	VF	XF	Unc	BU
2009 Proof	2,500	Value: 45.00				

KM# 673 5 DOLLARS
25.0000 g., 0.5000 Silver 0.4019 oz. ASW, 38.6 mm. **Ruler:** Elizabeth II **Rev:** Ferrari F-2008 Carbon

Date	Mintage	F	VF	XF	Unc	BU
2009 Proof	2,008	Value: 55.00				

KM# 674 5 DOLLARS
20.0000 g., 0.9250 Silver 0.5948 oz. ASW, 38.61 mm. **Ruler:** Elizabeth II **Subject:** Endangered Wildlife **Rev:** Giant Anteater

Date	Mintage	F	VF	XF	Unc	BU
2009 Proof	5,000	Value: 40.00				

KM# 675 5 DOLLARS
31.1050 g., 0.9250 Silver 0.9250 oz. ASW, 38.6 mm. **Ruler:** Elizabeth II **Series:** International Womens Day **Rev:** Roses and butterfly **Note:** Exclusive to the Russian Market

Date	Mintage	F	VF	XF	Unc	BU
2009 Proof	500	Value: 120				

KM# 676 5 DOLLARS
25.0000 g., 0.9250 Silver 0.7435 oz. ASW, 38.6 mm. **Ruler:** Elizabeth II **Rev:** Sir Lancelot, multicolor

Date	Mintage	F	VF	XF	Unc	BU
2009 Proof	2,500	Value: 75.00				

KM# 677 5 DOLLARS

0.9250 Silver **Ruler:** Elizabeth II **Subject:** Masters of Europe - Vermeer **Rev:** Girl with a pearl earing, multicolor **Shape:** Vertical rectangle

Date	Mintage	F	VF	XF	Unc	BU
2009 Proof	—	Value: 85.00				

KM# 678 5 DOLLARS

0.9250 Silver **Ruler:** Elizabeth II **Subject:** Masters of Europe - DaVinci **Rev:** Lady with an ermine, multicolor **Shape:** Vertical rectangle

Date	Mintage	F	VF	XF	Unc	BU
2009 Proof	—	Value: 95.00				

KM# 679 5 DOLLARS

0.9250 Silver **Ruler:** Elizabeth II **Subject:** Masters of Europe - Jan Matejko **Rev:** Wernyhora, multicolor **Shape:** Vertical rectangle

Date	Mintage	F	VF	XF	Unc	BU
2009 Proof	—	Value: 85.00				

KM# 680 5 DOLLARS

Silver **Ruler:** Elizabeth II **Subject:** 50th Anniversary of Space exploration, 40th Anniversary of Apollo 11 **Obv:** Moon **Rev:** Moonscape and moon rock implant

Date	Mintage	F	VF	XF	Unc	BU
2009 Matte	—	—	—	—	—	175

KM# 681 5 DOLLARS

25.0000 g., 0.9250 Silver copper plated 0.7435 oz. ASW **Ruler:** Elizabeth II **Subject:** 400th Anniversary of Mars observations **Obv:** Bust with tiara right **Rev:** Mars landscape

Date	Mintage	F	VF	XF	Unc	BU
2009 Matte	2,500	—	—	—	—	150

KM# 682 5 DOLLARS

25.0000 g., 0.9250 Silver 0.7435 oz. ASW, 38.61 mm. **Ruler:** Elizabeth II **Subject:** Year of the Ox **Rev:** Child riding oxen, partially gilt **Note:** Exclusive to the Russian market

Date	Mintage	F	VF	XF	Unc	BU
2009 Proof	1,000	Value: 200				

KM# 683 5 DOLLARS

25.0000 g., 0.9990 Silver 0.8029 oz. ASW **Ruler:** Elizabeth II **Subject:** World of Flowers - Pansey **Rev:** Pansey, multicolor cloisonne

Date	Mintage	F	VF	XF	Unc	BU
2009 Proof	2,500	Value: 85.00				

KM# 684 5 DOLLARS

25.0000 g., 0.9990 Silver 0.8029 oz. ASW, 38.6 mm. **Ruler:** Elizabeth II **Subject:** World of flowers - Poppy **Rev:** Poppy, multicolor closinne

Date	Mintage	F	VF	XF	Unc	BU
2009 Proof	2,500	Value: 85.00				

KM# 685 5 DOLLARS

25.0000 g., 0.9250 Silver 0.7435 oz. ASW, 30x43 mm. **Ruler:** Elizabeth II **Obv:** Bust right **Rev:** Easter chick, thermal image changing **Shape:** Egg

Date	Mintage	F	VF	XF	Unc	BU
2009 Proof	2,500	Value: 65.00				

KM# 686 5 DOLLARS

25.0000 g., 0.9250 Silver 0.7435 oz. ASW, 35x35 mm. **Ruler:** Elizabeth II **Rev:** Season's greetings, rocking horse **Shape:** Square

Date	Mintage	F	VF	XF	Unc	BU
2009 Proof	2,500	Value: 55.00				

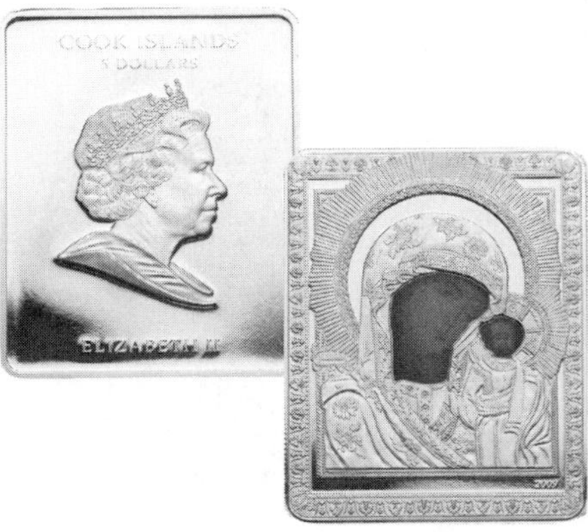

KM# 687 5 DOLLARS

25.0000 g., 0.9990 Silver 0.8029 oz. ASW, 30x38 mm. **Ruler:** Elizabeth II **Rev:** Kazan Virgin icon **Shape:** Vertical rectangle **Note:** Exclusive to the Russian market

Date	Mintage	F	VF	XF	Unc	BU
2009 Proof	2,500	Value: 125				

KM# 703 5 DOLLARS
25.0000 g., 0.9990 Silver 0.8029 oz. ASW, 38.6 mm. **Ruler:** Elizabeth II **Subject:** Nicolaus Copernicus **Rev:** Bust facing and orbit of the planets, crystal insert, partially gold plated

Date	Mintage	F	VF	XF	Unc	BU
2009 Proof	7,500	Value: 75.00				

KM# 782 5 DOLLARS
20.0000 g., 0.9990 Silver 0.6423 oz. ASW, 40 mm. **Ruler:** Elizabeth II **Subject:** Year of Astronomy **Rev:** Sun, multicolor

Date	Mintage	F	VF	XF	Unc	BU
2009	—	—	—	—	—	50.00

KM# 783 5 DOLLARS
20.0000 g., 0.9990 Silver 0.6423 oz. ASW, 40 mm. **Ruler:** Elizabeth II **Subject:** Year of Astronomy **Rev:** Mercury, multicolor

Date	Mintage	F	VF	XF	Unc	BU
2009	—	—	—	—	—	50.00

KM# 784 5 DOLLARS
20.0000 g., 0.9990 Silver 0.6423 oz. ASW, 40 mm. **Ruler:** Elizabeth II **Subject:** Year of Astronomy **Rev:** Venus, multicolor

Date	Mintage	F	VF	XF	Unc	BU
2009	—	—	—	—	—	50.00

KM# 785 5 DOLLARS
20.0000 g., 0.9990 Silver 0.6423 oz. ASW, 40 mm. **Ruler:** Elizabeth II **Subject:** Year of Astronomy **Rev:** Earth, multicolor

Date	Mintage	F	VF	XF	Unc	BU
2009	—	—	—	—	—	50.00

KM# 786 5 DOLLARS
20.0000 g., 0.9990 Silver 0.6423 oz. ASW, 40 mm. **Ruler:** Elizabeth II **Subject:** Year of Astronomy **Rev:** Mars, multicolor

Date	Mintage	F	VF	XF	Unc	BU
2009	—	—	—	—	—	50.00

KM# 787 5 DOLLARS
20.0000 g., 0.9990 Silver 0.6423 oz. ASW, 40 mm. **Ruler:** Elizabeth II **Subject:** Year of Astronomy **Rev:** Jupiter, multicolor

Date	Mintage	F	VF	XF	Unc	BU
2009	—	—	—	—	—	50.00

KM# 788 5 DOLLARS
20.0000 g., 0.9990 Silver 0.6423 oz. ASW, 40 mm. **Ruler:** Elizabeth II **Subject:** Year of Astronomy **Rev:** Saturn, multicolor

Date	Mintage	F	VF	XF	Unc	BU
2009	—	—	—	—	—	50.00

KM# 789 5 DOLLARS
20.0000 g., 0.9990 Silver 0.6423 oz. ASW, 40 mm. **Ruler:** Elizabeth II **Subject:** Year of Astronomy **Rev:** Uranus, multicolor

Date	Mintage	F	VF	XF	Unc	BU
2009	—	—	—	—	—	50.00

KM# 790 5 DOLLARS
20.0000 g., 0.9990 Silver 0.6423 oz. ASW, 40 mm. **Ruler:** Elizabeth II **Subject:** Year of Astronomy **Rev:** Neptune, multicolor

Date	Mintage	F	VF	XF	Unc	BU
2009	—	—	—	—	—	50.00

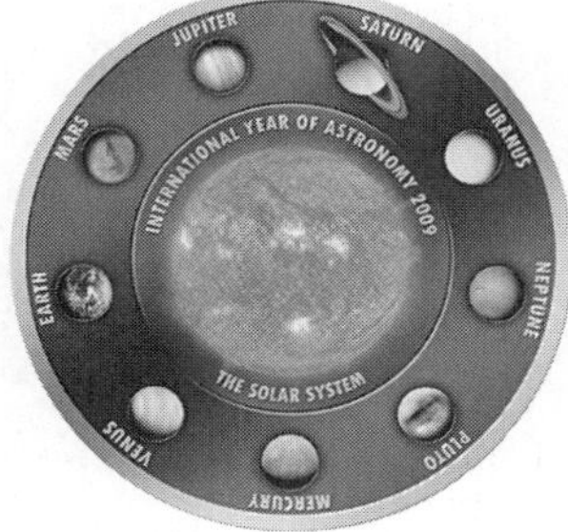

KM# 791 5 DOLLARS
20.0000 g., 0.9990 Silver 0.6423 oz. ASW, 40 mm. **Ruler:** Elizabeth II **Subject:** Year of Astronomy **Rev:** Solar System, multicolor

Date	Mintage	F	VF	XF	Unc	BU
2009	—	—	—	—	—	50.00

KM# 1225 5 DOLLARS
28.2800 g., 0.9250 Silver 0.8410 oz. ASW, 38.6 mm. **Ruler:** Elizabeth II **Subject:** Ikuko Shimizu's Hello Kitty **Rev:** Kitty and London Buss in multicolor

Date	Mintage	F	VF	XF	Unc	BU
2009 Proof	Est. 3,000	Value: 115				

KM# 1226 5 DOLLARS
28.2800 g., 0.9250 Silver 0.8410 oz. ASW, 38.6 mm. **Ruler:** Elizabeth II **Subject:** Ikuko Shimizu's Hello Kitty **Rev:** Kitty playing polo in multicolor

Date	Mintage	F	VF	XF	Unc	BU
2009 Proof	Est. 3,000	Value: 115				

KM# 1227 5 DOLLARS
28.2800 g., 0.9250 Silver 0.8410 oz. ASW, 38.6 mm. **Ruler:** Elizabeth II **Subject:** Ikuko Shimizu's Hello Kitty **Rev:** Kitty and Daniel with Tower Bridge in multicolor

Date	Mintage	F	VF	XF	Unc	BU
2009 Proof	Est. 3,000	Value: 115				

KM# 1236 5 DOLLARS
25.0000 g., 0.9250 Silver 0.7435 oz. ASW, 38.61 mm. **Ruler:** Elizabeth II **Subject:** Lady of the Lake

Date	Mintage	F	VF	XF	Unc	BU
2009 Proof	2,500	Value: 75.00				

KM# 1237 5 DOLLARS
25.0000 g., 0.9250 Silver 0.7435 oz. ASW, 38.61 mm. **Ruler:** Elizabeth II **Subject:** Excalibur

Date	Mintage	F	VF	XF	Unc	BU
2009 Proof	2,500	Value: 75.00				

KM# 1238 5 DOLLARS
25.0000 g., 0.9250 Silver 0.7435 oz. ASW, 38.61 mm. **Ruler:** Elizabeth II **Subject:** King Arthur

Date	Mintage	F	VF	XF	Unc	BU
2009 Proof	2,500	Value: 75.00				

KM# 1239 5 DOLLARS
25.0000 g., 0.9250 Silver 0.7435 oz. ASW, 38.61 mm. **Ruler:** Elizabeth II **Subject:** Sir Galahad

Date	Mintage	F	VF	XF	Unc	BU
2009 Proof	2,500	Value: 75.00				

KM# 1240 5 DOLLARS
25.0000 g., 0.9250 Silver 0.7435 oz. ASW, 38.61 mm. **Ruler:** Elizabeth II **Subject:** Round table theme

Date	Mintage	F	VF	XF	Unc	BU
2009 Proof	2,500	Value: 75.00				

KM# 723 5 DOLLARS
31.1050 g., 0.9990 Silver 0.9990 oz. ASW, 24x47 mm. **Ruler:** Elizabeth II **Subject:** War of 1812 **Rev:** Peter Bagraton

Date	Mintage	F	VF	XF	Unc	BU
2010 Antique finish	2,000	—	—	—	—	45.00

KM# 724 5 DOLLARS
31.1050 g., 0.9990 Silver 0.9990 oz. ASW **Ruler:** Elizabeth II **Subject:** War of 1812 **Rev:** Mikhail Kutuzov **Shape:** 24x47

Date	Mintage	F	VF	XF	Unc	BU
2010 Antique finish	2,000	—	—	—	—	45.00

KM# 725 5 DOLLARS
31.1050 g., 0.9990 Silver 0.9990 oz. ASW, 27x47 mm. **Ruler:** Elizabeth II **Subject:** War of 1812 **Rev:** Bikoly Raevsky

Date	Mintage	F	VF	XF	Unc	BU
2010 Antique finish	2,000	—	—	—	—	45.00

KM# 726 5 DOLLARS
20.0000 g., 0.9990 Silver 0.6423 oz. ASW, 30x43 mm. **Ruler:** Elizabeth II **Subject:** Imperial Eggs **Rev:** Blue egg

Date	Mintage	F	VF	XF	Unc	BU
2010 Proof	2,500	Value: 70.00				

KM# 727 5 DOLLARS
20.0000 g., 0.9990 Silver 0.6423 oz. ASW, 30x43 mm. **Ruler:** Elizabeth II **Subject:** Imperial Egg **Rev:** Green cloisonne

Date	Mintage	F	VF	XF	Unc	BU
2010 Proof	2,500	Value: 70.00				

KM# 728 5 DOLLARS
20.0000 g., 0.9990 Silver 0.6423 oz. ASW, 30x43 mm. **Ruler:** Elizabeth II **Subject:** Imperial Egg **Rev:** Yellow cloisonne and Bohemian crystals

Date	Mintage	F	VF	XF	Unc	BU
2010 Proof	2,500	Value: 70.00				

KM# 729 5 DOLLARS
25.0000 g., 0.9990 Silver 0.8029 oz. ASW, 38.6 mm. **Ruler:** Elizabeth II **Rev:** Martin Luther King, pointing **Note:** Fits together with KM#730.

Date	Mintage	F	VF	XF	Unc	BU
2010 Antique finish	2,500	—	—	—	—	55.00

KM# 730 5 DOLLARS
25.0000 g., 0.9990 Silver 0.8029 oz. ASW, 38.6 mm. **Ruler:** Elizabeth II **Rev:** Barack Obama, pointing **Note:** Fits together with KM#729.

Date	Mintage	F	VF	XF	Unc	BU
2010 Antique finish	2,500	—	—	—	—	55.00

KM# 731 5 DOLLARS
25.0000 g., 0.9250 Silver 0.7435 oz. ASW, 38.6 mm. **Ruler:** Elizabeth II **Subject:** Tender Love **Rev:** Rose in relief hologram

Date	Mintage	F	VF	XF	Unc	BU
2010 Proof	2,500	Value: 50.00				

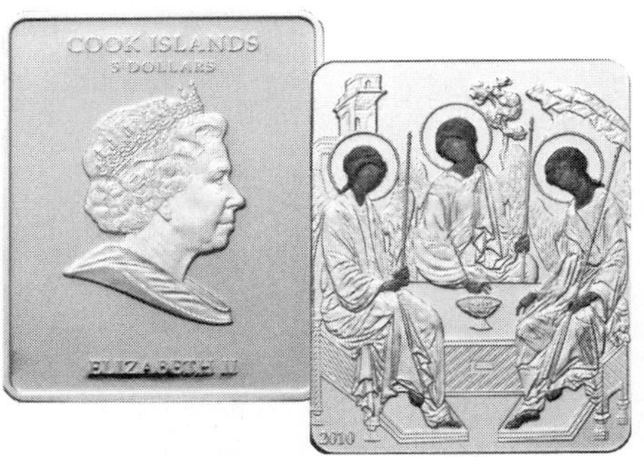

KM# 732 5 DOLLARS
25.0000 g., 0.9250 Silver 0.7435 oz. ASW, 30x38 mm. **Ruler:** Elizabeth II **Rev:** Holy Trinity icon

Date	Mintage	F	VF	XF	Unc	BU
2010 Proof	2,500	Value: 65.00				

KM# 771 5 DOLLARS
31.1050 g., 0.9990 Silver 0.9990 oz. ASW, 40 mm. **Ruler:** Elizabeth II **Subject:** Battle of Salams **Rev:** Trireame, multicolor insert

Date	Mintage	F	VF	XF	Unc	BU
2010 Proof	5,000	Value: 100				

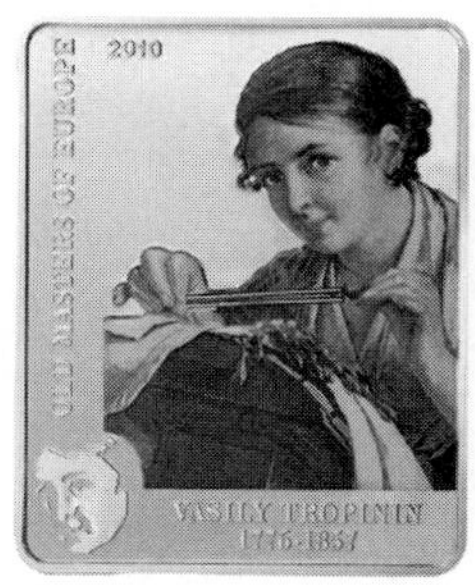

KM# 1244 5 DOLLARS
25.0000 g., 0.9250 Silver 0.7435 oz. ASW, 30x38 mm. **Ruler:** Elizabeth II **Subject:** Vasily Tropinin, 1776-1857 **Rev:** The Lacemaker, multicolor **Shape:** Vertical rectangle

Date	Mintage	F	VF	XF	Unc	BU
2010 Proof	2,500	Value: 65.00				

KM# 1245 5 DOLLARS
25.0000 g., 0.9250 Silver 0.7435 oz. ASW, 40.6 mm. **Ruler:** Elizabeth II **Subject:** Don Juan, Battle of Lepanto

Date	Mintage	F	VF	XF	Unc	BU
2010 Proof	1,000	Value: 75.00				

KM# 1247 5 DOLLARS
25.0000 g., 0.9990 Silver 0.8029 oz. ASW, 38.61 mm. **Ruler:** Elizabeth II **Subject:** Tender Love **Rev:** Rose in relief and with hologram

Date	Mintage	F	VF	XF	Unc	BU
2010 Proof	2,500	Value: 75.00				

KM# 1250 5 DOLLARS
26.0000 g., 0.9250 Silver 0.7732 oz. ASW, 30x38 mm. **Ruler:** Elizabeth II **Subject:** Peter Brandl **Shape:** Vertical rectangle

Date	Mintage	F	VF	XF	Unc	BU
2010 Proof	2,500	Value: 60.00				

KM# 1251 5 DOLLARS
25.0000 g., 0.9250 Silver 0.7435 oz. ASW, 30x38 mm. **Ruler:** Elizabeth II **Subject:** Michangelo's David **Shape:** Vertical rectangle

Date	Mintage	F	VF	XF	Unc	BU
2010 Proof	2,500	Value: 55.00				

KM# 1252 5 DOLLARS
25.0000 g., 0.9250 Silver 0.7435 oz. ASW, 38.61 mm. **Ruler:** Elizabeth II **Subject:** Hollywood Stars - Ginger Rogers

Date	Mintage	F	VF	XF	Unc	BU
2010 Proof	2,500	Value: 75.00				

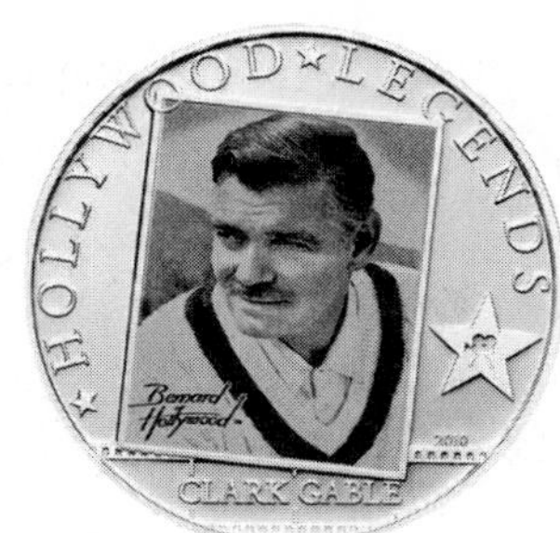

KM# 1254 5 DOLLARS
25.0000 g., 0.9250 Silver 0.7435 oz. ASW, 38.61 mm. **Ruler:** Elizabeth II **Subject:** Hollywood Stars - Clark Gable

Date	Mintage	F	VF	XF	Unc	BU
2010 Proof	2,500	Value: 75.00				

KM# 1255 5 DOLLARS
25.0000 g., 0.9250 Silver 0.7435 oz. ASW, 38.61 mm. **Ruler:** Elizabeth II **Subject:** Gdansk **Rev:** Town view, statue in copper **Note:** Antique patina.

Date	Mintage	F	VF	XF	Unc	BU
2010	1,000	Value: 50.00				

KM# 1281 5 DOLLARS
Silver, 27x47 mm. **Ruler:** Elizabeth II **Subject:** Ferrari 250 GTO and 599 GTO **Rev:** Yellow car right **Shape:** Vertical rectangle

Date	Mintage	F	VF	XF	Unc	BU
2010 Proof	1,010	Value: 135				

KM# 1253 5 DOLLARS
25.0000 g., 0.9250 Silver 0.7435 oz. ASW, 38.61 mm. **Ruler:** Elizabeth II **Subject:** Hollywood Stars - John Wayne

Date	Mintage	F	VF	XF	Unc	BU
2010 Proof	2,500	Value: 75.00				

KM# 1261 5 DOLLARS
25.0000 g., 0.9250 Silver 0.7435 oz. ASW, 38.61 mm. **Ruler:** Elizabeth II **Subject:** Flowers - Daisy

Date	Mintage	F	VF	XF	Unc	BU
2011 Proof	2,500	Value: 60.00				

KM# 1262 5 DOLLARS
25.0000 g., 0.9250 Silver 0.7435 oz. ASW, 38.61 mm. **Ruler:** Elizabeth II **Subject:** Hollywood Stars - Sophia Loren

Date	Mintage	F	VF	XF	Unc	BU
2011 Proof	2,500	Value: 75.00				

KM# 1263 5 DOLLARS
25.0000 g., 0.9250 Silver 0.7435 oz. ASW, 38.61 mm. **Ruler:** Elizabeth II **Subject:** Hollywood Stars - Elizabeth Taylor

Date	Mintage	F	VF	XF	Unc	BU
2011 Proof	2,500	Value: 75.00				

KM# 1264 5 DOLLARS
25.0000 g., 0.9250 Silver 0.7435 oz. ASW, 38.61 mm. **Ruler:** Elizabeth II **Subject:** Hollywood Stars - Marylin Monroe

Date	Mintage	F	VF	XF	Unc	BU
2011 Proof	2,500	Value: 75.00				

KM# 1265 5 DOLLARS
25.0000 g., 0.9250 Silver 0.7435 oz. ASW, 38.61 mm. **Ruler:** Elizabeth II **Subject:** Terminator-2, 20th Anniversary **Rev:** Walking through flames

Date	Mintage	F	VF	XF	Unc	BU
2011 Proof	—	Value: 75.00				

KM# 1266 5 DOLLARS
25.0000 g., 0.9250 Silver 0.7435 oz. ASW, 38.61 mm. **Ruler:** Elizabeth II **Subject:** Terminator-2, 20th Anniversary **Rev:** Riding motorcycle

Date	Mintage	F	VF	XF	Unc	BU
2011 Proof	—	Value: 60.00				

KM# 1267 5 DOLLARS
25.0000 g., 0.9250 Silver 0.7435 oz. ASW **Ruler:** Elizabeth II **Subject:** Terminator-2, 20th Anniversary **Rev:** Head shot **Shape:** 38.61

Date	Mintage	F	VF	XF	Unc	BU
2011 Proof	—	Value: 75.00				

KM# 1268 5 DOLLARS
25.0000 g., 0.9250 Silver 0.7435 oz. ASW, 38.61 mm. **Ruler:** Elizabeth II **Rev:** Koala and plant, scented

Date	Mintage	F	VF	XF	Unc	BU
2011	2,500	—	—	—	—	75.00

KM# 1273 5 DOLLARS
31.1050 g., 0.9990 Silver 0.9990 oz. ASW, 38.61 mm. **Ruler:** Elizabeth II **Subject:** Souzmultfilm, 75th Anniversary **Rev:** Crocodile Gena

Date	Mintage	F	VF	XF	Unc	BU
2011 Proof	2,000	Value: 100				

KM# 1274 5 DOLLARS
31.1050 g., 0.9990 Silver 0.9990 oz. ASW, 38.61 mm. **Ruler:** Elizabeth II **Subject:** Souzmultfilm, 75th Anniversary **Rev:** Cheburashka

Date	Mintage	F	VF	XF	Unc	BU
2011 Proof	2,000	Value: 100				

KM# 1275 5 DOLLARS
31.1050 g., 0.9990 Silver 0.9990 oz. ASW, 38.61 mm. **Ruler:** Elizabeth II **Subject:** Souzmultfilm, 75th Anniversary **Rev:** Shapoklyak

Date	Mintage	F	VF	XF	Unc	BU
2011 Proof	2,000	Value: 100				

KM# 1276 5 DOLLARS
31.1050 g., 0.9990 Silver 0.9990 oz. ASW, 38.61 mm. **Ruler:** Elizabeth II **Subject:** Souzmultfilm, 75th Anniversary **Rev:** Pooh with honey jar

Date	Mintage	F	VF	XF	Unc	BU
2011 Proof	2,000	Value: 100				

KM# 1277 5 DOLLARS
31.1050 g., 0.9990 Silver 0.9990 oz. ASW, 38.61 mm. **Ruler:** Elizabeth II **Subject:** Souzmultfilm, 75th Anniversary **Rev:** Eyore

Date	Mintage	F	VF	XF	Unc	BU
2011 Proof	2,000	Value: 100				

KM# 1278 5 DOLLARS
31.1050 g., 0.9990 Silver 0.9990 oz. ASW, 38.61 mm. **Ruler:** Elizabeth II **Subject:** Souzmultfilm, 75th Anniversary **Rev:** Piglett

Date	Mintage	F	VF	XF	Unc	BU
2011 Proof	2,000	Value: 100				

KM# 1279 5 DOLLARS
31.1050 g., 0.9990 Silver 0.9990 oz. ASW, 38.61 mm. **Ruler:** Elizabeth II **Subject:** Souzmultfilm, 75th Anniversary **Rev:** Pooh's Rabbit

Date	Mintage	F	VF	XF	Unc	BU
2011 Proof	2,000	Value: 100				

KM# 1280 5 DOLLARS
31.1050 g., 0.9990 Silver 0.9990 oz. ASW, 38.61 mm. **Ruler:** Elizabeth II **Subject:** Souzmultfilm, 75th Anniversary **Rev:** Pooh's owl

Date	Mintage	F	VF	XF	Unc	BU
2011 Proof	2,000	Value: 100				

KM# 473 10 DOLLARS
20.1200 g., Silver, 38.62 mm. **Ruler:** Elizabeth II **Subject:** 2004 Summer Olympics - Athens **Obv:** Crowned bust right **Rev:** Male discus thrower **Edge:** Reeded

Date	Mintage	F	VF	XF	Unc	BU
2001 Proof	—	Value: 35.00				

KM# 549 10 DOLLARS
10.0000 g., 0.9999 Gold 0.3215 oz. AGW, 25 mm. **Ruler:** Elizabeth II **Rev:** Multicolored Mikado Pheasant

Date	Mintage	F	VF	XF	Unc	BU
2001 Proof	1,000	Value: 500				

KM# 550 10 DOLLARS
10.0000 g., 0.9999 Gold 0.3215 oz. AGW, 25 mm. **Ruler:** Elizabeth II **Rev:** Multicolor black-faced spoonbill

Date	Mintage	F	VF	XF	Unc	BU
2001 Proof	1,000	Value: 500				

KM# 453 10 DOLLARS
186.8300 g., 0.9990 Silver Gilt 6.0005 oz. ASW, 89 mm. **Ruler:** Elizabeth II **Obv:** Crowned bust right, unique portrait for Cook Is. **Rev:** Queen Victoria standing with lion **Rev. Designer:** W. Wyon **Edge:** Reeded **Note:** Illustration reduced.

Date	Mintage	F	VF	XF	Unc	BU
2003 Proof	198	Value: 350				

KM# 1110 10 DOLLARS
1.2400 g., 0.9990 Gold 0.0398 oz. AGW **Ruler:** Elizabeth II **Rev:** Emblem

Date	Mintage	F	VF	XF	Unc	BU
2005 Proof	Est. 8,000	Value: 85.00				

KM# 1136 10 DOLLARS
1.2400 g., 0.9990 Gold 0.0398 oz. AGW, 13.92 mm. **Ruler:** Elizabeth II **Subject:** Star Wars, 30th Anniversary

Date	Mintage	F	VF	XF	Unc	BU
2005 Proof	9,999	Value: 85.00				

KM# 1176 10 DOLLARS
1.2400 g., 0.9990 Gold 0.0398 oz. AGW **Ruler:** Elizabeth II **Subject:** Marriage of Prince Charles and Camilla Parker-Bowles

Date	Mintage	F	VF	XF	Unc	BU
2005 Proof	Est. 25,000	Value: 85.00				

KM# 1178 10 DOLLARS
1.2400 g., 0.9990 Gold 0.0398 oz. AGW, 13.92 mm. **Ruler:** Elizabeth II **Rev:** Pope John Paul II

Date	Mintage	F	VF	XF	Unc	BU
2005 Proof	Est. 25,000	Value: 85.00				

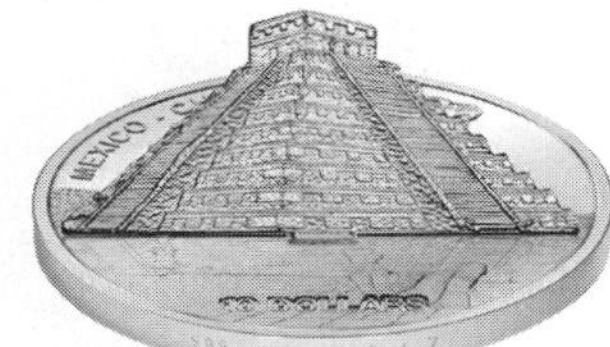

KM# 582 10 DOLLARS
31.1000 g., 0.9990 Silver 0.9988 oz. ASW, 38.6 mm. **Ruler:** Elizabeth II **Rev:** Chichen Itza gilt pop-up

Date	Mintage	F	VF	XF	Unc	BU
2007 Proof	5,000	Value: 65.00				

KM# 585 10 DOLLARS
31.1000 g., 0.9990 Silver 0.9988 oz. ASW, 38.6 mm. **Ruler:** Elizabeth II **Rev:** Easter Island status gilt pop-up

Date	Mintage	F	VF	XF	Unc	BU
2007 Proof	5,000	Value: 100				

KM# 587 10 DOLLARS
31.1000 g., 0.9990 Silver 0.9988 oz. ASW, 38.6 mm. **Ruler:** Elizabeth II **Rev:** Pyrmids gilt pop-up

Date	Mintage	F	VF	XF	Unc	BU
2007 Proof	5,000	Value: 65.00				

KM# 588 10 DOLLARS
31.1000 g., 0.9990 Silver 0.9988 oz. ASW, 38.6 mm. **Ruler:** Elizabeth II **Rev:** Golden Gate Bridge gilt pop-up

Date	Mintage	F	VF	XF	Unc	BU
2007 Proof	5,000	Value: 65.00				

KM# 589 10 DOLLARS
31.1000 g., 0.9990 Silver 0.9988 oz. ASW, 38.6 mm. **Ruler:** Elizabeth II **Rev:** Great Wall of China gilt pop-up

Date	Mintage	F	VF	XF	Unc	BU
2007 Proof	5,000	Value: 65.00				

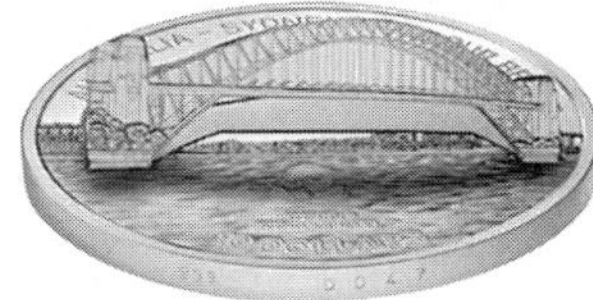

KM# 590 10 DOLLARS
31.1000 g., 0.9990 Silver 0.9988 oz. ASW, 38.6 mm. **Ruler:** Elizabeth II **Rev:** Sydney Harbor Bridge gilt pop-up

Date	Mintage	F	VF	XF	Unc	BU
2007 Proof	5,000	Value: 65.00				

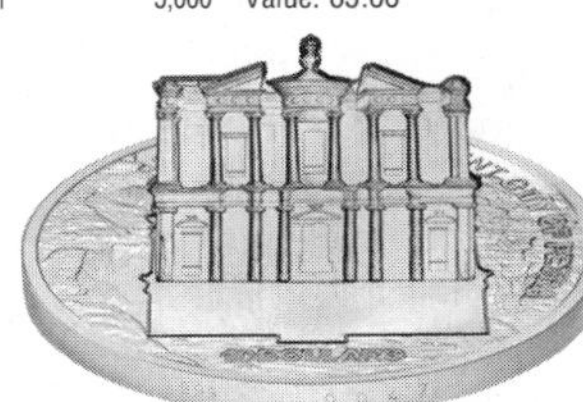

KM# 592 10 DOLLARS
31.1000 g., 0.9990 Silver 0.9988 oz. ASW, 38.6 mm. **Ruler:** Elizabeth II **Rev:** Petra Treasury gilt pop-up

Date	Mintage	F	VF	XF	Unc	BU
2007 Proof	5,000	Value: 65.00				

KM# 593 10 DOLLARS
31.1000 g., 0.9990 Silver 0.9988 oz. ASW, 38.6 mm. **Ruler:** Elizabeth II **Rev:** Taj mahal gilt pop-up

Date	Mintage	F	VF	XF	Unc	BU
2007 Proof	5,000	Value: 65.00				

KM# 1113 10 DOLLARS
0.5000 g., 0.9990 Gold 0.0161 oz. AGW, 11 mm. **Ruler:** Elizabeth II **Subject:** Treaty of rome, 50th Anniversary **Rev:** Monaco

Date	Mintage	F	VF	XF	Unc	BU
2007 Proof	Est. 5,000	Value: 50.00				

KM# 1171 10 DOLLARS
0.5000 g., 0.9990 Gold 0.0161 oz. AGW, 11 mm. **Ruler:** Elizabeth II **Subject:** Treaty of Rome, 50th Anniversary **Rev:** Vatican City

Date	Mintage	F	VF	XF	Unc	BU
2007 Proof	Est. 5,000	Value: 50.00				

KM# 1192 10 DOLLARS
1.2400 g., 0.9990 Gold 0.0398 oz. AGW, 13.92 mm. **Ruler:** Elizabeth II **Subject:** European Monarchs **Rev:** Elizabeth II

Date	Mintage	F	VF	XF	Unc	BU
2007 Proof	Est. 10,000	Value: 85.00				

KM# 1193 10 DOLLARS
1.2400 g., 0.9990 Gold 0.0398 oz. AGW **Ruler:** Elizabeth II **Subject:** European Monarchs **Rev:** Juan Carlos I

Date	Mintage	F	VF	XF	Unc	BU
2007 Proof	Est. 10,000	Value: 85.00				

KM# 1195 10 DOLLARS
1.2400 g., Gold, 13.92 mm. **Ruler:** Elizabeth II **Subject:** European Monarchs **Rev:** Beatrix

Date	Mintage	F	VF	XF	Unc	BU
2007 Proof	Est. 10,000	Value: 85.00				

KM# 1204 10 DOLLARS
1.2400 g., 0.9990 Gold 0.0398 oz. AGW, 13.92 mm. **Ruler:** Elizabeth II **Subject:** Christmas **Rev:** Cherib seated on rock

Date	Mintage	F	VF	XF	Unc	BU
2007 proof	Est. 15,000	Value: 85.00				

KM# 1194 10 DOLLARS
1.2400 g., 0.9990 Gold 0.0398 oz. AGW **Ruler:** Elizabeth II **Subject:** European Monarchs **Rev:** Carl XVI Gustaf

Date	Mintage	F	VF	XF	Unc	BU
2007 Proof	Est. 10,000	Value: 85.00				

KM# 619 10 DOLLARS
31.1000 g., 0.9990 Silver 0.9988 oz. ASW, 38.6 mm. **Ruler:** Elizabeth II **Rev:** Angor Wat temple gilt pop-up

Date	Mintage	F	VF	XF	Unc	BU
2008 Proof	5,000	Value: 65.00				

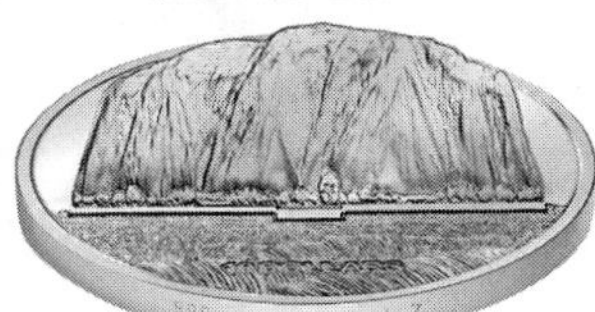

KM# 620 10 DOLLARS
31.1000 g., 0.9990 Silver 0.9988 oz. ASW, 38.6 mm. **Ruler:** Elizabeth II **Rev:** Ayer's Rock gilt pop-up

Date	Mintage	F	VF	XF	Unc	BU
2008 Proof	5,000	Value: 65.00				

KM# 621 10 DOLLARS
31.1000 g., 0.9990 Silver 0.9988 oz. ASW, 38.6 mm. **Ruler:** Elizabeth II **Rev:** Parliament Buildings and Big Ben pop-up

Date	Mintage	F	VF	XF	Unc	BU
2008 Proof	5,000	Value: 65.00				

KM# 622 10 DOLLARS
31.1000 g., 0.9990 Silver 0.9988 oz. ASW, 38.6 mm. **Ruler:** Elizabeth II **Rev:** Mt. Rushmore figures gilt pop-up

Date	Mintage	F	VF	XF	Unc	BU
2008 Proof	5,000	Value: 65.00				

KM# 623 10 DOLLARS
31.1000 g., 0.9990 Silver 0.9988 oz. ASW, 38.6 mm. **Ruler:** Elizabeth II **Rev:** Sydney Opera House gilt pop-up

Date	Mintage	F	VF	XF	Unc	BU
2008 Proof	5,000	Value: 65.00				

KM# 624 10 DOLLARS
31.1000 g., 0.9990 Silver 0.9988 oz. ASW, 38.6 mm. **Ruler:** Elizabeth II **Rev:** Malaysian Twin Towers gilt pop-up

Date	Mintage	F	VF	XF	Unc	BU
2008 Proof	5,000	Value: 65.00				

KM# 625 10 DOLLARS
31.1000 g., 0.9990 Silver 0.9988 oz. ASW, 38.6 mm. **Ruler:** Elizabeth II **Rev:** Sphinx gilt pop-up

Date	Mintage	F	VF	XF	Unc	BU
2008 Proof	5,000	Value: 65.00				

KM# 626 10 DOLLARS
31.1000 g., 0.9990 Silver 0.9988 oz. ASW, 38.6 mm. **Ruler:** Elizabeth II **Rev:** Stonehedge gilt pop-up

Date	Mintage	F	VF	XF	Unc	BU
2008 Proof	5,000	Value: 65.00				

KM# 627 10 DOLLARS
62.2050 g., 0.9990 Silver 1.9979 oz. ASW, 50 mm. **Ruler:** Elizabeth II **Rev:** Tsar Alexander II, multicolor **Note:** Exclusive to the Russian Market.

Date	Mintage	F	VF	XF	Unc	BU
2008 Proof	500	Value: 350				

KM# 628 10 DOLLARS
62.2050 g., 0.9990 Silver 1.9979 oz. ASW **Ruler:** Elizabeth II **Rev:** Tsar Alexi, multicolor **Note:** Exclusive to the Russian Market.

Date	Mintage	F	VF	XF	Unc	BU
2008 Proof	500	Value: 350				

KM# 629 10 DOLLARS
62.2050 g., 0.9990 Silver 1.9979 oz. ASW, 50 mm. **Ruler:** Elizabeth II **Rev:** Tsarina Anna, multicolor

Date	Mintage	F	VF	XF	Unc	BU
2008 Proof	500	Value: 350				

KM# 630 10 DOLLARS
62.2050 g., 0.9990 Silver 1.9979 oz. ASW, 50 mm. **Ruler:** Elizabeth II **Rev:** Tsarina Elizabeth, multicolor

Date	Mintage	F	VF	XF	Unc	BU
2008 Proof	500	Value: 350				

KM# 631 10 DOLLARS
62.2050 g., 0.9990 Silver 1.9979 oz. ASW, 50 mm. **Ruler:** Elizabeth II **Rev:** Tsar Mikhail, multicolor

Date	Mintage	F	VF	XF	Unc	BU
2008 Proof	500	Value: 350				

KM# 632 10 DOLLARS
62.2050 g., 0.9990 Silver 1.9979 oz. ASW, 50 mm. **Ruler:** Elizabeth II **Rev:** Tsar Paul I, multicolor

Date	Mintage	F	VF	XF	Unc	BU
2008 Proof	500	Value: 350				

KM# 633 10 DOLLARS
31.1000 g., 0.9990 Silver 0.9988 oz. ASW, 40 mm. **Ruler:** Elizabeth II **Rev:** Nathan Rothschild bust at right, partially gilt

Date	Mintage	F	VF	XF	Unc	BU
2008 Proof	10,000	Value: 55.00				

KM# 634 10 DOLLARS
31.1050 g., 0.9990 Silver 0.9990 oz. ASW, 40 mm. **Ruler:** Elizabeth II **Rev:** Henry Ford at left and Model-A car at right, partially gilt

Date	Mintage	F	VF	XF	Unc	BU
2008 Proof	10,000	Value: 55.00				

KM# 635 10 DOLLARS
31.1000 g., 0.9990 Silver 0.9988 oz. ASW, 40 mm. **Ruler:** Elizabeth II **Rev:** John D. Rockefeller Sr., bust right, oil derrick partially gilt.

Date	Mintage	F	VF	XF	Unc	BU
2008 Proof	10,000	Value: 55.00				

KM# 704 10 DOLLARS
1.0000 g., 0.9990 Gold 0.0321 oz. AGW, 13.9 mm. **Ruler:** Elizabeth II **Subject:** Gorch Fock **Rev:** Sailing vessel right

Date	Mintage	F	VF	XF	Unc	BU
2008 Proof	15,000	Value: 65.00				

KM# 705 10 DOLLARS
62.2100 g., 0.9990 Silver 1.9980 oz. ASW, 50 mm. **Ruler:** Elizabeth II **Subject:** Kiev Churches **Rev:** Lavra bell tower

Date	Mintage	F	VF	XF	Unc	BU
2008 Proof	500	—	—	—	—	120

KM# 1205 10 DOLLARS
1.0000 g., 0.9990 Gold 0.0321 oz. AGW, 13.92 mm. **Ruler:** Elizabeth II **Rev:** Gorch Fock I, 1933

Date	Mintage	F	VF	XF	Unc	BU
2008 Proof	—	Value: 65.00				

KM# 1206 10 DOLLARS
1.0000 g., 0.9990 Gold 0.0321 oz. AGW, 13.92 mm. **Ruler:** Elizabeth II **Subject:** Endangered Wildlife **Rev:** Polar Bear

Date	Mintage	F	VF	XF	Unc	BU
2008 Proof	Est. 25,000	Value: 65.00				

KM# 688 10 DOLLARS
31.1050 g., 0.9990 Silver 0.9990 oz. ASW, 38.6 mm. **Ruler:** Elizabeth II **Rev:** Statues of Ramesses II at Abu Simbel gilt pop-up

Date	Mintage	F	VF	XF	Unc	BU
2009 Proof	5,000	Value: 65.00				

KM# 689 10 DOLLARS
31.1050 g., 0.9990 Silver 0.9990 oz. ASW, 38.6 mm. **Ruler:** Elizabeth II **Rev:** Arc de Triumph gilt pop-up

Date	Mintage	F	VF	XF	Unc	BU
2009 Proof	5,000	Value: 65.00				

KM# 690 10 DOLLARS
31.1050 g., 0.9990 Silver 0.9990 oz. ASW, 38.6 mm. **Ruler:** Elizabeth II **Rev:** Hagia Sofia gilt pop-up

Date	Mintage	F	VF	XF	Unc	BU
2009 Proof	5,000	Value: 65.00				

KM# 691 10 DOLLARS
31.1050 g., 0.9990 Silver 0.9990 oz. ASW, 38.6 mm. **Ruler:** Elizabeth II **Rev:** Temple of Heaven gilt pop-up

Date	Mintage	F	VF	XF	Unc	BU
2009 Proof	5,000	Value: 65.00				

KM# 692 10 DOLLARS
31.1050 g., 0.9990 Silver 0.9990 oz. ASW, 38.6 mm. **Ruler:** Elizabeth II **Rev:** Holstein Gate gilt pop-up

Date	Mintage	F	VF	XF	Unc	BU
2009 Proof	5,000	Value: 65.00				

KM# 693 10 DOLLARS
31.1050 g., 0.9990 Silver 0.9990 oz. ASW, 38.6 mm. **Ruler:** Elizabeth II **Rev:** Ruins of Kaiser Church in Berlin, gilt pop-up

Date	Mintage	F	VF	XF	Unc	BU
2009 Proof	5,000	Value: 65.00				

KM# 694 10 DOLLARS
31.1050 g., 0.9990 Silver 0.9990 oz. ASW, 38.6 mm. **Ruler:** Elizabeth II **Rev:** Statue of Peter I gilt pop-up

Date	Mintage	F	VF	XF	Unc	BU
2009 Proof	5,000	Value: 65.00				

KM# 695 10 DOLLARS
31.1050 g., 0.9990 Silver 0.9990 oz. ASW, 38.6 mm. **Ruler:** Elizabeth II **Rev:** Bridge in Venice, gilt pop-up

Date	Mintage	F	VF	XF	Unc	BU
2009 Proof	5,000	Value: 65.00				

KM# 696 10 DOLLARS
31.1050 g., 0.9990 Silver 0.9990 oz. ASW, 38.6 mm. **Ruler:** Elizabeth II **Rev:** Opera house, gilt pop-up

Date	Mintage	F	VF	XF	Unc	BU
2009 Proof	—	Value: 65.00				

KM# 792 10 DOLLARS
31.1050 g., 0.9990 Silver 0.9990 oz. ASW, 40 mm. **Ruler:** Elizabeth II **Subject:** Tycoons - Alfred Nobel **Rev:** Nobel bust at right, Prize Medal partially gilt at right

Date	Mintage	F	VF	XF	Unc	BU
2009 Proof	10,000	Value: 55.00				

KM# 793 10 DOLLARS
31.1050 g., 0.9990 Silver 0.9990 oz. ASW, 40 mm. **Ruler:** Elizabeth II **Subject:** Tycoons **Rev:** Cecil Rhodes, partially gilt

Date	Mintage	F	VF	XF	Unc	BU
2009 Proof	10,000	Value: 55.00				

KM# 1228 10 DOLLARS
155.5000 g., 0.9250 Silver 4.6243 oz. ASW, 65 mm. **Ruler:** Elizabeth II **Subject:** Ikuko Shimizu's Hello Kitty **Rev:** Kitty and Buckingham Palace in multicolor

Date	Mintage	F	VF	XF	Unc	BU
2009 Proof	Est. 1,500	Value: 350				

KM# 1232 10 DOLLARS
1.2400 g., 0.9990 Gold 0.0398 oz. AGW, 13.92 mm. **Ruler:** Elizabeth II **Subject:** Knut Hamsun, 150th Anniversary of Birth

Date	Mintage	F	VF	XF	Unc	BU
2009 Proof	Est. 1,000	Value: 85.00				

KM# 1233 10 DOLLARS
1.2400 g., 0.9990 Gold 0.0398 oz. AGW, 13.92 mm. **Ruler:** Elizabeth II **Subject:** Sweedish King Oscar II

Date	Mintage	F	VF	XF	Unc	BU
2009 Proof	Est. 10,000	Value: 85.00				

KM# 1249 10 DOLLARS
31.1350 g., 0.9990 Silver 100000 oz. ASW, 45 mm. **Ruler:** Elizabeth II **Subject:** Albert Durer **Rev:** Rabbit illustration with crystals

Date	Mintage	F	VF	XF	Unc	BU
2010 Proof	3,000	Value: 75.00				

KM# 1258 10 DOLLARS
50.0000 g., 0.9250 Silver 1.4869 oz. ASW, 50 mm. **Ruler:** Elizabeth II **Subject:** Windows of Heaven **Rev:** Cologne Cathedral, stained glass windows, facade and ceiling arch plan

Date	Mintage	F	VF	XF	Unc	BU
2010 Proof	2,000	Value: 250				

KM# 1259 10 DOLLARS
50.0000 g., 0.9990 Silver 1.6059 oz. ASW, 50 mm. **Ruler:** Elizabeth II **Subject:** Windows of Heaven **Rev:** Westminister Abbey, stained glass windows, floor plan and facade

Date	Mintage	F	VF	XF	Unc	BU
2011 Proof	2,000	Value: 300				

KM# 1131 12 DOLLARS
10.0000 g., 0.9999 Gold 0.3215 oz. AGW, 26 mm. **Ruler:** Elizabeth II **Subject:** Full Gospel Business Men's Fellowship, 50th Anniversary **Rev:** Jesus Christ

Date	Mintage	F	VF	XF	Unc	BU
2003 Proof	Est. 4,999	Value: 550				

KM# 591 20 DOLLARS
31.1000 g., 0.9990 Silver 0.9988 oz. ASW, 38.6 mm. **Ruler:** Elizabeth II **Rev:** Machu Pichu gilt pop-up

Date	Mintage	F	VF	XF	Unc	BU
2007 Proof	5,000	Value: 65.00				

KM# 894 20 DOLLARS
31.1050 g., 0.9250 Silver 0.9250 oz. ASW **Ruler:** Elizabeth II **Rev:** Marco Pola visit the Khubla Khan in China

Date	Mintage
	— Value: 60.00

KM# 636 20 DOLLARS
93.3000 g., 0.9990 Silver 2.9965 oz. ASW, 55 mm. **Ruler:** Elizabeth II **Rev:** Michangelo, Creation of Adam, multicolor with crystal inserts

Date	Mintage	F	VF	XF	Unc	BU
2008 Proof	1,000	Value: 550				

KM# 637 20 DOLLARS
93.3000 g., 0.9990 Silver 2.9965 oz. ASW, 55 mm. **Ruler:** Elizabeth II **Rev:** DaVinci, Last Supper, multicolor with crystal inserts

Date	Mintage	F	VF	XF	Unc	BU
2008 Proof	1,000	Value: 650				

KM# 638 20 DOLLARS
93.3000 g., 0.9990 Silver 2.9965 oz. ASW, 55 mm. **Ruler:** Elizabeth II **Rev:** Raffaello, School of Athens, multicolor with crystal inserts

Date	Mintage	F	VF	XF	Unc	BU
2008 Proof	1,000	Value: 450				

KM# 639 20 DOLLARS
93.3000 g., 0.9990 Silver 2.9965 oz. ASW, 55 mm. **Ruler:** Elizabeth II **Rev:** Botticelli, Birth of Venus, multicolor with crystal inserts

Date	Mintage	F	VF	XF	Unc	BU
2008 Proof	1,458	Value: 375				

KM# 697 20 DOLLARS
93.3150 g., 0.9990 Silver 2.9970 oz. ASW, 55 mm. **Ruler:** Elizabeth II **Subject:** European Masters - DaVinci **Rev:** Mona Lisa, 12 crystals imbedded

Date	Mintage	F	VF	XF	Unc	BU
2009 Proof	999	Value: 1,350				

KM# 698 20 DOLLARS
93.3150 g., 0.9990 Silver 2.9970 oz. ASW, 55 mm. **Ruler:** Elizabeth II **Subject:** European Masters - Rembrandt **Rev:** The Night watch, crystals embedded

Date	Mintage	F	VF	XF	Unc	BU
2009 Proof	1,642	Value: 375				

KM# 699 20 DOLLARS
93.3150 g., 0.9990 Silver 2.9970 oz. ASW, 55 mm. **Ruler:** Elizabeth II **Subject:** European Masters - Raffaelo **Rev:** Sistine Chapel Madonna, crystals embedded

Date	Mintage	F	VF	XF	Unc	BU
2009 Proof	1,512	Value: 375				

KM# 700 20 DOLLARS
93.3150 g., 0.9990 Silver 2.9970 oz. ASW, 55 mm. **Ruler:** Elizabeth II **Subject:** European Masters - Spitzwig **Rev:** The Poor Poet, crystals embedded

Date	Mintage	F	VF	XF	Unc	BU
2009 Proof	—	Value: 550				

KM# 769 20 DOLLARS
93.3150 g., 0.9990 Silver partially gilt 2.9970 oz. ASW, 55 mm. **Ruler:** Elizabeth II **Rev:** Vetruvian man

Date	Mintage	F	VF	XF	Unc	BU
2010 Proof	—	Value: 550				

KM# 1246 20 DOLLARS
93.3000 g., 0.9990 Silver 2.9965 oz. ASW, 55 mm. **Ruler:** Elizabeth II **Subject:** Carlo Maratta **Rev:** Holy Night, color image of Mary and child, crystals

Date	Mintage	F	VF	XF	Unc	BU
2010	1,655	—	—	—	—	300

KM# 1248 20 DOLLARS
93.3000 g., 0.9990 Silver 2.9965 oz. ASW, 55 mm. **Ruler:** Elizabeth II **Subject:** Rembrandt **Rev:** Man in a Golden Helmet, plus crystals

Date	Mintage	F	VF	XF	Unc	BU
2010 Proof	1,655	Value: 300				

KM# 1145 25 DOLLARS
7.8700 g., 0.9999 Gold 0.2530 oz. AGW **Ruler:** Elizabeth II **Rev:** Edward "Ned"Kelley in color

Date	Mintage	F	VF	XF	Unc	BU
2004 proof	Est. 1,000	Value: 475				

KM# 1190 25 DOLLARS
155.5000 g., 0.9250 Silver 4.6243 oz. ASW, 65 mm. **Ruler:** Elizabeth II **Subject:** Elvis Presely, 30th Anniversary of death **Rev:** That's All right, Mama

Date	Mintage	F	VF	XF	Unc	BU
2007 Proof	Est. 1,977	Value: 350				

KM# 767 25 DOLLARS
155.5000 g., 0.9990 Silver 4.9942 oz. ASW, 65 mm. **Ruler:** Elizabeth II **Subject:** Year of the Ox **Rev:** Child riding back of ox, partially gilt

Date	Mintage	F	VF	XF	Unc	BU
2009 Proof	—	Value: 675				

KM# 1229 25 DOLLARS
7.9800 g., 0.9160 Gold 0.2350 oz. AGW, 22.05 mm. **Ruler:** Elizabeth II **Subject:** Ikuko Shimizu's Hello Kitty **Rev:** Kitty and Union Jack flag in multicolor

Date	Mintage	F	VF	XF	Unc	BU
2009 Proof	Est. 1,000	Value: 700				

KM# 1242 25 DOLLARS
4.0000 g., 0.9990 Gold 0.1285 oz. AGW, 14x23.3 mm. **Ruler:** Elizabeth II **Subject:** Shroud of Turin **Rev:** Image of the face of Jesus, 3 red crystals

Date	Mintage	F	VF	XF	Unc	BU
2010 Proof	2,000	Value: 500				

KM# 439 30 DOLLARS
10.0000 g., 0.9999 Gold 0.3215 oz. AGW, 16.1 mm. **Ruler:** Elizabeth II **Obv:** Crowned head right, date below **Rev:** Multicolor Peony flower and denomination **Edge:** Reeded

Date	Mintage	F	VF	XF	Unc	BU
2004	10,000	—	—	—	—	500

KM# 1128 35 DOLLARS
10.0210 g., 0.9990 Gold 0.3218 oz. AGW, 25 mm. **Ruler:** Elizabeth II **Rev:** James Cook and sailing ship

Date	Mintage	F	VF	XF	Unc	BU
2003 Proof	Est. 4,999	Value: 550				

KM# 440 35 DOLLARS
10.0000 g., 0.9999 Gold 0.3215 oz. AGW, 16.1 mm. **Ruler:** Elizabeth II **Obv:** Crowned head right, date below **Rev:** Multicolor Chinese man beating a tiger and denomination **Edge:** Reeded

Date	Mintage	F	VF	XF	Unc	BU
2004	6,000	—	—	—	—	500

KM# 441 35 DOLLARS
10.0000 g., 0.9999 Gold 0.3215 oz. AGW, 16.1 mm. **Ruler:** Elizabeth II **Obv:** Crowned head right, date below **Rev:** Multicolor Chinese man riding a horse and denomination **Edge:** Reeded

Date	Mintage	F	VF	XF	Unc	BU
2004	10,000	—	—	—	—	500

KM# 442 35 DOLLARS
10.0000 g., 0.9999 Gold 0.3215 oz. AGW, 25 x 15 mm. **Ruler:** Elizabeth II **Obv:** Crowned head right, date below **Rev:** Multicolor "Eight immortals crossing the sea" and denomination **Edge:** Plain **Shape:** Ingot

Date	Mintage	F	VF	XF	Unc	BU
2004	3,000	—	—	—	—	525

KM# 1132 50 DOLLARS
31.1050 g., 0.9999 Gold 0.9999 oz. AGW, 38.6 mm. **Ruler:** Elizabeth II **Subject:** Full Gospel Business Men's Fellowship, 50th Anniversary **Rev:** Jesus Christ

Date	Mintage	F	VF	XF	Unc	BU
2003 Proof	Est. 2,999	Value: 1,600				

KM# 1191 50 DOLLARS
7.7800 g., 0.7500 Gold 0.1876 oz. AGW, 26 mm. **Ruler:** Elizabeth II **Subject:** Elvis Presley, 30th Anniversary of death

Date	Mintage	F	VF	XF	Unc	BU
2007 Proof	500	Value: 420				

KM# 800 50 DOLLARS
155.5000 g., 0.9990 Silver 4.9942 oz. ASW, 65 mm. **Ruler:** Elizabeth II **Subject:** Tales of the Carribean **Rev:** Sea monster atacking Pirate ship

Date	Mintage	F	VF	XF	Unc	BU
2008	500	—	—	—	—	1,500

KM# 1230 50 DOLLARS
15.6100 g., 0.9990 Gold 0.5014 oz. AGW, 26.5 mm. **Ruler:** Elizabeth II **Subject:** Ikuko Shimizu's Hello Kitty **Rev:** Kitty and Daniel in automobile near Westminster and Big Ben in multicolor

Date	Mintage	F	VF	XF	Unc	BU
2009 Proof	Est. 1,000	Value: 1,250				

KM# 1234 50 DOLLARS
31.1050 g., 0.9990 Palladium 0.9990 oz., 38.6 mm. **Ruler:** Elizabeth II **Rev:** H.M.A.V. Bounty, as full hull model

Date	Mintage	F	VF	XF	Unc	BU
2009 Proof	—	—	—	—	—	1,000

KM# 738 50 DOLLARS
31.1050 g., 0.9999 Palladium 0.9999 oz. **Ruler:** Elizabeth II **Rev:** Ship model left

Date	Mintage	F	VF	XF	Unc	BU
2010	—	—	—	—	—	1,000

KM# 397 100 DOLLARS
23.3276 g., 0.9999 Gold Acrylic capsule center containing tiny diamonds, rubies and sapphires 0.7499 oz. AGW, 32.1 mm. **Ruler:** Elizabeth II **Subject:** Crown Jewels **Obv:** Crowned bust right, legend **Rev:** Crowns and royal regalia **Edge:** Reeded

Date	Mintage	F	VF	XF	Unc	BU
2002 Proof	5,000	Value: 1,350				

KM# 1129 100 DOLLARS
31.1620 g., 0.9990 Gold 1.0008 oz. AGW, 32 mm. **Ruler:** Elizabeth II **Rev:** James Cook and sailing ship

Date	Mintage	F	VF	XF	Unc	BU
2003 Proof	Est. 2,999	Value: 1,600				

KM# 503 100 DOLLARS
31.1030 g., 0.9999 Gold 0.9998 oz. AGW, 40.6 mm. **Ruler:** Elizabeth II **Subject:** WWI **Obv:** Head with tiara right **Rev:** Multicolor image of Australian WWI soldier in Europe **Edge:** Reeded

Date	Mintage	F	VF	XF	Unc	BU
2008 Proof	90	Value: 2,000				

KM# 505 100 DOLLARS
31.1030 g., 0.9999 Gold 0.9998 oz. AGW, 40.6 mm. **Ruler:** Elizabeth II **Subject:** WWI **Obv:** Head with tiara right **Rev:** Multicolor image of Australian WWI soldier in Mid-East scene **Edge:** Reeded

Date	Mintage	F	VF	XF	Unc	BU
2008 Proof	90	Value: 2,000				

KM# 737 100 DOLLARS
31.1050 g., 0.9999 Platinum 0.9999 oz. APW **Ruler:** Elizabeth II **Rev:** Ship model left

Date	Mintage	F	VF	XF	Unc	BU
2010	—	—	—	—	—	2,250

KM# 1212 200 DOLLARS
31.1620 g., 0.9999 Gold 1.0017 oz. AGW, 32 mm. **Ruler:** Elizabeth II **Subject:** John Marshall's Cow Parade **Rev:** Cow in multicolor

Date	Mintage	F	VF	XF	Unc	BU
2008	Est. 100	—	—	—	—	1,750

KM# 1213 200 DOLLARS
31.1620 g., 0.9990 Gold 1.0008 oz. AGW, 32 mm. **Ruler:** Elizabeth II **Subject:** John Marshall's Cow Parade **Rev:** African Moonlight Cow in multicolor

Date	Mintage	F	VF	XF	Unc	BU
2008	Est. 100	—	—	—	—	1,750

KM# 1214 200 DOLLARS
31.1650 g., 0.9990 Gold 1.0009 oz. AGW, 32 mm. **Ruler:** Elizabeth II **Subject:** John Marshall's Cow Parade **Rev:** Discownt Motivated in multicolor

Date	Mintage	F	VF	XF	Unc	BU
2008	Est. 100	—	—	—	—	1,750

KM# 1215 200 DOLLARS
31.1650 g., 0.9999 Gold 1.0018 oz. AGW **Ruler:** Elizabeth II **Subject:** John Marshall's Cow Parade **Rev:** Moodonna in multicolor

Date	Mintage	F	VF	XF	Unc	BU
2008	Est. 100	—	—	—	—	1,750

KM# 1216 200 DOLLARS
31.1650 g., 0.9990 Gold 1.0009 oz. AGW, 32 mm. **Ruler:** Elizabeth II **Subject:** John Marshall's Cow Parade **Rev:** Moodiba in multicolor

Date	Mintage	F	VF	XF	Unc	BU
2008	Est. 100	—	—	—	—	1,750

KM# 1217 200 DOLLARS
31.1650 g., 0.9999 Gold 1.0018 oz. AGW, 32 mm. **Ruler:** Elizabeth II **Subject:** John Marshall's Cow Parade **Rev:** Railbow Cowwow in multicolor

Date	Mintage	F	VF	XF	Unc	BU
2008	Est. 100	—	—	—	—	1,750

KM# 1218 200 DOLLARS
31.1650 g., 0.9999 Gold 1.0018 oz. AGW, 32 mm. **Ruler:** Elizabeth II **Subject:** John Marshall's Cow Parade **Rev:** Picowso in multicolor

Date	Mintage	F	VF	XF	Unc	BU
2008	Est. 100	—	—	—	—	1,750

KM# 1219 200 DOLLARS
31.1650 g., 0.9990 Gold 1.0009 oz. AGW, 32 mm. **Ruler:** Elizabeth II **Subject:** John Marshall's Cow Parade **Rev:** Location Cow in multicolor

Date	Mintage	F	VF	XF	Unc	BU
2008	Est. 100	—	—	—	—	1,750

KM# 1220 200 DOLLARS
31.1650 g., 0.9999 Gold 1.0018 oz. AGW, 32 mm. **Ruler:** Elizabeth II **Subject:** John Marshall's Cow Parade **Rev:** Milking in the Farmhouse in multicolor

Date	Mintage	F	VF	XF	Unc	BU
2008	Est. 100	—	—	—	—	1,750

KM# 1221 200 DOLLARS
31.1650 g., 0.9999 Gold 1.0018 oz. AGW, 32 mm. **Ruler:** Elizabeth II **Subject:** John Marshall's Cow Parade **Rev:** Evening Cows in multicolor

Date	Mintage	F	VF	XF	Unc	BU
2008	Est. 100	—	—	—	—	1,750

KM# 1222 200 DOLLARS
31.1650 g., 0.9999 Gold 1.0018 oz. AGW, 32 mm. **Ruler:** Elizabeth II **Subject:** John Marshall's Cow Parade **Rev:** Cultural Moosic Cow in multicolor

Date	Mintage	F	VF	XF	Unc	BU
2008	Est. 100	—	—	—	—	1,750

KM# 1223 200 DOLLARS
31.1650 g., 0.9999 Gold 1.0018 oz. AGW, 32 mm. **Ruler:** Elizabeth II **Subject:** John Marshall's Cow Parade **Rev:** Freedomoo Cow in multicolor

Date	Mintage	F	VF	XF	Unc	BU
2008	Est. 100	—	—	—	—	1,750

KM# 1224 200 DOLLARS
31.1650 g., 0.9999 Gold 1.0018 oz. AGW, 32 mm. **Ruler:** Elizabeth II **Subject:** John Marshall's Cow Parade **Rev:** Bovingham Palace Cow in multicolor

Date	Mintage	F	VF	XF	Unc	BU
2008	Est. 100	—	—	—	—	1,750

KM# 768 200 DOLLARS
31.1050 g., 0.9990 Gold 0.9990 oz. AGW, 40.6 mm. **Ruler:** Elizabeth II **Subject:** Year of the Ox **Rev:** Child riding back of ox

Date	Mintage	F	VF	XF	Unc	BU
2009 Proof	—	Value: 1,650				

KM# 389 500 DOLLARS
2000.0000 g., 0.9990 Silver 64.234 oz. ASW, 105. mm. **Ruler:** Elizabeth II **Subject:** Moby Dick **Obv:** Crowned head right **Rev:** Whale jumping over a six-man rowboat **Edge:** Plain **Note:** Illustration reduced.

Date	Mintage	F	VF	XF	Unc	BU
2001 Proof	—	Value: 2,500				

KM# 548 500 DOLLARS
113.0000 g., 1.0000 Gold 3.6328 oz. AGW, 50 mm. **Ruler:** Elizabeth II **Subject:** Jack Nicklaus **Rev:** Portrait facing - two golf poses flanking

Date	Mintage	F	VF	XF	Unc	BU
2006 Proof	113	Value: 5,500				

MAUNDY MONEY

Ceremonial Sterling Pence

KM# 449 PENNY
0.4800 g., 0.9990 Silver 0.0154 oz. ASW, 11.1 mm. **Ruler:** Elizabeth II **Subject:** Maundy **Obv:** Crowned bust right **Rev:** Crowned denomination divides date within wreath **Edge:** Plain

Date	Mintage	F	VF	XF	Unc	BU
2002 Proof	5,000	Value: 8.00				

KM# 450 2 PENCE
0.9400 g., 0.9990 Silver 0.0302 oz. ASW, 13.4 mm. **Ruler:** Elizabeth II **Subject:** Maundy **Obv:** Crowned bust right **Rev:** Crowned denomination divides date within wreath **Edge:** Plain

Date	Mintage	F	VF	XF	Unc	BU
2002 Proof	5,000	Value: 10.00				

KM# 451 3 PENCE
1.4400 g., 0.9990 Silver 0.0462 oz. ASW, 16.1 mm. **Ruler:** Elizabeth II **Subject:** Maundy **Obv:** Crowned bust right **Rev:** Crowned denomination divides date within wreath **Edge:** Plain

Date	Mintage	F	VF	XF	Unc	BU
2002 Proof	5,000	Value: 12.00				

KM# 452 4 PENCE
1.9300 g., 0.9990 Silver 0.0620 oz. ASW, 17.5 mm. **Ruler:** Elizabeth II **Subject:** Maundy **Obv:** Crowned bust right **Rev:** Crowned denomination divides date within wreath **Edge:** Plain

Date	Mintage	F	VF	XF	Unc	BU
2002 Proof	5,000	Value: 15.00				

PROOF SETS

KM#	Date	Mintage	Identification	Issue Price	Mkt Val
PS25	2002 (4)	5,000	KM#449-452 Maundy Set	—	45.00

COSTA RICA

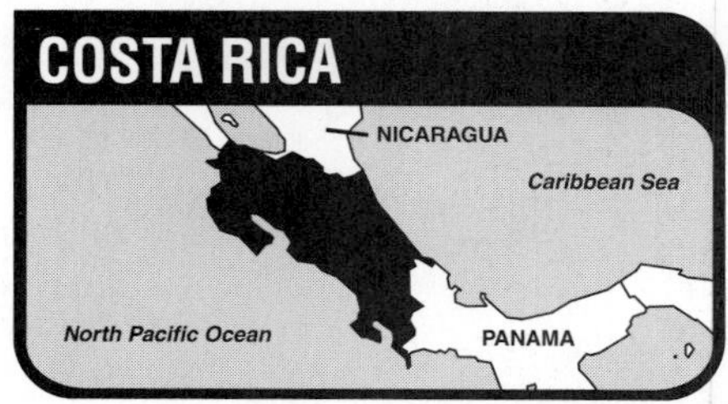

The Republic of Costa Rica, located in southern Central America between Nicaragua and Panama, has an area of 19,730 sq. mi. (51,100 sq. km.) and a population of 3.4 million. Capital: San Jose. Agriculture predominates; tourism and coffee, bananas, beef and sugar contribute heavily to the country's export earnings.

KEY TO MINT IDENTIFICATION

Key Letter	Mint
(a)	Armant Metalurgica, Santiago, Chile
(c)	Casa de Moneda, Mexico City Mint
(cc)	Casa de Moneda, Brazil
(co)	Colombia Republican Banko
(g)	Guatemala Mint
(i)	Italcambio Mint
(p) or (P)	Philadelphia Mint, USA
(r)	RCM – Royal Canadian Mint
(rm)	Royal Mint, London
(s)	San Francisco
(sj)	San Jose
(sm)	Sherrit Mint, Toronto
(v)	Vereingte Deutsche Metallwerke, Karlsruhe
(w)	Westain, Toronto

REPUBLIC

REFORM COINAGE

1920, 100 Centimos = 1 Colon

KM# 227a.2 5 COLONES

4.0000 g., Brass, 21.6 mm. **Obv:** National arms, date below, large letters in legend, large date, shield is not outlined **Rev:** Denomination above spray, B.C.C.R. below, thin '5' **Edge:** Segmented reeding

Date	Mintage	F	VF	XF	Unc	BU
2001(a)	—	—	—	—	0.65	1.00

KM# 227b 5 COLONES

0.9000 g., Aluminum, 21.4 mm. **Obv:** National arms **Obv. Legend:** REPUBLICA DE COSTA RICA **Rev:** Denomination above sprays, B.C.C.R. **Edge:** Plain

Date	Mintage	F	VF	XF	Unc	BU
2005	—	—	—	—	0.35	0.50
2008	—	—	—	—	0.35	0.50

KM# 228.2 10 COLONES

5.0000 g., Brass, 23.5 mm. **Obv:** National arms, date below, large legend and date, shield not outlined **Rev:** Denomination above spray, B.C.C.R. below, thick '1' **Edge:** Segmented reeding

Date	Mintage	F	VF	XF	Unc	BU
2002(a)	—	—	—	—	1.25	1.50

KM# 228b 10 COLONES

1.1300 g., Aluminum, 22.97 mm. **Obv:** National arms **Obv. Legend:** REPUBLICA DE COSTA RICA **Rev:** Denomination above sprays, B.C.C.R. **Edge:** Reeded

Date	Mintage	F	VF	XF	Unc	BU
2005	—	—	—	—	0.50	0.75
2008	—	—	—	—	0.50	0.75

KM# 229a 25 COLONES

7.0000 g., Brass, 25.4 mm. **Obv:** National arms **Obv. Legend:** REPUBLICA DE COSTA RICA **Rev:** Value above sprays, B.C.C.R. below **Edge:** Segmented reeding

Date	Mintage	F	VF	XF	Unc	BU
2001(a)	—	—	—	—	2.50	3.00
2003	—	—	—	—	2.50	3.00
2007	—	—	—	—	2.50	3.00

KM# 229a.1 25 COLONES

7.0000 g., Brass **Obv:** National arms, date below **Rev:** Value above sprays, B.C.C.R. below **Edge:** Plain

Date	Mintage	F	VF	XF	Unc	BU
2005	—	—	—	—	2.50	3.00

KM# 231.1a 50 COLONES

7.9200 g., Aluminum-Bronze, 27.5 mm. **Obv:** National arms, date below **Rev:** Value with spray below **Rev. Legend:** B. C. C. R. **Edge:** Segmented reeding

Date	Mintage	F	VF	XF	Unc	BU
2002	—	—	—	—	3.00	4.00

KM# 231.1b 50 COLONES

Brass Plated Steel, 27.5 mm. **Obv:** National arms above date **Rev:** Value above sprays, B.C.C.R. below

Date	Mintage	F	VF	XF	Unc	BU
2006 reeded edge	—	—	—	—	3.50	5.00
2007 plain edge	—	—	—	—	3.50	5.00

KM# 230a 100 COLONES

Brass, 29.5 mm. **Obv:** National arms, date below, large letters in legend and date, shield outlined **Rev:** Value above spray, B.C.C.R. below **Edge:** Segmented reeding

Date	Mintage	F	VF	XF	Unc	BU
2006(a)	—	—	—	—	4.50	6.00

KM# 240a 100 COLONES

8.8000 g., Brass Plated Steel, 29.4 mm. **Obv:** National arms above date **Rev:** Value above sprays **Edge:** Reeded

Date	Mintage	F	VF	XF	Unc	BU
2006	—	—	—	—	4.50	6.00
2007	—	—	—	—	4.50	6.00

KM# 239.1 500 COLONES

11.0000 g., Copper-Aluminum-Nickel, 32.9 mm. **Obv:** National arms **Obv. Legend:** REPUBLICA DE COSTA RICA **Rev:** Value above sprays, B.C.C.R. below, thick numerals **Edge:** Segmented reeding

Date	Mintage	F	VF	XF	Unc	BU
2003(a)	—	—	—	2.00	3.00	5.00
2005	—	—	—	2.00	3.00	5.00
2006	—	—	—	2.00	3.00	5.00

KM# 239.2 500 COLONES

Brass, 32.9 mm. **Obv:** National arms, date below **Obv. Legend:** REPUBLICA DE COSTA RICA **Rev:** Denomination above sprays, B.C.C.R. below, thin numerals **Edge:** Segmented reeding

Date	Mintage	F	VF	XF	Unc	BU
2003 Rare	100	—	—	—	—	250

KM# 239.1a 500 COLONES

Brass Plated Steel **Obv:** National arms, date below **Rev:** Value above sprays, B.C.C.R. below **Edge:** Segmented reeding

Date	Mintage	F	VF	XF	Unc	BU
2006	—	—	—	—	—	250
2007	—	—	—	—	—	250

The Republic of Croatia, (Hrvatska) bordered on the west by the Adriatic Sea and the northeast by Hungary, has an area of 21,829 sq. mi. (56,538 sq. km.) and a population of 4.7 million. Capital: Zagreb.

NOTE: Coin dates starting with 1994 are followed with a period. Example: 1994.

REPUBLIC

REFORM COINAGE

May 30, 1994 - 1000 Dinara = 1 Kuna; 100 Lipa = 1 Kuna

For the circulating minor coins, the reverse legend (name of item) is in Croatian for odd dated years and Latin for even dated years.

KM# 3 LIPA

0.7000 g., Aluminum, 17 mm. **Obv:** Denomination above crowned arms **Obv. Legend:** REPUBLIKA HRVATSKA **Rev:** Ears of corn, date below **Rev. Legend:** KUKURUZ **Edge:** Plain **Designer:** Kuzma Kovacic

Date	Mintage	F	VF	XF	Unc	BU
2001.	2,000,000	—	—	0.20	0.50	—
2001. Proof	1,000	Value: 2.50				
2003.	1,500,000	—	—	0.20	0.50	—
2003. Proof	1,000	Value: 2.50				
2005.	—	—	—	0.20	0.50	—
2005. Proof	—	Value: 2.00				
2007.	—	—	—	0.20	0.50	—
2007. Proof	—	Value: 2.00				
2009. In sets only	—	—	—	—	—	—

KM# 12 LIPA

0.7000 g., Aluminum, 17 mm. **Obv:** Denomination above crowned arms **Obv. Legend:** REPUBLIKA HRVATSKA **Rev:** Ears of corn, date below **Rev. Legend:** ZEA MAYS **Edge:** Plain

Date	Mintage	F	VF	XF	Unc	BU
2002.	3,000,000	—	—	0.40	1.00	—
2002. Proof	1,000	Value: 2.50				
2004.	2,000,000	—	—	0.40	1.00	—
2004. Proof	2,000	Value: 1.50				
2006.	—	—	—	0.40	1.00	—
2006. Proof	—	Value: 1.50				
2008.	—	—	—	0.40	1.00	—
2008. Proof	—	Value: 1.50				

KM# 4 2 LIPE

0.9200 g., Aluminum, 19 mm. **Obv:** Denomination above crowned arms on half braid **Obv. Legend:** REPUBLIKA HRVATSKA **Rev:** Grapevine, date below **Rev. Legend:** VINOVA LOZA **Edge:** Plain

Date	Mintage	F	VF	XF	Unc	BU
2001.	2,986,000	—	—	0.40	1.00	—
2001. Proof	1,000	Value: 3.00				
2003.	2,000,000	—	—	0.40	1.00	—
2003. Proof	1,000	Value: 3.00				
2005.	—	—	—	0.40	1.00	—
2005. Proof	—	Value: 3.00				
2007.	—	—	—	0.40	1.00	—
2007. Proof	—	Value: 3.00				
2009. In sets only	—	—	—	—	—	—

KM# 14 2 LIPE

0.9200 g., Aluminum, 19 mm. **Obv:** Denomination above crowned arms on half braid **Obv. Legend:** REPUBLIKA HRVATSKA **Rev:** Grapevine, date below **Rev. Legend:** VITIS VINIFERA **Edge:** Plain **Designer:** Kuzma Kovacic

Date	Mintage	F	VF	XF	Unc	BU
2002.	2,000,000	—	—	0.80	2.00	—
2002. Proof	1,000	Value: 3.00				
2004.	2,000,000	—	—	0.80	2.00	—
2004. Proof	2,000	Value: 2.50				
2006.	—	—	—	0.80	2.00	—
2006. Proof	—	Value: 2.50				
2008.	—	—	—	0.80	2.00	—
2008. Proof	—	Value: 2.50				

KM# 5 5 LIPA

2.5000 g., Brass Plated Steel, 18 mm. **Obv:** Denomination above crowned arms **Obv. Legend:** REPUBLIKA HRVATSKA **Rev:** Oak leaves, date below **Rev. Legend:** HRAST LUZNJAK **Edge:** Plain **Designer:** Kuzma Kovacic

Date	Mintage	F	VF	XF	Unc	BU
2001.	6,598,000	—	—	0.40	1.00	—
2001. Proof	1,000	Value: 4.00				
2003.	13,000,000	—	—	0.40	1.00	—
2003. Proof	2,000	Value: 3.50				
2005.	—	—	—	0.40	1.00	—
2005. Proof	—	Value: 3.50				
2007.	—	—	—	0.40	1.00	—
2007. Proof	—	Value: 3.50				
2009.	—	—	—	0.40	1.00	—

KM# 15 5 LIPA

2.5000 g., Brass Plated Steel, 18 mm. **Obv:** Denomination above crowned arms **Obv. Legend:** REPUBLIKA HRVATSKA **Rev:** Oak leaves, date below **Rev. Legend:** QUERCUS ROBUR **Edge:** Plain **Designer:** Kuzma Kovacic

Date	Mintage	F	VF	XF	Unc	BU
2002.	3,500,000	—	—	0.80	2.00	—
2002. Proof	1,000	Value: 4.00				
2004.	2,000,000	—	—	0.80	2.00	—
2004. Proof	2,000	Value: 3.00				
2006.	—	—	—	0.80	2.00	—
2006. Proof	—	Value: 3.00				
2008	—	—	—	0.80	2.00	—
2008. Proof	—	Value: 3.00				

KM# 6 10 LIPA

3.2500 g., Brass Plated Steel, 20 mm. **Obv:** Denomination above crowned arms **Obv. Legend:** REPUBLIKA HRVATSKA **Rev:** Tobacco plant, date below **Rev. Legend:** DUHAN **Edge:** Plain **Designer:** Kuzma Kovacic

Date	Mintage	F	VF	XF	Unc	BU
2001.	31,500,000	—	—	0.40	1.50	—
2001. Proof	1,000	Value: 5.00				
2003.	12,000,000	—	—	0.40	1.50	—
2003. Proof	1,000	Value: 5.00				
2005.	—	—	—	0.40	1.50	—
2005. Proof	—	Value: 5.00				
2007.	—	—	—	0.40	1.50	—
2007. Proof	—	Value: 5.00				
2009.	—	—	—	0.40	1.50	—

KM# 16 10 LIPA

3.2500 g., Brass Plated Steel, 20 mm. **Obv:** Denomination above crowned arms on half braid **Obv. Legend:** REPUBLIKA HRVATSKA **Rev:** Tobacco plant, date below **Rev. Legend:** NICOTIANA TABACUM **Edge:** Plain **Designer:** Kuzma Kovacic

Date	Mintage	F	VF	XF	Unc	BU
2002.	2,000,000	—	—	0.80	2.50	—
2002. Proof	1,000	Value: 5.00				
2004.	2,000,000	—	—	0.80	2.50	—
2004. Proof	2,000	Value: 4.50				
2006.	—	—	—	0.80	2.50	—
2006. Proof	—	Value: 4.50				
2008.	—	—	—	0.80	2.50	—
2008. Proof	—	Value: 4.50				

KM# 7 20 LIPA

2.9000 g., Nickel Plated Steel, 18.5 mm. **Obv:** Denomination above crowned arms on half braid **Obv. Legend:** REPUBLIKA HRVATSKA **Rev:** Olive branch, date below **Rev. Legend:** MASLINA **Edge:** Plain **Designer:** Kuzma Kovacic

Date	Mintage	F	VF	XF	Unc	BU
2001.	23,000,000	—	—	0.45	1.50	—
2001. Proof	1,000	Value: 5.00				
2003.	12,500,000	—	—	0.45	1.50	—
2003. Proof	1,000	Value: 5.00				
2005.	—	—	—	0.45	1.50	—
2005. Proof	—	Value: 5.00				
2007.	—	—	—	0.45	1.50	—
2007. Proof	—	Value: 5.00				
2009.	—	—	—	0.45	1.50	—

KM# 17 20 LIPA

2.9000 g., Nickel Plated Steel, 18.5 mm. **Obv:** Denomination above crowned arms on half braid **Obv. Legend:** REPUBLIKA HRVATSKA **Rev:** Olive branch, date below **Rev. Legend:** OLEA EUROPAEA **Edge:** Plain

Date	Mintage	F	VF	XF	Unc	BU
2002.	2,000,000	—	—	0.80	2.50	—
2002. Proof	1,000	Value: 5.00				
2004.	2,000,000	—	—	0.80	2.50	—
2004. Proof	2,000	Value: 4.50				
2006.	—	—	—	0.80	2.50	—
2006. Proof	—	Value: 4.50				
2008.	—	—	—	0.80	2.50	—
2008. Proof	—	Value: 4.50				

KM# 8 50 LIPA

3.6500 g., Nickel Plated Steel, 20.5 mm. **Obv:** Denomination above crowned arms on half braid **Obv. Legend:** REPUBLIKA HRVATSKA **Rev:** Flowers, date below **Rev. Legend:** VELEBITSKA DEGENIJA **Edge:** Plain **Designer:** Kuzma Kovacic

Date	Mintage	F	VF	XF	Unc	BU
2001.	5,500,000	—	—	0.60	1.50	—
2001. Proof	1,000	Value: 5.50				
2003.	8,000,000	—	—	0.60	1.50	—
2003. Proof	1,000	Value: 5.50				
2005.	—	—	—	0.60	1.50	—
2005. Proof	—	Value: 5.00				
2007.	—	—	—	0.60	1.50	—
2007. Proof	—	Value: 5.00				
2009.	—	—	—	0.60	1.50	—

KM# 19 50 LIPA

3.6500 g., Nickel Plated Steel, 20.5 mm. **Obv:** Denomination above crowned arms on half braid **Obv. Legend:** REPUBLIKA HRVATSKA **Rev:** Flowers, date below **Rev. Legend:** DEGENIA VELEBITICA **Edge:** Plain **Designer:** Kuzma Kovacic

Date	Mintage	F	VF	XF	Unc	BU
2002.	2,000,000	—	—	0.80	2.50	—
2002. Proof	1,000	Value: 5.00				
2004.	2,000,000	—	—	0.80	2.50	—
2004. Proof	2,000	Value: 4.50				
2006.	—	—	—	0.80	2.50	—
2006. Proof	—	Value: 4.50				
2008.	—	—	—	0.80	2.50	—
2008. Proof	—	Value: 4.50				

KM# 9.1 KUNA

5.0000 g., Copper-Nickel-Zinc, 22.5 mm. **Obv:** Marten back of numeral, arms divide branches below **Obv. Legend:** REPUBLIKA HRVATSKA **Rev:** Nightingale left, two dates **Rev. Legend:** SLAVUJ **Edge:** Reeded **Designer:** Kusma Kovacic

Date	Mintage	F	VF	XF	Unc	BU
2001.	1,000,000	—	—	0.75	1.65	2.00
2001. Proof	1,000	Value: 4.50				
2003.	2,000,000	—	—	0.75	1.65	2.00
2003. Proof	1,000	Value: 4.50				
2005.	—	—	—	0.75	1.65	2.00
2005. Proof	—	Value: 4.50				
2007.	—	—	—	0.75	1.65	2.00
2007. Proof	—	Value: 4.50				
2009.	—	—	—	0.75	1.65	2.00

KM# 9.2 KUNA

5.0000 g., Copper-Nickel-Zinc, 22.5 mm. **Obv:** Crowned arms flanked by sprays, denomination above on marten **Rev:** Nightingale, left, '1994' above, date below **Edge:** Reeded

Date	Mintage	F	VF	XF	Unc	BU
2001 Proof	—	Value: 4.00				

KM# 20.1 KUNA

5.0000 g., Copper-Nickel-Zinc, 22.5 mm. **Obv:** Marten back of numeral, arms divide branches below **Rev:** Nightingale left, date below **Rev. Legend:** Error spelling "LUSCINNIA" MEGARHYNCHOS **Edge:** Reeded **Designer:** Kuzma Kovacic **Note:** Formerly KM-20

Date	Mintage	F	VF	XF	Unc	BU
2002.	—	—	—	—	—	2.00

KM# 20.2 KUNA

5.0000 g., Copper-Nickel-Zinc, 22.5 mm. **Obv:** Marten back of numeral, arms divide branches below **Obv. Legend:** REPUBLIKA HRVATSKA **Rev:** Nightingale left, date below **Rev. Legend:** Correct spelling "LUSCINIA" MEGARHYNCHOS **Edge:** Reeded **Designer:** Kuzma Kovacic

Date	Mintage	F	VF	XF	Unc	BU
2002.	1,000,000	—	—	1.00	3.00	—
2002. Proof	1,000	Value: 5.00				
2006.	—	—	—	1.00	3.00	—
2006. Proof	—	Value: 5.00				
2008.	—	—	—	1.00	3.00	—
2008. Proof	—	Value: 5.00				

KM# 79 KUNA

5.0000 g., Copper-Nickel-Zinc, 22.5 mm. **Subject:** 10th Anniversary of National Currency **Obv:** Crowned arms flanked by sprays, denomination above on marten **Obv. Legend:** REPUBLIKA HRVATSKA **Rev:** Nightingale left, date below **Rev. Legend:** MEGARHYNCHOS **Edge:** Reeded

Date	Mintage	F	VF	XF	Unc	BU
ND(2004)	30,000	—	—	1.00	3.00	—
ND(2004) Proof	2,000	Value: 5.00				

KM# 10 2 KUNE

6.2000 g., Copper-Nickel-Zinc, 24.5 mm. **Obv:** Marten back of numeral, arms divide branches below **Obv. Legend:** REPUBLIKA HRVATSKA **Rev:** Bluefin tuna right, date below **Rev. Legend:** TUNJ **Edge:** Reeded **Designer:** Kuzma Kovacic

Date	Mintage	F	VF	XF	Unc	BU
2001.	1,250,000	—	—	1.00	2.00	—
2001. Proof	1,000	Value: 6.50				
2003.	7,250,000	—	—	1.00	2.00	—
2003. Proof	1,000	Value: 6.50				
2005.	—	—	—	1.00	2.00	—
2005. Proof	—	Value: 6.50				
2007.	—	—	—	1.00	2.00	—
2007. Proof	—	Value: 6.50				
2009.	—	—	—	1.00	2.00	—

KM# 21 2 KUNE

6.2000 g., Copper-Nickel-Zinc, 24.5 mm. **Obv:** Marten back of numeral, arms divide branches below **Obv. Legend:** REPUBLIKA HRVATSKA **Rev:** Bluefin tuna right, date below **Rev. Legend:** THUNNUS - THYNNUS **Edge:** Reeded **Designer:** Kuzma Kovacic

Date	Mintage	F	VF	XF	Unc	BU
2002.	1,000,000	—	—	1.50	3.00	—
2002. Proof	1,000	Value: 6.00				
2004.	2,000,000	—	—	1.50	3.00	—
2004. Proof	2,000	Value: 5.50				
2006.	—	—	—	1.50	3.00	—
2006. Proof	—	Value: 5.50				
2008.	—	—	—	1.50	3.00	—
2008. Proof	—	Value: 5.50				

KM# 11 5 KUNA

7.4500 g., Copper-Nickel-Zinc, 26.7 mm. **Obv:** Marten back of numeral, arms divide branches below **Obv. Legend:** REPUBLIKA HRVATSKA **Rev:** Brown bear left, date below **Rev. Legend:** MRKI MEDVJED **Edge:** Reeded

Date	Mintage	F	VF	XF	Unc	BU
2001.	17,300,000	—	—	1.50	5.00	10.00
2001. Proof	1,000	Value: 9.00				
2003.	1,000,000	—	—	1.50	5.00	10.00
2003. Proof	1,000	Value: 9.00				
2005.	—	—	—	1.50	5.00	10.00
2005. Proof	—	Value: 9.00				
2007.	—	—	—	1.50	5.00	10.00
2007. Proof	—	Value: 9.00				
2009.	—	—	—	1.50	5.00	10.00

KM# 23 5 KUNA

7.4500 g., Copper-Nickel-Zinc, 26.5 mm. **Obv:** Marten back of numeral, arms divide branches below **Obv. Legend:** REPUBLIKA HRVATSKA **Rev:** Brown bear left, date below **Rev. Legend:** URSUS ARCTOS **Edge:** Reeded

Date	Mintage	F	VF	XF	Unc	BU
2002.	2,000,000	—	—	2.00	5.00	9.00
2002. Proof	1,000	Value: 9.00				
2004.	2,000,000	—	—	2.00	5.00	9.00
2004. Proof	2,000	Value: 8.00				
2006.	—	—	—	2.00	5.00	9.00
2006. Proof	—	Value: 8.00				
2008.	—	—	—	2.00	5.00	9.00
2008. Proof	—	Value: 8.00				

KM# 66 25 KUNA

12.7500 g., Bi-Metallic Brass center in Copper-Nickel ring, 32 mm. **Subject:** 10th Anniversary of International Recognition **Obv:** Denomination in 3-D on outlined marten within circle, arms divide sprays below **Rev:** National map **Edge:** Plain **Shape:** 12-sided

Date	Mintage	F	VF	XF	Unc	BU
ND(2002)	200,000	—	—	—	8.50	—

KM# 78 25 KUNA

12.7500 g., Bi-Metallic Brass center in Copper-Nickel ring, 32 mm. **Subject:** Croatian European Union Candidacy **Obv:** Denomination in 3-D on outlined marten within circle, arms divide sprays below **Rev:** Joined squares within circle of stars **Edge:** Plain **Shape:** 12-sided

Date	Mintage	F	VF	XF	Unc	BU
ND (2004)	30,000	—	—	—	10.00	—
ND (2004) Proof	—	Value: 25.00				

KM# 83 150 KUNA

24.0000 g., 0.9250 Silver 0.7137 oz. ASW, 37 mm. **Subject:** 2006 Winter Olympics - Italy **Obv:** National arms below denomination **Rev:** Slalom skiing

Date	Mintage	F	VF	XF	Unc	BU
ND(2006) Proof	15,000	Value: 40.00				

KM# 84 150 KUNA

24.0000 g., 0.9250 Silver 0.7137 oz. ASW, 37 mm. **Subject:** 2006 World Soccer Championship - Germany **Obv:** National arms below denomination **Rev:** Soccer player

Date	Mintage	F	VF	XF	Unc	BU
ND(2006) Proof	50,000	Value: 35.00				

KM# 85 150 KUNA

24.0000 g., 0.9250 Silver 0.7137 oz. ASW, 37 mm. **Subject:** 2006 World Soccer Championship - Germany **Obv:** National arms above denomination **Rev:** Vignette

Date	Mintage	F	VF	XF	Unc	BU
ND(2006) Proof	10,000	Value: 45.00				

KM# 86 150 KUNA

24.0000 g., 0.9250 Silver 0.7137 oz. ASW, 37 mm. **Subject:** 150th Anniversary - Birth of Nikola Tesla **Obv:** National arms above induction motor and denomination **Rev:** Bust of Tesla

Date	Mintage	F	VF	XF	Unc	BU
ND(2006) Proof	5,000	Value: 50.00				

KM# 87 150 KUNA

24.0000 g., 0.9250 Silver 0.7137 oz. ASW, 37 mm. **Issuer:** Croatian National Bank **Subject:** 2008 Olympic Games - Peoples Republic of China **Obv:** National arms, value in laurel wreath **Rev:** T'ai-ho Tien gate in Beijing, athlete **Edge:** Plain **Edge Lettering:** Ag 925/1000 24 g 37 mm PP HNZ

Date	Mintage	F	VF	XF	Unc	BU
ND(2006) Proof	20,000	Value: 40.00				

KM# 88 150 KUNA

24.0000 g., 0.9250 Silver 0.7137 oz. ASW, 37 mm. **Subject:** Ican Mestrovic **Obv:** Squares and shamrocks **Obv. Designer:** Damir Matauzic **Rev:** Female kneeling with Irish harp

Date	Mintage	F	VF	XF	Unc	BU
2007	4,000	—	—	—	—	45.00

KM# 89 150 KUNA

24.0000 g., 0.9250 Silver 0.7137 oz. ASW, 37 mm. **Subject:** Benedikt Kotruljevic **Obv:** Pile of coins **Obv. Designer:** Damir Matausic **Rev:** Bust right

Date	Mintage	F	VF	XF	Unc	BU
2007	10,000	—	—	—	—	40.00

KM# 90 150 KUNA

24.0000 g., 0.9250 Silver 0.7137 oz. ASW, 37 mm. **Subject:** Historic Ships - Dubrovnik Karaka **Obv:** Sail within compass **Obv. Designer:** Matej Pasalic **Rev:** Ship

Date	Mintage	F	VF	XF	Unc	BU
2007	10,000	—	—	—	—	40.00

KM# 91 1000 KUNA

7.0000 g., 0.9860 Gold 0.2219 oz. AGW, 22 mm. **Subject:** Andrija Monorovicic, 150th Anniversary of Birth **Obv:** Globe bisected showing layers **Obv. Designer:** Stjipan Divkovic **Rev:** Bust facing

Date	Mintage	F	VF	XF	Unc	BU
2007	2,000	—	—	—	—	350

KM# 92 1000 KUNA

7.0000 g., 0.9860 Gold 0.2219 oz. AGW, 22 mm. **Subject:** Marin Drzic **Obv:** Shield flanked by comedy and tragedy masks **Rev:** Half-length figure right

Date	Mintage	F	VF	XF	Unc	BU
2008	2,000	—	—	—	—	350

MINT SETS

KM#	Date	Mintage	Identification	Issue Price	Mkt Val
MS2	2002 (9)	—	KM#12, 14-17, 19, 20.1, 21, 23	—	25.00

PROOF SETS

KM#	Date	Mintage	Identification	Issue Price	Mkt Val
PS32	2001 (9)	—	KM#3-8, 9.2, 10, 11	—	45.00
PS33	2003 (9)	—	KM#3-8, 9.1, 10, 11	—	45.00
PS34	2004 (9)	—	KM#12, 14-17, 19, 21, 23, 79	—	40.00
PS35	2005 (9)	—	KM#3-8, 9.1, 10-11	—	45.00
PS36	2006 (9)	—	KM#12, 14-17, 19, 20.2, 21, 23	—	40.00
PS37	2007 (9)	—	KM#3-8, 9.1, 10-11	—	45.00
PS38	2008 (9)	—	KM#12, 14-17, 19, 20.2, 21, 23	—	40.00

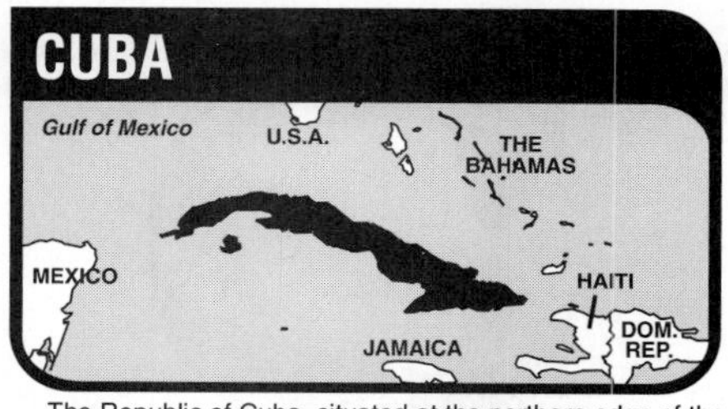

The Republic of Cuba, situated at the northern edge of the Caribbean Sea about 90 miles (145 km.) south of Florida, has an area of 42,804 sq. mi. (110,860 sq. km.) and a population of *11.2 million. Capital: Havana. The Cuban economy is based on the cultivation and refining of sugar, which provides 80 percent of export earnings.

MINT MARK

Key - Havana, 1977-

MONETARY SYSTEM

100 Centavos = 1 Peso

SECOND REPUBLIC

1962 - Present

DECIMAL COINAGE

KM# 33.3 CENTAVO

0.7500 g., Aluminum, 16.76 mm. **Obv:** Cuban arms within wreath, denomination below **Rev:** Roman denomination within circle of star, date below **Edge:** Plain **Note:** Shield varieties exist.

Date	Mintage	F	VF	XF	Unc	BU
2001	—	—	0.10	0.40	0.80	1.75
2003	—	—	0.10	0.40	0.80	1.75
2004	—	—	0.10	0.40	0.80	1.75
2005	—	—	0.10	0.40	0.80	1.75

KM# 34 5 CENTAVOS

1.5600 g., Aluminum, 21 mm. **Obv:** National arms within wreath, denomination below **Rev:** Roman denomination within circle of star, date below **Note:** Shield varieties exist.

Date	Mintage	F	VF	XF	Unc	BU
2001	6,703,331	—	0.10	0.25	0.75	1.50
2002	14,830,000	—	0.10	0.25	0.75	1.50
Note: High or low dates exist.						
2003	62,520,000	—	0.10	0.25	0.75	1.50
2004	62,520,000	—	0.10	0.25	0.75	1.50
2006	62,520,000	—	0.10	0.25	0.75	1.50
2007	62,520,000	—	0.10	0.25	0.75	1.50

KM# 35.2 20 CENTAVOS

Aluminum, 24 mm. **Obv:** National arms, revised shield **Rev:** Roman denomination within circle of star

Date	Mintage	F	VF	XF	Unc	BU
2002	—	4.00	7.00	10.00	15.00	—
Note: Large and small dates exist.						
2003	—	4.00	7.00	10.00	15.00	—
2005	—	4.00	7.00	10.00	15.00	—
2006	—	4.00	7.00	10.00	15.00	—

KM# 35.1 20 CENTAVOS

2.0000 g., Aluminum, 24 mm. **Obv:** Cuban arms within wreath, denomination below **Rev:** Roman denomination within circle of star, date below **Note:** Shield varieties exist.

Date	Mintage	F	VF	XF	Unc	BU
2002	25,000,000	—	0.50	1.00	2.00	4.00
2003	11,911,000	—	0.50	1.00	2.00	4.00
2005	—	—	0.50	1.00	2.00	4.00
2006	—	—	0.50	1.00	2.00	4.00
2007	—	—	0.50	1.00	2.00	4.00

KM# 834 PESO

Copper-Nickel, 32.65 mm. **Obv:** National arms **Rev:** Butterfly - multicolor **Rev. Legend:** FAUNA CUBANA - PAJERO CARPINTERO

Date	Mintage	F	VF	XF	Unc	BU
2001	—	—	—	—	—	15.00

KM# 844 PESO

26.0000 g., Copper-Nickel, 38 mm. **Subject:** Bolivar, 175th Anniversary of Liberation **Rev:** Bust

Date	Mintage	F	VF	XF	Unc	BU
2001	—	—	—	—	—	15.00

KM# 845 PESO

26.0000 g., Copper-Nickel, 38 mm. **Subject:** Bolivar - 175th Anniversary of Liberation **Rev:** Birthplace

Date	Mintage	F	VF	XF	Unc	BU
2001	—	—	—	—	—	15.00

KM# 846 PESO

Copper-Nickel, 38 mm. **Subject:** Boliver, 175th Anniversary of Liberation **Rev:** Battle scene

Date	Mintage	F	VF	XF	Unc	BU
2001	—	—	—	—	—	15.00

KM# 847 PESO

26.0000 g., Copper-Nickel, 38 mm. **Subject:** Cuban Fauna - Avellaneda Butterfly **Rev:** Butterfly

Date	Mintage	F	VF	XF	Unc	BU
2001	—	—	—	—	—	15.00

KM# 848 PESO

26.0000 g., Copper-Nickel, 38 mm. **Subject:** Global Conference Three

Date	Mintage	F	VF	XF	Unc	BU
2001	—	—	—	—	—	15.00

KM# 849 PESO

26.0000 g., Copper-Nickel, 38 mm. **Subject:** Monuments of Cuba **Rev:** Havana Cathedral

Date	Mintage	F	VF	XF	Unc	BU
2001	—	—	—	—	—	15.00

KM# 850 PESO

26.0000 g., Copper-Nickel, 38 mm. **Subject:** Monuments of Cuba **Rev:** Trinidad Cathedral

Date	Mintage	F	VF	XF	Unc	BU
2001	—	—	—	—	—	15.00

KM# 851 PESO

Copper-Nickel, 38 mm. **Subject:** Monuments of Cuba **Rev:** Templete

Date	Mintage	F	VF	XF	Unc	BU
2001	—	—	—	—	—	15.00

KM# 852 PESO

26.0000 g., Copper-Nickel, 38 mm. **Subject:** Playa Giron

Date	Mintage	F	VF	XF	Unc	BU
2001	—	—	—	—	—	15.00

KM# 829 PESO

13.0000 g., Copper-Nickel, 32.65 mm. **Obv:** National arms **Rev:** Carpenter bird perched - multicolor **Rev. Legend:** FAUNA CUBANA - PAJERO CARPINTERO **Edge:** Plain

Date	Mintage	F	VF	XF	Unc	BU
2001	—	—	—	—	15.00	—

KM# 347 PESO

5.5000 g., Brass Plated Steel, 24.4 mm. **Subject:** Jose Marti **Obv:** National arms within wreath, denomination below **Rev:** Smaller Bust facing, denomination at left **Rev. Legend:** PATRIA O MUERTE **Note:** Rim varieties exist.

Date	Mintage	F	VF	XF	Unc	BU
2001	—	—	—	1.00	2.00	4.00
2002	—	—	—	1.00	2.00	4.00

KM# 830 PESO

13.0000 g., Copper-Nickel, 32.65 mm. **Obv:** National arms **Rev:** Parrot perched - multicolor **Rev. Legend:** FAUNA CUBANA - COTORRA **Edge:** Plain

Date	Mintage	F	VF	XF	Unc	BU
2001	—	—	—	—	15.00	—

KM# 831 PESO

12.7000 g., Copper-Nickel, 32.5 mm. **Obv:** National arms **Rev:** Pink orchid - multicolor **Rev. Legend:** FLORA CUBANA - ORQUIDEAS **Edge:** Plain

Date	Mintage	F	VF	XF	Unc	BU
2001	—	—	—	—	20.00	—

KM# 832 PESO
12.7000 g., Copper-Nickel, 32.5 mm. **Obv:** National arms **Rev:** Yellow orchid - multicolor **Rev. Legend:** FLORA CUBANA - ORQUIDEAS **Edge:** Plain

Date	Mintage	F	VF	XF	Unc	BU
2001	—	—	—	—	20.00	—

KM# 833 PESO
12.7000 g., Copper-Nickel, 32.5 mm. **Obv:** National arms **Rev:** White orchid - multicolor **Rev. Legend:** FLORA CUBANA - ORQUIDEAS **Edge:** Plain

Date	Mintage	F	VF	XF	Unc	BU
2001	—	—	—	—	20.00	—

KM# 853 PESO
26.0000 g., Copper-Nickel, 38 mm. **Subject:** Engles

Date	Mintage	F	VF	XF	Unc	BU
2002	—	—	—	—	—	15.00

KM# 854 PESO
26.0000 g., Copper-Nickel, 38 mm. **Subject:** Lenin

Date	Mintage	F	VF	XF	Unc	BU
2002	—	—	—	—	—	15.00

KM# 855 PESO
26.0000 g., Copper-Nickel, 38 mm. **Subject:** Mao Tse Tung

Date	Mintage	F	VF	XF	Unc	BU
2002	—	—	—	—	—	15.00

KM# 856 PESO
26.0000 g., Copper-Nickel, 38 mm. **Subject:** Karl Marx

Date	Mintage	F	VF	XF	Unc	BU
2002	—	—	—	—	—	15.00

KM# 857 PESO
26.0000 g., Copper-Nickel, 38 mm. **Subject:** Che Guevara, 75th Anniversary of Birth

Date	Mintage	F	VF	XF	Unc	BU
2003	—	—	—	—	—	15.00

KM# 858 PESO
26.0000 g., Copper-Nickel, 38 mm. **Subject:** Che Guevara, 75th Anniversary of Birth

Date	Mintage	F	VF	XF	Unc	BU
2003	—	—	—	—	—	15.00

KM# 859 PESO
26.0000 g., Copper-Nickel, 38 mm. **Subject:** Fauna - Hawk Pilgrin

Date	Mintage	F	VF	XF	Unc	BU
2004	—	—	—	—	—	15.00

KM# 860 PESO
26.0000 g., Copper-Nickel, 38 mm. **Subject:** Fauna Iberian Lynx

Date	Mintage	F	VF	XF	Unc	BU
2004	—	—	—	—	—	15.00

KM# 861 PESO
26.0000 g., Copper-Nickel, 38 mm. **Subject:** Fauna - Imperial Eagle

Date	Mintage	F	VF	XF	Unc	BU
2004	—	—	—	—	—	15.00

KM# 862 PESO
26.0000 g., Copper-Nickel, 38 mm. **Subject:** Fauna Lobo Gris

Date	Mintage	F	VF	XF	Unc	BU
2004	—	—	—	—	—	15.00

KM# 863 PESO
26.0000 g., Copper-Nickel, 38 mm. **Subject:** Fauna - Oso Pards

Date	Mintage	F	VF	XF	Unc	BU
2004	—	—	—	—	—	15.00

KM# 864 PESO
26.0000 g., Copper-Nickel, 38 mm. **Subject:** Fauna - Osprey

Date	Mintage	F	VF	XF	Unc	BU
2004	—	—	—	—	—	15.00

KM# 865 PESO
Copper-Nickel, 38 mm. **Subject:** Cuban Tobacco

Date	Mintage	F	VF	XF	Unc	BU
2005	—	—	—	—	—	15.00

KM# 866 PESO
26.0000 g., Copper-Nickel, 38 mm. **Subject:** Tropical Fish - Pygoplites

Date	Mintage	F	VF	XF	Unc	BU
2005	—	—	—	—	—	15.00

KM# 867 PESO
26.0000 g., Copper-Nickel, 38 mm. **Subject:** Tropical Fish - Zanclus

Date	Mintage	F	VF	XF	Unc	BU
2005	—	—	—	—	—	15.00

KM# 868 PESO
26.0000 g., Copper-Nickel, 38 mm. **Subject:** Tropical Fish - Rhinecanthus

Date	Mintage	F	VF	XF	Unc	BU
2005	—	—	—	—	—	15.00

KM# 869 PESO
26.0000 g., Copper-Nickel, 38 mm. **Subject:** Toucan

Date	Mintage	F	VF	XF	Unc	BU
2006	—	—	—	—	—	15.00

KM# 870 PESO
26.0000 g., Copper-Nickel, 38 mm. **Subject:** 29th Summer Olympics

Date	Mintage	F	VF	XF	Unc	BU
2006	—	—	—	—	—	15.00

KM# 871 PESO
26.0000 g., Copper-Nickel, 38 mm. **Subject:** Che Guevara, 40th Anniversary of his Death

Date	Mintage	F	VF	XF	Unc	BU
2007	—	—	—	—	—	15.00

KM# 872 PESO
26.0000 g., Copper-Nickel, 38 mm. **Obv:** Che Guevara, 40th Anniversary of his Death

Date	Mintage	F	VF	XF	Unc	BU
2007	—	—	—	—	—	15.00

KM# 873 PESO
26.0000 g., Copper-Nickel **Subject:** Fauna - Buitre (Condor)

Date	Mintage	F	VF	XF	Unc	BU
2007	—	—	—	—	—	15.00

KM# 874 PESO
26.0000 g., Copper-Nickel, 38 mm. **Subject:** Fauna - Burro

Date	Mintage	F	VF	XF	Unc	BU
2007	—	—	—	—	—	15.00

KM# 875 PESO
26.0000 g., Copper-Nickel, 38 mm. **Subject:** Fauna - Cobra Montesa

Date	Mintage	F	VF	XF	Unc	BU
2007	—	—	—	—	—	15.00

KM# 876 PESO
26.0000 g., Copper-Nickel **Subject:** Fauna - Gato Montes

Date	Mintage	F	VF	XF	Unc	BU
2007	—	—	—	—	—	15.00

KM# 877 PESO
26.0000 g., Copper-Nickel, 38 mm. **Subject:** Fauma - Mastin Espanol

Date	Mintage	F	VF	XF	Unc	BU
2007	—	—	—	—	—	15.00

KM# 878 PESO
26.0000 g., Copper-Nickel, 26 mm. **Subject:** Fauna - Urogallo

Date	Mintage	F	VF	XF	Unc	BU
2007	—	—	—	—	—	15.00

KM# 879 PESO
26.0000 g., Copper-Nickel, 38 mm. **Subject:** Fortress - El Morro

Date	Mintage	F	VF	XF	Unc	BU
2007	—	—	—	—	—	15.00

KM# 880 PESO
26.0000 g., Copper-Nickel, 38 mm. **Subject:** Fortress - La Fuerza

Date	Mintage	F	VF	XF	Unc	BU
2007	—	—	—	—	—	15.00

KM# 881 PESO
26.0000 g., Copper-Nickel, 38 mm. **Subject:** Fortress - La Punta

Date	Mintage	F	VF	XF	Unc	BU
2007	—	—	—	—	—	15.00

KM# 882 PESO
26.0000 g., Copper-Nickel, 38 mm. **Subject:** Garibaldi

Date	Mintage	F	VF	XF	Unc	BU
2007	—	—	—	—	—	15.00

KM# 883 PESO
26.0000 g., Copper-Nickel, 38 mm. **Subject:** Santa Ana Ship

Date	Mintage	F	VF	XF	Unc	BU
2007	—	—	—	—	—	15.00

KM# 884 PESO
26.0000 g., Copper-Nickel, 38 mm. **Subject:** Sputnik

Date	Mintage	F	VF	XF	Unc	BU
2007	—	—	—	—	—	15.00

KM# 901 PESO
38.0000 g., Copper-Nickel, 38 mm. **Subject:** Ship - Principe Asturias

Date	Mintage	F	VF	XF	Unc	BU
2008	—	—	—	—	15.00	—

KM# 902 PESO
26.0000 g., Copper-Nickel, 38 mm. **Subject:** Ship San Carlos

Date	Mintage	F	VF	XF	Unc	BU
2008	—	—	—	—	15.00	—

KM# 903 PESO
38.0000 g., Copper-Nickel, 38 mm. **Subject:** Ship- San Hermene

Date	Mintage	F	VF	XF	Unc	BU
2008	—	—	—	—	—	15.00

KM# 907 PESO
26.0000 g., Copper-Nickel, 38 mm. **Subject:** Revolution, 50th Anniversary

Date	Mintage	F	VF	XF	Unc	BU
2009	—	—	—	—	—	15.00

KM# 908 PESO
26.0000 g., Copper-Nickel, 38 mm. **Subject:** Fidel & Raul Castro

Date	Mintage	F	VF	XF	Unc	BU
2009	—	—	—	—	—	15.00

KM# 909 PESO
26.0000 g., Copper-Nickel, 38 mm. **Subject:** Fidel and Raul Castro

Date	Mintage	F	VF	XF	Unc	BU
2009	—	—	—	—	—	15.00

KM# 910 PESO
26.0000 g., Copper-Nickel, 38 mm. **Subject:** Manatee

Date	Mintage	F	VF	XF	Unc	BU
2009	—	—	—	—	—	15.00

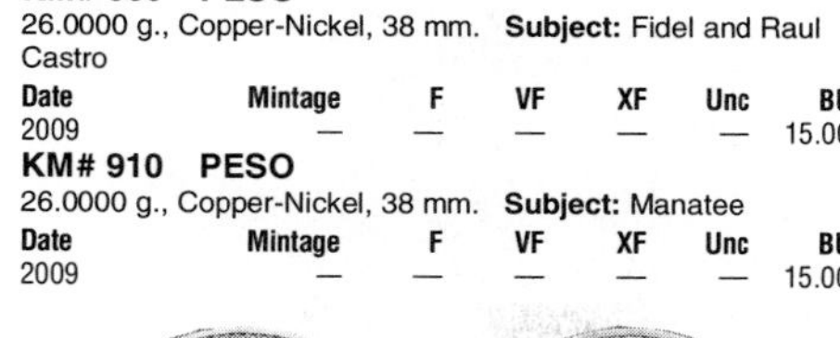

KM# 346a 3 PESOS
8.2000 g., Nickel Clad Steel, 26.3 mm. **Obv:** National arms within wreath, denomination below **Rev:** Head facing, date below **Note:** Shield varieties exist.

Date	Mintage	F	VF	XF	Unc	BU
2002	—	—	—	2.50	5.00	7.00

KM# 739 5 PESOS
1.2400 g., Gold, 14 mm. **Subject:** Wonders of the Ancient World **Obv:** Cuban arms **Rev:** Ancient lighthouse of Alexandria

Date	Mintage	F	VF	XF	Unc	BU
2005 Proof	5,000	Value: 85.00				

KM# 740 5 PESOS
1.2400 g., Gold, 14 mm. **Subject:** Wonders of the Ancient World **Obv:** Cuban arms **Rev:** Colossus of Rhodes

Date	Mintage	F	VF	XF	Unc	BU
2005 Proof	5,000	Value: 70.00				

KM# 741 5 PESOS
1.2400 g., Gold, 14 mm. **Subject:** Wonders of the Ancient World **Obv:** Cuban arms **Rev:** Hanging Gardens of Babylon

Date	Mintage	F	VF	XF	Unc	BU
2005 Proof	5,000	Value: 70.00				

KM# 742 5 PESOS
1.2400 g., Gold, 14 mm. **Subject:** Wonders of the Ancient World **Obv:** Cuban arms **Rev:** Egyptian Pyramids

Date	Mintage	F	VF	XF	Unc	BU
2005	5,000	Value: 70.00				

KM# 743 5 PESOS
1.2400 g., Gold, 14 mm. **Subject:** Wonders of the Ancient World **Obv:** Cuban arms **Rev:** Temple of Artemis

Date	Mintage	F	VF	XF	Unc	BU
2005 Proof	5,000	Value: 70.00				

KM# 744 5 PESOS
1.2400 g., Gold, 14 mm. **Subject:** Wonders of the Ancient World **Obv:** Cuban arms **Rev:** Statue of Jupiter

Date	Mintage	F	VF	XF	Unc	BU
2005	5,000	Value: 70.00				

KM# 745 5 PESOS
1.2400 g., Gold, 14 mm. **Subject:** Wonders of the Ancient World **Obv:** Cuban arms **Rev:** Mausoleum of Halicarnas

Date	Mintage	F	VF	XF	Unc	BU
2005 Proof	5,000	Value: 70.00				

KM# 746 5 PESOS
1.2400 g., Gold, 14 mm. **Obv:** Cuban arms **Rev:** Cortes, Montezuma and Aztec Pyramid

Date	Mintage	F	VF	XF	Unc	BU
2005 Proof	15,000	Value: 70.00				

KM# 885 5 PESOS
20.0000 g., Silver, 38 mm. **Subject:** Che Guevara, 40th Anniversary of his Death

Date	Mintage	F	VF	XF	Unc	BU
2007 Proof	—	Value: 45.00				

KM# 763 10 PESOS
20.0000 g., 0.9990 Silver 0.6423 oz. ASW, 38 mm. **Subject:** Third Globalization Conference **Obv:** Cuban arms **Rev:** World map

Date	Mintage	F	VF	XF	Unc	BU
2001 Proof	100	Value: 200				

KM# 764 10 PESOS
20.0000 g., 0.9990 Silver 0.6423 oz. ASW, 38 mm. **Subject:** 40th Anniversary - Battle of Giron **Obv:** Cuban arms **Rev:** Soldiers on tank

Date	Mintage	F	VF	XF	Unc	BU
2001 Proof	3,000	Value: 45.00				

KM# 765 10 PESOS
31.1035 g., 0.9990 Silver 0.9990 oz. ASW, 38 mm. **Subject:** 106th Anniversary - Jose Marti's **Obv:** Cuban arms **Rev:** Monument

Date	Mintage	F	VF	XF	Unc	BU
2001 Proof	2,000	Value: 50.00				

KM# 762 10 PESOS
31.1035 g., 0.9990 Silver 0.9990 oz. ASW, 38 mm. **Obv:** Cuban arms **Rev:** Two Bee hummingbirds

Date	Mintage	F	VF	XF	Unc	BU
2001 Proof	20,000	Value: 40.00				

KM# 766 10 PESOS
15.0000 g., 0.9990 Silver 0.4818 oz. ASW, 35 mm. **Subject:** Cuban Fauna **Obv:** Cuban arms **Rev:** Red-splashed Sulphur butterfly

Date	Mintage	F	VF	XF	Unc	BU
2001 Proof	5,000	Value: 40.00				

KM# 767 10 PESOS
15.0000 g., 0.9990 Silver 0.4818 oz. ASW, 35 mm. **Subject:** Cuban Fauna **Obv:** Cuban arms **Rev:** Cuban Parrot

Date	Mintage	F	VF	XF	Unc	BU
2001 Proof	5,000	Value: 40.00				

KM# 768 10 PESOS
15.0000 g., 0.9990 Silver 0.4818 oz. ASW, 35 mm. **Obv:** National arms **Rev:** Cuban (Green) woodpecker

Date	Mintage	F	VF	XF	Unc	BU
2001 Proof	5,000	Value: 40.00				

KM# 769 10 PESOS
15.0000 g., 0.9990 Silver 0.4818 oz. ASW, 35 mm. **Obv:** Cuban arms **Rev:** Multicolor white orchid

Date	Mintage	F	VF	XF	Unc	BU
2001 Proof	5,000	Value: 35.00				

KM# 770 10 PESOS
15.0000 g., 0.9990 Silver 0.4818 oz. ASW, 35 mm. **Subject:** Cuban Flora **Obv:** Cuban arms **Rev:** Multicolor yellow orchid

Date	Mintage	F	VF	XF	Unc	BU
2001 Proof	5,000	Value: 35.00				

KM# 771 10 PESOS
15.0000 g., 0.9990 Silver 0.4818 oz. ASW, 35 mm. **Subject:** Cuban Flora **Obv:** Cuban arms **Rev:** Multicolor pink orchid

Date	Mintage	F	VF	XF	Unc	BU
2001 Proof	5,000	Value: 35.00				

KM# 772 10 PESOS
31.1035 g., 0.9990 Silver 0.9990 oz. ASW, 38 mm. **Obv:** Cuban arms **Rev:** Multicolor Santa Maria

Date	Mintage	F	VF	XF	Unc	BU
2001 Proof	4,000	Value: 55.00				

KM# 773 10 PESOS
15.0000 g., 0.9990 Silver 0.4818 oz. ASW, 35 mm. **Subject:** World Cup Soccer Champions **Obv:** Cuban arms **Rev:** Soccer player and stadium

Date	Mintage	F	VF	XF	Unc	BU
2001 Proof	7,500	Value: 35.00				

KM# 774 10 PESOS
20.0000 g., 0.9990 Silver 0.6423 oz. ASW, 38 mm. **Subject:** Cuban Monuments **Obv:** Cuban arms **Rev:** Trinidad street view

Date	Mintage	F	VF	XF	Unc	BU
2001 Proof	5,000	Value: 45.00				

KM# 775 10 PESOS
20.0000 g., 0.9990 Silver 0.6423 oz. ASW, 38 mm. **Subject:** Cuban Monuments **Obv:** Cuban arms **Rev:** Havana Cathedral

Date	Mintage	F	VF	XF	Unc	BU
2001 Proof	5,000	Value: 45.00				

KM# 776 10 PESOS
20.0000 g., 0.9990 Silver 0.6423 oz. ASW, 38 mm. **Subject:** Cuban Monuments **Obv:** Cuban arms **Rev:** Template building

Date	Mintage	F	VF	XF	Unc	BU
2001 Proof	5,000	Value: 45.00				

KM# 777 10 PESOS
31.1035 g., 0.9990 Silver 0.9990 oz. ASW, 38 mm. **Obv:** Cuban arms **Rev:** Bolivar standing at his birthplace

Date	Mintage	F	VF	XF	Unc	BU
2001 Proof	5,000	Value: 50.00				

KM# 828 10 PESOS
20.0000 g., 0.9990 Silver 0.6423 oz. ASW **Subject:** XVII World Soccer Championship - Korea and Japan 2002 **Obv:** National arms

Date	Mintage	F	VF	XF	Unc	BU
2001 proof	—	Value: 50.00				

KM# 778 10 PESOS
31.1035 g., 0.9990 Silver 0.9990 oz. ASW, 38 mm. **Obv:** Cuban arms **Rev:** Bolivar and map of South America

Date	Mintage	F	VF	XF	Unc	BU
2001 Proof	5,000	Value: 50.00				

KM# 779 10 PESOS
31.1035 g., 0.9990 Silver 0.9990 oz. ASW, 38 mm. **Subject:** 180th Anniversary of the Battle of Carabobo **Obv:** Cuban arms **Rev:** Bolivar leading troops

Date	Mintage	F	VF	XF	Unc	BU
2001 Proof	5,000	Value: 50.00				

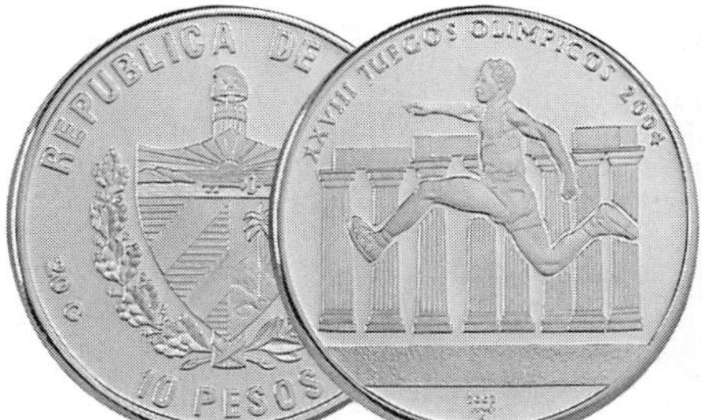

KM# 734 10 PESOS
20.0000 g., 0.9990 Silver 0.6423 oz. ASW, 37.9 mm. **Subject:** Olympics **Obv:** Cuban arms **Rev:** Runner and ancient ruins **Edge:** Reeded

Date	Mintage	F	VF	XF	Unc	BU
2002 Proof	—	Value: 40.00				

KM# 780 10 PESOS
20.0000 g., 0.9990 Silver 0.6423 oz. ASW, 38 mm. **Subject:** World Cup Soccer Champions **Obv:** Cuban arms **Rev:** Soccer player and map above "CHILE 1962"

Date	Mintage	F	VF	XF	Unc	BU
2002 Proof	7,500	Value: 40.00				

KM# 781 10 PESOS
20.0000 g., 0.9990 Silver 0.6423 oz. ASW, 38 mm. **Subject:** World Cup Soccer Champions **Obv:** Cuban arms **Rev:** Soccer player and Cuauhtemoc head below MEXICO 1970

Date	Mintage	F	VF	XF	Unc	BU
2002 Proof	7,500	Value: 40.00				

KM# 782 10 PESOS
20.0000 g., 0.9990 Silver 0.6423 oz. ASW, 38 mm. **Obv:** Cuban arms **Rev:** Vasco De Gama and ship

Date	Mintage	F	VF	XF	Unc	BU
2002 Proof	5,000	Value: 45.00				

KM# 783 10 PESOS
20.0000 g., 0.9990 Silver 0.6423 oz. ASW, 38 mm. **Obv:** Cuban arms **Rev:** Americo Vespucio and ship

Date	Mintage	F	VF	XF	Unc	BU
2002 Proof	5,000	Value: 45.00				

KM# 784 10 PESOS
31.1035 g., 0.9990 Silver 0.9990 oz. ASW, 38 mm. **Subject:** Leaders of Communism **Obv:** Cuban arms **Rev:** Head of Mao Tse Tung left

Date	Mintage	F	VF	XF	Unc	BU
2002 Proof	2,000	Value: 55.00				

KM# 785 10 PESOS
31.1035 g., 0.9990 Silver 0.9990 oz. ASW, 38 mm. **Subject:** Leaders of Communism **Obv:** Cuban arms **Rev:** Head of Karl Marx 3/4 left

Date	Mintage	F	VF	XF	Unc	BU
2002 Proof	2,000	Value: 55.00				

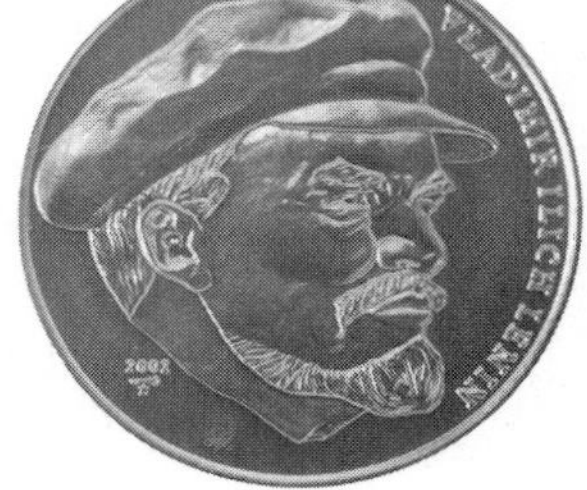

KM# 786 10 PESOS
31.1035 g., 0.9990 Silver 0.9990 oz. ASW, 38 mm. **Subject:** Leaders of Communism **Obv:** Cuban arms **Rev:** Head of Vladimir Lenin right

Date	Mintage	F	VF	XF	Unc	BU
2002 Proof	2,000	Value: 65.00				

KM# 787 10 PESOS
31.1035 g., 0.9990 Silver 0.9990 oz. ASW, 38 mm. **Subject:** Leaders of Communism **Obv:** Cuban arms **Rev:** Head of Federico Engels 3/4 right

Date	Mintage	F	VF	XF	Unc	BU
2002 Proof	2,000	Value: 55.00				

KM# 788 10 PESOS
27.0000 g., 0.9990 Silver 0.8672 oz. ASW, 40 mm. **Subject:** IBERO-AMERICA Series **Obv:** Circle of arms around Cuban arms **Rev:** Santisima Trinidad ship

Date	Mintage	F	VF	XF	Unc	BU
2002 Proof	14,000	Value: 50.00				

KM# 789 10 PESOS
31.1035 g., 0.9990 Silver 0.9990 oz. ASW, 38 mm. **Subject:** Jose Marti's 150th Birthday **Obv:** Cuban arms **Rev:** Numbered infield behind head right

Date	Mintage	F	VF	XF	Unc	BU
2003 Proof	150	Value: 150				

KM# 794 10 PESOS
20.0000 g., 0.9990 Silver 0.6423 oz. ASW, 38 mm. **Subject:** Endangered Wildlife **Obv:** Cuban arms **Rev:** Cuban Crocodile

Date	Mintage	F	VF	XF	Unc	BU
2003 Proof	5,000	Value: 50.00				

KM# 795 10 PESOS
20.0000 g., 0.9990 Silver 0.6423 oz. ASW, 38 mm. **Subject:** Endangered Wildlife **Obv:** Cuban arms **Rev:** Ocelot

Date	Mintage	F	VF	XF	Unc	BU
2003 Proof	5,000	Value: 50.00				

KM# 792 10 PESOS
20.0000 g., 0.9990 Silver 0.6423 oz. ASW, 38 mm. **Obv:** Cuban arms **Rev:** Che Guevara, 75th Anniversary of Birth

Date	Mintage	F	VF	XF	Unc	BU
2003 Proof	5,000	Value: 45.00				

KM# 791 10 PESOS
20.0000 g., 0.9990 Silver 0.6423 oz. ASW, 38 mm. **Obv:** Cuban arms **Rev:** Sailing ship, Sovereign of the Seas

Date	Mintage	F	VF	XF	Unc	BU
2003 Proof	5,000	Value: 45.00				

KM# 790 10 PESOS
20.0000 g., 0.9990 Silver 0.6423 oz. ASW, 38 mm. **Obv:** Cuban arms **Rev:** Ferdinand Magellan, ship, and astrolab

Date	Mintage	F	VF	XF	Unc	BU
2003 Proof	5,000	Value: 45.00				

KM# 793 10 PESOS
31.1000 g., 0.9990 Silver 0.9988 oz. ASW, 38 mm. **Subject:** World Cup Soccer - Germany 2006 **Obv:** Cuban arms **Rev:** 5 soccer players

Date	Mintage	F	VF	XF	Unc	BU
2003 Proof	50,000	Value: 45.00				

KM# 796 10 PESOS
20.0000 g., 0.9990 Silver 0.6423 oz. ASW, 38 mm. **Obv:** Cuban arms **Rev:** John Cabot's portrait in cameo above ship

Date	Mintage	F	VF	XF	Unc	BU
2004 Proof	5,000	Value: 45.00				

KM# 797 10 PESOS
15.0000 g., 0.9990 Silver 0.4818 oz. ASW, 35 mm. **Subject:** Hippocampus Kuda **Obv:** Cuban arms **Rev:** Spotted seahorse

Date	Mintage	F	VF	XF	Unc	BU
2004 Proof	5,000	Value: 50.00				

KM# 798 10 PESOS
20.0000 g., 0.9990 Silver 0.6423 oz. ASW, 38 mm. **Obv:** Cuban arms **Rev:** Murphy's Petrel bird on rock

Date	Mintage	F	VF	XF	Unc	BU
2004 Proof	5,000	Value: 50.00				

KM# 799 10 PESOS
20.0000 g., 0.9990 Silver 0.6423 oz. ASW, 38 mm. **Obv:** Cuban arms **Rev:** Cuban Rock Iguana on branch

Date	Mintage	F	VF	XF	Unc	BU
2004 Proof	5,000	Value: 50.00				

KM# 800 10 PESOS
31.1000 g., 0.9990 Silver 0.9988 oz. ASW, 38 mm. **Obv:** Cuban arms **Rev:** Imperial eagle perched on branch

Date	Mintage	F	VF	XF	Unc	BU
2004 Proof	1,000	Value: 60.00				

KM# 801 10 PESOS
31.1000 g., 0.9990 Silver 0.9988 oz. ASW, 38 mm. **Obv:** Cuban arms **Rev:** Bearded vulture in flight

Date	Mintage	F	VF	XF	Unc	BU
2004 Proof	1,000	Value: 60.00				

KM# 802 10 PESOS
31.1000 g., 0.9990 Silver 0.9988 oz. ASW, 38 mm. **Obv:** Cuban arms **Rev:** Iberian Lynx

Date	Mintage	F	VF	XF	Unc	BU
2004 Proof	1,000	Value: 60.00				

KM# 803 10 PESOS
31.1000 g., 0.9990 Silver 0.9988 oz. ASW, 38 mm. **Obv:** Cuban arms **Rev:** 2 grey wolves

Date	Mintage	F	VF	XF	Unc	BU
2004 Proof	1,000	Value: 65.00				

KM# 804 10 PESOS
31.1000 g., 0.9990 Silver 0.9988 oz. ASW, 38 mm. **Obv:** Cuban arms **Rev:** Brown bear

Date	Mintage	F	VF	XF	Unc	BU
2004 Proof	1,000	Value: 65.00				

KM# 805 10 PESOS
31.1000 g., 0.9990 Silver 0.9988 oz. ASW, 38 mm. **Obv:** Cuban arms **Rev:** Peregrine Falcon perches on branch

Date	Mintage	F	VF	XF	Unc	BU
2004 Proof	1,000	Value: 65.00				

KM# 806 10 PESOS
20.0000 g., 0.9990 Silver 0.6423 oz. ASW, 38 mm. **Subject:** Monuments of Cuba **Obv:** Cuban arms **Rev:** University of Havana building

Date	Mintage	F	VF	XF	Unc	BU
2004 Proof	1,500	Value: 50.00				

KM# 807 10 PESOS
20.0000 g., 0.9990 Silver 0.6423 oz. ASW, 38 mm. **Subject:** Monuments of Cuba **Obv:** Cuban arms **Rev:** Fountain of India

Date	Mintage	F	VF	XF	Unc	BU
2004 Proof	1,500	Value: 50.00				

KM# 808 10 PESOS
20.0000 g., 0.9990 Silver 0.6423 oz. ASW, 38 mm. **Subject:** Monuments of Cuba **Obv:** Cuban arms **Rev:** Plaza building

Date	Mintage	F	VF	XF	Unc	BU
2004 Proof	1,500	Value: 50.00				

KM# 809 10 PESOS
27.0000 g., 0.9250 Silver 0.8029 oz. ASW, 40 mm. **Obv:** Cuban arms within circle of arms **Rev:** Portions of the old Havana Wall

Date	Mintage	F	VF	XF	Unc	BU
2005 Proof	12,000	Value: 75.00				

KM# 810 10 PESOS
20.0000 g., 0.9990 Silver 0.6423 oz. ASW, 38 mm. **Subject:** Tobacco **Obv:** Cuban arms **Rev:** Indian showing tobacco to Columbus, ship in background

Date	Mintage	F	VF	XF	Unc	BU
2005 Proof	2,000	Value: 50.00				

KM# 811 10 PESOS
20.0000 g., 0.9250 Silver 0.5948 oz. ASW, 38 mm. **Subject:** Columbus' Ships **Obv:** Cuban arms **Rev:** The Santa Maria under sail

Date	Mintage	F	VF	XF	Unc	BU
2005 Proof	5,000	Value: 45.00				

KM# 812 10 PESOS
20.0000 g., 0.9250 Silver 0.5948 oz. ASW, 38 mm. **Subject:** Columbus' Ships **Obv:** Cuban arms **Rev:** The Nina under sail

Date	Mintage	F	VF	XF	Unc	BU
2005 Proof	5,000	Value: 45.00				

KM# 813 10 PESOS
20.0000 g., 0.9250 Silver 0.5948 oz. ASW, 38 mm. **Subject:** Columbus' Ships **Obv:** Cuban arms **Rev:** The Pinta under sail

Date	Mintage	F	VF	XF	Unc	BU
2005 Proof	5,000	Value: 45.00				

KM# 814 10 PESOS
20.0000 g., 0.9250 Silver 0.5948 oz. ASW, 38 mm. **Obv:** Cuban arms **Rev:** Cuban Solenodon on branch

Date	Mintage	F	VF	XF	Unc	BU
2005 Proof	5,000	Value: 45.00				

KM# 815 10 PESOS
15.0000 g., 0.9990 Silver 0.4818 oz. ASW, 35 mm. **Obv:** Cuban arms **Rev:** Multicolor Solenodon on branch

Date	Mintage	F	VF	XF	Unc	BU
2005 Proof	5,000	Value: 40.00				

KM# 816 10 PESOS
15.0000 g., 0.9250 Silver 0.4461 oz. ASW, 35 mm. **Subject:** Tropical Fish **Obv:** Cuban arms **Rev:** Picassofish (triggerfish)

Date	Mintage	F	VF	XF	Unc	BU
2005 Proof	2,000	Value: 40.00				

KM# 817 10 PESOS
15.0000 g., 0.9250 Silver 0.4461 oz. ASW, 35 mm. **Subject:** Tropical Fish **Obv:** Cuban arms **Rev:** Moorish Idol fish

Date	Mintage	F	VF	XF	Unc	BU
2005 Proof	2,000	Value: 40.00				

KM# 818 10 PESOS

15.0000 g., 0.9250 Silver 0.4461 oz. ASW, 35 mm. **Subject:** Tropical Fish **Obv:** Cuban arms **Rev:** Regal Angel fish

Date	Mintage	F	VF	XF	Unc	BU
2005 Proof	2,000	Value: 40.00				

KM# 819 10 PESOS

31.1000 g., 0.9250 Silver 0.9249 oz. ASW, 38 mm. **Subject:** 400 Years of Quijote **Obv:** Cuban arms **Rev:** Don Quijote and Sancho looking at two windmills

Date	Mintage	F	VF	XF	Unc	BU
2005 Proof	5,000	Value: 50.00				

KM# 820 10 PESOS

31.1000 g., 0.9990 Silver 0.9988 oz. ASW, 38 mm. **Subject:** Maximo Gomez Centennial of Death **Obv:** Cuban arms **Rev:** Bust 3/4 left, numbered behind neck

Date	Mintage	F	VF	XF	Unc	BU
2005 Proof	100	Value: 220				

KM# 821 10 PESOS

20.0000 g., 0.9250 Silver 0.5948 oz. ASW, 38 mm. **Subject:** XXIX Olympics **Obv:** Cuban arms **Rev:** Baseball player with bat, baseball background

Date	Mintage	F	VF	XF	Unc	BU
2006 Proof	15,000	Value: 45.00				

KM# 897 10 PESOS

20.0000 g., Silver, 38 mm. **Subject:** Hero - American Series - Javelin

Date	Mintage	F	VF	XF	Unc	BU
2007 Proof	—	Value: 45.00				

KM# 898 10 PESOS

20.0000 g., Silver, 38 mm. **Subject:** Spitnik

Date	Mintage	F	VF	XF	Unc	BU
2007 Proof	—	Value: 45.00				

KM# 886 10 PESOS

20.0000 g., Silver, 38 mm. **Subject:** Che Guevara, 40th Anniversary of his Death

Date	Mintage	F	VF	XF	Unc	BU
2007 Proof	—	Value: 45.00				

KM# 887 10 PESOS

20.0000 g., Silver, 38 mm. **Subject:** Fauna - Buitre (Condor)

Date	Mintage	F	VF	XF	Unc	BU
2007 Proof	—	Value: 45.00				

KM# 888 10 PESOS

20.0000 g., Silver **Subject:** Fauna Burro

Date	Mintage	F	VF	XF	Unc	BU
2007 Proof	—	Value: 45.00				

KM# 889 10 PESOS

20.0000 g., Silver, 38 mm. **Subject:** Fauna - Cobra Montesa

Date	Mintage	F	VF	XF	Unc	BU
2007 Proof	—	Value: 45.00				

KM# 890 10 PESOS

20.0000 g., Silver, 38 mm. **Subject:** Fauna - Gato Montes

Date	Mintage	F	VF	XF	Unc	BU
2007 Proof	—	—	—	—	—	45.00

KM# 891 10 PESOS

20.0000 g., Silver, 38 mm. **Subject:** Fauna - Mastin Espanol

Date	Mintage	F	VF	XF	Unc	BU
2007 Proof	—	Value: 40.00				

KM# 892 10 PESOS

20.0000 g., Silver, 38 mm. **Subject:** Fauna - Urogallo

Date	Mintage	F	VF	XF	Unc	BU
2007 Proof	—	Value: 45.00				

KM# 893 10 PESOS

20.0000 g., Silver, 38 mm. **Subject:** Fortress - El Morro

Date	Mintage	F	VF	XF	Unc	BU
2007 Proof	—	Value: 45.00				

KM# 894 10 PESOS

20.0000 g., Silver, 38 mm. **Subject:** Fortress - La Fuerza

Date	Mintage	F	VF	XF	Unc	BU
2007 Proof	—	Value: 45.00				

KM# 895 10 PESOS

20.0000 g., Silver, 38 mm. **Subject:** La Punta

Date	Mintage	F	VF	XF	Unc	BU
2007 Proof	—	Value: 45.00				

KM# 896 10 PESOS

20.0000 g., Silver, 20 mm. **Subject:** Garabaldi

Date	Mintage	F	VF	XF	Unc	BU
2007 Proof	—	Value: 45.00				

KM# 899 10 PESOS

20.0000 g., Silver, 38 mm. **Subject:** World Championship Soccer England

Date	Mintage	F	VF	XF	Unc	BU
2007 Proof	—	Value: 45.00				

KM# 904 10 PESOS

20.0000 g., Silver, 40 mm. **Subject:** Ship Principe Asturias

Date	Mintage	F	VF	XF	Unc	BU
2008 Proof	—	Value: 45.00				

KM# 905 10 PESOS

20.0000 g., Silver, 40 mm. **Subject:** Ship - San Carlos

Date	Mintage	F	VF	XF	Unc	BU
2008 Proof	—	Value: 45.00				

KM# 906 10 PESOS

20.0000 g., Copper-Nickel, 38 mm. **Subject:** Ship - San Hermene

Date	Mintage	F	VF	XF	Unc	BU
2008 Proof	—	Value: 45.00				

KM# 911 10 PESOS

Silver, 38 mm. **Subject:** Fidel and Raul Castro

Date	Mintage	F	VF	XF	Unc	BU
2009 Proof	—	Value: 45.00				

KM# 912 10 PESOS

20.0000 g., Silver, 38 mm. **Subject:** Manatee

Date	Mintage	F	VF	XF	Unc	BU
2009 Proof	—	Value: 45.00				

KM# 900 20 PESOS

40.0000 g., Silver, 45 mm. **Subject:** Che Guevara - 40th Anniversary of Death

Date	Mintage	F	VF	XF	Unc	BU
2007 Proof	—	Value: 100				

KM# 913 20 PESOS

Silver, 45 mm. **Subject:** Revolution 50th Anniversary

Date	Mintage	F	VF	XF	Unc	BU
2009 Proof	—	Value: 150				

KM# 822 100 PESOS

31.1000 g., 0.9990 Gold 0.9988 oz. AGW, 38 mm. **Subject:** 100th Anniversary - Death of Marti **Obv:** Cuban arms **Rev:** Monument

Date	Mintage	F	VF	XF	Unc	BU
2001 Proof	100	Value: 1,600				

PESO CONVERTIBLE SERIES

KM# 733 CENTAVO

0.7500 g., Aluminum, 16.75 mm. **Obv:** Cuban arms **Rev:** Tower and denomination **Edge:** Plain

Date	Mintage	F	VF	XF	Unc	BU
2001	—	—	—	—	2.00	—
2002	—	—	—	—	2.00	—
2003	—	—	—	—	2.00	—
2005	—	—	—	—	2.00	—

KM# 729 CENTAVO

1.7000 g., Copper Plated Steel, 15 mm. **Obv:** National arms within wreath, denomination below **Rev:** Tower and denomination **Edge:** Reeded

Date	Mintage	F	VF	XF	Unc	BU
2002	—	—	—	—	3.00	—

KM# 575.2 5 CENTAVOS

2.6500 g., Nickel Plated Steel, 18 mm. **Obv:** National arms **Rev:** Casa Colonial **Note:** Coin alignment, recut designs.

Date	Mintage	F	VF	XF	Unc	BU
2002	—	—	—	—	1.00	—
2006	—	—	—	—	1.00	—

KM# 576.2 10 CENTAVOS

3.9400 g., Nickel Plated Steel **Obv:** National arms **Rev:** Castillo de la Fuerza **Note:** Coin alignment, recut designs.

Date	Mintage	F	VF	XF	Unc	BU
2002	—	—	—	—	2.00	—
2008	—	—	—	—	2.00	—

KM# 577.2 25 CENTAVOS

5.7000 g., Nickel Plated Steel, 23 mm. **Obv:** National arms **Rev:** Trinidad **Note:** Coin alignment.

Date	Mintage	F	VF	XF	Unc	BU
2001	—	—	—	—	3.00	—
2002	—	—	—	—	3.00	—
2003	—	—	—	—	3.00	—
2006	—	—	—	—	3.00	—

KM# 578.2 50 CENTAVOS

7.5000 g., Nickel Plated Steel, 25 mm. **Obv:** Cuban arms **Rev:** Havana Cathedral **Note:** Coin alignment.

Date	Mintage	F	VF	XF	Unc	BU
2002	—	—	—	—	5.00	—

KM# 579.2 PESO

8.5000 g., Nickel Plated Steel, 27 mm. **Obv:** National arms **Rev:** Guama **Note:** Coin alignment.

Date	Mintage	F	VF	XF	Unc	BU
2001	—	—	—	—	5.00	—
2007	—	—	—	—	5.00	—

MINT SETS

KM#	Date	Mintage	Identification	Issue Price	Mkt Val
MS3	2001 (3)	—	KM#831-833	—	62.50

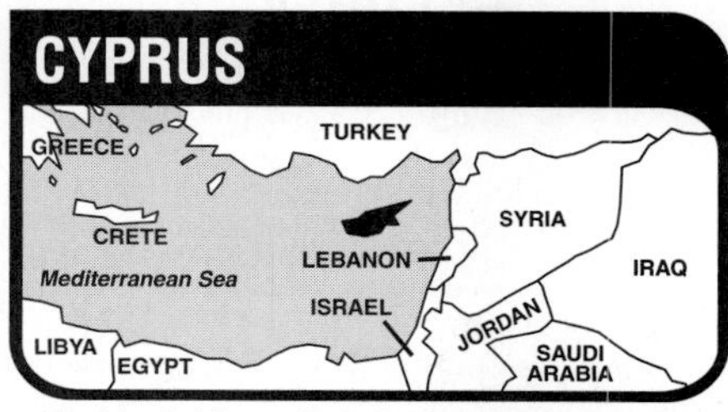

The island of Cyprus lies in the eastern Mediterranean Sea 44 miles (71 km.) south of Turkey and 60 miles (97 km.) off the Syrian coast. It is the third largest island in the Mediterranean Sea, having an area of 3,572 sq. mi. (9,251 sq. km.) and a population of 736,636. Capital: Nicosia. Agriculture, light manufacturing and tourism are the chief industries. Citrus fruit, potatoes, footwear and clothing are exported

Cyprus is a member of the Commonwealth of Nations. The president is Chief of State and Head of Government. Cyprus is also a member of the European Union since May 2004.

MINT MARKS

no mint mark - Royal Mint, London, England
H - Birmingham, England

REPUBLIC

REFORM COINAGE

100 Cents = 1 Pound

KM# 53.3 CENT

2.0000 g., Nickel-Brass, 16.5 mm. **Obv:** Shielded arms within altered wreath, date below **Rev:** Stylized bird on a branch, denomination at left **Edge:** Plain

Date	Mintage	F	VF	XF	Unc	BU
2003	5,000,000	—	—	0.10	0.20	0.30
2004 Narrow figures	12,000,000	—	—	0.10	0.20	0.30

KM# 54.3 2 CENTS

2.5000 g., Nickel-Brass, 19 mm. **Obv:** Shielded arms within altered wreath, date below **Rev:** Stylized goats, denomination upper right **Edge:** Plain

Date	Mintage	F	VF	XF	Unc	BU
2003	5,000,000	—	—	0.15	0.25	0.35
2004	7,000,000	—	—	0.15	0.25	0.35

KM# 55.3 5 CENTS

3.7500 g., Nickel-Brass, 22 mm. **Obv:** Altered wreath around arms **Rev:** Stylized bull's head above denomination **Edge:** Plain

Date	Mintage	F	VF	XF	Unc	BU
2001	15,000,000	—	—	0.20	0.50	0.75
2004	15,000,000	—	—	0.20	0.50	0.75

KM# 56.3 10 CENTS

5.5000 g., Nickel-Brass, 24.5 mm. **Obv:** Altered wreath around arms **Rev:** Decorative vase, denomination above **Edge:** Reeded

Date	Mintage	F	VF	XF	Unc	BU
2002	10,000,000	—	—	0.35	0.75	1.00
2004 Narrow figures	7,000,000	—	—	0.35	0.75	1.00

KM# 62.2 20 CENTS

7.7500 g., Nickel-Brass, 27.25 mm. **Obv:** Altered wreath around arms **Rev:** Head left, denomination at right **Edge:** Reeded

Date	Mintage	F	VF	XF	Unc	BU
2001	15,000,000	—	—	—	1.00	1.50
2004	4,000,000	—	—	—	1.00	1.50

KM# 66 50 CENTS

7.0000 g., Copper-Nickel, 26 mm. **Subject:** Abduction of Europa **Obv:** National arms, date below **Rev:** Female figure riding bull right within square, denomination below **Edge:** Plain **Shape:** 7-sided

Date	Mintage	F	VF	XF	Unc	BU
2002	7,000,000	—	—	—	2.50	3.25
2004	5,000,000	—	—	—	2.50	3.25

KM# 75 POUND

28.2800 g., Copper-Nickel, 38.6 mm. **Subject:** Cyprus Joins the European Union **Obv:** National arms **Rev:** Map in center with Triton trumpeting through a seashell **Edge:** Plain

Date	Mintage	F	VF	XF	Unc	BU
2004	3,000	—	—	—	25.00	50.00

KM# 75a POUND

28.2800 g., 0.9250 Silver 0.8410 oz. ASW, 38.6 mm. **Subject:** Cyprus Joins the European Union **Obv:** National arms **Rev:** Map and Triton trumpeting through a sea shell **Edge:** Plain

Date	Mintage	F	VF	XF	Unc	BU
2004 Proof	3,000	Value: 80.00				

KM# 76 POUND

28.2700 g., Copper-Nickel, 38.5 mm. **Obv:** National arms **Rev:** Mediterranean Monk Seal **Edge:** Plain

Date	Mintage	F	VF	XF	Unc	BU
2005 Proof	4,000	Value: 50.00				

KM# 76a POUND

28.2800 g., 0.9250 Silver 0.8410 oz. ASW **Obv:** National arms **Rev:** Mediterranean Monk Seal **Edge:** Plain

Date	Mintage	F	VF	XF	Unc	BU
2005	4,000	Value: 60.00				

KM# 77 POUND

28.2800 g., Copper-Nickel, 38.6 mm. **Obv:** National arms **Rev:** Akamas Centaurea flowers **Rev. Designer:** Spyros Chrysse Demetriades **Edge:** Plain

Date	Mintage	F	VF	XF	Unc	BU
2006 Prooflike	6,000	Value: 30.00				

KM# 77a POUND

28.2800 g., 0.9250 Silver 0.8410 oz. ASW **Obv:** National arms **Rev:** Akamas Centaurea flowers **Rev. Designer:** Spyros Chrysse Demetriades **Edge:** Plain

Date	Mintage	F	VF	XF	Unc	BU
2006	3,000	Value: 75.00				

KM# 86 POUND

28.2800 g., Copper-Nickel, 38.6 mm. **Subject:** 50th Anniversary Treaty of Rome **Obv:** National arms **Rev:** Open Treaty Book **Edge:** Plain

Date	Mintage	F	VF	XF	Unc	BU
2007 Prooflike	10,000	Value: 28.00				

KM# 87 20 POUNDS

7.9880 g., Gold, 22.05 mm. **Obv:** National arms **Rev:** Greek god Triton, trumpeter (messenger) of the deep sea below outlined map of Cyprus

Date	Mintage	F	VF	XF	Unc	BU
2004 Proof	1,500	Value: 1,000				

EURO COINAGE

European Union Issues

KM# 78 EURO CENT

2.2700 g., Copper Plated Steel, 16.2 mm. **Obv:** Two Mouflons **Rev:** Large value at left, globe at lower right **Edge:** Plain

Date	Mintage	F	VF	XF	Unc	BU
2008	40,000,000	—	—	—	0.35	0.50
2009	19,985,000	—	—	—	0.35	0.50

KM# 79 2 EURO CENT

3.0300 g., Copper Plated Steel, 18.7 mm. **Obv:** Two Mouflons **Rev:** Large value at left, globe at lower right **Edge:** Plain

Date	Mintage	F	VF	XF	Unc	BU
2008	100,000,000	—	—	—	0.50	0.75
2009	4,125,000	—	—	—	0.50	0.75

KM# 80 5 EURO CENT

3.8600 g., Copper Plated Steel, 21.2 mm. **Obv:** Two Mouflons **Rev:** Large value at left, globe at lower right **Edge:** Plain

Date	Mintage	F	VF	XF	Unc	BU
2008	59,930,000	—	—	—	1.00	1.25
2009	5,985,000	—	—	—	1.00	1.25

KM# 81 10 EURO CENT
4.0700 g., Brass, 19.7 mm. **Obv:** Early sailing boat **Rev:** Modified outline of Europe at left, large value at right

Date	Mintage	F	VF	XF	Unc	BU
2008	70,000,000	—	—	—	1.25	1.50
2009	985,000	—	—	—	1.25	1.50

KM# 82 20 EURO CENT
5.7300 g., Brass, 22.1 mm. **Obv:** Early sailing boat **Rev:** Modified outline of Europe at left, large value at right **Edge:** Notched

Date	Mintage	F	VF	XF	Unc	BU
2008	65,000,000	—	—	—	1.50	2.00
2009	985,000	—	—	—	1.50	2.00

KM# 83 50 EURO CENT
7.8100 g., Brass, 24.2 mm. **Obv:** Early sailing boat **Rev:** Modified outline of Europe at left, large value at right **Edge:** Reeded

Date	Mintage	F	VF	XF	Unc	BU
2008	30,000,000	—	—	—	2.00	2.50
2009	985,000	—	—	—	2.00	2.50

KM# 84 EURO
7.5000 g., Bi-Metallic Copper-Nickel center in Brass ring, 23.2 mm. **Obv:** Ancient cross shaped idol discovered in the village of Pomos in the distrct of Paphos. **Rev:** Large value at left, modified outline of Europe at right **Edge:** Segmented reeding

Date	Mintage	F	VF	XF	Unc	BU
2008	28,000,000	—	—	—	3.50	5.00
2009	3,985,000	—	—	—	3.50	5.00

KM# 85 2 EURO
8.5200 g., Bi-Metallic Brass center in Copper-Nickel ring, 25.7 mm. **Obv:** Ancient cross shaped idol discovered in the village of Pomos in the distrct of Paphos. **Rev:** Large value at left, modified outline of Europe at right

Date	Mintage	F	VF	XF	Unc	BU
2008	25,000,000	—	—	—	5.00	7.00
2009	4,985,000	—	—	—	5.00	7.00

KM# 89 2 EURO
8.5200 g., Bi-Metallic Brass center in Copper-Nickel ring, 25.74 mm. **Subject:** 10th Anniversary of Euro **Obv:** Ancient statue wearing a cross found in Solol **Rev:** Childs drawing of a stick figure and 2E

Date	Mintage	F	VF	XF	Unc	BU
2009	980,000	—	—	—	5.00	7.00
2009 Special Unc.	20,000	—	—	—	—	15.00
2009 Proof	—	Value: 25.00				

KM# 88 5 EURO
28.2800 g., 0.9250 Silver 0.8410 oz. ASW, 38.61 mm. **Subject:** Entry into Euro Zone **Obv:** National arms **Rev:** Euro band around outlined Europe and Cyprus **Edge:** Reeded

Date	Mintage	F	VF	XF	Unc	BU
2008 Proof	15,000	Value: 75.00				

KM# 94 5 EURO
28.2800 g., 0.9250 Silver 0.8410 oz. ASW, 38.61 mm. **Subject:** Republic of Cyprus, 50th Anniversary

Date	Mintage	F	VF	XF	Unc	BU
2010	—	—	—	—	—	55.00

KM# 95 20 EURO
7.9900 g., 0.9000 Gold 0.2312 oz. AGW, 22 mm. **Subject:** Republic of Cyprus, 50th Anniversary

Date	Mintage	F	VF	XF	Unc	BU
2010	—	—	—	—	—	375

CZECH REPUBLIC

The Czech Republic was formerly united with Slovakia as Czechoslovakia. It is bordered in the west by Germany, to the north by Poland, to the east by Slovakia and to the south by Austria. It consists of 3 major regions: Bohemia, Moravia and Silesia and has an area of 30,450 sq. mi. (78,864 sq. km.) and a population of 10.4 million. Capital: Prague (Praha). Agriculture and livestock are chief occupations while coal deposits are the main mineral resources.

MINT MARKS

(c) - castle = Hamburg
(cr) - cross = British Royal Mint
(l) - leaf = Royal Canadian
(m) - crowned *b* or *CM* = Jablonec nad Nisou
(mk) - *MK* in circle = Kremnica
(o) - broken circle = Vienna (Wien)

MONETARY SYSTEM

1 Czechoslovak Koruna (Kcs) = 1 Czech Koruna (Kc)
1 Koruna = 100 Haleru

REPUBLIC

STANDARD COINAGE

KM# 6 10 HALERU
0.6000 g., Aluminum, 15.5 mm. **Obv:** Crowned Czech lion left, date below **Rev:** Denomination and stylized river **Edge:** Plain **Designer:** Jiri Pradler **Note:** Two varieties of mint marks exist for 1994.

Date	Mintage	F	VF	XF	Unc	BU
2001(m)	40,525,000	—	—	—	0.20	—
2001(m) Proof	2,500	Value: 2.00				
2002(m)	81,496,000	—	—	—	0.20	—
2002(m) Proof	3,490	Value: 2.00				
2003(m)	3,022,350	—	—	—	0.20	—
2003(m) Proof	3,000	Value: 2.00				
2004(m)	—	—	—	—	0.20	—
2004(m) Proof	3,000	Value: 2.00				

KM# 2.3 20 HALERU
0.7400 g., Aluminum, 17 mm. **Obv:** Crowned Czech lion left, date above **Rev:** Open 2 in denomination, "h" above angle line **Edge:** Reeded **Note:** Medal alignment.

Date	Mintage	F	VF	XF	Unc	BU
2001(m)	44,425,000	—	—	—	0.30	—
2001(m) Proof	2,500	Value: 3.00				
2002(m)	20,000	—	—	—	0.30	—
2002(m) Proof	3,490	Value: 3.00				
2003(m)	22,200	—	—	—	0.30	—
2003(m) Proof	3,000	Value: 3.00				
2004(m)	—	—	—	—	0.30	—
2004(m) Proof	3,000	Value: 3.00				

KM# 3.2 50 HALERU
0.9000 g., Aluminum, 19 mm. **Obv:** Crowned Czech lion left, date below **Rev:** Large denomination **Edge:** Segmented reeding **Note:** Outlined lettering and larger mint mark

Date	Mintage	F	VF	XF	Unc	BU
2001(m)	21,425,000	—	—	—	0.50	—
2001(m) Proof	2,500	Value: 3.00				
2002(m)	26,246,298	—	—	—	0.50	—
2002(m) Proof	3,490	Value: 3.00				
2003(m)	41,548,000	—	—	—	0.50	—
2003(m) Proof	3,000	Value: 3.00				
2004(m)	931,145	—	—	—	0.50	—
2004(m) Proof	4,000	Value: 3.00				
2005(m)	36,800	—	—	—	0.50	—
2005(m) Proof	3,000	Value: 3.00				
2006(m)	40,000	—	—	—	0.50	—
2006(m) Proof	2,500	Value: 3.00				
2007(m)	—	—	—	—	0.50	—
2007(m) Proof	2,500	Value: 3.00				
2008(m)	—	—	—	—	0.50	—
2008(m) Proof	2,500	Value: 3.00				
2009(m)	—	—	—	—	0.50	—
2009(m) Proof	2,500	Value: 3.00				

KM# 3.1 50 HALERU
0.9000 g., Aluminum, 19 mm. **Obv:** Crowned Czech lion left, date below **Rev:** Large denomination **Edge:** Segmented reeding **Designer:** Vladimir Oppl **Note:** Prev. KM#3.

Date	Mintage	F	VF	XF	Unc	BU
2001(m)	21,425,000	—	—	—	0.50	—
2001(m) Proof	2,500	Value: 3.00				

KM# 7 KORUNA

3.6000 g., Nickel Plated Steel, 20 mm. **Obv:** Crowned Czech lion left, date below **Rev:** Denomination above crown **Edge:** Reeded **Designer:** Jarmila Truhlikova-Spevakova **Note:** Two varieties of mint marks exist for 1996. 2000-03 have two varieties in the artist monogram.

Date	Mintage	F	VF	XF	Unc	BU
2001(m)	15,938,353	—	—	—	0.60	—
2001(m) Proof	2,500	Value: 4.00				
2002(m)	26,244,666	—	—	—	0.60	—
2002(m) Proof	3,490	Value: 4.00				
2003(m)	36,877,440	—	—	—	0.60	—
2003(m) Proof	3,000	Value: 4.00				
2004(m)	30,500	—	—	—	0.60	—
2004(m) Proof	4,000	Value: 4.00				
2005(m)	—	—	—	—	0.60	—
2005(m) Proof	3,000	Value: 6.00				
2006(m)	35,864	—	—	—	0.60	—
2006(m) Proof	2,500	Value: 6.00				
2007(m)	—	—	—	—	0.60	—
2007(m) Proof	2,500	Value: 6.00				
2008(m)	—	—	—	—	0.60	—
2008(m) Proof	2,500	Value: 6.00				
2009(m)	—	—	—	—	0.60	—
2009(m) Proof	2,500	Value: 6.00				
2010(m)	—	—	—	—	0.60	—

KM# 9 2 KORUN

3.7000 g., Nickel Plated Steel, 21.5 mm. **Obv:** Crowned Czech lion left, date below **Rev:** Large denomination, pendant design at left **Edge:** Plain **Shape:** 11-sided **Designer:** Jarmila Truhlikova-Spevakova **Note:** Two varieties of designer monograms exist for 2001-04.

Date	Mintage	F	VF	XF	Unc	BU
2001(m)	26,117,000	—	—	—	0.65	—
2001(m) Proof	2,500	Value: 5.00				
2002(m)	20,941,084	—	—	—	0.65	—
2002(m) Proof	3,490	Value: 5.00				
2003(m)	20,955,000	—	—	—	0.65	—
2003(m) Proof	3,000	Value: 5.00				
2004(m)	15,658,556	—	—	—	0.65	—
2004(m) Proof	4,000	Value: 5.00				
2005(m)	—	—	—	—	0.65	—
2005(m) Proof	3,000	Value: 5.00				
2006(m)	—	—	—	—	0.65	—
2006(m) Proof	2,500	Value: 5.00				
2007(m)	—	—	—	—	0.65	—
2007(m) Proof	2,500	Value: 5.00				
2008(m)	—	—	—	—	0.65	—
2008(m) Proof	2,500	Value: 5.00				
2009(m)	—	—	—	—	0.65	—
2009(m) Proof	2,500	Value: 5.00				
2010(m)	—	—	—	—	0.65	—

KM# 8 5 KORUN

4.8000 g., Nickel Plated Steel, 23 mm. **Obv:** Crowned Czech lion left, date below **Rev:** Large denomination, Charles bridge and linden leaf **Edge:** Plain **Designer:** Jiri Harcuba

Date	Mintage	F	VF	XF	Unc	BU
2001(m)	25,000	—	—	—	1.00	—
2001(m) Proof	2,500	Value: 6.00				
2002(m)	21,344,995	—	—	—	1.00	—
2002(m) Proof	3,490	Value: 6.00				
2003(m)	22,000	—	—	—	1.00	—
2003(m) Proof	3,000	Value: 6.00				
2004(m)	34,940	—	—	—	1.00	—
2004(m) Proof	4,000	Value: 6.00				
2005(m)	—	—	—	—	1.00	—
2005(m) Proof	3,000	Value: 6.00				
2006(m)	25,000	—	—	—	1.00	—
2006(m) Proof	2,500	Value: 6.00				
2007(m)	—	—	—	—	1.00	—
2007(m) Proof	2,500	Value: 6.00				
2008(m)	—	—	—	—	1.00	—
2008(m) Proof	2,500	Value: 6.00				
2009(m)	—	—	—	—	1.00	—
2009(m) Proof	2,500	Value: 6.00				
2010(m)	—	—	—	—	1.00	—

KM# 4 10 KORUN

7.6200 g., Copper Plated Steel, 24.5 mm. **Obv:** Crowned Czech lion left, date below **Rev:** Brno Cathedral, denomination below **Edge:** Reeded **Designer:** Ladislav Kozak **Note:** Position of designer's initials on reverse change during the 1995 strike.

Date	Mintage	F	VF	XF	Unc	BU
2001(m)	25,000	—	—	—	1.50	—
2001(m) Proof	2,500	Value: 7.00				
2002(m)	20,156	—	—	—	1.50	—
2002(m) Proof	3,490	Value: 7.00				
2003(m)	18,747,000	—	—	—	1.50	—
2003(m) Proof	3,000	Value: 7.00				
2004(m)	2,255,740	—	—	—	1.50	—
2004(m) Proof	4,000	Value: 7.00				
2005(m)	—	—	—	—	1.50	—
2005(m) Proof	3,000	Value: 7.00				
2006(m)	—	—	—	—	1.50	—
2006(m) Proof	2,500	Value: 7.00				
2007(m)	—	—	—	—	1.50	—
2007(m) Proof	2,500	Value: 7.00				
2008(m)	—	—	—	—	1.50	—
2008(m) Proof	2,500	Value: 7.00				
2009(m)	—	—	—	—	1.50	—
2009(m) Proof	2,500	Value: 7.00				
2010(m)	—	—	—	—	1.50	—

KM# 5 20 KORUN

8.4300 g., Brass Plated Steel, 26 mm. **Obv:** Crowned Czech lion left, date below **Rev:** St. Wenceslas (Duke Vaclav) on horse **Edge:** Plain **Shape:** 13-sided **Designer:** Vladimir Oppl **Note:** Two varieties of mint marks and style of 9's exist for 1997.

Date	Mintage	F	VF	XF	Unc	BU
2001(m)	25,000	—	—	—	2.50	—
2001(m) Proof	2,500	Value: 10.00				
2002(m)	20,996,500	—	—	—	2.50	—
2002(m) Proof	3,490	Value: 10.00				
2003(m)	22,000	—	—	—	2.50	—
2003(m) Proof	3,000	Value: 10.00				
2004(m)	8,249,507	—	—	—	2.50	—
2004(m) Proof	4,000	Value: 10.00				
2005(m)	—	—	—	—	2.50	—
2005(m) Proof	3,000	Value: 10.00				
2006(m)	—	—	—	—	2.50	—
2006(m) Proof	2,500	Value: 10.00				
2007(m)	—	—	—	—	2.50	—
2007(m) Proof	2,500	Value: 10.00				
2008(m)	—	—	—	—	2.50	—
2008(m) Proof	2,500	Value: 10.00				
2009(m)	—	—	—	—	2.50	—
2009(m) Proof	2,500	Value: 10.00				
2010(m)	—	—	—	—	2.50	—

KM# 1 50 KORUN

9.7000 g., Bi-Metallic Brass Plated Steel center in Copper Plated Steel ring, 27.5 mm. **Obv:** Crowned Czech lion left **Rev:** Prague city view **Edge:** Plain **Designer:** Ladislav Kozak

Date	Mintage	F	VF	XF	Unc	BU
2001(m)	16,000	—	—	—	9.00	—
2001(m) Proof	2,500	Value: 20.00				
2002(m)	16,771	—	—	—	9.00	—
2002(m) Proof	3,490	Value: 20.00				
2003(m)	22,000	—	—	—	9.00	—
2003(m) Proof	3,000	Value: 20.00				
2004(m)	34,555	—	—	—	9.00	—
2004(m) Proof	4,000	Value: 20.00				
2005(m)	—	—	—	—	9.00	—
2005(m) Proof	3,000	Value: 20.00				
2006(m)	—	—	—	—	9.00	—
2006(m) Proof	2,500	Value: 20.00				
2007(m)	—	—	—	—	9.00	—
2007(m) Proof	2,500	Value: 20.00				
2008(m)	—	—	—	—	9.00	—
2008(m) Proof	2,500	Value: 20.00				
2009(m)	—	—	—	—	9.00	—
2009(m) Proof	2,500	Value: 20.00				
2010(m)	—	—	—	—	9.00	—

KM# 58 200 KORUN

13.0000 g., 0.9000 Silver 0.3761 oz. ASW, 31 mm. **Subject:** Frantisek Skroup **Obv:** Quartered, elongated arms above date **Rev:** Portrait and name **Designer:** Jiri Harcuba **Note:** 1,480 pieces uncirculated and 13 proof remelted.

Date	Mintage	F	VF	XF	Unc	BU
ND(2001)	12,909	—	—	—	16.00	18.00

Note: Reeded edge

Date	Mintage	F	VF	XF	Unc	BU
ND(2001) Proof	3,200	Value: 35.00				

Note: CESKA NARODNI BANKA * 0.900 *

KM# 51 200 KORUN

13.0000 g., 0.9000 Silver 0.3761 oz. ASW, 31 mm. **Subject:** Jaroslav Seifert **Obv:** Quartered arms above denomination **Rev:** Head right, dates at left **Designer:** Ladislav Kozak **Note:** 1,680 pieces uncirculated and 2 proof remelted.

Date	Mintage	F	VF	XF	Unc	BU
ND(2001)	12,870	—	—	—	16.00	18.00

Note: Reeded edge

Date	Mintage	F	VF	XF	Unc	BU
ND(2001) Proof	3,199	Value: 35.00				

Note: CESKA NARODNI BANKA * 0.900 *

KM# 53 200 KORUN

13.0000 g., 0.9000 Silver 0.3761 oz. ASW, 31 mm. **Subject:** 250th Anniversary - Death of Kilian Ignac Dientzenhofer **Obv:** Quartered arms, denomination at right **Rev:** Doorway and caliper **Designer:** Petr Pyciak **Note:** 1,840 pieces uncirculated and 104 proof remelted.

Date	Mintage	F	VF	XF	Unc	BU
ND(2001)	12,744	—	—	—	16.00	18.00

Note: Reeded edge

Date	Mintage	F	VF	XF	Unc	BU
ND(2001) Proof	3,373	Value: 35.00				

Note: CESKA NARODNI BANKA * 0.900 *

KM# 54 200 KORUN

13.0000 g., 0.9000 Silver 0.3761 oz. ASW, 31 mm. **Subject:** Euro Currency System **Obv:** National arms **Rev:** Prague gros coin design **Designer:** Josef Safarik **Note:** 134 pieces uncirculated and 1 proof remelted.

Date	Mintage	F	VF	XF	Unc	BU
ND(2001)	13,867	—	—	—	16.00	18.00
Note: Reeded edge						
ND(2001) Proof	4,000	Value: 30.00				
Note: CESKA NARODNI BANKA * 0.900 *						

KM# 52 200 KORUN

13.0000 g., 0.9000 Silver 0.3761 oz. ASW, 31 mm. **Subject:** Soccer **Obv:** Quartered arms on square, denomination below **Rev:** Rampant lion on soccer ball **Designer:** Milena Blaskova **Note:** 2,350 pieces uncirculated and 1 proof remelted.

Date	Mintage	F	VF	XF	Unc	BU
ND(2001)	13,324	—	—	—	16.00	18.00
Note: Reeded edge						
ND(2001) Proof	3,900	Value: 30.00				
Note: CESKA NARODNI BANKA * 0.900 *						

KM# 59 200 KORUN

13.0000 g., 0.9000 Silver 0.3761 oz. ASW, 31 mm. **Subject:** Mikolas Ales **Obv:** Four coats of arms above denomination **Rev:** Horse and rider **Edge:** Reeded **Designer:** Petr Pycian **Note:** 573 pieces uncirculated and 139 proof remelted.

Date	Mintage	F	VF	XF	Unc	BU
ND(2002)	12,473	—	—	—	16.00	18.00
ND(2002)(m) Proof	4,400	Value: 30.00				

KM# 57 200 KORUN

13.0000 g., 0.9000 Silver 0.3761 oz. ASW, 30.9 mm. **Subject:** Jiri of Podebrady **Obv:** Overlapped arms **Rev:** Head right **Designer:** Michal Vitanovswky **Note:** 1,200 pieces uncirculated and 5 proof remelted.

Date	Mintage	F	VF	XF	Unc	BU
ND(2002)	12,750	—	—	—	16.00	18.00
Note: Reeded edge						
ND(2002) Proof	3,600	Value: 30.00				
Note: CESKA NARDONI BANKA * 0.900 *						

KM# 56 200 KORUN

13.0000 g., 0.9000 Silver 0.3761 oz. ASW, 30.9 mm. **Subject:** Emil Holub **Obv:** National arms, eagles and lions, denomination below **Rev:** Traveler and African dancers **Designer:** Ladislav Kozak **Note:** 1,350 pieces uncirculated and 7 proof remelted.

Date	Mintage	F	VF	XF	Unc	BU
ND(2002)	12,635	—	—	—	16.00	18.00
Note: Reeded edge						
ND(2002) Proof	3,600	Value: 30.00				
Note: CESKA NARODNI BANKA * 0.900 *						

KM# 55 200 KORUN

13.0000 g., 0.9000 Silver 0.3761 oz. ASW, 31 mm. **Subject:** St. Zdislava **Obv:** Old and new arms form diamond above denomination **Rev:** Saint feeding sick person **Designer:** Michal Vitanovsky **Note:** 865 pieces uncirculated remelted.

Date	Mintage	F	VF	XF	Unc	BU
ND(2002)	12,706	—	—	—	16.00	18.00
Note: Reeded edge						
ND(2002) Proof	3,600	Value: 30.00				
Note: CESKA NARODNI BANKA * 0.900 *						

KM# 60 200 KORUN

13.1400 g., 0.9000 Silver 0.3802 oz. ASW, 31 mm. **Subject:** Jaroslav Vrchlicky **Obv:** Denomination and quill **Obv. Designer:** Jiri Harcuba **Rev:** Bust with hat facing **Rev. Designer:** Pavel Jekl **Note:** 889 pieces unciruclated and 5 proof remelted.

Date	Mintage	F	VF	XF	Unc	BU
ND(2003)	11,975	—	—	—	16.00	18.00
Note: Reeded						
ND(2003) Proof	3,700	Value: 30.00				
Note: Plain with CESKA NARODNI BANKA *Ag 0.900* 13g*						

KM# 62 200 KORUN

13.0000 g., 0.9000 Silver 0.3761 oz. ASW, 30.9 mm. **Subject:** Josef Thomayer **Obv:** National arms **Obv. Designer:** Ladislav Kozak **Rev:** Portrait **Rev. Designer:** Josef Oplistil **Edge:** Reeded **Note:** 783 uncirculated and 12 proof were remelted.

Date	Mintage	F	VF	XF	Unc	BU
ND(2003)	11,975	—	—	—	16.00	18.00
ND(2003) Proof	4,000	Value: 30.00				

KM# 63 200 KORUN

13.0000 g., 0.9000 Silver 0.3761 oz. ASW, 31 mm. **Subject:** Tabor-Bechyne Electric Railway **Obv:** Head left **Rev:** Railroad station scene **Designer:** Ladislav Kozak **Note:** 808 Uncirculated were remelted.

Date	Mintage	F	VF	XF	Unc	BU
ND(2003)	11,975	—	—	—	16.00	18.00
Note: Reeded edge						
ND(2003) Proof	4,100	Value: 30.00				
Note: Plain edge with CESKA NARODNI BANKA * Ag 0.900 * 13g						

KM# 64 200 KORUN

13.0000 g., 0.9000 Silver 0.3761 oz. ASW, 31 mm. **Subject:** Bohemian Skiers' Union **Obv:** Head 3/4 left **Rev:** Skier **Designer:** Ladislav Kozak **Note:** 680 Uncirculated and 13 proof were remelted.

Date	Mintage	F	VF	XF	Unc	BU
ND(2003)	11,975	—	—	—	16.00	18.00
Note: Reeded edge						
ND(2003) Proof	4,300	Value: 30.00				
Note: Plain edge with CESKA NARODNI BANKA * Ag 0.900 * 13g						

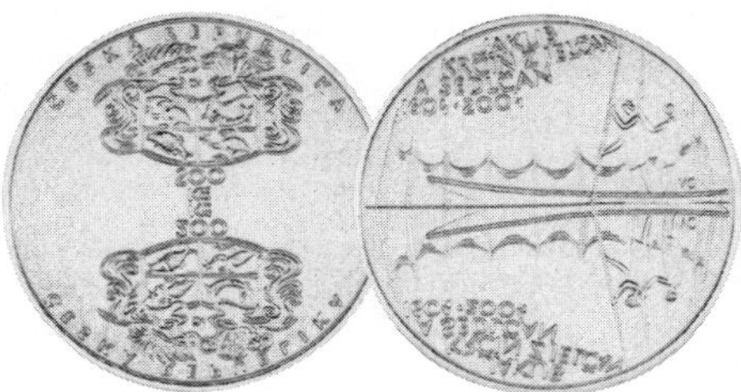

KM# 70 200 KORUN

13.1000 g., 0.9000 Silver 0.3790 oz. ASW, 30.8 mm. **Subject:** 300th Anniversary - Death of pond builder Jakub Krcin **Obv:** Coat of arms above value with reflected design below **Rev:** Two fishermen in boat with reflection on water below **Designer:** Vladimir Oppl **Note:** 656 uncirculated remelted.

Date	Mintage	F	VF	XF	Unc	BU
ND(2004)(m)	11,975	—	—	—	16.00	18.00
Note: Reeded						
ND(2004) Proof	4,000	Value: 30.00				
Note: Plain with CESKA NARODNI BANKA *Ag 0.900* 13g*						

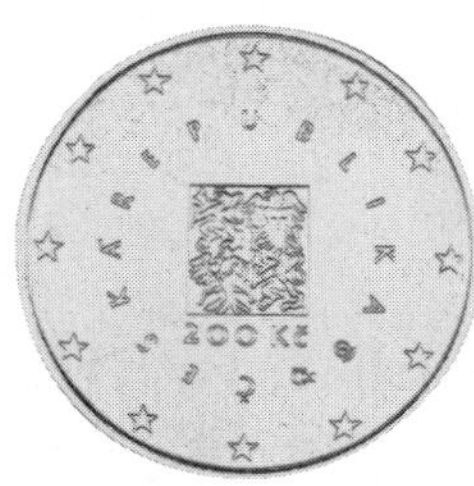

KM# 71 200 KORUN

13.1000 g., 0.9000 Silver 0.3790 oz. ASW **Subject:** Entry into the European Union

Date	Mintage	F	VF	XF	Unc	BU
2004	10,000	—	—	—	16.00	18.00
Note: Reeded						
2004 Proof	8,800	Value: 30.00				

KM# 72 200 KORUN

13.1000 g., 0.9000 Silver 0.3790 oz. ASW **Subject:** Prokop Divis

Date	Mintage	F	VF	XF	Unc	BU
2004	10,975	—	—	—	16.00	18.00
Note: Reeded						
2004 Proof	3,900	Value: 30.00				

KM# 73 200 KORUN

13.1000 g., 0.9000 Silver 0.3790 oz. ASW **Subject:** Leos Janacek

Date	Mintage	F	VF	XF	Unc	BU
2004	10,975	—	—	—	16.00	18.00
Note: Reeded						
2004 Proof	4,100	Value: 30.00				

KM# 74 200 KORUN

13.1000 g., 0.9000 Silver 0.3790 oz. ASW **Subject:** Kralice Bible

Date	Mintage	F	VF	XF	Unc	BU
2004	10,975	—	—	—	16.00	18.00
Note: Reeded						
2004 Proof	5,000	Value: 30.00				

KM# 77 200 KORUN

13.0000 g., 0.9000 Silver 0.3761 oz. ASW, 31 mm. **Rev:** Lightning Conductor

Date	Mintage	F	VF	XF	Unc	BU
2004	—	—	—	—	16.00	18.00
Note: Reeded						
2004 Proof	—	Value: 30.00				
Note: Plain edge with CESKA NARODNI BANKA * Ag 0.900 * 13g *						

KM# 78 200 KORUN

13.0000 g., 0.9000 Silver 0.3761 oz. ASW, 31 mm. **Subject:** 100th Anniversary of Jan Werich and Jiri Voskovec

Date	Mintage	F	VF	XF	Unc	BU
2005	—	—	—	—	16.00	18.00
2005 Proof	—	Value: 30.00				

KM# 79 200 KORUN

13.0000 g., 0.9000 Silver 0.3761 oz. ASW, 31 mm. **Subject:** 100th Anniversary of Production of 1st Car in Malada Boleslov

Date	Mintage	F	VF	XF	Unc	BU
2005	—	—	—	—	16.00	18.00
2006 Proof	—	Value: 30.00				

KM# 80 200 KORUN

13.0000 g., 0.9000 Silver 0.3761 oz. ASW, 31 mm. **Subject:** 450th Anniversary - Birth of Mikulas Dacicky

Date	Mintage	F	VF	XF	Unc	BU
2005	—	—	—	—	16.00	18.00
2005 Proof	—	Value: 30.00				

KM# 84 200 KORUN

13.0000 g., 0.9000 Silver 0.3761 oz. ASW, 31 mm. **Subject:** 700th Anniversary - Death of Wenceslas III **Obv:** Sword between two shields positioned top-to-top **Rev:** King Wenceslas III between two shields **Designer:** Vojtech Dostal

Date	Mintage	F	VF	XF	Unc	BU
2006	11,500	—	—	—	16.00	18.00
2006 Proof	7,500	Value: 30.00				

KM# 85 200 KORUN

13.0000 g., 0.9000 Silver 0.3761 oz. ASW, 31 mm. **Subject:** 100th Anniversary - Birth of Jaroslav Jezek **Obv:** Musical score **Rev:** Caricature looking at score **Designer:** Josef Oplistil

Date	Mintage	F	VF	XF	Unc	BU
2006(m)	11,500	—	—	—	16.00	18.00
2006(m) Proof	20,000	Value: 30.00				

KM# 81 200 KORUN

13.0000 g., 0.9000 Silver 0.3761 oz. ASW, 31 mm. **Subject:** 250th Anniversary - Birth of F.J. Gerstner

Date	Mintage	F	VF	XF	Unc	BU
2006	—	—	—	—	16.00	18.00
2006 Proof	—	Value: 30.00				

KM# 82 200 KORUN

13.0000 g., 0.9000 Silver 0.3761 oz. ASW, 31 mm. **Subject:** 150th Anniversary - School of Glass Making in Kamenicky Senov **Obv:** Image of National Arms within glass cube **Rev:** Artistic image within glass cube **Designer:** Zuzana Hubena

Date	Mintage	F	VF	XF	Unc	BU
2006	12,000	—	—	—	16.00	18.00
2006 Proof	7,500	Value: 30.00				

KM# 83 200 KORUN

13.0000 g., 0.9000 Silver 0.3761 oz. ASW, 31 mm. **Subject:** 500th Anniversary - Death of Matej Rejsek

Date	Mintage	F	VF	XF	Unc	BU
2006	—	—	—	—	16.00	18.00
2006 Proof	—	Value: 30.00				

KM# 91 200 KORUN

13.0000 g., 0.9000 Silver 0.3761 oz. ASW, 31 mm. **Subject:** Founding of Jednota Bratska

Date	Mintage	F	VF	XF	Unc	BU
2007	—	—	—	—	20.00	22.00
2007 Proof	—	Value: 32.00				

KM# 92 200 KORUN

13.0000 g., 0.9000 Silver 0.3761 oz. ASW, 31 mm. **Subject:** Charles Budge Cornerstone

Date	Mintage	F	VF	XF	Unc	BU
2007	—	—	—	—	20.00	22.00
2007 Proof	—	Value: 32.00				

KM# 93 200 KORUN

13.0000 g., 0.9000 Silver 0.3761 oz. ASW, 31 mm. **Subject:** Jarmila Novotná, birth

Date	Mintage	F	VF	XF	Unc	BU
2007	—	—	—	—	20.00	22.00
2007 Proof	—	Value: 32.00				

KM# 94 200 KORUN

13.0000 g., 0.9000 Silver 0.3761 oz. ASW, 31 mm. **Subject:** Earth Satellite Launch

Date	Mintage	F	VF	XF	Unc	BU
2007	—	—	—	—	20.00	22.00
2007 Proof	—	Value: 32.00				

KM# 97 200 KORUN

13.0000 g., 0.9000 Silver 0.3761 oz. ASW, 31 mm. **Subject:** Charles IV Vineyard Planting decresc

Date	Mintage	F	VF	XF	Unc	BU
2008	—	—	—	—	20.00	22.00
2008 Proof	—	Value: 32.00				

KM# 98 200 KORUN

13.0000 g., 0.9000 Silver 0.3761 oz. ASW **Subject:** Josef Hlavka Death Centennial **Obv:** Wing over architectural element **Rev:** Bearded portrait facing

Date	Mintage	F	VF	XF	Unc	BU
2008	—	—	—	—	20.00	22.00
2008 Proof	—	Value: 32.00				

KM# 99 200 KORUN

13.0000 g., 0.9000 Silver 0.3761 oz. ASW, 31 mm. **Subject:** Schengen Convention **Obv:** Arms **Obv. Designer:** Zbynek Fojtu

Date	Mintage	F	VF	XF	Unc	BU
2008	9,800	—	—	—	20.00	22.00
2008 Proof	16,000	Value: 32.00				

KM# 100 200 KORUN

13.0000 g., 0.9000 Silver 0.3761 oz. ASW, 31 mm. **Subject:** Viktor Ponrepo 150th Anniversary **Obv:** Tripod camera **Rev:** Mustache and top hat

Date	Mintage	F	VF	XF	Unc	BU
2008	—	—	—	—	20.00	22.00
2008 Proof	—	Value: 32.00				

KM# 101 200 KORUN

13.0000 g., 0.9000 Silver 0.3761 oz. ASW, 31 mm. **Subject:** National Technical Museum **Obv:** Steam Locomotive and driving wheel **Rev:** Museum façade and clock face

Date	Mintage	F	VF	XF	Unc	BU
2008	—	—	—	—	22.00	25.00
2008 Proof	—	Value: 35.00				

KM# 102 200 KORUN

13.0000 g., 0.9000 Silver 0.3761 oz. ASW, 31 mm. **Subject:** 100th Anniversary - Czech Ice Hockey Association **Obv:** Hockey Player **Obv. Designer:** Zbynek Fojtu **Rev:** Logo

Date	Mintage	F	VF	XF	Unc	BU
2008	10,600	—	—	—	20.00	22.00
2008 Proof	15,100	Value: 32.00				

KM# 105 200 KORUN

13.0000 g., 0.9000 Silver 0.3761 oz. ASW, 31 mm. **Subject:** Czech Presidency to Council of the European Union **Obv:** Arms in circle **Rev:** Czech flag and circle of stars

Date	Mintage	F	VF	XF	Unc	BU
2009	13,200	—	—	—	20.00	22.00

KM# 106 200 KORUN

13.0000 g., 0.9000 Silver 0.3761 oz. ASW, 31 mm. **Subject:** Nordic World Ski Championships in Liberec **Obv:** Logo with skis **Rev:** Cross country skiers and ski jumpers

Date	Mintage	F	VF	XF	Unc	BU
2009	11,000	—	—	—	20.00	22.00
2009	15,200	Value: 32.00				

KM# 107 200 KORUN

13.0000 g., 0.9000 Silver 0.3761 oz. ASW, 31 mm. **Subject:** North Pole Exploration **Obv:** Facing Explorer **Rev:** Sled and Northern Lights **Rev. Designer:** Jiri Venecek

Date	Mintage	F	VF	XF	Unc	BU
2009	10,500	—	—	—	20.00	22.00
2009 Proof	17,600	Value: 32.00				

KM# 108 200 KORUN

13.0000 g., 0.9000 Silver 0.3761 oz. ASW, 31 mm. **Subject:** Rabbi Jehuda Löw

Date	Mintage	F	VF	XF	Unc	BU
2009	—	—	—	—	20.00	22.00
2009 Proof	—	Value: 32.00				

KM# 109 200 KORUN

13.0000 g., 0.9000 Silver 0.3761 oz. ASW, 31 mm. **Subject:** Kepler's Planetary Motion Laws

Date	Mintage	F	VF	XF	Unc	BU
2009	—	—	—	—	20.00	22.00
2009 Proof	—	Value: 32.00				

KM# 112 200 KORUN

13.0000 g., 0.9000 Silver 0.3761 oz. ASW, 31 mm. **Subject:** Astronomical Clock, Prague **Obv:** Figures of saints **Rev:** Clock works

Date	Mintage	F	VF	XF	Unc	BU
2010	—	—	—	—	18.00	20.00
2010 Proof	—	Value: 30.00				

KM# 113 200 KORUN

13.0000 g., 0.9000 Silver 0.3761 oz. ASW, 31 mm. **Subject:** Gustav Mahler

Date	Mintage	F	VF	XF	Unc	BU
2010	—	—	—	—	18.00	20.00
2010 Proof	—	Value: 30.00				

KM# 114 200 KORUN

13.0000 g., 0.9000 Silver 0.3761 oz. ASW, 31 mm. **Subject:** Alfons Mucha

Date	Mintage	F	VF	XF	Unc	BU
2010	—	—	—	—	18.00	20.00
2010 Proof	—	Value: 30.00				

KM# 115 200 KORUN

13.0000 g., 0.9000 Silver 0.3761 oz. ASW, 31 mm. **Subject:** John of Luxenboug

Date	Mintage	F	VF	XF	Unc	BU
2010	—	—	—	—	18.00	20.00
2010 Proof	—	Value: 30.00				

KM# 116 200 KORUN

13.0000 g., 0.9000 Silver 0.3761 oz. ASW, 31 mm. **Subject:** Karel Zeman

Date	Mintage	F	VF	XF	Unc	BU
2010	—	—	—	—	18.00	20.00
2010 Proof	—	Value: 30.00				

GOLD BULLION COINAGE

KM# 65 2000 KORUN

6.2200 g., 0.9999 Gold 0.1999 oz. AGW, 20 mm. **Subject:** Romanesque - Znojmo Rotunda **Obv:** Three heraldic animals **Rev:** Farmer and round building **Designer:** Jiri Harcuba

Date	Mintage	F	VF	XF	Unc	BU
ND(2001)	2,500	—	—	—	—	300
Note: Reeded edge						
ND(2001) Proof	2,997	Value: 320				
Note: Plain edge						

KM# 66 2000 KORUN

6.2200 g., 0.9999 Gold 0.1999 oz. AGW, 20 mm. **Subject:** Gothic - Cloister of the Vyssi Brod Monastery **Obv:** Three heraldic animals above Gothic design **Rev:** Man holding church building model **Designer:** Michal Vitanovsky

Date	Mintage	F	VF	XF	Unc	BU
2001	2,197	—	—	—	—	300
Note: Reeded edge						
2001 Proof	2,997	Value: 320				
Note: Plain edge						

KM# 67 2000 KORUN

6.2200 g., 0.9999 Gold 0.1999 oz. AGW, 20 mm. **Subject:** Gothic - Fountain in Kutna Hora **Obv:** Three heraldic animals **Rev:** Fountain enclosure **Designer:** Josef Oplistil

Date	Mintage	F	VF	XF	Unc	BU
2002	2,197	—	—	—	—	300
Note: Reeded edge						
2002	2,997	Value: 320				
Note: Plain edge						

KM# 61 2000 KORUN

6.2200 g., 0.9999 Gold 0.1999 oz. AGW, 20 mm. **Subject:** Renaissance - Litomysl Castle **Obv:** Three heraldic animals above mermaid **Rev:** Aerial castle view and mythical creature **Designer:** Jiri Venecek

Date	Mintage	F	VF	XF	Unc	BU
2002	2,097	—	—	—	—	300
Note: Reeded edge						
2002 Proof	3,097	Value: 320				
Note: Plain edge						

KM# 68 2000 KORUN

6.2200 g., 0.9999 Gold 0.1999 oz. AGW, 20 mm. **Subject:** Renaissance - Slavonice House Gables **Obv:** Three heraldic animals above city view **Rev:** City arms **Designer:** Jiri Harcuba

Date	Mintage	F	VF	XF	Unc	BU
2003	1,997	—	—	—	—	300
Note: Reeded edge						
2003 Proof	1,497	Value: 335				
Note: Plain edge						

KM# 69 2000 KORUN

6.2200 g., 0.9999 Gold 0.1999 oz. AGW, 20 mm. **Subject:** Baroque - Buchlovice Palace **Obv:** Three heraldic animals above palace **Rev:** Palace view **Designer:** Jakub Venecek

Date	Mintage	F	VF	XF	Unc	BU
2003	1,997	—	—	—	—	300
Note: Reeded edge						
2003 Proof	3,197	Value: 320				
Note: Plain edge						

KM# 75 2000 KORUN

6.2200 g., 0.9999 Gold 0.1999 oz. AGW, 20 mm. **Obv:** Ornamental porch below three heraldic animals **Rev:** Hluboka Castle with coat of arms in foreground

Date	Mintage	F	VF	XF	Unc	BU
2004	2,500	—	—	—	—	300
Note: Reeded edge						
2004 Proof	3,500	Value: 320				
Note: Plain edge						

KM# 86 2000 KORUN

6.2200 g., 0.9990 Gold 0.1998 oz. AGW, 20 mm. **Subject:** Kacina Castle

Date	Mintage	F	VF	XF	Unc	BU
2004	—	—	—	—	—	300
2004 Proof	—	Value: 335				

KM# 87 2000 KORUN

6.2200 g., 0.9990 Gold 0.1998 oz. AGW, 20 mm. **Subject:** Lazne Bohdanec Spa

Date	Mintage	F	VF	XF	Unc	BU
2005	—	—	—	—	—	300
2005 Proof	—	Value: 320				

KM# 88 2000 KORUN

6.2200 g., 0.9990 Gold 0.1998 oz. AGW, 20 mm. **Subject:** Dancing house in Prague

Date	Mintage	F	VF	XF	Unc	BU
2005	—	—	—	—	—	300
2005 Proof	—	Value: 335				

KM# 76 2500 KORUN

31.1040 g., Bi-Metallic .9999 Gold 7.776g center in .999 Silver 23.328g ring, 40 mm. **Subject:** Czech entry into the European Union **Obv:** Value within circle of shields **Rev:** "1.5.2004" within circle of dates and text **Edge:** Lettered **Edge Lettering:** " CNB * Ag 0.999 * 23,328 g * Au 999.9 * 7,776g * "

Date	Mintage	F	VF	XF	Unc	BU
ND (2004) Proof	10,000	Value: 400				

KM# 89 2500 KORUN

7.7770 g., 0.9990 Gold 0.2498 oz. AGW, 22 mm. **Subject:** Hand Paper Mill at Velke Losiny

Date	Mintage	F	VF	XF	Unc	BU
2006	—	—	—	—	375	—
2006	—	Value: 400				

KM# 90 2500 KORUN

7.7850 g., 0.9990 Gold 0.2500 oz. AGW, 22 mm. **Subject:** Observatory at Prague Klementinum **Obv:** Sun's rays thru clouds **Obv. Designer:** Josef Oplistil **Rev:** Building tower, rays and moon **Rev. Designer:** Jesef Oplistil **Note:** Prev. KM #86.

Date	Mintage	F	VF	XF	Unc	BU
2006	2,100	—	—	—	—	375
2006 Proof	3,800	Value: 400				

KM# 95 2500 KORUN

7.7770 g., 0.9990 Gold 0.2498 oz. AGW, 22 mm. **Subject:** Serciny Mine at Phibram-Brezove Hory

Date	Mintage	F	VF	XF	Unc	BU
2007	—	—	—	—	375	—
2007 Proof	—	Value: 400				

KM# 96 2500 KORUN

7.7770 g., 0.9990 Gold 0.2498 oz. AGW, 22 mm. **Subject:** Water mill at Slup

Date	Mintage	F	VF	XF	Unc	BU
2007	—	—	—	—	375	—
2007 Proof	—	Value: 400				

KM# 103 2500 KORUN

7.7800 g., 0.9990 Gold 0.2499 oz. AGW, 22 mm. **Subject:** Stadlec Suspension Bridge **Obv:** Side view of bridge **Rev:** View of bridge thru arch

Date	Mintage	F	VF	XF	Unc	BU
2008	—	—	—	—	375	—
2008 Proof	—	Value: 400				

KM# 104 2500 KORUN

7.7800 g., 0.9990 Gold 0.2499 oz. AGW **Subject:** Pilzen Brewery **Obv:** View of copper vats **Rev:** View of façade and wooden barrels

Date	Mintage	F	VF	XF	Unc	BU
2008	—	—	—	—	375	—
2008 Proof	—	Value: 400				

KM# 110 2500 KORUN

7.7770 g., 0.9990 Gold 0.2498 oz. AGW, 22 mm. **Subject:** Elbe Sluice under Strelcov Castle

Date	Mintage	F	VF	XF	Unc	BU
2009	—	—	—	—	375	—
2009	—	Value: 400				

KM# 111 2500 KORUN

7.7770 g., 0.9990 Gold 0.2498 oz. AGW, 32 mm. **Subject:** Windmill at Ruprechtov

Date	Mintage	F	VF	XF	Unc	BU
2009	—	—	—	—	375	—
2009	—	Value: 400				

KM# 117 2500 KORUN

7.7700 g., 0.9990 Gold 0.2496 oz. AGW, 22 mm. **Subject:** Hammer Mill

Date	Mintage	F	VF	XF	Unc	BU
2010	—	—	—	—	—	375
2010 Proof	—	Value: 400				

KM# 118 2500 KORUN

7.7700 g., 0.9990 Gold 0.2496 oz. AGW, 22 mm. **Subject:** Michael Mine

Date	Mintage	F	VF	XF	Unc	BU
2010	—	—	—	—	—	375
2010 Proof	—	Value: 400				

MINT SETS

KM#	Date	Mintage	Identification	Issue Price	Mkt Val
MS13	2001 (9)	—	KM#1, 2.3, 3.2, 4-9 Tyn Church	—	17.50
MS14	2002 (9)	—	KM#1, 2.3, 3.2, 4-9 Nato Summit	—	17.50
MS15	2004 (8)	5,000	KM#1, 3.2, 4-5, 7-9, plus Smetna/Dvorak Medal and CD	—	17.50
MS16	2004 (7)	—	KM#1, 3.2, 4-5, 7-9 IIHF Hockey Year	—	16.00
MS17	2007 (7)	—	KM#1, 3.2, 4-5, 7-9. Unesco package	—	16.00
MS18	2007 (14)	10,000	KM#1, 3.2, 4-5, 7-9. Natural beauties with Slovakia coins	—	35.00
MS19	2008 (8)	6,000	KM#1, 3.2, 4-5, 7-9. Soccer medal and package	—	17.50
MS20	2009 (8)	10,000	KM#1, 3.2, 4-5, 7-9 plus brass medal Southern Bohemia	—	17.50

PROOF SETS

KM#	Date	Mintage	Identification	Issue Price	Mkt Val
PS6	2001 (9)	2,500	KM#1, 2.3, 3-9	35.00	65.00
PS7	2002 (9)	3,490	KM#1, 2.3, 3.2, 4-9	35.00	65.00
PS8	2003 (9)	3,000	KM#1, 2.3, 3.2, 4-9	35.00	65.00
PS10	2005 (7)	—	KM#1, 3.2, 4-5, 7-9, and silver strike of Czechoslovakia KM4	—	85.00
PS9	2004 (7)	4,000	KM#1, 3.2, 4-5, 7-9	35.00	60.00
PS11	2006 (7)	—	KM#1, 3.2, 4-5, 7-9, and silver strike of Czechoslovakia KM2	—	85.00
PS12	2007 (7)	—	KM#1, 3.2, 4-5, 7-9, and silver Unesco medal	—	85.00
PS13	2008 (7)	2,500	KM#1, 3.2, 4-5, 7-9 and silver medal	—	85.00
PS14	2009 (8)	2,500	KM#1, 3.2, 4-5, 7-9 and silver medal	—	85.00

DENMARK

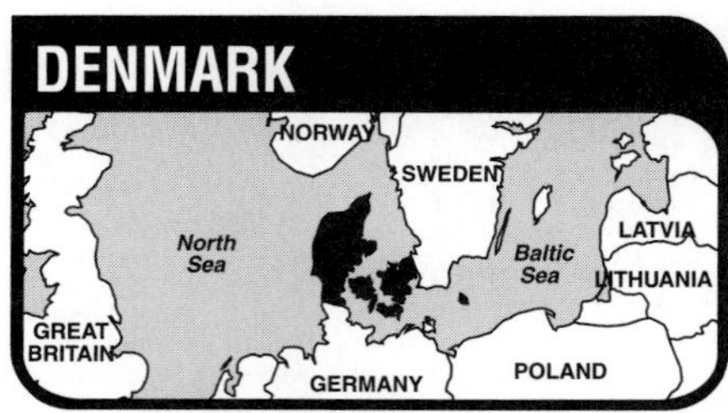

The Kingdom of Denmark (Danmark), a constitutional monarchy located at the mouth of the Baltic Sea, has an area of 16,639 sq. mi. (43,070 sq. km.) and a population of 5.2 million. Capital: Copenhagen. Most of the country is arable. Agriculture is conducted by large farms served by cooperatives. The largest industries are food processing, iron and metal, and shipping. Machinery, meats (chiefly bacon), dairy products and chemicals are exported.

As a result of a referendum held September 28, 2000, the currency of the European Monetary Union, the Euro, will not be introduced in Denmark in the foreseeable future.

RULER

Margrethe II, 1972—

MINT MARKS

(h) - Copenhagen, heart

MINT OFFICIALS' INITIALS

Copenhagen Mint

Letter	Date	Name
LG	1989-2001	Laust Grove

MONEYERS' INITIALS

Copenhagen Mint

Letter	Date	Name
A	1986-	Johan Alkjaer (designer)
HV	1986-	Hanne Varming (sculptor)
JP	1989-	Jan Petersen

MONETARY SYSTEM

100 Øre = 1 Krone

KINGDOM

DECIMAL COINAGE

100 Øre = 1 Krone; 1874-present

KM# 868.1 25 ORE

2.8000 g., Bronze, 17.5 mm. **Ruler:** Margrethe II **Obv:** Large crown divides date above, initial to right of country **Rev:** Denomination, small heart above, mint mark and initials LG-JP below **Note:** Beginning in 1996 and ending with 1998, the words "DANMARK" and "ØRE" have raised edges. Heart mint mark under "ØRE"; Prev. KM#868.

Date	Mintage	F	VF	XF	Unc	BU
2001 LG; JP; A	10,530,000	—	—	—	0.20	—

KM# 868.2 25 ORE

2.8000 g., Bronze, 17.5 mm. **Ruler:** Margrethe II **Obv:** Large crown divides date above **Rev:** Denomination, small heart above **Edge:** Plain **Note:** Without initials

Date	Mintage	F	VF	XF	Unc	BU
2002	12,000,000	—	—	—	0.15	—
2003	17,590,000	—	—	—	0.15	—
2004	7,040,304	—	—	—	0.15	2.00
2004 Proof	3,000	Value: 12.00				
2005	19,039,000	—	—	—	0.15	2.00
2005 Proof	2,650	Value: 12.00				
2006	16,796,000	—	—	—	0.15	2.00
2006 Proof	1,800	Value: 12.00				
2007	20,592,000	—	—	—	0.15	2.00
2007 Proof	1,400	Value: 12.00				
2008	2,049,000	—	—	—	2.00	3.00
2008 Proof	1,000	Value: 25.00				

KM# 866.2 50 ORE

4.3000 g., Bronze, 21.5 mm. **Ruler:** Margrethe II **Obv:** Large crown divides date above, initial to right of country name **Rev:** Large heart above value, mint mark and initials LG-JP below **Note:** Beginning in 1996 and ending with 1998, the words "DANMARK" and "ØRE" have raised edges. Heart mint mark under the word "ØRE".

Date	Mintage	F	VF	XF	Unc	BU
2001 LG; JP; A	12,270,000	—	—	—	0.35	—

KM# 866.3 50 ORE

4.3000 g., Bronze, 21.5 mm. **Ruler:** Margrethe II **Obv:** Large crown divides date above **Rev:** Small heart above denomination **Edge:** Plain **Note:** No initials

Date	Mintage	F	VF	XF	Unc	BU
2002	3,900,000	—	—	—	0.30	—
2003	8,817,000	—	—	—	0.30	—
2004	10,040,706	—	—	—	0.30	3.00
2004 Proof	3,000	Value: 15.00				
2005	12,037,000	—	—	—	0.25	3.00
2005 Proof	2,650	Value: 15.00				
2006	14,842,000	—	—	—	0.25	3.00
2006 Proof	1,800	Value: 15.00				
2007	10,198,000	—	—	—	0.25	3.00
2007 Proof	1,400	Value: 15.00				

Date	Mintage	F	VF	XF	Unc	BU
2008	2,573,000	—	—	—	0.25	3.00
2008 Proof	1,000	Value: 15.00				
2009 In sets only	25,700	—	—	—	0.25	4.00
2009 Proof	1,050	Value: 15.00				
2010 In sets only	—	—	—	—	0.25	3.00
2010 Proof	—	Value: 15.00				

KM# 873.1 KRONE

3.6000 g., Copper-Nickel, 20.25 mm. **Ruler:** Margrethe II **Obv:** 3 crowned MII monograms around center hole, date, mint mark, and initials LG-JP-A below **Rev:** Wave design surrounds center hole, value above, hearts flank **Edge:** Reeded **Note:** Prev. KM#873.

Date	Mintage	F	VF	XF	Unc	BU
2001 LG; JP; A	14,640,000	—	—	—	0.80	—

KM# 873.2 KRONE

3.6000 g., Copper-Nickel, 20.25 mm. **Ruler:** Margrethe II **Obv:** 3 crowned MII monograms around center hole, date below **Rev:** Design surounds center hole, value above, hearts flank **Edge:** Reeded **Note:** Without initials

Date	Mintage	F	VF	XF	Unc	BU
2002	9,000,000	—	—	—	0.60	—
2003	5,231,000	—	—	—	0.60	—
2004	16,139,596	—	—	—	0.60	4.00
2004 Proof	3,000	Value: 18.00				
2005	16,757,000	—	—	—	0.60	4.00
2005 Proof	2,650	Value: 18.00				
2006	21,026,000	—	—	—	0.60	4.00
2006 Proof	1,800	Value: 18.00				
2007	11,729,000	—	—	—	0.60	4.00
2007 Proof	1,400	Value: 18.00				
2008	13,339,000	—	—	—	0.60	4.00
2008 Proof	1,000	Value: 18.00				
2009 In sets only	624,000	—	—	—	1.50	5.00
2009 Proof	1,050	Value: 18.00				
2010 In sets only	—	—	—	—	0.60	4.00
2010 Proof	—	Value: 18.00				

KM# 874.1 2 KRONER

5.9000 g., Copper-Nickel, 24.5 mm. **Ruler:** Margrethe II **Obv:** 3 crowned MII monograms around center hole, date and initials LG-JP-A below **Rev:** Design surrounds center hole, denomination above, hearts flank **Edge:** Segmented reeding **Note:** Prev. KM#874.

Date	Mintage	F	VF	XF	Unc	BU
2001 LG; JP; A	11,180,000	—	—	—	0.80	—

KM# 874.2 2 KRONER

5.9000 g., Copper-Nickel, 24.5 mm. **Ruler:** Margrethe II **Obv:** 3 crowned MII monograms around center hole, date and initials LGpJP-A below **Rev:** Wave design surrounds center hole, denomination above, hearts flank **Edge:** Segmented reeding **Note:** Without initials

Date	Mintage	F	VF	XF	Unc	BU
2002	60,159,000	—	—	—	0.80	—
2004	7,381,531	—	—	—	0.80	4.00
2004 Proof	3,000	Value: 22.00				
2005	16,681,000	—	—	—	0.80	4.00
2005 Proof	2,650	Value: 22.00				
2006	7,329,000	—	—	—	0.80	4.00
2006 Proof	1,800	Value: 22.00				

Date	Mintage	F	VF	XF	Unc	BU
2007	22,059,000	—	—	—	0.80	4.00
2007 Proof	1,400	Value: 22.00				
2008	2,622,000	—	—	—	1.25	4.00
2008 Proof	1,000	Value: 22.00				
2009 In sets only	25,700	—	—	—	—	6.00
2009 Proof	1,050	Value: 22.00				
2010 In sets only	—	—	—	—	0.80	4.00
2010 Proof	—	Value: 22.00				

KM# 869.1 5 KRONER

9.2000 g., Copper-Nickel, 28.5 mm. **Ruler:** Margrethe II **Obv:** 3 crowned MII monograms around center hole, date and initials LG-JP-A below **Rev:** Wave design surrounds center hole, denomination above, hearts flank **Edge:** Reeded **Note:** Large and small date varieties exist.

Date	Mintage	F	VF	XF	Unc	BU
2001 LG; JP; A	5,700,000	—	—	—	2.50	—

KM# 869.2 5 KRONER

9.2000 g., Copper-Nickel, 28.5 mm. **Ruler:** Margrethe II **Obv:** 3 crowned MII monograms around center hole, date below **Rev:** Wave design surrounds center hole, denomination above, hearts flank **Edge:** Reeded **Note:** Without initials

Date	Mintage	F	VF	XF	Unc	BU
2002	5,980,000	—	—	—	2.25	—
2004	1,415,925	—	—	—	2.50	5.00
2004 Proof	3,000	Value: 30.00				
2005	7,073,000	—	—	—	2.25	5.00
2005 Proof	2,650	Value: 30.00				
2006	3,431,000	—	—	—	2.25	5.00
2006 Proof	1,800	Value: 30.00				
2007	4,983,000	—	—	—	2.25	5.00
2007 Proof	1,400	Value: 30.00				
2008	7,506,000	—	—	—	2.25	5.00
2008 Proof	1,000	Value: 30.00				
2009 In sets only	25,700	—	—	—	—	8.00
2009 Proof	1,050	Value: 30.00				
2010 In sets only	—	—	—	—	2.25	5.00
2010 Proof	—	Value: 30.00				

KM# 887.1 10 KRONER

7.0000 g., Aluminum-Bronze, 23.35 mm. **Ruler:** Margrethe II **Obv:** Crowned head right within inner circle, date, initials LG-JP-A below, mint mark after II in title **Obv. Legend:** MARGRETHE II - DANMARKS DRONNING **Obv. Designer:** Mogens Moller **Rev:** Crowned arms within inner circle above denomination **Edge:** Plain

Date	Mintage	F	VF	XF	Unc	BU
2001(h) LG; JP; A	4,800,000	—	—	—	4.00	—

KM# 887.2 10 KRONER

7.1000 g., Aluminum-Bronze, 23.35 mm. **Ruler:** Margrethe II **Obv:** Crowned bust right, mint mark after II in title **Obv. Legend:** MARGRETHE II - DANMARKS DRONNING **Obv. Designer:** Mogens Moller **Rev:** Crowned arms and denomination **Edge:** Plain **Note:** Without initials

Date	Mintage	F	VF	XF	Unc	BU
2002(h)	7,299,900	—	—	—	4.00	—

KM# 896 10 KRONER

7.0000 g., Aluminum-Bronze, 23.35 mm. **Ruler:** Margrethe II **Obv:** Crowned bust right within circle, date below **Obv. Legend:** MARGRETHE II - DANMARKS DRONNING **Rev:** Crowned arms above denomination **Edge:** Plain **Designer:** Mogens Moller

Date	Mintage	F	VF	XF	Unc	BU
2004(h)	5,835,426	—	—	—	4.00	7.00
2004(h) Proof	3,000	Value: 35.00				
2005(h)	2,614,000	—	—	—	4.00	7.00
2005(h) Proof	2,650	Value: 35.00				
2006(h)	3,530,000	—	—	—	4.00	7.00
2006(h) Proof	1,800	Value: 35.00				
2007(h)	3,294,000	—	—	—	4.00	7.00
2007(h) Proof	1,400	Value: 35.00				
2008(h)	2,258,000	—	—	—	3.25	7.00
2008(h) Proof	1,000	Value: 35.00				
2009(h)	1,701,000	—	—	—	3.50	7.00
2009(h) Proof	1,050	Value: 35.00				
2010(h) In sets only	—	—	—	—	3.50	7.00
2010(h) Proof	—	Value: 35.00				

KM# 898 10 KRONER

7.0000 g., Aluminum-Bronze, 23.35 mm. **Ruler:** Margrethe II **Series:** Fairy Tales **Subject:** Hans Christian Andersen's Ugly duckling story **Obv:** Crowned bust right within circle, date below **Obv. Legend:** MARGRETHE II - DANMARKS DRONNING **Rev:** Swan and reflection on water within circle, value below **Rev. Designer:** Hans Pauli Olsen **Edge:** Plain

Date	Mintage	F	VF	XF	Unc	BU
2005(h)	1,206,675	—	—	—	4.00	10.00

KM# 906 10 KRONER

31.1000 g., 0.9990 Silver 0.9988 oz. ASW, 38 mm. **Ruler:** Margrethe II **Series:** Fairy Tales **Subject:** Hans Christian Andersen's The Ugly Duckling **Obv:** Crowned bust right **Obv. Legend:** MARGRETHE II - DANMARKS DRONNING **Rev:** Swan and reflection on water **Rev. Designer:** Hans Pauli Olsen

Date	Mintage	F	VF	XF	Unc	BU
2005(h)	75,000	—	—	—	—	45.00

KM# 907 10 KRONER

8.6500 g., 0.9000 Gold 0.2503 oz. AGW, 22 mm. **Ruler:** Margrethe II **Series:** Fairy Tales **Subject:** Hans Christian Andersen's The Ugly Duckling **Obv:** Crowned bust right **Obv. Legend:** MARGRETHE II - DANMARKS DRONNING **Rev:** Swan and reflection on water **Rev. Designer:** Hans Pauli Olsen

Date	Mintage	F	VF	XF	Unc	BU
2005(h)	7,000	—	—	—	—	425

KM# 900 10 KRONER

7.0000 g., Aluminum-Bronze, 23.35 mm. **Ruler:** Margrethe II **Series:** Fairy Tales **Subject:** Hans Christian Andersen's Little Mermaid **Obv:** Crowned bust right within circle, date below **Obv. Legend:** MARGRETHE II - DANMARKS DRONNING **Rev:** Little Mermaid **Rev. Designer:** Tina Maria Nielsen **Edge:** Plain

Date	Mintage	F	VF	XF	Unc	BU
2005(h)	1,206,675	—	—	—	4.00	10.00

KM# 908 10 KRONER

31.1000 g., 0.9990 Silver 0.9988 oz. ASW, 38 mm. **Ruler:** Margrethe II **Series:** Fairy Tales **Subject:** Hans Christian Andersen's Little Mermaid **Obv:** Crowned bust right, date below **Obv. Legend:** MARGRETHE II - DANMARKS DRONNING **Rev:** Little Mermaid **Rev. Designer:** Tina Maria Nielsen

Date	Mintage	F	VF	XF	Unc	BU
2005(h)	40,220	—	—	—	—	45.00

KM# 911 10 KRONER

8.6500 g., 0.9000 Gold 0.2503 oz. AGW, 22 mm. **Ruler:** Margrethe II **Series:** Fairy Tales **Subject:** Hans Christian Andersen's Little Mermaid **Obv:** Crowned bust right **Obv. Legend:** MARGRETHE II - DANMARKS DRONNING **Rev:** Little Mermaid **Rev. Designer:** Tina Maria Nielsen

Date	Mintage	F	VF	XF	Unc	BU
2005(h)	4,220	—	—	—	—	500

KM# 903 10 KRONER

7.1000 g., Aluminum-Bronze, 23.35 mm. **Ruler:** Margrethe II **Series:** Fairy Tales **Subject:** H.C. Andersen's "The Shadow" **Obv:** Crowned bust right within circle, date below **Obv. Legend:** MARGRETHE II - DANMARKS DRONNING **Rev:** Stylized figures **Rev. Designer:** Bjørn Nørgaard **Edge:** Plain

Date	Mintage	F	VF	XF	Unc	BU
2006(h)	1,206,675	—	—	—	4.00	10.00

KM# 909 10 KRONER

31.1000 g., 0.9990 Silver 0.9988 oz. ASW, 38 mm. **Ruler:** Margrethe II **Series:** Fairy Tales **Subject:** H.C. Andersen's "Skyggen" (The Shadow) **Obv:** Crowned bust right **Obv. Legend:** MARGRETHE II - DANMARKS DRONNING **Rev:** Stylized figures **Rev. Designer:** Bjørn Nørgaard

Date	Mintage	F	VF	XF	Unc	BU
2006(h)	22,317	—	—	—	—	45.00

KM# 910 10 KRONER

8.6500 g., 0.9000 Gold 0.2503 oz. AGW, 22 mm. **Ruler:** Margrethe II **Series:** Fairy Tales **Subject:** H.C. Andersen's "Skyggen" (The Shadow) **Obv:** Crowned bust right **Obv. Legend:** MARGRETHE II - DANMARKS DRONNING **Rev:** Stylized figures **Rev. Designer:** Bjørn Nørgaard

Date	Mintage	F	VF	XF	Unc	BU
2006(h)	3,070	—	—	—	—	450

KM# 914a 10 KRONER

31.1000 g., 0.9990 Silver 0.9988 oz. ASW, 38 mm. **Ruler:** Margrethe II **Series:** Fairy Tales **Subject:** Hans Christian Andersen's Snow Queen **Obv:** Crowned bust right **Obv. Legend:** MARGRETHE II - DANMARKS DRONNING **Rev:** Ice pieces **Rev. Designer:** Øivind Nygaard

Date	Mintage	F	VF	XF	Unc	BU
2006(h)	25,758	—	—	—	—	45.00

KM# 914b 10 KRONER

8.6500 g., 0.9000 Gold 0.2503 oz. AGW, 22 mm. **Ruler:** Margrethe II **Series:** Fairy Tales **Subject:** The Snow Queen **Obv:** Crowned bust right **Obv. Legend:** MARGRETHE II - DANMARKS DRONNING **Obv. Designer:** Mogens Møller **Rev:** Ice pieces **Rev. Designer:** Øivind Nygaard

Date	Mintage	F	VF	XF	Unc	BU
2006(h)	3,075	—	—	—	—	450

KM# 914 10 KRONER

7.1000 g., Aluminum-Bronze, 23.35 mm. **Ruler:** Margrethe II **Series:** Fairy Tales **Subject:** Hans Christian Andersen's Snow Queen **Obv:** Crowned bust right **Obv. Legend:** MARGRETHE II - DANMARKS DRONNING **Rev:** Ice pieces **Rev. Designer:** Øivind Nygaard

Date	Mintage	F	VF	XF	Unc	BU
2006(h)	1,206,675	—	—	—	4.00	10.00

KM# 923a 10 KRONER

31.1000 g., 0.9990 Silver 0.9988 oz. ASW, 38 mm. **Ruler:** Margrethe II **Series:** Fairy Tales **Subject:** H.C. Anderson's 'The Nightengale' **Rev:** Bird **Rev. Designer:** Torben Ebbesen

Date	Mintage	F	VF	XF	Unc	BU
2007 Proof	18,117	Value: 45.00				

KM# 916 10 KRONER

7.1000 g., Aluminum-Bronze, 23.35 mm. **Ruler:** Margrethe II **Subject:** International Polar Year 2007-2009 **Obv:** Head with tiara right **Obv. Legend:** MARGRETHE II - DANMARKS DRONNING **Rev:** Polar bear facing, walking on ice flow **Rev. Legend:** POLARÅR 2007-2009 **Edge:** Plain

Date	Mintage	F	VF	XF	Unc	BU
2007(h)	1,200,000	—	—	—	5.00	10.00

KM# 923 10 KRONER

7.1000 g., Aluminum-Bronze, 23.35 mm. **Ruler:** Margrethe II **Series:** Fairy Tales **Subject:** H.C. Anderson's 'The Nightingale' **Rev:** Bird **Rev. Designer:** Torben Ebbesen

Date	Mintage	F	VF	XF	Unc	BU
2007	1,206,675	—	—	—	4.00	10.00

KM# 923b 10 KRONER

8.6500 g., 0.9000 Gold 0.2503 oz. AGW, 22 mm. **Ruler:** Margrethe II **Series:** Fairy Tales **Subject:** H.C. Anderson's 'The Nightengale' **Rev:** Bird **Rev. Designer:** Torben Ebbesen

Date	Mintage	F	VF	XF	Unc	BU
2007	2,964	—	—	—	—	450

KM# 925 10 KRONER

7.2000 g., Aluminum-Bronze, 23.35 mm. **Ruler:** Margrethe II **Series:** International Polar Year 2007-2009 **Obv:** Head with tiara right **Rev:** Outlined globe **Rev. Legend:** POLARÅR 2007-2009 **Edge:** Plain

Date	Mintage	F	VF	XF	Unc	BU
2008(h)	1,200,000	—	—	—	4.00	10.00

KM# 932 10 KRONER

7.1000 g., Aluminum-Bronze, 23.5 mm. **Ruler:** Margrethe II **Rev:** Ice scape, Northern Lights **Rev. Designer:** Morten Straede

Date	Mintage	F	VF	XF	Unc	BU
2009	1,200,000	—	—	—	4.00	10.00

KM# 888.1 20 KRONER

9.3000 g., Aluminum-Bronze, 27 mm. **Ruler:** Margrethe II **Obv:** Crowned bust right within circle, date and initials LG-JP-A below, mint mark after II in legend **Obv. Legend:** MARGRETHE II - DANMARKS DRONNING **Rev:** Crowned arms within ornaments and value **Edge:** Alternating reeded and plain sections **Designer:** Mogens Moller

Date	Mintage	F	VF	XF	Unc	BU
2001(h) LG; JP; A	2,900,000	—	—	—	6.25	10.00

KM# 889 20 KRONER

9.3000 g., Aluminum-Bronze, 27 mm. **Ruler:** Margrethe II **Series:** Danish Towers **Obv:** Crowned bust right within circle date below, mint mark after II in legend **Obv. Legend:** MARGRETHE II - DANMARKS DRONNING **Rev:** Aarhus City Hall **Rev. Designer:** Lis Nogel **Edge:** Reeded and plain sections

Date	Mintage	F	VF	XF	Unc	BU
2002(h)	1,208,600	—	—	—	6.50	10.00

KM# 888.2 20 KRONER
9.3000 g., Aluminum-Bronze, 27 mm. **Ruler:** Margrethe II **Obv:** Crowned bust right within circle, mint mark after II in legend **Obv. Legend:** MARGRETHE II - DANMARKS DRONNING **Rev:** Crowned arms within ornaments and value **Edge:** Alternate reeded and plain sections **Designer:** Mogens Møller **Note:** Without initials.

Date	Mintage	F	VF	XF	Unc	BU
2002(h)	5,500,000	—	—	—	6.00	10.00

KM# 890 20 KRONER
9.3000 g., Aluminum-Bronze, 27 mm. **Ruler:** Margrethe II **Series:** Danish towers **Obv:** Crowned bust right within circle, mint mark and date **Obv. Legend:** MARGRETHE II - DANMARKS DRONNING **Rev:** Copenhagen Old Stock Exchange spire with four intertwined dragon tails **Rev. Designer:** Karin Lorentzen **Edge:** Alternate reeded and plain sections

Date	Mintage	F	VF	XF	Unc	BU
2003(h)	1,208,600	—	—	—	6.00	10.00

KM# 891 20 KRONER
9.3000 g., Aluminum-Bronze, 27 mm. **Ruler:** Margrethe II **Obv:** Crowned bust right within circle, mint mark and date **Obv. Legend:** MARGRETHE II - DANMARKS DRONNING **Rev:** Crowned arms above denomination **Rev. Designer:** Mogens Møller **Edge:** Alternate reeded and plain sections

Date	Mintage	F	VF	XF	Unc	BU
2003(h)	5,720,000	—	—	—	6.00	10.00
2004(h)	6,922,182	—	—	—	6.00	10.00
2004(h) Proof	3,000	Value: 50.00				
2005(h)	4,194,000	—	—	—	6.00	10.00
2005(h) Proof	2,650	Value: 50.00				
2006(h)	3,051,000	—	—	—	6.00	10.00
2006(h) Proof	1,800	Value: 50.00				
2007(h)	2,409,000	—	—	—	6.00	10.00
2007(h) Proof	1,400	Value: 50.00				
2008(h)	1,982,000	—	—	—	6.00	10.00
2008(h) Proof	1,000	Value: 50.00				
2009(h)	2,021,000	—	—	—	6.00	10.00
2009(h) Proof	1,050	Value: 50.00				
2010(h) In sets only	—	—	—	—	6.00	10.00
2010(h) Proof	—	Value: 50.00				

KM# 892 20 KRONER
9.3100 g., Aluminum-Bronze, 27 mm. **Ruler:** Margrethe II **Series:** Danish towers **Obv:** Crowned bust right within circle, mint mark and date **Obv. Legend:** MARGRETHE II - DANMARKS DRONNING **Rev:** Christiansborg Castle (parliament) tower and Danish flag **Rev. Designer:** Hans Pauli Olsen **Edge:** Alternate reeded and plain sections

Date	Mintage	F	VF	XF	Unc	BU
2003(h)	1,208,600	—	—	—	6.00	10.00

KM# 893 20 KRONER
9.3100 g., Aluminum-Bronze, 27 mm. **Ruler:** Margrethe II **Series:** Danish Towers **Obv:** Crowned bust right within circle, date below **Obv. Legend:** MARGRETHE II - DANMARKS DRONNING **Rev:** Gåsetårnet tower **Rev. Designer:** Tina Maria Nielsen **Edge:** Alternate reeded and plain sections

Date	Mintage	F	VF	XF	Unc	BU
2004(h)	1,208,600	—	—	—	6.00	10.00

KM# 894 20 KRONER
9.3100 g., Aluminum-Bronze, 27 mm. **Ruler:** Margrethe II **Subject:** Crown Prince's Wedding **Obv:** Crowned bust right within circle, date below **Obv. Legend:** MARGRETHE II - DANMARKS DRONNING **Rev:** Crown Prince Frederik and Crown Princess Mary **Rev. Designer:** Karin Lorentzen **Edge:** Alternate reeded and plain sections

Date	Mintage	F	VF	XF	Unc	BU
2004(h)	1,200,000	—	—	—	7.00	10.00

KM# 897 20 KRONER
9.3100 g., Aluminum-Bronze, 27 mm. **Ruler:** Margrethe II **Series:** Danish Towers **Obv:** Crowned bust right within circle, date below **Obv. Legend:** MARGRETHE II - DANMARKS DRONNING **Rev:** Svaneke water tower, Bornholm **Rev. Designer:** Morten Straede **Edge:** Alternate reeded and plain sections

Date	Mintage	F	VF	XF	Unc	BU
2004(h)	1,208,600	—	—	—	6.00	10.00

KM# 899 20 KRONER
9.3000 g., Aluminum-Bronze, 27 mm. **Ruler:** Margrethe II **Series:** Danish Towers **Obv:** Crowned bust right within circle, date below **Obv. Legend:** MARGRETHE II - DANMARKS DRONNING **Rev:** Landet Kirke, with elements from the story of Elvira Madigan and Sixten Sparre, including a revolver among leaves of chestnut-trees **Rev. Designer:** Øivind Nygaard **Edge:** Segmented reeding

Date	Mintage	F	VF	XF	Unc	BU
2005(h)	1,208,600	—	—	—	6.00	10.00

KM# 901 20 KRONER
9.3000 g., Aluminum-Bronze, 27 mm. **Ruler:** Margrethe II **Series:** Danish Towers **Obv:** Crowned bust right within circle, date below **Obv. Legend:** MARGRETHE II - DANMARKS DRONNING **Rev:** Lighthouse of Nolsoy (Faeroe Islands) **Rev. Designer:** Hans Pauli Olsen **Edge:** Alternate plain and reeded segments

Date	Mintage	F	VF	XF	Unc	BU
2005(h)	1,208,600	—	—	—	6.00	10.00

KM# 902 20 KRONER
9.3300 g., Aluminum-Bronze, 27 mm. **Ruler:** Margrethe II **Series:** Danish Towers **Obv:** Crowned bust right within circle, date below **Obv. Legend:** MARGRETHE II - DANMARKS DRONNING **Rev:** Gråsten Castle Bell Tower **Rev. Designer:** Sys Hindsbo **Edge:** Segmented reeding

Date	Mintage	F	VF	XF	Unc	BU
2006(h)	1,208,600	—	—	—	6.00	10.00

KM# 913 20 KRONER
9.3000 g., Aluminum-Bronze, 27 mm. **Ruler:** Margrethe II **Series:** Danish Towers **Obv:** Crowned bust right within circle, date below **Obv. Legend:** MARGRETHE II - DANMARKS DRONNING **Rev:** The Greenland Cairns: Nukaritt/Three Brothers **Rev. Legend:** TRE BRØDRE **Rev. Designer:** Niels Motzfeldt **Edge:** Alternate plain and reeded segments

Date	Mintage	F	VF	XF	Unc	BU
2006(h)	1,208,600	—	—	—	6.00	10.00

KM# 919 20 KRONER
9.3000 g., Aluminum-Bronze, 27 mm. **Ruler:** Margrethe II **Series:** Danish Towers **Obv:** Bust with tiarra right **Obv. Legend:** MARGRETHE II - DANMARKS DRONNING **Rev:** City Hall in Copenhagen **Rev. Legend:** KØBENHAVNS RÅDHUS **Edge:** Alternate plain and reeded segments

Date	Mintage	F	VF	XF	Unc	BU
2007(h)	1,208,600	—	—	—	6.00	10.00

KM# 920 20 KRONER
9.3000 g., Aluminum-Bronze, 27 mm. **Ruler:** Margrethe II **Series:** Danish Ships **Obv:** Crowned bust right **Obv. Legend:** MARGRETHE II - DANMARKS DRONNING **Rev:** Sailing ship Jylland **Rev. Legend:** FREGATTEN - JYLLAND **Edge:** Segmented reeding

Date	Mintage	F	VF	XF	Unc	BU
2007(h)	1,200,000	—	—	—	7.00	10.00

KM# 921 20 KRONER
9.3000 g., Aluminum-Bronze, 27 mm. **Ruler:** Margrethe II **Series:** Danish ships **Subject:** The Galathea 3 expedition **Obv:** Crowned bust right **Obv. Legend:** MARGRETHE II - DANMARKS

DRONNING **Rev:** Ship Vaedderen, route map in background **Rev. Legend:** VAEDDEREN **Edge:** Segmented reeding

Date	Mintage	F	VF	XF	Unc	BU
2007(h)	1,200,000	—	—	—	6.00	10.00

KM# 926 20 KRONER

9.3000 g., Aluminum-Bronze, 27 mm. **Ruler:** Margrethe II **Series:** Danish Ships **Obv:** Head with tiara right **Rev:** World's first ocean-going diesel-engine merchant ship, built 1912 **Rev. Legend:** SELANDIA **Edge:** Segmented reeding

Date	Mintage	F	VF	XF	Unc	BU
2008(h)	1,200,000	—	—	—	6.00	9.00
2008(h) Proof	1,500	Value: 85.00				

KM# 927 20 KRONER

9.3000 g., Aluminum-Bronze, 27 mm. **Ruler:** Margrethe II **Series:** Danish Ships **Subject:** Voyage to Dublin, Irelend, with full size replica Viking ship, HAVHINGSTEN **Obv:** Crowned bust right **Obv. Legend:** MARGRETHE II - DANMARKS DRONNING **Rev:** Sailing vessel at sea **Rev. Legend:** HAVHINGSTEN / 20 KRONER **Rev. Designer:** Erik Varming **Edge:** Segmented reeding

Date	Mintage	F	VF	XF	Unc	BU
2008	1,200,000	—	—	—	6.00	9.00
2008 Proof	1,500	Value: 85.00				

KM# 928 20 KRONER

9.3000 g., Aluminum-Bronze, 27 mm. **Ruler:** Margrethe II **Series:** Danish Ships **Rev:** Royal Yacht Dannebrog **Rev. Designer:** Henrik Wiberg **Edge:** Segmented reeding

Date	Mintage	F	VF	XF	Unc	BU
2008	1,200,000	—	—	—	6.00	9.00
2008 Proof	1,500	Value: 85.00				

KM# 935 20 KRONER

9.3000 g., Aluminum-Bronze, 27 mm. **Ruler:** Margrethe II **Series:** Danish Ships **Obv:** Crowned bust right **Obv. Legend:** MARGRETHE II - DANMARKS DRONNING **Rev:** Lightship XVII (built 1895) on duty **Edge:** Segmented reeding

Date	Mintage	F	VF	XF	Unc	BU
2009	1,100,000	—	—	—	6.00	9.00
2009 Proof	1,500	Value: 85.00				

KM# 936 20 KRONER

9.3000 g., Aluminum-Bronze, 27 mm. **Ruler:** Margrethe II **Series:** Danish Ships **Obv:** Crowned bust facing right **Rev:** FAERØBÅD (Boat of Faeroe Islands) **Edge:** Segmented reeding **Designer:** Hans Pauli Olsen

Date	Mintage	F	VF	XF	Unc	BU
2009	900,000	—	—	—	6.00	9.00
2009 Proof	2,825	Value: 85.00				

KM# 937 20 KRONER

9.3000 g., Aluminum-Bronze, 27 mm. **Ruler:** Margrethe II **Subject:** Queen's 70th Birthday **Obv:** Head right **Rev:** Crowned shield against background of daisies

Date	Mintage	F	VF	XF	Unc	BU
2010	1,440,000	—	—	—	9.00	6.00
2010 Proof	4,100	Value: 25.00				

KM# 917 100 KRONER

31.0000 g., 0.9990 Silver 0.9956 oz. ASW, 38 mm. **Ruler:** Margrethe II **Subject:** International Polar Year 2007-2009 **Obv:** Crowned bust right **Obv. Legend:** MARGRETHE II - DANMARKS DRONNING **Rev:** Polar bear facing, walking on ice flow **Rev. Legend:** POLARÅR 2007-2009

Date	Mintage	F	VF	XF	Unc	BU
2007(h)	43,048	—	—	—	—	55.00

KM# 930 100 KRONER

31.1000 g., 0.9990 Silver 0.9988 oz. ASW, 38 mm. **Ruler:** Margrethe II **Subject:** International Polar Year 2007-2009 **Rev:** Globe and dog sled

Date	Mintage	F	VF	XF	Unc	BU
2008	15,631	—	—	—	—	50.00

KM# 933 100 KRONER

31.1000 g., 0.9990 Silver 0.9988 oz. ASW, 38 mm. **Ruler:** Margrethe II **Subject:** International Polar Year 2007-2009 **Rev:** Ice scape, Northern Lights **Rev. Designer:** Morten Straede

Date	Mintage	F	VF	XF	Unc	BU
2009	10,600	—	—	—	—	50.00

KM# 895 200 KRONER

31.1000 g., 0.9990 Silver 0.9988 oz. ASW, 38.3 mm. **Ruler:** Margrethe II **Subject:** Wedding of Crown Prince **Obv:** Crowned bust right within circle, date below **Obv. Legend:** MARGRETHE II - DANMARKS DRONNING **Rev:** Crown Prince Frederik and Crown Princess Mary **Rev. Designer:** Karin Lorentzen **Edge:** Plain **Note:** No initials.

Date	Mintage	F	VF	XF	Unc	BU
2004(h)	125,000	—	—	—	—	60.00

KM# 929 500 KRONUR

31.1000 g., 0.9990 Silver 0.9988 oz. ASW, 38 mm. **Ruler:** Margrethe II **Rev:** Royal Yacht Dannebrog **Rev. Designer:** Henrik Wiberg

Date	Mintage	F	VF	XF	Unc	BU
2008	31,700	—	—	—	—	115

KM# 938 500 KRONUR

31.1000 g., 0.9990 Silver 0.9988 oz. ASW, 38 mm. **Ruler:** Margrethe II **Subject:** Queen's 70th Birthday **Obv:** Head right **Rev:** Crowned shield against a background of daisies

Date	Mintage	F	VF	XF	Unc	BU
2010	—	—	—	—	—	95.00

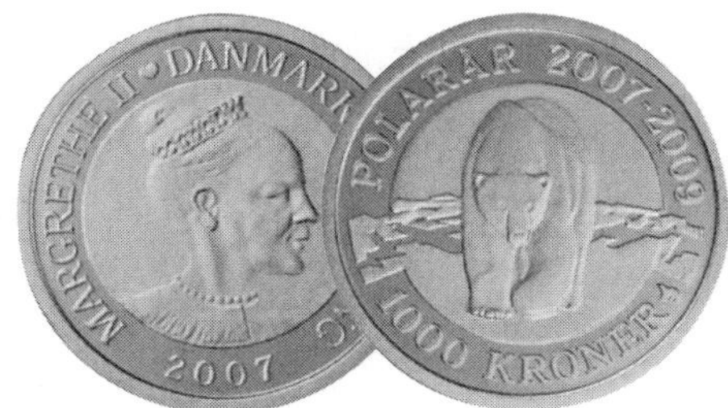

KM# 918 1000 KRONER

8.6500 g., 0.9000 Gold 0.2503 oz. AGW, 22 mm. **Ruler:** Margrethe II **Subject:** International Polar Year 2007-2009 **Obv:** Crowned bust right **Obv. Legend:** MARGRETHE II - DANMARKS DRONNING **Rev:** Polar bear facing, walking on ice flow **Rev. Legend:** POLARÅR 2007-2009 **Note:** Struck from gold from Greenland having a small polar bear to right of denomination.

Date	Mintage	F	VF	XF	Unc	BU
2007(h) Proof	6,000	Value: 475				

KM# 931 1000 KRONER

8.6500 g., 0.9000 Gold 0.2503 oz. AGW, 22 mm. **Ruler:** Margrethe II **Subject:** International Polar Year 2007-2009 **Rev:** Globe and dog sled

Date	Mintage	F	VF	XF	Unc	BU
2008 Proof	3,604	Value: 475				

KM# 934 1000 KRONER

8.6500 g., 0.9000 Gold 0.2503 oz. AGW, 22 mm. **Ruler:** Margrethe II **Subject:** International Polar Year 2007-2009 **Rev:** Ice scape, Northern Lights **Rev. Designer:** Morten Straede

Date	Mintage	F	VF	XF	Unc	BU
2009 Proof	2,400	Value: 475				

KM# 939 1000 KRONER

8.6500 g., 0.9000 Gold 0.2503 oz. AGW, 22 mm. **Ruler:** Margrethe II **Subject:** Queen's 70th Birthday **Obv:** Bust right **Rev:** Crowned shield against background of daisies

Date	Mintage	F	VF	XF	Unc	BU
2010	—	—	—	—	575	—

MINT SETS

KM#	Date	Mintage	Identification	Issue Price	Mkt Val
MS46	2001 (5)	28,000	KM866.2, 868, 869, 873, 874, 887, 888	15.00	37.50
MS47	2002 (7)	28,000	KM866.3, 868.2, 869.2, 873.2, 874.2, 887.2, 888.2	17.50	35.00
MS53	2002-07 (9)	8,600	KM#889, 890, 892, 893, 897, 899, 901, 902, 913, 919. (Tower coin set).	—	100
MS48	2003 (6)	30,000	KM866.3, 868.2, 873.2, 889, 890, 891	17.50	35.00
MS49	2004 (8)	33,000	KM#866.3, 868.2, 869.2, 873.2, 874.2, 891, 894, 896, plus Battle of KÅge Bay medal in Nordic gold	34.50	75.00
MS50	2005 (8)	26,700	KM#866.3, 868.2, 869.2, 873.2, 874.2, 891, 896, 898, plus Battle of Copenhagen medal in Nordic gold	34.50	50.00
MS54	2005-07 (6)	6,675	KM#898, 900, 903, 914, 923 plus Hans Christian Anderson medal in Nordic gold (Fairy tale coin set).	—	55.00
MS51	2006 (8)	25,000	KM#866.3, 868.2, 869.2, 873.2, 874.2, 891, 896, plus Floating Dock medal in Copenhagen sound medal in Nordic gold	40.00	42.00
MS52	2006 (8)	5,000	KM#866.3, 868.2, 869.2, 873.2, 874.2, 891, 896 plus children's medal in Nordic gold. (Children's coin set).	—	48.00
MS55	2007 (8)	23,000	KM#866.3, 868.2, 869.2, 873.2, 874.2, 891, 896 plus Galathea medal in Nordic gold.	—	42.00
MS56	2007 (7)	6,000	KM#866.3, 868.2, 869.2, 873.2, 874.2, 891, 896 plus Children's medal in Nordic gold (Children's coin set)	46.00	50.00
MS57	2008 (7)	1,050	KM#866.3, 868.2, 869.2, 873.2, 874.2, 891, 896 plus Children's medal in Nordic gold (Children's coin set).	—	50.00
MS58	2008 (8)	20,350	KM#866.3, 868.2, 869.2, 873.2, 874.2, 891, 896 plus Battle of Kronberg Castle Coast (Elsinore) medal in Nordic gold.	—	45.00
MS59	2009 (6)	1,450	KM#866.3, 869.2, 873.2, 874.2, 891, 896 plus Children's medal in Nordic gold (Children's coin set)	—	65.00
MS60	2009 (7)	24,250	KM#866.3, 869.2, 873.2, 874.2, 891, 896 plus Neptune admiring Naval fleet medal in Nordic gold.	—	60.00
MS61	2010 (7)	—	KM#866.3, 869.2, 873.2, 874.2, 891, 896 plus Danish Navy's first dry dock medal in Nordic gold	—	42.00
MS62	2010 (7)	—	KM#866.3, 869.2, 873.2, 874.2, 891, 896 plus Danish Navy's first dry dock medal in Nordic gold.	—	42.00

PROOF SETS

KM#	Date	Mintage	Identification	Issue Price	Mkt Val
PS1	2004 (8)	3,000	KM#866.3, 868.2, 869.2, 873.2, 874.2, 891, 896, plus Royal Wedding medal in .925 Silver	150	250
PS2	2005 (8)	2,650	KM866.3, 868.2, 869.2, 873.2, 874.2, 896, 891 plus 1801 Battle of Copenhagen medal in .925 Silver	150	185
PS3	2006 (8)	1,800	KM#866.3, 868.2, 869.2, 873.2, 874.2, 896, 891 plus 1691 Floating Dock medal in .925 Silver	160	185
PS4	2007 (8)	1,400	KM#866.3, 868.2, 869.2, 873.2, 874.2, 896, 891, plus Galathea medal in .925 silver	160	185
PS5	2008 (8)	1,000	KM#866.3, 868.2, 869.2, 873.2, 874.2, 896, 891, plus medal in .925 Silver	—	200
PS6	2009 (7)	1,050	KM#866.3, 869.2, 873.2, 874.2, 891, 896 plus Nepture admiring Naval fleet medal in .925 Silver.	—	250
PS7	2010 (7)	—	KM#866.3, 869.2, 873.2, 874.2, 891, 896 plus Danish Navy's first dry dock medal in .925 Silver.	—	185

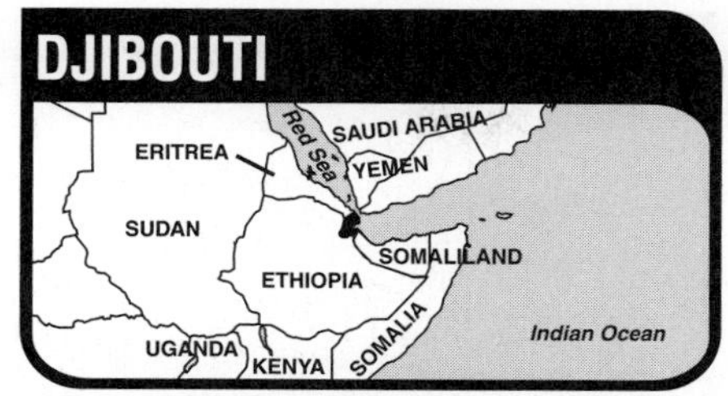

The Republic of Djibouti (formerly French Somaliland and the French Overseas Territory of Afars and Issas), located in northeast Africa at the Bab el Mandeb Strait connecting the Suez Canal and the Red Sea with the Gulf of Aden and the Indian Ocean, has an area of 8,950 sq. mi. (22,000 sq. km.) and a population of 421,320. Capital: Djibouti. The tiny nation has less than one sq. mi. of arable land, and no natural resources except salt, sand, and camels. The commercial activities of the transshipment port of Djibouti and the Addis Abada-Djibouti railroad are the basis of the economy. Salt, fish and hides are exported.

REPUBLIC

STANDARD COINAGE

KM# 34 10 FRANCS

3.4000 g., Copper-Nickel, 20.9 mm. **Obv:** National arms **Rev:** Chimpanzee **Edge:** Plain

Date	Mintage	F	VF	XF	Unc	BU
2003	—	—	—	—	2.00	4.00

KM# 23 10 FRANCS

3.0000 g., Aluminum-Bronze, 20 mm. **Obv:** National arms within wreath, date below **Rev:** Boats on water, denomination above **Rev. Designer:** Lucien Bazor **Note:** Varieties exist.

Date	Mintage	F	VF	XF	Unc	BU
2004(a)	—	—	—	—	2.50	4.50
2007(a)	—	—	—	—	2.50	4.50

KM# 24 20 FRANCS

4.0000 g., Aluminum-Bronze, 23.5 mm. **Obv:** National arms within wreath, date below **Rev:** Boats on water, denomination above **Rev. Designer:** Lucien Bazor **Note:** Varieties exist.

Date	Mintage	F	VF	XF	Unc	BU
2007(a)	—	—	—	—	2.50	4.50

KM# 25 50 FRANCS

7.0500 g., Copper-Nickel, 25.7 mm. **Obv:** National arms within wreath, date below **Rev:** Pair of dromedary camels right, denomination above **Rev. Designer:** Raymond Joly

Date	Mintage	F	VF	XF	Unc	BU
2007(a)	—	—	—	—	6.00	9.00

KM# 38 100 FRANCS

Nickel Possibly Copper-Nickel-Zinc, confirmation of magnetic quality requested, 35 mm. **Subject:** 25th Anniversary of Independence **Obv:** Small national arms on state flag **Obv. Legend:** REPUBLIQUE DE DJIBOUTI **Rev:** UNITÉ in color **Rev. Legend:** UNITÉ ... ÉGALITÉ ... PAIX

Date	Mintage	F	VF	XF	Unc	BU
ND(2002)	—	—	—	—	—	125

KM# 39 100 FRANCS

Nickel Possibly Copper-Nickel-Zinc, confirmation of magnetic quality requested, 35 mm. **Subject:** 25th Anniversary of Independence **Obv:** Small national arms on state flag **Obv. Legend:** REPUBLIQUE DE DJIBOUTI **Rev:** É/GAL/ITÉ in color **Rev. Legend:** UNITÉ ... ÉGALITÉ ... PAIX

Date	Mintage	F	VF	XF	Unc	BU
AH(2002)	—	—	—	—	—	125

KM# 40 100 FRANCS

Nickel Possibly Copper-Nickel-Zinc, confirmation of magnetic quality requested, 35 mm. **Subject:** 25th Anniversary of Independence **Obv:** Small national arms on state flag **Obv. Legend:** REPUBLIQUE DE DJIBOUTI **Rev:** PAI/X in color **Rev. Legend:** UNITÉ ... ÉGALITÉ ... PAIX

Date	Mintage	F	VF	XF	Unc	BU
ND(2002)	—	—	—	—	—	125

KM# 26 100 FRANCS

12.0000 g., Copper-Nickel, 30 mm. **Obv:** National arms within wreath, date below **Rev:** Pair of dromedary camels right, denomination above **Rev. Designer:** Raymond Joly

Date	Mintage	F	VF	XF	Unc	BU
2004(a)	—	—	—	2.50	7.00	9.00
2007(a)	—	—	—	2.50	7.00	9.00

KM# 41 250 FRANCS

22.2000 g., 0.9000 Silver 0.6423 oz. ASW **Obv:** National arms **Obv. Legend:** REPUBLIQUE DE DJIBOUTI **Rev:** Two dromedary camels right **Rev. Legend:** UNITÉ - ÉGALITÉ - PAIX

Date	Mintage	F	VF	XF	Unc	BU
2002(a) Proof	—	—	—	—	—	—

Note: Confirmation requested

The Dominican Republic, which occupies the eastern two-thirds of the island of Hispaniola, has an area of 18,704 sq. mi. (48,734 sq. km.) and a population of 7.9 million. Capital: Santo Domingo. The largely agricultural economy produces sugar, coffee, tobacco and cocoa. Tourism and casino gaming are also a rising source of revenue.

REPUBLIC

REFORM COINAGE

1937

100 Centavos = 1 Peso Oro

KM# 80.2 PESO

6.4900 g., Brass, 25 mm. **Subject:** Juan Pablo Duarte **Obv:** National arms and denomination **Rev:** DUARTE below bust, date below **Note:** Medal die alignment.

Date	Mintage	F	VF	XF	Unc	BU
2002	—	—	—	—	2.00	2.50
2005	—	—	—	—	2.00	2.50

KM# 90 PESO
12.5000 g., Copper-Nickel, 30.6 mm. **Obv:** Pan American Games logo **Rev:** National arms and denomination **Edge:** Reeded

Date	Mintage	F	VF	XF	Unc	BU
2003 Proof	—	Value: 15.00				

KM# 89 5 PESOS
6.0600 g., Bi-Metallic Stainless Steel center in Brass ring, 23 mm. **Subject:** Sanchez **Obv:** National arms and denomination **Rev:** Portrait facing within circle, date below **Edge:** Segmented reeding

Date	Mintage	F	VF	XF	Unc	BU
2002	—	—	—	—	2.50	3.00
2005	—	—	—	—	2.50	3.00
2007	—	—	—	—	2.50	3.00

KM# 106 10 PESOS
8.2000 g., Bi-Metallic Brass center in Copper-Nickel ring, 27 mm. **Obv:** Value at left of national arms **Obv. Legend:** • REPUBLICA DOMINICANA • **Rev:** Bust of General Mella facing **Rev. Legend:** BANCO CENTRAL DE LA REPUBLICA DOMINICANA **Edge:** Segmented reeding

Date	Mintage	F	VF	XF	Unc	BU
2005	—	—	—	—	6.00	8.00
2007	—	—	—	—	6.00	8.00
2008	—	—	—	—	6.00	8.00

KM# 107 25 PESOS
8.5600 g., Copper-Nickel, 28.82 mm. **Obv:** Value at left of national arms **Obv. Legend:** REPUBLICA DOMINICANA **Rev:** Bust of General Luperon facing **Rev. Legend:** BANCO CENTRAL DE LA REPUBLICA DOMINICANA **Rev. Inscription:** HEROE DE LA RESTAURACION **Edge:** Reeded

Date	Mintage	F	VF	XF	Unc	BU
2005	—	—	—	—	5.00	7.00
2008	—	—	—	—	5.00	7.00

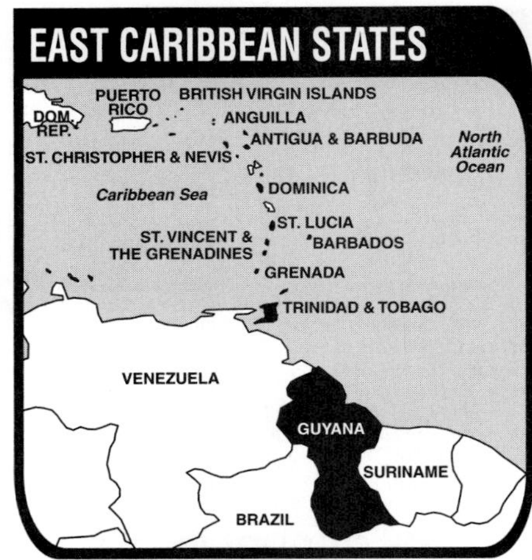

The East Caribbean States, formerly the British Caribbean Territories (Eastern Group), formed a currency board in 1950 to provide the constituent territories of Trinidad & Tobago, Barbados, British Guiana (now Guyana), British Virgin Islands, Anguilla, St. Kitts, Nevis, Antigua, Dominica, St. Lucia, St. Vincent and Grenada with a common currency, thereby permitting withdrawal of the regular British Pound currency. This was dissolved in 1965 and after the breakup, the East Caribbean Territories, a grouping including Barbados, the Leeward and Windward Islands, came into being. Coinage of the dissolved 'Eastern Group' continues to circulate. Paper currency of the East Caribbean Authority was first issued in 1965 and although Barbados withdrew from the group they continued using them prior to 1973 when Barbados issued a decimal coinage.

A series of 4-dollar coins tied to the FAO coinage program were released in 1970 under the name of the Caribbean Development Bank by eight loosely federated island groupings in the eastern Caribbean. These issues are listed individually in this volume under Antigua, Barbados, Dominica, Grenada, Montserrat, St. Kitts, St. Lucia and St. Vincent.

EAST CARIBBEAN STATES

STANDARD COINAGE

100 Cents = 1 Dollar

KM# 34 CENT
1.0300 g., Aluminum, 18.42 mm. **Ruler:** Elizabeth II **Obv:** Crowned head right **Obv. Designer:** Ian Rank-Broadley **Rev:** Denomination **Edge:** Plain

Date	Mintage	F	VF	XF	Unc	BU
2002	—	—	—	—	0.20	0.30
2004	—	—	—	—	0.20	0.30
2008	—	—	—	—	0.20	0.30

KM# 35 2 CENTS
1.4200 g., Aluminum, 21.46 mm. **Ruler:** Elizabeth II **Obv:** Crowned head right **Obv. Designer:** Ian Rank-Broadley **Rev:** Denomination **Edge:** Plain

Date	Mintage	F	VF	XF	Unc	BU
2002	—	—	—	—	0.25	0.35
2004	—	—	—	—	0.25	0.35

KM# 36 5 CENTS
1.7400 g., Aluminum, 23.11 mm. **Ruler:** Elizabeth II **Obv:** Crowned head right **Obv. Designer:** Ian Rank-Broadley **Rev:** Denomination **Edge:** Plain

Date	Mintage	F	VF	XF	Unc	BU
2002	—	—	—	—	0.30	0.45
2004	—	—	—	—	0.30	0.45
2008	—	—	—	—	0.30	0.45

KM# 37 10 CENTS
2.5900 g., Copper-Nickel, 18.06 mm. **Ruler:** Elizabeth II **Obv:** Crowned head right **Obv. Designer:** Ian Rank-Broadley **Rev:** Sir Francis Drake's Golden Hind and denomination **Edge:** Reeded

Date	Mintage	F	VF	XF	Unc	BU
2002	—	—	—	—	0.40	0.60
2004	—	—	—	—	0.40	0.60
2007	—	—	—	—	0.40	0.60

KM# 38 25 CENTS
6.4800 g., Copper-Nickel, 23.98 mm. **Ruler:** Elizabeth II **Obv:** Crowned head right **Obv. Designer:** Ian Rank-Broadley **Rev:** Sir Francis Drake's Golden Hind and denomination **Edge:** Reeded

Date	Mintage	F	VF	XF	Unc	BU
2002	—	—	—	—	0.50	0.75
2004	—	—	—	—	0.50	0.75
2007	—	—	—	—	0.50	0.75

KM# 39 DOLLAR
7.9800 g., Copper-Nickel, 26.5 mm. **Ruler:** Elizabeth II **Obv:** Crowned head right **Obv. Designer:** Ian Rank-Broadley **Rev:** Sir Francis Drake's Golden Hind and denomination **Edge:** Segmented reeding

Date	Mintage	F	VF	XF	Unc	BU
2002	—	—	—	—	2.00	3.00
2004	—	—	—	—	2.00	3.00
2007	—	—	—	—	2.00	3.00

KM# 40 DOLLAR
28.2800 g., Copper-Nickel Gilt, 38.6 mm. **Ruler:** Elizabeth II **Subject:** Golden Jubilee Monarchs **Obv:** Crowned head right **Obv. Designer:** Ian Rank-Broadley **Rev:** Henry III (1216-1277) **Edge:** Reeded

Date	Mintage	F	VF	XF	Unc	BU
2002	5,000	—	—	—	22.50	25.00

KM# 42 DOLLAR
28.2800 g., Copper-Nickel Gilt, 38.6 mm. **Ruler:** Elizabeth II **Subject:** Golden Jubilee Monarchs **Obv:** Crowned head right **Obv. Designer:** Ian Rank-Broadley **Rev:** Edward III (1327-1377) **Edge:** Reeded

Date	Mintage	F	VF	XF	Unc	BU
2002	5,000	—	—	—	22.50	25.00

KM# 44 DOLLAR
28.2800 g., Copper-Nickel Gilt, 38.6 mm. **Ruler:** Elizabeth II **Subject:** Golden Jubilee Monarchs **Obv:** Crowned head right **Obv. Designer:** Ian Rank-Broadley **Rev:** George III (1760-1820) **Edge:** Reeded

Date	Mintage	F	VF	XF	Unc	BU
2002	5,000	—	—	—	22.50	25.00

KM# 46 DOLLAR
28.2800 g., Copper-Nickel Gilt, 38.6 mm. **Ruler:** Elizabeth II **Subject:** Golden Jubilee Monarchs **Obv:** Crowned head right **Obv. Designer:** Ian Rank-Broadley **Rev:** Queen Victoria (1837-1901) **Edge:** Reeded

Date	Mintage	F	VF	XF	Unc	BU
2002	5,000	—	—	—	22.50	25.00

KM# 48 DOLLAR
28.2800 g., Copper-Nickel Gilt, 38.6 mm. **Ruler:** Elizabeth II **Subject:** Golden Jubilee Monarchs **Obv:** Crowned head right **Obv. Designer:** Ian Rank-Broadley **Rev:** Queen Elizabeth II (1952-) **Edge:** Reeded

Date	Mintage	F	VF	XF	Unc	BU
2002	5,000	—	—	—	22.50	25.00

KM# 86 DOLLAR

27.7300 g., Copper-Nickel, 38.5 mm. **Ruler:** Elizabeth II **Subject:** Coronation Jubilee **Obv:** Crowned head right **Obv. Designer:** Ian Rank-Broadley **Rev:** Fireworks display above building **Edge:** Reeded

Date	Mintage	F	VF	XF	Unc	BU
2002	—	—	—	—	10.00	12.00

KM# 58 DOLLAR

7.9800 g., Copper-Nickel, 26.5 mm. **Ruler:** Elizabeth II **Subject:** 25th Anniversary **Obv:** Head right **Rev:** Motto within wreath

Date	Mintage	F	VF	XF	Unc	BU
2008	500,000	—	—	—	—	5.00

KM# 51 2 DOLLARS

56.5600 g., Copper-Nickel Gilt, 38.6 mm. **Ruler:** Elizabeth II **Subject:** British Military Leaders **Obv:** Crowned head right **Obv. Designer:** Ian Rank-Broadley **Rev:** Wellington's portrait and battle scene **Edge:** Reeded

Date	Mintage	F	VF	XF	Unc	BU
2002 Proof	10,000	Value: 45.00				

KM# 54 2 DOLLARS

56.5600 g., Copper-Nickel Gilt, 38.6 mm. **Ruler:** Elizabeth II **Subject:** British Military Leaders **Obv:** Crowned head right **Obv. Designer:** Ian Rank-Broadley **Rev:** Admiral Nelson's portrait and naval battle scene **Edge:** Reeded

Date	Mintage	F	VF	XF	Unc	BU
2003 Proof	10,000	Value: 45.00				

KM# 57 2 DOLLARS

56.5600 g., Copper-Nickel Gilt, 38.6 mm. **Ruler:** Elizabeth II **Subject:** British Military Leaders **Obv:** Crowned head right **Obv. Designer:** Ian Rank-Broadley **Rev:** Churchill's portrait and air battle scene **Edge:** Reeded

Date	Mintage	F	VF	XF	Unc	BU
2003 Proof	10,000	Value: 45.00				

KM# 41 10 DOLLARS

28.2800 g., 0.9250 Silver with gold cameo 0.8410 oz. ASW, 38.6 mm. **Ruler:** Elizabeth II **Subject:** Golden Jubilee Monarchs **Obv:** Crowned head right **Obv. Designer:** Ian Rank-Broadley **Rev:** Henry III (1216-1272) **Edge:** Reeded

Date	Mintage	F	VF	XF	Unc	BU
2002 Proof	10,000	Value: 65.00				

KM# 41a 10 DOLLARS

39.9400 g., 0.9166 Gold 1.1770 oz. AGW, 38.6 mm. **Ruler:** Elizabeth II **Subject:** Golden Jubilee Monarchs **Obv:** Crowned head right **Obv. Designer:** Ian Rank-Broadley **Rev:** Henry III (1216-1272) **Edge:** Reeded

Date	Mintage	F	VF	XF	Unc	BU
2002 Proof	100	Value: 1,800				

KM# 43 10 DOLLARS

28.2800 g., 0.9250 Silver 0.8410 oz. ASW, 38.6 mm. **Ruler:** Elizabeth II **Subject:** Golden Jubile Monarchs **Obv:** Crowned head right **Obv. Designer:** Ian Rank-Broadley **Rev:** Edward III (1327-1377) **Edge:** Reeded

Date	Mintage	F	VF	XF	Unc	BU
2002 Proof	10,000	Value: 65.00				

KM# 43a 10 DOLLARS

39.9400 g., 0.9166 Gold 1.1770 oz. AGW, 38.6 mm. **Ruler:** Elizabeth II **Subject:** Golden Jubilee Monarchs **Obv:** Crowned head right **Obv. Designer:** Ian Rank-Broadley **Rev:** Edward III (1327-1377) **Edge:** Reeded

Date	Mintage	F	VF	XF	Unc	BU
2002 Proof	100	Value: 1,800				

KM# 45 10 DOLLARS

28.2800 g., 0.9250 Silver with gold cameo 0.8410 oz. ASW, 38.6 mm. **Subject:** Golden Jubilee Monarchs **Obv:** Crowned head right **Obv. Designer:** Ian Rank-Broadley **Rev:** George III (1760-1820) **Edge:** Reeded

Date	Mintage	F	VF	XF	Unc	BU
2002 Proof	10,000	Value: 65.00				

KM# 45a 10 DOLLARS

39.9400 g., 0.9166 Gold 1.1770 oz. AGW, 38.6 mm. **Ruler:** Elizabeth II **Subject:** Golden Jubilee Monarchs **Obv:** Crowned head right **Obv. Designer:** Ian Rank-Broadley **Rev:** George III (1760-1820) **Edge:** Reeded

Date	Mintage	F	VF	XF	Unc	BU
2002 Proof	100	Value: 1,800				

KM# 47 10 DOLLARS

28.2800 g., 0.9250 Silver with partial gold plating 0.8410 oz. ASW, 38.6 mm. **Ruler:** Elizabeth II **Subject:** Golden Jubilee Monarchs **Obv:** Crowned head right **Obv. Designer:** Ian Rank-Broadley **Rev:** Queen Victoria (1837-1901) **Edge:** Reeded

Date	Mintage	F	VF	XF	Unc	BU
2002 Proof	10,000	Value: 65.00				

KM# 47a 10 DOLLARS

39.9400 g., 0.9166 Gold 1.1770 oz. AGW, 38.6 mm. **Ruler:** Elizabeth II **Subject:** Golden Jubilee Monarchs **Obv:** Crowned head right **Obv. Designer:** Ian Rank-Broadley **Rev:** Queen Victoria (1837-1901) **Edge:** Reeded

Date	Mintage	F	VF	XF	Unc	BU
2002 Proof	100	Value: 1,800				

KM# 49 10 DOLLARS

28.2800 g., 0.9250 Silver with gold cameo 0.8410 oz. ASW, 38.6 mm. **Ruler:** Elizabeth II **Subject:** Golden Jubilee Monarchs **Obv:** Crowned head right **Obv. Designer:** Ian Rank-Broadley **Rev:** Queen Elizabeth II (1952-) **Edge:** Reeded

Date	Mintage	F	VF	XF	Unc	BU
2002 Proof	10,000	Value: 65.00				

KM# 49a 10 DOLLARS

39.9400 g., 0.9166 Gold 1.1770 oz. AGW, 38.6 mm. **Ruler:** Elizabeth II **Subject:** Golden Jubilee Monarchs **Obv:** Crowned head right **Obv. Designer:** Ian Rank-Broadley **Rev:** Queen Elizabeth II (1952-) **Edge:** Reeded

Date	Mintage	F	VF	XF	Unc	BU
2002 Proof	100	Value: 1,800				

KM# 59 10 DOLLARS

Silver partially gilt, 39 mm. **Ruler:** Elizabeth II **Obv:** Head right, partially gilt **Rev:** Fireworks display above building

Date	Mintage	F	VF	XF	Unc	BU
2002 Proof	—	Value: 50.00				

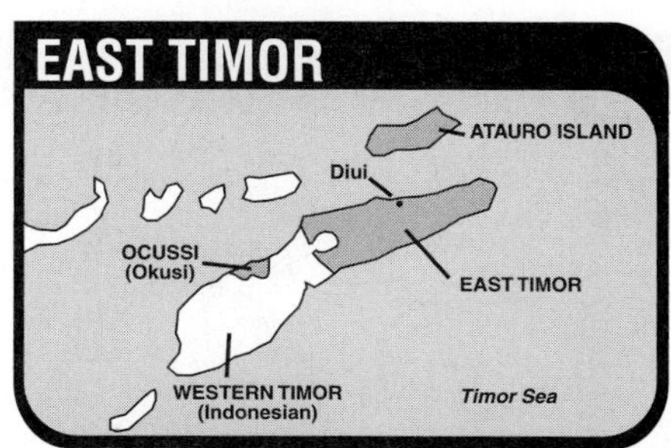

East Timor, population: 522,433, area: 7332 sq. miles, capital: Dili, is primarily located on the eastern half of the island of Timor, just northwest of Australia at the eastern end of the Indonesian archipelago. Formerly a Portuguese colony, Timor declared its independence from Portugal on November 28, 1975. After nine short days of fledgling autonomy, a guerilla faction sympathetic to the Indonesian territorial claim to East Timor seized the government. On July 17, 1976 the Provisional government enacted a law, which dissolved the free republic and made East Timor the 24th province of Indonesia. Violent rule and civil unrest plagued the province, with great loss of life and extreme damage to property and natural resources until independence was again achieved with United Nations assistance during a period from 1999 to 2002. Emerging as the Democratic Republic of Timor-Leste and commonly known as East Timor the country has worked, with international assistance to rebuild its decimated infrastructure. Natural resources waiting to be tapped include rich oil reserves, though current exports are most dependent on coffee, sandalwood and marble. The first coins of the new republic were issued in 2003.

DEMOCRATIC REPUBLIC OF TIMOR-LESTE

DECIMAL COINAGE

KM# 1 CENTAVO

3.1000 g., Nickel Clad Steel, 17 mm. **Obv:** Nautilus above date **Rev:** Denomination within circle **Edge:** Plain **Designer:** Jose Bandeira

Date	Mintage	F	VF	XF	Unc	BU
2003	1,500,000	—	—	—	1.50	2.50
2003 Proof	12,500	Value: 8.00				
2004	1,500,000	—	—	—	1.50	2.50

KM# 2 5 CENTAVOS

4.0500 g., Nickel Clad Steel, 18.8 mm. **Obv:** Rice plant above date **Rev:** Denomination within circle **Edge:** Plain **Designer:** Jose Bandeira

Date	Mintage	F	VF	XF	Unc	BU
2003	1,500,000	—	—	—	2.00	3.00
2003 Proof	12,500	Value: 10.00				
2004	1,500,000	—	—	—	2.00	3.00

KM# 3 10 CENTAVOS
5.1100 g., Nickel Clad Steel, 20.8 mm. **Obv:** Rooster left above date **Rev:** Denomination within circle **Edge:** Plain **Designer:** Jose Bandeira

Date	Mintage	F	VF	XF	Unc	BU
2003	2,500,000	—	—	—	2.50	4.00
2003 Proof	12,500	Value: 12.00				
2004	2,500,000	—	—	—	2.50	4.00

KM# 4 25 CENTAVOS
5.8700 g., Copper-Nickel-Zinc, 21.3 mm. **Obv:** Sail boat above date **Rev:** Denomination within circle **Edge:** Reeded **Designer:** Jose Bandeira

Date	Mintage	F	VF	XF	Unc	BU
2003	1,500,000	—	—	—	3.50	5.00
2003 Proof	12,500	Value: 16.00				
2004	1,500,000	—	—	—	3.50	5.00

KM# 5 50 CENTAVOS
6.5000 g., Copper-Nickel-Zinc, 25 mm. **Obv:** Coffee plant with beans above date **Rev:** Denomination within circle **Edge:** Reeded **Designer:** Jose Bandeira

Date	Mintage	F	VF	XF	Unc	BU
2003	1,000,000	—	—	—	5.00	7.00
2003 Proof	12,500	Value: 22.00				
2004	1,000,000	—	—	—	5.00	7.00

MINT SETS

KM#	Date	Mintage	Identification	Issue Price	Mkt Val
MS1	2003 (5)	25,000	KM#1-5	27.84	35.00

PROOF SETS

KM#	Date	Mintage	Identification	Issue Price	Mkt Val
PS1	2003 (5)	12,500	KM#1-5	57.25	70.00

ECUADOR

The Republic of Ecuador, located astride the equator on the Pacific Coast of South America, has an area of 105,037 sq. mi. (283,560 sq. km.) and a population of 10.9 million. Capital: Quito. Agriculture is the mainstay of the economy but there are appreciable deposits of minerals and petroleum. It is one of the world's largest exporters of bananas and balsa wood. Coffee, cacao, sugar and petroleum are also valuable exports.

REPUBLIC

REFORM COINAGE

100 Centavos = 1 Dollar

KM# 104 CENTAVO (Un)
2.5200 g., Brass, 19 mm. **Obv:** Map of the Americas within circle **Rev:** Denomination **Edge:** Plain

Date	Mintage	F	VF	XF	Unc	BU
2003	—	—	—	—	0.20	0.40
2004	—	—	—	—	0.20	0.40

KM# 104a CENTAVO (Un)
2.4200 g., Copper Plated Steel, 19 mm. **Obv:** Map of the Americas **Rev:** Denomination **Edge:** Plain

Date	Mintage	F	VF	XF	Unc	BU
2003	—	—	—	—	0.30	0.50

KM# 105 5 CENTAVOS (Cinco)
5.0000 g., Steel, 21.2 mm. **Subject:** Juan Montalvo **Obv:** Bust 3/4 facing and arms **Rev:** Denomination **Edge:** Plain

Date	Mintage	F	VF	XF	Unc	BU
2003	—	—	—	—	0.50	0.75

KM# 115 SUCRE (Un)
8.3600 g., 0.9000 Gold 0.2419 oz. AGW, 22 mm. **Subject:** Homage to Jefferson Pérez Quezada **Obv:** National arms **Obv. Legend:** BANCO CENTRAL DEL ECUADOR **Rev:** 3/4 length figure of Perez running **Rev. Legend:** BICAMPEON MUNDIAL - CAMPEON OLIMPICO ATLANTA 1996

Date	Mintage	F	VF	XF	Unc	BU
2006	—	Value: 400				

KM# 112 25000 SUCRES
27.1000 g., 0.9250 Silver 0.8059 oz. ASW, 40 mm. **Subject:** IBERO-AMERICA Series **Obv:** Coats of arms **Rev:** Balsawood sailing raft **Edge:** Reeded

Date	Mintage	F	VF	XF	Unc	BU
2002 Proof	—	Value: 65.00				

KM# 113 25000 SUCRES
27.0000 g., 0.9250 Silver 0.8029 oz. ASW, 40 mm. **Obv:** National arms **Rev:** Capital building in Quito **Edge:** Reeded

Date	Mintage	F	VF	XF	Unc	BU
2004 Proof	1,000	Value: 60.00				

KM# 114 25000 SUCRES
27.2000 g., 0.9250 Silver 0.8089 oz. ASW, 40 mm. **Subject:** 2006 World Cup Soccer **Obv:** National arms **Rev:** Ecuadorian Soccer player torso holding a soccer ball **Edge:** Reeded

Date	Mintage	F	VF	XF	Unc	BU
ND(2006) Proof	—	Value: 50.00				

EGYPT

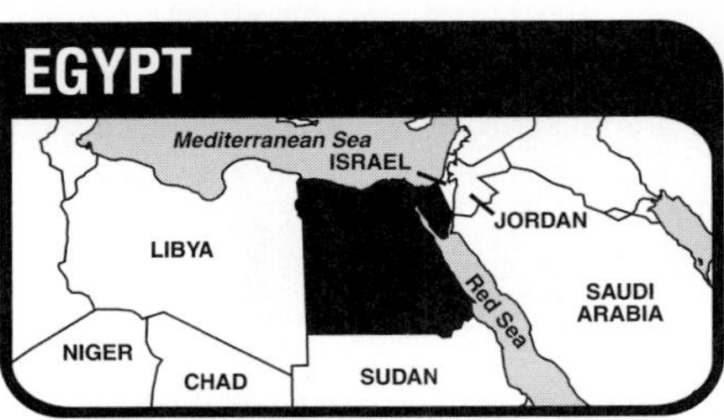

The Arab Republic of Egypt, located on the northeastern corner of Africa, has an area of 385,229 sq. mi. (1,1001,450 sq. km.) and a population of 62.4 million. Capital: Cairo. Although Egypt is an almost rainless expanse of desert, its economy is predominantly agricultural. Cotton, rice and petroleum are exported. Other main sources of income are revenues from the Suez Canal, remittances of Egyptian workers abroad and tourism.

ARAB REPUBLIC

AH1391- / 1971- AD

DECIMAL COINAGE

KM# 941 5 PIASTRES
1.9500 g., Brass, 18 mm. **Obv:** Denomination divides dates below, legend above **Rev:** Antique pottery vase **Edge:** Plain

Date	Mintage	F	VF	XF	Unc	BU
AH1425-2004	—	—	—	—	1.50	2.00

KM# 941a 5 PIASTRES
1.5000 g., Brass Plated Steel, 18 mm. **Rev:** Antique pottery vase

Date	Mintage	F	VF	XF	Unc	BU
AH1429/2008	—	—	—	—	1.50	2.00

KM# 922 10 PIASTRES
4.5200 g., Copper-Nickel, 24.8 mm. **Subject:** National Women's Council **Obv:** Value **Rev:** Woman standing next to Sphinx **Edge:** Reeded

Date	Mintage	F	VF	XF	Unc	BU
AH1425-2004	—	—	—	—	1.50	2.00

KM# 990 10 PIASTRES
3.4100 g., Nickel Plated Steel, 19.03 mm. **Obv:** Text, date and value **Rev:** Mosque

Date	Mintage	F	VF	XF	Unc	BU
AH1429 (2008)	—	—	—	—	1.00	1.50

KM# 923 20 PIASTRES
6.0000 g., Copper-Nickel, 26.8 mm. **Subject:** National Women's Council **Obv:** Value **Rev:** Woman standing next to Sphinx **Edge:** Reeded

Date	Mintage	F	VF	XF	Unc	BU
AH1425-2004	—	—	—	—	2.50	3.50

KM# 942.1 50 PIASTRES
6.5000 g., Brass, 25 mm. **Obv:** Value **Rev:** Bust of Cleopatra left **Edge:** Reeded **Note:** Non-magnetic.

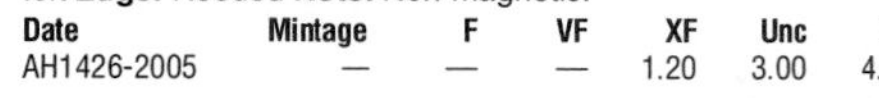

Date	Mintage	F	VF	XF	Unc	BU
AH1426-2005	—	—	—	1.20	3.00	4.00

KM# 942.2 50 PIASTRES
6.5000 g., Brass Plated Steel, 23 mm. **Rev:** Bust of Cleopatra left **Edge:** Reeded **Note:** Magnetic

Date	Mintage	F	VF	XF	Unc	BU
AH1428-2007	—	—	—	—	1.00	1.50

KM# 903 1/2 POUND
4.0000 g., 0.8750 Gold 0.1125 oz. AGW, 18 mm. **Subject:** Egyptian Museum Centennial **Obv:** Value **Rev:** Building **Edge:** Reeded

Date	Mintage	F	VF	XF	Unc	BU
AH1423-2002	—	—	—	—	250	270

KM# 930 POUND
15.0000 g., 0.7200 Silver 0.3472 oz. ASW, 35 mm. **Subject:** National Women's Council **Obv:** Value **Rev:** Woman standing next to Sphinx **Edge:** Reeded

Date	Mintage	F	VF	XF	Unc	BU
AH1421-2001	600	—	—	—	45.00	50.00

KM# 936 POUND
8.0000 g., 0.8750 Gold 0.2250 oz. AGW, 24 mm. **Subject:** 50th Anniversary of Egyptian Revolution **Obv:** Value **Rev:** Soldier with flag, pyramids and radiant sun **Edge:** Reeded

Date	Mintage	F	VF	XF	Unc	BU
AH1423-2002	400	—	—	—	375	400

KM# 938 POUND
8.0000 g., 0.8750 Gold 0.2250 oz. AGW, 24 mm. **Subject:** Alexandria Library **Obv:** Cufic text in center **Rev:** Arched inscription above slanted library roof **Edge:** Reeded

Date	Mintage	F	VF	XF	Unc	BU
AH1423-2002	750	—	—	—	375	400

KM# 904 POUND
15.0000 g., 0.7200 Silver 0.3472 oz. ASW, 35 mm. **Subject:** Egyptian Museum Centennial **Obv:** Value **Rev:** Building, centennial numerals in background **Edge:** Reeded

Date	Mintage	F	VF	XF	Unc	BU
AH1423-2002	1,500	—	—	—	35.00	40.00

KM# 905 POUND
8.0000 g., 0.8750 Gold 0.2250 oz. AGW, 24 mm. **Subject:** Egyptian Museum Centennial **Obv:** Value **Rev:** Building, centennial numerals in background **Edge:** Reeded

Date	Mintage	F	VF	XF	Unc	BU
AH1423-2002	300	—	—	—	375	400

KM# 909 POUND
15.0000 g., 0.7200 Silver 0.3472 oz. ASW, 35 mm. **Subject:** International Ear, Nose and Throat Conference **Obv:** King Tut's Gold Mask **Rev:** "IFOS" on world map **Edge:** Reeded

Date	Mintage	F	VF	XF	Unc	BU
AH1423-2002	2,500	—	—	—	30.00	35.00

KM# 910 POUND
15.0000 g., 0.7200 Silver 0.3472 oz. ASW, 35 mm. **Subject:** 50th Anniversary of Egyptian Revolution **Obv:** Value **Rev:** Soldier with flag **Edge:** Reeded

Date	Mintage	F	VF	XF	Unc	BU
AH1423-2002	1,500	—	—	—	35.00	40.00

KM# 912 POUND
15.0000 g., 0.7200 Silver 0.3472 oz. ASW, 35 mm. **Subject:** Alexandria Library **Obv:** Legend and inscription **Rev:** Inscribed arches above library roof **Edge:** Reeded

Date	Mintage	F	VF	XF	Unc	BU
AH1423-2002	8,000	—	—	—	30.00	35.00

KM# 913 POUND
15.0000 g., 0.7200 Silver 0.3472 oz. ASW, 35 mm. **Subject:** Body Building Championships **Obv:** Arabic and English legends **Rev:** Mr. Universe cartoon **Edge:** Reeded

Date	Mintage	F	VF	XF	Unc	BU
AH1423-2002	1,000	—	—	—	30.00	35.00

KM# 955 POUND
8.0000 g., 0.8750 Gold 0.2250 oz. AGW, 24 mm. **Subject:** Golden Jubilee Ein Shams University **Obv:** Value **Rev:** Obelisk with bird standing at left and right **Edge:** Reeded

Date	Mintage	F	VF	XF	Unc	BU
AH1422-2002	400	—	—	—	350	375

KM# 956 POUND
8.0000 g., 0.8750 Gold 0.2250 oz. AGW, 24 mm. **Subject:** Police Day **Obv:** Police eagle with wings spread, value **Rev:** Police badge **Edge:** Reeded

Date	Mintage	F	VF	XF	Unc	BU
AH1422-2002	400	—	—	—	350	375

KM# 957 POUND
8.0000 g., 0.8750 Gold 0.2250 oz. AGW, 24 mm. **Subject:** 30th Anniversary October War Victory **Obv:** Value **Rev:** Soldier holding flag on top of pyramid **Edge:** Reeded

Date	Mintage	F	VF	XF	Unc	BU
AH1424-2003	200	—	—	—	375	400

KM# 958 POUND
8.0000 g., 0.8750 Gold 0.2250 oz. AGW, 24 mm. **Series:** Value **Subject:** Radio and Television Festival **Obv:** Modern abstract design **Edge:** Reeded

Date	Mintage	F	VF	XF	Unc	BU
AH1424-2003	1,000	—	—	—	325	350

KM# 959 POUND
8.0000 g., 0.8750 Gold 0.2250 oz. AGW, 24 mm. **Subject:** 50th Anniversary El Gomhoreya Newspaper - Hosni Mubarak **Obv:** Value **Rev:** Bust facing at left, building in background **Edge:** Reeded

Date	Mintage	F	VF	XF	Unc	BU
AH1424-2003	400	—	—	—	350	375

KM# 915 POUND
15.0000 g., 0.7200 Silver 0.3472 oz. ASW, 35 mm. **Subject:** 30th Anniversary of the October War **Obv:** Value, dates and legend **Rev:** Soldier with flag above pyramids **Edge:** Reeded

Date	Mintage	F	VF	XF	Unc	BU
AH1424-2003	1,000	—	—	—	30.00	35.00

KM# 917 POUND
15.0000 g., 0.7200 Silver 0.3472 oz. ASW, 35 mm. **Subject:** 25th Anniversary of the Commerce Society **Obv:** Value, dates and legend **Rev:** Radiant sun above lattice work **Edge:** Reeded

Date	Mintage	F	VF	XF	Unc	BU
AH1424-2003	1,200	—	—	—	30.00	35.00

KM# 924 POUND
15.0000 g., 0.7200 Silver 0.3472 oz. ASW, 35 mm. **Subject:** 90th Anniversary Scouts **Obv:** Value **Rev:** Combined scouting badge **Edge:** Reeded

Date	Mintage	F	VF	XF	Unc	BU
AH1425-2004	2,000	—	—	—	30.00	35.00

KM# 960 POUND
8.0000 g., 0.8750 Gold 0.2250 oz. AGW, 24 mm. **Subject:** Golden Jubilee Military Production **Obv:** Value **Rev:** Ancient chariot, horse and rider left **Edge:** Reeded

Date	Mintage	F	VF	XF	Unc	BU
AH1425-2004	750	—	—	—	325	350

KM# 934 POUND
15.0000 g., 0.7250 Silver 0.3496 oz. ASW, 35 mm. **Subject:** Golden Jubilee - Military Production **Obv:** Value **Rev:** Ancient chariot, horse and rider **Edge:** Reeded

Date	Mintage	F	VF	XF	Unc	BU
AH1425-2004	1,000	—	—	—	30.00	35.00

KM# 940 POUND
8.5000 g., Bi-Metallic Brass center in Copper-Nickel ring, 25.1 mm. **Obv:** Value **Rev:** King Tutankhaman's gold mask **Edge:** Reeded

Date	Mintage	F	VF	XF	Unc	BU
AH1426-2005	—	—	—	—	3.00	5.00
AH1427-2006	—	—	—	—	3.00	5.00

KM# 965 POUND
15.0000 g., 0.7200 Silver 0.3472 oz. ASW, 35 mm. **Subject:** Golden Jubilee Suez Canal Nationalization **Obv:** Value **Rev:** Large "50" above government buildings **Edge:** Reeded

Date	Mintage	F	VF	XF	Unc	BU
AH1427-2006	1,750	—	—	—	35.00	40.00

KM# 966 POUND
15.0000 g., 0.7200 Silver 0.3472 oz. ASW, 35 mm. **Subject:** 60th Anniversary UNESCO **Obv:** Value **Rev:** Logo **Edge:** Reeded

Date	Mintage	F	VF	XF	Unc	BU
AH1427-2006	800	—	—	—	100	125

KM# 967 POUND
15.0000 g., 0.7200 Silver 0.3472 oz. ASW, 35 mm. **Subject:** 13th General Population Census **Obv:** Value **Rev:** Stylized couple leaning left at left **Edge:** Reeded

Date	Mintage	F	VF	XF	Unc	BU
AH1427-2006	2,000	—	—	—	45.00	50.00

KM# 961 POUND
8.0000 g., 0.8750 Gold 0.2250 oz. AGW, 24 mm. **Subject:** World Environment Day **Obv:** Value **Rev:** Stylized tree, emblem at left, bird standing at right **Edge:** Reeded

Date	Mintage	F	VF	XF	Unc	BU
AH1427-2006	200	—	—	—	375	400

KM# 962 POUND
8.0000 g., 0.8750 Gold 0.2250 oz. AGW, 24 mm. **Subject:** Golden Jubilee Suez Canal Nationalization **Obv:** Value **Rev:** Large "50" above government buildings **Edge:** Reeded

Date	Mintage	F	VF	XF	Unc	BU
AH1427-2006	1,000	—	—	—	325	350

KM# 963 POUND
8.0000 g., 0.8750 Gold 0.2250 oz. AGW, 24 mm. **Subject:** Silver Jubilee Egyptian Enviromental Protection **Obv:** Value **Rev:** World globe **Edge:** Reeded

Date	Mintage	F	VF	XF	Unc	BU
AH1428-2007	300	—	—	—	350	375

KM# 964 POUND
8.0000 g., 0.8750 Gold 0.2250 oz. AGW, 24 mm. **Subject:** Diamond Jubilee Air Force **Obv:** Value **Rev:** Air Force emblem **Edge:** Reeded

Date	Mintage	F	VF	XF	Unc	BU
AH1428-2007	130	—	—	—	550	—

KM# 968 POUND
15.0000 g., 0.7200 Silver 0.3472 oz. ASW, 35 mm. **Subject:** 100th Anniversary Ahly Club **Obv:** Value **Rev:** Large "100" with linked zeroes **Edge:** Reeded

Date	Mintage	F	VF	XF	Unc	BU
AH1428-2007	5,000	—	—	—	45.00	50.00

KM# 940a POUND
8.5000 g., Bi-Metallic Brass Plated Steel center in Nickel Plated Steel ring, 25.1 mm. **Obv:** Value at center **Rev:** King Tutankhaman's gold mask **Edge:** Reeded **Note:** Magnetic

Date	Mintage	F	VF	XF	Unc	BU
AH1428-2007	—	—	—	—	3.00	5.00

KM# 944 POUND
15.0000 g., 0.7200 Silver 0.3472 oz. ASW, 35.00 mm. **Subject:** Air Force Diamond Jubilee **Obv:** Value **Rev:** Air Force insignia **Edge:** Reeded

Date	Mintage	F	VF	XF	Unc	BU
AH1428-2007	—	—	—	—	45.00	50.00

KM# 931 5 POUNDS
17.5000 g., 0.7200 Silver 0.4051 oz. ASW, 37 mm. **Subject:** National Women's Council **Obv:** Value **Rev:** Woman standing next to Sphinx **Edge:** Reeded

Date	Mintage	F	VF	XF	Unc	BU
AH1421-2001	600	—	—	—	55.00	60.00

KM# 932 5 POUNDS
17.5000 g., 0.7200 Silver 0.4051 oz. ASW, 37 mm. **Subject:** 50th Anniversary of the National Police **Obv:** Value and police logo **Rev:** Ceremonial design **Edge:** Reeded

Date	Mintage	F	VF	XF	Unc	BU
AH1422-2002	750	—	—	—	45.00	50.00

KM# 906 5 POUNDS
17.5000 g., 0.7200 Silver 0.4051 oz. ASW, 37 mm. **Subject:** Egyptian Museum Centennial **Obv:** Value **Rev:** Building, centennial numerals in background **Edge:** Reeded

Date	Mintage	F	VF	XF	Unc	BU
AH1423-2002	1,500	—	—	—	40.00	45.00

KM# 907 5 POUNDS
26.0000 g., 0.8750 Gold 0.7314 oz. AGW, 33 mm. **Subject:** Egyptian Museum Centennial **Obv:** Value **Rev:** Building, centennial numerals in background **Edge:** Reeded

Date	Mintage	F	VF	XF	Unc	BU
AH1423-2002	250	—	—	—	1,100	1,150

KM# 911 5 POUNDS
17.5500 g., 0.9250 Silver 0.5219 oz. ASW, 37 mm. **Subject:** 50th Anniversary of the Egyptian Revolution **Obv:** Value **Rev:** Soldier with flag **Edge:** Reeded

Date	Mintage	F	VF	XF	Unc	BU
AH1423-2002	1,500	—	—	—	40.00	45.00

KM# 914 5 POUNDS
17.5000 g., 0.7200 Silver 0.4051 oz. ASW, 37 mm. **Subject:** Body Building Championships **Obv:** Arabic and English legends **Rev:** Mr. Universe cartoon **Edge:** Reeded

Date	Mintage	F	VF	XF	Unc	BU
AH1423-2002	800	—	—	—	35.00	40.00

KM# 916 5 POUNDS
17.5000 g., 0.7200 Silver 0.4051 oz. ASW, 37 mm. **Subject:** 30th Anniversary of the October War **Obv:** Value and legend **Rev:** Soldier with flag above pyramids **Edge:** Reeded

Date	Mintage	F	VF	XF	Unc	BU
AH1424-2003	800	—	—	—	35.00	40.00

KM# 918 5 POUNDS
17.5000 g., 0.7200 Silver 0.4051 oz. ASW, 37 mm. **Obv:** Value and legend **Rev:** Geo-Physical Institute **Edge:** Reeded

Date	Mintage	F	VF	XF	Unc	BU
AH1424-2003	800	—	—	—	35.00	40.00

KM# 919 5 POUNDS
17.5000 g., 0.7200 Silver 0.4051 oz. ASW, 37 mm. **Subject:** 50th Anniversary of the Republic **Obv:** Value and legend **Rev:** Portrait and building **Edge:** Reeded

Date	Mintage	F	VF	XF	Unc	BU
AH1424-2003	3,000	—	—	—	35.00	40.00

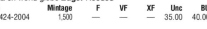

KM# 920 5 POUNDS
17.5000 g., 0.7200 Silver 0.4051 oz. ASW, 37 mm. **Subject:** 25th Anniversary of the Delta Bank **Obv:** Value and legend **Rev:** Delta on world globe **Edge:** Reeded

Date	Mintage	F	VF	XF	Unc	BU
AH1424-2004	1,500	—	—	—	35.00	40.00

KM# 925 5 POUNDS

17.5000 g., 0.7200 Silver 0.4051 oz. ASW, 37 mm. **Obv:** Value **Rev:** Balance scale **Edge:** Reeded

Date	Mintage	F	VF	XF	Unc	BU
AH1425-2004	3,300	—	—	—	35.00	40.00

KM# 974 5 POUNDS

17.5000 g., 0.7200 Silver 0.4051 oz. ASW, 37 mm. **Subject:** Golden Jubilee Cairo Mint **Obv:** Value **Rev:** National arms above mint building **Edge:** Reeded

Date	Mintage	F	VF	XF	Unc	BU
AH1425-2004	1,750	—	—	—	45.00	50.00

KM# 933 5 POUNDS

17.5000 g., 0.7200 Silver 0.4051 oz. ASW, 37 mm. **Subject:** 90th Anniversary - Egyptian Scouts Organization - 1914-2004 **Obv:** Value **Rev:** Combined scouting emblem **Edge:** Reeded

Date	Mintage	F	VF	XF	Unc	BU
AH1425-2004	—	—	—	—	35.00	40.00

KM# 935 5 POUNDS

17.5000 g., 0.7200 Silver 0.4051 oz. ASW, 37 mm. **Subject:** Golden Jubilee - Military Production **Obv:** Value **Rev:** Ancient chariot, horse and rider left **Edge:** Reeded

Date	Mintage	F	VF	XF	Unc	BU
AH1425-2004	800	—	—	—	35.00	40.00

KM# 975 5 POUNDS

17.5000 g., 0.7200 Silver 0.4051 oz. ASW, 37 mm. **Subject:** 60th Anniversary Arab League **Obv:** Value **Rev:** Logo in center of ornate background **Edge:** Reeded

Date	Mintage	F	VF	XF	Unc	BU
AH1426-2005	2,000	—	—	—	55.00	60.00

KM# 976 5 POUNDS

17.5000 g., 0.7200 Silver 0.4051 oz. ASW **Subject:** World Environment Day **Obv:** Value **Rev:** Stylized tree with logo at left, bird at right **Edge:** Reeded **Shape:** 37

Date	Mintage	F	VF	XF	Unc	BU
AH1427-2006	1,000	—	—	—	70.00	80.00

KM# 977 5 POUNDS

17.5000 g., 0.7200 Silver 0.4051 oz. ASW, 35 mm. **Subject:** Golden jubilee Suez Canal Nationalization **Obv:** Value **Rev:** Large "50" above government buildings **Edge:** Reeded

Date	Mintage	F	VF	XF	Unc	BU
AH1427-2006	1,750	—	—	—	45.00	50.00

KM# 978 5 POUNDS

17.5000 g., 0.7200 Silver 0.4051 oz. ASW, 37 mm. **Subject:** 60th Anniversary UNESCO **Obv:** Value **Rev:** Logo **Edge:** Reeded

Date	Mintage	F	VF	XF	Unc	BU
AH1427-2006	800	—	—	—	100	125

KM# 979 5 POUNDS

17.5000 g., 0.7200 Silver 0.4051 oz. ASW, 37 mm. **Subject:** Diamond Jubilee Academy of Arab Language **Obv:** Value **Rev:** Globe on open book **Edge:** Reeded

Date	Mintage	F	VF	XF	Unc	BU
AH1427-2006	1,000	—	—	—	70.00	80.00

KM# 980 5 POUNDS

17.5000 g., 0.7200 Silver 0.4051 oz. ASW, 37 mm. **Subject:** 13th General Population Census **Obv:** Circle with inscription in center **Rev:** Stylized couple leaning left at left **Edge:** Reeded

Date	Mintage	F	VF	XF	Unc	BU
AH1427-2006	1,500	—	—	—	65.00	75.00

KM# 981 5 POUNDS

17.5000 g., 0.7200 Silver 0.4051 oz. ASW, 37 mm. **Subject:** 100th Anniversary Ahly Club **Obv:** Value **Rev:** Large "100" With linked zeroes **Edge:** Reeded

Date	Mintage	F	VF	XF	Unc	BU
AH1428-2007	3,000	—	—	—	45.00	50.00

KM# 982 5 POUNDS

17.5000 g., 0.7200 Silver 0.4051 oz. ASW, 37 mm. **Subject:** Diamond Jubilee Court of Cassation **Obv:** Balance scale above inscriptions **Rev:** Court building **Edge:** Reeded

Date	Mintage	F	VF	XF	Unc	BU
AH1428-2007	450	—	—	—	125	150

KM# 983 5 POUNDS

17.5000 g., 0.7200 Silver 0.4051 oz. ASW, 37 mm. **Subject:** Silver Jubilee Enviromental Protection Agency **Obv:** Value **Rev:** World globe **Edge:** Reeded

Date	Mintage	F	VF	XF	Unc	BU
AH1428-2007	1,300	—	—	—	55.00	60.00

KM# 984 5 POUNDS

17.5000 g., 0.7200 Silver 0.4051 oz. ASW, 37 mm. **Subject:** 11th Arab Sports Championship - Egypt **Obv:** Value **Rev:** Stylized player on map of Arab countries **Edge:** Reeded

Date	Mintage	F	VF	XF	Unc	BU
AH1428-2007	6,300	—	—	—	45.00	50.00

KM# 943 5 POUNDS

17.5000 g., 0.7200 Silver 0.4051 oz. ASW, 37 mm. **Subject:** 11th Pan-Arab Games **Obv:** Value **Rev:** Logo with outlined map of Arab nations in background **Edge:** Reeded

Date	Mintage	F	VF	XF	Unc	BU
AH1428-2007	6,300	—	—	—	30.00	35.00

KM# 945 5 POUNDS

17.5000 g., 0.7200 Silver 0.4051 oz. ASW, 37 mm. **Subject:** Air Force Diamond Jubilee **Obv:** Value **Rev:** Air Force insignia **Edge:** Reeded

Date	Mintage	F	VF	XF	Unc	BU
AH1428-2007	600	—	—	—	55.00	60.00

KM# 908 10 POUNDS

40.0000 g., 0.8750 Gold 1.1252 oz. AGW, 37 mm. **Subject:** Egyptian Museum Centennial **Obv:** Denomination **Rev:** Building, centennial numerals in background **Edge:** Reeded

Date	Mintage	F	VF	XF	Unc	BU
AH1423-2002	150	—	—	—	1,700	1,750

KM# 989 10 POUNDS

40.0000 g., 0.8750 Gold 1.1252 oz. AGW, 37 mm. **Subject:** Golden Jubilee Police Day **Obv:** Eagle left with wings spread **Rev:** Police emblem **Edge:** Reeded

Date	Mintage	F	VF	XF	Unc	BU
AH1422-2002	150	—	—	—	1,700	1,750

KM# 985 10 POUNDS

40.0000 g., 0.8750 Gold 1.1252 oz. AGW, 37 mm. **Subject:** 50th Anniversary El Gomhoreya News **Obv:** Value **Rev:** Bust of Hosni Mubarak facing at left, building in background **Edge:** Reeded

Date	Mintage	F	VF	XF	Unc	BU
AH1424-2003	50	—	—	—	1,800	1,850

KM# 986 10 POUNDS

40.0000 g., 0.8750 Gold 1.1252 oz. AGW, 37 mm. **Subject:** Golden Jubilee Military Production **Obv:** Value **Rev:** Ancient chariot, horse and rider left **Edge:** Reeded

Date	Mintage	F	VF	XF	Unc	BU
AH1425-2004	85	—	—	—	1,750	1,800

KM# 987 10 POUNDS

40.0000 g., 0.8750 Gold 1.1252 oz. AGW, 37 mm. **Subject:** 60th Anniversary Arab League **Obv:** Value **Rev:** Emblem at center, ornate background **Edge:** Reeded

Date	Mintage	F	VF	XF	Unc	BU
AH1426-2005	50	—	—	—	1,800	1,850

KM# 988 10 POUNDS

40.0000 g., 0.8750 Gold 1.1252 oz. AGW, 37 mm. **Subject:** Diamond Jubilee Air Force **Obv:** Value **Rev:** Air Force emblem **Edge:** Reeded

Date	Mintage	F	VF	XF	Unc	BU
AH1428-2007	25	—	—	—	1,900	1,950

ESTONIA

The Republic of Estonia (formerly the Estonian Soviet Socialist Republic of the U.S.S.R.) is the northernmost of the three Baltic States in Eastern Europe. It has an area of 17,462 sq. mi. (45,100 sq. km.) and a population of 1.6 million. Capital: Tallinn. Agriculture and dairy farming are the principal industries. Butter, eggs, bacon, timber and petroleum are exported.

MODERN REPUBLIC

1991 - present

STANDARD COINAGE

KM# 22 10 SENTI

1.8500 g., Aluminum-Bronze, 17.1 mm. **Obv:** Three leopards divide date **Rev:** Denomination **Rev. Legend:** EESTI VABARIIK **Edge:** Plain

Date	Mintage	F	VF	XF	Unc	BU
2002	30,000,000	—	—	0.20	0.50	0.80
2006	—	—	—	0.20	0.50	0.80
2008	—	—	—	0.20	0.50	0.80

KM# 23a 20 SENTI

2.0000 g., Nickel Plated Steel, 18.9 mm. **Obv:** National arms divide date **Rev:** Denomination **Rev. Legend:** EESTI VABARIIK **Edge:** Plain

Date	Mintage	F	VF	XF	Unc	BU
2003	8,600,000	—	—	0.30	0.60	1.00
2004	—	—	—	0.30	0.60	1.00
2006	—	—	—	0.30	0.60	1.00

KM# 24 50 SENTI

2.9000 g., Aluminum-Bronze, 19.5 mm. **Obv:** National arms divide date **Rev:** Denomination **Rev. Legend:** EESTI VABARIIK **Edge:** Plain

Date	Mintage	F	VF	XF	Unc	BU
2004	—	—	—	0.40	1.00	1.50
2006	—	—	—	0.40	1.00	1.50
2007	—	—	—	0.40	1.00	1.50

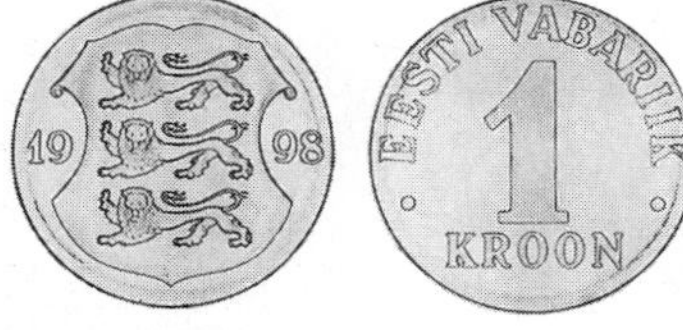

KM# 35 KROON

5.0000 g., Aluminum-Bronze, 23.5 mm. **Obv:** National arms **Rev:** Large, thick denomination **Rev. Legend:** EESTI VABARIIK **Edge:** Segmented reeding

Date	Mintage	F	VF	XF	Unc	BU
2001	15,000,000	—	—	0.50	1.00	1.50
2003	—	—	—	0.50	1.00	1.50
2006	—	—	—	0.50	1.00	1.50

KM# 44 KROON

4.8000 g., Brass, 23.21 mm. **Obv:** National arms **Rev:** Stylized plant in circle **Rev. Legend:** EESTI VABARIIK **Edge:** Segmented reeding

Date	Mintage	F	VF	XF	Unc	BU
2008	—	—	—	0.50	1.50	2.00

KM# 38 10 KROONI

28.2800 g., 0.9990 Silver 0.9083 oz. ASW, 38.6 mm. **Subject:** Tartu University **Obv:** National arms **Rev:** Building in oval, value at left **Edge:** Reeded

Date	Mintage	F	VF	XF	Unc	BU
2002 Proof	10,000	Value: 35.00				

KM# 40 10 KROONI

28.2800 g., 0.9990 Silver 0.9083 oz. ASW, 38.6 mm. **Subject:** Estonian Flag **Obv:** National arms **Rev:** Round multicolor flag design **Edge:** Reeded

Date	Mintage	F	VF	XF	Unc	BU
2004 Proof	10,000	Value: 35.00				

KM# 42 10 KROONI
28.2800 g., 0.9990 Silver 0.9083 oz. ASW, 38.6 mm. **Subject:** Torino Winter Olympics **Obv:** National arms **Rev:** Gold inset cross country skier in semi-circle above Olympic flame **Edge:** Reeded

Date	Mintage	F	VF	XF	Unc	BU
2006 Proof	5,000	Value: 45.00				

KM# 46 10 KROONI
28.2800 g., 0.9990 Silver 0.9083 oz. ASW, 38.61 mm. **Subject:** 90th Anniversary of Independence **Obv:** National arms **Obv. Legend:** EESTI VARBARIIK **Rev:** Wiiralt oak tree **Edge:** Plain **Designer:** Heino Prunsvelt

Date	Mintage	F	VF	XF	Unc	BU
2008 Proof	10,000	Value: 50.00				

KM# 48 10 KROONI
28.2800 g., 0.9990 Silver 0.9083 oz. ASW, 38.61 mm. **Subject:** Olympics **Obv:** Arms **Rev:** Torch and geometric patterns

Date	Mintage	F	VF	XF	Unc	BU
2008 Proof	—	Value: 42.50				

KM# 49 10 KROONI
24.1000 g., 0.9990 Silver 0.7740 oz. ASW, 38.61 mm. **Subject:** National Museum **Obv:** Shield in star **Rev:** Design in star

Date	Mintage	F	VF	XF	Unc	BU
2008 Proof	—	Value: 42.50				

KM# 51 10 KROONI
31.1050 g., 0.9990 Silver 0.9990 oz. ASW, 40.6 mm. **Subject:** Song and Dance Festival

Date	Mintage	F	VF	XF	Unc	BU
2009 Proof	—	Value: 42.50				

KM# 53 10 KROONI
28.2800 g., 0.9990 Silver 0.9083 oz. ASW, 38.61 mm. **Subject:** Vancouver Winter Olympics **Obv:** National arms within wreath, date below **Rev:** Two cross county skiers

Date	Mintage	F	VF	XF	Unc	BU
2010 Proof	—	Value: 45.00				

KM# 50 50 KROONI
8.6400 g., 0.9990 Gold 0.2775 oz. AGW, 22 mm. **Obv:** Shield **Rev:** Windmill

Date	Mintage	F	VF	XF	Unc	BU
2008 Proof	—	Value: 475				

KM# 39 100 KROONI
7.7760 g., 0.9999 Gold 0.2500 oz. AGW **Subject:** Monetary Reform **Obv:** National arms **Rev:** Cross design **Edge:** Reeded

Date	Mintage	F	VF	XF	Unc	BU
2002	2,000	—	—	—	—	425

KM# 41 100 KROONI
7.7760 g., 0.9999 Gold 0.2500 oz. AGW, 21.9 mm. **Subject:** Olympic Games **Obv:** National arms **Rev:** Olympic flame above rings in center **Edge:** Reeded

Date	Mintage	F	VF	XF	Unc	BU
2004	5,000	—	—	—	—	400

KM# 43 100 KROONI
28.2800 g., 0.9990 Silver 0.9083 oz. ASW, 38.6 mm. **Subject:** National Opera **Obv:** National arms **Rev:** Building front **Edge:** Plain

Date	Mintage	F	VF	XF	Unc	BU
2006 Proof	10,000	Value: 45.00				

KM# 45 100 KROONI
7.7800 g., 0.9999 Gold 0.2501 oz. AGW **Subject:** 15th Anniversary Reintroduction of the Estonian Kroon **Obv:** National arms **Obv. Legend:** EESTI VARBARIIK **Rev:** Cornflower **Rev. Legend:** KROONI TAAS- / KEHTESTAMISE / 15. AASTAPAEV **Edge:** Plain **Shape:** Triangular **Designer:** Ivar Sakk

Date	Mintage	F	VF	XF	Unc	BU
2007 Prooflike	6,000	—	—	—	—	500

KM# 47 100 KROONI
7.7750 g., 0.9990 Platinum 0.2497 oz. APW, 18 mm. **Subject:** 90th Anniversary of Republic **Rev:** Three buds on wire

Date	Mintage	F	VF	XF	Unc	BU
2008 Proof	3,000	Value: 600				

KM# 52 100 KROONI
7.7800 g., 0.9990 Gold 0.2499 oz. AGW, 22 mm. **Subject:** Song and dance festival **Obv:** Arms

Date	Mintage	F	VF	XF	Unc	BU
2009 Proof	—	Value: 425				

EURO COINAGE

KM# 61 EURO CENT
2.3000 g., Copper Plated Steel, 16.25 mm. **Obv:** Map of Estonia **Rev:** Denomination and globe

Date	Mintage	F	VF	XF	Unc	BU
2011	—	—	—	—	0.35	0.50

KM# 62 2 EURO CENT
3.0600 g., Copper Plated Steel, 18.75 mm. **Obv:** Map of Estonia **Rev:** Denomination and globe **Edge:** Grooved

Date	Mintage	F	VF	XF	Unc	BU
2011	—	—	—	—	0.50	0.75

KM# 63 5 EURO CENT
3.9200 g., Copper Plated Steel, 21.25 mm. **Obv:** Map of Estonia **Rev:** Denomination and globe

Date	Mintage	F	VF	XF	Unc	BU
2011	—	—	—	—	0.75	1.25

KM# 64 10 EURO CENT
4.1000 g., Brass, 19.75 mm. **Obv:** Map of Estonia **Rev:** Relief map of Western Europe, stars, line and value **Edge:** Reeded

Date	Mintage	F	VF	XF	Unc	BU
2011	—	—	—	—	1.25	2.00

KM# 65 20 EURO CENT
5.7400 g., Brass, 22.25 mm. **Obv:** Map of Estonia **Rev:** Relief map of Western Europe, stars, line and value **Edge:** Notched

Date	Mintage	F	VF	XF	Unc	BU
2011	—	—	—	—	1.00	1.50

KM# 66 50 EURO CENT
7.8000 g., Brass, 24.25 mm. **Obv:** Map of Estonia **Rev:** Relief map of Western Europe, stars, line and value **Edge:** Reeded

Date	Mintage	F	VF	XF	Unc	BU
2011	—	—	—	—	1.25	2.00

KM# 67 EURO
7.5000 g., Bi-Metallic Copper-Nickel center in Nickel-Brass ring, 23.35 mm. **Obv:** Map of Estonia **Rev:** Relief map of Western Europe, stars, lines and value **Edge:** Segmented reeding

Date	Mintage	F	VF	XF	Unc	BU
2011	—	—	—	—	2.75	4.00

KM# 68 2 EURO
8.5000 g., Bi-Metallic Nickel-Brass center in Copper-Nickel ring, 25.75 mm. **Obv:** Map of Estonia **Rev:** Relief map of Western Europe, stars, lines and value **Edge:** Reeded and lettered

Date	Mintage	F	VF	XF	Unc	BU
2011	—	—	—	—	3.75	6.00

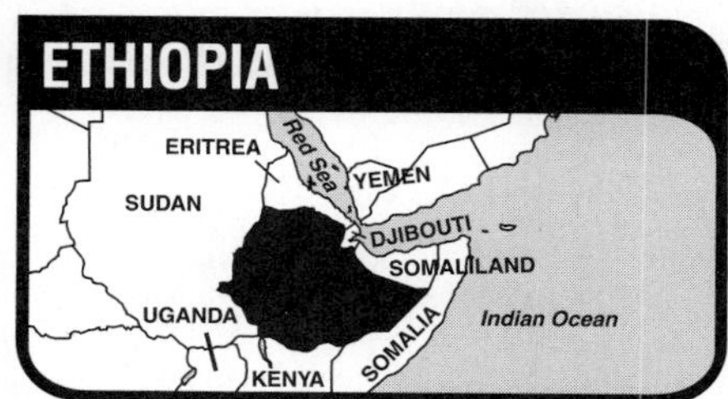

The People's Federal Republic of Ethiopia (formerly the Peoples Democratic Republic and the Empire of Ethiopia), Africa's oldest independent nation, faces the Red Sea in East-Central Africa. The country has an area of 424,214 sq. mi. (1,004,390 sq. km.) and a population of 56 million people who are divided among 40 tribes that speak some 270 languages and dialects. Capital: Addis Ababa. The economy is predominantly agricultural and pastoral. Gold and platinum are mined and petroleum fields are being developed. Coffee, oilseeds, hides and cereals are exported.

DATING

Ethiopian coinage is dated by the Ethiopian Era calendar (E.E.), which commenced 7 years and 8 months after the advent of A.D. dating.

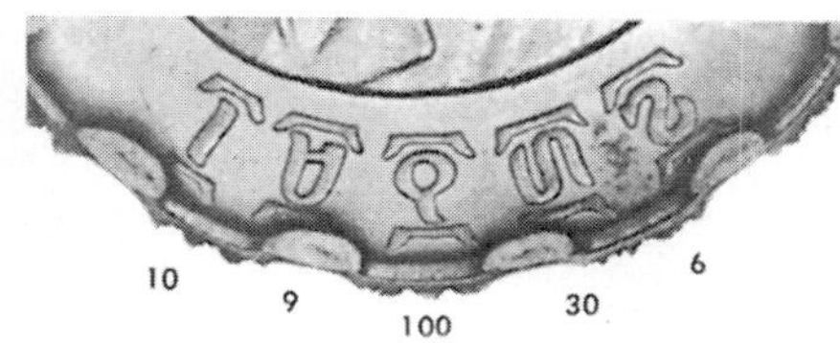

EXAMPLE

1900 (10 and 9 = 19 x 100)
36 (Add 30 and 6)
1936 E.E.
8 (Add)
1943/4 AD

PEOPLES DEMOCRATIC REPUBLIC

DECIMAL COINAGE

100 Santeems (Cents) = 1 Birr (Dollar)

100 Matonas = 100 Santeems

KM# 44.3 5 CENTS

3.0000 g., Brass, 20 mm. **Obv:** Large lion head, right **Rev:** Denomination left of figure **Designer:** Stuart Devlin

Date	Mintage	F	VF	XF	Unc	BU
EE1996(2004)	—	—	—	—	—	1.00

KM# 45.3 10 CENTS

4.5000 g., Brass, 23 mm. **Obv:** Large lion head right **Rev:** Mountain Nyala, denomination at right **Designer:** Stuart Devlin

Date	Mintage	F	VF	XF	Unc	BU
EE1996 (2004)	—	—	—	—	—	1.25
EE1997 (2005)	—	—	—	—	—	1.25

KM# 46.3 25 CENTS

3.7000 g., Copper-Nickel, 21.45 mm. **Obv:** Large lion head right **Rev:** Man and woman with arms raised divide denomination **Designer:** Stuart Devlin

Date	Mintage	F	VF	XF	Unc	BU
EE1996 (2004)	—	—	—	—	—	1.25

KM# 47.2 50 CENTS

6.0000 g., Copper-Nickel, 25 mm. **Obv:** Small lion head, two long chin whiskers at left nearly touch date **Rev:** People of the republic, denomination above

Date	Mintage	F	VF	XF	Unc	BU
EE1996 (2004)	—	—	—	1.50	3.00	—

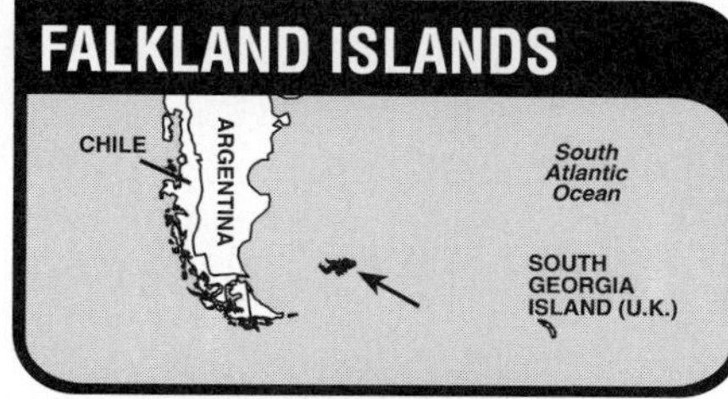

The Colony of the Falkland Islands and Dependencies, a British colony located in the South Atlantic about 500 miles northeast of Cape Horn, has an area of 4,700 sq. mi. (12,170 sq. km.) and a population of 2,121. East Falkland, West Falkland, South Georgia, and South Sandwich are the largest of the 200 islands. Capital: Stanley. Sheep grazing is the main industry. Wool, whale oil, and seal oil are exported.

RULER

British

MONETARY SYSTEM

100 Pence = 1 Pound

BRITISH COLONY

DECIMAL COINAGE

KM# 130 PENNY

Bronze Plated Steel, 20.3 mm. **Ruler:** Elizabeth II **Obv:** Head with tiara right **Obv. Legend:** QUEEN ELIZABETH THE SECOND **Rev:** Two Gentoo penguins flank value **Rev. Legend:** FALKLAND ISLANDS **Edge:** Plain

Date	Mintage	F	VF	XF	Unc	BU
2004	—	—	—	—	0.50	0.75

KM# 131 2 PENCE

Bronze Plated Steel, 25.9 mm. **Ruler:** Elizabeth II **Obv:** Head with tiara right **Obv. Legend:** QUEEN ELIZABETH THE SECOND **Rev:** Upland goose alighting, value above **Rev. Legend:** FALKLAND ISLANDS **Edge:** Plain

Date	Mintage	F	VF	XF	Unc	BU
2004	—	—	—	—	0.50	1.00

KM# 132 5 PENCE

Copper-Nickel, 18 mm. **Ruler:** Elizabeth II **Obv:** Head with tiara right **Obv. Legend:** QUEEN ELIZABETH THE SECOND **Rev:** Black-browed Albatross in flight, value below **Rev. Legend:** FALKLAND - ISLANDS **Edge:** Reeded

Date	Mintage	F	VF	XF	Unc	BU
2004	—	—	—	—	0.75	1.00

KM# 133 10 PENCE

Copper-Nickel, 24.5 mm. **Ruler:** Elizabeth II **Obv:** Head with tiara right **Obv. Legend:** QUEEN ELIZABETH THE SECOND **Rev:** Ursine seal with cub, value below **Rev. Legend:** FALKLAND ISLANDS

Date	Mintage	F	VF	XF	Unc	BU
2004	—	—	—	—	1.50	3.00

KM# 134 20 PENCE

Copper-Nickel, 21.4 mm. **Ruler:** Elizabeth II **Obv:** Head with tiara right **Obv. Legend:** QUEEN ELIZABETH THE SECOND **Rev:** Romney marsh sheep standing left, value above **Rev. Legend:** FALKLAND ISLANDS **Rev. Designer:** Robert Elderton **Edge:** Plain **Shape:** 7-sided

Date	Mintage	F	VF	XF	Unc	BU
2004	—	—	—	—	2.00	4.00

KM# 70 50 PENCE

29.1000 g., Copper-Nickel, 38.6 mm. **Ruler:** Elizabeth II **Subject:** Centennial of Queen Victoria's Death **Obv:** Crowned bust right, denomination below **Obv. Designer:** Raphael Maklouf **Rev:** Crowned head left, three dates **Edge:** Reeded

Date	Mintage	F	VF	XF	Unc	BU
2001	—	—	—	—	6.00	7.00

KM# 70a 50 PENCE

28.2800 g., 0.9250 Silver 0.8410 oz. ASW, 38.6 mm. **Ruler:** Elizabeth II **Obv:** Crowned bust right, denomination below **Rev:** Crowned head left, three dates **Edge:** Reeded

Date	Mintage	F	VF	XF	Unc	BU
2001 Proof	10,000	Value: 50.00				

KM# 70b 50 PENCE

47.5400 g., 0.9170 Gold 1.4015 oz. AGW, 38.61 mm. **Ruler:** Elizabeth II **Subject:** Centennial of Queen Victoria's Death **Obv:** Crowned bust right, denomination below **Rev:** Victoria's crowned bust left, three dates **Edge:** Reeded

Date	Mintage	F	VF	XF	Unc	BU
2001 Proof	100	Value: 2,150				

KM# 71 50 PENCE

29.1000 g., Copper-Nickel, 38.6 mm. **Ruler:** Elizabeth II

Subject: Queen Elizabeth's 75th Birthday **Obv:** Crowned bust right, denomination below **Obv. Designer:** Raphael Maklouf **Rev:** Bust of Queen Elizabeth II left **Edge:** Reeded

Date	Mintage	F	VF	XF	Unc	BU
2001	—	—	—	—	6.00	7.00

KM# 71b 50 PENCE

47.5400 g., 0.9170 Gold 1.4015 oz. AGW, 38.61 mm. **Ruler:** Elizabeth II **Subject:** Queen Elizabeth's 75th Birthday **Obv:** Crowned bust right, denomination below **Rev:** Bust of Queen Elizabeth II left

Date	Mintage	F	VF	XF	Unc	BU
2001 Proof	Est. 100	Value: 2,150				

KM# 86 50 PENCE

28.2800 g., Copper-Nickel, 38.6 mm. **Ruler:** Elizabeth II **Obv:** Crowned bust right, denomination below **Rev:** Edward IV (1461-83) with Rose Ryal gold coin design **Rev. Designer:** Willem Vis **Edge:** Reeded

Date	Mintage	F	VF	XF	Unc	BU
2001	—	—	—	—	9.00	10.00

KM# 86a 50 PENCE

28.2800 g., 0.9250 Silver 0.8410 oz. ASW, 38.6 mm. **Ruler:** Elizabeth II **Obv:** Crowned bust right, denomination below **Rev:** Edward IV (1461-83) with gold-plated Rose Ryal gold coin design **Edge:** Reeded

Date	Mintage	F	VF	XF	Unc	BU
2001 Proof	5,000	Value: 50.00				

KM# 87 50 PENCE

28.2800 g., Copper-Nickel, 38.6 mm. **Ruler:** Elizabeth II **Obv:** Crowned bust right, denomination below **Rev:** Henry VII (1485-1509) with 1489 Gold Sovereign coin design **Rev. Designer:** Willem Vis **Edge:** Reeded

Date	Mintage	F	VF	XF	Unc	BU
2001	—	—	—	—	9.00	10.00

KM# 87a 50 PENCE

28.2800 g., 0.9250 Silver 0.8410 oz. ASW, 38.6 mm. **Ruler:** Elizabeth II **Obv:** Crowned bust right, denomination below **Rev:** Henry VII (1485-1509) with gold-plated 1489 gold Sovereign coin design **Edge:** Reeded

Date	Mintage	F	VF	XF	Unc	BU
2001 Proof	5,000	Value: 50.00				

KM# 88 50 PENCE

28.2800 g., Copper-Nickel, 38.6 mm. **Ruler:** Elizabeth II **Obv:** Crowned bust right, denomination below **Rev:** Charles II (1660-85) with 1663 gold Guinea coin design **Rev. Designer:** Willem Vis **Edge:** Reeded

Date	Mintage	F	VF	XF	Unc	BU
2001	—	—	—	—	9.00	10.00

KM# 88a 50 PENCE

28.2800 g., 0.9250 Silver 0.8410 oz. ASW, 38.6 mm. **Ruler:** Elizabeth II **Obv:** Crowned bust right, denomination below **Rev:** Charles II (1660-85) with gold-plated Gold Guinea coin design **Edge:** Reeded

Date	Mintage	F	VF	XF	Unc	BU
2001 Proof	5,000	Value: 50.00				

KM# 89 50 PENCE

28.2800 g., Copper-Nickel, 38.6 mm. **Ruler:** Elizabeth II **Obv:** Crowned bust right, denomination below **Rev:** Queen Victoria with Gold Sovereign coin design **Rev. Designer:** Willem Vis **Edge:** Reeded

Date	Mintage	F	VF	XF	Unc	BU
2001	—	—	—	—	9.00	10.00

KM# 89a 50 PENCE

28.2800 g., 0.9250 Silver 0.8410 oz. ASW, 38.6 mm. **Ruler:** Elizabeth II **Obv:** Crowned bust right, denomination below **Rev:** Queen Victoria with gold-plated Gold Sovereign coin design **Edge:** Reeded

Date	Mintage	F	VF	XF	Unc	BU
2001 Proof	5,000	Value: 50.00				

KM# 73.1 50 PENCE

28.1300 g., Copper-Nickel, 38.6 mm. **Ruler:** Elizabeth II **Subject:** Queen's Golden Jubilee **Obv:** Crowned head right, denomination below **Rev:** Queen Elizabeth II on throne in inner circle below multicolor bunting **Edge:** Reeded

Date	Mintage	F	VF	XF	Unc	BU
2002(2001) Proof	—	Value: 8.00				

KM# 73.2 50 PENCE

Copper-Nickel **Ruler:** Elizabeth II **Subject:** Queen's Golden Jubilee **Obv:** Crowned bust right, denomination below **Rev:** With plain bunting

Date	Mintage	F	VF	XF	Unc	BU
2002	—	—	—	—	6.00	7.00

KM# 73a.1 50 PENCE

28.2800 g., 0.9250 Silver 0.8410 oz. ASW, 38.6 mm. **Ruler:** Elizabeth II **Subject:** Queen's Golden Jubilee **Obv:** Crowned bust right, denomination below **Rev:** Queen on throne below multicolor bunting **Edge:** Reeded

Date	Mintage	F	VF	XF	Unc	BU
2002 Proof	25,000	Value: 45.00				

KM# 73a.2 50 PENCE

28.2800 g., 0.9250 Silver 0.8410 oz. ASW, 38.61 mm. **Ruler:** Elizabeth II **Obv:** Crowned bust right, denomination below **Rev:** With plain bunting

Date	Mintage	F	VF	XF	Unc	BU
2002 Proof	—	Value: 45.00				

KM# 73b.1 50 PENCE

39.9400 g., 0.9170 Gold 1.1775 oz. AGW, 38.61 mm. **Ruler:** Elizabeth II **Obv:** Crowned bust right, denomination below **Rev:** Crowned queen with scepter and orb below multicolor bunting **Edge:** Reeded

Date	Mintage	F	VF	XF	Unc	BU
2002 Proof	150	Value: 1,800				

KM# 74.1 50 PENCE

28.1300 g., Copper-Nickel, 38.6 mm. **Ruler:** Elizabeth II **Subject:** Queen's Golden Jubilee **Obv:** Crowned bust right, denomination below **Obv. Designer:** Raphael Maklouf **Rev:** Queen on horse half left in inner circle below multicolor bunting **Edge:** Reeded

Date	Mintage	F	VF	XF	Unc	BU
2002(2001) Proof	—	Value: 8.00				

KM# 74.2 50 PENCE

Copper-Nickel **Ruler:** Elizabeth II **Subject:** Queen's Golden Jubilee **Obv:** Crowned bust right, denomination below **Rev:** With plain bunting

Date	Mintage	F	VF	XF	Unc	BU
2002	—	—	—	—	7.00	8.00

KM# 74a.1 50 PENCE

28.2800 g., 0.9250 Silver 0.8410 oz. ASW, 38.6 mm. **Ruler:** Elizabeth II **Subject:** Queen's Golden Jubilee **Obv:** Crowned bust right, denomination below **Rev. Designer:** Queen on horse below multicolor bunting **Edge:** Reeded

Date	Mintage	F	VF	XF	Unc	BU
2002 Proof	25,000	Value: 45.00				

KM# 74a.2 50 PENCE

28.2800 g., 0.9250 Silver 0.8410 oz. ASW, 38.61 mm. **Ruler:** Elizabeth II **Subject:** Queen's Golden Jubilee **Obv:** Crowned bust right, denomination below **Rev:** With plain bunting

Date	Mintage	F	VF	XF	Unc	BU
2002 Proof	—	Value: 45.00				

KM# 74b.1 50 PENCE

39.9400 g., 0.9170 Gold 1.1775 oz. AGW, 38.61 mm. **Ruler:** Elizabeth II **Subject:** Queen's Golden Jubilee **Obv:** Crowned bust right, denomination below **Rev:** Queen on horseback below multicolored bunting **Edge:** Reeded

Date	Mintage	F	VF	XF	Unc	BU
2002 Proof	150	Value: 1,800				

KM# 74b.2 50 PENCE

39.9400 g., 0.9170 Gold 1.1775 oz. AGW, 38.61 mm. **Ruler:** Elizabeth II **Obv:** Crowned bust right, denomination below **Rev:** With plain bunting

Date	Mintage	F	VF	XF	Unc	BU
2002 Proof	—	Value: 1,750				

KM# 75.1 50 PENCE

28.1300 g., Copper-Nickel, 38.6 mm. **Ruler:** Elizabeth II **Subject:** Queen's Golden Jubilee **Obv:** Crowned bust right, denomination below **Rev:** Queen Elizabeth II talking into microphone below multicolor bunting **Edge:** Reeded

Date	Mintage	F	VF	XF	Unc	BU
2002(2001) Proof	—	Value: 8.00				

KM# 75.2 50 PENCE
Copper-Nickel **Ruler:** Elizabeth II **Subject:** Queen's Golden Jubilee **Obv:** Crowned bust right, denomination below **Rev:** With plain bunting

Date	Mintage	F	VF	XF	Unc	BU
2002	—	—	—	—	6.00	7.00

KM# 75a.1 50 PENCE
28.2800 g., 0.9250 Silver 0.8410 oz. ASW, 38.6 mm. **Ruler:** Elizabeth II **Subject:** Queen's Golden Jubilee **Obv:** Crowned bust right, denomination below **Rev:** Queen speaking into a radio microphone below multicolored bunting **Edge:** Reeded

Date	Mintage	F	VF	XF	Unc	BU
2002 Proof	25,000	Value: 45.00				

KM# 75a.2 50 PENCE
28.2800 g., 0.9250 Silver 0.8410 oz. ASW, 38.61 mm. **Ruler:** Elizabeth II **Subject:** Queen's Golden Jubilee **Obv:** Crowned bust right, denomination below **Rev:** With plain bunting

Date	Mintage	F	VF	XF	Unc	BU
2002 Proof	—	Value: 45.00				

KM# 75b.1 50 PENCE
39.9400 g., 0.9170 Gold 1.1775 oz. AGW, 38.61 mm. **Ruler:** Elizabeth II **Subject:** Queen's Golden Jubilee **Obv:** Crowned bust right, denomination below **Rev:** Elizabeth speaking into a radio microphone below multicolored bunting **Edge:** Reeded

Date	Mintage	F	VF	XF	Unc	BU
2002 Proof	50	Value: 1,800				

KM# 75b.2 50 PENCE
39.9400 g., 0.9170 Gold 1.1775 oz. AGW, 38.61 mm. **Ruler:** Elizabeth II **Subject:** Queen's Golden Jubilee **Obv:** Crowned bust right, denomination below **Rev:** With plain bunting

Date	Mintage	F	VF	XF	Unc	BU
2002 Proof	—	Value: 1,750				

KM# 76.1 50 PENCE
28.1300 g., Copper-Nickel, 38.6 mm. **Ruler:** Elizabeth II **Subject:** Queen's Golden Jubilee **Obv:** Crowned bust right, denomination below **Rev:** Queen walking to left in front of a crowd below multicolored bunting **Edge:** Reeded

Date	Mintage	F	VF	XF	Unc	BU
2002(2001) Proof	—	Value: 8.00				

KM# 76.2 50 PENCE
Copper-Nickel **Ruler:** Elizabeth II **Subject:** Queen's Golden Jubilee **Obv:** Crowned bust right, denomination below **Rev:** With plain bunting

Date	Mintage	F	VF	XF	Unc	BU
2002	—	—	—	—	6.00	7.00

KM# 76a.1 50 PENCE
28.2800 g., 0.9250 Silver 0.8410 oz. ASW, 38.6 mm. **Ruler:** Elizabeth II **Subject:** Queen's Golden Jubilee **Obv:** Crowned bust right, denomination below **Rev:** Queen standing before crowd below multicolored bunting **Edge:** Reeded

Date	Mintage	F	VF	XF	Unc	BU
2002 Proof	15,000	Value: 45.00				

KM# 76a.2 50 PENCE
28.2800 g., 0.9250 Silver 0.8410 oz. ASW, 38.61 mm. **Ruler:** Elizabeth II **Subject:** Queen's Golden Jubilee **Obv:** Crowned bust right, denomination below **Rev:** With plain bunting

Date	Mintage	F	VF	XF	Unc	BU
2002 Proof	—	Value: 45.00				

KM# 76b.1 50 PENCE
39.9400 g., 0.9170 Gold 1.1775 oz. AGW, 38.61 mm. **Ruler:** Elizabeth II **Subject:** Queen's Golden Jubilee **Obv:** Crowned bust right, denomination below **Rev:** Queen standing before a crowd below multicolored bunting **Edge:** Reeded

Date	Mintage	F	VF	XF	Unc	BU
2002 Proof	50	Value: 1,800				

KM# 76b.2 50 PENCE
39.9400 g., 0.9170 Gold 1.1775 oz. AGW, 38.61 mm. **Ruler:** Elizabeth II **Subject:** Queen's Golden Jubilee **Obv:** Crowned bust right, denomination below **Rev:** With plain bunting

Date	Mintage	F	VF	XF	Unc	BU
2002 Proof	—	Value: 1,750				

KM# 77.1 50 PENCE
28.1300 g., Copper-Nickel, 38.6 mm. **Ruler:** Elizabeth II **Subject:** Queen's Golden Jubilee **Obv:** Crowned bust right, denomination below **Obv. Designer:** Raphael Maklouf **Rev:** Conjoined busts of Queen Elizabeth, Prince Charles, Prince William facing left in inner circle below multicolor bunting **Edge:** Reeded

Date	Mintage	F	VF	XF	Unc	BU
2002(2001) Proof	—	Value: 8.00				

KM# 77.2 50 PENCE
Copper-Nickel **Ruler:** Elizabeth II **Subject:** Queen's Golden Jubilee **Obv:** Crowned bust right, denomination below **Rev:** With plain bunting

Date	Mintage	F	VF	XF	Unc	BU
2002	—	—	—	—	6.00	7.00

KM# 77a.1 50 PENCE
28.2800 g., 0.9250 Silver 0.8410 oz. ASW, 38.6 mm. **Ruler:** Elizabeth II **Subject:** Queen's Golden Jubilee **Obv:** Crowned bust right, denomination below **Rev:** Queen, Prince Charles and Prince William below multicolor bunting **Edge:** Reeded

Date	Mintage	F	VF	XF	Unc	BU
2002 Proof	15,000	Value: 45.00				

KM# 77a.2 50 PENCE
28.2800 g., 0.9250 Silver 0.8410 oz. ASW, 38.61 mm. **Ruler:** Elizabeth II **Subject:** Queen's Golden Jubilee **Obv:** Crowned bust right, denomination below **Rev:** With plain bunting

Date	Mintage	F	VF	XF	Unc	BU
2002 Proof	—	Value: 45.00				

KM# 77b.1 50 PENCE
39.9400 g., 0.9170 Gold 1.1775 oz. AGW, 38.61 mm. **Ruler:** Elizabeth II **Subject:** Queen's Golden Jubilee **Obv:** Crowned bust right, denomination below **Rev:** Elizabeth II, Prince Charles and his son William below multicolored bunting **Edge:** Reeded

Date	Mintage	F	VF	XF	Unc	BU
2002 Proof	50	Value: 1,800				

KM# 77b.2 50 PENCE
39.9400 g., 0.9170 Gold 1.1775 oz. AGW, 38.61 mm. **Ruler:** Elizabeth II **Obv:** Crowned bust right, denomination below **Rev:** With plain bunting

Date	Mintage	F	VF	XF	Unc	BU
2002 Proof	—	Value: 1,750				

KM# 78.1 50 PENCE
28.1300 g., Copper-Nickel, 38.6 mm. **Ruler:** Elizabeth II **Subject:** Queen's Golden Jubilee **Obv:** Crowned bust right, denomination below **Rev:** Royal coach below multicolor bunting **Edge:** Reeded

Date	Mintage	F	VF	XF	Unc	BU
2002 Proof	—	Value: 8.00				

KM# 78.2 50 PENCE
Copper-Nickel **Ruler:** Elizabeth II **Subject:** Queen's Golden Jubilee **Obv:** Crowned bust right, denomination below **Rev:** With plain bunting

Date	Mintage	F	VF	XF	Unc	BU
2002	—	—	—	—	6.00	7.00

KM# 78a.1 50 PENCE
28.2800 g., 0.9250 Silver 0.8410 oz. ASW, 38.6 mm. **Ruler:** Elizabeth II **Subject:** Queen's Golden Jubilee **Obv:** Crowned bust right, denomination below **Rev:** Coronation coach below multicolor bunting **Edge:** Reeded

Date	Mintage	F	VF	XF	Unc	BU
2002 Proof	15,000	Value: 45.00				

KM# 78b.1 50 PENCE
39.9400 g., 0.9170 Gold 1.1775 oz. AGW, 38.61 mm. **Ruler:** Elizabeth II **Subject:** Queen's Golden Jubilee **Obv:** Crowned bust right, denomination below **Rev:** Coronation coach below multicolor bunting **Edge:** Reeded

Date	Mintage	F	VF	XF	Unc	BU
2002 Proof	150	Value: 1,800				

KM# 78b.2 50 PENCE
39.9400 g., 0.9170 Gold 1.1775 oz. AGW, 38.61 mm. **Ruler:** Elizabeth II **Subject:** Queen's Golden Jubilee **Obv:** Crowned bust right, denomination below **Rev:** With plain bunting

Date	Mintage	F	VF	XF	Unc	BU
2002 Proof	—	Value: 1,750				

KM# 79.1 50 PENCE
28.1300 g., Copper-Nickel, 38.6 mm. **Ruler:** Elizabeth II **Subject:** Queen's Golden Jubilee **Obv:** Crowned bust right, denomination below **Rev:** Scepter and orb below multicolor bunting **Edge:** Reeded

Date	Mintage	F	VF	XF	Unc	BU
2002 Proof	—	Value: 8.00				

KM# 79.2 50 PENCE
Copper-Nickel **Ruler:** Elizabeth II **Subject:** Queen's Golden Jubilee **Obv:** Crowned bust right, denomination below **Rev:** With plain bunting

Date	Mintage	F	VF	XF	Unc	BU
2002	—	—	—	—	6.00	7.00

KM# 79a.1 50 PENCE
28.2800 g., 0.9250 Silver 0.8410 oz. ASW, 38.6 mm. **Ruler:** Elizabeth II **Subject:** Queen's Golden Jubilee **Obv:** Crowned bust right, denomination below **Rev:** Orb and scepter below multicolor bunting **Edge:** Reeded

Date	Mintage	F	VF	XF	Unc	BU
2002 Proof	15,000	Value: 45.00				

KM# 79a.2 50 PENCE
28.2800 g., 0.9250 Silver 0.8410 oz. ASW, 38.61 mm. **Ruler:** Elizabeth II **Subject:** Queen's Golden Jubilee **Obv:** Crowned bust right, denomination below **Rev:** With plain bunting

Date	Mintage	F	VF	XF	Unc	BU
2002 Proof	—	Value: 45.00				

KM# 79b.1 50 PENCE
39.9400 g., 0.9170 Gold 1.1775 oz. AGW, 38.61 mm. **Ruler:** Elizabeth II **Subject:** Queen's Golden Jubilee **Obv:** Crowned bust right, denomination below **Rev:** Orb and scepter below multicolor bunting **Edge:** Reeded

Date	Mintage	F	VF	XF	Unc	BU
2002 Proof	150	Value: 1,800				

KM# 79b.2 50 PENCE
39.9400 g., 0.9170 Gold 1.1775 oz. AGW, 38.61 mm. **Ruler:** Elizabeth II **Subject:** Queen's Golden Jubilee **Obv:** Crowned bust right, denomination below **Rev:** With plain bunting

Date	Mintage	F	VF	XF	Unc	BU
2002 Proof	—	Value: 1,750				

KM# 80.1 50 PENCE
28.1300 g., Copper-Nickel, 38.6 mm. **Ruler:** Elizabeth II **Subject:** Queen's Golden Jubilee **Obv:** Crowned bust right, denomination below **Obv. Designer:** Raphael Maklouf **Rev:** Crown below multicolor bunting **Edge:** Reeded

Date	Mintage	F	VF	XF	Unc	BU
2002 Proof	—	Value: 8.00				

KM# 80.2 50 PENCE
Copper-Nickel **Ruler:** Elizabeth II **Subject:** Queen's Golden Jubilee **Obv:** Crowned bust right, denomination below **Rev:** With plain bunting

Date	Mintage	F	VF	XF	Unc	BU
2002	—	—	—	—	6.00	7.00

KM# 80a.1 50 PENCE
28.2800 g., 0.9250 Silver 0.8410 oz. ASW, 38.6 mm. **Ruler:** Elizabeth II **Subject:** Queen's Golden Jubilee **Obv:** Crowned bust right, denomination below **Rev:** Crown below multicolor bunting **Edge:** Reeded

Date	Mintage	F	VF	XF	Unc	BU
2002 Proof	15,000	Value: 45.00				

KM# 80a.2 50 PENCE
28.2800 g., 0.9250 Silver 0.8410 oz. ASW, 38.61 mm. **Ruler:** Elizabeth II **Subject:** Queen's Golden Jubilee **Obv:** Crowned bust right, denomination below **Rev:** With plain bunting

Date	Mintage	F	VF	XF	Unc	BU
2002 Proof	—	Value: 45.00				

KM# 80b.1 50 PENCE
39.9400 g., 0.9170 Gold 1.1775 oz. AGW, 38.61 mm. **Ruler:** Elizabeth II **Subject:** Queen's Golden Jubilee **Obv:** Crowned bust right, denomination below **Rev:** Crown below multicolor bunting **Edge:** Reeded

Date	Mintage	F	VF	XF	Unc	BU
2002 Proof	150	Value: 1,800				

KM# 80b.2 50 PENCE
39.9400 g., 0.9170 Gold 1.1775 oz. AGW, 38.61 mm. **Ruler:** Elizabeth II **Subject:** Queen's Golden Jubilee **Obv:** Crowned bust right, denomination below **Rev:** With plain bunting

Date	Mintage	F	VF	XF	Unc	BU
2002 Proof	—	Value: 1,750				

KM# 81.1 50 PENCE
28.1300 g., Copper-Nickel, 38.6 mm. **Ruler:** Elizabeth II **Subject:** Queen's Golden Jubilee **Obv:** Crowned bust right, denomination below **Rev:** Throne below multicolor bunting **Edge:** Reeded

Date	Mintage	F	VF	XF	Unc	BU
2002 Proof	—	Value: 8.00				

KM# 81.2 50 PENCE
Copper-Nickel **Ruler:** Elizabeth II **Subject:** Queen's Golden Jubilee **Obv:** Crowned bust right, denomination below **Rev:** With plain bunting

Date	Mintage	F	VF	XF	Unc	BU
2002	—	—	—	—	6.00	7.00

KM# 81a.1 50 PENCE
28.2800 g., 0.9250 Silver 0.8410 oz. ASW, 38.6 mm. **Ruler:** Elizabeth II **Subject:** Queen's Golden Jubilee **Obv:** Crowned bust right, denomination below **Rev:** Coronation throne below multicolor bunting **Edge:** Reeded

Date	Mintage	F	VF	XF	Unc	BU
2002 Proof	15,000	Value: 45.00				

KM# 81a.2 50 PENCE
Silver **Ruler:** Elizabeth II **Subject:** Queen's Golden Jubilee **Obv:** Crowned bust right, denomination below **Rev:** With plain bunting

Date	Mintage	F	VF	XF	Unc	BU
2002 Proof	—	Value: 45.00				

KM# 81b.1 50 PENCE
39.9400 g., 0.9170 Gold 1.1775 oz. AGW, 38.61 mm. **Ruler:** Elizabeth II **Subject:** Queen's Golden Jubilee **Obv:** Crowned bust right, denomination below **Rev:** Coronation Throne below multicolored bunting **Edge:** Reeded

Date	Mintage	F	VF	XF	Unc	BU
2002 Proof	150	Value: 1,800				

KM# 81b.2 50 PENCE
39.9400 g., 0.9170 Gold 1.1775 oz. AGW, 38.61 mm. **Ruler:** Elizabeth II **Obv:** Crowned bust right, denomination below **Rev:** With plain bunting

Date	Mintage	F	VF	XF	Unc	BU
2002 Proof	—	Value: 1,750				

KM# 82.1 50 PENCE
28.1300 g., Copper-Nickel, 38.6 mm. **Ruler:** Elizabeth II **Subject:** Queen's Golden Jubilee **Obv:** Crowned bust right, denomination below **Rev:** Queen on throne below multicolor bunting **Edge:** Reeded

Date	Mintage	F	VF	XF	Unc	BU
2002 Proof	—	—	—	—	6.00	7.00

KM# 82.2 50 PENCE
Copper-Nickel **Ruler:** Elizabeth II **Subject:** Queen's Golden Jubilee **Obv:** Crowned bust right, denomination below **Rev:** With plain bunting

Date	Mintage	F	VF	XF	Unc	BU
2002	—	—	—	—	6.00	7.00

KM# 82a.1 50 PENCE
28.2800 g., 0.9250 Silver 0.8410 oz. ASW, 38.6 mm. **Ruler:** Elizabeth II **Subject:** Queen's Golden Jubilee **Obv:** Crowned bust right, denomination below **Rev:** Queen on throne below multicolor bunting **Edge:** Reeded

Date	Mintage	F	VF	XF	Unc	BU
2002 Proof	15,000	Value: 45.00				

KM# 82a.2 50 PENCE
Silver **Ruler:** Elizabeth II **Subject:** Queen's Golden Jubilee **Obv:** Crowned bust right, denomination below **Rev:** With plain bunting

Date	Mintage	F	VF	XF	Unc	BU
2002 Proof	—	Value: 45.00				

KM# 82b.1 50 PENCE
39.9400 g., 0.9170 Gold 1.1775 oz. AGW, 38.61 mm. **Ruler:** Elizabeth II **Subject:** Queen's Golden Jubilee **Obv:** Crowned bust right, denomination below **Rev:** Queen seated on throne below multicolor bunting **Edge:** Reeded

Date	Mintage	F	VF	XF	Unc	BU
2002 Proof	50	Value: 1,800				

KM# 82b.2 50 PENCE
39.9400 g., 0.9170 Gold 1.1775 oz. AGW, 38.61 mm. **Ruler:** Elizabeth II **Subject:** Queen's Golden Jubilee **Obv:** Crowned bust right, denomination below **Rev:** With plain bunting

Date	Mintage	F	VF	XF	Unc	BU
2002 Proof	—	Value: 1,750				

KM# 83.1 50 PENCE
28.1300 g., Copper-Nickel, 38.6 mm. **Ruler:** Elizabeth II **Subject:** Queen's Golden Jubilee **Obv:** Crowned bust right, denomination below **Obv. Designer:** Raphael Maklouf **Rev:** Queen and young family below multicolor bunting **Edge:** Reeded

Date	Mintage	F	VF	XF	Unc	BU
2002 Proof	—	—	—	—	6.00	7.00

KM# 83a.1 50 PENCE

28.2800 g., 0.9250 Silver 0.8410 oz. ASW, 38.6 mm. **Ruler:** Elizabeth II **Subject:** Queen's Golden Jubilee **Obv:** Crowned bust right, denomination below **Rev:** Royal family below multicolor bunting **Edge:** Reeded

Date	Mintage	F	VF	XF	Unc	BU
2002 Proof	15,000	Value: 45.00				

KM# 83a.2 50 PENCE

Silver **Ruler:** Elizabeth II **Subject:** Queen's Golden Jubilee **Obv:** Crowned bust right, denomination below **Rev:** With plain bunting

Date	Mintage	F	VF	XF	Unc	BU
2002 Proof	—	Value: 45.00				

KM# 83b.1 50 PENCE

39.9400 g., 0.9170 Gold 1.1775 oz. AGW, 38.61 mm. **Ruler:** Elizabeth II **Subject:** Queen's Golden Jubilee **Obv:** Crowned bust right, denomination below **Rev:** Royal Family below multicolor bunting **Edge:** Reeded

Date	Mintage	F	VF	XF	Unc	BU
2002 Proof	50	Value: 1,800				

KM# 83b.2 50 PENCE

39.9400 g., 0.9170 Gold 1.1775 oz. AGW, 38.61 mm. **Ruler:** Elizabeth II **Subject:** Queen's Golden Jubilee **Obv:** Crowned bust right, denomination below **Rev:** With plain bunting

Date	Mintage	F	VF	XF	Unc	BU
2002 Proof	—	Value: 1,750				

KM# 84.1 50 PENCE

28.1300 g., Copper-Nickel, 38.6 mm. **Ruler:** Elizabeth II **Subject:** Queen's Golden Jubilee **Obv:** Crowned bust right, denomination below **Rev:** Queens head and tree house below multicolor bunting **Edge:** Reeded

Date	Mintage	F	VF	XF	Unc	BU
2002 Proof	—	Value: 8.00				

KM# 84.2 50 PENCE

Copper-Nickel **Ruler:** Elizabeth II **Subject:** Queen's Golden Jubilee **Obv:** Crowned bust right, denomination below **Rev:** With plain bunting

Date	Mintage	F	VF	XF	Unc	BU
2002	—	—	—	—	6.00	7.00

KM# 84a.1 50 PENCE

28.2800 g., 0.9250 Silver 0.8410 oz. ASW, 38.6 mm. **Ruler:** Elizabeth II **Subject:** Queen's Golden Jubilee **Obv:** Crowned bust right, denomination below **Rev:** Queen and tree house below multicolor bunting **Edge:** Reeded

Date	Mintage	F	VF	XF	Unc	BU
2002 Proof	25,000	Value: 45.00				

KM# 84a.2 50 PENCE

28.2800 g., 0.9250 Silver 0.8410 oz. ASW, 38.61 mm. **Ruler:** Elizabeth II **Subject:** Queen's Golden Jubilee **Obv:** Crowned bust right, denomination below **Rev:** With plain bunting

Date	Mintage	F	VF	XF	Unc	BU
2002 Proof	—	Value: 45.00				

KM# 84b.1 50 PENCE

39.9400 g., 0.9170 Gold 1.1775 oz. AGW, 38.61 mm. **Ruler:** Elizabeth II **Subject:** Queen's Golden Jubilee **Obv:** Crowned bust right, denomination below **Rev:** Queen and tree house below multicolor bunting **Edge:** Reeded

Date	Mintage	F	VF	XF	Unc	BU
2002 Proof	50	Value: 1,800				

KM# 84b.2 50 PENCE

39.9400 g., 0.9166 Gold 1.1770 oz. AGW, 38.61 mm. **Ruler:** Elizabeth II **Subject:** Queen's Golden Jubilee **Obv:** Crowned bust right, denomination below **Rev:** With plain bunting

Date	Mintage	F	VF	XF	Unc	BU
2002 Proof	—	Value: 1,750				

KM# 90 50 PENCE

28.2800 g., Copper-Nickel, 38.6 mm. **Ruler:** Elizabeth II **Obv:** Crowned bust right, denomination below **Rev:** Conjoined busts of Elizabeth and Philip below multicolor bunting **Edge:** Reeded

Date	Mintage	F	VF	XF	Unc	BU
2002	—	—	—	—	6.00	7.00

KM# 90a.1 50 PENCE

28.2800 g., 0.9250 Silver 0.8410 oz. ASW, 38.6 mm. **Ruler:** Elizabeth II **Obv:** Crowned bust right, denomination below **Rev:** Elizabeth and Philip below multicolor bunting **Edge:** Reeded

Date	Mintage	F	VF	XF	Unc	BU
2002 Proof	15,000	Value: 45.00				

KM# 90a.2 50 PENCE

28.2800 g., 0.9250 Silver 0.8410 oz. ASW, 38.6 mm. **Ruler:** Elizabeth II **Obv:** Crowned bust right, denomination below **Rev:** With plain bunting

Date	Mintage	F	VF	XF	Unc	BU
2002 Proof	—	Value: 45.00				

KM# 90b.1 50 PENCE

39.9400 g., 0.9170 Gold 1.1775 oz. AGW, 38.61 mm. **Ruler:** Elizabeth II **Obv:** Crowned bust right, denomination below **Rev:** Elizabeth and Philip below multicolor bunting **Edge:** Reeded

Date	Mintage	F	VF	XF	Unc	BU
2002 Proof	50	Value: 1,800				

KM# 90b.2 50 PENCE

39.9400 g., 0.9170 Gold 1.1775 oz. AGW, 38.61 mm. **Ruler:** Elizabeth II **Obv:** Crowned bust right, denomination below **Rev:** With plain bunting **Edge:** Reeded

Date	Mintage	F	VF	XF	Unc	BU
2002 Proof	—	Value: 1,750				

KM# 91 50 PENCE

28.2800 g., Copper-Nickel, 38.6 mm. **Ruler:** Elizabeth II **Obv:** Crowned bust right, denomination below **Rev:** Queen and Aborigine dancers below multicolor bunting **Edge:** Reeded

Date	Mintage	F	VF	XF	Unc	BU
2002	—	—	—	—	6.00	7.00

KM# 91a.1 50 PENCE

28.2800 g., 0.9250 Silver 0.8410 oz. ASW, 38.6 mm. **Ruler:** Elizabeth II **Obv:** Crowned bust right, denomination below **Rev:** Queen and Aborigine dancers below multicolor bunting **Edge:** Reeded

Date	Mintage	F	VF	XF	Unc	BU
2002 Proof	15,000	Value: 45.00				

KM# 91a.2 50 PENCE

28.2800 g., 0.9250 Silver 0.8410 oz. ASW, 38.6 mm. **Ruler:** Elizabeth II **Obv:** Crowned bust right, denomination below **Rev:** With plain bunting **Edge:** Reeded

Date	Mintage	F	VF	XF	Unc	BU
2002 Proof	—	Value: 45.00				

KM# 91b.1 50 PENCE

39.9400 g., 0.9170 Gold 1.1775 oz. AGW, 38.61 mm. **Ruler:** Elizabeth II **Obv:** Crowned bust right, denomination below **Rev:** Queen and Aborigine dancers below multicolor bunting **Edge:** Reeded

Date	Mintage	F	VF	XF	Unc	BU
2002 Proof	50	Value: 1,800				

KM# 91b.2 50 PENCE

39.9400 g., 0.9170 Gold 1.1775 oz. AGW, 38.61 mm. **Ruler:** Elizabeth II **Obv:** Crowned bust right, denomination below **Rev:** With plain bunting **Edge:** Reeded

Date	Mintage	F	VF	XF	Unc	BU
2002 Proof	—	Value: 1,750				

KM# 92 50 PENCE

28.2800 g., Copper-Nickel, 38.6 mm. **Ruler:** Elizabeth II **Obv:** Crowned bust right, denomination below **Rev:** Queen and St. Paul's Cathedral dome below multicolor bunting **Edge:** Reeded

Date	Mintage	F	VF	XF	Unc	BU
2002	—	—	—	—	6.00	7.00

KM# 92a.1 50 PENCE

28.2800 g., 0.9250 Silver 0.8410 oz. ASW, 38.6 mm. **Ruler:** Elizabeth II **Obv:** Crowned bust right, denomination below **Rev:** Queen and St. Paul's Cathedral dome below multicolor bunting **Edge:** Reeded

Date	Mintage	F	VF	XF	Unc	BU
2002 Proof	15,000	Value: 45.00				

KM# 92a.2 50 PENCE

28.2800 g., 0.9250 Silver 0.8410 oz. ASW, 38.6 mm. **Ruler:** Elizabeth II **Obv:** Crowned bust right, denomination below **Rev:** With plain bunting **Edge:** Reeded

Date	Mintage	F	VF	XF	Unc	BU
2002 Proof	—	Value: 45.00				

KM# 92b.1 50 PENCE

39.9400 g., 0.9170 Gold 1.1775 oz. AGW, 38.61 mm. **Ruler:** Elizabeth II **Obv:** Crowned bust right, denomination below **Rev:** Queen and St. Paul's Cathedral dome below multicolor bunting **Edge:** Reeded

Date	Mintage	F	VF	XF	Unc	BU
2002 Proof	50	Value: 1,800				

KM# 92b.2 50 PENCE

39.9400 g., 0.9170 Gold 1.1775 oz. AGW, 38.61 mm. **Ruler:** Elizabeth II **Obv:** Crowned bust right, denomination below **Rev:** With plain bunting **Edge:** Reeded

Date	Mintage	F	VF	XF	Unc	BU
2002 Proof	—	Value: 1,750				

KM# 93 50 PENCE

28.2800 g., Copper-Nickel, 38.6 mm. **Ruler:** Elizabeth II **Obv:** Crowned bust right, denomination below **Rev:** Elizabeth and Philip in coronation coach below multicolor bunting **Edge:** Reeded

Date	Mintage	F	VF	XF	Unc	BU
2002	—	—	—	—	6.00	7.00

KM# 93a.1 50 PENCE
28.2800 g., 0.9250 Silver 0.8410 oz. ASW, 38.6 mm. **Ruler:** Elizabeth II **Obv:** Crowned bust right, denomination below **Rev:** Elizabeth and Philip in coronation coach below multicolor bunting **Edge:** Reeded

Date	Mintage	F	VF	XF	Unc	BU
2002 Proof	15,000	Value: 45.00				

KM# 93a.2 50 PENCE
28.2800 g., 0.9250 Silver 0.8410 oz. ASW, 38.6 mm. **Ruler:** Elizabeth II **Obv:** Crowned bust right, denomination below **Rev:** With plain bunting **Edge:** Reeded

Date	Mintage	F	VF	XF	Unc	BU
2002 Proof	—	Value: 45.00				

KM# 93b.1 50 PENCE
39.9400 g., 0.9170 Gold 1.1775 oz. AGW, 38.61 mm. **Ruler:** Elizabeth II **Obv:** Crowned bust right, denomination below **Rev:** Elizabeth and Philip in coronation coach below multicolor bunting **Edge:** Reeded

Date	Mintage	F	VF	XF	Unc	BU
2002 Proof	50	Value: 1,800				

KM# 93b.2 50 PENCE
39.9400 g., 0.9170 Gold 1.1775 oz. AGW, 38.61 mm. **Ruler:** Elizabeth II **Obv:** Crowned bust right, denomination below **Rev:** With plain bunting **Edge:** Reeded

Date	Mintage	F	VF	XF	Unc	BU
2002 Proof	—	Value: 1,750				

KM# 94 50 PENCE
28.2800 g., Copper-Nickel, 38.6 mm. **Ruler:** Elizabeth II **Obv:** Crowned bust right, denomination below **Rev:** Elizabeth and Prince Charles at flower show below multicolor bunting **Edge:** Reeded

Date	Mintage	F	VF	XF	Unc	BU
2002	—	—	—	—	6.00	7.00

KM# 94a.1 50 PENCE
28.2800 g., 0.9250 Silver 0.8410 oz. ASW, 38.6 mm. **Ruler:** Elizabeth II **Obv:** Crowned bust right, denomination below **Rev:** Queen and Prince Charles at flower show below multicolor bunting **Edge:** Reeded

Date	Mintage	F	VF	XF	Unc	BU
2002 Proof	15,000	Value: 45.00				

KM# 94a.2 50 PENCE
28.2800 g., 0.9250 Silver 0.8410 oz. ASW, 38.6 mm. **Ruler:** Elizabeth II **Obv:** Crowned bust right, denomination below **Rev:** With plain bunting **Edge:** Reeded

Date	Mintage	F	VF	XF	Unc	BU
2002 Proof	—	Value: 45.00				

KM# 94b.1 50 PENCE
39.9400 g., 0.9170 Gold 1.1775 oz. AGW, 38.61 mm. **Ruler:** Elizabeth II **Obv:** Crowned bust right, denomination below **Rev:** Queen and Prince Charles at flower show below multicolor bunting **Edge:** Reeded

Date	Mintage	F	VF	XF	Unc	BU
2002 Proof	50	Value: 1,800				

KM# 94b.2 50 PENCE
39.9400 g., 0.9170 Gold 1.1775 oz. AGW, 38.61 mm. **Ruler:** Elizabeth II **Obv:** Crowned bust right, denomination below **Rev:** With plain bunting **Edge:** Reeded

Date	Mintage	F	VF	XF	Unc	BU
2002 Proof	—	Value: 1,750				

KM# 95 50 PENCE
28.2800 g., Copper-Nickel, 38.6 mm. **Ruler:** Elizabeth II **Obv:** Crowned bust right, denomination below **Rev:** Elizabeth and Philip on balcony below multicolor bunting **Edge:** Reeded

Date	Mintage	F	VF	XF	Unc	BU
2002	—	—	—	—	6.00	7.00

KM# 95a.1 50 PENCE
28.2800 g., 0.9250 Silver 0.8410 oz. ASW, 38.6 mm. **Ruler:** Elizabeth II **Obv:** Crowned bust right, denomination below **Rev:** Elizabeth and Philip on balcony below colored bunting **Edge:** Reeded

Date	Mintage	F	VF	XF	Unc	BU
2002 Proof	15,000	Value: 45.00				

KM# 95a.2 50 PENCE
28.2800 g., 0.9250 Silver 0.8410 oz. ASW, 38.6 mm. **Ruler:** Elizabeth II **Obv:** Crowned bust right, denomination below **Rev:** With plain bunting **Edge:** Reeded

Date	Mintage	F	VF	XF	Unc	BU
2002 Proof	—	Value: 45.00				

KM# 95b.1 50 PENCE
39.9400 g., 0.9170 Gold 1.1775 oz. AGW, 38.61 mm. **Ruler:** Elizabeth II **Obv:** Crowned bust right, denomination below **Rev:** Elizabeth and Philip on balcony below multicolor bunting **Edge:** Reeded

Date	Mintage	F	VF	XF	Unc	BU
2002 Proof	50	Value: 1,800				

KM# 95b.2 50 PENCE
39.9400 g., 0.9170 Gold 1.1775 oz. AGW, 38.61 mm. **Ruler:** Elizabeth II **Obv:** Crowned bust right, denomination below **Rev:** With plain bunting **Edge:** Reeded

Date	Mintage	F	VF	XF	Unc	BU
2002 Proof	—	Value: 1,750				

KM# 96 50 PENCE
28.2800 g., Copper-Nickel, 38.6 mm. **Ruler:** Elizabeth II **Obv:** Crowned bust right, denomination below **Rev:** Multicolor jets below multicolor bunting **Edge:** Reeded

Date	Mintage	F	VF	XF	Unc	BU
2002	—	—	—	—	6.00	7.00

KM# 96a.1 50 PENCE
28.2800 g., 0.9250 Silver 0.8410 oz. ASW, 38.6 mm. **Ruler:** Elizabeth II **Obv:** Crowned bust right, denomination below **Rev:** Multicolor jets below multicolor bunting **Edge:** Reeded

Date	Mintage	F	VF	XF	Unc	BU
2002 Proof	15,000	Value: 45.00				

KM# 96a.2 50 PENCE
28.2800 g., 0.9250 Silver 0.8410 oz. ASW, 38.6 mm. **Ruler:** Elizabeth II **Obv:** Crowned bust right, denomination below **Rev:** With plain bunting **Edge:** Reeded

Date	Mintage	F	VF	XF	Unc	BU
2002 Proof	—	Value: 45.00				

KM# 96b.1 50 PENCE
39.9400 g., 0.9170 Gold 1.1775 oz. AGW, 38.61 mm. **Ruler:** Elizabeth II **Obv:** Crowned bust right, denomination below **Rev:** Multicolor jets below multicolor bunting **Edge:** Reeded

Date	Mintage	F	VF	XF	Unc	BU
2002 Proof	50	Value: 1,800				

KM# 96b.2 50 PENCE
39.9400 g., 0.9170 Gold 1.1775 oz. AGW, 38.61 mm. **Ruler:** Elizabeth II **Obv:** Crowned bust right, denomination below **Rev:** With plain bunting **Edge:** Reeded

Date	Mintage	F	VF	XF	Unc	BU
2002 Proof	—	Value: 1,750				

KM# 97 50 PENCE
28.2800 g., Copper-Nickel, 38.6 mm. **Ruler:** Elizabeth II **Obv:** Crowned bust right, denomination below **Rev:** Queen and fireworks below multicolor bunting **Edge:** Reeded

Date	Mintage	F	VF	XF	Unc	BU
2002	—	—	—	—	6.00	7.00

KM# 97a.1 50 PENCE
28.2800 g., 0.9250 Silver 0.8410 oz. ASW, 38.61 mm. **Ruler:** Elizabeth II **Obv:** Crowned bust right, denomination below **Rev:** Queen and fireworks below multicolor bunting **Edge:** Reeded

Date	Mintage	F	VF	XF	Unc	BU
2002 Proof	15,000	Value: 45.00				

KM# 97a.2 50 PENCE
28.2800 g., 0.9250 Silver 0.8410 oz. ASW, 38.6 mm. **Ruler:** Elizabeth II **Obv:** Crowned bust right, denomination below **Rev:** With plain bunting **Edge:** Reeded

Date	Mintage	F	VF	XF	Unc	BU
2002 Proof	—	Value: 45.00				

KM# 97b.1 50 PENCE
39.9400 g., 0.9170 Gold 1.1775 oz. AGW, 38.61 mm. **Ruler:** Elizabeth II **Obv:** Crowned bust right, denomination below **Rev:** Queen and fireworks below multicolor bunting **Edge:** Reeded

Date	Mintage	F	VF	XF	Unc	BU
2002 Proof	50	Value: 1,800				

KM# 97b.2 50 PENCE
39.9400 g., 0.9170 Gold 1.1775 oz. AGW, 38.61 mm. **Ruler:** Elizabeth II **Obv:** Crowned bust right, denomination below **Rev:** With plain bunting **Edge:** Reeded

Date	Mintage	F	VF	XF	Unc	BU
2002 Proof	—	Value: 1,750				

KM# 98 50 PENCE
28.2800 g., Copper-Nickel, 38.6 mm. **Ruler:** Elizabeth II **Obv:** Crowned bust right, denomination below **Rev:** UK map and flags below multicolor bunting **Edge:** Reeded

Date	Mintage	F	VF	XF	Unc	BU
2002	—	—	—	—	6.00	7.00

KM# 98a.1 50 PENCE
28.2800 g., 0.9250 Silver 0.8410 oz. ASW, 38.6 mm. **Ruler:** Elizabeth II **Obv:** Crowned bust right, denomination below **Rev:** UK and four flags below multicolor bunting **Edge:** Reeded

Date	Mintage	F	VF	XF	Unc	BU
2002 Proof	15,000	Value: 45.00				

KM# 98a.2 50 PENCE
28.2800 g., 0.9250 Silver 0.8410 oz. ASW, 38.6 mm. **Ruler:** Elizabeth II **Obv:** Crowned bust right, denomination below **Rev:** With plain bunting **Edge:** Reeded

Date	Mintage	F	VF	XF	Unc	BU
2002 Proof	—	Value: 45.00				

KM# 98b.1 50 PENCE
39.9400 g., 0.9170 Gold 1.1775 oz. AGW, 38.61 mm. **Ruler:** Elizabeth II **Obv:** Crowned bust right, denomination below **Rev:** UK map and four flags below multicolor bunting **Edge:** Reeded

Date	Mintage	F	VF	XF	Unc	BU
2002 Proof	50	Value: 1,800				

KM# 98b.2 50 PENCE
39.9400 g., 0.9170 Gold 1.1775 oz. AGW, 38.61 mm. **Ruler:** Elizabeth II **Obv:** Crowned bust right, denomination below **Rev:** With plain bunting **Edge:** Reeded

Date	Mintage	F	VF	XF	Unc	BU
2002 Proof	—	Value: 1,750				

KM# 99 50 PENCE
28.2800 g., Copper-Nickel, 38.6 mm. **Ruler:** Elizabeth II **Obv:** Crowned bust right, denomination below **Rev:** Queen and two Commonwealth Games athletes below multicolor bunting **Edge:** Reeded

Date	Mintage	F	VF	XF	Unc	BU
2002	—	—	—	—	6.00	7.00

KM# 99a.1 50 PENCE
28.2800 g., 0.9250 Silver 0.8410 oz. ASW, 38.6 mm. **Ruler:** Elizabeth II **Obv:** Crowned bust right, denomination below **Rev:** Queen and two Commonwealth Games athletes below multicolor bunting **Edge:** Reeded

Date	Mintage	F	VF	XF	Unc	BU
2002 Proof	15,000	Value: 45.00				

KM# 99a.2 50 PENCE
28.2800 g., 0.9250 Silver 0.8410 oz. ASW, 38.6 mm. **Ruler:** Elizabeth II **Obv:** Crowned bust right, denomination below **Rev:** With plain bunting **Edge:** Reeded

Date	Mintage	F	VF	XF	Unc	BU
2002 Proof	—	Value: 45.00				

KM# 99b.1 50 PENCE
39.9400 g., 0.9170 Gold 1.1775 oz. AGW, 38.61 mm. **Ruler:** Elizabeth II **Obv:** Crowned bust right, denomination below **Rev:** Queen and two Commonwealth Games athletes below multicolor bunting **Edge:** Reeded

Date	Mintage	F	VF	XF	Unc	BU
2002 Proof	50	Value: 1,800				

KM# 99b.2 50 PENCE
39.9400 g., 0.9170 Gold 1.1775 oz. AGW, 38.61 mm. **Ruler:** Elizabeth II **Obv:** Crowned bust right, denomination below **Rev:** With plain bunting **Edge:** Reeded

Date	Mintage	F	VF	XF	Unc	BU
2002 Proof	—	Value: 1,750				

KM# 100 50 PENCE
28.2800 g., Copper-Nickel, 38.6 mm. **Ruler:** Elizabeth II **Obv:** Crowned bust right, denomination below **Rev:** Royal Ascot Carriage scene below multicolor bunting **Edge:** Reeded

Date	Mintage	F	VF	XF	Unc	BU
2002	—	—	—	—	6.00	7.00

KM# 100a.1 50 PENCE
28.2800 g., 0.9250 Silver 0.8410 oz. ASW, 38.6 mm. **Ruler:** Elizabeth II **Obv:** Crowned bust right, denomination below **Rev:** Royal Ascot Carriage scene below multicolor bunting **Edge:** Reeded

Date	Mintage	F	VF	XF	Unc	BU
2002 Proof	15,000	Value: 45.00				

KM# 100a.2 50 PENCE
28.2800 g., 0.9250 Silver 0.8410 oz. ASW, 38.6 mm. **Ruler:** Elizabeth II **Obv:** Crowned bust right, denomination below **Rev:** With plain bunting **Edge:** Reeded

Date	Mintage	F	VF	XF	Unc	BU
2002 Proof	—	Value: 45.00				

KM# 100b.1 50 PENCE
39.9400 g., 0.9170 Gold 1.1775 oz. AGW, 38.61 mm. **Ruler:** Elizabeth II **Obv:** Crowned bust right, denomination below **Rev:** Royal Ascot Carriage scene below multicolor bunting **Edge:** Reeded

Date	Mintage	F	VF	XF	Unc	BU
2002 Proof	50	Value: 1,800				

KM# 100b.2 50 PENCE
39.9400 g., 0.9170 Gold 1.1775 oz. AGW, 38.61 mm. **Ruler:** Elizabeth II **Obv:** Crowned bust right, denomination below **Rev:** With plain bunting **Edge:** Reeded

Date	Mintage	F	VF	XF	Unc	BU
2002 Proof	—	Value: 1,750				

KM# 101 50 PENCE
28.2800 g., Copper-Nickel, 38.6 mm. **Ruler:** Elizabeth II **Obv:** Crowned bust right, denomination below **Rev:** Queen and two hockey players below multicolor bunting **Edge:** Reeded

Date	Mintage	F	VF	XF	Unc	BU
2002	—	—	—	—	6.00	7.00

KM# 101a.1 50 PENCE
28.2800 g., 0.9250 Silver 0.8410 oz. ASW, 38.6 mm. **Ruler:** Elizabeth II **Obv:** Crowned bust right, denomination below **Rev:** Queen and two hockey players below multicolor bunting **Edge:** Reeded

Date	Mintage	F	VF	XF	Unc	BU
2002 Proof	15,000	Value: 45.00				

KM# 101a.2 50 PENCE
28.2800 g., 0.9250 Silver 0.8410 oz. ASW, 38.6 mm. **Ruler:** Elizabeth II **Obv:** Crowned bust right, denomination below **Rev:** With plain bunting **Edge:** Reeded

Date	Mintage	F	VF	XF	Unc	BU
2002 Proof	—	Value: 45.00				

KM# 101b.1 50 PENCE
39.9400 g., 0.9170 Gold 1.1775 oz. AGW, 38.61 mm. **Ruler:** Elizabeth II **Obv:** Crowned bust right, denomination below **Rev:** Queen and two hockey players below multicolor bunting **Edge:** Reeded

Date	Mintage	F	VF	XF	Unc	BU
2002 Proof	50	Value: 1,800				

KM# 101b.2 50 PENCE
39.9400 g., 0.9170 Gold 1.1775 oz. AGW, 38.61 mm. **Ruler:** Elizabeth II **Obv:** Crowned bust right, denomination below **Rev:** With plain bunting **Edge:** Reeded

Date	Mintage	F	VF	XF	Unc	BU
2002 Proof	—	Value: 1,750				

KM# 102 50 PENCE
28.2800 g., Copper-Nickel, 38.6 mm. **Ruler:** Elizabeth II **Obv:** Crowned bust right, denomination below **Obv. Designer:** Raphael Maklouf **Rev:** Queen Mother as a young lady and as an elderly lady **Rev. Designer:** Willem Vis **Edge:** Reeded

Date	Mintage	F	VF	XF	Unc	BU
ND(2002)	—	—	—	—	9.00	10.00

KM# 102a 50 PENCE
28.2800 g., 0.9250 Silver 0.8410 oz. ASW, 38.6 mm. **Ruler:** Elizabeth II **Obv:** Crowned bust right, denomination below **Rev:** Queen Mother as a young lady and as an elderly lady **Edge:** Reeded

Date	Mintage	F	VF	XF	Unc	BU
ND(2002) Proof	10,000	Value: 45.00				

KM# 135 50 PENCE
Copper-Nickel, 27.3 mm. **Ruler:** Elizabeth II **Obv:** Crowned bust right **Rev:** Fox standing right **Shape:** 7-sided

Date	Mintage	F	VF	XF	Unc	BU
2004	—	—	—	—	5.00	7.50

KM# 149 50 PENCE
28.2800 g., 0.9250 Silver 0.8410 oz. ASW, 38.6 mm. **Ruler:** Elizabeth II **Subject:** Queen's 80th Birthday **Obv:** Head with tiara right - gilt **Obv. Legend:** QUEEN ELIZABETH II - FALKLAND ISLANDS **Obv. Designer:** Ian Rank-Broadley **Rev:** Elizabeth seated at left, Queen Mother at right holding baby

Date	Mintage	F	VF	XF	Unc	BU
2006 Proof	—	Value: 45.00				

KM# 136 POUND
Nickel-Brass, 22.5 mm. **Ruler:** Elizabeth II **Obv:** Crowned bust right **Rev:** Shield

Date	Mintage	F	VF	XF	Unc	BU
2004	—	—	—	—	3.50	5.00

KM# 137 2 POUNDS
11.9800 g., Bi-Metallic Copper-Nickel center in Nickel-Brass ring, 28.4 mm. **Ruler:** Elizabeth II **Obv:** Head with tiara right **Obv. Legend:** QUEEN ELIZABETH THE SECOND **Rev:** Sun and map surrounded by wildlife **Rev. Designer:** Matthew Bonaccorsi **Edge:** Reeded and lettered **Edge Lettering:** 30 YEARS OF FALKLAND ISLANDS COINAGE

Date	Mintage	F	VF	XF	Unc	BU
2004	—	—	—	5.00	10.00	12.00

KM# 103 25 POUNDS
7.8100 g., 0.9999 Gold 0.2511 oz. AGW, 22 mm. **Ruler:** Elizabeth II **Obv:** Crowned bust right, denomination below **Obv. Designer:** Raphael Maklouf **Rev:** Queen Mother as a young lady and as an elderly lady **Rev. Designer:** Willem Vis **Edge:** Reeded

Date	Mintage	F	VF	XF	Unc	BU
ND(2002) Proof	1,000	Value: 400				

CROWN COINAGE

KM# 141 1/5 CROWN
6.2200 g., 0.9999 Gold 0.1999 oz. AGW **Ruler:** Elizabeth II **Subject:** Diamond Wedding Anniversary **Obv:** Conjoined busts with Prince Philip right **Obv. Legend:** QUEEN ELIZABETH II - FALKLAND ISLANDS **Rev:** Bride and groom standing facing at wedding cake; .01 carat x 1.3mm diamond embedded at top **Rev. Legend:** Diamond Wedding of H.M. Queen Elizabeth II & H.R.H. Prince Philip **Edge:** Reeded

Date	Mintage	F	VF	XF	Unc	BU
2007PM Proof	—	Value: 450				

KM# 129 CROWN
Copper-Nickel **Ruler:** Elizabeth II **Rev:** Nelson and the H.M.S. Victory

Date	Mintage	F	VF	XF	Unc	BU
2005	—	—	—	—	10.00	12.00

KM# 151 CROWN
Copper-Nickel, 39 mm. **Ruler:** Elizabeth II **Subject:** I. K. Burnel **Rev:** S. S. Great Britain sailing right

Date	Mintage	F	VF	XF	Unc	BU
2006PM	—	—	—	—	—	15.00

KM# 152 CROWN
Copper-Nickel, 39 mm. **Ruler:** Elizabeth II **Subject:** Artic and Antarctic - John Ross and James Clark Ross **Rev:** Ships Victory and Erebus

Date	Mintage	F	VF	XF	Unc	BU
2006PM	—	—	—	—	—	15.00

KM# 143a CROWN
0.9167 Silver **Ruler:** Elizabeth II **Subject:** Diamond Wedding Anniversary **Obv:** Conjoined busts with Prince Philip right **Obv. Legend:** QUEEN ELIZABETH II - FALKLAND ISLANDS **Rev:** Bride and groom standing facing at wedding cake **Rev. Legend:** Diamond Wedding of H.M. Queen Elizabeth II & H.R.H. Prince Philip **Edge:** Reeded

Date	Mintage	VG	F	VF	XF	Unc
2007PM Proof	—	Value: 40.00				

KM# 138 CROWN
Copper-Nickel **Ruler:** Elizabeth II **Rev:** Winston Churchill

Date	Mintage	F	VF	XF	Unc	BU
2007	—	—	—	—	15.00	17.50

KM# 139 CROWN
Copper-Nickel **Ruler:** Elizabeth II **Rev:** Queen Elizabeth I

Date	Mintage	F	VF	XF	Unc	BU
2007	—	—	—	—	15.00	17.50

KM# 140 CROWN
Copper-Nickel **Ruler:** Elizabeth II **Rev:** Charles Darwin

Date	Mintage	F	VF	XF	Unc	BU
2007	—	—	—	—	15.00	17.50

KM# 142 CROWN
Copper-Nickel **Ruler:** Elizabeth II **Subject:** Diamond Wedding Anniversary **Obv:** Conjoined busts with Prince Philip right **Obv. Legend:** QUEEN ELIZABETH II - FALKLAND ISLANDS **Rev:** King George VI standing at left giving Philip standing at right his consent to a contract of matrimony **Rev. Legend:** Diamond Wedding of H.M. Queen Elizabeth II & H.R.H. Prince Philip **Edge:** Reeded

Date	Mintage	F	VF	XF	Unc	BU
2007PM	—	—	—	—	17.00	20.00

KM# 142a CROWN
0.9167 Silver **Ruler:** Elizabeth II **Subject:** Diamond Wedding Anniversary **Obv:** Conjoined busts with Prince Philip right **Obv. Legend:** QUEEN ELIZABETH II - FALKLAND ISLANDS **Rev:** King George VI, standing at left, giving Philip, standing at right, his consent to a contract of matrimony **Rev. Legend:** Diamond Wedding of H.M. Queen Elizabeth II & H.R.H. Prince Philip **Edge:** Reeded

Date	Mintage	F	VF	XF	Unc	BU
2007PM	—	Value: 40.00				

KM# 143 CROWN
Copper-Nickel **Ruler:** Elizabeth II **Subject:** Diamond Wedding Anniversary **Obv:** Conjoined busts with Prince Philip right **Obv. Legend:** QUEEN ELIZABETH II - FALKLAND ISLANDS **Rev:** Bride and groom standing facing at wedding cake **Rev. Legend:** Diamond Wedding of H.M. Queen Elizabeth II & H.R.H. Prince Philip **Edge:** Reeded

Date	Mintage	F	VF	XF	Unc	BU
2007PM	—	—	—	—	17.00	20.00

KM# 144 CROWN
Copper-Nickel **Ruler:** Elizabeth II **Subject:** Diamond Wedding Anniversary **Obv:** Conjoined busts with Prince Philip right **Obv. Legend:** QUEEN ELIZABETH II - FALKLAND ISLANDS **Rev:** Bridesmaids and Page Boys **Rev. Legend:** Diamond Wedding of H.M. Queen Elizabeth II & H.R.H. Prince Philip **Edge:** Reeded

Date	Mintage	F	VF	XF	Unc	BU
2007PM	—	—	—	—	17.00	20.00

KM# 144a CROWN
0.9167 Silver **Ruler:** Elizabeth II **Subject:** Diamond Wedding Anniversary **Obv:** Conjoined busts with Prince Philip right **Obv. Legend:** QUEEN ELIZABETH II - FALKLAND ISLANDS **Rev:** Bridesmaids and Page Boys **Rev. Legend:** Diamond Wedding of H.M. Queen Elizabeth II & H.R.H. Prince Philip **Edge:** Reeded

Date	Mintage	F	VF	XF	Unc	BU
2007PM Proof	—	Value: 40.00				

KM# 145 CROWN
Copper-Nickel **Ruler:** Elizabeth II **Subject:** Diamond Wedding Anniversary **Obv:** Conjoined busts with Prince Philip right **Obv. Legend:** QUEEN ELIZABETH II - FALKLAND ISLANDS **Rev:** Buckingham Palace facade **Rev. Legend:** Diamond Wedding of H.M. Queen Elizabeth II & H.R.H. Prince Philip **Edge:** Reeded

Date	Mintage	F	VF	XF	Unc	BU
2007PM	—	—	—	—	17.00	20.00

KM# 146 CROWN
Copper-Nickel **Ruler:** Elizabeth II **Subject:** 10th Anniversary - Death of Princess Diana **Obv:** Bust with tiara right **Obv. Legend:** QUEEN ELIZABETH II - FALKLAND ISLANDS **Rev:** Bust of Princess Diana facing 3/4 right **Rev. Legend:** 1961 - 1997 • DIANA — PRINCESS OF WALES **Edge:** Reeded

Date	Mintage	F	VF	XF	Unc	BU
2007PM	—	—	—	—	17.00	20.00

KM# 146a CROWN
0.9167 Silver **Ruler:** Elizabeth II **Subject:** 10th Anniversary Death of Princess Diana **Obv:** Bust with tiara right **Obv. Legend:** QUEEN ELIZABETH II - FALKLAND ISLANDS **Rev:** Bust of Princess Diana facing 3/4 right **Rev. Legend:** 1961 - 1997 ? DIANA ? PRINCESS OF WALES **Edge:** Reeded

Date	Mintage	F	VF	XF	Unc	BU
2007PM Proof	—	Value: 75.00				

KM# 147 CROWN
Copper-Nickel, 38 mm. **Ruler:** Elizabeth II **Subject:** 20th Anniversary - Falkland Islands Fishery **Obv:** Bust right of Queen Elizabeth II **Rev:** Shortfin Squid (Illex Argentinca) **Edge:** Reeded

Date	Mintage	F	VF	XF	Unc	BU
2007PM	—	—	—	—	17.00	20.00

KM# 148 CROWN
Copper-Nickel, 39 mm. **Ruler:** Elizabeth II **Subject:** Scouting Centennial **Obv:** Crowned bust right **Obv. Legend:** QUEEN ELIZABETH II FALKLAND ISLANDS 2007 **Rev:** Baden-Powell bust 3/4 left, scout saluting, tent flanking within circle on animal tracks **Rev. Legend:** 1857 ROBERT BADEN-POWELL 1941 ONE CROWN **Edge:** Reeded

Date	Mintage	F	VF	XF	Unc	BU
2007PM	—	—	—	—	12.50	15.00

KM# 148a CROWN
28.2800 g., 0.9250 Silver 0.8410 oz. ASW, 38.5 mm. **Ruler:** Elizabeth II **Subject:** Scouting Centennial **Obv:** Crowned bust right **Obv. Legend:** QUEEN ELIZABETH II FALKLAND ISLANDS 2007 **Rev:** Baden-Powell bust 3/4 facing left, scout saluting and tent flanking, within circle of animal tracks and rope **Rev. Legend:** 1857 ROBERT BADEN-POWELL 1941 ONE CROWN **Edge:** Reeded

Date	Mintage	F	VF	XF	Unc	BU
2007PM Proof	10,000	Value: 65.00				

KM# 150 CROWN
28.2800 g., Copper-Nickel, 38.6 mm. **Ruler:** Elizabeth II **Subject:** Royal Air Force, 90th anniversary

Date	Mintage	F	VF	XF	Unc	BU
2008	—	—	—	—	—	12.00

PIEFORTS

KM#	Date	Mintage	Identification	Mkt Val
P4	2001	500	50 Pence. 0.9250 Silver. 56.5600 g. 38.6 mm. Reeded edge. Proof KM#86a.	90.00
P5	2001	500	50 Pence. 0.9250 Silver. 56.5600 g. 38.6 mm. Reeded edge. Proof KM#70a.	100
P6	2001	—	50 Pence. 0.9250 Silver. 56.5300 g. 38.6 mm. Queen's portrait. Edward's portrait with two gold plated coin designs. Reeded edge.	—
P7	2001	—	50 Pence. 0.9250 Silver. 56.5300 g. 38.6 mm. Queen's portrait. Henry's portrait with two gold plated coin designs. Reeded edge.	—
P8	2001	—	50 Pence. 0.9250 Silver. 56.5300 g. 38.6 mm. Queen's portrait. Charles' portrait with two gold plated coin designs. Reeded edge.	—
P9	2001	—	50 Pence. 0.9250 Silver. 56.5300 g. 38.6 mm. Queen's portrait. Victoria's portrait with two gold plated coin designs. Reeded edge.	—
P10	2001	500	50 Pence. 0.9250 Silver. 56.5600 g. 38.6 mm. Reeded edge.	90.00
P11	2001	500	50 Pence. 0.9250 Silver. 56.5600 g. 38.6 mm. Reeded edge.	90.00
P12	2001	500	50 Pence. 0.9250 Silver. 56.5600 g. 38.6 mm. Reeded edge.	90.00
P13	2001	500	50 Pence. 0.9250 Silver. 56.5600 g. 38.6 mm. Reeded edge.	100
P14	2002	500	50 Pence. 0.9250 Silver. 56.5600 g. 38.6 mm. Reeded edge. Proof KM#73a.	90.00
P15	2002	500	50 Pence. 0.9250 Silver. 56.5600 g. 38.6 mm. Reeded edge. Proof KM#74a.	90.00
P16	2002	500	50 Pence. 0.9250 Silver. 56.5600 g. 38.6 mm. Reeded edge. Proof KM#75a.	90.00
P17	2002	500	50 Pence. 0.9250 Silver. 56.5600 g. 38.6 mm. Reeded edge. Proof KM#76a.	90.00
P18	2002	500	50 Pence. 0.9250 Silver. 56.5600 g. 38.6 mm. Reeded edge. Proof KM#77a.	90.00

KM#	Date	Mintage	Identification	Mkt Val
P19	2002	500	50 Pence. 0.9250 Silver. 56.5600 g. 38.6 mm. Reeded edge. Proof KM#78a.	90.00
P20	2002	500	50 Pence. 0.9250 Silver. 56.5600 g. 38.6 mm. Reeded edge. Proof KM#79a.	90.00
P21	2002	500	50 Pence. 0.9250 Silver. 56.5600 g. 38.6 mm. Reeded edge. Proof KM#80a.	90.00
P22	2002	500	50 Pence. 0.9250 Silver. 56.5600 g. 38.6 mm. Reeded edge. Proof KM#81a.	90.00
P23	2002	500	50 Pence. 0.9250 Silver. 56.5600 g. 38.6 mm. Reeded edge. Proof KM#82a.	90.00
P24	2002	500	50 Pence. 0.9250 Silver. 56.5600 g. 38.6 mm. Reeded edge. Proof KM#83a.	90.00
P25	2002	500	50 Pence. 0.9250 Silver. 56.5600 g. 38.6 mm. Reeded edge. Proof KM#84a.	90.00
P26	ND(2002)	500	50 Pence. 0.9250 Silver. 56.5600 g. 38.6 mm. Reeded edge. Proof KM#102a.	90.00

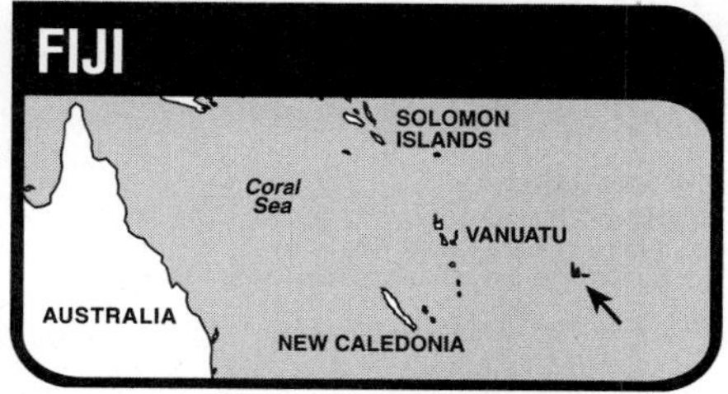

The Republic of Fiji consists of about 320 islands located in the southwestern Pacific 1,100 miles (1,770 km.) north of New Zealand. The islands have a combined area of 7,056 sq. mi. (18,274 sq. km.) and a population of 772,891. Capital: Suva. Fiji's economy is based on agriculture and mining. Sugar, coconut products, manganese, and gold are exported. Fiji is a member of the Commonwealth of Nations, but has been subject to periodic short suspensions.

MINT MARK

(o) - Royal Canadian Mint, Ottawa

REPUBLIC

British Administration until 1970

DECIMAL COINAGE

100 Cents = 1 Dollar

KM# 49a CENT

1.5800 g., Copper Plated Zinc, 17.53 mm. **Ruler:** Elizabeth II **Obv:** Crowned head right, date at right **Rev:** Tanoa kava bowl divides denomination

Date	Mintage	F	VF	XF	Unc	BU
2001(o)	—	—	—	—	0.20	0.65
2002(o)	5,880,000	—	—	—	0.20	0.65
2003(o)	8,030,000	—	—	—	0.20	0.65
2004(o)	8,840,000	—	—	—	0.20	0.65
2005(o)	9,720,000	—	—	—	0.20	0.65

KM# 50a 2 CENTS

3.1600 g., Copper Plated Zinc, 21.08 mm. **Ruler:** Elizabeth II **Obv:** Crowned head right, date at right **Rev:** Palm fan and denomination

Date	Mintage	F	VF	XF	Unc	BU
2001(o)	2,830,000	—	—	—	0.30	0.85
2002(o)	5,000,000	—	—	—	0.30	0.85
2003(o)	6,410,000	—	—	—	0.30	0.85
2004(o)	7,050,000	—	—	—	0.30	0.85
2005(o)	7,760,000	—	—	—	0.30	0.85

KM# 119 5 CENTS

2.3400 g., Nickel Bonded Steel, 19.5 mm. **Ruler:** Elizabeth II **Obv:** Crowned head right **Rev:** Fijian drum - Lali divides denomination **Edge:** Plain

Date	Mintage	F	VF	XF	Unc	BU
2009	—	—	—	—	0.75	1.00

KM# 52a 10 CENTS

4.7500 g., Nickel Plated Steel, 23.6 mm. **Ruler:** Elizabeth II **Obv:** Crowned head right **Rev:** Throwing club - ula tava tava divides value **Edge:** Reeded

Date	Mintage	F	VF	XF	Unc	BU
2006	—	—	—	—	1.00	1.25

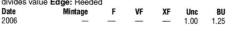

KM# 120 10 CENTS

3.5500 g., Nickel Plated Steel, 21.5 mm. **Ruler:** Elizabeth II **Obv:** Crowned head right **Rev:** Throwing club - ula tava tava divides value **Edge:** Reeded

Date	Mintage	F	VF	XF	Unc	BU
2009	—	—	—	—	1.00	1.25

KM# 95 20 CENTS

11.2400 g., Copper-Nickel, 28.5 mm. **Ruler:** Elizabeth II **Obv:** Crowned head right, date at right **Obv. Designer:** Raphael Maklouf **Rev:** South Pacific Games flame logo **Edge:** Reeded **Note:** Prooflike examples issued in special cards.

Date	Mintage	F	VF	XF	Unc	BU
2003	1,540,000	—	—	—	1.50	2.50
2003 Prooflike	—	—	—	—	—	6.00

KM# 121 20 CENTS

4.6800 g., Nickel Plated Steel, 24 mm. **Ruler:** Elizabeth II **Obv:** Crowned head right **Rev:** Tabua, a ceremonial whale's tooth divides denomination **Edge:** Segmented reeding

Date	Mintage	F	VF	XF	Unc	BU
2009	—	—	—	0.35	1.25	1.50

KM# 122 50 CENTS

6.5000 g., Nickel Plated Steel, 26.5 mm. **Ruler:** Elizabeth II **Obv:** Crowned head right **Rev:** Sailing canoe - Takia, denomination below **Edge:** Reeded

Date	Mintage	F	VF	XF	Unc	BU
2009	—	—	—	—	1.00	2.00

KM# 114 DOLLAR

31.1050 g., 0.9990 Silver 0.9990 oz. ASW, 40.7 mm. **Ruler:** Elizabeth II **Subject:** Sputnik I, 50th Anniversary **Rev:** Multicolor earth, satellite rocket

Date	Mintage	F	VF	XF	Unc	BU
2007 Prooflike	6,000	—	—	—	—	100

KM# 115 DOLLAR

31.1050 g., 0.9990 Silver 0.9990 oz. ASW **Ruler:** Elizabeth II **Subject:** Birds of Fiji **Rev:** Multicolor - blue crested broadbill

Date	Mintage	F	VF	XF	Unc	BU
2008 Prooflike	4,000	—	—	—	—	90.00

KM# 116 DOLLAR

31.1050 g., 0.9990 Silver 0.9990 oz. ASW **Ruler:** Elizabeth II **Subject:** Birds of Fiji **Rev:** Multicolor collared lory

Date	Mintage	F	VF	XF	Unc	BU
2008 Prooflike	4,000	—	—	—	—	90.00

KM# 117 DOLLAR

31.1050 g., 0.9990 Silver 0.9990 oz. ASW **Ruler:** Elizabeth II **Subject:** Birds of Fiji **Rev:** Multicolor - Island Thrush

Date	Mintage	F	VF	XF	Unc	BU
2008 Prooflike	4,000	—	—	—	—	90.00

KM# 118 DOLLAR

31.1050 g., 0.9990 Silver 0.9990 oz. ASW **Ruler:** Elizabeth II **Subject:** Birds of Fiji **Rev:** Multicolor white collared kingfisher

Date	Mintage	F	VF	XF	Unc	BU
2008 Prooflike	4,000	—	—	—	—	90.00

KM# 124 DOLLAR

Copper-Nickel **Ruler:** Elizabeth II **Subject:** Barack Obama elected U.S. President

Date	Mintage	F	VF	XF	Unc	BU
2009	—	—	—	—	—	15.00

KM# 130 DOLLAR

Copper-Nickel partially gilt, 40 mm. **Ruler:** Elizabeth II **Subject:** Pacific Explorers - Sir Francis Drake **Rev:** Ship, portrait in oval

Date	Mintage	F	VF	XF	Unc	BU
2009 Proof	—	Value: 15.00				

KM# 131 DOLLAR

Copper-Nickel partially gilt, 40 mm. **Ruler:** Elizabeth II **Subject:** Pacific Explorers - Ferdinand Magellan **Rev:** Ship, portrait in oval

Date	Mintage	F	VF	XF	Unc	BU
2009 Proof	—	Value: 15.00				

KM# 132 DOLLAR

Copper-Nickel partially gilt, 40 mm. **Ruler:** Elizabeth II **Subject:** Pacific Explorers - James Cook **Rev:** Ship, portrait in oval

Date	Mintage	F	VF	XF	Unc	BU
2009 Proof	—	Value: 15.00				

KM# 133 DOLLAR

Copper-Nickel partially gilt, 40 mm. **Ruler:** Elizabeth II **Subject:** Pacific Explorers - Abel Tasman **Rev:** Ship, portrait in oval

Date	Mintage	F	VF	XF	Unc	BU
2009 Proof	—	Value: 15.00				

KM# 134 DOLLAR
Copper-Nickel partially gilt **Ruler:** Elizabeth II **Subject:** Pacific Explorers - Jacob DeMare & William Schouten **Rev:** Ship, portraits in oval

Date	Mintage	F	VF	XF	Unc	BU
2009 Proof	—	Value: 15.00				

KM# 135 DOLLAR
Copper-Nickel partially gilt **Ruler:** Elizabeth II **Subject:** Pacific Explorers - William Bligh **Rev:** Ship, portrait in oval

Date	Mintage	F	VF	XF	Unc	BU
2009	—	—	—	—	—	15.00

KM# 137 DOLLAR
Copper-Nickel gilt **Ruler:** Elizabeth II **Subject:** Great animals of the World - Panda

Date	Mintage	F	VF	XF	Unc	BU
2009	—	—	—	—	—	15.00

KM# 138 DOLLAR
Copper-Nickel gilt **Ruler:** Elizabeth II **Subject:** Great animals of the World - Koi

Date	Mintage	F	VF	XF	Unc	BU
2009	—	—	—	—	—	15.00

KM# 139 DOLLAR
Copper-Nickel **Ruler:** Elizabeth II **Subject:** Great animals of the World - Zebra

Date	Mintage	F	VF	XF	Unc	BU
2009	—	—	—	—	—	15.00

KM# 140 DOLLAR
Copper-Nickel **Ruler:** Elizabeth II **Subject:** Great animals of the World - Elephant

Date	Mintage	F	VF	XF	Unc	BU
2009	—	—	—	—	—	15.00

KM# 141 DOLLAR
Copper-Nickel gilt **Ruler:** Elizabeth II **Subject:** Great animals of the World - Cheeta

Date	Mintage	F	VF	XF	Unc	BU
2009	—	—	—	—	—	15.00

KM# 142 DOLLAR
Copper-Nickel gilt **Ruler:** Elizabeth II **Subject:** Great animals of the World - Leopard

Date	Mintage	F	VF	XF	Unc	BU
2009	—	—	—	—	—	15.00

KM# 143 DOLLAR
Copper-Nickel **Ruler:** Elizabeth II **Subject:** Great animals of the World - Giraffe

Date	Mintage	F	VF	XF	Unc	BU
2009	—	—	—	—	—	15.00

KM# 144 DOLLAR
Copper-Nickel gilt **Ruler:** Elizabeth II **Subject:** Great animals of the World - Tiger

Date	Mintage	F	VF	XF	Unc	BU
2009	—	—	—	—	—	15.00

KM# 145 DOLLAR
Copper-Nickel silver plated **Ruler:** Elizabeth II **Subject:** Tropical fish - Yellow pointed nose

Date	Mintage	F	VF	XF	Unc	BU
2009	—	—	—	—	—	15.00

KM# 146 DOLLAR
Copper-Nickel silver plated **Ruler:** Elizabeth II **Subject:** Tropical fish - Albina yellow fish

Date	Mintage	F	VF	XF	Unc	BU
2009	—	—	—	—	—	15.00

KM# 147 DOLLAR
Copper-Nickel silver plated **Ruler:** Elizabeth II **Subject:** Tropical fish - Stripped Butterfly fish

Date	Mintage	F	VF	XF	Unc	BU
2009	—	—	—	—	—	15.00

KM# 148 DOLLAR
Copper-Nickel silver plated **Ruler:** Elizabeth II **Subject:** Tropical fish - Damsel fish

Date	Mintage	F	VF	XF	Unc	BU
2009	—	—	—	—	—	15.00

KM# 149 DOLLAR
Copper-Nickel silver plated **Ruler:** Elizabeth II **Subject:** Tropical fish - Surgern fish

Date	Mintage	F	VF	XF	Unc	BU
2009	—	—	—	—	—	15.00

KM# 150 DOLLAR
Copper-Nickel silver plated **Ruler:** Elizabeth II **Subject:** Tropical fish - Clown fish

Date	Mintage	F	VF	XF	Unc	BU
2009	—	—	—	—	—	15.00

KM# 126 DOLLAR
Silver **Ruler:** Elizabeth II **Subject:** H.C. Andersen - Steadfast Tin Soldier **Rev:** Multicolor toy soldier in flames

Date	Mintage	F	VF	XF	Unc	BU
2010 Proof	—	Value: 50.00				

KM# 127 DOLLAR
Silver **Ruler:** Elizabeth II **Subject:** H.C. Andersen - The Nightengale **Rev:** Multicolor bird

Date	Mintage	F	VF	XF	Unc	BU
2010 Proof	—	Value: 50.00				

KM# 128 DOLLAR
Silver **Ruler:** Elizabeth II **Subject:** H.C. Andersen - Thumbelina **Rev:** Multicolor Pixi

Date	Mintage	F	VF	XF	Unc	BU
2010 Proof	—	Value: 50.00				

KM# 129 DOLLAR
Silver **Ruler:** Elizabeth II **Subject:** H.C. Andersen - The little match girl **Rev:** Multicolor girl with match

Date	Mintage	F	VF	XF	Unc	BU
2010 Proof	—	Value: 50.00				

KM# 152 DOLLAR
31.1050 g., 0.9990 Silver 0.9990 oz. ASW, 46x29 mm. **Ruler:** Elizabeth II **Subject:** Siberian Tiger **Shape:** Irregular

Date	Mintage	F	VF	XF	Unc	BU
2010 Proof	10,000	Value: 50.00				

KM# 153 DOLLAR
31.1050 g., 0.9990 Silver 0.9990 oz. ASW, 46x29 mm. **Ruler:** Elizabeth II **Subject:** Bengal Tiger **Shape:** Irregular

Date	Mintage	F	VF	XF	Unc	BU
2010 Proof	10,000	Value: 50.00				

KM# 154 DOLLAR
Tri-Metallic Copper center, Brass inner ring, Copper-Nickel outer ring., 40 mm. **Ruler:** Elizabeth II **Subject:** FIAA World Cup - South Africa **Rev:** Pretoria stadium and animal

Date	Mintage	F	VF	XF	Unc	BU
2010	—	—	—	—	—	20.00

KM# 155 DOLLAR
Tri-Metallic Copper center, Brass inner ring, Copper-Nickel outer ring., 40 mm. **Ruler:** Elizabeth II **Subject:** FIAA World Cup - South Africa **Rev:** Kapstadt stadium and Zebra

Date	Mintage	F	VF	XF	Unc	BU
2010	—	—	—	—	—	20.00

KM# 156 DOLLAR
Tri-Metallic Copper center, Brass inner ring, Copper-Nickel outer ring., 40 mm. **Ruler:** Elizabeth II **Subject:** FIAA World Cup - South Africa **Rev:** Johannesburg Stadium and Rhino

Date	Mintage	F	VF	XF	Unc	BU
2010	—	—	—	—	—	20.00

KM# 157 DOLLAR
Tri-Metallic Copper center, Brass inner ring, Copper-Nickel outer ring., 40 mm. **Ruler:** Elizabeth II **Subject:** FIAA World Cup - South Africa **Rev:** Johannesburg Stadium and Leopard

Date	Mintage	F	VF	XF	Unc	BU
2010	—	—	—	—	—	20.00

KM# 158 DOLLAR
Tri-Metallic Copper center, Brass inner ring, Copper-Nickel outer ring., 40 mm. **Ruler:** Elizabeth II **Subject:** FIAA World Cup - South Africa **Rev:** Rustenburg Stadium and Lion

Date	Mintage	F	VF	XF	Unc	BU
2010	—	—	—	—	—	20.00

KM# 159 DOLLAR
Tri-Metallic Copper center, Brass inner ring, Copper-Nickel outer ring., 40 mm. **Ruler:** Elizabeth II **Subject:** FIAA World Cup - South Africa **Rev:** Durban and Giraffe

Date	Mintage	F	VF	XF	Unc	BU
2010	—	—	—	—	—	20.00

KM# 160 DOLLAR
Tri-Metallic Copper center, Brass inner ring, Copper-Nickel outer ring., 40 mm. **Ruler:** Elizabeth II **Subject:** FIAA World Cup - South Africa **Rev:** Polokwane and Elephant

Date	Mintage	F	VF	XF	Unc	BU
2010	—	—	—	—	—	20.00

KM# 161 DOLLAR
Tri-Metallic Copper center, Brass inner ring, Copper-Nickel outer ring., 40 mm. **Ruler:** Elizabeth II **Subject:** FIAA World Cup - South Africa **Rev:** Nelspruit stadium and Water buffalo

Date	Mintage	F	VF	XF	Unc	BU
2010	—	—	—	—	—	20.00

KM# 162 DOLLAR
Tri-Metallic Copper center, Brass inner ring, Copper-Nickel outer ring., 40 mm. **Ruler:** Elizabeth II **Subject:** FIAA World Cup - South Africa **Rev:** Bloemfontein stadium and Parrie Dog

Date	Mintage	F	VF	XF	Unc	BU
2010	—	—	—	—	—	20.00

KM# 163 DOLLAR
Tri-Metallic Copper center, Brass inner ring, Copper-Nickel outer ring., 40 mm. **Ruler:** Elizabeth II **Subject:** FIAA World Cup - South Africa **Rev:** Port Elizabeth stadium and Animal

Date	Mintage	F	VF	XF	Unc	BU
2010	—	—	—	—	—	20.00

KM# 108 2 DOLLARS
10.0000 g., 0.9250 Silver 0.2974 oz. ASW **Ruler:** Elizabeth II **Subject:** XVIII FIFA World Rootball Championship - Germany 2006 **Obv:** Crowned head right **Obv. Legend:** ELIZABETH II - FIJI **Rev:** World cup

Date	Mintage	F	VF	XF	Unc	BU
2004 Proof	50,000	Value: 22.00				

KM# 151 2 DOLLARS
31.1050 g., 0.9990 Silver 0.9990 oz. ASW, 40 mm. **Ruler:** Elizabeth II **Rev:** Hawksbill Taku Turtle

Date	Mintage	F	VF	XF	Unc	BU
2010 Proof	—	Value: 50.00				

KM# 151a 2 DOLLARS
31.1050 g., 0.9990 Silver partially gilt 0.9990 oz. ASW, 40 mm. **Ruler:** Elizabeth II **Rev:** Hawksbill Taku Turtle

Date	Mintage	F	VF	XF	Unc	BU
2010 Proof	—	Value: 50.00				

KM# 93 5 DOLLARS
1.5550 g., 0.9999 Gold 0.0500 oz. AGW **Ruler:** Elizabeth II **Obv:** Crowned head right, date at right **Rev:** Arms

Date	Mintage	F	VF	XF	Unc	BU
2002	3,000	Value: 85.00				

KM# 115A 5 DOLLARS
1.5600 g., 0.9999 Gold 0.0501 oz. AGW, 13.9 mm. **Ruler:** Elizabeth II **Rev:** Coat of Arms

Date	Mintage	F	VF	XF	Unc	BU
2002 Proof	3,000	Value: 220				

KM# 82 10 DOLLARS
31.6200 g., 0.9250 Silver 0.9403 oz. ASW, 38.6 mm. **Ruler:** Elizabeth II **Obv:** Crowned head right, date at right **Obv. Designer:** Raphael Maklouf **Rev:** William Bligh's - HMS Providence **Edge:** Reeded

Date	Mintage	F	VF	XF	Unc	BU
2001 Proof	—	Value: 40.00				

KM# 83 10 DOLLARS
28.2800 g., 0.9250 Silver 0.8410 oz. ASW, 38.6 mm. **Ruler:** Elizabeth II **Subject:** Queen Elizabeth II - 50 Years of Reign **Obv:** Queen's head right, gilded **Rev:** Cloth draped sword hilt, legend and denomination **Rev. Legend:** Defender of the Faith... **Rev. Designer:** Robert Low **Edge:** Reeded

Date	Mintage	F	VF	XF	Unc	BU
2002 Proof	15,000	Value: 40.00				

KM# 84 10 DOLLARS
28.2800 g., 0.9250 Silver 0.8410 oz. ASW, 38.6 mm. **Ruler:** Elizabeth II **Subject:** Queen Elizabeth II - 50th Year of Reign **Obv:** Head right, gilded **Rev:** Four man chorus, legend, and denomination **Rev. Legend:** Westminster Abbey June 1953. **Rev. Designer:** Robert Low **Edge:** Reeded

Date	Mintage	F	VF	XF	Unc	BU
2002 Proof	15,000	Value: 40.00				

KM# 94 10 DOLLARS
3.1100 g., 0.9999 Gold 0.1000 oz. AGW **Ruler:** Elizabeth II **Obv:** Crowned head right, date at right **Rev:** Arms **Edge:** Reeded

Date	Mintage	F	VF	XF	Unc	BU
2002 Proof	2,000	Value: 175				

KM# 101 10 DOLLARS
31.1000 g., 0.9990 Silver 0.9988 oz. ASW, 40 mm. **Ruler:** Elizabeth II **Series:** Save the Whales **Obv:** Crowned head right, date at right **Obv. Legend:** ELIZABETH II - FIJI **Rev:** Sperm Whale on mother-of-pearl inset **Edge:** Plain

Date	Mintage	F	VF	XF	Unc	BU
2002 Proof	2,000	Value: 85.00				

KM# 104 10 DOLLARS
28.2800 g., 0.9250 Silver 0.8410 oz. ASW, 38.6 mm. **Ruler:** Elizabeth II **Series:** Endangered Wildlife **Obv:** Crowned head right **Obv. Legend:** ELIZABETH II - FIJI **Rev:** Head of Peregrine Falcon right

Date	Mintage	F	VF	XF	Unc	BU
2002 Proof	—	Value: 45.00				

KM# 105 10 DOLLARS
28.2800 g., 0.9250 Silver 0.8410 oz. ASW, 38.6 mm. **Ruler:** Elizabeth II **Obv:** Crowned head right **Obv. Legend:** ELIZABETH II - FIJI **Rev:** Sailing ship "Vostok"

Date	Mintage	F	VF	XF	Unc	BU
2002 Proof	—	Value: 40.00				

KM# 106 10 DOLLARS
1.2400 g., 0.9999 Gold 0.0399 oz. AGW, 13.88 mm. **Ruler:** Elizabeth II **Obv:** Crowned head right **Obv. Legend:** ELIZABETH II - FIJI **Rev:** Sailing ship at left, naval bust 3/4 left at right **Rev. Legend:** HMS INVESTIGATOR * MATTHEW FLINDERS **Edge:** Reeded

Date	Mintage	F	VF	XF	Unc	BU
2002 Proof	—	Value: 65.00				

KM# 114A 10 DOLLARS
3.1100 g., 0.9999 Gold 0.1000 oz. AGW, 16 mm. **Ruler:** Elizabeth II **Rev:** Coat of Arms

Date	Mintage	F	VF	XF	Unc	BU
2002 Proof	2,000	Value: 350				

KM# 113 10 DOLLARS
1.2400 g., Gold, 13.91 mm. **Ruler:** Elizabeth II **Subject:** Lost Treasure of King Richard **Obv:** Crowned head right **Rev:** Bust of King Richard facing **Edge:** Reeded

Date	Mintage	F	VF	XF	Unc	BU
2003 Proof	—	Value: 65.00				

KM# 107 10 DOLLARS
28.2600 g., 0.9250 Silver 0.8404 oz. ASW, 38.61 mm. **Ruler:** Elizabeth II **Obv:** Crowned head right **Obv. Legend:** ELIZABETH II - FIJI **Obv. Designer:** Raphael Maklouf **Rev:** Sailing ship at left, naval bust 3/4 left at right **Rev. Legend:** HMS INVESTIGATOR * MATTHEW FLINDERS **Edge:** Reeded

Date	Mintage	F	VF	XF	Unc	BU
2003 Proof	—	Value: 40.00				

KM# 109 10 DOLLARS
Silver **Ruler:** Elizabeth II **Subject:** XXVIII Summer Olympics - Athens 2004 **Obv:** Crowned head right **Obv. Legend:** ELIZABETH II - FIJI **Rev:** Regatta

Date	Mintage	F	VF	XF	Unc	BU
2004 Proof	—	Value: 40.00				

KM# 110 10 DOLLARS
Copper-Nickel-Zinc, 38.6 mm. **Ruler:** Elizabeth II **Subject:** XVIII FIFA World Football Championship - Germany 2006 **Obv:** Crowned head right **Obv. Legend:** ELIZABETH II - FIJI **Rev:** Digital countdown clock

Date	Mintage	F	VF	XF	Unc	BU
2005	50,000	—	—	—	—	45.00

KM# 111 10 DOLLARS
1.2400 g., 0.9999 Gold 0.0399 oz. AGW **Ruler:** Elizabeth II **Subject:** 500th Anniversary Death of Christopher Columbus **Obv:** Crowned head right **Obv. Legend:** ELIZABETH II - FIJI **Rev:** Sailing ship "Santa Maria"

Date	Mintage	F	VF	XF	Unc	BU
2006 Proof	15,000	Value: 65.00				

KM# 125 10 DOLLARS
31.1050 g., 0.9990 Silver 0.9990 oz. ASW **Ruler:** Elizabeth II **Obv:** Crowned head right **Rev:** Yes we can!

Date	Mintage	F	VF	XF	Unc	BU
2009 Proof	—	Value: 50.00				

KM# 112 25 DOLLARS
155.5000 g., 0.9990 Silver 4.9942 oz. ASW **Ruler:** Elizabeth II **Obv:** Crowned head right **Obv. Legend:** ELIZABETH II - FIJI **Rev:** Sailing ship "Vostok"

Date	Mintage	F	VF	XF	Unc	BU
2002 Proof	—	Value: 200				

KM# 99 100 DOLLARS
7.7800 g., 0.5850 Gold 0.1463 oz. AGW **Ruler:** Elizabeth II **Subject:** 2006 FIFA World Cup - Germany **Obv:** Crowned head right, date at right **Rev:** World Cup **Edge:** Reeded

Date	Mintage	F	VF	XF	Unc	BU
2003 Proof	25,000	Value: 225				

KM# 136 100 DOLLARS
31.1050 g., 0.9990 Gold 0.9990 oz. AGW, 32 mm. **Ruler:** Elizabeth II **Rev:** Beach scene

Date	Mintage	F	VF	XF	Unc	BU
2009 Proof-like	—	—	—	—	—	1,500

The Republic of Finland, the third most northerly state of the European continent, has an area of 130,559 sq. mi. (338,127 sq. km.) and a population of 5.1 million. Capital: Helsinki. Lumbering, shipbuilding, metal and woodworking are the leading industries. Paper, timber, wood pulp, plywood and metal products are exported.

MONETARY SYSTEM
100 Pennia = 1 Markka

MINT MARKS
H - Birmingham 1921
Heart (h) - Copenhagen 1922
No mm – Helsinki
M – 1987-2006
FI – FINLAND – 2007-
Rampant lion in a circle – 2010-

MINT OFFICIALS' INITIALS

Letter	Date	Name
J-M	2002	Toivo Jaatinen & Raimo Makkonen
L-M	2000-03	Maija Lavonen & Raimo Makkonen
K-M	2004	Heli Kauhanen & Raimo Makkonen
K-M	2005-2006	Tapio Kettunen & Raimo Makkonen
M-M	2002-2006	Pertti Mäkinen & Raimo Makkonen
N-M	2001	Antti Neuvonen & Raimo Makkonen
P-M	2003	Matti Peltokangas & Raimo Makkonen
P-M	2001, 2005-07	Reijo Paavilainen & Raimo Makkonen
S-M	2003	Anneli Sigriläinen & Raimo Makkonen
VV-M	2002	Erkki Vainio & Hannu Veijalainen & Raimo Makkonen

REPUBLIC

REFORM COINAGE

KM# 65 10 PENNIA
1.8000 g., Copper-Nickel, 16.3 mm. **Obv:** Flower pods and stems, date at right **Rev:** Denomination to right of honeycombs **Designer:** Antti Neuvonen

Date	Mintage	F	VF	XF	Unc	BU
2001 M	25,000,000	—	—	—	1.00	1.50
2001 M Proof	—	Value: 7.00				

KM# 66 50 PENNIA
3.3000 g., Copper-Nickel, 19.7 mm. **Obv:** Polar bear, date below **Rev:** Denomination above flower heads **Edge:** Reeded **Designer:** Antti Neuvonen

Date	Mintage	F	VF	XF	Unc	BU
2001 M	200,000	—	—	0.20	1.00	1.50
2001 M Proof	—	Value: 8.00				

KM# 76 MARKKA
5.0000 g., Aluminum-Bronze, 22.2 mm. **Obv:** Rampant lion left within circle, date below **Rev:** Ornaments flank denomination within circle

Date	Mintage	F	VF	XF	Unc	BU
2001 M	200,000	—	—	0.35	0.75	1.00
2001 M Proof	—	Value: 10.00				

KM# 95 MARKKA
8.6400 g., 0.7500 Gold 0.2083 oz. AGW, 22 mm. **Subject:** Last Markka Coin **Obv:** Rampant lion with sword left **Rev:** Stylized tree with roots **Edge:** Reeded **Designer:** Reijo Paavilainen

Date	Mintage	F	VF	XF	Unc	BU
2001M P-M Proof	55,000	Value: 325				

KM# 106 MARKKA
6.1000 g., Copper-Nickel, 24 mm. **Subject:** Remembrance Markka **Obv:** Rampant lion with sword left **Rev:** Denomination and pine tree **Edge:** Plain **Designer:** Antti Neuvonen **Note:** This coin is encased in acrylic resin and sealed in a display card.

Date	Mintage	F	VF	XF	Unc	BU
2001M N-M	500,000	—	—	—	5.00	6.50

KM# 73 5 MARKKAA
5.5000 g., Copper-Aluminum-Nickel, 24.5 mm. **Obv:** Lake Saimaa ringed seal, date below **Rev:** Denomination, dragonfly and lily pad leaves

Date	Mintage	F	VF	XF	Unc	BU
2001 M	200,000	—	—	—	4.00	6.00
2001 M Proof	—	Value: 12.00				

KM# 77 10 MARKKAA
8.8000 g., Bi-Metallic Brass center in Copper-Nickel ring, 27.25 mm. **Obv:** Capercaillie bird within circle, date above **Rev:** Denomination and branches

Date	Mintage	F	VF	XF	Unc	BU
2001 M	200,000	—	—	3.00	5.00	6.00
2001 M Proof	—	Value: 18.00				

KM# 96 25 MARKKAA
20.2000 g., Bi-Metallic Brass center in Copper-Nickel ring, 35 mm. **Subject:** First Nordic Ski Championship, "Lahti 2001" **Obv:** Stylized woman's face **Rev:** Female torso, landscape **Edge:** Plain **Designer:** Jarkko Roth

Date	Mintage	F	VF	XF	Unc	BU
2001M Prooflike	100,000	—	—	—	—	30.00

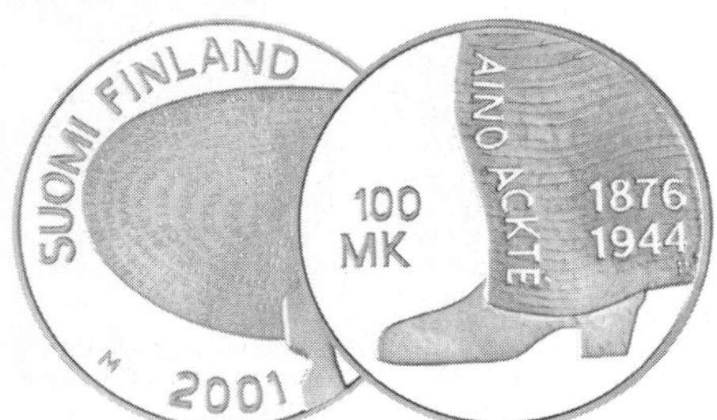

KM# 97 100 MARKKAA
31.0000 g., 0.9250 Silver 0.9219 oz. ASW, 35 mm. **Subject:** Aino Ackte **Obv:** Partial portrait **Rev:** High heel boot and trouser bottom **Edge:** Plain **Designer:** Timo Rytkönen.

Date	Mintage	F	VF	XF	Unc	BU
2001M	33,000	—	—	—	35.00	45.00
2001M Proof	12,000	Value: 60.00				

EURO COINAGE

European Union Issues

KM# 98 EURO CENT
2.3000 g., Copper Plated Steel, 16.3 mm. **Obv:** Rampant lion left surrounded by stars, date at left **Obv. Designer:** Heikki Häiväoja **Rev:** Denomination and globe **Rev. Designer:** Luc Luycx **Edge:** Plain

Date	Mintage	F	VF	XF	Unc	BU
2001M	500,000	—	—	—	10.00	—
2001M Proof	15,000	—	—	—	—	—
2002M	659,000	—	—	—	5.00	—
2002M Proof	13,000	Value: 15.00				
2003M	6,790,000	—	—	—	1.00	—
2003M Proof	14,500	Value: 15.00				
2004M	9,690,000	—	—	—	1.00	—
2004M Proof	5,000	Value: 15.00				
2005M	5,800,000	—	—	—	1.00	—
2005M Proof	3,000	Value: 15.00				
2006M	4,000,000	—	—	—	1.00	—
2006M Proof	3,300	Value: 15.00				
2007FI	3,000,000	—	—	—	1.00	—
2007FI Proof	—	Value: 15.00				
2008FI	1,500,000	—	—	—	1.00	—
2008FI Proof	—	Value: 15.00				
2009FI	—	—	—	—	1.00	—
2009FI Proof	—	Value: 15.00				
2010FI	—	—	—	—	1.00	—

KM# 99 2 EURO CENT
3.0000 g., Copper Plated Steel, 18.8 mm. **Obv:** Rampant lion surrounded by stars, date at left **Obv. Designer:** Heikki Häiväoja **Rev:** Denomination and globe **Rev. Designer:** Luc Luycx **Edge:** Grooved

Date	Mintage	F	VF	XF	Unc	BU
2001M	500,000	—	—	—	10.00	—
2001M Proof	15,000	Value: 15.00				
2002M	659,000	—	—	—	5.00	—
2002M Proof	13,000	Value: 15.00				
2003M	6,790,000	—	—	—	5.00	—
2003M Proof	14,500	Value: 15.00				
2004M	8,024,000	—	—	—	5.00	—
2004M Proof	5,000	Value: 15.00				
2005M	5,800,000	—	—	—	5.00	—
2005M Proof	3,000	Value: 15.00				
2006M	4,000,000	—	—	—	5.00	—
2006M Proof	3,300	Value: 15.00				
2007FI	3,000,000	—	—	—	5.00	—
2007FI Proof	—	Value: 15.00				
2008FI	1,500,000	—	—	—	5.00	—
2008FI Proof	—	Value: 15.00				
2009FI	—	—	—	—	5.00	—
2009FI Proof	—	Value: 15.00				
2010FI	—	—	—	—	5.00	—

KM# 100 5 EURO CENT
3.9400 g., Copper Plated Steel, 21.3 mm. **Obv:** Rampant lion left surrounded by stars, date at left **Obv. Designer:** Heikki Häiväoja **Rev:** Denomination and globe **Rev. Designer:** Luc Luycx **Edge:** Plain

Date	Mintage	F	VF	XF	Unc	BU
2001M	213,756,000	—	—	—	0.50	—
2001M Proof	15,000	Value: 15.00				
2002M	101,824,000	—	—	—	0.50	—
2002M Proof	13,000	Value: 15.00				
2003M	790,000	—	—	—	1.00	—
2003M Proof	14,500	Value: 15.00				
2004M	629,000	—	—	—	1.00	—
2004M Proof	5,000	Value: 15.00				
2005M	800,000	—	—	—	1.00	—
2005M Proof	3,000	Value: 15.00				
2006M	1,000,000	—	—	—	1.00	—
2006M Proof	3,000	Value: 15.00				
2007FI	1,000,000	—	—	—	1.00	—
2007FI Proof	—	Value: 15.00				
2008FI	1,000,000	—	—	—	1.00	—
2008FI Proof	—	Value: 15.00				
2009FI	—	—	—	—	1.00	—
2009M Proof	—	Value: 15.00				
2010FI	—	—	—	—	1.00	—

KM# 101 10 EURO CENT
4.0000 g., Brass, 19.7 mm. **Obv:** Rampant lion left surrounded by stars, date at left **Obv. Designer:** Heikki Häiväoja **Rev:** Denomination and map **Rev. Designer:** Luc Luycx **Edge:** Reeded

Date	Mintage	F	VF	XF	Unc	BU
2001M	14,730,000	—	—	—	10.00	—
2001M Proof	15,000	Value: 18.00				
2002M	1,499,000	—	—	—	2.50	—
2002M Proof	13,000	Value: 18.00				
2003M	790,000	—	—	—	2.50	—
2003M Proof	14,500	Value: 18.00				
2004M	629,000	—	—	—	2.50	—
2004M Proof	5,000	Value: 18.00				
2005M	800,000	—	—	—	2.50	—
2005M Proof	3,000	Value: 18.00				
2006M	1,000,000	—	—	—	2.50	—
2006M Proof	3,300	Value: 18.00				

KM# 126 10 EURO CENT
4.1000 g., Brass, 19.8 mm. **Obv:** Rampant lion surrounded by stars **Obv. Designer:** Heikki Häiväoja **Rev:** Relief map of Western Europe, stars, lines and value **Rev. Designer:** Luc Luycx **Edge:** Reeded

Date	Mintage	F	VF	XF	Unc	BU
2007FI	1,000,000	—	—	—	2.50	—
2007FI Proof	—	Value: 18.00				
2008FI	1,000,000	—	—	—	2.50	—
2008FI Proof	—	Value: 18.00				
2009FI	—	—	—	—	2.50	—
2009FI Proof	—	Value: 18.00				
2010FI	—	—	—	—	2.50	—

KM# 102 20 EURO CENT
5.7300 g., Brass, 22.2 mm. **Obv:** Rampant lion left surrounded by stars, date at left **Obv. Designer:** Heikki Häiväoja **Rev:** Denomination and map **Rev. Designer:** Luc Luycx **Edge:** Notched

Date	Mintage	F	VF	XF	Unc	BU
2001M	121,763,000	—	—	—	1.75	—
2001M Proof	15,000	Value: 20.00				
2002M	100,759,000	—	—	—	1.75	—
2002M Proof	13,000	Value: 20.00				
2003M	790,000	—	—	—	1.75	—
2003M Proof	14,500	Value: 20.00				
2004M	629,000	—	—	—	1.75	—
2004M Proof	5,000	Value: 20.00				
2005M	800,000	—	—	—	1.75	—
2005M Proof	3,000	Value: 20.00				
2006M	1,000,000	—	—	—	1.75	—
2006M Proof	3,300	Value: 20.00				

KM# 127 20 EURO CENT
5.7000 g., Brass, 22.3 mm. **Obv:** Rampant lion surrounded by stars **Obv. Designer:** Heikki Häiväoja **Rev:** Relief map of Western Europe, stars, lines and value **Rev. Designer:** Luc Luycx **Edge:** Notched

Date	Mintage	F	VF	XF	Unc	BU
2007FI	1,000,000	—	—	—	1.75	—
2007FI Proof	—	Value: 20.00				
2008FI	1,000,000	—	—	—	1.75	—
2008FI Proof	—	Value: 20.00				
2009FI	—	—	—	—	1.75	—
2009FI Proof	—	Value: 20.00				
2010FI	—	—	—	—	1.75	—

KM# 103 50 EURO CENT
7.8100 g., Brass, 24.2 mm. **Obv:** Rampant lion left surrounded by stars, date at left **Obv. Designer:** Heikki Häiväoja **Rev:** Denomination and map **Rev. Designer:** Luc Luycx **Edge:** Reeded

Date	Mintage	F	VF	XF	Unc	BU
2001M	4,432,000	—	—	—	7.50	—
2001M Proof	15,000	Value: 22.00				
2002M	1,147,000	—	—	—	5.00	—
2002M Proof	13,000	Value: 22.00				
2003M	790,000	—	—	—	5.00	—
2003M Proof	14,500	Value: 22.00				
2004M	629,000	—	—	—	5.00	—
2004M Proof	5,000	Value: 22.00				
2005M	4,800,000	—	—	—	5.00	—
2005M Proof	3,000	Value: 22.00				
2006M	6,850,000	—	—	—	5.00	—
2006M Proof	3,300	Value: 22.00				

KM# 128 50 EURO CENT
7.9000 g., Brass, 24.3 mm. **Obv:** Rampant lion surrounded by stars **Obv. Designer:** Heikki Häiväoja **Rev:** Relief map of Western Europe, stars, lines and value **Rev. Designer:** Luc Luycx **Edge:** Reeded

Date	Mintage	F	VF	XF	Unc	BU
2007FI	1,000,000	—	—	—	5.00	—
2007FI Proof	—	Value: 22.00				
2008FI	8,000,000	—	—	—	5.00	—
2008FI Proof	—	Value: 22.00				
2009FI	—	—	—	—	5.00	—
2009FI Proof	—	Value: 22.00				
2010FI	—	—	—	—	5.00	—

KM# 104 EURO
7.5000 g., Bi-Metallic Copper-Nickel center in Nickel-Brass ring, 23.2 mm. **Obv:** 2 flying swans, date below, surrounded by stars on outer ring **Obv. Designer:** Pertti Mäkinen **Rev:** Denomination and map **Rev. Designer:** Luc Luycx **Edge:** Segmented reeding

Date	Mintage	F	VF	XF	Unc	BU
2001M	13,862,000	—	—	—	3.00	—
2001M Proof	15,000	Value: 25.00				
2002M	14,114,000	—	—	—	6.50	—
2002M Proof	13,000	Value: 25.00				
2003M	790,000	—	—	—	6.50	—
2003M Proof	14,500	Value: 25.00				
2004M	5,529,000	—	—	—	6.50	—
2004M Proof	5,000	Value: 25.00				
2005M	7,935,000	—	—	—	6.50	—
2005M Proof	3,000	Value: 25.00				
2006M	1,705,000	—	—	—	6.50	—
2006M Proof	3,300	Value: 25.00				

KM# 129 EURO
7.5000 g., Bi-Metallic Copper-Nickel center in Nickel-Brass ring, 23.2 mm. **Obv:** 2 flying swans surrounded by stars on outer ring **Obv. Designer:** Pertti Mäekinen **Rev:** Relief map of western Europe, stars, lines and value **Rev. Designer:** Luc Luycx **Edge:** Segmented reeding

Date	Mintage	F	VF	XF	Unc	BU
2007FI	1,000,000	—	—	—	6.50	—
2007FI Proof	—	Value: 25.00				
2008FI	1,000,000	—	—	—	6.50	—
2008FI Proof	—	Value: 25.00				
2009FI	—	—	—	—	6.50	—
2009FI Proof	—	Value: 25.00				
2010FI	—	—	—	—	6.50	—

KM# 105 2 EURO
8.5000 g., Bi-Metallic Nickel-Brass center in Copper-Nickel ring, 25.75 mm. **Obv:** 2 cloudberry flowers surrounded by stars on outer ring **Obv. Designer:** Raimo Heino **Rev:** Denomination and map **Rev. Designer:** Luc Luycx **Edge:** Reeded and lettered **Edge Lettering:** SUOMI FINLAND

Date	Mintage	F	VF	XF	Unc	BU
2001M	29,132,000	—	—	—	4.00	—
2001M Proof	15,000	Value: 30.00				
2002M	1,386,000	—	—	—	7.50	—
2002M Proof	13,000	Value: 30.00				
2003M	9,080,000	—	—	—	5.00	—
2003M Proof	14,500	Value: 30.00				
2004M	10,029,000	—	—	—	5.00	—
2004M Proof	5,000	Value: 30.00				
2005M	10,800,000	—	—	—	5.00	—
2005M Proof	3,000	Value: 30.00				
2006M	11,000,000	—	—	—	5.00	—
2006M Proof	3,300	Value: 30.00				

KM# 114 2 EURO
8.5000 g., Bi-Metallic Nickel-Brass center in Copper-Nickel ring, 25.75 mm. **Subject:** EU Expansion **Obv:** Stylized flower **Obv. Designer:** Pertti Mäkinen **Rev:** Denomination and map **Rev. Designer:** Luc Luycx **Edge:** Reeded and lettered

Date	Mintage	F	VF	XF	Unc	BU
2004 M-M	1,000,000	—	—	—	10.00	11.50
2004 Proof	—	—	—	—	—	—

KM# 119 2 EURO
8.5000 g., Bi-Metallic Nickel-Brass center in Copper-Nickel ring, 25.75 mm. **Subject:** 60th Anniversary - Finland - UN **Obv:** Dove on a puzzle **Rev:** Denomination over map **Edge Lettering:** YK 1945-2005 FN

Date	Mintage	F	VF	XF	Unc	BU
2005M K-M	2,000,000	—	—	—	6.00	7.50

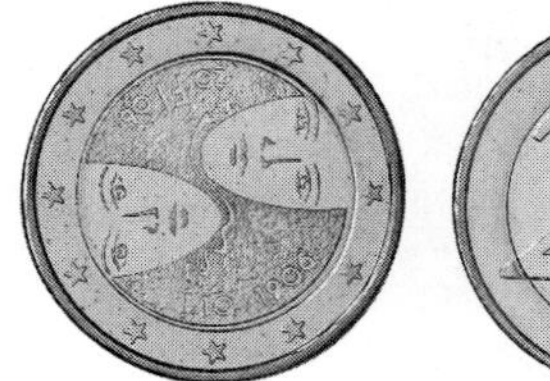

KM# 125 2 EURO
8.5000 g., Bi-Metallic Nickel-Brass center in Copper-Nickel ring, 25.75 mm. **Subject:** Centennial of Universal Suffrage **Obv:** Two faces **Obv. Designer:** Pertti Mäkinen **Rev:** Value and map **Rev. Designer:** Luc Luycx **Edge Lettering:** SUOMI FINLAND

Date	Mintage	F	VF	XF	Unc	BU
ND (2006)M M-M	2,500,000	—	—	—	6.00	7.50

KM# 130 2 EURO
8.5000 g., Bi-Metallic Nickel-Brass center in Copper-Nickel ring, 25.75 mm. **Obv:** 2 cloudberry flowers surrounded by stars on outer ring **Obv. Designer:** Raimo Heino **Rev:** Relief map of Western Europe, stars, lines and value **Rev. Designer:** Luc Luycx **Edge:** Reeded and lettered **Edge Lettering:** SUOMI FINLAND

Date	Mintage	F	VF	XF	Unc	BU
2007FI	8,600,000	—	—	—	6.00	7.50
2007FI Proof	—	Value: 30.00				
2008FI	9,800,000	—	—	—	6.00	7.50
2008FI Proof	—	Value: 30.00				
2009FI	—	—	—	—	6.00	7.50
2009FI Proof	—	Value: 30.00				
2010FI	—	—	—	—	6.00	7.50

KM# 138 2 EURO
8.5000 g., Bi-Metallic Nickel-Brass center in Copper-Nickel ring, 25.75 mm. **Subject:** 50th Anniversary Treaty of Rome **Obv:** Open treaty book **Rev:** Large value at left, modified outline of Europe at right **Edge:** Reeded and lettered

Date	Mintage	F	VF	XF	Unc	BU
2007	—	—	—	—	7.00	9.00
2007 Proof	—	Value: 75.00				

KM# 139 2 EURO
8.5000 g., Bi-Metallic Nickel-Brass center in Copper-Nickel ring, 25.75 mm. **Subject:** 90th Anniversary of Independence **Obv:** Longboat rowing together **Obv. Designer:** Reijo Paavilainen **Edge:** Reeded and lettered

Date	Mintage	F	VF	XF	Unc	BU
2007M	2,000,000	—	—	—	—	6.00
2007M Proof	20,000	Value: 20.00				

KM# 143 2 EURO
8.5000 g., Bi-Metallic Nickel-Brass center in Copper-Nickel ring, 25.75 mm. **Subject:** Universal Declaration of Human Rights **Obv:** Human figure within heart in landscape **Rev:** Segmented reeding

Date	Mintage	F	VF	XF	Unc	BU
2008	2,500,000	—	—	—	6.00	7.50
2008 Proof	—	Value: 25.00				

KM# 144 2 EURO
8.5000 g., Bi-Metallic Nickel-Brass center in Copper-Nickel ring, 25.75 mm. **Subject:** EMU 10th Anniversary **Obv:** Stick figure and E symbol **Edge:** Reeded and lettered

Date	Mintage	F	VF	XF	Unc	BU
2009	1,400,000	—	—	—	6.00	7.50
2009 Proof	25,000	—	—	—	—	—

KM# 149 2 EURO

8.5000 g., Bi-Metallic Nickel-Brass center in Copper-Nickel ring, 25.75 mm. **Subject:** Finnish Autonomy, 200th Anniversary **Obv:** Classical Pyramid **Edge:** Reeded and lettered

Date	Mintage	F	VF	XF	Unc	BU
2009	1,600,000	—	—	—	6.00	7.50

KM# 154 2 EURO

8.5000 g., Bi-Metallic Nickel-Brass center in Copper-Nickel ring, 25.6 mm. **Subject:** Finnish Currency, 150th Anniversary

Date	Mintage	F	VF	XF	Unc	BU
2010	—	—	—	—	6.00	7.50

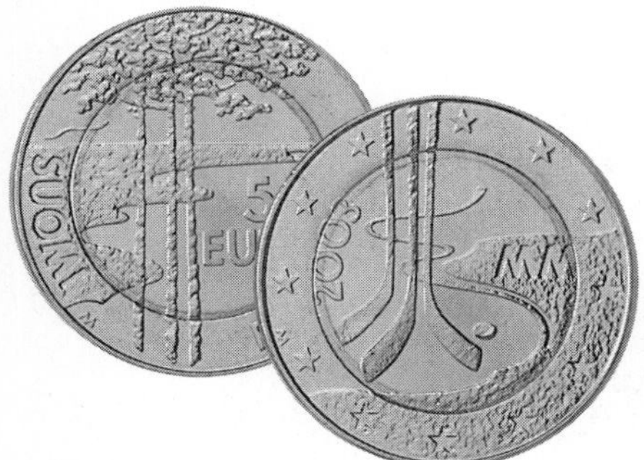

KM# 111 5 EURO

20.1000 g., Bi-Metallic Copper-Nickel center in Brass ring, 34.9 mm. **Subject:** Ice Hockey World Championships **Obv:** Summer landscape and denomination **Rev:** Three hockey sticks and a puck **Edge:** Plain **Designer:** Pertti Mäkinen

Date	Mintage	F	VF	XF	Unc	BU
2003M M-M	150,000	—	—	—	27.50	35.00

KM# 118 5 EURO

19.8000 g., Bi-Metallic Brass center in Copper-Nickel ring, 35 mm. **Subject:** 10th Anniversary - IAAF World Championships in Athletics **Obv:** Female javelin thrower, denomination **Rev:** Running feet **Edge:** Plain **Designer:** Tapio Kettunen

Date	Mintage	F	VF	XF	Unc	BU
2005M K-M	170,000	—	—	—	15.00	20.00
2005M K-M Proof	5,000	Value: 30.00				

KM# 123 5 EURO

18.7000 g., Copper, 35 mm. **Subject:** 150th Anniversary - Demilitarization of Aland **Obv:** Boat, Dove of Peace on the helm **Rev:** Tree **Edge Lettering:** AHVENANMAAN DEMILITARISOINTI 150 VUOTTA* **Designer:** Pertti Mäkinen

Date	Mintage	F	VF	XF	Unc	BU
2006 M-M	55,000	—	—	—	20.00	25.00

KM# 131 5 EURO

9.8100 g., Bi-Metallic Copper-Nickel center in Brass ring, 27.25 mm. **Subject:** Finland Presidency of European Union **Obv:** Letter decorations with 2006 and SUOMI-FINLAND **Rev:** 5 EURO below letter decoration **Designer:** Reijo Paavilainen

Date	Mintage	F	VF	XF	Unc	BU
2006M P-M	100,000	—	—	—	15.00	20.00

KM# 135 5 EURO

19.8000 g., Bi-Metallic Aluminum-Bronze center in Copper-Nickel ring, 35 mm. **Subject:** 90th Anniversary of Finland's Independence **Designer:** Reijo Paavilainen

Date	Mintage	F	VF	XF	Unc	BU
2007 P	130,000	—	—	—	15.00	20.00
2007 P Proof	20,000	Value: 30.00				

KM# 146 5 EURO

19.8000 g., Bi-Metallic, 35 mm. **Subject:** Independence, 90th Anniversary **Obv:** Petroglif of a longboat **Obv. Designer:** Reijo Paavilainen

Date	Mintage	F	VF	XF	Unc	BU
2007	130,000	—	—	—	—	15.00
2007 Proof	20,000	Value: 35.00				

KM# 141 5 EURO

19.6000 g., Bi-Metallic Copper-Nickel center in Brass ring, 35 mm. **Obv:** Science and Research

Date	Mintage	F	VF	XF	Unc	BU
2008	25,000	—	—	—	15.00	20.00
2008 Proof	20,000	Value: 30.00				

KM# 155 5 EURO

9.8000 g., Bi-Metallic Copper-Nickel center in Nickel-Brass ring, 27.5 mm. **Subject:** Historical Provincese - Varsinais - Suomi

Date	Mintage	F	VF	XF	Unc	BU
2010	90,000	—	—	—	—	15.00
2010 Proof	30,000	Value: 40.00				

KM# 156 5 EURO

19.8000 g., Bi-Metallic Copper-Nickel center in Nickel-Brass ring, 34.9 mm. **Subject:** Historical Provinces - Satakunta

Date	Mintage	F	VF	XF	Unc	BU
2010	—	—	—	—	—	20.00

KM# 107 10 EURO

27.4000 g., 0.9250 Silver 0.8148 oz. ASW, 38.6 mm. **Subject:** 50th Anniversary - Helsinki Olympics **Obv:** Flames and denomination above globe with map of Finland **Obv. Designer:** Erkki Vainio **Rev:** Tower and partial coin design **Rev. Designer:** Hannu Veijalainen **Edge:** Plain

Date	Mintage	F	VF	XF	Unc	BU
2002M VV-M	10,000	—	—	—	30.00	32.00
2002M VV-M Proof	34,800	Value: 35.00				

KM# 108 10 EURO

27.4000 g., 0.9250 Silver 0.8148 oz. ASW, 38.6 mm. **Subject:** Elias Lönnrot **Obv:** Ribbon with stars **Rev:** Quill and signature **Edge:** Plain **Designer:** Pertti Mäkinen.

Date	Mintage	F	VF	XF	Unc	BU
2002M M-M	40,000	—	—	—	30.00	32.00
2002M M-M Proof	40,000	Value: 35.00				

KM# 110 10 EURO

27.4000 g., 0.9250 Silver 0.8148 oz. ASW, 38.6 mm. **Subject:** Anders Chydenius **Obv:** Stylized design **Rev:** Name and book **Edge:** Plain **Designer:** Tero Lounas

Date	Mintage	F	VF	XF	Unc	BU
2003M L-M	30,000	—	—	—	32.00	35.00
2003M Proof	30,000	Value: 40.00				

KM# 112 10 EURO

27.4000 g., 0.9250 Silver 0.8148 oz. ASW, 38.6 mm. **Subject:** Mannerheim and St. Petersburg **Obv:** Head 3/4 facing **Rev:** Fortress, denomination at right **Designer:** Anneli Sipiläinen

Date	Mintage	F	VF	XF	Unc	BU
2003 S-M	6,000	—	—	—	35.00	37.50
2003 S-M Proof	29,000	Value: 55.00				

KM# 115 10 EURO

27.4000 g., 0.9250 Silver 0.8148 oz. ASW, 38.6 mm. **Subject:** 200th Birthday of Johan Ludwig Runeberg **Obv:** Head of Runeberg **Rev:** Text of 1831 Helsingfors Tidningar newspaper **Designer:** Heli Kauhanen

Date	Mintage	F	VF	XF	Unc	BU
2004 K-M	6,400	—	—	—	32.00	35.00
2004 K-M Proof	600	Value: 45.00				

KM# 116 10 EURO

27.4000 g., 0.9250 Silver 0.8148 oz. ASW, 38.6 mm. **Subject:** Tove Jansson **Obv:** Three "muumi" figures **Rev:** Head of Tove Jansson **Edge:** Pertti Mäkinen

Date	Mintage	F	VF	XF	Unc	BU
2004 M-M	50,000	—	—	—	32.00	35.00
2004 M-M Proof	20,000	Value: 45.00				

KM# 120 10 EURO

25.5000 g., 0.9250 Silver 0.7583 oz. ASW, 38.6 mm. **Subject:** 60 years of Peace **Obv:** Dove of peace **Rev:** Flowering plant **Designer:** Pertti Mäkinen

Date	Mintage	F	VF	XF	Unc	BU
2005 M-M	55,000	—	—	—	32.00	35.00
2005 Proof	5,000	Value: 45.00				

KM# 122 10 EURO

25.5000 g., 0.9250 Silver 0.7583 oz. ASW, 38.6 mm. **Subject:** Unknown Soldier and Finnish Film Art **Obv:** Trench **Rev:** Soldier with helmet on top of a film **Designer:** Reijo Paavilainen

Date	Mintage	F	VF	XF	Unc	BU
2005 P-M	25,000	—	—	—	35.00	37.50
2005 P-M Proof	15,000	Value: 50.00				

KM# 124 10 EURO

25.5000 g., 0.9250 Silver 0.7583 oz. ASW, 38.6 mm. **Subject:** 200th Birthday - Johan Vilhelm Snellman **Obv:** Sun rising over the lake **Rev:** Snellman **Designer:** Tapio Kettunen

Date	Mintage	F	VF	XF	Unc	BU
2006 K-M	—	—	—	—	32.00	35.00
2006 K-M Proof	—	Value: 45.00				

KM# 132 10 EURO

25.5000 g., 0.9250 Silver 0.7583 oz. ASW, 38.6 mm. **Subject:** 100th Anniversary of Parliamentary Reform **Obv:** Two stylist heads female and male with text SUOMI FINLAND 10 EURO **Rev:** Male and female fingers inserting ballot paper into ballot box with text 100V EDUSKUNTAUUDISTUS 2006 **Edge Lettering:** LANTDAGSREFORMEN 1906 **Designer:** Pertti Mäkinen

Date	Mintage	F	VF	XF	Unc	BU
2006M M-M	40,000	—	—	—	32.00	35.00
2006M M-M Proof	20,000	Value: 45.00				

KM# 134 10 EURO

25.5000 g., 0.9250 Silver 0.7583 oz. ASW, 38.6 mm. **Subject:** A.E. Nordenskiöld and the Northeast Passage **Rev:** Sailor at ship's wheel during foul weather **Designer:** Reijo Paavilainen

Date	Mintage	F	VF	XF	Unc	BU
2007M P	7,000	—	—	—	32.00	35.00
2007M P Proof	33,000	Value: 45.00				

KM# 136 10 EURO

25.5000 g., 0.9250 Silver 0.7583 oz. ASW, 38.6 mm. **Subject:** Mikael Agricola - Finnish Language **Obv:** Quill pen and lettering **Rev:** Alphabet Letters **Designer:** Reijo Paavilainen

Date	Mintage	F	VF	XF	Unc	BU
2007 P	6,000	—	—	—	32.00	35.00
2007 P Proof	24,000	Value: 45.00				

KM# 140 10 EURO

27.4000 g., 0.9250 Silver 0.8148 oz. ASW, 38.6 mm. **Subject:** Finnish Flag

Date	Mintage	F	VF	XF	Unc	BU
2008	9,000	—	—	—	32.00	30.00
2008 Proof	26,000	Value: 35.00				

KM# 142 10 EURO

27.4000 g., 0.9250 Silver 0.8148 oz. ASW, 36.8 mm. **Subject:** Mika Waltari

Date	Mintage	F	VF	XF	Unc	BU
2008	5,000	—	—	—	30.00	32.00
2008 Proof	15,000	Value: 35.00				

KM# 148 10 EURO

27.4000 g., 0.9250 Silver 0.8148 oz. ASW, 38.6 mm. **Subject:** Fredrik Pacius **Obv:** Opening notes to Kung Karls Jakt, first opera of Pacius **Rev:** Stage curtian opening

Date	Mintage	F	VF	XF	Unc	BU
2009	—	—	—	—	35.00	37.50

KM# 151 10 EURO

25.5000 g., 0.9250 Silver 0.7583 oz. ASW, 38.6 mm. **Subject:** Eero Saarinen, 100th Anniversary of Birth **Obv. Designer:** Juha Kauko **Rev:** St. Louis Arch **Rev. Designer:** Juha Kaulo

Date	Mintage	F	VF	XF	Unc	BU
2010	6,000	—	—	—	—	40.00
2010 Proof	20,000	Value: 50.00				

KM# 152 10 EURO

25.5000 g., 0.9250 Silver 0.7583 oz. ASW, 38.6 mm. **Subject:** Minna Carth, author

Date	Mintage	F	VF	XF	Unc	BU
2010	4,000	—	—	—	—	40.00
2010 Proof	16,000	Value: 50.00				

KM# 157 10 EURO

25.5000 g., 0.9250 Silver 0.7583 oz. ASW, 38.6 mm. **Subject:** Konsta Jylhan, 100th Anniversary of Birth

Date	Mintage	F	VF	XF	Unc	BU
2010	—	—	—	—	32.00	35.00

KM# 121 20 EURO

1.7300 g., 0.9000 Gold 0.0501 oz. AGW, 13.9 mm. **Subject:** 10th Anniversary - IAAF World Championships in Athletics **Obv:** Helsinki Stadium **Rev:** Two faces **Designer:** Pertti Mäkinen

Date	Mintage	F	VF	XF	Unc	BU
2005 M-M Proof	30,000	Value: 100				

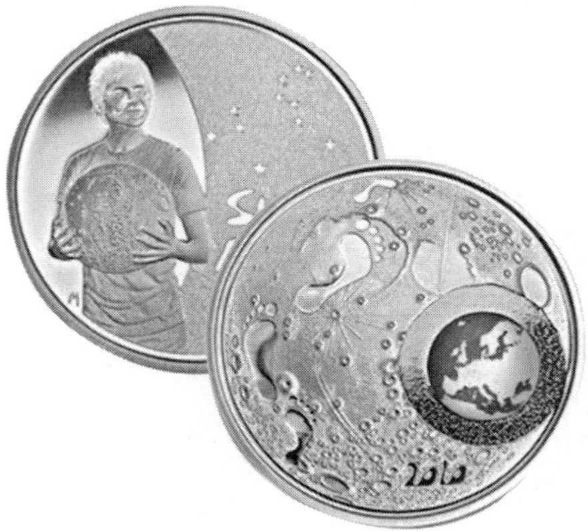

KM# 153 20 EURO

0.9250 Silver **Subject:** Children's creativity

Date	Mintage	F	VF	XF	Unc	BU
2010	—	—	—	—	—	40.00
2010 Proof	—	Value: 50.00				

KM# 113 50 EURO

13.2000 g., Bi-Metallic .750 Gold center in .925 Silver ring, 27.25 mm. **Subject:** Finnish art and design **Obv:** Snowflake design within box, beaded circle surrounds **Rev:** Snowflake design within beaded circle **Designer:** Matti Peltokangas

Date	Mintage	F	VF	XF	Unc	BU
2003 P-M Proof	10,600	Value: 350				

KM# 133 50 EURO

12.8000 g., Tri-Metallic 0.750 Gold 0.125 Silver 0.125 Copper center in 0.925 Silver and 0.075 Copper ring, 27.25 mm. **Subject:** Finland Presidency of European Union **Obv:** Letter decorations with 2006 and SUOMI-FINLAND **Rev:** 50 EURO below letter decoration **Designer:** Reijo Paavilainen

Date	Mintage	F	VF	XF	Unc	BU
2006M P-M Proof	8,000	Value: 350				

KM# 109 100 EURO

8.6400 g., 0.9000 Gold 0.2500 oz. AGW, 22 mm. **Subject:** Lapland **Obv:** Small tree and mountain stream **Rev:** Lake landscape beneath the midnight sun **Edge:** Plain with serial number **Designer:** Toivo Jaatinen

Date	Mintage	F	VF	XF	Unc	BU
2002M J-M Proof	25,000	Value: 375				

KM# 117 100 EURO

8.6400 g., 0.9000 Gold 0.2500 oz. AGW, 22 mm. **Subject:** 150th Birthday of Albert Edelfelt **Obv:** Flower **Rev:** Head of Edelfelt **Designer:** Pertti Mäkinen

Date	Mintage	F	VF	XF	Unc	BU
2004 M-M Proof	8,500	Value: 400				

KM# 137 100 EURO

8.4800 g., 0.9170 Gold 0.2500 oz. AGW **Subject:** 90th Anniversary of Finland's Independence **Obv:** Finland and the years of independence **Rev:** Abstract composition **Designer:** Reijo Paavilainen

Date	Mintage	F	VF	XF	Unc	BU
2007 P	—	—	—	—	385	375
2007 P Proof	—	Value: 400				

KM# 145 100 EURO

6.7800 g., 0.9170 Gold 0.1999 oz. AGW, 22 mm. **Subject:** Diet of Porvod

Date	Mintage	F	VF	XF	Unc	BU
2009 Proof	7,500	Value: 300				

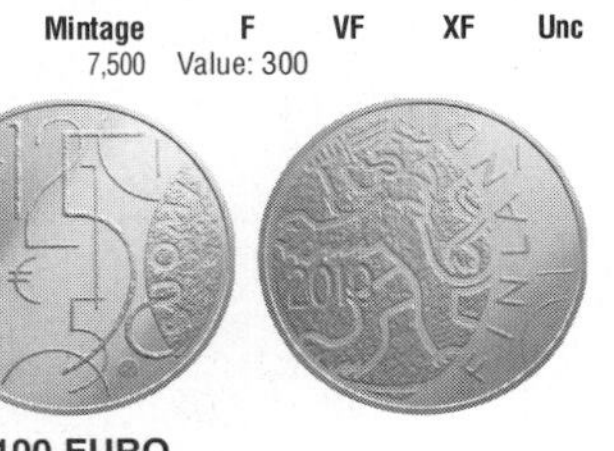

KM# 150 100 EURO

8.4800 g., 0.9170 Gold 0.2500 oz. AGW, 22 mm. **Subject:** Finland, 150th Anniversary

Date	Mintage	F	VF	XF	Unc	BU
2010 Proof	—	Value: 400				

MINT SETS

KM#	Date	Mintage	Identification	Issue Price	Mkt Val
MS58	2001 (5)	20,000	KM#65, 66, 73, 76, 77 plus 1865 coin design medal	18.00	22.50
MS59	2001 (5)	—	KM#65, 66, 73, 76, 77, medal (Johan Vilhelm Snellman)	—	22.50
MS60	2002 (8)	130,000	KM#98-105, Church medal	—	40.00
MS61	2003 (8)	170,000	KM#98-105, Golden Medal, goldpanning in Lappland	—	37.50
MS62	2002 (8)	2,000	KM#98-105, Baby	—	100
MS63	2003 (9)	8,000	KM#98-105, Silver medal, goldpanning in Lappland	—	125
MS64	2003 (8)	15,000	KM#98-105, Ice Hockey	—	60.00
MS65	2003 (9)	3,000	KM#98-105, medal and teddy bear	—	—
MS66	2003 (9)	5,000	KM#98-105, Baby, medal	—	37.50
MS67	2003 (9)	4,000	KM#98-105, Rose, medal	—	60.00
MS68	2003 (9)	30,000	KM#98-105, Christmas, golden medal	—	37.50
MS69	2004 (8)	55,000	KM#98-105, Euro zone, medal	—	40.00
MS70	2004 (8)	5,000	KM#98-105, 114, baby, medal	—	35.00
MS71	2004 (8)	18,000	KM#98-105, Tove Jansson, 90th Birthday	—	42.50
MS72	2004 (9)	4,000	KM#98-105, Music, medal	—	60.00
MS73	2005 (8)	40,000	KM#98-105, Wildlife, medal	—	42.50
MS74	2005 (9)	30,000	KM#98-105, 118, Paraolympics	—	55.00
MS75	2005 (9)	4,000	KM#98-105, Baby, medal	—	45.00
MS76	2005 (9)	3,000	KM#98-105, Music, medal	—	55.00
MS77	2006 (9)	40,000	KM#98-105, 119, Lighthouse	—	45.00
MS78	2006 (9)	20,000	KM#98-105, 125, Centennial of Parlament reform, suffrage	—	55.00
MS79	2006 (9)	3,200	KM#98-105, Music, medal	—	55.00
MS80	2006 (9)	4,000	KM#98-105, Wedding, medal	—	55.00
MS81	2006 (9)	4,600	KM#98-105, Baby, medal	—	55.00
MS82	2006 (9)	4,000	KM#98-105, Aland	—	45.00
MS83	2007 (9)	30,000	KM#98-100, 126-130, Lighthouse, medal	—	30.00
MS84	2007 (9)	3,000	KM#98-100, 126-130, Rose, medal	—	70.00
MS85	2007 (9)	3,000	KM#98-100, 126-130, Marriage, medal	—	55.00
MS86	2007 (9)	4,000	KM#98-100, 126-130, Baby, medal	—	65.00
MS87	2007 (10)	20,000	KM#98-100, 126-130, 138, European Song Festival, medal	—	45.00
MS88	2007 (8)	4,000	KM#98-100, 126-130, Aland	—	40.00
MS89	2007 (9)	20,000	KM#98-100, 126-130, 139, Swans	—	50.00
MS90	2007 (3)	—	KM98-100	—	10.00
MS91	2008 (9)	30,000	KM#98-100, 126-130, Lighthouse, medal	—	35.00
MS92	2008 (9)	3,000	KM#98-100, 126-130, Rose, medal	—	55.00
MS93	2008 (9)	3,000	KM#98-100, 126-130, Wedding, medal	—	45.00
MS94	2008 (9)	4,000	KM#98-100, 126-130, Baby, medal	—	50.00

PROOF SETS

KM#	Date	Mintage	Identification	Issue Price	Mkt Val
PS9	2001 (5)	—	KM#65-66, 73, 76-77, medal (Suomen Markka 1864-2001)	—	60.00
PS10	2002 (9)	5,000	KM#98-105, European Union gold medal	—	550
PS11	2002 (9)	8,000	KM#98-105, National Theater silver medal	—	185
PS12	2003 (9)	500	KM#98-105, Gold medal	—	350
PS13	2003 (9)	5,000	KM#98-105, Gold medal with diamond chip	—	500
PS14	2003 (9)	1,000	KM#98-105, Silver medal	—	400
PS15	2003 (9)	8,000	KM#98-105, Silver medal with diamond chip	—	150
PS16	2004 (10)	5,000	KM#98-105, 114, Silver medal	—	225
PS17	2005 (10)	3,000	KM#98-105, 118, Silver medal	—	200
PS18	2005 (2)	2,005	KM#118, 121 plus 2 older coins.	—	225
PS19	2006 (10)	3,300	KM#98-105, 125, Salmon medal	—	200
PS20	2007 (10)	2,500	KM#98-100, 126-130, 138, Silver medal.	—	150

FRANCE

The French Republic, largest of the West European nations, has an area of 210,026 sq. mi. (547,030 sq. km.) and a population of 58.1 million. Capital: Paris. Agriculture, manufacturing, tourist industry and financial services are the most important elements of France's diversified economy. Textiles and clothing, steel products, machinery and transportation equipment, chemicals, pharmaceuticals, nuclear electricity, agricultural products and wine are exported.

ENGRAVER GENERALS' PRIVY MARKS

Mark	Desc.	Date	Name
	Horseshoe	2000-2002	Gérard Buquoy
	SL Heart-shaped monogram	2002-2003	Serge Levet
	French horn w/starfish in water	2003	Hubert Lariviére

MINT DIRECTORS' PRIVY MARKS

Some modern coins struck from dies produced at the Paris Mint have the 'A' mint mark. In the absence of a mint mark, the cornucopia privy mark serves to attribute a coin to Paris design.

A – Paris, Central Mint

MODERN REPUBLICS

1870-

REFORM COINAGE

Commencing 1960

1 Old Franc = 1 New Centime;
100 New Centimes = 1 New Franc

KM# 928 CENTIME

1.6500 g., Stainless Steel, 15 mm. **Obv:** Cursive legend surrounds grain sprig **Rev:** Cursive denomination, date at top **Edge:** Plain **Designer:** Atelier de Paris **Note:** 1991-1993 dated coins, non-Proof, exist in both coin and medal alignment. Values given here are for medal alignment examples. Pieces struck in coin alignment have been traded for as much as $50.00.

Date	Mintage	F	VF	XF	Unc	BU
2001 In sets only	—	—	—	—	—	1.50
2001 Proof	—	Value: 2.00				

KM# 928a CENTIME

2.5000 g., 0.7500 Gold 0.0603 oz. AGW **Obv:** Cursive legend surrounds grain sprig, medallic alignment **Rev:** Cursive denomination, date above, medallic alignment **Edge:** Plain **Note:** Last Centime.

Date	Mintage	F	VF	XF	Unc	BU
2001	Est. 7,492	—	—	—	—	140

KM# 933 5 CENTIMES

2.0000 g., Aluminum-Bronze, 17 mm. **Obv:** Liberty bust left **Obv. Designer:** Henri Lagriffoul **Rev:** Denomination above date, grain sprig below, laurel branch at left **Rev. Designer:** Adrien Dieudonne **Edge:** Plain **Note:** 1991-1993 dated coins, non-Proof exist in both coin and medal alignment.

Date	Mintage	F	VF	XF	Unc	BU
2001 In sets only	—	—	—	—	1.50	2.50
2001 Proof	—	Value: 1.00				

KM# 929 10 CENTIMES

3.0000 g., Aluminum-Bronze, 20 mm. **Obv:** Liberty bust left **Obv. Designer:** Henri Lagriffoul **Rev:** Denomination above date, grain sprig below, laurel branch at left **Rev. Designer:** Adrien Dieudonne **Edge:** Plain **Note:** Without mint mark. 1991-1993 dated coins, non-Proof, exist in both coin and medal alignment.

Date	Mintage	F	VF	XF	Unc	BU
2001 In sets only	—	—	—	—	—	3.00
2001 Proof	—	Value: 1.00				

KM# 930 20 CENTIMES

4.0000 g., Aluminum-Bronze, 23.5 mm. **Obv:** Liberty bust left

Obv. Designer: Henri Lagriffoul **Rev:** Denomination above date, grain sprig below, laurel branch at left **Rev. Designer:** Adrien Dieudonne **Edge:** Plain **Note:** Without mint mark. 1991-1993 dated coins, non-Proof, exist in both coin and medal alignment.

Date	Mintage	F	VF	XF	Unc	BU
2001 In sets only	—	—	—	—	—	3.00
2001 Proof	—	Value: 1.00				

KM# 931.1 1/2 FRANC

4.5000 g., Nickel, 19.5 mm. **Obv:** The Seed Sower **Rev:** Laurel divides denomination and date **Edge:** Reeded **Designer:** Louis Oscar Roty **Note:** Without mint mark.

Date	Mintage	F	VF	XF	Unc	BU
2001 In sets only	—	—	—	—	2.00	3.00

KM# 931.2 1/2 FRANC

4.5000 g., Nickel, 19.5 mm. **Obv:** Modified sower, engraver's signature: "O. ROTY" preceded by "D'AP" **Rev:** Laurel divides date and denomination **Edge:** Plain

Date	Mintage	F	VF	XF	Unc	BU
2001	—	—	—	—	0.40	0.60
2001 Proof	—	Value: 1.50				

KM# 925.2 FRANC

6.0000 g., Nickel, 24 mm. **Obv:** Modified sower, engraver's signature: O. ROTY, preceded by D'AP **Rev:** Laurel divides date and denomination **Edge:** Plain

Date	Mintage	F	VF	XF	Unc	BU
2001	—	—	—	—	0.40	0.60
2001 Proof	—	Value: 2.50				

KM# 925.1a FRANC

8.0000 g., 0.7500 Gold 0.1929 oz. AGW, 24 mm. **Obv:** The Seed Sower **Rev:** Laurel divides date and denomination **Edge:** Reeded **Designer:** Louis Oscar Roty **Note:** Medallic alignment.

Date	Mintage	F	VF	XF	Unc	BU
2001	Est. 9,941	—	—	—	285	325

KM# 1290 FRANC

17.7700 g., 0.9800 Silver 0.5599 oz. ASW **Subject:** The Last Franc **Obv:** Legend on polished field **Obv. Legend:** UN ULTIME FRANC **Rev:** Number "1" on polished field **Edge Lettering:** REPUBLIQUE FRANCAISE STARCK LIBERTE EGALITE FRATERNITE (2001). **Note:** The coin is intentionally warped and the edge inscription is very faint. Struck at Paris Mint.

Date	Mintage	F	VF	XF	Unc	BU
2001 Matte	49,838	Value: 85.00				

KM# 1290a FRANC

26.1000 g., 0.7500 Gold 0.6293 oz. AGW **Subject:** The Last Franc **Obv:** Legend on polished field **Obv. Legend:** UN ULTIME FRANC **Rev:** Number "1" on polished field **Edge Lettering:** REPUBLIQUE FRANCAISE. STARCK. LIBERTE. EGALITE. FRATERNITE (cornucopia) 2001 **Note:** This coin has an intentionally warped surface and the edge inscription is very weak.

Date	Mintage	F	VF	XF	Unc	BU
2001 Matte	4,963	—	—	—	950	1,000

KM# 925.1 FRANC

6.0000 g., Nickel, 24 mm. **Obv:** The Seed Sower **Obv. Designer:** Louis Oscar Roty **Rev:** Laurel branch divides denomination and date **Edge:** Reeded **Note:** Without mint mark.

Date	Mintage	F	VF	XF	Unc	BU
2001	20,000,000	—	—	—	0.40	0.60

KM# 942.1 2 FRANCS

7.5000 g., Nickel, 26.5 mm. **Obv:** The Seed Sower **Rev:** Denomination on branches, date below **Edge:** Wide reeded **Designer:** Louis Oscar Roty

Date	Mintage	F	VF	XF	Unc	BU
2001 Bee	—	—	—	—	0.75	1.25

KM# 942.2 2 FRANCS

7.5000 g., Nickel, 26.5 mm. **Obv:** The Seed Sower **Rev:** Denomination on branches, date below **Edge:** Plain

Date	Mintage	F	VF	XF	Unc	BU
2001	—	—	—	—	0.75	1.25
2001 Proof	—	Value: 3.50				

KM# 926a.1 5 FRANCS

10.0000 g., Nickel Clad Copper-Nickel, 29 mm. **Obv:** The Seed Sower **Rev:** Branches divide denomination and date **Edge:** Reeded **Designer:** Raymond Joly

Date	Mintage	F	VF	XF	Unc	BU
2001 In sets only	—	—	—	—	5.00	7.50

KM# 926a.2 5 FRANCS

10.0000 g., Nickel, 29 mm. **Obv:** Modified sower, engraver's signature: "O. ROTY" preceded by "D'AP" **Rev:** Branches divide date and denomination **Edge:** Plain

Date	Mintage	F	VF	XF	Unc	BU
2001	—	—	—	—	1.65	2.50
2001 Proof	—	Value: 6.50				

KM# 1309 5 FRANCS

12.0000 g., 0.9000 Silver 0.3472 oz. ASW, 29 mm. **Subject:** Last Year of the Franc **Obv:** The Seed Sower **Rev:** Denomination and date **Edge:** Lettered **Edge Lettering:** "* LIBERTY * EGALITE * FRATERNITE * "

Date	Mintage	F	VF	XF	Unc	BU
2001	25,000	—	—	—	22.50	25.00

KM# 1265.1 6.55957 FRANCS

13.0000 g., 0.9000 Silver 0.3761 oz. ASW **Subject:** Last Year of the French Franc **Obv:** French and other European euro currency equivalents **Rev:** Europa allegorical portrait, date below, "last year of the franc" logo after the date **Edge:** Reeded

Date	Mintage	F	VF	XF	Unc	BU
2001	Est. 20,000	—	—	—	20.00	22.00

KM# 1265.2 6.55957 FRANCS

22.2000 g., 0.9000 Silver 0.6423 oz. ASW **Obv:** French and other European euro currency equivalents **Rev:** Europa allegorical portrait, date below, "last year of the franc" logo after the date **Edge:** Plain

Date	Mintage	F	VF	XF	Unc	BU
2001 Proof	Est. 10,000	Value: 45.00				

KM# 1276 6.55957 FRANCS

22.2000 g., 0.9000 Silver 0.6423 oz. ASW **Subject:** Mottos **Obv:** Denomination **Rev:** FRATERNITE in red letters **Edge:** Reeded

Date	Mintage	F	VF	XF	Unc	BU
2001 Proof	2,171	Value: 50.00				

KM# 1277 6.55957 FRANCS

22.2000 g., 0.9000 Silver 0.6423 oz. ASW **Subject:** Mottos **Obv:** Denomination **Rev:** EGALITE in white letters

Date	Mintage	F	VF	XF	Unc	BU
2001 Proof	2,190	Value: 50.00				

KM# 1278 6.55957 FRANCS

22.2000 g., 0.9000 Silver 0.6423 oz. ASW **Subject:** Mottos **Obv:** Denomination **Rev:** LIBERTE in white letters

Date	Mintage	F	VF	XF	Unc	BU
2001 Proof	2,259	Value: 50.00				

KM# 964.2 10 FRANCS

Aluminum-Bronze, 23 mm. **Obv:** Winged figure divides RF **Rev:** Patterned denomination above date **Edge:** Plain

Date	Mintage	F	VF	XF	Unc	BU
2001	—	—	—	—	6.00	7.50
2001 Proof	—	Value: 15.00				

KM# 1268 10 FRANCS

22.2000 g., 0.9000 Silver 0.6423 oz. ASW **Subject:** Monuments of France - Palace of Versailles **Obv:** Stylized French map **Rev:** 1/2 bust of Louis XIV at right, internal and external palace views at left **Edge:** Plain

Date	Mintage	F	VF	XF	Unc	BU
2001 Proof	Est. 2,561	Value: 50.00				

KM# 1270 10 FRANCS

22.2000 g., 0.9000 Silver 0.6423 oz. ASW **Subject:** Monuments of France - Arch of Triumph **Obv:** Stylized French map **Rev:** Arch of Triumph on the Champs Elysees partial close up and aerial views

Date	Mintage	F	VF	XF	Unc	BU
2001 Proof	Est. 2,882	Value: 50.00				

KM# 1272 10 FRANCS

22.2000 g., 0.9000 Silver 0.6423 oz. ASW **Subject:** Monuments of France - Notre Dame Cathedral **Obv:** Stylized French map **Rev:** Gargoyle at left, cathedral views at right

Date	Mintage	F	VF	XF	Unc	BU
2001 Proof	Est. 2,877	Value: 50.00				

KM# 1274 10 FRANCS

22.2000 g., 0.9000 Silver 0.6423 oz. ASW **Subject:** Monuments of France - Eiffel Tower **Obv:** Stylized French map **Rev:** Two tower views

Date	Mintage	F	VF	XF	Unc	BU
2001 Proof	Est. 3,888	Value: 45.00				

KM# 1008.2 20 FRANCS

9.0000 g., Tri-Metallic Copper-Aluminum-Nickel center, Nickel inner ring, Copper-Aluminum-Nickel outer ring, 27 mm. **Obv:** Mont St. Michel **Rev:** Patterned denomination above date **Edge:** 5 milled bands, reeded or plain

Date	Mintage	F	VF	XF	Unc	BU
2001	—	—	—	—	8.00	10.00
2001 Proof	—	Value: 25.00				

KM# 1266 65.5997 FRANCS
8.4500 g., 0.9200 Gold 0.2499 oz. AGW **Subject:** Last Year of the French Franc **Obv:** French and other European euro currency equivalents **Rev:** Europa allegorical portrait, date below, "last year of the franc" logo after the date **Edge:** Reeded

Date	Mintage	F	VF	XF	Unc	BU
2001 Proof	3,000	Value: 400				

KM# 1269 100 FRANCS
17.0000 g., 0.9200 Gold 0.5028 oz. AGW **Subject:** Palace of Versailles **Obv:** Stylized French map **Rev:** Louis XIV with internal and external palace views **Edge:** Plain

Date	Mintage	F	VF	XF	Unc	BU
2001 Proof	105	Value: 750				

KM# 1271 100 FRANCS
17.0000 g., 0.9200 Gold 0.5028 oz. AGW **Obv:** Champs-Elysees **Rev:** Arch of Triumph partial close up and aerial views

Date	Mintage	F	VF	XF	Unc	BU
2001 Proof	115	Value: 750				

KM# 1273 100 FRANCS
17.0000 g., 0.9200 Gold 0.5028 oz. AGW **Obv:** Notre-Dame Cathedral **Rev:** Gargoyle and cathedral views

Date	Mintage	F	VF	XF	Unc	BU
2001 Proof	116	Value: 775				

KM# 1275 100 FRANCS
17.0000 g., 0.9200 Gold 0.5028 oz. AGW **Obv:** Eiffel Tower **Rev:** Two tower views

Date	Mintage	F	VF	XF	Unc	BU
2001 Proof	170	Value: 750				

KM# 1267 655.957 FRANCS
31.1035 g., 0.9990 Gold 0.9990 oz. AGW **Subject:** Last Year of the French Franc **Obv:** French and other European euro currency equivalents **Rev:** Europa allegorical portrait, date below, "last year of the franc" logo after the date **Edge:** Plain

Date	Mintage	F	VF	XF	Unc	BU
2001 Proof	2,000	Value: 1,500				

KM# 1267.1 655.957 FRANCS
155.5175 g., 0.9990 Gold 4.9948 oz. AGW **Obv:** French and other European euro currency equivalents **Rev:** Europa allegorical portrait, date below, "last year of the franc" after the date **Edge:** Plain

Date	Mintage	F	VF	XF	Unc	BU
2001 Proof	99	Value: 7,500				

KM# 1279 655.957 FRANCS
17.0000 g., 0.9200 Gold 0.5028 oz. AGW **Subject:** Motto Series **Obv:** Denomination **Rev:** FRATERNITE **Edge:** Reeded

Date	Mintage	F	VF	XF	Unc	BU
2001 Proof	62	Value: 800				

KM# 1280 655.957 FRANCS
17.0000 g., 0.9200 Gold 0.5028 oz. AGW **Subject:** Motto Series **Obv:** Denomination **Rev:** EGALITE

Date	Mintage	F	VF	XF	Unc	BU
2001 Proof	64	Value: 800				

KM# 1281 655.957 FRANCS
17.0000 g., 0.9200 Gold 0.5028 oz. AGW **Subject:** Motto Series **Obv:** Denomination **Rev:** LIBERTE

Date	Mintage	F	VF	XF	Unc	BU
2001 Proof	63	Value: 800				

KM# 1617 20 EURO
163.8000 g., 0.9500 Silver 5.0028 oz. ASW, 50 mm. **Subject:** Unesco site - The Kremlin in Moscow **Obv:** Wall Tower and cathedral

Date	Mintage	F	VF	XF	Unc	BU
2009P Proof	500	Value: 250				

EURO COINAGE

European Union Issues

KM# 1282 EURO CENT
2.2700 g., Copper Plated Steel, 16.3 mm. **Obv:** Human face **Obv. Designer:** Fabienne Courtiade **Rev:** Denomination and globe **Rev. Designer:** Luc Luycx **Edge:** Plain

Date	Mintage	F	VF	XF	Unc	BU
2001	300,681,580	—	—	—	0.35	0.50
2001 Proof	15,000	Value: 10.00				
2002	200,000	—	—	—	—	10.00
2002 Proof	21,453	Value: 8.00				
2003	160,017,000	—	—	—	1.00	1.50
2003 Proof	40,000	Value: 8.00				
2004	400,032,000	—	—	—	0.35	0.50
2004 Proof	20,000	Value: 10.00				
2005	240,320,000	—	—	—	0.35	0.50
2005 Proof	10,000	Value: 12.00				
2006	343,078,000	—	—	—	0.35	0.50
2006 Proof	10,000	Value: 12.00				
2007	300,058,000	—	—	—	0.35	0.50
2007 Proof	7,500	Value: 14.00				
2008	462,757,000	—	—	—	0.35	0.50
2008 Proof	7,500	Value: 14.00				
2009	404,050,500	—	—	—	0.35	0.50
2009 Proof	7,500	Value: 14.00				
2010	—	—	—	—	0.35	0.50
2010 Proof	—	Value: 15.00				

KM# 1283 2 EURO CENT
3.0300 g., Copper Plated Steel, 18.7 mm. **Obv:** Human face **Obv. Designer:** Fabienne Courtiade **Rev:** Denomination and globe **Rev. Designer:** Luc Luycx **Edge:** Grooved

Date	Mintage	F	VF	XF	Unc	BU
2001	249,101,580	—	—	—	0.50	0.75
2001 Proof	15,000	Value: 10.00				
2002 In sets only	100,000	—	—	—	—	12.50
2002 Proof	21,453	Value: 8.00				
2003	160,175,000	—	—	—	1.25	2.00
2003 Proof	40,000	Value: 8.00				
2004	300,024,000	—	—	—	—	1.00
2004 Proof	20,000	Value: 10.00				
2005	2,603,202,000	—	—	—	—	1.00
2005 Proof	10,000	Value: 12.00				
2006	283,278,000	—	—	—	—	1.00
2006 Proof	10,000	Value: 12.00				
2007	213,258,000	—	—	—	—	1.00
2007 Proof	7,500	Value: 14.00				
2008	386,557,000	—	—	—	—	1.00
2008 Proof	7,500	Value: 14.00				
2009	317,050,500	—	—	—	—	1.00
2009 Proof	7,500	Value: 14.00				
2010	—	—	—	—	—	1.00
2010 Proof	—	Value: 14.00				

KM# 1284 5 EURO CENT
3.8600 g., Copper Plated Steel, 21.2 mm. **Obv:** Human face **Obv. Designer:** Fabienne Courtiade **Rev:** Denomination and globe **Rev. Designer:** Luc Luycx **Edge:** Plain

Date	Mintage	F	VF	XF	Unc	BU
2001	217,324,477	—	—	—	0.75	1.25
2001 Proof	15,000	Value: 12.00				
2002	186,400,000	—	—	—	0.75	1.25
2002 Proof	21,453	Value: 10.00				
2003	101,175,000	—	—	—	1.00	1.50
2003 Proof	40,000	Value: 10.00				
2004	60,162,000	—	—	—	—	1.25
2004 Proof	20,000	Value: 12.00				
2005	20,320,000	—	—	—	—	1.25
2005 Proof	10,000	Value: 14.00				
2006	132,078,000	—	—	—	—	1.25
2006 Proof	10,000	Value: 14.00				
2007	130,058,000	—	—	—	—	1.25
2007 Proof	7,500	Value: 16.00				
2008	218,257,000	—	—	—	—	1.25
2008 Proof	7,500	Value: 16.00				
2009	184,550,500	—	—	—	—	1.25
2009 Proof	7,500	Value: 16.00				
2010	—	—	—	—	—	1.25
2010 Proof	—	Value: 16.00				

KM# 1285 10 EURO CENT
4.0700 g., Brass, 19.7 mm. **Obv:** The seed sower divides date and RF **Obv. Designer:** Laurent Jorb **Rev:** Denomination and map **Rev. Designer:** Luc Luycx **Edge:** Reeded

Date	Mintage	F	VF	XF	Unc	BU
2001	144,513,261	—	—	—	1.25	2.00
2001 Proof	15,000	Value: 12.00				
2002	206,700,000	—	—	—	0.75	1.25
2002 Proof	21,453	Value: 10.00				
2003	180,875,000	—	—	—	1.25	2.00
2003 Proof	40,000	Value: 10.00				
2004	5,000,000	—	—	—	—	1.50
2004 In sets only	140,000	—	—	—	—	—
2004 Proof	20,000	Value: 12.00				
2005	45,120,000	—	—	—	—	1.50
2005 Proof	10,000	Value: 14.00				
2006	60,278,000	—	—	—	—	1.50
2006 Proof	10,000	Value: 14.00				

KM# 1410 10 EURO CENT
4.0700 g., Brass, 19.7 mm. **Obv:** Sower **Obv. Designer:** Laurent Jorb **Rev:** Relief map of Western Europe, stars, lines and value **Rev. Designer:** Luc Luycx **Edge:** Reeded

Date	Mintage	F	VF	XF	Unc	BU
2007	90,158,000	—	—	—	—	1.50
2007 Proof	7,500	Value: 14.00				
2008	178,757,000	—	—	—	—	1.50
2008 Proof	7,500	Value: 14.00				
2009	142,550,500	—	—	—	—	1.50
2009 Proof	7,500	Value: 14.00				
2010	—	—	—	—	—	1.50
2010 Proof	—	Value: 14.00				

KM# 1663 10 EURO CENT
12.0000 g., 0.9000 Silver 0.3472 oz. ASW, 29 mm. **Subject:** Midi - Pyrenees **Rev:** Value at center, wreath horizontal

Date	Mintage	F	VF	XF	Unc	BU
2010	7,690	—	—	—	—	—

KM# 1286 20 EURO CENT
5.7300 g., Brass, 22.2 mm. **Obv:** The seed sower divides date and RF **Obv. Designer:** Laurent Jorb **Rev:** Denomination and map **Rev. Designer:** Luc Luycx **Edge:** Notched

Date	Mintage	F	VF	XF	Unc	BU
2001	256,342,108	—	—	—	1.00	1.50
2001 Proof	15,000	Value: 14.00				
2002	192,100,000	—	—	—	1.00	1.50
2002 Proof	21,453	Value: 12.00				
2003 In sets only	180,000	—	—	—	—	9.50
2003 Proof	40,000	Value: 12.00				
2004 In sets only	160,000	—	—	—	—	9.50
2004 Proof	20,000	Value: 14.00				
2005 In sets only	120,000	—	—	—	—	9.50
2005 Proof	10,000	Value: 16.00				
2006 In sets only	67,600	—	—	—	—	9.50
2006 Proof	10,000	Value: 16.00				

KM# 1411 20 EURO CENT
5.7300 g., Brass, 22.2 mm. **Obv:** Sower **Obv. Designer:** Laurent Jorb **Rev:** Relief map of Western Europe, stars, lines and value **Rev. Designer:** Luc Luycx **Edge:** Notched

Date	Mintage	F	VF	XF	Unc	BU
2007	40,258,000	—	—	—	—	1.50
2007 Proof	7,500	Value: 14.00				
2008	25,557,000	—	—	—	—	1.50
2008 Proof	7,500	Value: 14.00				
2009	82,550,500	—	—	—	—	1.50
2009 Proof	7,500	Value: 14.00				
2010	—	—	—	—	—	1.50
2010 Proof	—	Value: 14.00				

KM# 1529 20 EURO CENT
163.8000 g., 0.9500 Silver 5.0028 oz. ASW, 50 mm. **Subject:** French Presidency of European Union **Obv:** Text within stars **Rev:** Europa head and flags

Date	Mintage	F	VF	XF	Unc	BU
2008 Proof	500	Value: 250				

KM# 1293 1/4 EURO
12.5000 g., Copper-Aluminum-Nickel, 30 mm. **Subject:** Childrens Design **Obv:** Euro globe with children **Rev:** Denomination and stars **Edge:** Plain

Date	Mintage	F	VF	XF	Unc	BU
2002	1,000,000	—	—	—	6.50	8.50

KM# 1300 1/4 EURO
13.0000 g., 0.9000 Silver 0.3761 oz. ASW, 30 mm. **Subject:** Europa **Obv:** Eight French euro coin designs **Rev:** Portrait and flags design of 6.55957 francs coin KM-1265 **Edge:** Reeded

Date	Mintage	F	VF	XF	Unc	BU
2002	20,000	—	—	—	20.00	22.00

KM# 1293a 1/4 EURO
13.0000 g., 0.9000 Silver 0.3761 oz. ASW, 30 mm. **Subject:** Childrens Design **Obv:** Euro globe with children **Rev:** Denomination **Edge:** Plain

Date	Mintage	F	VF	XF	Unc	BU
2002 Proof	10,000	Value: 45.00				

KM# 1331 1/4 EURO
3.1100 g., 0.9990 Gold 0.0999 oz. AGW, 15 mm. **Subject:** Children's Design **Obv:** Euro globe with children **Rev:** Denomination **Edge:** Plain

Date	Mintage	F	VF	XF	Unc	BU
2002 Proof	5,000	Value: 160				

KM# 1350 1/4 EURO
3.1100 g., 0.9999 Gold 0.1000 oz. AGW, 15 mm. **Obv:** Obverse design of first one franc coin **Rev:** Reverse design of first one franc coin **Edge:** Plain

Date	Mintage	F	VF	XF	Unc	BU
2003 Proof	5,000	Value: 160				

KM# 1372 1/4 EURO
22.2000 g., 0.9000 Silver 0.6423 oz. ASW, 37 mm. **Obv:** Samuel de Champlain **Rev:** Sail ship **Edge:** Plain

Date	Mintage	F	VF	XF	Unc	BU
2004	20,000	—	—	—	27.50	32.50

KM# 1390 1/4 EURO
13.0000 g., 0.9000 Silver 0.3761 oz. ASW, 30 mm. **Subject:** European Union Expansion **Obv:** Partial face and flags **Rev:** Puzzle map **Edge:** Plain

Date	Mintage	F	VF	XF	Unc	BU
2004	20,000	—	—	—	22.00	25.00

KM# 1402 1/4 EURO
11.0000 g., Copper-Aluminum-Nickel, 30 mm. **Subject:** Jules Verne **Obv:** Various scenes from Jules Verne's novels **Rev:** Jules Verne's portrait left of value and date

Date	Mintage	F	VF	XF	Unc	BU
2005	50,000	—	—	—	—	10.00

KM# 1442 1/4 EURO
22.2000 g., 0.9000 Silver 0.6423 oz. ASW, 37 mm. **Obv:** Bust of Franklin facing slightly right at left, his diplomatic and technical successes at right **Obv. Legend:** BENJAMIN FRANKLIN 1706-2006 **Obv. Inscription:** AMI DE LA FRANCE **Rev:** French flag at left, American flag at right **Rev. Inscription:** PHILOSOPHE / DIPLOMATE / ÉCRIVAIN / SAVANT

Date	Mintage	F	VF	XF	Unc	BU
2006	15,000	—	—	—	32.00	35.00

KM# 1445 1/4 EURO
22.2000 g., 0.9000 Silver 0.6423 oz. ASW, 37 mm. **Subject:** Marshall Bernadotte under Napoleon **Rev:** Military bust facing 3/4 right at left, building in backgound at right **Rev. Legend:** LIBERTÉ / ÉGALITÉ / FRATERNITÉ - KARL XIV JOHAN ROI DE SU?DE

Date	Mintage	F	VF	XF	Unc	BU
2006 Proof	10,000	—	—	—	32.00	35.00

KM# 1457 1/4 EURO
22.2000 g., 0.9000 Silver 0.6423 oz. ASW, 37 mm. **Subject:** Hèpitaux de France Foundation **Obv:** Foundation logo **Rev:** TGV train, money box on outlined map of France

Date	Mintage	F	VF	XF	Unc	BU
2006	50,000	—	—	—	28.00	30.00

KM# 1415 1/4 EURO
22.2000 g., 0.9000 Silver 0.6423 oz. ASW, 37 mm. **Obv:** Jean de la Fontaine, value, Chinese astrological animals, date, Paris mint privy marks but without national identification **Rev:** Dog in wreath **Edge:** Reeded **Note:** Anonymous coinage

Date	Mintage	F	VF	XF	Unc	BU
2006	10,000	—	—	—	32.00	35.00

KM# 1417 1/4 EURO
22.2000 g., 0.9000 Silver 0.6423 oz. ASW, 37 mm. **Obv:** Jean de la Fontaine, value, Chinese astrological animals, date, Paris mint privy marks but without national identification **Rev:** Pig in wreath **Edge:** Reeded **Note:** Anonymous issue.

Date	Mintage	F	VF	XF	Unc	BU
2007	10,000	—	—	—	32.00	35.00

KM# 1419 1/4 EURO
13.0000 g., 0.9000 Silver 0.3761 oz. ASW, 30 mm. **Obv:** Military bust of Lafayette facing 3/4 left **Obv. Legend:** LA FAYETTE. HÉROS DELA RÉVOLUTION AMÉRICAINE **Obv. Inscription:** 1757/1854 at left, RF monogram at right **Rev:** Sailing ship L' Hermione **Rev. Legend:** LA FAYETTE, HERO OF THE AMERICAN REVOLUTION **Edge:** Plain

Date	Mintage	F	VF	XF	Unc	BU
2007 (a) Proof-like	5,000	—	—	—	32.00	35.00

KM# 1421 1/4 EURO
15.0000 g., 0.9000 Silver 0.4340 oz. ASW **Subject:** 90th Anniversary Death of Degas **Obv:** Ballerina "The Star" at left **Obv. Inscription:** *Degas* **Rev:** Paint brushes and oils multicolor at left, self portrait at right **Rev. Inscription:** LIBERTÉ / ÉGALITÉ / FRATERNITÉ **Shape:** rectangular, 30 x 21 mm

Date	Mintage	F	VF	XF	Unc	BU
2007	5,000	—	—	—	42.00	45.00

KM# 1461 1/4 EURO
13.0000 g., 0.9000 Silver 0.3761 oz. ASW, 30 mm. **Subject:** Sebastien Le Prestre de Vauban, 300th Anniversary of Death **Obv:** Arms above funeral coach, book at left **Rev:** Vauban standing; plans of fortress

Date	Mintage	F	VF	XF	Unc	BU
2007 Proof	5,000	Value: 22.00				

KM# 1483 1/4 EURO
13.0000 g., 0.9000 Silver 0.3761 oz. ASW, 37 mm. **Subject:** 2007 Rugby World Cup **Obv:** Two Rugby players **Rev:** Logo and goal

Date	Mintage	F	VF	XF	Unc	BU
2007	5,000	—	—	—	32.00	35.00

KM# 1570 1/4 EURO
15.0000 g., 0.9000 Silver 0.4340 oz. ASW, 30 x 21 mm. **Subject:** Edward Manet **Obv:** Manet's "Olympia" painting **Rev:** Multicolor paint brushes and Manet's portrait **Shape:** Rectangle

Date	Mintage	F	VF	XF	Unc	BU
2008	10,000	—	—	—	—	65.00

KM# 1572 1/4 EURO
22.2000 g., 0.9000 Silver 0.6423 oz. ASW, 37 mm. **Subject:** Lunar New Year - Year of the Rat **Obv:** Bust of Jean de la Fontaine and twelve awards **Rev:** Rat within border

Date	Mintage	F	VF	XF	Unc	BU
2008	10,000	—	—	—	32.00	35.00

KM# 1287 50 EURO CENT
7.8100 g., Brass, 24.2 mm. **Obv:** The Seed Sower divides date and RF **Obv. Designer:** Laurent Jorb **Rev:** Denomination and map **Rev. Designer:** Luc Luycx **Edge:** Reeded

Date	Mintage	F	VF	XF	Unc	BU
2001	276,287,274	—	—	—	1.25	2.00
2001 Proof	15,000	Value: 15.00				
2002	226,500,000	—	—	—	1.25	2.00
2002 Proof	21,453	Value: 14.00				
2003 In sets only	180,000	—	—	—	—	11.50
2003 Proof	40,000	Value: 14.00				
2004 In sets only	160,000	—	—	—	—	11.50
2004 Proof	20,000	Value: 15.00				
2005 In sets only	120,000	—	—	—	—	11.50
2005 Proof	10,000	Value: 17.00				
2006 In sets only	67,600	—	—	—	—	11.50
2006 Proof	10,000	Value: 17.00				

KM# 1412 50 EURO CENT
7.8100 g., Brass, 24.2 mm. **Obv:** Sower **Obv. Designer:** Laurent Jorb **Rev:** Relief map of Western Europe, stars, lines and value **Rev. Designer:** Luc Luycx **Edge:** Reeded

Date	Mintage	F	VF	XF	Unc	BU
2007 In sets only	58,000	—	—	—	—	11.50
2007 Proof	7,500	Value: 16.00				
2008 In sets only	57,000	—	—	—	—	2.00
2008 Proof	7,500	Value: 16.00				
2009 In sets only	50,500	—	—	—	—	2.00
2009 Proof	7,500	Value: 16.00				
2010	—	—	—	—	—	2.00
2010 Proof	—	Value: 16.00				

KM# 1288 EURO
7.5000 g., Bi-Metallic Copper-Nickel center in Nickel-Brass ring, 23.3 mm. **Obv:** Stylized tree divides RF within circle, date below **Obv. Designer:** Joaquin Jimenez **Rev:** Denomination and map **Rev. Designer:** Luc Luycx **Edge:** Segmented reeding

Date	Mintage	F	VF	XF	Unc	BU
2001	150,251,624	—	—	—	2.75	4.00
2001 Proof	15,000	Value: 18.00				

Date	Mintage	F	VF	XF	Unc	BU
2002	129,400,000	—	—	—	2.50	3.75
2002 Proof	21,453	Value: 16.00				
2003 In sets only	100,000	—	—	—	8.00	12.50
2003 Proof	20,000	Value: 18.00				
2004 In sets only	160,000	—	—	—	—	2.50
2004 Proof	20,000	Value: 18.00				
2005 In sets only	120,000	—	—	—	—	2.50
2005 Proof	10,000	Value: 20.00				
2006 In sets only	78,000	—	—	—	—	2.50
2006 Proof	10,000	Value: 20.00				

KM# 1413 EURO

7.5000 g., Bi-Metallic Copper-Nickel center in Nickel-Brass ring, 23.3 mm. **Obv:** Stylized tree **Obv. Designer:** Joaquin Jimenz **Rev:** Relief map of Western Europe, stars, lines and value **Rev. Designer:** Luc Luycx **Edge:** Segmented reeding

Date	Mintage	F	VF	XF	Unc	BU
2007 In sets only	58,000	—	—	—	—	11.50
2007 Proof	7,500	Value: 20.00				
2008 In sets only	57,000	—	—	—	—	2.50
2008 Proof	7,500	Value: 20.00				
2009 In sets only	50,500	—	—	—	—	2.50
2009 Proof	7,500	Value: 20.00				
2010	—	—	—	—	—	2.50
2010 Proof	—	Value: 20.00				

KM# 1464 EURO

155.5500 g., 0.9500 Silver 4.7508 oz. ASW, 50 mm. **Subject:** Sebastien Le Prestre de Vauban, 300th Anniversary of Death

Date	Mintage	F	VF	XF	Unc	BU
2007 Proof	500	Value: 325				

KM# 1470 EURO

17.0000 g., 0.9200 Gold 0.5028 oz. AGW, 31 mm. **Subject:** Le Petit Prince, 60th Anniversary **Obv:** Prince standing with rabbit

Date	Mintage	F	VF	XF	Unc	BU
2007 Proof	2,000	Value: 750				

KM# 1486 EURO

17.0000 g., 0.9200 Gold 0.5028 oz. AGW, 31 mm. **Subject:** 2007 Rugby World Cup **Obv:** Two players and goal **Rev:** Logo and goal

Date	Mintage	F	VF	XF	Unc	BU
2007 Proof	500	Value: 800				

KM# 1490 EURO

22.0000 g., 0.9000 Silver 0.6366 oz. ASW **Subject:** Unesco **Obv:** Great Wall of China

Date	Mintage	F	VF	XF	Unc	BU
2007 Proof	5,000	Value: 60.00				

KM# 1491 EURO

8.4500 g., 0.9200 Gold 0.2499 oz. AGW, 22 mm. **Subject:** Unesco **Obv:** Crest Wall of China **Rev:** Unesco Building and emblem

Date	Mintage	F	VF	XF	Unc	BU
2007 Proof	500	Value: 400				

KM# 1492 EURO

22.2000 g., 0.9000 Silver 0.6423 oz. ASW, 37 mm. **Subject:** Point Neuf 400th Anniversary **Obv:** Monuments of France logo **Rev:** Point Neuf Bridge, Paris Mint Museum

Date	Mintage	F	VF	XF	Unc	BU
2007 Proof	3,000	Value: 80.00				

KM# 1493 EURO

8.4500 g., 0.9200 Gold 0.2499 oz. AGW, 22 mm. **Subject:** Point Neuf, 400th Anniversary **Obv:** Monuments of France logo **Rev:** Point Neuf Brudge, Paris Mint Building

Date	Mintage	F	VF	XF	Unc	BU
2007 Proof	500	Value: 425				

KM# 1495 EURO

8.4500 g., 0.9200 Gold 0.2499 oz. AGW, 22 mm. **Subject:** Cannes Film Festival **Obv:** Cinema screen and stage, Golden Palm Award

Date	Mintage	F	VF	XF	Unc	BU
2007 Proof	500	Value: 425				

KM# 1514 EURO

17.0000 g., 0.9200 Gold 0.5028 oz. AGW, 31 mm. **Subject:** Stanislas Lesczynski **Obv:** Bust, shield **Rev:** Palac Stanislas - Nancy

Date	Mintage	F	VF	XF	Unc	BU
2007 Proof	500	Value: 800				

KM# 1587 EURO

8.4500 g., 0.9200 Gold 0.2499 oz. AGW, 22 mm. **Subject:** Court of Human Rights, 50th Anniversary **Obv:** Sower left **Rev:** Text

Date	Mintage	F	VF	XF	Unc	BU
2009P Proof	500	Value: 425				

KM# 1332 1-1/2 EURO

22.2000 g., 0.9000 Silver 0.6423 oz. ASW, 37 mm. **Obv:** Victor Hugo, denomination and map **Rev:** Multicolor "Gavroche" **Edge:** Plain

Date	Mintage	F	VF	XF	Unc	BU
2002 Proof	10,000	Value: 55.00				

KM# 1301 1-1/2 EURO

22.2000 g., 0.9000 Silver 0.6423 oz. ASW, 37 mm. **Subject:** Europa **Obv:** Eight French euro coins design **Rev:** Portrait and flags design of 6.55957 francs KM-1265 **Edge:** Plain

Date	Mintage	F	VF	XF	Unc	BU
2002 Proof	50,000	Value: 45.00				

KM# 1305 1-1/2 EURO

22.2000 g., 0.9000 Silver 0.6423 oz. ASW, 37 mm. **Subject:** French Landmarks **Obv:** French map **Rev:** Le Mont St. Michel **Edge:** Plain

Date	Mintage	F	VF	XF	Unc	BU
2002 Proof	10,000	Value: 50.00				

KM# 1307 1-1/2 EURO

22.2000 g., 0.9000 Silver 0.6423 oz. ASW, 37 mm. **Subject:** French Landmarks **Obv:** French map **Rev:** La Butte Montmartre **Edge:** Plain

Date	Mintage	F	VF	XF	Unc	BU
2002 Proof	10,000	Value: 47.50				

KM# 1310 1-1/2 EURO

22.2000 g., 0.9000 Silver 0.6423 oz. ASW, 37 mm. **Subject:** First West to East Transatlantic Flight **Obv:** Denomination, map and Lindbergh portrait **Rev:** Spirit of St. Louis (airplane) and map **Edge:** Plain

Date	Mintage	F	VF	XF	Unc	BU
2002 Proof	10,000	Value: 50.00				

KM# 1321 1-1/2 EURO

22.2000 g., 0.9000 Silver 0.6423 oz. ASW, 37 mm. **Obv:** Tour de France logo **Rev:** Cyclist going left **Edge:** Plain

Date	Mintage	F	VF	XF	Unc	BU
2003 Proof	150,000	Value: 50.00				

KM# 1322 1-1/2 EURO

22.2000 g., 0.9000 Silver 0.6423 oz. ASW, 37 mm. **Obv:** Tour de France logo **Rev:** Group of cyclists and Arch de Triumph **Edge:** Plain

Date	Mintage	F	VF	XF	Unc	BU
2003 (Ht) Proof	150,000	Value: 50.00				

KM# 1323 1-1/2 EURO

22.2000 g., 0.9000 Silver 0.6423 oz. ASW, 37 mm. **Obv:** Tour de France logo **Rev:** Two cyclists and spectators **Edge:** Plain

Date	Mintage	F	VF	XF	Unc	BU
2003 (Ht) Proof	150,000	Value: 50.00				

KM# 1324 1-1/2 EURO

22.2000 g., 0.9000 Silver 0.6423 oz. ASW, 37 mm. **Obv:** Tour de France logo **Rev:** Two groups of cyclists **Edge:** Plain

Date	Mintage	F	VF	XF	Unc	BU
2003 (Ht) Proof	150,000	Value: 50.00				

KM# 1325 1-1/2 EURO

22.2000 g., 0.9000 Silver 0.6423 oz. ASW, 37 mm. **Obv:** Tour de France logo **Rev:** Cyclists, stopwatch and gears **Edge:** Plain

Date	Mintage	F	VF	XF	Unc	BU
2003 (Ht) Proof	150,000	Value: 50.00				

KM# 1336 1-1/2 EURO

22.2000 g., 0.9000 Silver 0.6423 oz. ASW, 37 mm. **Obv:** Jefferson and Napoleon with Louisiana Purchase map **Rev:** Jazz musician, mansion and river boat **Edge:** Plain

Date	Mintage	F	VF	XF	Unc	BU
2003 Proof	10,000	Value: 55.00				

KM# 1338 1-1/2 EURO

22.2000 g., 0.9000 Silver 0.6423 oz. ASW, 37 mm. **Obv:** Curved cross design with multiple values **Rev:** Goddess Europa and flags **Edge:** Plain

Date	Mintage	F	VF	XF	Unc	BU
2003 Proof	40,000	Value: 50.00				

KM# 1341 1-1/2 EURO

22.2000 g., 0.9000 Silver 0.6423 oz. ASW, 37 mm. **Obv:** Denomination and compass face **Rev:** SS Normandie and New York City **Edge:** Plain

Date	Mintage	F	VF	XF	Unc	BU
2003 Proof	15,000	Value: 55.00				

KM# 1343 1-1/2 EURO

22.2000 g., 0.9000 Silver 0.6423 oz. ASW, 37 mm. **Obv:** Denomination and compass face **Rev:** Airplane and Tokyo Geisha **Edge:** Plain

Date	Mintage	F	VF	XF	Unc	BU
2003 Proof	15,000	Value: 55.00				

KM# 1345 1-1/2 EURO

22.2000 g., 0.9000 Silver 0.6423 oz. ASW, 37 mm. **Obv:** Paul Gauguin **Rev:** Native woman **Edge:** Plain

Date	Mintage	F	VF	XF	Unc	BU
2003 Proof	15,000	Value: 55.00				

KM# 1351 1-1/2 EURO

22.2000 g., 0.9000 Silver 0.6423 oz. ASW, 37 mm. **Obv:** Obverse design of first one franc coin **Rev:** Reverse design of first one franc coin **Edge:** Plain

Date	Mintage	F	VF	XF	Unc	BU
2003 Proof	15,000	Value: 50.00				

KM# 1353 1-1/2 EURO

22.2000 g., 0.9000 Silver 0.6423 oz. ASW, 37 mm. **Obv:** Mona Lisa **Rev:** Leonardo da Vinci **Edge:** Plain

Date	Mintage	F	VF	XF	Unc	BU
2003 Proof	10,000	Value: 55.00				

KM# 1355 1-1/2 EURO

22.2000 g., 0.9000 Silver 0.6423 oz. ASW, 37 mm. **Obv:** Map and denomination **Rev:** Chateau Chambord **Edge:** Plain

Date	Mintage	F	VF	XF	Unc	BU
2003 Proof	10,000	Value: 50.00				

KM# 1357 1-1/2 EURO

22.2000 g., 0.9000 Silver 0.6423 oz. ASW, 37 mm. **Obv:** Denomination in swirling design **Rev:** Multicolor Hansel and Gretel, witch and house **Edge:** Plain

Date	Mintage	F	VF	XF	Unc	BU
2003 Proof	10,000	Value: 55.00				

KM# 1359 1-1/2 EURO

22.2000 g., 0.9000 Silver 0.6423 oz. ASW, 37 mm. **Obv:** Denomination in swirling design **Rev:** Multicolor Alice in Wonderland **Edge:** Plain

Date	Mintage	F	VF	XF	Unc	BU
2003 Proof	10,000	Value: 55.00				

KM# 1361 1-1/2 EURO

22.2000 g., 0.9000 Silver 0.6423 oz. ASW, 37 mm. **Obv:** Pierre de Coubertin **Rev:** Olympic runners **Edge:** Plain

Date	Mintage	F	VF	XF	Unc	BU
2003 Proof	50,000	Value: 50.00				

KM# 1364 1-1/2 EURO

22.2000 g., 0.9000 Silver 0.6423 oz. ASW, 37 mm. **Obv:** Map with denomination **Rev:** Avignon Popes Palace **Edge:** Plain

Date	Mintage	F	VF	XF	Unc	BU
2004 Proof	10,000	Value: 50.00				

KM# 1373 1-1/2 EURO

22.2000 g., 0.9000 Silver 0.6423 oz. ASW, 37 mm. **Obv:** Emile Loubet and King Edward VII **Rev:** Marianne and Britannia **Edge:** Plain

Date	Mintage	F	VF	XF	Unc	BU
2004 Proof	10,000	Value: 50.00				

KM# 1374 1-1/2 EURO

22.2000 g., 0.9000 Silver 0.6423 oz. ASW, 37 mm. **Obv:** Soccer ball and denomination **Rev:** Rooster and quill **Edge:** Plain

Date	Mintage	F	VF	XF	Unc	BU
2004 Proof	25,000	Value: 55.00				

KM# 1378 1-1/2 EURO

22.2000 g., 0.9000 Silver 0.6423 oz. ASW, 37 mm. **Obv:** Compass rose **Rev:** Ocean liner **Edge:** Plain

Date	Mintage	F	VF	XF	Unc	BU
2004 Proof	10,000	Value: 50.00				

KM# 1380 1-1/2 EURO

22.2000 g., 0.9000 Silver 0.6423 oz. ASW, 37 mm. **Obv:** Compass rose **Rev:** Trans-Siberian Railroad **Edge:** Plain

Date	Mintage	F	VF	XF	Unc	BU
2004 Proof	10,000	Value: 50.00				

KM# 1382 1-1/2 EURO
22.2000 g., 0.9000 Silver 0.6423 oz. ASW, 37 mm. **Obv:** Compass rose **Rev:** Half-track vehicle **Edge:** Plain

Date	Mintage	F	VF	XF	Unc	BU
2004 Proof	10,000	Value: 47.50				

KM# 1384 1-1/2 EURO
22.2000 g., 0.9000 Silver 0.6423 oz. ASW, 37 mm. **Obv:** Compass rose **Rev:** Biplane airliner **Edge:** Plain

Date	Mintage	F	VF	XF	Unc	BU
2004 Proof	10,000	Value: 47.50				

KM# 1386 1-1/2 EURO
22.2000 g., 0.9000 Silver 0.6423 oz. ASW, 37 mm. **Obv:** Statue of Liberty **Rev:** F.A. Bartholdi **Edge:** Plain

Date	Mintage	F	VF	XF	Unc	BU
2004 Proof	15,000	Value: 47.50				

KM# 1391 1-1/2 EURO
22.2000 g., 0.9000 Silver 0.6423 oz. ASW, 37 mm. **Subject:** European Union Expansion **Obv:** Partial face and flags **Rev:** Puzzle map **Edge:** Plain

Date	Mintage	F	VF	XF	Unc	BU
2004 Proof	40,000	Value: 42.50				

KM# 1366 1-1/2 EURO
22.2000 g., 0.9000 Silver 0.6423 oz. ASW, 37 mm. **Obv:** Book, eagle and denomination **Rev:** Napoleon and coronation scene in background **Edge:** Plain

Date	Mintage	F	VF	XF	Unc	BU
2004 Proof	20,000	Value: 45.00				

KM# 1369 1-1/2 EURO
22.2000 g., 0.9000 Silver 0.6423 oz. ASW, 37 mm. **Obv:** Soldiers and Normandy invasion scene **Rev:** "D-DAY" above denomination **Edge:** Plain

Date	Mintage	F	VF	XF	Unc	BU
2004 Proof	20,000	Value: 50.00				

KM# 1423 1-1/2 EURO
22.2000 g., 0.9000 Silver 0.6423 oz. ASW, 37 mm. **Subject:** Biathlon **Rev:** Skier at right facing 3/4 left, mountain peaks in background **Rev. Inscription:** JEUX D'HIVER

Date	Mintage	F	VF	XF	Unc	BU
2005 Proof	30,000	Value: 45.00				

KM# 1425 1-1/2 EURO
22.2000 g., 0.9000 Silver 0.6423 oz. ASW, 37 mm. **Series:** Jules Verne **Subject:** From the Earth to the Moon **Rev:** Crowd observing at lower left, volcano erupting above, moon at upper right, Verne in spaceship at lower right, factory chimneys belching smoke in bachground **Rev. Legend:** DE LA TERRE… LA LUNE

Date	Mintage	F	VF	XF	Unc	BU
2005 Proof	5,000	Value: 65.00				

KM# 1427 1-1/2 EURO
22.2000 g., 0.9000 Silver 0.6423 oz. ASW, 37 mm. **Rev:** Kitty and poodle at table at cafe, multicolor **Rev. Legend:** Hello Kitty

Date	Mintage	F	VF	XF	Unc	BU
2005 Proof	4,000	Value: 65.00				

KM# 1428 1-1/2 EURO
22.2000 g., 0.9000 Silver 0.6423 oz. ASW, 37 mm. **Rev:** Kitty on the Champs-Elysees, multicolor **Rev. Legend:** Hello Kitty

Date	Mintage	F	VF	XF	Unc	BU
2005 Proof	4,000	Value: 65.00				

KM# 1431 1-1/2 EURO
22.2000 g., 0.9000 Silver 0.6423 oz. ASW, 37 mm. **Subject:** Bicentennial Victory at Austerlitz **Rev:** Battle scene **Rev. Legend:** LIBERTÉ ÉGALITÉ FRATERNITÉ

Date	Mintage	F	VF	XF	Unc	BU
2005 Proof	15,000	Value: 50.00				

KM# 1434 1-1/2 EURO
22.2000 g., 0.9000 Silver 0.6423 oz. ASW, 37 mm. **Subject:** 50th Anniversary of the Europe flag **Rev:** Stars at left, partial flag at center right

Date	Mintage	F	VF	XF	Unc	BU
2005 Proof	15,000	Value: 50.00				

KM# 1436 1-1/2 EURO
, 37 mm. **Subject:** Centenary Law of Dec. 9, 1905 **Obv:** "Sower" left in ring of stars

Date	Mintage	F	VF	XF	Unc	BU
2005 Proof	15,000	Value: 50.00				
2006 Proof	10,000	Value: 50.00				

KM# 1438 1-1/2 EURO
22.2000 g., 0.9000 Silver 0.6423 oz. ASW, 37 mm. **Series:** Jules Verne **Subject:** 20,000 Leagues Under the Sea **Rev:** Submarine above plants and divers **Rev. Legend:** VINGT MILLE LIEUES SOUS LES MERS

Date	Mintage	F	VF	XF	Unc	BU
2005 Proof	5,000	Value: 65.00				

KM# 1440 1-1/2 EURO
22.2000 g., 0.9000 Silver 0.6423 oz. ASW, 37 mm. **Subject:** 150th Anniversary of Classification of Bordeaux Wines **Rev:** Stylized female with grapes between various names of wines at her feet

Date	Mintage	F	VF	XF	Unc	BU
2005 Proof	5,000	Value: 65.00				

KM# 1441 1-1/2 EURO
22.2000 g., 0.9000 Silver 0.6423 oz. ASW, 37 mm. **Subject:** 60th Anniversary - End of World War II **Rev:** Doves in flight **Rev. Inscription:** L'EUROPE FAIT LA PAIX

Date	Mintage	F	VF	XF	Unc	BU
2005 Proof	50,000	Value: 45.00				

KM# 1453 1-1/2 EURO
22.2000 g., 0.9000 Silver 0.6423 oz. ASW, 37 mm. **Subject:** 100th Anniversary - Death of Paul Cézanne **Obv:** Self portrait **Obv. Inscription:** PAUL / CÉZANNE **Rev:** "The Card Players" **Rev. Legend:** LIBERTÉ ÉGALITÉ FRATERNITÉ

Date	Mintage	F	VF	XF	Unc	BU
2006 Proof	5,000	Value: 65.00				

KM# 1455 1-1/2 EURO
22.2000 g., 0.9000 Silver 0.6423 oz. ASW, 37 mm. **Obv:** Map of the Basilica **Rev:** Bust of Pope Benoît with arms outstretched facing 3/4 right at lower left, Basilica in background **Rev. Legend:** 500 ANS de la BASILIQUE SAINT-PIERRE

Date	Mintage	F	VF	XF	Unc	BU
2006 Proof	5,000	Value: 65.00				

KM# 1456 1-1/2 EURO
22.2000 g., 0.9000 Silver 0.6423 oz. ASW, 37 mm. **Rev:** Half of Arc at left, eternal flame above WW I plaque at right **Rev. Legend:** ARC DE TRIOMPHE

Date	Mintage	F	VF	XF	Unc	BU
2006 Proof	10,000	Value: 50.00				

KM# 1458 1-1/2 EURO
22.2000 g., 0.9000 Silver 0.6423 oz. ASW, 37 mm. **Subject:** 300th Anniversary - Completion of the Dome of Les Invalides **Rev:** Dome between Jules-Hardouin Mansart at left, Louis XIV at right **Rev. Legend:** SAINT-LOUIS - DES INVALIDES **Rev. Inscription:** 28/AOÛT - 1706

Date	Mintage	F	VF	XF	Unc	BU
2006 Proof	10,000	Value: 50.00				

KM# 1444 1-1/2 EURO
22.2000 g., 0.9200 Silver 0.6566 oz. ASW, 37 mm. **Subject:** 100th Anniversary - French Grand Prix **Obv:** Steering wheel with early race car in upper segment, two gauges at lower left, R / F at lower right **Obv. Legend:** LE MANS 1906 - CENTENAIRE du 1er GRAND PRIX de l'AUTOMOBILE CLUB de FRANCE **Rev:** Modern racing car's steering wheel **Rev. Legend:** MAGNY-COURS

Date	Mintage	F	VF	XF	Unc	BU
2006 Proof	5,000	Value: 65.00				

KM# 1447 1-1/2 EURO
22.2000 g., 0.9000 Silver 0.6423 oz. ASW, 37 mm. **Obv:** Strogoff on horseback wielding sword, city at left, soldiers at lower left, calvalry at right **Obv. Legend:** MICHEL STROGOFF **Rev:** Head of Verne facing 3/4 right at left center, instruments and anchor in curved band **Rev. Legend:** 1828 JULES VERNE 1905 - LIBERTÉ . ÉGALITÉ . FRATERNITÉ

Date	Mintage	F	VF	XF	Unc	BU
2006 Proof	500	Value: 100				

KM# 1450 1-1/2 EURO
22.2000 g., 0.9000 Silver 0.6423 oz. ASW, 37 mm. **Subject:** Jules Verne **Obv:** Hot air balloon, parrots at left, native masks at lower left, foliage at right, native huts below, map of Africa in background **Obv. Legend:** CINQ SEMAINES EN BALLOON **Rev:** Head of Verne facing 3/4 right at left center, instruments and anchor in curved band **Rev. Legend:** 1828 JULES VERNE 1905

Date	Mintage	F	VF	XF	Unc	BU
2006 Proof	5,000	Value: 65.00				

KM# 1452 1-1/2 EURO
22.2000 g., 0.9000 Silver 0.6423 oz. ASW, 37 mm. **Subject:** Formula 1 World Championship **Obv:** Race car outline on checker board background **Obv. Legend:** LIBERTÉ ÉGALITÉ FRATERNITÉ **Rev:** Race car outline in victory sprays with star **Rev. Legend:** RENAULT - CHAMPION DU MONDE FIA 2005 DESCONSTRUCTEURS DE FORMULE 1

Date	Mintage	F	VF	XF	Unc	BU
2006 Proof	10,000	Value: 50.00				

KM# 1501 1-1/2 EURO
22.2000 g., 0.9000 Silver 0.6423 oz. ASW, 37 mm. **Subject:** Georges Pompendev Center, 30th Anniversary

Date	Mintage	F	VF	XF	Unc	BU
2007 Proof	—	Value: 50.00				

KM# 1484 1-1/2 EURO
22.2000 g., 0.9000 Silver 0.6423 oz. ASW, 37 mm. **Subject:** 2007 Rugby World Cup **Obv:** Two players and goal **Rev:** Logo and goal

Date	Mintage	F	VF	XF	Unc	BU
2007 Proof	5,000	Value: 50.00				

KM# 1462 1-1/2 EURO
22.0000 g., 0.9000 Silver 0.6366 oz. ASW, 37 mm. **Subject:** Sebastien Le Prestre de Vauban, 300th Anniversary of Death

Date	Mintage	F	VF	XF	Unc	BU
2007 Proof	30,000	Value: 40.00				

KM# 1465 1-1/2 EURO
22.2000 g., 0.9000 Silver 0.6423 oz. ASW, 37 mm. **Subject:** Le Petit Prince, 60th Anniversary **Obv:** Prince standing, multicolor

Date	Mintage	F	VF	XF	Unc	BU
2007 Proof	3,000	Value: 55.00				

KM# 1467 1-1/2 EURO
22.2000 g., 0.9000 Silver 0.6423 oz. ASW, 37 mm. **Subject:** Le Petit Prince, 60th Anniversary **Obv:** Prince lying in field, multicolor

Date	Mintage	F	VF	XF	Unc	BU
2007 Proof	3,000	Value: 55.00				

KM# 1469 1-1/2 EURO
22.2000 g., 0.9000 Silver 0.6423 oz. ASW, 37 mm. **Subject:** Le Petite Prince, 60th Anniversary **Obv:** Prince standing with rabbit, multicolor

Date	Mintage	F	VF	XF	Unc	BU
2007 Proof	—	Value: 55.00				

KM# 1473 1-1/2 EURO
22.2000 g., 0.9000 Silver 0.6423 oz. ASW, 37 mm. **Subject:** Paul E. Victor, 100th Birthday **Obv:** International Polar Year Logo **Rev:** Bust at left, Islands

Date	Mintage	F	VF	XF	Unc	BU
2007 Proof	5,000	Value: 55.00				

KM# 1475 1-1/2 EURO
22.2000 g., 0.9000 Silver 0.6423 oz. ASW, 37 mm. **Obv:** Formula 1 race car on checkered background **Rev:** Legend in wreath on checkered background

Date	Mintage	F	VF	XF	Unc	BU
2007//2006 Proof	5,000	Value: 55.00				

KM# 1477 1-1/2 EURO
22.2000 g., 0.9000 Silver 0.6423 oz. ASW, 37 mm. **Subject:** 29th Summer Olympic Games Beijing **Obv:** Rider on horseback, globe map of China **Rev:** Equestrian jump over orienteal fence

Date	Mintage	F	VF	XF	Unc	BU
2007 Proof	10,000	Value: 50.00				

KM# 1479 1-1/2 EURO
22.2000 g., 0.9000 Silver 0.6423 oz. ASW, 37 mm. **Subject:** Airbus A380 **Obv:** Airplane **Rev:** Europa head and flags

Date	Mintage	F	VF	XF	Unc	BU
2007 Proof	5,000	Value: 50.00				

KM# 1488 1-1/2 EURO
22.2000 g., 0.9000 Silver 0.6423 oz. ASW, 37 mm. **Obv:** Christian Dior bust **Rev:** Dior Museum building

Date	Mintage	F	VF	XF	Unc	BU
2007 Proof	3,000	Value: 75.00				

KM# 1505 1-1/2 EURO
22.2000 g., 0.9000 Silver 0.6423 oz. ASW, 37 mm. **Subject:** George Remir Centennial **Obv:** Wand and sparkles **Rev:** Tin Tin and the Professor calculus in multicolor

Date	Mintage	F	VF	XF	Unc	BU
2007 Proof	10,000	Value: 60.00				

KM# 1506 1-1/2 EURO
22.2000 g., 0.9000 Silver 0.6423 oz. ASW, 37 mm. **Subject:** Georges Remi Centennial **Obv:** Wand and sparkles **Rev:** Tin Tin and Captain Haddock in multicolor

Date	Mintage	F	VF	XF	Unc	BU
2007 Proof	10,000	Value: 65.00				

KM# 1507 1-1/2 EURO
22.2000 g., 0.9000 Silver 0.6423 oz. ASW, 37 mm. **Subject:** Georges Remi Centennial **Obv:** Wand and sparkles **Rev:** Tin Tin and Chang in multicolor

Date	Mintage	F	VF	XF	Unc	BU
2007 Proof	10,000	Value: 65.00				

KM# 1511 1-1/2 EURO
22.2000 g., 0.9000 Silver 0.6423 oz. ASW, 37 mm. **Subject:** Aristides de Sousa Mendes, Portuguese diplomat **Obv:** Bust right **Rev:** Plaque

Date	Mintage	F	VF	XF	Unc	BU
2007 Proof	3,000	Value: 55.00				

KM# 1516 1-1/2 EURO
22.2000 g., 0.9000 Silver 0.6423 oz. ASW, 37 mm. **Subject:** Asterix **Rev:** The Banquet

Date	Mintage	F	VF	XF	Unc	BU
2007 Proof	3,000	Value: 55.00				

KM# 1517 1-1/2 EURO
22.2000 g., 0.9000 Silver 0.6423 oz. ASW, 37 mm. **Subject:** Asterix **Rev:** The posion

Date	Mintage	F	VF	XF	Unc	BU
2007 Proof	3,000	Value: 55.00				

KM# 1518 1-1/2 EURO
22.2000 g., 0.9000 Silver 0.6423 oz. ASW, 37 mm. **Subject:** Asterix **Rev:** The Chase

Date	Mintage	F	VF	XF	Unc	BU
2007 Proof	3,000	Value: 55.00				

KM# 1527 1-1/2 EURO
22.2000 g., 0.9000 Silver 0.6423 oz. ASW, 37 mm. **Subject:** French Presidency of European Union **Obv:** Text written stars **Rev:** Europa head and flags

Date	Mintage	F	VF	XF	Unc	BU
2008 Proof	10,000	Value: 50.00				

KM# 1532 1-1/2 EURO
22.2000 g., 0.9000 Silver 0.6423 oz. ASW **Subject:** Eurpean Parliament, 50th Anniversary **Obv:** Map of EU within stars **Rev:** European Parliament Building in Strasboury **Shape:** 37

Date	Mintage	F	VF	XF	Unc	BU
2008 Proof	30,000	Value: 50.00				

KM# 1537 1-1/2 EURO
22.2000 g., 0.9000 Silver 0.6423 oz. ASW, 37 mm. **Subject:** 5th Republic, 50th Anniversasry **Obv:** Sower **Rev:** deGaulle head right

Date	Mintage	F	VF	XF	Unc	BU
2008 Proof	10,000	Value: 50.00				

KM# 1543 1-1/2 EURO
22.2000 g., 0.9000 Silver 0.6423 oz. ASW, 37 mm. **Subject:** 29th Summer Olympic Games - Beijing **Obv:** Swimmer and globe **Rev:** Diver and oriental screen

Date	Mintage	F	VF	XF	Unc	BU
2008 Proof	10,000	Value: 65.00				

KM# 1546 1-1/2 EURO
22.2000 g., 0.9000 Silver 0.6423 oz. ASW, 37 mm. **Subject:** UEFA **Obv:** French soccer team **Rev:** UEFA logo

Date	Mintage	F	VF	XF	Unc	BU
2008 Proof	5,000	Value: 55.00				

KM# 1548 1-1/2 EURO
22.2000 g., 0.9000 Silver 0.6423 oz. ASW, 37 mm. **Subject:** Franco - Japanese Relators, 150th Anniversary **Obv:** Eillfel Tower and Kimono forming logo **Rev:** Delacroix "La Liberte"

Date	Mintage	F	VF	XF	Unc	BU
2008 Proof	5,000	Value: 65.00				

KM# 1549 1-1/2 EURO
22.2000 g., 0.9000 Silver 0.6423 oz. ASW, 37 mm. **Subject:** Franco - Japanese Relators - 150th Anniversary **Obv:** Eillfel Tower and Kimono forming logo **Rev:** Ichikawa Ebizo IV portrait painting

Date	Mintage	F	VF	XF	Unc	BU
2008 Proof	5,000	Value: 65.00				

KM# 1550 1-1/2 EURO
22.2000 g., 0.9000 Silver 0.6423 oz. ASW, 37 mm. **Subject:** Franco - Japanese Relators - 150th Anniversary **Obv:** Eillfel Tower and Kimono forming logo **Rev:** Scenes of Paris and Tokyo - Eillfel Tower and Pagoda Sensoji

Date	Mintage	F	VF	XF	Unc	BU
2008 Proof	5,000	Value: 65.00				

KM# 1551 1-1/2 EURO
22.2000 g., 0.9000 Silver 0.6423 oz. ASW, 37 mm. **Subject:** Franco - Japanese Relators - 150th Anniversary **Obv:** Eiffel Tower and Kimono forming logo **Rev:** Japanese cash coin of "Kanei Tsuho"

Date	Mintage	F	VF	XF	Unc	BU
2008 Proof	5,000	Value: 65.00				

KM# 1555 1-1/2 EURO
22.2000 g., 0.9000 Silver 0.6423 oz. ASW, 37 mm. **Subject:** André Citronën **Obv:** First front wheel drive auto **Rev:** Bust 1/4 left

Date	Mintage	F	VF	XF	Unc	BU
2008 Proof	5,000	Value: 65.00				

KM# 1558 1-1/2 EURO
22.2000 g., 0.9000 Silver 0.6423 oz. ASW, 37 mm. **Subject:** Rouen Armada **Obv:** Cape Horn, sextant, hour glass **Rev:** Sailing ship

Date	Mintage	F	VF	XF	Unc	BU
2008 Proof	5,000	Value: 65.00				

KM# 1561 1-1/2 EURO
22.2000 g., 0.9000 Silver 0.6423 oz. ASW **Subject:** Lourdes, 150th Anniversary **Obv:** Church of Notre Dame at Lourdes **Rev:** Cross with Pope John Paul II, Pope Benedict XVI and Bernadette Soubirous in quadrants

Date	Mintage	F	VF	XF	Unc	BU
2008 Proof	15,000	Value: 60.00				

KM# 1574 1-1/2 EURO
22.2000 g., 0.9000 Silver 0.6423 oz. ASW, 37 mm. **Subject:** UNESCO - Grand Canyon **Obv:** Grand Canyon **Rev:** UNESCO logos

Date	Mintage	F	VF	XF	Unc	BU
2008 Proof	5,000	Value: 65.00				

KM# 1576 1-1/2 EURO
22.2000 g., 0.9000 Silver 0.6423 oz. ASW, 37 mm. **Subject:** International Polar Year **Obv:** IPY logo **Rev:** Emperor Penguin and map of Antartica

Date	Mintage	F	VF	XF	Unc	BU
2008 Proof	5,000	Value: 65.00				

KM# 1578 1-1/2 EURO
22.2000 g., 0.9000 Silver 0.6423 oz. ASW, 37 mm. **Subject:** Spirou, 70th Anniversary **Obv:** Character Spirou in thought **Rev:** 70th Anniversary logo

Date	Mintage	F	VF	XF	Unc	BU
2008 Proof	10,000	Value: 60.00				

KM# 1633 1-1/2 EURO
11.0000 g., Aluminum-Bronze, 30 mm. **Obv:** Stadium view, soccer player **Rev:** Shield of Olympique Lyonnais

Date	Mintage	F	VF	XF	Unc	BU
2009	25,000	—	—	—	15.00	20.00

KM# 1723 1-1/2 EURO
11.0000 g., Aluminum-Bronze, 30 mm. **Obv:** Soccer player **Rev:** Girondins de Bordeaux logo

Date	Mintage	F	VF	XF	Unc	BU
2010	25,000	—	—	—	15.00	20.00

KM# 1754 1-1/2 EURO
11.0000 g., Copper-Aluminum-Nickel, 30 mm. **Subject:** Olympique de Marseille **Obv:** Soccer player **Rev:** OM logo

Date	Mintage	F	VF	XF	Unc	BU
2011	25,000	—	—	—	—	15.00

KM# 1289 2 EURO
8.5200 g., Bi-Metallic Nickel-Brass center in Copper-Nickel ring, 25.6 mm. **Obv:** Stylized tree divides RF within circle, date below **Obv. Designer:** Joaquin Jimenez **Rev:** Denomination and map **Rev. Designer:** Luc Luycx **Edge:** Reeding with 2's and stars

Date	Mintage	F	VF	XF	Unc	BU
2001	237,950,793	—	—	—	3.75	6.00
2001 Proof	15,000	Value: 20.00				
2002	153,700,000	—	—	—	3.75	6.00
2002 Proof	21,453	Value: 18.00				
2003 In sets only	180,000	—	—	—	—	13.50
2003 Proof	40,000	Value: 20.00				
2004 In sets only	160,000	—	—	—	—	13.50
2004 Proof	20,000	Value: 20.00				
2005 In sets only	120,000	—	—	—	—	13.50
2005 Proof	10,000	Value: 20.00				
2006 In sets only	67,600	—	—	—	—	13.50
2006 Proof	10,000	Value: 20.00				

KM# 1414 2 EURO
8.5200 g., Bi-Metallic Nickel-Brass center in Copper-Nickel ring, 25.6 mm. **Obv:** Stylized tree **Obv. Designer:** Joaquin Jimenez **Rev:** Relief map of Western Europe, stars, lines and value **Rev. Designer:** Luc Luycx **Edge:** Reeding with 2's and stars

Date	Mintage	F	VF	XF	Unc	BU
2007 In sets only	58,000	—	—	—	—	15.00
2007 Proof	7,500	Value: 25.00				
2008 In sets only	57,000	—	—	—	—	6.00
2008 Proof	7,500	Value: 25.00				
2009 In sets only	50,500	—	—	—	—	6.00
2009 Proof	7,500	Value: 25.00				
2010	—	—	—	—	—	6.00
2010 Proof	—	Value: 25.00				

KM# 1460 2 EURO
8.5200 g., Bi-Metallic Nickel-Brass center in Copper-Nickel ring, 25.74 mm. **Subject:** Treaty of Rome 50th Anniversary

Date	Mintage	F	VF	XF	Unc	BU
2007	9,600,000	—	—	—	5.50	6.50

KM# 1459 2 EURO

8.5200 g., Bi-Metallic Nickel-Brass center in Copper-Nickel ring, 25.74 mm. **Subject:** European Union Presidency **Obv:** Inscription **Obv. Inscription:** PRÉSIDENCE / FRANÇAISE / UNION / EUROPÉENNE / RF **Rev:** Large value "2" at left, modified map of Europe at right **Edge:** Reeded with incuse stars

Date	Mintage	F	VF	XF	Unc	BU
2008(a)	20,100,000	—	—	—	5.50	6.50

KM# 1542 2 EURO

8.5000 g., Bi-Metallic Nickel-Brass center in Copper-Nickel ring, 25.75 mm. **Subject:** 5th Republic, 50th Anniversary **Obv:** Text within stars **Rev:** Value at left, relief map of the EU at right

Date	Mintage	F	VF	XF	Unc	BU
2008	10,000,000	—	—	—	6.50	7.50
2008 Sets only	20,000	—	—	—	—	20.00
2008 Proof	10,000	Value: 40.00				

KM# 1590 2 EURO

8.5000 g., Bi-Metallic Nickel-Brass center in Copper-Nickel ring, 25.7 mm. **Obv:** EMU 10th Anniversary **Rev:** Stick figure and E design

Date	Mintage	F	VF	XF	Unc	BU
2009P	—	—	—	—	8.00	10.00
2009P Proof	10,000	Value: 15.00				

KM# 1676 2 EURO

8.5000 g., Bi-Metallic Nickel-Brass center in Copper-Nickel ring, 25.75 mm. **Subject:** 70th Anniversary, June 18th Appeal **Obv:** General Charles DeGaulle giving BBC speech **Rev:** Value and map

Date	Mintage	F	VF	XF	Unc	BU
2010	20,000	—	—	—	8.00	10.00
2010 Proof	10,000	Value: 15.00				

KM# 1789 2 EURO

8.5000 g., Bi-Metallic Nickel-Brass center in Copper-Nickel ring, 25.75 mm. **Subject:** International Music Day, 30th Anniversary **Obv:** Youth jamming **Rev:** Value and map of Western Europe

Date	Mintage	F	VF	XF	Unc	BU
2011	10,000,000	—	—	—	5.00	—
2011 Special Unc.	20,000	—	—	—	—	8.00
2011 Proof	10,000	Value: 15.00				

KM# 1347 5 EURO

24.9000 g., 0.9000 Bi-Metallic .900 Silver 22.2g planchet with .750 Gold 2.7g insert 0.7205 oz., 37 mm. **Obv:** The Seed Sower on gold insert **Rev:** Denomination and map **Edge:** Plain

Date	Mintage	F	VF	XF	Unc	BU
2002 Proof	10,000	Value: 500				

KM# 1371 5 EURO

24.9000 g., Bi-Metallic .750 Gold 2.7 g insert on .900 Silver 22.2g planchet, 37 mm. **Obv:** The Seed Sower on gold insert **Rev:** French face map and denomination **Edge:** Plain

Date	Mintage	F	VF	XF	Unc	BU
2004 Proof	3,000	Value: 550				

KM# 1523 5 EURO

22.2000 g., 0.9000 Silver 0.6423 oz. ASW, 37 mm. **Subject:** Euro - 5th Anniversary **Obv:** The Seed Sower

Date	Mintage	F	VF	XF	Unc	BU
2007 Proof	5,000	Value: 55.00				

KM# 1524 5 EURO

163.8000 g., 0.9500 Silver 5.0028 oz. ASW, 50 mm. **Subject:** Euro 5th Anniversary **Obv:** Sower

Date	Mintage	F	VF	XF	Unc	BU
2007 Proof	500	Value: 325				

KM# 1525 5 EURO

1.2400 g., 0.9990 Gold 0.0398 oz. AGW, 14 mm. **Subject:** Euro 5th Anniversary **Obv:** The Seed Sower

Date	Mintage	F	VF	XF	Unc	BU
2007 Proof	20,000	Value: 75.00				

KM# 1526 5 EURO

31.1050 g., 0.9200 Gold 0.9200 oz. AGW, 31 mm. **Subject:** Euro 5th Anniversary **Obv:** The Seed Sower

Date	Mintage	F	VF	XF	Unc	BU
2007 Proof	500	Value: 1,400				

KM# 1534 5 EURO

10.0000 g., 0.5000 Silver 0.1607 oz. ASW, 27 mm. **Obv:** Sower, full length **Rev:** Value within hexagon design

Date	Mintage	F	VF	XF	Unc	BU
2008 Proof	2,000,000	Value: 15.00				

KM# 1538 5 EURO

1.2400 g., 0.9990 Gold 0.0398 oz. AGW, 13.9 mm. **Subject:** 5th Republic, 50th Anniversary **Obv:** Sower **Rev:** de Gaulle head right

Date	Mintage	F	VF	XF	Unc	BU
2008 Proof	20,000	Value: 75.00				

KM# 1566 5 EURO

22.2000 g., 0.9000 Silver 0.6423 oz. ASW, 37 mm. **Subject:** Gabrielle Chanel **Obv:** Bust right in hat **Rev:** Value on "Matelassé" pattern

Date	Mintage	F	VF	XF	Unc	BU
2008 Proof	10,000	Value: 65.00				

KM# 1567 5 EURO

8.4500 g., 0.9200 Gold 0.2499 oz. AGW, 22 mm. **Subject:** Gabrielle Chanel **Obv:** Portrait in hat, right **Rev:** Value on "Matelassé" pattern

Date	Mintage	F	VF	XF	Unc	BU
2008 Proof	500	Value: 400				

KM# 1568 5 EURO

163.8000 g., 0.9500 Silver 5.0028 oz. ASW, 50 mm. **Subject:** Gabrielle Chanel **Obv:** Portrait in hat, right **Rev:** Vlaue on "Matelassé" pattern

Date	Mintage	F	VF	XF	Unc	BU
2008 Proof	500	Value: 350				

KM# 1586 5 EURO

1.2400 g., 0.9990 Gold 0.0398 oz. AGW, 13.9 mm. **Subject:** Court of Human Rights, 50th Anniversary **Obv:** The Seed Sower left **Rev:** Text

Date	Mintage	F	VF	XF	Unc	BU
2009P Proof	10,000	Value: 70.00				

KM# 1625 5 EURO

15.0000 g., 0.9000 Silver 0.4340 oz. ASW, 30 x 21 mm. **Subject:** Monet **Obv:** Le Bassin Aux Nympheas, 1900 painting **Rev:** Multicolor pallet and brushes, portrait **Shape:** Rectangle

Date	Mintage	F	VF	XF	Unc	BU
2009P Proof	20,000	Value: 35.00				

KM# 1627 5 EURO

22.2000 g., 0.9000 Silver 0.6423 oz. ASW, 37 mm. **Subject:** Year of the Ox **Obv:** Oxen within Asia screen garden **Rev:** Portrait of La Fontaine

Date	Mintage	F	VF	XF	Unc	BU
2009P Proof	10,000	Value: 35.00				

KM# 1674 5 EURO

1.2400 g., 0.9990 Gold 0.0398 oz. AGW, 13.9 mm. **Obv:** The Seed Sower left **Rev:** Wheat and olive branch

Date	Mintage	F	VF	XF	Unc	BU
2010 Proof	10,000	Value: 75.00				

KM# 1680 5 EURO

0.5000 g., 0.9990 Gold 0.0161 oz. AGW, 11 mm. **Subject:** Cluny Abbey, 1100th Anniversary **Obv:** Europa head facing **Rev:** Cluny Abbey

Date	Mintage	F	VF	XF	Unc	BU
2010 Proof	20,000	Value: 45.00				

KM# 1715 5 EURO

22.2000 g., 0.9000 Silver 0.6423 oz. ASW, 37 mm. **Obv:** Tiger within border **Rev:** La Fontaine bust at left, animals at right

Date	Mintage	F	VF	XF	Unc	BU
2010 Proof	10,000	Value: 65.00				

KM# 1785 5 EURO

1.2440 g., 0.9990 Gold 0.0400 oz. AGW, 13.9 mm. **Subject:** Euro Starter Kit, 10th Anniversary **Obv:** Sower **Rev:** Euro starter kit

Date	Mintage	F	VF	XF	Unc	BU
2011 Proof	10,000	Value: 100				

KM# 1791 5 EURO

0.5000 g., 0.9990 Gold 0.0161 oz. AGW, 11 mm. **Subject:** International Music Day, 30th Anniversary **Obv:** Europa **Rev:** Youth jamming

Date	Mintage	F	VF	XF	Unc	BU
2011 Proof	20,000	—	—	—	—	100

KM# 1810 5 EURO

0.5000 g., 0.9990 Gold 0.0161 oz. AGW, 11 mm. **Subject:** UNESCO World Heritage Site - Palace of Versailles

Date	Mintage	F	VF	XF	Unc	BU
2011 Proof	20,000	Value: 100				

KM# 1833 5 EURO

22.2000 g., 0.9000 Silver 0.6423 oz. ASW, 37 mm. **Subject:** Year of the Rabbit **Obv:** Fontaine and animals **Rev:** Rabbit seated facing right

Date	Mintage	F	VF	XF	Unc	BU
2011 Proof	10,000	Value: 50.00				

KM# 1302 10 EURO

8.4500 g., 0.9990 Gold 0.2714 oz. AGW, 22 mm. **Subject:** Europa **Obv:** Eight French euro coin designs **Rev:** Portrait and flags design of 6.55957 francs KM-1265 **Edge:** Reeded

Date	Mintage	F	VF	XF	Unc	BU
2002 Proof	3,000	Value: 450				

KM# 1326 10 EURO

8.4500 g., 0.9200 Gold 0.2499 oz. AGW, 22 mm. **Obv:** Tour de France logo **Rev:** Cyclist going left **Edge:** Reeded

Date	Mintage	F	VF	XF	Unc	BU
2003 (Ht) Proof	5,000	Value: 400				

KM# 1348 10 EURO

8.4500 g., 0.9200 Gold 0.2499 oz. AGW, 22 mm. **Obv:** The seed sower **Rev:** Denomination and map **Edge:** Plain

Date	Mintage	F	VF	XF	Unc	BU
2003 Proof	15,000	Value: 375				

KM# 1352 10 EURO

8.4500 g., 0.9200 Gold 0.2499 oz. AGW, 22 mm. **Obv:** Obverse design of first one franc coin **Rev:** Reverse design of first one franc coin **Edge:** Plain

Date	Mintage	F	VF	XF	Unc	BU
2003 Proof	10,000	Value: 375				

KM# 1362 10 EURO
8.4500 g., 0.9200 Gold 0.2499 oz. AGW, 22 mm. **Obv:** Pierre de Coubertin **Rev:** Olympic runners **Edge:** Plain

Date	Mintage	F	VF	XF	Unc	BU
2003 Proof	15,000	Value: 375				

KM# 1367 10 EURO
6.4100 g., 0.9000 Gold 0.1855 oz. AGW, 22 mm. **Obv:** Book, denomination and eagle **Rev:** Napoleon and coronation scene **Edge:** Plain

Date	Mintage	F	VF	XF	Unc	BU
2004 Proof	5,000	Value: 400				

KM# 1375 10 EURO
8.4500 g., 0.9200 Gold 0.2499 oz. AGW, 22 mm. **Obv:** Half soccer ball and denomination **Rev:** Eiffel tower and soccer balls **Edge:** Plain

Date	Mintage	F	VF	XF	Unc	BU
2004 Proof	10,000	Value: 375				

KM# 1392 10 EURO
8.4500 g., 0.9200 Gold 0.2499 oz. AGW, 22 mm. **Subject:** European Union Expansion **Obv:** Partial face and flags **Rev:** Puzzle map **Edge:** Reeded

Date	Mintage	F	VF	XF	Unc	BU
2004 Proof	5,000	Value: 400				

KM# 1403 10 EURO
8.4500 g., 0.9200 Gold 0.2499 oz. AGW, 22 mm. **Subject:** Jules Verne **Obv:** Various scenes from Verne's novel "Around The World in 80 Days" **Rev:** Jules Verne's portrait left of value and date

Date	Mintage	F	VF	XF	Unc	BU
2005 Proof	2,000	Value: 400				

KM# 1424 10 EURO
8.4500 g., 0.9200 Gold 0.2499 oz. AGW, 22 mm. **Subject:** Biathlon **Rev:** Skier at right facing 3/4 left, mountain peaks in background **Rev. Inscription:** JEUX D'HIVER

Date	Mintage	F	VF	XF	Unc	BU
2005 Proof	—	Value: 400				

KM# 1426 10 EURO
8.4500 g., 0.9200 Gold 0.2499 oz. AGW, 22 mm. **Series:** Jules Verne **Subject:** From the earth to the moon **Rev:** Crowd observing at lower left, volcano erupting above, moon at upper right, Verne in spaceship at lower right, chimneys belching smoke in backgroud **Rev. Legend:** DE LA TERRE À LA LUNE

Date	Mintage	F	VF	XF	Unc	BU
2005 Proof	2,000	Value: 400				

KM# 1429 10 EURO
8.4500 g., 0.9200 Gold 0.2499 oz. AGW, 22 mm. **Rev:** Kitty at the Spectacle, multicolor **Rev. Legend:** Hello Kitty

Date	Mintage	F	VF	XF	Unc	BU
2005 Proof	1,000	Value: 425				

KM# 1432 10 EURO
6.4100 g., 0.9000 Gold 0.1855 oz. AGW, 21 mm. **Subject:** Bicentennial - Victory at Austerlitz **Rev:** Battle scene **Rev. Legend:** LIBERTÉ ÉGALITÉ FRATERNITÉ

Date	Mintage	F	VF	XF	Unc	BU
2005 Proof	3,000	Value: 400				

KM# 1435 10 EURO
8.4500 g., 0.9200 Gold 0.2499 oz. AGW, 22 mm. **Subject:** 50th Anniversary - Flag of Europe **Rev:** Stars at left, partial flag at center right

Date	Mintage	F	VF	XF	Unc	BU
2005 Proof	3,000	Value: 400				

KM# 1439 10 EURO
8.4500 g., 0.9200 Gold 0.2499 oz. AGW, 22 mm. **Series:** Jules Verne **Subject:** 20,000 Leagues Under the Sea **Rev:** Submarine above plants and divers **Rev. Legend:** VINGT MILLE LIEUES SOUS LES MERS

Date	Mintage	F	VF	XF	Unc	BU
2005 Proof	2,000	Value: 400				

KM# 1446 10 EURO
8.4500 g., 0.9200 Gold 0.2499 oz. AGW, 22 mm. **Subject:** Marshal Bernadotte under Napoleon **Rev:** Military bust facing 3/4 right at left, building in backgound at right **Rev. Legend:** LIBERTÉ GALITÉ FRATERNITÉ - KARL XIV JOHAN ROI DE SUÉDE11

Date	Mintage	F	VF	XF	Unc	BU
2006 Proof	1,000	Value: 425				

KM# 1448 10 EURO
8.4500 g., 0.9200 Gold 0.2499 oz. AGW, 22 mm. **Subject:** 20,000 Leagues Under the Sea **Obv:** Strogoff horseback wielding a sword, city at left, soldiers at lower left, calvary at right - the Tartars, Siberia and the Tsar's Army **Obv. Legend:** MICHEL STROGOFF **Rev:** Head of Verne facing 3/4 right at left center, instruments and anchor in curved band **Rev. Legend:** 1828 JULES VERNE 1905

Date	Mintage	F	VF	XF	Unc	BU
2006 Proof	500	Value: 450				

KM# 1449 10 EURO
8.4500 g., 0.9200 Gold 0.2499 oz. AGW, 22 mm. **Subject:** 20,000 Leagues Under the Sea **Obv:** Hot air balloon, parrots at left, native masks below left, foliage at right, huts below, map of Africa in background. **Obv. Legend:** CINQ SEMAINES EN BALLON **Rev:** Head of Verne facing 3/4 right at left center, instruments and anchor in curved band **Rev. Legend:** 1828 JULES VERNE 1905 - LIBERTÉ . ÉGALITÉ . FRATERNITÉ

Date	Mintage	F	VF	XF	Unc	BU
2006 Proof	500	Value: 450				

KM# 1451 10 EURO
8.4500 g., 0.9200 Gold 0.2499 oz. AGW, 22 mm. **Subject:** 100th Anniversary - French Grand Prix **Obv:** Steering wheel with early race car in upper segment, two gauges at lower left, R / F at lower right **Obv. Legend:** LE MANS 1906 - CENTENAIRE du 1er GRAND PRIX de l'AUTOMOBILE CLUB de FRANCE **Rev. Legend:** MAGNY-COURS

Date	Mintage	F	VF	XF	Unc	BU
2006 Proof	500	Value: 450				

KM# 1416 10 EURO
8.4500 g., 0.9200 Gold 0.2499 oz. AGW, 22 mm. **Obv:** Jean de la Fontaine, value, Chinese astrological animals, date, Paris mint privy marks but without national identification **Rev:** Dog in wreath **Edge:** Reeded **Note:** Anonymous issue

Date	Mintage	F	VF	XF	Unc	BU
2006 Proof	500	Value: 450				

KM# 1418 10 EURO
8.4500 g., 0.9200 Gold 0.2499 oz. AGW, 22 mm. **Obv:** Jean de la Fontaine, value, Chinese astrological animals, date, Paris mint privy marks but without national identification **Rev:** Pig in wreath **Edge:** Reeded **Note:** anonymous issue

Date	Mintage	F	VF	XF	Unc	BU
2007 Proof	500	Value: 450				

KM# 1420 10 EURO
8.4500 g., 0.9200 Gold 0.2499 oz. AGW, 22 mm. **Obv:** Military bust of Lafayette facing 3/4 left **Obv. Legend:** LA FAYETTE. HÉROS DELA RÉVOLUTION AMÉRICAINE **Obv. Inscription:** 1757/1854 at left, RF monogram at right **Rev:** Sailing ship L' Hermione **Rev. Legend:** LA FAYETTE, HERO OF THE AMERICAN REVOLUTION **Edge:** Plain

Date	Mintage	F	VF	XF	Unc	BU
2007 (a) Proof	500	Value: 450				

KM# 1502 10 EURO
8.4500 g., 0.9200 Gold 0.2499 oz. AGW, 22 mm. **Subject:** Georges Pompendev Center, 30th Anniversary

Date	Mintage	F	VF	XF	Unc	BU
2007 Proof	—	Value: 400				

KM# 1463 10 EURO
8.4500 g., 0.9200 Gold 0.2499 oz. AGW, 22 mm. **Subject:** Sebastien Le Prestre de Vauban, 300th Anniversary of Death

Date	Mintage	F	VF	XF	Unc	BU
2007 Proof	3,000	Value: 400				

KM# 1474 10 EURO
8.4500 g., 0.9200 Gold 0.2499 oz. AGW, 22 mm. **Subject:** Paul E. Victor, 100th birthday **Obv:** International polar year logo **Rev:** Bust at left, Islands

Date	Mintage	F	VF	XF	Unc	BU
2007	500	—	—	—	—	450

KM# 1476 10 EURO
8.4500 g., 0.9200 Gold 0.2499 oz. AGW, 22 mm. **Obv:** Formula 1 race car on checkered background **Rev:** Legend in wreath on checkered background

Date	Mintage	F	VF	XF	Unc	BU
2007//2006 Proof	500	Value: 450				

KM# 1478 10 EURO
8.4500 g., 0.9200 Gold 0.2499 oz. AGW, 22 mm. **Subject:** 29th Summer Olympic Games Beijing **Obv:** Rider on horseback, globe map of China **Rev:** Equestrian jump over oriental fence

Date	Mintage	F	VF	XF	Unc	BU
2007 Proof	500	Value: 450				

KM# 1480 10 EURO
8.4500 g., 0.9200 Gold 0.2499 oz. AGW, 22 mm. **Subject:** Airbus A380 **Obv:** Airplane **Rev:** Europa head and flags

Date	Mintage	F	VF	XF	Unc	BU
2007 Proof	1,000	Value: 425				

KM# 1485 10 EURO
8.4500 g., 0.9200 Gold 0.2499 oz. AGW, 22 mm. **Subject:** 2007 Rugby World Cup **Obv:** Two players and goal **Rev:** Logo and goal

Date	Mintage	F	VF	XF	Unc	BU
2007 Proof	500	Value: 450				

KM# 1489 10 EURO
8.4500 g., 0.9200 Gold 0.2499 oz. AGW, 22 mm. **Obv:** Christian Dior **Rev:** Dior Museum building

Date	Mintage	F	VF	XF	Unc	BU
2007 Proof	500	Value: 450				

KM# 1508 10 EURO
8.4500 g., 0.9200 Gold 0.2499 oz. AGW, 22 mm. **Subject:** Georges Remi Centennial **Obv:** Wand and sparkles **Rev:** Tin Tin raising cap

Date	Mintage	F	VF	XF	Unc	BU
2007 Proof	1,000	Value: 425				

KM# 1512 10 EURO
8.4500 g., 0.9200 Gold 0.2499 oz. AGW, 22 mm. **Subject:** Aristides de Sousa Mendes, Portuguese diplomat **Obv:** Bust right **Rev:** Plaque

Date	Mintage	F	VF	XF	Unc	BU
2007 Proof	500	Value: 450				

KM# 1519 10 EURO
8.4500 g., 0.9200 Gold 0.2499 oz. AGW, 22 mm. **Subject:** Asterix **Rev:** Character with torch

Date	Mintage	F	VF	XF	Unc	BU
2007 Proof	500	Value: 450				

KM# 1544 10 EURO
8.4500 g., 0.9200 Gold 0.2499 oz. AGW, 22 mm. **Subject:** 29th Summer Olympic Games - Beijing **Obv:** Swimmer and globe **Rev:** Diver and oriental screen

Date	Mintage	F	VF	XF	Unc	BU
2008 Proof	1,000	Value: 425				

KM# 1528 10 EURO
8.4500 g., 0.9200 Gold 0.2499 oz. AGW, 22 mm. **Subject:** French Presidency of European Union **Obv:** Text within stars **Rev:** Europa head and flags

Date	Mintage	F	VF	XF	Unc	BU
2008 Proof	1,000	Value: 425				

KM# 1533 10 EURO
8.4500 g., 0.9200 Gold 0.2499 oz. AGW, 22 mm. **Subject:** European Parliament, 50th Anniversary **Obv:** Map of EU within stars **Rev:** European Parliament Building in Strasbourg

Date	Mintage	F	VF	XF	Unc	BU
2008 Proof	3,000	Value: 400				

KM# 1539 10 EURO
8.4500 g., 0.9990 Gold 0.2714 oz. AGW, 22 mm. **Subject:** 5th Republic, 50th Anniversary **Obv:** The Seed Sower **Rev:** de Gaulle head right

Date	Mintage	F	VF	XF	Unc	BU
2008 Proof	1,000	Value: 425				

KM# 1547 10 EURO
8.4500 g., 0.9200 Gold 0.2499 oz. AGW, 22 mm. **Subject:** UEFA **Obv:** French soccer team **Rev:** UEFA logo

Date	Mintage	F	VF	XF	Unc	BU
2008 Proof	500	Value: 450				

KM# 1552 10 EURO
8.4500 g., 0.9200 Gold 0.2499 oz. AGW, 22 mm. **Subject:** Franco - Japanese Relators - 150th Anniversary **Obv:** Eiffel Tower and Kimono forming logo **Rev:** Delacroix's "La Liberte"

Date	Mintage	F	VF	XF	Unc	BU
2008 Proof	3,000	Value: 400				

KM# 1553 10 EURO
8.4500 g., 0.9200 Gold 0.2499 oz. AGW, 22 mm. **Subject:** Franco - Japanese Relators - 150th Anniversary **Obv:** Eiffel Tower and Kimono forming logo **Rev:** "Ichikawa Ebizo IV" portrait painting

Date	Mintage	F	VF	XF	Unc	BU
2008 Proof	3,000	Value: 400				

KM# 1554 10 EURO
8.4500 g., 0.9200 Gold 0.2499 oz. AGW, 22 mm. **Subject:** Franco - Japanese Relators - 150th Anniversary **Obv:** Eiffel Tower and Kimono forming logo **Rev:** Japanese cash coin from "Kanci Tsuho"

Date	Mintage	F	VF	XF	Unc	BU
2008 Proof	3,000	Value: 400				

KM# 1556 10 EURO
0.4500 g., 0.9200 Gold 0.0133 oz. AGW, 22 mm. **Subject:** André Citronë **Obv:** First front wheel drive auto **Rev:** Bust 1/4 left

Date	Mintage	F	VF	XF	Unc	BU
2008 Proof	500	Value: 450				

KM# 1559 10 EURO
8.4500 g., 0.9200 Gold 0.2499 oz. AGW, 22 mm. **Subject:** Rouen Armada **Obv:** Cape Hown, sextant, hour glass **Edge:** Sailing ship

Date	Mintage	F	VF	XF	Unc	BU
2008 Proof	500	Value: 450				

KM# 1562 10 EURO
8.4500 g., 0.9200 Gold 0.2499 oz. AGW, 22 mm. **Subject:** Lourdes, 150th Anniversary **Obv:** Church of Notre Dame at Lourdes **Rev:** Cross with Pope John Paul II, Pope Benedict XVI and Bernadette Soubirous in quadrants

Date	Mintage	F	VF	XF	Unc	BU
2008 Proof	1,000	Value: 425				

KM# 1573 10 EURO
8.4500 g., 0.9200 Gold 0.2499 oz. AGW, 22 mm. **Subject:** Lunar New Year - Year of the Rat **Obv:** Bust of Jean de la Fontaine and twelve awards **Rev:** Rat within border

Date	Mintage	F	VF	XF	Unc	BU
2008 Proof	500	Value: 450				

KM# 1575 10 EURO
8.4500 g., 0.9200 Gold 0.2499 oz. AGW, 22 mm. **Subject:** UNESCO - Grand Canyon **Obv:** Grand Canyon **Rev:** UNESCO logos

Date	Mintage	F	VF	XF	Unc	BU
2008 Proof	500	Value: 450				

KM# 1577 10 EURO
8.4500 g., 0.9200 Gold 0.2499 oz. AGW, 22 mm. **Subject:** International Polar Year **Obv:** IPY logo **Rev:** Emperor Penguin and map of Antartica

Date	Mintage	F	VF	XF	Unc	BU
2008 Proof	500	Value: 450				

KM# 1579 10 EURO
8.4500 g., 0.9200 Gold 0.2499 oz. AGW, 22 mm. **Subject:** Spirou, 70th Anniversary **Obv:** Character Spirou in thought **Rev:** 70th Aniversary logo

Date	Mintage	F	VF	XF	Unc	BU
2008 Proof	500	Value: 450				

KM# 1591 10 EURO
27.2000 g., 0.9000 Silver 0.7870 oz. ASW, 37 mm. **Subject:** Europa - Fall of Berlin Wall **Obv:** Brandenburg gate and doves in flight **Rev:** Head facing and flags

Date	Mintage	F	VF	XF	Unc	BU
2009P Proof	10,000	Value: 37.50				

KM# 1580 10 EURO
12.0000 g., 0.9000 Silver 0.3472 oz. ASW, 29 mm. **Obv:** Modernistic sower advancing right **Rev:** Wreath and value

Date	Mintage	F	VF	XF	Unc	BU
2009P	2,000,000	—	—	—	—	17.50

KM# 1584 10 EURO
22.2000 g., 0.9000 Silver 0.6423 oz. ASW, 37 mm. **Subject:** Court of Human Rights, 50th Anniversary **Obv:** Sower left **Rev:** Text

Date	Mintage	F	VF	XF	Unc	BU
2009P Proof	10,000	Value: 35.00				

KM# 1596 10 EURO
22.2000 g., 0.9000 Silver 0.6423 oz. ASW, 37 mm. **Subject:** Concorde 40th Anniversary **Obv:** Concorde in flight **Rev:** Tail emblems

Date	Mintage	F	VF	XF	Unc	BU
2009P Proof	3,000	Value: 40.00				

KM# 1601 10 EURO
20.8900 g., 0.9000 Silver 0.6044 oz. ASW, 37 mm. **Obv:** Eiffel Tower Structure **Rev:** Gustave Eiffel at left

Date	Mintage	F	VF	XF	Unc	BU
2009P Proof	10,000	Value: 35.00				

KM# 1606 10 EURO
27.2000 g., 0.9000 Silver 0.7870 oz. ASW, 37 mm. **Subject:** Bugatti 100th Anniversary **Obv:** Ettore Bugatti at left **Rev:** Race car and quilt motif

Date	Mintage	F	VF	XF	Unc	BU
2009P Proof	10,000	Value: 32.50				

KM# 1611 10 EURO
22.2000 g., 0.9000 Silver 0.6423 oz. ASW, 37 mm. **Subject:** Curie Institute, 100th Anniversary

Date	Mintage	F	VF	XF	Unc	BU
2009P Proof	10,000	Value: 35.00				

KM# 1616 10 EURO
27.2000 g., 0.9000 Silver 0.7870 oz. ASW, 37 mm. **Subject:** Unesco site - The Kremlin in Moscow **Obv:** Wall Tower and cathedral

Date	Mintage	F	VF	XF	Unc	BU
2009P Proof	20,000	Value: 37.50				

KM# 1621 10 EURO
22.2000 g., 0.9000 Silver 0.6423 oz. ASW, 37 mm. **Subject:** First Moon Landing, 40th Anniversary **Obv:** Footprint on the moon

Date	Mintage	F	VF	XF	Unc	BU
2009P Proof	10,000	Value: 35.00				

KM# 1629 10 EURO
22.2000 g., 0.9000 Silver 0.6423 oz. ASW, 37 mm. **Subject:** Comic strip heroes **Obv:** Wanted posted **Rev:** Lucky Luke on horseback

Date	Mintage	F	VF	XF	Unc	BU
2009P Proof	5,000	Value: 40.00				

KM# 1631 10 EURO
22.2000 g., 0.9000 Silver 0.6423 oz. ASW, 37 mm. **Obv:** Soccer player **Rev:** Shield of Stade Francais

Date	Mintage	F	VF	XF	Unc	BU
2009P Proof	5,000	Value: 40.00				

KM# 1634 10 EURO
27.2000 g., 0.9000 Silver 0.7870 oz. ASW, 37 mm. **Subject:** Alpine skiing **Obv:** Globe and downhill skier **Rev:** Downhill skier on mountainside

Date	Mintage	F	VF	XF	Unc	BU
2009P Proof	10,000	Value: 37.50				

KM# 1636 10 EURO
22.2000 g., 0.9000 Silver 0.6423 oz. ASW, 37 mm. **Subject:** FIFA World Cup, South Africa **Obv:** Soccer player on field **Rev:** Soccerball, map of Africa, Prorea flower

Date	Mintage	F	VF	XF	Unc	BU
2009P Proof	15,000	Value: 35.00				

KM# 1645 10 EURO
12.0000 g., 0.9000 Silver 0.3472 oz. ASW, 29 mm. **Subject:** Aquitaine **Rev:** Value at center, wreath horizontal

Date	Mintage	F	VF	XF	Unc	BU
2010	7,690	—	—	—	—	22.50

KM# 1646 10 EURO
12.0000 g., 0.9000 Silver 0.3472 oz. ASW, 29 mm. **Subject:** Auvergne **Rev:** Value at center, wreath horizontal

Date	Mintage	F	VF	XF	Unc	BU
2010	7,690	—	—	—	—	22.50

KM# 1647 10 EURO
12.0000 g., 0.9000 Silver 0.3472 oz. ASW, 29 mm. **Subject:** Basse - Normandie **Rev:** Value at center, wreath horizontal

Date	Mintage	F	VF	XF	Unc	BU
2010	7,690	—	—	—	—	22.50

KM# 1648 10 EURO
12.0000 g., 0.9000 Silver 0.3472 oz. ASW, 29 mm. **Subject:** Bretagne **Rev:** Value at center, wreath horizontal

Date	Mintage	F	VF	XF	Unc	BU
2010	7,690	—	—	—	—	22.50

KM# 1649 10 EURO
12.0000 g., 0.9000 Silver 0.3472 oz. ASW, 29 mm. **Subject:** Burgundy **Rev:** Value at center, wreath horizontal

Date	Mintage	F	VF	XF	Unc	BU
2010	7,690	—	—	—	—	22.50

KM# 1650 10 EURO
12.0000 g., 0.9000 Silver 0.3472 oz. ASW, 29 mm. **Subject:** Centre **Rev:** Value at center, wreath horizontal

Date	Mintage	F	VF	XF	Unc	BU
2010	7,690	—	—	—	—	22.50

KM# 1651 10 EURO
12.0000 g., 0.9000 Silver 0.3472 oz. ASW, 29 mm. **Subject:** Champagne - Ardenne **Rev:** Value at center, wreath horizontal

Date	Mintage	F	VF	XF	Unc	BU
2010	7,690	—	—	—	—	22.50

KM# 1652 10 EURO
12.0000 g., 0.9000 Silver 0.3472 oz. ASW, 29 mm. **Subject:** Alsace **Rev:** Value at center, wreath horizontal

Date	Mintage	F	VF	XF	Unc	BU
2010	7,690	—	—	—	—	22.50

KM# 1653 10 EURO
12.0000 g., 0.9000 Silver 0.3472 oz. ASW, 29 mm. **Subject:** French - Comte **Rev:** Value at center, wreath horizontal

Date	Mintage	F	VF	XF	Unc	BU
2010	7,690	—	—	—	—	22.50

KM# 1654 10 EURO
12.0000 g., 0.9000 Silver 0.3472 oz. ASW, 29 mm. **Subject:** French Guiana **Rev:** Value at center, wreath horizontal

Date	Mintage	F	VF	XF	Unc	BU
2010	7,690	—	—	—	—	22.50

KM# 1655 10 EURO
12.0000 g., 0.9000 Silver 0.3472 oz. ASW, 29 mm. **Subject:** Guadeloupe **Rev:** Value at center, wreath horizontal

Date	Mintage	F	VF	XF	Unc	BU
2010	7,690	—	—	—	—	22.50

KM# 1656 10 EURO
12.0000 g., 0.9000 Silver 0.3472 oz. ASW, 29 mm. **Subject:** Haute - Normandie **Rev:** Value at center, wreath horizontal

Date	Mintage	F	VF	XF	Unc	BU
2010	7,690	—	—	—	—	22.50

KM# 1657 10 EURO
12.0000 g., 0.9000 Silver 0.3472 oz. ASW, 29 mm. **Subject:** Ile-de-France **Rev:** Value at center, wreath horizontal

Date	Mintage	F	VF	XF	Unc	BU
2010	7,690	—	—	—	—	22.50

KM# 1658 10 EURO
12.0000 g., 0.9000 Silver 0.3472 oz. ASW, 29 mm. **Subject:** Corsica **Rev:** Value at center, wreath horizontal

Date	Mintage	F	VF	XF	Unc	BU
2010	7,690	—	—	—	—	22.50

KM# 1659 10 EURO
12.0000 g., 0.9000 Silver 0.3472 oz. ASW, 29 mm. **Subject:** Languedoc - Roussillon **Rev:** Value at center, wreath horizontal

Date	Mintage	F	VF	XF	Unc	BU
2010	7,690	—	—	—	—	22.50

KM# 1660 10 EURO
12.0000 g., 0.9000 Silver 0.3472 oz. ASW, 29 mm. **Subject:** Limousin **Rev:** Value at center, wreath horizontal

Date	Mintage	F	VF	XF	Unc	BU
2010	7,690	—	—	—	—	22.50

KM# 1661 10 EURO
12.0000 g., 0.9000 Silver 0.3472 oz. ASW, 29 mm. **Subject:** Lorroaine **Rev:** Value at center, wreath horizontal

Date	Mintage	F	VF	XF	Unc	BU
2010	7,690	—	—	—	—	22.50

KM# 1662 10 EURO
12.0000 g., 0.9000 Silver 0.3472 oz. ASW, 29 mm. **Subject:** Martinique **Rev:** Value at center, wreath horizontal

Date	Mintage	F	VF	XF	Unc	BU
2010	7,690	—	—	—	—	22.50

KM# 1664 10 EURO
12.0000 g., 0.9000 Silver 0.3472 oz. ASW, 29 mm. **Subject:** Nord - Pas de - Calais **Rev:** Value at center, wreath horizontal

Date	Mintage	F	VF	XF	Unc	BU
2010	7,690	—	—	—	—	22.50

KM# 1665 10 EURO
12.0000 g., 0.9000 Silver 0.3472 oz. ASW, 29 mm. **Subject:** Pays de la Loire **Rev:** Value at center, wreath horizontal

Date	Mintage	F	VF	XF	Unc	BU
2010	7,690	—	—	—	—	22.50

KM# 1666 10 EURO
12.0000 g., 0.9000 Silver 0.3472 oz. ASW, 29 mm. **Subject:** Picardie **Rev:** Value at center, wreath horizontal

Date	Mintage	F	VF	XF	Unc	BU
2010	7,690	—	—	—	—	22.50

KM# 1667 10 EURO
12.0000 g., 0.9000 Silver 0.3472 oz. ASW, 29 mm. **Subject:** Poitou - Charentes **Rev:** Value at center, wreath horizontal

Date	Mintage	F	VF	XF	Unc	BU
2010	7,690	—	—	—	—	22.50

KM# 1668 10 EURO
12.0000 g., 0.9000 Silver 0.3472 oz. ASW, 29 mm. **Subject:** Provence - Alpes - Cote d'Azur **Rev:** Value at center, wreath horizontal

Date	Mintage	F	VF	XF	Unc	BU
2010	7,690	—	—	—	—	22.50

KM# 1669 10 EURO
12.0000 g., 0.9000 Silver 0.3472 oz. ASW, 29 mm. **Subject:** Reunion **Rev:** Value at center, wreath horizontal

Date	Mintage	F	VF	XF	Unc	BU
2010	7,690	—	—	—	—	22.50

KM# 1670 10 EURO
12.0000 g., 0.9000 Silver 0.3472 oz. ASW, 29 mm. **Subject:** Rhone - Alpes **Rev:** Value at center, wreath horizontal

Date	Mintage	F	VF	XF	Unc	BU
2010	7,690	—	—	—	—	22.50

KM# 1675 10 EURO
22.2000 g., 0.9000 Silver 0.6423 oz. ASW, 37 mm. **Obv:** Sower left **Rev:** Wheat and olive branch

Date	Mintage	F	VF	XF	Unc	BU
2010 Proof	10,000	Value: 35.00				

KM# 1681 10 EURO
22.2000 g., 0.9990 Silver 0.7130 oz. ASW, 37 mm. **Subject:** Cluny Abbey, 1100th Anniversary **Obv:** Europa head facing **Rev:** Cluny Abbey

Date	Mintage	F	VF	XF	Unc	BU
2010 Proof	10,000	Value: 50.00				

KM# 1686 10 EURO
22.2000 g., 0.9000 Silver 0.6423 oz. ASW, 37 mm. **Obv:** Georges Pompidou Center design **Rev:** Design detail

Date	Mintage	F	VF	XF	Unc	BU
2010 Proof	30,000	Value: 40.00				

KM# 1691 10 EURO
Aeronotical alloy, 37 mm. **Obv:** Marcel Dassault **Rev:** Mirage III plane

Date	Mintage	F	VF	XF	Unc	BU
2010 Proof	20,000	Value: 45.00				

KM# 1695 10 EURO
22.2000 g., 0.9000 Silver 0.6423 oz. ASW, 37 mm. **Obv:** Mother Teresa and child **Rev:** Mother Teresa and Pope John Paul II

Date	Mintage	F	VF	XF	Unc	BU
2010 Proof	20,000	Value: 40.00				

KM# 1700 10 EURO
22.2000 g., 0.9000 Silver 0.6423 oz. ASW, 37 mm. **Obv:** Taj Mahal **Rev:** UNESCO offices

Date	Mintage	F	VF	XF	Unc	BU
2010 Proof	10,000	Value: 55.00				

KM# 1705 10 EURO
22.2000 g., 0.9000 Silver 0.6423 oz. ASW, 37 mm. **Obv:** Lille station and route map **Rev:** Three TGV trains

Date	Mintage	F	VF	XF	Unc	BU
2010 Proof	30,000	Value: 35.00				

KM# 1708 10 EURO
15.0000 g., 0.9000 Silver 0.4340 oz. ASW, 30x21 mm. **Rev:** Georges Braque **Shape:** Rectangle

Date	Mintage	F	VF	XF	Unc	BU
2010 Proof	20,000	Value: 37.50				

KM# 1713 10 EURO
15.0000 g., 0.9000 Silver 0.4340 oz. ASW, 30x21 mm. **Rev:** Picasso **Shape:** Rectangle

Date	Mintage	F	VF	XF	Unc	BU
2010 Proof	20,000	Value: 55.00				

KM# 1717 10 EURO
22.2000 g., 0.9000 Silver 0.6423 oz. ASW, 37 mm. **Obv:** Blake and Mortimer **Rev:** "Secret of the Swordfish" scene, arrest of Col. Olrik.

Date	Mintage	F	VF	XF	Unc	BU
2010 Proof	10,000	Value: 50.00				

KM# 1720 10 EURO
22.2000 g., 0.9000 Silver 0.6423 oz. ASW, 37 mm. **Obv:** Handball player and globe **Rev:** Handball player, net and Big Ben

Date	Mintage	F	VF	XF	Unc	BU
2010 Proof	10,000	Value: 40.00				

KM# 1721 10 EURO
8.4500 g., 0.9200 Gold 0.2499 oz. AGW, 22 mm. **Obv:** Soccer player **Rev:** Stade Toulousain logo, multicolor

Date	Mintage	F	VF	XF	Unc	BU
2010 Proof	500	Value: 450				

KM# 1722 10 EURO
22.2000 g., 0.9000 Silver 0.6423 oz. ASW, 37 mm. **Obv:** Soccer player **Rev:** Stade Toulousain logo, multicolor

Date	Mintage	F	VF	XF	Unc	BU
2010 Proof	5,000	Value: 50.00				

KM# 1726 10 EURO
10.0000 g., 0.5000 Silver 0.1607 oz. ASW, 29 mm. **Subject:** Mayotte **Obv:** Value at center, wreath horizontal

Date	Mintage	F	VF	XF	Unc	BU
2011	—	—	—	—	—	20.00

KM# 1727 10 EURO
10.0000 g., 0.5000 Silver 0.1607 oz. ASW, 29 mm. **Subject:** Aquitaine

Date	Mintage	F	VF	XF	Unc	BU
2011	—	—	—	—	—	20.00

KM# 1728 10 EURO
10.0000 g., 0.5000 Silver 0.1607 oz. ASW, 29 mm. **Subject:** Auvergne

Date	Mintage	F	VF	XF	Unc	BU
2011	—	—	—	—	—	20.00

KM# 1729 10 EURO
10.0000 g., 0.5000 Silver 0.1607 oz. ASW, 29 mm. **Subject:** Basse - Normindie

Date	Mintage	F	VF	XF	Unc	BU
2011	—	—	—	—	—	20.00

KM# 1730 10 EURO
10.0000 g., 0.5000 Silver 0.1607 oz. ASW, 29 mm. **Subject:** Bretagne

Date	Mintage	F	VF	XF	Unc	BU
2011	—	—	—	—	—	20.00

KM# 1731 10 EURO
10.0000 g., 0.5000 Silver 0.1607 oz. ASW, 29 mm. **Subject:** Burgundy

Date	Mintage	F	VF	XF	Unc	BU
2011	—	—	—	—	—	20.00

KM# 1732 10 EURO
10.0000 g., 0.5000 Silver 0.1607 oz. ASW, 29 mm. **Subject:** Centre

Date	Mintage	F	VF	XF	Unc	BU
2011	—	—	—	—	—	20.00

KM# 1733 10 EURO
10.0000 g., 0.5000 Silver 0.1607 oz. ASW, 29 mm. **Subject:** Campagne - Ardenne

Date	Mintage	F	VF	XF	Unc	BU
2011	—	—	—	—	—	20.00

KM# 1734 10 EURO
10.0000 g., 0.5000 Silver 0.1607 oz. ASW, 29 mm. **Subject:** Alsace

Date	Mintage	F	VF	XF	Unc	BU
2011	—	—	—	—	—	20.00

KM# 1735 10 EURO
10.0000 g., 0.5000 Silver 0.1607 oz. ASW, 29 mm. **Subject:** France - Comte

Date	Mintage	F	VF	XF	Unc	BU
2011	—	—	—	—	—	20.00

KM# 1736 10 EURO
10.0000 g., 0.5000 Silver 0.1607 oz. ASW, 29 mm. **Subject:** French Guiana

Date	Mintage	F	VF	XF	Unc	BU
2011	—	—	—	—	—	20.00

KM# 1737 10 EURO
10.0000 g., 0.5000 Silver 0.1607 oz. ASW, 29 mm. **Subject:** Guadeloupe

Date	Mintage	F	VF	XF	Unc	BU
2011	—	—	—	—	—	20.00

KM# 1738 10 EURO
10.0000 g., 0.5000 Silver 0.1607 oz. ASW, 29 mm. **Subject:** Haute - Normandie

Date	Mintage	F	VF	XF	Unc	BU
2011	—	—	—	—	—	20.00

KM# 1739 10 EURO
10.0000 g., 0.5000 Silver 0.1607 oz. ASW, 29 mm. **Subject:** Ile de France

Date	Mintage	F	VF	XF	Unc	BU
2011	—	—	—	—	—	20.00

KM# 1740 10 EURO
10.0000 g., 0.5000 Silver 0.1607 oz. ASW, 29 mm. **Subject:** Corsica

Date	Mintage	F	VF	XF	Unc	BU
2011	—	—	—	—	—	20.00

KM# 1741 10 EURO
10.0000 g., 0.5000 Silver 0.1607 oz. ASW, 29 mm. **Subject:** Lansuedoc - Rossillon

Date	Mintage	F	VF	XF	Unc	BU
2011	—	—	—	—	—	20.00

KM# 1742 10 EURO
10.0000 g., 0.5000 Silver 0.1607 oz. ASW, 29 mm. **Subject:** Limousin

Date	Mintage	F	VF	XF	Unc	BU
2011	—	—	—	—	—	20.00

KM# 1744 10 EURO
10.0000 g., 0.5000 Silver 0.1607 oz. ASW, 29 mm. **Subject:** Martinique

Date	Mintage	F	VF	XF	Unc	BU
2011	—	—	—	—	—	20.00

KM# 1745 10 EURO
10.0000 g., 0.5000 Silver 0.1607 oz. ASW, 29 mm. **Subject:** Nord Pas de Calais

Date	Mintage	F	VF	XF	Unc	BU
2011	—	—	—	—	—	20.00

KM# 1746 10 EURO
10.0000 g., 0.5000 Silver 0.1607 oz. ASW, 29 mm. **Subject:** Pays de la Loire

Date	Mintage	F	VF	XF	Unc	BU
2011	—	—	—	—	—	20.00

KM# 1747 10 EURO
10.0000 g., 0.5000 Silver 0.1607 oz. ASW, 29 mm. **Subject:** Picardie

Date	Mintage	F	VF	XF	Unc	BU
2011	—	—	—	—	—	20.00

KM# 1748 10 EURO
10.0000 g., 0.5000 Silver 0.1607 oz. ASW, 29 mm. **Subject:** Poitou - Charentes

Date	Mintage	F	VF	XF	Unc	BU
2011	—	—	—	—	—	20.00

KM# 1749 10 EURO
10.0000 g., 0.5000 Silver 0.1607 oz. ASW, 29 mm. **Subject:** Province - Alpes - Cote d'Azur

Date	Mintage	F	VF	XF	Unc	BU
2011	—	—	—	—	—	20.00

KM# 1750 10 EURO
10.0000 g., 0.5000 Silver 0.1607 oz. ASW, 29 mm. **Subject:** Reunion

Date	Mintage	F	VF	XF	Unc	BU
2011	—	—	—	—	—	20.00

KM# 1751 10 EURO
10.0000 g., 0.5000 Silver 0.1607 oz. ASW, 29 mm. **Subject:** Phone - Alpes

Date	Mintage	F	VF	XF	Unc	BU
2011	—	—	—	—	—	20.00

KM# 1752 10 EURO
10.0000 g., 0.5000 Silver 0.1607 oz. ASW, 29 mm. **Subject:** Midi - Pyreneis

Date	Mintage	F	VF	XF	Unc	BU
2011	—	—	—	—	—	20.00

KM# 1753 10 EURO
10.0000 g., 0.5000 Silver 0.1607 oz. ASW, 29 mm. **Subject:** Mayotte

Date	Mintage	F	VF	XF	Unc	BU
2011	—	—	—	—	—	20.00

KM# 1784 10 EURO
22.2000 g., 0.9000 Silver 0.6423 oz. ASW, 37 mm. **Subject:** Euro Starter Kit, 10th Anniversary **Obv:** Sower left **Rev:** Euro starter kit

Date	Mintage	F	VF	XF	Unc	BU
2011 Proof	10,000	Value: 40.00				

KM# 1790 10 EURO
22.2000 g., 0.9000 Silver 0.6423 oz. ASW, 37 mm. **Subject:** International Music Day, 30th Anniversary **Obv:** Europa **Rev:** Youth jamming

Date	Mintage	F	VF	XF	Unc	BU
2011 Proof	10,000	Value: 40.00				

KM# 1795 10 EURO
22.2000 g., 0.9000 Silver 0.6423 oz. ASW, 37 mm. **Subject:** Great Explorers - Jacques Cartier **Obv:** The Grand Hermine sailing away **Rev:** Cartier, globe and compass rose

Date	Mintage	F	VF	XF	Unc	BU
2011	30,000	Value: 50.00				

KM# 1800 10 EURO
22.2000 g., 0.9000 Silver 0.6423 oz. ASW, 37 mm. **Subject:** Colvis, 466-511 **Obv:** Crowned head left **Rev:** Hands over chalice, reign dates at left, value at right

Date	Mintage	F	VF	XF	Unc	BU
2011 Proof	20,000	Value: 50.00				

KM# 1802 10 EURO

22.2000 g., 0.9000 Silver 0.6423 oz. ASW, 37 mm. **Subject:** Charlemagne, 768-814 **Obv:** Crowned head left **Rev:** Cross on orb, reight dates at left, value at right

Date	Mintage	F	VF	XF	Unc	BU
2011 Proof	20,000	Value: 50.00				

KM# 1804 10 EURO

22.2000 g., 0.9000 Silver 0.6423 oz. ASW, 37 mm. **Subject:** Charles II, 823-877 **Obv:** Crowned head left

Date	Mintage	F	VF	XF	Unc	BU
2011 Proof	20,000	Value: 50.00				

KM# 1806 10 EURO

22.2000 g., 0.9000 Silver 0.6423 oz. ASW, 37 mm. **Subject:** WWF - Audouin's Gull **Obv:** Gull in flight right **Rev:** Gull standing right, WWF panda logo

Date	Mintage	F	VF	XF	Unc	BU
2011 Proof	20,000	Value: 50.00				

KM# 1809 10 EURO

22.2000 g., 0.9000 Silver 0.6423 oz. ASW, 37 mm. **Subject:** UNESCO World Heritage Site - Palace of Versailles **Obv:** Building and garden plan **Rev:** Top view of UNESCO's Paris headquarters

Date	Mintage	F	VF	XF	Unc	BU
2011 Proof	20,000	Value: 50.00				

KM# 1814 10 EURO

22.2000 g., 0.9000 Silver 0.6423 oz. ASW, 37 mm. **Obv:** Metz railroad station **Rev:** TGV and ICE trains

Date	Mintage	F	VF	XF	Unc	BU
2011 Proof	10,000	Value: 50.00				

KM# 1819 10 EURO

15.0000 g., 0.9000 Silver 0.4340 oz. ASW, 30x21 mm. **Subject:** Vassily Kandinsky **Shape:** Rectangle

Date	Mintage	F	VF	XF	Unc	BU
2011 Proof	10,000	Value: 50.00				

KM# 1823 10 EURO

15.0000 g., 0.9000 Silver 0.4340 oz. ASW, 30x21 mm. **Subject:** Andy Warhol **Shape:** Rectangle

Date	Mintage	F	VF	XF	Unc	BU
2011 proof	10,000	Value: 50.00				

KM# 1829 10 EURO

22.2000 g., 0.9000 Silver 0.6423 oz. ASW, 37 mm. **Obv:** Nana **Rev:** Emile Zola

Date	Mintage	F	VF	XF	Unc	BU
2011 Proof	5,000	Value: 50.00				

KM# 1831 10 EURO

22.2000 g., 0.9000 Silver 0.6423 oz. ASW, 37 mm. **Obv:** The Stranger **Rev:** Albert Camus

Date	Mintage	F	VF	XF	Unc	BU
2011 Proof	—	Value: 50.00				

KM# 1835 10 EURO

22.2000 g., 0.9000 Silver 0.6423 oz. ASW, 37 mm. **Subject:** Comic Strip XIII **Obv:** Profile left and large XIII **Rev:** Montage of characters

Date	Mintage	F	VF	XF	Unc	BU
2011 Proof	10,000	Value: 50.00				

KM# 1755 10 EURO

22.2000 g., 0.9000 Silver 0.6423 oz. ASW, 37 mm. **Obv:** Bicycle racer **Rev:** Metro 92 logo

Date	Mintage	F	VF	XF	Unc	BU
2011 Proof	5,000	Value: 50.00				

KM# 1838 10 EURO

22.2000 g., 0.9000 Silver 0.6423 oz. ASW, 37 mm. **Obv:** Female figure skater and globe **Rev:** Figure skating pair

Date	Mintage	F	VF	XF	Unc	BU
2011 Proof	10,000	Value: 50.00				

KM# 1743 10 EURO

10.0000 g., 0.5000 Silver 0.1607 oz. ASW, 29 mm. **Subject:** Lorroaine

Date	Mintage	F	VF	XF	Unc	BU
2011	—	—	—	—	—	20.00

KM# A1450 15 EURO

31.0000 g., 0.9000 Silver 0.8970 oz. ASW, 31 mm. **Rev:** Pantheon

Date	Mintage	F	VF	XF	Unc	BU
2007 Proof	7,500	Value: 75.00				

KM# 1535 15 EURO

15.0000 g., 0.9000 Silver 0.4340 oz. ASW, 31 mm. **Obv:** Sower, half length advancing right **Rev:** Value within hexagon

Date	Mintage	F	VF	XF	Unc	BU
2008 Proof	500,000	Value: 45.00				

KM# 1333 20 EURO

17.0000 g., 0.9200 Gold 0.5028 oz. AGW, 31 mm. **Obv:** Victor Hugo, denomination and map **Rev:** "Gavroche" **Edge:** Plain

Date	Mintage	F	VF	XF	Unc	BU
2002 Proof	2,000	Value: 750				

KM# 1306 20 EURO

17.0000 g., 0.9200 Gold 0.5028 oz. AGW, 31 mm. **Subject:** French Landmarks **Obv:** French map **Rev:** Le Mont St. Michel **Edge:** Plain

Date	Mintage	F	VF	XF	Unc	BU
2002 Proof	1,000	Value: 775				

KM# 1308 20 EURO

17.0000 g., 0.9200 Gold 0.5028 oz. AGW, 31 mm. **Subject:** French Landmarks **Obv:** French map **Rev:** La Butte Montmartre **Edge:** Plain

Date	Mintage	F	VF	XF	Unc	BU
2002 Proof	1,000	Value: 775				

KM# 1327 20 EURO

8.4500 g., 0.9200 Gold 0.2499 oz. AGW, 31 mm. **Obv:** Tour de France logo **Rev:** Group of cyclists and Arch de Triumph **Edge:** Reeded

Date	Mintage	F	VF	XF	Unc	BU
2003A Proof	5,000	Value: 375				

KM# 1328 20 EURO

8.4500 g., 0.9200 Gold 0.2499 oz. AGW, 31 mm. **Obv:** Tour de France logo **Rev:** Two cyclists and spectators **Edge:** Reeded

Date	Mintage	F	VF	XF	Unc	BU
2003A Proof	5,000	Value: 375				

KM# 1329 20 EURO

8.4500 g., 0.9200 Gold 0.2499 oz. AGW, 31 mm. **Obv:** Tour de France logo **Rev:** Two groups of cyclists **Edge:** Reeded

Date	Mintage	F	VF	XF	Unc	BU
2003A Proof	5,000	Value: 375				

KM# 1330 20 EURO

8.4500 g., 0.9200 Gold 0.2499 oz. AGW, 31 mm. **Obv:** Tour de France logo **Rev:** Cyclist, stop watch and gears **Edge:** Reeded

Date	Mintage	F	VF	XF	Unc	BU
2003A Proof	5,000	Value: 375				

KM# 1334 20 EURO

17.0000 g., 0.9200 Gold 0.5028 oz. AGW, 31 mm. **Obv:** Tour de France logo **Rev:** Cyclist going left **Edge:** Plain

Date	Mintage	F	VF	XF	Unc	BU
2003 Proof	5,000	Value: 750				

KM# 1337 20 EURO

17.0000 g., 0.9200 Gold 0.5028 oz. AGW, 31 mm. **Obv:** Jefferson and Napoleon with Louisiana Purchase map **Rev:** Jazz musician, mansion and river boat **Edge:** Plain

Date	Mintage	F	VF	XF	Unc	BU
2003 Proof	1,000	Value: 775				

KM# 1339 20 EURO

17.0000 g., 0.9200 Gold 0.5028 oz. AGW, 31 mm. **Obv:** Curved cross design with multiple values **Rev:** Goddess Europa and flags **Edge:** Plain

Date	Mintage	F	VF	XF	Unc	BU
2003 Proof	3,000	Value: 750				

KM# 1342 20 EURO

17.0000 g., 0.9200 Gold 0.5028 oz. AGW, 31 mm. **Obv:** Denomination and compass face **Rev:** SS Normandie and New York City skyline **Edge:** Plain

Date	Mintage	F	VF	XF	Unc	BU
2003 Proof	1,000	Value: 775				

KM# 1344 20 EURO

17.0000 g., 0.9200 Gold 0.5028 oz. AGW, 31 mm. **Obv:** Denomination and compass face **Rev:** Airplane and Tokyo Geisha **Edge:** Plain

Date	Mintage	F	VF	XF	Unc	BU
2003 Proof	1,000	Value: 775				

KM# 1346 20 EURO

17.0000 g., 0.9200 Gold 0.5028 oz. AGW, 31 mm. **Obv:** Paul Gauguin **Rev:** Native woman **Edge:** Plain

Date	Mintage	F	VF	XF	Unc	BU
2003 Proof	2,000	Value: 750				

KM# 1349 20 EURO

17.0000 g., 0.9200 Gold 0.5028 oz. AGW, 31 mm. **Obv:** The Seed Sower **Rev:** Denomination and map **Edge:** Plain

Date	Mintage	F	VF	XF	Unc	BU
2003 Proof	5,000	Value: 750				

KM# 1354 20 EURO

17.0000 g., 0.9200 Gold 0.5028 oz. AGW, 31 mm. **Obv:** Mona Lisa **Rev:** Leonardo da Vinci and denomination **Edge:** Plain

Date	Mintage	F	VF	XF	Unc	BU
2003 Proof	1,000	Value: 775				

KM# 1356 20 EURO

17.0000 g., 0.9200 Gold 0.5028 oz. AGW, 31 mm. **Obv:** Map and denomination **Rev:** Chateau Chambord **Edge:** Plain

Date	Mintage	F	VF	XF	Unc	BU
2003 Proof	1,000	Value: 775				

KM# 1358 20 EURO

17.0000 g., 0.9200 Gold 0.5028 oz. AGW, 31 mm. **Obv:** Denomination in swirling design **Rev:** Hansel and Gretel, witch and house **Edge:** Plain

Date	Mintage	F	VF	XF	Unc	BU
2003 Proof	1,000	Value: 775				

KM# 1360 20 EURO

17.0000 g., 0.9200 Gold 0.5028 oz. AGW, 31 mm. **Obv:** Denomination in swirling design **Rev:** Alice in Wonderland **Edge:** Plain

Date	Mintage	F	VF	XF	Unc	BU
2003 Proof	1,000	Value: 775				

KM# 1363 20 EURO

17.0000 g., 0.9200 Gold 0.5028 oz. AGW, 31 mm. **Obv:** Pierre de Coubertin **Rev:** Olympic runners **Edge:** Plain

Date	Mintage	F	VF	XF	Unc	BU
2003 Proof	3,000	Value: 750				

KM# 1365 20 EURO

17.0000 g., 0.9200 Gold 0.5028 oz. AGW, 31 mm. **Obv:** Map with denomination **Rev:** Avignon Popes Palace **Edge:** Plain

Date	Mintage	F	VF	XF	Unc	BU
2004 Proof	1,000	Value: 775				

KM# 1370 20 EURO

17.0000 g., 0.9200 Gold 0.5028 oz. AGW, 31 mm. **Obv:** Soldiers and Normandy invasion scene **Rev:** "D-DAY" above denomination **Edge:** Plain

Date	Mintage	F	VF	XF	Unc	BU
2004 Proof	2,000	Value: 750				

KM# 1376 20 EURO

17.0000 g., 0.9200 Gold 0.5028 oz. AGW, 31 mm. **Subject:** Centenary Law of Dec. 9, 1905 **Obv:** "Sower" left in ring of stars **Rev:** Denomination and French map face design **Edge:** Plain

Date	Mintage	F	VF	XF	Unc	BU
2004 Proof	3,000	Value: 750				
2006 Proof	1,000	Value: 775				

KM# 1379 20 EURO

17.0000 g., 0.9200 Gold 0.5028 oz. AGW, 31 mm. **Obv:** Compass rose **Rev:** Ocean liner **Edge:** Plain

Date	Mintage	F	VF	XF	Unc	BU
2004 Proof	1,000	Value: 775				

KM# 1381 20 EURO

17.0000 g., 0.9200 Gold 0.5028 oz. AGW, 31 mm. **Obv:** Compass rose **Rev:** Trans-Siberian Railroad **Edge:** Plain

Date	Mintage	F	VF	XF	Unc	BU
2004 Proof	1,000	Value: 775				

KM# 1383 20 EURO

17.0000 g., 0.9200 Gold 0.5028 oz. AGW, 31 mm. **Obv:** Compass rose **Rev:** Half-track vehicle **Edge:** Plain

Date	Mintage	F	VF	XF	Unc	BU
2004 Proof	1,000	Value: 775				

KM# 1385 20 EURO

17.0000 g., 0.9200 Gold 0.5028 oz. AGW, 31 mm. **Obv:** Compass rose **Rev:** Biplane airliner **Edge:** Plain

Date	Mintage	F	VF	XF	Unc	BU
2004 Proof	1,000	Value: 775				

KM# 1387 20 EURO
155.5000 g., 0.9500 Silver 4.7493 oz. ASW, 50 mm. **Obv:** Statue of Liberty **Rev:** F. A. Bartholdi **Edge:** Plain

Date	Mintage	F	VF	XF	Unc	BU
2004 Proof	999	Value: 200				

KM# 1388 20 EURO
17.0000 g., 0.9200 Gold 0.5028 oz. AGW, 31 mm. **Obv:** Statue of Liberty **Rev:** F. A. Bartholdi **Edge:** Plain

Date	Mintage	F	VF	XF	Unc	BU
2004 Proof	2,000	Value: 750				

KM# 1393 20 EURO
17.0000 g., 0.9200 Gold 0.5028 oz. AGW, 31 mm. **Subject:** European Union Expansion **Obv:** Partial face and flags **Rev:** Puzzle map **Edge:** Plain

Date	Mintage	F	VF	XF	Unc	BU
2004 Proof	3,000	Value: 750				

KM# 1433 20 EURO
17.0000 g., 0.9200 Gold 0.5028 oz. AGW, 31 mm. **Subject:** Bicentennial Victory at Austerlitz **Rev:** Battle scene **Rev. Legend:** LIBERTÉ ÉGALITÉ FRATERNITÉ

Date	Mintage	F	VF	XF	Unc	BU
2005 Proof	5,000	Value: 750				

KM# 1437 20 EURO
17.0000 g., 0.9200 Gold 0.5028 oz. AGW, 31 mm. **Subject:** Centenary - Law of Dec. 9, 1905 **Obv:** "Sower" at left in ring of stars

Date	Mintage	F	VF	XF	Unc	BU
2005 Proof	1,500	Value: 775				

KM# 1454 20 EURO
155.5000 g., 0.9500 Silver 4.7493 oz. ASW, 50 mm. **Subject:** 100th Anniversary - Paul Cézanne's death **Obv:** Self portrait **Rev:** "The Card Players" **Rev. Legend:** LIBERTÉ ÉGALITÉ FRATERNITÉ

Date	Mintage	F	VF	XF	Unc	BU
2006 Proof	500	Value: 225				

KM# 1443 20 EURO
155.5200 g., 0.9500 Silver 4.7499 oz. ASW, 50 mm. **Obv:** Bust of Franklin facing slightly right at left, his diplomatic and technical successes at right **Obv. Legend:** BENJAMIN FRANKLIN 1706-2006 **Obv. Inscription:** AMI DE LA FRANCE

Date	Mintage	F	VF	XF	Unc	BU
2006 Proof	500	Value: 225				

KM# 1520 20 EURO
155.5000 g., 0.9500 Silver 4.7493 oz. ASW, 50 mm. **Subject:** Asterix **Rev:** Character running downhill

Date	Mintage	F	VF	XF	Unc	BU
2007 Proof	500	Value: 325				

KM# 1468 20 EURO
17.0000 g., 0.9200 Gold 0.5028 oz. AGW, 31 mm. **Subject:** Le Petit Prince, 60th Anniversary **Obv:** Prince lying in field

Date	Mintage	F	VF	XF	Unc	BU
2007 Proof	2,000	Value: 750				

KM# 1471 20 EURO
155.5500 g., 0.9500 Silver 4.7508 oz. ASW, 50 mm. **Obv:** Two dragons in flight **Rev:** Merlin and Excalibur

Date	Mintage	F	VF	XF	Unc	BU
2007 Proof	500	Value: 300				

KM# 1472 20 EURO
17.0000 g., 0.9200 Gold 0.5028 oz. AGW, 31 mm. **Obv:** Two dragons in flight **Rev:** Merlin & Excalibur

Date	Mintage	F	VF	XF	Unc	BU
2007 Proof	500	Value: 800				

KM# 1494 20 EURO
155.5500 g., 0.9500 Silver 4.7508 oz. ASW, 50 mm. **Subject:** Point Neuf - 400th Anniversary **Obv:** Moments of France logo **Rev:** Point Neuf Bridge and Paris Mint Building

Date	Mintage	F	VF	XF	Unc	BU
2007 Proof	500	Value: 300				

KM# 1496 20 EURO
155.5500 g., 0.9500 Silver 4.7508 oz. ASW, 50 mm. **Subject:** Cannes Film Festival, 60th Anniversary **Obv:** Cinema screen and stage, Golden Palm Award

Date	Mintage	F	VF	XF	Unc	BU
2007 Proof	500	Value: 300				

KM# 1499 20 EURO
17.0000 g., 0.9200 Gold 0.5028 oz. AGW, 30 x 21 mm. **Subject:** Edgar Degas, 90th Anniversary of Seuth **Obv:** Degas painting of dancer **Rev:** Brushes and Degas portrait **Shape:** Rectangle

Date	Mintage	F	VF	XF	Unc	BU
2007 Proof	500	Value: 800				

KM# 1509 20 EURO
100.0000 g., 0.9500 Silver 3.0542 oz. ASW, 49 mm. **Subject:** Georges Remi Centennial **Rev:** Tin Tin and Snowy

Date	Mintage	F	VF	XF	Unc	BU
2007 Proof	500	Value: 325				

KM# 1513 20 EURO
155.5000 g., 0.9500 Silver 4.7493 oz. ASW, 50 mm. **Subject:** Stanislas Leszczynski **Obv:** Bust and shield **Rev:** Palace Stanislas - Nancy

Date	Mintage	F	VF	XF	Unc	BU
2007 Proof	500	Value: 325				

KM# 1521 20 EURO
17.0000 g., 0.9200 Gold 0.5028 oz. AGW, 31 mm. **Subject:** Asterix **Rev:** Asterix and Cleopatria

Date	Mintage	F	VF	XF	Unc	BU
2007 Proof	500	Value: 800				

KM# 1540 20 EURO
163.8000 g., 0.9500 Silver 5.0028 oz. ASW, 50 mm. **Subject:** 5th Republic, 50th Anniversary **Obv:** Sower **Rev:** de Gaulle head right

Date	Mintage	F	VF	XF	Unc	BU
2008 Proof	500	Value: 250				

KM# 1541 20 EURO
17.0000 g., 0.9205 Gold 0.5031 oz. AGW, 31 mm. **Subject:** 5th Republic, 50th Anniversary **Obv:** Sower **Rev:** de Gaulle head right

Date	Mintage	F	VF	XF	Unc	BU
2008 Proof	500	Value: 950				

KM# 1557 20 EURO
163.8000 g., 0.9500 Silver 5.0028 oz. ASW, 50 mm. **Subject:** André Citronë **Obv:** First front wheel drive auto **Rev:** Bust 1/4 left

Date	Mintage	F	VF	XF	Unc	BU
2008 Proof	500	Value: 325				

KM# 1560 20 EURO
163.8000 g., 0.9500 Silver 5.0028 oz. ASW, 50 mm. **Subject:** Rouen Armada **Obv:** Cape Horn, sextant, hourglass **Rev:** Sailing ship

Date	Mintage	F	VF	XF	Unc	BU
2008 Proof	—	Value: 350				

KM# 1563 20 EURO
163.8000 g., 0.9500 Silver 5.0028 oz. ASW, 50 mm. **Subject:** Lourdes, 150th Anniversary **Obv:** Church of Notre Dame at Lourdes **Rev:** Cross with Pope John Paul II, Pope Benedict XVI and Bernadette Soubirous in quadrants

Date	Mintage	F	VF	XF	Unc	BU
2008 Proof	500	Value: 300				

KM# 1571 20 EURO
17.0000 g., 0.9200 Gold 0.5028 oz. AGW, 30 x 21 mm. **Subject:** Edward Manet **Obv:** Manet's "Olympia" painting **Rev:** Paint brushes and Manet's portrait **Shape:** Rectangle

Date	Mintage	F	VF	XF	Unc	BU
2008 Proof	500	Value: 800				

KM# 1602 20 EURO
44.4000 g., 0.9000 Silver 1.2847 oz. ASW, 37 mm. **Obv:** Eiffel Tower Structure **Rev:** Gustave Eiffel at left

Date	Mintage	F	VF	XF	Unc	BU
2009P Proof	5,000	Value: 100				

KM# 1607 20 EURO
44.4000 g., 0.9000 Silver 1.2847 oz. ASW, 37 mm. **Subject:** Bugatti 100th Anniversary **Obv:** Ettore Bugatti at left **Rev:** Race car and grill motif

Date	Mintage	F	VF	XF	Unc	BU
2009P Proof	5,000	Value: 100				

KM# 1612 20 EURO
44.4000 g., 0.9000 Silver 1.2847 oz. ASW, 37 mm. **Subject:** Curie Institute, 100th Anniversary

Date	Mintage	F	VF	XF	Unc	BU
2009P Proof	5,000	Value: 70.00				

KM# 1690 20 EURO
44.4000 g., 0.9000 Silver 1.2847 oz. ASW, 37 mm. **Obv:** Marcel Dassault **Rev:** Mirage III plane

Date	Mintage	F	VF	XF	Unc	BU
2010 Proof	2,000	Value: 75.00				

KM# 1704 20 EURO
44.4000 g., 0.9000 Silver 1.2847 oz. ASW, 37 mm. **Obv:** Lille station and route map **Rev:** Three TGV trains

Date	Mintage	F	VF	XF	Unc	BU
2010 Proof	2,000	Value: 75.00				

KM# 1815 20 EURO
44.4000 g., 0.9000 Silver 1.2847 oz. ASW, 37 mm. **Obv:** Metz railroad station **Rev:** TGV and ICE trains

Date	Mintage	F	VF	XF	Unc	BU
2011 Proof	1,000	Value: 100				

KM# 1581 25 EURO
18.0000 g., 0.9000 Silver 0.5208 oz. ASW, 33 mm. **Obv:** Modernistic sower advancing right **Rev:** Value and wreath

Date	Mintage	F	VF	XF	Unc	BU
2009P	250,000	—	—	—	—	35.00

KM# 1303 50 EURO
31.0000 g., 0.9990 Gold 0.9956 oz. AGW, 37 mm. **Subject:** Europa **Obv:** Eight French euro coin designs **Rev:** Portrait and flags design of 6.55957 francs KM-1265 **Edge:** Plain

Date	Mintage	F	VF	XF	Unc	BU
2002 Proof	2,000	Value: 1,600				

KM# 1335 50 EURO
31.1000 g., 0.9990 Gold 0.9988 oz. AGW, 37 mm. **Obv:** Tour de France logo **Rev:** Cyclist going left **Edge:** Plain

Date	Mintage	F	VF	XF	Unc	BU
2003 Proof	5,000	Value: 1,550				

KM# 1340 50 EURO
1000.0000 g., 0.9500 Silver 30.541 oz. ASW, 100 mm. **Obv:** Curved cross design with multiple values **Rev:** Goddess Europa and flags **Edge:** Plain with three line inscription at six o'clock

Date	Mintage	F	VF	XF	Unc	BU
2003 Proof	2,000	Value: 1,150				

KM# 1368 50 EURO
31.1000 g., 0.9990 Gold 0.9988 oz. AGW, 37 mm. **Obv:** Book, denomination and eagle **Rev:** Napoleon and coronation scene **Edge:** Plain

Date	Mintage	F	VF	XF	Unc	BU
2004 Proof	2,000	Value: 1,600				

KM# 1394 50 EURO
31.1040 g., 0.9990 Gold 0.9990 oz. AGW, 37 mm. **Subject:** European Union Expansion **Obv:** Partial face and flags **Rev:** Puzzle map **Edge:** Plain

Date	Mintage	F	VF	XF	Unc	BU
2004 Proof	2,000	Value: 1,600				

KM# 1430 50 EURO
31.1040 g., 0.9990 Gold 0.9990 oz. AGW, 37 mm. **Rev:** Kitty and Daniel in Versailles **Rev. Legend:** Hello Kitty

Date	Mintage	F	VF	XF	Unc	BU
2005 Proof	1,000	Value: 1,650				

KM# 1466 50 EURO
31.1050 g., 0.9990 Gold 0.9990 oz. AGW, 37 mm. **Subject:** Le Petit Prince, 60th Anniversary **Obv:** Prince standing

Date	Mintage	F	VF	XF	Unc	BU
2007 Proof	2,000	Value: 1,600				

KM# 1481 50 EURO
31.1000 g., 0.9990 Gold 0.9988 oz. AGW, 37 mm. **Subject:** Airbus A380 **Obv:** Airplane **Rev:** Europa and flags

Date	Mintage	F	VF	XF	Unc	BU
2007 Proof	500	Value: 1,700				

KM# 1487 50 EURO
1000.0000 g., 0.9500 Silver 30.541 oz. ASW **Subject:** 2007 Rugby World Cup **Obv:** Two players and goal **Rev:** Logo and goal **Shape:** Oval

Date	Mintage	F	VF	XF	Unc	BU
2007 Proof	299	Value: 1,250				

KM# 1510 50 EURO
31.1050 g., 0.9990 Gold 0.9990 oz. AGW, 37 mm. **Subject:** Georges Remi Centennial **Obv:** Wand and sparkles **Rev:** Tin Tin and dog Snowy

Date	Mintage	F	VF	XF	Unc	BU
2007 Proof	500	Value: 1,700				

KM# 1522 50 EURO
31.0500 g., 0.9990 Gold 0.9972 oz. AGW, 37 mm. **Subject:** Asterix **Rev:** Asterix and the Butcher of Arverne

Date	Mintage	F	VF	XF	Unc	BU
2007 Proof	500	Value: 1,700				

KM# 1530 50 EURO
31.1040 g., 0.9990 Gold 0.9990 oz. AGW, 37 mm. **Subject:** French Presidency of the Euopean Union **Obv:** Text within stars **Rev:** Europa head within flags

Date	Mintage	F	VF	XF	Unc	BU
2008 Proof	500	Value: 1,750				

KM# 1564 50 EURO
31.1040 g., 0.9990 Gold 0.9990 oz. AGW, 37 mm. **Subject:** Lourdes, 150th Anniversary **Obv:** Church of Notre Dame at Lourdes **Rev:** Cross with Pope John Paul II, Pope Benedict XVI and Bernadette Soubirous in quadrants

Date	Mintage	F	VF	XF	Unc	BU
2008 Proof	500	Value: 1,750				

KM# 1597 50 EURO
163.8000 g., 0.9500 Silver 5.0028 oz. ASW, 50 mm. **Subject:** Concorde 40th Anniversary **Obv:** Concorde in flight **Rev:** Tail emblems

Date	Mintage	F	VF	XF	Unc	BU
2009P Proof	1,000	Value: 250				

KM# 1603 50 EURO
163.8000 g., 0.9500 Silver 5.0028 oz. ASW, 50 mm. **Obv:** Eiffel Tower Structure **Rev:** Gustave Eiffel at left

Date	Mintage	F	VF	XF	Unc	BU
2009P Proof	1,000	Value: 250				

KM# 1585 50 EURO
163.8000 g., 0.9500 Silver 5.0028 oz. ASW, 50 mm. **Subject:** Court of Human Rights, 50th Anniversary **Obv:** Sower left **Rev:** Text

Date	Mintage	F	VF	XF	Unc	BU
2009P Proof	500	Value: 275				

KM# 1592 50 EURO
8.4500 g., 0.9200 Gold 0.2499 oz. AGW, 22 mm. **Subject:** Europa - Fall of Berlin Wall **Obv:** Brandenburg gate and doves in flight **Rev:** Head facing and flags

Date	Mintage	F	VF	XF	Unc	BU
2009P	1,000	Value: 400				

KM# 1598 50 EURO
8.4500 g., 0.9200 Gold 0.2499 oz. AGW, 22 mm. **Subject:** Concorde 40th Anniversary **Obv:** Concorde in flight **Rev:** Tail emblems

Date	Mintage	F	VF	XF	Unc	BU
2009P Proof	3,000	Value: 375				

KM# 1604 50 EURO
8.4500 g., 0.9200 Gold 0.2499 oz. AGW, 22 mm. **Obv:** Eiffel Tower Structure **Rev:** Gustave Eiffel at left

Date	Mintage	F	VF	XF	Unc	BU
2009P Proof	1,000	Value: 400				

KM# 1608 50 EURO
163.8000 g., 0.9500 Silver 5.0028 oz. ASW, 50 mm. **Subject:** Bugatti 100th Anniversary **Obv:** Ettore Bugatti at left **Rev:** Race car and grill motif

Date	Mintage	F	VF	XF	Unc	BU
2009P Proof	500	Value: 275				

KM# 1609 50 EURO
8.4500 g., 0.9200 Gold 0.2499 oz. AGW, 22 mm. **Subject:** Bugatti 100th Anniversary **Obv:** Ettore Bugatti at left **Rev:** Race car and grill motif

Date	Mintage	F	VF	XF	Unc	BU
2009P Proof	1,000	Value: 400				

KM# 1613 50 EURO
163.8000 g., 0.9500 Silver 5.0028 oz. ASW, 30 mm. **Subject:** Curie Institute, 100th Anniversary

Date	Mintage	F	VF	XF	Unc	BU
2009P Proof	500	Value: 275				

KM# 1614 50 EURO
8.4500 g., 0.9200 Gold 0.2499 oz. AGW, 22 mm. **Subject:** Curie Institute, 100th Anniversary

Date	Mintage	F	VF	XF	Unc	BU
2009P Proof	1,000	Value: 400				

KM# 1618 50 EURO
8.4500 g., 0.9200 Gold 0.2499 oz. AGW, 22 mm. **Subject:** Unesco site - the Kremlin in Moscow **Obv:** Wall Tower and cathedral

Date	Mintage	F	VF	XF	Unc	BU
2009P Proof	1,000	Value: 400				

KM# 1622 50 EURO
163.8000 g., 0.9500 Silver 5.0028 oz. ASW, 50 mm. **Subject:** First Moon Landing, 40th Anniversary **Obv:** Footprint on the moon

Date	Mintage	F	VF	XF	Unc	BU
2009P Proof	500	Value: 275				

KM# 1623 50 EURO
8.4500 g., 0.9200 Gold 0.2499 oz. AGW, 22 mm. **Subject:** First Moon Landing, 40th Anniversary **Obv:** Footprint on the moon

Date	Mintage	F	VF	XF	Unc	BU
2009P Proof	1,000	Value: 400				

KM# 1628 50 EURO
8.4500 g., 0.9200 Gold 0.2499 oz. AGW, 22 mm. **Subject:** Year of the Ox **Obv:** Oxen within Asian screen **Rev:** Portrait of LaFontaine

Date	Mintage	F	VF	XF	Unc	BU
2009P Proof	500	Value: 425				

KM# 1630 50 EURO
8.4500 g., 0.9200 Gold 0.2499 oz. AGW, 22 mm. **Subject:** Comic strip heroes **Obv:** Wanted Poster **Rev:** Lucky Luke on horseback

Date	Mintage	F	VF	XF	Unc	BU
2009P Proof	1,000	Value: 400				

KM# 1632 50 EURO
8.4500 g., 0.9200 Gold 0.2499 oz. AGW, 22 mm. **Obv:** Rugby player **Rev:** State Francais

Date	Mintage	F	VF	XF	Unc	BU
2009P Proof	500	Value: 425				

KM# 1635 50 EURO
8.4500 g., 0.9200 Gold 0.2499 oz. AGW, 22 mm. **Subject:** Alpine skiing **Obv:** Globe and downhill skier **Rev:** Downhill skier on mountainside

Date	Mintage	F	VF	XF	Unc	BU
2009P Proof	1,000	Value: 400				

KM# 1637 50 EURO
163.8000 g., 0.9500 Silver 5.0028 oz. ASW, 50 mm. **Subject:** FIFA World Cup, South Africa 2010 **Obv:** Soccer player on field **Rev:** Soccerball, Map of Africa, Protrea flower

Date	Mintage	F	VF	XF	Unc	BU
2009P Proof	500	Value: 275				

KM# 1638 50 EURO
8.4500 g., 0.9200 Gold 0.2499 oz. AGW, 22 mm. **Subject:** FIFA World Cup, South Africa 2010 **Obv:** Soccer Player on field **Rev:** Soccerball, Map of Africa, Protea flower

Date	Mintage	F	VF	XF	Unc	BU
2009P Proof	7,500	Value: 375				

KM# 1644 50 EURO
36.0000 g., 0.9000 Silver 1.0416 oz. ASW, 36 mm. **Obv:** The Seed Sower advancing right, sun rays from above **Rev:** Value at center, wreath horizontal

Date	Mintage	F	VF	XF	Unc	BU
2010	100,000	—	—	—	—	45.00

KM# 1673 50 EURO
8.4500 g., 0.9200 Gold 0.2499 oz. AGW, 22 mm. **Obv:** The Seed Sower left **Rev:** Wheat and olive branch

Date	Mintage	F	VF	XF	Unc	BU
2010 Proof	500	Value: 425				

KM# 1679 50 EURO
8.4500 g., 0.9250 Gold 0.2513 oz. AGW, 22 mm. **Subject:** Cluny Abbey, 1100th Anniversary **Obv:** Europa head facing **Rev:** Cluney Abbey

Date	Mintage	F	VF	XF	Unc	BU
2010 Proof	1,000	Value: 400				

KM# 1684 50 EURO
8.4500 g., 0.9200 Gold 0.2499 oz. AGW, 22 mm. **Obv:** Georges Pompidou Center design **Rev:** Design detail

Date	Mintage	F	VF	XF	Unc	BU
2010 Proof	3,000	Value: 400				

KM# 1685 50 EURO
163.8000 g., 0.9500 Silver 5.0028 oz. ASW, 50 mm. **Obv:** Georges Pompidou Center design **Rev:** Design detail

Date	Mintage	F	VF	XF	Unc	BU
2010 Proof	1,000	Value: 225				

KM# 1688 50 EURO
8.4500 g., 0.9200 Gold 0.2499 oz. AGW, 22 mm. **Obv:** Marcel Dassault **Rev:** Mirage III plane

Date	Mintage	F	VF	XF	Unc	BU
2010 Proof	1,000	Value: 400				

KM# 1694 50 EURO
8.4500 g., 0.9200 Gold 0.2499 oz. AGW, 22 mm. **Obv:** Mother Teresa and child **Rev:** Mother Teresa and Pope John Paul II

Date	Mintage	F	VF	XF	Unc	BU
2010 Proof	1,000	Value: 400				

KM# 1699 50 EURO
8.4500 g., 0.9200 Gold 0.2499 oz. AGW, 22 mm. **Obv:** Taj Mahal **Rev:** UNESCO offices

Date	Mintage	F	VF	XF	Unc	BU
2010 Proof	1,000	Value: 400				

KM# 1702 50 EURO
8.4500 g., 0.9200 Gold 0.2499 oz. AGW, 22 mm. **Obv:** Lille station and route map **Rev:** Three TGV trains

Date	Mintage	F	VF	XF	Unc	BU
2010 Proof	1,000	Value: 400				

KM# 1703 50 EURO
163.8000 g., 0.9500 Silver 5.0028 oz. ASW, 50 mm. **Obv:** Lille station and route map **Rev:** Three TGV trains

Date	Mintage	F	VF	XF	Unc	BU
2010 Proof	500	Value: 275				

KM# 1714 50 EURO
8.4500 g., 0.9200 Gold 0.2499 oz. AGW, 22 mm. **Obv:** Tiger within border **Rev:** La Fontaine bust at left, animals at right

Date	Mintage	F	VF	XF	Unc	BU
2010 Proof	500	Value: 425				

KM# 1716 50 EURO
8.4500 g., 0.9200 Gold 0.2499 oz. AGW, 22 mm. **Obv:** Blake and Mortimer **Rev:** "Secret of the Swordfish" scene, the arrest of Col. Olrik

Date	Mintage	F	VF	XF	Unc	BU
2010 Proof	500	Value: 425				

KM# 1719 50 EURO
8.4500 g., 0.9200 Gold 0.2499 oz. AGW, 22 mm. **Obv:** Handball player on globe **Rev:** Handball player, net, Big Ben

Date	Mintage	F	VF	XF	Unc	BU
2010 Proof	1,000	Value: 400				

KM# 1786 50 EURO
8.4500 g., 0.9200 Gold 0.2499 oz. AGW, 22 mm. **Subject:** Euro Starter Kit, 10th Anniversary **Obv:** Sower **Rev:** Euro starter kit

Date	Mintage	F	VF	XF	Unc	BU
2011 Proof	3,000	Value: 450				

KM# 1792 50 EURO
8.4500 g., 0.9200 Gold 0.2499 oz. AGW, 22 mm. **Subject:** International Music Day, 30th Anniversary **Obv:** Europa **Rev:** Youth jamming

Date	Mintage	F	VF	XF	Unc	BU
2011 Proof	3,000	Value: 450				

KM# 1796 50 EURO
8.4500 g., 0.9200 Gold 0.2499 oz. AGW, 22 mm. **Subject:** Great Explorers - Jacques Cartier **Obv:** The Grande Hermine sailing away **Rev:** Carter, globe and compass rose

Date	Mintage	F	VF	XF	Unc	BU
2011 Proof	3,000	Value: 450				

KM# 1801 50 EURO
8.4500 g., 0.9200 Gold 0.2499 oz. AGW, 22 mm. **Subject:** Clovis, 466-511 **Obv:** Crowned head left **Rev:** Hands over chalice, riegn dates at left, value at right

Date	Mintage	F	VF	XF	Unc	BU
2011 Proof	1,500	Value: 450				

KM# 1803 50 EURO
8.4500 g., 0.9200 Gold 0.2499 oz. AGW, 22 mm. **Subject:** Charlemagne, 742-814 **Obv:** Crowned head left **Rev:** Cross on globe, reign dates at left, value at right

Date	Mintage	F	VF	XF	Unc	BU
2011 Proof	1,500	Value: 450				

KM# 1805 50 EURO
8.4500 g., 0.9200 Gold 0.2499 oz. AGW, 22 mm. **Subject:** Charles II, 823-877 **Obv:** Crowned head left

Date	Mintage	F	VF	XF	Unc	BU
2011 Proof	1,500	Value: 450				

KM# 1807 50 EURO
8.4500 g., 0.9200 Gold 0.2499 oz. AGW, 22 mm. **Subject:** WWF - Audouin's Gull **Obv:** Gull in flight right **Rev:** Gull standing right, WWF logo at right

Date	Mintage	F	VF	XF	Unc	BU
2011 Proof	1,000	Value: 450				

KM# 1811 50 EURO
8.4500 g., 0.9200 Gold 0.2499 oz. AGW, 22 mm. **Subject:** UNESCO World Heritage Site - Palace of Versailles

Date	Mintage	F	VF	XF	Unc	BU
2011 Proof	1,000	Value: 450				

KM# 1816 50 EURO
163.8000 g., 0.9500 Silver 5.0028 oz. ASW, 50 mm. **Obv:** Metz railroad station **Rev:** TGV and ICE trains

Date	Mintage	F	VF	XF	Unc	BU
2011 Proof	500	Value: 250				

KM# 1817 50 EURO
8.4500 g., 0.9200 Gold 0.2499 oz. AGW, 22 mm. **Obv:** Metz railroad station **Rev:** TGV and ICE trains

Date	Mintage	F	VF	XF	Unc	BU
2011 Proof	1,000	Value: 450				

KM# 1828 50 EURO
8.4500 g., 0.9200 Gold 0.2499 oz. AGW, 22 mm. **Obv:** Cosette - Les Miserables **Rev:** Victor Hugo

Date	Mintage	F	VF	XF	Unc	BU
2011 Proof	3,000	Value: 450				

KM# 1830 50 EURO
8.4500 g., 0.9200 Gold 0.2499 oz. AGW, 22 mm. **Obv:** Nana **Rev:** Emile Zola

Date	Mintage	F	VF	XF	Unc	BU
2011 Proof	1,000	Value: 450				

KM# 1832 50 EURO
8.4500 g., 0.9200 Gold 0.2499 oz. AGW, 22 mm. **Obv:** The Stranger **Rev:** Albert Camus

Date	Mintage	F	VF	XF	Unc	BU
2011 Proof	—	Value: 450				

KM# 1834 50 EURO
8.4500 g., 0.9200 Gold 0.2499 oz. AGW, 22 mm. **Subject:** Year of the Rabbit **Obv:** Fontaine and animals **Rev:** Rabbit seated facing right

Date	Mintage	F	VF	XF	Unc	BU
2011 Proof	500	Value: 450				

KM# 1837 50 EURO
8.4500 g., 0.9200 Gold 0.2499 oz. AGW, 22 mm. **Obv:** Profile left and XIII **Rev:** Comic Characters

Date	Mintage	F	VF	XF	Unc	BU
2011 Proof	1,000	Value: 450				

KM# 1756 50 EURO
8.4500 g., 0.9200 Gold 0.2499 oz. AGW, 22 mm. **Obv:** Bicycle racer **Rev:** Metro 92 logo

Date	Mintage	F	VF	XF	Unc	BU
2011 Proof	500	Value: 450				

KM# 1839 50 EURO
8.4500 g., 0.9200 Gold 0.2499 oz. AGW, 22 mm. **Obv:** Female figure skater on globe **Rev:** Figure skating pair

Date	Mintage	F	VF	XF	Unc	BU
2011 Proof	1,000	Value: 450				

KM# 1304 100 EURO
155.5175 g., 0.9990 Gold 4.9948 oz. AGW, 50 mm. **Subject:** Europa **Obv:** Eight French euro coin designs **Rev:** Portrait and flags design of 6.55957 francs KM-1265 **Edge:** Plain

Date	Mintage	F	VF	XF	Unc	BU
2002 Proof	99	Value: 7,750				

KM# 1377 100 EURO
155.5175 g., 0.9990 Gold 4.9948 oz. AGW, 50 mm. **Subject:** D-Day 60th Anniversary **Obv:** Soldiers and Normandy invasion scene **Rev:** "D-Day" inscription above denomination **Edge:** Plain

Date	Mintage	F	VF	XF	Unc	BU
2004 Proof	299	Value: 7,500				

KM# 1389 100 EURO
155.5000 g., 0.9990 Gold 4.9942 oz. AGW, 50 mm. **Obv:** Statue of Liberty **Rev:** F. A. Bartholdi **Edge:** Plain

Date	Mintage	F	VF	XF	Unc	BU
2004 Proof	99	Value: 7,750				

KM# 1395 100 EURO
155.5500 g., 0.9990 Gold 4.9958 oz. AGW, 50 mm. **Subject:** European Union Expansion **Obv:** Partial face and flags **Rev:** Puzzle map **Edge:** Plain

Date	Mintage	F	VF	XF	Unc	BU
2004 Proof	99	Value: 7,750				

KM# 1482 100 EURO
155.5500 g., 0.9990 Gold 4.9958 oz. AGW, 50 mm. **Subject:** Airbus A380 **Rev:** Europa head and flags

Date	Mintage	F	VF	XF	Unc	BU
2007 Proof	99	Value: 7,750				

KM# 1497 100 EURO
155.5000 g., 0.9990 Gold 4.9942 oz. AGW, 50 mm. **Subject:** Cannes Film Festival, 60th Anniversary **Obv:** Cinema screen and stage, Golden Palm Award

Date	Mintage	F	VF	XF	Unc	BU
2007 Proof	99	Value: 7,750				

KM# 1531 100 EURO
155.5000 g., 0.9990 Gold 4.9942 oz. AGW, 50 mm. **Subject:** French Presidency of the European Union **Obv:** Text within stars **Rev:** Europa head and flags

Date	Mintage	F	VF	XF	Unc	BU
2008 Proof	99	Value: 7,750				

KM# 1536 100 EURO
3.1000 g., 0.9990 Gold 0.0996 oz. AGW, 15 mm. **Obv:** The Seed Sower, full length **Rev:** Hexagon

Date	Mintage	F	VF	XF	Unc	BU
2008 Proof	—	Value: 175				

KM# 1545 100 EURO
155.5000 g., 0.9990 Gold 4.9942 oz. AGW, 50 mm. **Subject:** 29th Summer Olympic Games - Beijing **Obv:** Swimmer and globe **Rev:** Diver and oriental screen

Date	Mintage	F	VF	XF	Unc	BU
2008 Proof	99	Value: 7,750				

KM# 1565 100 EURO
155.5000 g., 0.9990 Gold 4.9942 oz. AGW, 50 mm. **Subject:** Lourdes, 150th Anniversary **Obv:** Church of Notre Dame at Lourdes **Rev:** Cross with Pope John Paul II, Pope Benedict XVI and Bernadette Soubirous in quadrants

Date	Mintage	F	VF	XF	Unc	BU
2008 Proof	99	Value: 7,750				

KM# 1582 100 EURO
3.1000 g., 0.9990 Gold 0.0996 oz. AGW, 15 mm. **Obv:** Modernistic sower advancing right **Rev:** Value and wreath

Date	Mintage	F	VF	XF	Unc	BU
2009P	50,000	—	—	—	—	175

KM# 1588 100 EURO
17.0000 g., 0.9200 Gold 0.5028 oz. AGW, 31 mm. **Subject:** Court of Human Rights, 50th Anniversary **Obv:** The Seed Sower left **Rev:** Text

Date	Mintage	F	VF	XF	Unc	BU
2009P Proof	500	Value: 800				

KM# 1626 100 EURO
17.0000 g., 0.9200 Gold 0.5028 oz. AGW, 30x21 mm. **Subject:** Renoir **Obv:** Le dejuner des canotiers, 1881 painting **Rev:** Brushes and portrait **Shape:** Rectangle

Date	Mintage	F	VF	XF	Unc	BU
2009P Proof	500	Value: 800				

KM# 1643 100 EURO
3.1000 g., 0.9990 Gold 0.0996 oz. AGW, 15 mm. **Obv:** The Seed Sower advancing right, sun rays from above **Rev:** Value in center, wreath horizontal

Date	Mintage	F	VF	XF	Unc	BU
2010	50,000	—	—	—	—	175

KM# 1672 100 EURO
17.0000 g., 0.9200 Silver 0.5028 oz. ASW, 31 mm. **Obv:** The Seed Sower left **Rev:** Wheat and olive branch

Date	Mintage	F	VF	XF	Unc	BU
2010 Proof	500	Value: 35.00				

KM# 1689 100 EURO
327.6000 g., 0.9500 Silver 10.005 oz. ASW, 65 mm. **Obv:** Marcel Dassault **Rev:** Mirage III plane

Date	Mintage	F	VF	XF	Unc	BU
2010 Proof	500	Value: 375				

KM# 1707 100 EURO
17.0000 g., 0.9200 Gold 0.5028 oz. AGW, 30x21 mm. **Rev:** Georges Braque **Shape:** Rectangle

Date	Mintage	F	VF	XF	Unc	BU
2010 Proof	500	Value: 800				

KM# 1711 100 EURO
17.0000 g., 0.9200 Gold 0.5028 oz. AGW, 30x21 mm. **Rev:** Picasso **Shape:** Rectangle

Date	Mintage	F	VF	XF	Unc	BU
2010 Proof	500	Value: 800				

KM# 1724 100 EURO
50.0000 g., 0.9000 Silver 1.4467 oz. ASW, 47 mm. **Obv:** Value at center, wreath horizontal **Rev:** Hercules goup

Date	Mintage	F	VF	XF	Unc	BU
2011	50,000	—	—	—	—	150

KM# 1787 100 EURO
17.0000 g., 0.9200 Gold 0.5028 oz. AGW, 31 mm. **Subject:** Euro Starter Kit, 10th Anniversary **Obv:** Sower **Rev:** Euro starter kit

Date	Mintage	F	VF	XF	Unc	BU
2011 Proof	500	Value: 800				

KM# 1820 100 EURO
17.0000 g., 0.9200 Gold 0.5028 oz. AGW, 30x21 mm. **Subject:** Vassily Kandinsky **Shape:** Rectangle

Date	Mintage	F	VF	XF	Unc	BU
2011 Proof	500	Value: 800				

KM# 1824 100 EURO
17.0000 g., 0.9200 Gold 0.5028 oz. AGW, 30x21 mm. **Subject:** Andy Warhol **Shape:** Rectangle

Date	Mintage	F	VF	XF	Unc	BU
2011 Proof	500	Value: 800				

KM# 1836 100 EURO
327.6000 g., 0.9500 Silver 10.005 oz. ASW, 75 mm. **Obv:** Profile left and XIII **Rev:** Comic Characters

Date	Mintage	F	VF	XF	Unc	BU
2011 Proof	500	Value: 400				

KM# 1589 200 EURO
31.1040 g., 0.9990 Gold 0.9990 oz. AGW, 37 mm. **Subject:** Court of Human Rights - 50th Anniversary **Obv:** The Seed Sower left **Rev:** Text

Date	Mintage	F	VF	XF	Unc	BU
2009P Proof	500	Value: 1,650				

KM# 1593 200 EURO
31.1040 g., 0.9990 Gold 0.9990 oz. AGW, 37 mm. **Subject:** Europa - Fall of Berlin Wall **Obv:** Brandenburg gate and doves in flight **Rev:** Head facing and flags

Date	Mintage	F	VF	XF	Unc	BU
2009P Proof	500	Value: 1,650				

KM# 1624 200 EURO
31.1040 g., 0.9990 Gold 0.9990 oz. AGW, 37 mm. **Subject:** First Moon Landing, 40th Anniversary **Obv:** Footprint on the moon

Date	Mintage	F	VF	XF	Unc	BU
2009P Proof	1,000	Value: 1,600				

KM# 1639 200 EURO
31.1040 g., 0.9990 Gold 0.9990 oz. AGW, 37 mm. **Subject:** FIFA World Cup, South Africa 2010 **Obv:** Soccer player on field **Rev:** Soccerball, Map of Africa, Protea flower **Shape:** 37

Date	Mintage	F	VF	XF	Unc	BU
2009P Proof	500	Value: 1,650				

KM# 1678 200 EURO
31.1040 g., 0.9990 Gold 0.9990 oz. AGW, 37 mm. **Subject:** Cluny Abbey, 1100th Anniversary **Obv:** Europa head facing **Rev:** Cluny Abbey

Date	Mintage	F	VF	XF	Unc	BU
2010 Proof	500	Value: 1,650				

KM# 1683 200 EURO
31.1040 g., 0.9990 Gold 0.9990 oz. AGW, 37 mm. **Obv:** Georges Pompidou Center design **Rev:** Design detail

Date	Mintage	F	VF	XF	Unc	BU
2010 Proof	500	Value: 1,650				

KM# 1693 200 EURO
31.1040 g., 0.9990 Gold 0.9990 oz. AGW, 37 mm. **Obv:** Mother Teresa and child **Rev:** Mother Teresa and Pope John Paul II

Date	Mintage	F	VF	XF	Unc	BU
2010 Proof	500	Value: 1,650				

KM# 1698 200 EURO
31.1040 g., 0.9990 Gold 0.9990 oz. AGW, 37 mm. **Obv:** Taj Mahal **Rev:** UNESCO offices

Date	Mintage	F	VF	XF	Unc	BU
2010 Proof	1,000	Value: 1,600				

KM# 1701 200 EURO
31.1040 g., 0.9990 Gold 0.9990 oz. AGW, 37 mm. **Obv:** Lille station and route map **Rev:** Three TGV trains

Date	Mintage	F	VF	XF	Unc	BU
2010 Proof	500	Value: 1,650				

KM# 1757 200 EURO
4.0000 g., 0.9990 Gold 0.1285 oz. AGW, 21 mm. **Subject:** Aquitaine

Date	Mintage	F	VF	XF	Unc	BU
2011	—	—	—	—	—	300

KM# 1758 200 EURO
4.0000 g., 0.9990 Gold 0.1285 oz. AGW, 21 mm. **Subject:** Auvergne

Date	Mintage	F	VF	XF	Unc	BU
2011	—	—	—	—	—	300

KM# 1759 200 EURO
4.0000 g., 0.9990 Gold 0.1285 oz. AGW, 21 mm. **Subject:** Basse - Normandie

Date	Mintage	F	VF	XF	Unc	BU
2011	—	—	—	—	—	300

KM# 1760 200 EURO
4.0000 g., 0.9990 Gold 0.1285 oz. AGW, 21 mm. **Subject:** Bretagne

Date	Mintage	F	VF	XF	Unc	BU
2011	—	—	—	—	—	300

KM# 1761 200 EURO
4.0000 g., 0.9990 Gold 0.1285 oz. AGW, 21 mm. **Rev. Designer:** Burgundy

Date	Mintage	F	VF	XF	Unc	BU
2011	—	—	—	—	—	300

KM# 1762 200 EURO
4.0000 g., 0.9990 Gold 0.1285 oz. AGW, 21 mm. **Subject:** Centre

Date	Mintage	F	VF	XF	Unc	BU
2011	—	—	—	—	—	300

KM# 1763 200 EURO
4.0000 g., 0.9990 Gold 0.1285 oz. AGW, 21 mm. **Subject:** Campaigne - Ardenne

Date	Mintage	F	VF	XF	Unc	BU
2011	—	—	—	—	—	300

KM# 1764 200 EURO
4.0000 g., 0.9990 Gold 0.1285 oz. AGW, 21 mm. **Subject:** Alsace

Date	Mintage	F	VF	XF	Unc	BU
2011	—	—	—	—	—	300

KM# 1765 200 EURO
4.0000 g., 0.9990 Gold 0.1285 oz. AGW, 21 mm. **Subject:** France - Comte

Date	Mintage	F	VF	XF	Unc	BU
2011	—	—	—	—	—	300

KM# 1766 200 EURO
4.0000 g., 0.9990 Gold 0.1285 oz. AGW, 21 mm. **Subject:** French Guiana

Date	Mintage	F	VF	XF	Unc	BU
2011	—	—	—	—	—	300

KM# 1767 200 EURO
4.0000 g., 0.9990 Gold 0.1285 oz. AGW, 21 mm. **Subject:** Guadeloupe

Date	Mintage	F	VF	XF	Unc	BU
2011	—	—	—	—	—	300

KM# 1768 200 EURO
4.0000 g., 0.9990 Gold 0.1285 oz. AGW, 21 mm. **Subject:** Haute - Normandie

Date	Mintage	F	VF	XF	Unc	BU
2011	—	—	—	—	—	300

KM# 1769 200 EURO
4.0000 g., 0.9990 Gold 0.1285 oz. AGW, 21 mm. **Subject:** Corsica

Date	Mintage	F	VF	XF	Unc	BU
2011	—	—	—	—	—	300

KM# 1770 200 EURO
4.0000 g., 0.9990 Gold 0.1285 oz. AGW, 21 mm. **Subject:** Lansuedoc Rossillon

Date	Mintage	F	VF	XF	Unc	BU
2011	—	—	—	—	—	300

KM# 1771 200 EURO
4.0000 g., 0.9990 Gold 0.1285 oz. AGW, 21 mm. **Subject:** Limousin

Date	Mintage	F	VF	XF	Unc	BU
2011	—	—	—	—	—	300

KM# 1772 200 EURO
4.0000 g., 0.9990 Gold 0.1285 oz. AGW, 21 mm. **Subject:** Lorraine

Date	Mintage	F	VF	XF	Unc	BU
2011	—	—	—	—	—	300

KM# 1773 200 EURO
4.0000 g., 0.9990 Gold 0.1285 oz. AGW, 21 mm. **Subject:** Martinique

Date	Mintage	F	VF	XF	Unc	BU
2011	—	—	—	—	—	300

KM# 1774 200 EURO
4.0000 g., 0.9990 Gold 0.1285 oz. AGW, 21 mm. **Subject:** Nord Pas de Calais

Date	Mintage	F	VF	XF	Unc	BU
2011	—	—	—	—	—	300

KM# 1775 200 EURO
4.0000 g., 0.9990 Gold 0.1285 oz. AGW, 21 mm. **Subject:** Pays de la Loire

Date	Mintage	F	VF	XF	Unc	BU
2011	—	—	—	—	—	300

KM# 1776 200 EURO
4.0000 g., 0.9990 Gold 0.1285 oz. AGW, 21 mm. **Subject:** Picardie

Date	Mintage	F	VF	XF	Unc	BU
2011	—	—	—	—	—	300

KM# 1777 200 EURO
4.0000 g., 0.9990 Gold 0.1285 oz. AGW, 21 mm. **Subject:** Poitou - Charentes

Date	Mintage	F	VF	XF	Unc	BU
2011	—	—	—	—	—	300

KM# 1778 200 EURO
4.0000 g., 0.9990 Gold 0.1285 oz. AGW, 21 mm. **Subject:** Province - Alpes - Cote d'Azur

Date	Mintage	F	VF	XF	Unc	BU
2011	—	—	—	—	—	300

KM# 1779 200 EURO
4.0000 g., 0.9990 Gold 0.1285 oz. AGW, 21 mm. **Subject:** Reunion

Date	Mintage	F	VF	XF	Unc	BU
2011	—	—	—	—	—	300

KM# 1780 200 EURO
4.0000 g., 0.9990 Gold 0.1285 oz. AGW, 21 mm. **Subject:** Phone - Alpes

Date	Mintage	F	VF	XF	Unc	BU
2011	—	—	—	—	—	300

KM# 1781 200 EURO
4.0000 g., 0.9990 Gold 0.1285 oz. AGW, 21 mm. **Subject:** Ile de France

Date	Mintage	F	VF	XF	Unc	BU
2011	—	—	—	—	—	300

KM# 1782 200 EURO
4.0000 g., 0.9990 Gold 0.1285 oz. AGW, 21 mm. **Subject:** Mayotte

Date	Mintage	F	VF	XF	Unc	BU
2011	—	—	—	—	—	300

KM# 1783 200 EURO
4.0000 g., 0.9990 Gold 0.1285 oz. AGW, 21 mm. **Subject:** Midi Pyrenees

Date	Mintage	F	VF	XF	Unc	BU
2011	—	—	—	—	—	300

KM# 1793 200 EURO
31.1040 g., 0.9990 Gold 0.9990 oz. AGW, 37 mm. **Subject:** International Music Day, 30th Anniversary **Obv:** Europa **Rev:** Youth jamming

Date	Mintage	F	VF	XF	Unc	BU
2011 Proof	500	Value: 1,600				

KM# 1797 200 EURO
31.1040 g., 0.9990 Gold 0.9990 oz. AGW, 37 mm. **Subject:** Great Explorers - Jacques Cartier **Obv:** The Grande Hermine sailing away **Rev:** Cartier, globe and compass rose

Date	Mintage	F	VF	XF	Unc	BU
2011 Proof	500	Value: 1,550				

KM# 1808 200 EURO
31.1040 g., 0.9990 Gold 0.9990 oz. AGW, 37 mm. **Subject:** WWF - Audouin's Gull **Obv:** Gull in flight right **Rev:** Gull standing right, WWF logo right

Date	Mintage	F	VF	XF	Unc	BU
2011 Proof	500	Value: 1,550				

KM# 1583 250 EURO
8.4500 g., 0.9200 Gold 0.2499 oz. AGW, 22 mm. **Obv:** Modernistic sower advancing right **Rev:** Value and wreath

Date	Mintage	F	VF	XF	Unc	BU
2009P	25,000	—	—	—	—	375

KM# 1671 250 EURO
62.2080 g., 0.9990 Gold 1.9979 oz. AGW, 37 mm. **Obv:** The Seed Sower left **Rev:** Wheat and olive branch

Date	Mintage	F	VF	XF	Unc	BU
2010 Proof	500	Value: 3,000				

KM# 1788 250 EURO
62.2080 g., 0.9990 Gold 1.9979 oz. AGW, 37 mm. **Subject:** Euro Starter Kit, 10th Anniversary **Obv:** Sower **Rev:** Euro starter kit **Note:** Thick planchet.

Date	Mintage	F	VF	XF	Unc	BU
2011 Proof	500	Value: 3,250				

KM# 1396 500 EURO
1000.0000 g., 0.9990 Gold 32.117 oz. AGW, 85 mm. **Subject:** European Union Expansion **Obv:** Partial face and flags **Rev:** Puzzle map **Edge:** Plain **Note:** Illustration reduced.

Date	Mintage	F	VF	XF	Unc	BU
2004 Proof, Rare	20	—	—	—	—	—

KM# 1594 500 EURO
155.5000 g., 0.9990 Gold 4.9942 oz. AGW, 50 mm. **Subject:** Europa - Fall of Berlin Wall **Obv:** Brandenburg gate and doves in flight **Rev:** Head facing and flags

Date	Mintage	F	VF	XF	Unc	BU
2009P Proof	99	Value: 7,750				

KM# 1599 500 EURO
155.5000 g., 0.9990 Gold 4.9942 oz. AGW, 50 mm. **Subject:** Concorde 40th Anniversary **Obv:** Concorde in flight **Rev:** Tail emblems

Date	Mintage	F	VF	XF	Unc	BU
2009P Proof	99	Value: 7,750				

KM# 1605 500 EURO
155.5000 g., 0.9990 Gold 4.9942 oz. AGW, 50 mm. **Obv:** Eiffel Tower Structure **Rev:** Gustave Eiffel at left

Date	Mintage	F	VF	XF	Unc	BU
2009P Proof	99	Value: 7,750				

KM# 1610 500 EURO
155.5000 g., 0.9990 Gold 4.9942 oz. AGW, 50 mm. **Subject:** Bugatti 100th Anniversary **Obv:** Ettore Bugatti at left **Rev:** Race car and grill motif

Date	Mintage	F	VF	XF	Unc	BU
2009P Proof	99	Value: 7,750				

KM# 1615 500 EURO
155.5000 g., 0.9990 Gold 4.9942 oz. AGW, 50 mm. **Subject:** Curie Institute, 100th Anniversary

Date	Mintage	F	VF	XF	Unc	BU
2009P Proof	99	Value: 7,750				

KM# 1619 500 EURO
155.5000 g., 0.9990 Gold 4.9942 oz. AGW, 50 mm. **Subject:** Unesco site - The Kremlin in Moscow **Obv:** Wall Tower and cathedral

Date	Mintage	F	VF	XF	Unc	BU
2009P Proof	99	Value: 7,750				

KM# 1640 500 EURO
155.5000 g., 0.9990 Gold 4.9942 oz. AGW, 50 mm. **Subject:** FIFA World Cup, South Africa 2010 **Obv:** Soccer player on field **Rev:** Soccerball, Map of Africa, Protea flower

Date	Mintage	F	VF	XF	Unc	BU
2009P Proof	99	Value: 7,750				

KM# 1642 500 EURO
12.0000 g., 0.9990 Gold 0.3854 oz. AGW, 31 mm. **Obv:** The Seed Sower advancing right, sun rays from below **Rev:** Value in center, wreath horizontal

Date	Mintage	F	VF	XF	Unc	BU
2010	25,000	—	—	—	—	625

KM# 1687 500 EURO
155.5000 g., 0.9990 Gold 4.9942 oz. AGW, 50 mm. **Obv:** Marcel Dassault **Rev:** Mirage III plane

Date	Mintage	F	VF	XF	Unc	BU
2010 Proof	99	Value: 7,750				

KM# 1692 500 EURO
155.5000 g., 0.9990 Gold 4.9942 oz. AGW, 50 mm. **Obv:** Mother Teresa and child **Rev:** Mother Teresa and Pope John Paul II

Date	Mintage	F	VF	XF	Unc	BU
2010 Proof	99	Value: 7,750				

KM# 1697 500 EURO
155.5000 g., 0.9990 Gold 4.9942 oz. AGW, 50 mm. **Obv:** Taj Mahal **Rev:** UNESCO offices

Date	Mintage	F	VF	XF	Unc	BU
2010 Proof	99	Value: 7,750				

KM# 1706 500 EURO
155.5000 g., 0.9990 Gold 4.9942 oz. AGW **Obv:** Doves **Rev:** Georges Baraque **Shape:** 50

Date	Mintage	F	VF	XF	Unc	BU
2010 Proof	99	Value: 7,750				

KM# 1710 500 EURO
155.5000 g., 0.9990 Gold 4.9942 oz. AGW, 50 mm. **Rev:** Picasso

Date	Mintage	F	VF	XF	Unc	BU
2010 Proof	99	Value: 7,750				

KM# 1712 500 EURO
1000.0000 g., 9.5000 Silver 305.41 oz. ASW, 100 mm. **Rev:** Picasso

Date	Mintage	F	VF	XF	Unc	BU
2010 Proof	500	Value: 1,250				

KM# 1718 500 EURO
155.5000 g., 0.9990 Gold 4.9942 oz. AGW, 50 mm. **Obv:** Handball player on globe **Rev:** Handball player, net, Big Ben

Date	Mintage	F	VF	XF	Unc	BU
2010 Proof	99	Value: 7,750				

KM# 1798 500 EURO
155.5000 g., 0.9990 Gold 4.9942 oz. AGW, 50 mm. **Subject:** Great Explorers - Jacques Cartier **Obv:** The Grande Hermine sailing away **Rev:** Cartier, globe and compass rose

Date	Mintage	F	VF	XF	Unc	BU
2011 Proof	99	Value: 8,000				

KM# 1812 500 EURO
155.5000 g., 0.9990 Gold 4.9942 oz. AGW, 50 mm. **Subject:** UNESCO World Heritage Site - Palace of Versailles

Date	Mintage	F	VF	XF	Unc	BU
2011 Proof	99	Value: 8,000				

KM# 1821 500 EURO
155.5000 g., 0.9990 Gold 4.9942 oz. AGW, 53x37 mm. **Subject:** Vassily Kandinsky **Shape:** Rectangle

Date	Mintage	F	VF	XF	Unc	BU
2011 Proof	99	Value: 8,000				

KM# 1825 500 EURO
155.5000 g., 0.9990 Gold 4.9942 oz. AGW, 53x37 mm. **Subject:** Andy Warhol **Shape:** Rectangle

Date	Mintage	F	VF	XF	Unc	BU
2011 Proof	99	Value: 8,000				

KM# 1595 1000 EURO
311.0000 g., 0.9990 Gold 9.9885 oz. AGW, 65 mm. **Subject:** Europa - Fall of Berlin Wall **Obv:** Brandenburg gate and doves in flight **Rev:** Head facing and flags

Date	Mintage	F	VF	XF	Unc	BU
2009P Proof	20	Value: 15,500				

KM# 1600 1000 EURO
311.0000 g., 0.9990 Gold 9.9885 oz. AGW, 65 mm. **Subject:** Concorde 40 Anniversary **Obv:** Concorde in flight **Rev:** Tail emblems

Date	Mintage	F	VF	XF	Unc	BU
2009P Proof	20	Value: 15,500				

KM# 1677 1000 EURO
31.1000 g., 0.9990 Gold 0.9988 oz. AGW, 65 mm. **Subject:** Cluny Abbey, 1100th Anniversary **Obv:** Europa head facing **Rev:** Cluny Abby view

Date	Mintage	F	VF	XF	Unc	BU
2010 Proof	39	Value: 15,500				

KM# 1682 1000 EURO
311.0000 g., 0.9990 Gold 9.9885 oz. AGW, 65 mm. **Obv:** Georges Pompidou Center design **Rev:** Design detail

Date	Mintage	F	VF	XF	Unc	BU
2010 Proof	39	Value: 15,500				

KM# 1725 1000 EURO
20.0000 g., 0.9990 Gold 0.6423 oz. AGW, 39 mm. **Obv:** Value at center, wreath horizontal **Rev:** Hercules goup

Date	Mintage	F	VF	XF	Unc	BU
2011	10,000	—	—	—	—	1,450

KM# 1794 1000 EURO
311.0000 g., 0.9990 Gold 9.9885 oz. AGW, 65 mm. **Subject:** International Music Day, 30th Anniversary **Obv:** Europa **Rev:** Youth jamming

Date	Mintage	F	VF	XF	Unc	BU
2011 Proof	39	Value: 16,000				

KM# 1799 1000 EURO
311.0000 g., 0.9990 Gold 9.9885 oz. AGW, 65 mm. **Subject:** Great Explorers - Jacques Cartier **Obv:** The Grande Hermine sailing away **Rev:** Cartier, globe and compass rose

Date	Mintage	F	VF	XF	Unc	BU
2011 Proof	39	Value: 15,000				

KM# 1620 5000 EURO
1000.0000 g., 0.9990 Gold 32.117 oz. AGW, 85 mm. **Subject:** Unesco site - The Kremlin in Moscow **Obv:** Wall Tower and cathedral

Date	Mintage	F	VF	XF	Unc	BU
2009P Proof	39	Value: 47,500				

KM# 1696 5000 EURO
1000.0000 g., 0.9990 Gold 32.117 oz. AGW, 85 mm. **Obv:** Taj Mahal and diamond inserts **Rev:** UNESCO offices

Date	Mintage	F	VF	XF	Unc	BU
2010 Proof	29	Value: 47,500				

KM# 1709 5000 EURO
1000.0000 g., 0.9990 Gold 32.117 oz. AGW, 85 mm. **Rev:** Picasso

Date	Mintage	F	VF	XF	Unc	BU
2010 Proof	29	Value: 47,500				

KM# 1813 5000 EURO
1000.0000 g., 0.9990 Gold 32.117 oz. AGW, 85 mm. **Subject:** UNESCO World Heritage Site - Palace of Versailles

Date	Mintage	F	VF	XF	Unc	BU
2011 Proof	29	Value: 48,000				

KM# 1822 5000 EURO
1000.0000 g., 0.9990 Gold 32.117 oz. AGW, 90x63 mm. **Subject:** Vassily Kandinsky **Shape:** Rectangle

Date	Mintage	F	VF	XF	Unc	BU
2011 Proof	29	Value: 48,000				

KM# 1826 5000 EURO
1000.0000 g., 0.9990 Gold 32.117 oz. AGW, 90x63 mm. **Subject:** Andy Warhol **Shape:** Rectangle

Date	Mintage	F	VF	XF	Unc	BU
2011 Proof	29	Value: 48,000				

MINT SETS

KM#	Date	Mintage	Identification	Issue Price	Mkt Val
MS20	2001 (2)	10,000	KM#925.1a, 928a	—	475
MS21	2001 (8)	35,000	KM#1282-1289	20.25	20.00
MS22	2002 (8)	35,000	KM#1282-1289	20.25	40.00
MS23	2003 (8)	—	KM#1282-89	—	55.00
MS24	2004 (8)	—	KM#1282-1289	—	45.00
MS25	2005 (8)	—	KM#1282-1289	—	45.00
MS26	2005 (8)	40,000	KM#1282-1289 Moebius set plus token	45.00	45.00
MS27	2005 (8)	10,000	KM1282-1289, French Memories - Bordeaux	45.00	45.00
MS28	2006 (8)	70,000	KM#1282-1289	36.50	42.50
MS29	2006 (8)	500	KM#1282-1289, Denver, Colorado special ANA Coin Convention Set	45.00	70.00
MS30	2006 (8)	500	KM#1282-1289, Berlin Coin Fair set	45.00	55.00
MS31	2006 (8)	500	KM1282-1289, Pierre Curie set	45.00	50.00
MS32	2006 (8)	500	KM#1282-1289, Musee de la Monnaie set	45.00	50.00
MS33	2006 (8)	500	KM#1282-1289, Journees du Patrimoine set	45.00	50.00
MS34	2006 (8)	500	KM#1282-1289, Bourgogne set	45.00	50.00
MS35	2006 (8)	500	KM#1282-1289, "Coree set" (Korea)	45.00	50.00
MS36	2006 (8)	500	KM#1282-1289, Nord Pas-de-Calais set	45.00	50.00
MS37	2006 (8)	500	KM#1282-1289, Jacques Chirac set	45.00	50.00
MS38	2006 (8)	500	KM#1282-1289, Mitterand & Khol	45.00	50.00
MS39	2006 (8)	500	KM#1282-1289, Birthday 1 set	45.00	45.00
MS40	2006 (8)	500	KM#1282-1289, Birthday 2 set	45.00	45.00
MS41	2006 (8)	500	KM#1282-1289, Tokyo set	45.00	50.00
MS42	2006 (8)	500	KM#1282-1289, Viaduc de Millau set	45.00	50.00
MS43	2006 (8)	500	KM#1282-1289, Ile-de-France set	45.00	50.00

PROOF SETS

KM#	Date	Mintage	Identification	Issue Price	Mkt Val
PS21	2001 (8)	15,000	KM#1282-1289	59.00	125
PS22	2002 (8)	40,000	KM#1282-1289	59.00	110
PS23	2003 (5)	150,000	KM#1321, 1322, 1323, 1324, 1325	—	260
PS24	2003 (5)	5,000	KM#1326, 1327, 1328, 1329, 1330	—	1,900

FRENCH POLYNESIA

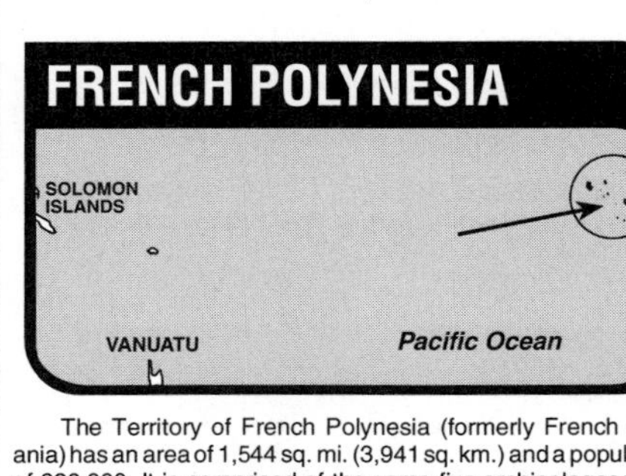
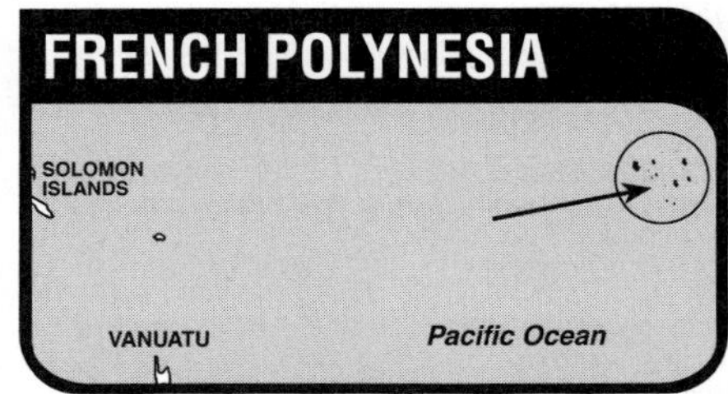

The Territory of French Polynesia (formerly French Oceania) has an area of 1,544 sq. mi. (3,941 sq. km.) and a population of 220,000. It is comprised of the same five archipelagoes that were grouped administratively to form French Oceania.

The colony of French Oceania became the Territory of French Polynesia by act of the French National Assembly in March, 1957. In Sept. of 1958 it voted in favor of the new constitution of the Fifth Republic, thereby electing to remain within the new French Community.

Picturesque, mountainous Tahiti, the setting of many tales of adventure and romance, is one of the most inspiringly beautiful islands in the world. Robert Louis Stevenson called it 'God's sweetest works'. It was there that Paul Gaugin, one of the pioneers of the Impressionist movement, painted the brilliant, exotic pictures that later made him famous. The arid coral atolls of Tuamotu comprise the most economically valuable area of French Polynesia. Pearl oysters thrive in the warm, limpid lagoons, and extensive portions of the atolls are valuable phosphate rock.

RULER
French

MINT MARK
(a) - Paris, privy marks only

MONETARY SYSTEM
100 Centimes = 1 Franc

FRENCH OVERSEAS TERRITORY

DECIMAL COINAGE

KM# 11 FRANC
1.3000 g., Aluminum, 23 mm. **Obv:** Seated Liberty with torch and cornucopia right, date below, legend added flanking figure's feet **Obv. Legend:** I. E. O. M. **Obv. Designer:** G.B.L. Bazor **Rev:** Legend and island scene divide denomination

Date	Mintage	F	VF	XF	Unc	BU
2001(a)	2,900,000	—	—	—	0.50	1.00
2002(a)	1,600,000	—	—	—	0.50	1.00
2003(a)	4,200,000	—	—	—	0.50	1.00
2004(a)	2,400,000	—	—	—	0.50	1.00
2005(a)	—	—	—	—	0.50	1.00
2006(a)	2,100,000	—	—	—	0.50	1.00
2007(a) Coin rotation	3,400,000	—	—	—	0.50	1.00
2007(a) Medal rotation	Inc. above	—	—	—	—	30.00
2008(a)	4,800,000	—	—	—	0.50	1.00

KM# 10 2 FRANCS
2.3000 g., Aluminum, 27 mm. **Obv:** Seated Liberty with torch and cornucopia right, date below, legend added flanking figure's feet **Obv. Legend:** I. E. O. M. **Obv. Designer:** G.B.L. Bazor **Rev:** Legend and island scene divide denomination

Date	Mintage	F	VF	XF	Unc	BU
2001(a)	2,400,000	—	—	—	0.75	1.50
2002(a)	2,500,000	—	—	—	0.75	1.50
2003(a)	3,200,000	—	—	—	0.75	1.50
2004(a)	3,000,000	—	—	—	0.75	1.50
2005(a)	900,000	—	—	—	0.75	1.50
2006(a)	1,600,000	—	—	—	0.75	1.50
2007(a)	640,000	—	—	—	0.75	1.50
2008(a)	1,900,000	—	—	—	0.75	1.50

KM# 12 5 FRANCS
3.7500 g., Aluminum, 31 mm. **Obv:** Seated Liberty with torch and cornucopia right, date below, legend added flanking figure's feet **Obv. Legend:** I. E. O. M. **Obv. Designer:** G.B.L. Bazor **Rev:** Legend and island divide denomination

Date	Mintage	F	VF	XF	Unc	BU
2001(a)	1,600,000	—	—	—	1.00	2.00
2002(a)	400,000	—	—	—	1.00	2.00
2003(a)	1,000,000	—	—	—	1.00	2.00
2004(a)	600,000	—	—	—	1.00	2.00
2005(a)	600,000	—	—	—	1.00	2.00
2006(a)	720,000	—	—	—	1.00	2.00
2007(a)	1,000,000	—	—	—	1.00	2.00
2008(a)	1,060,000	—	—	—	1.00	2.00

KM# 8 10 FRANCS
6.0000 g., Nickel, 24 mm. **Obv:** Capped head left, date and legend below **Obv. Legend:** I. E. O. M. **Obv. Designer:** R. Joly **Rev:** Native art, denomination below **Rev. Designer:** A. Guzman **Edge:** Reeded

Date	Mintage	F	VF	XF	Unc	BU
2001(a)	500,000	—	—	—	1.25	2.75
2002(a)	600,000	—	—	—	1.25	2.75
2003(a)	1,000,000	—	—	—	1.25	2.75
2004(a)	600,000	—	—	—	1.25	2.75
2005(a)	200,000	—	—	—	1.25	2.75

KM# 8a 10 FRANCS
6.0000 g., Copper-Nickel, 24 mm. **Obv:** Capped head left, date and legend below **Obv. Legend:** I. E. O. M. **Rev:** Native art, denomination below **Edge:** Reeded

Date	Mintage	F	VF	XF	Unc	BU
2006(a)	620,000	—	—	—	1.25	2.75
2007(a)	800,000	—	—	—	1.25	2.75
2008(a)	820,000	—	—	—	1.25	2.75

KM# 9 20 FRANCS
10.0000 g., Nickel, 28.3 mm. **Obv:** Capped head left, date and legend below **Obv. Legend:** I. E. O. M. **Obv. Designer:** R. Joly **Rev:** Flowers, vanilla shoots, bread fruit **Rev. Designer:** A. Guzman **Edge:** Reeded

Date	Mintage	F	VF	XF	Unc	BU
2001(a)	500,000	—	—	—	1.75	3.25
2002(a)	—	—	—	—	1.75	3.25
2003(a)	700,000	—	—	—	1.75	3.00
2004(a)	600,000	—	—	—	1.75	3.00
2005(a)	30,000	—	—	—	20.00	30.00

KM# 9a 20 FRANCS
10.0000 g., Copper-Nickel, 28.3 mm. **Obv:** Capped head left, date and legend below **Obv. Legend:** I. E. O. M. **Rev:** Flowers, vanilla shoots, bread fruit **Edge:** Reeded

Date	Mintage	F	VF	XF	Unc	BU
2006(a)	300,000	—	—	—	1.75	3.00
2007(a)	450,000	—	—	—	1.75	3.00
2008(a)	610,000	—	—	—	1.75	3.00

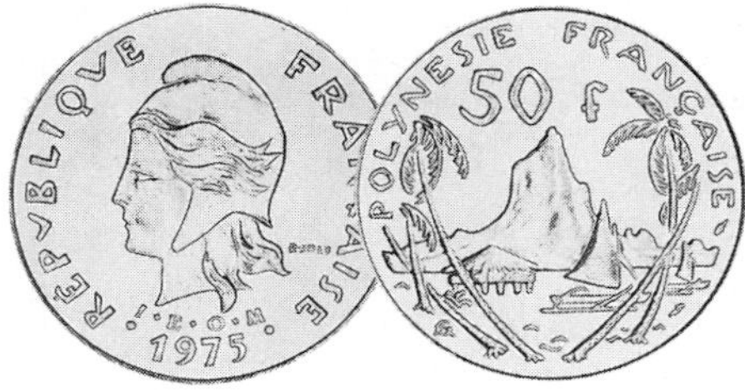

KM# 13 50 FRANCS
15.0000 g., Nickel, 33 mm. **Obv:** Capped head left, date and legend below **Obv. Legend:** I. E. O. M. **Obv. Designer:** R. Joly **Rev:** Denomination above Moorea Harbor **Rev. Designer:** A. Guzman **Edge:** Reeded

Date	Mintage	F	VF	XF	Unc	BU
2001(a)	300,000	—	—	—	2.00	4.00
2002(a)	—	—	—	—	2.00	4.00
2003(a)	240,000	—	—	—	2.00	4.00
2004(a)	100,000	—	—	—	2.00	4.00
2005(a)	100,000	—	—	—	2.00	4.00

KM# 13a 50 FRANCS
15.0000 g., Copper-Nickel, 33 mm. **Obv:** Capped head left, date and legend below **Obv. Legend:** I. E. O. M. **Rev:** Denomination above Moorea Harbor **Edge:** Reeded

Date	Mintage	F	VF	XF	Unc	BU
2006(a)	15,000	—	—	—	3.00	5.00
2007(a)	310,000	—	—	—	2.00	4.00
2008(a)	200,000	—	—	—	2.00	4.00
2009(a)	—	—	—	—	2.00	4.00

KM# 14 100 FRANCS
10.0000 g., Nickel-Bronze, 30 mm. **Obv:** Capped head left, date below **Obv. Designer:** R. Joly **Rev:** Denomination above Moorea Harbor **Rev. Designer:** A. Guzman **Edge:** Reeded

Date	Mintage	F	VF	XF	Unc	BU
2001(a)	200,000	—	—	—	3.00	5.00
2002(a)	—	—	—	—	3.00	5.00
2003(a)	600,000	—	—	—	2.75	5.00
2004(a)	450,000	—	—	—	2.75	5.00
2005(a)	300,000	—	—	—	2.75	5.00

KM# 14a 100 FRANCS
10.0000 g., Aluminum-Bronze, 30 mm. **Obv:** Capped head left, date below **Obv. Legend:** I. E. O. M. **Obv. Designer:** R. Joly **Rev:** Denomination above Moorea Harbor **Rev. Designer:** A. Guzman **Edge:** Reeded

Date	Mintage	F	VF	XF	Unc	BU
2006(a)	200,000	—	—	—	2.75	5.00
2007(a)	650,000	—	—	—	2.75	5.00
2008(a)	690,000	—	—	—	2.75	5.00
2009(a)	—	—	—	—	2.75	5.00

MINT SETS

KM#	Date	Mintage	Identification	Issue Price	Mkt Val
MS1	2001 (7)	3,000	KM#8-14	—	22.50
MS2	2002 (7)	5,000	KM#8-14	—	22.50
MS3	2003 (7)	3,000	KM#8-14	—	22.50

Georgia (formerly the Georgian Social Democratic Republic under the U.S.S.R.), is bounded by the Black Sea to the west and by Turkey, Armenia and Azerbaijan. It occupies the western part of Transcaucasia covering an area of 26,900 sq. mi. (69,700 sq. km.) and a population of 5.7 million. Capitol: Tbilisi. Hydro-electricity, minerals, forestry and agriculture are the chief industries.

Germano-- Georgian treaty was signed on May 28, 1918, followed by a Turko-Georgian peace treaty on June 4. The end of WW I and the collapse of the central powers allowed free The collapse of the U.S.S.R. allowed full transition to independence and on April 9, 1991 a unanimous vote declared the republic an independent state based on its original treaty of independence of May 1918.

MONETARY SYSTEM
100 Thetri = 1 Lari

INDEPENDENT STATE (C.I.S.)

STANDARD COINAGE

KM# 89 50 THETRI
6.5200 g., Copper-Nickel, 24 mm. **Obv:** National arms **Rev:** Value **Edge:** Reeded and lettered

Date	Mintage	F	VF	XF	Unc	BU
2006	—	—	—	—	3.00	4.00

KM# 90 LARI
7.8500 g., Copper-Nickel, 26.2 mm. **Obv:** National arms **Rev:** Value **Edge:** Reeded and lettered

Date	Mintage	F	VF	XF	Unc	BU
2006	—	—	—	—	5.00	6.50

KM# 95 LARI
28.2800 g., 0.9990 Silver 0.9083 oz. ASW **Subject:** World Cup Soccer **Obv:** Map of Georgia, flag **Rev:** World Cup trophy, two soccer players

Date	Mintage	F	VF	XF	Unc	BU
2006 Proof	50,000	Value: 45.00				

KM# 92 2 LARI
12.9200 g., Copper-Nickel, 31 mm. **Obv:** Trophy cup, value and date **Rev:** UFFA Winners Cup and soccer player **Edge:** Plain

Date	Mintage	F	VF	XF	Unc	BU
2006	10,000	—	—	—	—	18.00

KM# 94 2 LARI
8.0600 g., Bi-Metallic Brass center in Copper-Nickel ring, 27 mm. **Obv:** National arms **Rev:** Large value **Edge:** Reeded and lettered

Date	Mintage	F	VF	XF	Unc	BU
2006	—	—	—	—	7.50	9.00

KM# 103 2 LARI
28.2800 g., 0.9250 Silver 0.8410 oz. ASW, 38.61 mm. **Obv:** Trophy cup, value and date **Rev:** UFFA Winners Cup and soccer player

Date	Mintage	F	VF	XF	Unc	BU
2006 Proof	6,000	Value: 50.00				

KM# 93 3 LARI
12.8000 g., Copper-Nickel, 31 mm. **Obv:** Three oil wells **Rev:** Map with "Baku-Tbilisi-Ceyhan" route **Edge:** Lettered

Date	Mintage	F	VF	XF	Unc	BU
2006	3,000	—	—	—	—	25.00

KM# 102 3 LARI
28.2800 g., Silver, 38.61 mm. **Obv:** Three oil wells **Rev:** Map with "Baku-Tbilisi-Ceyhan" route

Date	Mintage	F	VF	XF	Unc	BU
2006 Proof	5,000	Value: 50.00				

KM# 106 10 LARI
28.2800 g., 0.9250 Silver 0.8410 oz. ASW, 38.61 mm. **Subject:** St. George's Day **Obv:** Drawing of church by Don Christoforo de Castelli **Rev:** Church of St. george in Ilora

Date	Mintage	F	VF	XF	Unc	BU
2009 Proof	1,500	Value: 50.00				

KM# 104 20 LARI
28.2800 g., 0.9250 Silver 0.8410 oz. ASW, 38.61 mm. **Obv:** Two classical runners **Rev:** Exterior of Bird's Nest Stadium, torch

Date	Mintage	F	VF	XF	Unc	BU
2008 Proof	1,500	Value: 50.00				

KM# 105 20 LARI
8.5000 g., 0.9000 Gold 0.2459 oz. AGW, 25 mm. **Obv:** Two classical runners **Rev:** Exterior of Bird's Nest Stadium, torch

Date	Mintage	F	VF	XF	Unc	BU
2008 Proof	—	Value: 450				

BULLION COINAGE

KM# 96 10 LARI
3.1100 g., 0.9990 Gold 0.0999 oz. AGW, 16 mm. **Obv:** Ancient sailing vessel, trade route **Rev:** Golden Fleece

Date	Mintage	F	VF	XF	Unc	BU
2006	4,000	—	—	—	—	175

KM# 97 25 LARI
7.7800 g., 0.9990 Gold 0.2499 oz. AGW, 22 mm. **Obv:** Ancient sailing ship trade route map **Rev:** Golden Feece

Date	Mintage	F	VF	XF	Unc	BU
2006	—	—	—	—	—	450

KM# 98 50 LARI
28.0000 g., 0.9990 Gold 0.8993 oz. AGW, 28 mm. **Obv:** Ancient sailing ship, trade route map **Rev:** Golden Fleece

Date	Mintage	F	VF	XF	Unc	BU
2006	—	—	—	—	—	1,400

KM# 99 100 LARI
31.1050 g., 0.9990 Gold 0.9990 oz. AGW, 37 mm. **Obv:** Ancient sailing ship, trade route map **Rev:** Golden Fleece

Date	Mintage	F	VF	XF	Unc	BU
2006	—	—	—	—	—	1,550

KM# 100 300 LARI
155.5000 g., 0.9990 Gold 4.9942 oz. AGW, 50 mm. **Obv:** Ancient sailing ship, trade route map **Rev:** Golden Fleece

Date	Mintage	F	VF	XF	Unc	BU
2006	—	—	—	—	—	7,500

KM# 101 1000 LARI
311.0000 g., 0.9990 Gold 9.9885 oz. AGW, 60 mm. **Obv:** Ancient sailing ship, trade route map **Rev:** Golden Fleece

Date	Mintage	F	VF	XF	Unc	BU
2006	—	—	—	—	—	15,500

1949-

The Federal Republic of Germany, located in north-central Europe, has an area of 137,744 sq. mi. (356,910sq. km.) and a population of 81.1 million. Capital: Berlin. The economy centers about one of the world's foremost industrial establishments. Machinery, motor vehicles, iron, steel, yarns and fabrics are exported.

MINT MARKS
A - Berlin
D - Munich
F - Stuttgart
G - Karlsruhe
J - Hamburg

MONETARY SYSTEM
100 Pfennig = 1 Deutsche Mark (DM)

FEDERAL REPUBLIC

STANDARD COINAGE

KM# 105 PFENNIG
2.0000 g., Copper Plated Steel, 16.5 mm. **Obv:** Five oak leaves, date below **Obv. Legend:** BUNDESREPUBLIK DEUTSCHLAND **Rev:** Denomination

Date	Mintage	F	VF	XF	Unc	BU
2001A In sets only	130,000	—	—	—	5.00	—
2001A Proof	78,000	Value: 5.00				
2001D In sets only	130,000	—	—	—	5.00	—
2001D Proof	78,000	Value: 5.00				
2001F In sets only	130,000	—	—	—	5.00	—
2001F Proof	78,000	Value: 5.00				
2001G In sets only	130,000	—	—	—	5.00	—
2001G Proof	78,000	Value: 5.00				
2001J In sets only	130,000	—	—	—	5.00	—
2001J Proof	78,000	Value: 5.00				

KM# 106a 2 PFENNIG
2.9000 g., Copper Plated Steel, 19.25 mm. **Obv:** Five oak leaves, date below **Rev:** Denomination

Date	Mintage	F	VF	XF	Unc	BU
2001A In sets only	130,000	—	—	—	5.00	—
2001A Proof	78,000	Value: 5.00				
2001D In sets only	130,000	—	—	—	5.00	—
2001D Proof	78,000	Value: 5.00				
2001F In sets only	130,000	—	—	—	5.00	—
2001F Proof	78,000	Value: 5.00				
2001G In sets only	130,000	—	—	—	5.00	—
2001G Proof	78,000	Value: 5.00				
2001J In sets only	130,000	—	—	—	5.00	—
2001J Proof	78,000	Value: 5.00				

KM# 107 5 PFENNIG

3.0000 g., Brass Clad Steel, 18.5 mm. **Obv:** Five oak leaves, date below **Obv. Legend:** BUNDESREPUBLIK DEUTSCHLAND **Rev:** Denomination

Date	Mintage	F	VF	XF	Unc	BU
2001A In sets only	130,000	—	—	—	5.00	—
2001A Proof	78,000	Value: 5.00				
2001D In sets only	130,000	—	—	—	5.00	—
2001D Proof	78,000	Value: 5.00				
2001F In sets only	130,000	—	—	—	5.00	—
2001F Proof	78,000	Value: 5.00				
2001G In sets only	130,000	—	—	—	5.00	—
2001G Proof	78,000	Value: 5.00				
2001J In sets only	130,000	—	—	—	5.00	—
2001J Proof	78,000	Value: 5.00				

KM# 108 10 PFENNIG

4.0000 g., Brass Clad Steel, 21.5 mm. **Obv:** Five oak leaves, date below **Obv. Legend:** BUNDESREPUBLIK DEUTSCHLAND **Rev:** Denomination **Edge:** Plain

Date	Mintage	F	VF	XF	Unc	BU
2001A In sets only	130,000	—	—	—	5.00	—
2001A Proof	78,000	Value: 5.00				
2001D In sets only	130,000	—	—	—	5.00	—
2001D Proof	78,000	Value: 5.00				
2001F In sets only	130,000	—	—	—	5.00	—
2001F Proof	78,000	Value: 5.00				
2001G In sets only	130,000	—	—	—	5.00	—
2001G Proof	78,000	Value: 5.00				
2001J In sets only	130,000	—	—	—	5.00	—
2001J Proof	78,000	Value: 5.00				

KM# 109.2 50 PFENNIG

3.5000 g., Copper-Nickel, 20 mm. **Obv:** Denomination **Obv. Legend:** BUNDESREPUBLIK DEUTSCHLAND **Rev:** Woman planting an oak seedling **Edge:** Plain

Date	Mintage	F	VF	XF	Unc	BU
2001A In sets only	130,000	—	—	—	10.00	—
2001A Proof	78,000	Value: 10.00				
2001D In sets only	130,000	—	—	—	10.00	—
2001D Proof	78,000	Value: 10.00				
2001F In sets only	130,000	—	—	—	10.00	—
2001F Proof	78,000	Value: 10.00				
2001G In sets only	130,000	—	—	—	10.00	—
2001G Proof	78,000	Value: 10.00				
2001J In sets only	130,000	—	—	—	10.00	—
2001J Proof	78,000	Value: 10.00				

KM# 110 MARK

5.5000 g., Copper-Nickel, 23.5 mm. **Obv:** Eagle **Rev:** Denomination flanked by oak leaves, date below

Date	Mintage	F	VF	XF	Unc	BU
2001A In sets only	130,000	—	—	—	15.00	—
2001A Proof	78,000	Value: 15.00				
2001D In sets only	130,000	—	—	—	15.00	—
2001D Proof	78,000	Value: 15.00				
2001F In sets only	130,000	—	—	—	15.00	—
2001F Proof	78,000	Value: 15.00				
2001G In sets only	130,000	—	—	—	15.00	—
2001G Proof	78,000	Value: 15.00				
2001J In sets only	130,000	—	—	—	15.00	—
2001J Proof	78,000	Value: 15.00				

KM# 203 MARK

11.8500 g., 0.9990 Gold 0.3806 oz. AGW, 23.5 mm. **Subject:** Retirement of the Mark Currency **Obv:** Eagle **Rev:** Denomination flanked by oak leaves, date below **Edge:** Arabeskes

Date	Mintage	F	VF	XF	Unc	BU
2001A Proof	200,000	Value: 600				
2001D Proof	200,000	Value: 600				
2001G Proof	200,000	Value: 600				
2001J Proof	200,000	Value: 600				
2001F Proof	200,000	Value: 600				

KM# 170 2 MARK

7.0000 g., Copper-Nickel Clad Nickel, 26.75 mm. **Subject:** Ludwig Erhard **Obv:** Eagle above denomination **Rev:** Head facing divides dates **Edge Lettering:** EINIGKEIT UND RECHT UND FREIHEIT

Date	Mintage	F	VF	XF	Unc	BU
2001A In sets only	130,000	—	—	—	10.00	—
2001A Proof	78,000	Value: 10.00				
2001D In sets only	130,000	—	—	—	10.00	—
2001D Proof	78,000	Value: 10.00				
2001F In sets only	130,000	—	—	—	10.00	—
2001F Proof	78,000	Value: 10.00				
2001G In sets only	130,000	—	—	—	10.00	—
2001G Proof	78,000	Value: 10.00				
2001J In sets only	130,000	—	—	—	10.00	—
2001J Proof	78,000	Value: 10.00				

KM# 175 2 MARK

7.0400 g., Copper-Nickel Clad Nickel, 26.8 mm. **Subject:** Franz Joseph Strauss **Obv:** Eagle above denomination **Rev:** Head left divides dates **Edge Lettering:** EINIGKEIT UND RECHT UND FREIHEIT

Date	Mintage	F	VF	XF	Unc	BU
2001A In sets only	130,000	—	—	—	10.00	—
2001A Proof	78,000	Value: 10.00				
2001D In sets only	130,000	—	—	—	10.00	—
2001D Proof	78,000	Value: 10.00				
2001F In sets only	130,000	—	—	—	10.00	—
2001F Proof	78,000	Value: 10.00				
2001G In sets only	130,000	—	—	—	10.00	—
2001G Proof	78,000	Value: 10.00				
2001J In sets only	130,000	—	—	—	10.00	—
2001J Proof	78,000	Value: 10.00				

KM# 183 2 MARK

7.0000 g., Copper-Nickel Clad Nickel, 26.75 mm. **Subject:** Willy Brandt **Obv:** Eagle above denomination **Rev:** Head facing divides dates **Edge Lettering:** EINIGKEIT UND RECHT UND FREIHEIT

Date	Mintage	F	VF	XF	Unc	BU
2001A In sets only	130,000	—	—	—	10.00	—
2001A Proof	78,000	Value: 10.00				
2001D In sets only	130,000	—	—	—	10.00	—
2001D Proof	78,000	Value: 10.00				
2001F In sets only	130,000	—	—	—	10.00	—
2001F Proof	78,000	Value: 10.00				
2001G In sets only	130,000	—	—	—	10.00	—
2001G Proof	78,000	Value: 10.00				

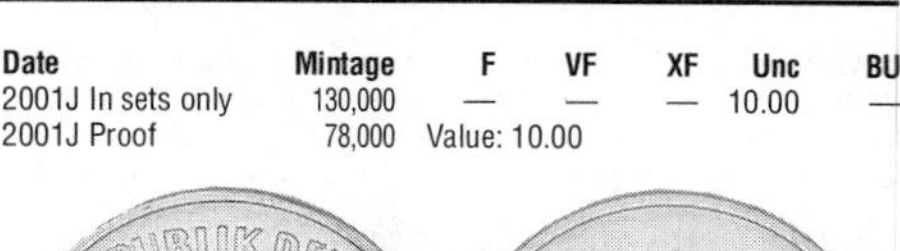

Date	Mintage	F	VF	XF	Unc	BU
2001J In sets only	130,000	—	—	—	10.00	—
2001J Proof	78,000	Value: 10.00				

KM# 140.1 5 MARK

10.0000 g., Copper-Nickel Clad Nickel, 29 mm. **Obv:** Denomination within rounded square **Rev:** Eagle above date **Edge Lettering:** EINIGKEIT UND RECHT UND FREIHEIT

Date	Mintage	F	VF	XF	Unc	BU
2001A In sets only	130,000	—	—	—	30.00	—
2001A Proof	78,000	Value: 30.00				
2001D In sets only	130,000	—	—	—	30.00	—
2001D Proof	78,000	Value: 30.00				
2001F In sets only	130,000	—	—	—	30.00	—
2001F Proof	78,000	Value: 30.00				
2001G In sets only	130,000	—	—	—	30.00	—
2001G Proof	78,000	Value: 30.00				
2001J In sets only	130,000	—	—	—	30.00	—
2001J Proof	78,000	Value: 30.00				

COMMEMORATIVE COINAGE

KM# 204 10 MARK

15.5000 g., 0.9250 Silver 0.4609 oz. ASW, 32.5 mm. **Obv:** Imperial eagle above denomination **Rev:** Naval Museum, Stralsund **Edge Lettering:** "OHNE WASSER KEIN LEBEN"

Date	Mintage	F	VF	XF	Unc	BU
2001A	2,500,000	—	—	—	16.50	17.50
2001A Proof	160,000	Value: 20.00				
2001D Proof	160,000	Value: 20.00				
2001F Proof	160,000	Value: 20.00				
2001G Proof	160,000	Value: 20.00				
2001J Proof	160,000	Value: 20.00				

KM# 205 10 MARK

15.5000 g., 0.9250 Silver 0.4609 oz. ASW, 32.5 mm. **Subject:** 200th Anniversary - Birth of Albert Gustav Lortzing **Obv:** Stylized eagle above denomination **Rev:** Portrait and music **Edge Lettering:** "WILDSCHUETZ * UNDINE" ZAR UND ZIMMERMANN"

Date	Mintage	F	VF	XF	Unc	BU
2001A Proof	160,000	Value: 20.00				
2001D Proof	160,000	Value: 20.00				
2001F Proof	160,000	Value: 20.00				
2001G Proof	160,000	Value: 20.00				
2001J	2,500,000	—	—	—	16.50	17.50
2001J Proof	160,000	Value: 20.00				

KM# 206 10 MARK

15.5000 g., 0.9250 Silver 0.4609 oz. ASW, 32.5 mm. **Subject:**

Federal Court of Constitution: 50th Anniversary **Obv:** Stylized eagle above denomination **Rev:** Justice holding books and scale **Edge:** Lettered

Date	Mintage	F	VF	XF	Unc	BU
2001A Proof	160,000	Value: 20.00				
2001D Proof	160,000	Value: 20.00				
2001F Proof	160,000	Value: 20.00				
2001G	2,500,000	—	—	—	16.50	17.50
2001G Proof	160,000	Value: 20.00				
2001J Proof	160,000	Value: 20.00				

EURO COINAGE

European Union Issues

KM# 207 EURO CENT

2.2700 g., Copper Plated Steel, 16.3 mm. **Obv:** Oak leaves **Obv. Designer:** Rolf Lederbogen **Rev:** Denomination and globe **Rev. Designer:** Luc Luycx **Edge:** Plain

Date	Mintage	F	VF	XF	Unc	BU
2002A	770,000,000	—	—	—	0.35	—
2002A Proof	130,000	Value: 1.00				
2002D	805,350,000	—	—	—	0.35	—
2002D Proof	130,000	Value: 1.00				
2002F	902,660,000	—	—	—	0.35	—
2002F Proof	130,000	Value: 1.00				
2002G	537,100,000	—	—	—	0.35	—
2002G Proof	130,000	Value: 1.00				
2002J	833,100,000	—	—	—	0.35	—
2002J Proof	130,000	Value: 1.00				
2003A In sets only	180,000	—	—	—	4.50	—
2003A Proof	150,000	Value: 1.00				
2003D In sets only	180,000	—	—	—	4.50	—
2003D Proof	150,000	Value: 1.00				
2003F In sets only	180,000	—	—	—	4.50	—
2003F Proof	150,000	Value: 1.00				
2003G In sets only	180,000	—	—	—	4.50	—
2003G Proof	150,000	Value: 1.00				
2003J In sets only	180,000	—	—	—	4.50	—
2003J Proof	150,000	Value: 1.00				
2004A	280,000,000	—	—	—	0.35	—
2004A Proof	—	Value: 1.00				
2004D	294,000,000	—	—	—	0.35	—
2004D Proof	—	Value: 1.00				
2004F	336,000,000	—	—	—	0.35	—
2004F Proof	—	Value: 1.00				
2004G	196,000,000	—	—	—	0.35	—
2004G Proof	—	Value: 1.00				
2004J	294,000,000	—	—	—	0.35	—
2004J Proof	—	Value: 1.00				
2005A	120,000,000	—	—	—	0.35	—
2005A Proof	—	Value: 1.00				
2005D	126,000,000	—	—	—	0.35	—
2005D Proof	—	Value: 1.00				
2005F	144,000,000	—	—	—	0.35	—
2005F Proof	—	Value: 1.00				
2005G	84,000,000	—	—	—	0.35	—
2005G Proof	—	Value: 1.00				
2005J	126,000,000	—	—	—	0.35	—
2005J Proof	—	Value: 1.00				
2006A In sets only	—	—	—	—	4.50	—
2006A Proof	—	Value: 1.00				
2006D In sets only	—	—	—	—	4.50	—
2006D Proof	—	Value: 1.00				
2006F In sets only	—	—	—	—	4.50	—
2006F Proof	—	Value: 1.00				
2006G In sets only	—	—	—	—	4.50	—
2006G Proof	—	Value: 1.00				
2006J In sets only	—	—	—	—	4.50	—
2006J Proof	—	Value: 1.00				
2007A	119,400,000	—	—	—	0.35	—
2007A Proof	—	Value: 1.00				
2007D	125,370,000	—	—	—	0.35	—
2007D Proof	—	Value: 1.00				
2007F	143,280,000	—	—	—	0.35	—
2007F Proof	—	Value: 1.00				
2007G	83,580,000	—	—	—	0.35	—
2007G Proof	—	Value: 1.00				
2007J	125,370,000	—	—	—	0.35	—
2007J Proof	—	Value: 1.00				
2008A	101,200,000	—	—	—	0.35	—
2008A Proof	—	Value: 1.00				
2008D	106,300,000	—	—	—	0.35	—
2008D Proof	—	Value: 1.00				
2008F	121,400,000	—	—	—	0.35	—
2008F Proof	—	Value: 1.00				
2008G	70,800,000	—	—	—	0.35	—
2008G Proof	—	Value: 1.00				
2008J	106,300,000	—	—	—	0.35	—
2008J Proof	—	Value: 1.00				
2009A	—	—	—	—	0.35	—
2009A Proof	—	Value: 1.00				
2009D	—	—	—	—	0.35	—
2009D Proof	—	Value: 1.00				
2009F	—	—	—	—	0.35	—
2009F Proof	—	Value: 1.00				
2009G	—	—	—	—	0.35	—
2009G Proof	—	Value: 1.00				
2009J	—	—	—	—	0.35	—
2009J Proof	—	Value: 1.00				
2010A	—	—	—	—	0.35	—
2010A Proof	—	Value: 1.00				
2010D	—	—	—	—	0.35	—
2010D Proof	—	Value: 1.00				
2010F	—	—	—	—	0.35	—
2010F Proof	—	Value: 1.00				
2010G	—	—	—	—	0.35	—
2010G Proof	—	Value: 1.00				
2010J	—	—	—	—	0.35	—
2010J Proof	—	Value: 1.00				

KM# 208 2 EURO CENT

3.1000 g., Copper Plated Steel, 18.8 mm. **Obv:** Oak leaves **Obv. Designer:** Rolf Lederbogen **Rev:** Denomination and globe **Rev. Designer:** Luc Luycx **Edge:** Grooved

Date	Mintage	F	VF	XF	Unc	BU
2002A	460,000,000	—	—	—	0.50	—
2002A Proof	130,000	Value: 1.50				
2002D	436,100,000	—	—	—	0.50	—
2002D Proof	130,000	Value: 1.50				
2002F	495,960,000	—	—	—	0.50	—
2002F Proof	130,000	Value: 1.50				
2002G	311,900,000	—	—	—	0.50	—
2002G Proof	130,000	Value: 1.50				
2002J	419,274,000	—	—	—	0.50	—
2002J Proof	130,000	Value: 1.50				
2003A	100,000,000	—	—	—	0.50	—
2003A Proof	150,000	Value: 1.50				
2003D	151,855,000	—	—	—	0.50	—
2003D Proof	150,000	Value: 1.50				
2003F	175,400,000	—	—	—	0.50	—
2003F Proof	150,000	Value: 1.50				
2003G	80,200,000	—	—	—	0.50	—
2003G Proof	150,000	Value: 1.50				
2003J	168,681,000	—	—	—	0.50	—
2003J Proof	150,000	Value: 1.50				
2004A	127,000,000	—	—	—	0.50	—
2004A Proof	—	Value: 1.50				
2004D	133,495,000	—	—	—	0.50	—
2004D Proof	—	Value: 1.50				
2004F	152,400,000	—	—	—	0.50	—
2004F Proof	—	Value: 1.50				
2004G	88,900,000	—	—	—	0.50	—
2004G Proof	—	Value: 1.50				
2004J	133,350,000	—	—	—	0.50	—
2004J Proof	—	Value: 1.50				
2005A	17,000,000	—	—	—	0.50	—
2005A Proof	—	Value: 1.50				
2005D	17,850,000	—	—	—	0.50	—
2005D Proof	—	Value: 1.50				
2005F	20,400,000	—	—	—	0.50	—
2005F Proof	—	Value: 1.50				
2005G	11,900,000	—	—	—	0.50	—
2005G Proof	—	Value: 1.50				
2005J	17,850,000	—	—	—	0.50	—
2005J Proof	—	Value: 1.50				
2006A	108,000,000	—	—	—	0.50	—
2006A Proof	—	Value: 1.50				
2006D	113,400,000	—	—	—	0.50	—
2006D Proof	—	Value: 1.50				
2006F	129,600,000	—	—	—	0.50	—
2006F Proof	—	Value: 1.50				
2006G	75,600,000	—	—	—	0.50	—
2006G Proof	—	Value: 1.50				
2006J	148,400,000	—	—	—	0.50	—
2006J Proof	—	Value: 1.50				
2007A	100,000,000	—	—	—	0.50	—
2007A Proof	—	Value: 1.50				
2007D	105,000,000	—	—	—	0.50	—
2007D Proof	—	Value: 1.50				
2007F	120,000,000	—	—	—	0.50	—
2007F Proof	—	Value: 1.50				
2007G	70,000,000	—	—	—	0.50	—
2007G Proof	—	Value: 1.50				
2007J	105,000,000	—	—	—	0.50	—
2007J Proof	—	Value: 1.50				
2008A	80,000,000	—	—	—	0.50	—
2008A Proof	—	Value: 1.50				
2008D	84,000,000	—	—	—	0.50	—
2008D Proof	—	Value: 1.50				
2008F	96,000,000	—	—	—	0.50	—
2008F Proof	—	Value: 1.50				
2008G	56,000,000	—	—	—	0.50	—
2008G Proof	—	Value: 1.50				
2008J	84,000,000	—	—	—	0.50	—
2008J Proof	—	Value: 1.50				
2009A	—	—	—	—	0.50	—
2009A Proof	—	Value: 1.50				
2009D	—	—	—	—	0.50	—
2009D Proof	—	Value: 1.50				
2009F	—	—	—	—	0.50	—
2009F Proof	—	Value: 1.50				
2009G	—	—	—	—	0.50	—
2009G Proof	—	Value: 1.50				
2009J	—	—	—	—	0.50	—
2009J Proof	—	Value: 1.50				
2010A	—	—	—	—	0.50	—
2010A Proof	—	Value: 1.50				
2010D	—	—	—	—	0.50	—
2010D Proof	—	Value: 1.50				
2010F	—	—	—	—	0.50	—
2010F Proof	—	Value: 1.50				
2010G	—	—	—	—	0.50	—
2010G Proof	—	Value: 1.50				
2010J	—	—	—	—	0.50	—
2010J Proof	—	Value: 1.50				

KM# 209 5 EURO CENT

4.0000 g., Copper Plated Steel, 21.3 mm. **Obv:** Oak leaves **Obv. Designer:** Rolf Lederbogen **Rev:** Denomination and globe **Rev. Designer:** Luc Luycx **Edge:** Plain

Date	Mintage	F	VF	XF	Unc	BU
2002A	475,000,000	—	—	—	0.75	—
2002A Proof	130,000	Value: 2.00				
2002D	495,700,000	—	—	—	0.75	—
2002D Proof	130,000	Value: 2.00				
2002F	563,710,000	—	—	—	0.75	—
2002F Proof	130,000	Value: 2.00				
2002G	328,400,000	—	—	—	0.75	—
2002G Proof	130,000	Value: 2.00				
2002J	501,850,000	—	—	—	0.75	—
2002J Proof	130,000	Value: 2.00				
2003A In sets only	180,000	—	—	—	4.50	—
2003A Proof	150,000	Value: 2.00				
2003D In sets only	180,000	—	—	—	4.50	—
2003D Proof	150,000	Value: 2.00				
2003F In sets only	180,000	—	—	—	4.50	—
2003F Proof	150,000	Value: 2.00				
2003G In sets only	180,000	—	—	—	4.50	—
2003G Proof	150,000	Value: 2.00				
2003J In sets only	180,000	—	—	—	4.50	—
2003J Proof	150,000	Value: 2.00				
2004A	112,000,000	—	—	—	0.75	—
2004A Proof	—	Value: 2.00				
2004D	117,600,000	—	—	—	0.75	—
2004D Proof	—	Value: 2.00				
2004F	134,400,000	—	—	—	0.75	—
2004F Proof	—	Value: 2.00				
2004G	78,400,000	—	—	—	0.75	—
2004G Proof	—	Value: 2.00				
2004J	117,600,000	—	—	—	0.75	—
2004J Proof	—	Value: 2.00				
2005A	44,000,000	—	—	—	0.75	—
2005A Proof	—	Value: 2.00				
2005D	46,200,000	—	—	—	0.75	—
2005D Proof	—	Value: 2.00				
2005F	52,800,000	—	—	—	0.75	—
2005F Proof	—	Value: 2.00				
2005G	30,800,000	—	—	—	0.75	—
2005G Proof	—	Value: 2.00				
2005J	46,200,000	—	—	—	0.75	—
2005J Proof	—	Value: 2.00				
2006A	27,000,000	—	—	—	0.75	—
2006A Proof	—	Value: 2.00				
2006D	28,350,000	—	—	—	0.75	—
2006D Proof	—	Value: 2.00				
2006F	32,400,000	—	—	—	0.75	—
2006F Proof	—	Value: 2.00				
2006G	18,900,000	—	—	—	0.75	—
2006G Proof	—	Value: 2.00				
2006J	28,350,000	—	—	—	0.75	—
2006J Proof	—	Value: 2.00				
2007A	52,400,000	—	—	—	0.75	—
2007A Proof	—	Value: 2.00				
2007D	55,020,000	—	—	—	0.75	—
2007D Proof	—	Value: 2.00				
2007F	62,880,000	—	—	—	0.75	—
2007F Proof	—	Value: 2.00				
2007G	38,680,000	—	—	—	0.75	—
2007G Proof	—	Value: 2.00				
2007J	55,020,000	—	—	—	0.75	—
2007J Proof	—	Value: 2.00				
2008A	29,200,000	—	—	—	0.75	—
2008A Proof	—	Value: 2.00				
2008D	30,700,000	—	—	—	0.75	—
2008D Proof	—	Value: 2.00				
2008F	35,000,000	—	—	—	0.75	—
2008F Proof	—	Value: 2.00				
2008G	20,400,000	—	—	—	0.75	—
2008G Proof	—	Value: 2.00				
2008J	30,700,000	—	—	—	0.75	—
2008J Proof	—	Value: 2.00				
2009A	—	—	—	—	0.75	—
2009A Proof	—	Value: 2.00				

Date	Mintage	F	VF	XF	Unc	BU
2009D	—	—	—	—	0.75	—
2009D Proof	—	Value: 2.00				
2009F	—	—	—	—	0.75	—
2009F Proof	—	Value: 2.00				
2009G	—	—	—	—	0.75	—
2009G Proof	—	Value: 2.00				
2009J	—	—	—	—	0.75	—
2009J Proof	—	Value: 2.00				
2010A	—	—	—	—	0.75	—
2010A Proof	—	Value: 2.00				
2010D	—	—	—	—	0.75	—
2010D Proof	—	Value: 2.00				
2010F	—	—	—	—	0.75	—
2010F Proof	—	Value: 2.00				
2010G	—	—	—	—	0.75	—
2010G Proof	—	Value: 2.00				
2010J	—	—	—	—	0.75	—
2010J Proof	—	Value: 2.00				

KM# 210 10 EURO CENT
4.0000 g., Brass, 19.7 mm. **Obv:** Brandenburg Gate **Obv. Designer:** Reinhard Heinsdorff **Rev:** Denomination and map **Rev. Designer:** Luc Luycx **Edge:** Reeded

Date	Mintage	F	VF	XF	Unc	BU
2002A	696,000,000	—	—	—	0.75	—
2002A Proof	130,000	Value: 2.00				
2002D	722,050,000	—	—	—	0.75	—
2002D Proof	130,000	Value: 2.00				
2002F	788,860,000	—	—	—	0.75	—
2002F Proof	130,000	Value: 2.00				
2002G	545,500,000	—	—	—	0.75	—
2002G Proof	130,000	Value: 2.00				
2002J	694,150,000	—	—	—	0.75	—
2002J Proof	130,000	Value: 2.00				
2003A	50,655,000	—	—	—	1.25	—
2003A Proof	150,000	Value: 2.00				
2003D	34,000,000	—	—	—	1.25	—
2003D Proof	150,000	Value: 2.00				
2003F	6,000,000	—	—	—	1.50	—
2003F Proof	150,000	Value: 2.00				
2003G	13,500,000	—	—	—	1.25	—
2003G Proof	150,000	Value: 2.00				
2003J	25,500,000	—	—	—	1.25	—
2003J Proof	150,000	Value: 2.00				
2004A In sets only	—	—	—	—	1.25	—
2004A Proof	—	Value: 2.00				
2004D	28,190,000	—	—	—	1.25	—
2004D Proof	—	Value: 2.00				
2004F	51,360,000	—	—	—	1.25	—
2004F Proof	—	Value: 2.00				
2004G	15,460,000	—	—	—	1.25	—
2004G Proof	—	Value: 2.00				
2004J In sets only	—	—	—	—	1.25	—
2004J Proof	—	Value: 2.00				
2005A In sets only	—	—	—	—	1.25	—
2005A Proof	—	Value: 2.00				
2005D In sets only	—	—	—	—	1.25	—
2005D Proof	—	Value: 2.00				
2005F In sets only	—	—	—	—	1.25	—
2005F Proof	—	Value: 2.00				
2005G In sets only	—	—	—	—	1.25	—
2005G Proof	—	Value: 2.00				
2005J In sets only	—	—	—	—	1.25	—
2005J Proof	—	Value: 2.00				
2006A In sets only	—	—	—	—	1.25	—
2006A Proof	—	Value: 2.00				
2006D In sets only	—	—	—	—	1.25	—
2006D Proof	—	Value: 2.00				
2006F In sets only	—	—	—	—	1.25	—
2006F Proof	—	Value: 2.00				
2006G In sets only	—	—	—	—	1.25	—
2006G Proof	—	Value: 2.00				
2006J In sets only	—	—	—	—	1.25	—
2006J Proof	—	Value: 2.00				

KM# 254 10 EURO CENT
4.0000 g., Brass, 19.7 mm. **Obv:** Brandenburg Gate **Obv. Designer:** Reinhard Heinsdorff **Rev:** Relief map of Western Europe, stars, lines and value **Rev. Designer:** Luc Luycx **Edge:** Reeded

Date	Mintage	F	VF	XF	Unc	BU
2007A In sets only	—	—	—	—	1.25	—
2007A Proof	—	Value: 2.00				
2007D In sets only	—	—	—	—	1.25	—
2007D Proof	—	Value: 2.00				
2007F In sets only	—	—	—	—	1.25	—
2007F Proof	—	Value: 2.00				
2007G In sets only	—	—	—	—	1.25	—
2007G Proof	—	Value: 2.00				
2007J In sets only	—	—	—	—	1.25	—
2007J Proof	—	Value: 2.00				
2008A In sets only	—	—	—	—	1.25	—
2008A Proof	—	Value: 2.00				
2008D In sets only	—	—	—	—	1.25	—
2008D Proof	—	Value: 2.00				
2008F In sets only	—	—	—	—	1.25	—
2008F Proof	—	Value: 2.00				
2008G In sets only	—	—	—	—	1.25	—
2008G Proof	—	Value: 2.00				
2008J In sets only	—	—	—	—	1.25	—
2008J Proof	—	Value: 2.00				
2009A	—	—	—	—	1.25	—
2009A Proof	—	Value: 2.00				
2009D	—	—	—	—	1.25	—
2009D Proof	—	Value: 2.00				
2009F	—	—	—	—	1.25	—
2009F Proof	—	Value: 2.00				
2009G	—	—	—	—	1.25	—
2009G Proof	—	Value: 2.00				
2009J	—	—	—	—	1.25	—
2009J Proof	—	Value: 2.00				
2010A	—	—	—	—	1.25	—
2010A Proof	—	Value: 2.00				
2010D	—	—	—	—	1.25	—
2010D Proof	—	Value: 2.00				
2010F	—	—	—	—	1.25	—
2010F Proof	—	Value: 2.00				
2010G	—	—	—	—	1.25	—
2010G Proof	—	Value: 2.00				
2010J	—	—	—	—	1.25	—
2010J Proof	—	Value: 2.00				

KM# 211 20 EURO CENT
5.7400 g., Brass, 22.2 mm. **Obv:** Brandenburg Gate **Obv. Designer:** Reinhard Heinsdorff **Rev:** Denomination and map **Rev. Designer:** Luc Luycx **Edge:** Notched

Date	Mintage	F	VF	XF	Unc	BU
2002A	378,000,000	—	—	—	1.00	—
2002A Proof	130,000	Value: 3.00				
2002D	367,100,000	—	—	—	1.00	—
2002D Proof	130,000	Value: 3.00				
2002F	423,760,000	—	—	—	1.00	—
2002F Proof	130,000	Value: 3.00				
2002G	252,100,000	—	—	—	1.00	—
2002G Proof	130,000	Value: 3.00				
2002J	441,000,000	—	—	—	1.00	—
2002J Proof	130,000	Value: 3.00				
2003A	42,000,000	—	—	—	1.00	—
2003A Proof	150,000	Value: 3.00				
2003D	24,100,000	—	—	—	1.00	—
2003D Proof	150,000	Value: 3.00				
2003F	82,000,000	—	—	—	1.00	—
2003F Proof	150,000	Value: 3.00				
2003G	24,829,000	—	—	—	1.00	—
2003G Proof	150,000	Value: 3.00				
2003J In sets only	180,000	—	—	—	4.50	—
2003J Proof	150,000	Value: 3.00				
2004A In sets only	—	—	—	—	4.50	—
2004A Proof	—	Value: 3.00				
2004D	33,600,000	—	—	—	2.50	—
2004D Proof	—	Value: 3.00				
2004F In sets only	—	—	—	—	4.50	—
2004F Proof	—	Value: 3.00				
2004G In sets only	—	—	—	—	4.50	—
2004G Proof	—	Value: 3.00				
2004J In sets only	—	—	—	—	4.50	—
2004J Proof	—	Value: 3.00				
2005A	8,000,000	—	—	—	1.00	—
2005A Proof	—	Value: 3.00				
2005D	24,700,000	—	—	—	1.00	—
2005D Proof	—	Value: 3.00				
2005F	9,600,000	—	—	—	1.00	—
2005F Proof	—	Value: 3.00				
2005G	5,600,000	—	—	—	1.00	—
2005G Proof	—	Value: 3.00				
2005J	8,400,000	—	—	—	1.00	—
2005J Proof	—	Value: 3.00				
2006A	39,000,000	—	—	—	1.00	—
2006A Proof	—	Value: 3.00				
2006D	40,950,000	—	—	—	1.00	—
2006D Proof	—	Value: 3.00				
2006F	46,800,000	—	—	—	1.00	—
2006F Proof	—	Value: 3.00				
2006G	27,300,000	—	—	—	1.00	—
2006G Proof	—	Value: 3.00				
2006J	40,950,000	—	—	—	1.00	—
2006J Proof	—	Value: 3.00				

KM# 255 20 EURO CENT
5.7300 g., Brass, 22.2 mm. **Obv:** Brandenburg Gate **Obv. Designer:** Reinhard Heinsdorff **Rev:** Relief map of Western Europe, stars, lines and value **Rev. Designer:** Luc Luycx **Edge:** Notched

Date	Mintage	F	VF	XF	Unc	BU
2007A	21,600,000	—	—	—	1.00	—
2007A Proof	—	Value: 3.00				
2007D	22,680,000	—	—	—	1.00	—
2007D Proof	—	Value: 3.00				
2007F	25,920,000	—	—	—	1.00	—
2007F Proof	—	Value: 3.00				
2007G	15,120,000	—	—	—	1.00	—
2007G Proof	—	Value: 3.00				
2007J	22,930,000	—	—	—	1.00	—
2007J Proof	—	Value: 3.00				
2008A	15,800,000	—	—	—	1.00	—
2008A Proof	—	Value: 3.00				
2008D	16,600,000	—	—	—	1.00	—
2008D Proof	—	Value: 3.00				
2008F	19,000,000	—	—	—	1.00	—
2008F Proof	—	Value: 3.00				
2008G	11,100,000	—	—	—	1.00	—
2008G Proof	—	Value: 3.00				
2008J	16,300,000	—	—	—	1.00	—
2008J Proof	—	Value: 3.00				
2009A	—	—	—	—	1.00	—
2009A Proof	—	Value: 3.00				
2009D	—	—	—	—	1.00	—
2009D Proof	—	Value: 3.00				
2009F	—	—	—	—	1.00	—
2009F Proof	—	Value: 3.00				
2009G	—	—	—	—	1.00	—
2009G Proof	—	Value: 3.00				
2009J	—	—	—	—	1.00	—
2009J Proof	—	Value: 3.00				
2010A	—	—	—	—	1.00	—
2010A Proof	—	Value: 3.00				
2010D	—	—	—	—	1.00	—
2010D Proof	—	Value: 3.00				
2010F	—	—	—	—	1.00	—
2010F Proof	—	Value: 3.00				
2010G	—	—	—	—	1.00	—
2010G Proof	—	Value: 3.00				
2010J	—	—	—	—	1.00	—
2010J Proof	—	Value: 3.00				

KM# 212 50 EURO CENT
7.8100 g., Brass, 24.2 mm. **Obv:** Brandenburg Gate **Obv. Designer:** Reinhard Heinsdorff **Rev:** Denomination and map **Rev. Designer:** Luc Luycx **Edge:** Reeded

Date	Mintage	F	VF	XF	Unc	BU
2002A	337,600,000	—	—	—	1.75	—
2002A Proof	130,000	Value: 4.00				
2002D	370,340,000	—	—	—	1.75	—
2002D Proof	130,000	Value: 4.00				
2002F	432,000,000	—	—	—	1.75	—
2002F Proof	130,000	Value: 4.00				
2002G	257,860,000	—	—	—	1.75	—
2002G Proof	130,000	Value: 4.00				
2002J	375,467,000	—	—	—	1.75	—
2002J Proof	130,000	Value: 4.00				
2003A In sets only	180,000	—	—	—	4.50	—
2003A Proof	150,000	Value: 4.00				
2003D In sets only	180,000	—	—	—	4.50	—
2003D Proof	150,000	Value: 4.00				
2003F In sets only	180,000	—	—	—	4.50	—
2003F Proof	150,000	Value: 4.00				
2003G In sets only	180,000	—	—	—	4.50	—
2003G Proof	150,000	Value: 4.00				
2003J	39,600,000	—	—	—	1.75	—
2003J Proof	150,000	Value: 4.00				
2004A	82,255,000	—	—	—	1.75	—
2004A Proof	—	Value: 4.00				
2004D	70,760,000	—	—	—	1.75	—
2004D Proof	—	Value: 4.00				
2004F	73,520,000	—	—	—	1.75	—
2004F Proof	—	Value: 4.00				
2004G	37,440,000	—	—	—	1.75	—
2004G Proof	—	Value: 4.00				
2004J In sets only	—	—	—	—	1.75	—
2004J Proof	—	Value: 4.00				

Date	Mintage	F	VF	XF	Unc	BU
2005A In sets only	—	—	—	—	1.50	—
2005A Proof	—	Value: 4.00				
2005D In sets only	—	—	—	—	1.50	—
2005D Proof	—	Value: 4.00				
2005F In sets only	—	—	—	—	1.50	—
2005F Proof	—	Value: 4.00				
2005G In sets only	—	—	—	—	1.50	—
2005G Proof	—	Value: 4.00				
2005J In sets only	—	—	—	—	1.50	—
2005J Proof	—	Value: 4.00				
2006A In sets only	—	—	—	—	1.50	—
2006A Proof	—	Value: 4.00				
2006D In sets only	—	—	—	—	1.50	—
2006D Proof	—	Value: 4.00				
2006F In sets only	—	—	—	—	1.50	—
2006F Proof	—	Value: 4.00				
2006G In sets only	—	—	—	—	1.50	—
2006G Proof	—	Value: 4.00				
2006J In sets only	—	—	—	—	1.50	—
2006J Proof	—	Value: 4.00				

KM# 256 50 EURO CENT

7.8100 g., Brass, 24.2 mm. **Obv:** Brandenburg Gate **Obv. Designer:** Reinhard Heinsdorff **Rev:** Relief map of Western Europe, stars, lines and value **Rev. Designer:** Luc Luycx **Edge:** Reeded

Date	Mintage	F	VF	XF	Unc	BU
2007A In sets only	—	—	—	—	1.50	—
2007A Proof	—	Value: 4.00				
2007D In sets only	—	—	—	—	1.50	—
2007D Proof	—	Value: 4.00				
2007F In sets only	—	—	—	—	1.50	—
2007F Proof	—	Value: 4.00				
2007G In sets only	—	—	—	—	1.50	—
2007G Proof	—	Value: 4.00				
2007J In sets only	—	—	—	—	1.50	—
2007J Proof	—	Value: 4.00				
2008A In sets only	—	—	—	—	1.50	—
2008A Proof	—	Value: 4.00				
2008D In sets only	—	—	—	—	1.50	—
2008D Proof	—	Value: 4.00				
2008F In sets only	—	—	—	—	1.50	—
2008F Proof	—	Value: 4.00				
2008G In sets only	—	—	—	—	1.50	—
2008G Proof	—	Value: 4.00				
2008J In sets only	—	—	—	—	1.50	—
2008J Proof	—	Value: 4.00				
2009A	—	—	—	—	1.50	—
2009A Proof	—	Value: 4.00				
2009D	—	—	—	—	1.50	—
2009D Proof	—	Value: 4.00				
2009F	—	—	—	—	1.50	—
2009F Proof	—	Value: 4.00				
2009G	—	—	—	—	1.50	—
2009G Proof	—	Value: 4.00				
2009J	—	—	—	—	1.50	—
2009J Proof	—	Value: 4.00				
2010A	—	—	—	—	1.50	—
2010A Proof	—	Value: 4.00				
2010D	—	—	—	—	1.50	—
2010D Proof	—	Value: 4.00				
2010F	—	—	—	—	1.50	—
2010F Proof	—	Value: 4.00				
2010G	—	—	—	—	1.50	—
2010G Proof	—	Value: 4.00				
2010J	—	—	—	—	1.50	—
2010J Proof	—	Value: 4.00				

KM# 213 EURO

7.5000 g., Bi-Metallic Copper-Nickel center in Nickel-Brass ring, 23.25 mm. **Obv:** Stylized eagle **Obv. Designer:** Heinz Sneschana Russewa-Hover **Rev:** Denomination over map **Rev. Designer:** Luc Luycx **Edge:** Segmented reeding

Date	Mintage	F	VF	XF	Unc	BU
2002A	367,750,000	—	—	—	2.50	—
2002A Proof	130,000	Value: 6.50				
2002D	372,700,000	—	—	—	2.50	—
2002D Proof	130,000	Value: 6.50				
2002F	440,910,000	—	—	—	2.50	—
2002F Proof	130,000	Value: 6.50				
2002G	266,975,000	—	—	—	2.50	—
2002G Proof	130,000	Value: 6.50				
2002J	433,000,000	—	—	—	2.50	—
2002J Proof	130,000	Value: 6.50				
2003A	50,250,000	—	—	—	2.50	—
2003A Proof	150,000	Value: 6.50				
2003D In sets only	180,000	—	—	—	5.50	—
2003D Proof	150,000	Value: 6.50				
2003F	375,000	—	—	—	5.50	—
2003F Proof	150,000	Value: 6.50				
2003G In sets only	180,000	—	—	—	5.50	—
2003G Proof	150,000	Value: 6.50				
2003J	29,850,000	—	—	—	2.50	—
2003J Proof	150,000	Value: 6.50				
2004A	21,855,000	—	—	—	2.50	—
2004A Proof	—	Value: 6.50				
2004D	93,825,000	—	—	—	2.50	—
2004D Proof	—	Value: 6.50				
2004F	88,200,000	—	—	—	2.50	—
2004F Proof	—	Value: 6.50				
2004G	41,650,000	—	—	—	2.50	—
2004G Proof	—	Value: 6.50				
2004J In sets only	—	—	—	—	2.50	—
2004J Proof	—	Value: 6.50				
2005A In sets only	—	—	—	—	2.50	—
2005A Proof	—	Value: 5.00				
2005D In sets only	—	—	—	—	2.50	—
2005D Proof	—	Value: 5.00				
2005F In sets only	—	—	—	—	2.50	—
2005F Proof	—	Value: 5.00				
2005G In sets only	—	—	—	—	2.50	—
2005G Proof	—	Value: 5.00				
2005J	59,840,000	—	—	—	2.50	—
2005J Proof	—	Value: 5.00				
2006A In sets only	—	—	—	—	2.50	—
2006A Proof	—	Value: 5.00				
2006D In sets only	—	—	—	—	2.50	—
2006D Proof	—	Value: 5.00				
2006F In sets only	—	—	—	—	2.50	—
2006F Proof	—	Value: 5.00				
2006G In sets only	—	—	—	—	2.50	—
2006G Proof	—	Value: 5.00				
2006J In sets only	—	—	—	—	2.50	—
2006J Proof	—	Value: 5.00				

KM# 257 EURO

7.5000 g., Bi-Metallic Copper-Nickel center in Nickel-Brass ring, 23.25 mm. **Obv:** Stylized eagle **Obv. Designer:** Heinz Sneschana Russewa-Hover **Rev:** Relief map of Western Europe, stars, lines and value **Rev. Designer:** Luc Luycx **Edge:** Segmented reeding

Date	Mintage	F	VF	XF	Unc	BU
2007A In sets only	—	—	—	—	2.50	—
2007A Proof	—	Value: 5.00				
2007D In sets only	—	—	—	—	2.50	—
2007D Proof	—	Value: 5.00				
2007F In sets only	—	—	—	—	2.50	—
2007F Proof	—	Value: 5.00				
2007G In sets only	—	—	—	—	2.50	—
2007G Proof	—	Value: 5.00				
2007J In sets only	—	—	—	—	2.50	—
2007J Proof	—	Value: 5.00				
2008A In sets only	—	—	—	—	2.50	—
2008A Proof	—	Value: 5.00				
2008D In sets only	—	—	—	—	2.50	—
2008D Proof	—	Value: 5.00				
2008F In sets only	—	—	—	—	2.50	—
2008F Proof	—	Value: 5.00				
2008G In sets only	—	—	—	—	2.50	—
2008G Proof	—	Value: 5.00				
2008J In sets only	—	—	—	—	2.50	—
2008J Proof	—	Value: 5.00				
2009A	—	—	—	—	2.50	—
2009A Proof	—	Value: 5.00				
2009D	—	—	—	—	2.50	—
2009D Proof	—	Value: 5.00				
2009F	—	—	—	—	2.50	—
2009F Proof	—	Value: 5.00				
2009G	—	—	—	—	2.50	—
2009G Proof	—	Value: 5.00				
2009J	—	—	—	—	2.50	—
2009J Proof	—	Value: 5.00				
2010A	—	—	—	—	2.50	—
2010A Proof	—	Value: 5.00				
2010D	—	—	—	—	2.50	—
2010D Proof	—	Value: 5.00				
2010F	—	—	—	—	2.50	—
2010F Proof	—	Value: 5.00				
2010G	—	—	—	—	2.50	—
2010G Proof	—	Value: 5.00				
2010J	—	—	—	—	2.50	—
2010J Proof	—	Value: 5.00				

KM# 214 2 EURO

8.5000 g., Bi-Metallic Nickel-Brass center in Copper-Nickel ring, 25.75 mm. **Obv:** Stylized eagle **Obv. Designer:** Heinz Sneschana Russewa-Hover **Rev:** Denomination and map **Rev. Designer:** Luc Luycx **Edge:** Reeded and "EINIGKEIT UND RECHT UND FREIHEIT"

Date	Mintage	F	VF	XF	Unc	BU
2002A	238,775,000	—	—	—	4.50	—
2002A Proof	130,000	Value: 12.50				
2002D	231,400,000	—	—	—	4.50	—
2002D Proof	130,000	Value: 12.50				
2002F	264,610,000	—	—	—	4.50	—
2002F Proof	130,000	Value: 12.50				
2002G	181,050,000	—	—	—	4.50	—
2002G Proof	130,000	Value: 12.50				
2002J	257,718,000	—	—	—	4.50	—
2002J Proof	130,000	Value: 12.50				
2003A	20,475,000	—	—	—	4.50	—
2003A Proof	150,000	Value: 12.50				
2003D	16,269,000	—	—	—	4.50	—
2003D Proof	150,000	Value: 12.50				
2003F	24,575,000	—	—	—	4.50	—
2003F Proof	150,000	Value: 12.50				
2003G	29,425,000	—	—	—	4.50	—
2003G Proof	150,000	Value: 12.50				
2003J	20,100,000	—	—	—	4.50	—
2003J Proof	150,000	Value: 12.50				
2004A	31,565,000	—	—	—	4.50	—
2004A Proof	—	Value: 12.50				
2004D	28,146,000	—	—	—	4.50	—
2004D Proof	—	Value: 12.50				
2004F In sets only	—	—	—	—	4.50	—
2004F Proof	—	Value: 12.50				
2004G In sets only	—	—	—	—	4.50	—
2004G Proof	—	Value: 12.50				
2004J	5,630,000	—	—	—	4.50	—
2004J Proof	—	Value: 12.50				
2005A In sets only	—	—	—	—	4.50	—
2005A Proof	—	Value: 10.00				
2005D In sets only	—	—	—	—	4.50	—
2005D Proof	—	Value: 10.00				
2005F In sets only	—	—	—	—	4.50	—
2005F Proof	—	Value: 10.00				
2005G In sets only	—	—	—	—	4.50	—
2005G Proof	—	Value: 10.00				
2005J In sets only	—	—	—	—	4.50	—
2005J Proof	—	Value: 10.00				
2006A In sets only	—	—	—	—	4.50	—
2006A Proof	—	Value: 10.00				
2006D In sets only	—	—	—	—	4.50	—
2006D Proof	—	Value: 10.00				
2006F In sets only	—	—	—	—	4.50	—
2006F Proof	—	Value: 10.00				
2006G In sets only	—	—	—	—	4.50	—
2006G Proof	—	Value: 10.00				
2006J In sets only	—	—	—	—	4.50	—
2006J Proof	—	Value: 10.00				

KM# 253 2 EURO

8.5000 g., Bi-Metallic Nickel-Brass center in Copper-Nickel ring, 25.75 mm. **Obv:** Schleswig Holstein castle **Obv. Legend:** BUNDESREPULIK DEUTSCHLAND **Obv. Inscription:** SCHLESWIG- / HOLSTEIN **Rev:** Denomination over map

Date	Mintage	F	VF	XF	Unc	BU
2006A	6,000,000	—	—	—	5.00	6.00
2006A Proof	70,000	Value: 10.00				
2006D	6,300,000	—	—	—	5.00	6.00
2006D Proof	70,000	Value: 10.00				
2006F	7,250,000	—	—	—	5.00	6.00
2006F Proof	70,000	Value: 10.00				
2006G	4,200,000	—	—	—	5.00	6.00
2006G Proof	70,000	Value: 10.00				
2006J	6,300,000	—	—	—	5.00	6.00
2006J Proof	70,000	Value: 10.00				

KM# 259 2 EURO

8.5000 g., Bi-Metallic Nickel-Brass center in Copper-Nickel ring, 25.75 mm. **Subject:** 50th Anniversary Treaty of Rome **Obv:** Open treaty book **Obv. Legend:** BUNDESREPUBLIK DEUTSCHLAND **Rev:** Large value at left, modified outline of Europe at right **Edge Lettering:** EINIGKEIT UND RECHT UND FREIHEIT

Date	Mintage	F	VF	XF	Unc	BU
2007A	1,000,000	—	—	—	4.00	5.00
2007A Proof	155,000	Value: 10.00				
2007D	14,500,000	—	—	—	4.00	5.50
2007D Prrof	155,000	Value: 10.00				
2007F	8,000,000	—	—	—	4.00	5.50
2007F Proof	155,000	Value: 10.00				
2007G	5,000,000	—	—	—	4.00	5.50

Date	Mintage	F	VF	XF	Unc	BU
2007G Proof	155,000	Value: 10.00				
2007J	1,500,000	—	—	—	4.00	5.50
2007J Proof	155,000	Value: 10.00				

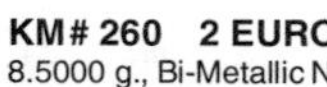

KM# 260 2 EURO

8.5000 g., Bi-Metallic Nickel-Brass center in Copper-Nickel ring, 25.75 mm. **Obv:** City buildings, Mecklenburg's Schwerin Castle **Obv. Legend:** BUNDESREPUBLIK DEUTSCHLAND **Obv. Inscription:** MECKLENBURG- / VORPOMMERN **Rev:** Large value at left, modified map of Europe at right **Edge Lettering:** EINIGKEIT UND RECHT UND FREIHEIT

Date	Mintage	F	VF	XF	Unc	BU
2007A	1,040,000	—	—	—	4.00	5.50
2007A Proof	70,000	Value: 10.00				
2007D	11,840,000	—	—	—	4.00	5.50
2007D Proof	70,000	Value: 10.00				
2007F	11,850,000	—	—	—	4.00	5.50
2007F Proof	70,000	Value: 10.00				
2007G	4,200,000	—	—	—	4.00	5.50
2007G Proof	70,000	Value: 10.00				
2007J	1,070,000	—	—	—	4.00	5.50
2007J Proof	70,000	Value: 10.00				

KM# 261 2 EURO

8.5000 g., Bi-Metallic Nickel-Brass center in Copper-Nickel ring, 25.75 mm. **Obv:** Hamburg Cathedral **Obv. Legend:** BUNDESREPUBLIK DEUTSCHLAND **Obv. Inscription:** HAMBURG **Rev:** Large value at left, modified outline of Europe at right **Edge Lettering:** EINIGKEIT UND RECHT UND FREIHEIT

Date	Mintage	F	VF	XF	Unc	BU
2008A	1,000,000	—	—	—	4.00	5.50
2008A Proof	—	Value: 10.00				
2008D	8,900,000	—	—	—	4.00	5.50
2008D Proof	—	Value: 10.00				
2008F	9,600,000	—	—	—	4.00	5.50
2008F Proof	—	Value: 10.00				
2008G	4,200,000	—	—	—	4.00	5.50
2008G Proof	—	Value: 10.00				
2008J	6,300,000	—	—	—	4.00	5.50
2008J Proof	—	Value: 10.00				

KM# 258 2 EURO

8.5000 g., Bi-Metallic Nickel-Brass center in Copper-Nickel ring, 25.75 mm. **Obv:** Stylized eagle **Obv. Designer:** Heinz Sneschana Russewa-Hover **Rev:** Relief map of Western Europe, stars, lines and value **Rev. Designer:** Luc Luycx **Edge Lettering:** EINIGKEIT UND RECHT UND FREIHEIT

Date	Mintage	F	VF	XF	Unc	BU
2008A In sets only	—	—	—	—	4.50	—
2008A Proof	—	Value: 10.00				
2008D In sets only	—	—	—	—	4.50	—
2008D Proof	—	Value: 10.00				
2008F In sets only	—	—	—	—	4.50	—
2008F Proof	—	Value: 10.00				
2008G In sets only	—	—	—	—	4.50	—
2008G Proof	—	Value: 10.00				
2008J In sets only	—	—	—	—	4.50	—
2008J Proof	—	Value: 10.00				
2009A	—	—	—	—	4.50	—
2009A Proof	—	Value: 10.00				
2009D	—	—	—	—	4.50	—
2009D Proof	—	Value: 10.00				
2009F	—	—	—	—	4.50	—

Date	Mintage	F	VF	XF	Unc	BU
2009F Proof	—	Value: 10.00				
2009G	—	—	—	—	4.50	—
2009G Proof	—	Value: 10.00				
2009J	—	—	—	—	4.50	—
2009J Proof	—	Value: 10.00				
2010A	—	—	—	—	4.50	—
2010A Proof	—	Value: 10.00				
2010D	—	—	—	—	4.50	—
2010D Proof	—	Value: 10.00				
2010F	—	—	—	—	4.50	—
2010F Proof	—	Value: 10.00				
2010G	—	—	—	—	4.50	—
2010G Proof	—	Value: 10.00				
2010J	—	—	—	—	4.50	—
2010J Proof	—	Value: 10.00				

KM# 277 2 EURO

8.5000 g., Bi-Metallic Nickel-Brass center in Copper-Nickel ring, 25.75 mm. **Subject:** EMU, 10th Anniversary **Obv:** Stick figure and E symbol

Date	Mintage	F	VF	XF	Unc	BU
2009A	—	—	—	—	4.50	5.00
2009A Proof	—	Value: 10.00				
2009D	—	—	—	—	4.50	5.00
2009D Proof	—	Value: 10.00				
2009F	—	—	—	—	4.50	5.00
2009F Proof	—	Value: 10.00				
2009G	—	—	—	—	4.50	5.00
2009G Proof	—	Value: 10.00				
2009J	—	—	—	—	4.50	5.00
2009J Proof	—	Value: 10.00				

KM# 276 2 EURO

8.5000 g., Bi-Metallic Nickel-Brass center in Copper-Nickel ring, 25.75 mm. **Obv:** Building in Saarland **Rev:** Value and map

Date	Mintage	F	VF	XF	Unc	BU
2009A	—	—	—	—	4.50	5.00
2009D	—	—	—	—	4.50	5.00
2009F	—	—	—	—	4.50	5.00
2009G	—	—	—	—	4.50	5.00
2009J	—	—	—	—	4.50	5.00

KM# 285 2 EURO

8.5000 g., Bi-Metallic Nickel-Brass center in Copper-Nickel ring, 25.75 mm. **Obv:** Bremen town hall and statue **Rev:** Value and map

Date	Mintage	F	VF	XF	Unc	BU
2010A	—	—	—	—	4.50	5.00
2010A Proof	—	Value: 10.00				
2010D	—	—	—	—	4.50	5.00
2010D Proof	—	Value: 10.00				
2010F	—	—	—	—	4.50	5.00
2010F Proof	—	Value: 10.00				
2010G	—	—	—	—	4.50	5.00
2010G Proof	—	Value: 10.00				
2010J	—	—	—	—	4.50	5.00
2010J Proof	—	Value: 10.00				

KM# 293 2 EURO

8.5000 g., Bi-Metallic Nickel-Brass center in Copper-Nickel ring, 25.75 mm. **Obv:** Cologne Cathedral

Date	Mintage	F	VF	XF	Unc	BU
2011A	—	—	—	—	5.00	7.50
2011D	—	—	—	—	5.00	7.50
2011F	—	—	—	—	5.00	7.50
2011G	—	—	—	—	5.00	7.50
2011J	—	—	—	—	5.00	7.50

KM# 215 10 EURO

18.0000 g., 0.9250 Silver 0.5353 oz. ASW, 32.5 mm. **Subject:** Introduction of the Euro Currency **Obv:** Stylized round eagle **Rev:** Euro symbol and map **Edge Lettering:** IM ZEICHEN DER EINIGUNG EUROPAS

Date	Mintage	F	VF	XF	Unc	BU
2002F	2,000,000	—	—	—	22.00	25.00
2002F Proof	400,000	Value: 30.00				

KM# 216 10 EURO

18.0000 g., 0.9250 Silver 0.5353 oz. ASW, 32.5 mm. **Subject:** Berlin Subway Centennial **Obv:** Stylized squarish eagle **Rev:** Elevated and subterranean train views **Edge Lettering:** HISTORISCH UND ZUKUNFTS WEISEND

Date	Mintage	F	VF	XF	Unc	BU
2002D	2,000,000	—	—	—	22.00	25.00
2002D Proof	400,000	Value: 30.00				

KM# 217 10 EURO

18.0000 g., 0.9250 Silver 0.5353 oz. ASW, 32.5 mm. **Subject:** Documenta Kassel Art Exposition **Obv:** Stylized eagle above inscription **Rev:** Exposition logo **Edge Lettering:** ART (in nine languages)

Date	Mintage	F	VF	XF	Unc	BU
2002J	2,000,000	—	—	—	22.00	25.00
2002J Proof	400,000	Value: 30.00				

KM# 218 10 EURO

18.0000 g., 0.9250 Silver 0.5353 oz. ASW, 32.5 mm. **Subject:** Museum Island, Berlin **Obv:** Stylized eagle **Rev:** Aerial view of museum complex **Edge Lettering:** FREISTÄTTE FUR KÜNST UND WISSENSCHAFT

Date	Mintage	F	VF	XF	Unc	BU
2002A	2,000,000	—	—	—	22.00	25.00
2002A Proof	280,000	Value: 30.00				

KM# 219 10 EURO

18.0000 g., 0.9250 Silver 0.5353 oz. ASW, 32.5 mm. **Subject:** 50 Years - German Television **Obv:** Stylized eagle silhouette **Rev:** Television screen silhouette **Edge Lettering:** BILDUNG UNTERHALTUNG INFORMATION

Date	Mintage	F	VF	XF	Unc	BU
2002G	2,000,000	—	—	—	22.00	25.00
2002G Proof	290,000	Value: 32.00				

KM# 222 10 EURO
18.0000 g., 0.9250 Silver 0.5353 oz. ASW, 32.5 mm. **Subject:** Justus von Liebig **Obv:** Eagle above denomination **Rev:** Liebig's portrait **Edge Lettering:** FORSCHEN • LEHREN • ANWENDEN •

Date	Mintage	F	VF	XF	Unc	BU
2003J	2,050,000	—	—	—	22.00	25.00
2003J Proof	350,000	Value: 30.00				

KM# 227 10 EURO
18.0000 g., 0.9250 Silver 0.5353 oz. ASW, 32.5 mm. **Obv:** Stylized eagle above denomination **Rev:** Gottfried Semper and floor plan **Edge Lettering:** ARCHITEKT • FORSCHER • KOSMOPOLIT • DEMOKRAT•

Date	Mintage	F	VF	XF	Unc	BU
2003G	2,050,000	—	—	—	20.00	22.00
2003G Proof	350,000	Value: 25.00				

KM# 223 10 EURO
18.0000 g., 0.9250 Silver 0.5353 oz. ASW, 32.5 mm. **Subject:** World Cup Soccer **Obv:** Stylized round eagle above denomination **Rev:** German map on soccer ball **Edge Lettering:** DIE WELT ZU GAST BEI FREUNDEN A • D • F • G • J • **Note:** Mint is determined by which letter "E" in the edge inscription has a short center bar. If the first letter "E" has the short center bar the coin is from the Berlin mint. Second "E"= Munich, third "E"=Stuttgart, fourth "E"=Karlsruhe, fifth "E"=Hamburg

Date	Mintage	F	VF	XF	Unc	BU
2003A	710,000	—	—	—	22.00	25.00
2003A Proof	80,000	Value: 32.00				
2003D	710,000	—	—	—	22.00	25.00
2003D Proof	80,000	Value: 32.00				
2003F	710,000	—	—	—	22.00	25.00
2003F Proof	80,000	Value: 32.00				
2003G	710,000	—	—	—	22.00	25.00
2003G Proof	80,000	Value: 32.00				
2003J	710,000	—	—	—	22.00	25.00
2003J Proof	80,000	Value: 32.00				

KM# 224 10 EURO
18.0000 g., 0.9250 Silver 0.5353 oz. ASW, 32.5 mm. **Subject:** Ruhr Industrial District **Obv:** Stylized eagle, denomination below **Rev:** Various city views **Edge Lettering:** RUHRPOTT KULTURLANDSCHAFT

Date	Mintage	F	VF	XF	Unc	BU
2003F	2,050,000	—	—	—	22.00	25.00
2003F Proof	350,000	Value: 30.00				

KM# 226 10 EURO
18.0000 g., 0.9250 Silver 0.5353 oz. ASW, 32.5 mm. **Subject:** 50th Anniversary of the Ill-fated East German Revolution **Obv:** Stylized eagle, denomination at left **Rev:** Tank tracks over slogans **Edge Lettering:** ERINNERUNG AN DEN VOLKSAUFSTAND IN DER DDR

Date	Mintage	F	VF	XF	Unc	BU
2003A	2,050,000	—	—	—	22.00	25.00
2003A Proof	350,000	Value: 30.00				

KM# 225 10 EURO
18.0000 g., 0.9250 Silver 0.5353 oz. ASW, 32.5 mm. **Subject:** German Museum München Centennial **Obv:** Stylized eagle, denomination at left **Rev:** Abstract design **Edge Lettering:** SAMMELN • AUSSTELLEN • FORSCHEN • BILDEN •

Date	Mintage	F	VF	XF	Unc	BU
2003D	2,050,000	—	—	—	22.00	25.00
2003D Proof	350,000	Value: 30.00				

KM# 230 10 EURO
18.0000 g., 0.9250 Silver 0.5353 oz. ASW, 32.5 mm. **Obv:** Stylized eagle, stars and denomination **Rev:** Bauhaus Dessau geometric shapes design **Edge Lettering:** KUNST TECHNIK LEHRE

Date	Mintage	F	VF	XF	Unc	BU
2004A	1,800,000	—	—	—	22.00	25.00
2004A Proof	300,000	Value: 30.00				

KM# 232 10 EURO
18.0000 g., 0.9250 Silver 0.5353 oz. ASW, 32.5 mm. **Obv:** Stylized eagle and denomination **Rev:** Geese flying over Wattenmeer National Park **Edge Lettering:** MEERESGRUND TRIFFT HORIZONT

Date	Mintage	F	VF	XF	Unc	BU
2004J	—	—	—	—	22.00	25.00
2004J Proof	—	Value: 30.00				

KM# 233 10 EURO
18.0000 g., 0.9250 Silver 0.5353 oz. ASW, 32.5 mm. **Obv:** Stylized eagle **Rev:** Eduard Moerike **Edge Lettering:** OHNE DAS SCHÖNE WAS SOLL DER GEWINN

Date	Mintage	F	VF	XF	Unc	BU
2004F	—	—	—	—	22.00	25.00
2004F Proof	—	Value: 30.00				

KM# 234 10 EURO
18.0000 g., 0.9250 Silver 0.5353 oz. ASW, 32.5 mm. **Obv:** Stylized eagle, denomination below **Rev:** Space station above the earth **Edge Lettering:** RAUMFAHRT VERBINDET DIE WELT

Date	Mintage	F	VF	XF	Unc	BU
2004D	1,800,000	—	—	—	22.00	25.00
2004D Proof	300,000	Value: 30.00				

KM# 231 10 EURO
18.0000 g., 0.9250 Silver 0.5353 oz. ASW, 32.5 mm. **Obv:** Stylized eagle above denomination **Rev:** European Union country names and dates **Edge Lettering:** FREUDE SCHÖNER GÖTTERFUNKEN

Date	Mintage	F	VF	XF	Unc	BU
2004F	—	—	—	—	22.00	25.00
2004F Proof	—	Value: 30.00				
2004G	—	—	—	—	22.00	25.00
2004G Proof	—	Value: 30.00				

KM# 229 10 EURO
18.0000 g., 0.9250 Silver 0.5353 oz. ASW, 32.5 mm. **Obv:** Stylized eagle, denomination below **Rev:** Soccer ball orbiting the earth **Edge Lettering:** DIE WELT ZU GAST BEI FREUNDEN A D F G J **Note:** Soccer Series: Mint determination same as KM-223

Date	Mintage	F	VF	XF	Unc	BU
2004A	800,000	—	—	—	22.00	25.00
2004A Proof	80,000	Value: 30.00				
2004D	800,000	—	—	—	22.00	25.00
2004D Proof	80,000	Value: 30.00				
2004F	800,000	—	—	—	22.00	25.00
2004F Proof	80,000	Value: 30.00				
2004G	800,000	—	—	—	22.00	25.00
2004G Proof	80,000	Value: 30.00				
2004J	800,000	—	—	—	22.00	25.00
2004J Proof	80,000	Value: 30.00				

KM# 238 10 EURO
18.0000 g., 0.9250 Silver 0.5353 oz. ASW, 32.5 mm. **Subject:** Albert Einstein **Obv:** Stylized eagle within circle, denomination below **Rev:** E=mc2 on a sphere resting on a net **Edge Lettering:** NICHT AUFHOREN ZU FRAGEN

Date	Mintage	F	VF	XF	Unc	BU
2005J	1,800,000	—	—	—	22.00	25.00
2005J Proof	300,000	Value: 30.00				

KM# 239 10 EURO
18.0000 g., 0.9250 Silver 0.5353 oz. ASW, 32.5 mm. **Subject:** Friedrich von Schiller **Obv:** Stylized eagle **Rev:** Schiller portrait **Edge Lettering:** ERNST IST DAS LEBEN. HEITER IST DIE KUNST

Date	Mintage	F	VF	XF	Unc	BU
2005G	1,800,000	—	—	—	20.00	22.00
2005G Proof	300,000	Value: 25.00				

KM# 240 10 EURO
18.0000 g., 0.9250 Silver 0.5353 oz. ASW, 32.5 mm. **Subject:** Magdeburg **Obv:** Stylized eagle, denomination below **Rev:** Church flanked by landmarks and objects **Edge Lettering:** MAGADOBURG 805 • MAGDEBURG 2005 •

Date	Mintage	F	VF	XF	Unc	BU
2005A	1,800,000	—	—	—	20.00	22.00
2005A Proof	300,000	Value: 25.00				

KM# 241 10 EURO
18.0000 g., 0.9250 Silver 0.5353 oz. ASW, 32.5 mm. **Subject:** Bavarian Forest National Park **Obv:** Stylized eagle **Rev:** Various park scenes **Edge:** Lettered

Date	Mintage	F	VF	XF	Unc	BU
2005D	1,800,000	—	—	—	20.00	22.00
2005D Proof	300,000	Value: 25.00				

KM# 242 10 EURO
18.0000 g., 0.9250 Silver 0.5353 oz. ASW, 32.5 mm. **Subject:** Bertha von Suttner **Obv:** Stylized eagle above stars **Rev:** Suttner's portrait **Edge Lettering:** EIPHNH PAX FRIEDEN twice

Date	Mintage	F	VF	XF	Unc	BU
2005F	1,800,000	—	—	—	20.00	22.00
2005F Proof	300,000	Value: 25.00				

KM# 243 10 EURO
18.0000 g., 0.9250 Silver 0.5353 oz. ASW, 32.5 mm. **Subject:** World Cup Soccer **Obv:** Round stylized eagle **Rev:** Ball and legs seen through a net **Edge Lettering:** DIE WELT ZU GAST BEI FREUNDEN

Date	Mintage	F	VF	XF	Unc	BU
2005A	800,000	—	—	—	20.00	22.00
2005A Proof	80,000	Value: 25.00				
2005D	800,000	—	—	—	20.00	22.00
2005D Proof	80,000	Value: 25.00				
2005F	800,000	—	—	—	20.00	22.00
2005F Proof	80,000	Value: 25.00				
2005G	800,000	—	—	—	20.00	22.00
2005G Proof	80,000	Value: 25.00				
2005J	800,000	—	—	—	20.00	22.00
2005J Proof	80,000	Value: 25.00				

KM# 245 10 EURO
18.0000 g., 0.9250 Silver 0.5353 oz. ASW, 32.5 mm. **Subject:** Karl Friedrich Schinkel **Obv:** Stylized eagle **Rev:** Kneeling brick layer **Edge Lettering:** DER MENSCH BILDE SICH IN ALLEM SCHÖN

Date	Mintage	F	VF	XF	Unc	BU
2006F	1,600,000	—	—	—	22.00	25.00
2006F Proof	300,000	Value: 30.00				

KM# 246 10 EURO
18.0000 g., 0.9250 Silver 0.5353 oz. ASW, 32.5 mm. **Subject:** Dresden **Obv:** Stylized eagle **Rev:** City view and reflection **Edge Lettering:** 1206 1485 1547 1697 1832 1945 1989 2006

Date	Mintage	F	VF	XF	Unc	BU
2006A	1,600,000	—	—	—	22.00	22.00
2006A Proof	300,000	Value: 25.00				

KM# 247 10 EURO
18.0000 g., 0.9250 Silver 0.5353 oz. ASW, 32.5 mm. **Subject:** Hanseatic League **Obv:** Stylized eagle **Rev:** Old sail boat **Edge Lettering:** Wandel durch Handel - von der Hanse nach Europa

Date	Mintage	F	VF	XF	Unc	BU
2006J	1,600,000	—	—	—	20.00	22.00
2006J Proof	300,000	Value: 25.00				

KM# 248 10 EURO
18.0000 g., 0.9250 Silver 0.5353 oz. ASW, 32.5 mm. **Subject:** Mozart **Obv:** Stylized eagle, music and denomination above **Rev:** Bust left, dates above **Edge Lettering:** -- MOZART -- DIE WELT HAT EINEN SINN

Date	Mintage	F	VF	XF	Unc	BU
2006D	1,600,000	—	—	—	20.00	22.00
2006D Proof	265,000	Value: 25.00				

KM# 249 10 EURO
18.0000 g., 0.9250 Silver 0.5353 oz. ASW, 32.5 mm. **Subject:** World Cup Soccer **Obv:** Stylized eagle **Rev:** Brandenburg Gate on ball on globe **Edge Lettering:** DIE WELT ZU GAST BEI FREUNDEN - ADFGJ **Note:** Mint is determined by which letter "E" in the edge inscription has a short center bar. If the first letter "E" has the short center bar the coin is from the Berlin mint. Second "E"= Munich, third "E"=Stuttgart, fourth "E"=Karlsruhe, fifth "E"=Hamburg

Date	Mintage	F	VF	XF	Unc	BU
2006A	800,000	—	—	—	20.00	22.00
2006A Proof	80,000	Value: 25.00				
2006D	800,000	—	—	—	20.00	22.00
2006D Proof	80,000	Value: 25.00				
2006F	800,000	—	—	—	20.00	22.00
2006F Proof	80,000	Value: 25.00				
2006G	800,000	—	—	—	20.00	22.00
2006G Proof	80,000	Value: 25.00				
2006J	800,000	—	—	—	20.00	22.00
2006J Proof	80,000	Value: 25.00				

KM# 263 10 EURO
18.0000 g., 0.9250 Silver 0.5353 oz. ASW, 32.5 mm. **Subject:** Saarland, 50th Anniversary of German control **Obv:** Eagle **Rev:** Modern town view, four stylized heads

Date	Mintage	F	VF	XF	Unc	BU
2007G	1,600,000	—	—	—	25.00	22.00
2007G Proof	300,000	Value: 30.00				

KM# 264 10 EURO

18.0000 g., 0.9250 Silver 0.5353 oz. ASW, 32.5 mm. **Subject:** Treaty of Rome, 50th Anniversary **Obv:** Eagle **Rev:** Map of Central Europe and stars

Date	Mintage	F	VF	XF	Unc	BU
2007F	1,600,000	—	—	—	25.00	22.00
2007F	300,000	Value: 30.00				

KM# 265 10 EURO

18.0000 g., 0.9250 Silver 0.5353 oz. ASW, 32.5 mm. **Subject:** Wilhelm Busch, 175th Anniversary of Birth **Obv:** Eagle within square **Rev:** Portrait of Busch, characters Helene, Max and Moritz flanking

Date	Mintage	F	VF	XF	Unc	BU
2007D	1,600,000	—	—	—	25.00	22.00
2007D	300,000	Value: 30.00				

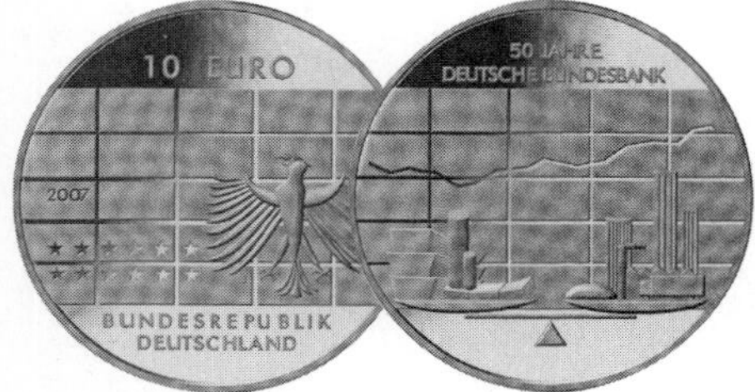

KM# 266 10 EURO

18.0000 g., 0.9250 Silver 0.5353 oz. ASW, 32.5 mm. **Subject:** Deutsche Bundesbank, 50th Aniversary **Obv:** Eagle on rectangle design **Rev:** Buildings on graph

Date	Mintage	F	VF	XF	Unc	BU
2007J	1,600,000	—	—	—	25.00	22.00
2007J Proof	300,000	Value: 30.00				

KM# 268 10 EURO

18.0000 g., 0.9250 Silver 0.5353 oz. ASW, 32.5 mm. **Subject:** Eagle **Rev:** St. Elisabeth von Thuringen

Date	Mintage	F	VF	XF	Unc	BU
2007A	150,000	—	—	—	25.00	22.00
2007A	70,000	Value: 30.00				

KM# 271 10 EURO

18.0000 g., 0.9250 Silver 0.5353 oz. ASW, 32.5 mm. **Subject:** Franz Kafka, 125th Anniversary of Birth **Obv:** Eagle **Rev:** Prague Cathedral, writings & portrait **Edge Lettering:** EIN KÄFIG GING EINEN VOGEL SUCHENS

Date	Mintage	F	VF	XF	Unc	BU
2008G	500,000	—	—	—	25.00	22.00
2008G Proof	260,000	Value: 30.00				

KM# 272 10 EURO

18.0000 g., 0.9250 Silver 0.5353 oz. ASW, 32.5 mm. **Subject:** Max Planck, 150th Anniversary of Birth **Obv:** Eagle **Rev:** Graph and portrait **Edge Lettering:** DEM ANWENDEN MUSS DAS + ERENNEN VORAUSGEHEN

Date	Mintage	F	VF	XF	Unc	BU
2008F	1,500,000	—	—	—	25.00	22.00
2008F Proof	260,000	Value: 30.00				

KM# 273 10 EURO

18.0000 g., 0.9250 Silver 0.5353 oz. ASW **Subject:** Carl Spitzweg - 200th Anniversary of Birth **Obv:** Eagle **Rev:** Spitzweg reclining in bed with books, umbrella above **Edge Lettering:** ACH, DIE VERGANGENHEIT IST SCHÖN **Shape:** 32.5

Date	Mintage	F	VF	XF	Unc	BU
2008D	1,500,000	—	—	—	25.00	22.00
2008D Proof	260,000	Value: 30.00				

KM# 274 10 EURO

18.0000 g., 0.9250 Silver 0.5353 oz. ASW, 32.5 mm. **Subject:** Gorch Fock II, 50th Anniversary **Obv:** Eagle **Rev:** Naval training sailing ship Gorch Fock II **Edge Lettering:** SEEFAHRT 1ST NOT

Date	Mintage	F	VF	XF	Unc	BU
2008J	—	—	—	—	25.00	22.00
2008J Proof	—	Value: 30.00				

KM# 294 10 EURO

18.0000 g., 0.9250 Silver 0.5353 oz. ASW, 32.5 mm. **Subject:** Archaology in Germany **Obv:** Eagle, stars flanking **Rev:** Sun, moon and star shield

Date	Mintage	F	VF	XF	Unc	BU
2008A	1,500,000	—	—	—	22.00	25.00
2008A Proof	260,000	Value: 30.00				

KM# 279 10 EURO

18.0000 g., 0.9250 Silver 0.5353 oz. ASW, 32.5 mm. **Subject:** IAAF World Championships - Berlin **Obv:** Eagle and value **Rev:** Female javelin thrower in stadium **Note:** Mint Marks letters are in Morse Code.

Date	Mintage	F	VF	XF	Unc	BU
2009A	—	—	—	—	22.00	20.00
2009A Proof	—	Value: 25.00				
2009D	—	—	—	—	22.00	20.00
2009D Proof	—	Value: 25.00				
2009F	—	—	—	—	22.00	20.00
2009F Proof	—	Value: 25.00				
2009G	—	—	—	—	22.00	20.00
2009G Proof	—	Value: 25.00				
2009J	—	—	—	—	22.00	20.00
2009J Proof	—	Value: 25.00				

KM# 280 10 EURO

18.0000 g., 0.9250 Silver 0.5353 oz. ASW, 32.5 mm. **Subject:** Kepler's Laws - 400th Anniversary **Obv:** Eagle above value **Rev:** Portrait and geometric diagram demonstrating planetary orbits

Date	Mintage	F	VF	XF	Unc	BU
2009F	1,500,000	—	—	—	22.00	20.00
2009F Proof	200,000	Value: 25.00				

KM# 281 10 EURO

18.0000 g., 0.9250 Silver 0.5353 oz. ASW, 32.5 mm. **Subject:** International Aerospace Expo, 100th Anniversary **Obv:** Eagle above value **Rev:** Plane landing, montage of plane development

Date	Mintage	F	VF	XF	Unc	BU
2009D	1,500,000	—	—	—	22.00	20.00
2009D Proof	200,000	Value: 25.00				

KM# 282 10 EURO

18.0000 g., 0.9250 Silver 0.5353 oz. ASW, 32.5 mm. **Subject:** Leipzig University - 600th Anniversary **Obv:** Eagle above value **Rev:** University seal, portrait of Gottfried Wilhelm Leibniz

Date	Mintage	F	VF	XF	Unc	BU
2009A	15,000,000	—	—	—	22.00	20.00
2009G Proof	200,000	Value: 25.00				

KM# 284 10 EURO

18.0000 g., 0.9250 Silver 0.5353 oz. ASW, 32.5 mm. **Subject:** Marion Countess Donhoff - 100th Anniversary of Birth **Obv:** Eagle and value **Rev:** Profile right

Date	Mintage	F	VF	XF	Unc	BU
2009J	1,500,000	—	—	—	22.00	20.00
2009J Proof	200,000	Value: 25.00				

KM# 281a 10 EURO

18.0000 g., 0.9250 Silver partially gilt 0.5353 oz. ASW, 32.5 mm. **Subject:** International Air Travel, 100th Anniversary **Obv:** Stylized eagle **Rev:** Airplanes, partially gilt

Date	Mintage	F	VF	XF	Unc	BU
2009D Proof	10,000	Value: 50.00				

KM# 283 10 EURO

18.0000 g., 0.9250 Silver 0.5353 oz. ASW, 32.5 mm. **Subject:** Youth hostels - 100th Anniversary **Obv:** Eagle and value **Rev:** Stylized mountain, Alternal hostel in Westphalia

Date	Mintage	F	VF	XF	Unc	BU
2009G	1,500,000	—	—	—	22.00	20.00
2009G Proof	200,000	Value: 25.00				

KM# 290 10 EURO

18.0000 g., 0.9250 Silver 0.5353 oz. ASW, 32.5 mm. **Subject:** German Unification, 20th Anniversary

Date	Mintage	F	VF	XF	Unc	BU
2010A	1,500,000	—	—	—	20.00	22.00
2010A Proof	200,000	Value: 25.00				

KM# 287 10 EURO

18.0000 g., 0.9250 Silver 0.5353 oz. ASW, 32.5 mm. **Subject:** Porcelain Production, 300th Anniversary

Date	Mintage	F	VF	XF	Unc	BU
2010F	1,500,000	—	—	—	20.00	22.00
2010F Proof	200,000	Value: 25.00				

KM# 288 10 EURO

18.0000 g., 0.9250 Silver 0.5353 oz. ASW, 32.5 mm. **Subject:** Robert Schumann - 200th Birth Anniversary

Date	Mintage	F	VF	XF	Unc	BU
2010J	1,500,000	—	—	—	20.00	22.00
2010J Proof	200,000	Value: 25.00				

KM# 289 10 EURO

18.0000 g., 0.9250 Silver 0.5353 oz. ASW, 32.5 mm. **Subject:** Konrad Zuse, 100th Birth Anniversary

Date	Mintage	F	VF	XF	Unc	BU
2010G	1,500,000	—	—	—	20.00	22.00
2010G Proof	200,000	Value: 25.00				

KM# 295 10 EURO

18.0000 g., 0.9250 Silver 0.5353 oz. ASW, 32.5 mm. **Subject:** Franz Liszt, 200th Anniversary of Birth

Date	Mintage	F	VF	XF	Unc	BU
2011	—	—	—	—	20.00	22.00
2011 Proof	—	Value: 30.00				

KM# 220 100 EURO

15.5500 g., 0.9990 Gold 0.4994 oz. AGW, 28 mm. **Subject:** Introduction of the Euro Currency **Obv:** Stylized round eagle **Rev:** Euro symbol and arches **Edge:** Reeded

Date	Mintage	F	VF	XF	Unc	BU
2002A Proof	100,000	Value: 750				
2002D Proof	100,000	Value: 750				
2002F Proof	100,000	Value: 750				
2002G Proof	100,000	Value: 750				
2002J Proof	100,000	Value: 750				

KM# 228 100 EURO

15.5500 g., 0.9999 Gold 0.4983 oz. AGW, 28 mm. **Obv:** Stylized eagle, denomination below **Rev:** Quedlinburg Abbey in monogram **Edge:** Reeded

Date	Mintage	F	VF	XF	Unc	BU
2003A Proof	100,000	Value: 750				
2003D Proof	100,000	Value: 750				
2003F Proof	100,000	Value: 750				
2003G Proof	100,000	Value: 750				
2003J Proof	100,000	Value: 750				

KM# 235 100 EURO

15.5500 g., 0.9999 Gold 0.4999 oz. AGW, 28 mm. **Obv:** Stylized eagle, denomination below **Rev:** Bamberg city view **Edge:** Reeded

Date	Mintage	F	VF	XF	Unc	BU
2004A Proof	80,000	Value: 750				
2004D Proof	80,000	Value: 750				
2004F Proof	80,000	Value: 750				
2004G Proof	80,000	Value: 750				
2004J Proof	80,000	Value: 750				

KM# 236 100 EURO

15.5500 g., 0.9990 Gold 0.4994 oz. AGW **Subject:** UNESCO - Weimar **Obv:** Stylized eagle **Rev:** Historical City of Weimar buildings **Edge:** Reeded

Date	Mintage	F	VF	XF	Unc	BU
2006A Proof	80,000	Value: 750				
2006D Proof	80,000	Value: 750				
2006F Proof	80,000	Value: 750				
2006G Proof	80,000	Value: 750				
2006J Proof	80,000	Value: 750				

KM# 237 100 EURO

15.5500 g., 0.9990 Gold 0.4994 oz. AGW, 28 mm. **Subject:** Soccer - Germany 2006 **Obv:** Round stylized eagle **Rev:** Aerial view of stadium

Date	Mintage	F	VF	XF	Unc	BU
2005A Proof	70,000	Value: 750				
2005D Proof	70,000	Value: 750				
2005F Proof	70,000	Value: 750				
2005G Proof	70,000	Value: 750				
2005J Proof	70,000	Value: 750				

KM# 267 100 EURO

15.5500 g., 0.9990 Gold 0.4994 oz. AGW, 28 mm. **Subject:** Lubeck - UNESCO Heritage site **Obv:** Eagle **Rev:** City view

Date	Mintage	F	VF	XF	Unc	BU
2007A	70,000	Value: 750				
2007D	70,000	Value: 750				
2007F	70,000	Value: 750				
2007G	70,000	Value: 750				
2007J	70,000	Value: 750				

KM# 270 100 EURO

15.5500 g., 0.9990 Gold 0.4994 oz. AGW, 28 mm. **Subject:** Goslar - UNESCO Heritage site **Obv:** Eagle **Edge:** Reeded

Date	Mintage	F	VF	XF	Unc	BU
2008A	64,000	Value: 750				
2008D	64,000	Value: 750				
2008F	64,000	Value: 750				
2008G	64,000	Value: 750				
2008J	64,000	Value: 750				

KM# 278 100 EURO

15.5500 g., 0.9990 Gold 0.4994 oz. AGW, 28 mm. **Subject:** Trier - UNESCO Heritage site **Obv:** Eagle and denomination **Rev:** Riverside montage of buildings **Edge:** Reeded

Date	Mintage	F	VF	XF	Unc	BU
2009A Proof	100,000	Value: 750				
2009D Proof	100,000	Value: 750				
2009F Proof	100,000	Value: 750				
2009G Proof	100,000	Value: 750				
2009J Proof	100,000	Value: 750				

KM# 286 100 EURO

15.5500 g., 0.9990 Gold 0.4994 oz. AGW, 28 mm. **Subject:** Wurzburg - UNESCO Heritage site **Rev:** Wurzburg residence and court garden

Date	Mintage	F	VF	XF	Unc	BU
2010A Proof	—	Value: 750				
2010D Proof	—	Value: 750				
2010F Proof	—	Value: 750				
2010G Proof	—	Value: 750				
2010J Proof	—	Value: 750				

KM# 221 200 EURO

31.1000 g., 0.9990 Gold 0.9988 oz. AGW, 32.5 mm. **Subject:** Introduction of the Euro Currency **Obv:** Stylized round eagle **Rev:** Euro symbol and arches **Edge Lettering:** IM ... ZEICHEN ... DER ... EINIGUNG ... EUROPAS

Date	Mintage	F	VF	XF	Unc	BU
2002A Proof	20,000	Value: 1,500				
2002D Proof	20,000	Value: 1,500				
2002F Proof	20,000	Value: 1,500				
2002G Proof	20,000	Value: 1,500				
2002J Proof	20,000	Value: 1,500				

GHANA

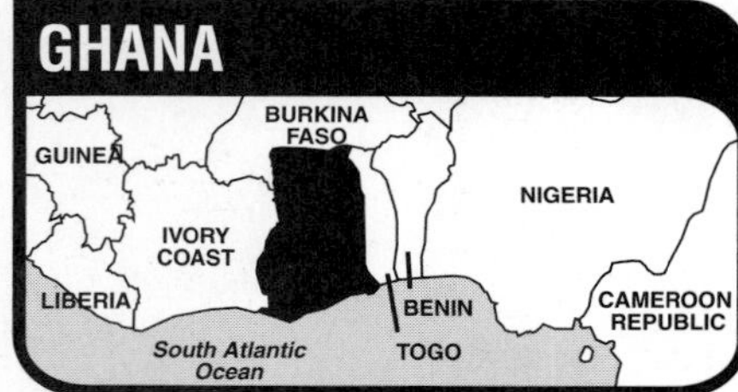

The Republic of Ghana, a member of the Commonwealth of Nations situated on the West Coast of Africa between Ivory Coast and Togo, has an area of 92,100 sq. mi. (238,540 sq. km.) and a population of 14 million, almost entirely African. Capital: Accra. Cocoa (the major crop), coconuts, palm kernels and coffee are exported. Mining, second in importance to agriculture, is concentrated on gold, manganese and industrial diamonds.

MONETARY SYSTEM

1 Cedi = 100 Pesewas, 1965-2007

1 (new) Cedi = 10,000 (old) Cedis, 2007-

REPUBLIC

DECIMAL COINAGE

KM# 36 10 CEDIS

4.4100 g., Copper-Nickel, 22.9 mm. **Obv:** National arms divides date and denomination **Rev:** Gorilla family **Edge:** Plain

Date	Mintage	F	VF	XF	Unc	BU
2003	—	—	—	—	1.50	2.00

REFORM COINAGE

2007-

KM# 37 PESEWA

1.8200 g., Copper Plated Steel, 17 mm. **Obv:** National arms **Obv. Legend:** GHANA **Rev:** Adomi Bridge **Edge:** Plain

Date	Mintage	F	VF	XF	Unc	BU
2007	—	—	—	—	—	0.75

KM# 38 5 PESEWAS

2.5000 g., Nickel Clad Steel, 18 mm. **Obv:** National arms **Obv. Legend:** GHANA **Rev:** Native male blowing horn **Edge:** Plain

Date	Mintage	F	VF	XF	Unc	BU
2007	—	—	—	—	—	1.25

KM# 39 10 PESEWAS

3.2300 g., Nickel Clad Steel, 20.4 mm. **Obv:** National arms **Obv. Legend:** GHANA **Rev:** Open book, pen **Edge:** Reeded

Date	Mintage	F	VF	XF	Unc	BU
2007	—	—	—	—	—	2.50

KM# 40 20 PESEWAS

4.4000 g., Nickel Plated Steel, 23.5 mm. **Obv:** National arms **Obv. Legend:** GHANA **Rev:** Split open cocoa pod **Edge:** Plain

Date	Mintage	F	VF	XF	Unc	BU
2007	—	—	—	—	—	3.50

KM# 41 50 PESEWAS

6.0800 g., Nickel Plated Steel, 26.4 mm. **Obv:** National arms **Obv. Legend:** GHANA **Rev:** 1/2 length figure of market woman facing **Edge:** Reeded

Date	Mintage	F	VF	XF	Unc	BU
2007	—	—	—	—	—	6.00

KM# 42 CEDI

7.4000 g., Bi-Metallic Brass center in Nickel Plated Steel ring, 28 mm. **Obv:** National arms **Obv. Legend:** GHANA **Rev:** Scale of Justice in sprays **Edge:** Segmented reeding

Date	Mintage	F	VF	XF	Unc	BU
2007	—	—	—	—	—	10.00

GIBRALTAR

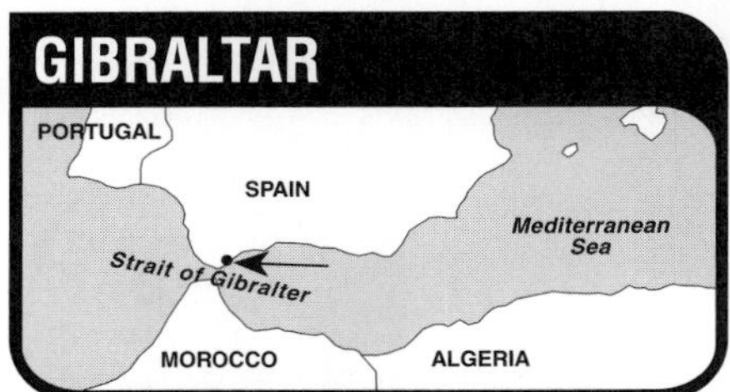

The British Colony of Gibraltar, located at the southernmost point of the Iberian Peninsula, has an area of 2.25 sq. mi. (6.5 sq. km.) and a population of 29,651. Capital (and only town): Gibraltar. Aside from its strategic importance as guardian of the western entrance to the Mediterranean Sea, Gibraltar is also a free port and a British naval base.

RULERS

British

MINT MARKS

PM - Pobjoy Mint

PMM – Pobjoy Mint (only appears on coins dated 2000)

NOTE: ALL coins for 1988 –2003 include the PM mint mark except the 2000 dated circulation pieces which instead have PMM.

MINT PRIVY MARKS

U - Unc finish

MONETARY SYSTEM

100 Pence = 1 Pound

BRITISH COLONY

DECIMAL COINAGE

100 Pence = 1 Pound

KM# 773 PENNY

3.5200 g., Bronze Plated Steel, 20.4 mm. **Ruler:** Elizabeth II **Obv:** Head with tiara right **Obv. Designer:** Ian Rank-Broadley **Rev:** Barbary partridge left divides denomination

Date	Mintage	F	VF	XF	Unc	BU
2001 AA	—	—	—	—	0.35	0.50
2002 AA	—	—	—	—	0.35	0.50
2003 AA	—	—	—	—	0.35	0.50

KM# 1046 PENNY

3.5400 g., Copper Plated Steel, 20.02 mm. **Ruler:** Elizabeth II **Subject:** 300th Anniversary **Obv:** Crowned bust right **Obv. Designer:** Raphael Maklouf **Rev:** Monkey **Rev. Designer:** Philip Nathan **Edge:** Plain

Date	Mintage	F	VF	XF	Unc	BU
2004	—	—	—	—	0.30	0.50

KM# 1079 PENNY

3.5400 g., Copper Plated Steel, 20.02 mm. **Ruler:** Elizabeth II **Obv:** Bust right **Rev:** Sceptre

Date	Mintage	F	VF	XF	Unc	BU
2005	—	—	—	—	0.35	0.50
2006	—	—	—	—	0.35	0.50
2007	—	—	—	—	0.35	0.50
2008	—	—	—	—	0.35	0.50
2009	—	—	—	—	0.35	0.50

KM# 774 2 PENCE

Bronze Plated Steel, 20.4 mm. **Ruler:** Elizabeth II **Obv:** Head with tiara right **Obv. Designer:** Ian Rank-Broadley

Date	Mintage	F	VF	XF	Unc	BU
2001 AA	—	—	—	—	0.50	0.85
2001PM AB	—	—	—	—	0.50	0.85
2003 AA	—	—	—	—	0.50	0.85

KM# 1044 2 PENCE
7.0400 g., Copper Plated Steel, 25.4 mm. **Ruler:** Elizabeth II **Subject:** 300th Anniversary **Obv:** Crowned bust right **Obv. Designer:** Ralphael Maklouf **Rev:** Four old keys **Rev. Designer:** Philip Nathan **Edge:** Plain

Date	Mintage	F	VF	XF	Unc	BU
2004	—	—	—	—	0.50	0.65

KM# 1065 2 PENCE
7.2000 g., Copper Plated Steel, 25.9 mm. **Ruler:** Elizabeth II **Subject:** Operation Torch, 1942 **Rev:** Three soldiers

Date	Mintage	F	VF	XF	Unc	BU
2005	—	—	—	—	0.50	0.65
2006	—	—	—	—	0.50	0.65
2007	—	—	—	—	0.50	0.65
2008	—	—	—	—	0.50	0.65
2009	—	—	—	—	0.50	0.65

KM# 1080 2 PENCE
25.4000 g., Copper Plated Steel, 25.4 mm. **Ruler:** Elizabeth II **Subject:** Diamond Wedding **Rev:** Conjoined busts of Elizabeth II and Philip

Date	Mintage	F	VF	XF	Unc	BU
2009	—	—	—	—	0.50	0.65

KM# 775 5 PENCE
3.1000 g., Copper-Nickel, 18 mm. **Ruler:** Elizabeth II **Obv:** Head with tiara right **Obv. Designer:** Ian Rank-Broadley **Rev:** Barbary Ape left divides denomination

Date	Mintage	F	VF	XF	Unc	BU
2001 AB	—	—	—	—	0.60	0.75
2002 AB	—	—	—	—	0.60	0.75
2003 AA	—	—	—	—	0.60	0.75

KM# 1049 5 PENCE
3.2500 g., Copper-Nickel, 18 mm. **Ruler:** Elizabeth II **Subject:** Tercentenary 1704-2004 **Obv:** Elizabeth II **Obv. Designer:** Raphael Maklouf **Rev:** British Royal Sceptre **Rev. Designer:** Philip Nathan **Edge:** Reeded

Date	Mintage	F	VF	XF	Unc	BU
2004	—	—	—	—	—	1.50

KM# 1081 5 PENCE
3.1000 g., Copper-Nickel, 18 mm. **Ruler:** Elizabeth II **Obv:** Bust in diadem right **Rev:** Barbary ape seated

Date	Mintage	F	VF	XF	Unc	BU
2005	—	—	—	—	0.60	0.75
2006	—	—	—	—	0.60	0.75
2007	—	—	—	—	0.60	0.75
2008	—	—	—	—	0.60	0.75
2009	—	—	—	—	0.60	0.75

KM# 776 10 PENCE
6.5000 g., Copper-Nickel, 24.5 mm. **Ruler:** Elizabeth II **Obv:** Head with tiara right, date below **Obv. Designer:** Ian Rank-Broadley **Rev:** Denomination below building

Date	Mintage	F	VF	XF	Unc	BU
2001 AA	—	—	—	—	1.00	1.25
2001 AB	—	—	—	—	1.00	1.25
2001 AC	—	—	—	—	1.00	1.25
2001 AE	—	—	—	—	1.00	1.25
2002 AC	—	—	—	—	1.00	1.25
2003 AA	—	—	—	—	1.00	1.25

KM# 1047 10 PENCE
6.4200 g., Copper-Nickel, 24.4 mm. **Ruler:** Elizabeth II **Subject:** 300th Anniversary **Obv:** Elizabeth II **Obv. Designer:** Raphael Maklouf **Rev:** Three military officers planning Operation Torch 1942 **Rev. Designer:** Philip Nathan **Edge:** Reeded

Date	Mintage	F	VF	XF	Unc	BU
2004	—	—	—	—	0.75	1.00

KM# 1082 10 PENCE
6.4200 g., Copper-Nickel, 24.4 mm. **Ruler:** Elizabeth II **Subject:** The Great Siege, 1779-1793 **Obv:** Bust in diadem right **Rev:** Cannon left

Date	Mintage	F	VF	XF	Unc	BU
2005	—	—	—	—	0.75	1.00
2006	—	—	—	—	0.75	1.00
2007	—	—	—	—	0.75	1.00
2008	—	—	—	—	0.75	1.00
2009	—	—	—	—	0.75	1.00

KM# 777 20 PENCE
5.0000 g., Copper-Nickel, 21.4 mm. **Ruler:** Elizabeth II **Obv:** Head with tiara right, date below **Obv. Designer:** Ian Rank-Broadley **Rev:** Our Lady of Europa, denomination below and right **Rev. Designer:** Alfred Ryman **Shape:** 7-sided

Date	Mintage	F	VF	XF	Unc	BU
2001 AA	—	—	—	—	1.50	2.00

KM# 1048 20 PENCE
4.9400 g., Copper-Nickel, 21.4 mm. **Ruler:** Elizabeth II **Subject:** 300th Anniversary **Obv:** Crowned buat right **Obv. Designer:** Raphael Maklouf **Rev:** Neanderthal skull found in Gibraltar in 1848 **Rev. Designer:** Philip Nathan **Edge:** Plain **Shape:** 7-sided

Date	Mintage	F	VF	XF	Unc	BU
2004	—	—	—	—	1.00	1.50

KM# 1083 20 PENCE
4.9400 g., Copper-Nickel, 21.4 mm. **Ruler:** Elizabeth II **Obv:** Bust in diadem right **Rev:** Keyring with four keys **Shape:** 7-sided

Date	Mintage	F	VF	XF	Unc	BU
2005	—	—	—	—	1.50	2.00
2006	—	—	—	—	1.50	2.00
2007	—	—	—	—	1.50	2.00
2008	—	—	—	—	1.50	2.00
2009	—	—	—	—	1.50	2.00

KM# 971 50 PENCE
8.0000 g., Copper-Nickel, 27.3 mm. **Ruler:** Elizabeth II **Subject:** Christmas **Obv:** Head with tiara right, date below **Obv. Designer:** Ian Rank-Broadley **Rev:** Three wise men **Edge:** Plain **Shape:** 7-sided

Date	Mintage	F	VF	XF	Unc	BU
2001 BB	30,000	—	—	—	10.00	12.00

KM# 971a 50 PENCE
8.0000 g., 0.9250 Silver 0.2379 oz. ASW, 27.3 mm. **Ruler:** Elizabeth II **Obv:** Head with tiara right, date below **Obv. Designer:** Ian Rank-Broadley **Rev:** Three wise men **Edge:** Plain **Shape:** 7-sided

Date	Mintage	F	VF	XF	Unc	BU
2001 Proof	5,000	Value: 35.00				

KM# 971b 50 PENCE
8.0000 g., 0.9167 Gold 0.2358 oz. AGW, 27.3 mm. **Ruler:** Elizabeth II **Obv:** Head with tiara right, date below **Obv. Designer:** Ian Rank-Broadley **Rev:** Three wise men **Edge:** Plain **Shape:** 7-sided

Date	Mintage	F	VF	XF	Unc	BU
2001 Proof	250	Value: 645				

KM# 778 50 PENCE
8.0000 g., Copper-Nickel, 27.3 mm. **Ruler:** Elizabeth II **Obv:** Head with tiara right **Obv. Designer:** Ian Rank-Broadley **Rev:** Dolphins surround denomination **Edge:** Plain **Shape:** 7-sided

Date	Mintage	F	VF	XF	Unc	BU
2001 AA	—	—	—	—	4.50	5.50
2001 AB	—	—	—	—	4.50	5.50
2003 AB	—	—	—	—	4.50	5.50

KM# 1026 50 PENCE
8.0000 g., Copper-Nickel, 27.3 mm. **Ruler:** Elizabeth II **Subject:** Christmas **Obv:** Head with tiara right, date below **Obv. Designer:** Ian Rank-Broadley **Rev:** Shepherds **Edge:** Plain **Shape:** 7-sided

Date	Mintage	F	VF	XF	Unc	BU
2002PM BB	30,000	—	—	—	10.00	12.00

KM# 1026a 50 PENCE
8.0000 g., 0.9250 Silver 0.2379 oz. ASW, 27.3 mm. **Ruler:** Elizabeth II **Subject:** Christmas **Obv:** Head with tiara right, date below **Obv. Designer:** Ian Rank-Broadley **Rev:** Two shepherds **Edge:** Plain **Shape:** 7-sided

Date	Mintage	F	VF	XF	Unc	BU
2002PM Proof	2,002	Value: 35.00				

KM# 1063a 50 PENCE
8.0000 g., 0.9250 Silver 0.2379 oz. ASW, 27.3 mm. **Ruler:** Elizabeth II **Subject:** Christmas **Obv. Designer:** Ian Rank-Broadley **Rev:** Joseph & Mary

Date	Mintage	F	VF	XF	Unc	BU
2003PM BB	—	—	—	—	12.00	14.00

KM# 1063 50 PENCE
8.0000 g., Copper-Nickel **Ruler:** Elizabeth II **Series:** Christmas **Obv:** Head with tiara right, date below **Obv. Designer:** Ian Rank-Broadley **Rev:** Joseph & Mary **Shape:** 27.3

Date	Mintage	F	VF	XF	Unc	BU
2003PM BB	—	—	—	—	10.00	12.00

KM# 1050 50 PENCE
8.0000 g., Copper-Nickel, 27.3 mm. **Ruler:** Elizabeth II **Subject:** Tercentenary 1704-2004 **Obv:** Elizabeth II **Obv. Designer:** Raphael Maklouf **Rev:** HMS Victory sailing past Gibraltar **Rev. Designer:** Philip Nathan **Edge:** Plain **Shape:** 7-sided

Date	Mintage	F	VF	XF	Unc	BU
2004	—	—	—	—	—	3.00

KM# 1066 50 PENCE
8.0000 g., Copper-Nickel, 27.3 mm. **Ruler:** Elizabeth II **Subject:** Christmas **Obv. Designer:** Raphael Maklouf **Rev:** Santa Claus walking left with sack over shoulder and waving **Shape:** 7-sided

Date	Mintage	F	VF	XF	Unc	BU
2004	—	—	—	—	10.00	12.00

KM# 1084 50 PENCE
8.0000 g., Copper-Nickel, 27.3 mm. **Ruler:** Elizabeth II **Subject:** Glorious 1st of June, 1794 **Rev:** Marines firing from deck of Naval ship **Shape:** 7-sided

Date	Mintage	F	VF	XF	Unc	BU
2004	—	—	—	—	10.00	12.00

KM# 1085 50 PENCE
8.0000 g., Copper-Nickel, 27.3 mm. **Ruler:** Elizabeth II **Subject:** Siege of Sebastopol, 1854 **Rev:** Troops in the Crimea **Shape:** 7-sided

Date	Mintage	F	VF	XF	Unc	BU
2004	—	—	—	—	10.00	12.00

KM# 1086 50 PENCE
8.0000 g., Copper-Nickel, 27.3 mm. **Ruler:** Elizabeth II **Subject:** World War I **Rev:** Troops advancing right **Shape:** 7-sided

Date	Mintage	F	VF	XF	Unc	BU
2004	—	—	—	—	10.00	12.00

KM# 1087 50 PENCE
8.0000 g., Copper-Nickel, 27.3 mm. **Ruler:** Elizabeth II **Subject:** World War II **Rev:** Troops in fox hole **Shape:** 7-sided

Date	Mintage	F	VF	XF	Unc	BU
2004	—	—	—	—	10.00	12.00

KM# 1088 50 PENCE
8.0000 g., Copper-Nickel, 27.3 mm. **Ruler:** Elizabeth II **Subject:** The Falklands, 1982 **Rev:** Troops advancing forward **Shape:** 7-sided

Date	Mintage	F	VF	XF	Unc	BU
2004	—	—	—	—	10.00	12.00

KM# 1067 50 PENCE
8.0000 g., Copper-Nickel, 27.3 mm. **Ruler:** Elizabeth II **Subject:** Christmas **Obv. Designer:** Raphael Maklouf **Rev:** Mary and child **Shape:** 7-sided

Date	Mintage	F	VF	XF	Unc	BU
2005	—	—	—	—	10.00	12.00

KM# 1074 50 PENCE
28.2800 g., Copper-Nickel, 27.13 mm. **Ruler:** Elizabeth II **Subject:** Capture of Gibraltar **Rev:** Naval Battle **Shape:** 7-sided

Date	Mintage	F	VF	XF	Unc	BU
2005	—	—	—	—	7.50	10.00

KM# 1089 50 PENCE
8.0000 g., Copper-Nickel, 27.3 mm. **Ruler:** Elizabeth II **Subject:** Capture of Gibraltar, 1704 **Rev:** Naval Battle **Shape:** 7-sided

Date	Mintage	F	VF	XF	Unc	BU
2006	—	—	—	—	4.50	5.50
2007	—	—	—	—	4.50	5.50
2008	—	—	—	—	4.50	5.50
2009	—	—	—	—	4.50	5.50

KM# 1068 50 PENCE
8.0000 g., Copper-Nickel, 27.3 mm. **Ruler:** Elizabeth II **Subject:** Christmas **Obv. Designer:** Raphael Maklouf **Rev:** Tree **Shape:** 7-sided

Date	Mintage	F	VF	XF	Unc	BU
2006	—	—	—	—	10.00	12.00

KM# 1069 50 PENCE
8.0000 g., Copper-Nickel, 27.3 mm. **Ruler:** Elizabeth II **Subject:** Christmas **Rev:** Santa, large face **Shape:** 7-sided

Date	Mintage	F	VF	XF	Unc	BU
2007	—	—	—	—	10.00	12.00

KM# 1070 50 PENCE
8.0000 g., Copper-Nickel, 27.3 mm. **Ruler:** Elizabeth II **Subject:** Christmas **Shape:** 7-sided

Date	Mintage	F	VF	XF	Unc	BU
2008	—	—	—	—	10.00	12.00

KM# 1090 50 PENCE
8.0000 g., Copper-Nickel, 27.3 mm. **Ruler:** Elizabeth II **Subject:** Our Lady of Europe **Rev:** Madonna and Child seated **Shape:** 7-sided

Date	Mintage	F	VF	XF	Unc	BU
2008	—	—	—	—	7.50	9.00

KM# 1071 50 PENCE
8.0000 g., Copper-Nickel, 27.3 mm. **Ruler:** Elizabeth II **Subject:** Christmas **Shape:** 7-sided

Date	Mintage	F	VF	XF	Unc	BU
2009	—	—	—	—	10.00	12.00

KM# 988 1/25 CROWN
1.2240 g., 0.9990 Gold 0.0393 oz. AGW, 13.92 mm. **Ruler:** Elizabeth II **Subject:** Peter Rabbit Centennial **Obv:** Crowned bust right **Rev:** Peter Rabbit **Edge:** Reeded

Date	Mintage	F	VF	XF	Unc	BU
2002 Proof	5,000	Value: 65.00				

KM# 988a 1/25 CROWN
1.2240 g., 0.9990 Platinum 0.0393 oz. APW, 13.92 mm. **Ruler:** Elizabeth II **Subject:** Peter Rabbit Centennial **Obv:** Crowned bust right **Rev:** Peter Rabbit **Edge:** Reeded

Date	Mintage	F	VF	XF	Unc	BU
2002 Proof	3,000	Value: 95.00				

KM# 1016 1/25 CROWN
1.2441 g., 0.9999 Gold 0.0400 oz. AGW, 13.92 mm. **Ruler:** Elizabeth II **Subject:** Peter Pan **Obv:** Crowned bust right **Rev:** Peter Pan and Tinkerbell flying above city **Edge:** Reeded

Date	Mintage	F	VF	XF	Unc	BU
2002 Proof	10,000	Value: 65.00				

KM# 989 1/10 CROWN
3.1100 g., 0.9990 Gold 0.0999 oz. AGW, 17.95 mm. **Ruler:** Elizabeth II **Subject:** Peter Rabbit Centennial **Obv:** Crowned bust right **Rev:** Peter Rabbit **Edge:** Reeded

Date	Mintage	F	VF	XF	Unc	BU
2002 Proof	5,000	Value: 150				

KM# 989a 1/10 CROWN
3.1100 g., 0.9990 Platinum 0.0999 oz. APW, 17395 mm. **Ruler:** Elizabeth II **Subject:** Peter Rabbit Centennial **Obv:** Crowned bust right **Rev:** Peter Rabbit **Edge:** Reeded

Date	Mintage	F	VF	XF	Unc	BU
2002 Proof	2,000	Value: 225				

KM# 1017 1/10 CROWN
3.1104 g., 0.9999 Gold 0.1000 oz. AGW, 17.95 mm. **Ruler:** Elizabeth II **Subject:** Peter Pan **Obv:** Crowned bust right **Rev:** Peter Pan and Tinkerbell flying above city **Edge:** Reeded

Date	Mintage	F	VF	XF	Unc	BU
2002 Proof	7,500	Value: 150				

KM# 902 1/5 CROWN
6.2200 g., 0.9999 Gold 0.1999 oz. AGW, 22 mm. **Ruler:** Elizabeth II **Subject:** Queen Mother **Obv:** Bust with tiara right **Obv. Designer:** Ian Rank-Broadley **Rev:** 1953 Coronation scene **Edge:** Reeded

Date	Mintage	F	VF	XF	Unc	BU
2001 Proof	5,000	Value: 300				

KM# 903 1/5 CROWN
6.2200 g., 0.9999 Gold 0.1999 oz. AGW **Ruler:** Elizabeth II **Obv:** Bust with tiara right **Obv. Designer:** Ian Rank-Broadley **Rev:** Queen Mother and Prince Charles in 1954

Date	Mintage	F	VF	XF	Unc	BU
2001 Proof	5,000	Value: 300				

KM# 909 1/5 CROWN
6.2200 g., 0.9999 Gold 0.1999 oz. AGW, 22 mm. **Ruler:** Elizabeth II **Series:** Victorian Era - Victoria's Coronation 1838 **Obv:** Bust with tiara right **Obv. Designer:** Ian Rank-Broadley **Rev:** 1838 Coronation scene **Edge:** Reeded

Date	Mintage	F	VF	XF	Unc	BU
2001 Proof	5,000	Value: 300				

KM# 909.1 1/5 CROWN
6.2200 g., 0.9999 Gold 0.1999 oz. AGW, 22 mm. **Ruler:** Elizabeth II **Series:** Victorian Era **Obv:** Bust with tiara right **Obv. Designer:** Ian Rank-Broadley **Rev:** 1838 Coronation scene with a tiny emerald set in the field below the 1838 date **Edge:** Reeded

Date	Mintage	F	VF	XF	Unc	BU
2001 Proof	2,001	Value: 320				

KM# 911.1 1/5 CROWN
6.2200 g., 0.9999 Gold 0.1999 oz. AGW, 22 mm. **Ruler:** Elizabeth II **Series:** Victorian Era - Empress of India 1876 **Obv:** Bust with tiara right **Obv. Designer:** Ian Rank-Broadley **Rev:** Crowned portrait of Victoria and two elephants **Edge:** Reeded

Date	Mintage	F	VF	XF	Unc	BU
2001 Proof	5,000	Value: 320				

KM# 911.2 1/5 CROWN
6.2200 g., 0.9999 Gold 0.1999 oz. AGW, 22 mm. **Ruler:** Elizabeth II **Series:** Victorian Era - Empress of India 1876 **Obv:** Bust with tiara right **Obv. Designer:** Ian Rank-Broadley **Rev:** Tiny ruby set in the field behind Victoria's head **Edge:** Reeded

Date	Mintage	F	VF	XF	Unc	BU
2001 Proof	2,001	Value: 320				

KM# 913.1 1/5 CROWN
6.2200 g., 0.9999 Gold 0.1999 oz. AGW, 22 mm. **Ruler:** Elizabeth II **Series:** Victorian Era - Diamond Jubilee 1897 **Obv:** Bust with tiara right **Obv. Designer:** Ian Rank-Broadley **Rev:** Victoria's cameo portrait above naval ships **Edge:** Reeded

Date	Mintage	F	VF	XF	Unc	BU
2001 Proof	5,000	Value: 300				

KM# 913.2 1/5 CROWN
6.2200 g., 0.9999 Gold 0.1999 oz. AGW, 22 mm. **Ruler:** Elizabeth II **Series:** Victorian Era - Diamond Jubilee 1897 **Obv:** Bust with tiara right **Obv. Designer:** Ian Rank-Broadley **Rev:** Tiny diamond set at the top of the fourth mast **Edge:** Reeded

Date	Mintage	F	VF	XF	Unc	BU
2001 Proof	2,001	Value: 320				

KM# 915.1 1/5 CROWN
6.2200 g., 0.9999 Gold 0.1999 oz. AGW, 22 mm. **Ruler:** Elizabeth II **Series:** Victorian Era - Victoria's Death 1901 **Obv:** Bust with tiara right **Obv. Designer:** Ian Rank-Broadley **Rev:** Victoria's cameo portrait and Osborne Manor **Edge:** Reeded

Date	Mintage	F	VF	XF	Unc	BU
2001 Proof	5,000	Value: 300				

KM# 915.2 1/5 CROWN
6.2200 g., 0.9999 Gold 0.1999 oz. AGW, 22 mm. **Ruler:** Elizabeth II **Series:** Victorian Era - Victoria's Death 1901 **Obv:** Bust with tiara right **Obv. Designer:** Ian Rank-Broadley **Rev:** Tiny sapphire set in the field between the towers **Edge:** Reeded

Date	Mintage	F	VF	XF	Unc	BU
2001 Proof	2,001	Value: 320				

KM# 917 1/5 CROWN
6.2200 g., 0.9999 Gold 0.1999 oz. AGW, 22 mm. **Ruler:** Elizabeth II **Series:** Victorian Era - Prince Albert and the Great Exhibition 1851 **Obv:** Bust with tiara right **Obv. Designer:** Ian Rank-Broadley **Rev:** Albert's cameo portrait and the exhibit hall **Edge:** Reeded

Date	Mintage	F	VF	XF	Unc	BU
2001 Proof	5,000	Value: 300				

KM# 919 1/5 CROWN
6.2200 g., 0.9999 Gold 0.1999 oz. AGW, 22 mm. **Ruler:** Elizabeth II **Series:** Victorian Era - Isambard K. Brunel **Obv:** Bust with tiara right **Obv. Designer:** Ian Rank-Broadley **Rev:** Portrait in top hat and railroad bridge **Edge:** Reeded

Date	Mintage	F	VF	XF	Unc	BU
2001 Proof	5,000	Value: 300				

KM# 921 1/5 CROWN
6.2200 g., 0.9999 Gold 0.1999 oz. AGW, 22 mm. **Ruler:** Elizabeth II **Series:** Victorian Era - Charles Dickens **Obv:** Bust with tiara right **Obv. Designer:** Ian Rank-Broadley **Rev:** Portrait and scene from "Oliver Twist" **Edge:** Reeded

Date	Mintage	F	VF	XF	Unc	BU
2001 Proof	5,000	Value: 300				

KM# 923 1/5 CROWN
6.2200 g., 0.9999 Gold 0.1999 oz. AGW, 22 mm. **Ruler:** Elizabeth II **Series:** Victorian Era - Charles Darwin **Obv:** Bust with tiara right **Obv. Designer:** Ian Rank-Broadley **Rev:** Portrait, ship and a squatting aboriginal figure **Edge:** Reeded

Date	Mintage	F	VF	XF	Unc	BU
2001 Proof	5,000	Value: 300				

KM# 925 1/5 CROWN
6.2200 g., 0.9999 Gold 0.1999 oz. AGW, 22 mm. **Ruler:** Elizabeth II **Series:** Mythology of the Solar System **Obv:** Queens portrait **Rev:** Standing goddess with snake basket **Edge:** Reeded

Date	Mintage	F	VF	XF	Unc	BU
2001 Proof	5,000	Value: 300				

KM# 926 1/5 CROWN
Bi-Metallic 0.925 Silver center in 0.999 Gold ring, 32.25 mm. **Ruler:** Elizabeth II **Series:** Mythology of the Solar System **Obv:** Bust with tiara right **Obv. Designer:** Ian Rank-Broadley **Rev:** Standing goddess with snake basket **Edge:** Reeded

Date	Mintage	F	VF	XF	Unc	BU
2001 In Proof sets only	999	Value: 400				

KM# 929.1 1/5 CROWN
6.2200 g., 0.9999 Gold 0.1999 oz. AGW, 22 mm. **Ruler:** Elizabeth II **Series:** Mythology of the Solar System - Sun **Obv:** Bust with tiara right **Obv. Designer:** Ian Rank-Broadley **Rev:** Helios in chariot and the sun **Edge:** Reeded

Date	Mintage	F	VF	XF	Unc	BU
2001 Proof	5,000	Value: 300				

KM# 929.2 1/5 CROWN
6.2200 g., 0.9999 Gold 0.1999 oz. AGW, 22 mm. **Ruler:** Elizabeth II **Series:** Mythology of the Solar System **Obv:** Bust with tiara right **Obv. Designer:** Ian Rank-Broadley **Rev:** Fiery hologram in the sun **Edge:** Reeded

Date	Mintage	F	VF	XF	Unc	BU
2001 In Proof sets only	999	Value: 375				

KM# 931.1 1/5 CROWN
6.2200 g., 0.9999 Gold 0.1999 oz. AGW, 22 mm. **Ruler:** Elizabeth II **Series:** Mythology of the Solar System - Moon **Obv:** Bust with tiara right **Obv. Designer:** Ian Rank-Broadley **Rev:** Goddess Diana and the moon **Edge:** Reeded

Date	Mintage	F	VF	XF	Unc	BU
2001 Proof	5,000	Value: 300				

KM# 931.2 1/5 CROWN
6.2200 g., 0.9999 Gold 0.1999 oz. AGW, 22 mm. **Ruler:** Elizabeth II **Series:** Mythology of the Solar System - Moon **Obv:** Bust with tiara right **Obv. Designer:** Ian Rank-Broadley **Rev:** Small pearl set in the moon **Edge:** Reeded

Date	Mintage	F	VF	XF	Unc	BU
2001 In Proof sets only	999	Value: 375				

KM# 933.1 1/5 CROWN
6.2200 g., 0.9999 Gold 0.1999 oz. AGW, 22 mm. **Ruler:** Elizabeth II **Series:** Mythology of the Solar System - Atlas **Obv:** Bust with tiara right **Obv. Designer:** Ian Rank-Broadley **Rev:** Atlas carrying the earth **Edge:** Reeded

Date	Mintage	F	VF	XF	Unc	BU
2001 Proof	5,000	Value: 300				

KM# 933.2 1/5 CROWN
6.2200 g., 0.9999 Gold 0.1999 oz. AGW, 22 mm. **Ruler:** Elizabeth II **Series:** Mythology of the Solar System - Atlas **Obv:** Bust with tiara right **Obv. Designer:** Ian Rank-Broadley **Rev:** Tiny diamond set in the earth **Edge:** Reeded

Date	Mintage	F	VF	XF	Unc	BU
2001 In Proof sets only	999	Value: 375				

KM# 935 1/5 CROWN
6.2200 g., 0.9999 Gold 0.1999 oz. AGW, 22 mm. **Ruler:** Elizabeth II **Series:** Mythology of the Solar System - Neptune **Obv:** Bust with tiara right **Obv. Designer:** Ian Rank-Broadley **Rev:** Seated god with trident and ringed planet **Edge:** Reeded

Date	Mintage	F	VF	XF	Unc	BU
2001 Proof	5,000	Value: 300				

KM# 937 1/5 CROWN
6.2200 g., 0.9999 Gold 0.1999 oz. AGW, 22 mm. **Ruler:** Elizabeth II **Series:** Mythology of the Solar System - Jupiter **Obv:** Bust with tiara right **Obv. Designer:** Ian Rank-Broadley **Rev:** Seated god with lightning bolts and a planet **Edge:** Reeded

Date	Mintage	F	VF	XF	Unc	BU
2001 Proof	5,000	Value: 300				

KM# 939 1/5 CROWN
6.2200 g., 0.9999 Gold 0.1999 oz. AGW, 22 mm. **Ruler:** Elizabeth II **Series:** Mythology of the Solar System - Mars **Obv:** Bust with tiara right **Obv. Designer:** Ian Rank-Broadley **Rev:** Standing Roman solider and a planet **Edge:** Reeded

Date	Mintage	F	VF	XF	Unc	BU
2001 Proof	5,000	Value: 300				

KM# 941 1/5 CROWN
6.2200 g., 0.9999 Gold 0.1999 oz. AGW, 22 mm. **Ruler:** Elizabeth II **Series:** Mythology of the Solar System - Mercury **Obv:** Bust with tiara right **Obv. Designer:** Ian Rank-Broadley **Rev:** Seated god with caduceus and a planet **Edge:** Reeded

Date	Mintage	F	VF	XF	Unc	BU
2001 Proof	5,000	Value: 300				

KM# 943 1/5 CROWN
6.2200 g., 0.9999 Gold 0.1999 oz. AGW, 22 mm. **Ruler:** Elizabeth II **Series:** Mythology of the Solar System - Uranus **Obv:** Bust with tiara right **Obv. Designer:** Ian Rank-Broadley **Rev:** Seated god with scepter **Edge:** Reeded

Date	Mintage	F	VF	XF	Unc	BU
2001 Proof	5,000	Value: 300				

KM# 945 1/5 CROWN
6.2200 g., 0.9999 Gold 0.1999 oz. AGW, 22 mm. **Ruler:** Elizabeth II **Series:** Mythology of the Solar System - Saturn **Obv:** Bust with tiara right **Obv. Designer:** Ian Rank-Broadley **Rev:** Seated god with long handled sickle and a ringed planet **Edge:** Reeded

Date	Mintage	F	VF	XF	Unc	BU
2001 Proof	5,000	Value: 300				

KM# 947 1/5 CROWN
6.2200 g., 0.9999 Gold 0.1999 oz. AGW, 22 mm. **Ruler:** Elizabeth II **Series:** Mythology of the Solar System - Pluto **Obv:** Bust with tiara right **Obv. Designer:** Ian Rank-Broadley **Rev:** Seated god with dogs and a planet **Edge:** Reeded

Date	Mintage	F	VF	XF	Unc	BU
2001 Proof	5,000	Value: 300				

KM# 949 1/5 CROWN
6.2200 g., 0.9999 Gold 0.1999 oz. AGW, 22 mm. **Ruler:** Elizabeth II **Series:** Mythology of the Solar System - Venus **Obv:** Bust with tiara right **Obv. Designer:** Ian Rank-Broadley **Rev:** Goddess seated on a half shell **Edge:** Reeded

Date	Mintage	F	VF	XF	Unc	BU
2001 Proof	5,000	Value: 300				

KM# 951 1/5 CROWN
6.2200 g., 0.9999 Gold 0.1999 oz. AGW, 22 mm. **Ruler:** Elizabeth II **Subject:** Queen's 76th Birthday **Obv:** Bust with tiara right **Obv. Designer:** Ian Rank-Broadley **Rev:** Queen in Order of the Garter robes with a tiny inset diamond **Edge:** Reeded

Date	Mintage	F	VF	XF	Unc	BU
2001 Proof	2,001	Value: 320				

KM# 954 1/5 CROWN
6.2200 g., 0.9999 Gold 0.1999 oz. AGW, 22 mm. **Ruler:** Elizabeth II **Series:** Victorian Age Part II - Victoria's Accession to the Throne **Obv:** Bust with tiara right **Obv. Designer:** Ian Rank-Broadley **Rev:** Victoria learning of her accession **Edge:** Reeded

Date	Mintage	F	VF	XF	Unc	BU
2001 Proof	5,000	Value: 300				

KM# 956 1/5 CROWN
6.2200 g., 0.9999 Gold 0.1999 oz. AGW, 22 mm. **Ruler:** Elizabeth II **Series:** Victorian Age Part II - Royal Family **Rev:** Victoria and Albert seated with children **Edge:** Reeded

Date	Mintage	F	VF	XF	Unc	BU
2001 Proof	5,000	Value: 300				

KM# 958 1/5 CROWN
6.2200 g., 0.9999 Gold 0.1999 oz. AGW, 22 mm. **Ruler:** Elizabeth II **Series:** Victorian Age Part II - Victoria in Scotland **Obv:** Bust with tiara right **Obv. Designer:** Ian Rank-Broadley **Rev:** Victoria on horse and servant **Edge:** Reeded

Date	Mintage	F	VF	XF	Unc	BU
2001 Proof	5,000	Value: 300				

KM# 960 1/5 CROWN
6.2200 g., 0.9999 Gold 0.1999 oz. AGW, 22 mm. **Ruler:** Elizabeth II **Series:** Victorian Age Part II **Obv:** Bust with tiara right **Obv. Designer:** Ian Rank-Broadley **Rev:** Portraits of Gladstone and Disaraeli **Edge:** Reeded

Date	Mintage	F	VF	XF	Unc	BU
2001 Proof	5,000	Value: 300				

KM# 962 1/5 CROWN
6.2200 g., 0.9999 Gold 0.1999 oz. AGW, 22 mm. **Ruler:** Elizabeth II **Series:** Victorian Age Part II **Obv:** Bust with tiara right **Obv. Designer:** Ian Rank-Broadley **Rev:** Florence Nightingale holding lantern **Edge:** Reeded

Date	Mintage	F	VF	XF	Unc	BU
2001 Proof	5,000	Value: 300				

KM# 964 1/5 CROWN
6.2200 g., 0.9999 Gold 0.1999 oz. AGW, 22 mm. **Ruler:** Elizabeth II **Series:** Victorian Age Part II **Obv:** Bust with tiara right **Obv. Designer:** Ian Rank-Broadley **Rev:** Lord Tennyson with the Light Brigade in background **Edge:** Reeded

Date	Mintage	F	VF	XF	Unc	BU
2001 Proof	5,000	Value: 300				

KM# 966 1/5 CROWN
6.2200 g., 0.9999 Gold 0.1999 oz. AGW, 22 mm. **Ruler:** Elizabeth II **Series:** Victorian Age Part II **Obv:** Bust with tiara right **Obv. Designer:** Ian Rank-Broadley **Rev:** Stanley meeting Dr. Livingstone **Edge:** Reeded

Date	Mintage	F	VF	XF	Unc	BU
2001 Proof	5,000	Value: 300				

KM# 968 1/5 CROWN
6.2200 g., 0.9999 Gold 0.1999 oz. AGW, 22 mm. **Ruler:** Elizabeth II **Series:** Victorian Age Part II **Obv:** Bust with tiara right **Rev:** Bronte sisters **Edge:** Reeded

Date	Mintage	F	VF	XF	Unc	BU
2001 Proof	5,000	Value: 300				

KM# 978 1/5 CROWN
6.2200 g., 0.9990 Gold 0.1998 oz. AGW, 22 mm. **Ruler:** Elizabeth II **Subject:** Queen Mother's Life **Obv:** Bust right **Rev:** Prince William's christening scene **Edge:** Reeded

Date	Mintage	F	VF	XF	Unc	BU
2002 Proof	5,000	Value: 300				

KM# 980 1/5 CROWN
6.2200 g., 0.9999 Gold 0.1999 oz. AGW, 22 mm. **Ruler:** Elizabeth II **Subject:** World Cup Soccer **Obv:** Bust right **Rev:** Two players about to collide **Edge:** Reeded

Date	Mintage	F	VF	XF	Unc	BU
2002 Proof	5,000	Value: 300				

KM# 982 1/5 CROWN
6.2200 g., 0.9999 Gold 0.1999 oz. AGW, 22 mm. **Ruler:** Elizabeth II **Subject:** World Cup Soccer **Obv:** Bust right **Rev:** Two players facing viewer **Edge:** Reeded

Date	Mintage	F	VF	XF	Unc	BU
2002 Proof	5,000	Value: 300				

KM# 984 1/5 CROWN
6.2200 g., 0.9999 Gold 0.1999 oz. AGW, 22 mm. **Ruler:** Elizabeth II **Subject:** World Cup Soccer **Obv:** Bust right **Rev:** Two horizontal players **Edge:** Reeded

Date	Mintage	F	VF	XF	Unc	BU
2002 Proof	5,000	Value: 300				

KM# 986 1/5 CROWN
6.2200 g., 0.9999 Gold 0.1999 oz. AGW, 22 mm. **Ruler:** Elizabeth II **Subject:** World Cup Soccer **Obv:** Bust right **Rev:** Two players moving to the left **Edge:** Reeded

Date	Mintage	F	VF	XF	Unc	BU
2002 Proof	5,000	Value: 300				

KM# 990 1/5 CROWN
6.2200 g., 0.9990 Gold 0.1998 oz. AGW, 22 mm. **Ruler:** Elizabeth II **Subject:** Peter Rabbit Centennial **Obv:** Bust right **Rev:** Peter Rabbit **Edge:** Reeded

Date	Mintage	F	VF	XF	Unc	BU
2002 Proof	3,500	Value: 300				

KM# 990a 1/5 CROWN
6.2200 g., 0.9990 Platinum 0.1998 oz. APW, 22 mm. **Ruler:** Elizabeth II **Subject:** Peter Rabbit Centennial **Obv:** Bust right **Rev:** Peter Rabbit **Edge:** Reeded

Date	Mintage	F	VF	XF	Unc	BU
2002 Proof	1,500	Value: 450				

KM# 993 1/5 CROWN
6.2200 g., 0.3750 Gold 0.0750 oz. AGW, 22 mm. **Ruler:** Elizabeth II **Subject:** Queen's Golden Jubilee **Obv:** Bust with tiara right **Obv. Designer:** Ian Rank-Broadley **Rev:** Royal couple and tree house **Edge:** Reeded

Date	Mintage	F	VF	XF	Unc	BU
2002 Proof	5,000	Value: 120				

KM# 993a 1/5 CROWN
6.2200 g., 0.9999 Gold 0.1999 oz. AGW, 22 mm. **Ruler:** Elizabeth II **Subject:** Queen's Golden Jubilee **Obv:** Bust with tiara right **Obv. Designer:** Ian Rank-Broadley **Rev:** Royal couple and tree house **Edge:** Reeded

Date	Mintage	F	VF	XF	Unc	BU
2002 Proof	2,002	Value: 300				

KM# 995 1/5 CROWN
6.2200 g., 0.3750 Gold 0.0750 oz. AGW, 22 mm. **Ruler:** Elizabeth II **Subject:** Queen's Golden Jubilee **Obv:** Bust with tiara right **Obv. Designer:** Ian Rank-Broadley **Rev:** Royal coach **Edge:** Reeded

Date	Mintage	F	VF	XF	Unc	BU
2002 Proof	5,000	Value: 120				

KM# 995a 1/5 CROWN
6.2200 g., 0.9999 Gold 0.1999 oz. AGW, 22 mm. **Ruler:** Elizabeth II **Subject:** Queen's Golden Jubilee **Obv:** Bust with tiara right **Obv. Designer:** Ian Rank-Broadley **Rev:** Royal coach **Edge:** Reeded

Date	Mintage	F	VF	XF	Unc	BU
2002 Proof	2,002	Value: 320				

KM# 997 1/5 CROWN
6.2200 g., 0.3750 Gold 0.0750 oz. AGW, 22 mm. **Ruler:** Elizabeth II **Subject:** Queen's Golden Jubilee **Obv:** Bust with tiara right **Obv. Designer:** Ian Rank-Broadley **Rev:** Queen holding baby **Edge:** Reeded

Date	Mintage	F	VF	XF	Unc	BU
2002 Proof	5,000	Value: 120				

KM# 997a 1/5 CROWN
6.2200 g., 0.9999 Gold 0.1999 oz. AGW, 22 mm. **Ruler:** Elizabeth II **Subject:** Queen's Golden Jubilee **Obv:** Bust with tiara right **Obv. Designer:** Ian Rank-Broadley **Rev:** Queen holding baby **Edge:** Reeded

Date	Mintage	F	VF	XF	Unc	BU
2002 Proof	2,002	Value: 320				

KM# 999 1/5 CROWN
6.2200 g., 0.3750 Gold 0.0750 oz. AGW, 22 mm. **Ruler:** Elizabeth II **Subject:** Queen's Golden Jubilee **Obv:** Bust with tiara right **Obv. Designer:** Ian Rank-Broadley **Rev:** Yacht under Tower bridge **Edge:** Reeded

Date	Mintage	F	VF	XF	Unc	BU
2002 Proof	5,000	Value: 120				

KM# 999a 1/5 CROWN
6.2200 g., 0.9999 Gold 0.1999 oz. AGW, 22 mm. **Ruler:** Elizabeth II **Subject:** Queen's Golden Jubilee **Obv:** Bust with tiara right **Obv. Designer:** Ian Rank-Broadley **Rev:** Yacht under Tower bridge **Edge:** Reeded

Date	Mintage	F	VF	XF	Unc	BU
2002 Proof	2,002	Value: 320				

KM# 1001 1/5 CROWN
6.2200 g., 0.9999 Gold 0.1999 oz. AGW, 22 mm. **Ruler:** Elizabeth II **Subject:** Queen's Golden Jubilee **Obv:** Bust with tiara right **Obv. Designer:** Ian Rank-Broadley **Rev:** Crown jewels inset with a tiny diamond, ruby, sapphire and emerald **Edge:** Reeded

Date	Mintage	F	VF	XF	Unc	BU
2002 Proof	2,002	Value: 320				

KM# 1003 1/5 CROWN
6.2200 g., Electrum Special alloy of equal parts of gold and silver, 22 mm. **Ruler:** Elizabeth II **Series:** Ancient Coins **Obv:** Bust with tiara right **Obv. Designer:** Ian Rank-Broadley **Rev:** Head of Athena left **Edge:** Reeded **Note:** From a Mysia electrum coin c.520BC.

Date	Mintage	F	VF	XF	Unc	BU
2002 Proof	3,500	Value: 125				

KM# 1005 1/5 CROWN
6.2200 g., Electrum Special alloy of equal parts of gold and silver., 22 mm. **Ruler:** Elizabeth II **Series:** Ancient Coins **Obv:** Bust with tiara right **Obv. Designer:** Ian Rank-Broadley **Rev:** Head of Hercules right **Edge:** Reeded **Note:** From a Lesbos coin c. 480-450 BC.

Date	Mintage	F	VF	XF	Unc	BU
2002 Proof	3,500	Value: 125				

KM# 1007 1/5 CROWN
6.2200 g., 0.9990 Electrum Special alloy of equal parts of gold and silver. 0.1998 oz., 22 mm. **Ruler:** Elizabeth II **Series:** Ancient Coins **Obv:** Bust with tiara right **Obv. Designer:** Ian Rank-Broadley **Rev:** Pegasus **Edge:** Reeded **Note:** From a Lampsakos electrum coin c. 450 BC.

Date	Mintage	F	VF	XF	Unc	BU
2002 Proof	3,500	Value: 120				

KM# 1009 1/5 CROWN
6.2200 g., Electrum Special Alloy of equal parts of gold and silver., 22 mm. **Ruler:** Elizabeth II **Series:** Ancient Coins **Obv:** Bust with tiara right **Obv. Designer:** Ian Rank-Broadley **Rev:** Lion and bull facing **Edge:** Reeded **Note:** From a Kroisos "sic" coin c. 560-546 BC.

Date	Mintage	F	VF	XF	Unc	BU
2002 Proof	3,500	Value: 125				

KM# 1012 1/5 CROWN
6.2200 g., 0.9999 Gold 0.1999 oz. AGW, 22 mm. **Ruler:** Elizabeth II **Subject:** Queen Mother **Obv:** Bust with tiara right **Obv. Designer:** Ian Rank-Broadley **Rev:** Queen Mother trout fishing **Edge:** Reeded

Date	Mintage	F	VF	XF	Unc	BU
2002 Proof	5,000	Value: 300				

KM# 1014 1/5 CROWN
6.2200 g., 0.9999 Gold 0.1999 oz. AGW, 22 mm. **Ruler:** Elizabeth II **Subject:** Princess Diana **Obv:** Bust right **Rev:** Diana's portrait **Edge:** Reeded

Date	Mintage	F	VF	XF	Unc	BU
2002 Proof	5,000	Value: 300				

KM# 1018 1/5 CROWN
6.2200 g., 0.9999 Gold 0.1999 oz. AGW, 22 mm. **Ruler:** Elizabeth II **Subject:** Peter Pan **Obv:** Bust right **Rev:** Peter Pan and Tinkerbell flying above city **Edge:** Reeded

Date	Mintage	F	VF	XF	Unc	BU
2002 Proof	5,000	Value: 300				

KM# 1020 1/5 CROWN
6.2200 g., 0.9999 Gold 0.1999 oz. AGW, 22 mm. **Ruler:** Elizabeth II **Subject:** Grand Masonic Lodge **Obv:** Bust right **Rev:** Masonic seal above Gibraltar **Edge:** Reeded

Date	Mintage	F	VF	XF	Unc	BU
2002 Proof	5,000	Value: 300				

KM# 991 1/2 CROWN
15.5500 g., 0.9990 Gold 0.4994 oz. AGW, 30 mm. **Ruler:** Elizabeth II **Subject:** Peter Rabbit Centennial **Obv:** Bust right **Rev:** Peter Rabbit **Edge:** Reeded

Date	Mintage	F	VF	XF	Unc	BU
2002 Proof	1,000	Value: 750				

KM# 1002 1/2 CROWN
15.5500 g., 0.9999 Gold 0.4999 oz. AGW, 30 mm. **Ruler:** Elizabeth II **Subject:** Queen's Golden Jubilee **Obv:** Bust with tiara right **Obv. Designer:** Ian Rank-Broadley **Rev:** Crown jewels inset with a tiny diamond, ruby, sapphire and emerald **Edge:** Reeded

Date	Mintage	F	VF	XF	Unc	BU
2002 Proof	999	Value: 750				

KM# 1004 1/2 CROWN
15.5500 g., Electrum Special alloy of equal parts of gold and silver., 32.2 mm. **Ruler:** Elizabeth II **Series:** Ancient Coins **Obv:** Bust with tiara right **Obv. Designer:** Ian Rank-Broadley **Rev:** Head of Athena left **Edge:** Reeded **Note:** From a Mysia electrum coin c. 520 BC.

Date	Mintage	F	VF	XF	Unc	BU
2002 Proof	2,000	Value: 250				

KM# 1006 1/2 CROWN
15.5500 g., Electrum Special alloy of equal parts of gold and silver., 32.2 mm. **Ruler:** Elizabeth II **Series:** Ancient Coins **Obv:** Bust with tiara right **Obv. Designer:** Ian Rank-Broadley **Rev:** Head of Hercules right **Edge:** Reeded **Note:** From a Lesbos coin c. 480-450 BC.

Date	Mintage	F	VF	XF	Unc	BU
2002 Proof	2,000	Value: 250				

KM# 1008 1/2 CROWN
15.5500 g., Gold With Silver Special alloy of equal parts of gold and silver., 32.2 mm. **Ruler:** Elizabeth II **Series:** Ancient Coins **Obv:** Bust with tiara right **Obv. Designer:** Ian Rank-Broadley **Rev:** Pegasus **Edge:** Reeded **Note:** From a Lampsakos electrum coin c. 450 BC.

Date	Mintage	F	VF	XF	Unc	BU
2002 Proof	2,000	Value: 250				

KM# 1010 1/2 CROWN
15.5500 g., Electrum Special alloy of equal parts of gold and silver., 32.2 mm. **Ruler:** Elizabeth II **Series:** Ancient Coins **Obv:** Bust with tiara right **Obv. Designer:** Ian Rank-Broadley **Rev:** Lion and bull facing **Edge:** Reeded **Note:** From a Kroisos [sic] coin c. 560-546 BC.

Date	Mintage	F	VF	XF	Unc	BU
2002 Proof	2,000	Value: 250				

KM# 1056 CROWN
31.1000 g., 0.9990 Tri-Metallic Center: silver, Ring: silver-gilt, Outer ring: silver-pearl black 0.9988 oz., 38.60 mm. **Ruler:** Elizabeth II **Subject:** 21st Century **Obv:** Crowned bust right **Obv. Legend:** GIBRALTER • ELIZABETH II **Rev:** Helmeted cross at center flanked by satellites, archaic sailing ship below **Rev. Legend:** 21st CENTURY **Edge:** Reeded

Date	Mintage	F	VF	XF	Unc	BU
2001 Proof	2,001	Value: 600				

KM# 904 CROWN
28.2800 g., Copper-Nickel, 38.6 mm. **Ruler:** Elizabeth II **Subject:** The Life of Queen Elizabeth - The Queen Mother **Obv:** Bust with tiara right **Obv. Designer:** Ian Rank-Broadley **Rev:** 1953 Coronation scene **Edge:** Reeded

Date	Mintage	F	VF	XF	Unc	BU
2001	—	—	—	—	10.00	12.00

KM# 904a CROWN
28.2800 g., 0.9250 Silver 0.8410 oz. ASW, 38.6 mm. **Ruler:** Elizabeth II **Subject:** The Life of Queen Elizabeth - The Queen Mother **Obv:** Bust with tiara right **Obv. Designer:** Ian Rank-Broadley **Rev:** 1953 Coronation scene **Edge:** Reeded

Date	Mintage	F	VF	XF	Unc	BU
2001 Proof	10,000	Value: 47.50				

KM# 905 CROWN

28.2800 g., Copper-Nickel, 38.6 mm. **Ruler:** Elizabeth II **Subject:** The Life of Queen Elizabeth - The Queen Mother **Obv:** Bust with tiara right **Obv. Designer:** Ian Rank-Broadley **Rev:** Queen Mother with Prince Charles in 1954 **Edge:** Reeded

Date	Mintage	F	VF	XF	Unc	BU
2001	—	—	—	—	10.00	12.00

KM# 905a CROWN

28.2800 g., 0.9250 Silver 0.8410 oz. ASW, 38.6 mm. **Ruler:** Elizabeth II **Subject:** The Life of Queen Elizabeth - The Queen Mother **Obv:** Bust with tiara right **Obv. Designer:** Ian Rank-Broadley **Rev:** Queen Mother with Prince Charles in 1954 **Edge:** Reeded

Date	Mintage	F	VF	XF	Unc	BU
2001 Proof	10,000	Value: 47.50				

KM# 906 CROWN

28.2800 g., Copper-Nickel, 38.6 mm. **Ruler:** Elizabeth II **Subject:** 21st Century **Obv:** Crowned bust right, date below **Obv. Designer:** Raphael Maklouf **Rev:** Celtic cross, Viking ship and modern technological items **Edge:** Reeded

Date	Mintage	F	VF	XF	Unc	BU
2001	—	—	—	—	10.00	12.00

KM# 906a CROWN

31.1035 g., 0.9990 Silver 0.9990 oz. ASW, 38.6 mm. **Ruler:** Elizabeth II **Subject:** 21st Century **Obv:** Crowned bust right, date below **Obv. Designer:** Raphael Maklouf **Rev:** Celtic cross, Viking ship and modern technological items **Edge:** Reeded **Note:** 31.1035 .999 Silver, 1.0000 ASW with a gold plated inner ring and a blackened outer ring.

Date	Mintage	F	VF	XF	Unc	BU
2001 Proof	2,001	Value: 75.00				

KM# 906b CROWN

31.1000 g., Tri-Metallic Center .9995 Platinum 5.2g. Inner Ring .9999 Gold 14.2g. Outer Ring .999 Silver 11.7g **Ruler:** Elizabeth II **Subject:** 21st Century **Obv:** Crowned bust right, date below **Obv. Designer:** Raphael Maklouf **Rev:** Celtic cross, Viking ship and modern technological items

Date	Mintage	F	VF	XF	Unc	BU
2001 Proof	999	Value: 750				

KM# 910 CROWN

28.2800 g., Copper-Nickel, 38.6 mm. **Ruler:** Elizabeth II **Series:** The Victorian Age **Obv:** Bust with tiara right **Obv. Designer:** Ian Rank-Broadley **Rev:** 1838 Coronation of Queen Victoria **Edge:** Reeded

Date	Mintage	F	VF	XF	Unc	BU
2001	—	—	—	—	10.00	12.00

KM# 910a CROWN

28.2800 g., 0.9250 Silver 0.8410 oz. ASW, 38.6 mm. **Ruler:** Elizabeth II **Series:** Victorian Era **Obv:** Bust with tiara right **Obv. Designer:** Ian Rank-Broadley **Rev:** 1838 Coronation scene **Edge:** Reeded

Date	Mintage	F	VF	XF	Unc	BU
2001 Proof	10,000	Value: 47.50				

KM# 912 CROWN

Copper-Nickel, 38.6 mm. **Ruler:** Elizabeth II **Series:** Victorian Era - Empress of India 1876 **Obv:** Bust with tiara right **Obv. Designer:** Ian Rank-Broadley **Rev:** Crowned portrait of Victoria and two elephants

Date	Mintage	F	VF	XF	Unc	BU
2001	—	—	—	—	10.00	12.00

KM# 912a CROWN

28.2800 g., 0.9250 Silver 0.8410 oz. ASW **Ruler:** Elizabeth II **Series:** The Victorian Age - Empress of India 1876 **Obv:** Bust with tiara right **Obv. Designer:** Ian Rank-Broadley **Rev:** Crowned portrait of Victoria and two elephants

Date	Mintage	F	VF	XF	Unc	BU
2001 Proof	10,000	Value: 47.50				

KM# 914 CROWN

Copper-Nickel, 38.6 mm. **Ruler:** Elizabeth II **Series:** Victorian Era - Diamond Jubilee **Obv:** Bust with tiara right **Obv. Designer:** Ian Rank-Broadley **Rev:** Victoria's cameo portrait above naval ships

Date	Mintage	F	VF	XF	Unc	BU
2001	—	—	—	—	10.00	12.00

KM# 914a CROWN

28.2800 g., 0.9250 Silver 0.8410 oz. ASW **Ruler:** Elizabeth II **Series:** The Victorian Age - Diamond Jubilee 1897 **Obv:** Bust with tiara right **Obv. Designer:** Ian Rank-Broadley **Rev:** Victoria's cameo above naval ships, Spithead Review

Date	Mintage	F	VF	XF	Unc	BU
2001 Proof	10,000	Value: 47.50				

KM# 916 CROWN

Copper-Nickel, 38.6 mm. **Ruler:** Elizabeth II **Series:** The Victorian Age - Victoria's Death 1901 **Obv:** Bust with tiara right **Obv. Designer:** Ian Rank-Broadley **Rev:** Victoria's cameo portrait and Osborne Manor

Date	Mintage	F	VF	XF	Unc	BU
2001	—	—	—	—	10.00	12.00

KM# 916a CROWN

28.2800 g., 0.9250 Silver 0.8410 oz. ASW, 38.6 mm. **Ruler:** Elizabeth II **Series:** The Victorian Age - Victoria's Death 1901 **Obv:** Bust with tiara right **Obv. Designer:** Ian Rank-Broadley **Rev:** Victoria's cameo portrait and Osborne Manor

Date	Mintage	F	VF	XF	Unc	BU
2001 Proof	10,000	Value: 47.50				

KM# 918 CROWN

Copper-Nickel, 38.6 mm. **Ruler:** Elizabeth II **Series:** The Victorian Age - Prince Albert and the Great Exhibition 1851 **Obv:** Bust with tiara right **Obv. Designer:** Ian Rank-Broadley **Rev:** Albert's cameo portrait and the exhibit hall

Date	Mintage	F	VF	XF	Unc	BU
2001 Proof	5,000	Value: 175				

KM# 918a CROWN

28.2800 g., 0.9250 Silver 0.8410 oz. ASW, 38.6 mm. **Ruler:** Elizabeth II **Series:** The Victorian Age - Prince Albert and the Great Exhibition 1851 **Obv:** Bust with tiara right **Obv. Designer:** Ian Rank-Broadley **Rev:** Albert's cameo portrait and the exhibit hall

Date	Mintage	F	VF	XF	Unc	BU
2001 Proof	10,000	Value: 47.50				

KM# 920 CROWN

Copper-Nickel, 38.6 mm. **Ruler:** Elizabeth II **Series:** The Victorian Age **Obv:** Bust with tiara right **Obv. Designer:** Ian Rank-Broadley **Rev:** 1/2 bust of Isambard K. Brunel half left in front of railroad bridge

Date	Mintage	F	VF	XF	Unc	BU
2001	—	—	—	—	10.00	12.00

KM# 920a CROWN

28.2800 g., 0.9250 Silver 0.8410 oz. ASW, 38.6 mm. **Ruler:** Elizabeth II **Series:** Victorian Era **Obv:** Bust with tiara right **Rev:** 1/2 bust of Isambard K. Brunel half left in front of railroad bridge

Date	Mintage	F	VF	XF	Unc	BU
2001 Proof	10,000	Value: 47.50				

KM# 922 CROWN
Copper-Nickel, 38.6 mm. **Ruler:** Elizabeth II **Series:** The Victorian Age **Obv:** Bust with tiara right **Obv. Designer:** Ian Rank-Broadley **Rev:** 1/2 length bust of Charles Dickens half left, scene from "Oliver Twist" in background

Date	Mintage	F	VF	XF	Unc	BU
2001	—	—	—	—	10.00	12.00

KM# 922a CROWN
28.2800 g., 0.9250 Silver 0.8410 oz. ASW, 38.6 mm. **Series:** The Victorian Age **Obv:** Bust with tiara right **Obv. Designer:** Ian Rank-Broadley **Rev:** 1/2 length bust of Charles Dickens half left, scene from "Oliver Twist" in background

Date	Mintage	F	VF	XF	Unc	BU
2001 Proof	10,000	Value: 47.50				

KM# 924 CROWN
Copper-Nickel, 38.6 mm. **Ruler:** Elizabeth II **Series:** The Victorian Age **Obv:** Bust with tiara right **Obv. Designer:** Ian Rank-Broadley **Rev:** 3/4-length figure of Charles Darwin right, ship and a squatting aboriginal figure

Date	Mintage	F	VF	XF	Unc	BU
2001	—	—	—	—	10.00	12.00

KM# 924a CROWN
28.2800 g., 0.9250 Silver 0.8410 oz. ASW, 38.6 mm. **Ruler:** Elizabeth II **Series:** The Victorian Age **Obv:** Bust with tiara right **Obv. Designer:** Ian Rank-Broadley **Rev:** 3/4-length figure of Charles Darwin right, ship and a squatting aboriginal figure

Date	Mintage	F	VF	XF	Unc	BU
2001 Proof	10,000	Value: 47.50				

KM# 927 CROWN
28.2800 g., Copper-Nickel, 38.6 mm. **Ruler:** Elizabeth II **Series:** Mythology of the Solar System **Obv:** Bust with tiara right **Obv. Designer:** Ian Rank-Broadley **Rev:** Standing goddess with snake basket **Edge:** Reeded

Date	Mintage	F	VF	XF	Unc	BU
2001	—	—	—	—	10.00	12.00

KM# 927a CROWN
28.2800 g., 0.9250 Silver 0.8410 oz. ASW, 38.6 mm. **Ruler:** Elizabeth II **Series:** Mythology of the Solar System **Obv:** Bust with tiara right **Obv. Designer:** Ian Rank-Broadley **Rev:** Standing goddess with snake basket **Edge:** Reeded

Date	Mintage	F	VF	XF	Unc	BU
2001 Proof	10,000	Value: 47.50				

KM# 928 CROWN
Bi-Metallic Titanium center in Silver ring, 32.25 mm. **Ruler:** Elizabeth II **Series:** Mythology of the Solar System **Obv:** Bust with tiara right **Obv. Designer:** Ian Rank-Broadley **Rev:** Standing goddess with snake basket **Edge:** Reeded

Date	Mintage	F	VF	XF	Unc	BU
2001 In Proof sets only	2,001	Value: 150				

KM# 930 CROWN
Copper-Nickel, 38.6 mm. **Ruler:** Elizabeth II **Series:** Mythology of the Solar System - Sun **Obv:** Bust with tiara right **Obv. Designer:** Ian Rank-Broadley **Rev:** Helios in chariot and the sun

Date	Mintage	F	VF	XF	Unc	BU
2001	—	—	—	—	10.00	12.00

KM# 930a CROWN
28.2800 g., 0.9250 Silver 0.8410 oz. ASW, 38.6 mm. **Ruler:** Elizabeth II **Series:** Mythology of the Solar System - Sun **Obv:** Bust with tiara right **Obv. Designer:** Ian Rank-Broadley **Rev:** Helios in chariot and the sun

Date	Mintage	F	VF	XF	Unc	BU
2001 Proof	10,000	Value: 47.50				

KM# 930a.1 CROWN
28.2800 g., 0.9250 Silver 0.8410 oz. ASW **Ruler:** Elizabeth II **Series:** Mythology of the Solar System - Sun **Obv:** Bust with tiara right **Obv. Designer:** Ian Rank-Broadley **Rev:** Fiery hologram in the sun

Date	Mintage	F	VF	XF	Unc	BU
2001 In Proof sets only	2,001	Value: 87.50				

KM# 932 CROWN
Copper-Nickel, 38.6 mm. **Ruler:** Elizabeth II **Series:** Mythology of the Solar System - Moon **Obv:** Bust with tiara right **Obv. Designer:** Ian Rank-Broadley **Rev:** Goddess Diana and the moon

Date	Mintage	F	VF	XF	Unc	BU
2001	—	—	—	—	10.00	12.00

KM# 932a CROWN
28.2800 g., 0.9250 Silver 0.8410 oz. ASW, 38.6 mm. **Ruler:** Elizabeth II **Series:** Mythology of the Solar System - Moon **Obv:** Bust with tiara right **Obv. Designer:** Ian Rank-Broadley **Rev:** Goddess Diana and the moon

Date	Mintage	F	VF	XF	Unc	BU
2001 Proof	10,000	Value: 47.50				

KM# 932a.1 CROWN
28.2800 g., 0.9250 Silver 0.8410 oz. ASW, 38.6 mm. **Ruler:** Elizabeth II **Series:** Mythology of the Solar System - Moon **Obv:** Bust with tiara right **Obv. Designer:** Ian Rank-Broadley **Rev:** Small pearl set in the moon

Date	Mintage	F	VF	XF	Unc	BU
2001 In Proof sets only	2,001	Value: 87.50				

KM# 934 CROWN
Copper-Nickel **Ruler:** Elizabeth II **Series:** Mythology of the Solar System - Atlas **Obv:** Bust with tiara right **Obv. Designer:** Ian Rank-Broadley **Rev:** Atlas carrying the earth

Date	Mintage	F	VF	XF	Unc	BU
2001	—	—	—	—	10.00	12.00

KM# 934a CROWN
28.2800 g., 0.9250 Silver 0.8410 oz. ASW, 38.6 mm. **Ruler:** Elizabeth II **Series:** Mythology of the Solar System - Atlas **Obv:** Bust with tiara right **Obv. Designer:** Ian Rank-Broadley **Rev:** Atlas carrying the earth

Date	Mintage	F	VF	XF	Unc	BU
2001 Proof	10,000	Value: 47.50				

KM# 934a.1 CROWN
28.2800 g., 0.9250 Silver 0.8410 oz. ASW, 38.6 mm. **Ruler:** Elizabeth II **Series:** Mythology of the Solar System - Atlas **Obv:** Bust with tiara right **Rev:** Fancy diamond set in the earth

Date	Mintage	F	VF	XF	Unc	BU
2001 In Proof sets only	2,001	Value: 87.50				

KM# 936 CROWN
Copper-Nickel, 38.6 mm. **Ruler:** Elizabeth II **Series:** Mythology of the Solar System **Obv:** Bust with tiara right **Obv. Designer:** Ian Rank-Broadley **Rev:** Seated Neptune with trident and ringed planet

Date	Mintage	F	VF	XF	Unc	BU
2001	—	—	—	—	10.00	12.00

KM# 936a CROWN
28.2800 g., 0.9250 Silver 0.8410 oz. ASW, 38.6 mm. **Ruler:** Elizabeth II **Series:** Mythology of the Solar System **Obv:** Bust with tiara right **Obv. Designer:** Ian Rank-Broadley **Rev:** Seated Neptune with trident and ringed planet

Date	Mintage	F	VF	XF	Unc	BU
2001 Proof	10,000	Value: 47.50				

KM# 938 CROWN
Copper-Nickel, 38.6 mm. **Ruler:** Elizabeth II **Series:** Mythology of the Solar System **Obv:** Bust with tiara right **Obv. Designer:** Ian Rank-Broadley **Rev:** Seated Jupiter with lightening bolts and a planet

Date	Mintage	F	VF	XF	Unc	BU
2001	—	—	—	—	10.00	12.00

KM# 938a CROWN
28.2800 g., 0.9250 Silver 0.8410 oz. ASW, 38.6 mm. **Ruler:** Elizabeth II **Series:** Mythology of the Solar System **Obv:** Bust with tiara right **Obv. Designer:** Ian Rank-Broadley **Rev:** Seated Jupiter with lightening bolts and a planet

Date	Mintage	F	VF	XF	Unc	BU
2001 Proof	10,000	Value: 47.50				

KM# 940 CROWN
Copper-Nickel, 38.6 mm. **Ruler:** Elizabeth II **Series:** Mythology of the Solar System - Mars **Obv:** Bust with tiara right **Obv. Designer:** Ian Rank-Broadley **Rev:** Standing Roman soldier and a planet

Date	Mintage	F	VF	XF	Unc	BU
2001	—	—	—	—	10.00	12.00

KM# 940a CROWN

28.2800 g., 0.9250 Silver 0.8410 oz. ASW, 38.6 mm. **Ruler:** Elizabeth II **Series:** Mythology of the Solar System - Mars **Obv:** Bust with tiara right **Obv. Designer:** Ian Rank-Broadley **Rev:** Standing Roman soldier and a planet

Date	Mintage	F	VF	XF	Unc	BU
2001 Proof	10,000	Value: 47.50				

KM# 942 CROWN

Copper-Nickel, 38.6 mm. **Ruler:** Elizabeth II **Series:** Mythology of the Solar System **Obv:** Bust with tiara right **Obv. Designer:** Ian Rank-Broadley **Rev:** Seated Mercury with caduceus and a planet

Date	Mintage	F	VF	XF	Unc	BU
2001	—	—	—	—	10.00	12.00

KM# 942a CROWN

28.2800 g., 0.9250 Silver 0.8410 oz. ASW, 38.6 mm. **Ruler:** Elizabeth II **Series:** Mythology of the Solar System **Obv:** Bust with tiara right **Obv. Designer:** Ian Rank-Broadley **Rev:** Seated Mercury with caduceus and a planet

Date	Mintage	F	VF	XF	Unc	BU
2001 Proof	10,000	Value: 47.50				

KM# 944 CROWN

Copper-Nickel, 38.6 mm. **Ruler:** Elizabeth II **Series:** Mythology of the Solar System **Obv:** Bust with tiara right **Obv. Designer:** Ian Rank-Broadley **Rev:** Seated Uranus with scepter

Date	Mintage	F	VF	XF	Unc	BU
2001	—	—	—	—	10.00	12.00

KM# 944a CROWN

28.2800 g., 0.9250 Silver 0.8410 oz. ASW, 38.6 mm. **Ruler:** Elizabeth II **Series:** Mythology of the Solar System **Obv:** Bust with tiara right **Obv. Designer:** Ian Rank-Broadley **Rev:** Seated Uranus with scepter

Date	Mintage	F	VF	XF	Unc	BU
2001 Proof	10,000	Value: 47.50				

KM# 946 CROWN

Copper-Nickel, 38.6 mm. **Ruler:** Elizabeth II **Series:** Mythology of the Solar System **Obv:** Bust with tiara right **Obv. Designer:** Ian Rank-Broadley **Rev:** Seated Saturn with long handled sickle and a ringed planet

Date	Mintage	F	VF	XF	Unc	BU
2001	—	—	—	—	10.00	12.00

KM# 946a CROWN

28.2800 g., 0.9250 Silver 0.8410 oz. ASW, 38.6 mm. **Ruler:** Elizabeth II **Series:** Mythology of the Solar System **Obv:** Bust with tiara right **Obv. Designer:** Ian Rank-Broadley **Rev:** Seated Saturn with long handled sickle and a ringed planet

Date	Mintage	F	VF	XF	Unc	BU
2001 Proof	10,000	Value: 47.50				

KM# 948 CROWN

Copper-Nickel, 38.6 mm. **Ruler:** Elizabeth II **Series:** Mythology of the Solar System **Obv:** Bust with tiara right **Obv. Designer:** Ian Rank-Broadley **Rev:** Seated Pluto with dogs and planet

Date	Mintage	F	VF	XF	Unc	BU
2001	—	—	—	—	10.00	12.00

KM# 948a CROWN

28.2800 g., 0.9250 Silver 0.8410 oz. ASW, 38.6 mm. **Ruler:** Elizabeth II **Series:** Mythology of the Solar System **Obv:** Bust with tiara right **Obv. Designer:** Ian Rank-Broadley **Rev:** Seated Pluto with dogs and planet

Date	Mintage	F	VF	XF	Unc	BU
2001 Proof	10,000	Value: 47.50				

KM# 950 CROWN

Copper-Nickel, 38.6 mm. **Ruler:** Elizabeth II **Series:** Mythology of the Solar System **Obv:** Bust with tiara right **Obv. Designer:** Ian Rank-Broadley **Rev:** Venus seated on a half shell

Date	Mintage	F	VF	XF	Unc	BU
2001	—	—	—	—	10.00	12.00

KM# 950a CROWN

28.2800 g., 0.9250 Silver 0.8410 oz. ASW, 38.6 mm. **Ruler:** Elizabeth II **Series:** Mythology of the Solar System **Obv:** Bust with tiara right **Obv. Designer:** Ian Rank-Broadley **Rev:** Venus seated on a half shell

Date	Mintage	F	VF	XF	Unc	BU
2001 Proof	10,000	Value: 47.50				

KM# 952 CROWN

28.2800 g., Copper-Nickel, 38.6 mm. **Ruler:** Elizabeth II **Subject:** Queen's 75th Birthday **Obv:** Bust with tiara right **Obv. Designer:** Ian Rank-Broadley **Rev:** Queen in Order of Garter robes **Edge:** Reeded

Date	Mintage	F	VF	XF	Unc	BU
2001	—	—	—	—	10.00	12.00

KM# 952a CROWN

28.2800 g., 0.9250 Silver 0.8410 oz. ASW, 38.6 mm. **Ruler:** Elizabeth II **Subject:** Queen's 75th Birthday **Obv:** Bust with tiara right **Obv. Designer:** Ian Rank-Broadley **Rev:** Queen in Order of Garter robes **Edge:** Reeded

Date	Mintage	F	VF	XF	Unc	BU
2001 Proof	10,000	Value: 47.50				

KM# 955 CROWN

28.2800 g., Copper-Nickel, 38.6 mm. **Ruler:** Elizabeth II **Series:** Victorian Age Part II **Obv:** Bust with tiara right **Obv. Designer:** Ian Rank-Broadley **Rev:** Victoria learning of her accession **Edge:** Reeded

Date	Mintage	F	VF	XF	Unc	BU
2001	—	—	—	—	10.00	12.00

KM# 955a CROWN

28.2800 g., 0.9250 Silver 0.8410 oz. ASW, 38.6 mm. **Ruler:** Elizabeth II **Series:** Victorian Age Part II **Obv:** Bust with tiara right **Obv. Designer:** Ian Rank-Broadley **Rev:** Victoria learning of her accession **Edge:** Reeded

Date	Mintage	F	VF	XF	Unc	BU
2001 Proof	10,000	Value: 47.50				

KM# 957 CROWN

Copper-Nickel, 38.6 mm. **Ruler:** Elizabeth II **Series:** Victorian Age Part II - Royal Family **Obv:** Bust with tiara right **Obv. Designer:** Ian Rank-Broadley **Rev:** Victoria and Albert seated with children **Edge:** Reeded

Date	Mintage	F	VF	XF	Unc	BU
2001	—	—	—	—	10.00	12.00

KM# 957a CROWN

28.2800 g., 0.9250 Silver 0.8410 oz. ASW, 38.6 mm. **Ruler:** Elizabeth II **Series:** Victorian Age Part II - Royal Family **Obv:** Bust with tiara right **Obv. Designer:** Ian Rank-Broadley **Rev:** Victoria and Albert seated with children **Edge:** Reeded

Date	Mintage	F	VF	XF	Unc	BU
2001 Proof	10,000	Value: 47.50				

KM# 959 CROWN

Copper-Nickel, 38.6 mm. **Ruler:** Elizabeth II **Series:** Victorian Age Part II - Victoria in Scotland **Obv:** Bust with tiara right **Obv. Designer:** Ian Rank-Broadley **Rev:** Victoria on horse with servant **Edge:** Reeded

Date	Mintage	F	VF	XF	Unc	BU
2001	2,001	—	—	—	10.00	12.00

KM# 959a CROWN

28.2800 g., 0.9250 Silver 0.8410 oz. ASW, 38.6 mm. **Ruler:** Elizabeth II **Series:** Victorian Age Part II - Victoria in Scotland **Obv:** Bust with tiara right **Obv. Designer:** Ian Rank-Broadley **Rev:** Victoria on horse with servant **Edge:** Reeded

Date	Mintage	F	VF	XF	Unc	BU
2001 Proof	10,000	Value: 47.50				

KM# 961 CROWN
Copper-Nickel, 38.6 mm. **Ruler:** Elizabeth II **Series:** Victorian Age Part II - Gladstone and Disraeli **Obv:** Bust with tiara right **Obv. Designer:** Ian Rank-Broadley **Rev:** Portraits of both politicians **Edge:** Reeded

Date	Mintage	F	VF	XF	Unc	BU
2001	—	—	—	—	10.00	12.00

KM# 961a CROWN
28.2800 g., 0.9250 Silver 0.8410 oz. ASW, 38.6 mm. **Ruler:** Elizabeth II **Series:** Victorian Age Part II - Gladstone and Disraeli **Obv:** Bust with tiara right **Obv. Designer:** Ian Rank-Broadley **Rev:** Portraits of both politicians **Edge:** Reeded

Date	Mintage	F	VF	XF	Unc	BU
2001 Proof	10,000	Value: 47.50				

KM# 963 CROWN
Copper-Nickel, 38.6 mm. **Ruler:** Elizabeth II **Series:** Victorian Age Part II **Obv:** Bust with tiara right **Obv. Designer:** Ian Rank-Broadley **Rev:** Florence Nightingale holding lantern **Edge:** Reeded

Date	Mintage	F	VF	XF	Unc	BU
2001	—	—	—	—	10.00	12.00

KM# 963a CROWN
28.2800 g., 0.9250 Silver 0.8410 oz. ASW, 38.6 mm. **Ruler:** Elizabeth II **Series:** Victorian Age Part II **Obv:** Bust with tiara right **Obv. Designer:** Ian Rank-Broadley **Rev:** Florence Nightingale holding lantern **Edge:** Reeded

Date	Mintage	F	VF	XF	Unc	BU
2001 Proof	10,000	Value: 47.50				

KM# 965 CROWN
Copper-Nickel, 38.6 mm. **Ruler:** Elizabeth II **Series:** Victorian Age Part II **Obv:** Bust with tiara right **Obv. Designer:** Ian Rank-Broadley **Rev:** Lord Tennyson with the Light Brigade in background **Edge:** Reeded

Date	Mintage	F	VF	XF	Unc	BU
2001	—	—	—	—	10.00	12.00

KM# 965a CROWN
28.2800 g., 0.9250 Silver 0.8410 oz. ASW, 38.6 mm. **Ruler:** Elizabeth II **Series:** Victorian Age Part II **Obv:** Bust with tiara right **Obv. Designer:** Ian Rank-Broadley **Rev:** Lord Tennyson with the Light Brigade in background **Edge:** Reeded

Date	Mintage	F	VF	XF	Unc	BU
2001 Proof	10,000	Value: 47.50				

KM# 967 CROWN
Copper-Nickel, 38.6 mm. **Ruler:** Elizabeth II **Series:** Victorian Age Part II **Obv:** Bust with tiara right **Obv. Designer:** Ian Rank-Broadley **Rev:** Stanley meeting Dr. Livingstone **Edge:** Reeded

Date	Mintage	F	VF	XF	Unc	BU
2001	—	—	—	—	10.00	12.00

KM# 967a CROWN
28.2800 g., 0.9250 Silver 0.8410 oz. ASW, 38.6 mm. **Ruler:** Elizabeth II **Series:** Victorian Age Part II **Obv:** Bust with tiara right **Obv. Designer:** Ian Rank-Broadley **Rev:** Stanley meeting Dr. Livingstone **Edge:** Reeded

Date	Mintage	F	VF	XF	Unc	BU
2001 Proof	10,000	Value: 47.50				

KM# 969 CROWN
Copper-Nickel, 38.6 mm. **Ruler:** Elizabeth II **Series:** Victorian Age Part II **Obv:** Bust with tiara right **Obv. Designer:** Ian Rank-Broadley **Rev:** Bronte sisters **Edge:** Reeded

Date	Mintage	F	VF	XF	Unc	BU
2001	—	—	—	—	10.00	12.00

KM# 969a CROWN
28.2800 g., 0.9250 Silver 0.8410 oz. ASW, 38.6 mm. **Ruler:** Elizabeth II **Series:** Victorian Age Part II **Obv:** Bust with tiara right **Obv. Designer:** Ian Rank-Broadley **Rev:** Bronte sisters **Edge:** Reeded

Date	Mintage	F	VF	XF	Unc	BU
2001 Proof	10,000	Value: 47.50				

KM# 1061 CROWN
31.1000 g., Electrum Special alloy of equal parts of gold and silver. **Ruler:** Elizabeth II **Series:** Ancient Coins **Obv:** Crowned bust right **Rev:** Lion and bull facing **Note:** From a Kroisos [sic] coin c. 560-546 BC.

Date	Mintage	F	VF	XF	Unc	BU
2002 Proof	—	Value: 650				

KM# 1060 CROWN
31.1000 g., Electrum Special alloy of equal parts of gold and silver. **Ruler:** Elizabeth II **Series:** Ancient Coins. **Obv:** Crowned bust right **Rev:** Lion and bull facing **Note:** From a Lampsakos electrum coin c. 450 BC.

Date	Mintage	F	VF	XF	Unc	BU
2002 Proof	—	Value: 650				

KM# 1059 CROWN
31.1000 g., Electrum Special alloy of equal parts of gold and silver. **Ruler:** Elizabeth II **Series:** Ancient Coins **Obv:** Crowned bust right **Rev:** Head of Hercules right **Note:** From a Lesbos coin c. 480-4501

Date	Mintage	F	VF	XF	Unc	BU
2002 Proof	—	Value: 650				

KM# 1058 CROWN
31.1000 g., 1.0000 Electrum Special alloy of equal parts of gold and silver. 0.9998 oz. **Ruler:** Elizabeth II **Series:** Ancient Coins **Obv:** Crowned head right **Rev:** Head of Athena left **Note:** From a Mysia electrum coin c. 520 BC.

Date	Mintage	F	VF	XF	Unc	BU
2002 Proof	—	Value: 650				

KM# 979 CROWN
28.2800 g., Copper-Nickel, 38.6 mm. **Ruler:** Elizabeth II **Subject:** Queen Mother's Life **Obv:** Bust with tiara right **Obv. Designer:** Ian Rank-Broadley **Rev:** Christening of Prince William **Edge:** Reeded

Date	Mintage	F	VF	XF	Unc	BU
2002	—	—	—	—	10.00	12.00

KM# 979a CROWN
28.2800 g., 0.9250 Silver 0.8410 oz. ASW, 38.6 mm. **Ruler:** Elizabeth II **Subject:** Queen Mother's Life **Obv:** Bust with tiara right **Obv. Designer:** Ian Rank-Broadley **Rev:** Prince William's christening **Edge:** Reeded

Date	Mintage	F	VF	XF	Unc	BU
2002 Proof	10,000	Value: 47.50				

KM# 981 CROWN
28.2800 g., Copper-Nickel, 38.6 mm. **Ruler:** Elizabeth II **Subject:** World Cup Soccer **Obv:** Bust with tiara right **Obv. Designer:** Ian Rank-Broadley **Rev:** Two players about to collide **Edge:** Reeded

Date	Mintage	F	VF	XF	Unc	BU
2002	—	—	—	—	10.00	11.50

KM# 981a CROWN
28.2800 g., 0.9250 Silver 0.8410 oz. ASW, 38.6 mm. **Ruler:** Elizabeth II **Subject:** World Cup Soccer **Obv:** Bust with tiara right **Obv. Designer:** Ian Rank-Broadley **Rev:** Two players about to collide **Edge:** Reeded

Date	Mintage	F	VF	XF	Unc	BU
2002 Proof	10,000	Value: 47.50				

KM# 983 CROWN
28.2800 g., Copper-Nickel, 38.6 mm. **Ruler:** Elizabeth II **Subject:** World Cup Soccer **Obv:** Bust with tiara right **Obv. Designer:** Ian Rank-Broadley **Rev:** Two players facing viewer **Edge:** Reeded

Date	Mintage	F	VF	XF	Unc	BU
2002	—	—	—	—	10.00	11.50

KM# 983a CROWN

28.2800 g., 0.9250 Silver 0.8410 oz. ASW, 38.6 mm. **Ruler:** Elizabeth II **Subject:** World Cup Soccer **Obv:** Bust with tiara right **Obv. Designer:** Ian Rank-Broadley **Rev:** Two players facing viewer **Edge:** Reeded

Date	Mintage	F	VF	XF	Unc	BU
2002 Proof	10,000	Value: 47.50				

KM# 985 CROWN

28.2800 g., Copper-Nickel, 38.6 mm. **Ruler:** Elizabeth II **Subject:** World Cup Soccer **Obv:** Bust with tiara right **Obv. Designer:** Ian Rank-Broadley **Rev:** Two horizontal players **Edge:** Reeded

Date	Mintage	F	VF	XF	Unc	BU
2002	—	—	—	—	10.00	11.50

KM# 985a CROWN

28.2800 g., 0.9250 Silver 0.8410 oz. ASW, 38.6 mm. **Ruler:** Elizabeth II **Subject:** World Cup Soccer **Obv:** Bust with tiara right **Obv. Designer:** Ian Rank-Broadley **Rev:** Two horizontal players **Edge:** Reeded

Date	Mintage	F	VF	XF	Unc	BU
2002 Proof	10,000	Value: 47.50				

KM# 987 CROWN

28.2800 g., Copper-Nickel, 38.6 mm. **Ruler:** Elizabeth II **Subject:** World Cup Soccer **Obv:** Bust with tiara right **Obv. Designer:** Ian Rank-Broadley **Rev:** Two players moving to left **Edge:** Reeded

Date	Mintage	F	VF	XF	Unc	BU
2002	—	—	—	—	10.00	11.50

KM# 987a CROWN

28.2800 g., 0.9250 Silver 0.8410 oz. ASW, 38.6 mm. **Ruler:** Elizabeth II **Subject:** World Cup Soccer **Obv:** Bust with tiara right **Obv. Designer:** Ian Rank-Broadley **Rev:** Two players moving to left **Edge:** Reeded

Date	Mintage	F	VF	XF	Unc	BU
2002 Proof	10,000	Value: 47.50				

KM# 992.1 CROWN

28.2800 g., Copper-Nickel, 38.6 mm. **Ruler:** Elizabeth II **Subject:** Peter Rabbit Centennial **Obv:** Bust with tiara right **Obv. Designer:** Ian Rank-Broadley **Rev:** Peter Rabbit **Edge:** Reeded

Date	Mintage	F	VF	XF	Unc	BU
2002	—	—	—	—	10.00	12.00

KM# 992a CROWN

28.2800 g., 0.9250 Silver 0.8410 oz. ASW, 38.6 mm. **Ruler:** Elizabeth II **Subject:** Peter Rabbit Centennial **Obv:** Bust with tiara right **Obv. Designer:** Ian Rank-Broadley **Rev:** Peter Rabbit **Edge:** Reeded

Date	Mintage	F	VF	XF	Unc	BU
2002 Proof	10,000	Value: 47.50				

KM# 992.2 CROWN

Copper-Nickel **Ruler:** Elizabeth II **Obv:** Bust with tiara right **Obv. Designer:** Ian Rank-Broadley **Rev:** Peter Rabbit in multi-color

Date	Mintage	F	VF	XF	Unc	BU
2002	—	—	—	—	10.00	12.00

KM# 994 CROWN

28.2800 g., Copper-Nickel, 38.6 mm. **Ruler:** Elizabeth II **Subject:** Queen's Golden Jubilee **Obv:** Bust with tiara right **Obv. Designer:** Ian Rank-Broadley **Rev:** Royal couple and tree house **Edge:** Reeded

Date	Mintage	F	VF	XF	Unc	BU
2002	—	—	—	—	10.00	12.00

KM# 994a CROWN

Yellow Brass, 38.6 mm. **Ruler:** Elizabeth II **Subject:** Queen's Golden Jubilee **Obv:** Bust with tiara right **Obv. Designer:** Ian Rank-Broadley **Rev:** Royal couple and tree house **Edge:** Reeded

Date	Mintage	F	VF	XF	Unc	BU
2002 Proof	15,000	Value: 20.00				

KM# 994b CROWN

28.2800 g., 0.9250 Gold Clad Silver 0.8410 oz., 38.6 mm. **Ruler:** Elizabeth II **Subject:** Queen's Golden Jubilee **Obv:** Bust with tiara right **Obv. Designer:** Ian Rank-Broadley **Rev:** Royal couple and tree house **Edge:** Reeded

Date	Mintage	F	VF	XF	Unc	BU
2002 Proof	10,000	Value: 55.00				

KM# 996 CROWN

28.2800 g., Copper-Nickel, 38.6 mm. **Ruler:** Elizabeth II **Subject:** Queen's Golden Jubilee **Obv:** Bust with tiara right **Obv. Designer:** Ian Rank-Broadley **Rev:** Royal coach **Edge:** Reeded

Date	Mintage	F	VF	XF	Unc	BU
2002	—	—	—	—	10.00	12.00

KM# 996a CROWN

Yellow Brass, 38.6 mm. **Ruler:** Elizabeth II **Subject:** Queen's Golden Jubilee **Obv:** Bust with tiara right **Obv. Designer:** Ian Rank-Broadley **Rev:** Royal coach **Edge:** Reeded

Date	Mintage	F	VF	XF	Unc	BU
2002 Proof	15,000	Value: 20.00				

KM# 996b CROWN

28.2800 g., 0.9250 Gold Clad Silver 0.8410 oz., 38.6 mm. **Ruler:** Elizabeth II **Subject:** Queen's Golden Jubilee **Obv:** Bust with tiara right **Obv. Designer:** Ian Rank-Broadley **Rev:** Royal coach **Edge:** Reeded

Date	Mintage	F	VF	XF	Unc	BU
2002 Proof	10,000	Value: 55.00				

KM# 998 CROWN

28.2800 g., Copper-Nickel, 38.6 mm. **Ruler:** Elizabeth II **Subject:** Queen's Golden Jubilee **Obv:** Bust with tiara right **Obv. Designer:** Ian Rank-Broadley **Rev:** Royal couple with baby **Edge:** Reeded

Date	Mintage	F	VF	XF	Unc	BU
2002	—	—	—	—	10.00	12.00

KM# 998a CROWN

Yellow Brass, 38.6 mm. **Ruler:** Elizabeth II **Subject:** Queen's Golden Jubilee **Obv:** Bust with tiara right **Obv. Designer:** Ian Rank-Broadley **Rev:** Royal couple with baby **Edge:** Reeded

Date	Mintage	F	VF	XF	Unc	BU
2002 Proof	15,000	Value: 20.00				

KM# 998b CROWN

28.2800 g., 0.9250 Gold Clad Silver 0.8410 oz., 38.6 mm. **Ruler:** Elizabeth II **Subject:** Queen's Golden Jubilee **Obv:** Bust with tiara right **Obv. Designer:** Ian Rank-Broadley **Rev:** Royal couple with baby **Edge:** Reeded

Date	Mintage	F	VF	XF	Unc	BU
2002 Proof	1,000	Value: 55.00				

KM# 1000 CROWN

28.2800 g., Copper-Nickel, 38.6 mm. **Ruler:** Elizabeth II **Subject:** Queen's Golden Jubilee **Obv:** Bust with tiara right **Obv. Designer:** Ian Rank-Broadley **Rev:** Royal yacht under Tower bridge **Edge:** Reeded

Date	Mintage	F	VF	XF	Unc	BU
2002	—	—	—	—	10.00	12.00

KM# 1000a CROWN

Yellow Brass, 38.6 mm. **Ruler:** Elizabeth II **Subject:** Queen's Golden Jubilee **Obv:** Bust with tiara right **Obv. Designer:** Ian Rank-Broadley **Rev:** Royal yacht under Tower bridge **Edge:** Reeded

Date	Mintage	F	VF	XF	Unc	BU
2002 Proof	15,000	Value: 20.00				

KM# 1000b CROWN

28.2800 g., 0.9250 Gold Clad Silver 0.8410 oz., 38.6 mm. **Ruler:** Elizabeth II **Subject:** Queen's Golden Jubilee **Obv:** Bust with tiara right **Obv. Designer:** Ian Rank-Broadley **Rev:** Royal yacht under Tower bridge **Edge:** Reeded

Date	Mintage	F	VF	XF	Unc	BU
2002 Proof	10,000	Value: 55.00				

KM# 1013 CROWN

28.2800 g., Copper-Nickel dark patina, 38.6 mm. **Ruler:** Elizabeth II **Subject:** Death of Queen Mother **Obv:** Bust with tiara right **Obv. Designer:** Ian Rank-Broadley **Rev:** Queen Mother trout fishing **Edge:** Reeded

Date	Mintage	F	VF	XF	Unc	BU
2002	—	—	—	—	10.00	12.00

KM# 1013a CROWN
28.2800 g., 0.9250 Silver 0.8410 oz. ASW, 38.6 mm. **Ruler:** Elizabeth II **Subject:** Queen Mother **Obv:** Bust with tiara right **Obv. Designer:** Ian Rank-Broadley **Rev:** Queen Mother trout fishing **Edge:** Reeded **Note:** Obv. and rev. have blackened legends.

Date	Mintage	F	VF	XF	Unc	BU
2002 Proof	5,000	Value: 175				

KM# 1015 CROWN
28.2800 g., Copper-Nickel, 38.6 mm. **Ruler:** Elizabeth II **Subject:** Princess Diana **Obv:** Bust with tiara right **Obv. Designer:** Ian Rank-Broadley **Rev:** Diana's portrait **Edge:** Reeded

Date	Mintage	F	VF	XF	Unc	BU
2002	—	—	—	—	10.00	12.00

KM# 1015a CROWN
28.2800 g., 0.9250 Silver 0.8410 oz. ASW, 38.6 mm. **Ruler:** Elizabeth II **Subject:** Princess Diana **Obv:** Bust with tiara right **Obv. Designer:** Ian Rank-Broadley **Rev:** Diana's portrait **Edge:** Reeded

Date	Mintage	F	VF	XF	Unc	BU
2002 Proof	10,000	Value: 47.50				

KM# 1019 CROWN
28.2800 g., Copper-Nickel, 38.6 mm. **Ruler:** Elizabeth II **Subject:** Peter Pan **Obv:** Bust with tiara right **Obv. Designer:** Ian Rank-Broadley **Rev:** Peter Pan and Tinkerbell flying above city **Edge:** Reeded

Date	Mintage	F	VF	XF	Unc	BU
2002	—	—	—	—	10.00	12.00

KM# 1019a CROWN
28.2800 g., 0.9250 Silver 0.8410 oz. ASW, 38.6 mm. **Ruler:** Elizabeth II **Subject:** Peter Pan **Obv:** Bust with tiara right **Obv. Designer:** Ian Rank-Broadley **Rev:** Peter Pan and Tinkerbell flying above city **Edge:** Reeded

Date	Mintage	F	VF	XF	Unc	BU
2002 Proof	10,000	Value: 47.50				

KM# 1021 CROWN
28.2800 g., Copper-Nickel, 38.6 mm. **Ruler:** Elizabeth II **Subject:** Grand Masonic Lodge **Obv:** Bust with tiara right **Obv. Designer:** Ian Rank-Broadley **Rev:** Masonic seal above Gibraltar **Edge:** Reeded

Date	Mintage	F	VF	XF	Unc	BU
2002 Proof	5,000	Value: 12.00				

KM# 1021a CROWN
28.2800 g., 0.9250 Silver 0.8410 oz. ASW, 38.6 mm. **Ruler:** Elizabeth II **Subject:** Grand Masonic Lodge **Obv:** Bust with tiara right **Obv. Designer:** Ian Rank-Broadley **Rev:** Masonic seal above Gibraltar **Edge:** Reeded

Date	Mintage	F	VF	XF	Unc	BU
2002 Proof	10,000	Value: 47.50				

KM# 1025 CROWN
28.2800 g., Copper-Nickel, 38.6 mm. **Ruler:** Elizabeth II **Subject:** Calpe Conference **Obv:** Bust with tiara right **Obv. Designer:** Ian Rank-Broadley **Rev:** Crossed flags and arms **Edge:** Reeded

Date	Mintage	F	VF	XF	Unc	BU
2002PM	—	—	—	—	10.00	12.00

KM# 1025a CROWN
28.2800 g., 0.9250 Silver 0.8410 oz. ASW, 38.6 mm. **Ruler:** Elizabeth II **Subject:** Calpe Conference **Obv:** Bust with tiara right **Obv. Designer:** Ian Rank-Broadley **Rev:** Crossed flags and arms **Edge:** Reeded

Date	Mintage	F	VF	XF	Unc	BU
2002PM Proof	10,000	Value: 47.50				

KM# 1052 CROWN
Copper-Nickel **Ruler:** Elizabeth II **Subject:** 2004 Athens Olympics **Rev:** Horse jumping left

Date	Mintage	F	VF	XF	Unc	BU
2003	—	—	—	—	10.00	12.00

KM# 1053 CROWN
Copper-Nickel **Ruler:** Elizabeth II **Subject:** 2004 Athens Olympics **Rev:** Javelin thrower

Date	Mintage	F	VF	XF	Unc	BU
2003	—	—	—	—	10.00	12.00

KM# 1054 CROWN
Copper-Nickel **Ruler:** Elizabeth II **Subject:** 2004 Athens Olympics **Rev:** Field Hockey

Date	Mintage	F	VF	XF	Unc	BU
2003	—	—	—	—	10.00	12.00

KM# 1055 CROWN
Copper-Nickel **Ruler:** Elizabeth II **Subject:** 2004 Athens Olympics **Rev:** Wrestlers

Date	Mintage	F	VF	XF	Unc	BU
2003	—	—	—	—	10.00	12.00

KM# 1035 CROWN
28.2800 g., Copper-Nickel, 38.6 mm. **Ruler:** Elizabeth II **Subject:** 1700th Anniversary - Death of St. George **Obv:** Bust with tiara right **Obv. Designer:** Ian Rank-Broadley **Rev:** St. George and the dragon **Edge:** Reeded

Date	Mintage	F	VF	XF	Unc	BU
2003	—	—	—	—	9.00	10.00

KM# 1035a CROWN
28.2800 g., 0.9250 Silver 0.8410 oz. ASW, 38.6 mm. **Ruler:** Elizabeth II **Subject:** 1700th Anniversary - Death of St. George **Obv:** Bust with tiara right **Obv. Designer:** Ian Rank-Broadley **Rev:** St. George and the dragon **Edge:** Reeded

Date	Mintage	F	VF	XF	Unc	BU
2003 Proof	10,000	Value: 47.50				

KM# 1039 CROWN
28.3000 g., Copper-Nickel, 38.6 mm. **Ruler:** Elizabeth II **Subject:** Peter Rabbit **Obv:** Bust with tiara right **Obv. Designer:** Ian Rank-Broadley **Rev:** Peter Rabbit holding carrot **Edge:** Reeded

Date	Mintage	F	VF	XF	Unc	BU
2003PM	—	—	—	—	9.00	10.00

KM# 1040 CROWN
28.2800 g., Copper-Nickel, 38.6 mm. **Ruler:** Elizabeth II **Subject:** Centennial of Powered Flight **Obv:** Queens portrait **Rev:** Stealth bomber within circles of WWI and WWII planes **Edge:** Reeded

Date	Mintage	F	VF	XF	Unc	BU
2003PM	—	—	—	—	10.00	12.00

KM# 1040a CROWN
31.1000 g., Tri-Metallic .9995 Platinum 5.2g center in .9999 Gold 14.2 g ring within .999 Silver 11.7 g outer ring, 38.6 mm. **Ruler:** Elizabeth II **Subject:** Centennial of Powered Flight **Obv:** Queens portrait **Rev:** Stealth bomber within circles of WWI and WWII planes **Edge:** Reeded

Date	Mintage	F	VF	XF	Unc	BU
2003PM Proof	999	Value: 1,500				

KM# 1041 CROWN
28.2800 g., Copper-Nickel, 38.6 mm. **Ruler:** Elizabeth II **Subject:** 50th Anniversary of Coronation **Obv:** Queens portrait **Rev:** Buckingham Palace **Edge:** Reeded

Date	Mintage	F	VF	XF	Unc	BU
2003PM	—	—	—	—	10.00	12.00

KM# 1075 CROWN
28.2800 g., Copper-Nickel, 38.6 mm. **Ruler:** Elizabeth II **Subject:** Trafalgar - First Shot **Rev:** Naval battle scene

Date	Mintage	F	VF	XF	Unc	BU
2005	—	—	—	—	10.00	12.00

KM# 1076 CROWN
28.2800 g., Copper-Nickel, 38.6 mm. **Ruler:** Elizabeth II **Subject:** Trafalgar - Breaking the line **Rev:** Naval battle

Date	Mintage	F	VF	XF	Unc	BU
2005	—	—	—	—	10.00	12.00

KM# 1077 CROWN
28.2800 g., Copper-Nickel, 38.6 mm. **Ruler:** Elizabeth II **Subject:** Trafalgar - Hardy **Rev:** Bust facing

Date	Mintage	F	VF	XF	Unc	BU
2005	—	—	—	—	10.00	12.00

KM# 1078 CROWN
28.2800 g., Copper-Nickel, 38.6 mm. **Ruler:** Elizabeth II **Subject:** Trafalgar - Nelson **Rev:** Bust facing

Date	Mintage	F	VF	XF	Unc	BU
2005	—	—	—	—	10.00	12.00

KM# 1034 2 CROWN
41.5000 g., Bi-Metallic .999 Silver 11.5g. star shaped center in Copper outer ring, 50 mm. **Ruler:** Elizabeth II **Subject:** Euro's First Anniversary **Obv:** Crowned bust right within star silhouette **Rev:** Europa riding a bull, stars and star silhouette in background **Edge:** Reeded

Date	Mintage	F	VF	XF	Unc	BU
2003PM Proof	3,500	Value: 125				

KM# 1034a 2 CROWN
50.0000 g., Bi-Metallic .9999 Gold 20g star shaped center in Copper outer ring, 50 mm. **Ruler:** Elizabeth II **Subject:** 1st Anniversary - Euro **Obv:** Crowned bust right within star silhouette **Rev:** Europa riding the bull, stars and star silhouette in background **Edge:** Reeded

Date	Mintage	F	VF	XF	Unc	BU
2003PM Proof	2,003	Value: 850				

KM# 1034b 2 CROWN
56.3000 g., Bi-Metallic .9999 Gold 20.8g star shaped center in a .999 Silver 35.5g outer ring, 50 mm. **Ruler:** Elizabeth II **Subject:** 1st Anniversary - Euro **Obv:** Crowned bust right within star silhouette **Rev:** Europa riding the bull, stars and star silhouette in background **Edge:** Reeded

Date	Mintage	F	VF	XF	Unc	BU
2003PM Proof	2,003	Value: 900				

KM# 907 5 CROWN
Tri-Metallic Center .9995 Platinum 26.9g. Inner Ring .9999 Gold 73.41g. Outer Ring .999 Silver 55.19g, 50 mm. **Ruler:** Elizabeth II **Subject:** 21st Century **Obv:** Crowned bust right, date below **Obv. Designer:** Raphael Maklouf **Rev:** Celtic cross, Viking ship and modern technological items **Edge:** Reeded

Date	Mintage	F	VF	XF	Unc	BU
2001 Proof	199	Value: 5,500				

KM# 1042 5 CROWN
155.5500 g., 0.9990 Silver 4.9958 oz. ASW, 65 mm. **Ruler:** Elizabeth II **Subject:** 50th Anniversary of Coronation **Obv:** Queens portrait **Rev:** Buckingham Palace with tiny .01ct ruby, diamond and sapphire inserts above the main entrance **Edge:** Reeded

Date	Mintage	F	VF	XF	Unc	BU
2003PM Proof	2,003	Value: 225				

KM# 1045 32 CROWNS
1000.0000 g., 0.9990 Silver 32.117 oz. ASW **Ruler:** Elizabeth II **Subject:** Beatrix Potter's Peter Rabbit **Obv:** Bust with tiara right **Obv. Designer:** Ian Rank-Broadley **Rev:** Multicolor Peter Rabbit holding carrot, with blue coat and red slippers

Date	Mintage	F	VF	XF	Unc	BU
2003 Proof	1,000	Value: 1,150				

KM# 869 POUND
9.5000 g., Nickel-Brass, 22.5 mm. **Ruler:** Elizabeth II **Obv:** Head with tiara right **Obv. Designer:** Ian Rank-Broadley **Rev:** Gibraltar castle and key

Date	Mintage	F	VF	XF	Unc	BU
2001 AA	—	—	—	—	3.50	4.50
2001 AB	—	—	—	—	3.50	4.50
2002 AC	—	—	—	—	3.50	4.50

KM# 1036 POUND
9.5000 g., Nickel-Brass, 22 mm. **Ruler:** Elizabeth II **Subject:** 1700th Anniversary - Death of St. George **Obv:** Bust with tiara right **Rev:** St. George and the dragon **Edge:** Reeded

Date	Mintage	F	VF	XF	Unc	BU
2003	—	—	—	—	9.00	10.00

KM# 1051 POUND
9.5000 g., Nickel-Brass, 22.5 mm. **Ruler:** Elizabeth II **Subject:** Tercentenary 1704-2004 **Obv:** Elizabeth II **Obv. Designer:** Raphael Maklouf **Rev:** Old cannon set for a downhill target **Rev. Designer:** Philip Nathan **Edge:** Reeded

Date	Mintage	F	VF	XF	Unc	BU
2004PM	—	—	—	—	—	4.00

KM# 1091 POUND
9.5000 g., Nickel-Brass, 22.5 mm. **Ruler:** Elizabeth II **Obv:** Bust in diadem right **Rev:** Neanderthal Skull

Date	Mintage	F	VF	XF	Unc	BU
2005	—	—	—	—	3.50	4.50
2006	—	—	—	—	3.50	4.50
2007	—	—	—	—	3.50	4.50
2008	—	—	—	—	3.50	4.50
2009	—	—	—	—	3.50	4.50

KM# 970 2 POUNDS
12.0600 g., Bi-Metallic Steel Copper-Nickel center in Brass ring, 28.4 mm. **Ruler:** Elizabeth II **Subject:** Bicentennial of the Union Jack **Obv:** Head with tiara right **Obv. Designer:** Ian Rank-Broadley **Rev:** Standing Britannia wearing flag as a cape **Edge:** Reeded

Date	Mintage	F	VF	XF	Unc	BU
2001 AA	—	—	—	—	10.00	12.00

KM# 970a 2 POUNDS

12.0000 g., 0.9990 Bi-Metallic Silver center in Gold plated Silver ring 0.3854 oz., 28.4 mm. **Ruler:** Elizabeth II **Subject:** Bicentennial of the Union Jack **Obv:** Head with tiara right **Obv. Designer:** Ian Rank-Broadley **Rev:** Standing Britannia wearing flag as a cape **Edge:** Reeded

Date	Mintage	F	VF	XF	Unc	BU
2001	7,500	—	—	—	35.00	40.00

KM# 1043 2 POUNDS

12.0600 g., Bi-Metallic Copper-Nickel center in Brass ring, 28.3 mm. **Ruler:** Elizabeth II **Obv:** Head with tiara right **Obv. Designer:** Ian Rank-Broadley **Rev:** Old cannon **Edge:** Reeded

Date	Mintage	F	VF	XF	Unc	BU
2003PM	—	—	—	—	10.00	12.00

KM# 1057 2 POUNDS

12.0600 g., Bi-Metallic Copper-Nickel center in Brass ring., 28.3 mm. **Ruler:** Elizabeth II **Subject:** Tercentenary 1704-2004 **Obv:** Elizabeth II **Obv. Designer:** Raphael Maklouf **Rev:** Naval Battle, capture of Gibraltar **Rev. Designer:** Philip Nathan **Edge:** Reeded

Date	Mintage	F	VF	XF	Unc	BU
2004PM	—	—	—	—	10.00	12.00

KM# 1072 2 POUNDS

12.0600 g., Bi-Metallic Copper-Nickel center in brass ring, 28.3 mm. **Ruler:** Elizabeth II **Subject:** Capture of Gibraltar **Rev:** Sea battle

Date	Mintage	F	VF	XF	Unc	BU
2004	—	—	—	—	10.00	12.00

KM# 1092 2 POUNDS

12.0600 g., Bi-Metallic, 28.3 mm. **Ruler:** Elizabeth II **Subject:** Battle of Trafalgar **Rev:** Two Naval vessels and rock in backbround

Date	Mintage	F	VF	XF	Unc	BU
2005	—	—	—	—	10.00	12.00
2006	—	—	—	—	10.00	12.00
2007	—	—	—	—	10.00	12.00
2008	—	—	—	—	10.00	12.00
2009	—	—	—	—	10.00	12.00

KM# 1073 2 POUNDS

12.0600 g., Bi-Metallic Copper-Nickel center in brass ring, 28.4 mm. **Ruler:** Elizabeth II **Subject:** Battle of Trafalgar **Rev:** Sea battle

Date	Mintage	F	VF	XF	Unc	BU
2005	—	—	—	—	10.00	12.00

KM# 1093 2 POUNDS

12.0600 g., Bi-Metallic, 28.3 mm. **Ruler:** Elizabeth II **Subject:** Diamond Wedding Anniversary **Obv:** Bust in diadem right **Rev:** Conjoined busts of Elizabelth and Philip

Date	Mintage	F	VF	XF	Unc	BU
2007	—	—	—	—	10.00	12.00

KM# 953 5 POUNDS

20.0000 g., Virenium, 36.1 mm. **Ruler:** Elizabeth II **Subject:** Gibraltar Chronicle 200 Years **Obv:** Head with tiara right **Obv. Designer:** Ian Rank-Broadley **Rev:** Naval battle scene with newspaper in background **Edge:** Reeded

Date	Mintage	F	VF	XF	Unc	BU
2001	—	—	—	—	17.00	20.00

KM# 953a 5 POUNDS

23.5000 g., 0.9250 Silver 0.6988 oz. ASW, 36.1 mm. **Ruler:** Elizabeth II **Subject:** Gibraltar Chronicle 200 Years **Obv:** Head with tiara right **Obv. Designer:** Ian Rank-Broadley **Rev:** Naval battle scene with newspaper in background **Edge:** Reeded

Date	Mintage	F	VF	XF	Unc	BU
2001 Proof	10,000	Value: 50.00				

KM# 953b 5 POUNDS

39.8300 g., 0.9167 Gold 1.1738 oz. AGW, 36.1 mm. **Ruler:** Elizabeth II **Subject:** Gibraltar Chronicle 200 Years **Obv:** Head with tiara right **Obv. Designer:** Ian Rank-Broadley **Rev:** Naval battle scene with newspaper in background **Edge:** Reeded

Date	Mintage	F	VF	XF	Unc	BU
2001 Proof	850	Value: 1,750				

KM# 1011 5 POUNDS

20.0000 g., Virenium, 36.1 mm. **Ruler:** Elizabeth II **Subject:** Queen's Golden Jubilee **Obv:** Head with tiara right **Obv. Designer:** Ian Rank-Broadley **Rev:** Coronation scene **Edge:** Reeded

Date	Mintage	F	VF	XF	Unc	BU
2002	—	—	—	—	17.00	20.00

KM# 1011a 5 POUNDS

23.5000 g., 0.9250 Silver 0.6988 oz. ASW, 36.1 mm. **Ruler:** Elizabeth II **Subject:** Queen's Golden Jubilee **Obv:** Head with tiara right **Obv. Designer:** Ian Rank-Broadley **Rev:** Coronation scene **Edge:** Reeded

Date	Mintage	F	VF	XF	Unc	BU
2002 Proof	10,000	Value: 50.00				

KM# 1011b 5 POUNDS

39.8300 g., 0.9166 Gold 1.1737 oz. AGW, 36.1 mm. **Ruler:** Elizabeth II **Subject:** Queen's Golden Jubilee **Obv:** Head with tiara right **Obv. Designer:** Ian Rank-Broadley **Rev:** Coronation scene **Edge:** Reeded

Date	Mintage	F	VF	XF	Unc	BU
2002 Proof	850	Value: 1,750				

KM# 1064 5 POUNDS

Silver, 38 mm. **Ruler:** Elizabeth II **Subject:** 200th Anniversary, Battle of Trafalgar **Rev:** Two naval vessels **Edge:** Reeded

Date	Mintage	F	VF	XF	Unc	BU
2005 Proof	—	Value: 45.00				

SOVEREIGN COINAGE

KM# 1037 1/5 SOVEREIGN

1.2200 g., 0.9999 Gold 0.0392 oz. AGW, 13.92 mm. **Ruler:** Elizabeth II **Subject:** Death of St. George **Obv:** Bust with tiara right **Obv. Designer:** Ian Rank-Broadley **Rev:** St. George and the dragon **Edge:** Reeded

Date	Mintage	F	VF	XF	Unc	BU
2003 Proof	10,000	Value: 65.00				

KM# 1038 SOVEREIGN

6.2200 g., 0.9999 Gold 0.1999 oz. AGW, 22 mm. **Ruler:** Elizabeth II **Subject:** Death of St. George **Obv:** Bust with tiara right **Obv. Designer:** Ian Rank-Broadley **Rev:** St. George and the dragon **Edge:** Reeded

Date	Mintage	F	VF	XF	Unc	BU
2003 Proof	5,000	Value: 300				

ROYAL COINAGE

KM# 896 1/25 ROYAL

1.2441 g., 0.9999 Gold 0.0400 oz. AGW, 13.92 mm. **Ruler:** Elizabeth II **Subject:** Bullion **Obv:** Bust with tiara right **Obv. Designer:** Ian Rank-Broadley **Rev:** Two cherubs **Edge:** Reeded

Date	Mintage	F	VF	XF	Unc	BU
2001	—	—	—	—	70.00	—
2001 Proof	1,000	Value: 60.00				

KM# 972 1/25 ROYAL

1.2440 g., 0.9990 Gold 0.0400 oz. AGW, 13.92 mm. **Ruler:** Elizabeth II **Subject:** Cherubs **Obv:** Bust with tiara right **Obv. Designer:** Ian Rank-Broadley **Rev:** Two cherubs shooting arrrows **Edge:** Reeded

Date	Mintage	F	VF	XF	Unc	BU
2002	—	—	—	—	—	60.00
2002 Proof	1,000	Value: 70.00				

KM# 1027 1/25 ROYAL

1.2440 g., 0.9999 Gold 0.0400 oz. AGW, 13.92 mm. **Ruler:** Elizabeth II **Obv:** Bust with tiara right **Obv. Designer:** Ian Rank-Broadley **Rev:** Cherub with crossed arms **Edge:** Reeded

Date	Mintage	F	VF	XF	Unc	BU
2003PM	—	—	—	—	60.00	—
2003PM Proof	—	Value: 70.00				

KM# 897 1/10 ROYAL

3.1100 g., 0.9999 Gold 0.1000 oz. AGW, 18 mm. **Ruler:** Elizabeth II **Subject:** Bullion **Obv:** Bust with tiara right **Obv. Designer:** Ian Rank-Broadley **Rev:** Two cherubs **Edge:** Reeded

Date	Mintage	F	VF	XF	Unc	BU
2001	—	—	—	—	—	150
2001 Proof	1,000	Value: 160				

KM# 973 1/10 ROYAL

3.1100 g., 0.9990 Gold 0.0999 oz. AGW, 17.95 mm. **Ruler:** Elizabeth II **Subject:** Cherubs **Obv:** Bust with tiara right **Obv. Designer:** Ian Rank-Broadley **Rev:** Two cherubs shooting arrows **Edge:** Reeded

Date	Mintage	F	VF	XF	Unc	BU
2002	—	—	—	—	—	150
2002 Proof	1,000	Value: 160				

KM# 1028 1/10 ROYAL

3.1100 g., 0.9999 Gold 0.1000 oz. AGW, 17.95 mm. **Ruler:** Elizabeth II **Obv:** Bust with tiara right **Obv. Designer:** Ian Rank-Broadley **Rev:** Cherub with crossed arms **Edge:** Reeded

Date	Mintage	F	VF	XF	Unc	BU
2003PM	—	—	—	—	—	150
2003PM Proof	—	Value: 160				

KM# 898 1/5 ROYAL

6.2200 g., 0.9990 Gold 0.1998 oz. AGW, 22 mm. **Ruler:** Elizabeth II **Subject:** Bullion **Obv:** Bust with tiara right **Obv. Designer:** Ian Rank-Broadley **Rev:** Two cherubs **Edge:** Reeded

Date	Mintage	F	VF	XF	Unc	BU
2001	—	—	—	—	—	300
2001 Proof	1,000	Value: 320				

KM# 974 1/5 ROYAL

6.2200 g., 0.9990 Gold 0.1998 oz. AGW, 22 mm. **Ruler:** Elizabeth II **Obv:** Bust with tiara right **Obv. Designer:** Ian Rank-Broadley **Rev:** Two cherubs shooting arrows **Edge:** Reeded

Date	Mintage	F	VF	XF	Unc	BU
2002	—	—	—	—	—	300
2002 Proof	1,000	Value: 320				

KM# 1029 1/5 ROYAL

6.2200 g., 0.9999 Gold 0.1999 oz. AGW, 22 mm. **Ruler:** Elizabeth II **Obv:** Bust with tiara right **Obv. Designer:** Ian Rank-Broadley **Rev:** Cherub with crossed arms **Edge:** Reeded

Date	Mintage	F	VF	XF	Unc	BU
2003PM	—	—	—	—	—	300
2003PM Proof	—	Value: 320				

KM# 899 1/2 ROYAL

15.5517 g., 0.9999 Gold 0.4999 oz. AGW, 30 mm. **Ruler:** Elizabeth II **Subject:** Bullion **Obv:** Bust with tiara right **Obv. Designer:** Ian Rank-Broadley **Rev:** Two cherubs **Edge:** Reeded

Date	Mintage	F	VF	XF	Unc	BU
2001	—	—	—	—	—	735
2001 Proof	1,000	Value: 750				

KM# 975 1/2 ROYAL

15.5510 g., 0.9990 Gold 0.4995 oz. AGW, 30 mm. **Ruler:** Elizabeth II **Obv:** Bust with tiara right **Obv. Designer:** Ian Rank-Broadley **Rev:** Two cherubs shooting arrows **Edge:** Reeded

Date	Mintage	F	VF	XF	Unc	BU
2002	—	—	—	—	—	730
2002 Proof	1,000	Value: 750				

KM# 1030 1/2 ROYAL

15.5510 g., 0.9999 Gold 0.4999 oz. AGW, 30 mm. **Ruler:** Elizabeth II **Obv:** Bust with tiara right **Obv. Designer:** Ian Rank-Broadley **Rev:** Cherub with crossed arms **Edge:** Reeded

Date	Mintage	F	VF	XF	Unc	BU
2003PM	—	—	—	—	—	730
2003PM Proof	—	Value: 750				

KM# 900 ROYAL

28.2800 g., Copper-Nickel, 38.6 mm. **Ruler:** Elizabeth II **Obv:** Bust with tiara right **Obv. Designer:** Ian Rank-Broadley **Rev:** Two cherubs **Edge:** Reeded

Date	Mintage	F	VF	XF	Unc	BU
2001	—	—	—	—	10.00	12.00

KM# 900a ROYAL

31.1035 g., 0.9990 Silver 0.9990 oz. ASW **Ruler:** Elizabeth II **Obv:** Bust with tiara right **Obv. Designer:** Ian Rank-Broadley **Rev:** Two cherubs

Date	Mintage	F	VF	XF	Unc	BU
2001 Proof	10,000	Value: 47.50				

KM# 901 ROYAL

31.1035 g., 0.9999 Gold 0.9999 oz. AGW, 32.7 mm. **Ruler:** Elizabeth II **Subject:** Bullion **Obv:** Bust with tiara right **Obv. Designer:** Ian Rank-Broadley **Rev:** Two cherubs **Edge:** Reeded

Date	Mintage	F	VF	XF	Unc	BU
2001	—	—	—	—	—	1,500
2001 Proof	1,000	Value: 1,550				

KM# 976 ROYAL

28.2800 g., Copper-Nickel, 38.6 mm. **Ruler:** Elizabeth II **Obv:** Bust with tiara right **Obv. Designer:** Ian Rank-Broadley **Rev:** Two cherubs shooting arrows **Edge:** Reeded

Date	Mintage	F	VF	XF	Unc	BU
2002	—	—	—	—	10.00	12.00

KM# 976a ROYAL

31.1035 g., 0.9990 Silver 0.9990 oz. ASW **Ruler:** Elizabeth II **Obv:** Bust with tiara right **Obv. Designer:** Ian Rank-Broadley **Rev:** Two cherubs shooting arrows **Edge:** Reeded

Date	Mintage	F	VF	XF	Unc	BU
2002 Proof	1,000	Value: 47.50				

KM# 977 ROYAL

31.1035 g., 0.9990 Gold 0.9990 oz. AGW, 32.7 mm. **Ruler:** Elizabeth II **Obv:** Bust with tiara right **Obv. Designer:** Ian Rank-Broadley **Rev:** Two cherubs shooting arrows **Edge:** Reeded

Date	Mintage	F	VF	XF	Unc	BU
2002	—	—	—	—	—	1,500
2002 Proof	1,000	Value: 1,550				

KM# 1031 ROYAL

28.2800 g., Copper-Nickel, 38.6 mm. **Ruler:** Elizabeth II **Obv:** Bust with tiara right **Obv. Designer:** Ian Rank-Broadley **Rev:** Cherub with crossed arms **Edge:** Reeded

Date	Mintage	F	VF	XF	Unc	BU
2003PM	—	—	—	—	10.00	12.00

KM# 1031a ROYAL

28.2800 g., 0.9990 Silver 0.9083 oz. ASW, 38.6 mm. **Ruler:** Elizabeth II **Obv:** Bust with tiara right **Obv. Designer:** Ian Rank-Broadley **Rev:** Cherub with crossed arms **Edge:** Reeded

Date	Mintage	F	VF	XF	Unc	BU
2003PM Proof	10,000	Value: 47.50				

KM# 1032 ROYAL

31.1035 g., 0.9999 Gold 0.9999 oz. AGW, 32.7 mm. **Ruler:** Elizabeth II **Obv:** Bust with tiara right **Obv. Designer:** Ian Rank-Broadley **Rev:** Cherub with crossed arms **Edge:** Reeded

Date	Mintage	F	VF	XF	Unc	BU
2003PM	—	—	—	—	—	1,500
2003PM Proof	—	Value: 1,550				

GREAT BRITAIN

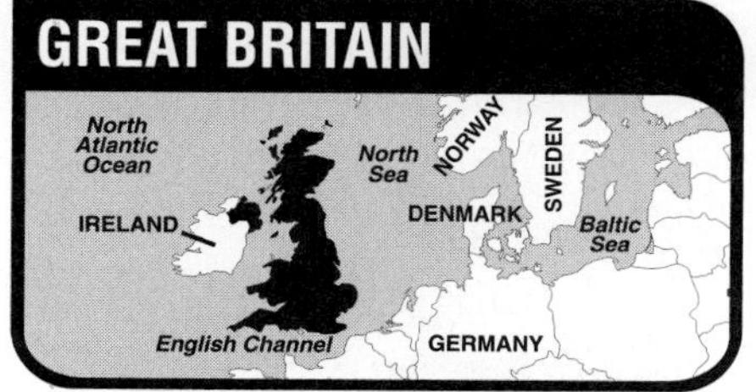

The United Kingdom of Great Britain and Northern Ireland, located off the northwest coast of the European continent, has an area of 94,227 sq. mi. (244,820 sq. km.) and a population of 54 million. Capital: London. The economy is based on industrial activity and trading. Machinery, motor vehicles, chemicals, and textile yarns and fabrics are exported.

By the mid-20th century, most of the territories formerly comprising the British Empire had gained independence, and the empire had evolved into the Commonwealth of Nations, an association of equal and autonomous states, which enjoy special trade interests. The Commonwealth is presently composed of 54 member nations, including the United Kingdom. All recognize the British monarch as head of the Commonwealth. Sixteen continue to recognize the British monarch as Head of State. They are: United Kingdom, Antigua and Barbuda, Australia, Bahamas, Barbados, Belize, Canada, Grenada, Jamaica, New Zealand, Papua New Guinea, St. Christopher & Nevis, Saint Lucia, Saint Vincent and the Grenadines, Solomon Islands, and Tuvalu. Elizabeth II is personally, and separately, the Queen of the sovereign, independent countries just mentioned. There is no other British connection between the several individual, national sovereignties, except that High Commissioners represent them each instead of ambassadors in each other's countries.

RULERS

Elizabeth II, 1952--

MINT MARKS

H - Heaton
KN - King's Norton

KINGDOM

PRE-DECIMAL COINAGE

KM# 898 PENNY

0.4713 g., 0.9250 Silver 0.0140 oz. ASW, 11 mm. **Ruler:** Elizabeth II **Obv:** Laureate bust right **Obv. Designer:** Mary Gillick **Rev:** Crowned value in sprays divides date within wreath **Edge:** Reeded

Date	Mintage	F	VF	XF	Unc	BU
2001 Prooflike	1,132	—	—	—	50.00	55.00
2002 Prooflike	1,681	—	—	—	50.00	55.00
2003 Prooflike	1,608	—	—	—	55.00	60.00
2004 Prooflike	1,613	—	—	—	55.00	60.00
2005 Prooflike	1,685	—	—	—	55.00	60.00
2006 Prooflike	1,811	—	—	—	55.00	60.00
2006 Proof	6,394	—	—	—	—	—
2007 Prooflike	1,985	—	—	—	55.00	60.00
2008 Prooflike	1,833	—	—	—	55.00	60.00
2009 Prooflike	1,602	—	—	—	55.00	60.00
2010 Prooflike	—	—	—	—	55.00	60.00
2011 Prooflike	—	—	—	—	55.00	60.00

KM# 898a PENNY

0.9167 Gold, 11 mm. **Ruler:** Elizabeth II **Obv:** Laureate bust right **Obv. Designer:** Mary Gillick **Rev:** Crowned denomination divides date within wreath

Date	Mintage	F	VF	XF	Unc	BU
2002 Proof	2,002	Value: 1,000				

KM# 899 2 PENCE

0.9426 g., 0.9250 Silver 0.0280 oz. ASW, 13 mm. **Ruler:** Elizabeth II **Obv:** Laureate bust right **Obv. Legend:** Without BRITT OMN **Obv. Designer:** Mary Gillick **Rev:** Crowned value in sprays divides date within wreath **Edge:** Reeded

Date	Mintage	F	VF	XF	Unc	BU
2001 Prooflike	1,132	—	—	—	55.00	60.00
2002 Prooflike	1,681	—	—	—	55.00	60.00
2003 Prooflike	1,608	—	—	—	60.00	65.00
2004 Prooflike	1,613	—	—	—	60.00	65.00
2005 Prooflike	1,685	—	—	—	60.00	65.00
2006 Prooflike	1,811	—	—	—	60.00	65.00
2006 Proof	6,394	—	—	—	—	—
2007 Prooflike	1,822	—	—	—	60.00	65.00
2008 Prooflike	1,999	—	—	—	60.00	65.00
2009 Prooflike	1,602	—	—	—	60.00	65.00
2010 Prooflike	—	—	—	—	60.00	65.00
2011 Prooflike	—	—	—	—	60.00	65.00

KM# 899a 2 PENCE

0.9167 Gold, 13 mm. **Ruler:** Elizabeth II **Series:** Maundy Sets **Obv:** Laureate bust right **Obv. Legend:** Without BRITT OMN **Obv. Designer:** Mary Gillick **Rev:** Crowned denomination divides date within wreath

Date	Mintage	F	VF	XF	Unc	BU
2002 Proof	2,002	Value: 1,100				

KM# 901 3 PENCE

1.4138 g., 0.9250 Silver 0.0420 oz. ASW, 16 mm. **Ruler:** Elizabeth II **Obv:** Laureate bust right **Obv. Legend:** without BRITT OMN **Obv. Designer:** Mary Gillick **Rev:** Crowned value in sprays divides date within wreath **Edge:** Reeded

Date	Mintage	F	VF	XF	Unc	BU
2001 Prooflike	1,132	—	—	—	58.00	62.00
2002 Prooflike	1,681	—	—	—	58.00	62.00
2003 Prooflike	1,608	—	—	—	60.00	65.00
2004 Prooflike	1,613	—	—	—	60.00	65.00
2005 Prooflike	1,685	—	—	—	60.00	65.00
2006 Prooflike	1,811	—	—	—	60.00	65.00
2006 Proof	6,394	—	—	—	—	—
2007 Prooflike	1,822	—	—	—	60.00	65.00
2008 Prooflike	1,833	—	—	—	60.00	65.00
2009 Prooflike	1,794	—	—	—	60.00	65.00
2010 Prooflike	—	—	—	—	60.00	65.00
2011 Prooflike	—	—	—	—	60.00	65.00

KM# 901a 3 PENCE

0.9167 Gold, 16 mm. **Ruler:** Elizabeth II **Obv:** Laureate bust right **Obv. Legend:** Without RITT OMN **Obv. Designer:** Mary Gillick **Rev:** Crowned denomination divides date within wreath

Date	Mintage	F	VF	XF	Unc	BU
2002 Proof	2,002	Value: 1,150				

KM# 902 4 PENCE (Groat)

1.8851 g., 0.9250 Silver 0.0561 oz. ASW, 18 mm. **Ruler:** Elizabeth II **Obv:** Laureate bust right **Obv. Legend:** without BRITT OMN **Rev:** Crowned denomination divides date within wreath **Edge:** Reeded

Date	Mintage	F	VF	XF	Unc	BU
2001 Prooflike	1,132	—	—	—	58.00	62.00
2002 Prooflike	1,681	—	—	—	58.00	62.00
2003 Prooflike	1,608	—	—	—	60.00	65.00
2004 Prooflike	1,613	—	—	—	60.00	65.00
2005 Prooflike	1,685	—	—	—	60.00	65.00
2006 Prooflike	1,811	—	—	—	60.00	65.00
2006 Proof	6,394	—	—	—	—	—
2007 Prooflike	1,822	—	—	—	60.00	65.00
2008 Prooflike	1,833	—	—	—	60.00	65.00
2009 Prooflike	1,602	—	—	—	60.00	65.00

Date	Mintage	F	VF	XF	Unc	BU
2010 Prooflike	—	—	—	—	60.00	65.00
2011 Prooflike	—	—	—	—	60.00	65.00

KM# 902a 4 PENCE

0.9167 Gold, 18 mm. **Ruler:** Elizabeth II **Obv:** Laureate bust right **Obv. Legend:** Without BRITT OMN **Rev:** Crowned denomination divides date within wreath

Date	Mintage	F	VF	XF	Unc	BU
2002 Proof	—	Value: 1,250				

DECIMAL COINAGE

1971-1981: 100 New Pence = 1 Pound;
1982-present: 100 Pence = 1 Pound

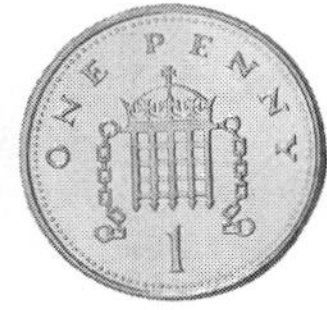

KM# 986 PENNY

3.5600 g., Copper Plated Steel, 20.32 mm. **Ruler:** Elizabeth II **Subject:** Badge of Henry VII **Obv:** Head with tiara right **Obv. Designer:** Ian Rank-Broadley **Rev:** Crowned portcullis with chains **Rev. Designer:** Christopher Ironside **Edge:** Plain

Date	Mintage	F	VF	XF	Unc	BU
2001	928,698,000	—	—	—	0.20	—
2002	601,446,000	—	—	—	0.20	—
2003	539,436,000	—	—	—	0.20	—
2003 Proof	43,513	Value: 3.25				
2004	739,764,000	—	—	—	0.20	—
2004 Proof	35,020	Value: 3.25				
2005	536,318,000	—	—	—	0.20	—
2005 Proof	40,563	Value: 3.25				
2006	524,605,000	—	—	—	0.20	—
2006 Proof	37,689	Value: 3.25				
2007	548,002,000	—	—	—	0.20	—
2007 Proof	38,215	Value: 3.25				
2008	180,600,000	—	—	—	—	2.00
2008 Proof	36,333	Value: 3.25				

KM# 986a PENNY

3.5000 g., Bronze, 20.3 mm. **Ruler:** Elizabeth II **Obv:** Head with tiara right **Obv. Designer:** Ian Rank-Broadley **Rev:** Crowned portcullis **Edge:** Plain

Date	Mintage	F	VF	XF	Unc	BU
2002 Proof	60,770	Value: 2.00				
2003 Proof	43,513	Value: 2.00				
2004 Proof	35,020	Value: 2.00				

KM# 986c PENNY

0.9167 Gold **Ruler:** Elizabeth II **Obv:** Head with tiara right **Obv. Designer:** Ian Rank-Broadley **Rev:** Crowned portcullis **Rev. Designer:** Christopher Ironside

Date	Mintage	F	VF	XF	Unc	BU
2002 Proof	—	Value: 750				
2008 Proof	2,008	Value: 550				

KM# 1107 PENNY

3.5900 g., Copper Plated Steel, 20.3 mm. **Ruler:** Elizabeth II **Obv:** Head with tiara right **Obv. Designer:** Ian Rank-Broadley **Rev:** Section of the Royal Arms - Lion and Harp **Rev. Designer:** Matthew Dent

Date	Mintage	F	VF	XF	Unc	BU
2008	507,952,000	—	—	—	—	0.20
2008 Proof	—	Value: 3.50				
2009	469,207,800	—	—	—	—	0.20
2009 Proof	—	Value: 3.50				
2010	—	—	—	—	—	0.20
2010 Proof	—	Value: 3.50				
2011	—	—	—	—	—	0.20
2011 Proof	—	Value: 3.50				

KM# 1107a PENNY

3.5600 g., 0.9250 Silver 0.1059 oz. ASW, 20.3 mm. **Ruler:** Elizabeth II **Obv:** Hear with tiara right **Obv. Designer:** Ian Rank-Broadley **Rev:** Section of the Royal Arms - Lion and Harp **Rev. Designer:** Matthew Dent

Date	Mintage	F	VF	XF	Unc	BU
2008 Proof	—	Value: 13.50				
2009	—	—	—	—	—	25.00
2009 Proof	—	Value: 25.00				
2010	—	—	—	—	—	25.00
2010 Proof	3,500	Value: 25.00				

KM# 986b PENNY

3.5600 g., 0.9250 Silver 0.1059 oz. ASW, 20.3 mm. **Ruler:** Elizabeth II **Obv:** Head with tiara right **Obv. Designer:** Ian Rank-Broadley **Rev:** Crowned portcullis **Rev. Designer:** Christopher Ironside **Edge:** Plain

Date	Mintage	F	VF	XF	Unc	BU
2008 Proof	10,000	Value: 16.50				

KM# 1107b PENNY

0.9167 Gold, 20.3 mm. **Ruler:** Elizabeth II **Obv:** Head with tiara right **Obv. Designer:** Ian rank-Broadley **Rev:** Section of the Royal Arms - Lion and Harp **Rev. Designer:** Matthew Dent

Date	Mintage	F	VF	XF	Unc	BU
2008 Proof	—	Value: 350				

KM# 1107c PENNY

Platinum APW, 20.3 mm. **Ruler:** Elizabeth II **Obv:** Head with tiara right **Obv. Designer:** Ian Rank-Broadley **Rev:** Section of the Royal Arms - Lion and Harp **Rev. Designer:** Matthew Dent

Date	Mintage	F	VF	XF	Unc	BU
2008 Proof	—	Value: 600				

KM# 987 2 PENCE

7.1400 g., Copper Plated Steel, 25.86 mm. **Ruler:** Elizabeth II **Obv:** Head with tiara right **Obv. Designer:** Ian Rank-Broadley **Rev:** Welsh plumes and crown **Rev. Designer:** Christopher Ironside **Edge:** Plain

Date	Mintage	F	VF	XF	Unc	BU
2001	551,880,000	—	—	—	0.25	—
2002	168,556,000	—	—	—	0.25	—
2003	260,225,000	—	—	—	0.25	—
2003 Proof	43,513	Value: 3.25				
2004	356,396,000	—	—	—	0.25	—
2004 Proof	35,020	Value: 3.25				
2005	280,396,000	—	—	—	0.25	—
2005 Proof	40,563	Value: 3.25				
2006	170,637,000	—	—	—	0.25	—
2006 Proof	37,689	Value: 3.25				
2007	254,500,000	—	—	—	0.25	—
2007 Proof	38,215	Value: 3.25				
2008	10,600,000	—	—	—	—	2.00

KM# 987a 2 PENCE

Bronze, 25.91 mm. **Ruler:** Elizabeth II **Obv:** Head with tiara right **Obv. Designer:** Ian Rank-Broadley **Rev:** Welsh plumes and crown **Rev. Designer:** Christopher Ironside

Date	Mintage	F	VF	XF	Unc	BU
2002 Proof	60,770	Value: 2.50				
2003 Proof	43,513	Value: 2.50				
2004 Proof	35,020	Value: 2.50				

KM# 987c 2 PENCE

0.9167 Gold, 25.91 mm. **Ruler:** Elizabeth II **Subject:** Queen's Golden Jubilee - 1952-2002 **Obv:** Head with tiara right **Obv. Designer:** Ian Rank-Broadley **Rev:** Welsh plumes and crown **Rev. Designer:** Christopher Ironside

Date	Mintage	F	VF	XF	Unc	BU
2002 Proof	—	Value: 850				
2008 Proof	2,008	Value: 650				

KM# 1108 2 PENCE

7.1000 g., Copper Plated Steel, 25.86 mm. **Ruler:** Elizabeth II **Obv:** Head with tiara right **Obv. Designer:** Ian Rank-Broadley **Rev:** Section of the Royal Arms - Lion **Rev. Designer:** Matthew Dent

Date	Mintage	F	VF	XF	Unc	BU
2008	241,679,000	—	—	—	—	0.25
2008 Proof	36,333	Value: 3.25				
2009	65,200,000	—	—	—	—	0.25
2009 Proof	40,000	Value: 3.25				
2010	—	—	—	—	—	0.25
2010 Proof	40,000	Value: 3.25				
2011	—	—	—	—	—	0.25
2011 Proof	—	Value: 3.25				

KM# 1108a 2 PENCE

7.1200 g., 0.9250 Silver 0.2117 oz. ASW, 25.86 mm. **Ruler:** Elizabeth II **Obv:** Head in tiara right **Obv. Designer:** Ian Rank-Broadley **Rev:** Section of the Royal Arms - Lion **Rev. Designer:** Matthew Dent

Date	Mintage	F	VF	XF	Unc	BU
2008 Proof	—	Value: 17.50				
2009 Proof	—	Value: 17.50				
2010 Proof	3,500	Value: 17.50				

KM# 987b 2 PENCE

7.1200 g., 0.9250 Silver 0.2117 oz. ASW, 25.9 mm. **Ruler:** Elizabeth II **Obv:** Head with tiara right **Obv. Designer:** Ian Rank-Broadley **Rev:** Welsh plumes and crown **Rev. Designer:** Christopher Ironside **Edge:** Plain

Date	Mintage	F	VF	XF	Unc	BU
2008 Proof	10,000	Value: 18.50				

KM# 1108b 2 PENCE

0.9167 Gold, 25.9 mm. **Ruler:** Elizabeth II **Obv:** Head in tiara right **Obv. Designer:** Ian Rank-Broadley **Rev:** Section of the Royal Arms - Lion **Rev. Designer:** Matthew Dent

Date	Mintage	F	VF	XF	Unc	BU
2008 Proof	—	Value: 700				

KM# 1108c 2 PENCE

Platinum APW, 25.9 mm. **Ruler:** Elizabeth II **Obv:** Head in tiara right **Obv. Designer:** Ian Rank-Broadley **Rev:** Section of Royal Arms - Lion **Rev. Designer:** Matthew Dent

Date	Mintage	F	VF	XF	Unc	BU
2008 Proof	—	Value: 1,100				

KM# 988 5 PENCE

3.2500 g., Copper-Nickel, 18 mm. **Ruler:** Elizabeth II **Obv:** Head with tiara right **Obv. Designer:** Ian Rank-Broadley **Rev:** Crowned thistle

Date	Mintage	F	VF	XF	Unc	BU
2001	337,930,000	—	—	—	0.30	—
2001 Proof	45,617	Value: 3.00				
2002	219,258,000	—	—	—	0.30	—
2002 Proof	60,770	Value: 3.00				
2003	333,230,000	—	—	—	0.30	—
2003 Proof	43,513	Value: 3.00				
2004	271,810,000	—	—	—	0.30	—
2004 Proof	35,020	Value: 3.00				
2005	236,212,000	—	—	—	0.30	—
2005 Proof	40,563	Value: 3.00				
2006	317,697,000	—	—	—	0.30	—
2006 Proof	37,689	Value: 3.00				
2007	246,720,000	—	—	—	0.30	—
2007 Proof	38,215	Value: 3.00				
2008	92,880,000	—	—	—	—	3.00

KM# 988b 5 PENCE

0.9167 Gold, 18 mm. **Ruler:** Elizabeth II **Obv:** Head with tiara right **Obv. Designer:** Ian Rank-Broadley **Rev:** Crowned thistle

Date	Mintage	F	VF	XF	Unc	BU
2002 Proof	—	Value: 450				
2008 Proof	—	Value: 400				

KM# 1109 5 PENCE

3.2500 g., Copper-Nickel, 18 mm. **Ruler:** Elizabeth II **Obv:** Head with tiara right **Obv. Designer:** Ian Rank-Broadley **Rev:** Section of the Royal Arms - Center of shield **Rev. Designer:** Matthew Dent

Date	Mintage	F	VF	XF	Unc	BU
2008	165,172,000	—	—	—	—	0.30
2008 Proof	36,333	Value: 3.00				
2009	125,520,300	—	—	—	—	0.30
2009 Proof	40,000	Value: 3.00				
2010	—	—	—	—	—	0.30
2010 Proof	40,000	Value: 3.00				

KM# 1109a 5 PENCE

3.2500 g., 0.9250 Silver 0.0966 oz. ASW, 18 mm. **Ruler:** Elizabeth II **Obv:** Head in tiara right **Obv. Designer:** Ian Rank-Broadley **Rev:** Section of Royal Arms - Center of shield **Rev. Designer:** Matthew Dent

Date	Mintage	F	VF	XF	Unc	BU
2008 Proof	—	Value: 20.00				
2009 Proof	—	Value: 20.00				
2010 Proof	3,500	Value: 20.00				

KM# 988a 5 PENCE
3.2500 g., 0.9250 Silver 0.0966 oz. ASW, 18 mm. **Ruler:** Elizabeth II **Obv:** Head with tiara right **Obv. Designer:** Ian Rank-Broadley **Rev:** Crowned thistle **Rev. Designer:** Christopher Ironside **Edge:** Reeded

Date	Mintage	F	VF	XF	Unc	BU
2008 Proof	10,000	Value: 22.50				

KM# 1109b 5 PENCE
0.9167 Gold, 18 mm. **Ruler:** Elizabeth II **Obv:** Head in tiara right **Obv. Designer:** Ian Rank-Broadley **Rev:** Section of Royal Arms - Center **Rev. Designer:** Matthew Dent

Date	Mintage	F	VF	XF	Unc	BU
2008 Proof	—	Value: 500				

KM# 1109c 5 PENCE
Platinum APW, 18 mm. **Ruler:** Elizabeth II **Obv:** Head in tiara right **Obv. Designer:** Ian Rank-Broadley **Rev:** Section of Royal Arms - Center **Rev. Designer:** Matthew Dent

Date	Mintage	F	VF	XF	Unc	BU
2008 Proof	—	Value: 800				

KM# 1109d 5 PENCE
3.2500 g., Nickel Plated Steel, 18 mm. **Ruler:** Elizabeth II **Obv:** Head with tiara right **Rev:** Section of Royal Arms - Center of shield **Rev. Designer:** Matthew Dent

Date	Mintage	F	VF	XF	Unc	BU
2011	—	—	—	—	—	0.50
2011 Proof	—	Value: 2.50				

KM# 989 10 PENCE
6.5000 g., Copper-Nickel, 24.5 mm. **Ruler:** Elizabeth II **Obv:** Head with tiara right **Obv. Designer:** Ian Rank-Broadley **Rev:** Crowned lion passant left **Rev. Designer:** Christopher Ironside

Date	Mintage	F	VF	XF	Unc	BU
2001	129,281,000	—	—	—	0.40	—
2001 Proof	45,617	Value: 3.25				
2002	80,934,000	—	—	—	0.40	—
2002 Proof	60,770	Value: 3.25				
2003	88,118,000	—	—	—	0.40	—
2003 Proof	43,513	Value: 3.25				
2004	99,602,000	—	—	—	0.40	—
2004 Proof	35,020	Value: 3.25				
2005	69,604,000	—	—	—	0.40	—
2005 Proof	40,563	Value: 3.25				
2006	118,803,000	—	—	—	0.40	—
2006 Proof	37,689	Value: 3.25				
2007	72,720,000	—	—	—	0.40	—
2007 Proof	38,215	Value: 3.25				
2008	9,720,000	—	—	—	—	3.00

KM# 989b 10 PENCE
0.9167 Gold, 24.5 mm. **Ruler:** Elizabeth II **Obv:** Head with tiara right **Obv. Designer:** Ian Rank-Broadley **Rev:** Crowned lion prancing left **Rev. Designer:** Christopher Ironside

Date	Mintage	F	VF	XF	Unc	BU
2002 Proof	—	Value: 650				
2008 Proof	2,008	Value: 550				

KM# 1110 10 PENCE
6.5000 g., Copper-Nickel, 24.5 mm. **Ruler:** Elizabeth II **Obv:** Head with tiara right **Obv. Designer:** Ian Rank-Broadley **Rev:** Section of the Royal Arms - two lions **Rev. Designer:** Matthew Dent

Date	Mintage	F	VF	XF	Unc	BU
2008	71,447,000	—	—	—	—	0.40
2008 Proof	36,333	Value: 3.25				
2009	60,000,000	—	—	—	—	0.40
2009 Proof	40,000	Value: 3.25				
2010	—	—	—	—	—	0.40
2010 Proof	40,000	Value: 3.25				

KM# 1110a 10 PENCE
6.5000 g., 0.9250 Silver 0.1933 oz. ASW, 24.5 mm. **Ruler:** Elizabeth II **Obv:** Head with tiara right **Obv. Designer:** Ian Rank-Broadley **Rev:** Section of the Royal Arms - two lions **Rev. Designer:** Matthew Dent

Date	Mintage	F	VF	XF	Unc	BU
2008 Proof	—	Value: 25.00				
2009 proof	—	Value: 25.00				
2010 Proof	3,500	Value: 25.00				

KM# 989a 10 PENCE
6.5000 g., 0.9250 Silver 0.1933 oz. ASW, 24.5 mm. **Ruler:** Elizabeth II **Obv:** Head with tiara right **Obv. Designer:** Ian Rank-Broadley **Rev:** Crowned lion prancing left **Rev. Designer:** Christopher Ironside **Edge:** Reeded

Date	Mintage	F	VF	XF	Unc	BU
2008 Proof	10,000	Value: 20.00				

KM# 1110b 10 PENCE
0.9167 Gold, 24.5 mm. **Ruler:** Elizabeth II **Obv:** Head in tiara right **Obv. Designer:** Ian Rank-Broadley **Rev:** Section of Royal Arms - two lions **Rev. Designer:** Matthew Dent

Date	Mintage	F	VF	XF	Unc	BU
2008 Proof	—	Value: 950				

KM# 1110c 10 PENCE
Platinum APW, 24.5 mm. **Ruler:** Elizabeth II **Obv:** Head in tiara right **Obv. Designer:** Iran Rank-Broadley **Rev:** Section of Royal Arms - two lions **Rev. Designer:** Matthew Dent

Date	Mintage	F	VF	XF	Unc	BU
2008 Proof	—	Value: 1,600				

KM# 1110d 10 PENCE
6.5000 g., Nickel Plated Steel, 24.5 mm. **Ruler:** Elizabeth II **Obv:** Head with tiara right **Rev:** Section of Royal Arms - two lions **Rev. Designer:** Matthew Dent

Date	Mintage	F	VF	XF	Unc	BU
2011	—	—	—	—	—	1.00
2011 Proof	—	Value: 4.00				

KM# 990 20 PENCE
5.0000 g., Copper-Nickel, 21.4 mm. **Ruler:** Elizabeth II **Obv:** Head with tiara right **Obv. Designer:** Ian Rank-Broadley **Rev:** Crowned double rose **Rev. Designer:** William Gardner **Shape:** 7-sided

Date	Mintage	F	VF	XF	Unc	BU
2001	148,122,500	—	—	—	0.60	—
2001 Proof	45,617	Value: 3.25				
2002	93,360,000	—	—	—	0.60	—
2002 Proof	60,770	Value: 3.25				
2003	153,383,750	—	—	—	0.60	—
2003 Proof	43,513	Value: 3.25				
2004	120,212,500	—	—	—	0.60	—
2004 Proof	35,020	Value: 3.25				
2005	124,488,750	—	—	—	0.60	—
2005 Proof	40,563	Value: 3.25				
2006	114,800,000	—	—	—	0.60	—
2006 Proof	37,689	Value: 3.25				
2007	117,075,000	—	—	—	0.60	—
2007 Proof	38,215	Value: 3.25				
2008	11,900,000	—	—	—	—	3.00

KM# 990b 20 PENCE
0.9167 Gold, 21.4 mm. **Ruler:** Elizabeth II **Obv:** Head with tiara right **Obv. Designer:** Ian Rank-Broadley **Rev:** Crowned double rose **Rev. Designer:** William Gardner **Shape:** 7-sided

Date	Mintage	F	VF	XF	Unc	BU
2002 Proof	—	Value: 550				
2008 Proof	2,008	Value: 500				

KM# 1111 20 PENCE
5.0000 g., Copper-Nickel, 21.4 mm. **Ruler:** Elizabeth II **Obv:** Head with tiara right **Obv. Designer:** Ian Rank-Broadley **Rev:** Section of the Royal Arms - lion's tails **Rev. Designer:** Matthew Dent **Shape:** 7-sided

Date	Mintage	F	VF	XF	Unc	BU
2008	115,022,000	—	—	—	—	0.60
2008 Proof	36,333	Value: 3.25				
2009	94,500,300	—	—	—	—	0.60
2009 Proof	40,000	Value: 3.25				
2010	—	—	—	—	—	0.60
2010 Proof	40,000	Value: 3.25				
2011	—	—	—	—	—	0.60
2011 Proof	—	Value: 3.25				

KM# 1111a 20 PENCE
5.0000 g., 0.9250 Silver 0.1487 oz. ASW, 21.4 mm. **Ruler:** Elizabeth II **Obv:** Head in tiara right **Obv. Designer:** Ian Rank-Broadley **Rev:** Section of the Royal Arms - lion's tails **Rev. Designer:** Matthew Dent **Shape:** 7-sided

Date	Mintage	F	VF	XF	Unc	BU
2008 Proof	—	Value: 35.00				
2009 Proof	—	Value: 35.00				
2010 Proof	—	Value: 35.00				

KM# 990a 20 PENCE
5.0000 g., 0.9250 Silver 0.1487 oz. ASW, 21.4 mm. **Ruler:** Elizabeth II **Obv:** Head with tiara right **Obv. Designer:** Ian Rank-Broadley **Rev:** Crowned double rose **Rev. Designer:** William Gardner **Edge:** Plain **Shape:** 7-sided

Date	Mintage	F	VF	XF	Unc	BU
2008 Proof	10,000	Value: 22.50				

KM# 1111b 20 PENCE
0.9167 Gold, 21.4 mm. **Ruler:** Elizabeth II **Obv:** Head in tiara right **Obv. Designer:** Ian Rank-Broadley **Rev:** Section of Royal Arms - lion's tails **Rev. Designer:** Matthew Dent **Shape:** 7-sided

Date	Mintage	F	VF	XF	Unc	BU
2008 Proof	—	Value: 700				

KM# 1111c 20 PENCE
Platinum APW, 21.4 mm. **Ruler:** Elizabeth II **Obv:** Head in tiara right **Obv. Designer:** Ian Rank-Broadley **Rev:** Section of Royal Arms - lion's tails **Rev. Designer:** Matthew Dent **Shape:** 7-sided

Date	Mintage	F	VF	XF	Unc	BU
2008 Proof	—	Value: 1,200				

KM# 1122 20 PENCE
5.0000 g., Copper-Nickel, 21.4 mm. **Ruler:** Elizabeth II **Obv:** Head right. Obverse of KM#990 **Rev:** Royal Arms part. Reverse of KM#1111 **Note:** Mule.

Date	Mintage	F	VF	XF	Unc	BU
ND(2008)	—	20.00	30.00	40.00	—	—

KM# 991 50 PENCE
8.0000 g., Copper-Nickel, 27.3 mm. **Ruler:** Elizabeth II **Obv:** Head with tiara right **Obv. Designer:** Ian Rank-Broadley **Rev:** Britannia seated right with shield, spear and lion **Rev. Designer:** Christopher Ironside **Shape:** 7-sided

Date	Mintage	F	VF	XF	Unc	BU
2001	84,998,500	—	—	—	1.75	—
2001 Proof	45,617	Value: 2.50				
2002	23,907,500	—	—	—	1.75	—
2002 Proof	60,770	Value: 2.50				
2003	23,583,000	—	—	—	1.75	—
2003 Proof	43,513	Value: 2.50				
2004	35,315,500	—	—	—	1.75	—
2004 Proof	35,020	Value: 2.50				
2005	25,363,500	—	—	—	1.75	—
2005 Proof	40,563	Value: 2.50				
2006	24,567,000	—	—	—	1.75	—
2006 Proof	37,689	Value: 2.50				
2007	11,200,000	—	—	—	1.75	—
2007 Proof	38,215	Value: 2.50				
2008	3,500,000	—	—	—	—	5.00

KM# 991b 50 PENCE
0.9167 Gold, 27.3 mm. **Ruler:** Elizabeth II **Obv:** Head with tiara right **Obv. Designer:** Ian Rank-Broadley **Rev:** Britannia seated right with shield, spear and lion **Rev. Designer:** Christopher Ironside **Shape:** 7-sided

Date	Mintage	F	VF	XF	Unc	BU
2002 Proof	—	Value: 700				
2008 Proof	—	Value: 650				

KM# 1036 50 PENCE
8.0000 g., Copper-Nickel, 27.3 mm. **Ruler:** Elizabeth II **Subject:** Woman's Social and Political Union, 100th Anniversary **Obv:** Head with tiara right **Obv. Designer:** Ian Rank-Broadley **Rev:** Standing suffragette chained to railings and holding banner **Rev. Designer:** Mary Milner Dickens **Edge:** Plain **Shape:** 7-sided

Date	Mintage	F	VF	XF	Unc	BU
2003	3,124,030	—	—	—	2.50	3.50
2003 Proof	35,513	Value: 9.50				

KM# 1036a 50 PENCE
8.0000 g., 0.9250 Silver 0.2379 oz. ASW, 27.3 mm. **Ruler:** Elizabeth II **Subject:** Woman's Social and Political Union, 100th Anniversary **Obv:** Head with tiara right **Obv. Designer:** Ian Rank-Broadley **Rev:** Standing suffragette chained to railings and holding banner **Rev. Designer:** Mary Milner Dickens **Edge:** Plain **Shape:** 7-sided

Date	Mintage	F	VF	XF	Unc	BU
2003 Proof	6,267	Value: 45.00				

KM# 1036b 50 PENCE
15.5000 g., 0.9166 Gold 0.4568 oz. AGW, 27.3 mm. **Ruler:** Elizabeth II **Subject:** Woman's Social and Political Union, 100th Anniversary **Obv:** Head with tiara right **Obv. Designer:** Ian Rank-Broadley **Rev:** Standing suffragette chained to railings and holding banner **Rev. Designer:** Mary Milner Dickens **Edge:** Plain **Shape:** 7-sided

Date	Mintage	F	VF	XF	Unc	BU
2003 Proof	942	Value: 750				

KM# 1047 50 PENCE
8.0000 g., Copper-Nickel, 27.3 mm. **Ruler:** Elizabeth II **Subject:** Roger Bannister, 50th Anniversary of the four minute mile **Obv:** Head with tiara right **Obv. Designer:** Ian Rank-Broadley **Rev:** Running legs, stop watch and value **Rev. Designer:** James Butler **Edge:** Plain

Date	Mintage	F	VF	XF	Unc	BU
2004	9,032,500	—	—	—	5.00	6.00
2004 Proof	35,020	Value: 7.50				

KM# 1050 50 PENCE
8.0000 g., Copper-Nickel, 27.3 mm. **Ruler:** Elizabeth II **Subject:** Samuel Johnson's Dictonary of the English Language, 250th Anniversary **Obv:** Head with tiara right **Obv. Designer:** Ian Rank-Broadley **Rev:** Dictonary entries for Fifty and Pence **Rev. Designer:** Tom Phillips **Edge:** Plain **Shape:** 7-sided

Date	Mintage	F	VF	XF	Unc	BU
2005	17,649,000	—	—	—	2.50	3.50
2005 Proof	40,563	Value: 6.00				

KM# 1050a 50 PENCE
8.0000 g., 0.9250 Silver 0.2379 oz. ASW, 27.3 mm. **Ruler:** Elizabeth II **Subject:** Samuel Johnson's Dictonary of the English Language, 250th Anniversary **Obv:** Head with tiara right **Obv. Designer:** Ian Rank-Broadley **Rev:** Dictonary entries for Fifty and Pence **Rev. Designer:** Tom Phillips **Edge:** Plain **Shape:** 7-sided

Date	Mintage	F	VF	XF	Unc	BU
2005 Proof	4,029	Value: 45.00				

KM# 1050b 50 PENCE
15.5000 g., 0.9167 Gold 0.4568 oz. AGW, 27.3 mm. **Ruler:** Elizabeth II **Subject:** Samuel Johnson's Dictonary of the English Language, 250th Anniversary **Obv:** Head with tiara right **Obv. Designer:** Ian Rank-Broadley **Rev:** Dictonary entries for Fifty and Pence **Rev. Designer:** Tom Phillips **Edge:** Plain **Shape:** 7-sided

Date	Mintage	F	VF	XF	Unc	BU
2005 Proof	1,000	Value: 750				

KM# 1057 50 PENCE
8.0000 g., Copper-Nickel, 27.3 mm. **Ruler:** Elizabeth II **Subject:** Victoria Cross, 150th Anniversary **Obv:** Head with tiara right **Obv. Designer:** Ian Rank-Broadley **Rev:** Victoria Cross Medal, obverse and reverse views **Rev. Designer:** Claire Aldridge **Edge:** Plain **Shape:** 7-sided

Date	Mintage	F	VF	XF	Unc	BU
2006	12,087,000	—	—	—	5.00	6.00
2006 Proof	Est. 50,000	Value: 7.50				
2007 Proof	—	Value: 7.50				

KM# 1058 50 PENCE
8.0000 g., Copper-Nickel, 27.3 mm. **Ruler:** Elizabeth II **Subject:** Victoria Cross, 150th Anniversary **Obv:** Head with tiara right **Obv. Designer:** Ian Rank-Broadley **Rev:** Heroic Act scene of a soldier carring a wounded comrade with outline of the Victoria Cross in the background **Rev. Designer:** Clive Duncan **Edge:** Plain **Shape:** 7-sided

Date	Mintage	F	VF	XF	Unc	BU
2006	10,000,500	—	—	—	5.00	6.00
2006 Proof	Est. 50,000	Value: 7.50				

KM# 1073 50 PENCE
8.0000 g., Copper-Nickel, 27.3 mm. **Ruler:** Elizabeth II **Subject:** Scouting Movement, 100th Anniversary **Obv:** Head with tiara right **Obv. Designer:** Ian Rank-Broadley **Rev:** Fleur-de-lis emblem superimposed on globe **Rev. Designer:** Kerry Jones **Edge:** Plain **Shape:** Seven sided

Date	Mintage	F	VF	XF	Unc	BU
2007	7,710,750	—	—	—	—	5.00
2007 Proof	Est. 50,000	Value: 7.50				

KM# 1073a 50 PENCE
8.0000 g., 0.9250 Silver 0.2379 oz. ASW, 27.3 mm. **Ruler:** Elizabeth II **Subject:** Scouting Movement, 100th Anniversary **Obv:** Head with tiara right **Obv. Designer:** Ian Rank-Broadley **Rev:** Fleur-de-lis emblem superimposed on globe **Rev. Designer:** Kerry Jones **Edge:** Plain **Shape:** 7-sided

Date	Mintage	F	VF	XF	Unc	BU
2007 Proof	12,500	Value: 60.00				

KM# 1073b 50 PENCE
15.5000 g., 0.9166 Gold 0.4568 oz. AGW, 27.3 mm. **Ruler:** Elizabeth II **Subject:** Scouting Movement, 100th Anniversary **Obv:** Head with tiara right **Obv. Designer:** Ian Rank-Broadley **Rev:** Fleur-de-lis emblem superimposed on globe **Rev. Designer:** Kerry Jones **Edge:** Plain **Shape:** 7-sided

Date	Mintage	F	VF	XF	Unc	BU
2007 Proof	1,250	Value: 775				

KM# 1112 50 PENCE
8.0000 g., Copper-Nickel, 27.3 mm. **Ruler:** Elizabeth II **Obv:** Head with tiara right **Obv. Designer:** Ian Rank-Broadley **Rev:** Section of the Royal Arms - bottom center **Rev. Designer:** Matthew Dent **Shape:** 7-sided

Date	Mintage	F	VF	XF	Unc	BU
2008	22,747,000	—	—	—	—	1.75
2008 Proof	36,333	Value: 3.50				
2009	—	—	—	—	—	1.75
2009 Proof	40,000	Value: 3.50				
2010	—	—	—	—	—	1.75
2010 Proof	40,000	Value: 3.50				
2011	—	—	—	—	—	1.75
2011 Proof	—	Value: 3.50				

KM# 1112a 50 PENCE
8.0000 g., 0.9250 Silver 0.2379 oz. ASW, 27.3 mm. **Ruler:** Elizabeth II **Obv:** Head in tiara right **Obv. Designer:** Ian Rank-Broadley **Rev:** Section of Royal Arms - bottom center **Rev. Designer:** Matthew Dent **Shape:** 7-sided

Date	Mintage	F	VF	XF	Unc	BU
2008 Proof	—	Value: 50.00				
2009 Proof	—	Value: 50.00				
2010 Proof	—	Value: 50.00				

KM# 1112b 50 PENCE
15.5000 g., 0.9167 Gold 0.4568 oz. AGW, 27.3 mm. **Ruler:** Elizabeth II **Obv:** Head in tiara right **Obv. Designer:** Ian Rank-Broadley **Rev:** Section of Royal Arms - bottom center **Rev. Designer:** Matthew Dent **Shape:** 7-sided

Date	Mintage	F	VF	XF	Unc	BU
2008 Proof	—	Value: 825				
2009 Proof	—	Value: 825				

KM# 1112c 50 PENCE
Platinum APW, 27.3 mm. **Ruler:** Elizabeth II **Obv:** Head in tiara right **Obv. Designer:** Ian Rank-Broadley **Rev:** Section of Royal Arms - bottom center **Rev. Designer:** Matthew Dent **Shape:** 7-sided

Date	Mintage	F	VF	XF	Unc	BU
2008 Proof	—	Value: 1,350				

KM# 1150 50 PENCE
8.0000 g., Copper-Nickel, 27.3 mm. **Ruler:** Elizabeth II **Subject:** London Olympics, 2012 - Athletics **Obv:** Head with tiara right **Obv. Designer:** Ian Rank-Broadley **Rev:** Youth's drawing of kid going over vault **Rev. Designer:** Florence Jackson **Edge:** Plain **Shape:** 7-sided

Date	Mintage	F	VF	XF	Unc	BU
2009	—	—	—	—	2.50	3.50
2009 Proof	—	Value: 7.50				
2011	—	—	—	—	2.50	3.50

KM# 1047a 50 PENCE
8.0000 g., 0.9250 Silver 0.2379 oz. ASW, 27.3 mm. **Ruler:** Elizabeth II **Subject:** Roger Bannister, 50th Anniversary four minute mile **Obv:** Head with tiara right **Obv. Designer:** Ian Rank-Broadley **Rev:** Running legs, stop watch and value **Rev. Designer:** James Butler **Shape:** 7-sided

Date	Mintage	F	VF	XF	Unc	BU
2009 Proof	4,924	Value: 50.00				

KM# 1114 50 PENCE
8.0000 g., Copper-Nickel, 27.3 mm. **Ruler:** Elizabeth II **Subject:** Royal Botanical Gardens at Kew, 250th Anniversary **Obv:** Head with tiara right **Obv. Designer:** Ian Rank-Broadley **Rev:** Pagoda and vine, 1759-2009 **Rev. Designer:** Christopher Le Brun **Edge:** Plain **Shape:** 7-sided

Date	Mintage	F	VF	XF	Unc	BU
2009	Est. 500,000	—	—	—	—	5.00
2009 Proof	—	Value: 7.50				

KM# 1114a 50 PENCE
8.0000 g., 0.9250 Silver 0.2379 oz. ASW, 27.3 mm. **Ruler:** Elizabeth II **Subject:** Royal Botanical Gardens at Kew, 250th Anniversary **Obv:** Head right **Obv. Designer:** Ian Rank-Broadley **Rev:** Pagoda and vine, 1759 2009 **Rev. Designer:** Christopher Le Brun **Edge:** Plain **Shape:** 7-sided

Date	Mintage	F	VF	XF	Unc	BU
2009 Proof	7,500	Value: 50.00				

KM# 1114b 50 PENCE
15.5000 g., 0.9160 Gold 0.4565 oz. AGW, 27.3 mm. **Ruler:** Elizabeth II **Subject:** Royal Botanical Gardens at Kew, 250th Anniversary **Obv:** Head right **Obv. Designer:** Ian Rank-Broadley **Rev:** Pagoda and vine, 1759 2009 **Rev. Designer:** Christopher Le Brun **Edge:** Plain **Shape:** 7-sided

Date	Mintage	F	VF	XF	Unc	BU
2009 Proof	1,000	Value: 750				

KM# 1150a 50 PENCE

8.0000 g., 0.9250 Silver 0.2379 oz. ASW, 27.3 mm. **Ruler:** Elizabeth II **Subject:** London Olympics, 2012 **Obv:** Head with tiara right **Rev:** Youth drawing of high jumper

Date	Mintage	F	VF	XF	Unc	BU
2009 Proof	—	Value: 50.00				

KM# 1165 50 PENCE

8.0000 g., Copper-Nickel, 27.3 mm. **Ruler:** Elizabeth II **Subject:** Girl Guides, 100th Anniversary **Obv:** Head with tiara right **Obv. Designer:** Ian Rank-Broadley **Rev:** Circle of six trifoils **Rev. Designer:** Jonathan Evans and Donna Hainan **Edge:** Plain **Shape:** 7-sided

Date	Mintage	F	VF	XF	Unc	BU
2010	—	—	—	—	4.00	5.00
2010 Proof	—	Value: 10.00				

KM# 1165a 50 PENCE

8.0000 g., 0.9250 Silver 0.2379 oz. ASW, 27.3 mm. **Ruler:** Elizabeth II **Subject:** Girl Guides, 100th Anniversary **Obv:** Head with tiara right **Obv. Designer:** Ian Rank-Broadley **Rev:** Circle of six trifoils **Rev. Designer:** Jonathan Evans and Donna Hainan **Edge:** Plain **Shape:** 7-sided

Date	Mintage	F	VF	XF	Unc	BU
2010 Proof	—	Value: 50.00				

KM# 1166 50 PENCE

8.0000 g., Copper-Nickel, 27.3 mm. **Ruler:** Elizabeth II **Subject:** 2012 London Olympics - Aquatics **Obv:** Head with tiara right **Obv. Designer:** Ian Rank-Broadley **Rev. Designer:** Jonathan Olliffe **Edge:** Plain **Shape:** 7-sided

Date	Mintage	F	VF	XF	Unc	BU
2011	—	—	—	—	—	6.00

KM# 1167 50 PENCE

8.0000 g., Copper-Nickel, 27.3 mm. **Ruler:** Elizabeth II **Subject:** 2012 London Paralympics - Archery **Obv:** Head with tirara right **Obv. Designer:** Ian Rank-Broadley **Rev. Designer:** Piota Powaga **Edge:** Plain **Shape:** 7-sided

Date	Mintage	F	VF	XF	Unc	BU
2011	—	—	—	—	—	6.00

KM# 1168 50 PENCE

8.0000 g., Copper-Nickel, 27.3 mm. **Ruler:** Elizabeth II **Subject:** 2012 London Olympics - Canoeing **Obv:** Head with tiara right **Obv. Designer:** Ian Rank-Broadley **Rev. Designer:** Timothy Lees **Edge:** Plain **Shape:** 7-sided

Date	Mintage	F	VF	XF	Unc	BU
2011	—	—	—	—	—	6.00

KM# 1169 50 PENCE

8.0000 g., Copper-Nickel, 27.3 mm. **Ruler:** Elizabeth II **Subject:** 2012 London Olympics - Cycling **Obv:** Head with tiara right **Obv. Designer:** Ian Rank-Broadley **Rev:** Cycle racing in a Velodrome **Rev. Designer:** Theo Crutchley-Mack **Edge:** Plain **Shape:** 7-sided

Date	Mintage	F	VF	XF	Unc	BU
2011	—	—	—	—	—	6.00

KM# 1170 50 PENCE

8.0000 g., Copper-Nickel, 27.3 mm. **Ruler:** Elizabeth II **Subject:** 2012 London Olympics - Gymnastics **Obv:** Head with tiara right **Obv. Designer:** Ian Rank-Broadley **Rev. Designer:** Jonathan Olliffe **Edge:** Plain **Shape:** 7-sided

Date	Mintage	F	VF	XF	Unc	BU
2011	—	—	—	—	—	6.00

KM# 1171 50 PENCE

8.0000 g., Copper-Nickel, 27.3 mm. **Ruler:** Elizabeth II **Subject:** 2012 London Olympics - Hockey **Obv:** Head with tiara right **Obv. Designer:** Ian Rank-Broadley **Rev. Designer:** Robert Evans **Edge:** Plain **Shape:** 7-sided

Date	Mintage	F	VF	XF	Unc	BU
2011	—	—	—	—	—	6.00

KM# 1172 50 PENCE

8.0000 g., Copper-Nickel, 27.3 mm. **Ruler:** Elizabeth II **Subject:** 2012 London Olympics - Rowing **Obv:** Head with tiara right **Obv. Designer:** Ian Rank-Broadley **Rev. Designer:** Davey Podmore **Edge:** Plain **Shape:** 7-sided

Date	Mintage	F	VF	XF	Unc	BU
2011	—	—	—	—	—	6.00

KM# 1173 50 PENCE

8.0000 g., Copper-Nickel, 27.3 mm. **Ruler:** Elizabeth II **Subject:** 2012 London Olympics - Triathlon **Obv:** Head with tiara right **Obv. Designer:** Ian Rank-Broadley **Rev. Designer:** Sarah Harvey **Edge:** Plain **Shape:** 7-sided

Date	Mintage	F	VF	XF	Unc	BU
2011	—	—	—	—	—	6.00

KM# 1174 50 PENCE

8.0000 g., Copper-Nickel, 27.3 mm. **Ruler:** Elizabeth II **Subject:** 2012 London Olympics - Badminton **Obv:** Head with tiara right **Obv. Designer:** Ian Rank-Broadley **Rev. Designer:** Emma Kelly **Edge:** Plain **Shape:** 7-sided

Date	Mintage	F	VF	XF	Unc	BU
2011	—	—	—	—	—	6.00

KM# 1175 50 PENCE

8.0000 g., Copper-Nickel, 27.3 mm. **Ruler:** Elizabeth II **Subject:** 2012 London Olympics - Boxing **Obv:** Head with tiara right **Obv. Designer:** Ian Rank-Broadley **Rev. Designer:** Shane Abery **Edge:** Plain **Shape:** 7-sided

Date	Mintage	F	VF	XF	Unc	BU
2011	—	—	—	—	—	6.00

KM# 1176 50 PENCE

8.0000 g., Copper-Nickel, 27.3 mm. **Ruler:** Elizabeth II **Subject:** 2012 London Olympics - Equestrian **Obv:** Head with tiara right **Obv. Designer:** Ian Rank-Broadley **Rev. Designer:** Thomas Babbage **Edge:** Plain **Shape:** 7-sided

Date	Mintage	F	VF	XF	Unc	BU
2011	—	—	—	—	—	6.00

KM# 1177 50 PENCE

8.0000 g., Copper-Nickel, 27.3 mm. **Ruler:** Elizabeth II **Subject:** 2012 London Olympics - Modern Pentathlon **Obv:** Head with tiara right **Obv. Designer:** Ian Rank-Broadley **Rev. Designer:** Daniel Brittain **Edge:** Plain **Shape:** 7-sided

Date	Mintage	F	VF	XF	Unc	BU
2011	—	—	—	—	—	6.00

KM# 1179 50 PENCE

8.0000 g., Copper-Nickel, 27.3 mm. **Ruler:** Elizabeth II **Subject:** 2012 London Olympics - Shooting **Obv:** Head with tiara right **Obv. Designer:** Ian Rank-Broadley **Rev. Designer:** Pravin Dewdhory **Edge:** Plain **Shape:** 7-sided

Date	Mintage	F	VF	XF	Unc	BU
2011	—	—	—	—	—	6.00

KM# 1180 50 PENCE

8.0000 g., Copper-Nickel, 27.3 mm. **Ruler:** Elizabeth II **Subject:** 2012 London Paralympics - Table Tennis **Obv:** Head with tiara right **Obv. Designer:** Ian Rank-Broadley **Rev. Designer:** Alan Linsdell **Edge:** Plain **Shape:** 7-sided

Date	Mintage	F	VF	XF	Unc	BU
2011	—	—	—	—	—	6.00

KM# 1181 50 PENCE

8.0000 g., Copper-Nickel, 27.3 mm. **Ruler:** Elizabeth II **Subject:** 2012 London Olympics - Volleyball **Obv. Designer:** Ian Rank-Broadley **Rev. Designer:** Daniela Boothman **Shape:** 7-sided

Date	Mintage	F	VF	XF	Unc	BU
2011	—	—	—	—	—	6.00

KM# 1182 50 PENCE
8.0000 g., Copper-Nickel, 27.3 mm. **Ruler:** Elizabeth II **Subject:** 2012 London Olympics - Canoeing **Obv. Designer:** Ian Rank-Broadley **Rev. Designer:** Timothy Lees **Shape:** 7-sided

Date	Mintage	F	VF	XF	Unc	BU
2011	—	—	—	—	—	6.00

KM# 1183 50 PENCE
8.0000 g., Copper-Nickel, 27.3 mm. **Ruler:** Elizabeth II **Subject:** 2012 London Paralympics - Goalball **Obv:** Head with tiara right **Obv. Designer:** Ian Rank-Broadley **Rev. Designer:** Jonathan Wren **Edge:** Plain **Shape:** 7-sided

Date	Mintage	F	VF	XF	Unc	BU
2011	—	—	—	—	—	6.00

KM# 1185 50 PENCE
8.0000 g., Copper-Nickel, 27.3 mm. **Ruler:** Elizabeth II **Subject:** 2012 London Olympics - Taekwondo **Obv:** Head with tiara right **Obv. Designer:** Ian Rank-Broadley **Rev. Designer:** David Gibbons **Edge:** Plain **Shape:** 7-sided

Date	Mintage	F	VF	XF	Unc	BU
2011	—	—	—	—	—	6.00

KM# 1186 50 PENCE
8.0000 g., Copper-Nickel, 27.3 mm. **Ruler:** Elizabeth II **Subject:** 2012 London Olympics - Weightlifting **Obv:** Head with tiara right **Obv. Designer:** Ian Rank-Broadley **Rev. Designer:** Rob Shakespeare **Edge:** Plain **Shape:** 7-sided

Date	Mintage	F	VF	XF	Unc	BU
2011	—	—	—	—	—	6.00

KM# 1187 50 PENCE
8.0000 g., Copper-Nickel, 27.3 mm. **Ruler:** Elizabeth II **Subject:** 2012 London Paralympics - Wheelchair Rugby **Obv:** Head with tiara right **Obv. Designer:** Ian Rank-Broadley **Rev. Designer:** Natasha Ratcliffe **Edge:** Plain **Shape:** 7-sided

Date	Mintage	F	VF	XF	Unc	BU
2011	—	—	—	—	—	6.00

KM# 1188 50 PENCE
8.0000 g., Copper-Nickel, 27.3 mm. **Ruler:** Elizabeth II **Subject:** 2012 Summer Olympics - Wrestling **Obv:** Head with tiara right **Obv. Designer:** Ian Rank-Broadley **Rev. Designer:** Roderick Enriquez **Edge:** Plain **Shape:** 7-sided

Date	Mintage	F	VF	XF	Unc	BU
2011	—	—	—	—	—	6.00

KM# 1189 50 PENCE
8.0000 g., Copper-Nickel, 27.3 mm. **Ruler:** Elizabeth II **Subject:** 2012 London Paralympics - Boccia **Obv:** Head with tiara right **Obv. Designer:** Ian Rank-Broadley **Rev. Designer:** Justin Chung **Edge:** Plain **Shape:** 7-sided

Date	Mintage	F	VF	XF	Unc	BU
2011	—	—	—	—	—	6.00

KM# 1190 50 PENCE
8.0000 g., Copper-Nickel, 27.3 mm. **Ruler:** Elizabeth II **Subject:** 2012 London Olympics - Basketball **Obv:** Head with tiara right **Obv. Designer:** Ian Rank-Broadley **Rev. Designer:** Sarah Payne **Edge:** Plain **Shape:** 7-sided

Date	Mintage	F	VF	XF	Unc	BU
2011	—	—	—	—	—	6.00

KM# 1191 50 PENCE
8.0000 g., Copper-Nickel, 27.3 mm. **Ruler:** Elizabeth II **Subject:** 2012 London Olympics - Fencing **Obv:** Head with tiara right **Obv. Designer:** Ian Rank-Broadley **Rev. Designer:** Ruth Summerfield **Edge:** Plain **Shape:** 7-sided

Date	Mintage	F	VF	XF	Unc	BU
2011	—	—	—	—	—	6.00

KM# 1192 50 PENCE
8.0000 g., Copper-Nickel, 27.3 mm. **Ruler:** Elizabeth II **Subject:** 2012 London Olympics - Handball **Obv:** Head with tiara right **Obv. Designer:** Ian Rank-Broadley **Rev. Designer:** Natasha Ratcliffe **Edge:** Plain **Shape:** 7-sided

Date	Mintage	F	VF	XF	Unc	BU
2011	—	—	—	—	—	6.00

KM# 1193 50 PENCE
8.0000 g., Copper-Nickel, 27.3 mm. **Ruler:** Elizabeth II **Subject:** 2012 London Olympics - Football (Soccer) **Obv:** Head with tiara right **Obv. Designer:** Ian Rank-Broadley **Rev. Designer:** Neil Wolfson **Edge:** Plain **Shape:** 7-sided

Date	Mintage	F	VF	XF	Unc	BU
2011	—	—	—	—	—	6.00

KM# 1194 50 PENCE
8.0000 g., Copper-Nickel, 27.3 mm. **Ruler:** Elizabeth II **Subject:** 2012 London Olympics - Tennis **Obv:** Head with tiara right **Obv. Designer:** Ian Rank-Broadley **Rev. Designer:** Tracy Baines **Edge:** Plain **Shape:** 7-sided

Date	Mintage	F	VF	XF	Unc	BU
2011	—	—	—	—	—	6.00

KM# 1195 50 PENCE
8.0000 g., Copper-Nickel, 27.3 mm. **Ruler:** Elizabeth II **Subject:** London Olympics - Sailing **Obv:** Head with tiara right **Obv. Designer:** Ian Rank-Broadley **Rev. Designer:** Bruce Rushin **Edge:** Plain **Shape:** 7-sided

Date	Mintage	F	VF	XF	Unc	BU
2011	—	—	—	—	3.00	4.00

KM# 1196a 50 PENCE
8.0000 g., 0.9250 Silver 0.2379 oz. ASW, 27.3 mm. **Ruler:** Elizabeth II **Subject:** World Wildlife Fund, 50th Anniversary **Obv:** Head with tiara right **Obv. Designer:** Ian Rank-Broadley **Rev:** Panda at center, animal shapes as blocks **Rev. Designer:** Matthew Dent **Edge:** Plain **Shape:** 7-sided

Date	Mintage	F	VF	XF	Unc	BU
2011 Proof	—	Value: 50.00				

KM# 1196 50 PENCE
8.0000 g., Copper-Nickel, 27.3 mm. **Ruler:** Elizabeth II **Subject:** World Wildlife Fund, 50th Anniversary **Obv:** Head with tiara right **Obv. Designer:** Ian Rank-Broadley **Rev:** Panda in center of animal shaped blocks **Rev. Designer:** Matthew Dent **Edge:** Plain **Shape:** 7-sided

Date	Mintage	F	VF	XF	Unc	BU
2011	—	—	—	—	5.00	6.00
2011 Proof	—	Value: 8.50				

KM# 1184 50 PENCE
8.0000 g., Copper-Nickel, 24.3 mm. **Ruler:** Elizabeth II **Subject:** 2012 London Olympics - Judo **Obv:** Head with tiara right **Obv. Designer:** Ian Rank-Broadley **Rev. Designer:** David Cornell **Edge:** Plain **Shape:** 7-sided

Date	Mintage	F	VF	XF	Unc	BU
2011	—	—	—	—	—	6.00

KM# 1178 50 PENCE
8.0000 g., Copper-Nickel, 27.3 mm. **Ruler:** Elizabeth II **Subject:** 2012 London Olympics - Sailing **Obv:** Head with tiara right **Obv. Designer:** Ian Rank-Broadley **Rev. Designer:** Bruce Rushin **Edge:** Plain **Shape:** 7-sided

Date	Mintage	F	VF	XF	Unc	BU
2012	—	—	—	—	—	6.00

KM# 1013 POUND

9.5000 g., Nickel-Brass, 22.5 mm. **Ruler:** Elizabeth II **Subject:** Northern Ireland **Obv:** Head with tiara right **Obv. Designer:** Ian Rank-Broadley **Rev:** Celtic cross with a pimpernel flower at the center **Rev. Designer:** Norman Sillman **Edge:** Reeded and lettered **Edge Lettering:** DECUS ET TUTAMEN

Date	Mintage	F	VF	XF	Unc	BU
2001	63,968,065	—	—	—	4.00	5.00
2001 Proof	45,617	Value: 6.00				

KM# 1013a POUND

9.5000 g., 0.9250 Silver 0.2825 oz. ASW, 22.5 mm. **Ruler:** Elizabeth II **Subject:** Northern Ireland **Obv:** Head with tiara right **Obv. Designer:** Ian Rank-Broadley **Rev:** Celtic cross with a pimpernel flower in the center **Rev. Designer:** Norman Sillman **Edge:** Reeded and lettered **Edge Lettering:** DECUS ET TUTAMEN

Date	Mintage	F	VF	XF	Unc	BU
2001 Proof	25,000	Value: 45.00				

KM# 1030 POUND

9.5000 g., Nickel-Brass, 22.5 mm. **Ruler:** Elizabeth II **Subject:** England **Obv:** Head with tiara right **Obv. Designer:** Ian Rank-Broadley **Rev:** Three lions passant left **Rev. Designer:** Norman Sillman **Edge:** Reeded and lettered **Edge Lettering:** DECUS ET TUTAMEN

Date	Mintage	F	VF	XF	Unc	BU
2002	77,818,000	—	—	—	5.00	6.00
2002 Proof	60,770	Value: 7.00				

KM# 1030a POUND

9.5000 g., 0.9250 Silver 0.2825 oz. ASW, 22.5 mm. **Ruler:** Elizabeth II **Subject:** England **Obv:** Head with tiara right **Obv. Designer:** Ian Rank-Broadley **Rev:** Three lions passant left **Rev. Designer:** Norman Sillman **Edge:** Reeded and lettered **Edge Lettering:** DECUS ET TUTAMEN

Date	Mintage	F	VF	XF	Unc	BU
2002 Proof	—	Value: 45.00				

KM# 1030b POUND

0.9167 Gold, 22.5 mm. **Ruler:** Elizabeth II **Subject:** England **Obv:** Head with tiara right **Obv. Designer:** Ian Rank-Broadley **Rev:** Three lions left passant left **Rev. Designer:** Norman Sillman **Edge:** Reeded and lettered **Edge Lettering:** DECUS ET TUTAMEN

Date	Mintage	F	VF	XF	Unc	BU
2002 Proof	—	Value: 850				

KM# 993 POUND

9.5000 g., Nickel-Brass, 22.5 mm. **Ruler:** Elizabeth II **Subject:** United Kingdom **Obv:** Head with tiara right **Obv. Designer:** Ian Rank-Broadley **Rev:** Royal Arms with supporters **Rev. Designer:** Eric Sewell **Edge:** Reeded and lettered **Edge Lettering:** DECUS ET TUTAMEN

Date	Mintage	F	VF	XF	Unc	BU
2003	61,596,500	—	—	—	5.00	6.00
2003 Proof	43,513	Value: 7.50				
2008	3,910,000	—	—	—	5.00	6.00

KM# 1048 POUND

9.5000 g., Nickel-Brass, 22.5 mm. **Ruler:** Elizabeth II **Obv:** Head with tiara right **Obv. Designer:** Ian Rank-Broadley **Rev:** Forth Rail Bridge in Scotland **Rev. Designer:** Edwina Ellis **Edge:** Reeded and ornamented

Date	Mintage	F	VF	XF	Unc	BU
2004	39,162,000	—	—	—	6.00	7.50
2004 Proof	35,020	Value: 9.00				

KM# 1048a POUND

9.5000 g., 0.9250 Silver 0.2825 oz. ASW, 22.5 mm. **Ruler:** Elizabeth II **Obv:** Head with tiara right **Obv. Designer:** Ian Rank-Broadley **Rev:** Forth Railway Bridge in Scotland **Rev. Designer:** Edwina Ellis **Edge:** Ornamented and reeded

Date	Mintage	F	VF	XF	Unc	BU
2004 Proof	Est. 20,000	Value: 45.00				

KM# 1048b POUND

19.6190 g., 0.9166 Gold 0.5781 oz. AGW, 22.5 mm. **Ruler:** Elizabeth II **Obv:** Head with tiara right **Obv. Designer:** Ian Rank-Broadley **Rev:** Forth Railway Bridge in Scotland **Rev. Designer:** Edwina Ellis **Edge:** Reeded and ornamented

Date	Mintage	F	VF	XF	Unc	BU
2004 Proof	Est. 1,500	Value: 850				

KM# 1051 POUND

9.5000 g., Nickel-Brass, 22.5 mm. **Ruler:** Elizabeth II **Obv:** Head with tiara right **Obv. Designer:** Ian Rank-Broadley **Rev:** Menai Bridge to the Isle of Anglesey **Rev. Designer:** Edwina Ellis **Edge:** Reeded and lettered **Edge Lettering:** PLEIDOL WYF I'M GWLAD

Date	Mintage	F	VF	XF	Unc	BU
2005	99,429,500	—	—	—	5.00	6.00
2005 Proof	40,563	Value: 10.00				

KM# 1051a POUND

9.5000 g., 0.9250 Silver 0.2825 oz. ASW, 22.5 mm. **Ruler:** Elizabeth II **Obv:** Head with tiara right **Obv. Designer:** Ian Rank-Broadley **Rev:** Menai Bridge to the Isle of Anglesey **Rev. Designer:** Edwina Ellis **Edge:** Reeded and lettered **Edge Lettering:** PLEIDOL WYF I'M GWLAD

Date	Mintage	F	VF	XF	Unc	BU
2005 Proof	Est. 15,000	Value: 45.00				

KM# 1051b POUND

19.6190 g., 0.9167 Gold 0.5782 oz. AGW, 22.5 mm. **Ruler:** Elizabeth II **Obv:** Head with tiara right **Obv. Designer:** Ian Rank-Broadley **Rev:** Menai Bridge to the Isle of Anglesey **Rev. Designer:** Edwina Ellis **Edge:** Reeded and lettered **Edge Lettering:** PLEIDOL WYF I'M GWLAD

Date	Mintage	F	VF	XF	Unc	BU
2005 Proof	Est. 1,500	Value: 850				

KM# 1051a.2 POUND

9.5000 g., 0.9250 Silver 0.2825 oz. ASW, 22.5 mm. **Ruler:** Elizabeth II **Obv:** Elizabeth II **Obv. Designer:** Ian Rank-Broadley **Rev:** Menai Bridge to the Isle of Anglesey **Rev. Designer:** Edwina Ellis **Edge:** Reeded and ornamented

Date	Mintage	F	VF	XF	Unc	BU
2005 Proof	Est. 20,000	Value: 45.00				

KM# 1051b.2 POUND

19.6190 g., 0.9166 Gold 0.5781 oz. AGW, 22.5 mm. **Ruler:** Elizabeth II **Obv:** Head with tiara right **Obv. Designer:** Ian Rank-Broadley **Rev:** Menai Bridge to the Isle of Anglesey **Rev. Designer:** Edwina Ellis **Edge:** Reeded and ornamented

Date	Mintage	F	VF	XF	Unc	BU
2005 Proof	Est. 1,500	Value: 850				

KM# 1059 POUND

9.6000 g., Nickel-Brass, 22.5 mm. **Ruler:** Elizabeth II **Obv:** Head with tiara right **Obv. Designer:** Ian Rank-Broadley **Rev:** Egyptian Arch Railway Bridge at Newry **Rev. Designer:** Edwina Ellis **Edge:** Reeded and lettered

Date	Mintage	F	VF	XF	Unc	BU
2006	38,938,000	—	—	—	8.00	9.00
2006 Proof	37,689	Value: 10.00				
2007 Proof	—	Value: 10.00				

KM# 1059a POUND

9.5000 g., 0.9250 Silver 0.2825 oz. ASW, 22.5 mm. **Ruler:** Elizabeth II **Obv:** Head with tiara right **Obv. Designer:** Ian Rank-Broadley **Rev:** Egyptian Arch Railway Bridge at Newry **Rev. Designer:** Edwina Ellis **Edge:** Reeded and lettered **Edge Lettering:** DECUS ET TUTAMEN

Date	Mintage	F	VF	XF	Unc	BU
2006 Proof	Est. 20,000	Value: 50.00				

KM# 1059a.2 POUND

9.5000 g., 0.9250 Silver 0.2825 oz. ASW, 22.5 mm. **Ruler:** Elizabeth II **Obv:** Head with tiara right **Obv. Designer:** Ian Rank-Broadley **Rev:** Egyptian Arch Railway Bridge at Newry **Rev. Designer:** Edwina Ellis **Edge:** Reeded and ornamented

Date	Mintage	F	VF	XF	Unc	BU
2006 Proof	Est. 20,000	Value: 45.00				

KM# 1059b POUND

19.6190 g., 0.9167 Gold 0.5782 oz. AGW, 22.5 mm. **Ruler:** Elizabeth II **Obv:** Head with tiara right **Obv. Designer:** Ian Rank-Broadley **Rev:** Egyptian Arch Railway Bridge at Newry **Rev. Designer:** Edwina Ellis **Edge:** Reeded and lettered **Edge Lettering:** DECUS ET TUTAMEN

Date	Mintage	F	VF	XF	Unc	BU
2006 Proof	—	Value: 875				

KM# 1059b.2 POUND

19.6190 g., 0.9166 Gold 0.5781 oz. AGW, 22.5 mm. **Ruler:** Elizabeth II **Obv:** Head with tiara right **Obv. Designer:** Ian Rank-Broadley **Rev:** Egyptian Arch Railway Bridge at Newry **Rev. Designer:** Edwina Ellis **Edge:** Reeded and ornamented

Date	Mintage	F	VF	XF	Unc	BU
2006 Proof	Est. 1,500	Value: 850				

KM# 1074 POUND

9.5000 g., Nickel-Brass, 22.5 mm. **Ruler:** Elizabeth II **Obv:** Head with tiara right **Obv. Designer:** Ian Rank-Broadley **Rev:** Millennium Bridge at Gateshead **Rev. Designer:** Edwina Ellis **Edge:** Reeded and ornamented

Date	Mintage	F	VF	XF	Unc	BU
2007	26,180,160	—	—	—	7.00	8.00
2007 Proof	38,215	Value: 10.00				

KM# 1074a POUND

9.5000 g., 0.9250 Silver 0.2825 oz. ASW, 22.5 mm. **Ruler:** Elizabeth II **Obv:** head with tiara right **Obv. Designer:** Ian Rank-Broadley **Rev:** Millennium Bridge at Gateshead **Rev. Designer:** Edwina Ellis **Edge:** Reeded and ornamented

Date	Mintage	F	VF	XF	Unc	BU
2007 Proof	Est. 20,000	Value: 45.00				

KM# 1074b POUND

19.6190 g., 0.9166 Gold 0.5781 oz. AGW, 22.5 mm. **Ruler:** Elizabeth II **Obv:** Head with tiara right **Obv. Designer:** Ian Rank-Broadley **Rev:** Millennium Bridge at Gateshead **Rev. Designer:** Edwina Ellis **Edge:** Reeded and ornamented

Date	Mintage	F	VF	XF	Unc	BU
2007 Proof	Est. 1,500	Value: 850				

KM# 993a POUND

9.5000 g., 0.9250 Silver 0.2825 oz. ASW, 22.5 mm. **Ruler:** Elizabeth II **Subject:** United Kingdom **Obv:** Head with tiara right **Obv. Designer:** Ian Rank-Broadley **Rev:** Royal Arms with supporters **Rev. Designer:** Eric Sewell **Edge:** Reeded and lettered **Edge Lettering:** DECUS ET TUTAMEN

Date	Mintage	F	VF	XF	Unc	BU
2008 Proof	Est. 10,000	Value: 45.00				

KM# 1113 POUND

9.5000 g., Nickel-Brass, 22.5 mm. **Ruler:** Elizabeth II **Obv:** Head with tiara right **Obv. Designer:** Ian Rank-Broadley **Rev:** Shield of the Royal Arms **Rev. Designer:** Matthew Dent **Edge:** Reeded and lettered **Edge Lettering:** DECUS ET TUTAMEN

Date	Mintage	F	VF	XF	Unc	BU
2008	43,827,300	—	—	—	4.00	5.00
2008 Proof	36,333	Value: 6.00				
2009	7,820,000	—	—	—	4.00	5.00
2009 Proof	40,000	Value: 6.00				
2010	—	—	—	—	4.00	5.00
2010 Proof	40,000	Value: 6.00				
2011	—	—	—	—	4.00	5.00
2011 Proof	—	Value: 6.00				

KM# 1113a POUND

9.5000 g., 0.9250 Silver 0.2825 oz. ASW, 22.5 mm. **Ruler:** Elizabeth II **Obv:** Head in tiara right **Obv. Designer:** Ian Rank-Broadley **Rev:** Shield of the Royal Arms **Rev. Designer:** Matthew Dent

Date	Mintage	F	VF	XF	Unc	BU
2008 Proof	5,000	Value: 50.00				
2009	50,000	—	—	—	—	50.00
2009 Proof	20,000	Value: 60.00				
2010	50,000	—	—	—	—	50.00
2010 Proof	20,000	Value: 60.00				

KM# 1113b POUND

16.6190 g., 0.9167 Gold 0.4898 oz. AGW, 22.5 mm. **Ruler:** Elizabeth II **Obv:** Head in tiara right **Obv. Designer:** Ian Rank-Broadley **Rev:** Shield of the Royal Arms **Rev. Designer:** Matthew Dent

Date	Mintage	F	VF	XF	Unc	BU
2008 Proof	860	Value: 1,100				
2009 Proof	1,000	Value: 1,050				

KM# 993b POUND

19.6000 g., 0.9167 Gold 0.5776 oz. AGW, 22.5 mm. **Ruler:** Elizabeth II **Subject:** United Kingdom **Obv:** Head with tiara right **Obv. Designer:** Ian Rank-Broadley **Rev:** Royal Arms with supporters **Rev. Designer:** Eric Sewell **Edge:** Reeded and lettered **Edge Lettering:** DECUS ET TUTAMEN

Date	Mintage	F	VF	XF	Unc	BU
2008 Proof	Est. 2,008	Value: 850				

KM# 1113c POUND

Platinum APW, 22.5 mm. **Ruler:** Elizabeth II **Obv:** Head in tiara right **Obv. Designer:** Ian Rank-Broadley **Rev:** Shield of the Royal Arms **Rev. Designer:** Matthew Dent

Date	Mintage	F	VF	XF	Unc	BU
2008 Proof	—	Value: 1,650				

KM# 1158 POUND

9.5000 g., Nickel-Brass, 22.5 mm. **Ruler:** Elizabeth II **Obv:** Head with tiara right **Obv. Designer:** Ian Rank-Broadley **Rev:** City of London arms, three smaller arms below **Rev. Designer:** Stuart Devlin **Edge:** Reeded and lettered **Edge Lettering:** DOMINE DIRIGE NOS

Date	Mintage	F	VF	XF	Unc	BU
2010	—	—	—	—	3.50	4.50
2010 Proof	—	Value: 10.00				

KM# 1158a POUND

9.5000 g., 0.9250 Silver 0.2825 oz. ASW, 22.5 mm. **Ruler:** Elizabeth II **Obv:** Head with tiara right **Obv. Designer:** Ian Rank-Broadley **Rev:** City of London arms, three smaller arms below **Rev. Designer:** Stuart Devlin

Date	Mintage	F	VF	XF	Unc	BU
2010 Proof	20,000	Value: 60.00				

KM# 1158b POUND

19.6190 g., 0.9167 Gold 0.5782 oz. AGW, 22.5 mm. **Ruler:** Elizabeth II **Obv:** Head with tiara right **Obv. Designer:** Ian Rank-Broadley **Rev:** City of London arms, three smaller arms below **Rev. Designer:** Stuart Devlin

Date	Mintage	F	VF	XF	Unc	BU
2010 Proof	2,500	Value: 1,100				

KM# 1159 POUND

9.5000 g., Nickel-Brass, 22.5 mm. **Ruler:** Elizabeth II **Obv:** Head with tiara right **Obv. Designer:** Ian Rank-Broadley **Rev:** City of Belfast arms, three smaller arms below **Rev. Designer:** Stuart Devlin **Edge:** Reeded and lettered **Edge Lettering:** PRO TANTO QUID RETRIBUAMUS

Date	Mintage	F	VF	XF	Unc	BU
2010	—	—	—	—	3.50	4.50
2010 Proof	—	Value: 10.00				

KM# 1159a POUND

9.5000 g., 0.9250 Silver 0.2825 oz. ASW, 22.5 mm. **Ruler:** Elizabeth II **Obv:** Head with tiara right **Obv. Designer:** Ian Rank-Broadley **Rev:** City of Belfast arms, three smaller arms below **Rev. Designer:** Stuart Devlin

Date	Mintage	F	VF	XF	Unc	BU
2010 Proof	20,000	Value: 60.00				

KM# 1159b POUND

19.6190 g., 0.9167 Gold 0.5782 oz. AGW, 22.5 mm. **Ruler:** Elizabeth II **Obv:** Head with tiara right **Obv. Designer:** Ian Rank-Broadley **Rev:** City of Belfast arms, three smaller arms below **Rev. Designer:** Stuart Devlin

Date	Mintage	F	VF	XF	Unc	BU
2010 Proof	2,500	Value: 1,100				

KM# 1197 POUND

9.5000 g., Nickel-Brass, 22.5 mm. **Ruler:** Elizabeth II **Obv:** Head with tiara right **Obv. Designer:** Ian Rank-Broadley **Rev:** Edinburgh city arms, three smaller arms below **Rev. Designer:** Stuart Devlin **Edge:** Reeded and lettered **Edge Lettering:** NISI DOMINUS FRUSTRA

Date	Mintage	F	VF	XF	Unc	BU
2011	—	—	—	—	5.00	6.00
2011 Proof	—	Value: 10.00				

KM# 1197a POUND

9.5000 g., 0.9250 Silver 0.2825 oz. ASW, 22.5 mm. **Ruler:** Elizabeth II **Obv:** Head with tiara right **Obv. Designer:** Ian Rank-Broadley **Rev:** Edinburgh City arms, three smaller arms below **Rev. Designer:** Stuart Devlin

Date	Mintage	F	VF	XF	Unc	BU
2011 Proof	—	Value: 45.00				

KM# 1198 POUND

9.5000 g., Nickel-Brass, 22.5 mm. **Ruler:** Elizabeth II **Obv:** Head with tiara right **Obv. Designer:** Ian Rank-Broadley **Rev:** Cardiff city arms, three smaller arms below **Rev. Designer:** Stuart Devlin **Edge:** Reeded and lettered **Edge Lettering:** DDRAIG GOCH DDYRY CYCHWYN

Date	Mintage	F	VF	XF	Unc	BU
2011	—	—	—	—	5.00	6.00
2011 Proof	—	Value: 10.00				

KM# 1198a POUND

9.5000 g., 0.9250 Silver 0.2825 oz. ASW, 22.5 mm. **Ruler:** Elizabeth II **Obv:** Head with tiara right **Obv. Designer:** Ian Rank-Broadley **Rev:** Cardiff city arms, three smaller arms below **Rev. Designer:** Stuart Devlin

Date	Mintage	F	VF	XF	Unc	BU
2011 Proof	—	Value: 45.00				

KM# 994 2 POUNDS

12.0000 g., Bi-Metallic Copper-Nickel center in Nickel-Brass ring, 28.4 mm. **Ruler:** Elizabeth II **Subject:** Technology **Obv:** Head with tiara right **Obv. Designer:** Ian Rank-Broadley **Rev:** Symbolic depiction in concentric circles of technological development from the Iron Age to the Internet **Rev. Designer:** Bruce Rushin **Edge Lettering:** STANDING ON THE SHOULDERS OF GIANTS

Date	Mintage	F	VF	XF	Unc	BU
2001	34,984,750	—	—	—	6.00	8.50
2001 Proof	—	Value: 10.00				
2002	13,024,750	—	—	—	6.00	8.50
2002 Proof	—	Value: 10.00				
2003	17,531,250	—	—	—	6.00	8.50
2003 Proof	43,513	Value: 10.00				
2004	11,981,500	—	—	—	6.00	8.50
2004 Proof	35,020	Value: 10.00				
2005	3,837,250	—	—	—	6.00	8.50
2005 Proof	40,563	Value: 10.00				
2006	16,715,000	—	—	—	6.00	8.50
2006 Proof	—	Value: 10.00				
2007	10,270,000	—	—	—	6.00	8.50
2007 Proof	—	Value: 10.00				
2008	29,197,000	—	—	—	6.00	8.00
2008 Proof	—	Value: 10.00				
2009	—	—	—	—	6.00	8.00
2009 Proof	—	Value: 10.00				
2010	—	—	—	—	6.00	8.00
2010 Proof	—	Value: 10.00				
2011	—	—	—	—	6.00	8.00
2011 Proof	—	Value: 10.00				

KM# 1014 2 POUNDS

11.9700 g., Bi-Metallic Copper-Nickel center in Nickel-Brass ring, 28.35 mm. **Ruler:** Elizabeth II **Subject:** First Transatlantic Radio Transmission **Obv:** Head with tiara right within circle **Obv. Designer:** Ian Rank-Broadley **Rev:** Symbolic design **Rev. Designer:** Robert Evans **Edge:** Reeded and inscribed **Edge Lettering:** WIRELESS BRIDGES THE ATLANTIC... MARCONI... 1901

Date	Mintage	F	VF	XF	Unc	BU
2001	4,558,000	—	—	—	6.00	7.00
2001 Proof	—	Value: 10.00				

KM# 1014a 2 POUNDS

12.0000 g., 0.9250 Silver Silver center in Gold plated ring 0.3569 oz. ASW, 28.4 mm. **Ruler:** Elizabeth II **Subject:** First Transatlantic Radio Transmission **Obv:** Head with tiara right within circle **Obv. Designer:** Ian Rank-Broadley **Rev:** Symbolic design **Rev. Designer:** Robert Evans **Edge Lettering:** WIRELESS BRIDGES THE ATLANTIC...MARCONI 1901...

Date	Mintage	F	VF	XF	Unc	BU
2001 Proof	6,759	Value: 45.00				

KM# 1014b 2 POUNDS

15.9700 g., 0.9166 Gold Yellow gold plated Red Gold center in Red Gold ring 0.4706 oz. AGW, 28.4 mm. **Ruler:** Elizabeth II **Subject:** First Transatlantic Radio Transmission **Obv:** Head with tiara right **Obv. Designer:** Ian Rank-Broadley **Rev:** Symbolic design **Rev. Designer:** Robert Evans

Date	Mintage	F	VF	XF	Unc	BU
2001 Proof	1,658	Value: 750				

KM# 994c 2 POUNDS

15.9800 g., 0.9167 Gold 0.4710 oz. AGW, 28.35 mm. **Ruler:** Elizabeth II **Subject:** Technology **Obv:** Head with tiara right **Obv. Designer:** Ian Rank-Broadley **Rev:** Symbolic depiction in concentric circles of technological development from the Iron Age to the Internet **Rev. Designer:** Bruce Rushin

Date	Mintage	F	VF	XF	Unc	BU
2002 Proof	—	Value: 800				

KM# 1031 2 POUNDS

12.0000 g., Bi-Metallic Copper-Nickel center in Nickel-Brass ring, 28.4 mm. **Ruler:** Elizabeth II **Subject:** 17th Commonwealth Games - Manchester, England **Obv:** Head with tiara right **Obv. Designer:** Ian Rank-Broadley **Rev:** Runner breaking ribbon at finish line, national flag of England in circle behind athlete **Rev. Designer:** Matthew Bonaccorsi **Edge:** Reeded and lettered **Edge Lettering:** SPIRIT OF FRIENDSHIP MANCHESTER 2002

Date	Mintage	F	VF	XF	Unc	BU
2002	650,500	—	—	—	6.00	7.00
2002 Proof	—	Value: 8.75				

KM# 1031a 2 POUNDS

12.0000 g., 0.9250 Silver Silver center in Gold plated ring 0.3569 oz. ASW, 28.4 mm. **Ruler:** Elizabeth II **Subject:** Commonwealth Games - England **Obv:** Head with tiara right **Obv. Designer:** Ian Rank-Broadley **Rev:** Runner breaking ribbon at finish line **Rev. Designer:** Matthew Bonaccorsi **Edge:** Reeded and lettered

Date	Mintage	F	VF	XF	Unc	BU
2002 Proof	10,000	Value: 45.00				

KM# 1031b 2 POUNDS

15.9800 g., 0.9160 Gold Yellow gold center in Red Gold ring 0.4706 oz. AGW, 28.4 mm. **Ruler:** Elizabeth II **Subject:** Commonwealth Games - England **Obv:** Head with tiara right **Obv. Designer:** Ian Rank-Broadley **Rev:** Runner breaking ribbon at finish line **Rev. Designer:** Matthew Bonaccorsi **Edge:** Reeded and lettered

Date	Mintage	F	VF	XF	Unc	BU
2002 Proof	500	Value: 750				

KM# 1032 2 POUNDS

12.0000 g., Bi-Metallic Copper-Nickel center in Nickel-Brass ring, 28.4 mm. **Ruler:** Elizabeth II **Subject:** 17th Commonwealth Games - Manchester, England **Obv:** Head with tiara right **Obv. Designer:** Ian Rank-Broadley **Rev:** Runner breaking ribbon at finish line, national flag of Scotland in circle behind athlete **Rev. Designer:** Matthew Bonaccorsi **Edge:** Reeded and lettered

Date	Mintage	F	VF	XF	Unc	BU
2002	771,750	—	—	—	5.00	6.00
2002 Proof	—	Value: 8.75				

KM# 1032a 2 POUNDS

12.0000 g., 0.9250 Silver Silver center with Gold plated ring 0.3569 oz. ASW, 28.4 mm. **Ruler:** Elizabeth II **Subject:** Commonwealth Games - Scotland **Obv:** Head with tiara right **Obv. Designer:** Ian Rank-Broadley **Rev:** Runner breaking ribbon at finish line **Rev. Designer:** Matthew Bonaccorsi **Edge:** Reeded and lettered

Date	Mintage	F	VF	XF	Unc	BU
2002 Proof	10,000	Value: 35.00				

KM# 1032b 2 POUNDS

15.9800 g., 0.9160 Gold Yellow gold center in Red Gold ring 0.4706 oz. AGW, 28.4 mm. **Ruler:** Elizabeth II **Subject:** Commonwealth Games - Scotland **Obv:** Head with tiara right **Obv. Designer:** Ian Rank-Broadley **Rev:** Runner breaking ribbon at finish line **Rev. Designer:** Matthew Bonaccorsi **Edge:** Reeded and lettered

Date	Mintage	F	VF	XF	Unc	BU
2002 Proof	500	Value: 750				

KM# 1033 2 POUNDS

12.0000 g., Bi-Metallic Copper-Nickel center in Nickel-Brass ring, 28.4 mm. **Ruler:** Elizabeth II **Subject:** 17th Commonwealth Games - Manchester, England **Obv:** Head with tiara right **Obv. Designer:** Ian Rank-Broadley **Rev:** Runner breaking ribbon at finish line, national flag of Wales in circle behind athlete **Rev. Designer:** Matthew Bonaccorsi **Edge:** Reeded and lettered **Edge Lettering:** SPIRIT OF FRIENDSHIP MANCHESTER 2002

Date	Mintage	F	VF	XF	Unc	BU
2002	588,500	—	—	—	6.00	7.00
2002 Proof	—	Value: 8.75				

KM# 1033a 2 POUNDS

12.0000 g., 0.9250 Silver Silver center in Gold plated ring 0.3569 oz. ASW, 28.4 mm. **Ruler:** Elizabeth II **Subject:** Commonwealth Games - Wales **Obv:** Head with tiara right **Obv. Designer:** Ian Rank-Broadley **Rev:** Runner breaking ribbon at finish line **Rev. Designer:** Matthew Bonaccorsi **Edge:** Reeded and lettered

Date	Mintage	F	VF	XF	Unc	BU
2002 Proof	10,000	Value: 35.00				

KM# 1033b 2 POUNDS

15.9800 g., 0.9160 Gold Yellow Gold center in Red Gold ring 0.4706 oz. AGW, 28.4 mm. **Ruler:** Elizabeth II **Subject:** Commonwealth Games - Wales **Obv:** Head with tiara right **Obv. Designer:** Ian Rank-Broadley **Rev:** Runner breaking ribbon at finish line **Rev. Designer:** Matthew Bonaccorsi **Edge:** Reeded and lettered

Date	Mintage	F	VF	XF	Unc	BU
2002 Proof	500	Value: 750				

KM# 1034 2 POUNDS

12.0000 g., Bi-Metallic Copper-Nickel center in Nickel-Brass ring, 28.4 mm. **Ruler:** Elizabeth II **Subject:** 17th Commonwealth Games - Manchester, England **Obv:** Head with tiara right **Obv. Designer:** Ian Rank-Broadley **Rev:** Runner breaking ribbon at finish line, national flag of Northern Ireland in circle behind athlete **Rev. Designer:** Matthew Bonaccorsi **Edge:** Reeded and lettered **Edge Lettering:** SPIRIT OF FRIENDSHIP MANCHESTER 2002

Date	Mintage	F	VF	XF	Unc	BU
2002	485,500	—	—	—	6.00	7.00
2002 Proof	—	Value: 8.75				

KM# 1034a 2 POUNDS

12.0000 g., 0.9250 Silver Silver center in Gold plated ring 0.3569 oz. ASW, 28.4 mm. **Ruler:** Elizabeth II **Subject:** Commonwealth Games - Northern Ireland **Obv:** Head with tiara right **Obv. Designer:** Ian Rank-Broadley **Rev:** Runner breaking ribbon at finish line **Rev. Designer:** Matthew Bonaccorsi **Edge:** Reeded and lettered

Date	Mintage	F	VF	XF	Unc	BU
2002 Proof	10,000	Value: 35.00				

KM# 1034b 2 POUNDS

15.9800 g., 0.9160 Gold Yellow Gold center in Red Gold ring 0.4706 oz. AGW, 28.4 mm. **Ruler:** Elizabeth II **Subject:** Commonwealth Games - Northern Ireland **Obv:** Head with tiara right **Obv. Designer:** Ian Rank-Broadley **Rev:** Runner breaking ribbon at finish line **Rev. Designer:** Matthew Bonaccorsi **Edge:** Reeded and lettered

Date	Mintage	F	VF	XF	Unc	BU
2002 Proof	500	Value: 750				

KM# 1037 2 POUNDS

12.0000 g., Bi-Metallic Copper-Nickel center in Nickel-Brass ring, 28.4 mm. **Ruler:** Elizabeth II **Subject:** 50th Anniversary of the Discovery of DNA **Obv:** Head with tiara right **Obv. Designer:** Ian Rank-Broadley **Rev:** DNA Double Helix **Rev. Designer:** John Mills **Edge:** Reeded and inscribed **Edge Lettering:** DEOXYRIBONUCLEIC ACID

Date	Mintage	F	VF	XF	Unc	BU
ND(2003)	4,299,000	—	—	—	7.00	8.00
ND(2003) Proof	43,513	Value: 10.00				

KM# 1037a 2 POUNDS

12.0000 g., 0.9250 Silver Silver center in Gold plated ring 0.3569 oz. ASW, 28.4 mm. **Ruler:** Elizabeth II **Obv:** Head with tiara right **Obv. Designer:** Ian Rank-Broadley **Rev:** DNA Double Helix **Rev. Designer:** John Mills **Edge:** Reeded and lettered

Date	Mintage	F	VF	XF	Unc	BU
ND(2003) Proof	11,204	Value: 35.00				

KM# 1037b 2 POUNDS

15.9800 g., 0.9167 Gold Yellow gold center in Red gold ring 0.4710 oz. AGW, 28.4 mm. **Ruler:** Elizabeth II **Obv:** Head with tiara right **Obv. Designer:** Ian Rank-Broadley **Rev:** DNA Double Helix **Rev. Designer:** John Mills **Edge:** Reeded and lettered

Date	Mintage	F	VF	XF	Unc	BU
ND2003 Proof	1,500	Value: 750				

KM# 1049 2 POUNDS

12.0000 g., Bi-Metallic Nickel-Brass center in Copper-Nickel ring, 28.4 mm. **Ruler:** Elizabeth II **Subject:** Richard Trevithick, Inventor of the First Steam Locomotive **Obv:** Head with tiara right **Obv. Designer:** Ian Rank-Broadley **Rev:** First steam locomotive **Rev. Legend:** 2004 R. TREVITHICK 1804 INVENTION-INDUSTRY-PROGRESS **Edge:** Incuse railway line motif

Date	Mintage	F	VF	XF	Unc	BU
2004	5,004,500	—	—	—	7.50	8.50
2004 Proof	35,020	Value: 10.00				

KM# 1049a 2 POUNDS

12.0000 g., 0.9250 Silver Silver center in Gold plated ring 0.3569 oz. ASW, 28.4 mm. **Ruler:** Elizabeth II **Obv:** Head with tiara right **Obv. Designer:** Ian Rank-Broadley **Rev:** First steam locomotive **Rev. Legend:** 2004 R. TREVITHICK 1804 INVENTION-INDUSTRY-PROGRESS **Edge:** Incuse railway line motif

Date	Mintage	F	VF	XF	Unc	BU
2004	1,923	—	—	—	—	40.00
2004 Proof	19,233	Value: 35.00				

KM# 1049b 2 POUNDS

15.9800 g., 0.9166 Gold Yellow Gold center in Red Gold ring 0.4709 oz. AGW, 28.4 mm. **Ruler:** Elizabeth II **Obv:** Head with tiara right **Obv. Designer:** Ian Rank-Broadley **Rev:** First steam locomotive **Rev. Legend:** 2004 R. TREVITHICK 1804 INVENTION-INDUSTRY-PROGRESS **Edge:** Incuse railway line motif

Date	Mintage	F	VF	XF	Unc	BU
2004 Proof	1,500	Value: 725				

KM# 1052 2 POUNDS

12.0000 g., Bi-Metallic Nickel-Brass center in Copper-Nickel ring, 28.4 mm. **Ruler:** Elizabeth II **Subject:** 400th Anniversary - The Gunpowder Plot **Obv:** Head with tiara right **Obv. Designer:** Ian Rank-Broadley **Rev:** Circular design of Royal scepters, swords and crosiers **Rev. Designer:** Peter Forster **Edge:** Reeded and lettered **Edge Lettering:** REMEMBER REMEMBER THE FIFTH OF NOVEMBER

Date	Mintage	F	VF	XF	Unc	BU
ND(2005)	5,140,500	—	—	—	6.00	7.00
ND(2005) Proof	40,563	Value: 9.00				

KM# 1056 2 POUNDS

Bi-Metallic Nickel-Brass center in Copper-Nickel ring, 28.4 mm. **Ruler:** Elizabeth II **Subject:** 60th Anniversary of the End of WW II **Obv:** Head with tiara right **Obv. Designer:** Ian Rank-Broadley **Rev:** St. Paul's Cathedral amid search light beams **Rev. Designer:** Robert Elderton **Edge:** Reeded and lettered **Edge Lettering:** IN VICTORY MAGNANIMITY IN PEACE GOODWILL

Date	Mintage	F	VF	XF	Unc	BU
ND (2005)	10,191,000	—	—	—	8.00	9.50

KM# 1056a 2 POUNDS

12.0000 g., 0.9250 Silver center in Gold-plated ring 0.3569 oz. ASW, 28.4 mm. **Ruler:** Elizabeth II **Subject:** 60th Anniversary of the End of WWII **Obv:** Crowned head right **Obv. Designer:** Ian Rank-Broadley **Rev:** St. Paul's Cathedral amid search light beams **Rev. Designer:** Robert Elderton **Edge:** Reeded and lettered **Edge Lettering:** IN VICTORY MAGNANIMITY IN PEACE GOODWILL

Date	Mintage	F	VF	XF	Unc	BU
ND(2005) Proof	21,734	Value: 35.00				

KM# 1056b 2 POUNDS

15.9700 g., 0.9167 Gold 0.4707 oz. AGW, 28.4 mm. **Ruler:** Elizabeth II **Subject:** 60th Anniversary of the End of WWII **Obv:** Crowned head right **Obv. Designer:** Ian Rank-Broadley **Rev:** St. Paul's Cathedral amid search light beams **Rev. Designer:** Robert Elderton **Edge:** Reeded and lettered **Edge Lettering:** IN VICTORY MAGNANIMITY IN PEACE GOODWILL

Date	Mintage	F	VF	XF	Unc	BU
ND(2005) Proof	2,924	Value: 725				

KM# 994a 2 POUNDS

12.0000 g., 0.9250 Silver 0.3569 oz. ASW, 28.35 mm. **Ruler:** Elizabeth II **Subject:** Technology **Obv:** Head with tiara right **Obv. Designer:** Ian Rank-Broadley **Rev:** Symbolic depiction in concentric circles of technological development from the Iron Age to the Internet **Rev. Designer:** Bruce Rushin **Note:** Gold plated silver ring, silver center.

Date	Mintage	F	VF	XF	Unc	BU
2006 Proof	—	Value: 45.00				

KM# 1060 2 POUNDS

12.0000 g., Bi-Metallic Copper-Nickel center in Nickel-Brass ring, 28.4 mm. **Ruler:** Elizabeth II **Subject:** 200th Birthday of Engineer Isambard Kingdom Brunel **Obv:** Head with tiara right **Obv. Designer:** Ian Rank-Broadley **Rev:** Isambard Brunel **Edge Lettering:** 1806-1859 ISAMBARD KINGDOM BRUNEL ENGINEER

Date	Mintage	F	VF	XF	Unc	BU
2006	7,925,250	—	—	—	16.00	18.00
2006 Proof	Est. 50,000	Value: 35.00				

KM# 1061 2 POUNDS

12.0000 g., Bi-Metallic Copper-Nickel center in Nickel-Brass ring, 28.4 mm. **Ruler:** Elizabeth II **Subject:** Engineering Achievements of Isambard Kingdom Brunel **Obv:** Head with tiara right **Obv. Designer:** Ian Rank-Broadley **Rev:** Paddington Station structural supports **Edge Lettering:** SO MANY IRONS IN THE FIRE

Date	Mintage	F	VF	XF	Unc	BU
2006	7,452,250	—	—	—	16.00	17.50
2006 Proof	Est. 50,000	Value: 20.00				

KM# 1060a 2 POUNDS

12.0000 g., 0.9250 Silver with gilt ring 0.3569 oz. ASW, 28.4 mm. **Ruler:** Elizabeth II **Subject:** Brunel's 200th Birthday **Obv:** Head with tiara right **Obv. Designer:** Ian Rank-Broadley **Rev:** Brunel and gears

Date	Mintage	F	VF	XF	Unc	BU
2006 Proof	—	Value: 55.00				

KM# 1060b 2 POUNDS

15.9800 g., 0.9160 Gold Yellow Gold center in Red Gold ring 0.4706 oz. AGW, 28.4 mm. **Ruler:** Elizabeth II **Subject:** Brunel's 200th Birthday **Obv:** Head with tiara right **Obv. Designer:** Ian Rank-Broadley **Rev:** Brunel and gears

Date	Mintage	F	VF	XF	Unc	BU
2006 Proof	—	Value: 765				

KM# 1061a 2 POUNDS

12.0000 g., 0.9250 Silver center in gilt ring 0.3569 oz. ASW, 28.4 mm. **Ruler:** Elizabeth II **Subject:** Brunel's engineering achievements **Obv:** Head with tiara right **Rev:** Archways

Date	Mintage	F	VF	XF	Unc	BU
2006 Proof	—	Value: 55.00				

KM# 1061b 2 POUNDS

15.9800 g., 0.9160 Gold Yellow Gold center in Red Gold ring 0.4706 oz. AGW, 28.4 mm. **Ruler:** Elizabeth II **Subject:** Brunel's engineering achievements **Obv:** Head with tiara right **Rev:** Archways

Date	Mintage	F	VF	XF	Unc	BU
2006 Proof	—	Value: 765				

KM# 1075 2 POUNDS

12.0000 g., Bi-Metallic Copper-Nickel center in Brass ring, 28.4 mm. **Ruler:** Elizabeth II **Subject:** 200th Anniversary of the Abolition of the Slave Trade **Obv:** Bust right **Obv. Designer:** Ian Rank-Broadley **Rev:** Chain crossing 1807 date **Edge:** Reeded and lettered **Edge Lettering:** AM I NOT A MAN AND A BROTHER

Date	Mintage	F	VF	XF	Unc	BU
2007	8,445,000	—	—	—	—	6.00
2007 Proof	Est. 50,000	Value: 9.00				

KM# 1075a 2 POUNDS

12.0000 g., 0.9250 Silver center in Gold plated ring 0.3569 oz. ASW, 28.4 mm. **Ruler:** Elizabeth II **Subject:** Abolition of the Slave Trade **Obv:** Elizabeth II right **Obv. Designer:** Ian Rank-Broadley **Rev:** Zero in 1807 date as a broken chain link **Edge:** Reeded and lettered **Edge Lettering:** AM I NOT A MAN AND A BROTHER

Date	Mintage	F	VF	XF	Unc	BU
2007 Proof	7,095	Value: 55.00				

KM# 1075b 2 POUNDS

15.9700 g., 0.9166 Gold Yellow Gold center in Red Gold ring 0.4706 oz. AGW, 28.4 mm. **Ruler:** Elizabeth II **Subject:** Abolition of the Slave Trade **Obv:** Head with tiara right **Obv. Designer:** Ian Rank-Broadley **Rev:** Zero in 1807 date as a broken chain link **Edge:** Reeded and lettered **Edge Lettering:** AM I NOT A MAN AND A BROTHER

Date	Mintage	F	VF	XF	Unc	BU
2007 Proof	1,000	Value: 765				

KM# 1076 2 POUNDS

12.0000 g., Bi-Metallic Copper-Nickel center in Nickel-Brass ring, 28.4 mm. **Ruler:** Elizabeth II **Subject:** 300th Anniversary of the Act of Union of England and Scotland **Obv:** Head with tiara right **Obv. Designer:** Ian Rank-Broadley **Rev:** Combination of British and Scottish arms **Edge:** Reeded and lettered **Edge Lettering:** UNITED INTO ONE KINGDOM

Date	Mintage	F	VF	XF	Unc	BU
2007	7,545,000	—	—	—	—	6.00
2007 Proof	Est. 50,000	Value: 9.00				

KM# 1076a 2 POUNDS

12.0000 g., 0.9250 Silver center in Gold Plated ring 0.3569 oz. ASW, 28.4 mm. **Ruler:** Elizabeth II **Subject:** 300th Anniv. Union of Scotland and England **Obv:** Head with tiara right **Obv. Designer:** Ian Rank-Broadley **Rev:** Combined English and Scottish arms **Edge:** Reeded and lettered

Date	Mintage	F	VF	XF	Unc	BU
2007 Proof	8,310	Value: 55.00				

KM# 1076b 2 POUNDS

15.9800 g., 0.9166 Gold Yellow Gold center in Red Gold ring 0.4709 oz. AGW, 28.4 mm. **Ruler:** Elizabeth II **Subject:** 300th Anniv. Union of Scotland and England **Obv:** Head with tiara right **Obv. Designer:** Ian Rank-Broadley **Rev:** Combined English and Scottish arms **Edge:** Reeded and lettered

Date	Mintage	F	VF	XF	Unc	BU
2007 Proof	750	Value: 765				

KM# 1105 2 POUNDS

12.0000 g., Bi-Metallic Copper-nickel center in brass ring, 28.4 mm. **Ruler:** Elizabeth II **Subject:** London 1908 - Olympics **Obv:** Head with tiara right **Obv. Designer:** Ian Rank-Braodley **Rev:** Sprint track **Rev. Designer:** Thomas T. Docherty **Edge:** Lettered and reeded **Edge Lettering:** THE 4TH OLYMPIAD LONDON

Date	Mintage	F	VF	XF	Unc	BU
2008	910,000	—	—	—	—	6.00
2008 Proof	—	Value: 9.00				

KM# 1106 2 POUNDS

12.0000 g., Bi-Metallic Copper-Nickel center in Brass ring, 28.4 mm. **Ruler:** Elizabeth II **Subject:** Beijing - London Olympic Flag handoff **Obv:** Head with tiara right **Obv. Designer:** Ian Rank-Broadley **Rev:** London 2012 Games Flag hand off **Edge Lettering:** I CALL UPON THE YOUTH OF THE WORLD

Date	Mintage	F	VF	XF	Unc	BU
2008	853,000	—	—	—	18.00	20.00
2008 Proof	Est. 250,000	Value: 45.00				

KM# 1106a 2 POUNDS

12.0000 g., 0.9250 Silver Silver center in Gilt ring 0.3569 oz. ASW, 28.4 mm. **Ruler:** Elizabeth II **Obv:** Head with tiara right **Rev:** Handoff of the Olympic Flag

Date	Mintage	F	VF	XF	Unc	BU
2008 Proof	—	Value: 55.00				

KM# 1115 2 POUNDS

12.0000 g., Bi-Metallic Copper-Nickel center in Nickel-Brass ring., 28.4 mm. **Ruler:** Elizabeth II **Subject:** Charles Darwin, 200th Anniversary of Birth **Obv:** Head with tiara right **Obv. Designer:** Ian Rank-Broadley **Rev:** Darwin and ape heads facing **Rev. Designer:** Suzie Zamit **Edge Lettering:** ON THE ORIGIN OF SPECIES 1859

Date	Mintage	F	VF	XF	Unc	BU
2009	Est. 300,000	—	—	—	16.00	18.00
2009 Proof	—	Value: 25.00				

KM# 1106b 2 POUNDS

15.9800 g., 0.9160 Gold 0.4706 oz. AGW, 28.4 mm. **Ruler:** Elizabeth II **Subject:** Countdown to 2010 London Olympics **Obv:** Head right **Obv. Designer:** Ian Rank-Broadley **Rev:** Handoff of the Olympic flag **Edge Lettering:** I CALL UPON THE YOUTH OF THE WORLD

Date	Mintage	F	VF	XF	Unc	BU
2009 Proof	3,000	Value: 725				

KM# 1115a 2 POUNDS

12.0000 g., 0.9250 Silver Silver center in Gilt ring 0.3569 oz. ASW, 28.4 mm. **Ruler:** Elizabeth II **Subject:** Charles Darwin, 200th Anniversary of Brith **Obv:** Head with tiara right **Obv. Designer:** Ian Rank-Broadley **Rev:** Darwin and ape heads facing **Rev. Designer:** Suzie Zamit

Date	Mintage	F	VF	XF	Unc	BU
2009 Proof	—	Value: 55.00				

KM# 1115b 2 POUNDS

15.9800 g., 0.9160 Gold Yellow Gold center in Red Gold ring 0.4706 oz. AGW, 28.4 mm. **Ruler:** Elizabeth II **Subject:** Charles Darwin, 200th Anniversary of Birth **Obv:** Head with tiara right **Obv. Designer:** Ian Rank-Broadley **Rev:** Darwin and ape heads facing **Rev. Designer:** Suzie Zamit

Date	Mintage	F	VF	XF	Unc	BU
2009 Proof	—	Value: 765				

KM# 1116 2 POUNDS

12.0000 g., Bi-Metallic Copper-Nickel center in Nickel-Brass ring, 28.4 mm. **Ruler:** Elizabeth II **Subject:** Robert Burns, 250th Anniversary of Birth **Obv:** Head with tiara right **Obv. Designer:** Ian Rank-Broadley **Rev:** Text **Edge:** Reeded and lettered **Edge Lettering:** SHOULD AULD ACQUAINTANCE BE FORGOT

Date	Mintage	F	VF	XF	Unc	BU
2009	300,000	—	—	—	16.00	18.00
2009 Proof	—	Value: 25.00				

KM# 1116a 2 POUNDS

12.0000 g., 0.9250 Silver Sivler center in Gilt ring 0.3569 oz. ASW, 28.4 mm. **Ruler:** Elizabeth II **Subject:** Robert Burns, 250th Anniversary of Birth **Obv:** Head with tiara right **Obv. Designer:** Ian Rank-Broadley **Rev:** Text

Date	Mintage	F	VF	XF	Unc	BU
2009 Proof	—	Value: 55.00				

KM# 1116b 2 POUNDS

15.9700 g., 0.9167 Gold Yellow Gold center in Red Gold ring 0.4707 oz. AGW, 28.4 mm. **Ruler:** Elizabeth II **Subject:** Robert Burns, 250th Anniversary of Birth **Obv:** Head with tiara right **Obv. Designer:** Ian Rank-Braodley **Rev:** Text

Date	Mintage	F	VF	XF	Unc	BU
2009 Proof	1,000	Value: 600				

KM# 1160 2 POUNDS

11.9700 g., Bi-Metallic Copper-Nickel center in Nickel-Brass ring, 28.35 mm. **Ruler:** Elizabeth II **Subject:** Florence Nightengale, 100th Anniversary of Death **Obv:** Head with tiara right **Obv. Designer:** Ian Rank-Broadley **Rev:** Hand taking pulse **Rev. Designer:** Gordon Summers **Edge Lettering:** 150 YEARS OF NURSING

Date	Mintage	F	VF	XF	Unc	BU
2010	—	—	—	—	6.00	8.50
2010 Proof	—	Value: 12.50				

KM# 1199 2 POUNDS

11.9700 g., Bi-Metallic Copper-Nickel center in Nickel-Brass ring, 28.4 mm. **Ruler:** Elizabeth II **Subject:** Mary Rose, 500th Anniversary **Obv:** Head with tiara right **Obv. Designer:** Ian Rank-Broadley **Rev:** H.M.S. Mary Rose under sail **Rev. Designer:** John Bergdahl **Edge:** Reeded and lettered **Edge Lettering:** YOUR NOBLEST SHIPPE 1511

Date	Mintage	F	VF	XF	Unc	BU
2011	—	—	—	—	7.00	8.50

KM# 1199a 2 POUNDS

12.0000 g., 0.9250 Silver center in Gilt ring 0.3569 oz. ASW, 28.4 mm. **Ruler:** Elizabeth II **Subject:** Mary Rose, 500th Anniversary **Obv:** Head with tiara right **Obv. Designer:** Ian Rank-Broadley **Rev:** H.M.S. Mary Rose under sail

Date	Mintage	F	VF	XF	Unc	BU
2011 Proof	—	Value: 55.00				

KM# 1199b 2 POUNDS

15.9800 g., 0.9166 Gold Yellow Gold center in Red Gold ring 0.4709 oz. AGW, 28.4 mm. **Ruler:** Elizabeth II **Subject:** Mary Rose, 500th Anniversary **Obv:** Head with tiara right **Obv. Designer:** Ian Rank-Broadley **Rev:** H.M.S. Mary Rose under sail **Rev. Designer:** John Bergdahl

Date	Mintage	F	VF	XF	Unc	BU
2011 Proof	—	Value: 725				

KM# 1200 2 POUNDS

11.9700 g., Bi-Metallic Copper-Nickel center in Nickel-Brass ring, 28.4 mm. **Ruler:** Elizabeth II **Subject:** King James Bible, 500th Anniversary **Obv:** Head in tiara right **Obv. Designer:** Ian Rank-Broadley **Rev:** Lead type and printed page of bible text **Rev. Designer:** Paul Stafford Benjamin Wright **Edge:** Reeded and lettered **Edge Lettering:** THE AUTHORIZED VERSION

Date	Mintage	F	VF	XF	Unc	BU
2011	—	—	—	—	7.00	8.50
2011 Proof	—	Value: 10.00				

KM# 1200a 2 POUNDS

12.0000 g., 0.9250 Silver center in Gilt ring 0.3569 oz. ASW, 28.4 mm. **Ruler:** Elizabeth II **Subject:** King James Bible, 500th Anniversary **Obv:** Head with tiara right **Obv. Designer:** Ian Rank-Braodley **Rev:** Lead type and printed page **Rev. Designer:** Paul Stafford Benjamin Wright

Date	Mintage	F	VF	XF	Unc	BU
2011 Proof	—	Value: 45.00				

KM# 1015 5 POUNDS

28.2800 g., Copper-Nickel, 38.6 mm. **Ruler:** Elizabeth II **Subject:** Centennial of Queen Victoria's death **Obv:** Head with tiara right **Obv. Designer:** Ian Rank-Broadley **Rev:** Young portrait from stamp, within industrial "V" **Rev. Designer:** Mary Milner Dickens, William Wyon **Edge:** Reeded

Date	Mintage	F	VF	XF	Unc	BU
2001	851,491	—	—	—	14.00	16.00
2001 Proof	—	Value: 20.00				

KM# 1015a 5 POUNDS

28.2800 g., 0.9250 Silver 0.8410 oz. ASW, 38.6 mm. **Ruler:** Elizabeth II **Subject:** Centennial of Queen Victoria **Obv:** Head with tiara right **Obv. Designer:** Ian Rank-Broadley **Rev:** Queen Victoria's portrait within "V" **Rev. Designer:** Mary Milner Dickens

Date	Mintage	F	VF	XF	Unc	BU
2001 Proof	—	Value: 65.00				

KM# 1015b 5 POUNDS

39.9400 g., 0.9167 Gold 1.1771 oz. AGW **Ruler:** Elizabeth II **Subject:** Centennial of Queen Victoria **Obv:** Head with tiara right **Obv. Designer:** Ian Rank-Broadley **Rev:** Queen Victoria's portrait within "V" **Rev. Designer:** Mary Milner Dickens

Date	Mintage	F	VF	XF	Unc	BU
2001 Proof	1,000	Value: 1,800				

KM# 1024 5 POUNDS

28.2800 g., Copper-Nickel, 38.6 mm. **Ruler:** Elizabeth II **Subject:** Queen's Golden Jubilee of Reign **Obv:** Crowned bust in royal garb right **Rev:** Queen on horse **Edge:** Reeded

Date	Mintage	F	VF	XF	Unc	BU
2002	3,469,243	—	—	—	12.50	14.50

Note: Mintage figure includes KM#1035

Date	Mintage	F	VF	XF	Unc	BU
2002 Proof	—	Value: 20.00				

KM# 1024a 5 POUNDS

28.2800 g., 0.9250 Silver 0.8410 oz. ASW, 38.6 mm. **Ruler:** Elizabeth II **Subject:** Queen's Golden Jubilee of Reign **Obv:** Crowned bust in royal garb right **Rev:** Queen on horse **Edge:** Reeded

Date	Mintage	F	VF	XF	Unc	BU
2002 Proof	—	Value: 60.00				

KM# 1024b 5 POUNDS

39.9400 g., 0.9167 Gold 1.1771 oz. AGW, 38.6 mm. **Ruler:** Elizabeth II **Subject:** Queen's Golden Jubilee of Reign **Obv:** Crowned bust in royal garb right **Rev:** Queen on horse left **Edge:** Reeded

Date	Mintage	F	VF	XF	Unc	BU
2002 Proof	—	Value: 1,750				

KM# 1035 5 POUNDS

28.2800 g., Copper-Nickel, 38.6 mm. **Ruler:** Elizabeth II **Subject:** Queen Mother **Obv:** Head with tiara right **Obv. Designer:** Ian Rank-Broadley **Rev:** Queen Mother's portrait in wreath **Rev. Designer:** Avril Vaughan **Edge:** Reeded

Date	Mintage	F	VF	XF	Unc	BU
ND(2002)	—	—	—	—	15.00	—

Note: Mintage included with KM#1024.

Date	Mintage	F	VF	XF	Unc	BU
ND(2002) Proof	—	Value: 20.00				

KM# 1035a 5 POUNDS

28.2800 g., Silver, 38.6 mm. **Ruler:** Elizabeth II **Subject:** Queen Mother **Obv:** Head with tiara right **Obv. Designer:** Ian Rank-Broadley **Rev:** Queen Mother's portrait in wreath **Rev. Designer:** Avril Vaughan **Edge:** Reeded

Date	Mintage	F	VF	XF	Unc	BU
ND(2002) Proof	25,000	Value: 60.00				

KM# 1035b 5 POUNDS

39.9400 g., 0.9167 Gold 1.1771 oz. AGW, 38.6 mm. **Ruler:** Elizabeth II **Subject:** Queen Mother **Obv:** Head with tiara right **Obv. Designer:** Ian Rank-Broadley **Rev:** Queen Mother's portrait in wreath **Rev. Designer:** Avril Vaughan **Edge:** Reeded

Date	Mintage	F	VF	XF	Unc	BU
ND(2002) Proof	3,000	Value: 1,750				

KM# 1038 5 POUNDS

28.2800 g., Copper-Nickel, 38.6 mm. **Ruler:** Elizabeth II **Subject:** Queen's Golden Jubilee **Obv:** Queen's stylized portrait **Rev:** Childlike lettering **Edge:** Reeded **Designer:** Tom Phillips

Date	Mintage	F	VF	XF	Unc	BU
2003	1,307,147	—	—	—	12.50	14.50
2003 Proof	43,513	Value: 20.00				

KM# 1038a 5 POUNDS

28.2800 g., 0.9250 Silver 0.8410 oz. ASW, 38.6 mm. **Ruler:** Elizabeth II **Subject:** Queen's Golden Jubilee **Obv:** Stylized Queens portrait **Rev:** Childlike lettering **Edge:** Reeded **Designer:** Tom Phillips

Date	Mintage	F	VF	XF	Unc	BU
2003 Proof	28,758	Value: 60.00				

KM# 1038b 5 POUNDS

39.9400 g., 0.9166 Gold 1.1770 oz. AGW, 38.6 mm. **Ruler:** Elizabeth II **Subject:** Queen's Golden Jubilee **Obv:** Stylized Queens portrait **Rev:** Childlike lettering **Edge:** Reeded **Designer:** Tom Phillips

Date	Mintage	F	VF	XF	Unc	BU
2003 Proof	1,896	Value: 1,750				

KM# 1055 5 POUNDS

28.2800 g., Copper-Nickel, 38.6 mm. **Ruler:** Elizabeth II **Subject:** Entente Cordiale **Obv:** Head with tiara right **Obv. Designer:** Ian Rank-Broadley **Rev:** Britannia and Marianne **Edge:** Reeded

Date	Mintage	F	VF	XF	Unc	BU
2004	1,205,594	—	—	—	15.00	17.50
2004 Proof	51,527	Value: 20.00				

KM# 1055a 5 POUNDS

28.2800 g., 0.9250 Silver 0.8410 oz. ASW, 38.6 mm. **Ruler:** Elizabeth II **Subject:** Entente Cordiale **Obv:** Head with tiara right **Obv. Designer:** Ian Rank-Broadley **Rev:** Britannia and Marianne **Edge:** Reeded

Date	Mintage	F	VF	XF	Unc	BU
2004 Proof	11,295	Value: 60.00				

KM# 1055b 5 POUNDS

39.9400 g., 0.9167 Gold 1.1771 oz. AGW, 38.6 mm. **Ruler:** Elizabeth II **Subject:** Entente Cordiale **Obv:** Head with tiara right **Obv. Designer:** Ian Rank-Broadley **Rev:** Britannia and Marianne **Edge:** Reeded

Date	Mintage	F	VF	XF	Unc	BU
2004 Proof	926	Value: 1,800				

KM# 1055c 5 POUNDS

94.2000 g., 0.9995 Platinum 3.0270 oz. APW, 38.6 mm. **Ruler:** Elizabeth II **Subject:** Entente Cordiale **Obv:** Head with tiara right **Obv. Designer:** Ian Rank-Broadley **Rev:** Britannia and Marianne **Edge:** Reeded

Date	Mintage	F	VF	XF	Unc	BU
2004 Proof	501	Value: 7,500				

KM# 1053 5 POUNDS

28.2800 g., Copper-Nickel, 38.6 mm. **Ruler:** Elizabeth II **Subject:** Battle of Trafalgar **Obv:** Head with tiara right **Obv. Legend:** ELIZABETH • II D • G • REG • F • D **Obv. Designer:** Ian Rank-Broadley **Rev:** HMS Victory and HMS Temeraire at Trafalgar **Rev. Legend:** TRAFALGAR **Rev. Designer:** Clive Duncan **Edge:** Reeded

Date	Mintage	F	VF	XF	Unc	BU
2005	1,075,516	—	—	—	12.50	16.50
2005 Proof	40,563	Value: 18.50				

KM# 1053a 5 POUNDS

28.2800 g., 0.9250 Silver 0.8410 oz. ASW, 38.6 mm. **Ruler:** Elizabeth II **Subject:** Battle of Trafalgar **Obv:** Head with tiara right **Obv. Legend:** ELIZABETH • II D • G • REG • F • D **Obv. Designer:** Ian Rank-Broadley **Rev:** Ships HMS Victory and Temeraire at Trafalgar **Rev. Legend:** TRAFALGAR **Rev. Designer:** Clive Duncan **Edge:** Reeded

Date	Mintage	F	VF	XF	Unc	BU
2005 Proof	21,448	Value: 65.00				

KM# 1053b 5 POUNDS

39.9400 g., 0.9167 Gold 1.1771 oz. AGW, 38.6 mm. **Ruler:** Elizabeth II **Subject:** Battle of Trafalgar **Obv:** Head with tiara right **Obv. Legend:** ELIZABETH • II D • G • REG • F • D **Obv. Designer:** Ian Rank-Broadley **Rev:** Ships HMS Victory and Temeraire at Trafalgar **Rev. Legend:** TRAFALGAR **Rev. Designer:** Clive Duncan **Edge:** Reeded

Date	Mintage	F	VF	XF	Unc	BU
2005 Proof	1,805	Value: 1,750				

KM# 1054 5 POUNDS

28.2800 g., Copper-Nickel, 38.6 mm. **Ruler:** Elizabeth II **Obv:** Head with tiara right **Obv. Legend:** ELIZABETH • II D • G • REG • F • D **Obv. Designer:** Ian Rank-Broadley **Rev:** Uniformed facing 1/2 bust of Admiral Horatio Nelson **Rev. Legend:** HORATIO NELSON **Edge:** Reeded

Date	Mintage	F	VF	XF	Unc	BU
2005	—	—	—	—	15.00	16.50

Date	Mintage	F	VF	XF	Unc	BU

Note: Mintage included with KM#1053b, 2005.

Date	Mintage	F	VF	XF	Unc	BU
2005 Proof	40,563	Value: 18.50				

KM# 1054a 5 POUNDS

28.2800 g., 0.9250 Silver 0.8410 oz. ASW, 38.6 mm. **Ruler:** Elizabeth II **Obv:** Queen's head with tiara right **Obv. Legend:** ELIZABETH • II D • G • REG • F • D **Obv. Designer:** Ian Rank-Broadley **Rev:** Uniformed facing 1/2 bust of Admiral Horatio Nelson **Rev. Legend:** HORATIO NELSON

Date	Mintage	F	VF	XF	Unc	BU
2005 Proof	12,852	Value: 65.00				

KM# 1054b 5 POUNDS

39.9400 g., 0.9167 Gold 1.1771 oz. AGW, 38.6 mm. **Ruler:** Elizabeth II **Subject:** Battle of Trafalgar **Obv:** Queen's head with tiara right **Obv. Legend:** ELIZABETH • II D • G • REG • F • D **Rev:** Uniformed facing 1/2 bust of Admiral Horatio Nelson **Rev. Legend:** HORATIO NELSON

Date	Mintage	F	VF	XF	Unc	BU
2005 Proof	1,700	Value: 1,750				

KM# 1062 5 POUNDS

28.2800 g., Copper-Nickel, 38.6 mm. **Ruler:** Elizabeth II **Obv:** Head with tiara right **Obv. Designer:** Ian Rank-Broadley **Rev:** Three bannered trumpets **Edge:** Reeded

Date	Mintage	F	VF	XF	Unc	BU
2006	—	—	—	—	20.00	22.00
2006 Proof	Est. 50,000	Value: 27.00				

KM# 1062a 5 POUNDS

28.2800 g., 0.9250 Silver 0.8410 oz. ASW **Ruler:** Elizabeth II **Subject:** Queen's 80th Birthday Celebration **Obv:** Queens head right **Obv. Legend:** ELIZABETH • II D • G • REG • F • D **Obv. Designer:** Ian Rank-Broadley **Rev:** Three bannered trumpets **Rev. Legend:** VIVAT REGINA **Edge:** Reeded

Date	Mintage	F	VF	XF	Unc	BU
2006 Proof	—	Value: 65.00				

KM# 1062b 5 POUNDS

39.9400 g., 0.9167 Gold 1.1771 oz. AGW, 38.6 mm. **Ruler:** Elizabeth II **Subject:** Queen's 80th Birthday Celebration **Obv:** Queen's head with tiara right **Obv. Legend:** ELIZABETH • II D • G • REG • F • D **Obv. Designer:** Ian Rank-Broadley **Rev:** Three bannered trumpets **Rev. Legend:** VIVAT REGINA **Edge:** Reeded

Date	Mintage	F	VF	XF	Unc	BU
2006 Proof	—	Value: 1,750				

KM# 1077 5 POUNDS

28.2800 g., Copper-Nickel, 38.6 mm. **Ruler:** Elizabeth II **Subject:** Queen's 60th Wedding Anniversary **Obv:** Conjoined busts of Queen Elizabeth II and Prince Philip **Rev:** Westminster Abbey's North Rose Window **Edge:** Reeded

Date	Mintage	F	VF	XF	Unc	BU
2007	—	—	—	—	—	20.00
2007 Proof	Est. 50,000	Value: 30.00				

KM# 1077a 5 POUNDS

28.2800 g., 0.9250 Silver 0.8410 oz. ASW, 38.6 mm. **Ruler:** Elizabeth II **Subject:** 60th Wedding Anniversary **Obv:** Conjoined busts of Queen Elizabeth II and Prince Philip **Rev:** Westminster Abbey's North Rose Window **Edge Lettering:** MY STRENGTH AND STAY

Date	Mintage	F	VF	XF	Unc	BU
ND (2007) Proof	Est. 35,000	Value: 70.00				

KM# 1077b 5 POUNDS

39.9400 g., 0.9166 Gold 1.1770 oz. AGW, 28.4 mm. **Ruler:** Elizabeth II **Subject:** 60th Wedding Anniversary **Obv:** Conjoined busts of Queen Elizabeth II and Prince Philip **Rev:** Westminster Abbey's North Rose Window **Edge Lettering:** MY STRENGTH AND STAY

Date	Mintage	F	VF	XF	Unc	BU
ND (2007) Proof	Est. 2,500	Value: 1,800				

KM# 1103 5 POUNDS

28.2800 g., Copper-Nickel, 38.6 mm. **Ruler:** Elizabeth II **Subject:** Charles, Prince of Wales 60th Birthday **Obv:** Head with tiara right **Rev:** Head right of Prince Charles

Date	Mintage	F	VF	XF	Unc	BU
2008	500,000	—	—	—	12.50	16.50
2008 Proof	—	Value: 18.50				

KM# 1104 5 POUNDS

28.2800 g., Copper-Nickel, 38.6 mm. **Ruler:** Elizabeth II **Subject:** Elizabeth I Accession 1558-2008 **Obv:** Head with tiara right **Rev:** Bust of Elizabeth I

Date	Mintage	F	VF	XF	Unc	BU
2008	500,000	—	—	—	12.50	16.50
2008 Proof	—	Value: 18.50				

KM# 1118 5 POUNDS

28.2800 g., Copper-Nickel, 38.6 mm. **Ruler:** Elizabeth II **Obv:** Head with tiara right **Rev:** Henry VIII standing, HR flanking

Date	Mintage	F	VF	XF	Unc	BU
2009 Proof	—	Value: 40.00				

KM# 1118a 5 POUNDS

28.2800 g., 0.9250 Silver 0.8410 oz. ASW, 38.6 mm. **Ruler:** Elizabeth II **Obv:** Head with tiara right **Rev:** Henry VIII standing, HR flanking

Date	Mintage	F	VF	XF	Unc	BU
2009 Proof	—	Value: 85.00				

KM# 1121 5 POUNDS

28.2800 g., Copper-Nickel, 38.61 mm. **Ruler:** Elizabeth II **Subject:** Countdown to 2012 London Olympics **Obv:** Bust right **Obv. Designer:** Ian Rank-Broadley **Rev:** Swimmer, stopwatch, 3 in center **Rev. Designer:** Claire Aldridge

Date	Mintage	F	VF	XF	Unc	BU
2009	500,000	—	—	—	—	20.00
2009 Proof	—	Value: 30.00				

KM# 1121a 5 POUNDS

28.2800 g., 0.9250 Silver 0.8410 oz. ASW, 38.61 mm. **Ruler:** Elizabeth II **Subject:** Countdown to the 2010 London Olympics **Obv:** Bust right **Obv. Designer:** Ian Rank-Broadley **Rev:** Swimmer, stopwatch, 3 in center **Rev. Designer:** Claire Aldridge

Date	Mintage	F	VF	XF	Unc	BU
2009 Proof	30,000	Value: 70.00				

KM# 1121b 5 POUNDS

Gold, 38.61 mm. **Ruler:** Elizabeth II **Subject:** Countdown to 2012 London Olympics **Rev:** 3 in large stopwatch, swimmer

Date	Mintage	F	VF	XF	Unc	BU
2009 Proof	—	Value: 1,750				

KM# 1140 5 POUNDS

28.2800 g., 0.9250 Silver 0.8410 oz. ASW, 38.6 mm. **Ruler:** Elizabeth II **Subject:** London Olympics, 2012 **Obv:** Head with tiara right **Rev:** Angel of the North, blue logo

Date	Mintage	F	VF	XF	Unc	BU
2009 Proof	95,000	Value: 85.00				

KM# 1141 5 POUNDS

28.2800 g., 0.9250 Silver 0.8410 oz. ASW, 38.6 mm. **Ruler:** Elizabeth II **Subject:** London Olympics, 2012 **Obv:** Head with tiara right **Rev:** Big Ben, blue logo

Date	Mintage	F	VF	XF	Unc	BU
2009 Proof	95,000	Value: 85.00				

KM# 1141a 5 POUNDS

28.2800 g., Copper-Nickel, 38.6 mm. **Ruler:** Elizabeth II **Subject:** London Olympics, 2012 **Obv:** Head in tiara right **Rev:** Big Ben, blue logo

Date	Mintage	F	VF	XF	Unc	BU
2009 Proof	—	Value: 40.00				

KM# 1142 5 POUNDS

28.2800 g., 0.9250 Silver 0.8410 oz. ASW, 38.6 mm. **Ruler:** Elizabeth II **Subject:** London Olympics, 2012 **Obv:** Head with tiara right **Rev:** Flying Scotsman, blue logo

Date	Mintage	F	VF	XF	Unc	BU
2009 Proof	95,000	Value: 85.00				

KM# 1143 5 POUNDS

28.2800 g., 0.9250 Silver 0.8410 oz. ASW, 38.6 mm. **Ruler:** Elizabeth II **Subject:** London Olympics, 2012 **Obv:** Head with tiara right **Rev:** Globe Theatre, blue logo

Date	Mintage	F	VF	XF	Unc	BU
2009 Proof	95,000	Value: 85.00				

KM# 1144 5 POUNDS

28.2800 g., 0.9250 Silver 0.8410 oz. ASW, 38.6 mm. **Ruler:** Elizabeth II **Subject:** London Olympics, 2012 **Obv:** Head with tiara right **Rev:** Man in leg braces, Issac Newton quote, blue logo

Date	Mintage	F	VF	XF	Unc	BU
2009 Proof	95,000	Value: 85.00				

KM# 1145 5 POUNDS

28.2800 g., 0.9250 Silver 0.8410 oz. ASW, 38.6 mm. **Ruler:** Elizabeth II **Series:** London Olympics, 2012 **Obv:** Head with tiara right **Rev:** Stonehenge, blue logo

Date	Mintage	F	VF	XF	Unc	BU
2009 Proof	95,000	Value: 85.00				

KM# 1139 5 POUNDS

28.2800 g., Copper-Nickel, 38.6 mm. **Ruler:** Elizabeth II **Obv:** Head with tiara right **Rev:** Runners and stopwatch, 2 in center

Date	Mintage	F	VF	XF	Unc	BU
2010	500,000	—	—	—	—	20.00
2010 Proof	—	Value: 30.00				

KM# 1139a 5 POUNDS

28.2800 g., 0.9250 Silver 0.8410 oz. ASW, 38.6 mm. **Ruler:** Elizabeth II **Obv:** Head with tiara right **Rev:** Runners and stopwatch, 2 in center

Date	Mintage	F	VF	XF	Unc	BU
2010 Proof	—	Value: 70.00				

KM# 1139b 5 POUNDS

39.9400 g., 0.9167 Gold 1.1771 oz. AGW, 38.61 mm. **Ruler:** Elizabeth II **Subject:** Countdown to the 2010 London Olympics **Obv:** Head with tiara right **Rev:** Runners and stopwatch, 2 in center

Date	Mintage	F	VF	XF	Unc	BU
2010 Proof	—	Value: 1,750				

KM# 1146 5 POUNDS

28.2800 g., 0.9250 Silver 0.8410 oz. ASW, 38.6 mm. **Ruler:** Elizabeth II **Subject:** London Olympics, 2012 **Obv:** Head with tiara right **Rev:** Churchill figure and quote, blue logo

Date	Mintage	F	VF	XF	Unc	BU
2010 Proof	95,000	Value: 85.00				

KM# 1146a 5 POUNDS

28.2800 g., Copper-Nickel, 38.6 mm. **Ruler:** Elizabeth II **Subject:** London Olympics, 2012 **Obv:** Head with tiara right **Rev:** Churchill figure and quote, blue logo

Date	Mintage	F	VF	XF	Unc	BU
2010 Proof	—	Value: 40.00				

KM# 1147 5 POUNDS

28.2800 g., 0.9250 Silver 0.8410 oz. ASW, 38.6 mm. **Ruler:** Elizabeth II **Subject:** London Olympics, 2012 **Obv:** Head with tiara right **Rev:** Unity, flora, blue logo

Date	Mintage	F	VF	XF	Unc	BU
2010 Proof	95,000	Value: 85.00				

KM# 1148 5 POUNDS

28.2800 g., 0.9990 Silver 0.9083 oz. ASW, 38.6 mm. **Ruler:** Elizabeth II **Subject:** London Olympics, 2012 **Obv:** Head with tiara right **Rev:** Buckingham Palace and the Mall, blue logo

Date	Mintage	F	VF	XF	Unc	BU
2010 Proof	95,000	Value: 85.00				

KM# 1148a 5 POUNDS

28.2800 g., Copper-Nickel, 38.6 mm. **Ruler:** Elizabeth II **Subject:** London Olympics, 2012 **Obv:** Head with tiara right **Rev:** Buckingham Palace and the Mall, blue logo

Date	Mintage	F	VF	XF	Unc	BU
2010 Proof	—	Value: 40.00				

KM# 1149 5 POUNDS

28.2800 g., 0.9250 Silver 0.8410 oz. ASW, 38.6 mm. **Ruler:** Elizabeth II **Subject:** London Olympics, 2010 **Obv:** Head with tiara right **Rev:** Music, blue logo

Date	Mintage	F	VF	XF	Unc	BU
2010 Proof	95,000	Value: 85.00				

KM# 1151 5 POUNDS

28.2800 g., Copper-Nickel, 38.6 mm. **Ruler:** Elizabeth II **Subject:** Restoration of the Monarchy, 1660 **Obv:** Head with tiara right

Date	Mintage	F	VF	XF	Unc	BU
2010	—	—	—	—	—	20.00

KM# 1151a 5 POUNDS

28.2800 g., 0.9250 Silver 0.8410 oz. ASW, 38.6 mm. **Ruler:** Elizabeth II **Subject:** Restoration of the Monarchy, 1660 **Obv:** Head with tiara right

Date	Mintage	F	VF	XF	Unc	BU
2010 Proof	—	Value: 85.00				

KM# 1152 5 POUNDS

28.2800 g., 0.9250 Silver 0.8410 oz. ASW, 38.6 mm. **Ruler:** Elizabeth II **Subject:** London Olympics, 2012 **Obv:** Head with tiara right **Rev:** Giants Causeway, orange logo

Date	Mintage	F	VF	XF	Unc	BU
2010 Proof	95,000	Value: 85.00				

KM# 1153 5 POUNDS

28.2800 g., 0.9250 Silver 0.8410 oz. ASW, 38.6 mm. **Ruler:** Elizabeth II **Subject:** London Olympics, 2012 **Obv:** Head with tiara right **Rev:** Coastline, orange logo

Date	Mintage	F	VF	XF	Unc	BU
2010 Proof	95,000	Value: 85.00				

KM# 1154 5 POUNDS

28.2800 g., 0.9250 Silver 0.8410 oz. ASW, 38.6 mm. **Ruler:** Elizabeth II **Subject:** London Olympics, 2012 **Obv:** Head with tiara right **Rev:** River Thames, orange logo

Date	Mintage	F	VF	XF	Unc	BU
2010 Proof	95,000	Value: 85.00				

KM# 1155 5 POUNDS

28.2800 g., 0.9250 Silver 0.8410 oz. ASW, 38.6 mm. **Ruler:** Elizabeth II **Subject:** London Olympics, 2012 **Obv:** Head with tiara right **Rev:** British flora, orange logo

Date	Mintage	F	VF	XF	Unc	BU
2010 Proof	95,000	Value: 85.00				

KM# 1156 5 POUNDS

28.2800 g., 0.9250 Silver 0.8410 oz. ASW, 38.6 mm. **Ruler:** Elizabeth II **Subject:** London Olympics, 2012 **Obv:** Head with tiara right **Rev:** Owl, orange logo

Date	Mintage	F	VF	XF	Unc	BU
2010 Proof	95,000	Value: 85.00				

KM# 1157 5 POUNDS

28.2800 g., 0.9250 Silver 0.8410 oz. ASW, 38.6 mm. **Ruler:** Elizabeth II **Subject:** London Olympics, 2012 **Obv:** Head with tiara right **Rev:** Weather vane, orange logo

Date	Mintage	F	VF	XF	Unc	BU
2010 Proof	95,000	Value: 85.00				

KM# 1201 5 POUNDS

28.2800 g., Copper-Nickel, 38.6 mm. **Ruler:** Elizabeth II **Subject:** Prince Philip's 90th Birthday **Obv:** Head with tiara right **Rev:** Large head of Prince Philip in profile right

Date	Mintage	F	VF	XF	Unc	BU
2011	—	—	—	—	—	20.00
2011 Proof	—	Value: 30.00				

KM# 1201a 5 POUNDS

28.2800 g., 0.9250 Silver 0.8410 oz. ASW, 38.6 mm. **Ruler:** Elizabeth II **Subject:** Prince Philip, 90th Birthday

Date	Mintage	F	VF	XF	Unc	BU
2011 Proof	—	Value: 60.00				

KM# 1202 5 POUNDS

28.2800 g., Copper-Nickel, 38.6 mm. **Ruler:** Elizabeth II **Subject:** Countdown to London Olympics, 2012 **Obv:** Head with tiara right **Rev:** 1 between wheels of cyclist traveling left

Date	Mintage	F	VF	XF	Unc	BU
2011	—	—	—	—	—	20.00
2011 Proof	—	Value: 30.00				

KM# 1202a 5 POUNDS

28.2800 g., 0.9250 Silver 0.8410 oz. ASW, 38.6 mm. **Ruler:** Elizabeth II **Subject:** Countdown to London Olympics, 2012 **Obv:** Head with tiara right **Rev:** 1 between wheels of cyclist traveling left

Date	Mintage	F	VF	XF	Unc	BU
2011 Proof	—	Value: 70.00				

KM# 1163 25 POUNDS

Gold **Ruler:** Elizabeth II **Subject:** London Olympics, 2012 **Obv:** Head with tiara right **Rev:** Mercury and cyclists

Date	Mintage	F	VF	XF	Unc	BU
2010 Proof	20,000	Value: 1,650				

KM# 1164 25 POUNDS

Gold **Ruler:** Elizabeth II **Subject:** London Olympics, 2012 **Obv:** Head with tiara right **Rev:** Diana and runners

Date	Mintage	F	VF	XF	Unc	BU
2010 Proof	20,000	Value: 1,650				

KM# 1162 100 POUNDS

31.1050 g., 0.9990 Gold 0.9990 oz. AGW **Ruler:** Elizabeth II **Subject:** London Olympics, 2012 **Obv:** Head with tiara right **Rev:** Neptune and sailing

Date	Mintage	F	VF	XF	Unc	BU
2010 Proof	7,500	Value: 1,650				

SOVEREIGN COINAGE

KM# 1117 1/4 SOVEREIGN

2.0000 g., 0.9170 Gold 0.0590 oz. AGW **Ruler:** Elizabeth II **Obv:** Head with tiara right **Rev:** St. George slaying dragon

Date	Mintage	F	VF	XF	Unc	BU
2009	—	—	—	—	—	90.00
2009 Proof	15,000	Value: 125				
2010	—	—	—	—	—	90.00
2010 Proof	15,000	Value: 125				
2011	—	—	—	—	—	90.00
2011 Proof	15,000	Value: 125				

KM# 1001 1/2 SOVEREIGN

3.9900 g., 0.9170 Gold 0.1176 oz. AGW **Ruler:** Elizabeth II **Obv:** Head with tiara right **Obv. Designer:** Ian Rank-Broadley **Rev:** St. George slaying the dragon

Date	Mintage	F	VF	XF	Unc	BU
2001	94,763	—	—	—	—	175
2001 Proof	10,000	Value: 205				
2002	61,347	—	—	—	—	175
2003	47,818	—	—	—	—	175
2003 Proof	14,750	Value: 205				
2004	34,924	—	—	—	—	175
2006	30,299	—	—	—	—	175
2006 Proof	8,500	Value: 205				
2007	75,000	—	—	—	—	175
2007 Proof	7,500	Value: 230				
2008	75,000	—	—	—	—	175
2008 Proof	7,500	Value: 230				
2009	75,000	—	—	—	—	175
2009 Proof	7,500	Value: 230				
2010	—	—	—	—	—	175
2010 Proof	7,500	Value: 230				

Date	Mintage	F	VF	XF	Unc	BU
2011	—	—	—	—	—	175
2011 Proof	7,500	Value: 230				

KM# 1025 1/2 SOVEREIGN
3.9900 g., 0.9167 Gold 0.1176 oz. AGW, 19.3 mm. **Ruler:** Elizabeth II **Subject:** Queen Elizabeth II's Golden Jubilee **Obv:** Head with tiara right **Obv. Designer:** Ian Rank-Broadley **Rev:** Crowned arms within wreath, date below **Edge:** Reeded

Date	Mintage	F	VF	XF	Unc	BU
2002 Proof	18,000	Value: 250				

KM# 1064 1/2 SOVEREIGN
3.9940 g., 0.9167 Gold 0.1177 oz. AGW, 19.3 mm. **Ruler:** Elizabeth II **Obv:** Head with tiara right **Obv. Designer:** Ian Rank-Broadley **Rev:** Knight fighting dragon with sword **Edge:** Reeded

Date	Mintage	F	VF	XF	Unc	BU
2005	30,299	—	—	—	—	180
2005 Proof	12,500	Value: 225				

KM# 1002 SOVEREIGN
7.9881 g., 0.9170 Gold 0.2355 oz. AGW **Ruler:** Elizabeth II **Obv:** Head with tiara right **Obv. Designer:** Ian Rank-Broadley **Rev:** St. George slaying the dragon

Date	Mintage	F	VF	XF	Unc	BU
2001	49,462	—	—	—	—	BV
2001 Proof	15,000	BV				
2002	75,264	—	—	—	—	BV
2003	43,230	—	—	—	—	BV
2003 Proof	19,750	BV				
2004	30,688	—	—	—	—	BV
2006	45,542	—	—	—	—	BV
2006 Proof	16,000	Value: 325				
2007	75,000	—	—	—	—	BV
2007 Proof	12,500	Value: 345				
2008	75,000	—	—	—	—	BV
2008 Proof	12,500	Value: 345				
2009	75,000	—	—	—	—	BV
2009 Proof	12,500	Value: 345				
2010	—	—	—	—	—	BV
2010 Proof	12,500	Value: 345				
2011	—	—	—	—	—	BV
2011 Proof	15,000	Value: 345				

KM# 1026 SOVEREIGN
7.9800 g., 0.9167 Gold 0.2352 oz. AGW, 22 mm. **Ruler:** Elizabeth II **Subject:** Queen Elizabeth II's Golden Jubilee **Obv:** Head with tiara right **Obv. Designer:** Ian Rank-Broadley **Rev:** Crowned arms within wreath, date below **Edge:** Reeded

Date	Mintage	F	VF	XF	Unc	BU
2002	71,815	—	—	—	—	BV
2002 Proof	20,500	Value: 320				

KM# 1065 SOVEREIGN
7.9880 g., 0.9176 Gold 0.2356 oz. AGW, 22.05 mm. **Ruler:** Elizabeth II **Obv:** Head with tiara right **Obv. Designer:** Ian Rank-Broadley **Rev:** Knight fighting dragon with sword **Edge:** Reeded

Date	Mintage	F	VF	XF	Unc	BU
2005	45,542	—	—	—	—	375
2005 Proof	17,500	BV				

KM# 1027 2 POUNDS
15.9700 g., 0.9167 Gold 0.4707 oz. AGW, 28.4 mm. **Ruler:** Elizabeth II **Subject:** Queen Elizabeth II's Golden Jubilee **Obv:** Head with tiara right **Obv. Designer:** Ian Rank-Broadley **Rev:** Crowned arms within wreath, date below **Edge:** Reeded

Date	Mintage	F	VF	XF	Unc	BU
2002 Proof	8,000	Value: 700				

KM# 1066 2 POUNDS
15.9760 g., 0.9167 Gold 0.4708 oz. AGW, 28.4 mm. **Ruler:** Elizabeth II **Obv:** Head with tiara right **Obv. Designer:** Ian Rank-Broadley **Rev:** Knight fighting dragon with sword **Edge:** Reeded

Date	Mintage	F	VF	XF	Unc	BU
2005 Proof	5,000	Value: 700				

KM# 1072 2 POUNDS
15.9700 g., 0.9167 Gold 0.4707 oz. AGW, 28.4 mm. **Ruler:** Elizabeth II **Obv:** Head with tiara right **Obv. Designer:** Ian Rank-Broadley **Rev:** St. George slaying the Dragon **Edge:** Reeded

Date	Mintage	F	VF	XF	Unc	BU
2006 Proof	3,500	Value: 700				
2007 Proof	2,500	Value: 725				
2008 Proof	2,500	Value: 725				
2009 Proof	2,500	Value: 725				
2010 Proof	2,500	Value: 725				
2011 Proof	2,950	Value: 725				

KM# 1003 5 POUNDS
39.9400 g., 0.9170 Gold 1.1775 oz. AGW, 36 mm. **Ruler:** Elizabeth II **Obv:** Head with tiara right **Obv. Designer:** Ian Rank-Broadley **Rev:** St. George slaying dragon **Edge:** Reeded

Date	Mintage	F	VF	XF	Unc	BU
2001 Proof	1,000	Value: 1,800				
2003 Proof	2,250	Value: 1,800				
2004	1,000	—	—	—	—	1,850
2006	1,000	—	—	—	—	1,800
2006 Proof	1,750	Value: 1,750				
2007 Proof	1,750	Value: 1,750				
2008 Proof	1,750	Value: 1,750				
2009 Proof	1,750	Value: 1,750				
2010	1,000	—	—	—	—	1,800
2010 Proof	—	Value: 1,750				
2011 Proof	2,000	Value: 1,750				

KM# 1028 5 POUNDS
39.9400 g., 0.9167 Gold 1.1771 oz. AGW, 36 mm. **Ruler:** Elizabeth II **Subject:** Queen Elizabeth II's Golden Jubilee **Obv:** Head with tiara right **Obv. Designer:** Ian Rank-Broadley **Rev:** Crowned arms within wreath **Edge:** Reeded

Date	Mintage	F	VF	XF	Unc	BU
2002 Proof	3,000	Value: 1,700				

KM# 1067 5 POUNDS
39.9400 g., 0.9167 Gold 1.1771 oz. AGW, 36 mm. **Ruler:** Elizabeth II **Obv:** Head with tiara right **Obv. Designer:** Ian Rank-Broadley **Rev:** Knight fighting dragon with sword **Edge:** Reeded

Date	Mintage	F	VF	XF	Unc	BU
2005 Proof	2,500	Value: 1,700				

BULLION COINAGE

All proof issues have designers name as P. Nathan. The uncirculated issues use only Nathan.

KM# 1016 20 PENCE
3.2400 g., 0.9584 Silver 0.0998 oz. ASW, 16.5 mm. **Ruler:** Elizabeth II **Subject:** Britannia Bullion **Obv:** Head with tiara right **Obv. Designer:** Ian Rank-Broadley **Rev:** Una and Lion **Edge:** Reeded

Date	Mintage	F	VF	XF	Unc	BU
2001 Proof	15,000	Value: 25.00				

KM# 1079 20 PENCE
3.2400 g., 0.9584 Silver 0.0998 oz. ASW, 16.5 mm. **Ruler:** Elizabeth II **Obv:** Head with tiara right **Rev:** Britannia standing **Edge:** Reeded

Date	Mintage	F	VF	XF	Unc	BU
2002 Proof	—	Value: 25.00				
2004 Proof	—	Value: 25.00				
2006 Proof	—	Value: 25.00				

KM# 1044 20 PENCE
3.2400 g., 0.9584 Silver 0.0998 oz. ASW, 16.5 mm. **Ruler:** Elizabeth II **Obv:** Head with tiara right **Obv. Designer:** Ian Rank-Broadley **Rev:** Britannia portrait behind wavy lines **Edge:** Reeded

Date	Mintage	F	VF	XF	Unc	BU
2003 Proof	5,000	Value: 35.00				

KM# 1085 20 PENCE
3.2400 g., 0.9584 Silver 0.0998 oz. ASW, 16.5 mm. **Ruler:** Elizabeth II **Obv:** Head with tiara right **Rev:** Britannia seated with shield left **Edge:** Reeded

Date	Mintage	F	VF	XF	Unc	BU
2005 Proof	—	Value: 25.00				

KM# 1088 20 PENCE
3.2400 g., 0.9584 Silver 0.0998 oz. ASW, 16.5 mm. **Ruler:** Elizabeth II **Obv:** Head with tiara right **Rev:** Britannia seated with reclining lion right **Edge:** Reeded

Date	Mintage	F	VF	XF	Unc	BU
2007 Proof	—	Value: 25.00				

KM# 1095 20 PENCE
3.2400 g., 0.9584 Silver 0.0998 oz. ASW, 16.5 mm. **Ruler:** Elizabeth II **Obv:** Head with tiara right **Rev:** Britannia standing facing left with trident, flowing garment, shield **Edge:** Reeded

Date	Mintage	F	VF	XF	Unc	BU
2008 Proof	—	Value: 35.00				

KM# 1123 20 PENCE
3.2400 g., 0.9580 Silver 0.0998 oz. ASW, 16.5 mm. **Ruler:** Elizabeth II **Obv:** Head right **Obv. Designer:** Ian Rank Broadley **Rev:** Britania in chariot right **Rev. Designer:** Philip Nathan

Date	Mintage	F	VF	XF	Unc	BU
2009 Proof	—	Value: 35.00				

KM# 1131 20 PENCE
3.2400 g., 0.9580 Silver 0.0998 oz. ASW, 16.5 mm. **Ruler:** Elizabeth II **Obv:** Head right **Obv. Designer:** Ian Rank Broadley **Rev:** Britannia bust right **Rev. Designer:** Suzie Zamit

Date	Mintage	F	VF	XF	Unc	BU
2010 Proof	8,000	Value: 35.00				

KM# 1017 50 PENCE
8.1100 g., 0.9584 Silver 0.2499 oz. ASW, 27.3 mm. **Ruler:** Elizabeth II **Subject:** Britannia Bullion **Obv:** Head with tiara right **Obv. Designer:** Ian Rank-Broadley **Rev:** Una and Lion **Edge:** Reeded

Date	Mintage	F	VF	XF	Unc	BU
2001 Proof	5,000	Value: 35.00				

KM# 1080 50 PENCE
8.1100 g., 0.9584 Silver 0.2499 oz. ASW, 22 mm. **Ruler:** Elizabeth II **Obv:** Head with tiara right **Rev:** Britannia standing **Edge:** Reeded

Date	Mintage	F	VF	XF	Unc	BU
2002 Proof	—	Value: 35.00				
2004 Proof	—	Value: 35.00				
2006 Proof	—	Value: 35.00				

KM# 1045 50 PENCE
8.1100 g., 0.9584 Silver 0.2499 oz. ASW, 22 mm. **Ruler:** Elizabeth II **Obv:** Head with tiara right **Obv. Designer:** Ian Rank-Broadley **Rev:** Britannia portrait behind wavy lines **Edge:** Reeded

Date	Mintage	F	VF	XF	Unc	BU
2003 Proof	5,000	Value: 35.00				

KM# 1086 50 PENCE
8.1100 g., 0.9584 Silver 0.2499 oz. ASW, 22 mm. **Ruler:** Elizabeth II **Obv:** Head with tiara right **Rev:** Britannia seated with shield left **Edge:** Reeded

Date	Mintage	F	VF	XF	Unc	BU
2005 Proof	—	Value: 35.00				

KM# 1089 50 PENCE
8.1100 g., 0.9584 Silver 0.2499 oz. ASW, 22 mm. **Ruler:** Elizabeth II **Obv:** Head with tiara right **Rev:** Britannia seated with reclining lion right **Edge:** Reeded

Date	Mintage	F	VF	XF	Unc	BU
2007 Proof	—	Value: 35.00				

KM# 1096 50 PENCE

8.1100 g., 0.9584 Silver 0.2499 oz. ASW, 22 mm. **Ruler:** Elizabeth II **Obv:** Head with tiara right **Rev:** Britannia standing facing left with trident, flowing garment, shield **Edge:** Reeded

Date	Mintage	F	VF	XF	Unc	BU
2008 Proof	—	Value: 45.00				

KM# 1124 50 PENCE

8.1100 g., 0.9580 Silver 0.2498 oz. ASW, 22 mm. **Ruler:** Elizabeth II **Obv:** Head right **Obv. Designer:** Ian Rank Broadley **Rev:** Britannia in chariot right **Rev. Designer:** Philip Nathan

Date	Mintage	F	VF	XF	Unc	BU
2009 Proof	—	Value: 50.00				

KM# 1132 50 PENCE

8.1100 g., 0.9580 Silver 0.2498 oz. ASW, 22 mm. **Ruler:** Elizabeth II **Obv:** Head right **Obv. Designer:** Ian Rank Broadley **Rev:** Britannia bust right **Rev. Designer:** Suzie Zamie

Date	Mintage	F	VF	XF	Unc	BU
2010 Proof	3,500	Value: 50.00				

KM# 1018 POUND

16.2200 g., 0.9584 Silver 0.4998 oz. ASW, 27 mm. **Ruler:** Elizabeth II **Subject:** Britannia Bullion **Obv:** Head with tiara right **Obv. Designer:** Ian Rank-Broadley **Rev:** Una and Lion" **Edge:** Reeded

Date	Mintage	F	VF	XF	Unc	BU
2001 Proof	5,000	Value: 50.00				

KM# 1081 POUND

16.2200 g., 0.9584 Silver 0.4998 oz. ASW, 27 mm. **Ruler:** Elizabeth II **Obv:** Head with tiara right **Rev:** Britannia standing **Edge:** Reeded

Date	Mintage	F	VF	XF	Unc	BU
2002 Proof	—	Value: 50.00				
2004 Proof	—	Value: 50.00				
2006 Proof	—	Value: 50.00				

KM# 1046 POUND

16.2200 g., 0.9584 Silver 0.4998 oz. ASW, 27 mm. **Ruler:** Elizabeth II **Obv:** Head with tiara right **Obv. Designer:** Ian Rank-Broadley **Rev:** Britannia portrait behind wavy lines **Edge:** Reeded

Date	Mintage	F	VF	XF	Unc	BU
2003 Proof	5,000	Value: 50.00				

KM# 1087 POUND

16.2200 g., 0.9584 Silver 0.4998 oz. ASW, 27 mm. **Ruler:** Elizabeth II **Obv:** Head with tiara right **Rev:** Britannia seated with shield left **Edge:** Reeded

Date	Mintage	F	VF	XF	Unc	BU
2005 Proof	—	Value: 50.00				

KM# 1090 POUND

16.2200 g., 0.9584 Silver 0.4998 oz. ASW, 27 mm. **Ruler:** Elizabeth II **Obv:** Head with tiara right **Rev:** Britannia seated with reclining lion right **Edge:** Reeded

Date	Mintage	F	VF	XF	Unc	BU
2007 Proof	—	Value: 50.00				

KM# 1097 POUND

16.2200 g., 0.9584 Silver 0.4998 oz. ASW, 27 mm. **Ruler:** Elizabeth II **Obv:** Head with tiara right **Rev:** Britannia standing facing left with trident, flowing garment, shield **Edge:** Reeded

Date	Mintage	F	VF	XF	Unc	BU
2008 Proof	—	Value: 60.00				

KM# 1125 POUND

16.2200 g., 0.9580 Silver 0.4996 oz. ASW, 27 mm. **Ruler:** Elizabeth II **Obv:** Head right **Obv. Designer:** Ian Rank Broadley **Rev:** Britannia in chariot right **Rev. Designer:** Philip Nathan

Date	Mintage	F	VF	XF	Unc	BU
2009 Proof	—	Value: 75.00				

KM# 1133 POUND

16.2200 g., 0.9580 Silver 0.4996 oz. ASW, 27 mm. **Ruler:** Elizabeth II **Obv:** Head right **Obv. Designer:** Ian Rank Broadley **Rev:** Britannia bust right **Rev. Designer:** Suzie Zamit

Date	Mintage	F	VF	XF	Unc	BU
2010 Proof	3,500	Value: 70.00				

KM# 1019 2 POUNDS

32.4500 g., 0.9584 Silver 0.9998 oz. ASW, 40 mm. **Ruler:** Elizabeth II **Subject:** Britannia Bullion **Obv:** Head with tiara right **Obv. Designer:** Ian Rank-Broadley **Rev:** Una and Lion **Edge:** Reeded

Date	Mintage	F	VF	XF	Unc	BU
2001	100,000	—	—	—	38.00	42.00
2001 Proof	10,000	Value: 65.00				

KM# 1029 2 POUNDS

32.5400 g., 0.9580 Silver 1.0022 oz. ASW, 40 mm. **Ruler:** Elizabeth II **Obv:** Head with tiara right **Obv. Designer:** Ian Rank-Broadley **Rev:** Standing Britannia **Rev. Designer:** Philip Nathan **Edge:** Reeded

Date	Mintage	F	VF	XF	Unc	BU
2002	36,543	—	—	—	—	38.00
2002 Proof	—	Value: 60.00				
2004	100,000	—	—	—	—	38.00
2004 Proof	2,174	Value: 60.00				
2006	100,000	—	—	—	—	38.00
2006 Proof	2,529	Value: 60.00				

KM# 1039 2 POUNDS

32.4500 g., 0.9580 Silver 0.9994 oz. ASW, 40 mm. **Ruler:** Elizabeth II **Subject:** Britannia Bullion **Obv:** Head with tiara right **Obv. Designer:** Ian Rank-Broadley **Rev:** Britannia portrait behind wavy puzzle-like lines **Rev. Designer:** Philip Nathan **Edge:** Reeded

Date	Mintage	F	VF	XF	Unc	BU
2003	73,271	—	—	—	—	38.00
2003 Proof	2,016	Value: 65.00				

KM# 1063 2 POUNDS

32.4500 g., 0.9580 Silver 0.9994 oz. ASW, 40 mm. **Ruler:** Elizabeth II **Obv:** Head with tiara right **Obv. Designer:** Ian Rank-Broadley **Rev:** Seated Britannia **Rev. Designer:** Philip Nathan **Edge:** Reeded

Date	Mintage	F	VF	XF	Unc	BU
2005	100,000	—	—	—	—	38.00
2005 Proof	1,539	Value: 70.00				

KM# 1029a 2 POUNDS

32.4500 g., 0.9580 Silver partially gilt 0.9994 oz. ASW, 40 mm. **Ruler:** Elizabeth II **Obv:** Head with tiara right **Obv. Designer:** Ian Rank-Broadley **Rev:** Britannia standing with shield, gilt **Edge:** Reeded

Date	Mintage	F	VF	XF	Unc	BU
2006 Proof	3,000	Value: 100				

KM# 1039a 2 POUNDS

32.4500 g., 0.9580 Silver partially gilt 0.9994 oz. ASW, 40 mm. **Ruler:** Elizabeth II **Obv:** Head with tiara right **Obv. Designer:** Ian Rank-Broadley **Rev:** Britannia head gilt **Edge:** Reeded

Date	Mintage	F	VF	XF	Unc	BU
2006 Proof	3,000	Value: 100				

KM# 1063a 2 POUNDS

32.4500 g., 0.9580 Silver partially gilt 0.9994 oz. ASW, 40 mm. **Ruler:** Elizabeth II **Obv:** Head with tiara right **Obv. Designer:** Ian Rank-Broadley **Rev:** Britannia seated, gilt **Edge:** Reeded

Date	Mintage	F	VF	XF	Unc	BU
2006 Proof	3,000	Value: 100				

KM# 1000a 2 POUNDS

32.4500 g., 0.9580 Silver partially gilt 0.9994 oz. ASW, 40 mm. **Ruler:** Elizabeth II **Obv:** Head with tiara right **Obv. Designer:** Ian Rank-Broadley **Rev:** Britannia in chariot, gilt **Rev. Designer:** Philip Nathan **Edge:** Reeded

Date	Mintage	F	VF	XF	Unc	BU
2006 Proof	3,000	Value: 100				

KM# 1019a 2 POUNDS
32.4500 g., 0.9580 Silver 0.9994 oz. ASW, 40 mm. **Ruler:** Elizabeth II **Subject:** Golden Silhouette Britannias **Obv:** Head with tiara right **Obv. Designer:** Ian Rank-Broadley **Rev:** Gold plated Britannia and Lion **Edge:** Reeded

Date	Mintage	F	VF	XF	Unc	BU
2006 Proof	3,000	Value: 100				

KM# 1078 2 POUNDS
32.4500 g., 0.9580 Silver 0.9994 oz. ASW, 40 mm. **Ruler:** Elizabeth II **Subject:** Britannia series **Obv:** Elizabeth II **Rev:** Seated, bareheaded Britannia with a recumbent lion at her feet **Edge:** Reeded

Date	Mintage	F	VF	XF	Unc	BU
2007	100,000	—	—	—	—	40.00
2007 Proof	2,500	Value: 65.00				

KM# 1098 2 POUNDS
32.4500 g., 0.9584 Silver 0.9998 oz. ASW, 40 mm. **Ruler:** Elizabeth II **Obv:** Head with tiara right **Rev:** Britannia standing facing left with trident, flowing garment, shield **Edge:** Reeded

Date	Mintage	F	VF	XF	Unc	BU
2008	—	—	—	—	—	40.00
2008 Proof	—	Value: 80.00				

KM# 1126 2 POUNDS
32.4500 g., 0.9580 Silver 0.9994 oz. ASW **Ruler:** Elizabeth II **Obv:** Head right **Obv. Designer:** Ian Rank-Broadley **Rev:** Britannia in chariot right **Rev. Designer:** Philip Nathan

Date	Mintage	F	VF	XF	Unc	BU
2009 Proof	—	Value: 90.00				

KM# 1000 2 POUNDS
32.5400 g., 0.9580 Silver 1.0022 oz. ASW, 40 mm. **Ruler:** Elizabeth II **Obv:** Head with tiara right **Obv. Designer:** Ian Rank-Broadley **Rev:** Britannia in chariot **Edge:** Reeded

Date	Mintage	F	VF	XF	Unc	BU
2009	—	—	—	—	—	40.00
2009 Proof	—	Value: 55.00				

KM# 1134 2 POUNDS
32.4500 g., 0.9580 Silver 0.9994 oz. ASW, 40 mm. **Ruler:** Elizabeth II **Obv:** Head right **Obv. Designer:** Ian Rank-Broadley **Rev:** Britannia bust right **Rev. Designer:** Britania bust right

Date	Mintage	F	VF	XF	Unc	BU
2010 Proof	8,000	Value: 90.00				

KM# 1020 10 POUNDS
3.4100 g., 0.9167 Gold 0.1005 oz. AGW, 16.5 mm. **Ruler:** Elizabeth II **Subject:** Britannia Bullion **Obv:** Head with tiara right **Obv. Designer:** Ian Rank-Broadley **Rev:** Stylized "Britannia and the Lion" **Rev. Designer:** Philip Nathan **Edge:** Reeded

Date	Mintage	F	VF	XF	Unc	BU
2001	1,100	—	—	—	BV+16%	—
2001 Proof	1,557	Value: 175				

KM# 1008 10 POUNDS
3.4100 g., 0.9167 Gold 0.1005 oz. AGW, 16.5 mm. **Ruler:** Elizabeth II **Obv:** Head with tiara right **Obv. Designer:** Ian Rank-Broadley **Rev:** Britannia standing **Rev. Designer:** Philip Nathan **Edge:** Reeded

Date	Mintage	F	VF	XF	Unc	BU
2002 Proof	1,500	Value: 175				
2004	—	—	—	—	—	BV+16%
2004 Proof	—	Value: 200				
2006	—	—	—	—	—	BV+16%
2006 Proof	—	Value: 175				

KM# 1040 10 POUNDS
3.4100 g., 0.9167 Gold 0.1005 oz. AGW, 16.5 mm. **Ruler:** Elizabeth II **Obv:** Head with tiara right **Obv. Designer:** Ian Rank-Broadley **Rev:** Britannia portrait behind wavy lines **Rev. Designer:** Philip Nathan **Edge:** Reeded

Date	Mintage	F	VF	XF	Unc	BU
2003	—	—	—	—	BV+16%	—
2003 Proof	4,000	Value: 175				

KM# 1068 10 POUNDS
3.4100 g., 0.9167 Gold 0.1005 oz. AGW, 16.5 mm. **Ruler:** Elizabeth II **Obv:** Head with tiara right **Obv. Designer:** Ian Rank-Broadley **Rev:** Seated Britannia **Rev. Designer:** Philip Nathan **Edge:** Reeded

Date	Mintage	F	VF	XF	Unc	BU
2005 Proof	1,225	Value: 185				

KM# 1091 10 POUNDS
3.4100 g., 0.9167 Gold 0.1005 oz. AGW, 16.5 mm. **Ruler:** Elizabeth II **Obv:** Head with tiara right **Rev:** Britannia seated with reclining lion right **Edge:** Reeded

Date	Mintage	F	VF	XF	Unc	BU
2007 Proof	—	Value: 195				

KM# 1091a 10 POUNDS
0.9999 Platinum APW **Ruler:** Elizabeth II **Obv:** Head with tiara right **Rev:** Britannia seated with reclining lion right **Edge:** Reeded **Edge Lettering:** 16.5

Date	Mintage	F	VF	XF	Unc	BU
2007 Proof	—	Value: 450				

KM# 1099 10 POUNDS
3.4100 g., 0.9167 Gold 0.1005 oz. AGW, 16.5 mm. **Ruler:** Elizabeth II **Obv:** Head with tiara right **Rev:** Britannia standing facing left with trident, flowing garment, shield **Edge:** Reeded

Date	Mintage	F	VF	XF	Unc	BU
2008 Proof	—	Value: 210				

KM# 1099a 10 POUNDS
0.9999 Platinum APW, 16.5 mm. **Ruler:** Elizabeth II **Obv:** Head with tiara right **Rev:** Britannia standing facing left with trident, flowing garment, shield **Edge:** Reeded

Date	Mintage	F	VF	XF	Unc	BU
2008 Proof	—	Value: 450				

KM# 1127 10 POUNDS
3.4100 g., 0.9160 Gold 0.1004 oz. AGW, 16.5 mm. **Ruler:** Elizabeth II **Obv:** Head right **Obv. Designer:** Ian Rank-Broadley **Rev:** Britannia in chariot right **Rev. Designer:** Philip Nathan

Date	Mintage	F	VF	XF	Unc	BU
2009 Proof	2,000	Value: 210				

KM# 1135 10 POUNDS
3.4100 g., 0.9160 Gold 0.1004 oz. AGW, 16.5 mm. **Ruler:** Elizabeth II **Obv:** Head right **Obv. Designer:** Ian Rank-Broadley **Rev:** Britannia bust right **Rev. Designer:** Sizie Zamit

Date	Mintage	F	VF	XF	Unc	BU
2010 Proof	750	Value: 200				

KM# 1021 25 POUNDS
8.5100 g., 0.9167 Gold 0.2508 oz. AGW, 22 mm. **Ruler:** Elizabeth II **Subject:** Britannia Bullion **Obv:** Head with tiara right **Obv. Designer:** Ian Rank-Broadley **Rev:** Stylized "Britannia and the Lion" **Rev. Designer:** Philip Nathan **Edge:** Reeded

Date	Mintage	F	VF	XF	Unc	BU
2001	1,100	—	—	—	BV+25%	—
2001 Proof	1,500	Value: 475				

KM# 1009 25 POUNDS
8.5100 g., 0.9167 Gold 0.2508 oz. AGW, 22 mm. **Ruler:** Elizabeth II **Obv:** Head with tiara right **Obv. Designer:** Ian Rank-Broadley **Rev:** Britannia standing **Rev. Designer:** Philip Nathan **Edge:** Reeded

Date	Mintage	F	VF	XF	Unc	BU
2002 Proof	750	Value: 475				
2004	—	—	—	—	BV+15%	—
2004 Proof	750	Value: 520				
2006	—	—	—	—	BV+15%	—
2006 Proof	1,000	Value: 520				

KM# 1041 25 POUNDS
8.5100 g., 0.9167 Gold 0.2508 oz. AGW, 22 mm. **Ruler:** Elizabeth II **Obv:** Head with tiara right **Obv. Designer:** Ian Rank-Broadley **Rev:** Britannia portrait behind wavy lines **Rev. Designer:** Philip Nathan **Edge:** Reeded

Date	Mintage	F	VF	XF	Unc	BU
2003	604	—	—	—	BV+25%	—
2003 Proof	3,250	Value: 475				

KM# 1069 25 POUNDS
8.5100 g., 0.9167 Gold 0.2508 oz. AGW, 22 mm. **Ruler:** Elizabeth II **Obv:** Head with tiara right **Obv. Designer:** Ian Rank-Broadley **Rev:** Seated Britannia **Rev. Designer:** Philip Nathan **Edge:** Reeded

Date	Mintage	F	VF	XF	Unc	BU
2005 Proof	2,750	Value: 500				

KM# 1092 25 POUNDS
8.5100 g., 0.9167 Gold 0.2508 oz. AGW, 22 mm. **Ruler:** Elizabeth II **Obv:** Head with tiara right **Rev:** Britannia seated with reclining lion right **Edge:** Reeded

Date	Mintage	F	VF	XF	Unc	BU
2007 Proof	—	Value: 500				

KM# 1092a 25 POUNDS
0.9999 Platinum APW, 22 mm. **Ruler:** Elizabeth II **Obv:** Head with tiara right **Rev:** Britannia seated with reclining lion right **Edge:** Reeded

Date	Mintage	F	VF	XF	Unc	BU
2007 Proof	—	Value: 750				

KM# 1100 25 POUNDS
8.5100 g., 0.9167 Gold 0.2508 oz. AGW, 22 mm. **Ruler:** Elizabeth II **Obv:** Head with tiara right **Rev:** Britannia standing facing left with trident, flowing garment, shield **Edge:** Reeded

Date	Mintage	F	VF	XF	Unc	BU
2008 Proof	—	Value: 525				

KM# 1100a 25 POUNDS
0.9999 Platinum APW, 22 mm. **Ruler:** Elizabeth II **Obv:** Head with tiara right **Rev:** Britannia standing facing left with trident, flowing garment, shield **Edge:** Reeded

Date	Mintage	F	VF	XF	Unc	BU
2008 Proof	—	Value: 750				

KM# 1128 25 POUNDS
8.5100 g., 0.9160 Gold 0.2506 oz. AGW, 22 mm. **Ruler:** Elizabeth II **Obv:** Head right **Obv. Designer:** Ian Rank-Broadley **Rev:** Britannia in chariot right **Rev. Designer:** Philip Nathan

Date	Mintage	F	VF	XF	Unc	BU
2009 Proof	2,250	Value: 500				

KM# 1136 25 POUNDS
8.5100 g., 0.9160 Gold 0.2506 oz. AGW, 22 mm. **Ruler:** Elizabeth II **Obv:** Head right **Obv. Designer:** Ian Rank-Broadley **Rev:** Britannia bust right **Rev. Designer:** Suzie Zamit

Date	Mintage	F	VF	XF	Unc	BU
2010 Proof	1,000	Value: 450				

KM# 1022 50 POUNDS
17.0200 g., 0.9167 Gold 0.5016 oz. AGW, 27 mm. **Ruler:** Elizabeth II **Subject:** Britannia Bullion **Obv:** Head with tiara right **Obv. Designer:** Ian Rank-Broadley **Rev:** Stylized "Britannia and the Lion" **Rev. Designer:** Philip Nathan **Edge:** Reeded

Date	Mintage	F	VF	XF	Unc	BU
2001	600	—	—	—	BV+25%	—
2001 Proof	1,000	Value: 850				

KM# 1010 50 POUNDS
17.0300 g., 0.9167 Gold 0.5019 oz. AGW, 27 mm. **Ruler:** Elizabeth II **Obv:** Head with tiara right **Obv. Designer:** Ian Rank-Broadley **Rev:** Britannia standing **Rev. Designer:** Philip Nathan **Edge:** Reeded

Date	Mintage	F	VF	XF	Unc	BU
2002 Proof	1,000	Value: 850				
2004	—	—	—	—	—	BV+15%
2004 Proof	—	Value: 875				
2006	—	—	—	—	—	BV+15%
2006 Proof	—	Value: 875				

KM# 1042 50 POUNDS
17.0200 g., 0.9167 Gold 0.5016 oz. AGW, 27 mm. **Ruler:** Elizabeth II **Obv:** Head with tiara right **Obv. Designer:** Ian Rank-Broadley **Rev:** Britannia portrait behind wavy lines **Rev. Designer:** Philip Nathan **Edge:** Reeded

Date	Mintage	F	VF	XF	Unc	BU
2003	—	—	—	—	BV+15%	—
2003 Proof	2,500	Value: 850				

KM# 1070 50 POUNDS
17.0300 g., 0.9167 Gold 0.5019 oz. AGW, 27 mm. **Ruler:** Elizabeth II **Obv:** Head with tiara right **Obv. Designer:** Ian Rank-Broadley **Rev:** Seated Britannia **Rev. Designer:** Philip Nathan **Edge:** Reeded

Date	Mintage	F	VF	XF	Unc	BU
2005 Proof	2,000	Value: 850				

KM# 1093 50 POUNDS
17.0250 g., 0.9167 Gold 0.5017 oz. AGW, 27 mm. **Ruler:** Elizabeth II **Obv:** Head with tiara right **Rev:** Britannia seated with reclining lion right **Edge:** Reeded

Date	Mintage	F	VF	XF	Unc	BU
2007 Proof	—	Value: 900				

KM# 1093a 50 POUNDS
0.9999 Platinum APW, 27 mm. **Ruler:** Elizabeth II **Obv:** Head with tiara right **Rev:** Britannia seated with reclining lion right **Edge:** Reeded

Date	Mintage	F	VF	XF	Unc	BU
2007 Proof	—	Value: 1,700				

KM# 1101 50 POUNDS
17.0250 g., 0.9167 Gold 0.5017 oz. AGW, 27 mm. **Ruler:** Elizabeth II **Obv:** Head with tiara right **Rev:** Britannia standing facing left with trident, flowing garment, shield **Edge:** Reeded

Date	Mintage	F	VF	XF	Unc	BU
2008 Proof	—	Value: 900				

KM# 1101a 50 POUNDS
0.9999 Platinum APW, 27 mm. **Ruler:** Elizabeth II **Obv:** Head with tiara right **Rev:** Britannia standing facing left with trident, flowing garment, shield **Edge:** Reeded

Date	Mintage	F	VF	XF	Unc	BU
2008 Proof	—	Value: 1,700				

KM# 1129 50 POUNDS
27.0000 g., 0.9160 Gold 0.7951 oz. AGW, 27 mm. **Ruler:** Elizabeth II **Obv:** Head right **Obv. Designer:** Ian Rank Broadley **Rev:** Britania in chariot right **Rev. Designer:** Philip Nathan

Date	Mintage	F	VF	XF	Unc	BU
2009 Proof	1,250	Value: 1,150				

KM# 1137 50 POUNDS
17.0200 g., 0.9160 Gold 0.5012 oz. AGW, 27 mm. **Ruler:** Elizabeth II **Obv:** Head right **Obv. Designer:** Ian Rank-Broadley **Rev:** Britannia bust right **Rev. Designer:** Suzie Zamit

Date	Mintage	F	VF	XF	Unc	BU
2010 Proof	1,250	Value: 750				

KM# 1023 100 POUNDS
34.0500 g., 0.9167 Gold 1.0035 oz. AGW, 32.7 mm. **Ruler:** Elizabeth II **Subject:** Britannia Bullion **Obv:** Head with tiara right **Obv. Designer:** Ian Rank-Broadley **Rev:** Stylized "Britannia and the Lion" **Rev. Designer:** Philip Nathan **Edge:** Reeded

Date	Mintage	F	VF	XF	Unc	BU
2001	900	—	—	—	BV+15%	—
2001 Proof	1,000	Value: 1,700				

KM# 1011 100 POUNDS
34.0500 g., 0.9167 Gold 1.0035 oz. AGW, 32.7 mm. **Ruler:** Elizabeth II **Obv:** Head with tiara right **Obv. Designer:** Ian Rank-Broadley **Rev:** Britannia standing **Rev. Designer:** Philip Nathan **Edge:** Reeded

Date	Mintage	F	VF	XF	Unc	BU
2002	—	—	—	—	—	BV+15%
2002 Proof	1,000	Value: 1,700				
2004	—	—	—	—	—	BV+15%
2004 Proof	—	Value: 1,700				
2006	—	—	—	—	—	BV+15%
2006 Proof	—	Value: 1,700				

KM# 1043 100 POUNDS
34.0500 g., 0.9167 Gold 1.0035 oz. AGW, 32.7 mm. **Ruler:** Elizabeth II **Obv:** Head with tiara right **Obv. Designer:** Ian Rank-Broadley **Rev:** Britannia portrait behind wavy lines **Rev. Designer:** Philip Nathan **Edge:** Reeded

Date	Mintage	F	VF	XF	Unc	BU
2003	—	—	—	—	BV+15%	—
2003 Proof	1,500	Value: 1,700				

KM# 1071 100 POUNDS
34.0500 g., 0.9167 Gold 1.0035 oz. AGW, 32.7 mm. **Ruler:** Elizabeth II **Obv:** Head with tiara right **Obv. Designer:** Ian Rank-Broadley **Rev:** Seated Britannia **Edge:** Reeded

Date	Mintage	F	VF	XF	Unc	BU
2005	—	—	—	—	BV+15%	—
2005 Proof	1,500	Value: 1,700				

KM# 1094 100 POUNDS
34.0500 g., 0.9167 Gold 1.0035 oz. AGW, 32.7 mm. **Ruler:** Elizabeth II **Obv:** Head with tiara right **Rev:** Britannia seated with reclining lion right **Edge:** Reeded

Date	Mintage	F	VF	XF	Unc	BU
2007	—	—	—	—	BV+15%	—
2007 Proof	—	Value: 1,700				

KM# 1094a 100 POUNDS
0.9999 Platinum APW, 32.7 mm. **Ruler:** Elizabeth II **Obv:** Head with tiara right **Rev:** Britannia seated with reclining lion right **Edge:** Reeded

Date	Mintage	F	VF	XF	Unc	BU
2007 Proof	—	Value: 2,900				

KM# 1102 100 POUNDS
34.0500 g., 0.9167 Gold 1.0035 oz. AGW, 32.7 mm. **Ruler:** Elizabeth II **Obv:** Head with tiara right **Rev:** Britannia standing facing left with trident, flowing garment, shield **Edge:** Reeded

Date	Mintage	F	VF	XF	Unc	BU
2008	—	—	—	—	BV+15%	—
2008 Proof	—	Value: 1,700				

KM# 1102a 100 POUNDS
0.9999 Platinum APW, 32.7 mm. **Ruler:** Elizabeth II **Obv:** Head with tiara right **Rev:** Britannia standing facing left with trident, flowing garment, shield **Edge:** Reeded

Date	Mintage	F	VF	XF	Unc	BU
2008 Proof	—	Value: 2,900				

KM# 1130 100 POUNDS
32.6900 g., 0.9160 Gold 0.9627 oz. AGW, 32.6 mm. **Ruler:** Elizabeth II **Obv:** Head right **Obv. Designer:** Ian Rank-Broadley **Rev:** Britannia in chariot right **Rev. Designer:** Philip Nathan

Date	Mintage	F	VF	XF	Unc	BU
2009 Proof	1,250	Value: 1,650				

KM# 1138 100 POUNDS
34.0500 g., 0.9160 Gold 1.0027 oz. AGW, 32.7 mm. **Ruler:** Elizabeth II **Obv:** Head right **Obv. Designer:** Ian Rank-Broadley **Rev:** Britannia bust right **Rev. Designer:** Suzie Zamit

Date	Mintage	F	VF	XF	Unc	BU
2010 Proof	1,250	Value: 1,700				

PIEFORTS

KM#	Date	Mintage	Identification	Mkt Val
P40	2003	6,795	50 Pence. 0.9250 Silver. 16.0000 g. KM#1036a.	—
P41	2003	9,871	Pound. 0.9250 Silver. 19.0000 g. KM#993a.	—
P42	2003	8,728	2 Pounds. 0.9250 Silver. 24.0000 g. KM#1037a.	—
P43	2004	4,054	50 Pence. 0.9250 Silver. 24.0000 g. KM#1047a.	—
P44	2004	7,013	Pound. 0.9250 Silver. 19.0000 g. KM#1048a.	—
P45	2004	5,303	2 Pounds. 0.9250 Silver. 24.0000 g. KM#1049a.	—
P46	2004	4,584	2 Pounds. 0.9250 Silver. 24.0000 g. KM#1052a.	—
P47	2004	2,500	5 Pounds. 0.9250 Silver. 56.5600 g. KM#1055a.	—
P48	2005	3,808	50 Pence. 0.9250 Silver. 16.0000 g. KM#1050a.	—
P49	2005	4,798	2 Pounds. 0.9250 Silver. 24.0000 g. KM#1056a.	—
P50	2005	6,007	Pound. 0.9250 Silver. 19.0000 g. KM#1051a.	—
P51	2005	—	5 Pounds. 0.9250 Silver. KM#1053a.	80.00
P52	2005	—	5 Pounds. 0.9250 Silver. KM#1054a.	80.00
P53	2006	3,532	50 Pence. 0.9250 Silver. 16.0000 g. KM#1057a.	—
P54	2006	3,415	50 Pence. 0.9250 Silver. 16.0000 g. KM#1058a.	—
P55	2006	5,129	Pound. 0.9250 Silver. 19.0000 g. KM#1051a.	—
P56	2006	3,199	2 Pounds. 0.9250 Silver. 24.0000 g. KM#1060a.	—
P57	2006	3,018	2 Pounds. 0.9250 Silver. 24.0000 g. KM#1061a.	—
P58	2006	—	5 Pounds. 0.9250 Silver. KM#1062a.	80.00
P59	2007	1,555	50 Pence. 0.9250 Silver. 16.0000 g. KM#1073a.	135
P60	2007	5,739	Pound. 0.9250 Silver. 19.0000 g. KM#1074a.	85.00
P61	2007	3,990	2 Pounds. 0.9250 Silver. 24.0000 g. KM#1075a.	90.00
P62	2007	4,000	2 Pounds. 0.9250 Silver. 24.0000 g. KM#1076a.	90.00
P63	2007	2,000	5 Pounds. 0.9250 Silver. 56.5600 g. KM#1075a.	135
P64	2007	250	5 Pounds. 0.9995 Platinum. 94.2000 g.	7,500
P65	2008	—	2 Pounds. 0.9250 Silver. 24.0000 g. KM#1106a.	—
P66	2008	—	2 Pounds. 0.9250 Silver. 24.0000 g. KM#1104.	—
P67	2008	—	5 Pounds. 0.9250 Silver. 56.5600 g. KM#1104.	—
P68	2008	—	5 Pounds. 0.9250 Silver. 56.5600 g. KM#1103.	—
P70	2009	—	5 Pounds. 0.9250 Silver. 56.5600 g. KM#1121a.	180
P75	2010	—	Pound. 0.9250 Silver. 19.0000 g. KM#1158a.	—
P76	2010	—	Pound. 0.9250 Silver. 19.0000 g.	—
P77	2011	—	Penny. 0.9250 Silver. KM#1107a.	—
P78	2011	—	2 Pence. 0.9250 Silver. KM#1108a.	—
P79	2011	—	5 Pence. 0.9250 Silver. KM#1109a.	—
P80	2011	—	10 Pence. 0.9250 Silver. KM#1110a.	—
P81	2011	—	20 Pence. 0.9250 Silver. KM#1111a.	—
P82	2011	—	50 Pence. 0.9250 Silver. KM#1112a.	—
P83	2011	—	Pound. 0.9250 Silver. KM#1113a.	—
P84	2011	—	Pound. 0.9250 Silver. 19.0000 g. KM#1197a.	—
P85	2011	—	Pound. 0.9250 Silver. 19.0000 g. KM#1198a.	—
P86	2011	—	50 Pence. 0.9250 Silver. 24.0000 g. KM#1196a.	—
P87	2011	—	2 Pounds. 0.9250 Silver. 24.0000 g. KM#1199a.	—
P88	2011	—	2 Pounds. 0.9250 Silver. 24.0000 g. KM#1200a.	—
P89	2011	—	5 Pounds. 0.9250 Silver. 56.5600 g. KM#1201a.	—

MAUNDY SETS

KM#	Date	Mintage	Identification	Issue Price	Mkt Val
MDS260	2001 (4)	1,132	KM#898-899, 901-902. Westminster Abbey	—	250
MDS261	2002 (4)	1,681	KM#898-899, 901-902. Canterbury Cathedral	—	250
MDS262	2003 (4)	1,601	KM#898-899, 901-902. Gloucester Cathedral	—	265
MDS263	2004 (4)	1,613	KM#898-899, 901-902. Liverpool Cathedral	—	265
MDS264	2005 (4)	1,685	KM#898-899, 901-902. Wakefield Cathedral	—	265
MDS265	2006 (4)	1,937	KM#898-899, 901-902. Guilford Cathedral	—	265
MDS266	2007 (4)	1,953	KM#898-899, 901-902. Manchester Cathedral	—	265
MDS267	2008 (4)	—	KM#898-899, 901-902. St. Patrick's Cathedral	—	265
MDS268	2009 (4)	—	KM#898-899, 901-902.	—	265
MDS269	2010 (4)	—	KM#898-899, 901-902.	—	265
MDS270	2011 (4)	—	KM#898-899, 901-902.	—	265

MINT SETS

KM#	Date	Mintage	Identification	Issue Price	Mkt Val
MS129	2001 (9)	57,741	KM#986-991, 994, 1013-1015 B.U. set	22.50	25.00
MS130	2001 (9)	—	KM#986-991, 994, 1013-1014 Wedding Collection	27.50	25.00
MS131	2001 (9)	—	KM#986-991, 994, 1013-1014 Baby Gift Set	27.50	25.00
MS132	2002 (8)	60,539	KM#986-991, 994, 1030	22.50	20.00
MS133	2002 (8)	—	KM#986-991, 994, 1030 Wedding Collection	27.50	20.00
MS134	2002 (8)	—	KM#986-991, 994, 1030 Baby Gift Set	27.50	20.00
MSA135	2004 (10)	46,032	KM#986-991, 994, 1047-1049 BU Set	—	35.00
MSB135	2004 (10)	4,214	KM#986-991, 994, 1047-1049, 1055 Wedding Collection	—	35.00
MSC135	2004 (10)	34,371	KM#986-991, 994, 1047-1049, 1055 Baby Gift Set	—	35.00
MS135	2003 (10)	—	KM#986-991, 993, 994, 1036-1037 BU Set	22.50	35.00

KM#	Date	Mintage	Identification	Issue Price	Mkt Val
MS136	2003 (10)	—	KM#986-991, 993, 994, 1036-1037 Wedding Collection	27.50	30.00
MS137	2003 (10)	—	KM#986-991, 993, 994, 1036-1037 Baby Gift Set	27.50	30.00
MS138	2005 (10)	—	KM#986-991, 994, 1050-1052	26.50	30.00
MS139	2005 (10)	—	KM#986-991, 994, 1050-1052 Baby Gift Set	36.50	35.00
MS140	2005 (3)	—	KM#1050-1052 New Coinage Set	16.25	17.50
MS141	2005 (2)	—	KM#1053-1054 Trafalgar Set	36.00	35.00
MS142	2006 (10)	—	KM#986-990, 1057-1061	30.00	60.00
MS143	2006 (10)	—	KM#986-990, 1057-1061 Baby Gift Set	38.50	60.00
MS144	2007 (6)	—	KM#986-991	—	10.00

PROOF SETS

KM#	Date	Mintage	Identification	Issue Price	Mkt Val
PS116	2001 (3)	1,500	KM#1001-1002, 1014a	795	525
PS117	2001 (4)	1,000	KM#1001-1003,1014a	1,645	2,250
PS118	2001 (4)	5,000	KM#1016-1019	—	175
PSA119	2001 (3)	1,500	KM#1001, 1002, 1014b	—	525
PSB119	2001 (4)	1,000	KM#1001, 1002, 1014b, 1015b	—	2,700
PS119	2001 (4)	1,000	KM#1020-1023	1,595	3,200
PS120	2002 (3)	5,000	KM#1025-1027	795	1,275
PS121	2002 (4)	3,000	KM#1025-1028	1,645	3,000
PS122	2002 (4)	3,358	KM#1031-1034; Standard Set	34.95	35.00
PS123	2002 (4)	673	KM#1031-1034; Display Set	44.95	40.00
PS124	2002 (4)	2,553	KM#1031a-1034a; Display Set	120	150
PS125	2002 (4)	315	KM#1031b-1034b; Display Set	1,675	3,000
PS126	2002 (4)	1,000	KM#1008-1011	1,600	3,200
PS127	2001 (10)	10,000	KM#986-991, 994, 1013-1015 Executive Proof Set in display case	115	80.00
PS128	2001 (10)	30,000	KM#986-991, 994, 1013-1015 Deluxe Proof Set in red leather case	72.50	80.00
PS129	2001 (10)	28,244	KM#986-991, 994, 1013-1015 Standard Proof Set in simple case	50.00	65.00
PS130	2001 (10)	1,351	KM#986-991, 994, 1013-1015 Gift Proof Set with a pack of occasion cards	65.00	65.00
PS131	2002 (9)	5,000	KM#986-991, 994, 1024, 1030 Executive Proof Set	100	60.00
PS132	2002 (9)	30,000	KM#986-991, 994, 1024, 1030 Deluxe Proof Set	70.00	55.00
PS133	2002 (9)	30,884	KM#986-991, 994, 1024, 1030 Standard Proof Set	48.00	55.00
PS134	2002 (9)	1,544	KM#986-991, 994, 1024, 1030 Gift Proof Set	62.40	55.00
PSA135	2002 (13)	—	KM#898a, 899a, 901a, 902a, 986c, 987c, 988b, 989b, 990b, 991b, 1030b, 994c, 1024b Queen Elizabeth II - Golden Jubilee 1952-2002, set is struck in gold (including Maundy set), in presentation box	—	11,250
PS135	2003 (11)	5,000	KM#986-991, 993, 994, 1036-1038 Executive Proof Set	100	85.00
PS136	2003 (11)	14,863	KM#986-991, 993, 994, 1036-1038 Deluxe Proof Set	72.00	80.00
PS137	2003 (11)	23,650	KM#986-991, 993, 994, 1036-1038 Standard Proof Set	50.00	80.00
PSA138	2003 (4)	3,669	KM#1039, 1044-1046	—	180
PSB138	2004 (11)	4,101	KM#986-991, 994, 1047-1049, 1055 Executive Proof Set	—	80.00
PSC138	2004 (11)	12,968	KM#986-991, 994, 1047-1049, 1055 Deluxe Proof Set	—	80.00
PSD138	2004 (11)	17,951	KM#986-991, 994, 1047-1049, 1055 Standard Proof Set	—	80.00
PS138	2005 (12)	4,290	KM#986-991, 994, 1050-1054 Executive Set	146	95.00
PS139	2005 (12)	14,899	KM#986-991, 994, 1050-1054 Deluxe Proof Set	80.00	95.00
PS140	2005 (12)	21,374	KM#986-991, 994, 1050-1054, Standard Proof Set	60.00	95.00
PS141	2005 (3)	417	KM#1068-1070	850	1,350
PS142	2005 (4)	1,439	KM#1068-1071	1,895	2,850
PS143	2005 (3)	2,500	KM#1064-1066	820	1,100
PS144	2005 (4)	2,500	KM#1064-1067	1,925	2,600
PS145	2005 (2)	—	P39, P40	—	175
PS146	2006 (13)	5,000	KM#986-991, 994, 1057-1062 Executive Proof Set, wooden case	—	140
PS147	2006 (13)	15,000	KM#986-991, 994, 1057-1062 Deluxe Proof Set	82.50	140
PS148	2006 (13)	30,000	KM#986-991, 994, 1057-1062 Standard Proof Set	65.00	140
PS149	2006 (5)	3,000	KM#1000a, 1012a, 1018a, 1039, 1063a	475	525
PS150	2006 (3)	1,750	KM#1001, 1002, 1072	1,015	1,150
PS151	2006 (4)	1,750	KM#1001-1003, 1072	2,091	2,650
PS152	2007 (13)	30,000	KM#986-991, 994, 1057-1062	65.00	140
PS153	2007 (4)	1,750	KM#1001-1003, 1072	—	2,850
PS154	2007 (3)	750	KM#1001-1002, 1072	—	1,200
PS155	2007 (2)	5,000	KM#1001-1002	—	550
PS156	2007 (5)	3,000	KM#P33, P35-P38	450	500
PS160	2002 (4)	—	KM#1029, 1079-1081	—	175
PS161	2003 (4)	1,250	KM#1040-1043	—	2,800
PS162	2004 (4)	—	KM#1029, 1079-1081	—	175
PS163	2004 (4)	973	KM#1008-1011	—	3,000
PS164	2005 (4)	2,360	KM#1063, 1085-1087	—	185
PS165	2006 (4)	—	KM#1029, 1079-1081	—	175
PS166	2006 (4)	—	KM#1008-1011	—	2,900
PS167	2007 (4)	—	KM#1078, 1088-1090	—	185
PS168	2007 (4)	—	KM#1091-1094	—	2,950
PS169	2007 (4)	—	KM#1091a-1094a	—	5,850
PS170	2008 (4)	—	KM#1095-1098	—	225
PS171	2008 (4)	—	KM#1099-1102	—	3,000
PS172	2008 (4)	—	KM#1099a-1102a	—	5,850

GREECE

The Hellenic (Greek) Republic is situated in southeastern Europe on the southern tip of the Balkan Peninsula. The republic includes many islands, the most important of which are Crete and the Ionian Islands. Greece (including islands) has an area of 50,944 sq. mi. (131,940 sq. km.) and a population of 10.3 million. Capital: Athens. Greece is still largely agricultural. Tobacco, cotton, fruit and wool are exported.

MINT MARKS

(a) - Paris, privy marks only
A - Paris
B - Vienna
BB – Strassburg
E – Madrid
F – Pessac, France
H - Heaton, Birmingham
K - Bordeaux
KN - King's Norton
(p) - Poissy – Thunderbolt
S – Vantaa (Suomi), Finland
(an) = Anthemion – Greek National Mint, Athens

MONETARY SYSTEM

Commencing 1831
100 Lepta = 1 Drachma

REPUBLIC

DECIMAL COINAGE

KM# 132 10 DRACHMES

7.5000 g., Copper-Nickel, 26 mm. **Subject:** Democritus **Obv:** Atom design **Rev:** Head left

Date	Mintage	F	VF	XF	Unc	BU
2002	—	—	0.25	0.50	1.25	2.50

EURO COINAGE

European Union Issues

The Greek Euro coinage series contains the denomination in Lepta as well.

KM# 181 EURO CENT

2.2700 g., Copper Plated Steel, 16.2 mm. **Obv:** Ancient Athenian trireme **Obv. Designer:** George Stamatopoulos **Rev:** Denomination and globe **Rev. Designer:** Luc Luycx **Edge:** Plain

Date	Mintage	F	VF	XF	Unc	BU
2002	101,000,000	—	—	—	0.35	—
2002 F in star	15,000,000	—	—	—	1.25	—
2003	35,200,000	—	—	—	0.35	—
2003 Proof	7,000,000	—	—	—	—	—
2004	50,000,000	—	—	—	0.35	—
2005	15,000,000	—	—	—	0.35	—
2006	45,000,000	—	—	—	0.35	—
2007	60,000,000	—	—	—	0.35	—
2008	24,000,000	—	—	—	0.35	—
2009	50,000,000	—	—	—	0.35	—
2010	27,000,000	—	—	—	0.35	—

KM# 182 2 EURO CENT

3.0300 g., Copper Plated Steel, 18.7 mm. **Obv:** Corvette sailing ship **Obv. Designer:** George Stamatopoulos **Rev:** Denomination and globe **Rev. Designer:** Luc Luycx **Edge:** Grooved

Date	Mintage	F	VF	XF	Unc	BU
2002	176,000,000	—	—	—	0.50	—
2002 F in star	18,000,000	—	—	—	1.00	—
2003	10,000,000	—	—	—	0.50	—
2003 Proof	500,000	—	—	—	—	—
2004	25,000,000	—	—	—	0.50	—
2005	15,000,000	—	—	—	0.50	—
2006	45,000,000	—	—	—	0.50	—
2007	25,000,103	—	—	—	0.50	—
2008	68,000,000	—	—	—	0.50	—
2009	16,000,000	—	—	—	0.50	—
2010	32,000,000	—	—	—	0.50	—

KM# 183 5 EURO CENT

3.8600 g., Copper Plated Steel, 21.2 mm. **Obv:** Freighter **Obv. Designer:** George Stamatopoulos **Rev:** Denomination and globe **Rev. Designer:** Luc Luycx **Edge:** Plain

Date	Mintage	F	VF	XF	Unc	BU
2002	211,000,000	—	—	—	1.00	—
2002 F in star	90,000,000	—	—	—	1.25	—
2003	750,000	—	—	—	1.00	—
2003 Proof	—	—	—	—	—	—
2004	250,000	—	—	—	1.00	—
2005	1,000,000	—	—	—	1.00	—
2006	50,000,000	—	—	—	1.00	—
2007	55,005,598	—	—	—	1.00	—
2008	50,000,000	—	—	—	1.00	—
2009	38,000,000	—	—	—	1.00	—
2010	5,000,000	—	—	—	1.00	—

KM# 184 10 EURO CENT

4.0700 g., Brass, 19.7 mm. **Obv:** Bust of Rhgas Feriaou's half right **Obv. Designer:** George Stamatopoulos **Rev:** Denomination and map **Rev. Designer:** Luc Luycx **Edge:** Reeded

Date	Mintage	F	VF	XF	Unc	BU
2002	138,000,000	—	—	—	1.25	—
2002 F in star	100,000,000	—	—	—	2.00	—
2003	600,000	—	—	—	1.25	—
2003 Proof	—	—	—	—	—	—
2004	10,000,000	—	—	—	1.25	—
2005	25,000,000	—	—	—	1.25	—
2006	45,000,000	—	—	—	1.25	—

KM# 211 10 EURO CENT

4.0700 g., Brass, 19.25 mm. **Obv:** Bust of Rhgas Feriaou's half right **Obv. Designer:** George Stamatopoulos **Rev:** Relief map of Western Europe, stars, lines and value **Rev. Designer:** Luc Luycx **Edge:** Reeded

Date	Mintage	F	VF	XF	Unc	BU
2007	63,000,000	—	—	—	1.25	—
2008	40,000,000	—	—	—	1.25	—
2009	46,000,000	—	—	—	1.25	—
2010	5,000,000	—	—	—	1.25	—

KM# 185 20 EURO CENT

5.7300 g., Brass, 22.25 mm. **Obv:** Bust of John Kapodistrias half right **Obv. Designer:** George Stamatopoulos **Rev:** Denomination and map **Rev. Designer:** Luc Luycx **Edge:** Notched

Date	Mintage	F	VF	XF	Unc	BU
2002	209,000,000	—	—	—	1.25	—
2002 E in star	120,000,000	—	—	—	2.25	—
2003	800,000	—	—	—	1.25	—
2003 Proof	—	—	—	—	—	—
2004	500,000	—	—	—	1.25	—
2005	1,000,000	—	—	—	1.25	—
2006	1,000,000	—	—	—	1.25	—

KM# 212 20 EURO CENT

5.7300 g., Brass, 22.1 mm. **Obv:** Bust of John Kapodistrias' half right **Obv. Designer:** George Stamatopoulos **Rev:** Relief map of Western Europe, stars, lines and value **Rev. Designer:** Luc Luycx **Edge:** Notched

Date	Mintage	F	VF	XF	Unc	BU
2007	1,000,000	—	—	—	1.25	—
2008	20,000,000	—	—	—	1.25	—
2009	24,000,000	—	—	—	1.25	—
2010	12,000,000	—	—	—	1.25	—

KM# 186 50 EURO CENT

7.8100 g., Brass, 24.2 mm. **Obv:** Bust of El. Venizelos half left **Obv. Designer:** George Stamatopoulos **Rev:** Denomination and map **Rev. Designer:** Luc Luycx **Edge:** Reeded

Date	Mintage	F	VF	XF	Unc	BU
2002	93,000,000	—	—	—	1.50	—
2002 F in star	70,000,000	—	—	—	2.50	—
2003	700,000	—	—	—	1.50	—
2003 Proof	—	—	—	—	—	—
2004	500,000	—	—	—	1.50	—
2005	1,000,000	—	—	—	1.50	—
2006	1,000,000	—	—	—	1.50	—

KM# 213 50 EURO CENT

7.8100 g., Brass, 24.2 mm. **Obv:** Bust of El. Venizelos half left **Obv. Designer:** George Stamatopoulos **Rev:** Relief map of Western Europe, stars, lines and value **Rev. Designer:** Luc Luycx **Edge:** Reeded

Date	Mintage	F	VF	XF	Unc	BU
2007	1,000,000	—	—	—	1.00	1.50
2008	10,000,000	—	—	—	1.00	1.50
2009	7,000,000	—	—	—	1.00	1.50
2010	6,000,000	—	—	—	1.00	1.50

KM# 187 EURO

7.5000 g., Bi-Metallic Copper-Nickel center in Nickel-Brass ring, 23.25 mm. **Obv:** Ancient Athenian coin design **Obv. Designer:** George Stamatopoulos **Rev:** Denomination and map **Rev. Designer:** Luc Luycx **Edge:** Segmented reeding

Date	Mintage	F	VF	XF	Unc	BU
2002	61,500,000	—	—	—	4.00	—
2002 S in star	50,000,000	—	—	—	6.00	—
2003	11,000,000	—	—	—	7.50	—
2003 Proof	—	—	—	—	—	—
2004	10,000,000	—	—	—	5.00	—
2005	10,000,000	—	—	—	5.00	—
2006	10,000,000	—	—	—	5.00	—

KM# 214 EURO

7.5000 g., Bi-Metallic Copper-Nickel center in Nickel-Brass ring, 23.25 mm. **Obv:** Ancient Athenian coin design **Obv. Designer:** George Stamatopoulos **Rev:** Relief map of Western Europe, stars, lines and value **Rev. Designer:** Luc Luycx **Edge:** Segmented reeding

Date	Mintage	F	VF	XF	Unc	BU
2007	24,000,000	—	—	—	3.00	4.00
2008	4,000,000	—	—	—	3.00	4.00
2009	18,000,000	—	—	—	3.00	4.00
2010	11,000,000	—	—	—	3.00	4.00

KM# 188 2 EURO

8.5000 g., Bi-Metallic Nickel-Brass center in Copper-Nickel ring, 25.75 mm. **Obv:** Europa seated on a bull **Obv. Designer:** George Stamatopoulos **Rev:** Denomination and map **Rev. Designer:** Luc Luycx **Edge:** Reeded with Greek legend and stars

Date	Mintage	F	VF	XF	Unc	BU
2002	75,400,000	—	—	—	4.00	—
2002 S in star	70,000,000	—	—	—	6.50	—
2003	550,000	—	—	—	20.00	—
2003 Proof	—	—	—	—	—	—
2004 In sets only	30,000	—	—	—	50.00	—
2005	1,000,000	—	—	—	4.00	—
2006	1,000,000	—	—	—	4.00	—

KM# 209 2 EURO

8.5000 g., Bi-Metallic Nickel-Brass center in Copper-Nickel ring., 25.75 mm. **Subject:** 2004 Olympics **Obv:** Discus thrower **Rev:** Denomination and map **Edge:** Reeded with Greek legend and stars

Date	Mintage	F	VF	XF	Unc	BU
2004	49,500,000	—	—	—	4.00	6.00
2004 Prooflike	500,000	—	—	—	—	15.00

KM# 215 2 EURO

8.5000 g., Bi-Metallic Nickel-Brass center in Copper-Nickel ring, 25.75 mm. **Obv:** Europa seated on a bull **Obv. Designer:** George Stamatopoulos **Rev:** Relief map of Western Europe, stars, lines and value **Rev. Designer:** Luc Luycx **Edge:** Reeded with Greek legend and stars

Date	Mintage	F	VF	XF	Unc	BU
2007 In sets only	15,000	—	—	—	—	25.00
2008	2,000,000	—	—	—	3.00	10.00
2009	982,000	—	—	—	3.00	5.00
2010	2,000,000	—	—	—	3.00	5.00

KM# 216 2 EURO

8.5000 g., Bi-Metallic Nickel-Brass center in Copper-Nickel ring, 25.75 mm. **Subject:** 50th Anniversary - Treaty of Rome **Obv:** Open treaty book **Rev:** Large value at left, modified outline of Europe at right **Edge:** Reeded with Greek legend and stars

Date	Mintage	F	VF	XF	Unc	BU
2007	4,000,000	—	—	—	—	9.00

KM# 227 2 EURO

8.5000 g., Bi-Metallic Nickel-Brass center in Copper-Nickel ring, 25.75 mm. **Subject:** European Monetary Union, 10th Anniversary **Obv:** Stick figure and Euro symbol **Edge:** Reeded with Greek legend and stars

Date	Mintage	F	VF	XF	Unc	BU
2009	4,000,000	—	—	—	—	7.00

KM# 236 2 EURO

8.5000 g., Bi-Metallic Nickel-Brass center in Copper-Nickel ring, 25.75 mm. **Subject:** Battle of Marathon, 2500th Anniversary **Rev:** Ancient Greek Warrior holding javelin running **Edge:** Reeded with Greek legend and stars

Date	Mintage	F	VF	XF	Unc	BU
2010	3,500,000	—	—	—	—	9.00

KM# 239 2 EURO

8.5000 g., Bi-Metallic Nickel-Brass center in Copper-Nickel ring, 25.75 mm. **Subject:** Special Olympics - Athens

Date	Mintage	F	VF	XF	Unc	BU
2011	—	—	—	—	6.00	7.50

KM# 191 10 EURO

34.0000 g., 0.9250 Silver 1.0111 oz. ASW, 40 mm. **Subject:** Olympics **Obv:** Olympic rings in wreath above value within circle of stars **Rev:** Ancient and modern discus throwers **Edge:** Plain

Date	Mintage	F	VF	XF	Unc	BU
ND(2003) Proof	68,000	Value: 60.00				

KM# 193 10 EURO

34.0000 g., 0.9250 Silver 1.0111 oz. ASW, 40 mm. **Subject:** Olympics **Obv:** Olympic rings in wreath above value within circle of stars **Rev:** Ancient and modern javelin throwers **Edge:** Plain

Date	Mintage	F	VF	XF	Unc	BU
ND(2003) Proof	68,000	Value: 60.00				

KM# 194 10 EURO

34.0000 g., 0.9250 Silver 1.0111 oz. ASW, 40 mm. **Subject:** Olympics **Obv:** Olympic rings in wreath above value within circle of stars **Rev:** Ancient and modern long jumpers **Edge:** Plain

Date	Mintage	F	VF	XF	Unc	BU
ND(2003) Proof	68,000	Value: 60.00				

KM# 196 10 EURO

34.0000 g., 0.9250 Silver 1.0111 oz. ASW, 40 mm. **Subject:** Olympics **Obv:** Olympic rings in wreath above value within circle of stars **Rev:** Ancient and modern relay runners **Edge:** Plain

Date	Mintage	F	VF	XF	Unc	BU
ND(2003) Proof	68,000	Value: 60.00				

KM# 197 10 EURO

34.0000 g., 0.9250 Silver 1.0111 oz. ASW, 40 mm. **Subject:** Olympics **Obv:** Olympic rings in wreath above value within circle of stars **Rev:** Ancient and modern horsemen **Edge:** Plain

Date	Mintage	F	VF	XF	Unc	BU
ND(2003) Proof	68,000	Value: 60.00				

KM# 199 10 EURO

34.0000 g., 0.9250 Silver 1.0111 oz. ASW, 40 mm. **Subject:** Olympics **Obv:** Olympic rings in wreath above value within circle of stars **Rev:** Modern ribbon dancer and two ancient female acrobats **Edge:** Plain

Date	Mintage	F	VF	XF	Unc	BU
ND(2003) Proof	68,000	Value: 60.00				

KM# 200 10 EURO

34.0000 g., 0.9250 Silver 1.0111 oz. ASW, 40 mm. **Subject:** Olympics **Obv:** Olympic rings in wreath above value within a circle of stars **Rev:** Ancient and modern female swimmers **Edge:** Plain

Date	Mintage	F	VF	XF	Unc	BU
ND(2003) Proof	68,000	Value: 60.00				

KM# 208 10 EURO

9.7500 g., 0.9250 Silver 0.2899 oz. ASW, 28.25 mm. **Subject:** Greek Presidency of E. U. **Obv:** National arms in wreath above value **Rev:** Stylized document design **Edge:** Notched

Date	Mintage	F	VF	XF	Unc	BU
2003 Proof	50,000	Value: 80.00				

KM# 190 10 EURO
34.0000 g., 0.9250 Silver 1.0111 oz. ASW, 40 mm. **Subject:** Olympics **Obv:** Olympic rings in wreath above value within circle of stars **Rev:** Ancient and modern runners **Edge:** Plain **Note:** Olympics

Date	Mintage	F	VF	XF	Unc	BU
ND (2003) Proof	68,000	Value: 60.00				

KM# 202 10 EURO
34.0000 g., 0.9250 Silver 1.0111 oz. ASW, 40 mm. **Subject:** Olympics **Obv:** Olympic rings in wreath above value within circle of stars **Rev:** Ancient and modern weight lifters **Edge:** Plain

Date	Mintage	F	VF	XF	Unc	BU
ND(2004) Proof	68,000	Value: 60.00				

KM# 203 10 EURO
34.0000 g., 0.9250 Silver 1.0111 oz. ASW, 40 mm. **Subject:** Olympics **Obv:** Olympic rings in wreath above value within circle of stars **Rev:** Ancient and modern wrestlers **Edge:** Plain

Date	Mintage	F	VF	XF	Unc	BU
ND(2004) Proof	68,000	Value: 60.00				

KM# 205 10 EURO
34.0000 g., 0.9250 Silver 1.0111 oz. ASW, 40 mm. **Subject:** Olympics **Obv:** Olympic rings in wreath above value within circle of stars **Rev:** Ancient and modern handball players **Edge:** Plain

Date	Mintage	F	VF	XF	Unc	BU
ND(2004) Proof	68,000	Value: 60.00				

KM# 206 10 EURO
34.0000 g., 0.9250 Silver 1.0111 oz. ASW, 40 mm. **Subject:** Olympics **Obv:** Olympic rings in wreath above value within circle of stars **Rev:** Ancient and modern soccer players **Edge:** Plain

Date	Mintage	F	VF	XF	Unc	BU
ND(2004) Proof	68,000	Value: 60.00				

KM# 230 10 EURO
34.0000 g., 0.9250 Silver 1.0111 oz. ASW **Obv:** Wreath **Rev:** Torch runner and map of Australia

Date	Mintage	F	VF	XF	Unc	BU
2004 Proof	10,000	Value: 110				

KM# 231 10 EURO
34.0000 g., 0.9250 Silver 1.0111 oz. ASW **Rev:** Torch runner and map of Asia

Date	Mintage	F	VF	XF	Unc	BU
2004 Proof	10,000	Value: 110				

KM# 232 10 EURO
34.0000 g., 0.9250 Silver 1.0111 oz. ASW **Rev:** Torch runner and map of Africa

Date	Mintage	F	VF	XF	Unc	BU
2004 Proof	10,000	Value: 110				

KM# 233 10 EURO
34.0000 g., 0.9250 Silver 1.0111 oz. ASW **Rev:** Torch runner and map of North and South America

Date	Mintage	F	VF	XF	Unc	BU
2004 Proof	10,000	Value: 110				

KM# 217 10 EURO
9.7500 g., 0.9250 Silver 0.2899 oz. ASW **Obv:** National arms above stylized flowers **Rev:** Four Titans above flowers in camp

Date	Mintage	F	VF	XF	Unc	BU
2005 Proof	25,000	Value: 45.00				

KM# 218 10 EURO
9.7500 g., 0.9250 Silver 0.2899 oz. ASW, 28.25 mm. **Subject:** PATRA - European Capitol of Culture - Achaia **Obv:** National arms at upper right, stylized bridge below **Rev:** PATRA logo **Edge:** Plain

Date	Mintage	F	VF	XF	Unc	BU
2006 Proof	—	Value: 50.00				

KM# 219 10 EURO
34.0000 g., 0.9250 Silver 1.0111 oz. ASW, 40.00 mm. **Obv:** National arms above stylizes flowers **Rev:** Outline of Greece at left, statue of Zeus, flowers at right **Edge:** Plain

Date	Mintage	F	VF	XF	Unc	BU
2006 Proof	5,000	Value: 55.00				

KM# 220 10 EURO
34.0000 g., 0.9250 Silver 1.0111 oz. ASW, 40.00 mm. **Subject:** National Parks - Mount Olympus - International Biosphere Reserve **Obv:** National arms above stylized flowers **Rev:** Archaeological outline of Dion City above landscape **Edge:** Plain

Date	Mintage	F	VF	XF	Unc	BU
2006 Proof	5,000	Value: 55.00				

KM# 221 10 EURO
34.0000 g., 0.9250 Silver 1.0111 oz. ASW, 40.00 mm. **Subject:** National Parks - Arkoudorema River in Southern Pindos - Valia Kalda **Obv:** National arms on stylized tree **Rev:** Outlined map at upper left, bird perched on stalk, flowers at center right **Edge:** Plain

Date	Mintage	F	VF	XF	Unc	BU
2007 Proof	5,000	Value: 60.00				

KM# 222 10 EURO
34.0000 g., 0.9250 Silver 1.0111 oz. ASW, 40.00 mm. **Subject:** National Parks - Valia Kalda - Southern Pindos **Obv:** National arms on stylized tree **Rev:** Tree line **Edge:** Plain

Date	Mintage	F	VF	XF	Unc	BU
2007 Proof	5,000	Value: 60.00				

KM# 223 10 EURO
9.7500 g., 0.9250 Silver 0.2899 oz. ASW, 28.25 mm. **Subject:** 30th Anniversary Death of Maria Callas, Operatic Soprano **Obv:** National arms above denomination, facsimile signature below, music scores in background **Rev:** Bust of Maria Callas right **Edge:** Plain **Shape:** Spanish Flower

Date	Mintage	F	VF	XF	Unc	BU
2007 Proof	5,000	Value: 50.00				

KM# 224 10 EURO
9.7500 g., 0.9250 Silver 0.2899 oz. ASW, 28.25 mm. **Subject:** 50th Anniversary death of Nikos Kazantzakis, Author **Obv:** National arms above denomination, facsimile signature below **Rev:** Head of N. Kazantzakis facing 3/4 left **Edge:** Plain **Shape:** Spanish Flower

Date	Mintage	F	VF	XF	Unc	BU
2007 Proof	5,000	Value: 50.00				

KM# 225 10 EURO
9.7500 g., 0.9250 Silver 0.2899 oz. ASW, 28.25 mm. **Subject:** Acropolis Museum **Obv:** Panoramic view of the Acropolis **Rev:** Pediment sculpture

Date	Mintage	F	VF	XF	Unc	BU
2008	10,000	—	—	—	—	50.00

KM# 226 10 EURO
9.7500 g., 0.9250 Silver 0.2899 oz. ASW **Subject:** Yannis Ritsas

Date	Mintage	F	VF	XF	Unc	BU
2009 Proof	—	Value: 50.00				

KM# 228 10 EURO
9.7500 g., 0.2899 Silver 0.0909 oz. ASW, 28.25 mm. **Subject:** International Year of Astronomy

Date	Mintage	F	VF	XF	Unc	BU
2009 Proof	—	Value: 45.00				

KM# 237 10 EURO
34.0000 g., 0.9250 Silver 1.0111 oz. ASW, 40 mm. **Subject:** Sofia Vempo, 100th Anniversary of Birth **Obv:** Sofia Vempo portrait **Rev:** Stave, national emblem and value **Shape:** Spanish flower

Date	Mintage	F	VF	XF	Unc	BU
2010 Proof	5,000	Value: 65.00				

KM# 238 10 EURO
9.7500 g., 0.9250 Silver 0.2899 oz. ASW, 28.25 mm. **Subject:** International Year of Biodiversity **Obv:** Various species of Biodiversity **Rev:** Nature's species, national emblem and value **Shape:** Spanish flower

Date	Mintage	F	VF	XF	Unc	BU
2010 Proof	5,000	Value: 50.00				

KM# 210 20 EURO
24.0000 g., 0.9250 Silver 0.7137 oz. ASW, 37 mm. **Subject:** Bank of Greece 75th Anniversary **Obv:** Value **Rev:** Flag

Date	Mintage	F	VF	XF	Unc	BU
2003 Proof	15,000	Value: 1,100				

KM# 192 100 EURO
10.0000 g., 0.9999 Gold 0.3215 oz. AGW, 25 mm. **Subject:** Olympics **Obv:** Olympic rings in wreath above value within circle of stars **Rev:** Knossos Palace **Edge:** Plain

Date	Mintage	F	VF	XF	Unc	BU
ND(2003) Proof	28,000	Value: 525				

KM# 195 100 EURO
10.0000 g., 0.9999 Gold 0.3215 oz. AGW, 25 mm. **Subject:** Olympics **Obv:** Olympic rings in wreath above value within circle of stars **Rev:** Krypte archway **Edge:** Plain

Date	Mintage	F	VF	XF	Unc	BU
ND(2003) Proof	28,000	Value: 525				

KM# 198 100 EURO
10.0000 g., 0.9999 Gold 0.3215 oz. AGW, 25 mm. **Subject:** Olympics **Obv:** Olympic rings in wreath above value within circle of stars **Rev:** Panathenean Stadium **Edge:** Plain

Date	Mintage	F	VF	XF	Unc	BU
ND(2003) Proof	28,000	Value: 525				

KM# 201 100 EURO
10.0000 g., 0.9999 Gold 0.3215 oz. AGW, 25 mm. **Subject:** Olympics **Obv:** Olympic rings in wreath above value within circle of stars **Rev:** Zappeion Mansion **Edge:** Plain

Date	Mintage	F	VF	XF	Unc	BU
ND(2003) Proof	28,000	Value: 525				

KM# 204 100 EURO
10.0000 g., 0.9999 Gold 0.3215 oz. AGW, 25 mm. **Subject:** Olympics **Obv:** Olympic rings in wreath above value within circle of stars **Rev:** Acropolis **Edge:** Plain

Date	Mintage	F	VF	XF	Unc	BU
ND(2004) Proof	28,000	Value: 525				

KM# 207 100 EURO
10.0000 g., 0.9999 Gold 0.3215 oz. AGW, 25 mm. **Subject:** Olympics **Obv:** Olympic rings in wreath above value within circle of stars **Rev:** Academy of Athens **Edge:** Plain

Date	Mintage	F	VF	XF	Unc	BU
ND(2004) Proof	28,000	Value: 525				

KM# 234 100 EURO
10.0000 g., 0.9990 Gold 0.3212 oz. AGW **Rev:** Classical female handing torch to kneeling runner

Date	Mintage	F	VF	XF	Unc	BU
2004 Proof	10,000	Value: 625				

KM# 235 100 EURO
10.0000 g., 0.9990 Gold 0.3212 oz. AGW **Rev:** Torch runner and flag

Date	Mintage	F	VF	XF	Unc	BU
2004 Proof	10,000	Value: 625				

KM# 229 200 EURO
17.0000 g., 0.9160 Gold 0.5006 oz. AGW, 28 mm. **Subject:** Bank of Greece, 75th Anniversary

Date	Mintage	F	VF	XF	Unc	BU
2003 Proof	1,000	Value: 7,000				

MINT SETS

KM#	Date	Mintage	Identification	Issue Price	Mkt Val
MS6	2002 (8)	50,000	KM#181-188	—	30.00
MS7	2002F (8)	5,000	KM#181-188 Issued by Ministry of Finance	—	300
MS8	2003 (8)	—	KM#181-188	—	40.00
MS9	2003 (9)	—	KM#181-188, 208	—	80.00
MS11	2004 (8)	20,000	KM#181-188 2004 Discobole commemorating Olympic Games in Athens	—	65.00
MS12	2005 (8)	25,000	KM#181-188	—	35.00
MS13	2005 (9)	25,000	KM#181-188, 220 Mount Olympus as a National Park	—	70.00
MS14	2006 (9)	25,000	KM#181-188 (2005), 220 Aegina - Korinth set	28.00	70.00
MS15	2006 (9)	25,000	KM#181-188, 218 Patras - Cultural Capital of Europe	50.00	70.00
MS16	2007 (8)	15,000	KM#181-183, 211-215 Ancient Coins of the Aegean Sea	—	50.00
MS17	2007 (9)	15,000	KM#181-183, 211-215, 224 Nikos Kazantzakis	50.00	75.00
MS18	2007 (9)	15,000	KM#181-183, 211-215, 223 Maria Callas	50.00	95.00
MS19	2008 (9)	15,000	KM#181-183, 211-215	28.00	40.00
MS20	2008 (9)	10,000	KM#181-183, 211-215, 225	45.00	55.00
MS21	2009 (8)	7,500	KM#181-183, 211-215	28.00	45.00
MS22	2009 (9)	5,000	KM#181-183, 211-215, 226	45.00	55.00
MS23	2009 (9)	5,000	KM#181-183, 211-215, 228	45.00	55.00
MS24	2010 (8)	7,500	KM#181-183, 211-215	28.00	30.00
MS25	2010 (8)	7,500	KM#181-183, 211-214, 236	28.00	30.00

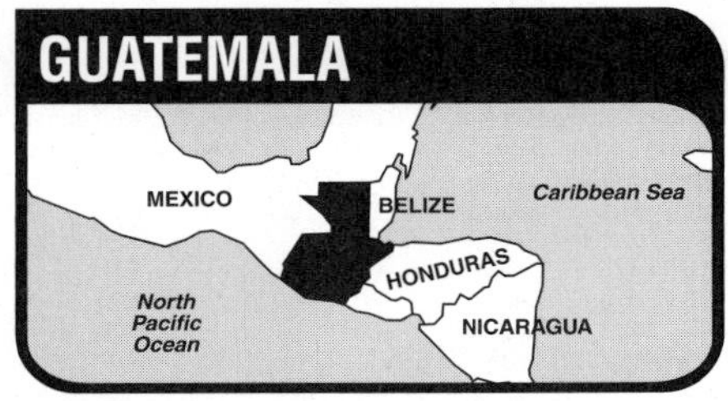

The Republic of Guatemala, the northernmost of the five Central American republics, has an area of 42,042 sq. mi. (108,890 sq. km.) and a population of 10.7 million. Capital: Guatemala City. The economy of Guatemala is heavily dependent on agriculture, however, the country is rich in nickel resources which are being developed. Coffee, cotton and bananas are exported.

Guatemala, once the site of an ancient Mayan civilization, was conquered by Pedro de Alvarado, the resourceful lieutenant of Cortes who undertook the conquest from Mexico. Cruel but strategically skillful, he progressed rapidly along the Pacific coastal lowlands to the highland plain of Quetzaltenango where the decisive battle for Guatemala was fought. After routing the Indian forces, he established the city of Guatemala in 1524. The Spanish Captaincy-General of Guatemala included all Central America but Panama. Guatemala declared its independence of Spain in 1821 and was absorbed into the Mexican empire of Augustin Iturbide (1822-23). From 1823 to 1839 Guatemala was a constituent state of the Central American Republic. Upon dissolution of that confederation, Guatemala proclaimed itself an independent republic. Like El Salvador, Guatemala suffered from internal strife between right-wing, US-backed military government and leftist indigenous peoples from ca. 1954 to ca. 1997.

MINT MARKS
(L) – London, Royal Mint

REPUBLIC

REFORM COINAGE

100 Centavos = 1 Quetzal

KM# 282 CENTAVO (Un)
0.8000 g., Aluminum, 19 mm. **Subject:** Fray Bartolome de las Casas **Obv:** National arms **Rev:** Bust left **Edge:** Plain **Note:** 7-sided interior field

Date	Mintage	F	VF	XF	Unc	BU
2007	—	—	—	0.15	0.25	0.50

KM# 276.6 5 CENTAVOS
1.6000 g., Copper-Nickel, 16 mm. **Obv:** National arms, smaller sized emblem, no dots by date **Obv. Legend:** REPUBLICA DE

GUATEMALA 1997 **Rev:** Kapok tree center, value at right, ground below **Edge:** Reeded **Note:** Varieties exist.

Date	Mintage	F	VF	XF	Unc	BU
2006	—	—	—	0.15	0.30	0.50

KM# 277.6 10 CENTAVOS

3.2000 g., Copper-Nickel, 21 mm. **Obv:** National arms, small letters in legend **Obv. Legend:** REPUBLICA DE GUATEMALA **Rev:** Monolith **Note:** Varieties exist.

Date	Mintage	F	VF	XF	Unc	BU
2006	—	—	0.15	0.25	0.75	1.00

KM# 283 50 CENTAVOS

5.5000 g., Nickel-Brass, 26.5 mm. **Obv:** National arms **Rev:** Whitenun orchid (lycaste skinneri var. alba orchidaceae) **Edge:** Reeded

Date	Mintage	F	VF	XF	Unc	BU
2001	—	—	—	0.50	1.25	1.75
2007	—	—	—	0.50	1.25	1.75

KM# 284 QUETZAL

11.0000 g., Nickel-Brass, 29 mm. **Obv:** National arms **Rev:** PAZ above stylized dove **Edge:** Reeded

Date	Mintage	F	VF	XF	Unc	BU
2001 Small letters	—	—	—	1.00	2.50	3.00
2006	—	—	—	1.00	2.50	3.00

KM# 287 QUETZAL

31.1035 g., 0.9999 Silver 0.9999 oz. ASW, 30 mm. **Subject:** Canonization of Brother Pedro Betancourt **Obv:** National arms **Rev:** Standing monk **Edge:** Plain

Date	Mintage	F	VF	XF	Unc	BU
ND(2002) Proof	6,000	Value: 60.00				

KM# 288 QUETZAL

31.1035 g., 0.9990 Silver 0.9990 oz. ASW **Subject:** Discovery of the Americas **Obv:** Shields around inner circle holding arms with date below **Rev:** Nature with fish in canoe

Date	Mintage	F	VF	XF	Unc	BU
2002 Proof	—	Value: 65.00				

GUERNSEY

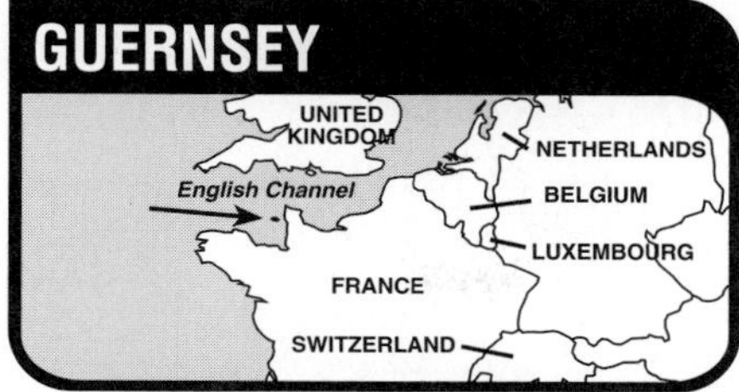

The Bailiwick of Guernsey, a British crown dependency located in the English Channel 30 miles (48 km.) west of Normandy, France, has an area of 30 sq. mi. (194 sq. km.)(including the isles of Alderney, Jethou, Herm, Brechou, and Sark), and a population of 54,000. Capital: St. Peter Port. Agriculture and cattle breeding are the main occupations.

Guernsey is administered by its own laws and customs. Unless the island is mentioned specifically, acts passed by the British Parliament are not applicable to Guernsey. During World War II, German troops occupied the island from June 30, 1940 till May 9,1945.

RULER
British

MONETARY SYSTEM
100 Pence = 1 Pound

BRITISH DEPENDENCY

STANDARD COINAGE

KM# 178 50 POUNDS

7.9800 g., 0.9160 Gold 0.2350 oz. AGW, 22.05 mm. **Ruler:** Elizabeth II **Subject:** Battle of Britain, 1940 **Rev:** Pilots scrrambling to planes, some in the sky **Edge:** Reeded

Date	Mintage	F	VF	XF	Unc	BU
2008 Proof	—	Value: 375				

DECIMAL COINAGE

100 Pence = 1 Pound

KM# 89 PENNY

3.5300 g., Copper Plated Steel, 20.3 mm. **Ruler:** Elizabeth II **Obv:** Head with tiara right **Obv. Designer:** Ian Rank-Broadley **Rev:** Edible crab **Rev. Designer:** Robert Elderton **Edge:** Plain

Date	Mintage	F	VF	XF	Unc	BU
2003	1,302,600	—	—	—	0.35	1.00
2006	1,731,000	—	—	—	0.35	0.75

KM# 96 2 PENCE

7.1200 g., Copper Plated Steel, 25.9 mm. **Ruler:** Elizabeth II **Obv:** Head with tiara, shield at left **Obv. Designer:** Ian Rank-Broadley **Rev:** Guernsey cows **Rev. Designer:** Robert Elderton **Edge:** Plain

Date	Mintage	F	VF	XF	Unc	BU
2003	662,600	—	—	—	0.50	1.00
2006	1,322,000	—	—	—	0.50	1.00

KM# 97 5 PENCE

3.2500 g., Copper-Nickel, 18 mm. **Ruler:** Elizabeth II **Obv:** Head with tiara right **Obv. Designer:** Ian Rank-Broadley **Rev:** Sailboat **Rev. Designer:** Robert Elderton **Edge:** Reeded

Date	Mintage	F	VF	XF	Unc	BU
2003	292,600	—	—	—	0.45	0.65
2006	1,217,000	—	—	—	0.45	0.65

KM# 149 10 PENCE

6.5000 g., Copper-Nickel, 24.5 mm. **Ruler:** Elizabeth II **Obv:** Crowned head right **Obv. Designer:** Ian Rank-Broadley **Rev:** Tomato plant **Rev. Designer:** Robert Elderton **Edge:** Reeded

Date	Mintage	F	VF	XF	Unc	BU
2003	32,600	—	—	—	0.60	0.85
2006	26,000	—	—	—	0.60	0.85

KM# 90 20 PENCE

5.1000 g., Copper-Nickel, 21.4 mm. **Ruler:** Elizabeth II **Obv:** Head with tiara right, small arms at left **Obv. Designer:** Ian Rank-Broadley **Rev:** Island map within cogwheel **Rev. Designer:** Robert Elderton **Shape:** 7-sided

Date	Mintage	F	VF	XF	Unc	BU
2003	732,600	—	—	—	0.90	1.25
2006	16,250	—	—	—	0.90	1.25
2009	—	—	—	—	0.90	1.25

KM# 145 50 PENCE

8.0000 g., Copper-Nickel, 27.3 mm. **Ruler:** Elizabeth II **Subject:** Coronation Jubilee **Obv:** Head with tiara right **Obv. Designer:** Ian Rank-Broadley **Rev:** Queen on horseback **Edge:** Plain **Shape:** 7-sided

Date	Mintage	F	VF	XF	Unc	BU
2003	—	—	—	—	1.50	2.50

KM# 145a 50 PENCE

8.1000 g., 0.9250 Silver 0.2409 oz. ASW, 27.3 mm. **Ruler:** Elizabeth II **Subject:** Coronation Jubilee **Obv:** Head with tiara right **Obv. Designer:** Ian Rank-Broadley **Rev:** Queen on horseback **Edge:** Plain **Shape:** 7-sided

Date	Mintage	F	VF	XF	Unc	BU
2003 Proof	—	Value: 25.00				

KM# 146 50 PENCE

8.0000 g., Copper-Nickel, 27.3 mm. **Ruler:** Elizabeth II **Subject:** Coronation Jubilee **Obv:** Head with tiara right **Rev:** Queen on throne **Edge:** Plain **Shape:** 7-sided

Date	Mintage	F	VF	XF	Unc	BU
2003	—	—	—	—	1.50	2.50

KM# 146a 50 PENCE

8.1000 g., 0.9250 Silver 0.2409 oz. ASW, 27.3 mm. **Ruler:** Elizabeth II **Subject:** Coronation Jubilee **Obv:** Head with tiara right **Rev:** Queen on throne **Edge:** Plain **Shape:** 7-sided

Date	Mintage	F	VF	XF	Unc	BU
2003 Proof	—	Value: 25.00				

KM# 147 50 PENCE

8.0000 g., Copper-Nickel, 27.3 mm. **Ruler:** Elizabeth II **Subject:** Coronation Jubilee **Obv:** Head with tiara right **Rev:** Crown **Edge:** Plain **Shape:** 7-sided

Date	Mintage	F	VF	XF	Unc	BU
2003	—	—	—	—	1.50	2.50

KM# 147a 50 PENCE

8.1000 g., 0.9250 Silver 0.2409 oz. ASW, 27.3 mm. **Ruler:** Elizabeth II **Subject:** Coronation Jubilee **Obv:** Head with tiara right **Rev:** Crown **Edge:** Plain **Shape:** 7-sided

Date	Mintage	F	VF	XF	Unc	BU
2003 Proof	—	Value: 25.00				

KM# 148 50 PENCE
8.0000 g., Copper-Nickel, 27.3 mm. **Ruler:** Elizabeth II **Subject:** Coronation Jubilee **Obv:** Head with tiara right **Rev:** Crowned ERII monogram **Edge:** Plain **Shape:** 7-sided

Date	Mintage	F	VF	XF	Unc	BU
2003	—	—	—	—	1.50	2.50

KM# 148a 50 PENCE
8.1000 g., 0.9250 Silver 0.2409 oz. ASW, 27.3 mm. **Ruler:** Elizabeth II **Subject:** Coronation Jubilee **Obv:** Head with tiara right **Rev:** Crowned ERII monogram **Edge:** Plain **Shape:** 7-sided

Date	Mintage	F	VF	XF	Unc	BU
2003 Proof	—	Value: 25.00				

KM# 156 50 PENCE
8.0000 g., Copper-Nickel, 27.3 mm. **Ruler:** Elizabeth II **Obv:** Head with tiara right **Rev:** Crossed flowers **Edge:** Plain **Shape:** 7-sided

Date	Mintage	F	VF	XF	Unc	BU
2003	—	—	—	—	1.75	2.75
2006	19,000	—	—	—	1.75	2.75
2008	—	—	—	—	1.75	2.75

KM# 110 POUND
9.5000 g., Nickel-Brass, 22.5 mm. **Ruler:** Elizabeth II **Subject:** Circulation Type **Obv:** Head with tiara right **Obv. Designer:** Ian Rank-Broadley **Rev:** Denomination **Edge:** Reeded

Date	Mintage	F	VF	XF	Unc	BU
2001	175,000	—	—	—	2.50	3.50
2003	46,600	—	—	—	2.50	3.50
2006	11,000	—	—	—	2.50	3.50

KM# 111 POUND
9.5000 g., 0.9250 Silver 0.2825 oz. ASW, 22.5 mm. **Subject:** Queen's 75th Birthday **Obv:** Head with tiara right **Rev:** Queen's portrait in wreath **Edge:** Reeded

Date	Mintage	F	VF	XF	Unc	BU
2001 Proof	50,000	Value: 28.00				

KM# 142 POUND
30.9300 g., 0.9250 Silver 0.9198 oz. ASW, 38.6 mm. **Ruler:** Elizabeth II **Obv:** Head with tiara right **Obv. Designer:** Ian Rank-Broadley **Rev:** 1/2-bust of William, Duke of Normandy holding sword at left **Edge:** Reeded

Date	Mintage	F	VF	XF	Unc	BU
2002	—	—	—	—	37.50	47.50

KM# 83 2 POUNDS
12.0000 g., Bi-Metallic Copper-Nickel center in Nickel-Brass ring, 28.35 mm. **Ruler:** Elizabeth II **Obv:** Head with tiara right **Obv. Designer:** Ian Rank-Broadley **Rev:** Latent image arms on cross **Rev. Designer:** Alan Copp **Edge:** BAILIWICK OF GUERNSEY

Date	Mintage	F	VF	XF	Unc	BU
2003	19,600	—	—	—	8.50	10.00
2006	9,500	—	—	—	8.50	10.00

KM# 106 5 POUNDS
28.2800 g., Copper-Nickel, 38.6 mm. **Ruler:** Elizabeth II **Subject:** Queen Victoria Centennial **Obv:** Head with tiara right **Obv. Designer:** Ian Rank-Broadley **Rev:** Bust of Queen Victoria left **Edge:** Reeded

Date	Mintage	F	VF	XF	Unc	BU
2001	12,754	—	—	—	7.50	8.50
2001 Proof	30,000	Value: 20.00				

KM# 106a 5 POUNDS
28.2800 g., 0.9250 Silver 0.8410 oz. ASW, 38.6 mm. **Ruler:** Elizabeth II **Subject:** Queen Victoria 1837-1901 **Obv:** Head with tiara right **Obv. Designer:** Ian Rank-Broadley **Rev:** Bust of Queen Victoria left **Edge:** Reeded

Date	Mintage	F	VF	XF	Unc	BU
2001 Proof	10,000	Value: 50.00				

KM# 108 5 POUNDS
28.2800 g., Copper-Nickel, 38.6 mm. **Ruler:** Elizabeth II **Subject:** Queen Elizabeth's 75th Birthday **Obv:** Head with tiara right **Obv. Designer:** Ian Rank-Broadley **Rev:** Queen's portrait in wreath **Edge:** Reeded

Date	Mintage	F	VF	XF	Unc	BU
2001	14,000	—	—	—	6.00	7.00

KM# 108a 5 POUNDS
28.2800 g., 0.9250 Silver 0.8410 oz. ASW, 38.6 mm. **Ruler:** Elizabeth II **Subject:** Queen's 75th Birthday **Obv:** Head with tiara right **Obv. Designer:** Ian Rank-Broadley **Rev:** Queen's portrait in wreath **Edge:** Reeded

Date	Mintage	F	VF	XF	Unc	BU
2001 Proof	20,000	Value: 55.00				

KM# 114 5 POUNDS
28.2800 g., Copper-Nickel, 38.6 mm. **Ruler:** Elizabeth II **Subject:** 19th Century Monarchy **Obv:** Head with tiara right **Obv. Designer:** Ian Rank-Broadley **Rev:** Four portraits **Edge:** Reeded

Date	Mintage	F	VF	XF	Unc	BU
2001	5,700	—	—	—	11.50	12.50

KM# 114a 5 POUNDS
28.2800 g., 0.9250 Silver 0.8410 oz. ASW, 38.6 mm. **Ruler:** Elizabeth II **Obv:** Head with tiara right **Obv. Designer:** Ian Rank-Broadley **Rev:** Four portraits **Edge:** Reeded

Date	Mintage	F	VF	XF	Unc	BU
2001 Proof	10,000	Value: 55.00				

KM# 115 5 POUNDS
1.1300 g., 0.9170 Gold 0.0333 oz. AGW, 13.9 mm. **Ruler:** Elizabeth II **Subject:** 19th Century Monarchy **Obv:** Head with tiara right **Obv. Designer:** Ian Rank-Broadley **Rev:** Four portraits **Edge:** Reeded

Date	Mintage	F	VF	XF	Unc	BU
2001 Proof	—	Value: 75.00				

KM# 117 5 POUNDS
1.1300 g., 0.9170 Gold 0.0333 oz. AGW, 13.9 mm. **Ruler:** Elizabeth II **Subject:** Queen Victoria 1837-1901 **Obv:** Head with tiara right **Obv. Designer:** Ian Rank-Broadley **Rev:** Queen Victoria's portrait **Edge:** Reeded

Date	Mintage	F	VF	XF	Unc	BU
2001 Proof	300	Value: 75.00				

KM# 118 5 POUNDS
1.1300 g., 0.9170 Gold 0.0333 oz. AGW, 13.9 mm. **Ruler:** Elizabeth II **Subject:** Queen's 75th Birthday **Obv:** Head with tiara right **Obv. Designer:** Ian Rank-Broadley **Rev:** Queen's portrait in wreath **Edge:** Reeded

Date	Mintage	F	VF	XF	Unc	BU
2001 Proof	250	Value: 75.00				

KM# 114b 5 POUNDS
39.9400 g., 0.9166 Gold 1.1770 oz. AGW, 38.6 mm. **Ruler:** Elizabeth II **Subject:** 19th Century Monarchy **Obv:** Head with tiara right **Obv. Designer:** Ian Rank-Broadley **Rev:** Four royal portraits **Edge:** Reeded

Date	Mintage	F	VF	XF	Unc	BU
2001 Proof	200	Value: 1,800				

KM# 119 5 POUNDS
27.7100 g., Copper-Nickel, 38.6 mm. **Ruler:** Elizabeth II **Subject:** The Golden Jubilee **Obv:** Head with tiara right **Obv. Designer:** Ian Rank-Broadley **Rev:** The queen in her coach **Edge:** Reeded

Date	Mintage	F	VF	XF	Unc	BU
2002	9,250	—	—	—	16.50	18.00

KM# 119a 5 POUNDS
28.2800 g., Base Metal Gilt Gold plated copper-nickel, 38.6 mm. **Ruler:** Elizabeth II **Subject:** Golden Jubilee **Obv:** Head with tiara right **Obv. Designer:** Ian Rank-Broadley **Rev:** Queen in coach **Edge:** Reeded

Date	Mintage	F	VF	XF	Unc	BU
2002	50,000	—	—	—	15.00	16.50

KM# 119b 5 POUNDS
28.2800 g., 0.9250 Silver 0.8410 oz. ASW, 38.6 mm. **Ruler:** Elizabeth II **Subject:** Queen's Golden Jubilee **Obv:** Head with tiara right **Obv. Designer:** Ian Rank-Broadley **Rev:** Queen in her coach **Edge:** Reeded **Note:** Prev. KM#119a.

Date	Mintage	F	VF	XF	Unc	BU
2002 Proof	20,000	Value: 50.00				

KM# 119c 5 POUNDS
39.9400 g., 0.9166 Gold 1.1770 oz. AGW, 38.6 mm. **Ruler:** Elizabeth II **Subject:** Golden Jubilee **Obv:** Head with tiara right **Obv. Designer:** Ian Rank-Broadley **Rev:** Queen in coach **Edge:** Reeded

Date	Mintage	F	VF	XF	Unc	BU
2002 Proof	250	Value: 1,800				

KM# 121 5 POUNDS
27.7100 g., Copper-Nickel, 38.6 mm. **Ruler:** Elizabeth II **Subject:** Queen's Golden Jubilee **Obv:** Head with tiara right **Obv. Designer:** Ian Rank-Broadley **Rev:** Trooping the Colors scene **Edge:** Reeded

Date	Mintage	F	VF	XF	Unc	BU
2002	2,000	—	—	—	17.50	20.00

KM# 121a 5 POUNDS
28.2800 g., 0.9250 Silver 0.8410 oz. ASW, 38.6 mm. **Ruler:** Elizabeth II **Subject:** Queen's Golden Jubilee **Obv:** Head with tiara right **Obv. Designer:** Ian Rank-Broadley **Rev:** Trooping the Colors scene **Edge:** Reeded

Date	Mintage	F	VF	XF	Unc	BU
2002 Proof	20,000	Value: 50.00				

KM# 121b 5 POUNDS
39.9400 g., 0.9166 Gold 1.1770 oz. AGW, 38.6 mm. **Ruler:** Elizabeth II **Subject:** Golden Jubilee **Obv:** Head with tiara right **Obv. Designer:** Ian Rank-Broadley **Rev:** Trooping the Colors scene **Edge:** Reeded

Date	Mintage	F	VF	XF	Unc	BU
2002 Proof	250	Value: 1,800				

KM# 122 5 POUNDS
28.2800 g., Copper-Nickel, 38.6 mm. **Ruler:** Elizabeth II **Subject:** Princess Diana **Obv:** Head with tiara right **Obv. Designer:** Ian Rank-Broadley **Rev:** World and children behind cameo portrait of Diana **Edge:** Reeded

Date	Mintage	F	VF	XF	Unc	BU
2002	4,231	—	—	—	13.50	15.00

KM# 122a 5 POUNDS
28.2800 g., 0.9250 Silver 0.8410 oz. ASW **Ruler:** Elizabeth II **Subject:** Princess Diana **Obv:** Head with tiara right **Obv. Designer:** Ian Rank-Broadley **Rev:** World and children behind Diana's cameo portrait **Edge:** Reeded

Date	Mintage	F	VF	XF	Unc	BU
2002 Proof	20,000	Value: 45.00				

KM# 122b 5 POUNDS
39.9400 g., 0.9167 Gold 1.1771 oz. AGW, 1.1771 mm. **Ruler:** Elizabeth II **Subject:** Princess Diana **Obv:** Head with tiara right **Obv. Designer:** Ian Rank-Broadley **Rev:** World and children behind Diana's cameo portrait **Edge:** Reeded

Date	Mintage	F	VF	XF	Unc	BU
2002 Proof	100	Value: 1,850				

KM# 124 5 POUNDS
28.2800 g., Copper-Nickel, 38.6 mm. **Ruler:** Elizabeth II **Subject:** 18th Century British Monarchy **Obv:** Head with tiara right **Obv. Designer:** Ian Rank-Broadley **Rev:** Five royal portraits **Edge:** Reeded

Date	Mintage	F	VF	XF	Unc	BU
2002	1,300	—	—	—	15.00	16.50

KM# 124a 5 POUNDS
28.2800 g., 0.9250 Silver 0.8410 oz. ASW, 38.6 mm. **Ruler:** Elizabeth II **Subject:** 18th Century British Monarchy **Obv:** Head with tiara right **Obv. Designer:** Ian Rank-Broadley **Rev:** Five royal portraits **Edge:** Reeded

Date	Mintage	F	VF	XF	Unc	BU
2002 Proof	10,000	Value: 50.00				

KM# 124b 5 POUNDS
39.9400 g., 0.9166 Gold 1.1770 oz. AGW, 38.6 mm. **Ruler:** Elizabeth II **Subject:** 18th Century British Monarchy **Obv:** Head with tiara right **Obv. Designer:** Ian Rank-Broadley **Rev:** Five royal portraits **Edge:** Reeded

Date	Mintage	F	VF	XF	Unc	BU
2002 Proof	200	Value: 1,800				

KM# 125 5 POUNDS
1.1300 g., 0.9166 Gold 0.0333 oz. AGW, 13.9 mm. **Ruler:** Elizabeth II **Subject:** 18th Century British Monarchy **Obv:** Head with tiara right **Obv. Designer:** Ian Rank-Broadley **Rev:** Five royal portraits **Edge:** Reeded **Note:** Prev. KM#124b.

Date	Mintage	F	VF	XF	Unc	BU
2002 Proof	55	Value: 80.00				

KM# 127 5 POUNDS
28.2800 g., Copper-Nickel, 38.6 mm. **Ruler:** Elizabeth II **Subject:** Queen Mother **Obv:** Head with tiara right **Obv. Designer:** Ian Rank-Broadley **Rev:** The late Queen Mother's portrait **Edge:** Reeded

Date	Mintage	F	VF	XF	Unc	BU
2002	1,750	—	—	—	15.00	16.50
2002 Proof	1,680	Value: 20.00				

KM# 127a 5 POUNDS
28.2800 g., 0.9250 Silver 0.8410 oz. ASW, 38.6 mm. **Ruler:** Elizabeth II **Subject:** Queen Mother **Obv:** Head with tiara right **Obv. Designer:** Ian Rank-Broadley **Rev:** The late Queen Mother's portrait **Edge:** Reeded

Date	Mintage	F	VF	XF	Unc	BU
2002 Proof	15,000	Value: 50.00				

KM# 127b 5 POUNDS
39.9400 g., 0.9166 Gold 1.1770 oz. AGW, 38.6 mm. **Ruler:** Elizabeth II **Subject:** Queen Mother **Obv:** Head with tiara right **Obv. Designer:** Ian Rank-Broadley **Rev:** Queen Mother's portrait **Edge:** Reeded

Date	Mintage	F	VF	XF	Unc	BU
2002 Proof	250	Value: 1,800				

KM# 128 5 POUNDS
1.1300 g., 0.9166 Gold 0.0333 oz. AGW, 13.9 mm. **Ruler:** Elizabeth II **Subject:** Queen Mother **Obv:** Head with tiara right **Obv. Designer:** Ian Rank-Broadley **Rev:** The late Queen Mother's portrait **Edge:** Reeded

Date	Mintage	F	VF	XF	Unc	BU
2002 Proof	—	Value: 75.00				

KM# 129 5 POUNDS
28.2800 g., Copper-Nickel, 38.6 mm. **Ruler:** Elizabeth II **Subject:** The Duke of Wellington **Obv:** Head with tiara right **Obv. Designer:** Ian Rank-Broadley **Rev:** Portrait with mounted dragoons in background **Edge:** Reeded

Date	Mintage	F	VF	XF	Unc	BU
2002	675	—	—	—	22.50	25.00

KM# 129a 5 POUNDS
28.2800 g., 0.9250 Silver 0.8410 oz. ASW, 38.6 mm. **Ruler:** Elizabeth II **Subject:** The Duke of Wellington **Obv:** Head with tiara right **Obv. Designer:** Ian Rank-Broadley **Rev:** Portrait with multicolor mounted dragoons in background **Rev. Designer:** Willem Vis **Edge:** Reeded

Date	Mintage	F	VF	XF	Unc	BU
2002 Proof	15,000	Value: 50.00				

KM# 129b 5 POUNDS
39.9400 g., 0.9166 Gold 1.1770 oz. AGW, 38.6 mm. **Ruler:** Elizabeth II **Subject:** Duke of Wellington **Obv:** Head with tiara right **Obv. Designer:** Ian Rank-Broadley **Rev:** Wellington's portrait with multicolor cavalry scene **Edge:** Reeded

Date	Mintage	F	VF	XF	Unc	BU
2002 Proof	200	Value: 1,800				

KM# 130 5 POUNDS
1.1300 g., 0.9166 Gold 0.0333 oz. AGW, 13.9 mm. **Ruler:** Elizabeth II **Subject:** The Duke of Wellington **Obv:** Head with tiara right **Obv. Designer:** Ian Rank-Broadley **Rev:** Portrait with mounted dragoons in background **Edge:** Reeded

Date	Mintage	F	VF	XF	Unc	BU
2002 Proof	—	Value: 75.00				

KM# 143 5 POUNDS
28.2800 g., Copper-Nickel, 38.6 mm. **Ruler:** Elizabeth II **Obv:** Head with tiara right **Obv. Designer:** Ian Rank-Broadley **Rev:** Prince William wearing sweater **Edge:** Reeded

Date	Mintage	F	VF	XF	Unc	BU
2003	3,700	—	—	—	17.50	20.00

KM# 143a 5 POUNDS
28.2800 g., 0.9250 Silver 0.8410 oz. ASW, 38.6 mm. **Ruler:** Elizabeth II **Obv:** Head with tiara right **Obv. Designer:** Ian Rank-Broadley **Rev:** Prince William wearing sweater **Edge:** Reeded

Date	Mintage	F	VF	XF	Unc	BU
2003 Proof	5,000	Value: 50.00				

KM# 143b 5 POUNDS
39.9400 g., 0.9166 Gold 1.1770 oz. AGW, 38.6 mm. **Ruler:** Elizabeth II **Obv:** Head with tiara right **Obv. Designer:** Ian Rank-Broadley **Rev:** Prince William wearing sweater **Edge:** Reeded

Date	Mintage	F	VF	XF	Unc	BU
2003 Proof	200	Value: 1,800				

KM# 158 5 POUNDS
28.2800 g., Copper-Nickel, 38.7 mm. **Ruler:** Elizabeth II **Subject:** Golden Hind **Obv:** Head with tiara right **Obv. Designer:** Ian Rank-Broadley **Rev:** The Golden Hind ship **Edge:** Reeded

Date	Mintage	F	VF	XF	Unc	BU
2003	300	—	—	—	—	25.00

KM# 159 5 POUNDS
Copper-Nickel **Ruler:** Elizabeth II **Subject:** 17th Century Monarchs **Obv:** Head with tiara right **Obv. Designer:** Ian Rank-Broadley

Date	Mintage	F	VF	XF	Unc	BU
2003	500	—	—	—	—	22.50

KM# 160 5 POUNDS
Copper-Nickel **Ruler:** Elizabeth II **Subject:** Royal Navy - H. Nelson **Obv:** Head with tiara right **Obv. Designer:** Ian Rank-Broadley

Date	Mintage	F	VF	XF	Unc	BU
2003	550	—	—	—	—	22.50

KM# 177 5 POUNDS
Copper-Nickel **Ruler:** Elizabeth II **Subject:** Coronation, 50th Anniversary

Date	Mintage	F	VF	XF	Unc	BU
2003	—	—	—	—	—	15.00

KM# 175 5 POUNDS
28.3200 g., Nickel-Brass, 38 mm. **Ruler:** Elizabeth II **Subject:** History of the Royal Navy **Rev:** Two naval vessels and Horatio Nelson, flag in color

Date	Mintage	F	VF	XF	Unc	BU
2003 Proof	—	Value: 40.00				

KM# 176 5 POUNDS
28.3200 g., Silver, 38 mm. **Ruler:** Elizabeth II **Subject:** History of the Royal Navy **Rev:** HMS Invincible, flag in color

Date	Mintage	F	VF	XF	Unc	BU
2004 Proof	—	Value: 50.00				

KM# 161 5 POUNDS
Copper-Nickel **Ruler:** Elizabeth II **Subject:** 16th Century Monarchs **Obv:** Head with tiara right **Obv. Designer:** Ian Rank-Broadley

Date	Mintage	F	VF	XF	Unc	BU
2004	500	—	—	—	—	22.50

KM# 162 5 POUNDS
Copper-Nickel **Ruler:** Elizabeth II **Subject:** Mallard Locomotive **Obv:** Head with tiara right **Obv. Designer:** Ian Rank-Broadley

Date	Mintage	F	VF	XF	Unc	BU
2004	2,193	—	—	—	—	17.50

KM# 163 5 POUNDS
Copper-Nickel **Ruler:** Elizabeth II **Subject:** City of Truro Train **Obv:** Head with tiara right **Obv. Designer:** Ian Rank-Broadley

Date	Mintage	F	VF	XF	Unc	BU
2004	500	—	—	—	—	22.50

KM# 164 5 POUNDS
Copper-Nickel **Ruler:** Elizabeth II **Subject:** The Boat Train **Obv:** Head with tiara right **Obv. Designer:** Ian Rank-Broadley

Date	Mintage	F	VF	XF	Unc	BU
2004	250	—	—	—	—	25.00

KM# 165 5 POUNDS
Copper-Nickel **Ruler:** Elizabeth II **Subject:** Train Spotter **Obv:** Head with tiara right **Obv. Designer:** Ian Rank-Broadley

Date	Mintage	F	VF	XF	Unc	BU
2004	300	—	—	—	—	25.00

KM# 166 5 POUNDS
Copper-Nickel **Ruler:** Elizabeth II **Subject:** Royal Navy - Henry VIII **Obv:** Head with tiara right **Obv. Designer:** Ian Rank-Broadley

Date	Mintage	F	VF	XF	Unc	BU
2004	300	—	—	—	—	25.00

KM# 167 5 POUNDS
Copper-Nickel **Ruler:** Elizabeth II **Subject:** Royal Navy - Invincible **Obv:** Head with tiara right **Obv. Designer:** Ian Rank-Broadley

Date	Mintage	F	VF	XF	Unc	BU
2004	300	—	—	—	—	25.00

KM# 150 5 POUNDS
28.2800 g., Copper-Nickel, 38.6 mm. **Ruler:** Elizabeth II **Subject:** D-Day **Obv:** Head with tiara right **Obv. Designer:** Ian Rank-Broadley **Rev:** British troops storming ashore **Edge:** Reeded

Date	Mintage	F	VF	XF	Unc	BU
2004	65,611	—	—	—	15.00	16.50

KM# 154 5 POUNDS
28.2800 g., 0.9250 Silver 0.8410 oz. ASW, 38.6 mm. **Ruler:** Elizabeth II **Subject:** D-Day **Obv:** Head with tiara right **Obv. Designer:** Ian Rank-Broadley **Rev:** British soldier advancing to left **Edge:** Reeded

Date	Mintage	F	VF	XF	Unc	BU
2004 Proof	10,000	Value: 85.00				

KM# 154a 5 POUNDS
39.9400 g., 0.9167 Gold 1.1771 oz. AGW, 38.6 mm. **Ruler:** Elizabeth II **Subject:** D-Day **Obv:** Head with tiara right **Obv. Designer:** Ian Rank-Broadley **Rev:** British soldier advancing to left **Edge:** Reeded

Date	Mintage	F	VF	XF	Unc	BU
2004 Proof	500	Value: 1,750				

KM# 155 5 POUNDS
28.2800 g., Copper-Nickel, 38.6 mm. **Ruler:** Elizabeth II **Subject:** 150th Anniversary of the Crimean War **Obv:** Head with tiara right **Obv. Designer:** Ian Rank-Broadley **Rev:** Sgt. Luke O'Connor , first army Victoria Cross winner, above Battle of Alma scene with multicolor flag **Edge:** Reeded

Date	Mintage	F	VF	XF	Unc	BU
2004 plain	—	—	—	—	25.00	27.50
2004 partial color	1,060	—	—	—	25.00	27.50

KM# 155a 5 POUNDS
28.2800 g., 0.9250 Silver 0.8410 oz. ASW, 38.6 mm. **Ruler:** Elizabeth II **Obv:** Head with tiara right **Obv. Designer:** Ian Rank-Broadley **Rev:** Sgt. Luke O'Conner, first army Victoria Cross winner, above Battle of Alma scene with multicolor flag **Edge:** Reeded

Date	Mintage	F	VF	XF	Unc	BU
2004 Proof	10,000	Value: 85.00				

KM# 155b 5 POUNDS
39.9400 g., 0.9166 Gold 1.1770 oz. AGW, 38.6 mm. **Ruler:** Elizabeth II **Obv:** Head with tiara right **Obv. Designer:** Ian Rank-Broadley **Rev:** Sgt. Luke O'Connor, first army Victoria Cross winner, above Battle of Alma scene with multicolor flag **Edge:** Reeded

Date	Mintage	F	VF	XF	Unc	BU
2004 Proof	500	Value: 1,750				

KM# 168a 5 POUNDS
28.2800 g., 0.9250 Silver 0.8410 oz. ASW, 38.6 mm. **Ruler:** Elizabeth II **Subject:** End of WWII **Obv:** Head with tiara right **Obv. Designer:** Ian Rank-Broadley **Rev:** Churchill and George VI **Edge:** Reeded

Date	Mintage	F	VF	XF	Unc	BU
2005 Proof	5,000	Value: 85.00				

KM# 168b 5 POUNDS
39.9400 g., 0.9167 Gold 1.1771 oz. AGW, 38.6 mm. **Ruler:** Elizabeth II **Subject:** End of WWII **Obv:** Head with tiara right **Obv. Designer:** Ian Rank-Broadley **Rev:** Churchill and George VI **Edge:** Reeded

Date	Mintage	F	VF	XF	Unc	BU
2005 Proof	150	Value: 1,800				

KM# 169a 5 POUNDS
39.9400 g., 0.9167 Gold 1.1771 oz. AGW, 38.6 mm. **Ruler:** Elizabeth II **Subject:** WWII Liberation **Obv:** Head with tiara right **Obv. Designer:** Ian Rank-Broadley **Rev:** Soldiers and waving crowd **Edge:** Reeded

Date	Mintage	F	VF	XF	Unc	BU
2005 Proof	150	Value: 1,800				

KM# 170 5 POUNDS
28.2800 g., 0.9250 Silver 0.8410 oz. ASW, 38.6 mm. **Ruler:** Elizabeth II **Subject:** Queen's 80th Birthday **Obv:** Head with tiara right - gilt **Obv. Legend:** ELIZABETH II BAILIWICK OF GUERNSEY **Obv. Designer:** Ian Rank-Broadley **Rev:** Bust at left looking upwards, tower and florals at upper right

Date	Mintage	F	VF	XF	Unc	BU
2006 Proof	—	Value: 45.00				

KM# 173 5 POUNDS
28.2800 g., 0.9250 Silver 0.8410 oz. ASW **Ruler:** Elizabeth II **Subject:** FIFA - XVIII World Football Championship - Germany 2006 **Rev:** Wembley Stadium

Date	Mintage	F	VF	XF	Unc	BU
2006 Proof	50,000	Value: 65.00				

KM# 116 10 POUNDS
141.7500 g., 0.9990 Silver 4.5526 oz. ASW, 65 mm. **Ruler:** Elizabeth II **Subject:** 19th Century Monarchy **Obv:** Head with tiara right **Obv. Designer:** Ian Rank-Broadley **Rev:** Four portraits **Edge:** Reeded

Date	Mintage	F	VF	XF	Unc	BU
2001 Proof	950	Value: 225				

KM# 126 10 POUNDS
155.5175 g., 0.9990 Silver 4.9948 oz. ASW, 65 mm. **Ruler:** Elizabeth II **Subject:** British Monarchy 18th Century **Obv:** Head with tiara right **Obv. Designer:** Ian Rank-Broadley **Rev:** Five royal portraits **Edge:** Reeded

Date	Mintage	F	VF	XF	Unc	BU
2002 Proof	950	Value: 225				

KM# 151 10 POUNDS
155.5170 g., 0.9250 Silver 4.6248 oz. ASW, 65 mm. **Ruler:** Elizabeth II **Subject:** D-Day **Obv:** Head with tiara right **Obv. Designer:** Ian Rank-Broadley **Rev:** British troops storming ashore **Edge:** Reeded

Date	Mintage	F	VF	XF	Unc	BU
2004 Proof	1,944	Value: 400				

KM# 107 25 POUNDS
7.8100 g., 0.9170 Gold 0.2302 oz. AGW, 22 mm. **Ruler:** Elizabeth II **Subject:** Queen Victoria Centennial **Obv:** Head with tiara right **Obv. Designer:** Ian Rank-Broadley **Rev:** Queen Victoria's portrait **Edge:** Reeded

Date	Mintage	F	VF	XF	Unc	BU
2001 Proof	2,500	Value: 400				

KM# 112 25 POUNDS
7.8100 g., 0.9170 Gold 0.2302 oz. AGW, 22 mm. **Ruler:** Elizabeth II **Subject:** Queen's 75th Birthday **Obv:** Head with tiara right **Obv. Designer:** Ian Rank-Broadley **Rev:** Queen's portrait in wreath **Edge:** Reeded

Date	Mintage	F	VF	XF	Unc	BU
2001 Proof	5,000	Value: 375				

KM# 123 25 POUNDS
7.9800 g., 0.9167 Gold 0.2352 oz. AGW, 22.05 mm. **Ruler:** Elizabeth II **Subject:** Princess Diana **Obv:** Head with tiara right **Obv. Designer:** Ian Rank-Broadley **Rev:** Diana's cameo portrait in wreath **Edge:** Reeded

Date	Mintage	F	VF	XF	Unc	BU
2002 Proof	2,500	Value: 400				

KM# 131 25 POUNDS
7.8100 g., 0.9166 Gold 0.2301 oz. AGW, 22 mm. **Ruler:** Elizabeth II **Subject:** The Duke of Wellington **Obv:** Head with tiara right **Obv. Designer:** Ian Rank-Broadley **Rev:** Portrait with mounted dragoons in the background **Edge:** Reeded

Date	Mintage	F	VF	XF	Unc	BU
2002 Proof	2,500	Value: 375				

KM# 139 25 POUNDS
7.9800 g., 0.9166 Gold 0.2352 oz. AGW, 22 mm. **Ruler:** Elizabeth II **Subject:** Golden Jubilee **Obv:** Head with tiara right **Obv. Designer:** Ian Rank-Broadley **Rev:** Queen in coach **Edge:** Reeded

Date	Mintage	F	VF	XF	Unc	BU
2002 Proof	5,000	Value: 400				

KM# 140 25 POUNDS
7.9800 g., 0.9166 Gold 0.2352 oz. AGW, 22 mm. **Ruler:** Elizabeth II **Subject:** Queen Mother **Obv:** Head with tiara right **Obv. Designer:** Ian Rank-Broadley **Rev:** Queen Mother's portrait **Edge:** Reeded

Date	Mintage	F	VF	XF	Unc	BU
2002 Proof	2,500	Value: 400				

KM# 141 25 POUNDS
7.9800 g., 0.9166 Gold 0.2352 oz. AGW, 22 mm. **Ruler:** Elizabeth II **Subject:** Golden Jubilee **Obv:** Head with tiara right **Obv. Designer:** Ian Rank-Broadley **Rev:** Trooping the Colors scene **Edge:** Reeded

Date	Mintage	F	VF	XF	Unc	BU
2003 Proof	5,000	Value: 400				

KM# 172 25 POUNDS
7.9800 g., 0.9166 Gold 0.2352 oz. AGW **Ruler:** Elizabeth II **Obv:** Head with tiara right **Rev:** Bust of Prince William facing **Edge:** Reeded

Date	Mintage	F	VF	XF	Unc	BU
2003 Proof	—	Value: 375				

KM# 152 25 POUNDS
7.9800 g., 0.9167 Gold 0.2352 oz. AGW, 22 mm. **Ruler:** Elizabeth II **Subject:** D-Day **Obv:** Head with tiara right **Obv. Designer:** Ian Rank-Broadley **Rev:** Advancing British soldier **Edge:** Reeded

Date	Mintage	F	VF	XF	Unc	BU
2004 Proof	500	Value: 425				

KM# 174 25 POUNDS
7.9800 g., 0.9166 Gold 0.2352 oz. AGW **Ruler:** Elizabeth II **Subject:** FIFA - XVIII World Football Championship - Germany 2006 **Rev:** Wembley Stadium

Date	Mintage	F	VF	XF	Unc	BU
2006 Proof	2,500	Value: 400				

KM# 144 50 POUNDS
1000.0000 g., 0.9250 Silver 29.738 oz. ASW, 100 mm. **Ruler:** Elizabeth II **Obv:** Head with tiara right **Obv. Designer:** Ian Rank-Broadley **Rev:** Prince William wearing sweater **Edge:** Reeded

Date	Mintage	F	VF	XF	Unc	BU
2003 Proof	500	Value: 1,250				

KM# 153 50 POUNDS
1000.0000 g., 0.9250 Silver 29.738 oz. ASW, 100 mm. **Ruler:** Elizabeth II **Subject:** D-Day **Obv:** Head with tiara right **Obv. Designer:** Ian Rank-Broadley **Rev:** British troops storming ashore **Edge:** Reeded

Date	Mintage	F	VF	XF	Unc	BU
2004 Proof	600	Value: 1,300				

PIEFORTS

KM#	Date	Mintage	Identification	Mkt Val
P3	2002	100	5 Pounds. 0.9166 Gold. 79.8900 g. 38.6 mm. Queen's portrait. Queen in coach. Reeded edge.	3,750

MINT SETS

KM#	Date	Mintage	Identification	Issue Price	Mkt Val
MS10	2003 (8)	—	KM#83, 89-90, 96-97, 110, 148-49	—	22.50
MS11	2004 (1)	—	Guernsey KM#155, Alderney KM#43, Jersey KM#126, 150th Anniversary of the Crimean War	—	80.00

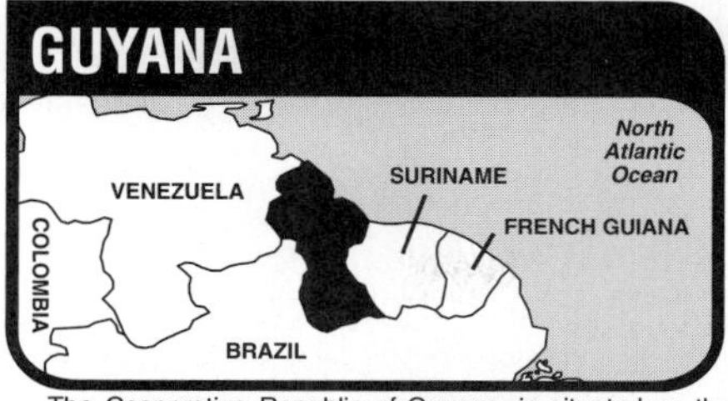

The Cooperative Republic of Guyana, is situated on the northeast coast of South America, has an area of 83,000 sq. mi. (214,970 sq. km.) and a population of 729,000. Capital: Georgetown. The economy is basically agrarian. Sugar, rice and bauxite are exported.

The original area of Essequibo and Demerary, which included present-day Suriname, French Guiana, and parts of Brazil and Venezuela was sighted by Columbus in 1498. Guyana became a republic on Feb. 23, 1970. It is a member of the Commonwealth of Nations. The president is the Chief of State. The prime minister is the Head of Government. Guyana is a member of the Caribbean Community and Common Market (CARICOM).

REPUBLIC

DECIMAL COINAGE

KM# 50 DOLLAR
2.4000 g., Copper Plated Steel, 17 mm. **Obv:** Helmeted and supported arms **Obv. Designer:** Sean Thomas **Rev:** Hand gathering rice **Rev. Designer:** Jean Thomas **Edge:** Reeded

Date	Mintage	F	VF	XF	Unc	BU
2001	—	—	—	0.30	0.50	0.65
2002	—	—	—	0.30	0.50	0.65
2005	—	—	—	0.30	0.50	0.65
2008	—	—	—	0.30	0.50	0.65

KM# 51 5 DOLLARS
3.7800 g., Copper Plated Steel, 20.5 mm. **Obv:** Helmeted and supported arms **Rev:** Sugar cane **Rev. Designer:** Selayn Cambridge **Edge:** Reeded

Date	Mintage	F	VF	XF	Unc	BU
2002	—	—	—	0.35	0.75	1.00
2005	—	—	—	0.35	0.75	1.00
2008	—	—	—	0.35	0.75	1.00
2009	—	—	—	0.35	0.75	1.00

KM# 52 10 DOLLARS
5.0000 g., Nickel Plated Steel, 23 mm. **Obv:** Helmeted and supported arms **Rev:** Gold mining scene **Rev. Designer:** Ignatias Adams **Edge:** Reeded **Shape:** 7-sided **Note:** Slightly different die for each date.

Date	Mintage	F	VF	XF	Unc	BU
2007	—	—	—	0.75	1.25	1.50
2009	—	—	—	0.75	1.25	1.50

KM# 54 1000 DOLLARS
28.2800 g., 0.9250 Silver partially gilt 0.8410 oz. ASW, 38.6 mm. **Subject:** Bank of Guyana, 40th Anniversary **Obv:** Arms **Rev:** Bank building, partially gilt

Date	Mintage	F	VF	XF	Unc	BU
2005 Proof	1,000	Value: 75.00				

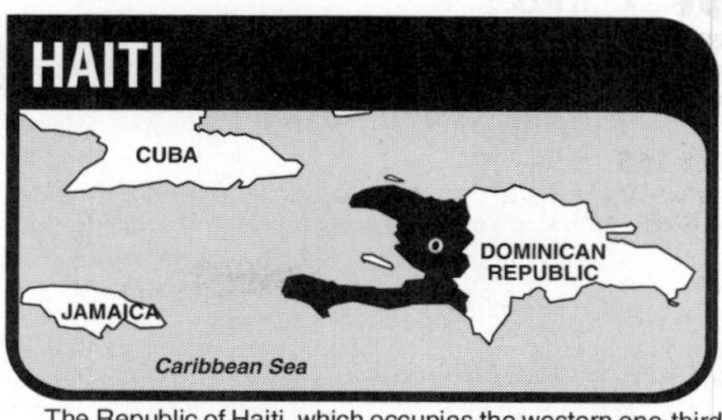

The Republic of Haiti, which occupies the western one-third of the island of Hispaniola in the Caribbean Sea between Puerto Rico and Cuba, has an area of 10,714 sq. mi. (27,750 sq. km.) and a population of 6.5 million. Capital: Port-au-Prince. The economy is based on agriculture; but light manufacturing and tourism are increasingly important. Coffee, bauxite, sugar, essential oils and handicrafts are exported.

The French language is used on Haitian coins although it is spoken by only about 10% of the populace. A form of Creole is the language of the Haitians.

MINT MARKS
A - Paris
(a) - Paris, privy marks only
R - Rome

MONETARY SYSTEM
100 Centimes = 1 Gourde

REPUBLIC

DECIMAL COINAGE

KM# 155 GOURDE
6.3000 g., Brass Plated Steel, 23 mm. **Obv:** Citadelle de Roi Christophe **Shape:** 7-sided

Date	Mintage	F	VF	XF	Unc	BU
2003	—	—	—	—	1.75	2.00

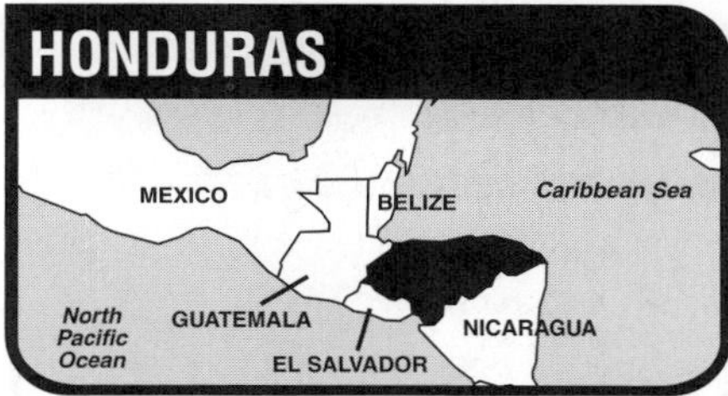

The Republic of Honduras, situated in Central America alongside El Salvador, between Nicaragua and Guatemala, has an area of 43,277 sq. mi. (112,090 sq. km.) and a population of 5.6 million. Capital: Tegucigalpa. Agriculture, mining (gold and silver), and logging are the major economic activities, with increasing tourism and emerging petroleum resource discoveries. Precious metals, bananas, timber and coffee are exported.

From 1933 to 1940 General Tiburcio Carias Andino was dictator president of the Republic. Since 1990 democratic practices have become more consistent.

MINT MARKS
T.G. - Yoro
T.L. – Comayagua

MONETARY SYSTEM
100 Centavos = 1 Lempira

REPUBLIC

REFORM COINAGE

KM# 72.4 5 CENTAVOS
3.2000 g., Brass, 21 mm. **Obv:** National arms **Rev:** Value in circle within sprays **Edge:** Plain

Date	Mintage	F	VF	XF	Unc	BU
2002	—	—	—	0.10	0.25	0.35
2003	—	—	—	0.10	0.25	0.35
2005	—	—	—	0.10	0.25	0.35
2006	—	—	—	0.10	0.25	0.35

KM# 76.3 10 CENTAVOS

6.0000 g., Brass, 26 mm. **Obv:** National arms, without clouds behind pyramid **Rev:** Denomination within circle, wreath surrounds **Edge:** Plain

Date	Mintage	F	VF	XF	Unc	BU
2002	—	—	0.10	0.20	0.45	0.65
2003	—	—	0.10	0.20	0.45	0.65
2005	—	—	0.10	0.20	0.45	0.65

KM# 76.4 10 CENTAVOS

6.2000 g., Brass, 26 mm. **Obv:** National arms, slightly larger legend, large date **Rev:** Value in circle within wreath **Edge:** Plain

Date	Mintage	F	VF	XF	Unc	BU
2006	—	—	—	0.15	0.35	0.45
2007	—	—	—	0.15	0.35	0.45

KM# 84a.2 50 CENTAVOS

5.0000 g., Nickel Plated Steel, 24 mm. **Obv:** National arms above date **Rev:** Chief Lempira head left within circle **Edge:** Reeded

Date	Mintage	F	VF	XF	Unc	BU
2005	—	—	0.15	0.35	0.90	1.25

HONG KONG

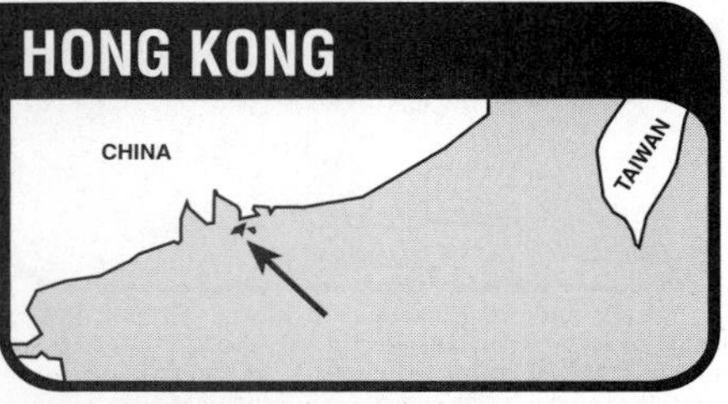

Hong Kong, a former British colony, reverted to control of the People's Republic of China on July 1, 1997 as a Special Administrative Region. It is situated at the mouth of the Canton or Pearl River 90 miles (145 km.) southeast of Canton, has an area of 403 sq. mi. (1,040 sq. km.) and an estimated population of 6.3 million. Capital: Victoria. The free port of Hong Kong, the commercial center of the Far East, is a trans-shipment point for goods destined for China and the countries of the Pacific Rim. Light manufacturing and tourism are important components of the economy.

SPECIAL ADMINISTRATION REGION (S.A.R.)

DECIMAL COINAGE

KM# 80 50 DOLLARS

35.4300 g., 0.9250 Silver Gold plated center 1.0536 oz. ASW, 40 mm. **Series:** Five Blessings **Obv:** Bauhinia flower **Rev:** Jade Ju-I

Date	Mintage	F	VF	XF	Unc	BU
2002 Proof	60,000	Value: 85.00				

KM# 81 50 DOLLARS

35.4300 g., 0.9250 Silver Gold plated center 1.0536 oz. ASW, 40 mm. **Series:** Five Blessings **Obv:** Bauhinia flower **Rev:** Fish

Date	Mintage	F	VF	XF	Unc	BU
2002 Proof	60,000	Value: 85.00				

KM# 82 50 DOLLARS

35.2500 g., 0.9250 Silver Gold plated center 1.0483 oz. ASW, 40 mm. **Series:** Five Blessings **Obv:** Bauhinia flower **Rev:** Horses

Date	Mintage	F	VF	XF	Unc	BU
2002 Proof	60,000	Value: 85.00				

KM# 83 50 DOLLARS

35.3400 g., 0.9250 Silver Gold plated center 1.0509 oz. ASW, 40 mm. **Series:** Five Blessings **Obv:** Bauhinia flower **Rev:** Peony flower

Date	Mintage	F	VF	XF	Unc	BU
2002 Proof	60,000	Value: 85.00				

KM# 84 50 DOLLARS

35.1400 g., 0.9250 Silver Gold plated center 1.0450 oz. ASW, 40 mm. **Series:** Five Blessings **Obv:** Bauhinia flower **Rev:** Windmills

Date	Mintage	F	VF	XF	Unc	BU
2002 Proof	60,000	Value: 85.00				

PROOF SETS

KM#	Date	Mintage	Identification	Issue Price	Mkt Val
PS8	2002 (5)	60,000	KM#80-84 plus 7.8g, .9999, AGW .2508, 25mm gold medal	370	800

HUNGARY

The Republic of Hungary, located in central Europe, has an area of 35,929 sq. mi. (93,030 sq. km.) and a population of 10.7 million. Capital: Budapest. The economy is based on agriculture, bauxite and a rapidly expanding industrial sector. Machinery, chemicals, iron and steel, and fruits and vegetables are exported.

MINT MARKS

BP - Budapest

MONETARY SYSTEM

Commencing 1946

100 Filler = 1 Forint

SECOND REPUBLIC

1989-present

DECIMAL COINAGE

KM# 692 FORINT

2.0500 g., Nickel-Brass, 16.5 mm. **Obv:** Crowned shield **Rev:** Denomination

Date	Mintage	F	VF	XF	Unc	BU
2001BP	—	—	—	—	0.10	0.25
2001BP Proof	3,000	Value: 3.75				
2002BP	—	—	—	—	0.10	0.25
2002BP Proof	3,000	Value: 3.75				
2003BP	—	—	—	—	0.10	0.25
2003BP Proof	7,000	Value: 3.50				
2004BP	—	—	—	—	0.10	0.25
2004BP Proof	7,000	Value: 3.50				
2005BP	—	—	—	—	0.10	0.25
2005BP Proof	—	Value: 3.50				
2006BP	—	—	—	—	0.10	0.25
2006BP Proof	—	Value: 3.50				
2007BP	—	—	—	—	0.10	0.25
2007BP Proof	—	Value: 3.50				
2008BP Proof	—	Value: 3.50				

KM# 693 2 FORINT

3.1000 g., Copper-Nickel, 19.2 mm. **Obv:** Native flower: Colchicum Hungaricum **Rev:** Denomination **Edge:** Reeded

Date	Mintage	F	VF	XF	Unc	BU
2001BP	—	—	—	—	0.20	0.35
2001BP Proof	3,000	Value: 4.25				
2002BP	—	—	—	—	0.20	0.35
2002BP Proof	3,000	Value: 4.25				
2003BP	—	—	—	—	0.20	0.35
2003BP Proof	7,000	Value: 4.00				
2004BP	—	—	—	—	0.20	0.35
2004BP Proof	7,000	Value: 4.00				
2005BP	—	—	—	—	0.20	0.35
2005BP Proof	—	Value: 4.00				
2006BP	—	—	—	—	0.20	0.35
2006BP Proof	—	Value: 4.00				
2007	—	—	—	—	0.20	0.35
2007 Proof	—	Value: 4.00				
2008 Proof	—	Value: 4.00				

KM# 694 5 FORINT
4.2000 g., Nickel-Brass, 21.2 mm. **Obv:** Great White Egret **Rev:** Denomination

Date	Mintage	F	VF	XF	Unc	BU
2001BP	—	—	—	—	1.00	1.50
2001BP Proof	3,000	Value: 5.00				
2002BP	—	—	—	—	1.00	1.50
2002BP Proof	3,000	Value: 5.00				
2003BP	—	—	—	—	1.00	1.50
2003BP Proof	7,000	Value: 4.50				
2004BP	—	—	—	—	1.00	1.50
2004BP Proof	7,000	Value: 4.50				
2005BP	—	—	—	—	1.00	1.50
2005BP Proof	—	Value: 4.50				
2006BP	—	—	—	—	1.00	1.50
2006BP Proof	—	Value: 4.50				
2007BP	—	—	—	—	1.00	1.50
2007BP Proof	—	Value: 4.50				
2008BP Proof	—	Value: 4.50				

KM# 695 10 FORINT
6.1000 g., Copper-Nickel, 24.8 mm. **Obv:** Crowned shield **Rev:** Denomination **Edge:** Segmented reeding

Date	Mintage	F	VF	XF	Unc	BU
2001BP	—	—	—	—	1.00	2.50
2001BP Proof	3,000	Value: 5.50				
2002BP	—	—	—	—	1.00	2.50
2002BP Proof	3,000	Value: 5.50				
2003BP	—	—	—	—	1.00	2.50
2003BP Proof	7,000	Value: 5.00				
2004BP	—	—	—	—	1.00	2.50
2004BP Proof	7,000	Value: 5.00				
2005BP	—	—	—	—	1.00	2.50
2005BP Proof	—	Value: 5.00				
2006BP	—	—	—	—	1.00	2.50
2006BP Proof	—	Value: 5.00				
2007	—	—	—	—	1.00	2.50
2007 Proof	—	Value: 5.00				
2008 Proof	—	Value: 5.00				

KM# 779 10 FORINT
6.1000 g., Copper-Nickel, 24.8 mm. **Obv:** Attila Jozsef **Rev:** Value **Edge:** Segmented reeding

Date	Mintage	F	VF	XF	Unc	BU
2005BP	20,000	—	—	—	2.50	3.00
2005BP Proof	7,000	Value: 3.50				

KM# 696 20 FORINT
6.9000 g., Nickel-Brass, 26.3 mm. **Obv:** Hungarian Iris **Rev:** Denomination **Edge:** Reeded

Date	Mintage	F	VF	XF	Unc	BU
2001BP	—	—	—	—	1.50	2.00
2001BP Proof	3,000	Value: 4.50				
2002BP	—	—	—	—	1.50	2.00
2002BP Proof	3,000	Value: 4.50				
2003BP	—	—	—	—	1.50	2.00
2003BP Proof	7,000	Value: 4.00				
2004BP	—	—	—	—	1.50	2.00
2004BP Proof	7,000	Value: 4.00				

Date	Mintage	F	VF	XF	Unc	BU
2005BP	—	—	—	—	1.50	2.00
2005BP Proof	—	Value: 4.00				
2006BP	—	—	—	—	1.50	2.00
2006BP Proof	—	Value: 4.00				
2007BP	—	—	—	—	1.50	2.00
2007BP Proof	—	Value: 4.00				
2008BP Proof	—	Value: 4.00				

KM# 768 20 FORINT
6.9000 g., Nickel-Brass, 26.3 mm. **Obv:** Ferenc Deak **Rev:** Denomination **Edge:** Reeded

Date	Mintage	F	VF	XF	Unc	BU
2003BP	993,000	—	—	—	1.50	2.00
2003BP Proof	7,000	Value: 4.00				

KM# 697 50 FORINT
7.6000 g., Copper-Nickel, 27.5 mm. **Obv:** Saker falcon **Rev:** Denomination

Date	Mintage	F	VF	XF	Unc	BU
2001BP	—	—	—	—	3.00	4.00
2001BP Proof	3,000	Value: 6.00				
2002BP	—	—	—	—	3.00	3.50
2002BP Proof	3,000	Value: 5.50				
2003BP	—	—	—	—	3.00	3.50
2003BP Proof	7,000	Value: 5.00				
2004BP	—	—	—	—	3.00	3.50
2004BP Proof	7,000	Value: 5.00				
2005BP	—	—	—	—	3.00	3.50
2005BP Proof	—	Value: 5.00				
2006BP	—	—	—	—	3.00	3.50
2006BP Proof	—	Value: 5.00				
2007BP	—	—	—	—	3.00	3.50
2007BP Proof	—	Value: 5.00				
2008BP Proof	—	Value: 5.00				

KM# 773 50 FORINT
7.7000 g., Copper-Nickel, 27.5 mm. **Obv:** National arms above Euro Union star circle **Rev:** Denomination **Edge:** Plain

Date	Mintage	F	VF	XF	Unc	BU
2004BP	993,000	—	—	—	3.00	3.50
2004BP Proof	7,000	Value: 6.00				

KM# 780 50 FORINT
7.7000 g., Copper-Nickel, 27.4 mm. **Subject:** International Childrens Safety Service **Obv:** Stylized crying child **Rev:** Denomination **Edge:** Plain

Date	Mintage	F	VF	XF	Unc	BU
2005BP	2,000,000	—	—	—	3.00	3.50

KM# 788 50 FORINT
7.7000 g., Copper-Nickel, 27.4 mm. **Obv:** Hungarian Red Cross 125th Anniversary seal above date and country name **Rev:** Value **Edge:** Plain

Date	Mintage	F	VF	XF	Unc	BU
2006BP	2,000,000	—	—	—	3.00	3.50

KM# 789 50 FORINT
7.7000 g., Copper-Nickel, 27.4 mm. **Subject:** 1956 Revolution **Obv:** Holed flag with Parliament building in background **Rev:** Value **Edge:** Plain

Date	Mintage	F	VF	XF	Unc	BU
2006BP	2,000,000	—	—	—	3.00	3.50

KM# 805 50 FORINT
7.7000 g., Copper-Nickel, 27.4 mm. **Subject:** Celebrating 50 years of the Treaty of Rome **Obv:** Book logo **Rev:** Value

Date	Mintage	F	VF	XF	Unc	BU
2007	2,000,000	—	—	—	1.50	2.00
2007 Proof	5,000	Value: 3.50				

KM# 760 100 FORINT
8.0000 g., Bi-Metallic Brass Plated Steel center in Stainless Steel ring, 23.7 mm. **Subject:** Lajos Kossuth **Obv:** Head right within circle **Rev:** Denomination within circle **Edge:** Reeded

Date	Mintage	F	VF	XF	Unc	BU
2002BP	997,000	—	—	—	2.00	2.50
2002BP Proof	3,000	Value: 5.00				

KM# 721 100 FORINT (Szaz)
Bi-Metallic Brass plated Steel center in Stainless Steel ring, 23.6 mm. **Obv:** Crowned shield **Rev:** Denomination

Date	Mintage	F	VF	XF	Unc	BU
2001BP	—	—	—	—	3.50	5.00
2001BP Proof	3,000	Value: 8.00				
2002BP	—	—	—	—	3.50	5.00
2002BP Proof	3,000	Value: 8.00				
2003BP	—	—	—	—	3.50	5.00
2003BP Proof	7,000	Value: 7.50				
2004BP	—	—	—	—	3.50	5.00
2004BP Proof	7,000	Value: 7.50				
2005BP	—	—	—	—	3.50	5.00
2005BP Proof	—	Value: 7.50				
2006BP	—	—	—	—	3.50	5.00
2006BP Proof	—	Value: 7.50				
2007 Proof	—	Value: 7.50				
2008 Proof	—	Value: 7.50				

KM# 754 200 FORINT
9.4000 g., Brass, 29.2 mm. **Subject:** Childrens Literature: Ludas Matyi **Obv:** Denomination **Rev:** Man holding a goose **Edge:** Plain

Date	Mintage	F	VF	XF	Unc	BU
2001BP	12,000	—	—	—	7.50	9.50
2001BP Proof	5,000	Value: 15.00				

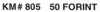

KM# 755 200 FORINT
Brass, 29.2 mm. **Subject:** Childrens Literature: Janos Vitez **Obv:** Denomination **Rev:** Soldier riding a flying bird **Edge:** Plain

Date	Mintage	F	VF	XF	Unc	BU
2001BP	12,000	—	—	—	7.50	9.50
2001BP Proof	5,000	Value: 15.00				

KM# 756 200 FORINT
Brass, 29.2 mm. **Subject:** Childrens Literature: Toldi **Obv:** Denomination **Rev:** Knight kicking a boat off the shore **Edge:** Plain

Date	Mintage	F	VF	XF	Unc	BU
2001BP	12,000	—	—	—	7.50	9.50
2001BP Proof	5,000	Value: 15.00				

KM# 757 200 FORINT
Brass, 29.2 mm. **Subject:** Childrens Literature: A Pal Utcai Fiuk **Obv:** Denomination **Rev:** Two men and cordwood **Edge:** Plain

Date	Mintage	F	VF	XF	Unc	BU
2001	12,000	—	—	—	7.50	9.50
2001 Proof	5,000	Value: 15.00				

KM# 826 200 FORINT
9.0000 g., Bi-Metallic Copper-Nickel center in Nickel-Brass ring, 28.3 mm. **Obv:** Suspension Bridge over the Danube **Rev:** Value **Edge:** Segmented reeding

Date	Mintage	F	VF	XF	Unc	BU
2009BP	—	—	—	—	4.00	5.00

KM# 764 500 FORINT
13.9000 g., Copper-Nickel **Subject:** Farkas Kempelen's Chess Machine **Obv:** Denomination, letters A-H and numbers 1-8 repeated along edges **Rev:** Robotic human form chess playing machine built in 1769 **Edge:** Plain **Shape:** Square, 28.43 x 28.43 mm

Date	Mintage	F	VF	XF	Unc	BU
2002BP	5,000	—	—	—	15.00	18.00
2002BP Proof	5,000	Value: 25.00				

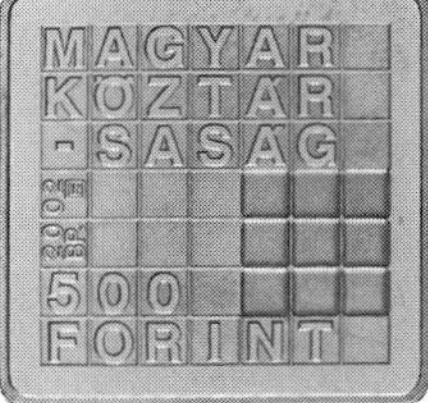

KM# 765 500 FORINT
13.8000 g., Copper-Nickel **Subject:** Rubik's Cube **Obv:** Inscription on Rubik's Cube design **Rev:** Rubik's Cube with inscription **Edge:** Plain **Shape:** Square, 28.43 x 28.43 mm

Date	Mintage	F	VF	XF	Unc	BU
2002BP	5,000	—	—	—	16.00	20.00
2002BP Proof	5,000	Value: 30.00				

KM# 781 500 FORINT
14.0000 g., Copper-Nickel **Obv:** Old wheel **Rev:** First Hungarian Post Office motor vehicle **Edge:** Plain **Shape:** Square **Note:** 28.43 x 28.43mm

Date	Mintage	F	VF	XF	Unc	BU
2005BP	5,000	—	—	—	16.00	20.00
2005BP Proof	10,000	Value: 30.00				

KM# 766 1000 FORINT
19.5000 g., Bronze Hollow coin unscrews to open **Obv:** Denomination and satellite dish **Rev:** Mercury

Date	Mintage	F	VF	XF	Unc	BU
2002BP	15,000	—	—	—	15.00	16.50

KM# 787 1000 FORINT
13.8100 g., Copper-Nickel, 28.3 mm. **Obv:** Value and partial front view of antique automobile **Rev:** Model T Ford **Edge:** Plain **Shape:** Square

Date	Mintage	F	VF	XF	Unc	BU
2006BP	10,000	—	—	—	15.00	18.00
2006BP Proof	10,000	Value: 25.00				

KM# 797 1000 FORINT
14.0000 g., Copper-Nickel, 28.43 x 28.43 mm. **Subject:** 125th Anniversary - Birth of János Adorján **Obv:** Early two cylinder aircraft motor with propeller **Obv. Legend:** MAGYAR / KOZTARSASAG **Obv. Designer:** Balozs Bi **Rev:** Early monoplane **Rev. Legend:** ADORJAN JANOS / AZ ELSO SIKERES MAGYAR / REPULOGEP TERVEZOJE **Edge:** Plain **Shape:** Square

Date	Mintage	F	VF	XF	Unc	BU
2007BP	10,000	—	—	—	15.00	18.00
2007BP Proof	10,000	Value: 25.00				

KM# 809 1000 FORINT
14.0000 g., Copper-Nickel, 28.43 x 28.43 mm. **Subject:** Telephone Herald **Edge:** Plain **Shape:** Square **Designer:** Áron Bohus

Date	Mintage	F	VF	XF	Unc	BU
2008	10,000	—	—	—	15.00	18.00
2008 Proof	15,000	Value: 25.00				

KM# 813 1000 FORINT
14.0000 g., Copper-Nickel, 28.4 x 28.4 mm. **Subject:** Donat Banki, 150th Anniversary of Birth **Obv:** Denomination view of crossflow turbine **Rev:** Portrait facing in suit **Shape:** Square

Date	Mintage	F	VF	XF	Unc	BU
2009BP	10,000	—	—	—	—	15.00
2009BP Proof	10,000	Value: 20.00				

KM# 818 1000 FORINT
14.0000 g., Copper-Nickel, 28.4 x 28.4 mm. **Subject:** Laszlo Jozsef Biro, Inventor of the ball point pen **Obv:** Ball point pen schematic **Obv. Designer:** Gyorgy Szabo **Rev:** Bust facing **Shape:** Square

Date	Mintage	F	VF	XF	Unc	BU
2010BP	10,000	—	—	—	12.00	15.00
2010BP Proof	10,000	Value: 25.00				

KM# 752 3000 FORINT
31.4600 g., 0.9250 Silver 0.9356 oz. ASW, 38.5 mm. **Subject:** Hungarian Silver Coinage Millennium **Obv:** Denomination in ornamental frame **Rev:** Thaler design circa 1500 portraying

Ladislaus I (1077-95) with the title of saint **Edge:** Reeding over "1001-2001" **Edge Lettering:** BP • NX • KB • HX • GY • F • AF • MM • C +

Date	Mintage	F	VF	XF	Unc	BU
2001BP	5,000	—	—	—	40.00	45.00
2001BP Proof	5,000	Value: 50.00				

KM# 759 3000 FORINT
31.8000 g., 0.9250 Silver 0.9457 oz. ASW, 38.7 mm. **Subject:** Centennial of First Hungarian Film "The Dance" **Obv:** Denomination **Rev:** Two dancers on film **Edge:** Reeded

Date	Mintage	F	VF	XF	Unc	BU
2001BP	3,500	—	—	—	42.00	47.50
2001BP Proof	3,500	Value: 55.00				

KM# 761 3000 FORINT
31.3300 g., 0.9250 Silver 0.9317 oz. ASW, 38.6 mm. **Subject:** Hortobagy National Park **Obv:** Landscape, denomination **Rev:** Hungarian Grey Longhorn bull **Edge:** Reeded

Date	Mintage	F	VF	XF	Unc	BU
2002BP	5,000	—	—	—	37.50	42.50
2002BP Proof	5,000	Value: 50.00				

KM# 767 3000 FORINT
31.4600 g., 0.9250 Silver 0.9356 oz. ASW **Subject:** 100th Anniversary - Birth of Kovacs Margit (1902-1977) **Obv:** Denomination **Rev:** The "Trumpet of Judgement Day"

Date	Mintage	F	VF	XF	Unc	BU
2002	4,000	—	—	—	40.00	45.00
2002 Proof	4,000	Value: 55.00				

KM# 762 3000 FORINT
31.4600 g., 0.9250 Silver 0.9356 oz. ASW, 38.5 mm. **Subject:** 200th Anniversary - National Library **Obv:** Small coat of arms in ornate frame **Rev:** Interior view of library **Edge:** Reeded

Date	Mintage	F	VF	XF	Unc	BU
2002BP	3,000	—	—	—	40.00	45.00
2002BP Proof	3,000	Value: 50.00				

KM# 763 3000 FORINT
31.4600 g., 0.9250 Silver 0.9356 oz. ASW, 38.5 mm. **Subject:** Janos Bolyai's publication of his "Appendix" **Obv:** Circular graph **Rev:** Signature above 7-line inscription, name and dates **Edge:** Reeded

Date	Mintage	F	VF	XF	Unc	BU
2002BP	3,000	—	—	—	40.00	45.00
2002BP Proof	3,000	Value: 50.00				

KM# 817 3000 FORINT
10.0000 g., 0.9250 Silver 0.2974 oz. ASW **Subject:** Ferenc Kazinczy, 250th Anniversary of Birth **Obv:** Quill pen and rolled document **Rev:** Bust facing **Rev. Designer:** E. Tamás Soltra

Date	Mintage	F	VF	XF	Unc	BU
2009	5,000	—	—	—	16.00	20.00
2009 Proof	5,000	Value: 30.00				

KM# 751 4000 FORINT
31.4600 g., 0.9250 Silver 0.9356 oz. ASW, 26.4 x 39.6 mm. **Subject:** Godollo Artist Colony Centennial **Obv:** Denomination **Rev:** "Sisters" stained glass window design **Edge:** Plain **Shape:** Vertical rectangle

Date	Mintage	F	VF	XF	Unc	BU
2001BP	4,000	—	—	—	40.00	45.00
2001BP Proof	4,000	Value: 50.00				

KM# 769 5000 FORINT
31.4600 g., 0.9250 Silver 0.9356 oz. ASW, 38.6 mm. **Subject:** Budapest Philharmonic Orchestra **Obv:** Crowned arms in wreath **Rev:** Four coin-like portraits of Erkel, Dohnanyi, Bartók and Kodaly **Edge:** Reeded

Date	Mintage	F	VF	XF	Unc	BU
2003BP	4,000	—	—	—	37.50	42.50
2003BP Proof	4,000	Value: 50.00				

KM# 770 5000 FORINT
31.4600 g., 0.9250 Silver 0.9356 oz. ASW, 38.6 mm. **Subject:** Janos Neumann, 100th Anniversary of Birth **Obv:** Denomination and binary number date **Rev:** Portrait and building **Edge:** Reeded

Date	Mintage	F	VF	XF	Unc	BU
2003BP	3,000	—	—	—	40.00	45.00
2003BP Proof	3,000	Value: 55.00				

KM# 771 5000 FORINT
31.4600 g., 0.9250 Silver 0.9356 oz. ASW, 38.6 mm. **Subject:** Rakoczi's War of Liberation **Obv:** Transylvanian ducat design above country name, value and date **Rev:** Kuruc cavalryman with sword and trumpet **Edge:** Reeded

Date	Mintage	F	VF	XF	Unc	BU
2003BP	3,000	—	—	—	45.00	50.00
2003BP Proof	3,000	Value: 60.00				

KM# 772 5000 FORINT
31.4600 g., 0.9250 Silver 0.9356 oz. ASW, 38.6 mm. **Subject:** World Heritage in Hungary - Holloko **Obv:** Holloko castle ruins above country name, value and date **Rev:** Village view behind woman in folk costume **Edge:** Reeded

Date	Mintage	F	VF	XF	Unc	BU
2003BP	5,000	—	—	—	42.50	45.00
2003BP Proof	5,000	Value: 50.00				

KM# 774 5000 FORINT
31.4600 g., 0.9250 Silver 0.9356 oz. ASW, 38.6 mm. **Obv:** Value **Rev:** Two Olympic boxers **Edge:** Reeded

Date	Mintage	F	VF	XF	Unc	BU
2004BP	3,000	—	—	—	45.00	47.50
2004BP Proof	9,000	Value: 50.00				

KM# 775 5000 FORINT
31.4600 g., 0.9250 Silver 0.9356 oz. ASW, 38.6 mm. **Obv:** "Solomon Tower" above value **Rev:** Visegrad Castle with the Solomon Tower **Edge:** Reeded

Date	Mintage	F	VF	XF	Unc	BU
2004BP	4,000	—	—	—	45.00	50.00
2004BP Proof	4,000	Value: 55.00				

KM# 776 5000 FORINT
31.4600 g., 0.9250 Silver 0.9356 oz. ASW, 38.6 mm. **Obv:** Value and country name above Euro Union stars **Rev:** Mythical stag seen through an ornate window **Edge:** Reeded

Date	Mintage	F	VF	XF	Unc	BU
2004BP Proof	10,000	Value: 50.00				

KM# 778 5000 FORINT
31.4600 g., 0.9250 Silver 0.9356 oz. ASW, 38.6 mm. **Subject:** Ancient Christian Necropolis at Pecs **Obv:** Value and ancient artifact **Rev:** Interior view of tomb **Edge:** Reeded

Date	Mintage	F	VF	XF	Unc	BU
2004BP	5,000	—	—	—	40.00	45.00
2004BP Proof	5,000	Value: 50.00				

KM# 782 5000 FORINT
31.4600 g., 0.9250 Silver 0.9356 oz. ASW, 38.6 mm. **Obv:** Bat flying above value **Rev:** Interior cave view **Edge:** Reeded

Date	Mintage	F	VF	XF	Unc	BU
2005BP	5,000	—	—	—	45.00	50.00
2005BP Proof	5,000	Value: 55.00				

KM# 783 5000 FORINT
31.4600 g., 0.9250 Silver 0.9356 oz. ASW, 38.6 mm. **Obv:** Hungarian National Bank building **Rev:** Ignac Alpar and life dates **Edge:** Reeded

Date	Mintage	F	VF	XF	Unc	BU
ND (2005)BP	3,000	—	—	—	45.00	50.00
ND (2005)BP Proof	3,000	Value: 55.00				

KM# 784 5000 FORINT
31.4600 g., 0.9250 Silver 0.9356 oz. ASW, 38.6 mm. **Obv:** Knight on horse with lance **Rev:** Diosgyor Castle **Edge:** Reeded

Date	Mintage	F	VF	XF	Unc	BU
2005BP	4,000	—	—	—	45.00	50.00
2005BP Proof	4,000	Value: 55.00				

KM# 785 5000 FORINT
31.4600 g., 0.9250 Silver 0.9356 oz. ASW, 38.6 mm. **Obv:** Large building above value **Rev:** Karoli Gaspar Reformed (Calvinist) University seal **Edge:** Reeded

Date	Mintage	F	VF	XF	Unc	BU
2005BP	3,000	—	—	—	45.00	50.00
2005BP Proof	3,000	Value: 55.00				

KM# 786 5000 FORINT
31.4600 g., 0.9250 Silver 0.9356 oz. ASW, 38.6 mm. **Obv:** Coin

design of a Transylvanian KM-10 thaler reverse dated 1605 **Rev:** Stephan Bocskai (1557-1606) **Edge:** Reeded

Date	Mintage	F	VF	XF	Unc	BU
2005BP	3,000	—	—	—	45.00	50.00
2005BP Proof	3,000	Value: 55.00				

KM# 790 5000 FORINT

31.4600 g., 0.9250 Silver 0.9356 oz. ASW, 38.61 mm. **Series:** Masterpieces of Ecclesiastical Architecture **Obv:** View of interior of dome **Obv. Legend:** MAGYAR KÖZTÁRSASÁG **Obv. Designer:** István Péter Bartos **Rev:** Basilica facade **Rev. Legend:** ESZTERGOMI BAZILIKA

Date	Mintage	F	VF	XF	Unc	BU
2006BP	2,500	—	—	—	55.00	50.00
2006BP Proof	3,500	Value: 60.00				

KM# 791 5000 FORINT

31.4600 g., 0.9250 Silver 0.9356 oz. ASW, 38.61 mm. **Subject:** 125th Anniversary - Birth of Béla Bartók **Obv:** Transylvanian woodcarving **Obv. Legend:** MAGYAR KÖZTÁRSASÁG **Obv. Designer:** György Kiss **Rev:** Bust of Bartók right, Euro star behind **Edge:** Reeded and lettered **Edge Lettering:** Bartók Béla repeated three times

Date	Mintage	F	VF	XF	Unc	BU
2006BP Proof	25,000	Value: 45.00				

KM# 792 5000 FORINT

31.4600 g., 0.9250 Silver 0.9356 oz. ASW, 38.61 mm. **Series:** Heritage Sites **Obv:** Great White Egret in flight **Obv. Legend:** MAGYAR - KÖZTÁRSASÁG **Obv. Designer:** Virág Szabó **Rev:** Landscape, Schneeberg Mountain above Esterházy palace facade

Date	Mintage	F	VF	XF	Unc	BU
2006BP	5,000	—	—	—	42.50	45.00
2006BP Proof	5,000	Value: 50.00				

KM# 793 5000 FORINT

31.4600 g., 0.9250 Silver 0.9356 oz. ASW, 38.61 mm. **Series:** Hungarian Castles **Subject:** Hungarian Castles **Obv:** Portrait of Ilona Zrinyi **Obv. Legend:** MAGYAR KÖZTÁRSASÁG **Obv. Designer:** Enikö Szöllössy **Rev:** Munkács Castle

Date	Mintage	F	VF	XF	Unc	BU
2006BP	4,000	—	—	—	42.50	45.00
2006BP Proof	4,000	Value: 50.00				

KM# 794 5000 FORINT

31.4600 g., 0.9250 Silver 0.9356 oz. ASW, 38.61 mm. **Subject:** 500th Anniversary - Victory in Nándorfehévár **Obv:** Decorative sword hilt **Obv. Legend:** MAGYAR KÖZTÁRSASÁG **Obv. Designer:** E. Tamás Soltra **Rev:** János Hunyadi in armor at left, John Capistrano in monk's garb at right **Rev. Inscription:** NÁNDORFEHÉRVÁRI / DIADAL

Date	Mintage	F	VF	XF	Unc	BU
2006BP	2,500	—	—	—	50.00	45.00
2006BP Proof	3,500	Value: 55.00				

KM# 795 5000 FORINT

31.4600 g., 0.9250 Silver 0.9356 oz. ASW, 38.61 mm. **Subject:** 50th Anniversary - Hungarian Revolution **Obv:** 1956 repeated in stone blocks at right **Obv. Legend:** MAGYAR KÖZTÁRSASÁG **Obv. Designer:** Attila Rónay **Rev:** 1956 repeated in stone blocks at left, freedom fighter's flag at center **Rev. Legend:** MAGYAR FORRADALOM ÉS SZABADSÁGHARC

Date	Mintage	F	VF	XF	Unc	BU
2006BP	5,000	—	—	—	42.50	45.00
2006BP Proof	5,000	Value: 50.00				

KM# 798 5000 FORINT

31.4600 g., 0.9250 Silver 0.9356 oz. ASW, 38.61 mm. **Series:** Hungarian Castles **Obv:** Walled tower **Obv. Inscription:** MAGYAR / KÖZTÁRSASÁG **Obv. Designer:** György Kiss **Rev:** Gyula castle **Rev. Inscription:** GYULAI / VÁR

Date	Mintage	F	VF	XF	Unc	BU
2007BP	4,000	—	—	—	50.00	55.00
2007BP Proof	4,000	Value: 60.00				

KM# 799 5000 FORINT

31.4600 g., 0.9250 Silver 0.9356 oz. ASW, 38.61 mm. **Subject:** 200th Anniversary - Birth of Count Lajos Batthyány **Obv:** Seal dated 1848 with crowned arms above Batthyány's autograph **Obv. Legend:** MAGYAR KÖZTÁRSASÁG **Obv. Designer:** Márta Csikai **Rev:** 1/2 length figure of Batthyány facing **Rev. Legend:** BATTHYÁNY LAJOS

Date	Mintage	F	VF	XF	Unc	BU
2007BP Proof	20,000	Value: 45.00				

KM# 800 5000 FORINT

31.4600 g., 0.9250 Silver 0.9356 oz. ASW, 38.61 mm. **Subject:** 125th Anniversary - Birth of Zoltán Kodály **Obv:** Gramaphone **Obv. Legend:** MAGYAR KÖZTÁRSASÁG **Obv. Designer:** Gábor Gáti **Rev:** Bust of Kodály facing 3/4 right

Date	Mintage	F	VF	XF	Unc	BU
2007BP	4,000	—	—	—	42.50	45.00
2007BP Proof	6,000	Value: 50.00				

KM# 802 5000 FORINT

31.4600 g., 0.9250 Silver 0.9356 oz. ASW, 38.61 mm. **Subject:** 8ooth Anniversary - Birth of St. Elizabeth **Obv:** Stylized image of St. Elizabeth feeding the hungry **Obv. Inscription:** Magyar / Köztárszág **Rev:** 3/4 length figure of St. Elizabeth seated facing holding roses and bread rolls in her lap

Date	Mintage	F	VF	XF	Unc	BU
2007BP	4,000	—	—	—	52.50	55.00
2007BP Proof	4,000	Value: 60.00				

KM# 804 5000 FORINT

31.4600 g., 0.9250 Silver 0.9356 oz. ASW, 38.61 mm. **Subject:** Great Reformed Church - Debrecen **Obv:** Church interior **Obv. Legend:** MAGYAR KOZTARSASAG **Rev:** Church facade **Rev. Legend:** DEBRECENI REFORMATUS NAGYTEMPLOM **Edge:** Plain **Shape:** 12-sided **Designer:** SZ.EGYED Emma

Date	Mintage	F	VF	XF	Unc	BU
2007BP	4,000	—	—	—	42.50	45.00
2007BP Proof	6,000	Value: 50.00				

KM# 811 5000 FORINT

31.4600 g., 0.9250 Silver 0.9356 oz. ASW, 38.6 mm. **Subject:** Europa heritage site Tokaj Wine Region **Obv:** Value within grape wreath **Rev:** Tokaj Hill and TV tower **Rev. Designer:** Gábor Gáti **Edge:** Reeded

Date	Mintage	F	VF	XF	Unc	BU
2008BP	5,000	—	—	—	—	45.00
2008BP Proof	15,000	Value: 55.00				

KM# 806 5000 FORINT

31.4600 g., 0.9250 Silver 0.9356 oz. ASW, 38.61 mm. **Obv:** Grape wreath rim with denomination, legend & mintmark inside **Rev:** Tokaj hill, TV tower, grapefield with a village & church **Edge:** Milled **Designer:** Gáti Gábor

Date	Mintage	F	VF	XF	Unc	BU
2008	5,000	—	—	—	—	45.00
2008 Proof	15,000	Value: 55.00				

KM# 807 5000 FORINT

31.4600 g., 0.9250 Silver 0.9356 oz. ASW, 38.61 mm. **Subject:** Castle of the Siklós **Obv:** Castle, tower, Franciscan monastery & church **Rev:** Castle of the Siklós **Designer:** Szöllössy Enikö

Date	Mintage	F	VF	XF	Unc	BU
2008	4,000	—	—	—	—	45.00
2008 Proof	6,000	Value: 50.00				

KM# 808 5000 FORINT

31.4600 g., 0.9250 Silver 0.9356 oz. ASW, 38.61 mm. **Subject:** 29th Summer Olympics **Obv:** Coat of arms over water **Rev:** Water polo player **Rev. Designer:** Gabór Kereszthury **Edge:** Milled

Date	Mintage	F	VF	XF	Unc	BU
2008	4,000	—	—	—	—	40.00
2008 Proof	14,000	Value: 45.00				

KM# 810 5000 FORINT

31.4600 g., 0.9250 Silver 0.9356 oz. ASW, 38.61 mm. **Subject:** Centenery birth of Ede Teller **Obv:** Diagram of Deuterium-tritium fusion reaction **Rev:** Portrait Ede Teller **Designer:** Mihály Fritz

Date	Mintage	F	VF	XF	Unc	BU
2008	4,000	—	—	—	—	45.00
2008 Proof	6,000	Value: 50.00				

KM# 812 5000 FORINT

31.4600 g., 0.9250 Silver 0.9356 oz. ASW **Subject:** Miklós Badnóti, 100th Anniversary of Birth **Obv:** Value **Rev:** Bust in suit facing **Rev. Designer:** Gábor Gáti

Date	Mintage	F	VF	XF	Unc	BU
2009	4,000	—	—	—	—	50.00
2009 Proof	4,000	Value: 55.00				

KM# 814 5000 FORINT

31.4600 g., 0.9250 Silver 0.9356 oz. ASW, 38.6 mm. **Subject:** Dohany Street Synagogue, 150th Anniversary **Obv:** Stained glass window **Obv. Designer:** György Szabó **Rev:** Synagogue facade **Shape:** 12-sided

Date	Mintage	F	VF	XF	Unc	BU
2009BP	4,000	—	—	—	—	45.00
2009BP Proof	4,000	Value: 65.00				

KM# 815 5000 FORINT

31.4600 g., 0.9250 Silver 0.9356 oz. ASW, 38.61 mm. **Subject:** Budapest - World Heritage Site **Obv:** Street scene **Rev:** Panoramic view of Danube and Parliament **Rev. Designer:** Mihály Fritz

Date	Mintage	F	VF	XF	Unc	BU
2009	5,000	—	—	—	—	50.00
2009 Proof	5,000	Value: 55.00				

KM# 827 5000 FORINT

31.4600 g., 0.9250 Silver 0.9356 oz. ASW, 38.6 mm. **Subject:** John Calvin, 500th Anniversary

Date	Mintage	F	VF	XF	Unc	BU
2009BP Proof	—	Value: 55.00				

KM# 819 5000 FORINT
31.4600 g., 0.9250 Silver 0.9356 oz. ASW, 38.6 mm. **Subject:** Kosztolanyi Dezso, 125th Anniversary of Birth **Obv:** Architectural element of stone **Rev:** Portrait

Date	Mintage	F	VF	XF	Unc	BU
2010BP	3,000	—	—	—	40.00	45.00
2010BP Proof	5,000	Value: 50.00				

KM# 820 5000 FORINT
31.4700 g., 0.9250 Silver 0.9359 oz. ASW, 39.6x26.4 mm. **Subject:** Orseg National Park **Obv:** Butterfly **Obv. Designer:** Gabor Gati **Rev:** Traditional rural buildings **Shape:** Rectangle

Date	Mintage	F	VF	XF	Unc	BU
2010BP	3,000	—	—	—	40.00	45.00
2010BP Proof	5,000	Value: 50.00				

KM# 821 5000 FORINT
31.4600 g., 0.9250 Silver 0.9356 oz. ASW, 38.6 mm. **Subject:** European Watersports Championships **Obv:** Value and waves **Obv. Designer:** Attila Ronay **Rev:** Swimmer with butterfly stroke

Date	Mintage	F	VF	XF	Unc	BU
2010BP	4,000	—	—	—	40.00	45.00
2010BP Proof	6,000	Value: 50.00				

KM# 822 5000 FORINT
0.5000 g., 0.9990 Gold 0.0161 oz. AGW, 11 mm. **Subject:** Ferenc Erkel - 200th Anniversary of Birth **Obv:** Denomination **Obv. Designer:** Laszlo Szlavics **Rev:** Large bust facing

Date	Mintage	F	VF	XF	Unc	BU
2010BP Proof	10,000	Value: 50.00				

KM# 823 5000 FORINT
31.4600 g., 0.9250 Silver 0.9356 oz. ASW, 38.6 mm. **Subject:** Ferenc Erkel, 200th Anniversary of Birth **Obv:** House **Obv. Designer:** Gyorgy Kiss **Rev:** Bust facing, signature below

Date	Mintage	F	VF	XF	Unc	BU
2010BP Proof	5,000	Value: 55.00				

KM# 753 20000 FORINT
6.9820 g., 0.9860 Gold 0.2213 oz. AGW, 22 mm. **Subject:** Hungarian Coinage Millennium **Obv:** Denomination **Rev:** Hammered coinage minting scene above old coin design **Edge:** Plain

Date	Mintage	F	VF	XF	Unc	BU
2001BP Proof	3,000	Value: 350				

KM# 777 50000 FORINT
13.9640 g., 0.9860 Gold 0.4426 oz. AGW, 25 mm. **Obv:** Value and country name above Euro Union stars **Rev:** Mythical stag seen through ornate window **Edge:** Reeded

Date	Mintage	F	VF	XF	Unc	BU
2004BP Proof	7,000	Value: 650				

KM# 803 50000 FORINT
10.0000 g., 0.9860 Gold 0.3170 oz. AGW, 25 mm. **Subject:** 550th Anniversary - Enthronement of Matthias Hunyadi **Obv:** Raven holding a ring in its beak **Rev:** Portrait of Mátyás Hunyadi based on a marble relief **Edge:** Smooth **Designer:** László Szlávics, Jr.

Date	Mintage	F	VF	XF	Unc	BU
2008 Proof	5,000	Value: 525				

KM# 816 50000 FORINT
10.0000 g., 0.9860 Gold 0.3170 oz. AGW, 25 mm. **Subject:** Ferenc Kazinczy, 250th Anniversary of Birth **Obv:** Value and classical facade **Obv. Designer:** Enikö Szölössy **Rev:** Bust at left

Date	Mintage	F	VF	XF	Unc	BU
2009 Proof	5,000	Value: 525				

KM# 825 50000 FORINT
6.9820 g., 0.9860 Gold 0.2213 oz. AGW, 22 mm. **Subject:** St. Stephen and St. Emeric **Obv:** Medieval document **Obv. Designer:** Eniko Szollossy **Rev:** St. Stephen and prince standing

Date	Mintage	F	VF	XF	Unc	BU
2010BP Proof	5,000	Value: 425				

KM# 758 100000 FORINT
31.1040 g., 0.9860 Gold 0.9860 oz. AGW, 37 mm. **Subject:** Saint Stephen **Obv:** Angels crowning coat of arms **Rev:** King seated on throne **Edge:** Reeded

Date	Mintage	F	VF	XF	Unc	BU
2001BP Proof	3,000	Value: 1,650				

KM# 796 100000 FORINT
20.9460 g., 0.9860 Gold 0.6640 oz. AGW, 38.61 mm. **Subject:** 50th Anniversary - Hungarian Revolution **Obv:** 1956 repeated in cut out stone **Rev:** 1956 repeated in cut out stone with two freedom fighter's flags

Date	Mintage	F	VF	XF	Unc	BU
2006BP Proof	5,000	Value: 1,100				

KM# 824 500,000 FORINT
63.8280 g., 0.9860 Gold 2.0233 oz. AGW, 46 mm. **Subject:** St. Stephan and St. Emeric **Obv:** Medieval document **Obv. Designer:** Eniko Szollossy **Rev:** King and prince standing **Note:** 18 Ducats

Date	Mintage	F	VF	XF	Unc	BU
2010BP Proof	500	Value: 3,500				

MINT SETS

KM#	Date	Mintage	Identification	Issue Price	Mkt Val
MS32	2001 (7)	—	KM#692-697, 721	—	16.50
MS33	2002 (8)	—	KM#692, 693, 694, 695, 696, 697, 721, 760	—	18.00
MS34	2003 (8)	—	KM#692, 693, 694, 695, 696, 697, 721, 768	—	17.50
MS35	2004 (8)	—	KM#692, 693, 694, 695, 696, 697, 721, 773	—	19.00
MS36	2005 (8)	—	KM#692-697, 721, 779 Magyarorszag Penzemei	—	20.00
MS37	2006 (7)	—	KM#692-697, 721, plus silver 1946 KM532	—	17.50

PROOF SETS

KM#	Date	Mintage	Identification	Issue Price	Mkt Val
PS26	2001 (7)	—	KM#692-697, 721	35.00	37.50
PS27	2002 (8)	—	KM#692-697, 721, 760	—	42.50
PS28	2003 (8)	—	KM#692-697, 721, 768	—	40.00
PS29	2004 (8)	—	KM#692-697, 721, 773	—	40.00
PS30	2005 (8)	7,000	KM#692-697, 721, 779	—	37.50
PS31	2006 (7)	—	KM#692-697, 721	—	35.00
PS32	2007 (8)	—	KM#692-697, 721, 805	—	40.00
PS33	2008 (7)	—	KM#692-697, 721	—	35.00

ICELAND

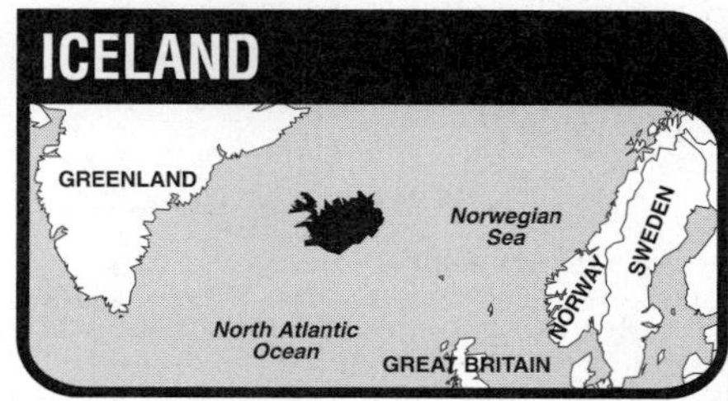

The Republic of Iceland, an island of recent volcanic origin in the North Atlantic east of Greenland and immediately south of the Arctic Circle, has an area of 39,768 sq. mi. (103,000 sq. km.) and a population of just over 300,000. Capital: Reykjavik. Fishing is the chief industry and accounts for a little less than 60 percent of the exports.

REPUBLIC

REFORM COINAGE

100 Old Kronur = 1 New Krona

KM# 27a KRONA
4.0000 g., Nickel Plated Steel, 21.5 mm. **Obv:** Giant facing **Rev:** Cod **Edge:** Reeded

Date	Mintage	F	VF	XF	Unc	BU
2003	5,144,000	—	—	—	0.75	1.50
2005	5,000,000	—	—	—	0.75	1.50
2006	10,000,000	—	—	—	0.75	1.50
2007	10,000,000	—	—	—	0.75	1.50

KM# 28a 5 KRONUR
5.6000 g., Nickel Clad Steel, 24.5 mm. **Obv:** Quartered design of Eagle, dragon, bull and giant **Rev:** Two dolphins leaping left **Edge:** Reeded

Date	Mintage	F	VF	XF	Unc	BU
2005	2,000,000	—	—	—	2.00	3.00
2007	10,000,000	—	—	—	2.00	3.00

KM# 29.1a 10 KRONUR
8.0000 g., Nickel Clad Steel, 27.5 mm. **Obv:** Quartered design of Eagle, dragon, bull and giant **Rev:** Four capelins left **Edge:** Reeded

Date	Mintage	F	VF	XF	Unc	BU
2004	2,000,000	—	—	—	1.75	2.50
2005	4,505,000	—	—	—	1.75	2.50
2006	7,800,000	—	—	—	1.75	2.50

KM# 31 50 KRONUR
8.2500 g., Nickel-Brass, 23 mm. **Obv:** Quartered design of eagle, dragon, bull and giant **Rev:** Crab **Edge:** Reeded **Designer:** Throstur Magnusson

Date	Mintage	F	VF	XF	Unc	BU
2001	2,000,000	—	—	—	4.00	5.00
2005	2,000,000	—	—	—	4.00	5.00

KM# 35 100 KRONUR
8.5000 g., Nickel-Brass, 25.5 mm. **Obv:** Quartered design of Eagle, dragon, bull and giant **Rev:** Lumpfish left **Edge:** Reeded **Designer:** Throstur Magnusson

Date	Mintage	F	VF	XF	Unc	BU
2001	2,140,000	—	—	—	6.00	7.00
2004	2,400,000	—	—	—	6.00	7.00
2006	2,000,000	—	—	—	6.00	7.00
2007	3,000,000	—	—	—	6.00	7.00

INDIA - REPUBLIC

The Republic of India, a subcontinent jutting southward from the mainland of Asia, has an area of 1,269,346 sq. mi. (3,287,590 sq. km.) and a population of over 900 million, second only to that of the People's Republic of China. Capital: New Delhi. India's economy is based on agriculture and industrial activity. Engineering goods, cotton apparel and fabrics, handicrafts, tea, iron and steel are exported.

The Republic of India is a member of the Common-wealth of Nations. The president is the Chief of State. The prime minister is the Head of Government.

MINT MARKS

(Mint marks usually appear directly below the date.)

B - Mumbai (Bombay), proof issues only
(B) - Mumbai (Bombay), diamond
(C) - Calcutta, no mint mark
(H) - Hyderabad, star (1963--)
M - Mumbai (Bombay), proof only after 1996
(N) - Noida, dot
(T) - Taegu (Korea), star below first or last date digit

REPUBLIC

DECIMAL COINAGE

KM# 54 25 PAISE
2.8200 g., Stainless Steel, 19 mm. **Obv:** Small Asoka lion pedestal **Rev:** Rhinoceros left **Edge:** Plain **Note:** Varieties of date size exist.

Date	Mintage	F	VF	XF	Unc	BU
2001(B)	—	—	0.10	0.20	1.00	—
2001(C)	—	—	0.10	0.20	1.00	—
2001(H)	—	—	0.15	0.25	1.00	—
2002(B)	—	—	0.15	0.25	1.00	—
2002(C)	—	—	0.15	0.25	1.00	—
2002(H)	—	—	0.25	0.40	1.00	—

KM# 69 50 PAISE
3.8000 g., Stainless Steel, 22 mm. **Subject:** Parliament Building in New Delhi **Obv:** Denomination **Rev:** Building

Date	Mintage	F	VF	XF	Unc	BU
2001(B)	—	—	0.15	0.25	0.50	—
2001(C)	—	—	0.15	0.25	0.50	—
2001(H)	—	—	0.20	0.40	0.75	—
2001(N)	—	—	0.15	0.25	0.50	—
2002(B)	—	—	0.15	0.25	0.50	—
2002(C)	—	—	0.15	0.25	0.50	—
2002(H)	—	—	0.15	0.25	0.50	—
2002(N)	—	—	0.15	0.25	0.50	—
2003(B)	—	—	0.15	0.25	0.50	—
2003(N)	—	—	0.15	0.25	0.50	—
2003(C)	—	—	0.15	0.25	0.50	—
2007(C)	—	—	0.15	0.25	0.50	—
2007(N)	—	—	0.15	0.25	0.50	—

KM# 374 50 PAISE
Stainless Steel, 23 mm. **Obv:** Asoka Pedestal **Rev:** Clenched fist and value

Date	Mintage	F	VF	XF	Unc	BU
2008(C)	—	—	—	—	0.50	0.75
2008(Hy)	—	—	—	—	0.50	0.75
2008(M)	—	—	—	—	0.50	0.75
2008(N)	—	—	—	—	0.50	0.75

KM# 92.2 RUPEE
4.9000 g., Stainless Steel, 25 mm. **Obv:** Asoka lion pedestal **Rev:** Denomination and date, grain ears flank **Edge:** Plain **Note:** Mint mark varieties exist.

Date	Mintage	F	VF	XF	Unc	BU
2001(B)	—	—	0.20	0.40	0.70	—
2001(C)	—	—	0.20	0.40	0.70	—
2001(K)	—	—	0.20	0.40	0.70	—
2001(N)	—	—	0.20	0.40	0.70	—
2001(H)	—	—	0.20	0.40	0.70	—

Note: Small and large mint mark exist, doubled left or right of wheat stalks

Date	Mintage	F	VF	XF	Unc	BU
2002(B)	—	—	0.20	0.40	0.70	—
2002(N)	—	—	0.20	0.40	0.70	—
2002(C)	—	—	0.20	0.40	0.70	—
2002(H)	—	—	0.20	0.40	0.70	—
2003(B)	—	—	0.20	0.40	0.70	—
2003(C)	—	—	0.20	0.40	0.70	—
2003(H)	—	—	0.20	0.40	0.70	—
2004(B)	—	—	0.20	0.40	0.70	—
2004(C)	—	—	0.20	0.40	0.70	—
2004(H)	—	—	0.20	0.40	0.70	—
2004(N)	—	—	0.20	0.40	0.70	—

KM# 313 RUPEE
4.9500 g., Stainless Steel, 25 mm. **Subject:** 100th Anniversary - Birth of Jaya Prakash Narayan **Obv:** Asoka column **Rev:** Bust of Jaya Prakash Narayan slightly left **Edge:** Plain

Date	Mintage	F	VF	XF	Unc	BU
2002(B)	—	—	0.45	0.75	1.00	—
2002(B) Proof	—	Value: 3.00				
2002(C)	—	—	0.45	0.75	1.00	—
2002(H)	—	—	0.45	0.75	1.00	—

KM# 314 RUPEE
4.9500 g., Stainless Steel, 25 mm. **Subject:** Maharana Pratap **Edge:** Plain

Date	Mintage	F	VF	XF	Unc	BU
2003(B)	—	—	0.45	0.75	1.00	—
2003(B) Proof	—	Value: 2.50				
2003(H)	—	—	0.45	0.75	1.00	—

KM# 316 RUPEE
4.8500 g., Stainless Steel, 25 mm. **Obv:** Asoka lions **Rev:** 3/4 length military figure Veer Durgadass with spear left **Edge:** Plain

Date	Mintage	F	VF	XF	Unc	BU
2003(B)	—	—	0.50	0.80	1.25	—
2003(B) Proof	—	Value: 2.50				
2003(H)	—	—	0.50	0.80	1.25	—

KM# 321 RUPEE
5.0000 g., Stainless Steel, 24.9 mm. **Subject:** 150th Anniversary of the Indian Postal Service **Obv:** Asoka lions above value **Rev:** Partial postage stamp design **Edge:** Grooved

Date	Mintage	F	VF	XF	Unc	BU
2004(C)	—	—	—	—	2.00	—
2004(C) Proof	—	Value: 3.50				

KM# 322 RUPEE
4.9500 g., Stainless Steel, 24.8 mm. **Obv:** Asoka lions and value **Rev:** Cross dividing four dots **Edge:** Plain

Date	Mintage	F	VF	XF	Unc	BU
2005(C)	—	—	—	—	2.00	—
2005(H)	—	—	—	—	0.20	—
2007(H)	—	—	—	—	2.00	—

KM# 331 RUPEE

4.9000 g., Stainless Steel, 25 mm. **Subject:** Bharata Natyam Dance Expressions **Obv:** Asoka lion pedestal **Rev:** Gesture of hand with thumb up **Edge:** Plain

Date	Mintage	F	VF	XF	Unc	BU
2007(C)	—	—	—	0.40	1.00	—
2007(H)	—	—	—	0.40	1.00	—
2007(N)	—	—	—	0.40	1.00	—
2008(B)	—	—	—	0.40	1.00	—
2008(C)	—	—	—	0.40	1.00	—
2008(Hy)	—	—	—	0.40	1.00	—
2008(N)	—	—	—	0.40	1.00	—
2008(M)	—	—	—	0.40	1.00	—
2009(B)	—	—	—	—	1.00	—
2009(C)	—	—	—	—	1.00	—
2009(Hy)	—	—	—	—	1.00	—
2009(M)	—	—	—	—	1.00	—
2009(N)	—	—	—	—	1.00	—

KM# 121.5 2 RUPEES

6.0600 g., Copper-Nickel, 26 mm. **Subject:** National Integration **Obv:** Type C **Rev:** Flag on map **Edge:** Plain **Note:** 11-sided

Date	Mintage	F	VF	XF	Unc	BU
2001(B)	—	—	0.40	0.70	1.50	—
2001(C)	—	—	0.40	0.70	1.50	—
2001(H)	—	—	0.40	0.70	1.50	—
2002(B)	—	—	0.40	0.70	1.50	—
2002(C)	—	—	0.40	0.70	1.50	—
2002(H)	—	—	0.40	0.70	1.50	—
2002(N)	—	—	0.40	0.70	1.50	—
2003(B)	—	—	—	0.70	1.50	—
2003(C)	—	—	—	0.70	1.50	—
2003(H)	—	—	—	0.70	1.50	—
2004(B)	—	—	—	0.70	1.50	—
2004(C)	—	—	—	0.70	1.50	—
2004(H)	—	—	—	0.70	1.50	—

KM# 121.3 2 RUPEES

6.0000 g., Copper-Nickel, 26 mm. **Subject:** National Integration **Obv:** Type A **Rev:** Flag on map **Edge:** Plain **Shape:** 11-sided **Note:** Reduced size, non magnetic.

Date	Mintage	F	VF	XF	Unc	BU
2001(B)	—	—	0.40	0.70	1.50	—
2001(C)	—	—	0.40	0.70	1.50	—
2002(C)	—	—	0.40	0.70	1.50	—
2003(C)	—	—	0.40	0.70	1.50	—
2003(H)	—	—	0.40	0.70	1.50	—

KM# 303 2 RUPEES

6.2400 g., Copper-Nickel, 25.7 mm. **Subject:** 100th Anniversary - Birth of Dr. Syama P. Mookerjee **Obv:** Asoka lion pedestal above denomination, type B **Rev:** Bust of Dr. Mookerjeeright **Edge:** Plain

Date	Mintage	F	VF	XF	Unc	BU
2001(B)	—	—	1.25	2.00	3.00	—
2001(C)	—	—	1.25	2.00	3.00	—
2001(C) Proof	—	Value: 7.50				
2001	—	—	1.25	2.00	3.00	—
2001(N)	—	—	1.25	2.00	3.00	—

KM# 305 2 RUPEES

6.1000 g., Copper-Nickel, 25.7 mm. **Subject:** Sant Tukaram (film about poet) **Obv:** Asoka column above value **Rev:** Seated musician **Shape:** Eleven sided

Date	Mintage	F	VF	XF	Unc	BU
2002(B)	—	—	—	1.25	2.00	—
2002(C)	—	—	—	1.25	2.00	—
2002(C)	—	Value: 5.00				

KM# 307 2 RUPEES

6.0500 g., Copper-Nickel **Subject:** 150th Anniversary - Indian Railways **Obv:** Asoka column above value **Rev:** Cartoon elephant holding railroad lantern **Edge:** Plain **Shape:** 11-sided

Date	Mintage	F	VF	XF	Unc	BU
2003(B)	—	—	—	1.25	2.00	—
2003(C)	—	—	—	1.25	2.00	—
2003(C) Proof	—	Value: 5.00				
2003(H)	—	—	—	1.75	2.00	—

KM# 334 2 RUPEES

6.0000 g., Copper-Nickel, 26 mm. **Subject:** 150th Anniversary - Telecommunications **Obv:** Asoka lions **Rev:** Cartoon bird standing holding cell phone **Edge:** Plain **Shape:** 11-sided

Date	Mintage	F	VF	XF	Unc	BU
2004(B)	—	—	—	—	2.00	—
2004(B) Proof	—	Value: 5.00				

KM# 326 2 RUPEES

5.8000 g., Stainless Steel **Obv:** Asoka Pillar and value in center **Rev:** Cross with U-shaped arms and dots **Edge:** Plain **Note:** Size varies 26.75 - 27.07 mm

Date	Mintage	F	VF	XF	Unc	BU
2005(B)	—	—	—	0.50	1.35	—
2005(C)	—	—	—	0.50	1.35	—
2005(H)	—	—	—	0.50	1.35	—
2005(N)	—	—	—	0.50	1.35	—
2006(B) small date	—	—	—	0.40	1.00	—
2006(B) large date	—	—	—	0.40	1.00	—
2006(H)	—	—	—	0.40	1.00	—
2006(N)	—	—	—	0.40	1.00	—
2007(B)	—	—	—	0.40	1.00	—
2007(H)	—	—	—	0.40	1.00	—

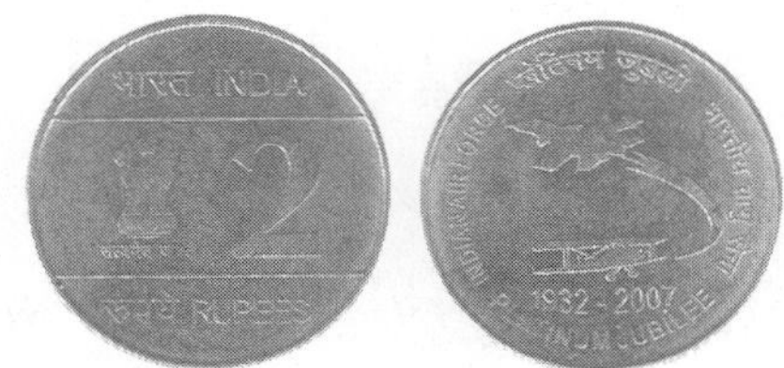

KM# 350 2 RUPEES

6.0000 g., Stainless Steel, 26.9 mm. **Subject:** 75th Anniversary Indian Air Force **Obv:** Asoka column **Rev:** Planes in flight **Edge:** Plain **Shape:** 11-sided

Date	Mintage	F	VF	XF	Unc	BU
2007(C)	—	—	—	2.00	3.00	—
2007(C) Proof	—	Value: 5.00				

KM# 327 2 RUPEES

5.8000 g., Stainless Steel, 27 mm. **Obv:** Asoka Pillar at center **Obv. Inscription:** INDIA in Hindi and English **Rev:** Hasta Mudra - hand gesture from the dance Bharata Natyam **Edge:** Plain

Date	Mintage	F	VF	XF	Unc	BU
2007(B)	—	—	—	0.50	1.25	—
Note: Mintmark position varies 1 or 2 mm below date.						
2007(C)	—	—	—	0.50	1.25	—
2007(H)	—	—	—	—	1.25	—
2008(B)	—	—	—	—	1.25	—
2008(C)	—	—	—	—	1.25	—
2008(H)	—	—	—	—	1.25	—
2008(N)	—	—	—	—	1.25	—
2009(B)	—	—	—	—	1.25	—
2009(C)	—	—	—	—	1.25	—
2009(H)	—	—	—	—	1.25	—
2009(N)	—	—	—	—	1.25	—

KM# 375 2 RUPEES

Stainless Steel, 27 mm. **Subject:** Natya Mudra **Obv:** Asoka Pedestal **Rev:** Value

Date	Mintage	F	VF	XF	Unc	BU
2008(C)	—	—	—	—	2.00	—
2008(Hy)	—	—	—	—	2.00	—
2008(M)	—	—	—	—	2.00	—
2008(N)	—	—	—	—	2.00	—
2009(C)	—	—	—	—	2.00	—
2009(Hy)	—	—	—	—	2.00	—
2009(M)	—	—	—	—	2.00	—
2009(N)	—	—	—	—	2.00	—

KM# 368 2 RUPEES

5.8000 g., Stainless Steel, 27 mm. **Subject:** Louis Braile, 200th Anniversary of Birth **Obv:** Asoka Pedestal **Rev:** Portrait

Date	Mintage	F	VF	XF	Unc	BU
2008(Hy) In sets only	—	—	—	—	—	1.25
2009(C)	—	—	—	—	0.50	1.25
2009(B)	—	—	—	—	0.50	1.25
2009(H)	—	—	—	—	0.50	1.25
2009(Hy)	—	—	—	—	0.50	1.25

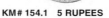

KM# 154.2 5 RUPEES

8.9100 g., Copper-Nickel, 23 mm. **Obv:** Asoka lion pedestal **Rev:** Denomination flanked by flowers **Edge:** Milled

Date	Mintage	F	VF	XF	Unc	BU
2001(C)	—	—	8.00	10.00	15.00	—
2002(C)	—	—	8.00	10.00	15.00	—
2003(C)	—	—	8.00	10.00	15.00	—

KM# 154.4 5 RUPEES

Copper-Nickel, 23 mm. **Obv:** Asoka lion pedestal as seen on 2 Rupees, KM#121.5 **Rev:** Denomination flanked by flowers

Date	Mintage	F	VF	XF	Unc	BU
2001(B)	—	—	0.40	0.70	1.50	—
2002(B)	—	—	0.40	0.70	1.50	—
2003(B)	—	—	0.40	0.70	1.50	—
2004(B)	—	—	0.40	0.70	1.50	—

KM# 154.1 5 RUPEES

9.3000 g., Copper-Nickel, 23.4 mm. **Obv:** Asoka lion pedestal **Rev:** Denomination flanked by flowers **Edge:** Security **Note:** (C) - Calcutta mint has issued 2 distinctly different security edge varieties every year 1992-2003 with large dots and thick center line, w/small dots and narrow center line.

Date	Mintage	F	VF	XF	Unc	BU
2001(B)	—	—	0.40	0.70	1.50	—
2001(C) Plain 1	—	—	0.40	0.70	1.50	—
2001(C) Serif 1	—	—	1.50	3.00	5.00	—
2001(H)	—	—	0.40	0.90	2.25	—
2002(C)	—	—	0.40	0.70	1.50	—
2002(N)	—	—	0.40	0.70	1.50	—
2003(C)	—	—	0.40	0.70	1.50	—

KM# 304 5 RUPEES
9.0700 g., Copper-Nickel, 23.19 mm. **Subject:** 2600th Anniversary Birth of Bhagwan Mahavir **Obv:** Asoka column above denomination **Rev:** Swastika above hand in irregular frame **Edge:** Security

Date	Mintage	F	VF	XF	Unc	BU
2001(B)	—	—	1.00	2.00	3.00	5.00
2001(B) Proof	—	Value: 6.50				
2001(N)	—	—	1.00	2.00	3.00	5.00

KM# 308 5 RUPEES
8.9200 g., Copper-Nickel, 23.1 mm. **Subject:** Dadabhai Naroji **Obv:** Asoka column above value **Rev:** Bust of Dadabhai Naroji 3/4 right **Edge:** Security

Date	Mintage	F	VF	XF	Unc	BU
ND(2003)(B)	—	—	—	1.75	3.00	5.00
ND(2003)(C)	—	—	—	1.75	3.00	5.00
ND(2003)(H)	—	—	—	1.75	3.00	5.00

KM# 317.1 5 RUPEES
8.8000 g., Copper-Nickel, 23.1 mm. **Obv:** Asoka lions **Rev:** K. Kamaraj above life dates **Edge:** Security

Date	Mintage	F	VF	XF	Unc	BU
ND(2003)(B)	—	—	1.00	1.75	3.00	5.00
ND(2003)(B) Proof	—	Value: 7.50				
ND(2003)(H)	—	—	1.25	2.00	3.50	5.50
ND(2003)(C)	—	—	1.00	1.75	3.00	5.00

KM# 317.2 5 RUPEES
8.8000 g., Copper-Nickel, 23.1 mm. **Obv:** Asoka lion pedestal **Rev:** K. Kamaraj above life dates **Edge:** Reeded

Date	Mintage	F	VF	XF	Unc	BU
ND (2003)(H)	—	—	5.00	7.00	11.00	—

KM# 329 5 RUPEES
9.0700 g., Bi-Metallic Brass center in Copper-Nickel ring, 23.25 mm. **Obv:** Asoka column, value below **Rev:** Bust of Shastri 3/4 left **Rev. Legend:** LALBAHADUR SHASTRI BIRTH CENTENARY **Edge:** Security

Date	Mintage	F	VF	XF	Unc	BU
ND(2004)	—	—	—	—	3.50	5.00

KM# 336 5 RUPEES
9.0000 g., Stainless Steel, 23 mm. **Subject:** 100th Anniversary Birth of Lal Bahadur Shastri **Obv:** Asoka lions **Rev:** Bust of Lal Bahadur Shastri 3/4 right **Edge:** Security

Date	Mintage	F	VF	XF	Unc	BU
ND(2004)(C)	—	—	—	—	3.50	5.00
ND(2004)(C) Proof	—	Value: 8.00				

KM# 325 5 RUPEES
8.8500 g., Copper-Nickel, 23 mm. **Subject:** 75th Anniversary Dandi March **Obv:** Asoka column **Rev:** Ghandi leading marchers **Edge:** Security type

Date	Mintage	F	VF	XF	Unc	BU
ND (2005)(B)	—	—	—	—	3.00	5.00
ND(2005)(B) Proof	—	Value: 7.50				

KM# 361 5 RUPEES
6.0300 g., Stainless Steel, 22.9 mm. **Subject:** Dandi March

Date	Mintage	F	VF	XF	Unc	BU
ND(2005)(B)	—	—	—	—	4.00	5.00

KM# 324 5 RUPEES
8.8500 g., Copper-Nickel, 23 mm. **Obv:** Asoka column **Rev:** Bust of Mahatma Basaveshwara slightly left **Edge:** Security

Date	Mintage	F	VF	XF	Unc	BU
ND(2006)(B)	—	—	0.40	1.00	3.00	5.00
ND(2006)(B) Proof	—	Value: 6.00				

KM# 324a 5 RUPEES
6.0000 g., Stainless Steel **Subject:** Mahatma Basveshwara

Date	Mintage	F	VF	XF	Unc	BU
ND(2006)(B)	—	—	—	—	—	2.50

KM# 354 5 RUPEES
6.0300 g., Stainless Steel, 22.8 mm. **Subject:** O.N.G.C., 50th Anniversary **Obv:** Asoka column above value

Date	Mintage	F	VF	XF	Unc	BU
ND(2006)(C)	—	—	—	—	4.00	5.00
ND(2006)(H)	—	—	—	—	4.00	5.00

KM# 355 5 RUPEES
9.5000 g., Copper-Nickel, 23.1 mm. **Subject:** Jagathguru Sree Narayana Guruden **Obv:** Asoka column **Rev:** Bust facing

Date	Mintage	F	VF	XF	Unc	BU
ND(2006)(B)	—	—	—	—	3.00	5.00

KM# 355a 5 RUPEES
6.0300 g., Stainless Steel, 22.9 mm. **Subject:** Jagadguru Shree Narayan Guru

Date	Mintage	F	VF	XF	Unc	BU
ND(2006)(B)	—	—	—	—	4.00	5.00

KM# 357 5 RUPEES
6.0300 g., Copper-Nickel, 22.9 mm. **Series:** Asoka column **Subject:** State Bank of India, 200th Anniversary

Date	Mintage	F	VF	XF	Unc	BU
ND(2006)(H)	—	—	—	—	4.00	5.00

KM# 328 5 RUPEES
9.5000 g., Copper-Nickel, 23.10 mm. **Subject:** 150th Anniversary Birth of L. B. G. Tilak **Obv:** Asoka Lion pedestal **Rev:** Bust of Tilak facing slightly right **Edge:** Security

Date	Mintage	F	VF	XF	Unc	BU
2007(B)	—	—	—	—	3.50	5.00

KM# 330 5 RUPEES
6.0300 g., Stainless Steel, 22.88 mm. **Subject:** Information

Technology **Obv:** Asoka column **Rev:** Waves below value **Edge:** Security

Date	Mintage	F	VF	XF	Unc	BU
2007(B)	—	—	—	—	4.00	5.00
2007(C)	—	—	—	—	4.00	5.00
2007(H)	—	—	—	—	4.00	5.00
2007(N)	—	—	—	—	4.00	5.00
2008(B)	—	—	—	—	4.00	5.00
2008(H)	—	—	—	—	4.00	5.00
2008(K)	—	—	—	—	4.00	5.00
2008(N)	—	—	—	—	4.00	5.00

KM# 356 5 RUPEES
6.0300 g., Copper-Nickel, 22.9 mm. **Subject:** Tilakji **Note:** Withdrawn.

Date	Mintage	F	VF	XF	Unc	BU
2007(N)	—	—	—	—	10.00	15.00

KM# 359 5 RUPEES
6.0300 g., Stainless Steel, 22.9 mm. **Subject:** First War of Independence

Date	Mintage	F	VF	XF	Unc	BU
ND(2007)(B)	—	—	—	—	4.00	5.00

KM# 360 5 RUPEES
6.0300 g., Stainless Steel, 22.9 mm. **Rev:** Ghandi seated facing

Date	Mintage	F	VF	XF	Unc	BU
2007	—	—	—	—	4.00	5.00

KM# 336a 5 RUPEES
6.0300 g., Stainless Steel, 22.9 mm. **Subject:** Lal Bahadur Shastri

Date	Mintage	F	VF	XF	Unc	BU
ND(2004)(C)	—	—	—	—	4.00	5.00
ND(2004)(H)	—	—	—	—	4.00	5.00

KM# 365 5 RUPEES
6.0300 g., Nickel-Bronze, 23 mm. **Subject:** St. Alphonsa, 100th Anniversary **Obv:** Asoka column **Rev:** Bust facing

Date	Mintage	F	VF	XF	Unc	BU
2009(B)	—	—	—	—	4.00	5.00

KM# 367 5 RUPEES
6.0300 g., Nickel-Bronze, 23 mm. **Subject:** C. N. Annadurai, 100th Anniversary of Birth **Obv:** Asoka pillar **Rev:** Portrait, signature below

Date	Mintage	F	VF	XF	Unc	BU
2009(B)	—	—	—	—	4.00	5.00

KM# 373 5 RUPEES
6.0000 g., Nickel-Brass, 23 mm. **Obv:** Ashoka Pillar **Rev:** Value flanked by flowers

Date	Mintage	F	VF	XF	Unc	BU
2009(C)	—	—	—	—	3.50	5.00
2009(M)	—	—	—	—	3.50	5.00
2009(Hy)	—	—	—	—	3.50	5.00

KM# 376 5 RUPEES
6.0300 g., Stainless Steel, 22.9 mm. **Subject:** 60th Anniversary of Commonwealth **Rev:** Building

Date	Mintage	F	VF	XF	Unc	BU
2009	—	—	—	—	4.00	5.00

KM# 377 5 RUPEES
Nickel-Brass, 23 mm. **Obv:** Askola column **Rev:** C. Subramaniam facing

Date	Mintage	F	VF	XF	Unc	BU
2010	—	—	—	—	4.00	5.00

KM# 378 5 RUPEES
Nickel-Brass, 23 mm. **Subject:** Brihadeeswarar Temple, 1000th Anniversary **Obv:** Askola column **Rev:** Statue of King Raja Rajan I

Date	Mintage	F	VF	XF	Unc	BU
2011	—	—	—	—	4.00	5.00

KM# 379 5 RUPEES
Nickel-Brass, 23 mm. **Subject:** Income Tax, 150th Anniversary **Obv:** Askola column **Rev:** Chanakya portrait at right

Date	Mintage	F	VF	XF	Unc	BU
2011	—	—	—	—	4.00	5.00

KM# 309 10 RUPEES
12.5000 g., Copper-Nickel, 31 mm. **Subject:** 100th Anniversary Birth of Dr. Syama P. Mookerjee **Obv:** Asoka lion pedestal **Rev:** Bust of Dr. Mookerjee 1/2 right **Edge:** Reeded

Date	Mintage	F	VF	XF	Unc	BU
2001(C)	—	—	—	—	9.00	10.00
2001(C) Proof	—	Value: 15.00				

KM# 344 10 RUPEES
12.5000 g., Copper-Nickel, 31 mm. **Subject:** 100th Anniversary Birth of Jaya Prakash Narayan **Obv:** Asoka column **Rev:** Bust of Jaya Prakash Narayan slightly left **Edge:** Reeded

Date	Mintage	F	VF	XF	Unc	BU
2002(B)	—	—	—	—	9.00	10.00
2002(B) Proof	—	Value: 15.00				

KM# 347 10 RUPEES
12.5000 g., Copper-Nickel, 31 mm. **Subject:** Sant Tukaram (film about poet) **Obv:** Asoka column **Edge:** Reeded

Date	Mintage	F	VF	XF	Unc	BU
2002(C)	—	—	—	—	9.00	10.00
2002(C) Proof	—	Value: 15.00				

KM# 319 10 RUPEES
12.5000 g., Copper-Nickel, 31 mm. **Obv:** Asoka lion pedestal **Rev:** Bust of Maharana Pratap left

Date	Mintage	F	VF	XF	Unc	BU
2003(B)	—	—	—	—	9.00	10.00
2003(B) Proof	—	Value: 15.00				

KM# 332 10 RUPEES
12.5000 g., Copper-Nickel, 31 mm. **Obv:** Asoka lions **Rev:** 3/4 length military figure Veer Durgadass with spear left **Edge:** Reeded

Date	Mintage	F	VF	XF	Unc	BU
2003(B)	—	—	—	—	9.00	10.00
2003(B) Proof	—	Value: 15.00				

KM# 353 10 RUPEES
7.7000 g., Bi-Metallic Copper-Nickel center in Brass ring, 27 mm. **Subject:** Unity in Diversity **Obv:** Asoka Pillar **Rev:** Four heads sharing a common body

Date	Mintage	F	VF	XF	Unc	BU
2005(N)	—	—	—	—	—	2.50
2006(N)	—	—	—	—	—	2.50
2007(N)	—	—	—	—	—	2.50

KM# 371 10 RUPEES
7.7000 g., Bi-Metallic Copper-Nickel center in Brass ring, 27 mm. **Subject:** Tercentenary of Gurta-Gaddi of Shri Guru Granth Sahibji **Obv:** Asoka Pillar and value

Date	Mintage	F	VF	XF	Unc	BU
2008(Hy) In sets only	—	—	—	—	—	10.00
2008(M) In sets only	—	—	—	—	—	10.00

KM# 363 10 RUPEES
7.7000 g., Bi-Metallic Copper-Nickel center in Brass ring, 27 mm. **Subject:** Connectivity and Information Technology **Obv:** Asoka column **Rev:** Large 10, wide rays above

Date	Mintage	F	VF	XF	Unc	BU
2008(N)	—	—	—	—	17.00	20.00
2009(N)	—	—	—	—	17.00	20.00

KM# 372 10 RUPEES
7.7000 g., Bi-Metallic Copper-Nickel center in Brass ring, 27 mm. **Subject:** Dr. Homi Bhabha - 100th Anniversary of Birth **Obv:** Asoka Pillar and value **Rev:** Portrait

Date	Mintage	F	VF	XF	Unc	BU
2009M	—	—	—	—	9.00	10.00

KM# 310 50 RUPEES
30.0000 g., Copper-Nickel, 39 mm. **Subject:** 100th Anniversary Birth of Dr. Syama P. Mookerjee **Obv:** Asoka lion pedestal **Rev:** Bust of Dr. Mookerjee 1/2 right **Edge:** Reeded

Date	Mintage	F	VF	XF	Unc	BU
2001(C)	—	—	—	—	17.00	20.00
2001(C) Proof	—	Value: 30.00				

KM# 348 50 RUPEES
30.0000 g., Copper-Nickel, 39 mm. **Subject:** Sant Tukaram (film about poet) **Obv:** Asoka column **Edge:** Reeded

Date	Mintage	F	VF	XF	Unc	BU
2002(C)	—	—	—	—	15.00	17.00
2002(C) Proof	—	Value: 35.00				

KM# 311 100 RUPEES
35.0000 g., 0.5000 Silver 0.5626 oz. ASW, 44 mm. **Subject:** 10th Anniversary Dr, Syama P. Mookerjee **Obv:** Asoka lion pedestal **Rev:** Bust of Dr. Mookerjee1/2 right **Edge:** Reeded

Date	Mintage	F	VF	XF	Unc	BU
2001(C)	—	—	—	—	50.00	55.00
2001(C) Proof	—	Value: 85.00				

KM# 312 100 RUPEES
35.0000 g., 0.5000 Silver 0.5626 oz. ASW, 44 mm. **Subject:** 2600th Anniversary Birth of Bhagwan Mahavir **Obv:** Asoka lion pedestal **Rev:** Swastika above hand in irregular frame **Edge:** Reeded

Date	Mintage	F	VF	XF	Unc	BU
2001(B)	—	—	—	—	50.00	55.00
2001(B) Proof	—	Value: 85.00				

KM# 345 100 RUPEES
35.0000 g., 0.5000 Silver 0.5626 oz. ASW, 44 mm. **Subject:** 100th Anniversary Birth of Jaya Prakash Narayan **Obv:** Asoka column **Rev:** Bust of Jaya Prakash Narayan slightly left **Edge:** Reeded

Date	Mintage	F	VF	XF	Unc	BU
2002(B)	—	—	—	—	55.00	50.00
2002(B) Proof	—	Value: 85.00				

KM# 349 100 RUPEES
35.0000 g., 0.5000 Silver 0.5626 oz. ASW, 44 mm. **Subject:** Sant Tukaram (film about poet) **Obv:** Asoka column **Edge:** Reeded

Date	Mintage	F	VF	XF	Unc	BU
2002(C)	—	—	—	—	55.00	50.00
2002(C) Proof	—	Value: 85.00				

KM# 340 100 RUPEES
35.0000 g., 0.5000 Silver 0.5626 oz. ASW, 44 mm. **Subject:** 150th Anniversary Indian Railways **Obv:** Asoka column **Rev:** Cartoon elephant holding railroad lantern **Edge:** Reeded

Date	Mintage	F	VF	XF	Unc	BU
2003(C)	—	—	—	—	55.00	50.00
2003(C) Proof	—	Value: 85.00				

KM# 318 100 RUPEES
35.0000 g., 0.5000 Silver 0.5626 oz. ASW, 44 mm. **Obv:** Asoka lion pedestal **Rev:** K. Kamaraj above life dates **Edge:** Reeded

Date	Mintage	F	VF	XF	Unc	BU
ND(2003)(B)	—	—	—	—	55.00	50.00
ND(2003)(B) Proof	—	Value: 85.00				

KM# 320 100 RUPEES
35.0000 g., 0.5000 Silver 0.5626 oz. ASW, 44 mm. **Obv:** Asoka lion pedestal **Rev:** Bust of Maharana Pratap left **Edge:** Reeded

Date	Mintage	F	VF	XF	Unc	BU
2003(B)	—	—	—	—	55.00	50.00
2003(B) Proof	—	Value: 85.00				

KM# 333 100 RUPEES
35.0000 g., 0.5000 Silver 0.5626 oz. ASW, 44 mm. **Obv:** Asoka lions **Rev:** 3/4 length military figure Veer Durgadass with spear left **Edge:** Reeded

Date	Mintage	F	VF	XF	Unc	BU
2003(B)	—	—	—	—	55.00	50.00
2003(B) Proof	—	Value: 85.00				

KM# 335 100 RUPEES
35.0000 g., 0.5000 Silver 0.5626 oz. ASW, 44 mm. **Subject:** 150th Anniversary Telecommunications **Obv:** Asoka lions **Rev:** Cartoon bird standing holding cell phone **Edge:** Reeded

Date	Mintage	F	VF	XF	Unc	BU
2004(B)	—	—	—	—	55.00	50.00
2004(B) Proof	—	Value: 85.00				

KM# 337 100 RUPEES
35.0000 g., 0.5000 Silver 0.5626 oz. ASW, 44 mm. **Subject:** 100th Anniversary Birth of Lal Bahadur Shasti **Obv:** Asoka lions **Rev:** Bust of Lal Bahadur Shastri 3/4 left **Edge:** Reeded

Date	Mintage	F	VF	XF	Unc	BU
ND(2004)(C)	—	—	—	—	55.00	50.00
ND(2004)(C) Proof	—	Value: 85.00				

KM# 343 100 RUPEES
35.0000 g., 0.5000 Silver 0.5626 oz. ASW, 44 mm. **Subject:** 150th Anniversary Indian Postal Service **Obv:** Asoka column **Rev:** Partial postage stamp design **Edge:** Reeded

Date	Mintage	F	VF	XF	Unc	BU
2004	—	—	—	—	55.00	50.00
2004 Proof	—	Value: 85.00				

KM# 338 100 RUPEES
35.0000 g., 0.5000 Silver 0.5626 oz. ASW, 44 mm. **Subject:** 75th Anniversary Dandi March **Obv:** Asoka lions **Rev:** Ghandi leading marchers **Edge:** Reeded

Date	Mintage	F	VF	XF	Unc	BU
ND(2005)(B)	—	—	—	—	55.00	50.00
ND(2005)(B) Proof	—	Value: 85.00				

KM# 339 100 RUPEES
35.0000 g., 0.5000 Silver 0.5626 oz. ASW, 44 mm. **Obv:** Asoka column **Rev:** Bust of Mahatma Basaveshwara slightly left **Edge:** Reeded

Date	Mintage	F	VF	XF	Unc	BU
ND(2006)B	—	—	—	—	55.00	50.00
ND(2006)B Proof	—	Value: 85.00				

KM# 351 100 RUPEES
35.0000 g., 0.5000 Silver 0.5626 oz. ASW, 44 mm. **Subject:** 75th Anniversary Indian Air Force **Obv:** Asoka column **Edge:** Reeded

Date	Mintage	F	VF	XF	Unc	BU
2007(C)	—	—	—	—	55.00	50.00
2007(C) Proof	—	Value: 85.00				

KM# 369 100 RUPEES
35.0000 g., 0.5000 Silver 0.5626 oz. ASW, 44 mm. **Subject:** Louis Braile, 200th Anniversary of Birth

Date	Mintage	F	VF	XF	Unc	BU
2009	—	—	—	—	50.00	55.00

PROOF SETS

KM#	Date	Mintage	Identification	Issue Price	Mkt Val
PS56	2001 (4)	—	KM#303, 309, 310, 311	—	125
PS57	2001 (2)	—	KM#304, 312	—	80.00
PS58	2002B (3)	—	KM#313, 344, 345	—	90.00
PS59	2002(C) (4)	—	KM#346-349	—	130
PS60	2003 (3)	—	KM#314, 319, 320	—	90.00
PS61	2003B (3)	—	KM#316, 332, 333	—	90.00
PS62	2003(C) (2)	—	KM#307, 340	—	80.00
PS63	ND(2003) (2)	—	KM#317.1,318	—	80.00
PS64	2004 (2)	—	KM#321, 343	—	75.00
PS65	2004B (2)	—	KM#334, 335	—	80.00
PS66	2004(C) (2)	—	KM#336, 337	—	80.00
PS67	2005B (2)	—	KM#325, 338	—	80.00
PS68	2006B (2)	—	KM#324, 339	—	80.00
PS69	2007 (2)	—	KM#350, 351	—	80.00

The Republic of Indonesia, the world's largest archipelago, extends for more than 3,000 miles (4,827 km.) along the equator from the mainland of southeast Asia to Australia. The 17,508 islands comprising the archipelago have a combined area of 788,425 sq. mi. (1,919,440 sq. km.) and a population of 205 million, including East Timor. On August 30, 1999, the Timorese majority voted for independence. The Inter FET (International Forces for East Timor) is now in charge of controlling the chaotic situation. Capitol: Jakarta. Petroleum, timber, rubber, and coffee are exported.

Modern coinage issued by the Republic of Indonesia includes separate series for West Irian and for the Riau Archipelago, an area of small islands between Singapore and Sumatra.

MONETARY SYSTEM
100 Sen = 1 Rupiah

REPUBLIC

STANDARD COINAGE

KM# 60 50 RUPIAH
1.3600 g., Aluminum, 19.95 mm. **Obv:** National emblem **Rev:** Black-naped Oriole **Edge:** Plain

Date	Mintage	F	VF	XF	Unc	BU
2001	—	—	—	—	0.30	1.00
2002	—	—	—	—	0.30	1.00

KM# 61 100 RUPIAH
1.7900 g., Aluminum, 23 mm. **Obv:** National emblem **Rev:** Palm Cockatoo **Edge:** Plain

Date	Mintage	F	VF	XF	Unc	BU
2001	—	—	—	—	0.75	1.25
2002	—	—	—	—	0.75	1.25
2003	—	—	—	—	0.75	1.25
2004	—	—	—	—	0.75	1.25
2005	—	—	—	—	0.75	1.25

KM# 66 200 RUPIAH
2.4000 g., Aluminum, 25 mm. **Obv:** National arms **Rev:** Balinese starling bird above value **Edge:** Plain

Date	Mintage	F	VF	XF	Unc	BU
2003	—	—	—	—	1.00	1.50

KM# 59 500 RUPIAH
5.3700 g., Aluminum-Bronze, 24 mm. **Obv:** National emblem **Rev:** Denomination

Date	Mintage	F	VF	XF	Unc	BU
2001	—	—	—	—	1.75	2.25

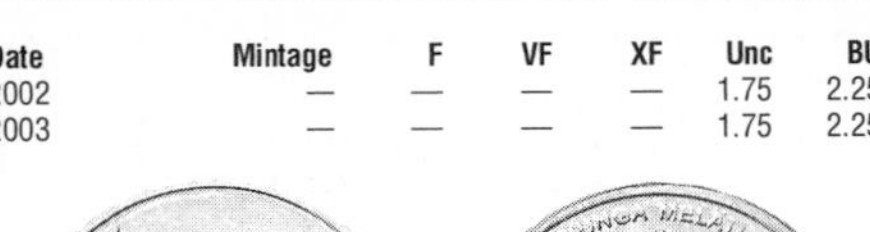

Date	Mintage	F	VF	XF	Unc	BU
2002	—	—	—	—	1.75	2.25
2003	—	—	—	—	1.75	2.25

KM# 67 500 RUPIAH
3.0500 g., Aluminum, 27.2 mm. **Obv:** National arms **Rev:** Jasmine flower above value **Edge:** Segmented reeding

Date	Mintage	F	VF	XF	Unc	BU
2003	—	—	—	—	2.00	2.50

KM# 64 25000 RUPIAH
28.2800 g., 0.9250 Silver 0.8410 oz. ASW, 38.6 mm. **Subject:** Centennial of Sukarno's Birth **Obv:** National arms **Rev:** Uniformed bust of Sukarno **Edge:** Reeded

Date	Mintage	F	VF	XF	Unc	BU
2001 Proof	500	Value: 120				

KM# 65 500,000 RUPIAH
15.0000 g., 0.9990 Gold 0.4818 oz. AGW, 28.2 mm. **Subject:** Centennial of Sukarno's Birth **Obv:** National arms **Rev:** Head left **Edge:** Reeded

Date	Mintage	F	VF	XF	Unc	BU
2001 Proof	500	Value: 850				

The Islamic Republic of Iran, located between the Caspian Sea and the Persian Gulf in southwestern Asia, has an area of 636,296 sq. mi. (1,648,000 sq. km.) and a population of 59.7 million. Capital: Tehran. Although predominantly an agricultural state, Iran depends heavily on oil for foreign exchange. Crude oil, carpets and agricultural products are exported.

In 1931 the Kingdom of Persia became known as the Kingdom of Iran. In 1979 the monarchy was toppled and an Islamic Republic proclaimed.

TITLES

دار الخلافة

Dar al-Khilafat

RULERS
Islamic Republic, SH1358-/1979-AD

MINT NAME

طهران

Tehran

تفليس
Tiflis

MINT MARKS
H - Heaton (Birmingham)
L - Leningrad (St. Petersburg)

COIN DATING

Iranian coins were dated according to the Moslem lunar calendar until March 21, 1925 (AD), when dating was switched to a new calendar based on the solar year, indicated by the notation SH. The monarchial calendar system was adopted in 1976 = MS2535 and was abandoned in 1978 = MS2537. The previously used solar year calendar was restored at that time.

MONETARY SYSTEM
20 Shahis = 1 Rial (100 Dinars)

ISLAMIC REPUBLIC

MILLED COINAGE

KM# 1260 50 RIALS
Copper-Nickel, 26 mm. **Subject:** Shrine of Hazrat Masumah **Obv:** Value and date **Rev:** Shrine within beaded circle **Edge:** Reeded

Date	Mintage	F	VF	XF	Unc	BU
SH1380 (2001)	—	—	2.50	3.50	5.00	—
SH1382 (2003)	—	—	2.50	3.50	5.00	—

KM# 1266 50 RIALS
3.5100 g., Aluminum-Bronze, 20.1 mm. **Obv:** Value and date **Rev:** Hazrat Masumah Shrine **Edge:** Reeded **Mint:** Tehran

Date	Mintage	F	VF	XF	Unc	BU
SH1382(2003)	—	—	—	—	50.00	—
SH1383(2004)	—	—	—	—	2.50	—
SH1384(2005)	—	—	—	—	2.50	—
SH1385(2006)	—	—	—	—	2.50	—

KM# 1261.2 100 RIALS
Copper-Nickel, 29 mm. **Obv:** Value and date **Rev:** Shrine within designed border **Note:** Thick denomination and numerals

Date	Mintage	F	VF	XF	Unc	BU
SH1380 (2001)	—	—	—	—	6.50	—
SH1382 (2003)	—	—	—	—	6.50	—

KM# 1267 100 RIALS
4.6200 g., Aluminum-Bronze, 22.9 mm. **Obv:** Value, date divides wreath below **Rev:** Imam Reza Shrine **Edge:** Reeded **Mint:** Tehran

Date	Mintage	F	VF	XF	Unc	BU
SH1382(2003)	—	—	—	—	50.00	—
SH1383(2004)	—	—	—	—	3.50	—
SH1384(2005)	—	—	—	—	3.50	—
SH1385(2006)	—	—	—	—	3.50	—

KM# 1262 250 RIALS
10.7000 g., Bi-Metallic Copper-Nickel center in Brass ring, 28.3 mm. **Obv:** Value within circle, inscription and date divide wreath **Rev:** Stylized flower within circle and wreath

Date	Mintage	F	VF	XF	Unc	BU
SH1381 (2002)	—	—	—	—	7.50	—
SH1382 (2003)	—	—	—	—	7.50	—

KM# 1268 250 RIALS
5.5000 g., Copper-Nickel, 24.6 mm. **Obv:** Value, date below divides sprays **Rev:** Stylized flower within sprays **Edge:** Plain **Mint:** Tehran

Date	Mintage	F	VF	XF	Unc	BU
SH1382(2003)	—	—	—	—	50.00	—
SH1383(2004)	—	—	—	—	4.50	—
SH1384(2005)	—	—	—	—	4.50	—
SH1385(2006)	—	—	—	—	4.50	—

KM# 1268a 250 RIALS
Aluminum-Bronze **Obv:** Value, date below divides sprays **Rev:** Stylized flower within sprays **Mint:** Tehran

Date	Mintage	F	VF	XF	Unc	BU
SH1386(2007)	—	—	—	—	4.50	—

KM# 1269 500 RIALS
8.9100 g., Bi-Metallic Aluminum-Bronze center in Copper-Nickel ring, 27.1 mm. **Obv:** Value **Rev:** Bird and flowers **Edge:** Reeded **Mint:** Tehran

Date	Mintage	F	VF	XF	Unc	BU
SH1382(2003)	—	—	—	—	50.00	—
SH1383(2004)	—	—	—	—	6.00	—
SH1384(2005)	—	—	—	—	6.00	—
SH1385(2006)	—	—	—	—	6.00	—

KM# 1269a 500 RIALS
Aluminum-Bronze **Obv:** Value in ornamental circle **Rev:** Bird and flowers **Mint:** Tehran

Date	Mintage	F	VF	XF	Unc	BU
SH1386(2007)	—	—	—	—	6.00	—

REFORM COINAGE

KM# 1270 250 RIALS
2.8000 g., Copper-Nickel, 18.5 mm. **Rev:** Feyziyeh School

Date	Mintage	F	VF	XF	Unc	BU
SH1388 (2009)	—	—	—	—	—	5.00

KM# 1271 500 RIALS
3.9000 g., Copper-Nickel, 20.6 mm. **Rev:** Saadi Tomb

Date	Mintage	F	VF	XF	Unc	BU
SH1388 (2009)	—	—	—	—	—	6.00

KM# 1272 1000 RIALS
5.8000 g., Copper-Nickel, 23.7 mm. **Rev:** Khajou Bridge in Isfahan

Date	Mintage	F	VF	XF	Unc	BU
SH1388 (2009)	—	—	—	—	—	12.00

BULLION COINAGE

Issued by the National Bank of Iran

KM# 1250.2 1/2 AZADI
4.0680 g., 0.9000 Gold 0.1177 oz. AGW **Obv:** Legend larger **Obv. Legend:** "Spring of Freedom"

Date	Mintage	F	VF	XF	Unc	BU
SH1381 (2002)	—	—	—	—	185	—
SH1383 (2004)	—	—	—	—	185	—

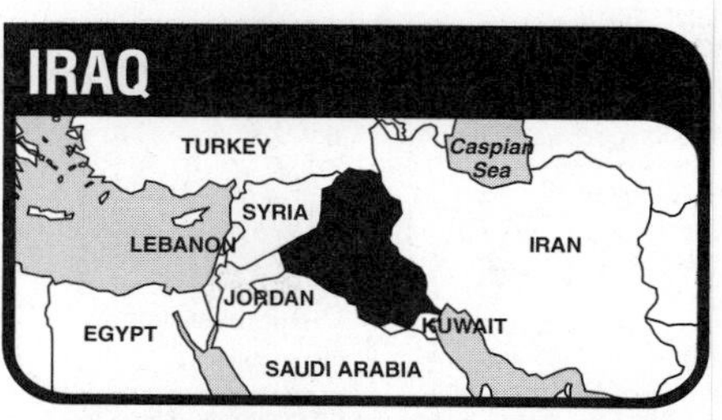

The Republic of Iraq, historically known as Mesopotamia, is located in the Near East and is bordered by Kuwait, Iran, Turkey, Syria, Jordan and Saudi Arabia. It has an area of 167,925 sq. mi. (434,920 sq. km.) and a population of 19 million. Capital: Baghdad. The economy of Iraq is based on agriculture and petroleum. Crude oil accounted for 94 percent of the exports before the war with Iran began in 1980.

Mesopotamia was the site of a number of flourishing civilizations of antiquity - Sumeria, Assyria, Babylonia, Parthia, Persia and the Biblical cities of Ur, Ninevehand and Babylon. Desired because of its favored location, which embraced the fertile alluvial plains of the Tigris and Euphrates Rivers, Mesopotamia - 'land between the rivers'- was conquered by Cyrus the Great of Persia, Alexander of Macedonia and by Arabs who made the legendary city of Baghdad the capital of the ruling caliphate. Suleiman the Magnificent conquered Mesopotamia for Turkey in1534, and it formed part of the Ottoman Empire until 1623, and from 1638 to 1917. Great Britain, given a League of Nations mandate over the territory in 1920, recognized Iraq as a kingdom in 1922. Iraq became an independent constitutional monarchy presided over by the Hashemite family, direct descendants of the prophet Mohammed, in 1932. In 1958, the army-led revolution of July 14 overthrew the monarchy and proclaimed a republic.

MONETARY SYSTEM

Falus, Fulus — Fals, Fils — Falsan

50 Fils = 1 Dirham
200 Fils = 1 Riyal
1000 Fils = 1 Dinar (Pound)

REPUBLIC

DECIMAL COINAGE

KM# 175 25 DINARS
2.5000 g., Copper Plated Steel, 17.4 mm. **Obv:** Value **Rev:** Map **Edge:** Plain

Date	Mintage	F	VF	XF	Unc	BU
AH1425-2004	—	—	—	0.30	0.75	1.00

KM# 176 50 DINARS
4.3400 g., Brass Plated Steel, 22 mm. **Obv:** Value and legend **Rev:** Map **Edge:** Plain

Date	Mintage	F	VF	XF	Unc	BU
AH1425-2004	—	—	—	0.50	1.20	1.60

KM# 177 100 DINARS
4.3000 g., Stainless Steel, 22 mm. **Obv:** Value **Rev:** Map **Edge:** Reeded

Date	Mintage	F	VF	XF	Unc	BU
AH1425-2004	—	—	—	0.80	2.00	2.50

IRELAND REPUBLIC

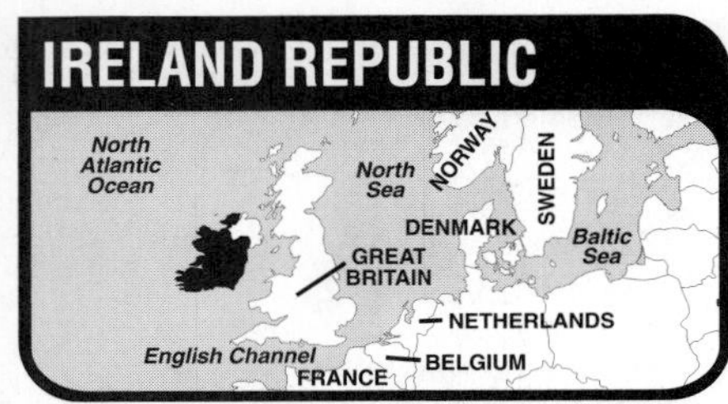

The Republic of Ireland, which occupies five-sixths of the island of Ireland located in the Atlantic Ocean west of Great Britain, has an area of 27,136 sq. mi. (70,280 sq. km.) and a population of 4.3 million. Capital: Dublin. Agriculture and dairy farming are the principal industries. Meat, livestock, dairy products and textiles are exported.

REPUBLIC

EURO COINAGE

European Union Issues

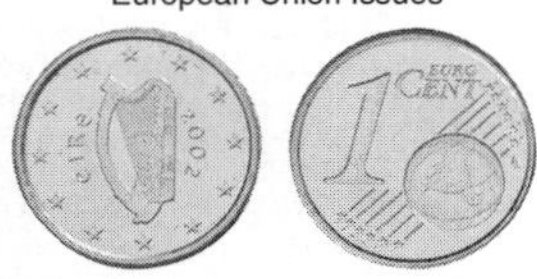

KM# 32 EURO CENT

2.2700 g., Copper Plated Steel, 16.25 mm. **Obv:** Harp **Obv. Designer:** Jarlath Hayes **Rev:** Denomination and globe **Rev. Designer:** Luc Luycx **Edge:** Plain

Date	Mintage	F	VF	XF	Unc	BU
2002	404,339,788	—	—	—	0.35	—
2003	67,902,182	—	—	—	0.35	—
2004	174,833,634	—	—	—	0.35	—
2005	126,964,391	—	—	—	0.35	—
2006	105,413,273	—	—	—	0.35	—
2006 Proof	5,000	Value: 15.00				
2007	18,515,843	—	—	—	0.35	—
2007 Proof	10,000	Value: 12.00				
2008	5,744,031	—	—	—	0.35	—
2009	—	—	—	—	0.35	—
2009 Proof	—	Value: 12.00				
2010	—	—	—	—	0.35	—

KM# 33 2 EURO CENT

3.0000 g., Copper Plated Steel, 18.75 mm. **Obv:** Harp **Obv. Designer:** Jarlath Hayes **Rev:** Denomination and globe **Rev. Designer:** Luc Luycx **Edge:** Plain with groove

Date	Mintage	F	VF	XF	Unc	BU
2002	354,643,386	—	—	—	0.50	—
2003	177,290,034	—	—	—	0.50	—
2004	143,004,694	—	—	—	0.50	—
2005	72,544,884	—	—	—	0.50	—
2006	26,568,597	—	—	—	0.50	—
2006 Proof	5,000	Value: 15.00				
2007	84,291,248	—	—	—	0.50	—
2007 Proof	10,000	Value: 12.00				
2008	52,068	—	—	—	0.50	—
2009	5,049,923	—	—	—	0.50	—
2009 Proof	—	Value: 12.00				
2010	—	—	—	—	0.50	—

KM# 34 5 EURO CENT

4.0000 g., Copper Plated Steel, 19.60 mm. **Obv:** Harp **Obv. Designer:** Jarlath Hayes **Rev:** Denomination and globe **Rev. Designer:** Luc Luycx **Edge:** Plain

Date	Mintage	F	VF	XF	Unc	BU
2002	456,270,848	—	—	—	0.75	—
2003	48,352,370	—	—	—	0.75	—
2004	80,354,322	—	—	—	0.75	—
2005	56,454,380	—	—	—	0.75	—
2006	88,003,370	—	—	—	0.75	—
2006 Proof	5,000	Value: 18.00				
2007	36,225,742	—	—	—	0.75	—
2007 Proof	10,000	Value: 15.00				
2008	50,000	—	—	—	0.75	—
2009	28,333,341	—	—	—	0.75	—
2009 Proof	—	Value: 15.00				
2010	—	—	—	—	0.75	—

KM# 35 10 EURO CENT

4.0700 g., Aluminum-Bronze, 19.75 mm. **Obv:** Harp **Obv. Designer:** Jarlath Hayes **Rev:** Denomination and map **Rev. Designer:** Luc Luycx **Edge:** Reeded

Date	Mintage	F	VF	XF	Unc	BU
2002	275,913,000	—	—	—	1.00	—
2003	133,815,907	—	—	—	1.00	—
2004	34,092,712	—	—	—	1.00	—
2005	4,652,786	—	—	—	1.00	—
2006	9,208,411	—	—	—	1.00	—
2006 Proof	5,000	Value: 18.00				

KM# 47 10 EURO CENT

4.0700 g., Aluminum-Bronze, 19.75 mm. **Obv:** Harp **Obv. Designer:** Jarlath Hayes **Rev:** Relief map of Western Europe, stars, lines and value **Rev. Designer:** Luc Luycz **Edge:** Reeded

Date	Mintage	F	VF	XF	Unc	BU
2007	54,434,307	—	—	—	1.00	—
2007 Proof	10,000	Value: 15.00				
2008	11,794,508	—	—	—	1.00	—
2009	10,850,328	—	—	—	1.00	—
2009 Proof	—	Value: 15.00				
2010	—	—	—	—	1.00	—

KM# 36 20 EURO CENT

5.7300 g., Aluminum-Bronze, 22.25 mm. **Obv:** Harp **Obv. Designer:** Jarlath Hayes **Rev:** Denomination and map **Rev. Designer:** Luc Luycx **Edge:** Notched

Date	Mintage	F	VF	XF	Unc	BU
2002	234,575,562	—	—	—	1.25	—
2003	57,142,221	—	—	—	1.25	—
2004	32,421,447	—	—	—	1.25	—
2005	37,798,942	—	—	—	1.25	—
2006	10,357,229	—	—	—	1.25	—
2006 Proof	5,000	Value: 20.00				

KM# 48 20 EURO CENT

5.7300 g., Aluminum-Bronze, 22.25 mm. **Obv:** Harp **Obv. Designer:** Jarlath Hayes **Rev:** Relief map of Western Europe, stars, lines and value **Rev. Designer:** Luc Luycz **Edge:** Notched

Date	Mintage	F	VF	XF	Unc	BU
2007	12,953,789	—	—	—	1.25	—
2007 Proof	10,000	Value: 18.00				
2008	14,786,835	—	—	—	1.25	—
2009	4,279,307	—	—	—	1.25	—
2009 Proof	—	Value: 18.00				
2010	—	Value: 18.00				

KM# 37 50 EURO CENT

7.8100 g., Aluminum-Bronze, 24.25 mm. **Obv:** Harp **Obv. Designer:** Jarlath Hayes **Rev:** Denomination and map **Edge:** Reeded

Date	Mintage	F	VF	XF	Unc	BU
2002	144,144,592	—	—	—	1.50	—
2003	11,811,926	—	—	—	1.50	—
2004	6,748,912	—	—	—	1.50	—
2005	17,253,568	—	—	—	1.50	—
2006	961,135	—	—	—	1.50	—
2006 Proof	5,000	—	—	—	—	—

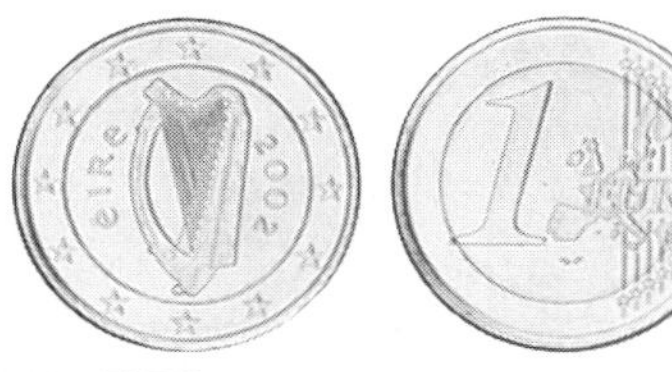

KM# 49 50 EURO CENT

7.8100 g., Aluminum-Bronze, 24.25 mm. **Obv:** Harp **Obv. Designer:** Jarlath Hayes **Rev:** Relief map of Western Europe, stars, lines and value **Rev. Designer:** Luc Luycx **Edge:** Reeded

Date	Mintage	F	VF	XF	Unc	BU
2007	4,991,002	—	—	—	1.50	—
2007 Proof	10,000	Value: 20.00				
2008	50,000	—	—	—	1.50	—
2009	1,866,011	—	—	—	1.50	—
2009 Proof	—	Value: 20.00				
2010	—	—	—	—	1.50	—

KM# 38 EURO

7.5000 g., Bi-Metallic Copper-Nickel center in Brass ring, 23.25 mm. **Obv:** Harp **Obv. Designer:** Jarlath Hayes **Rev:** Denomination and map **Rev. Designer:** Luc Luycx **Edge:** Reeded and plain sections

Date	Mintage	F	VF	XF	Unc	BU
2002	135,139,737	—	—	—	2.75	—
2003	2,520,000	—	—	—	2.75	—
2004	1,632,990	—	—	—	2.75	—
2005	6,769,777	—	—	—	2.75	—
2006	4,023,722	—	—	—	2.75	—
2006 Proof	5,000	Value: 25.00				

KM# 50 EURO

7.5000 g., Bi-Metallic Copper-Nickel center in Brass ring, 23.25 mm. **Obv:** Harp **Obv. Designer:** Jarlath Hayes **Rev:** Relief map of Western Europe, stars, lines and value **Rev. Designer:** Luc Luycz **Edge:** Reeded and plain sections

Date	Mintage	F	VF	XF	Unc	BU
2007	1,850,049	—	—	—	2.75	—
2007 Proof	10,000	Value: 22.00				
2008	2,609,757	—	—	—	2.75	—
2009	3,314,828	—	—	—	2.75	—
2009 Proof	—	Value: 22.00				
2010	—	—	—	—	2.75	—

KM# 39 2 EURO

8.5200 g., Bi-Metallic Brass center in Copper-Nickel ring, 25.7 mm. **Obv:** Harp **Obv. Designer:** Jarlath Hayes **Rev:** Denomination and map **Rev. Designer:** Luc Luycx **Edge:** Reeded with 2's and stars

Date	Mintage	F	VF	XF	Unc	BU
2002	90,548,166	—	—	—	4.00	—
2003	2,631,076	—	—	—	4.00	—
2004	3,738,186	—	—	—	4.00	—
2005	11,982,981	—	—	—	4.00	—
2006	3,860,519	—	—	—	4.00	—
2006 Proof	5,000	Value: 28.00				

KM# 51 2 EURO

8.5200 g., Bi-Metallic Brass center in Copper-Nickel ring, 25.7 mm. **Obv:** Harp **Obv. Designer:** Jarlath Hayes **Rev:** Relief map of Western Europe, stars, lines and value **Rev. Designer:** Luc Luycx **Edge:** Reeded with 2's and stars

Date	Mintage	F	VF	XF	Unc	BU
2007	—	—	—	—	4.00	—
2007 Proof	10,000	Value: 25.00				
2008	5,822,003	—	—	—	4.00	—
2009	30,063	—	—	—	4.00	—
2009 Proof	—	Value: 25.00				
2010	—	—	—	—	4.00	—

KM# 53 2 EURO
8.4500 g., Bi-Metallic Brass center in Copper-Nickel ring, 25.72 mm. **Subject:** 50th Anniversary Treaty of Rome **Obv:** Open treaty book **Rev:** Large value at left, modified outline of Europe at right **Edge:** Reeded with stars and 2's

Date	Mintage	F	VF	XF	Unc	BU
2007	4,605,112	—	—	—	5.00	10.00
2007 Special Unc.	35,000	—	—	—	—	20.00
2007 Proof	10,000	Value: 25.00				

KM# 62 2 EURO
8.5200 g., Bi-Metallic Brass center in Copper-Nickel ring, 25.72 mm. **Subject:** EMU, 10th Anniversary

Date	Mintage	F	VF	XF	Unc	BU
2009	5,000,000	—	—	—	—	10.00

KM# 40 5 EURO
14.1900 g., Copper-Nickel, 28.4 mm. **Subject:** Special Olympics **Obv:** Harp **Obv. Designer:** Jarlath Hayes **Rev:** Multicolor games logo **Edge:** Reeded

Date	Mintage	F	VF	XF	Unc	BU
2003	35,000	—	—	—	15.00	18.00
2003 Proof	25,000	Value: 25.00				

KM# 56 5 EURO
8.5200 g., 0.9250 Silver 0.2534 oz. ASW, 28 mm. **Subject:** International Polar Year **Obv:** Harp within wreath **Rev:** Ernest Shackleton, Tom Crean and The Endurance in distance **Rev. Designer:** Tom Ryan **Edge:** Reeded

Date	Mintage	F	VF	XF	Unc	BU
2008 Proof	5,000	Value: 90.00				

KM# 41 10 EURO
28.2800 g., 0.9250 Silver 0.8410 oz. ASW, 38.61 mm. **Subject:** Special Olympics **Obv:** Gold highlighted harp, 2003, Eire **Obv. Designer:** Jarlath Hayes **Rev:** Gold highlighted games logo **Edge:** Reeded

Date	Mintage	F	VF	XF	Unc	BU
2003 Proof	30,000	Value: 50.00				

KM# 42 10 EURO
28.2800 g., 0.9250 Silver 0.8410 oz. ASW, 38.61 mm. **Subject:** EU Presidency **Obv:** 2004, Eire, Harp **Rev:** Stylized Celtic swan **Rev. Designer:** Thomas Emmet Mullins **Edge:** Reeded

Date	Mintage	F	VF	XF	Unc	BU
2004 Proof	50,000	Value: 45.00				

KM# 44 10 EURO
28.2800 g., 0.9250 Silver 0.8410 oz. ASW, 38.6 mm. **Subject:** Sir William R. Hamilton **Obv:** Eire, 2005, Harp **Rev:** Triangle in circle of Greek letters used as math symbols **Rev. Designer:** Michael Guilfoyle **Edge:** Reeded

Date	Mintage	F	VF	XF	Unc	BU
2005 Proof	30,000	Value: 55.00				

KM# 45 10 EURO
28.2800 g., 0.9250 Silver 0.8410 oz. ASW, 38.61 mm. **Subject:** Samuel Beckett 1906-1989 **Obv:** 2006, Eire, Harp **Rev:** Face, value and play scene **Edge:** Reeded

Date	Mintage	F	VF	XF	Unc	BU
2006 Proof	35,000	Value: 50.00				

KM# 58 10 EURO
28.2800 g., 0.9250 Silver 0.8410 oz. ASW, 38.6 mm. **Subject:** European Culture - Ireland **Obv:** Irish map **Rev:** Celtic design **Rev. Designer:** Mary Gregoriy

Date	Mintage	F	VF	XF	Unc	BU
2007 Proof	35,000	Value: 55.00				

KM# 54 10 EURO
28.2800 g., 0.9250 Silver 0.8410 oz. ASW, 38.61 mm. **Subject:** Skellig Michael Island **Rev:** Birds and 12 stars above island **Rev. Legend:** SCEILIG MHICHIL **Rev. Designer:** Michael Guilfoyle

Date	Mintage	F	VF	XF	Unc	BU
2008 Proof	25,000	Value: 65.00				

KM# 60 10 EURO
28.2800 g., 0.9250 Silver 0.8410 oz. ASW, 38.61 mm. **Subject:** First currency, 80th Anniversary **Obv. Designer:** Emmet Mullins

Date	Mintage	F	VF	XF	Unc	BU
2009 Proof	15,000	Value: 55.00				

KM# 65 10 EURO
28.2800 g., 0.9250 Silver 0.8410 oz. ASW, 38.61 mm. **Subject:** The President's Award - Gaisce

Date	Mintage	F	VF	XF	Unc	BU
2010 Proof	8,000	Value: 60.00				

KM# 52 15 EURO
24.0000 g., 0.9250 Silver 0.7137 oz. ASW, 37 mm. **Obv:** Stylized clover with date and harp **Rev:** Ivan Mestroviae's Seated Woman with Harp design **Rev. Designer:** Damir Matavsic **Edge:** Plain **Note:** Illustration reduced.

Date	Mintage	F	VF	XF	Unc	BU
2007 Proof	10,000	Value: 85.00				

Note: 8,000 were sold in a single coin case. 1,000 were sold in a two coin set with the corresponding Croatian coin, as an Ireland set. An additional 1,000 were sold with the corresponding Croatian coin as a Croatia set. coins in both sets were the same but the packaging was different.

KM# 63 15 EURO
28.2800 g., 0.9250 Silver 0.8410 oz. ASW, 38.61 mm. **Subject:** Gaelic Athletics, 125 years

Date	Mintage	F	VF	XF	Unc	BU
2009 Proof	10,000	Value: 75.00				

KM# 64 15 EURO
24.0000 g., 0.9250 Silver 0.7137 oz. ASW, 38.61 mm. **Rev:** Foal and mare

Date	Mintage	F	VF	XF	Unc	BU
2010 Proof	15,000	Value: 75.00				

KM# 46 20 EURO
1.2400 g., 0.9990 Gold 0.0398 oz. AGW, 14 mm. **Subject:** Samuel Beckett 1906-1989 **Obv:** 2006, Eire, Harp **Rev:** Face, value and play **Edge:** Reeded

Date	Mintage	F	VF	XF	Unc	BU
2006 Proof	20,000	Value: 80.00				

KM# 59 20 EURO
1.2440 g., 0.9990 Gold 0.0400 oz. AGW, 14 mm. **Subject:** European Culture - Ireland **Obv:** Map **Rev:** Celtic design

Date	Mintage	F	VF	XF	Unc	BU
2007 Proof	25,000	Value: 90.00				

KM# 55 20 EURO
1.2440 g., 0.9990 Gold 0.0400 oz. AGW, 14 mm. **Subject:** Skellig Michael Island **Rev:** Birds and 12 stars above island **Rev. Legend:** SCEILIG MHICHIL

Date	Mintage	F	VF	XF	Unc	BU
2008 Proof	15,000	Value: 95.00				

KM# 61 20 EURO
1.2440 g., 0.9990 Gold 0.0400 oz. AGW, 14 mm. **Subject:** First currency, 80th Anniversary **Obv. Designer:** Emmet Mullins

Date	Mintage	F	VF	XF	Unc	BU
2009 Proof	15,000	Value: 85.00				

KM# 66 20 EURO
1.2400 g., 0.9990 Gold 0.0398 oz. AGW, 14 mm. **Subject:** The President's Award - Gaisce

Date	Mintage	F	VF	XF	Unc	BU
2010 Proof	6,000	Value: 85.00				

KM# 57 100 EURO
15.5500 g., 0.9990 Gold 0.4994 oz. AGW, 28 mm. **Subject:** International Polar Year **Obv:** Harp within wreath **Rev:** Ernest Shackleton, Tom Crean and The Endurance in distance **Rev. Designer:** Tom Ryan **Edge:** Reeded

Date	Mintage	F	VF	XF	Unc	BU
2008 Proof	2,000	Value: 850				

MINT SETS

KM#	Date	Mintage	Identification	Issue Price	Mkt Val
MS10	2002 (8)	20,000	KM#32-39	16.00	200
MS11	2003 (8)	30,000	KM#32-39	20.00	65.00
MS12	2003 (9)	35,000	KM#32-40 Special Olympics	25.00	90.00
MS13	2004 (8)	40,000	KM#32-39	25.00	45.00
MS14	2005 (8)	50,000	KM#32-39 Heywood Gardens	29.00	40.00
MS15	2006 (8)	40,000	KM#32-39 Glenveagh National Park and Castle	26.00	40.00
MS16	2006 (8)	—	KM#32-39 Boy Baby Set	35.00	42.50
MS17	2006 (8)	—	KM#32-39 Girl Baby Set	35.00	42.50
MS18	2007 (8)	20,000	KM#32-34, 47-51 Aran Islands	29.00	30.00
MS19	2007 (8)	—	KM#32-34, 47-51 Boy Baby Set	—	30.00
MS20	2007 (8)	—	KM#32-34, 47-51 Girl Baby Set	—	30.00
MS21	2007 (9)	20,000	KM#32-34, 47-51, 53	—	30.00
MS22	2008 (8)	30,000	KM#32-34, 47-51 Newgrange	—	30.00
MS23	2008 (8)	—	KM#32-34, 47-51 Boy Baby Set	—	30.00
MS24	2008 (8)	—	KM#32-34, 47-51 Girl Baby Set	—	30.00
MS25	2009 (8)	25,000	KM#32-34, 47-51 GAA 125th Anniversary	—	30.00
MS26	2009 (8)	—	KM#32-34, 47-51 Boy Baby Set	—	30.00
MS27	2009 (8)	—	KM#32-34, 47-51 Girl Baby Set	—	30.00
MS28	2010 (8)	20,000	KM#32-34, 47-51 Horse	—	30.00
MS29	2010 (8)	—	KM#32-34, 47-51 Baby Set	—	—

PROOF SETS

KM#	Date	Mintage	Identification	Issue Price	Mkt Val
PS6	2006 (8)	5,000	KM#32-39	125	165
PS7	2006 (2)	—	KM#45, 46	—	135
PS8	2007 (9)	10,000	KM#32-34, 47-51, 53	—	165
PS9	2007 (2)	—	KM#58-59	—	—
PS10	2008 (2)	—	KM#54-55	—	—
PS11	2008 (2)	—	KM#56-57	—	—
PS12	2009 (9)	—	KM#32-34, 47-51, 58 GAA 125th Anniversary	—	200
PS13	2009 (9)	5,000	KM#32-34, 47-51, 61.	—	225
PS14	2009 (2)	5,000	KM#60, 61. Ploughman Bank Note	—	150
PS15	2010 (2)	—	KM#65-66	—	—

ISLE OF MAN

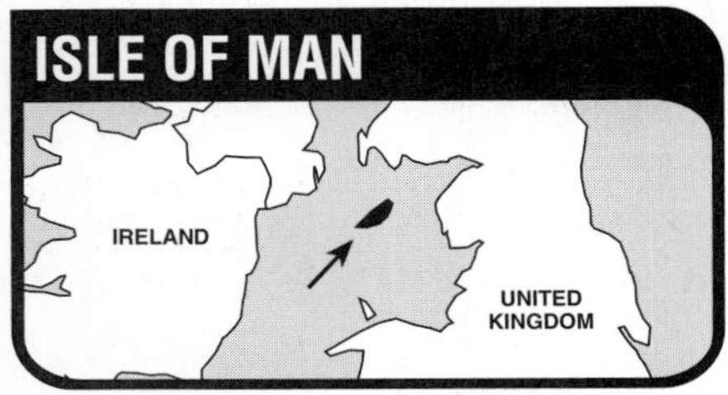

The Isle of Man, a dependency of the British Crown located in the Irish Sea equidistant from Ireland, Scotland and England, has an area of 227 sq. mi. (588 sq. km.) and a population of 68,000. Capital: Douglas. Agriculture, dairy farming, fishing and tourism are the chief industries.

MINT MARK

PM - Pobjoy Mint

BRITISH DEPENDENCY

DECIMAL COINAGE

100 Pence = 1 Pound

KM# 1036 PENNY

3.5600 g., Copper Plated Steel, 20.32 mm. **Ruler:** Elizabeth II **Obv:** Head with tiara right with small triskeles dividing legend **Obv. Designer:** Ian Rank-Broadley **Rev:** Ruins **Edge:** Plain

Date	Mintage	F	VF	XF	Unc	BU
2001PM AA	—	—	—	—	0.25	0.45
2001PM AC	—	—	—	—	0.25	0.45
2002PM AA	—	—	—	—	0.25	0.45
2002PM AE	—	—	—	—	0.25	0.45
2003PM AA	—	—	—	—	0.25	0.45
2003PM AE	—	—	—	—	0.25	0.45

KM# 1253 PENNY

3.5600 g., Copper Plated Steel, 20.3 mm. **Ruler:** Elizabeth II **Obv:** Head with tiara right **Rev:** Santon War Memorial

Date	Mintage	F	VF	XF	Unc	BU
2004PM AA	—	—	—	—	0.25	0.45
2004PM AB	—	—	—	—	0.25	0.45
2005PM AA	—	—	—	—	0.25	0.45
2005PM AB	—	—	—	—	0.25	0.45
2006PM AA	—	—	—	—	0.25	0.45
2006PM AB	—	—	—	—	0.25	0.45
2007PM AA	—	—	—	—	0.25	0.45
2007PM AB	—	—	—	—	0.25	0.45
2007PM BA	—	—	—	—	0.25	0.45
2008PM AA	—	—	—	—	0.25	0.45
2009PM AA	—	—	—	—	0.25	0.45
2010PM AA	—	—	—	—	0.25	0.45

KM# 1037 2 PENCE

7.1200 g., Copper Plated Steel, 25.9 mm. **Ruler:** Elizabeth II **Obv:** Head with tiara right **Obv. Designer:** Ian Rank-Broadley **Rev:** Sailboat **Edge:** Plain

Date	Mintage	F	VF	XF	Unc	BU
2001PM AA	—	—	—	—	0.40	0.60
2001PM AB	—	—	—	—	0.40	0.60
2001PM AC	—	—	—	—	0.40	0.60
2002PM AA	—	—	—	—	0.40	0.60
2002PM AB	—	—	—	—	0.40	0.60
2002PM AC	—	—	—	—	0.40	0.60
2002PM AF	—	—	—	—	0.40	0.60
2003PM AA	—	—	—	—	0.40	0.60
2003PM AF	—	—	—	—	0.40	0.60

KM# 1254 2 PENCE

7.1200 g., Copper Plated Steel, 25.9 mm. **Ruler:** Elizabeth II **Obv:** Head with tiara right **Obv. Designer:** Ian Rank-Broadley **Rev:** Albert Tower

Date	Mintage	F	VF	XF	Unc	BU
2004PM AA	—	—	—	—	0.40	0.60
2004PM AB	—	—	—	—	0.40	0.60
2005PM AA	—	—	—	—	0.40	0.60
2005PM AB	—	—	—	—	0.40	0.60
2006PM AA	—	—	—	—	0.40	0.60
2006PM AB	—	—	—	—	0.40	0.60
2007PM AA	—	—	—	—	0.40	0.60
2007PM AB	—	—	—	—	0.40	0.60
2007PM BA	—	—	—	—	0.40	0.60
2008PM AA	—	—	—	—	0.40	0.60
2009PM AA	—	—	—	—	0.40	0.60
2010PM AA	—	—	—	—	0.40	0.60

KM# 1038 5 PENCE

3.2500 g., Copper-Nickel, 18 mm. **Ruler:** Elizabeth II **Obv:** Head with tiara right **Obv. Designer:** Ian Rank-Broadley **Rev:** Gaut's Cross **Edge:** Reeded

Date	Mintage	F	VF	XF	Unc	BU
2001PM AA	—	—	—	—	0.75	1.00
2002PM AA	—	—	—	—	0.75	1.00
2002PM AC	—	—	—	—	0.75	1.00
2002PM AD	—	—	—	—	0.75	1.00
2002PM AE	—	—	—	—	0.75	1.00
2003PM AA	—	—	—	—	0.75	1.00
2003PM AB	—	—	—	—	0.75	1.00
2003PM AD	—	—	—	—	0.75	1.00

KM# 1255 5 PENCE

3.2500 g., Copper-Nickel, 18 mm. **Ruler:** Elizabeth II **Obv:** Head with tiara right **Obv. Designer:** Ian Rank-Broadley **Rev:** Tower of Refuge **Edge:** Reeded

Date	Mintage	F	VF	XF	Unc	BU
2004PM AA	—	—	—	—	0.75	1.00
2004PM AB	—	—	—	—	0.75	1.00
2005PM AA	—	—	—	—	0.75	1.00
2005PM AB	—	—	—	—	0.75	1.00
2006PM AA	—	—	—	—	0.75	1.00
2006PM AB	—	—	—	—	0.75	1.00
2007PM AA	—	—	—	—	0.75	1.00
2007PM AB	—	—	—	—	0.75	1.00
2008PM AA	—	—	—	—	0.75	1.00
2009PM AA	—	—	—	—	0.75	1.00
2010PM AA	—	—	—	—	0.75	1.00

KM# 1039 10 PENCE

6.5000 g., Copper-Nickel, 24.5 mm. **Ruler:** Elizabeth II **Obv:** Head with tiara right **Obv. Designer:** Ian Rank-Broadley **Rev:** Cathedral **Edge:** Reeded

Date	Mintage	F	VF	XF	Unc	BU
2001PM AA	—	—	—	—	1.00	1.50
2002PM AA	—	—	—	—	1.00	1.50
2003PM AA	—	—	—	—	1.00	1.50

KM# 1256 10 PENCE

6.5000 g., Copper-Nickel, 24.5 mm. **Ruler:** Elizabeth II **Obv:** Head with tiara right **Obv. Designer:** Ian Rank-Broadley **Rev:** Chicken Rock Lighthouse **Edge:** Reeded

Date	Mintage	F	VF	XF	Unc	BU
2004PM AA	—	—	—	—	1.00	1.50
2004PM AB	—	—	—	—	1.00	1.50
2005PM AA	—	—	—	—	1.00	1.50
2005PM AB	—	—	—	—	1.00	1.50
2006PM AA	—	—	—	—	1.00	1.50
2006PM AB	—	—	—	—	1.00	1.50
2007PM AA	—	—	—	—	1.00	1.50
2007PM AB	—	—	—	—	1.00	1.50
2008PM AA	—	—	—	—	1.00	1.50
2009PM AA	—	—	—	—	1.00	1.50
2010PM AA	—	—	—	—	1.00	1.50

KM# 1040 20 PENCE

5.0000 g., Copper-Nickel, 21.4 mm. **Ruler:** Elizabeth II **Subject:** Rushen Abbey **Obv:** Head with tiara right **Obv. Designer:** Ian Rank-Broadley **Rev:** Monk writing **Edge:** Plain **Shape:** 7-sided

Date	Mintage	F	VF	XF	Unc	BU
2001PM AA	—	—	—	—	1.50	2.00
2001PM AB	—	—	—	—	1.50	2.00
2002PM AA	—	—	—	—	1.50	2.00
2002PM AB	—	—	—	—	1.50	2.00
2002PM AC	—	—	—	—	1.50	2.00
2003PM AA	—	—	—	—	1.50	2.00
2003PM BA	—	—	—	—	1.50	2.00

KM# 1257 20 PENCE

5.0000 g., Copper-Nickel, 21.5 mm. **Ruler:** Elizabeth II **Obv:** Head with tiara right **Obv. Designer:** Ian Rank-Broadley **Rev:** Castle Rushen Clock **Edge:** Plain **Shape:** 7-sided

Date	Mintage	F	VF	XF	Unc	BU
2004PM AA	—	—	—	—	1.50	2.00
2004PM AB	—	—	—	—	1.50	2.00
2005PM AA	—	—	—	—	1.50	2.00
2005PM AB	—	—	—	—	1.50	2.00
2006PM AA	—	—	—	—	1.50	2.00
2006PM AB	—	—	—	—	1.50	2.00
2007PM AA	—	—	—	—	1.50	2.00
2007PM AB	—	—	—	—	1.50	2.00
2008PM AA	—	—	—	—	1.50	2.00
2009PM AA	—	—	—	—	1.50	2.00
2010PM AA	—	—	—	—	1.50	2.00

KM# 1041 50 PENCE

8.0000 g., Copper-Nickel, 27.3 mm. **Ruler:** Elizabeth II **Obv:** Head with tiara right **Obv. Designer:** Ian Rank-Broadley **Rev:** Stylized crucifix **Edge:** Plain **Shape:** 7-sided

Date	Mintage	F	VF	XF	Unc	BU
2001PM AA	—	—	—	—	2.25	2.75
2002PM AA	—	—	—	—	2.25	2.75
2003PM AA	—	—	—	—	2.25	2.75

KM# 1105 50 PENCE
8.0000 g., Copper-Nickel, 27.3 mm. **Ruler:** Elizabeth II **Subject:** Christmas **Obv:** Head with tiara right **Obv. Designer:** Ian Rank-Broadley **Rev:** Postman and children **Edge:** Plain **Shape:** 7-sided

Date	Mintage	F	VF	XF	Unc	BU
2001PM BB	30,000	—	—	—	4.50	6.00

KM# 1105a 50 PENCE
8.0000 g., 0.9250 Silver 0.2379 oz. ASW, 27.3 mm. **Ruler:** Elizabeth II **Obv:** Head with tiara right **Rev:** Postman and children **Edge:** Plain **Shape:** 7-sided

Date	Mintage	F	VF	XF	Unc	BU
2001PM Proof	5,000	Value: 35.00				

KM# 1105b 50 PENCE
8.0000 g., 0.9167 Gold 0.2358 oz. AGW, 27.3 mm. **Ruler:** Elizabeth II **Obv:** Head with tiara right **Rev:** Postman and children **Edge:** Plain **Shape:** 7-sided

Date	Mintage	F	VF	XF	Unc	BU
2001PM Proof	250	Value: 500				

KM# 1160 50 PENCE
8.0000 g., Copper-Nickel, 27.3 mm. **Ruler:** Elizabeth II **Subject:** Christmas **Obv:** Head with tiara right **Obv. Designer:** Ian Rank-Broadley **Rev:** Scrooge in bed **Edge:** Plain **Shape:** 7-sided

Date	Mintage	F	VF	XF	Unc	BU
2002BB PM	30,000	—	—	—	4.50	6.00

KM# 1160a 50 PENCE
8.0000 g., 0.9250 Silver 0.2379 oz. ASW, 27.3 mm. **Ruler:** Elizabeth II **Subject:** Christmas **Obv:** Head with tiara right **Rev:** Scrooge in bed **Edge:** Plain **Shape:** 7-sided

Date	Mintage	F	VF	XF	Unc	BU
2002PM Proof	5,000	Value: 35.00				

KM# 1160b 50 PENCE
8.0000 g., 0.9167 Gold 0.2358 oz. AGW, 27.3 mm. **Ruler:** Elizabeth II **Subject:** Christmas **Obv:** Head with tiara right **Rev:** Scrooge in bed **Edge:** Plain **Shape:** 7-sided

Date	Mintage	F	VF	XF	Unc	BU
2002PM Proof	250	Value: 500				

KM# 1183 50 PENCE
8.0000 g., Copper-Nickel, 27.3 mm. **Ruler:** Elizabeth II **Obv:** Head with tiara right **Obv. Designer:** Ian Rank-Broadley **Rev:** "The Snowman and James" **Edge:** Plain **Shape:** 7-sided

Date	Mintage	F	VF	XF	Unc	BU
2003PM BB	10,000	—	—	—	6.50	8.00
2008PM	—	—	—	—	6.50	8.00

KM# 1183a 50 PENCE
8.0000 g., 0.9250 Silver 0.2379 oz. ASW, 27.3 mm. **Ruler:** Elizabeth II **Subject:** Christmas **Obv:** Head with tiara right **Rev:** "The Snowman and James" **Edge:** Plain **Shape:** 7-sided

Date	Mintage	F	VF	XF	Unc	BU
2003PM Proof	3,000	Value: 35.00				

KM# 1183b 50 PENCE
8.0000 g., 0.9167 Gold 0.2358 oz. AGW, 27.3 mm. **Ruler:** Elizabeth II **Obv:** Head with tiara right **Rev:** "The Snowman and James" **Edge:** Plain **Shape:** 7-sided

Date	Mintage	F	VF	XF	Unc	BU
2003PM Proof	100	Value: 500				

KM# 1258 50 PENCE
8.0000 g., Copper-Nickel, 21.5 mm. **Ruler:** Elizabeth II **Obv:** Head with tiara right **Obv. Designer:** Ian Rank-Broadley **Rev:** Milner's Tower **Edge:** Plain **Shape:** 7-sided

Date	Mintage	F	VF	XF	Unc	BU
2004PM AA	—	—	—	—	2.25	2.75
2004PM AB	—	—	—	—	2.25	2.75
2005PM AA	—	—	—	—	2.25	2.75
2005PM AB	—	—	—	—	2.25	2.75
2006PM AA	—	—	—	—	2.25	2.75
2006PM AB	—	—	—	—	2.25	2.75
2007PM AA	—	—	—	—	2.25	2.75
2007PM AB	—	—	—	—	2.25	2.75
2008PM AA	—	—	—	—	2.25	2.75
2009PM AA	—	—	—	—	2.25	2.75
2010PM AA	—	—	—	—	2.25	2.75

KM# 1293 50 PENCE
Copper-Nickel **Ruler:** Elizabeth II **Obv:** Queen's new portrait **Rev:** Tourist Trophy Races

Date	Mintage	F	VF	XF	Unc	BU
2004PM AA	—	—	—	—	6.00	7.00
2007PM AA	—	—	—	—	6.00	7.00

KM# 1262 50 PENCE
8.0000 g., Copper-Nickel, 27.3 mm. **Ruler:** Elizabeth II **Subject:** Christmas **Obv:** Head with tiara right **Obv. Designer:** Ian Rank-Broadley **Rev:** Laxey Wheel **Edge:** Plain **Shape:** 7-sided

Date	Mintage	F	VF	XF	Unc	BU
2004PM AA	—	—	—	—	6.00	7.00
2004PM BA	30,000	—	—	—	6.00	7.00

KM# 1262a 50 PENCE
9.1852 g., 0.9250 Silver 0.2732 oz. ASW, 27.3 mm. **Ruler:** Elizabeth II **Subject:** Christmas **Obv:** Head with tiara right **Rev:** Laxey Wheel **Edge:** Plain **Shape:** 7-sided

Date	Mintage	F	VF	XF	Unc	BU
2004PM Proof	5,000	Value: 35.00				

KM# 1262b 50 PENCE
15.4074 g., 0.9167 Gold 0.4541 oz. AGW, 27.3 mm. **Ruler:** Elizabeth II **Subject:** Christmas **Obv:** Head with tiara right **Rev:** Laxey Wheel **Edge:** Plain **Shape:** 7-sided

Date	Mintage	F	VF	XF	Unc	BU
2004PM Proof	250	Value: 700				

KM# 1294 50 PENCE
Copper-Nickel **Ruler:** Elizabeth II **Obv:** Queen's new portrait **Rev:** Christmas scene

Date	Mintage	F	VF	XF	Unc	BU
2005	—	—	—	—	6.50	8.00

KM# 1320.1 50 PENCE
8.0000 g., Copper-Nickel, 27.3 mm. **Ruler:** Elizabeth II **Series:** 12 Days of Christmas **Obv:** Head with tiara right **Obv. Legend:** ISLE OF MAN - ELIZABETH II **Obv. Designer:** Ian Rank-Broadley **Rev:** Partridge in a Pear Tree **Rev. Legend:** CHRISTMAS **Edge:** Plain **Shape:** 7-sided

Date	Mintage	F	VF	XF	Unc	BU
2005PM AA	30,000	—	—	—	—	16.00

KM# 1320.2 50 PENCE
8.0000 g., Copper-Nickel, 27.3 mm. **Ruler:** Elizabeth II **Series:** 12 Days of Christmas **Obv:** Head with tiara right **Obv. Legend:** ISLE OF MAN - ELIZABETH II **Obv. Designer:** Ian Rank-Broadley **Rev:** Partidge in a Pear Tree multicolor **Rev. Legend:** CHRISTMAS **Edge:** Plain **Shape:** 7-sided

Date	Mintage	F	VF	XF	Unc	BU
2005PM	Inc. above	—	—	—	—	20.00

KM# 1320.1a 50 PENCE
9.1825 g., 0.9250 Silver 0.2731 oz. ASW, 27.3 mm. **Ruler:** Elizabeth II **Series:** 12 Days of Christmas **Obv:** Head with tiara right **Obv. Legend:** ISLE OF MAN - ELIZABETH II **Obv. Designer:** Ian Rank-Broadley **Rev:** Partridge in a Pear Tree **Rev. Legend:** CHRISTMAS **Edge:** Plain **Shape:** 7-sided

Date	Mintage	F	VF	XF	Unc	BU
2005PM Proof	—	Value: 35.00				

KM# 1320.2a 50 PENCE
8.0000 g., 0.9250 Silver 0.2379 oz. ASW, 27.3 mm. **Ruler:** Elizabeth II **Series:** 12 Days of Christmas **Obv:** Head with tiara right **Obv. Legend:** ISLE OF MAN - ELIZABETH II **Obv. Designer:** Ian Rank-Broadley **Rev:** Partridge in a Pear Tree multicolor **Rev. Legend:** CHRISTMAS **Edge:** Plain **Shape:** 7-sided

Date	Mintage	F	VF	XF	Unc	BU
2005PM Proof	—	Value: 35.00				

KM# 1320b 50 PENCE
0.9167 Gold, 27.3 mm. **Ruler:** Elizabeth II **Series:** 12 Days of Christmas **Obv:** Head with tiara right **Obv. Legend:** ISLE OF MAN - ELIZABETH II **Obv. Designer:** Ian Rank-Broadley **Rev:** Partridge in a Pear Tree **Rev. Legend:** CHRISTMAS **Edge:** Plain **Shape:** 7-sided

Date	Mintage	F	VF	XF	Unc	BU
2005PM Proof	—	Value: 700				

KM# 1321.1 50 PENCE
8.0000 g., Copper-Nickel, 27.3 mm. **Ruler:** Elizabeth II **Series:** 12 Days of Christmas **Obv:** Head with tiara right **Obv. Legend:** ISLE OF MAN - ELIZABETH II **Obv. Designer:** Ian Rank-Broadley **Rev:** Two Turtle Doves **Rev. Legend:** CHRISTMAS **Edge:** Plain **Shape:** 7-sided

Date	Mintage	F	VF	XF	Unc	BU
2006PM AA	—	—	—	—	6.00	7.00

KM# 1321.2 50 PENCE
8.0000 g., Copper-Nickel, 27.3 mm. **Ruler:** Elizabeth II **Series:** 12 Days of Christmas **Obv:** Head with tiara right **Obv. Legend:** ISLE OF MAN - ELIZABETH II **Obv. Designer:** Ian Rank-Broadley **Rev:** 2 Turtle Doves multicolor **Rev. Legend:** CHRISTMAS **Edge:** Plain **Shape:** 7-sided

Date	Mintage	F	VF	XF	Unc	BU
2006PM	—	—	—	—	8.00	10.00

KM# 1321.1a 50 PENCE
0.9250 Silver, 27.3 mm. **Ruler:** Elizabeth II **Series:** 12 Days of Christmas **Obv:** Head with tiara right **Obv. Legend:** ISLE OF MAN - ELIZABETH II **Obv. Designer:** Ian Rank-Broadley **Rev:** Two Turtle Doves **Rev. Legend:** CHRISTMAS **Edge:** Plain **Shape:** 7-sided

Date	Mintage	F	VF	XF	Unc	BU
2006PM Proof	—	Value: 35.00				

KM# 1321.2a 50 PENCE
0.9250 Silver, 27.3 mm. **Ruler:** Elizabeth II **Series:** 12 Days of Christmas **Obv:** Head with tiara right **Obv. Legend:** ISLE OF MAN - ELIZABETH II **Obv. Designer:** Ian Rank-Broadley **Rev:** 2 Turtle Doves multicolor **Rev. Legend:** CHRISTMAS **Edge:** Plain **Shape:** 7-sided

Date	Mintage	F	VF	XF	Unc	BU
2006PM Proof	—	Value: 40.00				

KM# 1321b 50 PENCE
0.9167 Gold, 27.3 mm. **Ruler:** Elizabeth II **Series:** 12 Days of Christmas **Obv:** Head with tiara right **Obv. Legend:** ISLE OF MAN - ELIZABETH II **Obv. Designer:** Ian Rank-Broadley **Rev:** 2 Turtle Doves **Rev. Legend:** CHRISTMAS **Edge:** Plain **Shape:** 7-sided

Date	Mintage	F	VF	XF	Unc	BU
2006PM Proof	—	Value: 700				

KM# 1322.1 50 PENCE
8.0000 g., Copper-Nickel, 27.3 mm. **Ruler:** Elizabeth II **Series:** 12 Days of Christmas **Obv:** Head with tiara right **Obv. Legend:** ISLE OF MAN - ELIZABETH II **Obv. Designer:** Ian Rank-Broadley **Rev:** 3 French Hens **Rev. Legend:** CHRISTMAS **Edge:** Plain **Shape:** 7-sided

Date	Mintage	F	VF	XF	Unc	BU
2007PM AA	—	—	—	—	6.00	7.00

KM# 1322.2 50 PENCE
8.0000 g., Copper-Nickel, 27.3 mm. **Ruler:** Elizabeth II **Series:** 12 Days of Christmas **Obv:** Head with tiara right **Obv. Legend:** ISLE OF MAN - ELIZABETH II **Obv. Designer:** Ian Rank-Broadley **Rev:** 3 French Hens multicolor **Rev. Legend:** CHRISTMAS **Edge:** Plain **Shape:** 7-sided

Date	Mintage	F	VF	XF	Unc	BU
2007PM	—	—	—	—	8.00	10.00

KM# 1322.1a 50 PENCE
0.9250 Silver, 27.3 mm. **Ruler:** Elizabeth II **Series:** 12 Days of Christmas **Obv:** Head with tiara right **Obv. Legend:** ISLE OF MAN - ELIZABETH II **Obv. Designer:** Ian Rank-Broadley **Rev:** 3 French Hens **Rev. Legend:** CHRISTMAS **Edge:** Plain **Shape:** 7-sided

Date	Mintage	F	VF	XF	Unc	BU
2007PM Proof	—	Value: 35.00				

KM# 1322.2a 50 PENCE
0.9250 Silver, 27.3 mm. **Ruler:** Elizabeth II **Series:** 12 Days of Christmas **Obv:** Head with tiara right **Obv. Legend:** ISLE OF MAN - ELIZABETH II **Obv. Designer:** Ian Rank-Broadley **Rev:** 3 French Hens multicolor **Rev. Legend:** CHRISTMAS **Edge:** Plain **Shape:** 7-sided

Date	Mintage	F	VF	XF	Unc	BU
2007PM Proof	—	Value: 40.00				

KM# 1322b 50 PENCE
0.9167 Gold, 27.3 mm. **Ruler:** Elizabeth II **Series:** 12 Days of Christmas **Obv:** Head with tiara right **Obv. Legend:** ISLE OF MAN - ELIZABETH II **Obv. Designer:** Ian Rank-Broadley **Rev:** 3 French Hens **Rev. Legend:** CHRISTMAS **Edge:** Plain **Shape:** 7-sided

Date	Mintage	F	VF	XF	Unc	BU
2007PM Proof	250	Value: 700				

KM# 1425 50 PENCE
8.0000 g., Copper-Nickel, 27.3 mm. **Ruler:** Elizabeth II **Subject:** TT Centennial **Obv:** Head with tiara right **Rev:** Two motorcyclists within wreath

Date	Mintage	F	VF	XF	Unc	BU
2007PM	—	—	—	—	8.00	10.00

KM# 1393.1 50 PENCE
8.0000 g., Copper-Nickel, 27.3 mm. **Ruler:** Elizabeth II **Subject:** Christmas **Rev:** Snowman **Shape:** 7-sided

Date	Mintage	F	VF	XF	Unc	BU
2008PM	—	—	—	—	10.00	12.00

KM# 1393.2 50 PENCE
8.0000 g., Copper-Nickel, 27.3 mm. **Ruler:** Elizabeth II **Subject:** Christmas **Rev:** Snowman, multicolored **Shape:** 7-sided

Date	Mintage	F	VF	XF	Unc	BU
2008PM	—	—	—	—	10.00	12.00

KM# 1372 50 PENCE
8.0000 g., Copper-Nickel, 27.3 mm. **Ruler:** Elizabeth II **Subject:** Honda, 50th Anniversary TT

Date	Mintage	F	VF	XF	Unc	BU
2009PM AA	—	—	—	—	—	9.00

KM# 1128 60 PENCE
Bi-Metallic Bronze finished base metal with a silver finished rotator on reverse., 38.6 mm. **Ruler:** Elizabeth II **Subject:** Euro Currency Converter **Obv:** Head with tiara right **Obv. Designer:** Ian Rank-Broadley **Rev:** Rotating map with cut out arrow revealing the Euro equivalent of the country's currency to which the arrow is pointed **Edge:** Reeded

Date	Mintage	F	VF	XF	Unc	BU
2002	15,000	—	—	—	20.00	22.50

KM# 1042 POUND
9.5000 g., Brass, 22.5 mm. **Ruler:** Elizabeth II **Subject:** Millennium Bells **Obv:** Head with tiara right **Obv. Designer:** Ian Rank-Broadley **Rev:** Triskeles and three bells **Edge:** Reeded and plain sections

Date	Mintage	F	VF	XF	Unc	BU
2001PM AA	—	—	—	—	4.00	5.00
2002PM AA	—	—	—	—	4.00	5.00
2003PM AA	—	—	—	—	4.00	5.00
2003PM BA	—	—	—	—	4.00	5.00

KM# 1259 POUND
9.5000 g., Nickel-Brass, 22.5 mm. **Ruler:** Elizabeth II **Obv:** Head with tiara right **Obv. Designer:** Ian Rank-Broadley **Rev:** St. John's Chapel **Edge:** Reeded and Plain Sections

Date	Mintage	F	VF	XF	Unc	BU
2004PM	—	—	—	—	4.00	5.00
2004PM AA	—	—	—	—	4.00	5.00
2004PM AB	—	—	—	—	4.00	5.00
2004PM AC	—	—	—	—	4.00	5.00
2005PM AA	—	—	—	—	4.00	5.00
2005PM AB	—	—	—	—	4.00	5.00
2006PM AA	—	—	—	—	4.00	5.00
2006PM AB	—	—	—	—	4.00	5.00
2007PM AA	—	—	—	—	4.00	5.00
2007PM BA	—	—	—	—	4.00	5.00
2007PM AB	—	—	—	—	4.00	5.00
2008PM AA	—	—	—	—	4.00	5.00
2008PM BA	—	—	—	—	4.00	5.00
2009PM AA	—	—	—	—	4.00	5.00
2010PM AA	—	—	—	—	4.00	5.00

KM# 1043 2 POUNDS
12.0000 g., Bi-Metallic Copper-Nickel center in Brass ring, 28.4 mm. **Ruler:** Elizabeth II **Subject:** Thorwald's Cross **Obv:** Head with tiara right within beaded circle **Obv. Designer:** Ian Rank-Broadley **Rev:** Ancient drawing within circle **Edge:** Reeded

Date	Mintage	F	VF	XF	Unc	BU
2001PM AA	—	—	—	—	6.50	7.50
2002PM AA	—	—	—	—	6.50	7.50
2003PM AA	—	—	—	—	6.50	7.50
2003PM AB	—	—	—	—	6.50	7.50

KM# 1260 2 POUNDS
12.0000 g., Bi-Metallic Copper-Nickel center in Brass ring, 28.4 mm. **Ruler:** Elizabeth II **Obv:** Head with tiara right **Obv. Designer:** Ian Rank-Broadley **Rev:** Round Tower of Peel Castle **Edge:** Reeded

Date	Mintage	F	VF	XF	Unc	BU
2004PM AA	—	—	—	—	6.50	7.50
2005PM AA	—	—	—	—	6.50	7.50
2006PM AA	—	—	—	—	6.50	7.50
2007PM AA	—	—	—	—	6.50	7.50
2007PM AB	—	—	—	—	6.50	7.50
2008PM AA	—	—	—	—	6.50	7.50
2009PM AA	—	—	—	—	6.50	7.50
2010PM AA	—	—	—	—	6.50	7.50

KM# 1044 5 POUNDS
20.1000 g., Virenium, 36.5 mm. **Ruler:** Elizabeth II **Subject:** St. Patrick's Hymn **Obv:** Head with tiara right **Obv. Designer:** Ian Rank-Broadley **Rev:** Stylized cross design **Edge:** Reeded and plain sections

Date	Mintage	F	VF	XF	Unc	BU
2001PM AA	—	—	—	—	15.00	16.50
2002PM AA	—	—	—	—	15.00	16.50
2003PM AA	—	—	—	—	15.00	16.50

KM# 1261 5 POUNDS
20.1000 g., Virenium, 36 mm. **Ruler:** Elizabeth II **Obv:** Head with tiara right **Obv. Designer:** Ian Rank-Broadley **Rev:** Laxey Wheel **Edge:** Reeded

Date	Mintage	F	VF	XF	Unc	BU
2004PM AA	—	—	—	—	15.00	16.50
2005PM AA	—	—	—	—	15.00	16.50
2006PM AA	—	—	—	—	15.00	16.50
2007PM AA	—	—	—	—	15.00	16.50
2007PM AB	—	—	—	—	15.00	16.50

CROWN SERIES

Pobjoy Mint Key

KM# 1129 1/32 CROWN
1.0000 g., 0.9720 Gold 0.0312 oz. AGW, 9.8 mm. **Ruler:** Elizabeth II **Subject:** Queen's Golden Jubilee **Obv:** Head with tiara right **Obv. Designer:** Ian Rank-Broadley **Rev:** Seated crowned Queen holding sceptre at her coronation **Edge:** Plain

Date	Mintage	F	VF	XF	Unc	BU
2002 Prooflike	—	—	—	—	—	55.00

KM# 1058 1/25 CROWN
1.2440 g., 0.9999 Gold 0.0400 oz. AGW, 13.92 mm. **Ruler:** Elizabeth II **Subject:** Year of the Snake **Obv:** Bust with tiara right **Obv. Designer:** Ian Rank-Broadley **Rev:** Snake **Edge:** Reeded

Date	Mintage	F	VF	XF	Unc	BU
2001 Proof	20,000	Value: 65.00				

KM# 1067 1/25 CROWN
1.2440 g., 0.9999 Gold 0.0400 oz. AGW, 13.9 mm. **Ruler:** Elizabeth II **Subject:** Somali Kittens **Obv:** Head with tiara right **Obv. Designer:** Ian Rank-Broadley **Rev:** Two kittens **Edge:** Reeded

Date	Mintage	F	VF	XF	Unc	BU
2001	—	—	—	—	—	65.00
2001 Proof	1,000	Value: 70.00				

KM# 1067a 1/25 CROWN
1.2441 g., 0.9995 Platinum 0.0400 oz. APW, 13.9 mm. **Ruler:** Elizabeth II **Subject:** Somali Kittens **Obv:** Head with tiara right **Obv. Designer:** Ian Rank-Broadley **Rev:** Two kittens **Edge:** Reeded

Date	Mintage	F	VF	XF	Unc	BU
2001	—	—	—	—	—	95.00

KM# 1086 1/25 CROWN
1.2441 g., 0.9999 Gold 0.0400 oz. AGW, 13.9 mm. **Ruler:** Elizabeth II **Subject:** Harry Potter **Obv:** Bust with tiara right **Obv. Designer:** Ian Rank-Broadley **Rev:** Boy with magic wand **Edge:** Reeded

Date	Mintage	F	VF	XF	Unc	BU
2001 Proof	10,000	Value: 65.00				

KM# 1088 1/25 CROWN
1.2441 g., 0.9999 Gold 0.0400 oz. AGW, 13.9 mm. **Ruler:** Elizabeth II **Series:** Harry Potter **Subject:** Journey to Hogwarts School **Obv:** Bust with tiara right **Obv. Designer:** Ian Rank-Broadley **Rev:** Boat full of children going to Hogwarts School **Edge:** Reeded

Date	Mintage	F	VF	XF	Unc	BU
2001 Proof	10,000	Value: 65.00				

KM# 1090 1/25 CROWN
1.2441 g., 0.9999 Gold 0.0400 oz. AGW, 13.9 mm. **Ruler:** Elizabeth II **Series:** Harry Potter **Subject:** First Quidditch Match **Obv:** Bust with tiara right **Obv. Designer:** Ian Rank-Broadley **Rev:** Harry flying a broom **Edge:** Reeded

Date	Mintage	F	VF	XF	Unc	BU
2001 Proof	10,000	Value: 65.00				

KM# 1092 1/25 CROWN
1.2441 g., 0.9999 Gold 0.0400 oz. AGW, 13.9 mm. **Ruler:** Elizabeth II **Series:** Harry Potter **Subject:** Birth of Norbert **Obv:** Bust with tiara right **Obv. Designer:** Ian Rank-Broadley **Edge:** Reeded

Date	Mintage	F	VF	XF	Unc	BU
2001 Proof	10,000	Value: 65.00				

KM# 1094 1/25 CROWN
1.2441 g., 0.9999 Gold 0.0400 oz. AGW, 13.9 mm. **Ruler:** Elizabeth II **Series:** Harry Potter **Subject:** School **Obv:** Bust with tiara right **Obv. Designer:** Ian Rank-Broadley **Rev:** Harry in Potions class **Edge:** Reeded

Date	Mintage	F	VF	XF	Unc	BU
2001 Proof	10,000	Value: 65.00				

KM# 1096 1/25 CROWN
1.2441 g., 0.9999 Gold 0.0400 oz. AGW, 13.9 mm. **Ruler:** Elizabeth II **Series:** Harry Potter **Subject:** Keys **Obv:** Bust with tiara right **Obv. Designer:** Ian Rank-Broadley **Rev:** Harry chasing the golden snitch **Edge:** Reeded

Date	Mintage	F	VF	XF	Unc	BU
2001 Proof	10,000	Value: 65.00				

KM# 1098 1/25 CROWN
1.2441 g., 0.9999 Gold 0.0400 oz. AGW, 13.9 mm. **Ruler:** Elizabeth II **Subject:** Year of the Horse **Obv:** Bust with tiara right **Obv. Designer:** Ian Rank-Broadley **Rev:** Two horses **Edge:** Reeded

Date	Mintage	F	VF	XF	Unc	BU
2002 Proof	20,000	Value: 65.00				

KM# 1107 1/25 CROWN
1.2440 g., 0.9990 Gold 0.0400 oz. AGW, 13.92 mm. **Ruler:** Elizabeth II **Subject:** Bengal Cat **Obv:** Head with tiara right **Obv. Designer:** Ian Rank-Broadley **Rev:** Cat and kitten **Edge:** Reeded

Date	Mintage	F	VF	XF	Unc	BU
2002	—	—	—	—	—	65.00
2002 Proof	1,000	Value: 70.00				

KM# 1107a 1/25 CROWN
1.2440 g., 0.9990 Platinum 0.0400 oz. APW, 13.92 mm. **Ruler:** Elizabeth II **Subject:** Bengal Cat **Obv:** Head with tiara right **Obv. Designer:** Ian Rank-Broadley **Rev:** Cat and kitten **Edge:** Reeded

Date	Mintage	F	VF	XF	Unc	BU
2002 Proof	—	Value: 95.00				

KM# 1145 1/25 CROWN
1.2440 g., 0.9999 Gold 0.0400 oz. AGW, 13.92 mm. **Ruler:** Elizabeth II **Subject:** Harry Potter Series **Obv:** Bust with tiara right **Obv. Designer:** Ian Rank-Broadley **Rev:** Harry and friends making Polyjuice potion **Edge:** Reeded

Date	Mintage	F	VF	XF	Unc	BU
2002PM Proof	10,000	Value: 65.00				

KM# 1143 1/25 CROWN
1.2440 g., 0.9999 Gold 0.0400 oz. AGW, 13.92 mm. **Ruler:** Elizabeth II **Subject:** Harry Potter **Obv:** Bust with tiara right **Obv. Designer:** Ian Rank-Broadley **Rev:** Tom Riddle twirling Harry's magic wand **Edge:** Reeded

Date	Mintage	F	VF	XF	Unc	BU
2002PM Proof	10,000	Value: 65.00				

KM# 1147 1/25 CROWN
1.2440 g., 0.9999 Gold 0.0400 oz. AGW **Ruler:** Elizabeth II **Subject:** Harry Potter **Obv:** Bust with tiara right **Obv. Designer:** Ian Rank-Broadley **Rev:** Harry arrives at the Burrow in a flying car **Edge:** Reeded

Date	Mintage	F	VF	XF	Unc	BU
2002PM Proof	10,000	Value: 65.00				

KM# 1149 1/25 CROWN
1.2440 g., 0.9999 Gold 0.0400 oz. AGW, 13.92 mm. **Ruler:** Elizabeth II **Subject:** Harry Potter Series **Obv:** Bust with tiara right **Obv. Designer:** Ian Rank-Broadley **Rev:** Harry retrieves Gryffindor sword from snake **Edge:** Reeded

Date	Mintage	F	VF	XF	Unc	BU
2002PM Proof	10,000	Value: 65.00				

KM# 1151 1/25 CROWN

1.2240 g., 0.9999 Gold 0.0393 oz. AGW, 13.92 mm. **Ruler:** Elizabeth II **Series:** Harry Potter **Obv:** Bust with tiara right **Obv. Designer:** Ian Rank-Broadley **Rev:** Harry and Ron encounter the spider Aragog **Edge:** Reeded

Date	Mintage	F	VF	XF	Unc	BU
2002PM Proof	10,000	Value: 65.00				

KM# 1153 1/25 CROWN

1.2440 g., 0.9999 Gold 0.0400 oz. AGW, 13.92 mm. **Ruler:** Elizabeth II **Series:** Harry Potter **Obv:** Bust with tiara right **Obv. Designer:** Ian Rank-Broadley **Rev:** Harry in hospital **Edge:** Reeded

Date	Mintage	F	VF	XF	Unc	BU
2002PM Proof	10,000	Value: 65.00				

KM# 1186 1/25 CROWN

1.2440 g., 0.9999 Gold 0.0400 oz. AGW, 13.9 mm. **Ruler:** Elizabeth II **Subject:** Lord of the Rings **Obv:** Bust with tiara right **Obv. Designer:** Ian Rank-Broadley **Rev:** Frodo Baggins with short sword **Edge:** Reeded

Date	Mintage	F	VF	XF	Unc	BU
2003PM Proof	6,000	Value: 65.00				

KM# 1161 1/25 CROWN

1.2440 g., 0.9999 Gold 0.0400 oz. AGW, 13.92 mm. **Ruler:** Elizabeth II **Subject:** Cat **Obv:** Head with tiara right **Obv. Designer:** Ian Rank-Broadley **Rev:** Two Balinese kittens **Edge:** Reeded

Date	Mintage	F	VF	XF	Unc	BU
2003PM	—	—	—	—	—	65.00
2003PM Proof	—	Value: 70.00				

KM# 1161a 1/25 CROWN

1.2440 g., 0.9995 Platinum 0.0400 oz. APW, 13.92 mm. **Ruler:** Elizabeth II **Subject:** Cat **Obv:** Head with tiara right **Obv. Designer:** Ian Rank-Broadley **Rev:** Two Balinese kittens **Edge:** Reeded

Date	Mintage	F	VF	XF	Unc	BU
2003PM Proof	—	Value: 95.00				

KM# 1167 1/25 CROWN

1.2441 g., 0.9999 Gold 0.0400 oz. AGW, 13.9 mm. **Ruler:** Elizabeth II **Subject:** Year of the Goat **Obv:** Head with tiara right **Obv. Designer:** Ian Rank-Broadley **Rev:** Three goats **Edge:** Reeded

Date	Mintage	F	VF	XF	Unc	BU
2003PM Proof	20,000	Value: 65.00				

KM# 1203 1/25 CROWN

1.2440 g., 0.9999 Gold 0.0400 oz. AGW, 14 mm. **Ruler:** Elizabeth II **Obv:** Bust with tiara right **Obv. Designer:** Ian Rank-Broadley **Rev:** Harry Potter and patron fighting off a spectre **Edge:** Reeded

Date	Mintage	F	VF	XF	Unc	BU
2004PM Proof	2,500	Value: 70.00				

KM# 1205 1/25 CROWN

1.2440 g., 0.9999 Gold 0.0400 oz. AGW, 14 mm. **Ruler:** Elizabeth II **Obv:** Bust with tiara right **Obv. Designer:** Ian Rank-Broadley **Rev:** Harry Potter in the shrieking shack **Edge:** Reeded

Date	Mintage	F	VF	XF	Unc	BU
2004PM Proof	2,500	Value: 70.00				

KM# 1207 1/25 CROWN

1.2440 g., 0.9999 Gold 0.0400 oz. AGW, 14 mm. **Ruler:** Elizabeth II **Obv:** Bust with tiara right **Obv. Designer:** Ian Rank-Broadley **Rev:** Harry Potter and Professor Dumbledore **Edge:** Reeded

Date	Mintage	F	VF	XF	Unc	BU
2004PM Proof	2,500	Value: 70.00				

KM# 1209 1/25 CROWN

1.2440 g., 0.9999 Gold 0.0400 oz. AGW, 14 mm. **Ruler:** Elizabeth II **Obv:** Bust with tiara right **Obv. Designer:** Ian Rank-Broadley **Rev:** Sirius Black on flying griffin **Edge:** Reeded

Date	Mintage	F	VF	XF	Unc	BU
2004PM Proof	2,500	Value: 70.00				

KM# 1211 1/25 CROWN

1.2440 g., 0.9999 Gold 0.0400 oz. AGW, 14 mm. **Ruler:** Elizabeth II **Obv:** Head with tiara right **Obv. Designer:** Ian Rank-Broadley **Rev:** Three Olympic Swimmers **Edge:** Reeded

Date	Mintage	F	VF	XF	Unc	BU
2004PM Proof	5,000	Value: 65.00				

KM# 1213 1/25 CROWN

1.2440 g., 0.9999 Gold 0.0400 oz. AGW, 14 mm. **Ruler:** Elizabeth II **Obv:** Head with tiara right **Obv. Designer:** Ian Rank-Broadley **Rev:** Three Olympic Cyclists **Edge:** Reeded

Date	Mintage	F	VF	XF	Unc	BU
2004PM Proof	5,000	Value: 65.00				

KM# 1215 1/25 CROWN

1.2440 g., 0.9999 Gold 0.0400 oz. AGW, 14 mm. **Ruler:** Elizabeth II **Obv:** Head with tiara right **Obv. Designer:** Ian Rank-Broadley **Rev:** Three Olympic Runners **Edge:** Reeded

Date	Mintage	F	VF	XF	Unc	BU
2004PM Proof	5,000	Value: 65.00				

KM# 1217 1/25 CROWN

1.2440 g., 0.9999 Gold 0.0400 oz. AGW, 14 mm. **Ruler:** Elizabeth II **Obv:** Head with tiara right **Obv. Designer:** Ian Rank-Broadley **Rev:** Three Olympic Sail Boarders **Edge:** Reeded

Date	Mintage	F	VF	XF	Unc	BU
2004PM Proof	5,000	Value: 65.00				

KM# 1240 1/25 CROWN

1.2440 g., 0.9999 Gold 0.0400 oz. AGW, 14 mm. **Ruler:** Elizabeth II **Obv:** Head with tiara right **Obv. Designer:** Ian Rank-Broadley **Rev:** Monkey **Edge:** Reeded

Date	Mintage	F	VF	XF	Unc	BU
2004PM Proof	20,000	Value: 65.00				

KM# 1247 1/25 CROWN

1.2440 g., 0.9999 Gold 0.0400 oz. AGW, 14 mm. **Ruler:** Elizabeth II **Obv:** Head with tiara right **Obv. Designer:** Ian Rank-Broadley **Rev:** Two Tonkinese cats **Edge:** Reeded

Date	Mintage	F	VF	XF	Unc	BU
2004PM	—	—	—	—	—	65.00
2004PM Proof	1,000	Value: 70.00				

KM# 1269 1/25 CROWN

1.2440 g., 0.9999 Gold 0.0400 oz. AGW, 13.92 mm. **Ruler:** Elizabeth II **Obv:** Bust with tiara right **Obv. Designer:** Ian Rank-Broadley **Rev:** Himalayan cat and two kittens **Edge:** Reeded

Date	Mintage	F	VF	XF	Unc	BU
2005PM Proof	—	Value: 70.00				

KM# 1269a 1/25 CROWN

1.2440 g., 0.9950 Platinum 0.0398 oz. APW, 13.92 mm. **Ruler:** Elizabeth II **Obv:** Bust with tiara right **Obv. Designer:** Ian Rank-Broadley **Rev:** Himalayan cat and two kittens **Edge:** Reeded

Date	Mintage	F	VF	XF	Unc	BU
2005PM Proof	—	Value: 90.00				

KM# 1340 1/25 CROWN

1.2441 g., 0.9999 Gold 0.0400 oz. AGW **Ruler:** Elizabeth II **Obv:** Bust with tiara right **Obv. Designer:** Ian Rank-Broadley **Rev:** Three Exotic Shorthair cats sitting facing **Edge:** Reeded

Date	Mintage	F	VF	XF	Unc	BU
2006PM	—	—	—	—	—	85.00

KM# 1343 1/25 CROWN

1.2441 g., 0.9999 Gold 0.0400 oz. AGW **Ruler:** Elizabeth II **Obv:** Bust with tiara right **Obv. Legend:** ELIZABETH II - ISLE OF MAN **Obv. Designer:** Ian Rank-Broadley **Rev:** Ragdoll cat with two kittens sitting facing **Edge:** Reeded

Date	Mintage	F	VF	XF	Unc	BU
2007PM	—	—	—	—	—	85.00

KM# 1349 1/25 CROWN

1.2440 g., 0.9999 Gold 0.0400 oz. AGW **Ruler:** Elizabeth II **Subject:** The Tale of Peter Rabbit **Obv:** Bust with tiara right **Obv. Legend:** ELIZABETH II - ISLE OF MAN **Obv. Designer:** Ian Rank-Broadley **Rev:** Peter walking with friends **Edge:** Reeded

Date	Mintage	F	VF	XF	Unc	BU
2007PM	—	—	—	—	—	110

KM# 1308 1/25 CROWN

1.2441 g., 0.9999 Gold 0.0400 oz. AGW **Ruler:** Elizabeth II **Subject:** 100th Anniversary of Scouting **Obv:** Bust with tiara right **Obv. Legend:** ELIZABETH II - ISLE OF MAN **Rev:** 3/4 length figure of Robert Baden-Powell standing facing 3/4 left, Fleur-de-lys below, images of scouting at left and right **Rev. Legend:** CENTENARY OF SCOUTING **Edge:** Reeded

Date	Mintage	F	VF	XF	Unc	BU
2007PM Proof	—	Value: 300				

KM# 1314 1/25 CROWN

1.2200 g., 0.9999 Gold AGW 0.0400 0.0392 oz. AGW, 13.92 mm. **Ruler:** Elizabeth II **Obv:** Bust with tiara right **Obv. Legend:** ELIZABETH II - ISLE OF MAN **Rev:** Two swans facing **Edge:** Reeded

Date	Mintage	F	VF	XF	Unc	BU
2007 Proof	10,000	Value: 65.00				

KM# 1383 1/25 CROWN

1.2400 g., 0.9999 Gold 0.0399 oz. AGW, 13.92 mm. **Ruler:** Elizabeth II **Obv:** Bust right **Rev:** Chinchilla cat and kitten

Date	Mintage	F	VF	XF	Unc	BU
2009	—	—	—	—	—	70.00
2009 Proof	1,000	Value: 85.00				

KM# 1387 1/25 CROWN

1.2400 g., 0.9950 Platinum 0.0397 oz. APW, 13.92 mm. **Ruler:** Elizabeth II **Obv:** Bust right **Rev:** Chinchilla cat and kitten

Date	Mintage	F	VF	XF	Unc	BU
2009	—	—	—	—	—	90.00

KM# 1059 1/10 CROWN

3.1100 g., 0.9999 Gold 0.1000 oz. AGW, 17.95 mm. **Ruler:** Elizabeth II **Subject:** Year of the Snake **Obv:** Bust with tiara right **Obv. Designer:** Ian Rank-Broadley **Rev:** Snake **Edge:** Reeded

Date	Mintage	F	VF	XF	Unc	BU
2001 Proof	15,000	Value: 150				

KM# 1068 1/10 CROWN

3.1100 g., 0.9999 Gold 0.1000 oz. AGW, 18 mm. **Ruler:** Elizabeth II **Obv:** Head with tiara right **Obv. Designer:** Ian Rank-Broadley **Rev:** Somali kittens **Edge:** Reeded

Date	Mintage	F	VF	XF	Unc	BU
2001	—	—	—	—	—	150
2001 Proof	1,000	Value: 155				

KM# 1068a 1/10 CROWN

3.1100 g., 0.9995 Platinum 0.0999 oz. APW, 18 mm. **Ruler:** Elizabeth II **Obv:** Head with tiara right **Obv. Designer:** Ian Rank-Broadley **Rev:** Somali kittens **Edge:** Reeded

Date	Mintage	F	VF	XF	Unc	BU
2001 Proof	—	Value: 200				

KM# 1328 1/10 CROWN

3.1100 g., 0.9990 Gold 0.0999 oz. AGW **Ruler:** Elizabeth II **Subject:** Harry Potter **Obv:** Bust right **Obv. Designer:** Ian Rank-Broadley **Rev:** Boy with magic wand **Edge:** Reeded

Date	Mintage	F	VF	XF	Unc	BU
2001 Proof	7,500	Value: 150				

KM# 1329 1/10 CROWN

3.1100 g., 0.9990 Gold 0.0999 oz. AGW **Ruler:** Elizabeth II **Subject:** Harry Potter - Journey to Hogwarts **Obv:** Bust right **Rev:** Boat full of children going to Hogwarts School **Edge:** Reeded

Date	Mintage	F	VF	XF	Unc	BU
2001 Proof	7,500	Value: 150				

KM# 1330 1/10 CROWN

3.1100 g., 0.9990 Gold 0.0999 oz. AGW **Ruler:** Elizabeth II **Subject:** Harry Potter **Obv:** Bust right **Obv. Designer:** Ian Rank-Broadley **Rev:** Harry flying on a broomstick **Edge:** Reeded

Date	Mintage	F	VF	XF	Unc	BU
2001 Proof	7,500	Value: 150				

KM# 1331 1/10 CROWN

3.1100 g., 0.9990 Gold 0.0999 oz. AGW **Ruler:** Elizabeth II **Subject:** Harry Potter **Obv:** Bust right **Obv. Designer:** Ian Rank-Broadley **Rev:** Birth of Norbert the dragon **Edge:** Reeded

Date	Mintage	F	VF	XF	Unc	BU
2001 Proof	7,500	Value: 150				

KM# 1332 1/10 CROWN

3.1100 g., 0.9990 Gold 0.0999 oz. AGW **Ruler:** Elizabeth II **Subject:** Harry Potter **Obv:** Bust right **Obv. Designer:** Ian Rank-Broadley **Rev:** Harry in Potions class **Edge:** Reeded

Date	Mintage	F	VF	XF	Unc	BU
2001 Proof	7,500	Value: 150				

KM# 1333 1/10 CROWN

3.1100 g., 0.9990 Gold 0.0999 oz. AGW **Ruler:** Elizabeth II **Subject:** Harry Potter **Obv:** Bust right **Obv. Designer:** Ian Rank-Broadley **Rev:** Harry chasing a snitch **Edge:** Reeded

Date	Mintage	F	VF	XF	Unc	BU
2001 Proof	7,500	Value: 150				

KM# 1099 1/10 CROWN

3.1100 g., 0.9999 Gold 0.1000 oz. AGW, 17.95 mm. **Ruler:** Elizabeth II **Subject:** Year of the Horse **Obv:** Bust with tiara right **Obv. Designer:** Ian Rank-Broadley **Rev:** Two horses **Edge:** Reeded

Date	Mintage	F	VF	XF	Unc	BU
2002 Proof	15,000	Value: 150				

KM# 1155 1/10 CROWN

3.1100 g., 0.9990 Gold 0.0999 oz. AGW, 17.95 mm. **Ruler:** Elizabeth II **Subject:** Queen's Golden Jubilee **Obv:** Queen's portrait **Rev:** Queen on horse **Edge:** Reeded

Date	Mintage	F	VF	XF	Unc	BU
2002PM Proof	500	Value: 150				

KM# 1108 1/10 CROWN

3.1100 g., 0.9990 Gold 0.0999 oz. AGW, 17.95 mm. **Ruler:** Elizabeth II **Subject:** Bengal Cat **Obv:** Head with tiara right **Obv. Designer:** Ian Rank-Broadley **Rev:** Cat and kitten **Edge:** Reeded

Date	Mintage	VG	F	VF	XF	Unc
2002	—	—	—	—	—	150
2002 Proof	—	Value: 155				

KM# 1108a 1/10 CROWN

3.1100 g., 0.9990 Platinum 0.0999 oz. APW, 17.95 mm. **Ruler:** Elizabeth II **Subject:** Bengal Cat **Obv:** Head with tiara right **Obv. Designer:** Ian Rank-Broadley **Rev:** Cat and kitten **Edge:** Reeded

Date	Mintage	F	VF	XF	Unc	BU
2002	—	—	—	—	—	210

KM# 1162 1/10 CROWN

3.1100 g., 0.9999 Gold 0.1000 oz. AGW, 17.95 mm. **Ruler:** Elizabeth II **Subject:** Cat **Obv:** Head with tiara right **Obv. Designer:** Ian Rank-Broadley **Rev:** Two Balinese kittens **Edge:** Reeded

Date	Mintage	F	VF	XF	Unc	BU
2003PM	—	—	—	—	—	150
2003PM Proof	—	Value: 155				

KM# 1162a 1/10 CROWN

3.1100 g., 0.9995 Platinum 0.0999 oz. APW, 17.95 mm. **Ruler:** Elizabeth II **Subject:** Cat **Obv:** Head with tiara right **Obv. Designer:** Ian Rank-Broadley **Rev:** Two Balinese kittens **Edge:** Reeded

Date	Mintage	F	VF	XF	Unc	BU
2003PM	—	—	—	—	—	210

KM# 1168 1/10 CROWN

3.1100 g., 0.9999 Gold 0.1000 oz. AGW, 17.95 mm. **Ruler:** Elizabeth II **Subject:** Year of the Goat **Obv:** Bust with tiara right **Obv. Designer:** Ian Rank-Broadley **Rev:** Three goats **Edge:** Reeded

Date	Mintage	F	VF	XF	Unc	BU
2003PM Proof	—	Value: 150				

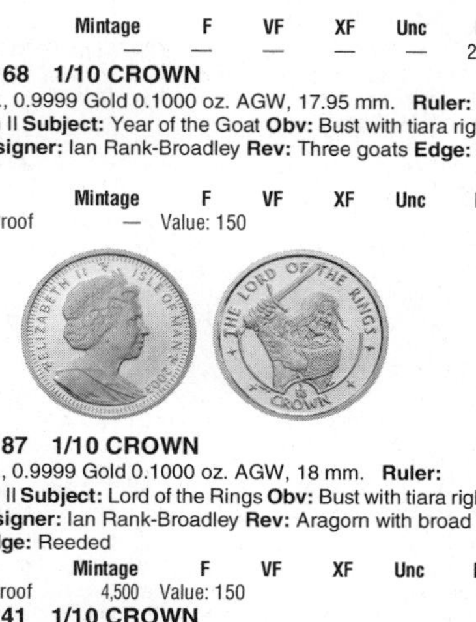

KM# 1187 1/10 CROWN

3.1100 g., 0.9999 Gold 0.1000 oz. AGW, 18 mm. **Ruler:** Elizabeth II **Subject:** Lord of the Rings **Obv:** Bust with tiara right **Obv. Designer:** Ian Rank-Broadley **Rev:** Aragorn with broad sword **Edge:** Reeded

Date	Mintage	F	VF	XF	Unc	BU
2003PM Proof	4,500	Value: 150				

KM# 1241 1/10 CROWN

3.1100 g., 0.9999 Gold 0.1000 oz. AGW, 18 mm. **Ruler:** Elizabeth II **Obv:** Head with tiara right **Obv. Designer:** Ian Rank-Broadley **Rev:** Monkey **Edge:** Reeded

Date	Mintage	F	VF	XF	Unc	BU
2004PM Proof	15,000	Value: 150				

KM# 1248 1/10 CROWN
3.1100 g., 0.9999 Gold 0.1000 oz. AGW, 18 mm. **Ruler:** Elizabeth II **Obv:** Head with tiara right **Obv. Designer:** Ian Rank-Broadley **Rev:** Two Tonkinese cats **Edge:** Reeded

Date	Mintage	F	VF	XF	Unc	BU
2004PM	—	—	—	—	—	150
2004PM Proof	1,000	Value: 155				

KM# 1270 1/10 CROWN
3.1100 g., 0.9999 Gold 0.1000 oz. AGW, 18 mm. **Ruler:** Elizabeth II **Obv:** Bust with tiara right **Obv. Designer:** Ian Rank-Broadley **Rev:** Himalayan cat and two kittens **Edge:** Reeded

Date	Mintage	F	VF	XF	Unc	BU
2005PM Proof	—	Value: 150				

KM# 1270a 1/10 CROWN
3.1100 g., 0.9950 Platinum 0.0995 oz. APW, 18 mm. **Ruler:** Elizabeth II **Obv:** Queen Elizabeth II **Rev:** Himalayan cat and two kittens **Edge:** Reeded

Date	Mintage	F	VF	XF	Unc	BU
2005PM Proof	—	Value: 235				

KM# 1341 1/10 CROWN
3.1100 g., 0.9999 Gold 0.1000 oz. AGW **Ruler:** Elizabeth II **Obv:** Bust with tiara right **Obv. Designer:** Ian Rank-Broadley **Rev:** Three Exotic Shorthair cats sitting facing **Edge:** Reeded

Date	Mintage	F	VF	XF	Unc	BU
2006PM	—	—	—	—	—	170

KM# 1350 1/10 CROWN
3.1100 g., 0.9999 Gold 0.1000 oz. AGW **Ruler:** Elizabeth II **Subject:** The Tale of Peter Rabbit **Obv:** Bust with tiara right **Obv. Legend:** ELIZABETH II - ISLE OF MAN **Obv. Designer:** Ian Rank-Broadley **Rev:** Peter walking with friends **Edge:** Reeded

Date	Mintage	F	VF	XF	Unc	BU
2007PM	—	—	—	—	—	180

KM# 1344 1/10 CROWN
3.1100 g., 0.9999 Gold 0.1000 oz. AGW **Ruler:** Elizabeth II **Obv:** Bust with tiara right **Obv. Legend:** ELIZABETH II - ISLE OF MAN **Obv. Designer:** Ian Rank-Broadley **Rev:** Ragdoll cat with two kittens sitting facing **Edge:** Reeded

Date	Mintage	F	VF	XF	Unc	BU
2007PM	—	—	—	—	—	170

KM# 1382 1/10 CROWN
3.1100 g., 0.9999 Gold 0.1000 oz. AGW, 17.95 mm. **Ruler:** Elizabeth II **Obv:** Bust right **Rev:** Chinchilla cat and kitten

Date	Mintage	F	VF	XF	Unc	BU
2009	—	—	—	—	—	155
2009 Proof	1,000	Value: 165				

KM# 1386 1/10 CROWN
3.1100 g., 0.9950 Platinum 0.0995 oz. APW, 17.95 mm. **Ruler:** Elizabeth II **Obv:** Bust right **Rev:** Chinchilla cat and kitten

Date	Mintage	F	VF	XF	Unc	BU
2009	—	—	—	—	—	200

KM# 1060 1/5 CROWN
6.2200 g., 0.9999 Gold 0.1999 oz. AGW, 22 mm. **Ruler:** Elizabeth II **Subject:** Year of the Snake **Obv:** Bust with tiara right **Obv. Designer:** Ian Rank-Broadley **Rev:** Snake **Edge:** Reeded

Date	Mintage	F	VF	XF	Unc	BU
2001 Proof	12,000	Value: 300				

KM# 1069 1/5 CROWN
6.2200 g., 0.9999 Gold 0.1999 oz. AGW, 22 mm. **Ruler:** Elizabeth II **Obv:** Head with tiara right **Obv. Designer:** Ian Rank-Broadley **Rev:** Two Somali kittens **Edge:** Reeded

Date	Mintage	F	VF	XF	Unc	BU
2001	—	—	—	—	—	300
2001 Proof	1,000	Value: 310				

KM# 1069a 1/5 CROWN
6.2200 g., 0.9995 Platinum 0.1999 oz. APW, 22 mm. **Ruler:** Elizabeth II **Obv:** Head with tiara right **Obv. Designer:** Ian Rank-Broadley **Rev:** Somali kittens **Edge:** Reeded

Date	Mintage	F	VF	XF	Unc	BU
2001	—	—	—	—	—	400

KM# 1074 1/5 CROWN
6.2200 g., 0.9999 Gold 0.1999 oz. AGW, 22 mm. **Ruler:** Elizabeth II **Subject:** Queen Mother **Obv:** Head with tiara right **Obv. Designer:** Ian Rank-Broadley **Rev:** 1948 Silver wedding anniversary **Edge:** Reeded

Date	Mintage	F	VF	XF	Unc	BU
2001 Proof	5,000	Value: 300				

KM# 1075 1/5 CROWN
6.2200 g., 0.9999 Gold 0.1999 oz. AGW, 22 mm. **Ruler:** Elizabeth II **Subject:** Queen Mother **Obv:** Head with tiara right **Obv. Designer:** Ian Rank-Broadley **Rev:** 1948 holding baby Prince Charles **Edge:** Reeded

Date	Mintage	F	VF	XF	Unc	BU
2001 Proof	5,000	Value: 300				

KM# 1078 1/5 CROWN
6.2200 g., 0.9999 Gold 0.1999 oz. AGW, 22 mm. **Ruler:** Elizabeth II **Subject:** Martin Frobisher **Obv:** Head with tiara right **Obv. Designer:** Ian Rank-Broadley **Rev:** Portrait, ship and map **Edge:** Reeded

Date	Mintage	F	VF	XF	Unc	BU
2001 Proof	5,000	Value: 300				

KM# 1079 1/5 CROWN
6.2200 g., 0.9999 Gold 0.1999 oz. AGW, 22 mm. **Ruler:** Elizabeth II **Subject:** Ronald Amundsen **Obv:** Head with tiara right **Obv. Designer:** Ian Rank-Broadley **Rev:** Portrait, ship and dirigible **Edge:** Reeded

Date	Mintage	F	VF	XF	Unc	BU
2001 Proof	5,000	Value: 300				

KM# 1082 1/5 CROWN
6.2200 g., 0.9999 Gold 0.1999 oz. AGW, 22 mm. **Ruler:** Elizabeth II **Subject:** Queen's 75th Birthday **Obv:** Head with tiara right **Obv. Designer:** Ian Rank-Broadley **Rev:** Flower bouquet with a tiny diamond mounted on the bow of the ribbon **Edge:** Reeded

Date	Mintage	F	VF	XF	Unc	BU
2001 Proof	2,000	Value: 325				

KM# 1339 1/5 CROWN
6.1500 g., 0.9990 Gold 0.1975 oz. AGW, 21.78 mm. **Ruler:** Elizabeth II **Subject:** Harry Potter **Obv:** Bust right **Obv. Designer:** Ian Rank-Broadley **Rev:** Harry chasing a jeweled snitch **Edge:** Reeded

Date	Mintage	F	VF	XF	Unc	BU
2001 Proof	5,000	Value: 300				

KM# 1334 1/5 CROWN
6.1500 g., 0.9990 Gold 0.1975 oz. AGW, 21.78 mm. **Ruler:** Elizabeth II **Subject:** Harry Potter **Obv:** Bust right **Obv. Designer:** Ian Rank-Broadley **Rev:** Harry with magic wand **Edge:** Reeded

Date	Mintage	F	VF	XF	Unc	BU
2001 Proof	5,000	Value: 300				

KM# 1335 1/5 CROWN
6.1500 g., 0.9990 Gold 0.1975 oz. AGW, 21.78 mm. **Ruler:** Elizabeth II **Subject:** Harry Potter - Journey to Hogwarts School **Obv:** Bust right **Obv. Designer:** Ian Rank-Broadley **Rev:** Boat full of children going to Hogwarts School **Edge:** Reeded

Date	Mintage	F	VF	XF	Unc	BU
2001 Proof	5,000	Value: 300				

KM# 1336 1/5 CROWN
6.1500 g., 0.9990 Gold 0.1975 oz. AGW, 21.78 mm. **Ruler:** Elizabeth II **Subject:** Harry Potter - First Quidditch Match **Obv:** Bust right **Obv. Designer:** Ian Rank-Broadley **Rev:** Harry flying a broom in a quidditch match **Edge:** Reeded

Date	Mintage	F	VF	XF	Unc	BU
2001 Proof	5,000	Value: 300				

KM# 1337 1/5 CROWN
6.1500 g., 0.9990 Gold 0.1975 oz. AGW, 21.78 mm. **Ruler:** Elizabeth II **Subject:** Harry Potter **Obv:** Bust right **Obv. Designer:** Ian Rank-Broadley **Rev:** Birth of Norbert, the dragon **Edge:** Reeded

Date	Mintage	F	VF	XF	Unc	BU
2001 Proof	5,000	Value: 300				

KM# 1338 1/5 CROWN
6.1500 g., 0.9990 Gold 0.1975 oz. AGW, 21.78 mm. **Ruler:** Elizabeth II **Subject:** Harry Potter **Obv:** Bust right **Obv. Designer:** Ian Rank-Broadley **Rev:** Harry in Potions class **Edge:** Reeded

Date	Mintage	F	VF	XF	Unc	BU
2001 Proof	5,000	Value: 300				

KM# 1156 1/5 CROWN
6.2200 g., 0.9990 Gold 0.1998 oz. AGW, 22 mm. **Ruler:** Elizabeth II **Subject:** Queen's Golden Jubilee **Obv:** Queen's portrait **Rev:** Queen on horse **Edge:** Reeded

Date	Mintage	F	VF	XF	Unc	BU
2002PM Proof	500	Value: 325				

KM# 1117 1/5 CROWN
6.2200 g., 0.9990 Gold 0.1998 oz. AGW, 22 mm. **Ruler:** Elizabeth II **Subject:** Queen Mother's Love of Horses **Obv:** Bust with tiara right **Obv. Designer:** Ian Rank-Broadley **Rev:** Queen Mother and horse **Edge:** Reeded

Date	Mintage	F	VF	XF	Unc	BU
2002 Proof	5,000	Value: 300				

KM# 1109 1/5 CROWN
6.2200 g., 0.9990 Gold 0.1998 oz. AGW, 22 mm. **Ruler:** Elizabeth II **Subject:** Bengal Cat **Obv:** Head with tiara right **Obv. Designer:** Ian Rank-Broadley **Rev:** Cat and kitten **Edge:** Reeded

Date	Mintage	VG	F	VF	XF	Unc
2002	—	—	—	—	—	—
2002 Proof	1,000	Value: 320				

KM# 1109a 1/5 CROWN
6.2200 g., 0.9990 Platinum 0.1998 oz. APW, 22 mm. **Ruler:** Elizabeth II **Subject:** Bengal Cat **Obv:** Head with tiara right **Obv. Designer:** Ian Rank-Broadley **Rev:** Cat and kitten **Edge:** Reeded

Date	Mintage	F	VF	XF	Unc	BU
2002	—	—	—	—	—	400

KM# 1100 1/5 CROWN
6.2200 g., 0.9999 Gold 0.1999 oz. AGW, 22 mm. **Ruler:** Elizabeth II **Subject:** Year of the Horse **Obv:** Bust with tiara right **Obv. Designer:** Ian Rank-Broadley **Rev:** Two horses **Edge:** Reeded

Date	Mintage	F	VF	XF	Unc	BU
2002 Proof	12,000	Value: 300				

KM# 1113 1/5 CROWN
6.2200 g., 0.9990 Gold 0.1998 oz. AGW, 22 mm. **Ruler:** Elizabeth II **Subject:** Olympics - Salt Lake City **Obv:** Bust with tiara right **Obv. Designer:** Ian Rank-Broadley **Rev:** Skier, torch and flag **Edge:** Reeded

Date	Mintage	F	VF	XF	Unc	BU
2002 Proof	5,000	Value: 300				

KM# 1114 1/5 CROWN
6.2200 g., 0.9990 Gold 0.1998 oz. AGW **Ruler:** Elizabeth II **Subject:** Olympics - Salt Lake City **Obv:** Bust with tiara right **Obv. Designer:** Ian Rank-Broadley **Rev:** Bobsled, torch and stadium **Edge:** Reeded

Date	Mintage	F	VF	XF	Unc	BU
2002 Proof	5,000	Value: 300				

KM# 1120 1/5 CROWN
6.2200 g., 0.9990 Gold 0.1998 oz. AGW, 22 mm. **Ruler:** Elizabeth II **Subject:** World Cup 2002 Japan - Korea **Obv:** Bust with tiara right **Obv. Designer:** Ian Rank-Broadley **Rev:** Player running right **Edge:** Reeded

Date	Mintage	F	VF	XF	Unc	BU
2002 Proof	5,000	Value: 300				

KM# 1122 1/5 CROWN
6.2200 g., 0.9990 Gold 0.1998 oz. AGW, 22 mm. **Ruler:** Elizabeth II **Subject:** World Cup 2002 Japan - Korea **Obv:** Bust with tiara right **Obv. Designer:** Ian Rank-Broadley **Rev:** Player kicking to right **Edge:** Reeded

Date	Mintage	F	VF	XF	Unc	BU
2002 Proof	5,000	Value: 300				

KM# 1124 1/5 CROWN
6.2200 g., 0.9990 Gold 0.1998 oz. AGW, 22 mm. **Ruler:** Elizabeth II **Subject:** World Cup 2002 Japan - Korea **Obv:** Head with tiara right **Obv. Designer:** Ian Rank-Broadley **Rev:** Player kicking to left **Edge:** Reeded

Date	Mintage	F	VF	XF	Unc	BU
2002 Proof	5,000	Value: 300				

KM# 1126 1/5 CROWN
6.2200 g., 0.9990 Gold 0.1998 oz. AGW, 22 mm. **Ruler:** Elizabeth II **Subject:** World Cup 2002 Japan - Korea **Obv:** Head with tiara right **Obv. Designer:** Ian Rank-Broadley **Rev:** Player running to left **Edge:** Reeded

Date	Mintage	F	VF	XF	Unc	BU
2002 Proof	5,000	Value: 300				

KM# 1130 1/5 CROWN
6.2200 g., 0.3750 Gold 0.0750 oz. AGW, 22 mm. **Ruler:** Elizabeth II **Subject:** Elizabeth II's Golden Jubilee **Obv:** Bust with tiara right **Obv. Designer:** Ian Rank-Broadley **Rev:** Seated crowned Queen holding scepter at her coronation **Edge:** Reeded

Date	Mintage	F	VF	XF	Unc	BU
2002 Proof	2,002	Value: 120				

KM# 1132 1/5 CROWN
6.2200 g., 0.3750 Gold 0.0750 oz. AGW, 22 mm. **Ruler:** Elizabeth II **Subject:** Elizabeth II's Golden Jubilee **Obv:** Bust with tiara right **Obv. Designer:** Ian Rank-Broadley **Rev:** Queen on horse **Edge:** Reeded

Date	Mintage	F	VF	XF	Unc	BU
2002 Proof	2,002	Value: 120				

KM# 1134 1/5 CROWN
6.2200 g., 0.3750 Gold 0.0750 oz. AGW, 22 mm. **Ruler:** Elizabeth II **Subject:** Elizabeth II's Golden Jubilee **Obv:** Head with tiara right **Obv. Designer:** Ian Rank-Broadley **Rev:** Queen with dog **Edge:** Reeded

Date	Mintage	F	VF	XF	Unc	BU
2002 Proof	2,002	Value: 120				

KM# 1136 1/5 CROWN
6.2200 g., 0.3750 Gold 0.0750 oz. AGW, 22 mm. **Ruler:** Elizabeth II **Subject:** Elizabeth II's Golden Jubilee **Obv:** Bust with tiara right **Obv. Designer:** Ian Rank-Broadley **Rev:** Queen at war memorial **Edge:** Reeded

Date	Mintage	F	VF	XF	Unc	BU
2002 Proof	2,002	Value: 120				

KM# 1138 1/5 CROWN
6.2200 g., 0.9990 Gold 0.1998 oz. AGW, 22 mm. **Ruler:** Elizabeth II **Subject:** Queen Mother **Obv:** Bust with tiara right **Obv. Designer:** Ian Rank-Broadley **Rev:** Queen Mother and Castle May **Edge:** Reeded

Date	Mintage	F	VF	XF	Unc	BU
2002 Proof	5,000	Value: 300				

KM# 1140 1/5 CROWN
6.2200 g., 0.9999 Gold 0.1999 oz. AGW, 22 mm. **Ruler:** Elizabeth II **Subject:** Princess Diana **Obv:** Bust with tiara right **Obv. Designer:** Ian Rank-Broadley **Rev:** Diana's portrait **Edge:** Reeded

Date	Mintage	F	VF	XF	Unc	BU
2002 Proof	5,000	Value: 300				

KM# 1163 1/5 CROWN
6.2200 g., 0.9999 Gold 0.1999 oz. AGW, 22 mm. **Ruler:** Elizabeth II **Subject:** Cat **Obv:** Head with tiara right **Obv. Designer:** Ian Rank-Broadley **Rev:** Two Balinese kittens **Edge:** Reeded

Date	Mintage	F	VF	XF	Unc	BU
2003PM	—	—	—	—	—	300
2003PM Proof	—	Value: 310				

KM# 1163a 1/5 CROWN
6.2200 g., 0.9995 Platinum 0.1999 oz. APW, 22 mm. **Ruler:** Elizabeth II **Subject:** Cat **Obv:** Head with tiara right **Obv. Designer:** Ian Rank-Broadley **Rev:** Two Balinese kittens **Edge:** Reeded

Date	Mintage	F	VF	XF	Unc	BU
2003PM	—	—	—	—	—	400

KM# 1169 1/5 CROWN
6.2200 g., 0.9999 Gold 0.1999 oz. AGW, 22 mm. **Ruler:** Elizabeth II **Subject:** Year of the Goat **Obv:** Bust with tiara right **Obv. Designer:** Ian Rank-Broadley **Rev:** Three goats **Edge:** Reeded

Date	Mintage	F	VF	XF	Unc	BU
2003PM Proof	—	Value: 300				

KM# 1175 1/5 CROWN
6.2200 g., 0.9999 Gold 0.1999 oz. AGW, 22 mm. **Ruler:** Elizabeth II **Subject:** Olympics **Obv:** Bust with tiara right **Obv. Designer:** Ian Rank-Broadley **Rev:** Swimmers **Edge:** Reeded

Date	Mintage	F	VF	XF	Unc	BU
2003PM Proof	5,000	Value: 300				

KM# 1177 1/5 CROWN
6.2200 g., 0.9999 Gold 0.1999 oz. AGW, 22 mm. **Ruler:** Elizabeth II **Subject:** Olympics **Obv:** Bust with tiara right **Obv. Designer:** Ian Rank-Broadley **Rev:** Runners **Edge:** Reeded

Date	Mintage	F	VF	XF	Unc	BU
2003PM Proof	5,000	Value: 300				

KM# 1179 1/5 CROWN
6.2200 g., 0.9999 Gold 0.1999 oz. AGW, 22 mm. **Ruler:** Elizabeth II **Subject:** Olympics **Obv:** Bust with tiara right **Obv. Designer:** Ian Rank-Broadley **Rev:** Bicyclists **Edge:** Reeded

Date	Mintage	F	VF	XF	Unc	BU
2003PM Proof	5,000	Value: 300				

KM# 1181 1/5 CROWN
6.2200 g., 0.9999 Gold 0.1999 oz. AGW, 22 mm. **Ruler:** Elizabeth II **Subject:** Olympics **Obv:** Head with tiara right **Obv. Designer:** Ian Rank-Broadley **Rev:** Sail Boarders **Edge:** Reeded

Date	Mintage	F	VF	XF	Unc	BU
2003PM Proof	—	Value: 300				

KM# 1188 1/5 CROWN
6.2200 g., 0.9999 Gold 0.1999 oz. AGW, 22 mm. **Ruler:** Elizabeth II **Subject:** Lord of the Rings **Obv:** Bust with tiara right **Obv. Designer:** Ian Rank-Broadley **Rev:** Legolas with bow and arrow **Edge:** Reeded

Date	Mintage	F	VF	XF	Unc	BU
2003PM Proof	3,500	Value: 300				

KM# 1223 1/5 CROWN
6.2200 g., 0.9999 Gold 0.1999 oz. AGW, 22 mm. **Ruler:** Elizabeth II **Obv:** Bust with tiara right **Obv. Designer:** Ian Rank-Broadley **Rev:** D-Day Invasion Plan Map **Edge:** Reeded

Date	Mintage	F	VF	XF	Unc	BU
2004PM Proof	5,000	Value: 300				

KM# 1225 1/5 CROWN
6.2200 g., 0.9999 Gold 0.1999 oz. AGW, 22 mm. **Ruler:** Elizabeth II **Obv:** Bust with tiara right **Obv. Designer:** Ian Rank-Broadley **Rev:** Victoria Cross and battle scene **Edge:** Reeded

Date	Mintage	F	VF	XF	Unc	BU
2004PM Proof	5,000	Value: 300				

KM# 1227 1/5 CROWN
6.2200 g., 0.9999 Gold 0.1999 oz. AGW, 22 mm. **Ruler:** Elizabeth II **Obv:** Bust with tiara right **Obv. Designer:** Ian Rank-Broadley **Rev:** Silver Star and battle scene **Edge:** Reeded

Date	Mintage	F	VF	XF	Unc	BU
2004PM Proof	5,000	Value: 300				

KM# 1229 1/5 CROWN
6.2200 g., 0.9999 Gold 0.1999 oz. AGW, 22 mm. **Ruler:** Elizabeth II **Obv:** Bust with tiara right **Obv. Designer:** Ian Rank-Broadley **Rev:** George Cross and rescue scene **Edge:** Reeded

Date	Mintage	F	VF	XF	Unc	BU
2004PM Proof	5,000	Value: 300				

KM# 1231 1/5 CROWN
6.2200 g., 0.9999 Gold 0.1999 oz. AGW, 22 mm. **Ruler:** Elizabeth II **Obv:** Bust with tiara right **Obv. Designer:** Ian Rank-Broadley **Rev:** White Rose of Finland Medal and battle scene **Edge:** Reeded

Date	Mintage	F	VF	XF	Unc	BU
2004PM Proof	5,000	Value: 300				

KM# 1233 1/5 CROWN
6.2200 g., 0.9999 Gold 0.1999 oz. AGW, 22 mm. **Ruler:** Elizabeth II **Obv:** Bust with tiara right **Obv. Designer:** Ian Rank-Broadley **Rev:** The Norwegian War Medal and naval battle scene **Edge:** Reeded

Date	Mintage	F	VF	XF	Unc	BU
2004PM Proof	5,000	Value: 300				

KM# 1235 1/5 CROWN
6.2200 g., 0.9999 Gold 0.1999 oz. AGW, 22 mm. **Ruler:** Elizabeth II **Obv:** Bust with tiara right **Obv. Designer:** Ian Rank-Broadley **Rev:** French Croix de Guerre and Partisan battle scene **Edge:** Reeded

Date	Mintage	F	VF	XF	Unc	BU
2004PM Proof	5,000	Value: 300				

KM# 1249.1 1/5 CROWN
6.2200 g., 0.9999 Gold 0.1999 oz. AGW, 22 mm. **Ruler:** Elizabeth II **Obv:** Head with tiara right **Obv. Designer:** Ian Rank-Broadley **Rev:** Two Tonkinese cats **Edge:** Reeded

Date	Mintage	F	VF	XF	Unc	BU
2004PM	—	—	—	—	—	300
2004PM Proof	1,000	Value: 310				

KM# 1249.2 1/5 CROWN
6.2200 g., 0.9999 Gold 0.1999 oz. AGW, 22 mm. **Ruler:** Elizabeth II **Obv:** Head with tiara right **Obv. Designer:** Ian Rank-Broadley **Rev:** Two multicolor Tonkinese cats **Edge:** Reeded

Date	Mintage	F	VF	XF	Unc	BU
2004PM Proof	—	Value: 300				

KM# 1198 1/5 CROWN
6.2200 g., 0.9990 Palladium 0.1998 oz., 22 mm. **Ruler:** Elizabeth II **Subject:** Palladium Bicentennial **Obv:** Head with tiara right **Obv. Designer:** Ian Rank-Broadley **Rev:** Athena **Edge:** Reeded

Date	Mintage	F	VF	XF	Unc	BU
2004PM Proof	999	Value: 200				

KM# 1271 1/5 CROWN
6.2200 g., 0.9999 Gold 0.1999 oz. AGW, 22 mm. **Ruler:** Elizabeth II **Obv:** Bust with tiara right **Obv. Designer:** Ian Rank-Broadley **Rev:** Himalayan cat and two kittens **Edge:** Reeded

Date	Mintage	F	VF	XF	Unc	BU
2005PM Proof	—	Value: 310				

KM# 1271a 1/5 CROWN
6.2200 g., 0.9950 Platinum 0.1990 oz. APW, 22 mm. **Ruler:** Elizabeth II **Obv:** Bust with tiara right **Obv. Designer:** Ian Rank-Broadley **Rev:** Himalayan cat and two kittens **Edge:** Reeded

Date	Mintage	F	VF	XF	Unc	BU
2005PM Proof	—	Value: 400				

KM# 1295 1/5 CROWN
6.2200 g., 0.9999 Gold 0.1999 oz. AGW, 22 mm. **Ruler:** Elizabeth II **Subject:** Battles that Changed the World **Obv:** Elizabeth II **Rev:** Trojan War scene **Edge:** Reeded

Date	Mintage	F	VF	XF	Unc	BU
2006PM Proof	5,000	Value: 300				

KM# 1297 1/5 CROWN
6.2200 g., 0.9999 Gold 0.1999 oz. AGW, 22 mm. **Ruler:** Elizabeth II **Subject:** Battles that Changed the World **Obv:** Elizabeth II **Rev:** Battle of Arbela scene **Edge:** Reeded

Date	Mintage	F	VF	XF	Unc	BU
2006PM Proof	5,000	Value: 300				

KM# 1299 1/5 CROWN
6.2200 g., 0.9999 Gold 0.1999 oz. AGW, 22 mm. **Ruler:** Elizabeth II **Subject:** Battles that Changed the World **Obv:** Elizabeth II **Rev:** Battle of Thapsus scene **Edge:** Reeded

Date	Mintage	F	VF	XF	Unc	BU
2006PM Proof	5,000	Value: 300				

KM# 1301 1/5 CROWN
6.2200 g., 0.9999 Gold 0.1999 oz. AGW, 22 mm. **Ruler:** Elizabeth II **Subject:** Battles that Changed the World **Obv:** Elizabeth II **Rev:** Battle of Cologne scene **Edge:** Reeded

Date	Mintage	F	VF	XF	Unc	BU
2006PM Proof	5,000	Value: 300				

KM# 1303 1/5 CROWN
6.2200 g., 0.9999 Gold 0.1999 oz. AGW, 22 mm. **Ruler:** Elizabeth II **Subject:** Battles that Changed the World **Obv:** Elizabeth II **Rev:** Siege of Valencia scene **Edge:** Reeded

Date	Mintage	F	VF	XF	Unc	BU
2006PM Proof	5,000	Value: 300				

KM# 1305 1/5 CROWN
6.2200 g., 0.9999 Gold 0.1999 oz. AGW, 22 mm. **Ruler:** Elizabeth II **Subject:** Battles that Changed the World **Obv:** Elizabeth II **Rev:** Battle of Agincourt scene **Edge:** Reeded

Date	Mintage	F	VF	XF	Unc	BU
2006PM Proof	5,000	Value: 300				

KM# 1342 1/5 CROWN
6.2200 g., 0.9999 Gold 0.1999 oz. AGW **Ruler:** Elizabeth II **Obv:** Bust with tiara right **Obv. Designer:** Ian Rank-Broadley **Rev:** Three Exotic Shorthair cats sitting facing **Edge:** Reeded

Date	Mintage	F	VF	XF	Unc	BU
2006PM	—	—	—	—	—	330

KM# 1345 1/5 CROWN
6.2200 g., 0.9999 Gold 0.1999 oz. AGW **Ruler:** Elizabeth II **Obv:** Bust with tiara right **Obv. Legend:** ELIZABETH II - ISLE OF MAN **Obv. Designer:** Ian Rank-Broadley **Rev:** Ragdoll cat with two kittens sitting facing **Edge:** Reeded

Date	Mintage	F	VF	XF	Unc	BU
2007PM	—	—	—	—	—	330

KM# 1351.1 1/5 CROWN
6.2200 g., 0.9999 Gold 0.1999 oz. AGW **Ruler:** Elizabeth II **Subject:** The Tale of Peter Rabbit **Obv:** Bust with tiara right **Obv. Legend:** ELIZABETH II - ISLE OF MAN **Obv. Designer:** Ian Rank-Broadley **Rev:** Peter walking with friends **Edge:** Reeded

Date	Mintage	F	VF	XF	Unc	BU
2007PM	—	—	—	—	—	340

KM# 1351.2 1/5 CROWN
6.2200 g., 0.9999 Gold 0.1999 oz. AGW **Ruler:** Elizabeth II **Subject:** The Tale of Peter Rabbit **Obv:** Bust with tiara right **Obv. Legend:** ELIZABETH II - ISLE OF MAN **Obv. Designer:** Ian Rank-Broadley **Rev:** Peter walking with friends **Edge:** Reeded

Date	Mintage	F	VF	XF	Unc	BU
2007PM	—	—	—	—	—	355

KM# 1309 1/5 CROWN
6.2200 g., 0.9999 Gold 0.1999 oz. AGW **Ruler:** Elizabeth II **Subject:** 100th Anniversary of Scouting **Obv:** Bust with tiara right **Obv. Legend:** ELIZABETH II - ISLE OF MAN **Rev:** 3/4 length figure of Robert Baden-Powell standing facing 3/4 left, Fleur-de-lys below, images of scouting at left and right **Rev. Legend:** CENTERARY OF SCOUTING **Edge:** Reeded

Date	Mintage	F	VF	XF	Unc	BU
2007 Proof	—	Value: 300				

KM# 1352 1/5 CROWN
6.2200 g., 0.9999 Gold 0.1999 oz. AGW, 22 mm. **Ruler:** Elizabeth II **Subject:** Prince Charles 60th Birthday **Obv:** Bust with tiara right **Obv. Legend:** ELIZABETH II - ISLE OF MAN **Obv. Designer:** Ian Rank-Broadley **Rev:** Heads of Charles, Princes William and Henry right **Edge:** Reeded

Date	Mintage	F	VF	XF	Unc	BU
2008PM Proof	5,000	Value: 310				

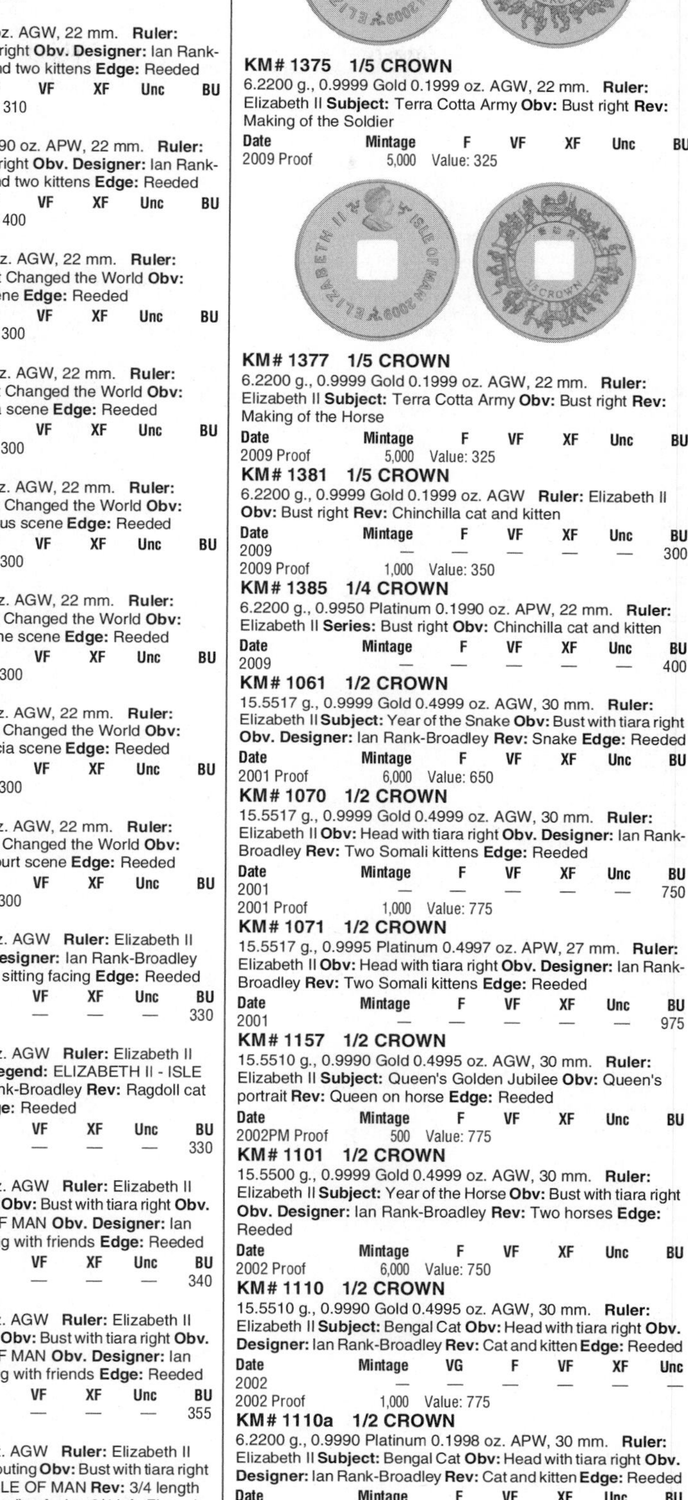

KM# 1375 1/5 CROWN
6.2200 g., 0.9999 Gold 0.1999 oz. AGW, 22 mm. **Ruler:** Elizabeth II **Subject:** Terra Cotta Army **Obv:** Bust right **Rev:** Making of the Soldier

Date	Mintage	F	VF	XF	Unc	BU
2009 Proof	5,000	Value: 325				

KM# 1377 1/5 CROWN
6.2200 g., 0.9999 Gold 0.1999 oz. AGW, 22 mm. **Ruler:** Elizabeth II **Subject:** Terra Cotta Army **Obv:** Bust right **Rev:** Making of the Horse

Date	Mintage	F	VF	XF	Unc	BU
2009 Proof	5,000	Value: 325				

KM# 1381 1/5 CROWN
6.2200 g., 0.9999 Gold 0.1999 oz. AGW **Ruler:** Elizabeth II **Obv:** Bust right **Rev:** Chinchilla cat and kitten

Date	Mintage	F	VF	XF	Unc	BU
2009	—	—	—	—	—	300
2009 Proof	1,000	Value: 350				

KM# 1385 1/4 CROWN
6.2200 g., 0.9950 Platinum 0.1990 oz. APW, 22 mm. **Ruler:** Elizabeth II **Series:** Bust right **Obv:** Chinchilla cat and kitten

Date	Mintage	F	VF	XF	Unc	BU
2009	—	—	—	—	—	400

KM# 1061 1/2 CROWN
15.5517 g., 0.9999 Gold 0.4999 oz. AGW, 30 mm. **Ruler:** Elizabeth II **Subject:** Year of the Snake **Obv:** Bust with tiara right **Obv. Designer:** Ian Rank-Broadley **Rev:** Snake **Edge:** Reeded

Date	Mintage	F	VF	XF	Unc	BU
2001 Proof	6,000	Value: 650				

KM# 1070 1/2 CROWN
15.5517 g., 0.9999 Gold 0.4999 oz. AGW, 30 mm. **Ruler:** Elizabeth II **Obv:** Head with tiara right **Obv. Designer:** Ian Rank-Broadley **Rev:** Two Somali kittens **Edge:** Reeded

Date	Mintage	F	VF	XF	Unc	BU
2001	—	—	—	—	—	750
2001 Proof	1,000	Value: 775				

KM# 1071 1/2 CROWN
15.5517 g., 0.9995 Platinum 0.4997 oz. APW, 27 mm. **Ruler:** Elizabeth II **Obv:** Head with tiara right **Obv. Designer:** Ian Rank-Broadley **Rev:** Two Somali kittens **Edge:** Reeded

Date	Mintage	F	VF	XF	Unc	BU
2001	—	—	—	—	—	975

KM# 1157 1/2 CROWN
15.5510 g., 0.9990 Gold 0.4995 oz. AGW, 30 mm. **Ruler:** Elizabeth II **Subject:** Queen's Golden Jubilee **Obv:** Queen's portrait **Rev:** Queen on horse **Edge:** Reeded

Date	Mintage	F	VF	XF	Unc	BU
2002PM Proof	500	Value: 775				

KM# 1101 1/2 CROWN
15.5500 g., 0.9999 Gold 0.4999 oz. AGW, 30 mm. **Ruler:** Elizabeth II **Subject:** Year of the Horse **Obv:** Bust with tiara right **Obv. Designer:** Ian Rank-Broadley **Rev:** Two horses **Edge:** Reeded

Date	Mintage	F	VF	XF	Unc	BU
2002 Proof	6,000	Value: 750				

KM# 1110 1/2 CROWN
15.5510 g., 0.9990 Gold 0.4995 oz. AGW, 30 mm. **Ruler:** Elizabeth II **Subject:** Bengal Cat **Obv:** Head with tiara right **Obv. Designer:** Ian Rank-Broadley **Rev:** Cat and kitten **Edge:** Reeded

Date	Mintage	VG	F	VF	XF	Unc
2002	—	—	—	—	—	—
2002 Proof	1,000	Value: 775				

KM# 1110a 1/2 CROWN
6.2200 g., 0.9990 Platinum 0.1998 oz. APW, 30 mm. **Ruler:** Elizabeth II **Subject:** Bengal Cat **Obv:** Head with tiara right **Obv. Designer:** Ian Rank-Broadley **Rev:** Cat and kitten **Edge:** Reeded

Date	Mintage	F	VF	XF	Unc	BU
2002	—	—	—	—	—	525

KM# 1164 1/2 CROWN
15.5510 g., 0.9999 Gold 0.4999 oz. AGW, 30 mm. **Ruler:** Elizabeth II **Subject:** Cat **Obv:** Head with tiara right **Obv. Designer:** Ian Rank-Broadley **Rev:** Two Balinese kittens **Edge:** Reeded

Date	Mintage	F	VF	XF	Unc	BU
2003PM	—	—	—	—	—	850
2003PM Proof	—	Value: 875				

KM# 1164a 1/2 CROWN
15.5510 g., 0.9995 Platinum 0.4997 oz. APW, 30 mm. **Ruler:** Elizabeth II **Subject:** Cat **Obv:** Head with tiara right **Obv. Designer:** Ian Rank-Broadley **Rev:** Two Balinese kittens **Edge:** Reeded

Date	Mintage	F	VF	XF	Unc	BU
2003PM	—	—	—	—	—	1,000

KM# 1170 1/2 CROWN
15.5500 g., 0.9999 Gold 0.4999 oz. AGW, 30 mm. **Ruler:** Elizabeth II **Subject:** Year of the Goat **Obv:** Bust with tiara right **Obv. Designer:** Ian Rank-Broadley **Rev:** Three goats **Edge:** Reeded

Date	Mintage	F	VF	XF	Unc	BU
2003PM Proof	—	Value: 875				

KM# 1189 1/2 CROWN
15.5510 g., 0.9999 Gold 0.4999 oz. AGW, 30 mm. **Ruler:** Elizabeth II **Subject:** Lord of the Rings **Obv:** Bust with tiara right **Obv. Designer:** Ian Rank-Broadley **Rev:** Gimli with two battle axes **Edge:** Reeded

Date	Mintage	F	VF	XF	Unc	BU
2003PM Proof	1,000	Value: 875				

KM# 1243 1/2 CROWN
15.5520 g., 0.9999 Gold 0.4999 oz. AGW, 30 mm. **Ruler:** Elizabeth II **Obv:** Head with tiara right **Obv. Designer:** Ian Rank-Broadley **Rev:** Monkey **Edge:** Reeded

Date	Mintage	F	VF	XF	Unc	BU
2004PM Proof	6,000	Value: 875				

KM# 1250 1/2 CROWN
15.5520 g., 0.9999 Gold 0.4999 oz. AGW, 30 mm. **Ruler:** Elizabeth II **Obv:** Head with tiara right **Obv. Designer:** Ian Rank-Broadley **Rev:** Two Tonkinese cats **Edge:** Reeded

Date	Mintage	F	VF	XF	Unc	BU
2004PM	—	—	—	—	—	855
2004PM Proof	1,000	Value: 875				

KM# 1199 1/2 CROWN
15.5500 g., 0.9990 Bi-Metallic .999 Palladium 6.3g center in .9999 Gold 9.25 g ring 0.4994 oz., 30 mm. **Ruler:** Elizabeth II **Subject:** Palladium Bicentennial **Obv:** Bust with tiara right **Obv. Designer:** Ian Rank-Broadley **Rev:** Athena **Edge:** Reeded

Date	Mintage	F	VF	XF	Unc	BU
2004PM Proof	500	Value: 975				

KM# 1272 1/2 CROWN
15.5510 g., 0.9999 Gold 0.4999 oz. AGW, 27 mm. **Ruler:** Elizabeth II **Obv:** Bust with tiara right **Obv. Designer:** Ian Rank-Broadley **Rev:** Himalayan cat and two kittens **Edge:** Reeded

Date	Mintage	F	VF	XF	Unc	BU
2005PM Proof	—	Value: 875				

KM# 1272a 1/2 CROWN
15.5510 g., 0.9950 Platinum 0.4975 oz. APW, 27 mm. **Ruler:** Elizabeth II **Obv:** Bust with tiara right **Obv. Designer:** Ian Rank-Broadley **Rev:** Himalayan cat and two kittens **Edge:** Reeded

Date	Mintage	F	VF	XF	Unc	BU
2005PM	—	—	—	—	—	975
2005PM Proof	—	Value: 1,000				

KM# 1346 1/2 CROWN
15.5500 g., 0.9999 Gold 0.4999 oz. AGW **Ruler:** Elizabeth II **Obv:** Bust with tiara right **Obv. Legend:** ELIZABETH II - ISLE OF MAN **Obv. Designer:** Ian Rank-Broadley **Rev:** Ragdoll cat with two kittens sitting facing **Edge:** Reeded

Date	Mintage	F	VF	XF	Unc	BU
2007PM	—	—	—	—	—	875

KM# 1396 1/2 CROWN
6.2200 g., 0.9999 Gold 0.1999 oz. AGW, 30x20 mm. **Ruler:** Elizabeth II **Rev:** Tut's golden mask

Date	Mintage	F	VF	XF	Unc	BU
2008PM	—	—	—	—	—	350

KM# 1399 1/2 CROWN
6.2200 g., 0.9999 Gold 0.1999 oz. AGW **Ruler:** Elizabeth II **Obv:** Bust with tiara right in Egyptian motif **Rev:** Statue standing **Shape:** Triangle

Date	Mintage	F	VF	XF	Unc	BU
2008PM Proof	—	Value: 350				

KM# 1400 1/2 CROWN
6.2200 g., 0.9999 Gold 0.1999 oz. AGW **Ruler:** Elizabeth II **Obv:** Bust with tiara right in Egyptian motif **Rev:** Statue standing, vile of sand above **Shape:** Triangle

Date	Mintage	F	VF	XF	Unc	BU
2008PM Proof	—	Value: 350				

KM# 1380 1/2 CROWN
15.5500 g., 0.9999 Gold 0.4999 oz. AGW, 30 mm. **Ruler:** Elizabeth II **Obv:** Bust right **Rev:** Chinchilla cat and kitten

Date	Mintage	F	VF	XF	Unc	BU
2009	—	—	—	—	—	850
2009 Proof	1,000	Value: 875				

KM# 1384 1/2 CROWN
15.5500 g., 0.9950 Platinum 0.4974 oz. APW, 27 mm. **Ruler:** Elizabeth II **Obv:** Bust right **Rev:** Chinchilla cat and kitten

Date	Mintage	F	VF	XF	Unc	BU
2009	—	—	—	—	—	1,000

KM# 1073 CROWN
31.1035 g., 0.9999 Gold 0.9999 oz. AGW, 32.7 mm. **Ruler:** Elizabeth II **Subject:** Somali Kittens **Obv:** Bust with tiara right **Obv. Designer:** Ian Rank-Broadley **Rev:** Two kittens **Edge:** Reeded

Date	Mintage	F	VF	XF	Unc	BU
2001	—	—	—	—	—	1,500
2001 Proof	1,000	Value: 1,550				

KM# 1076 CROWN
28.2800 g., Copper-Nickel, 38.6 mm. **Ruler:** Elizabeth II **Subject:** Queen Mother **Obv:** Bust with tiara right **Obv. Designer:** Ian Rank-Broadley **Rev:** 1948 Silver wedding anniversary **Edge:** Reeded

Date	Mintage	F	VF	XF	Unc	BU
2001	—	—	—	—	10.00	12.00

KM# 1076a CROWN
28.2800 g., 0.9250 Silver 0.8410 oz. ASW, 38.6 mm. **Ruler:** Elizabeth II **Subject:** Queen Mother **Obv:** Bust with tiara right **Obv. Designer:** Ian Rank-Broadley **Rev:** 1948 Silver wedding anniversary **Edge:** Reeded

Date	Mintage	F	VF	XF	Unc	BU
2001 Proof	10,000	Value: 47.50				

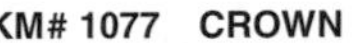

KM# 1077 CROWN
Copper-Nickel, 38.6 mm. **Ruler:** Elizabeth II **Subject:** Queen Mother **Obv:** Bust with tiara right **Obv. Designer:** Ian Rank-Broadley **Rev:** 1948 holding baby Prince Charles **Edge:** Reeded

Date	Mintage	F	VF	XF	Unc	BU
2001	—	—	—	—	10.00	12.00

KM# 1077a CROWN
28.2800 g., 0.9250 Silver 0.8410 oz. ASW, 38.6 mm. **Ruler:** Elizabeth II **Subject:** Queen Mother **Obv:** Head with tiara right **Obv. Designer:** Ian Rank-Broadley **Rev:** 1948 holding baby Prince Charles **Edge:** Reeded

Date	Mintage	F	VF	XF	Unc	BU
2001 Proof	10,000	Value: 47.50				

KM# 1080 CROWN
Copper-Nickel, 38.6 mm. **Ruler:** Elizabeth II **Subject:** Martin Frobisher **Obv:** Bust with tiara right **Obv. Designer:** Ian Rank-Broadley **Rev:** Bust at left, ship at right and map below **Edge:** Reeded

Date	Mintage	F	VF	XF	Unc	BU
2001	—	—	—	—	10.00	12.00

KM# 1080a CROWN
28.2800 g., 0.9250 Silver 0.8410 oz. ASW, 38.6 mm. **Ruler:** Elizabeth II **Subject:** Martin Frobisher **Obv:** Bust of Queen Elizabeth II right **Obv. Designer:** Ian Rank-Broadley **Edge:** Reeded

Date	Mintage	F	VF	XF	Unc	BU
2001 Proof	10,000	Value: 47.50				

KM# 1081 CROWN
Copper-Nickel, 38.6 mm. **Ruler:** Elizabeth II **Subject:** Roald Amundsen **Obv:** Bust with tiara right **Obv. Designer:** Ian Rank-Broadley **Rev:** Bust at right, ship at center, dirigible above at left **Edge:** Reeded

Date	Mintage	F	VF	XF	Unc	BU
2001	—	—	—	—	10.00	12.00

KM# 1081a CROWN
28.2800 g., 0.9250 Silver 0.8410 oz. ASW, 38.6 mm. **Ruler:** Elizabeth II **Subject:** Roald Amundsen **Obv:** Bust with tiara right **Obv. Designer:** Ian Rank-Broadley **Rev:** Bust at right, ship at center, dirigible at upper left **Edge:** Reeded

Date	Mintage	F	VF	XF	Unc	BU
2001 Proof	10,000	Value: 47.50				

KM# 1085 CROWN
28.2800 g., Copper-Nickel, 38.6 mm. **Ruler:** Elizabeth II **Subject:** Joey Dunlop (1952-2000) **Obv:** Bust with tiara right **Obv. Designer:** Ian Rank-Broadley **Rev:** Motorcycle racer **Edge:** Reeded

Date	Mintage	F	VF	XF	Unc	BU
2001 Black finish	—	—	—	—	10.00	12.00

KM# 1085a CROWN
28.2800 g., 0.9250 Silver 0.8410 oz. ASW, 38.6 mm. **Ruler:** Elizabeth II **Subject:** Joey Dunlop (1952-2000) **Obv:** Bust with tiara right **Obv. Designer:** Ian Rank-Broadley **Rev:** Motorcycle racer **Edge:** Reeded

Date	Mintage	F	VF	XF	Unc	BU
2001 Proof	10,000	Value: 47.50				

KM# 1083 CROWN

28.2800 g., Copper-Nickel, 38.6 mm. **Ruler:** Elizabeth II **Subject:** Queen's 75th Birthday **Obv:** Bust with tiara right **Obv. Designer:** Ian Rank-Broadley **Rev:** Flower bouquet **Edge:** Reeded

Date	Mintage	F	VF	XF	Unc	BU
2001	—	—	—	—	14.00	16.00

KM# 1083a CROWN

28.2800 g., 0.9250 Silver 0.8410 oz. ASW, 38.6 mm. **Ruler:** Elizabeth II **Subject:** Queen's 75th Birthday **Obv:** Bust with tiara right **Obv. Designer:** Ian Rank-Broadley **Rev:** Flower bouquet **Edge:** Reeded

Date	Mintage	F	VF	XF	Unc	BU
2001 Proof	10,000	Value: 50.00				

KM# 1087 CROWN

28.2800 g., Copper-Nickel, 38.6 mm. **Ruler:** Elizabeth II **Series:** Harry Potter **Obv:** Bust with tiara right **Obv. Designer:** Ian Rank-Broadley **Rev:** Harry with magic wand **Edge:** Reeded

Date	Mintage	F	VF	XF	Unc	BU
2001	—	—	—	—	10.00	12.00

KM# 1087a CROWN

28.2800 g., 0.9250 Silver 0.8410 oz. ASW, 38.6 mm. **Ruler:** Elizabeth II **Series:** Harry Potter **Obv:** Bust with tiara right **Obv. Designer:** Ian Rank-Broadley **Rev:** Harry with magic wand **Edge:** Reeded

Date	Mintage	F	VF	XF	Unc	BU
2001 Proof	15,000	Value: 47.50				

KM# 1089 CROWN

28.2800 g., Copper-Nickel, 38.6 mm. **Ruler:** Elizabeth II **Series:** Harry Potter **Subject:** Journey to Hogwart's **Obv:** Bust with tiara right **Obv. Designer:** Ian Rank-Broadley **Rev:** Boat full of children going to Hogwart's **Edge:** Reeded

Date	Mintage	F	VF	XF	Unc	BU
2001	—	—	—	—	10.00	12.00

KM# 1089a CROWN

28.2800 g., 0.9250 Silver 0.8410 oz. ASW, 38.6 mm. **Ruler:** Elizabeth II **Series:** Harry Potter **Obv:** Bust with tiara right **Obv. Designer:** Ian Rank-Broadley **Rev:** Boat full of children going to Hogwart's **Edge:** Reeded

Date	Mintage	F	VF	XF	Unc	BU
2001 Proof	15,000	Value: 47.50				

KM# 1091 CROWN

Copper-Nickel **Ruler:** Elizabeth II **Series:** Harry Potter **Subject:** First Quidditch Match **Obv:** Bust with tiara right **Obv. Designer:** Ian Rank-Broadley **Rev:** Harry flying his Nimbus 2000

Date	Mintage	F	VF	XF	Unc	BU
2001	—	—	—	—	10.00	12.00

KM# 1091a CROWN

28.2800 g., 0.9250 Silver 0.8410 oz. ASW **Ruler:** Elizabeth II **Series:** Harry Potter **Subject:** First Quidditch Match **Obv:** Bust with tiara right **Obv. Designer:** Ian Rank-Broadley **Rev:** Harry flying his Nimbus 2000

Date	Mintage	F	VF	XF	Unc	BU
2001 Proof	15,000	Value: 47.50				

KM# 1093 CROWN

Copper-Nickel **Ruler:** Elizabeth II **Series:** Harry Potter **Subject:** Birth of Norbert **Obv:** Bust with tiara right **Obv. Designer:** Ian Rank-Broadley **Rev:** Hagrid and children watching Norbert hatch

Date	Mintage	F	VF	XF	Unc	BU
2001	—	—	—	—	10.00	14.00

KM# 1093a CROWN

28.2800 g., 0.9250 Silver 0.8410 oz. ASW **Ruler:** Elizabeth II **Series:** Harry Potter **Subject:** Birth of Norbert **Obv:** Bust with tiara right **Obv. Designer:** Ian Rank-Broadley **Rev:** Hagrid and children watching Norbert hatch

Date	Mintage	F	VF	XF	Unc	BU
2001 Proof	15,000	Value: 47.50				

KM# 1095 CROWN

Copper-Nickel **Ruler:** Elizabeth II **Series:** Harry Potter **Subject:** School **Obv:** Bust with tiara right **Obv. Designer:** Ian Rank-Broadley **Rev:** Harry in Potions class

Date	Mintage	F	VF	XF	Unc	BU
2001	—	—	—	—	10.00	12.00

KM# 1095a CROWN

28.2800 g., 0.9250 Silver 0.8410 oz. ASW **Ruler:** Elizabeth II **Series:** Harry Potter **Subject:** School **Obv:** Bust with tiara right **Obv. Designer:** Ian Rank-Broadley **Rev:** Harry in Potions class

Date	Mintage	F	VF	XF	Unc	BU
2001 Proof	15,000	Value: 47.50				

KM# 1097 CROWN

Copper-Nickel, 38.72 mm. **Ruler:** Elizabeth II **Series:** Harry Potter **Obv:** Bust with tiara right **Obv. Designer:** Ian Rank-Broadley **Rev:** Harry catching the golden snitch **Edge:** Reeded

Date	Mintage	F	VF	XF	Unc	BU
2001	—	—	—	—	10.00	12.00

KM# 1097a CROWN

28.2800 g., 0.9250 Silver 0.8410 oz. ASW, 38.71 mm. **Ruler:** Elizabeth II **Series:** Harry Potter **Obv:** Bust with tiara right **Obv. Designer:** Ian Rank-Broadley **Rev:** Harry catching the golden snitch **Edge:** Reeded

Date	Mintage	F	VF	XF	Unc	BU
2001 Proof	15,000	Value: 47.50				

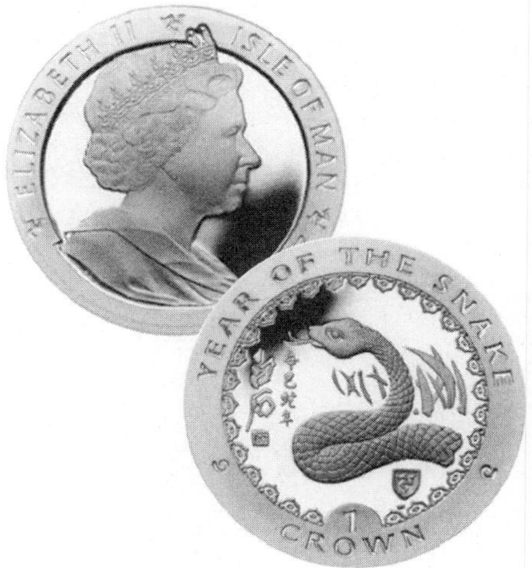

KM# 1062 CROWN

28.2800 g., Copper-Nickel, 38.6 mm. **Ruler:** Elizabeth II **Subject:** Year of the Snake **Obv:** Bust with tiara right **Obv. Designer:** Ian Rank-Broadley **Rev:** Snake **Edge:** Reeded

Date	Mintage	F	VF	XF	Unc	BU
2001	—	—	—	—	10.00	15.00

KM# 1062a CROWN

28.2800 g., 0.9250 Silver 0.8410 oz. ASW, 38.6 mm. **Ruler:** Elizabeth II **Subject:** Year of the Snake **Obv:** Head with tiara right **Obv. Designer:** Ian Rank-Broadley **Rev:** Snake **Edge:** Reeded

Date	Mintage	F	VF	XF	Unc	BU
2001 Proof	30,000	Value: 47.50				

KM# 1063 CROWN

31.1035 g., 0.9999 Gold 0.9999 oz. AGW, 32.7 mm. **Ruler:** Elizabeth II **Subject:** Year of the Snake **Obv:** Bust with tiara right **Obv. Designer:** Ian Rank-Broadley **Rev:** Snake **Edge:** Reeded

Date	Mintage	F	VF	XF	Unc	BU
2001 Proof	2,000	Value: 1,500				

KM# 1072 CROWN

28.2800 g., Copper-Nickel, 38.6 mm. **Ruler:** Elizabeth II **Subject:** Somali Kittens **Obv:** Bust with tiara right **Obv. Designer:** Ian Rank-Broadley **Rev:** Two kittens **Edge:** Reeded

Date	Mintage	F	VF	XF	Unc	BU
2001	—	—	—	—	11.00	15.00

KM# 1072a CROWN

31.1035 g., 0.9990 Silver 0.9990 oz. ASW, 38.6 mm. **Ruler:** Elizabeth II **Subject:** Somali Kittens **Obv:** Bust with tiara right **Obv. Designer:** Ian Rank-Broadley **Rev:** Two kittens **Edge:** Reeded

Date	Mintage	F	VF	XF	Unc	BU
2001 Proof	50,000	Value: 47.50				

KM# 1102 CROWN
28.2800 g., Copper-Nickel, 38.6 mm. **Ruler:** Elizabeth II **Subject:** Year of the Horse **Obv:** Bust with tiara right **Obv. Designer:** Ian Rank-Broadley **Rev:** Two horses **Edge:** Reeded

Date	Mintage	F	VF	XF	Unc	BU
2002	—	—	—	—	12.00	15.00

KM# 1102a CROWN
28.2800 g., 0.9250 Silver 0.8410 oz. ASW, 38.6 mm. **Ruler:** Elizabeth II **Subject:** Year of the Horse **Obv:** Bust with tiara right **Obv. Designer:** Ian Rank-Broadley **Rev:** Two horses **Edge:** Reeded

Date	Mintage	F	VF	XF	Unc	BU
2002 Proof	30,000	Value: 47.50				

KM# 1103 CROWN
31.1000 g., 0.9999 Gold 0.9997 oz. AGW **Ruler:** Elizabeth II **Subject:** Year of the Horse **Obv:** Bust with tiara right **Obv. Designer:** Ian Rank-Broadley

Date	Mintage	F	VF	XF	Unc	BU
2002 Proof	2,000	Value: 1,500				

KM# 1111 CROWN
28.2800 g., Copper-Nickel, 38.6 mm. **Ruler:** Elizabeth II **Subject:** Bengal Cat **Obv:** Bust with tiara right **Obv. Designer:** Ian Rank-Broadley **Rev:** Cat and kitten **Edge:** Reeded

Date	Mintage	F	VF	XF	Unc	BU
2002	—	—	—	—	12.50	14.00

KM# 1111a CROWN
31.1035 g., 0.9990 Silver 0.9990 oz. ASW, 38.6 mm. **Ruler:** Elizabeth II **Subject:** Bengal Cat **Obv:** Bust with tiara right **Obv. Designer:** Ian Rank-Broadley **Rev:** Cat and kitten **Edge:** Reeded

Date	Mintage	F	VF	XF	Unc	BU
2002 Proof	10,000	Value: 47.50				

KM# 1112 CROWN
31.1035 g., 0.9990 Gold 0.9990 oz. AGW, 33 mm. **Ruler:** Elizabeth II **Subject:** Bengal Cat **Obv:** Bust with tiara right **Obv. Designer:** Ian Rank-Broadley **Rev:** Cat and kitten **Edge:** Reeded

Date	Mintage	F	VF	XF	Unc	BU
2002	—	—	—	—	—	1,550
2002 Proof	1,000	Value: 1,600				

KM# 1115 CROWN
28.2800 g., Copper-Nickel, 38.6 mm. **Ruler:** Elizabeth II **Subject:** Olympics - Salt Lake City **Obv:** Bust with tiara right **Obv. Designer:** Ian Rank-Broadley **Rev:** Skier, torch and flag **Edge:** Reeded

Date	Mintage	F	VF	XF	Unc	BU
2002	—	—	—	—	10.00	12.00

KM# 1115a CROWN
28.2800 g., 0.9250 Silver 0.8410 oz. ASW, 38.6 mm. **Ruler:** Elizabeth II **Subject:** Olympics - Salt Lake City **Obv:** Bust with tiara right **Obv. Designer:** Ian Rank-Broadley **Rev:** Skier, torch and flag **Edge:** Reeded

Date	Mintage	F	VF	XF	Unc	BU
2002 Proof	10,000	Value: 47.50				

KM# 1116 CROWN
28.2800 g., Copper-Nickel, 38.6 mm. **Ruler:** Elizabeth II **Subject:** Olympics - Salt Lake City **Obv:** Bust with tiara right **Obv. Designer:** Ian Rank-Broadley **Rev:** Bobsled, torch and stadium **Edge:** Reeded

Date	Mintage	F	VF	XF	Unc	BU
2002	—	—	—	—	10.00	12.00

KM# 1116a CROWN
28.2800 g., 0.9250 Silver 0.8410 oz. ASW, 38.6 mm. **Ruler:** Elizabeth II **Subject:** Olympics - Salt Lake City **Obv:** Bust with tiara right **Obv. Designer:** Ian Rank-Broadley **Rev:** Bobsled, torch and stadium **Edge:** Reeded

Date	Mintage	F	VF	XF	Unc	BU
2002 Proof	10,000	Value: 47.50				

KM# 1118 CROWN
28.2800 g., Copper-Nickel, 38.6 mm. **Ruler:** Elizabeth II **Subject:** Queen Mother's Love of Horses **Obv:** Bust with tiara right **Obv. Designer:** Ian Rank-Broadley **Rev:** Queen Mother and horse **Edge:** Reeded

Date	Mintage	F	VF	XF	Unc	BU
2002	—	—	—	—	10.00	12.00

KM# 1118a CROWN
28.2800 g., Silver, 38.6 mm. **Ruler:** Elizabeth II **Subject:** Queen Mother's Love of Horses **Obv:** Bust with tiara right **Obv. Designer:** Ian Rank-Broadley **Rev:** Queen Mother and horse **Edge:** Reeded

Date	Mintage	F	VF	XF	Unc	BU
2002 Proof	10,000	Value: 47.50				

KM# 1119 CROWN
35.0000 g., 0.7500 Gold 0.8439 oz. AGW, 38.6 mm. **Ruler:** Elizabeth II **Subject:** Golden Jubilee **Obv:** Bust with tiara right **Obv. Designer:** Ian Rank-Broadley **Rev:** Queen Elizabeth II's young laureate bust right **Rev. Designer:** Mary Gillick **Edge:** Reeded **Note:** Red Gold center in a White Gold inner ring within a Yellow Gold outer ring.

Date	Mintage	F	VF	XF	Unc	BU
2002 Proof	999	Value: 1,350				

KM# 1121 CROWN
28.2800 g., Copper-Nickel, 38.6 mm. **Ruler:** Elizabeth II **Subject:** World Cup 2002 Japan - Korea **Obv:** Bust with tiara right **Obv. Designer:** Ian Rank-Broadley **Rev:** Player running right **Edge:** Reeded

Date	Mintage	F	VF	XF	Unc	BU
2002	—	—	—	—	10.00	12.00

KM# 1121a CROWN
28.2800 g., 0.9250 Silver 0.8410 oz. ASW, 38.6 mm. **Ruler:** Elizabeth II **Subject:** World Cup 2002 Japan - Korea **Obv:** Bust with tiara right **Obv. Designer:** Ian Rank-Broadley **Rev:** Player running right **Edge:** Reeded

Date	Mintage	F	VF	XF	Unc	BU
2002 Proof	10,000	Value: 47.50				

KM# 1123 CROWN
28.2800 g., Copper-Nickel, 38.6 mm. **Ruler:** Elizabeth II **Subject:** World Cup 2002 Japan - Korea **Obv:** Bust with tiara right **Obv. Designer:** Ian Rank-Broadley **Rev:** Player kicking to right **Edge:** Reeded

Date	Mintage	F	VF	XF	Unc	BU
2002	—	—	—	—	10.00	12.00

KM# 1123a CROWN
28.2800 g., 0.9250 Silver 0.8410 oz. ASW, 38.6 mm. **Ruler:** Elizabeth II **Subject:** World Cup 2002 Japan - Korea **Obv:** Bust with tiara right **Obv. Designer:** Ian Rank-Broadley **Rev:** Player kicking to right **Edge:** Reeded

Date	Mintage	F	VF	XF	Unc	BU
2002 Proof	10,000	Value: 47.50				

KM# 1125 CROWN

28.2800 g., Copper-Nickel, 38.6 mm. **Ruler:** Elizabeth II **Subject:** World Cup 2002 Japan - Korea **Obv:** Bust with tiara right **Obv. Designer:** Ian Rank-Broadley **Rev:** Player kicking to left **Edge:** Reeded

Date	Mintage	F	VF	XF	Unc	BU
2002	—	—	—	—	10.00	12.00

KM# 1125a CROWN

28.2800 g., 0.9250 Silver 0.8410 oz. ASW, 38.6 mm. **Ruler:** Elizabeth II **Subject:** World Cup 2002 Japan - Korea **Obv:** Bust with tiara right **Rev:** Player kicking to left **Edge:** Reeded

Date	Mintage	F	VF	XF	Unc	BU
2002 Proof	10,000	Value: 47.50				

KM# 1127 CROWN

28.2800 g., Copper-Nickel, 38.6 mm. **Ruler:** Elizabeth II **Subject:** World Cup 2002 Japan - Korea **Obv:** Bust with tiara right **Obv. Designer:** Ian Rank-Broadley **Rev:** Player running to left **Edge:** Reeded

Date	Mintage	F	VF	XF	Unc	BU
2002	—	—	—	—	10.00	12.00

KM# 1127a CROWN

28.2800 g., 0.9250 Silver 0.8410 oz. ASW, 38.6 mm. **Ruler:** Elizabeth II **Subject:** World Cup 2002 Japan - Korea **Obv:** Bust with tiara right **Obv. Designer:** Ian Rank-Broadley **Rev:** Player running to left **Edge:** Reeded

Date	Mintage	F	VF	XF	Unc	BU
2002 Proof	10,000	Value: 47.50				

KM# 1131 CROWN

28.2800 g., Copper-Nickel, 38.6 mm. **Ruler:** Elizabeth II **Subject:** Queen Elizabeth II's Golden Jubilee **Obv:** Bust with tiara right **Obv. Designer:** Ian Rank-Broadley **Rev:** Seated crowned Queen holding scepter at her coronation **Edge:** Reeded

Date	Mintage	F	VF	XF	Unc	BU
2002	—	—	—	—	10.00	12.00

KM# 1131a CROWN

28.2800 g., Gold Color Base Metal, 38.6 mm. **Ruler:** Elizabeth II **Subject:** Queen Elizabeth II's Golden Jubilee **Obv:** Bust with tiara right **Obv. Designer:** Ian Rank-Broadley **Rev:** Seated crowned Queen holding scepter at her coronation **Edge:** Reeded

Date	Mintage	F	VF	XF	Unc	BU
2002	15,000	—	—	—	10.00	12.00

KM# 1131b CROWN

28.2800 g., 0.9250 Gold Clad Silver 0.8410 oz., 38.6 mm. **Ruler:** Elizabeth II **Subject:** Queen Elizabeth II's Golden Jubilee **Obv:** Bust with tiara right **Obv. Designer:** Ian Rank-Broadley **Rev:** Seated crowned Queen holding scepter at her coronation **Edge:** Reeded

Date	Mintage	F	VF	XF	Unc	BU
2002 Proof	10,000	Value: 47.50				

KM# 1133 CROWN

28.2800 g., Copper-Nickel, 38.6 mm. **Ruler:** Elizabeth II **Subject:** Queen Elizabeth II's Golden Jubilee **Obv:** Bust with tiara right **Obv. Designer:** Ian Rank-Broadley **Rev:** Queen on horse **Edge:** Reeded

Date	Mintage	F	VF	XF	Unc	BU
2002	—	—	—	—	10.00	12.00

KM# 1133a CROWN

28.2800 g., Gold Color Base Metal, 38.6 mm. **Ruler:** Elizabeth II **Subject:** Queen Elizabeth II's Golden Jubilee **Obv:** Bust with tiara right **Obv. Designer:** Ian Rank-Broadley **Rev:** Queen on horse **Edge:** Reeded

Date	Mintage	F	VF	XF	Unc	BU
2002	15,000	—	—	—	10.00	12.00

KM# 1133b CROWN

28.2800 g., 0.9250 Gold Clad Silver 0.8410 oz., 38.6 mm. **Ruler:** Elizabeth II **Subject:** Queen Elizabeth II's Golden Jubilee **Obv:** Bust with tiara right **Obv. Designer:** Ian Rank-Broadley **Rev:** Queen on horse half left **Edge:** Reeded

Date	Mintage	F	VF	XF	Unc	BU
2002 Proof	10,000	Value: 47.50				

KM# 1135 CROWN

28.2800 g., Copper-Nickel, 38.6 mm. **Ruler:** Elizabeth II **Subject:** Queen Elizabeth II's Golden Jubilee **Obv:** Bust with tiara right **Obv. Designer:** Ian Rank-Broadley **Rev:** Queen with her pet Corgi **Edge:** Reeded

Date	Mintage	F	VF	XF	Unc	BU
2002	—	—	—	—	10.00	12.00

KM# 1135a CROWN

28.2800 g., Gold Color Base Metal, 38.6 mm. **Ruler:** Elizabeth II **Subject:** Queen Elizabeth II's Golden Jubilee **Obv:** Bust with tiara right **Obv. Designer:** Ian Rank-Broadley **Rev:** Seated Queen with her pet Corgi **Edge:** Reeded

Date	Mintage	F	VF	XF	Unc	BU
2002	15,000	—	—	—	10.00	12.00

KM# 1135b CROWN

28.2800 g., 0.9250 Gold Clad Silver 0.8410 oz., 38.6 mm. **Ruler:** Elizabeth II **Subject:** Queen Elizabeth II's Golden Jubilee **Obv:** Bust with tiara right **Obv. Designer:** Ian Rank-Broadley **Rev:** Queen with her pet Corgi **Edge:** Reeded

Date	Mintage	F	VF	XF	Unc	BU
2002 Proof	10,000	Value: 47.50				

KM# 1137 CROWN

28.2800 g., Copper-Nickel, 38.6 mm. **Ruler:** Elizabeth II **Subject:** Queen Elizabeth II's Golden Jubilee **Obv:** Bust with tiara right **Obv. Designer:** Ian Rank-Broadley **Rev:** Queen at war memorial **Edge:** Reeded

Date	Mintage	F	VF	XF	Unc	BU
2002	—	—	—	—	10.00	12.00

KM# 1137a CROWN

28.2800 g., Gold Color Base Metal, 38.6 mm. **Ruler:** Elizabeth II **Subject:** Queen Elizabeth II's Golden Jubilee **Obv:** Bust with tiara right **Obv. Designer:** Ian Rank-Broadley **Rev:** Queen at war memorial **Edge:** Reeded

Date	Mintage	F	VF	XF	Unc	BU
2002	15,000	—	—	—	10.00	12.00

KM# 1137b CROWN

28.2800 g., Gold Clad Silver, 38.6 mm. **Ruler:** Elizabeth II **Subject:** Queen Elizabeth II's Golden Jubilee **Obv:** Bust with tiara right **Obv. Designer:** Ian Rank-Broadley **Rev:** Queen at war memorial **Edge:** Reeded

Date	Mintage	F	VF	XF	Unc	BU
2002 Proof	10,000	Value: 47.50				

KM# 1139 CROWN

Copper-Nickel dark patina, 38.6 mm. **Ruler:** Elizabeth II **Subject:** Queen Mother **Obv:** Bust with tiara right **Obv. Designer:** Ian Rank-Broadley **Rev:** Queen Mother and Castle May **Edge:** Reeded

Date	Mintage	F	VF	XF	Unc	BU
2002	—	—	—	—	10.00	12.00

KM# 1139a CROWN

28.2800 g., 0.9250 Silver 0.8410 oz. ASW, 38.6 mm. **Ruler:** Elizabeth II **Obv:** Head with tiara right with blackened legends **Obv. Designer:** Ian Rank-Broadley **Rev:** Queen Mother standing at left in front of Castle May with blackened legends

Date	Mintage	F	VF	XF	Unc	BU
2002 Proof	10,000	Value: 47.50				

KM# 1141 CROWN

28.2800 g., Copper-Nickel, 38.6 mm. **Ruler:** Elizabeth II **Subject:** Princess Diana **Obv:** Bust with tiara right **Obv. Designer:** Ian Rank-Broadley **Rev:** Diana's bust facing **Edge:** Reeded

Date	Mintage	F	VF	XF	Unc	BU
2002	—	—	—	—	10.00	12.00

KM# 1141a CROWN

28.2800 g., 0.9250 Silver 0.8410 oz. ASW, 38.6 mm. **Ruler:** Elizabeth II **Subject:** Princess Diana **Obv:** Bust with tiara right **Obv. Designer:** Ian Rank-Broadley **Rev:** Diana facing **Edge:** Reeded

Date	Mintage	F	VF	XF	Unc	BU
2002 Proof	10,000	Value: 47.50				

KM# 1144 CROWN
28.2800 g., Copper-Nickel, 38.6 mm. **Ruler:** Elizabeth II **Series:** Harry Potter **Obv:** Bust with tiara right **Obv. Designer:** Ian Rank-Broadley **Rev:** Tom Riddle twirling Harry's magic wand **Edge:** Reeded

Date	Mintage	F	VF	XF	Unc	BU
2002PM	—	—	—	—	10.00	12.00

KM# 1144a CROWN
28.2800 g., 0.9250 Silver 0.8410 oz. ASW, 28.6 mm. **Ruler:** Elizabeth II **Series:** Harry Potter **Obv:** Bust with tiara right **Obv. Designer:** Ian Rank-Broadley **Rev:** Tom Riddle twirling Harry's magic wand **Edge:** Reeded

Date	Mintage	F	VF	XF	Unc	BU
2002PM Proof	15,000	Value: 50.00				

KM# 1146 CROWN
28.2800 g., Copper-Nickel, 38.6 mm. **Ruler:** Elizabeth II **Series:** Harry Potter **Obv:** Bust with tiara right **Obv. Designer:** Ian Rank-Broadley **Rev:** Harry and friends making Polyjuice potion **Edge:** Reeded

Date	Mintage	F	VF	XF	Unc	BU
2002PM	—	—	—	—	10.00	12.00

KM# 1146a CROWN
28.2800 g., 0.9250 Silver 0.8410 oz. ASW, 38.6 mm. **Ruler:** Elizabeth II **Series:** Harry Potter **Obv:** Bust with tiara right **Obv. Designer:** Ian Rank-Broadley **Rev:** Harry Potter and friends making Polyjuice potion **Edge:** Reeded

Date	Mintage	F	VF	XF	Unc	BU
2002PM Proof	15,000	Value: 50.00				

KM# 1148 CROWN
28.2800 g., Copper-Nickel, 38.6 mm. **Ruler:** Elizabeth II **Series:** Harry Potter **Obv:** Bust with tiara right **Obv. Designer:** Ian Rank-Broadley **Rev:** Harry arrives at the Burrow in a flying car **Edge:** Reeded

Date	Mintage	F	VF	XF	Unc	BU
2002PM	—	—	—	—	10.00	12.00

KM# 1148a CROWN
28.2800 g., 0.9250 Silver 0.8410 oz. ASW, 38.6 mm. **Ruler:** Elizabeth II **Series:** Harry Potter **Obv:** Bust with tiara right **Obv. Designer:** Ian Rank-Broadley **Rev:** Harry arrives at the Burrow in a flying car **Edge:** Reeded

Date	Mintage	F	VF	XF	Unc	BU
2002PM Proof	15,000	Value: 50.00				

KM# 1150 CROWN
28.2800 g., Copper-Nickel, 38.6 mm. **Ruler:** Elizabeth II **Series:** Harry Potter **Obv:** Bust with tiara right **Obv. Designer:** Ian Rank-Broadley **Rev:** Harry retrieves Gryffindor sword from sorting hat **Edge:** Reeded

Date	Mintage	F	VF	XF	Unc	BU
2002PM	—	—	—	—	10.00	12.00

KM# 1150a CROWN
28.2800 g., 0.9250 Silver 0.8410 oz. ASW, 38.6 mm. **Ruler:** Elizabeth II **Series:** Harry Potter **Obv:** Bust with tiara right **Obv. Designer:** Ian Rank-Broadley **Rev:** Harry retrieves Gryffindor sword from sorting hat **Edge:** Reeded

Date	Mintage	F	VF	XF	Unc	BU
2002PM Proof	15,000	Value: 50.00				

KM# 1152 CROWN
28.2800 g., Copper-Nickel, 38.6 mm. **Ruler:** Elizabeth II **Series:** Harry Potter **Obv:** Bust with tiara right **Obv. Designer:** Ian Rank-Broadley **Rev:** Harry and Ron encounter the spider Aragog **Edge:** Reeded

Date	Mintage	F	VF	XF	Unc	BU
2002PM	—	—	—	—	10.00	12.00

KM# 1152a CROWN
28.2800 g., 0.9250 Silver 0.8410 oz. ASW, 38.6 mm. **Ruler:** Elizabeth II **Series:** Harry Potter **Obv:** Bust with tiara right **Obv. Designer:** Ian Rank-Broadley **Rev:** Harry and Ron encounter the spider Aragog **Edge:** Reeded

Date	Mintage	F	VF	XF	Unc	BU
2002PM Proof	15,000	Value: 50.00				

KM# 1154 CROWN
28.2800 g., Copper-Nickel, 38.6 mm. **Ruler:** Elizabeth II **Series:** Harry Potter **Obv:** Bust with tiara right **Obv. Designer:** Ian Rank-Broadley **Rev:** Harry in hospital with Dobby **Edge:** Reeded

Date	Mintage	F	VF	XF	Unc	BU
2002PM	—	—	—	—	10.00	12.00

KM# 1154a CROWN
28.2800 g., 0.9250 Silver 0.8410 oz. ASW, 38.6 mm. **Ruler:** Elizabeth II **Series:** Harry Potter **Obv:** Bust with tiara right **Obv. Designer:** Ian Rank-Broadley **Rev:** Harry in hospital with Dobby **Edge:** Reeded

Date	Mintage	F	VF	XF	Unc	BU
2002PM Proof	15,000	Value: 50.00				

KM# 1185 CROWN
28.2800 g., Copper-Nickel, 38.6 mm. **Ruler:** Elizabeth II **Obv:** Bust with tiara right **Obv. Designer:** Ian Rank-Broadley **Rev:** Lord of the Rings characters **Edge:** Reeded

Date	Mintage	F	VF	XF	Unc	BU
2003PM	100,000	—	—	—	12.50	14.50

KM# 1185a CROWN
28.2800 g., 0.9250 Silver 0.8410 oz. ASW, 38.6 mm. **Ruler:** Elizabeth II **Obv:** Bust with tiara right **Obv. Designer:** Ian Rank-Broadley **Rev:** Lord of the Rings characters **Edge:** Reeded

Date	Mintage	F	VF	XF	Unc	BU
2003PM Proof	10,000	Value: 50.00				

KM# 1190 CROWN
31.1035 g., 0.9999 Gold 0.9999 oz. AGW, 32.7 mm. **Ruler:** Elizabeth II **Subject:** Lord of the Rings **Obv:** Bust with tiara right **Obv. Designer:** Ian Rank-Broadley **Rev:** Man on horse **Edge:** Reeded

Date	Mintage	F	VF	XF	Unc	BU
2003PM Proof	1,000	Value: 1,550				

KM# 1191 CROWN
28.2800 g., 0.9250 Silver 0.8410 oz. ASW, 38.6 mm. **Ruler:** Elizabeth II **Subject:** Lord of the Rings **Obv:** Bust with tiara right **Obv. Designer:** Ian Rank-Broadley **Rev:** Man with short sword **Edge:** Reeded

Date	Mintage	F	VF	XF	Unc	BU
2003PM Proof	5,000	Value: 47.50				

KM# 1192 CROWN
28.2800 g., 0.9250 Silver 0.8410 oz. ASW, 38.6 mm. **Ruler:** Elizabeth II **Subject:** Lord of the Rings **Obv:** Bust with tiara right **Obv. Designer:** Ian Rank-Broadley **Rev:** Aragorn with broadsword **Edge:** Reeded

Date	Mintage	F	VF	XF	Unc	BU
2003PM Proof	5,000	Value: 47.50				

KM# 1193 CROWN
28.2800 g., 0.9250 Silver 0.8410 oz. ASW, 38.6 mm. **Ruler:** Elizabeth II **Subject:** Lord of the Rings **Obv:** Bust with tiara right **Obv. Designer:** Ian Rank-Broadley **Rev:** Legolas **Edge:** Reeded

Date	Mintage	F	VF	XF	Unc	BU
2003PM Proof	5,000	Value: 47.50				

KM# 1194 CROWN
28.2800 g., 0.9250 Silver 0.8410 oz. ASW, 38.6 mm. **Ruler:** Elizabeth II **Subject:** Lord of the Rings **Obv:** Bust with tiara right **Obv. Designer:** Ian Rank-Broadley **Rev:** Gimli with two battle axes **Edge:** Reeded

Date	Mintage	F	VF	XF	Unc	BU
2003PM Proof	5,000	Value: 47.50				

KM# 1195 CROWN
28.2800 g., 0.9250 Silver 0.8410 oz. ASW, 38.6 mm. **Ruler:** Elizabeth II **Subject:** Lord of the Rings **Obv:** Bust with tiara right **Obv. Designer:** Ian Rank-Broadley **Rev:** Man on horse **Edge:** Reeded

Date	Mintage	F	VF	XF	Unc	BU
2003PM Proof	5,000	Value: 47.50				

KM# 1165 CROWN
28.2800 g., Copper-Nickel, 38.6 mm. **Ruler:** Elizabeth II **Subject:** Cat **Obv:** Bust with tiara right **Obv. Designer:** Ian Rank-Broadley **Rev:** Two Balinese kittens **Edge:** Reeded

Date	Mintage	F	VF	XF	Unc	BU
2003PM	—	—	—	—	12.00	14.00

KM# 1165a CROWN
31.1035 g., 0.9990 Silver 0.9990 oz. ASW, 38.6 mm. **Ruler:** Elizabeth II **Subject:** Cat **Obv:** Head with tiara right **Obv. Designer:** Ian Rank-Broadley **Rev:** Two Balinese kittens **Edge:** Reeded

Date	Mintage	F	VF	XF	Unc	BU
2003PM Proof	50,000	Value: 47.50				

KM# 1166 CROWN
31.1035 g., 0.9999 Gold 0.9999 oz. AGW, 32.7 mm. **Ruler:** Elizabeth II **Subject:** Cat **Obv:** Head with tiara right **Obv. Designer:** Ian Rank-Broadley **Rev:** Two Balinese kittens **Edge:** Reeded

Date	Mintage	F	VF	XF	Unc	BU
2003PM	—	—	—	—	—	1,550
2003PM Proof	—	Value: 1,600				

KM# 1171 CROWN
28.2800 g., Copper-Nickel, 38.6 mm. **Ruler:** Elizabeth II **Subject:** Year of the Goat **Obv:** Bust with tiara right **Obv. Designer:** Ian Rank-Broadley **Rev:** Three goats **Edge:** Reeded

Date	Mintage	F	VF	XF	Unc	BU
2003PM	—	—	—	—	12.00	14.00

KM# 1171a CROWN
28.2800 g., 0.9250 Silver 0.8410 oz. ASW, 38.6 mm. **Ruler:** Elizabeth II **Subject:** Year of the Goat **Obv:** Bust with tiara right **Obv. Designer:** Ian Rank-Broadley **Rev:** Three goats **Edge:** Reeded

Date	Mintage	F	VF	XF	Unc	BU
2003PM Proof	30,000	Value: 47.50				

KM# 1172 CROWN
31.1035 g., 0.9999 Gold 0.9999 oz. AGW, 32.7 mm. **Ruler:** Elizabeth II **Subject:** Year of the Goat **Obv:** Bust with tiara right **Obv. Designer:** Ian Rank-Broadley **Rev:** Three goats **Edge:** Reeded

Date	Mintage	F	VF	XF	Unc	BU
2003PM Proof	2,000	Value: 1,500				

KM# 1174 CROWN
28.5300 g., Copper-Nickel, 38.6 mm. **Ruler:** Elizabeth II **Obv:** Bust with tiara right **Obv. Designer:** Ian Rank-Broadley **Rev:** The Star of India sailing ship **Edge:** Reeded

Date	Mintage	F	VF	XF	Unc	BU
2003PM	—	—	—	—	10.00	12.00

KM# 1176 CROWN
28.2800 g., Copper-Nickel, 38.6 mm. **Ruler:** Elizabeth II **Subject:** Olympics **Obv:** Bust with tiara right **Obv. Designer:** Ian Rank-Broadley **Rev:** Swimmers **Edge:** Reeded

Date	Mintage	F	VF	XF	Unc	BU
2003PM	—	—	—	—	10.00	12.00

KM# 1176a CROWN
28.2800 g., 0.9250 Silver 0.8410 oz. ASW, 38.6 mm. **Ruler:** Elizabeth II **Subject:** Olympics **Obv:** Bust with tiara right **Obv. Designer:** Ian Rank-Broadley **Rev:** Swimmers **Edge:** Reeded

Date	Mintage	F	VF	XF	Unc	BU
2003PM Proof	10,000	Value: 47.50				

KM# 1178 CROWN
28.2800 g., Copper-Nickel, 38.6 mm. **Ruler:** Elizabeth II **Subject:** Olympics **Obv:** Bust with tiara right **Obv. Designer:** Ian Rank-Broadley **Rev:** Runners **Edge:** Reeded

Date	Mintage	F	VF	XF	Unc	BU
2003PM	—	—	—	—	10.00	12.00

KM# 1178a CROWN
28.2800 g., 0.9250 Silver 0.8410 oz. ASW, 38.6 mm. **Ruler:** Elizabeth II **Subject:** Olympics **Obv:** Bust with tiara right **Obv. Designer:** Ian Rank-Broadley **Rev:** Runners **Edge:** Reeded

Date	Mintage	F	VF	XF	Unc	BU
2003PM Proof	10,000	Value: 47.50				

KM# 1180 CROWN
28.2800 g., Copper-Nickel, 38.6 mm. **Ruler:** Elizabeth II **Subject:** Olympics **Obv:** Bust with tiara right **Obv. Designer:** Ian Rank-Broadley **Rev:** Bicyclists **Edge:** Reeded

Date	Mintage	F	VF	XF	Unc	BU
2003PM	—	—	—	—	10.00	12.00

KM# 1180a CROWN
28.2800 g., 0.9250 Silver 0.8410 oz. ASW, 38.6 mm. **Ruler:** Elizabeth II **Subject:** Olympics **Obv:** Bust with tiara right **Obv. Designer:** Ian Rank-Broadley **Rev:** Bicyclists **Edge:** Reeded

Date	Mintage	F	VF	XF	Unc	BU
2003PM Proof	10,000	Value: 47.50				

KM# 1182 CROWN
28.2800 g., Copper-Nickel, 38.6 mm. **Ruler:** Elizabeth II **Subject:** Olympics **Obv:** Bust with tiara right **Obv. Designer:** Ian Rank-Broadley **Rev:** Sail Boarders **Edge:** Reeded

Date	Mintage	F	VF	XF	Unc	BU
2003PM	—	—	—	—	10.00	12.00

KM# 1182a CROWN
28.2800 g., 0.9250 Silver 0.8410 oz. ASW, 38.6 mm. **Ruler:** Elizabeth II **Subject:** Olympics **Obv:** Bust with tiara right **Obv. Designer:** Ian Rank-Broadley **Rev:** Sail Boarders **Edge:** Reeded

Date	Mintage	F	VF	XF	Unc	BU
2003PM Proof	10,000	Value: 47.50				

KM# 1196 CROWN
28.4400 g., Copper-Nickel, 38.6 mm. **Ruler:** Elizabeth II **Obv:** Bust with tiara right **Obv. Designer:** Ian Rank-Broadley **Rev:** Four pre-1918 airplanes **Edge:** Reeded

Date	Mintage	F	VF	XF	Unc	BU
2003PM	—	—	—	—	10.00	12.00

KM# 1197 CROWN
28.4400 g., Copper-Nickel, 38.6 mm. **Obv:** Bust with tiara right **Obv. Designer:** Ian Rank-Broadley **Rev:** Propeller plain, Zeppelin and two jet airliners **Edge:** Reeded

Date	Mintage	F	VF	XF	Unc	BU
2003PM	—	—	—	—	10.00	12.00

KM# 1201 CROWN
28.2800 g., Copper-Nickel, 38.6 mm. **Ruler:** Elizabeth II **Obv:** Bust with tiara right **Obv. Designer:** Ian Rank-Broadley **Rev:** European Union map within hand held rope circle **Edge:** Reeded

Date	Mintage	F	VF	XF	Unc	BU
2004PM	—	—	—	—	10.00	12.00

KM# 1201a CROWN
28.2800 g., 0.9250 Silver 0.8410 oz. ASW, 38.6 mm. **Ruler:** Elizabeth II **Obv:** Bust with tiara right **Obv. Designer:** Ian Rank-Broadley **Rev:** European Union map within a hand held rope circle **Edge:** Reeded

Date	Mintage	F	VF	XF	Unc	BU
2004PM Proof	10,000	Value: 50.00				

KM# 1202 CROWN
28.2800 g., Copper-Nickel, 38.6 mm. **Ruler:** Elizabeth II **Obv:** Bust with tiara right **Obv. Designer:** Ian Rank-Broadley **Rev:** Harry Potter and patron fighting off a Deventer **Edge:** Reeded

Date	Mintage	F	VF	XF	Unc	BU
2004PM	—	—	—	—	15.00	17.00

KM# 1202a CROWN
28.2800 g., 0.9250 Silver 0.8410 oz. ASW, 38.6 mm. **Ruler:** Elizabeth II **Obv:** Bust with tiara right **Obv. Designer:** Ian Rank-Broadley **Rev:** Harry Potter and patron fighting off a Deventer **Edge:** Reeded

Date	Mintage	F	VF	XF	Unc	BU
2004PM Proof	10,000	Value: 50.00				

KM# 1204 CROWN
28.2800 g., Copper-Nickel, 38.6 mm. **Ruler:** Elizabeth II **Obv:** Bust with tiara right **Obv. Designer:** Ian Rank-Broadley **Rev:** Harry Potter in the shrieking shed **Edge:** Reeded

Date	Mintage	F	VF	XF	Unc	BU
2004PM	—	—	—	—	15.00	17.00

KM# 1204a CROWN

28.2800 g., 0.9250 Silver 0.8410 oz. ASW, 38.6 mm. **Ruler:** Elizabeth II **Obv:** Bust with tiara right **Obv. Designer:** Ian Rank-Broadley **Rev:** Harry Potter in the shrieking shack **Edge:** Reeded

Date	Mintage	F	VF	XF	Unc	BU
2004PM Proof	10,000	Value: 50.00				

KM# 1206 CROWN

28.2800 g., Copper-Nickel, 38.6 mm. **Ruler:** Elizabeth II **Obv:** Bust with tiara right **Obv. Designer:** Ian Rank-Broadley **Rev:** Harry Potter and Professor Dumbledore **Edge:** Reeded

Date	Mintage	F	VF	XF	Unc	BU
2004PM	—	—	—	—	15.00	17.00

KM# 1206a CROWN

28.2800 g., 0.9250 Silver 0.8410 oz. ASW, 38.6 mm. **Ruler:** Elizabeth II **Obv:** Bust with tiara right **Obv. Designer:** Ian Rank-Broadley **Rev:** Harry Potter and Professor Dumbledore **Edge:** Reeded

Date	Mintage	F	VF	XF	Unc	BU
2004PM Proof	10,000	Value: 50.00				

KM# 1208 CROWN

28.2800 g., Copper-Nickel, 38.6 mm. **Ruler:** Elizabeth II **Obv:** Bust with tiara right **Obv. Designer:** Ian Rank-Broadley **Rev:** Sirius Black on flying griffin **Edge:** Reeded

Date	Mintage	F	VF	XF	Unc	BU
2004PM	—	—	—	—	15.00	17.00

KM# 1208a CROWN

28.2800 g., 0.9250 Silver 0.8410 oz. ASW, 38.6 mm. **Ruler:** Elizabeth II **Obv:** Bust with tiara right **Obv. Designer:** Ian Rank-Broadley **Rev:** Sirius Black on flying griffin **Edge:** Reeded

Date	Mintage	F	VF	XF	Unc	BU
2004PM Proof	10,000	Value: 50.00				

KM# 1210 CROWN

28.2800 g., Copper-Nickel, 38.6 mm. **Ruler:** Elizabeth II **Obv:** Bust with tiara right **Obv. Designer:** Ian Rank-Broadley **Rev:** Three Olympic Swimmers **Edge:** Reeded

Date	Mintage	F	VF	XF	Unc	BU
2004PM	—	—	—	—	10.00	12.00

KM# 1210a CROWN

28.2800 g., 0.9250 Silver 0.8410 oz. ASW, 38.6 mm. **Ruler:** Elizabeth II **Obv:** Bust with tiara right **Obv. Designer:** Ian Rank-Broadley **Rev:** Three Olympic Swimmers **Edge:** Reeded

Date	Mintage	F	VF	XF	Unc	BU
2004PM Proof	10,000	Value: 50.00				

KM# 1212 CROWN

28.2800 g., Copper-Nickel, 38.6 mm. **Ruler:** Elizabeth II **Obv:** Bust with tiara right **Obv. Designer:** Ian Rank-Broadley **Rev:** Three Olympic Cyclists **Edge:** Reeded

Date	Mintage	F	VF	XF	Unc	BU
2004PM	—	—	—	—	10.00	12.00

KM# 1212a CROWN

28.2800 g., 0.9250 Silver 0.8410 oz. ASW, 38.6 mm. **Ruler:** Elizabeth II **Obv:** Bust with tiara right **Obv. Designer:** Ian Rank-Broadley **Rev:** Three Olympic Cyclists **Edge:** Reeded

Date	Mintage	F	VF	XF	Unc	BU
2004PM Proof	10,000	Value: 50.00				

KM# 1214 CROWN

28.2800 g., Copper-Nickel, 38.6 mm. **Ruler:** Elizabeth II **Obv:** Bust with tiara right **Obv. Designer:** Ian Rank-Broadley **Rev:** Three Olympic Runners **Edge:** Reeded

Date	Mintage	F	VF	XF	Unc	BU
2004PM	—	—	—	—	10.00	12.00

KM# 1214a CROWN

28.2800 g., 0.9250 Silver 0.8410 oz. ASW, 38.6 mm. **Ruler:** Elizabeth II **Obv:** Bust with tiara right **Obv. Designer:** Ian Rank-Broadley **Rev:** Three Olympic Runners **Edge:** Reeded

Date	Mintage	F	VF	XF	Unc	BU
2004PM Proof	10,000	Value: 50.00				

KM# 1216 CROWN

28.2800 g., Copper-Nickel, 38.6 mm. **Ruler:** Elizabeth II **Obv:** Bust with tiara right **Obv. Designer:** Ian Rank-Broadley **Rev:** Three Olympic Sail Boarders **Edge:** Reeded

Date	Mintage	F	VF	XF	Unc	BU
2004PM	—	—	—	—	10.00	12.00

KM# 1216a CROWN

28.2800 g., 0.9250 Silver 0.8410 oz. ASW, 38.6 mm. **Ruler:** Elizabeth II **Obv:** Bust with tiara right **Obv. Designer:** Ian Rank-Broadley **Rev:** Three Olympic Sail Boarders **Edge:** Reeded

Date	Mintage	F	VF	XF	Unc	BU
2004PM Proof	10,000	Value: 50.00				

KM# 1218 CROWN

28.2800 g., Copper-Nickel, 38.6 mm. **Ruler:** Elizabeth II **Obv:** Bust with tiara right **Obv. Designer:** Ian Rank-Broadley **Rev:** Ocean Liner Queen Mary 2 **Edge:** Reeded

Date	Mintage	F	VF	XF	Unc	BU
2004PM	—	—	—	—	15.00	17.00

KM# 1220 CROWN

28.2800 g., Copper-Nickel, 38.6 mm. **Ruler:** Elizabeth II **Obv:** Bust with tiara right **Obv. Designer:** Ian Rank-Broadley **Rev:** Lt. Quillan portrait above Battle of Trafalgar scene **Edge:** Reeded

Date	Mintage	F	VF	XF	Unc	BU
2004PM	—	—	—	—	15.00	17.00

KM# 1220a CROWN

28.2800 g., 0.9250 Silver 0.8410 oz. ASW, 38.6 mm. **Ruler:** Elizabeth II **Obv:** Bust with tiara right **Obv. Designer:** Ian Rank-Broadley **Rev:** Lt. Quillan portrait above Battle of Trafalgar scene **Edge:** Reeded

Date	Mintage	F	VF	XF	Unc	BU
2004PM Proof	10,000	Value: 50.00				

KM# 1221 CROWN

28.2800 g., Copper-Nickel, 38.6 mm. **Ruler:** Elizabeth II **Obv:** Bust with tiara right **Obv. Designer:** Ian Rank-Broadley **Rev:** Napoleon and Nelson portraits above Battle of Trafalgar scene **Edge:** Reeded

Date	Mintage	F	VF	XF	Unc	BU
2004PM	—	—	—	—	15.00	17.00

KM# 1221a CROWN

28.2800 g., 0.9990 Silver 0.9083 oz. ASW, 38.6 mm. **Ruler:** Elizabeth II **Obv:** Bust with tiara right **Obv. Designer:** Ian Rank-Broadley **Rev:** Napoleon and Nelson portraits above Battle of Trafalgar scene **Edge:** Reeded

Date	Mintage	F	VF	XF	Unc	BU
2004PM Proof	10,000	Value: 50.00				

KM# 1222 CROWN

28.2800 g., Copper-Nickel, 38.6 mm. **Ruler:** Elizabeth II **Obv:** Bust with tiara right **Obv. Designer:** Ian Rank-Broadley **Rev:** D-Day Invasion Plan Map **Edge:** Reeded

Date	Mintage	F	VF	XF	Unc	BU
2004PM	—	—	—	—	15.00	17.00

KM# 1222a CROWN

28.2800 g., 0.9250 Silver 0.8410 oz. ASW, 38.6 mm. **Ruler:** Elizabeth II **Obv:** Bust with tiara right **Obv. Designer:** Ian Rank-Broadley **Rev:** D-Day Invasion Plan Map **Edge:** Reeded

Date	Mintage	F	VF	XF	Unc	BU
2004PM Proof	10,000	Value: 50.00				

KM# 1224 CROWN

28.2800 g., Copper-Nickel, 38.6 mm. **Ruler:** Elizabeth II **Obv:** Bust with tiara right **Obv. Designer:** Ian Rank-Broadley **Rev:** Victoria Cross and battle scene **Edge:** Reeded

Date	Mintage	F	VF	XF	Unc	BU
2004PM	—	—	—	—	15.00	17.00

KM# 1224a CROWN

28.2800 g., 0.9250 Silver 0.8410 oz. ASW, 38.6 mm. **Ruler:** Elizabeth II **Obv:** Bust with tiara right **Obv. Designer:** Ian Rank-Broadley **Rev:** Victoria Cross and battle scene **Edge:** Reeded

Date	Mintage	F	VF	XF	Unc	BU
2004PM Proof	10,000	Value: 50.00				

KM# 1226 CROWN

28.2800 g., Copper-Nickel, 38.6 mm. **Ruler:** Elizabeth II **Obv:** Bust with tiara right **Obv. Designer:** Ian Rank-Broadley **Rev:** Silver Star and battle scene **Edge:** Reeded

Date	Mintage	F	VF	XF	Unc	BU
2004PM	—	—	—	—	15.00	17.00

KM# 1226a CROWN

28.2800 g., 0.9250 Silver 0.8410 oz. ASW, 38.6 mm. **Ruler:** Elizabeth II **Obv:** Bust with tiara right **Obv. Designer:** Ian Rank-Broadley **Rev:** Silver Star and battle scene **Edge:** Reeded

Date	Mintage	F	VF	XF	Unc	BU
2004PM Proof	10,000	Value: 50.00				

KM# 1228 CROWN

28.2800 g., Copper-Nickel, 38.6 mm. **Ruler:** Elizabeth II **Obv:** Bust with tiara right **Obv. Designer:** Ian Rank-Broadley **Rev:** George Cross and rescue scene **Edge:** Reeded

Date	Mintage	F	VF	XF	Unc	BU
2004PM	—	—	—	—	15.00	17.00

KM# 1228a CROWN

28.2800 g., 0.9250 Silver 0.8410 oz. ASW, 38.6 mm. **Ruler:** Elizabeth II **Obv:** Bust with tiara right **Obv. Designer:** Ian Rank-Broadley **Rev:** George Cross and rescue scene **Edge:** Reeded

Date	Mintage	F	VF	XF	Unc	BU
2004PM Proof	10,000	Value: 50.00				

KM# 1230 CROWN

28.2800 g., Copper-Nickel, 38.6 mm. **Ruler:** Elizabeth II **Obv:** Bust with tiara right **Obv. Designer:** Ian Rank-Broadley **Rev:** White Rose of Finland Medal and battle scene **Edge:** Reeded

Date	Mintage	F	VF	XF	Unc	BU
2004PM	—	—	—	—	15.00	17.00

KM# 1230a CROWN
28.2800 g., 0.9250 Silver 0.8410 oz. ASW, 38.6 mm. **Ruler:** Elizabeth II **Obv:** Bust with tiara right **Obv. Designer:** Ian Rank-Broadley **Rev:** White Rose of Finland Medal and battle scene **Edge:** Reeded

Date	Mintage	F	VF	XF	Unc	BU
2004PM Proof	10,000	Value: 50.00				

KM# 1232 CROWN
28.2800 g., Copper-Nickel, 38.6 mm. **Ruler:** Elizabeth II **Obv:** Bust with tiara right **Obv. Designer:** Ian Rank-Broadley **Rev:** The Norwegian War Medal and naval battle scene **Edge:** Reeded

Date	Mintage	F	VF	XF	Unc	BU
2004PM	—	—	—	—	15.00	17.00

KM# 1232a CROWN
28.2800 g., 0.9250 Silver 0.8410 oz. ASW, 38.6 mm. **Ruler:** Elizabeth II **Obv:** Bust with tiara right **Obv. Designer:** Ian Rank-Broadley **Rev:** The Norwegian War Medal and a naval battle scene **Edge:** Reeded

Date	Mintage	F	VF	XF	Unc	BU
2004PM Proof	10,000	Value: 50.00				

KM# 1234 CROWN
28.2800 g., Copper-Nickel, 38.6 mm. **Ruler:** Elizabeth II **Obv:** Bust with tiara right **Obv. Designer:** Ian Rank-Broadley **Rev:** French Croix de Guerre and partisan battle scene **Edge:** Reeded

Date	Mintage	F	VF	XF	Unc	BU
2004PM	—	—	—	—	15.00	17.00

KM# 1234a CROWN
28.2800 g., 0.9250 Silver 0.8410 oz. ASW, 38.6 mm. **Ruler:** Elizabeth II **Obv:** Bust with tiara right **Obv. Designer:** Ian Rank-Broadley **Rev:** French Croix de Guerre and partisan battle scene **Edge:** Reeded

Date	Mintage	F	VF	XF	Unc	BU
2004PM Proof	10,000	Value: 50.00				

KM# 1236 CROWN
28.2800 g., Copper-Nickel, 38.6 mm. **Ruler:** Elizabeth II **Obv:** Bust with tiara right **Obv. Designer:** Ian Rank-Broadley **Rev:** Multicolor cartoon soccer player **Edge:** Reeded

Date	Mintage	F	VF	XF	Unc	BU
2004PM	—	—	—	—	10.00	12.00

KM# 1236a CROWN
28.2800 g., 0.9250 Silver 0.8410 oz. ASW, 38.6 mm. **Ruler:** Elizabeth II **Obv:** Bust with tiara right **Obv. Designer:** Ian Rank-Broadley **Rev:** Multicolor cartoon soccer player **Edge:** Reeded

Date	Mintage	F	VF	XF	Unc	BU
2004PM Proof	7,500	Value: 50.00				

KM# 1237 CROWN
28.2800 g., Copper-Nickel, 38.6 mm. **Ruler:** Elizabeth II **Obv:** Bust with tiara right **Obv. Designer:** Ian Rank-Broadley **Rev:** Soccer ball in flight **Edge:** Reeded

Date	Mintage	F	VF	XF	Unc	BU
2004PM	—	—	—	—	10.00	12.00

KM# 1237a CROWN
28.2800 g., 0.9250 Silver 0.8410 oz. ASW, 38.6 mm. **Ruler:** Elizabeth II **Obv:** Bust with tiara right **Obv. Designer:** Ian Rank-Broadley **Rev:** Soccer ball in flight **Edge:** Reeded

Date	Mintage	F	VF	XF	Unc	BU
2004PM Proof	7,500	Value: 50.00				

KM# 1238 CROWN
28.2800 g., Copper-Nickel, 38.6 mm. **Ruler:** Elizabeth II **Obv:** Bust with tiara right **Obv. Designer:** Ian Rank-Broadley **Rev:** Gibbon monkey **Edge:** Reeded

Date	Mintage	F	VF	XF	Unc	BU
2004PM	—	—	—	—	10.00	15.00

KM# 1238a CROWN
28.2800 g., 0.9250 Silver 0.8410 oz. ASW, 38.6 mm. **Ruler:** Elizabeth II **Obv:** Bust with tiara right **Obv. Designer:** Ian Rank-Broadley **Rev:** Monkey **Edge:** Reeded

Date	Mintage	F	VF	XF	Unc	BU
2004PM Proof	30,000	Value: 50.00				

KM# 1239 CROWN
31.1035 g., 0.9999 Gold 0.9999 oz. AGW, 32.7 mm. **Ruler:** Elizabeth II **Obv:** Bust with tiara right **Obv. Designer:** Ian Rank-Broadley **Rev:** Monkey **Edge:** Reeded

Date	Mintage	F	VF	XF	Unc	BU
2004PM Proof	2,000	Value: 1,500				

KM# 1242 CROWN
6.2200 g., 0.9999 Gold 0.1999 oz. AGW, 22 mm. **Ruler:** Elizabeth II **Obv:** Bust with tiara right **Obv. Designer:** Ian Rank-Broadley **Rev:** Monkey **Edge:** Reeded

Date	Mintage	F	VF	XF	Unc	BU
2004PM Proof	12,000	Value: 300				

KM# 1245 CROWN
28.2800 g., Copper-Nickel, 38.6 mm. **Ruler:** Elizabeth II **Subject:** Lord of the Rings **Obv:** Bust with tiara right **Obv. Designer:** Ian Rank-Broadley **Rev:** Nine characters **Edge:** Reeded

Date	Mintage	F	VF	XF	Unc	BU
2004PM	100,000	—	—	—	15.00	17.00

KM# 1245a CROWN
28.2800 g., 0.9250 Silver 0.8410 oz. ASW, 38.6 mm. **Ruler:** Elizabeth II **Subject:** Lord of the Rings **Obv:** Bust with tiara right **Obv. Designer:** Ian Rank-Broadley **Rev:** Nine characters **Edge:** Reeded

Date	Mintage	F	VF	XF	Unc	BU
2004PM Proof	10,000	Value: 50.00				

KM# 1246.1 CROWN
28.2800 g., Copper-Nickel, 38.6 mm. **Ruler:** Elizabeth II **Obv:** Head with tiara right **Obv. Designer:** Ian Rank-Broadley **Rev:** Multicolor pair of Tonkinese cats **Edge:** Reeded

Date	Mintage	F	VF	XF	Unc	BU
2004PM	—	—	—	—	14.00	16.00

KM# 1246a.1 CROWN
31.1035 g., 0.9990 Silver 0.9990 oz. ASW, 38.6 mm. **Ruler:** Elizabeth II **Obv:** Head with tiara right **Obv. Designer:** Ian Rank-Broadley **Rev:** Two Tonkinese cats **Edge:** Reeded

Date	Mintage	F	VF	XF	Unc	BU
2004PM Proof	50,000	Value: 50.00				

KM# 1246a.2 CROWN
31.1035 g., 0.9990 Silver 0.9990 oz. ASW, 38.6 mm. **Ruler:** Elizabeth II **Obv:** Head with tiara right **Obv. Designer:** Ian Rank-Broadley **Rev:** Two multicolor Tonkinese cats **Edge:** Reeded

Date	Mintage	F	VF	XF	Unc	BU
2004PM Proof	—	Value: 55.00				

KM# 1251 CROWN
31.1035 g., 0.9999 Gold 0.9999 oz. AGW, 32.7 mm. **Ruler:** Elizabeth II **Obv:** Head with tiara right **Obv. Designer:** Ian Rank-Broadley **Rev:** Two Tonkinese cats **Edge:** Reeded

Date	Mintage	F	VF	XF	Unc	BU
2004PM	—	—	—	—	—	1,550
2004PM Proof	1,000	Value: 1,600				

KM# 1246.2 CROWN
28.2800 g., Copper-Nickel **Ruler:** Elizabeth II **Obv:** Head with tiara right **Obv. Designer:** Ian Rank-Broadley **Rev:** Two multicolor Tonkinese cats **Edge:** Reeded

Date	Mintage	F	VF	XF	Unc	BU
2004PM	—	—	—	—	14.00	16.00

KM# 1266 CROWN
28.3300 g., Copper-Nickel, 38.7 mm. **Ruler:** Elizabeth II **Obv:** Bust with tiara right **Obv. Designer:** Ian Rank-Broadley **Rev:** Himalayan cat with two kittens **Edge:** Reeded

Date	Mintage	F	VF	XF	Unc	BU
2005PM	—	—	—	—	12.00	14.00

KM# 1266a CROWN
31.1030 g., 0.9990 Silver 0.9989 oz. ASW, 38.6 mm. **Ruler:** Elizabeth II **Obv:** Bust with tiara right **Obv. Designer:** Ian Rank-Broadley **Rev:** Himalayan cat and two kittens **Edge:** Reeded

Date	Mintage	F	VF	XF	Unc	BU
2005PM Proof	50,000	Value: 50.00				

KM# 1268 CROWN
31.1030 g., 0.9999 Gold 0.9998 oz. AGW, 32.7 mm. **Ruler:** Elizabeth II **Obv:** Bust with tiara right **Obv. Designer:** Ian Rank-Broadley **Rev:** Himalayan cat and two kittens **Edge:** Reeded

Date	Mintage	F	VF	XF	Unc	BU
2005PM Proof	—	Value: 1,550				

KM# 1273 CROWN
28.2800 g., Copper-Nickel, 38.6 mm. **Ruler:** Elizabeth II **Obv:** Bust with tiara right **Obv. Designer:** Ian Rank-Broadley **Rev:** Harry Potter and the Hungarian Horn Tail, Tri-Wizard Tournament feat **Edge:** Reeded

Date	Mintage	F	VF	XF	Unc	BU
2005PM	—	—	—	—	15.00	17.00

KM# 1274 CROWN
28.2800 g., Copper-Nickel, 38.6 mm. **Ruler:** Elizabeth II **Subject:** 60th Anniversary - End of WW II **Obv:** Bust with tiara right **Obv. Designer:** Ian Rank-Broadley **Rev:** Sir Winston Churchill

Date	Mintage	F	VF	XF	Unc	BU
2005	—	—	—	—	10.00	12.00

KM# 1275 CROWN
28.2800 g., Copper-Nickel, 38.6 mm. **Ruler:** Elizabeth II **Subject:** 400th Anniversary - Gunpowder plot **Obv:** Bust with tiara right **Obv. Designer:** Ian Rank-Broadley **Rev:** Tower of London, Beefeaters

Date	Mintage	F	VF	XF	Unc	BU
2005	—	—	—	—	10.00	12.00

KM# 1276 CROWN
28.2800 g., Copper-Nickel, 38.6 mm. **Ruler:** Elizabeth II **Obv:** Bust with tiara right **Obv. Designer:** Ian Rank-Broadley **Rev:** Harry Potter and Tri-Wizard Tournament feat - Underwater retrieval

Date	Mintage	F	VF	XF	Unc	BU
2005	—	—	—	—	10.00	12.00

KM# 1277 CROWN
28.2800 g., Copper-Nickel, 38.6 mm. **Ruler:** Elizabeth II **Obv:** Bust with tiara right **Obv. Designer:** Ian Rank-Broadley **Rev:** Harry Potter and pensive

Date	Mintage	F	VF	XF	Unc	BU
2005	—	—	—	—	10.00	12.00

KM# 1278 CROWN
28.2800 g., Copper-Nickel, 38.6 mm. **Ruler:** Elizabeth II **Obv:** Bust with tiara right **Obv. Designer:** Ian Rank-Broadley **Rev:** Harry Potter and portkey

Date	Mintage	F	VF	XF	Unc	BU
2005	—	—	—	—	10.00	12.00

KM# 1291 CROWN
28.2800 g., Copper-Nickel, 38.6 mm. **Ruler:** Elizabeth II **Subject:** Trafalgar - 200th Anniversary **Obv:** Bust with tiara right **Obv. Designer:** Ian Rank-Broadley **Rev:** Nelson at Battle of Copenhagen

Date	Mintage	F	VF	XF	Unc	BU
2005	—	—	—	—	10.00	12.00

KM# 1279 CROWN
28.2800 g., Copper-Nickel, 38.6 mm. **Ruler:** Elizabeth II **Subject:** The Battle of Cape St. Vincent **Obv:** Bust with tiara right **Obv. Designer:** Ian Rank-Broadley **Rev:** Naval battle scene

Date	Mintage	F	VF	XF	Unc	BU
2005	—	—	—	—	10.00	12.00

KM# 1280 CROWN
28.2800 g., Copper-Nickel, 38.6 mm. **Ruler:** Elizabeth II **Subject:** Nelson Funeral Procession **Obv:** Bust with tiara right **Obv. Designer:** Ian Rank-Broadley **Rev:** Thames and Greenwich view

Date	Mintage	F	VF	XF	Unc	BU
2005	—	—	—	—	10.00	12.00

KM# 1281 CROWN
Copper-Nickel **Ruler:** Elizabeth II **Subject:** Battle of the Nile **Obv:** Bust with tiara right **Obv. Designer:** Ian Rank-Broadley **Rev:** Naval battle

Date	Mintage	F	VF	XF	Unc	BU
2005	—	—	—	—	10.00	12.00

KM# 1282 CROWN
28.2800 g., Copper-Nickel, 38.6 mm. **Ruler:** Elizabeth II **Subject:** Norway Independence **Obv:** Bust with tiara right **Obv. Designer:** Ian Rank-Broadley **Rev:** Three swords

Date	Mintage	F	VF	XF	Unc	BU
2005	—	—	—	—	10.00	12.00

KM# 1283 CROWN
28.2800 g., Copper-Nickel, 38.6 mm. **Ruler:** Elizabeth II **Subject:** Nelson - Trafalgar 300th Anniversary **Obv. Designer:** Ian Rank-Broadley **Rev:** Nelson portrait

Date	Mintage	F	VF	XF	Unc	BU
2005	—	—	—	—	10.00	12.00

KM# 1284 CROWN
28.2800 g., Copper-Nickel, 38.6 mm. **Ruler:** Elizabeth II **Subject:** Battle of Trafalgar **Obv. Designer:** Ian Rank-Broadley **Rev:** Naval battle scene

Date	Mintage	F	VF	XF	Unc	BU
2005	—	—	—	—	10.00	12.00

KM# 1285 CROWN
28.2800 g., Copper-Nickel, 38.6 mm. **Ruler:** Elizabeth II **Subject:** Steam Packet - King Orry III **Obv:** Bust with tiara right **Obv. Designer:** Ian Rank-Broadley **Rev:** Ship view

Date	Mintage	F	VF	XF	Unc	BU
2005	—	—	—	—	10.00	12.00

KM# 1286 CROWN
28.2800 g., Copper-Nickel, 38.6 mm. **Ruler:** Elizabeth II **Subject:** Isle of Man Steam Packet Company - 175th Anniversary **Obv:** Bust with tiara right **Obv. Designer:** Ian Rank-Broadley **Rev:** Modern and early ferry

Date	Mintage	F	VF	XF	Unc	BU
2005	—	—	—	—	10.00	12.00

KM# 1287 CROWN
28.2800 g., Copper-Nickel, 38.6 mm. **Ruler:** Elizabeth II **Rev:** Motorcycle right

Date	Mintage	F	VF	XF	Unc	BU
2005	—	—	—	—	10.00	12.00

KM# 1288 CROWN
28.2800 g., Copper-Nickel, 38.6 mm. **Ruler:** Elizabeth II **Rev:** Motorcycle forward

Date	Mintage	F	VF	XF	Unc	BU
2005	—	—	—	—	10.00	12.00

KM# 1289 CROWN
28.2800 g., Copper-Nickel, 38.6 mm. **Ruler:** Elizabeth II **Subject:** Ugly Duckling story **Obv:** Bust with tiara right **Obv. Designer:** Ian Rank-Broadley **Rev:** Farm animals

Date	Mintage	F	VF	XF	Unc	BU
2005	—	—	—	—	12.00	14.00

KM# 1290b CROWN
28.2800 g., 0.9250 Silver 0.8410 oz. ASW, 38.6 mm. **Ruler:** Elizabeth II **Obv:** Bust with tiara right **Obv. Designer:** Ian Rank-Broadley **Rev:** Three Exotic Shorthair cats sitting facing **Edge:** Reeded

Date	Mintage	F	VF	XF	Unc	BU
2006PM	—	—	—	—	15.00	25.00

KM# 1296 CROWN
28.2800 g., Copper-Nickel, 38.6 mm. **Ruler:** Elizabeth II **Subject:** Battles that Changed the World **Obv:** Elizabeth II **Rev:** Trojan War scene **Edge:** Reeded

Date	Mintage	F	VF	XF	Unc	BU
2006PM	—	—	—	—	10.00	12.00

KM# 1296a CROWN
28.2800 g., 0.9250 Silver 0.8410 oz. ASW, 38.6 mm. **Ruler:** Elizabeth II **Subject:** Battles that Changed the World **Obv:** Elizabeth II **Rev:** Trojan War scene **Edge:** Reeded

Date	Mintage	F	VF	XF	Unc	BU
2006PM Proof	10,000	Value: 47.50				

KM# 1298 CROWN
28.2800 g., Copper-Nickel, 38.6 mm. **Ruler:** Elizabeth II **Subject:** Battles that Changed the World **Obv:** Elizabeth II **Rev:** Battle of Arbela scene **Edge:** Reeded

Date	Mintage	F	VF	XF	Unc	BU
2006PM	—	—	—	—	10.00	12.00

KM# 1298a CROWN
28.2800 g., 0.9250 Silver 0.8410 oz. ASW, 38.6 mm. **Ruler:** Elizabeth II **Subject:** Battles that Changed the World **Obv:** Elizabeth II **Rev:** Battle of Arbela scene **Edge:** Reeded

Date	Mintage	F	VF	XF	Unc	BU
2006PM Proof	10,000	Value: 47.50				

KM# 1300 CROWN
28.2800 g., Copper-Nickel, 38.6 mm. **Ruler:** Elizabeth II **Subject:** Battles that Changed the World **Obv:** Elizabeth II **Rev:** Battle of Thapsus scene **Edge:** Reeded

Date	Mintage	F	VF	XF	Unc	BU
2006PM	—	—	—	—	10.00	12.00

KM# 1300a CROWN
28.2800 g., 0.9250 Silver 0.8410 oz. ASW, 38.6 mm. **Ruler:** Elizabeth II **Subject:** Battles that Changed the World **Obv:** Elizabeth II **Rev:** Battle of Thapsus scene **Edge:** Reeded

Date	Mintage	F	VF	XF	Unc	BU
2006PM Proof	10,000	Value: 47.50				

KM# 1302 CROWN
28.2800 g., Copper-Nickel, 38.6 mm. **Ruler:** Elizabeth II **Subject:** Battles that Changed the World **Obv:** Elizabeth II **Rev:** Battle of Cologne scene **Edge:** Reeded

Date	Mintage	F	VF	XF	Unc	BU
2006PM	—	—	—	—	10.00	12.00

KM# 1302a CROWN
28.2800 g., 0.9250 Silver 0.8410 oz. ASW, 38.6 mm. **Ruler:** Elizabeth II **Subject:** Battles that Changed the World **Obv:** Elizabeth II **Rev:** Battle of Cologne scene **Edge:** Reeded

Date	Mintage	F	VF	XF	Unc	BU
2006PM Proof	10,000	Value: 47.50				

KM# 1304 CROWN
28.2800 g., Copper-Nickel, 38.6 mm. **Ruler:** Elizabeth II **Subject:** Battles that Changed the World **Obv:** Elizabeth II **Rev:** Siege of Valencia scene **Edge:** Reeded

Date	Mintage	F	VF	XF	Unc	BU
2006PM	—	—	—	—	10.00	12.00

KM# 1304a CROWN
28.2800 g., 0.9250 Silver 0.8410 oz. ASW, 38.6 mm. **Ruler:** Elizabeth II **Subject:** Battles that Changed the World **Obv:** Elizabeth II **Rev:** Siege of Valencia scene **Edge:** Reeded

Date	Mintage	F	VF	XF	Unc	BU
2006PM Proof	10,000	Value: 47.50				

KM# 1306 CROWN
28.2800 g., Copper-Nickel, 38.6 mm. **Ruler:** Elizabeth II **Subject:** Battles that Changed the World **Obv:** Elizabeth II **Rev:** Battle of Agincourt scene **Edge:** Reeded

Date	Mintage	F	VF	XF	Unc	BU
2006PM	—	—	—	—	10.00	12.00

KM# 1306a CROWN
28.2800 g., 0.9250 Silver 0.8410 oz. ASW, 38.6 mm. **Ruler:** Elizabeth II **Subject:** Battles that Changed the World **Obv:** Elizabeth II **Rev:** Battle of Agincourt scene **Edge:** Reeded

Date	Mintage	F	VF	XF	Unc	BU
2006PM Proof	10,000	Value: 47.50				

KM# 1323.1 CROWN
28.2800 g., Copper-Nickel, 38.60 mm. **Ruler:** Elizabeth II **Subject:** Hans Christian Anderson's Fairy Tales **Obv:** Bust with tiarra right **Obv. Legend:** ELIZABETH II - ISLE OF MAN **Obv. Designer:** Ian Rank-Broadley **Rev:** Three bears startling Goldilocks in bed **Rev. Legend:** Goldilocks and the Three Bears **Edge:** Reeded

Date	Mintage	F	VF	XF	Unc	BU
2006PM	—	—	—	—	—	35.00

KM# 1323.2 CROWN
28.2800 g., Copper-Nickel, 38.60 mm. **Ruler:** Elizabeth II **Subject:** Hans Christian Anderson's Fairy Tales **Obv:** Bust with tiara right **Obv. Legend:** ELIZABETH II - ISLE OF MAN **Obv. Designer:** Ian Rank-Broadley **Rev:** Three bears startling Goldilocks in bed multicolor **Rev. Legend:** Goldilocks and the Three Bears **Edge:** Reeded

Date	Mintage	F	VF	XF	Unc	BU
2006PM	—	—	—	—	—	40.00

KM# 1323.1a CROWN
28.2800 g., 0.9250 Silver 0.8410 oz. ASW, 38.60 mm. **Ruler:** Elizabeth II **Subject:** Hans Christian Anderson's Fairy Tales **Obv:** Bust with tiara right **Obv. Legend:** ELIZABETH II - ISLE OF MAN **Obv. Designer:** Ian Rank-Broadley **Rev:** Three bears startling Goldilocks in bed **Rev. Legend:** Goldilocks and the Three Bears **Edge:** Reeded

Date	Mintage	F	VF	XF	Unc	BU
2006PM Proof	—	Value: 80.00				

KM# 1323.2a CROWN
28.2800 g., 0.9250 Silver 0.8410 oz. ASW, 38.60 mm. **Ruler:** Elizabeth II **Subject:** Hans Christian Anderson's Fairy Tales **Obv:** Bust with tiara right **Obv. Legend:** ELIZABETH II - ISLE OF MAN **Obv. Designer:** Ian-Rank-Broadley **Rev:** Three bears startling Goldilocks in bed multicolor **Rev. Legend:** Goldilocks and the Three Bears **Edge:** Reeded

Date	Mintage	F	VF	XF	Unc	BU
2006PM Proof	—	Value: 100				

KM# 1290a CROWN
28.2800 g., Copper-Nickel, 38.6 mm. **Ruler:** Elizabeth II **Obv:** Bust with tiara right **Obv. Designer:** Ian Rank-Broadley **Rev:** Three Exotic Shorthair cats sitting facing **Edge:** Reeded

Date	Mintage	F	VF	XF	Unc	BU
2006PM	—	—	—	—	12.00	14.00

KM# 1290c CROWN
31.1030 g., 0.9999 Gold 0.9998 oz. AGW **Ruler:** Elizabeth II **Obv:** Bust with tiara right **Obv. Designer:** Ian Rank-Broadley **Rev:** Three Exotic Shorthair cats sitting facing, multicolor **Edge:** Reeded

Date	Mintage	F	VF	XF	Unc	BU
2006PM	—	—	—	—	—	1,600

KM# 1423.1 CROWN
28.2800 g., Copper-Nickel, 38.6 mm. **Ruler:** Elizabeth II **Subject:** Concord, 30th Anniversary of transatlantic service **Obv:** Bust with tiara right **Rev:** Concord in flight, buildings below

Date	Mintage	F	VF	XF	Unc	BU
2006PM Proof	—	Value: 30.00				

KM# 1423.2 CROWN
28.2800 g., Copper-Nickel, 38.6 mm. **Ruler:** Elizabeth II **Subject:** Concorde, 30th Anniversary of transatlantic service **Obv:** Bust with tiara right **Rev:** Concorde in flight, multicolor

Date	Mintage	F	VF	XF	Unc	BU
2006PM Proof	—	Value: 50.00				

KM# 1347 CROWN
31.1030 g., 0.9999 Gold 0.9998 oz. AGW **Ruler:** Elizabeth II **Obv:** Bust with tiara right **Obv. Legend:** ELIZABETH II - ISLE OF MAN **Obv. Designer:** Ian Rank-Broadley **Rev:** Ragdoll cat with two kittens sitting facing **Edge:** Reeded

Date	Mintage	F	VF	XF	Unc	BU
2007PM	—	—	—	—	—	1,600

KM# 1348.1 CROWN
Copper-Nickel **Ruler:** Elizabeth II **Subject:** The Tale of Peter Rabbit **Obv:** Bust with tiara right **Obv. Legend:** ELIZABETH II - ISLE OF MAN **Obv. Designer:** Ian Rank-Broadley **Rev:** Peter walking with friends **Edge:** Reeded

Date	Mintage	F	VF	XF	Unc	BU
2007PM	—	—	—	—	—	30.00

KM# 1348.2 CROWN
Copper-Nickel **Ruler:** Elizabeth II **Subject:** The Tale of Peter Rabbit **Obv:** Bust with tiara right **Obv. Legend:** ELIZABETH II - ISLE OF MAN **Obv. Designer:** Ian Rank-Broadley **Rev:** Peter walking with friends, multicolor **Edge:** Reeded

Date	Mintage	F	VF	XF	Unc	BU
2007PM	—	—	—	—	—	35.00

KM# 1348.1a CROWN
0.9250 Silver **Ruler:** Elizabeth II **Subject:** The Tale of Peter Rabbit **Obv:** Bust with tiara right **Obv. Legend:** ELIZABETH II - ISLE OF MAN **Obv. Designer:** Ian Rank-Broadley **Rev:** Peter walking with friends **Edge:** Reeded

Date	Mintage	F	VF	XF	Unc	BU
2007PM Proof	—	Value: 85.00				

KM# 1348.2a CROWN
0.9250 Silver **Ruler:** Elizabeth II **Subject:** The Tale of Peter Rabbit **Obv:** Bust with tiara right **Obv. Legend:** ELIZABETH II - ISLE OF MAN **Obv. Designer:** Ian Rank-Broadley **Rev:** Peter walking with friends, multicolor **Edge:** Reeded

Date	Mintage	F	VF	XF	Unc	BU
2007PM Proof	—	Value: 100				

KM# 1307.1 CROWN
28.2800 g., Copper-Nickel, 38.6 mm. **Ruler:** Elizabeth II **Rev:** Ragdoll cat and kittens

Date	Mintage	F	VF	XF	Unc	BU
2007	—	—	—	—	15.00	18.00

KM# 1310 CROWN
28.2800 g., Copper-Nickel, 38.6 mm. **Ruler:** Elizabeth II **Subject:** 100th Anniversary of Scouting **Obv:** Bust with tiara right **Obv. Legend:** ELIZABETH II - ISLE OF MAN **Rev:** 3/4 length figure of Robert Baden-Powell standing facing 3/4 left, Fleur-de-lys below, images of scouting at left and right **Rev. Legend:** CENTENARY OF SCOUTING **Edge:** Reeded

Date	Mintage	F	VF	XF	Unc	BU
2007	—	—	—	—	17.00	20.00

KM# 1311 CROWN
28.2800 g., 0.9167 Silver 0.8334 oz. ASW **Ruler:** Elizabeth II **Subject:** 100th Anniversary of Scouting **Obv:** Bust with tiara right **Obv. Legend:** ELIZABETH II - ISLE OF MAN **Rev:** 3/4 length figure of Robert Baden-Powell standing facing 3/4 left, Fleur-de-lys below, images of scouting at left and right **Rev. Legend:** CENTENARY OF SCOUTING **Edge:** Reeded

Date	Mintage	F	VF	XF	Unc	BU
2007 Proof	—	Value: 75.00				

KM# 1312 CROWN
0.7500 Gold Yellow, white and red Gold **Ruler:** Elizabeth II **Subject:** Diamond Wedding Anniversary **Obv:** Bust with tiara right **Obv. Legend:** ELIZABETH II - ISLE OF MAN **Rev:** Crowned pair of doves surrounded by a leek, thistle, rose and shamrock **Edge:** Reeded

Date	Mintage	F	VF	XF	Unc	BU
2007 Proof	—	Value: 2,000				

KM# 1313 CROWN
28.2800 g., Copper-Nickel, 38.60 mm. **Ruler:** Elizabeth II **Obv:** Bust with tiara right **Obv. Legend:** ELIZABETH II - ISLE OF MAN **Rev:** Two swans facing **Edge:** Reeded

Date	Mintage	F	VF	XF	Unc	BU
2007	—	—	—	—	15.00	18.00

KM# 1315 CROWN
28.2800 g., 0.9167 Silver 0.8334 oz. ASW, 38.60 mm. **Ruler:** Elizabeth II **Obv:** Bust with tiara right **Obv. Legend:** ELIZABETH II - ISLE OF MAN **Rev:** Two swans facing **Edge:** Reeded

Date	Mintage	F	VF	XF	Unc	BU
2007 Proof	10,000	Value: 75.00				

KM# 1316 CROWN
28.2800 g., Copper-Nickel, 38.6 mm. **Ruler:** Elizabeth II **Subject:** Diamond Wedding Anniversary **Obv:** Conjoined busts with Philip right **Obv. Legend:** ELIZABETH II - ISLE OF MAN **Rev:** Bridal bouquet of white orchids **Rev. Legend:** Diamond Wedding of H.M. Queen Elizabeth II & H.R.H. Prince Philip **Edge:** Reeded

Date	Mintage	F	VF	XF	Unc	BU
2007	—	—	—	—	15.00	18.00

KM# 1316a CROWN

28.2800 g., 0.9167 Silver 0.8334 oz. ASW **Ruler:** Elizabeth II **Subject:** Diamond Wedding Anniversary **Obv:** Conjoined busts with Philip right **Obv. Legend:** ELIZABETH II - ISLE OF MAN **Rev:** Bridal bouquet of white orchids **Rev. Legend:** Diamond Wedding of H.M. Queen Elizabeth II & H.R.H. Prince Philip **Edge:** Reeded

Date	Mintage	F	VF	XF	Unc	BU
2007 Proof	—	Value: 75.00				

KM# 1317 CROWN

28.2800 g., Copper-Nickel **Ruler:** Elizabeth II **Subject:** Diamond Wedding Anniversary **Obv:** Conjoined busts with Philip right **Obv. Legend:** ELIZABETH II - ISLE OF MAN **Rev:** Westminster Abbey **Rev. Legend:** Diamond Wedding of H.M. Queen Elizabeth II & H.R.H. Prince Philip **Edge:** Reeded

Date	Mintage	F	VF	XF	Unc	BU
2007	—	—	—	—	15.00	18.00

KM# 1317a CROWN

28.2800 g., 0.9167 Silver 0.8334 oz. ASW **Ruler:** Elizabeth II **Subject:** Diamond Wedding Anniversary **Obv:** Conjoined busts with Philip right **Obv. Legend:** ELIZABETH II - ISLE OF MAN **Rev:** Westminster Abbey **Rev. Legend:** Diamond Wedding of H.M. Queen Elizabeth II & H.R.H. Prince Philip **Edge:** Reeded

Date	Mintage	F	VF	XF	Unc	BU
2007 Proof	—	Value: 75.00				

KM# 1318 CROWN

28.2800 g., Copper-Nickel, 38.6 mm. **Ruler:** Elizabeth II **Subject:** Diamond Wedding Anniversary **Obv:** Conjoined busts with Philip right **Obv. Legend:** ELIZABETH II - ISLE OF MAN **Rev:** Royal Family of five standing facing **Rev. Legend:** Diamond Wedding of H.M. Queen Elizabeth II & H.R.H. Prince Philip **Edge:** Reeded

Date	Mintage	F	VF	XF	Unc	BU
2007	—	—	—	—	15.00	18.00

KM# 1318a CROWN

28.2800 g., 0.9167 Silver 0.8334 oz. ASW, 38.6 mm. **Ruler:** Elizabeth II **Subject:** Diamond Wedding Anniversary **Obv:** Conjoined busts with Philip right **Obv. Legend:** ELIZABETH II - ISLE OF MAN **Rev:** Royal Family of five standing facing **Rev. Legend:** Diamond Wedding of H.M. Queen Elizabeth II & H.R.H. Prince Philip **Edge:** Reeded

Date	Mintage	F	VF	XF	Unc	BU
2007 Proof	—	Value: 75.00				

KM# 1319 CROWN

28.2800 g., Copper-Nickel, 38.6 mm. **Ruler:** Elizabeth II **Subject:** Diamond Wedding Anniversary **Obv:** Conjoined busts with Philip right **Obv. Legend:** ELIZABETH II - ISLE OF MAN **Rev:** Bride and groom standing facing **Rev. Legend:** Diamond Wedding of H.M. Queen Elizabeth II & H.R.H. Prince Philip **Edge:** Reeded

Date	Mintage	F	VF	XF	Unc	BU
2007	—	—	—	—	15.00	18.00

KM# 1319a CROWN

28.2800 g., 0.9167 Silver 0.8334 oz. ASW, 38.6 mm. **Ruler:** Elizabeth II **Subject:** Diamond Wedding Anniversary **Obv:** Conjoined busts with Philip right **Obv. Legend:** ELIZABETH II - ISLE OF MAN **Rev:** Bride and groom standing facing **Rev. Legend:** Diamond Wedding of H.M. Queen Elizabeth II & H.R.H. Prince Philip **Edge:** Reeded

Date	Mintage	F	VF	XF	Unc	BU
2007 Proof	—	Value: 75.00				

KM# 1325.1 CROWN

28.2800 g., Copper-Nickel, 38.60 mm. **Ruler:** Elizabeth II **Subject:** Hans Christian Anderson's Fairy Tales **Obv:** Bust with tiara right **Obv. Legend:** ELIZABETH II - ISLE OF MAN **Obv. Designer:** Ian Rank-Broadley **Rev:** Wolf at right trying to blow pig's house down, two pigs fleeing above in background **Rev. Legend:** Three Little Pigs **Edge:** Reeded

Date	Mintage	F	VF	XF	Unc	BU
2007PM	—	—	—	—	—	35.00

KM# 1325.2 CROWN

28.2800 g., Copper-Nickel, 38.60 mm. **Ruler:** Elizabeth II **Subject:** Hans Christian Anderson's Fairy Tales **Obv:** Bust with tiara right **Obv. Legend:** ELIZABETH II - ISLE OF MAN **Obv. Designer:** Ian Rank-Broadley **Rev:** Wolf at right trying to blow pig's house down, two pigs fleeing above in backgound multicolor **Rev. Legend:** Three Little Pigs **Edge:** Reeded

Date	Mintage	F	VF	XF	Unc	BU
2007PM	—	—	—	—	—	40.00

KM# 1325.1a CROWN

28.2800 g., 0.9250 Silver 0.8410 oz. ASW, 38.60 mm. **Ruler:** Elizabeth II **Subject:** Hans Christian Anderson's Fairy Tales **Obv:** Bust with tiara right **Obv. Legend:** ELIZABETH II - ISLE OF MAN **Obv. Designer:** Ian Rank-Broadley **Rev:** Wolf at right trying to blow pig's house down, two pigs fleeing above in background **Rev. Legend:** Three Little Pigs **Edge:** Reeded

Date	Mintage	F	VF	XF	Unc	BU
2007PM Proof	—	Value: 80.00				

KM# 1325.2a CROWN

28.2800 g., 0.9250 Silver 0.8410 oz. ASW, 38.60 mm. **Ruler:** Elizabeth II **Subject:** Hans Christian Anderson's Fairy Tales **Obv:** Bust with tiara right **Obv. Legend:** ELIZABETH II - ISLE OF MAN **Obv. Designer:** Ian Rank-Broadley **Rev:** Wolf at right trying to blow pig's house down, two pigs fleeing above in background multicolor **Rev. Legend:** Three Little Pigs **Edge:** Reeded

Date	Mintage	F	VF	XF	Unc	BU
2007PM Proof	—	Value: 100				

KM# 1307.2 CROWN

28.2800 g., Copper-Nickel, 38.6 mm. **Ruler:** Elizabeth II **Rev:** Three cats, multicolor

Date	Mintage	F	VF	XF	Unc	BU
2007PM	—	—	—	—	—	25.00

KM# 1324.1 CROWN

28.2800 g., Copper-Nickel, 38.60 mm. **Ruler:** Elizabeth II **Subject:** Hans Christian Anderson's Fairy Tales **Obv:** Bust with tiara right **Obv. Legend:** ELIZABETH II - ISLE OF MAN **Obv. Designer:** Ian Rank-Broadley **Rev:** Prince awakening Sleeping Beauty, castle in background **Rev. Legend:** Sleeping Beauty **Edge:** Reeded

Date	Mintage	F	VF	XF	Unc	BU
2007PM	—	—	—	—	—	35.00

KM# 1324.1a CROWN

28.2800 g., 0.9250 Silver 0.8410 oz. ASW, 38.60 mm. **Ruler:** Elizabeth II **Subject:** Hans Christian Anderson's Fairy Tales **Obv:** Bust with tiara right **Obv. Legend:** ELIZABETH II - ISLE OF MAN **Obv. Designer:** Ian Rank-Broadley **Rev:** Prince wakening Sleeping Beauty, castle in background **Rev. Legend:** Sleeping Beauty **Edge:** Reeded

Date	Mintage	F	VF	XF	Unc	BU
2007PM Proof	—	Value: 80.00				

KM# 1324.2 CROWN

28.2800 g., Copper-Nickel, 38.60 mm. **Ruler:** Elizabeth II **Subject:** Hans Christian Anderson's Fairy Tales **Obv:** Bust with tiara right **Obv. Legend:** ELIZABET II - ISLE OF MAN **Obv. Designer:** Ian Rank-Broadley **Rev:** Prince awakening Sleeping Beauty, castle in background multicolor **Rev. Legend:** Sleeping Beauty **Edge:** Reeded

Date	Mintage	F	VF	XF	Unc	BU
2007PM	—	—	—	—	—	40.00

KM# 1324.2a CROWN

28.2800 g., 0.9250 Silver 0.8410 oz. ASW, 38.60 mm. **Ruler:** Elizabeth II **Subject:** Hans Christian Anderson's Fairy Tales **Obv:** Bust with tiara right **Obv. Legend:** ELIZABETH II - ISLE OF MAN **Obv. Designer:** Ian Rank-Broadley **Rev:** Prince awakening Sleeping Beauty, castle in background multicolor **Rev. Legend:** Sleeping Beauty **Edge:** Reeded

Date	Mintage	F	VF	XF	Unc	BU
2007PM Proof	—	Value: 100				

KM# 1418 CROWN

28.2800 g., Copper-Nickel, 38.6 mm. **Ruler:** Elizabeth II **Subject:** TT Centennial **Obv:** Bust with tiara right **Rev:** Motorcyclist left

Date	Mintage	F	VF	XF	Unc	BU
2007PM	—	—	—	—	15.00	17.00

KM# 1419 CROWN

28.2800 g., Copper-Nickel, 38.6 mm. **Ruler:** Elizabeth II **Subject:** TT Centennial **Obv:** Bust with tiara right **Rev:** Motorcyclists Dunlop

Date	Mintage	F	VF	XF	Unc	BU
2007PM	—	—	—	—	15.00	17.00

KM# 1420 CROWN

28.2800 g., Copper-Nickel, 38.6 mm. **Ruler:** Elizabeth II **Subject:** TT Centennial **Obv:** Bust with tiara right **Rev:** Motorcyclists Woods

Date	Mintage	F	VF	XF	Unc	BU
2007PM	—	—	—	—	15.00	17.00

KM# 1421 CROWN

28.2800 g., Copper-Nickel, 38.6 mm. **Ruler:** Elizabeth II **Subject:** TT Centennial **Obv:** Bust with tiara right **Rev:** Motorcyclists Haliwood

Date	Mintage	F	VF	XF	Unc	BU
2007PM	—	—	—	—	15.00	17.00

KM# 1422 CROWN

28.2800 g., Copper-Nickel, 38.6 mm. **Ruler:** Elizabeth II **Subject:** TT Centennial **Obv:** Bust with tiara right **Rev:** Motorcyclists Colier

Date	Mintage	F	VF	XF	Unc	BU
2007PM	—	—	—	—	15.00	17.00

KM# 1353 CROWN

28.2800 g., Copper-Nickel, 38.6 mm. **Ruler:** Elizabeth II **Subject:** Prince Charles 60th Birthday **Obv:** Bust with tiara right **Obv. Legend:** ELIZABETH II - ISLE OF MAN **Obv. Designer:** Ian Rank-Broadley **Rev:** Heads of Charles, Princes William and Henry right **Edge:** Reeded

Date	Mintage	F	VF	XF	Unc	BU
2008PM	—	—	—	—	10.00	12.00

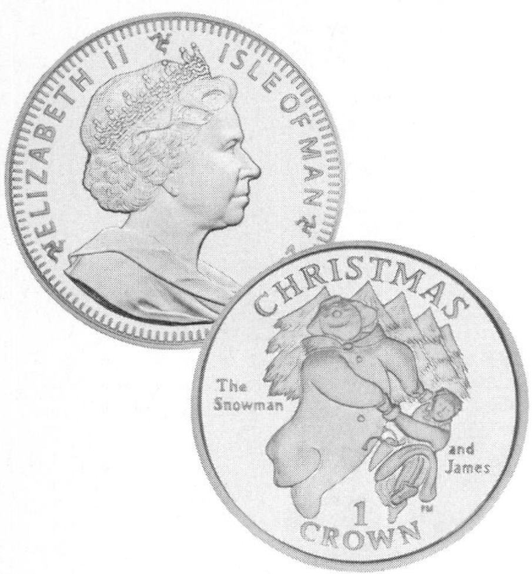

KM# 1394 CROWN

28.2800 g., Copper-Nickel, 38.6 mm. **Ruler:** Elizabeth II **Rev:** Snowman and James

Date	Mintage	F	VF	XF	Unc	BU
2008PM AA	—	—	—	—	—	20.00

KM# 1397 CROWN

0.9250 Silver, 56.2x40 mm. **Ruler:** Elizabeth II **Obv:** Bust with tiara right within Egyptian motif **Rev:** Seated figure and attendant **Shape:** Triangle

Date	Mintage	F	VF	XF	Unc	BU
2008PM Proof	2,500	Value: 95.00				

KM# 1398 CROWN

0.9250 Silver, 56.2x40 mm. **Ruler:** Elizabeth II **Obv:** Bust right in Tiaria within Egyptian motif **Rev:** Statue standing **Shape:** Triangle

Date	Mintage	F	VF	XF	Unc	BU
2008PM Proof	2,500	Value: 95.00				

KM# 1401 CROWN

28.2800 g., 0.9250 Silver 0.8410 oz. ASW, 38.6 mm. **Ruler:** Elizabeth II **Obv:** Bust with tiara right, multicolor band around **Rev:** Seated figures, multicolor band

Date	Mintage	F	VF	XF	Unc	BU
2008PM Proof	—	Value: 65.00				

KM# 1403 CROWN

28.2800 g., Copper-Nickel, 38.6 mm. **Ruler:** Elizabeth II **Subject:** Bejing Olympics **Obv:** Bust with tiara right **Rev:** Torch runner and Great Wall of China

Date	Mintage	F	VF	XF	Unc	BU
2008PM Proof	—	Value: 25.00				

KM# 1404 CROWN

28.2800 g., Copper-Nickel, 38.6 mm. **Ruler:** Elizabeth II **Obv:** Bust wiht tiara right **Rev:** Paddington Bear

Date	Mintage	F	VF	XF	Unc	BU
2008PM Proof	—	Value: 25.00				

KM# 1405 CROWN

0.9250 Silver **Ruler:** Elizabeth II **Obv:** Bust with tiara right **Rev:** Three figures standing, vile of sand above **Shape:** Triangle

Date	Mintage	F	VF	XF	Unc	BU
2008PM Proof	—	Value: 110				

KM# 1353a CROWN

28.2800 g., 0.9250 Silver 0.8410 oz. ASW, 38.6 mm. **Ruler:** Elizabeth II **Subject:** Prince Charles 60th Birthday **Obv:** Bust with tiara right **Obv. Legend:** ELIZABETH II - ISLE OF MAN **Obv. Designer:** Ian Rank-Broadley **Rev:** Heads of Charles, Princes William and Henry right **Edge:** Reeded

Date	Mintage	F	VF	XF	Unc	BU
2008PM Proof	10,000	Value: 50.00				

KM# 1424 CROWN

28.2800 g., Copper-Nickel, 38.6 mm. **Ruler:** Elizabeth II **Obv:** Bust with tiara right **Rev:** Two cats seated

Date	Mintage	F	VF	XF	Unc	BU
2008PM	—	—	—	—	15.00	17.00

KM# 1424a CROWN

31.1050 g., 0.9990 Silver 0.9990 oz. ASW, 38.6 mm. **Ruler:** Elizabeth II **Obv:** Bust with tiara right **Rev:** Two cats seated

Date	Mintage	F	VF	XF	Unc	BU
2008PM Proof	—	Value: 50.00				

KM# 1373 CROWN

28.2800 g., Copper-Nickel, 38.6 mm. **Ruler:** Elizabeth II **Rev:** Berlin Wall and Brandenburg Gate statue group

Date	Mintage	F	VF	XF	Unc	BU
2009	—	—	—	—	15.00	18.00

KM# 1373a CROWN

28.2800 g., 0.9250 Silver 0.8410 oz. ASW, 38.6 mm. **Ruler:** Elizabeth II **Rev:** Berlin Wall and Brandenberg Gate

Date	Mintage	F	VF	XF	Unc	BU
2009 Proof	10,000	Value: 40.00				

KM# 1374 CROWN

28.2800 g., Copper-Nickel, 38.6 mm. **Ruler:** Elizabeth II **Subject:** Terra Cotta Army **Obv:** Bust right **Rev:** Making of the Soldier

Date	Mintage	F	VF	XF	Unc	BU
2009	—	—	—	—	12.00	15.00

KM# 1374a CROWN

28.2800 g., 0.9250 Silver 0.8410 oz. ASW, 38.6 mm. **Ruler:** Elizabeth II **Subject:** Terra Cotta Army **Obv:** Bust right **Rev:** Making of the Soldier

Date	Mintage	F	VF	XF	Unc	BU
2009 Proof	10,000	Value: 40.00				

KM# 1376 CROWN
28.2800 g., 0.9250 Copper-Nickel 0.8410 oz., 38.6 mm. **Ruler:** Elizabeth II **Subject:** Terra Cotta Army **Obv:** Bust right **Rev:** Making of the Horse

Date	Mintage	F	VF	XF	Unc	BU
2009	—	—	—	—	12.00	15.00

KM# 1376a CROWN
28.2800 g., 0.9250 Silver 0.8410 oz. ASW, 38.6 mm. **Ruler:** Elizabeth II **Subject:** Terra Cotta Army **Obv:** Bust right **Rev:** Making of the Horse

Date	Mintage	F	VF	XF	Unc	BU
2009 Proof	10,000	Value: 40.00				

KM# 1378.1 CROWN
28.2800 g., Copper-Nickel, 38.6 mm. **Ruler:** Elizabeth II **Obv:** Bust right **Rev:** Chinchilla cat and kitten

Date	Mintage	F	VF	XF	Unc	BU
2009	—	—	—	—	15.00	18.00

KM# 1378.2 CROWN
28.2800 g., Copper-Nickel, 38.6 mm. **Ruler:** Elizabeth II **Obv:** Bust right **Rev:** Multicolor chinchilla cat and kitten

Date	Mintage	F	VF	XF	Unc	BU
2009	—	—	—	—	—	25.00

KM# 1378.1a CROWN
31.1000 g., 0.9990 Silver 0.9988 oz. ASW, 38.6 mm. **Ruler:** Elizabeth II **Obv:** Bust right **Rev:** Chinchilla cat and kitten

Date	Mintage	F	VF	XF	Unc	BU
2009 Proof	10,000	Value: 40.00				

KM# 1378.2a CROWN
31.1050 g., 0.9999 Silver 0.9999 oz. ASW, 38.6 mm. **Ruler:** Elizabeth II **Obv:** Bust right **Rev:** Multicolor chinchilla cat and kitten

Date	Mintage	F	VF	XF	Unc	BU
2009	—	—	—	—	—	40.00

KM# 1379 CROWN
31.1050 g., 0.9999 Gold 0.9999 oz. AGW, 32.7 mm. **Ruler:** Elizabeth II **Obv:** Bust right **Rev:** Chinchilla cat and kitten

Date	Mintage	F	VF	XF	Unc	BU
2009	—	—	—	—	—	1,550
2009 Proof	1,000	Value: 1,600				

KM# 1388 CROWN
31.1050 g., 0.9999 Gold 0.9999 oz. AGW, 45x31.1 mm. **Ruler:** Elizabeth II **Subject:** Howard Carter, 70th Anniversary of Death **Obv:** Bust right **Rev:** Pharoah and Anubis carving, encased with sand **Shape:** Pyramid

Date	Mintage	F	VF	XF	Unc	BU
2009 Proof	250	Value: 1,750				

KM# 1389 CROWN
31.1030 g., 0.9990 Silver 0.9989 oz. ASW, 56.2x40.7 mm. **Ruler:** Elizabeth II **Subject:** Howard Carter, 70th Anniversary of death **Obv:** Bust right **Rev:** Pharoah and Anubis, encased with sand **Shape:** Prymaid

Date	Mintage	F	VF	XF	Unc	BU
2009 Proof	3,000	Value: 125				

KM# 1390.1 CROWN
28.2800 g., Copper-Nickel, 38.6 mm. **Ruler:** Elizabeth II **Subject:** Concorde test flight, 40th Anniversary **Obv:** Bust right **Rev:** Concorde and five world landmarks

Date	Mintage	F	VF	XF	Unc	BU
2009	—	—	—	—	15.00	18.00

KM# 1390.1a CROWN
28.2800 g., 0.9250 Silver 0.8410 oz. ASW, 38.6 mm. **Ruler:** Elizabeth II **Subject:** Corcorde test flight, 40th Anniversary **Obv:** Bust right **Rev:** Concorde and five world landmarks

Date	Mintage	F	VF	XF	Unc	BU
2009 Proof	10,000	Value: 40.00				

KM# 1390.2 CROWN
28.2800 g., Copper-Nickel, 38.6 mm. **Ruler:** Elizabeth II **Subject:** 40th Anniversary of test flight **Rev:** Concorde in color

Date	Mintage	F	VF	XF	Unc	BU
2009PM	—	—	—	—	—	25.00

KM# 1391 CROWN
28.2800 g., Copper-Nickel, 38.6 mm. **Ruler:** Elizabeth II **Obv:** Bust right **Rev:** Henry VIII and portraits of wives

Date	Mintage	F	VF	XF	Unc	BU
2009	—	—	—	—	15.00	18.00

KM# 1391a CROWN
28.2800 g., 0.9250 Silver 0.8410 oz. ASW, 38.6 mm. **Ruler:** Elizabeth II **Obv:** Bust right **Rev:** Henry VIII

Date	Mintage	F	VF	XF	Unc	BU
2009 Proof	10,000	Value: 40.00				

KM# 1392 CROWN
28.2800 g., Copper-Nickel, 38.6 mm. **Ruler:** Elizabeth II **Subject:** FIFA World Cup - South Africa **Obv:** Bust right **Rev:** Two soccer players

Date	Mintage	F	VF	XF	Unc	BU
2009	—	—	—	—	15.00	18.00

KM# 1392a CROWN
28.2800 g., 0.9250 Silver 0.8410 oz. ASW, 38.6 mm. **Ruler:** Elizabeth II **Subject:** FIFA World Cup - South Africa **Obv:** Bust right

Date	Mintage	F	VF	XF	Unc	BU
2009 Proof	10,000	Value: 40.00				

KM# 1416 CROWN
28.2800 g., Copper-Nickel, 38.6 mm. **Ruler:** Elizabeth II **Obv:** Bust with tiara right **Rev:** Two cats

Date	Mintage	F	VF	XF	Unc	BU
2009PM	—	—	—	—	15.00	17.00

KM# 1406 CROWN
28.2800 g., Copper-Nickel, 38.6 mm. **Ruler:** Elizabeth II **Series:** London Olympics 2012 **Obv:** Bust wiht tiara right **Rev:** Three cyclists before Buckingham Palace

Date	Mintage	F	VF	XF	Unc	BU
2009PM Proof	—	Value: 25.00				

KM# 1407 CROWN
28.2800 g., Copper-Nickel, 38.6 mm. **Ruler:** Elizabeth II **Subject:** London Olympics, 2012 **Obv:** Bust with tiara right **Rev:** Rowers before Big Ben and Parliament

Date	Mintage	F	VF	XF	Unc	BU
2009PM Proof	—	Value: 25.00				

KM# 1408 CROWN
28.2800 g., Copper-Nickel, 38.6 mm. **Ruler:** Elizabeth II **Subject:** London Olympics, 2012 **Obv:** Bust with tiara right **Rev:** Swimmer before Tower of London

Date	Mintage	F	VF	XF	Unc	BU
2009PM Proof	—	Value: 25.00				

KM# 1409 CROWN
28.2800 g., Copper-Nickel, 38.6 mm. **Ruler:** Elizabeth II **Subject:** London Olympics, 2012 **Obv:** Bust with tiara right **Rev:** Two runners before St. Paul's Cathedral

Date	Mintage	F	VF	XF	Unc	BU
2009PM Proof	—	Value: 25.00				

KM# 1410 CROWN
28.2800 g., Copper-Nickel, 38.6 mm. **Ruler:** Elizabeth II **Subject:** London Olympics, 2012 **Obv:** Bust with tiara right **Rev:** Two sailboats before Tower Bridge

Date	Mintage	F	VF	XF	Unc	BU
2009PM Proof	—	Value: 25.00				

KM# 1411 CROWN
28.2800 g., Copper-Nickel, 38.6 mm. **Ruler:** Elizabeth II **Subject:** London Olympics, 2012 **Obv:** Bust with tiara right **Rev:** Two boxers before London Wheel and skyline

Date	Mintage	F	VF	XF	Unc	BU
2009PM Proof	—	Value: 25.00				

KM# 1412 CROWN
28.2800 g., Copper-Nickel, 38.6 mm. **Ruler:** Elizabeth II **Subject:** Vancouver Olympics, 2010 **Obv:** Bust with tiara right **Rev:** Torch at center of four sports, hockey, sled, figure skating and bobsled

Date	Mintage	F	VF	XF	Unc	BU
2009PM Proof	—	Value: 25.00				

KM# 1413 CROWN
28.2800 g., Copper-Nickel, 38.6 mm. **Ruler:** Elizabeth II **Subject:** Vancouver Olympics, 2010 **Obv:** Bust with tiara right **Rev:** Torch at center of four sports, ski jump, snoboardiong, biathlon and Salom

Date	Mintage	F	VF	XF	Unc	BU
2009PM Proof	—	Value: 25.00				

KM# 1414 CROWN
28.2800 g., Copper-Nickel, 38.6 mm. **Ruler:** Elizabeth II **Subject:** Bee Gee's 50th Anniversary **Obv:** Bust with tiara right **Rev:** Band name at center

Date	Mintage	F	VF	XF	Unc	BU
2009PM Proof	—	Value: 25.00				

KM# 1415 CROWN
28.2800 g., Copper-Nickel, 38.6 mm. **Ruler:** Elizabeth II **Subject:** First man on the Moon, 40th Anniversary **Obv:** Bust with tiara right **Rev:** Man in space suit with American Flag on moon

Date	Mintage	F	VF	XF	Unc	BU
2009PM Proof	—	Value: 25.00				

KM# 1416.a1 CROWN
31.1050 g., 0.9990 Silver 0.9990 oz. ASW, 38.6 mm. **Ruler:** Elizabeth II **Obv:** Bust with tiara right **Rev:** Two cats, multicolor

Date	Mintage	F	VF	XF	Unc	BU
2009PM Proof	—	Value: 50.00				

KM# 1416.a CROWN
31.1050 g., 0.9990 Silver 0.9990 oz. ASW, 38.6 mm. **Ruler:** Elizabeth II **Obv:** Bust with tiara right **Rev:** Two cats

Date	Mintage	F	VF	XF	Unc	BU
2009PM Proof	—	Value: 50.00				

KM# 1417 CROWN
0.9990 Silver **Ruler:** Elizabeth II **Obv:** Bust with tiara right within ornimentation **Rev:** Kubla Kahn standing **Shape:** Vertical rectangle

Date	Mintage	F	VF	XF	Unc	BU
2010PM Proof	—	Value: 50.00				

KM# 1426 CROWN
28.2800 g., Copper-Nickel, 38.6 mm. **Ruler:** Elizabeth II **Obv:** Bust with tiara right **Rev:** Cat standing right

Date	Mintage	F	VF	XF	Unc	BU
2010PM	—	—	—	—	15.00	17.00

KM# 1426a CROWN
31.1050 g., 0.9990 Silver 0.9990 oz. ASW, 38.6 mm. **Ruler:** Elizabeth II **Obv:** Bust with tiara right **Rev:** Cat standing right

Date	Mintage	F	VF	XF	Unc	BU
2010PM Proof	—	Value: 50.00				

KM# 1200 2 CROWNS
62.2000 g., 0.9990 Palladium 1.9977 oz., 40 mm. **Ruler:** Elizabeth II **Subject:** Discovery of Palladium Bicentennial **Obv:** Bust with tiara right **Obv. Designer:** Ian Rank-Broadley **Rev:** Pallas Athena left **Edge:** Reeded

Date	Mintage	F	VF	XF	Unc	BU
2004PM Proof	300	Value: 1,800				

KM# 1402 2 CROWNS
0.9250 Silver, 40 mm. **Ruler:** Elizabeth II **Obv:** Bust with tiara right **Rev:** Seven Wonders of the World, multicolor central item

Date	Mintage	F	VF	XF	Unc	BU
2008PM Proof	—	Value: 100				

KM# 1064 5 CROWN
155.5175 g., 0.9999 Gold 4.9993 oz. AGW, 65 mm. **Ruler:** Elizabeth II **Subject:** Year of the Snake **Obv:** Bust with tiara right **Obv. Designer:** Ian Rank-Broadley **Rev:** Snake **Edge:** Reeded

Date	Mintage	F	VF	XF	Unc	BU
2001 Proof	250	Value: 7,750				

KM# 1104 5 CROWN
155.5100 g., 0.9999 Gold 4.9991 oz. AGW, 65 mm. **Ruler:** Elizabeth II **Subject:** Year of the Horse **Obv:** Bust with tiara right **Obv. Designer:** Ian Rank-Broadley **Rev:** Two horses **Edge:** Reeded

Date	Mintage	F	VF	XF	Unc	BU
2002 Proof	250	Value: 7,750				

KM# 1173 5 CROWN
155.5100 g., 0.9999 Gold 4.9991 oz. AGW, 65 mm. **Ruler:** Elizabeth II **Subject:** Year of the Goat **Obv:** Bust with tiara right **Obv. Designer:** Ian Rank-Broadley **Rev:** Three goats **Edge:** Reeded

Date	Mintage	F	VF	XF	Unc	BU
2003PM Proof	250	Value: 7,750				

KM# 1244 5 CROWN
155.5175 g., 0.9999 Gold 4.9993 oz. AGW, 65 mm. **Ruler:** Elizabeth II **Obv:** Bust with tiara right **Obv. Designer:** Ian Rank-Broadley **Rev:** Monkey **Edge:** Reeded

Date	Mintage	F	VF	XF	Unc	BU
2004PM Proof	250	Value: 7,750				

KM# 1219 64 CROWNS
2000.0000 g., 0.9990 Silver 64.234 oz. ASW, 140 mm. **Ruler:** Elizabeth II **Obv:** Bust with tiara right **Obv. Designer:** Ian Rank-Broadley **Rev:** Ocean Liner Queen Mary 2 **Edge:** Reeded

Date	Mintage	F	VF	XF	Unc	BU
2004PM Proof	500	Value: 2,500				

KM# 1142 100 CROWNS

3000.0000 g., 0.9999 Silver 96.438 oz. ASW, 130 mm. **Ruler:** Elizabeth II **Subject:** Queen's Golden Jubilee **Obv:** Bust with tiara right **Obv. Designer:** Ian Rank-Broadley **Rev:** Queen on horse **Edge:** Reeded **Note:** Illustration reduced.

Date	Mintage	F	VF	XF	Unc	BU
2002 Proof	500	Value: 3,500				

KM# 1184 130 CROWNS

4000.0000 g., 0.9990 Silver 128.46 oz. ASW, 130 mm. **Ruler:** Elizabeth II **Obv:** Bust with tiara right **Obv. Designer:** Ian Rank-Broadley **Rev:** Gold clad cameo portrait of Elizabeth I with a .035ct ruby inset on her forehead all within a circle of portraits **Edge:** Reeded

Date	Mintage	F	VF	XF	Unc	BU
2003PM Proof	500	Value: 4,750				

GOLD BULLION COINAGE

Angel Issues

KM# 1106 1/20 ANGEL

1.5552 g., 0.9999 Gold 0.0500 oz. AGW, 15 mm. **Ruler:** Elizabeth II **Obv:** Bust with tiara right **Obv. Designer:** Ian Rank-Broadley **Rev:** St. Michael slaying dragon, three crown privy mark at right **Edge:** Reeded

Date	Mintage	F	VF	XF	Unc	BU
2001 (3c) Proof	1,000	Value: 85.00				
2002 Proof	—	Value: 85.00				
Note: With candy cane privy mark						

KM# 393 1/20 ANGEL

1.5551 g., 0.9999 Gold 0.0500 oz. AGW **Ruler:** Elizabeth II **Obv:** Crowned bust right **Obv. Designer:** Raphael Maklouf **Rev:** Archangel Michael slaying dragon right

Date	Mintage	F	VF	XF	Unc	BU
2001	—	—	—	—	—	85.00
2001 Proof	—	Value: 90.00				
2001 Proof	—	Value: 95.00				
Note: Privy mark: 3 Kings						
2002	—	—	—	—	—	85.00
2002 Proof	—	Value: 90.00				
2002 Proof	—	Value: 95.00				
Note: Privy mark: Candy						
2003	—	—	—	—	—	85.00
2003 Proof	—	Value: 90.00				
2003 Proof	—	Value: 95.00				
Note: Privy mark: Candy						
2004	—	—	—	—	—	85.00
2004 Proof	—	Value: 90.00				
2004 Proof	—	Value: 95.00				
Note: Privy mark: Partridge in a Pear Tree						
2005	—	—	—	—	—	85.00
2005 Proof	—	Value: 90.00				
2005 Proof	—	Value: 95.00				
Note: Privy mark: 2 Turtle doves						
2006	—	—	—	—	—	85.00
2006 Proof	—	Value: 90.00				
2006 Proof	—	Value: 95.00				
Note: Privy mark: 4 Calling birds						
2007	—	—	—	—	—	85.00
2007 Proof	—	Value: 90.00				
2007 Proof	—	Value: 95.00				
Note: Privy mark: 4 Calling birds						

KM# 1252 1/20 ANGEL

1.5550 g., 0.9999 Gold 0.0500 oz. AGW, 15 mm. **Ruler:** Elizabeth II **Obv:** Bust with tiara right **Obv. Designer:** Ian Rank-Broadley **Rev:** St. Michael and Christmas privy mark **Edge:** Reeded

Date	Mintage	F	VF	XF	Unc	BU
2004PM Proof	1,000	Value: 85.00				

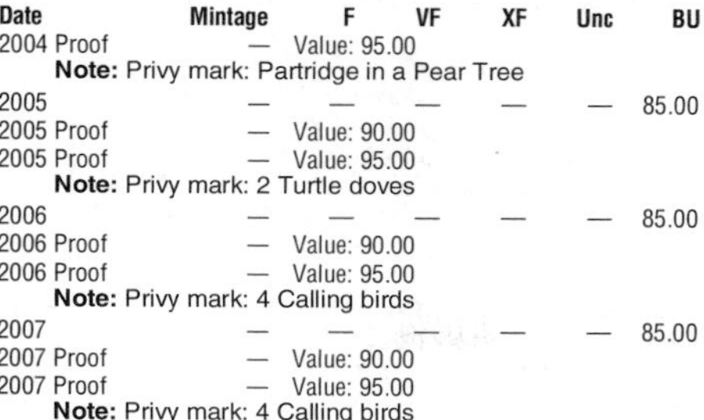

KM# 394 1/10 ANGEL

3.1103 g., 0.9999 Gold 0.1000 oz. AGW **Ruler:** Elizabeth II **Obv:** Crowned bust right **Obv. Designer:** Raphael Maklouf **Rev:** Archangel Michael

Date	Mintage	F	VF	XF	Unc	BU
2001	—	—	—	—	—	160
2001 Proof	—	Value: 165				
2002	—	—	—	—	—	160
2002 Proof	—	Value: 165				
2003	—	—	—	—	—	160
2003 Proof	—	Value: 165				
2004	—	—	—	—	—	160
2004 Proof	—	Value: 165				
2005	—	—	—	—	—	160
2005 Proof	—	Value: 165				

KM# 395 1/4 ANGEL

7.7758 g., 0.9999 Gold 0.2500 oz. AGW **Ruler:** Elizabeth II **Obv:** Crowned bust right **Obv. Designer:** Raphael Maklouf **Rev:** Archangel Michael slaying dragon

Date	Mintage	F	VF	XF	Unc	BU
2001	—	—	—	—	—	375
2001 Proof	—	Value: 385				
2002	—	—	—	—	—	375
2002 Proof	—	Value: 385				
2003	—	—	—	—	—	375
2003 Proof	—	Value: 385				
2004	—	—	—	—	—	375
2004 Proof	—	Value: 385				
2005	—	—	—	—	—	375
2005 Proof	—	Value: 385				

KM# 397 ANGEL

31.1035 g., 0.9999 Gold 0.9999 oz. AGW **Ruler:** Elizabeth II **Obv:** Crowned bust right **Obv. Designer:** Raphael Maklouf **Rev:** Archangel Michael slaying dragon right

Date	Mintage	F	VF	XF	Unc	BU
2001	—	—	—	—	—	1,500
2001 Proof	—	Value: 1,525				
2002	—	—	—	—	—	1,500
2002 Proof	—	Value: 1,525				
2003	—	—	—	—	—	1,500
2003 Proof	—	Value: 1,525				
2004	—	—	—	—	—	1,500
2004 Proof	—	Value: 1,525				
2005	—	—	—	—	—	1,500
2005 Proof	—	Value: 1,525				
2006	—	—	—	—	—	1,500
2006 Proof	500	Value: 1,525				
2007	—	—	—	—	—	1,500
2007 Proof	—	Value: 1,525				

KM# 397.1 ANGEL

31.1035 g., 0.9990 Gold 0.9990 oz. AGW **Ruler:** Elizabeth II **Obv:** Crowned bust right **Obv. Designer:** Raphael Maklouf **Rev:** Archangel Michael slaying dragon right

Date	Mintage	F	VF	XF	Unc	BU
2006 Proof, High Relief	Est. 1,000	Value: 1,500				
2007 Proof, High Relief	Est. 1,000	Value: 1,500				

MINT SETS

KM#	Date	Mintage	Identification	Issue Price	Mkt Val
MS30	2001 (8)	—	KM#1036-1043	—	22.50
MS31	2001 (9)	—	KM#1036-1044	—	40.00
MS32	2002 (8)	—	KM#1036-1043	—	22.50
MS33	2002 (9)	—	KM#1036-1044	—	40.00
MS34	2003 (8)	—	KM#1036-1043	—	22.50
MS35	2003 (9)	—	KM#1036-1044	—	40.00
MS36	2004 (8)	—	KM#1253-1260	—	25.00
MS37	2004 (9)	—	KM#1253-1261	—	40.00
MS38	2005 (8)	—	KM#1253-1260	—	22.50
MS39	2005 (9)	—	KM#1253-1261	—	40.00
MS40	2006 (8)	—	MS#1253-1260	35.00	25.00
MS41	2006 (9)	—	KM1253-1261	42.50	40.00
MS42	2007 (8)	—	KM#1253-1260	35.00	22.50
MS43	2007 (9)	—	KM1253-1261	42.50	40.00

PROOF SETS

KM#	Date	Mintage	Identification	Issue Price	Mkt Val
PS59	2001 (5)	1,000	KM#1067-1070, 1073	—	2,900
PS60	2003 (3)	—	KM#1186, 1187, 1188	—	525
PS61	2003 (5)	—	KM#1186, 1187, 1188, 1189, 1190 w/gold ring	—	3,000
PS62	2003 (5)	—	KM#1191-1195 w/gold-plated silver ring	—	245
PS63	2004 (5)	1,000	KM#1247, 1248, 1249.1, 1250, 1251	—	3,050

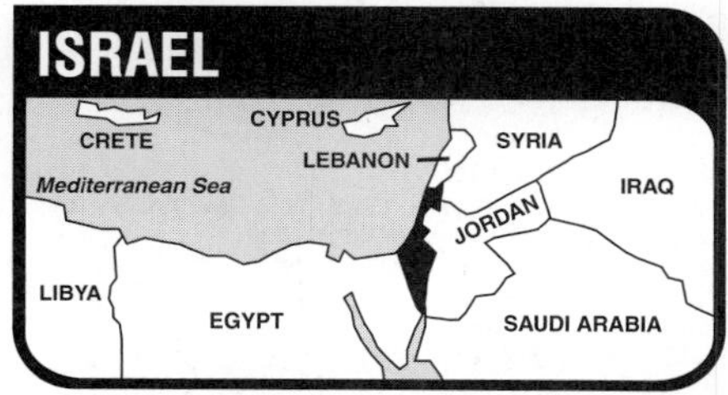

The state of Israel, a Middle Eastern republic at the eastern end of the Mediterranean Sea, bounded by Lebanon on the north, Syria on the northeast, Jordan on the east, and Egypt on the southwest, has an area of 9,000sq. mi. (20,770 sq. km.) and a population of 6 million. Capital: Jerusalem. Finished diamonds, chemicals, citrus, textiles, minerals, electronic and transportation equipment are exported.

HEBREW COIN DATING

Modern Israel's coins carry Hebrew dating formed from a combination of the 22 consonant letters of the Hebrew alphabet and read from right to left. The Jewish calendar dates back more than 5700 years; but five millenniums are assumed in the dating of coins (until 1981). Thus, the year 5735 (1975AD) appears as 735, with the first two characters from the right indicating the number of years in hundreds; tav (400), plus shin (300). The next is lamedh (30), followed by a separation mark which has the appearance of double quotation marks, then heh (5).

The Star of David is not a mintmark. It appears only on some coins sold by the Israel Government Coins and Medals Corporation Ltd., which is owned by the Israel government, and is a division of the Prime Minister's office and sole distributor to collectors. The Star of David was first used in 1971 on the science coin to signify that it was minted in Jerusalem, but was later used by different mint facilities.

AD Date		Jewish Era
2001	התשס"א	5761
2002	התשס"ב	5762
2003	התשס"ג	5763
2004	התשס"ד	5764

2005	התשס"ה	5765
2006	התשס"ו	5766
2007	התשס"ז	5767
2008	התשס"ח	5768
2009	התשס"ט	5769
2010	התש"ע	5770

MINT MARKS

(m) - Mem מ

(o) - Ottawa

(s) - San Francisco

None – Jerusalem

REPUBLIC

REFORM COINAGE

10 (old) Agorot = 1 New Agora; 100 New Agorot = 1 Sheqel

Commencing February 24, 1980-1985

KM# 163a NEW SHEQEL

Copper-Nickel, 18 mm. **Subject:** Hanukka **Obv:** Value, small menorah, country name in Hebrew, English and Arabic and inscription "HANUKKA" in Hebrew and English **Rev:** Lily, state emblem, ancient Hebrew inscription and Star of David mintmark

Date	Mintage	F	VF	XF	Unc	BU
JE5768 (2008)(u)	—	—	—	—	4.00	—
Note: In sets only.						

REFORM COINAGE

100 Agorot = 1 New Sheqel
1,000 Sheqalim = 1 New Sheqel

September 4, 1985

KM# 157 5 AGOROT

3.0000 g., Aluminum-Bronze, 19.45 mm. **Obv:** Ancient coin **Rev:** Value within lined square **Edge:** Plain

Date	Mintage	F	VF	XF	Unc	BU
JE5761 (2001)(sl)	6,144,000	—	—	—	0.15	—
JE5762 (2002)(sl)	6,144,000	—	—	—	0.15	—
JE5764 (2004)	—	—	—	—	0.15	—
JE5765 (2005)	—	—	—	—	0.15	—
JE5766 (2006)	—	—	—	—	0.15	—
JE5767 (2007)	—	—	—	—	0.15	—

KM# 172 5 AGOROT

3.0000 g., Aluminum-Bronze, 19.5 mm. **Subject:** Hanukka **Obv:** Ancient coin **Rev:** Value within lined square **Note:** JE5754-576 coins contain the Star of David mint mark; the JE5747-5753 coins do not.

Date	Mintage	F	VF	XF	Unc	BU
JE5761 (2001)(u)	4,000	—	—	—	2.50	—
Note: In sets only						
JE5762 (2002)(u)	4,000	—	—	—	2.50	—
Note: In sets only						
JE5763 (2003)(u)	3,000	—	—	—	3.00	—
Note: In sets only						
JE5764 (2004)(u)	3,000	—	—	—	3.00	—
Note: In sets only						
JE5765 (2005)(u)	2,500	—	—	—	3.00	—
Note: In sets only						
JE5766 (2006)(u)	3,000	—	—	—	3.00	—
Note: In sets only						
JE5767 (2007)(u)	3,000	—	—	—	3.00	—
Note: In sets only						
JE5768 (2008)(u)	3,000	—	—	—	3.00	—
Note: In sets only						

KM# 158 10 AGOROT

4.0000 g., Aluminum-Bronze, 22 mm. **Obv:** Menorah **Rev:** Value within lined square **Edge:** Plain

Date	Mintage	F	VF	XF	Unc	BU
JE5761 (2001)(sl)	46,140,000	—	—	—	0.20	—
Note: Sides of central part of zero are rounded.						
JE5761 (2001)(so)	32,256,000	—	—	—	0.20	—
Note: Sides of central part of zero are straight.						
JE5762 (2002)(w)	4,608,000	—	—	—	0.20	—
JE5763 (2003)(sl)	22,980,000	—	—	—	0.20	—
JE5764 (2004)	—	—	—	—	0.20	—
JE5765 (2005)	—	—	—	—	0.20	—
JE5766 (2006)	—	—	—	—	0.20	—
JE5767 (2007)	—	—	—	—	0.20	—
JE5768 (2008)	—	—	—	—	0.20	—
JE5769 (2009)	—	—	—	—	0.20	—
JE5770 (2010)	—	—	—	—	0.20	—

KM# 173 10 AGOROT

4.0000 g., Aluminum-Bronze, 22 mm. **Subject:** Hanukka **Obv:** Menorah **Rev:** Value within lined square **Note:** JE5754-5770 have the Star of David mint mark, JE5747-5753 coins do not.

Date	Mintage	F	VF	XF	Unc	BU
JE5761 (2001)(u)	4,000	—	—	—	3.00	—
Note: In sets only						
JE5762 (2002)(u)	4,000	—	—	—	3.00	—
Note: In sets only						
JE5763 (2003)(u)	3,000	—	—	—	3.00	—
Note: In sets only						
JE5764 (2004)(u)	3,000	—	—	—	3.00	—
Note: In sets only						
JE5765 (2005)(u)	2,500	—	—	—	3.00	—
Note: In sets only						
JE5766 (2006)(u)	3,000	—	—	—	3.00	—
Note: In sets only						
JE5767 (2007)(u)	3,000	—	—	—	3.00	—
Note: In sets only						
JE5768 (2008)(u)	3,000	—	—	—	3.00	—
Note: In sets only						
JE5769 (2009)(u)	1,800	—	—	—	3.50	—
Note: In sets only						
JE5770 (2010)(u) In sets only	1,800	—	—	—	3.50	—

KM# 174 1/2 NEW SHEQEL

6.5000 g., Aluminum-Bronze, 26 mm. **Subject:** Hanukka **Obv:** Value **Rev:** Lyre **Note:** Coins dated JE5754-5770 have the Star of David mint mark; the coins dated JE5747-5753 do not.

Date	Mintage	F	VF	XF	Unc	BU
JE5761 (2001)(u)	4,000	—	—	—	3.50	—
Note: In sets only						
JE5762 (2002)(u)	4,000	—	—	—	3.50	—
Note: In sets only						
JE5763 (2003)(u)	3,000	—	—	—	3.50	—
Note: In sets only						
JE5764 (2004)(u)	3,000	—	—	—	3.50	—
Note: In sets only						
JE5765 (2005)(u)	2,500	—	—	—	3.50	—
Note: In sets only						
JE5766 (2006)(u)	3,000	—	—	—	3.50	—
Note: In sets only						
JE5767 (2007)(u)	3,000	—	—	—	3.50	—
Note: In sets only						
JE5768 (2008)(u)	3,000	—	—	—	3.50	—
Note: In sets only						
JE5769 (2009)(u)	1,800	—	—	—	3.50	—
Note: In sets only						
JE5770 (2010)(u)	1,800	—	—	—	3.50	—
Note: In sets only						

KM# 354 1/2 NEW SHEQEL

6.5000 g., Copper-Aluminum-Nickel, 26 mm. **Subject:** Hanukka **Obv:** Denomination **Rev:** Curacao Hanukka lamp **Edge:** Plain **Shape:** 12-sided **Note:** Struck for sets only

Date	Mintage	F	VF	XF	Unc	BU
JE5761 (2001)(u)	4,000	—	—	—	11.00	—

KM# 159 1/2 NEW SHEQEL

6.5000 g., Aluminum-Bronze, 26 mm. **Obv:** Value **Rev:** Lyre **Edge:** Plain

Date	Mintage	F	VF	XF	Unc	BU
JE5762 (2002)(so)	2,880,000	—	—	—	0.75	—
JE5762 (2002)(v)	5,760,000	—	—	—	0.75	—
Note: Length of fraction line is 4 or 4.5 mm. but which mint produced which coin is not known.						
JE5763 (2003)	—	—	—	—	0.75	—
JE5764 (2004)(so)	2,640,000	—	—	—	0.75	—
JE5765 (2005)	—	—	—	—	0.75	—
JE5766 (2006)	—	—	—	—	0.75	—
JE5767 (2007)	—	—	—	—	0.75	—
JE5768 (2008)	—	—	—	—	0.75	—
JE5769 (2009)	—	—	—	—	0.60	—
JE5770 (2010)	—	—	—	—	0.60	—

KM# 355 1/2 NEW SHEQEL

6.5000 g., Copper-Aluminum-Nickel, 26 mm. **Obv:** Value **Rev:** Yemenite Hanukka Lamp **Edge:** Twelve plain sections **Note:** Struck for sets only

Date	Mintage	F	VF	XF	Unc	BU
JE5762 (2002)(u)	4,000	—	—	—	11.00	—

KM# 389 1/2 NEW SHEQEL

6.5000 g., Copper-Aluminum-Nickel, 26 mm. **Obv:** Value **Rev:** Polish Hanukka Lamp **Edge:** Plain **Shape:** 12-sided **Note:** Struck for sets only

Date	Mintage	F	VF	XF	Unc	BU
JE5763 (2003)(u)	3,000	—	—	—	12.00	—
Note: Even though not a proof, the coin has a mem						

KM# 390 1/2 NEW SHEQEL

6.5000 g., Copper-Aluminum-Nickel, 26 mm. **Obv:** Value **Rev:** Iraqi Hanukka Lamp **Edge:** Plain **Shape:** 12-sided **Note:** Struck for sets only

Date	Mintage	F	VF	XF	Unc	BU
JE5764 (2004)(u)	3,000	—	—	—	12.00	—

KM# 391 1/2 NEW SHEQEL

6.5000 g., Copper-Aluminum-Nickel, 26 mm. **Obv:** Value **Rev:** Syrian Hanukka Lamp **Edge:** Plain **Shape:** 12-sided **Note:** Struck for sets only

Date	Mintage	F	VF	XF	Unc	BU
JE5765 (2005)(u)	2,500	—	—	—	12.00	—

KM# 415 1/2 NEW SHEQEL

6.5000 g., Copper-Aluminum-Nickel, 26 mm. **Obv:** Value and mini-Hanukka Lamp **Rev:** Dutch Hanukka Lamp **Edge:** Plain **Shape:** 12-sided **Note:** Struck for sets only

Date	Mintage	F	VF	XF	Unc	BU
JE5766 (2006)(u)	3,000	—	—	—	12.00	—

KM# 422 1/2 NEW SHEQEL

6.5000 g., Copper-Aluminum-Nickel, 26 mm. **Obv:** Value and mini-Hanukka Lamp **Rev:** Corfu (Greek) Hanukka Lamp **Edge:** Plain **Shape:** 12-sided **Note:** Struck for sets only

Date	Mintage	F	VF	XF	Unc	BU
JE5767 (2007)(u)	3,000	—	—	—	12.00	—

KM# 434 1/2 NEW SHEQEL

6.5000 g., Copper-Aluminum-Nickel, 26 mm. **Subject:** Hanukka **Obv:** Value, date, inscriptions and menorah **Rev:** Egyptian Hanukka lamp **Shape:** 12-sided **Note:** Struck for sets only

Date	Mintage	F	VF	XF	Unc	BU
JE5768 (2008)(u)	3,000	—	—	—	12.00	—

KM# 466 1/2 NEW SHEQEL

6.5000 g., Copper-Aluminum-Nickel, 26 mm. **Subject:** Hanukka **Obv:** Value, date, inscriptions and menorah **Rev:** Algerian Hanukka Lamp **Edge:** Plain **Shape:** 12-sided **Note:** Struck for sets only

Date	Mintage	F	VF	XF	Unc	BU
JE5770 (2010)(u)	1,800	—	—	—	12.00	—
JE5770 (2010)(u)	1,800	—	—	—	12.00	—

KM# 436 1/2 NEW SHEQEL

6.5000 g., Copper-Aluminum-Nickel, 26 mm. **Subject:** Hanukka **Obv:** Value, date, inscriptions and menorah **Rev:** Prague Hanukka Lamp **Shape:** 12-sided **Note:** Struck for sets only

Date	Mintage	F	VF	XF	Unc	BU
JE5769(u)	1,800	—	—	—	12.00	—

KM# 160a NEW SHEQEL
3.4500 g., Nickel Clad Steel, 17.97 mm. **Obv:** Value **Rev:** Lily, state emblem and ancient Hebrew inscription **Edge:** Plain

Date	Mintage	F	VF	XF	Unc	BU
JE5761 (2001)(h)	9,648,000	—	—	—	1.00	—
JE5762 (2002)(h)	18,816,000	—	—	—	1.00	—
JE5763 (2003)(v)	10,198,500	—	—	—	1.00	—
JE5765 (2005)	—	—	—	—	1.00	—
JE5766 (2006)	—	—	—	—	1.00	—
Note: Coin alignment error exists. Value: $100 in Unc, $50 in XF.						
JE5767 (2007)	—	—	—	—	1.00	—
JE5768 (2008)	—	—	—	—	1.00	—
JE5769 (2009)	—	—	—	—	1.00	—
JE5770 (2010)	—	—	—	—	0.75	—

KM# 344 NEW SHEQEL
14.4000 g., 0.9250 Silver 0.4282 oz. ASW, 30 mm. **Series:** Independence Day **Subject:** Education **Obv:** Denomination **Rev:** Pomegranate full of symbols - Hebrew 'ABC-123', etc. **Rev. Designer:** Asher Kalderon **Edge:** Plain

Date	Mintage	F	VF	XF	Unc	BU
JE5761-2001(u) Prooflike	1,653	—	—	—	—	35.00

KM# 351 NEW SHEQEL
14.4000 g., 0.9250 Silver 0.4282 oz. ASW, 30 mm. **Series:** Art and the culture in Israel **Subject:** Music **Obv:** National arms and denomination **Rev:** Musical instruments **Edge:** Plain

Date	Mintage	F	VF	XF	Unc	BU
JE5761-2001(u) Prooflike	1,182	—	—	—	—	30.00

KM# 163 NEW SHEQEL
4.0000 g., Copper-Nickel, 18 mm. **Subject:** Hanukka **Obv:** Value **Rev:** Lily, state emblem and ancient Hebrew inscription. **Note:** Coins dated JE5754-5769 have the Star of David mint mark; the JE5746-5753 coins do not.

Date	Mintage	F	VF	XF	Unc	BU
JE5761 (2001)(u)	4,000	—	—	—	4.00	—
Note: In sets only						
JE5770 (2010)	1,800	—	—	—	4.00	—
JE5762 (2002)(u)	4,000	—	—	—	4.00	—
Note: In sets only						
JE5763 (2003)(u)	3,000	—	—	—	4.00	—
Note: In sets only						
JE5764 (2004)(u)	3,000	—	—	—	4.00	—
Note: In sets only						
JE5765 (2005)(u)	2,500	—	—	—	4.00	—
Note: In sets only						
JE5766 (2006)(u)	3,000	—	—	—	4.00	—
Note: In sets only						
JE5767 (2007)(u)	3,000	—	—	—	4.00	—
Note: In sets only						
JE5768 (2008)(u)	3,000	—	—	—	4.00	—
Note: In sets only.						
JE59769 (2009)	1,800	—	—	—	4.00	—
Note: In sets only						

KM# 356 NEW SHEQEL
14.4000 g., 0.9250 Silver 0.4282 oz. ASW, 30 mm. **Series:** Independence Day **Subject:** Volunteering **Obv:** Denomination **Rev:** Heart in hands **Edge:** Plain

Date	Mintage	F	VF	XF	Unc	BU
JE5762-2002(o) Prooflike	1,364	—	—	—	—	30.00

KM# 359 NEW SHEQEL
14.4000 g., 0.9250 Silver 0.4282 oz. ASW, 30 mm. **Series:** Biblical Art **Subject:** Tower of Babel **Obv:** National arms in spiral inscription **Rev:** Tower of Hebrew verses **Edge:** Plain

Date	Mintage	F	VF	XF	Unc	BU
JE5762 (2002)(o) Prooflike	1,312	—	—	—	—	50.00

KM# 371 NEW SHEQEL
14.4000 g., 0.9250 Silver 0.4282 oz. ASW, 30 mm. **Subject:** Space Exploration **Obv:** "Ofeq" satellite in orbit **Rev:** "Shavit" rocket **Edge Lettering:** Hebrew: "In memory of Ilan Ramon and his colleagues in the Columbia"

Date	Mintage	F	VF	XF	Unc	BU
JE5763-2003(v) Prooflike	1,233	—	—	—	—	40.00

KM# 374 NEW SHEQEL
14.4000 g., 0.9250 Silver 0.4282 oz. ASW, 30 mm. **Series:** Biblical Art **Subject:** Jacob and Rachel **Obv:** Value **Rev:** Jacob and Rachel floating in air **Edge:** Plain

Date	Mintage	F	VF	XF	Unc	BU
JE5763-2003(u) Prooflike	1,661	—	—	—	—	40.00

KM# 380 NEW SHEQEL
14.4000 g., 0.9250 Silver 0.4282 oz. ASW, 30 mm. **Series:** Independence Day **Obv:** Value **Rev:** Parent and child **Edge:** Plain

Date	Mintage	F	VF	XF	Unc	BU
JE5764-2004(u)	1,446	—	—	—	—	30.00

KM# 383 NEW SHEQEL
14.4000 g., 0.9250 Silver 0.4282 oz. ASW, 30 mm. **Subject:** 2004 Summer Olympics **Obv:** Four windsurfers, value and national arms **Rev:** Eight windsurfers **Edge:** Plain

Date	Mintage	F	VF	XF	Unc	BU
JE5764-2004(v) Prooflike	2,800	—	—	—	—	30.00

KM# 386 NEW SHEQEL
14.4000 g., 0.9250 Silver 0.4282 oz. ASW, 30 mm. **Series:** Biblical Art **Subject:** Burning Bush **Obv:** Burning twig and value **Rev:** Burning Bush **Edge:** Plain

Date	Mintage	F	VF	XF	Unc	BU
JE5764-2004(v)	1,274	—	—	—	—	55.00

KM# 377 NEW SHEQEL
14.4000 g., 0.9250 Silver 0.4282 oz. ASW, 30 mm. **Series:** Art and culture in Israel **Subject:** Architecture and design **Obv:** Value **Rev:** Architectural design **Edge:** Plain **Note:** With enamel.

Date	Mintage	F	VF	XF	Unc	BU
JE5764-2004(u)	930	—	—	—	—	30.00

KM# 405 NEW SHEQEL
1.2440 g., 0.9990 Gold 0.0400 oz. AGW, 13.92 mm. **Series:** Biblical Art **Subject:** Jacob and Rachel **Obv:** Value **Rev:** Jacob and Rachel floating in air **Edge:** Reeded

Date	Mintage	F	VF	XF	Unc	BU
JE5764 (2004)(u) Proof	6,057	Value: 75.00				

KM# 405a NEW SHEQEL
1.2440 g., 0.9990 Gold 0.0400 oz. AGW, 13.92 mm. **Series:** Biblical art **Subject:** Jacob and Rachel **Obv:** Value **Rev:** Jacob and Rachel floating in air. Arabic legend Israel is mispelled **Edge:** Reeded

Date	Mintage	F	VF	XF	Unc	BU
JE5764 (2004)(u) Proof	682	Value: 120				

KM# 406 NEW SHEQEL
14.4000 g., 0.9250 Silver 0.4282 oz. ASW, 30 mm. **Subject:** FIFA 2006 World Cup **Obv:** Value and soccer ball **Rev:** Map and soccer ball **Edge:** Plain

Date	Mintage	F	VF	XF	Unc	BU
JE5764-2004(u) Prooflike	Est. 2,800	—	—	—	—	40.00
Note: Issued in 2006						

KM# 412 NEW SHEQEL
14.4000 g., 0.9250 Silver 0.4282 oz. ASW, 30 mm. **Series:** Art and culture in Israel **Subject:** Naomi Shemer **Obv:** Value **Rev:** Portrait of Naomi Shemer **Edge:** Plain

Date	Mintage	F	VF	XF	Unc	BU
JE5765-2005(u) Prooflike	1,100	—	—	—	—	35.00

KM# 396 NEW SHEQEL
14.4000 g., 0.9250 Silver 0.4282 oz. ASW, 30 mm. **Subject:** Einstein's Relativity Theory **Obv:** Concentric circles above equation **Rev:** Value above signature

Date	Mintage	F	VF	XF	Unc	BU
JE5765-2005(v) Prooflike	Est. 1,100	—	—	—	—	40.00

KM# 399 NEW SHEQEL
14.4000 g., 0.9250 Silver 0.4282 oz. ASW, 30 mm. **Series:** Biblical Art **Subject:** Moses and the Ten Commandments **Obv:** Ten Commandments and value **Rev:** Moses and the Ten Commandments

Date	Mintage	F	VF	XF	Unc	BU
JE5765-2005(u) Prooflike	1,400	—	—	—	—	55.00

KM# 402 NEW SHEQEL
14.4000 g., 0.9250 Silver 0.4282 oz. ASW, 30 mm. **Subject:** Israel 57th Anniversary **Obv:** Value and olive branch **Rev:** Twisted olive tree

Date	Mintage	F	VF	XF	Unc	BU
JE5765-2005(u) Prooflike	Est. 1,100	—	—	—	—	45.00

KM# 409 NEW SHEQEL

14.4000 g., 0.9250 Silver 0.4282 oz. ASW, 30 mm. **Series:** Biblical Art **Subject:** Abraham and the Three Angels **Obv:** Value and stars **Rev:** Abraham and the three angels **Edge:** Reeded

Date	Mintage	F	VF	XF	Unc	BU
JE5766-2006(ig)	Est. 1,800	—	—	—	—	50.00

KM# 416 NEW SHEQEL

14.4000 g., 0.9250 Silver 0.4282 oz. ASW, 30 mm. **Series:** Independence Day **Subject:** Higher Education in Israel **Obv:** Value and design **Rev:** Symbols of Science, Humanities, Technology and Mathematics **Edge:** Plain

Date	Mintage	F	VF	XF	Unc	BU
JE5766-2006(ig)	737	—	—	—	—	50.00

KM# 419 NEW SHEQEL

14.4000 g., 0.9250 Silver 0.4282 oz. ASW, 30 mm. **Subject:** UNESCO World Heritage Site; White City of Tel Aviv **Obv:** Value and Bauhaus building **Rev:** Fall of Bauhaus style building and UNESCO symbol **Edge:** Plain

Date	Mintage	F	VF	XF	Unc	BU
JE5766-2006(ig)	Est. 1,200	—	—	—	—	50.00

KM# 423 NEW SHEQEL

14.4000 g., 0.9250 Silver 0.4282 oz. ASW, 30 mm. **Series:** Independence Day **Subject:** Performing Arts in Israel **Obv:** Value, state emblem and inscriptions **Rev:** Stylized actor, dancer and musician and inscription in Hebrew, English and Arabic, Performing Arts in Israel **Edge:** Plain

Date	Mintage	F	VF	XF	Unc	BU
JE5767-2007(ig) Prooflike	Est. 1,200	—	—	—	—	55.00

KM# 426 NEW SHEQEL

14.4000 g., 0.9250 Silver 0.4282 oz. ASW, 30 mm. **Subject:** 2008 Olympics - Judo **Obv:** Value, state emblem, judo belt and inscriptions **Rev:** 2 judo athletes and inscriptions in Hebrew, English and Arabic **Edge:** Plain

Date	Mintage	F	VF	XF	Unc	BU
JE5767-2007(u) Prooflike	Est. 2,800	—	—	—	—	50.00

KM# 429 NEW SHEQEL

14.4000 g., 0.9250 Silver 0.4282 oz. ASW, 30 mm. **Series:** Isaiah, Wolf with the Lamb **Subject:** Biblical Art **Obv:** Value, state emblem and inscriptions in Hebrew, English and Arabic **Obv. Inscription:** And the Wolf shall dwell with the Lamb **Rev:** Wolf and lamb lying together under a tree **Edge:** Plain

Date	Mintage	F	VF	XF	Unc	BU
JE5767-2007(v)	Est. 1,800	—	—	—	—	60.00

KM# 437 NEW SHEQEL

1.2440 g., 0.9990 Gold 0.0400 oz. AGW, 13.92 mm. **Series:** Biblical Art **Subject:** Abraham and the Angels **Obv:** Value, state emblem and Moses in Hebrew, English and Arabic **Rev:** Abraham greeting three angels **Edge:** Reeded

Date	Mintage	F	VF	XF	Unc	BU
JE5767-2007(v) Proof	Est. 5,000	Value: 92.00				

KM# 438 NEW SHEQEL

1.2440 g., 0.9990 Gold 0.0400 oz. AGW, 13.92 mm. **Series:** Biblical Art **Subject:** Moses and the Ten Commandments **Obv:** Value, state emblem and Moses in Hebrew **Rev:** Moses holding the Ten Commandments **Edge:** Reeded

Date	Mintage	F	VF	XF	Unc	BU
JE5767-2007 Proof	Est. 5,000	Value: 92.00				

KM# 439 NEW SHEQEL

14.4000 g., 0.9250 Silver 0.4282 oz. ASW, 30 mm. **Series:** Israeli Nobel Prize Laureates **Subject:** Shmuel Yosef Agnon **Obv:** Value, state emblem, outline of Agnon **Rev:** Portrait of Agnon **Edge:** Plain

Date	Mintage	F	VF	XF	Unc	BU
JE5768-2008(ig) Prooflike	Est. 666	—	—	—	—	55.00

KM# 440 NEW SHEQEL

1.2440 g., 0.9990 Gold 0.0400 oz. AGW, 13.92 mm. **Series:** Biblical Art **Subject:** Isaiah, Wolf with the Lamb **Obv:** Value, state emblem, and inscriptions **Rev:** Wolf and lamb lying under tree **Edge:** Reeded

Date	Mintage	F	VF	XF	Unc	BU
JE5768-2008(v) Proof	5,000	Value: 92.00				

KM# 441 NEW SHEQEL

14.4000 g., 0.9250 Silver 0.4282 oz. ASW, 30 mm. **Series:** Independence Day **Subject:** Israel's Sixtieth Anniversary **Obv:** Value, state emblem and inscriptions including "Independence Day" **Rev:** "60" the zero is shaped like a pomegranite and a dove

Date	Mintage	F	VF	XF	Unc	BU
JE5768-2008(v) Prooflike	Est. 1,800	—	—	—	—	60.00

KM# 442 NEW SHEQEL

14.4000 g., 0.9250 Silver 0.4282 oz. ASW, 30 mm. **Subject:** Israel Defense Forces Reserves **Obv:** Triangle, state emblem and inscription **Rev:** Teddy bear pendant over soldier's ID tag

Date	Mintage	F	VF	XF	Unc	BU
JE5768-2008(ig) Prooflike	Est. 1,200	—	—	—	—	60.00

KM# 443 NEW SHEQEL

1.2440 g., 0.9990 Gold 0.0400 oz. AGW, 13.92 mm. **Series:** Biblical Art **Subject:** Parting of the Red Sea **Obv:** Value, state emblem and inscriptions **Rev:** Israelites passing through the Red Sea **Edge:** Reeded

Date	Mintage	F	VF	XF	Unc	BU
JE5769-2008(v) Proof	Est. 5,000	Value: 100				

KM# 444 NEW SHEQEL

14.4000 g., 0.9250 Silver 0.4282 oz. ASW, 30 mm. **Series:** Biblical Art **Subject:** Parting of the Red Sea **Obv:** Value, state emblem and inscriptions **Rev:** Israelites passing through the Red Sea

Date	Mintage	F	VF	XF	Unc	BU
JE5769-2008(v) Prooflike	Est. 1,800	—	—	—	—	60.00

KM# 453 NEW SHEQEL

14.4000 g., 0.9250 Silver 0.4282 oz. ASW, 30 mm. **Series:** UNESCO World Heritage Sites **Subject:** Masada **Obv:** Value, state emblem, image of Masada **Rev:** View of Masada, UNESCO emblem, World Heritage Site emblem **Edge:** Plain

Date	Mintage	F	VF	XF	Unc	BU
JE5769 (2009)(u) Prooflike	Est. 1,800	—	—	—	—	60.00

KM# 456 NEW SHEQEL

14.4000 g., 0.9250 Silver 0.4282 oz. ASW, 30 mm. **Subject:** Israel's sixty-first anniversary **Obv:** Value, state emblem, finch **Rev:** Three birds, hoopoe, warbler and finch **Edge:** Plain

Date	Mintage	F	VF	XF	Unc	BU
JE5769 (2009)(u) Prooflike	1,800	—	—	—	—	60.00

KM# 459 NEW SHEQEL

14.4000 g., 0.9250 Silver 0.4282 oz. ASW, 30 mm. **Subject:** 2010 FIFA World Cup South Africa **Obv:** Soccer Player, ball, outline of globe, value, state emblem **Rev:** Soccer ball with design **Edge:** Plain

Date	Mintage	F	VF	XF	Unc	BU
JE5769 (2009)(u) Prooflike	Est. 1,800	—	—	—	—	55.00

KM# 462 NEW SHEQEL

1.2440 g., 0.9990 Gold 0.0400 oz. AGW, 13.92 mm. **Series:** Biblical Art **Subject:** Samson and the Lion **Obv:** Small stylized palm tree, value, state emblem **Rev:** Stylized Samson wrestling a lion and small stylized palm tree **Edge:** Reeded

Date	Mintage	F	VF	XF	Unc	BU
JE5769 (2009)(u) Proof	Est. 5,000	Value: 100				

KM# 463 NEW SHEQEL

14.4000 g., 0.9250 Silver 0.4282 oz. ASW, 30 mm. **Series:** Biblical Art **Subject:** Samson and the Lion **Obv:** Small stylized palm tree, value, state emblem **Rev:** Stylized Samson wrestling a lion and small stylized palm tree **Edge:** Plain

Date	Mintage	F	VF	XF	Unc	BU
JE5769 (2009)(u) Prooflike	Est. 1,800	—	—	—	—	60.00

KM# 468 NEW SHEQEL

14.4000 g., 0.9250 Silver 0.4282 oz. ASW, 30 mm. **Subject:** UNESCO World Sites, Old Akko (Acre) **Obv:** Fortress of Akko as seen agains backdrop of Mediterranean Sea, state emblem, value UNESCO logo **Rev:** Ancient fortress walls, Khan-el-Undan caravanseraie and its clock tower, underground Crussader Knights' hall, White Mosque and other buildings **Edge:** Plain

Date	Mintage	F	VF	XF	Unc	BU
JE5770 (2010)(h) Prooflike	Est. 1,800	—	—	—	—	60.00

KM# 471 NEW SHEQEL

14.4000 g., 0.9250 Silver 0.4282 oz. ASW, 30 mm. **Series:** Independence Day **Subject:** Independence Day, 62nd Anniversary **Obv:** Trail forming stylized 62, state emblem **Obv. Designer:** Meir Eshel **Rev:** Map of Isreal highlighting trail, boot, flowers **Rev. Designer:** Galia Erez **Edge:** Plain

Date	Mintage	F	VF	XF	Unc	BU
JE5770-2010(h) Prooflike	Est. 1,800	—	—	—	—	60.00

KM# 474 NEW SHEQEL

1.2440 g., 0.9990 Gold 0.0400 oz. AGW, 13.92 mm. **Subject:** Biblical Art - Jonah in the whale **Obv:** Small image of Jonah, value, state emblem **Rev:** Stylized Jonah in belly of whale **Edge:** Reeded

Date	Mintage	F	VF	XF	Unc	BU
JE5770-2010(v) Proof	Est. 5,000	Value: 125				

KM# 475 NEW SHEQEL

14.4000 g., 0.9250 Silver 0.4282 oz. ASW, 30 mm. **Subject:** Biblical Art - Jonah in the whale **Obv:** Small image of Jonah, value, state emblem **Rev:** Stylized Jonah in belly of whale **Edge:** Plain

Date	Mintage	F	VF	XF	Unc	BU
JE5770-2010(v) Prooflike	Est. 1,800	—	—	—	—	65.00

KM# 478 NEW SHEQEL

14.4000 g., 0.9250 Silver 0.4282 oz. ASW, 30 mm. **Subject:** Israeli Nobel Prize Laureates **Obv:** Menachem Begin, Jimmy Carter Anwar Sadat in triple handshake on White House lawn **Rev:** Portrait of Begin **Edge:** Plain

Date	Mintage	F	VF	XF	Unc	BU
JE5771-2010(u) Prooflike	Est. 2,800	—	—	—	—	65.00

KM# 476 2 SHEQALIM

28.8000 g., 0.9250 Silver 0.8565 oz. ASW, 38.7 mm. **Subject:** Biblical Art - Jonah in the Whale **Obv:** Small image of Jonah, value, state emblem **Rev:** Stylized Jonah in belly of whale **Edge:** Reeded

Date	Mintage	F	VF	XF	Unc	BU
JE5770-2010(v) Proof	Est. 2,800	Value: 95.00				

KM# 352 2 NEW SHEQALIM

28.8000 g., 0.9250 Silver 0.8565 oz. ASW, 38.7 mm. **Series:** Art and culture in Israel **Subject:** Music **Obv:** National arms and denomination **Rev:** Musical instruments **Edge:** Reeded

Date	Mintage	F	VF	XF	Unc	BU
JE5761-2001(u) Proof	1,747	Value: 50.00				

KM# 349 2 NEW SHEQALIM

28.8000 g., 0.9250 Silver 0.8565 oz. ASW, 38.7 mm. **Series:** Wildlife **Subject:** Wild goat and acacia tree **Obv:** Acacia tree **Rev:** Ibex **Edge:** Reeded

Date	Mintage	F	VF	XF	Unc	BU
JE5761-2000(u) Proof	2,000	Value: 55.00				

KM# 345 2 NEW SHEQALIM

28.8000 g., 0.9250 Silver 0.8565 oz. ASW, 38.7 mm. **Series:** Independence Day **Subject:** Education **Obv:** Denomination **Rev:** Pomegranate full of symbols **Edge:** Reeded **Designer:** Asher Kalderon

Date	Mintage	F	VF	XF	Unc	BU
JE5761-2001(u) Proof	1,847	Value: 55.00				

KM# 357 2 NEW SHEQALIM

28.8000 g., 0.9250 Silver 0.8565 oz. ASW, 38.7 mm. **Series:** Volunteering **Subject:** Independence Day **Obv:** Denomination **Rev:** Heart in hands **Edge:** Reeded

Date	Mintage	F	VF	XF	Unc	BU
JE5762-2002(o) Proof	1,426	Value: 60.00				

KM# 360 2 NEW SHEQALIM

28.8000 g., 0.9250 Silver 0.8565 oz. ASW, 38.7 mm. **Series:** Biblical Art **Subject:** Tower of Babel **Obv:** National arms in spiral inscription **Rev:** Tower of Hebrew verses **Edge:** Reeded

Date	Mintage	F	VF	XF	Unc	BU
JE5762-2002(o) Proof	1,295	Value: 90.00				

KM# 372 2 NEW SHEQALIM

28.8000 g., 0.9250 Silver 0.8565 oz. ASW, 38.7 mm. **Subject:** Space Exploration **Obv:** "Amos" satellite in orbit **Rev:** "Shavit" rocket **Edge Lettering:** Hebrew: "In memory of Ilan Ramon and his colleagues in the Columbia"

Date	Mintage	F	VF	XF	Unc	BU
JE5763-2003(v) Proof	1,249	Value: 65.00				

KM# 375 2 NEW SHEQALIM

28.8000 g., 0.9250 Silver 0.8565 oz. ASW, 38.7 mm. **Series:** Biblical Art **Subject:** Jacob and Rachel **Obv:** Value **Rev:** Figures floating in air above flower and sheep **Edge:** Reeded

Date	Mintage	F	VF	XF	Unc	BU
JE5763-2003(u) Proof	1,377	Value: 60.00				

KM# 378 2 NEW SHEQALIM
28.8000 g., 0.9250 Silver 0.8565 oz. ASW, 38.7 mm. **Series:** Art and culture in Israel **Subject:** Architecture and design **Obv:** Value and enameled shapes **Rev:** Architectural design **Edge:** Reeded

Date	Mintage	F	VF	XF	Unc	BU
JE5764-2004(u) Proof	1,084	Value: 60.00				

KM# 381 2 NEW SHEQALIM
28.8000 g., 0.9250 Silver 0.8565 oz. ASW, 38.7 mm. **Series:** Independence Day **Subject:** Parent and child **Obv:** Value and stylized human shapes **Rev:** Stylized parent and child **Edge:** Reeded

Date	Mintage	F	VF	XF	Unc	BU
JE5764-2004(u) Proof	1,182	Value: 60.00				

KM# 384 2 NEW SHEQALIM
28.8000 g., 0.9250 Silver 0.8565 oz. ASW, 38.7 mm. **Subject:** 2004 Summer Olympics **Obv:** Four windsurfers, value and national arms **Rev:** Eight windsurfers **Edge:** Reeded

Date	Mintage	F	VF	XF	Unc	BU
JE5764-2004(v) Proof	2,800	Value: 55.00				

KM# 387 2 NEW SHEQALIM
28.8000 g., 0.9250 Silver 0.8565 oz. ASW, 38.7 mm. **Series:** Burning Bush **Subject:** Biblical Art **Obv:** Burning twig and value **Rev:** Burning Bush **Edge:** Reeded

Date	Mintage	F	VF	XF	Unc	BU
JE5764-2004(v) Proof	1,354	Value: 90.00				

KM# 407 2 NEW SHEQALIM
28.8000 g., 0.9250 Silver 0.8565 oz. ASW, 38.7 mm. **Subject:** FIFA 2006 World Cup **Obv:** Value and soccer ball **Rev:** Map and soccer ball **Edge:** Reeded

Date	Mintage	F	VF	XF	Unc	BU
JE5764-2004(u) Proof	Est. 5,000	Value: 65.00				

Note: Issued in 2006

KM# 413 2 NEW SHEQALIM
28.8000 g., 0.9250 Silver 0.8565 oz. ASW, 38.7 mm. **Series:** Art and culture in Israel **Subject:** Noami Shemer **Obv:** Value **Rev:** Portrait of Naomi Shemer **Edge:** Reeded

Date	Mintage	F	VF	XF	Unc	BU
JE5765-2005(u) Proof	1,100	Value: 65.00				

KM# 397 2 NEW SHEQALIM
28.8000 g., 0.9250 Silver 0.8565 oz. ASW, 38.7 mm. **Subject:** Einstein's Relativity Theory **Obv:** Concentric circles above equation **Rev:** Value above signature

Date	Mintage	F	VF	XF	Unc	BU
JE5765-2005(v) Proof	Est. 1,600	Value: 75.00				

KM# 400 2 NEW SHEQALIM
28.8000 g., 0.9250 Silver 0.8565 oz. ASW, 38.7 mm. **Series:** Biblical Art **Subject:** Moses and Ten Commandments **Obv:** Ten Commandments and value **Rev:** Moses and Ten Commandments

Date	Mintage	F	VF	XF	Unc	BU
JE5765-2005(u) Proof	1,400	Value: 100				

KM# 403 2 NEW SHEQALIM
28.8000 g., 0.9250 Silver 0.8565 oz. ASW, 38.7 mm. **Series:** Independence Day **Subject:** Israel 57th Anniversary **Obv:** Value and olive branch **Rev:** Twisted olive tree **Edge:** Reeded

Date	Mintage	F	VF	XF	Unc	BU
JE5765-2005(u) Proof	1,100	Value: 60.00				

KM# 417 2 NEW SHEQALIM
28.8000 g., 0.9250 Silver 0.8565 oz. ASW, 38.7 mm. **Series:** Independence Day **Subject:** Higher Education in Israel **Obv:** Value and design **Rev:** Symbols of Science, Humanities, Technology and Mathematics **Edge:** Reeded

Date	Mintage	F	VF	XF	Unc	BU
JE5766-2006(ig) Proof	846	Value: 65.00				

KM# 410 2 NEW SHEQALIM
28.8000 g., 0.9250 Silver 0.8565 oz. ASW, 38.7 mm. **Series:** Biblical Art **Subject:** Abraham and the Three Angels **Obv:** Value and stars **Rev:** Abraham and the three angels **Edge:** Reeded

Date	Mintage	F	VF	XF	Unc	BU
JE5766-2006(ig) Proof	2,800	Value: 70.00				

KM# 420 2 NEW SHEQALIM
28.8000 g., 0.9250 Silver 0.8565 oz. ASW, 38.7 mm. **Series:** UNESCO World Heritage Site **Subject:** White Cityof Tel Aviv **Obv:** Value and Bauhaus building **Rev:** Fall of Bauhaus building and UNESCO symbol **Edge:** Reeded

Date	Mintage	F	VF	XF	Unc	BU
JE5766-2006(ig) Proof	Est. 1,200	Value: 75.00				

KM# 424 2 NEW SHEQALIM
28.8900 g., 0.9250 Silver 0.8591 oz. ASW, 38.7 mm. **Subject:** Performing Arts in Israel **Obv:** Value, state emblem and inscriptions **Rev:** Stylized actor, dancer and musician and inscription in Hebrew, English and Arabiv **Edge:** Reeded

Date	Mintage	F	VF	XF	Unc	BU
JE5767-2007(ig) Proof	Est. 1,200	Value: 75.00				

KM# 427 2 NEW SHEQALIM
28.8000 g., 0.9250 Silver 0.8565 oz. ASW, 38.7 mm. **Subject:** 2008 Olympics - Judo **Obv:** Value, state emblem, judo belt and inscriptions **Rev:** 2 judo athletes and inscriptions **Edge:** Reeded

Date	Mintage	F	VF	XF	Unc	BU
JE5767-2007(u) Proof	Est. 2,800	Value: 75.00				

KM# 430 2 NEW SHEQALIM
28.8000 g., 0.9250 Silver 0.8565 oz. ASW, 38.7 mm. **Subject:** Biblical Art - Isaiah, Wolf with the Lamb **Obv:** Value, state emblem and inscriptions in Hebrew, English and Arabic **Obv. Inscription:** And the Wolf shall dwell with the Lamb **Rev:** Wolf and lamb lying together under a tree **Edge:** Reeded

Date	Mintage	F	VF	XF	Unc	BU
JE5767-2007(v) Proof	Est. 2,800	Value: 80.00				

KM# 432 2 NEW SHEQALIM
5.7000 g., Nickel Plated Steel, 21.6 mm. **Subject:** Hanukka **Obv:** Value, date, inscriptions and menorah **Rev:** Double cornucopiae (horns of plenty) draped in ribbons and filled with fruit and grain including a pomegranate **Edge:** Plain with 4 notches

Date	Mintage	F	VF	XF	Unc	BU
JE5768 (2008)(u)	3,000	—	—	—	5.00	—
Note: In sets only						
JE5769-2009(u)	1,800	—	—	—	5.00	—
Note: In sets only						
JE5770 (2010)(u)	1,800	—	—	—	5.00	—
Note: In sets only						

KM# 433 2 NEW SHEQALIM
5.7000 g., Nickel Plated Steel, 21.6 mm. **Obv:** Value, date and inscriptions **Rev:** Double cornucopiae (horns of plenty) draped in ribbons and filled with fruit and grain including a pomegranate **Edge:** Plain with 4 notches

Date	Mintage	F	VF	XF	Unc	BU
JE5768 (2008)(u)	Est. 26,000,000	—	—	—	1.50	—
JE5769 (2009)(u)	—	—	—	—	1.50	—

KM# 445 2 NEW SHEQALIM
28.8000 g., 0.9250 Silver 0.8565 oz. ASW, 38.7 mm. **Series:** Israeli Nobel Prize Laureates **Subject:** Shmuel Yosef Agnon **Obv:** Value, state emblem and outline of Agnon **Rev:** Portrait of Agnon **Edge:** Reeded

Date	Mintage	F	VF	XF	Unc	BU
JE5768-2008(ig) Proof	666	Value: 80.00				

KM# 446 2 NEW SHEQALIM
28.8000 g., 0.8565 Silver 0.7930 oz. ASW, 38.7 mm. **Series:** Independence Day **Subject:** Israel's 60th Anniversary **Obv:** Value, state emblem and inscription "Independence Day" **Rev:** "60" the zero is shaped like a pomegranate and a dove

Date	Mintage	F	VF	XF	Unc	BU
JE5768-2008(v) Proof	1,800	Value: 85.00				

KM# 447 2 NEW SHEQALIM
28.8000 g., 0.9250 Silver 0.8565 oz. ASW, 38.7 mm. **Subject:** Israel Defense Forces Reserves **Obv:** Triangle, state emblem and inscription **Rev:** Teddy bear pendant over a soldier's ID tag

Date	Mintage	F	VF	XF	Unc	BU
JE5768-2008(ig) Proof	Est. 1,200	Value: 85.00				

KM# 448 2 NEW SHEQALIM
28.8000 g., 0.9250 Silver 0.8565 oz. ASW, 38.7 mm. **Series:** Biblical Art **Subject:** Parting of the Red Sea **Obv:** Value, state emblem and inscriptions **Rev:** Israelites passing through the Red Sea **Edge:** Reeded

Date	Mintage	F	VF	XF	Unc	BU
JE5769-2008(v) Proof	1,800	Value: 86.00				

KM# 454 2 NEW SHEQALIM
28.8000 g., 0.9250 Silver 0.8565 oz. ASW, 38.7 mm. **Series:** UNESCO World Heritage sites **Subject:** Masada **Obv:** Value, state emblem, image of Masada **Rev:** View of Masada, UNESCO emblem, World Heritage Site emblem **Edge:** Reeded

Date	Mintage	F	VF	XF	Unc	BU
JE5769 (2009)(u) Proof	Est. 1,800	Value: 90.00				

KM# 457 2 NEW SHEQALIM
28.8000 g., 0.9250 Silver 0.8565 oz. ASW, 38.7 mm. **Series:** Indepdence Day **Subject:** Israel's sixty-first anniversary **Obv:** Value, state emblem, hoopoe **Rev:** Three birds, hoopoe, warbler and finch **Edge:** Reeded

Date	Mintage	F	VF	XF	Unc	BU
JE5769 (2009)(u) Proof	Est. 2,800	Value: 90.00				

KM# 460 2 NEW SHEQALIM
28.8000 g., 0.9250 Silver 0.8565 oz. ASW, 38.7 mm. **Subject:** 2010 FIFA World Cup South Africa **Obv:** Soccer Player, ball, outline of globe **Rev:** Soccer player with design **Edge:** Reeded

Date	Mintage	F	VF	XF	Unc	BU
JE5769 (2009)(u) Proof	Est. 5,000	Value: 90.00				

KM# 464 2 NEW SHEQALIM
28.8000 g., 0.9250 Silver 0.8565 oz. ASW, 38.7 mm. **Series:** Biblical Art **Subject:** Samson and the Lion **Obv:** Small stylized palm tree, value, state emblem **Rev:** Stylized Samson wrestling with a lion and small stylized palm tree **Edge:** Reeded

Date	Mintage	F	VF	XF	Unc	BU
JE5769 (2009)(u) Proof	Est. 2,800	Value: 90.00				

KM# 469 2 NEW SHEQALIM
28.8000 g., 0.9250 Silver 0.8565 oz. ASW, 38.7 mm. **Subject:** UNESCO World Heritage site, Old Akko (Acre) **Obv:** Fortress of Akko as seen against backdrop of Mediterranean Sea, state emblem, value **Rev:** Ancient fortress walls, Khan-el-Umdan caravanseraie and its clock tower, underground Crusader Knights' Hall, White Mosque and other buildings **Edge:** Reeded

Date	Mintage	F	VF	XF	Unc	BU
JE5770 (2010)(h) Proof	Est. 2,800	Value: 90.00				

KM# 472 2 NEW SHEQALIM
28.8000 g., 0.9250 Silver 0.8565 oz. ASW, 38.7 mm. **Series:** Independence Day **Subject:** 62nd Anniversary **Obv:** Trail forming stylized 62, state emblem **Obv. Designer:** Meir Eshel **Rev:** Map of Israel highlighting national trail, boot, flowers **Rev. Designer:** Galia Erez **Edge:** Reeded

Date	Mintage	F	VF	XF	Unc	BU
JE5770-2010(h) Proof	Est. 1,800	Value: 90.00				

KM# 479 2 NEW SHEQALIM
28.8000 g., 0.9250 Silver 0.8565 oz. ASW, 28.8 mm. **Subject:** Israeli Nobel Pize Laureates - Menachem Begin **Obv:** Menachem Begin, Jimmy Carter and Anwar Sadat in triple handshake on White House lawn, state emblem **Rev:** Portrait of Menachem Begin **Edge:** Reeded

Date	Mintage	F	VF	XF	Unc	BU
JE5771-2010(u) Proof	Est. 2,800	Value: 95.00				

KM# 207 5 NEW SHEQALIM
8.2000 g., Copper-Nickel, 24 mm. **Obv:** Value **Rev:** Ancient column capitol **Edge:** Plain **Shape:** 12-sided

Date	Mintage	F	VF	XF	Unc	BU
JE5762 (2002)(o)	4,464,000	—	—	—	3.75	—
Note: The JE5762 coins are practically round.						
JE5765 (2005)	—	—	—	—	3.00	—
JE5766 (2006)	—	—	—	—	3.00	—
JE5768 (2008)	—	—	—	—	3.00	—
JE5769 (2009)	—	—	—	—	3.00	—

KM# 217 5 NEW SHEQALIM
8.2000 g., Copper-Nickel, 24 mm. **Obv:** Value, small menorah and inscription Hanukka **Rev:** Ancient column capitol **Note:** Coins dated JE5754-5770 have the Star of David mint mark; the JE5751-5753 coins do not.

Date	Mintage	F	VF	XF	Unc	BU
JE5762 (2002)(u)	4,000	—	—	—	7.00	—
Note: In sets only						
JE5763 (2003)(u)	3,000	—	—	—	8.00	—
Note: In sets only						
JE5764 (2004)(u)	3,000	—	—	—	8.00	—
Note: In sets only						
JE5765 (2005)(u)	2,500	—	—	—	8.00	—
Note: In sets only						
JE5766 (2006)(u)	3,000	—	—	—	8.00	—
Note: In sets only						
JE5767 (2007)(u)	3,000	—	—	—	8.00	—
Note: In sets only						
JE5768 (2008)(u)	3,000	—	—	—	8.00	—
Note: In sets only						
JE5769 (2009)(u)	1,800	—	—	—	8.00	—
Note: In sets only						
JE5770 (2010)(u)	1,800	—	—	—	8.00	—
Note: In sets only						

KM# 408 5 NEW SHEQALIM
7.7770 g., 0.9990 Gold 0.2498 oz. AGW, 27 mm. **Subject:** FIFA 2006 World Cup **Obv:** Value and soccer ball **Rev:** Map and soccer ball **Edge:** Reeded **Note:** Issued in 2006

Date	Mintage	F	VF	XF	Unc	BU
JE5764-2004(u) Proof	Est. 777	Value: 400				

KM# 461 5 NEW SHEQALIM
7.7700 g., 0.9990 Gold 0.2496 oz. AGW, 27 mm. **Subject:** 2010 FIFA World Cup South Africa **Obv:** Soccer Player, ball, outline of globe **Rev:** Soccer ball with design **Edge:** Reeded

Date	Mintage	F	VF	XF	Unc	BU
JE5769 (2009)(u) Proof	Est. 888	Value: 500				

KM# 315 10 NEW SHEQALIM
7.0000 g., Bi-Metallic Aureate bonded Bronze center in Nickel bonded Steel ring, 22.5 mm. **Subject:** Hanukka **Obv:** Value, text and menorah within circle and vertical lines **Rev:** Palm tree and baskets within half beaded circle

Date	Mintage	F	VF	XF	Unc	BU
JE5761 (2001)(u)	4,000	—	—	—	9.00	—
Note: In sets only						
JE5762 (2002)(u)	4,000	—	—	—	9.00	—
Note: In sets only						
JE5763 (2003)(u)	3,000	—	—	—	10.00	—
Note: In sets only						
JE5764 (2004)(u)	3,000	—	—	—	10.00	—
Note: In sets only						
JE5765 (2005)(u)	2,500	—	—	—	10.00	—
Note: In sets only						
JE5766 (2006)(u)	3,000	—	—	—	10.00	—
Note: In sets only						
JE5767 (2007)(u)	3,000	—	—	—	10.00	—
Note: In sets only						
JE5768 (2008)(u)	3,000	—	—	—	10.00	—
Note: In sets only						
JE5769 (2009)(u)	1,800	—	—	—	10.00	—
Note: In sets only						
JE5770 (2010)(u)	1,800	—	—	—	10.00	—
Note: In sets only						

KM# 346 10 NEW SHEQALIM
16.9600 g., 0.9170 Gold 0.5000 oz. AGW, 30 mm. **Subject:** Independence Day and Education **Obv:** Value **Rev:** Pomegranate full of symbols - Hebrew for 'ABC - 123', etc. **Edge:** Reeded **Designer:** Asher Kalderon

Date	Mintage	F	VF	XF	Unc	BU
JE5761-2001(u) Proof	660	Value: 775				

KM# 353 10 NEW SHEQALIM
16.9600 g., 0.9170 Gold 0.5000 oz. AGW, 30 mm. **Series:** Art and culture of Israel **Subject:** Music **Obv:** National arms and value **Rev:** Musical instruments **Edge:** Reeded

Date	Mintage	F	VF	XF	Unc	BU
JE5761-2001(u) Proof	766	Value: 775				

KM# 358 10 NEW SHEQALIM
16.9600 g., 0.9166 Gold 0.4998 oz. AGW, 30 mm. **Series:** Independence Day **Subject:** Volunteering **Obv:** Value **Rev:** Heart in hands **Edge:** Reeded

Date	Mintage	F	VF	XF	Unc	BU
JE5762-2002(o) Proof	617	Value: 800				

KM# 361 10 NEW SHEQALIM
16.9600 g., 0.9170 Gold 0.5000 oz. AGW, 30 mm. **Series:** Biblical Art **Subject:** Tower of Babel **Obv:** National arms in spiral inscription **Rev:** Tower of Hebrew verses **Edge:** Reeded

Date	Mintage	F	VF	XF	Unc	BU
JE5762-2002(o) Proof	750	Value: 825				

KM# 270 10 NEW SHEQALIM
7.0000 g., Bi-Metallic Aureate bonded Bronze center in Nickel bonded Steel ring, 22.95 mm. **Obv:** Value, vertical lines and text within circle **Rev:** Palm tree and baskets within half beaded circle **Edge:** Reeded

Date	Mintage	F	VF	XF	Unc	BU
JE5762 (2002)(h)	4,749,000	—	—	—	5.00	—
JE5765 (2005)	—	—	—	—	5.00	—
Note: Coin alignment error exists. Value: $200 in Unc, $100 in XF.						
JE5766 (2006)	—	—	—	—	5.00	—
JE5767 (2007)	—	—	—	—	5.00	—
JE5768 (2008)	—	—	—	—	5.00	—
JE5769 (2009)	—	—	—	—	5.00	—
JE5770 (2010)	—	—	—	—	5.00	—

KM# 373 10 NEW SHEQALIM
16.9600 g., 0.9170 Gold 0.5000 oz. AGW, 30 mm. **Subject:** Space Exploration **Obv:** "Eros" satellite in orbit **Rev:** "Shavit" rocket **Edge Lettering:** Hebrew: In memory of Ilan Ramon and his colleagues in the Columbia"

Date	Mintage	F	VF	XF	Unc	BU
JE5763-2003(v) Proof	573	Value: 825				

KM# 376 10 NEW SHEQALIM
16.9600 g., 0.9170 Gold 0.5000 oz. AGW, 30 mm. **Series:** Biblical Art **Subject:** Jacob and Rachel **Obv:** Value **Rev:** Jacob and Rachel floating in air above tree and sheep **Edge:** Reeded

Date	Mintage	F	VF	XF	Unc	BU
JE5763-2003(u) Proof	686	Value: 875				

KM# 379 10 NEW SHEQALIM
16.9600 g., 0.9170 Gold 0.5000 oz. AGW, 30 mm. **Series:** Art and culture in Israel **Subject:** Architecture and design **Obv:** Value **Rev:** Architectural design **Edge:** Reeded

Date	Mintage	F	VF	XF	Unc	BU
JE5764-2004(u) Proof	555	Value: 800				

KM# 382 10 NEW SHEQALIM
16.9600 g., 0.9170 Gold 0.5000 oz. AGW, 30 mm. **Series:** Independence Day **Obv:** Value **Rev:** Stylized parent and child **Edge:** Reeded

Date	Mintage	F	VF	XF	Unc	BU
JE5764-2004(u) Proof	539	Value: 800				

KM# 385 10 NEW SHEQALIM
16.9600 g., 0.9170 Gold 0.5000 oz. AGW, 30 mm. **Subject:** 2004 Summer Olympics **Obv:** Four windsurfers, value and national arms **Rev:** Eight windsurfers **Edge:** Reeded

Date	Mintage	F	VF	XF	Unc	BU
JE5764-2004(v) Proof	540	Value: 800				

KM# 388 10 NEW SHEQALIM
16.9600 g., 0.9170 Gold 0.5000 oz. AGW, 30 mm. **Series:** Biblical Art **Subject:** Burning Bush **Obv:** Burning twig and value **Rev:** Burning Bush **Edge:** Reeded

Date	Mintage	F	VF	XF	Unc	BU
JE5764-2004(v) Proof	555	Value: 825				

KM# 398 10 NEW SHEQALIM
16.9600 g., 0.9166 Gold 0.4998 oz. AGW, 30 mm. **Subject:** Einstein's Relativity Theory **Obv:** Concentric circles above equation **Rev:** Value above signature **Edge:** Reeded

Date	Mintage	F	VF	XF	Unc	BU
JE5765-2005(v) Proof	555	Value: 875				

KM# 401 10 NEW SHEQALIM
16.9600 g., 0.9166 Gold 0.4998 oz. AGW, 30 mm. **Series:** Biblical Art **Subject:** Moses and Ten Commandments **Obv:** Ten Commandments and value **Rev:** Moses and Ten Commandments **Edge:** Reeded

Date	Mintage	F	VF	XF	Unc	BU
JE5765-2005(u) Proof	555	Value: 850				

KM# 404 10 NEW SHEQALIM
16.9600 g., 0.9166 Gold 0.4998 oz. AGW, 30 mm. **Series:** Independence Day **Subject:** Israel 57th Anniversary - Golden years **Obv:** Value and olive branch **Rev:** Twisted olive tree **Edge:** Reeded

Date	Mintage	F	VF	XF	Unc	BU
JE5765-2005(u) Proof	485	Value: 825				

KM# 414 10 NEW SHEQALIM
16.9600 g., 0.9170 Gold 0.5000 oz. AGW, 30 mm. **Series:** Art and culture in Israel **Subject:** Naomi Shemer **Obv:** Value **Rev:** Portrait of Naomi Shemer **Edge:** Reeded

Date	Mintage	F	VF	XF	Unc	BU
JE5765-2005(u) Proof	455	Value: 800				

KM# 418 10 NEW SHEQALIM
16.9600 g., 0.9170 Gold 0.5000 oz. AGW, 30 mm. **Series:** Independence Day **Subject:** Higher Education in Israel **Obv:** Value and design **Rev:** Symbols of Science, Humanities, Technology and Mathematics **Edge:** Reeded

Date	Mintage	F	VF	XF	Unc	BU
JE5766-2006(ig) Proof	Est. 444	Value: 800				

KM# 411 10 NEW SHEQALIM
16.9600 g., 0.9170 Gold 0.5000 oz. AGW, 30 mm. **Series:** Biblical Art **Subject:** Abraham and the Three Angels **Obv:** Value and stars **Rev:** Abraham and the three angels **Edge:** Reeded

Date	Mintage	F	VF	XF	Unc	BU
JE5766-2006(ig) Proof	Est. 555	Value: 875				

KM# 421 10 NEW SHEQALIM
16.9600 g., 0.9170 Gold 0.5000 oz. AGW, 30 mm. **Series:** UNESCO World Heritage Site **Subject:** White City Tel Aviv **Obv:** Value and Bauhaus building **Rev:** Face of Bauhaus building and UNESCO symbol **Edge:** Reeded

Date	Mintage	F	VF	XF	Unc	BU
JE5766-2006(ig) Proof	Est. 555	Value: 800				

KM# 425 10 NEW SHEQALIM
16.9600 g., 0.9170 Gold 0.5000 oz. AGW, 30 mm. **Series:** Independence Day **Subject:** Performing Arts in Israel **Obv:** Value, state emblem and inscriptions **Rev:** Stylized actor, dancer and musician and inscription in Hebrew, English and Arabic, "Performing Arts in Israel" **Edge:** Reeded

Date	Mintage	F	VF	XF	Unc	BU
JE5767-2007(ig) Proof	Est. 444	Value: 825				

KM# 428 10 NEW SHEQALIM
16.9600 g., 0.9170 Gold 0.5000 oz. AGW, 30 mm. **Subject:** 2008 Olympics - Judo **Obv:** Value, state emblem, judo belt and inscriptions **Rev:** 2 judo athletes and inscriptions in Hebrew, English and Arabic **Edge:** Reeded

Date	Mintage	F	VF	XF	Unc	BU
JE5767 (2007)(u) Proof	Est. 555	Value: 800				

KM# 431 10 NEW SHEQALIM
16.9600 g., 0.9170 Gold 0.5000 oz. AGW, 30 mm. **Series:** Biblical Art **Subject:** Isaiah, Wolf with the Lamb **Obv:** Value, state emblem and inscriptions in Hebrew, English and Arabic **Obv. Inscription:** And the Wolf shall dwell with the Lamb **Rev:** Wolf and lamb lying together under a tree **Edge:** Reeded

Date	Mintage	F	VF	XF	Unc	BU
JE5767-2007(v) Proof	555	Value: 900				

KM# 452 10 NEW SHEQALIM
16.9600 g., 0.9170 Gold 0.5000 oz. AGW, 30 mm. **Series:** Biblical Art **Subject:** Parting of the Red Sea **Obv:** Value, state emblem and inscriptions **Rev:** Israelites passing through the Red Sea **Edge:** Reeded

Date	Mintage	F	VF	XF	Unc	BU
JE5769-2008(o) Proof	Est. 555	Value: 950				

KM# 449 10 NEW SHEQALIM
16.9600 g., 0.9170 Gold 0.5000 oz. AGW, 30 mm. **Series:** Israeli Nobel Prize Laureates **Subject:** Shmuel Yosef Agnon **Obv:** Value, state emblem and outline of Agnon **Rev:** Portrait of Agnon **Edge:** Reeded

Date	Mintage	F	VF	XF	Unc	BU
JE5768-2008(ig) Proof	Est. 444	Value: 825				

KM# 450 10 NEW SHEQALIM
16.9600 g., 0.9170 Gold 0.5000 oz. AGW, 30 mm. **Series:** Independence Day **Subject:** Israel's 60th Anniversary **Obv:** Value, state emblem and inscription "Independence Day" **Rev:** "60" the zero is shaped like a pomegranite and a dove **Edge:** Reeded

Date	Mintage	F	VF	XF	Unc	BU
JE5768-2008(v) Proof	444	Value: 850				

KM# 451 10 NEW SHEQALIM
16.9600 g., 0.9170 Gold 0.5000 oz. AGW, 30 mm. **Subject:** Israel Defense Force Reserves **Obv:** Value over a triangle, state emblem and inscriptions **Rev:** Teddy bear pendant over a soldier's ID tag **Edge:** Reeded

Date	Mintage	F	VF	XF	Unc	BU
JE5768-2008 Proof	Est. 444	Value: 850				

KM# 455 10 NEW SHEQALIM
16.9600 g., 0.9170 Gold 0.5000 oz. AGW, 30 mm. **Series:** UNESCO World Heritage Sites **Subject:** Masada **Obv:** Value, state emblem, image of Masada **Rev:** View of Masada, UNESCO emblem, World Heritage Site Emblem **Edge:** Reeded

Date	Mintage	F	VF	XF	Unc	BU
JE5679 (2009)(u) Proof	Est. 555	Value: 925				

KM# 458 10 NEW SHEQALIM
16.9600 g., 0.9170 Gold 0.5000 oz. AGW, 30 mm. **Subject:** Israel's sixty-first anniversary **Obv:** Value, state emblem, warbler **Rev:** Three birds, hoopoe, warbler and finch **Edge:** Reeded

Date	Mintage	F	VF	XF	Unc	BU
JE5769 (2009)(u) Proof	Est. 650	Value: 925				

KM# 465 10 NEW SHEQALIM
16.9600 g., 0.9170 Gold 0.5000 oz. AGW, 30 mm. **Series:** Biblical Art **Subject:** Samson and the Lion **Obv:** Small stylized palm tree, value, state emblem **Rev:** Stylized Samson wrestling a lion, stylized palm tree **Edge:** Reeded

Date	Mintage	F	VF	XF	Unc	BU
JE5769 (2009)(u) Proof	Est. 555	Value: 925				

KM# 470 10 NEW SHEQALIM
16.9600 g., 0.9170 Gold 0.5000 oz. AGW, 30 mm. **Series:** UNESCO World Heritage Site **Subject:** Old Akko (Acre) **Obv:** Fortress of Akko as seen against backdrop of Mediterranean Sea, state emblem, value **Rev:** Ancient fortress walls, Khan-el-Umdan caravanseraie and its clock tower, underground Crusader Knights' hall, White Mosque and other buildings **Edge:** Reeded

Date	Mintage	F	VF	XF	Unc	BU
JE5770 (2010)(h) Proof	Est. 555	Value: 925				

KM# 473 10 NEW SHEQALIM
16.9500 g., 0.9170 Gold 0.4997 oz. AGW, 30 mm. **Subject:** Independence Day, 62nd Anniversary **Obv:** Trail forming stylized 62, state emblem **Obv. Designer:** Meir Eskel **Rev:** Map of Israel highlighting trail, boot, flowers **Rev. Designer:** Galea Erez **Edge:** Reeded

Date	Mintage	F	VF	XF	Unc	BU
JE5770-2010(h) Proof	Est. 555	Value: 925				

KM# 477 10 NEW SHEQALIM
16.9600 g., 0.9170 Silver 0.5000 oz. ASW, 30 mm. **Subject:** Biblical Art - Jonah in the Whale **Obv:** Small image of Jonah, value, state emblem **Rev:** Stylized Jonah in belly of whale **Edge:** Reeded

Date	Mintage	F	VF	XF	Unc	BU
JE5770-2010 Proof	Est. 555	Value: 1,040				

KM# 480 10 NEW SHEQALIM
16.9600 g., 0.9170 Silver 0.5000 oz. ASW, 30 mm. **Subject:** Israeli Nobel Prize Laureates - Menachem Begin **Obv:** Menachem Begin, Jimmy Carter adn Anwar Sadat in triple handshake on White House lawn, state emblem **Rev:** Portrait of Menachem Begin **Edge:** Reeded

Date	Mintage	F	VF	XF	Unc	BU
JE5771-2010(u) Proof	Est. 888	Value: 1,040				

BULLION COINAGE

KM# 467 20 NEW SHEQALIM
31.1000 g., 0.9990 Gold 0.9988 oz. AGW, 32 mm. **Obv:** State emblem above lion of Megiddo **Rev:** Tower of David near the Jaffa Gate in Jerusalem

Date	Mintage	F	VF	XF	Unc	BU
JE5770 (2010)(u)	Est. 3,600	—	—	—	—	BV+20%

MINT SETS

KM#	Date	Mintage	Identification	Issue Price	Mkt Val
MS86	JE5761 (2001) (7)	4,000	KM#163b, 172-174, 217, 315, 354 (plastic case) 350th Anniversary of the Jewish Community of Curacao	24.00	37.00
MS88	JE5762 (2002) (7)	4,000	KM#163b, 172-174, 217, 315, 355 (plastic case) Yemenite Jewry	27.00	40.00
MS89	JE5761-5762 (2001-2002) (9)	3,000	KM#157, 158, 160a (JE5761), 157-159, 160a, 207, 270 (JE5762) plus Twin Towers medal (folder) Israel - New York	—	30.00
MS91	JE5763 (2003) (7)	3,000	KM#163b, 172-174, 217, 315, 389 (plastic case) The March of the Living into Poland	30.00	42.00
MS93	JE5764 (2004) (7)	3,000	KM#163b, 172-174, 217, 315, 390 (plastic case) Iraqi Jewry	—	40.00
MS94	JE5761-5763 (2001-2003) (6)	3,000	KM#157-159, 160a, 207, 270 (various dates) (folder) Bank of Israel Jubilee; (given or sold to Bank of Israel employees and VIP guests, not go to the general public)	—	45.00
MS96	JE5765 (2005) (7)	2,500	KM#163b, 172-174, 217, 315, 391 (plastic case) Syrian Jewry	—	42.00
MS97	JE5764-5765 (2004-2005) (6)	3,000	KM#158, 159 (JE5764), 157, 160a, 207, 270 (JE5765) (folder) Israel Today	37.00	35.00
MS98	JE5766 (2006) (7)	2,700	KM#163b, 172-174, 217, 315, 415 (folder) Dutch Jewry	45.00	45.00
MS99	JE5766 (2006) (7)	300	KM#163b, 172-174, 217, 315, 415 (plastic case) Dutch Jewry	—	45.00
MS100	JE5766 (2006) (6)	2,000	KM#157-159, 160a, 207, 270 (folder) To the North With Love	37.00	35.00
MS101	JE5767 (2007) (7)	3,000	KM#163b, 172-174, 217, 315, 422 (folder) Greek Jewry	43.00	42.00
MS102	JE5768 (2008) (8)	3,000	KM#163a, 172-174, 217, 315, 432, 434 (folder) Egyptian Jewry	43.00	45.00
MS103	JE5767-5768 (2007-2008) (8)	1,000	KM#157-159, 160a (JE5767), 158, 159, 207, 433 (JE5768) (folder) The Negev Shall Blossom	37.00	46.00
MS104	JE5769 (2009) (7)	1,800	KM#163b, 173, 174, 217, 315, 432, 436 (folder) Glorious Prague	43.00	45.00
MS105	JE5770 (2010) (7)	1,800	KM#163, 173, 174, 217, 315, 432, 466 (folder) Jews of Algeria	43.00	45.00
MS107	2009-2010 (6)	—	KM#160a, 207, 433 (JE5769), 158, 159, 270 (JE5770) (folder) 2010 Mint Set	29.95	30.00

MINT SETS NON-STANDARD METALS

KM#	Date	Mintage	Identification	Issue Price	Mkt Val
MS85	JE5761 (2001) (7)	4,000	KM#163b, 172-174, 217, 315, 354 (folder) 350th Anniversary of the Jewish Community of Curacao	32.00	38.00
MS87	JE5762 (2002) (7)	4,000	KM#163b, 172-174, 217, 315, 355 (folder) Yemenite Jewry	32.00	40.00
MS90	JE5763 (2003) (7)	3,000	KM#163b, 172-174, 217, 315, 389 (folder) The March of the Living into Poland	33.00	39.00
MS92	JE5764 (2004) (7)	3,000	KM#163b, 172-174, 217, 315, 390 (folder) Iraqi Jewry	39.00	40.00
MS95	JE5765 (2005) (7)	2,500	KM#163b, 172-174, 217, 315, 391 (folder) Syrian Jewry	39.00	40.00

The Italian Republic, a 700-mile-long peninsula extending into the heart of the Mediterranean Sea, has an area of 116,304 sq. mi. (301,230 sq. km.) and a population of 60 million. Capital: Rome. The economy centers around agriculture, manufacturing, forestry and fishing. Machinery, textiles, clothing and motor vehicles are exported.

MINT
R - Rome

REPUBLIC

DECIMAL COINAGE

KM# 91 LIRA
0.6200 g., Aluminum, 17 mm. **Obv:** Balance scales **Rev:** Cornucopia, value and date **Designer:** Giuseppe Romagnoli

Date	Mintage	F	VF	XF	Unc	BU
2001R	100,000	—	—	—	20.00	—
2001R Proof	10,000	Value: 40.00				

KM# 219 LIRA
11.0000 g., 0.8350 Silver 0.2953 oz. ASW, 29 mm. **Subject:** History of the Lira - Lira of 1946 (KM#87) **Obv:** Head with laureate left within circle **Rev:** Apple on branch within circle flanked by sprigs **Edge:** Reeded **Note:** This is a Lira Series reproducing an old coin design in the center of each coin.

Date	Mintage	F	VF	XF	Unc	BU
2001R	50,000	—	—	—	70.00	—
2001R Proof	6,100	Value: 220				

KM# 220 LIRA
6.0000 g., 0.8350 Silver 0.1611 oz. ASW, 24 mm. **Subject:** History of the Lira - Lira of 1951 (KM#91) **Obv:** Balance scale within circle **Rev:** Value and cornucopia within circle **Edge:** Reeded **Note:** This is a Lira Series reproducing an old coin design in the center of each coin.

Date	Mintage	F	VF	XF	Unc	BU
2001R	50,000	—	—	—	70.00	—
2001R Proof	6,100	Value: 220				

KM# 87a LIRA
8.0000 g., 0.9000 Gold 0.2315 oz. AGW, 21.6 mm. **Obv:** Ceres **Rev:** Orange on branch **Edge:** Plain **Note:** Official Restrike

Date	Mintage	F	VF	XF	Unc	BU
1946 (2006)R Proof	1,999	Value: 400				

KM# 91a LIRA
4.0000 g., 0.9000 Gold 0.1157 oz. AGW, 17.2 mm. **Obv:** Balance scale **Rev:** Cornucopia, date and value **Edge:** Plain **Note:** Official Restrike

Date	Mintage	F	VF	XF	Unc	BU
1951 (2006)R Proof	1,999	Value: 250				

KM# 94 2 LIRE
0.8000 g., Aluminum, 18 mm. **Obv:** Honey bee **Rev:** Olive branch and value **Edge:** Reeded **Designer:** G. Romagnoli **Note:** The 1968-1969 and 1982-2001 dates were issued in sets only.

Date	Mintage	F	VF	XF	Unc	BU
2001R	100,000	—	—	—	18.00	—
2001R Proof	10,000	Value: 40.00				

KM# 88a 2 LIRE
11.0000 g., 0.9000 Gold 0.3183 oz. AGW, 24.1 mm. **Obv:** Farmer plowing field **Rev:** Wheat ear **Edge:** Plain **Note:** Official Restrike

Date	Mintage	F	VF	XF	Unc	BU
1946 (2006)R Proof	1,999	Value: 700				

KM# 94a 2 LIRE
5.0000 g., 0.9000 Gold 0.1447 oz. AGW, 18.3 mm. **Obv:** Honey bee **Rev:** Olive branch **Edge:** Reeded **Note:** Official Restrike

Date	Mintage	F	VF	XF	Unc	BU
1953 (2006)R Proof	1,999	Value: 325				

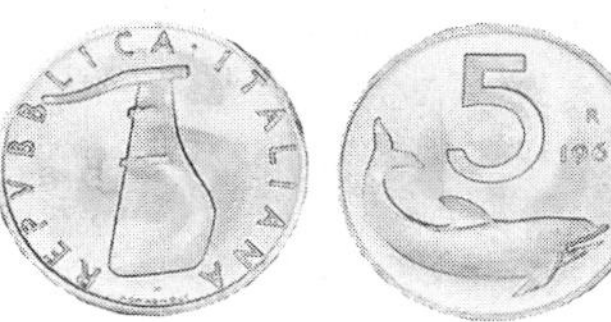

KM# 92 5 LIRE
1.0350 g., Aluminum, 20.12 mm. **Obv:** Rudder **Rev:** Dolphin and value **Edge:** Plain **Designer:** Giuseppe Romagnoli

Date	Mintage	F	VF	XF	Unc	BU
2001R	100,000	—	—	—	12.00	—
2001R Proof	10,000	Value: 20.00				

KM# 89a 5 LIRE
16.0000 g., 0.9000 Gold 0.4630 oz. AGW, 26.7 mm. **Obv:** Italia with torch **Rev:** Bunch of grapes **Edge:** Reeded **Note:** Official Restrike

Date	Mintage	F	VF	XF	Unc	BU
1946 (2006)R Proof	1,999	Value: 1,000				

KM# 92a 5 LIRE
6.0000 g., 0.9000 Gold 0.1736 oz. AGW, 20.2 mm. **Obv:** Rudder **Rev:** Dolphin and value **Edge:** Plain **Note:** Official Restrike

Date	Mintage	F	VF	XF	Unc	BU
1951 (2006)R Proof	1,999	Value: 425				

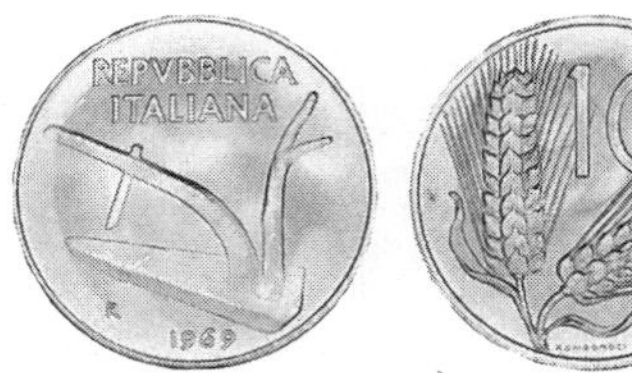

KM# 93 10 LIRE
1.6000 g., Aluminum, 23.25 mm. **Obv:** Plow **Rev:** Value within wheat ears **Edge:** Plain **Designer:** Giuseppe Romagnoli

Date	Mintage	F	VF	XF	Unc	BU
2001R	100,000	—	—	—	12.00	—
2001R Proof	10,000	Value: 35.00				

KM# 90a 10 LIRE
19.0000 g., 0.9000 Gold 0.5498 oz. AGW, 29 mm. **Obv:** Pegasus **Rev:** Olive branch **Edge:** Lettered **Edge Lettering:** REPVBBLICA ITALIANA **Note:** Official Restrike

Date	Mintage	F	VF	XF	Unc	BU
1946 (2006)R Proof	1,999	Value: 1,100				

KM# 93a 10 LIRE
10.0000 g., 0.9000 Gold 0.2893 oz. AGW, 23.3 mm. **Obv:** Plow **Rev:** Value within wheat ears **Edge:** Plain **Note:** Official Restrike

Date	Mintage	F	VF	XF	Unc	BU
1951 (2006)R Proof	1,999	Value: 600				

KM# 97.2 20 LIRE

3.6000 g., Aluminum-Bronze, 21.25 mm. **Obv:** Wheat sprigs within head left **Rev:** Oak leaves divide value and date **Edge:** Plain **Designer:** Pietro Giampaoli

Date	Mintage	F	VF	XF	Unc	BU
2001R	100,000	—	—	—	12.00	—
2001R Proof	10,000	Value: 35.00				

KM# 97.1a 20 LIRE

8.0000 g., 0.9000 Gold 0.2315 oz. AGW, 21.3 mm. **Obv:** Head laureate left **Rev:** Oak leaves divides date and value **Edge:** Reeded **Note:** Official Restrike

Date	Mintage	F	VF	XF	Unc	BU
1957 (2006)R Proof	1,999	Value: 500				

KM# 183 50 LIRE

4.5000 g., Copper-Nickel, 19 mm. **Obv:** Turreted head left **Rev:** Large value within wreath of produce **Designer:** L. Cretara

Date	Mintage	F	VF	XF	Unc	BU
2001R	100,000	—	—	—	10.00	—
2001R Proof	10,000	Value: 18.00				

KM# 95.1a 50 LIRE

14.0000 g., 0.9000 Gold 0.4051 oz. AGW, 24.8 mm. **Obv:** Italia **Rev:** Vulcan **Edge:** Reeded **Note:** Official Restrike

Date	Mintage	F	VF	XF	Unc	BU
1954 (2006)R Proof	1,999	Value: 750				

KM# 183a 50 LIRE

9.0000 g., 0.9000 Gold 0.2604 oz. AGW, 19.2 mm. **Obv:** Roma **Rev:** Value within wreath **Edge:** Plain **Note:** Official Restrike

Date	Mintage	F	VF	XF	Unc	BU
1996 (2006)R Proof	1,999	Value: 500				

KM# 159 100 LIRE

4.5000 g., Copper-Nickel, 22 mm. **Obv:** Turreted head left **Rev:** Large value within circle flanked by sprigs **Edge:** Segmented reeding **Designer:** Laura Cretara

Date	Mintage	F	VF	XF	Unc	BU
2001R	100,000	—	—	—	12.00	—
2001R Proof	10,000	Value: 35.00				

KM# 96.1a 100 LIRE

18.0000 g., 0.9000 Gold 0.5208 oz. AGW, 27.8 mm. **Obv:** Ancient athlete **Rev:** Minerva standing **Edge:** Reeded **Note:** Official Restrike

Date	Mintage	F	VF	XF	Unc	BU
1955 (2006)R Proof	1,999	Value: 1,000				

KM# 159a 100 LIRE

9.0000 g., 0.9000 Gold 0.2604 oz. AGW, 22 mm. **Obv:** Turreted head left **Rev:** Large value within circle flanked by sprigs **Edge:** Segmented reeding **Note:** Official Restrike

Date	Mintage	F	VF	XF	Unc	BU
1993 (2006)R Proof	1,999	Value: 500				

KM# 105 200 LIRE

5.0000 g., Aluminum-Bronze, 24 mm. **Obv:** Head right **Rev:** Value within gear **Edge:** Reeded **Designer:** M. Vallucci

Date	Mintage	F	VF	XF	Unc	BU
2001R	100,000	—	—	—	18.00	—
2001R Proof	10,000	Value: 40.00				

KM# 105a 200 LIRE

11.0000 g., 0.9000 Gold 0.3183 oz. AGW, 24 mm. **Obv:** Head right **Rev:** Value within gear **Edge:** Reeded **Note:** Official Restrike

Date	Mintage	F	VF	XF	Unc	BU
1977 (2006)R Proof	1,999	Value: 700				

KM# 98 500 LIRE

11.0000 g., 0.8350 Silver 0.2953 oz. ASW, 29.3 mm. **Obv:** Columbus' ships **Obv. Designer:** Guido Veroi **Rev:** Bust left within wreath **Rev. Designer:** Pietro Giampaoli **Edge:** Dates in raised lettering

Date	Mintage	F	VF	XF	Unc	BU
2001R	100,000	—	—	—	45.00	—
2001R Proof	10,000	Value: 205				

KM# 111 500 LIRE

6.8000 g., Bi-Metallic Aluminum-Bronze center in Stainless Steel ring, 25.8 mm. **Obv:** Head left within circle **Rev:** Plaza within circle flanked by sprigs **Edge:** Segmented reeding **Designer:** Cretara

Date	Mintage	F	VF	XF	Unc	BU
2001R	100,000	—	—	—	12.00	—
2001R Proof	10,000	Value: 35.00				

KM# 98a 500 LIRE

18.0000 g., 0.9000 Gold 0.5208 oz. AGW, 29 mm. **Obv:** Columbus' ships **Rev:** Bust left within wreath **Edge:** Lettered **Edge Lettering:** REPVBBLICA ITALIANA *** 1958*** **Note:** Official Restrike

Date	Mintage	F	VF	XF	Unc	BU
1958 (2006)R Proof	1,999	Value: 1,000				

KM# 99a 500 LIRE

18.0000 g., 0.9000 Gold 0.5208 oz. AGW, 29 mm. **Obv:** Seated Italia **Rev:** Lady **Edge:** Lettered **Edge Lettering:** "1 CENTENARIO VNITA'D'ITALIA * 1861-1961* " **Note:** Official Restrike

Date	Mintage	F	VF	XF	Unc	BU
1961 (2006)R Proof	1,999	Value: 1,000				

KM# 100a 500 LIRE

18.0000 g., 0.9000 Gold 0.5208 oz. AGW, 29 mm. **Obv:** Dante **Rev:** Hell **Edge:** Lettered **Edge Lettering:** "7 CENTENARIO DELLA NASCITA DI DANTE" **Note:** Official Restrike

Date	Mintage	F	VF	XF	Unc	BU
1965 (2006)R Proof	1,999	Value: 1,000				

KM# 111a 500 LIRE

14.0000 g., Bi-Metallic .750 Gold center in .900 Gold ring, 25.8 mm. **Obv:** Head left within circle **Rev:** Plaza within circle flanked by sprigs **Edge:** Segmented reeding **Note:** Official Restrike

Date	Mintage	F	VF	XF	Unc	BU
1982 (2006)R Proof	1,999	Value: 275				

KM# 194 1000 LIRE

Bi-Metallic Copper-Nickel center in Aluminum-Bronze ring, 27 mm. **Subject:** European Union **Obv:** Head left within circle **Obv. Designer:** Laura Cretara **Rev:** Corrected map with United Germany within globe design **Rev. Designer:** Pernazza

Date	Mintage	F	VF	XF	Unc	BU
2001R	100,000	—	—	—	10.00	—
2001R Proof	10,000	Value: 35.00				

KM# 236 1000 LIRE

14.6000 g., 0.8350 Silver 0.3919 oz. ASW, 31.4 mm. **Obv:** Giuseppe Verdi **Rev:** Building **Designer:** E. L. Frapiccini

Date	Mintage	F	VF	XF	Unc	BU
2001R	115,000	—	—	—	50.00	—
2001R Proof	10,000	Value: 100				

KM# 190a 1000 LIRE

17.0000 g., 0.9000 Gold 0.4919 oz. AGW, 27 mm. **Obv:** Roma **Rev:** European map **Edge:** Segmented reeding **Note:** Official Restrike

Date	Mintage	F	VF	XF	Unc	BU
1997 (2006)R Proof	1,999	Value: 800				

KM# 101a 1000 LIRE

24.0000 g., 0.9000 Gold 0.6944 oz. AGW, 31.2 mm. **Obv:** Concordia **Rev:** Geometric shape above value **Edge Lettering:** REPVBBLICA ITALIANA **Note:** Official restrike.

Date	Mintage	F	VF	XF	Unc	BU
1970 (2006)R Proof	1,999	Value: 1,250				

KM# 234 50000 LIRE

7.5000 g., 0.9000 Gold 0.2170 oz. AGW, 20 mm. **Subject:** 250th Anniversary - Palace of Caserta **Obv:** Front view of palace **Rev:** Fountain, date and denomination **Designer:** L. De Simoni

Date	Mintage	F	VF	XF	Unc	BU
2001R Proof	6,200	Value: 475				

KM# 233 100000 LIRE

15.0000 g., 0.9000 Gold 0.4340 oz. AGW, 25 mm. **Subject:** 700th Anniversary - Pulpit at the Church of St. Andrea a Pistoia **Obv:** Full pulpit **Rev:** Enlarged detail of the pulpit **Designer:** C. Momoni

Date	Mintage	F	VF	XF	Unc	BU
2001R Proof	4,500	Value: 850				

EURO COINAGE

European Union Issues

KM# 210 EURO CENT

2.3000 g., Copper Plated Steel, 16.3 mm. **Obv:** Castle del Monte **Obv. Designer:** Eugenio Drutti **Rev:** Value and globe **Rev. Designer:** Luc Luycx **Edge:** Plain

Date	Mintage	F	VF	XF	Unc	BU
2002R	1,348,899,500	—	—	—	0.25	—
2003R	9,629,000	—	—	—	0.35	—
2003R Proof	12,000	Value: 10.00				
2004R	100,000,000	—	—	—	0.25	—
2004R Proof	12,000	Value: 7.00				
2005R	180,000,000	—	—	—	0.35	—
2005R Proof	12,000	Value: 5.00				
2006R	159,000,000	—	—	—	0.25	—
2006R Proof	12,000	Value: 5.00				
2007R	215,000,000	—	—	—	0.25	—
2007R Proof	12,000	Value: 5.00				
2008R	180,000,000	—	—	—	0.25	—
2008R Proof	—	Value: 5.00				
2009R	—	—	—	—	0.25	—
2009R Proof	—	Value: 5.00				

KM# 211 2 EURO CENT

3.0300 g., Copper Plated Steel, 18.7 mm. **Obv:** Observation tower in Turin **Obv. Designer:** Luciana de Simoni **Rev:** Value and globe **Rev. Designer:** Luc Luycx **Edge:** Plain

Date	Mintage	F	VF	XF	Unc	BU
2002R	1,099,166,250	—	—	—	0.25	—
2003R	21,817,000	—	—	—	0.25	—
2003R Proof	12,000	Value: 10.00				
2004R	120,000,000	—	—	—	0.25	—
2004R Proof	12,000	Value: 7.00				
2005R	120,000,000	—	—	—	0.25	—
2005R Proof	12,000	Value: 5.00				
2006R	196,000,000	—	—	—	0.25	—
2006R Proof	12,000	Value: 5.00				
2007R	140,000,000	—	—	—	0.25	—
2007R Proof	12,000	Value: 5.00				
2008R	135,000,000	—	—	—	0.25	—
2008R Proof	—	Value: 5.00				
2009R	—	—	—	—	0.25	—
2009R Proof	—	Value: 5.00				

KM# 212 5 EURO CENT

3.9500 g., Copper Plated Steel, 19.64 mm. **Obv:** Colosseum **Obv. Designer:** Lorenzo Frapiccini **Rev:** Value and globe **Rev. Designer:** Luc Luycx **Edge:** Plain

Date	Mintage	F	VF	XF	Unc	BU
2002R	1,341,742,204	—	—	—	0.25	—
2003R	1,960,000	—	—	—	10.00	—
2003R Proof	12,000	Value: 20.00				
2004R	10,000,000	—	—	—	0.25	—
2004R Proof	12,000	Value: 8.00				
2005R	70,000,000	—	—	—	0.25	—
2005R Proof	12,000	Value: 6.00				
2006R	119,000,000	—	—	—	0.25	—

Date	Mintage	F	VF	XF	Unc	BU
2006R Proof	12,000	Value: 6.00				
2007R	85,000,000	—	—	—	0.25	—
2007R Proof	12,000	Value: 6.00				
2008R	90,000,000	—	—	—	0.25	—
2008R Proof	—	Value: 6.00				
2009R	—	—	—	—	0.25	—
2009R Proof	—	Value: 6.00				

KM# 213 10 EURO CENT

4.1000 g., Brass, 19.8 mm. **Obv:** Venus by Botticelli **Obv. Designer:** Claudia Momoni **Rev:** Value and map **Rev. Designer:** Luc Luycx **Edge:** Reeded

Date	Mintage	F	VF	XF	Unc	BU
2002R	1,142,383,000	—	—	—	0.25	—
2003R	29,976,000	—	—	—	0.50	—
2003R Proof	12,000	Value: 15.00				
2004R	5,000,000	—	—	—	10.00	—
2004R Proof	12,000	Value: 10.00				
2005R	100,000,000	—	—	—	0.50	—
2005R Proof	12,000	Value: 7.00				
2006R	180,000,000	—	—	—	0.50	—
2006R Proof	12,000	Value: 7.00				
2007R	105,000,000	—	—	—	0.50	—
2007R Proof	12,000	Value: 7.00				

KM# 247 10 EURO CENT

4.0700 g., Brass, 19.7 mm. **Obv:** Venus by Botticelli **Obv. Designer:** Claudia Momoni **Rev:** Relief Map of Western Europe, stars, lines and value **Rev. Designer:** Luc Luycx **Edge:** Reeded

Date	Mintage	F	VF	XF	Unc	BU
2008R	—	—	—	—	0.25	—
2009R	—	—	—	—	0.25	—

KM# 214 20 EURO CENT

5.7300 g., Brass, 22.1 mm. **Obv:** Futuristic sculpture **Obv. Designer:** Maria Cassol **Rev:** Value and map **Rev. Designer:** Luc Luycx **Edge:** Notched

Date	Mintage	F	VF	XF	Unc	BU
2002R	1,411,836,000	—	—	—	0.30	—
2003R	26,155,000	—	—	—	0.30	—
2003R Proof	12,000	Value: 16.00				
2004R	5,000,000	—	—	—	0.50	—
2004R Proof	12,000	Value: 14.00				
2005R	5,000,000	—	—	—	5.00	—
2005R Proof	12,000	Value: 8.00				
2006R	5,000,000	—	—	—	5.00	—
2006R Proof	12,000	Value: 8.00				
2007R	5,000,000	—	—	—	0.50	—
2007R Proof	12,000	Value: 8.00				

KM# 248 20 EURO CENT

5.7300 g., Brass, 22.1 mm. **Obv:** Futuristic sculpture **Obv. Designer:** Maria Cassoll **Rev:** Relief map of Western Europe, stars, lines and value **Rev. Designer:** Luc Luycx **Edge:** Reeded

Date	Mintage	F	VF	XF	Unc	BU
2008R	—	—	—	—	1.00	—
2009R	—	—	—	—	1.00	—

KM# 215 50 EURO CENT

7.8100 g., Brass, 24.2 mm. **Obv:** Sculpture of Marcus Aurelius on horseback **Obv. Designer:** Roberto Mauri **Rev:** Value and map **Rev. Designer:** Luc Luycx **Edge:** Reeded

Date	Mintage	F	VF	XF	Unc	BU
2002R	1,136,718,000	—	—	—	0.80	—
2003R	44,825,000	—	—	—	1.00	—
2003R Proof	12,000	Value: 18.00				
2004R	5,000,000	—	—	—	4.00	—
2004R Proof	12,000	Value: 16.00				
2005R	5,000,000	—	—	—	1.00	—
2005R Proof	12,000	Value: 10.00				
2006R	5,000,000	—	—	—	1.00	—
2006R Proof	12,000	Value: 10.00				
2007R	5,000,000	—	—	—	1.00	—
2007R Proof	12,000	Value: 10.00				

KM# 249 50 EURO CENT

7.8100 g., Brass, 24.2 mm. **Obv:** Sculpture of Marcus Aurelius on horseback **Obv. Designer:** Roberto Mauri **Rev:** Relief map of Western Europe, stars, lines and value **Rev. Designer:** Luc Luycx **Edge:** Reeded

Date	Mintage	F	VF	XF	Unc	BU
2008R	—	—	—	—	1.25	—
2009R	—	—	—	—	1.25	—

KM# 216 EURO

7.5000 g., Bi-Metallic Copper-Nickel center in Nickel-Brass ring, 23.2 mm. **Obv:** Male figure drawing by Leonardo da Vinci within circle of stars **Obv. Designer:** Laura Cretara **Rev:** Value and map within circle **Rev. Designer:** Luc Luycx **Edge:** Reeded and plain sections

Date	Mintage	F	VF	XF	Unc	BU
2002R	966,025,300	—	—	—	1.60	—
2003R	66,474,000	—	—	—	2.00	—
2003R Proof	12,000	Value: 20.00				
2004R	5,000,000	—	—	—	5.00	—
2004R Proof	12,000	Value: 18.00				
2005R	5,000,000	—	—	—	5.00	—
2005R Proof	12,000	Value: 15.00				
2006R	108,000,000	—	—	—	2.00	—
2006R Proof	12,000	Value: 15.00				
2007R	135,000,000	—	—	—	2.00	—
2007R Proof	12,000	Value: 15.00				

KM# 250 EURO

7.5000 g., Bi-Metallic Copper-Nickel center in Nickel-Brass ring, 23.2 mm. **Obv:** Male figure drawing by Leonardo da Vinci **Obv. Designer:** Laura Cretara **Rev:** Relief map of Western Europe, stars, lines and value **Rev. Designer:** Luc Luycx **Edge:** Reeded and plain sections

Date	Mintage	F	VF	XF	Unc	BU
2008R	—	—	—	—	2.50	—
2009R	—	—	—	—	2.50	—

KM# 217 2 EURO

8.5000 g., Bi-Metallic Nickel-Brass center in Copper-Nickel ring, 25.75 mm. **Obv:** Bust of Dante Aligheri left **Obv. Designer:** Maria Colanieri **Rev:** Value and map within circle **Rev. Designer:** Luc Luycx **Edge:** Reeded **Edge Lettering:** 2's and stars

Date	Mintage	F	VF	XF	Unc	BU
2002R	463,702,000	—	—	—	4.00	—
2003R	36,160,000	—	—	—	4.00	—
2003R Proof	12,000	Value: 25.00				
2004R	7,000,000	—	—	—	6.00	—
2004R Proof	12,000	Value: 22.00				
2005R	62,000,000	—	—	—	4.00	—
2005R Proof	12,000	Value: 20.00				
2006R	10,000,000	—	—	—	4.00	—
2006R Proof	12,000	Value: 20.00				
2007R	5,000,000	—	—	—	5.00	—
2007R Proof	12,000	Value: 20.00				

KM# 237 2 EURO

8.5000 g., Bi-Metallic Nickel-Brass center in Copper-Nickel ring, 25.75 mm. **Obv:** World Food Program globe within circle **Rev:** Value and map within circle **Edge:** Reeded and lettered **Edge Lettering:** 2's and stars

Date	Mintage	F	VF	XF	Unc	BU
2004R	16,000,000	—	—	—	5.00	6.00

KM# 245 2 EURO

8.5000 g., Bi-Metallic Nickel-Brass center in Copper-Nickel ring, 25.75 mm. **Subject:** European Constitution **Obv:** Europa holding an open book while sitting on a bull within circle **Rev:** Value and map within circle **Edge:** Reeding over stars and 2's

Date	Mintage	F	VF	XF	Unc	BU
2005R	18,000,000	—	—	—	4.00	5.00

KM# 246 2 EURO

8.5000 g., Bi-Metallic Nickel-Brass center in Copper-Nickel ring, 25.75 mm. **Subject:** Torino Winter Olympics **Obv:** Skier and other designs within circle **Rev:** Value and map within circle **Edge:** Reeded with stars and 2's

Date	Mintage	F	VF	XF	Unc	BU
2006R	40,000,000	—	—	—	4.00	5.00

KM# 280 2 EURO

8.5000 g., Bi-Metallic Nickel-Brass center in Copper-Nickel ring, 25.75 mm. **Subject:** Turin Olympics **Rev:** Value and map within circle

Date	Mintage	F	VF	XF	Unc	BU
2006R	—	Value: 5.00				

KM# 290 2 EURO

8.5200 g., Bi-Metallic Nickel-Brass center in Copper-Nickel ring, 25.75 mm.

Date	Mintage	F	VF	XF	Unc	BU
2007R	—	—	—	—	5.00	6.00

KM# 311 2 EURO

8.5000 g., Bi-Metallic Nickel-Brass center in Copper-Nickel ring, 25.75 mm. **Subject:** Treaty of Rome, 50th Anniversary

Date	Mintage	F	VF	XF	Unc	BU
2007R	5,000,000	—	—	—	4.00	5.00

KM# 251 2 EURO

8.5000 g., Bi-Metallic Nickel-Brass center in Copper-Nickel ring, 25.75 mm. **Obv:** Bust of Dante Aligheri **Obv. Designer:** Maria Colanieri **Rev:** Relief map of Western Europe, stars, lines and value **Rev. Designer:** Luc Luycx **Edge:** Reeded **Edge Lettering:** 2's and stars

Date	Mintage	F	VF	XF	Unc	BU
2008R	—	—	—	—	4.00	5.00
2009R	—	—	—	—	4.00	5.00

KM# 301 2 EURO

8.5000 g., Bi-Metallic Nickel-Brass center in Copper-Nickel ring, 25.75 mm. **Subject:** Declaration of Rights

Date	Mintage	F	VF	XF	Unc	BU
2008R	—	—	—	—	5.00	6.00

KM# 310 2 EURO

8.5000 g., Bi-Metallic Nickel-Brass center in Copper-Nickel ring, 25.75 mm. **Subject:** Louis Braille **Obv:** Hand reading book in braille font

Date	Mintage	F	VF	XF	Unc	BU
2009R	2,000,000	—	—	—	5.00	6.00

KM# 312 2 EURO

8.5000 g., Bi-Metallic Nickel-Brass center in Copper-Nickel ring, 25.75 mm. **Subject:** European Monetrary Union, 10th Anniversary **Obv:** Stick figure and Euro symbol

Date	Mintage	F	VF	XF	Unc	BU
2009R	2,000,000	—	—	—	4.00	5.00

KM# 328 2 EURO

8.5000 g., Bi-Metallic Nickel-Brass center in Copper-Nickel ring., 25.75 mm. **Subject:** Camillo Benso Count of Cavour **Obv:** Bust 3/4 right **Obv. Designer:** Claudia Momoni

Date	Mintage	F	VF	XF	Unc	BU
2010R Special Unc.	16,000	—	—	—	5.00	6.00

KM# 338 2 EURO

8.5000 g., Bi-Metallic Aluminum-Bronze center in Copper-Nickel ring, 25.75 mm. **Subject:** Italian Unification, 150th Anniversary

Date	Mintage	F	VF	XF	Unc	BU
2011R	—	—	—	—	6.00	7.50

KM# 252 5 EURO
18.0000 g., 0.9250 Silver 0.5353 oz. ASW, 32 mm. **Subject:** People in Europe

Date	Mintage	F	VF	XF	Unc	BU
2003R	25,000	Value: 40.00				
2003R Proof	8,000	Value: 65.00				

KM# 253 5 EURO
18.0000 g., 0.9250 Silver 0.5353 oz. ASW, 32 mm. **Subject:** Work in Europe

Date	Mintage	F	VF	XF	Unc	BU
2003R	50,000	—	—	—	35.00	40.00
2003R Proof	12,000	Value: 65.00				

KM# 238 5 EURO
18.0000 g., 0.9250 Silver 0.5353 oz. ASW, 32 mm. **Subject:** World Cup Soccer - Germany 2006 **Obv:** Santa Croce Square in Florence **Rev:** Soccer ball and world globe design

Date	Mintage	F	VF	XF	Unc	BU
2004R Proof	35,000	Value: 100				

KM# 239 5 EURO
18.0000 g., 0.9250 Silver 0.5353 oz. ASW, 32 mm. **Subject:** Madam Butterfly **Obv:** La Scala Opera House, where Madam Butterfly was first performed there in 1904 **Rev:** Geisha

Date	Mintage	F	VF	XF	Unc	BU
2004R	30,000	—	—	—	35.00	40.00
2004R Proof	12,000	Value: 60.00				

KM# 254 5 EURO
18.0000 g., 0.9250 Silver 0.5353 oz. ASW, 32 mm. **Subject:** 50th Anniversary of Italian Television

Date	Mintage	F	VF	XF	Unc	BU
2004R	40,000	—	—	—	35.00	40.00
2004R Proof	15,000	Value: 65.00				

KM# 255 5 EURO
18.0000 g., 0.9250 Silver 0.5353 oz. ASW, 32 mm. **Subject:** 85th Birthday of Federico Fellini

Date	Mintage	F	VF	XF	Unc	BU
2005R	35,000	—	—	—	30.00	35.00
2005R Proof	22,000	Value: 60.00				

KM# 256 5 EURO
18.0000 g., 0.9250 Silver 0.5353 oz. ASW, 32 mm. **Subject:** 2006 Olympic Winter Games Torino Ski Jump

Date	Mintage	F	VF	XF	Unc	BU
2005R	35,000	—	—	—	30.00	35.00
2005R Proof	40,000	Value: 60.00				

KM# 257 5 EURO
18.0000 g., 0.9250 Silver 0.5353 oz. ASW, 32 mm. **Subject:** 2006 Olympic Winter Games Cross Country Skiing

Date	Mintage	F	VF	XF	Unc	BU
2005R	35,000	—	—	—	30.00	35.00
2005R Proof	40,000	Value: 50.00				

KM# 266 5 EURO
18.0000 g., 0.9250 Silver 0.5353 oz. ASW, 32 mm. **Subject:** 2006 Olympic Games Torino Figure Skating

Date	Mintage	F	VF	XF	Unc	BU
2005	40,000	—	—	—	30.00	35.00
2005 Proof	—	Value: 50.00				

KM# 282 5 EURO
18.0000 g., 0.9250 Silver 0.5353 oz. ASW, 32 mm. **Subject:** FIFA World Cup

Date	Mintage	F	VF	XF	Unc	BU
2006R	—	—	—	—	60.00	62.00
2006R Proof	—	Value: 65.00				

KM# 294 5 EURO
18.0000 g., 0.9250 Silver 0.5353 oz. ASW, 32 mm. **Subject:** Arturo Toscani - 50th Aniversary Death

Date	Mintage	F	VF	XF	Unc	BU
2007R	—	—	—	—	60.00	62.00

KM# 291 5 EURO
18.0000 g., 0.9250 Silver 0.5353 oz. ASW, 32 mm. **Subject:** Kyoto Agreement - 5th Anniversary **Obv:** Allegorical representation of nature rebelling against pollution **Rev:** Allegorical representation of clear air with a spiral of vital energy

Date	Mintage	F	VF	XF	Unc	BU
2007R Special Unc	20,000	—	—	—	50.00	55.00
2007R Proof	7,000	Value: 100				

KM# 292 5 EURO
18.0000 g., 0.9250 Silver 0.5353 oz. ASW, 32 mm. **Subject:** Giuseppe Garibaldi - 200th Anniversary Birth **Obv:** Portrait facing **Rev:** Harbor Lympia in Nice

Date	Mintage	F	VF	XF	Unc	BU
2007R Special Unc.	8,000	—	—	—	35.00	40.00

KM# 293 5 EURO
18.0000 g., 0.9250 Silver 0.5353 oz. ASW, 32 mm. **Subject:** Aitero Spinelini 100th Birthday **Obv:** Bust 3/4 facing **Rev:** Representation of Ventotene island and Parliament hemicycle

Date	Mintage	F	VF	XF	Unc	BU
2007R Special Unc.	7,000	—	—	—	35.00	40.00

KM# 323 5 EURO
18.0000 g., 0.9250 Silver 0.5353 oz. ASW, 32 mm. **Subject:** Arturo Toscanini. 50th Death Anniversary **Obv:** Profile left **Rev:** Hand with baton, and musical instruments

Date	Mintage	F	VF	XF	Unc	BU
2007R Special Unc.	7,000	—	—	—	35.00	40.00

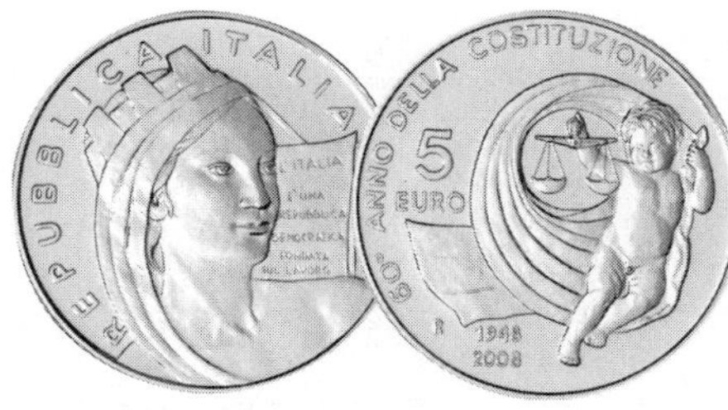

KM# 281 5 EURO
18.0000 g., 0.9250 Silver 0.5353 oz. ASW, 32 mm. **Subject:** Italian Republic - 60th Anniversary

Date	Mintage	F	VF	XF	Unc	BU
2008R	—	—	—	—	60.00	62.00
2008R Proof	—	Value: 65.00				

KM# 303 5 EURO
18.0000 g., 0.9250 Silver 0.5353 oz. ASW, 32 mm. **Subject:** Anna Magnani - 100th Birthday

Date	Mintage	F	VF	XF	Unc	BU
2008R	—	—	—	—	60.00	62.00

KM# 304 5 EURO
18.0000 g., 0.9250 Silver 0.5353 oz. ASW, 32 mm. **Subject:** Italian Constitution - 60th Anniversary

Date	Mintage	F	VF	XF	Unc	BU
2008	—	—	—	—	45.00	48.00

KM# 325 5 EURO
18.0000 g., 0.9250 Silver 0.5353 oz. ASW, 32 mm. **Series:** IFAD, 30th Anniversary

Date	Mintage	F	VF	XF	Unc	BU
2008R	—	—	—	—	62.00	65.00

KM# 326 5 EURO
18.0000 g., 0.9250 Silver 0.5353 oz. ASW, 32 mm. **Subject:** Antonio Meucci **Obv:** Bust 3/4 facing right

Date	Mintage	F	VF	XF	Unc	BU
2008R Proof	—	Value: 45.00				

KM# 313 5 EURO
18.0000 g., 0.9250 Silver 0.5353 oz. ASW, 32 mm. **Subject:** Giro d'Italy - Cycling Race Centennial **Obv:** Two cyclists **Rev:** Bicycle and map of Italy **Designer:** V. De Seta

Date	Mintage	F	VF	XF	Unc	BU
2009R Special Unc.	14,000	—	—	—	45.00	50.00

KM# 314 5 EURO
18.0000 g., 0.9250 Silver 0.5353 oz. ASW, 32 mm. **Subject:** World Aquatics Championships **Obv:** River God reclining **Rev:** Two swimmers

Date	Mintage	F	VF	XF	Unc	BU
2009R	5,500	—	—	—	45.00	50.00

KM# 315 5 EURO
18.0000 g., 0.9250 Silver 0.5353 oz. ASW, 32 mm. **Subject:** Herculaneum Discovery, 300th Anniversary **Obv:** Four dogs nipping at horse **Rev:** Marble relief of nymph drawing water with a horn **Designer:** M. C. Colaneri

Date	Mintage	F	VF	XF	Unc	BU
2009R Special Unc.	9,000	—	—	—	45.00	50.00

KM# 327 5 EURO
18.0000 g., 0.9250 Silver 0.5353 oz. ASW, 32 mm. **Subject:** FINA, 13th Anniversary **Obv:** Sculpture Allegory of the Tiber River

Rev: Swimmer Mosaics decorating the Foro Italico **Designer:** Roberto Mauri

Date	Mintage	F	VF	XF	Unc	BU
2009R Special Unc.	21,000	—	—	—	35.00	40.00
2009R Proof	5,500	Value: 65.00				

KM# 329 5 EURO
18.0000 g., 0.9250 Silver 0.5353 oz. ASW, 32 mm. **Subject:** Alfa Romeo 100th Anniversary **Obv:** Two Automobiles: 24HP in back, new Giulietta in front **Rev:** Company logo **Designer:** V. De Seta

Date	Mintage	F	VF	XF	Unc	BU
2010R Special Unc.	17,000	—	—	—	35.00	40.00
2010R Proof	5,500	Value: 60.00				

KM# 330 5 EURO
18.0000 g., 0.9250 Silver 0.5353 oz. ASW, 32 mm. **Subject:** Confindustria 100th Anniversary **Obv:** Female head left, mechanical gears within spiral at right **Rev:** Linear eagle and 100 logo **Designer:** L. De Simani

Date	Mintage	F	VF	XF	Unc	BU
2010R Special Unc.	7,500	—	—	—	35.00	37.00

KM# 331 5 EURO
18.0000 g., 0.9250 Silver 0.5353 oz. ASW, 32 mm. **Subject:** Santa Chiara in Naples **Obv:** Church facade **Rev:** Cloister interior

Date	Mintage	F	VF	XF	Unc	BU
2010R Proof	7,500	Value: 65.00				

KM# 258 10 EURO
22.0000 g., 0.9250 Silver 0.6542 oz. ASW, 34 mm. **Subject:** People In Europe

Date	Mintage	F	VF	XF	Unc	BU
2003	25,000	—	—	—	70.00	75.00
2003R Proof	8,000	Value: 120				

KM# 259 10 EURO
22.0000 g., 0.9250 Silver 0.6542 oz. ASW, 34 mm. **Subject:** Italian Presidency of E.U.

Date	Mintage	F	VF	XF	Unc	BU
2003R	40,000	—	—	—	45.00	50.00
2003R Proof	8,000	Value: 120				

KM# 240 10 EURO
22.0000 g., 0.9250 Silver 0.6542 oz. ASW, 34 mm. **Subject:** City of Genoa **Obv:** Sculpture and art works **Rev:** Tower and harbor map

Date	Mintage	F	VF	XF	Unc	BU
2004R	30,000	—	—	—	55.00	60.00
2004R Proof	12,000	Value: 70.00				

KM# 241 10 EURO
22.0000 g., 0.9250 Silver 0.6542 oz. ASW, 34 mm. **Subject:** Giacomo Puccini **Obv:** Puccini wearing hat **Rev:** Stage, music and quill

Date	Mintage	F	VF	XF	Unc	BU
2004R	30,000	—	—	—	70.00	75.00
2004R Proof	12,000	Value: 100				

KM# 260 10 EURO
22.0000 g., 0.9250 Silver 0.6542 oz. ASW, 34 mm. **Subject:** 2006 Olympic Winter Games Torino Alpine Skiing

Date	Mintage	F	VF	XF	Unc	BU
2005R	40,000	—	—	—	60.00	65.00
2005R Proof	40,000	Value: 85.00				

KM# 261 10 EURO
22.0000 g., 0.9250 Silver 0.6542 oz. ASW, 34 mm. **Subject:** 2006 Olympic Winter Games Torino Ice Hockey

Date	Mintage	F	VF	XF	Unc	BU
2005R	35,000	—	—	—	60.00	65.00
2005R Proof	40,000	Value: 85.00				

KM# 262 10 EURO
22.0000 g., 0.9250 Silver 0.6542 oz. ASW, 34 mm. **Subject:** 2006 Olympic Winter Games Torino Speed Skating

Date	Mintage	F	VF	XF	Unc	BU
2005R	35,000	—	—	—	60.00	65.00
2005R Proof	40,000	Value: 85.00				

KM# 268 10 EURO
22.0000 g., 0.9250 Silver 0.6542 oz. ASW, 34 mm. **Subject:** 60th Anniversary UN "ONU"

Date	Mintage	F	VF	XF	Unc	BU
2005	25,000	—	—	—	50.00	55.00

KM# 271 10 EURO
22.0000 g., 0.9250 Silver 0.6542 oz. ASW, 34 mm. **Subject:** Peace and Freedom In Europe

Date	Mintage	F	VF	XF	Unc	BU
2005 Proof	20,000	Value: 60.00				

KM# 283 10 EURO
22.0000 g., 0.9250 Silver 0.6542 oz. ASW, 34 mm. **Subject:** FIFA World Cup - Germany

Date	Mintage	F	VF	XF	Unc	BU
2006R	—	—	—	—	70.00	75.00

KM# 284 10 EURO
22.0000 g., 0.9250 Silver 0.6542 oz. ASW **Subject:** Andre Martenga - 500th Anniversary

Date	Mintage	F	VF	XF	Unc	BU
2006R	—	—	—	—	70.00	75.00

KM# 285 10 EURO
22.0000 g., 0.9250 Silver 0.6542 oz. ASW, 34 mm. **Subject:** Leonardo da Vinci

Date	Mintage	F	VF	XF	Unc	BU
2006R	—	—	—	—	70.00	75.00

KM# 286 10 EURO
22.0000 g., 0.9250 Silver 0.6542 oz. ASW, 34 mm. **Subject:** UNICEF 60th Anniversary

Date	Mintage	F	VF	XF	Unc	BU
2006R	—	—	—	—	70.00	75.00

KM# 295 10 EURO
22.0000 g., 0.9250 Silver 0.6542 oz. ASW, 34 mm. **Subject:** Treaty of Rome, 50th Anniversary

Date	Mintage	F	VF	XF	Unc	BU
2007R	—	—	—	—	70.00	75.00

KM# 296 10 EURO
22.0000 g., 0.9250 Silver 0.6542 oz. ASW, 34 mm. **Subject:** Antonia Canova - 250th Anniversary Birth **Obv:** Portrait facing **Rev:** Sculpture Eros and Psyche

Date	Mintage	F	VF	XF	Unc	BU
2007R Proof	8,000	Value: 65.00				

KM# 297 10 EURO
22.0000 g., 0.9250 Silver 0.6542 oz. ASW, 34 mm. **Subject:** Mint of Rome's School of Medallic Art - 100th Anniversary **Obv:** Sculptor designing medal, from a medal by Giuseppe Romagnoli **Rev:** School logo

Date	Mintage	F	VF	XF	Unc	BU
2007R Proof	8,000	Value: 65.00				

KM# 324 10 EURO
22.0000 g., 0.9250 Silver 0.6542 oz. ASW, 34 mm. **Subject:** Treaty of Rome, 50th Anniversary **Obv:** Pavement pattern from Capitol Square in Rome **Rev:** Steps leading up to Capitol

Date	Mintage	F	VF	XF	Unc	BU
2007R Proof	22,000	Value: 65.00				

KM# 305 10 EURO
22.0000 g., 0.9250 Silver 0.6542 oz. ASW, 34 mm. **Subject:** Andrea Palladio - 500th Birthday

Date	Mintage	F	VF	XF	Unc	BU
2008	—	—	—	—	70.00	75.00

KM# 306 10 EURO
22.0000 g., 0.9250 Silver 0.6542 oz. ASW, 34 mm. **Subject:** University of Perugia - 700th Anniversary

Date	Mintage	F	VF	XF	Unc	BU
2008	—	—	—	—	70.00	75.00

KM# 316 10 EURO
22.0000 g., 0.9250 Silver 0.6542 oz. ASW, 34 mm. **Subject:** International Year of Astronomy **Obv:** Head right, astrolabe at left **Rev:** Galilei's telescope, details of an astrolabe and sky **Designer:** L. De Simoni

Date	Mintage	F	VF	XF	Unc	BU
2009R Proof	9,000	Value: 75.00				

KM# 317 10 EURO
22.0000 g., 0.9250 Silver 0.6542 oz. ASW, 34 mm. **Subject:** Guglielmo Maroni's Nobel Prize in Physics **Obv:** Bust and yacht Elettra **Rev:** Radio receiver and antenna and radio waves **Designer:** U. Pemazza

Date	Mintage	F	VF	XF	Unc	BU
2009R Proof	18,000	Value: 75.00				

KM# 318 10 EURO
22.0000 g., 0.9250 Silver 0.6542 oz. ASW, 34 mm. **Subject:** Annibale Carracci, 400th Anniversary **Obv:** 1/2 length figure standing **Rev:** Historical cart **Designer:** U. Pemazza

Date	Mintage	F	VF	XF	Unc	BU
2009R Proof	9,000	Value: 75.00				

KM# 319 10 EURO
22.0000 g., 0.9250 Silver 0.6542 oz. ASW, 34 mm. **Subject:** Futurist movement, 100th Anniversary **Obv:** Building design **Rev:** Round sculpture **Designer:** Momoni

Date	Mintage	F	VF	XF	Unc	BU
2009R Proof	9,000	Value: 75.00				

KM# 337 10 EURO
22.0000 g., 0.9250 Silver 0.6542 oz. ASW, 34 mm. **Subject:** L'Aquila Earthquake, reconstruction

Date	Mintage	F	VF	XF	Unc	BU
2009R Proof	—	Value: 75.00				

KM# 332 10 EURO
22.0000 g., 0.9250 Silver 0.6542 oz. ASW, 34 mm. **Subject:** Caravaggio 400th Death Anniversary **Obv:** Bust 3/4 facing left, basket of fruit below **Rev:** Medussa head painting detail **Designer:** U. Pemazza

Date	Mintage	F	VF	XF	Unc	BU
2010R Proof	7,500	Value: 70.00				

KM# 333 10 EURO
22.0000 g., 0.9250 Silver 0.6542 oz. ASW, 34 mm. **Subject:** Giorgione, 500th Death Anniverdary **Obv:** Bust 3/4 left **Obv. Designer:** M C. Colaneri **Rev:** Detail from the painting "La Tempesta" **Rev. Designer:** M. C. Colaneri

Date	Mintage	F	VF	XF	Unc	BU
2010R Proof	7,500	Value: 70.00				

KM# 334 10 EURO
22.0000 g., 0.9250 Silver 0.6542 oz. ASW, 34 mm. **Subject:** Arts of Italy, Aquileia **Obv:** Basilica and architechtural floorplan **Rev:** Interpertation from the "Tabula Peuntigeriana" **Designer:** R. Mauri

Date	Mintage	F	VF	XF	Unc	BU
2010R Proof	7,500	Value: 70.00				

KM# 263 20 EURO
6.4510 g., 0.9000 Gold 0.1867 oz. AGW, 21 mm. **Subject:** Arts in Europe - Italy

Date	Mintage	F	VF	XF	Unc	BU
2003R Proof	6,000	Value: 370				

KM# 242 20 EURO
6.4510 g., 0.9000 Gold 0.1867 oz. AGW, 21 mm. **Obv:** Arts In Europe: Belgium **Rev:** Flying bird obscuring a man's face

Date	Mintage	F	VF	XF	Unc	BU
2004R Proof	6,000	Value: 350				

KM# 243 20 EURO
6.4510 g., 0.9000 Gold 0.1867 oz. AGW, 21 mm. **Subject:** World Cup Soccer - Germany 2006 **Obv:** Mascot **Rev:** Soccer ball and world globe

Date	Mintage	F	VF	XF	Unc	BU
2004R Proof	7,500	Value: 370				

KM# 265 20 EURO
6.4510 g., 0.9000 Gold 0.1867 oz. AGW, 54 mm. **Subject:** 2006 Olympic Winter Games Torino Porte Palatine Gate

Date	Mintage	F	VF	XF	Unc	BU
2005R Proof	10,000	Value: 350				

KM# 267 20 EURO
6.4510 g., 0.9000 Gold 0.1867 oz. AGW, 21 mm. **Subject:** 2006 Olympic Games Torino Madama Palace

Date	Mintage	F	VF	XF	Unc	BU
2005 Proof	10,000	Value: 350				

KM# 269 20 EURO
6.4510 g., 0.9000 Gold 0.1867 oz. AGW, 21 mm. **Subject:** 2006 Olympic Games Torino Stupinigi Palace

Date	Mintage	F	VF	XF	Unc	BU
2005 Proof	10,000	Value: 350				

KM# 272 20 EURO
6.4510 g., 0.9000 Gold 0.1867 oz. AGW, 21 mm. **Subject:** Art In Europe - Finland

Date	Mintage	F	VF	XF	Unc	BU
2005 Proof	5,000	Value: 400				

KM# 287 20 EURO
6.4510 g., 0.9000 Gold 0.1867 oz. AGW, 21 mm. **Subject:** FIFA World Cup

Date	Mintage	F	VF	XF	Unc	BU
2006R	—	—	—	—	—	450

KM# 288 20 EURO
6.4510 g., 0.9000 Gold 0.1867 oz. AGW, 21 mm. **Subject:** European Arts - Germany

Date	Mintage	F	VF	XF	Unc	BU
2006R	—	—	—	—	—	450

KM# 298 20 EURO
6.4510 g., 0.9000 Gold 0.1867 oz. AGW, 21 mm. **Subject:** Treaty of Rome - 50th Anniversary **Obv:** Pavement pattern in Capital Square in Rome **Rev:** Steps leading to Capital Building

Date	Mintage	F	VF	XF	Unc	BU
2007R Proof	4,000	Value: 450				

KM# 299 20 EURO
6.4510 g., 0.9000 Gold 0.1867 oz. AGW, 21 mm. **Subject:** European Art - Ireland **Obv:** Sailing ship **Rev:** Tara Brooch

Date	Mintage	F	VF	XF	Unc	BU
2007R Proof	3,500	Value: 450				

KM# 307 20 EURO
6.4510 g., 0.9000 Gold 0.1867 oz. AGW, 21 mm. **Subject:** Andrea Palladio - 500th Birthday **Obv:** Head left **Rev:** Building facase and floorplans

Date	Mintage	F	VF	XF	Unc	BU
2008	—	—	—	—	—	450

KM# 308 20 EURO
6.4510 g., 0.9000 Gold 0.1867 oz. AGW, 21 mm. **Subject:** Arts in Europe - Netherlands

Date	Mintage	F	VF	XF	Unc	BU
2008	—	—	—	—	—	450

KM# 320 20 EURO
6.4500 g., 0.9000 Gold 0.1866 oz. AGW, 21 mm. **Subject:** Guglielmo Marconi, 100th Anniversary of Nobel in Physics **Obv:** Bust and yacht Elettra **Rev:** Radio receiver with antenna and radio waves **Designer:** U. Pemazza

Date	Mintage	F	VF	XF	Unc	BU
2009R Proof	5,000	Value: 375				

KM# 321 20 EURO
6.4500 g., 0.9000 Gold 0.1866 oz. AGW, 21 mm. **Subject:** Arts in Europe - Great Britain **Obv:** Sailing ship **Rev:** Venus by Edward B. Jones **Designer:** E. L. Frapiccini

Date	Mintage	F	VF	XF	Unc	BU
2009R Proof	3,000	Value: 400				

KM# 335 20 EURO
6.4510 g., 0.9000 Gold 0.1867 oz. AGW, 21 mm. **Subject:** Arts of Europe - Sweden **Obv:** Sailing ship **Rev:** Viking Helmet **Designer:** E. L. Frapiccini

Date	Mintage	F	VF	XF	Unc	BU
2010R Proof	2,000	Value: 400				

KM# 264 50 EURO
16.1300 g., 0.9000 Gold 0.4667 oz. AGW, 28 mm. **Subject:** Arts in Europe - Austria

Date	Mintage	F	VF	XF	Unc	BU
2003R Proof	6,000	Value: 750				

KM# 244 50 EURO
16.1300 g., 0.9000 Gold 0.4667 oz. AGW, 28 mm. **Obv:** Arts In Europe: Denmark **Rev:** Angel carrying away two children

Date	Mintage	F	VF	XF	Unc	BU
2004R Proof	6,000	Value: 750				

KM# 270 50 EURO
16.1300 g., 0.9000 Gold 0.4667 oz. AGW, 28 mm. **Subject:** 2006 Olympic Games Torino Emanuele Filiberto

Date	Mintage	F	VF	XF	Unc	BU
2005 Proof	6,000	Value: 725				

KM# 273 50 EURO
16.1300 g., 0.9000 Gold 0.4667 oz. AGW, 28 mm. **Subject:** Art In Europe - France

Date	Mintage	F	VF	XF	Unc	BU
2005 Proof	5,000	Value: 750				

KM# 274 50 EURO
16.1300 g., 0.9000 Gold 0.4667 oz. AGW, 28 mm. **Subject:** 2006 Olympic Games Torino Olympic Torch

Date	Mintage	F	VF	XF	Unc	BU
2006 Proof	5,000	Value: 750				

KM# 289 50 EURO
16.1300 g., 0.9000 Gold 0.4667 oz. AGW, 28 mm. **Subject:** European Arts - Greece

Date	Mintage	F	VF	XF	Unc	BU
2006R	—	—	—	—	—	800

KM# 300 50 EURO
16.1300 g., 0.9000 Gold 0.4667 oz. AGW, 28 mm. **Subject:** European Art - Norway **Obv:** Sailing ship **Rev:** Painting "The Scream" by Edvard Munch

Date	Mintage	F	VF	XF	Unc	BU
2007R Proof	2,000	Value: 800				

KM# 309 50 EURO
16.1300 g., 0.9000 Gold 0.4667 oz. AGW, 28 mm. **Subject:** Arts in Europe - Portugal

Date	Mintage	F	VF	XF	Unc	BU
2008	—	—	—	—	—	800

KM# 322 50 EURO
6.1300 g., 0.9000 Gold 0.1774 oz. AGW, 28 mm. **Subject:** Arts in Europe - Spain **Obv:** Sailing ship **Rev:** Sagrada Familia of Antoni Gaudí **Designer:** E. L. Frapiccini

Date	Mintage	F	VF	XF	Unc	BU
2009R Proof	2,000	Value: 800				

KM# 336 50 EURO
16.1250 g., 0.9000 Gold 0.4666 oz. AGW, 28 mm. **Subject:** Arts of Europe - Hungary **Obv:** Sailing ship **Rev:** Detail of painting "Rozsi Szinyei Merse" by Pal Szinyel Merse **Designer:** E. L. Frapiccini

Date	Mintage	F	VF	XF	Unc	BU
2010R Proof	1,500	—	—	—	—	800

MINT SETS

KM#	Date	Mintage	Identification	Issue Price	Mkt Val
MS39	2001 (12)	125,200	KM#91-94, 97.2, 98, 105, 111, 159, 183, 194, 236	—	235
MS40	2002 (8)	50,000	KM#210-217	—	22.00
MS41	2003 (8)	50,000	KM#210-217	—	30.00
MS42	2003 (9)	50,000	KM#210-217, 253	—	70.00
MS43	2004 (8)	40,000	KM#210-217	—	35.00
MS44	2004 (9)	40,000	KM#210-217, 254	—	75.00
MS45	2005 (8)	35,000	KM#210-217	—	35.00
MS46	2005 (9)	35,000	KM#210-217, 255	—	75.00
MS47	2006 (8)	25,000	KM#210-217	—	30.00
MS48	2007 (8)	20,000	KM#210-217	—	30.00
MS49	2008 (8)	20,000	KM#210-216, 301	—	45.00
MS50	2008 (9)	5,000	KM#210-217, 281	—	125

PROOF SETS

KM#	Date	Mintage	Identification	Issue Price	Mkt Val
PS25	2001 (12)	10,000	KM#91-94, 97.2, 98, 105, 111, 159, 183, 194, 236	—	650
PS26	2003 (9)	12,000	KM#210-217, 253	—	200
PS27	2004 (9)	15,000	KM#210-217, 254	—	170
PS28	2005 (9)	12,000	KM#210-217, 255	—	140
PS29	2006 (8)	10,000	KM#210-217	—	80.00
PS30	2007 (8)	7,000	KM#210-217	—	80.00
PS31	2008 (9)	5,000	KM#210-217, 282	—	145

IVORY COAST

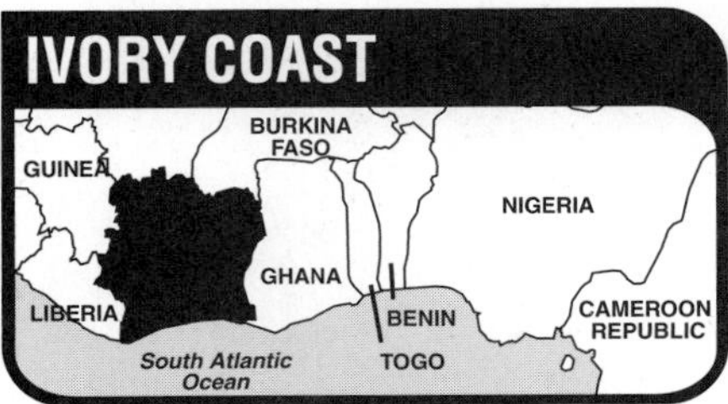

The Republic of the Ivory Coast, (Cote d'Ivoire), a former French Overseas territory located on the south side of the African bulge between Liberia and Ghana, has an area of 124,504 sq. mi. (322,463 sq. km.) and a population of 11.8 million. Capital: Yamoussoukro. The predominantly agricultural economy is one of Africa's most prosperous. Coffee, tropical woods, cocoa, and bananas are exported.

REPUBLIC

DECIMAL COINAGE

KM# 6 100 FRANCS
25.0000 g., 0.9250 Silver 0.7435 oz. ASW, 38.6 mm. **Rev:** Mamouth and embedded tooth fragment

Date	Mintage	F	VF	XF	Unc	BU
2010 Proof	2,500	Value: 75.00				

JAMAICA

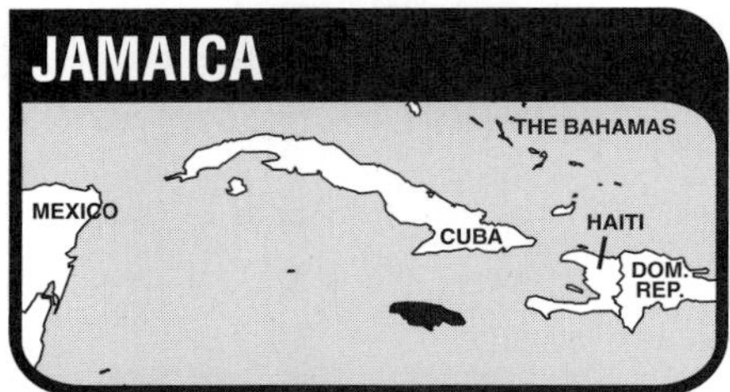

Jamaica is situated in the Caribbean Sea 90 miles south of Cuba, has an area of 4,244 sq. mi. (10,990 sq. km.) and a population of 2.1 million. Capital: Kingston. The economy is founded chiefly on mining, tourism and agriculture. Aluminum, bauxite, sugar, rum and molasses are exported.

Jamaica is a member of the Commonwealth of Nations. Elizabeth II is the Head of State, as Queen of Jamaica.

RULER
British, until 1962

MINT MARKS
C - Royal Canadian Mint, Ottawa
H - Heaton

MONETARY SYSTEM
100 Cents = 1 Dollar

COMMONWEALTH

DECIMAL COINAGE

KM# 64 CENT
1.2200 g., Aluminum, 21.08 mm. **Ruler:** Elizabeth II **Series:** F.A.O. **Obv:** National arms **Obv. Legend:** JAMAICA **Rev:** Ackee fruit above value **Edge:** Plain **Shape:** 12-sided **Designer:** Christopher Ironside

Date	Mintage	F	VF	XF	Unc	BU
2002	—	—	—	0.25	0.50	0.75
2002 Proof	500	Value: 1.00				

KM# 146.2 10 CENTS
2.4000 g., Copper Plated Steel, 17 mm. **Ruler:** Elizabeth II **Series:** National Heroes **Subject:** Paul Bogle **Obv:** National arms **Obv. Legend:** JAMAICA **Rev:** Bust facing **Edge:** Plain **Note:** Reduced size.

Date	Mintage	F	VF	XF	Unc	BU
2002	—	—	—	0.25	0.50	0.75
2002 Proof	500	Value: 2.00				
2003	—	—	—	0.25	0.50	0.75

KM# 167 25 CENTS
3.6000 g., Copper Plated Steel, 20 mm. **Ruler:** Elizabeth II **Series:** National Heroes **Subject:** Marcus Garvey **Obv:** National arms **Obv. Legend:** JAMAICA **Rev:** Head 1/4 right **Edge:** Plain

Date	Mintage	F	VF	XF	Unc	BU
2002	—	—	—	0.25	0.50	0.75
2002 Proof	500	Value: 3.00				
2003	—	—	—	0.25	0.50	0.75

KM# 164 DOLLAR
2.9100 g., Nickel Plated Steel, 18.5 mm. **Ruler:** Elizabeth II **Series:** National Heroes **Subject:** Sir Alexander Bustamante **Obv:** National arms **Obv. Legend:** JAMAICA **Rev:** Bust facing **Edge:** Plain **Shape:** 7-sided

Date	Mintage	F	VF	XF	Unc	BU
2002	—	—	—	0.40	1.00	1.50
2002 Proof	500	Value: 4.00				
2003	—	—	—	0.40	1.00	1.50
2005	—	—	—	0.40	1.00	1.50
2006	—	—	—	0.40	1.00	1.50

KM# 189 DOLLAR
2.9000 g., Nickel Clad Steel, 18.5 mm. **Ruler:** Elizabeth II **Rev:** Sir Alexander Bustamante

Date	Mintage	F	VF	XF	Unc	BU
2008	—	—	—	—	1.00	1.50
2009	—	—	—	—	1.00	1.50

KM# 163 5 DOLLARS
4.4000 g., Steel, 21.5 mm. **Ruler:** Elizabeth II **Series:** National Heroes **Subject:** Norman Manley **Obv:** National arms **Obv. Legend:** JAMAICA **Rev:** Head left **Edge:** Reeded

Date	Mintage	F	VF	XF	Unc	BU
2002	—	—	—	1.50	2.50	3.50
2002 Proof	500	Value: 5.00				

KM# 181 10 DOLLARS
5.9400 g., Nickel Plated Steel **Ruler:** Elizabeth II **Series:** National Heroes **Subject:** George William Gordon **Obv:** National arms **Obv. Legend:** JAMAICA / TEN DOLLARS - (date) **Rev:** Bust facing **Edge:** Plain **Shape:** Scalloped **Note:** Diameter varies: 24-24.6.

Date	Mintage	F	VF	XF	Unc	BU
2002	—	—	—	1.50	3.00	4.00

Date	Mintage	F	VF	XF	Unc	BU
2002 Proof	500	Value: 9.00				
2005	—	—	—	1.50	3.00	4.00

KM# 190 10 DOLLARS

5.9400 g., Stainless Steel, 24.6 mm. **Ruler:** Elizabeth II **Obv:** Arms **Obv. Legend:** JAMAICA / TEN DOLLARS (date) **Rev:** George William Gordon

Date	Mintage	F	VF	XF	Unc	BU
2008	—	—	—	—	6.00	7.50
2009	—	—	—	—	6.00	7.50

KM# 182 20 DOLLARS

7.8000 g., Bi-Metallic Copper-Nickel center in Nickel-Brass ring, 23 mm. **Ruler:** Elizabeth II **Series:** National Heroes **Subject:** Marcus Garvey **Obv:** Value above national arms within circle **Obv. Legend:** JAMAICA **Rev:** Head 1/4 right within circle **Edge:** Segmented reeding

Date	Mintage	F	VF	XF	Unc	BU
2001	—	—	—	1.50	3.00	4.00
2002	—	—	—	1.50	3.00	4.00
2002 Proof	500	Value: 15.00				

KM# 186 25 DOLLARS

28.2800 g., 0.9250 Silver 0.8410 oz. ASW, 38.6 mm. **Ruler:** Elizabeth II **Subject:** UNICEF **Obv:** Arms with supporters **Rev:** Two boys above "Pals" **Edge:** Reeded

Date	Mintage	F	VF	XF	Unc	BU
2001 Proof	—	Value: 60.00				

KM# 185 25 DOLLARS

28.2800 g., 0.9250 Silver 0.8410 oz. ASW, 38.6 mm. **Ruler:** Elizabeth II **Subject:** IAAF World Junior Championships **Obv:** Arms with supporters and value **Rev:** Female runner **Edge:** Reeded

Date	Mintage	F	VF	XF	Unc	BU
2002 Proof	5,500	Value: 65.00				

KM# 184 50 DOLLARS

28.4500 g., 0.9250 Silver 0.8461 oz. ASW, 38.6 mm. **Ruler:** Elizabeth II **Subject:** Millennium **Obv:** Arms with supporters **Rev:** Family within radiant sun **Edge:** Reeded

Date	Mintage	F	VF	XF	Unc	BU
ND(2002) Proof	5,000	Value: 55.00				

PROOF SETS

KM#	Date	Mintage	Identification	Issue Price	Mkt Val
PS33	2002 (8)	500	KM#64, 146.2, 163, 164, 167, 181, 182, 185	99.00	105

JAPAN

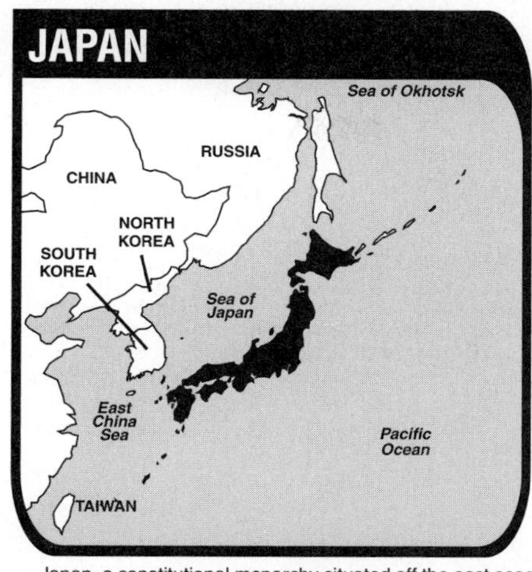

Japan, a constitutional monarchy situated off the east coast of Asia, has an area of 145,809 sq. mi. (377,835 sq. km.) and a population of 123.2 million. Capital: Tokyo. Japan, one of the major industrial nations of the world, exports machinery, motor vehicles, electronics and chemicals.

Japanese coinage of concern to this catalog includes those issued for the Ryukyu Islands (also called Liuchu), a chain of islands extending southwest from Japan toward Taiwan (Formosa), before the Japanese government converted the islands into a prefecture under the name Okinawa. Many of the provinces of Japan issued their own definitive coinage under the Shogunate.

RULERS

Emperors

Akihito (Heisei), 1989-

Years 1 – 平成

NOTE: The personal name of the emperor is followed by the name that he chose for his regnal era.

MONETARY UNITS

Yen 円 or 圓 or 圓

EMPIRE

REFORM COINAGE

Y# 95.2 YEN

1.0000 g., Aluminum, 20 mm. **Ruler:** Akihito **Obv:** Sprouting branch divides authority and value **Rev:** Value within circles above date **Edge:** Plain

Date	Mintage	F	VF	XF	Unc	BU
Yr,13(2001)	7,786,000	—	—	0.70	1.25	1.50
Yr.13(2001) Proof	238,000	Value: 3.00				
Yr.14(2002)	9,425,000	—	0.70	1.25	—	1.50
Yr.14(2002) Proof	242,000	Value: 5.00				
Yr.15(2003)	117,131,000	—	—	—	—	0.50
Yr.15(2003) Proof	275,000	Value: 3.00				
Yr.16(2004)	52,623,000	—	—	—	—	0.50
Yr.16(2004) Proof	280,000	Value: 3.00				
Yr.17(2005)	29,761,000	—	—	—	—	0.50
Yr.17(2005) Proof	258,000	Value: 3.00				
Yr.18(2006)	129,347,000	—	—	—	—	0.50
Yr.18(2006) Proof	247,000	Value: 3.00				
Yr.19(2007)	223,702,200	—	—	—	—	0.50
Yr.19(2007) Proof	201,800	Value: 3.00				
Yr.20(2008)	134,642,800	—	—	—	—	0.50
Yr.20(2008) Proof	168,200	Value: 3.00				
Yr.21(2009)	—	—	—	—	—	0.50
Yr.21(2009) Proof	—	Value: 3.00				
Yr.22(2010)	—	—	—	—	—	0.50
Yr.22(2010) Proof	—	Value: 3.00				

Y# 96.2 5 YEN

3.7500 g., Brass, 22 mm. **Ruler:** Akihito **Obv:** Hole in center flanked by a seed leaf with authority on top and date below **Rev:** Gear design around center hole with bending rice stalk above value in horizontal lines below

Date	Mintage	F	VF	XF	Unc	BU
Yr.13(2001)	77,787,000	—	—	—	—	0.35
Yr.13(2001) Proof	238,000	Value: 1.75				
Yr.14(2002)	143,420,000	—	—	—	—	0.35
Yr.14(2002) Proof	242,000	Value: 1.75				
Yr.15(2003)	102,031,000	—	—	—	—	0.35
Yr.15(2003) Proof	275,000	Value: 1.75				
Yr.16(2004)	70,623,000	—	—	—	—	0.35
Yr.16(2004) Proof	280,000	Value: 1.75				
Yr.17(2005)	15,761,000	—	—	0.50	0.75	1.00
Yr.17(2005) Proof	258,000	Value: 3.00				
Yr.18(2006)	9,347,000	—	—	0.75	1.25	1.50
Yr.18(2006) Proof	247,000	Value: 4.00				
Yr.19(2007)	9,702,200	—	—	—	1.25	1.50
Yr.19(2007) Proof	201,800	Value: 4.00				
Yr.20(2008)	9,642,800	—	—	0.75	1.25	1.50
Yr.20(2008) Proof	168,200	Value: 4.00				
Yr.21(2009)	—	—	—	—	—	0.35
Yr.21(2009) Proof	—	Value: 4.00				
Yr.22(2010)	—	—	—	—	—	0.35
Yr.22(2010) Proof	—	Value: 4.00				

Y# 97.2 10 YEN

4.5000 g., Bronze, 23.5 mm. **Ruler:** Akihito **Obv:** Temple divides authority and value **Rev:** Value within wreath

Date	Mintage	F	VF	XF	Unc	BU
Yr.13(2001)	541,786,000	—	—	—	—	0.45
Yr.13(2001) Proof	238,000	Value: 1.75				
Yr.14(2002)	455,425,000	—	—	—	—	0.45
Yr.14(2002) Proof	242,000	Value: 1.75				
Yr.15(2003)	551,131,000	—	—	—	—	0.45
Yr.15(2003) Proof	275,000	Value: 1.75				
Yr.16(2004)	592,623,000	—	—	—	—	0.45
Yr.16(2004) Proof	280,000	Value: 1.75				
Yr.17(2005)	503,761,000	—	—	—	—	0.45
Yr.17(2005) Proof	258,000	Value: 1.75				
Yr.18(2006)	440,347,000	—	—	—	—	0.45
Yr.18(2006) Proof	247,000	Value: 1.75				
Yr.19(2007)	388,702,200	—	—	—	—	0.45
Yr.19(2007) Proof	201,800	Value: 1.75				
Yr.20(2008)	362,642,800	—	—	—	—	0.45
Yr.20(2008) Proof	168,200	Value: 1.75				
Yr.21(2009)	—	—	—	—	—	0.45
Yr.21(2009) Proof	—	Value: 1.75				
Yr.22(2010)	—	—	—	—	—	0.45
Yr.22(2010) Proof	—	Value: 1.75				

Y# 101.2 50 YEN

4.0000 g., Copper-Nickel, 21 mm. **Ruler:** Akihito **Obv:** Center hole flanked by chrysanthemums, authority at top and value below **Rev:** Value above hole in center **Edge:** Reeded

Date	Mintage	F	VF	XF	Unc	BU
Yr.13(2001)	7,786,000	—	—	—	—	3.00
Yr.13(2001) Proof	238,000	Value: 4.00				
Yr.14(2002)	11,425,000	—	—	—	—	5.00
Yr.14(2002) Proof	242,000	Value: 7.00				
Yr.15(2003)	10,131,000	—	—	—	—	5.00
Yr.15(2003) Proof	275,000	Value: 7.00				
Yr.16(2004)	9,623,000	—	—	—	—	5.00
Yr.16(2004) Proof	280,000	Value: 7.00				
Yr.17(2005)	9,761,000	—	—	—	—	5.00
Yr.17(2005) Proof	258,000	Value: 7.00				
Yr.18(2006)	10,347,000	—	—	—	—	5.00
Yr.18(2006) Proof	247,000	Value: 7.00				
Yr.19(2007)	9,702,200	—	—	—	—	5.00
Yr.19(2007) Proof	201,800	Value: 7.00				
Yr.20(2008)	8,642,800	—	—	—	—	5.00
Yr.20(2008) Proof	168,200	Value: 7.00				

Date	Mintage	F	VF	XF	Unc	BU
Yr.21(2009)	—	—	—	—	—	5.00
Yr.21(2009) Proof	—	Value: 7.00				
Yr.22(2010)	—	—	—	—	—	5.00
Yr.22(2010) Proof	—	Value: 7.00				

Y# 98.2 100 YEN

4.8000 g., Copper-Nickel, 22.6 mm. **Ruler:** Akihito **Obv:** Cherry blossoms **Rev:** Large numeral 100, date in western numerals **Edge:** Reeded

Date	Mintage	F	VF	XF	Unc	BU
Yr.13(2001)	7,786,000	—	—	—	—	7.50
Yr.13(2001) Proof	238,000	Value: 10.00				
Yr.14(2002)	10,425,000	—	—	—	—	5.00
Yr.14(2002) Proof	242,000	Value: 8.00				
Yr.15(2003)	98,131,000	—	—	—	—	2.00
Yr.15(2003) Proof	275,000	Value: 5.00				
Yr.16(2004)	204,623,000	—	—	—	—	2.00
Yr.16(2004) Proof	280,000	Value: 5.00				
Yr.17(2005)	299,761,000	—	—	—	—	2.00
Yr.17(2005) Proof	258,000	Value: 5.00				
Yr.18(2006)	216,347,000	—	—	—	—	2.00
Yr.18(2006) Proof	247,000	Value: 5.00				
Yr.19(2007)	129,702,200	—	—	—	—	2.00
Yr.19(2007) Proof	201,800	Value: 5.00				
Yr.20(2008)	93,642,800	—	—	—	—	2.00
Yr.20(2008) Proof	168,200	Value: 5.00				
Yr.21(2009)	—	—	—	—	—	2.00
Yr.21(2009) Proof	—	Value: 5.00				
Yr.22(2010)	—	—	—	—	—	2.00
Yr.22(2010) Proof	—	Value: 5.00				

Y# 125 500 YEN

7.0000 g., Nickel-Brass, 26.5 mm. **Ruler:** Akihito **Obv:** Pawlownia flower and highlighted legends **Rev:** Value with latent zeros **Edge:** Slanted reeding

Date	Mintage	F	VF	XF	Unc	BU
Yr.13(2001)	607,813,000	—	—	—	—	9.00
Yr.13(2001) Proof	238,000	Value: 15.00				
Yr.14(2002)	504,419,000	—	—	—	—	9.00
Yr.14(2002) Proof	242,000	Value: 15.00				
Yr.15(2003)	438,130,000	—	—	—	—	9.00
Yr.15(2003) Proof	275,000	Value: 15.00				
Yr.16(2004)	356,623,000	—	—	—	—	9.00
Yr.16(2004) Proof	280,000	Value: 15.00				
Yr.17(2005)	334,762,000	—	—	—	—	9.00
Yr.17(2005) Proof	258,000	Value: 15.00				
Yr.18(2006)	381,346,000	—	—	—	—	9.00
Yr.18(2006) Proof	247,000	Value: 15.00				
Yr.19(2007)	401,701,200	—	—	—	—	9.00
Yr.19(2007) Proof	201,800	Value: 15.00				
Yr.20(2008)	432,642,800	—	—	—	—	9.00
Yr.20(2008) Proof	168,200	Value: 15.00				
Yr.21(2009)	—	—	—	—	—	9.00
Yr.21(2009) Proof	—	Value: 15.00				
Yr.22(2010)	—	—	—	—	—	9.00
Yr.22(2010) Proof	—	Value: 15.00				

Y# 126 500 YEN

7.0000 g., Copper-Nickel-Zinc, 26.5 mm. **Ruler:** Akihito **Subject:** World Cup Soccer - Europe & Africa **Obv:** Four players and map background **Rev:** Games logo within shooting star wreath **Edge:** Reeded

Date	Mintage	VG	F	VF	XF	BU
Yr.14(2002)	10,000,000	—	—	—	—	10.00

Y# 127 500 YEN

7.0000 g., Copper-Nickel-Zinc, 26.5 mm. **Ruler:** Akihito **Subject:** World Cup Soccer - Asia & Oceania **Obv:** Three players and map background **Rev:** Games logo within shooting star wreath **Edge:** Reeded

Date	Mintage	VG	F	VF	XF	BU
Yr. 14(2002)	10,000,000	—	—	—	—	10.00

Y# 128 500 YEN

7.0000 g., Copper-Nickel-Zinc, 26.5 mm. **Ruler:** Akihito **Subject:** World Cup Soccer - North & South America **Obv:** Four players and map background **Rev:** Games logo **Edge:** Reeded

Date	Mintage	VG	F	VF	XF	BU
Yr. 14 (2002)	10,000,000	—	—	—	—	10.00

Y# 133 500 YEN

7.0000 g., Copper-Nickel-Zinc, 26.5 mm. **Ruler:** Akihito **Subject:** Expo 2005 - Aichi, Japan **Obv:** Pacific map an globe **Rev:** Circular Expo logo

Date	Mintage	VG	F	VF	XF	BU
Yr. 17(2005)	8,241,000	—	—	—	—	10.00

Y# 134 500 YEN

15.6000 g., 0.9990 Silver 0.5010 oz. ASW, 28 mm. **Ruler:** Akihito **Subject:** Chubu International Airport **Obv:** Aircraft wing in flight over airport **Rev:** Aircraft silhouettes over maps

Date	Mintage	F	VF	XF	Unc	BU
Yr. 17(2005) Proof	50,000	Value: 85.00				

Y# 137 500 YEN

7.0000 g., Copper-Nickel-Zinc, 26.5 mm. **Ruler:** Akihito **Subject:** 50th Anniversary of Japanese Antarctic Research **Obv:** Ship and two dogs **Rev:** Map of Antarctica **Edge:** Helical ridges

Date	Mintage	F	VF	XF	Unc	BU
Yr.19(2007)	6,600,000	—	—	—	—	12.00

Y# 139 500 YEN

7.0000 g., Copper-Nickel-Zinc, 26.5 mm. **Ruler:** Akihito **Subject:** Centenary of Japanese immigration to Brazil/Japan-Brazil year of exchange **Obv:** Ship **Rev:** Crossed sprigs of cherry and coffee **Note:** Prev. #Y143.

Date	Mintage	F	VF	XF	Unc	BU
Yr. 20 (2008)	—	—	—	—	—	15.00

Y# 152 500 YEN

7.0000 g., Copper-Nickel-Zinc, 26.5 mm. **Ruler:** Akihito **Subject:** Japanese - Brazil Immigration Centennial **Obv:** Ship and map of Brazil **Rev:** Cherry Blosoms and grape cluster

Date	Mintage	F	VF	XF	Unc	BU
Yr.21(2008)	4,800,000	—	—	—	—	10.00

Y# 145 500 YEN

7.1000 g., Bi-Metallic Copper-nickel center in brass ring, 26.5 mm. **Ruler:** Akihito **Subject:** Shimane Prefecture **Obv:** Bell shaped bronze vessel, artifact from Kamoiwakura **Rev:** Cash coin

Date	Mintage	F	VF	XF	Unc	BU
Yr.20(2008)	1,940,000	—	—	—	15.00	17.50
Yr.20(2008)	30,000	Value: 50.00				

Y# 141 500 YEN

7.1000 g., Bi-Metallic Copper-Nickel center in brass ring, 26.5 mm. **Ruler:** Akihito **Subject:** Hokkaido Prefecture **Obv:** Lake Toya and the former Hokkaido Government Building

Date	Mintage	F	VF	XF	Unc	BU
Yr.20(2008)	2,070,000	—	—	—	15.00	17.50
Yr.20(2008)	30,000	Value: 50.00				

Y# 143 500 YEN

7.1000 g., Bi-Metallic Copper-nickel center in brass ring, 26.5 mm. **Ruler:** Akihito **Subject:** Kyoto Prefecture **Obv:** Scene from an antique illustrated version of the Tale of Genji **Rev:** Cash coin

Date	Mintage	F	VF	XF	Unc	BU
Yr.20(2008)	2,020,000	—	—	—	15.00	17.50
Yr20(2008)	30,000	Value: 50.00				

Y# 151 500 YEN

7.0000 g., Copper-Nickel-Zinc, 26.5 mm. **Ruler:** Akihito **Subject:** Japanese - Brazil Imigration Centennial **Obv:** Commemorative statue in Santos Port **Note:** Recalled

Date	Mintage	F	VF	XF	Unc	BU
yr.20(2008)	4,800,000	—	—	—	—	15.00

Y# 147 500 YEN

7.1000 g., Bi-Metallic Copper-Nickel center in brass ring, 26.5 mm. **Ruler:** Akihito **Subject:** Nagano Prefecture **Obv:** Zenkoji Temple and ox

Date	Mintage	F	VF	XF	Unc	BU
Yr.21(2009)	1,800,000	—	—	—	15.00	17.50
Yr.21(2009) Proof	30,000	Value: 50.00				

Y# 149 500 YEN

7.1000 g., Bi-Metallic Copper-Nickel center in brass ring, 26.5 mm. **Ruler:** Akihito **Subject:** Niigata Prefecture **Obv:** Two Japanese crested ibises and rice terrace

Date	Mintage	F	VF	XF	Unc	BU
Yr.21(2009)	1,810,000	—	—	—	15.00	17.50
Yr.21(2009) Proof	30,000	Value: 50.00				

Y# 153 500 YEN

7.1000 g., Bi-Metallic, 26.5 mm. **Ruler:** Akihito **Subject:** Ibaraki Prefecture **Obv:** Kairakuen Garden and plum tree **Rev:** Cast Japanese coin

Date	Mintage	F	VF	XF	Unc	BU
Yr.21(2009)	1,840,000	—	—	—	15.00	17.50
Yr.21(2009) Proof	30,000	Value: 50.00				

Y# 155 500 YEN

7.1000 g., Bi-Metallic Copper-Nickel center in brass ring, 26.5 mm. **Ruler:** Akihito **Subject:** Nara Prefecture **Obv:** Kentoshi-sen -Ship of the Japanese envoy to China in Tang Dynasty **Rev:** Cast Japanese coin

Date	Mintage	F	VF	XF	Unc	BU
Yr.21(2009)	1,770,000	—	—	—	15.00	17.50
Yr.21(2009) Proof	30,000	Value: 50.00				

Y# 157 500 YEN

7.0000 g., Nickel-Brass, 26.5 mm. **Ruler:** Akihito **Subject:** 20th Anniversary of Emperor's Enthronement **Obv:** Imperial chrysthantem crest **Rev:** Chrysthantem blosums

Date	Mintage	F	VF	XF	Unc	BU
Yr.21(2009)	9,950,000	—	—	—	—	12.50
Yr.21(2009) Proof	50,000	Value: 30.00				

Y# 159 500 YEN

7.1000 g., Bi-Metallic Copper-Nickel center in brass ring, 26.5 mm. **Ruler:** Akihito **Subject:** Local Autonomy commemorative - Kochi Prefecture **Obv:** SAKAMOTO Ryoma **Rev:** Legend for 47 prefectures coin program, and ancient coin design reading "local autonomy"

Date	Mintage	F	VF	XF	Unc	BU
Yr.22(2010)	—	—	—	—	15.00	17.50
Yr.22(2010) Proof	Est. 30,000	Value: 50.00				

Y# 161 500 YEN

7.1000 g., Bi-Metallic Copper-Nickel center in brass ring, 26.5 mm. **Ruler:** Akihito **Subject:** Local Autonomy commemorative - Gifu Prefecture **Obv:** Shirakawa village and Chinese milk vetch **Rev:** Legend for 47 prefectures coin program, and ancient coin design reading "local autonomy"

Date	Mintage	F	VF	XF	Unc	BU
Yr.22(2010)	—	—	—	—	15.00	17.50
Yr.22(2010) Proof	Est. 30,000	Value: 50.00				

Y# 163 500 YEN

7.1000 g., Bi-Metallic Copper-Nickel center in brass ring, 26.5 mm. **Ruler:** Akihito **Subject:** Local Autonomy commemorative - Fukui Prefecture **Obv:** Fukuiraptor (foreground) and Fukuisaurus **Rev:** Legend for 47 prefectures coin program, and ancient coin design reading "local autonomy"

Date	Mintage	F	VF	XF	Unc	BU
Yr.22(2010)	—	—	—	—	15.00	17.50
Yr.22(2010) Proof	Est. 30,000	Value: 50.00				

Y# 165 500 YEN

7.1000 g., Bi-Metallic Copper-Nickel center in brass ring, 26.5 mm. **Ruler:** Akihito **Subject:** Aichi Prefecture

Date	Mintage	F	VF	XF	Unc	BU
Yr.22 (2010)	—	—	—	—	15.00	17.50
Yr.22 (2010) Proof	—	Value: 50.00				

Y# 167 500 YEN

7.1000 g., Bi-Metallic Copper-Nickel center in brass ring, 26.5 mm. **Ruler:** Akihito **Subject:** Aomori Prefecture

Date	Mintage	F	VF	XF	Unc	BU
Yr.22 (2010)	—	—	—	—	15.00	17.50
Yr.22 (2010) Proof	—	Value: 50.00				

Y# 169 500 YEN

7.1000 g., Bi-Metallic Copper-Nickel center in brass ring, 26.5 mm. **Ruler:** Akihito **Subject:** Saga Prefecture

Date	Mintage	F	VF	XF	Unc	BU
Yr.22 (2010)	—	—	—	—	15.00	17.50
Yr.22 (2010) Proof	—	Value: 50.00				

Y# 129 1000 YEN

31.1000 g., 0.9990 Silver 0.9988 oz. ASW, 40 mm. **Ruler:** Akihito **Subject:** World Cup Soccer **Obv:** Trophy within flower sprigs **Rev:** Games logo flanked by players **Edge:** Reeded

Date	Mintage	F	VF	XF	Unc	BU
Yr. 14 (2002) Proof	100,000	Value: 200				

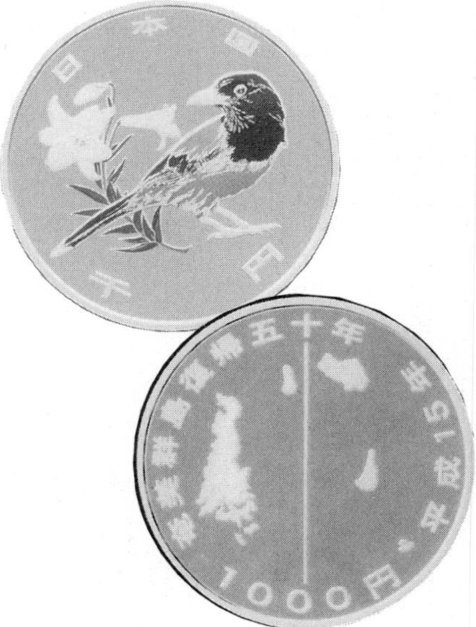

Y# 132 1000 YEN

31.1000 g., 0.9990 Silver 0.9988 oz. ASW, 40 mm. **Ruler:** Akihito **Subject:** 50th Anniversary of the reversion of the Amami Islands **Obv:** Lily and bird in multicolor enamel **Rev:** Map of the Amami-shoto

Date	Mintage	F	VF	XF	Unc	BU
Yr. 15 (2003) Proof	50,000	Value: 220				

Y# 131 1000 YEN
31.1000 g., 0.9990 Silver 0.9988 oz. ASW, 40 mm. **Ruler:** Akihito **Subject:** 5th Winter Asian Games, Aomori **Obv:** Skier and skater **Rev:** Three red apples and multicolor games logo

Date	Mintage	VG	F	VF	XF	BU
Yr.15 (2003) Proof	50,000	Value: 625				

Y# 135 1000 YEN
31.1000 g., 0.9990 Silver 0.9988 oz. ASW, 40 mm. **Ruler:** Akihito **Subject:** Expo 2005 **Obv:** Blue and white enamel Pacific map in wreath **Rev:** Expo logo

Date	Mintage	F	VF	XF	Unc	BU
Yr. 16(2004) Proof	70,000	Value: 165				

Y# 138 1000 YEN
31.1000 g., 1.0000 Silver 0.9998 oz. ASW, 40 mm. **Ruler:** Akihito **Subject:** 50th Anniversary of Japan's Entry into the United Nations **Obv:** Globe and plum blossom wreath (enameled blue, pink and green) **Rev:** UN emblem

Date	Mintage	F	VF	XF	Unc	BU
Yr.18(2006) Proof	70,000	Value: 165				

Y# 140 1000 YEN
31.1000 g., 0.9990 Silver 0.9988 oz. ASW, 40 mm. **Ruler:** Akihito **Obv:** Dual multicolor rainbows **Obv. Inscription:** SKILLS / 2007 **Rev:** Mount Fuji **Rev. Legend:** International Skills Festival for All, Japan **Edge:** Helical ridges **Note:** Prev. #Y142.

Date	Mintage	F	VF	XF	Unc	BU
Yr.19(2007) Proof	80,000	Value: 75.00				

Y# 142 1000 YEN
31.1000 g., 0.9990 Silver 0.9988 oz. ASW, 40 mm. **Ruler:** Akihito **Subject:** Hokkaido Prefecture **Obv:** Lake Toya and two multicolor red-crowned cranes in flight **Rev:** Cherry blossums and crescent

Date	Mintage	F	VF	XF	Unc	BU
Yr.20(2008) Proof	100,000	Value: 135				

Y# 144 1000 YEN
31.1000 g., 0.9990 Silver 0.9988 oz. ASW, 40 mm. **Ruler:** Akihito **Subject:** Kyoto Prefecture **Obv:** Multicolor scene from an antique illustrated version of the Tale of Genji **Rev:** Cherry blossums and crescent

Date	Mintage	F	VF	XF	Unc	BU
Yr.20(2008) Proof	100,000	Value: 120				

Y# 146 1000 YEN
31.1000 g., 0.9990 Silver 0.9988 oz. ASW, 40 mm. **Ruler:** Akihito **Subject:** Shimane Prefecture **Obv:** Multicolor peony flowers and Otoriosame chogin coin **Rev:** Cherry blossoms and crescent

Date	Mintage	F	VF	XF	Unc	BU
Yr.20(2008) Proof	100,000	Value: 115				

Y# 154 1000 YEN
31.1000 g., 0.9990 Silver 0.9988 oz. ASW **Ruler:** Akihito **Subject:** Ibaraki Prefecture **Obv:** Multicolor H-II launch vehicle and Mt. Tsukuba **Rev:** Snow crystal, moon and cherry blossom

Date	Mintage	F	VF	XF	Unc	BU
Yr.21(2008) Proof	100,000	Value: 100				

Y# 156 1000 YEN
31.1000 g., 0.9990 Silver 0.9988 oz. ASW **Ruler:** Akihito **Subject:** Nara Prefecture **Obv:** Daigokuden Audience Hall in multicolor, cherry blossoms and Kemari (ancient ball players) **Rev:** Snow crystal, moon and cherry blossoms

Date	Mintage	F	VF	XF	Unc	BU
Yr.21(2008) Proof	100,000	Value: 115				

Y# 148 1000 YEN
31.1000 g., 0.9990 Silver 0.9988 oz. ASW, 40 mm. **Ruler:**

Akihito **Subject:** Nagano Prefecture **Obv:** Multicolor Japan Alps and Kamikochi

Date	Mintage	F	VF	XF	Unc	BU
Yr.21(2009) Proof	100,000	Value: 115				

Y# 150 1000 YEN

31.1000 g., 0.9990 Silver 0.9988 oz. ASW, 40 mm. **Ruler:** Akihito **Subject:** Niigata Prefecture **Obv:** Two Japanese crested ibis and Sado Island

Date	Mintage	F	VF	XF	Unc	BU
Yr.21(2009) Proof	100,000	Value: 100				

Y# 160 1000 YEN

31.1000 g., 0.9990 Silver 0.9988 oz. ASW, 40 mm. **Ruler:** Akihito **Subject:** Local Autonomy commemorative - Kochi Prefecture **Obv:** SAKAMOTO Ryoma and Katsurahama Beach **Rev:** Snowflakes, cherry blossoms, and crescent moon with legend **Rev. Legend:** Local Autonomy 60 Years

Date	Mintage	F	VF	XF	Unc	BU
Yr.22(2010) Proof; colorized	100,000	Value: 130				

Y# 162 1000 YEN

31.1000 g., 0.9990 Silver 0.9988 oz. ASW, 40 mm. **Ruler:** Akihito **Subject:** Local Autonomy commemorative - Gifu Prefecture **Obv:** Cormorant fishing on the Nagara River **Rev:** Snowflakes, cherry blossoms, and crescent moon with legend **Rev. Legend:** Local Autonomy 60 Years

Date	Mintage	F	VF	XF	Unc	BU
Yr.22(2010) Proof; colorized	100,000	Value: 130				

Y# 164 1000 YEN

31.1000 g., 0.9990 Silver 0.9988 oz. ASW, 40 mm. **Ruler:** Akihito **Subject:** Local Autonomy commemorative - Fukui Prefecture **Obv:** Fukuiraptor and Tojinbo Cliffs **Rev:** Snowflakes, cherry blossoms, and crescent moon with legend **Rev. Legend:** Local Autonomy 60 Years

Date	Mintage	F	VF	XF	Unc	BU
Yr.22(2010) Proof; colorized	100,000	Value: 130				

Y# 166 1000 YEN

31.1000 g., 0.9990 Silver 0.9988 oz. ASW, 40 mm. **Ruler:** Akihito **Subject:** Aichi Prefecture

Date	Mintage	F	VF	XF	Unc	BU
Yr.22 (2010) Proof	100,000	Value: 80.00				

Y# 168 1000 YEN

31.1000 g., 0.9990 Silver 0.9988 oz. ASW, 40 mm. **Ruler:** Akihito **Subject:** Aomori Prefecture

Date	Mintage	F	VF	XF	Unc	BU
Yr.22 (2010) Proof	100,000	Value: 80.00				

Y# 170 1000 YEN

31.1000 g., 0.9990 Silver 0.9988 oz. ASW, 40 mm. **Ruler:** Akihito **Subject:** Saga Prefecture

Date	Mintage	F	VF	XF	Unc	BU
Yr.22 (2010) Proof	100,000	Value: 80.00				

Y# 130 10000 YEN

15.6000 g., 0.9990 Gold 0.5010 oz. AGW, 26 mm. **Ruler:** Akihito **Subject:** World Cup Soccer **Obv:** Two soccer players **Rev:** Games logo **Edge:** Reeded

Date	Mintage	F	VF	XF	Unc	BU
Yr.14(2002) Proof	100,000	Value: 750				

Y# 136 10000 YEN

15.6000 g., 0.9990 Gold 0.5010 oz. AGW, 26 mm. **Ruler:** Akihito **Subject:** Expo 2005 **Obv:** Two owls on globe **Rev:** Expo logo

Date	Mintage	F	VF	XF	Unc	BU
Yr. 16(2004) Proof	70,000	Value: 800				

Y# 158 10000 YEN

20.0000 g., 0.9990 Gold 0.6423 oz. AGW, 28 mm. **Ruler:** Akihito **Subject:** 20th Anniversary of Emperor's enthronment **Obv:** Imperial christaniumn crest **Rev:** Phoenix, an auspicious cloud, Niju-bashi bridge

Date	Mintage	F	VF	XF	Unc	BU
Yr.21(2009) Proof	50,000	Value: 950				

MINT SETS

KM#	Date	Mintage	Identification	Issue Price	Mkt Val
MS125	2001 (6)	8,000	Y#95.2-98.2, 101.2, 125 Mint exhibition in Fukuoka	16.00	30.00
MS126	2001 (6)	85,000	Y#95.2-98.2, 101.2, 125 Osaka cherry blossoms box	17.00	30.00
MS127	2001 (6)	10,000	Y#95.2-98.2, 101.2, 125 Hiroshima cherry blossoms box	17.00	33.00
MS128	2001 (6)	10,000	Y#95.2-98.2, 101.2, 125 12th Tokyo International Coin Convention	17.00	30.00
MS129	2001 (6)	5,000	Y#95.2-98.2, 101.2, 125 Beautiful Future Exposition	17.00	30.00
MS130	2001 (6)	8,000	Y#95.2-98.2, 101.2, 125 Kagoshima Coin and Stamp Show	17.00	30.00
MS131	2001 (6)	5,000	Y#95.2-98.2, 101.2, 125 Tokyo Mint Fair	17.00	33.00
MS132	2001 (6)	5,000	Y#95.2-98.2, 101.2, 125 Yamaguchi Exposition	17.00	40.00
MS133	2001 (6)	193,600	Y#95.2-98.2, 101.2, 125 21st Century Commemorative Respect for the Aged	17.00	27.00
MS134	2001 (6)	190,300	Y#95.2-98.2, 101.2, 125 Ryukyu World Cultural Sites	17.00	27.00
MS135	2001 (6)	8,300	Y#95.2-98.2, 101.2, 125 "Anniversary" folder	18.00	33.00
MS136	2001 (1)	4,000	Y#125 Mint Visit Commemorative	8.00	10.00
MS137	2001 (6)	224,000	Y#95.2-98.2, 101.2, 125 Mint Bureau Box	15.00	27.00
MS138	2001 (6)	7,300	Y#95.2-98.2, 101.2, 125 "Japan Coins"	17.00	30.00
MS139	2001 (2)	5,000	Y#96.2, 125 "Japan Coins" (short set)	8.50	13.00
MS140	2001 (6)	128,700	Y#95.2-98.2, 101.2, 125 World Intangible Heritage - Nogaku	17.00	27.00
MS141	2002 (1)	3,000	Y#125 Mint Visit Commemorative	7.50	10.00
MS142	2002 (6)	7,000	Y#95.2-98.2, 102.2, 125 "Anniversary" folder	18.00	27.00
MS143	2002 (2)	4,000	Y#96.2, 125. "Japan Coins" (short set)	8.50	13.00
MS144	2002 (6)	6,000	Y#95.2-98.2, 101.2, 125 "Japan Coins"	17.00	23.00
MS145	2002 (6)	4,000	Y#95.2-98.2, 101.2, 125 Mint exhibition in Takamatsu	16.00	33.00
MS146	2002 (6)	80,000	Y#95.2-98.2, 101.2, 125 Osaka cherry blossoms	16.00	20.00
MS147	2002 (6)	10,000	Y#95.2-98.2, 101.2, 125 Hiroshima cherry blossoms	16.00	23.00
MS148	2002 (6)	10,000	Y#95.2-98.2, 101.2, 125 13th Tokyo Int'l Coin Convention	16.00	20.00
MS149	2002 (6)	6,000	Y#95.2-98.2, 101.2, 125 Mint exhibition in Sendai	16.00	23.00
MS150	2002 (6)	194,000	Y#95.2-98.2, 101.2, 125 Respect for the Aged	19.00	20.00
MS151	2002 (6)	6,000	Y#95.2-98.2, 101.2, 125 Matsuyama Coin and Stamp Show	16.00	23.00
MS152	2002 (6)	3,000	Y395.2-98.2, 101.2, 125 Tokyo Mint Fair	16.00	120
MS153	2002 (6)	2,000	Y#95.2-98.2, 101,2, 125 Birthday folder (with sound recording function)	25.00	40.00
MS154	2002 (6)	214,800	Y395.2-98.2, 101.2, 125 Mint Bureau box	15.00	20.00
MSA141	2002 (3)	50,000	Y#126-128 World Cup soccer	26.00	35.00
MS155	2003 (6)	8,000	Y#95.2-98.2, 101,2, 125 "Japan Coins"	17.00	20.00
MS156	2003 (6)	7,000	Y#95.2-98.2, 101.2, 125 "Anniversary" folder	18.00	20.00

KM#	Date	Mintage	Identification	Issue Price	Mkt Val
MS157	2003 (6)	3,000	Y#95.2-98.2, 101.2, 125 "Anniversary" folder (with sound recording function)	25.00	27.00
MS158	2003 (6)	6,000	Y#95.2-98.2, 101.2, 125 Mint exhibition in Okayama	16.00	30.00
MS159	2003 (6)	80,000	Y#95.2-98.2, 101.2, 125 Osaka cherry blossoms	16.00	20.00
MS160	2003 (6)	10,000	Y#95.2-98.2, 101.2, 125 Hiroshima cherry blossoms	16.00	20.00
MS161	2003 (6)	10,000	Y#95.2-98.2, 101.2, 125 14th Tokyo Int'l Coin Convention	16.00	20.00
MS162	2003 (6)	6,000	Y#95.2-98.2, 101.2, 125 First Osaka Coin Show	16.00	20.00
MS163	2003 (6)	235,000	Y#95.2-98.2, 101.2, 125 Birth of Astro Boy	19.00	20.00
MS164	2003 (6)	130,000	Y#95.2-98.2, 101.2, 125 Respect for the Aged	19.00	17.00
MS165	2003 (6)	5,000	Y#95.2-98.2, 101.2, 125 Tokyo Mint Fair - Mint Collection in Omote-sando	17.00	30.00
MS166	2003 (6)	5,000	Y#95.2-98.2, 101.2, 125 Mint exhibition in Sapporo	17.00	27.00
MS167	2003 (6)	5,000	Y#95.2-98.2, 101.2, 125 Yonago Coin and Stamp Show	17.00	23.00
MS168	2003 (6)	205,000	Y#95.2-98.2, 101.2, 125 Mint Bureau box	17.00	16.00
MS169	2003 (6)	100,000	Y#95.2-98.2, 101.2, 125 2003 Central League Champions - Hanshin Tigers	22.00	27.00
MS170	2003 (6)	100,000	Y#95.2-98.2, 101.2, 125 2003 Pacific league Champions - Fukuoka Daiei Hawks	22.00	16.00
MS171	2003 (6)	5,000	Y#95.2-98.2, 101.2, 126 400th Anniversary of the Establishment of Government in Edo	22.00	200
MS172	2004 (6)	8,000	Y#95.2-98.2, 101.2, 125 "Japan Coin Set"	19.00	20.00
MS173	2004 (6)	5,000	Y#95.2-98.2, 101.2, 125 "Anniversary" folder	20.00	22.00
MS174	2004 (6)	5,000	Y#95.2-98.2, 101.2, 125 Anniversary folder (with sound recording function)	28.50	27.00
MS175	2004 (6)	4,000	Y#95.2-98.2, 101.2, 125 Mint exhibition in Fukui	18.00	53.00
MS176	2004 (6)	70,000	Y#95.2-98.2, 101.2, 125 Osaka cherry blossoms	18.00	20.00
MS177	2004 (6)	10,000	Y#95.2-98.2, 101.2, 125 Hiroshima cherry blossoms	18.00	20.00
MS178	2004 (6)	10,000	Y#95.2-98.2, 101.2, 125 15th Tokyo Int'l Coin Convention	18.00	20.00
MS179	2004 (6)	6,000	Y#95.2-98.2, 101.2, 125 Second Osaka Coin Show	18.00	20.00
MS180	2004 (6)	100,000	Y#95.2-98.2, 101.2, 125 World Intangible Heritage series: Bunraku puppets	19.00	20.00
MS181	2004 (6)	122,500	Y#95.2-98.2, 101.2, 125 Respect for the Aged	20.00	20.00
MS182	2004 (6)	5,000	Y#95.2-98.2, 101.2, 125 Mint exhibition in Tosu	18.00	23.00
MS183	2004 (6)	189,000	Y#95.2-98.2, 101.2, 125 Mint Bureau box	16.00	17.00
MS184	2004 (6)	5,000	Y#95.2-98.2, 101.2, 125 Gifu Coin and Stamp Show	17.00	23.00
MS185	2004 (6)	226,000	Y#95.2-98.2, 101.2, 125 30th Birthday of Hello Kitty (cartoon character)	22.00	23.00
MS186	2004 (6)	5,000	Y#95.2-98.2, 101.2, 125 Tokyo Mint Fair - 40th Anniversary - Issue of Commemorative Coins	17.00	33.00
MS187	2004 (6)	44,000	Y#95.2-98.2, 101.2, 125 2004 Central League Champions - Chunichi Dragons	21.00	17.00
MS188	2004 (6)	38,500	Y#95.2-98.2, 101.2, 125 2004 Pacific League Champions - Seibu Lions	21.00	17.00
MS189	2005 (6)	200,000	Y#95.2-98.2, 101.2, 133 Expo 2005, Aichi	22.00	23.00
MS190	2005 (6)	8,000	Y#95.2-98.2, 101.2, 125 "Japan Coin Set"	17.00	16.00
MS191	2005 (6)	5,000	Y#95.2-98.2, 101.2, 125 "Anniversary" folder	19.00	20.00
MS192	2005 (6)	2,000	Y#95.2-98.2, 101.2, 125 Anniversary folder (with sound recording function)	27.50	27.00
MS193	2005 (6)	5,000	Y#95.2-98.2, 101.2, 125 Mint exhibition in Shizuoka	17.00	33.00
MS194	2005 (6)	60,000	Y#95.2-98.2, 101.2, 125 Osaka cherry blossoms	17.00	23.00
MS195	2005 (6)	10,000	Y#95.2-98.2, 101.2, 125 Hiroshima Flower Tour	17.00	20.00
MS196	2005 (6)	10,000	Y#95.2-98.2, 101.2, 125 16th Tokyo International Coin Convention	17.00	20.00
MS197	2005 (6)	5,000	Y#95.2-98.2, 101.2, 125 Third Osaka Coin Show	17.00	20.00
MS198	2005 (6)	126,500	Y#95.2-98.2, 101.2, 125 World Cultural Heritage Series: Kii Hills Sacred Places and Pilgrimage Trails	18.00	20.00
MS199	2005 (6)	104,500	Y#95.2-98.2, 101.2, 125 Respect for the Aged	19.00	20.00
MS200	2005 (6)	5,000	Y#95.2-98.2, 101.2, 125 Mint Exhibition in Morioka	18.00	23.00
MS201	2005 (6)	5,000	Y#95.2-98.2, 101.2, 125 Koriyama Coin and Stamp Show	17.00	23.00
MS202	2005 (6)	182,000	Y#95.2-98.2, 101.2, 125 35th Anniversary of Doraemon (cartoon character)	17.00	30.00
MS203	2005 (6)	141,000	Y#95.2-98.2, 101.2, 125 Mint Bureau Box	16.00	18.00
MS204	2005 (6)	75,800	Y#95.2-98.2, 101.2, 125 World Natural Heritage	18.00	20.00
MS205	2005 (6)	5,000	Y#95.2-98.2, 101.2, 125 Mint Bureau Tokyo Fair / 50th Anniversary of One-Yen Aluminum Coin	17.00	40.00
MS206	2005 (6)	83,600	Y#95.2-98.2, 101.2, 125 2005 Central League Champions - Hanshin Tigers	21.00	20.00
MS207	2005 (6)	56,600	Y#95.2-98.2, 101.2, 125 2005 Pacific League Champions - Chiba Lotte Marines	21.00	20.00
MSA189	2005 (6)	1,000	Y#95.2-98.2, 101.2, 125 34th International Coin Convention, Basel	—	—
MS208	2006 (6)	5,000	Y#95.2-98.2, 101.2, 125 Mint exhibition in Oita	17.00	17.50
MS209	2006 (6)	9,000	Y#95.2-98.2, 101.2, 125 "Japan Coin Set"	18.00	18.00
MS210	2006 (6)	5,000	Y#95.2-98.2, 101.2, 125 "Anniversary" Folder	19.00	20.00
MS211	2006 (6)	189,400	Y#95.2-98.2, 101.2, 125 Mint Bureau box	16.00	17.00
MS212	2006 (6)	66,000	Y#95.2-98.2, 101.2, 125 World Intangible Heritage Series: Kabuki Theater	18.00	18.00
MS213	2006 (6)	60,000	Y#95.2-98.2, 101.2, 125 Osaka Cherry Blossoms	17.00	17.50
MS214	2006 (6)	8,000	Y#95.2-98.2, 101.2, 125 Hiroshima Flower Tour	17.00	17.50
MS215	2006 (6)	8,000	Y#95.2-98.2, 101.2, 125 17th Tokyo International Coin Convention	17.00	18.50
MS216	2006 (6)	85,500	Y#95.2-98.2, 101.2, 125 Respect for the Aged	19.00	20.00
MS217	2006 (6)	4,000	Y#95.2-98.2, 101.2, 125 Third Osaka Coin Show	17.00	18.50
MS218	2006 (6)	4,000	Y#95.2-98.2, 101.2, 125 Mint Exhibition in Kofu	17.00	17.50
MS219	2006 (6)	105,200	Y#95.2-98.2, 101.2, 125 80th Anniversary of Pooh-Bear	22.00	22.50
MS220	2006 (6)	3,500	Y#95.2-98.2, 101.2, 125 Nagasaki Coin and Stamp Show	17.00	17.50
MS221	2006 (6)	4,000	Y#95.2-98.2, 101.2, 125 Mint Bureau Tokyo Fair/"The Dawn of Modern Japan"	17.00	50.00
MS222	2006 (6)	49,600	Y#95.2-98.2, 101.2, 125 2006 Central League Champions - Chunichi Dragons	21.00	27.00
MS223	2006 (6)	56,600	Y#95.2-98.2, 101.2, 125 2006 Pacific League Champions - Japan Hamfighters	21.00	27.00
MS224	2007 (6)	180,000	Y#95.2-98.2, 101.2, 137 50th Anniversary of Japanese Antarctic Research	23.00	30.00
MS225	2007 (6)	4,000	Y#95.2-98.2, 101.2, 125 Mint exhibition in Tsukuba	17.00	18.00
MS226	2007 (6)	8,000	Y#95.2-98.2, 101.2, 125 "Japan Coin Set"	18.00	20.00
MS227	2007 (6)	5,700	Y#95.2-98.2, 101.2, 125 "Anniversary" folder	19.00	20.00
MS228	2007 (6)	150,000	Y#95.2-98.2, 101.2, 125 Mint Bureau box	16.00	18.00
MS229	2007 (6)	82,200	Y#95.2-98.2, 101.2, 125 "Gongitsune" 75th Anniversary of Publication	22.00	25.00
MS230	2007 (6)	7,000	Y#95.2-98.2, 101.2, 125 Hiroshima Flower Tour	18.00	—
MS231	2007 (6)	60,000	Y#95.2-98.2, 101.2, 125 Osaka cherry blossoms	17.00	18.00
MS232	2007 (6)	6,000	Y#95.2-98.2, 101.2, 125 18th Tokyo International Coin Convention	17.00	18.00
MS233	2007 (6)	4,000	Y#95.2-98.2, 101.2, 125 Fifth Osaka Coin Show	17.00	18.00
MS234	2007 (6)	76,500	Y#95.2-98.2, 101.2, 125 Rose of Versailles, Lady Oscar	22.00	25.00
MS235	2007 (6)	2,720	Y#95.2-98.2, 101.2, 125 Mint exhibition in Matsue	17.00	18.00
MS236	2007 (6)	4,000	Y#95.2-98.2, 101.2, 125 Nagoya Coin and Stamp Show	17.00	18.00
MS237	2007 (6)	69,000	Y#95.2-98.2, 101.2, 125 Respect for the Aged	19.00	20.00
MS238	2007 (6)	4,000	Y#95.2-98.2, 101.2, 125 Mint Bureau Tokyo Fair/50th anniversary of introduction of the 100-yen coin	17.00	18.00
MS239	2007 (6)	45,200	Y#95.2-98.2, 101.2, 125 2007 Central League Champions - Yomiuri Giants	21.00	22.00
MS240	2007 (6)	36,500	Y#95.2-98.2, 101.2, 125 2007 Pacific League Champions - Japan Hamfighters	21.00	22.00
MS241	2007 (6)	74,500	Y#95.2-98.2, 101.2, 125 World Cultural Heritage Series: Iwami Silver Mines Ruins and Cultural Landscape	18.00	20.00
MS242	2008 (6)	4,000	Y#95.2-98.2, 101.2, 125, Mint exhibition in Miyazaki	18.00	20.00
MS243	2008 (6)	15,100	Y95.2-98.2, 101.2, 125, "Japan Coin Set"	19.00	20.00
MS244	2008 (6)	7,500	Y95.2-98.2, 101.2, 125, "Anniversary" folder	20.00	20.00
MS245	2008 (6)	154,022	Y95.2-98.2, 101.2, 125, Mint Bureau Box	17.00	20.00
MS246	2008 (6)	4,500	Y95.2-98.2, 101.2, 125, Hiroshima Flower Tour	18.00	20.00
MS247	2008 (6)	60,000	Y95.2-98.2, 101.2, 125, Osaka cherry blossoms	18.00	20.00
MS248	2008 (6)	5,500	Y95.2-98.2, 101.2, 125, 19th Tokyo International Coin Convention	18.00	20.00
MS249	2008 (6)	4,000	Y25.2-98.2, 101.2, 125, G8 Finance Ministers' meeting, Osaka	18.00	18.00
MS250	2008 (6)	3,500	Y95.2-98.2, 101.2, 125, Sixth Osaka Coin Show.	18.00	20.00
MS251	2008 (6)	4,000	Y95.2-98.2, 101.2, 125, Kobe Coin and Stamp Exposition.	18.00	18.00
MS252	2008 (6)	142,000	Y95.2-98.2, 101.2, 125, Japan-Brazil Year of Exchange and Centenary of Japanese Immigration to Brazil	24.00	25.00
MS253	2008 (6)	100,000	Y95.2-98.2, 101.2, 125, Children's song coin set, Red Dragonfly.	23.00	25.00
MS254	2008 (6)	4,000	Y95.2-98.2, 101.2, 125 Mint Bureau Tokyo Fair/"Japan's Attractions"	20.00	—
MS255	2009 (6)	4,000	Y95.2-Y98.2, 101.2, 125 32nd World Money Festival, Nagoya	20.00	—
MS256	2009 (6)	—	Y95.2-Y98.2, 101.2, 125 Japan Coin Set	21.00	—
MS257	2009 (6)	—	Y95.2-Y98.2, 101.2, 125 Anniversary folder	22.00	—
MS258	2009 (6)	4,500	Y95.2-Y98.2, 101.2, 125 Hiroshima Flower Tour	20.00	—
MS259	2009 (6)	60,000	Y95.2-Y98.2, 101.2, 125 Osaka cherry blossoms	20.00	—
MS260	2009 (6)	5,500	Y95.2-Y98.2, 101.2, 125 20th Toyko International Coin Convention	20.00	—
MS261	2009 (6)	150,000	Y95.2-Y98.2, 101.2, 125 Mint Bureau box	19.00	—
MS262	2009 (6)	3,500	Y95.2-Y98.2, 101.2, 125 Mint exhibition in Niigata	20.00	—
MS263	2009 (6)	4,000	Y95.2-Y98.2, 101.2, 125 Seventh Osaka Coin Show	20.00	—
MS264	2009 (6)	5,000	Y95.2-Y98.2, 101.2, 125 Aqua Metropolis Osaka 2009	20.00	—
MS265	2009 (6)	3,500	Y95.2-Y98.2, 101.2, 125 Yamagata Coin and Stamp Exibition	20.00	—

PROOF SETS

KM#	Date	Mintage	Identification	Issue Price	Mkt Val
PS32	2001 (6)	138,000	Y#95.2-98.2, 101.2, 125 Mint Bureau Box	62.50	47.00
PS33	2001 (6)	100,000	Y#95.2-98.2, 101.2, 125 Old Type Coin Series (Trade dollar medallet)	62.50	53.00
PS38	2002 (2)	50,000	Y#129, 130 World Cup	385	550

KM#	Date	Mintage	Identification	Issue Price	Mkt Val
PS34	2002 (6)	144,000	Y#95.2-98.2, 101.2, 125 Mint Bureau box	62.50	53.00
PS35	2002 (6)	3,000	Y#95.2-98.2, 101.2, 125 15th Anniversary of Proof Sets	62.50	100
PS36	2002 (6)	95,000	Y#95.2-98.2, 101.2, 125 Techno medal set	62.50	53.00
PS39	2003 (6)	98,400	Y#95.2-98.2, 101.2, 125 Mint Bureau box, with date plaquette	67.50	53.00
PS40	2003 (6)	90,000	Y#95.2-98.2, 101.2, 125 Astro Boy	115	100
PS41	2003 (6)	5,000	Y#95.2-98.2, 101.2, 125 Tokyo Mint Fair - Mint Collection in Omote-Sando	67.50	100
PS42	2003 (6)	70,000	Y#95.2-98.2, 101.2, 125 Mickey Mouse	125	120
PS43	2003 (6)	5,000	Y#95.2-98.2, 101.2, 125 400th Anniversary - Establishment of Government in Edo	67.50	165
PS50	2004 (2)	35,000	Y#135-136 Expo 2005, Aichi	425	500
PS44	2004 (6)	94,900	Y#95.2-98.2, 101.2, 125 Mint Bureau box with date plaquette	71.00	60.00
PS45	2004 (6)	13,100	Y#95.2-98.2, 101.2, 125 Mint Bureau box without date plaquette	70.00	100
PS46	2004 (6)	60,000	Y#95.2-98.2, 101.2, 125 70h Anniversary - Pro Baseball	120	145
PS47	2004 (6)	60,000	Y#95.2-98.2, 101.2, 125 Techno Medal Series 2	71.00	60.00
PS48	2004 (6)	50,000	Y#95.2-98.2, 101.2, 125 30th Birthday of Hello Kitty (cartoon character)	120	150
PS49	2004 (6)	5,000	Y#95.2-98.2, 101.2, 125 Tokyo Mint Fair - 40th Anniversary - Issue of Commemorative Coins	71.00	100
PSA40	2003 (6)	6,600	Y#95.2-98.2, 101.2, 125 Mint Bureau Box without Date Plaquette	66.00	100
PS51	2005 (6)	76,700	Y#95.2-98.2, 101.2, 125 Mint Bureau Box with date plaquette	71.00	65.00
PS52	2005 (6)	10,000	Y#95.2-98.2, 101.2, 125 Mint Bureau Box without date plaquette	70.00	100
PS53	2005 (6)	60,000	Y#95.2-98.2, 101.2, 125 35th Anniversary of Doraemon (cartoon character)	125	170
PS54	2005 (6)	34,000	Y#95.2-98.2, 101.2, 125 50th Anniversary of One-Yen Aluminum Coin	125	170
PS55	2005 (6)	30,000	Y#95.2-98.2, 101.2, 125 50th Anniversary of the Pencil Rocket	125	100
PS56	2005 (6)	47,300	Y#95.2-98.2, 101.2, 125 Techno Medal Series #3	71.00	65.00
PS62	2006 (6)	4,000	Y#95.2-98.2, 101.2, 125 Mint Bureau Tokyo Fair/"The Dawn of Modern Japan"	71.00	150
PS57	2006 (6)	63,420	Y#95.2-98.2, 101.2, 125 Mint Bureau box with date plaquette	71.00	65.00
PS58	2006 (6)	8,700	Y#95.2-98.2, 101.2, 125 Mint Bureau Box without date plaquette	70.00	65.00
PS59	2006 (6)	35,000	Y#95.2-98.2, 101.2, 125 120th Anniversary of Cherry Blossom Viewing at the Mint	125	125
PS60	2006 (6)	46,000	Y#95.2-98.2, 101.2, 125 Australia-Japan Year of Exchange; includes Australian 1oz Silver coin KM#838	128	145
PS61	2006 (6)	49,900	Y#95.2-98.2, 101.2, 125 50th Anniversary of Debut of Ishihara Yujiro (film actor)	125	120
PS63	2007 (6)	40,000	Y#95.2-98.2, 101.2, 125 20-yen Gold Coin Memorial	125	150
PS64	2007 (6)	53,200	Y#95.2-98.2, 101.2, 125 Mint Bureau box, with date plaquette	71.00	75.00
PS65	2007 (6)	7,000	Y#95.2-98.2, 101.2, 125 Mint Bureau box, without date plaquette	70.00	75.00
PS66	2007 (6)	35,000	Y#95.2-98.2, 101.2, 125 60th Anniversary of Resumption of Cherry Blossom Viewing (at the Mint)	125	125
PS67	2007 (6)	40,100	Y#95.2-98.2, 101.2, 125 Sakamoto Ryohma (pre-Meiji loyalist, assassinated 1867)	125	125
PS68	2007 (6)	33,500	Y#95.2-98.2, 101.2, 125 11th IAAF World Championships in Athletics, Osaka (plus silver medal)	125	125
PS69	2007 (6)	3,000	Y#95.2-98.2, 101.2, 125 Mint Bureau Tokyo Fair/50th anniversary of introduction of the 100-yen coin	71.00	75.00
PS70	2007 (6)	30,000	Y#95.2-98.2, 101.2, 125 Japan-New Zealand Friendship (with NZ KM#232 coin)	125	125
PSA39	2007 (6)	7,000	Y#95.2-98.2, 101.2, 125 Mint Bureau box, without date plaquette	66.00	100
PS71	2008 (6)	55,200	Y95.2-95.2, 101.2, 125 Mint Bureau box with date plaquette	75.00	75.00
PS72	2008 (6)	6,000	Y95.2-98.2, 101.2, 125 Mint Bureau box without date plaquette	73.50	75.00
PS73	2008 (6)	27,000	Y95.2-98.2, 101.2, 125 Cherry blossom viewing (at the mint)	130	130
PS74	2008 (6)	44,000	Y95.2-Y98.2, 101.2, 125 150th Anniversary of Japanese-French relations (with French 1.5 euro coin KM1550.)	130	130
PS75	2008 (6)	33,000	Y95.2-98.2, 101.2, 125 1300th Anniversary of the Wado Kaichin coin (with a silver replica)	100	100
PS76	2008 (6)	3,000	Y95.2-Y98.2, 101.2, 125 Mint Bureau Tokyo Fair - Japan Attractions	79.00	—
PS77	2009 (6)	60,000	Y95.2-Y98.2, 101.2, 125 Mint Bureau box with date plaquette	79.00	—
PS78	2009 (6)	—	Y95.2-Y98.2, 101.2, 125 Mint Bureau box without date plaquette	77.50	—
PS79	2009 (6)	25,000	Y95.2-Y98.2, 101.2, 125 Cherry blossom viewing (at the mint)	136	—
PS80	2009 (6)	25,000	Y95.2-Y98.2, 101.2, 125 80 years of Japan/Canada Amity (with $5 Canadian coin on same subject)	136	—
PS81	2009 (6)	30,000	Y95.2-Y98.2, 101.2, 125 400 years of Japan/Dutch Commerce (with Dutch $5 coin, KM287 included)	136	—

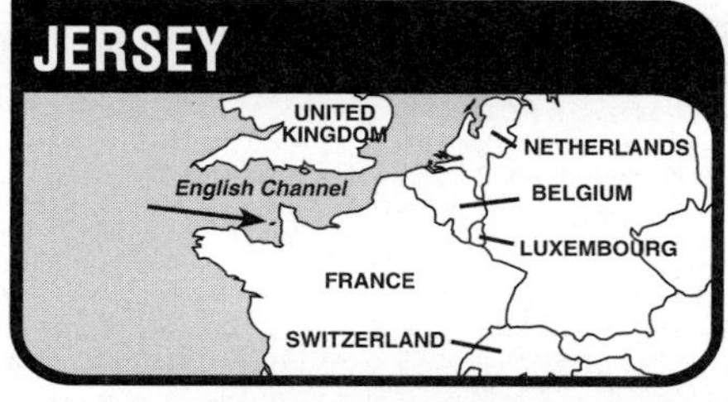

The Bailiwick of Jersey, a British Crown dependency located in the English Channel 12 miles (19 km.) west of Normandy, France, has an area of 45 sq. mi. (117 sq. km.) and a population of 74,000. Capital: St. Helier. The economy is based on agriculture and cattle breeding – the importation of cattle is prohibited to protect the purity of the island's world-famous strain of milk cows.

The island together with the Bailiwick of Guernsey, is the only part of the Dutchy of Normandy belonging to the British Crown, has been a possession of Britain since the Norman conquest of 1066. Jersey is administered by its own laws and customs. Unless the island is mentioned specifically, acts passed by the British Parliament are not applicable to Jersey. During WW II, German troops occupied the island from 1940 to 1945.

RULER
British

BRITISH DEPENDENCY

DECIMAL COINAGE

100 New Pence = 1 Pound

Many of the following coins are also struck in silver, gold, and platinum for collectors

KM# 103 PENNY

3.5000 g., Copper Plated Steel, 20.3 mm. **Ruler:** Elizabeth II **Obv:** Crowned head right **Obv. Designer:** Ian Rank-Broadley **Rev:** Le Hoeq Watchtower, St. Clement **Edge:** Plain

Date	Mintage	F	VF	XF	Unc	BU
2002	1,520,000	—	—	0.15	0.65	—
2003	1,575,000	—	—	0.15	0.65	—
2005	—	—	—	0.15	0.65	—
2006	585,000	—	—	0.15	0.65	—
2008	4,800,000	—	—	0.15	0.65	—

KM# 104 2 PENCE

7.1000 g., Copper Plated Steel, 25.91 mm. **Ruler:** Elizabeth II **Obv:** Head with tiara right **Obv. Designer:** Ian Rank-Broadley **Rev:** L'Hermitage, St. Helier **Edge:** Plain

Date	Mintage	F	VF	XF	Unc	BU
2002	1,259,000	—	—	0.20	0.65	—
2003	10,000	—	—	0.20	0.65	—
2005	400,000	—	—	0.20	0.65	—
2006	1,200,000	—	—	0.20	0.65	—
2008	2,459,000	—	—	0.20	0.65	—

KM# 105 5 PENCE

3.2900 g., Copper-Nickel, 18 mm. **Ruler:** Elizabeth II **Obv:** Head with tiara right **Obv. Designer:** Ian Rank-Broadley **Rev:** Seymour Tower, Grouville, L'Avathigon **Edge:** Reeded

Date	Mintage	F	VF	XF	Unc	BU
2002	1,200,000	—	—	0.20	0.65	—
2003	1,005,000	—	—	0.20	0.65	—
2006	1,200,000	—	—	0.20	0.65	—
2008	3,600,000	—	—	0.20	0.65	—

KM# 106 10 PENCE

Copper-Nickel, 24.5 mm. **Ruler:** Elizabeth II **Obv:** Head with tiara right **Obv. Designer:** Ian Rank-Broadley **Rev:** La Hougne Bie, Faldouet, St. Martin

Date	Mintage	F	VF	XF	Unc	BU
2002	500,000	—	—	—	1.25	—
2003	10,000	—	—	—	1.25	—
2006	—	—	—	—	1.25	—
2007	630,000	—	—	—	1.25	—

KM# 107 20 PENCE

Copper-Nickel, 21.4 mm. **Ruler:** Elizabeth II **Obv:** Head with tiara right **Obv. Designer:** Ian Rank-Broadley

Date	Mintage	F	VF	XF	Unc	BU
2002	975,500	—	—	—	1.00	1.25
2003	10,000	—	—	—	1.00	1.25
2005	500,000	—	—	—	1.00	1.25
2006	500,000	—	—	—	1.00	1.25
2007	780,000	—	—	—	1.00	1.25
2009	1,500,000	—	—	—	1.00	1.25

KM# 108 50 PENCE

Copper-Nickel, 27.3 mm. **Ruler:** Elizabeth II **Obv:** Crowned bust right **Obv. Designer:** Ian Rank-Broadley **Rev:** Gothic gate arch **Edge:** Plain

Date	Mintage	F	VF	XF	Unc	BU
2003	10,000	—	—	1.00	2.50	3.00
2005	200,000	—	—	1.00	2.50	3.00
2006	300,000	—	—	1.00	2.50	3.00
2009	480,000	—	—	1.00	2.50	3.00

KM# 123a 50 PENCE

8.0000 g., 0.9250 Silver 0.2379 oz. ASW, 27.3 mm. **Ruler:** Elizabeth II **Subject:** Coronation, 50th Anniversary **Obv:** Crowned head right **Rev:** Archbishop crowning Queen **Edge:** Plain **Shape:** 7-sided

Date	Mintage	F	VF	XF	Unc	BU
2003 Proof	15,000	Value: 25.00				

KM# 123 50 PENCE

8.0000 g., Copper-Nickel, 27.3 mm. **Ruler:** Elizabeth II **Subject:** Coronation, 50th Anniversary **Obv:** Crowned head right **Rev:** Archbishop crowning Queen **Edge:** Plain **Shape:** 7-sided

Date	Mintage	F	VF	XF	Unc	BU
2003	10,000	—	—	—	2.50	3.00

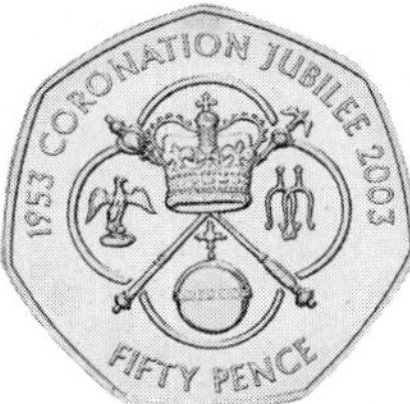

KM# 148 50 PENCE
8.0000 g., Copper-Nickel, 27.3 mm. **Ruler:** Elizabeth II **Subject:** Coronation, 50th Anniversary **Rev:** Regalia in quatrilobe **Shape:** 7-sided

Date	Mintage	F	VF	XF	Unc	BU
2003	—	—	—	—	2.50	3.50

KM# 148a 50 PENCE
8.0000 g., 0.9250 Silver 0.2379 oz. ASW, 27.3 mm. **Ruler:** Elizabeth II **Subject:** Coronation, 50th Anniversary **Rev:** Regalia in quatrilobe **Shape:** 7-sided

Date	Mintage	F	VF	XF	Unc	BU
2003 Proof	15,000	Value: 25.00				

KM# 149 50 PENCE
8.0000 g., Copper-Nickel, 27.3 mm. **Ruler:** Elizabeth II **Subject:** Coronation, 50th Anniversary **Rev:** Queen facing, seated on throne **Shape:** 7-sided

Date	Mintage	F	VF	XF	Unc	BU
2003	10,000	—	—	—	2.50	3.50

KM# 149a 50 PENCE
8.0000 g., 0.9250 Silver 0.2379 oz. ASW, 27.3 mm. **Ruler:** Elizabeth II **Subject:** Coronation, 50th Anniversary **Rev:** Queen facing, seated on throne **Shape:** 7-sided

Date	Mintage	F	VF	XF	Unc	BU
2003 Proof	15,000	Value: 25.00				

KM# 150 50 PENCE
8.0000 g., Copper-Nickel, 27.3 mm. **Ruler:** Elizabeth II **Subject:** Coronation, 50th Anniversary **Rev:** Crown, scepter and shield **Shape:** 7-sided

Date	Mintage	F	VF	XF	Unc	BU
2003	10,000	—	—	—	2.50	3.50

KM# 150a 50 PENCE
8.0000 g., 0.9250 Silver 0.2379 oz. ASW, 27.3 mm. **Ruler:** Elizabeth II **Subject:** Coronation, 50th Anniversary **Rev:** Crown, sceptre and shield **Shape:** 7-sided

Date	Mintage	F	VF	XF	Unc	BU
2003 Proof	15,000	Value: 25.00				

KM# 101 POUND
9.5000 g., Nickel-Brass, 22.5 mm. **Ruler:** Elizabeth II **Obv:** Head with tiara right **Obv. Designer:** Ian Rank-Broadley **Rev:** Schooner, Resolute **Rev. Designer:** Robert Evans **Edge Lettering:** CAESAREA INSULA

Date	Mintage	F	VF	XF	Unc	BU
2003	10,000	—	—	—	4.00	4.50
2005	200,000	—	—	—	4.00	4.50
2006	93,000	—	—	—	4.00	4.50

KM# 102 2 POUNDS
12.0000 g., Bi-Metallic Copper-Nickel center in Nickel-Brass ring, 28.35 mm. **Ruler:** Elizabeth II **Obv:** Head with tiara right **Obv. Designer:** Ian Rank-Broadley **Rev:** Latent image value within circle of assorted shields **Rev. Designer:** Alan Copp **Edge Lettering:** CAESAREA INSULA

Date	Mintage	F	VF	XF	Unc	BU
2003	10,000	—	—	—	10.00	12.00
2006	3,500	—	—	—	10.00	12.00

KM# 111 5 POUNDS
28.2800 g., Copper-Nickel, 38.6 mm. **Ruler:** Elizabeth II **Subject:** Princess Diana **Obv:** Crowned head right **Rev:** Diana's cameo above people **Edge:** Reeded

Date	Mintage	F	VF	XF	Unc	BU
2002	—	—	—	—	13.50	15.00

KM# 111a 5 POUNDS
28.2800 g., 0.9250 Silver 0.8410 oz. ASW, 38.6 mm. **Ruler:** Elizabeth II **Subject:** Princess Diana **Obv:** Crowned head right **Rev:** Diana's cameo above people **Edge:** Reeded

Date	Mintage	F	VF	XF	Unc	BU
2002 Proof	20,000	Value: 45.00				

KM# 111b 5 POUNDS
39.9400 g., 0.9167 Gold 1.1771 oz. AGW, 38.6 mm. **Ruler:** Elizabeth II **Subject:** Princess Diana **Obv:** Crowned head right **Rev:** Diana's cameo above people **Edge:** Reeded

Date	Mintage	F	VF	XF	Unc	BU
2002 Proof	100	Value: 1,850				

KM# 113 5 POUNDS
28.2800 g., Copper-Nickel, 38.6 mm. **Ruler:** Elizabeth II **Subject:** Queen Mother **Obv:** Crowned head right **Obv. Designer:** Ian Rank-Broadley **Rev:** Queen Mother's bust right (circa 1918) **Rev. Legend:** HER MAJESTY QUEEN ELIZABETH THE QUEEN MOTHER **Edge:** Reeded

Date	Mintage	F	VF	XF	Unc	BU
2002	—	—	—	—	13.50	15.00

KM# 113a 5 POUNDS
28.2800 g., 0.9250 Silver 0.8410 oz. ASW, 38.6 mm. **Ruler:** Elizabeth II **Subject:** Queen Mother **Obv:** Crowned head right **Obv. Designer:** Ian Rank-Broadley **Rev:** Queen Mother's bust right, (circa 1918) **Rev. Legend:** HER MAJESTY QUEEN ELIZABETH THE QUEEN MOTHER **Edge:** Reeded

Date	Mintage	F	VF	XF	Unc	BU
2002 Proof	15,000	Value: 50.00				

KM# 113b 5 POUNDS
39.9400 g., 0.9166 Gold 1.1770 oz. AGW, 38.6 mm. **Ruler:** Elizabeth II **Subject:** Queen Mother **Obv:** Crowned head right **Obv. Designer:** Ian Rank-Broadley **Rev:** Queen Mother's bust right, (circa 1918) **Rev. Legend:** HER MAJESTY QUEEN ELIZABETH THE QUEEN MOTHER **Edge:** Reeded

Date	Mintage	F	VF	XF	Unc	BU
2002 Proof	250	Value: 1,750				

KM# 115 5 POUNDS
28.2800 g., Copper-Nickel, 38.6 mm. **Ruler:** Elizabeth II **Subject:** Golden Jubilee **Obv:** Crowned head right **Rev:** Abbey procession scene **Rev. Designer:** Robert Evans **Edge:** Reeded

Date	Mintage	F	VF	XF	Unc	BU
2002	—	—	—	—	13.50	15.00

KM# 115a 5 POUNDS
28.2800 g., 0.9250 Silver 0.8410 oz. ASW, 38.6 mm. **Ruler:** Elizabeth II **Subject:** Golden Jubilee **Obv:** Crowned head right **Rev:** Abbey procession scene **Edge:** Reeded

Date	Mintage	F	VF	XF	Unc	BU
2002 Proof	20,000	Value: 50.00				

KM# 115b 5 POUNDS
39.9400 g., 0.9166 Gold 1.1770 oz. AGW, 38.6 mm. **Ruler:** Elizabeth II **Subject:** Golden Jubilee **Obv:** Crowned head right **Rev:** Abbey procession scene **Edge:** Reeded

Date	Mintage	F	VF	XF	Unc	BU
2002 Proof	100	Value: 1,850				

KM# 117 5 POUNDS
28.2800 g., Copper-Nickel, 38.6 mm. **Ruler:** Elizabeth II **Subject:** Duke of Wellington **Obv:** Crowned head right **Rev:** Wellington's portrait with multicolor infantry scene **Rev. Designer:** Willem Vis **Edge:** Reeded

Date	Mintage	F	VF	XF	Unc	BU
2002	—	—	—	—	13.50	15.00

KM# 117a 5 POUNDS
28.2800 g., 0.9250 Silver 0.8410 oz. ASW, 38.6 mm. **Ruler:** Elizabeth II **Subject:** Duke of Wellington **Obv:** Crowned head right **Rev:** Wellington's portrait with multicolor infantry scene **Edge:** Reeded

Date	Mintage	F	VF	XF	Unc	BU
2002 Proof	15,000	Value: 50.00				

KM# 117b 5 POUNDS
39.9400 g., 0.9166 Gold 1.1770 oz. AGW, 38.6 mm. **Ruler:** Elizabeth II **Subject:** Duke of Wellington **Obv:** Crowned head right **Rev:** Wellington's portrait with multicolor infantry scene **Edge:** Reeded

Date	Mintage	F	VF	XF	Unc	BU
2002 Proof	200	Value: 1,800				

KM# 119 5 POUNDS
28.2800 g., Copper-Nickel, 38.6 mm. **Ruler:** Elizabeth II **Subject:** Golden Jubilee **Obv:** Crowned head right **Rev:** Honor guard and memorial **Edge:** Reeded

Date	Mintage	F	VF	XF	Unc	BU
2003	—	—	—	—	13.50	15.00

KM# 119a 5 POUNDS
28.2800 g., 0.9250 Silver 0.8410 oz. ASW, 38.6 mm. **Ruler:** Elizabeth II **Subject:** Golden Jubilee **Obv:** Crowned head right **Rev:** Honor guard and monument **Edge:** Reeded

Date	Mintage	F	VF	XF	Unc	BU
2003 Proof	20,000	Value: 50.00				

KM# 119b 5 POUNDS
39.9400 g., 0.9166 Gold 1.1770 oz. AGW, 38.6 mm. **Ruler:** Elizabeth II **Subject:** Golden Jubilee **Obv:** Crowned head right **Rev:** Honor guard and monument **Edge:** Reeded

Date	Mintage	F	VF	XF	Unc	BU
2003 Proof	250	Value: 1,750				

KM# 121 5 POUNDS
28.2800 g., Copper-Nickel, 38.6 mm. **Ruler:** Elizabeth II **Obv:** Crowned head right **Rev:** Bust of Prince William facing and crowned arms with supporters **Edge:** Reeded

Date	Mintage	F	VF	XF	Unc	BU
2003	—	—	—	—	16.50	18.00

KM# 121a 5 POUNDS
28.2800 g., 0.9250 Silver 0.8410 oz. ASW, 38.6 mm. **Ruler:** Elizabeth II **Obv:** Crowned head right **Rev:** Bust of Prince William facing and crowned arms with supporters **Edge:** Reeded

Date	Mintage	F	VF	XF	Unc	BU
2003 Proof	5,000	Value: 47.50				

KM# 121b 5 POUNDS
39.9400 g., 0.9166 Gold 1.1770 oz. AGW, 38.6 mm. **Ruler:** Elizabeth II **Obv:** Crowned head right **Rev:** Bust of Prince William facing and crowned arms with supporters **Edge:** Reeded

Date	Mintage	F	VF	XF	Unc	BU
2003 Proof	200	Value: 1,800				

KM# 130 5 POUNDS
28.2800 g., 0.9250 Silver 0.8410 oz. ASW, 38.6 mm. **Ruler:** Elizabeth II **Subject:** Drake **Obv:** Crowned head right **Rev:** Naval leader Sir Francis Drake

Date	Mintage	F	VF	XF	Unc	BU
2003 Proof	—	Value: 75.00				

KM# 131 5 POUNDS
28.2800 g., 0.9250 Silver 0.8410 oz. ASW, 38.6 mm. **Ruler:** Elizabeth II **Subject:** Sovereign Of The Seas **Obv:** Crowned head right **Rev:** The Sovereign of the Seas ship

Date	Mintage	F	VF	XF	Unc	BU
2003 Proof	—	Value: 75.00				

KM# 132 5 POUNDS
28.2800 g., 0.9250 Silver 0.8410 oz. ASW, 38.6 mm. **Ruler:** Elizabeth II **Subject:** John Fisher **Obv:** Crowned head right **Rev:** WWI Naval leader Sir John Fisher

Date	Mintage	F	VF	XF	Unc	BU
2003 Proof	—	Value: 75.00				

KM# 133 5 POUNDS
28.2800 g., 0.9250 Silver 0.8410 oz. ASW, 38.6 mm. **Ruler:** Elizabeth II **Subject:** HMS Victory **Obv:** Crowned head right **Rev:** Nelson's flag ship HMS Victory, multicolor flag at top

Date	Mintage	F	VF	XF	Unc	BU
2004 Proof	—	Value: 75.00				

KM# 134 5 POUNDS
28.2800 g., 0.9250 Silver 0.8410 oz. ASW, 38.6 mm. **Ruler:** Elizabeth II **Subject:** Cunningham **Obv:** Crowned head right **Rev:** WWII Admiral Andrew B. Cunningham

Date	Mintage	F	VF	XF	Unc	BU
2003 Proof	—	Value: 75.00				

KM# 135 5 POUNDS
28.2800 g., 0.9250 Silver 0.8410 oz. ASW, 38.6 mm. **Ruler:** Elizabeth II **Subject:** Conqueror **Obv:** Crowned head right **Rev:** Submarine HMS Conqueror

Date	Mintage	F	VF	XF	Unc	BU
2003 Proof	—	Value: 75.00				

KM# 144 5 POUNDS
28.2800 g., 0.9250 Silver 0.8410 oz. ASW, 38.61 mm. **Ruler:** Elizabeth II **Subject:** History of the Royal Navy **Obv:** Head left with tiarra **Obv. Legend:** ELIZABETH II BALIWICK - OF JERSEY **Rev:** Five heads of King Alfred the Great, Sir Francis Drake, Admirals Horatio Nelson, John Fisher and John Woodward at five ships **Edge:** Reeded

Date	Mintage	F	VF	XF	Unc	BU
2003 Proof	—	Value: 75.00				

KM# 139 5 POUNDS
28.2800 g., 0.9250 Silver 0.8410 oz. ASW, 38.6 mm. **Ruler:** Elizabeth II **Subject:** Driver and Fireman **Obv:** Crowned head right **Rev:** Familiar image from the Golden Age of Steam: the driver and fireman

Date	Mintage	F	VF	XF	Unc	BU
2004 Proof	—	Value: 75.00				

KM# 124 5 POUNDS
28.2800 g., Copper-Nickel, 38.6 mm. **Ruler:** Elizabeth II **Obv:** Crowned head right **Rev:** British Horsa gliders in flight **Rev. Designer:** David Cornell **Edge:** Reeded **Note:** D-Day

Date	Mintage	F	VF	XF	Unc	BU
2004	—	—	—	—	15.00	17.00

KM# 124a 5 POUNDS
28.2800 g., 0.9250 Silver 0.8410 oz. ASW, 38.6 mm. **Ruler:** Elizabeth II **Obv:** Crowned head right **Rev:** British Horsa gliders in flight

Date	Mintage	F	VF	XF	Unc	BU
2004 Proof	10,000	Value: 85.00				

KM# 124b 5 POUNDS
39.9400 g., 0.9167 Gold 1.1771 oz. AGW, 38.6 mm. **Ruler:** Elizabeth II **Obv:** Crowned head right **Rev:** British Horsa gliders in flight

Date	Mintage	F	VF	XF	Unc	BU
2004 Proof	500	Value: 1,750				

KM# 126 5 POUNDS
28.2800 g., Copper-Nickel, 38.6 mm. **Ruler:** Elizabeth II **Subject:** 150th Anniversary of the Crimean War **Obv:** Crowned head right **Rev:** Charge of the Light Brigade scene with one blue uniform behind the Earl of Cardigan **Edge:** Reeded

Date	Mintage	F	VF	XF	Unc	BU
2004 plain	—	—	—	—	25.00	27.50

KM# 126a 5 POUNDS
28.2800 g., 0.9250 Silver 0.8410 oz. ASW, 38.6 mm. **Ruler:** Elizabeth II **Obv:** Crowned head right **Rev:** Charge of the Light Brigade scene with one blue uniform behind the Earl of Cardigan **Edge:** Reeded

Date	Mintage	F	VF	XF	Unc	BU
2004 Proof	10,000	Value: 85.00				

KM# 126b 5 POUNDS
39.9400 g., 0.9166 Gold 1.1770 oz. AGW, 38.6 mm. **Ruler:** Elizabeth II **Obv:** Crowned head right **Rev:** Charge of the Light Brigade scene with one blue uniform behind the Earl of Cardigan **Edge:** Reeded

Date	Mintage	F	VF	XF	Unc	BU
2004 Proof	500	Value: 1,750				

KM# 136 5 POUNDS
28.2800 g., 0.9250 Silver 0.8410 oz. ASW, 38.6 mm. **Ruler:** Elizabeth II **Subject:** Coronation **Obv:** Crowned head right **Rev:** The Pacific Class Coronation

Date	Mintage	F	VF	XF	Unc	BU
2004 Proof	—	Value: 75.00				

KM# 137 5 POUNDS
28.2800 g., 0.9250 Silver 0.8410 oz. ASW, 38.6 mm. **Ruler:** Elizabeth II **Subject:** Flying Scotsman **Obv:** Crowned head right **Rev:** Famous Flying Scotsman Locomotive, designed by Sir Nigel Gresley

Date	Mintage	F	VF	XF	Unc	BU
2004 Proof	—	Value: 75.00				

KM# 138 5 POUNDS
28.2800 g., 0.9250 Silver 0.8410 oz. ASW, 38.6 mm. **Ruler:** Elizabeth II **Subject:** Golden Arrow **Obv:** Crowned head right **Rev:** The Golden Arrow, which ran from London to Dover en route to Paris

Date	Mintage	F	VF	XF	Unc	BU
2004 Proof	—	Value: 75.00				

KM# 140 5 POUNDS
28.2800 g., 0.9250 Silver 0.8410 oz. ASW, 38.6 mm. **Ruler:** Elizabeth II **Subject:** Tunnel **Obv:** Crowned head right **Rev:** Familiar image from the Golden Age of Steam: A locomotive steaming out of a tunnel

Date	Mintage	F	VF	XF	Unc	BU
2004	—	Value: 75.00				

KM# 141 5 POUNDS
28.2800 g., 0.9250 Silver 0.8410 oz. ASW, 38.6 mm. **Ruler:** Elizabeth II **Subject:** Evening Star **Obv:** Crowned head right **Rev:** The Evening Star - representing the last British Rail Steam Locomotive

Date	Mintage	F	VF	XF	Unc	BU
2004 Proof	—	Value: 75.00				

KM# 127 5 POUNDS
Copper-Nickel **Ruler:** Elizabeth II **Subject:** Battle of Trafalgar **Obv:** Crowned head right

Date	Mintage	F	VF	XF	Unc	BU
2005	—	—	—	—	7.50	10.00

KM# 127a 5 POUNDS
28.2800 g., 0.9250 Silver 0.8410 oz. ASW, 38.6 mm. **Ruler:** Elizabeth II **Subject:** Nelson Trafalger **Obv:** Crowned head right **Rev:** 200th Anniversary of the Battle of Trafalgar, image of Nelson with a gilded ship in the background

Date	Mintage	F	VF	XF	Unc	BU
2005 Proof	—	Value: 75.00				

KM# 128 5 POUNDS
Copper-Nickel **Ruler:** Elizabeth II **Subject:** 60th Anniversary - End of WW II **Obv:** Crowned head right **Obv. Designer:** Ian Rank-Broadley **Rev:** Big Ben Tower

Date	Mintage	F	VF	XF	Unc	BU
2005	—	—	—	—	7.50	10.00

KM# 128a 5 POUNDS
28.2800 g., 0.9250 Silver 0.8410 oz. ASW, 38.6 mm. **Ruler:** Elizabeth II **Subject:** WWII Liberation **Obv:** Crowned head right **Rev:** Big Ben Tower **Edge:** Reeded

Date	Mintage	F	VF	XF	Unc	BU
2005 Proof	5,000	Value: 85.00				

KM# 128b 5 POUNDS
39.9400 g., 0.9167 Gold 1.1771 oz. AGW, 38.6 mm. **Ruler:** Elizabeth II **Subject:** WWII Liberation **Obv:** Crowned head right **Rev:** Big Ben Tower **Edge:** Reeded

Date	Mintage	F	VF	XF	Unc	BU
2005 Proof	150	Value: 1,800				

KM# 129 5 POUNDS
Copper-Nickel **Ruler:** Elizabeth II **Subject:** WW II Liberation **Obv:** Crowned head right **Rev:** Returning evacuees **Edge:** Reeded

Date	Mintage	F	VF	XF	Unc	BU
2005	—	—	—	—	7.50	10.00

KM# 129a 5 POUNDS
39.9400 g., 0.9167 Gold 1.1771 oz. AGW, 38.6 mm. **Ruler:** Elizabeth II **Subject:** WWII Liberation **Obv:** Crowned head right **Rev:** Returning evacuees **Edge:** Reeded

Date	Mintage	F	VF	XF	Unc	BU
2005 Proof	150	Value: 1,850				

KM# 142 5 POUNDS
28.2800 g., 0.9250 Silver 0.8410 oz. ASW, 38.6 mm. **Ruler:** Elizabeth II **Subject:** Queen's 80th Birthday **Obv:** Head with tiara right - gilt **Obv. Legend:** ELIZABETH II BAILIWICK - OF JERSEY **Obv. Designer:** Ian Rank-Broadley **Rev:** Queen horseback facing

Date	Mintage	F	VF	XF	Unc	BU
2006 Proof	—	Value: 45.00				

KM# 145 5 POUNDS
28.2800 g., 0.9250 Silver 0.8410 oz. ASW, 38.6 mm. **Ruler:** Elizabeth II **Subject:** Elizabeth II's 80th Birthday **Obv:** Head with tiara right **Obv. Legend:** ELIZABETH II BAILIWICK - OF JERSEY **Obv. Designer:** Ian Rank-Broadley **Rev:** Queen on horseback **Edge:** Reeded

Date	Mintage	F	VF	XF	Unc	BU
2006 Proof	—	Value: 45.00				

KM# 146 5 POUNDS
28.2800 g., 0.9250 Silver 0.8410 oz. ASW, 38.6 mm. **Ruler:** Elizabeth II **Subject:** Battle of Agincourt, 1415 **Obv:** Head right **Rev:** Archers and horsemen

Date	Mintage	F	VF	XF	Unc	BU
2009 Proof	2,500	Value: 55.00				

KM# 143 10 POUNDS
155.5000 g., 0.9250 Silver partially gilt 4.6243 oz. ASW, 65 mm. **Ruler:** Elizabeth II **Subject:** 50th Anniversary of Coronation **Obv:** Queens silver portrait on gold plated fields **Rev:** Crown and scepter above arms, gold plated **Rev. Designer:** Marcel Canioni

Date	Mintage	F	VF	XF	Unc	BU
2003	2,000	—	—	—	125	145

KM# 147 10 POUNDS
155.5000 g., 0.9250 Silver partially gilt 4.6243 oz. ASW, 65 mm. **Ruler:** Elizabeth II **Obv:** Head right **Rev:** St. George slaying dragon, partially gilt

Date	Mintage	F	VF	XF	Unc	BU
2009 Proof	450	Value: 350				

KM# 112 25 POUNDS
7.9800 g., 0.9167 Gold 0.2352 oz. AGW, 22.05 mm. **Ruler:** Elizabeth II **Subject:** Princess Diana **Obv:** Crowned head right **Rev:** Diana's portrait **Edge:** Reeded

Date	Mintage	F	VF	XF	Unc	BU
2002 Proof	2,500	Value: 375				

KM# 114 25 POUNDS
7.9800 g., 0.9166 Gold 0.2352 oz. AGW, 22 mm. **Ruler:** Elizabeth II **Subject:** Queen Mother **Obv:** Crowned head right **Rev:** Queen Mother's portrait circa 1918 **Edge:** Reeded

Date	Mintage	F	VF	XF	Unc	BU
2002 Proof	2,500	Value: 375				

KM# 116 25 POUNDS
7.9800 g., 0.9166 Gold 0.2352 oz. AGW, 22 mm. **Ruler:** Elizabeth II **Subject:** Golden Jubilee **Obv:** Crowned head right **Rev:** Abbey procession scene **Edge:** Reeded

Date	Mintage	F	VF	XF	Unc	BU
2002 Proof	2,500	Value: 375				

KM# 118 25 POUNDS
7.9800 g., 0.9166 Gold 0.2352 oz. AGW, 22 mm. **Ruler:** Elizabeth II **Subject:** Duke of Wellington **Obv:** Crowned head right **Rev:** Wellington's portrait with infantry scene **Edge:** Reeded

Date	Mintage	F	VF	XF	Unc	BU
2002 Proof	2,500	Value: 375				

KM# 120 25 POUNDS
7.9800 g., 0.9166 Gold 0.2352 oz. AGW, 22 mm. **Ruler:** Elizabeth II **Subject:** Golden Jubilee **Obv:** Crowned head right **Rev:** Honor guard and monument **Edge:** Reeded

Date	Mintage	F	VF	XF	Unc	BU
2003 Proof	5,000	Value: 350				

KM# 125 25 POUNDS
7.9800 g., 0.9167 Gold 0.2352 oz. AGW, 22 mm. **Ruler:** Elizabeth II **Subject:** D-Day **Obv:** Crowned head right **Rev:** British Horsa gliders in flight **Edge:** Reeded

Date	Mintage	F	VF	XF	Unc	BU
2004 Proof	500	Value: 400				

KM# 122 50 POUNDS
1000.0000 g., 0.9250 Silver 29.738 oz. ASW, 100 mm. **Ruler:** Elizabeth II **Obv:** Crowned head right **Rev:** Bust facing and crowned arms with supporters **Edge:** Reeded

Date	Mintage	F	VF	XF	Unc	BU
2003 Proof	500	Value: 1,150				

PIEFORTS

KM#	Date	Mintage	Identification	Mkt Val
P3	2002	100	5 Pounds. 0.9166 Gold. 56.5600 g. 38.6 mm. Queen's portrait. Abbey procession scene. Reeded edge. Underweight piefort	1,600

MINT SETS

KM#	Date	Mintage	Identification	Issue Price	Mkt Val
MS7	2004 (1)	—	Jersey KM#126, Guernsey KM#155, Alderney KM#43, 150th Anniversary of the Crimean War	—	100

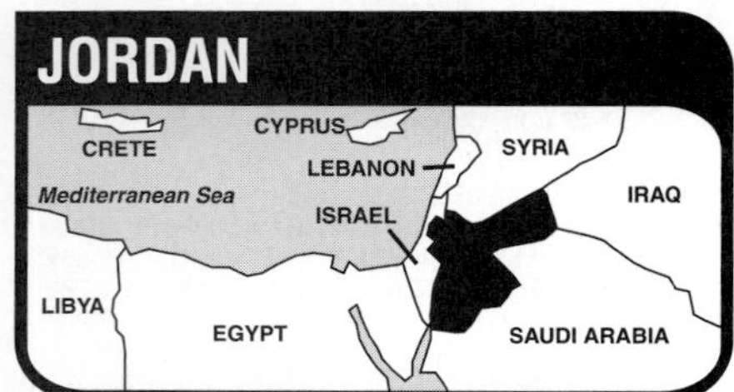

The Hashemite Kingdom of Jordan, a constitutional monarchy in southwest Asia, has an area of 37,738 sq. mi.(91,880 sq. km.) and a population of 3.5 million. Capital: Amman. Agriculture and tourism comprise Jordan's economic base. Chief exports are phosphates, tomatoes and oranges.

RULER
Abdullah Ibn Al-Hussein, 1999-

MONETARY SYSTEM
100 Piastres = 1 Dinar

KINGDOM

DECIMAL COINAGE

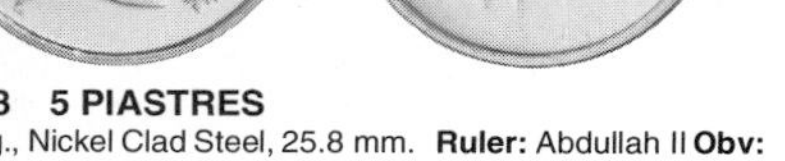

KM# 73 5 PIASTRES
5.0000 g., Nickel Clad Steel, 25.8 mm. **Ruler:** Abdullah II **Obv:** Bust right **Rev:** Value to left within lines below date with written value at lower right **Edge:** Milled

Date	Mintage	F	VF	XF	Unc	BU
AH1427-2006	—	—	—	—	1.50	2.00
AH1429-2008	—	—	—	—	1.50	2.00
AH1430-2009	—	—	—	—	1.50	2.00

KM# 74 10 PIASTRES
8.0000 g., Nickel Clad Steel, 28 mm. **Ruler:** Abdullah II **Obv:** Bust right **Rev:** Value at left within lines below date with written value at lower right **Edge:** Milled

Date	Mintage	F	VF	XF	Unc	BU
AH1425-2004	—	—	—	—	1.75	3.50
AH1425-2006	—	—	—	—	1.75	3.50
AH1429-2008	—	—	—	—	1.75	3.50
AH1430-2009	—	—	—	—	1.75	3.50

KM# 83 1/4 DINAR
7.4000 g., Nickel-Brass, 26.5 mm. **Ruler:** Abdullah II **Obv:** Bust right **Edge:** Plain **Shape:** 7-sided

Date	Mintage	F	VF	XF	Unc	BU
AH1425-2004	—	—	—	—	2.00	3.00
AH1427-2006	—	—	—	—	2.00	3.00
AH1429-2008	—	—	—	—	2.00	3.00
AH1430-2009	—	—	—	—	2.00	3.00

KM# 79 1/2 DINAR
9.6700 g., Bi-Metallic Copper-Nickel center in Brass ring, 29 mm. **Ruler:** Abdullah II **Obv:** Bust right within circle **Rev:** Value in center of circled wreath **Edge:** Plain **Shape:** 7-sided

Date	Mintage	F	VF	XF	Unc	BU
AH1427-2006	—	—	—	—	3.00	4.00
AH1428-2008	—	—	—	—	3.00	4.00
AH1430-2009	—	—	—	—	3.00	4.00

KM# 75 3 DINARS
28.5000 g., Brass, 40 mm. **Ruler:** Abdullah II **Subject:** Amman: Arabic Culture Capital **Obv:** Bust right **Rev:** Building **Edge:** Milled

Date	Mintage	F	VF	XF	Unc	BU
AH1423//2002	2,000	—	—	—	120	—

Note: Only 500 sold to collectors. Rest were taken by Amman municipality as official gifts

KM# 86 5 DINARS
120.0000 g., Bronze, 60 mm. **Ruler:** Abdullah **Subject:** Selection of Petra as one of the new Seven Wonders of the World **Obv:** King Abdullah II and Queen Rania **Rev:** Petra **Edge:** Milled

Date	Mintage	F	VF	XF	Unc	BU
AH1428-2008 Proof	500	Value: 160				

KM# 84 10 DINARS
120.0000 g., 0.9990 Silver 3.8541 oz. ASW, 60 mm. **Ruler:** Abdullah **Subject:** 60th Anniversary of Jordan's Independence **Obv:** King Abdullah I and Independence speech **Rev:** The National Assembly building **Edge:** Milled

Date	Mintage	F	VF	XF	Unc	BU
2006 Proof	250	Value: 250				

Note: Issued primarily for use as official state gifts

KM# 88 10 DINARS
31.1050 g., 0.9990 Silver 0.9990 oz. ASW, 40 mm. **Ruler:** Abdullah II **Subject:** Accession, 10th Anniversary **Obv:** Bust facing **Rev:** Crowned and mantled shield

Date	Mintage	F	VF	XF	Unc	BU
2009 Proof	2,250	Value: 150				

KM# 87 20 DINARS
120.0000 g., 0.9990 Silver 3.8541 oz. ASW, 60 mm. **Ruler:** Abdullah **Subject:** Selection of Petra as one of the new Seven Wonders of the World **Obv:** King Abdullah II and Queen Rania **Rev:** Petra **Edge:** Milled

Date	Mintage	F	VF	XF	Unc	BU
AH1428-2008 Proof	500	Value: 260				

KM# 89 50 DINARS
16.9600 g., 0.9990 Gold 0.5447 oz. AGW, 30 mm. **Ruler:** Abdullah II **Subject:** Accession, 10th Anniversary **Obv:** Bust **Rev:** Arms

Date	Mintage	F	VF	XF	Unc	BU
2009 Proof	1,750	Value: 800				

KM# 85 60 DINARS
72.7500 g., 0.9170 Gold 2.1447 oz. AGW, 40 mm. **Ruler:** Abdullah **Subject:** 60th Anniversary of Jordan's Independence **Obv:** King Abdullah II **Rev:** Treasury in Petra **Edge:** Milled

Date	Mintage	F	VF	XF	Unc	BU
2006 Proof	250	Value: 3,250				

Note: Issued primarily for use as official state gifts

MINT SETS

KM#	Date	Mintage	Identification	Issue Price	Mkt Val
MS4	2000-2004 (5)	—	KM#73-74, 78.1, 79, 83	—	20.00

PROOF SETS

KM#	Date	Mintage	Identification	Issue Price	Mkt Val
PS14	2006 (2)	250	KM#84-85	—	3,500
PS15	2008 (2)	—	KM#86-87	—	425

KAZAKHSTAN

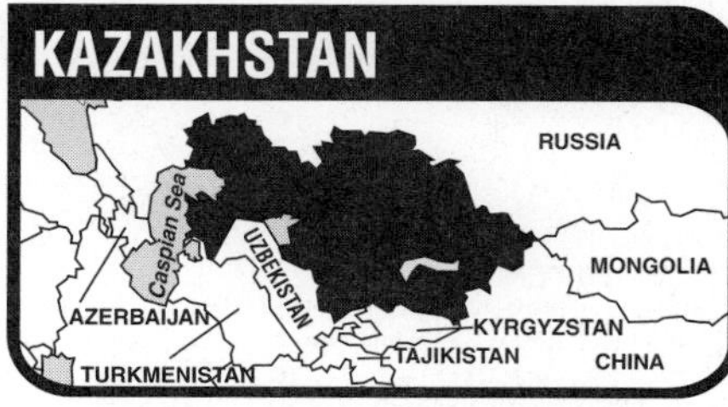

The Republic of Kazakhstan (formerly Kazakhstan S.S.R.) is bordered to the west by the Caspian Sea and Russia, to the north by Russia, in the east by the Peoples Republic of China and in the south by Uzbekistan and Kirghizia. It has an area of 1,049,155 sq. mi. (2,717,300 sq. km.) and a population of 16.7 million. Capital: Astana. Rich in mineral resources including coal, tungsten, copper, lead, zinc and manganese with huge oil and natural gas reserves. Agriculture is very important, (it previously represented 20 percent of the total arable acreage of the combined U.S.S.R.) Non-ferrous metallurgy, heavy engineering and chemical industries are leaders in its economy.

MONETARY SYSTEM
100 Tyin = 1 Tenge

REPUBLIC

DECIMAL COINAGE

KM# 23 TENGE
1.6000 g., Brass, 15 mm. **Obv:** National emblem **Rev:** Value flanked by designs **Edge:** Plain

Date	Mintage	F	VF	XF	Unc	BU
2002	—	—	—	—	0.50	0.85
2004	—	—	—	—	0.50	0.85
2005	—	—	—	—	0.50	0.85

KM# 64 2 TENGE
1.8200 g., Brass, 16 mm. **Obv:** National emblem **Rev:** Value flanked by designs **Edge:** Plain

Date	Mintage	F	VF	XF	Unc	BU
2005	—	—	—	—	0.65	1.20
2006	—	—	—	—	0.65	1.20

KM# 24 5 TENGE
2.2000 g., Brass, 17.3 mm. **Obv:** National emblem **Rev:** Value flanked by designs

Date	Mintage	F	VF	XF	Unc	BU
2002	—	—	—	—	0.50	0.85
2004	—	—	—	—	0.50	0.85
2005	—	—	—	—	0.50	0.85
2006	—	—	—	—	0.50	0.85
2010	—	—	—	—	0.50	0.85

KM# 25 10 TENGE
2.8000 g., Brass, 19.6 mm. **Obv:** National emblem **Rev:** Value above design

Date	Mintage	F	VF	XF	Unc	BU
2002	—	—	—	—	0.75	1.25
2004	—	—	—	—	0.75	1.25
2005	—	—	—	—	0.75	1.25
2006	—	—	—	—	0.75	1.25

KM# 26 20 TENGE
2.8600 g., Copper-Nickel, 18.3 mm. **Obv:** National emblem **Rev:** Value above design **Edge:** Segmented reeding **Edge Lettering:** * CTO TENGE * Y 3 TENGE

Date	Mintage	F	VF	XF	Unc	BU
2002	—	—	—	—	1.00	1.75
2004	—	—	—	—	1.00	1.75
2006	—	—	—	—	1.00	1.75
2010	—	—	—	—	1.00	1.75

KM# 40 50 TENGE
11.5000 g., Copper-Nickel, 31 mm. **Obv:** Eagle superimposed on ornate 10 **Edge:** Reeded and plain sections

Date	Mintage	F	VF	XF	Unc	BU
2001	—	—	—	—	4.00	6.50

KM# 41 50 TENGE
11.2000 g., Copper-Nickel, 31.1 mm. **Subject:** Gabiden Mustafin **Obv:** National emblem above value **Rev:** Bust 1/4 left **Edge:** Segmented reeding

Date	Mintage	F	VF	XF	Unc	BU
ND(2002)	—	—	—	—	4.00	6.50

KM# 69 50 TENGE
Copper-Nickel, 31 mm. **Subject:** Gabit Mosrepov **Obv:** Symbol and value **Rev:** Bust facing

Date	Mintage	F	VF	XF	Unc	BU
2002	—	—	—	—	4.00	6.50

KM# 27 50 TENGE
4.7000 g., Copper-Nickel, 23.1 mm. **Obv:** National emblem **Rev:** Value above design

Date	Mintage	F	VF	XF	Unc	BU
2002	—	—	—	—	2.00	3.50

KM# 70 50 TENGE

Copper-Nickel, 31 mm. **Subject:** 200th Anniversary of Makhambet Utemisov **Obv:** Symbol and value

Date	Mintage	F	VF	XF	Unc	BU
2003	—	—	—	—	4.00	6.50

KM# 54 50 TENGE

11.5000 g., Copper-Nickel, 31.1 mm. **Obv:** National emblem above value **Rev:** Painter Abylichan Kasteev (1904-1973) **Edge:** Reeded and plain sections

Date	Mintage	F	VF	XF	Unc	BU
2004	—	—	—	—	4.00	6.50

KM# 65 50 TENGE

11.5000 g., Copper-Nickel, 31.1 mm. **Subject:** Alken Margulan **Obv:** National emblem above value **Rev:** Bust facing **Edge:** Segmented reeding

Date	Mintage	F	VF	XF	Unc	BU
2004	—	—	—	—	4.00	6.50

KM# 58 50 TENGE

11.5000 g., Copper-Nickel, 31.1 mm. **Subject:** 10th Anniversary of the Constitution **Obv:** National emblem above value **Rev:** National emblem within circle above book **Edge:** Segmented reeding

Date	Mintage	F	VF	XF	Unc	BU
2005	—	—	—	—	4.00	6.50

KM# 71 50 TENGE

10.9500 g., Copper-Nickel, 31 mm. **Subject:** 60 Years Victory WWII **Obv:** Symbol and value

Date	Mintage	F	VF	XF	Unc	BU
2005	—	—	—	—	4.00	6.50

KM# 79 50 TENGE

11.2200 g., Copper-Nickel, 31 mm. **Subject:** 20th Anniversary **Obv:** National arms above value **Rev:** Happy woman **Edge:** Segmented reeding

Date	Mintage	F	VF	XF	Unc	BU
ND (2006)	—	—	—	—	4.00	6.50

KM# 73 50 TENGE

11.3700 g., Copper-Nickel, 31 mm. **Obv:** Human figure and solar system **Rev:** Astronaut and solar system **Edge:** Segmented reeding

Date	Mintage	F	VF	XF	Unc	BU
2006	50,000	—	—	—	4.00	6.00

KM# 74 50 TENGE

11.3700 g., Copper-Nickel, 31 mm. **Obv:** National arms on tapestry **Rev:** Woman with baby in cradle **Edge:** Segmented reeding

Date	Mintage	F	VF	XF	Unc	BU
2006	—	—	—	—	4.00	6.00

KM# 75 50 TENGE

11.3700 g., Copper-Nickel, 31 mm. **Obv:** National arms **Rev:** Altai Snowcock **Edge:** Segmented reeding

Date	Mintage	F	VF	XF	Unc	BU
2006	50,000	—	—	—	4.00	6.00

KM# 77 50 TENGE

11.3700 g., Copper-Nickel, 31 mm. **Obv:** National arms **Rev:** Altyn Kyran Order Breast Star **Edge:** Segmented reeding

Date	Mintage	F	VF	XF	Unc	BU
2006	50,000	—	—	—	4.00	6.00

KM# 78 50 TENGE

11.3700 g., Copper-Nickel, 31 mm. **Obv:** National arms **Rev:** Zhubanov bust and music score **Edge:** Segmented reeding

Date	Mintage	F	VF	XF	Unc	BU
2006	50,000	—	—	—	4.00	6.00

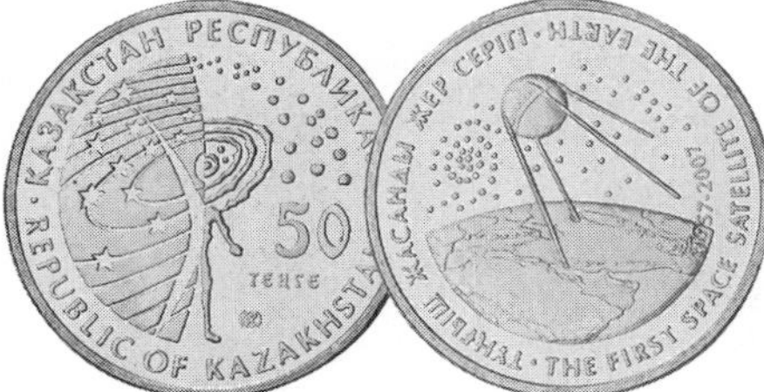

KM# 80 50 TENGE

10.8900 g., Copper-Nickel, 31.10 mm. **Subject:** 50th Anniversary Launch of Sputnik I **Obv:** Stylized view of solar system **Obv. Legend:** REPUBLIC OF KAZAKHSTAN **Rev:** Sputnik I in space, earth in background **Rev. Legend:** THE FIRST SPACE SATELLITE OF THE EARTH **Edge:** Segmented reeding

Date	Mintage	F	VF	XF	Unc	BU
ND(2007)	—	—	—	—	4.00	6.00

KM# 81 50 TENGE

11.1100 g., Copper-Nickel, 31 mm. **Obv:** National arms, value below **Obv. Legend:** КАЗАКСТАН.... **Rev:** Eurasian Spoonbill standing left **Rev. Legend:** ... • PLATALEA LEUCORODIA **Edge:** Segmented reeding

Date	Mintage	F	VF	XF	Unc	BU
2007	—	—	—	—	4.00	6.00

KM# 164 50 TENGE

11.3700 g., Copper-Nickel, 31 mm. **Obv:** National arms on tapestry **Rev:** Child and two men

Date	Mintage	F	VF	XF	Unc	BU
2007	—	—	—	—	4.00	6.00

KM# 165 50 TENGE

11.3700 g., Copper-Nickel, 31 mm. **Obv:** National arms above value **Rev:** Otan badge

Date	Mintage	F	VF	XF	Unc	BU
2007	—	—	—	—	4.00	6.00

KM# 86 50 TENGE

Copper-Nickel, 31 mm. **Obv:** National Arms

Date	Mintage	F	VF	XF	Unc	BU
2008 Prooflike	—	—	—	—	—	12.00

KM# 169 50 TENGE
11.3700 g., Copper-Nickel, 31 mm. **Obv:** National arms on tapersry background **Rev:** Two horsemen

Date	Mintage	F	VF	XF	Unc	BU
2008	—	—	—	—	4.00	6.00

KM# 170 50 TENGE
11.3700 g., Copper-Nickel, 31 mm. **Obv:** National arms above vlaue **Rev:** Dank Order Star

Date	Mintage	F	VF	XF	Unc	BU
2008	—	—	—	—	4.00	6.00

KM# 171 50 TENGE
11.3700 g., Copper-Nickel, 31 mm. **Obv:** National arms **Rev:** Aibyn Order Star

Date	Mintage	F	VF	XF	Unc	BU
2008	—	—	—	—	4.00	6.00

KM# 172 50 TENGE
11.3700 g., Copper-Nickel, 31 mm. **Subject:** Astana capital, 10th Anniversary **Obv:** National arms **Rev:** Architecture

Date	Mintage	F	VF	XF	Unc	BU
2008	—	—	—	—	4.00	6.00

KM# 132 50 TENGE
Copper-Nickel, 31 mm. **Subject:** Betashar **Obv:** Arms **Rev:** Two figures standing

Date	Mintage	F	VF	XF	Unc	BU
2009	50,000	—	—	—	—	10.00

KM# 135 50 TENGE
0.5000 g., 0.9990 Gold 0.0161 oz. AGW, 11 mm. **Obv:** Value **Rev:** Cat head sculpture

Date	Mintage	F	VF	XF	Unc	BU
2009 Proof	14,000	—	—	—	—	50.00

KM# 140 50 TENGE
Copper-Nickel, 31 mm. **Obv:** Arms **Rev:** Parassat medal insignia

Date	Mintage	F	VF	XF	Unc	BU
2009	50,000	—	—	—	—	10.00

KM# 141 50 TENGE
Copper-Nickel **Obv:** Arms **Rev:** Porcupine advancing right **Shape:** 31

Date	Mintage	F	VF	XF	Unc	BU
2009	50,000	—	—	—	—	15.00

KM# 144 50 TENGE
Copper-Nickel, 31 mm. **Obv:** Man standing in solar system **Rev:** Apollo-Soyoz space craft

Date	Mintage	F	VF	XF	Unc	BU
2009	50,000	—	—	—	—	10.00

KM# 145 50 TENGE
Copper-Nickel, 31 mm. **Obv:** Arms **Rev:** Star of the Order of Dostyk

Date	Mintage	F	VF	XF	Unc	BU
2009	50,000	—	—	—	—	10.00

KM# 146 50 TENGE
Copper-Nickel, 31 mm. **Subject:** T. Bassenov, 100th Anniversary of Birth **Obv:** Arms **Rev:** Bust at right, architectural column

Date	Mintage	F	VF	XF	Unc	BU
2009	50,000	—	—	—	—	10.00

KM# 152 50 TENGE
0.5000 g., 0.9990 Gold 0.0161 oz. AGW, 11 mm. **Subject:** Ahalavlinky Treasure **Obv:** Value **Rev:** Historical jewlery design

Date	Mintage	F	VF	XF	Unc	BU
2009 Proof	14,000	Value: 45.00				

KM# 174 50 TENGE
Copper-Nickel, 31 mm. **Subject:** Moon Exploration, 40th Anniversary **Obv:** Figure standing within solar system design **Rev:** Lunar Rover vehicle

Date	Mintage	F	VF	XF	Unc	BU
2010	—	—	—	—	—	5.00

KM# 175 50 TENGE
Copper-Nickel, 31 mm. **Subject:** Great Victory, 65th Anniversary **Obv:** National Emblem, value below **Rev:** Order star, 1945 above

Date	Mintage	F	VF	XF	Unc	BU
2010	—	—	—	—	—	5.00

KM# 39 100 TENGE
6.2300 g., Bi-Metallic Copper-Nickel center in Brass ring, 24.4 mm. **Obv:** National emblem **Rev:** Value within lined circle flanked by designs **Edge:** Reeding over incuse value

Date	Mintage	F	VF	XF	Unc	BU
2002	—	—	—	—	3.50	5.50
2004	—	—	—	—	3.50	5.50
2005	—	—	—	—	3.50	5.50
2006	—	—	—	—	3.50	5.50
2007	—	—	—	—	3.50	5.50

KM# 49 100 TENGE
6.4000 g., Bi-Metallic Copper-Nickel center in Brass ring, 24.5 mm. **Obv:** Stylized chicken **Rev:** Value within lined circle flanked by designs **Edge:** Reeded and lettered

Date	Mintage	F	VF	XF	Unc	BU
2003	100,000	—	—	—	4.00	6.50

KM# 50 100 TENGE
6.4000 g., Bi-Metallic Copper-Nickel center in Brass ring, 24.5 mm. **Obv:** Stylized panther **Rev:** Value within lined circle flanked by designs **Edge:** Reeded and lettered

Date	Mintage	F	VF	XF	Unc	BU
2003	100,000	—	—	—	4.00	6.50

KM# 51 100 TENGE
6.4000 g., Bi-Metallic Copper-Nickel center in Brass ring, 24.5 mm. **Obv:** Stylized wolf's head **Rev:** Value within lined circle flanked by designs **Edge:** Reeded and lettered

Date	Mintage	F	VF	XF	Unc	BU
2003	100,000	—	—	—	4.00	6.50

KM# 52 100 TENGE
6.4000 g., Bi-Metallic Copper-Nickel center in Brass ring,

24.5 mm. **Obv:** Stylized sheep's head **Rev:** Value within lined circle flanked by designs **Edge:** Reeded and lettered

Date	Mintage	F	VF	XF	Unc	BU
2003	100,000	—	—	—	4.00	6.50

KM# 116 100 TENGE
31.1000 g., 0.9250 Silver 0.9249 oz. ASW, 37 mm. **Subject:** Olympics **Obv:** Arms and stylized stadium **Rev:** Two cyclists

Date	Mintage	F	VF	XF	Unc	BU
2004 Proof	—	Value: 50.00				

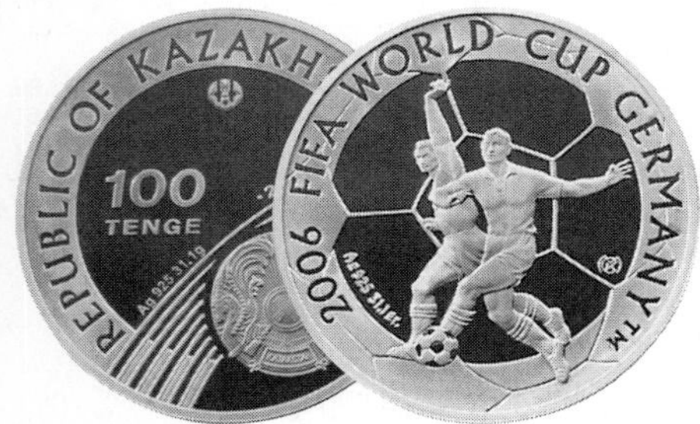

KM# 119 100 TENGE
31.1000 g., 0.9250 Silver 0.9249 oz. ASW, 37 mm. **Subject:** FIFA World Cup, Germany **Obv:** Arms and stylized stadium **Rev:** Two soccer players and large ball

Date	Mintage	F	VF	XF	Unc	BU
2004 Proof	—	Value: 50.00				

KM# 120 100 TENGE
1.2400 g., 0.9990 Gold 0.0398 oz. AGW, 13.92 mm. **Subject:** King Kroisos **Obv:** Arms **Rev:** Head left, coin, temple

Date	Mintage	F	VF	XF	Unc	BU
2004 Proof	—	Value: 75.00				

KM# 121 100 TENGE
1.2400 g., 0.9990 Gold 0.0398 oz. AGW, 13.92 mm. **Subject:** King Midas **Rev:** King Midas reclining on bench

Date	Mintage	F	VF	XF	Unc	BU
2004 Proof	—	Value: 75.00				

KM# 122 100 TENGE
1.2400 g., 0.9990 Gold 0.0398 oz. AGW, 13.92 mm. **Subject:** Ancient Turkestan **Obv:** Arms **Rev:** Camel caravan and building

Date	Mintage	F	VF	XF	Unc	BU
2004 Proof	—	Value: 75.00				

KM# 57 100 TENGE
6.4000 g., Bi-Metallic Copper-Nickel center in Brass ring, 24.5 mm. **Subject:** 60th Anniversary of the UN **Obv:** UN logo as part of the number 60 **Rev:** Value within lined circle flanked by designs **Edge:** Reeded and lettered

Date	Mintage	F	VF	XF	Unc	BU
2005	—	—	—	—	5.00	7.50

KM# 95 100 TENGE
31.1050 g., 0.9250 Silver 0.9250 oz. ASW, 38.61 mm. **Subject:** Baiturramman Mosque **Rev:** Mosque and reflecting pool

Date	Mintage	F	VF	XF	Unc	BU
2006 (2008) Proof	6,000	Value: 80.00				

KM# 98 100 TENGE
31.1050 g., 0.9250 Silver 0.9250 oz. ASW, 38.61 mm. **Subject:** Zahir Mosque **Rev:** Mosque

Date	Mintage	F	VF	XF	Unc	BU
2006 Proof	6,000	Value: 80.00				

KM# 166 100 TENGE
31.1000 g., 0.9250 Silver 0.9249 oz. ASW, 37 mm. **Subject:** Olympics - Pentathlon **Obv:** National arms and stylized stadium **Rev:** Five sports

Date	Mintage	F	VF	XF	Unc	BU
2007 Proof	—	Value: 50.00				

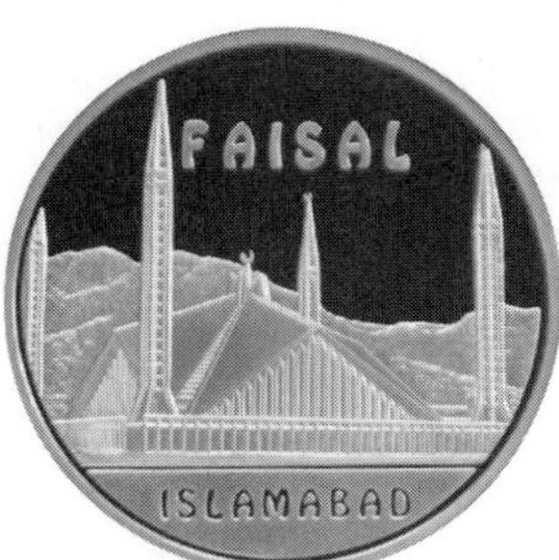

KM# 96 100 TENGE
31.1050 g., 0.9250 Silver 0.9250 oz. ASW, 38.61 mm. **Subject:** Faisal Mosque, Islamabad **Rev:** Mosque

Date	Mintage	F	VF	XF	Unc	BU
2006 (2008) Proof	6,000	Value: 80.00				

KM# 97 100 TENGE
31.1050 g., 0.9250 Silver 0.9250 oz. ASW, 38.61 mm. **Subject:** Hodja Akhmed Yassavi Mausoleum Turkestan **Rev:** Mausoleum

Date	Mintage	F	VF	XF	Unc	BU
2006 (2008) Proof	6,000	Value: 80.00				

KM# 110 100 TENGE
31.1050 g., 0.9250 Silver 0.9250 oz. ASW, 38.61 mm. **Subject:** Chingis Khan **Rev:** Khan on horseback facing

Date	Mintage	F	VF	XF	Unc	BU
2008 Proof	13,000	Value: 65.00				

KM# 125 100 TENGE
31.1050 g., 0.9250 Silver 0.9250 oz. ASW, 38.61 mm. **Subject:** Attila the Hun **Rev:** Medallic Profile right

Date	Mintage	F	VF	XF	Unc	BU
2009 Proof	13,000	Value: 75.00				

KM# 126 100 TENGE
31.1050 g., 0.9250 Silver 0.9250 oz. ASW, 38.61 mm. **Subject:** 2010 Olympics **Rev:** Ski jumper over Vancouver skyline

Date	Mintage	F	VF	XF	Unc	BU
2009 Proof	12,000	Value: 50.00				

KM# 134 100 TENGE
31.1000 g., 0.9990 Silver partially gilt 0.9988 oz. ASW **Subject:** Caracal **Obv:** Arms **Rev:** Caracal cat head facing, partially gilt

Date	Mintage	F	VF	XF	Unc	BU
2009 Proof	13,000	—	—	—	—	50.00

KM# 136 100 TENGE
1.2400 g., 0.9990 Gold 0.0398 oz. AGW, 13.92 mm. **Obv:** Value **Rev:** Cat head sculpture

Date	Mintage	F	VF	XF	Unc	BU
2009 Proof	9,500	—	—	—	—	80.00

KM# 147 100 TENGE
31.1000 g., 0.9250 Silver 0.9249 oz. ASW, 38.6 mm. **Obv:** Arms **Rev:** Tiger advancing right

Date	Mintage	F	VF	XF	Unc	BU
2009 Proof	13,000	Value: 40.00				

KM# 151 100 TENGE
31.1000 g., 0.9990 Silver 0.9988 oz. ASW, 38.61 mm. **Subject:** World Cup, South Africa **Obv:** Arms and stadium **Rev:** Soccer Player, gilt ball

Date	Mintage	F	VF	XF	Unc	BU
2009 Proof	—	Value: 45.00				

KM# 153 100 TENGE
1.2400 g., 0.9990 Gold 0.0398 oz. AGW, 13.92 mm. **Subject:** Zhalavlinky Treasure **Obv:** Arms **Rev:** Historic jewelery design

Date	Mintage	F	VF	XF	Unc	BU
2009 Proof	9,500	Value: 75.00				

KM# 176 100 TENGE
31.1000 g., 0.9250 Silver 0.9249 oz. ASW, 38.61 mm. **Obv:** State Emblem, gilt horsemen at right **Rev:** Queen Tomris

Date	Mintage	F	VF	XF	Unc	BU
2010 Proof	—	Value: 70.00				

KM# 66 500 TENGE
24.0000 g., 0.9250 Silver 0.7137 oz. ASW, 37 mm. **Obv:** Man seated under tree playing stringed instrument **Rev:** Stringed instrument, musical notes

Date	Mintage	F	VF	XF	Unc	BU
2001 Proof	—	Value: 50.00				

KM# 37 500 TENGE
23.9000 g., 0.9250 Silver 0.7107 oz. ASW, 37 mm. **Subject:** Wildlife **Obv:** Value **Rev:** Female Saiga with two calves **Edge:** Plain

Date	Mintage	F	VF	XF	Unc	BU
2001 Proof	3,000	Value: 90.00				

KM# 38 500 TENGE
23.8100 g., 0.9250 Silver 0.7081 oz. ASW, 36.9 mm. **Subject:** 10 Years of Independence **Obv:** Monument and flag **Rev:** National emblem within design above value **Edge:** Plain

Date	Mintage	F	VF	XF	Unc	BU
2001 Proof	3,000	Value: 125				

KM# 55 500 TENGE
24.0000 g., 0.9250 Silver 0.7137 oz. ASW, 37 mm. **Obv:** Value **Rev:** Altai Mountain petroglyph **Edge:** Plain

Date	Mintage	F	VF	XF	Unc	BU
2001 Proof	3,000	Value: 175				

KM# 112 500 TENGE
24.0000 g., 0.9250 Silver 0.7137 oz. ASW **Subject:** Applied art, stringed instrument **Obv:** Man seated under tree **Rev:** Stringed instrument and notes

Date	Mintage	F	VF	XF	Unc	BU
2001 Proof	—	Value: 40.00				

KM# 42 500 TENGE
23.9000 g., 0.9250 Silver 0.7107 oz. ASW, 37 mm. **Subject:** Music **Obv:** Musician and value divided by tree **Rev:** Musical instruments **Edge:** Plain

Date	Mintage	F	VF	XF	Unc	BU
2002 Proof	—	Value: 165				

KM# 43 500 TENGE
23.9000 g., 0.9250 Silver 0.7107 oz. ASW, 37 mm. **Subject:** Prehistoric Art **Obv:** Value **Rev:** Prehistoric cave art **Edge:** Plain

Date	Mintage	F	VF	XF	Unc	BU
2002 Proof	3,000	Value: 140				

KM# 44 500 TENGE
23.9000 g., 0.9250 Silver 0.7107 oz. ASW, 37 mm. **Subject:** Bighorn Sheep **Obv:** Value **Rev:** Kazakhstan Argali Ram **Edge:** Plain

Date	Mintage	F	VF	XF	Unc	BU
2002 Proof	3,000	Value: 120				

KM# 113 500 TENGE
24.0000 g., 0.9250 Silver 0.7137 oz. ASW, 37 mm. **Subject:** Petroglyph **Obv:** Value on traditional weave pattern **Rev:** Horse petroglyph

Date	Mintage	F	VF	XF	Unc	BU
2002 Proof	—	Value: 60.00				

KM# 53 500 TENGE
24.0000 g., 0.9250 Silver 0.7137 oz. ASW, 37 mm. **Obv:** Value **Rev:** Great Bustard bird standing on ground **Edge:** Plain

Date	Mintage	F	VF	XF	Unc	BU
2003 Proof	3,000	Value: 75.00				

KM# 56 500 TENGE
24.0000 g., 0.9250 Silver 0.7137 oz. ASW, 37 mm. **Subject:** Applied Arts **Obv:** Folk Dancer **Rev:** Cultural artifacts **Edge:** Plain

Date	Mintage	F	VF	XF	Unc	BU
2003 Proof	3,000	Value: 80.00				

KM# 59 500 TENGE
31.1000 g., 0.9250 Bi-Metallic Blackend silver center in proof silver ring 0.9249 oz., 38.6 mm. **Subject:** "Denga" **Obv:** Black square holed coin design above value **Rev:** Black square holed coin design and metal content statement **Edge:** Reeded

Date	Mintage	F	VF	XF	Unc	BU
2004 Proof	5,000	Value: 90.00				

KM# 117 500 TENGE
31.1000 g., 0.9250 Silver partially gilt 0.9249 oz. ASW, 38.6 mm. **Obv:** Three riders **Rev:** Golden deer ornament **Shape:** 12-sided

Date	Mintage	F	VF	XF	Unc	BU
2004 Proof	—	Value: 100				

KM# 60 500 TENGE
24.0000 g., 0.9250 Silver 0.7137 oz. ASW, 37 mm. **Obv:** Value **Rev:** Prehistoric art horseman **Edge:** Plain

Date	Mintage	F	VF	XF	Unc	BU
2005 Proof	3,000	Value: 70.00				

KM# 61 500 TENGE
24.0000 g., 0.9250 Silver 0.7137 oz. ASW, 37 mm. **Obv:** Value **Rev:** Two Goitered Gazelles **Edge:** Plain

Date	Mintage	F	VF	XF	Unc	BU
2005 Proof	3,000	Value: 70.00				

KM# 62 500 TENGE
31.1000 g., 0.9250 Silver 0.9249 oz. ASW, 38.6 mm. **Obv:** Horse race and value **Rev:** Gold plated tiger **Edge:** Plain **Shape:** 12-sided

Date	Mintage	F	VF	XF	Unc	BU
2005 Proof	5,000	Value: 120				

KM# 63 500 TENGE
31.1000 g., 0.9250 Bi-Metallic Blackened Silver center in proof Silver ring 0.9249 oz., 38.6 mm. **Subject:** "Drakhma" coin **Obv:** Old coin design **Rev:** Old coin design **Edge:** Reeded

Date	Mintage	F	VF	XF	Unc	BU
2005 Proof	5,000	Value: 65.00				

KM# 72 500 TENGE
31.1000 g., 0.9250 Silver 0.9249 oz. ASW, 38.6 mm. **Obv:** Horse race and value **Rev:** Gold plated rider **Edge:** Plain

Date	Mintage	F	VF	XF	Unc	BU
2005 Proof	5,000	Value: 100				

KM# 124 500 TENGE
24.0000 g., 0.9250 Silver 0.7137 oz. ASW, 37 mm. **Subject:** Zhoshi Khan Mausoleum **Rev:** 3/4 view of building facade

Date	Mintage	F	VF	XF	Unc	BU
2005 Proof	—	Value: 50.00				

KM# 162 500 TENGE
0.9990 Gold **Obv:** Archway **Rev:** Al-Baram Mosque in Mecca

Date	Mintage	F	VF	XF	Unc	BU
2006 Proof	—	Value: 500				

KM# 163 500 TENGE
0.9990 Gold **Obv:** Archway **Rev:** Al-Nabawi Mosque in Medina

Date	Mintage	F	VF	XF	Unc	BU
2006 Proof	—	—	—	—	—	—

KM# 76 500 TENGE
31.1000 g., 0.9250 Silver 0.9249 oz. ASW **Series:** Flora **Rev:** Tulopa Regeli in multicolor

Date	Mintage	F	VF	XF	Unc	BU
2006 Proof	—	Value: 150				

KM# 83 500 TENGE
24.0000 g., 0.9250 Silver 0.7137 oz. ASW, 38.7 mm. **Obv:** Value at center **Rev:** Tetraogallus Altalcus, Altai Snowcock

Date	Mintage	F	VF	XF	Unc	BU
2006 Proof	3,000	Value: 100				

KM# 84 500 TENGE
31.1000 g., 0.9250 Bi-Metallic Blackened Silver center in proof Silver ring. 0.9249 oz., 38.6 mm. **Subject:** "Dirkhem" coin **Obv:** Old coin design **Rev:** Old coin design **Edge:** Reeded

Date	Mintage	F	VF	XF	Unc	BU
2006 Proof	5,000	Value: 65.00				

KM# 168 500 TENGE
7.7700 g., 0.9990 Gold 0.2496 oz. AGW, 25 mm. **Obv:** Arms **Rev:** Lynx, crystal eyes **Rev. Legend:** FELIS LYNX

Date	Mintage	F	VF	XF	Unc	BU
2007 Proof	—	Value: 475				

KM# 82 500 TENGE
41.4000 g., Bi-Metallic Sterling Silver ring., 38.61 mm. **Subject:** 50th Anniversary Launch of Sputnik I **Obv:** Stylized view of our solar system, multicolor **Obv. Legend:** REPUBLIC OF KAZAKHSTAN **Rev:** Sputnik I in space, earth in background, multicolor **Rev. Legend:** THE FIRST SPACE SATELLITE OF THE EARTH **Edge:** Reeded

Date	Mintage	F	VF	XF	Unc	BU
ND(2007) Proof	4,000	Value: 100				

KM# 85 500 TENGE
31.1000 g., 0.9250 Bi-Metallic Blackened Silver center in proof Silver ring. 0.9249 oz., 38.6 mm. **Subject:** "Otyrar" coin **Obv:** Old coin design **Rev:** Old coin design **Edge:** Reeded

Date	Mintage	F	VF	XF	Unc	BU
2007 Proof	4,000	Value: 75.00				

KM# 87 500 TENGE
24.0000 g., 0.9250 Silver 0.7137 oz. ASW, 38.6 mm. **Obv:** Value **Rev:** Terekin Valley - noble deer petraglyph

Date	Mintage	F	VF	XF	Unc	BU
2007 Proof	3,000	Value: 90.00				

KM# 88 500 TENGE
31.1000 g., 0.9250 Silver 0.9249 oz. ASW **Subject:** Movement series - myth **Obv:** Value within square **Rev:** Design

Date	Mintage	F	VF	XF	Unc	BU
2007 Proof	4,000	Value: 80.00				

KM# 89 500 TENGE
31.1000 g., 0.9250 Silver 0.9249 oz. ASW, 38.6 mm. **Subject:** Gold of the Romans **Obv:** Four horseman **Rev:** Gilt Roman seal ring **Shape:** 12-sided

Date	Mintage	F	VF	XF	Unc	BU
2007 Proof	5,000	Value: 100				

KM# 90 500 TENGE
31.1000 g., 0.9250 Silver 0.9249 oz. ASW, 38.6 mm. **Obv:** State emblem **Rev:** Church

Date	Mintage	F	VF	XF	Unc	BU
2007 Proof	4,000	Value: 75.00				

KM# 91 500 TENGE
31.1000 g., 0.9250 Silver 0.9249 oz. ASW, 38.6 mm. **Obv:** State emblem **Rev:** Traditional family

Date	Mintage	F	VF	XF	Unc	BU
2007 Proof	4,000	Value: 70.00				

KM# 92 500 TENGE
31.1000 g., 0.9250 Silver 0.9249 oz. ASW, 38.6 mm. **Obv:** Leaves **Rev:** Tree growth rings, multicolor seeds

Date	Mintage	F	VF	XF	Unc	BU
2007 Proof	4,000	Value: 75.00				

KM# 93 500 TENGE
24.0000 g., 0.9250 Silver 0.7137 oz. ASW, 38.6 mm. **Subject:** Spoon billed duck **Obv:** Value **Rev:** Duck in reeds

Date	Mintage	F	VF	XF	Unc	BU
2007 Proof	3,000	Value: 85.00				

KM# 167 500 TENGE
7.7800 g., 0.9990 Gold 0.2499 oz. AGW, 25 mm. **Subject:** Olympics, high jump **Obv:** Arms and stylized stadium **Rev:** Female high jump

Date	Mintage	F	VF	XF	Unc	BU
2007 Proof	—	Value: 450				

KM# 94 500 TENGE
31.1050 g., 0.9250 Silver 0.9250 oz. ASW, 38.6 mm. **Subject:** National currency, 15th Anniversary **Obv:** Three coin designs

Date	Mintage	F	VF	XF	Unc	BU
2008 Proof	5,000	Value: 75.00				

KM# 99 500 TENGE
31.1050 g., 0.9250 Silver 0.9250 oz. ASW, 38.61 mm. **Subject:** Eurasic Capitals - Astana **Rev:** Skyline montage

Date	Mintage	F	VF	XF	Unc	BU
2008 Proof	5,000	Value: 75.00				

KM# 100 500 TENGE
24.0000 g., 0.9250 Silver 0.7137 oz. ASW, 38.61 mm. **Subject:** Tien Shan - Brown Bear **Rev:** Bear seated

Date	Mintage	F	VF	XF	Unc	BU
2008 Proof	3,000	Value: 85.00				

KM# 101 500 TENGE
31.1050 g., 0.9250 Silver 0.9250 oz. ASW, 38.61 mm. **Subject:** Nomad Gold **Rev:** Diadem fragment **Shape:** 12-sided

Date	Mintage	F	VF	XF	Unc	BU
2008 Proof	5,000	Value: 115				

KM# 102 500 TENGE
31.1050 g., 0.9250 Silver 0.9250 oz. ASW, 38.61 mm. **Subject:** Kalmykov **Rev:** Fantasy scene

Date	Mintage	F	VF	XF	Unc	BU
2008 Proof	4,000	Value: 80.00				

KM# 103 500 TENGE
31.1050 g., 0.9250 Silver 0.9250 oz. ASW, 38.61 mm. **Subject:** Kyz Kuu **Rev:** Two horseback riders

Date	Mintage	F	VF	XF	Unc	BU
2008 Proof	4,000	Value: 80.00				

KM# 104 500 TENGE
31.1050 g., 0.9250 Silver 0.9250 oz. ASW, 38.61 mm. **Subject:** Linum Olgae **Rev:** Flowers

Date	Mintage	F	VF	XF	Unc	BU
2008 Proof	4,000	Value: 100				

KM# 105 500 TENGE
31.1050 g., 0.9250 Silver 0.9250 oz. ASW, 38.61 mm. **Subject:** National Currency, 15th Anniversary **Rev:** Coin and bank note montage

Date	Mintage	F	VF	XF	Unc	BU
2008 Proof	5,000	Value: 75.00				

KM# 106 500 TENGE
24.0000 g., 0.9250 Silver 0.7137 oz. ASW, 38.6x28.8 mm. **Subject:** Papilio Alexanor **Rev:** Two butterflies **Shape:** oval

Date	Mintage	F	VF	XF	Unc	BU
2008 Proof	4,000	Value: 115				

KM# 107 500 TENGE
31.1050 g., 0.9250 Silver 0.9250 oz. ASW, 38.61 mm. **Subject:** Saraichik Coin **Rev:** Coin of the 14th Century

Date	Mintage	F	VF	XF	Unc	BU
2008 Proof	5,000	Value: 75.00				

KM# 108 500 TENGE
41.4000 g., Bi-Metallic Silver and Titanium, 38.61 mm. **Subject:** Vostok **Rev:** Space ship

Date	Mintage	F	VF	XF	Unc	BU
2008 Proof	4,000	Value: 110				

KM# 109 500 TENGE
31.1050 g., 0.9250 Silver 0.9250 oz. ASW, 38.61 mm. **Subject:** Zharkent Mosque **Rev:** Mosque

Date	Mintage	F	VF	XF	Unc	BU
2008 Proof	400	Value: 75.00				

KM# 118 500 TENGE
24.0000 g., 0.9250 Silver 0.7137 oz. ASW, 37 mm. **Subject:** Kazakhstan Railroads, 100th Anniversary **Obv:** Arms **Rev:** Modern train and Steam locomotive, country route map in background

Date	Mintage	F	VF	XF	Unc	BU
2008 Proof	—	Value: 55.00				

KM# 131 500 TENGE
31.1050 g., 0.9250 Silver 0.9250 oz. ASW, 38.61 mm. **Subject:** Almaty Aport **Rev:** Apple tree branch and flower

Date	Mintage	F	VF	XF	Unc	BU
2009 Proof	4,000	Value: 80.00				

KM# 149 500 TENGE
31.1050 g., 0.9250 Silver 0.9250 oz. ASW, 38.61 mm. **Subject:** Balkhash Tiger **Rev:** Tiger on the hunt

Date	Mintage	F	VF	XF	Unc	BU
2009 Proof	5,000	Value: 75.00				

KM# 133 500 TENGE
31.1050 g., 0.9990 Silver 0.9990 oz. ASW, 38.61 mm. **Subject:** Betashar **Rev:** Two figures standing

Date	Mintage	F	VF	XF	Unc	BU
2009 Proof	4,000	Value: 75.00				

KM# 139 500 TENGE
31.1050 g., 0.9250 Silver 0.9250 oz. ASW, 38.6 mm. **Subject:** Nur-Astana Mosque **Rev:** Mosque

Date	Mintage	F	VF	XF	Unc	BU
2009 Proof	4,000	Value: 75.00				

KM# 142 500 TENGE
24.0000 g., 0.9250 Silver 0.7137 oz. ASW, 38.61 mm. **Rev:** Porcupine left with quills raised

Date	Mintage	F	VF	XF	Unc	BU
2009 Proof	3,000	Value: 90.00				

KM# 143 500 TENGE
31.1050 g., 0.9990 Silver 0.9990 oz. ASW, 38.61 mm. **Rev:** Satir head facing **Shape:** 12-sided

Date	Mintage	F	VF	XF	Unc	BU
2009 Proof	5,000	Value: 100				

KM# 130 500 TENGE
41.1000 g., Bi-Metallic Silver and Titanium, 38.61 mm. **Subject:** Apollo - Soyoz Missions **Rev:** Spacecraft docked in orbit above the earth

Date	Mintage	F	VF	XF	Unc	BU
2009 Proof	4,000	Value: 115				

KM# 137 500 TENGE
31.1050 g., 0.9250 Silver 0.9250 oz. ASW, 38.61 mm. **Subject:** Coin of Almaty **Rev:** 13th Century coin

Date	Mintage	F	VF	XF	Unc	BU
2009 Proof	4,000	Value: 100				

KM# 127 500 TENGE
7.7800 g., 0.9990 Gold 0.2499 oz. AGW, 25 mm. **Subject:** Olympics - Biathlon **Obv:** Arms and stylized stadium **Rev:** Biathlon, 2 cross country skiers and shooter

Date	Mintage	F	VF	XF	Unc	BU
2009 Proof	5,000	Value: 385				

KM# 128 500 TENGE
31.1000 g., 0.9990 Gold 0.9988 oz. AGW, 38.6 mm. **Subject:** Almaty Aport **Obv:** Value and leaves **Rev:** Apples and flower

Date	Mintage	F	VF	XF	Unc	BU
2009 Proof	4,000	Value: 65.00				

KM# 129 500 TENGE
31.1000 g., 0.9250 Silver 0.9249 oz. ASW, 36.6 mm. **Subject:** Alpamys Batyr **Obv:** Arms **Rev:** Historical figure

Date	Mintage	F	VF	XF	Unc	BU
2009 Proof	5,000	Value: 55.00				

KM# 138 500 TENGE
24.0000 g., 0.9250 Silver 0.7137 oz. ASW, 28.61x28.81 mm.

Subject: Flamingo **Obv:** Partial butterfly **Rev:** Pair of flamings standing in holographic water **Shape:** Vertical oval

Date	Mintage	F	VF	XF	Unc	BU
2009 Proof	4,000	Value: 80.00				

KM# 148 500 TENGE

7.7800 g., 0.9990 Gold 0.2499 oz. AGW, 21.87 mm. **Rev:** Tiger walking right

Date	Mintage	F	VF	XF	Unc	BU
2009 Proof	3,000	Value: 400				

KM# 150 500 TENGE

7.7800 g., 0.9990 Gold 0.2499 oz. AGW, 25 mm. **Subject:** Uncia **Obv:** Arms **Rev:** Tiger head left

Date	Mintage	F	VF	XF	Unc	BU
2009 Proof	5,000	Value: 385				

KM# 179 500 TENGE

31.1000 g., 0.9250 Silver 0.9249 oz. ASW **Obv:** Three horsemen **Rev:** Buckle, gilt pair of seated raindeer **Shape:** 12-sided

Date	Mintage	F	VF	XF	Unc	BU
2010 Proof	5,000	Value: 85.00				

KM# 177 500 TENGE

31.1000 g., 0.9250 Silver 0.9249 oz. ASW **Obv:** Outline of three pelicans **Rev:** Pelecanus Crispus, pelican standing

Date	Mintage	F	VF	XF	Unc	BU
2010 Proof	5,000	Value: 75.00				

KM# 178 500 TENGE

31.1000 g., 0.9250 Silver 0.9249 oz. ASW, 38.6 mm. **Subject:** Otau Koteru **Obv:** National Emblem **Rev:** Horseman and large ceremonial umbrella

Date	Mintage	F	VF	XF	Unc	BU
2010 Proof	5,000	Value: 90.00				

KM# 180 500 TENGE

31.1000 g., 0.9250 Silver 0.9249 oz. ASW **Subject:** Flora **Rev:** Papaver Pavoninum in color

Date	Mintage	F	VF	XF	Unc	BU
2010 Proof	4,000	Value: 90.00				

KM# 181 500 TENGE

3.1100 g., 0.9990 Gold 0.0999 oz. AGW, 16 mm. **Obv:** Archway **Rev:** Dome of the Rock, Jerusalem

Date	Mintage	F	VF	XF	Unc	BU
2010 Proof	—	Value: 200				

KM# 182 500 TENGE

31.1000 g., 0.9250 Silver 0.9249 oz. ASW **Rev:** Musical instrument

Date	Mintage	F	VF	XF	Unc	BU
2010 Proof	—	Value: 75.00				

KM# 68 1000 TENGE

7.7800 g., 0.9990 Gold 0.2499 oz. AGW, 20 mm. **Obv:** Two winged ibexes **Rev:** Ancient warrior **Edge:** Reeded

Date	Mintage	F	VF	XF	Unc	BU
2001 Proof	—	Value: 385				

KM# 114 1000 TENGE

67.2500 g., 0.9250 Silver 1.9999 oz. ASW, 50 mm. **Subject:** National Currency, 10th Anniversary **Obv:** Flag, multicolor **Rev:** Coin and bank note designs

Date	Mintage	F	VF	XF	Unc	BU
2003 Proof	—	Value: 150				

KM# 115 1000 TENGE

67.2500 g., 0.9250 Silver 1.9999 oz. ASW, 50 mm. **Subject:** National Currency, 10th Anniversary **Obv:** Arms, gilt and blue enamel **Rev:** Coin montage

Date	Mintage	F	VF	XF	Unc	BU
2003 Proof	—	Value: 170				

KM# 67 5000 TENGE

1000.0000 g., 0.9250 Silver 29.738 oz. ASW, 100 mm. **Subject:** 10th Anniversary of Independence **Obv:** National arms above value **Rev:** Monument statue

Date	Mintage	F	VF	XF	Unc	BU
2001 Proof	—	Value: 1,150				

KM# 173 5000 TENGE

1000.0000 g., 0.9250 Silver 29.738 oz. ASW, 100 mm. **Subject:** Astana capitol, 10th anniversary **Obv:** National arms **Rev:** Architectural elements

Date	Mintage	F	VF	XF	Unc	BU
2008 Proof	—	Value: 1,250				

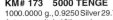

BULLION COINAGE

KM# 157 TENGE

3.1100 g., 0.9990 Gold 0.0999 oz. AGW **Obv:** Arms **Rev:** Tiger standing right on rock

Date	Mintage	F	VF	XF	Unc	BU
2009	—	—	—	—	—	200

KM# 161 TENGE

31.1050 g., 0.9990 Silver 0.9990 oz. ASW, 38.61 mm. **Obv:** Arms **Rev:** Tiger standing right on rock

Date	Mintage	F	VF	XF	Unc	BU
2009	—	—	—	—	—	65.00

KM# 160 2 TENGE

64.2100 g., 0.9990 Silver 2.0622 oz. ASW, 50 mm. **Obv:** Arms **Rev:** Tiger standing right on rock

Date	Mintage	F	VF	XF	Unc	BU
2009	—	—	—	—	—	125

KM# 159 5 TENGE

155.0000 g., 0.9990 Silver 4.9782 oz. ASW, 65 mm. **Obv:** Arms **Rev:** Tiger standing right on rock

Date	Mintage	F	VF	XF	Unc	BU
2009	—	—	—	—	—	250

KM# 158 10 TENGE
311.0500 g., 0.9990 Silver 9.9901 oz. ASW **Obv:** Arms **Rev:** Tiger standing right on rock

Date	Mintage	F	VF	XF	Unc	BU
2009	—	—	—	—	—	550

KM# 156 20 TENGE
7.7800 g., 0.9990 Gold 0.2499 oz. AGW **Obv:** Arms **Rev:** Tiger standing right on rock

Date	Mintage	F	VF	XF	Unc	BU
2009	—	—	—	—	—	400

KM# 155 50 TENGE
15.5500 g., 0.9990 Gold 0.4994 oz. AGW, 25 mm. **Obv:** Arms **Rev:** Tiger standing right on rock

Date	Mintage	F	VF	XF	Unc	BU
2009	—	—	—	—	—	775

KM# 154 100 TENGE
31.1050 g., 0.9990 Gold 0.9990 oz. AGW, 32 mm. **Obv:** Arms **Rev:** Tiger standing right on rock

Date	Mintage	F	VF	XF	Unc	BU
2009	—	—	—	—	—	1,550

KENYA

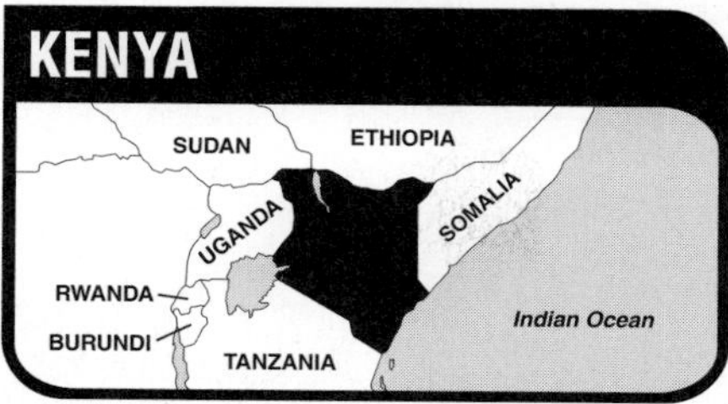

The Republic of Kenya, located on the east coast of Central Africa, has an area of 224,961 sq. mi (582,650 sq. km.) and a population of 20.1 million. Capital: Nairobi. The predominantly agricultural country exports coffee, tea and petroleum products.

Independence was attained on Dec. 12, 1963. Kenya became a republic in 1964. It is a member of the Commonwealth of Nations. The president is Chief of State and Head of Government.

MONETARY SYSTEM
100 Cents = 1 Shilling

REPUBLIC

STANDARD COINAGE

KM# 39 5 CENTS
Copper Clad Steel **Subject:** First President **Obv:** National arms **Rev:** Bust of Mzee Jomo Kenyatta left **Note:** Initially a planned issue, abandoned prior to release for circulation.

Date	Mintage	F	VF	XF	Unc	BU
2005	—	—	—	—	—	—

KM# 40 10 CENTS
Copper Clad Steel **Subject:** First President **Obv:** National arms **Rev:** Bust of Mzee Jomo Kenyatta left **Note:** Initially a planned issue, abandoned prior to release for circulation.

Date	Mintage	F	VF	XF	Unc	BU
2005	—	—	—	—	—	—

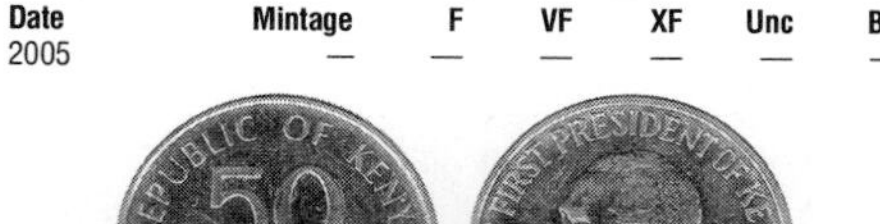

KM# 41 50 CENTS
Nickel Plated Steel **Subject:** First President **Obv:** National arms, value **Rev:** Bust of Mwee Jomo Kenyatta left

Date	Mintage	F	VF	XF	Unc	BU
2005	—	—	—	—	0.60	0.80

KM# 34 SHILLING
5.4600 g., Nickel Clad Steel, 23.9 mm. **Subject:** First President **Obv:** Value above national arms **Rev:** Bust of President Mzee Jomo Kenyata left **Edge:** Segmented reeding

Date	Mintage	F	VF	XF	Unc	BU
2005	—	—	—	—	0.80	1.20

KM# 37 5 SHILLINGS
3.7500 g., Bi-Metallic Aluminum-Bronze center in Copper-Nickel ring, 19.5 mm. **Subject:** First President **Obv:** Value above national arms **Obv. Legend:** REPUBLIC OF KENYA **Rev:** Bust of President Mzee Jomo Kenyatta left **Edge:** Reeded

Date	Mintage	F	VF	XF	Unc	BU
2005	—	—	—	0.60	1.50	2.00

KM# 35 10 SHILLINGS
5.0000 g., Bi-Metallic Copper-Nickel center in Aluminum-Bronze ring, 23 mm. **Subject:** First President **Obv:** Value above national arms **Obv. Legend:** REPUBLIC OF KENYA **Rev:** Bust of Mzee Jomo Kenyatta left **Edge:** Reeded

Date	Mintage	F	VF	XF	Unc	BU
2005	—	—	—	0.90	2.25	3.00

KM# 36 20 SHILLINGS
9.0000 g., Bi-Metallic Aluminum-Bronze center in copper-Nickel ring, 26 mm. **Subject:** First President **Obv:** Large value above national arms **Obv. Legend:** REPUBLIC OF KENYA **Rev:** Bust of President Mzee Jomo Kenyatta left **Edge:** Segmented reeding

Date	Mintage	F	VF	XF	Unc	BU
2005	—	—	—	1.20	3.00	4.00

KM# 33 40 SHILLINGS
11.0000 g., Bi-Metallic Copper-Nickel center in Aluminum-Bronze ring, 27.4 mm. **Obv:** Bust of H. E. Mwai Kibaki facing **Rev:** National arms, value below **Edge:** Reeded and lettered **Edge Lettering:** 40 YEARS OF INDEPENDENCE **Note:** Issued December 11, 2003.

Date	Mintage	F	VF	XF	Unc	BU
ND(2003)	—	—	—	—	6.00	7.50

KM# 38 1000 SHILLINGS
31.1030 g., 0.9250 Silver 0.9249 oz. ASW, 38.61 mm. **Subject:** 40th Anniversary Independence **Obv:** National arms **Rev:** Bust of President H. E. Mwai Kibaki facing

Date	Mintage	F	VF	XF	Unc	BU
ND(2003) Proof	—	Value: 65.00				

KIRIBATI

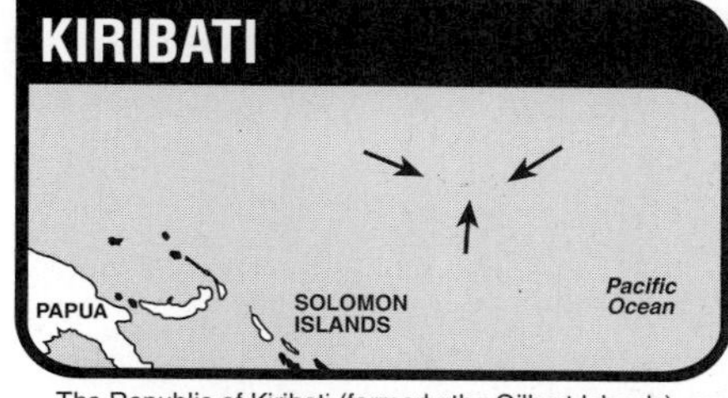

The Republic of Kiribati (formerly the Gilbert Islands), consists of 30 coral atolls and islands spread over more than one million sq. mi. (2,590,000 sq. km.) of the southwest Pacific Ocean, has an area of 332 sq. mi. (717 sq. km.) and a population of 64,200. Capital: Bairiki, on Tarawa. In addition to the Gilbert Islands proper, Kiribati includes Ocean Island, the Central and Southern Line Islands, and the Phoenix Islands, though possession of Canton and Enderbury of the Phoenix Islands is disputed with the United States. Most families engage in subsistence fishing. Copra and phosphates are exported, mostly to Australia and New Zealand.

Kiribati is a member of the Commonwealth of Nations. The President is the Head of State and Head of Government.

MONETARY SYSTEM
100 Cents = 1 Dollar

REPUBLIC

DECIMAL COINAGE

KM# 40 5 CENTS
4.2400 g., Brass, 22.9 mm. **Obv:** National arms **Rev:** Gorilla **Edge:** Reeded

Date	Mintage	F	VF	XF	Unc	BU
2003	—	—	—	—	1.00	1.50

The Democratic Peoples Republic of Korea, situated in northeastern Asia on the northern half of the Korean peninsula between the Peoples Republic of China and the Republic of Korea, has an area of 46,540 sq. mi. (120,540 sq. km.) and a population of 20 million. Capital: Pyongyang. The economy is based on heavy industry and agriculture. Metals, minerals and farm produce are exported.

MONETARY SYSTEM

100 Chon = 1 Won

MINT

Pyongyang

DATING

In the year 2001 the North Korean adopted the "Juche" dating system which is based on the birth year of Kim Il Sung, founder of North Korea. He was born in 1911. "Quel" refers to month and "Quil" refers to day. 9 Quel 3 Quil refers to September 3rd. The western dates on these coins follow the "Juche" date in parenthesis.

PEOPLES REPUBLIC

DECIMAL COINAGE

KM# 183 1/2 CHON

2.1600 g., Aluminum, 27.02 mm. **Obv:** State arms **Rev:** Horse **Edge:** Plain

Date	Mintage	F	VF	XF	Unc	BU
2002	—	—	—	—	1.25	1.50

KM# 184 1/2 CHON

2.1600 g., Aluminum, 27.02 mm. **Obv:** State arms **Rev:** Orangutan **Edge:** Plain

Date	Mintage	F	VF	XF	Unc	BU
2002	—	—	—	—	1.25	1.50

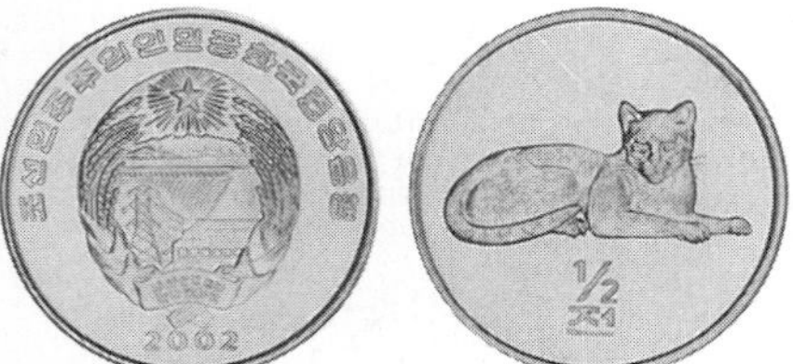

KM# 185 1/2 CHON

2.1600 g., Aluminum, 27.02 mm. **Obv:** State arms **Rev:** Leopard **Edge:** Plain

Date	Mintage	F	VF	XF	Unc	BU
2002	—	—	—	—	1.25	1.50

KM# 186 1/2 CHON

2.1600 g., Aluminum, 27.02 mm. **Obv:** State arms **Rev:** Two giraffes **Edge:** Plain

Date	Mintage	F	VF	XF	Unc	BU
2002	—	—	—	—	1.25	1.50

KM# 187 1/2 CHON

2.1600 g., Aluminum, 27.02 mm. **Obv:** State arms **Rev:** Helmeted guineafowl **Edge:** Plain

Date	Mintage	F	VF	XF	Unc	BU
2002	—	—	—	—	1.25	1.50

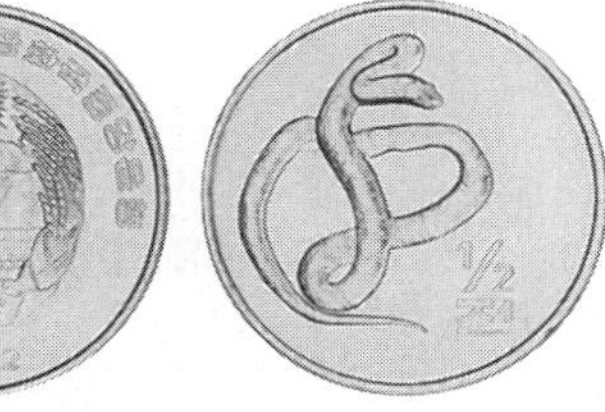

KM# 188 1/2 CHON

2.1600 g., Aluminum, 27.02 mm. **Obv:** State arms **Rev:** Mamushi pit viper **Edge:** Plain

Date	Mintage	F	VF	XF	Unc	BU
2002	—	—	—	—	1.25	1.50

KM# 189 1/2 CHON

2.1600 g., Aluminum, 27.02 mm. **Obv:** State arms **Rev:** Bighorn sheep **Edge:** Plain

Date	Mintage	F	VF	XF	Unc	BU
2002	—	—	—	—	1.25	1.50

KM# 190 1/2 CHON

2.1600 g., Aluminum, 27.02 mm. **Obv:** State arms **Rev:** Hippopotamus **Edge:** Plain

Date	Mintage	F	VF	XF	Unc	BU
2002	—	—	—	—	1.25	1.50

KM# 191 1/2 CHON

2.1600 g., Aluminum, 27.02 mm. **Subject:** FAO **Obv:** State arms **Rev:** Ancient ship **Edge:** Plain

Date	Mintage	F	VF	XF	Unc	BU
2002	—	—	—	—	1.25	1.50

KM# 192 1/2 CHON

2.1600 g., Aluminum, 27.02 mm. **Subject:** FAO **Obv:** State arms **Rev:** Archaic ship **Edge:** Plain

Date	Mintage	F	VF	XF	Unc	BU
2002	—	—	—	—	1.25	1.50

KM# 193 1/2 CHON

2.1600 g., Aluminum, 27.02 mm. **Subject:** FAO **Obv:** State arms **Rev:** Modern train **Edge:** Plain

Date	Mintage	F	VF	XF	Unc	BU
2002	—	—	—	—	1.25	1.50

KM# 194 1/2 CHON

2.1600 g., Aluminum, 27.02 mm. **Subject:** FAO **Obv:** State arms **Rev:** Jet airliner **Edge:** Plain

Date	Mintage	F	VF	XF	Unc	BU
2002	—	—	—	—	1.25	1.50

KM# 195 CHON

4.6300 g., Brass, 21.7 mm. **Subject:** FAO **Obv:** State arms **Rev:** Antique steam locomotive **Edge:** Plain

Date	Mintage	F	VF	XF	Unc	BU
2002	—	—	—	—	1.50	1.75

KM# 196 CHON

4.6300 g., Brass, 21.7 mm. **Subject:** FAO **Obv:** State arms **Rev:** Antique automobile **Edge:** Plain

Date	Mintage	F	VF	XF	Unc	BU
2002	—	—	—	—	1.50	1.75

KM# 197 2 CHON

6.0400 g., Copper-Nickel, 24.2 mm. **Subject:** FAO **Obv:** State arms **Rev:** Antique touring car **Edge:** Plain

Date	Mintage	F	VF	XF	Unc	BU
2002	—	—	—	—	2.00	2.50

KM# 162.2 WON

7.0000 g., Aluminum, 40 mm. **Obv:** State arms, date above value **Rev:** Radiant Korean map and landmarks **Edge:** Plain

Date	Mintage	F	VF	XF	Unc	BU
2001 Proof	—	Value: 15.00				

KM# 351 WON

7.0000 g., Aluminum, 40 mm. **Obv:** State arms, date and value below **Rev:** North Korean Arch of Triumph **Edge:** Plain

Date	Mintage	F	VF	XF	Unc	BU
2001 Proof	—	Value: 12.00				

KM# 352 WON

28.6000 g., Brass, 40.1 mm. **Obv:** State arms, value below **Rev:** North Korean Arch of Triumph **Edge:** Plain

Date	Mintage	F	VF	XF	Unc	BU
2001 Proof	—	Value: 15.00				

KM# 353 WON
6.4500 g., Aluminum, 40 mm. **Obv:** State arms, value below **Rev:** N. Korean landmarks and tourists above ship **Edge:** Plain

Date	Mintage	F	VF	XF	Unc	BU
2001 Proof	—	Value: 12.00				

KM# 354 WON
27.6300 g., Brass, 40 mm. **Obv:** State arms, date and value below **Rev:** N. Korean landmarks and tourists above ship **Edge:** Plain

Date	Mintage	F	VF	XF	Unc	BU
2001 Proof	—	Value: 15.00				

KM# 355 WON
6.7500 g., Aluminum, 40 mm. **Obv:** State arms, value below **Rev:** Temple of Heaven above Hong Kong city view below **Edge:** Plain

Date	Mintage	F	VF	XF	Unc	BU
ND Proof	—	Value: 12.00				

KM# 356 WON
28.1000 g., Brass, 40 mm. **Obv:** State arms, date and value below **Rev:** Temple of Heaven above, Hong Kong city view below **Edge:** Plain

Date	Mintage	F	VF	XF	Unc	BU
2001 Proof	—	Value: 15.00				

KM# 294a WON
6.7500 g., Aluminum, 40 mm. **Obv:** State arms **Rev:** Antique ceramics **Edge:** Plain

Date	Mintage	F	VF	XF	Unc	BU
2001 Proof	—	Value: 15.00				

KM# 358 WON
6.7500 g., Aluminum, 40 mm. **Obv:** State arms **Rev:** Old fort **Edge:** Plain

Date	Mintage	F	VF	XF	Unc	BU
2001 Proof	—	Value: 12.00				

KM# 358a WON
28.1000 g., Brass, 40 mm. **Obv:** State arms **Rev:** Old fort **Edge:** Plain

Date	Mintage	F	VF	XF	Unc	BU
2001 Proof	—	Value: 15.00				

KM# 359 WON
7.0000 g., Aluminum, 40.1 mm. **Obv:** State arms **Rev:** Old couple above dates1945-2000 **Edge:** Plain

Date	Mintage	F	VF	XF	Unc	BU
2001 Proof	—	Value: 12.00				

KM# 359a WON
27.8000 g., Brass, 40.1 mm. **Obv:** State arms **Rev:** Old couple above dates 1945-2000 **Edge:** Plain

Date	Mintage	F	VF	XF	Unc	BU
2001 Proof	—	Value: 15.00				

KM# 360 WON
27.8000 g., Brass, 40.1 mm. **Obv:** State arms **Rev:** Blue Dragon **Edge:** Plain

Date	Mintage	F	VF	XF	Unc	BU
2001 Proof	—	Value: 20.00				

KM# 361 WON
7.0000 g., Aluminum, 40.1 mm. **Obv:** State arms **Rev:** Head 3/4 left divides dates (1904-1997) flanked by sprigs **Edge:** Plain

Date	Mintage	F	VF	XF	Unc	BU
2001 Proof	—	Value: 12.00				

KM# 361a WON
27.8000 g., Brass, 40.1 mm. **Obv:** State arms **Rev:** Head 3/4 left divides dates(1904-1997) flanked by sprigs **Edge:** Plain

Date	Mintage	F	VF	XF	Unc	BU
2001 Proof	—	Value: 15.00				

KM# 362 WON
7.0000 g., Aluminum, 40.1 mm. **Obv:** State arms **Rev:** Children flying a kite **Edge:** Plain

Date	Mintage	F	VF	XF	Unc	BU
2001 Proof	—	Value: 15.00				

KM# 362a WON
27.8000 g., Brass, 40.1 mm. **Obv:** State arms **Rev:** Children flying a kite **Edge:** Plain

Date	Mintage	F	VF	XF	Unc	BU
2001 Proof	—	Value: 17.50				

KM# 363 WON
7.0000 g., Aluminum, 40.1 mm. **Obv:** State arms **Rev:** Children on seesaw **Edge:** Plain

Date	Mintage	F	VF	XF	Unc	BU
2001 Proof	—	Value: 15.00				

KM# 363a WON
27.8000 g., Brass, 40.1 mm. **Obv:** State arms **Rev:** Children on seesaw **Edge:** Plain

Date	Mintage	F	VF	XF	Unc	BU
2001 Proof	—	Value: 17.50				

KM# 364 WON
7.0000 g., Aluminum, 40.1 mm. **Obv:** State arms **Rev:** Children wrestling **Edge:** Plain

Date	Mintage	F	VF	XF	Unc	BU
2001 Proof	—	Value: 15.00				

KM# 364a WON
27.8000 g., Brass, 40.1 mm. **Obv:** State arms **Rev:** Children wrestling **Edge:** Plain

Date	Mintage	F	VF	XF	Unc	BU
2001 Proof	—	Value: 17.50				

KM# 365 WON
7.0000 g., Aluminum, 40.1 mm. **Obv:** State arms **Rev:** Girl on swing **Edge:** Plain

Date	Mintage	F	VF	XF	Unc	BU
2001 Proof	—	Value: 15.00				

KM# 365a WON
27.8000 g., Brass, 40.1 mm. **Obv:** State arms **Rev:** Girl on swing **Edge:** Plain

Date	Mintage	F	VF	XF	Unc	BU
2001 Proof	—	Value: 17.50				

KM# 366 WON
7.0000 g., Aluminum, 40.1 mm. **Obv:** State arms **Rev:** Girls jumping rope **Edge:** Plain

Date	Mintage	F	VF	XF	Unc	BU
2001 Proof	—	Value: 15.00				

KM# 366a WON
27.8000 g., Brass, 40.1 mm. **Obv:** State arms **Rev:** Girls jumping rope **Edge:** Plain

Date	Mintage	F	VF	XF	Unc	BU
2001 Proof	—	Value: 17.50				

KM# 367 WON
8.7000 g., Aluminum, 40.4 mm. **Obv:** State arms **Rev:** "Kumdang-2 Injection" in center square on leaves **Edge:** Plain

Date	Mintage	F	VF	XF	Unc	BU
2001 Proof	—	Value: 15.00				

KM# 367a WON
26.5400 g., Brass, 40.2 mm. **Obv:** State arms **Rev:** "Kumdang-2 Injection" in center square on leaves **Edge:** Plain

Date	Mintage	F	VF	XF	Unc	BU
2001 Proof	—	Value: 17.50				

KM# 368 WON

27.6100 g., Brass, 40.2 mm. **Obv:** State arms **Rev:** Bust facing divides dates(1912-1994) above sprigs **Edge:** Plain

Date	Mintage	F	VF	XF	Unc	BU
JU90-2001 Proof	—	Value: 17.50				

KM# 369 WON

6.5500 g., Aluminum, 40.4 mm. **Obv:** State arms **Rev:** Train at left, couple below jet plane at right **Edge:** Plain

Date	Mintage	F	VF	XF	Unc	BU
2001 Proof	—	Value: 15.00				

KM# 370 WON

27.5600 g., Brass, 40.1 mm. **Obv:** State arms **Rev:** Train at left, couple below jet plane at right **Edge:** Plain

Date	Mintage	F	VF	XF	Unc	BU
2001 Proof	—	Value: 17.50				

KM# 371 WON

5.0500 g., Aluminum, 35 mm. **Obv:** State arms **Rev:** Hong Kong city view **Edge:** Plain

Date	Mintage	F	VF	XF	Unc	BU
2001 Proof	—	Value: 10.00				

KM# 372 WON

6.4000 g., Aluminum, 40 mm. **Obv:** State arms **Rev:** Bust with beard facing flanked by text **Edge:** Plain

Date	Mintage	F	VF	XF	Unc	BU
2001 Proof	—	Value: 12.00				

KM# 372a WON

27.7000 g., Brass, 40 mm. **Obv:** State arms **Rev:** Bust with beard facing flanked by text **Edge:** Plain

Date	Mintage	F	VF	XF	Unc	BU
2001 Proof	—	Value: 15.00				

KM# 373 WON

6.9000 g., Aluminum, 40 mm. **Subject:** 1996 Olympics **Obv:** State arms **Rev:** Two green gymnasts and multicolor flame **Edge:** Plain

Date	Mintage	F	VF	XF	Unc	BU
2001 Proof	—	Value: 15.00				

KM# 374 WON

7.0000 g., Aluminum, 40 mm. **Obv:** State arms **Rev:** Taedong Gatehouse **Edge:** Plain

Date	Mintage	F	VF	XF	Unc	BU
2001 Proof	—	Value: 15.00				

KM# 375 WON

8.5000 g., Aluminum, 40.2 mm. **Obv:** State arms **Rev:** Tourists above volcano crater **Edge:** Plain

Date	Mintage	F	VF	XF	Unc	BU
JU90-2001 Proof	—	Value: 10.00				

KM# 238a WON

7.1400 g., Aluminum, 40.1 mm. **Obv:** State arms **Rev:** Tiger and cub **Edge:** Plain

Date	Mintage	F	VF	XF	Unc	BU
2001 Proof	—	Value: 17.00				

KM# 376 WON

7.1000 g., Aluminum, 40.1 mm. **Subject:** 1996 Olympics **Obv:** State arms **Rev:** Horse jumping **Edge:** Plain

Date	Mintage	F	VF	XF	Unc	BU
2001 Proof	—	Value: 15.00				

KM# 377 WON

7.0000 g., Aluminum, 40.1 mm. **Subject:** 1996 Olympics **Obv:** State arms **Rev:** Four runners **Edge:** Plain

Date	Mintage	F	VF	XF	Unc	BU
2001 Proof	—	Value: 15.00				

KM# 378 WON

6.8400 g., Aluminum, 40.1 mm. **Obv:** State arms **Rev:** Monument flanked by multicolor flags and flowers **Edge:** Plain

Date	Mintage	F	VF	XF	Unc	BU
2001 Proof	—	Value: 12.00				

KM# 379 WON

6.6000 g., Aluminum, 40.1 mm. **Obv:** State arms **Rev:** Olympic diver **Edge:** Plain

Date	Mintage	F	VF	XF	Unc	BU
2001 Proof	—	Value: 15.00				

KM# 380 WON

6.9100 g., Aluminum, 40.1 mm. **Obv:** State arms **Rev:** Olympic handball player **Edge:** Plain

Date	Mintage	F	VF	XF	Unc	BU
2001 Proof	—	Value: 15.00				

KM# 381 WON

7.1100 g., Aluminum, 40.2 mm. **Obv:** State arms **Rev:** Olympic high bar gymnast **Edge:** Plain

Date	Mintage	F	VF	XF	Unc	BU
2001 Proof	—	Value: 15.00				

KM# 381a WON

28.8200 g., Brass, 40.1 mm. **Obv:** State arms **Rev:** Olympic high bar gymnast **Edge:** Plain

Date	Mintage	F	VF	XF	Unc	BU
2001 Proof	—	Value: 17.50				

KM# 382 WON
6.5000 g., Aluminum, 40.1 mm. **Obv:** State arms **Rev:** Olympic archer **Edge:** Plain

Date	Mintage	F	VF	XF	Unc	BU
2001 Proof	—	Value: 15.00				

KM# 382a WON
27.4100 g., Brass, 40.2 mm. **Obv:** State arms **Rev:** Olympic archer **Edge:** Plain

Date	Mintage	F	VF	XF	Unc	BU
2001 Proof	—	Value: 17.50				

KM# 383 WON
7.1000 g., Aluminum, 40.1 mm. **Obv:** State arms **Rev:** Olympic hurdler **Edge:** Plain

Date	Mintage	F	VF	XF	Unc	BU
2001 Proof	—	Value: 15.00				

KM# 383a WON
28.0000 g., Brass, 40.1 mm. **Obv:** State arms **Rev:** Olympic hurdler **Edge:** Plain

Date	Mintage	F	VF	XF	Unc	BU
2001 Proof	—	Value: 17.50				

KM# 384 WON
7.1500 g., Aluminum, 40.1 mm. **Obv:** State arms **Rev:** Kim Il Sung's birthplace side view **Edge:** Plain

Date	Mintage	F	VF	XF	Unc	BU
JU90-2001 Proof	—	Value: 15.00				

KM# 385 WON
7.0000 g., Aluminum, 40.1 mm. **Obv:** State arms **Rev:** Mt. Kumgang Fairy playing flute **Edge:** Plain

Date	Mintage	F	VF	XF	Unc	BU
2001 Proof	—	Value: 12.00				

KM# 385a WON
28.1600 g., Brass, 40.2 mm. **Obv:** State arms **Rev:** Mt. Kumgang Fairy playing flute **Edge:** Plain

Date	Mintage	F	VF	XF	Unc	BU
2001 Proof	—	Value: 15.00				

KM# 452 WON
27.4400 g., Brass, 40 mm. **Obv:** State arms **Rev:** Early sailing ship **Rev. Legend:** • HISTORY OF SEAFARING • MERCHANTMAN - THE DPR KOREA . KORYO PERIOD . 918-1392 **Edge:** Plain

Date	Mintage	F	VF	XF	Unc	BU
2001 Proof	—	Value: 9.00				

KM# 157 WON
6.7000 g., Aluminum, 40 mm. **Subject:** Seafaring Ships **Obv:** State arms **Rev:** Cruise ship below stylized head left profile **Edge:** Plain

Date	Mintage	F	VF	XF	Unc	BU
JU90-2001 Proof	—	Value: 10.00				

KM# 157a WON
29.0500 g., Brass, 40.2 mm. **Obv:** State arms **Rev:** Cruise ship below stylized head profile left **Edge:** Plain

Date	Mintage	F	VF	XF	Unc	BU
2001 Proof	—	Value: 17.50				

KM# 158 WON
16.2000 g., Brass, 35 mm. **Subject:** First Nobel Prize Winner in Literature **Obv:** State arms **Rev:** Half length seated bust left flanked by shelves and books **Edge:** Plain

Date	Mintage	F	VF	XF	Unc	BU
ND(2001) Proof	—	Value: 10.00				

KM# 158a WON
17.0000 g., Copper-Nickel, 35 mm. **Subject:** First Nobel Prize Winner in Literature - Sully Prudhomme **Obv:** State arms **Rev:** Half length seated bust left flanked by shelves and books **Edge:** Plain

Date	Mintage	F	VF	XF	Unc	BU
ND(2001) Proof	2,000	Value: 100				

KM# 159 WON
16.2000 g., Brass, 35 mm. **Subject:** First Nobel Prize in Physics **Obv:** State arms **Rev:** Bust 3/4 right at left with same person seated in lab at right **Edge:** Plain

Date	Mintage	F	VF	XF	Unc	BU
ND(2001) Proof	—	Value: 10.00				

KM# 159a WON
17.0000 g., Copper-Nickel, 35 mm. **Subject:** First Nobel Prize Winner in Physics - Wilhelm C. Roentgen **Obv:** State arms **Rev:** Bust 3/4 right at left with same person seated in lab at right **Edge:** Plain

Date	Mintage	F	VF	XF	Unc	BU
ND(2001) Proof	2,000	Value: 100				

KM# 160 WON
16.2000 g., Brass, 35 mm. **Subject:** Nipponia Nippon **Obv:** State arms **Rev:** Two nest building Japanese ibis **Edge:** Plain

Date	Mintage	F	VF	XF	Unc	BU
JU90-2001 Proof	—	Value: 15.00				

KM# 160a WON
17.0000 g., Copper-Nickel, 35 mm. **Subject:** Wildlife **Obv:** State arms **Rev:** Two nesting Japanese Ibis birds **Edge:** Plain

Date	Mintage	F	VF	XF	Unc	BU
JU2001 Proof	200	Value: 100				

KM# 160b WON
5.3500 g., Aluminum, 35.1 mm. **Obv:** State arms **Rev:** Two nest building Japanese Ibis birds **Edge:** Plain

Date	Mintage	F	VF	XF	Unc	BU
JU90-2001 Proof	—	Value: 15.00				

KM# 202 WON
17.0000 g., Copper-Nickel, 35 mm. **Subject:** School Ships **Obv:** State arms **Rev:** SS Krusenstern **Edge:** Plain

Date	Mintage	F	VF	XF	Unc	BU
ND(2001) Proof	200	Value: 100				

KM# 204 WON
17.0000 g., Copper-Nickel, 35 mm. **Subject:** Wildlife **Obv:** State arms **Rev:** Two standing Japanese Ibis birds **Edge:** Plain

Date	Mintage	F	VF	XF	Unc	BU
JU90-2001 Proof	100	Value: 150				

KM# 207 WON
17.0000 g., Copper-Nickel, 35 mm. **Subject:** Wildlife **Obv:** State arms **Rev:** Two Korean Longtail Gorals **Edge:** Plain

Date	Mintage	F	VF	XF	Unc	BU
JU90-2001 Proof	200	Value: 100				

KM# 207a WON
16.0500 g., Brass, 35 mm. **Obv:** State arms **Rev:** Two Longtail Gorals **Edge:** Plain

Date	Mintage	F	VF	XF	Unc	BU
JU90-2001 Proof	—	Value: 12.50				

KM# 207b WON
5.3500 g., Aluminum, 35.1 mm. **Obv:** State arms **Rev:** Two Longtail Gorals **Edge:** Plain

Date	Mintage	F	VF	XF	Unc	BU
JU90-2001 Proof	—	Value: 10.00				

KM# 209 WON
17.0000 g., Copper-Nickel, 35 mm. **Subject:** First Nobel Prize Winner in Medicine - Emil A. von Behring **Obv:** State arms **Rev:** Lab beaker divides half length figures facing each other **Edge:** Plain

Date	Mintage	F	VF	XF	Unc	BU
ND(2001) Proof	2,000	Value: 100				

KM# 210 WON
17.0000 g., Copper-Nickel, 35 mm. **Subject:** First Nobel Prize Winner in Peace - Henri Dunant **Obv:** State arms **Rev:** Bust facing at left, war wounded at right **Edge:** Plain

Date	Mintage	F	VF	XF	Unc	BU
ND(2001) Proof	2,000	Value: 100				

KM# 211 WON
17.0000 g., Copper-Nickel, 35 mm. **Subject:** First Nobel Prize Winner in Chemistry - Jacobus Van't Hoff **Obv:** State arms **Rev:** Standing figures in lab scene **Edge:** Plain

Date	Mintage	F	VF	XF	Unc	BU
ND(2001) Proof	2,000	Value: 100				

KM# 212 WON
17.0000 g., Copper-Nickel, 35 mm. **Subject:** First Nobel Prize Winner in Peace - Frederic Passy **Obv:** State arms **Rev:** Head left at right with allegorical scene at left **Edge:** Plain

Date	Mintage	F	VF	XF	Unc	BU
ND(2001) Proof	2,000	Value: 100				

KM# 232 WON
28.1100 g., Brass, 40 mm. **Obv:** State arms **Rev:** White-bellied woodpecker **Edge:** Plain

Date	Mintage	F	VF	XF	Unc	BU
2001 Proof	—	Value: 27.50				

KM# 233 WON
28.1100 g., Brass, 40 mm. **Obv:** State arms **Rev:** Black grouse **Edge:** Plain

Date	Mintage	F	VF	XF	Unc	BU
2001 Proof	—	Value: 27.50				

KM# 234 WON
28.1100 g., Brass, 40 mm. **Obv:** State arms **Rev:** Sand grouse **Edge:** Plain

Date	Mintage	F	VF	XF	Unc	BU
2001 Proof	—	Value: 27.50				

KM# 235 WON
28.1100 g., Brass, 40 mm. **Obv:** State arms **Rev:** Fairy Pitta bird **Edge:** Plain

Date	Mintage	F	VF	XF	Unc	BU
2001 Proof	—	Value: 27.50				

KM# 236 WON
28.1100 g., Brass, 40 mm. **Obv:** State arms **Rev:** Mythical "Hyonmu" **Edge:** Plain

Date	Mintage	F	VF	XF	Unc	BU
2001 Proof	—	Value: 27.50				

KM# 236a WON
7.0000 g., Aluminum, 40 mm. **Obv:** State arms **Rev:** "Hyonmu" **Edge:** Plain

Date	Mintage	F	VF	XF	Unc	BU
2001 Proof	—	Value: 17.50				

KM# 237 WON
28.1100 g., Brass, 40 mm. **Obv:** State arms **Rev:** Blue Dragon **Edge:** Plain

Date	Mintage	F	VF	XF	Unc	BU
2001 Proof	—	Value: 27.50				

KM# 238 WON
28.1100 g., Brass, 40 mm. **Obv:** State arms **Rev:** Two tigers **Edge:** Plain

Date	Mintage	F	VF	XF	Unc	BU
2001 Proof	—	Value: 27.50				

KM# 239 WON
28.1100 g., Brass, 40 mm. **Obv:** State arms **Rev:** Brontosaurus **Edge:** Plain

Date	Mintage	F	VF	XF	Unc	BU
2001 Proof	—	Value: 27.50				

KM# 247 WON

26.9500 g., Brass, 40 mm. **Obv:** State arms **Rev:** Soldier watching an air raid on a Yalu River bridge **Edge:** Plain

Date	Mintage	F	VF	XF	Unc	BU
2001 Proof	—	Value: 20.00				

KM# 248 WON

7.0000 g., Aluminum, 40 mm. **Obv:** State arms **Rev:** Multicolor rabbit and hearts **Edge:** Plain **Note:** Year of the Rabbit

Date	Mintage	F	VF	XF	Unc	BU
2001 Proof	—	Value: 20.00				

KM# 290 WON

28.2000 g., Brass, 40.1 mm. **Obv:** State arms **Rev:** Bust facing above flower sprigs **Edge:** Plain

Date	Mintage	F	VF	XF	Unc	BU
JU90-2001 Proof	—	Value: 20.00				

KM# 291 WON

28.2000 g., Brass, 40.1 mm. **Obv:** State arms **Rev:** Bust facing divides dates (1917-1949) above flower sprigs **Edge:** Plain

Date	Mintage	F	VF	XF	Unc	BU
JU90-2001 Proof	—	Value: 20.00				

KM# 293 WON

28.2000 g., Brass, 40.2 mm. **Obv:** State arms **Rev:** Olympic runners **Edge:** Crude reeding

Date	Mintage	F	VF	XF	Unc	BU
2001 Proof	—	Value: 20.00				

KM# 294 WON

28.2000 g., Brass, 40.2 mm. **Obv:** State arms **Rev:** Antique porcelain objects **Edge:** Plain

Date	Mintage	F	VF	XF	Unc	BU
2001 Proof	—	Value: 20.00				

KM# 458 WON

Brass, 35 mm. **Subject:** Tall ships **Obv:** Arms **Rev:** Krugenstern

Date	Mintage	F	VF	XF	Unc	BU
2001 Proof	—	Value: 8.00				

KM# 459 WON

Brass, 35 mm. **Subject:** Return of Hong Kong **Obv:** Arms **Rev:** Architecture

Date	Mintage	F	VF	XF	Unc	BU
2001 Proof	—	Value: 6.50				

KM# 460 WON

Brass, 35 mm. **Subject:** Return of Hong Kong **Obv:** Skyline **Rev:** Dragon boat

Date	Mintage	F	VF	XF	Unc	BU
2001 Proof	—	Value: 12.00				

KM# 461 WON

Brass **Subject:** 2002 Olympics **Obv:** Arms **Rev:** Speedskater

Date	Mintage	F	VF	XF	Unc	BU
2001 Proof	—	Value: 10.00				

KM# 462 WON

Aluminum, 40 mm. **Subject:** Tae Kwon do **Obv:** Arms **Rev:** Two sportsmen

Date	Mintage	F	VF	XF	Unc	BU
2001 Proof	—	Value: 8.00				

KM# 463 WON

Aluminum, 40 mm. **Obv:** Arms **Rev:** Multicolor flowers

Date	Mintage	F	VF	XF	Unc	BU
2001 Proof	—	Value: 8.00				

KM# 464 WON

Aluminum, 40 mm. **Obv:** Arms **Rev:** Woodpecker on branch (Dryocopus Javensis)

Date	Mintage	F	VF	XF	Unc	BU
2001 Proof	—	Value: 8.00				

KM# 465 WON

Aluminum, 35 mm. **Obv:** Arms **Rev:** Zhou Enlai portrait facing

Date	Mintage	F	VF	XF	Unc	BU
2001 Proof	—	Value: 8.00				

KM# 466 WON

Aluminum, 40 mm. **Obv:** Arms **Rev:** Buddha seated, facing

Date	Mintage	F	VF	XF	Unc	BU
2001 Proof	—	Value: 7.00				

KM# 467 WON

Brass **Obv:** Arms **Rev:** Buddha seated, facing

Date	Mintage	F	VF	XF	Unc	BU
2001 Proof	—	Value: 10.00				

KM# 468 WON

Brass **Obv:** Arms **Rev:** Couple embracing, 1945-2000

Date	Mintage	F	VF	XF	Unc	BU
ND(2001) Proof	—	Value: 10.00				

KM# 470 WON

Brass, 35 mm. **Subject:** 2004 Olympics **Obv:** Arms **Rev:** Three Karate Sportsmen

Date	Mintage	F	VF	XF	Unc	BU
2002 Proof	—	Value: 6.50				

KM# 471 WON

Brass **Obv:** Arms **Rev:** Bridge

Date	Mintage	F	VF	XF	Unc	BU
2002 (91) Proof	—	Value: 7.50				

KM# 472 WON

Brass, 40 mm. **Obv:** Arms **Rev:** Tomb of King Kong Min

Date	Mintage	F	VF	XF	Unc	BU
2002 Proof	—	Value: 7.50				

KM# 473 WON

Aluminum, 40 mm. **Obv:** Arms **Rev:** Tomb of King Tong My Ong

Date	Mintage	F	VF	XF	Unc	BU
2002 Proof	—	Value: 7.50				

KM# 474 WON

Brass **Obv:** Arms **Rev:** Family about to hug

Date	Mintage	F	VF	XF	Unc	BU
2002 Proof	—	Value: 10.00				

KM# 475 WON

Brass, 40 mm. **Obv:** Arms **Rev:** Three people in group hug

Date	Mintage	F	VF	XF	Unc	BU
2002 Proof	—	Value: 10.00				

KM# 476 WON

Brass **Obv:** Arms **Rev:** Four dragons around map of North Korea

Date	Mintage	F	VF	XF	Unc	BU
2002 Proof	—	Value: 10.00				

KM# 305 WON

28.2000 g., Brass, 40.2 mm. **Obv:** State arms **Rev:** Tomb of King Kong Min **Edge:** Plain

Date	Mintage	F	VF	XF	Unc	BU
JU91-2002 Proof	—	Value: 20.00				

KM# 306 WON

7.1000 g., Aluminum, 40 mm. **Obv:** State arms **Rev:** Two horses within circle of animals **Edge:** Plain **Note:** Prev. KM#398.

Date	Mintage	F	VF	XF	Unc	BU
2002 Proof	—	Value: 20.00				

KM# 306a WON

28.2000 g., Brass, 40.2 mm. **Obv:** State arms **Rev:** Two horses within circle of animals **Edge:** Plain

Date	Mintage	F	VF	XF	Unc	BU
2002 Proof	—	Value: 20.00				

KM# 308 WON

6.9000 g., Aluminum, 40 mm. **Obv:** State arms **Rev:** Arirang dancer with cranes flying above **Edge:** Plain **Note:** Prev. KM#390.

Date	Mintage	F	VF	XF	Unc	BU
JU91-(2002) Proof	—	Value: 15.00				

KM# 308a WON

28.2000 g., Brass, 40.2 mm. **Subject:** Arirang **Obv:** State arms **Rev:** Performers and flying cranes **Edge:** Plain

Date	Mintage	F	VF	XF	Unc	BU
JU91-(2002) Proof	—	Value: 20.00				

KM# 313 WON

6.7000 g., Aluminum, 40 mm. **Obv:** State arms **Rev:** Arirang dancer **Edge:** Plain **Note:** Prev. KM#389.

Date	Mintage	F	VF	XF	Unc	BU
JU91-(2002) Proof	—	Value: 15.00				

KM# 313a WON

28.2000 g., Brass, 40.2 mm. **Subject:** Arirang **Obv:** State arms **Rev:** Dancer with upheld arms **Edge:** Plain

Date	Mintage	F	VF	XF	Unc	BU
JU91-(2002) Proof	—	Value: 20.00				

KM# 388 WON

7.1000 g., Aluminum, 40 mm. **Obv:** State arms **Rev:** Arirang dancer Silhouette **Edge:** Plain

Date	Mintage	F	VF	XF	Unc	BU
2002 Proof	—	Value: 15.00				

KM# 391 WON

7.1000 g., Aluminum, 40 mm. **Obv:** State arms **Rev:** Arirang ribbon dancer **Edge:** Plain

Date	Mintage	F	VF	XF	Unc	BU
JU91-2002 Proof	—	Value: 15.00				

KM# 392 WON

7.0000 g., Aluminum, 40 mm. **Obv:** State arms **Rev:** May Day Stadium **Edge:** Plain

Date	Mintage	F	VF	XF	Unc	BU
JU91-2002 Proof	—	Value: 12.00				

KM# 392a WON

28.5000 g., Brass, 40.1 mm. **Obv:** State arms **Rev:** May Day Stadium **Edge:** Plain

Date	Mintage	F	VF	XF	Unc	BU
JU91-2002 Proof	—	Value: 15.00				

KM# 393 WON

7.1000 g., Aluminum, 40 mm. **Obv:** State arms **Rev:** Woman floating above stadium **Edge:** Plain

Date	Mintage	F	VF	XF	Unc	BU
JU91-2002 Proof	—	Value: 15.00				

KM# 393a WON

28.2000 g., Brass, 40 mm. **Obv:** State arms **Rev:** Woman floating above stadium **Edge:** Plain

Date	Mintage	F	VF	XF	Unc	BU
JU91-2002 Proof	—	Value: 17.50				

KM# 394 WON

27.5000 g., Brass, 40 mm. **Obv:** State arms **Rev:** Ribbon dancer with Korea shaped ribbon **Edge:** Plain

Date	Mintage	F	VF	XF	Unc	BU
JU91-2002 Proof	—	Value: 17.50				

KM# 395 WON

27.5000 g., Brass, 40 mm. **Obv:** State arms **Rev:** Dancer in the shape of Korea **Edge:** Plain

Date	Mintage	F	VF	XF	Unc	BU
JU91-2002 Proof	—	Value: 17.50				

KM# 396 WON

7.0000 g., Aluminum, 40 mm. **Obv:** State arms **Rev:** Bust with hat facing divides dates(1337-1392) above building foundation **Edge:** Plain

Date	Mintage	F	VF	XF	Unc	BU
JU91-2002 Proof	—	Value: 15.00				

KM# 397 WON

7.0000 g., Aluminum, 40 mm. **Obv:** State arms **Rev:** Victorious athletes hugging **Edge:** Plain

Date	Mintage	F	VF	XF	Unc	BU
JU91-(2002) Proof	—	Value: 10.00				

KM# 397a WON

28.2400 g., Brass, 40 mm. **Obv:** State arms **Rev:** Victorious athletes hugging **Edge:** Plain

Date	Mintage	F	VF	XF	Unc	BU
JU91-(2002) Proof	—	Value: 12.50				

KM# 399 WON

4.8600 g., Aluminum, 35 mm. **Obv:** State arms **Rev:** Cantering horse **Edge:** Plain

Date	Mintage	F	VF	XF	Unc	BU
JU91-(2002) Proof	—	Value: 15.00				

KM# 399a WON

16.9300 g., Brass, 35 mm. **Obv:** State arms **Rev:** Cantering horse **Edge:** Plain

Date	Mintage	F	VF	XF	Unc	BU
JU91-(2002) Proof	—	Value: 15.00				

KM# 400 WON

5.1000 g., Aluminum, 35 mm. **Obv:** State arms **Rev:** Two wrestlers **Edge:** Plain

Date	Mintage	F	VF	XF	Unc	BU
JU91-(2002) Proof	—	Value: 12.50				

KM# 400a WON

16.5000 g., Brass, 35 mm. **Obv:** State arms **Rev:** Two wrestlers **Edge:** Plain

Date	Mintage	F	VF	XF	Unc	BU
JU91-(2002) Proof	—	Value: 15.00				

KM# 310 WON

Aluminum **Obv:** State arms **Rev:** Tomb of King Tongmyong

Date	Mintage	F	VF	XF	Unc	BU
2002 Proof	—	Value: 12.00				

KM# 310a WON
28.2000 g., Brass, 40.2 mm. **Obv:** State arms **Rev:** Tomb of King Tongmyong **Edge:** Plain

Date	Mintage	F	VF	XF	Unc	BU
JU91-2002 Proof	—	Value: 15.00				

KM# 319 WON
9.6200 g., Aluminum, 40 mm. **Obv:** State arms **Rev:** Helmeted head with two antenna-like horns on the helmet **Edge:** Plain

Date	Mintage	F	VF	XF	Unc	BU
JU92-2003 Proof	—	Value: 15.00				

KM# 264 WON
28.4700 g., Brass, 40 mm. **Obv:** State arms **Rev:** Sheep within circle of animals **Edge:** Plain

Date	Mintage	F	VF	XF	Unc	BU
2003 Proof	—	Value: 22.00				

KM# 319a WON
28.2000 g., Brass, 40.2 mm. **Obv:** State arms **Rev:** Helmeted head with two antenna-like horns on helmet **Edge:** Plain

Date	Mintage	F	VF	XF	Unc	BU
JU92-2003 Proof	—	Value: 17.50				

KM# 323 WON
6.9400 g., Aluminum, 40 mm. **Obv:** State arms **Rev:** Turtle shaped armoured ship of 1592 **Edge:** Plain

Date	Mintage	F	VF	XF	Unc	BU
JU92-2003 Proof	—	Value: 15.00				

KM# 323a WON
28.1000 g., Brass, 40.2 mm. **Obv:** State arms **Rev:** Turtle-shaped armoured ship of 1592 **Edge:** Plain

Date	Mintage	F	VF	XF	Unc	BU
JU92-2003 Proof	—	Value: 20.00				

KM# 403a WON
22.1000 g., Brass, 40 mm. **Obv:** State arms **Rev:** Armored bust facing wearing winged helmet (948-1031) **Edge:** Plain

Date	Mintage	F	VF	XF	Unc	BU
JU92-2003 Proof	—	Value: 17.50				

KM# 404 WON
9.6300 g., Aluminum, 40 mm. **Obv:** State arms **Rev:** Armored bust wearing a horned helmet **Edge:** Plain

Date	Mintage	F	VF	XF	Unc	BU
JU92-2003 Proof	—	Value: 15.00				

KM# 404a WON
22.2500 g., Brass, 40 mm. **Obv:** State arms **Rev:** Armored bust wearing a horned helmet **Edge:** Plain

Date	Mintage	F	VF	XF	Unc	BU
JU92-2003 Proof	—	Value: 17.50				

KM# 405 WON
7.0000 g., Aluminum, 40 mm. **Obv:** State arms **Rev:** Ram within circle of animals **Edge:** Plain

Date	Mintage	F	VF	XF	Unc	BU
2003 Proof	—	Value: 15.00				

KM# 405a WON
28.4400 g., Brass, 40 mm. **Obv:** State arms **Rev:** Ram within circle of animals **Edge:** Plain

Date	Mintage	F	VF	XF	Unc	BU
2003 Proof	—	Value: 17.50				

KM# 406 WON
10.1500 g., Aluminum, 40 mm. **Obv:** State arms **Rev:** Children kicking a shuttlecock **Edge:** Plain

Date	Mintage	F	VF	XF	Unc	BU
JU92-2003 Proof	—	Value: 15.00				

KM# 406a WON
24.6300 g., Brass, 40 mm. **Obv:** State arms **Rev:** Children kicking a shuttlecock **Edge:** Plain

Date	Mintage	F	VF	XF	Unc	BU
JU92-2003 Proof	—	Value: 17.50				

KM# 407a WON
23.1000 g., Brass, 40 mm. **Obv:** State arms **Rev:** Children playing jacks **Edge:** Plain

Date	Mintage	F	VF	XF	Unc	BU
JU92-2003 Proof	—	Value: 17.50				

KM# 408a WON

24.5600 g., Brass, 40 mm. **Obv:** State arms **Rev:** Children spinning tops **Edge:** Plain

Date	Mintage	F	VF	XF	Unc	BU
JU92-2003 Proof	—	Value: 17.50				

KM# 410a WON

24.6400 g., Brass, 40 mm. **Obv:** State arms **Rev:** Large dome building **Edge:** Plain

Date	Mintage	F	VF	XF	Unc	BU
JU92-2003 Proof	—	Value: 17.50				

KM# 265 WON

17.7000 g., Brass, 23.2 x 40.1 mm. **Obv:** State arms **Rev:** White-tufted-ear Marmoset **Edge:** Plain

Date	Mintage	F	VF	XF	Unc	BU
2004	—	Value: 27.50				

KM# 266 WON

17.7000 g., Brass, 23.2 x 40.1 mm. **Obv:** State arms **Rev:** Cercopjthecus Mitis monkey **Edge:** Plain

Date	Mintage	F	VF	XF	Unc	BU
2004 Proof	—	Value: 27.50				

KM# 267 WON

17.7000 g., Brass, 23.2 x 40.1 mm. **Obv:** State arms **Rev:** Two Saguinus Midas monkeys **Edge:** Plain

Date	Mintage	F	VF	XF	Unc	BU
2004 Proof	—	Value: 27.50				

KM# 330 WON

9.9200 g., Aluminum, 45 mm. **Obv:** State arms **Rev:** Mountain cabin **Edge:** Plain **Note:** Prev. KM#411.

Date	Mintage	F	VF	XF	Unc	BU
JU93-2004 Proof	—	Value: 15.00				

KM# 330a WON

26.4500 g., Brass, 45 mm. **Obv:** State arms **Rev:** Mountain cabin **Edge:** Plain

Date	Mintage	F	VF	XF	Unc	BU
JU93-2004 Proof	—	Value: 20.00				

KM# 331 WON

10.0000 g., Aluminum, 45 mm. **Obv:** State arms **Rev:** Kim Il Sung's birthplace, front view **Edge:** Plain **Note:** Prev. KM#412.

Date	Mintage	F	VF	XF	Unc	BU
JU93-2004 Proof	—	Value: 15.00				

KM# 331a WON

26.4500 g., Brass, 45 mm. **Obv:** State arms **Rev:** Sung's birth place, front view **Edge:** Plain

Date	Mintage	F	VF	XF	Unc	BU
JU93-2004 Proof	—	Value: 20.00				

KM# 332 WON

10.0000 g., Aluminum, 45 mm. **Obv:** State arms **Rev:** Kim Il Sung's birthplace, side view **Edge:** Plain **Note:** Prev. KM#413.

Date	Mintage	F	VF	XF	Unc	BU
JU93-2004 Proof	—	Value: 15.00				

KM# 332a WON

26.4500 g., Brass, 45 mm. **Obv:** State arms **Rev:** Sung's birthplace, side view **Edge:** Plain

Date	Mintage	F	VF	XF	Unc	BU
JU93-2004 Proof	—	Value: 20.00				

KM# 333 WON

26.4500 g., Brass, 45 mm. **Obv:** State arms **Rev:** Kim Jung Sook facing **Edge:** Plain

Date	Mintage	F	VF	XF	Unc	BU
JU93-2004 Proof	—	Value: 22.50				

KM# 334 WON

26.4500 g., Brass, 45 mm. **Obv:** State arms **Rev:** Uniformed bust facing **Edge:** Plain

Date	Mintage	F	VF	XF	Unc	BU
JU93-2004 Proof	—	Value: 22.50				

KM# 335 WON

26.4500 g., Brass, 45 mm. **Obv:** State arms **Rev:** Uniformed bust facing **Edge:** Plain

Date	Mintage	F	VF	XF	Unc	BU
JU93-2004 Proof	—	Value: 22.50				

KM# 336 WON

10.1000 g., Aluminum, 45 mm. **Obv:** State arms **Rev:** Kim Il Sung flower, orchid **Edge:** Plain **Note:** Prev. KM#414.

Date	Mintage	F	VF	XF	Unc	BU
JU93-2004 Proof	—	Value: 15.00				

KM# 336a WON

26.4500 g., Brass, 45 mm. **Obv:** State arms **Rev:** Orchids **Edge:** Plain

Date	Mintage	F	VF	XF	Unc	BU
JU93-2004 Proof	—	Value: 20.00				

KM# 337 WON

10.1000 g., Aluminum, 45 mm. **Obv:** State arms **Rev:** Kim Jong Il flower, peony **Edge:** Plain **Note:** Prev. KM#415.

Date	Mintage	F	VF	XF	Unc	BU
JU93-2004 Proof	—	Value: 15.00				

KM# 337a WON

26.4500 g., Brass, 45 mm. **Obv:** State arms **Rev:** Peony flower **Edge:** Plain

Date	Mintage	F	VF	XF	Unc	BU
JU93-2004 Proof	—	Value: 20.00				

KM# 338 WON

9.9300 g., Aluminum, 45 mm. **Obv:** State arms **Rev:** Jin Dal Lae flower, Rose of Sharon **Edge:** Plain **Note:** Prev. KM#416.

Date	Mintage	F	VF	XF	Unc	BU
JU93-2004 Proof	—	Value: 15.00				

KM# 338a WON

26.4500 g., Brass, 45 mm. **Obv:** State arms **Rev:** Rose of Sharon flowers **Edge:** Plain

Date	Mintage	F	VF	XF	Unc	BU
JU93-2004 Proof	—	Value: 20.00				

KM# 483 WON

Copper-Nickel **Subject:** Uzgn Monument **Obv:** Arms **Rev:** Map and building

Date	Mintage	F	VF	XF	Unc	BU
2008 Proof	—	Value: 15.00				

KM# 249 2 WON

7.0000 g., 0.9990 Silver 0.2248 oz. ASW, 30 mm. **Obv:** State arms **Rev:** Two multicolor pandas **Edge:** Plain

Date	Mintage	F	VF	XF	Unc	BU
2003 Proof	—	Value: 30.00				

KM# 417 2 WON

24.6600 g., Brass, 31.6x45.75 mm. **Obv:** State arms **Rev:** Half length uniformed figure standing in land rover saluting below dates 1904-2004 **Edge:** Plain **Shape:** Rectangle

Date	Mintage	F	VF	XF	Unc	BU
ND(2004) Proof	—	Value: 25.00				

KM# 339 3 WON

12.5500 g., Aluminum, 50.1 mm. **Obv:** Korean map **Rev:** Huh Jun Chosun doctor at left, books at right **Edge:** Plain

Date	Mintage	F	VF	XF	Unc	BU
JU93-2004 Proof	—	Value: 20.00				

KM# 339a 3 WON

40.5300 g., Brass, 50.2 mm. **Obv:** Korean map **Rev:** Huh Jun Chosun doctor at left, books at right **Edge:** Plain

Date	Mintage	F	VF	XF	Unc	BU
JU93-2004 Proof	—	Value: 25.00				

KM# 203 5 WON

15.0000 g., 0.9990 Silver 0.4818 oz. ASW, 35 mm. **Subject:** School Ships **Obv:** State arms **Rev:** SS Krusenstern **Edge:** Plain

Date	Mintage	F	VF	XF	Unc	BU
ND(2001) Proof	500	Value: 75.00				

KM# 205 5 WON

15.0000 g., 0.9990 Silver 0.4818 oz. ASW, 35 mm. **Subject:** Wildlife **Obv:** State arms **Rev:** Two standing Japanese Ibis birds **Edge:** Plain

Date	Mintage	F	VF	XF	Unc	BU
JU90-2001 Proof	100	Value: 200				

KM# 206 5 WON

15.0000 g., 0.9990 Silver 0.4818 oz. ASW, 35 mm. **Subject:** Wildlife **Obv:** State arms **Rev:** Two nesting Japanese Ibis birds **Edge:** Plain

Date	Mintage	F	VF	XF	Unc	BU
JU90-2001 Proof	3,000	Value: 50.00				

KM# 208 5 WON
15.0000 g., 0.9990 Silver 0.4818 oz. ASW, 35 mm. **Subject:** Wildlife **Obv:** State arms **Rev:** Two Korean Longtail Gorals **Edge:** Plain

Date	Mintage	F	VF	XF	Unc	BU
JU90-2001 Proof	3,000	Value: 50.00				

KM# 219 5 WON
14.9600 g., 0.9990 Silver 0.4805 oz. ASW, 35 mm. **Obv:** State arms **Rev:** Dragon ship **Edge:** Plain

Date	Mintage	F	VF	XF	Unc	BU
2001 Proof	5,000	Value: 35.00				

KM# 226 5 WON
20.0000 g., 0.9990 Silver 0.6423 oz. ASW, 33.8 mm. **Subject:** Olympics **Obv:** State arms **Rev:** Hurdler **Edge:** Reeded

Date	Mintage	F	VF	XF	Unc	BU
2001 Proof	—	Value: 35.00				

KM# 240 5 WON
14.9400 g., 0.9990 Silver 0.4798 oz. ASW, 35 mm. **Obv:** State arms **Rev:** "Orca" (Killer Whale) **Edge:** Plain

Date	Mintage	F	VF	XF	Unc	BU
2001 Proof	—	Value: 60.00				

KM# 241 5 WON
14.9200 g., 0.9990 Silver 0.4792 oz. ASW, 35 mm. **Obv:** State arms **Rev:** Orca and Eco-Tourists in boat **Edge:** Plain

Date	Mintage	F	VF	XF	Unc	BU
2001 Proof	—	Value: 60.00				

KM# 242 5 WON
14.8700 g., 0.9990 Silver 0.4776 oz. ASW, 35 mm. **Obv:** State arms **Rev:** "Pottwal" (Sperm Whale) **Edge:** Plain

Date	Mintage	F	VF	XF	Unc	BU
2001 Proof	—	Value: 60.00				

KM# 243 5 WON
14.9500 g., 0.9990 Silver 0.4802 oz. ASW, 35 mm. **Obv:** State arms **Rev:** "Buckelwal" (Humpback Whale) **Edge:** Plain

Date	Mintage	F	VF	XF	Unc	BU
2001 Proof	—	Value: 60.00				

KM# 244 5 WON
14.9300 g., 0.9990 Silver 0.4795 oz. ASW, 35 mm. **Obv:** State arms **Rev:** "Groenlandwal" (Greenland Right Whale) **Edge:** Plain

Date	Mintage	F	VF	XF	Unc	BU
2001 Proof	—	Value: 60.00				

KM# 245 5 WON
14.9500 g., 0.9990 Silver 0.4802 oz. ASW, 35 mm. **Obv:** State arms **Rev:** "Blauwal" (Blue Whale) **Edge:** Plain

Date	Mintage	F	VF	XF	Unc	BU
2001 Proof	—	Value: 60.00				

KM# 246 5 WON
14.9600 g., 0.9990 Silver 0.4805 oz. ASW, 35 mm. **Obv:** State arms **Rev:** "Grindwal" (Pilot Whale) **Edge:** Plain

Date	Mintage	F	VF	XF	Unc	BU
2001 Proof	—	Value: 60.00				

KM# 250 5 WON
14.9600 g., 0.9990 Silver 0.4805 oz. ASW, 35 mm. **Subject:** Return of Hong Kong to China **Obv:** State arms **Rev:** City view **Edge:** Plain

Date	Mintage	F	VF	XF	Unc	BU
2001 Proof	—	Value: 20.00				

KM# 251 5 WON
14.9000 g., 0.9990 Silver 0.4785 oz. ASW, 35 mm. **Subject:** Year of the Horse **Obv:** State arms **Rev:** Cantering horse **Edge:** Plain

Date	Mintage	F	VF	XF	Unc	BU
2002 Proof	—	Value: 30.00				

KM# 252 5 WON
14.9200 g., 0.9990 Silver 0.4792 oz. ASW, 35 mm. **Subject:** Korean Games **Obv:** State arms **Rev:** Two wrestlers **Edge:** Plain

Date	Mintage	F	VF	XF	Unc	BU
JU91-2002 Proof	—	Value: 20.00				

KM# 303 5 WON
15.0000 g., 0.9990 Silver 0.4818 oz. ASW, 35 mm. **Obv:** State arms **Rev:** Janggo dancer **Edge:** Segmented reeding

Date	Mintage	F	VF	XF	Unc	BU
JU91-2002 Proof	—	Value: 30.00				

KM# 304 5 WON

15.0000 g., 0.9990 Silver 0.4818 oz. ASW, 35 mm. **Obv:** State arms **Rev:** Armored Knight **Edge:** Segmented reeding

Date	Mintage	F	VF	XF	Unc	BU
JU91-2002 Proof	—	Value: 30.00				

KM# 327 5 WON

20.0000 g., 0.9990 Silver 0.6423 oz. ASW, 35 mm. **Obv:** State arms **Rev:** "Turtle Boat " of 1592 **Edge:** Segmented reeding

Date	Mintage	F	VF	XF	Unc	BU
JU92-2003 Proof	—	Value: 35.00				

KM# 328 5 WON

20.0000 g., 0.9990 Silver 0.6423 oz. ASW, 35 mm. **Obv:** State arms **Rev:** Olympic fencers **Edge:** Segmented reeding

Date	Mintage	F	VF	XF	Unc	BU
JU92-2003 Proof	—	Value: 35.00				

KM# 329 5 WON

20.0000 g., 0.9990 Silver 0.6423 oz. ASW, 35 mm. **Obv:** State arms **Rev:** Three wild horses **Edge:** Segmented reeding

Date	Mintage	F	VF	XF	Unc	BU
JU92-2003 Proof	—	Value: 35.00				

KM# 220 7 WON

20.0000 g., 0.9990 Silver 0.6423 oz. ASW, 38 mm. **Subject:** 2002 Olympics **Obv:** State arms **Rev:** Two speed skaters **Edge:** Plain

Date	Mintage	F	VF	XF	Unc	BU
2001 Proof	10,000	Value: 40.00				

KM# 221 7 WON

20.0000 g., 0.9990 Silver 0.6423 oz. ASW, 38 mm. **Subject:** Endangered Wildlife **Obv:** State arms **Rev:** White-tailed sea Eagle **Edge:** Plain

Date	Mintage	F	VF	XF	Unc	BU
2001 Proof	10,000	Value: 35.00				

KM# 477 7 WON

20.0000 g., Bi-Metallic Silver center in Brass ring. **Obv:** Arms **Rev:** Stadium along river

Date	Mintage	F	VF	XF	Unc	BU
2004 Proof	—	Value: 55.00				

KM# 292 10 WON

31.0000 g., 0.9990 Silver 0.9956 oz. ASW, 40.2 mm. **Obv:** State arms **Rev:** Bust facing flanked by dates (1912-1994) above flower sprigs **Edge:** Plain

Date	Mintage	F	VF	XF	Unc	BU
JU90-2001 Proof	—	Value: 45.00				

KM# 295 10 WON

31.0000 g., 0.9990 Silver 0.9956 oz. ASW, 40.2 mm. **Obv:** State arms **Rev:** Mountain cabin **Edge:** Plain

Date	Mintage	F	VF	XF	Unc	BU
JU90-2001 Proof	—	Value: 45.00				

KM# 296 10 WON

31.0000 g., 0.9990 Silver 0.9956 oz. ASW, 40.2 mm. **Obv:** State arms **Rev:** "KUMDANG - 2 INJECTION" in center of leaves **Edge:** Plain

Date	Mintage	F	VF	XF	Unc	BU
2001 Proof	—	Value: 50.00				

KM# 297 10 WON

31.0000 g., 0.9990 Silver 0.9956 oz. ASW, 40.2 mm. **Obv:** State arms **Rev:** Train scene and a couple below a jet liner **Rev. Legend:** ...1945 - 2001... **Edge:** Plain

Date	Mintage	F	VF	XF	Unc	BU
ND(2001) Proof	—	Value: 45.00				

KM# 298 10 WON

31.0000 g., 0.9990 Silver 0.9956 oz. ASW, 40.2 mm. **Obv:** State arms **Rev:** Cruise ship below stylized head left profile **Edge:** Plain

Date	Mintage	F	VF	XF	Unc	BU
JU90-2001 Proof	—	Value: 50.00				

KM# 299 10 WON

31.0000 g., 0.9990 Silver 0.9956 oz. ASW, 40.2 mm. **Obv:** State arms **Rev:** Old fortress **Edge:** Plain

Date	Mintage	F	VF	XF	Unc	BU
JU90-2001 Proof	—	Value: 47.50				

KM# 300 10 WON

31.0000 g., 0.9990 Silver 0.9956 oz. ASW, 40.2 mm. **Obv:** State arms **Rev:** Landmarks, flag and tourist couple above cruise ship **Edge:** Plain

Date	Mintage	F	VF	XF	Unc	BU
JU90-2001 Proof	—	Value: 45.00				

KM# 301 10 WON
31.0000 g., 0.9990 Silver 0.9956 oz. ASW, 40.2 mm. **Obv:** State arms **Rev:** 2 facing half length men shaking hands **Edge:** Plain

Date	Mintage	F	VF	XF	Unc	BU
JU90-2001 Proof	—	Value: 45.00				

KM# 302 10 WON
31.0000 g., 0.9990 Silver 0.9956 oz. ASW, 40.1 mm. **Obv:** State arms **Rev:** Great East Gate **Edge:** Plain

Date	Mintage	F	VF	XF	Unc	BU
JU90-2001 Proof	—	Value: 47.50				

KM# 357 10 WON
31.0000 g., 0.9990 Silver 0.9956 oz. ASW, 40.2 mm. **Obv:** State arms **Rev:** Antique ceramic items **Edge:** Plain

Date	Mintage	F	VF	XF	Unc	BU
2001 Proof	—	Value: 45.00				

KM# 386 10 WON
30.7600 g., 0.9990 Silver 0.9879 oz. ASW, 40.1 mm. **Obv:** State arms **Rev:** Kim Jung Sook facing flanked by dates (1917-1949) above flower sprigs **Edge:** Plain

Date	Mintage	F	VF	XF	Unc	BU
JU90-2001 Proof	—	Value: 47.50				

KM# 387 10 WON
30.7600 g., 0.9990 Silver 0.9879 oz. ASW, 40.1 mm. **Obv:** State arms **Rev:** Bust facing above flower sprigs **Edge:** Plain

Date	Mintage	F	VF	XF	Unc	BU
JU90-2001 Proof	—	Value: 47.50				

KM# 152 10 WON
31.0000 g., 0.9990 Silver 0.9956 oz. ASW, 39.8 mm. **Subject:** Asian Money Fair **Obv:** State arms **Rev:** Two snakes **Edge:** Reeded and plain sections

Date	Mintage	F	VF	XF	Unc	BU
2001 Proof	—	Value: 60.00				

KM# 153 10 WON
31.0000 g., 0.9990 Silver 0.9956 oz. ASW, 39.8 mm. **Subject:** Tortoise-Serpent **Obv:** State arms **Rev:** Mythical creature **Edge:** Reeded and plain sections

Date	Mintage	F	VF	XF	Unc	BU
2001 Proof	—	Value: 55.00				

KM# 227 10 WON
31.0600 g., 0.9250 Silver 0.9237 oz. ASW, 39.9 mm. **Subject:** General Ri Sun Sin **Obv:** State arms **Rev:** Helmeted head 1/4 left **Edge:** Reeded

Date	Mintage	F	VF	XF	Unc	BU
2001 Proof	—	Value: 47.50				

KM# 253 10 WON
31.1100 g., 0.9990 Silver 0.9992 oz. ASW, 40.2 mm. **Obv:** State arms **Rev:** Head 3/4 left flanked by dates (1904-1997) above flower sprigs **Edge:** Plain

Date	Mintage	F	VF	XF	Unc	BU
2001	—	Value: 45.00				

KM# 469 10 WON
31.1050 g., 0.9250 Silver 0.9250 oz. ASW **Obv:** Arms **Rev:** General Ri Sun Sin

Date	Mintage	F	VF	XF	Unc	BU
2001 Proof	—	Value: 50.00				

KM# 231 10 WON
31.0000 g., 0.9990 Silver 0.9956 oz. ASW, 39.9 mm. **Subject:** Kim Il Sung **Obv:** State arms **Rev:** Bust facing **Edge:** Segmented reeding

Date	Mintage	F	VF	XF	Unc	BU
JU91-2002 Proof	—	Value: 50.00				

KM# 254 10 WON
30.7700 g., 0.9990 Silver 0.9882 oz. ASW, 40.15 mm. **Obv:** State arms **Rev:** Bust facing and his tomb **Edge:** Plain

Date	Mintage	F	VF	XF	Unc	BU
JU91-2002 Proof	—	Value: 42.50				

KM# 255 10 WON
30.9400 g., 0.9990 Silver 0.9937 oz. ASW, 40.2 mm. **Subject:** Jongmongju and Sonjukgyo **Obv:** State arms **Rev:** Head with hat facing above building foundation **Edge:** Plain

Date	Mintage	F	VF	XF	Unc	BU
JU91-2002 Proof	—	Value: 42.50				

KM# 401 10 WON
31.0000 g., 0.9990 Silver 0.9956 oz. ASW, 40.1 mm. **Obv:** State arms **Rev:** Arirang dancer **Edge:** Plain

Date	Mintage	F	VF	XF	Unc	BU
JU91-2002 Proof	—	Value: 45.00				

KM# 402 10 WON
31.0000 g., 0.9990 Silver 0.9956 oz. ASW, 40.1 mm. **Obv:** State arms **Rev:** Arirang ribbon dancer **Edge:** Plain

Date	Mintage	F	VF	XF	Unc	BU
JU91-2002 Proof	—	Value: 45.00				

KM# 307 10 WON
31.0000 g., 0.9990 Silver 0.9956 oz. ASW, 40.1 mm. **Obv:** State arms **Rev:** Two horses within a circle of animals **Edge:** Plain

Date	Mintage	F	VF	XF	Unc	BU
2002 Proof	—	Value: 45.00				

KM# 309 10 WON
31.0000 g., 0.9990 Silver 0.9956 oz. ASW, 40.2 mm. **Subject:** Arirang **Obv:** State arms **Rev:** Performers and flying cranes **Edge:** Plain

Date	Mintage	F	VF	XF	Unc	BU
JU91-2002 Proof	—	Value: 45.00				

KM# 311 10 WON
31.0000 g., 0.9990 Silver 0.9956 oz. ASW, 40.2 mm. **Obv:** State arms **Rev:** Tomb of King Tongmyong **Edge:** Plain

Date	Mintage	F	VF	XF	Unc	BU
JU91-2002 Proof	—	Value: 45.00				

KM# 312 10 WON
31.0000 g., 0.9990 Silver 0.9956 oz. ASW, 40.2 mm. **Obv:** State arms **Rev:** Tomb of King Kong Min **Edge:** Plain

Date	Mintage	F	VF	XF	Unc	BU
JU91-2002 Proof	—	Value: 45.00				

KM# 314 10 WON
31.0000 g., 0.9990 Silver 0.9956 oz. ASW, 40.2 mm. **Subject:** Arirang **Obv:** State arms **Rev:** Stylized dancer **Edge:** Plain

Date	Mintage	F	VF	XF	Unc	BU
2002 Proof	—	Value: 45.00				

KM# 315 10 WON
31.0000 g., 0.9990 Silver 0.9956 oz. ASW, 40.2 mm. **Obv:** State arms **Rev:** Korean map shaped dancer **Edge:** Plain

Date	Mintage	F	VF	XF	Unc	BU
JU91-2002 Proof	—	Value: 47.50				

KM# 316 10 WON
31.0000 g., 0.9990 Silver 0.9956 oz. ASW, 40.2 mm. **Obv:** State arms **Rev:** Korean map shaped ribbon dancer **Edge:** Plain

Date	Mintage	F	VF	XF	Unc	BU
JU91-2002 Proof	—	Value: 47.50				

KM# 317 10 WON
31.0000 g., 0.9990 Silver 0.9956 oz. ASW, 40.2 mm. **Obv:** State arms **Rev:** Victorious athletes hugging **Edge:** Plain

Date	Mintage	F	VF	XF	Unc	BU
JU91-2002 Proof	—	Value: 45.00				

KM# 318 10 WON
31.0000 g., 0.9990 Silver 0.9956 oz. ASW, 40.2 mm. **Obv:** State arms **Rev:** Woman floating above arena **Edge:** Plain

Date	Mintage	F	VF	XF	Unc	BU
JU91-2002 Proof	—	Value: 45.00				

KM# 320 10 WON
31.0000 g., 0.9990 Silver 0.9956 oz. ASW, 40.2 mm. **Obv:** State arms **Rev:** Helmeted head with two antenna-like horns on helmet **Edge:** Plain

Date	Mintage	F	VF	XF	Unc	BU
JU92-2003 Proof	—	Value: 47.50				

KM# 321 10 WON
31.0000 g., 0.9990 Silver 0.9956 oz. ASW, 40.2 mm. **Obv:** State arms **Rev:** Helmeted head with horns **Edge:** Plain

Date	Mintage	F	VF	XF	Unc	BU
JU92-2003 Proof	—	Value: 47.50				

KM# 322 10 WON
31.0000 g., 0.9990 Silver 0.9956 oz. ASW, 40.2 mm. **Obv:** State arms **Rev:** Armored bust facing (948-1031) wearing winged helmet **Edge:** Plain

Date	Mintage	F	VF	XF	Unc	BU
JU92-2003 Proof	—	Value: 47.50				

KM# 324 10 WON
31.0000 g., 0.9990 Silver 0.9956 oz. ASW, 40.2 mm. **Obv:** State arms **Rev:** Turtle-shaped armoured ship of 1592 **Edge:** Plain

Date	Mintage	F	VF	XF	Unc	BU
JU92-2003 Proof	—	Value: 45.00				

KM# 325 10 WON
31.0000 g., 0.9990 Silver 0.9956 oz. ASW, 40.2 mm. **Obv:** State arms **Rev:** Children playing jacks **Edge:** Plain

Date	Mintage	F	VF	XF	Unc	BU
JU92-2003 Proof	—	Value: 45.00				

KM# 326 10 WON
31.0000 g., 0.9990 Silver 0.9956 oz. ASW, 40.2 mm. **Obv:** State arms **Rev:** Children kicking a shuttlecock **Edge:** Plain

Date	Mintage	F	VF	XF	Unc	BU
JU92-2003 Proof	—	Value: 45.00				

KM# 409 10 WON
30.9400 g., 0.9990 Silver 0.9937 oz. ASW, 40 mm. **Obv:** State arms **Rev:** Children spinning tops **Edge:** Plain

Date	Mintage	F	VF	XF	Unc	BU
JU92-2003 Proof	—	Value: 45.00				

KM# 453 10 WON
31.0000 g., 0.9990 Silver 0.9956 oz. ASW **Subject:** FIFA World Championship - Germany 2006 **Obv:** National arms **Rev:** Two hands holding up cup in rays at lower right, two smallplayers at left. **Rev. Legend:** WORLD CUP **Rev. Inscription:** FIFA

Date	Mintage	F	VF	XF	Unc	BU
JU92-2003 Proof	—	Value: 60.00				

KM# 418 10 WON
31.0000 g., 0.9990 Silver 0.9956 oz. ASW, 39.7 mm. **Obv:** State arms **Rev:** Ibis standing in water **Edge:** Segmented reeding

Date	Mintage	F	VF	XF	Unc	BU
JU93-2004 Proof	—	Value: 50.00				

KM# 342 10 WON
31.0000 g., 0.9990 Silver 0.9956 oz. ASW, 40 mm. **Obv:** State arms **Rev:** Domed building **Edge:** Plain

Date	Mintage	F	VF	XF	Unc	BU
JU93-2004 Proof	—	Value: 47.50				

KM# 343 10 WON
31.0000 g., 0.9990 Silver 0.9956 oz. ASW, 40 mm. **Obv:** State arms **Rev:** Pigeon on branch **Edge:** Segmented reeding

Date	Mintage	F	VF	XF	Unc	BU
JU93-2004 Proof	—	Value: 45.00				

KM# 344 10 WON
31.0000 g., 0.9990 Silver 0.9956 oz. ASW, 40 mm. **Obv:** State arms **Rev:** Two Leiothrix birds **Edge:** Segmented reeding

Date	Mintage	F	VF	XF	Unc	BU
JU93-2004 Proof	—	Value: 45.00				

KM# 345 10 WON
31.0000 g., 0.9990 Silver 0.9956 oz. ASW, 40 mm. **Obv:** State arms **Rev:** Two cranes standing in water **Edge:** Segmented reeding

Date	Mintage	F	VF	XF	Unc	BU
JU93-2004 Proof	—	Value: 47.50				

KM# 346 10 WON
31.0000 g., 0.9990 Silver 0.9956 oz. ASW, 40 mm. **Obv:** State arms **Rev:** Curlew bird **Edge:** Segmented reeding

Date	Mintage	F	VF	XF	Unc	BU
JU93-2004 Proof	—	Value: 45.00				

KM# 347 10 WON
31.0000 g., 0.9990 Silver 0.9956 oz. ASW, 40 mm. **Obv:** State arms **Rev:** Goshawk on branch **Edge:** Segmented reeding

Date	Mintage	F	VF	XF	Unc	BU
JU93-2004 Proof	—	Value: 45.00				

KM# 420 10 WON
30.9100 g., 0.9990 Silver 0.9927 oz. ASW, 40 mm. **Subject:** End of WWII 60th Anniversary **Obv:** State arms **Rev:** Multicolor radiant map, doves, rainbow and inscription **Edge:** Plain

Date	Mintage	F	VF	XF	Unc	BU
JU94-2005 Proof	—	Value: 45.00				

KM# 425 10 WON
1.6700 g., Aluminum, 23 mm. **Obv:** State arms **Rev:** Value

Date	Mintage	F	VF	XF	Unc	BU
JU94(2005)	—	—	—	—	1.00	1.25

KM# 256 20 WON
42.0600 g., 0.9990 Silver 1.3509 oz. ASW, 45.1 mm. **Obv:** State arms **Rev:** Rose of sharon flower **Edge:** Plain

Date	Mintage	F	VF	XF	Unc	BU
JU93-2004 Proof	—	Value: 60.00				

KM# 257 20 WON
42.2160 g., 0.9990 Silver 1.3492 oz. ASW, 45.1 mm. **Obv:** State arms **Rev:** Peony flower **Edge:** Plain

Date	Mintage	F	VF	XF	Unc	BU
JU93-2004 Proof	—	Value: 60.00				

KM# 258 20 WON
41.9200 g., 0.9990 Silver 1.3464 oz. ASW, 45.1 mm. **Obv:** State arms **Rev:** Orchid flowers **Edge:** Plain

Date	Mintage	F	VF	XF	Unc	BU
JU93-2004 Proof	—	Value: 60.00				

KM# 259 20 WON
42.0000 g., 0.9990 Silver 1.3489 oz. ASW, 45.1 mm. **Obv:** State arms **Rev:** Kim Il Sung's birth place, side view **Edge:** Plain

Date	Mintage	F	VF	XF	Unc	BU
JU93-2004 Proof	—	Value: 60.00				

KM# 260 20 WON
41.6200 g., 0.9990 Silver 1.3367 oz. ASW, 45.1 mm. **Obv:** State arms **Rev:** Mountain cabin **Edge:** Plain

Date	Mintage	F	VF	XF	Unc	BU
JU93-2004 Proof	—	Value: 60.00				

KM# 261 20 WON
41.9100 g., 0.9990 Silver 1.3460 oz. ASW, 45.1 mm. **Obv:** State arms **Rev:** Kim Il Sung's birth place, front view **Edge:** Plain

Date	Mintage	F	VF	XF	Unc	BU
JU93-2004 Proof	—	Value: 60.00				

KM# 340 20 WON
31.0000 g., 0.9990 Silver 0.9956 oz. ASW, 39.8 mm. **Obv:** State arms **Rev:** Conjoined half length figures facing shaking hands **Edge:** Segmented reeding

Date	Mintage	F	VF	XF	Unc	BU
2004 Proof	—	Value: 50.00				

KM# 341 20 WON
31.0000 g., 0.9990 Silver 0.9956 oz. ASW, 39.8 mm. **Obv:** State arms **Rev:** Bust facing **Edge:** Segmented reeding

Date	Mintage	F	VF	XF	Unc	BU
2004 Proof	—	Value: 50.00				

KM# 419 20 WON
31.0000 g., 0.9990 Silver 0.9956 oz. ASW, 39.75 mm. **Subject:** Historic Pyongyang Meeting **Obv:** State arms **Rev:** Half length figures facing each other shaking hands, English legend **Edge:** Segmented reeding

Date	Mintage	F	VF	XF	Unc	BU
2004 Proof	—	Value: 50.00				

KM# 478 20 WON
27.3000 g., Brass, 40 mm. **Obv:** Temple **Rev:** Multicolor rooster right

Date	Mintage	F	VF	XF	Unc	BU
2005 Proof	—	Value: 10.00				

KM# 479 20 WON
31.1050 g., 0.9990 Silver 0.9990 oz. ASW **Obv:** Arms **Rev:** A puppy, dog's head facing

Date	Mintage	F	VF	XF	Unc	BU
2005 Proof	—	Value: 45.00				

KM# 480 20 WON
23.7000 g., Brass, 40 mm. **Obv:** Temple **Rev:** Multicolor German shepard

Date	Mintage	F	VF	XF	Unc	BU
2006 Proof	—	Value: 10.00				

KM# 481 20 WON
Brass **Obv:** Arms **Rev:** Bejeweled female head

Date	Mintage	F	VF	XF	Unc	BU
2006 Proof	—	Value: 10.00				

KM# 482 20 WON
27.3000 g., Brass, 40 mm. **Obv:** Temple **Rev:** Multicolor pig and pigletts

Date	Mintage	F	VF	XF	Unc	BU
2007 Proof	—	Value: 10.00				

KM# 484 20 WON
27.3000 g., Brass, 40 mm. **Obv:** Temple **Rev:** Multicolor goat left

Date	Mintage	F	VF	XF	Unc	BU
2008 Proof	—	Value: 10.00				

KM# 485 20 WON
27.3000 g., Brass, 40 mm. **Obv:** Temple **Rev:** Multicolor snake and flowers

Date	Mintage	F	VF	XF	Unc	BU
2008 Proof	—	Value: 10.00				

KM# 486 20 WON
27.3000 g., Brass, 40 mm. **Obv:** Temple **Rev:** Multicolor, two rabbits

Date	Mintage	F	VF	XF	Unc	BU
2008 Proof	—	Value: 10.00				

KM# 487 20 WON
27.3000 g., Brass, 40 mm. **Obv:** Temple **Rev:** Multicolro two white rats

Date	Mintage	F	VF	XF	Unc	BU
2008 Proof	—	Value: 10.00				

KM# 488 20 WON
27.3000 g., Brass, 40 mm. **Obv:** Temple **Rev:** Multicolor monkey seated on branch

Date	Mintage	F	VF	XF	Unc	BU
2008 Proof	—	Value: 10.00				

KM# 489 20 WON
27.3000 g., Brass, 40 mm. **Obv:** Temple **Rev:** Multicolor tiger

Date	Mintage	F	VF	XF	Unc	BU
2008 Proof	—	Value: 10.00				

KM# 490 20 WON
27.3000 g., Brass, 40 mm. **Obv:** Temple **Rev:** Multicolor horse prancing right

Date	Mintage	F	VF	XF	Unc	BU
2008 Proof	—	Value: 10.00				

KM# 491 20 WON
27.3000 g., Brass, 40 mm. **Obv:** Temple **Rev:** Multicolor two oxen

Date	Mintage	F	VF	XF	Unc	BU
2008 Proof	—	Value: 10.00				

KM# 262 50 WON
69.6300 g., 0.9990 Silver 2.2363 oz. ASW, 50 mm. **Obv:** Korean map **Rev:** Huh Jun Chosun doctor at left, books at right **Edge:** Plain

Date	Mintage	F	VF	XF	Unc	BU
JU93-2004 Proof	—	Value: 95.00				

KM# 426 50 WON
2.0100 g., Aluminum, 25 mm. **Obv:** State arms **Rev:** Value

Date	Mintage	F	VF	XF	Unc	BU
JU94-2005	—	—	—	—	1.20	1.50

KM# 427 100 WON
2.2700 g., Aluminum, 27 mm. **Obv:** State arms **Rev:** Value

Date	Mintage	F	VF	XF	Unc	BU
JU94-2005	—	—	—	—	1.35	1.75

KM# 445 200 WON
5.1900 g., 0.9990 Silver 0.1667 oz. ASW, 30.00 mm. **Series:** Endangered Wildlife **Obv:** Fortress Gate **Rev:** Polar Bear standing facing **Rev. Legend:** URSUS MARITIMUS **Edge:** Plain

Date	Mintage	F	VF	XF	Unc	BU
2007 Proof	5,000	Value: 28.00				

KM# 441 500 WON
12.0000 g., 0.9990 Silver 0.3854 oz. ASW, 38.00 mm. **Subject:** 170th Anniversary First Public Railway St. Petersburg - Zarskoje Selo **Obv:** Fortress Gate **Rev:** First train arriving **Edge:** Plain

Date	Mintage	F	VF	XF	Unc	BU
ND(2007) Proof	5,000	Value: 70.00				

KM# 447 500 WON
12.0000 g., 0.9990 Silver 0.3854 oz. ASW, 38.00 mm. **Subject:** 150th Anniversay Birth of Ziolkowski and 50th Anniversary Launch of Sputnik I **Obv:** Fortress Gate **Rev:** Bust of Ziolkowski facing 3/4 right at lower left, Sputnik circling earth at upper right **Edge:** Plain

Date	Mintage	F	VF	XF	Unc	BU
ND(2007) Proof	5,000	Value: 65.00				

KM# 443 500 WON
12.0000 g., 0.9990 Silver 0.3854 oz. ASW, 38.00 mm. **Subject:** Lunar Year of the Rat **Obv:** Fortress Gate **Rev:** Two rats within circle of Lunar figures **Edge:** Plain

Date	Mintage	F	VF	XF	Unc	BU
2008	—	—	—	—	—	50.00
2008 Proof	5,000	Value: 70.00				

KM# 428 700 WON
15.5500 g., 0.9990 Silver 0.4994 oz. ASW, 30.00 mm. **Series:** European Union Euro Commemoratives **Obv:** National arms **Rev:** Schleswig-Holstein City gate in relief in tiger's-eye **Edge:** Plain

Date	Mintage	F	VF	XF	Unc	BU
2006 Proof	3,000	Value: 70.00				

KM# 429 700 WON
15.5500 g., 0.9990 Silver 0.4994 oz. ASW, 30.00 mm. **Series:** European Union Euro Commemoratives **Obv:** National arms **Rev:** Vatican in relief in tiger's-eye **Edge:** Plain

Date	Mintage	F	VF	XF	Unc	BU
2006 Proof	3,000	Value: 70.00				

KM# 430 700 WON
15.5500 g., 0.9990 Silver 0.4994 oz. ASW, 30.00 mm. **Series:** European Union Euro Commemoratives **Obv:** National arms **Rev:** Male Olympic statue - discus - Athens in relief in tiger's-eye **Edge:** Plain

Date	Mintage	F	VF	XF	Unc	BU
2006 Proof	3,000	Value: 70.00				

KM# 431 700 WON
15.5500 g., 0.9990 Silver 0.4994 oz. ASW, 30.00 mm. **Series:** European Union Euro Commemoratives **Obv:** National arms **Rev:** 50th Anniversary Austrian States Treaty in relief in tiger's-eye **Edge:** Plain

Date	Mintage	F	VF	XF	Unc	BU
2006 Proof	3,000	Value: 70.00				

KM# 432 700 WON
15.5500 g., 0.9990 Silver 0.4994 oz. ASW, 30.00 mm. **Series:** European Union Euro Commemoratives **Obv:** National arms **Rev:** Don Quixote in relief in tiger's-eye **Edge:** Plain

Date	Mintage	F	VF	XF	Unc	BU
2006 Proof	3,000	Value: 70.00				

KM# 433 700 WON
15.5500 g., 0.9990 Silver 0.4994 oz. ASW, 30.00 mm. **Series:** European Union Euro Commemoratives **Obv:** National arms **Rev:** Head of Henri, Grand Duke of Luxembourg at left facing right, crowned H at right in relief in tiger's-eye **Edge:** Plain

Date	Mintage	F	VF	XF	Unc	BU
2006 Proof	3,000	Value: 70.00				

KM# 434 700 WON
15.5500 g., 0.9990 Silver 0.4994 oz. ASW, 30 mm. **Series:** European Union Euro Commemoratives **Obv:** National arms **Rev:** Italian FAO logo in relief in tiger's-eye **Edge:** Plain

Date	Mintage	F	VF	XF	Unc	BU
2006 Proof	3,000	Value: 70.00				

KM# 435 700 WON
15.5500 g., 0.9990 Silver 0.4994 oz. ASW, 30 mm. **Series:** European Union Euro Commemoratives **Obv:** National arms **Rev:** Finland - stylized flower in relief in tiger's-eye **Edge:** Plain

Date	Mintage	F	VF	XF	Unc	BU
2006 Proof	3,000	Value: 70.00				

KM# 436 700 WON
15.5500 g., 0.9990 Silver 0.4994 oz. ASW, 30 mm. **Series:** European Union Euro Commemoratives **Obv:** National arms **Rev:** Conjoined heads of Grand Duke Henri of Luxembourg and King Albert of Belgium left in relief in tiger's-eye **Edge:** Plain

Date	Mintage	F	VF	XF	Unc	BU
2006 Proof	3,000	Value: 70.00				

KM# 437 700 WON
15.5500 g., 0.9990 Silver 0.4994 oz. ASW, 30 mm. **Series:** European Union Euro Commemoratives **Obv:** National arms **Rev:** San Marino - bust of Bartolomeo Borghesi slightly right in relief in tiger's-eye **Edge:** Plain

Date	Mintage	F	VF	XF	Unc	BU
2006 Proof	3,000	Value: 70.00				

KM# 438 700 WON
15.5500 g., 0.9990 Silver tigereye colored center 0.4994 oz. ASW, 30 mm. **Series:** European Union Euro Commemoratives **Obv:** National arms **Rev:** Vatican - World Youth Day in Cologne **Edge:** Plain

Date	Mintage	F	VF	XF	Unc	BU
2006 Proof	3,000	Value: 70.00				

KM# 439 700 WON
15.5500 g., 0.9990 Silver 0.4994 oz. ASW, 30 mm. **Series:** European Union Euro Commemoratives **Obv:** National arms **Rev:** San Marino - Year of Physics design in relief in tiger's-eye **Edge:** Plain

Date	Mintage	F	VF	XF	Unc	BU
2006 Proof	3,000	Value: 70.00				

KM# 440 1000 WON
20.0000 g., 0.9990 Silver 0.6423 oz. ASW, 38 mm. **Obv:** National arms **Rev:** Arctic animals with map of North Pole in background **Rev. Legend:** INTERNATIONAL POLAR YEAR / ARCTIC ANIMALS **Edge:** Plain

Date	Mintage	F	VF	XF	Unc	BU
ND(2007) Proof	—	Value: 85.00				

KM# 446 1000 WON
20.0000 g., 0.9990 Silver 0.6423 oz. ASW, 38 mm. **Series:** Endangered Wildlife **Obv:** Fortress Gate **Rev:** Polar Bear standing facing **Rev. Legend:** URSUS MAITIMUS **Edge:** Plain

Date	Mintage	F	VF	XF	Unc	BU
2007 Proof	5,000	Value: 70.00				

KM# 442 15000 WON
7.7800 g., 0.9990 Gold 0.2499 oz. AGW, 26 mm. **Subject:** 170th Anniversary First Public Railway St. Petersburg - Zarskoje Selo **Obv:** Fortress Gate **Rev:** First train arriving **Edge:** Plain

Date	Mintage	F	VF	XF	Unc	BU
ND(2007) Proof	2,000	Value: 450				

KM# 448 15000 WON
7.7800 g., 0.9990 Gold 0.2499 oz. AGW, 26 mm. **Subject:** 150th Anniversary Birth of Ziolkowski and 50th Anniversary Launch of Sputnik I **Obv:** Fortress Gate **Rev:** Bust of Ziolkowski facing 3/4 right at lower left, Sputnik circling earth at top right **Edge:** Plain

Date	Mintage	F	VF	XF	Unc	BU
ND(2007) Proof	2,000	Value: 450				

KM# 444 15000 WON
7.7800 g., 0.9990 Gold 0.2499 oz. AGW, 26 mm. **Subject:** Lunar Year of the Rat **Obv:** Fortress Gate **Rev:** Two rats within circle of Lunar figures **Edge:** Plain

Date	Mintage	F	VF	XF	Unc	BU
2008 Proof	2,000	Value: 450				

SOUTH KOREA

The Republic of Korea, situated in northeastern Asia on the southern half of the Korean peninsula between North Korea and the Korean Strait, has an area of 38,025 sq. mi. (98,480 sq. km.) and a population of 42.5 million. Capital: Seoul. The economy is based on agriculture and light and medium industry. Some of the world's largest oil tankers are built here. Automobiles, plywood, electronics, and textile products are exported.

NOTE: For earlier coinage see Korea.

MINT
KOMSCO - Korea Minting and Security Printing Corporation

REPUBLIC

REFORM COINAGE

10 Hwan = 1 Won

KM# 31 WON
0.7290 g., Aluminum, 17.2 mm. **Obv:** Rose of Sharon **Rev:** Value and date

Date	Mintage	F	VF	XF	Unc	BU
2001	130,000	—	—	—	0.15	0.25
2002	122,000	—	—	—	0.15	0.25
2003	20,000	—	—	—	0.15	0.25
2004	25,500	—	—	—	0.15	0.25
2005	38,000	—	—	—	0.15	0.25
2006	53,000	—	—	—	0.15	0.25
2007	53,000	—	—	—	0.15	0.25

KM# 32 5 WON
2.9500 g., Brass, 20.4 mm. **Obv:** Iron-clad turtle boat **Rev:** Value and date **Edge:** Plain

Date	Mintage	F	VF	XF	Unc	BU
2001	130,000	—	—	0.10	0.20	0.30
2002	120,000	—	—	0.10	0.20	0.30
2003	20,000	—	—	0.10	0.20	0.30
2004	25,500	—	—	0.10	0.20	0.30
2005	38,000	—	—	0.10	0.20	0.30
2006	53,000	—	—	0.10	0.20	0.30
2007	53,000	—	—	0.10	0.20	0.30

KM# 33.2 10 WON
4.0600 g., Brass **Obv:** Pagoda at Pul Guk Temple **Rev:** Thicker value below date

Date	Mintage	F	VF	XF	Unc	BU
2001	345,000,000	—	—	—	0.35	0.50
2002	100,000,000	—	—	—	0.35	0.50
2003	128,000,000	—	—	—	0.35	0.50
2004	135,000,000	—	—	—	0.35	0.50
2005	250,000,000	—	—	—	0.35	0.50

KM# 33.2a 10 WON
1.2200 g., Aluminum-Bronze, 18 mm. **Obv:** Pagoda at Pul Guk Temple **Rev:** Value below date

Date	Mintage	F	VF	XF	Unc	BU
2006	109,200,000	—	—	—	0.10	0.35
2007	—	—	—	—	0.10	0.35
2008	—	—	—	—	0.10	0.35

KM# 103 10 WON
1.3500 g., Copper Plated Aluminum, 18 mm. **Obv:** Pagoda at Pul Guk Temple **Rev:** Value below date **Edge:** Plain **Mint:** KOMSCO **Note:** Prev. KM #106.

Date	Mintage	F	VF	XF	Unc	BU
2006	40,800,000	—	—	0.10	0.20	0.25

Date	Mintage	F	VF	XF	Unc	BU
2007	210,000,000	—	—	0.10	0.20	0.25
2008	—	—	—	0.10	0.20	0.25
2009	—	—	—	0.10	0.20	0.25
2010	—	—	—	0.10	0.20	0.25

KM# 34 50 WON
4.1600 g., Copper-Nickel-Zinc, 21.6 mm. **Series:** F.A.O. **Obv:** Text below sagging oat sprig **Rev:** Value and date **Edge:** Reeded **Note:** Die varieties exist.

Date	Mintage	F	VF	XF	Unc	BU
2001	102,000,000	—	—	0.10	0.35	1.00
2002	100,000,000	—	—	0.10	0.35	0.50
2003	169,000,000	—	—	0.10	0.35	0.50
2004	100,000,000	—	—	0.10	0.45	1.00
2005	90,000,000	—	—	0.10	0.35	0.50
2006	120,000,000	—	—	0.10	0.35	0.50
2007	50,000,000	—	—	0.10	0.35	0.50
2008	—	—	—	0.10	0.35	0.50
2009	—	—	—	0.10	0.35	0.50
2010	—	—	—	0.10	0.35	0.50

KM# 35.2 100 WON
5.4200 g., Copper-Nickel, 24 mm. **Obv:** Bust with hat facing **Rev:** Value and date **Edge:** Reeded

Date	Mintage	F	VF	XF	Unc	BU
2001	470,000,000	—	0.25	0.50	1.00	3.00
2002	490,000,000	—	0.15	0.25	0.55	1.00
2003	415,000,000	—	0.15	0.25	0.55	1.00
2004	250,000,000	—	0.15	0.25	0.55	1.00
2005	205,000,000	—	0.15	0.25	0.55	1.00
2006	310,000,000	—	0.15	0.25	0.55	0.75
2007	240,000,000	—	0.15	0.25	0.55	0.75
2008	—	—	0.15	0.25	0.55	0.75
2009	—	—	0.15	0.25	0.55	0.75
2010	—	—	0.15	0.25	0.55	0.75

KM# 27 500 WON
7.7000 g., Copper-Nickel, 26.5 mm. **Obv:** Manchurian crane **Rev:** Value and date **Edge:** Reeded

Date	Mintage	F	VF	XF	Unc	BU
2001	113,000,000	—	—	1.00	2.50	5.00
2002	110,000,000	—	—	1.00	2.50	5.00
2003	122,000,000	—	—	1.00	2.50	5.00
2004	45,000,000	—	—	1.00	2.50	5.00
2005	105,000,000	—	—	1.00	2.50	5.00
2006	170,000,000	—	—	1.00	2.50	5.00
2007	70,000,000	—	—	1.00	2.50	5.00
2008	—	—	—	1.00	2.50	5.00
2009	—	—	—	1.00	2.50	5.00
2010	—	—	—	1.00	2.50	5.00

KM# 89 1000 WON
12.0000 g., Brass, 32 mm. **Series:** World Cup Soccer **Obv:** FIFA World Cup logo **Rev:** Mascot soccer player **Edge:** Reeded **Mint:** Seoul

Date	Mintage	F	VF	XF	Unc	BU
2001	102,000	—	—	—	10.00	12.00

KM# 90 10000 WON

31.1035 g., 0.9990 Silver 0.9990 oz. ASW, 35 mm. **Series:** World Cup Soccer **Subject:** Gwangju Stadium **Obv:** Multicolor soccer logo **Rev:** Player heading the ball **Edge:** Reeded **Mint:** Seoul

Date	Mintage	F	VF	XF	Unc	BU
2001 Proof	37,000	Value: 50.00				

KM# 91 10000 WON

31.1035 g., 0.9990 Silver 0.9990 oz. ASW, 35 mm. **Series:** World Sup Soccer **Subject:** Busan Stadium **Obv:** Multicolor soccer logo **Rev:** Player kicking the ball **Edge:** Reeded **Mint:** Seoul

Date	Mintage	F	VF	XF	Unc	BU
2001 Proof	37,000	Value: 50.00				

KM# 92 10000 WON

31.1035 g., 0.9990 Silver 0.9990 oz. ASW, 35 mm. **Series:** World Cup Soccer **Subject:** Daegu Stadium **Obv:** Multicolor soccer logo **Rev:** Player controlling the ball **Edge:** Reeded **Mint:** Seoul

Date	Mintage	F	VF	XF	Unc	BU
2001 Proof	37,000	Value: 50.00				

KM# 93 10000 WON

31.1035 g., 0.9990 Silver 0.9990 oz. ASW, 35 mm. **Series:** World Cup Soccer **Subject:** Suwon Stadium **Obv:** Multicolor soccer logo **Rev:** Player kicking the ball **Edge:** Reeded **Mint:** Seoul

Date	Mintage	F	VF	XF	Unc	BU
2001 Proof	37,000	Value: 50.00				

KM# 98 10000 WON

31.1035 g., 0.9990 Silver 0.9990 oz. ASW, 35 mm. **Obv:** Multicolor FIFA World Cup logo **Rev:** Player "Heading" ball **Edge:** Reeded **Mint:** Seoul

Date	Mintage	F	VF	XF	Unc	BU
2002 Proof	—	Value: 50.00				

KM# 99 10000 WON

31.1035 g., 0.9990 Silver 0.9990 oz. ASW, 35 mm. **Obv:** Multicolor FIFA World Cup logo **Rev:** Goalie catching ball **Edge:** Reeded **Mint:** Seoul

Date	Mintage	F	VF	XF	Unc	BU
2002 Proof	—	Value: 50.00				

KM# 100 10000 WON

31.1035 g., 0.9990 Silver 0.9990 oz. ASW, 35 mm. **Obv:** Multicolor FIFA World Cup logo **Rev:** Player's leg kicking ball **Edge:** Reeded **Mint:** Seoul

Date	Mintage	F	VF	XF	Unc	BU
2002 Proof	—	Value: 50.00				

KM# 101 10000 WON

31.1035 g., 0.9990 Silver 0.9990 oz. ASW, 35 mm. **Obv:** Multicolor FIFA World Cup logo **Rev:** Two players' legs and ball **Edge:** Reeded **Mint:** Seoul

Date	Mintage	F	VF	XF	Unc	BU
2002 Proof	—	Value: 50.00				

KM# 94 20000 WON

15.5518 g., 0.9990 Gold 0.4995 oz. AGW, 28 mm. **Series:** World Cup Soccer **Obv:** Soccer logo **Rev:** World Cup soccer trophy **Edge:** Reeded **Mint:** Seoul

Date	Mintage	F	VF	XF	Unc	BU
2001 Proof	20,000	Value: 750				

KM# 97 20000 WON

20.7000 g., Silver, 35 mm. **Obv:** Blue circle with APEC, 2005 Korea at bottom at upper center, Vista Pacific Economic Cooperation and value below **Rev:** APEC on World map at upper center, building below with Korean words below it

Date	Mintage	F	VF	XF	Unc	BU
2005 Proof	10,000	Value: 65.00				

KM# 102 20000 WON

20.7000 g., 0.9990 Silver 0.6648 oz. ASW **Subject:** 60th Anniversary of Independence **Obv:** Adult hand reaching out towards child's hand **Mint:** KOMSCO **Note:** Prev. KM #103.

Date	Mintage	F	VF	XF	Unc	BU
2005 Proof	10,000	Value: 65.00				

KM# 104 20000 WON

19.0000 g., 0.9990 Silver 0.6102 oz. ASW **Subject:** 560th Year of Hangeul - Alphabet **Obv:** Early alphabet characters **Obv. Legend:** THE BANK OF KOREA **Rev:** Modern alphabet characters **Shape:** Round with square center hole **Mint:** KOMSCO

Date	Mintage	F	VF	XF	Unc	BU
2006 Proof	—	Value: 75.00				

KM# 105 20000 WON

19.0000 g., 0.9990 Silver 0.6102 oz. ASW, 33.00 mm. **Series:** Traditional Folk Dance **Subject:** Talchum - Mask Dances **Obv:** Mask at center surrounded by 6 other masks **Obv. Legend:** THE BANK OF KOREA **Rev:** Mask dancer at left center **Edge:** Plain **Shape:** 12-sided **Mint:** KOMSCO **Note:** Prev. KM #102.

Date	Mintage	F	VF	XF	Unc	BU
2007 Proof	50,000	Value: 75.00				

KM# 106 20000 WON

19.0000 g., 0.9990 Silver 0.6102 oz. ASW, 33 mm. **Subject:** Mask dance **Rev:** Ganggangsullae ("Circle dance") **Shape:** 12-sided **Mint:** KOMSCO

Date	Mintage	F	VF	XF	Unc	BU
2008 Proof	50,000	Value: 75.00				

KM# 108 20000 WON

19.0000 g., 0.9000 Silver 0.5498 oz. ASW, 33 mm. **Subject:** Mask dance **Rev:** Youngsan Juldarigi (Tug of War) **Mint:** KOMSCO

Date	Mintage	F	VF	XF	Unc	BU
2009 Proof	50,000	Value: 75.00				

KM# 109 20000 WON

19.0000 g., 0.9990 Silver 0.6102 oz. ASW, 33 mm. **Subject:** Traditional Folk Games - Yeongsan Juldarigi (Tug of war) **Mint:** KOMSCO

Date	Mintage	F	VF	XF	Unc	BU
2009 Proof	50,000	Value: 55.00				

KM# 95 30000 WON

31.1035 g., 0.9990 Gold 0.9990 oz. AGW, 35 mm. **Series:** World Cup Soccer **Obv:** Soccer logo **Rev:** Nude soccer player flanked by other players **Edge:** Reeded **Mint:** Seoul

Date	Mintage	F	VF	XF	Unc	BU
2001 Proof	12,000	Value: 1,475				

KM# 107 30000 WON

Silver **Subject:** Flag, 60th Anniversary **Obv:** Flag **Rev:** Multicolor 60 logo **Mint:** KOMSCO

Date	Mintage	F	VF	XF	Unc	BU
2008 Proof	—	Value: 75.00				

KM# 110 30000 WON

19.0000 g., 0.9990 Silver 0.6102 oz. ASW, 33 mm. **Subject:** UNESCO World Heritage Site - Jongmyo Shrine **Obv:** Main Hall of the Jongmyo Shrine **Rev:** Scene of the Royal Ancestral Ritual in the shrine **Edge:** Reeded **Mint:** KOMSCO

Date	Mintage	F	VF	XF	Unc	BU
2010 Proof	50,000	Value: 60.00				

KM# 111 30000 WON

19.0000 g., 0.9990 Silver 0.6102 oz. ASW, 33 mm. **Subject:** G-20 Summit in Seoul **Obv:** Gwang-Hwa-Mun restored on Independence Day **Rev:** Multicolor lantern in national colors **Edge:** Reeded **Mint:** KOMSCO

Date	Mintage	F	VF	XF	Unc	BU
2010 Proof	50,000	Value: 55.00				

MINT SETS

KM#	Date	Mintage	Identification	Issue Price	Mkt Val
MS8	2001 (7)	—	KM#27, 31, 32, 33.2, 34, 35.2, 89	10.00	22.50

PROOF SETS

KM#	Date	Mintage	Identification	Issue Price	Mkt Val
PS10	2001 (6)	2,002	KM#90-95	—	2,500

KUWAIT

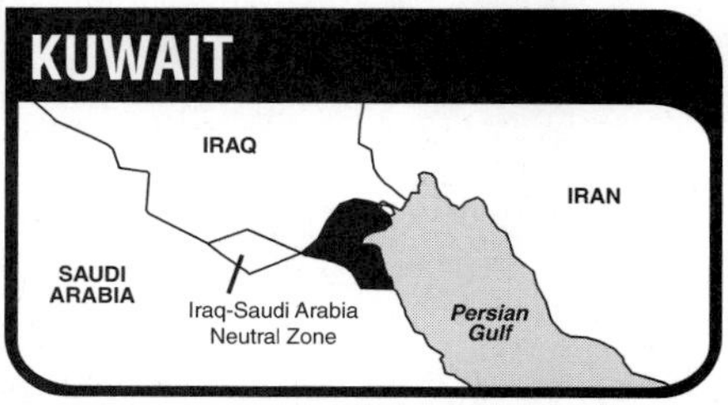

The State of Kuwait, a constitutional monarchy located on the Arabian Peninsula at the northwestern corner of the Persian Gulf, has an area of 6,880 sq. mi. (17,820 sq. km.) and a population of 1.7 million. Capital: Kuwait. Petroleum, the basis of the economy, provides 95 percent of the exports.

RULERS

Al Sabah Dynasty

Jabir Ibn Ahmad, 1977-2006

Sabah Al Ahmad Al Sabah, 2006-

MONETARY SYSTEM

1000 Fils = 1 Dinar

SOVEREIGN EMIRATE

MODERN COINAGE

KM# 9a FILS

2.4100 g., 0.9250 Silver 0.0717 oz. ASW, 17 mm. **Ruler:** Jabir Ibn Ahmad **Obv:** Value within circle **Rev:** Ship with sails

Date	Mintage	F	VF	XF	Unc	BU
AH1429-2008 Proof	—	Value: 65.00				

KM# 9c FILS

2.4100 g., 0.9250 Silver Gilt 0.0717 oz. ASW, 17 mm. **Obv:** Value within circle **Rev:** Dhow, dates below

Date	Mintage	F	VF	XF	Unc	BU
AH1429-2008 Proof	—	Value: 70.00				

KM# 10 5 FILS

2.5000 g., Nickel-Brass, 19.5 mm. **Ruler:** Jabir Ibn Ahmad **Obv:** Value within circle **Rev:** Dhow, dates below

Date	Mintage	F	VF	XF	Unc	BU
AH1422-2001	—	—	0.10	0.20	0.40	—
AH1424-2003	—	—	0.10	0.20	0.40	—
AH1426-2005	—	—	0.10	0.20	0.40	—
AH1429-2008	—	—	0.10	0.20	0.40	—

KM# 10a 5 FILS

3.0100 g., 0.9250 Silver 0.0895 oz. ASW, 19.5 mm. **Ruler:** Jabir Ibn Ahmad **Obv:** Value within circle **Rev:** Ship with sails

Date	Mintage	F	VF	XF	Unc	BU
AH1429-2008 Proof	—	Value: 70.00				

KM# 10c 5 FILS

3.0100 g., 0.9250 Silver Gilt 0.0895 oz. ASW, 19.5 mm. **Obv:** Value in circle **Rev:** Dhow, dates below

Date	Mintage	F	VF	XF	Unc	BU
AH1429-2008 Proof	—	Value: 75.00				

KM# 11 10 FILS

3.7500 g., Nickel-Brass, 21 mm. **Ruler:** Jabir Ibn Ahmad **Obv:** Value within circle **Rev:** Dhow, dates below

Date	Mintage	F	VF	XF	Unc	BU
AH1422-2001	—	—	—	0.25	0.75	—
AH1424-2003	—	—	—	0.25	0.75	—
AH1426-2005	—	—	—	0.25	0.75	—
AH1427-2006	—	—	—	0.25	0.75	—

KM# 11a 10 FILS

4.3500 g., 0.9250 Silver 0.1294 oz. ASW, 21 mm. **Ruler:** Jabir Ibn Ahmad **Obv:** Value within circle **Rev:** Ship with sails

Date	Mintage	F	VF	XF	Unc	BU
AH1429-2008 Proof	—	Value: 75.00				

KM# 11c 10 FILS

4.3500 g., 0.9250 Silver Gilt 0.1294 oz. ASW, 21 mm. **Obv:** Value within circle **Rev:** Dhow, dates below

Date	Mintage	F	VF	XF	Unc	BU
AH1429-2008 Proof	—	Value: 80.00				

KM# 12c 20 FILS

Stainless Steel, 20 mm. **Ruler:** Jabir Ibn Ahmad **Obv:** Value **Rev:** Dhow, dates below

Date	Mintage	F	VF	XF	Unc	BU
AH1422-2001	—	—	0.20	0.35	1.00	—
AH1424-2003	—	—	0.20	0.35	1.00	—
AH1426-2005	—	—	0.20	0.35	1.00	—

KM# 12 20 FILS

3.0000 g., Copper-Nickel, 20 mm. **Ruler:** Jabir Ibn Ahmad **Obv:** Value within circle **Rev:** Dhow, dates below **Edge:** Reeded **Note:** Varieties exist.

Date	Mintage	F	VF	XF	Unc	BU
AH1424-2003	—	—	0.20	0.45	2.00	—
AH1426-2005	—	—	0.20	0.45	2.00	—

KM# 12a 20 FILS

3.3700 g., 0.9250 Silver 0.1002 oz. ASW, 20 mm. **Ruler:** Jabir Ibn Ahmad **Obv:** Value within circle **Rev:** Dhow, dates below

Date	Mintage	F	VF	XF	Unc	BU
AH1429-2008 Proof	—	Value: 80.00				

KM# 12d 20 FILS

3.3700 g., 0.9250 Silver Gilt 0.1002 oz. ASW, 20 mm. **Obv:** Value within cricle **Rev:** Dhow, dates below

Date	Mintage	F	VF	XF	Unc	BU
1429-2008 Proof	—	Value: 85.00				

KM# 13 50 FILS

4.5000 g., Copper-Nickel, 23 mm. **Ruler:** Jabir Ibn Ahmad **Obv:** Value within circle **Rev:** Dhow, dates below **Edge:** Reeded

Date	Mintage	F	VF	XF	Unc	BU
AH1422-2001	—	—	0.25	0.35	1.25	—
AH1424-2003	—	—	0.25	0.35	1.00	—
AH1426-2005	—	—	0.25	0.35	1.00	—
AH1427-2006	—	—	0.25	0.35	1.00	—

KM# 13a 50 FILS

5.0700 g., 0.9250 Silver 0.1508 oz. ASW, 23 mm. **Ruler:** Jabir Ibn Ahmad **Obv:** Value within circle **Rev:** Ship with sails

Date	Mintage	F	VF	XF	Unc	BU
AH1429-2008 Proof	—	Value: 85.00				

KM# 13c 50 FILS

5.0700 g., 0.9250 Silver Gilt 0.1508 oz. ASW, 23 mm. **Obv:** Value within circle **Rev:** Dhow, dates below

Date	Mintage	F	VF	XF	Unc	BU
1429-2008 Proof	—	Value: 90.00				

KM# 14 100 FILS

6.5000 g., Copper-Nickel, 26 mm. **Ruler:** Jabir Ibn Ahmad **Obv:** Value within circle **Rev:** Dhow, dates below **Edge:** Reeded

Date	Mintage	F	VF	XF	Unc	BU
AH1424-2003	—	—	0.50	0.75	1.50	—
AH1426-2005	—	—	0.50	0.75	1.50	—
AH1428-2007	—	—	0.50	0.75	1.50	—

KM# 14a 100 FILS

7.3400 g., 0.9250 Silver 0.2183 oz. ASW, 26 mm. **Ruler:** Jabir Ibn Ahmad **Obv:** Value within circle **Rev:** Ship with sails

Date	Mintage	F	VF	XF	Unc	BU
AH1429-2008 Proof	—	Value: 90.00				

KM# 14c 100 FILS

7.3400 g., 0.9250 Silver Gilt 0.2183 oz. ASW, 26 mm. **Obv:** Value within circle **Rev:** Dhow, dates below

Date	Mintage	F	VF	XF	Unc	BU
1429-2008 Proof	—	Value: 100				

PROOF SETS

KM#	Date	Mintage	Identification	Issue Price	Mkt Val
PS5	2008 (6)	—	KM#9a-14a	—	475
PS6	2008 (6)	—	KM#9c-11c, 12d, 13c-14c	—	500

KYRGYZSTAN

The Republic of Kyrgyzstan, (formerly Kirghiz S.S.R., a Union Republic of the U.S.S.R.), is an independent state since Aug. 31, 1991, a member of the United Nations and of the C.I.S. It was the last state of the Union Republics to declare its sovereignty. Capital: Bishkek (formerly Frunze).

MONETARY SYSTEM

100 Tiyin = 1 Som

REPUBLIC

STANDARD COINAGE

KM# 11 TIYIN

1.0000 g., Aluminum-Bronze, 13.98 mm. **Obv:** National arms **Rev:** Flower at left of value **Edge:** Reeded **Note:** Prev. KM #8.

Date	Mintage	F	VF	XF	Unc	BU
2008 In sets only	95,000	—	—	—	0.65	1.00

KM# 12 10 TIYIN

1.3300 g., Brass Plated Steel, 14.94 mm. **Obv:** National arms **Rev:** Flower at left of value **Edge:** Plain **Note:** Prev. KM #9.

Date	Mintage	F	VF	XF	Unc	BU
2008	—	—	—	—	0.85	1.50

KM# 13 50 TIYIN

1.8600 g., Brass Plated Steel, 16.94 mm. **Obv:** National arms **Rev:** Flower at left of value **Edge:** Plain **Note:** Prev. KM #10.

Date	Mintage	F	VF	XF	Unc	BU
2008	—	—	—	—	1.25	2.00

KM# 19 SOM

12.0000 g., Copper-Nickel, 30 mm. **Series:** Great Silk Road **Subject:** Tashrabat **Obv:** Arms **Rev:** Fortress

Date	Mintage	F	VF	XF	Unc	BU
2008 Prooflike	5,000	—	—	—	10.00	15.00

KM# 14 SOM

2.5700 g., Nickel Plated Steel, 18.96 mm. **Obv:** National arms **Rev:** Symbol at left of denomination **Edge:** Reeded **Note:** Prev. KM #11.

Date	Mintage	F	VF	XF	Unc	BU
2008	—	—	—	—	1.50	2.25

KM# 20 SOM
28.2800 g., Copper-Nickel, 30 mm. **Series:** Great Silk Road **Subject:** Uzgen architecture complex

Date	Mintage	F	VF	XF	Unc	BU
2008 Prooflike	5,000	—	—	—	10.00	15.00

KM# 21 SOM
12.0000 g., Copper-Nickel, 30 mm. **Subject:** Uzgen Architectural Complex **Obv:** Arms **Rev:** Tower and building - map above

Date	Mintage	F	VF	XF	Unc	BU
2008 Prooflike	5,000	—	—	—	10.00	15.00

KM# 35 SOM
12.0000 g., Copper-Nickel, 30 mm. **Series:** Great Silk Road **Subject:** Burana Tower **Rev:** Tower and map

Date	Mintage	F	VF	XF	Unc	BU
2008 Prooflike	5,000	—	—	—	10.00	15.00

KM# 31 SOM
12.0000 g., Copper-Nickel, 30 mm. **Series:** Great Silk Road **Subject:** Suilaman Mountain

Date	Mintage	F	VF	XF	Unc	BU
2009 Prooflike	5,000	—	—	—	10.00	15.00

KM# 33 SOM
12.0000 g., Copper-Nickel, 30 mm. **Series:** Great Silk Road **Subject:** Lake Issykkul

Date	Mintage	F	VF	XF	Unc	BU
2009 Prooflike	5,000	—	—	—	10.00	15.00

KM# 15 3 SOM
3.1800 g., Nickel Plated Steel, 20.97 mm. **Obv:** National arms **Rev:** Symbol above right of denomination **Edge:** Reeded **Note:** Prev. KM #12.

Date	Mintage	F	VF	XF	Unc	BU
2008	—	—	—	—	1.25	2.00

KM# 16 5 SOM
4.2800 g., Nickel Plated Steel, 22.95 mm. **Obv:** National arms **Rev:** Symbol at right of value **Edge:** Reeded **Note:** Prev. KM #13.

Date	Mintage	F	VF	XF	Unc	BU
2008	—	—	—	—	1.50	2.50

KM# 4 10 SOM
28.2800 g., 0.9250 Silver 0.8410 oz. ASW, 38.6 mm. **Subject:** Tenth Anniversary of Republic **Obv:** National arms within circle **Rev:** Value and Khan Tengri mountain **Edge:** Reeded **Note:** Prev. KM #3.

Date	Mintage	F	VF	XF	Unc	BU
2001 Proof	1,000	Value: 175				

KM# 36 10 SOM
28.2800 g., 0.9250 Silver partially gilt 0.8410 oz. ASW, 38.6 mm. **Subject:** Som, 10th Anniversary **Obv:** National arms **Rev:** Som coin designs, some gilt

Date	Mintage	F	VF	XF	Unc	BU
2003 Proof	—	Value: 150				

KM# 5 10 SOM
28.2800 g., 0.9250 Silver 0.8410 oz. ASW, 38.6 mm. **Subject:** International Year of the mountains **Obv:** National arms **Rev:** Edelweiss flower and mountain **Edge:** Reeded **Note:** Prev. KM #4.

Date	Mintage	F	VF	XF	Unc	BU
2002 Proof	1,000	Value: 125				

KM# 6 10 SOM
28.2800 g., 0.9250 Silver 0.8410 oz. ASW, 38.6 mm. **Subject:** International Year of the Mountains **Obv:** National arms **Rev:** Argali Ram head and mountain **Edge:** Reeded **Note:** Prev. KM #5.

Date	Mintage	F	VF	XF	Unc	BU
2002 Proof	1,000	Value: 125				

KM# 7 10 SOM
28.2800 g., 0.9250 Silver partially gilt 0.8410 oz. ASW, 38.6 mm. **Subject:** Genesis of the Kyrgyz Statehood **Obv:** Arms **Rev:** Classical designs

Date	Mintage	F	VF	XF	Unc	BU
2003 Proof	1,000	Value: 250				

KM# 8 10 SOM
28.2800 g., 0.9250 Silver 0.8410 oz. ASW, 38.6 mm. **Subject:** 60 Years of Great Victory **Rev:** Figure of a mother, eternal light, Victory Memorial complex **Note:** Prev. KM #6.

Date	Mintage	F	VF	XF	Unc	BU
2005 Proof	1,000	Value: 110				

KM# 9 10 SOM
28.2800 g., 0.8250 Silver partially gilt 0.7501 oz. ASW, 38.6 mm. **Series:** Great Silk Road **Subject:** Tashrabat **Note:** Prev. KM #7.

Date	Mintage	F	VF	XF	Unc	BU
2005 Proof	1,500	Value: 100				

KM# 10 10 SOM
28.2800 g., 0.9250 Silver 0.8410 oz. ASW, 38.6 mm. **Subject:** Shanghai Cooperation **Obv:** Arms **Rev:** Multicolor logo of the Shanghai Cooperation Organization

Date	Mintage	F	VF	XF	Unc	BU
2007 Proof	1,000	Value: 180				

KM# 22 10 SOM
28.2800 g., 0.9250 Silver partially gilt 0.8410 oz. ASW, 38.6 mm. **Series:** Great Silk Road **Subject:** Uzgen Architectural Complex

Date	Mintage	F	VF	XF	Unc	BU
2007 Proof	1,500	Value: 120				

KM# 18 10 SOM
28.2800 g., 0.9250 Silver partially gilt 0.8410 oz. ASW, 38.6 mm. **Series:** Great Silk Road **Subject:** Burana Tower **Rev:** Buildings with partial gilting

Date	Mintage	F	VF	XF	Unc	BU
2008 Proof	1,500	Value: 110				

KM# 23 10 SOM
28.2800 g., 0.9250 Silver 0.8410 oz. ASW, 38.6 mm. **Series:** Capitals of the Eurasia Economic Community **Subject:** City of Bishkek **Obv:** National emblem **Rev:** Horseman statue, multicolor logo

Date	Mintage	F	VF	XF	Unc	BU
2008 Proof	2,500	Value: 90.00				

KM# 24 10 SOM
28.2800 g., 0.9250 Silver 0.8410 oz. ASW, 38.6 mm. **Rev:** Chynqyz Aytmatov

Date	Mintage	F	VF	XF	Unc	BU
2009 Proof	2,000	Value: 75.00				

KM# 25 10 SOM
28.2800 g., 0.9250 Silver 0.8410 oz. ASW, 38.6 mm. **Series:** Chinqiz Aitmatov's work's **Rev:** Jamila

Date	Mintage	F	VF	XF	Unc	BU
2009 Proof	3,000	Value: 75.00				

KM# 26 10 SOM
28.2800 g., 0.9250 Silver 0.8410 oz. ASW, 38.6 mm. **Series:** Chingiz Aitmatov's works **Rev:** Duishen

Date	Mintage	F	VF	XF	Unc	BU
2009 Proof	3,000	Value: 75.00				

KM# 27 10 SOM
28.2800 g., 0.9250 Silver 0.8410 oz. ASW, 38.6 mm. **Series:** Chinqiz Aitmatov's works **Rev:** Mother field

Date	Mintage	F	VF	XF	Unc	BU
2009 Proof	3,000	Value: 75.00				

KM# 28 10 SOM
28.2800 g., 0.9250 Silver 0.8410 oz. ASW, 38.5 mm. **Series:** Chinqiz Aitmatov's works **Rev:** Farewell, Gulsary!

Date	Mintage	F	VF	XF	Unc	BU
2009 Proof	3,000	Value: 75.00				

KM# 29 10 SOM
28.2800 g., 0.9250 Silver 0.8410 oz. ASW, 38.5 mm. **Series:** Chinqiz Aitmatov's works **Rev:** The white ship

Date	Mintage	F	VF	XF	Unc	BU
2009 Proof	3,000	Value: 75.00				

KM# 32 10 SOM
28.2800 g., 0.9250 Silver Partially gilt 0.8410 oz. ASW, 38.6 mm. **Series:** Great Silk Road **Subject:** Suliman Mountain

Date	Mintage	F	VF	XF	Unc	BU
2009 Proof	1,500	Value: 110				

KM# 34 10 SOM
28.2800 g., 0.9250 Silver partially gilt 0.8410 oz. ASW, 38.6 mm. **Series:** Great Silk Road **Subject:** Lake Issykkul

Date	Mintage	F	VF	XF	Unc	BU
2009 Proof	1,500	Value: 110				

KM# 38 10 SOM
28.2800 g., 0.9250 Silver 0.8410 oz. ASW, 38.6 mm. **Obv:** National arms at top of repeating motif **Rev:** Eagle in flight right

Date	Mintage	F	VF	XF	Unc	BU
2009 Proof	—	Value: 90.00				

KM# 41 10 SOM
31.1000 g., 0.9250 Silver 0.9249 oz. ASW, 38.6 mm. **Obv:** National emblem and linear design **Rev:** Two people riding deer, as in a cave painting; multicolor logo below

Date	Mintage	F	VF	XF	Unc	BU
2009 Proof	3,000	Value: 95.00				

KM# 39 10 SOM
31.1000 g., 0.9250 Silver 0.9249 oz. ASW, 38.6 mm. **Obv:** National Arms, multicolor design **Rev:** Frame construction of a Yurta

Date	Mintage	F	VF	XF	Unc	BU
2010 Proof	3,000	Value: 75.00				

KM# 40 10 SOM
31.1000 g., 0.9250 Silver 0.9249 oz. ASW, 38.6 mm. **Subject:** EurAsEC 10th Anniversary **Obv:** National arms and globe **Rev:** Five world sites, multicolor logo at center

Date	Mintage	F	VF	XF	Unc	BU
2010 Proof	2,000	Value: 75.00				

KM# 37 100 SOM
6.2200 g., 0.9990 Gold 0.1998 oz. AGW, 22 mm. **Rev:** Two horsemen

Date	Mintage	F	VF	XF	Unc	BU
2008 Proof	—	Value: 325				

KM# 42 100 SOM
31.1000 g., 0.9250 Silver 0.9249 oz. ASW, 38.61 mm. **Rev:** Panthera Tigris, gilt tiger

Date	Mintage	F	VF	XF	Unc	BU
2009 Proof	13,000	Value: 100				

MINT SETS

KM#	Date	Mintage	Identification	Issue Price	Mkt Val
MS1	2008 (6)	—	KM#11-16	—	30.00

LAO

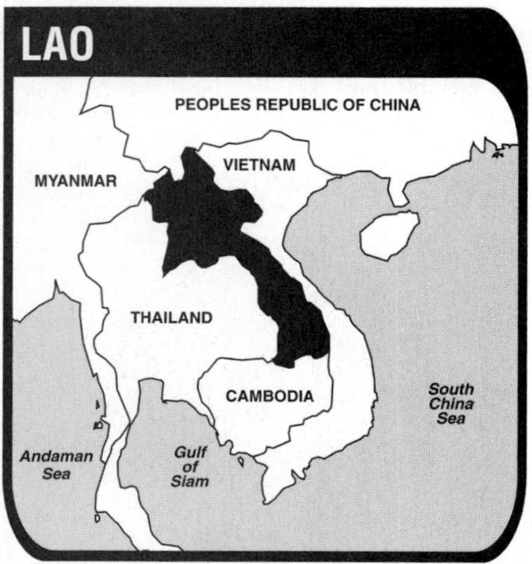

The Lao Peoples Democratic Republic, located on the Indo-Chinese Peninsula between the Socialist Republic of Vietnam and the Kingdom of Thailand, has an area of 91,428 sq. mi. (236,800 km.) and a population of 3.6 million. Capital Vientiane. Agriculture employs 95 per cent of the people. Tin, lumber and coffee are exported.

MONETARY SYSTEM
100 Att = 1 Kip

PEOPLES DEMOCRATIC REPUBLIC

STANDARD COINAGE

KM# 85 1000 KIP
31.5000 g., 0.9990 Silver 1.0117 oz. ASW, 38.5 mm. **Subject:** Olympics **Obv:** State emblem **Rev:** Freestyle skier **Edge:** Reeded

Date	Mintage	F	VF	XF	Unc	BU
2001 Proof	—	Value: 50.00				

KM# 96 1000 KIP
31.4500 g., 0.9990 Silver 1.0101 oz. ASW, 38.5 mm. **Obv:** State emblem **Rev:** Soccer player **Edge:** Reeded

Date	Mintage	F	VF	XF	Unc	BU
2001 Proof	—	Value: 50.00				

KM# 104 1000 KIP
36.4700 g., 0.9250 Silver 1.0846 oz. ASW, 38.6 mm. **Subject:** Terra Cotta Warriors **Obv:** Arms **Rev:** Gilt warrior standing, background warriors face right **Note:** Central gilt warrior is detachable and stands upright.

Date	Mintage	F	VF	XF	Unc	BU
2009 Proof	5,000	Value: 100				

KM# 105 1000 KIP
36.4700 g., 0.9250 Silver 1.0846 oz. ASW, 38.61 mm. **Subject:** Terra Cotta Warrior **Obv:** Arms **Rev:** Gilt standing warrior, warriors in background facing **Note:** Central gilt warrior is detachable and stands upright.

Date	Mintage	F	VF	XF	Unc	BU
2009 Proof	5,000	Value: 100				

KM# 106 1000 KIP
36.4700 g., 0.9250 Silver 1.0846 oz. ASW, 38.6 mm. **Subject:** Terra Cotta Warrior **Obv:** Arms **Rev:** Archer kneeling **Note:** Central gilt warrior is detachable and stands upright.

Date	Mintage	F	VF	XF	Unc	BU
2009 Proof	1,000	Value: 100				

KM# 107 1000 KIP
36.4700 g., 0.9250 Silver 1.0846 oz. ASW **Subject:** Terra Cotta Warrior **Obv:** Arms **Rev:** Gilt horse **Note:** Central gilt warrior is detachable and stands upright.

Date	Mintage	F	VF	XF	Unc	BU
2009 Proof	1,000	Value: 100				

KM# 86 15000 KIP
20.0000 g., 0.9250 Silver 0.5948 oz. ASW, 38.7 mm. **Subject:** Year of the Horse **Obv:** State emblem **Rev:** Multicolor horse **Edge:** Reeded

Date	Mintage	F	VF	XF	Unc	BU
2002 Proof	9,500	Value: 50.00				

KM# 87 15000 KIP
20.0000 g., 0.9250 Silver 0.5948 oz. ASW, 38.7 mm. **Subject:** Year of the Horse **Obv:** State emblem **Rev:** Horse with multicolor holographic background **Edge:** Reeded

Date	Mintage	F	VF	XF	Unc	BU
2002 Proof	9,500	Value: 55.00				

KM# 94 15000 KIP
20.0000 g., 0.9990 Silver 0.6423 oz. ASW, 38.7 mm. **Obv:** State emblem **Rev:** Multicolor Golden Monkey **Edge:** Reeded

Date	Mintage	F	VF	XF	Unc	BU
2004 Proof	2,300	Value: 55.00				

KM# 98 15000 KIP
Silver, 38.7 mm. **Issuer:** Bank of Lao PDR **Obv:** National arms **Obv. Legend:** THE LAO PEOPLE'S DEMOCRATIC REPUBLIC **Rev:** Statue of Mazu with stylized Phoenix at left and right **Rev. Legend:** GODDESS OF THE SEA **Edge:** Reeded

Date	Mintage	F	VF	XF	Unc	BU
2006 Proof	6,888	Value: 65.00				

KM# 88 60000 KIP
155.5175 g., 0.9250 Silver 4.6248 oz. ASW, 65 mm. **Subject:** Year of the Horse **Obv:** State emblem **Rev:** Multicolor horse **Edge:** Reeded

Date	Mintage	F	VF	XF	Unc	BU
2002 Proof	1,000	Value: 225				

KM# 89 100000 KIP
15.5518 g., 0.9999 Gold 0.4999 oz. AGW, 27 mm. **Subject:** Year of the Horse **Obv:** State emblem **Rev:** Horse **Edge:** Reeded

Date	Mintage	F	VF	XF	Unc	BU
2002	2,000	Value: 875				

KM# 95 100000 KIP
15.5518 g., 0.9990 Gold 0.4995 oz. AGW, 27 mm. **Obv:** State emblem **Rev:** Black Gibbon on holographic background **Edge:** Reeded

Date	Mintage	F	VF	XF	Unc	BU
2004 Proof	888	Value: 900				

KM# 103 100000 KIP
7.7750 g., 0.9990 Gold 0.2497 oz. AGW, 27 mm. **Subject:** President Print Souphanouvong, 100th Anniversary of Birth **Obv:** Bust facing **Rev:** Presidential Palace

Date	Mintage	F	VF	XF	Unc	BU
ND (2009) Proof	1,000	Value: 450				

KM# 102 100000 KIP
38.5000 g., 0.9250 Silver 1.1449 oz. ASW, 36.5 mm. **Subject:** President Print Souphanouvong, 100th Anniversary of Birth **Obv:** Bust facing **Rev:** Presidential Palace

Date	Mintage	F	VF	XF	Unc	BU
ND (2009) Proof	1,000	Value: 100				

KM# 90 1000000 KIP
155.5175 g., 0.9999 Gold 4.9993 oz. AGW, 55 mm. **Subject:** Year of the Horse **Obv:** State emblem **Rev:** Horse with multicolor holographic background **Edge:** Reeded

Date	Mintage	F	VF	XF	Unc	BU
2002 Proof	500	Value: 7,500				

KM# 99 1000000 KIP
155.5150 g., 0.9999 Gold 4.9992 oz. AGW, 55.0 mm. **Issuer:** Bank of Lao PDR **Obv:** National arms **Obv. Legend:** THE LAO PEOPLE'S DEMOCRATIC REPUBLIC **Rev:** Multi-latent color bust of Lord Buddha "Fo Guang Pu Zhao" facing with diamond insert in forehead **Edge:** Reeded

Date	Mintage	F	VF	XF	Unc	BU
2006 Proof	99	Value: 7,750				

PROOF SETS

KM#	Date	Mintage	Identification	Issue Price	Mkt Val
PS7	2000-2001 (3)	3,500	KM#74-76	138	200
PS8	2000-2001 (3)	500	KM#74-76	214	300
PS9	2000-2001 (2)	800	KM#78, 83	—	1,100

LATVIA

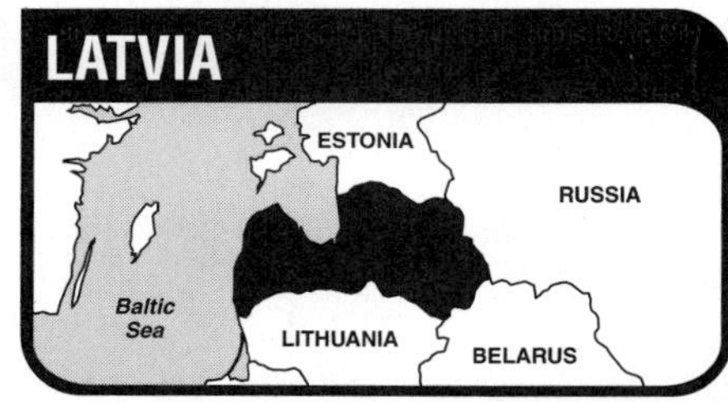

The Republic of Latvia, the central Baltic state in east Europe, has an area of 24,749 sq. mi. (43,601 sq. km.) and a population of *2.6 million. Capital: Riga. Livestock raising and manufacturing are the chief industries. Butter, bacon, fertilizers and telephone equipment are exported.

MONETARY SYSTEM
100 Santimu = 1 Lats

MODERN REPUBLIC

TANDARD COINAGE

KM# 15 SANTIMS
1.6000 g., Copper Clad Steel, 15.65 mm. **Obv:** National arms **Rev:** Value flanked by diamonds below lined arch **Edge:** Plain

Date	Mintage	F	VF	XF	Unc	BU
2003	30,000,000	—	—	0.10	0.30	0.40
2005	20,000,000	—	—	0.10	0.30	0.40
2007	25,000,000	—	—	0.10	0.30	0.40
2008	75,000,000	—	—	0.10	0.30	0.40

KM# 21 2 SANTIMI

1.9000 g., Copper Clad Steel, 17 mm. **Obv:** National arms **Rev:** Lined arch above value flanked by diamonds **Edge:** Plain

Date	Mintage	F	VF	XF	Unc	BU
2006	18,000,000	—	—	0.15	0.45	0.60
2007	30,000,000	—	—	0.15	0.45	0.60
2009	50,000,000	—	—	0.15	0.45	0.60

KM# 16 5 SANTIMI

2.5000 g., Nickel-Brass, 18.5 mm. **Obv:** National arms **Obv. Legend:** LATVIJAS REPUBLIKA **Rev:** Lined arch above value flanked by diamonds **Edge:** Plain

Date	Mintage	F	VF	XF	Unc	BU
2006	8,000,000	—	—	0.30	0.75	1.00
2007	15,000,000	—	—	0.30	0.75	1.00
2009	10,000,000	—	—	0.30	0.75	1.00

KM# 17 10 SANTIMU

3.2500 g., Nickel-Brass, 19.9 mm. **Obv:** National arms **Rev:** Lined arch above value flanked by diamonds

Date	Mintage	F	VF	XF	Unc	BU
2008	15,000,000	—	—	0.50	1.00	1.50

KM# 22.1 20 SANTIMU

4.0000 g., Nickel-Brass, 21.5 mm. **Obv:** National arms **Rev:** Lined arch above value flanked by diamonds **Edge:** Plain **Note:** 1.5mm thick.

Date	Mintage	F	VF	XF	Unc	BU
2007	15,000,000	—	—	0.50	1.00	2.00
2009	10,000,000	—	—	0.50	1.00	2.00

KM# 13 50 SANTIMU

3.5000 g., Copper-Nickel, 18.8 mm. **Obv:** National arms **Rev:** Triple sprig above value **Edge:** Reeded

Date	Mintage	F	VF	XF	Unc	BU
2007	4,000,000	—	—	2.00	3.00	4.00
2009	10,000,000	—	—	2.00	3.00	4.00

KM# 70 100 SANTIMU

31.4700 g., 0.9250 Silver 0.9359 oz. ASW, 38.6 mm. **Obv:** Baron von Muenchausen with chain of birds around a dog with a lantern hanging from its tail. **Rev:** Baron von Muenchausen and dog hunting a circle of animals **Edge Lettering:** LATVIJAS BANKA LATVIJAS REPUBLIKA

Date	Mintage	F	VF	XF	Unc	BU
2005 Proof	Est. 5,000	Value: 65.00				

KM# 49 LATS

31.4700 g., 0.9250 Silver 0.9359 oz. ASW, 38.6 mm. **Subject:** Hanseatic City of Cesis **Obv:** City arms **Rev:** Sailing ship above, inverted walled city view below **Edge Lettering:** LATVIJAS REPUBLIKA • LATVIJAS BANKA

Date	Mintage	F	VF	XF	Unc	BU
2001 Proof	Est. 15,000	Value: 70.00				

KM# 50 LATS

31.4700 g., 0.9250 Silver 0.9359 oz. ASW **Series:** Ice Hockey **Obv:** Arms with supporters **Rev:** Hockey player

Date	Mintage	F	VF	XF	Unc	BU
2001 Proof	Est. 25,000	Value: 90.00				

KM# 51 LATS

31.4700 g., 0.9250 Silver 0.9359 oz. ASW, 38.6 mm. **Series:** Roots - Heaven **Obv:** Stylized design **Rev:** Styilized woman holding sun **Edge:** Plain

Date	Mintage	F	VF	XF	Unc	BU
2001 Proof	Est. 5,000	Value: 55.00				

KM# 54 LATS

4.8000 g., Copper-Nickel, 21.75 mm. **Obv:** Arms with supporters **Rev:** Stork above value **Edge Lettering:** LATVIJAS BANKA • LATVIJAS BANKA

Date	Mintage	F	VF	XF	Unc	BU
2001	250,000	—	—	7.00	12.00	15.00

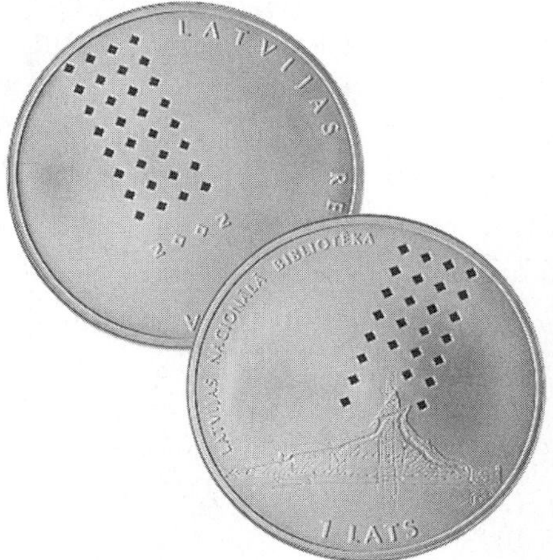

KM# 55 LATS

31.4700 g., 0.9250 Silver 0.9359 oz. ASW, 38.6 mm. **Subject:** National Library **Obv:** Country name and diamonds pattern **Rev:** Library building sketch and diamonds design **Edge Lettering:** GAISMU SAUCA - GAISMA AUSA

Date	Mintage	F	VF	XF	Unc	BU
2002 Proof	Est. 5,000	Value: 80.00				

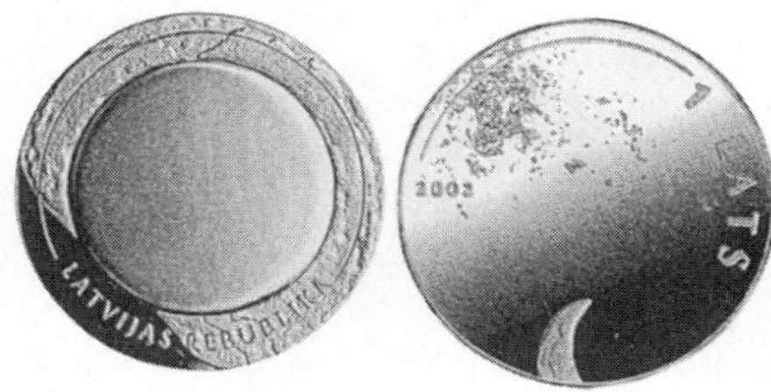

KM# 56 LATS

15.0000 g., 0.9250 Silver 0.4461 oz. ASW, 28 mm. **Subject:** "Fortune" **Obv:** Totally gold plated sun above country name **Rev:** Waning moon, date and value **Edge:** Plain

Date	Mintage	F	VF	XF	Unc	BU
2002 Proof	Est. 5,000	Value: 250				

KM# 52 LATS

31.4700 g., 0.9250 Silver 0.9359 oz. ASW, 38.6 mm. **Series:** Roots - Destiny **Obv:** Stylized design **Rev:** Apple tree and landscape **Edge:** Plain

Date	Mintage	F	VF	XF	Unc	BU
2002 Proof	Est. 5,000	Value: 85.00				

KM# 53 LATS
31.4700 g., 0.9250 Silver 0.9359 oz. ASW, 38.6 mm. **Subject:** Hanseatic City of Kuldiga **Obv:** City arms **Rev:** City view and ships **Edge:** Lettered

Date	Mintage	F	VF	XF	Unc	BU
2002 Proof	Est. 15,000	Value: 80.00				

KM# 57 LATS
31.4700 g., 0.9250 Silver 0.9359 oz. ASW, 38.6 mm. **Subject:** Olympics 2004 **Obv:** Arms with supporters **Rev:** Ancient wrestlers **Edge Lettering:** LATVIJAS BANKA • LATVIJAS BANKA

Date	Mintage	F	VF	XF	Unc	BU
2002 Proof	Est. 26,000	Value: 70.00				

KM# 60 LATS
31.4700 g., 0.9250 Silver 0.9359 oz. ASW, 38.6 mm. **Obv:** Crowned arms above partially built ship **Rev:** Hemp weighing scene with Iron foundry and brick wall in background **Edge Lettering:** REPUBLIKA LATVIJAS • BANKA LATVIJA

Date	Mintage	F	VF	XF	Unc	BU
2003 Proof	Est. 5,000	Value: 70.00				

KM# 71 LATS
31.4700 g., 0.9250 Silver 0.9359 oz. ASW, 38.6 mm. **Subject:** Vidzeme **Obv:** Crowned arms above horse drawn wagon **Rev:** Two men sawing wood **Edge Lettering:** Rahapaja Oy

Date	Mintage	F	VF	XF	Unc	BU
ND (2003) Proof	—	Value: 55.00				
2004 Proof	Est. 5,000	Value: 55.00				

KM# 72 LATS
31.4700 g., 0.9250 Silver 0.9359 oz. ASW, 38.6 mm. **Subject:** Latgale **Obv:** Madonna and Child above landscape **Rev:** Man sowing seeds and an angel **Edge Lettering:** Rahapaja Oy

Date	Mintage	F	VF	XF	Unc	BU
ND (2003) Proof	—	Value: 55.00				
2004 Proof	Est. 5,000	Value: 55.00				

KM# 75 LATS
31.4700 g., 0.9250 Silver 0.9359 oz. ASW, 38.61 mm. **Obv:** Coat of arms **Rev:** St. Simanis Church with VALMIERA and reflection of sailing ship **Edge:** LATVIJAS REPUBLIKA • LATVIJAS BANKA

Date	Mintage	F	VF	XF	Unc	BU
2003 Proof	Est. 15,000	Value: 55.00				

KM# 58 LATS
4.8000 g., Copper-Nickel, 21.75 mm. **Obv:** Arms with supporters **Rev:** Ant above value **Edge Lettering:** LATVIJAS BANKA • LATVIJAS BANKA

Date	Mintage	F	VF	XF	Unc	BU
2003	250,000	—	—	5.00	6.50	8.00

KM# 116 LATS
31.4700 g., 0.9250 Silver 0.9359 oz. ASW, 38.61 mm. **Obv:** Mideval Wolmar coin **Rev:** Church and ship

Date	Mintage	F	VF	XF	Unc	BU
2003 Proof	—	Value: 60.00				

KM# 64 LATS
31.4700 g., 0.9250 Silver 0.9359 oz. ASW, 38.6 mm. **Subject:** Latvian European Union Membership **Obv:** Arms with supporters **Rev:** P.S. LATVIJA-ES 2004 above value **Edge Lettering:** LATVIJAS BANKA • LATVIJAS BANKA

Date	Mintage	F	VF	XF	Unc	BU
2004 Proof	Est. 15,000	Value: 65.00				

KM# 61 LATS
4.8000 g., Copper-Nickel, 21.75 mm. **Obv:** Arms with supporters **Rev:** Spriditis with shovel above value **Edge Lettering:** LATVIJAS BANKA • LATVIJAS BANKA

Date	Mintage	F	VF	XF	Unc	BU
2004	500,000	—	—	3.00	4.00	6.00

KM# 62 LATS
17.1500 g., Bi-Metallic Dark Blue Niobium 7.15g center in .900 Silver 10g ring, 34 mm. **Obv:** Heraldic Rose **Rev:** Astronomical Clock **Edge:** Plain

Date	Mintage	F	VF	XF	Unc	BU
2004	Est. 5,000	—	—	—	75.00	85.00

KM# 63 LATS
31.4700 g., 0.9250 Silver 0.9359 oz. ASW, 38.6 mm. **Obv:** Arms with supporters **Rev:** World Cup Soccer player **Edge Lettering:** LATVIJA three times

Date	Mintage	F	VF	XF	Unc	BU
2004 Proof	Est. 50,000	Value: 70.00				

KM# 67 LATS
4.8000 g., Copper-Nickel, 21.75 mm. **Obv:** National arms **Obv. Legend:** LATVIJAS REPUBLIKA **Rev:** Mushroom above value **Edge Lettering:** LATVIJAS BANKA • LATVIJAS BANKA

Date	Mintage	F	VF	XF	Unc	BU
2004	500,000	—	—	3.00	4.00	5.00

KM# 68 LATS
31.4700 g., 0.9250 Silver 0.9359 oz. ASW, 38.6 mm. **Obv:** Mountains and value **Rev:** Laser picture of Janis Plieksans, pseudonym "Rainis" the mountain climbing poet, dramatist and patriot. **Edge Lettering:** LATVIJAS BANKA • LATVIJAS REPUBLIKA

Date	Mintage	F	VF	XF	Unc	BU
2005 Proof	Est. 5,000	Value: 45.00				

KM# 69 LATS
31.4700 g., 0.9250 Silver 0.9359 oz. ASW, 38.6 mm. **Obv:** National arms **Rev:** Bobsled **Edge Lettering:** LATVIJA repeated 3 times

Date	Mintage	F	VF	XF	Unc	BU
2005 Proof	Est. 15,000	Value: 45.00				

KM# 65 LATS
4.8000 g., Copper-Nickel, 21.75 mm. **Obv:** Arms with supporters **Rev:** Weathercock (from the spire of Riga's St. Peter Church) above value **Edge Lettering:** LATVIJAS BANKA • LATVIJAS BANKA

Date	Mintage	F	VF	XF	Unc	BU
2005	500,000	—	—	3.00	6.00	7.00

KM# 76 LATS
31.4700 g., 0.9250 Silver 0.9359 oz. ASW, 38.61 mm. **Obv:** Large coat of arms, date below **Rev:** Two hockey players viewed from above, RIGA 2006 on either side with hockey puck in center **Edge:** LATVIJA seperated by rhombic dots

Date	Mintage	F	VF	XF	Unc	BU
2005 Proof	Est. 5,000	Value: 55.00				

KM# 77 LATS
31.4700 g., 9.2500 Silver 9.3586 oz. ASW, 38.61 mm. **Obv:** Coat of arms **Rev:** Koknese castle on top with moon and sun on sides, reflection of Hanseatic Castle and ship on bottom **Edge Lettering:** LATVIJAS REPUBLIKA • LATVIJAS BANKA

Date	Mintage	F	VF	XF	Unc	BU
2005 Proof	Est. 15,000	Value: 45.00				

KM# 81 LATS
1.1500 g., Gold, 13.91 mm. **Obv:** Ribbon design **Obv. Legend:** RIGAS / LATVIJAS REPUBLIKA **Rev:** Stone face **Edge:** Reeded

Date	Mintage	F	VF	XF	Unc	BU
2005 Proof	—	Value: 70.00				

KM# 66 LATS
4.8000 g., Copper-Nickel, 21.75 mm. **Obv:** National arms **Obv. Legend:** LATVIJAS REPUBLIKA **Rev:** Pretzel above value **Edge Lettering:** LATVIJAS BANKA • LATVIJAS BANKA

Date	Mintage	F	VF	XF	Unc	BU
2005	500,000	—	—	3.00	4.00	6.00

KM# 73 LATS
4.8000 g., Copper-Nickel, 21.75 mm. **Subject:** Summer Solstice **Obv:** National arms **Rev:** Head wearing leaves above value **Edge Lettering:** LATVIJAS BANKA

Date	Mintage	F	VF	XF	Unc	BU
2006	500,000	—	—	3.00	4.00	6.00

KM# 74 LATS
4.8000 g., Copper-Nickel, 21.75 mm. **Obv:** National arms **Rev:** Pine cone above value **Edge Lettering:** LATVIJAS BANKA • LATVIJAS BANKA

Date	Mintage	F	VF	XF	Unc	BU
2006	1,000,000	—	—	3.00	5.00	6.00

KM# 78 LATS
31.4700 g., 0.9250 Silver 0.9359 oz. ASW, 38.61 mm. **Obv:** Stylized bonfire flames **Obv. Legend:** janvāris 1991 **Rev:** Latvian mythological hero with raised sword against the background of concrete block barricades, rising sun behind **Edge Lettering:** LATVIJAS BANKA

Date	Mintage	F	VF	XF	Unc	BU
2006 Proof	—	Value: 55.00				

KM# 79 LATS
31.4700 g., 0.9250 Silver 0.9359 oz. ASW, 38.61 mm. **Obv:** Starry sky on left with value on right side **Rev:** Portrait of Krisjanis Barons on right side and starry sky on left **Edge Lettering:** LATVIJAS BANKA • LATVIJAS REPUBLIKA

Date	Mintage	F	VF	XF	Unc	BU
2006 Proof	—	Value: 55.00				

KM# 80 LATS
31.4700 g., 0.9250 Silver 0.9359 oz. ASW, 38.61 mm. **Obv:** Seagul flying above water on left, value on right **Rev:** Portrait of Krisjanis Valdemars on right with sea on left **Edge Lettering:** LATVIJAS BANKA • LATVIJAS REPUBLIKA

Date	Mintage	F	VF	XF	Unc	BU
2006 Proof	—	Value: 55.00				

KM# 82 LATS
31.4700 g., 0.9250 Silver 0.9359 oz. ASW, 38.61 mm. **Obv:** Outline of Latvia with three stars above **Obv. Inscription:** LATVIJAS REPUBLIKA **Rev:** Two crossed swords outlined against the sun **Rev. Inscription:** NO ZOBENA SAULE LECA **Edge:** Plain

Date	Mintage	F	VF	XF	Unc	BU
2006 Proof	—	Value: 55.00				

KM# 83 LATS
31.4700 g., 0.9250 Silver 0.9359 oz. ASW, 38.61 mm. **Obv:** Coat of arms, date and value below **Obv. Inscription:** ROOP top, 1 LATS bottom **Rev:** Lielstraupe castle church top, reflection of Hanseatic ship with trees on both sides on bottom **Edge Lettering:** LATVIJAS REPUBLIKA • LATVIJAS BANKA

Date	Mintage	F	VF	XF	Unc	BU
2006 Proof	—	Value: 55.00				

KM# 84 LATS
27.0000 g., 0.9990 Silver 0.8672 oz. ASW, 38.61 mm. **Obv:** Arabic O in center of haptagon against an oriental background **Rev:** Roman I in center of heptagon **Shape:** 7-sided **Designer:** Ilmars Blumbergs and Janis Struplis

Date	Mintage	F	VF	XF	Unc	BU
2006 Proof	2,006	Value: 400				

KM# 115 LATS
31.4700 g., 0.9250 Silver 0.9359 oz. ASW, 38.61 mm. **Subject:** 2006 Rigo Ice Hockey World Championships **Obv:** National Arms **Rev:** Two Hockey players, as seen from above at a puck drop face-off

Date	Mintage	F	VF	XF	Unc	BU
2006 Proof	—	Value: 60.00				

KM# 12 LATS
4.8000 g., Copper-Nickel, 21.75 mm. **Obv:** Arms with supporters **Rev:** Salmon above value **Edge Lettering:** LATVIJAS BANKA

Date	Mintage	F	VF	XF	Unc	BU
2007	7,000,000	—	—	2.00	4.00	7.00
2008	25,000,000	—	—	2.00	4.00	7.00

KM# 85 LATS
4.8000 g., Copper-Nickel, 21.75 mm. **Obv:** National arms **Obv. Legend:** LATVIJAS REPUBLIKA **Rev:** Snowman **Edge Lettering:** LATVIJAS BANKA

Date	Mintage	F	VF	XF	Unc	BU
2007	1,000,000	—	—	3.00	4.00	6.00

KM# 86 LATS
4.8000 g., Copper-Nickel, 21.75 mm. **Obv:** National arms **Obv. Legend:** LATVIJAS REPUBLIKA **Rev:** Medieval owl figurine **Edge Lettering:** LATVIJAS BANKA

Date	Mintage	F	VF	XF	Unc	BU
2007	1,000,000	—	—	2.00	4.00	6.00

KM# 87 LATS
31.4700 g., 0.9250 Silver 0.9359 oz. ASW, 38.6 mm. **Obv:** Fragment of a large coat of arms **Rev:** Large coat of arms broken into fragments **Designer:** Ivo Grundulis and Ligita Franckevica

Date	Mintage	F	VF	XF	Unc	BU
2007 Proof	—	Value: 65.00				

KM# 88 LATS
31.4700 g., 0.9250 Silver 0.9359 oz. ASW, 38.6 mm. **Obv:** Large coat of arms **Rev:** Sun with its rays forming the red-white-red flag of the Republic **Designer:** Ivo Grundulis and Ligita Franckevica

Date	Mintage	F	VF	XF	Unc	BU
2007 Proof	—	Value: 65.00				

KM# 89 LATS
31.4700 g., 0.9250 Silver 0.9359 oz. ASW, 38.6 mm. **Obv:** Horse and sword within pendant **Rev:** Gauja Valley with the Turaida Castle and Sigulda Castle **Edge Lettering:** LATVIJAS REPUBLIKA • LATVIJAS BANKS **Designer:** Arvids Priedite and Janis Strupulis

Date	Mintage	F	VF	XF	Unc	BU
2007 Proof	—	Value: 65.00				

KM# 90 LATS
17.1500 g., Bi-Metallic Dark Purple, 34 mm. **Obv:** Heraldic rose at center **Rev:** Outer ring signs of the zodiac, inner circle different evolutionary stages of the plant world **Designer:** Laimonis Senbergs and Janis Strupulis

Date	Mintage	F	VF	XF	Unc	BU
2007	—	—	—	—	75.00	85.00

KM# 91 LATS
1.2442 g., 0.9990 Gold 0.0400 oz. AGW, 13.92 mm. **Obv:** Small coat of arms **Rev:** Logo of the publishing house Zelta abele **Designer:** Laimonis Senbergs and Janis Strupulis

Date	Mintage	F	VF	XF	Unc	BU
2007 Proof	—	Value: 65.00				

KM# 97 LATS
31.4700 g., 0.9250 Silver 0.9359 oz. ASW, 38.6 mm. **Subject:** Coin of life **Obv:** Golden heart-shaped leaves **Obv. Designer:** Ilmars Blumbergs and Ligita Franckevica **Rev:** Mother holding gilt wrapped child

Date	Mintage	F	VF	XF	Unc	BU
2007 Proof	—	Value: 80.00				

KM# 98 LATS
22.0000 g., 0.9250 Silver 0.6542 oz. ASW, 35 mm. **Subject:** Luckey Coin **Obv:** Cat on rooftop **Rev:** Man on ladder **Edge Lettering:** LATVIJAS BANKA (dots) LATVIJAS BANKA

Date	Mintage	F	VF	XF	Unc	BU
2008 Proof	5,000	Value: 55.00				

KM# 99 LATS
31.4700 g., 0.9250 Silver 0.9359 oz. ASW, 38.6 mm. **Subject:** 90th Anniversary of Statehood **Obv:** First Arms of the Republic **Rev:** Two children holding multicolor flag

Date	Mintage	F	VF	XF	Unc	BU
2008 Proof	5,000	Value: 80.00				

KM# 92 LATS
4.8000 g., Copper-Nickel, 21.75 mm. **Obv:** National arms **Obv. Legend:** LATVIJAS REPUBLIKA **Rev:** Water Lily **Edge Lettering:** LATVIJAS BANKA

Date	Mintage	F	VF	XF	Unc	BU
2008	1,000,000	—	—	3.00	4.00	6.00

KM# 93 LATS
12.4000 g., Copper-Nickel, 30 mm. **Obv:** Woman walking holding flowers **Rev:** Man walking holding wreath **Edge Lettering:** DZIESMAI SODIEN LIELA DIENA **Designer:** Arvids Priedite and Ligita Franckevica

Date	Mintage	F	VF	XF	Unc	BU
2008	—	—	—	—	7.00	9.00

KM# 93a LATS
31.4700 g., 0.9250 Silver 0.9359 oz. ASW, 38.61 mm. **Obv:** Woman walking holding flowers **Rev:** Man walking holding wreath **Edge Lettering:** DZIESMAI SODIEN LIELA DIENA **Designer:** Arvids Priedite and Ligita Franckevica

Date	Mintage	F	VF	XF	Unc	BU
2008 Proof	10,000	Value: 65.00				

KM# 94 LATS
31.4700 g., 0.9250 Silver 0.9359 oz. ASW **Obv:** Hanseatic city seal with coat of arms **Rev:** Limbazi Castle ruins and St. Johns Church with reflection of Hanseatic Ship on lower half **Edge Lettering:** LATVIJAS REPUBLIKA • LATVIJAS BANKA **Shape:** 38.61 **Designer:** Gunars Krollis and Janis Strupulis

Date	Mintage	F	VF	XF	Unc	BU
2008 Proof	5,000	Value: 65.00				

KM# 95 LATS
31.4700 g., 0.9250 Silver 0.9359 oz. ASW, 38.6 mm. **Obv:** Three stars and stylized basket ball design **Rev:** Two basketball players and a jump shot **Edge Lettering:** LATVIJAS BANKA • LATVIJAS REPUBLIKA **Designer:** Franceska Kirke and Ligita Franckevica

Date	Mintage	F	VF	XF	Unc	BU
2008 Proof	5,000	Value: 55.00				

KM# 107 LATS

4.8000 g., Copper-Nickel, 21.75 mm. **Obv:** National arms **Rev:** Chimney sweep standing with brush and ladder

Date	Mintage	F	VF	XF	Unc	BU
2008	—	—	—	—	4.00	6.00

KM# 101 LATS

4.8000 g., Copper-Nickel, 21.75 mm. **Subject:** Namejs ring **Obv:** National Arms **Rev:** Ring **Rev. Designer:** Ilze Libiete and Baiba Sime **Edge Lettering:** LATVIJAS BANKA

Date	Mintage	F	VF	XF	Unc	BU
2009	1,000,000	—	—	2.00	4.00	6.00

KM# 100 LATS

20.0000 g., 0.9250 Silver 0.5948 oz. ASW, 34 mm. **Subject:** My Dream Coin **Obv:** State Arms **Rev:** Piglet

Date	Mintage	F	VF	XF	Unc	BU
2009 Proof	—	Value: 60.00				

KM# 102 LATS

31.4700 g., 0.9250 Silver 0.9359 oz. ASW, 38.6 mm. **Subject:** Time of the Surveyors, Novel's 130th Anniversary **Obv:** Brali Kaudzites standing **Rev:** Six figures forming spokes of wheel **Edge Lettering:** LATVIJAS REPUBLICA LATVIJAS BANKA **Designer:** Laimonis Senbergs and Ligita Franckevica

Date	Mintage	F	VF	XF	Unc	BU
2009 Proof	—	Value: 55.00				

KM# 103 LATS

31.4700 g., 0.9250 Silver 0.9359 oz. ASW, 38.6 mm. **Subject:** University of Latvia **Obv:** Oak tree within wreath, partially multicolor **Rev:** Owl standing on open book, University building in background **Designer:** Arvids Predite and Ligita Frackevica

Date	Mintage	F	VF	XF	Unc	BU
2009 Proof	—	Value: 55.00				

KM# 104 LATS

26.0000 g., 0.9250 Silver 0.7732 oz. ASW, 32x32 mm. **Subject:** Coin of Water **Obv:** Water droplets **Rev:** Snowflake crystal **Shape:** Square **Designer:** Ilmars Blumbergs and Janis Strupulis

Date	Mintage	F	VF	XF	Unc	BU
2009 Proof	—	Value: 60.00				

KM# 105 LATS

4.8000 g., Copper-Nickel, 21.75 mm. **Subject:** Christmas Tree, 500th Anniversary **Obv:** Three children in folktale costumes **Rev:** Man walking with cut tree in moonlight, cat jumping from tree

Date	Mintage	F	VF	XF	Unc	BU
2009	1,000,000	—	—	—	4.00	8.00

KM# 106 LATS

4.8000 g., Copper-Nickel, 21.75 mm. **Obv:** National Arms **Rev:** Christmas tree, heart as ornament

Date	Mintage	F	VF	XF	Unc	BU
2009	—	—	—	—	4.00	6.00

KM# 108 LATS

4.8000 g., Copper-Nickel, 21.75 mm. **Obv:** National arms **Rev:** Toad

Date	Mintage	F	VF	XF	Unc	BU
2010	—	—	—	—	4.00	5.00

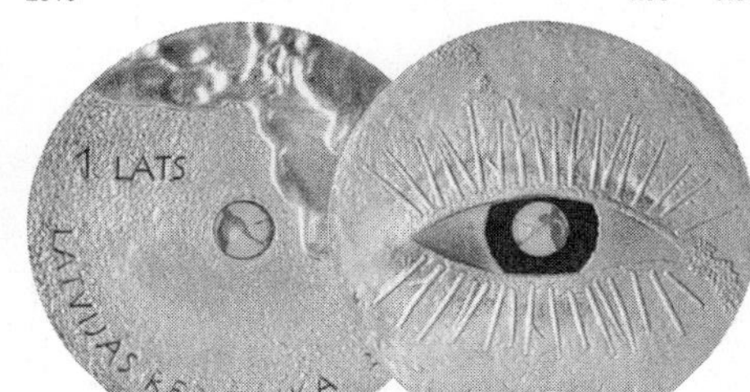

KM# 109 LATS

20.7000 g., 0.9250 Silver with amber insert 0.6156 oz. ASW, 35 mm. **Subject:** Amber **Obv:** Amber stone on seashore **Rev:** Eye with amber as pupil **Edge:** Plain

Date	Mintage	F	VF	XF	Unc	BU
2010 Proof	—	Value: 60.00				

KM# 110 LATS

12.4000 g., Copper-Nickel, 30 mm. **Subject:** The Latvian ABC Book **Obv:** Cock **Rev:** Teacher with students **Edge:** Lettered **Designer:** Arvids Priedite and Ligita Franckevica

Date	Mintage	F	VF	XF	Unc	BU
2010	—	—	—	—	—	10.00

KM# 111 LATS

31.4700 g., 0.9250 Silver 0.9359 oz. ASW, 38.61 mm. **Subject:** Latvian ABC Book **Obv:** Cock **Obv. Designer:** Arvids Priedite and Ligita Franckevica **Rev:** Teacher and students **Edge:** Lettered

Date	Mintage	F	VF	XF	Unc	BU
2010 Proof	—	Value: 65.00				

KM# 112 LATS

31.4700 g., 0.9250 Silver 0.9359 oz. ASW, 38.61 mm. **Subject:** Duke Jacob, 400th Anniversary of birth **Obv:** Bust right, value at bottom **Rev:** Arms **Edge:** Lettered

Date	Mintage	F	VF	XF	Unc	BU
2010 Proof	—	Value: 65.00				

KM# 113 LATS

31.4700 g., 0.9250 Silver 0.9359 oz. ASW, 38.61 mm. **Subject:** 20th Anniversary of Modern Republic **Obv:** Three small buds, red in color **Rev:** Elderly female with yoke of oppression **Edge:** Lettered **Designer:** Ilmars Blumbers and Ligita Franckevica

Date	Mintage	F	VF	XF	Unc	BU
2010 Proof	—	Value: 65.00				

KM# 114 LATS

17.1500 g., Bi-Metallic Niobium center within 10g of .900 Silver ring, 34 mm. **Subject:** Coin of Time III **Obv:** Heraldic Rose **Rev:** Forests, fields, rocks and water

Date	Mintage	F	VF	XF	Unc	BU
2010	—	—	—	—	—	60.00

KM# 38 2 LATI

9.5000 g., Bi-Metallic Nickel-Brass center in Copper-Nickel ring, 26.3 mm. **Obv:** Arms with supporters within circle **Rev:** Cow above value within circle **Edge Lettering:** LATVIJAS BANKA

Date	Mintage	F	VF	XF	Unc	BU
2003 In sets only	30,000	—	—	—	—	12.00
2009	2,000,000	—	—	7.00	8.00	9.00

KM# 59 5 LATI

1.2442 g., 0.9999 Gold 0.0400 oz. AGW, 13.92 mm. **Obv:** Bust right **Rev:** Arms with supporters above value **Edge:** Reeded **Note:** Remake of the popular KM-9 design

Date	Mintage	F	VF	XF	Unc	BU
2003 Proof	Est. 20,000	Value: 120				

KM# 96 20 LATI

10.0000 g., 0.9990 Gold 0.3212 oz. AGW, 22 mm. **Obv:** Woman's head covered with scarf **Rev:** Vessel with a milk bottle, apple, jug of milk, bread & knife on table **Designer:** Tedors Zalkalns and Ligita Franckevica

Date	Mintage	F	VF	XF	Unc	BU
2008	5,000	—	—	—	—	650

The Republic of Lebanon, situated on the eastern shore of the Mediterranean Sea between Syria and Israel, has an area of 4,015 sq. mi. (10,400 sq. km.) and a population of 3.5 million. Capital: Beirut. The economy is based on agriculture, trade and tourism. Fruit, other foodstuffs and textiles are exported.

MONETARY SYSTEM

100 Piastres = 1 Livre (Pound)

REPUBLIC

STANDARD COINAGE

KM# 40 25 LIVRES

2.8200 g., Nickel Plated Steel, 20.5 mm. **Obv:** Large value on cedar tree **Rev:** Value within square design **Rev. Legend:** BANQUE DU LIBAN **Edge:** Plain

Date	Mintage	F	VF	XF	Unc	BU
2002	—	—	—	0.30	0.80	1.20

KM# 37a 50 LIVRES

Nickel, 18.35 mm. **Obv:** Cedar tree with Arabic value superimposed. Arabic legend above, date below. **Rev:** Value in center.

Date	Mintage	F	VF	XF	Unc	BU
2006	—	—	—	0.50	1.20	1.80

KM# 38a 100 LIVRES

4.0500 g., Stainless Steel, 22.48 mm. **Obv:** Arabic legend above large value on cedar tree **Rev:** Stylized flag above large value "100" **Rev. Legend:** BANQUE DU LIBAN **Edge:** Plain

Date	Mintage	F	VF	XF	Unc	BU
2003	—	—	—	0.60	1.50	2.00

KM# 38b 100 LIVRES

4.0700 g., Copper Plated Steel, 22.49 mm. **Obv:** Arabic legend above large value on cedar tree **Rev:** Stylized flag above large value "100" **Rev. Legend:** BANQUE DU LIBAN **Edge:** Plain

Date	Mintage	F	VF	XF	Unc	BU
2006	—	—	—	0.60	1.50	2.00

KM# 38 100 LIVRES

4.0000 g., Brass, 22.5 mm. **Obv:** Arabic legend above large value on cedar tree **Rev:** Stylized flag above large value "100" **Rev. Legend:** BANQUE DU LIBAN **Edge:** Plain

Date	Mintage	F	VF	XF	Unc	BU
2006	—	—	—	0.65	1.50	2.00

KM# 36 250 LIVRES

5.0000 g., Aluminum-Bronze, 23.5 mm. **Obv:** Arabic legend above large value on cedar tree **Rev:** Large 250 within eliptical border design **Edge:** Reeded

Date	Mintage	F	VF	XF	Unc	BU
2003	—	—	—	0.75	1.85	2.50
2006	—	—	—	0.75	1.85	2.50
2009	—	—	—	0.75	1.85	2.50

KM# 39 500 LIVRES

6.0600 g., Nickel Plated Steel, 24.5 mm. **Obv:** Arabic legend above large value on cedar tree **Rev:** Large value "500", thick segmented circular border **Rev. Legend:** BANQUE DU LIBAN **Edge:** Plain

Date	Mintage	F	VF	XF	Unc	BU
2003	—	—	—	0.90	2.25	3.00
2006	—	—	—	0.90	2.25	3.00
2009	—	—	—	0.90	2.25	3.00

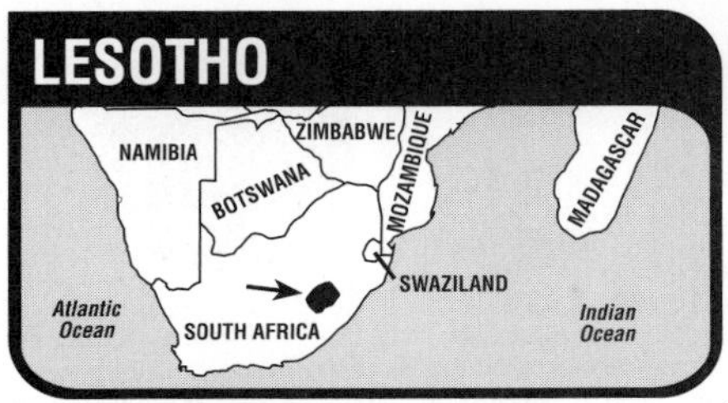

The Kingdom of Lesotho, a constitutional monarchy located within the east-central part of the Republic of South Africa, has an area of 11,720 sq. mi. (30,350 sq. km.) and a population of 1.5 million. Capital: Maseru. The economy is based on subsistence agriculture and livestock raising. Wool, mohair, and cattle are exported.

Lesotho (formerly Basutoland) was sparsely populated until the end of the 16th century. Between the 16th and 19th centuries an influx of refugees from tribal wars led to the development of a distinct Basotho group. During the reign of tribal chief Mashoeshoe I (1823-70), a series of wars with the Orange Free State resulted in the loss of large areas of territory to South Africa. Mashoeshoe appealed to the British for help, and Basutoland was constituted a native state under British protection. In 1871 it was annexed to Cape Colony, but was restored to direct control by the Crown in 1884. From 1884 to 1959 legislative and executive authority was vested in a British High Commissioner. The constitution of 1959 recognized the expressed wish of the people for independence, which was attained on Oct.4, 1966.

Lesotho is a member of the Commonwealth of Nations. The king is Head of State.

RULERS

Moshoeshoe II, 1966-1990
Letsie III, 1990-1995
Moshoeshoe II, 1995-

MONETARY SYSTEM

100 Licente/Lisente = 1 Maloti/Loti

KINGDOM

STANDARD COINAGE

KM# 62 5 LICENTE (Lisente)

1.6400 g., Brass Plated Steel, 15 mm. **Ruler:** Letsie III **Obv:** Arms with supporters **Rev:** Single pine tree among grass, hills and value

Date	Mintage	F	VF	XF	Unc	BU
2006	—	—	—	0.35	0.75	1.00

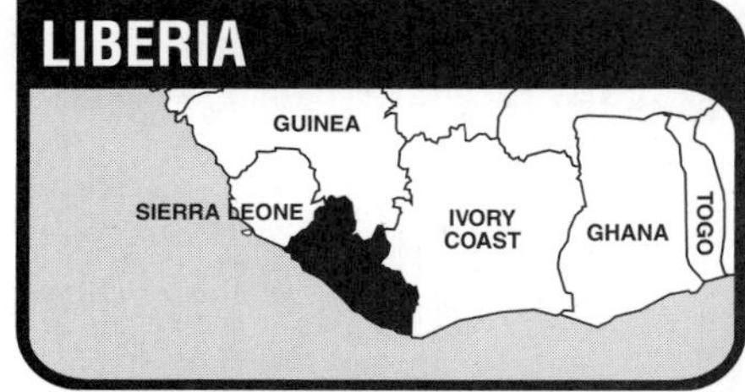

The Republic of Liberia, located on the southern side of the West African bulge between Sierra Leone and Ivory Coast, has an area of 38,250 sq. mi. (111,370 sq. km) and a population of 2.2 million. Capital: Monrovia. The major industries are agriculture, mining and lumbering. Iron ore, diamonds, rubber, coffee and coca are exported.

MINT MARKS

PM - Pobjoy Mint

MONETARY SYSTEM

100 Cents = 1 Dollar

REPUBLIC

STANDARD COINAGE

KM# 618 5 CENTS

5.0200 g., Copper-Nickel, 23.8 mm. **Obv:** National arms **Rev:** Chimpanzee family **Edge:** Plain

Date	Mintage	F	VF	XF	Unc	BU
2003	—	—	—	—	1.50	2.00

KM# 651 5 DOLLARS
14.5600 g., Copper-Nickel, 38 mm. **Obv:** National arms **Rev:** Japanese "Zero" flying over Pearl Harbor **Edge:** Reeded

Date	Mintage	F	VF	XF	Unc	BU
2001	—	—	—	—	10.00	12.00

KM# 568 5 DOLLARS
14.6300 g., Copper-Nickel, 33.1 mm. **Subject:** Battle of Gettysburg **Obv:** National arms **Rev:** Cannon and crossed flags divides busts facing **Edge:** Reeded **Note:** This also exists in an obverse denominated type for $2,000. Also see KM828.

Date	Mintage	F	VF	XF	Unc	BU
2001B	—	—	—	—	12.00	14.00

KM# 494 5 DOLLARS
8.5000 g., 0.9999 Silver 0.2732 oz. ASW, 30 mm. **Subject:** Soccer **Obv:** National arms **Rev:** Soccer player divides circle **Edge:** Reeded

Date	Mintage	F	VF	XF	Unc	BU
2002 Proof	3,000	Value: 30.00				

KM# 829 5 DOLLARS
14.9400 g., Copper-Nickel, 32.9 mm. **Subject:** 12th Anniversary Columbia Space Shuttle **Obv:** National arms **Rev:** Astronaut, space shuttle **Edge:** Reeded

Date	Mintage	F	VF	XF	Unc	BU
2003	—	—	—	—	8.00	10.00

KM# 831 5 DOLLARS
15.5500 g., 0.9990 Niobium 0.4994 oz., 38 mm. **Series:** From ancient to Modern Sports **Obv:** National arms **Rev:** Discus throwers **Edge:** Plain

Date	Mintage	F	VF	XF	Unc	BU
2004	2,004	—	—	—	—	25.00

KM# 832 5 DOLLARS
15.5500 g., 0.9990 Niobium 0.4994 oz., 38 mm. **Series:** From Ancient to Modern Sports **Obv:** National arms **Rev:** Javelin throwers **Edge:** Plain

Date	Mintage	F	VF	XF	Unc	BU
2004	2,004	—	—	—	—	25.00

KM# 833 5 DOLLARS
15.5500 g., 0.9990 Niobium 0.4994 oz., 38 mm. **Series:** From ancient to Modern Sports **Obv:** National arms **Rev:** Broad jumpers **Edge:** Plain

Date	Mintage	F	VF	XF	Unc	BU
2004	2,004	—	—	—	—	25.00

KM# 834 5 DOLLARS
15.5500 g., 0.9990 Niobium 0.4994 oz., 38 mm. **Series:** From Ancient to Modern Sports **Obv:** National arms **Rev:** Runners **Edge:** Plain

Date	Mintage	F	VF	XF	Unc	BU
2004	2,004	—	—	—	—	25.00

KM# 835 5 DOLLARS
15.5500 g., 0.9990 Niobium 0.4994 oz., 38 mm. **Series:** From Ancient to Modern Sports **Obv:** National arms **Rev:** Wrestlers **Edge:** Plain

Date	Mintage	F	VF	XF	Unc	BU
2004	2,004	—	—	—	—	25.00

KM# 664 5 DOLLARS
6.4000 g., Bi-Metallic Brass center in Copper-Nickel ring, 25.7 mm. **Obv:** National arms **Rev:** Pope and cathedral within circle **Edge:** Reeded

Date	Mintage	F	VF	XF	Unc	BU
2005	—	—	—	—	12.00	14.00

KM# 809 5 DOLLARS
25.9500 g., Silver, 39.97 mm. **Subject:** Papal visits to Africa **Obv:** National arms **Rev:** !/2 length multicolor figure of Pope John Paul II at center left, outlined map of Africa at center right in background **Edge:** Reeded

Date	Mintage	F	VF	XF	Unc	BU
2005 Proof	—	Value: 35.00				

KM# 810 5 DOLLARS
25.7200 g., Silver, 39.92 mm. **Obv:** National arms **Rev:** St. Peter's square in background, multicolor bust of Pope Benedict XVI in oval frame at upper right **Edge:** Reeded

Date	Mintage	F	VF	XF	Unc	BU
2005 Proof	—	Value: 40.00				

KM# 865 5 DOLLARS
7.7800 g., Niobium partially gilt, 35 mm. **Subject:** 10th Anniversary of the Euro - San Marino **Rev:** Castle

Date	Mintage	F	VF	XF	Unc	BU
2006 Proof	10,000	Value: 50.00				

KM# 866 5 DOLLARS
7.7800 g., Niobium partially gilt, 35 mm. **Subject:** 10th Anniversary of the Euro - Slovakia **Rev:** Bratislava Castle

Date	Mintage	F	VF	XF	Unc	BU
2006 Proof	10,000	Value: 50.00				

KM# 867 5 DOLLARS
7.7800 g., Niobium partially gilt, 35 mm. **Subject:** 10th Anniversary of the Euro - Latvia **Rev:** Old Buildings

Date	Mintage	F	VF	XF	Unc	BU
2006 Proof	10,000	Value: 50.00				

KM# 868 5 DOLLARS
7.7800 g., Niobium partially gilt, 35 mm. **Subject:** 10th Anniversary of the Euro - Monaco **Rev:** Ariel view of Principality

Date	Mintage	F	VF	XF	Unc	BU
2006 Proof	10,000	Value: 50.00				

KM# 869 5 DOLLARS
7.7800 g., Niobium partially gilt, 35 mm. **Subject:** 10th Anniversary of the Euro - Slovenia **Rev:** Hill-top buildings

Date	Mintage	F	VF	XF	Unc	BU
2006 Proof	10,000	Value: 50.00				

KM# 724 5 DOLLARS
26.3000 g., Silver Plated Bronze, 38.6 mm. **Obv:** National arms **Rev:** Multicolor Pope John Paul II with cross **Edge:** Reeded

Date	Mintage	F	VF	XF	Unc	BU
2007 Proof	—	Value: 30.00				

KM# 733 5 DOLLARS
27.0000 g., Copper-Nickel Silvered and Gilt, 38.61 mm. **Subject:** The Black Madonna of Czestochowa **Obv:** Arms **Obv. Legend:** REPUBLIC OF LIBERIA **Rev:** 1/2 length figure of Madonna facing with child

Date	Mintage	F	VF	XF	Unc	BU
2007 Proof	1,000	Value: 40.00				

KM# 958 5 DOLLARS
31.1050 g., Copper-Nickel Silver plated **Rev:** Martin van Buren multicolor applique

Date	Mintage	F	VF	XF	Unc	BU
2009	—	—	—	—	—	5.00

KM# 951 5 DOLLARS
31.1050 g., Copper-Nickel Silver plated **Rev:** George Washington multicolor applique

Date	Mintage	F	VF	XF	Unc	BU
2009	—	—	—	—	—	5.00

KM# 952 5 DOLLARS
31.1050 g., Copper-Nickel Silver plated **Rev:** John Adams multicolor applique

Date	Mintage	F	VF	XF	Unc	BU
2009	—	—	—	—	—	5.00

KM# 953 5 DOLLARS
31.1050 g., Copper-Nickel Silver plated **Rev:** Thomas Jefferson multicolor applique

Date	Mintage	F	VF	XF	Unc	BU
2009	—	—	—	—	—	5.00

KM# 954 5 DOLLARS
31.1050 g., Copper-Nickel Silver plated **Rev:** James Madison multicolor applique

Date	Mintage	F	VF	XF	Unc	BU
2009	—	—	—	—	—	5.00

KM# 955 5 DOLLARS
31.1050 g., Copper-Nickel Silver plated **Rev:** James Monroe multicolor applique

Date	Mintage	F	VF	XF	Unc	BU
2009	—	—	—	—	—	5.00

KM# 956 5 DOLLARS
31.1050 g., Copper-Nickel Silver plated **Rev:** John Quincey Adams multicolor applique

Date	Mintage	F	VF	XF	Unc	BU
2009	—	—	—	—	—	5.00

KM# 957 5 DOLLARS
31.1050 g., Copper-Nickel Silver plated **Rev:** Andrew Jackson multicolor applique

Date	Mintage	F	VF	XF	Unc	BU
2009	—	—	—	—	—	5.00

KM# 959 5 DOLLARS
31.1050 g., Copper-Nickel Silver plated **Rev:** William Henry Harrison multicolor applique

Date	Mintage	F	VF	XF	Unc	BU
2009	—	—	—	—	—	5.00

KM# 960 5 DOLLARS
31.1050 g., Copper-Nickel Silver plated **Rev:** John Tyler multicolor applique

Date	Mintage	F	VF	XF	Unc	BU
2009	—	—	—	—	—	5.00

KM# 961 5 DOLLARS
31.1050 g., Copper-Nickel Silver plated **Rev:** James K. Polk multicolor applique

Date	Mintage	F	VF	XF	Unc	BU
2009	—	—	—	—	—	5.00

KM# 962 5 DOLLARS
31.1050 g., Copper-Nickel Silver plated **Rev:** Zachary Taylor multicolor applique

Date	Mintage	F	VF	XF	Unc	BU
2009	—	—	—	—	—	5.00

KM# 963 5 DOLLARS
31.1050 g., Copper-Nickel Silver plated **Rev:** Millard Filmore multicolor applique

Date	Mintage	F	VF	XF	Unc	BU
2009	—	—	—	—	—	5.00

KM# 964 5 DOLLARS
31.1050 g., Copper-Nickel Silver plated **Rev:** Franklin Pierce multicolor applique

Date	Mintage	F	VF	XF	Unc	BU
2009	—	—	—	—	—	5.00

KM# 965 5 DOLLARS
31.1050 g., Copper-Nickel Silver plated **Rev:** James Buchanan multicolor applique

Date	Mintage	F	VF	XF	Unc	BU
2009	—	—	—	—	—	5.00

KM# 966 5 DOLLARS
31.1050 g., Copper-Nickel Silver plated **Rev:** Abraham Lincoln multicolor applique

Date	Mintage	F	VF	XF	Unc	BU
2009	—	—	—	—	—	5.00

KM# 967 5 DOLLARS
31.1050 g., Copper-Nickel Silver plated **Rev:** Andrew Johnson multicolor applique

Date	Mintage	F	VF	XF	Unc	BU
2009	—	—	—	—	—	5.00

KM# 968 5 DOLLARS
31.1050 g., Copper-Nickel Silver plated **Rev:** Ulysses S. Grant multicolor applique

Date	Mintage	F	VF	XF	Unc	BU
2009	—	—	—	—	—	5.00

KM# 969 5 DOLLARS
31.1050 g., Copper-Nickel Silver plated **Rev:** Rutherford B. Hayes multicolor applique

Date	Mintage	F	VF	XF	Unc	BU
2009	—	—	—	—	—	5.00

KM# 970 5 DOLLARS
31.1050 g., Copper-Nickel Silver plated **Rev:** James A. Garfield multicolor applique

Date	Mintage	F	VF	XF	Unc	BU
2009	—	—	—	—	—	5.00

KM# 971 5 DOLLARS
31.1050 g., Copper-Nickel Silver plated **Rev:** Chester Arthur multicolor underprint

Date	Mintage	F	VF	XF	Unc	BU
2009	—	—	—	—	—	5.00

KM# 972 5 DOLLARS
31.1050 g., Copper-Nickel Silver plated **Rev:** Grover Cleveland multicolor applique

Date	Mintage	F	VF	XF	Unc	BU
2009	—	—	—	—	—	5.00

KM# 973 5 DOLLARS
31.1050 g., Copper-Nickel Silver plated **Rev:** Benjamin Harrison multicolor applique

Date	Mintage	F	VF	XF	Unc	BU
2009	—	—	—	—	—	5.00

KM# 974 5 DOLLARS
31.1050 g., Copper-Nickel Silver plated **Rev:** William McKinley multicolor applique

Date	Mintage	F	VF	XF	Unc	BU
2009	—	—	—	—	—	5.00

KM# 975 5 DOLLARS
31.1050 g., Copper-Nickel Silver plated **Rev:** Theodore Roosevelt multicolor applique

Date	Mintage	F	VF	XF	Unc	BU
2009	—	—	—	—	—	5.00

KM# 976 5 DOLLARS
31.1050 g., Copper-Nickel Silver plated **Rev:** William Howard Taft multicolor applique

Date	Mintage	F	VF	XF	Unc	BU
2009	—	—	—	—	—	5.00

KM# 977 5 DOLLARS
31.1050 g., Copper-Nickel Silver plated **Rev:** Woodrow Wilson multicolor applique

Date	Mintage	F	VF	XF	Unc	BU
2009	—	—	—	—	—	5.00

KM# 978 5 DOLLARS
31.1050 g., Copper-Nickel Silver plated **Rev:** Warren G. Harding multicolor applique

Date	Mintage	F	VF	XF	Unc	BU
2009	—	—	—	—	—	5.00

KM# 979 5 DOLLARS
31.1050 g., Copper-Nickel Silver plated **Rev:** Calvin Collidge multicolor applique

Date	Mintage	F	VF	XF	Unc	BU
2009	—	—	—	—	—	5.00

KM# 980 5 DOLLARS
31.1050 g., Copper-Nickel Silver plated **Rev:** Herbert Hoover multicolor applique

Date	Mintage	F	VF	XF	Unc	BU
2009	—	—	—	—	—	5.00

KM# 981 5 DOLLARS
31.1050 g., Copper-Nickel Silver plated **Rev:** Franklin D. Roosevelt multicolor applique

Date	Mintage	F	VF	XF	Unc	BU
2009	—	—	—	—	—	5.00

KM# 982 5 DOLLARS
31.1050 g., Copper-Nickel Silver plated **Rev:** Harry S Truman multicolor applique

Date	Mintage	F	VF	XF	Unc	BU
2009	—	—	—	—	—	5.00

KM# 983 5 DOLLARS
31.1050 g., Copper-Nickel Silver plated **Rev:** Swight D. Eisenhower multicolor applique

Date	Mintage	F	VF	XF	Unc	BU
2009	—	—	—	—	—	5.00

KM# 984 5 DOLLARS
31.1050 g., Copper-Nickel Silver plated **Rev:** John F. Kennedy multicolor applique

Date	Mintage	F	VF	XF	Unc	BU
2009	—	—	—	—	—	5.00

KM# 985 5 DOLLARS
31.1050 g., Copper-Nickel Silver plated **Rev:** Lyndon B. Johnson multicolor applique

Date	Mintage	F	VF	XF	Unc	BU
2009	—	—	—	—	—	5.00

KM# 986 5 DOLLARS
31.1050 g., Copper-Nickel Silver plated **Rev:** Richard M. Nixon multicolor applique

Date	Mintage	F	VF	XF	Unc	BU
2009	—	—	—	—	—	5.00

KM# 987 5 DOLLARS
31.1050 g., Copper-Nickel Silver plated **Rev:** Gerald R. Ford multicolor applique

Date	Mintage	F	VF	XF	Unc	BU
2009	—	—	—	—	—	5.00

KM# 988 5 DOLLARS
31.1050 g., Copper-Nickel Silver plated **Rev:** Jimmy Carter multicolor applique

Date	Mintage	F	VF	XF	Unc	BU
2009	—	—	—	—	—	5.00

KM# 989 5 DOLLARS
31.1050 g., Copper-Nickel Silver plated **Rev:** Ronald Reagan multicolor applique

Date	Mintage	F	VF	XF	Unc	BU
2009	—	—	—	—	—	5.00

KM# 990 5 DOLLARS
31.1050 g., Copper-Nickel Silver plated **Rev:** George H. W. Bush multicolor applique

Date	Mintage	F	VF	XF	Unc	BU
2009	—	—	—	—	—	5.00

KM# 991 5 DOLLARS
31.1050 g., Copper-Nickel Silver plated **Rev:** Bill Clinton multicolor applique

Date	Mintage	F	VF	XF	Unc	BU
2009	—	—	—	—	—	5.00

KM# 992 5 DOLLARS
31.1050 g., Copper-Nickel Silver plated **Rev:** George W. Bush multicolor applique

Date	Mintage	F	VF	XF	Unc	BU
2009	—	—	—	—	—	5.00

KM# 993 5 DOLLARS
31.1050 g., Copper-Nickel Silver palted **Rev:** Barack Obama multicolor applique

Date	Mintage	F	VF	XF	Unc	BU
2009	—	—	—	—	—	5.00

KM# 513 10 DOLLARS
28.5000 g., Copper-Nickel, 38.6 mm. **Series:** Moments of Freedom **Subject:** Hungarian Revolution of 1848 **Obv:** National arms **Rev:** Multicolor heroic scene **Edge:** Reeded

Date	Mintage	F	VF	XF	Unc	BU
2001 Proof	9,999	Value: 12.00				

KM# 491 10 DOLLARS
25.2500 g., 0.9250 Silver 0.7509 oz. ASW, 36.8 mm. **Subject:** Illusion **Obv:** National arms **Rev:** Stylized head with glasses facing **Edge:** Plain **Shape:** 10-sided

Date	Mintage	F	VF	XF	Unc	BU
2001 Proof	5,000	Value: 37.50				

KM# 777 10 DOLLARS
14.5500 g., Copper-Nickel, 32 mm. **Subject:** 43rd President of USA **Obv:** National arms **Obv. Legend:** REPUBLIC OF LIBERIA **Rev:** George W. Bush, flag in background

Date	Mintage	F	VF	XF	Unc	BU
2001 Proof	—	Value: 12.00				

KM# 822 10 DOLLARS
1.2400 g., Gold, 13.68 mm. **Obv:** National arms **Rev:** Bust of Marlene Dietrich facing **Edge:** Reeded

Date	Mintage	F	VF	XF	Unc	BU
2001 Proof	—	Value: 65.00				

KM# 493 10 DOLLARS
770.0000 g., Copper, 100 mm. **Subject:** Wreck of the Princess Louisa **Obv:** National arms **Rev:** Sailing ship **Edge:** Reeded **Note:** Illustration reduced. With an encased glass shard recovered from the wreck site of the Princess Louisa.

Date	Mintage	F	VF	XF	Unc	BU
2001	2,000	—	—	—	225	—

KM# 510 10 DOLLARS
33.2400 g., Copper Gilt, 40.1 mm. **Obv:** National arms **Rev:** Multicolor holographic bald eagle **Edge:** Reeded

Date	Mintage	F	VF	XF	Unc	BU
2001	20,000	—	—	—	—	35.00

KM# 537 10 DOLLARS
28.5000 g., Copper-Nickel, 38.6 mm. **Subject:** Moments of Freedom **Obv:** National arms **Rev:** Multicolor Buddha, spelled "Budha" on the coin **Edge:** Reeded

Date	Mintage	F	VF	XF	Unc	BU
2001 Proof	9,999	Value: 12.00				

KM# 538 10 DOLLARS
28.5000 g., Copper-Nickel, 38.6 mm. **Subject:** Moments of Freedom **Obv:** National arms **Rev:** Multicolor Battle of Marathon scene **Edge:** Reeded

Date	Mintage	F	VF	XF	Unc	BU
2001 Proof	9,999	Value: 12.00				

KM# 539 10 DOLLARS
28.5000 g., Copper-Nickel, 38.6 mm. **Series:** Moments of Freedom **Obv:** National arms **Rev:** Multicolor founding of Liberia design **Edge:** Reeded

Date	Mintage	F	VF	XF	Unc	BU
2001 Proof	9,999	Value: 12.00				

KM# 540 10 DOLLARS
28.5000 g., Copper-Nickel, 38.6 mm. **Series:** Moments of Freedom **Obv:** National arms **Rev:** Multicolor portrait of Constantine I **Edge:** Reeded

Date	Mintage	F	VF	XF	Unc	BU
2001 Proof	9,999	Value: 12.00				

KM# 541 10 DOLLARS
28.5000 g., Copper-Nickel, 38.6 mm. **Series:** Moments of Freedom **Obv:** National arms **Rev:** Multicolor William Tell statue **Edge:** Reeded

Date	Mintage	F	VF	XF	Unc	BU
2001 Proof	9,999	Value: 12.00				

KM# 542 10 DOLLARS
28.5000 g., Copper-Nickel, 38.6 mm. **Series:** Moments of Freedom **Obv:** National arms **Rev:** Multicolor bust facing **Edge:** Reeded

Date	Mintage	F	VF	XF	Unc	BU
2001 Proof	9,999	Value: 12.00				

KM# 543 10 DOLLARS
28.5000 g., Copper-Nickel, 38.6 mm. **Series:** Moments of Freedom **Obv:** National arms **Rev:** Multicolor head with headdress and battle scene **Edge:** Reeded

Date	Mintage	F	VF	XF	Unc	BU
2001 Proof	9,999	Value: 12.00				

KM# 544 10 DOLLARS
28.5000 g., Copper-Nickel, 38.6 mm. **Series:** Moments of Freedom **Obv:** National arms **Rev:** Multicolor Brandenburg Gate scene **Edge:** Reeded

Date	Mintage	F	VF	XF	Unc	BU
2001 Proof	9,999	Value: 12.00				

KM# 545 10 DOLLARS
28.5000 g., Copper-Nickel, 38.6 mm. **Series:** Moments of Freedom **Obv:** National arms **Rev:** Multicolor half length figure facing **Edge:** Reeded

Date	Mintage	F	VF	XF	Unc	BU
2001 Proof	9,999	Value: 12.00				

KM# 546 10 DOLLARS
28.5000 g., Copper-Nickel, 38.6 mm. **Series:** Moments of Freedom **Obv:** National arms **Rev:** Multicolor Sitting Bull portrait **Edge:** Reeded

Date	Mintage	F	VF	XF	Unc	BU
2001 Proof	9,999	Value: 12.00				

KM# 547 10 DOLLARS
28.5000 g., Copper-Nickel, 38.6 mm. **Series:** Moments of Freedom **Obv:** National arms **Rev:** Multicolor Declaration of Independence scene **Edge:** Reeded

Date	Mintage	F	VF	XF	Unc	BU
2001 Proof	9,999	Value: 12.00				

KM# 548 10 DOLLARS
28.5000 g., Copper-Nickel, 38.6 mm. **Series:** Moments of Freedom **Obv:** National arms **Rev:** Multicolor allegorical woman **Edge:** Reeded

Date	Mintage	F	VF	XF	Unc	BU
2001 Proof	9,999	Value: 12.00				

KM# 549 10 DOLLARS
28.5000 g., Copper-Nickel, 38.6 mm. **Series:** Moments of Freedom **Obv:** National arms **Rev:** Multicolor bust of Gandhi looking down **Edge:** Reeded

Date	Mintage	F	VF	XF	Unc	BU
2001 Proof	9,999	Value: 12.00				

KM# 550 10 DOLLARS
28.5000 g., Copper-Nickel, 38.6 mm. **Series:** Moments of Freedom **Obv:** National arms **Rev:** Multicolor picture of a soldier at the moment he is shot in battle **Edge:** Reeded

Date	Mintage	F	VF	XF	Unc	BU
2001 Proof	9,999	Value: 12.00				

KM# 551 10 DOLLARS
28.5000 g., Copper-Nickel, 38.6 mm. **Series:** Moments of Freedom **Obv:** National arms **Rev:** Multicolor inmates behind wire fence scene **Edge:** Reeded

Date	Mintage	F	VF	XF	Unc	BU
2001 Proof	9,999	Value: 12.00				

KM# 552 10 DOLLARS
28.5000 g., Copper-Nickel, 38.6 mm. **Series:** Moments of Freedom **Obv:** National arms **Rev:** Multicolor Iwo Jima flag raising scene **Edge:** Reeded

Date	Mintage	F	VF	XF	Unc	BU
2001 Proof	9,999	Value: 12.00				

KM# 553 10 DOLLARS
28.5000 g., Copper-Nickel, 38.6 mm. **Series:** Moments of Freedom **Obv:** National arms **Rev:** Multicolor UN logo and dove **Edge:** Reeded

Date	Mintage	F	VF	XF	Unc	BU
2001 Proof	9,999	Value: 12.00				

KM# 554 10 DOLLARS
28.5000 g., Copper-Nickel, 38.6 mm. **Series:** Moments of Freedom **Obv:** National arms **Rev:** Multicolor Solzhenitsyn portrait **Edge:** Reeded

Date	Mintage	F	VF	XF	Unc	BU
2001 Proof	9,999	Value: 12.00				

KM# 555 10 DOLLARS
28.5000 g., Copper-Nickel, 38.6 mm. **Series:** Moments of Freedom **Obv:** National arms **Rev:** Multicolor Spartacus and troops **Edge:** Reeded

Date	Mintage	F	VF	XF	Unc	BU
2001 Proof	9,999	Value: 12.00				

KM# 556 10 DOLLARS
28.5000 g., Copper-Nickel, 38.6 mm. **Series:** Moments of Freedom **Obv:** National arms **Rev:** Multicolor Soviet tank in Prague **Edge:** Reeded

Date	Mintage	F	VF	XF	Unc	BU
2001 Proof	9,999	Value: 12.00				

KM# 557 10 DOLLARS
28.5000 g., Copper-Nickel, 38.6 mm. **Series:** Moments of Freedom **Obv:** National arms **Rev:** Multicolor Bastille scene **Edge:** Reeded

Date	Mintage	F	VF	XF	Unc	BU
2001 Proof	9,999	Value: 12.00				

KM# 558 10 DOLLARS
28.5000 g., Copper-Nickel, 38.6 mm. **Series:** Moments of Freedom **Obv:** National arms **Rev:** Multicolor Nelson Mandela and fist **Edge:** Reeded

Date	Mintage	F	VF	XF	Unc	BU
2001 Proof	9,999	Value: 12.00				

KM# 559 10 DOLLARS
28.5000 g., Copper-Nickel, 38.6 mm. **Series:** Moments of Freedom **Obv:** National arms **Rev:** Multicolor circuit board and world globe **Edge:** Reeded

Date	Mintage	F	VF	XF	Unc	BU
2001 Proof	9,999	Value: 12.00				

KM# 994 10 DOLLARS
0.9990 Gold, 12 mm. **Obv:** National Arms **Rev:** Franklin, Jefferson, Adams and Declaration of Independence

Date	Mintage	F	VF	XF	Unc	BU
2001 Proof	—	Value: 60.00				

KM# 654 10 DOLLARS
15.3300 g., Copper-Nickel, 33.2 mm. **Obv:** National arms **Rev:** "GEORGE W. BUSH..." No value at bottom **Edge:** Reeded

Date	Mintage	F	VF	XF	Unc	BU
2002	—	—	—	—	—	10.00

KM# 705 10 DOLLARS
31.1035 g., 0.9990 Silver 0.9990 oz. ASW, 38.6 mm. **Subject:** 2002 World Football Championship - Japan - South Korea **Obv:** National arms **Rev:** Pagoda superimposed on a soccer ball, legend around **Edge:** Reeded

Date	Mintage	F	VF	XF	Unc	BU
2002 Proof	—	Value: 45.00				

KM# 806 10 DOLLARS
14.3000 g., Copper-Nickel, 33.11 mm. **Obv:** National arms **Rev:** Bust of President Bush facing at left, soldier standing at right facing, flag in background **Rev. Legend:** America's Fight For Freedom **Edge:** Reeded

Date	Mintage	F	VF	XF	Unc	BU
2002	—	—	—	—	10.00	12.00

KM# 807 10 DOLLARS

26.3000 g., Copper-Nickel, 40.36 mm. **Subject:** America's First Ladies **Obv:** National arms **Rev:** Bust of Jacqueline Kennedy facing, small oval portrait of President John F. Kennedy at right **Edge:** Reeded

Date	Mintage	F	VF	XF	Unc	BU
2003 Proof	—	Value: 15.00				

KM# 824 10 DOLLARS

14.6000 g., Copper-Nickel, 33 mm. **Subject:** Abraham Lincoln **Obv:** National arms **Rev:** Bust facing at left, Lincoln Memorial in background **Edge:** Reeded

Date	Mintage	F	VF	XF	Unc	BU
2003 Proof	20,000	Value: 12.00				

KM# 708 10 DOLLARS

25.1000 g., 0.9250 Silver 0.7464 oz. ASW, 38.6 mm. **Obv:** National arms **Rev:** Clipper ship "Flying Cloud" **Edge:** Reeded

Date	Mintage	F	VF	XF	Unc	BU
2003 Proof	—	Value: 35.00				

KM# 602 10 DOLLARS

25.0000 g., 0.9250 Silver 0.7435 oz. ASW, 38.6 mm. **Obv:** National arms **Rev:** Icarus and Daedalus in flight **Edge:** Reeded

Date	Mintage	F	VF	XF	Unc	BU
2003 Proof	—	Value: 35.00				

KM# 603 10 DOLLARS

25.0000 g., 0.9250 Silver 0.7435 oz. ASW, 38.6 mm. **Obv:** National arms **Rev:** First parachute **Edge:** Reeded

Date	Mintage	F	VF	XF	Unc	BU
2003 Proof	—	Value: 35.00				

KM# 604 10 DOLLARS

25.0000 g., 0.9250 Silver 0.7435 oz. ASW, 38.6 mm. **Obv:** National arms **Rev:** Montgolfier ballon **Edge:** Reeded

Date	Mintage	F	VF	XF	Unc	BU
2003 Proof	—	Value: 35.00				

KM# 605 10 DOLLARS

25.0000 g., 0.9250 Silver 0.7435 oz. ASW, 38.6 mm. **Obv:** National arms **Rev:** Otto v. Lillenthal **Edge:** Reeded

Date	Mintage	F	VF	XF	Unc	BU
2003 Proof	—	Value: 35.00				

KM# 606 10 DOLLARS

25.0000 g., 0.9250 Silver 0.7435 oz. ASW, 38.6 mm. **Obv:** National arms **Rev:** Wright Brothers **Edge:** Reeded

Date	Mintage	F	VF	XF	Unc	BU
2003 Proof	—	Value: 35.00				

KM# 607 10 DOLLARS

25.0000 g., 0.9250 Silver 0.7435 oz. ASW, 38.6 mm. **Obv:** National arms **Rev:** Mach 1- Bell X **Edge:** Reeded

Date	Mintage	F	VF	XF	Unc	BU
2003 Proof	—	Value: 35.00				

KM# 608 10 DOLLARS

25.0000 g., 0.9250 Silver 0.7435 oz. ASW, 38.6 mm. **Obv:** National arms **Rev:** The Concorde **Edge:** Reeded

Date	Mintage	F	VF	XF	Unc	BU
2003 Proof	—	Value: 35.00				

KM# 823 10 DOLLARS

1.2300 g., Gold, 13.88 mm. **Subject:** 2006 World Football championship Gernany **Obv:** National arms **Rev:** Football at lower left, stadium at center **Rev. Legend:** DEUTSCHLAND 2006 **Edge:** Reeded

Date	Mintage	F	VF	XF	Unc	BU
2004 Proof	—	Value: 65.00				

KM# 611 10 DOLLARS

62.2070 g., 0.9990 Silver 1.9979 oz. ASW, 50 mm. **Obv:** National arms left of window design with Tiffany Glass inlay **Rev:** Window design with Tiffany Glass inlay **Edge:** Plain

Date	Mintage	F	VF	XF	Unc	BU
2004	999	—	—	—	—	200

KM# 740 10 DOLLARS

20.0000 g., 0.9990 Silver partially gilt 0.6423 oz. ASW, 38.00 mm. **Series:** Endangered Wildlife **Obv:** National arms **Obv. Legend:** REPUBLIC OF LIBERIA **Rev:** Gilt Siberian Tiger with diamonds inset in eyes **Rev. Legend:** RUSSIA **Edge:** Plain

Date	Mintage	F	VF	XF	Unc	BU
2004 Proof	5,000	Value: 175				

KM# 741 10 DOLLARS

20.0000 g., 0.9990 Silver partially gilt 0.6423 oz. ASW, 38.00 mm. **Series:** Endangered Wildlife **Obv:** National arms **Obv. Legend:** REPUBLIC OF LIBERIA **Rev:** Two gilt Hyacinth Macaws perched on branch with diamond insets in eyes **Rev. Legend:** BRAZIL **Edge:** Plain

Date	Mintage	F	VF	XF	Unc	BU
2004 Proof	5,000	Value: 175				

KM# 742 10 DOLLARS

20.0000 g., 0.9990 Silver partially gilt 0.6423 oz. ASW, 38.00 mm. **Series:** Endangered Wildlife **Obv:** National arms **Obv. Legend:** REPUBLIC OF LIBERIA **Rev:** Gilt young Giant Panda seated eating bamboo shoots **Rev. Legend:** CHINA **Edge:** Plain

Date	Mintage	F	VF	XF	Unc	BU
2004 Proof	5,000	Value: 175				

KM# 743 10 DOLLARS

20.0000 g., 0.9990 Silver partially gilt 0.6423 oz. ASW, 38.00 mm. **Subject:** Endangered Wildlife **Obv:** National arms **Obv. Legend:** REPUBLIC OF LIBERIA **Rev:** Two gilt Bald Eagles. one perched at left, one alighting at center right **Rev. Legend:** USA **Edge:** Plain

Date	Mintage	F	VF	XF	Unc	BU
2004 Proof	5,000	Value: 175				

KM# 744 10 DOLLARS
20.0000 g., 0.9990 Silver partially gilt 0.6423 oz. ASW, 38 mm. **Series:** Endangered Wildlife **Obv:** National arms **Obv. Legend:** REPUBLIC OF LIBERIA **Rev:** Gilt Puma standing with diamonds inset in eyes **Rev. Legend:** MEXICO **Edge:** Plain

Date	Mintage	F	VF	XF	Unc	BU
2004 Proof	5,000	Value: 175				

KM# 745 10 DOLLARS
20.0000 g., 0.9990 Silver partially gilt 0.6423 oz. ASW, 38 mm. **Series:** Endangered Wildlife **Obv:** National arms **Obv. Legend:** REPUBLIC OF LIBERIA **Rev:** Gilt Red-ruffed Lemur on branch with diamonds inset in eyes **Rev. Legend:** MADAGASCAR **Edge:** Plain

Date	Mintage	F	VF	XF	Unc	BU
2004 Proof	5,000	Value: 175				

KM# 746 10 DOLLARS
20.0000 g., 0.9990 Silver partially gilt 0.6423 oz. ASW, 38 mm. **Series:** Endangered Wildlife **Obv:** National arms **Obv. Legend:** REPUBLIC OF LIBERIA **Rev:** Two gilt Andean Condors, one lifting off at center, one perched at right **Rev. Legend:** CHILE **Edge:** Plain

Date	Mintage	F	VF	XF	Unc	BU
2004 Proof	5,000	Value: 175				

KM# 747 10 DOLLARS
20.0000 g., 0.9990 Silver partially gilt 0.6423 oz. ASW, 38 mm. **Series:** Endangered Wildlife **Obv:** National arms **Obv. Legend:** REPUBLIC OF LIBERIA **Rev:** Two gilt Yellow-eyed Penguins standing facing with diamonds inset in eyes **Rev. Legend:** NEW ZEALAND **Edge:** Plain

Date	Mintage	F	VF	XF	Unc	BU
2004 Proof	5,000	Value: 175				

KM# 748 10 DOLLARS
20.0000 g., 0.9990 Silver partially gilt 0.6423 oz. ASW, 38 mm. **Series:** Endangered Wildlife **Obv:** National arms **Obv. Legend:** REPUBLIC OF LIBERIA **Rev:** Gilt African lion standing facing with diamonds inset in eyes **Rev. Legend:** SOUTH AFRICA **Edge:** Plain

Date	Mintage	F	VF	XF	Unc	BU
2004 Proof	5,000	Value: 175				

KM# 749 10 DOLLARS
20.0000 g., 0.9990 Silver partially gilt 0.6423 oz. ASW, 38 mm. **Series:** Endangered Wildlife **Obv:** National arms **Obv. Legend:** REPUBLIC OF LIBERIA **Rev:** Two gilt perched Kookaburras with diamonds inset in eyes **Rev. Legend:** AUSTRALIA **Edge:** Plain

Date	Mintage	F	VF	XF	Unc	BU
2004 Proof	5,000	Value: 175				

KM# 750 10 DOLLARS
20.0000 g., 0.9990 Silver partially gilt 0.6423 oz. ASW, 38 mm. **Series:** Endangered Wildlife **Obv:** National arms **Obv. Legend:** REPUBLIC OF LIBERIA **Rev:** Gilt Polar Bear standing facing with diamonds inset in eyes **Rev. Legend:** CANADA **Edge:** Plain

Date	Mintage	F	VF	XF	Unc	BU
2004 Proof	5,000	Value: 175				

KM# 751 10 DOLLARS
20.0000 g., 0.9990 Silver partially gilt 0.6423 oz. ASW **Series:** Endangered Wildlife **Obv:** National arms **Obv. Legend:** REPUBLIC OF LIBERIA **Rev:** Gilt perched Blakiston's Fish-owl with diamonds inset in eyes **Rev. Legend:** JAPAN

Date	Mintage	F	VF	XF	Unc	BU
2004 Proof	5,000	Value: 175				

KM# 808 10 DOLLARS
14.5800 g., Copper-Nickel, 32.98 mm. **Obv:** National arms **Rev:** Bust of President Ronald Reagon facing, flag in background **Edge:** Reeded

Date	Mintage	F	VF	XF	Unc	BU
2004	—	—	—	—	8.00	10.00

KM# 830 10 DOLLARS
15.6200 g., Copper-Nickel, 33.3 mm. **Obv:** National arms **Rev:** Flag at left, bust of 43rd President George W. Bush facing at right **Edge:** Reeded

Date	Mintage	F	VF	XF	Unc	BU
2004	—	—	—	—	10.00	12.00

KM# 738 10 DOLLARS
27.1900 g., Copper-Nickel, 43 mm. **Subject:** Death of Pope John-Paul II **Edge:** Reeded

Date	Mintage	F	VF	XF	Unc	BU
2005	—	—	—	—	12.00	14.00

KM# 739.1 10 DOLLARS
25.0000 g., 0.9250 Silver 0.7435 oz. ASW **Subject:** Death of Pope John-Paul II **Rev:** Silhouette of John-Paul gilt, backgound in Ruthenium

Date	Mintage	F	VF	XF	Unc	BU
2005	7,500	—	—	—	—	60.00

KM# 739.2 10 DOLLARS
25.0000 g., 0.9250 Silver 0.7435 oz. ASW **Subject:** Death of Pope John-Paul II **Rev:** Silhouette of John-Paul gilt, blackened background

Date	Mintage	F	VF	XF	Unc	BU
2005	7,500	—	—	—	—	47.50

KM# 752 10 DOLLARS
20.0000 g., 0.9990 Silver partially gilt 0.6423 oz. ASW, 38 mm. **Series:** Endangered Wildlife **Obv:** National arms **Obv. Legend:** REPUBLIC OF LIBERIA **Rev:** Gilt Koala perched on branch with diamonds inset in eyes **Rev. Legend:** AUSTRALIA **Edge:** Plain

Date	Mintage	F	VF	XF	Unc	BU
2005 Proof	5,000	Value: 150				

KM# 753 10 DOLLARS
20.0000 g., 0.9990 Silver partially gilt 0.6423 oz. ASW, 38 mm. **Series:** Endangered Wildlife **Obv:** National arms **Obv. Legend:** REPUBLIC OF LIBERIA **Rev:** Two perched gilt Yellow-eared Conures with diamonds inset in eyes **Rev. Legend:** COLOMBIA **Edge:** Plain

Date	Mintage	F	VF	XF	Unc	BU
2005 Proof	5,000	Value: 150				

KM# 754 10 DOLLARS
20.0000 g., 0.9990 Silver partially gilt 0.6423 oz. ASW, 38 mm. **Series:** Endangered Wildlife **Obv:** National arms **Obv. Legend:** REPUBLIC OF LIBERIA **Rev:** Gilt Iberian Lynx standing facing with diamonds inset in eyes **Rev. Legend:** SPAIN **Edge:** Plain

Date	Mintage	F	VF	XF	Unc	BU
2005 Proof	5,000	Value: 150				

KM# 755 10 DOLLARS
20.0000 g., 0.9990 Silver partially gilt 0.6423 oz. ASW, 38 mm. **Series:** Endangered Wildlife **Obv:** National arms **Obv. Legend:** REPUBLIC OF LIBERIA **Rev:** Two perched gilt Yellow-crested Cockatoos **Rev. Legend:** INDONESIA **Edge:** Plain

Date	Mintage	F	VF	XF	Unc	BU
2005 Proof	5,000	Value: 150				

KM# 756 10 DOLLARS
20.0000 g., 0.9990 Silver partially gilt 0.6423 oz. ASW, 38 mm. **Series:** Endangered Wildlife **Obv:** National arms **Obv. Legend:** REPUBLIC OF LIBERIA **Rev:** Gilt Jaguar resting on branch with diamonds inset in eyes **Rev. Legend:** BELIZE **Edge:** Plain

Date	Mintage	F	VF	XF	Unc	BU
2005 Proof	5,000	Value: 150				

KM# 757 10 DOLLARS

20.0000 g., 0.9990 Silver partially gilt 0.6423 oz. ASW, 38 mm. **Series:** Endangered Wildlife **Obv:** National arms **Obv. Legend:** REPUBLIC OF LIBERIA **Rev:** Two perched gilt Plate-billed Mountain Toucans with diamonds inset in eyes **Rev. Legend:** ECUADOR **Edge:** Plain

Date	Mintage	F	VF	XF	Unc	BU
2005 Proof	5,000	Value: 150				

KM# 758 10 DOLLARS

20.0000 g., 0.9990 Silver partially gilt 0.6423 oz. ASW, 38 mm. **Series:** Endangered Wildlife **Obv:** National arms **Obv. Legend:** REPUBLIC OF LIBERIA **Rev:** Gilt Red Panda resting facing with diamonds inset in eyes **Rev. Legend:** INDIA **Edge:** Plain

Date	Mintage	F	VF	XF	Unc	BU
2005 Proof	5,000	Value: 150				

KM# 759 10 DOLLARS

20.0000 g., 0.9990 Silver partially gilt 0.6423 oz. ASW, 38 mm. **Series:** Endangered Wildlife **Obv:** National arms **Obv. Legend:** REPUBLIC OF LIBERIA **Rev:** Two perched gilt Resplendent Quetzals with diamonds inset in eyes **Rev. Legend:** GUATEMALA **Edge:** Plain

Date	Mintage	F	VF	XF	Unc	BU
2005 Proof	5,000	Value: 150				

KM# 760 10 DOLLARS

20.0000 g., 0.9990 Silver partially gilt 0.6423 oz. ASW, 38 mm. **Series:** Endangered Wildlife **Obv:** National arms **Obv. Legend:** REPUBLIC OF LIBERIA **Rev:** Gilt Snow Leopard standing left looking back with diamonds inset in eyes **Rev. Legend:** NEPAL **Edge:** Plain

Date	Mintage	F	VF	XF	Unc	BU
2005 Proof	5,000	Value: 150				

KM# 761 10 DOLLARS

20.0000 g., 0.9990 Silver partially gilt 0.6423 oz. ASW, 38 mm. **Series:** Endangered Wildlife **Obv:** National arms **Obv. Legend:** REPUBLIC OF LIBERIA **Rev:** Gilt Fossa standing right on branch facing with diamonds inset in eyes **Rev. Legend:** MADAGASCAR **Edge:** Plain

Date	Mintage	F	VF	XF	Unc	BU
2005 Proof	5,000	Value: 150				

KM# 762 10 DOLLARS

20.0000 g., 0.9990 Silver partially gilt 0.6423 oz. ASW, 38 mm. **Series:** Endangered Wildlife **Obv:** National arms **Obv. Legend:** REPUBLIC OF LIBERIA **Rev:** Two gilt Chilean Flamingos standing left with diamonds inset in eyes **Rev. Legend:** ARGENTINA **Edge:** Plain

Date	Mintage	F	VF	XF	Unc	BU
2005 Proof	5,000	Value: 150				

KM# 763 10 DOLLARS

20.0000 g., 0.9990 Silver partially gilt 0.6423 oz. ASW, 38 mm. **Series:** Endangered Wildlife **Obv:** National arms **Obv. Legend:** REPUBLIC OF LIBERIA **Rev:** Two gilt White-winged ducks, one standing, one swimming right with diamonds inset in eyes **Rev. Legend:** THAILAND **Edge:** Plain

Date	Mintage	F	VF	XF	Unc	BU
2005 Proof	5,000	Value: 150				

KM# 860 10 DOLLARS

25.0000 g., 0.9250 Silver 0.7435 oz. ASW, 38.6 mm. **Subject:** Poison frogs **Rev:** Green Frog, multicolor

Date	Mintage	F	VF	XF	Unc	BU
2005 Proof	2,500	Value: 50.00				

KM# 861 10 DOLLARS

25.0000 g., 0.9250 Silver 0.7435 oz. ASW, 38.6 mm. **Subject:** Poison frogs **Rev:** Red frog, multicolor

Date	Mintage	F	VF	XF	Unc	BU
2005 Proof	2,500	Value: 50.00				

KM# 862 10 DOLLARS

25.0000 g., 0.9250 Silver 0.7435 oz. ASW, 38.6 mm. **Subject:** Poison frogs **Rev:** Blue frog, multicolor

Date	Mintage	F	VF	XF	Unc	BU
2005 Proof	2,500	Value: 50.00				

KM# 864 10 DOLLARS

0.5000 g., 0.5850 Gold 0.0094 oz. AGW, 11 mm. **Subject:** 25th Anniversary of the Krugerrand **Obv:** Shield **Rev:** Paul Krueger bust left

Date	Mintage	F	VF	XF	Unc	BU
2005 Proof	—	Value: 35.00				

KM# 996 10 DOLLARS

62.2000 g., 0.9990 Silver 1.9977 oz. ASW, 50 mm. **Subject:** Romanesque Architecture **Rev:** Facade, Tiffany Glass insert

Date	Mintage	F	VF	XF	Unc	BU
2005 Antique finish	999	—	—	—	100	—

KM# 843 10 DOLLARS

0.7300 g., 0.9990 Gold 0.0234 oz. AGW, 11 mm. **Obv:** Arms **Rev:** John F. Kennedy head left

Date	Mintage	F	VF	XF	Unc	BU
2006 Proof	20,000	Value: 50.00				

KM# 764 10 DOLLARS

20.0000 g., 0.9990 Silver partially gilt 0.6423 oz. ASW, 38 mm. **Series:** Endangered Wildlife **Obv:** National arms **Obv. Legend:** REPUBLIC OF LIBERIA **Rev:** Gilt Crested Genet on branch facing with diamonds inset in eyes **Rev. Legend:** CAMEROON **Edge:** Plain

Date	Mintage	F	VF	XF	Unc	BU
2006 Proof	5,000	Value: 150				

KM# 765 10 DOLLARS

20.0000 g., 0.9990 Silver partially gilt 0.6423 oz. ASW, 38 mm. **Series:** Endangered Wildlife **Obv:** National arms **Obv. Legend:** REPUBLIC OF LIBERIA **Rev:** Two gilt Dalmatian Pelicans, one swimming, one standing with diamonds inset in eyes **Rev. Legend:** MONTENEGRO **Edge:** Plain

Date	Mintage	F	VF	XF	Unc	BU
2006 Proof	5,000	Value: 150				

KM# 766 10 DOLLARS

20.0000 g., 0.9990 Silver partially gilt 0.6423 oz. ASW, 38 mm. **Series:** Endangered Wildlife **Obv:** National arms **Obv. Legend:** REPUBLIC OF LIBERIA **Rev:** Gilt Hairy-bared Dwarf Lemue standing on branch with diamonds inset in eyes **Rev. Legend:** MADAGASCAR **Edge:** Plain

Date	Mintage	F	VF	XF	Unc	BU
2006 Proof	5,000	Value: 150				

KM# 767 10 DOLLARS

20.0000 g., 0.9990 Silver partially gilt 0.6423 oz. ASW, 38 mm. **Series:** Endangered Wildlife **Obv:** National arms **Obv. Legend:** REPUBLIC OF LIBERIA **Rev:** Two gilt Visayan Tarictics perched on branches with diamonds inset in eyes **Rev. Legend:** Philippines **Edge:** Plain

Date	Mintage	F	VF	XF	Unc	BU
2006 Proof	5,000	Value: 150				

KM# 768 10 DOLLARS

20.0000 g., 0.9990 Silver partially gilt 0.6423 oz. ASW, 38 mm. **Series:** Endangered Wildlife **Obv:** National arms **Obv. Legend:** REPUBLIC OF LIBERIA **Rev:** Two gilt Ethiopian Wolves, one seated, one laying with diamonds inset in eyes **Rev. Legend:** ETHIOPIA **Edge:** Plain

Date	Mintage	F	VF	XF	Unc	BU
2006 Proof	5,000	Value: 150				

KM# 769 10 DOLLARS

20.0000 g., 0.9990 Silver partially gilt 0.6423 oz. ASW, 38 mm. **Series:** Endangered Wildlife **Obv:** National arms **Obv. Legend:** REPUBLIC OF LIBERIA **Rev:** Two gilt Kakapos perched on a branch with diamonds inset in eyes **Rev. Legend:** NEW ZEALAND **Edge:** Plain

Date	Mintage	F	VF	XF	Unc	BU
2006 Proof	5,000	Value: 150				

KM# 770 10 DOLLARS

20.0000 g., 0.9990 Silver partially gilt 0.6423 oz. ASW, 38 mm. **Series:** Endangered Wildlife **Obv:** National arms **Obv. Legend:** REPUBLIC OF LIBERIA **Rev:** Gilt Spectacled Bear standing with diamonds inset in eyes **Rev. Legend:** BOLIVIA **Edge:** Plain

Date	Mintage	F	VF	XF	Unc	BU
2006 Proof	5,000	Value: 150				

KM# 771 10 DOLLARS

20.0000 g., 0.9990 Silver partially gilt 0.6423 oz. ASW, 38 mm. **Series:** Endangered Wildlife **Obv:** National arms **Obv. Legend:** REPUBLIC OF LIBERIA **Rev:** Two gilt Mauritius Kestrels perched on branch with diamonds inset in eyes **Rev. Legend:** MAURITIUS **Edge:** Plain

Date	Mintage	F	VF	XF	Unc	BU
2006 Proof	5,000	Value: 150				

KM# 772 10 DOLLARS

20.0000 g., 0.9990 Silver Partially gilt 0.6423 oz. ASW, 38 mm. **Series:** Endangered Wildlife **Obv:** National arms **Obv. Legend:** REPUBLIC OF LIBERIA **Rev:** Two gilt Mhorr Gazelles, one standing, one resting with diamonds inset in eyes **Rev. Legend:** MALI **Edge:** Plain

Date	Mintage	F	VF	XF	Unc	BU
2006 Proof	5,000	Value: 150				

KM# 773 10 DOLLARS

20.0000 g., 0.9990 Silver partially gilt 0.6423 oz. ASW, 38 mm. **Series:** Endangered Wildlife **Obv:** National arms **Obv. Legend:** REPUBLIC OF LIBERIA **Rev:** Two gilt Blue Lorikeets perched on branches with diamonds inset in eyes **Rev. Legend:** FRENCH POLYNESIA **Edge:** Plain

Date	Mintage	F	VF	XF	Unc	BU
2006 Proof	5,000	Value: 150				

KM# 774 10 DOLLARS

20.0000 g., 0.9990 Silver partially gilt 0.6423 oz. ASW, 38 mm. **Series:** Endangered Wildlife **Obv:** National arms **Obv. Legend:** REPUBLIC OF LIBERIA **Rev:** Gilt resting Arabian Leopard with diamonds inset in eyes **Rev. Legend:** SAUDI ARABIA **Edge:** Plain

Date	Mintage	F	VF	XF	Unc	BU
2006 Proof	5,000	Value: 150				

KM# 775 10 DOLLARS

20.0000 g., 0.9990 Silver partially gilt 0.6423 oz. ASW, 38 mm. **Series:** Endangered Wildlife **Obv:** National arms **Obv. Legend:** REPUBLIC OF LIBERIA **Rev:** Two gilt Hawaiian Geese standing with diamonds inset in eyes **Rev. Legend:** USA **Edge:** Plain

Date	Mintage	F	VF	XF	Unc	BU
2006 Proof	5,000	Value: 150				

KM# 827 10 DOLLARS

14.6000 g., Copper-Nickel, 33 mm. **Subject:** Abraham Lincoln **Obv:** National arms **Rev:** Bust facing 3/4 right **Edge:** Reeded

Date	Mintage	F	VF	XF	Unc	BU
2006 Proof	50,000	Value: 10.00				

KM# 725 10 DOLLARS

3.1100 g., 0.9990 Gold 0.0999 oz. AGW, 16 mm. **Obv:** National arms **Rev:** Leopard head **Edge:** Reeded

Date	Mintage	F	VF	XF	Unc	BU
2007 Proof	120	Value: 175				

KM# 734 10 DOLLARS

25.0000 g., 0.9250 Silver 0.7435 oz. ASW, 38.61 mm. **Subject:** The Black Madonna of Czestochowa **Obv:** Arms **Obv. Legend:** REPUBLIC OF LIBERIA **Rev:** 1/2 length figure of Madonna facing with child

Date	Mintage	F	VF	XF	Unc	BU
2007 Proof	1,000	Value: 70.00				

KM# 643 20 DOLLARS

15.5500 g., 0.9990 Silver 0.4994 oz. ASW, 30.4 mm. **Obv:** St. Peter's Basilica **Rev:** Bust of Pope facing **Edge:** Reeded

Date	Mintage	F	VF	XF	Unc	BU
2001S Proof	—	Value: 28.00				

KM# 650 20 DOLLARS

19.9100 g., 0.9990 Silver 0.6395 oz. ASW, 40 mm. **Obv:** National arms **Rev:** Bust of Charles Lindbergh facing and Spirit of St. Louis in background **Edge:** Reeded

Date	Mintage	F	VF	XF	Unc	BU
2001 Proof	—	Value: 40.00				

KM# 715 20 DOLLARS

20.0000 g., 0.9990 Silver 0.6423 oz. ASW, 40.3 mm. **Series:** American History **Obv:** National arms **Rev:** First Continental Congress in prayer **Edge:** Reeded

Date	Mintage	F	VF	XF	Unc	BU
2001 Proof	20,000	Value: 30.00				

KM# 716 20 DOLLARS

20.0000 g., 0.9990 Silver 0.6423 oz. ASW, 40.3 mm. **Series:** American History **Obv:** National arms **Rev:** U.S. Constitution Ratification, text in stars of folded flag **Edge:** Reeded

Date	Mintage	F	VF	XF	Unc	BU
2001 Proof	20,000	Value: 30.00				

KM# 717 20 DOLLARS

20.0000 g., 0.9990 Silver 0.6423 oz. ASW, 40.3 mm. **Series:** American History **Obv:** National arms **Rev:** Washington's Inauguration scene **Edge:** Reeded

Date	Mintage	F	VF	XF	Unc	BU
2001 Proof	20,000	Value: 30.00				

KM# 718 20 DOLLARS

20.0000 g., 0.9990 Silver 0.6423 oz. ASW, 40.3 mm. **Series:** American History **Obv:** National arms **Rev:** Appomattox Courthouse surrender scene with Lee and Grant **Edge:** Reeded

Date	Mintage	F	VF	XF	Unc	BU
2001 Proof	20,000	Value: 30.00				

KM# 719 20 DOLLARS

20.0000 g., 0.9990 Silver 0.6423 oz. ASW, 40.3 mm. **Series:** American History **Obv:** National arms **Rev:** Prohibition, hatchet, barrels and bottles destruction **Edge:** Reeded

Date	Mintage	F	VF	XF	Unc	BU
2001 Proof	20,000	Value: 30.00				

KM# 720 20 DOLLARS

20.0000 g., 0.9990 Silver 0.6423 oz. ASW, 40.3 mm. **Series:** American History **Obv:** National arms **Rev:** Cuban Missile Crisis, Castro, Khrushchev, Kennedy, missiles and map **Edge:** Reeded

Date	Mintage	F	VF	XF	Unc	BU
2001 Proof	20,000	Value: 30.00				

KM# 721 20 DOLLARS

20.0000 g., 0.9990 Silver 0.6423 oz. ASW, 40.3 mm. **Series:** American History **Obv:** National arms **Rev:** First Man on Moon, Armstrong and Lander **Edge:** Reeded

Date	Mintage	F	VF	XF	Unc	BU
2001 Proof	20,000	Value: 30.00				

KM# 722 20 DOLLARS

20.0000 g., 0.9990 Silver 0.6423 oz. ASW, 40.3 mm. **Series:** American History **Obv:** National arms **Rev:** Desert Storm, soldier, helicopter, rocket launcher etc. **Edge:** Reeded

Date	Mintage	F	VF	XF	Unc	BU
2001 Proof	20,000	Value: 30.00				

KM# 514 20 DOLLARS

31.1035 g., 0.9990 Silver 0.9990 oz. ASW, 38.2 mm. **Subject:** Bush-Cheney Inauguration **Obv:** White House **Rev:** Conjoined busts right **Edge:** Reeded

Date	Mintage	F	VF	XF	Unc	BU
2001 Proof	—	Value: 45.00				

KM# 616 20 DOLLARS

31.2000 g., 0.9990 Silver gilt 1.0021 oz. ASW, 38.7 mm. **Obv:** National arms **Rev:** Diamond studded scorpion (Scorpio) **Edge:** Reeded

Date	Mintage	F	VF	XF	Unc	BU
2002 Proof	—	Value: 60.00				

KM# 617 20 DOLLARS

31.2000 g., 0.9990 Silver gilt 1.0021 oz. ASW, 38.7 mm. **Obv:** National arms **Rev:** Diamond studded archer (Sagittarius) **Edge:** Reeded

Date	Mintage	F	VF	XF	Unc	BU
2002 Proof	—	Value: 60.00				

KM# 825 20 DOLLARS

20.0000 g., Silver, 40 mm. **Series:** America's First Ladies **Subject:** Mary Todd Lincoln **Obv:** National arms **Rev:** Bust facing slightly left at center left, oval portrait of Abraham Lincoln at right **Edge:** Reeded

Date	Mintage	F	VF	XF	Unc	BU
2003 Proof	20,000	Value: 32.50				

KM# 826 20 DOLLARS

20.0000 g., Silver, 40 mm. **Series:** History of America **Subject:** Emancipation Proclamation **Obv:** National arms **Rev:** Lincoln seated with seven politicians gathered **Edge:** Reeded

Date	Mintage	F	VF	XF	Unc	BU
2004 Proof	20,000	Value: 37.50				

KM# 634 25 DOLLARS

0.7300 g., 0.9990 Gold 0.0234 oz. AGW, 11.1 mm. **Obv:** National arms **Rev:** Joan of Arc **Edge:** Reeded

Date	Mintage	F	VF	XF	Unc	BU
2001 Proof	—	Value: 50.00				

KM# 666 25 DOLLARS

1.5200 g., Gold, 13.68 mm. **Subject:** Abraham Lincoln **Obv:** National arms **Rev:** Statue of Lincoln seated **Edge:** Reeded

Date	Mintage	F	VF	XF	Unc	BU
2001 Proof	—	Value: 80.00				

KM# 667 25 DOLLARS

0.7300 g., 0.9990 Gold 0.0234 oz. AGW, 11 mm. **Obv:** National arms **Rev:** Mount Rushmore **Edge:** Reeded

Date	Mintage	F	VF	XF	Unc	BU
2001 Proof	20,000	Value: 55.00				

KM# 995 25 DOLLARS

0.7300 g., 0.9990 Gold 0.0234 oz. AGW, 11 mm. **Obv:** National Arms **Rev:** Martin Luther King and Washington Monument

Date	Mintage	F	VF	XF	Unc	BU
2001 Proof	—	Value: 60.00				

KM# 669 25 DOLLARS

0.7300 g., 0.9990 Gold 0.0234 oz. AGW, 11 mm. **Subject:** Abraham Lincoln **Obv:** National arms **Rev:** Bust facing at right, Lincoln Memorial in background **Edge:** Reeded

Date	Mintage	F	VF	XF	Unc	BU
2002 Proof	20,000	Value: 55.00				

KM# 730 25 DOLLARS

0.0234 g., 0.9990 Gold 0.0008 oz. AGW **Obv:** Shield **Rev:** Map of Germany and stars

Date	Mintage	F	VF	XF	Unc	BU
2003B Proof	—	Value: 35.00				

KM# 804 25 DOLLARS

1.2500 g., 0.9990 Gold 0.0401 oz. AGW, 14.5 x 9 mm. **Subject:** R. M. S. Titanic - Expedition 2000 **Obv:** National arms **Obv. Legend:** REPUBLIC OF LIBERIA **Rev:** Titanic with small piece of recovered coal embedded in hull. **Edge:** Reeded **Shape:** Oval

Date	Mintage	F	VF	XF	Unc	BU
2005 Proof	—	Value: 70.00				

KM# 731 50 DOLLARS
222.0800 g., 0.9990 Silver 7.1326 oz. ASW, 80.04 mm. **Subject:** Japanese Attack on Pearl Harbor **Obv:** National arms **Obv. Legend:** REPUBLIC OF LIBERIA **Rev:** USA flag hologram at upper left, bust of Franklin D. Roosevelt facing above Japanese aircraft attacking ship in harbor **Rev. Legend:** REMEMBERING PEARL HARBOR - DECEMBER 7, 1941

Date	Mintage	F	VF	XF	Unc	BU
2001 Proof	—	Value: 250				

KM# 495 50 DOLLARS
907.0000 g., 0.9990 Silver 29.130 oz. ASW, 100 mm. **Subject:** Wreck of the Princess Louisa **Obv:** National arms and value **Rev:** Ship under sail **Edge:** Reeded **Note:** Each coin has a cob coin recovered from the wreck site encased in a hole with clear resin. Illustration reduced.

Date	Mintage	F	VF	XF	Unc	BU
2001	500	—	—	—	1,100	—

KM# 776 50 DOLLARS
93.3000 g., 0.9990 Silver partially gilt 2.9965 oz. ASW, 65.00 mm. **Series:** Endangered Wildlife **Obv:** National arms **Obv. Legend:** REPUBLIC OF LIBERIA **Rev:** Two gilt Cheetahs, one sitting, one resting with diamonds inset in eyes **Rev. Legend:** TANZANIA **Edge:** Plain

Date	Mintage	F	VF	XF	Unc	BU
2005 Proof	999	Value: 400				

KM# 726 50 DOLLARS
62.2070 g., 0.9990 Silver 1.9979 oz. ASW, 50 mm. **Obv:** National arms **Rev:** Leopard lying across a map of Africa **Edge:** Reeded

Date	Mintage	F	VF	XF	Unc	BU
2007 Proof	500	Value: 95.00				

KM# 844 100 DOLLARS
1000.0000 g., 0.9990 Silver 32.117 oz. ASW **Subject:** Tanks of World War II - T-34

Date	Mintage	F	VF	XF	Unc	BU
2008 Proof	1,000	Value: 1,500				

KM# 845 100 DOLLARS
1000.0000 g., 0.9990 Silver 32.117 oz. ASW **Subject:** Tanks of World War II - VI-Tiger

Date	Mintage	F	VF	XF	Unc	BU
2008 Proof	1,000	Value: 1,500				

KM# 846 100 DOLLARS
1000.0000 g., 0.9990 Silver 32.117 oz. ASW, 120 mm. **Obv:** Arms **Rev:** St. Paul standing, events of his life around

Date	Mintage	F	VF	XF	Unc	BU
2008 Proof	1,000	Value: 2,000				

KM# 727 2500 DOLLARS
155.5175 g., 0.9990 Gold 4.9948 oz. AGW, 60 mm. **Obv:** National arms **Rev:** Leopard lying across a map of Africa **Edge:** Reeded

Date	Mintage	F	VF	XF	Unc	BU
2007 Proof	48	Value: 7,750				

PATTERNS

Including off metal strikes

KM#	Date	Mintage	Identification	Mkt Val
Pn58	2001	—	10 Dollars. Copper-Nickel. 29.2500 g. 38.2 mm. National arms. "9-11" Flag raising scene. Plain edge.	125
Pn59	2001	—	20 Dollars. Silver Plated Base Metal. 5.3100 g. 20 mm. National arms. "9-11" Flag raising scene. Plain edge.	75.00
Pn60	2001	—	100 Dollars. Base Metal Gilt. 3.4200 g. 16 mm. National arms. "9-11" Flag raising scene. Plain edge.	50.00

LIBYA

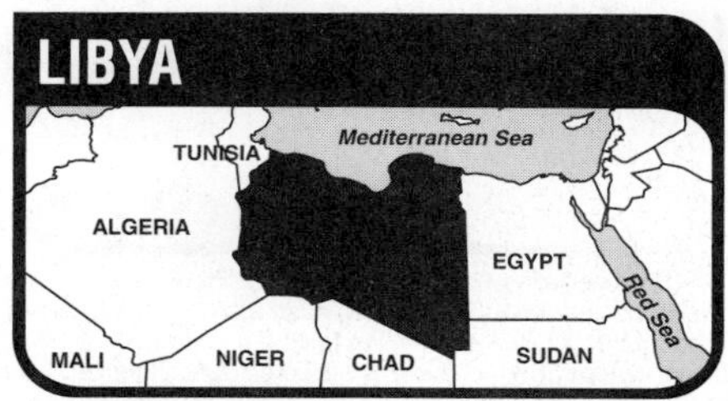

The Socialist People's Libyan Arab Jamahariya, located on the north-central coast of Africa between Tunisia and Egypt, has an area of 679,358 sq. mi. (1,759,540 sq. km.) and a population of 3.9 million. Capital: Tripoli. Crude oil, which accounts for 90 per cent of the export earnings, is the mainstay of the economy.

GREAT SOCIALIST PEOPLE'S LIBYAN ARAB JAMAHIRIYA

STANDARD COINAGE

10 Milliemes = 1 Piastre; 100 Piastres = 1 Pound

KM# 28 50 DIRHAMS
6.2500 g., Copper-Nickel, 25 mm. **Obv:** Armored equestrian **Rev:** Value at center **Shape:** Scalloped

Date	Mintage	F	VF	XF	Unc	BU
MD1377-2009	—	—	—	2.50	6.00	—

KM# 29 100 DIRHAMS
Copper-Nickel, 27 mm. **Obv:** Armored Equestrian **Rev:** Value at center

Date	Mintage	F	VF	XF	Unc	BU
MD1377-2009	—	—	—	4.50	9.00	—

KM# 30 1/4 DINAR
11.5000 g., Nickel-Brass, 28 mm. **Obv:** Armored horseman **Rev:** Value at center **Shape:** 10-sided

Date	Mintage	F	VF	XF	Unc	BU
MD1377-2009	—	—	—	9.00	12.50	—

KM# 31 1/2 DINAR
11.5000 g., Bi-Metallic Aluminum-Bronze center in Copper-Nickel ring, 30 mm. **Obv:** Armored horseman **Rev:** Value at center **Edge:** Reeded

Date	Mintage	F	VF	XF	Unc	BU
MD1377-2009	—	—	—	12.50	15.00	—

STANDARD COINAGE

1000 Dirhams = 1 Dinar

KM# 26 1/4 DINAR
11.1500 g., Nickel-Brass, 28 mm. **Obv:** Libyan knight on horse with gun 1/2 left surrounded by name of Libyan Arab Jamahiriya, ornamental legend with date **Rev:** Value in Arabic script above wheat ears in ornamented frame **Edge:** Ten alternating reeded and plain flat sections **Shape:** 10-sided

Date	Mintage	F	VF	XF	Unc	BU
MD1369	—	—	—	5.00	8.00	10.00

Note: Restruck in 2001-2002

KM# 27 1/2 DINAR
11.5000 g., Bi-Metallic Aluminumn bronze center in Copper-Nickel ring., 30 mm. **Obv:** Man on horse with gun 1/2 left, ornamental legend with date **Rev:** Value in Arabic script above wheat ears in ornamented frame **Edge:** Reeded

Date	Mintage	F	VF	XF	Unc	BU
MD1372	—	—	—	—	10.00	12.00

LIECHTENSTEIN

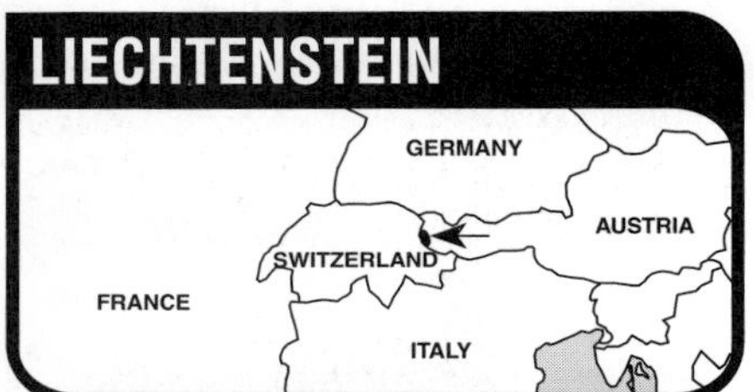

The Principality of Liechtenstein, located in central Europe on the east bank of the Rhine between Austria and Switzerland, has an area of 62 sq. mi. (160 sq. km.) and a population of 27,200. Capital: Vaduz. The economy is based on agriculture and light manufacturing. Canned goods, textiles, ceramics and precision instruments are exported.

RULERS
Prince Hans Adam II, 1990-

MINT MARKS
B - Bern

PRINCIPALITY

REFORM COINAGE

100 Rappen = 1 Frank

Y# 24 10 FRANKEN
29.9500 g., 0.9000 Silver 0.8666 oz. ASW, 37.3 mm. **Ruler:** Prince Hans Adam II **Subject:** 200 Years of Sovereignty **Obv:** Vertical inscription between crowned arms and value **Rev:** Johann I (1760-1836) **Edge:** Reeded

Date	Mintage	F	VF	XF	Unc	BU
ND (2006)B Proof	—	Value: 55.00				

Y# 25 50 FRANKEN
8.8800 g., 0.9990 Gold 0.2852 oz. AGW **Ruler:** Prince Hans Adam II **Subject:** 200th Anniversary of Sovereignty

Date	Mintage	F	VF	XF	Unc	BU
ND (2006)B Proof	—	Value: 475				

LITHUANIA

The Republic of Lithuania, southernmost of the Baltic states in east Europe, has an area of 25,174 sq. mi.(65,201 sq. km.) and a population of *3.6 million. Capital: Vilnius. The economy is based on livestock raising and manufacturing. Hogs, cattle, hides and electric motors are exported.

Lithuania declared its independence March 11, 1990 and it was recognized by the United States on Sept. 2, 1991, followed by the Soviet government in Moscow on Sept. 6. They were seated in the UN General Assembly on Sept. 17, 1991.

MODERN REPUBLIC

REFORM COINAGE

100 Centas = 1 Litas

KM# 106 10 CENTU
2.6000 g., Nickel-Brass, 17 mm. **Obv:** National arms **Rev:** Value **Edge:** Reeded

Date	Mintage	F	VF	XF	Unc	BU
2003 In sets only	—	—	—	—	—	0.60
2003 Proof	10,000	Value: 2.00				
2006	—	—	—	—	—	0.40
2006 Proof	2,000	Value: 45.00				
2007	—	—	—	—	—	0.40
2008	—	—	—	—	—	0.40
2008 Prooflike	200	—	—	—	—	5.00
2009	—	—	—	—	—	0.40
2009 Prooflike	500	—	—	—	—	20.00
2010	—	—	—	—	—	0.40

KM# 107 20 CENTU
4.8000 g., Nickel-Brass, 20.5 mm. **Obv:** National arms **Rev:** Value **Edge:** Reeded

Date	Mintage	F	VF	XF	Unc	BU
2003 In sets only	—	—	—	—	—	1.50
2003 Proof	10,000	Value: 2.00				
2007	—	—	—	—	—	1.00
2008	—	—	—	—	—	1.00
2008 Prooflike	200	—	—	—	—	5.00
2009	—	—	—	—	—	1.00
2009 Prooflike	500	—	—	—	—	3.00
2010	—	—	—	—	—	1.00

KM# 108 50 CENTU
6.0000 g., Nickel-Brass, 23 mm. **Obv:** National arms **Rev:** Value within designed circle **Edge:** Reeded

Date	Mintage	F	VF	XF	Unc	BU
2003 In sets only	—	—	—	—	—	4.00
2003 Proof	10,000	Value: 2.00				
2008	—	—	—	—	1.00	1.50
2008 Prooflike	200	—	—	—	—	30.00
2009 In sets only	5,000	—	—	—	—	10.00
2009 Prooflike	500	—	—	—	—	4.00
2010 In sets only	3,500	—	—	—	—	10.00

KM# 111 LITAS
6.2500 g., Copper-Nickel, 22.3 mm. **Obv:** National arms **Rev:** Value within circle above lined designs **Edge:** Reeded

Date	Mintage	F	VF	XF	Unc	BU
2001	—	—	—	—	1.50	2.00
2002	—	—	—	—	1.50	2.00
2003 In sets only	—	—	—	—	—	5.00
2003 Proof	10,000	Value: 8.00				
2008	—	—	—	—	1.50	2.00
2008 Prooflike	200	—	—	—	—	10.00
2009	—	—	—	—	1.50	2.00
2009 Prooflike	500	—	—	—	—	4.00
2010	—	—	—	—	1.50	2.00

KM# 137 LITAS
6.1500 g., Copper-Nickel, 22.2 mm. **Subject:** 425th Anniversary - University of Vilnius **Obv:** Knight on horse within rope wreath **Rev:** Building within court yard **Edge:** Segmented reeding

Date	Mintage	F	VF	XF	Unc	BU
2004	200,000	—	—	—	4.00	6.00

KM# 142 LITAS
6.4100 g., Copper-Nickel, 22.35 mm. **Obv:** Knight on horse within circle **Rev:** Palace **Edge:** Segmented reeding

Date	Mintage	F	VF	XF	Unc	BU
2005	1,000,000	—	—	—	4.00	5.00

KM# 162 LITAS
6.2500 g., Copper-Nickel, 22.3 mm. **Subject:** Vilnius - European Culture Capital **Obv:** National Arms **Rev:** Female figure standing at easel

Date	Mintage	F	VF	XF	Unc	BU
2009	1,000,000	—	—	—	4.00	5.00

KM# 112 2 LITAI
7.5000 g., Bi-Metallic Copper-Nickel center in Aluminum-Bronze ring, 25 mm. **Obv:** National arms within circle **Rev:** Value within circle **Edge:** Segmented reeding

Date	Mintage	F	VF	XF	Unc	BU
2001	—	—	—	—	3.00	6.00
2002	—	—	—	—	3.00	6.00
2003 In sets only	—	—	—	—	—	8.00
2003 Proof	10,000	Value: 3.50				
2008	—	—	—	—	2.25	3.00
2008 Prooflike	200	—	—	—	—	30.00
2009	—	—	—	—	3.00	6.00
2009 Prooflike	500	—	—	—	—	25.00
2010	—	—	—	—	3.00	6.00

KM# 132 5 LITAI
28.2800 g., 0.9250 Silver 0.8410 oz. ASW, 38.6 mm. **Series:** Endangered Wildlife **Obv:** Knight on horse **Rev:** Barn owl in flight **Edge Lettering:** LIETUVOS BANKAS

Date	Mintage	F	VF	XF	Unc	BU
2002 Proof	3,000	Value: 150				

KM# 113 5 LITAI
10.2600 g., Bi-Metallic Aluminum-Bronze center in Copper-Nickel ring, 22.5 mm. **Obv:** National arms within circle **Rev:** Value within circle **Edge Lettering:** PENKI LITAI

Date	Mintage	F	VF	XF	Unc	BU
2003 In sets only	—	—	—	—	—	14.00
2003 Proof	10,000	Value: 15.00				
2008 In sets only	3,800	—	—	—	—	15.00
2008 Prooflike	200	—	—	—	—	30.00
2009	—	—	—	—	5.00	7.50
2009 Prooflike	500	—	—	—	—	20.00
2010 In sets only	3,500	—	—	—	—	15.00

KM# 131 10 LITU
13.1500 g., Copper-Nickel, 28.7 mm. **Obv:** Knight on horse on shield within aerial harbor view **Rev:** Shield within city view **Edge Lettering:** KLAIPEDAI - 75 (twice)

Date	Mintage	F	VF	XF	Unc	BU
2002 Proof	5,000	Value: 25.00				

KM# 157 10 LITU
1.2440 g., 0.9990 Gold 0.0400 oz. AGW, 13.9 mm. **Obv:** Town gate **Rev:** Mathematical arc **Rev. Legend:** Sectio Aurea

Date	Mintage	F	VF	XF	Unc	BU
2007 Proof	7,000	Value: 120				

KM# 160 10 LITU
1.2400 g., 0.9990 Gold 0.0398 oz. AGW, 13.92 mm. **Obv:** Castle gate **Rev:** Geometric design

Date	Mintage	F	VF	XF	Unc	BU
2007LMK Proof	7,000	Value: 120				

KM# 169 10 LITU
11.4000 g., 0.9250 Silver 0.3390 oz. ASW, 28.7 mm. **Subject:** Lithuanian Culture - Music **Obv:** Vilnus **Rev:** Two chello and musical notations

Date	Mintage	F	VF	XF	Unc	BU
2010 Proof	10,000	Value: 45.00				

KM# 129 50 LITU
28.2800 g., 0.9250 Silver 0.8410 oz. ASW, 38.61 mm. **Subject:** Motiejus Valancius' 200th Birthday **Obv:** Knight on horse within shield above church and landscape **Rev:** Bust facing **Edge Lettering:** LIETUVISKAS ZODIS RASTAS IR TIKEJMAS TAUTOS GYVASTIS

Date	Mintage	F	VF	XF	Unc	BU
2001 Proof	2,000	Value: 200				

KM# 130 50 LITU
28.2800 g., 0.9250 Silver 0.8410 oz. ASW, 38.61 mm. **Subject:** Jonas Basanavicius (1851-1927) **Obv:** Knight on horse **Rev:** Jonas Basanavlcius **Edge Lettering:** KAD AUSRAI AUSTANT PRAVISTU IR LIETUVOS DVASIA

Date	Mintage	F	VF	XF	Unc	BU
2001 Proof	2,000	Value: 200				

KM# 134 50 LITU
28.2800 g., 0.9250 Silver 0.8410 oz. ASW, 38.6 mm. **Obv:** Knight on horse above value **Rev:** Vilnius Cathedral **Edge Lettering:** ISTORIJOS IR ARCHITEKTUROS PAMINKLAI

Date	Mintage	F	VF	XF	Unc	BU
2003 Proof	1,500	Value: 200				

KM# 135 50 LITU
28.2800 g., 0.9250 Silver 0.8410 oz. ASW, 38.6 mm. **Subject:** Olympics **Obv:** Knight on horse above value **Rev:** Stylized cyclists **Edge Lettering:** XXVIII OLIMPIADOS ZAIDYNEMS

Date	Mintage	F	VF	XF	Unc	BU
2003 Proof	2,000	Value: 140				

KM# 138 50 LITU
28.2800 g., 0.9250 Silver 0.8410 oz. ASW, 38.6 mm. **Series:** Historical Architecture **Subject:** 425th Anniversary - University of Vilnius **Obv:** Knight on horse **Rev:** Old university buildings **Edge:** Lettered **Edge Lettering:** ISTORIJOS IR ARCHITEKTUROS PAMINKLAI

Date	Mintage	F	VF	XF	Unc	BU
2004 Proof	2,000	Value: 120				

KM# 133 50 LITU
28.2800 g., 0.9250 Silver 0.8410 oz. ASW, 38.61 mm. **Series:** Historical Architecture **Obv:** Republic of Lithuania coat of arms **Rev:** Trakai Island Castle **Edge Lettering:** ISTORIJOS IR ARCHITEKTUROS PAMINKLAI

Date	Mintage	F	VF	XF	Unc	BU
2002 Proof	1,500	Value: 100				

KM# 139 50 LITU
28.2800 g., 0.9250 Silver 0.8410 oz. ASW, 38.6 mm. **Obv:** Knight on horse **Rev:** Pazaislis Monastery **Edge:** Lettered **Edge Lettering:** ISTORIJOS IR ARCHITEKTUROS PAMINKLAI

Date	Mintage	F	VF	XF	Unc	BU
2004 Proof	1,500	Value: 140				

KM# 140 50 LITU
28.2800 g., 0.9250 Silver 0.8410 oz. ASW, 38.6 mm. **Subject:** First Lithuanian Statute of 1529 **Obv:** Knight on horse **Rev:** Seated and kneeling figures **Edge:** Lettered **Edge Lettering:** "BUKIME TEISES VERGAI, KAD GALETUME NAUDOTIS LAISVEMIS"

Date	Mintage	F	VF	XF	Unc	BU
2004 Proof	1,000	Value: 200				

KM# 141 50 LITU
28.2800 g., 0.9250 Silver 0.8410 oz. ASW, 38.6 mm. **Subject:** Curonian Spit **Obv:** Knight on horse **Rev:** Shifting sand dunes design **Edge:** Ornamented pattern from Neringa emblem

Date	Mintage	F	VF	XF	Unc	BU
2004 Proof	2,000	Value: 170				

KM# 143 50 LITU
28.2800 g., 0.9250 Silver ASW 0.8410 0.8410 oz. ASW, 38.6 mm. **Series:** Historical Architecture **Obv:** Denar coin with Knight on horse **Rev:** Kernavė hill fort **Edge Lettering:** ISTORIJOS IR ARCHITEKTUROS PAMINKLAI

Date	Mintage	F	VF	XF	Unc	BU
2005 Proof	2,000	Value: 140				

KM# 147 50 LITU
28.2800 g., 0.9250 Silver 0.8410 oz. ASW, 38.6 mm. **Subject:** 1905 Lithuanian Congress **Obv:** Knight on horse **Rev:** Legend and inscription **Edge:** Ornamented

Date	Mintage	F	VF	XF	Unc	BU
2005 Proof	1,500	Value: 220				

KM# 144 50 LITU
28.2800 g., 0.9250 Silver 0.8410 oz. ASW, 38.6 mm. **Subject:** 150th Anniversary - National Museum **Obv:** Trio of ancient Lithuanian coins **Rev:** Man blowing horn **Edge Lettering:** PRO PUBLICO BONO

Date	Mintage	F	VF	XF	Unc	BU
2005 Proof	1,500	Value: 325				

KM# 145 50 LITU
28.2800 g., 0.9250 Silver 0.8410 oz. ASW, 38.6 mm. **Subject:** Knight on horse and cross **Rev:** Cardinal Vincentas Sladkevicius **Edge Lettering:** LET OUR LIFE BE BUILT ON GOODNESS AND HOPE

Date	Mintage	F	VF	XF	Unc	BU
2005 Proof	2,000	Value: 90.00				

KM# 148 50 LITU
28.2800 g., 0.9250 Silver 0.8410 oz. ASW, 38.6 mm. **Obv:** National arms on forest background **Rev:** Lynx prowling **Edge:** Stylized lynx paw prints

Date	Mintage	F	VF	XF	Unc	BU
2006 Proof	3,000	Value: 175				

KM# 149 50 LITU
28.2800 g., 0.9250 Silver 0.8410 oz. ASW, 38.6 mm. **Obv:** National arms against castle wall background **Rev:** Medininkai Castle **Edge Lettering:** ISTORIJOS IR ARCHITEKTUROS PAMINKLAI

Date	Mintage	F	VF	XF	Unc	BU
2006 Proof	2,500	Value: 200				

KM# 151 50 LITU
28.2800 g., 0.9250 Silver 0.8410 oz. ASW, 38.61 mm. **Subject:** 1831 Uprising **Obv:** Small national arms above battle scene **Obv. Legend:** LIETUVA **Rev:** Bust of Pliaterytė facing **Rev. Legend:** EMILIJA PLIATERYTĖ **Edge Lettering:** 1831 * SUKILIMAS **Designer:** Giedrius Paulauskis

Date	Mintage	F	VF	XF	Unc	BU
2006 Proof	2,500	Value: 200				

KM# 152 50 LITU
28.2800 g., 0.9250 Silver 0.8410 oz. ASW, 38.6 mm. **Subject:** XXIX Olympics 2008 - Beijing **Obv:** National arms **Obv. Legend:** LIETUVA **Rev:** Stylized swimmer right **Rev. Legend:** PEKINAS

Date	Mintage	F	VF	XF	Unc	BU
2007 Proof	5,000	Value: 150				

KM# 161 50 LITU
28.2800 g., 0.9250 Silver 0.8410 oz. ASW, 38.6 mm. **Subject:**

Panemune Castle **Obv:** Shield and fortress detail **Rev:** Castle towers

Date	Mintage	F	VF	XF	Unc	BU
2007LMK Proof	5,000	Value: 100				

KM# 153 50 LITU
28.2800 g., 0.9250 Silver 0.8410 oz. ASW, 38.6 mm. **Series:** European Cultural Heritage **Obv:** National arms surrounded by seven archaic crosses **Obv. Legend:** LIETUVA **Rev:** Circular latent image surrounded by seven archaic crosses

Date	Mintage	F	VF	XF	Unc	BU
2008 Proof	10,000	Value: 75.00				

KM# 155 50 LITU
28.2800 g., 0.9250 Silver 0.8410 oz. ASW, 38.6 mm. **Obv:** National arms **Obv. Legend:** LIETUVA **Rev:** Partial castle wall, towers **Rev. Legend:** KAUNO PILIS **Rev. Designer:** Giedrius Paulauskis

Date	Mintage	F	VF	XF	Unc	BU
2008 Proof	10,000	Value: 95.00				

KM# 154 50 LITU
28.2800 g., 0.9250 Silver 0.8410 oz. ASW, 38.6 mm. **Subject:** 550th Anniversary Birth of St. Casimer **Obv:** National arms on shield **Obv. Legend:** LIETUVA **Rev:** St. Casimer standing holding flowers **Rev. Legend:** SV. KAZIMIERAS **Rev. Designer:** Giedrius Paulauskis

Date	Mintage	F	VF	XF	Unc	BU
2008 Proof	5,000	Value: 200				

KM# 159 50 LITU
28.2800 g., 0.9250 Silver 0.8410 oz. ASW, 38.6 mm. **Subject:** Lithuania Nature **Obv:** National Arms **Rev:** Bee

Date	Mintage	F	VF	XF	Unc	BU
2008 Proof	10,000	Value: 170				

KM# 163 50 LITU
28.2800 g., 0.9250 Silver 0.8410 oz. ASW, 38.6 mm. **Subject:** Vilnius - European Culture Capital **Obv:** National Arms **Rev:** Female figure standing at easle

Date	Mintage	F	VF	XF	Unc	BU
2009 Proof	10,000	Value: 190				

KM# 164 50 LITU
28.2800 g., 0.9250 Silver 0.8410 oz. ASW, 38.6 mm. **Subject:** Tytuvenai **Obv:** National Arms in Shield **Rev:** Tytuvenai Church facade at left

Date	Mintage	F	VF	XF	Unc	BU
2009 Proof	10,000	Value: 200				

KM# 165 50 LITU
28.2800 g., 0.9250 Silver 0.8410 oz. ASW, 38.6 mm. **Subject:** Nature, Naktiziede **Obv:** Knight on horseback left **Rev:** Flowers

Date	Mintage	F	VF	XF	Unc	BU
2009LMK Proof	—	Value: 150				

KM# 170 50 LITU
28.2800 g., 0.9250 Silver 0.8410 oz. ASW **Subject:** Brazai Castle **Obv:** Viltus in shield **Rev:** Castle view and ariel plan

Date	Mintage	F	VF	XF	Unc	BU
2010 Proof	10,000	Value: 95.00				

KM# 171 50 LITU
28.2800 g., 0.9250 Silver 0.8410 oz. ASW, 38.61 mm. **Obv:** Vilnus **Rev:** Misgurnus Fossilis - European Weather Loach **Edge Lettering:** LIETUVOS GAMTA

Date	Mintage	F	VF	XF	Unc	BU
2010 Proof	10,000	Value: 75.00				

KM# 158 100 LITU
7.7800 g., 0.9990 Gold 0.2499 oz. AGW, 22.3 mm. **Subject:** Use of the Name Lithuania Millenium **Obv:** Linear National Arms **Rev:** Circular Legend

Date	Mintage	F	VF	XF	Unc	BU
2007 Proof	5,000	Value: 425				

KM# 156 100 LITU
7.7800 g., 0.9999 Gold 0.2501 oz. AGW, 22.3 mm. **Subject:** Millennium of name "Lithuania" **Obv:** Stylized national arms **Obv. Legend:** LIETUVA **Rev:** Partial parchment **Rev. Legend:** LIETUVOS DIDZIOJI KUNIGAIKSTYSTS

Date	Mintage	F	VF	XF	Unc	BU
2008 Proof	10,000	Value: 425				

KM# 166 100 LITU
7.7800 g., 0.9990 Gold 0.2499 oz. AGW, 22.3 mm. **Subject:** 1000th Anniversary of Name Lithuania **Obv:** Linear knight **Rev:** Timeline

Date	Mintage	F	VF	XF	Unc	BU
2009LMK Proof	10,000	Value: 425				

KM# 136 200 LITU
15.0000 g., Bi-Metallic .900 Gold 7.9g. center in a .925 Silver 7.1g. ring, 27 mm. **Subject:** 750th Anniversary - King Mindaugas **Obv:** Knight on horse **Obv. Legend:** LIETUVA **Rev:** Seated King **Rev. Legend:** MINDAUGO KARUNAVIMAS **Edge Lettering:** LIETUVOS KARALYSTE 1253

Date	Mintage	F	VF	XF	Unc	BU
2003 Proof	2,000	Value: 1,250				

KM# 146 500 LITU
31.1000 g., 0.9999 Gold 0.9997 oz. AGW, 32.5 mm. **Obv:** Knight on horse **Rev:** Palace **Edge:** Plain

Date	Mintage	F	VF	XF	Unc	BU
2005 Proof	1,000	Value: 1,500				

MINT SETS

KM#	Date	Mintage	Identification	Issue Price	Mkt Val
MS4	2003 (6)	10,000	KM#106-108, 111-113	7.50	35.00
MS5	2008 (9)	4,000	KM#85-87, 106-108, 111-113 KM#85-87 are dated 1991.	30.00	30.00

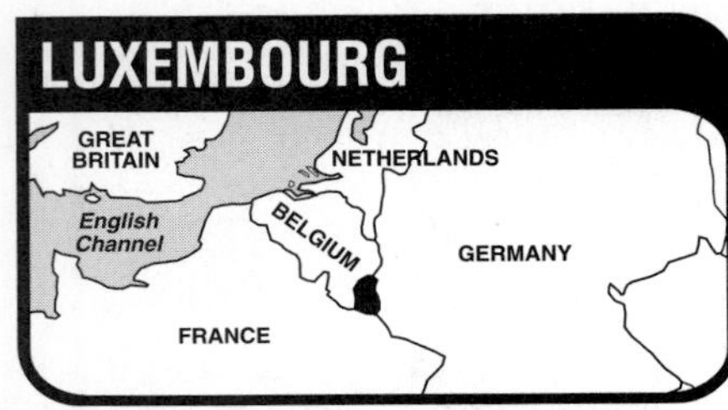

The Grand Duchy of Luxembourg is located in western Europe between Belgium, Germany and France, has an area of 1,103 sq. mi. (2,586 sq. km.) and a population of 377,100. Capital: Luxembourg. The economy is based on steel.

RULER

Henri, 2000-

MINT MARKS

A - Paris
(b) - Brussels, privy marks only
H – Gunzburg
(n) – lion - Namur
(u) - Utrecht, privy marks only

GRAND DUCHY

EURO COINAGE

European Economic Community Issues

KM# 75 EURO CENT

2.3000 g., Copper Plated Steel, 16.25 mm. **Ruler:** Henri **Obv:** Head right **Obv. Designer:** Yvette Gastauer-Claire **Rev:** Value and globe **Rev. Designer:** Luc Luycx **Edge:** Plain

Date	Mintage	F	VF	XF	Unc	BU
2002(u)	34,557,500	—	—	—	0.35	0.50
2002(u) Proof	1,500	Value: 3.00				
2003(u)	1,500,000	—	—	—	0.50	0.75
2003(u) Proof	1,500	Value: 3.00				
2004(u)	21,001,000	—	—	—	0.35	0.50
2004(u) Proof	1,500	Value: 3.00				
2005(u)	7,000,000	—	—	—	0.35	0.50
2005(u) Proof	1,500	Value: 3.00				
2006(u)	4,000,000	—	—	—	0.35	0.50
2006(u) Proof	2,000	Value: 4.00				
2007(a)	6,000,000	—	—	—	0.35	0.50
2007(a) Proof	2,500	Value: 4.00				
2008(a)	10,000,000	—	—	—	0.35	0.50
2008(a) Proof	2,500	Value: 4.00				
2009(a)	4,000,000	—	—	—	0.35	0.50
2009(a) Proof	2,500	Value: 4.00				
2010	6,000,000	—	—	—	0.35	0.50
2010 Proof	—	Value: 4.00				

KM# 76 2 EURO CENT

3.0200 g., Copper Plated Steel, 18.75 mm. **Ruler:** Henri **Obv:** Head right **Obv. Designer:** Yvette Gastauer-Claire **Rev:** Value and globe **Rev. Designer:** Luc Luycx **Edge:** Grooved

Date	Mintage	F	VF	XF	Unc	BU
2002(u)	35,917,500	—	—	—	0.50	0.75
2002(u) Proof	1,500	Value: 5.00				
2003(u)	1,500,000	—	—	—	0.65	0.85
2003(u) Proof	1,500	Value: 5.00				
2004(u)	20,001,000	—	—	—	0.50	0.75
2004(u) Proof	1,500	Value: 5.00				
2005(u)	13,000,000	—	—	—	0.50	0.75
2005(u) Proof	1,500	Value: 5.00				
2006(u)	4,000,000	—	—	—	0.50	0.75
2006(u) Proof	2,000	Value: 6.00				
2007(a)	8,000,000	—	—	—	0.50	0.75
2007(a) Proof	2,500	Value: 6.00				
2008(a)	12,000,000	—	—	—	0.50	0.75
2008(a) Proof	2,500	Value: 6.00				
2009(a)	3,000,000	—	—	—	0.50	0.75
2009(a) Proof	2,500	Value: 6.00				
2010(u)	8,000,000	—	—	—	0.50	0.75
2010(u) Proof	—	Value: 6.00				

KM# 77 5 EURO CENT

3.9000 g., Copper Plated Steel, 21.3 mm. **Ruler:** Henri **Obv:** Head right **Obv. Designer:** Yvette Gastauer-Claire **Rev:** Value and globe **Rev. Designer:** Luc Luycx **Edge:** Plain

Date	Mintage	F	VF	XF	Unc	BU
2002(u)	28,917,500	—	—	—	0.75	1.00
2002(u) Proof	1,500	Value: 7.00				
2003(u)	4,500,000	—	—	—	1.00	1.25
2003(u) Proof	1,500	Value: 7.00				
2004(u)	16,001,000	—	—	—	0.75	1.00
2004(u) Proof	1,500	Value: 7.00				
2005(u)	6,000,000	—	—	—	0.75	1.00
2005(u) Proof	1,500	Value: 7.00				
2006(u)	5,000,000	—	—	—	0.75	1.00
2006(u) Proof	2,000	Value: 8.00				
2007(a)	5,000,000	—	—	—	0.75	1.00
2007(a) Proof	2,500	Value: 9.00				
2008(a)	9,000,000	—	—	—	0.75	1.00
2008(a) Proof	2,500	Value: 9.00				
2009(a)	6,000,000	—	—	—	0.75	1.00
2009(a) Proof	2,500	Value: 9.00				
2010(u)	6,000,000	—	—	—	0.75	1.00
2010(u) Proof	—	Value: 9.00				

KM# 78 10 EURO CENT

4.0700 g., Brass, 19.7 mm. **Ruler:** Henri **Obv:** Grand Duke's portrait **Obv. Designer:** Yvette Gastauer-Claire **Rev:** Value and map **Rev. Designer:** Luc Luycx **Edge:** Reeded

Date	Mintage	F	VF	XF	Unc	BU
2002(u)	25,117,500	—	—	—	0.75	—
2002(u) Proof	1,500	Value: 14.00				
2003(u)	1,500,000	—	—	—	1.00	—
2003(u) Proof	1,500	Value: 14.00				
2004(u)	12,001,000	—	—	—	0.75	—
2004(u) Proof	1,500	Value: 14.00				
2005(u)	2,000,000	—	—	—	0.75	—
2005(u) Proof	1,500	Value: 14.00				
2006(u)	4,000,000	—	—	—	0.75	—
2006(u) Proof	2,000	Value: 14.00				

KM# 89 10 EURO CENT

4.1000 g., Brass, 19.8 mm. **Ruler:** Henri **Obv:** Prince's portrait **Obv. Designer:** Yvette Gastauer-Claire **Rev:** Relief map of Western Europe, stars, lines and value **Rev. Designer:** Luc Luycx **Edge:** Reeded

Date	Mintage	F	VF	XF	Unc	BU
2007(a)	5,000,000	—	—	—	0.75	1.00
2007(a) Proof	2,500	Value: 14.00				
2008(a)	5,000,000	—	—	—	0.75	1.00
2008(a) Proof	2,500	Value: 14.00				
2009(a)	4,000,000	—	—	—	0.75	1.00
2009(a) Proof	2,500	Value: 14.00				
2010(a)	4,000,000	—	—	—	0.75	1.00
2010(a) Proof	—	Value: 14.00				

KM# 79 20 EURO CENT

5.7300 g., Brass, 22.1 mm. **Ruler:** Henri **Obv:** Grand Duke's portrait **Obv. Designer:** Yvette Gastauer-Claire **Rev:** Value and map **Rev. Designer:** Luc Luycx **Edge:** Notched

Date	Mintage	F	VF	XF	Unc	BU
2002(u)	25,717,500	—	—	—	1.00	—
2002(u) Proof	1,500	Value: 16.00				
2003(u)	1,500,000	—	—	—	1.25	—
2003(u) Proof	1,500	Value: 16.00				
2004(u)	14,001,000	—	—	—	1.00	—
2004(u) Proof	1,500	Value: 16.00				
2005(u)	6,000,000	—	—	—	1.00	—
2005(u) Proof	1,500	Value: 16.00				
2006(u)	7,000,000	—	—	—	1.00	—
2006(u) Proof	2,000	Value: 16.00				

KM# 90 20 EURO CENT

5.7000 g., Brass, 22.3 mm. **Ruler:** Henri **Obv:** Prince's portrait **Obv. Designer:** Yvette Gastauer-Claire **Rev:** Relief map of Western Europe, stars, lines and value **Rev. Designer:** Luc Luycx **Edge:** Notched

Date	Mintage	F	VF	XF	Unc	BU
2007(a)	8,000,000	—	—	—	1.00	1.25
2007(a) Proof	2,500	Value: 16.00				
2008(a)	6,000,000	—	—	—	1.00	1.25
2008(a) Proof	2,500	Value: 16.00				
2009(a)	5,000,000	—	—	—	1.00	1.25
2009(a) Proof	2,500	Value: 16.00				
2010(a)	8,000,000	—	—	—	1.00	1.25
2010(a) Proof	—	Value: 16.00				

KM# 80 50 EURO CENT

7.8100 g., Brass, 24.1 mm. **Ruler:** Henri **Obv:** Grand Duke's portrait **Obv. Designer:** Yvette Gastauer-Claire **Rev:** Value and map **Rev. Designer:** Luc Luycx **Edge:** Reeded

Date	Mintage	F	VF	XF	Unc	BU
2002(u)	21,917,500	—	—	—	1.25	—
2002(u) Proof	1,500	Value: 18.00				
2003(u)	2,500,000	—	—	—	1.50	—
2003(u) Proof	1,500	Value: 18.00				
2004(u)	10,001,000	—	—	—	1.25	—
2004(u) Proof	1,500	Value: 18.00				
2005(u)	3,000,000	—	—	—	1.25	—
2005(u) Proof	1,500	Value: 18.00				
2006(u)	3,000,000	—	—	—	1.25	—
2006(u) Proof	2,000	Value: 18.00				

KM# 91 50 EURO CENT

7.8000 g., Brass, 24.3 mm. **Ruler:** Henri **Obv:** Prince's portrait **Obv. Designer:** Yvette Gastauer-Claire **Rev:** Relief map of Western Europe, stars, lines and value **Rev. Designer:** Luc Luycx **Edge:** Reeded

Date	Mintage	F	VF	XF	Unc	BU
2007(a)	4,000,000	—	—	—	1.25	1.50
2007(a) Proof	2,500	Value: 18.00				
2008(a)	4,000,000	—	—	—	1.25	1.50
2008(a) Proof	2,500	Value: 18.00				
2009(a)	2,000,000	—	—	—	1.25	1.50
2009(a) Proof	2,500	Value: 18.00				
2010(a)	5,000,000	—	—	—	1.25	1.50
2010(a) Proof	—	Value: 18.00				

KM# 81 EURO

7.5000 g., Bi-Metallic Copper-Nickel center in Brass ring, 23.2 mm. **Ruler:** Henri **Obv:** Grand Duke's portrait **Obv. Designer:** Yvette Gastauer-Claire **Rev:** Value and map within divided circle **Rev. Designer:** Luc Luycx **Edge:** Segmented reeding

Date	Mintage	F	VF	XF	Unc	BU
2002(u)	21,318,525	—	—	—	2.50	—
2002(u) Proof	1,500	Value: 18.00				
2003(u)	1,500,000	—	—	—	2.75	—
2003(u) Proof	1,500	Value: 18.00				
2004(u)	9,001,000	—	—	—	2.50	—

Date	Mintage	F	VF	XF	Unc	BU
2004(u) Proof	1,500	Value: 18.00				
2005(u)	2,000,000	—	—	—	2.50	—
2005(u) Proof	1,500	Value: 18.00				
2006(u)	1,000,000	—	—	—	2.50	—
2006(u) Proof	2,000	Value: 18.00				

KM# 92 EURO

7.5000 g., Bi-Metallic Copper-Nickel center in Brass ring, 23.3 mm. **Ruler:** Henri **Obv:** Prince's portrait **Obv. Designer:** Yvette Gastauer-Claire **Rev:** Relief map of Western Europe, stars, lines and value **Rev. Designer:** Luc Luycx **Edge:** Segmented reeding

Date	Mintage	F	VF	XF	Unc	BU
2007(a)	480,000	—	—	—	2.25	2.75
2007(a) Proof	2,500	Value: 24.00				
2008(a)	480,000	—	—	—	2.25	2.75
2008(a) Proof	2,500	Value: 24.00				
2009(a)	240,000	—	—	—	2.25	2.75
2009(a) Proof	2,500	Value: 24.00				
2010(a)	1,000,000	—	—	—	2.25	2.75
2010(a) Proof	—	Value: 24.00				

KM# 82 2 EURO

8.5200 g., Bi-Metallic Brass center in Copper-Nickel ring, 25.7 mm. **Ruler:** Henri **Obv:** Grand Duke's portrait **Obv. Designer:** Yvette Gastauer-Claire **Rev:** Value and map within divided circle **Rev. Designer:** Luc Luycx **Edge:** Reeded with 2's and stars

Date	Mintage	F	VF	XF	Unc	BU
2002(u)	18,517,500	—	—	—	3.75	—
2002(u) Proof	1,500	Value: 28.00				
2003(u)	3,500,000	—	—	—	4.50	—
2003(u) Proof	1,500	Value: 28.00				
2004(u)	7,553,200	—	—	—	4.00	—
2004(u) Proof	1,500	Value: 28.00				
2005(u)	3,500,000	—	—	—	4.00	—
2005(u) Proof	1,500	Value: 28.00				
2006(u)	2,000,000	—	—	—	4.00	—
2006(u) Proof	2,000	Value: 28.00				

KM# 85 2 EURO

8.5200 g., Bi-Metallic Brass center in Copper-Nickel ring, 25.7 mm. **Ruler:** Henri **Obv:** Head right and crowned monogram within 1/2 star circle **Rev:** Value and map within divided circle

Date	Mintage	F	VF	XF	Unc	BU
2004(u)	2,447,800	—	—	—	7.00	9.00
2004(u) Special Unc.	10,000	—	—	—	—	50.00
2004(u) Proof	4,000	Value: 50.00				

KM# 87 2 EURO

8.5200 g., Bi-Metallic Brass center in Copper-Nickel ring, 25.7 mm. **Ruler:** Henri **Obv:** Conjoined heads right within circle **Rev:** Value and map within divided circle **Edge:** Reeding over stars and 2's

Date	Mintage	F	VF	XF	Unc	BU
2005(u)	2,720,000	—	—	—	7.00	9.00
2005(u) Special Unc.	10,000	—	—	—	—	75.00
2005(u) Proof	4,000	Value: 50.00				

KM# 88 2 EURO

8.5000 g., Bi-Metallic Brass center in Copper-Nickel ring, 25.7 mm. **Ruler:** Henri **Obv:** Conjoined heads right within circle and star border **Rev:** Value and map within divided circle **Edge:** Reeding over 2's and stars

Date	Mintage	F	VF	XF	Unc	BU
2006(u)	1,052,000	—	—	—	7.00	9.00
2006(u) Prooflike	10,000	—	—	—	—	32.00
2006(u) Proof	4,500	Value: 50.00				

KM# 93 2 EURO

8.5000 g., Bi-Metallic Brass center in Copper-Nickel ring, 25.8 mm. **Ruler:** Henri **Obv:** Prince's portrait **Obv. Designer:** Yvette Gastauer-Claire **Rev:** Relief map of Western Europe, stars, lines and value **Rev. Designer:** Luc Luycx **Edge:** Reeded with 2's and stars

Date	Mintage	F	VF	XF	Unc	BU
2007(a)	4,000,000	—	—	—	4.00	5.00
2007(a) Proof	2,500	Value: 28.00				
2008(a)	6,000,000	—	—	—	4.00	5.00
2008(a) Proof	2,500	Value: 28.00				
2009(a)	240,000	—	—	—	6.00	7.50
2009(a) Proof	2,500	Value: 30.00				
2010(a)	3,500,000	—	—	—	4.00	5.00
2010(a) Proof	—	Value: 30.00				

KM# 94 2 EURO

Bi-Metallic Brass center in Copper-Nickel ring, 25.71 mm. **Ruler:** Henri **Subject:** 50th Anniversary Treaty of Rome **Obv:** Open treaty book with latent image on left hand page **Obv. Legend:** LËTZEBUERG **Rev:** Large value at left, modified outline of Europe at right **Edge:** Reeded with 2's and stars

Date	Mintage	F	VF	XF	Unc	BU
2007(a)	2,047,000	—	—	—	6.50	9.00
2007(a) Special Unc.	15,000	—	—	—	—	25.00
2007(a) Proof	5,000	Value: 30.00				

KM# 95 2 EURO

8.5400 g., Bi-Metallic Brass center in Copper-Nickel ring, 25.71 mm. **Ruler:** Henri **Obv:** Palace in background at left, head 3/4 left at right **Obv. Legend:** LETZEBUERG **Rev:** Large value at left, modified outline of Europe at right **Edge:** Reeded with 2's and stars

Date	Mintage	F	VF	XF	Unc	BU
2007(a)	1,000,000	—	—	—	6.50	9.00
2007(a) Special Unc.	15,000	—	—	—	—	25.00
2007(a) Proof	5,000	Value: 40.00				

KM# 96 2 EURO

8.5200 g., Bi-Metallic Brass center in Copper-Nickel ring, 25.71 mm. **Ruler:** Henri **Obv:** Head at left, Chateau de Berg at right **Obv. Legend:** LETZEBUERG **Rev:** Large value at left, modified outline of Europe at right **Edge:** Reeded with 2's and stars

Date	Mintage	F	VF	XF	Unc	BU
2008(a)	1,000,000	—	—	4.00	5.00	6.25

KM# 106 2 EURO

8.5000 g., Bi-Metallic Brass center in copper-nickel ring, 25.71 mm. **Ruler:** Henri **Subject:** 90th Anniversary of Grand Duchess Charlotte **Obv:** Conjoined busts of Charlotte and Henri

Date	Mintage	F	VF	XF	Unc	BU
2009	—	—	—	—	7.00	9.00
2009 Proof	—	Value: 15.00				

KM# 107 2 EURO

8.5000 g., Bi-Metallic Brass center in copper-nickel ring **Ruler:** Henri **Subject:** European Monetary Union - 10th Anniversary **Obv:** Stick figure and E emblem

Date	Mintage	F	VF	XF	Unc	BU
2009	—	—	—	—	5.00	6.00
2009 Proof	—	Value: 10.00				

KM# 115 2 EURO

8.5400 g., Bi-Metallic Brass center in Copper-Nickel ring, 25.75 mm. **Ruler:** Henri **Obv:** Henry head facing, crowned shield **Rev:** Large value at left, modified outline mape of Europe at right

Date	Mintage	F	VF	XF	Unc	BU
2010A	—	—	—	—	6.50	9.00

KM# 116 2 EURO

8.5000 g., Bi-Metallic Brass center in Copper-Nickel ring, 25.7 mm. **Ruler:** Henri **Subject:** Jean of Luxembourg - Nassau

Date	Mintage	F	VF	XF	Unc	BU
2011	—	—	—	—	7.00	9.00
2011 Proof	—	Value: 15.00				

KM# 84 5 EURO

6.2200 g., 0.9990 Gold 0.1998 oz. AGW, 20 mm. **Ruler:** Henri **Subject:** European Central Bank **Obv:** Grand Duke Henri **Rev:** Building

Date	Mintage	F	VF	XF	Unc	BU
2003(u) Proof	20,000	Value: 300				

KM# 108 5 EURO

Bi-Metallic Niobium center in Silver ring, 37 mm. **Ruler:** Henri **Subject:** Vianden Castle **Obv:** Head right **Rev:** Castle view

Date	Mintage	F	VF	XF	Unc	BU
2009	7,500	—	—	—	—	150

KM# 109 5 EURO

Bi-Metallic Nordic gold center in silver ring, 34 mm. **Ruler:** Henri **Subject:** Common Kestrel **Obv:** Head right **Rev:** Bird

Date	Mintage	F	VF	XF	Unc	BU
2009 Proof	3,000	Value: 60.00				

KM# 111 5 EURO

Bi-Metallic Nordic Gold center in Silver ring, 34 mm. **Ruler:** Henri **Subject:** Chateau d'Esch sur sure **Obv:** Head right **Rev:** Chateau view

Date	Mintage	F	VF	XF	Unc	BU
2010 Prooflike	3,000	—	—	—	—	100

KM# 112 5 EURO
Bi-Metallic Nordic Gold center in Silver ring, 34 mm. **Ruler:** Henri **Subject:** Flora and Fauna - Arnica Montana **Obv:** Head right **Rev:** Flowers

Date	Mintage	F	VF	XF	Unc	BU
2010 Proof	3,000	Value: 50.00				

KM# 117 5 EURO
Bi-Metallic Niobium center in .925 Silver ring **Ruler:** Henri **Subject:** Mersch Castle

Date	Mintage	F	VF	XF	Unc	BU
2011 Proof	—	Value: 100				

KM# 113 700 EURO CENTS
0.9250 Silver, 34 mm. **Ruler:** Henri **Subject:** 700th Anniversary - Marriage of John of Luxembourg

Date	Mintage	F	VF	XF	Unc	BU
2010 Proof	3,000	Value: 75.00				

KM# 97 10 EURO
3.1100 g., 0.9990 Gold 0.0999 oz. AGW, 25.71 mm. **Ruler:** Henri **Subject:** Culture **Obv:** Head right **Rev:** Hellenic sculpture head

Date	Mintage	F	VF	XF	Unc	BU
2004 Proof	5,000	Value: 175				

KM# 99 10 EURO
8.0000 g., Bi-Metallic Titanium center in silver ring, 26 mm. **Ruler:** Henri **Subject:** State Bank 150th Anniversary **Obv:** Head right **Rev:** Bank Plaza

Date	Mintage	F	VF	XF	Unc	BU
2006	7,500	—	—	—	—	150

KM# 101 10 EURO
3.1100 g., 0.9990 Gold 0.0999 oz. AGW, 16 mm. **Ruler:** Henri **Obv:** Head right **Rev:** Wild pig of Titelberg

Date	Mintage	F	VF	XF	Unc	BU
2006 Proof	5,000	Value: 175				

KM# 104 10 EURO
10.3700 g., 0.9990 Gold 0.3331 oz. AGW, 23 mm. **Ruler:** Henri **Subject:** Banque Central - 10th Anniversary **Obv:** Head right **Rev:** Old and new bank buildings

Date	Mintage	F	VF	XF	Unc	BU
2008 Proof	1,250	Value: 500				

KM# 110 10 EURO
3.1100 g., 0.9990 Gold 0.0999 oz. AGW, 16 mm. **Ruler:** Henri **Subject:** Deer of Orval's Refuge **Obv:** Head right **Rev:** Stag seated, flower in background

Date	Mintage	F	VF	XF	Unc	BU
2009 Proof	3,000	Value: 185				

KM# 114 10 EURO
Bi-Metallic .999 Titanium center in .925 Silver ring, 34 mm. **Ruler:** Henri **Subject:** Schengen Accord, 25th Anniversary **Obv:** Head right **Rev:** Building

Date	Mintage	F	VF	XF	Unc	BU
2010 Prooflike	3,000	—	—	—	—	125

KM# 118 10 EURO
14.9300 g., Bi-Metallic Nordic Gold center in .925 Silver ring, 37 mm. **Ruler:** Henri **Subject:** Flora and Fauna - Otter

Date	Mintage	F	VF	XF	Unc	BU
2011 Proof	—	Value: 50.00				

KM# 102 20 EURO
13.5000 g., Bi-Metallic Titanium center in silver ring, 34 mm. **Ruler:** Henri **Obv:** Three heads facing **Rev:** Council D'Etat building

Date	Mintage	F	VF	XF	Unc	BU
2006	4,000	—	—	—	—	120

KM# 83 25 EURO
22.8500 g., 0.9250 Silver 0.6795 oz. ASW, 37 mm. **Ruler:** Henri **Subject:** European Court System **Obv:** Grand Duke Henri **Rev:** Sword scale on law book

Date	Mintage	F	VF	XF	Unc	BU
2002(u) Proof	20,000	Value: 100				

KM# 86 25 EURO
22.8500 g., 0.9250 Silver 0.6795 oz. ASW, 37 mm. **Ruler:** Henri **Subject:** European Parliament **Obv:** Grand Duke Henri **Rev:** Parliament

Date	Mintage	F	VF	XF	Unc	BU
2004(u) Proof	20,000	Value: 100				

KM# 98 25 EURO
22.8000 g., 0.9250 Silver 0.6780 oz. ASW, 37 mm. **Ruler:** Henri **Subject:** EU Presidency **Obv:** Head right **Rev:** Conseil de l'Union building in Brussels

Date	Mintage	F	VF	XF	Unc	BU
2005 Proof	10,000	Value: 100				

KM# 100 25 EURO
22.8000 g., 0.9250 Silver 0.6780 oz. ASW, 37 mm. **Ruler:** Henri **Obv:** Head right **Rev:** European Commission building "Berlaymont" in Brussels

Date	Mintage	F	VF	XF	Unc	BU
2006 Proof	5,000	Value: 110				

KM# 103 25 EURO
22.8500 g., 0.9250 Silver 0.6795 oz. ASW, 37 mm. **Ruler:** Henri **Subject:** European Court of Auditors 30th Anniversary

Date	Mintage	F	VF	XF	Unc	BU
2007 Proof	3,000	Value: 80.00				

KM# 105 25 EURO
22.8500 g., 0.9250 Silver 0.6795 oz. ASW, 37 mm. **Ruler:** Henri **Subject:** European Investment Bank

Date	Mintage	F	VF	XF	Unc	BU
2008 Proof	4,000	Value: 275				

MINT SETS

KM#	Date	Mintage	Identification	Issue Price	Mkt Val
MS7	2002 (8)	35,000	KM#75-82	—	20.00
MS8	2002 (8)	—	KM#75-82	—	20.00
MS9	2003 (8)	50,000	KM#75-82, Adolph Brucke	—	30.00
MS10	2003 (8)	3,500	KM#75-82 plus stamps	—	75.00
MS11	2004 (8)	40,000	KM#75-82	—	50.00
MS12	2004 (8)	6,400	KM#75-82 plus stamps	—	50.00
MS13	2004 (8)	500	KM#75-82, Grand Duke	—	—
MS14	2004 (8)	500	KM#75-82, Ducal Palace	—	—
MS15	2005 (9)	20,000	KM#75-82, 87	40.00	65.00
MS16	2005 (8)	6,500	KM#75-82 plus stamps	—	55.00
MS17	2005 (8)	2,000	KM#75-82, Women and Myth, signed by Gastauer	—	75.00
MS18	2006 (9)	15,000	KM#75-82, 88	40.00	65.00
MS19	2006 (8)	2,000	KM#75-82 plus stamps	—	75.00
MS20	2007 (8)	11,000	KM#75-78, 89-93	—	50.00

PROOF SETS

KM#	Date	Mintage	Identification	Issue Price	Mkt Val
PS2	2002 (8)	1,500	KM#75-82	—	300
PS3	2003 (8)	1,500	KM#75-82	—	300
PS4	2004 (9)	1,500	KM#75-82, 85	—	300
PS5	2005 (9)	1,500	KM#75-82, 87	—	250
PS6	2006 (9)	2,000	KM#75-82, 88	—	200
PS7	2007 (10)	2,500	KM#75-77, 89-95	—	200
PS8	2008 (8)	2,500	KM#75-77, 89-93	—	250
PS9	2009 (8)	2,500	KM#75-77, 89-93	—	250
PS10	2010 (8)	2,500	KM#75-77, 89-93	—	250

MACAU

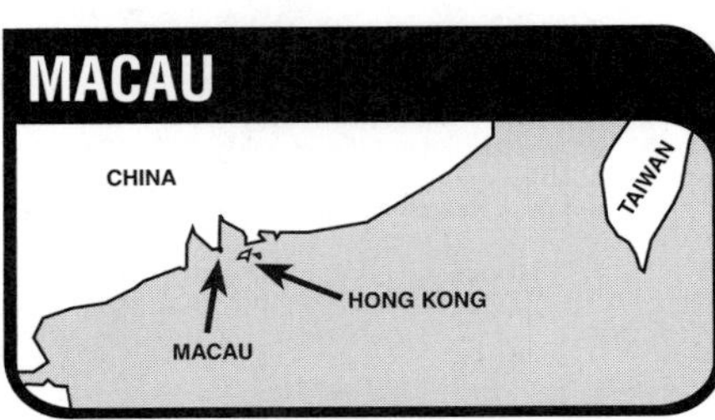

The Province of Macao, a Portuguese overseas province located in the South China Sea 40 miles southwest of Hong Kong, consists of the peninsula of Macao and the islands of Taipa and Coloane. It has an area of 6.2 sq. mi.(16 sq. km.) and a population of 500,000. Capital: Macao. Macao's economy is based on light industry, commerce, tourism, fishing, and gold trading - Macao is one of the entirely free markets for gold in the world. Cement, textiles, fireworks, vegetable oils, and metal products are exported.

In 1987, Portugal and China agreed that Macao would become a Chinese Territory in 1999. In December of 1999, Macao became a special administrative zone of China.

MINT MARKS
(p) - Pobjoy Mint
(s) - Singapore Mint

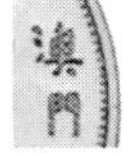
Pobjoy Mint

Singapore Mint

MONETARY SYSTEM
100 Avos = 1 Pataca

SPECIAL ADMINISTRATIVE REGION (S.A.R.)

STANDARD COINAGE

KM# 70 10 AVOS
1.3800 g., Brass, 17 mm. **Obv:** MACAU written at center with date below **Rev:** Crowned lion dance scene above value flanked by mint marks **Designer:** Justino Lei

Date	Mintage	F	VF	XF	Unc	BU
2005	—	—	—	—	0.75	1.25
2007	—	—	—	—	0.75	1.25

KM# 72 50 AVOS
4.5900 g., Brass, 23 mm. **Obv:** MACAU written across center of globe with date below **Rev:** The dragon dance led by a man **Designer:** Justino Lei

Date	Mintage	F	VF	XF	Unc	BU
2003	—	—	—	—	1.50	2.50
2005	—	—	—	—	1.50	2.50

KM# 57 PATACA
9.1800 g., Copper-Nickel, 25.98 mm. **Obv:** MACAU written across center of globe with date below **Rev:** Guia Fortress and Chapel of Our Lady of Guia **Edge:** Reeded **Designer:** Justino Lei

Date	Mintage	F	VF	XF	Unc	BU
2003	—	—	—	0.60	1.50	2.00
2005	—	—	—	0.60	1.50	2.00
2007	—	—	—	—	1.50	2.00

KM# 56 5 PATACAS
10.1000 g., Copper-Nickel **Obv:** MACAU written across center of globe with date below **Rev:** Chinese junk, ruins of St. Paul's Cathedral in background **Edge:** Plain **Shape:** 12-sided **Designer:** Justino Lei

Date	Mintage	F	VF	XF	Unc	BU
2003	—	—	—	—	6.50	10.00
2005	—	—	—	—	6.50	10.00
2007	—	—	—	—	6.50	10.00

KM# 142 20 PATACAS
31.1050 g., 0.9990 Silver 0.9990 oz. ASW, 40.7 mm. **Subject:** Year of the Rat **Obv:** A Ma Temple **Rev:** Rat, multicolor flowers at right

Date	Mintage	F	VF	XF	Unc	BU
2008 Proof	6,000	Value: 130				

KM# 145 20 PATACAS
31.1050 g., 0.9990 Silver 0.9990 oz. ASW, 40.7 mm. **Subject:** Year of the Ox **Obv:** Moorish Barracks **Rev:** Ox, multicolor flowers at right

Date	Mintage	F	VF	XF	Unc	BU
2009 Proof	—	Value: 60.00				

KM# 128 50 PATACAS
28.2800 g., 0.9250 Silver partially gilt 0.8410 oz. ASW **Subject:** 1st World Championship Grand Prix **Rev:** Two race cars - gilt

Date	Mintage	F	VF	XF	Unc	BU
2003 Proof	5,000	Value: 75.00				

KM# 102 100 PATACAS
28.2800 g., 0.9250 Silver 0.8410 oz. ASW **Subject:** Year of the Snake **Obv:** Church facade **Rev:** Snake

Date	Mintage	F	VF	XF	Unc	BU
2001 Proof	4,000	Value: 55.00				

KM# 107 100 PATACAS
28.2800 g., 0.9250 Silver 0.8410 oz. ASW, 38.6 mm. **Subject:** Year of the Horse **Obv:** Church facade flanked by stars **Rev:** Horse above value **Edge:** Reeded

Date	Mintage	F	VF	XF	Unc	BU
2002 Proof	4,000	Value: 45.00				

KM# 122 100 PATACAS
28.2800 g., 0.9250 Silver 0.8410 oz. ASW **Subject:** 5th Anniversary Return of Macao to China

Date	Mintage	F	VF	XF	Unc	BU
2004 Proof	10,000	Value: 60.00				

KM# 130 100 PATACAS
28.2800 g., 0.9250 Silver 0.8410 oz. ASW **Series:** Lunar **Subject:** Year of the Monkey

Date	Mintage	F	VF	XF	Unc	BU
2004	1,000	—	—	—	—	60.00
2004 Proof	4,000	Value: 75.00				

KM# 134 100 PATACAS
28.2800 g., 0.9250 Silver 0.8410 oz. ASW **Series:** Lunar **Subject:** Year of the Rooster **Rev:** Stylized rooster walking left

Date	Mintage	F	VF	XF	Unc	BU
2005 Proof	—	Value: 90.00				

KM# 137 100 PATACAS
28.2800 g., 0.9250 Silver 0.8410 oz. ASW **Subject:** IV East Asian Games - FRIENDSHIP

Date	Mintage	F	VF	XF	Unc	BU
2005 Proof	6,000	Value: 75.00				

KM# 139 100 PATACAS
28.2800 g., 0.9250 Silver 0.8410 oz. ASW **Series:** Lunar **Subject:** Year of the Dog **Rev:** Stylized dog standing left

Date	Mintage	F	VF	XF	Unc	BU
2006 Proof	—	Value: 90.00				

KM# 143 100 PATACAS
155.5000 g., 0.9990 Silver 4.9942 oz. ASW, 65 mm. **Subject:** Year of the Rat **Obv:** A Ma Temple **Rev:** Rat, multicolor flowers at right **Note:** Illustration reduced.

Date	Mintage	F	VF	XF	Unc	BU
2008 Proof	500	Value: 250				

KM# 146 100 PATACAS
155.5000 g., 0.9990 Silver 4.9942 oz. ASW, 65 mm. **Subject:** Year of the Ox **Obv:** Moorish Barracks **Rev:** Ox, multicolor flowers at right **Note:** Illustration reduced.

Date	Mintage	F	VF	XF	Unc	BU
2009 Proof	500	Value: 250				

KM# 123 200 PATACAS
28.2800 g., 0.9250 Silver partially gilt. 0.8410 oz. ASW **Subject:** 5th Anniversary Return of Macao to China

Date	Mintage	F	VF	XF	Unc	BU
2004 Proof	10,000	Value: 75.00				

KM# 138 200 PATACAS
28.2800 g., 0.9250 Silver partially gilt 0.8410 oz. ASW **Subject:** IV East Asian Games **Rev:** U-N-I-T-Y in blocks at left - bottom. logo at upper right

Date	Mintage	F	VF	XF	Unc	BU
2005 Proof	6,000	Value: 120				

KM# 103 250 PATACAS
3.9900 g., 0.9167 Gold 0.1176 oz. AGW **Subject:** Year of the Snake **Obv:** Church facade **Rev:** Snake

Date	Mintage	F	VF	XF	Unc	BU
2001 Proof	2,500	Value: 195				

KM# 108 250 PATACAS
3.9900 g., 0.9167 Gold 0.1176 oz. AGW, 19.3 mm. **Subject:** Year of the Horse **Obv:** Church of St. Paul facade **Rev:** Horse above value **Edge:** Reeded

Date	Mintage	F	VF	XF	Unc	BU
2002 Proof	2,500	Value: 195				

KM# 119 250 PATACAS
3.9900 g., 0.9167 Gold 0.1176 oz. AGW, 19.3 mm. **Subject:** Year of the Goat **Obv:** Church facade **Rev:** Goat above value **Edge:** Reeded

Date	Mintage	F	VF	XF	Unc	BU
2003 Proof	2,500	Value: 195				

KM# 131 250 PATACAS
3.9900 g., 0.9167 Gold 0.1176 oz. AGW **Series:** Lunar **Subject:** Year of the Monkey

Date	Mintage	F	VF	XF	Unc	BU
2004 Proof	2,500	Value: 255				

KM# 135 250 PATACAS
2.8300 g., 0.9990 Gold 0.0909 oz. AGW **Series:** Lunar **Subject:** Year of the Rooster **Rev:** Stylized rooster walking left

Date	Mintage	F	VF	XF	Unc	BU
2005 Proof	—	Value: 255				

KM# 140 250 PATACAS
3.1100 g., 0.9990 Gold 0.0999 oz. AGW **Series:** Lunar **Subject:** Year of the Dog **Rev:** Stylized dog standing left - multicolor

Date	Mintage	F	VF	XF	Unc	BU
2006 Proof	—	Value: 255				

KM# 148 250 PATACAS
7.7900 g., 0.9990 Gold 0.2502 oz. AGW **Subject:** Year of the Rat **Obv:** Temple **Rev:** Rat and multicolor flowers at right

Date	Mintage	F	VF	XF	Unc	BU
2008 Proof	—	Value: 385				

KM# 144 250 PATACAS
7.7700 g., 0.9990 Gold 0.2496 oz. AGW **Subject:** Year of the Rat **Obv:** A Ma Temple **Rev:** Rat, multicolor flowers at right

Date	Mintage	F	VF	XF	Unc	BU
2009 Proof	—	Value: 400				

KM# 147 250 PATACAS
7.7700 g., 0.9990 Gold 0.2496 oz. AGW **Subject:** Year of the Ox **Obv:** Moorish Barracks **Rev:** Ox, multicolor flowers at right

Date	Mintage	F	VF	XF	Unc	BU
2009 Proof	—	Value: 400				

KM# 104 500 PATACAS
7.9900 g., 0.9167 Gold 0.2355 oz. AGW **Subject:** Year of the Snake **Obv:** Church facade **Rev:** Snake

Date	Mintage	F	VF	XF	Unc	BU
2001 Proof	2,500	Value: 350				

KM# 109 500 PATACAS
7.9800 g., 0.9167 Gold 0.2352 oz. AGW, 22.05 mm. **Subject:** Year of the Horse **Obv:** Church facade **Rev:** Horse above value **Edge:** Reeded

Date	Mintage	F	VF	XF	Unc	BU
2002 Proof	2,500	Value: 350				

KM# 120 500 PATACAS
7.9800 g., 0.9167 Gold 0.2352 oz. AGW, 22 mm. **Subject:** Year of the Goat **Obv:** Church facade **Rev:** Goat above value **Edge:** Reeded

Date	Mintage	F	VF	XF	Unc	BU
2003 Proof	2,500	Value: 350				

KM# 129 500 PATACAS
7.9600 g., 0.9167 Gold 0.2346 oz. AGW **Subject:** 1st World Championship Grand Prix **Rev:** Two race cars

Date	Mintage	F	VF	XF	Unc	BU
2003 Proof	2,000	Value: 350				

KM# 124 500 PATACAS
62.2060 g., 0.9990 Silver partially gilt 1.9979 oz. ASW **Subject:** 5th Anniversary Return of Macao to China

Date	Mintage	F	VF	XF	Unc	BU
2004 Proof	1,000	Value: 120				

KM# 132 500 PATACAS
7.9800 g., 0.9167 Gold 0.2352 oz. AGW **Series:** Lunar **Subject:** Year of the Monkey

Date	Mintage	F	VF	XF	Unc	BU
2004 Proof	2,500	Value: 370				

KM# 136 500 PATACAS
7.9600 g., 0.9990 Gold 0.2557 oz. AGW **Series:** Lunar **Subject:** Year of the Rooster **Rev:** Stylized rooster walking left

Date	Mintage	F	VF	XF	Unc	BU
2005 Proof	—	Value: 400				

KM# 141 500 PATACAS
7.9600 g., 0.9990 Gold 0.2557 oz. AGW **Series:** Lunar **Subject:** Year of the Dog **Rev:** Stylized dog standing left

Date	Mintage	F	VF	XF	Unc	BU
2006 Proof	—	Value: 400				

KM# 105 1000 PATACAS
16.9760 g., 0.9167 Gold 0.5003 oz. AGW **Subject:** Year of the Snake **Obv:** Church facade flanked by stars **Rev:** Snake

Date	Mintage	F	VF	XF	Unc	BU
2001 Proof	4,000	Value: 775				

KM# 110 1000 PATACAS
15.9700 g., 0.9167 Gold 0.4707 oz. AGW, 28.4 mm. **Subject:** Year of the Horse **Obv:** Church facade **Rev:** Horse above value **Edge:** Reeded

Date	Mintage	F	VF	XF	Unc	BU
2002 Proof	4,000	Value: 750				

KM# 118 1000 PATACAS
28.2800 g., 0.9250 Silver 0.8410 oz. ASW, 38.6 mm. **Subject:** Year of the Goat **Obv:** Church facade **Rev:** Goat above value **Edge:** Reeded

Date	Mintage	F	VF	XF	Unc	BU
2003 Proof	4,000	Value: 45.00				

KM# 121 1000 PATACAS
15.9760 g., 0.9170 Gold 0.4710 oz. AGW **Subject:** Year of the Goat **Obv:** Church facade flanked by stars **Rev:** Goat above value **Edge:** Reeded

Date	Mintage	F	VF	XF	Unc	BU
2003 Proof	4,000	Value: 750				

KM# 125 1000 PATACAS
155.5150 g., 0.9990 Silver 4.9947 oz. ASW **Subject:** 5th Anniversary Return of Macao to China

Date	Mintage	F	VF	XF	Unc	BU
2004 Proof	3,000	Value: 310				

KM# 133 1000 PATACAS
15.9800 g., 0.9167 Gold 0.4710 oz. AGW **Series:** Lunar **Subject:** Year of the Monkey

Date	Mintage	F	VF	XF	Unc	BU
2004	500	—	—	—	775	—
2004 Proof	4,000	Value: 750				

KM# 126 2000 PATACAS
155.5150 g., 0.9990 Silver partially gilt 4.9947 oz. ASW **Subject:** 5th Anniversary Return of Macao to China

Date	Mintage	F	VF	XF	Unc	BU
2004 Proof	1,500	Value: 300				

PROOF SETS

KM#	Date	Mintage	Identification	Issue Price	Mkt Val
PS16	2001 (3)	2,500	KM#103-105	849	1,325
PS17	2002 (3)	4,000	KM#108-110	849	1,300
PS18	2003 (3)	2,500	KM#119-121	849	1,300

MACEDONIA

The Republic of Macedonia is land-locked, and is bordered in the north by Yugoslavia, to the east by Bulgaria, in the south by Greece and to the west by Albania and has an area of 9,781 sq. mi. (25,713 sq. km.) and a population at the 1991 census was 2,038,847, of which the predominating ethnic groups were Macedonians. The capital is Skopje.

On Nov. 20, 1991 parliament promulgated a new constitution, and declared its independence on Nov.20, 1992, but failed to secure EC and US recognition owing to Greek objections to use of the name *Macedonia*. On Dec. 11, 1992, the UN Security Council authorized the expedition of a small peacekeeping force to prevent hostilities spreading into Macedonia.

There is a 120-member single-chamber National Assembly.

REPUBLIC

STANDARD COINAGE

KM# 2 DENAR
5.1500 g., Brass, 23.7 mm. **Obv:** Pyrenean mountain dog **Obv. Legend:** РЕПУБЛИКА МАКЕДОНИЈА **Rev:** Radiant value **Edge:** Plain

Date	Mintage	F	VF	XF	Unc	BU
2001	12,874,000	—	0.20	0.35	1.50	4.00
2006	—	—	—	—	1.25	3.75

KM# 3 2 DENARI
5.1500 g., Brass, 23.7 mm. **Obv:** Trout above water **Obv. Legend:** РЕПУБЛИКА МАКЕДОНИЈА **Rev:** Radiant value **Edge:** Plain

Date	Mintage	F	VF	XF	Unc	BU
2001	11,672,000	—	—	0.50	1.25	3.00
2006	—	—	—	0.50	1.00	2.50
2008	—	—	—	—	1.00	2.50

KM# 4 5 DENARI
7.2500 g., Brass, 27.5 mm. **Obv:** European lynx **Obv. Legend:** РЕПУБЛИКА МАКЕДОНИЈА **Rev:** Radiant value **Edge:** Plain

Date	Mintage	F	VF	XF	Unc	BU
2001	6,921,000	—	0.35	0.75	1.75	3.50
2006	—	—	—	—	1.50	3.00
2008	—	—	—	—	1.50	3.00

KM# 13 10 DENARI
10.0000 g., 0.9160 Gold 0.2945 oz. AGW, 27 mm. **Subject:** 10th Anniversary of Independence **Obv:** Value in circle within radiant map **Rev:** Grape vine

Date	Mintage	F	VF	XF	Unc	BU
2001	1,000	—	—	—	450	475

KM# 31 10 DENARI
6.6000 g., Copper-Nickel-Zinc, 24.5 mm. **Obv:** Peacock **Rev:** Value within rays

Date	Mintage	F	VF	XF	Unc	BU
2008	—	—	—	—	—	2.00

KM# 32 50 DENARI
7.7000 g., Brass, 26.5 mm. **Obv:** Classical female bust right **Rev:** Value within rays

Date	Mintage	F	VF	XF	Unc	BU
2008	—	—	—	—	—	2.00

KM# 22 60 DENARI
6.0000 g., 0.9160 Gold 0.1767 oz. AGW, 23.8 mm. **Subject:** 100th Anniversary - Statehood **Obv:** Monument above value within circle **Rev:** Djorce Petrov

Date	Mintage	F	VF	XF	Unc	BU
2003	500	—	—	—	275	300

KM# 23 60 DENARI
6.0000 g., 0.9160 Gold 0.1767 oz. AGW, 23.8 mm. **Subject:** 100th Anniversary - Statehood **Obv:** Monument above value within circle **Rev:** Krste Petkov-Misirkov

Date	Mintage	F	VF	XF	Unc	BU
2003	500	—	—	—	275	300

KM# 24 60 DENARI
6.0000 g., 0.9160 Gold 0.1767 oz. AGW, 23.8 mm. **Subject:** 100th Anniversary - Statehood **Obv:** Monument above value within circle **Rev:** Metodije Andonov

Date	Mintage	F	VF	XF	Unc	BU
2003	500	—	—	—	275	300

KM# 25 60 DENARI
6.0000 g., 0.9160 Gold 0.1767 oz. AGW, 23.8 mm. **Subject:** 100th Anniversary - Statehood **Obv:** Monument above value within circle **Rev:** Mihailo Apostolski

Date	Mintage	F	VF	XF	Unc	BU
2003	500	—	—	—	275	300

KM# 26 60 DENARI
6.0000 g., 0.9160 Gold 0.1767 oz. AGW, 23.8 mm. **Subject:** 100th Anniversary - Statehood **Obv:** Monument above value within circle **Rev:** Blaze Koneski

Date	Mintage	F	VF	XF	Unc	BU
2003	500	—	—	—	275	300

KM# 21 60 DENARI
8.0000 g., 0.9160 Gold 0.2356 oz. AGW, 23.8 mm. **Subject:** 50th Anniversary of separation from Greece **Obv:** The Monifest **Rev:** Monastery

Date	Mintage	F	VF	XF	Unc	BU
2004	500	—	—	—	350	375

KM# 14 100 DENARI
16.0000 g., 0.9250 Silver 0.4758 oz. ASW, 32 mm. **Subject:** 100th Anniversary of Statehood **Obv:** Monument above value within circle **Rev:** Cherry tree cannon divides circle

Date	Mintage	F	VF	XF	Unc	BU
2003	500	—	—	—	700	725

KM# 14a 100 DENARI
18.0000 g., 0.9160 Gold 0.5301 oz. AGW, 32 mm. **Subject:** 100th Anniversary of Statehood **Obv:** Monument above value within circle **Rev:** Cherry tree cannon divides circle

Date	Mintage	F	VF	XF	Unc	BU
2003	500	—	—	—	775	800

KM# 15 100 DENARI
6.0000 g., 0.9160 Gold 0.1767 oz. AGW, 23.8 mm. **Subject:** 100th Anniversary of Statehood **Obv:** Monument above value within circle **Rev:** Bust facing within circle

Date	Mintage	F	VF	XF	Unc	BU
2003	500	—	—	—	275	300

KM# 16 100 DENARI
6.0000 g., 0.9160 Gold 0.1767 oz. AGW, 23.8 mm. **Subject:** 100th Anniversary of Statehood **Obv:** Monument above value within circle **Rev:** Head with hat facing within circle

Date	Mintage	F	VF	XF	Unc	BU
2003	500	—	—	—	275	300

KM# 17 100 DENARI
6.0000 g., 0.9160 Gold 0.1767 oz. AGW, 23.8 mm. **Subject:** 100th Anniversary of Statehood **Obv:** Monument above value within circle **Rev:** Head facing within circle

Date	Mintage	F	VF	XF	Unc	BU
2003	500	—	—	—	275	300

KM# 18 100 DENARI
6.0000 g., 0.9160 Gold 0.1767 oz. AGW, 23.8 mm. **Subject:** 100th Anniversary of Statehood **Obv:** Monument above value within circle **Rev:** Bust left within circle

Date	Mintage	F	VF	XF	Unc	BU
2003	500	—	—	—	275	300

KM# 19 100 DENARI
6.0000 g., 0.9160 Gold 0.1767 oz. AGW, 23.8 mm. **Subject:** 100th Anniversary of Statehood **Obv:** Monument above value within circle **Rev:** Bust right within circle

Date	Mintage	F	VF	XF	Unc	BU
2003	500	—	—	—	275	300

KM# 28 100 DENARI
7.0000 g., 0.9250 Silver 0.2082 oz. ASW **Obv:** Monument **Rev:** Jan Sandanski bust facing

Date	Mintage	F	VF	XF	Unc	BU
2003 Proof	1,000	Value: 60.00				

KM# 29 100 DENARI
7.0000 g., 0.9250 Silver 0.2082 oz. ASW **Obv:** Monument **Rev:** Nikola Karev bust facing

Date	Mintage	F	VF	XF	Unc	BU
2003 Proof	1,000	Value: 60.00				

KM# 30 100 DENARI
7.0000 g., 0.9250 Silver 0.2082 oz. ASW **Obv:** Monument **Rev:** Pitu Guli bust facing

Date	Mintage	F	VF	XF	Unc	BU
2003 Proof	1,000	Value: 60.00				

MADAGASCAR

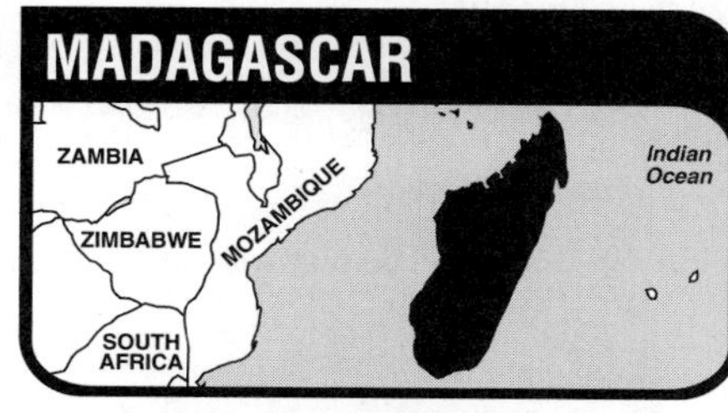

The Democratic Republic of Madagascar, an independent member of the French Community located in the Indian Ocean 250 miles (402 km.) off the southeast coast of Africa, has an area of 226,656 sq. mi. (587,040 sq. km.) and a population of 10 million. Capital: Antananarivo. The economy is primarily agricultural; large bauxite deposits are being developed. Coffee, vanilla, graphite, and rice are exported.

MONETARY SYSTEM
100 Centimes = 1 Franc

MINT MARKS
(a) - Paris, privy marks only
SA - Pretoria

MALAGASY REPUBLIC

STANDARD COINAGE

KM# 8 FRANC
2.4000 g., Stainless Steel **Obv:** Poinsettia **Rev:** Value within horns of ox head above sprigs

Date	Mintage	F	VF	XF	Unc	BU
2002(a)	—	0.15	0.20	0.40	1.45	—

REPUBLIC

Madagasikara Republic

STANDARD COINAGE

Madagasikara Republic 1 Ariary = 100 Iraimbilanja

KM# 28 10 FRANCS (2 Ariary)
4.3400 g., Bronze (Red To Yellow), 21.9 mm. **Obv:** Monkey **Obv. Legend:** BANKY FOIBEN'I MADAGASIKARA **Rev:** Value within steer horns flanked by sprigs **Edge:** Plain

Date	Mintage	F	VF	XF	Unc	BU
2003	—	—	—	1.00	2.50	3.50

KM# 29 ARIARY
4.9300 g., Stainless Steel, 22 mm. **Obv:** Flower **Obv. Legend:** BANKY FOIBEN'I MADAGASIKARA **Rev:** Value within steer horns above sprigs **Edge:** Plain

Date	Mintage	F	VF	XF	Unc	BU
2004(a)	—	—	—	0.90	2.25	3.00

KM# 30 2 ARIARY
3.2300 g., Copper Plated Steel, 21 mm. **Obv:** Plant **Obv. Legend:** BANKY FOIBEN'I MADAGASIKARA **Rev:** Value within steer horns flanked by sprigs **Edge:** Reeded

Date	Mintage	F	VF	XF	Unc	BU
2003	—	—	—	0.90	2.25	3.00

KM# 25.2 50 ARIARY
10.2600 g., Stainless Steel, 30.63 mm. **Obv:** Star above value within sprays **Rev:** Avenue of the Baobabs **Rev. Inscription:** Motto C **Edge:** Plain **Shape:** 11-sided

Date	Mintage	F	VF	XF	Unc	BU
2005	—	—	—	2.40	6.00	—

MALAWI

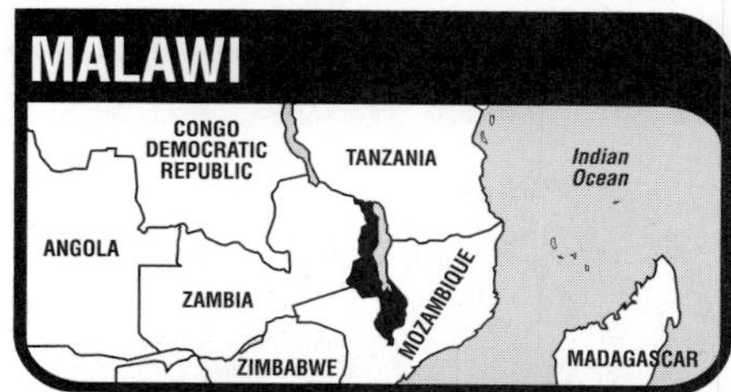

The Republic of Malawi (formerly Nyasaland), located in southeastern Africa to the west of Lake Malawi (Nyasa), has an area of 45,745 sq. mi. (118,480 sq. km.) and a population of 7 million. Capital: Lilongwe. The economy is predominantly agricultural. Tobacco, tea, peanuts and cotton are exported.

REPUBLIC

DECIMAL COINAGE

100 Tambala = 1 Kwacha

KM# 33a TAMBALA
Copper Plated Steel, 17.3 mm. **Obv:** Arms with supporters **Rev:** 2 Talapia fish **Edge:** Plain

Date	Mintage	F	VF	XF	Unc	BU
2003	—	—	—	—	1.00	1.50

KM# 34a 2 TAMBALA
Copper Plated Steel, 20.3 mm. **Obv:** Arms with supporters **Rev:** Paradise whydah bird divides date and value, designer's initials "P.V." **Edge:** Plain

Date	Mintage	F	VF	XF	Unc	BU
2003	—	—	—	—	1.00	1.50

KM# 32.2 5 TAMBALA
Nickel Plated Steel, 19.35 mm. **Obv:** Arms with supporters **Rev:** Purple heron, value, designer's initials "P.V."

Date	Mintage	F	VF	XF	Unc	BU
2003	—	—	—	—	2.50	3.00

KM# 27 10 TAMBALA
5.6200 g., Nickel Plated Steel, 23.6 mm. **Obv:** Bust right **Rev:** Bundled corn cobs divide date and value **Rev. Designer:** Paul Vincze

Date	Mintage	F	VF	XF	Unc	BU
2003	—	—	—	—	2.25	3.00

KM# 29 20 TAMBALA
7.5200 g., Nickel Clad Steel, 26.5 mm. **Obv:** Bust right **Rev:** Elephants **Rev. Designer:** Paul Vincze

Date	Mintage	F	VF	XF	Unc	BU
2003	—	—	—	—	3.75	4.50

KM# 30 50 TAMBALA
4.4000 g., Brass Plated Steel, 22 mm. **Obv:** Bust right **Rev:** Arms with supporters **Shape:** 7-sided

Date	Mintage	F	VF	XF	Unc	BU
2003	—	—	—	—	4.50	5.00

KM# 66 50 TAMBALA
4.4000 g., Brass Plated Steel, 22 mm. **Obv:** State arms and supporters with country name below **Rev:** Zebras with date above and value below **Shape:** 7-sided

Date	Mintage	F	VF	XF	Unc	BU
2004	—	—	—	—	4.50	5.00

KM# 28 KWACHA
9.0000 g., Brass Plated Steel, 26 mm. **Obv:** Bust right **Rev:** Fish eagle

Date	Mintage	F	VF	XF	Unc	BU
2003	—	—	—	—	7.00	10.00

KM# 65 KWACHA
Brass Plated Steel, 26 mm. **Obv:** State arms, country name **Rev:** Fish eagle, date

Date	Mintage	F	VF	XF	Unc	BU
2004	—	—	—	—	2.50	3.50

KM# 59 5 KWACHA
Brass, 45x27.5 mm. **Obv:** National arms, date and value **Rev:** USS Coral Sea aircraft carrier **Edge:** Plain

Date	Mintage	F	VF	XF	Unc	BU
2005 Proof	—	Value: 22.50				

KM# 62 5 KWACHA
Brass, 45x27.5 mm. **Obv:** National arms,date and value **Rev:** Ship USSR Molotov **Edge:** Plain

Date	Mintage	F	VF	XF	Unc	BU
2005 Proof	—	Value: 22.50				

KM# 63 5 KWACHA
Brass, 45x27.5 mm. **Obv:** National arms,date and value **Rev:** Ship USS Missouri **Edge:** Plain

Date	Mintage	F	VF	XF	Unc	BU
2005 Proof	—	Value: 22.50				

KM# 64 5 KWACHA
Brass, 45x27.5 mm. **Obv:** National arms,date and value **Rev:** Ship HMS Hood **Edge:** Plain

Date	Mintage	F	VF	XF	Unc	BU
2005 Proof	—	Value: 22.50				

KM# 98 5 KWACHA
29.1000 g., Copper-Nickel, 38.7 mm. **Obv:** Arms **Rev:** Pope John Paul II holding child

Date	Mintage	F	VF	XF	Unc	BU
2005 Proof	—	Value: 25.00				

KM# 44 5 KWACHA
22.0000 g., Silver Plated Copper-Nickel, 40 mm. **Subject:** Asian Zodiac Animals **Obv:** Queen Elizabeth II above Zambian arms **Rev:** Multicolor stylized rat **Edge:** Reeded

Date	Mintage	F	VF	XF	Unc	BU
2005 Prooflike	835	—	—	—	—	17.50

KM# 45 5 KWACHA
22.0000 g., Silver Plated Copper-Nickel, 40 mm. **Subject:** Asian Zodiac Animals **Obv:** Queen Elizabeth II above Zambian arms **Rev:** Multicolor stylized ox **Edge:** Reeded

Date	Mintage	F	VF	XF	Unc	BU
2005 Prooflike	835	—	—	—	—	17.50

KM# 46 5 KWACHA
22.0000 g., Silver Plated Copper-Nickel, 40 mm. **Subject:** Asian Zodiac Animals **Obv:** Queen Elizabeth II above Zambian arms **Rev:** Multicolor stylized tiger **Edge:** Reeded

Date	Mintage	F	VF	XF	Unc	BU
2005 Prooflike	835	—	—	—	—	17.50

KM# 47 5 KWACHA
22.0000 g., Silver Plated Copper-Nickel, 40 mm. **Subject:** Asian Zodiac Animals **Obv:** Queen Elizabeth II above Zambian arms **Rev:** Multicolor stylized rabbit **Edge:** Reeded

Date	Mintage	F	VF	XF	Unc	BU
2005 Prooflike	835	—	—	—	—	17.50

KM# 48 5 KWACHA
22.0000 g., Silver Plated Copper-Nickel, 40 mm. **Subject:** Asian Zodiac Animals **Obv:** Queen Elizabeth II above Zambian arms **Rev:** Multicolor stylized dragon **Edge:** Reeded

Date	Mintage	F	VF	XF	Unc	BU
2005 Prooflike	835	—	—	—	—	17.50

KM# 49 5 KWACHA
22.0000 g., Silver Plated Copper-Nickel, 40 mm. **Subject:** Asian Zodiac Animals **Obv:** Queen Elizabeth II above Zambian arms **Rev:** Multicolor stylized snake **Edge:** Reeded

Date	Mintage	F	VF	XF	Unc	BU
2005 Prooflike	835	—	—	—	—	17.50

KM# 50 5 KWACHA
22.0000 g., Silver Plated Copper-Nickel, 40 mm. **Subject:** Asian Zodiac Animals **Obv:** Queen Elizabeth II above Zambian arms **Rev:** Multicolor stylized horse **Edge:** Reeded

Date	Mintage	F	VF	XF	Unc	BU
2005 Prooflike	835	—	—	—	—	17.50

KM# 51 5 KWACHA
22.0000 g., Silver Plated Copper-Nickel, 40 mm. **Subject:** Asian Zodiac Animals **Obv:** Queen Elizabeth II above Zambian arms **Rev:** Multicolor stylized goat **Edge:** Reeded

Date	Mintage	F	VF	XF	Unc	BU
2005 Prooflike	835	—	—	—	—	17.50

KM# 52 5 KWACHA
22.0000 g., Silver Plated Copper-Nickel, 40 mm. **Subject:** Asian Zodiac Animals **Obv:** Queen Elizabeth II above Zambian arms **Rev:** Multicolor stylized monkey **Edge:** Reeded

Date	Mintage	F	VF	XF	Unc	BU
2005 Proolike	835	—	—	—	—	17.50

KM# 53 5 KWACHA
22.0000 g., Silver Plated Copper-Nickel, 40 mm. **Subject:** Asian Zodiac Animals **Obv:** Queen Elizabeth II above Zambian arms **Rev:** Multicolor stylized rooster **Edge:** Reeded

Date	Mintage	F	VF	XF	Unc	BU
2005 Prooflike	835	—	—	—	—	17.50

KM# 54 5 KWACHA
22.0000 g., Silver Plated Copper-Nickel, 40 mm. **Subject:** Asian Zodiac Animals **Obv:** Queen Elizabeth II above Zambian arms **Rev:** Multicolor stylized dog **Edge:** Reeded

Date	Mintage	F	VF	XF	Unc	BU
2005 Prooflike	835	—	—	—	—	17.50

KM# 55 5 KWACHA
22.0000 g., Silver Plated Copper-Nickel, 40 mm. **Subject:** Asian Zodiac Animals **Obv:** Queen Elizabeth II above Zambian arms **Rev:** Multicolor stylized pig **Edge:** Reeded

Date	Mintage	F	VF	XF	Unc	BU
2005 Prooflike	835	—	—	—	—	17.50

KM# 57 5 KWACHA
10.2500 g., Bi-Metallic Copper-Nickel ring and Nickel-Brass center, 27 mm. **Obv:** State arms and supporters with country name below **Obv. Legend:** MALAWI **Rev:** Fisherman at work with date above and value below **Edge:** Reeded

Date	Mintage	F	VF	XF	Unc	BU
2006	—	—	—	—	3.50	5.00

KM# 39 10 KWACHA
29.1000 g., Copper-Nickel, 38.7 mm. **Subject:** Soccer World Championship **Obv:** Arms with supporters **Rev:** Soccer players **Edge:** Reeded

Date	Mintage	F	VF	XF	Unc	BU
2002 Proof	—	Value: 50.00				

KM# 42 10 KWACHA
19.7400 g., 0.9990 Silver 0.6340 oz. ASW, 29.9 mm. **Subject:** XXVII Olympic Games - Athens 2004 **Obv:** Arms with supporters divides date **Obv. Legend:** REPUBLIC OF MALAWI **Rev:** Two rowers within circle flanked by sprigs **Edge:** Reeded

Date	Mintage	F	VF	XF	Unc	BU
2003 Proof	—	Value: 40.00				

KM# 80 10 KWACHA
24.0000 g., 0.9990 Silver 0.7708 oz. ASW, 38.5 mm. **Obv:** Arms **Rev:** Pope John Paul II in mitre and vestments

Date	Mintage	F	VF	XF	Unc	BU
2003 Proof	—	Value: 27.50				

KM# 102 10 KWACHA
19.3000 g., Silver, 38 mm. **Subject:** Antelopes of Africa **Obv:** National arms **Rev:** Eland

Date	Mintage	F	VF	XF	Unc	BU
2003 Proof	—	Value: 22.50				

KM# 103 10 KWACHA
19.3000 g., Silver, 38 mm. **Subject:** Antelopes of Africa **Obv:** National Arms **Rev:** Nyala

Date	Mintage	F	VF	XF	Unc	BU
2003 Proof	—	Value: 22.50				

KM# 104 10 KWACHA
19.3000 g., Silver, 38 mm. **Subject:** Antelopes of Africa **Obv:** National Arms **Rev:** Springbok

Date	Mintage	F	VF	XF	Unc	BU
2003 Proof	—	Value: 22.50				

KM# 105 10 KWACHA
19.3000 g., Silver, 38 mm. **Subject:** Antelopes of Africa **Obv:** National Arms **Rev:** Kudu

Date	Mintage	F	VF	XF	Unc	BU
2003 Proof	—	Value: 22.50				

KM# 106 10 KWACHA
19.3000 g., Silver, 38 mm. **Subject:** Antelopes of Africa **Obv:** National Arms **Rev:** Sable pair

Date	Mintage	F	VF	XF	Unc	BU
2003 Proof	—	Value: 22.50				

KM# 107 10 KWACHA
Bronze gilt **Obv:** Natural Arms **Rev:** John Paul II in mitre and vestments

Date	Mintage	F	VF	XF	Unc	BU
2003 Proof	—	Value: 7.50				

KM# 61 10 KWACHA
29.1500 g., Copper-Nickel silver plated, 38.7 mm. **Subject:** Endangered Wildlife **Obv:** National arms **Rev:** Multicolor Leopard with cub **Edge:** Reeded

Date	Mintage	F	VF	XF	Unc	BU
2004 Proof	—	Value: 10.00				

KM# 86 10 KWACHA
29.1500 g., Copper-Nickel silver plated, 38.7 mm. **Subject:** Endangered Wildlife **Obv:** National arms **Rev:** Multicolor Lion and cub **Edge:** Reeded

Date	Mintage	F	VF	XF	Unc	BU
2004 Proof	—	Value: 10.00				

KM# 60 10 KWACHA
29.1500 g., Copper-Nickel silver plated, 38.7 mm. **Subject:** Endangered Wildlife **Obv:** National arms **Rev:** Multicolor Zebra and colt **Edge:** Reeded

Date	Mintage	F	VF	XF	Unc	BU
2004 Proof	—	Value: 10.00				

KM# 84 10 KWACHA
29.1400 g., Copper-Nickel, 38.7 mm. **Obv:** National arms **Rev:** Multicolor elephant and calf **Edge:** Reeded

Date	Mintage	F	VF	XF	Unc	BU
2004 Proof	—	Value: 10.00				

KM# 89 10 KWACHA
29.1500 g., Copper-Nickel silver plated, 38.7 mm. **Obv:** National arms **Rev:** Multicolor Deer and fawn **Edge:** Reeded

Date	Mintage	F	VF	XF	Unc	BU
2004 Proof	—	Value: 10.00				

KM# 90 10 KWACHA
29.1500 g., Copper-Nickel silver plated, 38.7 mm. **Obv:** National arms **Rev:** Multicolor Giraffe and her calf **Edge:** Reeded

Date	Mintage	F	VF	XF	Unc	BU
2004 Proof	—	Value: 10.00				

KM# 81 10 KWACHA
Copper-Nickel silver plated **Obv:** Arms **Rev:** Chevrotain advancing left

Date	Mintage	F	VF	XF	Unc	BU
2005 Proof	—	Value: 12.50				

KM# 82 10 KWACHA
Copper-Nickel silver plated **Obv:** Arms **Rev:** Lemur on branch

Date	Mintage	F	VF	XF	Unc	BU
2005 Proof	—	Value: 12.50				

KM# 83 10 KWACHA
Copper-Nickel silver plated **Obv:** Arms **Rev:** Pigmy Hippo

Date	Mintage	F	VF	XF	Unc	BU
2005 Proof	—	Value: 12.50				

KM# 88 10 KWACHA
Copper-Nickel **Obv:** Arms **Rev:** Oryx in photo insert

Date	Mintage	F	VF	XF	Unc	BU
2005	—	—	—	—	—	20.00

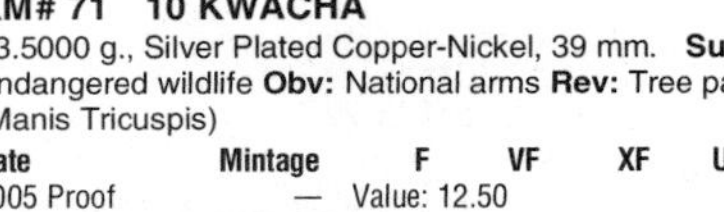

KM# 71 10 KWACHA
23.5000 g., Silver Plated Copper-Nickel, 39 mm. **Subject:** Endangered wildlife **Obv:** National arms **Rev:** Tree pangolin (Manis Tricuspis)

Date	Mintage	F	VF	XF	Unc	BU
2005 Proof	—	Value: 12.50				

KM# 87 10 KWACHA
Copper-Nickel **Obv:** Arms **Rev:** Monkies in photo insert

Date	Mintage	F	VF	XF	Unc	BU
2005 Proof	—	Value: 12.50				

KM# 58 10 KWACHA
15.1000 g., Bi-Metallic Copper-Nickel center with Nickel-Brass ring, 28 mm. **Obv:** State arms and supporters with country name below **Obv. Legend:** MALAWI **Rev:** Farm worker harvesting **Edge:** Coarse reeding

Date	Mintage	F	VF	XF	Unc	BU
2006	—	—	—	—	4.50	6.00

KM# 99 10 KWACHA
0.9990 Silver, 20x40 mm. **Obv:** Arms **Rev:** deRutter painting of ships

Date	Mintage	F	VF	XF	Unc	BU
2007 Proof	—	Value: 45.00				

KM# 100 10 KWACHA
Silver, 38.6 mm. **Obv:** Arms **Rev:** Puccini colorized

Date	Mintage	F	VF	XF	Unc	BU
2007 Proof	—	Value: 40.00				

KM# 110 10 KWACHA
62.2000 g., 0.9990 Silver 1.9977 oz. ASW, 42x42 mm. **Rev:** Lion with two crystal eyes

Date	Mintage	F	VF	XF	Unc	BU
2009 Proof	2,500	Value: 135				

KM# 91 10 KWACHA
23.5000 g., Silver Plated Copper-Nickel, 39 mm. **Subject:** Endangered Frogs - Blue Poison Arrowfrog **Rev:** Multicolor blue frog right

Date	Mintage	F	VF	XF	Unc	BU
2010 Proof	—	Value: 20.00				

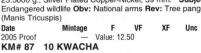

KM# 92 10 KWACHA
23.5000 g., Silver Plated Copper-Nickel, 39 mm. **Subject:** Endangered Frogs - Dyeing Poison Arrow frog **Rev:** Multicolor blue frog left

Date	Mintage	F	VF	XF	Unc	BU
2010 Proof	—	Value: 20.00				

KM# 93 10 KWACHA
23.5000 g., Silver Plated Copper-Nickel, 39 mm. **Subject:** Endangered Frogs - Darwin Frog **Rev:** Multicolor green frog right

Date	Mintage	F	VF	XF	Unc	BU
2010 Proof	—	Value: 20.00				

KM# 94 10 KWACHA
23.5000 g., Silver Plated Copper-Nickel, 39 mm. **Subject:** Endangered Frogs - Panamanian Spotted frog **Rev:** Multicolor orange and black frog

Date	Mintage	F	VF	XF	Unc	BU
2010 Proof	—	Value: 20.00				

KM# 95 10 KWACHA
23.5000 g., Silver Plated Copper-Nickel, 39 mm. **Subject:** Endangered Frogs - Purple frog **Rev:** Multicolor purple frog left

Date	Mintage	F	VF	XF	Unc	BU
2010 Proof	—	Value: 20.00				

KM# 96 10 KWACHA
23.5000 g., Silver Plated Copper-Nickel, 39 mm. **Subject:** Endangered Frogs - Carnileri Harlequin **Rev:** Multicolor red frog left

Date	Mintage	F	VF	XF	Unc	BU
2010 Proof	—	Value: 20.00				

KM# 97 10 KWACHA
23.5000 g., Silver Plated Copper-Nickel, 39 mm. **Subject:** Endangered Frogs - Tree frog **Rev:** Multicolor tree frog

Date	Mintage	F	VF	XF	Unc	BU
2010 Proof	—	Value: 20.00				

KM# 56 20 KWACHA
31.1000 g., 0.9990 Silver 0.9988 oz. ASW, 38.6 mm. **Series:** The Big Five **Obv:** National arms **Rev:** Two water buffalo on green malachite center insert **Edge:** Plain

Date	Mintage	F	VF	XF	Unc	BU
2004 Proof	3,000	Value: 55.00				

KM# 67 20 KWACHA
31.1000 g., 0.9990 Silver 0.9988 oz. ASW, 38.6 mm. **Series:** The Big Five **Obv:** National arms **Rev:** Elephant family on Haematite (blood stone) center insert **Edge:** Plain

Date	Mintage	F	VF	XF	Unc	BU
2004 Proof	3,000	Value: 55.00				

KM# 68 20 KWACHA
31.1000 g., 0.9990 Silver 0.9988 oz. ASW, 38.6 mm. **Series:** The Big Five **Obv:** National arms **Rev:** Leopard family on hawk or falcon-eye center insert **Edge:** Plain

Date	Mintage	F	VF	XF	Unc	BU
2004 Proof	3,000	Value: 55.00				

KM# 69 20 KWACHA
31.1000 g., 0.9990 Silver 0.9988 oz. ASW, 38.6 mm. **Series:** The Big Five **Obv:** National arms **Rev:** Lion family on tiger-eye center insert **Edge:** Plain

Date	Mintage	F	VF	XF	Unc	BU
2004 Proof	3,000	Value: 55.00				

KM# 70 20 KWACHA
31.1000 g., 0.9990 Silver 0.9988 oz. ASW, 38.6 mm. **Series:** The Big Five **Obv:** National arms **Rev:** Rhinoceros family on heliotrope center insert **Edge:** Plain

Date	Mintage	F	VF	XF	Unc	BU
2004 Proof	3,000	Value: 55.00				

KM# 74 20 KWACHA
0.5000 g., 0.9990 Gold 0.0161 oz. AGW **Subject:** Springbnok, 40 years, first design

Date	Mintage	F	VF	XF	Unc	BU
2007 Proof	—	Value: 70.00				

KM# 75 20 KWACHA
0.5000 g., 0.9990 Gold 0.0161 oz. AGW **Subject:** Springbok, 40th Anniversary, second desgin

Date	Mintage	F	VF	XF	Unc	BU
2007 Proof	—	Value: 70.00				

KM# 76 20 KWACHA
0.5000 g., 0.9990 Gold 0.0161 oz. AGW **Subject:** Springbok, 40th Anniversary, third design

Date	Mintage	F	VF	XF	Unc	BU
2007 Proof	—	Value: 70.00				

KM# 111 20 KWACHA
28.2800 g., 0.9250 Silver 0.8410 oz. ASW, 38.61 mm. **Subject:** Biosphere Reserves **Obv:** National Arms **Rev:** Goat on hillside, multicolor flower

Date	Mintage	F	VF	XF	Unc	BU
2010 Proof	8,000	Value: 60.00				

KM# 77 40 KWACHA
1.0000 g., 0.9990 Gold 0.0321 oz. AGW **Rev:** Springbok

Date	Mintage	F	VF	XF	Unc	BU
2008 Proof	—	Value: 100				

KM# 78 40 KWACHA
1.0000 g., 0.9990 Palladium 0.0321 oz. **Rev:** Springbok

Date	Mintage	F	VF	XF	Unc	BU
2008 Proof	—	Value: 75.00				

KM# 79 40 KWACHA
1.0000 g., 0.9990 Platinum 0.0321 oz. APW **Rev:** Springbok

Date	Mintage	F	VF	XF	Unc	BU
2008 Proof	—	Value: 125				

KM# 43 50 KWACHA
141.2100 g., Bronze with Gold Plated center and Silver Plated ring, 65 mm. **Subject:** Republic of China **Obv:** Large building above value within circle **Rev:** Conjoined busts facing within circle **Edge:** Reeded **Note:** Illustration reduced.

Date	Mintage	F	VF	XF	Unc	BU
2004 Proof	1,000	Value: 85.00				

KM# 108 50 KWACHA
Silver **Obv:** National Arms **Rev:** Soccer ball in flight from Germany to South Africa

Date	Mintage	F	VF	XF	Unc	BU
2006 Proof	—	Value: 45.00				

KM# 109 50 KWACHA
Silver **Obv:** National Arms **Rev:** Two female hurdlers

Date	Mintage	F	VF	XF	Unc	BU
2008 Proof	—	Value: 45.00				

KM# 85 50 KWACHA
62.2100 g., 0.9990 Silver 1.9980 oz. ASW, 42x42 mm. **Obv:** Arms **Rev:** White lion with crystal inserts in eyes **Shape:** Square

Date	Mintage	F	VF	XF	Unc	BU
2009 Proof	2,500	Value: 175				

PATTERNS

Including off metal strikes

KM#	Date	Mintage	Identification	Mkt Val
Pn2	2002	—	10 Kwacha. Copper-Nickel. 29.0200 g. 38.7 mm. National arms. Alexander the Great. Reeded edge.	—
Pn3	2002	—	10 Kwacha. Copper-Nickel. 29.0200 g. 38.7 mm. National arms. Olympic torch under two world globes. Reeded edge.	—
Pn4	2002	—	10 Kwacha. Copper-Nickel. 29.0200 g. 38.7 mm. National arms. "MILLENNIUM" above Mona Lisa like portrait. Reeded edge.	—
Pn9	2003	—	10 Kwacha. Silver Plated. 29.4500 g. 38 mm. Nyala antelope.	—
Pn5	2003	—	10 Kwacha. Silver Plated. 29.4500 g. 38.7 mm. National arms. Trans-Siberian Express train. Reeded edge.	—
Pn6	2003	—	10 Kwacha. Silver Plated. 29.4500 g. 38.7 mm. National arms. Blesbok antelope. Reeded edge.	—
Pn7	2003	—	10 Kwacha. Copper-Nickel. 29.0200 g. 38.7 mm. National arms. Eland antelope. Reeded edge.	—
Pn8	2003	—	10 Kwacha. Copper-Nickel. 29.0200 g. 38.7 mm. National arms. Kudu antelope. Reeded edge.	—
Pn15	ND (2004)	—	10 Kwacha. Silver Plated. 29.2200 g. 38.7 mm. National arms. Multicolor pair of birds with chick. Reeded edge.	15.00

MALAYSIA

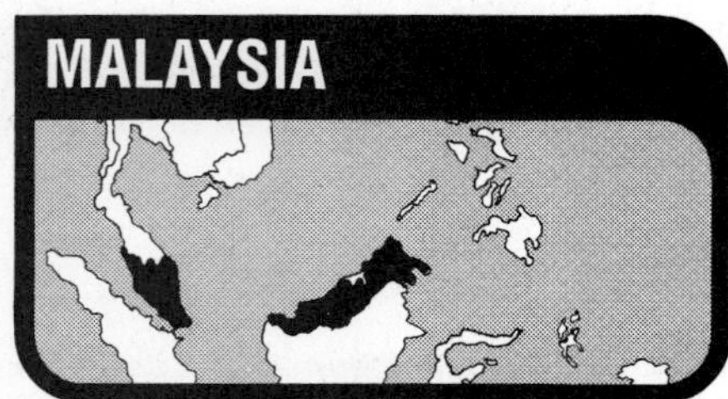

The independent limited constitutional monarchy of Malaysia, which occupies the southern part of the Malay Peninsula in Southeast Asia and the northern part of the island of Borneo, has an area of 127,316 sq. mi. (329,750 sq. km.) and a population of 15.4 million. Capital: Kuala Lumpur. The economy is based on agriculture, mining and forestry. Rubber, tin, timber and palm oil are exported.

Malaysia came into being on Sept. 16, 1963, as a federation of Malaya (Johore, Kelantan, Kedah, Perlis, Trengganu, Negri-Sembilan, Pahang, Perak, Selangor, Penang, Malacca), Singapore, Sabah (British North Borneo) and Sarawak. Following two serious racial riots involving Malays and Chinese, Singapore withdrew from the federation on Aug. 9, 1965. Malaysia is a member of the Commonwealth of Nations.

MINT MARK

FM - Franklin Mint, U.S.A.

CONSTITUTIONAL MONARCHY

STANDARD COINAGE

100 Sen = 1 Ringgit (Dollar)

KM# 49 SEN
1.8000 g., Bronze Clad Steel, 17.66 mm. **Obv:** Value divides date below flower blossom **Obv. Legend:** BANK NEGARA MALAYSIA **Rev:** Drum **Edge:** Plain

Date	Mintage	F	VF	XF	Unc	BU
2001	213,645,000	—	—	—	0.15	0.25
2002	185,220,000	—	—	—	0.15	0.25
2003	235,350,000	—	—	—	0.15	0.25
2004	227,700,000	—	—	—	0.15	0.25
2005	437,400,000	—	—	—	0.15	0.25
2006	328,050,000	—	—	—	0.15	0.25
2007	—	—	—	—	0.15	0.25

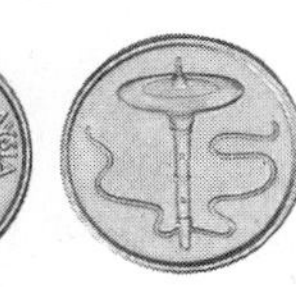

KM# 50 5 SEN
1.4000 g., Copper-Nickel, 16.28 mm. **Obv:** Value divides date below flower blossom **Obv. Legend:** BANK NEGARA MALAYSIA **Rev:** Top with string **Edge:** Reeded

Date	Mintage	F	VF	XF	Unc	BU
2001	94,617,472	—	—	—	0.15	0.25
2002	85,316,000	—	—	—	0.15	0.25
2003	75,690,000	—	—	—	0.15	0.25
2004	11,520,000	—	—	—	0.15	0.25
2005	119,520,000	—	—	—	0.15	0.25
2006	87,120,000	—	—	—	0.15	0.25
2007	97,200,338	—	—	—	0.15	0.25
2008	91,440,000	—	—	—	0.15	0.25
2009	125,172,842	—	—	—	0.15	0.25
2010	—	—	—	—	0.15	0.25

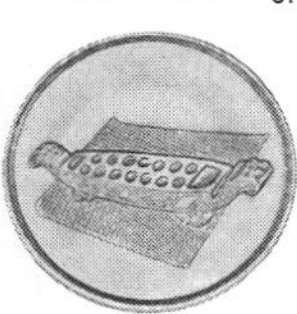

KM# 51 10 SEN
2.8200 g., Copper-Nickel, 19.43 mm. **Obv:** Value divides date below flower blossom **Obv. Legend:** BANK NEGARA MALAYSIA **Rev:** Ceremonial table **Edge:** Reeded

Date	Mintage	F	VF	XF	Unc	BU
2001	313,422,000	—	—	—	0.25	0.40
2002	290,451,948	—	—	—	0.25	0.40
2003	8,640,000	—	—	—	0.25	0.40
2004	170,640,000	—	—	—	0.25	0.40
2005	316,800,000	—	—	—	0.25	0.40
2006	304,560,000	—	—	—	0.25	0.40
2007	237,967,970	—	—	—	0.25	0.40
2008	241,560,000	—	—	—	0.25	0.40
2009	336,150,800	—	—	—	0.25	0.40
2010	—	—	—	—	0.25	0.40

KM# 52 20 SEN
5.6900 g., Copper-Nickel, 23.57 mm. **Obv:** Value divides date below flower blossom **Obv. Legend:** BANK NEGARA MALAYSIA **Rev:** Basket with food and utensils **Edge:** Reeded

Date	Mintage	F	VF	XF	Unc	BU
2001	278,802,000	—	—	—	0.35	0.50
2002	131,279,881	—	—	—	0.35	0.50
2003	—	—	—	—	0.35	0.50
2004	96,840,000	—	—	—	0.35	0.50
2005	209,700,000	—	—	—	0.35	0.50
2006	155,880,000	—	—	—	0.35	0.50
2007	212,897,236	—	—	—	0.35	0.50
2008	19,764,000	—	—	—	0.35	0.50
2009	—	—	—	—	0.35	0.50
2010	—	—	—	—	0.35	0.50

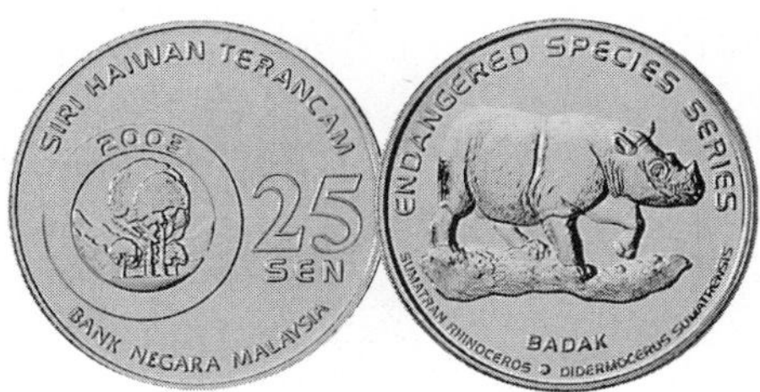

KM# 77 25 SEN
9.1400 g., Brass, 30 mm. **Series:** Endangered Species **Obv:** Logo left, value right **Rev:** Sumatran Rhinoceros **Edge:** Reeded

Date	Mintage	F	VF	XF	Unc	BU
2003	100,000	—	—	—	—	4.00

KM# 78 25 SEN
9.1400 g., Brass, 30 mm. **Series:** Endangered Species **Obv:** Logo left, value right **Rev:** Elephant **Edge:** Reeded

Date	Mintage	F	VF	XF	Unc	BU
2003	100,000	—	—	—	—	4.00

KM# 79 25 SEN
9.1400 g., Brass, 30 mm. **Series:** Endangered Species **Obv:** Logo left, value right **Rev:** Orangutan **Edge:** Reeded

Date	Mintage	F	VF	XF	Unc	BU
2003	100,000	—	—	—	—	4.00

KM# 80 25 SEN
9.1400 g., Brass, 30 mm. **Series:** Endangered Species **Obv:** Logo left, value right **Rev:** Sumatran Tiger **Edge:** Reeded

Date	Mintage	F	VF	XF	Unc	BU
2003	100,000	—	—	—	—	4.00

KM# 81 25 SEN
9.1400 g., Brass, 30 mm. **Series:** Endangered Species **Obv:** Logo left, value right **Rev:** Slow Loris on branch **Edge:** Reeded

Date	Mintage	F	VF	XF	Unc	BU
2003	100,000	—	—	—	—	4.00

KM# 82 25 SEN
9.1400 g., Brass, 30 mm. **Series:** Endangered Species **Obv:** Logo left, value right **Rev:** Barking Deer **Edge:** Reeded

Date	Mintage	F	VF	XF	Unc	BU
2003	100,000	—	—	—	—	4.00

KM# 83 25 SEN
9.1400 g., Brass, 30 mm. **Series:** Endangered Species **Obv:** Logo left, value right **Rev:** Malayan Tapir **Edge:** Reeded

Date	Mintage	F	VF	XF	Unc	BU
2003	100,000	—	—	—	—	4.00

KM# 84 25 SEN

9.1400 g., Brass, 30 mm. **Series:** Endangered Species **Obv:** Logo left, value right **Rev:** Serow **Edge:** Reeded

Date	Mintage	F	VF	XF	Unc	BU
2003	100,000	—	—	—	—	4.00

KM# 85 25 SEN

9.1400 g., Brass, 30 mm. **Series:** Endangered Species **Obv:** Logo left, value right **Rev:** Sambar Deer **Edge:** Reeded

Date	Mintage	F	VF	XF	Unc	BU
2003	100,000	—	—	—	—	4.00

KM# 86 25 SEN

9.1400 g., Brass, 30 mm. **Series:** Endangered Species **Obv:** Logo left, value right **Rev:** Seated Proboscis Monkey flanked by sprigs **Edge:** Reeded

Date	Mintage	F	VF	XF	Unc	BU
2003	100,000	—	—	—	—	4.00

KM# 87 25 SEN

9.1400 g., Brass, 30 mm. **Series:** Endangered Species **Obv:** Logo left, value right **Rev:** Gaur **Edge:** Reeded

Date	Mintage	F	VF	XF	Unc	BU
2003	100,000	—	—	—	—	4.00

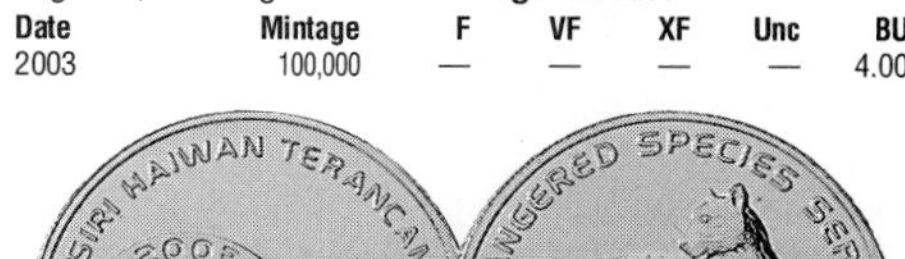

KM# 88 25 SEN

9.1400 g., Brass, 30 mm. **Series:** Endangered Species **Obv:** Logo left, value right **Rev:** Clouded Leopard **Edge:** Reeded

Date	Mintage	F	VF	XF	Unc	BU
2003	100,000	—	—	—	—	4.00

KM# 89 25 SEN

9.1400 g., Brass, 30 mm. **Series:** Endangered Species **Obv:** Logo left, value right **Obv. Legend:** BANK NEGARA MALAYSIA - SIRI HAIWAN TERANCAM **Rev:** Straw-headed Bulbul bird (Barau-Barau) **Edge:** Reeded

Date	Mintage	F	VF	XF	Unc	BU
2005	—	—	—	—	—	4.00

KM# 90 25 SEN

9.1400 g., Brass, 30 mm. **Series:** Endangered Species **Obv:** Logo left, value right **Obv. Legend:** BANK NEGARA MALAYSIA - SIRI HAIWAN TERANCAM **Rev:** Great Argus Pheasant (Kuang Raya) **Edge:** Reeded

Date	Mintage	F	VF	XF	Unc	BU
2005	40,000	—	—	—	—	4.00

KM# 91 25 SEN

9.1400 g., Brass, 30 mm. **Series:** Endangered Species **Obv:** Logo left, value right **Obv. Legend:** BANK NEGARA MALAYSIA - SIRI HAIWAN TERANCAM **Rev:** White-collared Kingfisher (Pekaka Sungai) **Edge:** Reeded

Date	Mintage	F	VF	XF	Unc	BU
2005	40,000	—	—	—	—	4.00

KM# 92 25 SEN

9.1400 g., Brass, 30 mm. **Series:** Endangered Species **Obv:** Logo left, value right **Obv. Legend:** BANK NEGARA MALAYSIA - SIRI HAIWAN TERANCAM **Rev:** White-bellied Sea Eagle (Lang Siput) perched on branch **Edge:** Reeded

Date	Mintage	F	VF	XF	Unc	BU
2005	40,000	—	—	—	—	4.00

KM# 93 25 SEN

9.1600 g., Brass, 30 mm. **Series:** Endangered Species **Obv:** Logo left, value right **Obv. Legend:** BANK NEGARA MALAYSIA - SIRI HAIWAN TERANCAM **Rev:** Asian Fairy Bluebird (Dendang Gajah) **Edge:** Reeded

Date	Mintage	F	VF	XF	Unc	BU
2005	40,000	—	—	—	—	4.00

KM# 94 25 SEN

9.1600 g., Brass, 30 mm. **Series:** Endangered Species **Obv:** Logo left, value right **Obv. Legend:** BANK NEGARA MALAYSIA - SIRI HAIWAN TERANCAM **Rev:** Rhinoceros Hornbill bird (Enggang Badak) **Edge:** Reeded

Date	Mintage	F	VF	XF	Unc	BU
2005	40,000	—	—	—	—	4.00

KM# 95 25 SEN

9.1600 g., Brass, 30 mm. **Series:** Endangered Species **Obv:** Logo left, value right **Obv. Legend:** BANK NEGARA MALAYSIA - SIRI HAIWAN TERANCAM **Rev:** Nicobar Pigeon (Merpati Emas) **Edge:** Reeded

Date	Mintage	F	VF	XF	Unc	BU
2005	40,000	—	—	—	—	4.00

KM# 96 25 SEN

9.1600 g., Brass, 30 mm. **Series:** Endangered Species **Obv:** Logo left, value right **Obv. Legend:** BANK NEGARA MALAYSIA - SIRI HAIWAN TERANCAM **Rev:** Two Crested Wood Partridges (Siul Berjambul) **Edge:** Reeded

Date	Mintage	F	VF	XF	Unc	BU
2005	40,000	—	—	—	—	4.00

KM# 97 25 SEN

9.1600 g., Brass, 30 mm. **Series:** Endangered Species **Obv:** Logo left, value right **Obv. Legend:** BANK NEGARA MALAYSIA - SIRI HAIWAN TERANCAM **Rev:** Black and Red Broadbill bird (Takau Rakit) **Edge:** Reeded

Date	Mintage	F	VF	XF	Unc	BU
2005	40,000	—	—	—	—	4.00

KM# 98 25 SEN

9.1600 g., Brass, 30 mm. **Series:** Endangered Species **Obv:** Logo left, value right **Obv. Legend:** BANK NEGARA MALAYSIA - SIRI HAIWAN TERANCAM **Rev:** Green Imperial Pigeon (Pergam Besar) on branch **Edge:** Reeded

Date	Mintage	F	VF	XF	Unc	BU
2005	40,000	—	—	—	—	4.00

KM# 99 25 SEN

9.1600 g., Brass, 30 mm. **Series:** Endangered Species **Obv:** Logo left, value right **Obv. Legend:** BANK NEGARA MALAYSIA - SIRI HAIWAN TERANCAM **Rev:** Great Egret (Bangau Besar) **Edge:** Reeded

Date	Mintage	F	VF	XF	Unc	BU
2005	40,000	—	—	—	—	4.00

KM# 100 25 SEN

9.1600 g., Brass, 30 mm. **Series:** Endangered Species **Obv:** Logo left, value right **Obv. Legend:** BANK NEGARA MALAYSIA - SIRI HAIWAN TERANCAM **Rev:** Brown Shrike (Tirjup Tanah) on branch **Edge:** Reeded

Date	Mintage	F	VF	XF	Unc	BU
2005	40,000	—	—	—	—	4.00

KM# 104 25 SEN

Brass, 34 mm. **Series:** Endangered Species **Obv:** Logo and value **Obv. Legend:** BANK NEGARA MALAYSIA - SIRI HAIWAN TERANCAM **Rev:** Hawksbill turtle (Penyu Karah)

Date	Mintage	F	VF	XF	Unc	BU
2006	40,000	—	—	—	—	4.00

KM# 103 25 SEN

Brass, 34 mm. **Series:** Endangered Species **Obv:** Logo and value **Obv. Legend:** BANK NEGARA MALAYSIA - SIRI HAIWAN TERANCAM **Rev:** Green turtle (Penyu Agar)

Date	Mintage	F	VF	XF	Unc	BU
2006	40,000	—	—	—	—	4.00

KM# 102 25 SEN

Brass, 34 mm. **Series:** Endangered Species **Obv:** Logo and value **Obv. Legend:** BANK NEGARA MALAYSIA - SIRI HAIWAN TERANCAM **Rev:** Leatherback turtle (Penyu Belimbing)

Date	Mintage	F	VF	XF	Unc	BU
2006	40,000	—	—	—	—	4.00

KM# 101 25 SEN

Brass, 34 mm. **Series:** Endangered Species **Obv:** Logo and value **Obv. Legend:** BANK NEGARA MALAYSIA - SIRI HAIWAN TERANCAM **Rev:** Olive Ridley Turtle (Pengu Lipas)

Date	Mintage	F	VF	XF	Unc	BU
2006	40,000	—	—	—	—	4.00

KM# 105 25 SEN

15.5000 g., Brass, 34 mm. **Series:** Endangered Species **Obv:** Logo and value **Obv. Legend:** BANK NEGARA MALAYSIA - SIRI HAIWAN TERANCAM **Rev:** Dugong manatee **Edge:** Reeded

Date	Mintage	F	VF	XF	Unc	BU
2006	40,000	—	—	—	—	4.00

KM# 106 25 SEN

15.5000 g., Brass, 34 mm. **Series:** Endangered Species **Obv:** Logo and value **Obv. Legend:** BANK NEGARA MALAYSIA - SIRI HAIWAN TERANCAM **Rev:** Whale Shark (Jerung Paus) **Edge:** Reeded

Date	Mintage	F	VF	XF	Unc	BU
2006	40,000	—	—	—	—	4.00

KM# 107 25 SEN

15.5000 g., Brass, 34 mm. **Series:** Endangered Species **Obv:** Logo and value **Obv. Legend:** BANK NEGARA MALAYSIA - SIRI HAIWAN TERANCAM **Rev:** Irraddy Dolphin (Lumba-Lumba Empesut) **Edge:** Reeded

Date	Mintage	F	VF	XF	Unc	BU
2006	40,000	—	—	—	—	4.00

KM# 108 25 SEN

15.5000 g., Brass, 34 mm. **Series:** Endangered Species **Obv:** Logo and value **Obv. Legend:** BANK NEGARA MALAYSIA - SIRI HAIWAN TERANCAM **Rev:** Bottlenose Dolphin (Lumba Lumba) **Edge:** Reeded

Date	Mintage	F	VF	XF	Unc	BU
2006	40,000	—	—	—	—	4.00

KM# 109 25 SEN

15.5000 g., Brass, 34 mm. **Series:** Endangered Species **Obv:** Logo and value **Obv. Legend:** BANK NEGARA MALAYSIA - SIRI HAIWAN TERANCAM **Rev:** Siamese Crocodile (Buaya Siam) **Edge:** Reeded

Date	Mintage	F	VF	XF	Unc	BU
2006	40,000	—	—	—	—	4.00

KM# 110 25 SEN

15.5000 g., Brass, 34 mm. **Series:** Endangered Species **Obv:** Logo and value **Obv. Legend:** BANK NEGARA MALAYSIA - SIRI HAIWAN TERANCAM **Rev:** Indopacific Crocodile (Buaya Tembaga) **Edge:** Reeded

Date	Mintage	F	VF	XF	Unc	BU
2006	40,000	—	—	—	—	4.00

KM# 111 25 SEN

15.5000 g., Brass, 34 mm. **Series:** Endangered Species **Obv:** Logo and value **Obv. Legend:** BANK NEGARA MALAYSIA - SIRI HAIWAN TERANCAM **Rev:** Malayan Gharial (Buaya Julong) **Edge:** Reeded

Date	Mintage	F	VF	XF	Unc	BU
2006	40,000	—	—	—	—	4.00

KM# 112 25 SEN

15.5000 g., Brass, 34 mm. **Series:** Endangered Species **Obv:** Logo and value **Obv. Legend:** BANK NEGARA MALAYSIA - SIRI HAIWAN TERANCAM **Rev:** Painted Terrapin turtle (Tuntung Laut) **Edge:** Reeded

Date	Mintage	F	VF	XF	Unc	BU
2006	40,000	—	—	—	—	4.00

KM# 53 50 SEN

9.2800 g., Copper-Nickel, 27.78 mm. **Obv:** Value divides date below flower blossom **Obv. Legend:** BANK NEGARA MALAYSIA **Rev:** Ceremonial kite **Edge Lettering:** BANK NEGARA MALAYSIA (twice)

Date	Mintage	F	VF	XF	Unc	BU
2001	67,371,000	—	—	—	0.65	0.85
2002	61,928,000	—	—	—	0.65	0.85
2003	32,580,000	—	—	—	0.65	0.85
2004	37,890,000	—	—	—	0.65	0.85
2005	691,680,006	—	—	—	0.65	0.85
2006	19,480,006	—	—	—	0.65	0.85
2007	—	—	—	—	0.65	0.85
2008	61,380,000	—	—	—	0.65	0.85
2009	94,691,783	—	—	—	0.65	0.85
2010	—	—	—	—	0.65	0.85

KM# 71 RINGGIT

16.8000 g., Copper-Nickel, 33.7 mm. **Subject:** XXI SEA Games **Obv:** Games logo **Rev:** Cartoon mascot **Edge:** Reeded

Date	Mintage	F	VF	XF	Unc	BU
2001	200,000	—	—	—	3.00	5.00

KM# 165 RINGGIT

10.4000 g., Copper Plated Zinc, 26 mm. **Subject:** 10th Men's Hockey World Cup **Obv:** Logo **Obv. Legend:** BANK NEGARA MALAYSIA **Rev:** 2 stylized players **Rev. Legend:** KEJOHANAN HOKI LELAKI PIALA DUNIA **Edge:** Reeded

Date	Mintage	F	VF	XF	Unc	BU
2002	100,000	—	—	—	—	10.00

KM# 168 RINGGIT

Brass **Subject:** 45th National Day **Obv:** Buildings, tower, metro liner **Obv. Legend:** BANK NEGARA MALAYSIA **Rev:** Stylized waving flag **Rev. Legend:** 45 TAHUN MERDEKA

Date	Mintage	F	VF	XF	Unc	BU
2002	10,000	—	—	—	—	8.00

KM# 74 RINGGIT

16.8000 g., Copper-Nickel, 33.7 mm. **Subject:** Coronation of Agong XII **Obv:** Head with headdress facing **Rev:** Arms with supporters within sprigs **Edge:** Reeded **Note:** Prev. KM#72.

Date	Mintage	F	VF	XF	Unc	BU
ND(2002)	100,000	—	—	—	4.00	6.00

KM# 171 RINGGIT

Brass **Subject:** XIII NAM Summit **Obv:** Modern building, plaza **Obv. Legend:** MALAYSIA - BANK NEGARA MALAYSIA **Rev:** Stylized dove in rays **Rev. Legend:** XIII CONFERENCE OF HEADS OF STATE OR GOVERNMENT OF THE NON-ALIGNED MOVEMENT

Date	Mintage	F	VF	XF	Unc	BU
2003 Proof	9,400	Value: 8.00				

KM# 174 RINGGIT

Brass **Subject:** LIMA - 7th Bi-annual Langkawi Island Trade Fair **Obv:** Jet fighter plane above naval missile corvette **Obv. Legend:** BANK NEGARA MALAYSIA **Rev:** Logo **Rev. Legend:** LANGKAWI INTERNATIONAL MARITIME & AEROSPACE

Date	Mintage	F	VF	XF	Unc	BU
2003	25,000	—	—	—	—	8.00

KM# 177 RINGGIT

Brass **Subject:** 10th Session Islamic Summit Conference **Obv:** Circular Arabic text **Obv. Legend:** BANK NEGARA MALAYSIA **Rev:** Symmetrical design **Rev. Legend:** PERSIDANGAN KETUA-KETUA NEGARASLAM

Date	Mintage	F	VF	XF	Unc	BU
2003	25,000	—	—	—	—	8.00

KM# 114 RINGGIT

Copper-Nickel **Subject:** Century of Tunku Abdul Rahman **Obv:** National arms **Obv. Legend:** BANK NEGARA MALAYSIA - BAPA KEMERDEKAAN **Rev:** 3/4 length figure of Tunku Abdul Rahman left with right hand raised **Rev. Legend:** Y. T. M. TUNKU ABDUL RAHMAN PUTRA AL-HAJ

Date	Mintage	F	VF	XF	Unc	BU
2005	25,000	—	—	—	—	8.00

KM# 132 RINGGIT

Brass **Subject:** 30th Annual Meeting Islamic Development Bank **Obv:** Circular Arabic text **Obv. Legend:** BANK NEGARA MALYSIA - MESYUARAT TAHUNAN BANK PEMBANCUNAN ISLAM KE - 30 **Rev:** Logo

Date	Mintage	F	VF	XF	Unc	BU
2005	20,000	—	—	—	—	8.00

KM# 135 RINGGIT

Copper-Nickel **Subject:** 11th ASEAN Summit **Obv:** Twin towers center right **Obv. Legend:** BANK NEGARA MALAYSIA - SIDANG KEMUNCAK ASEAN KE-11 **Rev:** Logo

Date	Mintage	F	VF	XF	Unc	BU
2005	20,000	—	—	—	—	6.00

KM# 138 RINGGIT
Bi-Metallic **Subject:** Songket - The Regal Heritage **Obv:** Stylized flower - Bunga Ketola **Obv. Legend:** BANK NEGARA MALAYSIA **Rev:** Floral pattern below inscription

Date	Mintage	F	VF	XF	Unc	BU
2005	20,000	—	—	—	—	6.00

KM# 141 RINGGIT
Brass **Subject:** 50th Anniversary Mara Technology University **Obv:** Large "50" with horizontal lines in background **Obv. Legend:** BANK NEGARA MALAYSIA - JUBLI EMAS UITM **Rev:** Logo **Rev. Legend:** Universiti Teknologi Mara

Date	Mintage	F	VF	XF	Unc	BU
ND(2006)	12,050	—	—	—	—	6.00

KM# 144 RINGGIT
Brass **Subject:** 50th Anniversary P. Felda **Obv:** 1/2 length figure of Felda 3/4 right **Obv. Legend:** BANK NEGARA MALYSIA **Rev:** Two opposed hands holding symbol **Rev. Legend:** MENEMPA KEJAYAAN

Date	Mintage	F	VF	XF	Unc	BU
2006	10,000	—	—	—	—	6.00

KM# 147 RINGGIT
Brass **Subject:** 9th Malaysian Plan **Obv:** Bust 3/4 right **Obv. Legend:** BANK NEGARA MALAYSIA - CEMERLANG GEMILANG TERBILANg **Rev:** Globe logo **Rev. Legend:** RANCANGAN MALAYSIA KE SEMBILAN

Date	Mintage	F	VF	XF	Unc	BU
2006	10,000	—	—	—	—	6.00

KM# 162 RINGGIT
Brass **Subject:** 200th Anniversary Malaysian Police Force **Obv:** Police badge **Obv. Legend:** BANK NEGARA MALAYSIA **Rev:** Two hands clasped in sprays

Date	Mintage	F	VF	XF	Unc	BU
2007	20,000	—	—	—	—	5.50

KM# 182 RINGGIT
8.8000 g., Aluminum-Bronze, 30 mm. **Subject:** Installation of Agong XIII **Obv:** National arms within wreath **Rev:** Facing portrait

Date	Mintage	F	VF	XF	Unc	BU
2007	10,000	—	—	—	—	5.00
2007 Proof	600	—	—	—	—	—

KM# 185 RINGGIT
8.8000 g., Aluminum-Bronze, 30 mm. **Subject:** Independence, 50th Anniversary **Obv:** National Arms **Rev:** 50 above city skyline

Date	Mintage	F	VF	XF	Unc	BU
2007	10,000	—	—	—	—	5.00
2007 Proof	2,000	—	—	—	—	—

KM# 188 RINGGIT
8.8000 g., Aluminum-Bronze, 30 mm. **Subject:** Royal Malaysian Air Force, 50th Anniversary **Obv:** Air Force insignia **Rev:** Old and modern plane

Date	Mintage	F	VF	XF	Unc	BU
2008	10,000	—	—	—	—	5.00
2008 Proof	350	—	—	—	—	—

KM# 191 RINGGIT
8.8000 g., Aluminum-Bronze, 30 mm. **Subject:** St. John's Ambulance, 100th Anniversary **Obv:** St. John's insignia in wreath above valye **Rev:** Cliernt being loaded into ambulance

Date	Mintage	F	VF	XF	Unc	BU
2008	10,000	—	—	—	—	5.00
2008 Proof	350	—	—	—	—	—

KM# 155 RINGGIT
8.8000 g., Brass, 30 mm. **Subject:** Bank Negara Malaysia, 50th Anniversary **Obv:** Bank logo **Rev:** 14-pointed star

Date	Mintage	F	VF	XF	Unc	BU
2009	13,700	—	—	—	—	6.00
2009 Proof	3,300	—	—	—	—	—

KM# 159 RINGGIT
8.0000 g., Brass, 30 mm. **Subject:** Parliament, 50th Anniversary **Obv:** National Arms and 2 maces **Rev:** Parliament Building

Date	Mintage	F	VF	XF	Unc	BU
2009	10,000	—	—	—	—	6.00
2009 Proof	450	—	—	—	—	—

KM# 194 RINGGIT
8.8000 g., Aluminum-Bronze, 30 mm. **Subject:** International Year of Astronomy **Obv:** Adult and Child looking to the heavens **Rev:** Langkawi National Observatory

Date	Mintage	F	VF	XF	Unc	BU
2009	10,000	—	—	—	—	5.00
2009 Proof	350	—	—	—	—	—

KM# 197 RINGGIT
8.8000 g., Aluminum-Bronze, 30 mm. **Subject:** Royal Malaysian Navy, 75th Anniversary **Obv:** Submarine **Rev:** Navy insignia

Date	Mintage	F	VF	XF	Unc	BU
2009	10,000	—	—	—	—	5.00
2009 Proof	450	—	—	—	—	—

KM# 72 10 RINGGIT
21.7000 g., 0.9250 Silver 0.6453 oz. ASW, 35.7 mm. **Subject:** XXI SEA Games **Obv:** Games logo **Rev:** Cartoon mascot **Edge:** Reeded

Date	Mintage	F	VF	XF	Unc	BU
2001 Proof	3,000	Value: 70.00				

KM# 75 10 RINGGIT
21.7000 g., 0.9250 Silver 0.6453 oz. ASW, 35.7 mm. **Subject:** Coronation of Agong XII **Obv:** Head with headdress facing **Rev:** Arms with supporters within sprigs **Edge:** Reeded

Date	Mintage	F	VF	XF	Unc	BU
ND(2002) Proof	10,000	Value: 100				

KM# 166 10 RINGGIT
16.8000 g., 0.9250 Silver 0.4996 oz. ASW, 32 mm. **Subject:** 10th Men's Hockey World Cup **Obv:** Official logo of the World Cup games **Obv. Legend:** BANK NEGARA MALAYSIA **Rev:** 2 stylized players in front of the Kuala Lumpur skyline **Rev. Legend:** KEJOHANAN HOKI LELAKI PIALA

Date	Mintage	F	VF	XF	Unc	BU
2002 Proof	3,000	Value: 120				

KM# 169 10 RINGGIT
0.9250 Silver **Subject:** 45th National Day **Obv:** Buildings, tower, metro liner **Obv. Legend:** BANK NEGARA MALAYSIA **Rev:** Stylized waving flag **Rev. Legend:** 45 TAHUN MERDEKA

Date	Mintage	F	VF	XF	Unc	BU
2002 Proof	1,800	Value: 90.00				

KM# 172 10 RINGGIT
0.9250 Silver **Subject:** XIII NAM Summit **Obv:** Modern building, plaza **Obv. Legend:** MALAYSIA - BANK NEGARA MALAYSIA **Rev:** Stylized dove in rays **Rev. Legend:** XIII CONFERENCE OF HEADS OF STATE OR GOVERNMENT OF THE NON-ALIGNED MOVEMENT

Date	Mintage	F	VF	XF	Unc	BU
2003 Proof	2,400	Value: 90.00				

KM# 175 10 RINGGIT
0.9250 Silver **Subject:** LIMA - 7th bi-annual Langkawi Island Trade Fair **Obv:** Jet fighter plane above naval missile corvette **Obv. Legend:** BANK NEGARA MALAYSIA **Rev:** Logo **Rev. Legend:** LANGKAWI INTERNATIONAL MARITIME & SPACE

Date	Mintage	F	VF	XF	Unc	BU
2003 Proof	—	Value: 90.00				

KM# 178 10 RINGGIT
0.9250 Silver **Subject:** 10th Session Islamic Summit Conference **Obv:** Circular Arabic Text **Obv. Legend:** BANK NEGARA MALAYSIA **Rev:** Symmetrical pattern **Rev. Legend:** PERSIDANGAN KETUA - KETUA NEGARA ISLAM

Date	Mintage	F	VF	XF	Unc	BU
2003 Proof	300	Value: 90.00				

KM# 115 10 RINGGIT
0.9250 Silver **Subject:** Century of Tunku Abdul Rahman **Obv:** National arms **Obv. Legend:** BANK NEGARA MALAYSIA - BAPA KEMERDEKAAN **Rev:** 3/4 length figure of Tunku Abdul Rahman left with right hand raised **Rev. Legend:** Y. T. M. TUNKU ABDUL RAHMAN PUTRA AL-HAJ

Date	Mintage	F	VF	XF	Unc	BU
2005 Proof	200	Value: 90.00				

KM# 136 10 RINGGIT
21.7000 g., Silver, 35.7 mm. **Subject:** 11th ASEAN Summit **Obv:** Twin towers center right **Obv. Legend:** BANK NEGARA MALAYSIA - SIDANG KEMUNCAK ASEAN KE-11 **Rev:** Logo

Date	Mintage	F	VF	XF	Unc	BU
2005 Proof	250	Value: 90.00				

KM# 139 10 RINGGIT
21.7000 g., Silver, 35.7 mm. **Subject:** Songket - The Regal Heritage **Obv:** Uniform pattern - Bunga Bintang **Obv. Legend:** BANK NEGARA MALAYSIA **Rev:** Floral pattern below inscription

Date	Mintage	F	VF	XF	Unc	BU
2005 Proof	250	Value: 90.00				

KM# 142 10 RINGGIT
21.7000 g., Silver, 35.7 mm. **Subject:** 50th Anniversary Mara Technology Universit **Obv:** Large "50" with horizontal lines in background **Obv. Legend:** BANK NEGARA MALAYSIA - JUBLI EMAS UITM **Rev:** Logo **Rev. Legend:** Universiti Teknologi Mara

Date	Mintage	F	VF	XF	Unc	BU
ND(2006) Proof	500	Value: 90.00				

KM# 145 10 RINGGIT
31.1100 g., Silver, 40 mm. **Subject:** 50th Anniversary P. Felda **Obv:** Outlined map of South East Asia above logo **Obv. Legend:** BANK NEGARA MALAYSIA **Rev:** Monument at left, Felda with 4 others at right **Rev. Legend:** MENEMPA KEJAYAAN

Date	Mintage	F	VF	XF	Unc	BU
2006 Proof	300	Value: 80.00				

KM# 148 10 RINGGIT
21.0000 g., Silver, 35.7 mm. **Subject:** 9th Malaysian Plan **Obv:** Bust 3/4 right **Obv. Legend:** BANK NEGARA MALAYSIA - CEMERLANG GEMILANG TERBILANG **Rev:** Globe logo **Rev. Legend:** RANCANGAN MALAYSIA KE SEMBILAN

Date	Mintage	F	VF	XF	Unc	BU
2006 Proof	300	Value: 80.00				

KM# 163 10 RINGGIT
21.0000 g., Silver, 35.70 mm. **Subject:** 200th Anniversary Malaysian Police Force **Obv:** Police badge **Obv. Legend:** BANK NEGARA MALAYSIA **Rev:** Two hands clasped in sprays

Date	Mintage	F	VF	XF	Unc	BU
2007 Proof	500	Value: 80.00				

KM# 183 10 RINGGIT
21.0000 g., 0.9250 Silver 0.6245 oz. ASW, 35.7 mm. **Subject:** Installation of Agong XIII **Obv:** National arms in wreath **Rev:** Portrait facing

Date	Mintage	F	VF	XF	Unc	BU
2007 Proof	800	Value: 70.00				

KM# 186 10 RINGGIT
21.0000 g., 0.9250 Silver 0.6245 oz. ASW, 35.7 mm. **Subject:** Independence, 50th Anniversary **Obv:** National Arms **Rev:** 50 above city skyline

Date	Mintage	F	VF	XF	Unc	BU
2007 Proof	2,200	Value: 100				

KM# 189 10 RINGGIT
21.0000 g., 0.9250 Silver 0.6245 oz. ASW, 35.7 mm. **Subject:** Royal Malaysian Air Force, 50th Anniversary **Obv:** Air Force insignia **Rev:** Old and new plane

Date	Mintage	F	VF	XF	Unc	BU
2008 Proof	700	Value: 70.00				

KM# 192 10 RINGGIT
21.0000 g., 0.9250 Silver 0.6245 oz. ASW, 35.7 mm. **Subject:** St. John's Ambulance **Obv:** St. John's emblem in wreath above vlaue **Rev:** Client being loaded into ambulance

Date	Mintage	F	VF	XF	Unc	BU
2008 Proof	700	Value: 70.00				

KM# 156 10 RINGGIT
21.0000 g., 0.9250 Silver 0.6245 oz. ASW, 35.7 mm. **Subject:** Bank Negara Malaysia, 50th Anniversary **Obv:** Bank logo **Rev:** 14-pointed star

Date	Mintage	F	VF	XF	Unc	BU
2009 Proof	3,700	Value: 80.00				

KM# 160 10 RINGGIT
21.0000 g., 0.9250 Silver 0.6245 oz. ASW, 35.7 mm. **Subject:** Parliament, 50th Anniversary **Obv:** National Arms and 2 maces **Rev:** Parliament Building

Date	Mintage	F	VF	XF	Unc	BU
2009 Proof	750	Value: 90.00				

KM# 195 10 RINGGIT
21.0000 g., 0.9250 Silver 0.6245 oz. ASW, 35.7 mm. **Subject:** International Year of Astronomy **Obv:** Adult and child looking to the heavens **Rev:** Langkawi Naitonal Observatory

Date	Mintage	F	VF	XF	Unc	BU
2009 Proof	700	Value: 75.00				

KM# 198 10 RINGGIT
21.0000 g., 0.9250 Silver 0.6245 oz. ASW, 35.7 mm. **Subject:** Royal Malaysian navy, 75th Anniversary **Obv:** Submarine **Rev:** Navy insignia

Date	Mintage	F	VF	XF	Unc	BU
2009 Proof	650	Value: 85.00				

KM# 133 20 RINGGIT
31.1000 g., Silver, 40 mm. **Subject:** 30th Annual Meeting Islamic Development Bank **Obv:** Mosque **Obv. Legend:** BANK NEGARA MALAYSIA **Rev:** Logo

Date	Mintage	F	VF	XF	Unc	BU
2005 Proof	1,000	Value: 90.00				

KM# 157 50 RINGGIT
10.0700 g., 0.9990 Gold 0.3234 oz. AGW, 25 mm. **Subject:** Bank Negara Malaysia, 50th Anniversary **Obv:** Bank logo **Rev:** 14-pointed star

Date	Mintage	F	VF	XF	Unc	BU
2009 Proof	500	Value: 900				

KM# 73 100 RINGGIT
8.6000 g., 0.9160 Gold 0.2533 oz. AGW, 22 mm. **Subject:** XXI SEA Games **Obv:** Games logo **Rev:** Cartoon mascot **Edge:** Reeded

Date	Mintage	F	VF	XF	Unc	BU
2001 Proof	500	Value: 650				

KM# 76 100 RINGGIT
8.6000 g., 0.9160 Gold 0.2533 oz. AGW, 22 mm. **Subject:** Coronation of Agong XII **Obv:** Head with headdress facing **Rev:** Arms with supporters within sprigs **Edge:** Reeded

Date	Mintage	F	VF	XF	Unc	BU
ND(2002) Proof	300	Value: 700				

KM# 167 100 RINGGIT
9.0000 g., 0.9000 Gold 0.2604 oz. AGW, 22 mm. **Subject:** 10th Men's Hockey World Cup **Obv:** Logo **Obv. Legend:** BANK NEGARA MALAYSIA **Rev:** 2 stylized players in front of Kuala Lumpur skyline **Rev. Legend:** KEJOHANAN HOKI LELAKI PIALA

Date	Mintage	F	VF	XF	Unc	BU
2002 Proof	1,000	Value: 600				

KM# 170 100 RINGGIT
8.6000 g., 0.9999 Gold 0.2765 oz. AGW **Subject:** 45th National Day **Obv:** Buildings, tower, metro liner **Obv. Legend:** BANK NEGARA MALAYSIA **Rev:** Stylized waving flag **Rev. Legend:** 45 TAHUN MERDEKA

Date	Mintage	F	VF	XF	Unc	BU
2002 Proof	300	Value: 700				

KM# 173 100 RINGGIT
8.6000 g., 0.9999 Gold 0.2765 oz. AGW, 22 mm. **Subject:** XIII NAM Summit **Obv:** Modern building, plaza **Obv. Legend:** MALAYSIA - BANK NEGARA MALAYSIA **Rev:** Stylized dove in rays **Rev. Legend:** XIII CONFERENCE OF HEADS OF STATE OR GOVERNMENT OF THE NON-ALIGNED MOVEMENT

Date	Mintage	F	VF	XF	Unc	BU
2003 Proof	—	Value: 700				

KM# 176 100 RINGGIT
8.6000 g., 0.9999 Gold 0.2765 oz. AGW, 22 mm. **Subject:** LIMA - 7th bi-annual Langkawi Island Trade Fair **Obv:** Jet fighter plane above naval missile corvette **Obv. Legend:** BANK NEGARA MALAYSIA **Rev:** Logo **Rev. Legend:** LANGKAWI INTERNATIONAL MARITIME & AEROSPACE

Date	Mintage	F	VF	XF	Unc	BU
2003 Proof	50	Value: 1,100				

KM# 179 100 RINGGIT
8.6000 g., 0.9999 Gold 0.2765 oz. AGW, 22 mm. **Obv:** Circular Arabic text **Obv. Legend:** BANK NEGARA MALAYSIA **Rev:** Symmetrical design **Rev. Legend:** PERSIDANGAN KETUA - KETUA NEGARA ISLAM

Date	Mintage	F	VF	XF	Unc	BU
2003 Proof	200	Value: 750				

KM# 116 100 RINGGIT

0.9999 Gold **Subject:** Century of Tunku Abdul Rahman **Obv:** National arms **Obv. Legend:** BANK NEGARA MALAYSIA - BAPA KEMERDEKAAN **Rev:** 3/4 length figure of Tunku Abdul Rahman left with right hand raised **Rev. Legend:** Y. T. M. TUNKU ABDUL RAHMAN PUTRA AL-HAJ

Date	Mintage	F	VF	XF	Unc	BU
2005 Proof	100	Value: 750				

KM# 137 100 RINGGIT

8.6000 g., Gold, 22 mm. **Subject:** 11th ASEAN Summit **Obv:** Twin towers center right **Obv. Legend:** BANK NEGARA MALAYSIA - SIDANG KEMUNCAK ASEAN KE-11 **Rev:** Logo

Date	Mintage	F	VF	XF	Unc	BU
2005 Proof	150	Value: 750				

KM# 140 100 RINGGIT

8.6000 g., Gold, 22 mm. **Subject:** Songket - The Regal Heritage **Obv:** Uniform pattern - Tampur Kesemak **Obv. Legend:** BANK NEGARA MALAYSIA **Rev:** Floral pattern below inscription

Date	Mintage	F	VF	XF	Unc	BU
2005 Proof	150	Value: 750				

KM# 143 100 RINGGIT

8.6000 g., Gold, 22 mm. **Subject:** 50th Anniversary Mara Technology University **Obv:** Large "50" with horizontal lines in background **Obv. Legend:** BANK NEGARA MALAYSIA - JUBLI EMAS UITM **Rev:** Logo **Rev. Legend:** Universiti Teknologi Mara

Date	Mintage	F	VF	XF	Unc	BU
ND(2006) Proof	300	Value: 750				

KM# 146 100 RINGGIT

9.0000 g., Gold, 22 mm. **Subject:** 50th Anniversary P. Felda **Obv:** 1/2 length figure of Felda 3/4 right **Obv. Legend:** BANK NEGARA MALAYSIA **Rev:** Stylized palm tree at left, rubber tree trunk at right **Rev. Legend:** MENEMPA KEJAYAAN

Date	Mintage	F	VF	XF	Unc	BU
2006 Proof	200	Value: 750				

KM# 149 100 RINGGIT

7.9600 g., Gold, 22 mm. **Subject:** 9th Malaysian Plan **Obv:** Bust 3/4 right **Obv. Legend:** BANK NEGARA MALAYSIA - CEMERLANG GEMILANG TERBILANG **Rev:** Globe logo **Rev. Legend:** RANCANGAN MALAYSIA KE SEMBILAN

Date	Mintage	F	VF	XF	Unc	BU
2006 Proof	500	Value: 700				

KM# 164 100 RINGGIT

7.9600 g., Gold, 22 mm. **Subject:** 200th Anniversary Malaysian Police Force **Obv:** Police badge **Obv. Legend:** BANK NEGARA MALAYSIA **Rev:** Two hands clasped in sprays

Date	Mintage	F	VF	XF	Unc	BU
2007 Proof	500	Value: 700				

KM# 184 100 RINGGIT

7.9600 g., 0.9999 Gold 0.2559 oz. AGW, 22 mm. **Obv:** National Arms within wreath **Rev:** Facing portrait

Date	Mintage	F	VF	XF	Unc	BU
2007 Proof	400	Value: 560				

KM# 187 100 RINGGIT

7.9600 g., 0.9999 Gold 0.2559 oz. AGW, 22 mm. **Subject:** Independence, 50th Anniversary **Obv:** National Arms **Rev:** 50 above city skyline

Date	Mintage	F	VF	XF	Unc	BU
2007 Proof	1,100	Value: 600				

KM# 190 100 RINGGIT

7.9600 g., 0.9999 Gold 0.2559 oz. AGW, 22 mm. **Subject:** Royal Malaysian Air Force, 50th Anniversary **Obv:** Royal Airforce insignia **Rev:** Old and new plane

Date	Mintage	F	VF	XF	Unc	BU
2008 Proof	250	Value: 600				

KM# 193 100 RINGGIT

7.9600 g., 0.9999 Gold 0.2559 oz. AGW, 22 mm. **Subject:** St. John's Ambulance, 100th Anniversary **Obv:** St. John's insignia in wreath above value **Rev:** Client being loaded into ambulance

Date	Mintage	F	VF	XF	Unc	BU
2008 Proof	250	Value: 600				

KM# 158 100 RINGGIT

7.9600 g., 0.9990 Gold 0.2557 oz. AGW, 22 mm. **Subject:** Bank Negara Malaysia, 50th Anniversary **Obv:** Bank logo **Rev:** 14-pointed star

Date	Mintage	F	VF	XF	Unc	BU
2009 Proof	350	Value: 900				

KM# 180 100 RINGGIT

7.9600 g., 0.9999 Gold 0.2559 oz. AGW, 22 mm. **Subject:** Parliament, 50th Anniversary **Obv:** National arms above mace and sceptre **Rev:** Parliament buildings, sunburst

Date	Mintage	F	VF	XF	Unc	BU
2009 Proof	550	Value: 550				

KM# 196 100 RINGGIT

7.9600 g., 0.9999 Gold 0.2559 oz. AGW, 22 mm. **Subject:** International Year of Astronomy **Obv:** Adult and child looking to the ehavens **Rev:** Langkawi National Observatory

Date	Mintage	F	VF	XF	Unc	BU
2009 Proof	450	Value: 550				

KM# 199 100 RINGGIT

7.9600 g., 0.9999 Gold 0.2559 oz. AGW, 22 mm. **Subject:** Royal Malaysian Navy, 75th Anniversary **Obv:** Submarine **Rev:** Navy insignia

Date	Mintage	F	VF	XF	Unc	BU
2009 Proof	450	Value: 550				

KM# 134 200 RINGGIT

15.5500 g., Gold, 28 mm. **Subject:** 30th Annual Meeting Islamic Development Bank **Obv:** Mosque in rays **Obv. Legend:** BANK NEGARA MALAYSIA **Rev:** Logo

Date	Mintage	F	VF	XF	Unc	BU
2005 Proof	500	Value: 775				

PROOF SETS

KM#	Date	Mintage	Identification	Issue Price	Mkt Val
PS19	2003 (2)	300	KM#171, 172	—	120
PS20	2003 (3)	300	KM#171-173	—	800
PS21	2003 (2)	300	KM#174, 175	—	150
PS22	2003 (3)	100	KM#174-176	—	1,200
PS23	2003 (2)	500	KM#177, 178	—	100
PS24	2003 (3)	250	KM#177-179	—	850
PS25	2005 (2)	300	KM#114, 115	—	120
PS26	2005 (3)	100	KM#114-116	—	1,000
PS27	2005 (2)	1,000	KM#132, 133	—	100
PS28	2005 (3)	500	KM#132-134	—	950
PS29	2005 (2)	200	KM#135, 136	—	120
PS30	2005 (3)	150	KM#135-137	—	950
PS31	2006 (2)	150	KM#138, 139	—	120
PS32	2005 (3)	150	KM#138-140	—	900
PS33	2006 (2)	300	KM#141, 142	—	120
PS34	2006 (3)	300	KM#141-143	—	900
PS35	2006 (2)	500	KM#144, 145	—	110
PS36	2006 (3)	500	KM#144-146	—	850
PS37	2006 (2)	300	KM#147, 148	—	110
PS38	2006 (3)	500	KM#147-149	—	700
PS39	2007 (2)	200	KM#162, 163	—	120
PS40	2007 (3)	200	KM#162-164	—	700

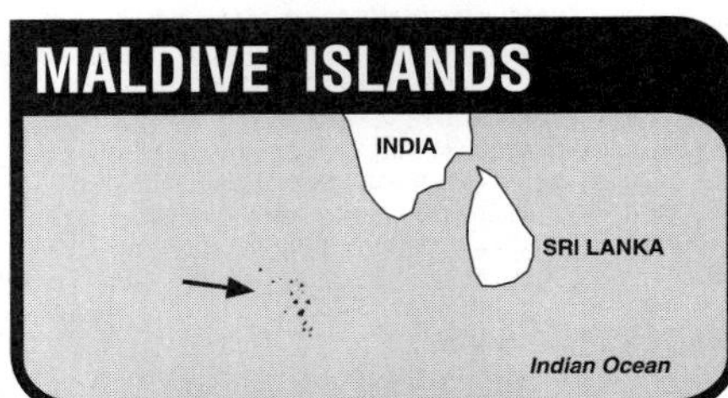

The Republic of Maldives, an archipelago of 2,000 coral islets in the northern Indian Ocean 417 miles (671 km.) west of Ceylon, has an area of 116 sq. mi. (298 sq. km.)and a population of 189,000. Capital: Male. Fishing employs 95% of the male work force. Dried fish, copra and coir yarn are exported.

The Maldive Islands were visited by Arab traders and converted to Islam in 1153. After being harassed in the16th and 17th centuries by Mopla pirates of the Malabar coast and Portuguese raiders, the Maldivians voluntarily placed themselves under the suzeraignty of Ceylon. In 1887 the islands became an internally self-governing British protectorate and a nominal dependency of Ceylon. Traditionally a sultanate, the Maldives became a republic in 1953 but restored the sultanate in 1954. The Sultanate of the Maldive Islands attained complete internal and external autonomy on July 26, 1965, and on Nov. 11, 1968, again became a republic. The Maldives is a member of the Commonwealth of Nations.

MONETARY SYSTEM

100 Lari = 1 Rupee (Rufiyaa)

2ND REPUBLIC

STANDARD COINAGE

KM# 68 LAARI

0.4700 g., Aluminum, 18.2 mm. **Obv:** Value **Rev:** Palm tree within circle **Rev. Designer:** Maizan Hassan Manik and Ahmed Abbas **Edge:** Plain

Date	Mintage	F	VF	XF	Unc	BU
AH1423-2002	—	—	—	0.10	0.15	0.20

KM# 70 10 LAARI

1.9500 g., Aluminum, 23 mm. **Obv:** Value **Rev:** Maldivian sailing ship - Odi **Rev. Designer:** Maizan Hassan Manik and Ahmed Abbas **Shape:** Scalloped

Date	Mintage	F	VF	XF	Unc	BU
AH1422-2001	—	—	—	0.10	0.20	0.30

KM# 73b RUFIYAA

6.5400 g., Nickel Plated Steel, 25.8 mm. **Obv:** Value **Obv. Legend:** REPUBLIC OF MALDIVES **Rev:** National arms **Edge:** Reeded

Date	Mintage	F	VF	XF	Unc	BU
AH1428-2007	—	—	—	0.50	2.00	3.00

KM# 88 2 RUFIYAA

11.7000 g., Brass, 25.47 mm. **Obv:** Value **Rev:** Pacific triton sea shell **Edge:** Reeded and lettered **Edge Lettering:** REPUBLIC OF MALDIVES

Date	Mintage	F	VF	XF	Unc	BU
AH1428-2007	—	—	—	2.25	5.50	7.50

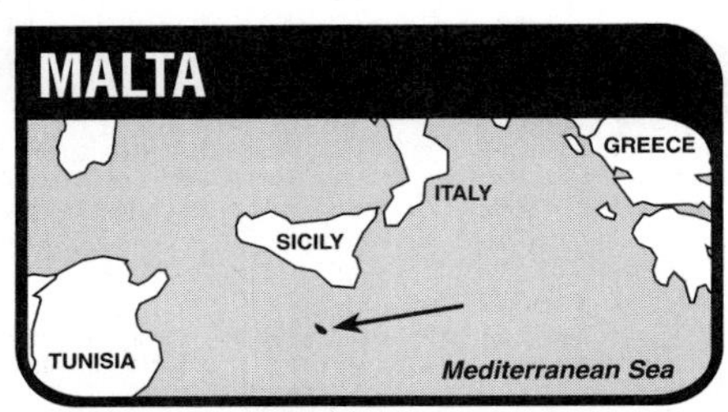

The Republic of Malta, an independent parliamentary democracy, is situated in the Mediterranean Sea between Sicily and North Africa. With the islands of Gozo and Comino, Malta has an area of 124 sq. mi. (320 sq. km.) and a population of 386,000. Capital: Valletta. Malta has no proven mineral resources, an agriculture insufficient to its needs, and a small, but expanding, manufacturing facility. Clothing, textile yarns and fabrics, and knitted wear are exported.

For more than 3,500 years Malta was ruled, in succession by Phoenicians, Carthaginians, Romans, Arabs, Normans, the Knights of Malta, France and Britain. Napoleon seized Malta by treachery in 1798. The French were ousted by a Maltese insurrection assisted by Britain, and in 1814 Malta, of its own free will, became a part of the British Empire. Malta obtained full independence in Sept., 1964; electing to remain within the Commonwealth with the British monarch as the nominal head of state.

Malta became a republic on Dec. 13, 1974, but remained a member of the Commonwealth of Nations. The president is Chief of State. The prime minister is the Head of Government.

RULER

British, until 1964

REPUBLIC

DECIMAL COINAGE

10 Mils = 1 Cent; 100 Cents = 1 Pound

KM# 5 2 MILS

0.9500 g., Aluminum, 20.3 mm. **Obv:** Maltese cross **Rev:** Value within 3/4 wreath **Shape:** Scalloped **Designer:** Envin Cremona

Date	Mintage	F	VF	XF	Unc	BU
2005 In sets only	—	—	—	—	—	4.00
2006 In sets only	—	—	—	—	—	4.00
2007 In sets only	—	—	—	—	—	4.00

REFORM COINAGE

1982 - Present

10 Mils = 1 Cent; 100 Cents = 1 Lira = (Pound)

KM# 93 CENT

2.8100 g., Nickel-Brass, 18.51 mm. **Obv:** Crowned shield within sprigs **Obv. Designer:** Galea Bason **Rev:** Common Weasel (ballottra) below value **Edge:** Plain

Date	Mintage	F	VF	XF	Unc	BU
2001	—	—	0.40	0.50	1.00	—
2002 In sets only	—	—	—	—	1.00	—
2004	—	—	0.40	0.50	0.75	—
2005 In sets only	—	—	—	—	1.00	—
2006 In sets only	—	—	—	—	1.00	—
2007 In sets only	—	—	—	—	1.00	—

KM# 94 2 CENTS

2.2600 g., Copper-Nickel, 17.78 mm. **Obv:** Crowned shield within sprigs **Obv. Designer:** Galea Bason **Rev:** Zebbuga branch and value **Edge:** Reeded

Date	Mintage	F	VF	XF	Unc	BU
2002	—	—	0.75	1.00	1.25	—
2004	—	—	0.75	1.00	1.25	—
2005	—	—	—	—	1.25	—
2006 In sets only	—	—	—	—	1.25	—
2007 In sets only	—	—	—	—	1.25	—

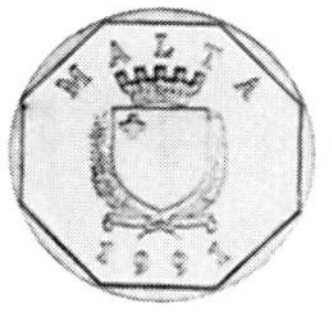 

KM# 95 5 CENTS

3.5100 g., Copper-Nickel, 19.78 mm. **Obv:** Crowned shield within sprigs **Obv. Designer:** Galea Bason **Rev:** Freshwater Crab (il-Qobru) and value **Edge:** Reeded

Date	Mintage	F	VF	XF	Unc	BU
2001	—	—	0.75	1.00	1.25	2.00
2005 In sets only	—	—	—	—	—	2.00
2006 In sets only	—	—	—	—	—	2.00
2007 In sets only	—	—	—	—	—	2.00

KM# 96 10 CENTS

5.0100 g., Copper-Nickel, 21.78 mm. **Obv:** Crowned shield within sprigs **Obv. Designer:** Galea Bason **Rev:** Lampuka and value **Edge:** Reeded

Date	Mintage	F	VF	XF	Unc	BU
2005	—	—	1.25	1.50	2.00	—
2006 In sets only	—	—	—	—	2.00	—
2007 In sets only	—	—	—	—	2.00	—

KM# 97 25 CENTS

6.1900 g., Copper-Nickel, 24.95 mm. **Obv:** Crowned shield within sprigs **Obv. Designer:** Galea Bason **Rev:** Ghirlanda flower and value

Date	Mintage	F	VF	XF	Unc	BU
2001	—	—	2.25	2.50	3.00	—
2005	—	—	2.25	2.50	3.00	—
2006 In sets only	—	—	—	—	3.00	—
2007 In sets only	—	—	—	—	3.00	—

KM# 98 50 CENTS

8.0000 g., Copper-Nickel, 27 mm. **Obv:** Crowned shield within sprigs **Obv. Designer:** Galea Bason **Rev:** Tulliera plant and value **Edge Lettering:** BANK CENTRALI TA' MALTA

Date	Mintage	F	VF	XF	Unc	BU
2001	—	—	2.50	5.00	10.00	—
2005 In sets only	—	—	—	—	10.00	—
2006 In sets only	—	—	—	—	10.00	—
2007 In sets only	—	—	—	—	10.00	—

KM# 99 LIRA

13.0000 g., Nickel, 29.82 mm. **Obv:** Crowned shield within sprigs **Obv. Designer:** Galea Bason **Rev:** Merill bird and value **Rev. Designer:** Noel Galea **Edge Lettering:** BANK CENTRALI TA' MALTA

Date	Mintage	F	VF	XF	Unc	BU
2005	—	—	—	4.50	6.50	12.00
2006 In sets only	—	—	—	—	—	12.00
2007 In sets only	—	—	—	—	—	12.00

KM# 117 5 LIRI

28.2800 g., 0.9250 Silver 0.8410 oz. ASW, 38.6 mm. **Obv:** Crowned shield within sprigs **Rev:** Enrico Mizzi right **Edge:** Reeded

Date	Mintage	F	VF	XF	Unc	BU
2001 Proof	2,000	Value: 80.00				

KM# 118 5 LIRI

28.2800 g., 0.9250 Silver 0.8410 oz. ASW, 38.6 mm. **Obv:** Crowned shield within sprigs **Rev:** Nicolo Isouard left **Edge:** Reeded

Date	Mintage	F	VF	XF	Unc	BU
2002 Proof	2,000	Value: 80.00				

KM# 120 5 LIRI

28.2800 g., 0.9250 Silver 0.8410 oz. ASW, 38.6 mm. **Obv:** Crowned shield within sprigs **Rev:** Sir Adriano Dingli as Grand Commander of the St. Michael and George Order **Edge:** Reeded

Date	Mintage	F	VF	XF	Unc	BU
2003 Proof	2,000	Value: 80.00				

KM# 121 5 LIRI

28.2800 g., 0.9250 Silver 0.8410 oz. ASW, 38.6 mm. **Obv:** Crowned shield within sprigs **Rev:** Painter Giuseppe Cali with palette **Edge:** Reeded

Date	Mintage	F	VF	XF	Unc	BU
2004 Proof	2,000	Value: 120				

KM# 123 5 LIRI

28.2800 g., 0.9250 Silver 0.8410 oz. ASW, 38.61 mm. **Subject:** 450th Anniversary of Jean de la Valette appointed Grand master **Rev:** de la Vallete standing facing left, city of Valletta map at lower left

Date	Mintage	F	VF	XF	Unc	BU
ND(2007) Proof	25,000	Value: 75.00				

KM# 119 10 LIRI

1.2400 g., 0.9990 Gold 0.0398 oz. AGW, 13.92 mm. **Obv:** Crowned shield within sprigs **Rev:** Xprunara sailboat **Edge:** Reeded

Date	Mintage	F	VF	XF	Unc	BU
2002 Prooflike	Est. 25,000	—	—	—	—	130

KM# 122 25 LIRI

3.9940 g., 0.9167 Gold 0.1177 oz. AGW, 19.3 mm. **Subject:** Accession to the European Union **Obv:** Crowned shield within sprigs **Rev:** Maltese flag under European Union star circle **Edge:** Reeded

Date	Mintage	F	VF	XF	Unc	BU
2004 Proof	6,000	Value: 290				

KM# 124 25 LIRI

6.5000 g., 0.9200 Gold 0.1923 oz. AGW, 21 mm. **Subject:** 450th Anniversary Jean de la Valette Appointed as Grand Master **Rev:** de la Valette standing facing left, city of Valletta map at lower left

Date	Mintage	F	VF	XF	Unc	BU
ND(2007) Proof	2,500	Value: 350				

EURO COINAGE

KM# 125 EURO CENT

2.3000 g., Copper Plated Steel, 16.25 mm. **Obv:** Doorway **Rev:** Denomination and globe **Edge:** Plain

Date	Mintage	F	VF	XF	Unc	BU
2008	—	—	—	—	—	1.00

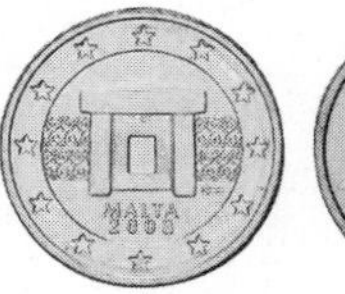 

KM# 126 2 EURO CENT

3.0600 g., Copper Plated Steel, 18.75 mm. **Obv:** Doorway **Rev:** Denomination and globe **Edge:** Grooved

Date	Mintage	F	VF	XF	Unc	BU
2008	—	—	—	—	—	0.70

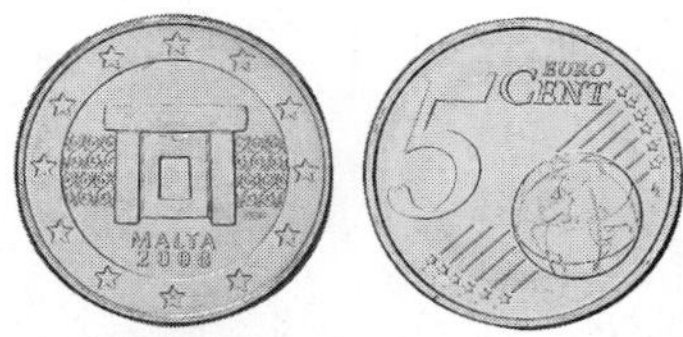

KM# 127 5 EURO CENT

3.9200 g., Copper Plated Steel, 21.25 mm. **Obv:** Doorway **Rev:** Denomination and globe

Date	Mintage	F	VF	XF	Unc	BU
2008	—	—	—	—	—	0.70

KM# 128 10 EURO CENT

4.1000 g., Brass, 19.75 mm. **Obv:** Crowned shield within wreath **Rev:** Value and relief map of Europe **Edge:** Notched

Date	Mintage	F	VF	XF	Unc	BU
2008	—	—	—	—	—	1.00

KM# 129 20 EURO CENT

5.7500 g., Brass, 22.25 mm. **Obv:** Crowned shield within wreath **Rev:** Denomination and Map of Western Europe **Edge:** Notched

Date	Mintage	F	VF	XF	Unc	BU
2008	—	—	—	—	—	1.50

KM# 130 50 EURO CENT

7.8000 g., Brass, 24.25 mm. **Obv:** Crowned shield within wreath **Rev:** Relief map of Western Europe **Edge:** Reeded

Date	Mintage	F	VF	XF	Unc	BU
2008	—	—	—	—	—	2.00

KM# 131 EURO

7.5000 g., Bi-Metallic Copper-Nickel center in Nickel-Brass ring, 23.25 mm. **Obv:** Maltese Cross **Rev:** Value and relief map of Europe **Edge:** Segmented reeding

Date	Mintage	F	VF	XF	Unc	BU
2008	—	—	—	—	—	4.00

KM# 132 2 EURO
8.5000 g., Bi-Metallic Nickel-Brass center in Copper-Nickel ring, 25.75 mm. **Obv:** Maltese Cross **Rev:** Value and Relief Map of Western Europe **Edge:** Reeded with 2s and Maltese Crosses

Date	Mintage	F	VF	XF	Unc	BU
2008	—	—	—	—	—	6.00

KM# 134 2 EURO
8.5000 g., Bi-Metallic Nickel-Brass center in Copper-Nickel ring, 25.75 mm. **Subject:** E.M.U., 10th Anniversary **Obv:** Stick figure and large E symbol **Rev:** Value and relief map of Western Europe **Edge:** Segmented reeding

Date	Mintage	F	VF	XF	Unc	BU
2009	—	—	—	—	—	6.00

KM# 136 10 EURO
28.2800 g., 0.9250 Silver 0.8410 oz. ASW, 38.6 mm. **Subject:** Auberge de Castille **Rev:** Building tower

Date	Mintage	F	VF	XF	Unc	BU
2008 Proof	18,000	Value: 60.00				

KM# 133 10 EURO
28.2800 g., 0.9250 Silver 0.8410 oz. ASW, 38.6 mm. **Rev:** La Castellania, Merchant's Street, Valletta

Date	Mintage	F	VF	XF	Unc	BU
2009 Proof	15,000	Value: 60.00				

KM# 137 50 EURO
6.5000 g., 0.9160 Gold 0.1914 oz. AGW, 21 mm. **Subject:** Auberge de Castille **Rev:** Building tower

Date	Mintage	F	VF	XF	Unc	BU
2008 Proof	3,000	Value: 325				

KM# 135 50 EURO
6.5000 g., 0.9160 Gold 0.1914 oz. AGW, 21 mm. **Rev:** La Castellania, Merchant's Street, Valletta

Date	Mintage	F	VF	XF	Unc	BU
2009 Proof	3,000	Value: 325				

MINT SETS

KM#	Date	Mintage	Identification	Issue Price	Mkt Val
MS26	2005 (8)	—	KM#5, 93-99	—	35.00
MS27	2006 (8)	—	KM#5, 93-99	—	37.50
MS28	2007 (8)	—	KM#5, 93-99	—	45.00
MS29	2008 (8)	40,000	KM#125-132, wooden box	—	70.00
MS30	2008 (8)	30,000	KM#125-132, Malta Post and Lombard Bank card	—	45.00

MARSHALL ISLANDS

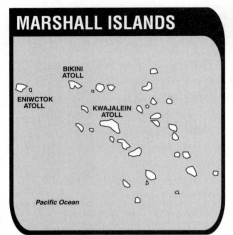

The Republic of the Marshall Islands, an archipelago which is one of the four island groups that make up what is commonly known as Micronesia, consists of 33 coral atolls comprised of over 1,150 islands or islets. It is located east of the Caroline Islands and west-northwest of the Gilbert Islands halfway between Hawaii and Australia. The Ratak chain to the east and the Ralik chain to the west comprise a total land area of 70 sq. mi. (181 sq. km.) with a population of 25,000 of which about 10 % includes Americans who work at the Kwajalein Missile Range. Majuro Atoll is the government and commercial center of the Republic.

A constitutional government was formed on May 1,1979 with Amata Kabua being elected as the head of the government. On October 1, 1986, the United States notified the United Nations that the Marshall Islands were to be recognized as a separate nation.

The USA dollar is the current monetary system. Recently, the coinage has had limited redemption policies enforced.

MINT MARKS
M - Medallic Art Co.
R - Roger Williams Mint, Rhode Island
S - Sunshine Mining Co. Mint, Idaho

REPUBLIC

NON-CIRCULATING COLLECTOR COINAGE

The USA dollar is the current monetary system. Recently, the coinage has had limited redemption policies enforced.

KM# 495 50 DOLLARS
31.1600 g., 0.9990 Silver 1.0008 oz. ASW, 39 mm. **Obv:** State seal **Rev:** Long-snouted Spinner Dolphins **Edge:** Reeded **Note:** Legal tender status questionable

Date	Mintage	F	VF	XF	Unc	BU
2002S Proof	—	Value: 60.00				

MAURITANIA

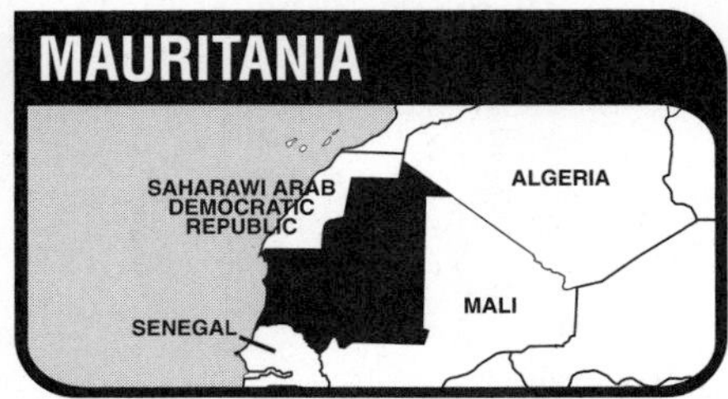

The Islamic Republic of Mauritania, located in northwest Africa bounded by Western Sahara, Mali, Algeria, Senegal and the Atlantic Ocean, has an area of 397,955 sq. mi.(1,030,700 sq. km.) and a population of 1.9 million. Capital: Nouakchott. The economy centers on herding, agriculture, fishing and mining. Iron ore, copper concentrates and fish products are exported.

The indigenous Negroid inhabitants were driven out of Mauritania by Berber invaders of the Islamic faith in the 11th century. The Berbers in turn were conquered by Arab invaders, the Beni Hassan, in the 16th century. Arab traders carried on a gainful trade in gum arabic, gold and slaves with Portuguese, Dutch, English and French traders until late in the 19th century when France took control of the area and made it a part of French West Africa, in 1920.Mauritania became a part of the French Union in 1946 and was made an autonomous republic within the new French Community in 1958, when the Islamic Republic of Mauritania was proclaimed. The republic became independent on November 28, 1960, and withdrew from the French Community in 1966.

On June 28, 1973, in a move designed to emphasize its nonalignment with France, Mauritania converted its currency from the old French-supported C.F.A. franc unit to a new unit called the Ouguiya.

MONETARY SYSTEM
5 Khoums = 1 Ouguiya

REPUBLIC

STANDARD COINAGE

KM# 6 OUGUIYA
3.6000 g., Copper-Nickel-Aluminum, 21 mm. **Obv:** National emblem divides date above value **Obv. Legend:** BANQUE CENTRALE DE MAURITANIE **Rev:** Star and crescent divide sprigs with legend below value, all within circle **Edge:** Reeded

Date	Mintage	F	VF	XF	Unc	BU
AH1423//2003	—	—	—	0.50	1.25	2.00

KM# 3 5 OUGUIYA
5.8800 g., Copper-Nickel-Aluminum, 25 mm. **Obv:** National emblem divides date above value **Obv. Legend:** BANQUE CENTRALE DE MAURITANIE **Rev:** Star and crescent divide sprigs below value within circle **Edge:** Plain

Date	Mintage	F	VF	XF	Unc	BU
AH1423//2003	—	—	—	1.75	3.50	5.00
AH1425//2004	—	—	—	1.75	3.50	5.00

KM# 3a 5 OUGUIYA
5.4600 g., Copper Plated Steel, 24.5 mm. **Obv:** National emblem divides date above value **Obv. Legend:** BANQUE CENTRALE DE MAURITANIE **Rev:** Star and crescent divides sprigs below value within circle **Edge:** Plain

Date	Mintage	F	VF	XF	Unc	BU
AH1425//2004	—	—	0.50	1.00	2.00	3.00
AH1426//2005	—	—	0.50	1.00	2.00	3.00

KM# 4 10 OUGUIYA
6.0000 g., Copper-Nickel, 25 mm. **Obv:** National emblem divides date above value **Obv. Legend:** BANQUE CENTRALE DE MAURITANIE **Rev:** Crescent and star divide sprigs below value within circle **Edge:** Reeded

Date	Mintage	F	VF	XF	Unc	BU
AH1423//2003	—	—	—	2.00	4.00	5.50
AH1425//2004	—	—	—	2.00	4.00	5.50

KM# 4a 10 OUGUIYA
5.8000 g., Nickel Plated Steel, 24.5 mm. **Obv:** National emblem divides date above value **Obv. Legend:** BANQUE CENTRALE DE MAURITANIE **Rev:** Crescent and star divides sprigs below value within circle **Edge:** Reeded

Date	Mintage	F	VF	XF	Unc	BU
AH1425//2004	—	—	—	1.25	3.00	4.50
AH1426//2005	—	—	—	1.25	3.00	4.50

KM# 5 20 OUGUIYA
8.0000 g., Copper-Nickel, 28 mm. **Obv:** National emblem divides date above value **Obv. Legend:** BANQUE CENTRALE DE MAURITANIE **Rev:** Star and crescent divide sprigs below value within circle **Edge:** Reeded

Date	Mintage	F	VF	XF	Unc	BU
AH1423//2003	—	—	—	3.00	6.00	8.00
AH1425//2004	—	—	—	3.00	6.00	8.00

KM# 5a 20 OUGUIYA
7.8000 g., Nickel Plated Steel, 28.05 mm. **Obv:** National emblem divides date above value **Obv. Legend:** BANQUE CENTRALE DE MAURITANIE **Rev:** Star and crescent divide sprigs below value within circle **Edge:** Reeded

Date	Mintage	F	VF	XF	Unc	BU
AH1425//2004	—	—	—	2.00	4.00	6.00
AH1426//2005	—	—	—	2.00	4.00	6.00
AH1430//2009	—	—	—	2.00	4.00	6.00

KM# 8 20 OUGUIYA
Bi-Metallic **Obv:** Value within wreath

Date	Mintage	F	VF	XF	Unc	BU
2009	—	—	—	—	6.00	7.50

MAURITIUS

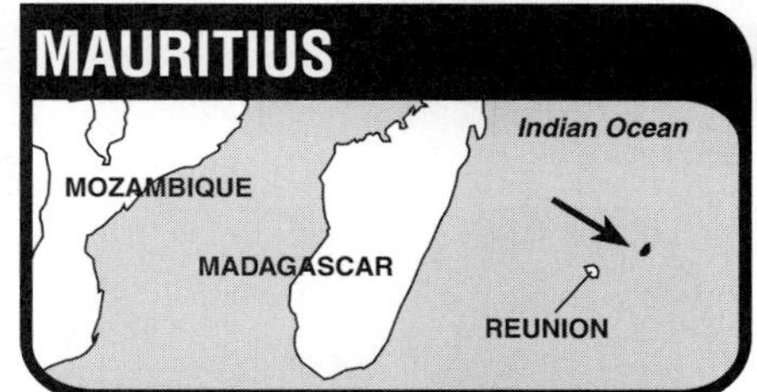

The Republic of Mauritius, is located in the Indian Ocean 500 miles (805 km.) east of Madagascar, has an area of 790 sq. mi. (1,860 sq. km.) and a population of 1 million. Capital: Port Louis. Sugar provides 90 percent of the export revenue.

Mauritius became independent on March 12, 1968. It is a member of the Commonwealth of Nations.

MONETARY SYSTEM
100 Cents = 1 Rupee

REPUBLIC

STANDARD COINAGE

KM# 52 5 CENTS
3.0000 g., Copper Plated Steel **Obv:** Value within beaded circle **Rev:** Bust of Sir Seewoosagur Ramgoolam 3/4 right

Date	Mintage	F	VF	XF	Unc	BU
2003	—	—	—	0.10	0.35	0.50
2004	—	—	—	0.10	0.35	0.50
2005	—	—	—	0.10	0.35	0.50
2007	—	—	—	0.10	0.35	0.50

KM# 53 20 CENTS
3.0000 g., Nickel Plated Steel, 19 mm. **Obv:** Value within beaded circle **Rev:** Bust of Sir Seewoosagur Ramgoolam 3/4 right

Date	Mintage	F	VF	XF	Unc	BU
2001	—	—	—	0.20	0.50	0.75
2003	—	—	—	0.20	0.50	0.75
2004	—	—	—	0.20	0.50	0.75
2005	—	—	—	0.20	0.50	0.75
2007	—	—	—	0.20	0.50	0.75

KM# 54 1/2 RUPEE
5.9000 g., Nickel Plated Steel, 23.6 mm. **Obv:** Stag left **Rev:** Bust of Sir Seewoosagur Ramgoolam 3/4 right **Rev. Designer:** G. E. Kruger-Gray

Date	Mintage	F	VF	XF	Unc	BU
2002	—	—	—	0.60	1.50	2.00
2003	—	—	—	0.60	1.50	2.00
2004	—	—	—	0.60	1.50	2.00
2005	—	—	—	0.60	1.50	2.00
2007	—	—	—	0.60	1.50	2.00

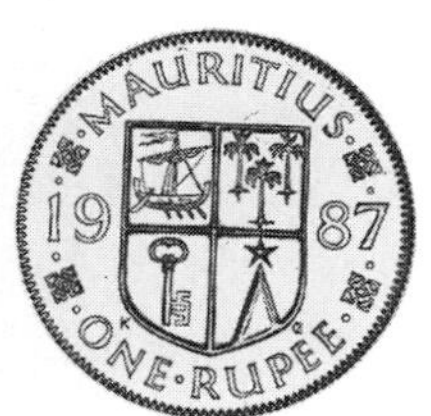

KM# 55 RUPEE
7.5000 g., Copper-Nickel, 26.6 mm. **Obv:** Shield divides date above value **Rev:** Bust of Sir Seewoosagur Ramgoolam 3/4 right **Rev. Designer:** G.E. Kruger-Gray

Date	Mintage	F	VF	XF	Unc	BU
2002	—	—	—	0.65	1.65	2.75
2004	—	—	—	0.65	1.65	2.75
2005	—	—	—	0.65	1.65	2.75
2007	—	—	—	0.65	1.65	2.75
2008	—	—	—	0.65	1.65	2.75

KM# 66 20 RUPEES
10.1000 g., Bi-Metallic Copper-Nickel center in Aluminum-Bronze ring, 27.96 mm. **Obv:** Modern tower **Rev:** Bust of Sir Seewoosagur Ramgoolam KT 3/4 right **Edge:** Reeded

Date	Mintage	F	VF	XF	Unc	BU
2007	—	—	—	2.00	5.00	7.00

KM# 65 100 RUPEES
36.5700 g., 0.9250 Silver 1.0875 oz. ASW, 43.9 mm. **Obv:** National arms, date below **Obv. Legend:** MAURITIUS ONE HUNDRED RUPEES **Rev:** Bust of Gandhi 3/4 right **Rev. Legend:** MAHATMA GANDHI CENTENARY OF ARRIVAL IN MAURITIUS **Edge:** Reeded

Date	Mintage	F	VF	XF	Unc	BU
2001 Proof	—	Value: 125				

REFORM COINAGE

KM# 67 1500 RUPEES
7.7800 g., 0.9990 Platinum 0.2499 oz. APW, 25 mm. **Subject:** Sir Seewoosagur Ramgoolan **Obv:** Portrait **Rev:** State House **Edge:** Plain

Date	Mintage	F	VF	XF	Unc	BU
2009 Proof	—	Value: 500				

MEXICO

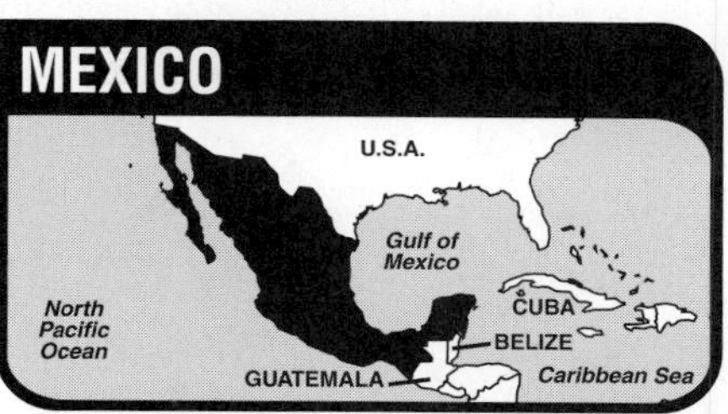

The United States of Mexico, located immediately south of the United States has an area of 759,529 sq. mi. (1,967,183 sq. km.) and an estimated population of 100 million. Capital: Mexico City. The economy is based on agriculture, manufacturing and mining. Oil, cotton, silver, coffee, and shrimp are exported.

UNITED STATES

REFORM COINAGE

1 New Peso = 1000 Old Pesos;
100 centavos = 1 New Peso; 100 Centavos = 1 Peso

KM# 546 5 CENTAVOS
1.5800 g., Stainless Steel, 15.5 mm. **Obv:** National arms **Rev:** Large value **Edge:** Plain

Date	Mintage	F	VF	XF	Unc	BU
2001Mo	34,811,000	—	—	0.15	0.20	0.50
2002Mo	14,901,000	—	—	0.15	0.20	0.50

KM# 547 10 CENTAVOS
2.0800 g., Stainless Steel, 17 mm. **Obv:** National arms, eagle left **Rev:** Large value

Date	Mintage	F	VF	XF	Unc	BU
2001Mo	618,061,000	—	—	0.20	0.25	0.30
2002Mo	463,968,000	—	—	0.20	0.25	0.30
2003Mo	378,938,000	—	—	0.20	0.25	0.30
2004Mo	393,705,000	—	—	0.20	0.25	0.30
2005Mo	488,594,000	—	—	0.20	0.25	0.30
2006Mo	473,261,000	—	—	0.20	0.25	0.30
2007Mo	473,261,000	—	—	0.20	0.25	0.30
2008Mo	433,951,000	—	—	0.20	0.25	0.30
2009Mo	90,968,000	—	—	0.20	0.25	0.30

KM# 548 20 CENTAVOS
3.0400 g., Aluminum-Bronze, 19.5 mm. **Obv:** National arms, eagle left **Rev:** Value and date within 3/4 wreath **Shape:** 12-sided

Date	Mintage	F	VF	XF	Unc	BU
2001Mo	234,360,000	—	—	0.25	0.35	0.40
2002Mo	229,256,000	—	—	0.25	0.35	0.40

Date	Mintage	F	VF	XF	Unc	BU
2003Mo	149,518,000	—	—	0.25	0.35	0.40
2004Mo	174,351,000	—	—	0.25	0.35	0.40
2005Mo	204,426,000	—	—	0.25	0.35	0.40
2006Mo	234,263,000	—	—	0.25	0.35	0.40
2007Mo	234,301,000	—	—	0.25	0.35	0.40
2008Mo	214,303,000	—	—	0.25	0.35	0.40
2009Mo	41,167,000	—	—	0.25	0.35	0.40

KM# 549 50 CENTAVOS

4.3900 g., Aluminum-Bronze, 22 mm. **Obv:** National arms, eagle left **Rev:** Value and date within 1/2 designed wreath **Shape:** 12-sided

Date	Mintage	F	VF	XF	Unc	BU
2001Mo	199,006,000	—	—	0.45	0.75	1.00
2002Mo	94,552,000	—	—	0.45	0.75	1.00
2003Mo	124,522,000	—	—	0.45	0.75	1.00
2004Mo	154,434,000	—	—	0.45	0.75	1.00
2005Mo	179,296,000	—	—	0.45	0.75	1.00
2006Mo	234,142,000	—	—	0.45	0.75	1.00
2007Mo	253,634,000	—	—	0.45	0.75	1.00
2008Mo	249,279,000	—	—	0.45	0.75	1.00
2009Mo	90,602,000	—	—	0.45	0.75	1.00

KM# 603 PESO

3.9500 g., Bi-Metallic Aluminum-Bronze center in Stainless Steel ring, 21 mm. **Obv:** National arms, eagle left within circle **Rev:** Value and date within circle **Note:** Similar to KM#550 but without N.

Date	Mintage	F	VF	XF	Unc	BU
2001Mo	208,576,000	—	—	—	1.25	2.75
2002Mo	119,514,000	—	—	—	1.25	2.75
2003Mo	169,320,000	—	—	—	1.25	2.75
2004Mo	208,611,000	—	—	—	1.25	2.75
2005Mo	253,923,000	—	—	—	1.25	2.75
2006Mo	289,834,000	—	—	—	1.25	2.75
2007Mo	368,408,000	—	—	—	1.25	2.75
2008Mo	393,878,000	—	—	—	1.25	2.75
2009Mo	239,229,000	—	—	—	1.25	2.75
2010Mo	—	—	—	—	0.75	1.25

KM# 604 2 PESOS

5.1900 g., Bi-Metallic Aluminum-Bronze center in Stainless Steel ring, 23 mm. **Obv:** National arms, eagle left within circle **Rev:** Value and date within center circle of assorted emblems **Note:** Similar to KM#551, but denomination without N.

Date	Mintage	F	VF	XF	Unc	BU
2001Mo	74,563,000	—	—	—	2.35	4.00
2002Mo	74,547,000	—	—	—	2.35	4.00
2003Mo	39,814,000	—	—	—	2.35	4.00
2004Mo	89,496,000	—	—	—	2.35	4.00
2005Mo	94,532,000	—	—	—	2.35	4.00
2006Mo	144,123,000	—	—	—	2.35	4.00
2007Mo	129,422,000	—	—	—	2.35	4.00
2008Mo	134,235,000	—	—	—	2.35	4.00
2009Mo	6,465,000	—	—	—	2.35	4.00
2010Mo	—	—	—	—	1.00	1.50

KM# 651 5 PESOS

31.1710 g., 0.9990 Silver 1.0011 oz. ASW, 40 mm. **Series:** Endangered Wildlife **Obv:** National arms in center of past and present arms **Rev:** Manatee, value and date **Edge:** Reeded

Date	Mintage	F	VF	XF	Unc	BU
2001Mo	30,000	—	—	—	40.00	50.00

KM# 653 5 PESOS

31.1710 g., 0.9990 Silver 1.0011 oz. ASW, 40 mm. **Series:** Endangered Wildlife **Subject:** Aguila Arpia **Obv:** National arms in center of past and present arms **Rev:** Crowned Harpy Eagle perched on branch, value and date

Date	Mintage	F	VF	XF	Unc	BU
2001Mo	30,000	—	—	—	40.00	50.00

KM# 654 5 PESOS

31.1710 g., 0.9990 Silver 1.0011 oz. ASW, 40 mm. **Series:** Endangered Wildlife **Subject:** Oso Negro **Obv:** National arms in center of past and present arms **Rev:** Black bear, value and date

Date	Mintage	F	VF	XF	Unc	BU
2001Mo	30,000	—	—	—	40.00	50.00

KM# 658 5 PESOS

31.1710 g., 0.9990 Silver 1.0011 oz. ASW, 40 mm. **Series:** Endangered Wildlife **Obv:** National arms in center of past and present arms **Rev:** Jaguar, value and date

Date	Mintage	F	VF	XF	Unc	BU
2001Mo	30,000	—	—	—	40.00	50.00

KM# 659 5 PESOS

31.1710 g., 0.9990 Silver 1.0011 oz. ASW, 40 mm. **Series:** Endangered Wildlife **Obv:** National arms in center of past and present arms **Rev:** Prairie dog, value and date

Date	Mintage	F	VF	XF	Unc	BU
2001Mo	30,000	—	—	—	40.00	50.00

KM# 660 5 PESOS

31.1710 g., 0.9990 Silver 1.0011 oz. ASW, 40 mm. **Series:** Endangered Wildlife **Obv:** National arms in center of past and present arms **Rev:** Volcano rabbit, value and date

Date	Mintage	F	VF	XF	Unc	BU
2001Mo	30,000	—	—	—	40.00	50.00

KM# 605 5 PESOS

7.0700 g., Bi-Metallic Aluminum-Bronze center in Stainless Steel ring, 25.5 mm. **Obv:** National arms, eagle left within circle **Rev:** Value within circle **Note:** Similar to KM#552 but denomination without N.

Date	Mintage	F	VF	XF	Unc	BU
2001Mo	79,169,000	—	—	3.00	5.00	7.50
2002Mo	34,754,000	—	—	3.00	5.00	7.50
2003Mo	54,676,000	—	—	3.00	5.00	7.50
2004Mo	89,518,000	—	—	3.00	5.00	7.50
2005Mo	94,482,000	—	—	3.00	5.00	7.50
2006Mo	89,447,000	—	—	3.00	5.00	7.50
2007Mo	123,382,000	—	—	3.00	5.00	7.50
2008Mo	9,939,000	—	—	3.00	5.00	7.50
2009Mo	9,898,000	—	—	3.00	5.00	7.50
2010Mo	—	—	—	1.00	2.00	2.50

KM# 678 5 PESOS

27.0000 g., 0.9250 Silver 0.8029 oz. ASW, 40 mm. **Subject:** Ibero-America: Acapulco Galleon **Obv:** National arms in center of past and present arms **Rev:** Spanish galleon with Pacific Ocean background and trading scene in foreground **Edge:** Reeded

Date	Mintage	F	VF	XF	Unc	BU
2003Mo Proof	5,000	Value: 90.00				

KM# 765 5 PESOS

31.1035 g., 0.9250 Silver 0.9250 oz. ASW, 40 mm. **Subject:** Palacio de Bellas Artes **Obv:** Mexican Eagle and Snake **Rev:** Palace of Fine Arts **Edge:** Reeded

Date	Mintage	F	VF	XF	Unc	BU
2005Mo Proof	—	Value: 90.00				

KM# 769 5 PESOS

15.5518 g., 0.9990 Silver 0.4995 oz. ASW, 33 mm. **Subject:** Monetary Reform of 1905 **Obv:** Mexican Eagle and Snake **Rev:** Cap and rays coin design

Date	Mintage	F	VF	XF	Unc	BU
2005Mo Proof	1,505	Value: 45.00				

KM# 770 5 PESOS

31.1035 g., 0.9990 Silver 0.9990 oz. ASW, 40 mm. **Subject:** World Cup Soccer **Obv:** Mexican Eagle and Snake **Rev:** Mayan Pelota player and soccer ball

Date	Mintage	F	VF	XF	Unc	BU
2006Mo Proof	40,000	Value: 65.00				

KM# 805 5 PESOS

31.1050 g., 0.9250 Silver 0.9250 oz. ASW **Obv:** Eagle on cactus **Rev:** Mayan ball game

Date	Mintage	F	VF	XF	Unc	BU
2006Mo Proof	—	Value: 75.00				

KM# 894 5 PESOS

7.0700 g., Bi-Metallic Aluminum-bronze center in stainless steel ring, 25.5 mm. **Subject:** Independence, 200th Anniversary **Obv:** National Arms - Eagle left **Rev:** Ignacio Rayon bust left

Date	Mintage	F	VF	XF	Unc	BU
2008Mo	9,934,397	—	—	0.75	1.50	—
2008Mo Prooflike	4,267	—	—	—	—	7.50

KM# 895 5 PESOS

7.0700 g., Bi-Metallic Aluminum-bronze center in stainless steel ring, 25.5 mm. **Subject:** Revolution 100th Anniversary **Obv:** National Arms - Eagle left **Rev:** Alvaro Obregon bust 3/4 facing left

Date	Mintage	F	VF	XF	Unc	BU
2008Mo	9,948,722	—	—	0.75	1.50	—
2008Mo Prooflike	4,727	—	—	—	—	7.50

KM# 896 5 PESOS

7.0700 g., Bi-Metallic Aluninum-bronze in stainless steel ring, 25.5 mm. **Subject:** Independence 200th Anniversary **Obv:** National Arms - Eagle left **Rev:** Carlos Maria de Bustamante bust left

Date	Mintage	F	VF	XF	Unc	BU
2008Mo	9,941,302	—	—	0.75	1.50	—
2008Mo Prooflike	4,852	—	—	—	—	7.50

KM# 897 5 PESOS

7.0700 g., Bi-Metallic Aluminum-bronze center in stainless steel ring, 25.5 mm. **Subject:** Revolution 100th Anniversary **Obv:** National Arms - Eagle left **Rev:** Jose Vasconcelos bust left

Date	Mintage	F	VF	XF	Unc	BU
2008Mo	9,939,839	—	—	0.75	1.50	—
2008Mo Prooflike	4,767	—	—	—	—	7.50

KM# 898 5 PESOS

7.0700 g., Bi-Metallic Aluminum-bronze center in stainless steel ring, 25.5 mm. **Subject:** Independence 200th Anniversary **Obv:** National Arms - Eagle left **Rev:** Francisco Mina bust 3/4 facing left

Date	Mintage	F	VF	XF	Unc	BU
2008Mo	9,914,938	—	—	0.75	1.50	—
2008Mo Prooflike	4,523	—	—	—	—	7.50

KM# 899 5 PESOS

7.0700 g., Bi-Metallic Aluminum-bronze center in stainless steel ring, 25.5 mm. **Subject:** Revolution 100th Anniversary **Obv:** National Arms - Eagle left **Rev:** Francisco Villa on horseback left

Date	Mintage	F	VF	XF	Unc	BU
2008Mo	—	—	—	0.75	1.50	—
2008Mo Prooflike	4,866	—	—	—	—	7.50

KM# 900 5 PESOS

7.0700 g., Bi-Metallic Aluminum-Bronze center in Stainless Steel ring, 25.5 mm. **Subject:** Independence 200th Anniversary **Obv:** National Arms - Eagle left **Rev:** Francisco Verdad y Rames bust right

Date	Mintage	F	VF	XF	Unc	BU
2008Mo	9,937,000	—	—	0.75	1.50	—
2008Mo Prooflike	3,279	—	—	—	—	7.50

KM# 901 5 PESOS

7.0700 g., Bi-Metallic Aluminum-Bronze center in Stainless Steel ring, 25.5 mm. **Subject:** Revolution 100th Anniversary **Obv:** National Arms - Eagle left **Rev:** Heriberto Jara bust 3/4 left

Date	Mintage	F	VF	XF	Unc	BU
2008Mo	9,936,333	—	—	0.75	1.50	—
2008Mo Prooflike	4,870	—	—	—	—	7.50

KM# 902 5 PESOS

7.0700 g., Bi-Metallic Aluminum-Bronze center in Stainless Steel ring, 25.5 mm. **Subject:** Independence 200th Anniversary **Obv:** National Arms - Eagle left **Rev:** Mariano Matamoros bust 3/4 facing right

Date	Mintage	F	VF	XF	Unc	BU
2008Mo	9,947,802	—	—	0.75	1.50	—
2008Mo Prooflike	4,820	—	—	—	—	7.50

KM# 903 5 PESOS

7.0700 g., Bi-Metallic Aluminum-Bronze center Stainless Steel ring, 25.5 mm. **Subject:** Revolution 100th Anniversary **Obv:** National Arms - Eagle left **Rev:** Ricardo Magon bust right

Date	Mintage	F	VF	XF	Unc	BU
2008Mo	9,940,278	—	—	0.75	1.50	—
2008Mo Prooflike	4,690	—	—	—	—	7.50

KM# 904 5 PESOS

7.0700 g., Bi-Metallic Aluminum-Bronze center in Stainless Steel ring, 25.5 mm. **Subject:** Independence 200th Anniversary **Obv:** National Arms - Eagle left **Rev:** Miguel Arizpe bust right

Date	Mintage	F	VF	XF	Unc	BU
2008Mo	9,927,433	—	—	0.75	1.50	—
2008Mo Prooflike	4,863	—	—	—	—	7.50

KM# 905 5 PESOS

7.0700 g., Bi-Metallic Aluminum-Bronze center in Stainless Steel ring, 25.5 mm. **Subject:** Revolution 100th Anniversary **Obv:** National arms, eagle left **Rev:** Francisco Mugica bust 3/4 facing left

Date	Mintage	F	VF	XF	Unc	BU
2008Mo	9,926,537	—	—	0.75	1.50	—
2008Mo Prooflike	4,588	—	—	—	—	7.50

KM# 906 5 PESOS

7.0700 g., Bi-Metallic Aluminum-Bronze center in Stainless Steel ring, 25.5 mm. **Subject:** Independence 200th Anniversary **Obv:** National Arms, eagle left **Rev:** Hermenegildo Galeana bust 3/4 facing left

Date	Mintage	F	VF	XF	Unc	BU
2008Mo	9,935,901	—	—	0.75	1.50	—
2008Mo Prooflike	4,966	—	—	—	—	7.50

KM# 907 5 PESOS

7.0700 g., Bi-Metallic Aluminum-Bronze center in Stainless Steel ring., 25.5 mm. **Subject:** Revolution, 100th Anniversary **Obv:** National arms, eagle left **Rev:** Filomeno Mata bust facing.

Date	Mintage	F	VF	XF	Unc	BU
2009Mo	9,935,689	—	—	0.75	1.50	—
2009Mo Prooflike	4,920	—	—	—	—	7.50

KM# 908 5 PESOS

7.0700 g., Bi-Metallic Aluminum-Bronze cetner in Stainless Steel ring., 25.5 mm. **Obv:** National arms, eagle left. **Rev:** Jose Maria Cos bust right

Date	Mintage	F	VF	XF	Unc	BU
2009Mo	9,935,040	—	—	0.75	1.50	—
2009Mo Prooflike	4,950	—	—	—	—	7.50

KM# 909 5 PESOS

7.0700 g., Bi-Metallic Aluminum-Bronze center in Stainless Steel ring, 25.5 mm. **Subject:** Revolution 100th Anniversary **Obv:** National Amrs, Eagle left **Rev:** Carmen Serdan bust facing

Date	Mintage	F	VF	XF	Unc	BU
2009Mo	7,160,841	—	—	0.75	1.50	—
2009Mo Prooflike	4,787	—	—	—	—	7.50

KM# 910 5 PESOS

7.0700 g., Bi-Metallic Aluminum-Bronze center in Stainless Steel ring, 25.5 mm. **Subject:** Independence, 200th Anniversary **Obv:** National arms, eagle left **Rev:** Pedro Moreno bust 3/4 right

Date	Mintage	F	VF	XF	Unc	BU
2009Mo	6,942,480	—	—	0.75	1.50	—
2009Mo Prooflike	4,940	—	—	—	—	7.50

KM# 911 5 PESOS

7.0700 g., Bi-Metallic Aluminum-Bronze center in Stainless Steel ring, 25.5 mm. **Subject:** Revolution 100th Anniversary **Obv:** National arms, eagle left **Rev:** Andres Enriquezs bust 3/4 right

Date	Mintage	F	VF	XF	Unc	BU
2009Mo	6,942,763	—	—	0.75	1.50	—
2009Mo Prooflike	4,666	—	—	—	—	7.50

KM# 912 5 PESOS

7.0700 g., Bi-Metallic Aluminum-Bronze center in Stainless Steel ring, 25.5 mm. **Subject:** Independence, 200th Anniversary **Obv:** National arms, eagle left **Rev:** Agustin de Iturbide bust left

Date	Mintage	F	VF	XF	Unc	BU
2009Mo	6,944,222	—	—	0.75	1.50	—
2009Mo Prooflike	4,838	—	—	—	—	7.50

KM# 913 5 PESOS

7.0700 g., Bi-Metallic Aluminumn-Bronze center in Stainless Steel ring, 25.5 mm. **Subject:** Revolution 100th Anniversary **Obv:** National Arms, eagle left **Rev:** Luis Cabrera bust 3/4 facing left

Date	Mintage	F	VF	XF	Unc	BU
2009Mo	—	—	—	0.75	1.50	—
2009Mo Prooflike	4,656	—	—	—	—	7.50

KM# 914 5 PESOS

7.0700 g., Bi-Metallic Aluminum-Bronze center Stainless Steel ring, 25.5 mm. **Subject:** Independence, 200th Anniversary **Obv:** National Arms, Eagle left **Rev:** Nicolas Bravo bust 3/4 facing left

Date	Mintage	F	VF	XF	Unc	BU
2009Mo	—	—	—	0.75	0.50	—
2009Mo Prooflike	4,780	—	—	—	—	7.50

KM# 915 5 PESOS

7.0700 g., Bi-Metallic Aluminum-bronze center in Stainless steel ring, 25.5 mm. **Subject:** Revolution 100th Anniversary **Obv:** National Arms, eagle left **Rev:** Eulalio Gutierrez bust 3/4 right

Date	Mintage	F	VF	XF	Unc	BU
2009Mo	6,908,760	—	—	0.75	1.50	—
2009Mo Prooflike	4,862	—	—	—	—	7.50

KM# 916 5 PESOS

7.0700 g., Bi-Metallic Aluminum-Bronze center in Stainless Steel ring, 25.5 mm. **Subject:** Independence 200th Anniversary **Obv:** National Arms, eagle left **Rev:** Servando de Mier bust left

Date	Mintage	F	VF	XF	Unc	BU
2009Mo	6,937,421	—	—	0.75	1.50	—
2009Mo Prooflike	4,675	—	—	—	—	7.50

KM# 917 5 PESOS

7.0700 g., Bi-Metallic Aluminum-Bronze center in Stainless Steel ring, 25.5 mm. **Subject:** Revolution 100th Anniversary **Obv:** National Arms, eagle left **Rev:** Otilio Montano bust left

Date	Mintage	F	VF	XF	Unc	BU
2009Mo	6,890,052	—	—	0.75	1.50	—
2009Mo Prooflike	4,923	—	—	—	—	7.50

KM# 918 5 PESOS

7.0700 g., Bi-Metallic Aluminum-Bronze center in Stainless Steel ring, 25.5 mm. **Series:** Revolution 100th Anniversary **Obv:** National Arms, eagle left **Rev:** Belisario Dominquez bust 3/4 left

Date	Mintage	F	VF	XF	Unc	BU
2009Mo	6,926,606	—	—	0.75	1.50	—
2009Mo Prooflike	4,773	—	—	—	—	7.50

KM# 919 5 PESOS

7.0700 g., Bi-Metallic Aluminum-Bronze center in Stainless Steel ring, 25.5 mm. **Subject:** Independence 200th Anniversary **Obv:** National Arms, eagle left **Rev:** Leona Vicario bust left

Date	Mintage	F	VF	XF	Unc	BU
2009Mo	6,937,872	—	—	0.75	1.50	—
2009Mo Prooflike	4,730	—	—	—	—	7.50

KM# 920 5 PESOS

7.0700 g., Bi-Metallic Aluminumn-Bronze center in Stainless Steel ring, 25.5 mm. **Subject:** Independence 200th Anniversary **Obv:** National Arms, eagle left **Rev:** Hildalgo bust

Date	Mintage	F	VF	XF	Unc	BU
2010Mo	6,932,486	—	—	0.75	1.50	—
2010Mo Prooflike	4,763	—	—	—	—	7.50

KM# 922 5 PESOS

7.0700 g., Bi-Metallic Aluminum-Bronze center in Stainless Steel ring, 25.5 mm. **Subject:** Revolution 100th Anniversary **Rev:** Francisco I. Madero head facing 1/4 left

Date	Mintage	F	VF	XF	Unc	BU
2010	6,930,998	—	—	0.75	1.50	—
2010 Prooflike	4,750	—	—	—	—	7.50

KM# 923 5 PESOS

7.0700 g., Bi-Metallic Aluminum-Bronze center in Stainless Steel ring., 25.5 mm. **Subject:** Independence 200th Anniversary **Rev:** Jose Maria Morelos y Pavon head facing 1/2 right

Date	Mintage	F	VF	XF	Unc	BU
2010	—	—	—	0.75	1.50	—
2010 Prooflike	—	—	—	—	—	7.50

KM# 924 5 PESOS

7.0700 g., Bi-Metallic Aluminum-Bronze center in Stainless Steel ring., 25.5 mm. **Subject:** Revolution 100th Anniversary **Rev:** Emiliano Zapata head 1/4 facing left

Date	Mintage	F	VF	XF	Unc	BU
2010	—	—	—	0.75	1.50	—
2010 Prooflike	—	—	—	—	—	7.50

KM# 925 5 PESOS

7.0700 g., Bi-Metallic Aluminum-Bronze center in Stainless Steel ring., 25.5 mm. **Subject:** Independence 200th Anniversary **Rev:** Vicente Guerrero head facing 1/4 left

Date	Mintage	F	VF	XF	Unc	BU
2010	—	—	—	0.75	1.50	—
2010 Prooflike	—	—	—	—	—	7.50

KM# 926 5 PESOS

7.0700 g., Bi-Metallic Aluminum-Bronze center in Stainless Steel ring., 25.5 mm. **Subject:** Revolution 100th Anniversary **Rev:** Venustiano Carranza head 1/4 facing left

Date	Mintage	F	VF	XF	Unc	BU
2010	—	—	—	0.75	1.50	—
2010 Prooflike	—	—	—	—	—	7.50

KM# 927 5 PESOS

7.0700 g., Bi-Metallic Aluminum-Bronze center in Stainless Steel ring., 25.5 mm. **Subject:** Independence 200th Anniversary **Rev:** Ignacio Allende head facing 1/2 left

Date	Mintage	F	VF	XF	Unc	BU
2010	—	—	—	0.75	1.50	—
2010 Prooflike	—	—	—	—	—	7.50

KM# 928 5 PESOS

7.0700 g., Bi-Metallic Aluminum-Bronze center in Stainless Steel ring., 25.5 mm. **Subject:** Revolution 100th Anniversary **Rev:** Female soldier's head facing 1/4 left

Date	Mintage	F	VF	XF	Unc	BU
2010	—	—	—	0.75	1.50	—
2010 Prooflike	—	—	—	—	—	7.50

KM# 929 5 PESOS

7.0700 g., Bi-Metallic Aluminum-Bronze center in Stainless Steel ring., 25.5 mm. **Subject:** Indpendence 200th Anniversary **Rev:** Guadalupe Victoria head 1/4 facing left

Date	Mintage	F	VF	XF	Unc	BU
2010	—	—	—	0.75	1.50	—
2010 Prooflike	—	—	—	—	—	7.50

KM# 930 5 PESOS

7.0700 g., Bi-Metallic Aluminum-Bronze center in Stainless Steel ring., 25.5 mm. **Subject:** Revolution 100th Anniversary **Rev:** Jose Mario Pino Suarez head

Date	Mintage	F	VF	XF	Unc	BU
2010	—	—	—	0.75	1.50	—
2010 Prooflike	—	—	—	—	—	7.50

KM# 931 5 PESOS

7.0700 g., Bi-Metallic Aluminum-Bronze center in Stainless Steel ring., 25.5 mm. **Subject:** Independence 200th Anniversary **Rev:** Josefa Ortiz de Dominguez head right

Date	Mintage	F	VF	XF	Unc	BU
2010	—	—	—	0.75	1.50	—
2010 Prooflike	—	—	—	—	—	7.50

KM# 636 10 PESOS

10.3300 g., Bi-Metallic Copper-Nickel-Zinc center in Aluminum-Bronze ring, 28 mm. **Series:** Millennium **Obv:** National arms **Obv. Legend:** ESTADOS UNIDOS MEXICANOS **Rev:** Aztec carving **Edge Lettering:** ANO (year) repeated 3 times

Date	Mintage	F	VF	XF	Unc	BU
2001Mo	44,768,000	—	—	5.00	7.50	10.00

KM# 616 10 PESOS

10.3300 g., Bi-Metallic Copper-Nickel-Zinc center in Aluminum-Bronze ring, 28 mm. **Obv:** National arms **Obv. Legend:** ESTADOS UNIDOS MEXICANOS **Rev:** Aztec design

Date	Mintage	F	VF	XF	Unc	BU
2002Mo	44,721,000	—	—	5.00	8.00	12.00
2004Mo	74,739,000	—	—	5.00	8.00	12.00
2005Mo	64,635,000	—	—	5.00	8.00	12.00
2006Mo	84,575,000	—	—	5.00	8.00	12.00
2007Mo	89,678,000	—	—	5.00	8.00	12.00
2008Mo	24,896,000	—	—	5.00	8.00	12.00
2009Mo	—	—	—	5.00	8.00	12.00
2010Mo	—	—	—	5.00	8.00	12.00

KM# 679 10 PESOS

31.1040 g., 0.9990 Silver 0.9990 oz. ASW, 39.9 mm. **Series:** First **Subject:** 180th Anniversary of Federation **Obv:** National arms **Obv. Legend:** ESTADOS UNIDOS MEXICANOS **Rev:** State Arms **Rev. Legend:** ESTADO DE ZACATECAS **Edge:** Reeded

Date	Mintage	F	VF	XF	Unc	BU
2003Mo Proof	10,000	Value: 70.00				

KM# 680 10 PESOS

31.1040 g., 0.9990 Silver 0.9990 oz. ASW, 39.9 mm. **Series:** First **Subject:** 180th Anniversary of Federation **Obv:** National arms **Obv. Legend:** ESTADO UNIDOS MEXICANOS **Rev:** State arms **Rev. Legend:** ESTADO DE YUCATÁN **Edge:** Reeded

Date	Mintage	F	VF	XF	Unc	BU
2003Mo Proof	10,000	Value: 70.00				

KM# 681 10 PESOS

31.1040 g., 0.9990 Silver 0.9990 oz. ASW, 39.9 mm. **Series:** First **Subject:** 180th Anniversary of Federation **Obv:** National arms **Obv. Legend:** ESTADOS UNIDOS MEXICANOS **Rev:** State arms **Rev. Legend:** ESTADO DE VERACRUZ-LLAVE **Edge:** Reeded

Date	Mintage	F	VF	XF	Unc	BU
2003Mo Proof	10,000	Value: 70.00				

KM# 682 10 PESOS
31.1040 g., 0.9990 Silver 0.9990 oz. ASW, 39.9 mm. **Series:** First **Subject:** 180th Anniversary of Frederation **Obv:** National arms **Obv. Legend:** ESTADOS UNIDOS MEXICANOS **Rev:** State arms **Rev. Legend:** ESTADO DE TLAXCALA **Edge:** Reeded

Date	Mintage	F	VF	XF	Unc	BU
2003Mo Proof	10,000	Value: 70.00				

KM# 683 10 PESOS
31.1040 g., 0.9990 Silver 0.9990 oz. ASW, 39.9 mm. **Series:** First **Subject:** 180th Anniversary of Federation **Obv:** National arms **Obv. Legend:** ESTADOS UNIDOS MEXICANOS **Rev:** State arms **Rev. Legend:** ESTADO DE TAMAULIPAS **Edge:** Reeded

Date	Mintage	F	VF	XF	Unc	BU
2004Mo Proof	10,000	Value: 70.00				

KM# 684 10 PESOS
31.1040 g., 0.9990 Silver 0.9990 oz. ASW, 39.9 mm. **Series:** First **Subject:** 180th Anniversary of Federation **Obv:** National arms **Obv. Legend:** ESTADOS UNIDOS DE MEXICANOS **Rev:** State arms **Rev. Legend:** ESTADO DE TABASCO **Edge:** Reeded

Date	Mintage	F	VF	XF	Unc	BU
2004Mo Proof	10,000	Value: 70.00				

KM# 685 10 PESOS
31.1040 g., 0.9990 Silver 0.9990 oz. ASW, 39.9 mm. **Series:** First **Subject:** 180th Anniversary of Federation **Obv:** National arms **Obv. Legend:** ESTADOS UNIDOS MEXICANOS **Rev:** State arms **Rev. Legend:** ESTADO DE SONORA **Edge:** Reeded **Note:** Mexican States: Sonora

Date	Mintage	F	VF	XF	Unc	BU
2004Mo Proof	10,000	Value: 70.00				

KM# 686 10 PESOS
31.1040 g., 0.9990 Silver 0.9990 oz. ASW, 39.9 mm. **Series:** First **Subject:** 180th Anniversary of Federation **Obv:** National arms **Obv. Legend:** ESTADOS UNIDOS DE MEXICANOS **Rev:** State arms **Rev. Legend:** ESTADO DE SINALOA **Edge:** Reeded **Note:** Mexican States: Sinaloa

Date	Mintage	F	VF	XF	Unc	BU
2004Mo Proof	10,000	Value: 70.00				

KM# 687 10 PESOS
31.1040 g., 0.9990 Silver 0.9990 oz. ASW, 39.9 mm. **Series:** First **Subject:** 180th Anniversary of Federation **Obv:** National arms **Obv. Legend:** ESTADOS UNIDOS MEXICANOS **Rev:** State arms **Rev. Legend:** ESTADO DE SAN LUIS POTOSÍ **Edge:** Reeded

Date	Mintage	F	VF	XF	Unc	BU
2004Mo Proof	10,000	Value: 70.00				

KM# 735 10 PESOS
31.1040 g., 0.9990 Silver 0.9990 oz. ASW, 39.9 mm. **Series:** First **Subject:** 180th Anniversary of Federation **Obv:** National arms **Obv. Legend:** ESTADOS UNIDOS MEXICANOS **Rev:** State arms **Rev. Legend:** ESTADO DE QUINTANA ROO

Date	Mintage	F	VF	XF	Unc	BU
2004 Proof	10,000	Value: 70.00				

KM# 733 10 PESOS
31.1040 g., 0.9990 Silver 0.9990 oz. ASW, 39.9 mm. **Series:** First **Subject:** 180th Anniversary of Federation **Obv:** National arms **Obv. Legend:** ESTADOS UNIDOS MEXICANOS **Rev:** State arms **Rev. Legend:** ESTADO DE QUERÉTARO ARTEAGA **Edge:** Reeded

Date	Mintage	F	VF	XF	Unc	BU
2004 Proof	10,000	Value: 70.00				

KM# 737 10 PESOS
31.1040 g., 0.9990 Silver 0.9990 oz. ASW, 39.9 mm. **Series:** First **Subject:** 180th Anniversary of Federation **Obv:** National arms **Obv. Legend:** ESTADOS UNIDOS MEXICANOS **Rev:** State arms **Rev. Legend:** ESTADO DE PUEBLA **Edge:** Reeded

Date	Mintage	F	VF	XF	Unc	BU
2004Mo Proof	10,000	Value: 70.00				

KM# 739 10 PESOS
31.1040 g., 0.9990 Bi-Metallic 0.9990 oz., 39.9 mm. **Series:** First **Subject:** 180th Anniversary of Federation **Obv:** National arms **Obv. Legend:** ESTADOS UNIDOS MEXICANOS **Rev:** State arms **Rev. Legend:** ESTADO DE OAXACA **Edge:** Reeded

Date	Mintage	F	VF	XF	Unc	BU
2004Mo Proof	10,000	Value: 70.00				

KM# 741 10 PESOS
31.1040 g., 0.9990 Silver 0.9990 oz. ASW, 39.9 mm. **Series:** First **Subject:** 180th Anniversary of Federation **Obv:** National arms **Obv. Legend:** ESTADOS UNIDOS MEXICANOS **Rev:** State arms **Rev. Legend:** ESTADO DE NUEVO LEÓN **Edge:** Reeded

Date	Mintage	F	VF	XF	Unc	BU
2004Mo Proof	10,000	Value: 70.00				

KM# 743 10 PESOS
31.1040 g., 0.9990 Silver 0.9990 oz. ASW, 39.9 mm. **Series:** First **Subject:** 180th Anniversary of Federation **Obv:** National

arms **Obv. Legend:** ESTADOS UNIDOS MEXICANOS **Rev:** State arms **Rev. Legend:** ESTADO DE NAYARIT **Edge:** Reeded

Date	Mintage	F	VF	XF	Unc	BU
2004Mo Proof	10,000	Value: 70.00				

KM# 745 10 PESOS

31.1040 g., 0.9990 Silver 0.9990 oz. ASW, 39.9 mm. **Series:** First **Subject:** 180th Anniversary of Federation **Obv:** National arms **Obv. Legend:** ESTADOS UNIDOS MEXICANOS **Rev:** State arms **Rev. Legend:** ESTADO DE MORELOS **Edge:** Reeded

Date	Mintage	F	VF	XF	Unc	BU
2004Mo Proof	10,000	Value: 70.00				

KM# 796 10 PESOS

31.1040 g., 0.9990 Silver 0.9990 oz. ASW, 39.9 mm. **Series:** First **Subject:** 180th Anniversary of Federation **Obv:** National arms **Obv. Legend:** ESTADOS UNIDOS MEXICANOS **Rev:** State arms **Rev. Legend:** ESTADO DE MICHOACÁN DE OCAMPO **Edge:** Reeded

Date	Mintage	F	VF	XF	Unc	BU
2004Mo Proof	10,000	Value: 70.00				

KM# 747 10 PESOS

31.1040 g., 0.9990 Silver 0.9990 oz. ASW, 39.9 mm. **Series:** First **Subject:** 180th Anniversary of Federation **Obv:** National arms **Obv. Legend:** ESTADOS UNIDOS MEXICANOS **Rev:** State arms **Rev. Legend:** ESTADO DE MÉXICO **Edge:** Reeded

Date	Mintage	F	VF	XF	Unc	BU
2004Mo Proof	10,000	Value: 70.00				

KM# 749 10 PESOS

31.1040 g., 0.9990 Silver 0.9990 oz. ASW, 39.9 mm. **Series:** First **Subject:** 180th Anniversary of Federation **Obv:** National arms **Obv. Legend:** ESTADOS UNIDOS MEXICANOS **Rev:** State arms **Rev. Legend:** ESTADO DE JALISCO **Edge:** Reeded

Date	Mintage	F	VF	XF	Unc	BU
2004Mo Proof	10,000	Value: 70.00				

KM# 766 10 PESOS

31.1035 g., 0.9990 Silver 0.9990 oz. ASW, 40 mm. **Subject:** Cervantes Festival **Obv:** Mexican Eagle and Snake **Rev:** Don Quixote **Edge:** Reeded

Date	Mintage	F	VF	XF	Unc	BU
2005Mo Proof	1,205	Value: 75.00				

KM# 768 10 PESOS

31.1035 g., 0.9990 Silver 0.9990 oz. ASW, 40 mm. **Subject:** 470th Anniversary - Mexico City Mint **Obv:** Mexican Eagle and Snake **Rev:** Antique coin press

Date	Mintage	F	VF	XF	Unc	BU
2005Mo Proof	2,005	Value: 65.00				

KM# 711 10 PESOS

31.1040 g., 0.9990 Silver 0.9990 oz. ASW, 39.9 mm. **Series:** First **Subject:** 180th Anniversary of Federation **Obv:** National arms **Obv. Legend:** ESTADOS UNIDOS MEXICANOS **Rev:** State arms **Rev. Legend:** ESTADO DE HIDALGO **Edge:** Reeded

Date	Mintage	F	VF	XF	Unc	BU
2005Mo Proof	10,000	Value: 70.00				

KM# 710 10 PESOS

31.1040 g., 0.9990 Silver 0.9990 oz. ASW, 39.9 mm. **Series:** First **Subject:** 180th Anniversary of Federation **Obv:** National arms **Obv. Legend:** ESTADOS UNIDOS MEXICANOS **Rev:** State arms **Rev. Legend:** ESTADO DE GUERRERO **Edge:** Reeded

Date	Mintage	F	VF	XF	Unc	BU
2005Mo Proof	10,000	Value: 70.00				

KM# 709 10 PESOS

31.1040 g., 0.9990 Silver 0.9990 oz. ASW, 39.9 mm. **Series:** First **Subject:** 180th Anniversary of Federation **Obv:** National arms **Obv. Legend:** ESTADOS UNIDOS MEXICANOS **Rev:** State arms **Rev. Legend:** ESTADO DE GUANAJUATO **Edge:** Reeded

Date	Mintage	F	VF	XF	Unc	BU
2005Mo Proof	10,000	Value: 70.00				

KM# 708 10 PESOS

31.1040 g., 0.9990 Silver 0.9990 oz. ASW, 39.9 mm. **Series:** First **Subject:** 180th Anniversary of Federation **Obv:** National arms **Obv. Legend:** ESTADOS UNIDOS MEXICANOS **Rev:** State arms **Rev. Legend:** ESTADO DE DURANGO **Edge:** Reeded

Date	Mintage	F	VF	XF	Unc	BU
2005Mo Proof	10,000	Value: 70.00				

KM# 707 10 PESOS

31.1040 g., 0.9990 Silver 0.9990 oz. ASW, 39.9 mm. **Series:** First **Subject:** 180th Anniversary of Federation **Obv:** National arms **Obv. Legend:** ESTADOS UNIDOS MEXICANOS **Rev:** Federal District arms **Rev. Legend:** DISTRITO FEDERAL **Edge:** Reeded

Date	Mintage	F	VF	XF	Unc	BU
2005Mo Proof	10,000	Value: 70.00				

KM# 753 10 PESOS

31.1040 g., 0.9990 Silver 0.9990 oz. ASW, 39.9 mm. **Series:** First **Subject:** 180th Anniversary of Federation **Obv:** National arms **Obv. Legend:** ESTADOS UNIDOS MEXICANOS **Rev:** State arms **Rev. Legend:** ESTADO DE CHIHUAHUA **Edge:** Reeded

Date	Mintage	F	VF	XF	Unc	BU
2005Mo Proof	10,000	Value: 70.00				

KM# 706 10 PESOS

31.1040 g., 0.9990 Silver 0.9990 oz. ASW, 39.9 mm. **Series:** First **Subject:** 180th Anniversary of Federation **Obv:** National arms **Obv. Legend:** ESTADOS UNIDOS MEXICANOS **Rev:** State arms **Rev. Legend:** ESTADO DE CHIAPAS **Edge:** Reeded

Date	Mintage	F	VF	XF	Unc	BU
2005Mo Proof	10,000	Value: 70.00				

KM# 728 10 PESOS
31.1040 g., 0.9990 Silver 0.9990 oz. ASW, 39.9 mm. **Series:** First **Subject:** 180th Anniversary of Federation **Obv:** National arms **Obv. Legend:** ESTADOS UNIDOS MEXICANOS **Rev:** State arms **Rev. Legend:** ESTADO DE COLIMA **Edge:** Reeded

Date	Mintage	F	VF	XF	Unc	BU
2005Mo Proof	10,000	Value: 70.00				

KM# 751 10 PESOS
31.1040 g., 0.9990 Silver 0.9990 oz. ASW, 39.9 mm. **Series:** First **Subject:** 180th Anniversary of Federation **Obv:** National arms **Obv. Legend:** ESTADOS UNIDOS MEXICANOS **Rev:** State arms **Rev. Legend:** ESTADO DE COAHUILA DE ZARAGOZA **Edge:** Reeded

Date	Mintage	F	VF	XF	Unc	BU
2005Mo Proof	10,000	Value: 70.00				

KM# 726 10 PESOS
31.1040 g., 0.9990 Silver 0.9990 oz. ASW, 39.9 mm. **Series:** First **Subject:** 180th Anniversary of Federation **Obv:** National arms **Obv. Legend:** ESTADOS UNIDOS MEXICANOS **Rev:** State arms **Rev. Legend:** ESTADO DE CAMPECHE **Edge:** Reeded

Date	Mintage	F	VF	XF	Unc	BU
2005Mo Proof	10,000	Value: 70.00				

KM# 724 10 PESOS
31.1040 g., 0.9990 Silver 0.9990 oz. ASW, 39.9 mm. **Series:** First **Subject:** 180th Anniversary of Federation **Obv:** National arms **Obv. Legend:** ESTADOS UNIDOS MEXICANOS **Rev:** State arms **Rev. Legend:** ESTADO DE BAJA CALIFORNIA SUR **Edge:** Reeded

Date	Mintage	F	VF	XF	Unc	BU
2005Mo Proof	10,000	Value: 70.00				

KM# 722 10 PESOS
31.1040 g., 0.9990 Silver 0.9990 oz. ASW, 39.9 mm. **Series:** First **Subject:** 180th Anniversary of Federation **Obv:** National arms **Obv. Legend:** ESTADOS UNIDOS MEXICANOS **Rev:** State arms **Rev. Legend:** ESTADO DE BAJA CALIFORNIA **Edge:** Reeded

Date	Mintage	F	VF	XF	Unc	BU
2005Mo Proof	10,000	Value: 70.00				

KM# 720 10 PESOS
31.1040 g., 0.9990 Silver 0.9990 oz. ASW, 39.9 mm. **Series:** First **Subject:** 180th Anniversary of Federation **Obv:** National arms **Obv. Legend:** ESTADOS UNIDOS MEXICANOS **Rev:** State arms **Rev. Legend:** ESTADO DE AGUASCALIENTES **Edge:** Reeded

Date	Mintage	F	VF	XF	Unc	BU
2005Mo Proof	10,000	Value: 70.00				

KM# 718 10 PESOS
31.1040 g., 0.9990 Silver 0.9990 oz. ASW, 40 mm. **Series:** Second **Obv:** National arms **Obv. Legend:** ESTADOS UNIDOS MEXICANOS **Rev:** Facade of the San Marcos garden above sculpture of national emblem at left, San Antonio Temple at right **Rev. Legend:** AGUASCALIENTES **Edge:** Reeded

Date	Mintage	F	VF	XF	Unc	BU
2005Mo Proof	6,000	Value: 65.00				

KM# 757 10 PESOS
31.1040 g., 0.9990 Silver 0.9990 oz. ASW, 40 mm. **Series:** Second **Obv:** National arms **Obv. Legend:** ESTADOS UNIDOS MEXICANOS **Rev:** Rams head, mountain outline in background **Rev. Legend:** BAJA CALIFORNIA - GOBIERNO DEL ESTADO **Edge:** Reeded

Date	Mintage	F	VF	XF	Unc	BU
2005Mo Proof	6,000	Value: 65.00				

KM# 755 10 PESOS
31.1040 g., 0.9990 Silver 0.9990 oz. ASW, 40 mm. **Obv:** National arms **Rev:** Baja California del Norte arms

Date	Mintage	F	VF	XF	Unc	BU
2005Mo Proof	—	Value: 75.00				

KM# 763 10 PESOS
31.1040 g., 0.9990 Silver 0.9990 oz. ASW, 40 mm. **Obv:** National arms **Rev:** Benito Juarez **Edge:** Reeded

Date	Mintage	F	VF	XF	Unc	BU
2006Mo Proof	—	Value: 75.00				

KM# 761 10 PESOS
31.1040 g., 0.9990 Silver 0.9990 oz. ASW, 40 mm. **Series:** Second **Obv:** National arms **Obv. Legend:** ESTADOS UNIDOS MEXICANOS **Rev:** Outlined map of peninsula at center, cave painting of deer behind, cactus at right **Rev. Legend:** ESTADO DE BAJA CALIFORNIA SUR **Edge:** Reeded

Date	Mintage	F	VF	XF	Unc	BU
2006Mo Proof	6,000	Value: 65.00				

KM# 759 10 PESOS
31.1040 g., 0.9990 Silver 0.9990 oz. ASW, 40 mm. **Series:** Second **Obv:** National arms **Obv. Legend:** ESTADOS UNIDOS MEXICANOS **Rev:** Jade mask - Calakmul, Campeche **Rev. Legend:** ESTADO DE CAMPECHE **Edge:** Reeded

Date	Mintage	F	VF	XF	Unc	BU
2006Mo Proof	6,000	Value: 65.00				

KM# 780 10 PESOS
31.1040 g., 0.9990 Silver 0.9990 oz. ASW, 40 mm. **Series:** Second **Obv:** National arms **Obv. Legend:** ESTADOS UNIDOS MEXICANOS **Rev:** Outlined map with turtle, mine cart above grapes at center, Friendship dam above Christ of the Nodas at left, chimneys above crucibles and bell tower of Santiago's cathedral at right **Rev. Inscription:** COAHUILA DE ZARAGOZA **Edge:** Reeded

Date	Mintage	F	VF	XF	Unc	BU
2006Mo Proof	6,000	Value: 65.00				

KM# 776 10 PESOS

31.1040 g., 0.9990 Silver 0.9990 oz. ASW, 40 mm. **Series:** Second **Obv:** National arms **Obv. Legend:** ESTADOS UNIDOS MEXICANOS **Rev:** State arms at lower center, Nevado de Colima and Volcan de Fuego volcanos in background **Rev. Legend:** *Colima* **Rev. Inscription:** GENEROSO **Edge:** Reeded

Date	Mintage	F	VF	XF	Unc	BU
2006Mo Proof	6,000	Value: 65.00				

KM# 772 10 PESOS

31.1040 g., 0.9990 Silver 0.9990 oz. ASW, 40 mm. **Series:** Second **Obv:** National arms **Obv. Legend:** ESTADOS UNIDOS MEXICANOS **Rev:** Head of Pakal, ancient Mayan king, Palenque **Rev. Legend:** ESTADO DE CHIAPAS - CABEZA MAYA DEL REY PAKAL, PALENQUE **Edge:** Reeded

Date	Mintage	F	VF	XF	Unc	BU
2006Mo Proof	6,000	Value: 65.00				

KM# 774 10 PESOS

31.1040 g., 0.9990 Silver 0.9990 oz. ASW, 40 mm. **Series:** Second **Obv:** National arms **Obv. Legend:** ESTADOS UNIDOS MEXICANOS **Rev:** Angel of Liberty **Rev. Legend:** MÉXICO - ANGEL DE LA LIBERTAD, CHIHUAHUA **Edge:** Reeded

Date	Mintage	F	VF	XF	Unc	BU
2006Mo Proof	6,000	Value: 65.00				

KM# 778 10 PESOS

31.1040 g., 0.9990 Silver 0.9990 oz. ASW, 40 mm. **Series:** Second **Obv:** National arms **Obv. Legend:** ESTADOS UNIDOS MEXICANOS **Rev:** National Palace **Rev. Legend:** DISTRITO FEDERAL - ANTIGUO AYUNTAMIENTO **Edge:** Reeded

Date	Mintage	F	VF	XF	Unc	BU
2006Mo Proof	6,000	Value: 65.00				

KM# 786 10 PESOS

31.1040 g., 0.9990 Silver 0.9990 oz. ASW, 40 mm. **Series:** Second **Obv:** National arms **Obv. Legend:** ESTADOS UNIDOS MEXICANOS **Rev:** Tree **Rev. Legend:** PRIMERA RESERVA NACIONAL FORESTAL - DURANGO **Edge:** Reeded

Date	Mintage	F	VF	XF	Unc	BU
2006Mo Proof	6,000	Value: 65.00				

KM# 788 10 PESOS

31.1040 g., 0.9990 Silver 0.9990 oz. ASW, 40 mm. **Series:** Second **Obv:** National arms **Obv. Legend:** ESTADOS UNIDOS MEXICANOS **Rev:** State arms at center, statue of Miguel Hidalgo at left, monument to Pípila at lower right **Rev. Inscription:** *Guanajuato* **Edge:** Reeded

Date	Mintage	F	VF	XF	Unc	BU
2006Mo Proof	6,000	Value: 65.00				

KM# 790 10 PESOS

31.1040 g., 0.9990 Silver 0.9990 oz. ASW, 40 mm. **Series:** Second **Obv:** National arms **Obv. Legend:** ESTADOS UNIDOS MEXICANOS **Rev:** Stylized portrait of Vicente Guerrero at left, church of Taxco at upper center, Acapulco's la Quebrada with diver above Christmas Eve flower and mask **Rev. Legend:** GUERRERO **Edge:** Reeded

Date	Mintage	F	VF	XF	Unc	BU
2006Mo Proof	6,000	Value: 65.00				

KM# 792 10 PESOS

31.1040 g., 0.9990 Silver 0.9990 oz. ASW, 40 mm. **Series:** Second **Obv:** National arms **Obv. Legend:** ESTADOS UNIDOS MEXICANOS **Rev:** Monument of Pachuca Hidalgo **Rev. Inscription:** *RELOJ / MONUMENTAL / DE / PACHUCA / HIDALGO - La / Bella / Airosa* **Edge:** Reeded

Date	Mintage	F	VF	XF	Unc	BU
2006Mo Proof	6,000	Value: 65.00				

KM# 794 10 PESOS

31.1040 g., 0.9990 Silver 0.9990 oz. ASW, 40 mm. **Series:** Second **Obv:** National arms **Obv. Legend:** ESTADOS UNIDOS MEXICANOS **Rev:** Hospicio Cabañas orphanage **Rev. Legend:** ESTADO DE JALISCCO **Edge:** Reeded

Date	Mintage	F	VF	XF	Unc	BU
2006Mo Proof	6,000	Value: 65.00				

KM# 830 10 PESOS

31.1040 g., 0.9990 Silver 0.9990 oz. ASW, 40 mm. **Series:** Second **Obv:** National arms **Obv. Legend:** ESTADOS UNIDOS MEXICANOS **Rev:** Pyramid de la Loona (Moon) **Rev. Legend:** ESTADO DE MÉXICO **Edge:** Reeded

Date	Mintage	F	VF	XF	Unc	BU
2006Mo Proof	6,000	Value: 65.00				

KM# 831 10 PESOS

31.1040 g., 0.9990 Silver 0.9990 oz. ASW, 40 mm. **Series:** Second **Obv:** National arms **Obv. Legend:** ESTADOS UNIDOS MEXICANOS **Rev:** Four Monarch butterflies **Rev. Legend:** ESTADO DE MICHOACÁN **Edge:** Reeded

Date	Mintage	F	VF	XF	Unc	BU
2006Mo Proof	6,000	Value: 65.00				

KM# 832 10 PESOS

31.1040 g., 0.9990 Silver 0.9990 oz. ASW, 40 mm. **Series:** Second **Obv:** National arms **Obv. Legend:** ESTADOS UNIDOS MEXICANOS **Rev:** 1/2 length figure of Chinelo (local dancer) at right, Palacio de Cortes in background **Rev. Inscription:** ESTADO DE / MORELOS **Edge:** Reeded

Date	Mintage	F	VF	XF	Unc	BU
2006Mo Proof	6,000	Value: 65.00				

KM# 833 10 PESOS

31.1040 g., 0.9990 Silver 0.9990 oz. ASW, 40 mm. **Series:** Second **Obv:** National arms **Obv. Legend:** ESTADOS UNIDOS

MEXICANOS **Rev:** Isle de Mexcaltitlán **Rev. Legend:** ESTADO DE NAYARIT **Edge:** Reeded

Date	Mintage	F	VF	XF	Unc	BU
2007Mo Proof	6,000	Value: 65.00				

KM# 834 10 PESOS
31.1040 g., 0.9990 Silver 0.9990 oz. ASW, 40 mm. **Series:** Second **Obv:** National arms **Obv. Legend:** ESTADOS UNIDOS MEXICANOS **Rev:** Old foundry in Pargue Fundidora (public park) at right, Cerro de la Silla (Saddle Hill) in background **Rev. Legend:** ESTADO DE NUEVO LEÓN **Edge:** Reeded

Date	Mintage	F	VF	XF	Unc	BU
2007Mo Proof	6,000	Value: 65.00				

KM# 835 10 PESOS
31.1040 g., 0.9990 Silver 0.9990 oz. ASW, 40 mm. **Series:** Second **Obv:** National arms **Obv. Legend:** ESTADOS UNIDOS MEXICANOS **Rev:** Teatro Macedonio Alcala (theater) **Rev. Legend:** OAXACA **Edge:** Reeded

Date	Mintage	F	VF	XF	Unc	BU
2007Mo Proof	6,000	Value: 65.00				

KM# 836 10 PESOS
31.1040 g., 0.9990 Silver 0.9990 oz. ASW, 40 mm. **Series:** Second **Obv:** National arms **Obv. Legend:** ESTADOS UNIDOS MEXICANOS **Rev:** Talavera porcelain dish **Rev. Legend:** ESTADO DE PUEBLA **Edge:** Reeded

Date	Mintage	F	VF	XF	Unc	BU
2007Mo Proof	6,000	Value: 65.00				

KM# 837 10 PESOS
31.1040 g., 0.9990 Silver 0.9990 oz. ASW, 40 mm. **Series:** Second **Obv:** National arms **Obv. Legend:** ESTADOS UNIDOS MEXICANOS **Rev:** Mask at left, rays above state arms at center, Mayan ruins at right **Rev. Legend:** QUINTANA ROO **Edge:** Reeded

Date	Mintage	F	VF	XF	Unc	BU
2007Mo Proof	6,000	Value: 65.00				

KM# 838 10 PESOS
31.1040 g., 0.9990 Silver 0.9990 oz. ASW, 40 mm. **Series:** Second **Obv:** National arms **Obv. Legend:** ESTADOS UNIDOS MEXICANOS **Rev:** Acqueduct of Querétaro at left, church of Santa Rosa de Viterbo at right **Rev. Legend:** ESTADO DE QUERÉTARO ARTEAGA **Edge:** Reeded

Date	Mintage	F	VF	XF	Unc	BU
2007Mo Proof	6,000	Value: 65.00				

KM# 839 10 PESOS
31.1040 g., Silver, 40 mm. **Series:** Second **Obv:** National arms **Obv. Legend:** ESTADOS UNIDOS MEXICANOS **Rev:** Facade of Caja Real **Rev. Legend:** • SAN LUIS POTOSÍ • **Edge:** Reeded

Date	Mintage	F	VF	XF	Unc	BU
2007Mo Proof	6,000	Value: 65.00				

KM# 840 10 PESOS
31.1040 g., 0.9990 Silver 0.9990 oz. ASW, 40 mm. **Series:** Second **Obv:** National arms **Obv. Legend:** ESTADOS UNIDOS MEXICANOS **Rev:** Shield on pile of cactus fruits **Rev. Legend:** ESTADO DE SINALOA - LUGAR DE PITAHAYAS **Edge:** Reeded

Date	Mintage	F	VF	XF	Unc	BU
2007Mo Proof	6,000	Value: 65.00				

KM# 841 10 PESOS
31.1040 g., 0.9990 Silver 0.9990 oz. ASW, 40 mm. **Series:** Second **Obv:** National arms **Obv. Legend:** ESTADOS UNIDOS MEXICANOS **Rev:** Local in Dance of the Deer at left, cactus at right, mountains in background **Rev. Legend:** ESTADO DE SONORA **Edge:** Reeded

Date	Mintage	F	VF	XF	Unc	BU
2007Mo Proof	6,000	Value: 65.00				

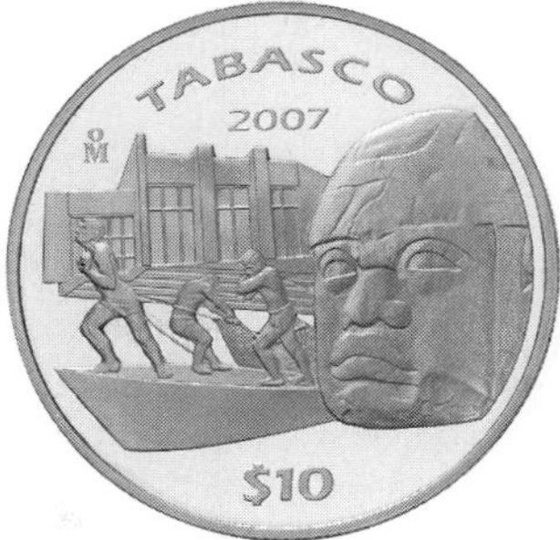

KM# 842 10 PESOS
31.1040 g., 0.9990 Silver 0.9990 oz. ASW, 40 mm. **Series:** Second **Obv:** National arms **Obv. Legend:** ESTADOS UNIDOS MEXICANOS **Rev:** Fuente de los Pescadores (fisherman fountain) at lower left, giant head from the Olmec-pre-Hispanic culture at right, Planetario Tabasco in background **Rev. Legend:** TABASCO **Edge:** Reeded

Date	Mintage	F	VF	XF	Unc	BU
2007Mo Proof	6,000	Value: 65.00				

KM# 843 10 PESOS
31.1040 g., 0.9990 Silver 0.9990 oz. ASW, 40 mm. **Series:** Second **Obv:** National arms **Obv. Legend:** ESTADOS UNIDOS MEXICANOS **Rev:** Ridge - Cerro Del Bernal, Gonzáles **Rev. Legend:** TAMAULIPAS **Edge:** Reeded

Date	Mintage	F	VF	XF	Unc	BU
2007Mo Proof	6,000	Value: 65.00				

KM# 844 10 PESOS
31.1040 g., 0.9990 Silver 0.9990 oz. ASW, 40 mm. **Series:** Second **Obv:** National arms **Obv. Legend:** ESTADOS UNIDOS MEXICANOS **Rev:** Basilica de Ocotlán at left, state arms above Capilla Abierta, Plaza de Toros Ranchero Aguilar below, Exconvento de San Francisco at right **Rev. Legend:** ESTADO DE TLAXCALA **Edge:** Reeded

Date	Mintage	F	VF	XF	Unc	BU
2007Mo Proof	6,000	Value: 65.00				

KM# 845 10 PESOS
31.1040 g., 0.9990 Silver 0.9990 oz. ASW, 40 mm. **Series:** Second **Obv:** National arms **Obv. Legend:** ESTADOS UNIDOS MEXICANOS **Rev:** Pyramid of El Tajín **Rev. Legend:** • VERACRUZ • - • DE IGNACIO DE LA LLAVE • **Edge:** Reeded

Date	Mintage	F	VF	XF	Unc	BU
2007Mo Proof	6,000	Value: 65.00				

KM# 846 10 PESOS
31.1030 g., 0.9990 Silver 0.9989 oz. ASW, 40 mm. **Series:** Second **Obv:** National arms **Obv. Legend:** ESTADOS UNIDOS MEXICANOS **Rev:** Stylized pyramid of Chichén-Itzá **Rev. Legend:** Castillo de Chichén Itzá **Rev. Inscription:** YUCATÁN **Edge:** Reeded

Date	Mintage	F	VF	XF	Unc	BU
2007Mo Proof	6,000	Value: 65.00				

KM# 847 10 PESOS
31.1040 g., 0.9990 Silver 0.9990 oz. ASW, 40 mm. **Series:** Second **Obv:** National arms **Obv. Legend:** ESTADOS UNIDOS MEXICANOS **Rev:** Cable car above Monumento al Minero at left, Cathedral de Zacatecas at center right **Rev. Legend:** Zacatecas **Edge:** Reeded

Date	Mintage	F	VF	XF	Unc	BU
2007Mo Proof	6,000	Value: 65.00				

KM# 637 20 PESOS
Bi-Metallic Copper-Nickel center within Brass ring, 32 mm. **Subject:** Xiuhtecuhtli **Obv:** National arms, eagle left within circle **Rev:** Aztec with torch within spiked circle

Date	Mintage	F	VF	XF	Unc	BU
2001Mo	2,478,000	—	—	—	16.00	18.00

KM# 638 20 PESOS
Bi-Metallic Copper-Nickel center within Brass ring, 32 mm. **Subject:** Octavio Paz **Obv:** National arms, eagle left within circle **Rev:** Head 1/4 right within circle

Date	Mintage	F	VF	XF	Unc	BU
2001Mo	2,515,000	—	—	—	16.00	18.50

KM# 704 20 PESOS
62.4000 g., 0.9990 Silver 2.0041 oz. ASW, 48.1 mm. **Subject:** 400th Anniversary of Don Quijote de la Manchia **Obv:** National arms **Rev:** Skeletal figure horseback with spear galloping right **Edge:** Plain

Date	Mintage	F	VF	XF	Unc	BU
ND(2005)Mo Proof	10,000	Value: 85.00				

KM# 767 20 PESOS
62.4000 g., 0.9990 Silver 2.0041 oz. ASW, 48 mm. **Subject:** 80th Anniversary - Bank of Mexico **Obv:** National arms **Rev:** 100 Peso banknote design of 1925

Date	Mintage	F	VF	XF	Unc	BU
2005Mo	—	—	—	—	—	70.00
2005Mo Proof	3,005	Value: 90.00				

KM# 688 100 PESOS
33.9400 g., Bi-Metallic .925 Silver 20.1753g center in Aluminum-Bronze ring, 39.04 mm. **Series:** First **Subject:** 180th Anniversary of Federation **Obv:** National arms **Obv. Legend:** ESTADOS UNIDOS MEXICANOS **Rev:** State arms **Rev. Legend:** ESTADO DE ZACATECAS **Edge:** Segmented reeding

Date	Mintage	F	VF	XF	Unc	BU
2003Mo	244,900	—	—	—	40.00	50.00

KM# 696 100 PESOS
29.1690 g., Bi-Metallic .999 Gold 17.154g center in .999 Silver 12.015g ring, 34.5 mm. **Series:** First **Subject:** 180th Anniversary of Federation **Obv:** National arms **Obv. Legend:** ESTADOS UNIDOS MEXICANOS **Rev:** State arms **Rev. Legend:** ESTADO DE ZACATECAS **Edge:** Segmented reeding

Date	Mintage	F	VF	XF	Unc	BU
2003Mo Proof	1,000	Value: 850				

KM# 689 100 PESOS
33.9400 g., Bi-Metallic .925 Silver 20.1753g center in Aluminum-Bronze ring, 39.04 mm. **Series:** First **Subject:** 180th Anniversary of Federation **Obv:** National arms **Obv. Legend:** ESTADOS UNIDOS MEXICANOS **Rev:** State arms **Rev. Legend:** ESTADO DE YUCATÁN **Edge:** Segmented reeding

Date	Mintage	F	VF	XF	Unc	BU
2003Mo	235,763	—	—	—	40.00	50.00

KM# 697 100 PESOS
29.1690 g., Bi-Metallic .999 Gold 17.154g center in .999 Silver 12.015g ring, 34.5 mm. **Series:** First **Subject:** 180th Anniversary of Federation **Obv:** National arms **Obv. Legend:** ESTADOS UNIDOS MEXICANOS **Rev:** State arms **Rev. Legend:** ESTADO DE YUCATÁN **Edge:** Segmented reeding

Date	Mintage	F	VF	XF	Unc	BU
2003Mo Proof	1,000	Value: 850				

KM# 690 100 PESOS
33.9400 g., Bi-Metallic .925 Silver 20.1753g center in Aluminum-Bronze ring, 39.04 mm. **Series:** First **Subject:** 180th Anniversary of Federation **Obv:** National arms **Obv. Legend:** ESTADOS UNIDOS MEXICANOS **Rev:** State arms **Rev. Legend:** ESTADO DE VERACRUZ-LLAVE **Edge:** Segmented reeding

Date	Mintage	F	VF	XF	Unc	BU
2003Mo	248,810	—	—	—	40.00	50.00

KM# 698 100 PESOS
29.1690 g., Bi-Metallic .999 Gold 17.154g center in .999 Silver 12.015g ring, 34.5 mm. **Series:** First **Subject:** 180th Anniversary of Federation **Obv:** National arms **Obv. Legend:** ESTADOS UNIDOS MEXICANOS **Rev:** State arms **Rev. Legend:** ESTADO DE VERACRUZ-LLAVE **Edge:** Segmented reeding

Date	Mintage	F	VF	XF	Unc	BU
2003Mo Proof	1,000	Value: 850				

KM# 691 100 PESOS
33.9400 g., Bi-Metallic .925 Silver 20.1753g center in Aluminum-Bronze ring, 39.9 mm. **Series:** First **Subject:** 180th Anniversary of Federation **Obv:** National arms **Obv. Legend:** ESTADOS UNIDOS MEXICANOS **Rev:** State arms **Rev. Legend:** ESTADO DE TLAXCALA **Edge:** Segmented reeding

Date	Mintage	F	VF	XF	Unc	BU
2003Mo	248,976	—	—	—	35.00	40.00

KM# 699 100 PESOS
29.1690 g., Bi-Metallic .999 Gold 17.154g center in .999 Silver 12.015g ring, 34.5 mm. **Series:** First **Subject:** 180th Anniversary of Federation **Obv:** National arms **Obv. Legend:** ESTADOS UNIDOS MEXICANOS **Rev:** State arms **Rev. Legend:** ESTADO DE TLAXCALA **Edge:** Segmented reeding

Date	Mintage	F	VF	XF	Unc	BU
2003Mo Proof	1,000	Value: 850				

KM# 692 100 PESOS
33.9400 g., Bi-Metallic .925 Silver 20.1753g center in Aluminum-Bronze ring, 39.04 mm. **Series:** First **Subject:** 180th Anniversay of Federation **Obv:** National arms **Obv. Legend:** ESTADOS UNIDOS MEXICANOS **Rev:** State arms **Rev. Legend:** ESTADO DE TAMAULIPAS **Edge:** Segmented reeding

Date	Mintage	F	VF	XF	Unc	BU
2004Mo	249,398	—	—	—	35.00	40.00

KM# 700 100 PESOS
29.1690 g., Bi-Metallic .999 Gold 17.154g center in .999 Silver 12.015g ring, 34.5 mm. **Series:** First **Subject:** 180th Anniversary of Federation **Obv:** National arms **Obv. Legend:** ESTADOS UNIDOS MEXICANOS **Rev:** State arms **Rev. Legend:** ESTADO DE TAMAULIPAS **Edge:** Segmented reeding

Date	Mintage	F	VF	XF	Unc	BU
2004Mo Proof	1,000	Value: 850				

KM# 693 100 PESOS
33.9400 g., Bi-Metallic .925 Silver 20.1753g center in Aluminum-Bronze ring, 39.04 mm. **Series:** First **Subject:** 180th Anniversary of Federation **Obv:** National arms **Obv. Legend:** ESTADOS UNIDOS MEXICANOS **Rev:** State arms **Rev. Legend:** ESTADO DE TABASCO **Edge:** Segmented reeding

Date	Mintage	F	VF	XF	Unc	BU
2004Mo	249,318	—	—	—	35.00	40.00

KM# 701 100 PESOS
29.1690 g., Bi-Metallic .999 Gold 17.154g center in .999 Silver 12.015g ring, 34.5 mm. **Series:** First **Subject:** 180th Anniversary of Federation **Obv:** National arms **Obv. Legend:** ESTADOS UNIDOS MEXICANOS **Rev:** State arms **Rev. Legend:** ESTADO DE TABASCO **Edge:** Segmented reeding

Date	Mintage	F	VF	XF	Unc	BU
2004Mo Proof	1,000	Value: 850				

KM# 694 100 PESOS
33.9400 g., Bi-Metallic .925 Silver 20.1753g center in Aluminum-Bronze ring, 39.04 mm. **Series:** First **Subject:** 180th Anniversary of Federation **Obv:** National arms **Obv. Legend:** ESTADOS UNIDOS MEXICANOS **Rev:** State arms **Rev. Legend:** ESTADO DE SONORA **Edge:** Segmented reeding

Date	Mintage	F	VF	XF	Unc	BU
2004Mo	249,300	—	—	—	35.00	40.00

KM# 702 100 PESOS
29.1690 g., Bi-Metallic .999 Gold 17.154g center in .999 Silver 12.015g ring, 34.5 mm. **Series:** First **Subject:** 180th Anniversary of Federation **Obv:** National arms **Obv. Legend:** ESTADOS UNIDOS MEXICANOS **Rev:** State arms **Rev. Legend:** ESTADO DE SONORA **Edge:** Segmented reeding

Date	Mintage	F	VF	XF	Unc	BU
2004Mo Proof	1,000	Value: 850				

KM# 695 100 PESOS
33.9400 g., Bi-Metallic .925 Silver 20.1753g center in Aluminum-Bronze ring, 39.04 mm. **Series:** First **Subject:** 180th Anniversary of Federation **Obv:** National arms **Obv. Legend:** ESTADOS UNIDOS MEXICANOS **Rev:** State arms **Rev. Legend:** ESTADO DE SINALOA **Edge:** Segmented reeding

Date	Mintage	F	VF	XF	Unc	BU
2004Mo	244,722	—	—	—	35.00	40.00

KM# 703 100 PESOS
29.1690 g., Bi-Metallic .999 Gold 17.154g center in .999 Silver 12.015g ring, 34.5 mm. **Series:** First **Subject:** 180th Anniversary of Federation **Obv:** National arms **Obv. Legend:** ESTADOS UNIDOS MEXICANOS **Rev:** State arms **Rev. Legend:** ESTADO DE SINALOA **Edge:** Segmented reeding

Date	Mintage	F	VF	XF	Unc	BU
2004Mo Proof	1,000	Value: 850				

KM# 803 100 PESOS
33.9400 g., Bi-Metallic .925 Silver 20.1753g center in Aluminum-Bronze ring, 39.04 mm. **Series:** First **Subject:** 180th Anniversary of Federation **Obv:** National arms **Obv. Legend:** ESTADOS UNIDOS MEXICANOS **Rev:** State arms **Rev. Legend:** ESTADO DE SAN LUIS POTOSÍ **Edge:** Segmented reeding

Date	Mintage	F	VF	XF	Unc	BU
2004Mo	249,662	—	—	—	35.00	40.00

KM# 806 100 PESOS
29.1690 g., Bi-Metallic .999 Gold 17.154g center in .999 silver 12.015 ring, 34.5 mm. **Series:** First **Subject:** 180th Anniversary of Federation **Obv:** National arms **Obv. Legend:** ESTADOS UNIDOS MEXICANOS **Rev:** State arms **Rev. Legend:** ESTADO DE SAN LUIS POTOSÍ **Edge:** Segmented reeding

Date	Mintage	F	VF	XF	Unc	BU
2004Mo Proof	1,000	Value: 850				

KM# 736 100 PESOS
33.9400 g., Bi-Metallic .925 Silver 20.1753g center in Aluminum-Bronze ring, 39.04 mm. **Series:** First **Subject:** 180th Anniversary of Federation **Obv:** National arms **Obv. Legend:** ESTADOS UNIDOS MEXICANOS **Rev:** State arms **Rev. Legend:** ESTADO DE QUINTANA ROO **Edge:** Segmented reeding

Date	Mintage	F	VF	XF	Unc	BU
2004Mo	249,134	—	—	—	35.00	40.00

KM# 807 100 PESOS
29.1690 g., Bi-Metallic .999 Gold 17.154g center in .999 Silver 12.015g ring, 34.5 mm. **Series:** First **Subject:** 180th Anniversary of Federation **Obv:** National arms **Obv. Legend:** ESTADOS UNIDOS MEXICANOS **Rev:** State arms **Rev. Legend:** ESTADO DE QUINTANA ROO **Edge:** Segmented reeding

Date	Mintage	F	VF	XF	Unc	BU
2004Mo Proof	1,000	Value: 850				

KM# 734 100 PESOS
33.9400 g., Bi-Metallic .925 Silver 20.1753g center in Aluminum-Bronze ring, 39.04 mm. **Series:** First **Subject:** 180th Anniversary of Federation **Obv:** National arms **Obv. Legend:** ESTADOS UNIDOS MEXICANOS **Rev:** State arms **Rev. Legend:** ESTADO DE QUERÉTARO ARTEAGA **Edge:** Segmented reeding

Date	Mintage	F	VF	XF	Unc	BU
2004Mo	249,263	—	—	—	35.00	40.00

KM# 808 100 PESOS
29.1690 g., Bi-Metallic .999 Gold 17.154g center in .999 Silver 12.015g ring, 34.5 mm. **Series:** First **Subject:** 180th Anniversary of Federation **Obv:** National arms **Obv. Legend:** ESTADOS UNIDOS MEXICANOS **Rev:** State arms **Rev. Legend:** ESTADO DE QUERÉTARO ARTEAGA **Edge:** Segmented reeding

Date	Mintage	F	VF	XF	Unc	BU
2004Mo Proof	1,000	Value: 850				

KM# 738 100 PESOS
33.9400 g., Bi-Metallic .925 Silver 20.1753g center in Aluminum-Bronze ring, 39.04 mm. **Series:** First **Subject:** 180th Anniversary of Federation **Obv:** National arms **Obv. Legend:** ESTADOS UNIDOS MEXICANOS **Rev:** State arms **Rev. Legend:** ESTADO DE PUEBLA **Edge:** Segmented reeding

Date	Mintage	F	VF	XF	Unc	BU
2004Mo	248,850	—	—	—	35.00	40.00

KM# 809 100 PESOS
Bi-Metallic .999 Gold 17.154g center in .999 Silver 12.015g ring, 34.5 mm. **Series:** First **Subject:** 180th Anniversary of Federation **Obv:** National arms **Obv. Legend:** ESTADOS UNIDOS MEXICANOS **Rev:** State arms **Rev. Legend:** ESTADO DE PUEBLA **Edge:** Segmented reeding

Date	Mintage	F	VF	XF	Unc	BU
2004Mo Proof	1,000	Value: 850				

KM# 740 100 PESOS
33.9400 g., Bi-Metallic .925 Silver 20.1753g center in Aluminum-Bronze ring, 39.04 mm. **Series:** First **Subject:** 180th Anniversary of Federation **Obv:** National arms **Obv. Legend:** ESTADOS UNIDOS MEXICANOS **Rev:** State arms **Rev. Legend:** ESTADO DE OAXACA **Edge:** Segmented reeding

Date	Mintage	F	VF	XF	Unc	BU
2004Mo	249,589	—	—	—	35.00	40.00

KM# 810 100 PESOS
29.1690 g., Bi-Metallic .999 Gold 17.154g center in .999 Silver 12.015g ring, 34.5 mm. **Series:** First **Subject:** 180th Anniversary of Federation **Obv:** National arms **Obv. Legend:** ESTADOS UNIDOS MEXICANOS **Rev:** State arms **Rev. Legend:** ESTADO DE OAXACA **Edge:** Segmented reeding

Date	Mintage	F	VF	XF	Unc	BU
2004Mo Proof	1,000	Value: 850				

KM# 742 100 PESOS
33.9400 g., Bi-Metallic .925 Silver 20.1753g center in Aluminum-Bronze ring, 39.04 mm. **Series:** First **Subject:** 180th Anniversary of Federation **Obv:** National arms **Obv. Legend:** ESTADOS UNIDOS MEXICANOS **Rev:** State arms **Rev. Legend:** ESTADO DE NUEVO LEÓN **Edge:** Segmented reeding

Date	Mintage	F	VF	XF	Unc	BU
2004Mo	249,199	—	—	—	35.00	40.00

KM# 811 100 PESOS
29.1690 g., Bi-Metallic .999 Gold 17.154g center in .999 Silver 12.015g ring, 34.5 mm. **Series:** First **Subject:** 180th Anniversary of Federation **Obv:** National arms **Obv. Legend:** ESTADOS UNIDOS MEXICANOS **Rev:** State arms **Rev. Legend:** ESTADO DE NUEVO LEÓN **Edge:** Segmented reeding

Date	Mintage	F	VF	XF	Unc	BU
2004Mo Proof	1,000	Value: 850				

KM# 744 100 PESOS
33.9400 g., Bi-Metallic .925 Silver 20.1753g center in Aluminum-Bronze ring, 39.04 mm. **Series:** First **Subject:** 180th Anniversary of Federation **Obv:** National arms **Obv. Legend:** ESTADOS UNIDOS MEXICANOS **Rev:** State arms **Rev. Legend:** ESTADO DE NAYARIT **Edge:** Segmented reeding

Date	Mintage	F	VF	XF	Unc	BU
2004Mo	248,305	—	—	—	35.00	40.00

KM# 812 100 PESOS
29.1690 g., Bi-Metallic .999 Gold 17.154g center in .999 Silver 12.015g ring, 34.5 mm. **Series:** First **Subject:** 180th Anniversary of Federation **Obv:** National arms **Obv. Legend:** ESTADOS UNIDOS MEXICANOS **Rev:** State arms **Rev. Legend:** ESTADO DE NAYARIT **Edge:** Segmented reeding

Date	Mintage	F	VF	XF	Unc	BU
2004Mo Proof	1,000	Value: 850				

KM# 746 100 PESOS
33.9400 g., Bi-Metallic .925 Silver 20.1753g center in Aluminum-Bronze ring, 39.04 mm. **Series:** First **Subject:** 180th Anniversary of Federation **Obv:** National arms **Obv. Legend:** ESTADOS UNIDOS MEXICANOS **Rev:** State arms **Rev. Legend:** ESTADO DE MORELOS **Edge:** Segmented reeding

Date	Mintage	F	VF	XF	Unc	BU
2004Mo	249,260	—	—	—	35.00	40.00

KM# 813 100 PESOS
29.1690 g., Bi-Metallic .999 Gold 17.154g center in .999 Silver 12.015g ring, 34.5 mm. **Series:** First **Subject:** 180th Anniversary of Federation **Obv:** National arms **Obv. Legend:** ESTADOS UNIDOS MEXICANOS **Rev:** State arms **Rev. Legend:** ESTADO DE MORELOS **Edge:** Segmented reeding

Date	Mintage	F	VF	XF	Unc	BU
2004Mo Proof	1,000	Value: 850				

KM# 804 100 PESOS
33.9400 g., Bi-Metallic o.925 Silver 20.1763g center in Aluminum-Bronze ring, 39.04 mm. **Series:** First **Subject:** 180th Anniversary of Federation **Obv:** National arms **Obv. Legend:** ESTADOS UNIDOS MEXICANOS **Rev:** State arms **Rev. Legend:** ESTADO DE MICHOACÁN DE OCAMPO **Edge:** Segmented reeding

Date	Mintage	F	VF	XF	Unc	BU
2004Mo	249,492	—	—	—	35.00	40.00

KM# 814 100 PESOS
29.1690 g., Bi-Metallic .999 Gold 17.154g center in .999 12.015g ring, 34.5 mm. **Series:** First **Subject:** 180th Anniversary of Federation **Obv:** National arms **Obv. Legend:** ESTADOS UNIDOS MEXICANOS **Rev:** State arms **Rev. Legend:** ESTADO DE MICHOACÁN DE OCAMPO **Edge:** Segmented reeding

Date	Mintage	F	VF	XF	Unc	BU
2004Mo Proof	1,000	Value: 850				

KM# 748 100 PESOS
33.9400 g., Bi-Metallic .925 Silver 20.1753g center in Aluminum-Bronze ring, 39.04 mm. **Series:** First **Subject:** 180th Anniversary of Federation **Obv:** National arms **Obv. Legend:** ESTADOS UNIDOS MEXICANOS **Rev:** State arms **Rev. Legend:** ESTADO DE MÉXICO **Edge:** Segmented reeding

Date	Mintage	F	VF	XF	Unc	BU
2004Mo	249,800	—	—	—	35.00	40.00

KM# 815 100 PESOS
29.1690 g., Bi-Metallic .999 Gold 17.154 center in .999 Silver 12.015 ring, 34.5 mm. **Series:** First **Subject:** 180th Anniversary of Federation **Obv:** National arms **Obv. Legend:** ESTADOS UNIDOS MEXICANOS **Rev:** State arms **Rev. Legend:** ESTADO DE MÉXICO **Edge:** Segmented reeding

Date	Mintage	F	VF	XF	Unc	BU
2004Mo Proof	1,000	Value: 850				

KM# 750 100 PESOS
33.9400 g., Bi-Metallic .925 Silver 20.1753g center in Aluminum-Bronze ring, 39.04 mm. **Series:** First **Subject:** 180th Anniversary of Federation **Obv:** National arms **Obv. Legend:** ESTADOS UNIDOS MEXICANOS **Rev:** State arms **Rev. Legend:** ESTADO DE JALISCO **Edge:** Segmented reeding

Date	Mintage	F	VF	XF	Unc	BU
2004Mo	249,115	—	—	—	35.00	40.00

KM# 816 100 PESOS
29.1690 g., Bi-Metallic .999 Gold 17.154g center in .999 Silver 12.015g ring, 34.5 mm. **Series:** First **Subject:** 180th Anniversary of Federation **Obv:** National arms **Obv. Legend:** ESTADOS UNIDOS MEXICANOS **Rev:** State arms **Rev. Legend:** ESTADO DE JALISCO **Edge:** Segmented reeding

Date	Mintage	F	VF	XF	Unc	BU
2004Mo Proof	1,000	Value: 850				

KM# 705 100 PESOS
33.7400 g., Bi-Metallic .925 Silver center in Aluminum-Bronze ring, 39 mm. **Subject:** 400th Anniversary of Don Quijote de la Manchia **Obv:** National arms **Obv. Legend:** ESTADOS UNIDOS MEXICANOS **Rev:** Skeletal figure on horseback with spear galloping right **Edge:** Segmented reeding

Date	Mintage	F	VF	XF	Unc	BU
2005Mo	726,833	—	—	—	25.00	32.00
2005Mo Proof	3,761	Value: 75.00				

KM# 730 100 PESOS
33.8250 g., Bi-Metallic .925 Silver 20.1753g center in Aluminum-Bronze ring, 39.9 mm. **Subject:** Monetary Reform Centennial **Obv:** National arms **Rev:** Radiant Liberty Cap divides date above value within circle **Edge:** Segmented reeding

Date	Mintage	F	VF	XF	Unc	BU
2005Mo	49,716	—	—	—	40.00	45.00
2005Mo Proof	—	Value: 75.00				

KM# 731 100 PESOS
33.8250 g., Bi-Metallic .925 Silver 20.1753g center in Aluminum-Bronze ring, 39.9 mm. **Subject:** Mexico City Mint's 470th Anniversary **Obv:** National arms **Rev:** Screw press, value and date within circle **Edge:** Segmented reeding

Date	Mintage	F	VF	XF	Unc	BU
2005Mo	49,895	—	—	—	40.00	45.00
2005Mo Proof	—	Value: 95.00				

KM# 732 100 PESOS
33.8250 g., Bi-Metallic .925 Silver 20.1753g center in Aluminum-Bronze ring, 39.9 mm. **Subject:** Bank of Mexico's 80th Anniversary **Obv:** National arms **Rev:** Back design of the 1925 hundred peso note **Edge:** Segmented reeding

Date	Mintage	F	VF	XF	Unc	BU
2005Mo	49,712	—	—	—	40.00	45.00
2005Mo Proof	—	Value: 95.00				

KM# 717 100 PESOS
33.9400 g., Bi-Metallic .925 Silver center in Brass ring, 39.04 mm. **Series:** First **Subject:** 180th Anniversary of Federation **Obv:** National arms **Obv. Legend:** ESTADOS UNIDOS MEXICANOS **Rev:** State arms **Rev. Legend:** ESTADO DE HIDALGO **Edge:** Segmented reeding

Date	Mintage	F	VF	XF	Unc	BU
2005Mo	249,820	—	—	—	35.00	40.00

KM# 817 100 PESOS
29.1690 g., Bi-Metallic .999 Gold 17.154g center in .999 Silver 12.015g ring, 34.5 mm. **Series:** First **Subject:** 180th Anniversary of Federation **Obv:** National arms **Obv. Legend:** ESTADOS UNIDOS MEXICANOS **Rev:** State arms **Rev. Legend:** ESTADO DE HIDALGO **Edge:** Segmented reeding

Date	Mintage	F	VF	XF	Unc	BU
2005Mo Proof	1,000	Value: 850				

KM# 716 100 PESOS
33.9400 g., Bi-Metallic .925 Silver center in Brass ring, 39.04 mm. **Series:** First **Subject:** 180th Anniversary of Federation **Obv:** National arms **Obv. Legend:** ESTADOS UNIDOS MEXICANOS **Rev:** State arms **Rev. Legend:** ESTADO DE GUERRERO **Edge:** Segmented reeding

Date	Mintage	F	VF	XF	Unc	BU
2005Mo	248,850	—	—	—	35.00	40.00

KM# 818 100 PESOS
29.1690 g., Bi-Metallic .999 Gold 17.154g center in .999 Silver 12.015 ring, 34.5 mm. **Series:** First **Subject:** 180th Anniversary of Federation **Obv:** National arms **Obv. Legend:** ESTADOS UNIDOS MEXICANOS **Rev:** State arms **Rev. Legend:** ESTADO DE GUERRERO **Edge:** Segmented reeding

Date	Mintage	F	VF	XF	Unc	BU
2005Mo Proof	1,000	Value: 850				

KM# 715 100 PESOS
33.9400 g., Bi-Metallic .925 Silver center in Brass ring, 39.04 mm. **Series:** First **Subject:** 180th Anniversary of Federation **Obv:** National arms **Obv. Legend:** ESTADOS UNIDOS MEXICANOS **Rev:** State arms **Rev. Legend:** ESTADO DE GUANAJUATO **Edge:** Segmented reeding

Date	Mintage	F	VF	XF	Unc	BU
2005Mo	249,489	—	—	—	35.00	40.00

KM# 819 100 PESOS
29.1690 g., Bi-Metallic .999 Gold 17.154g center in .999 Silver 12.015g ring, 34.5 mm. **Series:** First **Subject:** 180th Anniversary of Federation **Obv:** National arms **Obv. Legend:** ESTADOS UNIDOS MEXICANOS **Rev:** State arms **Rev. Legend:** ESTADO DE GUANAJUATO **Edge:** Segmented reeding

Date	Mintage	F	VF	XF	Unc	BU
2005Mo Proof	1,000	Value: 850				

KM# 714 100 PESOS
33.9400 g., Bi-Metallic .925 Silver center in Brass ring, 39.04 mm. **Series:** First **Subject:** 180th Anniversary of Federation **Obv:** National arms **Obv. Legend:** ESTADOS UNIDOS MEXICANOS **Rev:** State arms **Rev. Legend:** ESTADO DE DURANGO **Edge:** Segmented reeding

Date	Mintage	F	VF	XF	Unc	BU
2005Mo	249,774	—	—	—	35.00	40.00

KM# 820 100 PESOS
29.1690 g., Bi-Metallic .999 Gold 17.154g center in .999 silver 12.015g ring, 34.5 mm. **Series:** First **Subject:** 180th Anniversary of Federation **Obv:** National arms **Obv. Legend:** ESTADOS UNIDOS MEXICANOS **Rev:** State arms **Rev. Legend:** ESTADO DE DURANGO **Edge:** Segmented reeding

Date	Mintage	F	VF	XF	Unc	BU
2005Mo Proof	1,000	Value: 850				

KM# 713 100 PESOS
33.9400 g., Bi-Metallic .925 Silver 20.1753g center in Brass ring, 39.04 mm. **Series:** First **Subject:** 180th Anniversary of Federation **Obv:** National arms **Obv. Legend:** ESTADOS UNIDOS MEXICANOS **Rev:** Federal District arms **Rev. Legend:** DISTRITO FEDERAL **Edge:** Segmented reeding

Date	Mintage	F	VF	XF	Unc	BU
2005Mo	249,461	—	—	—	35.00	40.00

KM# 821 100 PESOS
29.1690 g., Bi-Metallic .999 Gold 17.154g center in .999 Silver 12.015g ring, 34.5 mm. **Series:** First **Subject:** 180th Anniversary of Federation **Obv:** National arms **Obv. Legend:** ESTADOS UNIDOS MEXICANOS **Rev:** Federal District arms **Rev. Legend:** DISTRITO FEDERAL **Edge:** Segmented reeding

Date	Mintage	F	VF	XF	Unc	BU
2005Mo Proof	1,000	Value: 850				

KM# 754 100 PESOS
33.9400 g., Bi-Metallic .925 Silver 20.1753g center in Aluminum-Bronze ring, 39.04 mm. **Series:** First **Subject:** 180th Anniversary of Federation **Obv:** National arms **Obv. Legend:** ESTADOS UNIDOS MEXICANOS **Rev:** State arms **Rev. Legend:** ESTADO DE CHIHUAHUA **Edge:** Segmented reeding

Date	Mintage	F	VF	XF	Unc	BU
2005Mo	249,102	—	—	—	35.00	40.00

KM# 822 100 PESOS
29.1690 g., Bi-Metallic .999 Gold 17.154g center in .999 Silver 12.015g ring, 34.5 mm. **Series:** First **Subject:** 180th Anniversary of Federation **Obv:** National arms **Obv. Legend:** ESTADOS UNIDOS MEXICANOS **Rev:** State arms **Rev. Legend:** ESTADO DE CHIHUAHUA **Edge:** Segmented reeding

Date	Mintage	F	VF	XF	Unc	BU
2005Mo Proof	1,000	Value: 850				

KM# 712 100 PESOS
33.9400 g., Bi-Metallic .925 Silver 20.1753g center in Brass ring, 39.04 mm. **Series:** First **Subject:** 180th Anniversary of Federation **Obv:** National arms **Obv. Legend:** ESTADOS UNIDOS MEXICANOS **Rev:** State arms **Rev. Legend:** ESTADO DE CHIAPAS **Edge:** Segmented reeding

Date	Mintage	F	VF	XF	Unc	BU
2005Mo	249,417	—	—	—	35.00	40.00

KM# 823 100 PESOS
29.1690 g., Bi-Metallic .999 Gold 17.154g center in .999 Silver 12.015g ring, 34.5 mm. **Series:** First **Subject:** 180th Anniversary of Federation **Obv:** National arms **Obv. Legend:** ESTADOS UNIDOS MEXICANOS **Rev:** State arms **Rev. Legend:** ESTADO DE CHIAPAS **Edge:** Segmented reeding

Date	Mintage	F	VF	XF	Unc	BU
2005Mo Proof	1,000	Value: 850				

KM# 729 100 PESOS
33.8250 g., Bi-Metallic .925 Silver 20.1753g center in Aluminum-Bronze ring, 39.04 mm. **Series:** First **Subject:** 180th Anniversary of Federation **Obv:** National arms **Obv. Legend:** ESTADOS UNIDOS MEXICANOS **Rev:** State arms **Rev. Legend:** ESTADO DE COLIMA **Edge:** Segmented reeding

Date	Mintage	F	VF	XF	Unc	BU
2005Mo	248,850	—	—	—	35.00	40.00

KM# 824 100 PESOS
29.1690 g., Bi-Metallic .999 Gold 17.154g center in .999 Silver 12.015g ring, 34.5 mm. **Series:** First **Subject:** 180th Anniversary of Federation **Obv:** National arms **Obv. Legend:** ESTADOS UNIDOS MEXICANOS **Rev:** State arms **Rev. Legend:** ESTADO DE COLIMA **Edge:** Segmented reeding

Date	Mintage	F	VF	XF	Unc	BU
2005Mo Proof	1,000	Value: 850				

KM# 752 100 PESOS

33.9400 g., Bi-Metallic .925 Silver 20.1753g center in Aluminum-Bronze ring, 39.04 mm. **Series:** First **Subject:** 180th Anniversary of Federation **Obv:** National arms **Obv. Legend:** ESTADOS UNIDOS MEXICANOS **Rev:** State arms **Rev. Legend:** ESTADO DE COAHUILA DE ZARAGOZA **Edge:** Segmented reeding

Date	Mintage	F	VF	XF	Unc	BU
2005Mo	247,991	—	—	—	35.00	40.00

KM# 825 100 PESOS

29.1690 g., Bi-Metallic .999 Gold 17.154g center in .999 Silver 12.015g ring, 34.5 mm. **Series:** First **Subject:** 180th Anniversary of Federation **Obv:** National arms **Obv. Legend:** ESTADOS UNIDOS MEXICANOS **Rev:** State arms **Rev. Legend:** ESTADO DE COAHUILA DE ZARAGOZA **Edge:** Segmented reeding

Date	Mintage	F	VF	XF	Unc	BU
2005Mo Proof	1,000	Value: 850				

KM# 727 100 PESOS

33.9400 g., Bi-Metallic .925 Silver 20.1753g center in Aluminum-Bronze ring, 39.04 mm. **Series:** First **Subject:** 180th Anniversary of Federation **Obv:** National arms **Obv. Legend:** ESTADOS UNIDOS MEXICANOS **Rev:** State arms **Rev. Legend:** ESTADO DE CAMPECHE **Edge:** Segmented reeding

Date	Mintage	F	VF	XF	Unc	BU
2005Mo	249,040	—	—	—	35.00	40.00

KM# 826 100 PESOS

29.1690 g., Bi-Metallic .999 Gold 17.154g center in .999 Silver 12.015g ring, 34.5 mm. **Series:** First **Subject:** 180th Anniversary of Federation **Obv:** National arms **Obv. Legend:** ESTADOS UNIDOS MEXICANOS **Rev:** State arms **Rev. Legend:** ESTADO DE CAMPECHE **Edge:** Segmented reeding

Date	Mintage	F	VF	XF	Unc	BU
2005Mo Proof	1,000	Value: 850				

KM# 725 100 PESOS

33.9400 g., Bi-Metallic .925 Silver 20.1753g center in Aluminum-Bronze ring, 39.04 mm. **Series:** First **Subject:** 180th Anniversary of Federation **Obv:** National arms **Obv. Legend:** ESTADOS UNIDOS MEXICANOS **Rev:** State arms **Rev. Legend:** ESTADO DE BAJA CALIFORNIA SUR **Edge:** Segmented reeding

Date	Mintage	F	VF	XF	Unc	BU
2005Mo	249,585	—	—	—	35.00	40.00

KM# 827 100 PESOS

29.1690 g., Bi-Metallic .999 Gold 17.154g center in .999 Silver 12.015g ring, 34.5 mm. **Series:** First **Subject:** 180th Anniversary of Federation **Obv:** National arms **Obv. Legend:** ESTADOS UNIDOS MEXICANOS **Rev:** State arms **Rev. Legend:** ESTADO DE BAJA CALIFORNIA SUR **Edge:** Segmented reeding

Date	Mintage	F	VF	XF	Unc	BU
2005Mo Proof	—	Value: 850				

KM# 723 100 PESOS

33.9400 g., Bi-Metallic .925 Silver 20.1753g center in Aluminum-Bronze ring, 39.04 mm. **Series:** First **Subject:** 180th Anniversary of Federation **Obv:** National arms **Obv. Legend:** ESTADOS UNIDOS MEXICANOS **Rev:** State arms **Rev. Legend:** ESTADO DE BAJA CALIFORNIA **Edge:** Segmented reeding

Date	Mintage	F	VF	XF	Unc	BU
2005Mo	249,263	—	—	—	35.00	40.00

KM# 828 100 PESOS

29.1690 g., Bi-Metallic .999 Gold 17.154g center in .999 Silver 12.015g ring, 34.5 mm. **Series:** First **Subject:** 180th Anniversary of Federation **Obv:** National arms **Obv. Legend:** ESTADOS UNIDOS MEXICANOS **Rev:** State arms **Rev. Legend:** ESTADO DE BAJA CALIFORNIA **Edge:** Segmented reeding

Date	Mintage	F	VF	XF	Unc	BU
2005Mo Proof	1,000	Value: 850				

KM# 721 100 PESOS

33.9400 g., Bi-Metallic .925 Silver 20.1753g center in Aluminum-Bronze ring, 39.04 mm. **Series:** First **Subject:** 180th Anniversary of Federation **Obv:** National arms **Obv. Legend:** ESTADOS UNIDOS MEXICANOS **Rev:** Estados de Aguascalientes state arms **Rev. Legend:** ESTADO DE AGUASCALIENTES **Edge:** Segmented reeding

Date	Mintage	F	VF	XF	Unc	BU
2005Mo	248,410	—	—	—	35.00	40.00

KM# 829 100 PESOS

29.1690 g., Bi-Metallic .999 Gold 17.154g center in .999 Silver 12.015g ring, 34.5 mm. **Series:** First **Subject:** 180th Anniversary of Federation **Obv:** National arms **Obv. Legend:** ESTADOS UNIDOS MEXICANOS **Rev:** State arms **Rev. Legend:** ESTADO DE AGUASCALIENTES **Edge:** Segmented reeding

Date	Mintage	F	VF	XF	Unc	BU
2005Mo Proof	1,000	Value: 850				

KM# 719 100 PESOS

33.8250 g., Bi-Metallic .925 Silver 20.1753g center in Aluminum-Bronze ring, 39.04 mm. **Series:** Second **Obv:** National arms **Obv. Legend:** ESTADOS UNIDOS MEXICANOS **Rev:** Facade of the San Marcos garden above sculpture of national emblem at left, San Antonio Temple at right **Rev. Legend:** AGUASCALIENTES **Edge:** Segmented reeding

Date	Mintage	F	VF	XF	Unc	BU
2005Mo	149,705	—	—	—	25.00	30.00

KM# 862 100 PESOS

29.1690 g., Bi-Metallic .999 Gold 17.154g center in .999 Silver 12.015g ring, 34.5 mm. **Series:** Second **Obv:** National arms **Obv. Legend:** ESTADOS UNIDOS MEXICANOS **Rev:** Facade of the San Marcos garden above sculpture of national emblem at left, San Antonio temple at right **Rev. Legend:** AGUASCALIENTES **Edge:** Segmented reeding

Date	Mintage	F	VF	XF	Unc	BU
2005Mo Proof	600	Value: 875				

KM# 758 100 PESOS

33.9400 g., Bi-Metallic .925 Silver 20.1753g center in Aluminum-Bronze ring, 39.04 mm. **Series:** Second **Obv:** National arms **Obv. Legend:** ESTADOS UNIDOS MEXICANOS **Rev:** Ram's head and value within circle **Rev. Legend:** BAJA CALIFORNIA - GOBIERNO DEL ESTADO **Edge:** Segmented reeding

Date	Mintage	F	VF	XF	Unc	BU
2005Mo	—	—	—	—	25.00	30.00

KM# 863 100 PESOS

29.1690 g., Bi-Metallic .999 Gold 17.154g center in .999 Silver 12.015g ring, 34.5 mm. **Series:** Second **Obv:** National arms **Obv. Legend:** ESTTADOS UNIDOS MEXICANOS **Rev:** Ram's head, mountain outline in background **Rev. Legend:** BAJA CALIFORNIA - GOBIERNO DEL ESTADO **Edge:** Segmented reeding

Date	Mintage	F	VF	XF	Unc	BU
2005Mo Proof	600	Value: 875				

KM# 762 100 PESOS

33.9400 g., Bi-Metallic .925 Silver 20.175g center in Aluminum-Bronze ring, 39.04 mm. **Series:** Second **Obv:** National arms **Obv. Legend:** ESTADOS UNIDOS MEXICANOS **Rev:** Outlined map of peninsula at center, cave painting of deer behind, cactus at right **Rev. Legend:** ESTADO DE BAJA CALIFORNIA SUR **Edge:** Segmented reeding

Date	Mintage	F	VF	XF	Unc	BU
2005Mo	149,152	—	—	—	25.00	30.00

KM# 764 100 PESOS

33.7000 g., Bi-Metallic .925 Silver 20.1753g center in Aluminum-Bronze ring **Subject:** 200th Anniversary Birth of Benito Juarez Garcia **Obv:** National arms **Rev:** Bust 1/4 left within circle

Date	Mintage	F	VF	XF	Unc	BU
2006Mo	49,913	—	—	—	40.00	45.00

KM# 864 100 PESOS

29.1690 g., Bi-Metallic .999 Gold 17.154g center in .999 Silver 12.015g ring, 34.5 mm. **Series:** Second **Obv:** National arms **Obv. Legend:** ESTADOS UNIDOS MEXICANOS **Rev:** Outlined map of peninsula at center, cave painting of deer behind, cactus at right **Rev. Legend:** ESTADO DE BAJA CALIFORNIA SUR **Edge:** Segmented reeding

Date	Mintage	F	VF	XF	Unc	BU
2006Mo Proof	600	Value: 875				

KM# 760 100 PESOS

33.9400 g., Bi-Metallic .925 Silver 20.1753g center in Aluminum-Bronze ring, 39.04 mm. **Series:** Second **Subject:** Estado de Campeche **Obv:** National arms **Obv. Legend:** ESTADOS UNIDOS MEXICANOS **Rev:** Jade mask - Calakmul, Campeche **Rev. Legend:** ESTADO DE CAMPECHE **Edge:** Segmented reeding

Date	Mintage	F	VF	XF	Unc	BU
2006Mo	—	—	—	—	25.00	30.00

KM# 865 100 PESOS

29.1690 g., Bi-Metallic .999 Gold 17.154g center in .999 Silver 12.015g ring, 34.5 mm. **Series:** Second **Obv:** National arms **Obv. Legend:** ESTADOS UNIDOS MEXICANOS **Rev:** Jade mask - Calakmul, Campeche **Rev. Legend:** ESTADO DE CAMPECHE **Edge:** Segmented reeding

Date	Mintage	F	VF	XF	Unc	BU
2006Mo Proof	600	Value: 875				

KM# 781 100 PESOS

33.7000 g., Bi-Metallic .925 Silver 20.1753g center in Aluminum-Bronze ring, 39.04 mm. **Series:** Second **Obv:** National arms **Obv. Legend:** ESTADOS UNIDOS MEXICANOS **Rev:** Outlined map with turtle, mine cart above grapes at center, Friendship Dam above Christ of the Nodas at left, chimneys above crucibles and bell tower of Santiago's cathedral at right **Rev. Legend:** COAHUILA DE ZARAGOZA **Edge:** Segmented reeding

Date	Mintage	F	VF	XF	Unc	BU
2006Mo	—	—	—	—	25.00	30.00

KM# 866 100 PESOS

29.1690 g., Bi-Metallic .999 Gold 17.154g center in .999 Silver 12.015g ring, 34.5 mm. **Series:** Second **Obv:** National arms **Obv. Legend:** ESTADOS UNIDOS MEXICANOS **Rev:** Outlined map with turtle, mine cart above grapes at center, Friendship dam above Christ of the Nodas at left, chimneys above crucibles and bell tower of Santiago's cathedral at right **Rev. Inscription:** COAHUILA DE ZARAGOZA **Edge:** Segmented reeding

Date	Mintage	F	VF	XF	Unc	BU
2006Mo Proof	600	Value: 875				

KM# 777 100 PESOS

33.9400 g., Bi-Metallic .925 Silver 20.1753g center in Aluminum-Bronze ring, 39.04 mm. **Series:** Second **Obv:** National arms **Obv. Legend:** ESTADOS UNIDOS MEXICANOS **Rev:** State arms at lower center, Nevado de Colima and Volcan de Fuego volcanos in background **Rev. Legend:** *Colima* **Rev. Inscription:** GENEROSO **Edge:** Segmented reeding

Date	Mintage	F	VF	XF	Unc	BU
2006Mo	149,041	—	—	—	25.00	30.00

KM# 867 100 PESOS

29.1690 g., Bi-Metallic .999 Gold 17.154g center in .999 Silver 12.015 ring, 34.5 mm. **Series:** Second **Obv:** National arms **Obv. Legend:** ESTADOS UNIDOS MEXICANOS **Rev:** State arms at lower center, Nevado de Colima and Volcan de Fuego volcanos in background **Rev. Legend:** *Colima* **Rev. Inscription:** GENEROSO **Edge:** Segmented reeding

Date	Mintage	F	VF	XF	Unc	BU
2006Mo Proof	600	Value: 875				

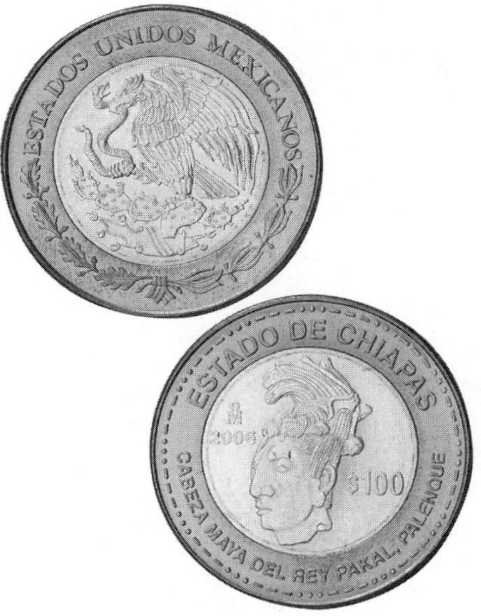

KM# 773 100 PESOS

33.9400 g., Bi-Metallic .925 Silver 20.1753g center in Aluminum-Bronze ring, 39.04 mm. **Series:** Second **Obv:** National arms **Obv. Legend:** ESTADOS UNIDOS MEXICANOS **Rev:** Head of Pakal, ancient Mayan king, Palenque **Rev. Legend:** ESTADO DE CHIAPAS - CABEZA MAYA DEL REY PAKAL, PALENQUE **Edge:** Segmented reeding

Date	Mintage	F	VF	XF	Unc	BU
2006Mo	149,491	—	—	—	25.00	30.00

KM# 868 100 PESOS

29.1690 g., Bi-Metallic .999 Gold 17.154g center in .999 Silver 12.015g ring, 34.5 mm. **Series:** Second **Obv:** National arms **Obv. Legend:** ESTADOS UNIDOS MEXICANOS **Rev:** Head of Pakal, ancient Mayan king, Palenque **Rev. Legend:** ESTADO DE CHIAPAS - CABEZA MAYA DEL REY PAKAL, PALENQUE **Edge:** Segmented reeding

Date	Mintage	F	VF	XF	Unc	BU
2006Mo Proof	600	Value: 875				

KM# 775 100 PESOS

33.9400 g., Bi-Metallic .925 Silver 20.1753g center in Aluminum-Bronze ring, 39.04 mm. **Series:** Second **Obv:** National arms **Obv. Legend:** ESTADOS UNIDOS MEXICANOS **Rev:** Angel of Liberty **Rev. Legend:** MÉXICO - ANGEL DE LA LIBERTAD, CHIHUAHUA **Edge:** Segmented reeding

Date	Mintage	F	VF	XF	Unc	BU
2006Mo	149,557	—	—	—	25.00	30.00

KM# 869 100 PESOS

29.1690 g., Bi-Metallic .999 Gold 17.154g center in .999 Silver 12.015g ring, 34.5 mm. **Series:** Second **Obv:** National arms **Obv. Legend:** ESTADOS UNIDOS MEXICANOS **Rev:** Angel of Liberty **Rev. Legend:** MÉXICO - ANGEL DE LA LIBERTAD, CHIHUAHUA **Edge:** Segmented reeding

Date	Mintage	F	VF	XF	Unc	BU
2006Mo Proof	600	Value: 875				

KM# 779 100 PESOS

33.9400 g., Bi-Metallic .925 Silver 20.1753g center in Aluminum-Bronze ring, 39.04 mm. **Series:** Second **Obv:** National arms **Obv. Legend:** ESTADOS UNIDOS MEXICANOS **Rev:** National Palace **Rev. Legend:** DISTRITO FEDERAL - ANTIGUO AYUNTAMIENTO **Edge:** Segmented reeding

Date	Mintage	F	VF	XF	Unc	BU
2006Mo	149,525	—	—	—	25.00	30.00

KM# 870 100 PESOS

29.1690 g., Bi-Metallic .999 Gold 17.154g center in .999 Silver 12.015g ring, 34.5 mm. **Series:** Second **Obv:** National arms **Obv. Legend:** ESTADOS UNIDOS MEXICANOS **Rev:** National palace **Rev. Legend:** DISTRITO FEDERAL - ANTIGUO AYUNTAMIENTO **Edge:** Segmented reeding

Date	Mintage	F	VF	XF	Unc	BU
2006Mo Proof	600	Value: 875				

KM# 787 100 PESOS

33.9400 g., Bi-Metallic .925 Silver 20.1753g center in Brass ring, 39.04 mm. **Series:** Second **Obv:** National arms **Obv. Legend:** ESTADOS UNIDOS MEXICANOS **Rev:** Tree **Rev. Legend:** PRIMERA RESERVA NACIONAL FORESTAL - DURANGO **Edge:** Segmented reeding

Date	Mintage	F	VF	XF	Unc	BU
2006Mo	149,034	—	—	—	25.00	30.00

KM# 871 100 PESOS

29.1690 g., Bi-Metallic .999 Gold 17.154g center in .999 Silver 12.015g ring, 34.5 mm. **Series:** Second **Obv:** National arms **Obv. Legend:** ESYADOS UNIDOS MEXICANOS **Rev:** Tree **Rev. Legend:** PRIMERA RESERVA NACIONAL RORESTAL - DURANGO **Edge:** Segmented reeding

Date	Mintage	F	VF	XF	Unc	BU
2006Mo Proof	600	Value: 875				

KM# 789 100 PESOS

33.9400 g., Bi-Metallic .925 Silver 20.1753g center in Brass ring, 39.04 mm. **Series:** Second **Obv:** National arms **Obv. Legend:** ESTADOS UNIDOS MEXICANOS **Rev:** State arms at center, statue of Miguel Hidalgo at left, monument to Pipla at lower right **Rev. Inscription:** *Guanajuato* **Edge:** Segmented reeding

Date	Mintage	F	VF	XF	Unc	BU
2006Mo	149,921	—	—	—	25.00	30.00

KM# 872 100 PESOS

29.1690 g., Bi-Metallic .999 Gold 17.154g center in .999 Silver 12.015g ring, 34.50 mm. **Series:** Second **Obv:** National arms **Obv. Legend:** ESTADOS UNIDOS MEXICANOS **Rev:** State arms at lower center, statue of Miguel Hidalgo at left, monument to Pipila at lower right **Rev. Inscription:** *Guanajauto* **Edge:** Segmented reeding

Date	Mintage	F	VF	XF	Unc	BU
2006Mo Proof	600	Value: 875				

KM# 791 100 PESOS
33.9400 g., Bi-Metallic .925 Silver 20.1753g center in Brass ring, 39.04 mm. **Series:** Second **Obv:** National arms **Obv. Legend:** ESTADOS UNIDOS MEXICANOS **Rev:** Stylized portrait of Vicente Guerrero at left, church of Taxco at upper center, Acapulco's la Quebrada with diver above Christmas Eve flower and mask **Rev. Legend:** GUERRERO **Edge:** Segmented reeding

Date	Mintage	F	VF	XF	Unc	BU
2006Mo	149,675	—	—	—	25.00	30.00

KM# 873 100 PESOS
29.1690 g., Bi-Metallic .999 Gold 17.154g center in .999 Silver 12.015g ring, 34.5 mm. **Series:** Second **Obv:** National arms **Obv. Legend:** ESTADOS UNIDOS MEXICANOS **Rev:** Stylized portrait of Vicente Guerrero at left, church of Taxco at upper center, Acapulco's la Quebrada with diver over Christmas Eve flower and mask **Rev. Legend:** GUERRERO **Edge:** Segmented reeding

Date	Mintage	F	VF	XF	Unc	BU
2006Mo Proof	600	Value: 875				

KM# 793 100 PESOS
33.9400 g., Bi-Metallic .925 Silver 20.1753g center in Aluminum-Bronze ring, 39.04 mm. **Series:** Second **Obv:** National arms **Obv. Legend:** ESTADOS UNIDOS MEXICANOS **Rev:** Monument of Pachuca Hidalgo **Rev. Inscription:** *RELOJ / MONUMENTAL / DE / PACHUCA / HIDALGO - La / Bella / Airosa* **Edge:** Segmented reeding

Date	Mintage	F	VF	XF	Unc	BU
2006Mo	149,273	—	—	—	25.00	30.00

KM# 874 100 PESOS
29.1690 g., Bi-Metallic .999 Gold 17.154g center in .999 Silver 12.015g ring, 34.5 mm. **Series:** Second **Obv:** National arms **Obv. Legend:** ESTADOS UNIDOS MEXICANOS **Rev:** Monument of Pachuca Hidalgo **Rev. Inscription:** *RELOJ / MONUMENTAL / DE / PACHUCA / HIDALGO* **Edge:** Segmented reeding

Date	Mintage	F	VF	XF	Unc	BU
2006Mo Proof	600	Value: 875				

KM# 795 100 PESOS
33.9400 g., Bi-Metallic .925 Silver 20.1753g center in Brass ring, 39.04 mm. **Series:** Second **Obv:** National arms **Obv. Legend:** ESTADOS UNIDOS MEXICANOS **Rev:** Hospicio Cabañas orphanage **Rev. Legend:** ESTADO DE JALISCO **Edge:** Segmented reeding

Date	Mintage	F	VF	XF	Unc	BU
2006Mo	149,750	—	—	—	25.00	30.00

KM# 875 100 PESOS
29.1690 g., Bi-Metallic .999 Gold 17.154g center in .999 Silver 12.015g ring, 34.5 mm. **Series:** Second **Obv:** National arms **Obv. Legend:** ESTADOS UNIDOS MEXICANOS **Rev:** Hospicio Cabañas orphanage **Rev. Legend:** ESTADO DE JALISCO **Edge:** Segmented reeding

Date	Mintage	F	VF	XF	Unc	BU
2006Mo Proof	600	Value: 875				

KM# 802 100 PESOS
33.9400 g., Bi-Metallic .925 Silver 20.1753g center in Aluminum-Bronze ring, 33.7, 39.04 mm. **Series:** Second **Obv:** National arms **Obv. Legend:** ESTADOS UNIDOS MEXICANOS **Rev:** Pyramid de la Loona (moon) **Rev. Legend:** ESTADO DE MÉXICO **Edge:** Segmented reeding

Date	Mintage	F	VF	XF	Unc	BU
2006Mo	149,377	—	—	—	25.00	30.00

KM# 876 100 PESOS
29.1690 g., Bi-Metallic .999 Gold 17.154g center in .999 Silver 12.015g ring, 34.5 mm. **Series:** Second **Obv:** National arms **Obv. Legend:** ESTADOS UNIDOS MEXICANOS **Rev:** Pyramid de la Looona (moon) **Rev. Legend:** ESTADO DE MÉXICO **Edge:** Segmented reeding

Date	Mintage	F	VF	XF	Unc	BU
2006Mo Proof	600	Value: 875				

KM# 785 100 PESOS
33.9400 g., Bi-Metallic .925 Silver 20.1753g center in Aluminum-Bronze ring, 33.7, 39.04 mm. **Series:** Second **Obv:** National arms **Obv. Legend:** ESTADOS UNIDOS MEXICANOS **Rev:** Four Monarch butterflies **Rev. Legend:** ESTADO DE MICHOACÁN **Edge:** Segmented reeding

Date	Mintage	F	VF	XF	Unc	BU
2006Mo	149,730	—	—	—	25.00	30.00

KM# 877 100 PESOS
29.1690 g., Bi-Metallic .999 Gold 17.154g center in .999 Silver 12.015g ring, 34.5 mm. **Series:** Second **Obv:** National arms **Obv. Legend:** ESTADOS UNIDOS MEXICANOS **Rev:** Four Monarch butterflies **Rev. Legend:** ESTADO DE MICHOACÁN **Edge:** Segmented reeding

Date	Mintage	F	VF	XF	Unc	BU
2006Mo Proof	600	Value: 875				

KM# 800 100 PESOS
33.9400 g., Bi-Metallic .925 Silver 20.1753g center in Aluminum-Bronze ring, 33.7, 39.04 mm. **Series:** Second **Obv:** National arms **Obv. Legend:** ESTADOS UNIDOS MEXICANOS **Rev:** 1/2 length figure of Chinelo (local dancer) at right, Palacio de Cortes in background **Rev. Inscription:** ESTADO DE / MORELOS **Edge:** Segmented reeding

Date	Mintage	F	VF	XF	Unc	BU
2006Mo	149,648	—	—	—	25.00	30.00

KM# 878 100 PESOS
29.1690 g., Bi-Metallic .999 Gold 17.154g center in .999 Silver 12.015g ring, 34.5 mm. **Series:** Second **Obv:** National arms **Obv. Legend:** ESTADOS UNIDOS MEXICANOS **Rev:** 1/2 length figure of Chinelo (local dancer) at right, Palacio de Cortes in background **Rev. Inscription:** ESTADO DE / MORELOS **Edge:** Segmented reeding

Date	Mintage	F	VF	XF	Unc	BU
2006Mo Proof	600	Value: 875				

KM# 798 100 PESOS
33.9400 g., 33.8250 Bi-Metallic 0.925 Silver 20.1753g center in Aluminum-Bronze ring 36.908 oz., 39.04 mm. **Series:** Second **Obv:** National arms **Obv. Legend:** ESTADOS UNIDOS MEXICANOS **Rev:** Isle de Mexcaltitlán **Rev. Legend:** ESTADO DE NAYARIT **Edge:** Segmented reeding

Date	Mintage	F	VF	XF	Unc	BU
2007Mo	149,560	—	—	—	25.00	30.00

KM# 879 100 PESOS
29.1690 g., Bi-Metallic .999 Gold 17.154g center in .999 12.015g ring, 34.5 mm. **Series:** Second **Obv:** National arms **Obv. Legend:** ESTADOS UNIDOS MEXICANOS **Rev:** Isle de Mexcaltitlán **Rev. Legend:** ESTADO DE NAYARIT **Edge:** Segmented reeding

Date	Mintage	F	VF	XF	Unc	BU
2007Mo Proof	600	Value: 875				

KM# 848 100 PESOS
33.9400 g., Bi-Metallic .925 Silver 20.1753 center in Aluminum-Bronze ring, 39.04 mm. **Series:** Second **Obv:** National arms **Obv. Legend:** ESTADOS UNIDOS MEXICANOE **Rev:** Old foundry in Parque Fundidora (public park) at right, Cerro de la Silla (Saddle Hill) in background **Rev. Legend:** ESTADO DE NUEVO LÉON **Edge:** Segmented reeding

Date	Mintage	F	VF	XF	Unc	BU
2007Mo	149,425	—	—	—	25.00	30.00

KM# 880 100 PESOS
29.1690 g., Bi-Metallic .999 Gold 17.154g center in .999 Silver 12.015g ring, 34.5 mm. **Series:** Second **Obv:** National arms **Obv. Legend:** ESTADOS UNIDOS MEXICANOS **Rev:** Old foundry in Parque Fundidora (public park) at right, Cerro de la Silla (Saddle hill) in background **Rev. Legend:** ESTADO DE NUEVO LEÓN **Edge:** Segmented reeding

Date	Mintage	F	VF	XF	Unc	BU
2007Mo Proof	600	Value: 875				

KM# 849 100 PESOS
33.9400 g., Bi-Metallic .925 Silver 20.1753g center in Aluminum-Bronze ring, 39.04 mm. **Series:** Second **Obv:** National arms **Obv. Legend:** ESTADOS UNIDOS MEXICANOS **Rev:** Teatro Macedonio Alcala (theater) **Rev. Legend:** OAXACA **Edge:** Segmented reeding

Date	Mintage	F	VF	XF	Unc	BU
2007Mo	149,892	—	—	—	25.00	30.00

KM# 881 100 PESOS

29.1690 g., Bi-Metallic .999 Gold 17.154g center in .999 Silver 12.015g ring, 34.50 mm. **Series:** Second **Obv:** National arms **Obv. Legend:** ESTADOS UNIDOS MEXICANOS **Rev:** Teatro Macedonio Alcala (theater) **Rev. Legend:** OAXACA **Edge:** Segmented reeding

Date	Mintage	F	VF	XF	Unc	BU
2007Mo Proof	600	Value: 875				

KM# 850 100 PESOS

33.9400 g., Bi-Metallic .925 Silver 20.1753g center in Aluminum-Bronze ring, 39.04 mm. **Series:** Second **Obv:** National arms **Obv. Legend:** ESTADOS UNIDOS MEXICANOS **Rev:** Talavera porcelain dish **Rev. Legend:** ESTADO DE PUEBLA **Edge:** Segmented reeding

Date	Mintage	F	VF	XF	Unc	BU
2007Mo	149,474	—	—	—	25.00	30.00

KM# 882 100 PESOS

29.1690 g., Bi-Metallic .999 Gold 17.154g center in .999 Silver 12.015g ring, 34.5 mm. **Series:** Second **Obv:** National arms **Obv. Legend:** ESTADOS UNIDOS MEXICANOS **Rev:** Talavera porcelain dish **Rev. Legend:** ESTADO DE PUEBLA **Edge:** Segmented reeding

Date	Mintage	F	VF	XF	Unc	BU
2007Mo Proof	600	Value: 875				

KM# 851 100 PESOS

33.9400 g., Bi-Metallic .925 Silver 20.1753g center in Aluminum-Bronze ring, 39.04 mm. **Series:** Second **Obv:** National arms **Obv. Legend:** ESTADOS UNIDOS MEXICANOS **Rev:** Mask at left, rays above state arms at center, Mayan ruins at right **Rev. Legend:** QUINTANA ROO **Edge:** Segmented reeding

Date	Mintage	F	VF	XF	Unc	BU
2007Mo	149,582	—	—	—	25.00	30.00

KM# 883 100 PESOS

29.1690 g., Bi-Metallic .999 Gold 17.154g center in .999 Silver 12.015g ring, 34.5 mm. **Series:** Second **Obv:** National arms **Obv. Legend:** ESTADOS UNIDOS MEXICANOS **Rev:** Mask at left, rays above state arms at center, Mayan ruins at right **Rev. Legend:** QUINTANA ROO **Edge:** Segmented reeding

Date	Mintage	F	VF	XF	Unc	BU
2007Mo Proof	600	Value: 875				

KM# 852 100 PESOS

33.9400 g., Bi-Metallic .925 Silver 20.1753 center in Aluminum-Bronze ring, 39.04 mm. **Series:** Second **Obv:** National arms **Obv. Legend:** ESTADOS UNIDOS MEXICANOS **Rev:** Aqueduct of Querétaro at left, church of Santa Rosa de Viterbo at right **Rev. Legend:** ESTADO DE QUERÉTARO ARTEAGA **Edge:** Segmented reeding

Date	Mintage	F	VF	XF	Unc	BU
2007Mo	149,127	—	—	—	25.00	30.00

KM# 884 100 PESOS

29.1690 g., Bi-Metallic .999 Gold 17.154g center in .999 Silver 12.015g ring, 34.5 mm. **Series:** Second **Obv:** National arms **Obv. Legend:** ESTADOS UNIDOS MEXICANOS **Rev:** Aqueduct of Querétaro at left, church of Santa Rosa de Viterbo at right **Rev. Legend:** ESTADO DE QUERÉTARO ARTEAGA **Edge:** Segmented reeding

Date	Mintage	F	VF	XF	Unc	BU
2007Mo Proof	600	Value: 875				

KM# 853 100 PESOS

33.9400 g., Bi-Metallic .925 Silver 20.1753g center in Aluminum-Bronze ring, 39.04 mm. **Series:** Second **Obv:** National arms **Obv. Legend:** ESTADOS UNIDOS MEXICANOS **Rev:** Facade of Caja Real **Rev. Legend:** • SAN LUIS POTOSÍ • **Edge:** Segmented reeding

Date	Mintage	F	VF	XF	Unc	BU
2007Mo	148,750	—	—	—	25.00	30.00

KM# 885 100 PESOS

29.1690 g., Bi-Metallic .999 Gold 17.154g center in .999 Silver 12.015 ring, 34.5 mm. **Series:** Second **Obv:** National arms **Obv. Legend:** ESTADOS UNIDOS MEXICANOS **Rev:** Facade of Caja Real **Rev. Legend:** • SAN LUIS POTOSÍ • **Edge:** Segmented reeding

Date	Mintage	F	VF	XF	Unc	BU
2007Mo Proof	600	Value: 875				

KM# 854 100 PESOS

33.9400 g., Bi-Metallic .925 Silver 20.1753g center in Aluminum-Bronze ring, 39.04 mm. **Series:** Second **Obv:** National arms **Obv. Legend:** ESTADOS UNIDOS MEXICANOS **Rev:** Shield on pile of cactus fruits **Rev. Legend:** ESTADO DE SINALOA - LUGAR DE PITAHAYAS **Edge:** Segmented reeding

Date	Mintage	F	VF	XF	Unc	BU
2007Mo	149,032	—	—	—	25.00	30.00

KM# 886 100 PESOS

29.1690 g., Bi-Metallic .999 Gold 17.154 center in .999 Silver 12.015g ring, 34.5 mm. **Series:** Second **Obv:** National arms **Obv. Legend:** ESTADOS UNIDOS MEXICANOS **Rev:** Shield on pile of cactus fruits **Rev. Legend:** ESTADO DE SINALOA - LUGAR DE PITAHAYES **Edge:** Segmented reeding

Date	Mintage	F	VF	XF	Unc	BU
2007Mo Proof	600	Value: 875				

KM# 855 100 PESOS

33.9400 g., Bi-Metallic .925 Silver 20.1753g center in Aluminum-Bronze ring, 39.04 mm. **Series:** Second **Obv:** National arms **Obv. Legend:** ESTADOS UNIDOS MEXICANOS **Rev:** Local in Dance of the Deer at left, cactus at right, mountains in background **Rev. Legend:** ESTADO DE SONORA **Edge:** Segmented reeding

Date	Mintage	F	VF	XF	Unc	BU
2007Mo	149,891	—	—	—	25.00	30.00

KM# 887 100 PESOS

29.1690 g., Bi-Metallic .999 Gold 17.154g center in .999 Silver 12.015g ring, 34.5 mm. **Series:** Second **Obv:** National arms **Obv. Legend:** ESTADOS UNIDOS MEXICANOS **Rev:** Local in Dance of the Deer at left, cactus at right, mountains in background **Rev. Legend:** ESTADO DE SONORA **Edge:** Segmented reeding

Date	Mintage	F	VF	XF	Unc	BU
2007Mo Proof	600	Value: 875				

KM# 856 100 PESOS

33.9400 g., Bi-Metallic .925 Silver 20.1753 center in Aluminum-Bronze ring, 39.04 mm. **Series:** Second **Obv:** National arms **Obv. Legend:** ESTADOS UNIDOS MEXICANOS **Rev:** Fuente de los Pescadores (fisherman fountain) at lower left, giant head from the Olmec-pre-Hispanic culture at right, Planetario Tabasco in background **Rev. Legend:** TABASCO **Edge:** Segmented reeding

Date	Mintage	F	VF	XF	Unc	BU
2007Mo	149,715	—	—	—	25.00	30.00

KM# 888 100 PESOS

29.1690 g., Bi-Metallic .999 Gold 17.154g center in .999 Silver 12.015g ring, 34.5 mm. **Series:** Second **Obv:** National arms **Obv. Legend:** ESTADOS UNIDOS MEXICANOS **Rev:** Fuente de los Pescadores (fisherman fountain) at lower left, giant head from the Olmec-pre-Hispanic culture at right, Planetario Tabasco in background **Rev. Legend:** TABASCO **Edge:** Segmented reeding

Date	Mintage	F	VF	XF	Unc	BU
2007Mo Proof	600	Value: 875				

KM# 857 100 PESOS

33.9400 g., Bi-Metallic .925 Silver 20.1753g center in Aluminum-Bronze ring, 39.04 mm. **Series:** Second **Obv:** National arms **Obv. Legend:** ESTADOS UNIDOS MEXICANOS **Rev:** Ridge - Cerro Del Bermal, Gonzáles **Rev. Legend:** TAMAULIPAS **Edge:** Segmented reeding

Date	Mintage	F	VF	XF	Unc	BU
2007Mo	149,776	—	—	—	25.00	30.00

KM# 889 100 PESOS

29.1690 g., Bi-Metallic .999 Gold 17.154g center in .999 Silver 12.015g ring, 34.5 mm. **Series:** Second **Obv:** National arms **Obv. Legend:** ESTADOS DE MEXICANOS **Rev:** Ridge - Cerro Del Bemal, Gonzáles **Rev. Legend:** TAMAULIPAS **Edge:** Segmented reeding

Date	Mintage	F	VF	XF	Unc	BU
2007Mo Proof	600	Value: 875				

KM# 858 100 PESOS

33.9400 g., Bi-Metallic .925 Silver 20.1753g center in Aluminum-Bronze ring, 39.04 mm. **Series:** Second **Obv:** National arms **Obv. Legend:** ESTADOS UNIDOS MEXICANOS **Rev:** Basilica de Ocotlán at left, state arms above Capilla Abierta, Plaza de Toros Ranchero Aguilar below, Exconvento de San Francisco at right **Rev. Legend:** ESTADO DE TLAXCALA **Edge:** Segmented reeding

Date	Mintage	F	VF	XF	Unc	BU
2007Mo	149,465	—	—	—	25.00	30.00

KM# 890 100 PESOS

29.1690 g., Bi-Metallic .999 Gold 17.154g center in .999 Silver 12.015g ring, 34.5 mm. **Series:** Second **Obv:** National arms **Obv. Legend:** ESTADOS UNIDOS MEXICANOS **Rev:** Basilica de Ocotlán at left, state arms above Capilla Abierta, Plaza de Toros Aguilar below, Exconvento de San Francisco at right **Rev. Legend:** ESTADO DE TLAXCALA **Edge:** Segmented reeding

Date	Mintage	F	VF	XF	Unc	BU
2007Mo Proof	600	Value: 875				

KM# 859 100 PESOS

33.9400 g., Bi-Metallic .912 Silver 20.1753g center in Aluminum-Bronze ring, 39.04 mm. **Series:** Second **Obv:** National arms **Obv. Legend:** ESTADOS UNIDOS MEXICANOS **Rev:** Pyramid of El Tajín **Rev. Legend:** • VERACRUZ • - • DE IGNACIO DE LA LLAVE • **Edge:** Segmented reeding

Date	Mintage	F	VF	XF	Unc	BU
2007Mo	149,703	—	—	—	25.00	30.00

KM# 891 100 PESOS

29.1690 g., Bi-Metallic .999 Gold 17.154g center in .999 Silver 12.015g ring, 34.5 mm. **Series:** Second **Obv:** National arms **Obv. Legend:** ESTADOS UNIDOS MEXICANOS **Rev:** Pyramid of El Tajin **Rev. Legend:** • VERACRUZ • - • DE IGNACIO DE LA LLAVE • **Edge:** Segmented reeding

Date	Mintage	F	VF	XF	Unc	BU
2007Mo Proof	600	Value: 875				

KM# 860 100 PESOS

33.9400 g., Bi-Metallic .925 Silver 20.1753 center in Aluminum-Bronze ring, 39.04 mm. **Series:** Second **Obv:** National arms **Obv. Legend:** ESTADOS UNIDOS MEXICANOS **Rev:** Stylized pyramid of Chichén Itzá **Rev. Legend:** Castillo de Chichén Itzá **Edge:** Segmented reeding

Date	Mintage	F	VF	XF	Unc	BU
2007Mo	149,579	—	—	—	25.00	30.00

KM# 892 100 PESOS

29.1690 g., Bi-Metallic .999 Gold 17.154g center in .999 Silver 12.015g ring, 34.5 mm. **Series:** Second **Obv:** National arms **Obv. Legend:** ESTADOS UNIDOS MEXICANOS **Rev:** Stylized pyramid of Chichén-Itzá **Rev. Inscription:** YUCATÁN **Edge:** Segmented reeding

Date	Mintage	F	VF	XF	Unc	BU
2007Mo Proof	600	Value: 875				

KM# 861 100 PESOS

33.9400 g., Bi-Metallic .925 Silver 20.1753g center in Aluminum-Bronze ring, 39.04 mm. **Series:** Second **Obv:** National arms **Obv. Legend:** ESTADOS UNIDOS MEXICANOS **Rev:** Cable car above Monumento al Minero at left, Cathedral de Zacatecas at center right **Rev. Legend:** ZACATECAS **Edge:** Segmented reeding

Date	Mintage	F	VF	XF	Unc	BU
2007Mo	148,833	—	—	—	25.00	30.00

KM# 893 100 PESOS

29.1690 g., Bi-Metallic .999 Gold 17.154g center in .999 Silver 12.015g ring, 34.5 mm. **Series:** Second **Obv:** National arms **Obv. Legend:** ESTADOS UNIDOS MEXICANOS **Rev:** Cable car above Monumento al Minero at left, Cathedral de Zacatecas at center right **Rev. Legend:** Zacatecas **Edge:** Segmented reeding

Date	Mintage	F	VF	XF	Unc	BU
2007Mo Proof	600	Value: 875				

KM# 771 50000 PESOS

7.7700 g., 0.9990 Gold 0.2496 oz. AGW, 23 mm. **Subject:** World Cup Soccer **Obv:** Mexican Eagle and Snake **Rev:** Kneeling Mayan Pelota player and soccer ball

Date	Mintage	F	VF	XF	Unc	BU
2006Mo Proof	9,505	Value: 600				

SILVER BULLION COINAGE

Libertad Series

KM# 921 100 PESOS

1000.0000 g., 0.9990 Silver 32.117 oz. ASW **Obv:** National arms in center of past and present arms **Rev:** Aztec Calendar **Edge:** Plain

Date	Mintage	F	VF	XF	Unc	BU
2010Mo	1,000	—	—	—	—	2,000

KM# 609 1/20 ONZA (1/20 Troy Ounce of Silver)

1.5551 g., 0.9990 Silver 0.0499 oz. ASW **Obv:** National arms, eagle left **Rev:** Winged Victory

Date	Mintage	F	VF	XF	Unc	BU
2001Mo	25,000	—	—	—	—	25.00
2001Mo Proof	45,000	Value: 30.00				
2002Mo	2,800	—	—	—	—	16.00
2002Mo Proof	50,000	Value: 25.00				
2003Mo	4,400	—	—	—	—	16.00
2003Mo Proof	30,000	Value: 25.00				
2004Mo	2,700	—	—	—	—	16.00
2004Mo Proof	15,000	Value: 25.00				
2005Mo	2,600	—	—	—	—	16.00
2005Mo Proof	1,500	Value: 25.00				
2006Mo	20,000	—	—	—	—	16.00
2006Mo Proof	3,500	Value: 25.00				
2007Mo	4,000	—	—	—	—	16.00
2007Mo Proof	7,000	Value: 25.00				
2008Mo	3,300	—	—	—	—	16.00
2008Mo Proof	10,000	Value: 25.00				
2009Mo	5,000	—	—	—	—	16.00
2009Mo Proof	—	Value: 25.00				
2010Mo	—	—	—	—	—	16.00
2010Mo Proof	—	Value: 25.00				
2011Mo	—	—	—	—	—	16.00
2011Mo Proof	—	Value: 25.00				

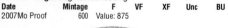

KM# 610 1/10 ONZA (1/10 Troy Ounce of Silver)

3.1103 g., 0.9990 Silver 0.0999 oz. ASW **Obv:** National arms, eagle left **Rev:** Winged Victory

Date	Mintage	F	VF	XF	Unc	BU
2001Mo	25,000	—	—	—	—	27.50
2001Mo Proof	1,500	Value: 36.00				
2002Mo	35,000	—	—	—	—	20.00
2002Mo Proof	2,800	Value: 30.00				
2003Mo	20,000	—	—	—	—	20.00
2003Mo Proof	4,900	Value: 30.00				
2004Mo	15,000	—	—	—	—	20.00
2004Mo Proof	2,500	Value: 30.00				
2005Mo	9,277	—	—	—	—	20.00
2005Mo Proof	3,000	Value: 27.50				
2006Mo	15,000	—	—	—	—	20.00
2006Mo Proof	3,000	Value: 27.50				
2007Mo	3,500	—	—	—	—	20.00
2007Mo Proof	4,000	Value: 27.50				
2008Mo	10,000	—	—	—	—	20.00
2008Mo Proof	5,000	Value: 27.50				
2009Mo	10,000	—	—	—	—	20.00
2009Mo Proof	5,000	Value: 27.50				
2010Mo	—	—	—	—	—	20.00
2010Mo Proof	—	Value: 27.50				
2011Mo	—	—	—	—	—	20.00
2011Mo Proof	—	Value: 27.50				

KM# 611 1/4 ONZA (1/4 Troy Ounce of Silver)

7.7758 g., 0.9990 Silver 0.2497 oz. ASW **Obv:** National arms, eagle left **Rev:** Winged Victory

Date	Mintage	F	VF	XF	Unc	BU
2001Mo	25,000	—	—	—	—	36.00
2001Mo Proof	1,000	Value: 44.00				
2002Mo	35,000	—	—	—	—	27.50
2002Mo Proof	2,800	Value: 40.00				
2003Mo	22,000	—	—	—	—	27.50
2003Mo Proof	3,900	Value: 40.00				
2004Mo	15,000	—	—	—	—	27.50
2004Mo Proof	2,500	Value: 40.00				
2005Mo	15,000	—	—	—	—	27.50
2005Mo Proof	2,400	Value: 37.00				
2006Mo	15,000	—	—	—	—	25.00
2006Mo Proof	2,900	Value: 37.00				
2007Mo	3,500	—	—	—	—	25.00
2007Mo Proof	3,000	Value: 37.00				
2008Mo	9,000	—	—	—	—	25.00
2008Mo Proof	2,800	Value: 37.00				
2009Mo	10,000	—	—	—	—	25.00
2009Mo Proof	3,000	Value: 37.00				
2010Mo	—	—	—	—	—	25.00
2010Mo Proof	—	Value: 37.00				
2011Mo	—	—	—	—	—	25.00
2011Mo Proof	—	Value: 37.00				

KM# 612 1/2 ONZA (1/2 Troy Ounce of Silver)

15.5517 g., 0.9990 Silver 0.4995 oz. ASW **Obv:** National arms, eagle left **Rev:** Winged Victory

Date	Mintage	F	VF	XF	Unc	BU
2001Mo	20,000	—	—	—	—	44.00
2001Mo Proof	1,000	Value: 60.00				
2002Mo	35,000	—	—	—	—	36.00
2002Mo Proof	2,800	Value: 50.00				
2003Mo	28,000	—	—	—	—	36.00
2003Mo Proof	3,400	Value: 50.00				
2004Mo	20,000	—	—	—	—	36.00
2004Mo Proof	2,500	Value: 50.00				
2005Mo	10,000	—	—	—	—	36.00
2005Mo Proof	2,800	Value: 44.00				
2006Mo	15,000	—	—	—	—	36.00
2006Mo Proof	2,900	Value: 44.00				
2007Mo	3,500	—	—	—	—	36.00
2007Mo Proof	1,500	Value: 44.00				
2008Mo	9,000	—	—	—	—	36.00
2008Mo Proof	2,500	Value: 44.00				
2009Mo	10,000	—	—	—	—	36.00
2009Mo Proof	3,000	Value: 44.00				
2010Mo	—	—	—	—	—	36.00
2010Mo Proof	—	Value: 44.00				
2011Mo	—	—	—	—	—	36.00
2011Mo Proof	—	Value: 44.00				

KM# 639 ONZA (Troy Ounce of Silver)
31.1000 g., 0.9990 Silver 0.9988 oz. ASW **Subject:** Libertad **Obv:** National arms, eagle left within center of past and present arms **Rev:** Winged Victory **Edge:** Reeded

Date	Mintage	F	VF	XF	Unc	BU
2001Mo	725,000	—	—	—	—	60.00
2001Mo Proof	2,000	Value: 140				
2002Mo	854,000	—	—	—	—	55.00
2002Mo Proof	3,800	Value: 150				
2003Mo	805,000	—	—	—	—	55.00
2003Mo Proof	5,400	Value: 130				
2004Mo	450,000	—	—	—	—	75.00
2004Mo Proof	3,000	Value: 130				
2005Mo	698,281	—	—	—	—	90.00
2005Mo Proof	3,300	Value: 150				
2006Mo	300,000	—	—	—	—	55.00
2006Mo Proof	4,000	Value: 140				
2007Mo	200,000	—	—	—	—	95.00
2007Mo Proof	5,800	Value: 150				
2008Mo	950,000	—	—	—	—	65.00
2008Mo Proof	11,000	Value: 150				
2009Mo	1,650,000	—	—	—	—	75.00
2009Mo Proof	10,000	Value: 150				
2010Mo	—	—	—	—	—	75.00
2010Mo Proof	—	Value: 140				
2011Mo	—	—	—	—	—	75.00
2011Mo Proof	—	Value: 140				

KM# 614 2 ONZAS (2 Troy Ounces of Silver)
62.2070 g., 0.9990 Silver 1.9979 oz. ASW, 48 mm. **Subject:** Libertad **Obv:** National arms, eagle left within center of past and present arms **Rev:** Winged Victory **Edge:** Reeded

Date	Mintage	F	VF	XF	Unc	BU
2001Mo	6,700	—	—	—	—	120
2001Mo Proof	500	Value: 160				
2002Mo	8,700	—	—	—	—	110
2002Mo Proof	1,000	Value: 190				
2003Mo	9,500	—	—	—	—	110
2003Mo Proof	800	Value: 190				
2004Mo	8,000	—	—	—	—	100
2004Mo Proof	1,000	Value: 160				
2005Mo	3,549	—	—	—	—	100
2005Mo Proof	600	Value: 150				
2006Mo	5,800	—	—	—	—	100
2006Mo Proof	1,100	Value: 150				
2007Mo	8,000	—	—	—	—	100
2007Mo Proof	500	Value: 170				
2008Mo	17,000	—	—	—	—	110
2008Mo Proof	1,000	Value: 170				
2009Mo	46,000	—	—	—	—	110
2009Mo Proof	6,200	Value: 170				
2010Mo	—	—	—	—	—	110
2010Mo Proof	—	Value: 190				
2011Mo	—	—	—	—	—	110
2011Mo Proof	—	Value: 190				

KM# 615 5 ONZAS (5 Troy Ounces of Silver)
155.5175 g., 0.9990 Silver 4.9948 oz. ASW, 65 mm. **Subject:** Libertad **Obv:** National arms, eagle left within center of past and present arms **Rev:** Winged Victory **Edge:** Reeded **Note:** Illustration reduced.

Date	Mintage	F	VF	XF	Unc	BU
2001Mo	4,000	—	—	—	—	180
2001Mo Proof	600	Value: 325				
2002Mo	5,200	—	—	—	—	180
2002Mo Proof	1,000	Value: 325				
2003Mo	6,000	—	—	—	—	165
2003Mo Proof	1,500	Value: 250				
2004Mo	3,923	—	—	—	—	165
2004Mo Proof	800	Value: 225				
2005Mo	2,401	—	—	—	—	205
2005Mo Proof	1,000	Value: 225				
2006Mo	3,000	—	—	—	—	165
2006Mo Proof	700	Value: 265				
2007Mo	3,000	—	—	—	—	165
2007Mo Proof	500	Value: 205				
2008Mo	9,000	—	—	—	—	205
2008Mo Proof	900	Value: 270				
2009Mo	21,000	—	—	—	—	225
2009Mo Proof	5,000	Value: 270				

KM# 677 KILO (32.15 Troy Ounces of Silver)
999.9775 g., 0.9990 Silver 32.116 oz. ASW, 110 mm. **Subject:** Collector Bullion **Obv:** National arms in center of past and present arms **Rev:** Winged Victory **Edge:** Reeded

Date	Mintage	F	VF	XF	Unc	BU
2001Mo Prooflike	—	—	—	—	—	2,200
2002Mo Prooflike	1,100	—	—	—	—	1,750
2003Mo Prooflike	2,234	—	—	—	—	1,650
2004Mo Prooflike	500	—	—	—	—	1,800
2005Mo Prooflike	874	—	—	—	—	1,750
2006Mo Prooflike	—	—	—	—	—	1,650
2007Mo Prooflike	—	—	—	—	—	1,650
2008Mo Prooflike	—	—	—	—	—	1,650
2009Mo Prooflike	—	—	—	—	—	1,650

GOLD BULLION COINAGE

KM# 932 200 PESOS
41.6666 g., 0.9000 Gold 1.2056 oz. AGW, 37 mm. **Subject:** Independence 200th Anniversary **Obv:** National Arms **Rev:** Winged Victory

Date	Mintage	F	VF	XF	Unc	BU
2010Mo	—	—	—	—	—	BV+5%
2010Mo Proof	—	BV+6%				

KM# 671 1/20 ONZA (1/20 Ounce of Pure Gold)
1.5551 g., 0.9990 Gold 0.0499 oz. AGW, 13 mm. **Obv:** National arms, eagle left **Rev:** Winged Victory **Edge:** Reeded **Note:** Design similar to KM#609. Value estimates do not include the high taxes and surcharges added to the issue prices by the Mexican Government.

Date	Mintage	F	VF	XF	Unc	BU
2002Mo	5,000	—	—	—	—	BV+30%
2003Mo	800	—	—	—	—	BV+32%
2004Mo	7,000	—	—	—	—	BV+30%
2005Mo	3,200	—	—	—	—	BV+30%
2005Mo Proof	400	BV+35%				
2006Mo	3,200	—	—	—	—	BV+30%
2006Mo Proof	3,000	BV+35%				
2007Mo	1,200	—	—	—	—	BV+30%
2007Mo Proof	500	BV+35%				
2008Mo	800	—	—	—	—	BV+30%
2008Mo Proof	500	—	—	—	—	BV+35%
2009Mo	2,000	—	—	—	—	BV+30%
2009Mo Proof	600	—	—	—	—	BV+35%

KM# 672 1/10 ONZA (1/10 Ounce of Pure Gold)
3.1103 g., 0.9990 Gold 0.0999 oz. AGW, 16 mm. **Obv:** National arms, eagle left **Rev:** Winged Victory **Edge:** Reeded **Note:** Design similar to KM#610. Value estimates do not include the high taxes and surcharges added to the issue prices by the Mexican Government.

Date	Mintage	F	VF	XF	Unc	BU
2002Mo	5,000	—	—	—	—	BV+20%
2003Mo	300	—	—	—	—	BV+22%
2004Mo	2,000	—	—	—	—	BV+20%
2005Mo	500	—	—	—	—	BV+20%
2005Mo Proof	400	BV+22%				
2006Mo	2,500	—	—	—	—	BV+20%
2006Mo Proof	520	BV+22%				
2007Mo	1,200	—	—	—	—	BV+20%
2007Mo Proof	500	BV+22%				
2008Mo	2,500	—	—	—	—	BV+20%
2008Mo Proof	500	BV+22%				
2009Mo	9,000	—	—	—	—	BV+20%
2009Mo Proof	600	BV+22%				

KM# 673 1/4 ONZA (1/4 Ounce of Pure Gold)
7.7758 g., 0.9990 Gold 0.2497 oz. AGW, 23 mm. **Obv:** National arms, eagle left **Rev:** Winged Victory **Edge:** Reeded **Note:** Design similar to KM#611. Value estimates do not include the high taxes and surcharges added to the issue prices by the Mexican Government.

Date	Mintage	F	VF	XF	Unc	BU
2002Mo	5,000	—	—	—	—	BV+12%
2003Mo	300	—	—	—	—	BV+14%
2004Mo	1,500	—	—	—	—	BV+12%
2004Mo Proof	1,000	BV+15%				
2005Mo	500	—	—	—	—	BV+12%
2005Mo Proof	2,600	BV+15%				
2006Mo	1,500	—	—	—	—	BV+12%
2006Mo Proof	2,120	BV+15%				
2007Mo	500	—	—	—	—	BV+12%
2007Mo Proof	1,500	BV+15%				
2008Mo	800	—	—	—	—	BV+12%
2008Mo Proof	800	BV+15%				
2009Mo	3,000	—	—	—	—	BV+12%
2009Mo Proof	1,700	BV+15%				

KM# 674 1/2 ONZA (1/2 Ounce of Pure Gold)
15.5517 g., 0.9990 Gold 0.4995 oz. AGW, 29 mm. **Obv:** National arms, eagle left **Rev:** Winged Victory **Edge:** Reeded **Note:** Design similar to KM#612. Value estimates do not include the high taxes and surcharges added to the issue prices by the Mexican Government.

Date	Mintage	F	VF	XF	Unc	BU
2002Mo	5,000	—	—	—	—	BV+8%
2003Mo	300	—	—	—	—	BV+10%
2004Mo	500	—	—	—	—	BV+8%
2005Mo	500	—	—	—	—	BV+8%
2005Mo Proof	400	BV+12%				
2006Mo	500	—	—	—	—	BV+8%
2006Mo Proof	520	BV+12%				
2007Mo	500	—	—	—	—	BV+8%
2007Mo Proof	500	BV+12%				
2008Mo	300	—	—	—	—	BV+8%
2008Mo Proof	500	BV+12%				
2009Mo	3,000	—	—	—	—	BV+8%
2009Mo Proof	600	BV+12%				

KM# 675 ONZA (Ounce of Pure Gold)
31.1035 g., 0.9990 Gold 0.9990 oz. AGW, 34.5 mm. **Obv:** National arms, eagle left **Rev:** Winged Victory **Edge:** Reeded **Note:** Design similar to KM#639. Value estimates do not include the high taxes and surcharges added to the issue prices by the Mexican Government.

Date	Mintage	F	VF	XF	Unc	BU
2002Mo	15,000	—	—	—	—	BV+3%
2003Mo	500	—	—	—	—	BV+4%
2004Mo	3,000	—	—	—	—	BV+3%
2004Mo Proof	150	BV+5%				
2005Mo	3,000	—	—	—	—	BV+3%
2005Mo Proof	250	BV+5%				
2006Mo	4,000	—	—	—	—	BV+3%
2006Mo Proof	520	BV+5%				
2007Mo	2,500	—	—	—	—	BV+3%
2007Mo Proof	500	BV+5%				
2008Mo	800	—	—	—	—	BV+3%
2008Mo Proof	500	BV+5%				
2009Mo	6,200	—	—	—	—	BV+3%
2009Mo Proof	600	BV+5%				

BANK SETS

Hard Case Sets unless otherwise noted.

KM#	Date	Mintage	Identification	Issue Price	Mkt Val
BS38	2001 (10)	—	KM#546-549, 603-605, 636-638 Set in folder	—	65.00
BS39	2002 (8)	—	KM#546-549, 603-605, 616 Set in folder	—	30.00
BS40	2003 (6)	—	KM#547-549, 603-605 Set in folder	—	30.00

The Republic of Moldova (formerly the Moldavian S.S.R.) is bordered in the north, east and south by the Ukraine and on the west by Romania. It has an area of 13,000 sq.mi. (33,700 sq.km.) and a population of 4.4 million. The capital is Chisinau. Agricultural products are mainly cereals, grapes, tobacco, sugar beets and fruits. Food processing, clothing, building materials and agricultural machinery manufacturing dominate industry.

MONETARY SYSTEM
100 Bani = 1 Leu

REPUBLIC

DECIMAL COINAGE

KM# 1 BAN

0.6800 g., Aluminum, 14.5 mm. **Obv:** National arms **Rev:** Value divides date above monogram **Edge:** Plain

Date	Mintage	F	VF	XF	Unc	BU
2004	—	—	—	—	0.25	0.50
2006	—	—	—	—	0.25	0.50

KM# 2 5 BANI

0.8000 g., Aluminum, 16 mm. **Obv:** National arms **Rev:** Monogram divides sprigs below value and date **Edge:** Plain

Date	Mintage	F	VF	XF	Unc	BU
2001	—	—	—	0.15	0.35	0.50
2002	—	—	—	0.15	0.35	0.50
2003	—	—	—	0.15	0.35	0.50
2004	—	—	—	0.15	0.35	0.50
2005	—	—	—	0.15	0.35	0.50
2006	—	—	—	0.15	0.35	0.50
2008	—	—	—	0.15	0.35	0.50

KM# 7 10 BANI

0.8400 g., Aluminum, 16.6 mm. **Obv:** National arms **Rev:** Value, date and monogram **Edge:** Plain

Date	Mintage	F	VF	XF	Unc	BU
2001	—	—	—	—	0.40	0.60
2002	—	—	—	—	0.40	0.60
2003	—	—	—	—	0.40	0.60
2004	—	—	—	—	0.40	0.60
2005	—	—	—	—	0.40	0.60
2006	—	—	—	—	0.40	0.60
2008	—	—	—	—	0.40	0.60
2010	—	—	—	—	0.40	0.60

KM# 3 25 BANI

0.9200 g., Aluminum, 17.5 mm. **Obv:** National arms **Rev:** Monogram divides sprigs below value and date **Edge:** Plain

Date	Mintage	F	VF	XF	Unc	BU
2001	—	—	—	0.20	0.50	0.75
2002	—	—	—	0.20	0.50	0.75
2003	—	—	—	0.20	0.50	0.75
2004	—	—	—	0.20	0.50	0.75
2005	—	—	—	0.20	0.50	0.75
2006	—	—	—	0.20	0.50	0.75
2008	—	—	—	0.20	0.50	0.75
2010	—	—	—	0.20	0.50	0.75

KM# 10 50 BANI

3.1000 g., Brass Clad Steel, 19 mm. **Obv:** National arms **Rev:** Value and date within grapevine **Edge:** Reeded

Date	Mintage	F	VF	XF	Unc	BU
2003	—	—	—	—	1.50	2.00
2005	—	—	—	—	1.50	2.00
2008	—	—	—	—	1.50	2.00

KM# 12 10 LEI

13.5000 g., 0.9250 Silver 0.4015 oz. ASW, 24.5 mm. **Obv:** National arms above value **Rev:** European wildcat within circle **Edge:** Plain

Date	Mintage	F	VF	XF	Unc	BU
2001 Proof	1,000	Value: 65.00				

KM# 13 10 LEI

13.5000 g., 0.9250 Silver 0.4015 oz. ASW, 24.5 mm. **Obv:** National arms above value **Rev:** Green Woodpecker on tree within circle **Edge:** Plain

Date	Mintage	F	VF	XF	Unc	BU
2001 Proof	1,000	Value: 60.00				

KM# 19 10 LEI

13.4500 g., 0.9250 Silver 0.4000 oz. ASW, 24.5 mm. **Obv:** National arms above value **Rev:** European Mink within circle **Edge:** Plain

Date	Mintage	F	VF	XF	Unc	BU
2003 Proof	500	Value: 65.00				

KM# 20 10 LEI

13.4500 g., 0.9250 Silver 0.4000 oz. ASW, 24.5 mm. **Obv:** National arms above value **Rev:** Black Storks within circle **Edge:** Plain

Date	Mintage	F	VF	XF	Unc	BU
2003 Proof	500	Value: 65.00				

KM# 25 10 LEI

25.0000 g., Nickel Plated Brass, 30 mm. **Subject:** Wine Holiday **Obv:** National arms above value **Rev:** Wine grapes, goblet and flask **Edge:** Plain

Date	Mintage	F	VF	XF	Unc	BU
2003 Proof	—	Value: 12.50				

KM# 22 10 LEI

13.5000 g., 0.9250 Silver 0.4015 oz. ASW, 24.5 mm. **Obv:** National arms above value **Rev:** Pine Marten within circle **Edge:** Plain

Date	Mintage	F	VF	XF	Unc	BU
2004 Proof	500	Value: 65.00				

KM# 29 10 LEI

25.0000 g., Nickel Plated Brass, 30 mm. **Subject:** European Women's Chess Championship **Obv:** Arms, date at top, value at bottom **Obv. Legend:** REPUBLICA - 2005 - MOLDOVA **Rev:** 2 chess figures on board at left, map at right **Rev. Inscription:** 2005 CHISINAU **Edge:** Plain

Date	Mintage	F	VF	XF	Unc	BU
2005 Proof	—	Value: 12.50				

KM# 30 10 LEI

13.5000 g., 0.9250 Silver 0.4015 oz. ASW, 24.5 mm. **Obv:** Arms, value below **Obv. Legend:** REPUBLICA MOLDOVA **Rev:** Imperial eagle on branch, legend follows the coin circumference **Edge:** Plain

Date	Mintage	F	VF	XF	Unc	BU
2005 Proof	500	Value: 65.00				

KM# 33 10 LEI

13.5000 g., 0.9250 Silver 0.4015 oz. ASW, 24.5 mm. **Obv:** Arms, value below **Obv. Legend:** REPUBLICA - 2006 - MOLDOVA **Rev:** Bustard on vegetal background, legend around circumference using Latin name **Edge:** Plain

Date	Mintage	F	VF	XF	Unc	BU
2006 Proof	500	Value: 65.00				

KM# 38 10 LEI

13.5000 g., 0.9250 Silver 0.4015 oz. ASW, 24.5 mm. **Rev:** Common ground squirrel

Date	Mintage	F	VF	XF	Unc	BU
2006 Proof	500	Value: 65.00				

KM# 43 10 LEI

13.5000 g., 0.9250 Silver 0.4015 oz. ASW, 24.5 mm. **Rev:** White water lilly

Date	Mintage	F	VF	XF	Unc	BU
2008 Proof	500	Value: 60.00				

KM# 47 20 LEI

13.5000 g., 0.9250 Silver 0.4015 oz. ASW, 22 mm. **Subject:** Assumption of the Virgin Mary

Date	Mintage	F	VF	XF	Unc	BU
2009 Proof	1,000	Value: 40.00				

KM# 36 50 LEI

16.5000 g., 0.9250 Silver 0.4907 oz. ASW, 30 mm. **Subject:** Vazile Alecsandri, 180th Anniversary **Obv:** Arms **Rev:** Bust and landscape

Date	Mintage	F	VF	XF	Unc	BU
2001 Proof	1,000	Value: 40.00				

KM# 17 50 LEI

16.5000 g., 0.9250 Silver 0.4907 oz. ASW, 30 mm. **Obv:** National arms above value **Rev:** Constantin Brancusi and building **Edge:** Plain

Date	Mintage	F	VF	XF	Unc	BU
2001 Proof	1,000	Value: 65.00				

KM# 18 50 LEI

16.5000 g., 0.9250 Silver 0.4907 oz. ASW, 30 mm. **Obv:** National arms above value **Rev:** Vasile Alecsandri with book and landscape **Edge:** Plain

Date	Mintage	F	VF	XF	Unc	BU
2001 Proof	1,000	Value: 65.00				

KM# 21 50 LEI
16.5000 g., 0.9250 Silver 0.4907 oz. ASW, 29.8 mm. **Subject:** Effigy of Dimitrie Cantemir **Obv:** National arms above value **Rev:** Bust facing flanked by dates and scroll **Edge:** Plain

Date	Mintage	F	VF	XF	Unc	BU
2003 Proof	500	Value: 165				

KM# 14 50 LEI
16.5500 g., 0.9250 Silver 0.4922 oz. ASW, 29.9 mm. **Subject:** Effigy of Miron Costin **Obv:** National arms above value **Rev:** Bust with hat 1/4 right flanked by dates and books **Edge:** Plain

Date	Mintage	F	VF	XF	Unc	BU
2003 Proof	500	Value: 165				

KM# 23 50 LEI
16.5000 g., 0.9250 Silver 0.4907 oz. ASW, 30 mm. **Obv:** National arms above value **Rev:** Bust of Bishop facing holding scepter **Edge:** Plain

Date	Mintage	F	VF	XF	Unc	BU
2004 Proof	500	Value: 90.00				

KM# 31 50 LEI
16.5000 g., 0.9250 Silver 0.4907 oz. ASW, 30 mm. **Subject:** 415th Anniversary - Birth of Grigore Ureche **Obv:** Arms, date divides legend at top, value below, **Obv. Legend:** REPUBLICA MOLDOVA **Rev:** Bust faces right, scroll with feather pen at right, inscription on scroll **Rev. Legend:** GRIGORE URECHE **Rev. Inscription:** Letopisetul Tarii Moldovei **Edge:** Plain

Date	Mintage	F	VF	XF	Unc	BU
2005 Proof	—	Value: 120				

KM# 34 50 LEI
16.5000 g., 0.9250 Silver 0.4907 oz. ASW, 30 mm. **Subject:** 200th Anniversary - Birth of Alexandru Donici **Obv:** Arms, date divides legend above, value below **Obv. Legend:** REPUBLICA MOLDOVA **Rev:** Bust of Donici facing, life dates on ribbon below **Rev. Legend:** ALEXANDRU DONICI

Date	Mintage	F	VF	XF	Unc	BU
2006 Proof	—	Value: 120				

KM# 40 50 LEI
16.5000 g., 0.9250 Silver 0.4907 oz. ASW, 30 mm. **Subject:** Metropolitian Varilaam **Rev:** Bust 3/4 right

Date	Mintage	F	VF	XF	Unc	BU
2007 Proof	500	Value: 120				

KM# 41 50 LEI
16.5000 g., 0.9250 Silver 0.4907 oz. ASW, 30 mm. **Subject:** Pottery Tradition **Rev:** Hand modeling clay vessel on pottery wheel

Date	Mintage	F	VF	XF	Unc	BU
2007 Proof	500	Value: 60.00				

KM# 44 50 LEI
16.5000 g., 0.9250 Silver 0.4907 oz. ASW, 30 mm. **Subject:** Oak tree in Stefan **Rev:** Oak tree

Date	Mintage	F	VF	XF	Unc	BU
2008 Proof	500	Value: 75.00				

KM# 45 50 LEI
16.5000 g., 0.9250 Silver 0.4907 oz. ASW, 30 mm. **Subject:** Cooper trade **Rev:** Barrell maker

Date	Mintage	F	VF	XF	Unc	BU
2008 Proof	500	Value: 55.00				

KM# 48 50 LEI
16.5000 g., 0.9250 Silver 0.4907 oz. ASW, 30 mm. **Subject:** Geodezic arc of Struve **Rev:** Map

Date	Mintage	F	VF	XF	Unc	BU
2009 Proof	500	Value: 75.00				

KM# 49 50 LEI
16.5000 g., 0.9250 Silver 0.4907 oz. ASW, 30 mm. **Subject:** Rule of Vasile Lupu **Rev:** Open book and coat-of-arms

Date	Mintage	F	VF	XF	Unc	BU
2009 Proof	500	Value: 75.00				

KM# 50 50 LEI
16.5000 g., 0.9250 Silver 0.4907 oz. ASW, 30 mm. **Subject:** Traditional weaving **Rev:** Woman seated at weaving frame

Date	Mintage	F	VF	XF	Unc	BU
2009 Proof	500	Value: 70.00				

KM# 16 100 LEI
31.1000 g., 0.9250 Silver 0.9249 oz. ASW, 37 mm. **Subject:** 10th Anniversary of Independence **Obv:** National arms above value **Rev:** Arch monument within circle above value and sprigs **Edge:** Plain

Date	Mintage	F	VF	XF	Unc	BU
2001 Proof	1,000	Value: 220				

KM# 26 100 LEI
7.8000 g., 0.9999 Gold 0.2507 oz. AGW, 24 mm. **Obv:** National arms above value **Rev:** King Stephan the Great (1456-1504) **Edge:** Plain

Date	Mintage	F	VF	XF	Unc	BU
2004 Proof	—	Value: 400				

KM# 32 100 LEI
31.1000 g., 0.9250 Silver 0.9249 oz. ASW, 37 mm. **Subject:** Burebista - King of Dacians **Obv:** Arms, date divides legend at top, value below **Obv. Legend:** REPUBLICA MOLDOVA **Rev:** Bust of Burebista at left, battle scene of Geto-Dacians with Romans at right **Rev. Legend:** BUREBISTA REGELE DACILOR **Edge:** Plain

Date	Mintage	F	VF	XF	Unc	BU
2005 Proof	500	Value: 300				

KM# 35 100 LEI
31.1000 g., 0.9250 Silver 0.9249 oz. ASW, 37 mm. **Subject:** 15th Anniversary - Independence Proclamation of the Republic of Moldova **Obv:** Arms, date divides legend above, value below **Obv. Legend:** REPUBLICA MOLDOVA **Rev:** Map of Moldova within stars in inner circle, legend around **Rev. Legend:** PROCLAMAREA INDEPENDENTEI / 1991-2006 **Edge:** Plain

Date	Mintage	F	VF	XF	Unc	BU
2006 Proof	500	Value: 500				

KM# 37 100 LEI
31.1050 g., 0.9250 Silver 0.9250 oz. ASW, 37 mm. **Subject:** National Bank, 15th Anniversary **Obv:** Arms **Rev:** Bank building and coins

Date	Mintage	F	VF	XF	Unc	BU
2006 Proof	500	Value: 140				

KM# 39 100 LEI
31.1050 g., 0.9990 Silver 0.9990 oz. ASW, 37 mm. **Subject:** National Bank, 15th Anniversary **Rev:** Bank building

Date	Mintage	F	VF	XF	Unc	BU
2006 Proof	500	Value: 140				

KM# 42 100 LEI
31.1050 g., 0.9250 Silver 0.9250 oz. ASW, 37 mm. **Subject:** Petru Rares **Rev:** Bust 3/4 right

Date	Mintage	F	VF	XF	Unc	BU
2007 Proof	500	Value: 450				

KM# 46 100 LEI
31.1050 g., 0.9250 Silver 0.9250 oz. ASW, 37 mm. **Subject:** Antioh Cantemir **Rev:** Half-length figure standing 3/4 left

Date	Mintage	F	VF	XF	Unc	BU
2008 Proof	1,000	Value: 100				

KM# 51 100 LEI
22.5000 g., 0.9250 Silver 0.6691 oz. ASW, 34 mm. **Subject:** Moldovan Chronicals, 15-18 Centuries **Rev:** Man seated writing

Date	Mintage	F	VF	XF	Unc	BU
2009 Proof	1,000	Value: 90.00				

MONACO

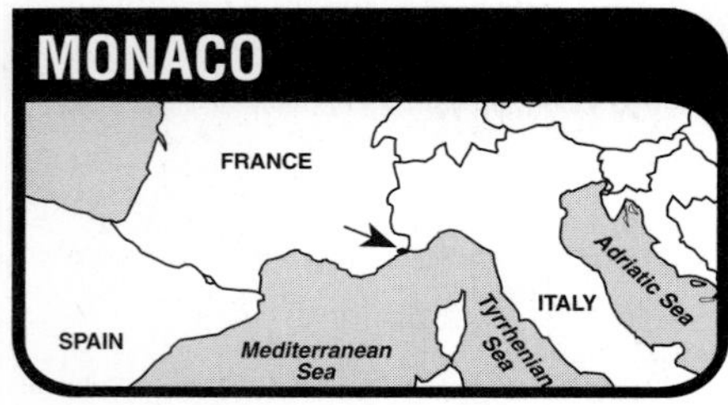

The Principality of Monaco, located on the Mediterranean coast nine miles from Nice, has an area of 0.58 sq. mi. (1.9 sq. km.) and a population of 26,000. Capital: Monaco-Ville. The economy is based on tourism and the manufacture of cosmetics, gourmet foods and highly specialized electronics. Monaco also derives its revenue from a tobacco monopoly and the sale of postage stamps for philatelic purpose. Gambling in Monte Carlo accounts for only a small fraction of the country's revenue.

RULERS
Rainier III, 1949-2005
Albert II, 2005-

MINT PRIVY MARKS
(a) - Paris (privy marks only)
Horseshoe - 2001 and 2002
Heart – 2002-2003
French Horn with starfish in water – 2003-
(p) - Thunderbolt - Poissy

MONETARY SYSTEM
100 Euro Cents = 1 Euro

PRINCIPALITY

EURO COINAGE

KM# 167 EURO CENT
2.3000 g., Copper Plated Steel, 16.25 mm. **Ruler:** Rainier III **Obv:** Crowned arms **Obv. Designer:** Robert Cochet **Rev:** Value and globe **Rev. Designer:** Luc Luycx **Edge:** Plain

Date	Mintage	F	VF	XF	Unc	BU
2001(a)	327,200	—	—	—	20.00	35.00
2001(a) Proof	3,500	Value: 75.00				
2002(a) In sets only	40,000	—	—	—	—	75.00
2003(a)	—	—	—	—	—	10.00
2004(a) Proof	14,999	Value: 25.00				
2005(a) Proof	35,000	Value: 50.00				

KM# 188 EURO CENT
2.3000 g., Copper Plated Steel, 16.25 mm. **Ruler:** Albert II **Obv:** Crowned arms within circle of stars **Rev:** Value and globe

Date	Mintage	F	VF	XF	Unc	BU
2006 Proof	11,180	Value: 30.00				
2007	—	—	—	—	—	30.00
2009 In sets only	8,020	—	—	—	—	30.00

KM# 168 2 EURO CENT
3.0600 g., Copper Plated Steel, 18.75 mm. **Ruler:** Rainier III **Obv:** Crowned arms **Obv. Designer:** Robert Cochet **Rev:** Value and globe **Rev. Designer:** Luc Luycx **Edge:** Grooved

Date	Mintage	F	VF	XF	Unc	BU
2001(a)	393,400	—	—	—	15.00	30.00
2001(a) Proof	3,500	Value: 85.00				
2002(a) In sets only	40,000	—	—	—	—	85.00
2003(a)	—	—	—	—	—	10.00
2004(a) Proof	14,999	Value: 35.00				
2005(a) Proof	35,000	Value: 50.00				

KM# 189 2 EURO CENT
3.0600 g., Copper Plated Steel, 18.75 mm. **Ruler:** Albert II **Obv:** Crowned arms within circle of stars **Rev:** Value and globe **Edge:** Grooved

Date	Mintage	F	VF	XF	Unc	BU
2006 Proof	11,260	Value: 25.00				
2007	—	—	—	—	—	25.00
2009 In sets only	8,020	—	—	—	—	25.00

KM# 169 5 EURO CENT
3.9200 g., Copper Plated Steel, 21.25 mm. **Ruler:** Rainier III **Obv:** Crowned arms **Obv. Designer:** Robert Cochet **Rev:** Value and globe **Rev. Designer:** Luc Luycx **Edge:** Plain

Date	Mintage	F	VF	XF	Unc	BU
2001(a)	320,000	—	—	—	20.00	35.00
2001(a) Proof	3,500	Value: 95.00				
2002(a) In sets only	40,000	—	—	—	—	85.00
2003(a)	—	—	—	—	—	15.00
2004(a) Proof	14,999	Value: 45.00				
2005(a) Proof	35,000	Value: 55.00				

KM# 190 5 EURO CENT
3.9200 g., Copper Plated Steel, 21.25 mm. **Ruler:** Albert II **Obv:** Crowned arms within circle of stars **Rev:** Value and globe

Date	Mintage	F	VF	XF	Unc	BU
2006 Proof	11,180	Value: 30.00				
2007	—	—	—	—	—	30.00
2009 In sets only	8,020	—	—	—	—	30.00

KM# 170 10 EURO CENT
4.1000 g., Brass, 19.75 mm. **Ruler:** Rainier III **Obv:** Knight on horse **Obv. Designer:** R. Baron **Rev:** Value and map **Rev. Designer:** Luc Luycx **Edge:** Reeded

Date	Mintage	F	VF	XF	Unc	BU
2001(a)	320,000	—	—	—	15.00	25.00
2001(a) Proof	3,500	Value: 110				
2002(a)	407,200	—	—	—	8.00	12.00
2003(a)	100,800	—	—	—	12.00	16.00
2004(a) Proof	14,999	Value: 50.00				

KM# 181 10 EURO CENT
4.1000 g., Brass, 19.75 mm. **Ruler:** Albert II **Obv:** Crowned AA monogram **Rev:** Relief map of Western Europe, stars, lines and value **Rev. Designer:** Luc Luycx **Edge:** Reeded

Date	Mintage	F	VF	XF	Unc	BU
2006(a) Proof	11,180	Value: 50.00				

KM# 191 10 EURO CENT
4.1000 g., Brass, 19.75 mm. **Ruler:** Albert II **Obv:** Crowned AA monogram **Rev:** Relief map of western Europe, stars, lines and value **Edge:** Reeded

Date	Mintage	F	VF	XF	Unc	BU
2007(a)	—	—	—	—	—	30.00
2009(a) In sets only	8,020	—	—	—	—	30.00

KM# 171 20 EURO CENT
5.7400 g., Brass, 22.25 mm. **Ruler:** Rainier III **Obv:** Knight on horse **Rev:** Value and map **Edge:** Notched **Designer:** R. Baron

Date	Mintage	F	VF	XF	Unc	BU
2001(a)	386,400	—	—	—	15.00	20.00
2001(a) Proof	3,500	Value: 120				
2002(a)	376,000	—	—	—	12.00	16.00
2003(a)	100,000	—	—	—	12.00	16.00
2004(a) Proof	14,999	Value: 60.00				

KM# 182 20 EURO CENT
5.7400 g., Brass, 22.25 mm. **Ruler:** Albert II **Obv:** Crowned AA monogram **Obv. Designer:** R. Baron **Rev:** Relief map of Western Europe, stars, lines and value **Edge:** Notched

Date	Mintage	F	VF	XF	Unc	BU
2006(a) Proof	11,180	Value: 60.00				

KM# 192 20 EURO CENT
5.7400 g., Brass, 22.25 mm. **Ruler:** Albert II **Obv:** Crowned AA monogram **Rev:** Relief map of western Europe, stars, lines and value **Edge:** Notched

Date	Mintage	F	VF	XF	Unc	BU
2007(a)	—	—	—	—	—	30.00
2009(a) In sets only	8,020	—	—	—	—	30.00

KM# 172 50 EURO CENT
7.8000 g., Brass, 24.25 mm. **Ruler:** Rainier III **Obv:** Knight on horse **Obv. Designer:** R. Baron **Rev:** Value and map **Rev. Designer:** Luc Luycx **Edge:** Reeded

Date	Mintage	F	VF	XF	Unc	BU
2001 (a)	320,000	—	—	—	15.00	30.00
2001 (a) Proof	3,500	Value: 130				
2002 (a)	364,000	—	—	—	8.00	12.00
2003 (a)	100,000	—	—	—	12.00	16.00
2004 (a) Proof	14,999	Value: 65.00				

KM# 183 50 EURO CENT
7.8000 g., Brass, 24.25 mm. **Ruler:** Albert II **Obv:** Crowned AA monogram **Obv. Designer:** R. Baron **Rev:** Relief map of Western Europe, stars, lines and value **Rev. Designer:** Luc Luycx **Edge:** Reeded

Date	Mintage	F	VF	XF	Unc	BU
2006(a) Proof	11,180	Value: 65.00				

KM# 193 50 EURO CENT
7.8000 g., Brass, 24.25 mm. **Ruler:** Albert II **Obv:** Crowned AA monogram **Rev:** Relief map of western Europe, stars, lines and values **Edge:** Reeded

Date	Mintage	F	VF	XF	Unc	BU
2007(a)	—	—	—	—	—	30.00
2009(a) In sets only	8,020	—	—	—	—	30.00

KM# 173 EURO
7.5000 g., Bi-Metallic Copper-Nickel center in Nickel-Brass ring, 23.25 mm. **Ruler:** Rainier III **Obv:** Conjoined heads of Prince Ranier and Crown Prince Albert right within circle **Obv. Designer:** Henri Thiebaud **Rev:** Value and map **Rev. Designer:** Luc Luycx **Edge:** Segmented reeding

Date	Mintage	F	VF	XF	Unc	BU
2001(a)	991,100	—	—	—	10.00	12.00
2001(a) Proof	3,500	Value: 145				
2002(a)	512,500	—	—	—	11.00	14.00
2003(a)	135,000	—	—	—	13.50	18.50
2004(a) Proof	14,999	Value: 75.00				

KM# 184 EURO

7.5000 g., Bi-Metallic Copper-Nickel center in Nickel-Brass ring, 23.25 mm. **Ruler:** Albert II **Obv:** Head right of Prince Albert **Rev:** Relief map of Western Europe, stars, lines and value **Rev. Designer:** Luc Luycx **Edge:** Segmented reeding

Date	Mintage	F	VF	XF	Unc	BU
2006(a) Proof	11,180	Value: 75.00				

KM# 194 EURO

7.5000 g., Bi-Metallic Copper-Nickel center in Nickel-Brass ring, 23.25 mm. **Ruler:** Albert II **Obv:** Head right **Rev:** Relief map of western Europe, stars, lines and value **Edge:** Segmented reeding

Date	Mintage	F	VF	XF	Unc	BU
2007(a)	100,000	—	—	—	—	18.00
2009(a) In sets only	8,020	—	—	—	—	30.00

KM# 174 2 EURO

8.5000 g., Bi-Metallic Nickel-Brass center in Copper-Nickel ring, 25.75 mm. **Ruler:** Rainier III **Obv:** Head right within circle flanked by stars **Obv. Designer:** Pierre Givaudin **Rev:** Value and map **Rev. Designer:** Luc Luycx **Edge:** Reeded with 2s and stars

Date	Mintage	F	VF	XF	Unc	BU
2001(a)	919,800	—	—	—	14.00	25.00
2001(a) Proof	3,500	Value: 165				
2002(a)	496,000	—	—	—	15.00	18.00
2003(a)	228,000	—	—	—	17.50	22.50
2004(a) Proof	14,999	Value: 95.00				

KM# 185 2 EURO

8.5000 g., Bi-Metallic Nickel-Brass center in Copper-Nickel ring, 25.75 mm. **Ruler:** Albert II **Obv:** Prince Albert's head right **Rev:** Relief map of Western Europe, stars, lines and value **Rev. Designer:** Luc Luycx **Edge:** Reeded with 2's and stars

Date	Mintage	F	VF	XF	Unc	BU
2006(a) Proof	11,180	Value: 120				

KM# 186 2 EURO

8.5000 g., Bi-Metallic Nickel-Brass center in Copper-Nickel ring., 25.75 mm. **Ruler:** Albert II **Subject:** Princess Grace, 25th Anniversary of Death **Obv:** Head of Princess Grace left **Rev:** Relief map of Western Europe, stars, lines and value **Edge:** Reeded with 2s and stars

Date	Mintage	F	VF	XF	Unc	BU
2007(a)	20,000	—	—	—	850	1,250

KM# 195 2 EURO

8.5000 g., Bi-Metallic Nickel-Brass center in Copper-Nickel ring, 25.75 mm. **Ruler:** Albert II **Obv:** Head right **Rev:** Relief map of western Europe, stars, lines and values **Edge:** Reeded with 2's and stars

Date	Mintage	F	VF	XF	Unc	BU
2007(a)	—	—	—	—	—	65.00
2009(a)	250,000	—	—	—	—	35.00
2010(a)	25,000	Value: 300				

KM# 180 5 EURO

12.0000 g., 0.9000 Silver 0.3472 oz. ASW, 29 mm. **Ruler:** Rainier III **Obv:** Bust right **Rev:** Saint standing

Date	Mintage	F	VF	XF	Unc	BU
2004 (a) Proof	14,999	Value: 150				

KM# 178 10 EURO

25.0000 g., 0.9250 Silver 0.7435 oz. ASW, 37 mm. **Ruler:** Rainier III **Obv:** Conjoined busts of Prince Ranier and Crown Prince Albert right **Rev:** Arms

Date	Mintage	F	VF	XF	Unc	BU
2003(a) Proof	4,000	Value: 465				

KM# 187 10 EURO

3.2200 g., 0.9000 Gold 0.0932 oz. AGW **Ruler:** Albert II **Subject:** Death of Rainier III **Obv:** Principality arms **Rev:** Head of Rainier III right

Date	Mintage	F	VF	XF	Unc	BU
2005(a) Proof	3,313	Value: 550				

KM# 177 20 EURO

18.0000 g., 0.9250 Gold 0.5353 oz. AGW, 32 mm. **Ruler:** Rainier III **Obv:** Bust right **Rev:** Arms

Date	Mintage	F	VF	XF	Unc	BU
2002(a) Proof	10,000	Value: 1,100				

KM# 179 100 EURO

29.0000 g., 0.9000 Gold 0.8391 oz. AGW **Ruler:** Rainier III **Obv:** Bust right **Rev:** Knight on horse

Date	Mintage	F	VF	XF	Unc	BU
2003(a) Proof	1,000	Value: 3,250				

MINT SETS

KM#	Date	Mintage	Identification	Issue Price	Mkt Val
MS1	2001 (8)	20,000	KM#167-174, exercise caution, privately packaged and deceptively false sets exist	35.00	225
MS2	2002 (8)	40,000	KM#167-174, exercise caution, privately packaged and deceptively false sets exist	35.00	325

PROOF SETS

KM#	Date	Mintage	Identification	Issue Price	Mkt Val
PS1	2001 (8)	3,500	KM#167-174	—	1,000
PS2	2004 (9)	14,999	KM#167-174, 180	—	600
PS3	2005 (3)	35,000	KM#167-169	—	155
PS4	2006 (8)	11,180	KM#181-185, 188-190	—	475

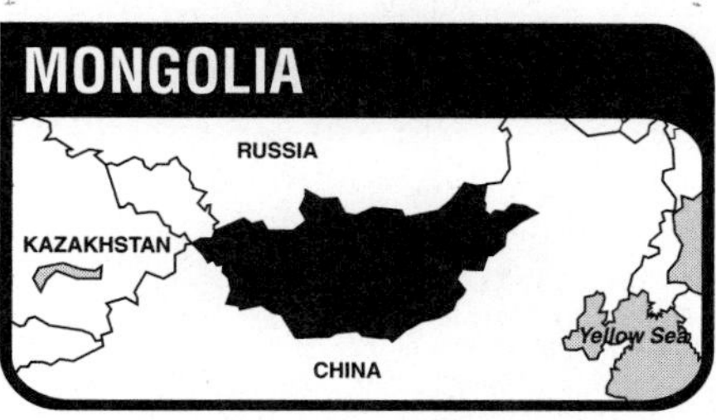

The State of Mongolia, (formerly the Mongolian Peoples Republic) a landlocked country in central Asia between Russia and the People's Republic of China, has an area of 604,250 sq. mi. (1,565,000 sq. km.) and a population of 2.26 million. Capital: Ulaan Baator. Animal herds and flocks are the chief economic asset. Wool, cattle, butter, meat and hides are exported.

For earlier issues see Russia - Tannu Tuva.

MONETARY SYSTEM

100 Mongo = 1 Tugrik

STATE

DECIMAL COINAGE

KM# 302 100 TUGRIK

Silver **Subject:** XXVI Summer Olympics, Atlanta **Obv:** Arms **Rev:** 1904 St. Louis World's Fair Program Cover

Date	Mintage	F	VF	XF	Unc	BU
2002 Proof	—	Value: 20.00				

KM# 254 100 TUGRIK

25.0000 g., 0.9250 Silver 0.7435 oz. ASW **Obv:** Arms **Rev:** Yin-Yang symbol

Date	Mintage	F	VF	XF	Unc	BU
2007 Proof	—	Value: 25.00				

KM# 306 100 TUGRIK

26.0000 g., 0.9250 Silver 0.7732 oz. ASW, 38.5 mm. **Subject:** Wonders of the World **Obv:** National emblem **Rev:** Rome's Colosseum

Date	Mintage	F	VF	XF	Unc	BU
2008 Prooflike	—	—	—	—	—	35.00

KM# 307 100 TUGRIK

26.4000 g., 0.9250 Silver 0.7851 oz. ASW, 38.5 mm. **Subject:** Wonders of the World **Obv:** National Emblem **Rev:** Chichen Itza pyramid

Date	Mintage	F	VF	XF	Unc	BU
2008 Prooflike	—	—	—	—	—	35.00

KM# 308 100 TUGRIK

25.0000 g., 0.9250 Silver 0.7435 oz. ASW **Obv:** National emblem **Rev:** Treasury at Petra

Date	Mintage	F	VF	XF	Unc	BU
2008 Proof	—	Value: 75.00				

KM# 282 250 TUGRIK

15.5000 g., 0.9250 Silver 0.4609 oz. ASW, 33 mm. **Subject:** Zodiac - Capricorn **Rev:** Seated goat left, partially gilt

Date	Mintage	F	VF	XF	Unc	BU
2007	7,000	—	—	—	—	25.00

KM# 283 250 TUGRIK

15.5000 g., 0.9250 Silver 0.4609 oz. ASW, 33 mm. **Subject:** Zodiac - Aquarius **Rev:** Man pouring water, partially gilt

Date	Mintage	F	VF	XF	Unc	BU
2007	7,000	—	—	—	—	25.00

KM# 284 250 TUGRIK

15.5000 g., 0.9250 Silver 0.4609 oz. ASW, 33 mm. **Subject:** Zodiac - Piceis **Rev:** Two fish partially gilt

Date	Mintage	F	VF	XF	Unc	BU
2007	7,000	—	—	—	—	25.00

KM# 285 250 TUGRIK

15.5000 g., 0.9250 Silver 0.4609 oz. ASW, 33 mm. **Subject:** Zodiac - Aries **Rev:** Ram seated partially gilt

Date	Mintage	F	VF	XF	Unc	BU
2007	7,000	—	—	—	—	25.00

KM# 286 250 TUGRIK

15.5000 g., 0.9250 Silver 0.4609 oz. ASW, 33 mm. **Subject:** Zodiac - Taurus **Rev:** Bull, partially gilt

Date	Mintage	F	VF	XF	Unc	BU
2007	7,000	—	—	—	—	25.00

KM# 287 250 TUGRIK

15.5000 g., 0.9250 Silver 0.4609 oz. ASW, 33 mm. **Subject:** Zodiac - Gemini **Rev:** Twins, partially gilt

Date	Mintage	F	VF	XF	Unc	BU
2007	7,000	—	—	—	—	25.00

KM# 288 250 TUGRIK
15.5000 g., 0.9250 Silver 0.4609 oz. ASW, 33 mm. **Subject:** Zodiac - Cancer **Rev:** Crab - partially gilt

Date	Mintage	F	VF	XF	Unc	BU
2007	7,000	—	—	—	—	25.00

KM# 289 250 TUGRIK
15.5000 g., 0.9250 Silver 0.4609 oz. ASW, 33 mm. **Subject:** Zodiac - Leo **Rev:** Lion walking left, partially gilt

Date	Mintage	F	VF	XF	Unc	BU
2007	7,000	—	—	—	—	25.00

KM# 290 250 TUGRIK
15.5000 g., 0.9250 Silver 0.4609 oz. ASW, 33 mm. **Subject:** Zodiac - Virgo **Rev:** Female, partially gilt

Date	Mintage	F	VF	XF	Unc	BU
2007	7,000	—	—	—	—	25.00

KM# 291 250 TUGRIK
15.5000 g., 0.9250 Silver 0.4609 oz. ASW, 33 mm. **Subject:** Zodiac - Libra **Rev:** Scales, partially gilt

Date	Mintage	F	VF	XF	Unc	BU
2007	7,000	—	—	—	—	25.00

KM# 292 250 TUGRIK
15.5000 g., 0.9250 Silver 0.4609 oz. ASW, 33 mm. **Subject:** Zodiac - Scorpio **Rev:** Scorpion, partially gilt

Date	Mintage	F	VF	XF	Unc	BU
2007	7,000	—	—	—	—	25.00

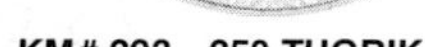

KM# 293 250 TUGRIK
15.5000 g., 0.9250 Silver 0.4609 oz. ASW, 33 mm. **Subject:** Zodiac - Sagittarius **Rev:** Centar, partailly gilt

Date	Mintage	F	VF	XF	Unc	BU
2007	7,000	—	—	—	—	25.00

KM# 300 250 TUGRIK
15.5000 g., 0.9990 Silver 0.4978 oz. ASW, 33 mm. **Subject:** Moscow Waterworks **Rev:** Building in multicolor, aqueduct in background

Date	Mintage	F	VF	XF	Unc	BU
2007	1,000	—	—	—	—	45.00

KM# 301 250 TUGRIK
15.5000 g., 0.9990 Silver 0.4978 oz. ASW, 33 mm. **Subject:** Moscow Metro **Rev:** Subway train, multicolor

Date	Mintage	F	VF	XF	Unc	BU
2007	1,000	—	—	—	—	45.00

KM# 270 250 TUGRIK
15.5500 g., 0.9250 Silver 0.4624 oz. ASW, 37 mm. **Subject:** Baby Boy **Obv:** Arms **Rev:** Baby seated on flower, multicolor **Shape:** Heart

Date	Mintage	F	VF	XF	Unc	BU
2008 Proof	2,500	Value: 40.00				

KM# 271 250 TUGRIK
15.5500 g., 0.9250 Silver 0.4624 oz. ASW, 37 mm. **Subject:** Baby Girl **Obv:** Arms **Rev:** Baby Girl on flower **Shape:** Heart

Date	Mintage	F	VF	XF	Unc	BU
2008 Proof	2,500	Value: 40.00				

KM# 189 500 TUGRIK
25.0000 g., 0.9250 Silver 0.7435 oz. ASW, 38.7 mm. **Obv:** National emblem above value **Rev:** Protoceratops Andrewsi **Edge:** Reeded

Date	Mintage	F	VF	XF	Unc	BU
2001 Proof	2,500	Value: 45.00				

KM# 190 500 TUGRIK
25.0000 g., 0.9250 Silver 0.7435 oz. ASW **Obv:** National emblem above value **Rev:** Velociraptor Mongoliensis

Date	Mintage	F	VF	XF	Unc	BU
2001 Proof	2,500	Value: 45.00				

KM# 191 500 TUGRIK
25.0000 g., 0.9250 Silver 0.7435 oz. ASW **Series:** Olympics **Obv:** National emblem above value **Rev:** Speed skater

Date	Mintage	F	VF	XF	Unc	BU
2001 Proof	15,000	Value: 32.00				

KM# 192 500 TUGRIK
25.0000 g., 0.9250 Silver 0.7435 oz. ASW **Series:** Olympics **Obv:** National emblem above value **Rev:** Cross-country skiers

Date	Mintage	F	VF	XF	Unc	BU
2001 Proof	20,000	Value: 30.00				

KM# 195 500 TUGRIK
Copper-Nickel, 22.1 mm. **Subject:** Sukhe-Bataar **Obv:** National emblem and value **Rev:** Crowned head facing **Edge:** Plain

Date	Mintage	F	VF	XF	Unc	BU
2001	—	—	—	—	2.50	3.00

KM# 238 500 TUGRIK
20.0000 g., 0.9250 Silver 0.5948 oz. ASW **Subject:** Gobi Desert Brown Bear **Obv:** Arms **Rev:** Bear standing on rock in stream

Date	Mintage	F	VF	XF	Unc	BU
2001 Proof	—	Value: 25.00				

KM# 239 500 TUGRIK
31.1050 g., 0.9990 Silver 0.9990 oz. ASW, 38.5 mm. **Subject:** Year of the Snake **Rev:** Snake

Date	Mintage	F	VF	XF	Unc	BU
2001 Proof	—	Value: 65.00				

KM# 239a 500 TUGRIK
31.1050 g., 0.9990 Silver partially gilt 0.9990 oz. ASW **Subject:** Year of the Snake **Obv:** Arms **Rev:** Snake, gilt

Date	Mintage	F	VF	XF	Unc	BU
2001 Proof	—	Value: 75.00				

KM# 241 500 TUGRIK
31.1050 g., 0.9990 Silver 0.9990 oz. ASW, 38.5 mm. **Subject:** Year of the Horse **Obv:** Arms **Rev:** Horse

Date	Mintage	F	VF	XF	Unc	BU
2002 Proof	—	Value: 65.00				

KM# 241a 500 TUGRIK
31.1050 g., 0.9990 Silver partially gilt 0.9990 oz. ASW, 38.5 mm. **Subject:** Year of the Horse **Rev:** Horse, gilt

Date	Mintage	F	VF	XF	Unc	BU
2002 Proof	—	Value: 75.00				

KM# 200 500 TUGRIK
25.5700 g., 0.9250 Silver 0.7604 oz. ASW, 38.5 mm. **Subject:** Marco Polo, Homeward **Obv:** National emblem above value **Rev:** Five-masted sailing junk **Edge:** Reeded

Date	Mintage	F	VF	XF	Unc	BU
2003 Proof	5,000	Value: 45.00				

KM# 205 500 TUGRIK
25.0000 g., 0.9250 Silver 0.7435 oz. ASW, 38.6 mm. **Obv:** National emblem above value **Rev:** Medallion divides busts **Edge:** Reeded

Date	Mintage	F	VF	XF	Unc	BU
2003 Proof	5,000	Value: 65.00				

KM# 206 500 TUGRIK
1.2440 g., 0.9999 Gold 0.0400 oz. AGW, 13.92 mm. **Obv:** National emblem above value **Rev:** Five masted sailing junk **Edge:** Reeded

Date	Mintage	F	VF	XF	Unc	BU
2003 Proof	25,000	Value: 65.00				

KM# 207 500 TUGRIK
1.2440 g., 0.9999 Gold 0.0400 oz. AGW, 13.92 mm. **Obv:** National emblem above value **Rev:** Medallion divides busts **Edge:** Reeded

Date	Mintage	F	VF	XF	Unc	BU
2003 Proof	25,000	Value: 70.00				

KM# 204 500 TUGRIK
25.0000 g., 0.9250 Silver 0.7435 oz. ASW, 38 mm. **Obv:** National emblem above value **Rev:** Wolf within full moon **Edge:** Reeded

Date	Mintage	F	VF	XF	Unc	BU
2003 Proof	10,000	Value: 60.00				

KM# 229 500 TUGRIK
31.1050 g., 0.9990 Silver 0.9990 oz. ASW **Obv:** Arms above legend **Rev:** Ram standing left

Date	Mintage	F	VF	XF	Unc	BU
2003	—	—	—	—	—	65.00

KM# 229a 500 TUGRIK
31.1050 g., 0.9990 Silver partialy gilt 0.9990 oz. ASW, 38.5 mm. **Subject:** Year of the Ram **Obv:** Arms **Rev:** Ram standing left, gilt

Date	Mintage	F	VF	XF	Unc	BU
2003 Proof	—	Value: 75.00				

KM# 208 500 TUGRIK
25.0000 g., 0.9250 Silver 0.7435 oz. ASW, 38 mm. **Obv:** National emblem above value **Rev:** Holographic Osprey catching fish **Edge:** Reeded

Date	Mintage	F	VF	XF	Unc	BU
2004 Proof	5,000	Value: 50.00				

KM# 218 500 TUGRIK
31.2400 g., 0.9990 Silver 1.0033 oz. ASW, 38.59 mm. **Series:** Chinese Lunar **Subject:** Year of the Monkey **Obv:** National emblem **Rev:** Monkey seated on branch - gilt, border of scampering monkeys **Edge:** Reeded

Date	Mintage	F	VF	XF	Unc	BU
ND(2004) Proof	20,000	Value: 45.00				

KM# 219 500 TUGRIK
1.2400 g., 0.9999 Gold 0.0399 oz. AGW **Series:** Chinese Lunar **Subject:** Year of the Monkey **Obv:** National emblem **Rev:** Monkey seated on branch

Date	Mintage	F	VF	XF	Unc	BU
ND(2004) Proof	—	Value: 65.00				

KM# 244 500 TUGRIK
31.1050 g., 0.9990 Silver 0.9990 oz. ASW, 38.5 mm. **Subject:** Year of the Monkey **Obv:** Arms **Rev:** Monkey

Date	Mintage	F	VF	XF	Unc	BU
2004 Proof	—	Value: 65.00				

KM# 244a 500 TUGRIK
31.1050 g., 0.9990 Silver partially gilt 0.9990 oz. ASW, 38.5 mm. **Subject:** Year of the Monkey **Obv:** Arms **Rev:** Monkey, gilt

Date	Mintage	F	VF	XF	Unc	BU
2004 Proof	—	Value: 75.00				

KM# 209 500 TUGRIK
24.9300 g., 0.9250 Bi-Metallic with .925 Silver oval in center 0.7414 oz., 30 mm. **Obv:** National emblem above value, niobium leopard in oval center **Rev:** Snow Leopard **Edge:** Reeded **Shape:** Oval

Date	Mintage	F	VF	XF	Unc	BU
2005 Proof	5,000	Value: 85.00				

KM# 210 500 TUGRIK
31.1035 g., 0.9990 Silver 0.9990 oz. ASW, 35x35 mm. **Obv:** Bronze plated horse and rider on antiqued silver with national emblem and value **Rev:** Bronze plated horse and rider on antiqued silver above date **Edge:** Reeded **Shape:** Square

Date	Mintage	F	VF	XF	Unc	BU
2005	2,500	—	—	—	65.00	70.00

KM# 210a 500 TUGRIK
31.1035 g., 0.9990 Silver 0.9990 oz. ASW, 35x35 mm. **Obv:** Gold plated horse and rider with national emblem and value **Rev:** Gold plated horse and rider above date **Edge:** Reeded

Date	Mintage	F	VF	XF	Unc	BU
2005 Proof	2,500	Value: 80.00				

KM# 304 500 TUGRIK
31.1000 g., 0.9990 Silver 0.9988 oz. ASW **Obv:** National emblem **Rev:** Sumo Wrestler Yokozuna Ounomatsu in color

Date	Mintage	F	VF	XF	Unc	BU
2005 Proof	—	Value: 125				

KM# 246 500 TUGRIK
31.1050 g., 0.9990 Silver 0.9990 oz. ASW, 38.5 mm. **Subject:** Year of the Rooster **Obv:** Arms **Rev:** Rooster standing right

Date	Mintage	F	VF	XF	Unc	BU
2005 Proof	—	Value: 65.00				

KM# 246a 500 TUGRIK
31.1050 g., 0.9990 Silver 0.9990 oz. ASW, 38.5 mm. **Subject:** Year of the Rooster **Obv:** Arms **Rev:** Rooster, gilt

Date	Mintage	F	VF	XF	Unc	BU
2005 Proof	—	Value: 75.00				

KM# 230 500 TUGRIK
25.0000 g., 0.9250 Silver 0.7435 oz. ASW **Rev:** Swan with crystal insert

Date	Mintage	F	VF	XF	Unc	BU
2006 Proof	—	Value: 90.00				

KM# 231 500 TUGRIK
25.0000 g., 0.9250 Silver 0.7435 oz. ASW **Rev:** Gobi bear head with crystal inserts

Date	Mintage	F	VF	XF	Unc	BU
2006 Proof	—	Value: 120				

KM# 248 500 TUGRIK
25.0000 g., 0.9250 Silver 0.7435 oz. ASW **Subject:** Long Eared Jerboa **Obv:** Arms **Rev:** Long eared jerboa, crystal eyes **Shape:** 38.6

Date	Mintage	F	VF	XF	Unc	BU
2006 Proof	2,500	Value: 120				

KM# 249 500 TUGRIK
25.0000 g., 0.9250 Silver 0.7435 oz. ASW, 38.6 mm. **Obv:** Arms **Rev:** Scorpion, crystal tail point

Date	Mintage	F	VF	XF	Unc	BU
2006 Proof	2,500	Value: 120				

KM# 250 500 TUGRIK
25.0000 g., 0.9250 Silver 0.7435 oz. ASW, 38.6 mm. **Rev:** Tiger, head facing, crystal eyes

Date	Mintage	F	VF	XF	Unc	BU
2006 Proof	2,500	Value: 120				

KM# 251 500 TUGRIK
31.1050 g., 0.9990 Silver 0.9990 oz. ASW, 38.5 mm. **Subject:** Year of the Dog **Obv:** Arms **Rev:** Dog standing

Date	Mintage	F	VF	XF	Unc	BU
2006 Proof	—	Value: 55.00				

KM# 251a 500 TUGRIK
31.1050 g., 0.9990 Silver 0.9990 oz. ASW, 38.5 mm. **Subject:** Year of the Dog **Obv:** Arms **Rev:** Dog standing, gilt

Date	Mintage	F	VF	XF	Unc	BU
2006 Proof	—	Value: 65.00				

KM# 260 500 TUGRIK
25.0000 g., 0.9250 Silver 0.7435 oz. ASW, 38.6 mm. **Subject:** Great Mongolian State, 800th Anniversary **Obv:** Arms **Rev:** Chinggis Khan and black pennant

Date	Mintage	F	VF	XF	Unc	BU
2006 Proof	2,500	Value: 70.00				

KM# 261 500 TUGRIK
25.0000 g., 0.9250 Silver 0.7435 oz. ASW, 38.61 mm. **Subject:** Great Mongolian State, 800th Anniversary **Obv:** Arms **Rev:** Nine white pennants

Date	Mintage	F	VF	XF	Unc	BU
2006 Proof	2,500	Value: 70.00				

KM# 212 500 TUGRIK
31.1050 g., 0.9990 Silver 0.9990 oz. ASW, 38 mm. **Obv:** Arms and value **Rev:** Wolverine head facing with diamonds in eyes **Rev. Inscription:** WILDLIFE PROTECTION GULO GULO

Date	Mintage	F	VF	XF	Unc	BU
2007	—	—	—	—	—	120

KM# 265 500 TUGRIK
31.1050 g., 0.9990 Silver 0.9990 oz. ASW, 38.61 mm. **Subject:** Society Space exploration **Obv:** Arms **Rev:** Sputnik, rocket, three figures

Date	Mintage	F	VF	XF	Unc	BU
2007 Proof	1,000	Value: 75.00				

KM# 266 500 TUGRIK
31.1050 g., 0.9990 Silver 0.9990 oz. ASW, 38.61 mm. **Subject:** Soviet Space Exploration **Rev:** Laika, first dog in space

Date	Mintage	F	VF	XF	Unc	BU
2007 Proof	500	Value: 85.00				

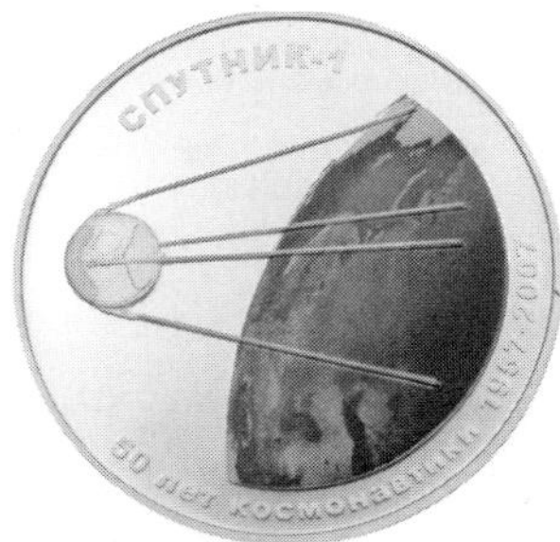

KM# 267 500 TUGRIK
31.1050 g., 0.9990 Silver 0.9990 oz. ASW, 38.61 mm. **Subject:** Soviet Space Exploration **Obv:** Arms **Rev:** Sputnik

Date	Mintage	F	VF	XF	Unc	BU
2007 Proof	500	Value: 85.00				

KM# 268 500 TUGRIK
31.1050 g., 0.9990 Silver 0.9990 oz. ASW, 38.61 mm. **Subject:** Soviet Space Exploration **Obv:** Arms **Rev:** Yuri Gagarian

Date	Mintage	F	VF	XF	Unc	BU
2007 Proof	500	Value: 85.00				

KM# 269 500 TUGRIK
31.1050 g., 0.9990 Silver 0.9990 oz. ASW, 38.61 mm. **Subject:** Soviet Space Exploration **Obv:** Arms **Rev:** Mir space station

Date	Mintage	F	VF	XF	Unc	BU
2007 Proof	1,000	Value: 85.00				

KM# 222 500 TUGRIK
25.0000 g., 0.9250 Silver 0.7435 oz. ASW, 38.61 mm. **Subject:** Wonders of the World **Obv:** Arms **Rev:** Multicolor Chichen Itza

Date	Mintage	F	VF	XF	Unc	BU
2008	2,500	—	—	—	—	75.00

KM# 223 500 TUGRIK
25.0000 g., 0.9250 Silver 0.7435 oz. ASW, 38.6 mm. **Subject:** Wonders of the World **Obv:** Arms **Rev:** Multicolor Treasury at Petra

Date	Mintage	F	VF	XF	Unc	BU
2008	2,500	—	—	—	—	75.00

KM# 224 500 TUGRIK
25.0000 g., 0.9250 Silver 0.7435 oz. ASW, 38.61 mm. **Subject:** Wonders of the World **Obv:** Arms **Rev:** Multicolor Taj Mahal

Date	Mintage	F	VF	XF	Unc	BU
2008	2,500	—	—	—	—	75.00

KM# 225 500 TUGRIK
25.0000 g., 0.9250 Silver 0.7435 oz. ASW, 38.61 mm. **Subject:** Wonders of the World **Obv:** Arms **Rev:** Multicolor Machu Picchu

Date	Mintage	F	VF	XF	Unc	BU
2008	2,500	—	—	—	—	75.00

KM# 226 500 TUGRIK
25.0000 g., 0.9250 Silver 0.7435 oz. ASW, 38.61 mm. **Subject:** Wonders of the World **Obv:** Arms **Rev:** Multicolor Great Wall of China

Date	Mintage	F	VF	XF	Unc	BU
2008	2,500	—	—	—	—	75.00

KM# 227 500 TUGRIK
25.0000 g., 0.9250 Silver 0.7435 oz. ASW, 38.61 mm. **Subject:** Wonders of the World **Obv:** Arms **Rev:** Multicolor Colosseum in Rome

Date	Mintage	F	VF	XF	Unc	BU
2008	2,500	—	—	—	—	75.00

KM# 228 500 TUGRIK
25.0000 g., 0.9250 Silver 0.7435 oz. ASW, 38.61 mm. **Subject:** Wonders of the World **Obv:** Arms **Rev:** Multicolor Christ the Redeemer statue in Rio

Date	Mintage	F	VF	XF	Unc	BU
2008	2,500	—	—	—	—	75.00

KM# 213 500 TUGRIK
31.1000 g., 0.9990 Silver 0.9988 oz. ASW, 39mm mm. **Subject:** Year of the Rat **Obv:** National emblem, value below **Rev:** Three rats in grass **Edge:** Reeded

Date	Mintage	F	VF	XF	Unc	BU
2008	20,000	—	—	—	—	40.00

KM# 213a 500 TUGRIK
31.1000 g., 0.9990 Silver 0.9988 oz. ASW, 39.0 mm. **Subject:** Year of the Rat **Obv:** National emblem, value below **Rev:** Three gilt rats in grass **Edge:** Reeded

Date	Mintage	F	VF	XF	Unc	BU
2008 Proof	5,000	Value: 50.00				

KM# 255 500 TUGRIK
25.0000 g., 0.9250 Silver 0.7435 oz. ASW, 38.6 mm. **Subject:** Frederic Chopin **Obv:** Arms **Rev:** Bust right, color keyboard vertical in center

Date	Mintage	F	VF	XF	Unc	BU
2008 Proof	1,000	Value: 90.00				

KM# 256 500 TUGRIK
31.1050 g., 0.9990 Silver 0.9990 oz. ASW, 38.6 mm. **Subject:** Year of the Rat **Obv:** Arms **Rev:** Two mice

Date	Mintage	F	VF	XF	Unc	BU
2008 Proof	—	Value: 55.00				

KM# 256a 500 TUGRIK
31.1050 g., 0.9990 Silver partially gilt 0.9990 oz. ASW, 38.6 mm. **Subject:** Year of the Rat **Obv:** Arms **Rev:** Two mice, gilt

Date	Mintage	F	VF	XF	Unc	BU
2008 Proof	—	Value: 65.00				

KM# 272 500 TUGRIK
25.0000 g., 0.9250 Silver 0.7435 oz. ASW, 38.6 mm. **Series:** Mongolian Olympians, Baatarjav **Obv:** Arms

Date	Mintage	F	VF	XF	Unc	BU
2008 Proof	2,500	Value: 50.00				

KM# 273 500 TUGRIK
25.0000 g., 0.9250 Silver 0.7435 oz. ASW, 38.61 mm. **Subject:** Mongolian Olympians - Badar-Uugan

Date	Mintage	F	VF	XF	Unc	BU
2008 Proof	2,500	Value: 50.00				

KM# 274 500 TUGRIK
25.0000 g., 0.9990 Silver 0.8029 oz. ASW, 38.61 mm. **Subject:** Mongolian Olympians - Serdamba

Date	Mintage	F	VF	XF	Unc	BU
2008 Proof	2,500	Value: 50.00				

KM# 275 500 TUGRIK
25.0000 g., 0.9250 Silver 0.7435 oz. ASW, 38.61 mm. **Subject:** Mongolian Olympians - Tuvshinbayar

Date	Mintage	F	VF	XF	Unc	BU
2008 Proof	2,500	Value: 50.00				

KM# 276 500 TUGRIK
25.0000 g., 0.9250 Silver 0.7435 oz. ASW, 38.61 mm. **Subject:** Mongolian Olympians - Gundegmaa

Date	Mintage	F	VF	XF	Unc	BU
2008 Proof	2,500	Value: 50.00				

KM# 279 500 TUGRIK
0.5000 g., 0.9990 Gold 0.0161 oz. AGW, 11 mm. **Subject:** Mongolian Olympic Sports - Archery

Date	Mintage	F	VF	XF	Unc	BU
2008 Proof	15,000	—	—	—	—	50.00

KM# 280 500 TUGRIK
25.0000 g., 0.9250 Silver 0.7435 oz. ASW, 38.61 mm. **Obv:** Arms **Rev:** Two snow leopards, multicolor

Date	Mintage	F	VF	XF	Unc	BU
2008 Proof	2,500	Value: 45.00				

KM# 281 500 TUGRIK
25.0000 g., 0.9250 Silver 0.7435 oz. ASW, 38.61 mm. **Obv:** Arms **Rev:** The Almas, multicolor changing insert

Date	Mintage	F	VF	XF	Unc	BU
2008 Proof	2,500	Value: 45.00				

KM# 305 500 TUGRIK
25.0000 g., 0.9250 Silver 0.7435 oz. ASW, 38.61 mm. **Subject:** Frederic Chopin **Obv:** National emblem **Rev:** Piano keys in color, bust at right

Date	Mintage	F	VF	XF	Unc	BU
2008 Proof	—	Value: 75.00				

KM# 312 500 TUGRIK
25.0000 g., 0.9250 Silver 0.7435 oz. ASW, 38.6 mm. **Obv:** National Emblem **Rev:** Treasury at Petra, rocks in color

Date	Mintage	F	VF	XF	Unc	BU
2008	2,500	—	—	—	—	75.00

KM# 258 500 TUGRIK
31.1050 g., 0.9990 Silver 0.9990 oz. ASW, 38.6 mm. **Subject:** Year of the Ox **Obv:** Arms **Rev:** Ox

Date	Mintage	F	VF	XF	Unc	BU
2009 Proof	—	Value: 55.00				

KM# 258a 500 TUGRIK
31.1050 g., 0.9990 Silver partially gilt 0.9990 oz. ASW, 38.6 mm. **Subject:** Year of the Ox **Obv:** Arms **Rev:** Ox, gilt

Date	Mintage	F	VF	XF	Unc	BU
2009 Proof	—	Value: 65.00				

KM# 309 500 TUGRIK
31.1000 g., 0.9250 Silver 0.9249 oz. ASW, 38.6 mm. **Subject:** Endangered Wildlife **Obv:** National Emblem **Rev:** Owl's head facing (Strix Uralensis) crystal insert eyes

Date	Mintage	F	VF	XF	Unc	BU
2011 Antique finish	2,500	—	—	—	—	125

KM# 310 500 TUGRIK
0.5000 g., 0.9990 Gold 0.0161 oz. AGW, 11 mm. **Subject:** Endangered Wildlife **Obv:** National emblem **Rev:** Ural Owl (Strix Uralersis) standing left

Date	Mintage	F	VF	XF	Unc	BU
2011 Proof	15,000	—	—	—	—	75.00

KM# 199 1000 TUGRIK
31.1100 g., 0.9250 Silver 0.9252 oz. ASW, 38.6 mm. **Obv:** National emblem above value **Obv. Inscription:** Denomination spelled "TOGROG" **Rev:** Head facing **Edge:** Reeded

Date	Mintage	F	VF	XF	Unc	BU
2002	17,000	—	—	—	40.00	45.00

KM# 303 1000 TUGRIK
Copper-Nickel, 38 mm. **Obv:** National emblem **Rev:** Two soccer players

Date	Mintage	F	VF	XF	Unc	BU
2003 Prooflike	2,000	—	—	—	—	10.00

KM# 233 1000 TUGRIK
Gold **Rev:** Snow leopard

Date	Mintage	F	VF	XF	Unc	BU
2005 Proof	—	Value: 85.00				

KM# 253 1000 TUGRIK
1.2400 g., 0.9990 Gold 0.0398 oz. AGW **Subject:** Mozart **Obv:** Arms **Rev:** Portrait and profile heads above building

Date	Mintage	F	VF	XF	Unc	BU
2006 Proof	—	Value: 70.00				

KM# 262 1000 TUGRIK
1.2400 g., 0.9990 Gold 0.0398 oz. AGW, 13.92 mm. **Obv:** Arms **Rev:** Scorpion

Date	Mintage	F	VF	XF	Unc	BU
2006 Proof	25,000	Value: 85.00				

KM# 263 1000 TUGRIK
1.2400 g., 0.9990 Silver 0.0398 oz. ASW, 13.9 mm. **Obv:** Arms **Rev:** Long-eared Jerboa

Date	Mintage	F	VF	XF	Unc	BU
2006 Proof	—	Value: 85.00				

KM# 264 1000 TUGRIK
1.2400 g., 0.9990 Gold 0.0398 oz. AGW, 13.9 mm. **Obv:** Arms **Rev:** Gobi Bear

Date	Mintage	F	VF	XF	Unc	BU
2006 Proof	25,000	Value: 85.00				

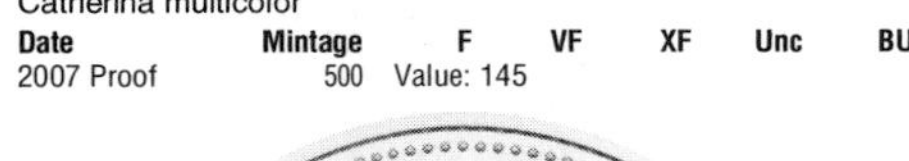

KM# 294 1000 TUGRIK
62.2000 g., 0.9990 Silver 1.9977 oz. ASW, 50 mm. **Rev:** Tsarina Catherina multicolor

Date	Mintage	F	VF	XF	Unc	BU
2007 Proof	500	Value: 145				

KM# 295 1000 TUGRIK
62.2000 g., 0.9990 Silver 1.9977 oz. ASW, 50 mm. **Rev:** Tsar Nicholas I, multicolor

Date	Mintage	F	VF	XF	Unc	BU
2007 Proof	500	Value: 145				

KM# 296 1000 TUGRIK
62.2000 g., 0.9990 Silver 1.9977 oz. ASW, 50 mm. **Rev:** Tsar Nicholas II

Date	Mintage	F	VF	XF	Unc	BU
2007 Proof	500	Value: 145				

KM# 297 1000 TUGRIK
62.2000 g., 0.9990 Silver 1.9977 oz. ASW, 50 mm. **Rev:** Tsar Ivan IV, multicolor

Date	Mintage	F	VF	XF	Unc	BU
2007 Proof	500	Value: 145				

KM# 298 1000 TUGRIK
62.2000 g., 0.9990 Silver 1.9977 oz. ASW, 50 mm. **Rev:** Tsar Peter I, multicolor

Date	Mintage	F	VF	XF	Unc	BU
2007 Proof	500	Value: 145				

KM# 299 1000 TUGRIK
62.2000 g., 0.9990 Silver 1.9977 oz. ASW, 50 mm. **Rev:** Tsar Yuri

Date	Mintage	F	VF	XF	Unc	BU
2007 Proof	500	Value: 145				

KM# 214 1000 TUGRIK
1.2400 g., 0.9990 Gold 0.0398 oz. AGW, 14.0 mm. **Subject:** Year of the Rat **Obv:** National emblem, value below **Edge:** Reeded

Date	Mintage	F	VF	XF	Unc	BU
2008 Proof	10,000	Value: 70.00				

KM# 277 1000 TUGRIK

1.2400 g., 0.9990 Gold 0.0398 oz. AGW, 13.92 mm. **Subject:** Mongolian Olympic Sports - Boxing **Rev:** Two fighters in the ring

Date	Mintage	F	VF	XF	Unc	BU
2008 Proof	15,000	Value: 80.00				

KM# 278 1000 TUGRIK

1.2400 g., 0.9990 Gold 0.0398 oz. AGW, 13.92 mm. **Subject:** Mongolian Olympic Sports - Judo **Rev:** Judo athlete getting fliped

Date	Mintage	F	VF	XF	Unc	BU
2008 Proof	15,000	Value: 80.00				

KM# 311 1000 TUGRIK

1.2400 g., 0.9990 Gold 0.0398 oz. AGW, 13.92 mm. **Subject:** Frederic Chopin **Obv:** National Emblem **Rev:** Piano keyboard vertical at left, bust at right

Date	Mintage	F	VF	XF	Unc	BU
2011 Proof	—	Value: 100				

KM# 240 2500 TUGRIK

7.7700 g., 0.9990 Gold 0.2496 oz. AGW **Subject:** Year of the Snake **Obv:** Arms **Rev:** Snake

Date	Mintage	F	VF	XF	Unc	BU
2001 Proof	2,000	Value: 400				

KM# 242 2500 TUGRIK

7.7000 g., 0.9990 Gold 0.2473 oz. AGW **Subject:** Year of the Horse **Obv:** Arms **Rev:** Year of the Horse

Date	Mintage	F	VF	XF	Unc	BU
2002 Proof	—	Value: 400				

KM# 243 2500 TUGRIK

155.5000 g., 0.9990 Silver partially gilt 4.9942 oz. ASW, 65 mm. **Subject:** Year of the Ram **Obv:** Arms **Rev:** Ram standing left, gilt

Date	Mintage	F	VF	XF	Unc	BU
2003 Proof	4,000	Value: 325				

KM# 245 2500 TUGRIK

155.5000 g., 0.9990 Silver partially gilt 4.9942 oz. ASW, 65 mm. **Subject:** Year of the Monkey **Obv:** Arms **Rev:** Monkey, gilt

Date	Mintage	F	VF	XF	Unc	BU
2004 Proof	4,000	Value: 325				

KM# 220 2500 TUGRIK

7.7800 g., 0.9999 Gold 0.2501 oz. AGW **Series:** Chinese Lunar **Subject:** Year of the Monkey **Obv:** National emblem **Rev:** Monkey seated on branch **Edge:** Reeded

Date	Mintage	F	VF	XF	Unc	BU
ND(2004) Proof	2,000	Value: 425				

KM# 247 2500 TUGRIK

155.5000 g., 0.9990 Silver partially gilt 4.9942 oz. ASW, 65 mm. **Subject:** Year of the Rooster **Obv:** Arms **Rev:** Rooster, gilt

Date	Mintage	F	VF	XF	Unc	BU
2005 Proof	4,000	Value: 325				

KM# 252 2500 TUGRIK

155.5000 g., 0.9990 Silver partially gilt 4.9942 oz. ASW, 65 mm. **Subject:** Year of the Dog **Obv:** Arms **Rev:** Dog standing, gilt

Date	Mintage	F	VF	XF	Unc	BU
2006 Proof	—	Value: 325				

KM# 257 2500 TUGRIK

155.5000 g., 0.9990 Silver partially gilt 4.9942 oz. ASW, 65 mm. **Subject:** Year of the Rat **Obv:** Arms **Rev:** Two mice, gilt

Date	Mintage	F	VF	XF	Unc	BU
2008 Proof	—	Value: 325				

KM# 259 2500 TUGRIK

155.5000 g., 0.9990 Silver partially gilt 4.9942 oz. ASW, 65 mm. **Subject:** Year of the Ox **Obv:** Arms **Rev:** Ox, gilt

Date	Mintage	F	VF	XF	Unc	BU
2009 Proof	—	Value: 325				

KM# 198 5000 TUGRIK

155.5000 g., 0.9990 Silver 4.9942 oz. ASW, 40x90 mm. **Subject:** Year of the Horse **Obv:** National emblem above value to left of Palace Museum **Rev:** Five multicolor running horses **Edge:** Plain **Note:** Round-cornered rectangle. Photo reduced.

Date	Mintage	F	VF	XF	Unc	BU
2002 Proof	—	Value: 225				

KM# 232 5000 TUGRIK

155.5000 g., 0.9990 Silver 4.9942 oz. ASW, 40x90 mm. **Rev:** Three sumo wrestlers, multicolor **Shape:** Rectangle **Note:** Illustration reduced.

Date	Mintage	F	VF	XF	Unc	BU
2005 Proof	—	Value: 300				

KM# 221 100000 TUGRIK

3000.0000 g., 0.9990 Silver 96.351 oz. ASW **Series:** Chinese Lunar **Subject:** Year of the Monkey **Obv:** National emblem **Rev:** Monkey seated on branch

Date	Mintage	F	VF	XF	Unc	BU
ND(2004) Proof	—	Value: 3,500				

KM# 215 100000 TUGRIK

3000.0000 g., 0.9990 Silver 96.351 oz. ASW, 130.0 mm. **Subject:** Year of the Rat **Obv:** National emblem, value below **Rev:** Three rats in grass **Edge:** Reeded **Note:** Serial number on edge.

Date	Mintage	F	VF	XF	Unc	BU
2008 Proof	500	Value: 3,500				

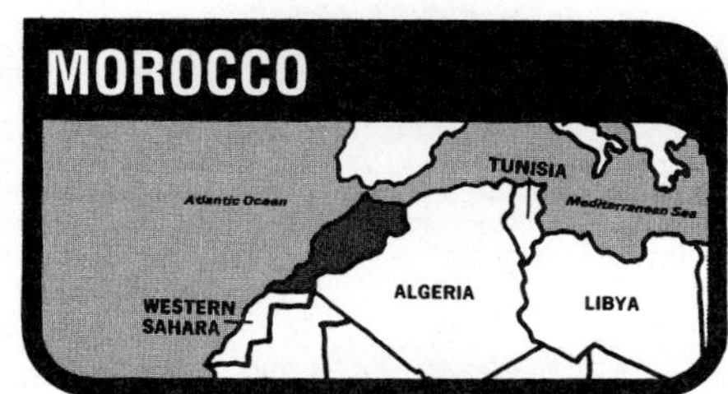

The Kingdom of Morocco, situated on the northwest corner of Africa, has an area of 432,620 sq. mi. (710,850 sq. km.) and a population of 36 million. Capital: Rabat. The economy is essentially agricultural. Phosphates, fresh and preserved vegetables, canned fish, and raw materials are exported.

KINGDOM
1956-

Mohammed VI
AH1420/1999AD

REFORM COINAGE

100 Santimat = 1 Dirham

Y# 116 1/2 DIRHAM

4.0000 g., Copper-Nickel, 21 mm. **Obv:** Crowned arms with supporters **Rev:** Value, design theme "telecommunications and new technologies" **Edge:** Reeded

Date	Mintage	F	VF	XF	Unc	BU
AH1423-2002	—	—	—	—	2.00	3.00

Y# 117 DIRHAM

6.0000 g., Copper-Nickel, 24 mm. **Obv:** Head 3/4 left **Rev:** Crowned arms with supporters above value **Edge:** Reeded

Date	Mintage	F	VF	XF	Unc	BU
AH1423-2002	—	—	—	—	3.00	5.00

Y# 112 5 SANTIMAT

2.0000 g., Aluminum-Bronze, 17.5 mm. **Obv:** Crowned arms with supporters **Rev:** Value, flower and dates **Edge:** Plain

Date	Mintage	F	VF	XF	Unc	BU
AH1423-2002	—	—	—	—	0.50	1.00

Y# 114 10 SANTIMAT

3.0000 g., Aluminum-Bronze, 20 mm. **Obv:** Crowned arms with supporters **Rev:** Value, design of "sport and solidarity" **Edge:** Reeded

Date	Mintage	F	VF	XF	Unc	BU
AH1423-2002	—	—	—	—	1.00	2.00

Y# 115 20 SANTIMAT

4.0000 g., Aluminum-Bronze, 23 mm. **Obv:** Crowned arms with supporters **Rev:** Value, design of "tourist and craftsmen trade" **Edge:** Reeded

Date	Mintage	F	VF	XF	Unc	BU
AH1423-2002	—	—	—	—	1.50	3.00

Y# 118 2 DIRHAMS

7.3000 g., Copper-Nickel, 25.9 mm. **Obv:** Head 3/4 left within octagon shape **Rev:** Crowned arms with supporters above value within octagon shape **Edge:** Reeded

Date	Mintage	F	VF	XF	Unc	BU
AH1423-2002	—	—	—	—	4.00	6.00

Y# 109 5 DIRHAMS

7.5300 g., Bi-Metallic Brass center in Copper-Nickel ring, 25 mm. **Obv:** Head 3/4 left **Rev:** Crowned arms with supporters above value **Edge:** Segmented reeding

Date	Mintage	F	VF	XF	Unc	BU
AH1423-2002	—	—	—	—	6.00	9.00

Y# 110 10 DIRHAMS

9.0000 g., Bi-Metallic Copper-Nickel center in Brass ring, 26.9 mm. **Obv:** Head 3/4 left **Rev:** Crowned arms with supporters above value **Edge:** Reeded

Date	Mintage	F	VF	XF	Unc	BU
AH1423-2002	—	—	—	—	10.00	15.00

Y# 107 250 DIRHAMS

25.0000 g., 0.9250 Silver 0.7435 oz. ASW, 37 mm. **Subject:** Inauguration of Mohammed VI 2nd Anniversary **Obv:** Head 3/4 left **Rev:** Crowned arms with supporters above value **Edge:** Reeded

Date	Mintage	F	VF	XF	Unc	BU
AH1422-2001	—	—	—	—	55.00	70.00

Y# 95 250 DIRHAMS

25.0000 g., 0.9250 Silver 0.7435 oz. ASW, 37 mm. **Subject:** World Children's Day **Obv:** Head 3/4 left **Rev:** Children standing on open book within globe **Edge:** Reeded

Date	Mintage	F	VF	XF	Unc	BU
AH1422-2001	—	—	—	—	55.00	70.00
AH1422-2001 Proof	—	Value: 90.00				

Y# 95a 250 DIRHAMS

25.0000 g., 0.9999 Gold 0.8037 oz. AGW, 37 mm. **Subject:** World Children's Day **Obv:** Head 3/4 left **Rev:** Two children standing on an open book within globe **Edge:** Reeded **Note:** Prev. Y#95.

Date	Mintage	F	VF	XF	Unc	BU
AH1422-2001 Proof	2,800	Value: 1,250				

Y# 108 250 DIRHAMS

25.0000 g., 0.9250 Silver 0.7435 oz. ASW, 37 mm. **Subject:** Mohammed VI's Inauguration 3rd Anniversary **Obv:** Head 3/4 left **Rev:** Crowned arms with supporters above value **Edge:** Reeded **Note:** Slightly different legend of Y-107

Date	Mintage	F	VF	XF	Unc	BU
AH1423-2002	—	—	—	—	55.00	70.00
AH1423-2002 Proof	—	Value: 90.00				

Y# 113 250 DIRHAMS

25.0000 g., 0.9250 Silver 0.7435 oz. ASW, 37 mm. **Subject:** Marriage of King Mohammed VI, July 12, 2002 **Obv:** Head 3/4 left **Rev:** Crown above radiant flowers **Edge:** Reeded

Date	Mintage	F	VF	XF	Unc	BU
ND (2002) Proof	—	Value: 90.00				

Y# 119 250 DIRHAMS

25.0000 g., Silver, 37 mm. **Subject:** Birth of Crown Prince Moulay Al Hassan **Obv:** Head 3/4 left **Rev:** Crowned arms with supporters above value

Date	Mintage	F	VF	XF	Unc	BU
ND(2003) Proof	—	Value: 90.00				

Y# 120 250 DIRHAMS

25.0000 g., Silver, 37 mm. **Subject:** 50th Anniversary - Kingdom **Obv:** Conjoined heads right **Rev:** Crowned arms with supporters above value

Date	Mintage	F	VF	XF	Unc	BU
AH1424-2003	—	—	—	—	55.00	70.00
AH1424-2003 Proof	—	Value: 90.00				

Y# 111 250 DIRHAMS

25.0000 g., 0.9250 Silver 0.7435 oz. ASW, 37 mm. **Subject:** Mohammed VI's Inauguration 4th Anniversary **Obv:** Head 3/4 left **Rev:** Crowned arms with supporters above value **Edge:** Reeded **Note:** Virtually identical to Y-107 and Y-108.

Date	Mintage	F	VF	XF	Unc	BU
AH1424-2003	—	—	—	—	55.00	70.00

Y# 122 250 DIRHAMS

25.0000 g., 0.9250 Silver 0.7435 oz. ASW, 37 mm. **Subject:** 5th Anniversary of Mohammed VI's Reign **Obv:** Head 3/4 left, national arms **Rev:** Crowned arms with supporters above value **Edge:** Reeded **Note:** Vitually identical to Y-107, 108 and 111.

Date	Mintage	F	VF	XF	Unc	BU
AH1425-2004	—	—	—	—	55.00	70.00

Y# 121 250 DIRHAMS

25.0000 g., Silver, 37 mm. **Subject:** Year of Handicapped Persons **Obv:** Head 3/4 left **Rev:** Stylized figures

Date	Mintage	F	VF	XF	Unc	BU
AH1425-2004	—	—	—	—	55.00	70.00

Y# 123 250 DIRHAMS

25.0000 g., Silver, 37 mm. **Subject:** 30th Anniversary - Green March **Obv:** Head 3/4 left **Rev:** Men marching left with flags aloft

Date	Mintage	F	VF	XF	Unc	BU
AH1426-2005	—	—	—	—	55.00	70.00

Y# 124 250 DIRHAMS

25.0000 g., 0.9250 Silver 0.7435 oz. ASW, 37 mm. **Subject:** 6th Anniversary of Mohammed VI's Reign **Obv:** Head 3/4 left **Rev:** Crowned arms with supporters above value **Edge:** Reeded **Note:** Virtually identical to Y-107, 108, 111 and 122

Date	Mintage	F	VF	XF	Unc	BU
AH1426-2005	—	—	—	—	55.00	70.00

Y# 125 250 DIRHAMS

25.0000 g., 0.9250 Silver 0.7435 oz. ASW, 37 mm. **Subject:** 6th Anniversary of Mohammed VI's Reign **Obv:** Head 3/4 left **Rev:** Crowned arms with supporters above value **Edge:** Reeded **Note:** Virtually identical to Y-107, 108, 111 and 122

Date	Mintage	F	VF	XF	Unc	BU
AH1427-2006	—	—	—	—	55.00	70.00

Y# 126 250 DIRHAMS

25.0000 g., 0.9250 Silver 0.7435 oz. ASW, 37 mm. **Subject:** 8th Anniversary of Mohammed VI's reign **Obv:** Head 3/4 left **Rev:** Corwned arms with supporters, value below **Edge:** Reeded

Date	Mintage	F	VF	XF	Unc	BU
AH1428/2007	—	—	—	—	55.00	70.00

Y# 127 250 DIRHAMS

25.0000 g., 0.9250 Silver 0.7435 oz. ASW, 37 mm. **Subject:** 9th Anniversary of Mohammed VI's reign **Obv:** Head 3/4 left **Rev:** Crowned arms with supporters above value **Edge:** Reeded

Date	Mintage	F	VF	XF	Unc	BU
AH1429-2008 Proof	1,000	Value: 70.00				

Y# 128 250 DIRHAMS

25.0000 g., 0.9250 Silver 0.7435 oz. ASW, 37 mm. **Subject:** 12 Centuries of Monarchy

Date	Mintage	F	VF	XF	Unc	BU
AH1429-2008 Proof	5,000	Value: 70.00				

Y# 133 250 DIRHAMS

6.4500 g., 0.9000 Gold 0.1866 oz. AGW, 21 mm. **Subject:** 12 Centuries of Monarchy

Date	Mintage	F	VF	XF	Unc	BU
AH1429-2008	3,000	Value: 350				

Y# 129 250 DIRHAMS

25.0000 g., 0.9250 Silver 0.7435 oz. ASW, 37 mm. **Subject:** 10th Anniversary of Mohammed VI's reign **Obv:** Head 3/4 left **Rev:** Crowned arms with supporters above value **Edge:** Reeded

Date	Mintage	F	VF	XF	Unc	BU
AH1430-2009 Proof	1,500	Value: 70.00				

Y# 130 250 DIRHAMS

25.0000 g., 0.9250 Silver 0.7435 oz. ASW, 37 mm. **Subject:** Central Bank, 50th Anniversary

Date	Mintage	F	VF	XF	Unc	BU
AH1430-2009 Proof	—	Value: 70.00				

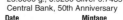

Y# 131 250 DIRHAMS
25.0000 g., 0.9250 Silver 0.7435 oz. ASW, 37 mm. **Subject:** 11th Anniversary of Mohammed VI's reign **Obv:** Head 3/4 left **Rev:** Crowned arms with supporters above value **Edge:** Reeded

Date	Mintage	F	VF	XF	Unc	BU
AH1431-2010 Proof	1,500	Value: 70.00				

Y# 132 250 DIRHAMS
25.0000 g., 0.9250 Silver 0.7435 oz. ASW, 37 mm. **Subject:** Green March, 35th Anniversary **Edge:** Reeded

Date	Mintage	F	VF	XF	Unc	BU
AH1431-2010 Proof	1,000	Value: 70.00				

KM# 135 500 DIRHAMS
Bi-Metallic **Obv:** Head left **Rev:** Building

Date	Mintage	F	VF	XF	Unc	BU
AH1430-2009 Proof	—	—	—	—	—	—

MOZAMBIQUE

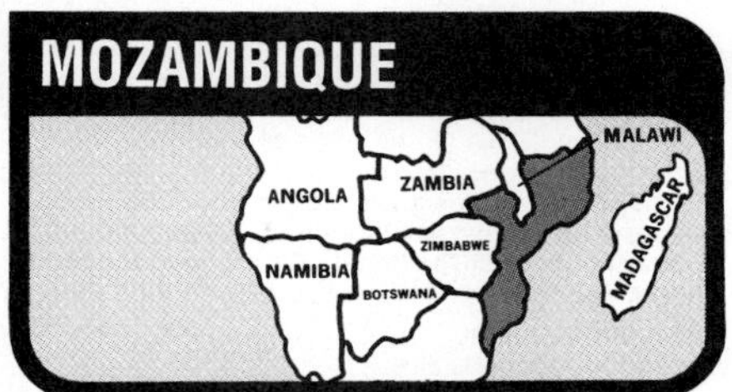

The Republic of Mozambique, a former overseas province of Portugal, stretches for 1,430 miles (2,301 km.) along the southeast coast of Africa, has an area of 302,330 sq. mi. (801,590 sq. km.) and a population of 14.1 million, 99 % of whom are native Africans of the Bantu tribes. Capital: Maputo. Agriculture is the chief industry. Cashew nuts, cotton, sugar, copra and tea are exported.

Mozambique became a member of the Commonwealth of Nations in November 1995. The President is Head of State; the Prime Minister is Head of Government.

REPUBLIC

REFORM COINAGE

100 Centavos = 1 Metical; 1994

KM# 130 1000 METICAIS
25.7100 g., 0.9800 Silver 0.8100 oz. ASW, 38.5 mm. **Subject:** Pedro De Covilha, 1498 **Obv:** National arms within circle **Rev:** Sailing ship within circle **Edge:** Reeded

Date	Mintage	F	VF	XF	Unc	BU
2003 Proof	—	Value: 45.00				

KM# 131 10000 METICAIS
8.0400 g., Bi-Metallic Stainless Steel center in Brass ring, 26.6 mm. **Obv:** National arms within circle **Rev:** Rhino within circle **Edge:** Segmented reeding

Date	Mintage	F	VF	XF	Unc	BU
2003	—	—	3.50	5.00	7.50	12.00

REFORM COINAGE

(New) Metical = 1,000 Meticals; 2005

KM# 132 CENTAVO
2.0000 g., Copper Plated Steel, 15 mm. **Obv:** Bank logo, date **Obv. Legend:** BANCO DE MOÇAMBIQUE **Rev:** Rhinoceros standing left, value **Rev. Designer:** Michael Guilfoyle **Edge:** Reeded

Date	Mintage	F	VF	XF	Unc	BU
2006	—	—	—	—	0.15	0.25

KM# 133 5 CENTAVOS
2.3000 g., Copper Plated Steel, 19 mm. **Obv:** Bank logo, date **Obv. Legend:** BANCO DE MOÇAMBIQUE **Rev:** Cheetah standing left, value **Rev. Designer:** Michael Guilfoyle **Edge:** Reeded

Date	Mintage	F	VF	XF	Unc	BU
2006	—	—	—	0.10	0.25	0.35

KM# 134 10 CENTAVOS
3.0600 g., Brass Plated Steel, 17 mm. **Obv:** Bank logo, date **Obv. Legend:** BANCO DE MOÇAMBIQUE **Rev:** Farmer cultivating with tractor, value **Rev. Designer:** Michael Guilfoyle **Edge:** Reeded

Date	Mintage	F	VF	XF	Unc	BU
2006	—	—	—	0.15	0.35	0.50

KM# 135 20 CENTAVOS
4.1000 g., Brass Plated Steel, 20 mm. **Obv:** Bank logo, date **Obv. Legend:** BANCO DE MOÇAMBIQUE **Rev:** Cotton plant, value **Rev. Designer:** Michael Guilfoyle **Edge:** Reeded

Date	Mintage	F	VF	XF	Unc	BU
2006	—	—	—	0.20	0.50	0.75

KM# 136 50 CENTAVOS
5.7400 g., Brass Plated Steel, 23 mm. **Obv:** Bank logo, date **Obv. Legend:** BANCO DE MOÇAMBIQUE **Rev:** Giant Kingfisher perched on branch, value **Rev. Designer:** Michael Guilfoyle **Edge:** Reeded

Date	Mintage	F	VF	XF	Unc	BU
2006	—	—	—	0.50	1.25	1.75

KM# 137 METICAL
5.3000 g., Nickel Plated Steel, 21 mm. **Obv:** Bank logo, date **Obv. Legend:** BANCO DE MOÇAMBIQUE **Rev:** Young woman seated left writing, value **Rev. Designer:** Michael Guilfoyle **Edge:** Plain **Shape:** 7-sided

Date	Mintage	F	VF	XF	Unc	BU
2006	—	—	—	0.45	1.10	1.50

KM# 138 2 METICAIS
6.0000 g., Nickel Plated Steel, 24 mm. **Obv:** Bank logo, date **Obv. Legend:** BANCO DE MOÇAMBIQUE **Rev:** Coelacanth fish, value **Rev. Designer:** Michael Guilfoyle **Edge:** Segmented reeding

Date	Mintage	F	VF	XF	Unc	BU
2006	—	—	—	0.75	1.80	2.50

KM# 139 5 METICAIS
6.5000 g., Nickel Plated Steel, 27 mm. **Obv:** Bank logo, date **Obv. Legend:** BANCO DE MOÇAMBIQUE **Rev:** Timbila (similar to a xylophone), value **Rev. Designer:** Michael Guilfoyle **Edge:** Reeded

Date	Mintage	F	VF	XF	Unc	BU
2006	—	—	—	1.20	3.00	4.00

KM# 140 10 METICAIS
7.5100 g., Bi-Metallic Nickel Clad Steel center in Brass ring., 24.92 mm. **Obv:** Bank logo **Obv. Legend:** BANCO • DE • MOCAMBIQUE **Rev:** Modern bank building, value below **Rev. Designer:** Michael Guilfoyle **Edge:** Reeded

Date	Mintage	F	VF	XF	Unc	BU
2006	—	—	—	1.50	3.75	5.00

NAGORNO-KARABAKH

Nagorno-Karabakh, an ethnically Armenian enclave inside Azerbaijan (pop., 1991 est.: 193,000), SW region. It occupies an area of 1,700 sq mi (4,400 square km) on the NE flank of the Karabakh Mountain Range, with the capital city of Stepanakert.

Russia annexed the area from Persia in 1813, and in 1923 it was established as an autonomous province of the Azerbaijan S.S.R. In 1988 the region's ethnic Armenian majority demonstrated against Azerbaijani rule, and in 1991, after the breakup of the U.S.S.R. brought independence to Armenia and Azerbaijan, war broke out between the two ethnic groups. On January 8, 1992 the leaders of Nagorno-Karabakh declared independence as the Republic of Mountainous Karabakh (RMK). Since 1994, following a cease-fire, ethnic Armenians have held Karabakh, though officially it remains part of Azerbaijan. Karabakh remains sovereign, but the political and military condition is volatile and tensions frequently flare into skirmishes.

Its marvelous nature and geographic situation, have all facilitated Karabakh to be a center of science, poetry and, especially, of the musical culture of Azerbaijan.

MONETARY SYSTEM

100 Luma = 1 Dram

REPUBLIC

STANDARD COINAGE

KM# 6 50 LUMA
0.9500 g., Aluminum, 19.8 mm. **Obv:** National arms **Rev:** Horse cantering left **Edge:** Plain

Date	Mintage	F	VF	XF	Unc	BU
2004	—	—	—	—	1.00	1.25

KM# 7 50 LUMA
0.9500 g., Aluminum, 19.8 mm. **Obv:** National arms **Rev:** Gazelle **Edge:** Plain

Date	Mintage	F	VF	XF	Unc	BU
2004	—	—	—	—	1.00	1.25

KM# 8 DRAM
1.1300 g., Aluminum, 21.7 mm. **Obv:** National arms **Rev:** Pheasant **Edge:** Plain

Date	Mintage	F	VF	XF	Unc	BU
2004	—	—	—	—	1.00	1.25

KM# 9 DRAM
1.1200 g., Aluminum, 21.7 mm. **Obv:** National arms **Rev:** 1/2-length Saint facing **Edge:** Plain

Date	Mintage	F	VF	XF	Unc	BU
2004	—	—	—	—	1.25	1.50

KM# 10 DRAM
1.1300 g., Aluminum, 21.7 mm. **Obv:** National arms **Rev:** Cheetah facing **Edge:** Plain

Date	Mintage	F	VF	XF	Unc	BU
2004	—	—	—	—	1.00	1.25

KM# 11 5 DRAMS
4.4000 g., Brass, 21.8 mm. **Obv:** National arms **Rev:** Church **Edge:** Plain

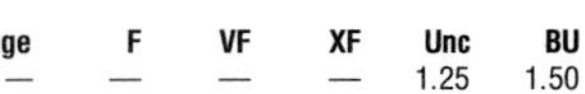

Date	Mintage	F	VF	XF	Unc	BU
2004	—	—	—	—	1.25	1.50

KM# 12 5 DRAMS
4.5000 g., Brass, 21.8 mm. **Obv:** National arms **Rev:** Monument faces **Edge:** Plain

Date	Mintage	F	VF	XF	Unc	BU
2004	—	—	—	—	1.00	1.25

KM# 23 1000 DRAMS
31.4300 g., 0.9990 Silver 1.0094 oz. ASW, 38.9 mm. **Obv:** National arms **Rev:** Archer **Edge:** Plain

Date	Mintage	F	VF	XF	Unc	BU
2003 Proof	—	Value: 75.00				

KM# 24 1000 DRAMS
31.3300 g., 0.9990 Silver 1.0062 oz. ASW, 38.39 mm. **Series:** Armenian architectural sculpture **Obv:** National arms **Rev:** Church of the Holy Cross at Aghthamar, Turkey **Edge:** Plain

Date	Mintage	F	VF	XF	Unc	BU
2003 Proof	—	Value: 75.00				

KM# 25 1000 DRAMS
31.3000 g., 0.9990 Silver 1.0053 oz. ASW, 38.92 mm. **Obv:** National arms **Rev:** Bust of Kevork Chavoush 3/4 left **Edge:** Plain

Date	Mintage	F	VF	XF	Unc	BU
2004 Proof	—	Value: 75.00				

KM# 19 1000 DRAMS
31.3700 g., 0.9990 Silver 1.0075 oz. ASW, 38.9 mm. **Obv:** National arms **Rev:** Leopard head facing **Edge:** Plain

Date	Mintage	F	VF	XF	Unc	BU
2004 Proof	—	Value: 65.00				

KM# 19a 1000 DRAMS
31.3700 g., 0.9990 Silver Gilt 1.0075 oz. ASW, 38.9 mm. **Obv:** National arms **Rev:** Leopard head facing **Edge:** Plain

Date	Mintage	F	VF	XF	Unc	BU
2004 Proof	—	Value: 75.00				

KM# 20 1000 DRAMS
31.3700 g., 0.9990 Silver 1.0075 oz. ASW, 38.9 mm. **Obv:** National arms **Rev:** Standing Brown Bear **Edge:** Plain

Date	Mintage	F	VF	XF	Unc	BU
2004 Proof	—	Value: 75.00				

KM# 20a 1000 DRAMS
31.3700 g., 0.9990 Silver Gilt 1.0075 oz. ASW, 38.9 mm. **Obv:** National arms **Rev:** Standing Brown Bear **Edge:** Plain

Date	Mintage	F	VF	XF	Unc	BU
2004 Proof	—	Value: 85.00				

KM# 21 1000 DRAMS
31.3700 g., 0.9990 Silver 1.0075 oz. ASW, 38.9 mm. **Obv:** National arms **Rev:** Eagle head within circle **Edge:** Plain

Date	Mintage	F	VF	XF	Unc	BU
2004 Proof	—	Value: 75.00				

KM# 21a 1000 DRAMS
31.3700 g., 0.9990 Silver Gilt 1.0075 oz. ASW, 38.9 mm. **Obv:** National arms **Rev:** Eagle head within circle **Edge:** Plain

Date	Mintage	F	VF	XF	Unc	BU
2004 Proof	—	Value: 85.00				

KM# 22 1000 DRAMS
31.1200 g., 0.9990 Silver 0.9995 oz. ASW, 38.9 mm. **Obv:** National arms **Rev:** 1918 Genocide Victims Monument **Edge:** Plain

Date	Mintage	F	VF	XF	Unc	BU
2004 Proof	—	Value: 65.00				

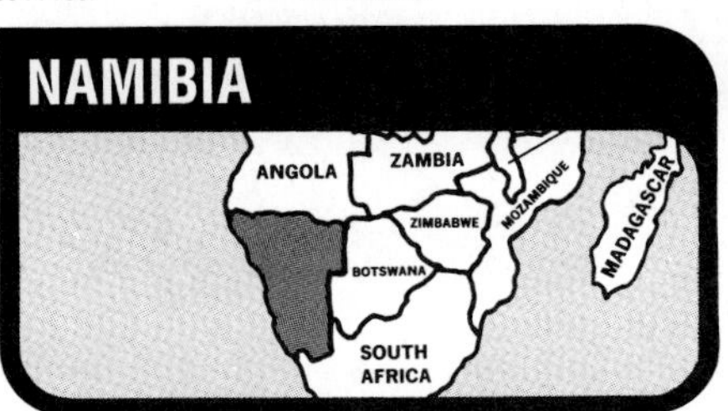

The Republic of Namibia, once the German colonial territory of German South West Africa, and later South West Africa, is situated on the Atlantic coast of southern Africa, bounded on the north by Angola, on the east by Botswana, and on the south by South Africa. It has an area of 318,261 sq. mi. (824,290 sq. km.) and a population of *1.4 million. Capital: Windhoek. Diamonds, copper, lead, zinc, and cattle are exported.

On June 17, 1985 the Transitional Government of National Unity was installed. Negotiations were held in 1988 between Angola, Cuba, and South Africa reaching a peaceful settlement on Aug. 5, 1988. By April 1989 Cuban troops were to withdraw from Angola and South African troops from Namibia. The Transitional Government resigned on Feb. 28, 1988 for the upcoming elections of the constituent assembly in Nov. 1989. Independence was finally achieved on March 12, 1990 within the Commonwealth of Nations. The President is the Head of State; the Prime Minister is Head of Government.

MONETARY SYSTEM
100 Cents = 1 Namibia Dollar

REPUBLIC

1990 - present

DECIMAL COINAGE

KM# 1 5 CENTS
2.2000 g., Nickel Plated Steel, 17 mm. **Obv:** National arms **Rev:** Value left, aloe plant within 3/4 sun design

Date	Mintage	F	VF	XF	Unc	BU
2002	—	—	—	0.20	0.50	0.75
2007	—	—	—	0.20	0.50	0.75
2009	—	—	—	0.20	0.50	0.75

KM# 2 10 CENTS
3.4000 g., Nickel Plated Steel, 21.5 mm. **Obv:** National arms **Rev:** Camelthorn tree right, partial sun design left, value below

Date	Mintage	F	VF	XF	Unc	BU
2002	—	—	—	0.35	1.00	1.25

KM# 3 50 CENTS
4.4300 g., Nickel Plated Steel, 24 mm. **Obv:** National arms **Rev:** Quiver tree right, partial sun design upper left, value below

Date	Mintage	F	VF	XF	Unc	BU
2008	—	—	—	—	1.75	2.00

KM# 4 DOLLAR
5.0000 g., Brass, 22.4 mm. **Obv:** National arms **Rev:** Value divides Bateleur eagle at right, partial sun design at left

Date	Mintage	F	VF	XF	Unc	BU
2002	—	—	—	1.25	3.50	6.00
2006	—	—	—	1.25	3.50	6.00

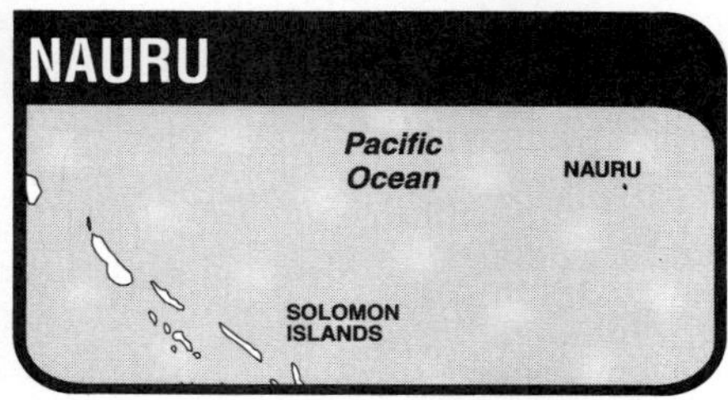

The Republic of Nauru, formerly Pleasant Island, is an island republic in the western Pacific Ocean west of the Gilbert Islands. It has an area of 8-1/2 sq. mi. and a population of 7,254. It is known for its phosphate deposits. Nauru is a special member of the Commonwealth of Nations.

RULER
British, until 1968

MONETARY SYSTEM
100 Cents = 1 (Australian) Dollar

REPUBLIC

DECIMAL COINAGE

KM# 38 DOLLAR
27.0000 g., Silver Plated Copper, 38.6 mm. **Subject:** Guardian Angel **Obv:** Arms **Rev:** Angel standing, swarovski crystals in hair

Date	Mintage	F	VF	XF	Unc	BU
2009 Proof	10,000	Value: 35.00				

KM# 36 5 DOLLARS
0.5000 g., 0.9990 Gold 0.0161 oz. AGW, 11 mm. **Subject:** Kaiser Wilhelm **Obv:** Arms **Rev:** Bust right

Date	Mintage	F	VF	XF	Unc	BU
2008 Proof	—	Value: 65.00				

KM# 37 5 DOLLARS
0.5000 g., 0.9990 Gold 0.0161 oz. AGW, 11 mm. **Subject:** Christmas **Obv:** Arms **Rev:** Bells ringing

Date	Mintage	F	VF	XF	Unc	BU
2008 Proof	—	Value: 65.00				

KM# 39 5 DOLLARS
0.5000 g., 0.9990 Gold 0.0161 oz. AGW **Issuer:** 11 **Subject:** Christmas **Obv:** Arms **Rev:** Teddy bear seated

Date	Mintage	F	VF	XF	Unc	BU
2009 Proof	—	Value: 55.00				

KM# 18 10 DOLLARS
31.1000 g., 0.9990 Silver 0.9988 oz. ASW **Subject:** Discontinuation of the German Mark **Obv:** National arms **Obv. Legend:** BANK OF NAURU

Date	Mintage	F	VF	XF	Unc	BU
2001 Proof	—	Value: 80.00				

KM# 13 10 DOLLARS
31.2500 g., 0.9990 Silver 71.5 x 72 1.0037 oz. ASW, 72 mm. **Subject:** First Euro Coinage **Obv:** National arms, matte finish **Rev:** Denomination, inscription and partially gold-plated 1 Euro reverse coin design, Proof finish **Edge:** Plain **Shape:** Like a map

Date	Mintage	F	VF	XF	Unc	BU
2002 Proof	—	Value: 80.00				

KM# 15 10 DOLLARS
31.1000 g., 0.9990 Silver 0.9988 oz. ASW, 40 mm. **Series:** Save the Whales **Obv:** National arms **Obv. Legend:** BANK OF NAURU **Rev:** Blue Whale on mother-of-pearl insert **Edge:** Plain

Date	Mintage	F	VF	XF	Unc	BU
2002 Proof	2,000	Value: 85.00				

KM# 14 10 DOLLARS
34.6000 g., 0.9250 Silver with gold plated or gold attachment 1.0289 oz. ASW, 38.5 mm. **Subject:** Brandenburg Gate **Obv:** National arms **Rev:** Brandenburg Gate **Edge:** Plain **Note:** Gold color 1mm thick

Date	Mintage	F	VF	XF	Unc	BU
2002 Proof/Matte	—	Value: 150				

KM# 19 10 DOLLARS
31.1000 g., 0.9990 Silver 0.9988 oz. ASW **Subject:** European Union - Mark and Euro **Obv:** National arms **Obv. Legend:** BANK OF NAURU

Date	Mintage	F	VF	XF	Unc	BU
2003 Proof	5,000	Value: 75.00				

KM# 20 10 DOLLARS
1.2400 g., 0.9990 Gold 0.0398 oz. AGW, 13.92 mm. **Subject:** First Anniversary of the Euro **Obv:** National arms **Obv. Legend:** BANK OF NAURU **Rev:** Euro symbol **Edge:** Reeded

Date	Mintage	F	VF	XF	Unc	BU
2003 Proof	—	Value: 75.00				

KM# 21 10 DOLLARS
1.2400 g., 0.9990 Gold 0.0398 oz. AGW **Subject:** Treasure of Priamos in Troja **Obv:** National arms **Obv. Legend:** BANK OF NAURU

Date	Mintage	F	VF	XF	Unc	BU
2003 Proof	—	Value: 85.00				

KM# 22 10 DOLLARS
1.2400 g., 0.9990 Gold 0.0398 oz. AGW **Subject:** Treasure of Nibelungen **Obv:** National arms **Obv. Legend:** BANK OF NAURU

Date	Mintage	F	VF	XF	Unc	BU
2003 Proof	—	Value: 85.00				

KM# 23 10 DOLLARS
30.9500 g., Silver With removable gold or gilt 2.6g Reichstag building attachment with 2004/ NAURU 0077 on reverse **Subject:** European Monuments **Obv:** National arms **Obv. Legend:** BANK OF NAURU **Rev. Legend:** GERMANY - DEUTSCHER REICHSTAG **Edge:** Plain

Date	Mintage	F	VF	XF	Unc	BU
2003 Proof/Matte	—	Value: 150				

KM# 24 10 DOLLARS
Silver With removable gold or gilt attachment **Series:** European Monuments **Subject:** Palazzo Pubblico in San Marino **Obv:** National arms **Obv. Legend:** BANK OF NAURU **Edge:** Plain

Date	Mintage	F	VF	XF	Unc	BU
2005 Proof/Matte	—	Value: 150				

KM# 25 10 DOLLARS
1.2400 g., 0.9990 Gold 0.0398 oz. AGW **Subject:** East Gothic stylized eagle broach from Domagnano, Italy in National Museum in Nuremburg **Obv:** National arms **Obv. Legend:** BANK OF NAURU

Date	Mintage	F	VF	XF	Unc	BU
2005 Proof	25,000	Value: 85.00				

KM# 35 10 DOLLARS
31.1050 g., 0.9990 Silver 0.9990 oz. ASW **Subject:** German Railways, 150th Anniversary **Obv:** National Arms **Rev:** Baureihi "01"

Date	Mintage	F	VF	XF	Unc	BU
2005 Proof	—	Value: 60.00				

KM# 40 10 DOLLARS
1.2400 g., 0.9990 Gold 0.0398 oz. AGW, 13.92 mm. **Obv:** National Arms **Rev:** Ludwig Erhard

Date	Mintage	F	VF	XF	Unc	BU
2005 Proof	—	Value: 85.00				

KM# 26 10 DOLLARS
1.2400 g., 0.9990 Gold 0.0398 oz. AGW **Subject:** Angela Dorothea Merkel, Chancellor of Germany **Obv:** National arms **Obv. Legend:** BANK OF NAURU

Date	Mintage	F	VF	XF	Unc	BU
2005 Proof	—	Value: 85.00				

KM# 41 10 DOLLARS
31.1000 g., 0.9990 Silver 0.9988 oz. ASW, 38.61 mm. **Rev:** Tower Bridge, gilt

Date	Mintage	F	VF	XF	Unc	BU
2005	2,000	Value: 200				

KM# 27 10 DOLLARS
1.2400 g., 0.9990 Gold 0.0398 oz. AGW **Subject:** Konrad Adenauer at 1949 demonstration **Obv:** National arms **Obv. Legend:** BANK OF NAURU

Date	Mintage	F	VF	XF	Unc	BU
2006 Proof	15,000	Value: 85.00				

KM# 28 10 DOLLARS
1.2400 g., 0.9990 Gold 0.0398 oz. AGW **Subject:** Volkswagen **Obv:** National arms **Obv. Legend:** BANK OF NAURU

Date	Mintage	F	VF	XF	Unc	BU
2006 Proof	—	Value: 85.00				

KM# 29 10 DOLLARS
1.2400 g., 0.9990 Gold 0.0398 oz. AGW **Subject:** Conrad Schumann in Berlin 1961 **Obv:** National arms **Obv. Legend:** BANK OF NAURU

Date	Mintage	F	VF	XF	Unc	BU
2006 Proof	—	Value: 85.00				

KM# 30 10 DOLLARS
1.2400 g., 0.9990 Gold 0.0398 oz. AGW **Subject:** Olympic Stadium in Munich 1972 **Obv:** National arms **Obv. Legend:** BANK OF NAURU

Date	Mintage	F	VF	XF	Unc	BU
2006 Proof	—	Value: 85.00				

KM# 31 10 DOLLARS
1.2400 g., 0.9990 Gold 0.0398 oz. AGW **Subject:** Independent Activists 1980 **Obv:** National arms **Obv. Legend:** BANK OF NAURU

Date	Mintage	F	VF	XF	Unc	BU
2006 Proof	—	Value: 85.00				

KM# 32 10 DOLLARS
1.2400 g., 0.9990 Gold 0.0398 oz. AGW **Subject:** Brandenburg Gate in Berlin 1990 **Obv. Legend:** BANK OF NAURU

Date	Mintage	F	VF	XF	Unc	BU
2006 Proof	—	Value: 85.00				

KM# 33 10 DOLLARS
1.2400 g., 0.9990 Gold 0.0398 oz. AGW **Subject:** European Union 2002 **Obv:** National arms **Obv. Legend:** BANK OF NAURU

Date	Mintage	F	VF	XF	Unc	BU
2006 Proof	—	Value: 85.00				

KM# 34 10 DOLLARS
1.2400 g., 0.9990 Gold 0.0398 oz. AGW **Subject:** Johannes Rau, German President, 1999-2004 **Obv:** National arms **Obv. Legend:** BANK OF NAURU

Date	Mintage	F	VF	XF	Unc	BU
2006 Proof	—	Value: 85.00				

KM# 42 10 DOLLARS
31.1000 g., 0.9990 Silver 0.9988 oz. ASW, 38.61 mm. **Rev:** Tower of Pisa, gilt

Date	Mintage	F	VF	XF	Unc	BU
2006 Proof	2,000	Value: 200				

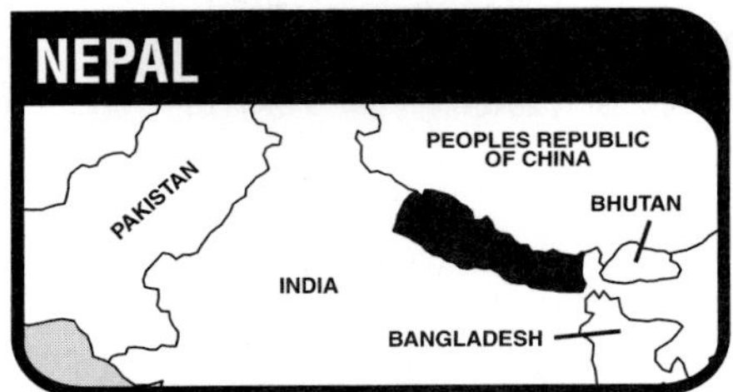

The Kingdom of Nepal, the world's only surviving Hindu kingdom, is a landlocked country occupying the southern slopes of the Himalayas. It has an area of 56,136 sq. mi. (140,800 sq. km.) and a population of 18 million. Capital: Kathmandu. Nepal has deposits of coal, copper, iron and cobalt, but they are largely unexploited. Agriculture is the principal economic activity. Rice, timber and jute are exported, with tourism being the other major foreign exchange earner.

On June 2, 2001 tragedy struck the royal family when Crown Prince Dipendra used an assault rifle to kill his father, mother and other members of the royal family as the result of a dispute over his current lady friend. He died 48 hours later, as King, from self inflicted gunshot wounds. Gyanendra began his second reign as King (his first was a short time as a toddler, 1950-51).

DATING

Bikram Samvat Era (VS)

From 1888AD most copper coins were dated in the Bikram Samvat (VS) era. To convert take VS date - 57 =AD date. Coins with this era have VS before the year in the listing. Tthis era is used for all coins struck in Nepal since 1911AD.

RULER

SHAH DYNASTY

ज्ञानेन्द्र वीर विक्रम

Gyanendra Bir Bikram
VS2058-/2001-AD

NUMERALS

Nepal has used more variations of numerals on their coins than any other nation. The most common are illustrated in the numeral chart in the introduction. The chart below illustrates some variations encompassing the last four centuries.

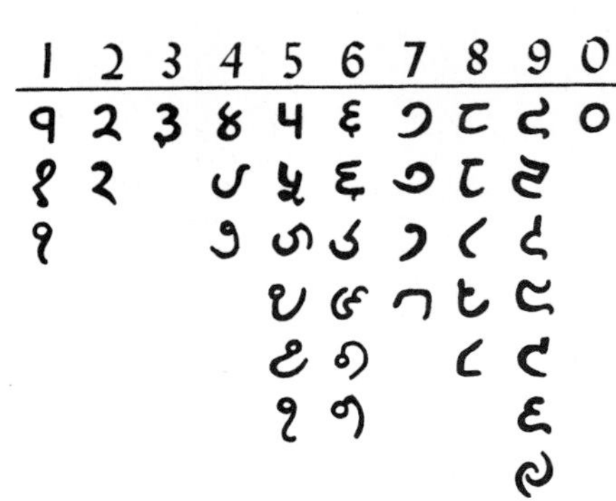

NUMERICS

One	एक
Two	दुइ
Ten	दसा
Twenty-five	पचीसा
Fifty	पचासा
Hundred	सय

DENOMINATIONS

Rupee	रुपैयाँ

Legend on reverse

श्री श्री श्री गोरषनाथ

Shri Shri Shri Gorakhanatha in 8 petals

KINGDOM

Gyanendra Bir Bikram
VS2058-2064 / 2001- 2007AD

DECIMAL COINAGE

100 Paisa = 1 Rupee

KM# 1173 10 PAISA
Aluminum, 17 mm. **Obv:** Royal crown **Edge:** Plain

Date	Mintage	F	VF	XF	Unc	BU
VS2058 (2001)	—	—	—	—	1.00	1.50

KM# 1148 25 PAISA
Aluminum, 20 mm. **Obv:** Royal crown **Edge:** Plain

Date	Mintage	F	VF	XF	Unc	BU
VS2058 (2001)	—	—	—	—	0.50	0.75
VS2059 (2002)	—	—	—	—	0.50	0.75
VS2060 (2003)	—	—	—	—	0.50	0.75

KM# 1149 50 PAISA
Aluminum, 22.5 mm. **Obv:** Royal crown **Rev:** Swayambhunath **Edge:** Plain

Date	Mintage	F	VF	XF	Unc	BU
VS2058 (2001)	—	—	—	—	0.50	0.75
VS2059 (2002)	—	—	—	—	0.50	0.75

KM# 1179 50 PAISA
1.4100 g., Aluminum, 22.5 mm. **Obv:** Crown above crossed flags **Rev:** Swayambhunath **Edge:** Plain

Date	Mintage	F	VF	XF	Unc	BU
VS2060 (2003)	—	—	—	—	0.40	0.50
VS2061 (2004)	—	—	—	—	0.40	0.50

KM# 1150.2 RUPEE
Brass Plated Steel **Obv:** Traditional design **Rev:** Small (7mm high) temple, small (4mm) "1" **Edge:** Plain **Note:** Magnetic.

Date	Mintage	F	VF	XF	Unc	BU
VS2058 (2001)	—	—	—	—	1.00	1.50
VS2059 (2002)	—	—	—	—	1.00	1.50
VS2060 (2003)	—	—	—	—	1.00	1.50

KM# 1150.1 RUPEE
Brass Plated Steel **Rev:** Large (8.5mm) temple, medium '1' (4.5mm) **Edge:** Reeded **Note:** Non-magnetic.

Date	Mintage	F	VF	XF	Unc	BU
VS2058 (2001)	—	—	—	—	1.00	1.50

KM# 1150.3 RUPEE
3.9600 g., Brass, 20 mm. **Obv:** Traditional design **Rev:** Small (6.5mm high) temple, small (4mm) "1" **Edge:** Plain

Date	Mintage	F	VF	XF	Unc	BU
VS2058 (2001)	—	—	—	—	0.50	0.75

KM# 1150.4 RUPEE
3.9600 g., Brass Plated Steel, 20 mm. **Obv:** Traditional design **Rev:** Small (7mm high) temple, large (4.5mm) "1" **Note:** Magnetic.

Date	Mintage	F	VF	XF	Unc	BU
VS2059 (2002)	—	—	—	—	1.00	1.50
VS2060 (2003)	—	—	—	—	1.00	1.50

KM# 1180 RUPEE
3.9600 g., Brass Plated Steel, 20 mm. **Obv:** Traditional design **Rev:** Wagheshwari Temple **Edge:** Plain **Note:** "1" in denomination of a different style.

Date	Mintage	F	VF	XF	Unc	BU
VS2061 (2004)	—	—	—	—	0.75	1.00

KM# 1181 RUPEE
3.9400 g., Brass Plated Steel, 19.95 mm. **Obv:** Traditional design **Rev:** Sri Talbarahi Temple with outline mountain scene behind **Edge:** Plain

Date	Mintage	F	VF	XF	Unc	BU
VS2062(2005)	—	—	—	0.50	1.20	1.60

KM# 1170 2 RUPEES
4.9400 g., Brass, 25 mm. **Obv:** Traditional square design **Rev:** People with flag celebrating 50 Years of Democracy **Edge:** Plain

Date	Mintage	F	VF	XF	Unc	BU
VS2058(2001)	—	—	—	—	0.50	0.75

KM# 1151.2 2 RUPEES
Brass, 25 mm. **Obv:** Traditional design **Rev:** Three domed building **Edge:** Plain

Date	Mintage	F	VF	XF	Unc	BU
VS2058 (2001)	—	—	—	—	1.50	2.00
VS2059 (2002)	—	—	—	—	1.50	2.00
VS2060 (2003)	—	—	—	—	1.50	2.00

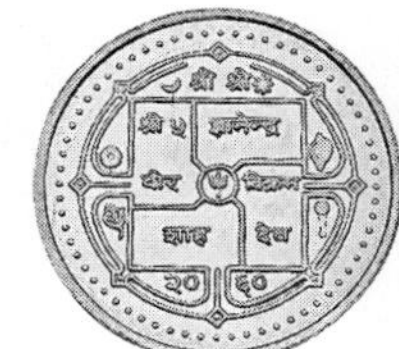

KM# 1151.1 2 RUPEES
5.0700 g., Brass Plated Steel, 25 mm. **Obv:** Traditional design **Rev:** Three domed building **Edge:** Plain **Note:** Edge varieties exist. Prev. KM#1151. Magnetic.

Date	Mintage	F	VF	XF	Unc	BU
VS2060 (2003)	—	—	—	—	1.50	2.00

KM# 1151.1a 2 RUPEES
6.7000 g., Silver, 25 mm. **Obv:** Traditional design **Rev:** Three domed building **Edge:** Plain

Date	Mintage	F	VF	XF	Unc	BU
VS2060(2003)	—	—	—	—	100	—

KM# 1159 25 RUPEE
8.3600 g., Copper-Nickel, 29.1 mm. **Obv:** Crowned bust right **Rev:** Traditional design **Edge:** Plain

Date	Mintage	F	VF	XF	Unc	BU
VS2058 (2001)	—	—	—	—	4.00	5.00
VS2059 (2002)	—	—	—	—	4.00	5.00

KM# 1164 25 RUPEE
8.6000 g., Copper-Nickel, 29.1 mm. **Subject:** Silver Jubilee **Obv:** Traditional design **Rev:** Stylized face design **Edge:** Plain

Date	Mintage	F	VF	XF	Unc	BU
VS2060 (2003)	—	—	—	—	4.00	5.00

KM# 1183 25 RUPEE
8.5500 g., Copper-Nickel, 29.1 mm. **Subject:** World Hindu Federation **Obv:** Traditional design **Edge:** Plain

Date	Mintage	F	VF	XF	Unc	BU
VS2062 (2005)	—	—	—	—	4.00	5.00

KM# 1160 50 RUPEE
20.1000 g., Brass, 37.7 mm. **Subject:** 50th Anniversary of Scouting in Nepal **Obv:** Traditional design **Rev:** Scouting emblem within beaded wreath **Edge:** Plain

Date	Mintage	F	VF	XF	Unc	BU
VS2059 (2002)	—	—	—	—	9.00	10.00

KM# 1182 50 RUPEE
8.6000 g., Copper-Nickel, 29 mm. **Subject:** Golden Jubilee of Supreme Court **Obv:** Traditional design **Rev:** Supreme Court building **Edge:** Plain

Date	Mintage	F	VF	XF	Unc	BU
VS2063 (2006)	—	—	—	—	6.00	9.00

KM# 1157 100 RUPEE
20.0000 g., Brass, 38.7 mm. **Subject:** Buddha **Obv:** Traditional design **Rev:** Seated Buddha teaching five seated monks **Edge:** Reeded

Date	Mintage	F	VF	XF	Unc	BU
VS2058 (2001)	30,000	—	—	—	10.00	12.00

KM# 1162 200 RUPEE
18.1000 g., 0.5000 Silver 0.2910 oz. ASW, 29.6 mm. **Subject:** 50th Anniversary of Civil Service **Obv:** Traditional design **Rev:** Crown above flags and value **Edge:** Plain

Date	Mintage	F	VF	XF	Unc	BU
VS2058 (2001)	—	—	—	—	20.00	25.00

KM# 1161 200 RUPEE
18.1000 g., 0.5000 Silver 0.2910 oz. ASW, 29.6 mm. **Subject:** 50th Anniversary of the Nepal Chamber of Commerce **Obv:** Traditional design **Rev:** Swastika within rotary gear **Edge:** Plain

Date	Mintage	F	VF	XF	Unc	BU
VS2059 (2002)	—	—	—	—	20.00	25.00

KM# 1171 250 RUPEE
18.0000 g., 0.5000 Silver 0.2893 oz. ASW, 29 mm. **Subject:** 2600th Anniversary of Bhagawan Mahavir **Obv:** Traditional design **Rev:** Haloed head above value **Edge:** Plain

Date	Mintage	F	VF	XF	Unc	BU
VS2058 (2001)	—	—	—	—	25.00	30.00

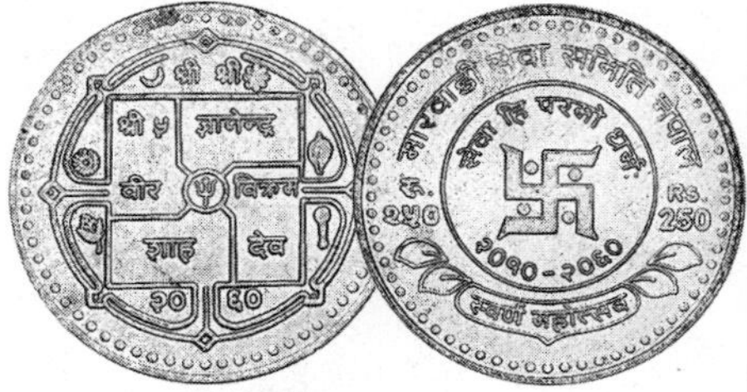

KM# 1176 250 RUPEE
17.8300 g., 0.5000 Silver 0.2866 oz. ASW, 31.6 mm. **Subject:** Marwadi, non-profit making organization **Obv:** Traditional design **Rev:** Swastika within circle **Edge:** Reeded

Date	Mintage	F	VF	XF	Unc	BU
VS2060 (2003)	—	—	—	—	25.00	30.00

KM# 1184 250 RUPEE
18.0000 g., Silver, 32 mm. **Subject:** 400th Anniversary of Guru Granth Sahib **Obv:** Traditional design **Rev:** Holy Book of Sikhs **Edge:** Reeded

Date	Mintage	F	VF	XF	Unc	BU
VS2061 (2004)	—	—	—	—	25.00	30.00

KM# 1174 300 RUPEE
22.5000 g., 0.5000 Silver 0.3617 oz. ASW, 31.8 mm. **Subject:** Economic Growth Through Export **Obv:** Traditional design **Rev:** Two joined hands in front of globe **Edge:** Reeded

Date	Mintage	F	VF	XF	Unc	BU
VS2060 (2003)	—	—	—	—	22.00	28.00

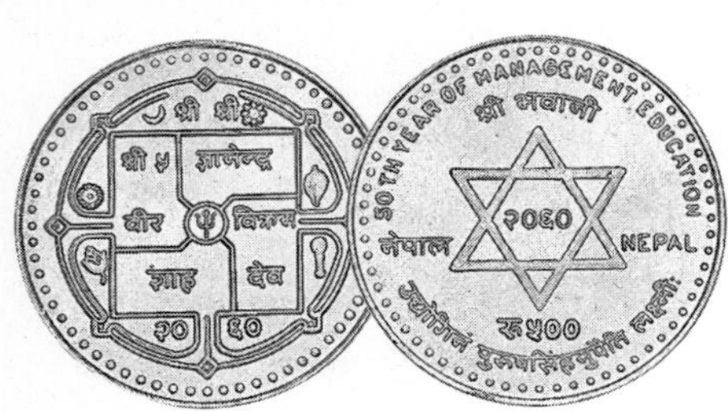

KM# 1177 500 RUPEE
23.0000 g., 0.9000 Silver 0.6655 oz. ASW, 31.7 mm. **Subject:** Management Education 50th Anniversary **Obv:** Traditional design **Rev:** Six point star outline **Edge:** Reeded

Date	Mintage	F	VF	XF	Unc	BU
VS2060 (2003)	—	—	—	—	30.00	35.00

KM# 1163 500 RUPEE
23.3400 g., 0.9000 Silver 0.6753 oz. ASW, 32 mm. **Subject:** 50th Anniversary of the Conquest of Mt. Everest **Obv:** Traditional design **Rev:** Mountain and map above value **Edge:** Reeded

Date	Mintage	F	VF	XF	Unc	BU
VS2060 (2003)	—	—	—	—	30.00	35.00

KM# 1185 500 RUPEE
20.1000 g., Silver, 32 mm. **Subject:** 50th Anniversary of Nepal-United Nations **Obv:** Traditional design **Rev:** Head of the late King Mahendra Bir Birkam **Edge:** Reeded

Date	Mintage	F	VF	XF	Unc	BU
VS2062	—	—	—	—	25.00	30.00

KM# 1175 1000 RUPEE
35.0000 g., Silver, 40 mm. **Subject:** 100 Years - Rotary Club **Edge:** Reeded

Date	Mintage	F	VF	XF	Unc	BU
VS2062 (2005)	—	—	—	—	45.00	50.00

KM# 1178 1000 RUPEE
35.2000 g., 0.5000 Silver 0.5658 oz. ASW, 40 mm. **Subject:** Rastriya Bank 50th Anniversary **Obv:** Traditional square design **Rev:** Bank seal above value **Edge:** Reeded

Date	Mintage	F	VF	XF	Unc	BU
VS2062 (2005)	—	—	—	—	25.00	30.00

KM# 1158 1500 RUPEE
20.0000 g., 0.9250 Silver 0.5948 oz. ASW, 38.7 mm. **Subject:** Buddha **Obv:** Traditional design **Rev:** Seated Buddha teaching five seated monks **Edge:** Reeded

Date	Mintage	F	VF	XF	Unc	BU
VS2058 (2001) Proof	15,000	Value: 32.50				

KM# 1172 2000 RUPEE
31.2000 g., 0.7200 Silver 0.7222 oz. ASW, 40 mm. **Subject:** Gyanendra's Accession to the Throne **Obv:** Crowned bust right **Rev:** Upright sword above value in circular design **Edge:** Reeded

Date	Mintage	F	VF	XF	Unc	BU
VS2058 (2001)	—	—	—	—	40.00	45.00

KM# 1201 2000 RUPEE
31.1050 g., 0.9990 Silver 0.9990 oz. ASW, 40 mm. **Subject:** Conquest of Mt. Everest 50th Anniversary **Rev:** Sir Edmond Hillary and Tenzing Norgay at Summit

Date	Mintage	F	VF	XF	Unc	BU
VS2061 (2003) Proof	8,000	Value: 80.00				

KM# 1191 2000 RUPEE
31.2000 g., 0.9250 Silver 0.9278 oz. ASW, 38.61 mm. **Subject:** 2006 FIFA World Cup - Germany **Obv:** Traditional design

Date	Mintage	F	VF	XF	Unc	BU
VS2063 (2006) (2006)	—	—	—	—	45.00	50.00

ASARFI GOLD COINAGE

(Asarphi)

Fractional designations are approximate for this series. Actual Gold Weight (AGW) is used to identify each type.

KM# 1200 ASARPHI
7.7700 g., 0.9999 Gold 0.2498 oz. AGW, 22 mm. **Subject:** Conquest of Mt. Everest **Rev:** Sir Edward Hillary and Tenzing Norgay at Summit

Date	Mintage	F	VF	XF	Unc	BU
VS2060 (2003)	2,000	—	—	—	800	—

KM# 1153 0.3G ASARPHI
0.3000 g., 0.9999 Gold 0.0096 oz. AGW, 7 mm. **Subject:** Buddha **Obv:** Traditional design **Rev:** Seated Buddha **Edge:** Plain

Date	Mintage	VG	F	VF	XF	BU
VS2058 (2001)	30,000	—	—	—	—	20.00

KM# 1154 1/25-OZ. ASARFI
1.2441 g., 0.9999 Gold 0.0400 oz. AGW, 13.92 mm. **Subject:** Buddha **Obv:** Traditional design **Rev:** Seated Buddha **Edge:** Reeded

Date	Mintage	VG	F	VF	XF	BU
VS2058 (2001)	25,000	—	—	—	—	65.00

KM# 1155 1/10-OZ. ASARFI
3.1104 g., 0.9999 Gold 0.1000 oz. AGW, 17.95 mm. **Subject:** Buddha **Obv:** Traditional design **Rev:** Seated Buddha **Edge:** Reeded

Date	Mintage	VG	F	VF	XF	BU
VS2058 (2001)	15,000	—	—	—	—	150

KM# 1156 1/2-OZ. ASARFI
15.5518 g., 0.9999 Gold 0.4999 oz. AGW, 27 mm. **Subject:** Buddha **Obv:** Traditional design **Rev:** Seated Buddha **Edge:** Reeded

Date	Mintage	VG	F	VF	XF	BU
VS2058 (2001) Proof	2,500	Value: 750				

SECULAR STATE

Gyanendra Bir Bikram

VS2058-2064 / 2001- 2007AD

DECIMAL COINAGE

100 Paisa = 1 Rupee

KM# 1186 25 RUPEE
8.5000 g., Copper-Nickel, 29 mm. **Subject:** 125th Anniversary - First Nepal Postal Stamp Issue **Obv:** Features image of legendary 1 Anna stamp **Rev:** Traditional mailman on the reverse

Date	Mintage	F	VF	XF	Unc	BU
VS2063 (2006)	—	—	—	—	7.00	9.00
VS2064 (2006)	—	—	—	—	7.00	9.00

DEMOCRATIC REPUBLIC

DECIMAL COINAGE

100 Paisa = 1 Rupee

KM# 1204 RUPEE
Brass Plated Steel, 19 mm. **Obv:** Mt. Everest within square **Rev:** Map of Nepal

Date	Mintage	F	VF	XF	Unc	BU
VS2064	—	—	—	—	2.00	3.50

KM# 1188 2 RUPEES
5.0000 g., Brass Plated Steel, 24.93 mm. **Obv:** Farmer plowing with water buffalos **Rev:** Mount Everest **Edge:** Plain

Date	Mintage	F	VF	XF	Unc	BU
VS2063(2006)	—	—	—	1.50	2.75	3.50

KM# 1189 50 RUPEE
8.6000 g., Copper-Nickel, 29 mm. **Subject:** 250th Anniversary Hindu festival "Kimari Jatra" **Obv:** Kumari Temple at Durbar Square in Kathmandu **Rev:** Bust of Goddess Kumari facing **Edge:** Plain

Date	Mintage	F	VF	XF	Unc	BU
VS2064 (2006)	—	—	—	—	8.00	10.00

KM# 1190 500 RUPEE
14.1900 g., 0.5000 Silver 0.2281 oz. ASW, 32 mm. **Subject:** 250th Anniversary Hindu festival "Kimari Jatra" **Obv:** Kumari Temple at Durbar Square in Kathmandu **Rev:** Bust of Goddess Kumari facing **Edge:** Reeded

Date	Mintage	F	VF	XF	Unc	BU
VS2064 (2007)	—	—	—	—	25.00	30.00

MINT SETS

KM#	Date	Mintage	Identification	Issue Price	Mkt Val
MSA19	1996, 1995, 2011 (3)	—	KM#709.2 (1996); 711 (1995); 737 (2011)	—	8.00

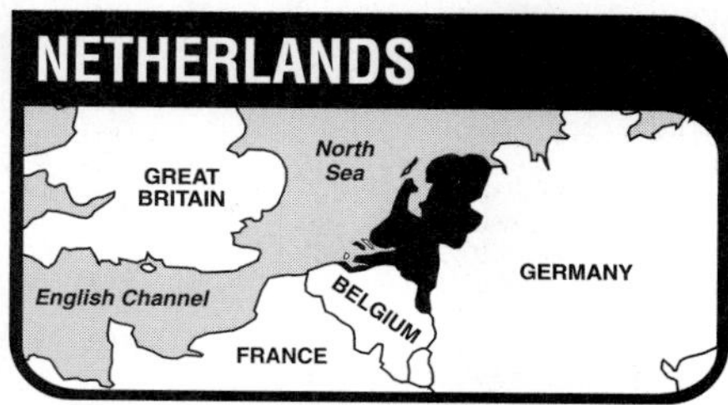

The Kingdom of the Netherlands, a country of western Europe fronting on the North Sea and bordered by Belgium and Germany, has an area of 15,770 sq. mi. (41,500 sq. km.) and a population of 16.4 million. Capital: Amsterdam, but the seat of government is at The Hague. The economy is based on dairy farming and a variety of industrial activities. Chemicals, yarns and fabrics, and meat products are exported.

NOTE: Excepting the World War II issues struck at U.S. mints, all of the modern coins were struck at the Utrecht Mint and bear the caduceus mint mark of that facility. They also bear the mintmasters' marks.

RULERS

KINGDOM OF THE NETHERLANDS

Beatrix, 1980—

MINT PRIVY MARKS

Utrecht

Date	Privy Mark
1806-present	Caduceus

MINTMASTERS' PRIVY MARKS

Utrecht Mint

Date	Privy Mark
2001	Wine tendril w/grapes
2002	Wine tendril w/grapes and star
2003	Sails of a clipper

NOTE: A star adjoining the privy mark indicates that the piece was struck at the beginning of the term of office of a successor. (The star was used only if the successor had not chosen his own mark yet.)

NOTE: Since October 1999, the Dutch Mint has taken the title of Royal Dutch Mint.

MONETARY SYSTEM

Until January 29, 2002

100 Cents = 1 Gulden

Since January 1, 2002

100 Euro Cents = 1 Euro

KINGDOM

DECIMAL COINAGE

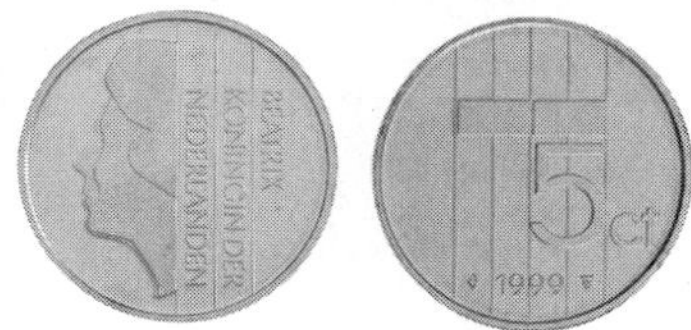

KM# 202 5 CENTS

3.5000 g., Bronze, 21 mm. **Ruler:** Beatrix **Obv:** Head left with vertical inscription **Rev:** Value within vertical lines **Edge:** Plain **Designer:** Bruno Ninaber Van Eyben

Date	Mintage	F	VF	XF	Unc	BU
2001	15,815,000	—	—	—	—	0.70
2001 Proof	17,000	Value: 4.00				

KM# 203 10 CENTS

1.5000 g., Nickel, 15 mm. **Ruler:** Beatrix **Obv:** Head left with vertical inscription **Rev:** Value and vertical lines **Edge:** Reeded **Designer:** Bruno Ninaber Van Eyben

Date	Mintage	F	VF	XF	Unc	BU
2001	25,600,000	—	—	—	0.45	0.75
2001 Proof	17,000	Value: 4.00				

KM# 204 25 CENTS

3.0000 g., Nickel, 19 mm. **Ruler:** Beatrix **Obv:** Head left with vertical inscription **Obv. Inscription:** Beatrix/Konincin Der/Nederlanden **Rev:** Value within vertical and horizontal lines **Edge:** Reeded **Designer:** Bruno Ninaber van Eyben

Date	Mintage	F	VF	XF	Unc	BU
2001	11,515,000	—	—	—	0.20	0.75
2001 Proof	17,000	Value: 6.00				

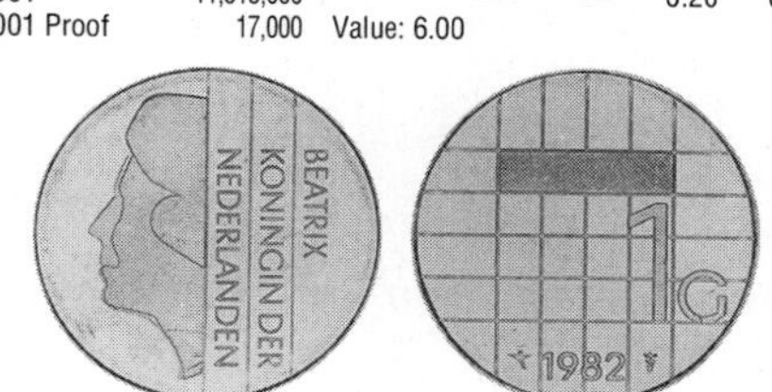

KM# 205 GULDEN

6.0000 g., Nickel, 25 mm. **Ruler:** Beatrix **Obv:** Head left with vertical inscription **Rev:** Value within vertical and horizontal lines **Edge Lettering:** GOD * ZIJ * MET * ONS * **Designer:** Bruno Ninaber von Eyben

Date	Mintage	F	VF	XF	Unc	BU
2001	6,414,500	—	—	—	—	1.25
2001 Proof	17,000	Value: 7.50				

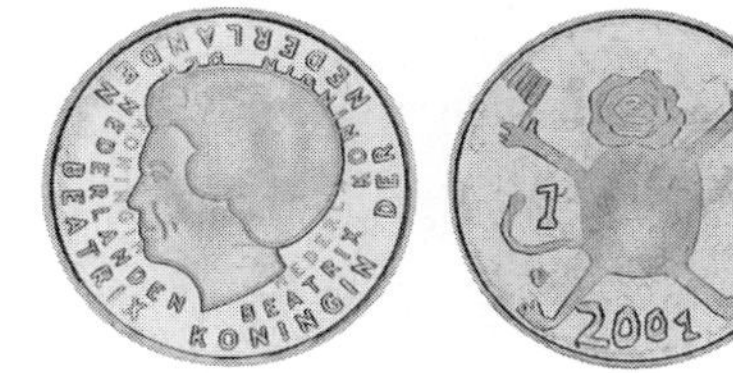

KM# 233 GULDEN

6.0000 g., Nickel, 25 mm. **Ruler:** Beatrix **Obv:** Head left within inscription **Obv. Designer:** Geerten Verheus and Michael Raedecker **Rev:** Child art design **Rev. Designer:** Tim van Melis **Edge Lettering:** GOD * ZIJ * MET * ONS *

Date	Mintage	F	VF	XF	Unc	BU
2001	16,009,000	—	—	—	—	4.00
2001 Prooflike	32,000	—	—	—	—	6.00

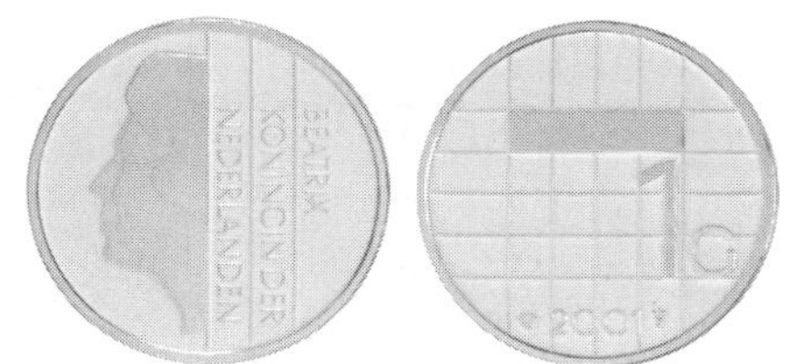

KM# 205a GULDEN

7.1000 g., 0.9250 Silver 0.2111 oz. ASW **Ruler:** Beatrix **Obv:** Head left with vertical inscription **Rev:** Value within vertical and horizontal lines **Edge Lettering:** GOD*ZIJ*MET*OMS*

Date	Mintage	F	VF	XF	Unc	BU
2001 Prooflike	200,000	—	—	—	—	10.00

KM# 205c GULDEN

13.2000 g., 0.9990 Gold 0.4239 oz. AGW **Ruler:** Beatrix **Obv:** Head left with vertical inscription **Rev:** Value within vertical and horizontal lines **Edge:** Plain, missing lettering

Date	Mintage	F	VF	XF	Unc	BU
2001 Prooflike	Est. 500	—	—	—	—	650

KM# 205b GULDEN

13.2000 g., 0.9990 Gold 0.4239 oz. AGW **Ruler:** Beatrix **Obv:** Head left with vertical inscription **Rev:** Value within vertical and horizontal lines **Edge Lettering:** GOD*ZIJ*MET*ONS* **Note:** Prev. KM#205a.

Date	Mintage	F	VF	XF	Unc	BU
2001 Prooflike	25,500	—	—	—	—	625

Note: Mintage includes KM#205c.

KM# 233a GULDEN

7.1000 g., 0.9250 Silver 0.2111 oz. ASW, 25 mm. **Ruler:** Beatrix **Obv:** Head left within inscription **Rev:** Child art design **Edge Lettering:** GOD * ZIJ * MET * ONS *

Date	Mintage	F	VF	XF	Unc	BU
2001 Prooflike	360	—	—	—	—	2,400

Note: Given as gifts to workers at the mint

KM# 233b GULDEN

13.2000 g., 0.9990 Gold 0.4239 oz. AGW, 25 mm. **Ruler:** Beatrix **Obv:** Head left within inscription **Obv. Designer:** G. Verheus and M. Raedecker **Rev:** Child art design **Rev. Designer:** T. van Melis **Note:** 98 of 100 pieces melted down, with 2 known in museum collections.

Date	Mintage	F	VF	XF	Unc	BU
2001 Prooflike; Rare	100	—	—	—	—	—

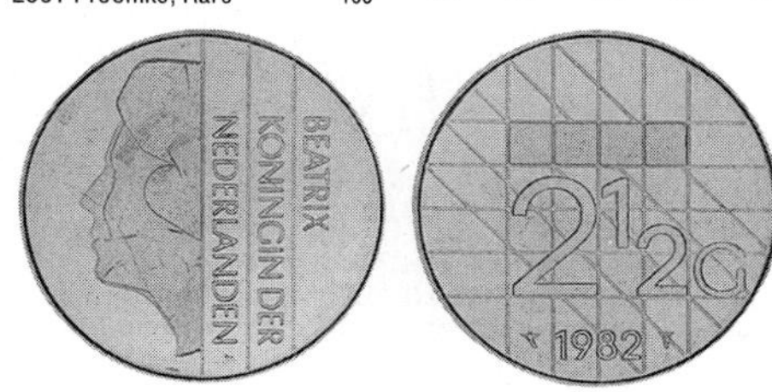

KM# 206 2-1/2 GULDEN

10.0000 g., Nickel, 29 mm. **Ruler:** Beatrix **Obv:** Head left with vertical inscription **Rev:** Value within horizontal, vertical and diagonal lines **Edge Lettering:** GOD * ZIJ * MET * ONS * **Designer:** Bruno Ninaber van Eyben

Date	Mintage	F	VF	XF	Unc	BU
2001	315,000	—	—	—	6.00	10.00
2001 Proof	17,000	Value: 16.00				

KM# 210 5 GULDEN

9.2500 g., Bronze Clad Nickel, 23.5 mm. **Ruler:** Beatrix **Obv:** Head left with vertical inscription **Rev:** Value within horizontal, vertical and diagonal lines **Edge:** GOD * ZIJ * MET * ONS * **Designer:** Bruno Ninaber van Eyben

Date	Mintage	F	VF	XF	Unc	BU
2001	115,000	—	—	—	6.00	10.00
2001 Proof	17,000	Value: 15.50				

EURO COINAGE

European Union Issues

KM# 234 EURO CENT

2.3000 g., Copper Plated Steel, 16.2 mm. **Ruler:** Beatrix **Obv:** Head left among stars **Obv. Designer:** Bruno Ninaber van Eyben **Rev:** Value and globe **Rev. Designer:** Luc Luycx **Edge:** Plain

Date	Mintage	F	VF	XF	Unc	BU
2001	179,300,000	—	—	—	0.35	0.50
2001 Proof	16,500	—	—	—	—	—
2002	800,000	—	—	—	3.00	1.25
2002 Proof	16,500	Value: 5.00				
2003	58,100,000	—	—	—	0.50	0.75
2003 Proof	13,000	Value: 4.00				
2004	113,900,000	—	—	—	0.50	0.75
2004 Proof	5,000	Value: 4.00				
2005	413,000	—	—	—	1.50	2.00
2005 Proof	5,000	Value: 4.00				
2006	200,000	—	—	—	1.50	2.00
2006 Proof	3,500	Value: 4.00				
2007	225,000	—	—	—	1.50	2.00
2007 Proof	10,000	Value: 3.50				
2008	162,500	—	—	—	1.50	2.00
2008 Proof	10,000	Value: 3.50				
2009	200,000	—	—	—	1.50	2.00
2009 Proof	75,000	Value: 3.50				
2010	—	—	—	—	1.50	2.00
2010 Proof	5,000	Value: 3.50				
2011	—	—	—	—	1.50	2.00
2011 Proof	—	Value: 3.50				

KM# 235 2 EURO CENT

3.0600 g., Copper Plated Steel, 18.7 mm. **Ruler:** Beatrix **Obv:** Head left among stars **Obv. Designer:** Bruno Ninaber van Eyben **Rev:** Value and globe **Rev. Designer:** Luc Luycx **Edge:** Grooved

Date	Mintage	F	VF	XF	Unc	BU
2001	145,800,000	—	—	—	0.50	0.75
2001 Proof	16,500	—	—	—	—	—
2002	53,100,000	—	—	—	0.75	1.00
2002 Proof	16,500	—	—	—	—	—
2003	151,200,000	—	—	—	0.50	0.75
2003 Proof	13,000	—	—	—	—	—
2004	115,622,000	—	—	—	0.50	0.75
2004 Proof	5,000	Value: 4.00				
2005	413,000	—	—	—	1.50	2.00
2005 Proof	5,000	Value: 4.00				
2006	200,000	—	—	—	1.50	2.00
2006 Proof	3,500	Value: 4.00				
2007	225,000	—	—	—	1.50	2.00
2007 Proof	10,000	Value: 3.50				
2008	162,500	—	—	—	1.50	2.00
2008 Proof	10,000	Value: 3,50				
2009	200,000	—	—	—	1.50	2.00
2009 Proof	75,000	Value: 3.50				
2010	—	—	—	—	1.50	2.00
2010 Proof	5,000	Value: 3.50				
2011	—	—	—	—	1.50	2.00
2011 Proof	—	Value: 3.50				

KM# 236 5 EURO CENT

3.9200 g., Copper Plated Steel, 21.25 mm. **Ruler:** Beatrix **Obv:** Head left among stars **Obv. Designer:** Bruno Ninaber van Eyben **Rev:** Value and globe **Rev. Designer:** Luc Luycx **Edge:** Plain

Date	Mintage	F	VF	XF	Unc	BU
2001	205,900,000	—	—	—	0.50	0.75
2001 Proof	16,500	—	—	—	—	—
2002	900,000	—	—	—	1.75	3.50
2002 Proof	16,500	—	—	—	—	—
2003	1,400,000	—	—	—	1.50	5.00
2003 Proof	13,000	—	—	—	—	—
2004	306,000	—	—	—	2.00	2.50
2004 Proof	5,000	Value: 4.00				
2005	80,413,000	—	—	—	1.00	1.25
2005 Proof	5,000	Value: 4.00				
2006	60,100,000	—	—	—	1.00	1.25
2006 Proof	3,500	Value: 4.00				
2007	78,625,000	—	—	—	1.00	1.25
2007 Proof	10,000	Value: 3.50				
2008	—	—	—	—	1.00	1.25
2008 Proof	10,000	Value: 3.50				
2009	40,200,000	—	—	—	1.00	1.25
2009 Proof	75,000	Value: 3.50				
2010	—	—	—	—	1.00	1.25
2010 Proof	5,000	Value: 3.50				
2011	—	—	—	—	1.00	1.25
2011 Proof	—	Value: 3.50				

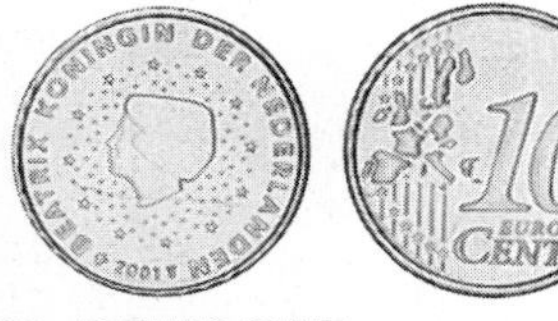

KM# 237 10 EURO CENT

4.1000 g., Brass, 19.7 mm. **Ruler:** Beatrix **Obv:** Head left among stars **Obv. Designer:** Bruno Ninaber van Eyben **Rev:** Value and map **Rev. Designer:** Luc Luycx

Date	Mintage	F	VF	XF	Unc	BU
2001	193,500,000	—	—	—	0.75	1.00
2001 Proof	16,500	—	—	—	—	—
2002	800,000	—	—	—	1.50	5.00
2002 Proof	16,500	—	—	—	—	—
2003	1,200,000	—	—	—	1.50	2.00
2003 Proof	13,000	—	—	—	—	—
2004	262,000	—	—	—	2.00	2.50
2004 Proof	5,000	Value: 6.00				
2005	363,000	—	—	—	1.75	2.00
2005 Proof	5,000	Value: 6.00				
2006	150,000	—	—	—	1.75	2.50
2006 Proof	3,500	Value: 6.00				

KM# 268 10 EURO CENT

4.1000 g., Brass, 19.7 mm. **Ruler:** Beatrix **Obv:** Head of Queen Beatrix left **Obv. Designer:** Bruno Ninaber van Eybew **Rev:** Relief map of Western Europe, stars, lines and value **Rev. Designer:** Luc Luycx

Date	Mintage	F	VF	XF	Unc	BU
2007	180,000	—	—	—	1.75	2.50
2007 Proof	10,000	Value: 5.00				
2008	130,000	—	—	—	1.75	2.75
2008 Proof	10,000	Value: 5.00				
2009	200,000	—	—	—	1.75	2.50
2009 Proof	7,500	Value: 5.00				
2010	—	—	—	—	1.75	2.50
2010 Proof	5,000	Value: 5.00				
2011	—	—	—	—	1.75	2.50
2011 Proof	—	Value: 5.00				

KM# 238 20 EURO CENT

5.7400 g., Brass, 22.2 mm. **Ruler:** Beatrix **Obv:** Head left among stars **Obv. Designer:** Bruno Ninaber van Eyben **Rev:** Value and map **Rev. Designer:** Luc Luycx **Edge:** Notched

Date	Mintage	F	VF	XF	Unc	BU
2001	97,600,000	—	—	—	1.00	1.25
2001 Proof	16,500	—	—	—	—	—
2002	51,200,000	—	—	—	1.00	1.25
2002 Proof	16,500	—	—	—	—	—
2003	58,200,000	—	—	—	1.00	1.25
2003 Proof	13,000	—	—	—	—	—
2004	20,430,000	—	—	—	1.00	1.50
2004 Proof	5,000	Value: 8.00				
2005	363,000	—	—	—	2.00	3.00
2005 Proof	5,000	Value: 8.00				
2006	150,000	—	—	—	2.00	3.00
2006 Proof	3,500	Value: 8.00				

KM# 269 20 EURO CENT

5.7000 g., Brass, 22.2 mm. **Ruler:** Beatrix **Obv:** Head of Queen Beatrix left **Obv. Designer:** Bruno Ninaber van Eybew **Rev:** Relief map of Western Europe, stars, lines and value **Rev. Designer:** Luc Luycx **Edge:** Notched

Date	Mintage	F	VF	XF	Unc	BU
2007	180,000	—	—	—	2.00	3.00
2007 Proof	10,000	Value: 7.00				
2008	130,000	—	—	—	2.50	3.00
2008 Proof	10,000	Value: 7.00				
2009	200,000	—	—	—	2.00	3.00
2009 Proof	7,500	Value: 7.00				
2010	—	—	—	—	2.50	3.00
2010 Proof	5,000	Value: 7.00				
2011	—	—	—	—	2.50	3.00
2011 Proof	—	Value: 7.00				

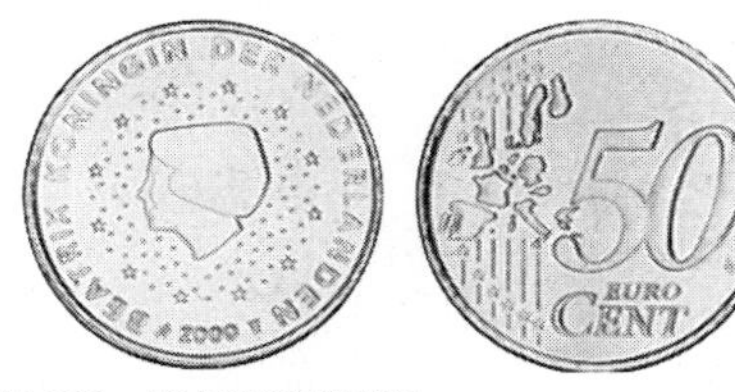

KM# 239 50 EURO CENT

7.8000 g., Brass, 24.2 mm. **Ruler:** Beatrix **Obv:** Head left among stars **Obv. Designer:** Bruno Ninaber van Eyben **Rev:** Value and map **Rev. Designer:** Luc Luycx **Edge:** Notched

Date	Mintage	F	VF	XF	Unc	BU
2001	94,500,000	—	—	—	1.25	1.50
2001 Proof	16,500	—	—	—	—	—
2002	80,900,000	—	—	—	1.25	1.50
2002 Proof	16,500	—	—	—	—	—
2003	1,200,000	—	—	—	2.00	2.50
2003 Proof	13,000	—	—	—	—	—
2004	269,000	—	—	—	2.25	3.00
2004 Proof	5,000	Value: 10.00				
2005	363,000	—	—	—	2.00	2.50
2005 Proof	5,964	Value: 10.00				
2006	150,000	—	—	—	2.00	2.50
2006 Proof	3,500	Value: 10.00				

KM# 270 50 EURO CENT

7.8000 g., Brass, 24.2 mm. **Ruler:** Beatrix **Obv:** Head of Quen Beatrix left **Obv. Designer:** Bruno Ninaber van Eybew **Rev:** Relief map of Western Europe, stars, lines and value **Rev. Designer:** Luc Luycx **Edge:** Notched

Date	Mintage	F	VF	XF	Unc	BU
2007	180,000	—	—	—	2.00	2.75
2007 Proof	10,000	Value: 9.00				
2008	162,500	—	—	—	2.00	2.75
2008 Proof	10,000	Value: 9.00				
2009	200,000	—	—	—	2.00	2.75
2009 Proof	7,500	Value: 9.00				
2010	—	—	—	—	2.00	2.75
2010 Proof	5,000	Value: 9.00				
2011	—	—	—	—	2.00	2.75
2011 Proof	—	Value: 9.00				

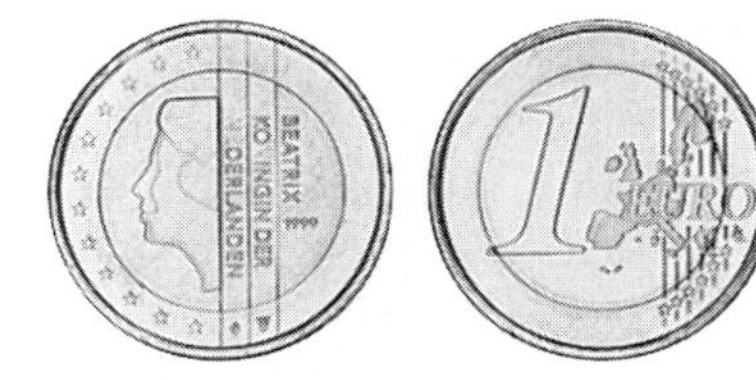

KM# 240 EURO

7.5000 g., Bi-Metallic Copper-Nickel center in Brass ring, 23.2 mm. **Ruler:** Beatrix **Obv:** Half head left within 1/2 circle and star border, name within vertical lines **Obv. Designer:** Bruno Ninaber van Eyben **Rev:** Value and map within circle **Rev. Designer:** Luc Luycx **Edge:** Segmented reeding

Date	Mintage	F	VF	XF	Unc	BU
2001	67,900,000	—	—	—	2.50	3.00
2001 Proof	16,500	—	—	—	—	—
2002	20,100,000	—	—	—	2.50	3.00
2002 Proof	16,500	—	—	—	—	—
2003	1,400,000	—	—	—	3.50	4.00
2003 Proof	13,000	—	—	—	—	—
2004	235,000	—	—	—	5.00	6.00
2004 Proof	5,000	Value: 15.00				
2005	288,000	—	—	—	4.00	5.00
2005 Proof	5,964	Value: 15.00				
2006	100,000	—	—	—	4.00	5.00
2006 Proof	3,500	Value: 15.00				

KM# 271 EURO

7.5000 g., Bi-Metallic Copper-Nickel center in Brass ring, 23.2 mm. **Ruler:** Beatrix **Obv:** Queen's profile left **Obv. Designer:** Bruno Ninaber van Eybew **Rev:** Relief map of Western Europe, stars, lines and value **Edge:** Segmented reeding

Date	Mintage	F	VF	XF	Unc	BU
2007	112,500	—	—	—	3.50	4.00
2007 Proof	10,000	Value: 14.50				
2008	81,250	—	—	—	3.50	4.00
2008 Proof	10,000	Value: 14.50				
2009	100,000	—	—	—	3.50	4.00
2009 Proof	7,500	Value: 14.50				
2010	—	—	—	—	3.50	4.00
2010 Proof	5,000	Value: 14.50				
2011	—	—	—	—	3.50	4.00
2011 Proof	—	Value: 14.50				

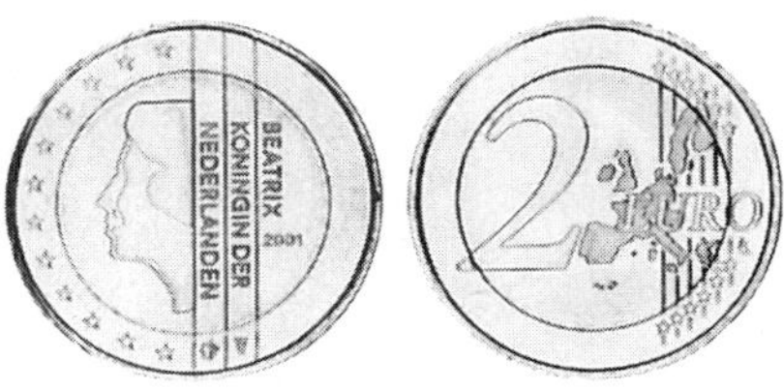

KM# 241 2 EURO

8.5000 g., Bi-Metallic Brass center in Copper-Nickel ring, 25.7 mm. **Ruler:** Beatrix **Obv:** Profile left within 1/2 circle and star border, name within vertical lines **Obv. Designer:** Bruno Ninaber van Eyben **Rev:** Value and map within circle **Rev. Designer:** Luc Luycx **Edge Lettering:** GOD * ZIJ * MET * ONS *

Date	Mintage	F	VF	XF	Unc	BU
2001	140,500,000	—	—	—	4.00	4.50
2001 Proof	16,500	—	—	—	—	—
2002	37,200,000	—	—	—	4.50	12.00
2002 Proof	16,500	—	—	—	—	—
2003	1,200,000	—	—	—	5.50	8.00
2003 Proof	13,000	—	—	—	—	—
2004	245,000	—	—	—	7.00	12.00
2004 Proof	5,000	Value: 18.00				
2005	288,000	—	—	—	6.00	8.00
2005 Proof	5,964	Value: 18.00				
2006	100,000	—	—	—	6.00	10.00
2006 Proof	3,500	Value: 18.00				

KM# 272 2 EURO

8.5000 g., Bi-Metallic Brass center in Copper-Nickel ring, 25.7 mm. **Ruler:** Beatrix **Obv:** Queen's profile left **Obv. Designer:** Bruno Ninaber van Eybew **Rev:** Relief map of Western Europe, stars, lines and value **Rev. Designer:** Luc Luycx **Edge Lettering:** GOD * ZIJ * MET * ONS *

Date	Mintage	F	VF	XF	Unc	BU
2007	112,500	—	—	—	6.00	8.00
2007 Proof	10,000	—	—	—	—	—
2008	81,250	—	—	—	6.00	8.00
2008 Proof	10,000	—	—	—	—	—
2009	100,000	—	—	—	6.00	8.00
2009 Proof	7,500	—	—	—	—	—
2010	—	—	—	—	6.00	8.00
2010 Proof	5,000	—	—	—	—	—
2011	—	—	—	—	6.00	8.00
2011 Proof	—	—	—	—	—	—

KM# 273 2 EURO
8.5000 g., Bi-Metallic Brass center in Copper-Nickel ring, 25.69 mm. **Ruler:** Beatrix **Subject:** 50th Anniversary Treaty of Rome **Obv:** Open treaty book **Rev:** Large value at left, modified outline of Europe at right **Edge Lettering:** GOD * ZU * MET * ONS * **Note:** 15,000 BU coins are in a Benelux set

Date	Mintage	F	VF	XF	Unc	BU
2007	6,515,000	—	—	—	6.00	15.00
2007 Proof	10,000	Value: 22.00				

KM# 281 2 EURO
8.5000 g., Bi-Metallic Brass center in copper-nickel ring, 25.69 mm. **Ruler:** Beatrix **Subject:** European Monetary Union, 10th Anniversary **Rev:** Stick figure and euro symbol **Edge Lettering:** *GOD *ZIJ *MET *ONS

Date	Mintage	F	VF	XF	Unc	BU
2009	5,300,000	—	—	—	4.50	15.00
2009 Proof	9,500	Value: 60.00				

KM# 245 5 EURO
11.9000 g., 0.9250 Silver 0.3539 oz. ASW, 29 mm. **Ruler:** Beatrix **Subject:** Vincent Van Gogh **Obv:** Head facing **Rev:** Tilted head facing **Edge Lettering:** GOD * ZIJ * MET * ONS * **Designer:** K. Martens

Date	Mintage	F	VF	XF	Unc	BU
ND(2003)	1,000,000	—	—	—	BV	12.50
ND(2003) Prooflike	100,000	—	—	—	—	25.00

KM# 252 5 EURO
11.9000 g., 0.9250 Silver 0.3539 oz. ASW **Ruler:** Beatrix **Subject:** New EEC member countries **Obv:** Head left **Obv. Designer:** M. Mieras and H. Mieras **Rev:** Names of old and new member countries **Edge Lettering:** GOD * ZIJ * MET * ONS *

Date	Mintage	F	VF	XF	Unc	BU
2004	600,000	—	—	—	12.50	14.50
2004 Proof	55,000	Value: 65.00				

KM# 253 5 EURO
11.9000 g., 0.9250 Silver 0.3539 oz. ASW **Ruler:** Beatrix **Subject:** 50th Anniversary - End of colonization of Netherlands Antilles **Obv:** Head left **Obv. Designer:** R. Luijters **Rev:** Fruit and date within beaded circle **Edge Lettering:** GOD * ZIJ * MET * ONS *

Date	Mintage	F	VF	XF	Unc	BU
2004	650,000	—	—	—	12.50	14.50
2004 Proof	26,900	Value: 35.00				

KM# 254 5 EURO
11.9100 g., 0.9250 Silver 0.3542 oz. ASW, 29 mm. **Ruler:** Beatrix **Subject:** 60th Anniversary of Liberation **Obv:** Queen's image **Rev:** Value and dots **Edge Lettering:** GOD * ZIJ * MET * ONS * **Designer:** Suzan Drummen

Date	Mintage	F	VF	XF	Unc	BU
2005	630,000	—	—	—	12.50	15.00
2005 Proof	40,000	Value: 45.00				

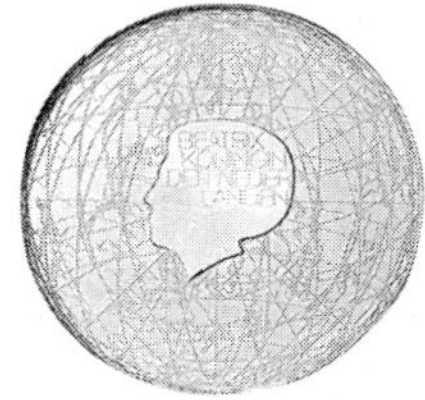

KM# 255 5 EURO
11.9000 g., 0.9250 Silver 0.3539 oz. ASW, 29 mm. **Ruler:** Beatrix **Obv:** Queen's silhouette centered on a world globe **Rev:** Value above Australia on a world globe **Edge Lettering:** GOD * ZIJ * MET * ONS * **Designer:** Irma Boom

Date	Mintage	F	VF	XF	Unc	BU
2006	500,000	—	—	—	12.50	15.00
2006 Proof	22,500	Value: 45.00				

KM# 266 5 EURO
11.9000 g., 0.9250 Silver 0.3539 oz. ASW, 28.9 mm. **Ruler:** Beatrix **Obv:** Queen Beatrix **Rev:** Rembrandt **Edge Lettering:** GOD * Z IJ * MET * ONS * **Designer:** Berend Strik

Date	Mintage	F	VF	XF	Unc	BU
ND(2006)	655,000	—	—	—	12.50	15.00
ND(2006) Proof	35,000	Value: 35.00				

KM# 267 5 EURO
11.9000 g., 0.9250 Silver 0.3539 oz. ASW, 29 mm. **Ruler:** Beatrix **Subject:** Tax Service, 200th Anniversary **Obv:** Queen's portrait **Rev:** Circles with dates 1806-2006 **Edge Lettering:** GOD * ZIJ * MET * ONS * **Designer:** Hennie Bouwe

Date	Mintage	F	VF	XF	Unc	BU
2006	359,189	—	—	—	12.50	20.00
2006 Prooflike	40,000	—	—	—	—	25.00
2006 Proof	15,000	Value: 50.00				

KM# 277 5 EURO
11.9000 g., 0.9250 Silver 0.3539 oz. ASW, 29 mm. **Ruler:** Beatrix **Subject:** Admiral M.A. de Ruyter, 400th Anniversary of Birth **Obv:** Queen's head 1/4 left **Obv. Designer:** Martyn Engelbregt **Rev:** deRuyter's head 1/4 right **Edge Lettering:** GOD * ZIJ * MET * ONS *

Date	Mintage	F	VF	XF	Unc	BU
2007	520,500	—	—	—	12.50	15.00
2007 Proof	17,500	Value: 40.00				

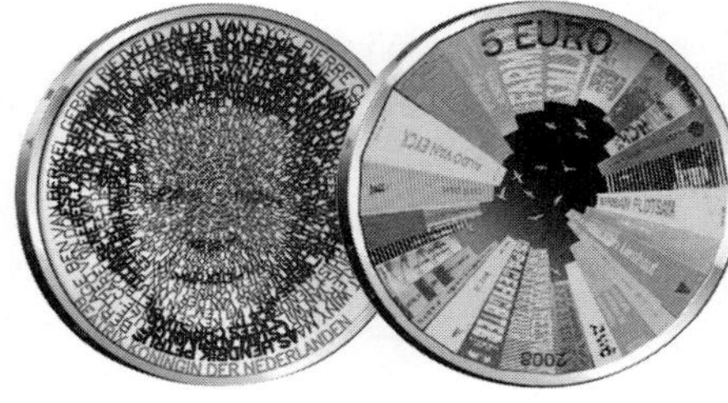

KM# 279 5 EURO
15.5000 g., 0.9250 Silver 0.4609 oz. ASW, 33 mm. **Ruler:** Beatrix **Subject:** Architecture **Obv:** Portrait facing in names of famous architects **Rev:** Books around map of the Netherlands **Edge Lettering:** GOD * ZIJ * MET * ONS * **Designer:** Stani Michiels

Date	Mintage	F	VF	XF	Unc	BU
2008 Proof	24,505	Value: 45.00				

KM# 279a 5 EURO
10.5000 g., Silver Plated Copper, 29 mm. **Ruler:** Beatrix **Subject:** Architecture **Obv:** Portrait facing in names of famous Architects **Rev:** Architecture books around map of the Netherlands

Date	Mintage	F	VF	XF	Unc	BU
2008	350,000	—	—	—	10.00	12.50

KM# 282 5 EURO
15.5000 g., 0.9250 Silver 0.4609 oz. ASW, 33 mm. **Ruler:** Beatrix **Subject:** Manhattan 400th Anniversary **Obv:** Bottom tip of Manhattan Island today **Rev:** Bottom tip of Manhattan Island in 1609 **Edge Lettering:** GOD * ZIJ * MET * ONS * **Designer:** Ronald van Tienhoven

Date	Mintage	F	VF	XF	Unc	BU
2009 Proof	20,000	Value: 45.00				

KM# 282a 5 EURO
10.5000 g., Silver Plated Copper, 29 mm. **Ruler:** Beatrix **Subject:** Manhattan 400th Anniversary **Obv:** Tip of Manhattan Island today **Rev:** Tip of Manhattan Island in 1609 **Designer:** Ronald van Tienhoven

Date	Mintage	F	VF	XF	Unc	BU
2009	303,209	—	—	—	10.00	12.50

KM# 287 5 EURO
15.5000 g., 0.9250 Silver 0.4609 oz. ASW, 33 mm. **Ruler:** Beatrix **Subject:** Netherlands-Japanese Friendship **Obv:** Guilder of 1982 with Queen **Rev:** Value and date **Edge Lettering:** GOD * ZIJ * MET * ONS * **Designer:** Richard Niessen and Esther de Uries

Date	Mintage	F	VF	XF	Unc	BU
2009 Proof	45,000	Value: 40.00				

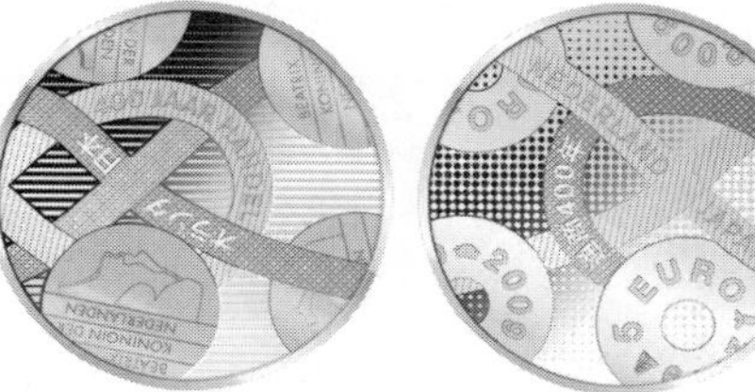

KM# 287a 5 EURO
10.5000 g., Silver Plated Copper, 29 mm. **Ruler:** Beatrix **Subject:** Netherlands-Japanese Friendship

Date	Mintage	F	VF	XF	Unc	BU
2009	343,859	—	—	—	8.00	10.00

KM# 294 5 EURO
11.9000 g., 0.9250 Silver 0.3539 oz. ASW, 33 mm. **Ruler:** Beatrix **Subject:** Max Havelaar, 150th Anniversary **Obv:** Queen **Rev:** Ink pen, words in spiral, figures walking around edge **Edge Lettering:** GOD * ZIJ * MET * ONS * **Designer:** Eelco Brand

Date	Mintage	F	VF	XF	Unc	BU
2010 Proof	15,000	Value: 45.00				

KM# 294a 5 EURO
10.5000 g., Silver Plated Copper, 29 mm. **Ruler:** Beatrix **Subject:** Max Havelaar, 150th Anniversary of Birth **Obv:** Queen **Rev:** Ink pen, words in spiral, figures walking around edge **Edge Lettering:** GOD * ZIJ * MET * ONS * **Designer:** Eelco Brand

Date	Mintage	F	VF	XF	Unc	BU
2010	350,000	—	—	—	9.00	12.00

KM# 296 5 EURO
15.5000 g., 0.9250 Silver 0.4609 oz. ASW, 33 mm. **Ruler:** Beatrix **Subject:** Waterland **Obv:** Queen's bust facing, and reflected in water **Rev:** Map of the Netherlands, partly reflected

Date	Mintage	F	VF	XF	Unc	BU
2010	17,500	Value: 45.00				

KM# 296a 5 EURO
10.5000 g., Silver Plated Copper, 29 mm. **Ruler:** Beatrix **Subject:** Waterland **Obv:** Queens bust facing and reflected in water **Rev:** Map of the Netherlands, partly reflected

Date	Mintage	F	VF	XF	Unc	BU
2010	300,000	—	—	—	—	10.00

KM# 243 10 EURO
17.8000 g., 0.9250 Silver 0.5293 oz. ASW, 33 mm. **Ruler:** Beatrix **Subject:** Wedding of Willem-Alexander and Maxima **Obv:** Queen's head left **Rev:** Conjoined busts left **Edge Lettering:** GOD * ZIJ * MET * ONS * **Designer:** H. van Houwelingen

Date	Mintage	F	VF	XF	Unc	BU
2002	990,800	—	—	—	15.00	40.00
2002 Proof	80,000	Value: 55.00				

KM# 244 10 EURO
6.7200 g., 0.9000 Gold 0.1944 oz. AGW, 22.5 mm. **Ruler:** Beatrix **Subject:** Crown Prince's Wedding **Obv:** Head left **Rev:** Two facing silhouettes **Edge:** Reeded **Designer:** J. van Houwelingen

Date	Mintage	F	VF	XF	Unc	BU
2002 Prooflike	33,000	—	—	—	—	300

KM# 246 10 EURO
6.7200 g., 0.9000 Gold 0.1944 oz. AGW, 22.5 mm. **Ruler:** Beatrix **Subject:** Vincent Van Gogh **Obv:** Head facing **Rev:** Tilted head facing **Edge:** Reeded **Designer:** K. Martens

Date	Mintage	F	VF	XF	Unc	BU
ND(2003) Prooflike	20,000	—	—	—	—	300

KM# 248 10 EURO
17.8000 g., 0.9250 Silver 0.5293 oz. ASW, 33 mm. **Ruler:** Beatrix **Obv:** Head left **Rev:** Multi-views of Prince Willem-Alexander, Princess Catherina-Amalia and Princess Maxima

Date	Mintage	F	VF	XF	Unc	BU
2004	1,000,000	—	—	—	—	18.00
2004 Proof	50,000	Value: 40.00				

KM# 247 10 EURO
6.7200 g., 0.9000 Gold 0.1944 oz. AGW, 22.5 mm. **Ruler:** Beatrix **Subject:** New EEC members **Obv:** Head left **Rev:** Value and legend **Edge:** Reeded **Designer:** M. Mieras and H. Mieras

Date	Mintage	F	VF	XF	Unc	BU
2004 Proof	6,000	Value: 650				

KM# 251 10 EURO
6.7200 g., 0.9000 Gold 0.1944 oz. AGW, 22.5 mm. **Ruler:** Beatrix **Subject:** 50 Years of Domestic Autonomy, 1954-2004 (for Netherlands Antilles) **Obv:** Small head left **Rev:** Fruit and date within beaded circle **Edge:** Reeded **Designer:** Rudy Luijters

Date	Mintage	F	VF	XF	Unc	BU
2004 Proof	3,800	Value: 550				

KM# 261 10 EURO
17.8000 g., 0.9250 Silver 0.5293 oz. ASW, 33 mm. **Ruler:** Beatrix **Subject:** Silver Jubilee of Reign **Obv:** Queen's photo **Rev:** Queen taking oath photo **Edge Lettering:** GOD * ZIJ * MET * ONS * **Designer:** Germaine Kruip

Date	Mintage	F	VF	XF	Unc	BU
2005	1,000,000	—	—	—	—	20.00
2005 Proof	59,754	Value: 40.00				

KM# 264 10 EURO
6.7200 g., 0.9000 Gold 0.1944 oz. AGW, 22.5 mm. **Ruler:** Beatrix **Subject:** 60th Anniversary of Liberation **Obv:** Queen and dots **Rev:** Value and dots **Edge:** Reeded **Designer:** Suzan Drummen

Date	Mintage	F	VF	XF	Unc	BU
2005 Proof	6,000	Value: 500				

KM# 289 10 EURO
6.7200 g., 0.9000 Gold 0.1944 oz. AGW, 22.5 mm. **Ruler:** Beatrix **Series:** Tax Services, 200th Anniversary **Obv:** Queen's portrait **Rev:** Florin of 1807 **Edge:** Reeded

Date	Mintage	F	VF	XF	Unc	BU
2006 Proof	5,500	Value: 500				

KM# 290 10 EURO
6.7200 g., 0.9000 Gold 0.1944 oz. AGW, 22.5 mm. **Ruler:** Beatrix **Subject:** Netherlands-Australian Friendship, 400th Anniversary **Obv:** Queens portrait within lines of a globe **Rev:** Australia, value and dates **Edge:** Reeded

Date	Mintage	F	VF	XF	Unc	BU
2006 Proof	3,500	Value: 700				

KM# 291 10 EURO
6.7200 g., 0.9000 Gold 0.1944 oz. AGW, 22.5 mm. **Ruler:** Beatrix **Subject:** Rembrant, 400th Anniversary of Birth **Obv:** Queen's portrait **Rev:** Self-portrait **Edge:** Reeded

Date	Mintage	F	VF	XF	Unc	BU
2006 Proof	8,500	Value: 300				

KM# 278 10 EURO
6.7200 g., 0.9000 Gold 0.1944 oz. AGW, 22.5 mm. **Ruler:** Beatrix **Subject:** Admiral M.A. de Ruyter, 400th Birthday **Obv:** Head 1/4 left **Rev:** Head 1/4 right **Edge:** Reeded **Designer:** Martyn Engelbregt

Date	Mintage	F	VF	XF	Unc	BU
2007 Proof	7,000	Value: 300				

KM# 280 10 EURO
6.7200 g., 0.9000 Gold 0.1944 oz. AGW, 22.5 mm. **Ruler:** Beatrix **Subject:** Architecture **Obv:** Portrait facing in names of famous architects **Rev:** Architecture books around map of the Netherlands **Edge:** Reeded **Designer:** Stani Michiels

Date	Mintage	F	VF	XF	Unc	BU
2008 Proof	8,000	Value: 300				

KM# 283 10 EURO
6.7200 g., 0.9000 Gold 0.1944 oz. AGW, 22.5 mm. **Ruler:** Beatrix **Subject:** Dutch settlement of Manhattan, NY 400th Anniversary **Obv:** Bottom tip of Manhattan Island today **Rev:** Bottom tip of Manhattan Island in 1609 **Edge:** Reeded **Designer:** Ronald van Tienhoven

Date	Mintage	F	VF	XF	Unc	BU
2009 Proof	6,500	Value: 350				

KM# 288 10 EURO
6.7200 g., 0.9000 Gold 0.1944 oz. AGW, 22.5 mm. **Ruler:** Beatrix **Subject:** Netherlands-Japanese Friendship **Edge:** Reeded

Date	Mintage	F	VF	XF	Unc	BU
2009 Proof	9,000	Value: 300				

KM# 295 10 EURO
6.7200 g., 0.9000 Gold 0.1944 oz. AGW, 22.5 mm. **Ruler:** Beatrix **Subject:** Max Havelaar, 150th Anniversary of Birth **Rev:** Ink pen, words in spiral, firgures walking around edge **Edge:** Reeded

Date	Mintage	F	VF	XF	Unc	BU
2010 Proof	5,500	Value: 375				

KM# 297 10 EURO
6.7200 g., 0.9000 Gold 0.1944 oz. AGW, 22.5 mm. **Ruler:** Beatrix **Subject:** Waterland **Obv:** Bust of Queen facing and reflected in water **Rev:** Map of the Netherlands, partly reflected

Date	Mintage	F	VF	XF	Unc	BU
2010 Proof	4,500	Value: 375				

KM# 249 20 EURO
8.5000 g., 0.9000 Gold 0.2459 oz. AGW, 25 mm. **Ruler:** Beatrix **Subject:** Birth of Crown-Princess - Catharina-Amalia - July 12, 2003 **Obv:** Bust left **Rev:** Holographic images: left, Princess Maxima; front, Princess Catharina-Amalia; right, Prince Willem-Alexander **Edge:** Reeded

Date	Mintage	F	VF	XF	Unc	BU
2004 Proof	5,345	Value: 530				

KM# 262 20 EURO
8.5000 g., 0.9000 Gold 0.2459 oz. AGW, 25 mm. **Ruler:** Beatrix **Subject:** Silver Jubilee of Reign **Obv:** Queen's photo **Rev:** Queen taking oath photo **Edge:** Reeded **Designer:** Germaine Kruip

Date	Mintage	F	VF	XF	Unc	BU
2005 Proof	5,001	Value: 530				

KM# 250 50 EURO
13.4400 g., 0.9000 Gold 0.3889 oz. AGW, 27 mm. **Ruler:** Beatrix **Subject:** Birth of Crown-Princess - Catharina-Amalia - July 12, 2003 **Obv:** Bust left **Rev:** Holographic images: left, Princess Maxima; front, Princess Catharina-Amalia; right, Prince Willem-Alexander **Edge:** Reeded

Date	Mintage	F	VF	XF	Unc	BU
2004 Proof	3,500	Value: 675				

KM# 263 50 EURO
13.4400 g., 0.9000 Gold 0.3889 oz. AGW, 27 mm. **Ruler:** Beatrix **Subject:** Silver Jubilee of Reign **Obv:** Queen's photo **Rev:** Queen taking oath photo **Edge:** Reeded **Designer:** Germaine Kruip

Date	Mintage	F	VF	XF	Unc	BU
2005 Proof	3,500	Value: 675				

TRADE COINAGE

KM# 190.2 DUCAT
3.4940 g., 0.9830 Gold 0.1104 oz. AGW **Ruler:** Beatrix **Obv:** Knight divides date with larger letters in legend **Rev:** Inscription within decorated square

Date	Mintage	F	VF	XF	Unc	BU
2001 Proof	7,500	Value: 185				
2002 Proof	3,400	Value: 185				
2003 Proof	3,800	Value: 185				
2004 Proof	2,120	Value: 400				
2005 Proof	2,243	Value: 185				
2006 Proof	2,097	Value: 250				
2007 Proof	2,250	Value: 185				
2008 Proof	3,260	Value: 185				
2009 Proof	3,500	Value: 185				
2010 Proof	—	Value: 185				

KM# 211 2 DUCAT
6.9880 g., 0.9830 Gold 0.2208 oz. AGW, 26 mm. **Ruler:** Beatrix **Obv:** Knight divides date within beaded circle **Rev:** Inscription within decorated square

Date	Mintage	F	VF	XF	Unc	BU
2002 Proof	6,650	Value: 350				
2003 Proof	4,500	Value: 350				
2004 Proof	2,015	Value: 400				
2005 Proof	3,500	Value: 350				
2006 Proof	1,800	Value: 400				
2007 Proof	2,000	Value: 350				
2008 Proof	2,100	Value: 350				
2009 Proof	2,500	Value: 350				
2010 Proof	—	Value: 350				

SILVER BULLION COINAGE

KM# 242 SILVER DUCAT
28.2500 g., 0.8730 Silver 0.7929 oz. ASW, 40 mm. **Ruler:** Beatrix **Obv:** Crowned shield **Rev:** Armored knight with sword divides date and circle, shield in front **Edge:** Reeded **Note:** Utrecht coin design circa 1659 based on KM#48.

Date	Mintage	F	VF	XF	Unc	BU
2001 Proof	9,000	Value: 35.00				

KM# 256 SILVER DUCAT
28.2500 g., 0.8730 Silver 0.7929 oz. ASW, 40 mm. **Ruler:** Beatrix **Obv:** Crowned shield **Rev:** Armored knight with Gelderland arms **Edge:** Reeded

Date	Mintage	F	VF	XF	Unc	BU
2002 Proof	9,400	Value: 35.00				

KM# 257 SILVER DUCAT
28.2500 g., 0.8730 Silver 0.7929 oz. ASW, 40 mm. **Ruler:** Beatrix **Obv:** Crowned shield **Rev:** Armored knight with sword holding arms of Holland **Edge:** Reeded

Date	Mintage	F	VF	XF	Unc	BU
2003 Proof	4,100	Value: 45.00				

KM# 258 SILVER DUCAT
28.2500 g., 0.8730 Silver 0.7929 oz. ASW, 40 mm. **Ruler:** Beatrix **Obv:** Crowned shield **Rev:** Armored knight holding sword with Zeeland arms **Edge:** Reeded

Date	Mintage	F	VF	XF	Unc	BU
2004 Proof	4,109	Value: 45.00				

KM# 259 SILVER DUCAT
28.2500 g., 0.8730 Silver 0.7929 oz. ASW, 40 mm. **Ruler:** Beatrix **Obv:** Crowned shield **Rev:** Armored knight holding sword with Friesland arms **Edge:** Reeded

Date	Mintage	F	VF	XF	Unc	BU
2005 Proof	4,000	Value: 45.00				

KM# 260 SILVER DUCAT
28.2500 g., 0.8730 Silver 0.7929 oz. ASW, 40 mm. **Ruler:** Beatrix **Obv:** Crowned shield **Rev:** Armored knight holding sword with Groningen arms **Edge:** Reeded

Date	Mintage	F	VF	XF	Unc	BU
2006 Proof	4,000	Value: 45.00				

KM# 275 SILVER DUCAT
28.2500 g., 0.8730 Silver 0.7929 oz. ASW, 40 mm. **Ruler:** Beatrix **Obv:** Crowned shield **Rev:** Armored knight holding sword with Overyssel arms **Edge:** Reeded

Date	Mintage	F	VF	XF	Unc	BU
2007 Proof	3,500	Value: 45.00				

KM# 292 SILVER DUCAT
28.2500 g., 0.8730 Silver 0.7929 oz. ASW, 40 mm. **Ruler:** Beatrix **Subject:** Northern Brabant **Obv:** Crowned shield **Rev:** John I, Count of Brabant standing with shield **Edge:** Reeded

Date	Mintage	F	VF	XF	Unc	BU
2008 Proof	—	Value: 55.00				

KM# 284 SILVER DUCAT
28.2500 g., 0.8730 Silver 0.7929 oz. ASW, 40 mm. **Ruler:** Beatrix **Rev:** Jan I standing with sword and Gelderland arms

Date	Mintage	F	VF	XF	Unc	BU
2009 Proof	3,000	Value: 55.00				

KM# 293 SILVER DUCAT
28.2500 g., 0.8730 Silver 0.7929 oz. ASW, 40 mm. **Ruler:** Beatrix **Subject:** Limburg **Obv:** Crowned shield **Rev:** Philip II of Montmorency, Count of Horne, standing **Edge:** Reeded

Date	Mintage	F	VF	XF	Unc	BU
2009 Proof	—	Value: 55.00				

KM# 285 SILVER DUCAT
28.2500 g., 0.8750 Silver 0.7947 oz. ASW, 40 mm. **Ruler:** Beatrix **Obv:** William of Orange standing with Zuid-Holland arms

Date	Mintage	F	VF	XF	Unc	BU
2010 Proof	—	Value: 55.00				

KM# 286 SILVER DUCAT
28.2500 g., 0.8750 Silver 0.7947 oz. ASW, 40 mm. **Ruler:** Beatrix **Obv:** Frederik Hendrik standing with Gelderland arms

Date	Mintage	F	VF	XF	Unc	BU
2010 Proof	—	Value: 55.00				

PATTERNS

Including off metal strikes

KM#	Date	Mintage	Identification	Mkt Val
Pn164	2001	—	Gulden. Nickel. Medal rotation	—
Pn165	2001	—	2 Euro Cent. Nickel.	100
Pn166	2001	—	Euro. Brass. KM240	150

MINT SETS

KM#	Date	Mintage	Identification	Issue Price	Mkt Val
MS4	2001 (6)	85,000	KM#202-206, 210	12.00	8.00
MS5	2001 (8)	68,000	KM#234-241 Charity set, Disabled Sports	15.00	8.00
MS6	2002 (8)	105,000	KM#234-241 Charity set, Blind Escort Dogs Fund	15.00	10.00
MS7	2002 (8)	59,500	KM#234-241 Last FDC set	15.00	10.00
MS8	2002 (8)	25,000	KM#234-241 plus bear medal Baby set	15.50	25.00
MS9	2002 (8)	10,000	KM#234-241 plus medal Wedding Set	15.50	35.00
MS10	2002 (8)	3,500	KM#234-241 plus medal Queen Beatrix set	20.00	110
MS11	2002 (8)	2,002	KM#234-241 plus medal 10th Day of the Mint	22.00	150
MS12	2002 (8)	10,000	KM#234-241 plus medal VOC set I	22.00	20.00
MS13	2002 (8)	10,000	KM#234-241 plus medal VOC set II	22.00	20.00
MS14	2002 (9)	10,000	KM#234-241 plus medal VOC set III	22.00	20.00
MS15	2002 (8)	10,000	KM#234-241 plus medal VOC set IV	22.00	20.00
MS16	2002 (8)	3,000	KM#234-241 plus medal BVC	30.00	40.00
MS17A	2002 (8)	2,500	KM#234-241 VVV - Irisgitftset	20.00	40.00
MS17	2002 (1)	9,200	KM#243 plus stamp	30.00	30.00
MS18	2002 (8)	1,000	KM#234-241 plus medal Theo Peters (Christmas)	99.00	60.00
MS19	2003 (8)	75,000	KM#234-241 Charity set, Epilepsy fund	15.50	10.00
MS20	2003 (8)	15,000	KM#234-241 Information set Denmark	20.00	40.00
MS21	2003 (9)	10,000	KM#234-241 VVV - Irisgiftset	15.50	20.00
MS22	2003 (8)	10,000	KM#234-241 plus medal VOC set V	22.00	25.00
MS23	2003 (8)	10,000	KM#234-241 plus medal VOC set VI	42.00	45.00
MS24	2003 (7)	2,003	KM#234-241 plus medal Day of the Mint	25.00	100
MS25	2003 (8)	1,000	KM#234-241 plus bi-color medal Theo Peters Jubilee set	—	20.00
MS26	2003 (7)	100	KM#234-241 plus silver medal Theo Peters Jubilee set	70.00	50.00
MS27	2003 (8)	25	KM#234-241 plus golden medal Theo Peters Jubilee set	400	250
MS28	2003 (8)	25,000	KM#234-241 plus bear medal Baby set	20.00	25.00
MS29	2003 (8)	15,000	KM#234-241 plus medal Wedding set	20.00	25.00
MS30	2003 (8)	1,000	KM#234-241 plus silver medal Theo Peters Christmas set	—	20.00
MS31	2003 (8)	150	KM#234-241 plus silver medal Theo Peters Christmas set	70.00	50.00
MS32	2003 (8)	50	KM#234-241 plus golden medal Theo Peters Christmas set	400	275
MS33	2003 (8)	3,500	KM#234-241 plus medal Mintmasters I	20.00	60.00
MS34	2003 (8)	1,000	KM#234-241 World Money Fair	20.00	100
MS35	2003 (8)	15,000	KM234-241 Information Set Hungaria	20.00	25.00
MS36	2003 (8)	20,000	KM#234-241 plus silver medal Royal Birth of Princess Catharina-Amalia	22.00	25.00
MS37	2003 (16)	10,000	KM#234-241 and Luxembourg KM#75-81, 40 Benelux Set	40.00	45.00
MS38	2003 (40)	10,000	KM#224-231 plus Germany KM#207-214 plus Spain KM#1040-1047 plus Belgium KM#224-231 and Austria KM#3082-3089 Charles V Set	85.00	85.00
MS39	2004 (8)	3,500	KM#234-241 plus medal Mintmasters II	20.00	60.00
MS40	2004 (8)	10,000	KM#234-241 Wedding set plus medal	18.00	—
MS41	2004 (9)	20,000	KM#234-241 Baby set plus bear medal	20.00	25.00
MS42	2004 (8)	1,000	KM#234-241 Basel World Money Fair	20.00	110
MS43	2004 (24)	35,000	KM#234-241 and Luxembourg KM#75-81 plus Belgium KM#224-231 Benelux set with silver medal	60.00	60.00
MS44	2004 (10)	10,000	KM#234-241 Queen Juliana set plus silver guilder, KM#184 and 30mm silver medal	25.00	28.00
MS45	2004 (9)	1,500	KM#234-241 Theo Peters Christmas set plus bi-color medal	30.00	30.00
MS46	2004 (8)	3,500	KM#234-241 VVV - Iris gift set	20.00	25.00
MS47	2004 (9)	150	KM#234-241 Theo Peters Christmas set plus silver medal	100	100
MS48	2004 (9)	50	KM#234-241 Theo Peters Christmas set plus golden medal	500	500
MS49	2004 (8)	50,000	KM#234-241 Fire - Burn Centre Charity set	18.00	22.00
MS50	2004 (9)	—	KM#234-241 Day of the Mint plus medal	25.00	150
MS51	2005 (9)	3,500	KM#234-241 Mintmasters III plus medal	20.00	60.00
MS52	2005 (9)	—	KM#234-241 Day of the Mint plus medal	25.00	150
MS53	2005 (9)	10,000	KM#234-241 Wedding set plus medal	18.00	20.00
MS54	2005 (9)	20,000	KM#234-241 Baby set plus bear medal	20.00	25.00
MS55	2005 (9)	20,000	KM#234-241 Nijntje set (Dick Bruna) plus medal	18.00	20.00
MS56	2005 (8)	55,000	KM#234-241 Charity set: Princess Beatrix Fonds	18.00	22.00

KM#	Date	Mintage	Identification	Issue Price	Mkt Val
MS57	2005 (24)	20,000	KM#234-241, Belgium 224-231, Luxembourg 75-81 Benelux set: Belgium, Netherlands plus Luxembourg with silver medal	60.00	60.00
MS58	2005 (8)	1,000	KM#234-241 World Money Fair, Basel	25.00	110
MS59	2005 (8)	15,000	KM#234-241 60th Anniversary Liberation plus Canadian 25 cent	35.00	35.00
MS60	2005 (9)	1,000	KM#234-241 Theo Peters Christmas set plus bi-color medal	30.00	30.00
MS61	2005 (9)	100	KM#234-241 Theo Peters Christmas set plus silver medal	120	80.00
MS62	2005 (9)	25	KM#234-241 Theo Peters Christmas set plus golden medal	550	300
MS63	2006 (10)	3,500	KM#234-241 Mintmasters IV plus medal	20.00	40.00
MS64	2006 (10)	4,000	KM#234-241 5 sets plus a Rembrandt silver medal and 1 set with a Rembrandt 5 Euro coin (6x8)	250	210
MS65	2006 (10)	500	KM#234-241 5 sets with Rembrandt silver medal and one set with Rembrandt 10 euro coin (6x8)	900	900
MS66	2006 (8)	45,000	KM#234-241 Charity set: Kika	18.00	10.00
MS67	2006 (9)	2,750	KM#231-241 Baby set boy plus bear medal	20.00	25.00
MS68	2006 (9)	100	KM#234-241 Baby set boy plus silver medal	—	95.00
MS69	2006 (8)	25	KM#234-241 Baby set boy plus gold medal	—	500
MS70	2006 (9)	2,750	KM#234-241 Baby set girl plus bear medal	20.00	25.00
MS71	2006 (8)	100	KM#234-241 Baby set girl plus silver medal	—	95.00
MS72	2006 (9)	25	KM#234-241 Baby set girl, plus gold medal	—	500
MS73	2006 (9)	15,000	KM#234-241 Benelux set: Belgium, 224-231, Luxembourg 75-81 plus Netherlands	65.00	65.00
MS74	2006 (9)	1,050	KM#234-241 Wedding set plus medal	22.00	25.00
MS75	2006 (8)	1,500	KM#234-241 Royal Dutch Mint Christmas set	30.00	25.00
MS76	2006 (9)	600	KM#234-241 Theo Peters Christmas set plus bi-color medal	35.00	40.00
MS77	2006 (9)	100	KM#234-241 Christmas set plus silver medal	150	100
MS78	2006 (9)	25	KM#234-241 Christmas set plus golden medal	650	400
MS79	2006 (8)	1,000	KM#234-241 Berlin Coin Fair	25.00	45.00
MS80	2006 (9)	—	KM#234-241 Day of the Mint set plus medal	25.00	120
MS81	2006 (8)	10,000	KM#234-241 200 Years of Coins in Kingdom of Holland	25.00	20.00
MS82	2007 (9)	3,500	KM#234-236, 268-272 Mintmasters V plus medal	20.00	40.00
MS83	2007 (9)	100	KM#234-236, 268-272 Mintmasters V plus silver medal	—	500
MS84	2007 (8)	3,500	KM#234-236, 268-272 Michiel de Ruyter sets, 1 plus silver medal and 1 set with Ruyter's 5 euro coin	—	250
MS85	2007 (8)	500	KM#234-236, 268-272 Michiel de Ruyter sets, 1 set with silver medal and 1 set with Ruyter's 10 euro coin	900	900
MS86	2007 (8)	40,000	KM#234-236, 268-272 National set	18.00	22.00
MS87	2007 (9)	3,000	KM#234-236, 268-272 Baby set boy plus bear medal	20.00	25.00
MS88	2007 (9)	100	KM#234-236, 268-272 Baby set boy plus silver medal	—	95.00
MS89	2007 (9)	3,000	KM#234-236, 268-272 Baby set girl plus bear medal	20.00	25.00
MS90	2007 (9)	100	KM#234-236, 268-272 Baby set girl plus silver medal	—	95.00
MS92	2007 (9)	1,050	KM#234-236, 268-272 Wedding set plus medal	22.00	25.00
MS93	2007 (9)	1,000	KM#234-236, 268-272 Christmas set plus bi-color medal	35.00	40.00
MS94	2007 (9)	100	KM#234-236, 268-272 Christmas set plus silver medal	150	150
MS95	2007 (9)	25	KM#234-236, 268-272 Christmas set plus golden medal	650	650
MS96	2007 (8)	1,000	KM#234-236, 268-272 Berlin Coin Fair	25.00	75.00
MS97	2007 (9)	—	KM#234-236, 268-272 Day of the Mint plus medal	25.00	100
MS98	2007 (8)	5,000	KM#234-236, 268-272 200 Years of Royal Predicate	25.00	28.00
MS109	2001 (6)	120,000	KM#202-206, 210 Introduction Euro-coins, no medal	15.00	16.00
MS110	2001 (6)	3,400	KM#202-206, 210 Queen Juliana	17.50	40.00
MS111	2001 (6)	100	KM#202-206, 210 Queen Juliana (error) in these sets are 5 or 25 cents or 5 guilden coins dated 2000	17.50	150
MS112	2001 (6)	1,000	KM#202-206, 210 BOLEGO-VOK	—	60.00
MS113	2001 (6)	1,000	KM#202-206, 210 De Akerendam II, with a silver 2 stuiver coin from the wreck	125	145
MS114	2001 (6)	1,000	KM#202-206, 210 United Seven Provinces Groningen	40.00	40.00
MS115	2001 (6)	1,000	KM#202-206, 210 United Seven Provinces Utrecht	40.00	40.00
MS116	2001 (6)	21,000	KM#202-206, 210 Baby set + bear medal	15.50	17.50
MS117	2001 (6)	1,015	KM#202-206, 210 Onderlinge "s-Grdevenhage"	—	70.00
MS121	2001 (8)	68,000	KM#234-241 Charity set, disabled sport	15.00	17.00
MS122	2002 (8)	105,000	KM#234-241 Charity set, blind escort dogs fund	15.00	17.00
MS123	2002 (8)	59,500	KM#234-241 Last FDS-set	15.00	17.00
MS124	2002 (8)	25,000	KM#234-241 Baby set + bear medal	15.50	25.00
MS125	2002 (8)	10,000	KM#234-241 Wedding-set + medal	15.50	35.00
MS126	2002 (8)	3,500	KM#234-241 Queen Beatrix + medal	20.00	110
MS127	2002 (8)	2,002	KM#234-241 10th day of the Mint + medal	22.00	175
MS128	2002 (8)	10,000	KM#234-241 VOC set I + medal	22.00	35.00
MS129	2002 (8)	10,000	KM#234-241 VOC set II + medal	22.00	25.00
MS130	2002 (8)	10,000	KM#234-241 VOC set III + medal	22.00	25.00
MS131	2002 (8)	10,000	KM#234-241 VOC set IV + medal	22.00	25.00
MS132	2002 (8)	3,000	KM#234-241 BVC + medal	30.00	40.00
MS133	2002 (8)	9,200	KM#234-241 10 Euro + poststamp	30.00	30.00
MS134	2002 (8)	2,500	KM#234-241VVV-Iris gift set	20.00	40.00
MS135	2002 (8)	1,000	KM#234-241 Theo Peters (Christmas) + medal	99.00	90.00
MS136	2003 (8)	75,000	KM#234-241 Charity set, epilepsy fund	15.50	17.00
MS137	2003 (8)	15,000	KM#234-241 Information set Denmark	20.00	40.00
MS138	2003 (8)	10,000	KM#234-241 VVV-Iris gift set	20.00	25.00
MS139	2003 (8)	10,000	KM#234-241 VOC set V + medal	22.00	25.00
MS140	2003 (8)	10,000	KM#234-241 VOC set VI + medal	42.00	45.00
MS141	2003 (8)	2,003	KM#234-241 Day of the mint + medal	25.00	140
MS142	2003 (8)	1,000	KM#234-241 Theo Peters jubilee set + bi-colour medal	—	30.00
MS143	2003 (8)	100	KM#234-241 Theo Peters jubilee set + silver medal	70.00	70.00
MS144	2003 (8)	25	KM#234-241 Theo Peters jubilee set + golden medal	400	410
MS145	2003 (8)	25,000	KM#234-241 Baby set + bear medal	20.00	25.00
MS146	2003 (8)	15,000	KM#234-241 Wedding-set + medal	20.00	25.00
MS147	2003 (8)	1,000	KM#234-241 Theo Peters Christmas set + bi-colour medal	—	30.00
MS148	2003 (8)	150	KM#234-241 Theo Peters Christmas set + silver medal	70.00	70.00
MS149	2003 (8)	50	KM#234-241 Theo Peters Christmas set + golden medal	400	400
MS150	2003 (8)	3,500	KM#234-241 Mint masters I + medal	20.00	60.00
MS151	2003 (8)	1,000	KM#234-241 World Money Fair Basel	20.00	130
MS152	2003 (8)	15,000	KM#234-241 Information set Hungaria	20.00	40.00
MS153	2003 (8)	20,000	KM#234-241 Royal birthset of Princess Catharina-Amalia December 7 + silver medal	22.00	25.00
MS154	2003 (8)	10,000	KM#234-241 Benelux set, with Belgium (8) KM#224-231 and Luxembourg (8) KM#75-81	40.00	45.00
MS155	2003 (8)	10,000	KM#234-241 Charles V set + medal, with Germany (8) KM#207-214, Spain (8) KM#1040-1047, Belgium (8) KM#224-231, and Austria (8) KM#3082-3089	85.00	85.00
MS156	2004 (8)	3,500	KM#234-241 Mintmasters II + medal	20.00	60.00
MS157	2004 (8)	10,000	KM#234-241 Wedding-set + medal	18.00	20.00
MS158	2004 (8)	20,000	KM#234-241 Baby set + bear medal	20.00	25.00
MS159	2004 (8)	1,000	KM#234-241 World Money Fair Basel	20.00	110
MS160	2004 (8)	35,000	KM#234-241 Benelux: Belgium, Netherlands + Luxembourg. With silver medal	60.00	60.00
MS161	2004 (8)	10,000	KM#234-241 Queen Juliana-set + silver guilder KM#184 and 30mm silver medal	25.00	28.00
MS162	2004 (8)	1,500	KM#234-241 Theo Peters Christmas set + bi-colour medal	30.00	30.00
MS163	2004 (8)	3,500	KME234-241 VVV-Iris gift set	20.00	25.00
MS164	2004 (8)	150	KM#234-241 Theo Peters Christmas set + silver medal	100	100
MS165	2004 (8)	50	KM#234-241 Theo Peters Christmas set + golden medal	500	500
MS166	2004 (8)	50,000	KM#234-241 Charity set, Fire-burn Centre	18.00	22.00
MS167	2004 (8)	2,004	KM#234-241 Day of the Mint + medal	25.00	150
MS168	2005 (8)	3,500	KM#234-241 Mintmasters III + medal	20.00	60.00
MS169	2005 (8)	2,005	KM#234-241 Day of the Mint + medal	25.00	150
MS170	2005 (8)	10,000	KM#234-241 Wedding-set + medal	18.00	—
MS171	2005 (8)	20,000	KM#234-241 Baby set + bear medal	20.00	25.00
MS172	2005 (8)	20,000	KM#234-241 Nijntje-set (Dick Bruna) + medal	18.00	20.00
MS173	2005 (8)	55,000	KM#234-241 Charity set: Princess Beatrix Fonds	18.00	22.00
MS174	2005 (8)	20,000	KM#234-241 Beneluz: Belgium, Netherlands + Luxembourg. With silver medal	60.00	60.00
MS175	2005 (8)	1,000	KM#234-241 World Money Fair Basel	25.00	110
MS176	2005 (8)	15,000	KM#234-241 60th Anniversary Liberation + Canadian 25 ct	35.00	35.00
MS177	2005 (8)	1,000	KM#234-241 Theo Peters Christmas set + bi-colour medal	30.00	30.00
MS178	2005 (8)	100	KM#234-241 Theo Peters Christmas set + silver medal	120	120
MS179	2005 (8)	25	KM#234-241 Theo Peters Christmas set + golden medal	550	550
MS180	2006 (8)	3,500	KM#234-241 Mintmasters IV + medal	20.00	40.00
MS181	2006 (8)	4,000	KM#234-241 5 sets with a Rembrandt silver medal and one set with the Rembrandt 5 euro coin	250	250
MS182	2006 (8)	500	KM#234-241 5 sets with a Rembrandt silver medal and one set with the Rembrandt 10 euro coin	900	900
MS183	2006 (8)	45,000	KM#234-241 Charity set: (Kika)	18.00	22.00
MS184	2006 (8)	2,750	KM#234-241 Baby set boy + bear medal	20.00	25.00
MS185	2006 (8)	100	KM#234-241 Baby set boy + silver medal	—	95.00
MS186	2006 (8)	25	KM#234-241 Baby set boy + gold medal	—	500
MS187	2006 (8)	2,750	KM#234-241 Baby set girl + bear medal	20.00	25.00
MS188	2006 (8)	100	KM#234-241 Baby set girl + silver medal	—	95.00
MS189	2006 (8)	25	KM#234-241 Baby set girl + gold medal	—	500
MS190	2006 (8)	15,000	KM#234-241 Beneluz: Belgium, Netherlands + Luxembourg. With silver medal	65.00	65.00
MS192	2006 (8)	1,050	KM#234-241 Wedding-set + medal	22.00	25.00

KM#	Date	Mintage	Identification	Issue Price	Mkt Val
MS193	2006 (8)	1,500	KM#234-241 Christmas set Royal Dutch Mint	30.00	30.00
MS194	2006 (8)	600	KM#234-241 Theo Peters Christmas set + bi-colour medal	35.00	40.00
MS195	2006 (8)	100	KM#234-241 Christmas set + silver medal	150	150
MS196	2006 (8)	25	KM#234-241 Christmas set + golden medal	650	650
MS197	2006 (8)	1,000	KM#234-241 Berlin Coin Fair	25.00	45.00
MS198	2006 (8)	2,006	KM#234-241 Day of the Mint + medal	25.00	120
MS199	2006 (8)	10,000	KM#234-241 200 years coins in Kingdom Holland	25.00	20.00
MS200	2007 (8)	3,500	KM#234-236, 268-272 Mintmasters V + medal	20.00	40.00
MS201	2007 (8)	100	KM#234-236, 268-272 Mintmasters V + silver medal	—	600
MS202	2007 (8)	3,500	KM#234-236, 268-272 5 sets Michiel de Ruyter + silver medal and one set with the Michiel de Ruyter 5 euro coin BU	250	250
MS203	2007 (8)	500	KM#234-236, 268-272 5 sets Michiel de Ruyter + silver medal and one set with the Michiel de Ruyter 10 euro coin	900	900
MS204	2007 (8)	40,000	KM#234-236, 268-272 Charity set	18.00	22.00
MS205	2007 (8)	3,000	KM#234-236, 268-272 Baby set boy + bear medal	20.00	25.00
MS206	2007 (8)	100	KM#234-236, 268-272 Baby set boy + silver medal	—	95.00
MS207	2007 (8)	3,000	KM#234-236, 268-272 Baby set girl + bear medal	20.00	25.00
MS208	2007 (8)	100	KM#234-236, 268-272 Baby set girl + silver medal	—	95.00
MS209	2007 (8)	15,000	KM#234-236, 268-272 Benelux: Belgium, Netherlands + Luxembourg. With silver medal + 3x 2 Euro Rome Treaty	75.00	75.00
MS210	2007 (8)	1,050	KM#234-236, 268-272 Wedding-set + medal	22.00	25.00
MS211	2007 (8)	1,000	KM#234-236, 268-272 Christmas set + bi-colour medal	35.00	40.00
MS212	2007 (8)	100	KM#234-236, 268-272 Christmas set + silver medal	150	150
MS213	2007 (8)	25	KM#234-236, 268-272 Christmas set + golden medal	650	650
MS214	2007 (8)	500	KM#234-236, 268-272 Berlin Coin Fair	25.00	90.00
MS215	2007 (8)	2,007	KM#234-236, 268-272 Day of the Mint + medal	25.00	100
MS216	2007 (8)	5,000	KM#234-236, 268-272 200 years of Royal predicate	25.00	28.00
MS224	2008 (8)	12,500	KM#234-236, 268-272 Benelux: Belgium, Netherlands + Luxembourg. With silver medal	75.00	75.00
MS217	2008 (8)	3,500	KM#234-236, 268-272 Mintmasters VI + medal	20.00	40.00
MS218	2008 (8)	100	KM#234-236, 268-272 Mintmasters VI + silver medal	20.00	500
MS219	2008 (8)	40,000	KM#234-236, 268-272 National set	20.00	22.00
MS220	2008 (8)	2,500	KM#234-236, 268-272 Baby set boy + bear medal	25.00	25.00
MS221	2008 (8)	100	KM#234-236, 268-272 Baby set boy + silver medal	65.00	65.00
MS222	2008 (8)	2,500	KM#234-236, 268-272 Baby set girl + bear medal	25.00	25.00
MS223	2008 (8)	100	KM#234-236, 268-272 Baby set girl + silver medal	65.00	65.00
MS225	2008 (8)	1,250	KM#234-236, 268-272 Wedding-set + medal	22.00	25.00
MS226	2008 (8)	500	KM#234-236, 268-272 Christmas set + bi-colour medal	35.00	40.00
MS227	2008 (8)	50	KM#234-236, 268-272 Christmas set + silver medal	130	135
MS228	2008 (8)	25	KM#234-236, 268-272 Christmas set + golden medal	850	850
MS229	2008 (8)	500	KM#234-236, 268-272 Berlin Coin Fair	25.00	75.00
MS230	2008 (8)	2,008	KM#234-236, 268-272 Day of the Mint + medal	25.00	80.00
MS231	2008 (8)	5,000	KM#234-236, 268-272 150 year Queen Emma + silver medal	32.00	35.00
MS232	2008 (8)	500	KM#234-236, 268-272 Theo Peters Jubilation set + bi-colour medal	35.00	40.00
MS233	2008 (8)	50	KM#234-236, 268-272 Theo Peters Jubilation set + silver medal	130	135
MS234	2008 (8)	25	KM#234-236, 268-272 Theo Peters Jubilation set + golden medal	850	850
MS235	2008 (8)	500	KM#234-236, 268-272 5 sets "2 centuries Amsterdam capitol of the Netherlands" + gold plated silver medals and one set with the golden Arctecture 10 euro coin	900	850

PROOF SETS

KM#	Date	Mintage	Identification	Issue Price	Mkt Val
PS54	2001 (6)	17,000	KM#202-206, 210 Booklet 5 Guilder	50.00	50.00
PS55	2001 (2)	500	KM#190.2, 242 Gold and Silver Ducat	50.00	120
PS56	2002 (2)	—	KM#190.2, 211 Golden Ducats	—	230
PS57	2002 (3)	—	KM#190.2, 211, 232 Golden Ducats and Silver Ducat	—	270
PS58	2003 (2)	—	KM#190.2, 211 Golden ducats in wooden box	230	230
PS59	2003 (8)	2,000	KM#234-241 Frigate "The Netherland" and silver medal and numbered ingot	85.00	125
PS63	2001 (7)	17,000	KM#202-207, 210 Booklet 5 guilder	50.00	60.00
PS64	2001 (2)	500	KM#190.2, 242 Gold + silver ducat	—	230
PS65	2002 (2)	—	KM#190.2, 211 Golden ducats	—	230
PS66	2002 (3)	—	KM#190.2, 211, 256 Golden ducats + silver ducat	—	270
PS67	2003 (2)	—	KM#190.2, 211 Golden ducats in wooden box	230	230
PS68	2004 (8)	5,000	KM#234-241 Proofset in wooden box	60.00	65.00
PS69	2005 (8)	5,000	KM#234-241 Proofset in wooden box	60.00	65.00
PS70	2005 (2)	2,500	KM#254, 264 60 years of freedom 5 Euro (silver) and 10 Euro (gold)	—	180
PS71	2006 (8)	3,500	KM#234-241	—	60.00
PS72	2006	—	5 Euro KM#255, Australian $5	90.00	—
PS73	2006	—	5 Euro KM#255, 10 Euro, Australian $5 and $10	—	550
PS74	2007 (8)	10,000	KM#234-236, 268-272 Proofset, including 2 Euro Rome Treaty KM#273	—	60.00
PS75	2008 (8)	10,000	KM#234-236, 268-272	—	60.00
PS76	2003 (8)	2,000	KM#234-241 Frigateship "The Netherland" + silver medal and numbered ingot. "Mintmaster Set" in wooden box	125	125
PS77	2004 (8)	1,000	KM#234-241 Value transport over sea during the eighty year of war + silver medal and numbered ingot. "Mintmaster Set" in wooden box	125	125
PS78	2005 (8)	1,000	KM#234-241 Value transport over sea 1650-1750 + silver medal and numbered ingot. "Mintmaster Set" in wooden box	125	125
PS79	2006 (8)	1,500	KM#234-241 Plus silver medal and numbered ingot. "Mintmaster Set" in wooden box	125	125

PROOF-LIKE SETS (PL)

KM#	Date	Mintage	Identification	Issue Price	Mkt Val
PL3	2001 (8)	16,500	KM#234-241	50.00	40.00
PL4	2002 (2)	—	KM#243, 244 Wedding set (10 Euro in silver and gold) in plastic box	145	250
PL5	2002 (2)	—	KM#243, 244 Wedding set in wooden box	145	200
PL6	2002 (8)	15,500	KM#234-241	50.00	40.00
PL7	2003 (8)	10,000	KM#234-241	50.00	40.00
PL8	2004 (8)	10,000	KM#234-241	—	50.00
PL9	2005 (8)	10,000	KM#234-241	—	50.00
PL12	2001 (8)	16,500	KM#234-241	50.00	40.00
PL13	2002 (2)	—	KM#243-244 Wedding set (10 Euro silver and gold) in plastic box	145	150
PL14	2002 (2)	—	KM#243-244 Wedding set in wooden box	145	160
PL15	2002 (8)	16,500	KM#234-241	50.00	40.00
PL16	2003 (8)	16,500	KM#234-241	50.00	40.00

SELECT SETS (FLEUR DE COIN)

KM#	Date	Mintage	Identification	Issue Price	Mkt Val
SS90	2001 (6)	120,000	KM#202-206, 210 Introduction to Euro Coins	15.00	10.00
SS91	2001 (6)	3,400	KM#202-206, 210 Queen Julianna Medal	17.50	30.00
SS92	2001 (6)	100	KM#202-206, 210 Queen Julianna Medal; some coins dated 2000 in error	17.50	150
SS93	2001 (6)	1,000	KM#202-206, 210 BOLEGO - VOK	—	60.00
SS94	2001 (6)	1,000	KM#202-206, 210, 2 Stuiver coin from the wreck of the De Akerendam II	125	60.00
SS95	2001 (6)	1,000	KM#202-206, 210 United Provinces, Groningen Medal	40.00	25.00
SS96	2001 (6)	21,000	KM#202-206, 210 Baby set plus bear medal	15.50	17.50
SS97	2001 (6)	1,015	KM#202-206, 210 Onderlinge "'s-Gravenhage"	70.00	100

SPECIMEN FDC SETS (FLEUR DE COIN)

KM#	Date	Mintage	Identification	Issue Price	Mkt Val
SS95A	2001 (6)	1,000	KM202-206, 210 United Provinces, Utrecht Medal	40.00	40.00

NETHERLANDS ANTILLES

The Netherlands Antilles, comprises two groups of islands in the West Indies: Aruba (until 1986), Bonaire and Curacao and their dependencies near the Venezuelan coast and St. Eustatius, Saba, and the southern part of St. Martin (*St. Maarten*) southeast of Puerto Rico. The island group has an area of 371 sq. mi. (960 sq. km.) and a population of 225,000. Capital: Willemstad. Chief industries are the refining of crude oil and tourism. Petroleum products and phosphates are exported.

RULERS

Beatrix, 1980-

MINT MARKS

Y – York Mint

Utrecht Mint
(privy marks only)

Date	Privy Mark
2001	Wine tendril with grapes
2002	Wine tendril with grapes and star
2003	Sails of a clipper

MONETARY SYSTEM

100 Cents = 1 Gulden

DUTCH ADMINISTRATION

DECIMAL COINAGE

KM# 32 CENT

0.7000 g., Aluminum, 14 mm. **Ruler:** Beatrix **Obv:** Orange blossom within circle **Rev:** Value within circle of geometric designed border **Edge:** Reeded

Date	Mintage	F	VF	XF	Unc	BU
2001(u)	12,806,500	—	—	0.10	0.20	0.50
2002(u) In sets only	6,000	—	—	—	—	1.25
2003(u)	19,604,000	—	—	0.10	0.20	0.50
2004(u) In sets only	7,100	—	—	—	—	1.00
2005(u)	—	—	—	0.10	0.20	0.50
2006(u)	—	—	—	0.10	0.20	0.50
2007(u)	—	—	—	0.10	0.20	0.50
2008(u)	—	—	—	0.10	0.20	0.50
2009(u)	—	—	—	0.10	0.20	0.50
2010(u)	—	—	—	—	—	—

KM# 33 5 CENTS

1.1600 g., Aluminum, 16 mm. **Ruler:** Beatrix **Obv:** Orange blossom within circle **Rev:** Value within circle, geometric designed border **Edge:** Reeded

Date	Mintage	F	VF	XF	Unc	BU
2001	2,006,500	—	—	0.20	0.60	0.75
2002 In sets only	6,000	—	—	—	—	2.50
2003	3,104,000	—	—	0.30	0.60	0.75
2004	2,402,100	—	—	0.30	0.50	0.75
2005	—	—	—	0.30	0.50	0.75
2006	—	—	—	0.30	0.50	0.75
2007	—	—	—	0.30	0.50	0.75
2008	—	—	—	0.30	0.50	0.75
2009	—	—	—	0.30	0.50	0.75
2010	—	—	—	—	—	—

KM# 34 10 CENTS

3.0000 g., Nickel Bonded Steel, 18 mm. **Ruler:** Beatrix **Obv:** Orange blossom within circle **Rev:** Value within circle, geometric designed border **Edge:** Reeded

Date	Mintage	F	VF	XF	Unc	BU
2001 In sets only	11,500	—	—	—	—	3.00
2002 In sets only	6,000	—	—	—	—	3.00
2003	2,104,000	—	—	0.50	1.00	1.75
2004	2,202,100	—	—	0.50	1.00	1.75
2005	—	—	—	0.50	1.00	1.75
2006	—	—	—	0.50	1.00	1.75
2007	—	—	—	0.50	1.00	1.75
2008	—	—	—	0.50	1.00	1.75
2009	—	—	—	0.50	1.00	1.75
2010	—	—	—	—	—	—

KM# 35 25 CENTS

3.5000 g., Nickel Bonded Steel, 20.2 mm. **Ruler:** Beatrix **Obv:** Orange blossom within circle **Rev:** Value within circle, geometric designed border **Edge:** Reeded

Date	Mintage	F	VF	XF	Unc	BU
2001 In sets only	11,500	—	—	—	—	3.00
2002 In sets only	6,000	—	—	—	—	3.00
2003	1,404,000	—	—	0.50	1.25	1.50
2004	1,502,100	—	—	0.50	1.25	1.50
2005	—	—	—	0.50	1.25	1.50
2006	—	—	—	0.50	1.25	1.50
2007	—	—	—	0.50	1.25	1.50
2008	—	—	—	0.50	1.25	1.50
2009	—	—	—	0.50	1.25	1.50
2010	—	—	—	—	—	—

KM# 36 50 CENTS

5.0000 g., Aureate Steel, 24 mm. **Ruler:** Beatrix **Obv:** Orange blossom within circle, designed border **Rev:** Value within circle of pearls and shell border **Edge:** Plain **Shape:** 4-sided

Date	Mintage	F	VF	XF	Unc	BU
2001 In sets only	11,500	—	—	—	—	4.00
2002 In sets only	6,000	—	—	—	—	6.00
2003 In sets only	9,000	—	—	—	—	4.00
2004 In sets only	7,100	—	—	—	—	4.00
2005	—	—	—	0.75	3.00	4.00
2006	—	—	—	0.75	3.00	4.00
2007	—	—	—	0.75	3.00	4.00
2008	—	—	—	0.75	3.00	4.00
2009	—	—	—	0.75	3.00	4.00
2010	—	—	—	—	—	—

KM# 37 GULDEN

6.0000 g., Aureate Steel, 24 mm. **Ruler:** Beatrix **Obv:** Head left **Rev:** Crowned shield divides value above date and ribbon **Edge Lettering:** GOD * ZIJ * MET * ONS *

Date	Mintage	F	VF	XF	Unc	BU
2001 In sets only	11,500	—	—	—	—	4.00
2002 In sets only	6,000	—	—	—	—	6.00
2003	504,000	—	—	0.75	3.00	5.00
2004 In sets only	7,100	—	—	—	—	6.00
2005	—	—	—	0.75	3.00	5.00
2006	—	—	—	0.75	3.00	5.00
2007	—	—	—	0.75	3.00	5.00
2008	—	—	—	0.75	3.00	5.00
2009	—	—	—	0.75	3.00	5.00
2010	—	—	—	—	—	—

KM# 38 2-1/2 GULDEN

9.0000 g., Aureate Steel, 28 mm. **Ruler:** Beatrix **Obv:** Head left **Rev:** Crowned shield divides value above date and ribbon **Edge Lettering:** GOD * ZIJ * MET * ONS *

Date	Mintage	F	VF	XF	Unc	BU
2001 In sets only	11,500	—	—	—	—	6.00
2002 In sets only	6,000	—	—	—	—	8.00
2003 In sets only	9,000	—	—	—	—	6.00
2004 In sets only	7,100	—	—	—	—	6.00
2005	—	—	—	1.00	5.00	6.00
2006	—	—	—	1.00	5.00	6.00
2007	—	—	—	1.00	5.00	6.00
2008	—	—	—	1.00	5.00	6.00
2009	—	—	—	1.00	5.00	6.00
2010	—	—	—	—	—	—

KM# 43 5 GULDEN

14.0000 g., Aureate Bonded Steel, 26 mm. **Ruler:** Beatrix **Obv:** Head left **Rev:** Crowned shield divides value above date and ribbon **Edge Lettering:** GOD * ZIJ * MET * ONS *

Date	Mintage	F	VF	XF	Unc	BU
2001 In sets only	9,500	—	—	—	—	7.50
2002 In sets only	6,000	—	—	—	—	7.50
2003 In sets only	7,000	—	—	—	—	7.50
2004	102,100	—	—	1.00	4.00	5.00
2005	—	—	—	1.00	4.00	5.00
2006	—	—	—	1.00	4.00	5.00
2007	—	—	—	1.00	4.00	5.00
2008	—	—	—	1.00	4.00	5.00
2009	—	—	—	1.00	4.00	5.00
2010	—	—	—	—	—	—

KM# 74 5 GULDEN

11.9000 g., 0.9250 Silver 0.3539 oz. ASW, 29 mm. **Ruler:** Beatrix **Subject:** 50th Anniversary - Charter for the Kingdom of Netherlands including Aruba as third party **Obv:** Head left **Rev:** Triangular design with hands writing signatures around value **Edge Lettering:** GOD * ZIJ * MET * ONS * **Designer:** Ans Mezas-Hummelink

Date	Mintage	F	VF	XF	Unc	BU
2004(u) Proof	4,000	Value: 30.00				

KM# 74.1 5 GULDEN

11.0000 g., Aureate Bonded Steel, 26 mm. **Ruler:** Beatrix **Subject:** 50th Anniversary - End To Dutch Colonial Rule **Obv:** Head left **Rev:** Triangular signatures around value **Edge Lettering:** GOD * ZIJ * MET * ONS *

Date	Mintage	F	VF	XF	Unc	BU
2004	10,000	—	—	—	7.00	10.00

KM# 76 5 GULDEN

11.9000 g., 0.9250 Silver 0.3539 oz. ASW, 29 mm. **Ruler:** Beatrix **Subject:** Queen's Silver Jubilee **Obv:** Head left **Rev:** Child art and value **Edge Lettering:** GOD * ZIJ * MET * ONS *

Date	Mintage	F	VF	XF	Unc	BU
2005(u) Proof	4,000	Value: 32.00				

KM# 76.1 5 GULDEN

11.0000 g., Aureate Bonded Steel, 26 mm. **Ruler:** Beatrix **Subject:** Queen's Silver Jubilee **Obv:** Head left **Rev:** Child art and value **Edge Lettering:** GOD * ZIJ * MET * ONS *

Date	Mintage	F	VF	XF	Unc	BU
2005	10,000	—	—	—	7.00	10.00

KM# 80 5 GULDEN

11.9000 g., 0.9250 Silver 0.3539 oz. ASW, 29 mm. **Ruler:** Beatrix **Subject:** 50 Years Brishopric Willemstad **Obv:** Logo Brishopric **Rev:** Cathedral **Edge Lettering:** GOD * Z'J * MET * ONS * **Designer:** Tirzo Martha

Date	Mintage	F	VF	XF	Unc	BU
2007 Proof	—	Value: 30.00				

KM# 79 5 GULDEN

11.9000 g., 0.9250 Silver 0.3539 oz. ASW, 29 mm. **Ruler:** Beatrix **Obv:** Antoine Maduro **Rev:** Crowned shield divides value **Edge Lettering:** GOD * ZIJ * MET * ONS *

Date	Mintage	F	VF	XF	Unc	BU
2009 Proof	1,250	Value: 35.00				

KM# 49 10 GULDEN

31.1035 g., 0.9250 Silver 0.9250 oz. ASW, 40 mm. **Ruler:** Beatrix **Subject:** Gold Trade Coins: Sulla Aureus **Obv:** Crowned shield divides value above date and ribbon **Rev:** Bust facing with two gold coins at lower left **Edge:** Plain

Date	Mintage	F	VF	XF	Unc	BU
2001(u) Proof	589	Value: 65.00				

KM# 50 10 GULDEN

31.1035 g., 0.9250 Silver 0.9250 oz. ASW, 40 mm. **Ruler:** Beatrix **Subject:** Gold Trade Coins: Constantin I Solidus **Obv:** Crowned shield divides value above date and ribbon **Rev:** Bust facing with two gold coins at lower right **Edge:** Plain

Date	Mintage	F	VF	XF	Unc	BU
2001(u) Proof	578	Value: 65.00				

KM# 51 10 GULDEN

31.1035 g., 0.9250 Silver 0.9250 oz. ASW, 40 mm. **Ruler:** Beatrix **Subject:** Gold Trade Coins: Clovis I Tremissis fiorino d'oro **Obv:** Crowned shield divides value above date and ribbon **Rev:** Bust facing with two gold coins **Edge:** Plain

Date	Mintage	F	VF	XF	Unc	BU
2001(u) Proof	566	Value: 65.00				

KM# 52 10 GULDEN

31.1035 g., 0.9250 Silver 0.9250 oz. ASW, 40 mm. **Ruler:** Beatrix **Subject:** Gold Trade Coins: Cosimo de'Medici Fiorino d'oro **Obv:** Crowned shield divides value above date and ribbon **Rev:** Bust facing with two gold coins **Edge:** Plain

Date	Mintage	F	VF	XF	Unc	BU
2001(u) Proof	575	Value: 65.00				

KM# 53 10 GULDEN

31.1035 g., 0.9250 Silver 0.9250 oz. ASW, 40 mm. **Ruler:** Beatrix **Subject:** Gold Trade Coins: Dandolo Ducato d'Oro **Obv:** Crowned shield divides value above date and ribbon **Rev:** Bust facing with two gold coins **Edge:** Plain

Date	Mintage	F	VF	XF	Unc	BU
2001(u) Proof	490	Value: 65.00				

KM# 54 10 GULDEN
31.1035 g., 0.9250 Silver 0.9250 oz. ASW, 40 mm. **Ruler:** Beatrix **Subject:** Gold Trade Coins: Philips IV Ecu d'or la chaise **Obv:** Crowned shield divides value above date and ribbon **Rev:** Bust facing with two gold coins **Edge:** Plain

Date	Mintage	F	VF	XF	Unc	BU
2001(u) Proof	460	Value: 65.00				

KM# 55 10 GULDEN
31.1035 g., 0.9250 Silver 0.9250 oz. ASW, 40 mm. **Ruler:** Beatrix **Subject:** Gold Trade Coins: Edward III Nobel **Obv:** Crowned shield divides value above date and ribbon **Rev:** Crowned bust facing with two gold coins **Edge:** Plain

Date	Mintage	F	VF	XF	Unc	BU
2001(u) Proof	575	Value: 65.00				

KM# 56 10 GULDEN
31.1035 g., 0.9250 Silver 0.9250 oz. ASW, 40 mm. **Ruler:** Beatrix **Subject:** Gold Trade Coins: Carolus IV Rhine Gold Guilder **Obv:** Crowned shield divides value above date and ribbon **Rev:** Bust facing with two gold coins **Edge:** Plain

Date	Mintage	F	VF	XF	Unc	BU
2001(u) Proof	430	Value: 75.00				

KM# 57 10 GULDEN
31.1035 g., 0.9250 Silver 0.9250 oz. ASW, 40 mm. **Ruler:** Beatrix **Subject:** Gold Trade Coins: John II Franc d'or a cheval **Obv:** Crowned shield divides value above date and ribbon **Rev:** Bust facing with two gold coins **Edge:** Plain

Date	Mintage	F	VF	XF	Unc	BU
2001(u) Proof	464	Value: 65.00				

KM# 58 10 GULDEN
31.1035 g., 0.9250 Silver 0.9250 oz. ASW, 40 mm. **Ruler:** Beatrix **Subject:** Gold Trade Coins: Philip the Good Adriesguilder **Obv:** Crowned shield divides value above date and ribbon **Rev:** Bust facing with two gold coins **Edge:** Plain

Date	Mintage	F	VF	XF	Unc	BU
2001(u) Proof	250	Value: 110				

KM# 59 10 GULDEN
31.1035 g., 0.9250 Silver 0.9250 oz. ASW, 40 mm. **Ruler:** Beatrix **Subject:** Gold Trade Coins: Louis XI Ecu d'or au soleil **Obv:** Crowned shield divides value above date and ribbon **Rev:** Bust facing with two gold coins **Edge:** Plain

Date	Mintage	F	VF	XF	Unc	BU
2001(u) Proof	450	Value: 65.00				

KM# 60 10 GULDEN
31.1035 g., 0.9250 Silver 0.9250 oz. ASW, 40 mm. **Ruler:** Beatrix **Subject:** Gold Trade Coins: Elisabeth I Sovereign **Obv:** Crowned shield divides value above date and ribbon **Rev:** Bust facing with two gold coins **Edge:** Plain

Date	Mintage	F	VF	XF	Unc	BU
2001(u) Proof	450	Value: 65.00				

KM# 61 10 GULDEN
31.1035 g., 0.9250 Silver 0.9250 oz. ASW, 40 mm. **Ruler:** Beatrix **Subject:** Gold Trade Coins: Carolus V Carolus Guilder **Obv:** Crowned shield divides value above date and ribbon **Rev:** Bust facing with two gold coins **Edge:** Plain

Date	Mintage	F	VF	XF	Unc	BU
2001(u) Proof	440	Value: 65.00				

KM# 62 10 GULDEN
31.1035 g., 0.9250 Silver 0.9250 oz. ASW, 40 mm. **Ruler:** Beatrix **Subject:** Gold Trade Coins: Philips II Real **Obv:** Crowned shield divides value above date and ribbon **Rev:** Bust facing with two gold coins **Edge:** Plain

Date	Mintage	F	VF	XF	Unc	BU
2001(u) Proof	440	Value: 65.00				

KM# 63 10 GULDEN
31.1035 g., 0.9250 Silver 0.9250 oz. ASW, 40 mm. **Ruler:** Beatrix **Subject:** Gold Trade Coins: Maurits Ducat **Obv:** Crowned shield divides value above date and ribbon **Rev:** Bust facing with two gold coins **Edge:** Plain

Date	Mintage	F	VF	XF	Unc	BU
2001(u) Proof	443	Value: 65.00				

KM# 64 10 GULDEN
31.1035 g., 0.9250 Silver 0.9250 oz. ASW, 40 mm. **Ruler:** Beatrix **Subject:** Gold Trade Coins: Isabella and Albrecht Double Albertin **Obv:** Crowned shield divides value above date and ribbon **Rev:** Conjoined busts facing with two gold coins **Edge:** Plain

Date	Mintage	F	VF	XF	Unc	BU
2001(u) Proof	490	Value: 65.00				

KM# 65 10 GULDEN
31.1035 g., 0.9250 Silver 0.9250 oz. ASW, 40 mm. **Ruler:** Beatrix **Subject:** Gold Trade Coins: William III Golden Rider **Obv:** Crowned shield divides value above date and ribbon **Rev:** Bust facing with two gold coins **Edge:** Plain

Date	Mintage	F	VF	XF	Unc	BU
2001(u) Proof	440	Value: 65.00				

KM# 66 10 GULDEN
31.1035 g., 0.9250 Silver 0.9250 oz. ASW, 40 mm. **Ruler:** Beatrix **Subject:** Gold Trade Coins: Louis XIII Louis d'or **Obv:** Crowned shield divides value above date and ribbon **Rev:** Bust facing with two gold coins **Edge:** Plain

Date	Mintage	F	VF	XF	Unc	BU
2001(u) Proof	440	Value: 65.00				

KM# 67 10 GULDEN
31.1035 g., 0.9250 Silver 0.9250 oz. ASW, 40 mm. **Ruler:** Beatrix **Subject:** Gold Trade Coins: Catharina the Great Rubel **Obv:** Crowned shield divides value above date and ribbon **Rev:** Crowned laureate bust facing with two gold coins **Edge:** Plain

Date	Mintage	F	VF	XF	Unc	BU
2001(u) Proof	560	Value: 75.00				

KM# 68 10 GULDEN
31.1035 g., 0.9250 Silver 0.9250 oz. ASW, 40 mm. **Ruler:** Beatrix **Subject:** Gold Trade Coins: Maria Theresia Double Sovereign **Obv:** Crowned shield divides value above date and ribbon **Rev:** Bust facing with two gold coins **Edge:** Plain

Date	Mintage	F	VF	XF	Unc	BU
2001(u) Proof	440	Value: 65.00				

KM# 69 10 GULDEN
31.1035 g., 0.9250 Silver 0.9250 oz. ASW, 40 mm. **Ruler:** Beatrix **Subject:** Gold Trade Coins: Napolean Bonaparte 20 Franc **Obv:** Crowned shield divides value above date and ribbon **Rev:** Bust facing with two gold coins **Edge:** Plain

Date	Mintage	F	VF	XF	Unc	BU
2001(u) Proof	555	Value: 65.00				

KM# 70 10 GULDEN
31.1035 g., 0.9250 Silver 0.9250 oz. ASW, 40 mm. **Ruler:** Beatrix **Series:** Gold Trade Coins: Wilhelmina Golden 10 Guilder **Obv:** Crowned shield divides value above date and ribbon **Rev:** Bust facing with two gold coins **Edge:** Plain

Date	Mintage	F	VF	XF	Unc	BU
2001(u) Proof	440	Value: 65.00				

KM# 71 10 GULDEN
31.1035 g., 0.9250 Silver 0.9250 oz. ASW, 40 mm. **Ruler:** Beatrix **Subject:** Gold Trade Coins: George III Sovereign **Obv:** Crowned shield divides value above date and ribbon **Rev:** Bust facing with two gold coins **Edge:** Plain

Date	Mintage	F	VF	XF	Unc	BU
2001(u) Proof	440	Value: 65.00				

KM# 72 10 GULDEN
31.1035 g., 0.9250 Silver 0.9250 oz. ASW, 40 mm. **Ruler:** Beatrix **Subject:** Gold Trade Coins: Albert I Belgium 20 Franc **Obv:** Crowned shield divides value above date and ribbon **Rev:** Bust facing with two gold coins **Edge:** Plain

Date	Mintage	F	VF	XF	Unc	BU
2001(u) Proof	490	Value: 65.00				

KM# 84 10 GULDEN
17.0000 g., 0.9250 Silver 0.5055 oz. ASW, 33 mm. **Ruler:** Beatrix **Subject:** Mariage of Willem-Alexander and Maxima **Obv:** Queen's head left **Rev:** Conjoined busts left **Edge Lettering:** GOD * ZIJ * MET * ONS * **Designer:** G. Colley

Date	Mintage	F	VF	XF	Unc	BU
2002(u) Proof	1,500	Value: 40.00				

KM# 75 10 GULDEN
6.7200 g., 0.9000 Gold 0.1944 oz. AGW **Ruler:** Beatrix **Subject:** 50th Anniversary - End to Dutch Colonial Rule **Obv:** Head left **Rev:** Triangular signatures around value **Edge:** Reeded **Designer:** Ans Mezas-Hummelink

Date	Mintage	F	VF	XF	Unc	BU
2004 Proof	1,000	Value: 275				

KM# 77 10 GULDEN
6.7200 g., 0.9000 Gold 0.1944 oz. AGW, 22.5 mm. **Ruler:** Beatrix **Subject:** Queen's Silver Jubilee **Obv:** Head left **Rev:** Child art and value **Edge:** Reeded

Date	Mintage	F	VF	XF	Unc	BU
2005(u) Proof	1,500	Value: 275				

KM# 78 10 GULDEN
1.2442 g., 0.9990 Gold 0.0400 oz. AGW, 13.92 mm. **Ruler:** Beatrix **Subject:** Year of the dolphin **Obv:** Head left **Obv. Legend:** BEATRIX KONINGIN DER NEDERLANDEN **Rev:** Stylized outlines of birds above dolphins at sunset **Rev. Legend:** NEDERLANDSE ANTILLEN - JAAR VAN DE DOLFIJN **Edge:** Reeded

Date	Mintage	F	VF	XF	Unc	BU
2007(u) Proof	5,000	Value: 80.00				

KM# 82 25 GULDEN
25.0000 g., 0.9250 Silver 0.7435 oz. ASW, 38 mm. **Ruler:** Beatrix **Obv:** 175 year Bank of the Netherlands Antilles **Rev:** Sailing ship

Date	Mintage	F	VF	XF	Unc	BU
2003 Prooflike	1,500	—	—	—	—	45.00

KM# 83 25 GULDEN
25.0000 g., 0.9250 Silver 0.7435 oz. ASW, 38 mm. **Ruler:** Beatrix **Obv:** 50 years of monument care **Rev:** Folker FXVIII plane over route map **Edge Lettering:** GOD * ZIJ * MET * ONS *

Date	Mintage	F	VF	XF	Unc	BU
2004 Proof	—	Value: 45.00				

MINT SETS

KM#	Date	Mintage	Identification	Issue Price	Mkt Val
MS22	2001 (8)	6,500	KM#32-38, 43	15.00	30.00
MS23	2002 (8)	6,000	KM#32-38, 43	15.00	40.00
MS24	2003 (8)	4,000	KM#32-38, 43	15.00	30.00
MS25	2004 (8)	2,100	KM32-38, 43	15.00	30.00
MS26	2005 (8)	3,500	KM32-38, 43	17.00	25.00
MS27	2006 (8)	2,000	KM#32-38, 43	20.00	25.00
MS28	2007 (8)	2,000	KM#32-38, 43	20.00	25.00
MS29	2008 (8)	2,000	KM#32-38, 43	21.00	25.00
MS30	2009 (8)	2,000	KM#32-38, 43	27.00	27.00
MS31	2010 (8)	2,000	KM#32-38, 43	28.00	28.00

NEW CALEDONIA

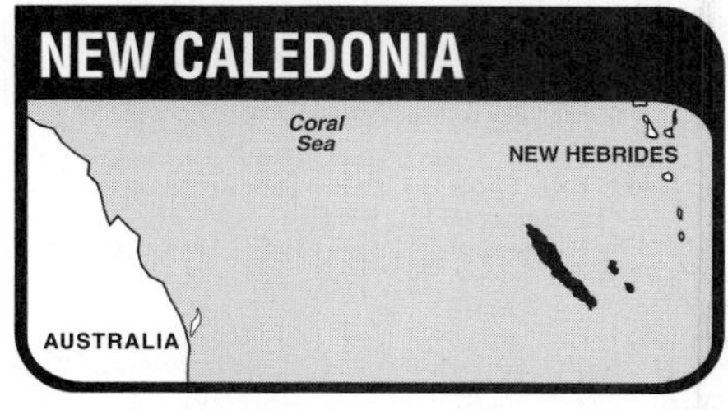

The French Associated State of New Caledonia is a group of about 25 islands in the South Pacific. They are situated about 750 miles (1,207 km.) east of Australia. The territory, which includes the dependencies of Isle des Pins, Loyalty Islands, Isle Huon, Isles Belep, Isles Chesterfield, Isle Walpole, Wallis and Futuna Islands and has a total land area of 7,358 sq. mi.(19,060 sq. km.) and a population of *156,000. Capital: Noumea. The islands are rich in minerals; New Caledonia has some of the world's largest known deposit of nickel. Nickel, nickel castings, coffee and copra are exported.

MINT MARK

Paris, privy marks only

MONETARY SYSTEM

100 Centimes = 1 Franc

FRENCH OVERSEAS TERRITORY
1958-1998

DECIMAL COINAGE

KM# 10 FRANC

1.3000 g., Aluminum, 23 mm. **Obv:** Seated figure holding torch, legend added **Obv. Legend:** I. E. O. M. **Rev:** Kagu bird within sprigs below value **Designer:** G.B.L. Bazor

Date	Mintage	F	VF	XF	Unc	BU
2001(a)	100,000	—	—	0.15	0.50	1.25
2002(a)	1,200,000	—	—	0.15	0.50	1.25
2003(a)	2,000,000	—	—	0.15	0.50	1.25
2004(a)	1,200,000	—	—	0.15	0.50	1.25
2005(a)	700,000	—	—	0.15	0.50	1.25
2006(a)	1,600,000	—	—	—	0.50	1.25
2007(a)	2,000,000	—	—	—	0.50	1.25
2008(a)	2,800,000	—	—	—	0.50	1.25
2009(a)	—	—	—	—	0.50	1.25

KM# 14 2 FRANCS

2.2000 g., Aluminum, 27 mm. **Obv:** Seated figure holding torch, legend added **Obv. Legend:** I. E. O. M. **Rev:** Kagu bird and value within sprigs

Date	Mintage	F	VF	XF	Unc	BU
2001(a)	800,000	—	—	0.25	0.75	1.50
2002(a)	1,200,000	—	—	0.25	0.75	1.50
2003(a)	2,400,000	—	—	0.20	0.65	1.50
2004(a)	200,000	—	—	0.20	0.65	1.50
2005(a)	530,000	—	—	0.20	0.65	1.50
2006(a)	1,200,000	—	—	—	0.65	1.50
2007(a)	600,000	—	—	—	0.65	1.50
2008(a)	2,400,000	—	—	—	0.65	1.50

KM# 16 5 FRANCS

3.7500 g., Aluminum, 31 mm. **Obv:** Seated figure holding torch, legend added **Obv. Legend:** I. E. O. M. **Rev:** Kagu bird and value within sprigs **Designer:** G.B.L. Bazor

Date	Mintage	F	VF	XF	Unc	BU
2001(a)	600,000	—	—	0.50	1.00	2.00
2002(a)	480,000	—	—	0.50	1.00	2.00
2003(a)	700,000	—	—	0.40	1.00	2.00
2004(a)	1,000,000	—	—	0.40	1.00	2.00
2005(a)	360,000	—	—	0.40	1.00	2.00
2006(a)	480,000	—	—	0.40	1.00	2.00
2007(a)	960,000	—	—	—	1.00	2.00
2008(a)	1,700,000	—	—	—	1.00	2.00
2009(a)	—	—	—	—	1.00	2.00

KM# 11 10 FRANCS

6.0000 g., Nickel, 24 mm. **Obv:** Liberty head left **Obv. Legend:** I. E. O. M. **Rev:** Sailboat above value **Designer:** R. Joly

Date	Mintage	F	VF	XF	Unc	BU
2001(a)	100,000	—	—	0.65	1.25	2.75
2002(a)	200,000	—	—	0.65	1.25	2.75
2003(a)	800,000	—	—	0.65	1.25	2.75
2004(a)	600,000	—	—	0.65	1.25	2.75
2005(a)	64,000	—	—	0.65	1.25	2.75

KM# 12 20 FRANCS

10.0000 g., Nickel, 28.5 mm. **Obv:** Liberty head left **Obv. Legend:** I. O. E. M. **Rev:** Three ox heads above value **Designer:** R. Joly

Date	Mintage	F	VF	XF	Unc	BU
2001(a)	150,000	—	—	1.00	1.75	3.25
2002(a)	250,000	—	—	1.00	1.75	3.25
2003(a)	250,000	—	—	1.00	1.75	3.25
2004(a)	500,000	—	—	1.00	1.75	3.25
2005(a)	300,000	—	—	1.00	1.75	3.25

KM# 13 50 FRANCS

15.0000 g., Nickel, 33 mm. **Obv:** Liberty head left **Obv. Legend:** I. E. O. M. **Rev:** Hut above value in center of palm and pine trees **Designer:** R. Joly

Date	Mintage	F	VF	XF	Unc	BU
2001(a)	100,000	—	—	1.25	2.00	4.00
2002(a)	—	—	—	1.25	2.00	4.00
2003(a)	75,000	—	—	1.25	2.00	4.00
2004(a)	150,000	—	—	1.25	2.00	4.00
2005(a)	54,000	—	—	1.25	2.00	4.00

KM# 15 100 FRANCS

10.0000 g., Nickel-Bronze, 30 mm. **Obv:** Liberty head left **Rev:** Hut above value in center of palm and pine trees **Designer:** R. Joly

Date	Mintage	F	VF	XF	Unc	BU
2001(a)	100,000	—	—	1.50	3.00	5.00
2002(a)	620,000	—	—	1.50	3.00	6.00
2003(a)	500,000	—	—	1.50	3.00	5.00
2004(a)	500,000	—	—	1.50	3.00	5.00
2005(a)	180,000	—	—	1.50	3.00	5.00

FRENCH ASSOCIATED STATE
1998-

DECIMAL COINAGE

KM# 11a 10 FRANCS

6.0000 g., Copper-Nickel **Obv:** Liberty head left **Rev:** Sailboat above value **Shape:** 24

Date	Mintage	F	VF	XF	Unc	BU
2006(a)	60,000	—	—	0.65	1.25	2.75
2007(a)	1,000,000	—	—	0.65	1.25	2.75
2008(a)	1,200,000	—	—	—	1.25	2.75
2009(a)	—	—	—	—	1.25	2.75

KM# 12a 20 FRANCS

10.0000 g., Copper-Nickel, 28.5 mm. **Obv:** Liberty head left **Rev:** Three ox heads above value

Date	Mintage	F	VF	XF	Unc	BU
2006(a)	300,000	—	—	1.00	1.75	3.25
2007(a)	800,000	—	—	—	1.75	3.25
2008(a)	800,000	—	—	—	1.75	3.25

KM# 13a 50 FRANCS

15.0000 g., Silver **Obv:** Liberty head left **Rev:** Hut in center of palm and pine trees, value below

Date	Mintage	F	VF	XF	Unc	BU
2006(a)	75,000	—	—	1.25	2.00	4.00
2007(a)	225,000	—	—	—	2.00	4.00
2008(a)	375,000	—	—	—	2.00	4.00

KM# 15a 100 FRANCS

9.9000 g., Nickel-Aluminum-Copper, 30 mm. **Obv:** Liberty head left **Rev:** Hut above value in center of palm and pine trees **Designer:** R. Joly

Date	Mintage	F	VF	XF	Unc	BU
2006(a)	300,000	—	—	1.50	3.00	5.00
2007(a)	800,000	—	—	—	3.00	5.00
2008(a)	1,100,000	—	—	—	3.00	5.00

MINT SETS

KM#	Date	Mintage	Identification	Issue Price	Mkt Val
MS1	2001 (7)	3,000	KM#10-16	—	30.00
MS2	2002 (7)	5,000	KM#10-16	—	25.00
MS3	2004 (7)	3,000	KM#10-16	—	30.00

NEW ZEALAND

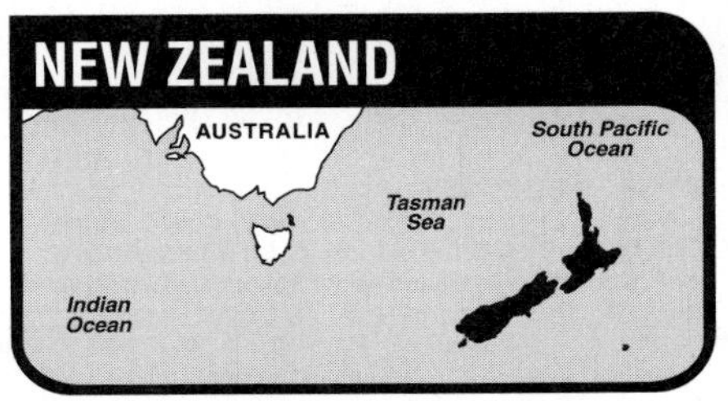

New Zealand, a parliamentary state located in the Southwest Pacific 1,250 miles (2,011 km.) east of Australia, has an area of 103,883 sq. mi. (268,680 sq. km.) and a population of *3.4 million. Capital: Wellington. Wool, meat, dairy products and some manufactured items are exported.

Decimal Currency was introduced in 1967 with special sets commemorating the last issues of pound sterling (1965) and the first of the decimal issues. Since then dollars and sets of coins have been issued nearly every year.

New Zealand is a founding member of the Commonwealth of Nations. Elizabeth II is the Head of State as the Queen of New Zealand; the Prime Minister is the Head of Government.

RULER
British

STATE
1907 - present

DECIMAL COINAGE

100 Cents = 1 Dollar

(c) Royal Australian Mint, Canberra

(l) Royal Mint, Llantrisant

(o) Royal Canadian Mint, Ottawa or Winnipeg

(m) B.H. Mayer, Germany

(n) Norwegian Mint, Kongsberg

(p) South African Mint, Pretoria

(v) Valcambi SA, Switzerland

(w) Perth Mint, Western Australia

KM# 116 5 CENTS

2.8300 g., Copper-Nickel, 19.41 mm. **Ruler:** Elizabeth II **Obv:** Head with tiara right **Obv. Designer:** Ian Rank-Broadley **Rev:** Value below tuatara **Rev. Designer:** James Berry **Edge:** Reeded
Note: Many recalled and melted in 2006.

Date	Mintage	F	VF	XF	Unc	BU
2001(l)	20,000,000	—	—	0.10	0.50	1.00
2001(c) In sets only	2,910	—	—	—	4.00	5.00
2001(c) Proof	1,364	Value: 3.00				
2002(l)	40,500,000	—	—	0.10	0.50	1.00
2002(c) In sets only	3,000	—	—	—	5.00	6.00
2002(c) Proof	1,500	Value: 3.00				
2003(l)	30,000,000	—	—	—	0.50	1.00
2003(c) In sets only	1,496	—	—	—	5.00	6.00
2003 Proof	3,000	Value: 3.00				
2004(l)	15,000,000	—	—	—	2.00	3.00

Note: All but 48,000 melted. Many of these survivors have recently come onto the NZ market in bulk.

Date	Mintage	F	VF	XF	Unc	BU
2004(c) In sets only	2,800	—	—	—	20.00	30.00
2004(c) Proof	1,750	Value: 3.00				
2005(c) In sets only	3,000	—	—	—	8.00	12.00
2005(c) Proof	2,250	Value: 3.00				
2006(c) In sets only	—	—	—	—	8.00	12.00
2006(c) Proof	—	Value: 3.00				

KM# 117 10 CENTS
5.6500 g., Copper-Nickel, 23.6 mm. **Ruler:** Elizabeth II **Obv:** Head with tiara right **Obv. Designer:** Ian Rank-Broadley **Rev:** Value above koruru **Rev. Designer:** James Berry **Edge:** Reeded **Note:** Many recalled and melted in 2006.

Date	Mintage	F	VF	XF	Unc	BU
2001(l)	10,000,000	—	—	0.10	0.30	0.50
2001(c) In sets only	2,910	—	—	—	6.00	8.00
2001(c) Proof	1,364	Value: 4.00				
2002(l)	10,000,000	—	—	0.10	0.30	0.50
2002(c) In sets only	3,000	—	—	—	3.00	5.00
2002(c) Proof	1,500	Value: 4.00				
2003(l)	13,000,000	—	—	0.10	0.30	0.50
2003(c) In sets only	3,000	—	—	—	5.00	8.00
2003(l) Proof	1,496	Value: 4.00				
2004(l)	6,500,000	—	—	—	0.30	0.50
2004(c) In sets only	—	—	—	—	5.00	8.00
2004(c) Proof	1,750	Value: 4.00				
2005	2,000,000	—	—	—	30.00	40.00
Note: All but 28,000 melted						
2005(c) In sets only	3,000	—	—	—	20.00	30.00
2005(c) Proof	2,250	Value: 4.00				
2006(c) In sets only	3,000	—	—	—	10.00	15.00
2006(c) Proof	2,100	Value: 4.00				

KM# 117a 10 CENTS
3.3100 g., Copper Plated Steel, 20.5 mm. **Ruler:** Elizabeth II **Obv:** Head with tiara right **Obv. Designer:** Ian Rank-Broadley **Rev:** Value above koruru

Date	Mintage	F	VF	XF	Unc	BU
2006(o)	140,200,000	—	—	—	0.20	0.40
2007(o)	15,000,000	—	—	—	—	—
2007(c) In sets only	5,000	—	—	—	—	5.00
2007(c) Proof	3,500	Value: 4.00				
2008(l) In sets only	4,000	—	—	—	—	5.00
2008(l) Proof	3,000	Value: 4.00				
2009(o)	30,000,000	—	—	—	0.20	0.40
2009(w) In Sets only	2,000	—	—	—	—	5.00
2009(w) Proof	1,500	Value: 4.00				

KM# 234 10 CENTS
3.3100 g., Copper Plated Steel, 20.5 mm. **Ruler:** Elizabeth II **Obv:** Head with tiara right **Obv. Designer:** Ian Rank-Broadley **Rev:** Tuatara right **Edge:** Plain

Date	Mintage	F	VF	XF	Unc	BU
2007(c) In sets only	15,000	—	—	—	0.50	5.00

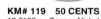

KM# 118 20 CENTS
11.3100 g., Copper-Nickel, 28.58 mm. **Ruler:** Elizabeth II **Obv:** Head with tiara right **Obv. Designer:** Ian Rank-Broadley **Rev:** Value below Pukaki **Rev. Designer:** R.M. Conly **Edge:** Reeded **Note:** Many recalled and melted in 2006.

Date	Mintage	F	VF	XF	Unc	BU
2001(c) In sets only	2,910	—	—	—	—	4.00
2001(c) Proof	1,364	Value: 10.00				
2002(l)	7,000,000	—	—	—	0.50	—
2002(c) In sets only	3,000	—	—	—	—	5.00
2002(c) Proof	1,500	Value: 10.00				
2003(c) In sets only	3,000	—	—	—	—	4.00
2003(c) Proof	3,000	Value: 10.00				
2004(l)	8,500,000	—	—	—	0.50	—
2004(c) In sets only	2,800	—	—	—	—	5.00
2004(c) Proof	1,750	Value: 10.00				
2005(l)	4,000,000	—	—	—	—	15.00
Note: All but 178,000 melted						
2005(c) In sets only	3,000	—	—	—	—	5.00
2005(c) Proof	2,250	Value: 10.00				
2006(c) In sets only	3,000	—	—	—	—	5.00
2006(c) Proof	2,100	Value: 10.00				

KM# 118a 20 CENTS
4.0000 g., Nickel Plated Steel, 21.75 mm. **Ruler:** Elizabeth II **Obv:** Head with tiara right **Obv. Designer:** Ian Rank-Broadley **Rev:** Value below Pukaki **Rev. Designer:** R.M. Conly **Shape:** Scalloped

Date	Mintage	F	VF	XF	Unc	BU
2006(o)	116,600,000	—	—	—	0.40	0.65
2007(c) In sets only	5,000	—	—	—	—	7.00
2007(c) Proof	4,000	Value: 8.00				
2008(o)	80,000,000	—	—	—	0.40	0.65
2008(l) In sets only	4,000	—	—	—	—	7.00
2008(l) Proof	3,000	Value: 8.00				
2009(w) In sets only	2,000	—	—	—	—	7.00
2009(w) Proof	1,500	Value: 8.00				

KM# 119 50 CENTS
13.6100 g., Copper-Nickel, 31.75 mm. **Ruler:** Elizabeth II **Obv:** Head with tiara right **Obv. Designer:** Ian Rank-Broadley **Rev:** H.M.S. Endeavour and value **Rev. Designer:** James Berry **Edge:** Segmented reeding **Note:** Many recalled and melted in 2006.

Date	Mintage	F	VF	XF	Unc	BU
2001(l)	5,000,000	—	—	—	1.00	—
2001(c) In sets only	2,910	—	—	—	—	4.00
2001(c) Proof	1,364	Value: 5.00				
2002(l)	3,000,000	—	—	0.50	1.00	—
2002(c) In sets only	3,000	—	—	—	—	4.00
2002(c) Proof	1,500	Value: 5.00				
2003(l)	2,500,000	—	—	0.50	1.00	—
2003(c) In sets only	3,000	—	—	—	—	4.00
2003(c) Proof	1,496	Value: 5.00				
2004(l)	2,000,000	—	—	—	1.00	—
2004(c) In sets only	2,800	—	—	—	—	4.00
2004(c) Proof	1,750	Value: 5.00				
2005(l)	1,000,000	—	—	—	7.50	—
Note: All but 503,800 melted						
2005(c) In sets only	3,000	—	—	—	—	4.00
2005(c) Proof	2,250	Value: 5.00				
2006(c) In sets only	3,000	—	—	—	—	4.00
2006(c) Proof	2,100	Value: 5.00				

KM# 135 50 CENTS
13.6100 g., Copper-Nickel, 31.75 mm. **Ruler:** Elizabeth II **Subject:** Lord of the Rings **Obv:** Head with tiara right **Obv. Designer:** Ian Rank-Broadley **Rev:** Frodo's head facing to left of vine and value **Rev. Designer:** Matthew Bonaccorsi **Edge:** Reeded

Date	Mintage	F	VF	XF	Unc	BU
2003(l)	41,221	—	—	—	—	15.00

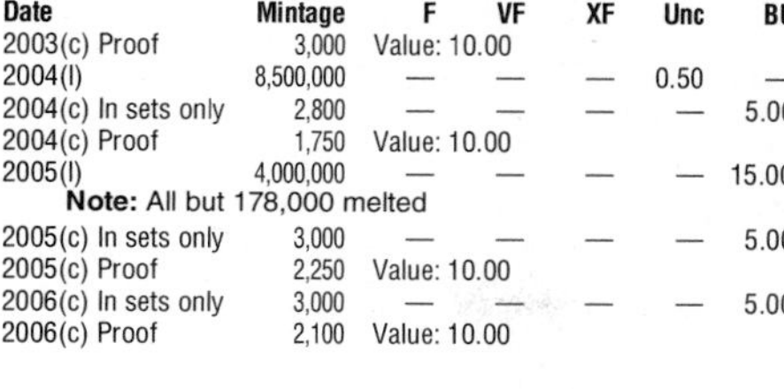

KM# 136 50 CENTS
13.6100 g., Copper-Nickel, 31.75 mm. **Ruler:** Elizabeth II **Subject:** Lord of the Rings **Obv:** Head with tiara right **Obv. Designer:** Ian Rank-Broadley **Rev:** Head of Gandalf with hat facing and value **Rev. Designer:** Matthew Bonaccorsi **Edge:** Reeded

Date	Mintage	F	VF	XF	Unc	BU
2003(l)	41,221	—	—	—	—	15.00

KM# 137 50 CENTS
13.6100 g., Copper-Nickel, 31.75 mm. **Ruler:** Elizabeth II **Subject:** Lord of the Rings **Obv:** Head with tiara right **Obv. Designer:** Ian Rank-Broadley **Rev:** Head of Aragorn facing and value **Rev. Designer:** Matthew Bonaccorsi **Edge:** Reeded

Date	Mintage	F	VF	XF	Unc	BU
2003(l)	41,221	—	—	—	—	15.00

KM# 138 50 CENTS
13.6100 g., Copper-Nickel, 31.75 mm. **Ruler:** Elizabeth II **Subject:** Lord of the Rings **Obv:** Head with tiara right **Obv. Designer:** Ian Rank-Broadley **Rev:** Head of Gollum facing and value **Rev. Designer:** Matthew Bonaccorsi **Edge:** Reeded

Date	Mintage	F	VF	XF	Unc	BU
2003(l)	38,400	—	—	—	—	15.00

KM# 139 50 CENTS
13.6100 g., Copper-Nickel, 31.75 mm. **Ruler:** Elizabeth II **Subject:** Lord of the Rings **Obv:** Head with tiara right **Obv. Designer:** Ian Rank-Broadley **Rev:** Saruman, value **Rev. Designer:** Matthew Bonaccorsi **Edge:** Reeded

Date	Mintage	F	VF	XF	Unc	BU
2003(l)	38,400	—	—	—	—	15.00

KM# 140 50 CENTS
13.6100 g., Copper-Nickel, 31.75 mm. **Ruler:** Elizabeth II **Subject:** Lord of the Rings **Obv:** Head with tiara right **Obv. Designer:** Ian Rank-Broadley **Rev:** Head of Sauron left and value **Rev. Designer:** Matthew Bonaccorsi **Edge:** Reeded

Date	Mintage	F	VF	XF	Unc	BU
2003(l)	38,400	—	—	—	—	15.00

KM# 235 50 CENTS
13.6100 g., Copper-Nickel, 31.75 mm. **Ruler:** Elizabeth II **Subject:** Lord of the Rings **Obv:** Head with tiara right **Obv. Designer:** Ian Rank-Broadley **Rev:** Boromir **Rev. Designer:** Matthew Bonaccorsi

Date	Mintage	F	VF	XF	Unc	BU
2003(l)	6,889	—	—	—	—	18.00

KM# 236 50 CENTS
13.6100 g., Copper-Nickel, 31.75 mm. **Ruler:** Elizabeth II **Subject:** Lord of the Rings **Obv:** Head with tiara right **Obv. Designer:** Ian Rank-Broadley **Rev:** Gimli **Rev. Designer:** Matthew Bonaccorsi

Date	Mintage	F	VF	XF	Unc	BU
2003(l)	6,889	—	—	—	—	18.00

KM# 237 50 CENTS
13.6100 g., Copper-Nickel, 31.75 mm. **Ruler:** Elizabeth II **Subject:** Lord of the Rings **Obv:** Head with tiara right **Obv. Designer:** Ian Rank-Broadley **Rev:** Legolas **Rev. Designer:** Matthew Bonaccorsi

Date	Mintage	F	VF	XF	Unc	BU
2003(l)	6,889	—	—	—	—	18.00

KM# 238 50 CENTS
13.6100 g., Copper-Nickel, 31.75 mm. **Ruler:** Elizabeth II **Subject:** Lord of the Rings **Obv:** Head with tiara right **Obv. Designer:** Ian Rank-Broadley **Rev:** Merry **Rev. Designer:** Matthew Bonaccorsi

Date	Mintage	F	VF	XF	Unc	BU
2003(l)	6,889	—	—	—	—	18.00

KM# 239 50 CENTS
13.6100 g., Copper-Nickel, 31.75 mm. **Ruler:** Elizabeth II **Subject:** Lord of the Rings **Obv:** Head with tiara right **Obv. Designer:** Ian Rank-Broadley **Rev:** Pippin **Rev. Designer:** Matthew Bonaccorsi

Date	Mintage	F	VF	XF	Unc	BU
2003(l)	6,889	—	—	—	—	18.00

KM# 240 50 CENTS

13.6100 g., Copper-Nickel, 31.75 mm. **Ruler:** Elizabeth II **Subject:** Lord of the Rings **Obv:** Head with tiara right **Obv. Designer:** Ian Rank-Broadley **Rev:** Sam **Rev. Designer:** Matthew Bonaccorsi

Date	Mintage	F	VF	XF	Unc	BU
2003(l)	6,889	—	—	—	—	18.00

KM# 241 50 CENTS

13.6100 g., Copper-Nickel, 31.75 mm. **Ruler:** Elizabeth II **Subject:** Lord of the Rings **Obv:** Head with tiara right **Obv. Designer:** Ian Rank-Broadley **Rev:** Arwen **Rev. Designer:** Matthew Bonaccorsi

Date	Mintage	F	VF	XF	Unc	BU
2003(l)	4,068	—	—	—	—	20.00

KM# 242 50 CENTS

13.6100 g., Copper-Nickel, 31.75 mm. **Ruler:** Elizabeth II **Subject:** Lord of the Rings **Obv:** Head with tiara right **Obv. Designer:** Ian Rank-Broadley **Rev:** Elrond **Rev. Designer:** Matthew Bonaccorsi

Date	Mintage	F	VF	XF	Unc	BU
2003(l)	4,068	—	—	—	—	20.00

KM# 243 50 CENTS

13.6100 g., Copper-Nickel, 31.75 mm. **Ruler:** Elizabeth II **Subject:** Lord of the Rings **Obv:** Head with tiara right **Obv. Designer:** Ian Rank-Broadley **Rev:** Eowyn **Rev. Designer:** Matthew Bonaccorsi

Date	Mintage	F	VF	XF	Unc	BU
2003(l)	4,068	—	—	—	—	20.00

KM# 244 50 CENTS

13.6100 g., Copper-Nickel, 31.75 mm. **Ruler:** Elizabeth II **Subject:** Lord of the Rings **Obv:** Head with tiara right **Obv. Designer:** Ian Rank-Broadley **Rev:** Galadriel **Rev. Designer:** Matthew Bonaccorsi

Date	Mintage	F	VF	XF	Unc	BU
2003(l)	4,068	—	—	—	—	20.00

KM# 245 50 CENTS

13.6100 g., Copper-Nickel, 31.75 mm. **Ruler:** Elizabeth II **Subject:** Lord of the Rings **Obv:** Head with tiara right **Obv. Designer:** Ian Rank-Broadley **Rev:** An Orc **Rev. Designer:** Matthew Bonaccorsi

Date	Mintage	F	VF	XF	Unc	BU
2003(l)	4,068	—	—	—	—	20.00

KM# 246 50 CENTS

13.6100 g., Copper-Nickel, 31.75 mm. **Ruler:** Elizabeth II **Subject:** Lord of the Rings **Obv:** Head with tiara right **Obv. Designer:** Ian Rank-Broadley **Rev:** Treebeard **Rev. Designer:** Matthew Bonaccorsi

Date	Mintage	F	VF	XF	Unc	BU
2003(l)	4,068	—	—	—	—	20.00

KM# 119a 50 CENTS

5.0000 g., Nickel Plated Steel, 24.75 mm. **Ruler:** Elizabeth II **Obv:** Head with tiara right **Rev:** Ship, H.M.S. Endeavour **Rev. Designer:** James Berry

Date	Mintage	F	VF	XF	Unc	BU
2006(o)	70,200,000	—	—	—	0.75	1.00
2007(c) In sets only	5,000	—	—	—	—	8.00
2007(c) Proof	3,500	Value: 10.00				
2008(l) In sets only	4,000	—	—	—	—	8.00
2008(l) Proof	3,000	Value: 10.00				
2009(o)	20,000,000	—	—	—	0.75	1.00
2009(w) In sets only	2,000	—	—	—	—	8.00
2009(w) Proof	1,500	Value: 10.00				

KM# 279 50 CENTS

Aluminum-Bronze, 38.74 mm. **Ruler:** Elizabeth II **Subject:** Narnia **Obv:** Head with tiara right **Obv. Designer:** Ian Rank-Broadley **Rev:** Peter **Rev. Designer:** W. Pietranik

Date	Mintage	F	VF	XF	Unc	BU
2006(c)	20,000	—	—	—	—	6.00

KM# 280 50 CENTS

Aluminum-Bronze, 38.74 mm. **Ruler:** Elizabeth II **Subject:** Narnia **Obv:** Head with tiara right **Obv. Designer:** Ian Rank-Broadley **Rev:** Susan **Rev. Designer:** W. Pietranik

Date	Mintage	F	VF	XF	Unc	BU
2006(c)	20,000	—	—	—	—	6.00

KM# 281 50 CENTS

Aluminum-Bronze, 38.74 mm. **Ruler:** Elizabeth II **Subject:** Narnia **Obv:** Head with tiara right **Obv. Designer:** Ian Rank-Broadley **Rev:** Edmund **Rev. Designer:** W. Pietranik

Date	Mintage	F	VF	XF	Unc	BU
2006(c)	20,000	—	—	—	—	6.00

KM# 282 50 CENTS

Aluminum-Bronze, 38.74 mm. **Ruler:** Elizabeth II **Subject:** Narnia **Obv:** Head with tiara right **Obv. Designer:** Ian Rank-Broadley **Rev:** Lucy **Rev. Designer:** W. Pietranik

Date	Mintage	F	VF	XF	Unc	BU
2006(c)	20,000	—	—	—	—	6.00

KM# 283 50 CENTS

Aluminum-Bronze, 38.74 mm. **Ruler:** Elizabeth II **Subject:** Narnia **Obv:** Head with tiara right **Obv. Designer:** Ian Rank-Broadley **Rev:** Mr. Tumnus **Rev. Designer:** W. Pietranik

Date	Mintage	F	VF	XF	Unc	BU
2006(c)	20,000	—	—	—	—	6.00

KM# 284 50 CENTS

Aluminum-Bronze, 38.74 mm. **Ruler:** Elizabeth II **Subject:** Narnia **Obv:** Head with tiara right **Obv. Designer:** Ian Rank-Broadley **Rev:** Ginarrbrik **Rev. Designer:** W. Pietranik

Date	Mintage	F	VF	XF	Unc	BU
2006(c)	20,000	—	—	—	—	6.00

KM# 120 DOLLAR

8.0000 g., Aluminum-Bronze, 23 mm. **Ruler:** Elizabeth II **Obv:** Head with tiara right **Obv. Designer:** Ian Rank-Broadley **Rev:** Kiwi bird within sprigs, value below **Rev. Designer:** R. Maurice Conly **Edge:** Segmented reeding

Date	Mintage	F	VF	XF	Unc	BU
2001(c) In sets only	2,910	—	—	—	—	4.00
2001(c) Proof	1,364	Value: 5.00				
2002(l)	8,000,000	—	—	—	1.00	2.50
2002(c) In sets only	4,000	—	—	—	—	4.00
2002(c) Proof	1,500	Value: 5.00				
2003(l)	4,000,000	—	—	—	1.00	2.50
2003(c) In sets only	5,000	—	—	—	—	4.00
2003(c) Proof	1,750	Value: 5.00				
2004(l)	2,700,000	—	—	—	1.00	2.50
2004(c) In sets only	3,500	—	—	—	—	4.00
2004(c) Proof	2,250	Value: 5.00				
2005(l)	2,000,000	—	—	—	1.00	2.50
2005(c) In sets only	4,000	—	—	—	—	4.00
2005(c) Proof	2,250	Value: 5.00				
2006(c) In sets only	3,000	—	—	—	—	4.00
2006(c) Proof	2,100	Value: 5.00				
2007(c)	—	—	—	—	—	4.00
2007(c) Proof	—	Value: 5.00				
2008(l)	6,000,000	—	—	—	1.00	2.50
2008(l) In sets only	4,000	—	—	—	—	4.00
2008(l) Proof	3,000	Value: 5.00				
2009(w) In sets only	2,000	—	—	—	—	4.00
2009(w) Proof	1,500	Value: 5.00				

KM# 141 DOLLAR

28.2800 g., Aluminum-Bronze, 38.61 mm. **Ruler:** Elizabeth II **Subject:** Lord of the Rings **Obv:** Head with tiara right **Obv. Designer:** Ian Rank-Broadley **Rev:** Inscribed ring around value **Rev. Designer:** Matthew Bonaccorsi **Edge:** Reeded

Date	Mintage	F	VF	XF	Unc	BU
2003(l)	30,081	—	—	—	—	15.00

Note: Mintage includes 10,454 in sets.

KM# 141a DOLLAR

28.2800 g., 0.9250 Silver 0.8410 oz. ASW, 38.61 mm. **Ruler:** Elizabeth II **Obv:** Head with tiara right **Obv. Designer:** Ian Rank-Broadley **Rev:** Gold-plated ring and edge **Edge:** Reeded

Date	Mintage	F	VF	XF	Unc	BU
2003(l) Proof	39,244	Value: 70.00				

KM# 142 DOLLAR

28.2800 g., Aluminum-Bronze, 38.61 mm. **Ruler:** Elizabeth II **Subject:** Lord of the Rings **Obv:** Head with tiara right **Obv. Designer:** Ian Rank-Broadley **Rev:** Head of Frodo looking down above inscription **Rev. Designer:** Matthew Bonaccorsi **Edge:** Reeded

Date	Mintage	F	VF	XF	Unc	BU
2003(l)	10,454	—	—	—	—	10.00

KM# 143 DOLLAR

28.2800 g., Aluminum-Bronze, 38.61 mm. **Ruler:** Elizabeth II **Subject:** Lord of the Rings **Obv:** Head with tiara right **Obv. Designer:** Ian Rank-Broadley **Rev:** View of Sauron, value **Rev. Designer:** Matthew Bonaccorsi **Edge:** Reeded

Date	Mintage	F	VF	XF	Unc	BU
2003(l)	10,454	—	—	—	—	10.00

KM# 247 DOLLAR

28.2800 g., 0.9250 Silver 0.8410 oz. ASW, 38.61 mm. **Ruler:** Elizabeth II **Subject:** Lord of the Rings **Obv:** Head with tiara right **Obv. Designer:** Ian Rank-Broadley **Rev:** Aragorn's Coronation **Rev. Designer:** Matthew Bonaccorsi

Date	Mintage	F	VF	XF	Unc	BU
2003(l) Proof	3,057	Value: 70.00				

KM# 248 DOLLAR

28.2800 g., 0.9250 Silver 0.8410 oz. ASW, 38.61 mm. **Ruler:** Elizabeth II **Subject:** Lord of the Rings **Obv:** Head with tiara right **Obv. Designer:** Ian Rank-Broadley **Rev:** King Theoden **Rev. Designer:** Matthew Bonaccorsi

Date	Mintage	F	VF	XF	Unc	BU
2003(l) Proof	2,022	Value: 70.00				

KM# 249 DOLLAR

28.2800 g., 0.9250 Silver 0.8410 oz. ASW, 38.61 mm. **Ruler:** Elizabeth II **Subject:** Lord of the Rings **Obv:** Head with tiara right **Obv. Designer:** Ian Rank-Broadley **Rev:** Flight to the Ford **Rev. Designer:** Matthew Bonaccorsi

Date	Mintage	F	VF	XF	Unc	BU
2003(l) Proof	2,020	Value: 70.00				

KM# 250 DOLLAR

28.2800 g., 0.9250 Silver 0.8410 oz. ASW, 38.61 mm. **Ruler:** Elizabeth II **Subject:** Lord of the Rings **Obv:** Head with tiara right **Obv. Designer:** Ian Rank-Broadley **Rev:** Mirror of Galadriel **Rev. Designer:** Matthew Bonaccorsi

Date	Mintage	F	VF	XF	Unc	BU
2003(I) Proof	2,036	Value: 70.00				

KM# 251 DOLLAR

28.2800 g., 0.9250 Silver 0.8410 oz. ASW, 38.61 mm. **Ruler:** Elizabeth II **Subject:** Lord of the Rings **Obv:** Head with tiara right **Obv. Designer:** Ian Rank-Broadley **Rev:** Frodo offering ring to Nazgul **Rev. Designer:** Matthew Bonaccorsi

Date	Mintage	F	VF	XF	Unc	BU
2003(I) Proof	1,784	Value: 70.00				

KM# 252 DOLLAR

28.2800 g., 0.9250 Silver 0.8410 oz. ASW, 38.61 mm. **Ruler:** Elizabeth II **Subject:** Lord of the Rings **Obv:** Head with tiara right **Obv. Designer:** Ian Rank-Broadley **Rev:** Bridge of Kazad-Dum **Rev. Designer:** Matthew Bonaccorsi

Date	Mintage	F	VF	XF	Unc	BU
2003(I) Proof	952	Value: 70.00				

KM# 253 DOLLAR

28.2800 g., 0.9250 Silver 0.8410 oz. ASW, 38.61 mm. **Ruler:** Elizabeth II **Subject:** Lord of the Rings **Obv:** Head with tiara right **Obv. Designer:** Ian Rank-Broadley **Rev:** Shelob's Lair **Rev. Designer:** Matthew Bonaccorsi

Date	Mintage	F	VF	XF	Unc	BU
2003(I) Proof	917	Value: 70.00				

KM# 254 DOLLAR

28.2800 g., 0.9250 Silver 0.8410 oz. ASW, 38.61 mm. **Ruler:** Elizabeth II **Subject:** Lord of the Rings **Obv:** Head with tiara right **Obv. Designer:** Ian Rank-Broadley **Rev:** Taming of Smeagol **Rev. Designer:** Matthew Bonaccorsi

Date	Mintage	F	VF	XF	Unc	BU
2003(I) Proof	1,017	Value: 70.00				

KM# 255 DOLLAR

28.2800 g., 0.9250 Silver 0.8410 oz. ASW, 38.61 mm. **Ruler:** Elizabeth II **Subject:** Lord of the Rings **Obv:** Head with tiara right **Obv. Designer:** Ian Rank-Broadley **Rev:** Dark Lord's Tower and the Eye **Rev. Designer:** Matthew Bonaccorsi

Date	Mintage	F	VF	XF	Unc	BU
2003(I) Proof	1,002	Value: 70.00				

KM# 256 DOLLAR

28.2800 g., 0.9250 Silver 0.8410 oz. ASW, 38.61 mm. **Ruler:** Elizabeth II **Subject:** Lord of the Rings **Obv:** Head with tiara right **Obv. Designer:** Ian Rank-Broadley **Rev:** Knife in the Dark **Rev. Designer:** Matthew Bonaccorsi

Date	Mintage	F	VF	XF	Unc	BU
2003(I) Proof	967	Value: 70.00				

KM# 257 DOLLAR

28.2800 g., 0.9250 Silver 0.8410 oz. ASW, 38.61 mm. **Ruler:** Elizabeth II **Subject:** Lord of the Rings **Obv:** Head with tiara right **Obv. Designer:** Ian Rank-Broadley **Rev:** Gandalf and Saruman **Rev. Designer:** Matthew Bonaccorsi

Date	Mintage	F	VF	XF	Unc	BU
2003(I) Proof	867	Value: 70.00				

KM# 258 DOLLAR

28.2800 g., 0.9250 Silver 0.8410 oz. ASW, 38.61 mm. **Ruler:** Elizabeth II **Subject:** Lord of the Rings **Obv:** Head with tiara right **Obv. Designer:** Ian Rank-Broadley **Rev:** Council of Elrond **Rev. Designer:** Matthew Bonaccorsi

Date	Mintage	F	VF	XF	Unc	BU
2003(I) Proof	1,204	Value: 70.00				

KM# 259 DOLLAR

28.2800 g., 0.9250 Silver 0.8410 oz. ASW, 38.61 mm. **Ruler:** Elizabeth II **Subject:** Lord of the Rings **Obv:** Head with tiara right **Obv. Designer:** Ian Rank-Broadley **Rev:** Helm's Deep **Rev. Designer:** Matthew Bonaccorsi

Date	Mintage	F	VF	XF	Unc	BU
2003(I) Proof	967	Value: 70.00				

KM# 260 DOLLAR

28.2800 g., 0.9250 Silver 0.8410 oz. ASW, 38.61 mm. **Ruler:** Elizabeth II **Subject:** Lord of the Rings **Obv:** Head with tiara right **Obv. Designer:** Ian Rank-Broadley **Rev:** Frodo & Co. at Mt. Doom **Rev. Designer:** Matthew Bonaccorsi

Date	Mintage	F	VF	XF	Unc	BU
2003(I) Proof	917	Value: 70.00				

KM# 261 DOLLAR

28.2800 g., 0.9250 Silver 0.8410 oz. ASW, 38.61 mm. **Ruler:** Elizabeth II **Subject:** Lord of the Rings **Obv:** Head with tiara right **Obv. Designer:** Ian Rank-Broadley **Rev:** Departure of Boromir **Rev. Designer:** Matthew Bonaccorsi

Date	Mintage	F	VF	XF	Unc	BU
2003(I) Proof	917	Value: 70.00				

KM# 262 DOLLAR

28.2800 g., 0.9250 Silver 0.8410 oz. ASW, 38.61 mm. **Ruler:** Elizabeth II **Subject:** Lord of the Rings **Obv:** Head with tiara right **Obv. Designer:** Ian Rank-Broadley **Rev:** Meeting of Treebeard **Rev. Designer:** Matthew Bonaccorsi

Date	Mintage	F	VF	XF	Unc	BU
2003(I) Proof	867	Value: 70.00				

KM# 263 DOLLAR

28.2800 g., 0.9250 Silver 0.8410 oz. ASW, 38.61 mm. **Ruler:** Elizabeth II **Subject:** Lord of the Rings **Obv:** Head with tiara right **Obv. Designer:** Ian Rank-Broadley **Rev:** Battle of Minas Tirith / Pelenor Fields **Rev. Designer:** Matthew Bonaccorsi

Date	Mintage	F	VF	XF	Unc	BU
2003(I) Proof	867	Value: 70.00				

KM# 264 DOLLAR

28.2800 g., 0.9250 Silver 0.8410 oz. ASW, 38.61 mm. **Ruler:** Elizabeth II **Subject:** Lord of the Rings **Obv:** Head with tiara right **Obv. Designer:** Ian Rank-Broadley **Rev:** Gandalf Reappears **Rev. Designer:** Matthew Bonaccorsi

Date	Mintage	F	VF	XF	Unc	BU
2003(I) Proof	967	Value: 70.00				

KM# 265 DOLLAR

28.2800 g., 0.9250 Silver 0.8410 oz. ASW, 38.61 mm. **Ruler:** Elizabeth II **Subject:** Lord of the Rings **Obv:** Head with tiara right **Obv. Designer:** Ian Rank-Broadley **Rev:** Army of the Dead **Rev. Designer:** Matthew Bonaccorsi

Date	Mintage	F	VF	XF	Unc	BU
2003(I) Proof	917	Value: 70.00				

KM# 266 DOLLAR

28.2800 g., 0.9250 Silver 0.8410 oz. ASW, 38.61 mm. **Ruler:** Elizabeth II **Subject:** Lord of the Rings **Obv:** Head with tiara right **Obv. Designer:** Ian Rank-Broadley **Rev:** Travel to the Undying Lands **Rev. Designer:** Matthew Bonaccorsi

Date	Mintage	F	VF	XF	Unc	BU
2003(I) Proof	867	Value: 70.00				

KM# 267 DOLLAR

28.2800 g., 0.9250 Silver 0.8410 oz. ASW, 38.61 mm. **Ruler:** Elizabeth II **Subject:** Lord of the Rings **Obv:** Head with tiara right **Obv. Designer:** Ian Rank-Broadley **Rev:** Great River **Rev. Designer:** Matthew Bonaccorsi

Date	Mintage	F	VF	XF	Unc	BU
2003(I) Proof	867	Value: 70.00				

KM# 268 DOLLAR

28.2800 g., 0.9250 Silver 0.8410 oz. ASW, 38.61 mm. **Ruler:** Elizabeth II **Subject:** Lord of the Rings **Obv:** Head with tiara right **Obv. Designer:** Ian Rank-Broadley **Rev:** Death of the Witch King **Rev. Designer:** Matthew Bonaccorsi

Date	Mintage	F	VF	XF	Unc	BU
2003(I) Proof	867	Value: 70.00				

KM# 269 DOLLAR

28.2800 g., 0.9250 Silver 0.8410 oz. ASW, 38.61 mm. **Ruler:** Elizabeth II **Subject:** Lord of the Rings **Obv:** Head with tiara right **Obv. Designer:** Ian Rank-Broadley **Rev:** March of the Oliphants **Rev. Designer:** Matthew Bonaccorsi

Date	Mintage	F	VF	XF	Unc	BU
2003(I) Proof	867	Value: 70.00				

KM# 152 DOLLAR

31.1350 g., 0.9990 Silver 100000 oz. ASW, 40 mm. **Ruler:** Elizabeth II **Obv:** Crowned head right **Rev:** Little spotted kiwi **Edge:** Reeded

Date	Mintage	F	VF	XF	Unc	BU
2004(c)	2,500	—	—	—	—	45.00
2004(c) Proof	2,000	Value: 50.00				

Note: Includes 500 struck in 2008 for sets.

KM# 157 DOLLAR

Aluminum-Bronze, 38.74 mm. **Ruler:** Elizabeth II **Subject:** ANZAC **Obv:** Crowned head right **Rev:** Soldiers from Chun uk Bair battle with rifles and bayonets **Edge:** Reeded

Date	Mintage	F	VF	XF	Unc	BU
2005 Proof	15,000	Value: 25.00				

KM# 153 DOLLAR

31.6350 g., 0.9990 Silver 1.0160 oz. ASW, 40.6 mm. **Ruler:** Elizabeth II **Obv:** Crowned head right **Obv. Designer:** Ian Rank-Broadley **Rev:** Rowi Kiwi **Edge:** Reeded

Date	Mintage	F	VF	XF	Unc	BU
2005(w)	10,000	—	—	—	—	40.00
2005(w)	4,000	Value: 60.00				

KM# 153a DOLLAR

31.6350 g., 0.9990 Silver 1.0160 oz. ASW, 38.74 mm. **Ruler:** Elizabeth II **Rev:** Kiwi

Date	Mintage	F	VF	XF	Unc	BU
2005(w) Proof	2,700	Value: 80.00				

Note: Mintage includes 500 struck in 2008 for sets.

Date	Mintage	F	VF	XF	Unc	BU
2005(w) Proof	5,000	Value: 50.00				

Note: Each has different packaging.

KM# 154 DOLLAR

31.1350 g., 0.9990 Silver 100000 oz. ASW, 40 mm. **Ruler:** Elizabeth II **Subject:** ANZAC **Obv:** Crowned head right **Rev:** Soldiers seated, multicolor flag in background **Edge:** Reeded

Date	Mintage	F	VF	XF	Unc	BU
2005 P Proof	15,000	Value: 110				

KM# 156 DOLLAR

28.2800 g., Aluminum-Bronze, 38.61 mm. **Ruler:** Elizabeth II **Subject:** Lions Rugby Tour **Obv:** Crowned head right **Rev:** Rugby player, Lions crest and New Zealand map **Rev. Designer:** Michael Guilfoyle

Date	Mintage	F	VF	XF	Unc	BU
2005(l)	15,000	—	—	—	—	20.00

KM# 156a DOLLAR

28.2800 g., 0.9250 Silver 0.8410 oz. ASW, 38.61 mm. **Ruler:** Elizabeth II **Series:** Rugby player, Lions crest & New Zealand map **Subject:** Lions Rugby Tour **Obv:** Crowned head right **Obv. Designer:** Ian Rank-Broadley **Rev. Designer:** Michael Guilfoyle **Edge:** Reeded

Date	Mintage	F	VF	XF	Unc	BU
2005(l) Proof	5,000	Value: 50.00				

KM# 159 DOLLAR

20.0000 g., Aluminum-Bronze, 38.74 mm. **Ruler:** Elizabeth II **Subject:** King Kong **Obv:** Crowned head right **Obv. Designer:** Ian Rank-Broadley **Rev:** King Kong **Edge:** Reeded

Date	Mintage	F	VF	XF	Unc	BU
2005(w)	7,000	—	—	—	—	20.00

KM# 160 DOLLAR

20.0000 g., Aluminum-Bronze, 38.74 mm. **Ruler:** Elizabeth II **Subject:** King Kong **Obv:** Crowned head right **Rev:** Multicolored King Kong **Edge:** Reeded

Date	Mintage	F	VF	XF	Unc	BU
2005(w)	4,000	—	—	—	—	35.00

KM# 161 DOLLAR

20.0000 g., Aluminum-Bronze, 38.74 mm. **Ruler:** Elizabeth II **Subject:** King Kong **Obv:** Crowned head right **Rev:** Carl Denham and camera in multicolor **Edge:** Reeded

Date	Mintage	F	VF	XF	Unc	BU
2005	4,000	—	—	—	—	35.00

KM# 162 DOLLAR

20.0000 g., Aluminum-Bronze, 38.74 mm. **Ruler:** Elizabeth II **Subject:** King Kong **Obv:** Crowned head right **Rev:** Ann Darrow and Jack Driscoll multicolored **Edge:** Reeded

Date	Mintage	F	VF	XF	Unc	BU
2005	4,000	—	—	—	—	35.00

KM# 164 DOLLAR

31.1350 g., 0.9990 Silver partially gold plated 100000 oz. ASW, 40.6 mm. **Ruler:** Elizabeth II **Obv:** Crowned head right **Rev:** King Kong partially gold plated

Date	Mintage	F	VF	XF	Unc	BU
2005(w) Proof	3,000	Value: 70.00				

KM# 276 DOLLAR

20.0000 g., Aluminum-Bronze, 38.74 mm. **Ruler:** Elizabeth II **Subject:** Emblem **Obv:** Head with tiara right **Obv. Designer:** Ian Rank-Broadley **Rev:** Rowi and chick inside patterned ring

Date	Mintage	F	VF	XF	Unc	BU
2005(w)	20,000	—	—	—	—	25.00

KM# 158 DOLLAR

28.2800 g., 0.9990 Silver 0.9083 oz. ASW, 38.61 mm. **Ruler:** Elizabeth II **Subject:** FIFA **Obv:** Crowned head right **Obv. Designer:** Ian Rank-Broadley **Rev:** Soccer player, silver fern and map **Rev. Designer:** Michael McHalick

Date	Mintage	F	VF	XF	Unc	BU
2006(v) Proof	7,500	Value: 50.00				

KM# 285 DOLLAR

31.1000 g., 0.9990 Silver with gold highlights 0.9988 oz. ASW, 40 mm. **Ruler:** Elizabeth II **Subject:** Narnia **Obv:** Head with tiara right **Obv. Designer:** Ian Rank-Broadley **Rev:** White Witch

Date	Mintage	F	VF	XF	Unc	BU
2006(c) Proof	2,000	Value: 70.00				

KM# 286 DOLLAR

20.0000 g., Aluminum-Bronze, 38.74 mm. **Ruler:** Elizabeth II **Subject:** Narnia **Obv:** Head with tiara right **Obv. Designer:** Ian Rank-Broadley **Rev:** Asian, lion standing right

Date	Mintage	F	VF	XF	Unc	BU
2006(c)	8,000	—	—	—	—	20.00

KM# 287 DOLLAR

31.1350 g., 0.9990 Silver With Gold highlights 100000 oz. ASW, 40 mm. **Ruler:** Elizabeth II **Subject:** Narnia **Obv:** Head with tiara right **Obv. Designer:** Ian Rank-Broadley **Rev:** Asian

Date	Mintage	F	VF	XF	Unc	BU
2006(c) Proof	4,320	Value: 70.00				

KM# 288 DOLLAR

31.1350 g., 0.9990 Silver 100000 oz. ASW, 40 mm. **Ruler:** Elizabeth II **Subject:** Narnia **Obv:** Head with tiara right **Obv. Designer:** Ian Rank-Broadley **Rev:** Wardrobe from the Lion, Witch and Wardrobe series

Date	Mintage	F	VF	XF	Unc	BU
2006(c) Proof	1,000	Value: 70.00				

KM# 289 DOLLAR

20.0000 g., Aluminum-Bronze, 38.74 mm. **Ruler:** Elizabeth II **Subject:** Queen's 80th birthday **Obv:** Head with tiara right **Obv. Designer:** Ian Rank-Broadley **Rev:** Heraldic arms **Rev. Designer:** Philip O'Shea

Date	Mintage	F	VF	XF	Unc	BU
2006	2,000	—	—	—	—	30.00

KM# 290 DOLLAR

31.1350 g., 0.9990 Silver 100000 oz. ASW, 38.74 mm. **Ruler:** Elizabeth II **Subject:** Queen's 80th birthday **Obv:** Head with tiara right **Obv. Designer:** Ian Rank-Broadley **Rev:** Heraldic arms **Rev. Designer:** Philip O'Shea

Date	Mintage	F	VF	XF	Unc	BU
2006 Proof	1,500	—	—	—	—	—

KM# 291 DOLLAR

31.1350 g., 0.9990 Silver 100000 oz. ASW, 40 mm. **Ruler:** Elizabeth II **Obv:** Head with tiara right **Obv. Designer:** Ian Rank-Broadley **Rev:** North Island Brown Kiwi **Edge:** Reeded

Date	Mintage	F	VF	XF	Unc	BU
2006(w)	3,000	—	—	—	—	50.00

KM# 291a DOLLAR

31.1350 g., 0.9990 Silver 100000 oz. ASW, 40 mm. **Ruler:** Elizabeth II **Obv:** Head with tiara right **Obv. Designer:** Ian Rank-Broadley **Rev:** North Island Brown Kiwi **Edge:** Reeded

Date	Mintage	F	VF	XF	Unc	BU
2006(w) Proof	2,000	Value: 80.00				

Note: Mintage includes 500 struck in 2008 for sets.

KM# 293 DOLLAR

20.0000 g., Aluminum-Bronze, 38.74 mm. **Ruler:** Elizabeth II **Subject:** NZ Gold Rushes - West Coast **Obv:** Head with tiara right **Obv. Designer:** Ian Rank-Broadley **Rev:** 1860s miners

Date	Mintage	F	VF	XF	Unc	BU
2006(w)	1,500	—	—	—	—	30.00

KM# 294 DOLLAR

31.1350 g., 0.9990 Silver with gold highlights 100000 oz. ASW, 40.60 mm. **Ruler:** Elizabeth II **Subject:** NZ Gold Rushes - Thames/Coromandel **Obv:** Head with tiara right **Obv. Designer:** Ian Rank-Broadley **Rev:** Gold panning

Date	Mintage	F	VF	XF	Unc	BU
2006(w) Proof	3,000	Value: 90.00				

KM# 232 DOLLAR

31.1350 g., 0.9990 Silver 100000 oz. ASW, 40 mm. **Ruler:** Elizabeth II **Subject:** Aoraki - Mount Cook, Japanese Friendship **Obv:** Head with tiara right **Obv. Legend:** NEW ZEALAND - ELIZABETH II **Rev:** Flowers in bloom, Mount Cook in background multicolor **Note:** Also released in a Japanese proof set.

Date	Mintage	F	VF	XF	Unc	BU
2007(j) Proof	70,000	Value: 90.00				

KM# 296 DOLLAR

1.2440 g., 0.9990 Gold 0.0400 oz. AGW, 13.92 mm. **Ruler:** Elizabeth II **Subject:** 50th anniversary of Scott Base **Obv:** Head with tiara right **Obv. Designer:** Ian Rank-Broadley **Rev:** Scott Base, Antarctica and International Polar Year logo

Date	Mintage	F	VF	XF	Unc	BU
2007(m) Proof	10,000	Value: 100				

KM# 297 DOLLAR

31.1350 g., 0.9990 Silver 100000 oz. ASW, 40 mm. **Ruler:** Elizabeth II **Subject:** 50th anniversary of Scott Base **Obv:** Head with tiara right **Obv. Designer:** Ian Rank-Broadley **Rev:** Scott Base, Antarctica and International Polar Year logo

Date	Mintage	F	VF	XF	Unc	BU
2007(m) Proof	10,000	Value: 80.00				

KM# 298 DOLLAR

28.2800 g., 0.9250 Silver 0.8410 oz. ASW, 38.61 mm. **Ruler:** Elizabeth II **Subject:** Scouting centenary **Obv:** Head with tiara right **Obv. Designer:** Ian Rank-Broadley

Date	Mintage	F	VF	XF	Unc	BU
2007(l) Proof	1,500	Value: 80.00				

KM# 299 DOLLAR

28.2800 g., Copper-Nickel, 38.61 mm. **Ruler:** Elizabeth II **Subject:** Scouting centenary **Obv:** Head with tiara right **Obv. Designer:** Ian Rank-Broadley

Date	Mintage	F	VF	XF	Unc	BU
2007(l)	1,900	—	—	—	—	50.00

KM# 300 DOLLAR

31.1350 g., 0.9990 Silver 100000 oz. ASW, 40 mm. **Ruler:** Elizabeth II **Obv:** Head with tiara right **Obv. Designer:** Ian Rank-Broadley **Rev:** Great Spotted Kiwi **Rev. Designer:** Chris Waind **Edge:** Reeded

Date	Mintage	F	VF	XF	Unc	BU
2007(m)	4,000	—	—	—	—	50.00

KM# 300a DOLLAR

31.1350 g., 0.9990 Silver 100000 oz. ASW, 40 mm. **Ruler:** Elizabeth II **Obv:** Head with tiara right **Obv. Designer:** Ian Rank-Broadley **Rev:** Great Spotted Kiwi **Rev. Designer:** Chris Waind **Edge:** Reeded

Date	Mintage	F	VF	XF	Unc	BU
2007(m) Proof	3,000	Value: 100				

Note: Mintage includes 500 struck in 2008 for sets.

KM# 302 DOLLAR

31.1350 g., Copper-Nickel, 40 mm. **Ruler:** Elizabeth II **Subject:** Elizabeth & Philip Diamond Wedding **Obv:** Head with tiara right **Obv. Designer:** Ian Rank-Broadley **Rev:** Royal crests **Rev. Designer:** Phillip O'Shea **Edge:** Reeded

Date	Mintage	F	VF	XF	Unc	BU
2007(m)	1,600	—	—	—	—	30.00

KM# 302a DOLLAR

31.1050 g., 0.9990 Silver 0.9990 oz. ASW, 40 mm. **Ruler:** Elizabeth II **Subject:** Elizabeth & Philip Diamond Wedding **Obv:** Head with tiara right **Obv. Designer:** Ian Rank-Broadley **Rev:** Royal crests **Rev. Designer:** Phillip O'Shea **Edge:** Reeded

Date	Mintage	F	VF	XF	Unc	BU
2007(m) Proof	1,500	Value: 80.00				

KM# 321 DOLLAR

30.8000 g., Brass, 30 mm. **Ruler:** Elizabeth II **Rev:** Sir Edmond Hillary with Mt. Everest **Edge:** Reeded **Note:** Sold in a PNC cover only

Date	Mintage	F	VF	XF	Unc	BU
2008(w)	4,000	—	—	—	—	20.00

KM# 309 DOLLAR

31.1350 g., 0.9990 Silver 100000 oz. ASW, 40 mm. **Ruler:** Elizabeth II **Obv:** Head with tiara right **Obv. Designer:** Ian Rank-Broadley **Rev:** Haast Tokoeka Kiwi

Date	Mintage	F	VF	XF	Unc	BU
2008(w)	8,000	—	—	—	—	60.00

KM# 309a DOLLAR

31.1350 g., 0.9990 Silver 100000 oz. ASW, 40 mm. **Ruler:** Elizabeth II **Obv:** Head with tiara right **Obv. Designer:** Ian Rank-Broadley **Rev:** Haast Tokoeka Kiwi

Date	Mintage	F	VF	XF	Unc	BU
2008(w) Proof	5,000	Value: 85.00				

Note: Includes 500 for 2004-2008 sets.

KM# 311 DOLLAR

31.1350 g., 0.9990 Silver 100000 oz. ASW, 40.6 mm. **Ruler:** Elizabeth II **Subject:** Sir Edmund Hillary **Obv:** Head with tiara right **Obv. Designer:** Ian Rank-Broadley **Rev:** Hillary with Mt. Everest in background

Date	Mintage	F	VF	XF	Unc	BU
2008(w) Proof	10,000	Value: 90.00				

KM# 322 DOLLAR

31.1350 g., 0.9990 Silver 100000 oz. ASW, 40 mm. **Ruler:** Elizabeth II **Subject:** Icons of New Zealand **Rev:** Kiwi with map of New Zealand **Edge:** Reeded

Date	Mintage	F	VF	XF	Unc	BU
2009(m)	10,000	—	—	—	—	50.00
2009(m) Proof	7,500	Value: 80.00				

KM# 323 DOLLAR

31.1350 g., 0.9990 Silver 100000 oz. ASW, 40 mm. **Ruler:** Elizabeth II **Obv:** Bust right **Obv. Designer:** Ian Rank-Broadley **Rev:** Southern Right Whale **Rev. Designer:** Ken Wright **Edge:** Reeded

Date	Mintage	F	VF	XF	Unc	BU
2009(m) Prooflike	11,500	—	—	—	—	70.00

KM# 324 DOLLAR

31.1350 g., 0.9990 Silver 100000 oz. ASW, 40 mm. **Ruler:** Elizabeth II **Rev:** Haast's Eagle **Rev. Designer:** Ken Wright

Date	Mintage	F	VF	XF	Unc	BU
2009(m) Prooflike	11,500	—	—	—	—	80.00

KM# 325 DOLLAR

31.1350 g., 0.9990 Silver 100000 oz. ASW, 40 mm. **Ruler:** Elizabeth II **Rev:** Giant Moa **Rev. Designer:** Ken Wright

Date	Mintage	F	VF	XF	Unc	BU
2009(m) Prooflike	1,500	—	—	—	—	80.00

KM# 326 DOLLAR

31.1350 g., 0.9990 Silver 100000 oz. ASW, 40 mm. **Ruler:** Elizabeth II **Rev:** Colossal squid **Edge:** Reeded

Date	Mintage	F	VF	XF	Unc	BU
2009(m) Prooflike	1,500	—	—	—	—	80.00

KM# 327 DOLLAR

31.1350 g., 0.9990 Silver 100000 oz. ASW, 40 mm. **Ruler:** Elizabeth II **Rev:** Giant Weta **Rev. Designer:** Ken Wright **Edge:** Reeded

Date	Mintage	F	VF	XF	Unc	BU
2009(m) Prooflike	1,500	—	—	—	—	80.00

KM# 328 DOLLAR

26.4500 g., Copper-Nickel, 39.19 mm. **Ruler:** Elizabeth II **Subject:** Reserve Bank of New Zealand, 75th Anniversary **Rev:** Tui and Kowhai as on 1940-65 bronze penny

Date	Mintage	F	VF	XF	Unc	BU
2009(o)	2,000	—	—	—	—	30.00

KM# 331 DOLLAR

31.1050 g., 0.9990 Silver 0.9990 oz. ASW, 40 mm. **Ruler:** Elizabeth II **Subject:** Icons of New Zealand **Obv. Designer:** Ian Rank Broadley **Rev:** Kiwi and Southern Cross **Edge:** Reeded

Date	Mintage	F	VF	XF	Unc	BU
2010(m)	Est. 12,500	—	—	—	—	60.00
2010(m) Proof	Est. 8,500	Value: 90.00				

KM# 333 DOLLAR

31.1050 g., 0.9990 Silver 0.9990 oz. ASW, 40 mm. **Ruler:** Elizabeth II **Subject:** 2010 FIFA World Cup **Obv. Designer:** Ian Rank Broadley **Rev:** Soccer player with stylized NS koru **Edge:** Reeded

Date	Mintage	F	VF	XF	Unc	BU
2010	10,000	—	—	—	—	100

Note: Mintage includes 1500 in NZ Post packaging.

KM# 335 DOLLAR

31.1050 g., 0.9990 Silver 0.9990 oz. ASW, 40 mm. **Ruler:** Elizabeth II **Obv:** Head in tiara right **Rev:** Kiwi and fern

Date	Mintage	F	VF	XF	Unc	BU
2011 Proof	7,000	Value: 75.00				

KM# 121 2 DOLLARS

10.0000 g., Aluminum-Bronze, 26.5 mm. **Ruler:** Elizabeth II **Obv:** Head with tiara right **Obv. Designer:** Ian Rank-Broadley **Rev:** White heron (kotuku) above value **Rev. Designer:** R. Maurice Conly

Date	Mintage	F	VF	XF	Unc	BU
2001(l)	3,000,000	—	—	—	2.50	5.00
2001(c) In sets only	2,910	—	—	—	—	6.00
2001(c) Proof	2,000	Value: 7.50				
2002(l)	6,000,000	—	—	—	2.50	5.00
2002(c) In sets only	3,000	—	—	—	—	6.00
2002(c) Proof	2,000	Value: 7.50				
2003(l)	6,000,000	—	—	—	2.50	5.00
2003(c) In sets only	3,000	—	—	—	—	6.00
2003(c) Proof	3,000	Value: 7.50				
2004(c) In sets only	2,800	—	—	—	—	5.00
2004 Proof	3,500	Value: 7.50				
2005(l)	5,000,000	—	—	—	2.50	5.00
2005(c) In sets only	3,000	—	—	—	—	6.00
2005(c) Proof	3,000	Value: 7.50				
2006(c) In sets only	3,000	—	—	—	—	6.00
2006(c) Proof	2,100	Value: 7.50				
2007(c)	—	—	—	—	—	6.00
2007(c) Proof	4,000	Value: 7.50				
2008(l) In sets only	4,000	—	—	—	—	6.00
2008(l) Proof	3,000	Value: 7.50				
2009(w) In sets only	2,000	—	—	—	—	6.00
2009(w) Proof	1,500	Value: 7.50				

KM# 128 5 DOLLARS

28.2800 g., Copper-Nickel, 38.6 mm. **Ruler:** Elizabeth II **Subject:** Kereru Bird **Obv:** Head with tiara right **Obv. Designer:** Ian Rank-Broadley **Rev:** Wood Pigeon on branch **Edge:** Reeded

Date	Mintage	F	VF	XF	Unc	BU
2001(l)	1,500	—	—	—	25.00	—

KM# 128a 5 DOLLARS

28.2800 g., 0.9990 Silver 0.9083 oz. ASW **Ruler:** Elizabeth II **Obv:** Head with tiara right **Obv. Designer:** Ian Rank-Broadley **Rev:** Pigeon on branch

Date	Mintage	F	VF	XF	Unc	BU
2001 Proof	1,000	Value: 80.00				

KM# 149 5 DOLLARS

28.2800 g., Copper-Nickel, 38.6 mm. **Ruler:** Elizabeth II **Subject:** Royal Visit (canceled after coin issue) **Obv:** Crowned head right **Obv. Designer:** Ian Rank-Broadley **Rev:** Queen with flowers and two girls **Edge:** Reeded

Date	Mintage	F	VF	XF	Unc	BU
2001	—	—	—	—	—	20.00

KM# 149a 5 DOLLARS

28.2800 g., 0.9250 Silver 0.8410 oz. ASW, 38.6 mm. **Ruler:** Elizabeth II **Subject:** Royal Visit (canceled after coin issue) **Obv:** Head with tiara right **Obv. Designer:** Ian Rank-Broadley **Rev:** Queen with flowers and two girls **Edge:** Reeded

Date	Mintage	F	VF	XF	Unc	BU
2001 Proof	2,000	Value: 100				

Note: 200 issued in stamp cover

KM# 131 5 DOLLARS

28.2800 g., Copper-Nickel, 38.6 mm. **Ruler:** Elizabeth II **Subject:** Architectural Heritage **Obv:** Head with tiara right **Obv. Designer:** Ian Rank-Broadley **Rev:** Auckland Sky Tower **Edge:** Reeded

Date	Mintage	F	VF	XF	Unc	BU
2002(l)	3,000	—	—	—	12.50	—

Note: 500 pieces were housed in a stamp cover

KM# 131a 5 DOLLARS

28.2800 g., 0.9250 Silver 0.8410 oz. ASW, 38.6 mm. **Ruler:** Elizabeth II **Subject:** Architectural Heritage **Obv:** Head with tiara right **Obv. Designer:** Ian Rank-Broadley **Rev:** Auckland Sky Tower **Edge:** Reeded

Date	Mintage	F	VF	XF	Unc	BU
2002(l)	2,000	Value: 37.50				

Note: 500 pieces were housed in a stamp cover

KM# 145 5 DOLLARS

27.2200 g., Copper-Nickel, 38.74 mm. **Ruler:** Elizabeth II **Obv:** Head with tiara right **Obv. Designer:** Ian Rank-Broadley **Rev:** Hector's Dolphins jumping out of the water **Rev. Designer:** Michael McHalick **Edge:** Reeded

Date	Mintage	F	VF	XF	Unc	BU
2002(c)	4,000	—	—	—	35.00	—

Note: 500 pieces were housed in a stamp covers

KM# 145a 5 DOLLARS

27.2220 g., 0.9990 Silver 0.8743 oz. ASW **Ruler:** Elizabeth II **Obv:** Head with tiara right **Obv. Designer:** Ian Rank-Broadley **Rev:** Two Hector's Dolphins jumping out of the water **Edge:** Reeded

Date	Mintage	F	VF	XF	Unc	BU
2002(c)	Est. 2,000	—	—	—	—	100

Note: 500 in stamp covers

KM# 151 5 DOLLARS

28.2800 g., 0.9250 Silver Gilt 0.8410 oz. ASW, 38.61 mm. **Ruler:** Elizabeth II **Subject:** Queen's Jubilee **Obv:** Gilt head with tiara right **Obv. Designer:** Ian Rank-Broadley **Rev:** Scepter with "Great Star of Africa' at left of vertical band with crowns and shields **Rev. Designer:** Robert Lowe **Edge:** Reeded

Date	Mintage	F	VF	XF	Unc	BU
2002(l) Proof	25,000	Value: 80.00				

Note: 100 pieces were housed in a stamp cover, value $85

KM# 272a 5 DOLLARS

28.2800 g., 0.9250 Silver 0.8410 oz. ASW, 38.61 mm. **Ruler:** Elizabeth II **Subject:** America's Cup **Obv:** Head with tiara right **Obv. Designer:** Ian Rank-Broadley **Rev:** Yachts **Rev. Designer:** Michael McHalick

Date	Mintage	F	VF	XF	Unc	BU
2002(l) Proof	4,000	Value: 50.00				

Note: Includes 500 in stamp cover, value $50.

KM# 272 5 DOLLARS

28.2800 g., Copper-Nickel, 38.61 mm. **Ruler:** Elizabeth II **Subject:** America's cup **Rev. Designer:** Michael McHalick

Date	Mintage	F	VF	XF	Unc	BU
2002(l)	6,000	—	—	—	—	20.00

KM# 132 5 DOLLARS

26.7000 g., Copper-Nickel, 38.6 mm. **Ruler:** Elizabeth II **Obv:** Head with tiara right **Rev:** Giant Kokopu fish divides circle **Edge:** Reeded **Designer:** Michael McHalick

Date	Mintage	F	VF	XF	Unc	BU
2003(c)	2,400	—	—	—	12.00	27.50

Note: Includes 400 issued in a stamp cover.

KM# 132a 5 DOLLARS

28.2800 g., 0.9990 Silver Gold plated 0.9083 oz. ASW, 38.6 mm. **Ruler:** Elizabeth II **Obv:** Head with tiara right **Obv. Designer:** Ian Rank-Broadley **Rev:** Giant Kokopu fish **Edge:** Reeded

Date	Mintage	F	VF	XF	Unc	BU
2003(c) Proof	1,700	Value: 75.00				

Note: Includes 200 issued in a stamp cover

KM# 133 5 DOLLARS

26.7200 g., Copper-Nickel, 38.6 mm. **Ruler:** Elizabeth II **Subject:** Chatham Island Taiko **Obv:** Head with tiara right **Obv. Designer:** Ian Rank-Broadley **Rev:** Magenta Petrel **Edge:** Reeded

Date	Mintage	F	VF	XF	Unc	BU
2004(2003)	1,350	—	—	—	—	35.00

KM# 147 5 DOLLARS

28.2300 g., 0.9250 Silver 0.8395 oz. ASW, 38.6 mm. **Ruler:** Elizabeth II **Subject:** 50th Anniversary of Coronation **Obv:** Gold plated crowned head right **Obv. Designer:** Ian Rank-Broadley **Rev:** Crown above fern and flowers **Edge:** Reeded

Date	Mintage	F	VF	XF	Unc	BU
2003 Proof	25,000	Value: 80.00				

Note: Includes 100 issued in a stamp cover

KM# 133a 5 DOLLARS

28.2800 g., 0.9990 Silver 0.9083 oz. ASW, 38.74 mm. **Ruler:** Elizabeth II **Obv:** Head with tiara right **Obv. Designer:** Ian Rank-Broadley **Rev:** Chatham Island Taiko

Date	Mintage	F	VF	XF	Unc	BU
2004 Proof	1,300	Value: 60.00				

KM# 146 5 DOLLARS

27.2200 g., Copper-Nickel, 38.74 mm. **Ruler:** Elizabeth II **Obv:**

Head with tiara right **Obv. Designer:** Ian Rank-Broadley **Rev:** Fiordland Crested Penguin **Edge:** Reeded

Date	Mintage	F	VF	XF	Unc	BU
2005(2004)	4,000	—	—	—	25.00	30.00

KM# 146a 5 DOLLARS
27.2200 g., 0.9990 Silver 0.8742 oz. ASW, 38.74 mm. **Ruler:** Elizabeth II **Obv:** Head with tiara right **Obv. Designer:** Ian Rank-Broadley **Rev:** Fiordland Crested Penguin **Edge:** Reeded

Date	Mintage	F	VF	XF	Unc	BU
2005	3,500	—	—	—	—	50.00

KM# 148 5 DOLLARS
27.2200 g., Copper-Nickel, 38.74 mm. **Ruler:** Elizabeth II **Obv:** Head with tiara right **Obv. Designer:** Ian Rank-Broadley **Rev:** Falcon on tree stump **Edge:** Reeded

Date	Mintage	F	VF	XF	Unc	BU
2006	4,000	—	—	—	—	30.00

KM# 148a 5 DOLLARS
28.2800 g., 0.9990 Silver 0.9083 oz. ASW, 38.74 mm. **Ruler:** Elizabeth II **Obv:** Head with tiara right **Obv. Designer:** Ian Rank-Broadley **Rev:** New Zealand Falcon on tree stump **Edge:** Reeded

Date	Mintage	F	VF	XF	Unc	BU
2006 Proof	2,500	Value: 50.00				

KM# 150 5 DOLLARS
27.2200 g., Copper-Nickel, 38.74 mm. **Ruler:** Elizabeth II **Subject:** Tuatara **Obv:** Head with tiara right **Obv. Designer:** Ian Rank-Broadley **Rev:** Tuatara (Sphenodon punctatus), a lizard-like reptile **Edge:** Reeded

Date	Mintage	F	VF	XF	Unc	BU
2007(c)	3,000	—	—	—	—	30.00

KM# 150a 5 DOLLARS
28.2800 g., 0.9990 Silver 0.9083 oz. ASW, 38.74 mm. **Ruler:** Elizabeth II **Subject:** Tuatara **Obv:** Head with tiara right **Obv. Designer:** Ian Rank-Broadley **Rev:** Tuatara right **Edge:** Reeded

Date	Mintage	F	VF	XF	Unc	BU
2007(c) Proof	4,000	Value: 80.00				

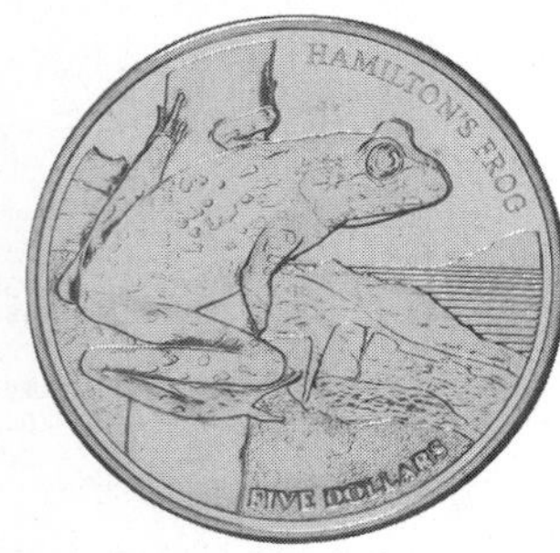

KM# 233 5 DOLLARS
28.2800 g., 0.9990 Silver 0.9083 oz. ASW, 38.6 mm. **Ruler:** Elizabeth II **Subject:** Hamilton's frog **Obv:** Head with tiara right **Obv. Legend:** NEW ZEALAND - ELIZABETH II **Obv. Designer:** Ian Rank-Broadley **Rev:** Frog perched on branch at left center **Rev. Designer:** Chris Waind

Date	Mintage	F	VF	XF	Unc	BU
2008	4,000	—	—	—	—	40.00

KM# 233a 5 DOLLARS
28.2800 g., 0.9990 Silver 0.9083 oz. ASW, 38.61 mm. **Ruler:** Elizabeth II **Rev:** Hamilton's frog **Rev. Designer:** Chris Waind **Edge:** Reeded

Date	Mintage	F	VF	XF	Unc	BU
2008(l) Proof	4,000	Value: 90.00				

Note: Mintage includes 1500 struck in 2009

KM# 329 5 DOLLARS
22.0000 g., Copper-Nickel, 38.60 mm. **Ruler:** Elizabeth II **Obv. Designer:** Ian Rank-Broadley **Rev:** Kakapo **Rev. Designer:** Ken Wright **Edge:** Reeded

Date	Mintage	F	VF	XF	Unc	BU
2009(w)	2,000	—	—	—	—	30.00

KM# 329a 5 DOLLARS
31.1350 g., 0.9990 Silver 100000 oz. ASW, 38.61 mm. **Ruler:** Elizabeth II **Rev:** Kakapo **Rev. Designer:** Ken Wright

Date	Mintage	F	VF	XF	Unc	BU
2009(w) Proof	4,000	Value: 90.00				

KM# 334 5 DOLLARS
31.1000 g., Copper-Nickel, 38.7 mm. **Ruler:** Elizabeth II **Series:** Maui's Dolphin, subspecies of the Hector Dolphin **Rev:** Dolphin jumping right **Edge:** Reeded

Date	Mintage	F	VF	XF	Unc	BU
2010	2,000	—	—	—	—	35.00

KM# 129 10 DOLLARS
3.8879 g., 0.9990 Gold 0.1249 oz. AGW, 18 mm. **Ruler:** Elizabeth II **Obv:** Head with tiara right **Obv. Designer:** Ian Rank-Broadley **Rev:** Salvage ship above value **Edge:** Reeded

Date	Mintage	F	VF	XF	Unc	BU
2001 Proof	600	Value: 155				

KM# 130 10 DOLLARS
7.7759 g., 0.9990 Gold 0.2497 oz. AGW, 22 mm. **Ruler:** Elizabeth II **Obv:** Head with tiara right **Obv. Designer:** Ian Rank-Broadley **Rev:** Ship above value **Edge:** Reeded

Date	Mintage	F	VF	XF	Unc	BU
2001 Proof	600	Value: 315				

KM# 273 10 DOLLARS
Nickel-Brass gold plated, 28.4 mm. **Ruler:** Elizabeth II **Subject:** America's Cup **Obv:** Head with tiara right **Obv. Designer:** Ian Rank-Broadley **Rev:** Map, cup and yachts **Rev. Designer:** Michael McHalick

Date	Mintage	F	VF	XF	Unc	BU
2002(l)	5,000	—	—	—	—	45.00

KM# 274 10 DOLLARS
15.5520 g., 0.9990 Gold 0.4995 oz. AGW, 28.4 mm. **Ruler:** Elizabeth II **Subject:** America's Cup **Obv:** Head with tiara right **Obv. Designer:** Ian Rank-Broadley **Rev:** Map, cup and yachts **Rev. Designer:** Michael McHalick

Date	Mintage	F	VF	XF	Unc	BU
2002(l) Proof	900	Value: 625				

KM# 144 10 DOLLARS
39.9400 g., 0.9170 Gold 1.1775 oz. AGW, 38.61 mm. **Ruler:** Elizabeth II **Subject:** Lord of the Rings **Obv:** Head with tiara right **Obv. Designer:** Ian Rank-Broadley **Rev:** The One Ring **Rev. Designer:** Matthew Bonaccorsi **Edge:** Reeded

Date	Mintage	F	VF	XF	Unc	BU
2003(l) Proof	1,198	Value: 1,500				

KM# 270 10 DOLLARS
39.9400 g., 0.9170 Gold 1.1775 oz. AGW, 38.61 mm. **Ruler:** Elizabeth II **Subject:** Lord of the Rings **Obv:** Head with tiara right **Obv. Designer:** Ian Rank-Broadley **Rev:** Frodo **Rev. Designer:** Matthew Bonaccorsi **Edge:** Reeded

Date	Mintage	F	VF	XF	Unc	BU
2003(l) Proof	142	Value: 1,500				

KM# 271 10 DOLLARS
39.9400 g., 0.9170 Gold 1.1775 oz. AGW, 38.61 mm. **Ruler:** Elizabeth II **Subject:** Lord of the Rings **Obv:** Head with tiara right **Obv. Designer:** Ian Rank-Broadley **Rev:** Sauron **Rev. Designer:** Matthew Bonaccorsi **Edge:** Reeded

Date	Mintage	F	VF	XF	Unc	BU
2003(l) Proof	142	Value: 1,500				

KM# 275 10 DOLLARS
38.5000 g., 0.9170 Gold 1.1350 oz. AGW, 38.61 mm. **Ruler:** Elizabeth II **Subject:** Pukaki **Obv:** Head with tiara right **Obv. Designer:** Ian Rank-Broadley **Rev:** Statue of Pukaki **Edge:** Reeded

Date	Mintage	F	VF	XF	Unc	BU
2004(l) Proof	300	Value: 3,500				
2004(l) NW RB Proof	2	—	—	—	—	—

Note: Initials added for presention to Ngati Whakaue (Maori tribe) and the Reserve Bank.

KM# 165 10 DOLLARS
7.9880 g., 0.9170 Gold 0.2355 oz. AGW, 22.05 mm. **Ruler:** Elizabeth II **Subject:** Lions Rugby Tour **Obv:** Crowned head right **Edge:** Reeded

Date	Mintage	F	VF	XF	Unc	BU
2005(l) Proof	1,000	Value: 300				

KM# 155 10 DOLLARS
7.7500 g., 0.9990 Gold 0.2489 oz. AGW, 17.53 mm. **Ruler:** Elizabeth II **Subject:** ANZAC **Obv:** Crowned head right **Rev:** New Zealand soldier playing bugle in front of War Memorial **Edge:** Reeded

Date	Mintage	F	VF	XF	Unc	BU
2005	1,000	—	—	—	—	400

KM# 295 10 DOLLARS
31.1350 g., 0.9990 Gold 100000 oz. AGW, 34 mm. **Ruler:** Elizabeth II **Subject:** Narnia **Obv:** Head with tiara right **Obv. Designer:** Ian Rank-Broadley **Rev:** Asian

Date	Mintage	F	VF	XF	Unc	BU
2006 Proof	365	Value: 1,600				

KM# 307 10 DOLLARS
7.7770 g., 0.9990 Gold 0.2498 oz. AGW, 20 mm. **Ruler:** Elizabeth II **Subject:** Queen's 80th birthday **Obv:** Head with tiara right **Obv. Designer:** Ian Rank-Broadley **Rev:** Heraldic arms **Rev. Designer:** Phillip O'Shea

Date	Mintage	F	VF	XF	Unc	BU
2006 Proof	500	Value: 325				

KM# 308 10 DOLLARS
15.5540 g., 0.9990 Gold 0.4996 oz. AGW, 25.10 mm. **Ruler:** Elizabeth II **Subject:** Gold Rushes - Otago **Obv:** Head with tiara right **Obv. Designer:** Ian Rank-Broadley **Rev:** Picks, shovels and nuggets

Date	Mintage	F	VF	XF	Unc	BU
2006(w) Proof	500	Value: 625				

KM# 304 10 DOLLARS
7.7750 g., 0.9990 Gold 0.2497 oz. AGW, 26 mm. **Ruler:** Elizabeth II **Subject:** Elizabeth & Philip Diamond Wedding Anniversary **Obv:** Head with tiara right **Obv. Designer:** Ian Rank-Broadley **Rev:** Royal crests **Rev. Designer:** Phillip O'Shea

Date	Mintage	F	VF	XF	Unc	BU
2007(m) Proof	300	Value: 500				

KM# 305 10 DOLLARS
31.1350 g., 0.9170 Gold 0.9179 oz. AGW, 38.61 mm. **Ruler:** Elizabeth II **Subject:** Scouting centenary **Obv:** Head with tiara right **Obv. Designer:** Ian Rank-Broadley

Date	Mintage	F	VF	XF	Unc	BU
2007(l) Proof	150	Value: 1,800				

KM# 306 10 DOLLARS
7.7855 g., 0.9990 Gold 0.2500 oz. AGW, 20.6 mm. **Ruler:** Elizabeth II **Subject:** Sir Edmund Hilary **Obv:** Head with tiara right **Obv. Designer:** Ian Rank-Broadley **Rev:** Ed Hilary with Mt. Everest in background

Date	Mintage	F	VF	XF	Unc	BU
2008(w) Proof	1,953	Value: 520				

KM# 330 10 DOLLARS
7.7750 g., 0.9990 Gold 0.2497 oz. AGW, 26 mm. **Ruler:** Elizabeth II **Subject:** Icons of New Zealand **Rev:** Kiwi and map of New Zealand **Edge:** Reeded

Date	Mintage	F	VF	XF	Unc	BU
2009(m) Proof	1,500	Value: 575				

KM# 332 10 DOLLARS
7.7750 g., 0.9990 Gold 0.2497 oz. AGW, 26. mm. **Ruler:** Elizabeth II **Subject:** Icons of New Zealand **Obv. Designer:** Ian Rank Broadley **Rev:** Kiwi and Southern Cross **Edge:** Reeded

Date	Mintage	F	VF	XF	Unc	BU
2010(m) Proof	1,800	—	—	—	—	650

MINT SETS

KM#	Date	Mintage	Identification	Issue Price	Mkt Val
MS50	2001 (7)	2,910	KM#116-121, 128	18.50	70.00
MS51	2002 (7)	3,000	KM#116-121, 145. Hector's dolphin.	18.00	60.00
MS52	2003 (7)	3,000	KM#116-121, 132. Giant Kokopu.	18.00	120
MS53	2003 (6)	34,332	KM#135-140. Lord of the Rings, Light vs. Dark set.	19.95	100
MS54	2003 (9)	2,821	KM#135-137; 235-240. Fellowship of the Ring.	—	175
MS55	2003 (18)	4,068	KM#135-140; 235-246. Lord of the Rings. Character collection.	—	325
MS56	2003 (3)	10,454	KM#141, 142, 143. Lord of the Rings. Battle for the Ring set.	29.95	35.00
MS57	2004 (7)	2,800	KM#116-121, 133. Taiko.	33.00	150
MS58	2005 (7)	3,000	KM#116-121; 146. Crested Penguin.	33.00	120
MS59	2006 (7)	3,000	KM#116-121; 148. Falcon.	33.00	110
MS60	2003-5-6 (7)	5,000	Mixed Set for Change over to smaller size coins. KM#116 (2003); 117-119 (2005); KM#117a-119a (2006).	7.50	70.00
MS61	2007 (6)	5,000	KM#117a-119a; 120-121; 150. Tuatara.	33.00	55.00
MS62	2008 (6)	4,000	KM#117a-119a; 120-121; 233. Hamilton's frog.	37.50	50.00
MS63	2009 (6)	2,000	KM#117a-119a; 120-121; 329. Kakapo.	—	50.00
MS64	2009 (5)	1,500	KM#323-327. Giants of New Zealand.	—	400

PROOF SETS

KM#	Date	Mintage	Identification	Issue Price	Mkt Val
PS45	2001 (7)	1,366	KM#116-121, 128a	49.25	200
PS46	2001 (2)	600	KM#129-130	400	475
PS47	2001 (7)	1,500	KM#116-121, 128a	60.00	250
PS48	2003 (1)	810	KM#141a and 5 others.	—	—
PS49	2003	—	Five coins as per PS48, less 141a	—	—
PS50	2003 (3)	133	KM#144; 270; 271. Lord of the Rings. Gold set.	—	4,200
PS51	2003 (2)	9	KM#270; 271. Lord of the Rings.	—	2,800
PS52	2003 (7)	1,496	KM#116-121, 132a.	60.00	230
PS53	2004 (7)	1,750	KM#116-121, 133. Chatham Islands Taiko	—	200
PS54	2005 (7)	2,250	KM#116-121; 146a. Crested Penguin.	88.00	120
PS55	2006 (7)	2,100	KM#116-121; 148a. Falcon.	90.00	125
PS56	2006 (3)	1,000	KM#285; 287; 288.	—	225
PS57	2007 (6)	3,500	KM#117a-119a; 120-121; 150a. Tuatara.	88.00	90.00
PS58	2007 (7)	69,000	KM#232, NZ Aoraki dollar and Japan 95.2; 96.2; 97.2; 98.2; 101.2; 125.	115	—
PS59	2008 (6)	3,000	KM#117a-119a; 120-121; 233a. Hamilton's frog.	94.00	95.00
PS60	2004-08 (5)	500	KM#152; 153a; 291a; 300a; 309a. Kiwi.	375	500
PS61	2009 (6)	1,500	KM#117a-119a; 120-121; 329a. Kakapo.	—	95.00

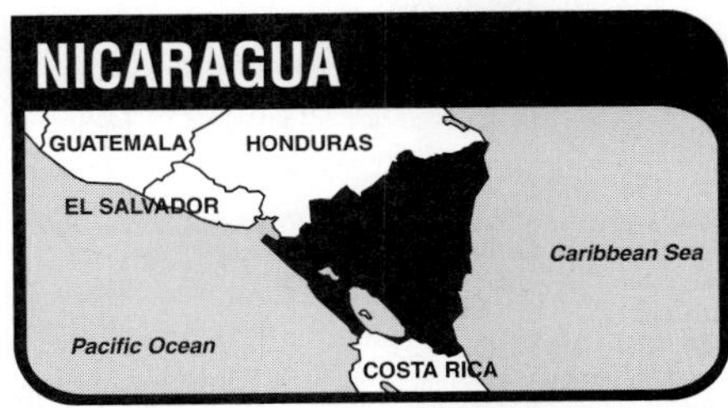

The Republic of Nicaragua, situated in Central America between Honduras and Costa Rica, has an area of 50,193 sq. mi. (129,494 sq. km.) and a population of *3.7 million. Capital: Managua. Agriculture, mining (gold and silver) and hardwood logging are the principal industries. Cotton, meat, coffee and sugar are exported.

MONETARY SYSTEM

100 Centavos = 1 Cordoba

REPUBLIC

DECIMAL COINAGE

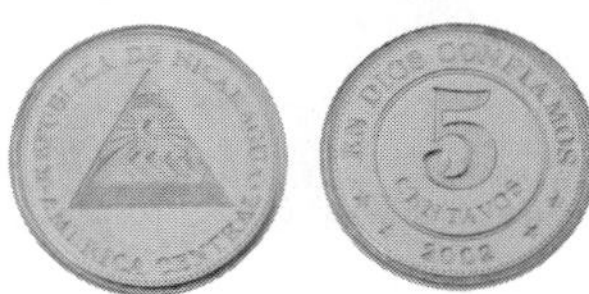

KM# 97 5 CENTAVOS

3.0000 g., Copper Plated Steel, 18.5 mm. **Obv:** National arms **Rev:** Value within circle **Edge:** Plain

Date	Mintage	F	VF	XF	Unc	BU
2002	—	—	—	—	0.25	0.50

KM# 98 10 CENTAVOS

4.0000 g., Brass Plated Steel, 20.5 mm. **Obv:** National arms **Rev:** Value within circle **Edge:** Reeded and plain sections

Date	Mintage	F	VF	XF	Unc	BU
2002	—	—	—	—	0.45	0.85

KM# 99 25 CENTAVOS

5.0000 g., Brass Plated Steel, 23.25 mm. **Obv:** National arms **Rev:** Value within circle **Edge:** Reeded and plain sections

Date	Mintage	F	VF	XF	Unc	BU
2002	—	—	—	—	0.65	1.25

KM# 104 25 CENTAVOS

Brass **Obv:** Arms **Rev:** Value at center **Rev. Legend:** EN DIOS CONFIAMOS

Date	Mintage	F	VF	XF	Unc	BU
2007	—	—	—	—	1.50	2.50

KM# 89 CORDOBA

6.2000 g., Nickel Clad Steel, 25 mm. **Obv:** National emblem **Rev:** Value above sprigs within circle **Edge:** Reeded

Date	Mintage	F	VF	XF	Unc	BU
2002	—	—	—	—	2.50	3.00

KM# 101 CORDOBA

6.2700 g., Nickel Clad Steel, 24.9 mm. **Obv:** National arms **Rev:** Large value "1" **Rev. Legend:** EN DIOS CONFIAMOS **Edge:** Reeded

Date	Mintage	F	VF	XF	Unc	BU
2002	—	—	0.35	0.90	2.25	3.00

KM# 100 10 CORDOBAS

27.1200 g., 0.9250 Silver 0.8065 oz. ASW, 40 mm. **Subject:** Ibero-America **Obv:** National arms in circle of arms **Rev:** Sail boat **Edge:** Reeded

Date	Mintage	F	VF	XF	Unc	BU
2002 Proof	—	Value: 45.00				

KM# 102 10 CORDOBAS

8.4700 g., Brass Plated Steel, 26.5 mm. **Obv:** National arms **Rev:** Value at upper left, circular latent image BCN below, statue of Andrés Castro at right **Edge Lettering:** B C N repeated 4 times

Date	Mintage	F	VF	XF	Unc	BU
2007	—	—	—	—	—	4.00

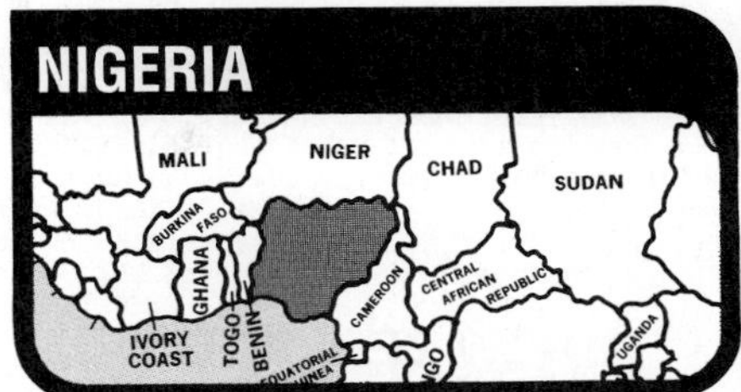

Nigeria, situated on the Atlantic coast of West Africa has an area of 356,669 sq. mi. (923,770 sq. km.). Nigeria is a member of the Commonwealth of Nations. The President is the Head of State and the Head of Government.

FEDERAL REPUBLIC

DECIMAL COINAGE

100 Kobo = 1 Naira

KM# 17 KOBO

4.6700 g., Brass, 23.2 mm. **Obv:** Arms with supporters **Rev:** Monkey musicians below value **Edge:** Reeded

Date	Mintage	F	VF	XF	Unc	BU
2003	—	—	—	—	15.00	20.00

KM# 13.3 50 KOBO

3.5000 g., Nickel Clad Steel, 19.44 mm. **Obv:** Arms with supporters **Obv. Legend:** FEDERAL REPUBLIC of NIGERIA **Rev:** Value at left, corn cob and stalk at right **Edge:** Plain **Note:** Reduced size.

Date	Mintage	F	VF	XF	Unc	BU
2006	—	—	—	—	1.00	1.35

KM# 18 NAIRA

5.4300 g., Bi-Metallic Brass center in Stainless Steel ring, 21.48 mm. **Obv:** National arms **Obv. Legend:** FEDERAL REPUBLIC OF NIGERIA **Rev:** Small bust of Herbert Macaulay above value **Edge:** Plain

Date	Mintage	F	VF	XF	Unc	BU
2006	—	—	—	—	2.00	3.00

KM# 19 2 NAIRA

7.4800 g., Bi-Metallic Stainless Steel center in Copper-Brass ring, 25.99 mm. **Obv:** National arms **Obv. Legend:** FEDERAL REPUBLIC OF NIGERIA **Rev:** Large value, National Assembly in background **Edge:** Coarse reeding

Date	Mintage	F	VF	XF	Unc	BU
2006	—	—	—	—	3.00	4.00

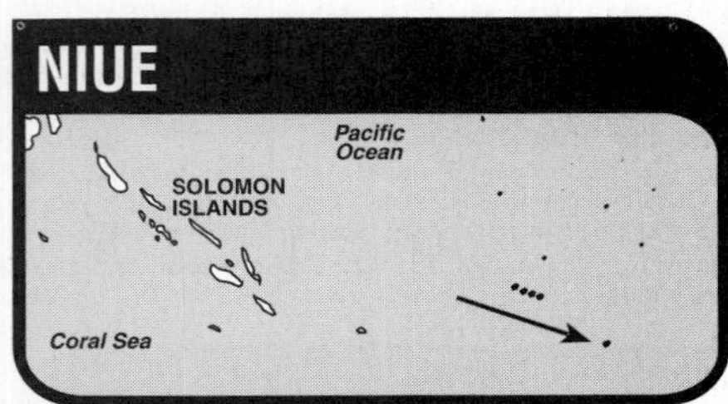

Niue, or Savage Island, a dependent state of New Zealand is located in the Pacific Ocean east of Tonga and southeast of Samoa. The size is 100 sq. mi. (260 sq. km.) with a population of *2,000. Chief village and port is Alofi. Bananas and copra are exported.

MINT MARK

PM - Pobjoy Mint

NEW ZEALAND DEPENDENT STATE

DECIMAL COINAGE

KM# 193 5 CENTS

4.3000 g., Copper Plated Bronze, 19 mm. **Ruler:** Elizabeth II **Obv:** Head right **Rev:** Two whales

Date	Mintage	F	VF	XF	Unc	BU
2009	—	—	—	—	1.00	2.00
2010	—	—	—	—	1.00	2.00

KM# 194 10 CENTS

5.8000 g., Copper Plated Bronze, 22 mm. **Ruler:** Elizabeth II **Obv:** Head right **Rev:** Coconut crab **Edge:** Reeded

Date	Mintage	F	VF	XF	Unc	BU
2009	—	—	—	—	1.50	2.00
2010	—	—	—	—	1.50	2.00

KM# 195 20 CENTS

7.3000 g., Nickel Plated Bronze, 25 mm. **Ruler:** Elizabeth II **Obv:** Head right **Rev:** Two scuba divers and coral

Date	Mintage	F	VF	XF	Unc	BU
2009	—	—	—	—	2.00	4.00
2010	—	—	—	—	2.00	4.00

KM# 263 50 CENTS

15.5500 g., 0.9990 Silver 0.4994 oz. ASW, 35 mm. **Ruler:** Elizabeth II **Series:** Year of the Rooster **Rev:** Multicolor rooster standing right, sunrise

Date	Mintage	F	VF	XF	Unc	BU
2005	—	Value: 20.00				

KM# 292 50 CENTS

15.5500 g., 0.9990 Silver 0.4994 oz. ASW, 35 mm. **Ruler:** Elizabeth II **Subject:** Year of the Dog **Rev:** Multicolor dog

Date	Mintage	F	VF	XF	Unc	BU
2005 Proof	—	Value: 25.00				

KM# 189 50 CENTS

15.5000 g., 0.9990 Silver 0.4978 oz. ASW, 28 mm. **Ruler:** Elizabeth II **Subject:** Year of the Pig **Obv:** Head right **Rev:** Multicolor pig

Date	Mintage	F	VF	XF	Unc	BU
2007 Proof	—	Value: 50.00				

KM# 196 50 CENTS

9.3000 g., Nickel Plated Bronze, 28 mm. **Ruler:** Elizabeth II **Obv:** Head right **Rev:** Outrigger canoe **Edge:** Segmented reeding

Date	Mintage	F	VF	XF	Unc	BU
2009	—	—	—	—	5.00	7.50
2010	—	—	—	—	5.00	7.50

KM# 462 1/33 DOLLAR

42.5000 g., 0.9990 Silver 1.3650 oz. ASW, 41.7x40 mm. **Ruler:** Elizabeth II **Rev:** Sistine Chapel Corner featuring Haman's punishment

Date	Mintage	F	VF	XF	Unc	BU
2010 Proof	500	Value: 60.00				

KM# 463 1/33 DOLLAR

42.5000 g., 0.9990 Silver 1.3650 oz. ASW, 41.7x40 mm. **Ruler:** Elizabeth II **Rev:** Sistine Chapel Arch featuring the Prophet Jonah

Date	Mintage	F	VF	XF	Unc	BU
2010 Proof	500	Value: 60.00				

KM# 464 1/33 DOLLAR

42.5000 g., 0.9990 Silver 1.3650 oz. ASW, 41.7x40 mm. **Ruler:** Elizabeth II **Rev:** Sistine Chapel Corner Spandrel featuring the Brazen Serpent

Date	Mintage	F	VF	XF	Unc	BU
2010 Proof	500	Value: 60.00				

KM# 465 1/33 DOLLAR

26.8000 g., 0.9990 Silver 0.8607 oz. ASW, 29x36.1 mm. **Ruler:** Elizabeth II **Rev:** Sistine Chapel Arch featuring the Prophet Jeremiah

Date	Mintage	F	VF	XF	Unc	BU
2010 Proof	500	Value: 40.00				

KM# 466 1/33 DOLLAR

26.8000 g., 0.9990 Silver 0.8607 oz. ASW, 29x36.1 mm. **Ruler:** Elizabeth II **Rev:** Sistine Chapel Arch with Salmon

Date	Mintage	F	VF	XF	Unc	BU
2010 Proof	500	Value: 40.00				

KM# 467 1/33 DOLLAR

26.8000 g., 0.9990 Silver 0.8607 oz. ASW, 29x36.1 mm. **Ruler:** Elizabeth II **Rev:** Sistine Chapel Arch with Persian Sibyl

Date	Mintage	F	VF	XF	Unc	BU
2010 Proof	500	Value: 40.00				

KM# 468 1/33 DOLLAR

21.0000 g., 0.9990 Silver 0.6745 oz. ASW, 23x36.1 mm. **Ruler:** Elizabeth II **Rev:** Sistine Chapel Arch with Roboam

Date	Mintage	F	VF	XF	Unc	BU
2010 Proof	500	—	—	—	—	30.00

KM# 469 1/33 DOLLAR

26.8000 g., 0.9990 Silver 0.8607 oz. ASW, 29x36.1 mm. **Ruler:** Elizabeth II **Rev:** Sistine Chapel Arch with Prophet Ezekiel

Date	Mintage	F	VF	XF	Unc	BU
2010 Proof	500	Value: 40.00				

KM# 470 1/33 DOLLAR

26.8000 g., 0.9990 Silver 0.8607 oz. ASW, 29x36.1 mm. **Ruler:** Elizabeth II **Rev:** Sistine Chapel Arch with Ozias

Date	Mintage	F	VF	XF	Unc	BU
2010 Proof	500	Value: 40.00				

KM# 471 1/33 DOLLAR

21.0000 g., 0.9990 Silver 0.6745 oz. ASW, 23x36.1 mm. **Ruler:** Elizabeth II **Rev:** Sistine Chapel Arch with Erythraean Sibyl

Date	Mintage	F	VF	XF	Unc	BU
2010 Proof	500	Value: 30.00				

KM# 472 1/33 DOLLAR

26.8000 g., 0.9990 Silver 0.8607 oz. ASW, 29x36.1 mm. **Ruler:** Elizabeth II **Rev:** Sistine Chapel Arch with Zorobabel

Date	Mintage	F	VF	XF	Unc	BU
2010 Proof	500	Value: 40.00				

KM# 473 1/33 DOLLAR

21.0000 g., 0.9990 Silver 0.6745 oz. ASW, 23x36.1 mm. **Ruler:** Elizabeth II **Rev:** Sistine Chapel Arch with Prophel Joel

Date	Mintage	F	VF	XF	Unc	BU
2010 Proof	500	Value: 30.00				

KM# 474 1/33 DOLLAR

35.5000 g., 0.9990 Silver 1.1402 oz. ASW, 29x47.8 mm. **Ruler:** Elizabeth II **Rev:** Sistine Chapel vault depicting Genesis creation story of Separation of Light from Darkness

Date	Mintage	F	VF	XF	Unc	BU
2010 Proof	500	Value: 50.00				

KM# 475 1/33 DOLLAR

35.5000 g., 0.9990 Silver 1.1402 oz. ASW, 29x47.8 mm. **Ruler:** Elizabeth II **Rev:** Sistine Chapel vault depecting Genesis story of Creation of Sun and Moon

Date	Mintage	F	VF	XF	Unc	BU
2010 Proof	500	Value: 50.00				

KM# 476 1/33 DOLLAR

35.5000 g., 0.9990 Silver 1.1402 oz. ASW, 29x47.8 mm. **Ruler:** Elizabeth II **Rev:** Sistine Chapel vault depicting Genesis creation story of the Separation of Land and Water

Date	Mintage	F	VF	XF	Unc	BU
2010 Proof	500	Value: 50.00				

KM# 477 1/33 DOLLAR

28.0000 g., 0.9990 Silver 0.8993 oz. ASW, 23x47.8 mm. **Ruler:** Elizabeth II **Rev:** Sistine Chapel vault depicting Genesis story of the Creation of Adam

Date	Mintage	F	VF	XF	Unc	BU
2010 Proof	500	Value: 45.00				

KM# 478 1/33 DOLLAR

35.5000 g., 0.9990 Silver 1.1402 oz. ASW, 29x47.8 mm. **Ruler:** Elizabeth II **Rev:** Sistine Chapel vault depicting the story of the Creation of Eve

Date	Mintage	F	VF	XF	Unc	BU
2010 Proof	500	Value: 50.00				

KM# 479 1/33 DOLLAR

28.0000 g., 0.9990 Silver 0.8993 oz. ASW, 23x47.8 mm. **Ruler:** Elizabeth II **Rev:** Sistine Chapel vault depicting the Genesis story of Original Sin

Date	Mintage	F	VF	XF	Unc	BU
2010 Proof	500	Value: 45.00				

KM# 480 1/33 DOLLAR

35.5000 g., 0.9990 Silver 1.1402 oz. ASW, 29x47.7 mm. **Ruler:** Elizabeth II **Rev:** Sistine Chapel vault depicting the Genesis story of the Sacrifice of Noah

Date	Mintage	F	VF	XF	Unc	BU
2010 Proof	500	Value: 50.00				

KM# 481 1/33 DOLLAR

28.0000 g., 0.9990 Silver 0.8993 oz. ASW, 23x47.8 mm. **Ruler:** Elizabeth II **Rev:** Sistine Chapel vault depicting the Genesis story of the Flood

Date	Mintage	F	VF	XF	Unc	BU
2010 Proof	500	Value: 45.00				

KM# 482 1/33 DOLLAR

35.5000 g., 0.9990 Silver 1.1402 oz. ASW, 29x47.8 mm. **Ruler:** Elizabeth II **Rev:** Sistine Chapel vault depicting the Genesis story of the Drunkenness of Noah

Date	Mintage	F	VF	XF	Unc	BU
2010 Proof	500	Value: 50.00				

KM# 483 1/33 DOLLAR

26.8000 g., 0.9990 Silver 0.8607 oz. ASW, 29x36.1 mm. **Ruler:** Elizabeth II **Rev:** Sistine Chapel Arch depicting the Libyan Sibyl

Date	Mintage	F	VF	XF	Unc	BU
2010 Proof	500	Value: 40.00				

KM# 484 1/33 DOLLAR

26.8000 g., 0.9990 Silver 0.8607 oz. ASW, 29x36.1 mm. **Ruler:** Elizabeth II **Rev:** Sistine Chapel Arch depicting Jesse

Date	Mintage	F	VF	XF	Unc	BU
2010 Proof	500	Value: 40.00				

KM# 485 1/33 DOLLAR

26.8000 g., 0.9990 Silver 0.8607 oz. ASW, 29x36.1 mm. **Ruler:** Elizabeth II **Rev:** Sistine Chapel Arch depicting the Prophet Daniel

Date	Mintage	F	VF	XF	Unc	BU
2010 Proof	500	Value: 40.00				

KM# 486 1/33 DOLLAR

21.0000 g., 0.9990 Silver 0.6745 oz. ASW, 23x36.1 mm. **Ruler:** Elizabeth II **Rev:** Sistine Chapel Arch depicting Asa

Date	Mintage	F	VF	XF	Unc	BU
2010 Proof	500	Value: 30.00				

KM# 487 1/33 DOLLAR

26.8000 g., 0.9990 Silver 0.8607 oz. ASW, 29x36.1 mm. **Ruler:** Elizabeth II **Rev:** Sistine Chapel Arch depicting the Cumaean Sibyl

Date	Mintage	F	VF	XF	Unc	BU
2010 Proof	500	Value: 40.00				

KM# 488 1/33 DOLLAR

21.0000 g., 0.9990 Silver 0.6745 oz. ASW, 23x36.1 mm. **Ruler:** Elizabeth II **Rev:** Sistine Chapel Arch depicting Ezxekias

Date	Mintage	F	VF	XF	Unc	BU
2010 Proof	500	Value: 30.00				

KM# 489 1/33 DOLLAR

26.8000 g., 0.9990 Silver 0.8607 oz. ASW, 29x.36.1 mm. **Ruler:** Elizabeth II **Rev:** Sistine Chapel Arch depicting the Prophet Isiah

Date	Mintage	F	VF	XF	Unc	BU
2010 Proof	500	Value: 40.00				

KM# 490 1/33 DOLLAR

26.8000 g., 0.9990 Silver 0.8607 oz. ASW, 29x36.1 mm. **Ruler:** Elizabeth II **Rev:** Sistine Chapel Arch depicting Josias

Date	Mintage	F	VF	XF	Unc	BU
2010 Proof	500	Value: 40.00				

KM# 491 1/33 DOLLAR

21.0000 g., 0.9990 Silver 0.6745 oz. ASW, 23x36.1 mm. **Ruler:** Elizabeth II **Rev:** Sistine Chapel Arch depicting the Delphic Sibyl

Date	Mintage	F	VF	XF	Unc	BU
2010 Proof	500	Value: 30.00				

KM# 492 1/33 DOLLAR

42.5000 g., 0.9990 Silver 1.3650 oz. ASW, 41.7x40 mm. **Ruler:** Elizabeth II **Rev:** Sistine Chapel corner spandrel depicting David & Goliath

Date	Mintage	F	VF	XF	Unc	BU
2010 Proof	500	Value: 60.00				

KM# 493 1/33 DOLLAR

42.5000 g., 0.9990 Silver 1.3650 oz. ASW, 41.7x40 mm. **Ruler:** Elizabeth II **Rev:** Sistine Chapel Arch vault depicting the Prophet Zechariah

Date	Mintage	F	VF	XF	Unc	BU
2010 Proof	500	Value: 60.00				

KM# 494 1/33 DOLLAR

42.5000 g., 0.9990 Silver 1.3650 oz. ASW, 41.7x40 mm. **Ruler:** Elizabeth II **Rev:** Sistine Chapel corner spandrel depicting Judith & Holofornes

Date	Mintage	F	VF	XF	Unc	BU
2010 Proof	500	Value: 60.00				

KM# 526 1/24 DOLLAR

42.5000 g., 0.9990 Silver 1.3650 oz. ASW, 41.7x40 mm. **Ruler:** Elizabeth II **Obv:** Head with tiara right **Rev:** Partial DaVinci drawing

Date	Mintage	F	VF	XF	Unc	BU
2011 Proof	500	Value: 60.00				

KM# 527 1/24 DOLLAR

42.5000 g., 0.9990 Silver 1.3650 oz. ASW, 41.7x40 mm. **Ruler:** Elizabeth II **Obv:** Head with tiara right **Rev:** Partial DaVinci drawing

Date	Mintage	F	VF	XF	Unc	BU
2011 Proof	500	Value: 60.00				

KM# 528 1/24 DOLLAR

42.5000 g., 0.9990 Silver 1.3650 oz. ASW, 41.7x40 mm. **Ruler:** Elizabeth II **Obv:** Head with tiara right **Rev:** Partial DaVinci drawing

Date	Mintage	F	VF	XF	Unc	BU
2011 Proof	500	Value: 60.00				

KM# 529 1/24 DOLLAR

42.5000 g., 0.9990 Silver 1.3650 oz. ASW, 41.7x40 mm. **Ruler:** Elizabeth II **Obv:** Head with tiara right **Rev:** Partial DaVinci drawing

Date	Mintage	F	VF	XF	Unc	BU
2011 Proof	500	Value: 60.00				

KM# 530 1/24 DOLLAR

42.5000 g., 0.9990 Silver 1.3650 oz. ASW, 41.7x40 mm. **Ruler:** Elizabeth II **Obv:** Head with tiara right **Rev:** Partial DaVinci drawing

Date	Mintage	F	VF	XF	Unc	BU
2011 Proof	500	Value: 60.00				

KM# 531 1/24 DOLLAR

42.5000 g., 0.9990 Silver 1.3650 oz. ASW, 41.7x40 mm. **Ruler:** Elizabeth II **Obv:** Head with tiara right **Rev:** Partial DaVinci drawing

Date	Mintage	F	VF	XF	Unc	BU
2011 Proof	500	Value: 60.00				

KM# 534 1/24 DOLLAR

42.5000 g., 0.9990 Silver 1.3650 oz. ASW, 41.7x40 mm. **Ruler:** Elizabeth II **Obv:** Head with tiara right **Rev:** Partial DaVinci drawing

Date	Mintage	F	VF	XF	Unc	BU
2011 Proof	500	Value: 60.00				

KM# 532 1/24 DOLLAR

42.5000 g., 0.9990 Silver 1.3650 oz. ASW, 41.7x40 mm. **Ruler:** Elizabeth II **Obv:** Head with tiara right **Rev:** Partial DaVinci drawing

Date	Mintage	F	VF	XF	Unc	BU
2011 Proof	500	Value: 60.00				

KM# 533 1/24 DOLLAR

42.5000 g., 0.9990 Silver 1.3650 oz. ASW **Ruler:** Elizabeth II **Obv:** Head in tiara right **Rev:** Partial DaVinci drawing

Date	Mintage	F	VF	XF	Unc	BU
2011 Proof	500	Value: 60.00				

KM# 535 1/24 DOLLAR

42.5000 g., 0.9990 Silver 1.3650 oz. ASW, 41.7x40 mm. **Ruler:** Elizabeth II **Obv:** Head with tiara right **Rev:** Partial DaVinci drawing

Date	Mintage	F	VF	XF	Unc	BU
2011 Proof	500	Value: 60.00				

KM# 536 1/24 DOLLAR

42.5000 g., 0.9990 Silver 1.3650 oz. ASW, 41.7x40 mm. **Ruler:** Elizabeth II **Obv:** Head in tiara right **Rev:** Partial DaVinci drawing

Date	Mintage	F	VF	XF	Unc	BU
2011 Proof	500	Value: 60.00				

KM# 537 1/24 DOLLAR

42.5000 g., 0.9990 Silver 1.3650 oz. ASW, 41.7x40 mm. **Ruler:** Elizabeth II **Obv:** Head with tiara right **Rev:** Partial DaVinci drawing

Date	Mintage	F	VF	XF	Unc	BU
2011 Proof	500	Value: 60.00				

KM# 538 1/24 DOLLAR

42.5000 g., 0.9990 Silver 1.3650 oz. ASW, 41.7x40 mm. **Ruler:** Elizabeth II **Obv:** Head with tiara right **Rev:** Partial DaVinci drawing

Date	Mintage	F	VF	XF	Unc	BU
2011 Proof	500	Value: 60.00				

KM# 539 1/24 DOLLAR

42.5000 g., 0.9990 Silver 1.3650 oz. ASW, 41.7x40 mm. **Ruler:** Elizabeth II **Obv:** Head with tiara right **Rev:** Partial DaVinci drawing

Date	Mintage	F	VF	XF	Unc	BU
2011 Proof	500	Value: 60.00				

KM# 540 1/24 DOLLAR

42.5000 g., 0.9990 Silver 1.3650 oz. ASW, 41.7x40 mm. **Ruler:** Elizabeth II **Obv:** Head with tiara right **Rev:** Partial DaVinci drawing

Date	Mintage	F	VF	XF	Unc	BU
2011 Proof	500	Value: 60.00				

KM# 541 1/24 DOLLAR

42.5000 g., 0.9990 Silver 1.3650 oz. ASW, 41.7x40 mm. **Ruler:** Elizabeth II **Obv:** Head with tiara right **Rev:** Partial DaVinci drawing

Date	Mintage	F	VF	XF	Unc	BU
2011 Proof	500	Value: 60.00				

KM# 542 1/24 DOLLAR

42.5000 g., 0.9990 Silver 1.3650 oz. ASW, 41.7x40 mm. **Ruler:** Elizabeth II **Obv:** Head with tiara right **Rev:** Partial DaVinci drawing

Date	Mintage	F	VF	XF	Unc	BU
2011 Proof	500	Value: 60.00				

KM# 543 1/24 DOLLAR

42.5000 g., 0.9990 Silver 1.3650 oz. ASW, 41.7x40 mm. **Ruler:** Elizabeth II **Obv:** Head with tiara right **Rev:** Partial DaVinci drawing

Date	Mintage	F	VF	XF	Unc	BU
2011 Proof	500	Value: 60.00				

KM# 544 1/24 DOLLAR

42.5000 g., 0.9990 Silver 1.3650 oz. ASW, 41.7x40 mm. **Ruler:** Elizabeth II **Obv:** Head with tiara right **Rev:** Partial DaVinci drawing

Date	Mintage	F	VF	XF	Unc	BU
2011 Proof	500	Value: 60.00				

KM# 545 1/24 DOLLAR

42.5000 g., 0.9990 Silver 1.3650 oz. ASW, 41.7x40 mm. **Ruler:** Elizabeth II **Obv:** Head with tiara right **Rev:** Partial DaVinci drawing

Date	Mintage	F	VF	XF	Unc	BU
2011 Proof	500	Value: 60.00				

KM# 546 1/24 DOLLAR

42.5000 g., 0.9990 Silver 1.3650 oz. ASW, 41.7x40 mm. **Ruler:** Elizabeth II **Obv:** Head with tiara right **Rev:** Partial DaVinci drawing

Date	Mintage	F	VF	XF	Unc	BU
2011 Proof	500	Value: 60.00				

KM# 547 1/24 DOLLAR

42.5000 g., 0.9990 Silver 1.3650 oz. ASW, 41.7x40 mm. **Ruler:** Elizabeth II **Obv:** Head with tiara right **Rev:** Partial DaVinci drawing

Date	Mintage	F	VF	XF	Unc	BU
2011 Proof	500	—	—	—	—	—

KM# 548 1/24 DOLLAR

42.5000 g., 0.9990 Silver 1.3650 oz. ASW, 41.7x40 mm. **Ruler:** Elizabeth II **Obv:** Head with tiara right **Rev:** Partial DaVinci drawing

Date	Mintage	F	VF	XF	Unc	BU
2011 Proof	500	Value: 60.00				

KM# 549 1/24 DOLLAR

42.5000 g., 0.9990 Silver 1.3650 oz. ASW, 41.7x40 mm. **Ruler:** Elizabeth II **Obv:** Head with tiara right **Rev:** Partial DaVinci drawing

Date	Mintage	F	VF	XF	Unc	BU
2011 Proof	500	Value: 60.00				

KM# 123 DOLLAR

28.2800 g., Copper-Nickel, 38.6 mm. **Ruler:** Elizabeth II **Subject:** Snoopy as an Ace **Obv:** Crowned head right **Rev:** Snoopy flying his dog house **Edge:** Reeded

Date	Mintage	F	VF	XF	Unc	BU
2001	100,000	—	—	—	3.00	4.50

KM# 128 DOLLAR

28.2800 g., Copper-Nickel, 38.6 mm. **Ruler:** Elizabeth II **Series:** Pokemon **Obv:** Crowned shield within sprigs **Rev:** Bulbasaur **Edge:** Reeded

Date	Mintage	F	VF	XF	Unc	BU
2001	100,000	—	—	—	12.00	14.00

KM# 129 DOLLAR

7.7700 g., 0.9990 Silver 0.2496 oz. ASW, 22 mm. **Ruler:** Elizabeth II **Series:** Pokemon **Obv:** Crowned shield within sprigs **Rev:** Bulbasaur **Edge:** Reeded

Date	Mintage	F	VF	XF	Unc	BU
2001 Proof	20,000	Value: 8.00				

KM# 131 DOLLAR

28.2800 g., Copper-Nickel, 38.6 mm. **Ruler:** Elizabeth II **Series:** Pokemon **Obv:** Crowned shield within sprigs **Rev:** Charmander **Edge:** Reeded

Date	Mintage	F	VF	XF	Unc	BU
2001	100,000	—	—	—	12.00	14.00

KM# 132 DOLLAR

7.7700 g., 0.9990 Silver 0.2496 oz. ASW, 22 mm. **Ruler:** Elizabeth II **Series:** Pokemon **Obv:** Crowned shield within sprigs **Rev:** Charmander **Edge:** Reeded

Date	Mintage	F	VF	XF	Unc	BU
2001 Proof	20,000	Value: 8.00				

KM# 134 DOLLAR

28.2800 g., Copper-Nickel, 38.6 mm. **Ruler:** Elizabeth II **Series:** Pokemon **Obv:** Crowned shield within sprigs **Rev:** Meowth **Edge:** Reeded

Date	Mintage	F	VF	XF	Unc	BU
2001	100,000	—	—	—	12.00	14.00

KM# 135 DOLLAR

7.7700 g., 0.9990 Silver 0.2496 oz. ASW, 22 mm. **Ruler:** Elizabeth II **Series:** Pokemon **Obv:** Crowned shield within sprigs **Rev:** Meowth **Edge:** Reeded

Date	Mintage	F	VF	XF	Unc	BU
2001 Proof	20,000	Value: 8.00				

KM# 137 DOLLAR

28.2800 g., Copper-Nickel, 38.6 mm. **Ruler:** Elizabeth II **Series:** Pokemon **Obv:** Crowned shield within sprigs **Rev:** Pikachu **Edge:** Reeded

Date	Mintage	F	VF	XF	Unc	BU
2001	100,000	—	—	—	12.00	14.00

KM# 138 DOLLAR

7.7700 g., 0.9990 Silver 0.2496 oz. ASW, 22 mm. **Ruler:** Elizabeth II **Series:** Pokemon **Obv:** Crowned shield within sprigs **Rev:** Pikachu **Edge:** Reeded

Date	Mintage	F	VF	XF	Unc	BU
2001 Proof	20,000	Value: 8.00				

KM# 140 DOLLAR

28.2800 g., Copper-Nickel, 38.6 mm. **Ruler:** Elizabeth II **Series:** Pokemon **Obv:** Crowned shield within sprigs **Rev:** Squirtle **Edge:** Reeded

Date	Mintage	F	VF	XF	Unc	BU
2001	100,000	—	—	—	12.00	14.00

KM# 141 DOLLAR

7.7700 g., 0.9990 Silver 0.2496 oz. ASW, 22 mm. **Ruler:** Elizabeth II **Series:** Pokemon **Obv:** Crowned shield within sprigs **Rev:** Squirtle **Edge:** Reeded

Date	Mintage	F	VF	XF	Unc	BU
2001 Proof	20,000	Value: 8.00				

KM# 146 DOLLAR

28.2800 g., Copper-Nickel, 38.6 mm. **Ruler:** Elizabeth II **Subject:** Pokemon Series **Obv:** Crowned shield within sprigs **Rev:** Pikachu **Edge:** Reeded

Date	Mintage	F	VF	XF	Unc	BU
2002PM	100,000	—	—	—	3.00	4.50

KM# 151 DOLLAR

28.2800 g., Copper-Nickel, 38.6 mm. **Ruler:** Elizabeth II **Subject:** Pokemon Series **Obv:** Crowned shield within sprigs **Rev:** Pichu **Edge:** Reeded

Date	Mintage	F	VF	XF	Unc	BU
2002PM	100,000	—	—	—	3.00	4.50

KM# 156 DOLLAR

28.2800 g., Copper-Nickel, 38.6 mm. **Ruler:** Elizabeth II **Subject:** Pokemon Series **Obv:** Crowned shield within sprigs **Rev:** Mewtwo **Edge:** Reeded

Date	Mintage	F	VF	XF	Unc	BU
2002PM	100,000	—	—	—	3.00	4.50

KM# 161 DOLLAR

28.2800 g., Copper-Nickel, 38.6 mm. **Ruler:** Elizabeth II **Subject:** Pokemon Series **Obv:** Crowned shield within sprigs **Rev:** Entei **Edge:** Reeded

Date	Mintage	F	VF	XF	Unc	BU
2002PM	100,000	—	—	—	3.00	4.50

KM# 166 DOLLAR

28.2800 g., Copper-Nickel, 38.6 mm. **Ruler:** Elizabeth II **Subject:** Pokemon Series **Obv:** Crowned shield within sprigs **Rev:** Celebi **Edge:** Reeded

Date	Mintage	F	VF	XF	Unc	BU
2002PM	100,000	—	—	—	3.00	4.50

KM# 264 DOLLAR

31.1000 g., 0.9990 Silver 0.9988 oz. ASW, 45 mm. **Ruler:** Elizabeth II **Subject:** Year of the Rooster **Rev:** Multicolor rooster standing right, sunrise

Date	Mintage	F	VF	XF	Unc	BU
2005 Proof	—	Value: 30.00				

KM# 293 DOLLAR

31.1050 g., 0.9990 Silver 0.9990 oz. ASW, 45 mm. **Ruler:** Elizabeth II **Subject:** Year of the Dog **Rev:** Multicolor dog

Date	Mintage	F	VF	XF	Unc	BU
2005 Proof	—	Value: 40.00				

KM# 186 DOLLAR

31.1050 g., 0.9990 Silver 0.9990 oz. ASW **Ruler:** Elizabeth II **Subject:** Marshalls of China's Army, 50th Anniversary **Obv:** Head right **Rev:** Multicolor scene of military men

Date	Mintage	F	VF	XF	Unc	BU
2005	1,000	—	—	—	—	50.00

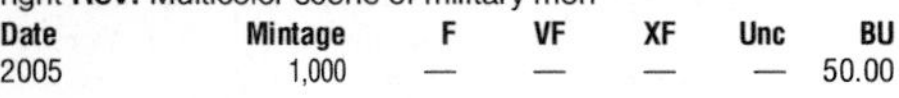

KM# 187 DOLLAR

31.1050 g., 0.9990 Silver 0.9990 oz. ASW **Ruler:** Elizabeth II **Subject:** World War II, 60th Anniversary **Obv:** Bust right **Rev:** Multicolor badge

Date	Mintage	F	VF	XF	Unc	BU
2005	1,000	—	—	—	—	50.00

KM# 188 DOLLAR

31.1050 g., 0.9990 Silver 0.9990 oz. ASW **Ruler:** Elizabeth II **Series:** Bust right **Obv:** Multicolor image of two astronauts, rocket and map of China

Date	Mintage	F	VF	XF	Unc	BU
2005 Proof	—	Value: 65.00				

KM# 262 DOLLAR

Bronze partially silvered, 38.61 mm. **Ruler:** Elizabeth II **Subject:** Thomas Alva Edison **Rev:** Lightbulb

Date	Mintage	F	VF	XF	Unc	BU
2005	—	—	—	—	—	27.50

KM# 262a DOLLAR

31.1050 g., 0.9990 Silver partially gilt 0.9990 oz. ASW **Ruler:** Elizabeth II **Subject:** Thomas Alva Edison **Rev:** Lightbulb, partailly gilt

Date	Mintage	F	VF	XF	Unc	BU
2005 Proof	Est. 2,500	Value: 55.00				

KM# 275 DOLLAR

31.1050 g., 0.9990 Silver 0.9990 oz. ASW **Ruler:** Elizabeth II **Subject:** 60th Anniversary, China

Date	Mintage	F	VF	XF	Unc	BU
2005 Proof	Est. 1,000	Value: 55.00				

KM# 276 DOLLAR

31.1050 g., 0.9990 Silver 0.9990 oz. ASW **Ruler:** Elizabeth II **Subject:** Mao Zedong and the Red Army in Bejing

Date	Mintage	F	VF	XF	Unc	BU
2005 Proof	—	Value: 55.00				

KM# 277 DOLLAR

31.1050 g., 0.9990 Silver 0.9990 oz. ASW, 45 mm. **Ruler:** Elizabeth II **Subject:** Chinese space acheivements **Rev:** Multicolor rocket, flag, map

Date	Mintage	F	VF	XF	Unc	BU
2005 Proof	Est. 5,000	Value: 65.00				

KM# 300 DOLLAR

31.1050 g., 0.9990 Silver 0.9990 oz. ASW, 45 mm. **Ruler:** Elizabeth II **Subject:** Dogs of the World **Rev:** Multicolor Bichon standing before the Louvre

Date	Mintage	F	VF	XF	Unc	BU
2006 Proof	Est. 3,000	Value: 50.00				

KM# 301 DOLLAR

31.1050 g., 0.9990 Silver 0.9990 oz. ASW, 45 mm. **Ruler:** Elizabeth II **Subject:** Dogs of the World **Rev:** Multicolor Welsh Corgi before Buckingham Palace

Date	Mintage	F	VF	XF	Unc	BU
2006 Proof	Est. 3,000	Value: 50.00				

KM# 302 DOLLAR

31.1050 g., 0.9990 Silver 0.9990 oz. ASW, 45 mm. **Ruler:** Elizabeth II **Subject:** Dogs of the World **Rev:** Poodle before the Palace at Versailles

Date	Mintage	F	VF	XF	Unc	BU
2006 Proof	Est. 3,000	Value: 50.00				

KM# 303 DOLLAR

31.1050 g., 0.9990 Silver 0.9990 oz. ASW, 45 mm. **Ruler:** Elizabeth II **Subject:** Dogs of the World **Rev:** Bare dog before the Potala Plast

Date	Mintage	F	VF	XF	Unc	BU
2006 Proof	Est. 3,000	Value: 50.00				

KM# 304 DOLLAR

31.1050 g., 0.9990 Silver 0.9990 oz. ASW, 45 mm. **Ruler:** Elizabeth II **Subject:** Dogs of the World **Rev:** Pekineese before the Palastmuseum

Date	Mintage	F	VF	XF	Unc	BU
2006 Proof	Est. 3,000	Value: 50.00				

KM# 305 DOLLAR

31.1050 g., 0.9990 Silver 0.9990 oz. ASW, 45 mm. **Ruler:** Elizabeth II **Subject:** Dogs of the World **Rev:** Malteser before the Schonbrunn

Date	Mintage	F	VF	XF	Unc	BU
2006 Proof	Est. 3,000	Value: 50.00				

KM# 306 DOLLAR

31.1050 g., 0.9990 Silver 0.9990 oz. ASW, 45 mm. **Ruler:** Elizabeth II **Subject:** Dogs of the World **Rev:** Japanese Chin before Emeror's palace inKyoto

Date	Mintage	F	VF	XF	Unc	BU
2006 Proof	Est. 3,000	Value: 50.00				

KM# 307 DOLLAR

31.1050 g., 0.9990 Silver 0.9990 oz. ASW, 45 mm. **Ruler:** Elizabeth II **Subject:** Dogs of the World **Rev:** King Charles Spaniel before Westminster Abbey

Date	Mintage	F	VF	XF	Unc	BU
2006 Proof	Est. 3,000	Value: 50.00				

KM# 308 DOLLAR

31.1050 g., 0.9990 Silver 0.9990 oz. ASW, 45 mm. **Ruler:** Elizabeth II **Subject:** Dogs of the World **Rev:** Butterfly dog before the Kings Palace in Madrid

Date	Mintage	F	VF	XF	Unc	BU
2006 Proof	Est. 3,000	Value: 50.00				

KM# 309 DOLLAR

31.1050 g., 0.9990 Silver 0.9990 oz. ASW, 45 mm. **Ruler:** Elizabeth II **Subject:** Olympics **Rev:** Discus thrower

Date	Mintage	F	VF	XF	Unc	BU
ND Proof	Est. 2,008	Value: 60.00				

KM# 310 DOLLAR

31.1050 g., 0.9990 Silver 0.9990 oz. ASW, 45 mm. **Ruler:** Elizabeth II **Subject:** Olympics **Rev:** Sprinter

Date	Mintage	F	VF	XF	Unc	BU
ND Proof	Est. 2,008	Value: 60.00				

KM# 311 DOLLAR

31.1050 g., 0.9990 Silver 0.9990 oz. ASW, 45 mm. **Ruler:** Elizabeth II **Subject:** Olympics **Rev:** Long Jump

Date	Mintage	F	VF	XF	Unc	BU
ND Proof	Est. 2,008	Value: 60.00				

KM# 312 DOLLAR

31.1050 g., 0.9990 Silver 0.9990 oz. ASW, 45 mm. **Ruler:** Elizabeth II **Subject:** Olympics **Rev:** Javelin Thrower

Date	Mintage	F	VF	XF	Unc	BU
ND Proof	Est. 2,008	Value: 60.00				

KM# 313 DOLLAR

31.1050 g., 0.9990 Silver 0.9990 oz. ASW, 45 mm. **Ruler:** Elizabeth II **Subject:** Olympics **Rev:** Weightlifter

Date	Mintage	F	VF	XF	Unc	BU
ND Proof	Est. 2,008	Value: 60.00				

KM# 314 DOLLAR

31.1050 g., 0.9990 Silver 0.9990 oz. ASW, 45 mm. **Ruler:** Elizabeth II **Subject:** Olympics **Rev:** Hammer Throw

Date	Mintage	F	VF	XF	Unc	BU
ND Proof	Est. 2,008	—	—	—	—	—

KM# 315 DOLLAR

31.1050 g., 0.9990 Silver 0.9990 oz. ASW, 45 mm. **Ruler:** Elizabeth II **Subject:** Olympics **Rev:** Archery

Date	Mintage	F	VF	XF	Unc	BU
ND Proof	Est. 2,008	Value: 60.00				

KM# 316 DOLLAR

31.1050 g., 0.9990 Silver 0.9990 oz. ASW, 45 mm. **Ruler:** Elizabeth II **Subject:** Olympics **Rev:** Lacrosse player

Date	Mintage	F	VF	XF	Unc	BU
ND Proof	Est. 2,008	Value: 60.00				

KM# 317 DOLLAR

31.1050 g., 0.9990 Silver 0.9990 oz. ASW, 45 mm. **Ruler:** Elizabeth II **Subject:** Olympics **Rev:** Soccer player

Date	Mintage	F	VF	XF	Unc	BU
ND Proof	Est. 2,008	Value: 60.00				

KM# 318 DOLLAR

31.1050 g., 0.9990 Silver 0.9990 oz. ASW, 45 mm. **Ruler:** Elizabeth II **Subject:** Olympics **Rev:** Boxer

Date	Mintage	F	VF	XF	Unc	BU
ND Proof	Est. 2,008	Value: 60.00				

KM# 320 DOLLAR

31.1050 g., 0.9990 Silver 0.9990 oz. ASW, 45 mm. **Ruler:** Elizabeth II **Subject:** Olympics **Rev:** Wrestler

Date	Mintage	F	VF	XF	Unc	BU
ND Proof	Est. 2,008	Value: 60.00				

KM# 321 DOLLAR

31.1050 g., 0.9990 Silver 0.9990 oz. ASW, 35x46 mm. **Ruler:** Elizabeth II **Subject:** Life of Christ **Rev:** Radiant Mary **Shape:** Vertical rectangle

Date	Mintage	F	VF	XF	Unc	BU
2006 Proof	Est. 1,000	Value: 1,000				

KM# 322 DOLLAR

31.1050 g., 0.9990 Silver 0.9990 oz. ASW, 35x46 mm. **Ruler:** Elizabeth II **Subject:** Life of Christ **Rev:** Mary and Child (1483) **Shape:** Vertical rectangle

Date	Mintage	F	VF	XF	Unc	BU
2006 Proof	Est. 1,000	Value: 60.00				

KM# 323 DOLLAR

31.1050 g., 0.9990 Silver 0.9990 oz. ASW, 35x46 mm. **Ruler:** Elizabeth II **Subject:** Life of Christ **Rev:** Christ in the Jrodan (1478) **Shape:** Vertical rectangle

Date	Mintage	F	VF	XF	Unc	BU
2006 Proof	Est. 1,000	Value: 60.00				

KM# 324 DOLLAR

31.1050 g., 0.9990 Silver 0.9990 oz. ASW, 35x46 mm. **Ruler:** Elizabeth II **Subject:** Life of Christ **Rev:** Jesus Christ (1481) **Shape:** Vertical rectangle

Date	Mintage	F	VF	XF	Unc	BU
2006 Proof	Est. 1,000	Value: 60.00				

KM# 325 DOLLAR

31.1050 g., 0.9990 Silver 0.9990 oz. ASW, 35x46 mm. **Ruler:** Elizabeth II **Subject:** Life of Christ **Rev:** betrayal of Judas (1303) **Shape:** Vertical rectangle

Date	Mintage	F	VF	XF	Unc	BU
2006 Proof	Est. 1,000	Value: 60.00				

KM# 326 DOLLAR

31.1050 g., 0.9990 Silver 0.9990 oz. ASW, 35x46 mm. **Ruler:** Elizabeth II **Subject:** Life of Christ **Rev:** Stations of the Cross (1517) **Shape:** Vertical rectangle

Date	Mintage	F	VF	XF	Unc	BU
2006 Proof	Est. 1,000	Value: 60.00				

KM# 327 DOLLAR

31.1050 g., 0.9990 Silver 0.9990 oz. ASW, 35x46 mm. **Ruler:** Elizabeth II **Subject:** Life of Christ **Rev:** Jesus on the Cross (1558) **Shape:** Vertical rectangle

Date	Mintage	F	VF	XF	Unc	BU
2006 Proof	Est. 1,000	Value: 60.00				

KM# 329 DOLLAR

31.1050 g., 0.9990 Silver 0.9990 oz. ASW, 35x45 mm. **Ruler:** Elizabeth II **Subject:** Life of Christ **Rev:** Heaven **Shape:** Vertical rectangle

Date	Mintage	F	VF	XF	Unc	BU
2006 Proof	Est. 1,000	Value: 60.00				

KM# 328 DOLLAR

31.1050 g., 0.9990 Silver 0.9990 oz. ASW, 35x46 mm. **Ruler:** Elizabeth II **Subject:** Life of Christ **Rev:** Ascension (1520) **Shape:** Vertical rectangle

Date	Mintage	F	VF	XF	Unc	BU
2006 Proof	Est. 1,000	Value: 60.00				

KM# 319 DOLLAR

31.1050 g., 0.9990 Silver 0.9990 oz. ASW, 45 mm. **Ruler:** Elizabeth II **Subject:** Olympics **Rev:** Equestrian

Date	Mintage	F	VF	XF	Unc	BU
ND Proof	Est. 2,008	Value: 60.00				

KM# 176 DOLLAR

28.2800 g., 0.9250 Silver 0.8410 oz. ASW **Ruler:** Elizabeth II

Obv: Tiarra head of Elizabeth II right at left, multicolor Van Gogh's painting "Starry Night" with 3 zircon crystals as stars at center right. **Obv. Inscription:** ELIZABETH II - NIUE ISLAND **Rev:** Van Gogh's painting "Vase with Twelve Sunflowers" at left, self portrait of artist with brush at upper right **Rev. Inscription:** VAN GOGH / Vincent **Edge:** Plain **Shape:** Rectangular, 39.94 x 27.97 mm

Date	Mintage	F	VF	XF	Unc	BU
2007 Proof	10,000	Value: 85.00				

KM# 331 DOLLAR

28.2800 g., 0.9250 Silver 0.8410 oz. ASW **Ruler:** Elizabeth II **Subject:** Year of the Pig

Date	Mintage	F	VF	XF	Unc	BU
2007 Proof	Est. 5,000	Value: 30.00				

KM# 332 DOLLAR

28.2800 g., 0.9250 Silver 0.8410 oz. ASW **Ruler:** Elizabeth II **Subject:** Year of the Pig **Rev:** Three little pigs dancing, brick house, wolf

Date	Mintage	F	VF	XF	Unc	BU
2007	—	—	—	—	—	50.00

KM# 334 DOLLAR

28.2800 g., 0.9250 Silver 0.8410 oz. ASW, 38.61 mm. **Ruler:** Elizabeth II **Rev:** Female advancing left with long dress **Rev. Legend:** Change Flies to the Moon

Date	Mintage	F	VF	XF	Unc	BU
2007	Est. 5,000	—	—	—	—	50.00

KM# 335 DOLLAR

28.2800 g., 0.9250 Silver 0.8410 oz. ASW, 38.61 mm. **Ruler:** Elizabeth II **Rev:** Man weiding axe against tree **Rev. Legend:** Wu Gang cuts the sweet-scented osmanthus tree

Date	Mintage	F	VF	XF	Unc	BU
2007	Est. 5,000	—	—	—	—	50.00

KM# 336 DOLLAR

28.2800 g., 0.9250 Silver 0.8410 oz. ASW, 38.61 mm. **Ruler:** Elizabeth II **Rev:** Group visiting palace **Rev. Legend:** Emperor Mint of Tang Dynasty visit the Moon Palace at Night

Date	Mintage	F	VF	XF	Unc	BU
2007	Est. 5,000	—	—	—	—	50.00

KM# 337 DOLLAR

28.2800 g., 0.9250 Silver 0.8410 oz. ASW, 38.61 mm. **Ruler:** Elizabeth II **Rev:** Rabbit with mortar and pestile in house yard **Rev. Legend:** The jade rabbit pounds the medicine of immortality

Date	Mintage	F	VF	XF	Unc	BU
2007 Proof	Est. 5,000	—	—	—	—	50.00

KM# 212 DOLLAR

Silver **Ruler:** Elizabeth II **Rev:** Ox seated multicolor lotus flower

Date	Mintage	F	VF	XF	Unc	BU
2008 Antique finish	—	—	—	—	—	—

KM# 192 DOLLAR

31.1050 g., 0.9990 Silver 0.9990 oz. ASW **Ruler:** Elizabeth II **Subject:** Year of the Ox **Obv:** Head right **Rev:** Multicolor ox

Date	Mintage	F	VF	XF	Unc	BU
2008//2009 Proof	10,000	Value: 70.00				

KM# 201 DOLLAR

28.2800 g., 0.9250 Silver 0.8410 oz. ASW, 38.61 mm. **Ruler:** Elizabeth II **Subject:** Amber Road **Obv:** Roman cart and map, Elizabeth II head at lower left **Rev:** Church, goblet, ancient coin, amber insert **Rev. Legend:** ELBLAG SZLAK BURSZTYNOWY

Date	Mintage	F	VF	XF	Unc	BU
2008 Antique finish	10,000	—	—	—	—	80.00

KM# 202 DOLLAR

28.2800 g., 0.9250 Silver 0.8410 oz. ASW, 38.61 mm. **Ruler:** Elizabeth II **Subject:** Amber Road **Obv:** Roman cart, map, Elizabeth II head at lower left **Rev:** Antonius Pius coins, Nepture statue, mine shaft, amber insert **Rev. Legend:** GDANSK SZLAK BURSZTYNOWY

Date	Mintage	F	VF	XF	Unc	BU
2008 Antique finish	10,000	—	—	—	—	80.00

KM# 203 DOLLAR

28.2800 g., 0.9250 Silver 0.8410 oz. ASW, 38.61 mm. **Ruler:** Elizabeth II **Subject:** Amber Road **Obv:** Roman cart, map, Elizabeth II head at lower left **Rev:** Castle, roman coin, squid, amber insert **Rev. Legend:** KALINGRAD SZLAK BURSZTYNOWY

Date	Mintage	F	VF	XF	Unc	BU
2008 Antique finish	10,000	—	—	—	—	140

KM# 204 DOLLAR

28.2800 g., 0.9990 Silver 0.9083 oz. ASW, 38.61 mm. **Ruler:** Elizabeth II **Subject:** Amber Road **Rev:** Kalingrad, amber insert **Rev. Legend:** SZLAK BURSZTYNOWY KALINGRAD

Date	Mintage	F	VF	XF	Unc	BU
2008 Antique finish	10,000	—	—	—	—	125

KM# 211 DOLLAR

28.2800 g., 0.9250 Silver 0.8410 oz. ASW, 28x40 mm. **Ruler:** Elizabeth II **Obv:** Head of Elizabeth II at lower left, Portrait of Lautrec at top right **Rev:** Toulouse-Lautrec and can-can girl

Date	Mintage	F	VF	XF	Unc	BU
2008 Proof	15,000	Value: 65.00				

KM# 338 DOLLAR

31.1050 g., 0.9990 Silver 0.9990 oz. ASW, 45 mm. **Ruler:** Elizabeth II **Subject:** Year of the Rat **Rev:** Rat in field, sun rays above

Date	Mintage	F	VF	XF	Unc	BU
2008	Est. 8,000	—	—	—	—	50.00

KM# 339 DOLLAR

31.1050 g., 0.9990 Silver 0.9990 oz. ASW, 45 mm. **Ruler:** Elizabeth II **Subject:** Year of the Rat **Rev:** Rat left before house

Date	Mintage	F	VF	XF	Unc	BU
2008	Est. 8,000	—	—	—	—	50.00

KM# 340 DOLLAR

31.1050 g., 0.9990 Silver 0.9990 oz. ASW, 45 mm. **Ruler:** Elizabeth II **Subject:** Year of the Rat **Rev:** Rat standing on hind legs sniffing flora

Date	Mintage	F	VF	XF	Unc	BU
2008	Est. 8,000	—	—	—	—	55.00

KM# 341 DOLLAR

, 45 mm. **Ruler:** Elizabeth II **Rev:** Multicolor Happy mouse

Date	Mintage	F	VF	XF	Unc	BU
2008 Proof	—	Value: 50.00				

KM# 342 DOLLAR

31.1050 g., 0.9990 Silver 0.9990 oz. ASW, 45 mm. **Ruler:** Elizabeth II **Rev:** Multicolor wealthy rat

Date	Mintage	F	VF	XF	Unc	BU
2008 Proof	—	Value: 50.00				

KM# 343 DOLLAR

31.1050 g., 0.9990 Silver 0.9990 oz. ASW, 45 mm. **Ruler:** Elizabeth II **Rev:** Multicolor happy rat

Date	Mintage	F	VF	XF	Unc	BU
2008 Proof	—	Value: 50.00				

KM# 344 DOLLAR

31.1050 g., 0.9990 Silver 0.9990 oz. ASW, 45 mm. **Ruler:** Elizabeth II **Rev:** Multicolor successful rat

Date	Mintage	F	VF	XF	Unc	BU
2008 Proof	—	Value: 50.00				

KM# 345 DOLLAR

31.1050 g., 0.9990 Silver 0.9990 oz. ASW, 45 mm. **Ruler:** Elizabeth II **Rev:** Multicolor rat holding charm

Date	Mintage	F	VF	XF	Unc	BU
2008 Proof	Est. 10,000	Value: 50.00				

KM# 346 DOLLAR

3.1100 g., 0.9990 Gold 0.0999 oz. AGW, 18 mm. **Ruler:** Elizabeth II **Rev:** Rate in garden

Date	Mintage	F	VF	XF	Unc	BU
2008 Proof	Est. 10,000	Value: 175				

KM# 347 DOLLAR

28.2800 g., 0.9250 Silver 0.8410 oz. ASW, 38.61 mm. **Ruler:** Elizabeth II **Rev:** Rate standing infront of multicolor cut cheese wheel

Date	Mintage	F	VF	XF	Unc	BU
2008 Proof	Est. 10,000	Value: 40.00				

KM# 348 DOLLAR

28.2800 g., 0.9250 Silver 0.8410 oz. ASW, 38.61 mm. **Ruler:** Elizabeth II **Rev:** Multicolor dancince mice in garland

Date	Mintage	F	VF	XF	Unc	BU
2008 Proof	—	Value: 40.00				

KM# 197 DOLLAR

17.3000 g., Aluminum-Brass, 32 mm. **Ruler:** Elizabeth II **Obv:** Head right **Rev:** Swordfish **Edge:** Reeded

Date	Mintage	F	VF	XF	Unc	BU
2009	—	—	—	—	7.50	12.50

KM# 231 DOLLAR

31.1030 g., 0.9990 Silver 0.9989 oz. ASW, 38.6 mm. **Ruler:** Elizabeth II **Subject:** Year of the Tiger **Rev:** Tiger cub in basket playing with ball

Date	Mintage	F	VF	XF	Unc	BU
2009 Proof	6,000	Value: 80.00				

KM# 232 DOLLAR

31.1030 g., 0.9990 Silver 0.9989 oz. ASW, 38.6 mm. **Ruler:** Elizabeth II **Subject:** Year of the Tiger **Rev:** Tiger advancing left

Date	Mintage	F	VF	XF	Unc	BU
2009 Proof	6,000	Value: 80.00				

KM# 198 DOLLAR

17.3000 g., Copper Plated Bronze, 32 mm. **Ruler:** Elizabeth II **Obv:** Head right **Rev:** Taro leaves **Edge:** Reeded

Date	Mintage	F	VF	XF	Unc	BU
2010	—	—	—	—	7.50	12.50

KM# 234 DOLLAR

28.2800 g., 0.9250 Silver 0.8410 oz. ASW, 40x40 mm. **Ruler:** Elizabeth II **Obv:** Head right, footprints in field **Rev:** Antilocapra Americana, two antelope running right **Shape:** Square

Date	Mintage	F	VF	XF	Unc	BU
2010 Proof	9,000	Value: 90.00				

KM# 235 DOLLAR
28.2800 g., 0.9250 Silver 0.8410 oz. ASW, 36.8 mm. **Ruler:** Elizabeth II **Obv:** Head right **Rev:** Lycaena Virgavreae multicolor butterfly

Date	Mintage	F	VF	XF	Unc	BU
2010 Proof	8,000	Value: 80.00				

KM# 236 DOLLAR
14.1400 g., 0.9250 Silver 0.4205 oz. ASW, 25x28 mm. **Ruler:** Elizabeth II **Obv:** Head right on musical score **Rev:** Chopin bust at left, score **Shape:** Square

Date	Mintage	F	VF	XF	Unc	BU
2010 Proof	6,000	Value: 60.00				

KM# 238 DOLLAR
28.2800 g., 0.9250 Silver 0.8410 oz. ASW, 36.81 mm. **Ruler:** Elizabeth II **Subject:** Fire **Obv:** Head right, images of early man **Rev:** Volcano and men around fire in multicolor

Date	Mintage	F	VF	XF	Unc	BU
2010 Proof	6,000	Value: 80.00				

KM# 239 DOLLAR
28.2800 g., 0.9250 Silver 0.8410 oz. ASW, 40x28 mm. **Ruler:** Elizabeth II **Obv:** Head right, aircraft propeller, wing schematic **Rev:** Greek warrior shield and multicolor Icarus in flight **Shape:** Rectangle

Date	Mintage	F	VF	XF	Unc	BU
2010 Proof	6,000	Value: 80.00				

KM# 240 DOLLAR
28.2800 g., 0.9250 Silver 0.8410 oz. ASW, 28x40 mm. **Ruler:** Elizabeth II **Obv:** Head right, propeller, wing schematic **Rev:** Montgolfier brothers and balloon **Shape:** Rectangle

Date	Mintage	F	VF	XF	Unc	BU
2010 Proof	6,000	Value: 60.00				

KM# 241 DOLLAR
28.2800 g., 0.9250 Silver 0.8410 oz. ASW, 40x28 mm. **Ruler:** Elizabeth II **Obv:** Head right, Monet painting **Rev:** Claude Monet portrait and painting **Shape:** Rectangle

Date	Mintage	F	VF	XF	Unc	BU
2010 Proof	15,000	Value: 80.00				

KM# 242 DOLLAR
28.2800 g., 0.9250 Silver 0.8410 oz. ASW, 38.61 mm. **Ruler:** Elizabeth II **Obv:** Head right, three men on horseback in multicolor **Rev:** Napoleon and troop in multicolor

Date	Mintage	F	VF	XF	Unc	BU
2010 Proof	10,000	Value: 80.00				

KM# 243 DOLLAR
28.2800 g., 0.9250 Silver 0.8410 oz. ASW, 38.6 mm. **Ruler:** Elizabeth II **Subject:** 65th Anniversary - End of World War II **Obv:** Head right at top, three Soviet medals below **Rev:** Soviet flat, rose and eternal light

Date	Mintage	F	VF	XF	Unc	BU
2010 Proof	7,000	Value: 80.00				

KM# 244 DOLLAR
28.2800 g., 0.9250 Silver 0.8410 oz. ASW, 38.6 mm. **Ruler:** Elizabeth II **Obv:** Head at left, ship, coins, artifacts **Rev:** Stupsk

Date	Mintage	F	VF	XF	Unc	BU
2010 Proof	8,000	Value: 80.00				

KM# 251 DOLLAR
31.1050 g., 0.9990 Silver 0.9990 oz. ASW, 38.6 mm. **Ruler:** Elizabeth II **Subject:** Peanuts 60th Anniversary **Rev:** Snoopy as conductor with flowers, Woodstock with red ribbon

Date	Mintage	F	VF	XF	Unc	BU
2010 Prooflike	3,000	—	—	—	—	80.00

KM# 365 DOLLAR
28.2800 g., 0.9250 Silver 0.8410 oz. ASW, 38.61 mm. **Ruler:** Elizabeth II **Subject:** WWII, 65th Anniversary **Obv:** Elizabeth II head, WWI medal and two stars below **Rev:** Russian flag and medal ribbon

Date	Mintage	F	VF	XF	Unc	BU
2010 Proof	7,000	Value: 50.00				

KM# 366 DOLLAR
28.2800 g., 0.9250 Silver 0.8410 oz. ASW, 38.61 mm. **Ruler:** Elizabeth II **Obv:** Englarged butterfly wing **Rev:** Butterfly - Parnassius Apollo

Date	Mintage	F	VF	XF	Unc	BU
2010 Proof	8,000	Value: 50.00				

KM# 367 DOLLAR
28.2800 g., 0.9250 Silver 0.8410 oz. ASW, 38.61 mm. **Ruler:** Elizabeth II **Subject:** Amber Route - Stare Hradisko **Rev:** Ambert insert, old coin

Date	Mintage	F	VF	XF	Unc	BU
2010 Antique finish	10,000	—	—	—	—	50.00

KM# 369 DOLLAR
14.1400 g., 0.9250 Silver 0.4205 oz. ASW, 32 mm. **Ruler:** Elizabeth II **Subject:** Cartoon Characters - Mis Uszatek **Obv:** Elizabeth II head left, movie film **Rev:** Image of rabbits and bear

Date	Mintage	F	VF	XF	Unc	BU
2010 Proof	8,000	Value: 30.00				

KM# 370 DOLLAR
28.2800 g., 0.9250 Silver 0.8410 oz. ASW **Ruler:** Elizabeth II **Obv:** Elizabeth II head right, Cupid **Rev:** Romeo and Juliet about to kiss

Date	Mintage	F	VF	XF	Unc	BU
2010 Proof	9,000	Value: 50.00				

KM# 392 DOLLAR
14.1400 g., 0.9250 Silver 0.4205 oz. ASW, 32 mm. **Ruler:** Elizabeth II **Subject:** Cartoon Characters - Wolf and the Hare **Rev:** Wolf and Hare characters in multicolor

Date	Mintage	F	VF	XF	Unc	BU
2010 Proof	8,000	Value: 30.00				

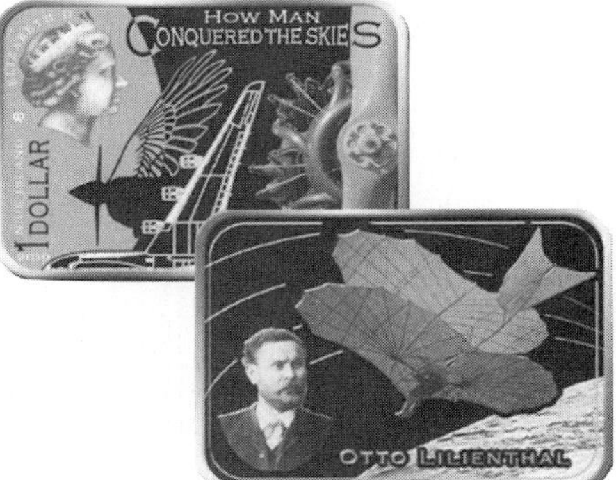

KM# 393 DOLLAR
28.2800 g., 0.9250 Silver 0.8410 oz. ASW, 40x28 mm. **Ruler:** Elizabeth II **Obv:** Queen's head at top left, three airplane views **Rev:** Otto Lilienthal and the glider **Shape:** Rectangle

Date	Mintage	F	VF	XF	Unc	BU
2010 Proof	6,000	Value: 50.00				

KM# 394 DOLLAR
28.2800 g., 0.9250 Silver 0.8410 oz. ASW, 38.8 mm. **Ruler:** Elizabeth II **Obv:** Queen's head right within star pattern **Rev:** Two portraits of Sitting Bull in multicolor

Date	Mintage	F	VF	XF	Unc	BU
2010 Proof	6,000	Value: 60.00				

KM# 395 DOLLAR
28.2800 g., 0.9250 Silver 0.8410 oz. ASW, 40x40 mm. **Ruler:** Elizabeth II **Obv:** Head in tiara right within diamond, footprints in background **Rev:** Platypus (Ornithorhynchus anatinus) **Shape:** Square

Date	Mintage	F	VF	XF	Unc	BU
2010 Proof	9,000	Value: 50.00				

KM# 396 DOLLAR
28.2800 g., 0.9250 Silver with amber insert 0.8410 oz. ASW, 38.61 mm. **Ruler:** Elizabeth II **Subject:** Amber Route - Carnuntum **Rev:** Arches, ancient coin and statue

Date	Mintage	F	VF	XF	Unc	BU
2010 Antique patina	10,000	Value: 50.00				

KM# 398 DOLLAR
28.2800 g., 0.9250 Silver with amber insert 0.8410 oz. ASW, 38.61 mm. **Ruler:** Elizabeth II **Subject:** Amber Route - Szombathely **Rev:** Cathedral, ancient coin

Date	Mintage	F	VF	XF	Unc	BU
2010 Antique patina	10,000	Value: 50.00				

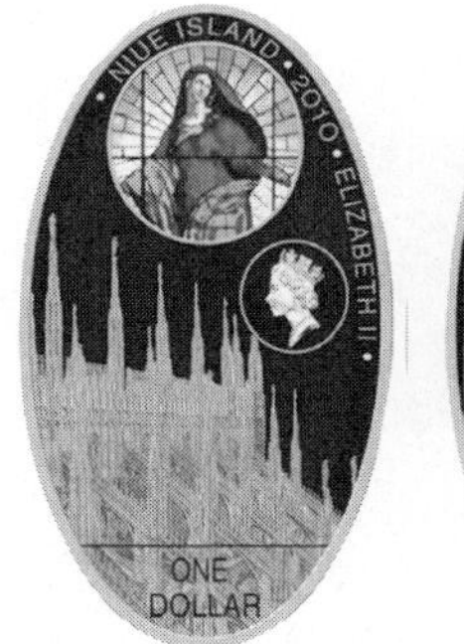

KM# 400 DOLLAR
28.2800 g., 0.9250 Silver 0.8410 oz. ASW, 27x45 mm. **Ruler:** Elizabeth II **Subject:** Milan Cathedral **Obv:** Cathedral's flying buttresses, stained glass colored inset **Rev:** Front facade of cathedral, stained glass colored inset **Shape:** Vertical oval

Date	Mintage	F	VF	XF	Unc	BU
2010 Proof	5,000	Value: 60.00				

KM# 401 DOLLAR
28.2800 g., 0.9250 Silver 0.8410 oz. ASW, 27x45 mm. **Ruler:** Elizabeth II **Subject:** Cologne Cathedral **Obv:** Cathedral side exterior, stained glass colored inset **Rev:** Cathedral floor plan and facade, stained glass colored inset **Shape:** Vertical oval

Date	Mintage	F	VF	XF	Unc	BU
2010 Proof	5,000	Value: 60.00				

KM# 402 DOLLAR
28.2800 g., 0.9250 Silver 0.8410 oz. ASW, 27x45 mm. **Ruler:** Elizabeth II **Subject:** Notre Dame Cathedral **Obv:** Cathedral side view, stained glass colored inset **Rev:** Linear cathedral interior view, cathedral facade, stained glass colored inset **Shape:** Vertical oval

Date	Mintage	F	VF	XF	Unc	BU
2010 Proof	5,000	Value: 60.00				

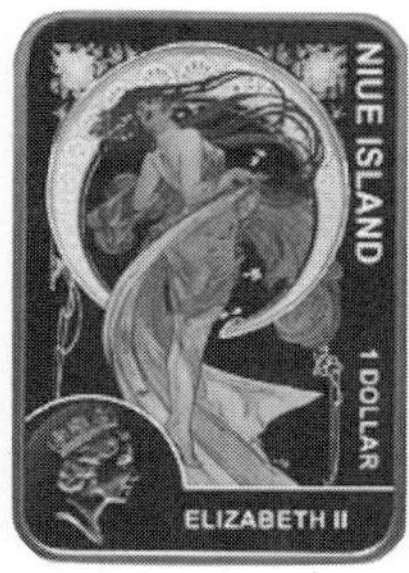

KM# 403 DOLLAR
28.2800 g., 0.9250 Silver 0.8410 oz. ASW, 28x40 mm. **Ruler:** Elizabeth II **Subject:** Alfons Mucha, 150th Anniversary of Birth **Obv:** Standing Female in multicolor **Rev:** Female portrait and Mucha portrait in multicolor **Shape:** Vertical Rectangle

Date	Mintage	F	VF	XF	Unc	BU
2010 Proof	5,000	Value: 60.00				

KM# 404 DOLLAR
28.2800 g., 0.9250 Silver 0.8410 oz. ASW, 28x40 mm. **Ruler:** Elizabeth II **Subject:** Carl Brullov **Obv:** Female on horseback in color **Rev:** Two females with grape wreath above, Brullov portrait, Three nuns singing below; all in color **Shape:** Vertical Rectangle

Date	Mintage	F	VF	XF	Unc	BU
2010 Proof	5,000	Value: 60.00				

KM# 406 DOLLAR
28.2800 g., 0.9250 Silver 0.8410 oz. ASW, 40x40 mm. **Ruler:** Elizabeth II **Obv:** Head with tiara right, in diamond, footprints in background **Rev:** Venus Flytrap in color **Shape:** Square

Date	Mintage	F	VF	XF	Unc	BU
2010 Proof	9,000	Value: 60.00				

KM# 407 DOLLAR
28.2800 g., 0.9250 Silver 0.8410 oz. ASW, 41. mm. **Ruler:** Elizabeth II **Subject:** Good Luck **Obv:** Head with tiara right, horseshoes below **Rev:** horshoes and clover

Date	Mintage	F	VF	XF	Unc	BU
2010 Proof	10,000	Value: 60.00				

KM# 412 DOLLAR
28.2800 g., 0.9250 Silver 0.8410 oz. ASW, 38.61 mm. **Ruler:** Elizabeth II **Subject:** Siberia **Obv:** Head with tiara right **Rev:** Khanty-Mansiysk

Date	Mintage	F	VF	XF	Unc	BU
2010 Proof-like	4,000	—	—	—	—	40.00

KM# 413 DOLLAR
28.2800 g., 0.9250 Silver 0.8410 oz. ASW, 38.61 mm. **Ruler:** Elizabeth II **Subject:** Siberia **Obv:** Head with tiara right **Rev:** Uray

Date	Mintage	F	VF	XF	Unc	BU
2010 Proof-like	4,000	—	—	—	—	40.00

KM# 414 DOLLAR
28.2800 g., 0.9250 Silver 0.8410 oz. ASW, 38.61 mm. **Ruler:** Elizabeth II **Subject:** Siberia **Obv:** Head with tiara right **Rev:** Surgut

Date	Mintage	F	VF	XF	Unc	BU
2010 Proof-like	4,000	—	—	—	—	40.00

KM# 415 DOLLAR
28.2800 g., 0.9250 Silver 0.8410 oz. ASW, 38.61 mm. **Ruler:** Elizabeth II **Subject:** Siberia **Obv:** Head with tiara right **Rev:** Nizhnevartovsk

Date	Mintage	F	VF	XF	Unc	BU
2010 Proof-like	4,000	—	—	—	—	40.00

KM# 417 DOLLAR
28.2800 g., 0.9250 Silver 0.8410 oz. ASW, 38.61 mm. **Ruler:** Elizabeth II **Subject:** Famous Love Stories - Samson and Dalilah **Obv:** Head with tiara right, Cupid below **Rev:** Portraits of Samson and Dalilah

Date	Mintage	F	VF	XF	Unc	BU
2010 Proof	9,000	Value: 60.00				

KM# 418 DOLLAR
31.1000 g., 0.9990 Silver 0.9988 oz. ASW, 40 mm. **Ruler:** Elizabeth II **Subject:** Jaroslawl, 100th Anniversary **Obv:** Head with tiara right **Rev:** Banner in color

Date	Mintage	F	VF	XF	Unc	BU
2010 Proof	2,000	Value: 60.00				

KM# 419 DOLLAR
31.1000 g., 0.9990 Silver 0.9988 oz. ASW, 40 mm. **Ruler:** Elizabeth II **Subject:** Jaroslawl, 1000th Anniversary **Obv:** Head with tiara right **Rev:** Three church towers in color

Date	Mintage	F	VF	XF	Unc	BU
2010 Proof	9,000	Value: 60.00				

KM# 420 DOLLAR
31.1000 g., 0.9990 Silver 0.9988 oz. ASW, 40 mm. **Ruler:** Elizabeth II **Subject:** Jaroslawl, 1000th Anniversary **Obv:** Head in tiara right **Rev:** Town square in color

Date	Mintage	F	VF	XF	Unc	BU
2010 Proof	9,000	Value: 60.00				

KM# 421 DOLLAR
28.2800 g., 0.9250 Silver 0.8410 oz. ASW, 36.81 mm. **Ruler:** Elizabeth II **Subject:** Cultural Achievements **Obv:** Head with tiara at center **Rev:** Bow and arrows, Bow and firestarting kit

Date	Mintage	F	VF	XF	Unc	BU
2010 Proof	6,000	Value: 60.00				

KM# 422 DOLLAR
28.2800 g., 0.9250 Silver 0.8410 oz. ASW, 44 mm. **Ruler:** Elizabeth II **Subject:** Christmas star **Obv:** Head with tiara right, snowflakes around **Rev:** Children before christmas tree in color **Shape:** 7-pointed star

Date	Mintage	F	VF	XF	Unc	BU
2010 Proof	15,000	Value: 60.00				

KM# 426 DOLLAR
28.2800 g., 0.9250 Silver 0.8410 oz. ASW, 41 mm. **Ruler:** Elizabeth II **Subject:** Four Leaf Clover **Obv:** Head with titara right, clovers **Rev:** four clovers and ripple background

Date	Mintage	F	VF	XF	Unc	BU
2010 Proof	10,000	Value: 60.00				

KM# 427 DOLLAR
28.2800 g., 0.9250 Silver 0.8410 oz. ASW, 38.61 mm. **Ruler:** Elizabeth II **Subject:** Veliky Novgorod **Obv:** Head with tiara right, montage of ship and coins at right **Rev:** Market scene, Church; city arms below

Date	Mintage	F	VF	XF	Unc	BU
2010 Proof	8,000	Value: 60.00				

KM# 428 DOLLAR
28.2800 g., 0.9250 Silver 0.8410 oz. ASW, 38.61 mm. **Ruler:** Elizabeth II **Subject:** Year of the Rabbit **Obv:** Head with tiara right **Rev:** Rabbit seated in field

Date	Mintage	F	VF	XF	Unc	BU
2010 Proof	3,000	Value: 60.00				

KM# 429 DOLLAR
28.2800 g., 0.9250 Silver 0.8410 oz. ASW, 38.61 mm. **Ruler:** Elizabeth II **Subject:** Year of the Rabbit **Obv:** Head with tiara right **Rev:** Two rabbits holding heart at center

Date	Mintage	F	VF	XF	Unc	BU
2010 Proof	3,000	Value: 60.00				

KM# 432 DOLLAR
28.2800 g., 0.9250 Silver 0.8410 oz. ASW, 40x28 mm. **Ruler:** Elizabeth II **Subject:** Francisco Goya **Obv:** Head with tiara right at left, painting of man and woman at right **Rev:** Goya and Clothed female reclining **Shape:** Rectangle

Date	Mintage	F	VF	XF	Unc	BU
2010 Proof	10,000	Value: 60.00				

KM# 433 DOLLAR
28.2800 g., 0.9250 Silver 0.8410 oz. ASW, 38.61 mm. **Ruler:** Elizabeth II **Subject:** Peter the Great **Obv:** Head with tiara right above ship and city view **Rev:** Half-length figure holding coins, map in background

Date	Mintage	F	VF	XF	Unc	BU
2010 Proof	4,000	Value: 60.00				

KM# 434 DOLLAR
28.2800 g., 0.9250 Silver 0.8410 oz. ASW, 38.61 mm. **Ruler:** Elizabeth II **Subject:** Sea of Love **Obv:** Head in tiara right above sunset at sea with heart at center **Rev:** Two white doves in flight over sea, within heart

Date	Mintage	F	VF	XF	Unc	BU
2010 Proof	7,000	Value: 60.00				

KM# 435 DOLLAR
15.5500 g., 0.9250 Silver 0.4624 oz. ASW, 35 mm. **Ruler:** Elizabeth II **Subject:** Prehistoric art - Chauvet cave **Rev:** Two figures of cats

Date	Mintage	F	VF	XF	Unc	BU
2010 Proof	1,000	Value: 40.00				

KM# 436 DOLLAR
15.5500 g., 0.9250 Silver 0.4624 oz. ASW, 35 mm. **Ruler:** Elizabeth II **Subject:** Prehistoric art - Altamira cave **Rev:** Bison artwork

Date	Mintage	F	VF	XF	Unc	BU
2010 Proof	1,000	Value: 40.00				

KM# 437 DOLLAR
15.5500 g., 0.9250 Silver 0.4624 oz. ASW, 35 mm. **Ruler:** Elizabeth II **Subject:** Prehistoric art - Lascaux cave **Rev:** Horse art

Date	Mintage	F	VF	XF	Unc	BU
2010 Proof	1,000	Value: 40.00				

KM# 438 DOLLAR
15.5500 g., 0.9250 Silver 0.4624 oz. ASW, 35 mm. **Ruler:** Elizabeth II **Subject:** Prehistoric art - Jabbaren cave **Rev:** Male figure with bow

Date	Mintage	F	VF	XF	Unc	BU
2010 Proof	1,000	Value: 40.00				

KM# 439 DOLLAR
15.5500 g., 0.9250 Silver 0.4624 oz. ASW, 35 mm. **Ruler:** Elizabeth II **Subject:** Prehistoric art - Tadrart cave **Rev:** Elephant art

Date	Mintage	F	VF	XF	Unc	BU
2010 Proof	1,000	Value: 40.00				

KM# 440a DOLLAR
28.2800 g., Copper-Nickel, 38.61 mm. **Ruler:** Elizabeth II **Subject:** Lifetime of Service **Obv:** Head in tiara right **Rev:** Conjoined busts of Elizabeth II and Prince Philip

Date	Mintage	F	VF	XF	Unc	BU
2010	—	—	—	—	—	20.00

KM# 440b DOLLAR
28.2800 g., 0.9250 Silver 0.8410 oz. ASW, 38.61 mm. **Ruler:** Elizabeth II **Subject:** Lifetime of Service **Obv:** Head with tiara right **Rev:** Conjoined busts of Elizabeth II and Prince Philip

Date	Mintage	F	VF	XF	Unc	BU
2010 Proof	19,500	Value: 50.00				

KM# 441 DOLLAR
31.1000 g., 0.9990 Silver 0.9988 oz. ASW, 38.61 mm. **Ruler:** Elizabeth II **Subject:** Slovic mythology - Perun **Rev:** Two warriors, tree in background

Date	Mintage	F	VF	XF	Unc	BU
2010 Proof	1,000	Value: 60.00				

KM# 454 DOLLAR
Silver **Ruler:** Elizabeth II **Rev:** Michail Ktzov stadium

Date	Mintage	F	VF	XF	Unc	BU
2010 Proof	—	Value: 50.00				

KM# 455 DOLLAR
Silver **Ruler:** Elizabeth II **Subject:** Polish Stadiums **Rev:** Gdansk

Date	Mintage	F	VF	XF	Unc	BU
2010 Proof	—	Value: 50.00				

KM# 456 DOLLAR
31.1030 g., 0.9990 Silver 0.9989 oz. ASW, 40 mm. **Ruler:** Elizabeth II **Subject:** Giah Thong - safe conduct pass **Obv:** Head with tiara right **Rev:** Two soldiers below Viet Nam flag

Date	Mintage	F	VF	XF	Unc	BU
2010 Prooflike	—	—	—	—	—	50.00

KM# 495 DOLLAR
28.2800 g., 0.9250 Silver 0.8410 oz. ASW, 38.61 mm. **Ruler:** Elizabeth II **Subject:** Zodiac Mucha Paintings **Rev:** Aries

Date	Mintage	F	VF	XF	Unc	BU
2010 Proof	10,000	Value: 50.00				

KM# 496 DOLLAR
28.2800 g., 0.9250 Silver 0.8410 oz. ASW, 38.61 mm. **Ruler:** Elizabeth II **Subject:** Zodiac Mucha Paintings **Rev:** Taurus

Date	Mintage	F	VF	XF	Unc	BU
2010 Proof	10,000	Value: 50.00				

KM# 497 DOLLAR

28.2800 g., 0.9250 Silver 0.8410 oz. ASW, 38.61 mm. **Ruler:** Elizabeth II **Subject:** Zodiac Mucha Paintings **Rev:** Gemini

Date	Mintage	F	VF	XF	Unc	BU
2010 Proof	10,000	Value: 50.00				

KM# 498 DOLLAR

28.2800 g., 0.9250 Silver 0.8410 oz. ASW, 38.61 mm. **Ruler:** Elizabeth II **Subject:** Zodiac Mucha Paintings **Rev:** Cancer

Date	Mintage	F	VF	XF	Unc	BU
2010 Proof	10,000	Value: 50.00				

KM# 499 DOLLAR

28.2800 g., 0.9250 Silver 0.8410 oz. ASW **Ruler:** Elizabeth II **Subject:** Zodiac Mucha Paintings **Rev:** Leo

Date	Mintage	F	VF	XF	Unc	BU
2010 Proof	10,000	Value: 50.00				

KM# 500 DOLLAR

28.2500 g., 0.9250 Silver 0.8401 oz. ASW, 38.61 mm. **Ruler:** Elizabeth II **Subject:** Zodiac Mucha Paintings **Rev:** Virgo

Date	Mintage	F	VF	XF	Unc	BU
2010 Proof	10,000	Value: 50.00				

KM# 501 DOLLAR

28.2800 g., 0.9250 Silver 0.8410 oz. ASW, 38.61 mm. **Ruler:** Elizabeth II **Subject:** Zodiac Mucha Paintings **Rev:** Libra

Date	Mintage	F	VF	XF	Unc	BU
2010 Proof	10,000	Value: 50.00				

KM# 502 DOLLAR

28.2800 g., 0.9250 Silver 0.8410 oz. ASW, 38.61 mm. **Ruler:** Elizabeth II **Subject:** Zodiac Mucha Paintings **Rev:** Scorpio

Date	Mintage	F	VF	XF	Unc	BU
2010 Proof	10,000	Value: 50.00				

KM# 503 DOLLAR

28.2800 g., 0.9250 Silver 0.8410 oz. ASW, 38.61 mm. **Ruler:** Elizabeth II **Subject:** Zodiac Mucha Paintings **Rev:** Sagittarius

Date	Mintage	F	VF	XF	Unc	BU
2010 Proof	10,000	Value: 50.00				

KM# 504 DOLLAR

28.2800 g., 0.9250 Silver 0.8410 oz. ASW, 38.61 mm. **Ruler:** Elizabeth II **Subject:** Zodiac Mucha Paintings **Rev:** Capricorn

Date	Mintage	F	VF	XF	Unc	BU
2011 Proof	10,000	Value: 50.00				

KM# 505 DOLLAR

28.2800 g., 0.9250 Silver 0.8410 oz. ASW, 38.61 mm. **Ruler:** Elizabeth II **Subject:** Zodiac Mucha Painting **Rev:** Aquarius

Date	Mintage	F	VF	XF	Unc	BU
2011 Proof	10,000	Value: 50.00				

KM# 506 DOLLAR

28.2800 g., 0.9250 Silver 0.8410 oz. ASW, 38.61 mm. **Ruler:** Elizabeth II **Subject:** Zodiac Mucha Paintings **Rev:** Pisces

Date	Mintage	F	VF	XF	Unc	BU
2011 Proof	10,000	Value: 50.00				

KM# 508 DOLLAR

Silver **Ruler:** Elizabeth II **Subject:** Russian Cartoons

Date	Mintage	F	VF	XF	Unc	BU
2011 Proof	—	Value: 50.00				

KM# 509 DOLLAR

Silver **Ruler:** Elizabeth II **Subject:** Russian Cartoons

Date	Mintage	F	VF	XF	Unc	BU
2011 Proof	—	Value: 50.00				

KM# 510 DOLLAR

28.2800 g., 0.9250 Silver 0.8410 oz. ASW **Ruler:** Elizabeth II **Subject:** Year of the Rabbit **Rev:** Rabbit in the snow **Shape:** Horizontal oval

Date	Mintage	F	VF	XF	Unc	BU
2011 Proof	5,000	Value: 50.00				

KM# 514 DOLLAR

31.1050 g., Silver Plated Copper-Nickel, 40 mm. **Ruler:** Elizabeth II **Subject:** Royal Engagement **Obv:** Head with tiara right **Rev:** Prince William and Catherine Middleton facing

Date	Mintage	F	VF	XF	Unc	BU
2011 Proof	10,000	Value: 25.00				

KM# 515 DOLLAR

31.1000 g., Silver Plated Copper, 40 mm. **Ruler:** Elizabeth II **Subject:** Diana - A wife, Princess, Mother, Legend

Date	Mintage	F	VF	XF	Unc	BU
2011 Proof	10,000	Value: 20.00				

KM# 516 DOLLAR

31.1000 g., Silver Plated Copper, 40 mm. **Ruler:** Elizabeth II **Subject:** Diana - Wedding to Charles

Date	Mintage	F	VF	XF	Unc	BU
2011 Proof	10,000	Value: 20.00				

KM# 517 DOLLAR

31.1000 g., Silver Plated Copper, 40 mm. **Ruler:** Elizabeth II **Subject:** Diana - Engaement to Prince Charles

Date	Mintage	F	VF	XF	Unc	BU
2011 Proof	10,000	Value: 20.00				

KM# 518 DOLLAR

31.1000 g., Silver Plated Copper, 40 mm. **Ruler:** Elizabeth II **Subject:** Diana - Quote

Date	Mintage	F	VF	XF	Unc	BU
2011 Proof	10,000	Value: 20.00				

KM# 519 DOLLAR

31.1000 g., Silver, 40 mm. **Ruler:** Elizabeth II **Subject:** Diana - Mother Teresa

Date	Mintage	F	VF	XF	Unc	BU
2011 Proof	10,000	Value: 20.00				

KM# 520 DOLLAR

31.1000 g., Silver Plated Copper, 40 mm. **Ruler:** Elizabeth II **Subject:** Diana - We will always remember

Date	Mintage	F	VF	XF	Unc	BU
2011 Proof	10,000	Value: 20.00				

KM# 265 2 DOLLARS

62.2100 g., 0.9990 Silver 1.9980 oz. ASW, 55 mm. **Ruler:** Elizabeth II **Subject:** Year of the Rooster **Rev:** Multicolor rooster standing right, sunrise

Date	Mintage	F	VF	XF	Unc	BU
2005 Proof	—	Value: 60.00				

KM# 294 2 DOLLARS

62.2000 g., 0.9990 Silver 1.9977 oz. ASW, 55 mm. **Ruler:** Elizabeth II **Subject:** Year of the Dog **Rev:** Multicolor dog

Date	Mintage	F	VF	XF	Unc	BU
2005 Proof	—	Value: 80.00				

KM# 269 2 DOLLARS

1.2400 g., 0.9990 Gold 0.0398 oz. AGW, 14 mm. **Ruler:** Elizabeth II **Subject:** Year of the Rooster

Date	Mintage	F	VF	XF	Unc	BU
2005 Proof	—	Value: 65.00				

KM# 270 2 DOLLARS

1.5600 g., 0.9990 Gold 0.0501 oz. AGW, 18 mm. **Ruler:** Elizabeth II **Subject:** Year of the Rooster

Date	Mintage	F	VF	XF	Unc	BU
2005 Proof	—	Value: 85.00				

KM# 271 2 DOLLARS

3.1100 g., 0.9990 Gold 0.0999 oz. AGW, 18 mm. **Ruler:** Elizabeth II **Subject:** Year of the Rooster

Date	Mintage	F	VF	XF	Unc	BU
2005 Proof	—	Value: 150				

KM# 278 2 DOLLARS

3.1100 g., 0.9990 Gold 0.0999 oz. AGW, 18 mm. **Ruler:** Elizabeth II **Subject:** Chinese space acheivements **Rev:** Multicolor rocket, flag, map

Date	Mintage	F	VF	XF	Unc	BU
2005 Proof	Est. 3,000	Value: 165				

KM# 279 2 DOLLARS

31.1050 g., 0.9990 Silver 0.9990 oz. ASW, 35x46 mm. **Ruler:** Elizabeth II **Subject:** Impressionist paintings **Rev:** Multicolor painting of a bridge **Shape:** Vertical rectangle

Date	Mintage	F	VF	XF	Unc	BU
2005 Proof	Est. 2,005	Value: 40.00				

KM# 280 2 DOLLARS

31.1050 g., 0.9990 Silver 0.9990 oz. ASW, 35x46 mm. **Ruler:** Elizabeth II **Subject:** Impressionist paintings **Rev:** Multicolor painting of a female **Shape:** Vertical rectangle

Date	Mintage	F	VF	XF	Unc	BU
2005 Proof	Est. 2,005	Value: 40.00				

KM# 281 2 DOLLARS

31.1050 g., 0.9990 Silver 0.9990 oz. ASW, 35x46 mm. **Ruler:** Elizabeth II **Subject:** Impressionists paintings **Rev:** Multicolor painting of a village **Shape:** Vertical rectangle

Date	Mintage	F	VF	XF	Unc	BU
2005 Proof	Est. 2,005	Value: 40.00				

KM# 282 2 DOLLARS

31.1050 g., 0.9990 Silver 0.9990 oz. ASW, 35x46 mm. **Ruler:** Elizabeth II **Subject:** Impressionists paintings **Rev:** Multicolor painting of a seaside **Shape:** Vertical rectangle

Date	Mintage	F	VF	XF	Unc	BU
2005 Proof	Est. 2,005	Value: 40.00				

KM# 283 2 DOLLARS

31.1050 g., 0.9990 Silver 0.9990 oz. ASW, 35x46 mm. **Ruler:** Elizabeth II **Subject:** Impressionists paintings **Rev:** Multicolor painting of Paris **Shape:** Vertical rectangle

Date	Mintage	F	VF	XF	Unc	BU
2005 Proof	Est. 2,005	Value: 40.00				

KM# 284 2 DOLLARS

31.1050 g., 0.9990 Silver 0.9990 oz. ASW, 35x46 mm. **Ruler:** Elizabeth II **Subject:** Impressionists paintings **Rev:** Multicolor painting of female **Shape:** Vertical rectangle

Date	Mintage	F	VF	XF	Unc	BU
2005 Proof	Est. 2,005	Value: 40.00				

KM# 285 2 DOLLARS

31.1050 g., 0.9990 Silver 0.9990 oz. ASW, 35x46 mm. **Ruler:** Elizabeth II **Subject:** Impressionist paintings **Rev:** Multicolor painting of dancers **Shape:** Vertical rectangle

Date	Mintage	F	VF	XF	Unc	BU
2005 Proof	Est. 2,005	Value: 40.00				

KM# 286 2 DOLLARS

31.1050 g., 0.9990 Silver 0.9990 oz. ASW, 35x46 mm. **Ruler:** Elizabeth II **Subject:** Impressionists paintings **Rev:** Multicolor painting of Fifer **Shape:** Vertical rectangle

Date	Mintage	F	VF	XF	Unc	BU
2005 Proof	Est. 2,005	Value: 40.00				

KM# 287 2 DOLLARS

31.1050 g., 0.9990 Silver 0.9990 oz. ASW, 35x46 mm. **Ruler:** Elizabeth II **Subject:** Impressionists paintings **Rev:** Multicolor painting of boats **Shape:** Vertical rectangle

Date	Mintage	F	VF	XF	Unc	BU
2005 Proof	Est. 2,005	Value: 40.00				

KM# 288 2 DOLLARS

31.1050 g., 0.9990 Silver 0.9990 oz. ASW, 35x46 mm. **Ruler:** Elizabeth II **Subject:** Impressionists paintings **Obv:** Multicolor painting of Paris scene **Shape:** Vertical rectangle

Date	Mintage	F	VF	XF	Unc	BU
2005 Proof	Est. 2,005	Value: 40.00				

KM# 289 2 DOLLARS

31.1050 g., 0.9990 Silver 0.9990 oz. ASW, 35x46 mm. **Ruler:** Elizabeth II **Subject:** Impressionists paintings **Rev:** Multicolor painting of a maiden **Shape:** Vertical rectangle

Date	Mintage	F	VF	XF	Unc	BU
2005 Proof	Est. 2,005	Value: 40.00				

KM# 290 2 DOLLARS

31.1050 g., 0.9990 Silver 0.9990 oz. ASW, 35x46 mm. **Ruler:** Elizabeth II **Subject:** Impresionists paintings **Rev:** Multicolor painting of an artist **Shape:** Vertical rectangle

Date	Mintage	F	VF	XF	Unc	BU
2005 Proof	Est. 2,005	Value: 40.00				

KM# 291 2 DOLLARS

31.1050 g., 0.9990 Silver 0.9990 oz. ASW, 35x46 mm. **Ruler:** Elizabeth II **Subject:** Impressionists paintings **Rev:** Multicolor painting of Canada **Shape:** Vertical rectangle

Date	Mintage	F	VF	XF	Unc	BU
2005 Proof	Est. 2,005	Value: 40.00				

KM# 298 2 DOLLARS

1.5600 g., 0.9990 Gold 0.0501 oz. AGW, 16 mm. **Ruler:** Elizabeth II **Subject:** Year of the Dog **Rev:** Multicolor dog

Date	Mintage	F	VF	XF	Unc	BU
2005 Proof	—	Value: 80.00				

KM# 299 2 DOLLARS

3.1100 g., 0.9990 Gold 0.0999 oz. AGW, 18 mm. **Ruler:** Elizabeth II **Subject:** Year of the Dog **Rev:** Multicolor dog

Date	Mintage	F	VF	XF	Unc	BU
2005 Proof	—	Value: 150				

KM# 330 2 DOLLARS

62.2000 g., 0.9990 Silver 1.9977 oz. ASW, 30x70 mm. **Ruler:** Elizabeth II **Subject:** Life of Christ **Rev:** Last Supper (1495) **Shape:** Vertical rectangle

Date	Mintage	F	VF	XF	Unc	BU
2006 Proof	Est. 1,000	Value: 175				

KM# 190 2 DOLLARS

1.5000 g., 0.9990 Gold 0.0482 oz. AGW **Ruler:** Elizabeth II **Subject:** Year of the Pig **Obv:** Head right **Rev:** Multicolor pig

Date	Mintage	F	VF	XF	Unc	BU
2007 Proof	—	Value: 90.00				

KM# 205 2 DOLLARS

31.1050 g., 0.9990 Silver 0.9990 oz. ASW, 40.7 mm. **Ruler:** Elizabeth II **Subject:** Peoples Republic of China, 60th Anniversary **Rev:** Dragon and scenes of China in multicolor

Date	Mintage	F	VF	XF	Unc	BU
2008 Proof	6,888	Value: 150				

KM# 214 2 DOLLARS

62.2100 g., 0.9990 Silver 1.9980 oz. ASW, 63x27 mm. **Ruler:** Elizabeth II **Subject:** Feng Shui **Rev:** Multicolor blossoming peonies **Shape:** Vertical rectangle

Date	Mintage	F	VF	XF	Unc	BU
2009 Prooflike	16,888	—	—	—	—	200

KM# 185 2 DOLLARS

31.1050 g., 0.9990 Silver Partially gilt 0.9990 oz. ASW, 40 mm. **Ruler:** Elizabeth II **Subject:** Year of the Ox **Rev:** Gilt ox advancing left

Date	Mintage	F	VF	XF	Unc	BU
2009 Proof	20,000	Value: 75.00				

KM# 199 2 DOLLARS

25.0000 g., 0.9250 Silver 0.7435 oz. ASW, 38.6 mm. **Ruler:** Elizabeth II **Rev:** Two spinner dolphins leaping, swarovski crystal chip in eye

Date	Mintage	F	VF	XF	Unc	BU
2009 Proof	2,500	Value: 45.00				

KM# 200 2 DOLLARS

0.5000 g., 0.9990 Gold 0.0161 oz. AGW, 11 mm. **Ruler:** Elizabeth II **Rev:** Two spinner dolphins leaping out of the water

Date	Mintage	F	VF	XF	Unc	BU
2009 Proof	10,000	Value: 50.00				

KM# 209 2 DOLLARS

1.0000 g., 0.9000 Gold 0.0289 oz. AGW **Ruler:** Elizabeth II **Subject:** Frederic Chopin **Obv:** Elizabeth II head right **Rev:** Chopin bust and autograph

Date	Mintage	F	VF	XF	Unc	BU
2009 Proof	10,000	Value: 100				

KM# 210 2 DOLLARS

31.1050 g., 0.9990 Silver 0.9990 oz. ASW, 40.7 mm. **Ruler:** Elizabeth II **Obv:** Head right **Rev:** Two black swans, multicolor **Rev. Designer:** LOVE IS PRECIOUS

Date	Mintage	F	VF	XF	Unc	BU
2009 Proof	10,000	Value: 80.00				

KM# 215 2 DOLLARS

31.1050 g., 0.9990 Silver 0.9990 oz. ASW, 40 mm. **Ruler:** Elizabeth II **Subject:** Russian Ballet **Rev:** Anna Pavlova in multicolor

Date	Mintage	F	VF	XF	Unc	BU
2009 Prooflike	5,000	—	—	—	—	90.00

KM# 216 2 DOLLARS

31.1030 g., 0.9990 Silver 0.9989 oz. ASW, 40.7 mm. **Ruler:** Elizabeth II **Subject:** Russian Ballet **Rev:** Matilda Kshesinskaya in multicolor

Date	Mintage	F	VF	XF	Unc	BU
2009 Prooflike	10,000	—	—	—	—	80.00

KM# 217 2 DOLLARS

31.1050 g., 0.9990 Silver 0.9990 oz. ASW, 40.7 mm. **Ruler:** Elizabeth II **Subject:** Russian Ballet **Rev:** Sergey Lefar in multicolor

Date	Mintage	F	VF	XF	Unc	BU
2009 Prooflike	10,000	—	—	—	—	80.00

KM# 218 2 DOLLARS

31.1050 g., 0.9990 Silver 0.9990 oz. ASW, 40.7 mm. **Ruler:** Elizabeth II **Subject:** Russian Ballet **Rev:** Sergi Daighilev in multicolor

Date	Mintage	F	VF	XF	Unc	BU
2009 Prooflike	10,000	—	—	—	—	80.00

KM# 219 2 DOLLARS

31.1030 g., 0.9990 Silver 0.9989 oz. ASW, 40.7 mm. **Ruler:** Elizabeth II **Subject:** Russian Ballet **Rev:** Vaslav Fomich Nijinsky

Date	Mintage	F	VF	XF	Unc	BU
2009 Prooflike	10,000	—	—	—	—	80.00

KM# 220 2 DOLLARS

31.1050 g., 0.9990 Silver 0.9990 oz. ASW, 40.7 mm. **Ruler:** Elizabeth II **Subject:** Panagyurishte Treasure **Rev:** Vessel in the shape of a female head right

Date	Mintage	F	VF	XF	Unc	BU
2009	5,000	—	—	—	—	80.00

KM# 221 2 DOLLARS

31.1050 g., 0.9990 Silver 0.9990 oz. ASW, 40.7 mm. **Ruler:** Elizabeth II **Subject:** Panagyurishte Treasure **Rev:** Vessel in shape of female head left

Date	Mintage	F	VF	XF	Unc	BU
2009	5,000	—	—	—	—	80.00

KM# 222 2 DOLLARS

31.1050 g., 0.9990 Silver 0.9990 oz. ASW, 40.7 mm. **Ruler:** Elizabeth II **Subject:** Panagyurishte Treasure **Rev:** Vessel in shape of ram's head

Date	Mintage	F	VF	XF	Unc	BU
2009	5,000	—	—	—	—	80.00

KM# 223 2 DOLLARS

31.1050 g., 0.9990 Silver 0.9990 oz. ASW, 40 mm. **Ruler:** Elizabeth II **Subject:** Peoples Republic of China, 60th Anniversary **Rev:** Multicolor background, astronaut, olympic flame and dragon motifs

Date	Mintage	F	VF	XF	Unc	BU
2009 Prooflike	6,888	—	—	—	—	90.00

KM# 224 2 DOLLARS

31.1050 g., 0.9990 Silver 0.9990 oz. ASW, 40.7 mm. **Ruler:** Elizabeth II **Series:** Soviet Automobiles **Rev:** GAZ 12 ZIM in multicolor

Date	Mintage	F	VF	XF	Unc	BU
2009 Prooflike	15,000	—	—	—	—	80.00

KM# 225 2 DOLLARS

31.1050 g., 0.9990 Silver 0.9990 oz. ASW, 40.7 mm. **Ruler:** Elizabeth II **Subject:** Soviet Automobiles **Rev:** GAZ M290 Pobeda in multicolor

Date	Mintage	F	VF	XF	Unc	BU
2009 Prooflike	15,000	—	—	—	—	80.00

KM# 226 2 DOLLARS

31.1050 g., 0.9990 Silver 0.9990 oz. ASW, 40.7 mm. **Ruler:** Elizabeth II **Subject:** Soviet Automobiles **Rev:** GAZ M21 Volga

Date	Mintage	F	VF	XF	Unc	BU
2009 Prooflike	15,000	—	—	—	—	80.00

KM# 227 2 DOLLARS

31.1050 g., 0.9990 Silver 0.9990 oz. ASW, 40.7 mm. **Ruler:** Elizabeth II **Subject:** Soviet Automobiles **Rev:** Moskvich 400

Date	Mintage	F	VF	XF	Unc	BU
2009 Prooflike	15,000	—	—	—	—	80.00

KM# 229 2 DOLLARS

31.1050 g., 0.9990 Silver partially gilt 0.9990 oz. ASW, 40 mm. **Ruler:** Elizabeth II **Subject:** Year of the Ox **Rev:** Ox, partially gilt

Date	Mintage	F	VF	XF	Unc	BU
2009 Proof	2,000	Value: 100				

KM# 350 2 DOLLARS

25.0000 g., 0.9990 Silver 0.8029 oz. ASW, 38.61 mm. **Ruler:** Elizabeth II **Rev:** Partridge in a pair tree

Date	Mintage	F	VF	XF	Unc	BU
2009	1,500	Value: 50.00				

KM# 351 2 DOLLARS

25.0000 g., 0.9990 Silver 0.8029 oz. ASW, 38.61 mm. **Ruler:** Elizabeth II **Rev:** Two turtle doves

Date	Mintage	F	VF	XF	Unc	BU
2009 Proof	1,500	Value: 50.00				

KM# 352 2 DOLLARS

25.0000 g., 0.9990 Silver 0.8029 oz. ASW, 38.61 mm. **Ruler:** Elizabeth II **Rev:** Three French hens

Date	Mintage	F	VF	XF	Unc	BU
2009 Proof	1,500	Value: 50.00				

KM# 353 2 DOLLARS

25.0000 g., 0.9990 Silver 0.8029 oz. ASW, 38.61 mm. **Ruler:** Elizabeth II **Rev:** Four Colly Birds

Date	Mintage	F	VF	XF	Unc	BU
2009 Proof	1,500	Value: 50.00				

KM# 354 2 DOLLARS

25.0000 g., 0.9990 Silver 0.8029 oz. ASW, 38.61 mm. **Ruler:** Elizabeth II **Rev:** Five golden rings

Date	Mintage	F	VF	XF	Unc	BU
2009 Proof	1,500	Value: 50.00				

KM# 355 2 DOLLARS

25.0000 g., 0.9990 Silver 0.8029 oz. ASW, 38.61 mm. **Ruler:** Elizabeth II **Rev:** Six Geese a-laying

Date	Mintage	F	VF	XF	Unc	BU
2009 Proof	1,500	Value: 50.00				

KM# 356 2 DOLLARS

25.0000 g., 0.9990 Silver 0.8029 oz. ASW, 38.61 mm. **Ruler:** Elizabeth II **Rev:** Seven swans a-swimming

Date	Mintage	F	VF	XF	Unc	BU
2009 Proof	1,500	Value: 50.00				

KM# 357 2 DOLLARS

25.0000 g., 0.9990 Silver 0.8029 oz. ASW, 38.61 mm. **Ruler:** Elizabeth II **Rev:** Eight maids a-milking

Date	Mintage	F	VF	XF	Unc	BU
2009 Proof	1,500	Value: 50.00				

KM# 358 2 DOLLARS

25.0000 g., 0.9990 Silver 0.8029 oz. ASW, 38.61 mm. **Ruler:** Elizabeth II **Rev:** Nine ladies dancing

Date	Mintage	F	VF	XF	Unc	BU
2009 Proof	1,500	Value: 50.00				

KM# 359 2 DOLLARS

25.0000 g., 0.9990 Silver 0.8029 oz. ASW, 38.61 mm. **Ruler:** Elizabeth II **Rev:** Ten Lords a-leaping

Date	Mintage	F	VF	XF	Unc	BU
2009 Proof	1,500	Value: 50.00				

KM# 360 2 DOLLARS

25.0000 g., 0.9990 Silver 0.8029 oz. ASW, 38.61 mm. **Ruler:** Elizabeth II **Rev:** Eleven Pipers Piping

Date	Mintage	F	VF	XF	Unc	BU
2009 Proof	1,500	Value: 50.00				

KM# 361 2 DOLLARS

25.0000 g., 0.9990 Silver 0.8029 oz. ASW, 38.61 mm. **Ruler:** Elizabeth II **Rev:** Twelve drummers drumming

Date	Mintage	F	VF	XF	Unc	BU
2009 Proof	1,500	Value: 50.00				

KM# 362 2 DOLLARS

62.2000 g., 0.9990 Silver 1.9977 oz. ASW, 63x27 mm. **Ruler:** Elizabeth II **Rev:** Flowers **Shape:** Vertical rectangle

Date	Mintage	F	VF	XF	Unc	BU
2009 Proof	16,888	Value: 100				

KM# 363 2 DOLLARS

1.0000 g., 0.9990 Gold 0.0321 oz. AGW, 12 mm. **Ruler:** Elizabeth II **Rev:** Chopin bust

Date	Mintage	F	VF	XF	Unc	BU
2009 Proof	10,000	Value: 80.00				

KM# 206 2 DOLLARS

31.1050 g., 0.9990 Silver 0.9990 oz. ASW, 40.7 mm. **Ruler:** Elizabeth II **Rev:** Two white swans, red heart in background

Date	Mintage	F	VF	XF	Unc	BU
2010 Proof	20,000	—	—	—	—	50.00

KM# 213 2 DOLLARS
56.6000 g., 0.9250 Silver 1.6832 oz. ASW, 55.6x41.6 mm. **Ruler:** Elizabeth II **Subject:** Coronation Egg **Obv:** Open egg - Queen Elizabeth head right **Rev:** Faberge Egg and coach **Shape:** Vertical oval

Date	Mintage	F	VF	XF	Unc	BU
2010	5,000	—	—	—	—	100

KM# 228 2 DOLLARS
31.1050 g., 0.9990 Silver 0.9990 oz. ASW, 40 mm. **Ruler:** Elizabeth II **Subject:** Gai Thong Hanh, Safe Conduct Pass **Rev:** Viet Nam flag and soldiers, partially gilt

Date	Mintage	F	VF	XF	Unc	BU
2010 Proof	5,000	Value: 140				

KM# 233 2 DOLLARS
62.2100 g., 0.9990 Silver partially gilt 1.9980 oz. ASW, 40 mm. **Ruler:** Elizabeth II **Subject:** Year of the Tiger **Rev:** Tiger partially gilt

Date	Mintage	F	VF	XF	Unc	BU
2010 Proof	20,000	Value: 100				

KM# 237 2 DOLLARS
1.0000 g., 0.9000 Gold 0.0289 oz. AGW, 12 mm. **Ruler:** Elizabeth II **Obv:** Head right **Rev:** Copernicus bust 3/4 left

Date	Mintage	F	VF	XF	Unc	BU
2010 Proof	5,000	Value: 75.00				

KM# 245 2 DOLLARS
31.1030 g., 0.9990 Silver 0.9989 oz. ASW, 40.7 mm. **Ruler:** Elizabeth II **Subject:** Famous express trains **Rev:** Steam train traveling left, multicolor

Date	Mintage	F	VF	XF	Unc	BU
2010 Proof	15,000	Value: 80.00				

KM# 246 2 DOLLARS
31.1030 g., 0.9990 Silver 0.9989 oz. ASW, 40.7 mm. **Ruler:** Elizabeth II **Subject:** Famous express trains **Rev:** Steam train left, multicolor

Date	Mintage	F	VF	XF	Unc	BU
2010 Proof	15,000	Value: 80.00				

KM# 247 2 DOLLARS
31.1030 g., 0.9990 Silver 0.9989 oz. ASW, 40.7 mm. **Ruler:** Elizabeth II **Subject:** Famous express trains **Rev:** Steam train left, multicolor

Date	Mintage	F	VF	XF	Unc	BU
2010 Proof	15,000	Value: 80.00				

KM# 248 2 DOLLARS
31.1030 g., 0.9990 Silver 0.9989 oz. ASW, 40.7 mm. **Ruler:** Elizabeth II **Subject:** Famous Express trains - 20th Century Limited **Rev:** Streamlined steam train left, multicolored

Date	Mintage	F	VF	XF	Unc	BU
2010 Proof	15,000	Value: 80.00				

KM# 249 2 DOLLARS
31.1050 g., 0.9990 Silver 0.9990 oz. ASW, 40.7 mm. **Ruler:** Elizabeth II **Subject:** Love is precious **Rev:** Two white swans and red floral heart

Date	Mintage	F	VF	XF	Unc	BU
2010 Proof	20,000	Value: 90.00				

KM# 252 2 DOLLARS
31.1050 g., 0.9990 Silver 0.9990 oz. ASW, 38.6 mm. **Ruler:** Elizabeth II **Subject:** Peanuts 60th Anniversary **Rev:** Charlie Brown with Snoopy and birthday cake

Date	Mintage	F	VF	XF	Unc	BU
2010 Prooflike	3,000	—	—	—	—	80.00

KM# 253 2 DOLLARS
31.1050 g., 0.9990 Silver 0.9990 oz. ASW, 38.6 mm. **Ruler:** Elizabeth II **Subject:** Peanuts 60th Anniversary **Rev:** Schroeder and Lucy by piano

Date	Mintage	F	VF	XF	Unc	BU
2010 Prooflike	3,000	—	—	—	—	80.00

KM# 371 2 DOLLARS
56.5600 g., 0.9250 Silver 1.6820 oz. ASW, 55.6x41.6 mm. **Ruler:** Elizabeth II **Subject:** Faberge egg - Lily of the Valley **Obv:** Elizabeth II head right, open egg **Rev:** Egg on stand **Shape:** Oval

Date	Mintage	F	VF	XF	Unc	BU
2010 Proof	7,000	Value: 100				

KM# 373 2 DOLLARS
31.1050 g., 0.9990 Silver 0.9990 oz. ASW, 37.1x31.9 mm. **Ruler:** Elizabeth II **Subject:** Kiki Lala **Shape:** Heart with ribbon

Date	Mintage	F	VF	XF	Unc	BU
2010 Proof	Est. 3,000	Value: 50.00				

KM# 374 2 DOLLARS
31.1050 g., 0.9990 Silver 0.9990 oz. ASW, 37.1x31.9 mm. **Ruler:** Elizabeth II **Subject:** My Melo **Shape:** Heart with ribbon

Date	Mintage	F	VF	XF	Unc	BU
2010 Proof	Est. 3,000	Value: 50.00				

KM# 381 2 DOLLARS
31.1050 g., 0.9990 Silver 0.9990 oz. ASW, 40.2 mm. **Ruler:** Elizabeth II **Subject:** Russian Musicians **Rev:** Viktor Tsoy at lower right in multicolor

Date	Mintage	F	VF	XF	Unc	BU
2010 Proof	2,000	Value: 50.00				

KM# 382 2 DOLLARS
31.1050 g., 0.9990 Silver 0.9990 oz. ASW, 40.2 mm. **Ruler:** Elizabeth II **Subject:** Russian Musicians **Rev:** Vladimir Vysotsky at lower right in multicolor

Date	Mintage	F	VF	XF	Unc	BU
2010 Proof	2,000	Value: 50.00				

KM# 383 2 DOLLARS
31.1050 g., 0.9990 Silver 0.9990 oz. ASW **Ruler:** Elizabeth II **Rev:** Portrait in multicolor

Date	Mintage	F	VF	XF	Unc	BU
2010 Proof	Est. 2,000	Value: 50.00				

KM# 384 2 DOLLARS
31.1050 g., 0.9990 Silver 0.9990 oz. ASW, 38.61 mm. **Ruler:** Elizabeth II **Subject:** Miffy with friends

Date	Mintage	F	VF	XF	Unc	BU
2010 Proof	Est. 3,000	Value: 50.00				

KM# 385 2 DOLLARS
31.1050 g., 0.9990 Silver 0.9990 oz. ASW, 38.61 mm. **Ruler:** Elizabeth II **Subject:** Miffy on turtle

Date	Mintage	F	VF	XF	Unc	BU
2010 Proof	Est. 3,000	Value: 50.00				

KM# 386 2 DOLLARS
31.1050 g., 0.9990 Silver 0.9990 oz. ASW, 38.61 mm. **Ruler:** Elizabeth II **Subject:** Miffy celebration

Date	Mintage	F	VF	XF	Unc	BU
2010 Proof	Est. 3,000	Value: 50.00				

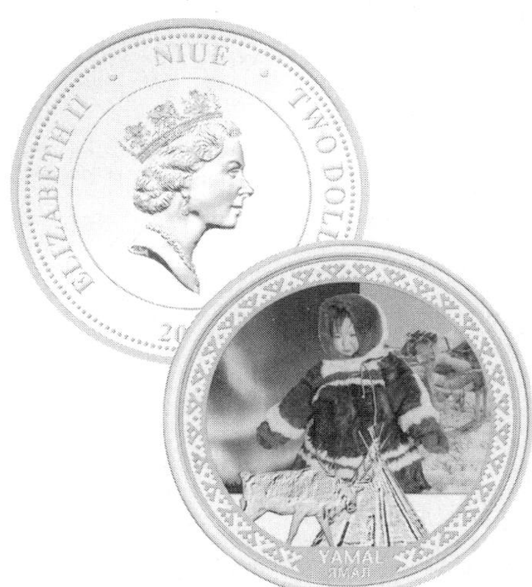

KM# 390 2 DOLLARS
31.1030 g., 0.9990 Silver 0.9989 oz. ASW, 40.7 mm. **Ruler:** Elizabeth II **Subject:** Yamal **Rev:** Child wearing fur coat in multicolor

Date	Mintage	F	VF	XF	Unc	BU
2010 Proof	5,000	Value: 50.00				

KM# 391 2 DOLLARS
31.1030 g., 0.9990 Silver 0.9989 oz. ASW, 40.7 mm. **Ruler:** Elizabeth II **Subject:** Yamal **Rev:** Gas and Oil exploration in multicolor

Date	Mintage	F	VF	XF	Unc	BU
2010 Proof	5,000	Value: 50.00				

KM# 408 2 DOLLARS
31.1030 g., 0.9990 Silver 0.9989 oz. ASW, 40.7 mm. **Ruler:** Elizabeth II **Series:** Russian Transport **Obv:** Head with tiara right **Rev:** Bus in multicolor

Date	Mintage	F	VF	XF	Unc	BU
2010 Proof	15,000	Value: 60.00				

KM# 409 2 DOLLARS
31.1030 g., 0.9990 Silver 0.9989 oz. ASW, 40.7 mm. **Ruler:** Elizabeth II **Subject:** Russian Transport **Obv:** Head with tiara right **Rev:** Trolley Bus in multicolor

Date	Mintage	F	VF	XF	Unc	BU
2010 Proof	15,000	Value: 60.00				

KM# 410 2 DOLLARS
31.1030 g., 0.9990 Silver 0.9989 oz. ASW, 40.7 mm. **Ruler:** Elizabeth II **Subject:** Russian Transport **Obv:** Head with tiara right **Rev:** Metro in color

Date	Mintage	F	VF	XF	Unc	BU
2010 Proof	15,000	Value: 60.00				

KM# 411 2 DOLLARS
31.1030 g., 0.9990 Silver 0.9989 oz. ASW, 40.7 mm. **Ruler:** Elizabeth II **Subject:** Russian Transport **Obv:** Head with tiara right **Rev:** Tram in color

Date	Mintage	F	VF	XF	Unc	BU
2010 Proof	15,000	Value: 60.00				

KM# 416 2 DOLLARS
28.2800 g., 0.9250 Silver 0.8410 oz. ASW, 38.61 mm. **Ruler:** Elizabeth II **Obv:** Head with tiara right **Rev:** Kirovo Chepetsk

Date	Mintage	F	VF	XF	Unc	BU
2010 Proof	2,000	Value: 60.00				

KM# 424 2 DOLLARS
56.5600 g., 0.9250 Silver 1.6820 oz. ASW, 41.6x55.6 mm. **Ruler:** Elizabeth II **Subject:** Faberge Imperial Eggs - Clover Leaf **Obv:** Head with tiara right above opened egg **Rev:** Egg on stand in color **Shape:** Vertical oval

Date	Mintage	F	VF	XF	Unc	BU
2010 Proof	7,000	Value: 125				

KM# 431 2 DOLLARS

1.0000 g., 0.9000 Silver 0.0289 oz. ASW, 12 mm. **Ruler:** Elizabeth II **Subject:** Tadeusz Kosciuszko **Obv:** Head with tiara right **Rev:** Head left, signature below

Date	Mintage	F	VF	XF	Unc	BU
2010 Proof	5,000	Value: 35.00				

KM# 442 2 DOLLARS

25.0000 g., 0.9250 Silver 0.7435 oz. ASW, 38.61 mm. **Ruler:** Elizabeth II **Subject:** Twelve days of Christmas **Rev:** Partidge in a pear tree

Date	Mintage	F	VF	XF	Unc	BU
2010 Proof	1,500	Value: 50.00				

KM# 443 2 DOLLARS

25.0000 g., 0.9250 Silver 0.7435 oz. ASW, 38.61 mm. **Ruler:** Elizabeth II **Subject:** Twelve days of Christmas **Rev:** Turtle dove

Date	Mintage	F	VF	XF	Unc	BU
2010 Proof	1,500	Value: 50.00				

KM# 444 2 DOLLARS

25.0000 g., 0.9250 Silver 0.7435 oz. ASW, 38.61 mm. **Ruler:** Elizabeth II **Subject:** Twelve days of Christmas **Rev:** French hen

Date	Mintage	F	VF	XF	Unc	BU
2010 Proof	1,500	Value: 50.00				

KM# 445 2 DOLLARS

25.0000 g., 0.9250 Silver 0.7435 oz. ASW **Ruler:** Elizabeth II **Subject:** Twelve days of Christmas **Rev:** Calling bird

Date	Mintage	F	VF	XF	Unc	BU
2010 Proof	1,500	Value: 50.00				

KM# 446 2 DOLLARS

25.0000 g., 0.9250 Silver 0.7435 oz. ASW, 38.61 mm. **Ruler:** Elizabeth II **Subject:** Twelve days of Christmas **Rev:** Golden rings

Date	Mintage	F	VF	XF	Unc	BU
2010 Proof	1,500	Value: 50.00				

KM# 447 2 DOLLARS

25.0000 g., 0.9250 Silver 0.7435 oz. ASW, 38.61 mm. **Ruler:** Elizabeth II **Subject:** Twelve days of Christmas **Rev:** Geese a laying

Date	Mintage	F	VF	XF	Unc	BU
2010 Proof	1,500	Value: 50.00				

KM# 448 2 DOLLARS

25.0000 g., 0.9250 Silver 0.7435 oz. ASW, 38.61 mm. **Ruler:** Elizabeth II **Subject:** Twelve days of Christmas **Rev:** Swans a swimming

Date	Mintage	F	VF	XF	Unc	BU
2010 Proof	1,500	Value: 50.00				

KM# 449 2 DOLLARS

25.0000 g., 0.9250 Silver 0.7435 oz. ASW, 38.61 mm. **Ruler:** Elizabeth II **Subject:** Twelve days of Christmas **Rev:** Maids a milking

Date	Mintage	F	VF	XF	Unc	BU
2010 Proof	1,500	Value: 50.00				

KM# 450 2 DOLLARS

25.0000 g., 0.9250 Silver 0.7435 oz. ASW, 38.61 mm. **Ruler:** Elizabeth II **Subject:** Twelve days of Christmas **Rev:** Ladies dancing

Date	Mintage	F	VF	XF	Unc	BU
2010 Proof	1,500	Value: 50.00				

KM# 451 2 DOLLARS

25.0000 g., 0.9250 Silver 0.7435 oz. ASW, 38.61 mm. **Ruler:** Elizabeth II **Subject:** Twelve days of Christmas **Rev:** Lords a leaping

Date	Mintage	F	VF	XF	Unc	BU
2010 Proof	1,500	Value: 50.00				

KM# 452 2 DOLLARS

25.0000 g., 0.9250 Silver 0.7435 oz. ASW, 38.61 mm. **Ruler:** Elizabeth II **Subject:** Twelve days of Christmas **Rev:** Pipers piping

Date	Mintage	F	VF	XF	Unc	BU
2010 Proof	1,500	Value: 50.00				

KM# 453 2 DOLLARS

25.0000 g., 0.9250 Silver 0.7435 oz. ASW, 38.61 mm. **Ruler:** Elizabeth II **Subject:** Twelve days of Christmas **Rev:** Drummers drumming

Date	Mintage	F	VF	XF	Unc	BU
2010 Proof	1,500	Value: 50.00				

KM# 457 2 DOLLARS

31.1030 g., 0.9990 Silver 0.9989 oz. ASW, 38.61 mm. **Ruler:** Elizabeth II **Subject:** Bulgarian theme roses - Survachka **Rev:** Figure-8 floral arangement

Date	Mintage	F	VF	XF	Unc	BU
2010 Proof	3,000	Value: 50.00				

KM# 458 2 DOLLARS

31.1030 g., 0.9990 Silver 0.9989 oz. ASW, 38.61 mm. **Ruler:** Elizabeth II **Subject:** Bulgarian rose **Rev:** Top view into rose

Date	Mintage	F	VF	XF	Unc	BU
2010	6,000	Value: 50.00				

KM# 459 2 DOLLARS

31.1030 g., 0.9990 Silver 0.9989 oz. ASW, 38.61 mm. **Ruler:** Elizabeth II **Subject:** Bulgarian rose theme - Martenitsa **Rev:** tassle like device

Date	Mintage	F	VF	XF	Unc	BU
2010 Proof	3,000	Value: 50.00				

KM# 460 2 DOLLARS

31.1030 g., 0.9990 Silver 0.9989 oz. ASW, 38.61 mm. **Ruler:** Elizabeth II **Rev:** Saint Peter icon

Date	Mintage	F	VF	XF	Unc	BU
2010 Proof	2,000	Value: 50.00				

KM# 461 2 DOLLARS

31.1030 g., 0.9990 Silver 0.9989 oz. ASW, 38.61 mm. **Ruler:** Elizabeth II **Rev:** Saint Paul icon

Date	Mintage	F	VF	XF	Unc	BU
2010 Proof	2,000	Value: 50.00				

KM# 372 2 DOLLARS

31.1050 g., 0.9990 Silver 0.9990 oz. ASW, 37.1x31.9 mm. **Ruler:** Elizabeth II **Subject:** Hello Kitty **Shape:** Heart with ribbon

Date	Mintage	F	VF	XF	Unc	BU
2010 Proof	Est. 3,000	Value: 50.00				

KM# 507 2 DOLLARS

31.1000 g., 0.9990 Silver 0.9988 oz. ASW, 40.7 mm. **Ruler:** Elizabeth II **Subject:** Love is precious **Rev:** Two white swans within heart

Date	Mintage	F	VF	XF	Unc	BU
2011 Proof	20,000	Value: 50.00				

KM# 521 2 DOLLARS

31.1000 g., 0.9990 Silver 0.9988 oz. ASW **Ruler:** Elizabeth II **Subject:** The Evangelists - St. Mathew and angel **Rev:** Icon in color

Date	Mintage	F	VF	XF	Unc	BU
2011 Proof	2,000	Value: 50.00				

KM# 522 2 DOLLARS

31.1000 g., 0.9990 Silver 0.9988 oz. ASW **Ruler:** Elizabeth II **Subject:** The Evangelists - St Mark with lion **Rev:** Icon in color

Date	Mintage	F	VF	XF	Unc	BU
2011 Proof	2,000	Value: 50.00				

KM# 523 2 DOLLARS

31.1000 g., 0.9990 Silver 0.9988 oz. ASW **Ruler:** Elizabeth II **Subject:** The Evangelists - Luke and oxen **Rev:** Icon in color

Date	Mintage	F	VF	XF	Unc	BU
2011 Proof	2,000	Value: 50.00				

KM# 524 2 DOLLARS

31.1000 g., 0.9990 Silver 0.9988 oz. ASW **Ruler:** Elizabeth II **Subject:** The Evangelists - John and eagle **Rev:** Icon in color

Date	Mintage	F	VF	XF	Unc	BU
2011 Proof	2,000	Value: 50.00				

KM# 525 2 DOLLARS

31.1000 g., 0.9990 Silver 0.9988 oz. ASW **Ruler:** Elizabeth II **Subject:** Eternal Love **Rev:** Two white doves within flora and scrolls

Date	Mintage	F	VF	XF	Unc	BU
2011 Proof	5,000	Value: 50.00				

KM# 295 5 DOLLARS

155.5000 g., 0.9990 Silver 4.9942 oz. ASW, 70 mm. **Ruler:** Elizabeth II **Subject:** Year of the Dog **Rev:** Multicolor dog

Date	Mintage	F	VF	XF	Unc	BU
2005 Proof	—	Value: 150				

KM# 266 5 DOLLARS

155.5000 g., 0.9990 Silver 4.9942 oz. ASW, 70 mm. **Ruler:** Elizabeth II **Subject:** Year of the Rooster **Rev:** Multicolor rooster standing right, sunrise

Date	Mintage	F	VF	XF	Unc	BU
2005 Proof	—	Value: 150				

KM# 272 5 DOLLARS

6.2200 g., 0.9990 Gold 0.1998 oz. AGW, 25 mm. **Ruler:** Elizabeth II **Subject:** Year of the Rooster

Date	Mintage	F	VF	XF	Unc	BU
2005 Proof	—	Value: 300				

KM# 273 5 DOLLARS

15.5500 g., 0.9990 Gold 0.4994 oz. AGW, 33 mm. **Ruler:** Elizabeth II **Subject:** Year of the Rooster

Date	Mintage	F	VF	XF	Unc	BU
2005 Proof	—	Value: 675				

KM# 333 5 DOLLARS

15.5000 g., 0.9170 Gold 0.4570 oz. AGW, 27 mm. **Ruler:** Elizabeth II **Subject:** Amber Road - Gdansk **Rev:** Nepture statue, castle, amber insert

Date	Mintage	F	VF	XF	Unc	BU
2007	—	—	—	—	—	650

KM# 191 5 DOLLARS

15.5000 g., 0.9000 Gold 0.4485 oz. AGW, 27 mm. **Ruler:** Elizabeth II **Subject:** Amber road **Obv:** Bust and Roman cart **Rev:** Kaliningrad Castle, Roman coin, Amber insert

Date	Mintage	F	VF	XF	Unc	BU
2008 Proof	2,000	Value: 575				

KM# 230 5 DOLLARS

62.2100 g., 0.9990 Silver 1.9980 oz. ASW, 50x32 mm. **Ruler:** Elizabeth II **Subject:** Battleship: Tripitz **Shape:** Rectangle

Date	Mintage	F	VF	XF	Unc	BU
2009	1,000	—	—	—	—	140

KM# 349 5 DOLLARS

15.5000 g., 0.9000 Gold 0.4485 oz. AGW, 27 mm. **Ruler:** Elizabeth II **Subject:** Amber Road - Elblag **Rev:** Amber insert

Date	Mintage	F	VF	XF	Unc	BU
2009 Proof	—	Value: 625				

KM# 364 5 DOLLARS

77.7000 g., 0.9990 Silver 2.4955 oz. ASW, 50x32 mm. **Ruler:** Elizabeth II **Rev:** Battleship Tirpitz sailing left **Shape:** Wavy rectangle

Date	Mintage	F	VF	XF	Unc	BU
2009 Proof	1,000	Value: 125				

KM# 250 5 DOLLARS

0.5000 g., 0.9990 Gold 0.0161 oz. AGW, 11 mm. **Ruler:** Elizabeth II **Rev:** Ned Kelly, multicolor

Date	Mintage	F	VF	XF	Unc	BU
2010 Proof	—	Value: 75.00				

KM# 368 5 DOLLARS

15.5000 g., 0.9000 Gold 0.4485 oz. AGW, 27 mm. **Ruler:** Elizabeth II **Subject:** Amber road - Stare Hradisko **Rev:** Amber insert

Date	Mintage	F	VF	XF	Unc	BU
2010	2,000	—	—	—	—	700

KM# 376 5 DOLLARS

2.5000 g., 0.9990 Gold 0.0803 oz. AGW, 14x26.7 mm. **Ruler:** Elizabeth II **Subject:** Kitty **Shape:** Vertical rectangle

Date	Mintage	F	VF	XF	Unc	BU
2010 Proof	Est. 2,000	Value: 150				

KM# 377 5 DOLLARS

2.5000 g., 0.9990 Gold 0.0803 oz. AGW, 14x26.7 mm. **Ruler:** Elizabeth II **Subject:** Kiki Lala **Shape:** Vertical rectangle

Date	Mintage	F	VF	XF	Unc	BU
2010 Proof	Est. 2,000	Value: 150				

KM# 378 5 DOLLARS

2.5000 g., 0.9990 Gold 0.0803 oz. AGW, 14x26.7 mm. **Ruler:** Elizabeth II **Subject:** My Melo **Shape:** Vertical rectangle

Date	Mintage	F	VF	XF	Unc	BU
2010 Proof	Est. 2,000	Value: 150				

KM# 397 5 DOLLARS

15.5000 g., 0.9000 Gold 0.4485 oz. AGW, 27 mm. **Ruler:** Elizabeth II **Subject:** Amber Road - Carnuntum **Rev:** Arches, ancient coin, statue

Date	Mintage	F	VF	XF	Unc	BU
2010	2,000	Value: 750				

KM# 399 5 DOLLARS

15.5000 g., 0.9000 Gold 0.4485 oz. AGW, 27 mm. **Ruler:** Elizabeth II **Subject:** Amber Route - Szombathely **Rev:** Cathedral, ancient coin

Date	Mintage	F	VF	XF	Unc	BU
2010 Matte finish	2,000	Value: 750				

KM# 423 5 DOLLARS

15.5000 g., 0.9000 Gold 0.4485 oz. AGW, 27 mm. **Ruler:** Elizabeth II **Subject:** Christmas Star **Obv:** Head with tiara right, snowflakes around **Rev:** Three children and christmas tree, crystal insets

Date	Mintage	F	VF	XF	Unc	BU
2010 Proof	2,000	Value: 750				

KM# 430 5 DOLLARS

15.5000 g., 0.9000 Gold 0.4485 oz. AGW, 27 mm. **Ruler:** Elizabeth II **Obv:** Head with tiara right, wing enlargment as background **Rev:** Butterfly - Lycaena Virgaureae

Date	Mintage	F	VF	XF	Unc	BU
2010 Proof	1,000	Value: 700				

KM# 513 5 DOLLARS

50.0000 g., 0.9990 Silver 1.6059 oz. ASW, 35.2x35.2 mm. **Ruler:** Elizabeth II **Subject:** The three kings of 1936 **Obv:** Head with tiara right **Rev:** Busts left of George V, Edward VIII and George VI

Date	Mintage	F	VF	XF	Unc	BU
2011 Proof	2,500	Value: 100				

KM# 267 15 DOLLARS

500.0000 g., 0.9990 Silver 16.058 oz. ASW, 100 mm. **Ruler:** Elizabeth II **Subject:** Year of the Rooster **Rev:** Multicolor rooster standing right, sunrise

Date	Mintage					
	—	Value: 400				

KM# 296 15 DOLLARS
500.0000 g., 0.9990 Silver 16.058 oz. ASW, 100 mm. **Ruler:** Elizabeth II **Subject:** Year of the Dog **Rev:** Multicolor dog

Date	Mintage	F	VF	XF	Unc	BU
2005 Proof	—	Value: 400				

KM# 124 10 DOLLARS
28.2800 g., 0.9250 Silver 0.8410 oz. ASW, 38.6 mm. **Ruler:** Elizabeth II **Subject:** Snoopy as an Ace **Obv:** Crowned head right **Rev:** Snoopy flying his dog house **Edge:** Reeded

Date	Mintage	F	VF	XF	Unc	BU
2001 Proof	10,000	Value: 18.50				

KM# 130 10 DOLLARS
28.2800 g., 0.9250 Silver 0.8410 oz. ASW, 38.6 mm. **Ruler:** Elizabeth II **Series:** Pokeman **Obv:** Crowned shield within sprigs **Rev:** Bulbasaur **Edge:** Reeded

Date	Mintage	F	VF	XF	Unc	BU
2001 Proof	10,000	Value: 17.50				

KM# 133 10 DOLLARS
28.2800 g., 0.9250 Silver 0.8410 oz. ASW, 38.6 mm. **Ruler:** Elizabeth II **Series:** Pokeman **Obv:** Crowned shield within sprigs **Rev:** Charmander **Edge:** Reeded

Date	Mintage	F	VF	XF	Unc	BU
2001 Proof	10,000	Value: 17.50				

KM# 136 10 DOLLARS
28.2800 g., 0.9250 Silver 0.8410 oz. ASW, 38.6 mm. **Ruler:** Elizabeth II **Series:** Pokeman **Obv:** Crowned shield within sprigs **Rev:** Meowth **Edge:** Reeded

Date	Mintage	F	VF	XF	Unc	BU
2001 Proof	10,000	Value: 17.50				

KM# 139 10 DOLLARS
28.2800 g., 0.9250 Silver 0.8410 oz. ASW, 38.6 mm. **Ruler:** Elizabeth II **Series:** Pokeman **Obv:** Crowned shield within sprigs **Rev:** Pikachu **Edge:** Reeded

Date	Mintage	F	VF	XF	Unc	BU
2001 Proof	10,000	Value: 17.50				

KM# 142 10 DOLLARS
28.2800 g., 0.9250 Silver 0.8410 oz. ASW, 38.6 mm. **Ruler:** Elizabeth II **Series:** Pokeman **Obv:** Crowned shield within sprigs **Rev:** Squirtle **Edge:** Reeded

Date	Mintage	F	VF	XF	Unc	BU
2001 Proof	10,000	Value: 17.50				

KM# 147 10 DOLLARS
28.2800 g., 0.9250 Silver 0.8410 oz. ASW, 38.6 mm. **Ruler:** Elizabeth II **Subject:** Pokémon Series **Obv:** Crowned shield within sprigs **Rev:** Pikachu **Edge:** Reeded

Date	Mintage	F	VF	XF	Unc	BU
2002PM Proof	10,000	Value: 17.50				

KM# 152 10 DOLLARS
28.2800 g., 0.9250 Silver 0.8410 oz. ASW, 38.6 mm. **Ruler:** Elizabeth II **Subject:** Pokémon Series **Obv:** Crowned shield within sprigs **Rev:** Pichu **Edge:** Reeded

Date	Mintage	F	VF	XF	Unc	BU
2002PM Proof	10,000	Value: 17.50				

KM# 157 10 DOLLARS
28.2800 g., 0.9250 Silver 0.8410 oz. ASW, 38.6 mm. **Ruler:** Elizabeth II **Subject:** Pokémon Series **Obv:** Crowned shield within sprigs **Rev:** Mewtwo **Edge:** Reeded

Date	Mintage	F	VF	XF	Unc	BU
2002PM Proof	10,000	Value: 17.50				

KM# 162 10 DOLLARS
28.2800 g., 0.9250 Silver 0.8410 oz. ASW, 38.6 mm. **Ruler:** Elizabeth II **Subject:** Pokémon Series **Obv:** Crowned shield within sprigs **Rev:** Entei **Edge:** Reeded

Date	Mintage	F	VF	XF	Unc	BU
2002PM Proof	10,000	Value: 17.50				

KM# 167 10 DOLLARS
28.2800 g., 0.9250 Silver 0.8410 oz. ASW, 38.6 mm. **Ruler:** Elizabeth II **Subject:** Pokémon Series **Obv:** Crowned shield within sprigs **Rev:** Celebi **Edge:** Reeded

Date	Mintage	F	VF	XF	Unc	BU
2002PM Proof	10,000	Value: 17.50				

KM# 274 10 DOLLARS
31.1050 g., 0.9990 Gold 0.9990 oz. AGW, 38.6 mm. **Ruler:** Elizabeth II **Subject:** Year of the Rooster

Date	Mintage	F	VF	XF	Unc	BU
2005 Proof	—	Value: 1,300				

KM# 254 10 DOLLARS
155.5000 g., 0.9990 Silver 4.9942 oz. ASW, 65 mm. **Ruler:** Elizabeth II **Subject:** Peanuts 60th Anniversary **Rev:** Peanut character heads around a central Snoopy

Date	Mintage	F	VF	XF	Unc	BU
2010 Prooflike	1,000	—	—	—	—	200

KM# 375 10 DOLLARS
100.0000 g., 0.9990 Silver 3.2117 oz. ASW, 64x54.2 mm. **Ruler:** Elizabeth II **Subject:** Kitty and friends **Shape:** Heart

Date	Mintage	F	VF	XF	Unc	BU
2010 Proof	Est. 1,000	Value: 150				

KM# 387 10 DOLLARS
155.5000 g., 0.9990 Silver 4.9942 oz. ASW, 65 mm. **Ruler:** Elizabeth II **Subject:** Miffy with cake

Date	Mintage	F	VF	XF	Unc	BU
2010 Proof	Est. 1,500	Value: 200				

KM# 125 20 DOLLARS
1.2400 g., 0.9999 Gold 0.0399 oz. AGW, 13.9 mm. **Ruler:** Elizabeth II **Subject:** Snoopy as an Ace **Obv:** Crowned head right **Rev:** Snoopy flying his dog house **Edge:** Reeded

Date	Mintage	F	VF	XF	Unc	BU
2001 Proof	10,000	Value: 50.00				

KM# 148 20 DOLLARS
1.2400 g., 0.9999 Gold 0.0399 oz. AGW, 13.92 mm. **Ruler:** Elizabeth II **Subject:** Pokémon Series **Obv:** Crowned shield within sprigs **Rev:** Pikachu **Edge:** Reeded

Date	Mintage	F	VF	XF	Unc	BU
2002PM Proof	10,000	Value: 50.00				

KM# 153 20 DOLLARS
1.2400 g., 0.9999 Gold 0.0399 oz. AGW, 13.9 mm. **Ruler:** Elizabeth II **Subject:** Pokémon Series **Obv:** Crowned shield within sprigs **Rev:** Pichu **Edge:** Reeded

Date	Mintage	F	VF	XF	Unc	BU
2002PM Proof	10,000	Value: 50.00				

KM# 158 20 DOLLARS
1.2400 g., 0.9999 Gold 0.0399 oz. AGW, 13.92 mm. **Ruler:** Elizabeth II **Subject:** Pokémon Series **Obv:** Crowned shield within sprigs **Rev:** Mewtwo **Edge:** Reeded

Date	Mintage	F	VF	XF	Unc	BU
2002PM Proof	10,000	Value: 50.00				

KM# 163 20 DOLLARS
1.2400 g., 0.9999 Gold 0.0399 oz. AGW, 13.9 mm. **Ruler:** Elizabeth II **Subject:** Pokémon Series **Obv:** Crowned shield within sprigs **Rev:** Entei **Edge:** Reeded

Date	Mintage	F	VF	XF	Unc	BU
2002PM Proof	10,000	Value: 50.00				

KM# 168 20 DOLLARS
1.2400 g., 0.9999 Gold 0.0399 oz. AGW, 13.9 mm. **Ruler:** Elizabeth II **Subject:** Pokémon Series **Obv:** Crowned shield within sprigs **Rev:** Celebi **Edge:** Reeded

Date	Mintage	F	VF	XF	Unc	BU
2002PM Proof	10,000	Value: 50.00				

KM# 379 20 DOLLARS
0.9170 Gold, 13.9x16.7 mm. **Ruler:** Elizabeth II **Subject:** Hello Kitty **Shape:** Face **Note:** Center part to KM#380.

Date	Mintage	F	VF	XF	Unc	BU
2010 Proof	Est. 1,000	Value: 250				

KM# 255 25 DOLLARS
15.5500 g., 0.9990 Gold 0.4994 oz. AGW, 22 mm. **Ruler:** Elizabeth II **Subject:** Peanuts 60th Anniversary **Rev:** Snoopy dancing, Charlie Brown's zig-zag shirt pattern in background

Date	Mintage	F	VF	XF	Unc	BU
2010 Prooflike	1,000	—	—	—	—	800

KM# 388 25 DOLLARS
7.7700 g., 0.9990 Gold 0.2496 oz. AGW, 22 mm. **Ruler:** Elizabeth II **Subject:** Miffy with key

Date	Mintage	F	VF	XF	Unc	BU
2010 Proof	1,000	Value: 400				

KM# 268 30 DOLLARS
1000.0000 g., 0.9990 Silver 32.117 oz. ASW, 120 mm. **Ruler:** Elizabeth II **Subject:** Year of the Rooster **Rev:** Multicolor rooster standing right, sunrise

Date	Mintage	F	VF	XF	Unc	BU
2005 Proof	—	Value: 750				

KM# 297 30 DOLLARS
1000.0000 g., 0.9990 Silver 32.117 oz. ASW, 120 mm. **Ruler:** Elizabeth II **Subject:** Year of the Dog **Rev:** Multicolor dog

Date	Mintage	F	VF	XF	Unc	BU
2005 Proof	—	Value: 750				

KM# 380 30 DOLLARS
0.9170 Gold, 30 mm. **Ruler:** Elizabeth II **Subject:** Bears **Note:** Outer ring for KM#379

Date	Mintage	F	VF	XF	Unc	BU
2010 Proof	Est. 1,000	Value: 400				

KM# 126 50 DOLLARS
3.1100 g., 0.9999 Gold 0.1000 oz. AGW, 17.9 mm. **Ruler:** Elizabeth II **Subject:** Snoopy as an Ace **Obv:** Crowned head right **Rev:** Snoopy flying his dog house **Edge:** Reeded

Date	Mintage	F	VF	XF	Unc	BU
2001 Proof	7,500	Value: 125				

KM# 149 50 DOLLARS
3.1100 g., 0.9999 Gold 0.1000 oz. AGW, 17.9 mm. **Ruler:** Elizabeth II **Subject:** Pokémon Series **Obv:** Crowned shield within sprigs **Rev:** Pikachu **Edge:** Reeded

Date	Mintage	F	VF	XF	Unc	BU
2002PM Proof	7,500	Value: 125				

KM# 154 50 DOLLARS
3.1100 g., 0.9999 Gold 0.1000 oz. AGW, 17.9 mm. **Ruler:** Elizabeth II **Subject:** Pokémon Series **Obv:** Crowned shield within sprigs **Rev:** Pichu **Edge:** Reeded

Date	Mintage	F	VF	XF	Unc	BU
2002PM Proof	7,500	Value: 125				

KM# 159 50 DOLLARS
3.1100 g., 0.9999 Gold 0.1000 oz. AGW, 17.9 mm. **Ruler:** Elizabeth II **Subject:** Pokémon Series **Obv:** Crowned shield within sprigs **Rev:** Mewtwo **Edge:** Reeded

Date	Mintage	F	VF	XF	Unc	BU
2002PM Proof	7,500	Value: 125				

KM# 164 50 DOLLARS
3.1100 g., 0.9999 Gold 0.1000 oz. AGW, 17.9 mm. **Ruler:** Elizabeth II **Subject:** Pokémon Series **Obv:** Crowned shield within sprigs **Rev:** Entei **Edge:** Reeded

Date	Mintage	F	VF	XF	Unc	BU
2002PM Proof	7,500	Value: 125				

KM# 169 50 DOLLARS
3.1100 g., 0.9999 Gold 0.1000 oz. AGW, 17.9 mm. **Ruler:** Elizabeth II **Subject:** Pokémon Series **Obv:** Crowned shield within sprigs **Rev:** Celebi **Edge:** Reeded

Date	Mintage	F	VF	XF	Unc	BU
2002PM Proof	7,500	Value: 125				

KM# 256 50 DOLLARS
15.5500 g., 0.9990 Gold 0.4994 oz. AGW, 30 mm. **Ruler:** Elizabeth II **Subject:** Peanuts 60th Anniversary **Rev:** Snoopy as a king

Date	Mintage	F	VF	XF	Unc	BU
2010 Prooflike	1,000	—	—	—	—	800

KM# 389 50 DOLLARS
15.5500 g., 0.9990 Gold 0.4994 oz. AGW, 30 mm. **Ruler:** Elizabeth II **Subject:** Miffy in flowers

Date	Mintage	F	VF	XF	Unc	BU
2010 Proof	Est. 1,000	Value: 800				

KM# 127 100 DOLLARS
6.2200 g., 0.9999 Gold 0.1999 oz. AGW, 22 mm. **Ruler:** Elizabeth II **Subject:** Snoopy as an Ace **Obv:** Crowned head right **Rev:** Snoopy flying his dog house **Edge:** Reeded

Date	Mintage	F	VF	XF	Unc	BU
2001 Proof	5,000	Value: 250				

KM# 150 100 DOLLARS
6.2200 g., 0.9999 Gold 0.1999 oz. AGW, 22 mm. **Ruler:** Elizabeth II **Subject:** Pokémon Series **Obv:** Crowned shield within sprigs **Rev:** Pikachu **Edge:** Reeded

Date	Mintage	F	VF	XF	Unc	BU
2002PM Proof	5,000	Value: 250				

KM# 155 100 DOLLARS
6.2200 g., 0.9999 Gold 0.1999 oz. AGW, 22 mm. **Ruler:** Elizabeth II **Subject:** Pokémon Series **Obv:** Crowned shield within sprigs **Rev:** Pichu **Edge:** Reeded

Date	Mintage	F	VF	XF	Unc	BU
2002PM Proof	5,000	Value: 250				

KM# 160 100 DOLLARS
6.2200 g., 0.9999 Gold 0.1999 oz. AGW, 22 mm. **Ruler:** Elizabeth II **Subject:** Pokémon Series **Obv:** Crowned shield within sprigs **Rev:** Mewtwo **Edge:** Reeded

Date	Mintage	F	VF	XF	Unc	BU
2002PM Proof	5,000	Value: 250				

KM# 165 100 DOLLARS
6.2200 g., 0.9999 Gold 0.1999 oz. AGW, 22 mm. **Ruler:** Elizabeth II **Subject:** Pokémon Series **Obv:** Crowned shield within sprigs **Rev:** Entei **Edge:** Reeded

Date	Mintage	F	VF	XF	Unc	BU
2002PM Proof	5,000	Value: 250				

KM# 170 100 DOLLARS
6.2200 g., 0.9999 Gold 0.1999 oz. AGW, 22 mm. **Ruler:** Elizabeth II **Subject:** Pokémon Series **Obv:** Crowned shield within sprigs **Rev:** Celebi **Edge:** reeded

Date	Mintage	F	VF	XF	Unc	BU
2002PM Proof	5,000	Value: 250				

KM# 425 100 DOLLARS
93.3000 g., 0.9000 Gold 2.6996 oz. AGW, 41.6x55.6 mm. **Ruler:** Elizabeth II **Subject:** Imperial Faberge Egg - Coronation Egg **Obv:** Head with tiara right above opened egg **Rev:** Coronation egg and coach **Shape:** Vertical oval

Date	Mintage	F	VF	XF	Unc	BU
2010 Proof	222	Value: 4,000				

KM# 511 100 DOLLARS
31.1030 g., 0.9990 Gold 0.9989 oz. AGW, 38.61 mm. **Ruler:** Elizabeth II **Obv:** Head with tiara right **Rev:** Tasmanian tiger in color

Date	Mintage	F	VF	XF	Unc	BU
2011 Proof	200	Value: 1,550				

KM# 512 200 DOLLARS
62.2000 g., 0.9990 Gold 1.9977 oz. AGW, 35.2x35.2 mm. **Ruler:** Elizabeth II **Subject:** Three kings of 1935 **Obv:** Head with tiara right **Rev:** Head left of George V, Edward VIII and George VI

Date	Mintage	F	VF	XF	Unc	BU
2011 Proof	250	Value: 3,000				

KM# 405 3000 DOLLARS
500.0000 g., 0.9999 Gold 16.073 oz. AGW, 67.35x90 mm. **Ruler:** Elizabeth II **Subject:** Russian Royal Family **Obv:** Seven figures as Orthodox Saints, Elizabeth head with tiara below **Rev:** Oval portaits of Nicholas II and his family **Shape:** Vertical Oval

Date	Mintage	F	VF	XF	Unc	BU
2010 Proof	23	Value: 23,750				

MINT SETS

KM#	Date	Mintage	Identification	Issue Price	Mkt Val
MS1	2009 (5)	20,000	KM#193-197	—	30.00
MS2	2010 (5)	10,000	KM193-196, 198	—	30.00

NORWAY

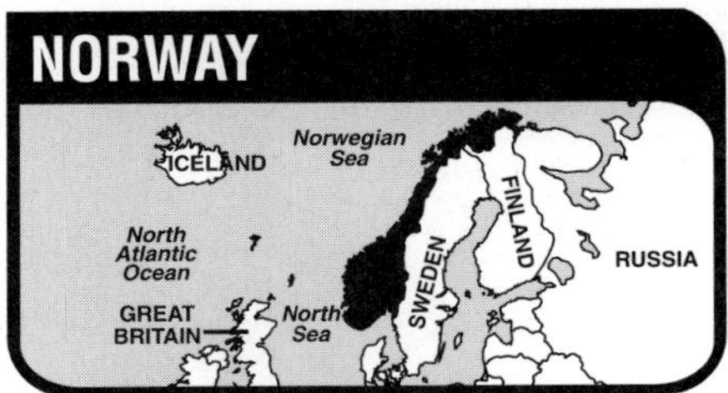

The Kingdom of Norway (*Norge, Noreg*), a constitutional monarchy located in northwestern Europe, has an area of 150,000sq. mi. (324,220 sq. km.), including the island territories of Spitzbergen (Svalbard) and Jan Mayen, and a population of *4.2 million. Capital: Oslo (Christiania). The diversified economic base of Norway includes shipping, fishing, forestry, agriculture, and manufacturing. Nonferrous metals, paper and paperboard, paper pulp, iron, steel and oil are exported.

RULER
Harald V, 1991-

MINT MARK
(h) - Crossed hammers – Kongsberg

MONETARY SYSTEM
100 Ore = 1 Krone

KINGDOM

DECIMAL COINAGE

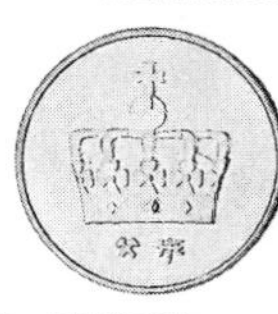

KM# 460 50 ORE
3.6000 g., Bronze, 18.5 mm. **Ruler:** Harald V **Obv:** Crown **Rev:** Stylized animal and value **Edge:** Plain **Designer:** Grazyna Jolanta Linday

Date	Mintage	VG	F	VF	XF	BU
2001 without star	16,848,250	—	—	—	—	0.40
2001 with star	13,291,750	—	—	—	—	0.40
2001 Proof	—	Value: 10.00				
2002	28,293,000	—	—	—	—	0.40
2002 Proof	—	Value: 10.00				
2003	15,533,000	—	—	—	—	0.40
2003 Proof	—	Value: 10.00				
2004	14,807,000	—	—	—	—	0.40
2004 Proof	—	Value: 10.00				
2005	4,963,000	—	—	—	—	0.40
2005 Proof	—	Value: 10.00				
2006	30,227,000	—	—	—	—	0.40
2006 Proof	—	Value: 10.00				
2007	20,117,000	—	—	—	—	0.40
2007 Proof	—	Value: 10.00				
2008	19,391,000	—	—	—	—	0.40
2008 Proof	—	Value: 10.00				
2009	9,903,000	—	—	—	—	0.40
2009 Proof	—	Value: 10.00				
2010	—	—	—	—	—	0.40
2010 Proof	—	Value: 10.00				

KM# 462 KRONE
4.3500 g., Copper-Nickel, 21 mm. **Ruler:** Harald V **Obv:** Crowned monograms form cross within circle with center hole **Rev:** Bird on vine above center hole date and value below

Date	Mintage	VG	F	VF	XF	BU
2001 without star	43,128,650	—	—	—	—	0.65
2001 with star	7,355,350	—	—	—	—	0.75
2001 Proof	—	Value: 10.00				
2002	21,313,000	—	—	—	—	0.65
2002 Proof	—	Value: 10.00				
2003	24,093,000	—	—	—	—	0.65
2003 Proof	—	Value: 10.00				
2004	25,151,000	—	—	—	—	0.65
2004 Proof	—	Value: 10.00				
2005	25,648,000	—	—	—	—	0.65
2005 Proof	—	Value: 10.00				
2006	63,129,000	—	—	—	—	0.65
2006 Proof	—	Value: 10.00				
2007	47,108,000	—	—	—	—	0.65
2007 Proof	—	Value: 10.00				
2008	46,047,000	—	—	—	—	0.65
2008 Proof	—	Value: 10.00				
2009	50,055,000	—	—	—	—	0.65
2009 Proof	—	Value: 10.00				

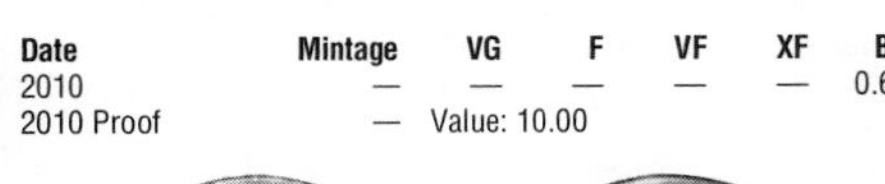

Date	Mintage	VG	F	VF	XF	BU
2010	—	—	—	—	—	0.65
2010 Proof	—	Value: 10.00				

KM# 463 5 KRONER
7.8500 g., Copper-Nickel, 26 mm. **Ruler:** Harald V **Subject:** Order of St. Olaf **Obv:** Hole at center of order chain **Rev:** Center hole divides sprigs, value above and date below **Edge:** Reeded

Date	Mintage	VG	F	VF	XF	BU
2001	480,000	—	—	—	—	2.00
2001 Proof	—	Value: 12.50				
2002	3,622,000	—	—	—	—	1.50
2002 Proof	—	Value: 12.50				
2003	827,000	—	—	—	—	1.50
2003 Proof	—	Value: 12.50				
2004	503,000	—	—	—	—	1.50
2004 Proof	—	Value: 12.50				
2005	503,000	—	—	—	—	1.50
2005 Proof	—	Value: 12.50				
2006	509,000	—	—	—	—	1.50
2006 Proof	—	Value: 12.50				
2007	9,152,000	—	—	—	—	1.50
2007 Proof	—	Value: 12.50				
2008	5,502,000	—	—	—	—	1.50
2008 Proof	—	Value: 12.50				
2009	10,020,000	—	—	—	—	1.50
2009 Proof	—	Value: 12.50				
2010	—	—	—	—	—	1.50
2010 Proof	—	Value: 12.50				

KM# 457 10 KRONER
6.8000 g., Nickel-Brass, 24 mm. **Ruler:** Harald V **Obv:** Head right **Rev:** Stylized church rooftop, value and date **Edge:** Segmented reeding **Designer:** Ingrid Austlid Rise

Date	Mintage	VG	F	VF	XF	BU
2001 without star	9,854,000	—	—	—	—	3.50
2001 with star	10,000	—	—	—	—	7.50
2001 Proof	—	Value: 10.00				
2002	1,123,000	—	—	—	—	3.50
2002 Proof	—	Value: 10.00				
2003	957,000	—	—	—	—	3.50
2003 Proof	—	Value: 10.00				
2004	503,000	—	—	—	—	3.50
2004 Proof	—	Value: 10.00				
2005	466,000	—	—	—	—	3.50
2005 Proof	—	Value: 10.00				
2006	497,000	—	—	—	—	3.50
2006 Proof	—	Value: 10.00				
2007	474,000	—	—	—	—	3.50
2007 Proof	—	Value: 10.00				
2008	565,000	—	—	—	—	3.50
2008 Proof	—	Value: 10.00				
2009	475,000	—	—	—	—	3.50
2009 Proof	—	Value: 10.00				
2010	—	—	—	—	—	3.50
2010 Proof	—	Value: 10.00				

KM# 482 10 KRONER
6.8000 g., Copper-Nickel-Zinc, 24 mm. **Ruler:** Harald V **Subject:** Henrik Vergeland **Obv:** Head right **Rev:** Spectacles and vertical signature

Date	Mintage	F	VF	XF	Unc	BU
2008	4,628,000	—	—	—	—	3.50

KM# 453 20 KRONER
9.9000 g., Nickel-Brass, 27.5 mm. **Ruler:** Harald V **Obv:** Head right **Rev:** Value above 1/2 ancient boat **Designer:** Ingrid Austlid Rise

Date	Mintage	VG	F	VF	XF	BU
2001	4,194,000	—	—	—	—	6.50
2001 Proof	—	Value: 25.00				

Date	Mintage	VG	F	VF	XF	BU
2002	20,463,000	—	—	—	—	6.50
2002 Proof	—	Value: 25.00				
2003	30,061,000	—	—	—	—	6.50
2003 Proof	—	Value: 25.00				
2004	499,000	—	—	—	—	6.50
2004 Proof	—	Value: 25.00				
2005	553,000	—	—	—	—	6.50
2005 Proof	—	Value: 25.00				
2006	1,000,000	—	—	—	—	6.50
2006 Proof	—	Value: 22.50				
2007	493,000	—	—	—	—	6.50
2007 Proof	—	Value: 25.00				
2008	481,000	—	—	—	—	6.50
2008 Proof	—	Value: 25.00				
2009	473,000	—	—	—	—	6.50
2009 Proof	—	Value: 25.00				
2010	—	—	—	—	—	6.50
2010 Proof	—	Value: 25.00				

KM# 471 20 KRONER

9.7300 g., Nickel-Brass, 27.4 mm. **Ruler:** Harald V **Subject:** Niels Henrik Abel **Obv:** Head right **Rev:** Pair of glasses, dates and value within mathematical graphs **Edge:** Plain

Date	Mintage	F	VF	XF	Unc	BU
2002	—	—	—	—	10.00	12.50

KM# 478 20 KRONER

9.9000 g., Copper-Nickel-Zinc, 27.5 mm. **Ruler:** Harald V **Subject:** First Norwegian Railroad **Obv:** Head right **Rev:** Railroad track switch and value **Edge:** Plain

Date	Mintage	F	VF	XF	Unc	BU
2004	10,000	—	—	—	17.50	20.00
2004 Proof	—	Value: 25.00				

KM# 479 20 KRONER

9.9000 g., Copper-Nickel-Zinc, 27.5 mm. **Ruler:** Harald V **Obv:** Head right **Rev:** Henrik Ibsen caricature walking left, signature **Rev. Designer:** Nina Sundbye **Edge:** Plain

Date	Mintage	F	VF	XF	Unc	BU
2006	10,000	—	—	—	10.00	12.50

KM# 469 100 KRONER

33.6000 g., 0.9250 Silver 0.9992 oz. ASW, 39 mm. **Ruler:** Harald V **Subject:** Nobel Peace Prize Centennial **Obv:** Rampant crowned lion left holding axe **Rev:** Head left **Edge:** Plain

Date	Mintage	F	VF	XF	Unc	BU
2001 Proof	Est. 50,000	Value: 85.00				

KM# 472 100 KRONER

33.8000 g., 0.9250 Silver 1.0052 oz. ASW, 39 mm. **Ruler:** Harald V **Subject:** 1905 Independence from Sweden **Obv:** Three kings **Rev:** Farm field **Edge:** Plain

Date	Mintage	F	VF	XF	Unc	BU
2003 Proof	65,000	Value: 70.00				

KM# 474 100 KRONER

33.8000 g., 0.9250 Silver 1.0052 oz. ASW, 39 mm. **Ruler:** Harald V **Subject:** 1905 Liberation **Obv:** Three kings **Rev:** Off shore ocean oil well **Edge:** Plain

Date	Mintage	F	VF	XF	Unc	BU
2004 Proof	65,000	Value: 70.00				

KM# 476 100 KRONER

33.8000 g., 0.9250 Silver 1.0052 oz. ASW, 39 mm. **Ruler:** Harald V **Obv:** Three kings **Rev:** Circuit board **Edge:** Plain

Date	Mintage	F	VF	XF	Unc	BU
2005 Proof	—	Value: 70.00				

KM# 480 200 KRONER

16.8500 g., 0.9250 Silver 0.5011 oz. ASW, 32 mm. **Ruler:** Harald V **Subject:** Henrik Wergeland, 200th Birth Anniversary **Obv:** Head right **Rev:** Spectacles and signature **Rev. Designer:** Enzo Finger

Date	Mintage	F	VF	XF	Unc	BU
2008 Proof	40,000	Value: 100				

KM# 481 200 KRONER

16.8500 g., 0.9250 Silver 0.5011 oz. ASW, 32 mm. **Ruler:** Harald V **Subject:** Knut Hamsun 150th Birth Anniversary **Obv:** Crowned shield **Rev:** Streppled portrait, novel text and signature **Rev. Designer:** Enzo Finger

Date	Mintage	F	VF	XF	Unc	BU
2009 Proof	40,000	Value: 100				

KM# 470 1500 KRONER

16.9600 g., 0.9170 Gold 0.5000 oz. AGW, 27 mm. **Ruler:** Harald V **Subject:** Nobel Peace Prize Centennial **Obv:** Head right **Rev:** Reverse design of the prize medal **Edge:** Plain

Date	Mintage	VG	F	VF	XF	BU
ND(2001) Matte Proof	7,500	Value: 650				

KM# 473 1500 KRONER

16.9600 g., 0.9170 Gold 0.5000 oz. AGW, 27 mm. **Ruler:** Harald V **Subject:** 1905 Liberation **Obv:** Three kings **Rev:** Various leaf types **Edge:** Plain

Date	Mintage	F	VF	XF	Unc	BU
2003 Proof	10,000	Value: 625				

KM# 475 1500 KRONER

16.9600 g., 0.9170 Gold 0.5000 oz. AGW, 27 mm. **Ruler:** Harald V **Subject:** 1905 Liberation **Obv:** Three kings **Rev:** Liquid drops on hard surface **Edge:** Plain

Date	Mintage	F	VF	XF	Unc	BU
2004 Proof	10,000	Value: 625				

KM# 477 1500 KRONER

16.9600 g., 0.9170 Gold 0.5000 oz. AGW, 27 mm. **Ruler:** Harald V **Obv:** Three kings **Rev:** Binary language **Edge:** Plain

Date	Mintage	F	VF	XF	Unc	BU
2005 Proof	—	Value: 625				

MINT SETS

KM#	Date	Mintage	Identification	Issue Price	Mkt Val
MS59	2001 (5)	55,000	KM453, 457, 460, 462, 463. Folder.	20.00	25.00
MS60	2001 (5)	30,000	KM453, 457, 460, 462, 463. Baby gift set.	18.00	30.00
MS61	2001 (5)	2,000	KM453, 457, 460, 462, 463 plus medal.	27.00	27.00
MS62	2001 (5)	—	KM453, 457, 460, 462, 463. Sandhill.	—	30.00
MS63	2002 (6)	55,000	KM#453, 457, 460, 462, 463, 471	—	32.00
MS64	2003 (5)	55,000	KM#453, 457, 460, 462, 463	—	30.00
MS65	2004 (6)	55,000	KM#453, 457, 460, 462, 463, 478	—	32.00
MS66	2005 (5)	55,000	KM#453, 457, 460, 462, 463	—	30.00

PROOF SETS

KM#	Date	Mintage	Identification	Issue Price	Mkt Val
PS13	2002 (6)	10,000	KM#453, 457, 460, 462, 463, 471	—	110
PS14	2003 (5)	10,000	KM#453, 457, 460, 462, 463	—	100
PS15	2004 (6)	10,000	KM#453, 457, 460, 462, 463, 478	—	110
PS16	2005 (5)	10,000	KM#453, 457, 460, 462, 463	—	100

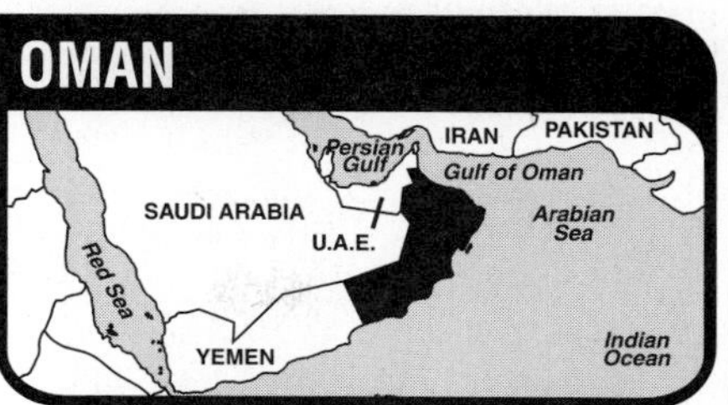

The Sultanate of Oman (formerly Muscat and Oman), an independent monarchy located in the southeastern part of the Arabian Peninsula, has an area of 82,030 sq. mi. (212,460 sq. km.) and a population of *1.3 million. Capital: Muscat. The economy is based on agriculture, herding and petroleum. Petroleum products, dates, fish and hides are exported.

RULER:

Qaboos ibn al-Sa'id, AH1390-/1970AD-

SULTANATE

REFORM COINAGE

1000 Baisa = 1 Omani Rial

KM# 150 5 BAISA

2.6500 g., Bronze Clad Steel, 19 mm. **Ruler:** Qabus bin Sa'id AH1390-/1970AD- **Obv:** National arms **Rev:** Value and dates

Date	Mintage	F	VF	XF	Unc	BU
AH1429-2008	—	—	—	0.20	0.50	0.75

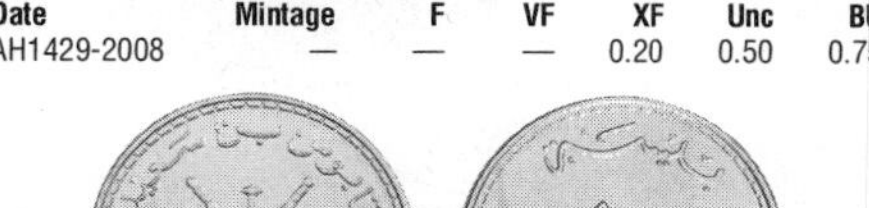

KM# 151 10 BAISA

4.0400 g., Bronze Clad Steel, 22.5 mm. **Ruler:** Qabus bin Sa'id AH1390-/1970AD- **Obv:** National arms **Rev:** Value with both dates

Date	Mintage	F	VF	XF	Unc	BU
AH1429-2008	—	—	—	0.30	0.75	1.00

KM# 152 25 BAISA

3.0300 g., Copper-Nickel, 18 mm. **Ruler:** Qabus bin Sa'id AH1390-/1970AD- **Obv:** National arms **Rev:** Value and both dates **Edge:** Plain

Date	Mintage	F	VF	XF	Unc	BU
AH1428-2008	—	—	0.15	0.35	0.90	1.25
AH1429-2009	—	—	0.15	0.35	0.90	1.25

KM# 152a 25 BAISA

2.6300 g., Nickel Clad Steel, 17.95 mm. **Ruler:** Qabus bin Sa'id AH1390-/1970AD- **Obv:** National arms **Rev:** Value with both dates **Edge:** Reeded

Date	Mintage	F	VF	XF	Unc	BU
AH1428-2008	—	—	—	0.35	0.90	1.25

KM# 153 50 BAISA

6.4000 g., Copper-Nickel, 24 mm. **Ruler:** Qabus bin Sa'id

AH1390-/1970AD- **Obv:** National arms **Rev:** Value with both dates **Edge:** Reeded

Date	Mintage	F	VF	XF	Unc	BU
AH1429-2008	—	—	0.25	0.60	1.50	2.00

KM# 153a 50 BAISA

5.5700 g., Nickel Clad Steel, 23.96 mm. **Ruler:** Qabus bin Sa'id AH1390-/1970AD- **Obv:** National arms **Rev:** Value with both dates **Edge:** Reeded

Date	Mintage	F	VF	XF	Unc	BU
AH1428-2008	—	—	—	0.60	1.50	2.00

KM# 154 OMANI RIAL

28.2800 g., 0.9250 Silver 0.8410 oz. ASW, 38.6 mm. **Ruler:** Qabus bin Sa'id AH1390-/1970AD- **Subject:** 31st National Day and Environment Year **Obv:** National arms **Rev:** Multicolor map design **Edge:** Reeded

Date	Mintage	F	VF	XF	Unc	BU
2001	500	—	—	—	90.00	—
2001 Proof	105	Value: 150				

KM# 154a OMANI RIAL

37.8000 g., 0.9160 Gold 1.1132 oz. AGW, 38.6 mm. **Ruler:** Qabus bin Sa'id AH1390-/1970AD- **Subject:** 31st National Day and Environment Year **Obv:** National arms **Rev:** Multicolor map design **Edge:** Reeded

Date	Mintage	F	VF	XF	Unc	BU
2001	350	—	—	—	1,700	—
2001 Proof	105	Value: 1,850				

KM# 156 OMANI RIAL

28.2800 g., 0.9250 Silver 0.8410 oz. ASW, 38.7 mm. **Ruler:** Qabus bin Sa'id AH1390-/1970AD- **Series:** Environment Collection **Obv:** National arms **Rev:** Hoopoe bird standing right multicolor

Date	Mintage	F	VF	XF	Unc	BU
2002 Proof	1,000	Value: 75.00				

KM# 157 OMANI RIAL

28.2800 g., 0.9250 Silver 0.8410 oz. ASW, 38.7 mm. **Ruler:** Qabus bin Sa'id AH1390-/1970AD- **Series:** Environment Collection **Obv:** National arms **Rev:** Dolphin right multicolor

Date	Mintage	F	VF	XF	Unc	BU
2002 Proof	1,000	Value: 75.00				

KM# 158 OMANI RIAL

28.2800 g., 0.9250 Silver 0.8410 oz. ASW, 38.7 mm. **Ruler:** Qabus bin Sa'id AH1390-/1970AD- **Series:** Environment Collection **Obv:** National arms **Rev:** Turtle left multicolor

Date	Mintage	F	VF	XF	Unc	BU
2002 Proof	1,000	Value: 75.00				

KM# 159 OMANI RIAL

28.2800 g., 0.9250 Silver 0.8410 oz. ASW, 38.7 mm. **Ruler:** Qabus bin Sa'id AH1390-/1970AD- **Series:** Environment Collection **Obv:** National arms **Rev:** Flower multicolor

Date	Mintage	F	VF	XF	Unc	BU
2002 Proof	1,000	Value: 75.00				

KM# 160 OMANI RIAL

28.2800 g., 0.9250 Silver 0.8410 oz. ASW, 38.7 mm. **Ruler:** Qabus bin Sa'id AH1390-/1970AD- **Series:** Environment Collection **Obv:** National arms **Rev:** Ibex standing left multicolor

Date	Mintage	F	VF	XF	Unc	BU
2002 Proof	1,000	Value: 75.00				

KM# 161 OMANI RIAL

28.2800 g., 0.9250 Silver 0.8410 oz. ASW, 38.7 mm. **Ruler:** Qabus bin Sa'id AH1390-/1970AD- **Series:** Environment Collection **Obv:** National arms **Rev:** Butterfly multicolor

Date	Mintage	F	VF	XF	Unc	BU
2002 Proof	1,000	Value: 75.00				

KM# 162 OMANI RIAL

28.2800 g., 0.9250 Silver 0.8410 oz. ASW, 38.7 mm. **Ruler:** Qabus bin Sa'id AH1390-/1970AD- **Subject:** Population Census - December, 2003

Date	Mintage	F	VF	XF	Unc	BU
2003 Rare	—	—	—	—	—	—

KM# 155 OMANI RIAL

28.2800 g., 0.9250 Silver 0.8410 oz. ASW, 38.6 mm. **Ruler:** Qabus bin Sa'id AH1390-/1970AD- **Subject:** The Sindibad Voyage, 1980/1981 **Obv:** National arms **Rev:** Sailing ship below map within circle **Edge:** Reeded

Date	Mintage	F	VF	XF	Unc	BU
2003 Proof	—	Value: 65.00				

KM# 163 OMANI RIAL

28.2800 g., 0.9250 Silver 0.8410 oz. ASW, 38.7 mm. **Ruler:** Qabus bin Sa'id AH1390-/1970AD- **Subject:** 35th National Day **Obv:** Oman Map

Date	Mintage	F	VF	XF	Unc	BU
AH1427-2005	—	—	—	—	100	120

KM# 164 OMANI RIAL

28.2800 g., 0.9250 Silver 0.8410 oz. ASW, 38.7 mm. **Ruler:** Qabus bin Sa'id AH1390-/1970AD- **Subject:** 40th Anniversary of First Oil Export from Oman

Date	Mintage	F	VF	XF	Unc	BU
2007	—	—	—	—	90.00	100

KM# 165 OMANI RIAL

28.2800 g., 0.9250 Silver 0.8410 oz. ASW, 38.7 mm. **Ruler:** Qabus bin Sa'id AH1390-/1970AD- **Subject:** 29th GCC Summit held in Muscat in December 2008

Date	Mintage	F	VF	XF	Unc	BU
2008	—	—	—	—	100	120

KM# 166 OMANI RIAL

28.2800 g., 0.9250 Silver 0.8410 oz. ASW, 38.7 mm. **Ruler:** Qabus bin Sa'id AH1390-/1970AD- **Subject:** 19th Arabian Gulf Cup

Date	Mintage	F	VF	XF	Unc	BU
2008	—	—	—	—	250	—

PAKISTAN

The Islamic Republic of Pakistan, located on the Indian subcontinent between India and Afghanistan, has an area of 310,404 sq. mi. (803,940 sq. km.) and a population of 130 million. Capital: Islamabad. Pakistan is mainly an agricultural land although the industrial base is expanding rapidly. Yarn, textiles, cotton, rice, medical instruments, sports equipment and leather are exported.

TITLE

Pakistan

ISLAMIC REPUBLIC

DECIMAL COINAGE

100 Paisa = 1 Rupee

KM# 62 RUPEE

4.0000 g., Bronze, 20 mm. **Obv:** Head of Jinnah facing left **Rev:** Mosque above value **Edge:** Reeded

Date	Mintage	F	VF	XF	Unc	BU
2001	—	0.20	0.25	0.35	0.65	0.75
2002	—	0.20	0.25	0.35	0.65	0.75
2003	—	0.20	0.25	0.35	0.65	0.75

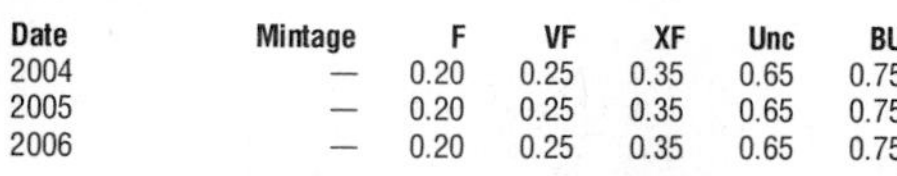

Date	Mintage	F	VF	XF	Unc	BU
2004	—	0.20	0.25	0.35	0.65	0.75
2005	—	0.20	0.25	0.35	0.65	0.75
2006	—	0.20	0.25	0.35	0.65	0.75

KM# 67 RUPEE

1.7500 g., Aluminum, 20 mm. **Obv:** Head left **Rev:** Mosque

Date	Mintage	F	VF	XF	Unc	BU
2007	—	—	—	—	—	2.00
2008	—	—	—	—	—	2.00
2009	—	—	—	—	—	2.00
2010	—	—	—	—	—	2.00

KM# 64 2 RUPEES

5.0000 g., Nickel-Brass, 22.5 mm. **Obv:** Crescent, star and date above sprigs **Rev:** Value below mosque and clouds **Edge:** Reeded

Date	Mintage	F	VF	XF	Unc	BU
2001	—	0.20	0.30	0.45	0.85	1.00
2002	—	0.20	0.30	0.45	0.85	1.00
2003	—	0.20	0.30	0.45	0.85	1.00
2004	—	0.20	0.30	0.45	0.85	1.00
2005	—	0.20	0.30	0.45	0.85	1.00
2006	—	0.20	0.30	0.45	0.85	1.00

KM# 68 2 RUPEES

Aluminum **Obv:** Star and crescent, wheat ears below **Rev:** Mosque

Date	Mintage	F	VF	XF	Unc	BU
2007	—	—	—	—	—	2.00
2008	—	—	—	—	—	2.00
2009	—	—	—	—	—	2.00
2010	—	—	—	—	—	2.00

KM# 65 5 RUPEES

6.5000 g., Copper-Nickel, 24 mm. **Obv:** Cresent, star and date above sprays **Rev:** Value within star design and sprigs **Edge:** Reeded

Date	Mintage	F	VF	XF	Unc	BU
2002	—	0.50	1.00	1.50	3.00	3.25
2003	—	0.50	1.00	1.50	3.00	3.25
2004	—	0.50	—	1.50	3.00	3.25
2005	—	0.50	—	—	3.00	3.25
2006	—	—	—	—	3.00	3.25

KM# 66 10 RUPEES

7.5000 g., Copper-Nickel, 27.5 mm. **Obv:** Cresent, star and date above sprays **Rev:** Flowers and inscription **Rev. Inscription:** Year of Fatima Jinnah **Edge:** Reeded

Date	Mintage	F	VF	XF	Unc	BU
2003	200,000	—	—	4.00	6.50	7.50

KM# 69 10 RUPEES

8.2500 g., Copper-Nickel, 27.5 mm. **Subject:** Benazir Bhutto **Obv:** Star and crescent, wheat wreath below **Rev:** Bust facing, Urdu script legend above

Date	Mintage	F	VF	XF	Unc	BU
2007	—	—	—	—	—	5.00
2008	300,000	—	—	—	—	5.00

KM# 70 10 RUPEES

8.2500 g., Copper-Nickel, 27.5 mm. **Subject:** Pakistan - China Friendship, 60 years of Peoples' Republic of China **Obv:** Crescent and star **Rev:** Pakistan and Chinese flags, clasped hands below

Date	Mintage	F	VF	XF	Unc	BU
2009	100,000	—	—	—	3.00	5.00

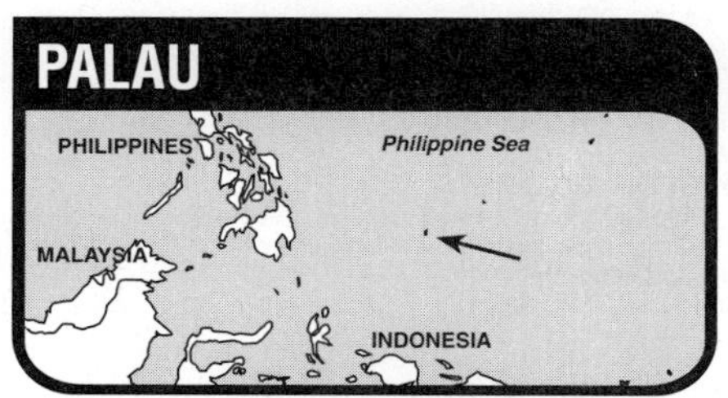

The Republic of Palau, a group of about 100 islands and islets, is generally considered a part of the Caroline Islands. It is located about 1,000 miles southeast of Manila and about the same distance southwest of Saipan and has an area of 179 sq. mi. and a population of 12,116. Capital: Koror.

REPUBLIC

MILLED COINAGE

KM# 86 DOLLAR

1.2441 g., 0.9999 Gold 0.0400 oz. AGW, 13.94 mm. **Subject:** Marine Life Protection **Obv:** Prone Mermaid **Rev:** Two fish

Date	Mintage	F	VF	XF	Unc	BU
2001 Proof	—	Value: 65.00				

KM# 87 DOLLAR

1.2441 g., 0.9999 Gold 0.0400 oz. AGW, 13.94 mm. **Subject:** Marine Life Protection **Obv:** Seated Mermaid with raised arm above value **Rev:** Two glittering fish

Date	Mintage	F	VF	XF	Unc	BU
2001 Proof	—	Value: 65.00				

KM# 88 DOLLAR

1.2441 g., 0.9999 Gold 0.0400 oz. AGW, 13.94 mm. **Subject:** Marine Life Protection **Obv:** Figurehead Mermaid and value **Rev:** Moorish Idol fish

Date	Mintage	F	VF	XF	Unc	BU
2001 Proof	—	Value: 65.00				

KM# 89 DOLLAR

1.2441 g., 0.9999 Gold 0.0400 oz. AGW, 13.94 mm. **Subject:** Marine Life Protection **Obv:** Figurehead Mermaid and value **Rev:** Moorish Idol fish

Date	Mintage	F	VF	XF	Unc	BU
2001 Proof	—	Value: 65.00				

KM# 60 DOLLAR

26.8000 g., Copper-Nickel, 37.2 mm. **Subject:** Marine Life Protection **Obv:** Seated Mermaid with raised arm above value **Rev:** Two glittering fish **Edge:** Reeded

Date	Mintage	F	VF	XF	Unc	BU
2001 Proof	—	Value: 30.00				

KM# 61 DOLLAR

26.8000 g., Copper-Nickel, 37.2 mm. **Subject:** Marine Life Protection **Obv:** Prone Mermaid above value **Rev:** Two glittering fish **Edge:** Reeded

Date	Mintage	F	VF	XF	Unc	BU
2001 Proof	—	Value: 32.50				

KM# 62 DOLLAR

26.8000 g., Copper-Nickel, 37.2 mm. **Subject:** Marine Life Protection **Obv:** Figurehead mermaid and value **Rev:** Moorish-Idol fish **Edge:** Reeded

Date	Mintage	F	VF	XF	Unc	BU
2001 Proof	—	Value: 30.00				

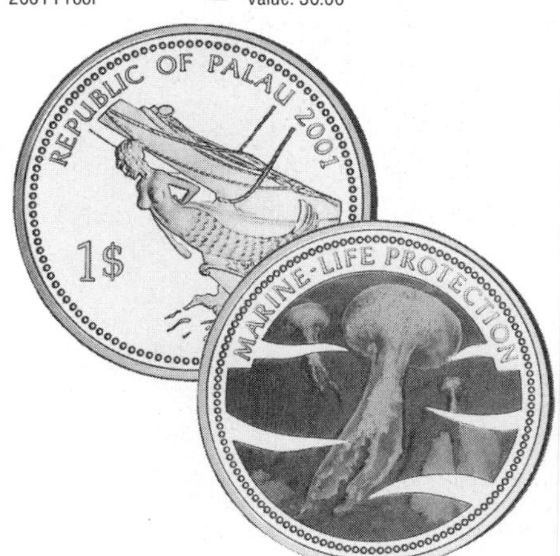

KM# 52 DOLLAR

26.8600 g., Copper-Nickel, 37.3 mm. **Subject:** Marine Life Protection **Obv:** Mermaid figurehead and value **Rev:** Multicolor jellyfish **Edge:** Reeded

Date	Mintage	F	VF	XF	Unc	BU
2001 Proof	—	Value: 30.00				

KM# 253 DOLLAR
1.2500 g., 0.9990 Gold 0.0401 oz. AGW, 13.9 mm. **Obv:** Mermaid body-surfing wave **Rev:** Blue angelfish

Date	Mintage	F	VF	XF	Unc	BU
2001 Proof	—	Value: 65.00				

KM# 254 DOLLAR
1.2400 g., 0.9990 Gold 0.0398 oz. AGW, 13.9 mm. **Obv:** Large breasted mermaid on beach **Rev:** Emperor Angelfish

Date	Mintage	F	VF	XF	Unc	BU
2001 Proof	—	Value: 65.00				

KM# 287 DOLLAR
35.0000 g., Copper-Nickel, 50 mm. **Obv:** National Arms **Rev:** Cut card corners, Queens of Hearts, Clubs

Date	Mintage	F	VF	XF	Unc	BU
ND (2001) Antique finish	—	—	—	—	—	25.00

KM# 288 DOLLAR
35.0000 g., Copper-Nickel, 50 mm. **Obv:** National arms **Rev:** Cut card corner, Queen of Spades, diamonds

Date	Mintage	F	VF	XF	Unc	BU
ND (2001) Antique finish	—	—	—	—	—	25.00

KM# 56 DOLLAR
26.8000 g., Copper-Nickel, 37.2 mm. **Subject:** Marine Life Protection **Obv:** Mermaid figurehead and value **Rev:** Multicolor fish scene **Edge:** Reeded

Date	Mintage	F	VF	XF	Unc	BU
2002 Proof	—	Value: 32.50				

KM# 57 DOLLAR
26.8000 g., Copper-Nickel, 37.2 mm. **Subject:** Marine Life Protection **Obv:** Mermaid figurehead on approaching ship **Rev:** Multicolor reflective fish scene under an acrylic layer **Edge:** Reeded

Date	Mintage	F	VF	XF	Unc	BU
2002 Proof	—	Value: 37.50				

KM# 63 DOLLAR
26.8000 g., Copper-Nickel, 37.2 mm. **Subject:** Marine Life Protection **Obv:** Figurehead mermaid and value **Rev:** Blue Tang Fish **Edge:** Reeded

Date	Mintage	F	VF	XF	Unc	BU
2002 Proof	—	Value: 37.50				

KM# 64 DOLLAR
26.8000 g., Copper-Nickel, 37.2 mm. **Subject:** Marine Life Protection **Obv:** Figurehead mermaid and value **Rev:** Multicolor whales **Edge:** Reeded

Date	Mintage	F	VF	XF	Unc	BU
2002 Proof	—	Value: 37.50				

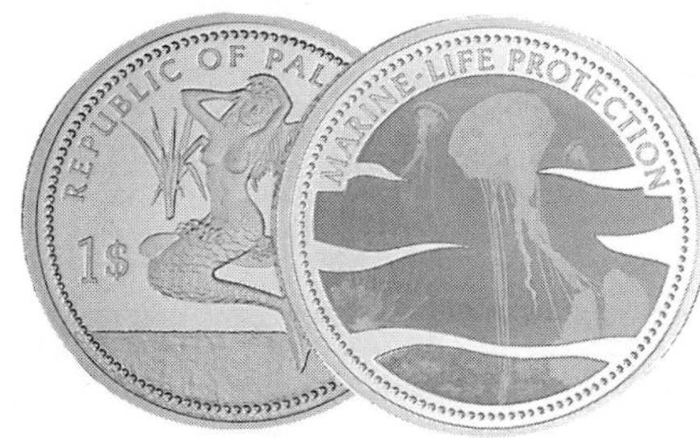

KM# 65 DOLLAR
26.8000 g., Copper-Nickel, 37.2 mm. **Subject:** Marine Life Protection **Obv:** Mermaid washing hair and value **Rev:** Multicolor jellyfish **Edge:** Reeded

Date	Mintage	F	VF	XF	Unc	BU
2002 Proof	—	Value: 37.50				

KM# 90 DOLLAR
1.2441 g., 0.9999 Gold 0.0400 oz. AGW, 13.94 mm. **Subject:** Marine Life Protection **Obv:** Figurehead Mermaid and value **Rev:** Multicolor whales

Date	Mintage	F	VF	XF	Unc	BU
2002 Proof	—	Value: 65.00				

KM# 91 DOLLAR
1.2441 g., 0.9999 Gold 0.0400 oz. AGW, 13.94 mm. **Subject:** Marine Life Protection **Obv:** Figurehead Mermaid and value **Rev:** Pufferfish

Date	Mintage	F	VF	XF	Unc	BU
2002 Proof	—	Value: 65.00				

KM# 92 DOLLAR
1.2441 g., 0.9999 Gold 0.0400 oz. AGW, 13.94 mm. **Subject:** Marine Life Protection **Obv:** Seated Mermaid with both arms raised and value **Rev:** Jellyfish

Date	Mintage	F	VF	XF	Unc	BU
2002 Proof	—	Value: 65.00				

KM# 93 DOLLAR
1.2441 g., 0.9999 Gold 0.0400 oz. AGW, 13.94 mm. **Subject:** Marine Life Protection **Obv:** Figurehead Mermaid and value **Rev:** Blue Tang Fish

Date	Mintage	F	VF	XF	Unc	BU
2002 Proof	—	Value: 65.00				

KM# 94 DOLLAR
1.2441 g., 0.9999 Gold 0.0400 oz. AGW, 13.94 mm. **Subject:** Marine Life Protection **Obv:** Figurehead mermaid and value **Rev:** Lionfish

Date	Mintage	F	VF	XF	Unc	BU
2002 Proof	—	Value: 65.00				

KM# 95 DOLLAR
1.2441 g., 0.9999 Gold 0.0400 oz. AGW, 13.94 mm. **Subject:** Marine Life Protection **Obv:** Mermaid riding dolphin and value **Rev:** Starfish

Date	Mintage	F	VF	XF	Unc	BU
2003 Proof	—	Value: 65.00				

KM# 96 DOLLAR
1.2441 g., 0.9999 Gold 0.0400 oz. AGW, 13.94 mm. **Subject:** Marine Life Protection **Obv:** Seated Mermaid on shell and value **Rev:** Multicolor Orca **Edge:** Reeded Proof

Date	Mintage	F	VF	XF	Unc	BU
2003 Proof	—	Value: 65.00				

KM# 97 DOLLAR
1.2441 g., 0.9999 Gold 0.0400 oz. AGW, 13.94 mm. **Subject:** Marine Life Protection **Obv:** Mermaid under radiant sun and value **Rev:** Crab

Date	Mintage	F	VF	XF	Unc	BU
2003 Proof	—	Value: 65.00				

KM# 98 DOLLAR
1.2441 g., 0.9999 Gold 0.0400 oz. AGW, 13.94 mm. **Subject:** Marine Life Protection **Obv:** Mermaid riding turtle and value **Rev:** Two glittering fish

Date	Mintage	F	VF	XF	Unc	BU
2003 Proof	—	Value: 65.00				

KM# 66 DOLLAR
26.8000 g., Copper-Nickel, 37.2 mm. **Subject:** Marine Life Protection **Obv:** Mermaid under sun and value **Rev:** Orange crab **Edge:** Reeded

Date	Mintage	F	VF	XF	Unc	BU
2003 Proof	—	Value: 37.50				

KM# 67 DOLLAR
26.8000 g., Copper-Nickel, 37.2 mm. **Subject:** Marine Life Protection **Obv:** Mermaid riding turtle and value **Rev:** Two glittering fish **Edge:** Reeded

Date	Mintage	F	VF	XF	Unc	BU
2003 Proof	—	Value: 37.50				

KM# 68 DOLLAR
26.8000 g., Copper-Nickel, 37.2 mm. **Subject:** Marine Life Protection **Obv:** Seated Mermaid on shell and value **Rev:** Multicolor Orca **Edge:** Reeded

Date	Mintage	F	VF	XF	Unc	BU
2003 Proof	—	Value: 37.50				

KM# 69 DOLLAR
26.8000 g., Copper-Nickel, 37.2 mm. **Subject:** Marine Life Protection **Obv:** Mermaid playing shell guitar and value **Rev:** Green fish **Edge:** Reeded

Date	Mintage	F	VF	XF	Unc	BU
2003 Proof	—	Value: 37.50				

KM# 256 DOLLAR
Copper-Nickel, 38.6 mm. **Obv:** Mermaid on dolphin **Rev:** Red starfish - multicolor

Date	Mintage	F	VF	XF	Unc	BU
2003	—	—	—	—	—	25.00

KM# 70 DOLLAR
26.8000 g., Copper-Nickel, 37.2 mm. **Subject:** Marine Life Protection **Obv:** Seated Mermaid on rock and value **Rev:** School of blue fish **Edge:** Reeded

Date	Mintage	F	VF	XF	Unc	BU
2004 Proof	—	Value: 37.50				

KM# 71 DOLLAR
26.8000 g., Copper-Nickel, 37.2 mm. **Subject:** Marine Life Protection **Obv:** Side view of Mermaid facing right and value **Rev:** Clownfish **Edge:** Reeded

Date	Mintage	F	VF	XF	Unc	BU
2004 Proof	—	Value: 37.50				

KM# 72 DOLLAR
26.8000 g., Copper-Nickel, 37.2 mm. **Subject:** Marine Life Protection **Obv:** Mermaid flanked by dolphins **Rev:** Multicolor dolphin head **Edge:** Reeded

Date	Mintage	F	VF	XF	Unc	BU
2004 Proof	—	Value: 37.50				

KM# 123 DOLLAR
Copper-Nickel, 37.2 mm. **Subject:** Marine Life Protection **Obv:** Mermaid seated inside a giant conch shell **Rev:** Puffer fish **Edge:** Reeded

Date	Mintage	F	VF	XF	Unc	BU
2004 Proof	—	Value: 35.00				

KM# 124 DOLLAR
Copper-Nickel, 37.2 mm. **Subject:** Marine Life Protection **Obv:** Seated Mermaid **Rev:** Sea turtle **Edge:** Reeded

Date	Mintage	F	VF	XF	Unc	BU
2004 Proof	—	Value: 50.00				

KM# 99 DOLLAR
1.2441 g., 0.9999 Gold 0.0400 oz. AGW, 13.94 mm. **Subject:** Marine Life Protection **Obv:** Mermaid under radiant sun and value **Rev:** Clownfish

Date	Mintage	F	VF	XF	Unc	BU
2004 Proof	—	Value: 65.00				

KM# 100 DOLLAR
1.2441 g., 0.9999 Gold 0.0400 oz. AGW, 13.94 mm. **Subject:** Marine Life Protection **Obv:** Mermaid flanked by dolphins **Rev:** Multicolor dolphin head

Date	Mintage	F	VF	XF	Unc	BU
2004 Proof	—	Value: 65.00				

KM# 101 DOLLAR
1.2441 g., 0.9999 Gold 0.0400 oz. AGW, 13.94 mm. **Subject:** Marine Life Protection **Obv:** Mermaid sitting in a shell listening to a conch shell **Rev:** Sea Horse

Date	Mintage	F	VF	XF	Unc	BU
2005 Proof	—	Value: 65.00				

KM# 139 DOLLAR
26.8000 g., Copper-Nickel, 37.2 mm. **Subject:** Marine Life - Protection **Obv:** Mermaid fixing hair, dolphin jumping **Rev:** School of fish

Date	Mintage	F	VF	XF	Unc	BU
2005	—	—	—	—	—	37.50

KM# 140 DOLLAR
26.8000 g., Copper-Nickel, 37.2 mm. **Subject:** Marine Life - Protection **Obv:** Mermaid seated in shell, listening to shell **Rev:** Multicolor sea horse

Date	Mintage	F	VF	XF	Unc	BU
2005	—	—	—	—	—	37.50

KM# 141 DOLLAR
26.8000 g., Copper-Nickel **Subject:** Marine Life - Protection **Obv:** Mermaid and dolphin **Rev:** Multicolor fish scene

Date	Mintage	F	VF	XF	Unc	BU
2005	—	—	—	—	—	37.50

KM# 255 DOLLAR
Copper-Nickel, 38.6 mm. **Obv:** Mermaid seated on rock **Rev:** Stingray - multicolor

Date	Mintage	F	VF	XF	Unc	BU
2005	—	—	—	—	—	25.00

KM# 125 DOLLAR
Copper-Nickel, 37.2 mm. **Subject:** Marine Life Protection **Obv:** Mermaid with head tilted back **Rev:** Barracuda

Date	Mintage	F	VF	XF	Unc	BU
2006 Proof	—	Value: 37.50				

KM# 126 DOLLAR
Copper-Nickel, 37.2 mm. **Subject:** Marine Life Protection **Obv:** Two mermaids **Rev:** Parrot fish

Date	Mintage	F	VF	XF	Unc	BU
2006 Proof	—	Value: 50.00				

KM# 127 DOLLAR
Copper-Nickel, 37.2 mm. **Subject:** Marine Life Protection **Obv:** Mermaid swimming downward **Rev:** Hog Fish **Edge:** Reeded

Date	Mintage	F	VF	XF	Unc	BU
2006 Proof	—	Value: 32.50				

KM# 128 DOLLAR
Copper-Nickel, 37.2 mm. **Subject:** Marine Life Protection **Obv:** Seated mermaid with bird perched on outstretched hand **Rev:** Mahi Mahi **Edge:** Reeded

Date	Mintage	F	VF	XF	Unc	BU
2006 Proof	—	Value: 47.50				

KM# 129 DOLLAR
Copper-Nickel, 37.2 mm. **Subject:** Marine Life Protection **Obv:** Mermaid, sailing ship and sun **Rev:** Box Fish **Edge:** Reeded

Date	Mintage	F	VF	XF	Unc	BU
2006 Proof	—	Value: 45.00				

KM# 142 DOLLAR
20.0000 g., 0.9990 Silver 0.6423 oz. ASW **Obv:** Arms **Rev:** Snowflake with blue crystal **Shape:** 38.6

Date	Mintage	F	VF	XF	Unc	BU
2006 Proof	2,500	Value: 65.00				

KM# 257 DOLLAR
25.0000 g., 0.9250 Silver 0.7435 oz. ASW, 38.6 mm. **Obv:** Arms **Rev:** White pearl in shell **Shape:** Heart

Date	Mintage	F	VF	XF	Unc	BU
2006 Proof	500	Value: 125				

KM# 144 DOLLAR
27.0000 g., 0.9250 Silver 0.8029 oz. ASW **Obv:** Shield **Rev:** Multicolor John Paul II waving

Date	Mintage	F	VF	XF	Unc	BU
2007 Proof	—	Value: 45.00				

KM# 145 DOLLAR
1.2440 g., 0.9990 Gold 0.0400 oz. AGW, 13.92 mm. **Subject:** Marine Life - Protection **Obv:** Neptune and mermaid seated on rocks **Rev:** Tropical fish

Date	Mintage	F	VF	XF	Unc	BU
2007 Proof	—	Value: 75.00				

KM# 150 DOLLAR
25.0000 g., 0.9250 Silver 0.7435 oz. ASW **Subject:** Pacific Wildlife **Obv:** Shield **Rev:** Multicolor seahorse

Date	Mintage	F	VF	XF	Unc	BU
2007 Proof	—	Value: 70.00				

KM# 116 DOLLAR
25.7300 g., Silver Plated Bronze, 38.6 mm. **Obv:** National arms **Rev:** Multicolor Pope John Paul II with cross **Edge:** Reeded

Date	Mintage	F	VF	XF	Unc	BU
2007 Proof	—	Value: 37.50				

KM# 118 DOLLAR
27.0000 g., Copper-Nickel, 38.61 mm. **Series:** Marine Life Protection **Obv:** Neptune reclining with trident, mermaid at his side **Obv. Legend:** REPUBLIC OF PALAU **Rev:** Multicolor Doctor Fish

Date	Mintage	F	VF	XF	Unc	BU
2007 Proof	5,000	Value: 35.00				

KM# 121 DOLLAR
27.0000 g., Copper-Nickel, 38.61 mm. **Obv:** Shield with Neptune holding trident, mermaid reclining at his side, RAINBOW'S / END below **Obv. Legend:** REPUBLIC OF PALAU **Rev:** Red racing car 3/4 left **Rev. Legend:** FERRARI - 60 YEARS ANNIVERSARY

Date	Mintage	F	VF	XF	Unc	BU
ND(2007) Proof	5,000	Value: 35.00				

KM# 120 DOLLAR
0.5000 g., 0.9990 Gold 0.0161 oz. AGW, 11.0 mm. **Obv:** Shield with Neptune holding trident, mermaid reclining at his side, RAINBOW'S / END below **Obv. Legend:** REPUBLIC OF PALAU **Shape:** 4-leaf clover **Note:** Uniface

Date	Mintage	F	VF	XF	Unc	BU
2007 Proof	25,000	Value: 50.00				

KM# 258 DOLLAR
25.0000 g., 0.9990 Silver 0.8029 oz. ASW **Subject:** Pacific Wildlife **Rev:** Seahorse - prism

Date	Mintage	F	VF	XF	Unc	BU
2007 Proof	—	Value: 50.00				

KM# 154 DOLLAR
26.8000 g., Copper-Nickel silver plated, 38.61 mm. **Subject:** 150th Anniversary of the Appriations **Obv:** Shield **Rev:** Statue of Our Lady of Lourdes and holy water vile

Date	Mintage	F	VF	XF	Unc	BU
2008 Proof	—	Value: 22.50				

KM# 155 DOLLAR
26.8000 g., Copper-Nickel, 37.2 mm. **Subject:** Dealer Button **Obv:** Shield **Rev:** Vegas Chips and cards, Ace of Clubs corner cut

Date	Mintage	F	VF	XF	Unc	BU
2008	—	—	—	—	—	25.00

KM# 156 DOLLAR
26.8000 g., Copper-Nickel, 37.2 mm. **Subject:** Dealer Buttons **Obv:** Shield **Rev:** Vegas Chips and cards, Ace of Diamonds corner cut

Date	Mintage	F	VF	XF	Unc	BU
2008	—	—	—	—	—	25.00

KM# 157 DOLLAR
26.8000 g., Copper-Nickel, 37.2 mm. **Subject:** Dear Buttons **Obv:** Shield **Rev:** Vegas Chips and cards, Ace of Heats corner cut

Date	Mintage	F	VF	XF	Unc	BU
2008	—	—	—	—	—	25.00

KM# 158 DOLLAR
26.8000 g., Copper-Nickel, 37.2 mm. **Obv:** Shield **Rev:** Vegas chips and cards, Ace of Spades corner cut

Date	Mintage	F	VF	XF	Unc	BU
2008	—	—	—	—	—	25.00

KM# 159 DOLLAR
1.2400 g., 0.9990 Gold 0.0398 oz. AGW, 13.9 mm. **Subject:** St. Francis of Assisi **Obv:** Shield **Rev:** Bust facing

Date	Mintage	F	VF	XF	Unc	BU
2008 Proof	—	Value: 75.00				

KM# 160 DOLLAR
1.2440 g., 0.9900 Gold 0.0396 oz. AGW, 13.9 mm. **Subject:** St, Francis of Assisi **Obv:** Shield **Rev:** Multicolor bust facing

Date	Mintage	F	VF	XF	Unc	BU
2008	—	—	—	—	—	80.00

KM# 161 DOLLAR
0.5000 g., 0.9990 Gold 0.0161 oz. AGW, 11 mm. **Obv:** Shield **Rev:** Multicolor poppy **Shape:** Irregular

Date	Mintage	F	VF	XF	Unc	BU
2008	—	—	—	—	—	60.00

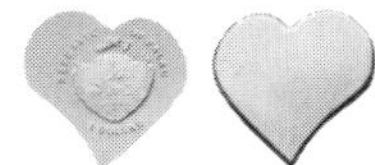

KM# 162 DOLLAR
0.5000 g., 0.9990 Gold 0.0161 oz. AGW, 11 mm. **Subject:** Everlasting love **Obv:** Shield **Rev:** Heart **Shape:** Heart

Date	Mintage	F	VF	XF	Unc	BU
2008	—	—	—	—	—	60.00

KM# 163 DOLLAR
1.2440 g., 0.9990 Gold 0.0400 oz. AGW **Subject:** Marine Life-Protection **Obv:** Neptune and mermaid seated on rock **Rev:** Grey reef shark

Date	Mintage	F	VF	XF	Unc	BU
2008 Proof	1,500	Value: 85.00				

KM# 164 DOLLAR
26.8000 g., Copper-Nickel, 37.2 mm. **Subject:** Endangered Wildlife **Obv:** Shield **Rev:** Multicolor Tiger shark

Date	Mintage	F	VF	XF	Unc	BU
2008	—	—	—	—	—	35.00

KM# 165 DOLLAR
26.8000 g., Copper-Nickel, 37.2 mm. **Subject:** Endangered Wildlife **Obv:** Shield **Rev:** Multicolor Hawksbill turtle

Date	Mintage	F	VF	XF	Unc	BU
2008	—	—	—	—	—	35.00

KM# 166 DOLLAR
26.8000 g., Copper-Nickel, 37.2 mm. **Subject:** Endangered Wildlife **Obv:** Shield **Rev:** Multicolored Regal angelfish swimming right

Date	Mintage	F	VF	XF	Unc	BU
2008 Proof	—	Value: 30.00				

KM# 167 DOLLAR

26.8000 g., Copper-Nickel, 37.2 mm. **Subject:** Endangered Wildlife **Obv:** Shield **Rev:** Multicolor Spiny lobster

Date	Mintage	F	VF	XF	Unc	BU
2008 Proof	—	Value: 30.00				

KM# 259 DOLLAR

0.5000 g., 0.9990 Gold 0.0161 oz. AGW, 11 mm. **Subject:** Sitting bull **Obv:** Shield **Rev:** Portrait facing

Date	Mintage	F	VF	XF	Unc	BU
2008 Proof	—	Value: 60.00				

KM# 177 DOLLAR

1.2440 g., 0.9990 Gold 0.0400 oz. AGW, 13.9 mm. **Obv:** Shield **Rev:** Madonna and child

Date	Mintage	F	VF	XF	Unc	BU
ND(2009) Proof	25,000	Value: 80.00				

KM# 178 DOLLAR

1.2440 g., 0.9990 Gold 0.0400 oz. AGW, 13.9 mm. **Subject:** FIAA World Cup - South Africa **Obv:** Shield **Rev:** Soccer ball, South African flag and Water Buffalo

Date	Mintage	F	VF	XF	Unc	BU
2009 Proof	—	Value: 75.00				

KM# 222 DOLLAR

27.0000 g., Silver Plated Copper, 38.6 mm. **Rev:** Lighthouse of Alexandria, multicolor

Date	Mintage	F	VF	XF	Unc	BU
2009 Prooflike	5,000	—	—	—	—	20.00

KM# 223 DOLLAR

27.0000 g., Silver Plated Copper, 38.6 mm. **Rev:** Zeus statue, multicolor

Date	Mintage	F	VF	XF	Unc	BU
2009 Prooflike	—	—	—	—	—	20.00

KM# 224 DOLLAR

27.0000 g., Silver Plated Copper, 38.6 mm. **Rev:** Hanging Garden of Babylon, multicolor

Date	Mintage	F	VF	XF	Unc	BU
2009 Prooflike	5,000	—	—	—	—	20.00

KM# 225 DOLLAR

27.0000 g., Silver Plated Copper, 38.6 mm. **Rev:** Mausoleum, multicolor

Date	Mintage	F	VF	XF	Unc	BU
2009 Prooflike	5,000	—	—	—	—	20.00

KM# 226 DOLLAR

27.0000 g., Silver Plated Copper, 38.6 mm. **Rev:** Pyramids, multicolor

Date	Mintage	F	VF	XF	Unc	BU
2009 Prooflike	5,000	—	—	—	—	20.00

KM# 227 DOLLAR

27.0000 g., Silver Plated Copper, 38.6 mm. **Rev:** Artemis temple, multicolor

Date	Mintage	F	VF	XF	Unc	BU
2009 Prooflike	5,000	—	—	—	—	20.00

KM# 228 DOLLAR

27.0000 g., Silver Plated Copper, 38.6 mm. **Rev:** Colosus of Rhodes, multicolor

Date	Mintage	F	VF	XF	Unc	BU
2009 Prooflike	5,000	—	—	—	—	20.00

KM# 229 DOLLAR

27.0000 g., Silver Plated Copper, 38.6 mm. **Subject:** Ducati - Casey Stoner **Rev:** Motorcycle left, multicolor

Date	Mintage	F	VF	XF	Unc	BU
2009 Prooflike	2,008	—	—	—	—	25.00

KM# 230 DOLLAR

27.0000 g., Silver Plated Copper, 38.6 mm. **Subject:** Ducati - Troy Bayliss **Rev:** Motorcycle, multicolor

Date	Mintage	F	VF	XF	Unc	BU
2009 Prooflike	2,008	—	—	—	—	25.00

KM# 233 DOLLAR

27.0000 g., Copper-Nickel, 38.6 mm. **Subject:** Marine Life Protection **Obv:** Neptune standing, two mermaids below **Rev:** Lionfish, multicolor

Date	Mintage	F	VF	XF	Unc	BU
2009 Prooflike	5,000	—	—	—	—	25.00

KM# 234 DOLLAR

1.0000 g., 0.9990 Gold 0.0321 oz. AGW, 13.9 mm. **Subject:** Marine Life Protection **Rev:** Lionfish

Date	Mintage	F	VF	XF	Unc	BU
2009 Proof	25,000	Value: 65.00				

KM# 235 DOLLAR

0.5000 g., 0.9990 Gold 0.0161 oz. AGW, 11.8 mm. **Subject:** Augustus Aureus **Rev:** Head laureate right

Date	Mintage	F	VF	XF	Unc	BU
MMIX (2009)	15,000	—	—	—	—	40.00

KM# 236 DOLLAR

0.5000 g., 0.9990 Gold 0.0161 oz. AGW, 11.8 mm. **Subject:** Germanicus Dupondius **Rev:** General in quadriga right

Date	Mintage	F	VF	XF	Unc	BU
MMIX (2009)	15,000	—	—	—	—	40.00

KM# 237 DOLLAR

0.5000 g., 0.9990 Gold 0.0161 oz. AGW, 11.8 mm. **Subject:** Julius Caesar Denarius **Rev:** Head laureate right

Date	Mintage	F	VF	XF	Unc	BU
MMIX (2009)	15,000	—	—	—	—	40.00

KM# 238 DOLLAR

0.5000 g., 0.9990 Gold 0.0161 oz. AGW, 11.8 mm. **Subject:** Brutus Denarius **Rev:** Cap flanked by two daggers

Date	Mintage	F	VF	XF	Unc	BU
MMIX (2009)	15,000	—	—	—	—	40.00

KM# 239 DOLLAR

1.2400 g., 0.9990 Gold 0.0398 oz. AGW, 13.9 mm. **Subject:** Salesian Order, 150th Anniversary **Rev:** Don Bosco facing

Date	Mintage	F	VF	XF	Unc	BU
2009 Proof	15,000	Value: 65.00				

KM# 240 DOLLAR

0.5000 g., 0.9990 Gold 0.0161 oz. AGW, 11 mm. **Rev:** Pebbled **Shape:** 5-pointed star

Date	Mintage	F	VF	XF	Unc	BU
ND (2009)	25,000	—	—	—	—	40.00

KM# 241 DOLLAR

1.2400 g., 0.9990 Gold 0.0398 oz. AGW, 13.9 mm. **Subject:** Fontana de Trevi **Rev:** Fountain and building facade

Date	Mintage	F	VF	XF	Unc	BU
2009 Proof	15,000	—	—	—	—	65.00

KM# 244 DOLLAR

0.5000 g., 0.9990 Gold 0.0161 oz. AGW, 11.8 mm. **Subject:** First didrachm **Rev:** Twins sucking at she-wolf

Date	Mintage	F	VF	XF	Unc	BU
MMIX (2009)	15,000	—	—	—	—	40.00

KM# 245 DOLLAR

0.5000 g., 0.9990 Gold 0.0161 oz. AGW, 11.8 mm. **Subject:** Claudius aureus **Rev:** Head laureate right

Date	Mintage	F	VF	XF	Unc	BU
MMIX (2009)	15,000	—	—	—	—	40.00

KM# 246 DOLLAR

0.5000 g., 0.9990 Gold 0.0161 oz. AGW, 11.8 mm. **Subject:** Tiberius aureus **Rev:** Head laureate right

Date	Mintage	F	VF	XF	Unc	BU
MMIX (2009)	15,000	—	—	—	—	40.00

KM# 247 DOLLAR

0.5000 g., 0.9990 Gold 0.0161 oz. AGW, 11.8 mm. **Subject:** Caligula aureus **Rev:** Head laureate right

Date	Mintage	F	VF	XF	Unc	BU
MMIX (2009)	15,000	—	—	—	—	40.00

KM# 260 DOLLAR

Silver Plated Copper **Subject:** 2000th Anniversary Teutobury Forest Battle **Obv:** Shield **Rev:** Warrior in forest battle, multicolor

Date	Mintage	F	VF	XF	Unc	BU
MMIX (2009) Proof	2,500	Value: 30.00				

KM# 261 DOLLAR

25.0000 g., 0.9990 Silver 0.8029 oz. ASW, 38.6 mm. **Subject:** Pacific Wildlife **Obv:** Arms **Rev:** Barn Swallow - prism

Date	Mintage	F	VF	XF	Unc	BU
2009 Proof	2,500	Value: 50.00				

KM# 262 DOLLAR

25.0000 g., 0.9990 Silver 0.8029 oz. ASW, 38.6 mm. **Subject:** Pacific Wildlife **Obv:** Arms **Rev:** Gecko on rock - prism

Date	Mintage	F	VF	XF	Unc	BU
2009 Proof	2,500	Value: 50.00				

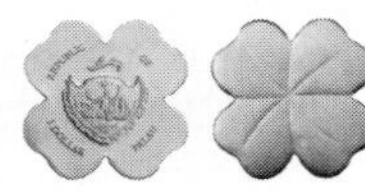

KM# 263 DOLLAR

0.5000 g., 0.9990 Gold 0.0161 oz. AGW, 11 mm. **Rev:** 4-leaf clover, green

Date	Mintage	F	VF	XF	Unc	BU
2009	—	—	—	—	—	65.00

KM# 269 DOLLAR

Copper-Nickel, 37.2 mm. **Subject:** Protect Wildlife - Angelfish **Rev:** Angelfish - Prisim

Date	Mintage	F	VF	XF	Unc	BU
2009	—	—	—	—	—	35.00

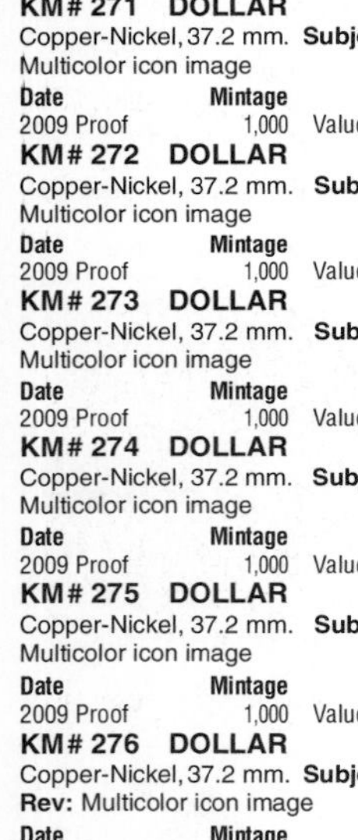

KM# 270 DOLLAR

Copper-Nickel, 37.2 mm. **Subject:** Apostles - Peter **Rev:** Multicolor icon image

Date	Mintage	F	VF	XF	Unc	BU
2009 Proof	1,000	Value: 25.00				

KM# 271 DOLLAR

Copper-Nickel, 37.2 mm. **Subject:** Apostles - James Minor **Rev:** Multicolor icon image

Date	Mintage	F	VF	XF	Unc	BU
2009 Proof	1,000	Value: 25.00				

KM# 272 DOLLAR

Copper-Nickel, 37.2 mm. **Subject:** Apostles - John **Rev:** Multicolor icon image

Date	Mintage	F	VF	XF	Unc	BU
2009 Proof	1,000	Value: 25.00				

KM# 273 DOLLAR

Copper-Nickel, 37.2 mm. **Subject:** Apostle - Simon **Rev:** Multicolor icon image

Date	Mintage	F	VF	XF	Unc	BU
2009 Proof	1,000	Value: 25.00				

KM# 274 DOLLAR

Copper-Nickel, 37.2 mm. **Subject:** Apostles - Matthaeus **Rev:** Multicolor icon image

Date	Mintage	F	VF	XF	Unc	BU
2009 Proof	1,000	Value: 25.00				

KM# 275 DOLLAR

Copper-Nickel, 37.2 mm. **Subject:** Apostles - Thomas **Rev:** Multicolor icon image

Date	Mintage	F	VF	XF	Unc	BU
2009 Proof	1,000	Value: 25.00				

KM# 276 DOLLAR

Copper-Nickel, 37.2 mm. **Subject:** Apostles - Judas Thaddaeus **Rev:** Multicolor icon image

Date	Mintage	F	VF	XF	Unc	BU
2009 Proof	1,000	Value: 25.00				

KM# 277 DOLLAR

Copper-Nickel, 37.2 mm. **Subject:** Apostles - Bartholomew **Rev:** Multicolor icon image

Date	Mintage	F	VF	XF	Unc	BU
2009 Proof	1,000	Value: 25.00				

KM# 278 DOLLAR

Copper-Nickel, 37.2 mm. **Subject:** Apostles - Philip **Rev:** Multicolor icon image

Date	Mintage	F	VF	XF	Unc	BU
2009 Proof	1,000	Value: 25.00				

KM# 279 DOLLAR

Copper-Nickel, 37.2 mm. **Subject:** Apostles - John Major **Rev:** Multicolor icon image

Date	Mintage	F	VF	XF	Unc	BU
2009 Proof	1,000	Value: 25.00				

KM# 280 DOLLAR

Copper-Nickel **Subject:** Apostles - Andrew **Rev:** Multicolor icon image **Shape:** 37.2

Date	Mintage	F	VF	XF	Unc	BU
2009 Proof	1,000	Value: 25.00				

KM# 281 DOLLAR

Copper-Nickel, 37.2 mm. **Subject:** Apostles - Judas Iscariot **Rev:** Multicolor icon image

Date	Mintage	F	VF	XF	Unc	BU
2009 Proof	1,000	Value: 25.00				

KM# 282 DOLLAR

26.8000 g., Copper-Nickel, 37.2 mm. **Subject:** Endangered Wildlife - Orange Lined Tigerfish **Rev:** Multicolor fish left

Date	Mintage	F	VF	XF	Unc	BU
2009 Proof	—	Value: 37.50				

KM# 283 DOLLAR

26.8000 g., Copper-Nickel, 37.2 mm. **Subject:** Endangered Wildlife - Blue Grilled Angelfish **Rev:** Multicolor fish

Date	Mintage	F	VF	XF	Unc	BU
2009 Proof	—	Value: 37.50				

KM# 284 DOLLAR

26.8000 g., Copper-Nickel, 37.2 mm. **Subject:** Endangered Wildlife - Green Turtle **Rev:** Multicolor turtle

Date	Mintage	F	VF	XF	Unc	BU
2009 Proof	—	Value: 37.50				

KM# 285 DOLLAR

26.8000 g., Copper-Nickel, 37.2 mm. **Subject:** Endangered Wildlife - Sailfin Tang fish **Rev:** Multicolor fish right

Date	Mintage	F	VF	XF	Unc	BU
2009 Proof	—	Value: 37.50				

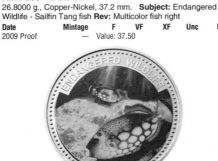

KM# 286 DOLLAR

26.8000 g., Copper-Nickel, 37.2 mm. **Subject:** Endangered Wildlife - Clown Trigger fish **Rev:** Multicolor fish left

Date	Mintage	F	VF	XF	Unc	BU
2009 Proof	—	Value: 37.50				

KM# 266 DOLLAR

25.0000 g., 0.9250 Silver 0.7435 oz. ASW **Subject:** Battle of Grimwald **Rev:** Vyautas and Jagiello busts **Shape:** Square

Date	Mintage	F	VF	XF	Unc	BU
2010 Proof	—	Value: 50.00				

KM# 267 DOLLAR

25.0000 g., 0.9990 Silver 0.8029 oz. ASW **Subject:** Battle of Grimwald **Rev:** Warrior on horseback, multicolor **Shape:** Square

Date	Mintage	F	VF	XF	Unc	BU
2010 Proof	2,500	Value: 55.00				

KM# 268 DOLLAR

25.0000 g., 0.9990 Silver 0.8029 oz. ASW **Subject:** Battle of Grimwald **Rev:** Knight kneeling, multicolor **Shape:** Square

Date	Mintage	F	VF	XF	Unc	BU
2010 Proof	2,500	Value: 55.00				

KM# 130 2 DOLLARS

10.0000 g., 0.9990 Silver 0.3212 oz. ASW, 30.0 mm. **Obv:** Shield with Neptune holding trident, mermaid reclining at his side **Obv. Legend:** REPUBLIC OF PALAU **Rev:** Red racing car 3/4 right **Rev. Legend:** FERRARI - 60 YEARS ANNIVERSARY

Date	Mintage	F	VF	XF	Unc	BU
ND(2007) Proof	2,500	Value: 55.00				

KM# 131 2 DOLLARS

10.0000 g., 0.9990 Silver 0.3212 oz. ASW, 30.0 mm. **Obv:** Shield with Neptune holding trident, mermaid reclining at his side **Obv. Legend:** REPUBLIC OF PALAU **Rev:** Red racing car 3/4 right **Rev. Legend:** FERRARI - 60 YEARS ANNIVERSARY

Date	Mintage	F	VF	XF	Unc	BU
ND(2007) Proof	2,500	Value: 55.00				

KM# 132 2 DOLLARS

10.0000 g., 0.9990 Silver 0.3212 oz. ASW, 30.00 mm. **Obv:** Shield with Neptune holding trident, mermaid reclining at his side **Obv. Legend:** REPUBLIC OF PALAU **Rev:** Red racing car front view **Rev. Legend:** FERRARI - 60 YEARS ANNIVERSARY

Date	Mintage	F	VF	XF	Unc	BU
ND(2007) Proof	2,500	Value: 55.00				

KM# 133 2 DOLLARS

10.0000 g., 0.9990 Silver 0.3212 oz. ASW, 30.0 mm. **Obv:** Shield with Neptune holding trident, mermaid reclining at his side **Obv. Legend:** REPUBLIC OF PALAU **Rev:** Looking down on red racing car approaching in turn **Rev. Legend:** FERRARI - 60 YEARS ANNIVERSARY

Date	Mintage	F	VF	XF	Unc	BU
ND(2007) Proof	2,500	Value: 55.00				

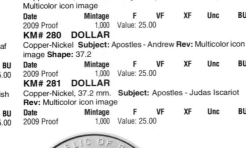

KM# 134 2 DOLLARS
10.0000 g., 0.9990 Silver 0.3212 oz. ASW, 30.0 mm. **Obv:** Shield with Neptune holding trident, reclining mermaid at his side **Obv. Legend:** REPUBLIC OF PALAU **Rev:** Front view of red racing car **Rev. Legend:** FERRARI - 60 YEARS ANNIVERSARY

Date	Mintage	F	VF	XF	Unc	BU
ND(2007) Proof	2,500	Value: 55.00				

KM# 135 2 DOLLARS
10.0000 g., 0.9990 Silver 0.3212 oz. ASW, 30.0 mm. **Obv:** Shield with Neptune holding trident, mermaid reclining at his side **Obv. Legend:** REPUBLIC OF PALAU **Rev:** Red racing car approaching 3/4 right **Rev. Legend:** FERRARI - 60 YEARS ANNIVERSARY

Date	Mintage	F	VF	XF	Unc	BU
ND(2007) Proof	2,500	Value: 100				

KM# 53 5 DOLLARS
25.0000 g., 0.9000 Silver 0.7234 oz. ASW, 37.2 mm. **Series:** Marine Life Protection **Obv:** Neptune **Rev:** Multicolor jellyfish **Edge:** Reeded

Date	Mintage	F	VF	XF	Unc	BU
2001 Proof	—	Value: 75.00				

KM# 75 5 DOLLARS
25.0000 g., 0.9000 Silver 0.7234 oz. ASW, 37.2 mm. **Subject:** Marine Life Protection **Obv:** Neptune behind Polynesian ship and value **Rev:** Moorish-Idol fish **Edge:** Reeded

Date	Mintage	F	VF	XF	Unc	BU
2001 Proof	—	Value: 75.00				

KM# 76 5 DOLLARS
Silver, 37.2 mm. **Subject:** Marine Life Protection **Obv:** Neptune riding seahorse and value **Rev:** Fish **Edge:** Reeded

Date	Mintage	F	VF	XF	Unc	BU
2001 Proof	—	Value: 75.00				

KM# 115 5 DOLLARS
25.0000 g., 0.9000 Silver 0.7234 oz. ASW, 37.2 mm. **Subject:** Marine Life Protection **Obv:** Neptune waist deep in water above value with mermaid to the left and behind **Rev:** Multicolor iridescent fish scene **Edge:** Reeded

Date	Mintage	F	VF	XF	Unc	BU
2001 Proof	—	Value: 70.00				

KM# 77 5 DOLLARS
25.0000 g., 0.9000 Silver 0.7234 oz. ASW, 37.2 mm. **Subject:** Marine Life Protection **Obv:** Neptune in shell boat **Rev:** Blue Tang Fish **Edge:** Reeded

Date	Mintage	F	VF	XF	Unc	BU
2002 Proof	—	Value: 75.00				

KM# 78 5 DOLLARS
25.0000 g., 0.9000 Silver 0.7234 oz. ASW, 37.2 mm. **Subject:** Marine Life Protection **Obv:** Neptune in sea chariot **Rev:** Multicolor whales **Edge:** Reeded

Date	Mintage	F	VF	XF	Unc	BU
2002 Proof	—	Value: 75.00				

KM# 79 5 DOLLARS
25.0000 g., 0.9000 Silver 0.7234 oz. ASW, 37.2 mm. **Subject:** Marine Life Protection **Obv:** Zeus and value **Rev:** Multicolor puffer fish **Edge:** Reeded

Date	Mintage	F	VF	XF	Unc	BU
2002 Proof	—	Value: 75.00				

KM# 80 5 DOLLARS
25.0000 g., 0.9000 Silver 0.7234 oz. ASW, 37.2 mm. **Subject:** Marine Life Protection **Obv:** Neptune standing behind Polynesian ship **Rev:** Multicolor Jellyfish **Edge:** Reeded

Date	Mintage	F	VF	XF	Unc	BU
2002 Proof	—	Value: 70.00				

KM# 102 5 DOLLARS
25.0000 g., 0.9000 Silver 0.7234 oz. ASW, 32 mm. **Subject:** Marine Life Protection **Obv:** Neptune in sea chariot with two merhorses **Rev:** Two multicolor reflective fish

Date	Mintage	F	VF	XF	Unc	BU
2002 Proof	—	Value: 60.00				

KM# 103 5 DOLLARS
25.0000 g., 0.9000 Silver 0.7234 oz. ASW, 32 mm. **Subject:** Marine Life Protection **Obv:** Neptune standing in waves **Rev:** Multicolor starfish

Date	Mintage	F	VF	XF	Unc	BU
2003 Proof	—	Value: 60.00				

KM# 104 5 DOLLARS
25.0000 g., 0.9000 Silver 0.7234 oz. ASW, 32 mm. **Subject:** Marine Life Protection **Obv:** Neptune standing in sea chariot **Rev:** Two multicolor reflective fish

Date	Mintage	F	VF	XF	Unc	BU
2003 Proof	—	Value: 60.00				

KM# 105 5 DOLLARS
25.0000 g., 0.9000 Silver 0.7234 oz. ASW, 32 mm. **Subject:** Marine Life Protection **Rev:** Multicolor Orca

Date	Mintage	F	VF	XF	Unc	BU
2003 Proof	—	Value: 60.00				

KM# 106 5 DOLLARS
25.0000 g., 0.9000 Silver 0.7234 oz. ASW, 32 mm. **Subject:** Marine Life Protection **Obv:** Neptune in sea chariot **Rev:** Multicolor Napoleon Fish

Date	Mintage	F	VF	XF	Unc	BU
2003 Proof	—	Value: 60.00				

KM# 107 5 DOLLARS
25.0000 g., 0.9000 Silver 0.7234 oz. ASW, 32 mm. **Subject:** Marine Life Protection **Obv:** Neptune seated behind mermaid **Rev:** Multicolor school of sweetlips fish

Date	Mintage	F	VF	XF	Unc	BU
2004 Proof	—	Value: 60.00				

KM# 108 5 DOLLARS
25.0000 g., 0.9000 Silver 0.7234 oz. ASW, 32 mm. **Subject:** Marine Life Protection **Obv:** Standing Neptune and ship **Rev:** Multicolor Porcupine fish

Date	Mintage	F	VF	XF	Unc	BU
2004 Proof	—	Value: 75.00				

KM# 109 5 DOLLARS
25.0000 g., 0.9000 Silver 0.7234 oz. ASW, 32 mm. **Subject:** Marine Life Protection **Obv:** Neptune in sea chariot **Rev:** Multicolor Loggerhead turtle

Date	Mintage	F	VF	XF	Unc	BU
2004 Proof	—	Value: 75.00				

KM# 110 5 DOLLARS
25.0000 g., 0.9000 Silver 0.7234 oz. ASW, 32 mm. **Subject:** Marine Life Protection **Obv:** Neptune and merhorse **Rev:** Multicolor dolphin head

Date	Mintage	F	VF	XF	Unc	BU
2004 Proof	—	Value: 75.00				

KM# 81 5 DOLLARS
25.0000 g., 0.9000 Silver 0.7234 oz. ASW, 37.2 mm. **Subject:** Marine Life Protection **Obv:** Neptune with treasure chest **Rev:** Clownfish **Edge:** Reeded

Date	Mintage	F	VF	XF	Unc	BU
2004 Proof	—	Value: 75.00				

KM# 111 5 DOLLARS
25.0000 g., 0.9000 Silver 0.7234 oz. ASW, 32 mm. **Subject:** Marine Life Protection **Obv:** Neptune flanked by mermaids **Rev:** Multicolor sea horse

Date	Mintage	F	VF	XF	Unc	BU
2005 Proof	—	Value: 75.00				

KM# 113 5 DOLLARS
25.0000 g., 0.9000 Silver 0.7234 oz. ASW, 32 mm. **Subject:** Marine Life Protection **Obv:** Neptune flanked by mermaids **Rev:** Multicolor fish with ring-like stripes **Edge:** Reeded

Date	Mintage	F	VF	XF	Unc	BU
2005 Proof	—	Value: 75.00				

KM# 114 5 DOLLARS
25.0000 g., 0.9000 Silver 0.7234 oz. ASW, 32 mm. **Subject:** Marine Life Protection **Obv:** Neptune in shell boat talking to a dolphin **Rev:** Multicolor reef fish scene **Edge:** Reeded

Date	Mintage	F	VF	XF	Unc	BU
2006 Proof	—	Value: 75.00				

KM# 143 5 DOLLARS
25.0000 g., 0.9250 Silver with meteorite insert. 0.7435 oz. ASW **Subject:** Nantan Meteorite fall, May 1516 **Obv:** Shield **Rev:** Farmer and oxen plowing field, meteorite insert

Date	Mintage	F	VF	XF	Unc	BU
2006 Proof	2,500	Value: 100				

KM# 185 5 DOLLARS
24.8500 g., 0.9990 Silver 0.7981 oz. ASW, 38.6 mm. **Rev:** Black pearl oyster

Date	Mintage	F	VF	XF	Unc	BU
2006 Proof	2,500	Value: 300				

KM# 186 5 DOLLARS
25.0000 g., 0.9990 Silver 0.8029 oz. ASW, 38.61 mm. **Subject:** Pacific Wildlife **Rev:** Rainbow Lorikeet head left

Date	Mintage	F	VF	XF	Unc	BU
2006 Proof	5,000	Value: 55.00				

KM# 187 5 DOLLARS
25.0000 g., 0.9990 Silver 0.8029 oz. ASW, 38.61 mm. **Subject:** Pacific Wildlife **Rev:** Eclectus Parrot head right

Date	Mintage	F	VF	XF	Unc	BU
2006 Proof	5,000	Value: 55.00				

KM# 188 5 DOLLARS
25.0000 g., 0.9990 Silver 0.8029 oz. ASW, 38.61 mm. **Subject:** Pacific Wildlife **Rev:** Fruit dove head right

Date	Mintage	F	VF	XF	Unc	BU
2006 Proof	5,000	Value: 55.00				

KM# 189 5 DOLLARS
31.1050 g., 0.9990 Silver 0.9990 oz. ASW, 38.61 mm. **Subject:** One ounce of luck **Rev:** Four-leaf clover

Date	Mintage	F	VF	XF	Unc	BU
2006 Proof	5,000	Value: 65.00				

KM# 190 5 DOLLARS
25.0000 g., 0.9250 Silver 0.7435 oz. ASW, 38.61 mm. **Subject:** Dream Island **Rev:** Pacific island scene - beach, boat and sunset

Date	Mintage	F	VF	XF	Unc	BU
2006 Proof	5,000	Value: 50.00				

KM# 151 5 DOLLARS
25.0000 g., 0.9250 Silver 0.7435 oz. ASW, 38.6 mm. **Subject:** Pacific Wildlife **Obv:** Shield **Rev:** Multicolor nautilus shell

Date	Mintage	F	VF	XF	Unc	BU
2007 Proof	—	Value: 70.00				

KM# 152 5 DOLLARS
25.0000 g., 0.9250 Silver 0.7435 oz. ASW **Subject:** Pacific Wildlife **Obv:** Shield **Rev:** Multicolor starfish

Date	Mintage	F	VF	XF	Unc	BU
2007 Proof	—	Value: 70.00				

KM# 153 5 DOLLARS
25.0000 g., 0.9250 Silver 0.7435 oz. ASW **Subject:** Good heavens! **Obv:** Multicolor devil and angel child **Shape:** Heart

Date	Mintage	F	VF	XF	Unc	BU
2007 Proof	2,500	Value: 65.00				

KM# 119 5 DOLLARS
25.0000 g., 0.9000 Silver 0.7234 oz. ASW, 38.61 mm. **Series:** Marine Life Protection **Obv:** Neptune reclining with trident, mermaid at his side **Obv. Legend:** REPUBLIC OF PALAU **Rev:** Multicolor Doctor Fish

Date	Mintage	F	VF	XF	Unc	BU
2007 Proof	1,500	Value: 120				

KM# 122 5 DOLLARS
25.0000 g., 0.5000 Silver 0.4019 oz. ASW, 38.61 mm. **Obv:** Shield with Neptune holding trident, mermaid reclining at his side, RAINBOW'S / End below **Obv. Legend:** REPUBLIC OF PALAU **Rev:** Red racing car 3/4 right **Rev. Legend:** FERRARI - 60 YEARS ANNIVERSARY

Date	Mintage	F	VF	XF	Unc	BU
ND(2007) Proof	2,500	Value: 75.00				

KM# 136 5 DOLLARS
25.0000 g., 0.9250 Silver 0.7435 oz. ASW, 38.61 mm. **Series:** Pacific Wildlife **Obv:** National arms **Obv. Legend:** REPUBLIC OF PALAU **Rev:** Saltwater Crocodile with green crystal eye

Date	Mintage	F	VF	XF	Unc	BU
2007 Proof	2,500	Value: 75.00				

KM# 138 5 DOLLARS
24.7000 g., Silver, 38.6 mm. **Series:** Marine Life Protection **Obv:** National arms with Neptune and mermaid **Rev:** Pearl in oyster shell - multicolor **Edge:** Reeded

Date	Mintage	F	VF	XF	Unc	BU
2007 Proof	2,500	Value: 185				

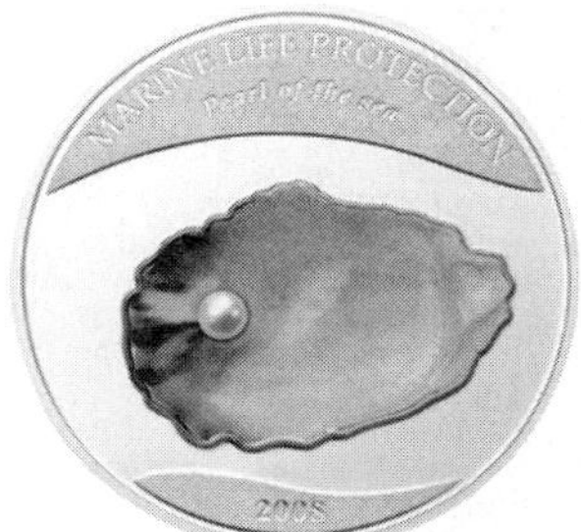

KM# 137 5 DOLLARS
24.7000 g., 0.9250 Silver 0.7345 oz. ASW, 38.5 mm. **Obv:** Outrigger canoe above shield **Obv. Legend:** REPUBLIC OF PALAU **Rev:** Pearl in colorized shell **Rev. Legend:** MARINE LIFE PROTECTION / Pearl of the sea **Edge:** Reeded

Date	Mintage	F	VF	XF	Unc	BU
2008 Proof	2,500	Value: 125				

KM# 168 5 DOLLARS
25.0000 g., 0.9250 Silver 0.7435 oz. ASW, 30x45 mm. **Obv:** Shield **Rev:** Don Quiote in armor **Shape:** Vertical oval

Date	Mintage	F	VF	XF	Unc	BU
2008 Proof	—	Value: 70.00				

KM# 169 5 DOLLARS
25.0000 g., 0.9250 Silver 0.7435 oz. ASW **Subject:** Pacific Wildlife **Obv:** Shield **Rev:** Multicolor hologram, blue butterfly (Papilio Pericles) **Shape:** 37.2

Date	Mintage	F	VF	XF	Unc	BU
2008 Proof	2,500	Value: 60.00				

KM# 170 5 DOLLARS
25.0000 g., 0.9250 Silver 0.7435 oz. ASW, 37.2 mm. **Subject:** Pacific Wildlife **Obv:** Shield **Rev:** Multicolor sulphur butterfly (Hebomoia Leucippe)

Date	Mintage	F	VF	XF	Unc	BU
2008 Proof	2,500	Value: 60.00				

KM# 171 5 DOLLARS
25.0000 g., 0.9250 Silver 0.7435 oz. ASW, 37.2 mm. **Subject:** Pacific Wildlife **Obv:** Shield **Rev:** Multicolor hologram, butterfly

Date	Mintage	F	VF	XF	Unc	BU
2008 Proof	2,500	Value: 60.00				

KM# 172 5 DOLLARS
25.0000 g., 0.9250 Silver 0.7435 oz. ASW, 38.6 mm. **Subject:** Telescope, 400th Anniversary **Obv:** Shield **Rev:** Hans Lippersheg, lens insert

Date	Mintage	F	VF	XF	Unc	BU
2008 Matte finish	1,608	—	—	—	—	70.00

KM# 173 5 DOLLARS
25.0000 g., 0.9250 Silver 0.7435 oz. ASW, 38.6 mm. **Subject:** Telescope, 400th Anniversary **Obv:** Shield **Rev:** The Hubble Telescope, lens insert

Date	Mintage	F	VF	XF	Unc	BU
2008 Matte finish	1,608	—	—	—	—	70.00

KM# 174 5 DOLLARS
Copper-Nickel, 38.6 mm. **Subject:** Endangered Wildlife **Obv:** Shield **Rev:** Multicolor yellow fish

Date	Mintage	F	VF	XF	Unc	BU
2008 Proof	—	—	—	—	—	25.00

KM# 175 5 DOLLARS
25.0000 g., 0.9250 Silver 0.7435 oz. ASW, 38.6 mm. **Subject:** Everything for you **Obv:** Shield **Rev:** Multicolor, outstretched hand, ribbon above **Shape:** Heart

Date	Mintage	F	VF	XF	Unc	BU
2008 Proof	2,500	Value: 100				

KM# 192 5 DOLLARS
25.0000 g., 0.9250 Silver partially gilt 0.7435 oz. ASW, 30x45 mm. **Subject:** Illusion Autum Leaves **Rev:** Gilt leaf **Shape:** Oval

Date	Mintage	F	VF	XF	Unc	BU
2008 Proof	2,500	Value: 75.00				

KM# 179 5 DOLLARS
25.0000 g., 0.9250 Silver 0.7435 oz. ASW, 38.61 mm. **Subject:** Scent of Paradise **Obv:** Shield **Rev:** Multicolor open coconut, scented

Date	Mintage	F	VF	XF	Unc	BU
2009	2,500	—	—	—	—	65.00

KM# 180 5 DOLLARS
25.0000 g., 0.9250 Silver 0.7435 oz. ASW, 38.5 mm. **Subject:** Jewels of the Sea **Obv:** Shield **Rev:** Multicolor blue oyster with inset pearl

Date	Mintage	F	VF	XF	Unc	BU
2009 Proof	2,500	Value: 150				

KM# 181 5 DOLLARS
25.0000 g., 0.9250 Silver 0.7435 oz. ASW, 38.5 mm. **Subject:** Louis Braile, 200th Anniversary of Birth **Obv:** Shield **Rev:** Portrait of Braile

Date	Mintage	F	VF	XF	Unc	BU
2009 Matte finish	2,500	—	—	—	—	45.00

KM# 182 5 DOLLARS

25.0000 g., 0.9250 Silver 0.7435 oz. ASW **Subject:** Missing you **Obv:** Shield **Rev:** Two angels, multicolor, crystal insert **Shape:** Heart

Date	Mintage	F	VF	XF	Unc	BU
2009 Proof	2,500	Value: 55.00				

KM# 196 5 DOLLARS

25.0000 g., 0.9250 Silver 0.7435 oz. ASW, 38.61 mm. **Subject:** Pacific Wildlife **Rev:** Angelfish

Date	Mintage	F	VF	XF	Unc	BU
2009 Proof	2,500	Value: 60.00				

KM# 197 5 DOLLARS

25.0000 g., 0.9250 Silver 0.7435 oz. ASW, 38.61 mm. **Subject:** Pacific Wildlife **Rev:** Barn Swallow

Date	Mintage	F	VF	XF	Unc	BU
2009 Proof	2,500	Value: 60.00				

KM# 198 5 DOLLARS

25.0000 g., 0.9250 Silver 0.7435 oz. ASW, 38.61 mm. **Subject:** Pacific Wildlife **Rev:** Gecko

Date	Mintage	F	VF	XF	Unc	BU
2009 Proof	2,500	Value: 60.00				

KM# 199 5 DOLLARS

25.0000 g., 0.9250 Silver 0.7435 oz. ASW, 38.61 mm. **Subject:** Exceptional Animals **Rev:** Bird of Paradise

Date	Mintage	F	VF	XF	Unc	BU
2009 Proof	2,500	Value: 55.00				

KM# 200 5 DOLLARS

25.0000 g., 0.9250 Silver 0.7435 oz. ASW, 38.61 mm. **Subject:** Exceptional Animals **Rev:** Peacock

Date	Mintage	F	VF	XF	Unc	BU
2009 Proof	2,500	Value: 55.00				

KM# 201 5 DOLLARS

25.0000 g., 0.9250 Silver 0.7435 oz. ASW, 38.61 mm. **Subject:** Marine Life Protection **Rev:** Lionfish

Date	Mintage	F	VF	XF	Unc	BU
2009 Proof	1,500	Value: 65.00				

KM# 202 5 DOLLARS

25.0000 g., 0.9990 Silver 0.8029 oz. ASW, 38.61 mm. **Subject:** Fall of the Berlin Wall **Rev:** Brandenberg Gate, half with and half without wall

Date	Mintage	F	VF	XF	Unc	BU
2009 Proof	2,009	Value: 110				

KM# 203 5 DOLLARS

20.0000 g., 0.9250 Silver 0.5948 oz. ASW, 38.61 mm. **Rev:** Sail training vessel Pamir

Date	Mintage	F	VF	XF	Unc	BU
2009 Proof	2,500	Value: 50.00				

KM# 204 5 DOLLARS

25.0000 g., 0.9250 Silver 0.7435 oz. ASW, 38.61 mm. **Subject:** Wonders of the Ancient World **Rev:** Lighthouse at Alexandria

Date	Mintage	F	VF	XF	Unc	BU
2009 Proof	2,500	Value: 65.00				

KM# 205 5 DOLLARS

25.0000 g., 0.9250 Silver 0.7435 oz. ASW **Subject:** Wonders of the Ancient World **Rev:** Statue of Zeus

Date	Mintage	F	VF	XF	Unc	BU
2009 Proof	2,500	Value: 65.00				

KM# 206 5 DOLLARS

25.0000 g., 0.9250 Silver 0.7435 oz. ASW, 38.61 mm. **Subject:** Wonders of the Ancient World **Rev:** Hanging Gardens of Babylon

Date	Mintage	F	VF	XF	Unc	BU
2009 Proof	2,500	Value: 65.00				

KM# 207 5 DOLLARS

25.0000 g., 0.9250 Silver 0.7435 oz. ASW, 38.61 mm. **Subject:** Wonders of the Ancient World **Rev:** Mausoleum of Halicarnassus

Date	Mintage	F	VF	XF	Unc	BU
2009 Proof	2,500	Value: 65.00				

KM# 208 5 DOLLARS

25.0000 g., 0.9250 Silver 0.7435 oz. ASW, 38.61 mm. **Subject:** Wonders of the Ancient World **Rev:** Pyramids of Giza

Date	Mintage	F	VF	XF	Unc	BU
2009 Proof	2,500	Value: 65.00				

KM# 209 5 DOLLARS

25.0000 g., 0.9250 Silver 0.7435 oz. ASW, 38.61 mm. **Subject:** Wonders of the Ancient World **Rev:** Temple of Artemis

Date	Mintage	F	VF	XF	Unc	BU
2009 Proof	2,500	Value: 65.00				

KM# 210 5 DOLLARS

25.0000 g., 0.9250 Silver 0.7435 oz. ASW, 38.61 mm. **Subject:** Wonders of the Ancient World **Rev:** Colossus of Rhodes

Date	Mintage	F	VF	XF	Unc	BU
2009 Proof	2,500	Value: 65.00				

KM# 211 5 DOLLARS

25.0000 g., 0.9250 Silver 0.7435 oz. ASW, 38.6 mm. **Subject:** Flora and Mountains of the Alps **Rev:** Zugspitze and blue flower

Date	Mintage	F	VF	XF	Unc	BU
2009 Proof	2,500	Value: 65.00				

KM# 212 5 DOLLARS

25.0000 g., 0.9250 Silver 0.7435 oz. ASW, 38.61 mm. **Subject:** Flora and Mountains of the Alps **Rev:** Grossglockner and white flower

Date	Mintage	F	VF	XF	Unc	BU
2009 Proof	2,500	Value: 65.00				

KM# 213 5 DOLLARS

25.0000 g., 0.9250 Silver 0.7435 oz. ASW, 38.61 mm. **Subject:** Flora and Mountains of the Alps **Rev:** Matterhorn and pink flower

Date	Mintage	F	VF	XF	Unc	BU
2009 Proof	2,500	Value: 65.00				

KM# 214 5 DOLLARS

25.0000 g., 0.9250 Silver 0.7435 oz. ASW, 38.61 mm. **Subject:** Flora and Mountains of the Alps **Rev:** Dachstein and purple flower

Date	Mintage	F	VF	XF	Unc	BU
2009 Proof	2,500	Value: 65.00				

KM# 215 5 DOLLARS

25.0000 g., 0.9250 Silver 0.7435 oz. ASW, 38.61 mm. **Subject:** Flora and Mountains of the Alps **Rev:** Mont Blanc and orange flower

Date	Mintage	F	VF	XF	Unc	BU
2009 Proof	2,500	Value: 65.00				

KM# 216 5 DOLLARS

25.0000 g., 0.9250 Silver 0.7435 oz. ASW, 38.61 mm. **Subject:** Flora and Mountains of the Alps **Rev:** Watzmann and purple flower

Date	Mintage	F	VF	XF	Unc	BU
2009 Proof	2,500	Value: 65.00				

KM# 217 5 DOLLARS

25.0000 g., 0.9250 Silver 0.7435 oz. ASW, 38.61 mm. **Subject:** Flora and Mountains of the Alps **Rev:** Oetscher and yellow flower

Date	Mintage	F	VF	XF	Unc	BU
2009 Proof	2,500	Value: 65.00				

KM# 218 5 DOLLARS

25.0000 g., 0.9250 Silver 0.7435 oz. ASW, 38.61 mm. **Subject:** Flora and Mountains of the Alps **Rev:** Piz Buin and pink flower

Date	Mintage	F	VF	XF	Unc	BU
2009 Proof	2,500	Value: 65.00				

KM# 242 5 DOLLARS

20.0000 g., 0.9250 Silver 0.5948 oz. ASW, 38.6 mm. **Subject:** Finnish icebreaker Tarmo **Rev:** Ship left in ice pack

Date	Mintage	F	VF	XF	Unc	BU
2009 Proof	2,500	Value: 40.00				

KM# 264 5 DOLLARS

25.0000 g., 0.9250 Silver 0.7435 oz. ASW, 38.61 mm. **Subject:** Treasures of the World - Emeralds **Rev:** Mule mine cart and emerald insert

Date	Mintage	F	VF	XF	Unc	BU
2009 Antique	2,000	Value: 85.00				

KM# 265 5 DOLLARS

25.0000 g., 0.9250 Silver 0.7435 oz. ASW, 38.6 mm. **Obv:** Arms **Rev:** Our Lady of the Gate of Dawn, partially gilt

Date	Mintage	F	VF	XF	Unc	BU
2009 Proof	1,000	Value: 75.00				

KM# 248 5 DOLLARS

25.0000 g., 0.9250 Silver 0.7435 oz. ASW, 38.6 mm. **Subject:** Marine Life Protection **Rev:** Blue freshwater pearl set within multicolor shell

Date	Mintage	F	VF	XF	Unc	BU
2010 Proof	2,500	Value: 75.00				

KM# 249 5 DOLLARS

25.0000 g., 0.9250 Silver 0.7435 oz. ASW, 38.6 mm. **Subject:** Scent of Paradise - Sea breeze fragrance **Rev:** Female surfboarder in multicolor wave

Date	Mintage	F	VF	XF	Unc	BU
2010	2,500	—	—	—	—	60.00

KM# 191 10 DOLLARS

62.2050 g., 0.9990 Silver 1.9979 oz. ASW, 50 mm. **Subject:** Tiffany Art **Rev:** Renaissance doorway

Date	Mintage	F	VF	XF	Unc	BU
2007 Matte Proof	999	Value: 500				

KM# 193 10 DOLLARS

62.2100 g., 0.9990 Silver 1.9980 oz. ASW, 50 mm. **Subject:** Tiffany Art **Rev:** Mannerism, staircase design

Date	Mintage	F	VF	XF	Unc	BU
2008 Matte Proof	999	Value: 450				

KM# 194 10 DOLLARS

62.2100 g., 0.9990 Silver 1.9980 oz. ASW, 42x42 mm. **Subject:** WWII Battleships **Rev:** Japan's Yamato

Date	Mintage	F	VF	XF	Unc	BU
2008 Proof	1,000	Value: 300				

KM# 195 10 DOLLARS

62.2100 g., 0.9990 Silver 1.9980 oz. ASW, 42x42 mm. **Subject:** WWII Battleships **Rev:** USS Missouri, gilt eagle above

Date	Mintage	F	VF	XF	Unc	BU
2008 Proof	1,000	Value: 175				

KM# 184 10 DOLLARS

62.2500 g., 0.9990 Silver 1.9993 oz. ASW, 42x42 mm. **Subject:** WWII Battleships **Obv:** Shield **Rev:** Bismarck, gilt Iron Cross above **Shape:** Square

Date	Mintage	F	VF	XF	Unc	BU
2009 Proof	—	Value: 165				

KM# 219 10 DOLLARS

62.2100 g., 0.9990 Silver 1.9980 oz. ASW, 50 mm. **Subject:** Tiffany Art **Rev:** Baroque facade

Date	Mintage	F	VF	XF	Unc	BU
2009 Matte Proof	—	Value: 400				

KM# 220 10 DOLLARS

62.2100 g., 0.9990 Silver 1.9980 oz. ASW, 50 mm. **Rev:** Amber insert

Date	Mintage	F	VF	XF	Unc	BU
2009 Matte Proof	2,500	Value: 275				

KM# 221 10 DOLLARS

62.2100 g., 0.9990 Silver 1.9980 oz. ASW, 42x42 mm. **Subject:** WWII Battleship **Rev:** Britains's HMS Prince of Wales, gilt Union Jack above

Date	Mintage	F	VF	XF	Unc	BU
2009 Proof	1,000	Value: 145				

KM# 250 10 DOLLARS

62.2000 g., 0.9990 Silver 1.9977 oz. ASW, 42x42 mm. **Subject:** Russian Battleship Marat **Rev:** Battleship sailing left

Date	Mintage	F	VF	XF	Unc	BU
2010 Proof	1,000	Value: 80.00				

KM# 252 10 DOLLARS

64.2100 g., 0.9990 Silver 2.0622 oz. ASW, 50 mm. **Subject:** Tiffany Art - Rococo **Obv:** Arms at lower right, glass insert **Rev:** Cherus at left, glass insert

Date	Mintage	F	VF	XF	Unc	BU
2010 Antique	999	—	—	—	—	325

KM# 176 20 DOLLARS

164.0000 g., 0.9990 Silver 5.2672 oz. ASW, 63 mm. **Obv:** Auto steering wheel **Rev:** Side sillouette of Corvette 206

Date	Mintage	F	VF	XF	Unc	BU
2008 Proof	—	Value: 200				

KM# 183 500 DOLLARS

77.7000 g., 0.9990 Gold 2.4955 oz. AGW, 42x42 mm. **Obv:** Shield **Rev:** Battleship Bismark

Date	Mintage	F	VF	XF	Unc	BU
2009 Proof	77	Value: 4,000				

KM# 243 500 DOLLARS

77.7500 g., 0.9990 Gold 2.4971 oz. AGW, 42x42 mm. **Subject:** H.M.S. Prince of Wales **Rev:** Battleship right, Royal Navy flag above

Date	Mintage	F	VF	XF	Unc	BU
2009 Proof	77	Value: 4,000				

KM# 251 500 DOLLARS

77.7500 g., 0.9990 Gold 2.4971 oz. AGW, 42x42 mm. **Subject:** Battleship Marat **Rev:** Battleship sailing left

Date	Mintage	F	VF	XF	Unc	BU
2010 Proof	77	Value: 4,000				

PROOF SETS

KM#	Date	Mintage	Identification	Issue Price	Mkt Val
PS4	2007 (6)	2,500	KM#130-135	—	375

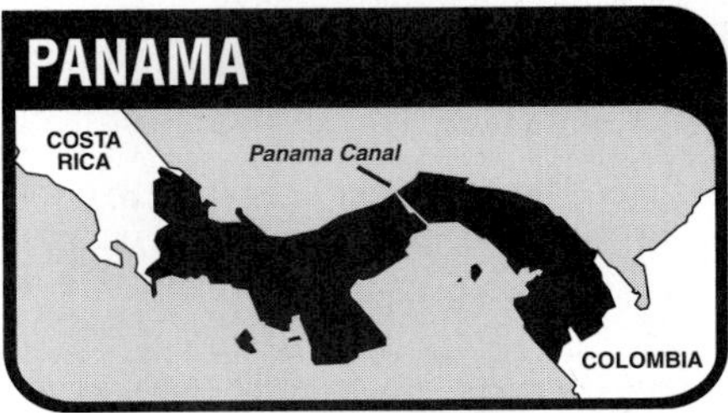

The Republic of Panama, a Central American country situated between Costa Rica and Colombia, has an area of 29,762 sq. mi. (78,200 sq. km.) and a population of *2.4 million. Capital: Panama City. The Panama Canal is the country's biggest asset; servicing world related transit trade and international commerce. Bananas, refined petroleum, sugar and shrimp are exported.

MONETARY SYSTEM

100 Centesimos = 1 Balboa

REPUBLIC

DECIMAL COINAGE

KM# 125 CENTESIMO

2.4400 g., Copper Plated Zinc, 18.96 mm. **Obv:** Written value **Obv. Legend:** REPUBLICA DE PANAMA **Rev:** Native Urraca bust left **Edge:** Plain

Date	Mintage	F	VF	XF	Unc	BU
2001(c)	160,000,000	—	—	—	0.15	0.35
2008(c)	—	—	—	—	0.15	0.35

KM# 133 5 CENTESIMOS

5.0000 g., Copper-Nickel, 21.15 mm. **Subject:** Sara Sotillo **Obv:** National coat of arms **Obv. Legend:** REPUBLICA DE PANAMA **Rev:** Head of Sotillo 3/4 right **Edge:** Plain

Date	Mintage	F	VF	XF	Unc	BU
2001(c)	8,000,000	—	—	—	0.30	0.50
2008(c)	—	—	—	—	0.30	0.50

KM# 127 1/10 BALBOA

2.2680 g., Copper-Nickel Clad Copper, 17.91 mm. **Obv:** National coat of arms **Obv. Legend:** REPUBLICA DE PANAMA **Rev:** Armored bust of Balboa left **Edge:** Reeded

Date	Mintage	F	VF	XF	Unc	BU
2001(c)	15,000,000	—	—	0.75	1.00	2.00
2008(c)	28,000,000	—	—	0.75	1.00	2.00

KM# 135 25 CENTESIMOS

5.6700 g., Copper-Nickel Clad Copper, 24.26 mm. **Obv:** National coat of arms **Obv. Legend:** REPUBLICA DE PANAMA **Rev:** Tower and Spanish ruins **Edge:** Reeded **Note:** Released in 2004

Date	Mintage	F	VF	XF	Unc	BU
2003(c)	6,000,000	—	—	0.30	1.00	2.00
2003(c) Proof	2,000	Value: 20.00				

KM# 136 25 CENTESIMOS

5.6700 g., Copper-Nickel Clad Copper, 24.26 mm. **Obv:** National coat of arms **Obv. Legend:** REPUBLICA DE PANAMA **Rev:** King's Bridge **Rev. Legend:** Puente Del Rey **Edge:** Reeded

Date	Mintage	F	VF	XF	Unc	BU
2005(c)	3,000,000	—	—	—	1.00	1.50
2005(c) Proof	2,000	Value: 12.00				

KM# 128 1/4 BALBOA

5.6700 g., Copper-Nickel Clad Copper, 24.26 mm. **Obv:** National coat of arms **Obv. Legend:** REPUBLICA DE PANAMA **Rev:** Armored bust of Balboa left **Edge:** Reeded

Date	Mintage	F	VF	XF	Unc	BU
2001(c)	12,000,000	—	—	0.35	0.75	2.00

KM# 137 1/4 BALBOA

5.6700 g., Copper-Nickel Clad Copper, 24.26 mm. **Subject:** Breast Cancer Awareness **Obv:** National coat of arms **Obv. Legend:** REPUBLICA DE PANAMA **Rev:** Ribbon **Rev. Legend:** Protegete Mujer **Edge:** Reeded

Date	Mintage	F	VF	XF	Unc	BU
2008(c)	14,000,000	—	—	—	1.00	2.00

Note: Also available in a laminated Breast Cancer Awareness pink bookmark

KM# 137a 1/4 BALBOA

5.6700 g., Copper-Nickel Clad Copper, 24.26 mm. **Subject:** Breast Cancer Awareness **Obv:** National coat of arms **Obv. Legend:** REPUBLICA DE PANAMA **Rev:** Pink Ribbon **Rev. Legend:** Protegete Mujer **Edge:** Reeded

Date	Mintage	F	VF	XF	Unc	BU
2008(c) Proof, pink colored ribbon	2,500	Value: 100				

Note: Pink ribbon proof issued in red plush case with black cardboard sleeve with printed pink ribbon

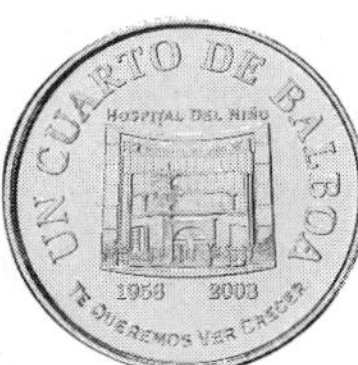

KM# 138 1/4 BALBOA

5.6700 g., Copper-Nickel Clad Copper, 24.26 mm. **Subject:** 50th Anniversary of the Children's Hospital **Obv:** National coat of arms **Obv. Legend:** REPUBLICA DE PANAMA **Rev:** Children's Hospital **Edge:** Reeded

Date	Mintage	F	VF	XF	Unc	BU
2008	6,000,000	—	—	—	2.00	3.00

KM# 138a 1/4 BALBOA

5.6700 g., Copper-Nickel Clad Copper, 24.26 mm. **Subject:** 50th Anniversary of the Children's Hospital **Obv:** National coat of arms **Obv. Legend:** REPUBLICA DE PANAMA **Rev:** Children's Hospital **Edge:** Reeded

Date	Mintage	F	VF	XF	Unc	BU
2008(c) Proof	1,000	Value: 30.00				

KM# 139 50 CENTESIMOS

11.3400 g., Copper-Nickel Clad Copper, 30.6 mm. **Subject:** Centenary of the National Bank of Panama **Obv:** National coat of arms **Obv. Legend:** REPUBLICA DE PANAMA **Rev:** BNP Building - Banco National de Panama **Rev. Legend:** BANCO NACIONAL DE PANAMA CENTENARIO **Edge:** Reeded

Date	Mintage	F	VF	XF	Unc	BU
2009(c)	4,000,000	—	—	—	2.00	3.00

KM# 139a 50 CENTESIMOS

11.3400 g., Copper-Nickel Clad Copper, 30.61 mm. **Subject:** Centenary - National Bank of Panama **Obv:** National coat of arms **Obv. Legend:** REPUBLICA DE PANAMA **Rev:** BNP building - 1904-2004 **Rev. Legend:** BANCO NACIONAL DE PANAMA CENTENARIO **Edge:** Reeded

Date	Mintage	F	VF	XF	Unc	BU
2009(c) Proof	2,000	Value: 50.00				

KM# 129 1/2 BALBOA

11.3000 g., Copper-Nickel Clad Copper, 30.54 mm. **Obv:** National coat of arms **Obv. Legend:** REPUBLICA DE PANAMA **Rev:** Armored bust of Balboa left **Edge:** Reeded

Date	Mintage	F	VF	XF	Unc	BU
2001(c)	600,000	—	—	1.00	2.25	4.00
2008(c)	5,800,000	—	—	0.75	1.25	2.00

KM# 140 1/2 BALBOA

11.3400 g., Copper-Nickel Clad Copper, 30.6 mm. **Subject:** Convent of the Conception **Obv:** National arms **Rev:** Building ruins **Edge:** Reeded

Date	Mintage	F	VF	XF	Unc	BU
2010(c)	3,000,000	—	—	—	4.00	5.00

KM# 134 BALBOA

22.6800 g., Copper-Nickel, 38 mm. **Obv:** Bust of President Mireya Moscoso left, flanked by dates of her presidency **Rev:** Flag and canal scene **Edge:** Reeded

Date	Mintage	F	VF	XF	Unc	BU
2004(c)	348,000	—	—	2.00	4.00	12.00
2004(c) Proof	2,000	Value: 60.00				

Papua New Guinea occupies the eastern half of the island of New Guinea. It lies north of Australia near the equator and borders on West Irian. The country, which includes nearby Bismark archipelago, Buka and Bougainville, has an area of 178,260 sq. mi. (461,690 sq. km.) and a population of 3.7 million that is divided into more than 1,000 separate tribes, speaking more than 700 mutually unintelligible languages. Capital: Port Moresby. The economy is agricultural, and exports copra, rubber, cocoa, coffee, tea, gold and copper

Papua New Guinea is a member of the Commonwealth of Nations. Elizabeth II is Head of State, as Queen of Papua New Guinea.

CONSTITUTIONAL MONARCHY

Commonwealth of Nations

STANDARD COINAGE

KM# 1 TOEA

2.0000 g., Bronze, 17.65 mm. **Obv:** National emblem **Obv. Designer:** Richard Renninger **Rev:** Butterfly and value **Rev. Designer:** Herman de Roos **Edge:** Plain

Date	Mintage	F	VF	XF	Unc	BU
2001	—	—	—	0.25	1.00	10.00
2002	—	—	—	0.15	1.00	10.00
2004	—	—	—	0.10	1.00	10.00

KM# 2 2 TOEA

4.1000 g., Bronze, 21.6 mm. **Obv:** National emblem **Obv. Designer:** Richard Renninger **Rev:** Lion fish **Rev. Designer:** William Shoyer **Edge:** Plain

Date	Mintage	F	VF	XF	Unc	BU
2001	—	—	—	0.30	0.75	12.00
2002	—	—	—	0.25	0.60	12.00
2004	—	—	—	0.15	0.45	12.00

KM# 3a 5 TOEA

2.5500 g., Nickel Plated Steel, 19.53 mm. **Obv:** National emblem **Rev:** Plateless turtle **Edge:** Reeded

Date	Mintage	F	VF	XF	Unc	BU
2002	—	—	—	0.50	1.25	2.50
2005	—	—	—	0.40	1.00	2.00

KM# 4 10 TOEA

5.6700 g., Copper-Nickel, 23.72 mm. **Obv:** National emblem **Obv. Designer:** Richard Renninger **Rev:** Cuscus and value **Rev. Designer:** Herman DeRoos **Edge:** Reeded

Date	Mintage	F	VF	XF	Unc	BU
2001	—	Value: 2.50				

KM# 4a 10 TOEA

5.1600 g., Nickel Plated Steel, 23.72 mm. **Obv:** National emblem **Rev:** Cuscus and value **Edge:** Reeded

Date	Mintage	F	VF	XF	Unc	BU
2002	—	—	—	0.80	2.00	3.00
2004	—	—	—	0.80	2.00	3.00
2005	—	—	—	6.00	1.50	3.00
2006	—	—	—	0.60	1.50	2.50

KM# 5a 20 TOEA

10.1300 g., Nickel Plated Steel, 28.65 mm. **Obv:** National emblem **Rev:** Bennett's Cassowary and value **Edge:** Reeded

Date	Mintage	F	VF	XF	Unc	BU
2004	—	—	—	0.80	2.00	3.00
2005	—	—	—	0.80	2.00	3.00
2006	—	—	—	0.60	1.50	2.50

KM# 6a KINA

14.6100 g., Nickel Plated Steel, 33.28 mm. **Obv:** Native design **Obv. Designer:** Richard Renninger **Rev:** Two Salt Water Crocodiles **Rev. Designer:** William Shoyer **Edge:** Reeded

Date	Mintage	F	VF	XF	Unc	BU
2002	—	—	—	1.60	4.00	5.00
2004	—	—	—	1.40	3.50	4.50

KM# 6b KINA

11.1300 g., Nickel Plated Steel, 30 mm. **Obv:** Native design **Obv. Designer:** Richard Renninger **Rev:** Two Salt Water Crocodiles **Rev. Designer:** William Shoyer **Edge:** Reeded

Date	Mintage	F	VF	XF	Unc	BU
2005	—	—	—	1.20	3.00	4.00

KM# 51 2 KINA

Bi-Metallic Brass center in Copper-Nickel ring **Subject:** 35th Anniversary **Obv:** Bird of Pariaise

Date	Mintage	F	VF	XF	Unc	BU
2008	—	—	—	—	—	5.00

The Republic of Paraguay, a landlocked country in the heart of South America surrounded by Argentina, Bolivia and Brazil, has an area of 157,048 sq. mi. (406,750 sq. km.) and a population of *4.5 million, 95 percent of whom are of mixed Spanish and Indian descent. Capital: Asuncion. The country is predominantly agrarian, with no important mineral deposits or oil reserves. Meat, timber, hides, oilseeds, tobacco and cotton account for 70 percent of Paraguay's export revenue.

During the Triple Alliance War (1864-1870) in which Paraguay faced Argentina, Brazil and Uruguay, Asuncion's ladies gathered in an Assembly on Feb. 24, 1867 and decided to give up their jewelry in order to help the national defense. The President of the Republic, Francisco Solano Lopez accepted the offering and ordered one twentieth of it be used to mint the first Paraguayan gold coins according to the Decree of the 11th of Sept.1867.

Two dies were made, one by Bouvet, and another by an American, Leonard Charles, while only the die made by Bouvet was eventually used.

MINT MARK
HF – LeLocle (Swiss)

REPUBLIC

REFORM COINAGE

100 Centimos = 1 Guarani

KM# 197 GUARANI
27.0000 g., 0.9250 Silver 0.8029 oz. ASW, 39.7 mm. **Subject:** 50th Anniversary of the Central Bank **Obv:** Naval gunship **Obv. Legend:** REPUBLICA DEL PARAGUAY **Obv. Inscription:** CAÑONERO PARAGUAY **Rev:** Bank building within circle **Rev. Legend:** BANCO CENTRAL DEL PARAGUAY **Edge:** Reeded

Date	Mintage	F	VF	XF	Unc	BU
2002 Proof	3,000	Value: 75.00				

KM# 199 GUARANI
26.8600 g., 0.9250 Silver 0.7988 oz. ASW, 40.03 mm. **Series:** 5th Ibero-America **Subject:** Encounter of the Two Worlds **Obv:** National arms in center with ten national arms in outer circle **Obv. Legend:** REPUBLICA DEL PARAGUAY **Rev:** Native in canoe with outline of South America in background at left, early sailing ship at lower right. **Rev. Legend:** ENCUENTRO DE DOS MUNDOS **Edge:** Reeded

Date	Mintage	F	VF	XF	Unc	BU
2002 Proof	—	Value: 60.00				

KM# 200 GUARANI
27.0000 g., 0.9250 Silver 0.8029 oz. ASW **Subject:** 60th Anniversary of Currency Reform **Obv:** National arms **Obv. Legend:** REPUBLICA DEL PARAGUAY **Rev:** Outline map of Paraguay **Edge:** Reeded

Date	Mintage	F	VF	XF	Unc	BU
2003 Proof	—	Value: 80.00				

KM# 201 GUARANI
26.9000 g., 0.9250 Silver 0.8000 oz. ASW, 40.04 mm. **Subject:** FIFA - XVIII World Football Championship - Germany 2006 **Obv:** National arms **Obv. Legend:** REPUBLICA DEL PARAGUAY **Rev:** Two opponents after ball **Rev. Legend:** COPA MUNDIAL DE LA FIFA - ALEMANIA **Edge:** Reeded

Date	Mintage	F	VF	XF	Unc	BU
2003 Proof	50,000	Value: 50.00				

KM# 202 GUARANI
27.0000 g., 0.9250 Silver 0.8029 oz. ASW **Subject:** FIFA - XVIII World Football Championship - Germany 2006 **Obv:** National arms **Obv. Legend:** REPUBLICA DEL PARAGUAY **Rev:** Ball in goal **Edge:** Reeded

Date	Mintage	F	VF	XF	Unc	BU
2004 Proof	50,000	Value: 50.00				

KM# 204 GUARANI
27.0000 g., 0.9250 Silver 0.8029 oz. ASW **Series:** 6th Ibero-America **Subject:** Encounter of the Two Worlds **Obv:** National arms in center with ten national arms in outer circle **Obv. Legend:** REPUBLICA DEL PARAGUAY **Rev:** Church of the Most Holy, Trinidad in Yaguarón **Rev. Legend:** ENCUENTRO DE DOS MUNDOS - IGLESIA DE LA SANTISIMA TRINIDAD **Edge:** Reeded

Date	Mintage	F	VF	XF	Unc	BU
2005 Proof	—	Value: 65.00				

KM# 191a 50 GUARANIES
Brass Plated Steel **Obv:** Uniformed bust facing **Rev:** Value above river dam **Note:** Magnetic

Date	Mintage	F	VF	XF	Unc	BU
2005	10,000,000	—	—	—	0.75	1.00

KM# 191b 50 GUARANIES
1.0100 g., Aluminum, 18.98 mm. **Obv:** Bust of Major General J.F. Estigarribia facing **Obv. Legend:** REPUBLICA DEL PARAGUAY **Rev:** Acaray River Dam **Rev. Inscription:** REPRESA ACARAY **Edge:** Plain **Note:** Reduced size

Date	Mintage	F	VF	XF	Unc	BU
2006	25,000,000	—	—	—	1.00	2.00
2008	—	—	—	—	1.00	2.00

KM# 177a 100 GUARANIES
5.4500 g., Brass Plated Steel **Obv:** Bust of General Jose E. Dias facing **Obv. Legend:** REPUBLICA DEL PARAGUAY **Rev:** Ruins of Humaita **Rev. Inscription:** RUINAS DE HUMAITA 1865/70 **Note:** Reduced weight and thickness.

Date	Mintage	F	VF	XF	Unc	BU
2004	15,000,000	—	—	—	1.50	2.00
2005	10,000,000	—	—	—	1.50	2.00

KM# 177b 100 GUARANIES
3.6600 g., Nickel-Steel, 20.94 mm. **Obv:** Bust of General Jose E. Dias facing **Obv. Legend:** REPUBLICA DEL PARAGUAY **Rev:** Ruins of Humaita **Rev. Inscription:** RUINAS DE HUMAITA 1865/70 **Edge:** Plain

Date	Mintage	F	VF	XF	Unc	BU
2006	30,000,000	—	—	—	1.50	2.00
2007	25,000,000	—	—	—	1.50	2.00
2008	—	—	—	—	1.50	2.00

KM# 195 500 GUARANIES
7.8200 g., Brass Plated Steel **Obv:** Head of General Bernardino Caballero facing **Obv. Legend:** REPUBLICA DEL PARAGUAY **Rev:** Bank above value within circle **Rev. Legend:** BANCO CENTRAL DEL PARAGUAY

Date	Mintage	F	VF	XF	Unc	BU
2002	15,000,000	—	—	—	2.50	3.00
2005	5,000,000	—	—	—	2.50	3.00

KM# 195a 500 GUARANIES
4.8000 g., Nickel-Steel, 23 mm. **Obv:** Head of General Bernardino Caballero facing **Obv. Legend:** REPUBLICA DEL PARAGUAY **Rev:** Bank above value in circle **Rev. Legend:** BANCO CENTRAL DEL PARAGUAY **Edge:** Plain

Date	Mintage	F	VF	XF	Unc	BU
2006	12,000,000	—	—	—	2.00	2.50
2007	25,000,000	—	—	—	2.00	2.50
2008	—	—	—	—	2.00	2.50

KM# 198 MIL (1000) GUARANIES
6.0700 g., Nickel-Steel, 25 mm. **Obv:** Bust of Major General Francisco Solano Lopez facing **Obv. Legend:** REPUBLICA DEL PARAGUAY **Rev:** National Heroes Pantheon **Rev. Legend:** BANCO CENTRAL DEL PARAGUAY **Rev. Inscription:** PANTEON NACIONAL / DE LOS HEROES **Edge:** Plain

Date	Mintage	F	VF	XF	Unc	BU
2006	25,000,000	—	—	—	3.00	4.00
2007	35,000,000	—	—	—	3.00	4.00
2008	—	—	—	—	3.00	4.00

KM# 203 1500 GUARANIES
6.7000 g., 0.9990 Gold 0.2152 oz. AGW **Subject:** XVIII World Football Championship - Germany 2006 **Obv:** National arms **Obv. Legend:** REPUBLICA DEL PARAGUAY **Rev:** Ball in goal

Date	Mintage	F	VF	XF	Unc	BU
2004 Proof	25,000	Value: 450				

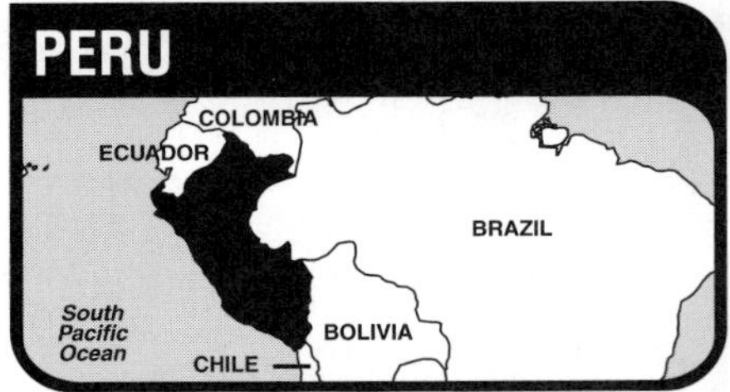

The Republic of Peru, located on the Pacific coast of South America, has an area of 496,225 sq. mi. (1,285,220sq. km.) and a population of *21.4 million. Capital: Lima. The diversified economy includes mining, fishing and agriculture. Fishmeal, copper, sugar, zinc and iron ore are exported.

REPUBLIC

REFORM COINAGE

1/M Intis = 1 Nuevo Sol; 100 (New) Centimos = 1 Nuevo Sol

KM# 303.4 CENTIMO
1.8800 g., Brass, 15.9 mm. **Obv:** National arms, accent mark

above "u" **Rev:** Without Braille dots, no Chavez **Edge:** Plain **Note:** LIMA monogram is mint mark.

Date	Mintage	F	VF	XF	Unc	BU
2001LIMA	—	—	—	—	0.25	0.40
2002LIMA	—	—	—	—	0.25	0.40
2004LIMA	—	—	—	—	0.25	0.40
2005LIMA	—	—	—	—	0.25	0.40
2006LIMA	—	—	—	—	0.25	0.40

KM# 303.4a CENTIMO

0.8300 g., Aluminum, 16 mm. **Obv:** National arms **Rev:** Value flanked by designs **Edge:** Plain **Note:** LIMA monogram is mint mark.

Date	Mintage	F	VF	XF	Unc	BU
2005LIMA	—	—	—	—	0.25	0.40
2006LIMA	—	—	—	—	0.50	0.75
2007LIMA	—	—	—	—	0.50	0.75
2008LIMA	—	—	—	—	0.50	0.75
2009LIMA	—	—	—	—	0.50	0.75
2010LIMA	—	—	—	—	0.50	0.75

KM# 304.4 5 CENTIMOS

2.6900 g., Brass, 18 mm. **Obv:** National arms, accent above "u" **Rev:** Value flanked by designs. Without Braille dots, with accent above "e" **Edge:** Plain **Note:** LIMA monogram is mint mark.

Date	Mintage	F	VF	XF	Unc	BU
2001LIMA	—	—	—	—	0.35	0.50
2002LIMA	—	—	—	—	0.35	0.50
2005LIMA	—	—	—	—	0.35	0.50
2006LIMA	—	—	—	—	0.35	0.50
2007LIMA	—	—	—	—	0.35	0.50

KM# 304.4a 5 CENTIMOS

1.0200 g., Aluminum, 18 mm. **Obv:** National arms **Rev:** Value flanked by designs **Edge:** Plain **Note:** LIMA monogram is mint mark.

Date	Mintage	F	VF	XF	Unc	BU
2007LIMA	—	—	—	—	0.50	0.75
2008LIMA	—	—	—	—	0.50	0.75
2009LIMA	—	—	—	—	0.50	0.75
2010LIMA	—	—	—	—	0.50	0.75

KM# 305.4 10 CENTIMOS

3.5000 g., Brass, 20.5 mm. **Obv:** National arms, accent above "u" **Rev:** Without braille dots, accent above "e" **Edge:** Plain **Note:** LIMA monogram is mint mark.

Date	Mintage	F	VF	XF	Unc	BU
2001LIMA	—	—	—	—	0.65	0.85
2002LIMA	—	—	—	—	0.65	0.85
2003LIMA	—	—	—	—	0.65	0.85
2004LIMA	—	—	—	—	0.65	0.85
2005LIMA	—	—	—	—	0.65	0.85
2006LIMA	—	—	—	—	0.65	0.85
2007LIMA	—	—	—	—	0.65	0.85
2008LIMA	—	—	—	—	0.65	0.85
2009LIMA	—	—	—	—	0.65	0.85
2010LIMA	—	—	—	—	0.65	0.85

KM# 306.4 20 CENTIMOS

4.4000 g., Brass, 23 mm. **Obv:** National arms, accent above "u" **Rev:** Without braille dots, accent above "e" **Edge:** Plain **Note:** LIMA monogram is mint mark.

Date	Mintage	F	VF	XF	Unc	BU
2001LIMA	—	—	—	—	0.85	1.20
2002LIMA	—	—	—	—	0.85	1.20
2004LIMA	—	—	—	—	0.85	1.20
2006LIMA	—	—	—	—	0.85	1.20
2007LIMA	—	—	—	—	0.85	1.20
2008LIMA	—	—	—	—	0.85	1.20
2009LIMA	—	—	—	—	0.85	1.20
2010LIMA	—	—	—	—	0.85	1.20

KM# 307.4 50 CENTIMOS

5.4500 g., Copper-Nickel-Zinc, 22 mm. **Obv:** National arms, accent above "u" **Rev:** Without braille, accent above "e" **Edge:** Reeded **Note:** LIMA monogram is mint mark.

Date	Mintage	F	VF	XF	Unc	BU
2001LIMA	—	—	—	—	1.50	1.75
2002LIMA	—	—	—	—	1.50	1.75
2003LIMA	—	—	—	—	1.50	1.75
2004LIMA	—	—	—	—	1.50	1.75
2005LIMA	—	—	—	—	1.50	1.75
2006LIMA	—	—	—	—	1.50	1.75
2007LIMA	—	—	—	—	1.50	1.75
2008LIMA	—	—	—	—	1.50	1.75
2009LIMA	—	—	—	—	1.50	1.75
2010LIMA	—	—	—	—	1.50	1.75

KM# 345 SOL

7.3000 g., Copper-Nickel, 25.5 mm. **Obv:** National arms **Rev:** Chullpas de Sillustan ruins

Date	Mintage	F	VF	XF	Unc	BU
2011	10,000,000	—	—	—	2.50	3.00

KM# 308.4 NUEVO SOL

7.3200 g., Copper-Nickel-Zinc, 25.5 mm. **Obv:** National arms, accent above "u" **Rev:** Without braille, accent above "e" **Edge:** Reeded **Note:** LIMA monogram is mint mark.

Date	Mintage	F	VF	XF	Unc	BU
2001LIMA	—	—	—	—	2.50	3.00
2002LIMA	—	—	—	—	2.50	3.00
2003LIMA	—	—	—	—	2.50	3.00
2004LIMA	—	—	—	—	2.50	3.00
2005LIMA	—	—	—	—	2.50	3.00
2006LIMA	—	—	—	—	2.50	3.00
2007LIMA	—	—	—	—	2.50	3.00
2008LIMA	—	—	—	—	2.50	3.00
2009LIMA	—	—	—	—	2.50	3.00

KM# 329 NUEVO SOL

33.6250 g., 0.9250 Silver 0.9999 oz. ASW, 37 mm. **Subject:** 450th Anniversary - San Marcos University **Obv:** National arms **Rev:** University seal and building **Edge:** Reeded **Note:** LIMA monogram is mint mark.

Date	Mintage	F	VF	XF	Unc	BU
2001 Proof	—	Value: 60.00				

KM# 330 NUEVO SOL

33.6250 g., 0.9250 Silver 0.9999 oz. ASW, 37 mm. **Subject:** 50th Anniversary - Numismatic Society of Peru **Obv:** National arms **Rev:** Stylized design within circle **Edge:** Reeded **Note:** LIMA monogram is mint mark.

Date	Mintage	F	VF	XF	Unc	BU
2001 Proof	—	Value: 50.00				

KM# 331 NUEVO SOL

33.6250 g., 0.9250 Silver 0.9999 oz. ASW, 37 mm. **Subject:** 200th Anniversary - von Humboldt's visit to Peru **Obv:** National arms **Rev:** Seated figure 1/4 left **Edge:** Reeded **Note:** LIMA monogram is mint mark.

Date	Mintage	F	VF	XF	Unc	BU
2002 Proof	—	Value: 60.00				

KM# 334 NUEVO SOL

27.0800 g., 0.9250 Silver 0.8053 oz. ASW, 40 mm. **Series:** Fifth Ibero-America **Obv:** National arms in center with ten national arms in outer circle **Obv. Legend:** BANCO CENTRAL DE RESERVA DEL PERÚ **Rev:** Ceramic - Indians in reed boats **Rev. Legend:** PERÚ **Edge:** Reeded

Date	Mintage	F	VF	XF	Unc	BU
2002 Proof	—	Value: 65.00				

KM# 332 NUEVO SOL

33.6250 g., 0.9250 Silver 0.9999 oz. ASW, 37 mm. **Subject:** 125th Anniversary of the Inmaculate Jesuitas - Lima College **Obv:** National arms **Rev:** Statue and 3/4 crowned shield **Edge:** Reeded **Note:** LIMA monogram is mint mark.

Date	Mintage	F	VF	XF	Unc	BU
2003 Proof	—	Value: 55.00				

KM# 333 NUEVO SOL
33.6250 g., 0.9250 Silver 0.9999 oz. ASW, 37 mm. **Subject:** 180th Anniversary of Peru's Congress **Obv:** National arms **Rev:** Statue in front of building **Edge:** Reeded **Note:** LIMA monogram is mint mark.

Date	Mintage	F	VF	XF	Unc	BU
2003 Proof	—	Value: 60.00				

KM# 335 NUEVO SOL
Silver **Subject:** FIFA World Cup Soccer **Obv:** Arms within wreath **Rev:** Action scene beneath globe **Edge:** Reeded

Date	Mintage	F	VF	XF	Unc	BU
2004 Proof	—	Value: 60.00				

KM# 339 NUEVO SOL
27.0000 g., 0.9250 Silver 0.8029 oz. ASW, 40 mm. **Series:** 6th Ibero-America **Subject:** Lost city of the Incas **Obv:** National arms in center with ten national arms in outer ring **Obv. Legend:** BANCO CENTRAL DE RESERVA DEL PERÚ **Rev:** Village ruins **Rev. Legend:** MACHU PICCHU . PERÚ **Edge:** Reeded

Date	Mintage	F	VF	XF	Unc	BU
2005 Proof	—	Value: 60.00				

KM# 340 NUEVO SOL
7.3200 g., Copper-Nickel-Zinc, 25.5 mm. **Series:** Wealth and pride of Peru **Obv:** National arms **Rev:** Tumi de oro **Edge:** Reeded

Date	Mintage	F	VF	XF	Unc	BU
2010	10,000,000	—	—	—	2.50	3.00

KM# 341 NUEVO SOL
7.3200 g., Copper-Nickel-Zinc, 25.5 mm. **Series:** Wealth and pride of Peru **Obv:** National arms **Rev:** Sarcophagus of Karajia

Date	Mintage	F	VF	XF	Unc	BU
2010	10,000,000	—	—	—	2.50	3.00

KM# 342 NUEVO SOL
7.3200 g., Copper-Nickel-Zinc, 25.5 mm. **Obv:** National Arms **Rev:** Estela de Ramondi

Date	Mintage	F	VF	XF	Unc	BU
2010LIMA	10,000,000	—	—	—	2.50	3.00

KM# 313 2 NUEVOS SOLES
5.5800 g., Bi-Metallic Nickel-Brass center in Stainless Steel ring, 22.2 mm. **Obv:** National arms within circle **Rev:** Stylized bird in flight to left of value within circle **Edge:** Plain **Note:** LIMA monogram is mint mark.

Date	Mintage	F	VF	XF	Unc	BU
2002LIMA	—	—	—	—	4.50	5.00
2003LIMA	—	—	—	—	4.50	5.00
2004LIMA	—	—	—	—	4.50	5.00
2005LIMA	—	—	—	—	4.50	5.00
2006LIMA	—	—	—	—	4.50	5.00
2007LIMA	—	—	—	—	4.50	5.00
2008LIMA	—	—	—	—	4.50	5.00

KM# 343 2 NUEVOS SOLES
5.5800 g., Bi-Metallic Brass center in Stainless Steel ring, 22.2 mm. **Obv:** National Arms **Rev:** The Hummingbird from the Inca Lines, large value at right

Date	Mintage	F	VF	XF	Unc	BU
2010LIMA	—	—	—	—	4.50	5.00

KM# 316 5 NUEVOS SOLES
6.6700 g., Bi-Metallic Nickel-Brass center in Stainless Steel ring, 24.3 mm. **Obv:** National arms within circle **Rev:** Stylized bird in flight to left of value within circle **Edge:** Reeded **Note:** LIMA monogram is mint mark.

Date	Mintage	F	VF	XF	Unc	BU
2001LIMA	—	—	—	—	6.50	7.00
2002LIMA	—	—	—	—	6.50	7.00
2004LIMA	—	—	—	—	6.50	7.00
2005LIMA	—	—	—	—	6.50	7.00
2006LIMA	—	—	—	—	6.50	7.00
2007LIMA	—	—	—	—	6.50	7.00
2008LIMA	—	—	—	—	6.50	7.00

KM# 344 5 NUEVOS SOLES
6.6700 g., Bi-Metallic Brass center in Stainless Steel ring, 24.27 mm. **Obv:** National Arms **Rev:** Frigate bird from the Nasca lines, large value at right

Date	Mintage	F	VF	XF	Unc	BU
2010LIMA	—	—	—	—	6.50	7.00

PHILIPPINES

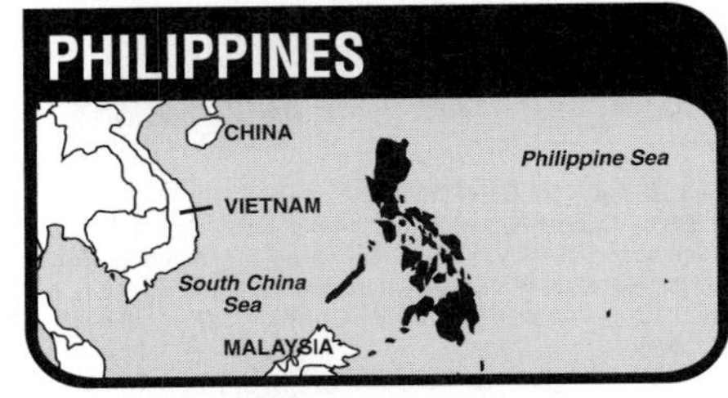

The Republic of the Philippines, an archipelago in the western Pacific 500 miles (805 km.) from the southeast coast of Asia, has an area of 115,830 sq. mi. (300,000 sq. km.) and a population of *64.9 million. Capital: Manila. The economy of the 7,000-island group is based on agriculture, forestry and fishing. Timber, coconut products, sugar and hemp are exported.

MINT MARKS
BSP - Bangko Sentral Pilipinas
M, MA - Manila

REPUBLIC

REFORM COINAGE

100 Sentimos = 1 Piso

KM# 273 SENTIMO
2.0000 g., Copper Plated Steel **Obv:** Value and date **Rev:** Central bank seal within circle and gear design, 1993 (date Central Bank was established) below **Rev. Legend:** BANGKO SENTRAL NG PILIPINAS - 1993

Date	Mintage	F	VF	XF	Unc	BU
2001	—	—	—	—	0.10	0.15
2002	—	—	—	—	0.10	0.15
2004	—	—	—	—	0.10	0.15
2005	—	—	—	—	0.10	0.15
2006	—	—	—	—	0.10	0.15
2007	—	—	—	—	0.10	0.15
2008	—	—	—	—	0.10	0.15
2009	—	—	—	—	0.10	0.15

KM# 268 5 SENTIMOS
1.9000 g., Copper Plated Steel, 15.43 mm. **Obv:** Numeral value around center hole **Rev:** Hole in center with date, bank and name around border, 1993 (date Central Bank was established) below **Rev. Legend:** BANGKO CENTRAL NG PILIPINAS - 1993 **Edge:** Plain

Date	Mintage	F	VF	XF	Unc	BU
2001	—	—	—	0.10	0.20	0.25
2002	—	—	—	0.10	0.20	0.25
2004	—	—	—	0.10	0.50	1.00
2005	—	—	—	0.10	0.20	0.25
2006	—	—	—	0.10	0.20	0.25
2007	—	—	—	0.10	0.20	0.25
2008	—	—	—	0.10	0.20	0.25
2009	—	—	—	0.10	0.20	0.25

KM# 270.1 10 SENTIMOS
2.5000 g., Copper Plated Steel, 17 mm. **Obv:** Value and date **Rev:** Central Bank seal within circle and gear design, 1993 (date Central Bank was established) below **Rev. Legend:** BANGKO SENTRAL NG PILIPINAS - 1993 **Edge:** Reeded

Date	Mintage	F	VF	XF	Unc	BU
2001	—	—	—	0.10	0.30	0.40
2002	—	—	—	0.10	0.30	0.40
2004	—	—	—	0.75	1.50	2.50
2005	—	—	—	0.10	0.30	0.40

KM# 270.2 10 SENTIMOS
2.5000 g., Copper Plated Steel, 17 mm. **Obv:** Value high on coin, different font, date **Rev:** Central Bank seal within circle and gear design **Rev. Legend:** BANGKO SENTRAL NG PILIPINAS - 1993 **Edge:** Reeded

Date	Mintage	F	VF	XF	Unc	BU
2006	—	—	—	0.10	0.30	0.40
2007	—	—	—	0.10	0.30	0.40
2008	—	—	—	0.10	0.30	0.40
2009	—	—	—	0.10	0.30	0.40

KM# 271 25 SENTIMOS
3.8000 g., Brass, 20 mm. **Obv:** Value and date **Rev:** Central Bank seal within circle and gear design, 1993 (date Central Bank was established) below **Rev. Legend:** BANGKO SENTRAL NG PILIPINAS - 1993 **Edge:** Plain

Date	Mintage	F	VF	XF	Unc	BU
2001	—	—	0.10	0.25	0.60	0.80
2002	—	—	0.10	0.25	0.60	0.80
2003	—	—	0.10	0.25	0.60	0.80

KM# 271a 25 SENTIMOS
3.6000 g., Brass Plated Steel, 20 mm. **Obv:** Value and date **Rev:** Central Bank seal within circle and gear design **Rev. Legend:** BANGKO SENTRAL NG PILIPINAS - 1993 **Edge:** Plain

Date	Mintage	F	VF	XF	Unc	BU
2004	—	—	—	0.25	2.00	2.50
2005	—	—	—	0.25	1.00	1.25
2006	—	—	—	0.25	1.00	1.25
2007	—	—	—	0.25	1.00	1.25
2008	—	—	—	0.25	0.50	1.00
2009	—	—	—	0.25	0.50	1.00

KM# 269 PISO
6.1000 g., Copper-Nickel, 24 mm. **Obv:** Head of Jose Rizal right, value and date **Rev:** Bank seal within circle and gear design, 1993 (date Central Bank was established) below **Rev. Legend:** BANGKO SENTRAL NG PILIPINAS - 1993 **Edge:** Reeded

Date	Mintage	F	VF	XF	Unc	BU
2001	—	—	0.25	0.50	1.25	1.75
2002	—	—	0.25	0.50	1.25	1.75
2003 Non Magnetic	—	—	—	—	—	10.00

KM# 269a PISO
5.4000 g., Nickel Plated Steel, 24 mm. **Obv:** Head of Jose Rizal right, value and date **Rev:** Bank seal within circle and gear design **Rev. Legend:** BANGKO SENTRAL NG PILIPINAS - 1993 **Edge:** Reeded

Date	Mintage	F	VF	XF	Unc	BU
2003	—	—	—	1.00	2.00	3.00
2004	—	—	—	0.45	5.00	7.00
2005	—	—	—	0.45	1.10	1.50
2006	—	—	—	0.45	1.10	1.50
2007	—	—	—	0.45	1.10	1.50
2008	—	—	—	0.45	1.10	1.50
2009	—	—	—	0.45	1.10	1.50

KM# 272 5 PISO
7.7000 g., Nickel-Brass, 27 mm. **Obv:** Head of Emilio Aguinaldo right, value and date within scalloped border **Rev:** Central Bank seal within circle and gear design within scalloped border, 1993 (date Central Bank was established) below **Rev. Legend:** BANGKO SENTRAL NG PILIPINAS - 1993 **Edge:** Plain

Date	Mintage	F	VF	XF	Unc	BU
2001BSP	—	—	1.00	2.00	3.00	4.50
2002	—	—	0.35	0.70	1.75	3.00
2003	—	—	0.35	0.70	1.75	3.00
2004	—	—	0.50	1.00	5.00	6.00
2005	—	—	0.35	0.70	1.75	4.00
2006	—	—	0.35	0.70	1.75	3.00
2007	—	—	0.35	0.70	1.75	3.00
2008	—	—	0.35	0.70	1.75	3.00
2009	—	—	0.35	0.70	1.75	3.00

KM# 278 10 PISO
8.7000 g., Bi-Metallic Aluminum-Bronze center in Copper-Nickel ring, 26.5 mm. **Obv:** Conjoined heads right within circle **Rev:** Bank seal within circle and gear design, 1993 (date Central Bank was established) below **Rev. Legend:** BANGKO SENTRAL NG PILIPINAS - 1993 **Edge:** Segmented reeding

Date	Mintage	F	VF	XF	Unc	BU
2001	—	—	0.70	1.40	3.50	5.50
2002	—	—	0.60	1.20	2.00	3.00
2003	—	—	0.60	1.20	3.00	4.00
2004	—	—	0.80	2.00	5.00	8.00
2005	—	—	0.75	1.50	3.75	5.00
2006	—	—	0.60	1.20	3.00	4.00
2007	—	—	0.75	1.50	3.75	5.00
2008	—	—	0.75	1.50	3.75	5.00
2009	—	—	0.75	1.50	3.75	5.00

MINT SETS

KM#	Date	Mintage	Identification	Issue Price	Mkt Val
MS39	2005 (7)	—	KM#268-273, 278 plus medal	10.00	15.00
MS40	2006 (7)	—	KM#268-273, 278	10.00	12.50

PITCAIRN ISLANDS

A small volcanic island, along with the uninhabited islands of Oeno, Henderson, and Ducie, constitute the British Colony of Pitcairn Islands. The main island has an area of about 2 sq. mi. (5 sq. km.) and a population of *68. It is located 1350 miles southeast of Tahiti. The islanders subsist on fishing, garden produce and crops. The sale of postage stamps and carved curios to passing ships brings cash income.

New Zealand currency has been used since July 10, 1967.

BRITISH COLONY

REGULAR COINAGE

KM# 54 5 CENTS
3.4000 g., Copper Plated Bronze, 19 mm. **Ruler:** Elizabeth II **Obv:** Head right **Rev:** Anchor from the H.M.A.V. Bounty

Date	Mintage	F	VF	XF	Unc	BU
2009	20,000	—	—	—	—	2.00
2010	20,000	—	—	—	—	2.00

KM# 55 10 CENTS
4.6000 g., Copper Plated Bronze, 22 mm. **Ruler:** Elizabeth II **Obv:** Head right **Rev:** Bell from H.M.A.V. Bounty **Edge:** Reeded

Date	Mintage	F	VF	XF	Unc	BU
2009	20,000	—	—	—	—	3.00
2010	20,000	—	—	—	—	3.00

KM# 56 20 CENTS
6.5000 g., Nickel Plated Bronze, 25 mm. **Ruler:** Elizabeth II **Obv:** Head right **Rev:** Bible from H.M.A.V. Bounty

Date	Mintage	F	VF	XF	Unc	BU
2009	20,000	—	—	—	—	5.00
2010	20,000	—	—	—	—	5.00

KM# 57 50 CENTS
8.0000 g., Copper-Nickel **Ruler:** Elizabeth II **Obv:** Head right **Rev:** Pitcairn Longboat

Date	Mintage	F	VF	XF	Unc	BU
2009	—	—	—	—	—	8.00
2010	—	—	—	—	—	8.00

KM# 14 DOLLAR
Copper-Nickel, 38.8 mm. **Ruler:** Elizabeth II **Obv:** Bust facing right **Rev:** Queen Mum, Elizabeth II and Margaret facing **Rev. Legend:** 80th Birthday of H.M. Queen Elizabeth II

Date	Mintage	F	VF	XF	Unc	BU
2006	—	—	—	—	10.00	12.00

KM# 58 DOLLAR
16.3000 g., Aluminum-Brass, 32 mm. **Ruler:** Elizabeth II **Obv:** Head right **Rev:** Cannon from H.A.M.V. Bounty **Edge:** Reeded

Date	Mintage	F	VF	XF	Unc	BU
2009	20,000	—	—	—	—	12.00
2010	20,000	—	—	—	—	12.00

KM# 45 2 DOLLARS
31.1050 g., 0.9990 Silver 0.9990 oz. ASW, 40.7 mm. **Ruler:** Elizabeth II **Subject:** Year of the Rat **Rev:** Multicolor rat seated right

Date	Mintage	F	VF	XF	Unc	BU
2008 Prooflike	30,000	—	—	—	—	65.00

KM# 46 2 DOLLARS
31.1050 g., 0.9990 Silver 0.9990 oz. ASW, 40.7 mm. **Ruler:** Elizabeth II **Rev:** Multicolor HMAV Bounty under full sail right

Date	Mintage	F	VF	XF	Unc	BU
2008 Prooflike	5,000	—	—	—	—	75.00

KM# 47 2 DOLLARS
31.1050 g., 0.9990 Silver Partially gilt 0.9990 oz. ASW, 40.7 mm. **Ruler:** Elizabeth II **Rev:** HMAV Bounty under full sail right

Date	Mintage	F	VF	XF	Unc	BU
2008 Proof	1,500	Value: 85.00				

KM# 59 2 DOLLARS
19.5000 g., Aluminum-Brass, 35 mm. **Ruler:** Elizabeth II **Obv:** Head right **Rev:** Helm (wheel) from H.M.A.V. Bounty **Edge:** Seqmented reeding

Date	Mintage	F	VF	XF	Unc	BU
2009	20,000	—	—	—	—	15.00

KM# 51 2 DOLLARS
31.1050 g., 0.9990 Silver partially gilt 0.9990 oz. ASW, 40.7 mm. **Ruler:** Elizabeth II **Rev:** Captain William Bligh

Date	Mintage	F	VF	XF	Unc	BU
2009 Proof	1,500	Value: 75.00				

KM# 60 2 DOLLARS
Brass, 36 mm. **Ruler:** Elizabeth II **Rev:** H.M.A.V. Bounty at sail **Edge:** Segmented reeding

Date	Mintage	F	VF	XF	Unc	BU
2010	20,000	—	—	—	—	15.00

KM# 61 2 DOLLARS
15.5000 g., 0.9250 Silver 0.4609 oz. ASW, 35 mm. **Ruler:** Elizabeth II **Subject:** Deep sea fish **Rev:** Black sea devil (Melanocetus Johnsonii) in color

Date	Mintage	F	VF	XF	Unc	BU
2010 Proof	1,000	Value: 75.00				

KM# 62 2 DOLLARS
15.5500 g., 0.9250 Silver 0.4624 oz. ASW, 35 mm. **Ruler:** Elizabeth II **Subject:** Deep sea fish **Rev:** White spotted jellyfish in color

Date	Mintage	F	VF	XF	Unc	BU
2010 Proof	—	Value: 75.00				

KM# 63 2 DOLLARS
15.5500 g., 0.9250 Silver 0.4624 oz. ASW, 35 mm. **Ruler:** Elizabeth II **Subject:** Deep sea fish **Rev:** Laternfish (Mychtophios) in color

Date	Mintage	F	VF	XF	Unc	BU
2010 Proof	1,000	Value: 75.00				

KM# 64 2 DOLLARS
31.1050 g., 0.9990 Silver 0.9990 oz. ASW, 40.7 mm. **Ruler:** Elizabeth II **Subject:** Alice in Wonderland **Rev:** March Hare within backward clock face

Date	Mintage	F	VF	XF	Unc	BU
2011 Proof	15,000	Value: 85.00				

KM# 12 5 DOLLARS
31.1000 g., 0.9990 Silver with Mother-of-Pearl inset 0.9988 oz. ASW, 40 mm. **Ruler:** Elizabeth II **Series:** Save the Whales **Obv:** Crowned bust right **Obv. Legend:** ELIZABETH II • PITCAIRN ISLANDS **Rev:** Humpback Whale and date on mother-of-pearl inset **Edge:** Plain

Date	Mintage	F	VF	XF	Unc	BU
2002 Proof	2,000	Value: 85.00				

KM# 50 5 DOLLARS
1.2700 g., 0.9999 Gold 0.0408 oz. AGW, 13.92 mm. **Ruler:** Elizabeth II **Obv:** Crowned bust right **Obv. Legend:** Elizabeth II Pitcairn Islands **Rev:** Bounty Bible and ship

Date	Mintage	F	VF	XF	Unc	BU
2005 Proof	—	Value: 75.00				

KM# 48 10 DOLLARS
1.2440 g., 0.9999 Gold 0.0400 oz. AGW, 22 mm. **Ruler:** Elizabeth II **Rev:** HMAV Bounty under full sail right

Date	Mintage	F	VF	XF	Unc	BU
2008 Proof	10,000	Value: 75.00				

KM# 49 25 DOLLARS
7.7700 g., 0.9990 Gold 0.2496 oz. AGW, 22 mm. **Ruler:** Elizabeth II **Rev:** HMAV Bounty under full sail right

Date	Mintage	F	VF	XF	Unc	BU
2008 Proof	1,000	Value: 400				

The Republic of Poland, located in central Europe, has an area of 120,725 sq. mi. (312,680 sq. km.) and a population of *38.2 million. Capital: Warszawa (Warsaw). The economy is essentially agricultural, but industrial activity provides the products for foreign trade. Machinery, coal, coke, iron, steel and transport equipment are exported.

MINT MARKS

MV, MW, MW-monogram - Warsaw Mint, 1965-
CHI - Valcambi, Switzerland

Other letters appearing with date denote the Mintmaster at the time the coin was struck.

REPUBLIC

REFORM COINAGE

Y# 276 GROSZ

1.6400 g., Brass, 15.5 mm. **Obv:** National arms **Obv. Legend:** RZECZPOSPOLITA POLSKA **Rev:** Drooping oak leaf over value **Edge:** Reeded

Date	Mintage	F	VF	XF	Unc	BU
2001MW	210,000,020	—	—	—	0.10	0.20
2002MW	240,000,000	—	—	—	0.10	0.20
2003MW	250,000,000	—	—	—	0.10	0.20
2004MW	300,000,000	—	—	—	0.10	0.20
2005MW	375,000,000	—	—	—	0.10	0.20
2006MW	184,000,000	—	—	—	0.10	0.20
2007MW	330,000,000	—	—	—	0.10	0.20
2008MW	—	—	—	—	0.10	0.20
2009MW	—	—	—	—	0.10	0.20
2010MW	—	—	—	—	0.10	0.20

Y# 277 2 GROSZE

2.1300 g., Brass, 17.5 mm. **Obv:** National arms **Obv. Legend:** RZECZPOSPOLITA POLSKA **Rev:** Drooping oak leaves above value **Edge:** Plain

Date	Mintage	F	VF	XF	Unc	BU
2001MW	86,100,000	—	—	—	0.15	0.25
2002MW	83,910,000	—	—	—	0.15	0.25
2003MW	80,000,000	—	—	—	0.15	0.25
2004MW	100,000,000	—	—	—	0.15	0.25
2005MW	163,003,250	—	—	—	0.15	0.25
2006MW	105,000,000	—	—	—	0.15	0.25
2007MW	160,000,000	—	—	—	0.15	0.25
2008MW	—	—	—	—	0.15	0.25
2009MW	—	—	—	—	0.15	0.25
2010MW	—	—	—	—	0.15	0.25

Y# 278 5 GROSZY

2.5900 g., Brass, 19.5 mm. **Obv:** National arms **Obv. Legend:** RZECZPOSPOLITA POLSKA **Rev:** Value at upper left of oak leaves **Edge:** Segmented reeding

Date	Mintage	F	VF	XF	Unc	BU
2001MW	67,368,000	—	—	—	0.25	0.45
2002MW	67,200,000	—	—	—	0.25	0.45
2003MW	48,000,000	—	—	—	0.25	0.45
2004MW	62,500,000	—	—	—	0.25	0.45
2005MW	113,000,000	—	—	—	0.25	0.45
2006MW	54,000,000	—	—	—	0.25	0.45
2007MW	116,000,000	—	—	—	0.25	0.45
2008MW	—	—	—	—	0.25	0.45
2009MW	—	—	—	—	0.25	0.45
2010MW	—	—	—	—	0.25	0.45

Y# 279 10 GROSZY

2.5500 g., Copper-Nickel, 16.5 mm. **Obv:** National arms **Obv. Legend:** RZECZPOSPOLITA POLSKA **Rev:** Value within wreath

Date	Mintage	F	VF	XF	Unc	BU
2001MW	62,820,000	—	—	—	0.40	0.60
2002MW	10,500,000	—	—	—	0.40	0.60
2003MW	31,500,000	—	—	—	0.40	0.60
2004MW	70,500,000	—	—	—	0.40	0.60
2005MW	94,000,000	—	—	—	0.40	0.60
2006MW	40,000,000	—	—	—	0.40	0.60
2007MW	100,000,000	—	—	—	0.40	0.60
2008MW	—	—	—	—	0.40	0.60
2009MW	—	—	—	—	0.40	0.60
2010MW	—	—	—	—	0.40	0.60

Y# 280 20 GROSZY

3.2200 g., Copper-Nickel, 18.5 mm. **Obv:** National arms **Obv. Legend:** RZECZPOSPOLITA POLSKA **Rev:** Value within artistic design **Edge:** Reeded

Date	Mintage	F	VF	XF	Unc	BU
2001MW	41,980,001	—	—	—	0.65	0.85
2002MW	10,500,000	—	—	—	0.65	0.85
2003MW	20,400,000	—	—	—	0.65	0.85
2004MW	40,000,025	—	—	—	0.65	0.85
2005MW	37,000,000	—	—	—	0.65	0.85
2006MW	35,000,000	—	—	—	0.65	0.85
2007MW	68,000,000	—	—	—	0.65	0.85
2008MW	—	—	—	—	0.65	0.85
2009MW	—	—	—	—	0.65	0.85
2010MW	—	—	—	—	0.65	0.85

Y# 281 50 GROSZY

3.9400 g., Copper-Nickel, 20.5 mm. **Obv:** National arms **Obv. Legend:** RZECZPOSPOLITA POLSKA **Rev:** Value to right of sprig **Edge:** Reeded

Date	Mintage	F	VF	XF	Unc	BU
2008MW	—	—	—	—	1.00	1.25
2009MW	—	—	—	—	1.00	1.25
2010MW	—	—	—	—	1.00	1.25

Y# 282 ZLOTY

5.0300 g., Copper-Nickel, 23 mm. **Obv:** National arms **Obv. Legend:** RZECZPOSPOLITA POLSKA **Rev:** Value within wreath **Edge:** Segmented reeding

Date	Mintage	F	VF	XF	Unc	BU
2008MW	—	—	—	—	1.75	2.00
2009MW	—	—	—	—	1.75	2.00
2010MW	—	—	—	—	1.75	2.00

Y# 408 2 ZLOTE

8.1500 g., Brass, 27 mm. **Subject:** Wieliczka Salt Mine **Obv:** Crowned eagle with wings open **Rev:** Ancient salt miners

Date	Mintage	F	VF	XF	Unc	BU
2001	500,000	—	—	3.50	7.00	12.00

Y# 410 2 ZLOTE

8.1500 g., Brass, 27 mm. **Subject:** Amber Route **Obv:** Crowned eagle with wings open **Rev:** Ancient Roman coin and map with route marked in stars

Date	Mintage	F	VF	XF	Unc	BU
2001	500,000	—	—	3.50	7.00	12.00

Y# 412 2 ZLOTE

8.1500 g., Brass, 27 mm. **Subject:** 15 Years of the Constitutional Court **Obv:** Crowned eagle with wings open **Rev:** Crowned eagle head and scale **Edge:** * NBP * eight times

Date	Mintage	F	VF	XF	Unc	BU
2001MW	500,000	—	—	—	3.00	5.00

Y# 414 2 ZLOTE

8.1500 g., Brass, 27 mm. **Obv:** Crowned eagle with wings open **Rev:** Butterfly **Edge:** * NBP * eight times

Date	Mintage	F	VF	XF	Unc	BU
2001MW	600,000	—	—	4.00	8.00	15.00

Y# 418 2 ZLOTE

8.1500 g., Brass, 27 mm. **Subject:** Cardinal Stefan Wyszynski **Obv:** Crowned eagle with wings open **Rev:** Bust left wearing mitre **Edge:** "NBP" eight times

Date	Mintage	F	VF	XF	Unc	BU
2001MW	1,200,000	—	—	—	3.00	5.00

Y# 421 2 ZLOTE

8.1500 g., Brass, 27 mm. **Subject:** Michal Siedlecki **Obv:** Crowned eagle with wings open **Rev:** Bust left and art work **Edge:** NBP eight times

Date	Mintage	F	VF	XF	Unc	BU
2001MW	600,000	—	—	—	3.00	5.00

Y# 422 2 ZLOTE

8.1500 g., Brass, 27 mm. **Subject:** Koledicy **Obv:** Crowned eagle with wings open **Rev:** Christmas celebration scene

Date	Mintage	F	VF	XF	Unc	BU
2001MW	600,000	—	—	—	3.00	5.00

Y# 423 2 ZLOTE

8.1500 g., Brass, 27 mm. **Subject:** Jan III Sobieski **Obv:** Crowned eagle with wings open **Rev:** Bust facing **Edge Lettering:** * NBP * eight times

Date	Mintage	F	VF	XF	Unc	BU
2001MW	500,000	—	—	3.50	7.00	12.00

Y# 426 2 ZLOTE
8.1500 g., Brass, 27 mm. **Subject:** Henryk Wieniawski **Obv:** Crowned eagle with wings open **Rev:** Bust left and violin **Edge Lettering:** * NBP * eight times

Date	Mintage	F	VF	XF	Unc	BU
2001MW	600,000	—	—	—	3.00	5.00

Y# 427 2 ZLOTE
8.1500 g., Brass, 27 mm. **Obv:** Crowned eagle with wings open **Rev:** European Pond Turtles **Edge Lettering:** * NBP * eight times

Date	Mintage	F	VF	XF	Unc	BU
2002MW	750,000	—	—	3.50	7.00	12.00

Y# 431 2 ZLOTE
8.1500 g., Brass, 27 mm. **Subject:** Bronislaw Malinowski **Obv:** Crowned eagle with wings open **Rev:** Bust facing and Trobriand Islanders **Edge Lettering:** * NBP * eight times

Date	Mintage	F	VF	XF	Unc	BU
2002MW	680,000	—	—	—	3.50	5.50

Y# 433 2 ZLOTE
8.1500 g., Brass, 27 mm. **Subject:** World Cup Soccer **Obv:** National arms **Rev:** Soccer players **Edge Lettering:** * NBP * eight times

Date	Mintage	F	VF	XF	Unc	BU
2002MW	1,000,000	—	—	—	3.00	5.00

Y# 439 2 ZLOTE
8.1000 g., Brass, 26.8 mm. **Subject:** August II (1697-1706, 1709-1733) **Obv:** National arms **Rev:** Head facing **Edge Lettering:** * NBP * eight times

Date	Mintage	F	VF	XF	Unc	BU
2002MW	620,000	—	—	—	4.00	7.00

Y# 440 2 ZLOTE
8.1500 g., Brass, 27 mm. **Subject:** Gen. Wladyslaw Anders **Obv:** Crowned eagle with wings open **Rev:** Uniformed bust facing and cross **Edge Lettering:** * NBP * eight times

Date	Mintage	F	VF	XF	Unc	BU
2002MW	680,000	—	—	—	3.00	5.00

Y# 443 2 ZLOTE
8.1500 g., Brass, 27 mm. **Subject:** Malbork Castle **Obv:** Crowned eagle with wings open **Rev:** Castle **Edge Lettering:** * NBP * eight times

Date	Mintage	F	VF	XF	Unc	BU
2002MW	680,000	—	—	—	3.00	5.00

Y# 444 2 ZLOTE
8.1500 g., Brass, 27 mm. **Subject:** Jan Matejko **Obv:** Denomination, crowned eagle and artist's palette **Rev:** Jester behind portrait **Edge Lettering:** * NBP * eight times

Date	Mintage	F	VF	XF	Unc	BU
2002MW	700,000	—	—	—	3.00	5.00

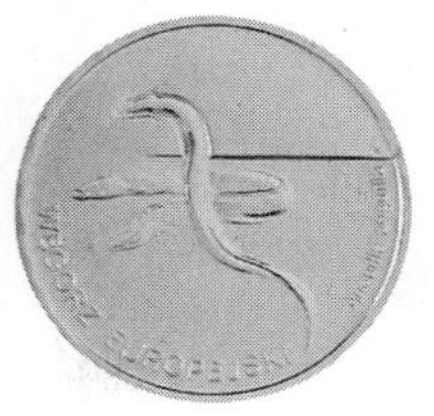

Y# 445 2 ZLOTE
8.1500 g., Brass, 27 mm. **Subject:** Eels **Obv:** Crowned eagle with wings open **Rev:** Two European eels **Edge Lettering:** * NBP * eight times

Date	Mintage	F	VF	XF	Unc	BU
2003MW	450,000	—	—	6.00	12.00	20.00

Y# 446 2 ZLOTE
7.7500 g., Brass, 27 mm. **Subject:** Children **Obv:** Children and square design above crowned eagle, date and value **Rev:** Children on square design **Edge Lettering:** * NBP * eight times **Note:** Center hole.

Date	Mintage	F	VF	XF	Unc	BU
2003MW	2,500,000	—	—	—	4.50	6.50

Y# 447 2 ZLOTE
8.1500 g., Brass, 27 mm. **Subject:** City of Poznan (Posen) **Obv:** Crowned eagle with wings open **Rev:** Clock face and tower flanked by goat heads **Edge Lettering:** * NBP * eight times

Date	Mintage	F	VF	XF	Unc	BU
2003MW	600,000	—	—	—	5.00	8.00

Y# 451 2 ZLOTE
8.1500 g., Brass, 27 mm. **Subject:** Easter Monday Festival **Obv:** Crowned eagle with wings open **Rev:** Festival scene **Edge Lettering:** * NBP * eight times

Date	Mintage	F	VF	XF	Unc	BU
2003MW	600,000	—	—	—	4.00	7.00

Y# 455 2 ZLOTE
8.1500 g., Brass, 27 mm. **Subject:** Petroleum and Gas Industry 150th Anniversary **Obv:** Crowned eagle with wings open **Rev:** Portrait and refinery **Edge Lettering:** * NBP * eight times

Date	Mintage	F	VF	XF	Unc	BU
2003MW	600,000	—	—	—	3.50	5.50

Y# 456 2 ZLOTE
8.1500 g., Brass, 27 mm. **Subject:** General B. S. Maczek **Obv:** Crowned eagle with wings open **Rev:** Military uniformed portrait **Edge Lettering:** * NBP * eight times

Date	Mintage	F	VF	XF	Unc	BU
2003MW	700,000	—	—	—	3.00	5.00

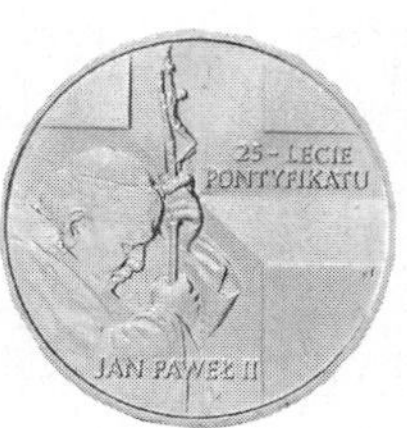

Y# 465 2 ZLOTE
8.1500 g., Aluminum-Bronze, 27 mm. **Subject:** Pope JohnPaul II **Obv:** Small national arms at lower right with cross in background **Obv. Legend:** RZECZPOSPOLITA POLSKA **Rev:** Pope in prayer at left, cross in background **Edge Lettering:** * NBP * eight times

Date	Mintage	F	VF	XF	Unc	BU
2003MW	2,000,000	—	—	—	3.00	5.00

Y# 473 2 ZLOTE
8.1500 g., Brass, 27 mm. **Obv:** Crowned eagle with wings open **Rev:** Stanislaus Leszcywski **Edge Lettering:** * NBP * eight times

Date	Mintage	F	VF	XF	Unc	BU
2003MW	600,000	—	—	—	3.50	5.50

Y# 477 2 ZLOTE
8.1500 g., Brass, 27 mm. **Obv:** Crowned eagle with wings open and artist's palette **Rev:** Self portrait of Jacek Malczewski **Edge Lettering:** * NBP * eight times

Date	Mintage	F	VF	XF	Unc	BU
2003MW	600,000	—	—	—	3.50	5.50

Y# 479 2 ZLOTE
8.1500 g., Brass, 27 mm. **Subject:** 80th Anniversary of the Modern Zloty Currency **Obv:** Crowned eagle with wings open above value **Rev:** Bust left **Edge Lettering:** * NBP * eight times

Date	Mintage	F	VF	XF	Unc	BU
2004MW	800,000	—	—	—	3.00	5.00

Y# 481 2 ZLOTE
8.1500 g., Brass, 27 mm. **Subject:** Poland Joining the European Union **Obv:** Crowned eagle with wings open above value **Rev:** Map and stars **Edge Lettering:** * NBP * eight times

Date	Mintage	F	VF	XF	Unc	BU
2004MW	1,000,000	—	—	—	3.00	5.00

Y# 484 2 ZLOTE
8.1500 g., Brass, 27 mm. **Subject:** Dolnoslaskie (Lower Silesian) District **Obv:** Crowned eagle with wings open on map **Rev:** Silesian eagle on shield **Edge Lettering:** * NBP * eight times

Date	Mintage	F	VF	XF	Unc	BU
2004MW	700,000	—	—	—	4.00	6.00

Y# 485 2 ZLOTE
8.1500 g., Brass, 27 mm. **Subject:** Kujawsko-Pomorskie District

Obv: Crowned eagle with wings open on map **Rev:** Shield with crowned half eagle and griffin **Edge Lettering:** * NBP * eight times

Date	Mintage	F	VF	XF	Unc	BU
2004MW	750,000	—	—	—	7.00	12.00

Y# 486 2 ZLOTE

8.1500 g., Brass, 27 mm. **Subject:** Lubuskie District **Obv:** Crowned eagle with wings open on map **Rev:** Shield with stag left **Edge Lettering:** * NBP * eight times

Date	Mintage	F	VF	XF	Unc	BU
2004MW	820,000	—	—	—	3.00	5.00

Y# 487 2 ZLOTE

8.1500 g., Brass, 27 mm. **Subject:** Lodzkie District **Obv:** Crowned eagle with wings open on map **Rev:** Shield with two creatures above an eagle **Edge Lettering:** * NBP * eight times

Date	Mintage	F	VF	XF	Unc	BU
2004MW	920,000	—	—	—	3.00	5.00

Y# 488 2 ZLOTE

8.1500 g., Brass, 27 mm. **Subject:** Malopolskie District **Obv:** Crowned eagle with wings open on map **Rev:** Shield with crowned eagle **Edge Lettering:** * NBP * eight times

Date	Mintage	F	VF	XF	Unc	BU
2004MW	920,000	—	—	—	3.00	5.00

Y# 489 2 ZLOTE

8.1500 g., Brass, 27 mm. **Subject:** Mazowieckie District **Obv:** Crowned eagle with wings open on map **Rev:** Eagle on shield **Edge Lettering:** * NBP * eight times

Date	Mintage	F	VF	XF	Unc	BU
2004MW	920,000	—	—	—	3.00	5.00

Y# 490 2 ZLOTE

8.1500 g., Brass, 27 mm. **Subject:** Podkarpackie District **Obv:** Crowned eagle with wings open on map **Rev:** Shield with iron cross above griffin and lion **Edge Lettering:** * NBP * eight times

Date	Mintage	F	VF	XF	Unc	BU
2004MW	920,000	—	—	—	3.00	5.00

Y# 491 2 ZLOTE

8.1500 g., Brass, 27 mm. **Subject:** Podlaskie District **Obv:** Crowned eagle with wings open on map **Rev:** Shield with Polish eagle above Lithuanian knight **Edge Lettering:** * NBP * eight times

Date	Mintage	F	VF	XF	Unc	BU
2004MW	900,000	—	—	—	3.00	5.00

Y# 492 2 ZLOTE

8.1500 g., Brass, 27 mm. **Subject:** Pomorskie District **Obv:** Crowned eagle with wings open on map **Rev:** Griffin on shield **Edge Lettering:** * NBP * eight times

Date	Mintage	F	VF	XF	Unc	BU
2004MW	900,000	—	—	—	3.00	5.00

Y# 493 2 ZLOTE

8.1500 g., Brass, 27 mm. **Subject:** Slaskie (Silesia) District **Obv:** Crowned eagle with wings open on map **Rev:** Eagle on shield **Edge Lettering:** * NBP * eight times

Date	Mintage	F	VF	XF	Unc	BU
2004MW	960,000	—	—	—	3.00	5.00

Y# 496 2 ZLOTE

8.1500 g., Brass, 27 mm. **Subject:** Warsaw Uprising 60th Anniversary **Obv:** Crowned eagle with wings open **Rev:** Resistance symbol on brick wall **Edge Lettering:** * NBP * eight times

Date	Mintage	F	VF	XF	Unc	BU
2004MW	900,000	—	—	—	3.00	5.00

Y# 499 2 ZLOTE

8.1500 g., Brass, 27 mm. **Obv:** Crowned eagle with wings open **Rev:** Gen. Stanislaw F. Sosabowski **Edge Lettering:** * NBP * eight times

Date	Mintage	F	VF	XF	Unc	BU
2004MW	850,000	—	—	—	3.00	5.00

Y# 501 2 ZLOTE

8.1500 g., Brass, 27 mm. **Subject:** Polish Police 85th Anniversary **Obv:** Crowned eagle with wings open **Rev:** Police badge **Edge Lettering:** * NBP * eight times

Date	Mintage	F	VF	XF	Unc	BU
2004MW	760,000	—	—	—	3.00	5.00

Y# 503 2 ZLOTE

8.1500 g., Brass, 27 mm. **Subject:** Polish Senate **Obv:** Crowned eagle with wings open **Rev:** Senate eagle and speaker's staff **Edge Lettering:** * NBP * eight times

Date	Mintage	F	VF	XF	Unc	BU
2004MW	760,000	—	—	—	3.00	5.00

Y# 505 2 ZLOTE

8.1500 g., Brass, 27 mm. **Obv:** Crowned eagle with wings open **Rev:** Aleksander Czekanowski (1833-1876) **Edge Lettering:** * NBP * eight times

Date	Mintage	F	VF	XF	Unc	BU
2004MW	700,000	—	—	—	3.00	5.00

Y# 507 2 ZLOTE

8.1500 g., Brass, 27 mm. **Obv:** National arms **Obv. Legend:** RZECZPOSPOLITA POLSKA **Rev:** Harvest fest couple in folk costume at left, large group in background at right **Rev. Legend:** DOZYNKI **Edge Lettering:** * NBP * eight times

Date	Mintage	F	VF	XF	Unc	BU
2004MW	850,000	—	—	—	3.00	5.00

Y# 509 2 ZLOTE

8.1500 g., Brass, 27 mm. **Subject:** Warsaw Fine Arts Academy Centennial **Obv:** Crowned eagle with wings open **Rev:** Painter's hands **Edge Lettering:** * NBP * eight times

Date	Mintage	F	VF	XF	Unc	BU
2004MW	850,000	—	—	—	3.00	5.00

Y# 516 2 ZLOTE

8.1500 g., Brass, 27 mm. **Subject:** Olympics **Obv:** Crowned eagle with wings open **Rev:** Ancient runners **Edge Lettering:** * NBP * eight times

Date	Mintage	F	VF	XF	Unc	BU
2004MW	1,000,000	—	—	—	3.00	5.00

Y# 607 2 ZLOTE

8.1500 g., Brass, 27 mm. **Obv:** National arms on outlined map **Obv. Legend:** RZECZPOSPOLITA POLSKA **Rev:** Region arms **Rev. Legend:** WOJEWODZTWO - OPOLSKIE **Edge Lettering:** * NBP * eight times

Date	Mintage	F	VF	XF	Unc	BU
2004MW	900,000	—	—	—	3.00	5.00

Y# 464 2 ZLOTE

8.1500 g., Brass, 27 mm. **Obv:** Crowned eagle with wings open **Rev:** Harbor Porpoises **Edge Lettering:** * NBP * eight times

Date	Mintage	F	VF	XF	Unc	BU
2004MW	800,000	—	—	3.50	7.00	12.00

Y# 512 2 ZLOTE

8.1500 g., Brass, 27 mm. **Obv:** Crowned eagle with wings open and artist's palette **Rev:** Stanislaw Wyspianski (1869-1907) **Edge Lettering:** * NBP * eight times

Date	Mintage	F	VF	XF	Unc	BU
2004MW	900,000	—	—	—	3.00	5.00

Y# 514 2 ZLOTE

8.1500 g., Brass, 27 mm. **Obv:** National arms on outlined map **Rev:** Wojewodztwo-Lubelskie arms with stag on shield **Edge Lettering:** * NBP * eight times

Date	Mintage	F	VF	XF	Unc	BU
2004MW	820,000	—	—	—	—	7.50

Y# 283 2 ZLOTE

5.2100 g., Bi-Metallic Copper-Nickel center in Aluminum-Bronze ring, 21.5 mm. **Obv:** National arms within circle **Obv. Legend:** RZECZPOSPOLITA POLSKA **Rev:** Value flanked by oak leaves **Edge:** Plain

Date	Mintage	F	VF	XF	Unc	BU
2005MW	5,000,000	—	—	—	4.00	4.50
2006MW	5,000,000	—	—	—	4.00	4.50
2007MW	20,000,000	—	—	—	4.00	4.50
2008MW	—	—	—	—	4.00	4.50
2009MW	—	—	—	—	4.00	4.50
2010MW	—	—	—	—	4.00	4.50

Y# 520 2 ZLOTE

8.1500 g., Brass, 27 mm. **Obv:** National arms **Rev:** Owl perched on nest with owlets **Rev. Legend:** PUCHACZ - Bubo-bubo **Edge Lettering:** * NBP * eight times

Date	Mintage	F	VF	XF	Unc	BU
2005MW	990,000	—	—	—	4.00	7.00

Y# 521 2 ZLOTE

8.1500 g., Brass, 27 mm. **Obv:** Crowned eagle with wings open **Rev:** Ship within circle **Edge Lettering:** * NBP * eight times

Date	Mintage	F	VF	XF	Unc	BU
2005MW	920,000	—	—	—	3.50	5.50

Y# 522 2 ZLOTE

8.1500 g., Brass, 26.8 mm. **Subject:** Japan's Aichi Expo **Obv:** Crowned eagle with wings open **Rev:** Two cranes flying over Mt. Fuji with rising sun background **Edge Lettering:** * NBP * eight times

Date	Mintage	F	VF	XF	Unc	BU
2005MW	1,000,000	—	—	—	3.50	5.50

Y# 524 2 ZLOTE

8.1500 g., Brass, 27 mm. **Subject:** Obrony Jasnej Gory **Obv:** Crowned eagle with wings open **Rev:** Half length figure left and bombarded city scene **Edge Lettering:** * NBP * eight times

Date	Mintage	F	VF	XF	Unc	BU
2005MW	1,000,000	—	—	—	4.00	6.00

Y# 525 2 ZLOTE

8.1500 g., Brass, 27 mm. **Subject:** Pope John-Paul II **Obv:** National arms **Obv. Legend:** RZECZPOSPOLITA POLSKA **Rev:** Bust right at left, outline of church steeple at center right **Edge Lettering:** * NBP * eight times

Date	Mintage	F	VF	XF	Unc	BU
2005MW	4,000,000	—	—	—	4.00	6.00

Y# 527 2 ZLOTE

8.1500 g., Brass, 27 mm. **Obv:** Crowned eagle with wings open **Rev:** Bust 1/4 left with horse head and goose at left **Edge Lettering:** * NBP * eight times

Date	Mintage	F	VF	XF	Unc	BU
2005MW	850,000	—	—	—	3.00	5.00

Y# 528 2 ZLOTE

8.1500 g., Brass, 27 mm. **Obv:** Crowned eagle above wall **Rev:** Kolobrzeg Lighthouse **Edge Lettering:** * NBP * eight times

Date	Mintage	F	VF	XF	Unc	BU
2005MW	1,100,000	—	—	—	3.00	5.00

Y# 529 2 ZLOTE

8.1500 g., Brass, 27 mm. **Obv:** National arms above gateway **Rev:** Wloclawek Cathedral **Edge Lettering:** * NBP * eight times

Date	Mintage	F	VF	XF	Unc	BU
2005MW	1,100,000	—	—	—	3.00	5.00

Y# 530 2 ZLOTE

8.1500 g., Brass, 27 mm. **Obv:** National arms **Rev:** Bust of King Stanislaus Poniatowski right **Edge Lettering:** * NBP * eight times

Date	Mintage	F	VF	XF	Unc	BU
2005MW	990,000	—	—	—	3.00	5.00

Y# 541 2 ZLOTE

8.1500 g., Brass, 27 mm. **Obv:** Eagle, value, palette and paint brushes **Rev:** Painter Tadeusz Makowski **Edge Lettering:** * NBP * eight times

Date	Mintage	F	VF	XF	Unc	BU
2005MW	900,000	—	—	—	3.00	5.00

Y# 558 2 ZLOTE

8.1500 g., Brass, 27 mm. **Subject:** 60th Anniversary of WWII **Obv:** National arms **Edge Lettering:** * NBP * eight times

Date	Mintage	F	VF	XF	Unc	BU
2005MW	1,000,000	—	—	—	3.00	5.00

Y# 560 2 ZLOTE

8.1500 g., Brass, 27 mm. **Obv:** National arms on outline map **Obv. Legend:** RZECZPOSPOLITA POLSKA **Rev:** Region arms **Rev. Legend:** WOJEWOZTWO SWIETOKRZYSKIE **Edge Lettering:** * NBP * eight times

Date	Mintage	F	VF	XF	Unc	BU
2005MW	900,000	—	—	—	3.00	5.00

Y# 562 2 ZLOTE

8.1500 g., Brass, 27 mm. **Obv:** National arms **Rev:** Region Wielkopolskie **Edge Lettering:** * NBP * eight times

Date	Mintage	F	VF	XF	Unc	BU
2005MW	940,000	—	—	—	3.00	5.00

Y# 563 2 ZLOTE

8.1500 g., Brass, 27 mm. **Obv:** National arms on outlined map **Obv. Legend:** RZECZPOSPOLITA POLSKA **Rev:** Region arms **Rev. Legend:** WOJEWODZTWO ZACHODIOPOMORSKIE **Edge Lettering:** * NBP * eight times

Date	Mintage	F	VF	XF	Unc	BU
2005	—	—	—	—	3.00	5.00

Y# 564 2 ZLOTE

8.1500 g., Brass, 27 mm. **Obv:** National arms **Rev:** City of Gniezno **Edge Lettering:** * NBP * eight times

Date	Mintage	F	VF	XF	Unc	BU
2005	1,250,000	—	—	—	3.00	5.00

Y# 565 2 ZLOTE

8.1500 g., Brass, 27 mm. **Obv:** National arms **Rev:** Solidarity **Edge Lettering:** * NBP * eight times

Date	Mintage	F	VF	XF	Unc	BU
2005MW	1,000,000	—	—	—	3.00	5.00

Y# 608 2 ZLOTE
8.1500 g., Brass, 27 mm. **Subject:** 500th Anniversary Birth of Nikolaja Reja **Obv:** National arms **Obv. Legend:** RZECZPOSPOLITA POLSKA **Rev:** Bust of Reja facing 3/4 right **Edge Lettering:** NBP eight times

Date	Mintage	F	VF	XF	Unc	BU
2005	850,000	—	—	—	3.00	5.00

Y# 614 2 ZLOTE
8.1500 g., Brass, 27 mm. **Obv:** National arms on outlined map **Obv. Legend:** RZECZPOSPOLITA POLSKA **Rev:** Region arms **Rev. Legend:** WOJEWÓDZTWO WARMINSKO - MAZURSKIE **Edge Lettering:** * NBP * eight times

Date	Mintage	F	VF	XF	Unc	BU
2005MW	900,000	—	—	—	3.00	5.00

Y# 753 2 ZLOTE
8.1500 g., Brass, 27 mm. **Subject:** Cizsyn **Rev:** Round tower

Date	Mintage	F	VF	XF	Unc	BU
2005MW	—	—	—	—	3.00	5.00

Y# 532 2 ZLOTE
8.1500 g., Brass, 27 mm. **Obv:** National arms **Rev:** St. John's Night dancer **Edge Lettering:** * NBP * eight times

Date	Mintage	F	VF	XF	Unc	BU
2006MW	1,000,000	—	—	—	2.50	4.00

Y# 534 2 ZLOTE
8.1500 g., Brass, 27 mm. **Obv:** National arms **Rev:** Alpine Marmot standing **Edge Lettering:** * NBP * eight times

Date	Mintage	F	VF	XF	Unc	BU
2006MW	1,400,000	—	—	—	3.00	6.00

Y# 543 2 ZLOTE
8.1500 g., Brass, 27 mm. **Obv:** Polish Eagle above castle gate **Rev:** Bochnia church **Edge Lettering:** * NBP * eight times

Date	Mintage	F	VF	XF	Unc	BU
2006MW	1,100,000	—	—	—	3.00	5.00

Y# 544 2 ZLOTE
8.1500 g., Brass, 27 mm. **Obv:** Polish Eagle above castle gate **Rev:** Chelm church **Edge Lettering:** * NBP * eight times

Date	Mintage	F	VF	XF	Unc	BU
2006MW	1,100,000	—	—	—	3.00	5.00

Y# 545 2 ZLOTE
8.1500 g., Brass, 27 mm. **Obv:** Polish Eagle above castle gate **Rev:** Chelmno Palace **Edge Lettering:** * NBP * eight times

Date	Mintage	F	VF	XF	Unc	BU
2006MW	1,100,000	—	—	—	3.00	5.00

Y# 546 2 ZLOTE
8.1500 g., Brass, 27 mm. **Obv:** Polish Eagle above castle gate **Rev:** Elblag tower **Edge Lettering:** * NBP * eight times

Date	Mintage	F	VF	XF	Unc	BU
2006MW	1,100,000	—	—	—	3.00	5.00

Y# 547 2 ZLOTE
8.1500 g., Brass, 27 mm. **Obv:** Polish Eagle above castle gate **Rev:** Castle **Rev. Legend:** KOSCIOL W. HACZOWIE **Edge Lettering:** * NBP * eight times

Date	Mintage	F	VF	XF	Unc	BU
2006MW	1,000,000	—	—	—	3.00	5.00

Y# 548 2 ZLOTE
8.1500 g., Brass, 27 mm. **Obv:** National arms above gateway **Rev:** Legnica tower and building **Edge Lettering:** * NBP * eight times

Date	Mintage	F	VF	XF	Unc	BU
2006MW	1,100,000	—	—	—	3.00	5.00

Y# 549 2 ZLOTE
8.1500 g., Brass, 27 mm. **Obv:** Polish Eagle above castle gate **Rev:** Pszczyna palace **Edge Lettering:** * NBP * eight times

Date	Mintage	F	VF	XF	Unc	BU
2006MW	1,100,000	—	—	—	3.00	5.00

Y# 550 2 ZLOTE
8.1500 g., Brass, 27 mm. **Obv:** Polish Eagle above castle gate **Rev:** Sandomierz palace **Edge Lettering:** * NBP * eight times

Date	Mintage	F	VF	XF	Unc	BU
2006MW	1,100,000	—	—	—	3.00	5.00

Y# 566 2 ZLOTE
8.1500 g., Brass, 27 mm. **Obv:** National arms **Rev:** City of Jaroslaw **Edge Lettering:** * NBP * eight times

Date	Mintage	F	VF	XF	Unc	BU
2006MW	1,200,000	—	—	—	3.00	5.00

Y# 569 2 ZLOTE
8.1500 g., Brass, 27 mm. **Obv:** National arms **Rev:** Castle Zagan **Edge Lettering:** * NBP * eight times

Date	Mintage	F	VF	XF	Unc	BU
2006MW	1,100,000	—	—	—	3.00	5.00

Y# 570 2 ZLOTE
815.0000 g., Brass, 27 mm. **Obv:** National arms above gateway **Rev:** City of Nysa **Edge Lettering:** * NBP * eight times

Date	Mintage	F	VF	XF	Unc	BU
2006MW	1,100,000	—	—	—	5.00	3.00

Y# 571 2 ZLOTE
8.1500 g., Brass, 27 mm. **Subject:** 30th Anniversary of June 1976 **Obv:** National arms **Edge Lettering:** * NBP * eight times

Date	Mintage	F	VF	XF	Unc	BU
2006MW	1,000,000	—	—	—	3.00	5.00

Y# 573 2 ZLOTE
8.1500 g., Brass, 27 mm. **Obv:** Polish eagle above wall **Rev:** Nowy Sacz church **Edge Lettering:** * NBP * eight times

Date	Mintage	F	VF	XF	Unc	BU
2006MW	1,100,000	—	—	—	3.00	5.00

Y# 574 2 ZLOTE
8.1500 g., Brass, 27 mm. **Subject:** 500th Anniversary of the Publication of the Statute by Laski **Obv:** National arms above value **Rev:** Jan Laski and book **Edge Lettering:** * NBP * eight times

Date	Mintage	F	VF	XF	Unc	BU
2006MW	1,000,000	—	—	—	3.00	5.00

Y# 575 2 ZLOTE
8.1500 g., Brass, 27 mm. **Subject:** Aleksander Gierymski (painter) **Obv:** Palette, brushes at left, national arms at right **Obv. Legend:** RZECZPOSPOLITA POLSKA **Rev:** Bust of Gierymski facing at left, coastline village in background **Edge Lettering:** * NBP * eight times

Date	Mintage	F	VF	XF	Unc	BU
2006MW	1,000,000	—	—	—	3.00	5.00

Y# 576 2 ZLOTE
8.1500 g., Brass, 27 mm. **Obv:** National arms **Rev:** Knight on horseback **Edge Lettering:** * NBP * eight times

Date	Mintage	F	VF	XF	Unc	BU
2006MW	1,000,000	—	—	—	3.00	5.00

Y# 580 2 ZLOTE
8.1500 g., Brass, 27 mm. **Obv:** Polish eagle above wall **Rev:** Kalisz building **Edge Lettering:** * NBP * eight times

Date	Mintage	F	VF	XF	Unc	BU
2006MW	1,100,000	—	—	—	3.00	5.00

Y# 582 2 ZLOTE
8.1500 g., Brass, 27 mm. **Obv:** National arms **Obv. Legend:** RZECZPOSPOLITA POLSKA **Rev:** Queen's head left as on KM-20, coin design from 1932 **Edge Lettering:** * NBP * eight times

Date	Mintage	F	VF	XF	Unc	BU
2006MW	1,000,000	—	—	—	3.00	5.00

Y# 605 2 ZLOTE
8.1500 g., Brass, 27 mm. **Obv:** National arms **Obv. Legend:** RZECZPOSPOLITA POLSKA **Rev:** Skier and marksman standing **Rev. Legend:** XX ZIMOWE IGAZYSKA OLIMPIJSKIE - TURYN **Edge Lettering:** * NBP * eight times

Date	Mintage	F	VF	XF	Unc	BU
2006MW	1,200,000	—	—	—	3.00	5.00

Y# 606 2 ZLOTE
8.1500 g., Brass, 27 mm. **Obv:** National arms **Obv. Legend:** RZECZPOSPOLITA POLSKA **Rev:** Large soccer ball with fancy linked date 2006 **Rev. Legend:** MISTRZOSTWA SWIATA W PItCE NOZNEJ NIEMCY - FIFA **Edge Lettering:** * NBP * eight times

Date	Mintage	F	VF	XF	Unc	BU
2006MW	1,200,000	—	—	—	3.00	5.00

Y# 609 2 ZLOTE

8.1500 g., Brass, 27 mm. **Subject:** 100th Anniversary - Warsaw School of Economics **Obv:** National arms **Obv. Legend:** RZECZPOSPOLITA POLSKA **Rev:** School facade **Rev. Legend:** SZKOLA CLOWNA HANDLOWA W WARSZAWIE **Rev. Inscription:** Large SGH **Edge Lettering:** * NBP * eight times

Date	Mintage	F	VF	XF	Unc	BU
2006MW	1,000,000	—	—	—	3.00	5.00

Y# 577 2 ZLOTE

8.1500 g., Brass, 27 mm. **Obv:** Crowned eagle **Rev:** Kwidzyn Castle **Edge Lettering:** * NBP * eight times

Date	Mintage	F	VF	XF	Unc	BU
2007MW	1,000,000	—	—	—	3.00	5.00

Y# 578 2 ZLOTE

8.1500 g., Brass, 27 mm. **Obv:** Crowned eagle **Rev:** Grey Seal and silhouette **Edge Lettering:** * NBP * eight times

Date	Mintage	F	VF	XF	Unc	BU
2007MW	1,000,000	—	—	—	4.00	7.00

Y# 586 2 ZLOTE

8.1500 g., Brass, 27 mm. **Subject:** 75th Anniversary Breaking the Enigma Code **Obv:** National arms **Obv. Legend:** RZECZPOSPOLITA POLSKA **Rev:** Enigma machine wheel **Edge Lettering:** * NBP * eight times

Date	Mintage	F	VF	XF	Unc	BU
2007MW	900,000	—	—	—	3.00	5.00

Y# 590 2 ZLOTE

8.1500 g., Brass, 27 mm. **Obv:** National arms **Obv. Legend:** RZECZPOSPOLITA POLSKA **Rev:** Bust of Domeyko facing **Rev. Legend:** IGNACY DOMEYKO 1802 - 1889 **Edge Lettering:** * NBP * eight times

Date	Mintage	F	VF	XF	Unc	BU
2007MW	900,000	—	—	—	3.00	5.00

Y# 592 2 ZLOTE

8.1500 g., Brass, 27 mm. **Subject:** History of Zloty **Obv:** Nike at left, obverse of 5 Zlotych, Y#18, national arms below **Obv. Legend:** RZECZPOLPOLITA POLSKA **Rev:** Spray at left of reverse of 5 Zlotych, Y# 18 **Edge Lettering:** * NBP * eight times

Date	Mintage	F	VF	XF	Unc	BU
2007MW	900,000	—	—	—	3.00	5.00

Y# 594 2 ZLOTE

8.1500 g., Brass, 27 mm. **Subject:** 750th Anniversary Municipality of Krakau **Obv:** National arms **Obv. Legend:** RZECZPOSPOLITA POLSKA **Rev:** Knight standing facing with spear and shield **Edge Lettering:** * NBP * eight times

Date	Mintage	F	VF	XF	Unc	BU
2007MW	900,000	—	—	—	3.00	5.00

Y# 610 2 ZLOTE

8.1500 g., Brass, 27 mm. **Subject:** Artic Explorers Antoni B. Dombrowolski and Henryk Arctowski **Obv:** National arms **Obv. Legend:** RZCEZPOSPOLITA POLSKA **Rev:** Explorer's bust facing at bottom, sailing ship in background **Edge Lettering:** * NBP * eight times

Date	Mintage	F	VF	XF	Unc	BU
2007MW	900,000	—	—	—	3.00	5.00

Y# 611 2 ZLOTE

8.1500 g., Brass, 27 mm. **Obv:** National arms **Obv. Legend:** RZECZPOSPOLITA POLSKA **Rev:** Ciezkozbrojny in armor, horseback left **Rev. Legend:** RYCERZ CIEZKOZBROJNY-XV **Edge Lettering:** * NBP * eight times

Date	Mintage	F	VF	XF	Unc	BU
2007MW	900,000	—	—	—	3.00	5.00

Y# 612 2 ZLOTE

8.1500 g., Brass, 27 mm. **Subject:** 70th Anniversary Death of Szymanowski **Obv:** National arms **Obv. Legend:** RZECZPOSPOLITA POLSKA **Rev:** Bust facing 3/4 right at left, music score in background **Rev. Legend:** ROCZNICA URODZIN KAROLA SYMANOWSKIEGO **Edge Lettering:** * NBP * eight times

Date	Mintage	F	VF	XF	Unc	BU
2007MW	900,000	—	—	—	3.00	5.00

Y# 613 2 ZLOTE

8.1500 g., Brass, 27 mm. **Obv:** National arms above gateway **Obv. Legend:** RZECZPOSPOLITA POLSKA **Rev:** Buildings **Rev. Legend:** STARGARD - SZCZECINSKI **Edge Lettering:** * NBP * eight times

Date	Mintage	F	VF	XF	Unc	BU
2007MW	1,000,000	—	—	—	3.00	5.00

Y# 615 2 ZLOTE

8.1500 g., Brass, 27 mm. **Obv:** National arms above gateway **Obv. Legend:** RZECZPOSPOLITA POLSKA **Rev:** Building with branches at left and right **Rev. Legend:** BRZEG **Edge Lettering:** * NBP * eight times

Date	Mintage	F	VF	XF	Unc	BU
2007MW	1,000,000	—	—	—	3.00	5.00

Y# 616 2 ZLOTE

8.1500 g., Brass, 27 mm. **Obv:** National arms above gateway **Obv. Legend:** RZECZPOSPOLITA POLSKA **Rev:** Church **Rev. Legend:** LOMZA **Edge Lettering:** * NBP alternating normal and inverted 4x

Date	Mintage	F	VF	XF	Unc	BU
2007MW	1,000,000	—	—	—	3.00	5.00

Y# 617 2 ZLOTE

8.1500 g., Brass, 27 mm. **Obv:** National arms above gateway **Obv. Legend:** RZECZPOSPOLITA POLSKA **Rev:** Church **Rev. Legend:** PLOCK **Edge Lettering:** * NBP * eight times

Date	Mintage	F	VF	XF	Unc	BU
2007MW	1,000,000	—	—	—	3.00	5.00

Y# 618 2 ZLOTE

8.1500 g., Brass, 27 mm. **Obv:** National arms above gateway **Obv. Legend:** RZECZPOSPOLITA POLSKA **Rev:** Church **Rev. Legend:** PRZEMYSL **Edge Lettering:** * NBP * eight times

Date	Mintage	F	VF	XF	Unc	BU
2007MW	1,000,000	—	—	—	3.00	5.00

Y# 619 2 ZLOTE

8.1500 g., Brass, 27 mm. **Obv:** National arms above gateway **Obv. Legend:** RZECZPOSPOLITA POLSKA **Rev:** Towered gateway **Rev. Legend:** RACIBÓRZ **Edge Lettering:** * NBP * eight times

Date	Mintage	F	VF	XF	Unc	BU
2007MW	1,000,000	—	—	—	3.00	5.00

Y# 620 2 ZLOTE

8.1500 g., Brass, 27 mm. **Obv:** National arms above gateway **Obv. Legend:** RZECZPOSPOLITA POLSKA **Rev:** Church **Rev. Legend:** SLUPSK **Edge Lettering:** NBP repeated

Date	Mintage	F	VF	XF	Unc	BU
2007MW	1,000,000	—	—	—	3.00	5.00

Y# 621 2 ZLOTE

8.1500 g., Brass, 27 mm. **Obv:** National arms above gateway **Obv. Legend:** RZECZPOSPOLITA POLSKA **Rev:** Church **Rev. Legend:** SWIDNICA **Edge Lettering:** * NBP * eight times

Date	Mintage	F	VF	XF	Unc	BU
2007MW	1,000,000	—	—	—	3.00	5.00

Y# 622 2 ZLOTE

8.1500 g., Brass, 27 mm. **Obv:** National arms **Obv. Legend:** RZECZPOSPOLITA POLSKE **Rev:** Town view **Rev. Legend:** MIASTO SREDNIOWIECZNE - W TORUNIU **Edge Lettering:** * NBP * eight times

Date	Mintage	F	VF	XF	Unc	BU
2007MW	900,000	—	—	—	3.00	5.00

Y# 623 2 ZLOTE

8.1500 g., Brass, 27 mm. **Obv:** National arms above gateway **Obv. Legend:** RZECZPOSPOLITA POLSKA **Rev:** Church **Rev. Legend:** GORZÓW WIELKOPOLSKI **Edge Lettering:** * NBP * eight times

Date	Mintage	F	VF	XF	Unc	BU
2007MW	1,000,000	—	—	—	3.00	5.00

Y# 624 2 ZLOTE

8.1500 g., Brass, 27 mm. **Obv:** National arms above gateway **Obv. Legend:** RZECZPOSPOLITA POLSKA **Rev:** Church at lower right, houses to left, fortress in upper background **Rev. Legend:** KLODZKO **Edge Lettering:** * NBP * eight times

Date	Mintage	F	VF	XF	Unc	BU
2007MW	1,000,000	—	—	—	3.00	5.00

Y# 625 2 ZLOTE

8.1500 g., Brass, 27 mm. **Obv:** National arms above gateway **Obv. Legend:** RZECZPOSPOLITA POLSKE **Rev:** Church **Rev. Legend:** TARNOW **Edge Lettering:** * NBP * eight times

Date	Mintage	F	VF	XF	Unc	BU
2007MW	1,000,000	—	—	—	3.00	5.00

Y# 626 2 ZLOTE

8.1500 g., Brass, 27 mm. **Subject:** Leon Wyczolkowski **Obv:** Artist's palette, brushes at left, national arms at right **Obv. Legend:** RZECZPOSPOLITA POLSKA **Rev:** Bust facing **Edge Lettering:** * NBP * eight times

Date	Mintage	F	VF	XF	Unc	BU
2007MW	900,000	—	—	—	3.00	5.00

Y# 755 2 ZLOTE

815.0000 g., Brass, 27 mm. **Subject:** Joseph Conrad **Rev:** Portrait, signature and ship

Date	Mintage	F	VF	XF	Unc	BU
2007	—	—	—	—	3.00	5.00

Y# 629 2 ZLOTE

8.1500 g., Brass, 27 mm. **Subject:** 40th Anniversary "Rocznica" March **Obv:** National arms above value **Obv. Legend:** RZECZPOSPOLITA POLSKA **Obv. Designer:** Ewa Tyc-Karpinska **Rev:** University of Warsaw coat of arms above political protest marchers **Rev. Designer:** Andrzej Nowakowski **Edge Lettering:** * NBP * eight times

Date	Mintage	F	VF	XF	Unc	BU
2008MW	1,400,000	—	—	0.90	2.25	3.00

Y# 630 2 ZLOTE

8.1500 g., Brass, 27 mm. **Obv:** National arms above gateway **Obv. Legend:** RZECZPOSPOLITA POLSKA **Rev:** Building **Rev. Legend:** LOWICZ **Edge Lettering:** * NBP * eight times

Date	Mintage	F	VF	XF	Unc	BU
2008MW	1,100,000	—	—	0.90	2.25	3.00

Y# 631 2 ZLOTE

8.1500 g., Brass, 27 mm. **Obv:** National arms above gateway **Obv. Legend:** RZECZPOSPOLITA POLSKA **Rev:** Monument **Rev. Legend:** KONIN **Edge Lettering:** * NBP * eight times

Date	Mintage	F	VF	XF	Unc	BU
2008MW	1,100,000	—	—	0.90	2.25	3.00

Y# 633 2 ZLOTE

8.1500 g., Brass, 27 mm. **Subject:** 65th Anniversary Warsaw Uprising **Obv:** National arms **Obv. Legend:** RZECZPOSPOLITA POLSKA **Rev:** Star of David in barbed wire, female freedom fighter at right. **Rev. Legend:** POWSTANIA W GETCIE WARSZAWSKIM 65. ROCZNICA **Edge Lettering:** * NBP * eight times

Date	Mintage	F	VF	XF	Unc	BU
2008MW	1,750,000	—	—	—	3.00	5.00

Y# 634 2 ZLOTE

8.1500 g., Brass, 27 mm. **Subject:** Zbigniew Herbert **Obv:** National arms **Obv. Legend:** RZECZPOSPOLITA POLSKA **Rev:** Head of Herbert right **Edge Lettering:** * NBP * eight times

Date	Mintage	F	VF	XF	Unc	BU
2008MW	1,510,000	—	—	—	3.00	4.00

Y# 638 2 ZLOTE

8.1500 g., Brass, 27 mm. **Subject:** Siberian Exiles **Obv:** National arms **Obv. Legend:** RZECZPOSPOLITA POLSKA **Rev:** Bleak forest **Rev. Inscription:** SYBIRACY **Edge Lettering:** * NBP * eight times

Date	Mintage	F	VF	XF	Unc	BU
2008MW	1,500,000	—	—	—	3.00	4.00

Y# 641 2 ZLOTE

8.1500 g., Brass, 27 mm. **Subject:** Kazimierz Dolny **Obv:** National arms **Obv. Legend:** RZECZPOSPOLITA POLSKA **Obv. Designer:** Ewa Tyc-Karpinska **Rev:** City view **Rev. Designer:** Ewa Olszewska-Borys **Edge Lettering:** * NBP * eight times

Date	Mintage	F	VF	XF	Unc	BU
2008MW	1,380,000	—	—	—	3.00	4.00

Y# 627 2 ZLOTE

8.1500 g., Brass, 27 mm. **Obv:** National arms above flags **Obv. Legend:** RZECZPOSPOLITA POLSKA **Obv. Designer:** Ewa Tyc-Karpinska **Rev:** Peregrine Falcon perched on branch **Rev. Legend:** SOKOL WEDROWNY - Falco peregrinus **Rev. Designer:** Roussanka Nowakowska **Edge Lettering:** * NBP * eight times

Date	Mintage	F	VF	XF	Unc	BU
2008MW	1,600,000	—	—	—	3.00	4.00

Y# 628 2 ZLOTE

8.1500 g., Brass, 27 mm. **Obv:** National arms above gateway **Obv. Legend:** RZECZPOSPOLITA POLSKA **Rev:** National arms ar upper left, Piotrków Tribunal building at lower right **Rev. Legend:** PIOTRKÓW - TRYBUNALSKI **Edge Lettering:** * NBP * eight times

Date	Mintage	F	VF	XF	Unc	BU
2008MW	1,100,000	—	—	0.90	2.25	3.00

Y# 644 2 ZLOTE

8.1500 g., Brass, 27 mm. **Subject:** 29th Olympic Games Beijing 2008 **Obv:** Eagle **Obv. Designer:** Ewa Tyc-Karpinska **Rev:** Two rowers in boat & a square **Rev. Designer:** Urszula Walerzak **Edge Lettering:** * NBP * eight times

Date	Mintage	F	VF	XF	Unc	BU
2008	2,000,000	—	—	—	3.00	4.00

Y# 648 2 ZLOTE

8.1500 g., Brass, 27 mm. **Subject:** Polish Travellers & Explorers **Obv:** Eagle **Obv. Designer:** Ewa Tyc-Karpinska **Rev:** Bust of Bronislaw Pilsudski **Rev. Designer:** Roussanka Nowakowska **Edge Lettering:** * NBP * eight times

Date	Mintage	F	VF	XF	Unc	BU
2008	1,100,000	—	—	—	3.00	4.00

Y# 650 2 ZLOTE

8.1500 g., Brass, 27 mm. **Subject:** 90th Anniversary of Regaining Freedom **Obv:** Eagle **Obv. Designer:** Ewa Tyc-Karpinska **Rev:** Order of Polonia Restituta **Rev. Designer:** Ewa Olszewska-Borys **Edge Lettering:** * NBP * eight times

Date	Mintage	F	VF	XF	Unc	BU
2008	1,200,000	—	—	—	3.00	4.00

Y# 656 2 ZLOTE

8.1500 g., Brass, 27 mm. **Subject:** 450th Anniversary of the Polish Post **Obv:** Eagle **Obv. Designer:** Ewa Tyc-Karpinska **Rev:** Post rider on horse **Rev. Designer:** Robert Kotowicz **Edge:** NBP

Date	Mintage	F	VF	XF	Unc	BU
2008	1,400,000	—	—	—	3.00	4.00

Y# 659 2 ZLOTE

8.1500 g., Brass, 27 mm. **Subject:** 400th Anniversary of Polish settlement in North America **Obv:** Eagle **Obv. Designer:** Ewa Tyc-Karpinska **Rev:** Man blowing glassware **Rev. Designer:** Roussanka Nowakowska **Edge Lettering:** * NBP * eight times

Date	Mintage	F	VF	XF	Unc	BU
2008	1,200,000	—	—	—	3.00	4.00

Y# 662 2 ZLOTE

8.1500 g., Brass, 27 mm. **Subject:** 90th Anniversary of the Greater Poland Uprising **Obv:** Eagle **Obv. Designer:** Ewa Tyc-Karpinska **Rev:** Bust of Igancy Jan Paderewski, soldiers at bottom **Rev. Designer:** Urszula Walerzak **Edge Lettering:** * NBP * eight times

Date	Mintage	F	VF	XF	Unc	BU
2008	1,100,000	—	—	—	3.00	4.00

Y# 663 2 ZLOTE

8.1500 g., Brass, 27 mm. **Subject:** Belsko - Biala **Obv:** National arms above gateway **Rev:** Building

Date	Mintage	F	VF	XF	Unc	BU
2008MW	—	—	—	—	3.00	4.00

Y# 670 2 ZLOTE

8.1500 g., Brass, 27 mm. **Subject:** Polish Cavalry **Obv:** National arms above value **Rev:** Hussar Knights, XVII Century

Date	Mintage	F	VF	XF	Unc	BU
2009MW	1,400,000	—	—	—	3.00	4.00

Y# 673 2 ZLOTE

8.1500 g., Brass, 27 mm. **Subject:** Supreme Chamber of Control, 100th Anniversary **Obv:** National arms above value **Rev:** Building

Date	Mintage	F	VF	XF	Unc	BU
2009MW	1,200,000	—	—	—	3.00	4.00

Y# 675 2 ZLOTE
8.1500 g., Brass, 27 mm. **Subject:** Central Banking, 180th Anniversary **Obv:** National arms above value **Rev:** Five coins

Date	Mintage	F	VF	XF	Unc	BU
2009MW	1,300,000	—	—	—	3.00	4.00

Y# 678 2 ZLOTE
8.1500 g., Brass, 27 mm. **Subject:** Green Lizards **Obv:** National arms above value **Rev:** Two green lizards on rocks (lacerta viridis) **Rev. Legend:** JASZCZURKA

Date	Mintage	F	VF	XF	Unc	BU
2009MW	1,700,000	—	—	—	3.00	4.00

Y# 680 2 ZLOTE
8.1500 g., Brass, 27 mm. **Subject:** General Elections of 1989 **Obv:** National arms above eagle **Rev:** Election notice within wreath

Date	Mintage	F	VF	XF	Unc	BU
2009MW	1,300,000	—	—	—	3.00	4.00

Y# 684 2 ZLOTE
8.1500 g., Brass, 27 mm. **Subject:** Czeslaw Niemen **Obv:** National arms above value **Rev:** Two dimensional facing portrait

Date	Mintage	F	VF	XF	Unc	BU
2009MW	1,400,000	—	—	—	3.00	4.00

Y# 687 2 ZLOTE
8.1500 g., Brass, 27 mm. **Subject:** Poets of the Warsaw uprising, 65th Anniversary **Obv:** National arms above eagle

Date	Mintage	F	VF	XF	Unc	BU
2009MW	1,400,000	—	—	—	3.00	4.00

Y# 690 2 ZLOTE
8.1500 g., Brass, 27 mm. **Subject:** First Cadre March **Obv:** National arms above value **Rev:** Military badge

Date	Mintage	F	VF	XF	Unc	BU
2009MW	1,000,000	—	—	—	3.00	4.00

Y# 692 2 ZLOTE
8.1500 g., Brass, 27 mm. **Subject:** Liquidation of Lodz Ghetto **Obv:** National arms above value **Rev:** Silhouette of Ghetto

Date	Mintage	F	VF	XF	Unc	BU
2009MW	1,000,000	—	—	—	3.00	4.00

Y# 694 2 ZLOTE
8.1500 g., Brass, 27 mm. **Subject:** Westerplatte **Obv:** National arms above value **Rev:** Three soldiers and map

Date	Mintage	F	VF	XF	Unc	BU
2009	1,400,000	—	—	—	3.00	4.00

Y# 697 2 ZLOTE
8.1500 g., Brass, 27 mm. **Subject:** Tatar Mountain Rescue **Obv:** National arms above value **Rev:** Mountain climber

Date	Mintage	F	VF	XF	Unc	BU
2009MW	1,400,000	—	—	—	3.00	4.00

Y# 700 2 ZLOTE
8.1500 g., Brass, 27 mm. **Subject:** Fr. Jerzy Popieluszko, 25th Anniversary of Murder **Obv:** National arms above value **Rev:** Portrait and candle memorial

Date	Mintage	F	VF	XF	Unc	BU
2009MW	1,500,000	—	—	—	3.00	4.00

Y# 703 2 ZLOTE
8.1500 g., Brass, 27 mm. **Subject:** Poles saving Jews **Obv:** National arms above value **Rev:** Broken brick wall

Date	Mintage	F	VF	XF	Unc	BU
2009MW	1,400,000	—	—	—	3.00	4.00

Y# 705 2 ZLOTE
8.1500 g., Brass, 27 mm. **Subject:** Wald Strzeminski **Obv:** Artist palette and National arms **Rev:** Portrait at left

Date	Mintage	F	VF	XF	Unc	BU
2009MW	1,300,000	—	—	—	3.00	4.00

Y# 707 2 ZLOTE
8.1500 g., Brass, 27 mm. **Subject:** Polish Underground **Obv:** National arms above value **Rev:** Monogram of resistance and map of Poland

Date	Mintage	F	VF	XF	Unc	BU
2009MW	1,000,000	—	—	—	3.00	4.00

Y# 709 2 ZLOTE
8.1500 g., Brass, 27 mm. **Subject:** Czestochowa **Rev:** Church

Date	Mintage	F	VF	XF	Unc	BU
2009MW	—	—	—	—	3.00	4.00

Y# 710 2 ZLOTE
8.1500 g., Brass, 27 mm. **Subject:** Jedrzejow Cistercian Monastery **Rev:** Church

Date	Mintage	F	VF	XF	Unc	BU
2009MW	—	—	—	—	3.00	4.00

Y# 711 2 ZLOTE
8.1500 g., Brass, 27 mm. **Subject:** Trzebnica **Rev:** Building

Date	Mintage	F	VF	XF	Unc	BU
2009MW	—	—	—	—	3.00	4.00

Y# 712 2 ZLOTE
8.1500 g., Brass, 27 mm. **Subject:** Liberation of Auschwitz **Obv:** National arms above value **Rev:** Three prisoners and camp gate sign

Date	Mintage	F	VF	XF	Unc	BU
2010MW	1,000,000	—	—	—	3.00	4.00

Y# 715 2 ZLOTE
8.1500 g., Brass, 27 mm. **Subject:** Vancouver Winter Olympics **Obv:** National arms above value **Rev:** Ski jump athlete

Date	Mintage	F	VF	XF	Unc	BU
2010MW	1,400,000	—	—	—	3.00	4.00

Y# 718 2 ZLOTE
8.1500 g., Brass, 27 mm. **Subject:** Imperial Guard **Obv:** National arms above value **Rev:** Napoleonic era mounted soldier

Date	Mintage	F	VF	XF	Unc	BU
2010MW	1,400,000	—	—	—	3.00	4.00

Y# 721 2 ZLOTE
8.1500 g., Brass, 27 mm. **Subject:** Katyn Crime **Obv:** National arms above value **Rev:** City name above cap

Date	Mintage	F	VF	XF	Unc	BU
2010MW	1,000,000	—	—	—	3.00	4.00

Y# 723 2 ZLOTE
8.1500 g., Brass, 27 mm. **Obv:** National arms above value **Rev:** Bat

Date	Mintage	F	VF	XF	Unc	BU
2010	—	—	—	—	3.00	4.00

Y# 725 2 ZLOTE
8.1500 g., Brass, 27 mm. **Subject:** Polish Scouting Centennial

Date	Mintage	F	VF	XF	Unc	BU
2010MW	1,100,000	—	—	—	3.00	4.00

Y# 727 2 ZLOTE
8.1500 g., Brass, 27 mm. **Subject:** Popular Music - Marek Grechuta

Date	Mintage	F	VF	XF	Unc	BU
2010MW	1,400,000	—	—	—	3.00	4.00

Y# 730 2 ZLOTE
8.1500 g., Brass, 27 mm. **Subject:** Jan Twardowski

Date	Mintage	F	VF	XF	Unc	BU
2010MW	1,000,000	—	—	—	3.00	4.00

Y# 732 2 ZLOTE
8.1500 g., Brass, 27 mm. **Subject:** Battles of Grunwald and Kluszyn

Date	Mintage	F	VF	XF	Unc	BU
2010MW	1,400,000	—	—	—	3.00	4.00

Y# 735 2 ZLOTE
8.1500 g., Brass **Subject:** Battle of Warsaw

Date	Mintage	F	VF	XF	Unc	BU
2010MW	1,200,000	—	—	—	3.00	4.00

Y# 737 2 ZLOTE
8.1500 g., Brass, 27 mm. **Subject:** August of 1980

Date	Mintage	F	VF	XF	Unc	BU
2010MW	1,400,000	—	—	—	3.00	4.00

Y# 742 2 ZLOTE
8.1500 g., Brass, 27 mm. **Subject:** Polish Explorers - Benedykt Dybowski

Date	Mintage	F	VF	XF	Unc	BU
2010MW Proof	1,200,000	—	—	—	3.00	4.00

Y# 744 2 ZLOTE
8.1500 g., Brass, 27 mm. **Subject:** Krzeszow

Date	Mintage	F	VF	XF	Unc	BU
2010MW	1,000,000	—	—	—	3.00	4.00

Y# 746 2 ZLOTE
8.1500 g., Brass **Subject:** Arthur Grottger **Shape:** 27

Date	Mintage	F	VF	XF	Unc	BU
2010MW	1,300,000	—	—	—	3.00	4.00

Y# 749 2 ZLOTE
8.1500 g., Brass, 27 mm. **Subject:** August of 1980, second issue

Date	Mintage	F	VF	XF	Unc	BU
2010MW	—	—	—	—	3.00	4.00

Y# 751 2 ZLOTE
8.1500 g., Brass, 27 mm. **Subject:** City of Warsaw

Date	Mintage	F	VF	XF	Unc	BU
2010MW	—	—	—	—	3.00	4.00

Y# 752 2 ZLOTE
815.0000 g., Brass, 27 mm. **Subject:** City of Trzemeszno

Date	Mintage	F	VF	XF	Unc	BU
2010	—	—	—	—	3.00	4.00

Y# 756 2 ZLOTE
8.1500 g., Brass, 27 mm. **Subject:** Kalwaria Zebrzydowska **Obv:** National Arms above value **Rev:** Statue of Saint, Church in background

Date	Mintage	F	VF	XF	Unc	BU
2010	1,000,000	—	—	—	3.00	4.00

Y# 757 2 ZLOTE
8.1500 g., Brass, 27 mm. **Subject:** Benedykt Dybowski **Obv:** National Arms above value **Rev:** Bust facing

Date	Mintage	F	VF	XF	Unc	BU
2010	1,200,000	—	—	—	3.00	4.00

Y# 759 2 ZLOTE
8.1500 g., Brass, 27 mm. **Subject:** Gorlice **Obv:** National Arms above value **Rev:** City view

Date	Mintage	F	VF	XF	Unc	BU
2010	1,000,000	—	—	—	3.00	4.00

Y# 760 2 ZLOTE
8.1500 g., Brass, 27 mm. **Subject:** Meichow **Obv:** National Arms above value **Rev:** Building tower

Date	Mintage	F	VF	XF	Unc	BU
2010	1,000,000	—	—	—	3.00	4.00

Y# 761 2 ZLOTE
8.1500 g., Brass, 27 mm. **Subject:** Katowice **Obv:** National Arms above value **Rev:** Town factory view

Date	Mintage	F	VF	XF	Unc	BU
2010	1,000,000	—	—	—	3.00	4.00

Y# 762 2 ZLOTE
8.1500 g., Brass, 27 mm. **Subject:** Borsuk **Obv:** National Arms above value **Rev:** Badger

Date	Mintage	F	VF	XF	Unc	BU
2011	1,500,000	—	—	—	3.00	4.00

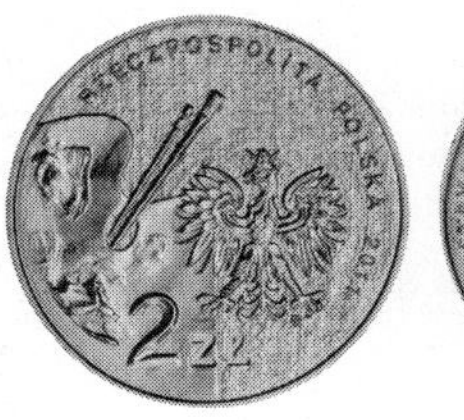

Y# 764 2 ZLOTE
8.1500 g., Brass, 27 mm. **Subject:** Zofia Stryjenska **Obv:** National arms, value and artist pallet with brushes **Rev:** Portrait facing

Date	Mintage	F	VF	XF	Unc	BU
2011	1,000,000	—	—	—	3.00	4.00

Y# 284 5 ZLOTYCH
6.5400 g., Bi-Metallic Aluminum-Bronze center in Copper-Nickel ring, 24 mm. **Obv:** National arms within circle **Obv. Legend:** RZECZPOSPOLITA POLSKA **Rev:** Value within circle flanked by oak leaves

Date	Mintage	F	VF	XF	Unc	BU
2008MW	—	—	—	—	7.00	8.00
2009MW	—	—	—	—	7.00	8.00
2010MW	—	—	—	—	7.00	8.00

Y# 406 10 ZLOTYCH
14.1400 g., 0.9250 Silver 0.4205 oz. ASW **Subject:** Year 2001 **Obv:** Crowned eagle with wings open **Rev:** Printed circuit board

Date	Mintage	F	VF	XF	Unc	BU
2001MW Proof	35,000	Value: 75.00				

Y# 413 10 ZLOTYCH
14.1400 g., 0.9250 Silver 0.4205 oz. ASW, 32 mm. **Subject:** 15 Years of the Constitutional Court **Obv:** Crowned eagle suspended from a judge's neck chain **Rev:** Crowned eagle head and balance scale **Edge Lettering:** TRYBUNAL KONSTYTUCYJNY W SLUZBIE PANSTWA PRAWA

Date	Mintage	F	VF	XF	Unc	BU
2001MW Proof	25,000	Value: 65.00				

Y# 419 10 ZLOTYCH
14.1400 g., 0.9250 Silver 0.4205 oz. ASW, 32 mm. **Subject:** Cardinal Stefan Wyszynski **Obv:** Crowned eagle with wings open above ribbon **Rev:** Half length figure facing with raised hands **Edge Lettering:** 100 • ROCZNIA URODZIN

Date	Mintage	F	VF	XF	Unc	BU
2001MW Proof	60,000	Value: 30.00				

Y# 425 10 ZLOTYCH

14.2100 g., 0.9250 Silver 0.4226 oz. ASW, 32 mm. **Subject:** Jan III Sobieski **Obv:** Crowned eagle with wings open **Rev:** 3/4 armored bust facing with army in background **Edge:** Plain

Date	Mintage	F	VF	XF	Unc	BU
2001MW Proof	24,000	Value: 120				

Y# 458 10 ZLOTYCH

14.1400 g., 0.9250 Silver 0.4205 oz. ASW, 32 mm. **Obv:** Crowned eagle with wings open **Rev:** Jan Sobieski, type II **Edge:** Plain

Date	Mintage	F	VF	XF	Unc	BU
2001MW Proof	17,000	Value: 175				

Y# 459 10 ZLOTYCH

14.1400 g., 0.9250 Silver 0.4205 oz. ASW, 32 mm. **Obv:** Three violins **Rev:** Henryk Wieniawski **Edge:** Plain

Date	Mintage	F	VF	XF	Unc	BU
2001MW Proof	28,000	Value: 60.00				

Y# 460 10 ZLOTYCH

14.1400 g., 0.9250 Silver 0.4205 oz. ASW, 32 mm. **Obv:** Crowned eagle with wings open above fish **Rev:** Michal Siedlecki **Edge:** Plain

Date	Mintage	F	VF	XF	Unc	BU
2001MW Proof	26,000	Value: 60.00				

Y# 432 10 ZLOTYCH

14.1400 g., 0.9250 Silver 0.4205 oz. ASW, 32 mm. **Subject:** Bronislaw Malinowski **Obv:** Small crowned eagle with wings open to right of bust facing **Rev:** Trobriand Islands village scene **Edge Lettering:** etnolog, antropolog kultury

Date	Mintage	F	VF	XF	Unc	BU
2002MW Proof	33,500	Value: 35.00				

Y# 434 10 ZLOTYCH

14.1400 g., 0.9250 Silver 0.4205 oz. ASW, 32 mm. **Subject:** World Cup Soccer **Obv:** Crowned eagle with wings open **Rev:** Soccer player **Edge Lettering:** etnolog, antropolog kultury

Date	Mintage	F	VF	XF	Unc	BU
2002MW Proof	55,000	Value: 27.50				

Y# 435 10 ZLOTYCH

14.1400 g., 0.9250 Silver 0.4205 oz. ASW, 32 mm. **Subject:** World Cup Soccer **Obv:** Amber soccer ball inset entering goal net **Rev:** Two soccer players with amber soccer ball inset **Edge Lettering:** etnolog, antropolog kultury

Date	Mintage	F	VF	XF	Unc	BU
2002MW Proof	65,000	Value: 75.00				

Y# 437 10 ZLOTYCH

14.1400 g., 0.9250 Silver 0.4205 oz. ASW, 32 mm. **Subject:** Pope John Paul II **Obv:** Crowned eagle with wings open within two views of praying Pope **Rev:** Pope facing radiant Holy Door **Edge:** Plain

Date	Mintage	F	VF	XF	Unc	BU
2002MW Proof	80,000	Value: 45.00				

Y# 441 10 ZLOTYCH

14.2000 g., 0.9250 Silver 0.4223 oz. ASW, 32 mm. **Subject:** Gen. Wladyslaw Anders **Obv:** Crowned eagle with wings open, cross and multicolor flowers **Rev:** Uniformed bust right **Edge:** Plain

Date	Mintage	F	VF	XF	Unc	BU
2002MW Proof	40,000	Value: 120				

Y# 450 10 ZLOTYCH

14.1400 g., 0.9250 Silver 0.4205 oz. ASW, 32 mm. **Subject:** August II (1697-1706, 1709-1735) **Obv:** Crowned eagle with wings open **Rev:** Portrait and Order of the White Eagle **Edge:** Plain

Date	Mintage	F	VF	XF	Unc	BU
2002MW Proof	30,000	Value: 90.00				

Y# 453 10 ZLOTYCH

14.1400 g., 0.9250 Silver 0.4205 oz. ASW, 32 mm. **Subject:** Great Orchestra of Christmas Charity **Obv:** Large inscribed heart above crowned eagle with wings open **Rev:** Boy playing flute **Edge:** Plain

Date	Mintage	F	VF	XF	Unc	BU
2003MW Proof	47,000	Value: 45.00				

Y# 468 10 ZLOTYCH

14.1400 g., 0.9250 Silver 0.4205 oz. ASW, 32 mm. **Obv:** Tanks on battlefield **Rev:** General Maczek **Edge:** Plain

Date	Mintage	F	VF	XF	Unc	BU
2003MW Proof	44,000	Value: 35.00				

Y# 469 10 ZLOTYCH

14.1400 g., 0.9250 Silver 0.4205 oz. ASW, 32 mm. **Subject:** Gas and Oil Industry **Obv:** Crowned eagle and highway leading to city view **Rev:** Portrait and refinery **Edge:** Plain

Date	Mintage	F	VF	XF	Unc	BU
2003MW Proof	43,000	Value: 35.00				

Y# 474 10 ZLOTYCH

14.1400 g., 0.9250 Silver 0.4205 oz. ASW, 32 mm. **Obv:** Crowned eagle with wings open **Rev:** Stanislaus I and wife's portrait **Edge:** Plain

Date	Mintage	F	VF	XF	Unc	BU
2003MW Proof	45,000	Value: 35.00				

Y# 475 10 ZLOTYCH

14.1400 g., 0.9250 Silver 0.4205 oz. ASW, 32 mm. **Obv:** Crowned eagle with wings open **Rev:** Half-length figure of Stanislaus I with his wife in background **Edge:** Plain

Date	Mintage	F	VF	XF	Unc	BU
2003MW Proof	40,000	Value: 45.00				

Y# 448 10 ZLOTYCH

14.1400 g., 0.9250 Silver 0.4205 oz. ASW, 32 mm. **Subject:** City of Poznan (Posen) **Obv:** Old coin design and arched door **Rev:** Old coin design and city view **Edge:** Plain

Date	Mintage	F	VF	XF	Unc	BU
2003MW Proof	39,000	Value: 75.00				

Y# 480 10 ZLOTYCH

14.1400 g., 0.9250 Silver 0.4205 oz. ASW, 32 mm. **Subject:** 80th Anniversary of the Modern Zloty Currency **Obv:** Man wearing glasses behind crowned eagle with wings open **Rev:** Bust left **Edge:** Plain

Date	Mintage	F	VF	XF	Unc	BU
2004MW Proof	55,000	Value: 35.00				

Y# 482 10 ZLOTYCH

14.1400 g., 0.9250 Silver 0.4205 oz. ASW, 32 mm. **Subject:** Poland Joining the European Union **Obv:** Crowned eagle in blue circle with yellow stars **Rev:** Multicolor European Union and Polish flags **Edge:** Plain

Date	Mintage	F	VF	XF	Unc	BU
2004MW Proof	78,000	Value: 65.00				

Y# 497 10 ZLOTYCH

14.1400 g., 0.9250 Silver 0.4205 oz. ASW, 32 mm. **Subject:** Warsaw Uprising 60th Anniversary **Obv:** Crowned eagle and value on resistance symbol **Rev:** Polish soldier wearing captured German helmet **Edge:** Plain

Date	Mintage	F	VF	XF	Unc	BU
2004MW Proof	92,000	Value: 30.00				

Y# 500 10 ZLOTYCH

14.1400 g., 0.9250 Silver 0.4205 oz. ASW, 32 mm. **Obv:** Polish paratrooper badge **Rev:** Gen. Sosabowski and descending paratrooper **Edge:** Plain

Date	Mintage	F	VF	XF	Unc	BU
2004MW Proof	56,000	Value: 30.00				

Y# 502 10 ZLOTYCH

14.1400 g., 0.9250 Silver 0.4205 oz. ASW, 32 mm. **Subject:** Polish Police 85th Anniversary **Obv:** Crowned eagle with wings open **Rev:** Seal partially overlapping police badge **Edge:** Plain

Date	Mintage	F	VF	XF	Unc	BU
2004MW Proof	65,000	Value: 30.00				

Y# 506 10 ZLOTYCH

14.1400 g., 0.9250 Silver 0.4205 oz. ASW, 32 mm. **Obv:** Siberian landscape above crowned eagle and value **Rev:** Aleksander Czekanowski (1833-1876) **Edge:** Plain

Date	Mintage	F	VF	XF	Unc	BU
2004MW Proof	45,000	Value: 30.00				

Y# 510 10 ZLOTYCH

14.1400 g., 0.9250 Silver 0.4205 oz. ASW, 32 mm. **Subject:** Warsaw Fine Arts Academy Centennial **Obv:** Crowned eagle with wings open within city square **Rev:** Art studio **Edge:** Plain

Date	Mintage	F	VF	XF	Unc	BU
2004MW Proof	75,000	Value: 30.00				

Y# 517 10 ZLOTYCH

14.1400 g., 0.9250 Silver 0.4205 oz. ASW, 32 mm. **Subject:** Olympics **Obv:** Crowned eagle with wings open and woman **Rev:** Fencers in front of Parthenon **Edge:** Plain

Date	Mintage	F	VF	XF	Unc	BU
2004MW Proof	70,000	Value: 30.00				

Y# 518 10 ZLOTYCH

14.1400 g., 0.9250 Silver 0.4205 oz. ASW, 32 mm. **Subject:** Olympics **Obv:** Crowned eagle with wings open within gold plated center **Rev:** Ancient athlete within gold plated circle **Edge:** Plain

Date	Mintage	F	VF	XF	Unc	BU
2004MW Proof	90,000	Value: 35.00				

Y# 523 10 ZLOTYCH
14.2300 g., 0.9250 Silver 0.4232 oz. ASW, 43.2 x 29.2 mm. **Subject:** Japan's Aichi Expo **Obv:** Monument **Rev:** Two cranes **Edge:** Plain **Shape:** Quarter of circle

Date	Mintage	F	VF	XF	Unc	BU
2005MW Proof	80,000	Value: 45.00				

Y# 526 10 ZLOTYCH
14.1400 g., 0.9250 Silver partially gilt 0.4205 oz. ASW, 32.1 mm. **Obv:** Crowned eagle with wings open above date and grasping hands **Rev:** Gold plated bust right and church **Edge:** Plain

Date	Mintage	F	VF	XF	Unc	BU
2005MW Proof	—	Value: 30.00				

Y# 537 10 ZLOTYCH
14.1400 g., 0.9250 Silver 0.4205 oz. ASW, 32 mm. **Obv:** Horse drawn carriage **Rev:** Green duck and Konstanty Ildefons Galczynski in top hat **Edge:** Plain

Date	Mintage	F	VF	XF	Unc	BU
2005MW Proof	62,000	Value: 30.00				

Y# 539 10 ZLOTYCH
14.1400 g., 0.9250 Silver 0.4205 oz. ASW, 32 mm. **Obv:** Baptismal font and Polish eagle **Rev:** Pope John Paul II and St. Peter's Basilica **Edge:** Plain

Date	Mintage	F	VF	XF	Unc	BU
2005MW Proof	170,000	Value: 32.00				

Y# 552 10 ZLOTYCH
14.1400 g., 0.9250 Silver 0.4205 oz. ASW, 32 mm. **Obv:** Crowned eagle above value **Rev:** Stanislaw August Poniatowski and shadow **Edge:** Plain

Date	Mintage	F	VF	XF	Unc	BU
2005MW Proof	60,000	Value: 35.00				

Y# 553 10 ZLOTYCH
14.1400 g., 0.9250 Silver 0.4205 oz. ASW, 32 mm. **Obv:** Crowned eagle above value **Rev:** Stanislaw August Poniatowski and crowned monogram **Edge:** Plain

Date	Mintage	F	VF	XF	Unc	BU
2005MW Proof	60,000	Value: 35.00				

Y# 554 10 ZLOTYCH
14.1400 g., 0.9250 Silver 0.4205 oz. ASW, 32 mm. **Subject:** End of WWII 60th Anniversary **Obv:** Crowned eagle above soldier silhouettes and value **Rev:** City view in ruins above bird with green sprig **Edge:** Plain

Date	Mintage	F	VF	XF	Unc	BU
2005MW Proof	70,000	Value: 40.00				

Y# 568 10 ZLOTYCH
14.1400 g., 0.9250 Silver 0.4205 oz. ASW, 32 mm. **Obv:** Sail ship and obverse design of Y-31 **Rev:** Reverse design of Y-31 on radiant design **Edge:** Lettered

Date	Mintage	F	VF	XF	Unc	BU
2005MW Proof	61,000	Value: 35.00				

Y# 596 10 ZLOTYCH
14.1800 g., 0.9250 Silver 0.4217 oz. ASW, 32 mm. **Subject:** 500th Anniversary - Birth of M. Reja **Obv:** National arms in oval, value below **Obv. Legend:** RZECZPOSPOLITA POLSKA **Rev:** Bust of Reja 3/4 right **Rev. Legend:** 500. ROCZNICA URODZIN MIKOLAJA REJA **Edge:** Plain

Date	Mintage	F	VF	XF	Unc	BU
2005MW Proof	60,000	Value: 30.00				

Y# 556 10 ZLOTYCH
14.1400 g., 0.9250 Silver 0.4205 oz. ASW, 32.03 mm. **Subject:** 2006 Winter Olympics **Obv:** Small national arms at left, figure skating couple at center **Obv. Legend:** RZECZPOSPOLITA POLSKA **Rev:** Female figure skater **Rev. Legend:** XX ZIMOWE IGRZYSKA OLIMPIJSKIE **Edge:** Plain

Date	Mintage	F	VF	XF	Unc	BU
2006MW Proof	72,000	Value: 32.00				

Y# 599 10 ZLOTYCH
14.1800 g., 0.9250 Silver 0.4217 oz. ASW, 32 mm. **Series:** History of the Zloty **Obv:** National arms at upper left, 1932 dated 10 Zlotych obverse at lower right, building facade in background **Obv. Legend:** RZECZPOSPOLITA POLSKA **Rev:** Reverse of 1932 dated coin with head of Queen Jadwiga **Rev. Legend:** DZIEJE ZLOTEGO **Edge:** Plain

Date	Mintage	F	VF	XF	Unc	BU
2006MW Proof	61,000	Value: 40.00				

Y# 555 10 ZLOTYCH
14.1400 g., 0.9250 Silver 0.4205 oz. ASW, 32 mm. **Subject:** 2006 Winter Olympics **Obv:** Snow boarder above crowned eagle **Rev:** Snow boarder **Edge:** Plain

Date	Mintage	F	VF	XF	Unc	BU
2006MW Proof	71,400	Value: 30.00				

Y# 598 10 ZLOTYCH
14.1500 g., 0.9250 Silver 0.4208 oz. ASW, 32 mm. **Subject:** 30th Anniversary June 1976 **Obv:** National arms divides denomination, split railroad tracks below **Obv. Legend:** RZECZPOSPOLITA POLSKA **Rev:** 3/4 length woman standing with child, outlined row of shielded forces in background **Rev. Legend:** 30. ROCZNICA - CZERWCA 1976 **Edge:** Plain

Date	Mintage	F	VF	XF	Unc	BU
2006MW Proof	56,000	Value: 32.00				

Y# 754 10 ZLOTYCH
14.1400 g., Bi-Metallic, 32 mm. **Subject:** World Cup soccer **Obv:** Eagle within net **Rev:** Player kicking ball, sun

Date	Mintage	F	VF	XF	Unc	BU
2006 Proof	—	Value: 75.00				

Y# 600 10 ZLOTYCH
14.1000 g., 0.9250 Silver 0.4193 oz. ASW, 32 mm. **Subject:** 125th Anniversary - Birth of Szymanowskiego **Obv:** Piano keys at left, national arms on music score at right **Obv. Legend:** RZECZPOSPOLITA POLSKA **Rev:** Bust of Szymanowskiego 3/4 left, music composition at back of head and over upper body, dates as hologram at left **Rev. Legend:** 125. ROCZNICA URODZIN KAROLA SZYMANOWSKIEGO **Edge:** Plain

Date	Mintage	F	VF	XF	Unc	BU
2007MW Proof	55,000	Value: 35.00				

Y# 601 10 ZLOTYCH
14.3000 g., 0.9250 Silver 0.4253 oz. ASW, 14 mm. **Subject:** Arctic Explorers **Obv:** Sailing ship at center, national arms at right with denomination below **Obv. Legend:** RZECZPOSPOLITA POLSKA **Rev:** Busts of Henryk Arctowski and Antoni Dobrowolski facing, polar outline map at lower left **Edge:** Plain

Date	Mintage	F	VF	XF	Unc	BU
2007MW Proof	60,000	Value: 35.00				

Y# 602 10 ZLOTYCH
14.0500 g., 0.9250 Silver 0.4178 oz. ASW, 31.95 x 22.39 mm. **Obv:** Helmeted national arms, sword and denomination below **Obv. Legend:** RZECZPOSPOLITA - POLSKA **Rev:** Chivalrous knight on horseback jousting right **Rev. Inscription:** RYCERZ - CIEZKOZBROJNY **Edge:** Plain **Shape:** Rectangular

Date	Mintage	F	VF	XF	Unc	BU
2007MW Proof	57,000	Value: 45.00				

Y# 585 10 ZLOTYCH
14.1400 g., 0.9250 Silver 0.4205 oz. ASW, 32 mm. **Obv:** Mountains, Polish Eagle and value **Rev:** Ignacy Domeyko **Edge:** Plain

Date	Mintage	F	VF	XF	Unc	BU
2007MW Proof	55,000	Value: 32.00				

Y# 587 10 ZLOTYCH
14.1400 g., 0.9250 Silver 0.4205 oz. ASW, 32 mm. **Subject:** 75th Anniversary - Breaking the Enigma Code **Obv:** Polish Eagle on circuit board **Rev:** Segmented letters **Edge:** Lettered

Date	Mintage	F	VF	XF	Unc	BU
2007MW Proof	55,000	Value: 50.00				

Y# 589 10 ZLOTYCH
14.1400 g., 0.9250 Silver 0.4205 oz. ASW, 32 mm. **Obv:** Angel, Polish Eagle and obverse coin design of Y-18 **Rev:** Reverse coin design of Y-18 on wheat ears **Edge:** Plain

Date	Mintage	F	VF	XF	Unc	BU
2007MW Proof	57,000	Value: 40.00				

Y# 595 10 ZLOTYCH
14.1400 g., 0.9250 Silver ASW 0.4205 0.4205 oz. ASW **Subject:** 750th Anniversary Munincipality of Krakau **Obv:** City gate tower, national arms at lower right **Obv. Legend:** RZECZPOSPOLITA POLSKA **Rev:** Knight with shield standing facing

Date	Mintage	F	VF	XF	Unc	BU
2007MW Proof	58,000	Value: 50.00				

Y# 632 10 ZLOTYCH
14.1400 g., 0.9250 Silver 0.4205 oz. ASW, 32 mm. **Subject:**

40th Anniversary "Rocznica" March **Obv:** National arms at upper right, manuscript pages fluttering at left **Obv. Legend:** RZECZPOSPOLITA POLSKA **Rev:** Student protesters in front of gates of Warsaw University, military police in silhouette in foreground **Designer:** Andrzej Nowakowski

Date	Mintage	F	VF	XF	Unc	BU
2008MW Proof	118,000	Value: 50.00				

Y# 635 10 ZLOTYCH

14.1000 g., Silver, 32.03 mm. **Subject:** Zbigniew Herbert **Obv:** Bust of Herbert 3/4 right at left, national arms at lower right **Rev:** Statue of Nike **Edge:** Plain

Date	Mintage	F	VF	XF	Unc	BU
2008MW Proof	—	Value: 40.00				

Y# 645 10 ZLOTYCH

14.4000 g., Silver center gold plated, 32 mm. **Subject:** The 29th Olympic Games Beijing 2008 **Obv:** Chinese ornament & dragon **Rev:** Swimmer **Designer:** Robert Kotowicz

Date	Mintage	F	VF	XF	Unc	BU
2008 Proof	140,000	Value: 50.00				

Y# 639 10 ZLOTYCH

14.1400 g., 0.9250 Silver 0.4205 oz. ASW, 32 mm. **Subject:** Siberian Exiles **Obv:** Small national arms at left, human outlines at right **Obv. Legend:** RZECZPOSPOLITA POLSKA **Rev:** Tree lines with imbedded triangular crystal below **Rev. Inscription:** SYBIRACY **Edge:** Plain **Designer:** Ewa Tyc-Karpinska

Date	Mintage	F	VF	XF	Unc	BU
2008MW Proof	135,000	Value: 35.00				

Y# 646 10 ZLOTYCH

14.1400 g., Silver, 32 mm. **Subject:** The 29th Olympic Games Beijing 2008 **Obv:** Square hole & an eagle **Rev:** Square hole & a windsurfer **Designer:** Urszula Walerzak

Date	Mintage	F	VF	XF	Unc	BU
2008 Proof	150,000	Value: 30.00				

Y# 649 10 ZLOTYCH

14.1400 g., Silver, 32 mm. **Subject:** Polish Travellers & Explorers **Obv:** Man & woman holding child **Obv. Designer:** Roussanka Nowakowska **Rev:** Bust of Bronislaw Pilsudski **Rev. Designer:** Roussanks Nowakowska

Date	Mintage	F	VF	XF	Unc	BU
2008 Proof	99,000	Value: 32.00				

Y# 655 10 ZLOTYCH

14.1400 g., Silver, 32 mm. **Subject:** 450th Anniversary of the Polish Post **Obv:** Eatle on top right, post stamp in center with man on horse **Rev:** Post courier **Designer:** Robert Kotowicz

Date	Mintage	F	VF	XF	Unc	BU
2008 Proof	135,000	Value: 35.00				

Y# 658 10 ZLOTYCH

14.1400 g., Silver, 32 mm. **Subject:** 400th Anniversary - Polish Settlement in North America **Obv:** Man blowing glassware left **Rev:** Man blowing glassware right **Designer:** Robert Kotowicz

Date	Mintage	F	VF	XF	Unc	BU
2008 Proof	126,000	Value: 35.00				

Y# 661 10 ZLOTYCH

14.1400 g., Silver, 32 mm. **Subject:** 90th Anniversary of the Greater Poland Uprising **Obv:** Eagle at top, Commander riding horse followed by soldiers **Rev:** Rose at left, Bust of Igancy Jan Paderewski at right **Designer:** Urszula Walerzak

Date	Mintage	F	VF	XF	Unc	BU
2008 Proof	107,000	Value: 40.00				

Y# 695 10 ZLOTYCH

14.1400 g., 0.9250 Silver 0.4205 oz. ASW, 32 mm. **Subject:** 70th Anniversary of the start of World War II **Obv:** Eagle and map of Nazi and Soviet invasion **Rev:** Planes dropping bombs on Wielun

Date	Mintage	F	VF	XF	Unc	BU
2009MW Proof	100,000	Value: 45.00				

Y# 671 10 ZLOTYCH

14.4000 g., 0.9250 Silver 0.4282 oz. ASW, 22x32 mm. **Obv:** Eagle, flag and armor **Rev:** Hussar Knights, XVII Century **Shape:** Vertical rectangle

Date	Mintage	F	VF	XF	Unc	BU
2009 Proof	100,000	Value: 50.00				

Y# 688 10 ZLOTYCH

14.1400 g., 0.9250 Silver Gold plated center in silver ring 0.4205 oz. ASW, 27 mm. **Subject:** Poets of the Uprising **Obv:** National arms **Rev:** Tadeusz Gajcy portrait

Date	Mintage	F	VF	XF	Unc	BU
2009MW Proof	100,000	Value: 45.00				

Y# 674 10 ZLOTYCH

14.4000 g., 0.9250 Silver 0.4282 oz. ASW, 32 mm. **Subject:** Supreme Chamber, 90th Anniversary **Obv:** Building **Rev:** Monogram hologram

Date	Mintage	F	VF	XF	Unc	BU
2009MW Proof	100,000	Value: 55.00				

Y# 676 10 ZLOTYCH

14.4000 g., 0.9250 Silver 0.4282 oz. ASW, 32 mm. **Subject:** Central Banking, 180th Anniversary **Obv:** National arms above building **Rev:** Portrait above banknote

Date	Mintage	F	VF	XF	Unc	BU
2009MW Proof	92,000	Value: 45.00				

Y# 681 10 ZLOTYCH

14.1400 g., 0.9250 Silver 0.4205 oz. ASW, 32 mm. **Subject:** General Elections of 1989 **Obv:** Eagle **Rev:** Pope John Paul II and Solidarity banner in color

Date	Mintage	F	VF	XF	Unc	BU
2009MW Proof	100,000	Value: 35.00				

Y# 685 10 ZLOTYCH

14.1400 g., 0.9250 Silver 0.4205 oz. ASW, 29x29 mm. **Subject:** Czeslaw Niemen **Obv:** National arms and large portrait **Rev:** Female crying **Shape:** Square

Date	Mintage	F	VF	XF	Unc	BU
2009MW Proof	100,000	Value: 45.00				

Y# 686 10 ZLOTYCH

14.1400 g., 0.9250 Silver 0.4205 oz. ASW, 32 mm. **Subject:** Cezeslaw Neiman **Obv:** National arms and portrait **Rev:** Abstract painting

Date	Mintage	F	VF	XF	Unc	BU
2009MW Proof	100,000	Value: 45.00				

Y# 689 10 ZLOTYCH

14.1400 g., 0.9250 Silver Silver center in gold plated ring 0.4205 oz. ASW, 32 mm. **Subject:** Poets of the uprising **Obv:** National arms **Rev:** Krzystof Baczynski portrait facing

Date	Mintage	F	VF	XF	Unc	BU
2009MW Proof	100,000	Value: 45.00				

Y# 691 10 ZLOTYCH

14.1400 g., 0.9250 Silver 0.4205 oz. ASW, 32 mm. **Subject:** First Cadre Company March **Obv:** National arms and eagle atop stelle monument **Rev:** Troops marching, song and music

Date	Mintage	F	VF	XF	Unc	BU
2009MW Proof	50,000	Value: 50.00				

Y# 698 10 ZLOTYCH

14.1400 g., 0.9250 Silver 0.4205 oz. ASW, 32 mm. **Series:** Tatar Rescues, 100th Anniversary **Obv:** National arms and logo colorized **Rev:** Mountains and figure of Karlowicz

Date	Mintage	F	VF	XF	Unc	BU
2009MW Proof	100,000	Value: 45.00				

Y# 701 10 ZLOTYCH

14.1400 g., 0.9250 Silver 0.4205 oz. ASW, 32 mm. **Subject:** Fr. Jerzy Popielosko, 25th Anniversary of Murder **Obv:** Rose on monument **Rev:** Statue and tear drop on map of Poland

Date	Mintage	F	VF	XF	Unc	BU
2009MW Proof	100,000	Value: 45.00				

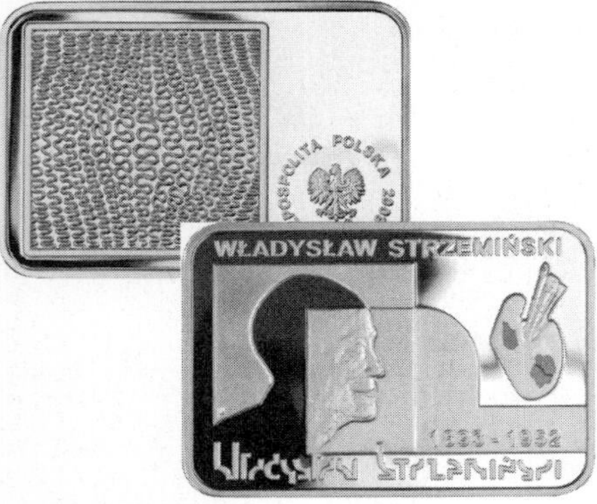

Y# 706 10 ZLOTYCH

28.2800 g., 0.9250 Silver 0.8410 oz. ASW, 40x28 mm. **Subject:** Wald Strzeminski **Obv:** Portrait and multicolor palette **Rev:** Artwork **Shape:** Rectangle

Date	Mintage	F	VF	XF	Unc	BU
2009MW Proof	100,000	Value: 45.00				

Y# 708 10 ZLOTYCH

14.1400 g., 0.9250 Silver 0.4205 oz. ASW, 32 mm. **Subject:** Polish Underground State **Obv:** National arms and monogram and cloth flag **Rev:** Figure and cloth flag

Date	Mintage	F	VF	XF	Unc	BU
2009MW Proof	50,000	Value: 55.00				

Y# 713 10 ZLOTYCH

14.1400 g., 0.9250 Silver 0.4205 oz. ASW, 32 mm. **Subject:** Auschwitz liberation **Obv:** National arms, camp sign and barbed wire fence **Rev:** Prisoner and barbed wire fence

Date	Mintage	F	VF	XF	Unc	BU
2010MW Proof	80,000	Value: 45.00				

Y# 716 10 ZLOTYCH

14.1400 g., 0.9250 Silver 0.4205 oz. ASW, 32 mm. **Subject:** Vancouver Winter Olympics **Obv:** Speedskaters **Rev:** Biathlon

Date	Mintage	F	VF	XF	Unc	BU
2010MW Proof	80,000	Value: 45.00				

Y# 719 10 ZLOTYCH

14.1400 g., 0.9250 Silver 0.4205 oz. ASW, 32x22 mm. **Subject:** Napoleonic Imperial Guard **Obv:** National arms and helmet **Rev:** Mounted Napoleonic Guard member **Shape:** Vertical rectangle

Date	Mintage	F	VF	XF	Unc	BU
2010MW Proof	100,000	Value: 45.00				

Y# 722 10 ZLOTYCH

14.1400 g., 0.9250 Silver 0.4205 oz. ASW, 32 mm. **Subject:** Katyn Crime **Obv:** National emblem and silhouette of a badge **Rev:** Field of crosses

Date	Mintage	F	VF	XF	Unc	BU
2010MW Antiqued	80,000	—	—	—	50.00	—

Y# 724 10 ZLOTYCH

28.2800 g., 0.9250 Silver 0.8410 oz. ASW, 38.61 mm. **Subject:** Horseshoe Bat

Date	Mintage	F	VF	XF	Unc	BU
2010MW Proof	100,000	Value: 37.50				

Y# 726 10 ZLOTYCH

14.1400 g., 0.9250 Silver 0.4205 oz. ASW, 32 mm. **Subject:** Polish Scouting Centennial

Date	Mintage	F	VF	XF	Unc	BU
2010MW Proof	90,000	Value: 30.00				

Y# 728 10 ZLOTYCH

14.1400 g., 0.9250 Silver 0.4205 oz. ASW, 32 mm. **Subject:** Popular Music - Marke Grechuta

Date	Mintage	F	VF	XF	Unc	BU
2010MW Proof	100,000	Value: 30.00				

Y# 729 10 ZLOTYCH

14.1400 g., 0.9250 Silver 0.4205 oz. ASW, 28.2x28.2 mm. **Subject:** Popular Music - Marek Grechuta **Shape:** Square

Date	Mintage	F	VF	XF	Unc	BU
2010MW Proof	100,000	Value: 35.00				

Y# 731 10 ZLOTYCH

14.1400 g., 0.9250 Silver 0.4205 oz. ASW, 32 mm. **Subject:** Jan Twardowski

Date	Mintage	F	VF	XF	Unc	BU
2010MW Proof	80,000	Value: 35.00				

Y# 733 10 ZLOTYCH

14.1400 g., 0.9250 Silver 0.4205 oz. ASW, 40x26 mm. **Subject:** Battles of Grunwald, Kluszyn

Date	Mintage	F	VF	XF	Unc	BU
2010MW Proof	100,000	Value: 35.00				

Y# 736 10 ZLOTYCH

28.2800 g., 0.9250 Silver 0.8410 oz. ASW, 38.6 mm. **Subject:** Battle of Warsaw

Date	Mintage	F	VF	XF	Unc	BU
2010MW Proof	100,000	Value: 40.00				

Y# 738 10 ZLOTYCH

14.1400 g., 0.9250 Silver 0.4205 oz. ASW, 32 mm. **Subject:** August of 1980

Date	Mintage	F	VF	XF	Unc	BU
2010MW Proof	100,000	Value: 35.00				

Y# 743 10 ZLOTYCH

14.1400 g., 0.9250 Silver 0.4205 oz. ASW, 32 mm. **Subject:** Polish Explorers - Benedykt Dybowski

Date	Mintage	F	VF	XF	Unc	BU
2010MW Proof	100,000	Value: 35.00				

Y# 745 10 ZLOTYCH

28.2800 g., 0.9250 Silver 0.8410 oz. ASW **Subject:** Krzeszow

Date	Mintage	F	VF	XF	Unc	BU
2010MW Proof	80,000	Value: 40.00				

Y# 747 10 ZLOTYCH

28.2800 g., 0.9250 Silver 0.8410 oz. ASW, 40x28 mm. **Subject:** Arthur Grottger

Date	Mintage	F	VF	XF	Unc	BU
2010MW Proof	100,000	Value: 40.00				

Y# 750 10 ZLOTYCH

14.1400 g., 0.9250 Silver 0.4205 oz. ASW, 40x26 mm. **Subject:** Battle of Grunwald **Shape:** Oval

Date	Mintage	F	VF	XF	Unc	BU
2010MW Proof	100,000	Value: 45.00				

Y# 758 10 ZLOTYCH

14.1400 g., 0.9250 Silver 0.4205 oz. ASW, 32 mm. **Subject:** Benedykt Dybowski **Obv:** Books **Rev:** Bust facing, map in background

Date	Mintage	F	VF	XF	Unc	BU
2010 Proof	60,000	Value: 55.00				

Y# 409 20 ZLOTYCH

28.2800 g., 0.9250 Silver 0.8410 oz. ASW, 38.6 mm. **Subject:** Wieliezce Salt Mine **Obv:** Crowned eagle with wings open in center of rock **Rev:** Ancient salt miners **Edge:** Plain

Date	Mintage	F	VF	XF	Unc	BU
2001MW Proof	25,000	Value: 250				

Y# 415 20 ZLOTYCH

28.2800 g., 0.9250 Silver 0.8410 oz. ASW, 38.6 mm. **Obv:** Crowned eagle with wings open flanked by flags **Rev:** European Swallowtail Butterfly **Edge:** Plain

Date	Mintage	F	VF	XF	Unc	BU
2001MW Proof	27,000	Value: 300				

Y# 411 20 ZLOTYCH

28.2800 g., 0.9250 Silver 0.8410 oz. ASW, 38.6 mm. **Subject:** Amber Route **Obv:** Crowned eagle and two ancient Roman silver cups **Rev:** Piece of amber mounted above an ancient Roman coin design and map with the route marked with stars **Edge:** Plain **Note:** Antiqued patina

Date	Mintage	F	VF	XF	Unc	BU
2001MW	30,000	—	—	—	750	—

Y# 424 20 ZLOTYCH

28.7700 g., 0.9250 Silver 0.8556 oz. ASW, 38.6 mm. **Subject:** Christmas **Obv:** Ornate city view **Rev:** Celebration scene including an attached zirconia star **Edge:** Plain **Note:** Antiqued patina.

Date	Mintage	F	VF	XF	Unc	BU
2001MW	55,000	—	—	—	225	—

Y# 457 20 ZLOTYCH

28.2800 g., 0.9250 Silver 0.8410 oz. ASW, 38.6 mm. **Obv:** National arms at lower left, castle complex in background **Rev:** Malborku castle, reddish-brown ceramic applique, **Rev. Legend:** ZAMEK W MALBORKU **Edge:** Plain **Note:** Antiqued patina.

Date	Mintage	F	VF	XF	Unc	BU
2002MW Antiqued finish	51,000	—	—	—	100	—

Y# 442 20 ZLOTYCH
28.0500 g., 0.9250 Silver 0.8342 oz. ASW **Subject:** Jan Matejko **Obv:** Seated figure with crowned eagle at lower right **Rev:** Head facing with multicolor artist's palette **Edge:** Plain **Shape:** Rectangular **Note:** Actual size 40 x 37.9mm.

Date	Mintage	F	VF	XF	Unc	BU
2002MW Proof	57,000	Value: 200				

Y# 428 20 ZLOTYCH
28.2800 g., 0.9250 Silver 0.8410 oz. ASW, 38.6 mm. **Obv:** Crowned eagle with wings open flanked by flags **Rev:** European Pond Turtles **Edge:** Plain

Date	Mintage	F	VF	XF	Unc	BU
2002 Proof	35,000	Value: 175				

Y# 449 20 ZLOTYCH
28.4700 g., 0.9250 Silver 0.8466 oz. ASW, 38.6 mm. **Obv:** Crowned eagle with wings open **Rev:** European Eels and world globe **Edge:** Plain

Date	Mintage	F	VF	XF	Unc	BU
2003MW Proof	—	Value: 250				

Y# 452 20 ZLOTYCH
28.2800 g., 0.9250 Silver 0.8410 oz. ASW, 38.6 mm. **Subject:** Easter Monday Festival **Obv:** Crowned eagle on lace curtain above lamb and multicolor Easter eggs **Rev:** Festival scene **Edge:** Plain

Date	Mintage	F	VF	XF	Unc	BU
2003MW Proof	44,000	Value: 100				

Y# 471 20 ZLOTYCH
28.2800 g., 0.9250 Silver 0.8410 oz. ASW, 40 x 40 mm. **Obv:** Standing Pope John Paul II **Rev:** Pope"s portrait **Edge:** Plain **Shape:** Square

Date	Mintage	F	VF	XF	Unc	BU
2003MW Proof	83,000	Value: 75.00				

Y# 478 20 ZLOTYCH
28.2800 g., 0.9250 Silver 0.8410 oz. ASW **Obv:** "Death" allegory closing an old man's eyes, national arms at lower right **Rev:** Self portrait of Jacek Malczewski, palette at lower right multicolor **Edge:** Plain **Shape:** Rectangular **Note:** 27.93 x 39.94 mm.

Date	Mintage	F	VF	XF	Unc	BU
2003MW Proof	64,000	Value: 65.00				

Y# 498 20 ZLOTYCH
28.2800 g., 0.9250 Silver 0.8410 oz. ASW, 38.6 mm. **Subject:** Lodz Ghetto (1940-1944) **Obv:** Silhouette on wall **Rev:** Child with a pot **Edge:** Plain

Date	Mintage	F	VF	XF	Unc	BU
2004MW Matte	64,000	—	—	—	—	45.00

Y# 504 20 ZLOTYCH
28.2800 g., 0.9250 Silver 0.8410 oz. ASW, 38.6 mm. **Subject:** Polish Senate **Obv:** Crowned eagle above Senate chamber **Rev:** Senate eagle and speaker's staff **Edge:** Plain

Date	Mintage	F	VF	XF	Unc	BU
2004MW Proof	67,000	Value: 75.00				

Y# 508 20 ZLOTYCH
28.2800 g., 0.9250 Silver 0.8410 oz. ASW, 38.6 mm. **Obv:** Crowned eagle in harvest wreath **Rev:** Harvest fest parade **Edge:** Plain

Date	Mintage	F	VF	XF	Unc	BU
2004MW Proof	74,000	Value: 45.00				

Y# 513 20 ZLOTYCH
28.2800 g., 0.9250 Silver 0.8410 oz. ASW, 40x28 mm. **Obv:** Mother and children **Rev:** Stanislaw Wyspianski (1869-1907) **Edge:** Plain

Date	Mintage	F	VF	XF	Unc	BU
2004MW Proof	80,000	Value: 55.00				

Y# 515 20 ZLOTYCH
28.2800 g., 0.9250 Silver 0.8410 oz. ASW, 38.6 mm. **Obv:** National arms **Obv. Legend:** RZECZPOSPOLITA POLSKA **Rev:** 2 Harbor Porpoises **Rev. Legend:** MORSWIN - Phocoena phocoena **Edge:** Plain

Date	Mintage	F	VF	XF	Unc	BU
2004MW Proof	56,000	Value: 175				

Y# 531 20 ZLOTYCH
28.8400 g., 0.9250 Silver 0.8576 oz. ASW, 38.6 mm. **Obv:** Polish eagle above value **Rev:** Eagle Owl with nestlings **Edge:** Plain

Date	Mintage	F	VF	XF	Unc	BU
2005MW Proof	61,000	Value: 150				

Y# 542 20 ZLOTYCH
28.2800 g., 0.9250 Silver 0.8410 oz. ASW, 28 x 40 mm. **Obv:** Sneak thief stealing from a miser **Rev:** Painter Tadeusz Makowski **Edge:** Plain **Shape:** Rectangular

Date	Mintage	F	VF	XF	Unc	BU
2005MW Proof	70,000	Value: 60.00				

Y# 597 20 ZLOTYCH
28.5000 g., 0.9250 Silver 0.8475 oz. ASW, 38.5 mm. **Subject:** 350 Years, Defence of Góry **Obv:** National arms to right of outlined Góry **Obv. Legend:** RZECZPOSPOLITA POLSKA **Obv. Inscription:** Tutaj zawsze / bylismy woini / JAN PAWEL II **Rev:** 1/2 length figure of man at lower right, Góry under bombardment in background **Rev. Legend:** 350 - LECIE OBRONY JASNEJ GÓRY **Edge:** Lettered **Edge Lettering:** CZESTOCHOWA 2005 repeated three times

Date	Mintage	F	VF	XF	Unc	BU
2005MW Proof	69,000	Value: 55.00				

Y# 535 20 ZLOTYCH
28.8400 g., 0.9250 Silver 0.8576 oz. ASW, 38.6 mm. **Obv:** Polish eagle above value **Rev:** Alpine Marmot standing **Edge:** Plain

Date	Mintage	F	VF	XF	Unc	BU
2006MW Proof	60,000	Value: 125				

Y# 533 20 ZLOTYCH
28.8400 g., 0.9250 Silver 0.8576 oz. ASW, 38.6 mm. **Obv:** Polish eagle above value **Rev:** Multicolor holographic spider web **Edge:** Plain

Date	Mintage	F	VF	XF	Unc	BU
2006MW Proof	65,000	Value: 115				

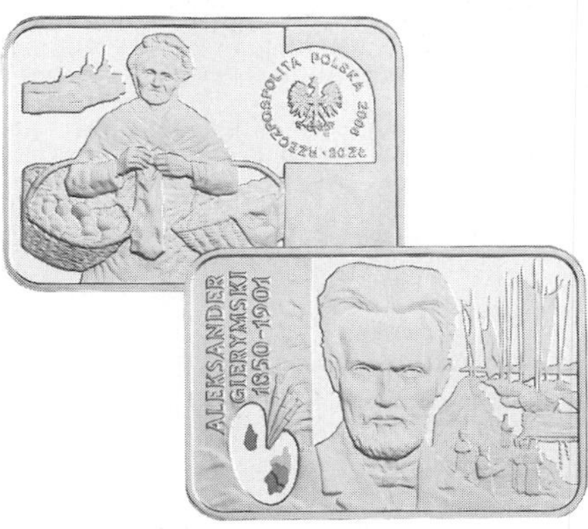

Y# 604 20 ZLOTYCH
28.1400 g., Silver **Subject:** Aleksander Gierymski **Obv:** National arms at upper right, painting of elderly woman carrying baskets **Rev:** Bust of Gierymski facing at center, harbor scene at right, painter's palette at lower left multicolor **Edge:** Plain **Shape:** Rectangular **Note:** 39.95 x 27.97 mm.

Date	Mintage	F	VF	XF	Unc	BU
2006MW Proof	66,000	Value: 65.00				

Y# 584 20 ZLOTYCH

28.4700 g., 0.9250 Silver 0.8466 oz. ASW, 38.6 mm. **Obv:** Polish Eagle on old wood **Rev:** Multi-color wood behind Haczowie church **Edge:** Plain

Date	Mintage	F	VF	XF	Unc	BU
2006MW Proof	—	Value: 60.00				

Y# 579 20 ZLOTYCH

28.2800 g., 0.9250 Silver 0.8410 oz. ASW, 38.6 mm. **Obv:** Crowned eagle **Rev:** Two Grey Seal females and pup with two silhouettes in background **Edge:** Plain

Date	Mintage	F	VF	XF	Unc	BU
2007MW Proof	58,000	Value: 125				

Y# 603 20 ZLOTYCH

28.2500 g., 0.9250 Silver 0.8401 oz. ASW, 38.5 mm. **Subject:** Medieval Principality of Sredniowieczne in Torin **Obv:** City arms at right, national arms below walled city gate in background **Obv. Legend:** RZECZPOSPOLITA POLSKA **Rev:** City view **Rev. Legend:** MIASTO SREDNIOWIECZNE W TORUNIU **Edge:** Plain

Date	Mintage	F	VF	XF	Unc	BU
2007MW Proof	58,000	Value: 70.00				

Y# 636 20 ZLOTYCH

28.3800 g., Silver, 38.6 mm. **Subject:** 65th Anniversary Warsaw Ghetto Uprising **Obv:** Small national arms at left, flames, shattered wall **Obv. Legend:** RZECZPOSPOLITA POLSKA **Rev:** Tree, Star of David, wall in backgound **Rev. Inscription:** 65. ROCZNICA POWSTANIA / W GETCIE WARSZAWSKIM **Edge:** Plain

Date	Mintage	F	VF	XF	Unc	BU
2008MW Proof	—	Value: 60.00				

Y# 642 20 ZLOTYCH

28.2800 g., Silver, 38.61 mm. **Subject:** Kazimierez Dolny **Obv:** Part of a wall and an eagle **Rev:** Houses and a well **Designer:** Ewa Olszewska-Borys

Date	Mintage	F	VF	XF	Unc	BU
2008 Proof	125,000	Value: 50.00				

Y# 637 20 ZLOTYCH

28.2800 g., 0.9250 Silver 0.8410 oz. ASW, 38.61 mm. **Obv:** National arms **Obv. Legend:** RZECZPOSPOLITA POLSKA **Obv. Designer:** Ewa Tyc-Karpinska **Rev:** Peregrine Falcon by 2 chicks in nest at right **Rev. Legend:** SOKOL WEDROWNY - Falco peregrinus **Rev. Designer:** Roussanka Nowakowska **Edge:** Plain

Date	Mintage	F	VF	XF	Unc	BU
2008MW Proof	107,000	Value: 80.00				

Y# 651 20 ZLOTYCH

28.2800 g., Silver, 38.61 mm. **Subject:** 90th Anniversary of Regaining Freedom **Obv:** War decoration left side, eagle top right **Rev:** 3 generals **Designer:** Ewa Olszewska-Borys

Date	Mintage	F	VF	XF	Unc	BU
2008 Proof	110,000	Value: 55.00				

Y# 679 20 ZLOTYCH

28.2800 g., 0.9250 Silver 0.8410 oz. ASW, 38.6 mm. **Subject:** Green Lizard **Obv:** National arms above value **Rev:** Two green lizards in nature

Date	Mintage	F	VF	XF	Unc	BU
2009MW Proof	100,000	Value: 45.00				

Y# 693 20 ZLOTYCH

28.2800 g., 0.9250 Silver 0.8410 oz. ASW, 38.6 mm. **Subject:** Liquidation of the Lotz Ghetto **Obv:** New oak sprig amongst broken bricks **Rev:** Oak tree, bare and with leaves, star of David within

Date	Mintage	F	VF	XF	Unc	BU
2009MW Antiqued	50,000	—	—	—	45.00	—

Y# 704 20 ZLOTYCH

28.2800 g., 0.9250 Silver 0.8410 oz. ASW, 38.6 mm. **Subject:** Poles who saved Jews **Obv:** National arms above broken brick wall **Rev:** Three portraits

Date	Mintage	F	VF	XF	Unc	BU
2009MW Proof	100,000	Value: 40.00				

Y# 763 20 ZLOTYCH

28.8400 g., 0.9250 Silver 0.8576 oz. ASW, 38.6 mm. **Subject:** Borsuk **Obv:** National Arms above value **Rev:** Two small bear

Date	Mintage	F	VF	XF	Unc	BU
2011 Proof	80,000	Value: 60.00				

Y# 765 20 ZLOTYCH

28.2800 g., 0.9250 Silver 0.8410 oz. ASW, 40x28 mm. **Subject:** Zofia Stryjenska **Obv:** Horseback scene, National Arms at right **Rev:** Portrait with artist pallet with brushes

Date	Mintage	F	VF	XF	Unc	BU
2011 Proof	50,000	Value: 55.00				

Y# 682 25 ZLOTYCH

1.0000 g., 0.9000 Gold 0.0289 oz. AGW, 12 mm. **Subject:** General Elections of 1989 **Obv:** National arms above value **Rev:** Solidarity logo

Date	Mintage	F	VF	XF	Unc	BU
2009MW Proof	40,000	Value: 65.00				

Y# 740 25 ZLOTYCH

1.0000 g., 0.9000 Gold 0.0289 oz. AGW, 12 mm. **Subject:** Constitutional Tribunal

Date	Mintage	F	VF	XF	Unc	BU
2010MW Proof	10,000	Value: 75.00				

Y# 739 30 ZLOTYCH

1.7000 g., 0.9000 Gold 0.0492 oz. AGW, 16 mm. **Subject:** August of 1980

Date	Mintage	F	VF	XF	Unc	BU
2010MW Proof	50,000	Value: 100				

Y# 702 37 ZLOTYCH

1.7500 g., 0.9000 Gold 0.0506 oz. AGW, 16 mm. **Subject:** Fr. Jorzy Popieluszko, 25th Anniversary of Murder **Obv:** National arms above large 37 **Rev:** Many hands holding crosses

Date	Mintage	F	VF	XF	Unc	BU
2009MW Proof	60,000	Value: 90.00				

Y# 652 50 ZLOTYCH

3.1300 g., Gold, 18 mm. **Subject:** 90th Annniversary of Regaining Freedom **Obv:** Tomb of the unknown soldier **Rev:** Mounted Commander-In-Chief Jósef Pilsudski **Designer:** Ewa Olszewska-Borys

Date	Mintage	F	VF	XF	Unc	BU
2008 Proof	8,800	Value: 125				

Y# 416 100 ZLOTYCH

8.0000 g., 0.9000 Gold 0.2315 oz. AGW, 21 mm. **Subject:** Wladyslaw I (1320-33) **Obv:** Crowned eagle with wings open **Rev:** Crowned bust facing **Edge:** Plain

Date	Mintage	F	VF	XF	Unc	BU
2001MW Proof	2,000	Value: 875				

Y# 417 100 ZLOTYCH

8.0000 g., 0.9000 Gold 0.2315 oz. AGW, 21 mm. **Subject:** Boleslaw III (1102-1138) **Obv:** Crowned eagle with wings open **Rev:** Pointed crowned bust facing **Edge:** Plain

Date	Mintage	F	VF	XF	Unc	BU
2001MW Proof	2,000	Value: 875				

Y# 462 100 ZLOTYCH

8.0000 g., 0.9000 Gold 0.2315 oz. AGW, 21 mm. **Obv:** Crowned eagle with wings open **Rev:** Jan Sobieski III **Edge:** Plain

Date	Mintage	F	VF	XF	Unc	BU
2001MV Proof	2,200	Value: 875				

Y# 436 100 ZLOTYCH

8.0000 g., 0.9000 Gold 0.2315 oz. AGW, 21 mm. **Subject:** World Cup Soccer **Obv:** Crowned eagle with wings open and world background **Rev:** Soccer player **Edge:** Plain

Date	Mintage	F	VF	XF	Unc	BU
2002MW Proof	4,500	Value: 375				

Y# 429 100 ZLOTYCH

8.0000 g., 0.9000 Gold 0.2315 oz. AGW, 21 mm. **Obv:** Crowned eagle with wings open **Rev:** Crowned bust facing **Edge:** Plain

Date	Mintage	F	VF	XF	Unc	BU
2002MW Proof	2,400	Value: 875				

Y# 430 100 ZLOTYCH

8.0000 g., 0.9000 Gold 0.2315 oz. AGW, 21 mm. **Obv:** Crowned eagle with wings open **Rev:** Crowned bust 1/4 left **Edge:** Plain

Date	Mintage	F	VF	XF	Unc	BU
2002MW Proof	2,200	Value: 875				

Y# 454 100 ZLOTYCH

8.0000 g., 0.9000 Gold 0.2315 oz. AGW, 21 mm. **Obv:** Crowned eagle with wings open **Rev:** Uniformed bust 1/4 left **Edge:** Plain

Date	Mintage	F	VF	XF	Unc	BU
2003MW Proof	2,000	Value: 1,000				

Y# 466 100 ZLOTYCH

8.0000 g., 0.9000 Gold 0.2315 oz. AGW, 21 mm. **Subject:** 750th Anniversary - City Charter **Obv:** Door knocker and church **Rev:** Clock face and tower **Edge:** Plain

Date	Mintage	F	VF	XF	Unc	BU
2003MW Proof	2,100	Value: 750				

Y# 467 100 ZLOTYCH

8.0000 g., 0.9000 Gold 0.2315 oz. AGW, 21 mm. **Obv:** Crowned eagle with wings open **Rev:** Kazimierz IV (1447-1492) **Edge:** Plain

Date	Mintage	F	VF	XF	Unc	BU
2003MW Proof	2,300	Value: 750				

Y# 476 100 ZLOTYCH

8.0000 g., 0.9000 Gold 0.2315 oz. AGW, 21 mm. **Obv:** Crowned eagle with wings open **Rev:** Stanislaus I and eagle **Edge:** Plain

Date	Mintage	F	VF	XF	Unc	BU
2003MW Proof	2,500	Value: 750				

Y# 494 100 ZLOTYCH

8.0000 g., 0.9000 Gold 0.2315 oz. AGW, 21 mm. **Obv:** Crowned eagle with wings open **Rev:** King Przemysl II (1295-1296) **Edge:** Plain

Date	Mintage	F	VF	XF	Unc	BU
2004MW Proof	3,400	Value: 550				

Y# 495 100 ZLOTYCH

8.0000 g., 0.9000 Gold 0.2315 oz. AGW, 21 mm. **Obv:** Crowned eagle with wings open **Rev:** King Zygmunt I (1506-1548) **Edge:** Plain

Date	Mintage	F	VF	XF	Unc	BU
2004MW Proof	3,400	Value: 550				

Y# 540 100 ZLOTYCH

8.0000 g., 0.9000 Gold 0.2315 oz. AGW, 21 mm. **Obv:** St. Peters Basilica dome **Rev:** Pope John Paul II and baptismal font **Edge:** Plain

Date	Mintage	F	VF	XF	Unc	BU
2005MW Proof	18,700	Value: 450				

Y# 581 100 ZLOTYCH

8.0000 g., 0.9000 Gold 0.2315 oz. AGW, 21 mm. **Obv:** Line of soccer players on soccer ball surface with Polish eagle in one of the sections **Rev:** Two soccer players **Edge:** Plain

Date	Mintage	F	VF	XF	Unc	BU
2006MW Proof	—	Value: 375				

Y# 640 100 ZLOTYCH

8.0000 g., 0.9000 Gold 0.2315 oz. AGW, 21 mm. **Subject:** Siberian Exiles **Obv:** Small national arms at left, bleak forest at right **Obv. Legend:** RZECZPOSPOLITA POLSKA **Rev:** Grieving mother with child by tree at lower right, building in background at left **Rev. Legend:** SYBIRACY

Date	Mintage	F	VF	XF	Unc	BU
2008MW Proof	12,000	Value: 350				

Y# 657 100 ZLOTYCH

8.0000 g., 0.9000 Gold 0.2315 oz. AGW, 21 mm. **Subject:** 400th Anniversary of Polish Settlement in North America **Obv:** Eagle in center against wind rose. Outline of Europe & North America. **Obv. Designer:** Roussanka Nowakowska **Rev:** Center wind rose surrounded by 4 men working **Rev. Designer:** Roussanks Nowakowska

Date	Mintage	F	VF	XF	Unc	BU
2008 Proof	9,500	Value: 425				

Y# 699 100 ZLOTYCH

8.0000 g., 0.9000 Gold 0.2315 oz. AGW, 21 mm. **Subject:** Tatar Rescue, 100th Anniversary **Obv:** Figure of Mariusz Zaruski **Rev:** Mountains and reszue helicopter image

Date	Mintage	F	VF	XF	Unc	BU
2009MW Proof	10,000	Value: 350				

Y# 714 100 ZLOTYCH

8.0000 g., 0.9000 Gold 0.2315 oz. AGW, 21 mm. **Subject:** Auschwitz liberation **Obv:** Prisoner and railroad track entrance **Rev:** Buildings

Date	Mintage	F	VF	XF	Unc	BU
2010MW Proof	8,000	Value: 400				

Y# 741 100 ZLOTYCH

8.0000 g., 0.9000 Gold 0.2315 oz. AGW, 21 mm. **Subject:** Constitutional Tribunal

Date	Mintage	F	VF	XF	Unc	BU
2010MW Proof	5,000	Value: 425				

KM# 766 100 ZLOTYCH

8.0000 g., 0.9000 Gold 0.2315 oz. AGW, 21 mm. **Subject:** President Lech Kaczynski and wife Maria

Date	Mintage	F	VF	XF	Unc	BU
2010 Proof	—	Value: 475				

Y# 407 200 ZLOTYCH

Tri-Metallic Gold with Palladium center, Gold with Silver ring, Gold with Copper outer limit, 27 mm. **Subject:** Year 2001 **Obv:** Crowned eagle with wings open within a swirl **Rev:** Couple looking into the future **Edge:** Plain

Date	Mintage	F	VF	XF	Unc	BU
2001MW Proof	4,000	Value: 450				

Y# 420 200 ZLOTYCH

15.5000 g., 0.9000 Gold 0.4485 oz. AGW, 27 mm. **Subject:** Cardinal Stefan Wyszynski **Obv:** Pillar divides arms and eagle **Rev:** Bust left within arch **Edge Lettering:** 100 ROCZNIA URODZIN

Date	Mintage	F	VF	XF	Unc	BU
2001MW Proof	4,500	Value: 700				

Y# 463 200 ZLOTYCH

15.5000 g., 0.9000 Gold 0.4485 oz. AGW, 27 mm. **Obv:** Standing violinist **Rev:** Henryk Wieniawski **Edge Lettering:** XII MIEDZYNARODOWY KONKURS SKRZYPCOWY IM HENRYKA WIENIAWSKIEGO

Date	Mintage	F	VF	XF	Unc	BU
2001MW Proof	2,000	Value: 1,150				

Y# 438 200 ZLOTYCH

15.5000 g., 0.9000 Gold 0.4485 oz. AGW, 27 mm. **Subject:** Pope John Paul II **Obv:** Bust left and small eagle with wings open **Rev:** Pope facing radiant Holy Door **Edge:** Plain

Date	Mintage	F	VF	XF	Unc	BU
2002MW Proof	5,000	Value: 1,200				

Y# 470 200 ZLOTYCH

15.5000 g., 0.9000 Gold 0.4485 oz. AGW, 27 mm. **Subject:** Gas and Oil Industry **Obv:** Crowned eagle, oil wells and refinery **Rev:** Scientist at work **Edge:** Plain

Date	Mintage	F	VF	XF	Unc	BU
2003MW Proof	2,100	Value: 1,250				

Y# 472 200 ZLOTYCH

15.5000 g., 0.9000 Gold 0.4485 oz. AGW, 27 mm. **Obv:** Standing Pope John Paul II **Rev:** Seated Pope **Edge:** Plain

Date	Mintage	F	VF	XF	Unc	BU
2003MW Proof	4,900	Value: 1,300				

Y# 483 200 ZLOTYCH

15.5000 g., 0.9000 Gold 0.4485 oz. AGW, 27 mm. **Subject:** Poland Joining the European Union **Obv:** Polish euro coin design elements **Rev:** Polish euro coin design elements **Edge:** Plain

Date	Mintage	F	VF	XF	Unc	BU
2004MW Proof	4,400	Value: 750				

Y# 511 200 ZLOTYCH

15.5000 g., 0.9000 Gold 0.4485 oz. AGW, 27 mm. **Subject:** Warsaw Fine Arts Academy Centennial **Obv:** Campus view **Rev:** Statue and building **Edge:** Plain

Date	Mintage	F	VF	XF	Unc	BU
2004MW Proof	5,000	Value: 575				

Y# 519 200 ZLOTYCH

15.5000 g., 0.9000 Gold 0.4485 oz. AGW, 27 mm. **Subject:** Olympics **Obv:** Woman and crowned eagle **Rev:** Ancient runners painted on pottery **Edge:** Plain

Date	Mintage	F	VF	XF	Unc	BU
2004MW Proof	6,000	Value: 675				

Y# 538 200 ZLOTYCH

15.5000 g., 0.9000 Gold 0.4485 oz. AGW, 27 mm. **Obv:** Horse drawn carriage **Rev:** Konstanty Ildefons Galczynski in top hat **Edge:** Plain

Date	Mintage	F	VF	XF	Unc	BU
2005MW Proof	3,500	Value: 775				

Y# 536 200 ZLOTYCH

15.5000 g., 0.9000 Gold 0.4485 oz. AGW, 27 mm. **Obv:** Chopin **Rev:** Nagoya Castle roof tops and Mt. Fuji **Edge:** Plain **Note:** Aichi Expo Japan

Date	Mintage	F	VF	XF	Unc	BU
2005MW Proof	4,200	Value: 700				

Y# 672 200 ZLOTYCH

15.5000 g., 0.9000 Gold 0.4485 oz. AGW, 27 mm. **Obv:** Helmet and breastplate **Rev:** Knight of the 15th Century

Date	Mintage	F	VF	XF	Unc	BU
2007 Proof	10,500	Value: 750				

Y# 643 200 ZLOTYCH

15.5000 g., Gold, 27 mm. **Subject:** Zbigniew Herbert **Obv:** Eagle and Zbigniew Herbert **Rev:** Mounted statue of Marcus Aurelius **Designer:** Dominika Karpinska-Kopiec

Date	Mintage	F	VF	XF	Unc	BU
2008 Proof	11,200	Value: 775				

Y# 647 200 ZLOTYCH

15.5000 g., Gold, 27 mm. **Series:** The 29th Olympic Games Beijing 2008 **Obv:** Two kites and an eagle **Rev:** Female pole vault jumper **Designer:** Robert Kotowicz

Date	Mintage	F	VF	XF	Unc	BU
2008	—	—	—	—	—	750

Y# 653 200 ZLOTYCH

15.5000 g., Gold, 27 mm. **Subject:** 90th Anniversary of Regaining Freedom **Obv:** Tomb of the unknown soldier **Rev:** Mounted Commander-In-Chief Jozef Pilsudski **Designer:** Ewa Olszewska-Borys

Date	Mintage	F	VF	XF	Unc	BU
2008 Proof	10,000	Value: 725				

Y# 654 200 ZLOTYCH

15.5000 g., Gold, 27 mm. **Subject:** 450 years of the Polish Post **Obv:** Eagle right, bottom against post stamp **Rev:** Horse with rider crossing bridge **Designer:** Robert Kotowicz

Date	Mintage	F	VF	XF	Unc	BU
2008 Proof	11,000	Value: 725				

Y# 660 200 ZLOTYCH

15.5000 g., Gold, 27 mm. **Subject:** 90th Anniversary of the Greater Poland Uprising **Obv:** Eagle at left, eagle at right with chain **Rev:** Charging cavalrymen and German soldiers firing at them **Designer:** Urszula Walerzak

Date	Mintage	F	VF	XF	Unc	BU
2008 Proof	9,400	Value: 725				

Y# 664 200 ZLOTYCH
15.5000 g., 0.9000 Gold 0.4485 oz. AGW, 27 mm. **Subject:** Warsaw Ghetto **Obv:** Building on fire, Naitonal arms **Rev:** Face looking out from broken brick wall

Date	Mintage	F	VF	XF	Unc	BU
2008MW Proof	12,000	Value: 700				

Y# 665 200 ZLOTYCH
8.0000 g., 0.9000 Gold 0.2315 oz. AGW, 21 mm. **Subject:** Poles in the US, 400th Anniversary **Obv:** National Arms, North America and Europe map, compass **Rev:** Four glass maker views

Date	Mintage	F	VF	XF	Unc	BU
2008MW Proof	9,500	Value: 375				

Y# 696 200 ZLOTYCH
15.1500 g., 0.9000 Gold 0.4384 oz. AGW, 27 mm. **Obv:** Eagle and statue, flames in background **Rev:** Stefan Starzonski, Warsaw Mayor; Burning of the Clock Tower

Date	Mintage	F	VF	XF	Unc	BU
2009 Proof	10,500	Value: 750				

Y# 677 200 ZLOTYCH
15.5000 g., 0.9000 Gold 0.4485 oz. AGW, 27 mm. **Subject:** Central Banking, 180th Anniversary **Obv:** National arms above crowned shield **Rev:** Building and portrait

Date	Mintage	F	VF	XF	Unc	BU
2009MW Proof	8,500	Value: 675				

Y# 683 200 ZLOTYCH
15.5000 g., 0.9000 Gold 0.4485 oz. AGW, 27 mm. **Subject:** General election of 1989 **Obv:** National arms above shipyard scene **Rev:** Lech Walesa silhouette before crowd

Date	Mintage	F	VF	XF	Unc	BU
2009MW Proof	10,000	Value: 675				

Y# 717 200 ZLOTYCH
15.5000 g., 0.9000 Gold 0.4485 oz. AGW, 27 mm. **Subject:** Vancouver Winter Olympics **Obv:** Downhill skiing **Rev:** Cross Country skiing

Date	Mintage	F	VF	XF	Unc	BU
2010MW Proof	8,000	Value: 675				

Y# 720 200 ZLOTYCH
15.5000 g., 0.9000 Gold 0.4485 oz. AGW, 27 mm. **Subject:** Napoleonic Imperial Guard **Obv:** Pile of arms **Rev:** Galloping guardsman

Date	Mintage	F	VF	XF	Unc	BU
2010MW Proof	10,500	Value: 675				

Y# 734 200 ZLOTYCH
15.5000 g., 0.9000 Gold 0.4485 oz. AGW, 27 mm. **Subject:** Battles of Grunwald and Kluszyn

Date	Mintage	F	VF	XF	Unc	BU
2010MW Proof	10,500	Value: 700				

GOLD BULLION COINAGE

Y# 292 50 ZLOTYCH
3.1000 g., 0.9999 Gold 0.0997 oz. AGW, 18 mm. **Obv:** Crowned eagle with wings open, all within circle **Rev:** Golden eagle

Date	Mintage	F	VF	XF	Unc	BU
2002	500	—	—	—	BV	220
2004	2,000	—	—	—	BV	160
2006	1,600	—	—	—	BV	170
2007	2,000	—	—	—	BV	160
2008	—	—	—	—	BV	160

Y# 293 100 ZLOTYCH
7.7800 g., 0.9999 Gold 0.2501 oz. AGW, 22 mm. **Obv:** Crowned eagle with wings open, all within circle **Rev:** Golden eagle

Date	Mintage	F	VF	XF	Unc	BU
2002	800	—	—	—	BV	400
2004	1,000	—	—	—	BV	375
2006	900	—	—	—	BV	400
2007	1,500	—	—	—	BV	375
2008	—	—	—	—	BV	375

Y# 294 200 ZLOTYCH
15.5000 g., 0.9000 Gold 0.4485 oz. AGW, 27 mm. **Obv:** Crowned eagle with wings open within beaded circle **Rev:** Golden eagle

Date	Mintage	F	VF	XF	Unc	BU
2002	1,000	—	—	—	BV	675
2004	1,000	—	—	—	BV	675
2006	900	—	—	—	BV	675
2007	1,500	—	—	—	BV	675
2008	—	—	—	—	BV	675

Y# 295 500 ZLOTYCH
31.1035 g., 0.9999 Gold 0.9999 oz. AGW **Obv:** Crowned eagle with wings open within beaded circle **Rev:** Golden eagle

Date	Mintage	F	VF	XF	Unc	BU
2002	1,000	—	—	—	BV	1,550
2004	2,500	—	—	—	BV	1,500
2006	600	—	—	—	BV	1,600
2007	2,500	—	—	—	BV	1,500
2008	—	—	—	—	BV	1,500

MINT SETS

KM#	Date	Mintage	Identification	Issue Price	Mkt Val
MS5	2007 (11)	2,000	Y#276-284, 465, 525, mixed date set - 1995-2007	39.95	37.50

PORTUGAL

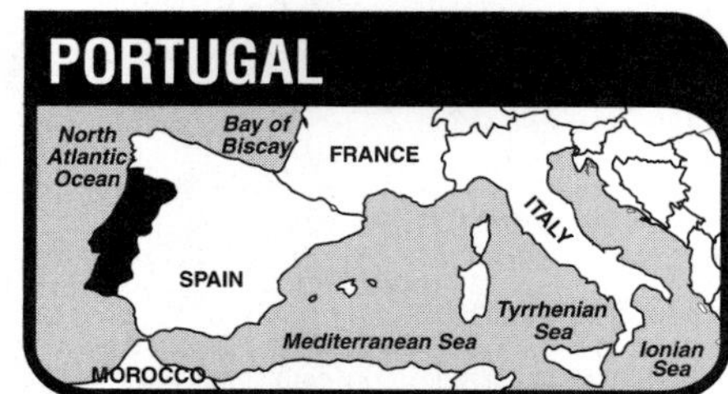

The Portuguese Republic, located in the western part of the Iberian Peninsula in southwestern Europe, has an area of 35,553 sq. mi. (92,080 sq. km.) and a population of *10.5 million. Capital: Lisbon. Portugal's economy is based on agriculture, tourism, minerals, fisheries and a rapidly expanding industrial sector. Textiles account for 33% of the exports and Portuguese wine is world famous. Portugal has become Europe's number one producer of copper and the world's largest producer of cork.

RULER
Republic, 1910 to date

MONETARY SYSTEM
100 Cents = 1 Euro

REPUBLIC

DECIMAL COINAGE

KM# 631a ESCUDO
4.6000 g., 0.9167 Gold 0.1356 oz. AGW, 16 mm. **Subject:** Last Escudo **Obv:** Design above shield with "Au" above top left corner of shield **Rev:** Flower design above value **Edge:** Plain

Date	Mintage	F	VF	XF	Unc	BU
2001INCM	50,000	—	—	—	210	225

KM# 634.1 20 ESCUDOS
6.9000 g., Copper-Nickel, 26.5 mm. **Obv:** Shield divides date with value below **Obv. Legend:** REPUBLICA PORTUGUESA **Rev:** Nautical windrose **Designer:** Euclides Vaz

Date	Mintage	F	VF	XF	Unc	BU
2001INCM	Est. 250,000	—	—	—	2.75	3.50

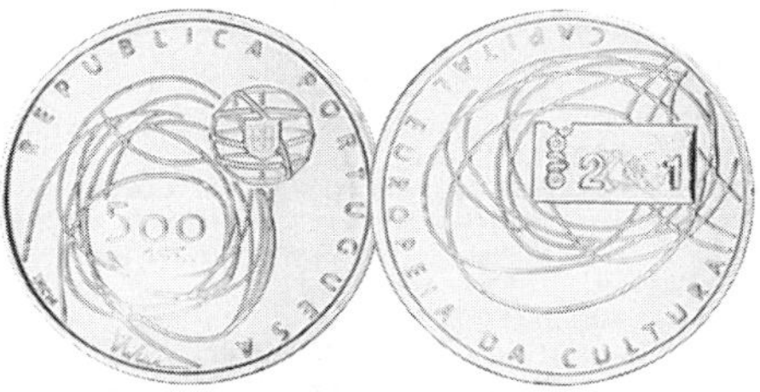

KM# 733 500 ESCUDOS
13.9600 g., 0.5000 Silver 0.2244 oz. ASW, 30.1 mm. **Subject:** Porto, European Culture Capital **Obv:** National arms and value **Rev:** Stylized design **Edge:** Reeded

Date	Mintage	F	VF	XF	Unc	BU
2001INCM	—	—	—	—	9.50	8.50
2001INCM Proof	10,000	Value: 60.00				

KM# 733a 500 ESCUDOS
Gold **Subject:** Porto, European Culture Capital **Obv:** National arms and value **Rev:** Stylized design **Edge:** Reeded

Date	Mintage	F	VF	XF	Unc	BU
2001INCM Proof	5,000	Value: 550				

KM# 734 1000 ESCUDOS
26.9500 g., 0.5000 Silver 0.4332 oz. ASW, 40 mm. **Obv:** National arms and value **Obv. Legend:** REPUBLICA PORTUGUESA 2001 **Rev:** Soccer ball within net **Rev. Legend:** 10º Campeonato Europeu de Futebol - UEFA Euro 2004 Portugal **Edge:** Reeded

Date	Mintage	F	VF	XF	Unc	BU
2001INCM	50,000	—	—	—	16.50	18.50
2001INCM Proof	—	Value: 75.00				

EURO COINAGE

European Union Issues

KM# 740 EURO CENT
2.3000 g., Copper Plated Steel, 16.25 mm. **Obv:** Royal seal of 1134 with country name and cross **Obv. Designer:** Vitor Santos **Rev:** Value and globe **Rev. Designer:** Luc Luycx **Edge:** Plain

Date	Mintage	F	VF	XF	Unc	BU
2002	278,106,172	—	—	—	0.35	0.50
2002 Proof	15,000	Value: 7.00				
2003	50,000	—	—	—	0.35	0.50
2003 Proof	15,000	Value: 7.00				
2004	75,000,000	—	—	—	0.35	0.50
2004 Proof	15,000	Value: 7.00				
2005	40,000,000	—	—	—	0.35	0.50

Date	Mintage	F	VF	XF	Unc	BU
2005 Proof	10,000	Value: 7.00				
2006	30,000,000	—	—	—	0.35	0.50
2006 Proof	3,000	Value: 7.00				
2007	105,000,000	—	—	—	0.35	0.50
2007 Proof	—	Value: 7.00				
2008	75,000,000	—	—	—	0.35	0.50
2008 Proof	—	Value: 7.00				
2009	60,000,000	—	—	—	0.35	0.50
2009 Proof	—	Value: 7.00				
2010	—	—	—	—	0.35	0.50
2010 Proof	—	Value: 7.00				

KM# 741 2 EURO CENT

3.0300 g., Copper Plated Steel, 18.7 mm. **Obv:** Royal seal of 1134 with country name and cross **Obv. Designer:** Vitor Santos **Rev:** Value and globe **Rev. Designer:** Luc Luycx **Edge:** Grooved

Date	Mintage	F	VF	XF	Unc	BU
2002	324,376,590	—	—	—	0.50	0.65
2002 Proof	15,000	Value: 9.00				
2003	50,000	—	—	—	—	2.50
Note: In sets only						
2003 Proof	15,000	Value: 9.00				
Note: In sets only						
2004	1,000,000	—	—	—	0.50	0.65
2004 Proof	15,000	Value: 9.00				
2005	10,000,000	—	—	—	0.50	0.65
2005 Proof	10,000	Value: 9.00				
2006	1,000,000	—	—	—	0.50	0.65
2006 Proof	3,000	Value: 9.00				
2007	10,000,000	—	—	—	0.50	0.65
2007 Proof	—	Value: 9.00				
2008	35,000,000	—	—	—	0.50	0.65
2008 Proof	—	Value: 9.00				
2009	45,000,000	—	—	—	0.50	0.65
2009 Proof	—	Value: 9.00				
2010	—	—	—	—	0.50	0.65
2010 Proof	—	Value: 9.00				

KM# 742 5 EURO CENT

3.8600 g., Copper Plated Steel, 21.2 mm. **Obv:** Royal seal of 1134 with country name and cross **Obv. Designer:** Vitor Santos **Rev:** Value and globe **Rev. Designer:** Luc Luycx **Edge:** Plain

Date	Mintage	F	VF	XF	Unc	BU
2002	234,512,047	—	—	—	0.75	1.00
2002 Proof	15,000	Value: 10.00				
2003	50,000	—	—	—	—	4.00
Note: In sets only						
2003 Proof	15,000	Value: 10.00				
Note: In sets only						
2004	40,000,000	—	—	—	0.75	1.00
2004 Proof	15,000	Value: 10.00				
2005	30,000,000	—	—	—	0.75	1.00
2005 Proof	10,000	Value: 10.00				
2006	20,000,000	—	—	—	0.75	1.00
2006 Proof	3,000	Value: 10.00				
2007	25,000,000	—	—	—	0.75	1.00
2007 Proof	—	Value: 10.00				
2008	25,000,000	—	—	—	0.75	1.00
2008 Proof	—	Value: 10.00				
2009	25,000,000	—	—	—	0.75	1.00
2009 Proof	—	Value: 10.00				
2010	—	—	—	—	0.75	1.00
2010 Proof	—	Value: 10.00				

KM# 743 10 EURO CENT

4.0700 g., Brass, 19.7 mm. **Obv:** Royal seal of 1142, country name in circular design **Obv. Designer:** Vitor Santos **Rev:** Value and map **Rev. Designer:** Luc Luycx **Edge:** Reeded

Date	Mintage	F	VF	XF	Unc	BU
2002	220,289,835	—	—	—	0.75	1.00
2002 Proof	15,000	Value: 12.00				
2003	6,332,000	—	—	—	1.00	1.50
2003 Proof	15,000	Value: 12.00				
Note: In sets only						
2004	1,000,000	—	—	—	1.50	2.00
2004 Proof	15,000	Value: 12.00				
2005	1,000,000	—	—	—	1.50	2.00
2005 Proof	10,000	Value: 12.00				
2006	1,000,000	—	—	—	1.50	2.00
2006 Proof	3,000	Value: 12.00				

KM# 763 10 EURO CENT

4.0700 g., Brass, 19.7 mm. **Obv:** Royal seal of 1142, country name in circular design **Obv. Designer:** Vitor Santos **Rev:** Relief map of Western Europe, stars, lines and value **Rev. Designer:** Luc Luycx **Edge:** Reeded

Date	Mintage	F	VF	XF	Unc	BU
2008	1,000,000	—	—	—	1.50	2.00
2008 Proof	—	Value: 12.00				
2009	10,000,000	—	—	—	1.50	2.00
2009 Proof	—	Value: 12.00				
2010	—	—	—	—	1.50	2.00
2010 Proof	—	Value: 12.00				

KM# 744 20 EURO CENT

5.7300 g., Brass, 22.1 mm. **Obv:** Royal seal of 1142, country name in circular design **Obv. Designer:** Vitor Santos **Rev:** Value and map **Rev. Designer:** Luc Luycx **Edge:** Notched

Date	Mintage	F	VF	XF	Unc	BU
2002	147,411,038	—	—	—	1.00	1.25
2002 Proof	15,000	Value: 14.00				
2003	9,493,600	—	—	—	1.25	1.50
2003 Proof	15,000	Value: 14.00				
2004	1,000,000	—	—	—	1.50	2.00
2004 Proof	15,000	Value: 14.00				
2005	25,000,000	—	—	—	1.50	2.00
2005 Proof	10,000	Value: 14.00				
2006	20,000,000	—	—	—	1.50	2.00
2006 Proof	3,000	Value: 14.00				

KM# 764 20 EURO CENT

5.7300 g., Brass, 22.1 mm. **Obv:** Royal seal of 1142, country name in circular design **Obv. Designer:** Vitor Santos **Rev:** Relief map of Western Europe, stars, lines and value **Rev. Designer:** Luc Luycx **Edge:** Notched

Date	Mintage	F	VF	XF	Unc	BU
2008	1,000,000	—	—	—	1.50	2.00
2008 Proof	—	Value: 14.00				
2009	20,000,000	—	—	—	1.50	2.00
2009 Proof	—	Value: 14.00				
2010	—	—	—	—	1.50	2.00
2010 Proof	—	Value: 14.00				

KM# 777 1/4 EURO

1.5600 g., 0.9990 Gold 0.0501 oz. AGW, 14 mm. **Series:** Portugal Universal **Subject:** King Alfons I, the Conqueror **Obv:** National arms, value **Obv. Legend:** REPÚBLICA PORTUGUESA **Rev:** Stylized 3/4 length armored figure standing facing **Rev. Legend:** D. AFONSO HENRIQUES **Edge:** Reeded **Note:** Each coin is numbered.

Date	Mintage	F	VF	XF	Unc	BU
2006INCM FDC	30,000	—	—	—	—	145

KM# 787 1/4 EURO

1.5600 g., 0.9990 Gold 0.0501 oz. AGW, 14 mm. **Subject:** Vasco da Gama

Date	Mintage	F	VF	XF	Unc	BU
2009 Proof	30,000	Value: 125				

KM# 794 1/4 EURO

1.5600 g., 0.9000 Gold 0.0451 oz. AGW, 14 mm. **Subject:** Luis Vaz de Camoes

Date	Mintage	F	VF	XF	Unc	BU
2010INCM	—	—	—	—	—	145

KM# 745 50 EURO CENT

7.8100 g., Brass, 24.2 mm. **Obv:** Royal seal of 1142, country name in circular design **Obv. Designer:** Vitor Santos **Rev:** Value and map **Rev. Designer:** Luc Luycx **Edge:** Reeded

Date	Mintage	F	VF	XF	Unc	BU
2002	151,947,133	—	—	—	1.50	2.00
2002 Proof	15,000	Value: 16.00				
2003	10,353,000	—	—	—	1.50	2.00
2003 Proof	15,000	Value: 16.00				
Note: In sets only						
2004	1,000,000	—	—	—	2.50	3.00
2004 Proof	15,000	Value: 16.00				
2005	1,000,000	—	—	—	2.50	3.00
2005 Proof	10,000	Value: 16.00				
2006	1,000,000	—	—	—	2.50	3.00
2006 Proof	3,000	Value: 16.00				

KM# 765 50 EURO CENT

7.8100 g., Brass, 24.2 mm. **Obv:** Royal seal of 1142, country name in circular design **Obv. Designer:** Vitor Santos **Rev:** Relief map of Western Europe, stars, lines and value **Rev. Designer:** Luc Luycx **Edge:** Reeded

Date	Mintage	F	VF	XF	Unc	BU
2008	5,000,000	—	—	—	2.50	3.00
2008 Proof	—	Value: 16.00				
2009	20,000,000	—	—	—	2.50	3.00
2009 Proof	—	Value: 16.00				
2010	—	—	—	—	2.50	3.00
2010 Proof	—	Value: 16.00				

KM# 746 EURO

7.5000 g., Bi-Metallic Copper-Nickel center in Brass ring, 23.25 mm. **Obv:** Royal seal of 1144, country name in looped design **Obv. Designer:** Vitor Santos **Rev:** Value and map **Rev. Designer:** Luc Luycx **Edge:** Alternating plain and milled.

Date	Mintage	F	VF	XF	Unc	BU
2002	100,228,135	—	—	—	2.00	2.50
Note: Variety in the edge milling, 28 or 29.						
2002 Proof	15,000	Value: 18.00				
2003	16,206,875	—	—	—	2.00	2.50
2003 Proof	15,000	Value: 18.00				
2004	20,000,000	—	—	—	2.00	2.50
2004 Proof	15,000	Value: 18.00				
2005	20,000,000	—	—	—	2.00	2.50
2005 Proof	10,000	Value: 18.00				
2006	20,000,000	—	—	—	2.00	2.50
2006 Proof	3,000	Value: 18.00				
2007	4,935,400	—	—	—	2.00	2.50

KM# 766 EURO

7.5000 g., Bi-Metallic Copper-Nickel center in Brass ring, 23.25 mm. **Obv:** Royal seal of 1144, country name in looped design **Obv. Designer:** Vitor Santos **Rev:** Relief map of Western Europe, stars, lines and value **Rev. Designer:** Luc Luycx **Edge:** Reeded and plain sections

Date	Mintage	F	VF	XF	Unc	BU
2008	5,000,000	—	—	—	2.75	3.50
2008 Proof	—	Value: 18.00				
2009	20,000,000	—	—	—	2.75	3.50
2009 Proof	—	Value: 18.00				
2010	—	—	—	—	2.75	3.50
2010 Proof	—	Value: 18.00				

KM# 788 1-1/2 EURO

10.3700 g., 0.9990 Gold 0.3331 oz. AGW, 26.5 mm. **Subject:** Numismatics - Marabitino of Sancho II **Obv:** Cross of shields **Rev:** King on horseback

Date	Mintage	F	VF	XF	Unc	BU
2009 Proof	2,500	Value: 650				

KM# 789 1-1/2 EURO

Copper-Nickel, 26.5 mm. **Obv:** Numismatics - Marabitino of Sancho II

Date	Mintage	F	VF	XF	Unc	BU
2009 Proof	150,000	—	—	—	5.00	6.00

KM# 795 1-1/2 EURO

10.0000 g., 0.9250 Silver 0.2974 oz. ASW, 26.5 mm. **Subject:** Against Famine

Date	Mintage	F	VF	XF	Unc	BU
2010INCM Proof	5,000	Value: 55.00				

KM# 795a 1-1/2 EURO

8.0000 g., Copper-Nickel, 26.5 mm. **Subject:** Against Famine

Date	Mintage	F	VF	XF	Unc	BU
2010INCM	100,000	—	—	—	5.00	6.00

KM# 747 2 EURO

8.5200 g., Bi-Metallic Brass center in Copper-Nickel ring, 25.7 mm. **Obv:** Royal seal of 1144, country name in looped design **Obv. Designer:** Vitor Santos **Rev:** Value and map **Rev. Designer:** Luc Luycx **Edge:** Reeding over castles and shields

Date	Mintage	F	VF	XF	Unc	BU
2002	61,930,775	—	—	—	3.50	4.00
2002 Proof	15,000	Value: 22.00				
2003	5,979,750	—	—	—	4.25	5.00
2003 Proof	15,000	Value: 22.00				
Note: In sets only						
2004	1,000,000	—	—	—	5.50	6.00
2004 Proof	15,000	Value: 22.00				
2005	1,000,000	—	—	—	5.50	6.00
2005 Proof	10,000	Value: 22.00				
2006	1,000,000	—	—	—	5.50	6.00
2006 Proof	3,000	Value: 22.00				

KM# 771 2 EURO

8.4700 g., Bi-Metallic Brass center in Copper-Nickel ring, 25.74 mm. **Subject:** 50th Anniversary Treaty of Rome **Obv:** Open treaty book **Rev:** Large value at left, modified outline of Europe at right **Edge:** Reeded and lettered

Date	Mintage	F	VF	XF	Unc	BU
2007	1,500,000	—	—	—	4.50	6.00
2007 Prooflike	15,000	—	—	—	—	12.50
2007 Proof	5,000	Value: 25.00				

KM# 772 2 EURO

8.4000 g., Bi-Metallic Brass center in Copper-Nickel ring, 25.73 mm. **Subject:** European Union President **Obv:** Large tree, small national arms at lower left **Obv. Inscription:** POR / TV / GAL **Rev:** Large value at left, revised map of Europe at right **Edge:** Reeded with repeated symbols

Date	Mintage	F	VF	XF	Unc	BU
2007	1,250,000	—	—	—	4.50	6.00
2007 Prooflike	15,000	—	—	—	—	12.50
2007 Proof	5,000	Value: 25.00				

KM# 767 2 EURO

8.5200 g., Bi-Metallic Brass center in Copper-Nickel ring, 25.7 mm. **Obv:** Royal seal of 1144, country name in looped design **Obv. Designer:** Vitor Santos **Rev:** Relief map of Western Europe, stars, lines and value **Rev. Designer:** Luc Luycx **Edge:** Reeding over castles and shields

Date	Mintage	F	VF	XF	Unc	BU
2008INCM In sets only	—	—	—	—	—	6.00
2008INCM Proof	—	Value: 22.00				
2009INCM In sets only	—	—	—	—	—	6.00
2009INCM Proof	—	Value: 22.00				
2010INCM	—	—	—	—	—	6.00
2010INCM Proof	—	Value: 22.00				

KM# 784 2 EURO

8.5500 g., Bi-Metallic Brass center in Copper-Nickel ring, 25.72 mm. **Subject:** Declaration of Human Rights, 60th Anniversary **Obv:** Seal above field

Date	Mintage	F	VF	XF	Unc	BU
2008INCM	1,000,000	—	—	—	4.00	5.00

KM# 785 2 EURO

8.5500 g., Bi-Metallic Brass center in Copper-Nickel ring, 25.72 mm. **Subject:** European monetary Union, 10th Anniversary **Obv:** Stick figure and Euro symbol

Date	Mintage	F	VF	XF	Unc	BU
2009	1,285,000	—	—	—	4.00	5.00

KM# 786 2 EURO

8.5500 g., Bi-Metallic Brass center in Copper-Nickel ring, 25.75 mm. **Subject:** Lusofonia Games **Rev:** Figure with long flowing ribbon

Date	Mintage	F	VF	XF	Unc	BU
2009INCM	1,275,000	—	—	—	—	5.00

KM# 796 2 EURO

8.5000 g., Bi-Metallic Brass center in Copper-Nickel ring, 25.72 mm. **Subject:** Portuguese Republic, 100th Anniversary

Date	Mintage	F	VF	XF	Unc	BU
2010INCM	—	—	—	—	6.00	7.00

KM# 783 2-1/2 EURO

9.8500 g., Copper-Nickel, 28 mm. **Obv:** Small national arms on stringed instrument at right **Rev:** Fado musician at lower left **Edge:** Coarse reeding

Date	Mintage	F	VF	XF	Unc	BU
2008	150,000	—	—	—	6.00	9.00

KM# 783a 2-1/2 EURO

12.0000 g., 0.9250 Silver 0.3569 oz. ASW, 28 mm. **Obv:** Small national arms on stringed instrument at right **Rev:** Fado musician at lower left

Date	Mintage	F	VF	XF	Unc	BU
2008 Proof	20,000	Value: 60.00				

KM# 790 2-1/2 EURO

Copper-Nickel, 28 mm. **Subject:** Bejing Olympics

Date	Mintage	F	VF	XF	Unc	BU
2008	—	—	—	—	6.00	7.00

KM# 791 2-1/2 EURO

Copper-Nickel, 28 mm. **Subject:** Portugese Literature

Date	Mintage	F	VF	XF	Unc	BU
2009	—	—	—	—	6.00	7.00

KM# 792 2-1/2 EURO

Copper-Nickel, 28 mm. **Subject:** Hieronymites Monastery - Belém

Date	Mintage	F	VF	XF	Unc	BU
2009	150,000	—	—	—	6.00	7.00

KM# 793 2-1/2 EURO

Copper-Nickel, 28 mm. **Rev. Designer:** Belém Unesco Heritage Site

Date	Mintage	F	VF	XF	Unc	BU
2009	150,000	—	—	—	6.00	7.00

KM# 797 2-1/2 EURO

12.0000 g., 0.9250 Silver 0.3569 oz. ASW, 28 mm. **Subject:** FIFA Soccer - South Africa

Date	Mintage	F	VF	XF	Unc	BU
2010INCM Proof	12,500	Value: 55.00				

KM# 797a 2-1/2 EURO

10.0000 g., Copper-Nickel, 28 mm. **Subject:** FIFA Soccer - South Africa

Date	Mintage	F	VF	XF	Unc	BU
2010INCM	120,000	—	—	—	6.00	7.00

KM# 798 2-1/2 EURO

12.0000 g., 0.9250 Silver 0.3569 oz. ASW, 28 mm. **Subject:** Palace Square, Lisbon

Date	Mintage	F	VF	XF	Unc	BU
2010INCM Proof	15,000	Value: 55.00				

KM# 798a 2-1/2 EURO

10.0000 g., Copper-Nickel, 28 mm. **Subject:** Palace Square, Lisbon

Date	Mintage	F	VF	XF	Unc	BU
2010INCM	120,000	—	—	—	6.00	7.00

KM# 799 2-1/2 EURO

15.5500 g., 0.9990 Gold 0.4994 oz. AGW, 28 mm. **Subject:** Palace Square, Lisbon

Date	Mintage	F	VF	XF	Unc	BU
2010INCM Proof	2,500	Value: 750				

KM# 800 2-1/2 EURO

12.0000 g., 0.9250 Silver 0.3569 oz. ASW, 28 mm. **Subject:** Torres Defence Line, 200th Anniversary

Date	Mintage	F	VF	XF	Unc	BU
2010INCM Proof	—	Value: 55.00				

KM# 800a 2-1/2 EURO

10.0000 g., Copper-Nickel, 28 mm. **Subject:** Torres Defence Line, 200th Anniversary

Date	Mintage	F	VF	XF	Unc	BU
2010INCM	—	—	—	—	6.00	7.00

KM# 801 2-1/2 EURO

12.0000 g., Silver, 28 mm. **Subject:** UNESCO World Cultural Heritage Site - Coa Valley

Date	Mintage	F	VF	XF	Unc	BU
2010INCM Proof	5,000	—	—	—	—	—

KM# 801a 2-1/2 EURO

10.0000 g., Copper-Nickel, 28 mm. **Subject:** UNESCO World Cultural Heritage site - Coa Valley

Date	Mintage	F	VF	XF	Unc	BU
2010INCM	120,000	—	—	—	6.00	7.00

KM# 749 5 EURO

14.0000 g., 0.5000 Silver 0.2250 oz. ASW, 30 mm. **Subject:** 150th Anniversary - First Portuguese Postage Stamp **Obv:** National arms and value within partial stamp design **Rev:** Partial postal stamp design **Edge:** Reeded

Date	Mintage	F	VF	XF	Unc	BU
2003INCM	300,000	—	—	—	30.00	32.50
2003INCM Prooflike	—	—	—	—	—	45.00

KM# 749a 5 EURO

14.0000 g., 0.9250 Silver 0.4163 oz. ASW, 30 mm. **Obv:** National arms and value within partial stamp design **Rev:** Partial postal stamp design

Date	Mintage	F	VF	XF	Unc	BU
2003INCM Proof	20,000	Value: 55.00				

KM# 749b 5 EURO

17.5000 g., 0.9166 Gold 0.5157 oz. AGW, 30 mm. **Obv:** National arms and value within partial stamp design **Rev:** Partial postal stamp design

Date	Mintage	F	VF	XF	Unc	BU
2003INCM Proof	—	Value: 850				

KM# 754 5 EURO

14.0000 g., 0.5000 Silver 0.2250 oz. ASW, 30 mm. **Subject:** Convent of Christ **Obv:** National arms above value flanked by designs **Rev:** Ornate convent window **Edge:** Reeded

Date	Mintage	F	VF	XF	Unc	BU
2004INCM	300,000	—	—	—	30.00	32.50

KM# 754a 5 EURO

14.0000 g., 0.9250 Silver 0.4163 oz. ASW, 30 mm. **Subject:** Convent of Christ **Obv:** National arms above value flanked by designs **Rev:** Ornate convent window **Edge:** Reeded

Date	Mintage	F	VF	XF	Unc	BU
2004INCM Proof	10,000	Value: 60.00				

KM# 755 5 EURO

14.0000 g., 0.5000 Silver 0.2250 oz. ASW, 30 mm. **Subject:** Historic City of Evora **Obv:** National arms and value on city map silhouette **Rev:** Architectural highlights **Edge:** Reeded

Date	Mintage	F	VF	XF	Unc	BU
2004INCM	300,000	—	—	—	30.00	32.50

KM# 755a 5 EURO

14.0000 g., 0.9250 Silver 0.4163 oz. ASW, 30 mm. **Subject:** Historic City of Evora **Obv:** National arms and value on city map silhouette **Rev:** Architectural highlights **Edge:** Reeded

Date	Mintage	F	VF	XF	Unc	BU
2004INCM Proof	10,000	Value: 60.00				

KM# 762 5 EURO

14.0000 g., 0.5000 Silver 0.2250 oz. ASW, 30 mm. **Subject:** 800th Anniversary Birth of Pope John XXI **Obv:** National arms at lower right with archways in backgound **Obv. Legend:** REPUBLICA PORTUGUESA **Rev:** 1/2 length figure of Pope facing at right with staff dividing dates, small shield at left **Edge:** Reeded

Date	Mintage	F	VF	XF	Unc	BU
2005INCM	300,000	—	—	—	30.00	32.50

KM# 762a 5 EURO

14.0000 g., 0.9250 Silver 0.4163 oz. ASW, 30 mm. **Subject:** 800th Anniversary Birth of Pope John XXI **Obv:** National arms at lower right with archways in backgound **Obv. Legend:** REPUBLICA PORTUGUESA **Rev:** 1/2 length figure of Pope facing at right with staff dividing dates, small shield at left **Edge:** Reeded

Date	Mintage	F	VF	XF	Unc	BU
2005INCM Proof	15,000	Value: 65.00				

KM# 762b 5 EURO

17.5000 g., 0.9167 Gold 0.5157 oz. AGW, 30 mm. **Subject:** 800th Anniversary Birth of Pope John XXI **Obv:** National arms at lower right, archways in background **Obv. Legend:** REPUBLICA PORTUGUESA **Edge:** Reeded

Date	Mintage	F	VF	XF	Unc	BU
2005INCM Proof	7,500	Value: 850				

KM# 760 5 EURO

14.0000 g., 0.5000 Silver 0.2250 oz. ASW, 30 mm. **Obv:** National arms within circle **Obv. Legend:** REPUBLICA POTUGUESA **Rev:** Angra do Heroismo - Azores Terceira, emblem above **Rev. Legend:** CENTRO HISTÓRICO DE ANGRA DO HEROISMA **Edge:** Reeded

Date	Mintage	F	VF	XF	Unc	BU
2005	300,000	—	—	—	30.00	32.50

KM# 760a 5 EURO

14.0000 g., 0.9250 Silver 0.4163 oz. ASW, 30 mm. **Obv:** National arms within circle **Obv. Legend:** REPUBLICA PORTUGUESA **Rev:** Angra do Heroisma - Azores Terceira, emblem above **Rev. Legend:** CENTRO HISTÓRICO DE ANGRA DO HEROISMA **Edge:** Reeded

Date	Mintage	F	VF	XF	Unc	BU
2005 Proof	10,000	Value: 60.00				

KM# 761 5 EURO

14.0000 g., 0.5000 Silver 0.2250 oz. ASW, 30 mm. **Obv:** Design divides national arms and value **Obv. Legend:** REPUBLICA PORTUGUESA **Rev:** Batalha monastery and emblem **Rev. Legend:** MONTEIRO DA BATALHA **Edge:** Reeded

Date	Mintage	F	VF	XF	Unc	BU
2005	300,000	—	—	—	30.00	32.50

KM# 761a 5 EURO

14.0000 g., 0.9250 Silver 0.4163 oz. ASW, 30 mm. **Obv:** Design divides national arms and value **Obv. Legend:** REPUBLICA PORTUGUESA **Rev:** Batalha monastery and emblem **Rev. Legend:** MONTEIRO DA BATALHA **Edge:** Reeded

Date	Mintage	F	VF	XF	Unc	BU
2005 Proof	10,000	Value: 60.00				

KM# 769 5 EURO

14.0000 g., 0.5000 Silver 0.2250 oz. ASW, 30 mm. **Subject:** UNESCO - Cultural preservation **Obv:** National arms above value **Obv. Legend:** REPUBLICA PORTUGUESA **Rev:** Outlined view **Rev. Legend:** PAISAGEM CULTURAL DE SINTRA **Edge:** Reeded

Date	Mintage	F	VF	XF	Unc	BU
2006INCM	300,000	—	—	—	30.00	32.50

KM# 769a 5 EURO

14.0000 g., 0.9250 Silver 0.4163 oz. ASW, 30 mm. **Subject:** UNESCO - Cultural preservation **Obv:** National arms above value **Obv. Legend:** REPUBLICA PORTUGUESA **Rev:** Outlined view **Rev. Legend:** PAISAGEM CULTURAL DE SINTRA **Edge:** Reeded

Date	Mintage	F	VF	XF	Unc	BU
2006INCM Proof	10,000	Value: 60.00				

KM# 779 5 EURO

14.0000 g., 0.5000 Silver 0.2250 oz. ASW **Subject:** Alcobaça Monastery **Obv:** National arms **Obv. Legend:** REPÚBLICA PORTUGUESA **Edge:** Reeded

Date	Mintage	F	VF	XF	Unc	BU
2006INCM	300,000	—	—	—	25.00	27.50

KM# 779a 5 EURO

14.0000 g., 0.9250 Silver 0.4163 oz. ASW **Subject:** Alcobaça Monestary **Obv:** National arms **Obv. Legend:** REPÚBLICA PORTUGUESA **Edge:** Reeded

Date	Mintage	F	VF	XF	Unc	BU
2006INCM Proof	10,000	Value: 60.00				

KM# 770a 5 EURO

14.0000 g., 0.9250 Silver 0.4163 oz. ASW, 30 mm. **Subject:** World Scouting Centennial **Obv:** National arms, World Scouting emblem **Obv. Legend:** REPUBLICA PORTUGUESA 1907 - 2007 CENTENARIO DO ESCUTISMO MUNDIAL **Rev:** Linear portrait of Lord Robert Baden-Powell **Rev. Legend:** UM MUNDO UMA PROMESA **Edge:** Reeded **Designer:** Joao Calvina

Date	Mintage	F	VF	XF	Unc	BU
ND(2007) Proof	10,000	Value: 60.00				

KM# 781 5 EURO

14.0400 g., 0.5000 Silver 0.2257 oz. ASW, 30 mm. **Subject:** Equal Opportunities **Obv:** Small national arms above moon shaped arc **Obv. Legend:** República Portuguesa **Rev:** Small 3 persons logo above 12 stars along rim **Rev. Legend:** Ano Europeu da Igualdade de Oportunidades para Todos **Edge:** Reeded

Date	Mintage	F	VF	XF	Unc	BU
2007INCM	75,000	—	—	—	25.00	27.50

KM# 781a 5 EURO

14.0000 g., 0.9250 Silver 0.4163 oz. ASW, 30 mm. **Subject:** Equal Opportunities **Obv:** Small national arms above moon shaped arc **Obv. Legend:** República Portuguesa **Rev:** Small 3 persons logo above 12 stars along rim **Rev. Legend:** Ano Europeu da Igualdade de Oportunidades para Todos **Edge:** Reeded

Date	Mintage	F	VF	XF	Unc	BU
2007INCM Proof	6,000	Value: 65.00				

KM# 770 5 EURO

14.0000 g., 0.5000 Silver 0.2250 oz. ASW, 30 mm. **Subject:** World Scouting Centennial **Obv:** Portuguese Arms, World Scouting emblem **Obv. Legend:** REPUBLICA PORTUGUESA 1907-2007 CENTENARIO DO ESCUTISMO MUNDIAL **Rev:** Linear portrait of Lord Robert Baden-Powell **Rev. Legend:** UM MUNDO UMA PROMESA **Edge:** Reeded **Designer:** Joao Calvino

Date	Mintage	F	VF	XF	Unc	BU
ND(2007)	70,000	—	—	—	25.00	27.50

KM# 782 5 EURO

13.9500 g., 0.5000 Silver 0.2242 oz. ASW, 30 mm. **Series:** UNESCO - World Heritage **Subject:** National Forest Reserve in Madeira Nature Park **Obv:** National arms **Obv. Legend:** REPÚBLICA PORTUGUESA **Rev:** Foliage with small UNESCO World Heritage logo at lower right **Rev. Legend:** FLORESTA LAURISSILVA DA MADEIRA **Edge:** Reeded

Date	Mintage	F	VF	XF	Unc	BU
2007INCM	75,000	—	—	—	25.00	27.50

KM# 782a 5 EURO

14.0000 g., 0.9250 Silver 0.4163 oz. ASW, 30 mm. **Series:** UNESCO - World Heritage **Subject:** National Forest Reserve in Madeira Nature Park **Obv:** National arms **Obv. Legend:** REPÚBLICA PORTUGUESA **Rev:** Foliage with small UNESCO World Heritage logo at lower right **Rev. Legend:** FLORESTA LAURISSILVA DA MADEIRA **Edge:** Reeded

Date	Mintage	F	VF	XF	Unc	BU
2007INCM Proof	6,000	Value: 65.00				

KM# 802 5 EURO

15.5500 g., 0.9990 Gold 0.4994 oz. AGW, 30 mm. **Subject:** Numismatic Treasurers - Justo of John II

Date	Mintage	F	VF	XF	Unc	BU
2010INCM Proof	—	Value: 850				

KM# 802a 5 EURO

14.0000 g., Copper-Nickel, 30 mm. **Subject:** NUmismatic Treasurers - Justo of John II

Date	Mintage	F	VF	XF	Unc	BU
2010INCM	—	—	—	—	12.00	15.00

KM# 750a 8 EURO

31.1000 g., 0.9250 Silver 0.9249 oz. ASW, 36 mm. **Obv:** National arms, value and flag-covered globe **Rev:** Flag-covered globe and "Euro 2004" soccer games logo

Date	Mintage	F	VF	XF	Unc	BU
2003INCM Prooflike	30,000	—	—	—	—	100
2003INCM Proof	15,000	Value: 165				

KM# 750 8 EURO

21.1000 g., 0.5000 Silver 0.3392 oz. ASW, 36 mm. **Obv:** National arms, value and flag-covered globe **Rev:** Flag-covered globe and "Euro 2004" soccer games logo **Edge:** Reeded

Date	Mintage	F	VF	XF	Unc	BU
2003INCM	1,500,000	—	—	—	35.00	37.50

KM# 750b 8 EURO

31.1000 g., 0.9166 Gold 0.9165 oz. AGW, 36 mm. **Obv:** National arms, value and flag-covered globe **Rev:** Flag-covered globe and "Euro 2004" soccer games logo

Date	Mintage	F	VF	XF	Unc	BU
2003INCM Proof	10,000	Value: 1,850				

KM# 751 8 EURO
21.1000 g., 0.5000 Silver 0.3392 oz. ASW, 36 mm. **Obv:** National arms and value below many bubbles **Rev:** "Euro 2004" soccer games logo below many hearts **Edge:** Reeded

Date	Mintage	F	VF	XF	Unc	BU
2003INCM	1,500,000	—	—	—	35.00	37.50

KM# 751a 8 EURO
31.1000 g., 0.9250 Silver 0.9249 oz. ASW, 36 mm. **Obv:** National arms and value below many bubbles **Rev:** "Euro 2004" soccer games logo below many hearts

Date	Mintage	F	VF	XF	Unc	BU
2003INCM Prooflike	—	—	—	—	—	100
2003INCM Proof	15,000	Value: 165				

KM# 751b 8 EURO
31.1000 g., 0.9166 Gold 0.9165 oz. AGW, 36 mm. **Obv:** National arms and value below many bubbles **Rev:** "Euro 2004" soccer games logo below many hearts

Date	Mintage	F	VF	XF	Unc	BU
2003INCM Proof	10,000	Value: 1,850				

KM# 752 8 EURO
21.1000 g., 0.5000 Silver 0.3392 oz. ASW, 36 mm. **Obv:** National arms and value **Rev:** "Euro 2004" soccer games logo in center with partial text background **Edge:** Reeded

Date	Mintage	F	VF	XF	Unc	BU
2003INCM	1,500,000	—	—	—	35.00	37.50

KM# 752a 8 EURO
31.1000 g., 0.9250 Silver 0.9249 oz. ASW, 36 mm. **Obv:** National arms and value **Rev:** "Euro 2004" soccer games logo in center with partial text background

Date	Mintage	F	VF	XF	Unc	BU
2003INCM Prooflike	—	—	—	—	—	100
2003INCM Proof	15,000	Value: 165				

KM# 752b 8 EURO
31.1000 g., 0.9166 Gold 0.9165 oz. AGW, 36 mm. **Obv:** National arms and value **Rev:** "Euro 2004" soccer games logo in center with partial text background

Date	Mintage	F	VF	XF	Unc	BU
2003INCM Proof	10,000	Value: 1,850				

KM# 753 8 EURO
21.2200 g., 0.5000 Silver 0.3411 oz. ASW, 36 mm. **Subject:** Expansion of the European Union **Obv:** Radiant national arms and value **Rev:** European map **Edge:** Reeded

Date	Mintage	F	VF	XF	Unc	BU
2004INCM	300,000	—	—	—	25.00	27.50

KM# 753a 8 EURO
31.1000 g., 0.9250 Silver 0.9249 oz. ASW, 36 mm. **Subject:** Expansion of the European Union **Obv:** Radiant national arms and value **Rev:** European map **Edge:** Reeded

Date	Mintage	F	VF	XF	Unc	BU
2004INCM Proof	35,000	Value: 60.00				

KM# 756 8 EURO
21.0000 g., 0.5000 Silver 0.3376 oz. ASW, 36 mm. **Subject:** Euro 2004 Soccer **Obv:** National arms **Rev:** Stylized goal keeper **Edge:** Reeded

Date	Mintage	F	VF	XF	Unc	BU
2004INCM	1,500,000	—	—	—	25.00	27.50

KM# 756a 8 EURO
31.1000 g., 0.9250 Silver 0.9249 oz. ASW, 36 mm. **Subject:** Euro 2004 Soccer **Obv:** National arms **Rev:** Stylized goal keeper **Edge:** Reeded

Date	Mintage	F	VF	XF	Unc	BU
2004INCM	30,000	—	—	—	—	80.00
2004INCM Proof	15,000	Value: 150				

KM# 756b 8 EURO
31.1000 g., 0.9166 Gold 0.9165 oz. AGW, 36 mm. **Subject:** Euro 2004 Soccer **Obv:** National arms **Rev:** Stylized goal keeper **Edge:** Reeded

Date	Mintage	F	VF	XF	Unc	BU
2004INCM Proof	10,000	Value: 1,850				

KM# 757 8 EURO
21.0000 g., 0.9250 Silver 0.6245 oz. ASW, 36 mm. **Subject:** Euro 2004 Soccer **Obv:** National arms **Rev:** Face of player making shot **Edge:** Reeded

Date	Mintage	F	VF	XF	Unc	BU
2004INCM	1,500,000	—	—	—	25.00	27.50

KM# 757a 8 EURO
31.1000 g., 0.9250 Silver 0.9249 oz. ASW, 36 mm. **Subject:** Euro 2004 Soccer **Obv:** National arms **Rev:** Face of player making a shot **Edge:** Reeded

Date	Mintage	F	VF	XF	Unc	BU
2004INCM	30,000	—	—	—	—	80.00
2004INCM Proof	15,000	Value: 150				

KM# 757b 8 EURO
31.1000 g., 0.9166 Gold 0.9165 oz. AGW, 36 mm. **Subject:** Euro 2004 Soccer **Obv:** National arms **Rev:** Face of player making a shot **Edge:** Reeded

Date	Mintage	F	VF	XF	Unc	BU
2004INCM Proof	10,000	Value: 1,850				

KM# 758 8 EURO
21.0000 g., 0.5000 Silver 0.3376 oz. ASW, 36 mm. **Subject:** Euro 2004 Soccer **Obv:** National arms **Rev:** Symbolic explosion of a goal **Edge:** Reeded

Date	Mintage	F	VF	XF	Unc	BU
2004INCM	1,500,000	—	—	—	25.00	27.50

KM# 758a 8 EURO
31.1000 g., 0.9250 Silver 0.9249 oz. ASW, 36 mm. **Subject:** Euro 2004 Soccer **Obv:** National arms **Rev:** Symbolic explosion of a goal **Edge:** Reeded

Date	Mintage	F	VF	XF	Unc	BU
2004INCM	30,000	—	—	—	—	80.00
2004INCM Proof	15,000	Value: 150				

KM# 758b 8 EURO
31.1000 g., 0.9166 Gold 0.9165 oz. AGW, 36 mm. **Subject:** Euro 2004 Soccer **Obv:** National arms **Rev:** Symbolic explosion of a goal **Edge:** Reeded

Date	Mintage	F	VF	XF	Unc	BU
2004INCM Proof	10,000	Value: 1,850				

KM# 773 8 EURO
21.0000 g., 0.5000 Silver 0.3376 oz. ASW, 36 mm. **Subject:** 60th Anniversary End of WW II **Obv:** Quill pens horizontal at left center, national arms at lower righr **Obv. Inscription:** REPÚBLICA PORTUGUESA **Rev:** Four quill pens upright, outlined map of Europe in background **Rev. Inscription:** FIM DA II GUERRA MUNDIAL **Edge:** Reeded

Date	Mintage	F	VF	XF	Unc	BU
2005INCM	300,000	—	—	—	30.00	32.50

KM# 773a 8 EURO
31.1000 g., 0.9250 Silver 0.9249 oz. ASW, 36 mm. **Subject:** 60th Anniversary End of WW II **Obv:** Quill pens horizontal at left center, national arms at lower right **Obv. Inscription:** REPÚBLICA PORTUGUESA **Rev:** Four quill pens upright, outlined map of Europe in background **Rev. Inscription:** FIM DA II GUERRA MUNDIAL **Edge:** Reeded

Date	Mintage	F	VF	XF	Unc	BU
2005INCM Proof	35,000	Value: 70.00				

KM# 776 8 EURO
20.8000 g., 0.5000 Silver 0.3344 oz. ASW, 36 mm. **Series:** Famous Europeans **Subject:** Prince Henry the Navigator **Obv:** Small national arms and shield **Obv. Legend:** REPÚBLICA PORTUGUESA **Rev:** Tiny bust 3/4 right **Edge:** Reeded

Date	Mintage	F	VF	XF	Unc	BU
2006INCM	100,000	—	—	—	30.00	32.50

KM# 776a 8 EURO
31.1000 g., 0.9250 Silver 0.9249 oz. ASW, 36 mm. **Series:** Famous Europeans **Subject:** Prince Henry the Navigator **Obv:** Small national arms and shield **Obv. Legend:** REPÚBLICA PORTUGUESA **Rev:** Tiny bust 3/4 right **Edge:** Reeded

Date	Mintage	F	VF	XF	Unc	BU
2006INCM Proof	35,000	Value: 65.00				

KM# 778 8 EURO
21.0000 g., 0.5000 Silver 0.3376 oz. ASW, 36 mm. **Subject:** 150th Anniversary Railroad Lisbon - Carregado **Obv:** National arms on wavy flag **Obv. Legend:** REPÚBLICA PORTUGUESA **Rev:** Vertical railroad track divides two shields **Rev. Legend:** 150 ANOS DA PRIMEIRA LINHA FERREA LISBOA CARREGADO **Edge:** Reeded

Date	Mintage	F	VF	XF	Unc	BU
2006INCM	100,000	—	—	—	32.50	35.00

KM# 778a 8 EURO
31.1000 g., 0.9250 Silver 0.9249 oz. ASW, 36 mm. **Subject:** 150th Anniversary Railroad Lisbon - Carregado **Obv:** National srms on wavy flag **Obv. Legend:** REPÚBLICA PORTUGUESA **Rev:** Vertical railroad track divides two shields **Rev. Legend:** 150 ANOSDA PRIMEIRA LINHA FERREA LISBOA CARREGADO **Edge:** Reeded

Date	Mintage	F	VF	XF	Unc	BU
2006INCM Proof	35,000	Value: 75.00				

KM# 748 10 EURO
27.0000 g., 0.5000 Silver 0.4340 oz. ASW, 40 mm. **Subject:** Nautica **Obv:** National arms within circle of assorted shields **Rev:** Sailing ship and sextant **Edge:** Reeded

Date	Mintage	F	VF	XF	Unc	BU
2003INCM	350,000	—	—	—	22.50	25.00

KM# 748a 10 EURO
27.0000 g., 0.9250 Silver 0.8029 oz. ASW, 40 mm. **Obv:** National arms within circle of assorted shields **Rev:** Sailing ship and sextant **Edge:** Reeded

Date	Mintage	F	VF	XF	Unc	BU
2003INCM Proof	10,000	Value: 70.00				

KM# 759 10 EURO
27.0000 g., 0.5000 Silver 0.4340 oz. ASW, 40 mm. **Subject:**

Olympics **Obv:** National arms above stylized value **Rev:** Stylized sail above Olympic rings **Edge:** Reeded

Date	Mintage	F	VF	XF	Unc	BU
2004INCM	350,000	—	—	—	25.00	27.50

KM# 759a 10 EURO

27.0000 g., 0.9250 Silver 0.8029 oz. ASW, 40 mm. **Subject:** Olympics **Obv:** National arms above stylized value **Rev:** Stylized sail above Olympic rings **Edge:** Reeded

Date	Mintage	F	VF	XF	Unc	BU
2004INCM Proof	15,000	Value: 65.00				

KM# 768 10 EURO

27.0000 g., 0.5000 Silver 0.4340 oz. ASW, 40 mm. **Obv:** National arms above value in circle of multi-national coats of arms **Rev:** Church **Edge:** Reeded

Date	Mintage	F	VF	XF	Unc	BU
2005INCM	—	—	—	—	—	30.00
2005INCM Proof	300,000	Value: 75.00				

KM# 774 10 EURO

27.0000 g., 0.5000 Silver 0.4340 oz. ASW, 40 mm. **Subject:** XVIII World Championship Football Games - Germany 2006 **Obv:** National arms above stadium **Obv. Legend:** REPÚBLICA PORTUGUESA **Rev:** Circular legend above sticks representing stadium fans **Rev. Legend:** CAMPEONATO DO MUNDO DE FUTEBOL FIFA ALEMANHA 2006 **Edge:** Reeded

Date	Mintage	F	VF	XF	Unc	BU
2006INCM	100,000	—	—	—	37.50	40.00

KM# 774a 10 EURO

27.0000 g., 0.9250 Silver 0.8029 oz. ASW, 40 mm. **Subject:** XVIII World Championship Football Games - Germany 2006 **Obv:** National arms above stadium **Obv. Inscription:** REPÚBLICA PORTUGUESA **Rev:** Circular legend above sticks representing stadium fans **Edge:** Reeded

Date	Mintage	F	VF	XF	Unc	BU
2006INCM Proof	25,000	Value: 85.00				

KM# 775 10 EURO

27.0000 g., 0.5000 Silver 0.4340 oz. ASW, 40 mm. **Subject:** 20th Anniversary of Spain and Portugal's membership in the European Union **Obv:** National arms **Obv. Legend:** REPÚBLICA PORTUGUESA **Rev:** Viaduct, outlined map of Europe above **Rev. Legend:** ADESÃO AS COMUNIDADES EUROPIAS **Edge:** Reeded

Date	Mintage	F	VF	XF	Unc	BU
2006INCM	100,000	—	—	—	27.50	30.00

KM# 775a 10 EURO

27.0000 g., 0.9250 Silver 0.8029 oz. ASW, 40 mm. **Subject:** 20th Anniversary of Spain and Portugal's membership in European Union **Obv:** National arms **Obv. Legend:** REPÚBLICA PORTUGUESA **Rev:** Viaduct, outlined map of Europe above **Rev. Legend:** ADESÃO AS COMUNIDADES EUROPIAS **Edge:** Reeded

Date	Mintage	F	VF	XF	Unc	BU
2006INCM Proof	25,000	Value: 70.00				

KM# 803 10 EURO

27.0000 g., 0.9250 Silver 0.8029 oz. ASW, 40 mm. **Subject:** The Escudo

Date	Mintage	F	VF	XF	Unc	BU
2010INCM	100,000	—	—	—	32.50	35.00

KM# 803a 10 EURO

27.0000 g., 0.5000 Silver 0.4340 oz. ASW, 40 mm. **Subject:** The Escudo

Date	Mintage	F	VF	XF	Unc	BU
2010INCM Proof	12,000	Value: 85.00				

MINT SETS

KM#	Date	Mintage	Identification	Issue Price	Mkt Val
MS32	2002 (8)	50,000	KM#740-747	—	50.00
MS33	2003 (8)	50,000	KM#740-747	—	50.00
MS34	2004 (8)	50,000	KM#740-747	—	45.00
MS35	2005 (8)	30,000	KM#740-747	—	45.00
MS36	2006 (8)	12,500	KM#740-747	—	45.00

PROOF SETS

KM#	Date	Mintage	Identification	Issue Price	Mkt Val
PS45	2002 (8)	15,000	KM#740-747	—	120
PS46	2003 (8)	15,000	kM#740-747	—	110
PS47	2004 (8)	15,000	KM#740-747	—	110
PS48	2005 (8)	10,000	KM#740-747	—	110
PS49	2006 (8)	3,000	KM#740-747	—	110

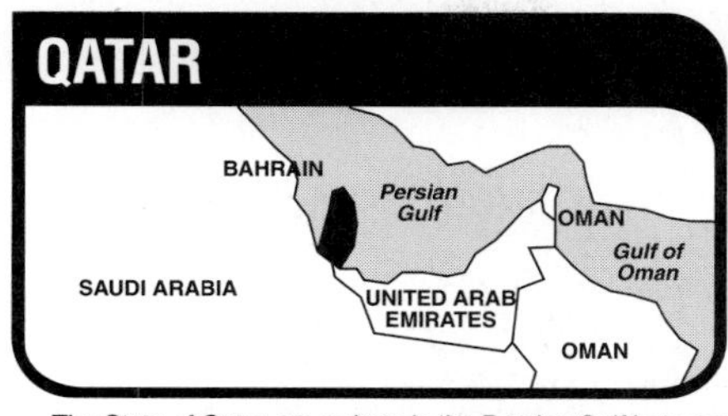

The State of Qatar, an emirate in the Persian Gulf between Bahrain and Trucial Oman, has an area of 4,247sq. mi. (11,000 sq. km.) and a population of *469,000. Capital: Doha. Oil is the chief industry and export.

TITLES

Daulat Qatar

RULERS

Al-Thani Dynasty

Hamad bin Khalifah, 1995-

MONETARY SYSTEM

100 Dirhem = 1 Riyal

STATE

STANDARD COINAGE

KM# 12 5 DIRHAMS

3.8000 g., Bronze, 21.9 mm. **Ruler:** Hamad bin Khalifa **Obv:** Arms **Rev:** Value **Edge:** Plain

Date	Mintage	F	VF	XF	Unc	BU
AH1427-2006	—	—	—	0.35	0.90	1.25

KM# 13 10 DIRHAMS

7.5000 g., Bronze, 27 mm. **Ruler:** Hamad bin Khalifa **Obv:** National arms **Rev:** Value **Edge:** Plain

Date	Mintage	F	VF	XF	Unc	BU
AH1427-2006	—	—	—	0.60	1.50	2.00

KM# 8 25 DIRHAMS

3.5000 g., Copper-Nickel, 20 mm. **Ruler:** Hamad bin Khalifa **Obv:** Sail boat and palm trees flanked by beads **Obv. Legend:** STATE OF QATAR **Rev:** Value **Rev. Designer:** Norman Sillman **Edge:** Reeded

Date	Mintage	F	VF	XF	Unc	BU
AH1424-2003	—	—	0.30	0.65	1.50	2.50

KM# 14 25 DIRHAMS

3.5000 g., Copper-Nickel, 20 mm. **Ruler:** Hamad bin Khalifa **Obv:** National arms **Rev:** Value **Edge:** Reeded

Date	Mintage	F	VF	XF	Unc	BU
AH1427-2006	—	—	—	0.75	1.85	2.50

KM# 9 50 DIRHAMS

6.5000 g., Copper-Nickel, 25 mm. **Ruler:** Hamad bin Khalifa **Obv:** National arms **Obv. Designer:** Norman Sillman **Rev:** Value **Edge:** Reeded

Date	Mintage	F	VF	XF	Unc	BU
AH1424-2003	—	—	—	—	2.00	3.00

KM# 15 50 DIRHAMS

6.5000 g., Copper-Nickel, 25 mm. **Ruler:** Hamad bin Khalifa **Obv:** National arms **Rev:** Value **Edge:** Reeded

Date	Mintage	F	VF	XF	Unc	BU
AH1427-2006	—	—	—	0.80	2.00	2.75

KM# 16 RIYAL

Aluminum-Bronze **Ruler:** Hamad bin Khalifa **Subject:** 15th Asian Games **Obv:** Arms above value **Rev:** Multicolor Fox on Bicycle, cartoon character

Date	Mintage	F	VF	XF	Unc	BU
2006	—	—	—	—	—	25.00

KM# 34 RIYAL

Aluminum-Bronze, 38.74 mm. **Ruler:** Hamad bin Khalifa **Subject:** 15th Asian Games **Obv:** Arms **Rev:** Multicolor mascot with flag

Date	Mintage	F	VF	XF	Unc	BU
2006	25,000	—	—	—	—	25.00

KM# 35 RIYAL

Aluminum-Bronze, 38.74 mm. **Ruler:** Hamad bin Khalifa **Subject:** 15th Asian Games **Obv:** Arms **Rev:** Multicolor mascot kicking soccer ball

Date	Mintage	F	VF	XF	Unc	BU
2006	25,000	—	—	—	—	25.00

KM# 36 RIYAL

Aluminum-Bronze, 38.74 mm. **Ruler:** Hamad bin Khalifa **Subject:** 15th Asian Games **Obv:** Arms **Rev:** Three multicolor torches

Date	Mintage	F	VF	XF	Unc	BU
2006	25,000	—	—	—	—	25.00

KM# 37 RIYAL

Aluminum-Bronze, 38.74 mm. **Ruler:** Hamad bin Khalifa **Subject:** 15th Asian Games **Obv:** Arms **Rev:** Two figures with linked arms

Date	Mintage	F	VF	XF	Unc	BU
2006	25,000	—	—	—	—	25.00

KM# 38 RIYAL

Aluminum-Bronze, 38.74 mm. **Ruler:** Hamad bin Khalifa **Subject:** 15th Asian Games **Obv:** Arms **Rev:** Figure with outstretched arms

Date	Mintage	F	VF	XF	Unc	BU
2006	25,000	—	—	—	—	25.00

KM# 25 10 RIYALS

31.1035 g., 0.9990 Silver 0.9990 oz. ASW, 40.5 mm. **Ruler:**

Hamad bin Khalifa **Subject:** 15th Asian Games **Obv:** Arms **Rev:** Runner trailing green color

Date	Mintage	F	VF	XF	Unc	BU
2006 Proof	25,000	Value: 110				

KM# 26 10 RIYALS

31.1035 g., 0.9990 Silver 0.9990 oz. ASW, 40.5 mm. **Ruler:** Hamad bin Khalifa **Subject:** 15th Asian Games **Obv:** Arms **Rev:** Cyclist trailing red color

Date	Mintage	F	VF	XF	Unc	BU
2006 Proof	25,000	Value: 110				

KM# 27 10 RIYALS

31.1035 g., 0.9990 Silver 0.9990 oz. ASW, 40.5 mm. **Ruler:** Hamad bin Khalifa **Subject:** 15th Asian Games **Obv:** Arms **Rev:** Soccer player legs on green color

Date	Mintage	F	VF	XF	Unc	BU
2006 Proof	25,000	Value: 110				

KM# 28 10 RIYALS

31.1035 g., 0.9990 Silver 0.9990 oz. ASW, 40.5 mm. **Ruler:** Hamad bin Khalifa **Subject:** 15th Asian Games **Obv:** Arms **Rev:** Ribbon dancer trailing red color

Date	Mintage	F	VF	XF	Unc	BU
2006 Proof	25,000	Value: 110				

KM# 29 10 RIYALS

31.1035 g., 0.9990 Silver 0.9990 oz. ASW, 40.5 mm. **Ruler:** Hamad bin Khalifa **Subject:** 15th Asian Games **Obv:** Arms **Rev:** Karate contestants and dark yellow color

Date	Mintage	F	VF	XF	Unc	BU
2006 Proof	25,000	Value: 110				

KM# 30 10 RIYALS

31.1035 g., 0.9990 Silver 0.9990 oz. ASW, 40.5 mm. **Ruler:** Hamad bin Khalifa **Subject:** 15th Asian Games **Obv:** Arms **Rev:** Swimmer in aqua colored water

Date	Mintage	F	VF	XF	Unc	BU
2006 Proof	25,000	Value: 110				

KM# 31 10 RIYALS

31.1035 g., 0.9990 Silver 0.9990 oz. ASW, 40.5 mm. **Ruler:** Hamad bin Khalifa **Subject:** 15th Asian Games **Obv:** Arms **Rev:** Table tennis player and orange-brownish color

Date	Mintage	F	VF	XF	Unc	BU
2006 Proof	25,000	Value: 110				

KM# 32 10 RIYALS

31.1035 g., 0.9990 Silver 0.9990 oz. ASW, 40.5 mm. **Ruler:** Hamad bin Khalifa **Subject:** 15th Asian Games **Obv:** Arms **Rev:** Tennis player and aqua color

Date	Mintage	F	VF	XF	Unc	BU
2006 Proof	25,000	Value: 110				

KM# 33 10 RIYALS

31.1035 g., 0.9990 Silver 0.9990 oz. ASW, 40.5 mm. **Ruler:** Hamad bin Khalifa **Subject:** 15th Asian Games **Obv:** Arms **Rev:** Volleyball player trailing purple color

Date	Mintage	F	VF	XF	Unc	BU
2006 Proof	25,000	Value: 110				

KM# 17 100 RIYALS

Gold **Ruler:** Hamad bin Khalifa **Subject:** 15th Asian Games **Obv:** Arms above value **Rev:** Games mascot Fox on Bicycle cartoon character

Date	Mintage	F	VF	XF	Unc	BU
2006 Proof	Est. 10,000	Value: 550				

KM# 18 100 RIYALS

17.0000 g., 0.9200 Gold 0.5028 oz. AGW, 31 mm. **Ruler:** Hamad bin Khalifa **Obv:** Arms **Rev:** Central Bank building **Edge:** Reeded

Date	Mintage	F	VF	XF	Unc	BU
2006 Proof	300	Value: 1,500				

KM# 19 100 RIYALS

10.0000 g., 0.9999 Gold 0.3215 oz. AGW, 24.5 mm. **Ruler:** Hamad bin Khalifa **Subject:** 15th Asian Games **Obv:** Arms **Rev:** Khalifa Stadium **Edge:** Reeded

Date	Mintage	F	VF	XF	Unc	BU
2006 Proof	—	Value: 650				

KM# 20 100 RIYALS

10.0000 g., 0.9999 Gold 0.3215 oz. AGW, 24.5 mm. **Ruler:** Hamad bin Khalifa **Subject:** 15th Asian Games **Obv:** Arms **Rev:** Two fighting oryxes **Edge:** Reeded

Date	Mintage	F	VF	XF	Unc	BU
2006 Proof	—	Value: 650				

KM# 21 100 RIYALS

10.0000 g., 0.9999 Gold 0.3215 oz. AGW, 24.5 mm. **Ruler:** Hamad bin Khalifa **Subject:** 15th Asian Games **Obv:** Arms **Rev:** Falcon bust **Edge:** Reeded

Date	Mintage	F	VF	XF	Unc	BU
2006 Proof	—	Value: 650				

KM# 22 100 RIYALS

10.0000 g., 0.9999 Gold 0.3215 oz. AGW, 24.5 mm. **Ruler:** Hamad bin Khalifa **Subject:** 15th Asian Games **Obv:** Arms **Rev:** Coffee pot **Edge:** Reeded

Date	Mintage	F	VF	XF	Unc	BU
2006 Proof	—	Value: 650				

KM# 23 100 RIYALS

10.0000 g., 0.9999 Gold 0.3215 oz. AGW, 24.5 mm. **Ruler:** Hamad bin Khalifa **Subject:** 15th Asian Games **Obv:** Arms **Rev:** Radiant sun **Edge:** Reeded

Date	Mintage	F	VF	XF	Unc	BU
2006 Proof	—	Value: 650				

KM# 11 250 RIYALS

Silver **Ruler:** Hamad bin Khalifa **Subject:** 4th WTO Conference **Obv:** National arms **Rev:** WTO logo, value, date, and legend in English and Islamic

Date	Mintage	F	VF	XF	Unc	BU
AH1422 (2001) Proof	1,000	Value: 650				

KM# 39 300 RIYALS

1000.0000 g., 0.9990 Silver 32.117 oz. ASW, 100.0 mm. **Ruler:** Hamad bin Khalifa **Obv:** National arms **Obv. Legend:** STATE OF QATAR **Rev:** Sports montage around game's logo **Rev. Inscription:** 15TH ASIAN GAMES / DOHA 2006 **Edge:** Plain

Date	Mintage	F	VF	XF	Unc	BU
2006 Proof	5,000	Value: 1,250				

KM# 24 10000 RIYALS

1000.0000 g., 0.9999 Gold 32.146 oz. AGW, 75.3 mm. **Ruler:** Hamad bin Khalifa **Subject:** 15th Asian Games **Obv:** Arms **Rev:** Radiant sun **Edge:** Reeded **Note:** Illustration reduced.

Date	Mintage	F	VF	XF	Unc	BU
2006 Proof	—	Value: 48,000				

Romania (formerly the Socialist Republic of Romania), a country in southeast Europe, has an area of 91,699 sq. mi. (237,500 sq. km.) and a population of 23.2 million. Capital: Bucharest. Machinery, foodstuffs, raw minerals and petroleum products are exported. Heavy industry and oil have become increasingly important to the economy since 1959. Romania joined the European Union in January 2007.

MONETARY SYSTEM

100 Bani = 1 Leu

REPUBLIC

STANDARD COINAGE

KM# 115 LEU

2.5200 g., Copper Plated Steel, 19 mm. **Obv:** Value flanked by sprigs **Rev:** Shield divides date

Date	Mintage	F	VF	XF	Unc	BU
2002 Proof	1,500	Value: 5.00				
2003 Proof	2,000	Value: 5.00				
2004 Proof	2,000	Value: 5.00				
2005	—	—	—	—	1.00	—
2005 Proof	—	Value: 6.00				
2006 Proof	1,000	Value: 6.00				

KM# 199 LEU

23.5000 g., Copper Plated Tombac, 37 mm. **Subject:** 130th Anniversary of Proclamation of Independence **Obv:** Shield and "The Smardan Assault" painting by Nicolae Grigoresuv **Rev:** Meeting of the Parliament

Date	Mintage	F	VF	XF	Unc	BU
2007 Proof	130	Value: 250				

KM# 114 5 LEI

3.3000 g., Nickel Plated Steel, 21 mm. **Obv:** Value flanked by oak leaves **Rev:** Shield divides date **Edge:** Plain

Date	Mintage	F	VF	XF	Unc	BU
2002 Proof	1,500	Value: 5.00				
2003 Proof	2,000	Value: 5.00				
2004 Proof	—	Value: 5.00				
2005 Proof	—	Value: 5.00				

KM# 200 5 LEI

15.5500 g., 0.9990 Silver 0.4994 oz. ASW, 30 mm. **Subject:**

130th Anniversary of Proclamation of Independence **Obv:** Shield and "The Smardan Assault" painting by Nicolae Grigoresuv **Rev:** Meeting of the Parliament

Date	Mintage	F	VF	XF	Unc	BU
2007 Proof	130	Value: 500				

KM# 116 10 LEI

4.7000 g., Nickel Clad Steel, 23 mm. **Obv:** Value within sprigs **Rev:** Shield divides date **Edge:** Plain

Date	Mintage	F	VF	XF	Unc	BU
2002 Proof	1,500	Value: 6.00				
2003 Proof	2,000	Value: 6.00				

KM# 233 10 LEI

31.1030 g., Silver, 37 mm. **Subject:** Snagov Monastery **Obv:** Shield and saints **Obv. Designer:** Christian Ciomai and Vasile Gabor **Rev:** Monastery Building

Date	Mintage	F	VF	XF	Unc	BU
2007 Proof	500	Value: 160				

KM# 234 10 LEI

31.1030 g., 0.9990 Silver 0.9989 oz. ASW, 37 mm. **Subject:** Romanian Oil Industry, 150th Anniversary **Obv:** Shield, Mehedinteanu Refinery **Obv. Designer:** Cristian Ciomet and Vasile Gabor **Rev:** Drilling well and pump jack

Date	Mintage	F	VF	XF	Unc	BU
2007 Proof	500	Value: 140				

KM# 231 10 LEI

31.1030 g., 0.9989 Silver 0.9988 oz. ASW, 37 mm. **Subject:** 80th Anniversary Romanian Broadcasting Co. **Obv:** Radio Romania, years 1928 and 2008, coat of arms **Rev:** Radio set from 30's, logo of Radio Romania, headphones **Edge:** Reeded

Date	Mintage	F	VF	XF	Unc	BU
2008 Proof	500	Value: 300				

KM# 232 10 LEI

1.2240 g., 0.9990 Gold 0.0393 oz. AGW, 13.9 mm. **Subject:** Hoard of Hinova **Obv:** Romanian Coat of Arms, necklace parts **Rev:** Necklace parts, four bell shaped necklace parts, muff **Edge:** Reeded

Date	Mintage	F	VF	XF	Unc	BU
2008 Proof	500	Value: 135				

KM# 109 20 LEI

5.0000 g., Brass Clad Steel, 24 mm. **Obv:** Crowned bust of Prince Stefan Cel Mare facing, flanked by dots **Rev:** Value and date within half sprigs and dots **Edge:** Plain **Designer:** Constantin Dumitrescu **Note:** Date varieties exist.

Date	Mintage	F	VF	XF	Unc	BU
2002 Proof	1,500	Value: 7.50				
2003 Proof	2,000	Value: 7.50				

KM# 159 50 LEI

15.5510 g., 0.9990 Silver 0.4995 oz. ASW, 31.1 mm. **Series:** Romanian Aviation **Obv:** AVIONUL VUIA 1 - 1906 airplane **Rev:** Traian Vuia **Edge:** Plain **Shape:** Octagonal

Date	Mintage	F	VF	XF	Unc	BU
2001 Proof	500	Value: 165				

KM# 160 50 LEI

15.5510 g., 0.9990 Silver 0.4995 oz. ASW, 31.1 mm. **Series:** Romanian Aviation **Obv:** Avionul Coanda 1910, world's first (?) jet airplane **Rev:** Portrait of Henri Coanda **Edge:** Plain **Shape:** Octagonal

Date	Mintage	F	VF	XF	Unc	BU
2001 Proof	500	Value: 165				

KM# 161 50 LEI

15.5510 g., 0.9990 Silver 0.4995 oz. ASW, 27 mm. **Series:** Romanian Aviation **Obv:** IAR CV-11 airplane **Rev:** Elie Carafoli **Edge:** Plain **Shape:** Octagonal

Date	Mintage	F	VF	XF	Unc	BU
2001 Proof	500	Value: 165				

KM# 110 50 LEI

5.9000 g., Brass Clad Steel, 26 mm. **Obv:** Bust left flanked by dots **Rev:** Sprig divides date and value **Edge:** Plain **Designer:** Vasile Gabor

Date	Mintage	F	VF	XF	Unc	BU
2002 Proof	1,500	Value: 8.00				
2003 Proof	2,000	Value: 8.00				

KM# 167 50 LEI

15.5510 g., 0.9990 Silver 0.4995 oz. ASW, 29.5 mm. **Subject:** National Parks: Retezat **Obv:** National arms in triangular design **Rev:** Chamois **Edge:** Plain **Shape:** Rounded triangle

Date	Mintage	F	VF	XF	Unc	BU
2002 Proof	500	Value: 200				

KM# 168 50 LEI

15.5510 g., 0.9990 Silver 0.4995 oz. ASW, 29.5 mm. **Subject:** National Parks: Pictrosul Mare **Obv:** National arms in triangular design **Rev:** Eagle **Edge:** Plain **Shape:** Rounded triangle

Date	Mintage	F	VF	XF	Unc	BU
2002 Proof	500	Value: 200				

KM# 169 50 LEI

15.5510 g., 0.9990 Silver 0.4995 oz. ASW, 29.5 mm. **Subject:** National Parks: Piatra Craiului **Obv:** National arms in triangular design **Rev:** Lynx **Edge:** Plain **Shape:** Rounded triangle

Date	Mintage	F	VF	XF	Unc	BU
2002 Proof	500	Value: 200				

KM# 186 50 LEI

15.5510 g., 0.9990 Silver 0.4995 oz. ASW, 27 mm. **Subject:** Birds **Obv:** Stylized water drop **Rev:** Dalmatian Pelicans within circle **Edge:** Plain

Date	Mintage	F	VF	XF	Unc	BU
2003 Proof	500	Value: 100				

KM# 187 50 LEI

15.5510 g., 0.9990 Silver 0.4995 oz. ASW, 27 mm. **Subject:** Birds **Obv:** Stylized water drop **Rev:** Great Egret within circle **Edge:** Plain

Date	Mintage	F	VF	XF	Unc	BU
2003 Proof	500	Value: 100				

KM# 188 50 LEI

15.5510 g., 0.9990 Silver 0.4995 oz. ASW, 27 mm. **Subject:** Birds **Obv:** Stylized water drop **Rev:** Common Kingfisher within circle **Edge:** Plain

Date	Mintage	F	VF	XF	Unc	BU
2003 Proof	500	Value: 100				

KM# 111 100 LEI

8.7500 g., Nickel Plated Steel, 29 mm. **Obv:** Bust with headdress 1/4 right **Rev:** Value within sprigs **Edge Lettering:** ROMANIA **Designer:** Vasile Gabor

Date	Mintage	F	VF	XF	Unc	BU
2002 Proof	1,500	Value: 8.00				
2003 Proof	2,000	Value: 8.00				
2004 Proof	2,000	Value: 8.00				
2005	—	—	—	—	2.50	—
2005 Proof	2,000	Value: 9.00				
2006 Proof	1,000	Value: 9.00				

KM# 165 100 LEI

1.2240 g., 0.9990 Gold 0.0393 oz. AGW, 13.9 mm. **Subject:** History of Gold - "The Apahida Eagle" **Obv:** National arms in ornamental circle above value **Edge:** Plain

Date	Mintage	F	VF	XF	Unc	BU
2003 Proof	2,000	Value: 125				

KM# 198 100 LEI

1.2240 g., 0.9990 Gold 0.0393 oz. AGW, 13.93 mm. **Obv:** National arms in wreath **Obv. Legend:** ROMANIA **Rev:** Medieval helmet - "COIF POTANA COTOFENESTI" **Edge:** Reeded

Date	Mintage	F	VF	XF	Unc	BU
2003 Proof	—	Value: 85.00				

KM# 166 100 LEI

1.2240 g., 0.9990 Gold 0.0393 oz. AGW, 14 mm. **Subject:** History of Gold - Engolpion **Obv:** National arms and country name above two stylized birds and value **Rev:** Jeweled double headed eagle pendant

Date	Mintage	F	VF	XF	Unc	BU
2004 Proof	1,000	Value: 165				

KM# 201 100 LEI

6.4520 g., 0.9000 Gold 0.1867 oz. AGW, 21 mm. **Subject:** 130th Anniversary of Proclamation of Independence **Obv:** Shield and "The Smardan Assault" painting by Nicole Grigorescu **Rev:** Meeting of the Parliament

Date	Mintage	F	VF	XF	Unc	BU
2007 Proof	130	Value: 1,500				

KM# 235 100 LEI

6.4520 g., 0.9990 Gold 0.2072 oz. AGW, 21 mm. **Subject:** Battles of Marasti, Marasesti, Oituz 90th Anniversary **Obv:** Mausoleum of Marasesti **Obv. Designer:** Cristian Ciomei and Vasile Gabor **Rev:** Group of soldiers at Battle of Marasti

Date	Mintage	F	VF	XF	Unc	BU
2007 Proof	250	Value: 550				

KM# 176 500 LEI

6.2200 g., 0.9990 Gold 0.1998 oz. AGW, 23.2 mm. **Subject:** Christian Monuments **Rev:** Mogosoaia Palace **Shape:** Square

Date	Mintage	F	VF	XF	Unc	BU
2001	250	—	—	—	—	550

KM# 170 500 LEI

6.2200 g., 0.9990 Gold 0.1998 oz. AGW, 11.75 mm. **Subject:** History of Gold - Treasure of Pietroasa **Rev:** "Big Clip" of Pietroasa

Date	Mintage	F	VF	XF	Unc	BU
	250	—	—	—	—	700

KM# 171 500 LEI

6.2200 g., 0.9990 Gold 0.1998 oz. AGW, 11.75 mm. **Subject:** History of Gold - Treasure of Pietroasa **Rev:** "Medium Clip" of Pietroasa

Date	Mintage	F	VF	XF	Unc	BU
2001	250	—	—	—	—	700

KM# 172 500 LEI
6.2200 g., 0.9990 Gold 0.1998 oz. AGW, 11.75 mm. **Subject:** History of Gold - Treasure of Pietroasa **Rev:** 12-sided golden bowl

Date	Mintage	F	VF	XF	Unc	BU
2001	250	—	—	—	—	700

KM# 173 500 LEI
6.2200 g., 0.9990 Gold 0.1998 oz. AGW, 11.75 mm. **Subject:** History of Gold - Treasure of Pietroasa **Rev:** Pitcher

Date	Mintage	F	VF	XF	Unc	BU
2001	250	—	—	—	—	700

KM# 145 500 LEI
3.7000 g., Aluminum, 25 mm. **Obv:** Shield within sprigs **Rev:** Value within 3/4 wreath **Edge:** Lettered **Edge Lettering:** ROMANIA (three times)

Date	Mintage	F	VF	XF	Unc	BU
2001	—	—	—	0.75	2.00	—
2002 Proof	1,500	Value: 7.00				
2003 Proof	2,000	Value: 7.00				
2004 Proof	2,000	Value: 7.00				
2005	—	—	—	—	3.00	—
2005 Proof	1,000	Value: 8.00				
2006	—	—	—	—	3.00	—
2006 Proof	—	Value: 8.00				

KM# 174 500 LEI
6.2200 g., 0.9990 Gold 0.1998 oz. AGW, 23.2 mm. **Subject:** Christian Monuments **Rev:** Bistritz Monastery

Date	Mintage	F	VF	XF	Unc	BU
2002	250	—	—	—	—	550

KM# 175 500 LEI
6.2200 g., 0.9990 Gold 0.1998 oz. AGW, 23.2 mm. **Subject:** Christian Monuments **Rev:** Coltea Church

Date	Mintage	F	VF	XF	Unc	BU
2002	250	—	—	—	—	550

KM# 177 500 LEI
31.1030 g., 0.9990 Silver 0.9989 oz. ASW, 37 mm. **Subject:** 150th Anniversary - Birth of Ciprian Porumbescu, Composer **Obv:** Partial piano and violin left of National arms and value **Rev:** Portrait and musical score **Edge:** Plain

Date	Mintage	F	VF	XF	Unc	BU
2003 Proof	500	Value: 160				

KM# 178 500 LEI
31.1030 g., 0.9990 Silver 0.9989 oz. ASW, 37 mm. **Subject:** 500th Anniversary - Establishment of Bishopric of Ramnic **Obv:** National arms and value above inscription **Rev:** Bishopric's coat-of-arms **Edge:** Plain

Date	Mintage	F	VF	XF	Unc	BU
2003 Proof	500	Value: 160				

KM# 179 500 LEI
31.1030 g., 0.9990 Silver 0.9989 oz. ASW, 37 mm. **Subject:** Romanian Numismatic Society Centennial **Obv:** Cornucopia pouring forth coins, value below **Rev:** Minerva and torch **Rev. Legend:** CENTENARUL SOCIETATII NUMISMATICE ROMANE, 1903-2003 **Edge:** Plain

Date	Mintage	F	VF	XF	Unc	BU
2003 Proof	1,000	Value: 150				

KM# 180 500 LEI
31.1030 g., 0.9990 Silver 0.9989 oz. ASW, 37 mm. **Subject:** 140th Anniversary - University of Bucharest **Obv:** Vertical inscription divides National arms, value and date at left. University emblem at right **Obv. Inscription:** ROMANIA **Rev:** Cameo at right and crowned arms at left above University Building **Rev. Inscription:** Upper: UNIVERSITATEA DIN BUCURESTI / 140 DE ANI; Lower: INTEMEIATA LA 1864 DE / AL IOAN CUZA **Edge:** Plain

Date	Mintage	F	VF	XF	Unc	BU
2004 Proof	500	Value: 180				

KM# 193 500 LEI
31.1035 g., 0.9990 Silver 0.9990 oz. ASW, 37 mm. **Subject:** 150th Anniversary - Birth of Anghel Saligny **Obv:** Arms at left above Cernavoda bridge, inscription, date, and value below **Obv. Inscription:** PODUL DE LA CERNAVODA **Rev:** Bust of bridge builder Anghel Saligny half right, life dates at right, his signature below at left **Edge:** Plain

Date	Mintage	F	VF	XF	Unc	BU
2004 Proof	500	Value: 350				

KM# 163 500 LEI
31.1030 g., 0.9990 Silver 0.9989 oz. ASW, 37 mm. **Subject:** Christian Feudal Art Monuments **Obv:** National arms, date and value at left, belfry tower of church at right **Rev:** Cotroceni Monastery church **Edge:** Plain **Shape:** 10-sided

Date	Mintage	F	VF	XF	Unc	BU
2004 Proof	500	Value: 150				

KM# 164 500 LEI
31.1030 g., 0.9990 Silver 0.9989 oz. ASW, 37 mm. **Subject:** Christian Feudal Art Monuments **Obv:** National arms, bell and value **Rev:** St. Trei Ierarhi church in Iasi **Edge:** Plain **Shape:** 10-sided

Date	Mintage	F	VF	XF	Unc	BU
2004 Proof	500	Value: 150				

KM# 194 500 LEI
31.1035 g., 0.9990 Silver 0.9990 oz. ASW, 37 mm. **Subject:** 125th Anniversary - National Bank **Obv:** National arms and coin design of 5 Lei dated 1880 **Rev:** Bank building **Edge:** Plain

Date	Mintage	F	VF	XF	Unc	BU
2005 Proof	—	Value: 1,000				

KM# 233a 500 LEI
31.1030 g., 0.9990 Gold 0.9989 oz. AGW, 35 mm. **Subject:** Union of 1918 - 90 years

Date	Mintage	F	VF	XF	Unc	BU
2008 Proof	3,000	Value: 1,500				

KM# 153 1000 LEI
2.0000 g., Aluminum, 22 mm. **Subject:** Constantin Brancoveanu **Obv:** Value above shield within lined circle **Rev:** Bust with headdress facing **Edge:** Plain with serrated sections

Date	Mintage	VG	F	VF	XF	Unc
2001	—	—	—	—	0.25	2.50
2002	—	—	—	—	0.25	2.50
2002 Proof	1,500	Value: 12.00				
2003	—	—	—	—	0.25	2.50
2003 Proof	2,000	Value: 12.00				
2004	—	—	—	—	0.25	2.50
2004 Proof	2,000	Value: 12.00				
2005	—	—	—	—	0.25	2.50
2005 Proof	—	Value: 13.00				
2006 Proof	1,000	Value: 13.00				

KM# 156 1000 LEI
15.5510 g., 0.9990 Gold 0.4995 oz. AGW, 27 mm. **Subject:** 1900th Anniversary of the First Roman-Dacian War **Obv:** Traian's column and shield **Rev:** Monument divides cameos **Edge:** Plain

Date	Mintage	VG	F	VF	XF	Unc
2001 Proof	500	Value: 900				

KM# 181 2000 LEI
25.0000 g., Bi-Metallic .999 Silver, 10g center in .999 Gold, 15g ring, 35 mm. **Subject:** Ion Heliade Radulescu (1802-1872) **Obv:** Lyre at left, national arms at right in divided circle design **Rev:** Ion Heliade Radulescu above signature **Edge:** Reeded

Date	Mintage	F	VF	XF	Unc	BU
2002 Proof	500	Value: 1,000				

KM# 158 5000 LEI
2.5000 g., Aluminum, 24 mm. **Obv:** Value and country name **Rev:** Sprig divides date and shield **Edge:** Plain **Shape:** 12-sided

Date	Mintage	F	VF	XF	Unc	BU
2001	—	—	—	—	0.50	—
2002	—	—	—	—	0.50	—
2002 Proof	1,500	Value: 15.00				
2003	—	—	—	—	0.25	—
2003 Proof	2,000	Value: 15.00				
2004	—	—	—	—	0.25	—
2004 Proof	2,000	Value: 16.00				
2005	—	—	—	—	0.25	—
2005 Proof	2,000	Value: 17.00				
2006 Proof	1,000	Value: 17.00				

KM# 162 5000 LEI
31.1035 g., 0.9990 Gold 0.9990 oz. AGW, 35 mm. **Subject:** Constantin Brancusi 125th Anniversary of Birth **Obv:** National arms, value and sculpture **Rev:** Bearded portrait and signature **Edge:** Plain

Date	Mintage	F	VF	XF	Unc	BU
2001 Proof	500	Value: 2,250				

KM# 183 5000 LEI
31.1030 g., 0.9990 Gold 0.9989 oz. AGW, 35 mm. **Subject:** Ion Luca Caragiale, playright (1852-1912) **Obv:** National arms, value and masks of Comedy and Tragedy **Rev:** Portrait **Edge:** Plain

Date	Mintage	F	VF	XF	Unc	BU
2002 Proof	250	Value: 2,500				

KM# 184 5000 LEI
31.1030 g., 0.9990 Gold 0.9989 oz. AGW, 35 mm. **Subject:** Bran Castle (1378-2003) **Obv:** Two coats of arms on shield above value **Rev:** Castle view **Edge:** Plain

Date	Mintage	F	VF	XF	Unc	BU
2003 Proof	250	Value: 2,000				

KM# 185 5000 LEI
31.1030 g., 0.9990 Gold 0.9989 oz. AGW, 35 mm. **Subject:** Stephen the Great **Obv:** National arms, value above coin design in wall **Rev:** Portrait of Stephen and Putna Monastery

Date	Mintage	F	VF	XF	Unc	BU
2004 Proof	250	Value: 2,000				

REFORM COINAGE - 2005

10,000 Old Leu = 1 New Leu

KM# 189 BAN
2.4000 g., Brass Plated Steel, 16.8 mm. **Subject:** Monetary Reform of 2005 **Obv:** National arms flanked by stars **Rev:** Value **Edge:** Plain

Date	Mintage	F	VF	XF	Unc	BU
2005	—	—	—	—	0.30	0.50
2005 Proof	—	Value: 2.50				
2006	—	—	—	—	0.30	0.50
2006 Proof	—	Value: 2.50				
2007	—	—	—	—	0.30	0.50
2007 Proof	—	Value: 2.50				
2008	—	—	—	—	0.30	0.50
2008 Proof	—	Value: 2.50				
2009	—	—	—	—	0.30	0.50
2010	—	—	—	—	0.30	0.50

KM# 190 5 BANI
2.8000 g., Copper Plated Steel, 18.25 mm. **Subject:** Monetary Reform of 2005 **Obv:** National arms flanked by stars **Obv. Legend:** ROMANIA **Rev:** Value **Edge:** Reeded

Date	Mintage	F	VF	XF	Unc	BU
2005	—	—	—	—	0.50	0.75
2005 Proof	—	Value: 5.00				
2006	—	—	—	—	0.50	0.75
2006 Proof	—	Value: 5.00				
2007	—	—	—	—	0.50	0.75
2007 Proof	—	Value: 5.00				
2008	—	—	—	—	0.50	0.75
2008 Proof	—	Value: 5.00				
2009	—	—	—	—	0.50	0.75
2010	—	—	—	—	0.50	0.75

KM# 191 10 BANI
4.0000 g., Nickel Plated Steel, 20.4 mm. **Subject:** Monetary Reform of 2005 **Obv:** National arms flanked by stars **Obv. Legend:** ROMANIA **Rev:** Value **Edge:** Segmented reeding

Date	Mintage	F	VF	XF	Unc	BU
2005	—	—	—	—	0.65	0.85
2005 Proof	—	Value: 7.00				
2006	—	—	—	—	0.60	0.80
2006 Proof	—	Value: 7.00				
2007	—	—	—	—	0.50	0.75
2007 Proof	—	Value: 7.00				
2008	—	—	—	—	0.50	0.70
2008 Proof	—	Value: 7.00				
2009	—	—	—	—	0.50	0.70
2010	—	—	—	—	0.50	0.70

KM# 192 50 BANI
6.1000 g., Nickel-Brass, 23.75 mm. **Subject:** Monetary Reform of 2005 **Obv:** National arms flanked by stars **Obv. Legend:** ROMANIA **Rev:** Value **Edge:** Lettered **Edge Lettering:** ROMANIA twice

Date	Mintage	F	VF	XF	Unc	BU
2005	—	—	—	—	0.85	1.00
2005 Proof	—	Value: 10.00				
2006	—	—	—	—	0.75	0.85
2006 Proof	—	Value: 10.00				
2007	—	—	—	—	0.65	0.75
2007 Proof	—	Value: 10.00				
2008	—	—	—	—	0.65	0.75
2008 Proof	—	Value: 10.00				
2009	—	—	—	—	0.65	0.75
2010	—	—	—	—	0.65	0.75

KM# 209 LEU
23.5000 g., Copper Plated Tombac, 37 mm. **Subject:** 140th Anniversary Founding Romanian Academy **Edge:** Plain

Date	Mintage	F	VF	XF	Unc	BU
2006 Proof	35	Value: 750				

KM# 220 LEU
23.5000 g., Copper Plated Tombac, 37 mm. **Subject:** Centennial - Birth of Mircea Eliade **Obv:** Shield and value **Rev:** Portrait facing **Edge:** Reeded

Date	Mintage	F	VF	XF	Unc	BU
2007 Proof	250	Value: 150				

KM# 223 LEU
23.5000 g., Copper Plated Tombac, 37 mm. **Subject:** Dimitrie Cantemir, (Prince of Moldavia 1710-1711), Scientist **Edge:** Reeded

Date	Mintage	F	VF	XF	Unc	BU
2007 Proof	250	Value: 150				

KM# 226 LEU
23.5000 g., Copper Plated Tombac, 37 mm. **Subject:** Stephan the Great **Edge:** Reeded

Date	Mintage	F	VF	XF	Unc	BU
2007 Proof	250	Value: 150				

KM# 258 LEU
23.5000 g., Copper Plated Tombac, 37 mm. **Subject:** Bucharest, 550th Anniversary **Obv:** Vlad Tepes **Rev:** Buildings

Date	Mintage	F	VF	XF	Unc	BU
2009 Proof	250	Value: 150				

KM# 208 5 LEI
31.1000 g., 0.9990 Silver 0.9988 oz. ASW, 37 mm. **Subject:** 100th Anniversary - Birth of Grigore Vasiliu-Birlic **Edge:** Plain

Date	Mintage	F	VF	XF	Unc	BU
2005 Proof	150	Value: 1,200				

KM# 210 5 LEI
31.1000 g., 0.9990 Silver 0.9988 oz. ASW, 37 mm. **Subject:** 140th Anniversary Founding Romanian Academy **Edge:** Plain

Date	Mintage	F	VF	XF	Unc	BU
2006 Proof	500	Value: 300				

KM# 212 5 LEI
31.1000 g., 0.9990 Silver 0.9988 oz. ASW, 37 mm. **Subject:** Christian Feudal Art - "Wooden Church from Ieud-Deal" **Obv:** Fragment of mural in Ieud Church depicting Isaac, Abraham and Jacob at top, inscription, value and date in lower half **Obv. Inscription:** ROMANIA **Rev:** Front view of Ieud Church against frosted background **Rev. Inscription:** BISERICA DE LEMN IEUD DEAL **Edge:** Plain **Designer:** Cristian Ciornci, Vasilc Gabor

Date	Mintage	F	VF	XF	Unc	BU
2006 Proof	500	Value: 170				

KM# 213 5 LEI
31.1030 g., Silver, 37 mm. **Subject:** 150th Anniversary - Establishment of the European Commission of the Danube **Edge:** Plain

Date	Mintage	F	VF	XF	Unc	BU
2006 Proof	500	Value: 170				

KM# 216 5 LEI
31.1030 g., 0.9990 Silver 0.9989 oz. ASW, 37 mm. **Subject:** Church from Densus **Obv:** 14th century icon on which "The Holy Trinity of Densus" was painted at left, arms with value below at center, inscription at right **Obv. Inscription:** ROMANIA **Obv. Designer:** Cristian Ciornei and Vasile Gabor **Rev:** Image of Densus Church as from the altar apse, central pillar at right **Rev. Inscription:** BISERICA DE LA DENSUS **Edge:** Plain

Date	Mintage	F	VF	XF	Unc	BU
2006 Proof	500	Value: 170				

KM# 236 5 LEI
31.1050 g., 0.9990 Silver 0.9990 oz. ASW, 37 mm. **Subject:** Wooden Church of Ievd Deal **Obv:** Fragment of mural painting **Rev:** Front view of church

Date	Mintage	F	VF	XF	Unc	BU
2006 Proof	500	Value: 160				

KM# 217 5 LEI
31.1030 g., 0.9990 Silver 0.9989 oz. ASW, 37 mm. **Subject:** Designation of Sibiu as the "European Capital of Culture in 2007" **Obv:** 2 city towers in Sibiu at left, fortress wall connecting them, Potter's Tower in background, coat of arms at right **Obv. Inscription:** ROMANIA **Obv. Designer:** Cristian Ciornci and Vasile Gabor **Rev:** City of Sibiu's logo at bottom, 2 line inscription at left, 3 line inscription at right, 4 famous edifices at center **Rev. Inscription:** SIBIU/2007 and CAPITALA / CULTURALA / EUROPEANA **Edge:** Plain

Date	Mintage	F	VF	XF	Unc	BU
2007 Proof	500	Value: 400				

KM# 221 5 LEI
15.5500 g., 0.9990 Silver 0.4994 oz. ASW, 30 mm. **Subject:** Centennial - Birth of Mircea Eliade **Obv:** Shield and value **Rev:** Portrait facing **Edge:** Reeded

Date	Mintage	F	VF	XF	Unc	BU
2007 Proof	250	Value: 300				

KM# 224 5 LEI
15.5500 g., 0.9000 Silver 0.4499 oz. ASW, 30 mm. **Subject:** Dimitrie Cantemir, (Prince of Moldavia 1710-1711), Scientist **Edge:** Reeded

Date	Mintage	F	VF	XF	Unc	BU
2007 Proof	250	Value: 300				

KM# 227 5 LEI
15.5000 g., 0.9990 Silver 0.4978 oz. ASW, 30 mm. **Subject:** Stephan the Great **Edge:** Reeded

Date	Mintage	F	VF	XF	Unc	BU
2007 Proof	250	Value: 300				

KM# 242 5 LEI
15.5500 g., 0.9990 Silver 0.4994 oz. ASW, 30 mm. **Subject:** Ovidivs Naso **Rev:** Half-length figure

Date	Mintage	F	VF	XF	Unc	BU
2008 Proof	500	Value: 170				

KM# 207 10 LEI
1.2200 g., 0.9990 Gold 0.0392 oz. AGW, 13.92 mm. **Subject:** History of Gold - The Persinari Hoard **Edge:** Plain

Date	Mintage	F	VF	XF	Unc	BU
2005 Proof	1,000	Value: 200				

KM# 203 10 LEI
1.2240 g., 0.9990 Gold 0.0393 oz. AGW, 13.92 mm. **Subject:** Histoy of Gold - The Cuculeni Báiceni Hoard **Obv:** Romania's Coat of Arms with denomination **Rev:** Cheekpiece of the gold helmet in the Cucuteni-Baiceni hoard **Edge:** Milled **Designer:** Cristian Ciornei

Date	Mintage	F	VF	XF	Unc	BU
2006 Proof	500	Value: 250				

KM# 229 10 LEI
31.1030 g., 0.9990 Silver 0.9989 oz. ASW, 37 mm. **Subject:** 50th Anniversary - Treaty of Rome **Edge:** Reeded

Date	Mintage	F	VF	XF	Unc	BU
2007 Proof	500	Value: 400				

KM# 240 10 LEI
31.1050 g., 0.9990 Silver 0.9990 oz. ASW, 37 mm. **Subject:** Petroleum Industry, 150th Anniversary **Rev:** Oil derrick and pump

Date	Mintage	F	VF	XF	Unc	BU
2007 Proof	500	Value: 150				

KM# 241 10 LEI
31.1050 g., 0.9990 Silver 0.9990 oz. ASW, 37 mm. **Subject:** Snagov Monastery **Rev:** Building and bust

Date	Mintage	F	VF	XF	Unc	BU
2007 Proof	500	Value: 170				

KM# 230 10 LEI
31.1000 g., 0.9990 Silver 0.9988 oz. ASW, 37 mm. **Subject:** 150th Anniversary of First Postage Stamp **Rev:** "Cap de Bour" (bull's head) stamp **Edge:** Reeded

Date	Mintage	F	VF	XF	Unc	BU
2008 Proof	1,000	Value: 175				

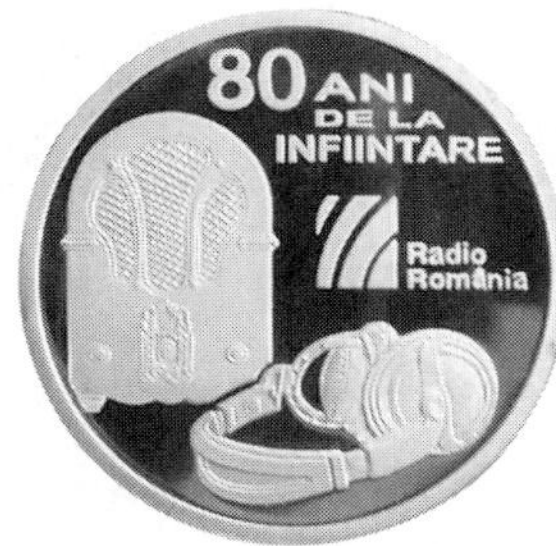

KM# 243 10 LEI
31.1050 g., 0.9990 Silver 0.9990 oz. ASW, 37 mm. **Subject:** Romanian Broadcast Company, 80th anniversary **Rev:** Radio and headset

Date	Mintage	F	VF	XF	Unc	BU
2008 Proof	500	Value: 250				

KM# 244 10 LEI
31.1050 g., 0.9990 Silver 0.9990 oz. ASW, 37 mm. **Subject:** Constin Kirtescu **Rev:** Bust facing

Date	Mintage	F	VF	XF	Unc	BU
2008 Proof	500	Value: 170				

KM# 245 10 LEI
31.1050 g., 0.9990 Silver 0.9990 oz. ASW, 37 mm. **Subject:** First printed book in Walachia, 500th Anniversary **Rev:** Building and printers at press

Date	Mintage	F	VF	XF	Unc	BU
2008 Proof	500	Value: 170				

KM# 246 10 LEI
31.1050 g., 0.9990 Silver 0.9990 oz. ASW, 37 mm. **Subject:** Simon Barnutiu **Rev:** Bust facing

Date	Mintage	F	VF	XF	Unc	BU
2008 Proof	500	Value: 150				

KM# 247 10 LEI

31.1050 g., 0.9990 Silver 0.9990 oz. ASW, 37 mm. **Subject:** Cozia Monastery **Rev:** Church building

Date	Mintage	F	VF	XF	Unc	BU
2008 Proof	500	Value: 165				

KM# 248 10 LEI

31.1050 g., 0.9990 Silver 0.9990 oz. ASW, 37 mm. **Subject:** Sambata des Sus Monastery **Rev:** Church building

Date	Mintage	F	VF	XF	Unc	BU
2008 Proof	500	Value: 165				

KM# 249 10 LEI

31.1050 g., 0.9990 Silver 0.9990 oz. ASW, 37 mm. **Subject:** Voronet Monastery **Rev:** Church building

Date	Mintage	F	VF	XF	Unc	BU
2008 Proof	500	Value: 165				

KM# 250 10 LEI

31.1050 g., 0.9990 Silver 0.9990 oz. ASW, 37 mm. **Subject:** European Monitary Union, 10th Anniversary **Rev:** Stick figure and Euro symbol

Date	Mintage	F	VF	XF	Unc	BU
2009 Proof	1,000	Value: 150				

KM# 251 10 LEI

31.1050 g., 0.9990 Silver 0.9990 oz. ASW, 37 mm. **Subject:** Alexander Macedonski **Rev:** Bust left

Date	Mintage	F	VF	XF	Unc	BU
2009 Proof	500	Value: 150				

KM# 252 10 LEI

31.1050 g., 0.9990 Silver 0.9990 oz. ASW, 37 mm. **Subject:** Walachia's establishment as an Archdiocese, 650th Anniversary **Rev:** Archbishop and Cathedral

Date	Mintage	F	VF	XF	Unc	BU
2009 Proof	500	Value: 170				

KM# 253 10 LEI

31.1050 g., 0.9990 Silver 0.9990 oz. ASW, 37 mm. **Subject:** Statistical Office, 150th Anniversary **Rev:** Two busts and document

Date	Mintage	F	VF	XF	Unc	BU
2009 Proof	500	Value: 150				

KM# 254 10 LEI

31.1050 g., 0.9990 Silver 0.9990 oz. ASW, 37 mm. **Subject:** Bucharest - Giurgiv Railway, 150th Anniversary **Rev:** Steam train

Date	Mintage	F	VF	XF	Unc	BU
2009 Proof	500	Value: 170				

KM# 255 10 LEI

31.1050 g., 0.9990 Silver 0.9990 oz. ASW, 37 mm. **Subject:** Bucharest, 550th Anniversary **Rev:** Architectural elements

Date	Mintage	F	VF	XF	Unc	BU
2009 Proof	500	Value: 160				

KM# 256 10 LEI

31.1050 g., 0.9990 Silver 0.9990 oz. ASW, 37 mm. **Subject:** Constanta Harbor, 100th Anniversary **Rev:** Ship and buildings

Date	Mintage	F	VF	XF	Unc	BU
2009 Proof	500	Value: 160				

KM# 257 10 LEI

31.1050 g., 0.9990 Silver 0.9990 oz. ASW, 37 mm. **Subject:** Tropaeum Traiani, 1900th Anniversary **Rev:** Ancient Roman building, Emperor Trajan

Date	Mintage	F	VF	XF	Unc	BU
2009 Proof	500	Value: 150				

KM# 211 50 LEI

6.4500 g., 0.9000 Gold 0.1866 oz. AGW, 21 mm. **Subject:** 140th Anniversary Founding Romanian Academy **Edge:** Plain

Date	Mintage	F	VF	XF	Unc	BU
2006 Proof	35	Value: 3,000				

KM# 222 100 LEI

6.4500 g., 0.9000 Gold 0.1866 oz. AGW, 21 mm. **Subject:** Centennial - Birth of Mircea Eliade **Obv:** Shield and value **Rev:** Portrait facing **Edge:** Reeded

Date	Mintage	F	VF	XF	Unc	BU
2007 Proof	250	Value: 900				

KM# 225 100 LEI

6.4500 g., 0.9000 Gold 0.1866 oz. AGW, 21 mm. **Subject:** Dimitrie Cantemir, (Prince of Moldavia 1710-1711), Scientist **Edge:** Reeded

Date	Mintage	F	VF	XF	Unc	BU
2007 Proof	250	Value: 900				

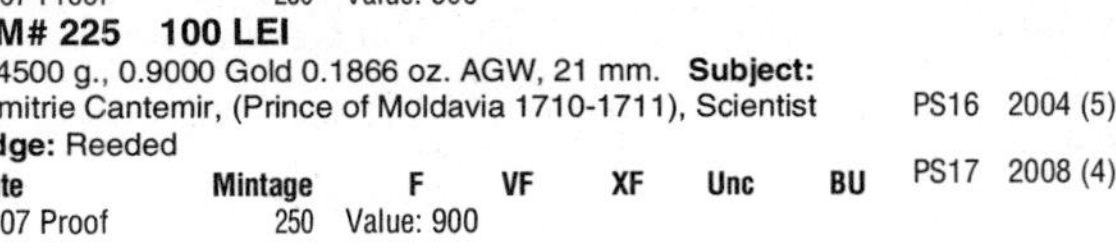

KM# 228 100 LEI

6.4520 g., 0.9000 Gold 0.1867 oz. AGW, 21 mm. **Subject:** 550th Anniversary - Ascension Prince Stephen the Great into Moldavia **Edge:** Reeded

Date	Mintage	F	VF	XF	Unc	BU
2007 Proof	250	Value: 900				

KM# 206 500 LEI

31.1000 g., 0.9990 Gold 0.9988 oz. AGW, 35 mm. **Subject:** 50th Anniversary - Death of George Enescu **Edge:** Plain

Date	Mintage	F	VF	XF	Unc	BU
2005 Proof	250	Value: 2,250				

KM# 214 500 LEI

31.1030 g., 0.9990 Gold 0.9989 oz. AGW, 35 mm. **Subject:** 350th Anniversary - Establishment of the Patriarchal Cathedral **Edge:** Plain

Date	Mintage	F	VF	XF	Unc	BU
2006 Proof	250	Value: 3,000				

KM# 204 500 LEI

31.1035 g., 0.9990 Gold 0.9990 oz. AGW, 35 mm. **Subject:** Romania's Accession to European Union, January 1 2007 **Obv:** Romania's Coat of Arms surrounded by 12 stars of European Union **Rev:** Map of the European Union including Romania **Edge:** Plain **Designer:** Cristian Ciornei

Date	Mintage	F	VF	XF	Unc	BU
2007 Proof	250	Value: 3,000				

KM# 205 500 LEI

31.1035 g., 0.9990 Gold 0.9990 oz. AGW, 35 mm. **Subject:** Nicolae Balcescu (1819-1852) **Obv:** Romania's Coat of Arms and **Obv. Inscription:** Justice and Brotherhood **Rev:** Portrait of Nicolae Balcescu **Edge:** Plain

Date	Mintage	F	VF	XF	Unc	BU
2007 Proof	250	Value: 2,250				

MINT SETS

KM#	Date	Mintage	Identification	Issue Price	Mkt Val
MS6	2005 (4)	—	KM#189-192	—	50.00
MS4	2006 (4)	—	KM189-192, plus medal	—	75.00
MS5	2007 (4)	1,000	KM189-192, plus medal	—	60.00

PROOF SETS

KM#	Date	Mintage	Identification	Issue Price	Mkt Val
PS4	2001 (3)	500	KM#159, 160, 161	80.00	525
PS5	2002 (9)	1,500	KM#109-111, 114-116, 145, 153, 158	20.00	75.00
PS6	2003 (9)	2,000	KM#109-111, 114-116, 145, 153, 158	20.00	75.00
PS7	2003 (3)	500	KM#186, 187, 188	—	325
PS8	2004 (2)	500	KM#163, 164	—	325
PS9	2005 (10)	—	KM#111, 115, 145, 153, 158, 189-192 plus medal	—	80.00
PS10	2006 (10)	—	KM#111, 115, 145, 153, 158, 189-192	—	80.00
PS11	2006 (3)	—	KM#209, 210, 211	—	4,050
PS12	2007 (3)	—	KM#220, 221, 222	—	1,350
PS13	2007 (3)	—	KM#223, 224, 225	—	1,350
PS14	2007 (3)	—	KM#226, 227, 228	—	1,350
PS15	2007 (5)	—	KM#189-192 plus Silver 75th Anniversary of Rodna Mountains National Park medal	—	50.00
PS16	2004 (5)	—	KM#111, 115, 145, 153, 158	—	50.00
PS17	2008 (4)	—	KM#189-192 plus silver medal Antipa Museum	—	50.00

Russia, formerly the central power of the Union of Soviet Socialist Republics and now of the Commonwealth of Independent States occupies the northern part of Asia and the eastern part of Europe, has an area of 17,075,400 sq. km. Capital: Moscow. Exports include iron and steel, crude oil, timber, and nonferrous metals.

In the fall of 1991, events moved swiftly in the Soviet Union. Estonia, Latvia and Lithuania won their independence and were recognized by Moscow, Sept. 6. The Commonwealth of Independent States was formed Dec. 8, 1991 in Mensk by Belarus, Russia and Ukraine. It was expanded at a summit Dec. 21, 1991 to include 11 of the 12 remaining republics (excluding Georgia) of the old U.S.S.R.

RUSSIAN FEDERATION

Issued by БАНК РОССИИ (Bank of Russia)

REFORM COINAGE

January 1, 1998

1,000 Old Roubles = 1 New Rouble

Y# 600 KOPEK

1.5000 g., Copper-Nickel Plated Steel, 15.5 mm. **Obv:** St. George **Obv. Legend:** БАНК РОССИИ **Rev:** Value above vine sprig **Edge:** Plain

Date	Mintage	F	VF	XF	Unc	BU
2001M	—	—	—	—	0.30	0.40
2001CП	—	—	—	—	0.30	0.40
2002M	—	—	—	—	0.30	0.40
2002CП	—	—	—	—	0.30	0.40
2003M	—	—	—	—	0.30	0.40
2003CП	—	—	—	—	0.30	0.40
2004M	—	—	—	—	0.30	0.40
2004CП	—	—	—	—	0.30	0.40
2005M	—	—	—	—	0.30	0.40
2005CП	—	—	—	—	0.30	0.40
2006M	—	—	—	—	0.30	0.40
2006CП	—	—	—	—	0.30	0.40
2007M	—	—	—	—	0.30	0.40
2007CП	—	—	—	—	0.30	0.40
2008M	—	—	—	—	0.30	0.40
2008CП	—	—	—	—	0.30	0.40
2009M	—	—	—	—	0.30	0.40
2009CП	—	—	—	—	0.30	0.40

Y# 601 5 KOPEKS

2.6000 g., Copper-Nickel Clad Steel, 18.5 mm. **Obv:** St. George **Obv. Legend:** БАНК РОССИИ **Rev:** Value above vine sprig **Edge:** Plain

Date	Mintage	F	VF	XF	Unc	BU
2001M	—	—	—	—	0.40	0.60
2001CП	—	—	—	—	0.40	0.60
2002	—	—	80.00	95.00	120	—
2002M	—	—	—	—	0.40	0.60
2002CП	—	—	—	—	0.40	0.60
2003	—	—	10.00	15.00	25.00	—
2003M	—	—	—	—	0.35	0.50
2003CП	—	—	—	—	0.35	0.50
2004M	—	—	—	—	0.35	0.50
2004CП	—	—	—	—	0.35	0.50
2005M	—	—	—	—	0.35	0.50
2005CП	—	—	—	—	0.35	0.50
2006M	—	—	—	—	0.35	0.50
2006CП	—	—	—	—	0.35	0.50
2007M	—	—	—	—	0.35	0.50
2007CП	—	—	—	—	0.35	0.50
2008M	—	—	—	—	0.35	0.50
2008CП	—	—	—	—	0.35	0.50
2009M	—	—	—	—	0.35	0.50
2009CП	—	—	—	—	0.35	0.50

Y# 601a 5 KOPEKS

Brass Plated Steel **Obv:** St. George on horseback slaying dragon right **Obv. Legend:** БАНК РОССИИ **Rev:** Value above vine sprig **Edge:** Plain

Date	Mintage	F	VF	XF	Unc	BU
2006CП	—	—	—	—	300	—

Y# 602 10 KOPEKS

1.9500 g., Brass, 17.5 mm. **Obv:** St. George horseback right slaying dragon **Rev:** Value above vine sprig **Edge:** Reeded

Date	Mintage	F	VF	XF	Unc	BU
2001M	—	—	—	—	0.50	0.80
2001CП	—	—	—	—	0.50	0.80
2002M	—	—	—	—	0.50	0.80
2002CП	—	—	—	—	0.50	0.80
2003M	—	—	—	—	0.50	0.80
2003CП	—	—	—	—	0.50	0.80
2004M	—	—	—	—	0.50	0.80
2004CП	—	—	—	—	0.50	0.80
2005M	—	—	—	—	0.50	0.80
2005CП	—	—	—	—	0.50	0.80
2006M	—	—	—	—	0.50	0.80
2006CП	—	—	—	—	0.50	0.80

Y# 602a 10 KOPEKS

1.8500 g., Tombac Plated Steel, 17.5 mm. **Obv:** St. George on horseback slaying dragon to right **Obv. Legend:** БАНК РОССИИ **Rev:** Denomination above vine sprig **Edge:** Plain

Date	Mintage	F	VF	XF	Unc	BU
2006M	—	—	—	—	0.50	0.80
2006CП	—	—	—	—	0.50	0.80
2007M	—	—	—	—	0.50	0.80
2007CП	—	—	—	—	0.50	0.80
2008M	—	—	—	—	0.50	0.80
2008CП	—	—	—	—	0.50	0.80
2009M	—	—	—	—	0.50	0.80
2009CП	—	—	—	—	0.50	0.80
2010M	—	—	—	—	0.50	0.80
2010CП	—	—	—	—	0.50	0.80

Y# 603 50 KOPEKS

2.9000 g., Brass, 19.5 mm. **Obv:** St. George on horseback slaying dragon right **Rev:** Value above vine sprig **Edge:** Reeded

Date	Mintage	F	VF	XF	Unc	BU
2001M Rare	—	—	—	5,000	—	—
2002M	—	—	—	—	1.50	3.00
2002CП	—	—	—	—	1.50	3.00
2003M	—	—	—	—	0.80	1.00
2003CП	—	—	—	—	0.80	1.00
2004M	—	—	—	—	0.80	1.00
2004CП	—	—	—	—	0.80	1.00
2005M	—	—	—	—	0.80	1.00
2005CП	—	—	—	—	0.80	1.00
2006M	—	—	—	—	0.80	1.00
2006CП	—	—	—	—	0.80	1.00

Y# 603a 50 KOPEKS

2.7500 g., Tombac Plated Steel, 19.5 mm. **Obv:** St. George on horseback slaying dragon right **Rev:** Value above vine sprig **Edge:** Plain

Date	Mintage	F	VF	XF	Unc	BU
2006M	—	—	—	—	0.80	1.00
2006CП	—	—	—	—	0.80	1.00
2007M	—	—	—	—	0.80	1.00
2007CП	—	—	—	—	0.80	1.00
2008M	—	—	—	—	0.80	1.00
2008CП	—	—	—	—	0.80	1.00
2009M	—	—	—	—	0.80	1.00
2009CП	—	—	—	—	0.80	1.00
2010M	—	—	—	—	0.80	1.00
2010CП	—	—	—	—	0.80	1.00

Y# 745 ROUBLE

17.4000 g., 0.9000 Silver 0.5035 oz. ASW, 32.8 mm. **Obv:** Double-headed eagle within beaded circle **Rev:** Altai argalia sheep **Edge:** Reeded

Date	Mintage	F	VF	XF	Unc	BU
2001(sp) Proof	7,500	Value: 45.00				

Y# 746 ROUBLE

17.4000 g., 0.9000 Silver 0.5035 oz. ASW, 32.8 mm. **Obv:** Double-headed eagle within beaded circle **Rev:** Beavers **Edge:** Reeded

Date	Mintage	F	VF	XF	Unc	BU
2001(sp) Proof	7,500	Value: 45.00				

Y# 604 ROUBLE

3.2500 g., Copper-Nickel-Zinc, 20.5 mm. **Obv:** Double-headed eagle **Rev:** Value **Edge:** Reeded

Date	Mintage	F	VF	XF	Unc	BU
2001M Rare	—	—	—	—	—	—

Y# 731 ROUBLE

3.2100 g., Copper-Nickel, 20.7 mm. **Obv:** Double-headed eagle **Rev:** Stylized design above hologram **Edge:** Reeded

Date	Mintage	F	VF	XF	Unc	BU
2001СПМД	100,000,000	—	—	—	1.50	2.00

Y# 732 ROUBLE

17.4300 g., 0.9000 Silver 0.5043 oz. ASW, 32.8 mm. **Subject:** Sturgeon **Obv:** Double-headed eagle within beaded circle **Rev:** Sakhalin sturgeon and other fish **Edge:** Reeded

Date	Mintage	F	VF	XF	Unc	BU
2001 Proof	7,500	Value: 45.00				

Y# 758 ROUBLE

17.4400 g., 0.9000 Silver 0.5046 oz. ASW, 33 mm. **Obv:** Double-headed eagle within beaded circle **Rev:** Chinese Goral **Edge:** Reeded

Date	Mintage	F	VF	XF	Unc	BU
2002(sp) Proof	10,000	Value: 30.00				

Y# 759 ROUBLE

17.4400 g., 0.9000 Silver 0.5046 oz. ASW, 33 mm. **Obv:** Double-headed eagle within beaded circle **Rev:** Sei Whale **Edge:** Reeded

Date	Mintage	F	VF	XF	Unc	BU
2002(sp) Proof	10,000	Value: 30.00				

Y# 760 ROUBLE

17.4400 g., 0.9000 Silver 0.5046 oz. ASW, 33 mm. **Subject:** Golden Eagle **Obv:** Double-headed eagle within beaded circle **Rev:** Golden Eagle with nestling **Edge:** Reeded

Date	Mintage	F	VF	XF	Unc	BU
2002(sp) Proof	10,000	Value: 30.00				

Y# 770 ROUBLE

8.5300 g., 0.9250 Silver 0.2537 oz. ASW, 25 mm. **Subject:** Ministry of Education **Obv:** Double-headed eagle within beaded circle **Rev:** Seedling within open book **Edge:** Reeded

Date	Mintage	F	VF	XF	Unc	BU
2002(m) Proof	3,000	Value: 50.00				

Y# 771 ROUBLE

8.5300 g., 0.9250 Silver 0.2537 oz. ASW, 25 mm. **Subject:** Ministry of Finances **Obv:** Double-headed eagle within beaded circle **Rev:** Caduceus in monogram **Edge:** Reeded

Date	Mintage	F	VF	XF	Unc	BU
2002(sp) Proof	3,000	Value: 50.00				

Y# 772 ROUBLE

8.5300 g., 0.9250 Silver 0.2537 oz. ASW, 25 mm. **Subject:** Ministry of Economic Development **Obv:** Double-headed eagle within beaded circle **Rev:** Crowned double-headed eagle with cornucopia and caduceus **Edge:** Reeded

Date	Mintage	F	VF	XF	Unc	BU
2002(sp) Proof	3,000	Value: 50.00				

Y# 773 ROUBLE

8.5300 g., 0.9250 Silver 0.2537 oz. ASW, 25 mm. **Subject:** Ministry of Foreign Affairs **Obv:** Double-headed eagle within beaded circle **Rev:** Crowned two-headed eagle above crossed sprigs **Edge:** Reeded

Date	Mintage	F	VF	XF	Unc	BU
2002(sp) Proof	3,000	Value: 50.00				

Y# 774 ROUBLE

8.5300 g., 0.9250 Silver 0.2537 oz. ASW, 25 mm. **Subject:** Ministry of Internal Affairs **Obv:** Double-headed eagle within beaded circle **Rev:** Crowned two-headed eagle with round breast **Edge:** Reeded

Date	Mintage	F	VF	XF	Unc	BU
2002(sp) Proof	3,000	Value: 50.00				

Y# 775 ROUBLE

8.5300 g., 0.9250 Silver 0.2537 oz. ASW, 25 mm. **Subject:** Ministry of Justice **Obv:** Double-headed eagle within beaded circle **Rev:** Crowned double-headed eagle with column on breast shield **Edge:** Reeded

Date	Mintage	F	VF	XF	Unc	BU
2002(sp) Proof	3,000	Value: 50.00				

Y# 776 ROUBLE

8.5300 g., 0.9250 Silver 0.2537 oz. ASW, 25 mm. **Subject:** Russian Armed Forces **Obv:** Double-headed eagle within beaded circle **Rev:** Double-headed eagle with crowned top pointed breast shield **Edge:** Reeded

Date	Mintage	F	VF	XF	Unc	BU
2002(m) Proof	3,000	Value: 50.00				

Y# 833 ROUBLE

3.2500 g., Copper-Nickel-Zinc, 20.5 mm. **Obv:** Two headed eagle, curved bank name and date below **Rev:** Value and flower **Edge:** Reeded

Date	Mintage	F	VF	XF	Unc	BU
2002(m) Mint sets only	15,000	—	—	—	—	—
2002(sp) Mint sets only	15,000	—	—	—	—	—
2003(sp)	15,000	—	—	300	400	500
2005(m)	—	—	—	—	2.00	3.00
2005(sp)	—	—	—	—	2.00	3.00
2006(m)	—	—	—	—	2.00	3.00
2006(sp)	—	—	—	—	2.00	3.00
2007(m)	—	—	—	—	2.00	3.00
2007(sp)	—	—	—	—	2.00	3.00
2008(m)	—	—	—	—	2.00	3.00
2008(sp)	—	—	—	—	2.00	3.00
2009(m)	—	—	—	—	2.00	3.00
2009(sp)	—	—	—	—	2.00	3.00

Y# A834 ROUBLE

7.7800 g., 0.9250 Silver 0.2314 oz. ASW, 0.25 mm. **Subject:** St. Petersburg **Obv:** Double-headed eagle within beaded circle **Rev:** Angel on steeple of Cathedral in fortress

Date	Mintage	F	VF	XF	Unc	BU
2002 Proof	5,000	Value: 25.00				

Y# 835 ROUBLE

7.7800 g., 0.9250 Silver 0.2314 oz. ASW, 25 mm. **Subject:** St. Petersburg **Obv:** Double-headed eagle within beaded circle **Rev:** Sphinx

Date	Mintage	F	VF	XF	Unc	BU
2002 Proof	5,000	Value: 25.00				

Y# 836 ROUBLE

7.7800 g., 0.9250 Silver 0.2314 oz. ASW, 25 mm. **Subject:** St. Petersburg **Obv:** Double-headed eagle within beaded circle **Rev:** Small ship

Date	Mintage	F	VF	XF	Unc	BU
2002 Proof	5,000	Value: 25.00				

Y# 837 ROUBLE

7.7800 g., 0.9250 Silver 0.2314 oz. ASW, 25 mm. **Subject:** St. Petersburg **Obv:** Double-headed eagle within beaded circle **Rev:** Lion

Date	Mintage	F	VF	XF	Unc	BU
2002 Proof	5,000	Value: 25.00				

Y# 838 ROUBLE

7.7800 g., 0.9250 Silver 0.2314 oz. ASW, 25 mm. **Subject:** St. Petersburg **Obv:** Double-headed eagle within beaded circle **Rev:** Horse sculpture

Date	Mintage	F	VF	XF	Unc	BU
2002 Proof	5,000	Value: 25.00				

Y# 839 ROUBLE

7.7800 g., 0.9250 Silver 0.2314 oz. ASW, 25 mm. **Subject:** St. Petersburg **Obv:** Double-headed eagle within beaded circle **Rev:** Griffin

Date	Mintage	F	VF	XF	Unc	BU
2002 Proof	5,000	Value: 25.00				

Y# 814 ROUBLE

17.4000 g., 0.9000 Silver 0.5035 oz. ASW, 32.8 mm. **Obv:** Double-headed eagle within beaded circle **Rev:** Arctic foxes **Edge:** Reeded

Date	Mintage	F	VF	XF	Unc	BU
2003(sp) Proof	10,000	Value: 30.00				

Y# 816 ROUBLE

17.4000 g., 0.9000 Silver 0.5035 oz. ASW, 32.8 mm. **Obv:** Double-headed eagle within beaded circle **Rev:** Pygmy Cormorant drying its wings **Edge:** Reeded

Date	Mintage	F	VF	XF	Unc	BU
2003(sp) Proof	10,000	Value: 30.00				

Y# 815 ROUBLE

17.4000 g., 0.9000 Silver 0.5035 oz. ASW, 32.8 mm. **Obv:** Double-headed eagle within beaded circle **Rev:** Chinese Softshell turtle **Edge:** Reeded

Date	Mintage	F	VF	XF	Unc	BU
2003(sp) Proof	10,000	Value: 35.00				

Y# 828 ROUBLE

17.2800 g., 0.9000 Silver 0.5000 oz. ASW, 33 mm. **Obv:** Two headed eagle within beaded circle **Rev:** Amur Forest Cat on branch **Edge:** Reeded

Date	Mintage	F	VF	XF	Unc	BU
2004(sp) Proof	10,000	Value: 30.00				

Y# 1029 ROUBLE

16.8000 g., 0.9250 Silver 0.4996 oz. ASW, 32.8 mm. **Subject:** The Great Bustard

Date	Mintage	F	VF	XF	Unc	BU
2004 Proof	—	Value: 30.00				

Y# 881 ROUBLE

17.2800 g., 0.5000 Silver 0.2778 oz. ASW, 32.8 mm. **Obv:** Double-headed eagle within beaded circle **Rev:** Rush Toad **Edge:** Reeded

Date	Mintage	F	VF	XF	Unc	BU
2004 Proof	—	Value: 45.00				

Y# 882 ROUBLE

16.8100 g., 0.4999 Silver 0.2702 oz. ASW, 32.8 mm. **Obv:** Double-headed eagle within beaded circle **Rev:** Two Marbled Murrelet sea birds **Edge:** Reeded

Date	Mintage	F	VF	XF	Unc	BU
2005 Proof	—	Value: 30.00				

Y# 883 ROUBLE

16.8100 g., 0.4999 Silver 0.2702 oz. ASW, 32.8 mm. **Obv:** Double-headed eagle within beaded circle **Rev:** Asiatic Wild Dog **Edge:** Reeded

Date	Mintage	F	VF	XF	Unc	BU
2005 Proof	—	Value: 45.00				

Y# 884 ROUBLE

16.8100 g., 0.4999 Silver 0.2702 oz. ASW, 32.8 mm. **Obv:** Double-headed eagle within beaded circle **Rev:** Volkhov Whitefish **Edge:** Reeded

Date	Mintage	F	VF	XF	Unc	BU
2005 Proof	—	Value: 30.00				

Y# 916 ROUBLE

8.5300 g., 0.9250 Silver 0.2537 oz. ASW, 25 mm. **Obv:** Double-headed eagle **Rev:** Russian Navy Emblem **Edge:** Reeded

Date	Mintage	F	VF	XF	Unc	BU
2005 Proof	10,000	Value: 25.00				

Y# 917 ROUBLE

8.5300 g., 0.9250 Silver 0.2537 oz. ASW, 25 mm. **Obv:** Double-headed eagle **Rev:** Russian Marine circa 1705 **Edge:** Reeded

Date	Mintage	F	VF	XF	Unc	BU
2005 Proof	10,000	Value: 25.00				

Y# 918 ROUBLE

8.5300 g., 0.9250 Silver 0.2537 oz. ASW, 25 mm. **Obv:** Double-headed eagle **Rev:** Russian Marine circa 2005 **Edge:** Reeded

Date	Mintage	F	VF	XF	Unc	BU
2005 Proof	10,000	Value: 25.00				

Y# 981 ROUBLE

15.5500 g., 0.9250 Silver 0.4624 oz. ASW, 33 mm. **Obv:** Double headed eagle **Rev:** Mongolian Gazelle **Edge:** Reeded

Date	Mintage	F	VF	XF	Unc	BU
2006 Proof	—	Value: 50.00				

Y# 1058 ROUBLE

33.9000 g., 0.9250 Silver 1.0081 oz. ASW, 39 mm. **Subject:** Swan Goose

Date	Mintage	F	VF	XF	Unc	BU
2006 Proof	—	Value: 40.00				

Y# 1059 ROUBLE

33.9000 g., 0.9250 Silver 1.0081 oz. ASW, 39 mm. **Subject:** Ussury Clawed Newt

Date	Mintage	F	VF	XF	Unc	BU
2006 Proof	—	Value: 40.00				

Y# 1069 ROUBLE
7.7800 g., 0.9250 Silver 0.2314 oz. ASW, 22.6 mm. **Subject:** Airborne Troops

Date	Mintage	F	VF	XF	Unc	BU
2006 Proof	—	Value: 25.00				

Y# 1070 ROUBLE
7.7800 g., 0.9250 Silver 0.2314 oz. ASW, 22.6 mm. **Subject:** Airborne Troops

Date	Mintage	F	VF	XF	Unc	BU
2006 Proof	—	Value: 25.00				

Y# 1071 ROUBLE
7.7800 g., 0.9250 Silver 0.2314 oz. ASW, 22.6 mm. **Subject:** Airborne Troops

Date	Mintage	F	VF	XF	Unc	BU
2006 Proof	—	Value: 25.00				

Y# 1072 ROUBLE
7.7800 g., 0.9250 Silver 0.2314 oz. ASW, 22.6 mm. **Subject:** Submarine Forces

Date	Mintage	F	VF	XF	Unc	BU
2006 Proof	—	Value: 25.00				

Y# 1073 ROUBLE
7.7800 g., 0.9250 Silver 0.2314 oz. ASW, 22.6 mm. **Subject:** Submarine Forces

Date	Mintage	F	VF	XF	Unc	BU
2006 Proof	—	Value: 25.00				

Y# 1074 ROUBLE
7.7800 g., Silver, 22.6 mm. **Subject:** Submarine Forces

Date	Mintage	F	VF	XF	Unc	BU
2006 Proof	—	Value: 25.00				

Y# 1075 ROUBLE
Silver **Subject:** Bogolyvbovo Township

Date	Mintage	F	VF	XF	Unc	BU
2006 Proof	—	Value: 25.00				

Y# 961 ROUBLE
15.5500 g., 0.9250 Silver 0.4624 oz. ASW, 33 mm. **Obv:** Double headed eagle **Rev:** Red banded snake **Edge:** Reeded

Date	Mintage	F	VF	XF	Unc	BU
2007 Proof	—	Value: 30.00				

Y# 962 ROUBLE
15.5500 g., 0.9250 Silver 0.4624 oz. ASW, 33 mm. **Obv:** Double headed eagle **Rev:** Pallid Harrier in flight

Date	Mintage	F	VF	XF	Unc	BU
2007 Proof	—	Value: 50.00				

Y# 1109 ROUBLE
33.9000 g., 0.9250 Silver 1.0081 oz. ASW, 39 mm. **Subject:** Ringed seal

Date	Mintage	F	VF	XF	Unc	BU
2007 Proof	—	Value: 40.00				

Y# 1110 ROUBLE
7.7800 g., 0.9250 Silver 0.2314 oz. ASW, 33 mm. **Subject:** Space Force

Date	Mintage	F	VF	XF	Unc	BU
2007 Proof	—	Value: 30.00				

Y# 1112 ROUBLE
33.9000 g., 0.9250 Silver 1.0081 oz. ASW, 3 mm. **Subject:** Space Force

Date	Mintage	F	VF	XF	Unc	BU
2007 Proof	—	Value: 30.00				

Y# 1111 ROUBLE
7.7800 g., 0.9250 Silver 0.2314 oz. ASW, 33 mm. **Subject:** Space Force

Date	Mintage	F	VF	XF	Unc	BU
2007 Proof	—	Value: 30.00				

Y# 1146 ROUBLE
16.8000 g., 0.9250 Silver 0.4996 oz. ASW **Subject:** Emperor Dragon Fly **Shape:** 33

Date	Mintage	F	VF	XF	Unc	BU
2008 Proof	—	Value: 30.00				

Y# 1151 ROUBLE
16.8000 g., 0.9250 Silver 0.4996 oz. ASW, 32.8 mm. **Subject:** City of Moscow

Date	Mintage	F	VF	XF	Unc	BU
2008 Proof	—	Value: 25.00				

Y# 833a ROUBLE
3.0000 g., Nickel Plated Steel, 20.5 mm. **Obv:** Two headed eagle, curved bank name and date below

Date	Mintage	F	VF	XF	Unc	BU
2009ММД	—	—	—	—	0.75	1.50
2009СПМД	—	—	—	—	0.75	1.50
2010ММД	—	—	—	—	0.75	1.50
2010СПМД	—	—	—	—	0.75	1.50

Y# 1204 ROUBLE
16.8000 g., 0.9250 Silver 0.4996 oz. ASW, 33 mm. **Subject:** Air Force

Date	Mintage	F	VF	XF	Unc	BU
2009 Proof	—	Value: 30.00				

Y# 1205 ROUBLE
16.8000 g., 0.9250 Silver 0.4996 oz. ASW, 33 mm. **Subject:** Air Force

Date	Mintage	F	VF	XF	Unc	BU
2009 Proof	—	Value: 30.00				

Y# 1206 ROUBLE
16.8000 g., 0.9250 Silver 0.4996 oz. ASW, 33 mm. **Subject:** Air Force

Date	Mintage	F	VF	XF	Unc	BU
2009 Proof	—	Value: 30.00				

Y# 1244 ROUBLE
7.7800 g., 0.9250 Silver 0.2314 oz. ASW, 33 mm. **Subject:** Armored Forces

Date	Mintage	F	VF	XF	Unc	BU
2010 Proof	—	Value: 30.00				

Y# 1245 ROUBLE
7.7800 g., 0.9250 Silver 0.2314 oz. ASW, 33 mm. **Subject:** Armored Force

Date	Mintage	F	VF	XF	Unc	BU
2010 Proof	—	Value: 30.00				

Y# 1246 ROUBLE
7.7800 g., 0.9250 Silver 0.2314 oz. ASW, 33 mm. **Subject:** Armored Force

Date	Mintage	F	VF	XF	Unc	BU
2010 Proof	—	—	—	—	—	30.00

Y# 1253 ROUBLE
7.7800 g., 0.9250 Silver 0.2314 oz. ASW, 22.6 mm. **Subject:** Russian Aviation

Date	Mintage	F	VF	XF	Unc	BU
2010 Proof	—	Value: 30.00				

Y# 1254 ROUBLE
7.7800 g., 0.9250 Silver 0.2314 oz. ASW, 33 mm. **Subject:** Russian Aviation

Date	Mintage	F	VF	XF	Unc	BU
2010 Proof	—	Value: 30.00				

Y# 605 2 ROUBLES
5.1000 g., Copper-Nickel-Zinc, 23 mm. **Obv:** Double-headed eagle **Rev:** Value and vine sprig **Edge:** Segmented reeding

Date	Mintage	F	VF	XF	Unc	BU
2001M Rare	—	—	—	—	—	—

Y# 730 2 ROUBLES
17.0000 g., 0.9250 Silver 0.5055 oz. ASW, 33 mm. **Subject:** V.I. Dal **Obv:** Double-headed eagle **Rev:** Portrait, book, signature, figures **Edge:** Reeded

Date	Mintage	F	VF	XF	Unc	BU
2001(m) Proof	7,500	Value: 40.00				

Y# 675 2 ROUBLES
5.1000 g., Copper-Nickel, 23 mm. **Subject:** Yuri Gagarin **Obv:** Value and date to left of vine sprig **Rev:** Uniformed bust facing **Edge:** Segmented reeding

Date	Mintage	F	VF	XF	Unc	BU
2001	—	—	100	125	175	—
2001ММД	10,000,000	—	—	—	2.00	4.00
2001СПМД	10,000,000	—	—	—	2.00	4.00

Y# 1002 2 ROUBLES
16.8100 g., 0.9250 Silver 0.4999 oz. ASW, 33 mm. **Subject:** V. I. Dal. 200th Anniversary of birth

Date	Mintage	F	VF	XF	Unc	BU
2001 Proof	—	Value: 30.00				

Y# 742 2 ROUBLES
17.0000 g., 0.9250 Silver 0.5055 oz. ASW, 33 mm. **Subject:** Zodiac Signs **Obv:** Double-headed eagle within beaded circle **Rev:** Leo **Edge:** Reeded

Date	Mintage	F	VF	XF	Unc	BU
2002(m) Proof	20,000	Value: 35.00				

Y# 834 2 ROUBLES
5.1000 g., Copper-Nickel-Zinc, 23 mm. **Obv:** Two headed eagle above curved inscription **Rev:** Value and flower **Edge:** Segmented reeding

Date	Mintage	F	VF	XF	Unc	BU
2002ММД Mint sets only	15,000	—	—	—	—	—
2002СПМД Mint sets only	15,000	—	—	—	—	—
2003ММД	15,000	—	—	300	400	500
2006ММД	—	—	—	—	4.00	5.00
2006СПМД	—	—	—	—	4.00	5.00
2007ММД	—	—	—	—	4.00	5.00
2007СПМД	—	—	—	—	4.00	5.00
2008ММД	—	—	—	—	4.00	5.00
2008СПМД	—	—	—	—	4.00	5.00
2009ММД	—	—	—	—	4.00	5.00
2009СПМД	—	—	—	—	4.00	5.00

Y# 747 2 ROUBLES
17.0000 g., 0.9250 Silver 0.5055 oz. ASW, 33 mm. **Subject:** Zodiac Signs **Obv:** Double-headed eagle within beaded circle **Rev:** Virgo and stars **Edge:** Reeded

Date	Mintage	F	VF	XF	Unc	BU
2002(m) Proof	20,000	Value: 30.00				

Y# 761 2 ROUBLES
17.0000 g., 0.9250 Silver 0.5055 oz. ASW, 33 mm. **Subject:** Zodiac Signs **Obv:** Double-headed eagle within beaded circle **Rev:** Capricorn **Edge:** Reeded

Date	Mintage	F	VF	XF	Unc	BU
2002(sp) Proof	20,000	Value: 35.00				

Y# 762 2 ROUBLES
17.0000 g., 0.9250 Silver 0.5055 oz. ASW, 33 mm. **Subject:** Zodiac Signs **Obv:** Double-headed eagle within beaded circle **Rev:** Sagittarius **Edge:** Reeded

Date	Mintage	F	VF	XF	Unc	BU
2002(sp) Proof	20,000	Value: 30.00				

Y# 766 2 ROUBLES
17.0000 g., 0.9250 Silver 0.5055 oz. ASW, 33 mm. **Subject:** Zodiac Signs **Obv:** Double-headed eagle within beaded circle **Rev:** Scorpion **Edge:** Reeded

Date	Mintage	F	VF	XF	Unc	BU
2002(m) Proof	20,000	Value: 35.00				

Y# 768 2 ROUBLES
17.0000 g., 0.9250 Silver 0.5055 oz. ASW, 33 mm. **Subject:** Zodiac Signs **Obv:** Double-headed eagle **Rev:** Balance scale **Edge:** Reeded

Date	Mintage	F	VF	XF	Unc	BU
2002(sp) Proof	20,000	Value: 30.00				

Y# 793 2 ROUBLES
17.0000 g., 0.9250 Silver 0.5055 oz. ASW, 33 mm. **Subject:** L.P. Orlova **Obv:** Double-headed eagle **Rev:** Head facing **Edge:** Reeded

Date	Mintage	F	VF	XF	Unc	BU
2002(m) Proof	10,000	Value: 25.00				

Y# 803 2 ROUBLES
17.1000 g., 0.9250 Silver 0.5085 oz. ASW, 32.8 mm. **Subject:** Zodiac signs **Obv:** Double-headed eagle within beaded circle **Rev:** Pisces **Edge:** Reeded

Date	Mintage	F	VF	XF	Unc	BU
2003(sp) Proof	20,000	Value: 35.00				

Y# 804 2 ROUBLES
17.1000 g., 0.9250 Silver 0.5085 oz. ASW, 32.8 mm. **Subject:** Zodiac signs **Obv:** Double-headed eagle within beaded circle **Rev:** Aquarius **Edge:** Reeded

Date	Mintage	F	VF	XF	Unc	BU
2003(m) Proof	20,000	Value: 35.00				

Y# 820 2 ROUBLES
17.0000 g., 0.9250 Silver 0.5055 oz. ASW, 33 mm. **Subject:** Zodiac signs **Obv:** Double-headed eagle within beaded circle **Rev:** Cancer Crayfish **Edge:** Reeded

Date	Mintage	F	VF	XF	Unc	BU
2003(sp) Proof	20,000	Value: 35.00				

Y# 840 2 ROUBLES
16.8100 g., 0.9250 Silver 0.4999 oz. ASW, 33 mm. **Rev:** Guil Yarovsky

Date	Mintage	F	VF	XF	Unc	BU
2003(m) Proof	10,000	Value: 20.00				

Y# 841 2 ROUBLES
16.8100 g., 0.9250 Silver 0.4999 oz. ASW, 33 mm. **Rev:** Fedor Tyutchev

Date	Mintage	F	VF	XF	Unc	BU
2003(sp) Proof	10,000	Value: 20.00				

Y# 844 2 ROUBLES
17.0000 g., 0.9250 Silver 0.5055 oz. ASW, 33 mm. **Subject:** Zodiac Signs **Obv:** Double-headed eagle within beaded circle **Rev:** Aries

Date	Mintage	F	VF	XF	Unc	BU
2003 Proof	20,000	Value: 25.00				

Y# 845 2 ROUBLES
17.0000 g., 0.9250 Silver 0.5055 oz. ASW **Subject:** Zodiac Signs **Obv:** Double-headed eagle within beaded circle **Rev:** Taurus

Date	Mintage	F	VF	XF	Unc	BU
2003 Proof	20,000	Value: 25.00				

Y# 846 2 ROUBLES
17.0000 g., 0.9250 Silver 0.5055 oz. ASW, 33 mm. **Subject:** Zodiac Signs **Obv:** Double-headed eagle within beaded circle **Rev:** Gemini

Date	Mintage	F	VF	XF	Unc	BU
2003 Proof	20,000	Value: 22.50				

Y# 842 2 ROUBLES
16.8100 g., 0.9250 Silver 0.4999 oz. ASW, 33 mm. **Rev:** V. P. Tchkalov

Date	Mintage	F	VF	XF	Unc	BU
2004(m) Proof	7,000	Value: 20.00				

Y# 843 2 ROUBLES
16.8100 g., 0.9250 Silver 0.4999 oz. ASW, 33 mm. **Rev:** Mikhail Glinka

Date	Mintage	F	VF	XF	Unc	BU
2004(m) Proof	7,000	Value: 20.00				

Y# 1021 2 ROUBLES
16.8000 g., 0.9250 Silver 0.4996 oz. ASW, 33 mm. **Subject:** Sini Rerikh, 100th Anniversary of Birth

Date	Mintage	F	VF	XF	Unc	BU
2004 Proof	—	Value: 30.00				

Y# 897 2 ROUBLES
17.0000 g., 0.9250 Silver 0.5055 oz. ASW, 33 mm. **Obv:** Double-headed eagle **Rev:** Gemini twins **Edge:** Reeded

Date	Mintage	F	VF	XF	Unc	BU
2005 Proof	20,000	Value: 30.00				

Y# 899 2 ROUBLES
17.0000 g., 0.9250 Silver 0.5055 oz. ASW, 33 mm. **Obv:** Double-headed eagle **Rev:** Cancer Crayfish **Edge:** Reeded

Date	Mintage	F	VF	XF	Unc	BU
2005 Proof	20,000	Value: 30.00				

Y# 901 2 ROUBLES
17.0000 g., 0.9250 Silver 0.5055 oz. ASW, 33 mm. **Obv:** Double-headed eagle **Rev:** Leo lion **Edge:** Reeded

Date	Mintage	F	VF	XF	Unc	BU
2005 Proof	20,000	Value: 30.00				

Y# 905 2 ROUBLES
17.0000 g., 0.9250 Silver 0.5055 oz. ASW, 33 mm. **Obv:** Double-headed eagle **Rev:** Mikhail Sholokhov with pen in hand **Edge:** Reeded

Date	Mintage	F	VF	XF	Unc	BU
2005 Proof	10,000	Value: 25.00				

Y# 909 2 ROUBLES
17.0000 g., 0.9250 Silver 0.5055 oz. ASW, 33 mm. **Obv:** Double-headed eagle **Rev:** Peter Klodt viewing man and horse statue **Edge:** Reeded

Date	Mintage	F	VF	XF	Unc	BU
2005 Proof	10,000	Value: 25.00				

Y# 914 2 ROUBLES
17.0000 g., 0.9250 Silver 0.5055 oz. ASW, 33 mm. **Obv:** Double-headed eagle **Rev:** Virgo standing lady **Edge:** Reeded

Date	Mintage	F	VF	XF	Unc	BU
2005 Proof	20,000	Value: 30.00				

Y# 919 2 ROUBLES
17.0000 g., 0.9250 Silver 0.5055 oz. ASW, 33 mm. **Obv:** Double-headed eagle **Rev:** Libra - 2 stylized birds forming a balance scale **Edge:** Reeded

Date	Mintage	F	VF	XF	Unc	BU
2005 Proof	20,000	Value: 30.00				

Y# 921 2 ROUBLES
17.0000 g., 0.9250 Silver 0.5055 oz. ASW, 33 mm. **Obv:** Double-headed eagle **Rev:** Scorpio scorpion **Edge:** Reeded

Date	Mintage	F	VF	XF	Unc	BU
2005 Proof	25	Value: 30.00				

Y# 926 2 ROUBLES
17.0000 g., 0.9250 Silver 0.5055 oz. ASW, 33 mm. **Obv:** Double-headed eagle **Rev:** Sagittarius the archer **Edge:** Reeded

Date	Mintage	F	VF	XF	Unc	BU
2005 Proof	20,000	Value: 30.00				

Y# 928 2 ROUBLES
17.0000 g., 0.9250 Silver 0.5055 oz. ASW, 33 mm. **Obv:** Double-headed eagle **Rev:** Capricorn as half goat and fish **Edge:** Reeded

Date	Mintage	F	VF	XF	Unc	BU
2005 Proof	20,000	Value: 30.00				

Y# 930 2 ROUBLES
17.0000 g., 0.9250 Silver 0.5055 oz. ASW, 33 mm. **Obv:** Double-headed eagle **Rev:** Pisces as catfish and sturgeon **Edge:** Reeded

Date	Mintage	F	VF	XF	Unc	BU
2005 Proof	20,000	Value: 30.00				

Y# 932 2 ROUBLES
17.0000 g., 0.9250 Silver 0.5055 oz. ASW, 33 mm. **Obv:** Double-headed eagle **Rev:** Aries ram **Edge:** Reeded

Date	Mintage	F	VF	XF	Unc	BU
2005 Proof	20,000	Value: 30.00				

Y# 934 2 ROUBLES
17.0000 g., 0.9250 Silver 0.5055 oz. ASW, 33 mm. **Obv:** Double-headed eagle **Rev:** Taurus bull **Edge:** Reeded

Date	Mintage	F	VF	XF	Unc	BU
2005 Proof	20,000	Value: 30.00				

Y# 936 2 ROUBLES
17.0000 g., 0.9250 Silver 0.5055 oz. ASW, 33 mm. **Obv:** Double-headed eagle **Rev:** Aquarius water carrier **Edge:** Reeded

Date	Mintage	F	VF	XF	Unc	BU
2005 Proof	20,000	Value: 30.00				

Y# 1054 2 ROUBLES
16.8000 g., 0.9250 Silver 0.4996 oz. ASW, 33 mm. **Subject:** O. K. Antonov, 100th Anniversary of Birth

Date	Mintage	F	VF	XF	Unc	BU
2006 Proof	—	Value: 35.00				

Y# 1055 2 ROUBLES
16.8000 g., 0.9250 Silver 0.4996 oz. ASW, 33 mm. **Subject:** M. A. Vrubel, 150th Anniversary of Birth

Date	Mintage	F	VF	XF	Unc	BU
2006 Proof	—	Value: 35.00				

Y# 1056 2 ROUBLES
16.8000 g., 0.9250 Silver 0.4996 oz. ASW, 33 mm. **Subject:** A. A. Ivanov, 200th Anniversary of Birth

Date	Mintage	F	VF	XF	Unc	BU
2006 Proof	—	Value: 35.00				

Y# 1057 2 ROUBLES
16.8000 g., 0.9250 Silver 0.4996 oz. ASW, 33 mm. **Subject:** D. D. Shostakovich, 100th Anniversary of Birth

Date	Mintage	F	VF	XF	Unc	BU
2006 Proof	—	Value: 35.00				

Y# 967 2 ROUBLES
17.0000 g., 0.9250 Silver 0.5055 oz. ASW, 33.0 mm. **Subject:** 100th Anniversary Birth of Gerasimov **Obv:** Two-headed eagle **Rev:** Gerasimov recreating a man's face **Rev. Legend:** М. М. ГЕРАСИМОВ

Date	Mintage	F	VF	XF	Unc	BU
2007(m) Proof	10,000	Value: 35.00				

Y# 968 2 ROUBLES
17.0000 g., 0.9250 Silver 0.5055 oz. ASW, 33.0 mm. **Subject:** 150th Anniversary Birth of Tsiolkovsky **Rev:** Bust of Tsiolkovsky 3/4 right at left, scheme of two flight vehicles with earth in background at upper right **Rev. Legend:** К. Э. ЦИОЛКОВСКИЈ **Edge:** Reeded

Date	Mintage	F	VF	XF	Unc	BU
2007(m) Proof	10,000	Value: 35.00				

Y# 1104 2 ROUBLES
16.8000 g., 0.9250 Silver 0.4996 oz. ASW, 33 mm. **Subject:** S.P. Korolyov, 100th Anniversary of Birth

Date	Mintage	F	VF	XF	Unc	BU
2007 Proof	—	Value: 35.00				

Y# 1105 2 ROUBLES
16.8000 g., 0.9250 Silver 0.4996 oz. ASW, 33 mm. **Subject:** V.M. Bekhterev, 150th Anniversary of Birth

Date	Mintage	F	VF	XF	Unc	BU
2007 Proof	—	Value: 35.00				

Y# 1106 2 ROUBLES
16.8000 g., 0.9250 Silver 0.4996 oz. ASW, 33 mm. **Subject:** L. Euler, 300th Anniversary of Birth

Date	Mintage	F	VF	XF	Unc	BU
2007 Proof	—	Value: 35.00				

Y# 1107 2 ROUBLES
16.8000 g., 0.9250 Silver 0.4996 oz. ASW, 33 mm. **Subject:** V. P. Soloviev - Sedoy, 100th Anniversary of Birth

Date	Mintage	F	VF	XF	Unc	BU
2007 Proof	—	Value: 35.00				

Y# 979 2 ROUBLES
15.5500 g., 0.9250 Silver 0.4624 oz. ASW, 33 mm. **Obv:** Double headed eagle **Rev:** Black caped marmot **Edge:** Reeded

Date	Mintage	F	VF	XF	Unc	BU
2008 Proof	—	Value: 32.00				

Y# 980 2 ROUBLES
15.5500 g., 0.9250 Silver 0.4624 oz. ASW, 33 mm. **Obv:** Double headed eagle **Rev:** Shemaya fish **Edge:** Reeded

Date	Mintage	F	VF	XF	Unc	BU
2008 Proof	—	Value: 32.00				

Y# 1131 2 ROUBLES
16.8000 g., 0.9250 Silver 0.4996 oz. ASW, 33 mm. **Subject:** L. D. Landau, 100th Anniversary of Birth

Date	Mintage	F	VF	XF	Unc	BU
2008 Proof	—	Value: 35.00				

Y# 1132 2 ROUBLES
16.8000 g., 0.9250 Silver 0.4996 oz. ASW, 33 mm. **Subject:** V. P. Glushko, 100th Anniversary of Birth

Date	Mintage	F	VF	XF	Unc	BU
2008 Proof	—	Value: 35.00				

Y# 1133 2 ROUBLES
16.8000 g., 0.9250 Silver 0.4996 oz. ASW, 33 mm. **Subject:** D. F. Oistrakh, 100th Anniversary of Birth

Date	Mintage	F	VF	XF	Unc	BU
2008 Proof	—	Value: 35.00				

Y# 1134 2 ROUBLES
16.8000 g., 0.9250 Silver 0.4996 oz. ASW, 33 mm. **Subject:** I. M. Frank. 100th Anniversary of Birth

Date	Mintage	F	VF	XF	Unc	BU
2008 Proof	—	Value: 35.00				

Y# 1135 2 ROUBLES
16.8000 g., 0.9250 Silver 0.4996 oz. ASW, 33 mm. **Subject:** N. N. Nosoc, 100th Anniversary of Birth

Date	Mintage	F	VF	XF	Unc	BU
2008 Proof	—	Value: 35.00				

Y# 1136 2 ROUBLES
16.8000 g., 0.9250 Silver 0.4996 oz. ASW, 33 mm. **Subject:** V. I. Nemirovich, 100th Anniversary of Birth

Date	Mintage	F	VF	XF	Unc	BU
2008 Proof	—	Value: 35.00				

Y# 1137 2 ROUBLES
16.8000 g., 0.9250 Silver 0.4996 oz. ASW, 33 mm. **Subject:** E. V. Vuchetich, 100th Anniversary of Birth

Date	Mintage	F	VF	XF	Unc	BU
2008 Proof	—	Value: 35.00				

Y# 834a 2 ROUBLES
5.0000 g., Nickel Plated Steel, 23 mm. **Obv:** Two headed eagle, curved bank name and denomination below **Edge:** Segmented reeding

Date	Mintage	F	VF	XF	Unc	BU
2009ММД	—	—	—	—	0.50	0.75
2009СПМД	—	—	—	—	0.50	0.75
2010ММД	—	—	—	—	0.50	0.75
2010СПМД	—	—	—	—	0.50	0.75

Y# 1158 2 ROUBLES
16.8000 g., 0.9250 Silver 0.4996 oz. ASW **Subject:** D. I. Mendeleyev, 175th Anniversary of Birth

Date	Mintage	F	VF	XF	Unc	BU
2009 Proof	—	Value: 35.00				

Y# 1190 2 ROUBLES
16.8000 g., 0.9250 Silver 0.4996 oz. ASW, 33 mm. **Subject:** A. V. Koltsov, 200th Anniversary of Birth

Date	Mintage	F	VF	XF	Unc	BU
2009 Proof	—	Value: 35.00				

Y# 1191 2 ROUBLES
16.8000 g., 0.9250 Silver 0.4996 oz. ASW, 33 mm. **Subject:** A. N. Voronikhin, 250th Anniversary of Birth

Date	Mintage	F	VF	XF	Unc	BU
2009 Proof	—	Value: 35.00				

Y# 1192 2 ROUBLES
16.8000 g., 0.9250 Silver 0.4996 oz. ASW, 33 mm. **Subject:** G. S. Ulanova, 100th Anniversary of Birth

Date	Mintage	F	VF	XF	Unc	BU
2009 Proof	—	Value: 35.00				

Y# 1193 2 ROUBLES
16.8000 g., 0.9250 Silver 0.4996 oz. ASW, 33 mm. **Subject:** L. I. Yashin, Soccer player

Date	Mintage	F	VF	XF	Unc	BU
2009 Proof	—	Value: 45.00				

Y# 1194 2 ROUBLES
16.8000 g., 0.9250 Silver 0.4996 oz. ASW, 33 mm. **Subject:** E. I. Beskov, Soccer player

Date	Mintage	F	VF	XF	Unc	BU
2009 Proof	—	Value: 45.00				

Y# 1195 2 ROUBLES
16.8000 g., 0.9250 Silver 0.4996 oz. ASW, 33 mm. **Subject:** E. A. Stresov, Soccer player

Date	Mintage	F	VF	XF	Unc	BU
2009 Proof	—	Value: 45.00				

Y# 1196 2 ROUBLES
16.8000 g., 0.9250 Silver 0.4996 oz. ASW, 33 mm. **Subject:** V. M. Bobrov, Hockey player

Date	Mintage	F	VF	XF	Unc	BU
2009 Proof	—	Value: 45.00				

Y# 1197 2 ROUBLES
16.8000 g., 0.9250 Silver 0.4996 oz. ASW, 33 mm. **Subject:** A. N. Maltzev, Hockey player

Date	Mintage	F	VF	XF	Unc	BU
2009 Proof	—	Value: 45.00				

Y# 1198 2 ROUBLES
16.8000 g., 0.9250 Silver 0.4996 oz. ASW, 33 mm. **Subject:** V. B. Kharlamov, Hockey player

Date	Mintage	F	VF	XF	Unc	BU
2009 Proof	—	Value: 45.00				

Y# 1216 2 ROUBLES
16.8000 g., 0.9250 Silver 0.4996 oz. ASW, 33 mm. **Subject:** N. I. Pirogov, 200th Anniversary of Birth

Date	Mintage	F	VF	XF	Unc	BU
2010 Proof	—	Value: 35.00				

Y# 1217 2 ROUBLES
16.8000 g., 0.9250 Silver 0.4996 oz. ASW, 33 mm. **Subject:** I. I. Levitan, 150th Anniversary of Birth

Date	Mintage	F	VF	XF	Unc	BU
2010 Proof	—	Value: 35.00				

Y# 1218 2 ROUBLES
16.8000 g., 0.9250 Silver 0.4996 oz. ASW, 33 mm. **Subject:** G. S. Ulanova, 100th Anniversary of Birth

Date	Mintage	F	VF	XF	Unc	BU
2010 Proof	—	Value: 35.00				

Y# 1248 2 ROUBLES
16.8000 g., 0.9250 Silver 0.4996 oz. ASW, 33 mm. **Subject:** Sika Deer

Date	Mintage	F	VF	XF	Unc	BU
2010 Proof	—	Value: 32.00				

Y# 1249 2 ROUBLES
16.8000 g., 0.9250 Silver 0.4996 oz. ASW, 33 mm. **Subject:** Short tailed albatross

Date	Mintage	F	VF	XF	Unc	BU
2010 Proof	—	Value: 32.00				

Y# 1250 2 ROUBLES
16.8000 g., 0.9250 Silver 0.4996 oz. ASW, 33 mm. **Subject:** Gjursa

Date	Mintage	F	VF	XF	Unc	BU
2010 Proof	—	Value: 32.00				

Y# 1269 2 ROUBLES
16.8000 g., 0.9250 Silver 0.4996 oz. ASW, 33 mm. **Subject:** I. K. Rodnina, Figure skater

Date	Mintage	F	VF	XF	Unc	BU
2010 Proof	—	Value: 40.00				

Y# 1270 2 ROUBLES
16.8000 g., 0.9250 Silver 0.4996 oz. ASW, 33 mm. **Subject:** A. G. Zaitsev, figure skater

Date	Mintage	F	VF	XF	Unc	BU
2010 Proof	—	Value: 40.00				

Y# 1271 2 ROUBLES
16.8000 g., 0.9250 Silver 0.4996 oz. ASW, 33 mm. **Subject:** L. A. Pakhomova, Figure skater

Date	Mintage	F	VF	XF	Unc	BU
2010 Proof	—	Value: 40.00				

Y# 1272 2 ROUBLES
16.8000 g., 0.9250 Silver 0.4996 oz. ASW, 33 mm. **Subject:** A. G. Gorshkov, Figure skater

Date	Mintage	F	VF	XF	Unc	BU
2010 Proof	—	Value: 40.00				

Y# 677 3 ROUBLES
34.8800 g., 0.9000 Silver 1.0092 oz. ASW, 39 mm. **Subject:** 225 Years - Bolshoi Theater **Obv:** Double-headed eagle **Rev:** Standing figures facing **Edge:** Reeded

Date	Mintage	F	VF	XF	Unc	BU
2001 Proof	7,500	Value: 55.00				

Y# 680 3 ROUBLES
34.8800 g., 0.9000 Silver 1.0092 oz. ASW, 39 mm. **Subject:** 40th Anniversary of Manned Space Flight - Yuri Gagarin **Obv:** Double-headed eagle **Rev:** Uniformed bust holding dove **Edge:** Reeded

Date	Mintage	F	VF	XF	Unc	BU
2001 Proof	7,500	Value: 55.00				

Y# 682 3 ROUBLES
34.8800 g., 0.9000 Silver 1.0092 oz. ASW, 39 mm. **Subject:**

Siberian Exploration **Obv:** Double-headed eagle **Rev:** Men riding horses, deer and sleds **Edge:** Reeded

Date	Mintage	F	VF	XF	Unc	BU
2001 Proof	5,000	Value: 70.00				

Y# 733 3 ROUBLES

34.8800 g., 0.9000 Silver 1.0092 oz. ASW, 39 mm. **Subject:** 200th Anniversary of Navigation School **Obv:** Double-headed eagle **Rev:** Navigational tools and building **Edge:** Reeded

Date	Mintage	F	VF	XF	Unc	BU
2001 Proof	5,000	Value: 70.00				

Y# 734 3 ROUBLES

34.8800 g., 0.9000 Silver 1.0092 oz. ASW, 39 mm. **Subject:** First Moscow Savings Bank **Obv:** Double-headed eagle **Rev:** Beehive above building within circle **Edge:** Reeded

Date	Mintage	F	VF	XF	Unc	BU
2001 Proof	17,500	Value: 45.00				

Y# 735 3 ROUBLES

34.8800 g., 0.9000 Silver 1.0092 oz. ASW, 39 mm. **Subject:** State Labor Savings Bank **Obv:** Double-headed eagle **Rev:** Dam, passbook and tractor **Edge:** Reeded

Date	Mintage	F	VF	XF	Unc	BU
2001 Proof	17,500	Value: 45.00				

Y# 736 3 ROUBLES

34.8800 g., 0.9000 Silver 1.0092 oz. ASW, 39 mm. **Subject:** Savings Bank of the Russian Federation **Obv:** Double-headed eagle **Rev:** Chevrons above building **Edge:** Reeded

Date	Mintage	F	VF	XF	Unc	BU
2001 Proof	17,500	Value: 45.00				

Y# 737 3 ROUBLES

34.8800 g., 0.9000 Silver 1.0092 oz. ASW, 39 mm. **Subject:** 10th Anniversary - Commonwealth of Independent States **Obv:** Double-headed eagle **Rev:** Hologram below logo **Edge:** Reeded

Date	Mintage	F	VF	XF	Unc	BU
2001 Proof	7,500	Value: 50.00				

Y# 738 3 ROUBLES

34.8800 g., 0.9000 Silver 1.0092 oz. ASW, 39 mm. **Subject:** Olympics **Obv:** Double-headed eagle **Rev:** Cross-country skiers **Edge:** Reeded

Date	Mintage	F	VF	XF	Unc	BU
2002 Proof	25,000	Value: 50.00				

Y# 744 3 ROUBLES

34.8800 g., 0.9000 Silver 1.0092 oz. ASW, 39 mm. **Subject:** St. John's Nunnery, St. Petersburg **Obv:** Double-headed eagle **Rev:** Nunnery and cameo **Edge:** Reeded

Date	Mintage	F	VF	XF	Unc	BU
2002 Proof	5,000	Value: 55.00				

Y# 778 3 ROUBLES

34.8800 g., 0.9000 Silver 1.0092 oz. ASW, 39 mm. **Subject:** Kideksha **Obv:** Double-headed eagle **Rev:** Three churches on river bank **Edge:** Reeded

Date	Mintage	F	VF	XF	Unc	BU
2002(sp) Proof	10,000	Value: 60.00				

Y# 779 3 ROUBLES

34.8800 g., 0.9000 Silver 1.0092 oz. ASW, 39 mm. **Subject:** Iversky Monastery, Valdaiy **Obv:** Double-headed eagle **Rev:** Building complex on an island in Lake Valdaiy **Edge:** Reeded

Date	Mintage	F	VF	XF	Unc	BU
2002(sp) Proof	10,000	Value: 60.00				

Y# 780 3 ROUBLES

34.8800 g., 0.9000 Silver 1.0092 oz. ASW, 39 mm. **Subject:** Miraculous Savior Church **Obv:** Double-headed eagle **Rev:** Church with separate bell tower **Edge:** Reeded

Date	Mintage	F	VF	XF	Unc	BU
2002(m) Proof	5,000	Value: 55.00				

Y# 781 3 ROUBLES

34.8800 g., 0.9000 Silver 1.0092 oz. ASW, 39 mm. **Subject:** Works of Dionissy **Obv:** Double-headed eagle **Rev:** "The Crucifix" **Edge:** Reeded

Date	Mintage	F	VF	XF	Unc	BU
2002(sp) Proof	10,000	Value: 45.00				

Y# 755 3 ROUBLES

34.8800 g., 0.9000 Silver 1.0092 oz. ASW, 39 mm. **Subject:** Admiral Nakhimov **Obv:** Double-headed eagle **Rev:** Monument, Admiral with cannon and naval battle scene **Edge:** Reeded

Date	Mintage	F	VF	XF	Unc	BU
2002(sp) Proof	10,000	Value: 45.00				

Y# 787 3 ROUBLES

34.8800 g., 0.9000 Silver 1.0092 oz. ASW, 39 mm. **Subject:** World Cup Soccer **Obv:** Double-headed eagle **Rev:** Soccer ball within circle of players **Edge:** Reeded

Date	Mintage	F	VF	XF	Unc	BU
2002(sp) Proof	25,000	Value: 40.00				

Y# 756 3 ROUBLES

34.8800 g., 0.9000 Silver 1.0092 oz. ASW, 39 mm. **Subject:** Hermitage **Obv:** Double-headed eagle **Rev:** Statues and arch **Edge:** Reeded

Date	Mintage	F	VF	XF	Unc	BU
2002(sp) Proof	10,000	Value: 50.00				

Y# 885 3 ROUBLES

34.8000 g., 0.9000 Silver 1.0069 oz. ASW, 38.7 mm. **Subject:** City of Pskov 1100th Anniversary **Obv:** Double-headed eagle **Rev:** Walled city view **Edge:** Reeded

Date	Mintage	F	VF	XF	Unc	BU
2003(sp) Proof	—	Value: 55.00				

Y# 801 3 ROUBLES

34.8000 g., 0.9000 Silver 1.0069 oz. ASW, 38.7 mm. **Subject:** Veborg **Obv:** Double-headed eagle **Rev:** Sailing ships and buildings **Edge:** Reeded

Date	Mintage	F	VF	XF	Unc	BU
2003(sp) Proof	10,000	Value: 55.00				

Y# 802 3 ROUBLES
34.7500 g., 0.9000 Silver 1.0055 oz. ASW, 38.7 mm. **Subject:** Lunar Calendar **Obv:** National emblem **Rev:** Mountain goat in crescent **Edge:** Reeded

Date	Mintage	F	VF	XF	Unc	BU
2003(m) Proof	15,000	Value: 50.00				

Y# 805 3 ROUBLES
34.8400 g., 0.9000 Silver 1.0081 oz. ASW, 38.8 mm. **Subject:** Zodiac signs **Obv:** Double-headed eagle within beaded circle **Rev:** Leo **Edge:** Reeded

Date	Mintage	F	VF	XF	Unc	BU
2003(m) Proof	30,000	Value: 50.00				

Y# 806 3 ROUBLES
34.7400 g., 0.9000 Silver 1.0052 oz. ASW, 38.8 mm. **Subject:** St. Daniel's Monastery **Obv:** Double-headed eagle **Rev:** Statue and monastery **Edge:** Reeded

Date	Mintage	F	VF	XF	Unc	BU
2003(m) Proof	10,000	Value: 50.00				

Y# 807 3 ROUBLES
34.7400 g., 0.9000 Silver 1.0052 oz. ASW, 38.8 mm. **Subject:** World Biathlon Championships **Obv:** Double-headed eagle **Rev:** Rifleman and archer on skis **Edge:** Reeded

Date	Mintage	F	VF	XF	Unc	BU
2003(m) Proof	7,500	Value: 50.00				

Y# 808 3 ROUBLES
34.7400 g., 0.9000 Silver 1.0052 oz. ASW, 38.8 mm. **Obv:** Double-headed eagle **Rev:** Monastery **Edge:** Reeded

Date	Mintage	F	VF	XF	Unc	BU
2003(m) Proof	10,000	Value: 45.00				

Y# 809 3 ROUBLES
34.7400 g., 0.9000 Silver 1.0052 oz. ASW, 38.8 mm. **Subject:** First Kamchatka Expedition **Obv:** Double-headed eagle **Rev:** Natives, fish and ship **Edge:** Reeded

Date	Mintage	F	VF	XF	Unc	BU
2003(sp) Proof	10,000	Value: 45.00				

Y# 810 3 ROUBLES
34.7400 g., 0.9000 Silver 1.0052 oz. ASW, 38.8 mm. **Subject:** Zodiac signs **Obv:** Double-headed eagle within beaded circle **Rev:** Virgo **Edge:** Reeded

Date	Mintage	F	VF	XF	Unc	BU
2003(sp)	30,000	Value: 40.00				

Y# 811 3 ROUBLES
34.7400 g., 0.9000 Silver 1.0052 oz. ASW, 38.8 mm. **Subject:** Zodiac signs **Obv:** Double-headed eagle within beaded circle **Rev:** Libra **Edge:** Reeded

Date	Mintage	F	VF	XF	Unc	BU
2003(m) Proof	30,000	Value: 45.00				

Y# 812 3 ROUBLES
34.7400 g., 0.9000 Silver 1.0052 oz. ASW, 38.8 mm. **Subject:** Diveyevsky Monastery **Obv:** Double-headed eagle **Rev:** Cameo above churches **Edge:** Reeded

Date	Mintage	F	VF	XF	Unc	BU
2003(sp) Proof	10,000	Value: 45.00				

Y# 813 3 ROUBLES
34.7400 g., 0.9000 Silver 1.0052 oz. ASW, 38.8 mm. **Subject:** Zodiac Signs **Obv:** Double-headed eagle within beaded circle **Rev:** Scorpio **Edge:** Reeded

Date	Mintage	F	VF	XF	Unc	BU
2003(m) Proof	30,000	Value: 40.00				

Y# 847 3 ROUBLES
34.5600 g., 0.9000 Silver 100000 oz. ASW, 39 mm. **Rev:** St. Trinity Monastery

Date	Mintage	F	VF	XF	Unc	BU
2003(sp) Proof	10,000	Value: 45.00				

Y# 848 3 ROUBLES
34.5600 g., 0.9000 Silver 100000 oz. ASW, 39 mm. **Subject:** Zodiac Signs **Obv:** Double-headed eagle within beaded circle **Rev:** Sagittarius

Date	Mintage	F	VF	XF	Unc	BU
2003(sp) Proof	30,000	Value: 40.00				

Y# 849 3 ROUBLES
34.5600 g., 0.9000 Silver 100000 oz. ASW, 39 mm. **Subject:** Zodiac Signs **Obv:** Double-headed eagle within beaded circle **Rev:** Capricorn

Date	Mintage	F	VF	XF	Unc	BU
2003(m) Proof	30,000	Value: 40.00				

Y# 1012 3 ROUBLES
33.9000 g., 0.9250 Silver 1.0081 oz. ASW, 39 mm. **Subject:** Year of the Goat

Date	Mintage	F	VF	XF	Unc	BU
2003 Proof	—	Value: 50.00				

Y# 850 3 ROUBLES
34.5600 g., 0.9000 Silver 100000 oz. ASW, 39 mm. **Subject:** Lunar Calendar **Rev:** Monkey

Date	Mintage	F	VF	XF	Unc	BU
2004(m) Proof	15,000	Value: 45.00				

Y# 851 3 ROUBLES
34.5600 g., 0.9000 Silver 100000 oz. ASW, 39 mm. **Subject:** Zodiac Signs **Obv:** Double-headed eagle within beaded circle **Rev:** Aquarius

Date	Mintage	F	VF	XF	Unc	BU
2004(sp) Proof	30,000	Value: 40.00				

Y# 852 3 ROUBLES
34.5600 g., 0.9000 Silver 100000 oz. ASW, 39 mm. **Rev:** Tomsk

Date	Mintage	F	VF	XF	Unc	BU
2004(m) Proof	8,000	Value: 55.00				

Y# 853 3 ROUBLES
34.5600 g., 0.9000 Silver 100000 oz. ASW, 39 mm. **Subject:** Zodiac Signs **Obv:** Double-headed eagle within beaded circle **Rev:** Pisces

Date	Mintage	F	VF	XF	Unc	BU
2004(m) Proof	30,000	Value: 40.00				

Y# 854 3 ROUBLES
34.5600 g., 0.9000 Silver 100000 oz. ASW, 39 mm. **Rev:** Epiphany Cathedral, Moscow

Date	Mintage	F	VF	XF	Unc	BU
2004(m) Proof	8,000	Value: 55.00				

Y# 855 3 ROUBLES
34.5600 g., 0.9000 Silver 100000 oz. ASW, 39 mm. **Subject:** Zodiac Signs **Obv:** Double-headed eagle within beaded circle **Rev:** Aries

Date	Mintage	F	VF	XF	Unc	BU
2004(sp) Proof	30,000	Value: 40.00				

Y# 856 3 ROUBLES
34.5600 g., 0.9000 Silver 100000 oz. ASW, 39 mm. **Rev:** Soccer

Date	Mintage	F	VF	XF	Unc	BU
2004(sp) Proof	10,000	Value: 40.00				

Y# 857 3 ROUBLES
34.5600 g., 0.9000 Silver 100000 oz. ASW, 39 mm. **Subject:** Zodiac Signs **Obv:** Double-headed eagle within beaded circle **Rev:** Taurus

Date	Mintage	F	VF	XF	Unc	BU
2004(sp) Proof	30,000	Value: 40.00				

Y# 858 3 ROUBLES
34.5600 g., 0.9000 Silver 100000 oz. ASW, 39 mm. **Rev:** Olympic torch

Date	Mintage	F	VF	XF	Unc	BU
2004(m) Proof	20,000	Value: 50.00				

Y# 859 3 ROUBLES
34.5600 g., 0.9000 Silver 100000 oz. ASW, 39 mm. **Subject:** Zodiac Signs **Obv:** Double-headed eagle within beaded circle **Rev:** Gemini

Date	Mintage	F	VF	XF	Unc	BU
2004(m) Proof	30,000	Value: 40.00				

Y# 860 3 ROUBLES
34.5600 g., 0.9000 Silver 100000 oz. ASW, 39 mm. **Subject:** Zodiac Signs **Obv:** Double-headed eagle within beaded circle **Rev:** Cancer

Date	Mintage	F	VF	XF	Unc	BU
2004(sp) Proof	30,000	Value: 40.00				

Y# 861 3 ROUBLES
34.5600 g., 0.9000 Silver 100000 oz. ASW, 39 mm. **Rev:** Church of the Sign of the Holy Mother of God

Date	Mintage	F	VF	XF	Unc	BU
2004(m) Proof	8,000	Value: 55.00				

Y# 862 3 ROUBLES
34.5600 g., 0.9000 Silver 100000 oz. ASW, 39 mm. **Rev:** Transfiguration icon

Date	Mintage	F	VF	XF	Unc	BU
2004(m) Proof	8,000	Value: 55.00				

Y# 863 3 ROUBLES
34.5600 g., 0.9000 Silver 100000 oz. ASW, 39 mm. **Rev:** Peter I's monetary reform

Date	Mintage	F	VF	XF	Unc	BU
2004(sp) Proof	8,000	Value: 75.00				

Y# 1013 3 ROUBLES
33.9000 g., 0.9250 Silver 1.0081 oz. ASW, 39 mm. **Subject:** 2nd Kamchatka Expedition, 1733-43

Date	Mintage	F	VF	XF	Unc	BU
2004 Proof	—	Value: 65.00				

Y# 1015 3 ROUBLES
33.9000 g., 0.9250 Silver 1.0081 oz. ASW, 39 mm. **Subject:** Theophanes the Greek

Date	Mintage	F	VF	XF	Unc	BU
2004 Proof	—	Value: 65.00				

Y# 1020 3 ROUBLES
33.9000 g., 0.9250 Silver 1.0081 oz. ASW, 39 mm. **Subject:** Church of the Virgin Nativity in Gordniya

Date	Mintage	F	VF	XF	Unc	BU
2004 Proof	—	Value: 65.00				

Y# 1022 3 ROUBLES
33.9000 g., 0.9250 Silver 1.0081 oz. ASW, 39 mm. **Subject:** Reindeer

Date	Mintage	F	VF	XF	Unc	BU
2004 Proof	—	Value: 70.00				

Y# 892 3 ROUBLES
33.9400 g., 0.9250 Silver 1.0093 oz. ASW, 39 mm. **Obv:** Double-headed eagle **Rev:** Rooster and crescent moon **Edge:** Reeded

Date	Mintage	F	VF	XF	Unc	BU
2005 Proof	15,000	Value: 45.00				

Y# 893 3 ROUBLES
33.9400 g., 0.9250 Silver 1.0093 oz. ASW, 39 mm. **Subject:** 60th Anniversary - Victory Over Germany **Obv:** Double-headed eagle **Rev:** Soldier and wife circa 1945 **Edge:** Reeded

Date	Mintage	F	VF	XF	Unc	BU
2005 Proof	35,000	Value: 40.00				

Y# 903 3 ROUBLES
33.9400 g., 0.9250 Silver 1.0093 oz. ASW, 39 mm. **Obv:** Double-headed eagle **Rev:** St. Nicholas Cathedral in Kaliningrad **Edge:** Reeded

Date	Mintage	F	VF	XF	Unc	BU
2005 Proof	10,000	Value: 50.00				

Y# 904 3 ROUBLES
33.9400 g., 0.9250 Silver 1.0093 oz. ASW, 39 mm. **Obv:** Double-headed eagle **Rev:** Kropotkin Metro Station in Moscow **Edge:** Reeded

Date	Mintage	F	VF	XF	Unc	BU
2005 Proof	10,000	Value: 50.00				

Y# 906 3 ROUBLES
33.9400 g., 0.9250 Silver 1.0093 oz. ASW, 39 mm. **Subject:** Helsinki Games **Obv:** Double-headed eagle **Rev:** Stylized track and field athletes **Edge:** Reeded

Date	Mintage	F	VF	XF	Unc	BU
2005 Proof	10,000	Value: 45.00				

Y# 908 3 ROUBLES
33.9400 g., 0.9250 Silver 1.0093 oz. ASW, 39 mm. **Obv:** Double-headed eagle **Rev:** Virgin Monastery in Raifa, Tatarstan **Edge:** Reeded

Date	Mintage	F	VF	XF	Unc	BU
2005 Proof	10,000	Value: 45.00				

Y# 910 3 ROUBLES
33.9400 g., 0.9250 Silver 1.0093 oz. ASW, 39 mm. **Obv:** Double-headed eagle **Rev:** Kazan Theater Building **Edge:** Reeded

Date	Mintage	F	VF	XF	Unc	BU
2005 Proof	10,000	Value: 50.00				

Y# 923 3 ROUBLES
33.9400 g., 0.9250 Silver 1.0093 oz. ASW, 39 mm. **Subject:** 625th Anniversary - Battle of Kulikovo **Obv:** Double-headed eagle **Rev:** Carved Lion and Griffin between opposing armies **Edge:** Reeded

Date	Mintage	F	VF	XF	Unc	BU
2005 Proof	10,000	Value: 50.00				

Y# 955 3 ROUBLES
33.9400 g., 0.9250 Silver 1.0093 oz. ASW, 39 mm. **Subject:** Moscow's Lomonosov University **Obv:** Two headed eagle **Rev:** Lomonosov statue before university building and Moscow skyline **Edge:** Reeded

Date	Mintage	F	VF	XF	Unc	BU
2005(m) Proof	10,000	Value: 40.00				

Y# 1038 3 ROUBLES
33.9000 g., 0.9250 Silver 1.0081 oz. ASW **Subject:** I. V. Russakov, House of Culture **Shape:** 39

Date	Mintage	F	VF	XF	Unc	BU
2005 Proof	—	Value: 60.00				

Y# 1039 3 ROUBLES
33.9000 g., 0.9250 Silver 1.0081 oz. ASW, 39 mm. **Subject:** Novosibirsk State Academic Opera & Ballet

Date	Mintage	F	VF	XF	Unc	BU
2005 Proof	—	Value: 60.00				

Y# 1040 3 ROUBLES
33.9000 g., 0.9250 Silver 1.0081 oz. ASW, 39 mm. **Subject:** Year of the Rooster

Date	Mintage	F	VF	XF	Unc	BU
2006 Proof	—	Value: 60.00				

Y# 1041 3 ROUBLES
33.9000 g., 0.9250 Silver 1.0081 oz. ASW, 39 mm. **Subject:** Parliament, 100th Anniversary

Date	Mintage	F	VF	XF	Unc	BU
2006 Proof	—	Value: 60.00				

Y# 1046 3 ROUBLES
33.9000 g., 0.9250 Silver 1.0081 oz. ASW, 39 mm. **Subject:** Tretyakov State Gallery, 150th Anniversary

Date	Mintage	F	VF	XF	Unc	BU
2006 Proof	—	Value: 60.00				

Y# 1048 3 ROUBLES
33.9000 g., 0.9250 Silver 1.0081 oz. ASW **Subject:** Russia Savings **Shape:** 39

Date	Mintage	F	VF	XF	Unc	BU
2006 Proof	—	Value: 60.00				

Y# 1052 3 ROUBLES
169.0000 g., 0.9250 Silver 5.0258 oz. ASW, 60 mm. **Subject:** State bank Building, Nizhny Novgorod

Date	Mintage	F	VF	XF	Unc	BU
2006 Proof	—	Value: 275				

Y# 1060 3 ROUBLES
33.9000 g., 0.9250 Silver 1.0081 oz. ASW, 33 mm. **Subject:** Moscow's Kremlin and Red Square

Date	Mintage	F	VF	XF	Unc	BU
2006 Proof	—	Value: 70.00				

Y# 1065 3 ROUBLES
33.9000 g., 0.9250 Silver 1.0081 oz. ASW, 39 mm. **Subject:** XX Winter Olympics, Torino

Date	Mintage	F	VF	XF	Unc	BU
2006 Proof	12,500	Value: 95.00				

Y# 1066 3 ROUBLES
33.9000 g., 0.9250 Silver 1.0081 oz. ASW, 39 mm. **Subject:** FIFA World Cup, Germany

Date	Mintage	F	VF	XF	Unc	BU
2006 Proof	—	Value: 75.00				

Y# 1079 3 ROUBLES
33.9000 g., 0.9250 Silver 1.0081 oz. ASW, 39 mm. **Subject:** Year of the Dog

Date	Mintage	F	VF	XF	Unc	BU
2006 Proof	—	Value: 60.00				

Y# 966 3 ROUBLES
33.9400 g., 0.9250 Silver 1.0093 oz. ASW, 39.0 mm. **Subject:** 250th Anniversary Academy of the Arts **Obv:** Two-headed eagle **Rev:** Relief image of Minerva group **Rev. Legend:** РОССИЙСКАЯ - АКАДЕМИЯ ХУДОЖЕСТВ **Edge:** Reeded

Date	Mintage	F	VF	XF	Unc	BU
2007(m) Proof	10,000	Value: 50.00				

Y# 1080 3 ROUBLES
33.9000 g., 0.9250 Silver 1.0081 oz. ASW, 39 mm. **Subject:** International Arctic Year

Date	Mintage	F	VF	XF	Unc	BU
2007 Proof	—	Value: 60.00				

Y# 1086 3 ROUBLES
33.9000 g., 0.9250 Silver 1.0081 oz. ASW, 39 mm. **Subject:** Academy of Arts, 250th Anniversary

Date	Mintage	F	VF	XF	Unc	BU
2007 Proof	—	Value: 60.00				

Y# 1087 3 ROUBLES
33.9000 g., 0.9250 Silver 1.0081 oz. ASW **Subject:** First Artificial Earth Satellite, 50th Anniversary

Date	Mintage	F	VF	XF	Unc	BU
2007 Proof	—	Value: 60.00				

Y# 1088 3 ROUBLES
33.9000 g., 0.9250 Silver 1.0081 oz. ASW, 39 mm. **Subject:** Andrew Rublyov

Date	Mintage	F	VF	XF	Unc	BU
2007 Proof	—	Value: 60.00				

Y# 1092 3 ROUBLES
33.9000 g., 0.9250 Silver 1.0081 oz. ASW, 39 mm. **Subject:** Bashkira, 450th Anniversary of annexation by Russia

Date	Mintage	F	VF	XF	Unc	BU
2007 Proof	—	Value: 60.00				

Y# 1100 3 ROUBLES
33.9000 g., 0.9250 Silver 1.0081 oz. ASW **Subject:** Nevyansk inclined tower, Sverdlorsk Region

Date	Mintage	F	VF	XF	Unc	BU
2007 Proof	—	Value: 60.00				

Y# 1103 3 ROUBLES

33.9000 g., 0.9250 Silver 1.0081 oz. ASW, 39 mm. **Subject:** Kazan Railway Station, Moscow

Date	Mintage	F	VF	XF	Unc	BU
2007 Proof	—	Value: 60.00				

Y# 1114 3 ROUBLES

33.9000 g., 0.9250 Silver 1.0081 oz. ASW, 39 mm. **Subject:** Year of the Rat

Date	Mintage	F	VF	XF	Unc	BU
2007 Proof	—	Value: 60.00				

Y# 1113 3 ROUBLES

33.9000 g., 0.9250 Silver 1.0081 oz. ASW, 39 mm. **Subject:** Year of the Boar

Date	Mintage	F	VF	XF	Unc	BU
2008 Proof	—	Value: 60.00				

Y# 1115 3 ROUBLES

33.9000 g., 0.9250 Silver 1.0081 oz. ASW, 39 mm. **Subject:** Russian Postage Stamp - 150th Anniversary of Introduction

Date	Mintage	F	VF	XF	Unc	BU
2008 Proof	—	Value: 60.00				

Y# 1118 3 ROUBLES

33.9000 g., 0.9250 Silver 1.0081 oz. ASW, 39 mm. **Subject:** I. M. Schenov Medical Academy, 250th Anniversary

Date	Mintage	F	VF	XF	Unc	BU
2008 Proof	—	Value: 60.00				

Y# 1119 3 ROUBLES

33.9000 g., 0.9250 Silver 1.0081 oz. ASW, 39 mm. **Subject:** Udmurtiya, 450th Anniversary of annexation into Russia

Date	Mintage	F	VF	XF	Unc	BU
2008 Proof	—	Value: 60.00				

Y# 1124 3 ROUBLES

33.9000 g., 0.9250 Silver 1.0081 oz. ASW, 39 mm. **Subject:** Cathedral of St. Demetrius, Vladimir

Date	Mintage	F	VF	XF	Unc	BU
2008 Proof	—	Value: 60.00				

Y# 1126 3 ROUBLES

33.9000 g., 0.9250 Silver 1.0081 oz. ASW, 39 mm. **Subject:** N. I. Sevastyanov, House of Trade Unions

Date	Mintage	F	VF	XF	Unc	BU
2008 Proof	—	Value: 60.00				

Y# 1127 3 ROUBLES

33.9000 g., 0.9250 Silver 1.0081 oz. ASW, 39 mm. **Subject:** Cathedral of the Nativity of our Lady, Snetogorsk

Date	Mintage	F	VF	XF	Unc	BU
2008 Proof	—	Value: 60.00				

Y# 1128 3 ROUBLES

33.9000 g., 0.9250 Silver 1.0081 oz. ASW, 39 mm. **Subject:** Assumption Church (Admiralty's)

Date	Mintage	F	VF	XF	Unc	BU
2008 Proof	—	Value: 60.00				

Y# 1129 3 ROUBLES

33.9000 g., 0.9250 Silver 1.0081 oz. ASW, 39 mm. **Subject:** St. Nicholas Cathedral, Yakutsk

Date	Mintage	F	VF	XF	Unc	BU
2008 Proof	—	Value: 60.00				

Y# 1130 3 ROUBLES

33.9000 g., 0.9250 Silver 1.0081 oz. ASW, 39 mm. **Subject:** St. Vladimir Cathedral, Zadonsk

Date	Mintage	F	VF	XF	Unc	BU
2008 Proof	—	Value: 60.00				

Y# 1138 3 ROUBLES

33.9000 g., 0.9250 Silver 1.0081 oz. ASW, 39 mm. **Subject:** European Beaver

Date	Mintage	F	VF	XF	Unc	BU
2008 Proof	—	Value: 60.00				

Y# 1147 3 ROUBLES

33.9000 g., 0.9250 Silver 1.0081 oz. ASW, 39 mm. **Subject:** Kamchatka Volcano

Date	Mintage	F	VF	XF	Unc	BU
2008 Proof	—	Value: 60.00				

Y# 1150 3 ROUBLES

33.9000 g., 0.9250 Silver 1.0081 oz. ASW, 39 mm. **Subject:** World walking Race Cup, Cheboksary

Date	Mintage	F	VF	XF	Unc	BU
2008 Proof	—	Value: 60.00				

Y# 1152 3 ROUBLES

33.9000 g., 0.9250 Silver 1.0081 oz. ASW, 39 mm. **Subject:** 29th Summer Olympics Bejing

Date	Mintage	F	VF	XF	Unc	BU
2008 Proof	—	Value: 60.00				

Y# 992 3 ROUBLES

Silver, 39 mm. **Subject:** Year of the Bull **Obv:** Double headed eagle **Rev:** Stylized bull

Date	Mintage	F	VF	XF	Unc	BU
2009 Proof	—	Value: 50.00				

Y# 1159 3 ROUBLES

33.9000 g., 0.9250 Silver 1.0081 oz. ASW, 39 mm. **Subject:** Moon research, 50th Anniversary

Date	Mintage	F	VF	XF	Unc	BU
2009 Proof	—	Value: 60.00				

Y# 1161 3 ROUBLES

33.9000 g., 0.9250 Silver 1.0081 oz. ASW, 39 mm. **Subject:** Russian Currency

Date	Mintage	F	VF	XF	Unc	BU
2009 Proof	—	Value: 60.00				

Y# 1166 3 ROUBLES

33.9000 g., 0.9250 Silver 1.0081 oz. ASW, 39 mm. **Subject:** A. P. Chekhov, 150th Anniversary of Birth

Date	Mintage	F	VF	XF	Unc	BU
2009 Proof	—	Value: 60.00				

Y# 1170 3 ROUBLES

33.9000 g., 0.9250 Silver 1.0081 oz. ASW, 39 mm. **Subject:** Kalmyk Peoples, 400th Anniversary of annexation into Russia

Date	Mintage	F	VF	XF	Unc	BU
2009 Proof	—	Value: 60.00				

Y# 1173 3 ROUBLES

33.9000 g., 0.9250 Silver 1.0081 oz. ASW, 39 mm. **Subject:** N. V. Gogol, 200th Anniversary of Birth

Date	Mintage	F	VF	XF	Unc	BU
2009 Proof	—	Value: 60.00				

Y# 1177 3 ROUBLES

33.9000 g., 0.9250 Silver 1.0081 oz. ASW, 39 mm. **Subject:** Poltava Battle, 300th Anniversary

Date	Mintage	F	VF	XF	Unc	BU
2009 Proof	—	Value: 60.00				

Y# 1180 3 ROUBLES

33.9000 g., 0.9250 Silver 1.0081 oz. ASW, 39 mm. **Subject:** St. George the victorious

Date	Mintage	F	VF	XF	Unc	BU
2009 Proof	—	Value: 60.00				

Y# 1182 3 ROUBLES

33.9000 g., 0.9250 Silver 1.0081 oz. ASW, 39 mm. **Subject:** Vitebsky Railway Station, St. Petersburg

Date	Mintage	F	VF	XF	Unc	BU
2009 Proof	—	Value: 60.00				

Y# 1183 3 ROUBLES

33.9000 g., 0.9250 Silver 1.0081 oz. ASW, 39 mm. **Subject:** Tula Kremlin

Date	Mintage	F	VF	XF	Unc	BU
2009 Proof	—	Value: 60.00				

Y# 1185 3 ROUBLES

33.9000 g., 0.9250 Silver 1.0081 oz. ASW, 39 mm. **Subject:** Odygitriya Church

Date	Mintage	F	VF	XF	Unc	BU
2009 Proof	—	Value: 60.00				

Y# 1188 3 ROUBLES

33.9000 g., 0.9250 Silver 1.0081 oz. ASW, 39 mm. **Subject:** Intercession Cathedral, Voronezsh

Date	Mintage	F	VF	XF	Unc	BU
2009 Proof	—	Value: 60.00				

Y# 1189 3 ROUBLES

33.9000 g., 0.9250 Silver 1.0081 oz. ASW, 39 mm. **Subject:** Tales of the Russian People

Date	Mintage	F	VF	XF	Unc	BU
2009 Proof	—	Value: 60.00				

Y# 1199 3 ROUBLES

33.9000 g., 0.9250 Silver 1.0081 oz. ASW, 39 mm. **Subject:** Velikly Novgorod

Date	Mintage	F	VF	XF	Unc	BU
2009 Proof	—	Value: 60.00				

Y# 1207 3 ROUBLES

33.9000 g., 0.9250 Silver 1.0081 oz. ASW, 39 mm. **Subject:** Fauna - Bear

Date	Mintage	F	VF	XF	Unc	BU
2009 Proof	—	Value: 60.00				

Y# 1208 3 ROUBLES

33.9000 g., 0.9250 Silver 1.0081 oz. ASW, 39 mm. **Series:** Year of the Tiger

Date	Mintage	F	VF	XF	Unc	BU
2009 Proof	—	Value: 60.00				

Y# 1214 3 ROUBLES

31.1050 g., 0.9990 Silver 0.9990 oz. ASW **Subject:** St. George the Victorious

Date	Mintage	F	VF	XF	Unc	BU
2010 Proof	—	Value: 55.00				

Y# 1219 3 ROUBLES

33.9000 g., 0.9250 Silver 1.0081 oz. ASW, 39 mm. **Subject:** Savior's Transfiguration Cathedral, Bolkhov

Date	Mintage	F	VF	XF	Unc	BU
2010 Proof	—	Value: 55.00				

Y# 1220 3 ROUBLES

33.9000 g., 0.9250 Silver 1.0081 oz. ASW, 39 mm. **Subject:** Vovnushki Battle tower

Date	Mintage	F	VF	XF	Unc	BU
2010 Proof	—	Value: 55.00				

Y# 1221 3 ROUBLES

16.8000 g., 0.9250 Silver 0.4996 oz. ASW, 33 mm. **Subject:** Holy Trinity Church, St. Petersburg

Date	Mintage	F	VF	XF	Unc	BU
2010 Proof	—	Value: 35.00				

Y# 1222 3 ROUBLES

33.9000 g., 0.9250 Silver 1.0081 oz. ASW, 39 mm. **Subject:** Round Square, Petrozavodsk

Date	Mintage	F	VF	XF	Unc	BU
2010 Proof	—	Value: 55.00				

Y# 1228 3 ROUBLES

33.9000 g., 0.9250 Silver 1.0081 oz. ASW, 39 mm. **Subject:** Bank of Russia, 150th Anniversary

Date	Mintage	F	VF	XF	Unc	BU
2010 Proof	—	Value: 55.00				

Y# 1232 3 ROUBLES

33.9000 g., 0.9250 Silver 1.0081 oz. ASW, 39 mm. **Subject:** UNESCO Heritage Site - Yaroslav

Date	Mintage	F	VF	XF	Unc	BU
2010 Proof	—	Value: 55.00				

Y# 1237 3 ROUBLES

33.9000 g., 0.9250 Silver 1.0081 oz. ASW, 39 mm. **Subject:** A. P. Chekhov, 200th Anniversary of Birth

Date	Mintage	F	VF	XF	Unc	BU
2010 Proof	—	Value: 55.00				

Y# 1241 3 ROUBLES

31.1000 g., 0.9250 Silver 0.9249 oz. ASW **Subject:** Great Patriotic War, 65th Anniversary

Date	Mintage	F	VF	XF	Unc	BU
2010 Proof	—	Value: 55.00				

Y# 1242 3 ROUBLES

33.9000 g., 0.9250 Silver 1.0081 oz. ASW, 39 mm. **Subject:** Great Patrotic War, 65th Anniversary

Date	Mintage	F	VF	XF	Unc	BU
2010 Proof	—	Value: 55.00				

Y# 1243 3 ROUBLES

33.9000 g., 0.9250 Silver 1.0081 oz. ASW, 39 mm. **Subject:** Great Patrotic War, 65th Anniversary

Date	Mintage	F	VF	XF	Unc	BU
2010 Proof	—	Value: 55.00				

Y# 1247 3 ROUBLES

33.9000 g., 0.9250 Silver 1.0081 oz. ASW, 39 mm. **Subject:** Year of the Rabbit

Date	Mintage	F	VF	XF	Unc	BU
2010 Proof	—	Value: 55.00				

Y# 1251 3 ROUBLES

33.9000 g., 0.9250 Silver 1.0081 oz. ASW, 39 mm. **Subject:** EAEC, 10th Anniversary

Date	Mintage	F	VF	XF	Unc	BU
2010 Proof	—	Value: 55.00				

Y# 1252 3 ROUBLES

33.9000 g., 0.9250 Silver 1.0081 oz. ASW, 39 mm. **Subject:** EAEC, National Costumes

Date	Mintage	F	VF	XF	Unc	BU
2010 Proof	—	Value: 55.00				

Y# 1265 3 ROUBLES

31.1000 g., 0.9250 Silver 0.9249 oz. ASW **Subject:** Russian Census

Date	Mintage	F	VF	XF	Unc	BU
2010 Proof	—	Value: 55.00				

Y# 1273 3 ROUBLES

33.9000 g., 0.9250 Silver 1.0081 oz. ASW, 39 mm. **Subject:** 39th World Chess Olympics

Date	Mintage	F	VF	XF	Unc	BU
2010 Proof	—	Value: 55.00				

Y# 799 5 ROUBLES

6.4500 g., Copper-Nickel Clad Copper, 25 mm. **Obv:** Two headed eagle, curved bank name and denomination below **Edge:** Segmented reeding

Date	Mintage	F	VF	XF	Unc	BU
2002ММД In sets only	15,000	—	—	—	—	—
2002СПМД In sets only	15,000	—	—	—	—	—
2003ММД	15,000	—	—	150	200	250
2008ММД	—	—	—	—	3.00	4.00
2008СПМД	—	—	—	—	3.00	4.00
2009ММД	—	—	—	—	3.00	4.00
2009СПМД	—	—	—	—	3.00	4.00

Y# 829 5 ROUBLES

47.2400 g., Bi-Metallic .900 Silver 21.34g center in .900 Gold 25.9g ring, 39.5 mm. **Obv:** Double-headed eagle **Rev:** Uglich city view **Edge:** Reeded

Date	Mintage	F	VF	XF	Unc	BU
2004(sp) Proof	5,000	Value: 950				

Y# 1076 5 ROUBLES

47.2400 g., 0.9000 Silver .900 Silver 21.34g center in .900 Gold 25.9g ring 1.3669 oz. ASW, 39.5 mm. **Subject:** City of Turyev-Polsky

Date	Mintage	F	VF	XF	Unc	BU
2006 Proof	250	Value: 950				

Y# 1154 5 ROUBLES

47.2400 g., 0.9000 Silver .900 Silver 21.34g center in .900 Gold 25.9g ring 1.3669 oz. ASW, 39.5 mm. **Subject:** Pereslavl Zalessky

Date	Mintage	F	VF	XF	Unc	BU
2008 Proof	1,000	Value: 1,150				

Y# 1155 5 ROUBLES

47.2400 g., 0.9000 Silver .900 Silver 21.34g center in .900 Gold 25.9g ring 1.3669 oz. ASW, 39.5 mm. **Subject:** Alexandrov

Date	Mintage	F	VF	XF	Unc	BU
2008 Proof	—	Value: 1,150				

Y# 799a 5 ROUBLES

6.0000 g., Nickel Plated Steel, 25 mm. **Obv:** Two headed eagle, curved bank name and denomination below

Date	Mintage	F	VF	XF	Unc	BU
2009ММД	—	—	—	—	2.00	3.00
2009СПМД	—	—	—	—	2.00	3.00
2010ММД	—	—	—	—	2.00	3.00
2010СПМД	—	—	—	—	2.00	3.00

Y# 676 10 ROUBLES

8.2200 g., Bi-Metallic Copper-Nickel center in Brass ring, 27 mm. **Subject:** Yuri Gagarin **Obv:** Value with latent image in zero within circle and sprigs **Rev:** Helmeted bust 1/4 right **Edge:** Reeding over denomination

Date	Mintage	F	VF	XF	Unc	BU
2001ММД	10,000,000	—	—	—	4.00	5.00
2001СПМД	10,000,000	—	—	—	4.00	5.00

Y# 686 10 ROUBLES

1.6100 g., 0.9990 Gold 0.0517 oz. AGW, 12 mm. **Subject:** Bolshoi Theater 225 Years **Obv:** Double-headed eagle within circle **Rev:** Building above number 225 **Edge:** Reeded

Date	Mintage	F	VF	XF	Unc	BU
2001 Proof	3,000	Value: 95.00				

Y# 739 10 ROUBLES

8.2200 g., Bi-Metallic Copper-Nickel center in Brass ring, 27 mm. **Subject:** Ancient Towns - Derbent **Obv:** Value with latent image in zero within circle and sprigs **Rev:** Shield above walled city view **Edge:** Reeding over denomination

Date	Mintage	F	VF	XF	Unc	BU
2002ММД	5,000,000	—	—	—	4.00	5.00

Y# 740 10 ROUBLES

8.2200 g., Bi-Metallic Copper-Nickel center in Brass ring, 27 mm. **Subject:** Ancient Towns - Kostroma **Obv:** Value with latent image in zero within circle and sprigs **Rev:** Cupola, shield and river view **Edge:** Reeding over denomination

Date	Mintage	F	VF	XF	Unc	BU
2002СПМД	5,000,000	—	—	—	4.00	6.00

Y# 741 10 ROUBLES

8.2200 g., Bi-Metallic Copper-Nickel center in Brass ring, 27 mm. **Subject:** Ancient Towns - Staraya Russa **Obv:** Value with latent image in zero within circle and sprigs **Rev:** Shield and cathedral **Edge:** Reeding over denomination

Date	Mintage	F	VF	XF	Unc	BU
2002СПМД	5,000,000	—	—	—	4.00	6.00

Y# 748 10 ROUBLES

8.2200 g., Bi-Metallic Copper-Nickel center in Brass ring, 27 mm. **Subject:** Ministry of Education **Obv:** Value with latent image in zero within circle and sprigs **Rev:** Seedling within open book **Edge:** Reeding over denomination

Date	Mintage	F	VF	XF	Unc	BU
2002ММД	5,000,000	—	—	—	4.00	6.00

Y# 749 10 ROUBLES

8.2200 g., Bi-Metallic Copper-Nickel center in Brass ring, 27 mm. **Subject:** Ministry of Finance **Obv:** Value with latent image in zero within circle and sprigs **Rev:** Caduceus within monogram **Edge:** Reeding over denomination

Date	Mintage	F	VF	XF	Unc	BU
2002СПМД	5,000,000	—	—	—	4.00	6.00

Y# 750 10 ROUBLES

8.2200 g., Bi-Metallic Copper-Nickel center in Brass ring, 27 mm. **Subject:** Ministry of Economic Development and Trade **Obv:** Value with latent image in zero within circle and sprigs **Rev:** Crowned double-headed eagle with cornucopia and caduceus **Edge:** Reeding over denomination

Date	Mintage	F	VF	XF	Unc	BU
2002СПМД	5,000,000	—	—	—	4.00	6.00

Y# 751 10 ROUBLES

8.2200 g., Bi-Metallic Copper-Nickel center in Brass ring, 27 mm. **Subject:** Ministry of Foreign Affairs **Obv:** Value with latent image in zero within circle and sprigs **Rev:** Crowned double-headed eagle above crossed sprigs **Edge:** Reeding over denomination

Date	Mintage	F	VF	XF	Unc	BU
2002СПМД	5,000,000	—	—	—	4.00	6.00

Y# 752 10 ROUBLES

8.2200 g., Bi-Metallic Copper-Nickel center in Brass ring, 27 mm. **Subject:** Ministry of Internal Affairs **Obv:** Value with latent image in zero within circle and sprigs **Rev:** Crowned double-headed eagle with round breast shield **Edge:** Reeding over denomination

Date	Mintage	F	VF	XF	Unc	BU
2002ММД	5,000,000	—	—	—	4.00	6.00

Y# 753 10 ROUBLES

8.2200 g., Bi-Metallic Copper-Nickel center in Brass ring, 27 mm. **Subject:** Ministry of Justice **Obv:** Value with latent image in zero within circle and sprigs **Rev:** Crowned double-headed eagle with column on breast shield **Edge:** Reeding over denomination

Date	Mintage	F	VF	XF	Unc	BU
2002СПМД	5,000,000	—	—	—	4.00	6.00

Y# 754 10 ROUBLES

8.2200 g., Bi-Metallic Copper-Nickel center in Brass ring, 27 mm. **Subject:** Russian Armed Forces **Obv:** Value with latent image in zero within circle and sprigs **Rev:** Crowned double-headed eagle with crowned pointed top shield **Edge:** Reeding over denomination

Date	Mintage	F	VF	XF	Unc	BU
2002ММД	5,000,000	—	—	—	4.00	6.00

Y# 817 10 ROUBLES

8.3400 g., Bi-Metallic Copper-Nickel center in Brass ring, 27 mm. **Obv:** Value with latent image in zero within circle and sprigs **Rev:** Murom city view and tilted oval shields within circle **Edge:** Reeded and lettered

Date	Mintage	F	VF	XF	Unc	BU
2003(sp)	5,000,000	—	—	—	4.00	6.00

Y# 800 10 ROUBLES

8.4400 g., Bi-Metallic Copper-Nickel center in Brass ring, 27.1 mm. **Subject:** Pskov **Obv:** Value with latent image in zero within circle and sprigs **Rev:** Shield above walled city **Edge:** Reeding over lettering

Date	Mintage	F	VF	XF	Unc	BU
2003СПМД	5,000,000	—	—	—	4.00	6.00

Y# 818 10 ROUBLES

8.3400 g., Bi-Metallic Copper-Nickel center in Brass ring, 27 mm. **Obv:** Value with latent image in zero within circle and sprigs **Rev:** Kasimov city view and shield within circle **Edge:** Reeded and lettered

Date	Mintage	F	VF	XF	Unc	BU
2003СПМД	5,000,000	—	—	—	4.00	6.00

Y# 819 10 ROUBLES
8.3400 g., Bi-Metallic Copper-Nickel center in Brass ring, 27 mm. **Subject:** Dorogobuzh **Obv:** Value with latent image in zero within circle and sprigs **Rev:** Monument, city view and shield within circle **Edge:** Reeded and lettered

Date	Mintage	F	VF	XF	Unc	BU
2003ММД	5,000,000	—	—	—	4.00	6.00

Y# 824 10 ROUBLES
8.4600 g., Bi-Metallic Copper-Nickel center in Brass ring, 27.1 mm. **Subject:** Town of Ryazhsk **Obv:** Value with latent image in zero within circle and sprigs **Obv. Legend:** БАНК РОССИИ **Rev:** City view and crowned shield within circle **Edge:** Reeded and lettered

Date	Mintage	F	VF	XF	Unc	BU
2004ММД	—	—	—	—	4.00	6.00

Y# 825 10 ROUBLES
8.4600 g., Bi-Metallic Copper-Nickel center in Brass ring, 27.1 mm. **Subject:** Town of Dmitrov **Obv:** Value with latent image in zero within circle and sprigs **Obv. Legend:** БАНК РОССИИ **Rev:** City view and crowned shield within circle **Edge:** Reeded and lettered

Date	Mintage	F	VF	XF	Unc	BU
2004ММД	5,000,000	—	—	—	4.00	6.00

Y# 826 10 ROUBLES
8.4600 g., Bi-Metallic Copper-Nickel center in Brass ring, 27.1 mm. **Subject:** Town of Kem **Obv:** Value with latent image in zero within circle and sprigs **Obv. Legend:** БАНК РОССИИ **Rev:** City view and crowned shield within circle **Edge:** Reeded and lettered

Date	Mintage	F	VF	XF	Unc	BU
2004СПМД	5,000,000	—	—	—	4.00	6.00

Y# 827 10 ROUBLES
8.4000 g., Bi-Metallic Copper-Nickel center in brass ring, 27 mm. **Subject:** Great Victory, 60th Anniversary **Obv:** Value with latent image in zero within circle and sprigs **Rev:** WWII eternal flame monument above date and sprig within circle **Edge:** Reeded and Lettered

Date	Mintage	F	VF	XF	Unc	BU
2005ММД	30,000,000	—	—	—	4.00	6.00
2005СПМД	30,000,000	—	—	—	4.00	6.00

Y# 886 10 ROUBLES
8.2300 g., Bi-Metallic Copper-Nickel center in Brass ring, 27 mm. **Obv:** Value with latent image in zero within circle and sprigs **Rev:** Moscow coat of arms within circle **Edge:** Reeded and lettered

Date	Mintage	F	VF	XF	Unc	BU
2005ММД	10,000,000	—	—	—	4.00	6.00

Y# 887 10 ROUBLES
8.2300 g., Bi-Metallic Copper-Nickel center in Brass ring, 27 mm. **Obv:** Value with latent image in zero within circle and sprigs **Rev:** Leningrad Oblast coat of arms within circle **Edge:** Reeded and lettered

Date	Mintage	F	VF	XF	Unc	BU
2005СПМД	10,000,000	—	—	—	4.00	6.00

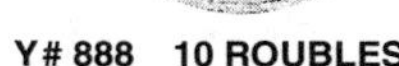

Y# 888 10 ROUBLES
8.2300 g., Bi-Metallic Copper-Nickel center in Brass ring, 27 mm. **Obv:** Value with latent image in zero within circle and sprigs **Rev:** Tverskaya arms within circle **Edge:** Reeded and lettered

Date	Mintage	F	VF	XF	Unc	BU
2005ММД	10,000,000	—	—	—	4.00	6.00

Y# 889 10 ROUBLES
8.2300 g., Bi-Metallic Copper-Nickel center in Brass ring, 27 mm. **Obv:** Value with latent image in zero within circle and sprigs **Rev:** Krasnodarskiy Kray coat of arms **Edge:** Reeded and lettered

Date	Mintage	F	VF	XF	Unc	BU
2005(m)	10,000,000	—	—	—	4.00	6.00

Y# 890 10 ROUBLES
8.2300 g., Bi-Metallic Copper-Nickel center in Brass ring, 27 mm. **Obv:** Value with latent image in zero within circle and sprigs **Rev:** Orlovskaya Oblast coat of arms within circle **Edge:** Reeded and lettered

Date	Mintage	F	VF	XF	Unc	BU
2005(m)	10,000,000	—	—	—	4.00	6.00

Y# 891 10 ROUBLES
8.2300 g., Bi-Metallic Copper-Nickel center in Brass ring, 27 mm. **Obv:** Value with latent image in zero within circle and sprigs **Rev:** Tatarstan Republic coat of arms within circle **Edge:** Reeded and lettered

Date	Mintage	F	VF	XF	Unc	BU
2005СПМД	10,000,000	—	—	—	4.00	6.00

Y# 943 10 ROUBLES
8.2300 g., Bi-Metallic Copper-Nickel center in Brass ring, 27.1 mm. **Obv:** Large value **Rev:** City of Kazan and arms

Date	Mintage	F	VF	XF	Unc	BU
2005СПМД	5,000,000	—	—	—	4.00	6.00

Y# 944 10 ROUBLES
8.2300 g., Bi-Metallic Copper-Nickel center in Brass ring, 27.1 mm. **Obv:** Large value **Rev:** City of Borovsk and arms

Date	Mintage	F	VF	XF	Unc	BU
2005СПМД	5,000,000	—	—	—	4.00	6.00

Y# 945 10 ROUBLES
8.2300 g., Bi-Metallic Copper-Nickel center in Brass ring, 27.1 mm. **Obv:** Large value **Rev:** City of Mzensk and shield

Date	Mintage	F	VF	XF	Unc	BU
2005ММД	5,000,000	—	—	—	4.00	6.00

Y# 946 10 ROUBLES
8.2300 g., Bi-Metallic Copper-Nickel center in Brass ring, 27.1 mm. **Obv:** Large value **Rev:** City of Kaliningrad and shield

Date	Mintage	F	VF	XF	Unc	BU
2005ММД	5,000,000	—	—	—	4.00	6.00

Y# 938 10 ROUBLES

8.2300 g., Bi-Metallic Copper-Nickel center in Brass ring, 27 mm. **Obv:** Value with latent image in zero within circle and sprigs **Rev:** Republic of Altai arms **Edge:** Lettered and reeded

Date	Mintage	F	VF	XF	Unc	BU
2006СПМД	10,000,000	—	—	—	4.00	6.00

Y# 939 10 ROUBLES

8.2300 g., Bi-Metallic Copper-Nickel center in Brass ring, 27 mm. **Obv:** Value with latent image in zero within circle and sprigs **Rev:** Chita Region arms **Edge:** Lettered and reeded

Date	Mintage	F	VF	XF	Unc	BU
2006СПМД	10,000,000	—	—	—	4.00	6.00

Y# 940 10 ROUBLES

8.2300 g., Bi-Metallic Copper-Nickel center in Brass ring, 27 mm. **Obv:** Value with latent image in zero within circle and sprigs **Rev:** Primorskij Kraj Maritime Territory coat of arms **Edge:** Lettered and reeded

Date	Mintage	F	VF	XF	Unc	BU
2006ММД	10,000,000	—	—	—	4.00	6.00

Y# 941 10 ROUBLES

8.2300 g., Bi-Metallic Copper-Nickel center in Brass ring, 27 mm. **Obv:** Value with latent image in zero within circle and sprigs **Rev:** Sakha (Yakutiya) Republic coat of arms **Edge:** Lettered and reeded

Date	Mintage	F	VF	XF	Unc	BU
2006СПМД	10,000,000	—	—	—	4.00	6.00

Y# 942 10 ROUBLES

8.2300 g., Bi-Metallic Copper-Nickel center in Brass ring, 27 mm. **Obv:** Value with latent image in zero within circle and sprigs **Rev:** Sakhalinskaya Oblast coat of arms **Edge:** Lettered and reeded

Date	Mintage	F	VF	XF	Unc	BU
2006ММД	10,000,000	—	—	—	4.00	6.00

Y# 947 10 ROUBLES

8.2300 g., Bi-Metallic Copper-Nickel center in Brass ring, 27.1 mm. **Obv:** Large value **Rev:** City of Belgorod and shield

Date	Mintage	F	VF	XF	Unc	BU
2006ММД	5,000,000	—	—	—	4.00	6.00

Y# 948 10 ROUBLES

8.2300 g., Bi-Metallic Copper-Nickel center in Brass ring, 27.1 mm. **Obv:** Large value **Rev:** City of Kargopol and shield

Date	Mintage	F	VF	XF	Unc	BU
2006ММД	5,000,000	—	—	—	4.00	6.00

Y# 949 10 ROUBLES

8.2300 g., Bi-Metallic Copper-Nickel center in Brass ring, 27.1 mm. **Obv:** Large value **Rev:** City of Turzhok and shield

Date	Mintage	F	VF	XF	Unc	BU
2006СПМД	5,000,000	—	—	—	4.00	6.00

Y# 963 10 ROUBLES

8.3000 g., Bi-Metallic Copper-Nickel center in Brass ring, 27 mm. **Obv:** Value with latent image in zero within circle and sprays **Rev:** Vologda church **Edge:** Reeded and lettered **Edge Lettering:** Denomination repeated

Date	Mintage	F	VF	XF	Unc	BU
2007ММД	2,500,000	—	—	—	4.00	6.00
2007СПМД	2,500,000	—	—	—	4.00	6.00

Y# 964 10 ROUBLES

8.3000 g., Bi-Metallic Copper-Nickel center in Brass ring, 27 mm. **Obv:** Value with latent image in zero within circle and sprays **Rev:** Veliky Ustyug city view **Edge:** Reeded and lettered **Edge Lettering:** Denomination repeated

Date	Mintage	F	VF	XF	Unc	BU
2007ММД	2,500,000	—	—	—	4.00	6.00
2007СПМД	2,500,000	—	—	—	4.00	6.00

Y# 965 10 ROUBLES

8.3000 g., Bi-Metallic Copper-Nickel center in Brass ring, 27 mm. **Obv:** Value with latent image in zero within circle and sprays **Rev:** Gdov church **Edge:** Reeded and lettered **Edge Lettering:** Denomination repeated

Date	Mintage	F	VF	XF	Unc	BU
2007ММД	2,500,000	—	—	—	4.00	6.00
2007СПМД	2,500,000	—	—	—	4.00	6.00

Y# 970 10 ROUBLES

8.5700 g., Bi-Metallic Copper-Nickel center in Brass ring, 27.08 mm. **Obv:** Value with latent image in zero within circle and sprays **Obv. Legend:** БАНК РОССИИ **Rev:** Rostovskaya Oblast arms **Edge:** Reeded and lettered **Edge Lettering:** Denomination repeated

Date	Mintage	F	VF	XF	Unc	BU
2007СПМД	10,000,000	—	—	—	4.00	6.00

Y# 971 10 ROUBLES

8.5700 g., Bi-Metallic Copper-Nickel center in Brass ring, 27.08 mm. **Obv:** Value with latent image in zero within circle and sprays **Obv. Legend:** БАНК РОССИИ **Rev:** Khakassia Republic arms **Edge:** Reeded and lettered **Edge Lettering:** Denomination repeated

Date	Mintage	F	VF	XF	Unc	BU
2007СПМД	10,000,000	—	—	—	4.00	6.00

Y# 972 10 ROUBLES

8.5700 g., Bi-Metallic Copper-Nickel center in Brass ring, 27.08 mm. **Obv:** Value with latent image in zero within circle and sprays **Obv. Legend:** БАНК РОССИИ **Rev:** Bashkortostan Republic arms **Edge:** Reeded and lettered **Edge Lettering:** Denomination repeated

Date	Mintage	F	VF	XF	Unc	BU
2007ММД	10,000,000	—	—	—	4.00	6.00

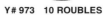

Y# 973 10 ROUBLES

8.5700 g., Bi-Metallic Copper-Nickel center in Brass ring, 27.08 mm. **Obv:** Value with latent image in zero within circle and sprays **Obv. Legend:** БАНК РОССИИ **Rev:** Archangelskaya Oblast arms **Edge:** Reeded and lettered **Edge Lettering:** Denomination repeated

Date	Mintage	F	VF	XF	Unc	BU
2007СПМД	10,000,000	—	—	—	4.00	6.00

Y# 974 10 ROUBLES

8.5700 g., Bi-Metallic Copper-Nickel center in brass ring., 27.08 mm. **Obv:** Value with latent image in zero within circle and sprays **Obv. Legend:** БАНК РОССИИ **Rev:** Novosibirskaya Oblast arms **Edge:** Reeded and lettered **Edge Lettering:** Denomination repeated

Date	Mintage	F	VF	XF	Unc	BU
2007ММД	10,000,000	—	—	—	4.00	6.00

Y# 993 10 ROUBLES

Bi-Metallic Copper-Nickel center in Brass ring **Subject:** Lipetskaya Oblast

Date	Mintage	F	VF	XF	Unc	BU
2007ММД	10,000,000	—	—	—	2.00	3.50

Y# 975 10 ROUBLES

8.2000 g., Bi-Metallic Copper-Nickel center in brass ring., 27.1 mm. **Obv:** Value with latent image in zero within circle and sprays **Obv. Legend:** БАНК РОССИИ **Rev:** Udmurtia Republic arms **Rev. Legend:** УДМУРТСКАЯ РЕСПУБЛИКА **Edge:** Reeded and lettered **Edge Lettering:** Denomination repeated

Date	Mintage	F	VF	XF	Unc	BU
2008ММД	5,000,000	—	—	0.90	2.25	3.00
2008СПМД	5,000,000	—	—	0.90	2.25	3.00

Y# 976 10 ROUBLES

8.2800 g., Bi-Metallic Copper-Nickel center in brass ring., 27.1 mm. **Series:** Ancient cities **Subject:** Vladimir **Obv:** Value with latent image in zero within circle and sprays **Obv. Legend:** БАНК РОССИИ **Rev:** Small shield at upper left above city view **Rev. Legend:** ВЛАДИМИР **Edge:** Reeded and lettered **Edge Lettering:** Denomination repeated

Date	Mintage	F	VF	XF	Unc	BU
2008ММД	2,500,000	—	—	0.90	2.25	3.00
2008СПМД	2,500,000	—	—	0.90	2.25	3.00

Y# 977 10 ROUBLES

8.2300 g., Bi-Metallic Copper-Nickel center in Brass ring, 27 mm. **Obv:** Value with latent image in zero within circle and sprays **Obv. Legend:** БАНК РОССИИ **Rev:** Astrakhanskaya Oblast arms **Edge:** Reeded and lettered **Edge Lettering:** Denomination repeated

Date	Mintage	F	VF	XF	Unc	BU
2008ММД	5,000,000	—	—	0.90	2.25	3.00
2008СПМД	5,000,000	—	—	0.90	2.25	3.00

Y# 978 10 ROUBLES

8.1600 g., Bi-Metallic Copper-Nickel center in brass ring, 27 mm. **Obv:** Value with latent image in zero within circle and sprays **Obv. Legend:** БАНК РОССИИ **Rev:** Sverdlovskaya Oblast arms **Edge:** Reeded and lettered **Edge Lettering:** Denomination repeated

Date	Mintage	F	VF	XF	Unc	BU
2008ММД	5,000,000	—	—	0.90	2.25	3.00
2008СПМД	5,000,000	—	—	0.90	2.25	3.00

Y# 986 10 ROUBLES

8.0800 g., Bi-Metallic Copper-Nickel center in Brass ring, 27 mm. **Rev:** Azov town view

Date	Mintage	F	VF	XF	Unc	BU
2008ММД	2,500,000	—	—	—	2.00	3.50
2008СПМД	2,500,000	—	—	—	2.00	3.50

Y# 991 10 ROUBLES

8.0800 g., Bi-Metallic Copper-Nickel center in Brass ring, 27 mm. **Rev:** Kabardino-Balkaria Republic Arms

Date	Mintage	F	VF	XF	Unc	BU
2008ММД	5,000,000	—	—	—	2.00	3.50
2008СПМД	5,000,000	—	—	—	2.00	3.50

Y# 994 10 ROUBLES

Bi-Metallic Copper-Nickel center in Brass ring **Subject:** Priozersk

Date	Mintage	F	VF	XF	Unc	BU
2008ММД	2,500,000	—	—	—	2.00	3.50
2008СПМД	2,500,000	—	—	—	2.00	3.50

Y# 995 10 ROUBLES

Bi-Metallic Copper-Nickel center in Brass ring **Subject:** Smolensk

Date	Mintage	F	VF	XF	Unc	BU
2008ММД	2,500,000	—	—	—	2.00	3.50
2008СПМД	2,500,000	—	—	—	2.00	3.50

Y# 998 10 ROUBLES

5.6300 g., Brass Plated Steel, 22 mm. **Obv:** Double headed eagle **Rev:** Value

Date	Mintage	F	VF	XF	Unc	BU
2009ММД	—	—	—	—	2.50	4.00
2010ММД	—	—	—	—	2.50	4.00
2010СПМД	—	—	—	—	2.50	4.00

Y# 982 10 ROUBLES

8.0800 g., Bi-Metallic Copper-Nickel center in Brass ring, 27 mm. **Rev:** Kaluga town view

Date	Mintage	F	VF	XF	Unc	BU
2009ММД	2,500,000	—	—	—	2.00	3.50
2009СПМД	2,500,000	—	—	—	2.00	3.50

Y# 983 10 ROUBLES

8.0800 g., Bi-Metallic Copper-Nickel center in Brass ring, 27 mm. **Rev:** Vyborg town view

Date	Mintage	F	VF	XF	Unc	BU
2009ММД	2,500,000	—	—	—	2.00	3.50
2009СПМД	2,500,000	—	—	—	2.00	3.50

Y# 984 10 ROUBLES

8.0800 g., Bi-Metallic Copper-Nickel center in Brass ring, 27 mm. **Rev:** Galich town view

Date	Mintage	F	VF	XF	Unc	BU
2009ММД	2,500,000	—	—	—	2.00	3.50
2009СПМД	2,500,000	—	—	—	2.00	3.50

Y# 985 10 ROUBLES

8.0800 g., Bi-Metallic Copper-Nickel center in Brass ring, 27 mm. **Rev:** Kalmykiya Republic arms

Date	Mintage	F	VF	XF	Unc	BU
2009ММД	5,000,000	—	—	—	2.00	3.50
2009СПМД	5,000,000	—	—	—	2.00	3.50

Y# 987 10 ROUBLES

8.0800 g., Bi-Metallic Copper-Nickel center in Brass ring, 27 mm. **Rev:** Adygeya Republic arms

Date	Mintage	F	VF	XF	Unc	BU
2009ММД	5,000,000	—	—	—	2.00	3.50
2009СПМД	5,000,000	—	—	—	2.00	3.50

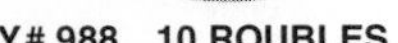

Y# 988 10 ROUBLES

8.0800 g., Bi-Metallic Copper-Nickel center in Brass ring, 27 mm. **Rev:** Veliky Novgorod arms

Date	Mintage	F	VF	XF	Unc	BU
2009ММД	2,500,000	—	—	—	2.00	3.50
2009СПМД	2,500,000	—	—	—	2.00	3.50

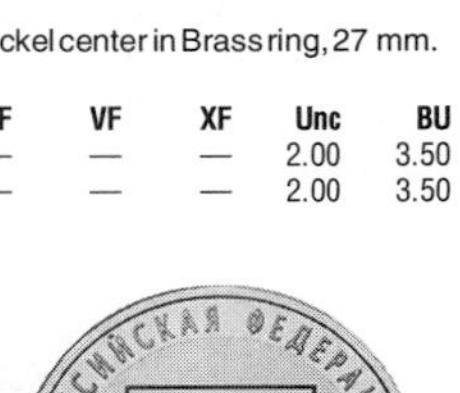

Y# 989 10 ROUBLES

8.0800 g., Bi-Metallic Copper-Nickel center in Brass ring, 27 mm. **Rev:** Jewish Autonomous Oblast Arms

Date	Mintage	F	VF	XF	Unc	BU
2009ММД	5,000,000	—	—	—	2.00	3.50
2009СПМД	5,000,000	—	—	—	2.00	3.50

Y# 996 10 ROUBLES

Bi-Metallic Copper-Nickel center in Brass ring **Subject:** Komi Republic

Date	Mintage	F	VF	XF	Unc	BU
2009СПМД	10,000,000	—	—	—	2.00	3.50

Y# 997 10 ROUBLES

Bi-Metallic Copper-Nickel center in Brass ring **Subject:** Kirovskaya Oblast

Date	Mintage	F	VF	XF	Unc	BU
2009СПМД	10,000,000	—	—	—	2.00	3.50

Y# 1274 10 ROUBLES

Bi-Metallic Copper-Nickel center in Brass ring, 27 mm. **Subject:** Russian Census

Date	Mintage	F	VF	XF	Unc	BU
2010	10,000,000	—	—	—	4.00	6.00

Y# 1275 10 ROUBLES

Bi-Metallic Copper-Nickel center in Brass ring, 27 mm. **Subject:** Bryansk

Date	Mintage	F	VF	XF	Unc	BU
2010	10,000,000	—	—	—	4.00	6.00

Y# 1276 10 ROUBLES

Bi-Metallic Copper-Nickel center in Brass ring, 27 mm. **Subject:** Yurevets, Ivanovo Region

Date	Mintage	F	VF	XF	Unc	BU
2010	10,000,000	—	—	—	4.00	6.00

Y# 1277 10 ROUBLES

Bi-Metallic Copper-Nickel in Brass ring, 27 mm. **Series:** Perm Krai

Date	Mintage	F	VF	XF	Unc	BU
2010	200,000	—	—	—	4.00	6.00

Y# 1278 10 ROUBLES

Bi-Metallic Copper-Nickel center in Brass ring, 27 mm. **Subject:** Nenets Autonomous Region

Date	Mintage	F	VF	XF	Unc	BU
2010	10,000,000	—	—	—	4.00	6.00

Y# 1279 10 ROUBLES

Bi-Metallic Copper-Nickel center in Brass ring, 27 mm. **Subject:** Chechen Republic

Date	Mintage	F	VF	XF	Unc	BU
2010	10,000,000	—	—	—	4.00	6.00

Y# 1280 10 ROUBLES

Bi-Metallic Copper-Nickel center in Brass ring, 27 mm. **Subject:** Yamal-nevets Autonomous Area

Date	Mintage	F	VF	XF	Unc	BU
2010	10,000,000	—	—	—	4.00	6.00

Y# 678 25 ROUBLES

173.2900 g., 0.9000 Silver 5.0141 oz. ASW, 60 mm. **Subject:** Bolshoi Theater 225 Years **Obv:** Double-headed eagle **Rev:** Dancing couple scene **Edge:** Reeded **Note:** Illustration reduced.

Date	Mintage	F	VF	XF	Unc	BU
2001 Proof	2,000	Value: 285				

Y# 683 25 ROUBLES

173.2900 g., 0.9000 Silver 5.0141 oz. ASW, 60 mm. **Subject:** Siberian Exploration **Obv:** Double-headed eagle **Rev:** Standing king and river boats **Edge:** Reeded **Note:** Illustration reduced.

Date	Mintage	F	VF	XF	Unc	BU
2001 Proof	1,000	Value: 350				

Y# 794 25 ROUBLES

173.1300 g., 0.9000 Silver 5.0094 oz. ASW, 60.2 mm. **Subject:** Foundation of Russian Savings Banks **Obv:** Double-headed eagle **Rev:** Czar Nicholas I and document **Edge:** Reeded

Date	Mintage	F	VF	XF	Unc	BU
2001(m) Proof	10,500	Value: 225				

Y# 687 25 ROUBLES

3.2000 g., 0.9990 Gold 0.1028 oz. AGW, 16 mm. **Subject:** Bolshoi Theater **Obv:** Double-headed eagle **Rev:** Ballerina **Edge:** Reeded

Date	Mintage	F	VF	XF	Unc	BU
2001 Proof	2,500	Value: 175				

Y# 999 25 ROUBLES

169.0000 g., 0.9250 Silver 5.0258 oz. ASW, 60 mm. **Subject:** Bolshoi Theater, 225th Anniversary

Date	Mintage	F	VF	XF	Unc	BU
2001 Proof	—	Value: 285				

Y# 1000 25 ROUBLES

169.0000 g., 0.9250 Silver 5.0258 oz. ASW, 60 mm. **Subject:** Savings Bank

Date	Mintage	F	VF	XF	Unc	BU
2001 Proof	—	Value: 285				

Y# 1001 25 ROUBLES

169.0000 g., 0.9250 Silver 5.0258 oz. ASW, 60 mm. **Subject:** Siberia - Development and Exploration

Date	Mintage	F	VF	XF	Unc	BU
2001 Proof	—	Value: 285				

Y# 777 25 ROUBLES

173.2900 g., 0.9000 Silver 5.0141 oz. ASW, 60 mm. **Subject:** Czar Alexander I **Obv:** Double-headed eagle **Rev:** Head right and crowned double-headed eagle above document text **Edge:** Reeded **Note:** Illustration reduced.

Date	Mintage	F	VF	XF	Unc	BU
2002(m) Proof	1,500	Value: 300				

Y# 785 25 ROUBLES
173.2900 g., 0.9000 Silver 5.0141 oz. ASW, 60 mm. **Subject:** Admiral Nakhimov **Obv:** Double-headed eagle **Rev:** Admiral watching naval battle **Edge:** Reeded **Note:** Illustration reduced.

Date	Mintage	F	VF	XF	Unc	BU
2002(sp) Proof	2,000	Value: 250				

Y# 790 25 ROUBLES
173.2900 g., 0.9000 Silver 5.0141 oz. ASW, 60 mm. **Subject:** Hermitage **Obv:** Double-headed eagle **Rev:** Staircase viewed through doorway **Edge:** Reeded **Note:** Illustration reduced.

Date	Mintage	F	VF	XF	Unc	BU
2002(sp) Proof	2,000	Value: 250				

Y# 743 25 ROUBLES
3.2000 g., 0.9990 Gold 0.1028 oz. AGW, 16 mm. **Subject:** Zodiac Signs: **Obv:** Double-headed eagle within beaded circle **Rev:** Leo **Edge:** Reeded

Date	Mintage	F	VF	XF	Unc	BU
2002 Proof	10,000	Value: 175				

Y# 763 25 ROUBLES
3.2000 g., 0.9990 Gold 0.1028 oz. AGW, 16 mm. **Subject:** Zodiac Signs **Obv:** Double-headed eagle within beaded circle **Rev:** Capricorn **Edge:** Reeded

Date	Mintage	F	VF	XF	Unc	BU
2002(m)	10,000	—	—	—	—	200

Y# 764 25 ROUBLES
3.2000 g., 0.9990 Gold 0.1028 oz. AGW, 16 mm. **Subject:** Zodiac Signs **Obv:** Double-headed eagle within beaded circle **Rev:** Virgo **Edge:** Reeded

Date	Mintage	F	VF	XF	Unc	BU
2002(sp)	10,000	—	—	—	—	200

Y# 765 25 ROUBLES
3.2000 g., 0.9990 Gold 0.1028 oz. AGW, 16 mm. **Subject:** Zodiac Signs **Obv:** Double-headed eagle within beaded circle **Rev:** Sagittarius **Edge:** Reeded

Date	Mintage	F	VF	XF	Unc	BU
2002(SP)	10,000	—	—	—	—	200

Y# 767 25 ROUBLES
3.2000 g., 0.9990 Gold 0.1028 oz. AGW, 16 mm. **Subject:** Zodiac signs **Obv:** Double-headed eagle within beaded circle **Rev:** Scorpio **Edge:** Reeded

Date	Mintage	F	VF	XF	Unc	BU
2002(m)	10,000	—	—	—	—	200

Y# 769 25 ROUBLES
3.2000 g., 0.9990 Gold 0.1028 oz. AGW **Subject:** Zodiac Signs **Obv:** Double-headed eagle within beaded circle **Rev:** Libra **Edge:** Reeded

Date	Mintage	F	VF	XF	Unc	BU
2002(sp)	10,000	—	—	—	—	200

Y# 821 25 ROUBLES
3.2000 g., 0.9990 Gold 0.1028 oz. AGW, 16 mm. **Subject:** Zodiac signs **Obv:** Double-headed eagle within beaded circle **Rev:** Cancer **Edge:** Reeded

Date	Mintage	F	VF	XF	Unc	BU
2003(sp)	50,000	—	—	—	—	200

Y# 864 25 ROUBLES
172.8000 g., 0.9000 Silver 4.9999 oz. ASW, 60 mm. **Rev:** St. Sercius Monastery

Date	Mintage	F	VF	XF	Unc	BU
2003 Proof	2,000	Value: 285				

Y# 865 25 ROUBLES
172.8000 g., 0.9000 Silver 4.9999 oz. ASW, 60 mm. **Rev:** Shlisselburg

Date	Mintage	F	VF	XF	Unc	BU
2003(m) Proof	2,000	Value: 285				

Y# 866 25 ROUBLES
172.8000 g., 0.9000 Silver 4.9999 oz. ASW, 60 mm. **Rev:** Kamchatka

Date	Mintage	F	VF	XF	Unc	BU
2003	2,000	Value: 285				

Y# 1003 25 ROUBLES
169.0000 g., 0.9250 Silver 5.0258 oz. ASW, 60 mm. **Subject:** Aquarius

Date	Mintage	F	VF	XF	Unc	BU
2003 Proof	—	Value: 285				

Y# 1004 25 ROUBLES
169.0000 g., 0.9250 Silver 5.0258 oz. ASW, 60 mm. **Subject:** Pisces

Date	Mintage	F	VF	XF	Unc	BU
2003 Proof	—	Value: 285				

Y# 1005 25 ROUBLES
169.0000 g., 0.9250 Silver 5.0258 oz. ASW, 60 mm. **Subject:** Aries

Date	Mintage	F	VF	XF	Unc	BU
2003 Proof	—	Value: 285				

Y# 1006 25 ROUBLES
169.0000 g., 0.9250 Silver 5.0258 oz. ASW, 60 mm. **Subject:** Taurus

Date	Mintage	F	VF	XF	Unc	BU
2003 Proof	—	Value: 285				

Y# 830 25 ROUBLES
177.9600 g., 0.9000 Bi-Metallic .900 Silver 172.78g planchet with .900 Gold 5.18g insert 5.1492 oz., 60 mm. **Subject:** Monetary reform of Peter the Great **Obv:** Double-headed eagle **Rev:** Gold insert replicating the obverse and reverse designs of a 1704 one rouble coin **Edge:** Reeded **Note:** Illustration reduced.

Date	Mintage	F	VF	XF	Unc	BU
2004(sp) Proof	1,000	Value: 950				

Y# 867 25 ROUBLES
172.8000 g., 0.9000 Silver 4.9999 oz. ASW, 60 mm. **Rev:** Valaam Church

Date	Mintage	F	VF	XF	Unc	BU
2004	1,500	Value: 300				

Y# 1014 25 ROUBLES
169.0000 g., 0.9250 Silver 5.0258 oz. ASW, 60 mm. **Subject:** 2nd Kamchatka Expedition, 1733-43

Date	Mintage	F	VF	XF	Unc	BU
2004 Proof	—	Value: 285				

Y# 1019 25 ROUBLES
169.0000 g., 0.9250 Silver 5.0258 oz. ASW, 60 mm. **Subject:** Holy Trinity - St. Sergius Lavra in Sergiev Posad

Date	Mintage	F	VF	XF	Unc	BU
2004 Proof	—	Value: 285				

Y# 1023 25 ROUBLES
169.0000 g., 0.9250 Silver 5.0258 oz. ASW, 60 mm. **Subject:** Reindeer

Date	Mintage	F	VF	XF	Unc	BU
2004 Proof	—	Value: 285				

Y# 898 25 ROUBLES
3.2000 g., 0.9990 Gold 0.1028 oz. AGW, 16 mm. **Obv:** Double-headed eagle **Rev:** Gemini twins **Edge:** Reeded

Date	Mintage	F	VF	XF	Unc	BU
2005	10,000	—	—	—	—	200

Y# 900 25 ROUBLES
3.2000 g., 0.9990 Gold 0.1028 oz. AGW, 16 mm. **Obv:** Double-headed eagle **Rev:** Cancer crawfish **Edge:** Reeded

Date	Mintage	F	VF	XF	Unc	BU
2005 Proof	10,000	Value: 175				

Y# 902 25 ROUBLES
3.2000 g., 0.9990 Gold 0.1028 oz. AGW, 16 mm. **Obv:** Double-headed eagle **Rev:** Leo lion **Edge:** Reeded

Date	Mintage	F	VF	XF	Unc	BU
2005	10,000	—	—	—	—	200

Y# 915 25 ROUBLES
3.2000 g., 0.9990 Gold 0.1028 oz. AGW, 16 mm. **Obv:** Double-headed eagle **Rev:** Virgos standing lady **Edge:** Reeded

Date	Mintage	F	VF	XF	Unc	BU
2005 Proof	10,000	Value: 175				

Y# 920 25 ROUBLES
3.2000 g., 0.9990 Gold 0.1028 oz. AGW, 16 mm. **Obv:** Double-headed eagle **Rev:** Two stylized birds forming balance scale **Edge:** Reeded

Date	Mintage	F	VF	XF	Unc	BU
2005	10,000	—	—	—	—	200

Y# 922 25 ROUBLES
3.2000 g., 0.9990 Gold 0.1028 oz. AGW, 16 mm. **Obv:** Double-headed eagle **Rev:** Scorpio scorpion **Edge:** Reeded

Date	Mintage	F	VF	XF	Unc	BU
2005	10,000	—	—	—	—	200

Y# 927 25 ROUBLES
3.2000 g., 0.9990 Gold 0.1028 oz. AGW, 16 mm. **Obv:** Double-headed eagle **Rev:** Sagittarius the archer **Edge:** Reeded

Date	Mintage	F	VF	XF	Unc	BU
2005	10,000	—	—	—	—	200

Y# 929 25 ROUBLES
3.2000 g., 0.9990 Gold 0.1028 oz. AGW, 16 mm. **Obv:** Double-headed eagle **Rev:** Capricorn as half goat and fish **Edge:** Reeded

Date	Mintage	F	VF	XF	Unc	BU
2005	10,000	—	—	—	—	200

Y# 931 25 ROUBLES
3.2000 g., 0.9990 Gold 0.1028 oz. AGW, 16 mm. **Obv:** Double-headed eagle **Rev:** Pisces as catfish and sturgeon **Edge:** Reeded

Date	Mintage	F	VF	XF	Unc	BU
2005	10,000	—	—	—	—	200

Y# 933 25 ROUBLES
3.2000 g., 0.9990 Gold 0.1028 oz. AGW, 16 mm. **Obv:** Double-headed eagle **Rev:** Aries ram **Edge:** Reeded

Date	Mintage	F	VF	XF	Unc	BU
2005	10,000	—	—	—	—	200

Y# 935 25 ROUBLES
3.2000 g., 0.9990 Gold 0.1028 oz. AGW, 16 mm. **Obv:** Double-headed eagle **Rev:** Taurus bull **Edge:** Reeded

Date	Mintage	F	VF	XF	Unc	BU
2005	10,000	—	—	—	—	200

Y# 937 25 ROUBLES
3.2000 g., 0.9990 Gold 0.1028 oz. AGW, 16 mm. **Obv:** Double-headed eagle **Rev:** Aquarius water carrier **Edge:** Reeded

Date	Mintage	F	VF	XF	Unc	BU
2005	10,000	—	—	—	—	200

Y# 924 25 ROUBLES
169.0000 g., 0.9250 Silver 5.0258 oz. ASW, 60 mm. **Subject:** 625th Anniversary - Battle of Kulikovo **Obv:** Double-headed eagle **Rev:** Mounted warriors above and below crossed swords **Edge:** Reeded **Note:** Illustration reduced.

Date	Mintage	F	VF	XF	Unc	BU
2005 Proof	1,500	Value: 300				

Y# 1047 25 ROUBLES
169.0000 g., 0.9250 Silver 5.0258 oz. ASW, 60 mm. **Subject:** Tretyakov State Galler, 150th Anniversary

Date	Mintage	F	VF	XF	Unc	BU
2006 Proof	—	Value: 285				

Y# 1050 25 ROUBLES
169.0000 g., 0.9250 Silver 5.0258 oz. ASW, 60 mm. **Subject:** Malye Korely

Date	Mintage	F	VF	XF	Unc	BU
2006 Proof	—	Value: 285				

Y# 1051 25 ROUBLES
169.0000 g., 0.9250 Silver 5.0258 oz. ASW, 60 mm. **Subject:** Tikhvin Monastery, Dome of the Mother of God

Date	Mintage	F	VF	XF	Unc	BU
2006 Proof	—	Value: 285				

Y# 1053 25 ROUBLES
169.0000 g., 0.9250 Silver 5.0258 oz. ASW, 60 mm. **Subject:** Konevsky Monastery of St. Virgin's Nativity

Date	Mintage	F	VF	XF	Unc	BU
2006 Proof	—	Value: 285				

Y# 969 25 ROUBLES
169.0000 g., 0.9250 Silver 5.0258 oz. ASW, 60.00 mm. **Obv:** Two-headed eagle **Rev:** Vyatka St. Trifon Monastery of the Assumption, Kirov **Edge:** Reeded **Note:** Illustration reduced

Date	Mintage	F	VF	XF	Unc	BU
2007(sp) Proof	2,000	Value: 285				

Y# 1083 25 ROUBLES
169.0000 g., 0.9250 Silver 5.0258 oz. ASW, 60 mm. **Subject:** Russian Railways, 150th Anniversary

Date	Mintage	F	VF	XF	Unc	BU
2007 Proof	—	Value: 285				

Y# 1084 25 ROUBLES
169.0000 g., 0.9250 Silver 5.0258 oz. ASW, 60 mm. **Subject:** F. A. Golovin, first Order of St. Andrew awardee

Date	Mintage	F	VF	XF	Unc	BU
2007 Proof	—	Value: 285				

Y# 1101 25 ROUBLES
169.0000 g., 0.9250 Silver 5.0258 oz. ASW, 60 mm. **Subject:** St. Artemy Verkolsky Monastery, Arkhamgelsk

Date	Mintage	F	VF	XF	Unc	BU
2007 Proof	—	Value: 285				

Y# 1102 25 ROUBLES
169.0000 g., 0.9250 Silver 5.0258 oz. ASW, 60 mm. **Subject:** Pskov-Pechersky Holy Monastery of the Assumption

Date	Mintage	F	VF	XF	Unc	BU
2007 Proof	—	Value: 285				

Y# 1116 25 ROUBLES
169.0000 g., 0.9250 Silver 5.0258 oz. ASW, 60 mm. **Subject:** Goznak, 190th Anniversary

Date	Mintage	F	VF	XF	Unc	BU
2008 Proof	—	Value: 285				

Y# 1125 25 ROUBLES
169.0000 g., 0.9250 Silver 5.0258 oz. ASW, 60 mm. **Subject:** Astrakhan Kremlin

Date	Mintage	F	VF	XF	Unc	BU
2008 Proof	—	Value: 325				

Y# 1139 25 ROUBLES
169.0000 g., 0.9250 Silver 5.0258 oz. ASW, 60 mm. **Subject:** European Beaver

Date	Mintage	F	VF	XF	Unc	BU
2008 Proof	—	Value: 325				

Y# 1160 25 ROUBLES
168.0000 g., 0.9250 Silver 4.9960 oz. ASW, 60 mm. **Subject:** Alexander I Monument, 175th Anniversary

Date	Mintage	F	VF	XF	Unc	BU
2009 Proof	—	Value: 285				

Y# 1178 25 ROUBLES
168.0000 g., 0.9250 Silver 4.9960 oz. ASW, 60 mm. **Subject:** Poltava Battle, 300th Anniversary

Date	Mintage	F	VF	XF	Unc	BU
2009 Proof	—	Value: 285				

Y# 1184 25 ROUBLES
168.0000 g., 0.9250 Silver 4.9960 oz. ASW, 60 mm. **Subject:** Arkhangelskoye Museum

Date	Mintage	F	VF	XF	Unc	BU
2009 Proof	—	Value: 285				

Y# 1186 25 ROUBLES
168.0000 g., 0.9250 Silver 4.9960 oz. ASW, 60 mm. **Subject:** St. Trinity Monastery, Pensu Region

Date	Mintage	F	VF	XF	Unc	BU
2009 Proof	—	Value: 285				

Y# 1187 25 ROUBLES
168.0000 g., 0.9250 Silver 4.9960 oz. ASW, 60 mm. **Subject:** St. Nikolas Monastary, Staraya Ladoga

Date	Mintage	F	VF	XF	Unc	BU
2009 Proof	—	Value: 285				

Y# 1200 25 ROUBLES
168.0000 g., 0.9250 Silver 4.9960 oz. ASW, 60 mm. **Subject:** Velikly Novgorod

Date	Mintage	F	VF	XF	Unc	BU
2009 Proof	—	Value: 285				

Y# 1223 25 ROUBLES
168.0000 g., 0.9250 Silver 4.9960 oz. ASW, 60 mm. **Subject:** Khmelita, Griboyedov family estate

Date	Mintage	F	VF	XF	Unc	BU
2010 Proof	—	Value: 285				

Y# 1224 25 ROUBLES
168.0000 g., 0.9250 Silver 4.9960 oz. ASW, 60 mm. **Subject:** Kirillo Belosersk Monastery

Date	Mintage	F	VF	XF	Unc	BU
2010 Proof	—	Value: 285				

Y# 1225 25 ROUBLES
168.0000 g., 0.9250 Silver 4.9960 oz. ASW, 60 mm. **Subject:** Alezxandro - Svirsky Monestary

Date	Mintage	F	VF	XF	Unc	BU
2010 Proof	—	Value: 285				

Y# 1226 25 ROUBLES
168.0000 g., 0.9250 Silver 4.9960 oz. ASW, 60 mm. **Subject:** Sanaksarsky Monestary

Date	Mintage	F	VF	XF	Unc	BU
2010 Proof	—	Value: 285				

Y# 1227 25 ROUBLES
31.1000 g., 0.9990 Gold 0.9988 oz. AGW **Subject:** Warship - Goto Predestination

Date	Mintage	F	VF	XF	Unc	BU
2010 Proof	—	Value: 1,500				

Y# 1229 25 ROUBLES
168.0000 g., 0.9250 Silver 4.9960 oz. ASW, 60 mm. **Subject:** Bank of Russia, 150th Anniversary

Date	Mintage	F	VF	XF	Unc	BU
2010 Proof	—	Value: 285				

Y# 1233 25 ROUBLES
169.0000 g., 0.9250 Silver 5.0258 oz. ASW, 60 mm. **Subject:** UNESCO Heritage Site - Yaroslav

Date	Mintage	F	VF	XF	Unc	BU
2010 Proof	—	Value: 285				

Y# 679 50 ROUBLES
8.7500 g., 0.9990 Gold 0.2810 oz. AGW, 22.6 mm. **Subject:** Bolshoi Theater **Obv:** Double-headed eagle within beaded circle **Rev:** Dueling figures **Edge:** Reeded

Date	Mintage	F	VF	XF	Unc	BU
2001 Proof	2,000	Value: 450				

Y# 684 50 ROUBLES
8.7500 g., 0.9000 Gold 0.2532 oz. AGW, 22.6 mm. **Subject:** Siberian Exploration **Obv:** Double-headed eagle within beaded circle **Rev:** Head with hat 1/4 right and boat **Edge:** Reeded

Date	Mintage	F	VF	XF	Unc	BU
2001 Proof	1,500	Value: 400				

Y# 757 50 ROUBLES
8.6444 g., 0.9000 Gold 0.2501 oz. AGW, 22.6 mm. **Subject:** Olympics **Obv:** Double-headed eagle within beaded circle **Rev:** Figure skater and flying eagle **Edge:** Reeded

Date	Mintage	F	VF	XF	Unc	BU
2002 Proof	3,000	Value: 375				

Y# 782 50 ROUBLES
7.8900 g., 0.9990 Gold 0.2534 oz. AGW, 22.6 mm. **Subject:** Works of Dionissy **Obv:** Double-headed eagle within beaded circle **Rev:** Half-length figure holding child flanked by double headed eagle and church **Edge:** Reeded

Date	Mintage	F	VF	XF	Unc	BU
2002(m) Proof	1,500	Value: 400				

Y# 786 50 ROUBLES
8.7500 g., 0.9000 Gold 0.2532 oz. AGW, 22.6 mm. **Subject:** Admiral Nakhimov **Obv:** Double-headed eagle within beaded circle **Rev:** Bust facing within circle above flags and anchor **Edge:** Reeded

Date	Mintage	F	VF	XF	Unc	BU
2002(sp) Proof	1,500	Value: 400				

Y# 788 50 ROUBLES
8.7500 g., 0.9000 Gold 0.2532 oz. AGW, 22.6 mm. **Subject:** World Cup Soccer **Obv:** Double-headed eagle within beaded circle **Rev:** Stylized player kicking soccer ball **Edge:** Reeded

Date	Mintage	F	VF	XF	Unc	BU
2002(m) Proof	3,000	Value: 375				

Y# 822 50 ROUBLES
7.8900 g., 0.9990 Gold 0.2534 oz. AGW, 22.6 mm. **Subject:** Zodiac Signs **Obv:** Double-headed eagle within beaded circle **Rev:** Virgo **Edge:** Reeded

Date	Mintage	F	VF	XF	Unc	BU
2003(sp)	30,000	—	—	—	—	375

Y# 823 50 ROUBLES
7.8900 g., 0.9990 Gold 0.2534 oz. AGW, 22.6 mm. **Subject:** Zodiac signs **Obv:** Double-headed eagle within beaded circle **Rev:** Libra **Edge:** Reeded

Date	Mintage	F	VF	XF	Unc	BU
2003(m)	30,000	—	—	—	—	375

Y# 868 50 ROUBLES
8.6400 g., 0.9000 Gold 0.2500 oz. AGW, 23 mm. **Rev:** Peter I monetary reform

Date	Mintage	F	VF	XF	Unc	BU
2003(m) Proof	1,500	Value: 400				

Y# 869 50 ROUBLES
8.6400 g., 0.9000 Gold 0.2500 oz. AGW, 23 mm. **Rev:** Ski race

Date	Mintage	F	VF	XF	Unc	BU
2003(m) Proof	1,500	Value: 400				

Y# 1007 50 ROUBLES
169.0000 g., 0.9250 Silver 5.0258 oz. ASW, 60 mm. **Subject:** Leo

Date	Mintage	F	VF	XF	Unc	BU
2003 Proof	—	Value: 285				

Y# 1008 50 ROUBLES
169.0000 g., 0.9250 Silver 5.0258 oz. ASW, 60 mm. **Subject:** Leo

Date	Mintage	F	VF	XF	Unc	BU
2003 Proof	—	Value: 285				

Y# 1009 50 ROUBLES
7.7900 g., 0.9990 Gold 0.2502 oz. AGW, 22.6 mm. **Subject:** Scorpion

Date	Mintage	F	VF	XF	Unc	BU
2003 Proof	—	Value: 400				

Y# 1010 50 ROUBLES
7.7800 g., 0.9990 Gold 0.2499 oz. AGW, 22.6 mm. **Subject:** Sagatarius

Date	Mintage	F	VF	XF	Unc	BU
2003 Proof	—	Value: 400				

Y# 1011 50 ROUBLES
7.7800 g., 0.9990 Gold 0.2499 oz. AGW, 22.6 mm. **Subject:** Capricorn

Date	Mintage	F	VF	XF	Unc	BU
2003 Proof	—	Value: 400				

Y# 870 50 ROUBLES
8.6400 g., 0.9000 Gold 0.2500 oz. AGW, 23 mm. **Rev:** Soccer player

Date	Mintage	F	VF	XF	Unc	BU
2004(sp) Proof	1,000	Value: 400				

Y# 871 50 ROUBLES
8.6400 g., 0.9000 Gold 0.2500 oz. AGW, 23 mm. **Rev:** Olympic athletes

Date	Mintage	F	VF	XF	Unc	BU
2004(m) Proof	2,000	Value: 375				

Y# 872 50 ROUBLES
8.6400 g., 0.9000 Gold 0.2500 oz. AGW, 23 mm. **Rev:** Virgin of the Son Icon

Date	Mintage	F	VF	XF	Unc	BU
2004(m) Proof	1,500	Value: 400				

Y# 1016 50 ROUBLES
7.7800 g., 0.9990 Gold 0.2499 oz. AGW, 22.6 mm. **Subject:** Theophanes the Greek

Date	Mintage	F	VF	XF	Unc	BU
2004 Proof	—	Value: 400				

Y# 1025 50 ROUBLES
7.7800 g., 0.9990 Gold 0.2499 oz. AGW, 22.6 mm. **Subject:** Reindeer

Date	Mintage	F	VF	XF	Unc	BU
2004 Proof	—	Value: 400				

Y# 1030 50 ROUBLES
7.7800 g., 0.9990 Gold 0.2499 oz. AGW, 22.6 mm. **Subject:** Aquarius

Date	Mintage	F	VF	XF	Unc	BU
2004 Proof	—	Value: 400				

Y# 1031 50 ROUBLES
7.7800 g., 0.9990 Gold 0.2499 oz. AGW, 22.6 mm. **Rev. Designer:** Pisces

Date	Mintage	F	VF	XF	Unc	BU
2004 Proof	—	Value: 375				

Y# 1032 50 ROUBLES
7.7800 g., 0.9990 Gold 0.2499 oz. AGW, 22.6 mm. **Subject:** Aries

Date	Mintage	F	VF	XF	Unc	BU
2004 Proof	—	Value: 400				

Y# 1033 50 ROUBLES
7.7800 g., 0.9990 Gold 0.2499 oz. AGW, 22.6 mm. **Subject:** Taurus

Date	Mintage	F	VF	XF	Unc	BU
2004 Proof	—	Value: 375				

Y# 1034 50 ROUBLES
7.7800 g., 0.9990 Gold 0.2499 oz. AGW, 22.6 mm. **Subject:** Gemni

Date	Mintage	F	VF	XF	Unc	BU
2004 Proof	—	Value: 400				

Y# 1035 50 ROUBLES
7.7800 g., 0.9990 Gold 0.2499 oz. AGW, 22.6 mm. **Subject:** Cancer

Date	Mintage	F	VF	XF	Unc	BU
2004 Proof	—	Value: 400				

Y# 894 50 ROUBLES
7.8900 g., 0.9990 Gold 0.2534 oz. AGW, 22.6 mm. **Subject:** 60th Anniversary - Victory Over Germany **Obv:** Double-headed eagle **Rev:** 60th Anniversary - Victory Over Germany medal **Edge:** Reeded

Date	Mintage	F	VF	XF	Unc	BU
2005 Proof	7,000	Value: 375				

Y# 907 50 ROUBLES
7.8900 g., 0.9990 Gold 0.2534 oz. AGW, 22.6 mm. **Subject:** Helsinki Games **Obv:** Double-headed eagle **Rev:** Stylized track and field athletes **Edge:** Reeded

Date	Mintage	F	VF	XF	Unc	BU
2005 Proof	1,500	Value: 400				

Y# 911 50 ROUBLES
7.8900 g., 0.9990 Gold 0.2534 oz. AGW, 22.6 mm. **Obv:** Double-headed eagle **Rev:** Kazan University Building **Edge:** Reeded

Date	Mintage	F	VF	XF	Unc	BU
2005 Proof	1,500	Value: 400				

Y# 1049 50 ROUBLES
7.7800 g., 0.9990 Gold 0.2499 oz. AGW, 22.6 mm. **Subject:** St. George the Victorious

Date	Mintage	F	VF	XF	Unc	BU
2006 Proof	—	Value: 400				

Y# 1063 50 ROUBLES
7.7800 g., 0.9990 Gold 0.2499 oz. AGW, 22.6 mm. **Subject:** Moscow's Kremlin and Red Square

Date	Mintage	F	VF	XF	Unc	BU
2006 Proof	—	Value: 400				

Y# 1067 50 ROUBLES
7.7800 g., 0.9990 Gold 0.2499 oz. AGW, 22.6 mm. **Subject:** XX Winter Olympics, Torino

Date	Mintage	F	VF	XF	Unc	BU
2006 Proof	—	Value: 400				

Y# 1068 50 ROUBLES
7.7800 g., 0.9990 Gold 0.2499 oz. AGW, 22.6 mm. **Subject:** FIFA World Cup, Germany

Date	Mintage	F	VF	XF	Unc	BU
2006 Proof	—	Value: 400				

Y# 1090 50 ROUBLES
7.7800 g., 0.9990 Gold 0.2499 oz. AGW, 22.6 mm. **Subject:** Andrew Rublyov

Date	Mintage	F	VF	XF	Unc	BU
2007 Proof	—	Value: 400				

Y# 1094 50 ROUBLES
7.7800 g., 0.9250 Gold 0.2314 oz. AGW, 22.6 mm. **Subject:** Bashkiria, 450th Anniversary of of annexation by Russia

Date	Mintage	F	VF	XF	Unc	BU
2007 Proof	—	Value: 375				

Y# 1097 50 ROUBLES
7.7800 g., 0.9990 Gold 0.2499 oz. AGW, 22.6 mm. **Subject:** Khakassia, 300th Anniversary of of annexation by Russia

Date	Mintage	F	VF	XF	Unc	BU
2007 Proof	—	Value: 375				

Y# 1099 50 ROUBLES
7.7800 g., 0.9990 Gold 0.2499 oz. AGW, 22.6 mm. **Subject:** St. George the Victorious

Date	Mintage	F	VF	XF	Unc	BU
2007 Proof	—	Value: 375				

Y# 1121 50 ROUBLES
7.7800 g., 0.9990 Gold 0.2499 oz. AGW, 22.6 mm. **Subject:** Udmurtiya, 450th Anniversary of annexation into Russia

Date	Mintage	F	VF	XF	Unc	BU
2008 Proof	—	Value: 375				

Y# 1123 50 ROUBLES
7.7800 g., 0.9990 Gold 0.2499 oz. AGW, 22.6 mm. **Subject:** St. George the Victorious

Date	Mintage	F	VF	XF	Unc	BU
2008 Proof	—	Value: 400				

Y# 1141 50 ROUBLES
7.7800 g., 0.9990 Gold 0.2499 oz. AGW, 22.6 mm. **Subject:** European Beaver

Date	Mintage	F	VF	XF	Unc	BU
2008 Proof	—	Value: 400				

Y# 1153 50 ROUBLES
7.7800 g., 0.9990 Gold 0.2499 oz. AGW, 22.6 mm. **Subject:** 29th Summer Olympics, Bejing

Date	Mintage	F	VF	XF	Unc	BU
2008 Proof	—	Value: 400				

Y# 1168 50 ROUBLES
7.7800 g., 0.9990 Gold 0.2499 oz. AGW, 22.6 mm. **Subject:** A. P. Chekhov, 150th Anniversary of Birth

Date	Mintage	F	VF	XF	Unc	BU
2009 Proof	—	Value: 400				

Y# 1172 50 ROUBLES
7.7800 g., 0.9990 Gold 0.2499 oz. AGW, 22.6 mm. **Subject:** Kalmyk Peoples, 400th Anniversary of annexation into Russia

Date	Mintage	F	VF	XF	Unc	BU
2009 Proof	—	Value: 400				

Y# 1175 50 ROUBLES
7.7800 g., 0.9990 Gold 0.2499 oz. AGW, 22.6 mm. **Subject:** N. V. Gogol, 200th Anniversary of Birth

Date	Mintage	F	VF	XF	Unc	BU
2009 Proof	—	Value: 400				

Y# 1181 50 ROUBLES
7.7800 g., 0.9990 Gold 0.2499 oz. AGW, 22.6 mm. **Subject:** St. George the victorious

Date	Mintage	F	VF	XF	Unc	BU
2009 Proof	—	Value: 400				

Y# 1202 50 ROUBLES
7.7800 g., 0.9990 Gold 0.2499 oz. AGW, 22.6 mm. **Subject:** Velikly Novgorod

Date	Mintage	F	VF	XF	Unc	BU
2009 Proof	—	Value: 400				

Y# 1215 50 ROUBLES
7.7800 g., 0.9990 Gold 0.2499 oz. AGW, 22.6 mm. **Subject:** St. George the victorious

Date	Mintage	F	VF	XF	Unc	BU
2010 Proof	—	Value: 400				

Y# 1230 50 ROUBLES
7.7800 g., 0.9990 Gold 0.2499 oz. AGW, 22.6 mm. **Subject:** Bank of Russia, 150th Anniversary

Date	Mintage	F	VF	XF	Unc	BU
2010 Proof	—	Value: 400				

Y# 1235 50 ROUBLES
7.7800 g., 0.9990 Gold 0.2499 oz. AGW, 22.6 mm. **Subject:** UNESCO Heritage Site - Yaroslav

Date	Mintage	F	VF	XF	Unc	BU
2010 Proof	—	Value: 400				

Y# 1239 50 ROUBLES
7.7800 g., 0.9990 Gold 0.2499 oz. AGW, 22.6 mm. **Subject:** A. P. Chekhov, 200th Anniversary of birth

Date	Mintage	F	VF	XF	Unc	BU
2010 Proof	—	Value: 400				

Y# 795 100 ROUBLES
1111.1200 g., 0.9000 Silver 32.149 oz. ASW, 100 mm. **Subject:** The Bark Sedov **Obv:** Double-headed eagle **Rev:** Ship flanked by compass and cameo **Edge:** Reeded **Note:** Illustration reduced.

Date	Mintage	F	VF	XF	Unc	BU
2001(m) Proof	500	Value: 2,000				

Y# 681 100 ROUBLES
1111.1000 g., 0.9000 Silver 32.149 oz. ASW, 100 mm. **Subject:** 40th Anniversary of Manned Space Flight - Yuri Gagarin **Obv:** Double-headed eagle **Rev:** Astronaut and rocket in space **Edge:** Reeded

Date	Mintage	F	VF	XF	Unc	BU
2001 Proof	750	Value: 1,800				

Y# 689 100 ROUBLES
1111.1000 g., 0.9000 Silver 32.149 oz. ASW, 100 mm. **Subject:** Bolshoi Theater 225 Years **Obv:** Double-headed eagle **Rev:** Casino gambling scene **Edge:** Reeded **Note:** Illustration reduced.

Date	Mintage	F	VF	XF	Unc	BU
2001 Proof	500	Value: 1,850				

Y# 685 100 ROUBLES
17.4500 g., 0.9000 Gold 0.5049 oz. AGW, 30 mm. **Subject:** Siberian Exploration **Obv:** Double-headed eagle within beaded circle **Rev:** Head and silhouette left, sailboat and other designs **Edge:** Reeded

Date	Mintage	F	VF	XF	Unc	BU
2001 Proof	1,000	Value: 750				

Y# 688 100 ROUBLES
15.7200 g., 0.9990 Gold 0.5049 oz. AGW, 30 mm. **Subject:** Bolshoi Theater 225 Years **Obv:** Double-headed eagle within beaded circle **Rev:** Three dancers with swords **Edge:** Reeded

Date	Mintage	F	VF	XF	Unc	BU
2001 Proof	1,500	Value: 750				

Y# 783 100 ROUBLES
1111.1200 g., 0.9000 Silver 32.149 oz. ASW, 100 mm. **Subject:** Works of Dionissy **Obv:** Double-headed eagle **Rev:** St. Ferapont Monastery in the center of a fresco covered cross **Edge:** Reeded **Note:** Illustration reduced.

Date	Mintage	F	VF	XF	Unc	BU
2002(sp) Prooflike	500	—	—	—	—	1,350

Y# 789 100 ROUBLES
1111.1200 g., 0.9000 Silver 32.149 oz. ASW, 100 mm. **Subject:** World Cup Soccer **Obv:** Double-headed eagle **Rev:** Soccer ball design with map and players **Edge:** Reeded

Date	Mintage	F	VF	XF	Unc	BU
2002(sp) Proof	500	Value: 1,850				

Y# 791 100 ROUBLES
1111.1200 g., 0.9000 Silver 32.149 oz. ASW, 100 mm. **Subject:** Hermitage **Obv:** Double-headed eagle **Rev:** Statues and arches **Edge:** Reeded **Note:** Illustration reduced.

Date	Mintage	F	VF	XF	Unc	BU
2002(sp) Proof	1,000	Value: 1,500				

Y# 792 100 ROUBLES
17.4500 g., 0.9000 Gold 0.5049 oz. AGW, 30 mm. **Subject:** Hermitage **Obv:** Double-headed eagle within beaded circle **Rev:** Ancient battle scene sculpted on comb **Edge:** Reeded

Date	Mintage	F	VF	XF	Unc	BU
2002(sp) Proof	1,000	Value: 900				

Y# 873 100 ROUBLES
1111.1200 g., 0.9000 Silver 32.149 oz. ASW, 100 mm. **Rev:** St. Petersburg

Date	Mintage	F	VF	XF	Unc	BU
2003(m) Proof	1,000	Value: 1,650				

Y# 874 100 ROUBLES
17.4500 g., 0.9000 Gold 0.5049 oz. AGW, 30 mm. **Rev:** Petrozavodsk

Date	Mintage	F	VF	XF	Unc	BU
2003(m) Proof	1,000	Value: 900				

Y# 875 100 ROUBLES
17.4500 g., 0.9000 Gold 0.5049 oz. AGW, 30 mm. **Rev:** Kamchatka

Date	Mintage	F	VF	XF	Unc	BU
2003(sp) Proof	1,500	Value: 850				

Y# 832 100 ROUBLES
17.2800 g., 0.9000 Gold 0.5000 oz. AGW, 30 mm. **Subject:** 2nd Kamchatka Expedition **Obv:** Double-headed eagle **Rev:** Shaman and two seated men **Edge:** Reeded

Date	Mintage	F	VF	XF	Unc	BU
2004(sp) Proof	1,500	Value: 850				

Y# 831 100 ROUBLES
1000.0000 g., 0.9000 Silver 28.934 oz. ASW, 100 mm. **Obv:** Double-headed eagle **Rev:** Panel of icons painted by Theophanes the Greek **Edge:** Reeded **Note:** Illustration reduced.

Date	Mintage	F	VF	XF	Unc	BU
2004(sp) Proof	500	Value: 1,850				

Y# 876 100 ROUBLES
1111.1200 g., 0.9000 Silver 32.149 oz. ASW, 100 mm. **Rev:** Annunciation Cathedral Iconostasis

Date	Mintage	F	VF	XF	Unc	BU
2004(sp) Proof	500	Value: 2,000				

Y# 1024 100 ROUBLES
1000.0000 g., 0.9250 Silver 29.738 oz. ASW, 100 mm. **Subject:** Reindeer

Date	Mintage	F	VF	XF	Unc	BU
2004 Proof	—	Value: 1,750				

Y# 1026 100 ROUBLES
1000.0000 g., 0.9990 Silver 32.117 oz. ASW, 100 mm. **Subject:** Reindeer

Date	Mintage	F	VF	XF	Unc	BU
2004 Proof	—	Value: 1,750				

Y# 1036 100 ROUBLES
1046.0000 g., 0.9250 Silver 31.106 oz. ASW, 100 mm. **Subject:** Rostov

Date	Mintage	F	VF	XF	Unc	BU
2004 Proof	—	Value: 1,750				

Y# 895 100 ROUBLES
1083.7400 g., 0.9250 Silver 32.228 oz. ASW, 100 mm. **Subject:** 60th Anniversary Victory Over Germany **Obv:** Double-headed eagle **Rev:** Decorated locomotive returning soldiers circa 1945 **Edge:** Reeded

Date	Mintage	F	VF	XF	Unc	BU
2005 Proof	2,000	Value: 1,750				

Y# 912 100 ROUBLES
1083.7400 g., 0.9250 Silver 32.228 oz. ASW, 100 mm. **Obv:** Double-headed eagle **Rev:** Kazan city view with mausoleums **Edge:** Reeded **Note:** Illustration reduced.

Date	Mintage	F	VF	XF	Unc	BU
2005 Proof	500	Value: 1,850				

Y# 925 100 ROUBLES
1083.7400 g., 0.9250 Silver 32.228 oz. ASW, 100 mm. **Subject:** 625th Anniversary - Battle of Kulikovo **Obv:** Double-headed eagle **Rev:** Battle of Kulikovo beginning scene **Edge:** Reeded **Note:** Illustration reduced.

Date	Mintage	F	VF	XF	Unc	BU
2005 Proof	500	Value: 1,850				

Y# 1078 100 ROUBLES
1046.0000 g., 0.9250 Silver 31.106 oz. ASW, 100 mm. **Subject:** Yuryev Polsky

Date	Mintage	F	VF	XF	Unc	BU
2006	—	Value: 1,750				

Y# 1044 100 ROUBLES
1046.0000 g., 0.9250 Silver 31.106 oz. ASW, 100 mm. **Subject:** Frigate Myr

Date	Mintage	F	VF	XF	Unc	BU
2006 Proof	—	Value: 1,350				

Y# 1061 100 ROUBLES
1046.0000 g., 0.9250 Silver 31.106 oz. ASW, 100 mm. **Subject:** Moscow's Kremlin and Red Square

Date	Mintage	F	VF	XF	Unc	BU
2006 Proof	—	Value: 1,350				

Y# 1077 100 ROUBLES
1046.0000 g., 0.9250 Silver 31.106 oz. ASW, 100 mm. **Subject:** Bogolyubovo Township

Date	Mintage	F	VF	XF	Unc	BU
2006 Proof	—	Value: 1,750				

Y# 1081 100 ROUBLES
1046.0000 g., 0.9250 Silver 31.106 oz. ASW, 100 mm. **Subject:** International Artic Year

Date	Mintage	F	VF	XF	Unc	BU
2007 Proof	—	Value: 1,750				

Y# 1085 100 ROUBLES
1046.0000 g., 0.9250 Silver 31.106 oz. ASW, 100 mm. **Subject:** Russian railways, 175th Anniversary

Date	Mintage	F	VF	XF	Unc	BU
2007 Proof	—	Value: 1,750				

Y# 1089 100 ROUBLES
1046.0000 g., 0.9250 Silver 31.106 oz. ASW, 100 mm. **Subject:** Andrew Rublyov

Date	Mintage	F	VF	XF	Unc	BU
2007 Proof	—	Value: 1,750				

Y# 1093 100 ROUBLES
169.0000 g., 0.9250 Silver 5.0258 oz. ASW, 60 mm. **Subject:** Bashkiria, 450th Anniversary of Annexation by Russia

Date	Mintage	F	VF	XF	Unc	BU
2007 Proof	—	Value: 285				

Y# 1096 100 ROUBLES
1046.0000 g., 0.9250 Silver 31.106 oz. ASW, 100 mm. **Subject:** Khakassia, 300th Anniversary of Annexation by Russia

Date	Mintage	F	VF	XF	Unc	BU
2007 Proof	—	Value: 1,750				

Y# 1120 100 ROUBLES
1046.0000 g., 0.9250 Silver 31.106 oz. ASW, 100 mm. **Subject:** Udmurtiya, 450th Anniversary of Annexation into Russia

Date	Mintage	F	VF	XF	Unc	BU
2008 Proof	—	Value: 1,750				

Y# 1140 100 ROUBLES
1046.0000 g., 0.9250 Silver 31.106 oz. ASW, 100 mm. **Subject:** European Beaver

Date	Mintage	F	VF	XF	Unc	BU
2008 Proof	—	Value: 1,750				

Y# 1142 100 ROUBLES
15.5600 g., 0.9990 Gold 0.4997 oz. AGW **Subject:** European Beaver

Date	Mintage	F	VF	XF	Unc	BU
2008 Proof	—	Value: 775				

Y# 1143 100 ROUBLES
1046.0000 g., 0.9250 Silver 31.106 oz. ASW, 100 mm. **Subject:** European Beaver

Date	Mintage	F	VF	XF	Unc	BU
2008 Proof	—	Value: 1,350				

Y# 1156 100 ROUBLES
1046.0000 g., 0.9250 Silver 31.106 oz. ASW, 100 mm. **Subject:** Pereslaval Zalessky

Date	Mintage	F	VF	XF	Unc	BU
2008 Proof	—	Value: 1,750				

Y# 1157 100 ROUBLES
1046.0000 g., 0.9990 Silver 33.594 oz. ASW, 100 mm. **Subject:** Alexandrov

Date	Mintage	F	VF	XF	Unc	BU
2008 Proof	—	Value: 1,750				

Y# 1148 100 ROUBLES
1046.0000 g., 0.9250 Silver 31.106 oz. ASW, 100 mm. **Subject:** Kamchatka Volcano

Date	Mintage	F	VF	XF	Unc	BU
2008 Proof	—	Value: 1,750				

Y# 1162 100 ROUBLES
168.0000 g., 0.9250 Silver 4.9960 oz. ASW, 60 mm. **Subject:** Russian Currency

Date	Mintage	F	VF	XF	Unc	BU
2009 Proof	—	Value: 285				

Y# 1163 100 ROUBLES
168.0000 g., 0.9250 Silver 4.9960 oz. ASW, 60 mm. **Subject:** Russian Currency

Date	Mintage	F	VF	XF	Unc	BU
2009 Proof	—	Value: 285				

Y# 1167 100 ROUBLES
168.0000 g., 0.9250 Silver 4.9960 oz. ASW, 60 mm. **Subject:** A. P. Chekhov, 150th Anniversary of Birth

Date	Mintage	F	VF	XF	Unc	BU
2009 Proof	—	Value: 285				

Y# 1171 100 ROUBLES
1046.0000 g., 0.9990 Silver 33.594 oz. ASW, 100 mm. **Subject:** Kalmyk Peoples, 400th Anniversary of annexation into Russia

Date	Mintage	F	VF	XF	Unc	BU
2009 Proof	—	Value: 1,750				

Y# 1174 100 ROUBLES
33.9000 g., 0.9250 Silver 1.0081 oz. ASW, 39 mm. **Subject:** N. V. Gogol, 200th Anniversary of Birth

Date	Mintage	F	VF	XF	Unc	BU
2009 Proof	—	Value: 60.00				

Y# 1179 100 ROUBLES
1048.0000 g., 0.9250 Silver 31.165 oz. ASW, 100 mm. **Subject:** Poltava Battle, 300th Anniversary

Date	Mintage	F	VF	XF	Unc	BU
2009 Proof	—	Value: 1,750				

Y# 1238 100 ROUBLES
1046.0000 g., 0.9250 Silver 31.106 oz. ASW, 100 mm. **Subject:** A. P. Chekhov, 200th Anniversary of Birth

Date	Mintage	F	VF	XF	Unc	BU
2010 Prooflike	—	—	—	—	—	1,350

Y# 877 200 ROUBLES
3342.3899 g., 0.9000 Silver 96.710 oz. ASW, 130 mm. **Rev:** Peter I monetary reform

Date	Mintage	F	VF	XF	Unc	BU
2003(sp) Proof	300	Value: 5,250				

Y# 1027 200 ROUBLES
31.1050 g., 0.9990 Gold 0.9990 oz. AGW **Subject:** Reindeer

Date	Mintage	F	VF	XF	Unc	BU
2004 Proof	500	Value: 3,250				

Y# 1042 200 ROUBLES
31.1000 g., 0.9990 Gold 0.9988 oz. AGW **Subject:** Parliament, 100th Anniversary

Date	Mintage	F	VF	XF	Unc	BU
2006 Proof	750	Value: 1,500				

Y# 1062 200 ROUBLES
3138.0000 g., 0.9250 Silver 93.318 oz. ASW, 100 mm. **Subject:** Moscow's Kremlin and Red Square

Date	Mintage	F	VF	XF	Unc	BU
2006 Proof	200	Value: 6,500				

Y# 1144 200 ROUBLES
31.1050 g., 0.9990 Gold 0.9990 oz. AGW **Subject:** European Beaver

Date	Mintage	F	VF	XF	Unc	BU
2008 Proof	500	Value: 3,250				

Y# 1169 200 ROUBLES
31.1050 g., 0.9990 Gold 0.9990 oz. AGW **Subject:** A. P. Chekhov, 150th Anniversary of Birth

Date	Mintage	F	VF	XF	Unc	BU
2009 Proof	500	Value: 1,750				

Y# 1176 200 ROUBLES
3120.0000 g., 0.9250 Silver 92.783 oz. ASW **Subject:** N. V. Gogol, 200th Anniversary of Birth **Edge:** 100

Date	Mintage	F	VF	XF	Unc	BU
2009 Proof	—	Value: 6,500				

Y# 1201 200 ROUBLES
31.1050 g., 0.9990 Gold 0.9990 oz. AGW **Subject:** Velikly Novgorod

Date	Mintage	F	VF	XF	Unc	BU
2009 Proof	200	Value: 7,500				

Y# 1209 200 ROUBLES
31.1050 g., 0.9990 Gold 0.9990 oz. AGW **Series:** Speed Skating

Date	Mintage	F	VF	XF	Unc	BU
2009 Proof	500	Value: 1,650				

Y# 1210 200 ROUBLES
31.1000 g., 0.9990 Gold 0.9988 oz. AGW **Subject:** Ski Jumping

Date	Mintage	F	VF	XF	Unc	BU
2009 Proof	500	Value: 1,650				

Y# 1211 200 ROUBLES
31.1000 g., 0.9990 Gold 0.9988 oz. AGW **Subject:** Luge

Date	Mintage	F	VF	XF	Unc	BU
2009 Proof	500	Value: 1,650				

Y# 1213 200 ROUBLES
31.1050 g., 0.9990 Gold 0.9990 oz. AGW **Subject:** Figure Skating

Date	Mintage	F	VF	XF	Unc	BU
2009 Proof	500	Value: 1,650				

Y# 1212 200 ROUBLES
31.1050 g., 0.9990 Gold 0.9990 oz. AGW **Subject:** Biathlon

Date	Mintage	F	VF	XF	Unc	BU
2009 Proof	500	Value: 1,650				

Y# 1234 200 ROUBLES
3130.0000 g., 0.9250 Silver 93.080 oz. ASW **Subject:** UNESCO Heritage Site - Yaroslav

Date	Mintage	F	VF	XF	Unc	BU
2010 Proof	200	Value: 6,000				

Y# 1240 200 ROUBLES
31.1000 g., 0.9990 Gold 0.9988 oz. AGW **Subject:** A. P. Chekhov, 200th Anniversary of Birth

Date	Mintage	F	VF	XF	Unc	BU
2010 Proof	500	Value: 1,750				

Y# 1255 200 ROUBLES
31.1000 g., 0.9990 Gold 0.9988 oz. AGW **Subject:** Hockey

Date	Mintage	F	VF	XF	Unc	BU
2010 Proof	—	Value: 1,650				

Y# 1256 200 ROUBLES
31.1000 g., 0.9990 Gold 0.9988 oz. AGW **Subject:** Ski Race

Date	Mintage	F	VF	XF	Unc	BU
2010 Proof	500	Value: 1,650				

Y# 1257 200 ROUBLES
31.1000 g., 0.9990 Gold 0.9988 oz. AGW **Subject:** Nordic Combined

Date	Mintage	F	VF	XF	Unc	BU
2010 Proof	500	Value: 1,650				

Y# 1258 200 ROUBLES
31.1000 g., 0.9990 Gold 0.9988 oz. AGW **Subject:** Freestyle Skiing

Date	Mintage	F	VF	XF	Unc	BU
2010 Proof	500	Value: 1,650				

Y# 1259 200 ROUBLES
31.1000 g., 0.9990 Gold 0.9988 oz. AGW **Subject:** Short Track Speed Skating

Date	Mintage	F	VF	XF	Unc	BU
2010 Proof	500	Value: 1,650				

Y# 1260 200 ROUBLES
31.1000 g., 0.9990 Gold 0.9988 oz. AGW **Subject:** Curling

Date	Mintage	F	VF	XF	Unc	BU
2010 Proof	500	Value: 1,650				

Y# 1261 200 ROUBLES
31.1000 g., 0.9990 Gold 0.9988 oz. AGW **Subject:** Snowboarding

Date	Mintage	F	VF	XF	Unc	BU
2010 Proof	500	Value: 1,650				

Y# 1262 200 ROUBLES
31.1000 g., 0.9990 Gold 0.9988 oz. AGW **Subject:** Skeleton

Date	Mintage	F	VF	XF	Unc	BU
2010 Proof	500	Value: 1,650				

Y# 1263 200 ROUBLES
31.1000 g., 0.9990 Gold 0.9988 oz. AGW **Subject:** Bobsled

Date	Mintage	F	VF	XF	Unc	BU
2010 Proof	500	Value: 1,650				

Y# 1264 200 ROUBLES
31.1000 g., 0.9990 Gold 0.9988 oz. AGW **Subject:** Mountain Skiing

Date	Mintage	F	VF	XF	Unc	BU
2010 Proof	500	Value: 1,650				

Y# 796 1000 ROUBLES
156.4000 g., 0.9990 Gold 5.0231 oz. AGW, 50 mm. **Subject:** The Bark Sedov **Obv:** Double-headed eagle **Rev:** Four-masted sailing ship **Edge:** Reeded

Date	Mintage	F	VF	XF	Unc	BU
2001(m) Proof	250	Value: 7,500				

Y# 878 1000 ROUBLES
156.4000 g., 0.9990 Gold 5.0231 oz. AGW, 50 mm. **Rev:** Cronstadt

Date	Mintage	F	VF	XF	Unc	BU
2003(m) Proof	250	Value: 7,500				

Y# 1037 1000 ROUBLES
1046.0000 g., 0.9250 Silver 31.106 oz. ASW, 100 mm. **Subject:** Uglich

Date	Mintage	F	VF	XF	Unc	BU
2004 Proof	—	Value: 1,750				

Y# 1045 1000 ROUBLES
1000.0000 g., 0.9990 Gold 32.117 oz. AGW, 100 mm. **Subject:** Frigate Myr

Date	Mintage	F	VF	XF	Unc	BU
2006 Proof	—	Value: 47,500				

Y# 1082 1000 ROUBLES
156.0000 g., 0.9990 Gold 5.0103 oz. AGW, 100 mm. **Subject:** International Artic Year

Date	Mintage	F	VF	XF	Unc	BU
2007 Proof	—	Value: 7,500				

Y# 1164 1000 ROUBLES
156.0000 g., 0.9990 Gold 5.0103 oz. AGW, 100 mm. **Subject:** Russian Currency

Date	Mintage	F	VF	XF	Unc	BU
2009 Proof	—	Value: 7,500				

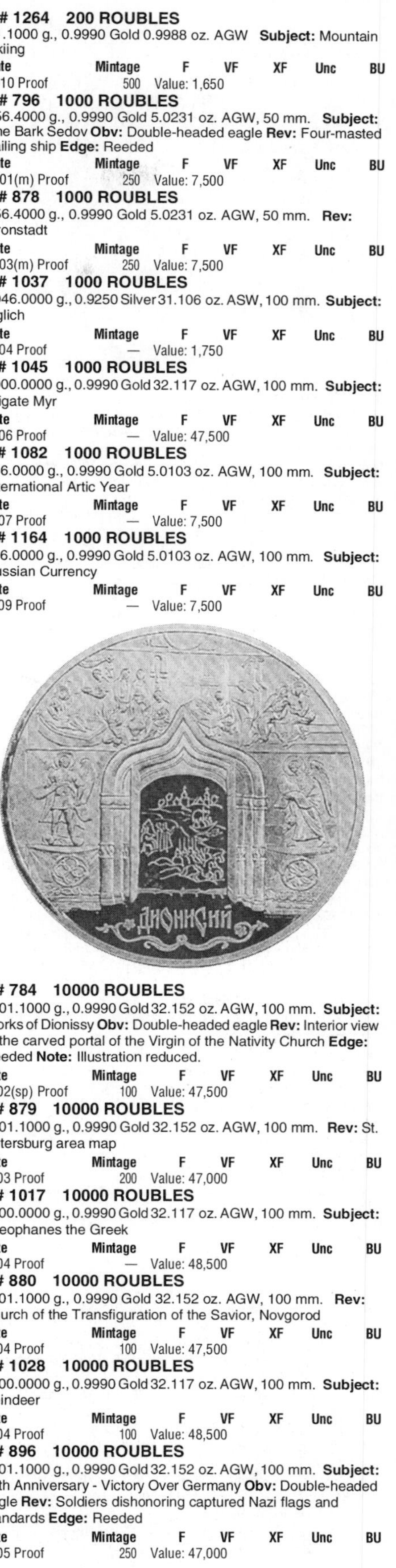

Y# 784 10000 ROUBLES
1001.1000 g., 0.9990 Gold 32.152 oz. AGW, 100 mm. **Subject:** Works of Dionissy **Obv:** Double-headed eagle **Rev:** Interior view of the carved portal of the Virgin of the Nativity Church **Edge:** Reeded **Note:** Illustration reduced.

Date	Mintage	F	VF	XF	Unc	BU
2002(sp) Proof	100	Value: 47,500				

Y# 879 10000 ROUBLES
1001.1000 g., 0.9990 Gold 32.152 oz. AGW, 100 mm. **Rev:** St. Petersburg area map

Date	Mintage	F	VF	XF	Unc	BU
2003 Proof	200	Value: 47,000				

Y# 1017 10000 ROUBLES
1000.0000 g., 0.9990 Gold 32.117 oz. AGW, 100 mm. **Subject:** Theophanes the Greek

Date	Mintage	F	VF	XF	Unc	BU
2004 Proof	—	Value: 48,500				

Y# 880 10000 ROUBLES
1001.1000 g., 0.9990 Gold 32.152 oz. AGW, 100 mm. **Rev:** Church of the Transfiguration of the Savior, Novgorod

Date	Mintage	F	VF	XF	Unc	BU
2004 Proof	100	Value: 47,500				

Y# 1028 10000 ROUBLES
1000.0000 g., 0.9990 Gold 32.117 oz. AGW, 100 mm. **Subject:** Reindeer

Date	Mintage	F	VF	XF	Unc	BU
2004 Proof	100	Value: 48,500				

Y# 896 10000 ROUBLES
1001.1000 g., 0.9990 Gold 32.152 oz. AGW, 100 mm. **Subject:** 60th Anniversary - Victory Over Germany **Obv:** Double-headed eagle **Rev:** Soldiers dishonoring captured Nazi flags and standards **Edge:** Reeded

Date	Mintage	F	VF	XF	Unc	BU
2005 Proof	250	Value: 47,000				

Y# 913 10000 ROUBLES
1001.1000 g., 0.9990 Gold 32.152 oz. AGW, 100 mm. **Obv:** Two headed eagle **Rev:** Kazan Kremlin view **Edge:** Reeded **Note:** Illustration reduced.

Date	Mintage	F	VF	XF	Unc	BU
2005 Proof	150	Value: 47,500				

Y# 1043 10000 ROUBLES
1000.0000 g., 0.9990 Gold 32.117 oz. AGW, 100 mm. **Subject:** Parliament, 100th Anniversary

Date	Mintage	F	VF	XF	Unc	BU
2006 Proof	100	Value: 47,500				

Y# 1064 10000 ROUBLES
1000.0000 g., 0.9990 Gold 32.117 oz. AGW, 100 mm. **Subject:** Moscow's Kremlin and Red Square

Date	Mintage	F	VF	XF	Unc	BU
2006 Proof	—	Value: 48,500				

Y# 1091 10000 ROUBLES
1000.0000 g., 0.9990 Gold 32.117 oz. AGW, 100 mm. **Subject:** Andrew Rublyov

Date	Mintage	F	VF	XF	Unc	BU
2007 Proof	—	Value: 48,500				

Y# 1095 10000 ROUBLES
1000.0000 g., 0.9990 Gold 32.117 oz. AGW, 100 mm. **Subject:** Bashkiria, 450th Anniversary of Annexation by Russia

Date	Mintage	F	VF	XF	Unc	BU
2007 Proof	—	Value: 47,500				

Y# 1098 10000 ROUBLES
1000.0000 g., 0.9990 Gold 32.117 oz. AGW, 100 mm. **Subject:** Khakassia, 300th Anniversary of Annexation by Russia

Date	Mintage	F	VF	XF	Unc	BU
2007 Proof	—	Value: 48,500				

Y# 1122 10000 ROUBLES
1000.0000 g., 0.9990 Gold 32.117 oz. AGW, 100 mm. **Subject:** Udmurtiya, 450th Anniversary of Annexation into Russia

Date	Mintage	F	VF	XF	Unc	BU
2008 Proof	—	—	—	—	—	48,500

Y# 1145 10000 ROUBLES
1000.0000 g., 0.9990 Gold 32.117 oz. AGW, 100 mm. **Subject:** European Beaver

Date	Mintage	F	VF	XF	Unc	BU
2008 Proof	—	Value: 48,500				

Y# 1149 10000 ROUBLES
1000.0000 g., 0.9990 Gold 32.117 oz. AGW, 100 mm. **Subject:** Kamchatka Volcano

Date	Mintage	F	VF	XF	Unc	BU
2008 Proof	—	Value: 48,500				

Y# 1203 10000 ROUBLES
1000.0000 g., 0.9990 Gold 32.117 oz. AGW, 100 mm. **Subject:** Velikly Novgorod

Date	Mintage	F	VF	XF	Unc	BU
2009 Proof	—	Value: 48,500				

Y# 1236 10000 ROUBLES
1000.0000 g., 0.9990 Gold 32.117 oz. AGW, 100 mm. **Subject:** UNESCO Heritage Site - Yaroslav

Date	Mintage	F	VF	XF	Unc	BU
2010 Prooflike	—	—	—	—	—	47,500

Y# 1117 25000 ROUBLES
1000.0000 g., 0.9990 Gold 32.117 oz. AGW, 100 mm. **Subject:** Goznak, 190th Anniversary

Date	Mintage	F	VF	XF	Unc	BU
2008 Proof	—	Value: 48,000				

Y# 1165 25000 ROUBLES
1000.0000 g., 0.9990 Gold 32.117 oz. AGW, 100 mm. **Subject:** Russian Currency

Date	Mintage	F	VF	XF	Unc	BU
2009 Proof	—	Value: 48,000				

Y# 1231 50000 ROUBLES
5000.0000 g., 0.9990 Gold 160.58 oz. AGW **Subject:** Bank of Russia, 150th Anniversary

Date	Mintage	F	VF	XF	Unc	BU
2010 Prooflike	—	—	—	—	—	235,000

MINT SETS

KM#	Date	Mintage	Identification	Issue Price	Mkt Val
MS44	2002 (7)	—	Y#600-603, 797-799, plus mint medal	7.50	15.00

RWANDA

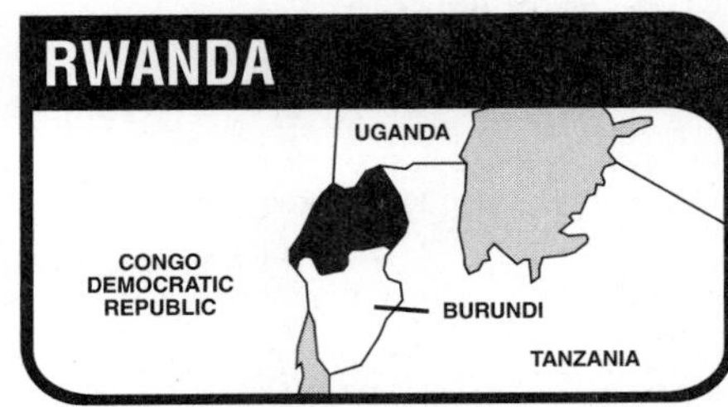

The Republic of Rwanda, located in central Africa between the Republic of the Congo and Tanzania, has an area of 10,169 sq. mi. (26,340 sq. km.) and a population of 7.3 million. Capital: Kigali. The economy is based on agriculture and mining. Coffee and tin are exported.

For earlier coinage see Belgian Congo, and Rwanda and Burundi.

MINT MARKS
(a) - Paris, privy marks only
(b) - Brussels, privy marks only

MONETARY SYSTEM
100 Centimes = 1 Franc

REPUBLIC

STANDARD COINAGE

KM# 22 FRANC
0.0700 g., Aluminum, 16 mm. **Obv:** National arms **Rev:** Sorghum plant **Edge:** Plain

Date	Mintage	F	VF	XF	Unc	BU
2003	—	—	—	0.25	0.65	1.00

KM# 23 5 FRANCS
2.9600 g., Brass Plated Steel, 20 mm. **Obv:** National arms **Rev:** Coffee plant **Edge:** Plain

Date	Mintage	F	VF	XF	Unc	BU
2003	—	—	—	0.25	0.65	1.00

KM# 24 10 FRANCS
5.0000 g., Brass Plated Steel, 23.9 mm. **Obv:** National arms **Rev:** Banana tree **Edge:** Plain

Date	Mintage	F	VF	XF	Unc	BU
2003	—	—	—	0.45	1.00	1.50

KM# 25 20 FRANCS
3.5000 g., Nickel Clad Steel, 20 mm. **Obv:** National arms **Rev:** Coffee plant seedling **Edge:** Reeded

Date	Mintage	F	VF	XF	Unc	BU
2003	—	—	—	—	1.75	2.00

KM# 26 50 FRANCS
5.8000 g., Nickel Clad Steel, 24 mm. **Obv:** National arms **Rev:** Ear of corn within husks **Edge:** Reeded

Date	Mintage	F	VF	XF	Unc	BU
2003(a)	—	—	—	—	2.50	4.00

KM# 32 100 FRANCS
Bi-Metallic, 27 mm. **Obv:** Shield **Rev:** Value

Date	Mintage	F	VF	XF	Unc	BU
2007	—	—	—	—	5.00	6.50

KM# 28 200 FRANCS
1.0000 g., 0.9990 Gold 0.0321 oz. AGW, 13.9 mm. **Subject:** 75th Birthday Dian Fossey **Obv:** National arms **Obv. Legend:** BANKI NASIYONALI Y'U RWANDA **Rev:** Fossey facing holding monkey **Edge:** Plain

Date	Mintage	F	VF	XF	Unc	BU
2007 Proof	15,000	Value: 85.00				

KM# 30 500 FRANCS
22.2000 g., 0.9000 Silver 0.6423 oz. ASW **Obv:** National arms **Obv. Legend:** BANQUE NATIONALE DU RWANDA **Rev:** Stalk of bananas on leaves

Date	Mintage	F	VF	XF	Unc	BU
2002(a) Proof	500	Value: 115				

KM# 31 500 FRANCS
22.2000 g., 0.9000 Silver 0.6423 oz. ASW **Subject:** Euro Parity **Obv:** Arms **Rev:** Plant

Date	Mintage	F	VF	XF	Unc	BU
2002 Proof	500	Value: 115				

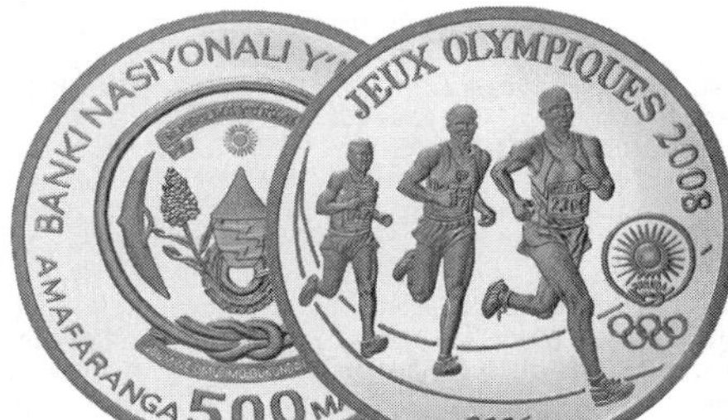

KM# 27 500 FRANCS
20.0000 g., 0.9990 Silver 0.6423 oz. ASW, 38 mm. **Subject:** Olympic Games 2008 - Peking, marathon races **Obv:** National arms **Obv. Legend:** BANKI NASIYONALI Y'U RWANDA **Rev:** Three male marathon runners, Rwanda Olympic logo at right **Rev. Legend:** JEUX OLYMPIQUES **Edge:** Plain

Date	Mintage	F	VF	XF	Unc	BU
2006 Proof	—	Value: 110				

KM# 29 1000 FRANCS
93.3000 g., 0.9990 Silver And Gold 2.9965 oz., 65 mm. **Obv:** National arms **Obv. Legend:** BANKI NASIYONALI Y'U RWANDA **Rev:** Gilt elephant family of four with diamonds inset in eyes **Rev. Legend:** AFRICAN ELEPHANT **Edge:** Plain **Note:** Illustration reduced.

Date	Mintage	F	VF	XF	Unc	BU
2007	1,500	—	—	—	—	650
2007 Proof	500	Value: 1,000				

SAHARAWI ARAB D.R.

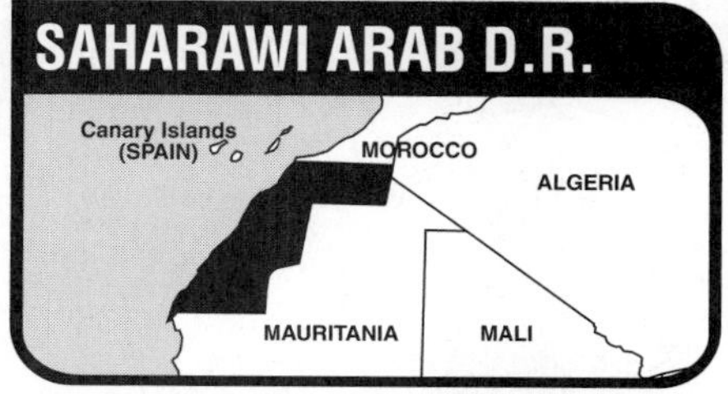

The Saharawi Arab Democratic Republic, located in northwest Africa has an area of 102,703 sq. mi. and a population (census taken 1974) of 76,425. Formerly known as Spanish Sahara, the area is bounded on the north by Morocco, on the east and southeast by Mauritania, on the northeast by Algeria, and on the west by the Atlantic Ocean. Capital: El Aaium. Agriculture, fishing and mining are the three main industries. Exports are barley, livestock and phosphates. The SADR is a "government in exile". It currently controls about 20% of its claimed territory, the former Spanish colony of Western Sahara; Morocco controls and administers the majority of the territory as its Southern Provinces. SADR claims control over a zone largely bordering Mauritania, described as "the Free Zone," although characterized by Morocco as a buffer zone.

DEMOCRATIC REPUBLIC

STANDARD COINAGE

KM# 54 1000 PESETAS

19.9400 g., 0.9990 Silver 0.6404 oz. ASW, 38.1 mm. **Obv:** National arms **Rev:** Soccer player and stadium **Edge:** Plain

Date	Mintage	F	VF	XF	Unc	BU
2002 Proof	—	Value: 35.00				

SAINT HELENA

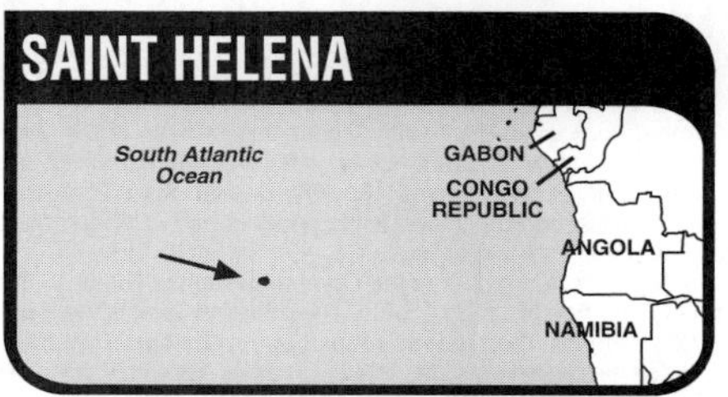

Saint Helena, a British colony located about 1,150 miles (1,850 km.) from the west coast of Africa, has an area of 47 sq. mi. (410 sq. km.) and a population of *7,000. Capital: Jamestown. Flax, lace, and rope are produced for export. Ascension and Tristan da Cunha are dependencies of Saint Helena.

MONETARY SYSTEM

100 Pence = 1 Pound

BRITISH COLONY

STANDARD COINAGE

KM# 19 50 PENCE

38.6000 g., Copper-Nickel, 38.6 mm. **Ruler:** Elizabeth II **Subject:** 75th Birthday of Queen Elizabeth II **Obv:** Crowned bust right **Obv. Designer:** Raphael Maklouf **Rev:** Bust facing within circle and rose sprigs **Edge:** Reeded

Date	Mintage	VG	F	VF	XF	Unc
2001	—	—	—	—	—	8.00

KM# 19a 50 PENCE

28.2800 g., 0.9250 Silver 0.8410 oz. ASW, 38.6 mm. **Ruler:** Elizabeth II **Subject:** 75th Birthday of Queen Elizabeth II **Obv:** Crowned bust right **Rev:** Bust facing within circle and rose sprigs **Edge:** Reeded

Date	Mintage	F	VF	XF	Unc	BU
2001 Proof	10,000	Value: 45.00				

KM# 19b 50 PENCE

47.5400 g., 0.9166 Gold 1.4009 oz. AGW, 38.6 mm. **Ruler:** Elizabeth II **Subject:** 75th Birthday of Queen Elizabeth II **Obv:** Crowned bust right **Rev:** Bust facing within circle and rose sprigs **Edge:** Reeded

Date	Mintage	F	VF	XF	Unc	BU
2001 Proof	75	Value: 2,250				

KM# 20 50 PENCE

28.5500 g., Copper-Nickel, 38.6 mm. **Ruler:** Elizabeth II **Subject:** Queen Victoria's Death **Obv:** Crowned bust right **Obv. Designer:** Raphael Maklouf **Rev:** Half-length figure facing and ship within circle **Edge:** Reeded

Date	Mintage	VG	F	VF	XF	Unc
2001	—	—	—	—	—	8.00

KM# 20a 50 PENCE

28.2800 g., 0.9250 Silver 0.8410 oz. ASW, 38.6 mm. **Ruler:** Elizabeth II **Subject:** Centennial - Death of Queen Victoria **Obv:** Crowned bust right **Rev:** Half-length figure facing and ship within circle **Edge:** Reeded

Date	Mintage	F	VF	XF	Unc	BU
2001 Proof	10,000	Value: 45.00				

KM# 20b 50 PENCE

47.5400 g., 0.9166 Gold 1.4009 oz. AGW, 38.6 mm. **Ruler:** Elizabeth II **Subject:** Centennial - Death of Queen Victoria **Obv:** Crowned bust right **Rev:** Half-length figure facing and ship within circle **Edge:** Reeded

Date	Mintage	F	VF	XF	Unc	BU
2001 Proof	100	Value: 2,200				

KM# 23 50 PENCE

28.2800 g., Copper-Nickel, 38.6 mm. **Ruler:** Elizabeth II **Subject:** 50th Anniversary - Queen Elizabeth II's Accession **Obv:** Crowned bust right **Obv. Designer:** Raphael Maklouf **Rev:** Crown on pillow within circle **Edge:** Reeded

Date	Mintage	F	VF	XF	Unc	BU
ND(2002)	—	—	—	—	8.00	10.00

KM# 23a 50 PENCE

28.2800 g., 0.9250 Silver 0.8410 oz. ASW, 38.6 mm. **Ruler:** Elizabeth II **Subject:** 50th Anniversary - Queen Elizabeth's Accession **Obv:** Crowned bust right **Rev:** Crown on pillow within circle **Edge:** Reeded

Date	Mintage	F	VF	XF	Unc	BU
ND(2002) Proof	10,000	Value: 40.00				

KM# 24 50 PENCE

28.2800 g., Copper-Nickel, 38.6 mm. **Ruler:** Elizabeth II **Subject:** To Celebrate a Life of Duty, Dignity and Love, 1900-2002 **Obv:** Crowned bust right **Obv. Designer:** Raphael Maklouf **Rev:** Conjoined busts right **Rev. Designer:** Willem Vis **Edge:** Reeded

Date	Mintage	F	VF	XF	Unc	BU
ND(2002)	—	—	—	—	8.00	10.00

KM# 24a 50 PENCE

28.2800 g., 0.9250 Silver 0.8410 oz. ASW, 38.6 mm. **Ruler:** Elizabeth II **Subject:** To Celebrate a Life of Duty, Dignity and Love, 1900-2002 **Obv:** Crowned bust right **Rev:** Conjoined busts right **Edge:** Reeded

Date	Mintage	F	VF	XF	Unc	BU
ND(2002) Proof	10,000	Value: 40.00				

KM# 25 50 PENCE

28.2800 g., Copper-Nickel, 38.6 mm. **Ruler:** Elizabeth II **Subject:** 500th Anniversary - Discovery of St. Helena **Obv:** Crowned bust right **Obv. Designer:** Raphael Maklouf **Rev:** Half length figure right and ship above 1502 date **Rev. Designer:** Willem Vis **Edge:** Reeded

Date	Mintage	F	VF	XF	Unc	BU
ND(2002)	—	—	—	—	10.00	12.00

KM# 25a 50 PENCE

28.2800 g., 0.9250 Silver 0.8410 oz. ASW, 38.6 mm. **Ruler:** Elizabeth II **Subject:** 500th Anniversary - Discovery of St. Helena **Obv:** Crowned bust right **Rev:** Half length figure right and ship above 1502 date **Edge:** Reeded

Date	Mintage	F	VF	XF	Unc	BU
ND(2002) Proof	5,000	Value: 50.00				

KM# 26 50 PENCE

28.2800 g., Copper-Nickel, 38.6 mm. **Ruler:** Elizabeth II **Obv:** Crowned bust right **Obv. Designer:** Raphael Maklouf **Rev:** Bust 1/4 left, ship HMS Paramour and a comet **Rev. Designer:** Willem Vis **Edge:** Reeded

Date	Mintage	F	VF	XF	Unc	BU
ND(2002)	—	—	—	—	10.00	12.00

KM# 26a 50 PENCE

28.2800 g., 0.9250 Silver 0.8410 oz. ASW, 38.6 mm. **Ruler:** Elizabeth II **Obv:** Crowned bust right **Rev:** Bust 1/4 left, ship HMS Paramour and a comet **Edge:** Reeded

Date	Mintage	F	VF	XF	Unc	BU
ND(2002) Proof	5,000	Value: 50.00				

KM# 27 50 PENCE

28.2800 g., Copper-Nickel, 38.6 mm. **Ruler:** Elizabeth II **Obv:** Crowned bust right **Obv. Designer:** Raphael Maklouf **Rev:** Bust 1/4 right and the HMS Resolution **Rev. Designer:** Willem Vis **Edge:** Reeded

Date	Mintage	F	VF	XF	Unc	BU
ND(2002)	—	—	—	—	10.00	12.00

KM# 27a 50 PENCE

28.2800 g., 0.9250 Silver 0.8410 oz. ASW, 38.6 mm. **Ruler:** Elizabeth II **Obv:** Crowned bust right **Rev:** Bust 1/4 right and the HMS Resolution **Edge:** Reeded

Date	Mintage	F	VF	XF	Unc	BU
ND(2002) Proof	5,000	Value: 50.00				

KM# 28 50 PENCE

28.2800 g., Copper-Nickel, 38.6 mm. **Ruler:** Elizabeth II **Obv:** Crowned bust right **Obv. Designer:** Raphael Maklouf **Rev:** Half length figure facing and the ship HMS Northumberland **Rev. Designer:** Willem Vis **Edge:** Reeded

Date	Mintage	F	VF	XF	Unc	BU
ND(2002)	—	—	—	—	10.00	12.00

KM# 28a 50 PENCE

28.2800 g., 0.9250 Silver 0.8410 oz. ASW, 38.6 mm. **Ruler:** Elizabeth II **Obv:** Queen Elizabeth II **Rev:** Napoleon and the ship HMS Northumberland **Edge:** Reeded

Date	Mintage	F	VF	XF	Unc	BU
ND(2002) Proof	5,000	Value: 50.00				

KM# 29 50 PENCE

28.2800 g., Copper-Nickel, 38.6 mm. **Ruler:** Elizabeth II **Obv:** Crowned bust right **Obv. Designer:** Raphael Maklouf **Rev:** Four conjoined busts left plus the HMS Vanguard **Rev. Designer:** Willem Vis **Edge:** Reeded

Date	Mintage	F	VF	XF	Unc	BU
ND(2002)	—	—	—	—	8.00	10.00

KM# 29a 50 PENCE

28.2800 g., 0.9250 Silver 0.8410 oz. ASW, 38.6 mm. **Ruler:** Elizabeth II **Obv:** Crowned bust right **Rev:** Four conjoined busts left plus the HMS Vanguard **Edge:** Reeded

Date	Mintage	F	VF	XF	Unc	BU
ND(2002) Proof	5,000	Value: 45.00				

KM# 30 50 PENCE
28.2800 g., Copper-Nickel, 38.6 mm. **Ruler:** Elizabeth II **Subject:** 50th Anniversary of Queen Elizabeth's Coronation **Obv:** Crowned bust right **Obv. Designer:** Raphael Maklouf **Rev:** Crowned Queen facing with scepter and orb **Edge:** Reeded

Date	Mintage	F	VF	XF	Unc	BU
ND(2003)	—	—	—	—	10.00	12.00

KM# 30a 50 PENCE
28.2800 g., 0.9250 Silver 0.8410 oz. ASW, 38.6 mm. **Ruler:** Elizabeth II **Subject:** 50th Anniversary - Queen Elizabeth's Coronation **Obv:** Crowned bust right **Rev:** Crowned Queen facing with scepter and orb **Edge:** Reeded

Date	Mintage	F	VF	XF	Unc	BU
ND(2003) Proof	5,000	Value: 50.00				

KM# 30b 50 PENCE
39.9400 g., 0.9166 Gold 1.1770 oz. AGW, 38.6 mm. **Ruler:** Elizabeth II **Subject:** 50th Anniversary of Queen's Coronation **Obv:** Crowned bust right **Rev:** Crowned Queen facing with scepter and orb **Edge:** Reeded

Date	Mintage	F	VF	XF	Unc	BU
ND(2003) Proof	50	Value: 2,000				

KM# 31 50 PENCE
28.2800 g., Copper-Nickel, 38.6 mm. **Ruler:** Elizabeth II **Subject:** 50th Anniversary of Coronation **Obv:** Crowned bust right **Obv. Designer:** Raphael Maklouf **Rev:** Coronation implements **Edge:** Reeded

Date	Mintage	F	VF	XF	Unc	BU
ND(2003)	—	—	—	—	10.00	12.00

KM# 31a 50 PENCE
28.2800 g., 0.9250 Silver 0.8410 oz. ASW, 38.6 mm. **Ruler:** Elizabeth II **Subject:** 50th Anniversary - Queen Elizabeth II's Coronation **Obv:** Crowned bust right **Rev:** Coronation implements **Edge:** Reeded

Date	Mintage	F	VF	XF	Unc	BU
ND(2003) Proof	5,000	Value: 50.00				

KM# 31b 50 PENCE
39.9400 g., 0.9166 Gold 1.1770 oz. AGW, 38.6 mm. **Ruler:** Elizabeth II **Subject:** 50th Anniversary of Coronation **Obv:** Crowned bust right **Rev:** Coronation implements **Edge:** Reeded

Date	Mintage	F	VF	XF	Unc	BU
ND(2003) Proof	50	Value: 2,000				

PIEFORTS

KM#	Date	Mintage	Identification	Mkt Val
P3	ND(2002)	500	50 Pence. 0.9250 Silver. 56.5600 g. 38.6 mm. Reeded edge. Proof.	120

SAINT HELENA & ASCENSION

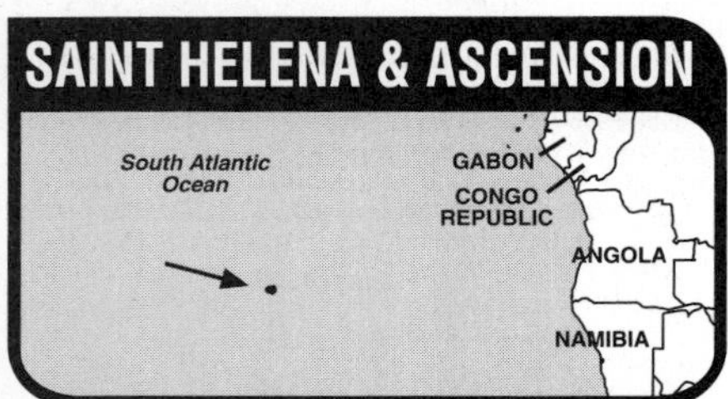

Saint Helena, a British colony located about 1,150 miles (1,850 km.) from the west coast of Africa, has an area of 47 sq. mi. (410 sq. km.) and a population of *7,000. Capital: Jamestown. Flax, lace, and rope are produced for export. Ascension and Tristan da Cunha are dependencies of Saint Helena.

MONETARY SYSTEM
100 Pence = 1 Pound

BRITISH OVERSEAS TERRITORY

STANDARD COINAGE

100 Pence = 1 Pound

KM# 13a PENNY
3.5000 g., Copper Plated Steel, 20.28 mm. **Ruler:** Queen Elizabeth II **Obv:** Crowned head right **Obv. Designer:** Raphael David Maklouf **Rev:** Tuna above value **Rev. Designer:** Michael Hibbit **Edge:** Plain

Date	Mintage	F	VF	XF	Unc	BU
2003	—	—	—	0.15	0.35	0.75

KM# 12a 2 PENCE
Copper Plated Steel, 25.9 mm. **Ruler:** Queen Elizabeth II **Obv:** Crowned head right **Obv. Designer:** Raphael David Maklouf **Rev:** Value below donkey **Rev. Designer:** Mike Hibbit

Date	Mintage	F	VF	XF	Unc	BU
2003	—	—	—	0.20	0.60	1.25
2006	—	—	—	0.20	0.60	1.25

KM# 22 5 PENCE
3.2500 g., Copper-Nickel, 18 mm. **Ruler:** Queen Elizabeth II **Obv:** Crowned head right **Rev:** Giant tortoise **Rev. Designer:** Robert Elderton

Date	Mintage	F	VF	XF	Unc	BU
2003	—	—	—	1.00	2.50	5.00

KM# 23 10 PENCE
6.5000 g., Copper-Nickel, 24.5 mm. **Ruler:** Queen Elizabeth II **Obv:** Crowned head right **Obv. Designer:** Raphael David Maklouf **Rev:** Dolphins **Rev. Designer:** Robert Elderton

Date	Mintage	F	VF	XF	Unc	BU
2003	—	—	—	2.00	4.00	6.00
2006	—	—	—	2.00	4.00	6.00

KM# 21 20 PENCE
5.0000 g., Copper-Nickel, 21.4 mm. **Ruler:** Queen Elizabeth II **Obv:** Crowned head right **Rev:** Ebony flower **Rev. Designer:** Robert Elderton **Shape:** 7-sided

Date	Mintage	F	VF	XF	Unc	BU
2003	—	—	—	0.75	1.50	2.50

KM# 16 50 PENCE
13.5000 g., Copper-Nickel, 30 mm. **Ruler:** Queen Elizabeth II **Obv:** Crowned head right **Obv. Designer:** Raphael David Maklouf **Rev:** Green sea turtle **Rev. Designer:** Michael Hibbit **Shape:** 7-sided

Date	Mintage	F	VF	XF	Unc	BU
2003	—	—	—	1.50	4.00	6.00
2006	—	—	—	1.50	4.00	6.00

KM# 17 POUND
9.5000 g., Nickel-Brass, 22.5 mm. **Ruler:** Queen Elizabeth II **Obv:** Crowned head right **Obv. Designer:** Raphael David Maklouf **Rev:** Sooty terns (Wideawake birds) **Rev. Designer:** Michael Hibbit

Date	Mintage	F	VF	XF	Unc	BU
2003	—	—	—	2.25	5.00	8.00
2006	—	—	—	2.25	5.00	8.00

KM# 26 2 POUNDS
11.8100 g., Nickel-Brass, 28.3 mm. **Ruler:** Queen Elizabeth II **Obv:** Crowned bust right **Obv. Designer:** Raphael Maklouf **Rev:** National arms above value **Edge:** Reeded and lettered **Edge Lettering:** 500TH ANNIVERSARY

Date	Mintage	F	VF	XF	Unc	BU
2002	—	—	—	6.00	10.00	12.50

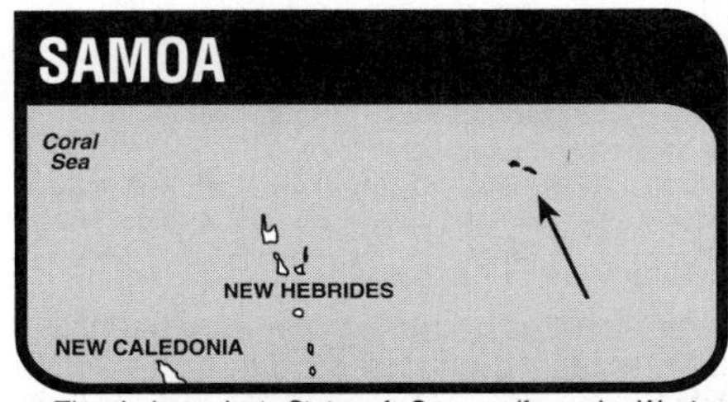

KM# 25 2 POUNDS
12.0000 g., Bi-Metallic Copper-Nickel center in Brass ring, 28.4 mm. **Ruler:** Queen Elizabeth II **Obv:** Crowned bust right **Obv. Designer:** Raphael Maklouf **Rev:** National Arms **Edge:** Reeded and lettered **Edge Lettering:** LOYAL AND FAITHFUL

Date	Mintage	F	VF	XF	Unc	BU
2003	—	—	—	9.00	15.00	17.50
2006	—	—	—	9.00	15.00	17.50

SAMOA

Coral Sea
NEW HEBRIDES
NEW CALEDONIA

The Independent State of Samoa (formerly Western Samoa), located in the Pacific Ocean 1,600 miles (2,574 km.) northeast of New Zealand, has an area of 1,097 sq. mi. (2,860 sq. km.) and a population of *182,000. Capital: Apia. The economy is based on agriculture, fishing and tourism. Copra, cocoa and bananas are exported.

Samoa is a member of the Commonwealth of Nations. The Chief Executive is Chief of State. The prime minister is the Head of Government. The present Head of State, Malietoa Tanumafili II, holds his position for life. The Legislative Assembly will elect future Heads of State for 5-year terms.

Samoa, which had used New Zealand coinage, converted to a decimal coinage in 1967.

RULER
Malietoa Tanumafili II, 1962-2007
Tuiatua Tupua Tamasese Efi, 2007-

MONETARY SYSTEM
100 Sene = 1 Tala

CONSTITUTIONAL MONARCHY
Commonwealth of Nations

STANDARD COINAGE

KM# 131 5 SENE
2.8400 g., Copper-Nickel, 19.5 mm. **Obv:** Head left **Obv. Designer:** T.H. Paget **Rev:** Pineapple and value **Rev. Designer:** James Berry **Edge:** Reeded **Note:** "Western" dropped from country name

Date	Mintage	F	VF	XF	Unc	BU
2002	—	—	—	0.30	0.50	0.75
2006	—	—	—	0.30	0.50	0.75

KM# 167 5 SENE

Nickel Plated Steel

Date	Mintage	F	VF	XF	Unc	BU
2010	—	—	—	—	0.50	0.75

KM# 132 10 SENE

5.6500 g., Copper-Nickel, 23.6 mm. **Obv:** Head left **Rev:** Taro leaves and value **Rev. Designer:** James Berry **Edge:** Reeded **Note:** "Western" dropped from country name

Date	Mintage	F	VF	XF	Unc	BU
2002	—	—	—	0.45	0.75	1.00

KM# 168 10 SENE

Nickel Plated Steel

Date	Mintage	F	VF	XF	Unc	BU
2010	—	—	—	—	0.75	1.00

KM# 133 20 SENE

11.4000 g., Copper-Nickel, 28.45 mm. **Obv:** Head left **Obv. Designer:** T.H. Paget **Rev:** Breadfruits and value **Rev. Designer:** James Berry **Edge:** Reeded **Note:** "Western" dropped from country name

Date	Mintage	F	VF	XF	Unc	BU
2002	—	—	—	0.60	1.00	1.50
2006	—	—	—	0.60	1.00	1.50

KM# 169 20 SENE

Nickel Plated Steel

Date	Mintage	F	VF	XF	Unc	BU
2010	—	—	—	—	1.00	1.50

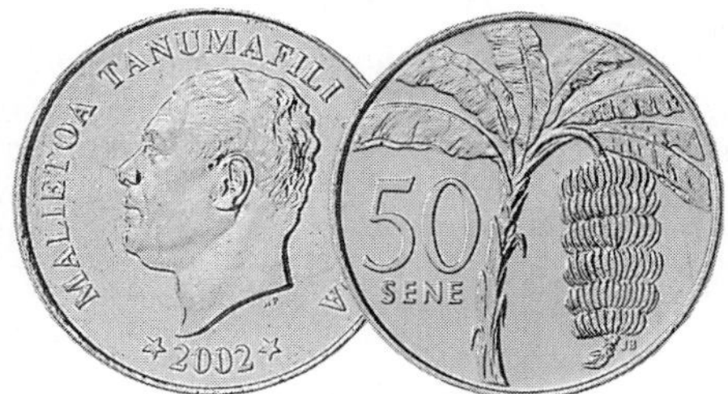

KM# 134 50 SENE

14.1300 g., Copper-Nickel, 32.3 mm. **Obv:** Head left **Rev:** Banana tree and value **Edge:** Reeded **Note:** "Western" dropped from country name

Date	Mintage	F	VF	XF	Unc	BU
2002	—	—	—	1.00	1.75	2.00

KM# 170 50 SENE

Nickel Plated Steel

Date	Mintage	F	VF	XF	Unc	BU
2010	—	—	—	—	1.75	2.00

KM# 135 TALA

9.5000 g., Brass, 30 mm. **Obv:** Head left **Obv. Designer:** T.H. Paget **Rev:** National arms above value and banner flanked by sprigs **Rev. Designer:** Nelson Eustis **Edge:** Reeded **Note:** "Western" dropped from country name

Date	Mintage	F	VF	XF	Unc	BU
2002	—	—	—	1.50	2.50	3.00

KM# 150 TALA

Goldine Plated Metal **Subject:** Thomas Mann **Obv:** Arms **Rev:** Bust facing

Date	Mintage	F	VF	XF	Unc	BU
2009	—	—	—	—	—	30.00

KM# 151 TALA

Goldine Plated Metal **Subject:** Hercules & Hydra

Date	Mintage	F	VF	XF	Unc	BU
2009	—	—	—	—	—	25.00

KM# 152 TALA

Goldine Plated Metal **Subject:** Alhambra

Date	Mintage	F	VF	XF	Unc	BU
2009	—	—	—	—	—	25.00

KM# 153 TALA

Goldine Plated Metal **Rev:** Golden horn

Date	Mintage	F	VF	XF	Unc	BU
2009	—	—	—	—	—	25.00

KM# 154 TALA

Goldine Plated Metal **Rev:** Sphinx

Date	Mintage	F	VF	XF	Unc	BU
2009	—	—	—	—	—	25.00

KM# 155 TALA

Goldine Plated Metal **Rev:** Kaiser Wilhelm II

Date	Mintage	F	VF	XF	Unc	BU
2009	—	—	—	—	—	25.00

KM# 156 TALA

Goldine Plated Metal **Rev:** Hagia Sophia

Date	Mintage	F	VF	XF	Unc	BU
2009	—	—	—	—	—	25.00

KM# 171 TALA

Aluminum-Bronze

Date	Mintage	F	VF	XF	Unc	BU
2010	—	—	—	—	2.50	3.00

KM# 165 5 TALA

28.2800 g., 0.9250 Silver 0.8410 oz. ASW, 38.61 mm. **Obv:** National Arms **Rev:** Steam Locomotive centennial

Date	Mintage	F	VF	XF	Unc	BU
2007 Proof	Est. 5,000	Value: 75.00				

KM# 166 5 TALA

31.1050 g., 0.9990 Silver 0.9990 oz. ASW, 38.6 mm. **Obv:** National arms **Rev:** John Paul II at right and as figure in flames

Date	Mintage	F	VF	XF	Unc	BU
2009 Proof	Est. 2,000	Value: 85.00				

KM# 137 10 TALA

31.1000 g., 0.9990 Silver with Mother-of-Pearl insert 0.9988 oz. ASW, 40 mm. **Series:** Save the Whales **Obv:** National arms above value and banner flanked by sprigs **Obv. Legend:** SAMOA I SISIFO **Rev:** Bowhead Whale on mother-of-pearl insert **Edge:** Plain

Date	Mintage	F	VF	XF	Unc	BU
2002 Proof	2,000	Value: 85.00				

KM# 139 10 TALA

31.4700 g., 0.9250 Silver 0.9359 oz. ASW **Subject:** XXVIII Summer Olympics - Athens **Obv:** National arms **Obv. Legend:** SAMOA I SISIFO **Rev:** Swimming - two divers

Date	Mintage	F	VF	XF	Unc	BU
2003 Proof	—	Value: 60.00				

KM# 146 10 TALA

1.2300 g., Gold, 13.89 mm. **Obv:** National arms **Obv. Legend:** SAMOA SISIFO **Rev:** Bust of Fletcher Christian 3/4 left at left, sailing ship "H. M. S. Bounty" at right **Edge:** Reeded

Date	Mintage	F	VF	XF	Unc	BU
2003 Proof	—	Value: 65.00				

KM# 140 10 TALA

1.2400 g., 0.9990 Gold 0.0398 oz. AGW **Series:** World Statesmen **Subject:** Mahatma Gandhi **Obv:** National arms **Obv. Legend:** SAMOA I SISIFO

Date	Mintage	F	VF	XF	Unc	BU
2003 Proof	—	Value: 80.00				

KM# 141 10 TALA

1.2400 g., 0.9990 Gold 0.0398 oz. AGW **Series:** World Statesmen **Subject:** Konrad Adenauer **Obv:** National arms **Obv. Legend:** SAMOA I SISIFO

Date	Mintage	F	VF	XF	Unc	BU
2003 Proof	—	Value: 80.00				

KM# 159 10 TALA

1.2400 g., 0.9990 Gold 0.0398 oz. AGW, 13.92 mm. **Obv:** National arms **Rev:** Theodore Roosevelt

Date	Mintage	F	VF	XF	Unc	BU
2003 Proof	Est. 2,000	Value: 70.00				

KM# 160 10 TALA

1.2400 g., 0.9990 Gold 0.0398 oz. AGW, 13.92 mm. **Obv:** National arms **Rev:** Winston Churchill

Date	Mintage	F	VF	XF	Unc	BU
2003 Proof	Est. 2,000	Value: 70.00				

KM# 161 10 TALA

1.2400 g., 0.9990 Gold 0.0398 oz. AGW, 13.92 mm. **Obv:** National arms **Rev:** Charles de Gaulle

Date	Mintage	F	VF	XF	Unc	BU
2003 Proof	Est. 2,000	Value: 70.00				

KM# 162 10 TALA

1.2400 g., 0.9990 Gold 0.0398 oz. AGW, 13.92 mm. **Obv:** National arms **Rev:** John F. Kennedy

Date	Mintage	F	VF	XF	Unc	BU
2003 Proof	Est. 2,000	Value: 70.00				

KM# 143 10 TALA

28.5800 g., Silver, 38.61 mm. **Obv:** National arms **Obv. Legend:** SAMOA I SISIFO **Rev:** Sailing ship "La Récherche" **Rev. Legend:** JEAN FRANCOIS GALAUP - COMTE DE LA PEROUSE **Edge:** Reeded

Date	Mintage	F	VF	XF	Unc	BU
2004 Proof	—	Value: 55.00				

KM# 142 10 TALA

1.2400 g., 0.9990 Gold 0.0398 oz. AGW **Subject:** Death of Pope John-Paul II **Obv:** National arms

Date	Mintage	F	VF	XF	Unc	BU
2005	15,000	—	—	—	—	65.00
2005 Proof	3,300	Value: 75.00				

KM# 163 10 TALA

1.2400 g., 0.9990 Gold 0.0398 oz. AGW, 13.92 mm. **Obv:** National arms **Rev:** 2006 FIFA World Cup Germany logo

Date	Mintage	F	VF	XF	Unc	BU
2005 Proof	Est. 25,000	Value: 65.00				

KM# 164 10 TALA

1.2400 g., 0.9990 Gold 0.0398 oz. AGW, 13.92 mm. **Obv:** National arms **Rev:** Pope Benedict XVI in robes and mitre giving blessing

Date	Mintage	F	VF	XF	Unc	BU
2006 Proof	—	Value: 65.00				

SAN MARINO

The Republic of San Marino, the oldest and smallest republic in the world is located in north central Italy entirely surrounded by the Province of Emilia-Romagna. It has an area of 24 sq. mi. (60 sq. km.) and a population of *23,000. Capital: San Marino. The principal economic activities are farming, livestock raising, cheese making, tourism and light manufacturing. Building stone, lime, wheat, hides and baked goods are exported. The government derives most of its revenue from the sale of postage stamps for philatelic purposes.

San Marino has its own coinage, but Italian and Vatican City coins and currency are also in circulation.

MINT MARKS

R - Rome

MONETARY SYSTEM

100 Centesimi = 1 Lira

REPUBLIC

STANDARD COINAGE

KM# 424 10 LIRE

1.6000 g., Aluminum, 23.3 mm. **Obv:** Three towers within circle **Rev:** Wheat stalks and value **Edge:** Plain

Date	Mintage	F	VF	XF	Unc	BU
2001R	—	—	—	—	0.35	0.50

KM# 425 20 LIRE
3.6000 g., Aluminum-Bronze, 21.8 mm. **Obv:** Three towers within circle **Rev:** Two dolphins and value **Edge:** Plain

Date	Mintage	F	VF	XF	Unc	BU
2001R	—	—	—	—	1.00	2.00

KM# 426 50 LIRE
4.5000 g., Copper-Nickel, 19 mm. **Obv:** Three towers within circle **Rev:** Tree and value **Edge:** Plain

Date	Mintage	F	VF	XF	Unc	BU
2001R	—	—	—	—	0.85	1.50

KM# 427 100 LIRE
4.5000 g., Copper-Nickel, 22 mm. **Obv:** Three towers within circle **Rev:** Grasping hands and value **Edge:** Plain and reeded sections

Date	Mintage	F	VF	XF	Unc	BU
2001R	—	—	—	—	1.25	2.00

KM# 428 200 LIRE
5.0000 g., Aluminum-Bronze, 24 mm. **Obv:** Three towers within circle **Rev:** Broken chain, leaves, vines and value **Edge:** Reeded

Date	Mintage	F	VF	XF	Unc	BU
2001R	—	—	—	—	1.50	2.50

KM# 429 500 LIRE
Bi-Metallic Aluminum-Bronze center in Stainless Steel ring, 25.8 mm. **Obv:** Three towers within circle **Rev:** Three different plant stalks and value **Edge:** Reeded and plain sections **Note:** 6.8 grams.

Date	Mintage	F	VF	XF	Unc	BU
2001R	—	—	—	—	3.00	3.50

KM# 430 1000 LIRE
8.8000 g., Bi-Metallic Stainless-Steel center in Aluminum-Bronze ring, 27 mm. **Obv:** Three towers within circle **Rev:** Value within circle of birds **Edge:** Reeded and plain sections

Date	Mintage	F	VF	XF	Unc	BU
2001R	—	—	—	—	7.50	10.00

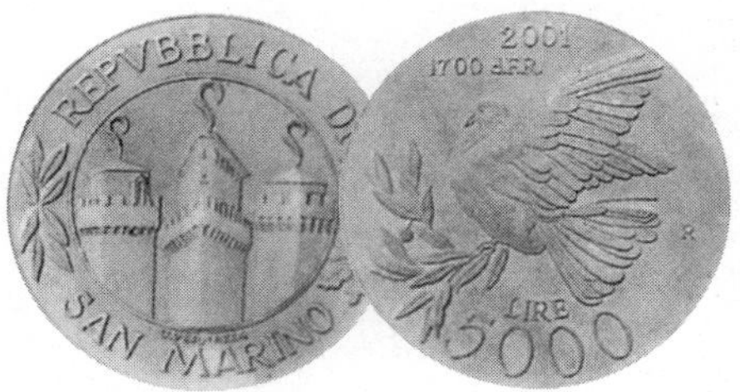

KM# 431 5000 LIRE
18.0000 g., 0.8350 Silver 0.4832 oz. ASW, 32 mm. **Obv:** Three towers within circle **Rev:** Dove on laurel branch above value **Edge:** Reeded and plain sections

Date	Mintage	F	VF	XF	Unc	BU
2001R	—	—	—	—	22.50	27.50

KM# 436 5000 LIRE
18.0000 g., 0.8350 Silver 0.4832 oz. ASW, 32 mm. **Subject:** Last Lire Coinage **Obv:** Crowned arms within sprigs **Rev:** Feather above six old coin designs with value below, all within beaded border **Edge:** Lettered

Date	Mintage	F	VF	XF	Unc	BU
2001R Proof	20,000	Value: 25.00				

KM# 432 10000 LIRE
22.0000 g., 0.8350 Silver 0.5906 oz. ASW, 34 mm. **Subject:** Ferrari **Obv:** Crowned arms within sprigs **Rev:** Race car with "FERRARI" background **Edge:** Reeded and plain sections

Date	Mintage	F	VF	XF	Unc	BU
2001R Proof	20,000	Value: 45.00				

KM# 437 10000 LIRE
22.0000 g., 0.8350 Silver 0.5906 oz. ASW, 34 mm. **Subject:** Last Lire Coinage **Obv:** Crowned arms within sprigs **Rev:** Feather above six old coin designs with value below, all within star border **Edge:** Reeded and plain sections

Date	Mintage	F	VF	XF	Unc	BU
2001R Proof	20,000	Value: 42.00				

KM# 438 10000 LIRE
22.0000 g., 0.8350 Silver 0.5906 oz. ASW, 34 mm. **Subject:** 2nd International Chambers of Commerce Convention **Obv:** Crowned arms within sprigs **Rev:** Mercury running by a computer **Edge:** Reeded and plain sections.

Date	Mintage	F	VF	XF	Unc	BU
2001R Proof	20,000	Value: 42.00				

KM# 433 1/2 SCUDO
1.6100 g., 0.9000 Gold 0.0466 oz. AGW, 13.8 mm. **Subject:** Cavaliere **Obv:** Crowned arms within sprigs **Rev:** Horse and rider **Edge:** Reeded

Date	Mintage	F	VF	XF	Unc	BU
2001R Proof	4,500	Value: 75.00				

KM# 434 SCUDO
3.2200 g., 0.9000 Gold 0.0932 oz. AGW, 16 mm. **Subject:** Tiziano **Obv:** Crowned arms within sprigs **Rev:** Bearded bust left **Edge:** Reeded

Date	Mintage	F	VF	XF	Unc	BU
2001R Proof	4,500	Value: 150				

KM# 435 2 SCUDI
6.4400 g., 0.9000 Gold 0.1863 oz. AGW, 21 mm. **Subject:** Flora **Obv:** Crowned arms within sprigs **Rev:** Bust 1/4 left and value **Edge:** Reeded

Date	Mintage	F	VF	XF	Unc	BU
2001R Proof	4,500	Value: 275				

KM# 457 2 SCUDI
6.4516 g., 0.9000 Gold 0.1867 oz. AGW, 21 mm. **Obv:** Crowned arms within sprigs **Rev:** Madonna and Child **Edge:** Reeded

Date	Mintage	F	VF	XF	Unc	BU
2002R Proof	3,000	Value: 280				

KM# 459 2 SCUDI
6.4516 g., 0.9000 Gold 0.1867 oz. AGW, 21 mm. **Obv:** Crowned arms within sprigs **Rev:** Nostradamus above value **Edge:** Reeded

Date	Mintage	F	VF	XF	Unc	BU
2003R Proof	7,500	Value: 275				

KM# 464 2 SCUDI
6.4516 g., 0.9000 Gold 0.1867 oz. AGW, 21 mm. **Subject:** The Domagnano Treasure **Obv:** Crowned arms within sprigs **Rev:** Gothic Eagle Brooch, 5 Mark coin of 1952 **Edge:** Reeded

Date	Mintage	F	VF	XF	Unc	BU
2004R Proof	6,500	Value: 275				

KM# 493 2 SCUDI
6.4100 g., 0.9000 Gold 0.1855 oz. AGW, 21 mm. **Subject:** Pompeo Batoni, 300th Anniversary of Brith **Obv:** Arms **Rev:** Batoni's "San Marino Risolleva la Republica"

Date	Mintage	F	VF	XF	Unc	BU
2008R Proof	2,100	Value: 300				

KM# 439 5 SCUDI
16.9655 g., 0.9166 Gold 0.4999 oz. AGW, 28 mm. **Subject:** San Marino's World Bank Membership **Obv:** Crowned arms within sprigs **Rev:** Orchid and bee within globe **Edge:** Reeded

Date	Mintage	F	VF	XF	Unc	BU
2001R Proof	4,000	Value: 750				

EURO COINAGE

KM# 440 EURO CENT
2.2700 g., Copper Plated Steel, 16.2 mm. **Obv:** "Il Montale" **Obv. Designer:** M. Frantisek Chochola **Rev:** Value and globe **Rev. Designer:** Luc Luycx **Edge:** Plain

Date	Mintage	F	VF	XF	Unc	BU
2002R	125,000	—	—	—	—	40.00
2003R In sets only	70,000	—	—	—	—	42.00
2004R	1,500,000	—	—	—	—	20.00
2005R In sets only	70,000	—	—	—	—	20.00
2006R	2,730,000	—	—	8.00	—	12.00
2007R	—	—	—	8.00	—	12.00
2008R	—	—	—	8.00	—	12.00
2008R Proof	13,000	Value: 10.00				
2009R	—	—	—	8.00	—	12.00
2009R Proof	13,500	Value: 10.00				

KM# 441 2 EURO CENT
3.0300 g., Copper Plated Steel, 18.7 mm. **Obv:** Stefano Gallietti, Liberty fighter **Obv. Designer:** M. Frantisek Chochola **Rev:** Value and globe **Rev. Designer:** Luc Luycx **Edge:** Grooved

Date	Mintage	F	VF	XF	Unc	BU
2002R	125,000	—	—	—	—	40.00
2003R In sets only	70,000	—	—	—	—	42.00
2004R	1,395,000	—	—	—	—	20.00
2005R In sets only	150,000	—	—	—	—	20.00
2006R	2,730,000	—	—	—	8.00	12.00
2007R	—	—	—	—	8.00	12.00
2008R	—	—	—	—	8.00	12.00
2008R Proof	13,000	Value: 10.00				
2009R	—	—	—	—	8.00	12.00
2009R Proof	13,500	Value: 10.00				

KM# 442 5 EURO CENT
3.8600 g., Copper Plated Steel, 21.2 mm. **Obv:** "Guaita" tower **Obv. Designer:** M. Frantisek Chochola **Rev:** Value and globe **Rev. Designer:** Luc Luycx **Edge:** Plain

Date	Mintage	F	VF	XF	Unc	BU
2002R	125,000	—	—	—	—	40.00
2003R In sets only	70,000	—	—	—	—	42.00
2004R	1,000,000	—	—	—	—	20.00
2005R In sets only	70,000	—	—	—	—	20.00
2006R	2,880,000	—	—	—	8.00	12.00
2007R	—	—	—	—	8.00	12.00
2008R	—	—	—	—	8.00	12.00
2008R Proof	13,000	Value: 10.00				
2009R	—	—	—	—	8.00	12.00
2009R Proof	13,500	Value: 10.00				

KM# 443 10 EURO CENT
4.0700 g., Brass, 19.7 mm. **Obv:** Building Basilica del Santo Marinus **Obv. Designer:** M. Frantisek Chochola **Rev:** Map and value **Rev. Designer:** Luc Luycx **Edge:** Reeded

Date	Mintage	F	VF	XF	Unc	BU
2002R	125,000	—	—	—	—	40.00
2003R In sets only	70,000	—	—	—	—	42.00
2004R	180,000	—	—	—	—	22.00
2005R In sets only	70,000	—	—	—	—	22.00
2006R In sets only	65,000	—	—	—	—	20.00
2007R	—	—	—	—	—	18.00

KM# 482 10 EURO CENT
4.0700 g., Brass, 19.7 mm. **Obv:** Basilica de Santo Marinus facade **Rev:** Relief maps of Western Europe, value and stars

Date	Mintage	F	VF	XF	Unc	BU
2008R	—	—	—	—	8.00	12.00
2008R Proof	13,000	Value: 12.00				
2009R	—	—	—	—	8.00	12.00
2009R Proof	13,500	Value: 12.00				

KM# 444 20 EURO CENT
5.7300 g., Brass, 22.1 mm. **Obv:** St. Marinus from a portrait by van Guercino **Obv. Designer:** M. Frantisek Chochola **Rev:** Map and value **Rev. Designer:** Luc Luycx **Edge:** Notched

Date	Mintage	F	VF	XF	Unc	BU
2002R	267,400	—	—	—	18.00	20.00
2003R	430,000	—	—	—	15.00	18.00
2004R In sets only	70,000	—	—	—	15.00	18.00
2005R	310,000	—	—	—	15.00	18.00
2006R In sets only	70,000	—	—	—	15.00	18.00
2007R	—	—	—	—	14.00	16.00

KM# 483 20 EURO CENT
5.7300 g., Brass **Obv:** Saint holding Monte Titano **Rev:** Relief map of Western Europe, value and stars

Date	Mintage	F	VF	XF	Unc	BU
2008R	—	—	—	—	8.00	12.00
2008R Proof	13,000	Value: 15.00				
2009R	—	—	—	—	8.00	12.00
2009R Proof	13,500	Value: 15.00				

KM# 445 50 EURO CENT
7.8100 g., Brass, 24.2 mm. **Obv:** Fortress of San Marino **Obv. Designer:** M. Frantisek Chochola **Rev:** Map and value **Rev. Designer:** Luc Luycx **Edge:** Reeded

Date	Mintage	F	VF	XF	Unc	BU
2002R	230,400	—	—	—	20.00	22.50
2003R	415,000	—	—	—	17.50	20.00
2004R In sets only	70,000	—	—	—	17.50	20.00
2005R	179,000	—	—	—	17.50	20.00
2006R	343,880	—	—	—	15.00	18.00
2007R	—	—	—	—	14.00	16.00

KM# 484 50 EURO CENT
7.8000 g., Brass, 24.2 mm. **Obv:** Buildings on hill top **Rev:** Relief map of Western Europe, value and stars

Date	Mintage	F	VF	XF	Unc	BU
2008R	—	—	—	—	10.00	12.00
2008R Proof	13,000	Value: 13.00				
2009R	—	—	—	—	10.00	12.00
2009R Proof	13,500	Value: 13.00				

KM# 446 EURO
7.5000 g., Bi-Metallic Copper-Nickel center in Nickel-Brass ring, 23.25 mm. **Obv:** Crowned arms within sprigs and circle within star border **Obv. Designer:** M. Frantisek Chochola **Rev:** Value and map **Rev. Designer:** Luc Luycx **Edge:** Segmented reeding

Date	Mintage	F	VF	XF	Unc	BU
2002R	360,800	—	—	—	22.00	25.00
2003R In sets only	70,000	—	—	—	—	45.00
2004R	180,000	—	—	—	—	25.00
2005R In sets only	70,000	—	—	—	—	25.00
2006R In sets only	220,000	—	—	—	—	20.00
2007R	—	—	—	—	—	18.00

KM# 485 EURO
7.5000 g., Bi-Metallic Copper-Nickel center in Nickel-Brass ring, 23.25 mm. **Obv:** Covered arms within wreath and stars **Rev:** Relief map of Western Europe, value and stars **Edge:** Segmented reeding

Date	Mintage	F	VF	XF	Unc	BU
2008R	—	—	—	—	12.00	15.00
2008R Proof	13,000	Value: 15.00				
2009R	—	—	—	—	12.00	15.00
2009R Proof	13,500	Value: 15.00				

KM# 447 2 EURO
8.5000 g., Bi-Metallic Nickel-Brass center in Copper-Nickel ring, 25.75 mm. **Obv:** Government building **Obv. Designer:** M. Frantisek Chochola **Rev:** Value and map **Rev. Designer:** Luc Luycx **Edge:** Reeded with 2's and stars

Date	Mintage	F	VF	XF	Unc	BU
2002R	255,760	—	—	—	25.00	28.00
2003R In sets only	70,000	—	—	—	—	45.00
2004R In sets only	70,000	—	—	—	—	28.00
2005R In sets only	210,000	—	—	—	—	28.00
2006R In sets only	190,000	—	—	—	—	22.00
2007R	—	—	—	—	—	20.00

KM# 467 2 EURO
8.5000 g., Bi-Metallic Nickel-Brass center in Copper-Nickel ring, 25.75 mm. **Obv:** Crowned arms within sprigs **Rev:** Bartolomeo Borghesi **Edge:** Alternating stars and 2's

Date	Mintage	F	VF	XF	Unc	BU
2004R	110,000	—	—	—	20.00	30.00

KM# 469 2 EURO
8.5000 g., Bi-Metallic Nickel-Brass center in Copper-Nickel ring, 25.75 mm. **Obv:** Galileo Galilei at telescope

Date	Mintage	F	VF	XF	Unc	BU
2005R	130,000	—	—	—	35.00	45.00

KM# 478 2 EURO
8.5000 g., Bi-Metallic Nickel-Brass center in Copper-Nickel ring, 25.75 mm. **Subject:** Christopher Columbus, 500th Anniversary of Death **Obv:** Head of Columbus within border of stars **Rev:** Map and value

Date	Mintage	F	VF	XF	Unc	BU
2006R	120,000	—	—	—	55.00	60.00

KM# 481 2 EURO
8.5000 g., Bi-Metallic Nickel-Brass center in Copper-Nickel ring, 25.75 mm. **Subject:** Giuseppe Garibaldi, 200th Anniversary of Birth **Obv:** Half length bust facing **Rev:** Relief map of Western Europe, value and stars

Date	Mintage	F	VF	XF	Unc	BU
2007R	130,000	—	—	—	50.00	55.00

KM# 486 2 EURO

8.5000 g., Bi-Metallic Nickel-Brass center in Copper-Nickel ring, 25.75 mm. **Obv:** Palace **Rev:** Relief map of Western Europe, value and stars

Date	Mintage	F	VF	XF	Unc	BU
2008R	—	—	—	—	24.00	28.00
2008R Proof	13,000	Value: 20.00				
2009R	—	—	—	—	24.00	28.00
2009R Proof	13,500	Value: 20.00				

KM# 487 2 EURO

8.5000 g., Bi-Metallic Nickel-Brass center in Copper-Nickel ring, 25.75 mm. **Subject:** European year of Intercultural Dialogue **Obv:** Five figures with arms outstretched, books below **Rev:** Relief map of Western Europe, value and stars

Date	Mintage	F	VF	XF	Unc	BU
2008R	130,000	—	—	—	20.00	25.00

KM# 490 2 EURO

8.5000 g., Bi-Metallic Nickel-Brass center in Copper-Nickel ring, 25.75 mm. **Subject:** Creativitiy and Innovation **Obv:** Chemical flasks and book

Date	Mintage	F	VF	XF	Unc	BU
2009R	—	—	—	—	20.00	30.00

KM# 494 2 EURO

8.5000 g., Bi-Metallic Nickel-Brass center in Copper-Nickel ring, 25.75 mm. **Subject:** Sandra Botticeli, 500th Anniversary of Death

Date	Mintage	F	VF	XF	Unc	BU
2010R	—	—	—	—	20.00	30.00

KM# 500 2 EURO

8.5000 g., Bi-Metallic Nickel-Brass center in Copper-Nickel ring, 25.75 mm. **Subject:** Hgiorgio Vasari, 500th Anniversary of Birth

Date	Mintage	F	VF	XF	Unc	BU
2011R	—	—	—	—	20.00	30.00

KM# 448 5 EURO

18.0000 g., 0.9250 Silver 0.5353 oz. ASW, 32 mm. **Subject:** Welcome Euro **Obv:** Three plumed towers **Rev:** Circle of roses

Date	Mintage	F	VF	XF	Unc	BU
2002R Proof	37,000	Value: 75.00				

KM# 450 5 EURO

18.0000 g., 0.9250 Silver 0.5353 oz. ASW, 32 mm. **Subject:** 1600th Anniversary of Ravenna **Obv:** National arms **Rev:** Bas-relief wall design **Edge:** Reeded

Date	Mintage	F	VF	XF	Unc	BU
2002R Proof	—	Value: 60.00				

KM# 453 5 EURO

18.0000 g., 0.9250 Silver 0.5353 oz. ASW, 32 mm. **Subject:** 2004 Olympics **Obv:** Stylized three towers **Rev:** Ancient Olympians **Edge:** Reeded

Date	Mintage	F	VF	XF	Unc	BU
2003R Proof	37,766	Value: 50.00				

KM# 452 5 EURO

18.0000 g., 0.9250 Silver 0.5353 oz. ASW, 32 mm. **Obv:** National arms **Rev:** Allegorical depiction of Independence, Tolerance and Liberty

Date	Mintage	F	VF	XF	Unc	BU
2003R	—	—	—	—	35.00	40.00

KM# 468 5 EURO

18.0000 g., 0.9250 Silver 0.5353 oz. ASW, 32 mm. **Obv:** Three towers **Rev:** Antonio Onofri and value

Date	Mintage	F	VF	XF	Unc	BU
2004R	—	—	—	—	45.00	50.00
2005R	—	—	—	—	45.00	50.00

KM# 458 5 EURO

18.0000 g., 0.9250 Silver 0.5353 oz. ASW, 32 mm. **Obv:** National arms **Rev:** Value behind Bartolomeo Borghesi

Date	Mintage	F	VF	XF	Unc	BU
2004R	—	—	—	—	—	35.00
2004R Proof	—	Value: 45.00				

KM# 462 5 EURO

18.0000 g., 0.9250 Silver 0.5353 oz. ASW, 32 mm. **Obv:** Three stylized plumed towers **Rev:** Two soccer players

Date	Mintage	F	VF	XF	Unc	BU
2004R Proof	35,000	Value: 45.00				

KM# 472 5 EURO

18.0000 g., 0.9250 Silver 0.5353 oz. ASW, 32 mm. **Obv:** Portrait of Melchiorie Delfico

Date	Mintage	F	VF	XF	Unc	BU
2006R	65,000	—	—	—	30.00	35.00

KM# 476 5 EURO

18.0000 g., 0.9250 Silver 0.5353 oz. ASW, 32 mm. **Subject:** Andrea Mantegna, 500th Anniversary of Death **Obv:** Three towers **Rev:** Statue of soldier and naked femal

Date	Mintage	F	VF	XF	Unc	BU
2006R Proof	19,000	Value: 40.00				

KM# 473 5 EURO

18.0000 g., 0.9250 Silver 0.5353 oz. ASW, 32 mm. **Subject:** Equal Opportunity between the sexes **Obv:** Three plumed towers **Obv. Legend:** REPUBLICA DI SAN MARINO **Rev:** Nude female at left, nude male at right, ribbon across symbols within circle above, value below **Rev. Inscription:** PARI OPPORTITA **Edge:** Reeded

Date	Mintage	F	VF	XF	Unc	BU
2007R	—	—	—	—	30.00	35.00

KM# 474 5 EURO

18.0000 g., 0.9250 Silver 0.5353 oz. ASW, 32 mm. **Subject:** 50th Anniversary Death of Toscanini **Obv:** Stylized national arms **Obv. Legend:** REPUBBLICA DI SAN MARINO **Rev:** Head of Toscanini left **Edge:** Reeded

Date	Mintage	F	VF	XF	Unc	BU
ND(2007)R Proof	18,000	Value: 35.00				

KM# 506 5 EURO

18.0000 g., 0.9250 Silver 0.5353 oz. ASW, 32 mm. **Subject:** Kepler **Obv:** Kepler bust and globe **Rev:** Planets orbit around central sun **Designer:** Maria Angela Cassol

Date	Mintage	F	VF	XF	Unc	BU
2009R Proof	—	Value: 35.00				

KM# 495 5 EURO

18.0000 g., 0.9250 Silver 0.5353 oz. ASW, 32 mm. **Subject:** Shanghai Expo

Date	Mintage	F	VF	XF	Unc	BU
2010R	—	—	—	—	30.00	35.00

KM# 496 5 EURO

18.0000 g., 0.9250 Silver 0.5353 oz. ASW, 32 mm. **Subject:** Michelangelo Caravaggio, 500th Anniverdary of Death

Date	Mintage	F	VF	XF	Unc	BU
2010R	—	—	—	—	30.00	35.00

KM# 501 5 EURO

18.0000 g., 0.9250 Silver 0.5353 oz. ASW, 32 mm. **Subject:** European Discoveries

Date	Mintage	F	VF	XF	Unc	BU
2011R	—	—	—	—	30.00	35.00

KM# 502 5 EURO

18.0000 g., 0.9250 Silver 0.5353 oz. ASW, 32 mm. **Subject:** First Manned Space Flight, 50th Anniversary

Date	Mintage	F	VF	XF	Unc	BU
2011R	—	—	—	—	30.00	35.00

KM# 449 10 EURO

22.0000 g., 0.9250 Silver 0.6542 oz. ASW, 34 mm. **Subject:** Welcome Euro **Obv:** Three plumed towers **Rev:** Infant sleeping in flower

Date	Mintage	F	VF	XF	Unc	BU
2002R Proof	37,000	Value: 100				

KM# 451 10 EURO

22.0000 g., 0.9250 Silver 0.6542 oz. ASW, 34 mm. **Subject:** 1600th Anniversary of Ravenna **Obv:** National arms **Rev:** Wall painting

Date	Mintage	F	VF	XF	Unc	BU
2002R Proof	—	Value: 95.00				

KM# 454 10 EURO

22.0000 g., 0.9250 Silver 0.6542 oz. ASW, 34 mm. **Subject:** 2004 Olympics **Obv:** Three stylized towers **Rev:** Modern Olympians **Edge:** Segmented reeding

Date	Mintage	F	VF	XF	Unc	BU
2003R Proof	37,766	Value: 75.00				

KM# 463 10 EURO

22.0000 g., 0.9250 Silver 0.6542 oz. ASW, 34 mm. **Obv:** Three stylized plumed towers **Rev:** Two soccer players

Date	Mintage	F	VF	XF	Unc	BU
2004R Proof	30,000	Value: 70.00				

KM# 477 10 EURO

22.0000 g., 0.9250 Silver 0.6542 oz. ASW, 34 mm. **Subject:** Antonio Canova **Obv:** Three towers **Rev:** The Three Graces

Date	Mintage	F	VF	XF	Unc	BU
2006R Proof	19,000	Value: 65.00				

KM# 475 10 EURO

22.0000 g., 0.9250 Silver 0.6542 oz. ASW, 34 mm. **Subject:** 100th Anniversary - Birthday of Giosuè Carducci **Obv:** Stylized national arms **Obv. Legend:** REPUBBLICA DI SAN MARINO **Rev:** 1/2 length figure of Carducci facing with quill pen in hand at table **Rev. Legend:** CARDUCCI **Edge:** Segmented reeding

Date	Mintage	F	VF	XF	Unc	BU
ND(2007)R Proof	16,000	Value: 55.00				

KM# 497 10 EURO

22.0000 g., 0.9250 Silver 0.6542 oz. ASW, 34 mm. **Subject:** Robert Schumann, 200th Anniversary of Birth

Date	Mintage	F	VF	XF	Unc	BU
2010R Proof	—	Value: 55.00				

KM# 503 10 EURO

22.0000 g., 0.9250 Silver 0.6542 oz. ASW, 34 mm. **Subject:** Euro Coins and Banknotes, 10th Anniversary

Date	Mintage	F	VF	XF	Unc	BU
2011R Proof	—	Value: 60.00				

KM# 460 20 EURO

6.4510 g., 0.9000 Gold 0.1867 oz. AGW, 21 mm. **Subject:** 1600th Anniversary of Ravenna **Obv:** National arms **Rev:** Bas-relief wall design **Edge:** Reeded

Date	Mintage	F	VF	XF	Unc	BU
2002R Proof	4,550	Value: 375				

KM# 455 20 EURO

6.4516 g., 0.9000 Gold 0.1867 oz. AGW, 21 mm. **Obv:** Three plumes **Rev:** Giotto's "Presentation of Jesus at the Temple" **Edge:** Reeded

Date	Mintage	F	VF	XF	Unc	BU
2003R Proof	7,300	Value: 275				

KM# 465 20 EURO

6.4510 g., 0.9000 Gold 0.1867 oz. AGW, 21 mm. **Obv:** Three plumes **Rev:** Marco Polo meeting Kublai Khan **Edge:** Reeded

Date	Mintage	F	VF	XF	Unc	BU
2004R Proof	7,300	Value: 275				

KM# 470 20 EURO

6.4510 g., 0.9000 Gold 0.1867 oz. AGW, 21 mm. **Subject:** International Day of Peace **Obv:** Stylized faces and leaves

Date	Mintage	F	VF	XF	Unc	BU
2005R Proof	5,300	Value: 300				

KM# 479 20 EURO

6.4500 g., 0.9000 Gold 0.1866 oz. AGW, 21 mm. **Subject:** Giovan Battista Belluzzi, 500th Birthday **Obv:** Crowned shield **Rev:** Fortification plan **Designer:** Guido Veroi

Date	Mintage	F	VF	XF	Unc	BU
2006R Proof	4,500	Value: 300				

KM# 491 20 EURO

6.4500 g., 0.9000 Gold 0.1866 oz. AGW **Subject:** Roman Antiquities **Obv:** Arms **Rev:** Small statue of Mercury

Date	Mintage	F	VF	XF	Unc	BU
2008R Proof	2,100	Value: 300				

KM# 498 20 EURO

6.4510 g., 0.9000 Gold 0.1867 oz. AGW, 21 mm. **Subject:** Treasurers from San Marino - Wooden bust of St. Agata

Date	Mintage	F	VF	XF	Unc	BU
2010R Proof	—	Value: 325				

KM# 504 20 EURO

6.4510 g., 0.9000 Gold 0.1867 oz. AGW, 21 mm. **Subject:** Treasures from San Marino

Date	Mintage	F	VF	XF	Unc	BU
2011R Proof	—	Value: 325				

KM# 461 50 EURO

16.1290 g., 0.9000 Gold 0.4667 oz. AGW, 28 mm. **Subject:** 1600th Anniversary of Ravenna **Obv:** National arms **Rev:** Wall painting **Edge:** Reeded

Date	Mintage	F	VF	XF	Unc	BU
2002R Proof	4,550	Value: 775				

KM# 456 50 EURO

16.1290 g., 0.9000 Gold 0.4667 oz. AGW, 28 mm. **Obv:** Three plumes **Rev:** Giotto's "The Pentecost" **Edge:** Reeded

Date	Mintage	F	VF	XF	Unc	BU
2003R Proof	7,300	Value: 700				

KM# 466 50 EURO

16.1290 g., 0.9000 Gold 0.4667 oz. AGW, 28 mm. **Obv:** Three plumes **Rev:** Marco Polo **Edge:** Reeded

Date	Mintage	F	VF	XF	Unc	BU
2004R Proof	7,300	Value: 700				

KM# 471 50 EURO

16.1290 g., 0.9000 Gold 0.4667 oz. AGW, 28 mm. **Subject:** International Day of Peace **Obv:** Group of people gathering

Date	Mintage	F	VF	XF	Unc	BU
2005R Proof	5,300	Value: 750				

KM# 480 50 EURO
16.1300 g., 0.9000 Gold 0.4667 oz. AGW, 28 mm. **Subject:** Giovan Batista Belluzzi **Obv:** Crowned shield **Rev:** Bust right **Designer:** Guido Veroi

Date	Mintage	F	VF	XF	Unc	BU
2006R Proof	4,500	Value: 750				

KM# 492 50 EURO
16.1300 g., 0.9000 Gold 0.4667 oz. AGW, 28 mm. **Subject:** Antiquities **Obv:** Arms **Rev:** Two bronze fibulae

Date	Mintage	F	VF	XF	Unc	BU
2008R Proof	2,100	Value: 800				

KM# 499 50 EURO
16.1290 g., 0.9000 Gold 0.4667 oz. AGW, 28 mm. **Subject:** Treasurers from San marino - Saint Marinus

Date	Mintage	F	VF	XF	Unc	BU
2010R Proof	—	Value: 825				

KM# 505 50 EURO
16.1290 g., 0.9000 Gold 0.4667 oz. AGW, 28 mm. **Subject:** Treasures from San Marino

Date	Mintage	F	VF	XF	Unc	BU
2011R Proof	—	Value: 825				

MINT SETS

KM#	Date	Mintage	Identification	Issue Price	Mkt Val
MS61	2001 (8)	2,000	KM424-431	18.00	50.00
MS62	2002 (8)	120,000	KM440 - 447	—	275
MS63	2003 (9)	—	KM#440-447, 452	55.00	350
MS64	2004 (9)	—	KM#440-447, 458	55.00	220
MS65	2005 (9)	—	KM#440-447, 468	55.00	225
MS66	2006 (9)	65,000	KM#440-447, 472	—	185
MS67	2007 (3)	—	KM#443, 444, 447	27.50	55.00
MS68	2007 (9)	—	KM#440-447, 473	120	160

PROOF SETS

KM#	Date	Mintage	Identification	Issue Price	Mkt Val
PS14	2001 (3)	4,500	KM433-435	179	500
PSA15	2001 (2)	—	KM#436, 437	—	70.00
PS15	2002 (2)	37,000	KM448-449	—	175
PS16	2002 (2)	4,550	KM#460-461	—	1,150
PS17	2003 (2)	7,300	KM#455-456	—	975
PS18	2004 (2)	7,300	KM#465-466	—	975
PS19	2005 (2)	5,300	KM#470-471	—	1,050
PS20	2008 (8)	13,000	KM#440-442, 482-486.	—	135
PS21	2009 (8)	13,500	KM#440-443, 482-486.	—	135

SAUDI ARABIA

UNITED KINGDOMS

The Kingdom of Saudi Arabia, an independent and absolute hereditary monarchy comprising the former sultanate of Nejd, the old kingdom of Hejaz, Asir and Al Hasa, occupies four-fifths of the Arabian peninsula. The kingdom has an area of 830,000 sq. mi. (2,149,690 sq. km.) and a population of *16.1 million. Capital: Riyadh. The economy is based on oil, which provides 85 percent of Saudi Arabia's revenue.

TITLES

العربية السعودية

Al-Arabiya(t) as-Sa'udiya(t)

المملكة العربية السعودية

Al-Mamlaka(t) al-'Arabiya(t) as-Sa'udiya(t)

RULERS

al Sa'ud Dynasty

Fahad bin Abd Al-Aziz, AH1403-1426/1982-2005AD
Abdullah bin Abdul Aziz, AH1426-/2005AD

KINGDOM

REFORM COINAGE

5 Halala = 1 Ghirsh; 100 Halala = 1 Riyal

KM# 69 5 HALALA (Ghirsh)
Copper-Nickel **Ruler:** Abdullah bin Abdul Aziz AH1426-/2005-AD **Obv:** National emblem at center **Rev:** Legend above inscription in circle, dividing value, date below

Date	Mintage	F	VF	XF	Unc	BU
AH1430(2009)	—	—	0.30	0.60	1.50	2.00

KM# 62 10 HALALA (2 Ghirsh)
4.0000 g., Copper-Nickel, 21 mm. **Ruler:** Fahad Bin Abd Al-Aziz AH1403-1426/1982-2005AD **Obv:** National emblem at center, legend above and below **Rev:** Legend above inscription in circle dividing value, date below **Edge:** Reeded

Date	Mintage	F	VF	XF	Unc	BU
AH1423 (2002)	—	—	0.15	0.35	0.90	1.00

KM# 70 10 HALALA (2 Ghirsh)
Copper-Nickel **Ruler:** Abdullah bin Abdul Aziz AH1426-/2005-AD **Obv:** National emblem at center **Rev:** Legend above inscription in circle, dividing value, date below

Date	Mintage	F	VF	XF	Unc	BU
AH1430(2009)	—	—	0.30	0.60	1.50	2.50

KM# 63 25 HALALA (1/4 Riyal)
5.0000 g., Copper-Nickel, 23 mm. **Ruler:** Fahad Bin Abd Al-Aziz AH1403-1426/1982-2005AD **Obv:** National emblem at center, legend above and below **Rev:** Legend above inscription in circle dividing value, date below **Edge:** Reeded

Date	Mintage	F	VF	XF	Unc	BU
AH1423 (2002)	—	—	0.20	0.45	1.10	1.50

KM# 71 25 HALALA (1/4 Riyal)
Bi-Metallic **Ruler:** Abdullah bin Abdul Aziz AH1426-/2005-AD **Obv:** National emblem at center **Rev:** Legend above inscription in circle, divides value, date below

Date	Mintage	F	VF	XF	Unc	BU
AH1430(2009)	—	0.10	0.20	0.45	1.10	1.50

KM# 64 50 HALALA (1/2 Riyal)
6.5000 g., Copper-Nickel, 26 mm. **Ruler:** Fahad Bin Abd Al-Aziz AH1403-1426/1982-2005AD **Obv:** National emblem at center, legend above and below **Rev:** Legend above inscription in circle dividing value, date below **Edge:** Reeded

Date	Mintage	F	VF	XF	Unc	BU
AH1423 (2002)	—	0.15	0.30	0.75	1.50	2.00

KM# 68 50 HALALA (1/2 Riyal)
6.5000 g., Copper-Nickel **Ruler:** Abdullah bin Abdul Aziz AH1426-/2005-AD **Obv:** National emblem at center **Rev:** Legend above inscription in circle, dividing value, date below

Date	Mintage	F	VF	XF	Unc	BU
AH1427(2006)	—	0.15	0.30	0.60	1.50	2.00
AH1428 (2007)	—	0.15	0.30	0.60	1.50	2.00

KM# 72 100 HALALA (1 Riyal)
Bi-Metallic Brass center in Copper-Nickel ring, 23 mm. **Ruler:** Abdullah bin Abdul Aziz AH1426-/2005-AD **Obv:** National emblem at center **Rev:** Legend above inscription, divides value, date below **Edge:** Reeded

Date	Mintage	F	VF	XF	Unc	BU
AH1427(2006)	—	—	0.45	0.90	2.25	3.00
AH1429(2008)	—	—	0.45	0.90	2.25	3.00

SERBIA

Serbia, a former inland Balkan kingdom has an area of 34,116 sq. mi. (88,361 sq. km.). Capital: Belgrade.

MINT MARKS

A - Paris
(a) - Paris, privy mark only
H - Birmingham
V - Vienna
БП - (BP) Budapest

MONETARY SYSTEM

100 Para = 1 Dinara

DENOMINATIONS

ПАРА = Para
ПАРЕ = Pare
ДИНАР = Dinar
ДИНАРА = Dinara

REPUBLIC

STANDARD COINAGE

KM# 34 DINAR
4.3400 g., Copper-Nickel-Zinc, 20 mm. **Obv:** National Bank emblem within circle **Rev:** Bank building and value **Edge:** Reeded

Date	Mintage	F	VF	XF	Unc	BU
2003	10,320,000	—	—	0.25	1.00	1.50
2004	—	—	—	0.25	1.00	1.50
2005	—	—	—	0.25	1.00	1.50

KM# 39 DINAR
4.2600 g., Nickel-Brass, 20 mm. **Obv:** Crowned and mantled arms **Rev:** National Bank and value **Edge:** Segmented reeding

Date	Mintage	F	VF	XF	Unc	BU
2006	—	—	—	0.25	1.00	1.50
2007	—	—	—	0.25	1.00	1.50
2008	—	—	—	0.25	1.00	1.50
2009	—	—	—	0.25	1.00	1.50

KM# 48 DINAR
4.2000 g., Copper Plated Steel, 20 mm. **Obv:** Arms **Rev:** National Bank and value

Date	Mintage	F	VF	XF	Unc	BU
2009	—	—	—	—	1.00	1.50

KM# 35 2 DINARA
5.2400 g., Copper-Nickel-Zinc, 22 mm. **Obv:** National Bank

emblem within circle **Rev:** Gracanica Monastery and value **Edge:** Reeded

Date	Mintage	F	VF	XF	Unc	BU
2003	4,688,500	—	—	0.50	2.00	2.50

KM# 46 2 DINARA

5.1500 g., Nickel-Brass, 22 mm. **Obv:** Crowned and mantled arms **Rev:** Gracanica Monastery and value **Edge:** Segmented reeding

Date	Mintage	F	VF	XF	Unc	BU
2006	—	—	—	0.50	2.00	2.50
2007	—	—	—	0.50	2.00	2.50
2008	—	—	—	0.50	2.00	2.50
2009	—	—	—	0.50	2.00	2.50

KM# 49 2 DINARA

5.0500 g., Copper Plated Steel, 22 mm. **Obv:** Arms **Rev:** Gracanica Monastery and value

Date	Mintage	F	VF	XF	Unc	BU
2009	—	—	—	0.50	2.00	2.50

KM# 36 5 DINARA

6.2300 g., Copper-Nickel-Zinc, 22 mm. **Obv:** National Bank emblem within circle **Rev:** Krusedol Monastery and value **Edge:** Reeded

Date	Mintage	F	VF	XF	Unc	BU
2003	15,170,000	—	0.50	1.00	2.25	3.50

KM# 40 5 DINARA

6.1300 g., Nickel-Brass, 24 mm. **Obv:** Crowned and mantled arms **Rev:** Krusedol Monastery and value **Edge:** Segmented reeding

Date	Mintage	F	VF	XF	Unc	BU
2005	—	—	—	0.75	2.00	3.50
2006	—	—	—	0.75	2.00	3.50
2007	—	—	—	0.75	2.00	3.50
2008	—	—	—	0.75	2.00	3.50
2009	—	—	—	0.75	2.00	3.50

KM# 50 5 DINARA

Copper Plated Steel **Obv:** Arms **Rev:** Krusedol Monastery and value

Date	Mintage	F	VF	XF	Unc	BU
2009	—	—	—	0.75	2.00	3.50

KM# 37 10 DINARA

7.7700 g., Copper-Nickel-Zinc, 26 mm. **Obv:** National Bank emblem within circle **Rev:** Studenica Monastery and value **Edge:** Reeded

Date	Mintage	F	VF	XF	Unc	BU
2003	10,160,500	—	0.50	1.00	2.50	3.50

KM# 41 10 DINARA

7.7700 g., Copper-Nickel-Zinc, 26 mm. **Obv:** Crowned and mantled arms **Rev:** Studenica Monastery and value **Edge:** Segmented reeding

Date	Mintage	F	VF	XF	Unc	BU
2005	—	—	—	0.75	2.25	4.00
2006	—	—	—	0.75	2.25	4.00
2007	—	—	—	0.75	2.00	4.00
2009	—	—	—	0.75	2.00	4.00

KM# 51 10 DINARA

7.7700 g., Copper-Nickel-Zinc, 26 mm. **Subject:** 25th Summer Universiade, Belgrade **Obv:** Arms **Rev:** Logo

Date	Mintage	F	VF	XF	Unc	BU
2009	500,000	—	—	1.00	3.00	5.00

KM# 38 20 DINARA

9.0000 g., Copper-Nickel-Zinc, 28 mm. **Obv:** National Bank emblem within circle **Rev:** Temple of St. Sava and value **Edge:** Reeded

Date	Mintage	F	VF	XF	Unc	BU
2003	25,491,500	—	—	0.75	2.25	4.00

KM# 42 20 DINARA

9.0000 g., Copper-Nickel-Zinc, 28 mm. **Obv:** Crowned and mantled Serbian royal arms **Rev:** Nikola Tesla **Edge:** Segmented reeding

Date	Mintage	F	VF	XF	Unc	BU
2006	1,000,000	—	—	0.75	2.25	4.00

KM# 47 20 DINARA

9.0000 g., Copper-Nickel-Zinc, 28 mm. **Subject:** Dositej Obradovic, 1742-1811 **Obv:** National arms **Obv. Legend:** РЕПУБЛИКА СРБИЈА - REPUBLIKA SRBIJA **Rev:** Bust facing slightly left **Edge:** Segmented reeding

Date	Mintage	F	VF	XF	Unc	BU
2007	—	—	—	1.00	2.50	4.50

KM# 52 20 DINARA

9.0000 g., Copper-Nickel-Zinc, 28 mm. **Obv:** National arms **Rev:** Milutin Milankovic profile 3/4 left

Date	Mintage	F	VF	XF	Unc	BU
2009	500,000	—	—	—	2.00	3.50

KM# 43 1000 DINARA

13.0000 g., 0.9250 Silver 0.3866 oz. ASW, 30 mm. **Obv:** Crowned and mantled Serbian royal arms **Rev:** Nikola Tesla **Edge:** Segmented reeding

Date	Mintage	F	VF	XF	Unc	BU
2006 Proof	2,000	Value: 40.00				

KM# 44 5000 DINARA

3.4550 g., 0.9000 Gold 0.1000 oz. AGW, 20 mm. **Obv:** Crowned and mantled Serbian royal arms **Rev:** Nikola Tesla

Date	Mintage	F	VF	XF	Unc	BU
2006 Proof	2,000	Value: 185				

KM# 45 10000 DINARA

8.6400 g., 0.9000 Gold 0.2500 oz. AGW, 25 mm. **Obv:** Crowned and mantled Serbian royal arms **Rev:** Nikola Tesla

Date	Mintage	F	VF	XF	Unc	BU
2006 Proof	1,000	Value: 425				

MINT SETS

KM#	Date	Mintage	Identification	Issue Price	Mkt Val
MS1	2003 (5)	—	KM34-38	—	15.00
MS2	2005 (3)	—	KM39-41	—	10.00
MS3	2006 (5)	—	KM#39-42, 46	—	16.00

PROOF SETS

KM#	Date	Mintage	Identification	Issue Price	Mkt Val
PS1	2006 (3)	—	KM#43-45	—	650

SEYCHELLES

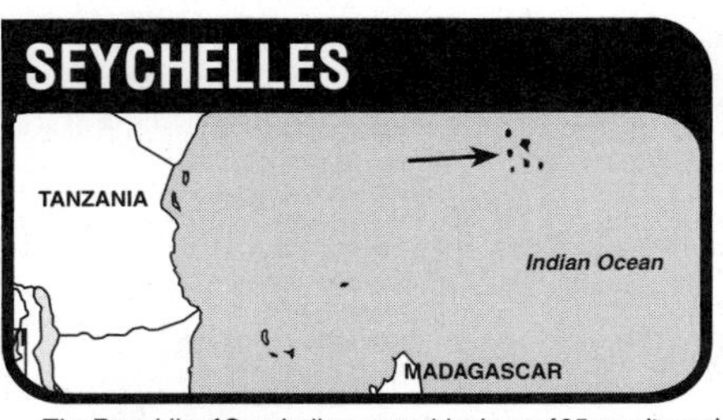

The Republic of Seychelles, an archipelago of 85 granite and coral islands situated in the Indian Ocean 600 miles (965 km.) northeast of Madagascar, has an area of 156 sq. mi. (455 sq. km.) and a population of *70,000. Among these islands are the Aldabra Islands, the Farquhar Group, and Ile Desroches, which the United Kingdom ceded to the Seychelles upon its independence. Capital: Victoria, on Mahe. The economy is based on fishing, a plantation system of agriculture, and tourism. Copra, cinnamon and vanilla are exported.

Seychelles is a member of the Commonwealth of Nations. The president is the Head of State and of the Government.

MINT MARKS

(sa) - M in oval – South African Mint Co.
(starting in 2000, not PM)
None - British Royal Mint

MONETARY SYSTEM

100 Cents = 1 Rupee

REPUBLIC

STANDARD COINAGE

KM# 46.2 CENT

1.4300 g., Brass, 16.03 mm. **Obv:** Altered coat of arms **Rev:** Mud Crab **Rev. Designer:** Robert Elderton **Edge:** Plain

Date	Mintage	F	VF	XF	Unc	BU
2004	—	—	—	0.15	0.25	0.35

KM# 47.2 5 CENTS

2.0000 g., Brass, 18 mm. **Obv:** Altered coat of arms **Rev:** Tapioca plant **Rev. Designer:** Robert Elderton

Date	Mintage	F	VF	XF	Unc	BU
2003	—	—	—	0.10	0.30	0.50

KM# 47a 5 CENTS

1.9700 g., Brass Plated Steel, 17.97 mm. **Obv:** National arms **Rev:** Tapioca plant **Rev. Designer:** Robert Elderton **Edge:** Plain

Date	Mintage	F	VF	XF	Unc	BU
2007PM	—	—	—	0.10	0.30	0.50

KM# 48.2 10 CENTS

3.3400 g., Brass, 21 mm. **Obv:** Altered coat of arms **Rev:** Yellowfin tuna **Rev. Designer:** Robert Elderton **Edge:** Plain

Date	Mintage	F	VF	XF	Unc	BU
2003	—	—	0.10	0.35	1.00	1.50

KM# 48a 10 CENTS

3.3700 g., Brass Plated Steel, 21 mm. **Obv:** National arms **Rev:** Black parrot, value **Edge:** Plain

Date	Mintage	F	VF	XF	Unc	BU
2007PM	—	—	0.15	0.30	0.75	1.00

KM# 49a 25 CENTS
2.9700 g., Nickel Clad Steel, 18.9 mm. **Obv:** National arms **Rev:** Black Parrot and value **Edge:** Plain

Date	Mintage	F	VF	XF	Unc	BU
2003PM	—	—	0.15	0.40	1.00	1.25
2007PM	—	—	0.15	0.40	1.00	1.25

KM# 50.2 RUPEE
6.1800 g., Copper-Nickel, 25.46 mm. **Obv:** Altered coat of arms **Rev:** Triton Conch Shell **Rev. Designer:** Suzanne Danielli **Edge:** Reeded

Date	Mintage	F	VF	XF	Unc	BU
2007	—	—	0.25	0.45	1.10	1.50

KM# 118 5 RUPEES
28.2800 g., Copper-Nickel, 38.6 mm. **Subject:** John Paul II memorial **Obv:** National Arms **Rev:** John Paul II in mitre waving

Date	Mintage	F	VF	XF	Unc	BU
2005	—	—	—	—	8.00	10.00

KM# 119 5 RUPEES
28.2800 g., Copper-Nickel, 38.6 mm. **Obv:** National Arms **Rev:** Benedict XVI blessing crowd at St. Peter's Square

Date	Mintage	F	VF	XF	Unc	BU
2005	—	—	—	—	10.00	12.00

KM# 51.2 5 RUPEES
9.0000 g., Copper-Nickel, 29 mm. **Obv:** Altered arms **Rev:** Fruit tree divides value **Rev. Designer:** Frederick Mogford **Edge:** Reeded

Date	Mintage	F	VF	XF	Unc	BU
2007	—	—	0.30	0.70	1.75	2.25

KM# 121 25 RUPEES
28.2800 g., 0.9250 Silver 0.8410 oz. ASW, 38.6 mm. **Obv:** National arms **Rev:** Benedict XVI blessing crowd at St. Peter's Square **Edge:** Reeded

Date	Mintage	F	VF	XF	Unc	BU
2005	—	Value: 55.00				

KM# 120 25 RUPEES
28.2800 g., 0.9250 Silver 0.8410 oz. ASW, 38.6 mm. **Obv:** National arms **Rev:** Description John Paul II in mitre waving **Edge:** Reeded

Date	Mintage	F	VF	XF	Unc	BU
2005 Proof	—	Value: 55.00				

KM# 122 250 RUPEES
6.2200 g., 0.9999 Gold 0.1999 oz. AGW, 22 mm. **Obv:** National arms **Rev:** Description John Paul II in mitre waving **Edge:** Reeded

Date	Mintage	F	VF	XF	Unc	BU
2005 Proof	—	Value: 300				

KM# 123 250 RUPEES
6.2200 g., 0.9999 Gold 0.1999 oz. AGW, 22 mm. **Obv:** National arms **Rev:** Benedict XVI blessing crowd at St. Peter's Square **Edge:** Reeded

Date	Mintage	F	VF	XF	Unc	BU
2005 Proof	—	Value: 300				

The Republic of Sierra Leone is located in western Africa between Guinea and Liberia, has an area of 27,699 sq. mi. (71,740 sq. km.) and a population of *4.1 million. Capital: Freetown. The economy is predominantly agricultural but mining contributes significantly to export revenues. Diamonds, iron ore, palm kernels, cocoa, and coffee are exported.

Sierra Leone is a member of the Commonwealth of Nations. The president is Chief of State and Head of Government.

MONETARY SYSTEM

Beginning 1964

100 Cents = 1 Leone

NOTE: Sierra Leone's official currency is the Leone. For previously listed Dollar Denominated Coinage, see the 5th Edition of Unusual World Coins.

REPUBLIC

STANDARD COINAGE

KM# 295 20 LEONES
3.9200 g., Copper-Nickel, 21.7 mm. **Obv:** Value within fish and beaded circle **Rev:** Chimpanzee facing **Edge:** Plain

Date	Mintage	F	VF	XF	Unc	BU
2003	—	—	—	—	0.50	1.25

KM# 302 100 LEONES
28.2800 g., Copper-Nickel, 38.6 mm. **Subject:** 40th Anniversary - Bank of Sierra Leone **Obv:** Bank President Kabbah **Rev:** Lion **Edge:** Reeded

Date	Mintage	F	VF	XF	Unc	BU
ND (2004)PM	5,000	—	—	—	15.00	18.00

KM# 296 500 LEONES
7.2000 g., Bi-Metallic Stainless Steel center in Brass ring, 24 mm. **Obv:** Building within circle **Rev:** Bust with hat facing within circle **Edge:** Plain **Shape:** 10-sided

Date	Mintage	F	VF	XF	Unc	BU
2004	—	—	—	—	7.50	9.00

KM# 346 500 LEONES
28.2800 g., Bronze, 38.6 mm. **Subject:** 40th Anniversary - Bank of Sierra Leone **Obv:** Bank President Kabbah **Rev:** Lion, denomination as "Le 500" **Edge:** Reeded

Date	Mintage	F	VF	XF	Unc	BU
ND(2004)PM	10,000	—	—	—	15.00	18.00

DOLLAR DENOMINATED COINAGE

KM# 222 DOLLAR
28.4900 g., Copper-Nickel, 38.5 mm. **Series:** The Big Five **Obv:** National arms **Rev:** Rhino **Edge:** Reeded

Date	Mintage	F	VF	XF	Unc	BU
2001PM	—	—	—	—	12.50	15.00

KM# 225 DOLLAR
28.4900 g., Copper-Nickel, 38.6 mm. **Series:** The Big Five **Obv:** National arms **Rev:** Lion **Edge:** Reeded

Date	Mintage	F	VF	XF	Unc	BU
2001PM	—	—	—	—	10.00	14.00

KM# 228 DOLLAR
28.4900 g., Copper-Nickel, 38.6 mm. **Series:** The Big Five **Obv:** National arms **Rev:** Leopard **Edge:** Reeded

Date	Mintage	F	VF	XF	Unc	BU
2001PM	—	—	—	—	10.00	14.00

KM# 231 DOLLAR
28.4900 g., Copper-Nickel, 38.6 mm. **Series:** The Big Five **Obv:** National arms **Rev:** Elephants **Edge:** Reeded

Date	Mintage	F	VF	XF	Unc	BU
2001PM	—	—	—	—	10.00	14.00

KM# 234 DOLLAR
28.4900 g., Copper-Nickel, 38.6 mm. **Series:** The Big Five **Obv:** National arms **Rev:** Buffalo **Edge:** Reeded

Date	Mintage	F	VF	XF	Unc	BU
2001PM	—	—	—	—	10.00	14.00

KM# 237 DOLLAR
28.4900 g., Copper-Nickel, 38.5 mm. **Series:** The Big Five **Obv:** National arms **Rev:** All five animals **Edge:** Reeded

Date	Mintage	F	VF	XF	Unc	BU
2001PM	—	—	—	—	10.00	14.00

KM# 241.1 DOLLAR
28.5400 g., Copper-Nickel, 38.65 mm. **Series:** Big Cats **Obv:** National arms **Rev:** Male and female lions **Edge:** Reeded

Date	Mintage	F	VF	XF	Unc	BU
2001PM	—	—	—	—	12.50	15.00

KM# 241.2 DOLLAR
28.5400 g., Copper-Nickel, 38.65 mm. **Series:** Big Cats **Obv:** National arms **Rev:** Multi-colored male and female lions **Edge:** Reeded

Date	Mintage	F	VF	XF	Unc	BU
2001PM	—	—	—	—	15.00	17.50

KM# 242.1 DOLLAR
28.5400 g., Copper-Nickel, 38.65 mm. **Series:** Big Cats **Obv:** National arms **Rev:** Tiger **Edge:** Reeded

Date	Mintage	F	VF	XF	Unc	BU
2001PM	—	—	—	—	10.00	14.00

KM# 242.2 DOLLAR
28.5400 g., Copper-Nickel, 38.65 mm. **Series:** Big Cats **Obv:** National arms **Rev:** Multi-colored Tiger **Edge:** Reeded

Date	Mintage	F	VF	XF	Unc	BU
2001PM	—	—	—	—	15.00	17.50

KM# 243.1 DOLLAR
28.5400 g., Copper-Nickel, 38.65 mm. **Series:** Big Cats **Obv:** National arms **Rev:** Cheetah **Edge:** Reeded

Date	Mintage	F	VF	XF	Unc	BU
2001PM	—	—	—	—	12.50	15.00

KM# 243.2 DOLLAR
28.5400 g., Copper-Nickel, 38.65 mm. **Series:** Big Cats **Obv:** National arms **Rev:** Multi-colored Cheetah **Edge:** Reeded

Date	Mintage	F	VF	XF	Unc	BU
2001PM	—	—	—	—	15.00	17.50

KM# 244.1 DOLLAR

28.5400 g., Copper-Nickel, 38.65 mm. **Series:** Big Cats **Obv:** National arms **Rev:** Cougar **Edge:** Reeded

Date	Mintage	F	VF	XF	Unc	BU
2001PM	—	—	—	—	10.00	14.00

KM# 244.2 DOLLAR

28.5400 g., Copper-Nickel, 38.65 mm. **Series:** Big Cats **Obv:** National arms **Rev:** Multi-colored Cougar **Edge:** Reeded

Date	Mintage	F	VF	XF	Unc	BU
2001PM	—	—	—	—	15.00	17.50

KM# 245.1 DOLLAR

28.5400 g., Copper-Nickel, 38.65 mm. **Series:** Big Cats **Obv:** National arms **Rev:** Black panther **Edge:** Reeded

Date	Mintage	F	VF	XF	Unc	BU
2001PM	—	—	—	—	10.00	14.00

KM# 245.2 DOLLAR

28.5400 g., Copper-Nickel, 38.65 mm. **Series:** Big Cats **Obv:** National arms **Rev:** Multi-colored Black Panther **Edge:** Reeded

Date	Mintage	F	VF	XF	Unc	BU
2001PM	—	—	—	—	15.00	17.50

KM# 198 DOLLAR

28.2800 g., Copper-Nickel, 38.6 mm. **Subject:** Year of the Snake **Obv:** National arms **Rev:** Snake **Edge:** Reeded

Date	Mintage	F	VF	XF	Unc	BU
2001	—	—	—	—	10.00	14.00

KM# 206 DOLLAR

Copper-Nickel, 38.6 mm. **Subject:** P'an Ku **Obv:** National arms **Rev:** Dragon

Date	Mintage	F	VF	XF	Unc	BU
2001	—	—	—	—	10.00	14.00

KM# 214 DOLLAR

Copper-Nickel, 38.6 mm. **Subject:** P'an Ku **Obv:** National arms **Rev:** Dragon and three animals

Date	Mintage	F	VF	XF	Unc	BU
2001	—	—	—	—	10.00	14.00

KM# 256 DOLLAR

28.2800 g., Copper-Nickel, 38.6 mm. **Subject:** Year of the Horse **Obv:** National arms **Rev:** Horse **Edge:** Reeded

Date	Mintage	F	VF	XF	Unc	BU
2002	—	—	—	—	12.50	15.00

KM# 264 DOLLAR

28.2800 g., Copper-Nickel, 38.6 mm. **Subject:** RMS Titanic **Obv:** National arms **Rev:** Titanic at dock **Edge:** Reeded

Date	Mintage	F	VF	XF	Unc	BU
2002	—	—	—	—	10.00	12.00

KM# 268 DOLLAR

28.2800 g., Copper-Nickel, 38.6 mm. **Subject:** Queen's Golden Jubilee **Obv:** National arms **Rev:** Queen Elizabeth II and Prince Philip visiting blacksmiths in Sierra Leone **Edge:** Reeded

Date	Mintage	F	VF	XF	Unc	BU
2002	—	—	—	—	10.00	12.00

KM# 269 DOLLAR

28.2800 g., Copper-Nickel, 38.6 mm. **Subject:** Queen's Golden Jubilee **Obv:** National arms **Rev:** Queen, Prince Charles and Princess Anne **Edge:** Reeded

Date	Mintage	F	VF	XF	Unc	BU
2002	—	—	—	—	10.00	12.00

KM# 276 DOLLAR

28.2800 g., Copper-Nickel, 38.6 mm. **Subject:** British Queen Mother **Obv:** National arms **Rev:** Queen Mother with dog in garden **Edge:** Reeded

Date	Mintage	F	VF	XF	Unc	BU
2002	—	—	—	—	10.00	12.00

KM# 279 DOLLAR

28.2800 g., Copper-Nickel, 38.6 mm. **Subject:** Queen Mother **Obv:** National arms **Rev:** Queen Mother with daughters **Edge:** Reeded

Date	Mintage	F	VF	XF	Unc	BU
2002	—	—	—	—	10.00	12.00

KM# 282 DOLLAR

28.2800 g., Copper-Nickel, 38.6 mm. **Subject:** Queen's Golden Jubilee **Obv:** National arms **Rev:** Queen Elizabeth and a young Prince Charles **Edge:** Reeded

Date	Mintage	F	VF	XF	Unc	BU
2002	—	—	—	—	10.00	12.00

KM# 285 DOLLAR

28.2800 g., Copper-Nickel, 38.6 mm. **Subject:** Queen's Golden Jubilee **Obv:** National arms **Rev:** Queen Elizabeth and Prince Philip **Edge:** Reeded

Date	Mintage	F	VF	XF	Unc	BU
2002	—	—	—	—	10.00	12.00

KM# 288 DOLLAR

28.2800 g., Copper-Nickel, 38.6 mm. **Subject:** Olympics **Obv:** National arms **Rev:** Victory goddess Nike **Edge:** Reeded

Date	Mintage	F	VF	XF	Unc	BU
2003	—	—	—	—	10.00	12.00
2004	—	—	—	—	10.00	12.00

KM# 291 DOLLAR

28.2800 g., Copper-Nickel, 38.6 mm. **Subject:** Olympics **Obv:** National arms **Rev:** Ancient archer **Edge:** Reeded

Date	Mintage	F	VF	XF	Unc	BU
2003	—	—	—	—	10.00	12.00
2004	—	—	—	—	10.00	12.00

KM# 297 DOLLAR

28.2800 g., Copper-Nickel, 38.6 mm. **Obv:** National arms **Rev:** Nelson Mandela **Edge:** Reeded

Date	Mintage	F	VF	XF	Unc	BU
2004	—	—	—	—	15.00	16.50

KM# 300 DOLLAR

28.2800 g., Copper-Nickel, 38.6 mm. **Obv:** National arms **Rev:** Ronald Reagan **Edge:** Reeded

Date	Mintage	F	VF	XF	Unc	BU
2004	—	—	—	—	15.00	16.50

KM# 304 DOLLAR

28.4200 g., Copper-Nickel, 38.6 mm. **Obv:** National arms **Rev:** Giraffe **Edge:** Reeded

Date	Mintage	F	VF	XF	Unc	BU
2005	—	—	—	—	12.00	16.00

KM# 305 DOLLAR

28.4200 g., Copper-Nickel, 38.6 mm. **Obv:** National arms **Rev:** Crocodile **Edge:** Reeded

Date	Mintage	F	VF	XF	Unc	BU
2005	—	—	—	—	12.00	16.00

KM# 306 DOLLAR

28.4200 g., Copper-Nickel, 38.6 mm. **Obv:** National arms **Rev:** Hippo in water **Edge:** Reeded

Date	Mintage	F	VF	XF	Unc	BU
2005	—	—	—	—	12.00	16.00

KM# 345 DOLLAR

28.5000 g., Copper-Nickel, 38.58 mm. **Subject:** Death of Prince Rainier III **Obv:** National arms **Rev:** Bust left, small knight horseback right on neck **Edge:** Reeded

Date	Mintage	F	VF	XF	Unc	BU
2005	—	—	—	—	7.00	9.00

KM# 317 DOLLAR

Copper-Nickel **Series:** 60th Anniversary End of WW II **Subject:** Battle of El Alamein **Obv:** National arms **Obv. Legend:** REPUBLIC OF SIERRA LEONE **Rev:** Tank, plane and ground troops

Date	Mintage	F	VF	XF	Unc	BU
2005	—	—	—	—	10.00	12.00

KM# 316 DOLLAR

Copper-Nickel **Series:** 60th Anniversary End of WW II **Subject:** The Battle of the Atlantic **Obv:** National arms **Obv. Legend:** REPUBLIC OF SIERRA LEONE **Rev:** Plane and ship convoy

Date	Mintage	F	VF	XF	Unc	BU
2005	—	—	—	—	10.00	12.00

KM# 319 DOLLAR

Copper-Nickel **Series:** 60th Anniversary End of WW II **Subject:** The Battle of Berlin **Obv:** National arms **Obv. Legend:** REPUBLIC OF SIERRA LEONE **Rev:** Berlin city view, tank

Date	Mintage	F	VF	XF	Unc	BU
2005	—	—	—	—	10.00	12.00

KM# 315 DOLLAR

Copper-Nickel **Series:** 60th Anniversary End of WW II **Subject:** Battle of Britian **Obv:** National arms **Obv. Legend:** REPUBLIC OF SIERRA LEONE **Rev:** Planes in flight

Date	Mintage	F	VF	XF	Unc	BU
2005	—	—	—	—	10.00	12.00

KM# 318 DOLLAR

Copper-Nickel **Series:** 60th Anniversay End of WW II **Subject:** Battle of the Bulge **Obv:** National arms **Obv. Legend:** REPUBLIC OF SIERRA LEONE **Rev:** Forest battle scene

Date	Mintage	F	VF	XF	Unc	BU
2005	—	—	—	—	10.00	12.00

KM# 320 DOLLAR

Copper-Nickel **Series:** 60th Anniversary End of WW II **Subject:** The Heavy Water Raids **Obv:** National arms **Obv. Legend:** REPUBLIC OF SIERRA LEONE **Rev:** Troops on skies, factory in ruins

Date	Mintage	F	VF	XF	Unc	BU
2005	—	—	—	—	10.00	12.00

KM# 321 DOLLAR

Copper-Nickel **Obv:** National Arms **Rev:** Mountain Gorillia

Date	Mintage	F	VF	XF	Unc	BU
2005	—	—	—	—	12.00	16.00

KM# 322 DOLLAR

Copper-Nickel **Rev:** John Paul II head left, within ring of the Stations of the Cross

Date	Mintage	F	VF	XF	Unc	BU
2005	—	—	—	—	10.00	12.00

KM# 323 DOLLAR

Copper-Nickel **Rev:** Benedict XVI and St. Peter's

Date	Mintage	F	VF	XF	Unc	BU
2005	—	—	—	—	10.00	12.00

KM# 324 DOLLAR
Copper-Nickel **Obv:** National Arms **Rev:** Brontosaurus

Date	Mintage	F	VF	XF	Unc	BU
2006	—	—	—	—	14.00	16.00

KM# 308 DOLLAR
28.3700 g., Copper-Nickel, 38.5 mm. **Obv:** National arms **Rev:** Stegosaurus **Edge:** Reeded

Date	Mintage	F	VF	XF	Unc	BU
2006	—	—	—	—	14.00	16.00

KM# 309 DOLLAR
28.3700 g., Copper-Nickel, 38.5 mm. **Obv:** National arms **Rev:** Tyrannosaurus Rex **Edge:** Reeded

Date	Mintage	F	VF	XF	Unc	BU
2006	—	—	—	—	14.00	16.00

KM# 310 DOLLAR
28.3700 g., Copper-Nickel, 38.5 mm. **Obv:** National arms **Rev:** Triceratops **Edge:** Reeded

Date	Mintage	F	VF	XF	Unc	BU
2006	—	—	—	—	14.00	16.00

KM# 311 DOLLAR
28.3700 g., Copper-Nickel, 38.5 mm. **Obv:** National arms **Rev:** Lion **Edge:** Reeded

Date	Mintage	F	VF	XF	Unc	BU
2006	—	—	—	—	12.00	16.00

KM# 312 DOLLAR
28.3700 g., Copper-Nickel, 38.5 mm. **Obv:** National arms **Rev:** Dromedary Camel **Edge:** Reeded

Date	Mintage	F	VF	XF	Unc	BU
2006	—	—	—	—	12.00	16.00

KM# 313 DOLLAR
28.3700 g., Copper-Nickel, 38.63 mm. **Obv:** National arms **Rev:** Chimpanzee **Edge:** Reeded

Date	Mintage	F	VF	XF	Unc	BU
2006	—	—	—	—	12.00	16.00

KM# 314 DOLLAR
28.3700 g., Copper-Nickel, 38.5 mm. **Obv:** National arms **Rev:** Impala **Edge:** Reeded

Date	Mintage	F	VF	XF	Unc	BU
2006	—	—	—	—	12.00	16.00

KM# 326 DOLLAR
Copper-Nickel **Rev:** Cheetah

Date	Mintage	F	VF	XF	Unc	BU
2007	—	—	—	—	14.00	17.00

KM# 327 DOLLAR
Copper-Nickel **Rev:** Zebra

Date	Mintage	F	VF	XF	Unc	BU
2007	—	—	—	—	14.00	17.00

KM# 328 DOLLAR
Copper-Nickel **Rev:** Rhino

Date	Mintage	F	VF	XF	Unc	BU
2007	—	—	—	—	14.00	17.00

KM# 329 DOLLAR
Copper-Nickel **Obv:** Arms **Rev:** African elephant

Date	Mintage	F	VF	XF	Unc	BU
2007	—	—	—	—	15.00	18.00

KM# 347 DOLLAR
28.3700 g., Copper-Nickel, 38.6 mm. **Series:** Nocturnal Creatures of Africa **Obv:** National arms **Rev:** Duiker Antelope standing left, facing **Edge:** Reeded **Note:** Blackened finish.

Date	Mintage	F	VF	XF	Unc	BU
2008	—	—	—	—	17.50	20.00

KM# 348 DOLLAR
28.3700 g., Copper-Nickel, 38.6 mm. **Series:** Nocturnal Creatures of Africa **Obv:** National arms **Rev:** Bush Baby on tree limb **Edge:** Reeded **Note:** Blackened finish.

Date	Mintage	F	VF	XF	Unc	BU
2008	—	—	—	—	17.50	20.00

KM# 349 DOLLAR
28.3700 g., Copper-Nickel, 38.6 mm. **Series:** Nocturnal Creatures of Africa **Obv:** National arms **Rev:** Honey Badger **Edge:** Reeded **Note:** Blackened finish

Date	Mintage	F	VF	XF	Unc	BU
2008	—	—	—	—	17.50	20.00

KM# 350 DOLLAR
28.3700 g., Copper-Nickel, 38.6 mm. **Series:** Nocturnal Creatures of Africa **Obv:** National arms. **Rev:** Pygmy Hippopotamus in water facing **Edge:** Reeded **Note:** Blackened finish.

Date	Mintage	F	VF	XF	Unc	BU
2008	—	—	—	—	17.50	20.00

KM# 223 10 DOLLARS
28.2800 g., 0.9250 Silver 0.8410 oz. ASW, 38.6 mm. **Series:** The Big Five **Obv:** National arms **Rev:** Rhino and value within circle **Edge:** Reeded

Date	Mintage	F	VF	XF	Unc	BU
2001 Proof	—	Value: 45.00				

KM# 226 10 DOLLARS
28.2800 g., 0.9250 Silver 0.8410 oz. ASW, 38.6 mm. **Series:** The Big Five **Obv:** National arms **Rev:** Lion head and value within circle

Date	Mintage	F	VF	XF	Unc	BU
2001 Proof	Est. 10,000	Value: 45.00				

KM# 229 10 DOLLARS
28.2800 g., 0.9250 Silver 0.8410 oz. ASW, 38.6 mm. **Series:** The Big Five **Obv:** National arms **Rev:** Leopard and value within circle

Date	Mintage	F	VF	XF	Unc	BU
2001 Proof	Est. 10,000	Value: 45.00				

KM# 232 10 DOLLARS
28.2800 g., 0.9250 Silver 0.8410 oz. ASW, 38.6 mm. **Series:** The Big Five **Obv:** National arms **Rev:** Elephants and value within circle

Date	Mintage	F	VF	XF	Unc	BU
2001 Proof	Est. 10,000	Value: 45.00				

KM# 235 10 DOLLARS
28.2800 g., 0.9250 Silver 0.8410 oz. ASW, 38.6 mm. **Series:** The Big Five **Obv:** National arms **Rev:** Buffalo and value within circle

Date	Mintage	F	VF	XF	Unc	BU
2001 Proof	Est. 10,000	Value: 45.00				

KM# 238 10 DOLLARS
28.2800 g., 0.9250 Silver 0.8410 oz. ASW, 38.6 mm. **Series:** The Big Five **Obv:** National arms **Rev:** All five animals within circle

Date	Mintage	F	VF	XF	Unc	BU
2001 Proof	Est. 10,000	Value: 45.00				

KM# 246.1 10 DOLLARS
28.2800 g., 0.9250 Silver 0.8410 oz. ASW, 38.6 mm. **Series:** Big Cats **Obv:** National arms **Rev:** Male and female lions **Edge:** Reeded

Date	Mintage	F	VF	XF	Unc	BU
2001 Proof	10,000	Value: 45.00				

KM# 246.2 10 DOLLARS
28.2800 g., 0.9250 Silver 0.8410 oz. ASW, 38.6 mm. **Series:** Big Cats **Obv:** National arms **Rev:** Multi-colored male and female lions **Edge:** Reeded

Date	Mintage	F	VF	XF	Unc	BU
2001 Proof	—	Value: 55.00				

KM# 247.1 10 DOLLARS
28.2800 g., 0.9250 Silver 0.8410 oz. ASW, 38.6 mm. **Series:** Big Cats **Obv:** National arms **Rev:** Tiger **Edge:** Reeded

Date	Mintage	F	VF	XF	Unc	BU
2001 Proof	—	Value: 45.00				

KM# 247.2 10 DOLLARS
28.2800 g., 0.9250 Silver 0.8410 oz. ASW, 38.6 mm. **Series:** Big Cats **Obv:** National arms **Rev:** Multi-colored Tiger **Edge:** Reeded

Date	Mintage	F	VF	XF	Unc	BU
2001 Proof	—	Value: 55.00				

KM# 248.1 10 DOLLARS
28.2800 g., 0.9250 Silver 0.8410 oz. ASW, 38.6 mm. **Series:** Big Cats **Obv:** National arms **Rev:** Cheetah head facing **Edge:** Reeded

Date	Mintage	F	VF	XF	Unc	BU
2001 Proof	10,000	Value: 45.00				

KM# 248.2 10 DOLLARS
28.2800 g., 0.9250 Silver 0.8410 oz. ASW, 38.6 mm. **Series:** Big Cats **Obv:** National arms **Rev:** Multi-colored Cheetah head facing **Edge:** Reeded

Date	Mintage	F	VF	XF	Unc	BU
2001 Proof	—	Value: 55.00				

KM# 249.1 10 DOLLARS
28.2800 g., 0.9250 Silver 0.8410 oz. ASW, 38.6 mm. **Series:** Big Cats **Obv:** National arms **Rev:** Cougar **Edge:** Reeded

Date	Mintage	F	VF	XF	Unc	BU
2001 Proof	10,000	Value: 45.00				

KM# 249.2 10 DOLLARS
28.2800 g., 0.9250 Silver 0.8410 oz. ASW, 38.6 mm. **Series:** Big Cats **Obv:** National arms **Rev:** Multi-colored Cougar **Edge:** Reeded

Date	Mintage	F	VF	XF	Unc	BU
2001 Proof	—	Value: 55.00				

KM# 250.1 10 DOLLARS
28.2800 g., 0.9250 Silver 0.8410 oz. ASW, 38.6 mm. **Series:** Big Cats **Obv:** National arms **Rev:** Leopard **Edge:** Reeded

Date	Mintage	F	VF	XF	Unc	BU
2001 Proof	10,000	Value: 45.00				

KM# 199 10 DOLLARS

28.2800 g., 0.9250 Silver 0.8410 oz. ASW, 38.6 mm. **Subject:** Year of the Snake **Obv:** National arms **Rev:** Snake on bamboo **Edge:** Reeded

Date	Mintage	F	VF	XF	Unc	BU
2001 Proof	Est. 25,000	Value: 55.00				

KM# 207 10 DOLLARS

28.2800 g., 0.9250 Silver 0.8410 oz. ASW, 38.6 mm. **Subject:** P'an Ku **Obv:** National arms **Rev:** Dragon

Date	Mintage	F	VF	XF	Unc	BU
2001 Proof	Est. 5,000	Value: 55.00				

KM# 215 10 DOLLARS

28.2800 g., 0.9250 Silver 0.8410 oz. ASW, 38.6 mm. **Subject:** P'an Ku **Obv:** National arms **Rev:** Dragon and three animals

Date	Mintage	F	VF	XF	Unc	BU
2001 Proof	Est. 5,000	Value: 55.00				

KM# 250.2 10 DOLLARS

28.2800 g., 0.9250 Silver 0.8410 oz. ASW, 38.6 mm. **Series:** Big Cats **Obv:** National arms **Rev:** Multi-colored Leopard **Edge:** Reeded

Date	Mintage	F	VF	XF	Unc	BU
2001 Proof	—	Value: 55.00				

KM# 277 10 DOLLARS

28.2800 g., 0.9250 Silver Gold clad 0.8410 oz. ASW, 38.6 mm. **Subject:** British Queen Mother **Obv:** National arms **Rev:** Bust facing in garden with dog within sprigs **Edge:** Reeded

Date	Mintage	F	VF	XF	Unc	BU
2002 Proof	10,000	Value: 55.00				

KM# 280 10 DOLLARS

28.2800 g., 0.9250 Silver Gold clad 0.8410 oz. ASW, 38.6 mm. **Subject:** British Queen Mother **Obv:** National arms **Rev:** Conjoined busts facing within sprigs **Edge:** Reeded

Date	Mintage	F	VF	XF	Unc	BU
2002 Proof	10,000	Value: 55.00				

KM# 257 10 DOLLARS

28.2800 g., 0.9250 Silver 0.8410 oz. ASW, 38.6 mm. **Subject:** Year of the Horse **Obv:** National arms **Rev:** Horse divides circle **Edge:** Reeded

Date	Mintage	F	VF	XF	Unc	BU
2002 Proof	5,000	Value: 60.00				

KM# 265 10 DOLLARS

28.2800 g., 0.9250 Silver 0.8410 oz. ASW, 38.6 mm. **Subject:** RMS Titanic **Obv:** National arms **Rev:** Titanic at dock **Edge:** Reeded

Date	Mintage	F	VF	XF	Unc	BU
2002 Proof	10,000	Value: 55.00				

KM# 270 10 DOLLARS

28.2800 g., 0.9250 Silver Gold clad 0.8410 oz. ASW, 38.6 mm. **Subject:** Queen's Golden Jubilee **Obv:** National arms **Rev:** Queen Elizabeth II and Prince Philip visiting blacksmiths in Sierra Leone **Edge:** Reeded

Date	Mintage	F	VF	XF	Unc	BU
2002 Proof	10,000	Value: 55.00				

KM# 271 10 DOLLARS

28.2800 g., 0.9250 Silver Gold clad 0.8410 oz. ASW, 38.6 mm. **Subject:** Queen's Golden Jubilee **Obv:** National arms **Rev:** Queen Elizabeth II, Prince Charles and Princess Anne **Edge:** Reeded

Date	Mintage	F	VF	XF	Unc	BU
2002 Proof	10,000	Value: 52.00				

KM# 283 10 DOLLARS

28.2800 g., 0.9250 Silver Gold clad 0.8410 oz. ASW, 38.6 mm. **Subject:** Queen Elizabeth's Golden Jubilee **Obv:** National arms **Rev:** Queen and young Prince Charles **Edge:** Reeded

Date	Mintage	F	VF	XF	Unc	BU
2002 Proof	10,000	Value: 50.00				

KM# 286 10 DOLLARS

28.2800 g., 0.9250 Silver Gold clad 0.8410 oz. ASW, 38.6 mm. **Subject:** Queen Elizabeth's Golden Jubilee **Obv:** National arms **Rev:** Queen and Prince Philip **Edge:** Reeded

Date	Mintage	F	VF	XF	Unc	BU
2002 Proof	10,000	Value: 50.00				

KM# 292 10 DOLLARS

28.2800 g., 0.9250 Silver 0.8410 oz. ASW, 38.6 mm. **Subject:** Olympics **Obv:** National arms **Rev:** Ancient archer **Edge:** Reeded

Date	Mintage	F	VF	XF	Unc	BU
2003 Proof	10,000	Value: 50.00				
2004 Proof	10,000	Value: 50.00				

KM# 289 10 DOLLARS

28.2800 g., 0.9250 Silver 0.8410 oz. ASW, 38.6 mm. **Subject:** Olympics **Obv:** National arms **Rev:** Victory goddess Nike **Edge:** Reeded **Note:** The leone is the official currency of Sierra Leone

Date	Mintage	F	VF	XF	Unc	BU
2003 Proof	10,000	Value: 50.00				
2004 Proof	10,000	Value: 50.00				

KM# 298 10 DOLLARS

28.2800 g., 0.9250 Silver 0.8410 oz. ASW, 38.6 mm. **Obv:** National arms **Rev:** Nelson Mandela **Edge:** Reeded

Date	Mintage	F	VF	XF	Unc	BU
2004 Proof	10,000	Value: 55.00				

KM# 301 10 DOLLARS

28.2800 g., 0.9250 Silver 0.8410 oz. ASW, 38.6 mm. **Obv:** National arms **Rev:** Ronald Reagan **Edge:** Reeded

Date	Mintage	F	VF	XF	Unc	BU
2004 Proof	10,000	Value: 55.00				

KM# 307 DOLLAR

28.6200 g., 0.9250 Silver 0.8511 oz. ASW, 38.5 mm. **Obv:** National arms **Rev:** Giraffe **Edge:** Reeded

Date	Mintage	F	VF	XF	Unc	BU
2005 Proof	—	Value: 50.00				

KM# 342 10 DOLLARS

0.9250 Silver **Series:** 60th Anniversary End of WW II **Subject:** Battle of the Bulge **Obv:** National arms **Obv. Legend:** REPUBLIC OF SIERRA LEONE **Rev:** Forest battle scene

Date	Mintage	F	VF	XF	Unc	BU
2005 Proof	—	Value: 50.00				

KM# 339 10 DOLLARS

0.9250 g., Silver **Series:** 60th Anniversary of WW II **Subject:** Battle of Britain **Obv:** National arms **Obv. Legend:** REPUBLIC OF SIERRA LEONE **Rev:** Planes in flight

Date	Mintage	F	VF	XF	Unc	BU
2005 Proof	—	Value: 50.00				

KM# 340 10 DOLLARS

0.9250 Silver **Series:** 60th Anniversary End of WW II **Subject:** The Battle of the Atlantic **Obv:** National arms **Obv. Legend:** REPUBLIC OF SIERRA LEONE **Rev:** Plane and ship convoy

Date	Mintage	F	VF	XF	Unc	BU
2005 Proof	—	Value: 50.00				

KM# 341 10 DOLLARS

0.9250 Silver **Series:** 60th Anniversary End of WW II **Subject:** Battle of El Alamein **Obv:** National arms **Obv. Legend:** REPUBLIC OF SIERRA LEONE **Rev:** Tank, plane and ground troops

Date	Mintage	F	VF	XF	Unc	BU
2005 Proof	—	Value: 50.00				

KM# 343 10 DOLLARS

0.9250 Silver **Series:** 60th Anniversary End of WW II **Subject:** Battle of Berlin **Obv:** National arms **Obv. Legend:** REPUBLIC OF SIERRA LEONE **Rev:** Berlin city view, tank

Date	Mintage	F	VF	XF	Unc	BU
2005 Proof	—	Value: 50.00				

KM# 344 10 DOLLARS

0.9250 Silver **Series:** 60th Anniversary End of WW II **Subject:** The Heavy Water Raids **Obv:** National arms **Obv. Legend:** REPUBLIC OF SIERRA LEONE **Rev:** Troops on skies, factory in ruins

Date	Mintage	F	VF	XF	Unc	BU
2005 Proof	—	Value: 50.00				

KM# 330 10 DOLLARS

0.9167 Silver **Series:** Crown Jewels **Obv:** Arms **Obv. Legend:** REPUBLIC OF SIERRA LEONE **Rev:** Imperial State crown with ruby setting **Rev. Legend:** CROWN JEWELS **Edge:** Reeded

Date	Mintage	F	VF	XF	Unc	BU
2006 Proof	—	Value: 120				

KM# 331 10 DOLLARS

0.9167 Silver **Series:** Crown Jewels **Obv:** Arms **Obv. Legend:** REPUBLIC OF SIERRA LEONE **Rev:** Sword of State with sapphire setting **Rev. Legend:** CROWN JEWELS **Edge:** Reeded

Date	Mintage	F	VF	XF	Unc	BU
2006 Proof	—	Value: 120				

KM# 332 10 DOLLARS

0.9167 Silver **Series:** Crown Jewels **Obv:** Arms **Obv. Legend:** REPUBLIC OF SIERRA LEONE **Rev:** St. Edward's Crown with emerald setting **Rev. Legend:** CROWN JEWELS **Edge:** Reeded

Date	Mintage	F	VF	XF	Unc	BU
2006 Proof	—	Value: 120				

KM# 333 10 DOLLARS
0.9167 Silver **Series:** Crown Jewels **Obv:** Arms **Obv. Legend:** REPUBLIC OF SIERRA LEONE **Rev:** Orb and Sceptre with the cross with diamond setting **Rev. Legend:** CROWN JEWELS **Edge:** Reeded

Date	Mintage	F	VF	XF	Unc	BU
2006 Proof	—	Value: 120				

KM# 334 10 DOLLARS
Copper-Nickel **Subject:** 80th Birthday of Queen Elizabeth II **Obv:** Arms **Obv. Legend:** REPUBLIC OF SIERRA LEONE **Rev:** Elizabeth II seated giving Christmas message **Rev. Legend:** 80th Birthday of H.M. Queen Elizabeth II **Edge:** Reeded

Date	Mintage	F	VF	XF	Unc	BU
2006	—	—	—	—	16.50	18.50

KM# 334a 10 DOLLARS
Silver **Subject:** 80th Birthday of Queen Elizabeth II **Obv:** Arms **Obv. Legend:** REPUBLIC OF SIERRA LEONE **Rev:** Elizabeth II seated giving Christmas Message **Rev. Legend:** 80th Birthday of H.M. Queen Elizabeth II **Edge:** Reeded

Date	Mintage	F	VF	XF	Unc	BU
2006 Proof	—	Value: 75.00				

KM# 335 10 DOLLARS
Copper-Nickel **Subject:** 80th Bithday of Queen Elizabeth II **Obv:** Arms **Obv. Legend:** REPUBLIC OF SIERRA LEONE **Rev:** Elizabeth II at 2002 Golden Jubilee celebrations in London, Concorde and Red Arrows doing flypass over Buckingham Palace **Rev. Legend:** 80th Birthday of H.M. Queen Elizabeth II **Edge:** Reeded

Date	Mintage	F	VF	XF	Unc	BU
2006	—	—	—	—	16.50	18.50

KM# 335a 10 DOLLARS
0.9167 Silver **Subject:** 80th Birthday of Queen Elizabeth Ii **Obv:** Arms **Obv. Legend:** RIPUBLIC OF SIERRA LEONE **Rev:** Elizabeth II at 2002 Golden Jubilee celebrations in London, Concorde and Red Arrows doing flypass over Buckingham Palace **Rev. Legend:** 80th Birthday of H.M. Queen Elizabeth II **Edge:** Reeded

Date	Mintage	F	VF	XF	Unc	BU
2006 Proof	—	Value: 75.00				

KM# 336 10 DOLLARS
Copper-Nickel **Subject:** 80th Birthday of Queen Elizabeth II **Obv:** Arms **Obv. Legend:** REPUBLIC OF SIERRA LEONE **Rev:** Elizabeth II presenting 1966 Football World Cup to English team **Rev. Legend:** 80th Birthday of H.M. Queen Elizabeth II **Edge:** Reeded

Date	Mintage	F	VF	XF	Unc	BU
2006	—	—	—	—	16.50	18.50

KM# 336a 10 DOLLARS
0.9167 Silver **Subject:** 80th Birthday of Queen Elizabeth II **Obv:** Arms **Obv. Legend:** REPUBLIC OF SIERRA LEONE **Rev:** Elizabeth II presenting 1966 Football World Cup to English team **Rev. Legend:** 80th Birthday of H.M. Queen Elizabeth II **Edge:** Reeded

Date	Mintage	F	VF	XF	Unc	BU
2006 Proof	—	Value: 75.00				

KM# 337 10 DOLLARS
Copper-Nickel **Subject:** 80th Birthday of Queen Elizabeth II **Obv:** Arms **Obv. Legend:** REPUBLIC OF SIERRA LEONE **Rev:** Investiture of Charles as Prince of Wales in 1969 **Rev. Legend:** 80th Birthday of H.M. Queen Elizabeth II **Edge:** Reeded

Date	Mintage	F	VF	XF	Unc	BU
2006	—	—	—	—	16.50	18.50

KM# 337a 10 DOLLARS
0.9167 Silver **Subject:** 80th Birthday of Queen Elizabeth II **Obv:** Arms **Obv. Legend:** REPUBLIC OF SIERRA LEONE **Rev:** Investiture of Charles as Prince of Wales in 1969 **Rev. Legend:** 80th Birthday of H.M. Queen Elizabeth II **Edge:** Reeded

Date	Mintage	F	VF	XF	Unc	BU
2006 Proof	—	Value: 75.00				

KM# 338 10 DOLLARS
Copper-Nickel **Subject:** 10th Anniversary Death of Princess Diana **Obv:** Arms **Obv. Legend:** REPUBLIC OF SIERRA LEONE **Rev:** Diana with sons, Prince William and Prince Harry facing **Rev. Legend:** DIANA — PRINCESS OF WALES **Edge:** Reeded

Date	Mintage	F	VF	XF	Unc	BU
2007	—	—	—	—	16.50	18.50

KM# 338a 10 DOLLARS
0.9167 Silver **Subject:** 10th Anniversary Death of Princess Diana **Obv:** Arms **Obv. Legend:** REPUBLIC OF SIERRA LEONE **Rev:** Diana with sons, Prince William and Prince Harry facing **Rev. Legend:** DIANA — PRINCESS OF WALES **Edge:** Reeded

Date	Mintage	F	VF	XF	Unc	BU
2007 Proof	—	Value: 75.00				

KM# 200 20 DOLLARS
1.2441 g., 0.9990 Gold 0.0400 oz. AGW, 13.9 mm. **Subject:** Year of the Snake **Obv:** National arms **Rev:** Snake **Edge:** Reeded

Date	Mintage	F	VF	XF	Unc	BU
2001 Proof	Est. 50,000	Value: 70.00				

KM# 208 20 DOLLARS
1.2441 g., 0.9990 Gold 0.0400 oz. AGW, 13.9 mm. **Subject:** P'an Ku **Obv:** National arms **Rev:** Dragon

Date	Mintage	F	VF	XF	Unc	BU
2001 Proof	Est. 5,000	Value: 70.00				

KM# 216 20 DOLLARS
1.2441 g., 0.9990 Gold 0.0400 oz. AGW, 13.9 mm. **Subject:** P'an Ku **Obv:** National arms **Rev:** Dragon and three animals

Date	Mintage	F	VF	XF	Unc	BU
2001 Proof	Est. 5,000	Value: 70.00				

KM# 258 20 DOLLARS
1.2400 g., 0.9990 Gold 0.0398 oz. AGW, 13.92 mm. **Subject:** Year of the Horse **Obv:** National arms **Rev:** Horse **Edge:** Reeded

Date	Mintage	F	VF	XF	Unc	BU
2002 Proof	5,000	Value: 70.00				

KM# 272 30 DOLLARS
6.2200 g., 0.3750 Gold 0.0750 oz. AGW, 22 mm. **Subject:** Queen's Golden Jubilee **Obv:** National arms **Rev:** Queen Elizabeth II and Prince Philip **Edge:** Reeded

Date	Mintage	F	VF	XF	Unc	BU
2002 Proof	5,000	Value: 120				

KM# 273 30 DOLLARS
6.2200 g., 0.3750 Gold 0.0750 oz. AGW, 22 mm. **Subject:** Queen's Golden Jubilee **Obv:** National arms **Rev:** Queen Elizabeth II, Prince Charles and Princess Anne **Edge:** Reeded

Date	Mintage	F	VF	XF	Unc	BU
2002 Proof	5,000	Value: 120				

KM# 201 50 DOLLARS
3.1103 g., 0.9990 Gold 0.0999 oz. AGW, 18 mm. **Subject:** Year of the Snake **Obv:** National arms **Rev:** Snake **Edge:** Reeded

Date	Mintage	F	VF	XF	Unc	BU
2001 Proof	Est. 10,000	Value: 150				

KM# 209 50 DOLLARS
3.1103 g., 0.9990 Gold 0.0999 oz. AGW, 18 mm. **Subject:** P'an Ku **Obv:** National arms **Rev:** Dragon

Date	Mintage	F	VF	XF	Unc	BU
2001 Proof	Est. 5,000	Value: 150				

KM# 217 50 DOLLARS
3.1103 g., 0.9990 Gold 0.0999 oz. AGW, 18 mm. **Subject:** P'an Ku **Obv:** National arms **Rev:** Dragon and three animals

Date	Mintage	F	VF	XF	Unc	BU
2001 Proof	Est. 5,000	Value: 150				

KM# 266 50 DOLLARS
155.5500 g., 0.9999 Silver 5.0003 oz. ASW, 65 mm. **Subject:** RMS Titanic **Obv:** National arms **Rev:** Titanic at dock **Edge:** Reeded

Date	Mintage	F	VF	XF	Unc	BU
2002 Proof	2,000	Value: 220				

KM# 259 50 DOLLARS
3.1100 g., 0.9990 Gold 0.0999 oz. AGW, 18 mm. **Subject:** Year of the Horse **Obv:** National arms **Rev:** Horse **Edge:** Reeded

Date	Mintage	F	VF	XF	Unc	BU
2002 Proof	5,000	Value: 150				

KM# 202 100 DOLLARS
6.2200 g., 0.9990 Gold 0.1998 oz. AGW, 22 mm. **Subject:** Year of the Snake **Obv:** National arms **Rev:** Snake **Edge:** Reeded

Date	Mintage	F	VF	XF	Unc	BU
2001 Proof	—	Value: 300				

KM# 210 100 DOLLARS
6.2200 g., 0.9990 Gold 0.1998 oz. AGW, 22 mm. **Subject:** P'an Ku **Obv:** National arms **Rev:** Dragon

Date	Mintage	F	VF	XF	Unc	BU
2001 Proof	Est. 10,000	Value: 300				

KM# 218 100 DOLLARS
6.2200 g., 0.9990 Gold 0.1998 oz. AGW, 22 mm. **Subject:** P'an Ku **Obv:** National arms **Rev:** Dragon and three animals

Date	Mintage	F	VF	XF	Unc	BU
2001 Proof	Est. 10,000	Value: 300				

KM# 224 100 DOLLARS
6.2200 g., 0.9990 Gold 0.1998 oz. AGW, 22 mm. **Series:** The Big Five **Obv:** National arms **Rev:** Rhino **Edge:** Reeded

Date	Mintage	F	VF	XF	Unc	BU
2001 Proof	Est. 5,000	Value: 300				

KM# 227 100 DOLLARS
6.2200 g., 0.9990 Gold 0.1998 oz. AGW, 22 mm. **Series:** The Big Five **Obv:** National arms **Rev:** Lion

Date	Mintage	F	VF	XF	Unc	BU
2001 Proof	Est. 5,000	Value: 300				

KM# 230 100 DOLLARS
6.2200 g., 0.9990 Gold 0.1998 oz. AGW, 22 mm. **Series:** The Big Five **Obv:** National arms **Rev:** Leopard

Date	Mintage	F	VF	XF	Unc	BU
2001 Proof	Est. 5,000	Value: 300				

KM# 233 100 DOLLARS
6.2200 g., 0.9990 Gold 0.1998 oz. AGW, 22 mm. **Series:** The Big Five **Obv:** National arms **Rev:** Elephants

Date	Mintage	F	VF	XF	Unc	BU
2001 Proof	Est. 5,000	Value: 300				

KM# 236 100 DOLLARS
6.2200 g., 0.9990 Gold 0.1998 oz. AGW, 22 mm. **Series:** The Big Five **Obv:** National arms **Rev:** Buffalo

Date	Mintage	F	VF	XF	Unc	BU
2001 Proof	Est. 5,000	Value: 300				

KM# 239 100 DOLLARS
6.2200 g., 0.9990 Gold 0.1998 oz. AGW, 22 mm. **Series:** The Big Five **Obv:** National arms **Rev:** All five animals

Date	Mintage	F	VF	XF	Unc	BU
2001 Proof	Est. 5,000	Value: 300				

KM# 251 100 DOLLARS
6.2200 g., 0.9990 Gold 0.1998 oz. AGW, 22 mm. **Series:** Big Cats **Obv:** National arms **Rev:** Male and female lions **Edge:** Reeded

Date	Mintage	F	VF	XF	Unc	BU
2001 Proof	5,000	Value: 300				

KM# 252 100 DOLLARS
6.2200 g., 0.9990 Gold 0.1998 oz. AGW, 22 mm. **Series:** Big Cats **Rev:** Tiger **Edge:** Reeded

Date	Mintage	F	VF	XF	Unc	BU
2001 Proof	5,000	Value: 300				

KM# 253 100 DOLLARS
6.2200 g., 0.9990 Gold 0.1998 oz. AGW, 22 mm. **Series:** Big Cats **Rev:** Cheetah **Edge:** Reeded

Date	Mintage	F	VF	XF	Unc	BU
2001 Proof	5,000	Value: 300				

KM# 254 100 DOLLARS
6.2200 g., 0.9990 Gold 0.1998 oz. AGW, 22 mm. **Series:** Big Cats **Rev:** Cougar **Edge:** Reeded

Date	Mintage	F	VF	XF	Unc	BU
2001 Proof	5,000	Value: 300				

KM# 255 100 DOLLARS
6.2200 g., 0.9990 Gold 0.1998 oz. AGW, 22 mm. **Series:** Big Cats **Rev:** Black panther **Edge:** Reeded

Date	Mintage	F	VF	XF	Unc	BU
2001 Proof	5,000	Value: 300				

KM# 274 100 DOLLARS
6.2200 g., 0.9999 Gold 0.1999 oz. AGW, 22 mm. **Subject:** Queen's Golden Jubilee **Obv:** National arms **Rev:** Queen Elizabeth II and Prince Philip **Edge:** Reeded

Date	Mintage	F	VF	XF	Unc	BU
2002 Proof	2,002	Value: 320				

KM# 275 100 DOLLARS
6.2200 g., 0.9999 Gold 0.1999 oz. AGW, 22 mm. **Subject:** Queen's Golden Jubilee **Obv:** National arms **Rev:** Queen Elizabeth II, Prince Charles and Princess Anne **Edge:** Reeded

Date	Mintage	F	VF	XF	Unc	BU
2002 Proof	5,000	Value: 300				

KM# 284 100 DOLLARS
6.2200 g., 0.9999 Gold 0.1999 oz. AGW, 22 mm. **Subject:** Queen Elizabeth's Golden Jubilee **Obv:** National arms **Rev:** Queen and young Prince Charles **Edge:** Reeded

Date	Mintage	F	VF	XF	Unc	BU
2002 Proof	2,002	Value: 320				

KM# 287 100 DOLLARS
6.2200 g., 0.9999 Gold 0.1999 oz. AGW, 22 mm. **Subject:** Queen Elizabeth's Golden Jubilee **Obv:** National arms **Rev:** Queen and Prince Philip **Edge:** Reeded

Date	Mintage	F	VF	XF	Unc	BU
2002 Proof	2,002	Value: 320				

KM# 278 100 DOLLARS
6.2200 g., 0.9999 Gold 0.1999 oz. AGW, 22 mm. **Subject:** British Queen Mother **Obv:** National arms **Rev:** Queen Mother in garden with dog **Edge:** Reeded

Date	Mintage	F	VF	XF	Unc	BU
2002 Proof	2,000	Value: 320				

KM# 281 100 DOLLARS
6.2200 g., 0.9999 Gold 0.1999 oz. AGW, 22 mm. **Subject:** British Queen Mother **Obv:** National arms **Rev:** Queen Mother with daughters **Edge:** Reeded

Date	Mintage	F	VF	XF	Unc	BU
2002 Proof	2,000	Value: 320				

KM# 260 100 DOLLARS
6.2200 g., 0.9990 Gold 0.1998 oz. AGW, 22 mm. **Subject:** Year of the Horse **Obv:** National arms **Rev:** Horse **Edge:** Reeded

Date	Mintage	F	VF	XF	Unc	BU
2002 Proof	2,000	Value: 320				

KM# 290 100 DOLLARS
6.2200 g., 0.9999 Gold 0.1999 oz. AGW, 22 mm. **Subject:** Olympics **Obv:** National arms **Rev:** Victory goddess Nike **Edge:** Reeded

Date	Mintage	F	VF	XF	Unc	BU
2003 Proof	5,000	Value: 300				
2004 Proof	5,000	Value: 300				

KM# 293 100 DOLLARS
6.2200 g., 0.9999 Gold 0.1999 oz. AGW, 22 mm. **Subject:** Olympics **Obv:** National arms **Rev:** Ancient archer **Edge:** Reeded

Date	Mintage	F	VF	XF	Unc	BU
2003 Proof	5,000	Value: 300				
2004 Proof	5,000	Value: 300				

KM# 267 150 DOLLARS
1000.0000 g., 0.9999 Silver 32.146 oz. ASW, 85 mm. **Subject:** RMS Titanic **Obv:** National arms **Rev:** Titanic at dock **Edge:** Reeded

Date	Mintage	F	VF	XF	Unc	BU
2002 Proof	500	Value: 1,350				

KM# 203 250 DOLLARS
15.5118 g., 0.9990 Gold 0.4982 oz. AGW, 30 mm. **Subject:** Year of the Snake **Obv:** National arms **Rev:** Snake **Edge:** Reeded

Date	Mintage	F	VF	XF	Unc	BU
2001 Proof	Est. 5,000	Value: 750				

KM# 211 250 DOLLARS
15.5518 g., 0.9990 Gold 0.4995 oz. AGW, 30 mm. **Subject:** P'an Ku **Obv:** National arms **Rev:** Dragon

Date	Mintage	F	VF	XF	Unc	BU
2001 Proof	Est. 2,000	Value: 775				

KM# 219 250 DOLLARS
15.5518 g., 0.9990 Gold 0.4995 oz. AGW, 30 mm. **Subject:** P'an Ku **Obv:** National arms **Rev:** Dragon and three animals

Date	Mintage	F	VF	XF	Unc	BU
2001 Proof	Est. 2,000	Value: 775				

KM# 261 250 DOLLARS
15.5500 g., 0.9990 Gold 0.4994 oz. AGW, 30 mm. **Subject:** Year of the Horse **Obv:** National arms **Rev:** Horse **Edge:** Reeded

Date	Mintage	F	VF	XF	Unc	BU
2002 Proof	2,000	Value: 775				

KM# 204 500 DOLLARS
31.1035 g., 0.9990 Gold 0.9990 oz. AGW, 32.7 mm. **Subject:** Year of the Snake **Obv:** National arms **Rev:** Snake **Edge:** Reeded

Date	Mintage	F	VF	XF	Unc	BU
2001 Proof	Est. 1,000	Value: 1,600				

KM# 212 500 DOLLARS

31.1035 g., 0.9990 Gold 0.9990 oz. AGW, 32.7 mm. **Subject:** P'an Ku **Obv:** National arms **Rev:** Dragon

Date	Mintage	F	VF	XF	Unc	BU
2001 Proof	Est. 1,000	Value: 1,550				

KM# 220 500 DOLLARS

31.1035 g., 0.9990 Gold 0.9990 oz. AGW, 32.7 mm. **Subject:** P'an Ku **Obv:** National arms **Rev:** Dragon and three animals

Date	Mintage	F	VF	XF	Unc	BU
2001 Proof	Est. 1,000	Value: 1,550				

KM# 262 500 DOLLARS

31.1000 g., 0.9990 Gold 0.9988 oz. AGW, 32.7 mm. **Subject:** Year of the Horse **Obv:** National arms **Rev:** Horse **Edge:** Reeded

Date	Mintage	F	VF	XF	Unc	BU
2002 Proof	1,000	Value: 1,550				

KM# 294 500 DOLLARS

31.1000 g., 0.9999 Gold 0.9997 oz. AGW, 32.7 mm. **Obv:** National arms **Rev:** Multicolor Astro Boy cartoon **Edge:** Reeded

Date	Mintage	F	VF	XF	Unc	BU
2003 Proof	2,003	Value: 1,500				

KM# 299 500 DOLLARS

31.1035 g., 0.9999 Gold 0.9999 oz. AGW, 32.7 mm. **Obv:** National arms **Rev:** Nelson Mandela **Edge:** Reeded

Date	Mintage	F	VF	XF	Unc	BU
2004 Proof	—	Value: 1,550				

KM# 205 2500 DOLLARS

155.5175 g., 0.9990 Gold 4.9948 oz. AGW, 50 mm. **Subject:** Year of the Snake **Obv:** National arms **Rev:** Snake **Edge:** Reeded

Date	Mintage	F	VF	XF	Unc	BU
2001 Proof	Est. 250	Value: 7,500				

KM# 213 2500 DOLLARS

155.5175 g., 0.9990 Gold 4.9948 oz. AGW, 50 mm. **Subject:** P'an Ku **Obv:** National arms **Rev:** Dragon

Date	Mintage	F	VF	XF	Unc	BU
2001 Proof	Est. 250	Value: 7,500				

KM# 263 2500 DOLLARS

155.5100 g., 0.9990 Gold 4.9946 oz. AGW, 50 mm. **Subject:** Year of the Horse **Obv:** National arms **Rev:** Horse **Edge:** Reeded

Date	Mintage	F	VF	XF	Unc	BU
2002 Proof	250	Value: 7,500				

MINT SETS

KM#	Date	Mintage	Identification	Issue Price	Mkt Val
MS2	2006 (4)	—	KM# 334-337	65.00	75.00

PROOF SETS

KM#	Date	Mintage	Identification	Issue Price	Mkt Val
PS7	2006 (4)	—	KM# 330-333	450	480
PS8	2006 (4)	—	KM# 334a-337a	300	300

SINGAPORE

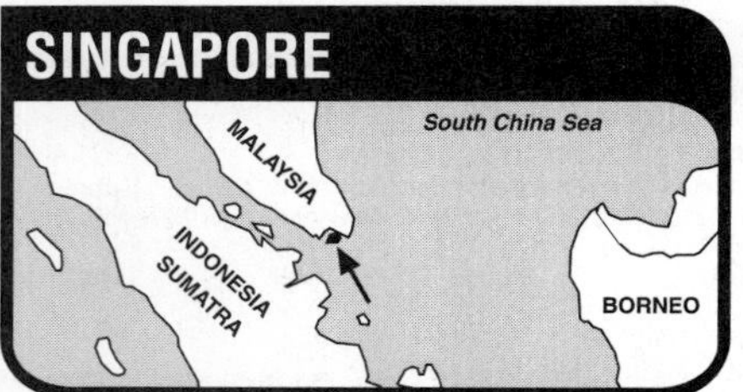

The Republic of Singapore, a member of the Commonwealth of Nations situated off the southern tip of the Malay peninsula, has an area of 224 sq. mi. (633 sq. km.) and a population of *2.7 million. Capital: Singapore. The economy is based on entrepôt trade, manufacturing and oil. Rubber, petroleum products, machinery and spices are exported.

The President is Chief of State. The prime minister is Head of Government.

MINT MARK

sm = "*sm*" - Singapore Mint monogram

MONETARY SYSTEM

100 Cents = 1 Dollar

REPUBLIC

STANDARD COINAGE

100 Cents = 1 Dollar

KM# 98a CENT

1.8100 g., 0.9250 Silver 0.0538 oz. ASW, 15.9 mm. **Obv:** National arms **Rev:** Value divides plants

Date	Mintage	F	VF	XF	Unc	BU
2001sm Proof	10,000	Value: 2.50				
2002sm Proof	10,000	Value: 2.50				
2003sm Proof	—	Value: 2.50				
2004sm Proof	—	Value: 2.50				
2005sm Proof	—	Value: 2.50				
2006sm Proof	—	Value: 2.50				
2007sm Proof	—	Value: 2.50				
2008sm Proof	—	Value: 2.50				
2009sm Proof	—	Value: 2.50				

KM# 98 CENT

1.2400 g., Copper Plated Zinc, 15.9 mm. **Obv:** National arms **Rev:** Value divides plants **Edge:** Plain **Note:** Similar to KM#49 but motto ribbon on arms curves down at center.

Date	Mintage	F	VF	XF	Unc	BU
2001	56,220,000	—	—	—	0.10	0.15
2002	19,003,000	—	—	—	0.10	0.15
2003	—	—	—	—	0.10	0.15
2003 Proof	—	Value: 2.00				
2004	—	—	—	—	0.10	0.15
2004 Proof	20,000	Value: 2.00				
2005	—	—	—	—	0.10	0.15
2006	—	—	—	—	0.10	0.15
2007	—	—	—	—	0.10	0.15
2008	—	—	—	—	0.10	0.15
2009	—	—	—	—	0.10	0.15

KM# 99a 5 CENTS

2.0000 g., 0.9250 Silver 0.0595 oz. ASW, 16.75 mm. **Obv:** National arms **Rev:** Fruit salad plant

Date	Mintage	F	VF	XF	Unc	BU
2001sm Proof	10,000	Value: 2.75				
2002sm Proof	10,000	Value: 2.75				
2003sm Proof	—	Value: 2.75				
2004sm Proof	—	Value: 2.75				
2005sm Proof	—	Value: 2.75				
2006sm Proof	—	Value: 2.75				
2007sm Proof	—	Value: 2.75				
2008sm Proof	—	Value: 2.75				
2009sm Proof	—	Value: 2.75				

KM# 99 5 CENTS

1.5600 g., Aluminum-Bronze, 16.75 mm. **Obv:** National arms **Rev:** Fruit salad plant **Edge:** Reeded **Note:** Similar to KM#50 but motto ribbon on arms curves down at center.

Date	Mintage	F	VF	XF	Unc	BU
2001	35,005,000	—	—	—	0.20	0.30
2002	33,556,000	—	—	—	0.20	0.30
2003	35,930,000	—	—	—	0.20	0.30
2003 Proof	—	Value: 3.00				
2004	38,040,000	—	—	—	0.20	0.30
2004 Proof	20,000	Value: 3.00				
2005	56,832,000	—	—	—	0.20	0.30
2006	—	—	—	—	0.20	0.30
2007	—	—	—	—	0.20	0.30
2008	—	—	—	—	0.20	0.30
2009	—	—	—	—	0.20	0.30

KM# 100a 10 CENTS

3.0500 g., 0.9250 Silver 0.0907 oz. ASW, 18.5 mm. **Obv:** National arms **Rev:** Star Jasmine plant **Edge:** Reeded

Date	Mintage	F	VF	XF	Unc	BU
2001sm Proof	10,000	Value: 4.00				
2002sm Proof	10,000	Value: 4.00				
2003sm Proof	—	Value: 4.00				
2004sm Proof	—	Value: 4.00				
2005sm Proof	—	Value: 4.00				
2006sm Proof	—	Value: 4.00				
2007sm Proof	—	Value: 4.00				
2008sm Proof	—	Value: 4.00				
2009sm Proof	—	Value: 4.00				

KM# 100 10 CENTS

2.6000 g., Copper-Nickel, 18.5 mm. **Obv:** National arms **Rev:** Star Jasmine plant **Edge:** Reeded **Note:** Similar to KM#51 but motto ribbon on arms curves down at center.

Date	Mintage	F	VF	XF	Unc	BU
2001	70,600,000	—	—	—	0.20	0.30
2002	61,670,000	—	—	—	0.20	0.30
2003	58,990,000	—	—	—	0.20	0.30
2003 Proof	—	Value: 4.00				
2004	59,670,000	—	—	—	0.20	0.30
2004 Proof	20,000	Value: 4.00				
2005	49,960,000	—	—	—	0.20	0.30
2006	—	—	—	—	0.20	0.30
2007	—	—	—	—	0.20	0.30
2008	—	—	—	—	0.20	0.30
2009	—	—	—	—	0.20	0.30

KM# 101a 20 CENTS

5.2400 g., 0.9250 Silver 0.1558 oz. ASW, 21.36 mm. **Obv:** National arms **Rev:** Powder puff plant above value **Edge:** Reeded

Date	Mintage	F	VF	XF	Unc	BU
2001sm Proof	10,000	Value: 7.00				
2002sm Proof	10,000	Value: 7.00				
2003sm Proof	—	Value: 7.00				
2004sm Proof	—	Value: 7.00				
2005sm Proof	—	Value: 7.00				
2006sm Proof	—	Value: 7.00				
2007sm Proof	—	Value: 7.00				

KM# 101 20 CENTS

4.5000 g., Copper-Nickel, 21.36 mm. **Obv:** National arms **Rev:** Powder-puff plant above value **Edge:** Reeded **Note:** Similar to KM#52 but motto ribbon on arms curves down at center.

Date	Mintage	F	VF	XF	Unc	BU
2001	52,050,000	—	—	—	0.60	0.75
2002	48,120,000	—	—	—	0.60	0.75
2003	45,470,000	—	—	—	0.60	0.75
2003	—	Value: 5.00				
2004	44,870,000	—	—	—	0.60	0.75
2004	20,000	Value: 5.00				
2005	—	—	—	—	0.60	0.75
2006	23,310,000	—	—	—	0.60	0.75
2007	—	—	—	—	0.60	0.75
2008	—	—	—	—	0.60	0.75
2009	—	—	—	—	0.60	0.75

KM# 102a 50 CENTS

8.5600 g., 0.9250 Silver 0.2546 oz. ASW, 24.66 mm. **Obv:** National arms **Rev:** Yellow Allamanda plant above value

Date	Mintage	F	VF	XF	Unc	BU
2001sm Proof	10,000	Value: 12.00				
2002sm Proof	10,000	Value: 12.00				
2003sm Proof	—	Value: 12.00				
2004sm Proof	—	Value: 12.00				
2005sm Proof	—	Value: 12.00				
2006sm Proof	—	Value: 12.00				
2007sm Proof	—	Value: 12.00				

KM# 102 50 CENTS

7.2900 g., Copper-Nickel, 24.66 mm. **Obv:** National arms **Rev:** Yellow Allamanda plant above value **Edge Lettering:** REPUBLIC OF SINGAPORE (lion's head) **Note:** Similar to KM#53 but motto ribbon on arms curves down at center.

Date	Mintage	F	VF	XF	Unc	BU
2001	30,020,000	—	—	—	0.75	1.00
2002	27,420,000	—	—	—	0.75	1.00
2003	23,650,000	—	—	—	0.75	1.00
2003 Proof	—	Value: 6.00				
2004	24,640,000	—	—	—	0.75	1.00
2004 Proof	20,000	Value: 6.00				
2005	24,996,000	—	—	—	0.75	1.00
2006	—	—	—	—	0.75	1.00
2007	7,680,000	—	—	—	0.75	1.00
2008	—	—	—	—	0.75	1.00
2009	—	—	—	—	0.75	1.00

KM# 103a DOLLAR

8.0500 g., 0.9250 Silver 0.2394 oz. ASW, 22.4 mm. **Obv:** National arms **Rev:** Periwinkle flower

Date	Mintage	F	VF	XF	Unc	BU
2001sm Proof	10,000	Value: 15.00				
2002sm Proof	10,000	Value: 15.00				
2003sm Proof	—	Value: 15.00				
2004sm Proof	—	Value: 15.00				
2005sm Proof	—	Value: 15.00				
2006sm Proof	—	Value: 15.00				
2007sm Proof	—	Value: 15.00				

KM# 103 DOLLAR

6.3000 g., Aluminum-Bronze, 22.4 mm. **Obv:** National arms **Rev:** Periwinkle flower **Edge:** Reeded **Note:** Similar to KM#54 but motto ribbon on arms curves down at center.

Date	Mintage	F	VF	XF	Unc	BU
2001	40,840,000	—	—	—	1.50	2.25
2002	35,660,000	—	—	—	1.50	2.25
2003	31,900,000	—	—	—	1.50	2.25
2003 Proof	—	Value: 10.00				
2004	34,380,000	—	—	—	1.50	2.25
2004 Proof	20,000	Value: 10.00				
2005	—	—	—	—	1.50	2.25
2006	25,488,000	—	—	—	1.50	2.25
2007	—	—	—	—	1.50	2.25
2008	—	—	—	—	1.50	2.25
2009	—	—	—	—	1.50	2.25

KM# 184 DOLLAR

Copper-Nickel, 24.6 mm. **Subject:** Old World Charm - Balestier **Obv:** Arms with supporters **Rev:** Old buildings **Edge:** Reeded

Date	Mintage	F	VF	XF	Unc	BU
2004sm Prooflike	—	—	—	—	—	10.00

KM# 184a DOLLAR

0.9990 Silver, 24.6 mm. **Subject:** Old World Charm - Balestier **Obv:** Arms with supporters **Rev:** Old buildings

Date	Mintage	F	VF	XF	Unc	BU
2004sm Proof	8,000	Value: 27.50				

KM# 190 DOLLAR

Copper-Nickel, 24.6 mm. **Subject:** Old World Charm - Jalan Besar

Date	Mintage	F	VF	XF	Unc	BU
2004sm Prooflike	—	—	—	—	—	10.00

KM# 190a DOLLAR

0.9990 Silver, 24.6 mm. **Subject:** Old World Charm - Jalan Besar

Date	Mintage	F	VF	XF	Unc	BU
2004sm Proof	8,000	Value: 27.50				

KM# 191 DOLLAR

Copper-Nickel, 24.6 mm. **Subject:** Old World Charm - Joo Chiat

Date	Mintage	F	VF	XF	Unc	BU
2004sm Prooflike	—	—	—	—	—	10.00

KM# 191a DOLLAR

0.9990 Silver, 24.6 mm. **Subject:** Old World Charm - Joo Chiat

Date	Mintage	F	VF	XF	Unc	BU
2004sm Proof	8,000	Value: 27.50				

KM# 192 DOLLAR

Copper-Nickel, 24.6 mm. **Subject:** Old World Charm - Tanjong Katong

Date	Mintage	F	VF	XF	Unc	BU
2004sm Prooflike	—	—	—	—	—	10.00

KM# 192a DOLLAR

0.9990 Silver, 24.6 mm. **Subject:** Old World Charm - Tanjong Katong

Date	Mintage	F	VF	XF	Unc	BU
2004sm Proof	8,000	Value: 27.50				

KM# 244 DOLLAR

Copper-Nickel **Series:** Urban Redevelopment **Obv:** National arms **Rev:** Anak Bukit

Date	Mintage	F	VF	XF	Unc	BU
2005sm Prooflike	—	Value: 12.00				

KM# 244a DOLLAR

0.9999 Silver **Series:** Urban Redevelopment **Obv:** National arms **Rev:** Anak Bukit - multicolor

Date	Mintage	F	VF	XF	Unc	BU
2005sm Proof	8,000	Value: 45.00				

KM# 245 DOLLAR

Copper-Nickel **Series:** Urban Redevelopment **Obv:** National arms **Rev:** Coronation

Date	Mintage	F	VF	XF	Unc	BU
2005sm Prooflike	—	Value: 12.00				

KM# 245a DOLLAR

0.9999 Silver **Series:** Urban Redevelopment **Obv:** National arms **Rev:** Coronation - multicolor

Date	Mintage	F	VF	XF	Unc	BU
2005sm Proof	8,000	Value: 45.00				

KM# 246 DOLLAR

Copper-Nickel **Series:** Urban Redevelopment **Obv:** National arms **Rev:** Jalan Leban and Casuarina Road

Date	Mintage	F	VF	XF	Unc	BU
2005sm Prooflike	—	Value: 12.00				

KM# 246a DOLLAR

0.9999 Silver **Series:** Urban Redevelopment **Obv:** National arms **Rev:** Jalan Leban and Casuarina Road - multicolor

Date	Mintage	F	VF	XF	Unc	BU
2005sm Proof	8,000	Value: 45.00				

KM# 247 DOLLAR

Copper-Nickel **Series:** Urban Redevelopment **Obv:** National arms **Rev:** Springleaf

Date	Mintage	F	VF	XF	Unc	BU
2005sm Prooflike	—	Value: 12.00				

KM# 247a DOLLAR

0.9999 Silver **Series:** Urban Redevelopment **Obv:** National arms **Rev:** Springleaf - multicolor

Date	Mintage	F	VF	XF	Unc	BU
2005sm Proof	8,000	Value: 45.00				

KM# 248 DOLLAR

Copper-Nickel **Series:** Urban Redevelopment **Obv:** National arms **Rev:** Thomson Village

Date	Mintage	F	VF	XF	Unc	BU
2005sm Prooflike	—	Value: 12.00				

KM# 248a DOLLAR

0.9999 Silver **Series:** Urban Redevelopment **Obv:** National arms **Rev:** Thomson Village - multicolor

Date	Mintage	F	VF	XF	Unc	BU
2005sm Proof	8,000	Value: 45.00				

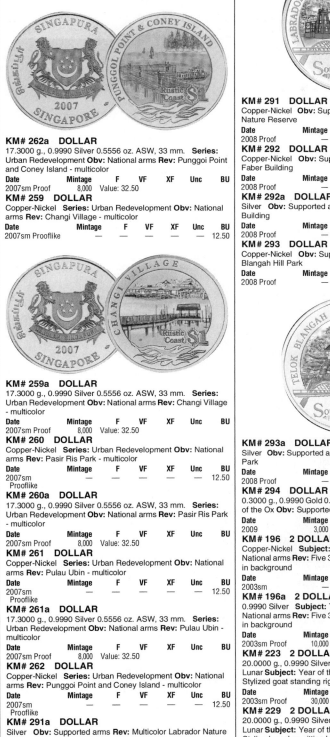

KM# 262a DOLLAR

17.3000 g., 0.9990 Silver 0.5556 oz. ASW, 33 mm. **Series:** Urban Redevelopment **Obv:** National arms **Rev:** Punggoi Point and Coney Island - multicolor

Date	Mintage	F	VF	XF	Unc	BU
2007sm Proof	8,000	Value: 32.50				

KM# 259 DOLLAR

Copper-Nickel **Series:** Urban Redevelopment **Obv:** National arms **Rev:** Changi Village - multicolor

Date	Mintage	F	VF	XF	Unc	BU
2007sm Prooflike	—	—	—	—	—	12.50

KM# 259a DOLLAR

17.3000 g., 0.9990 Silver 0.5556 oz. ASW, 33 mm. **Series:** Urban Redevelopment **Obv:** National arms **Rev:** Changi Village - multicolor

Date	Mintage	F	VF	XF	Unc	BU
2007sm Proof	8,000	Value: 32.50				

KM# 260 DOLLAR

Copper-Nickel **Series:** Urban Redevelopment **Obv:** National arms **Rev:** Pasir Ris Park - multicolor

Date	Mintage	F	VF	XF	Unc	BU
2007sm Prooflike	—	—	—	—	—	12.50

KM# 260a DOLLAR

17.3000 g., 0.9990 Silver 0.5556 oz. ASW, 33 mm. **Series:** Urban Redevelopment **Obv:** National arms **Rev:** Pasir Ris Park - multicolor

Date	Mintage	F	VF	XF	Unc	BU
2007sm Proof	8,000	Value: 32.50				

KM# 261 DOLLAR

Copper-Nickel **Series:** Urban Redevelopment **Obv:** National arms **Rev:** Pulau Ubin - multicolor

Date	Mintage	F	VF	XF	Unc	BU
2007sm Prooflike	—	—	—	—	—	12.50

KM# 261a DOLLAR

17.3000 g., 0.9990 Silver 0.5556 oz. ASW, 33 mm. **Series:** Urban Redevelopment **Obv:** National arms **Rev:** Pulau Ubin - multicolor

Date	Mintage	F	VF	XF	Unc	BU
2007sm Proof	8,000	Value: 32.50				

KM# 262 DOLLAR

Copper-Nickel **Series:** Urban Redevelopment **Obv:** National arms **Rev:** Punggoi Point and Coney Island - multicolor

Date	Mintage	F	VF	XF	Unc	BU
2007sm Prooflike	—	—	—	—	—	12.50

KM# 291a DOLLAR

Silver **Obv:** Supported arms **Rev:** Multicolor Labrador Nature Reserve

Date	Mintage	F	VF	XF	Unc	BU
2008 Proof	—	Value: 37.50				

KM# 290 DOLLAR

Copper-Nickel **Obv:** Supported arms **Rev:** Multicolor Kent Ridge Park

Date	Mintage	F	VF	XF	Unc	BU
2008 Proof	—	Value: 10.00				

KM# 290a DOLLAR

Silver **Obv:** Supported arms **Rev:** Multicolor Kent Ridge Park

Date	Mintage	F	VF	XF	Unc	BU
2008 Proof	—	Value: 37.50				

KM# 291 DOLLAR

Copper-Nickel **Obv:** Supported arms **Rev:** Multicolor Labrador Nature Reserve

Date	Mintage	F	VF	XF	Unc	BU
2008 Proof	—	Value: 10.00				

KM# 292 DOLLAR

Copper-Nickel **Obv:** Supported arms **Rev:** Multicolor Mount Faber Building

Date	Mintage	F	VF	XF	Unc	BU
2008 Proof	—	Value: 10.00				

KM# 292a DOLLAR

Silver **Obv:** Supported arms **Rev:** Multicolor Mount Faber Building

Date	Mintage	F	VF	XF	Unc	BU
2008 Proof	—	Value: 37.50				

KM# 293 DOLLAR

Copper-Nickel **Obv:** Supported arms **Rev:** Multicolor Telok Blangah Hill Park

Date	Mintage	F	VF	XF	Unc	BU
2008 Proof	—	Value: 10.00				

KM# 293a DOLLAR

Silver **Obv:** Supported arms **Rev:** Multicolor Telok Blangah Hill Park

Date	Mintage	F	VF	XF	Unc	BU
2008 Proof	—	Value: 37.50				

KM# 294 DOLLAR

0.3000 g., 0.9990 Gold 0.0096 oz. AGW, 7 mm. **Subject:** Year of the Ox **Obv:** Supported arms **Rev:** Ox

Date	Mintage	F	VF	XF	Unc	BU
2009	3,000	—	—	—	30.00	35.00

KM# 196 2 DOLLARS

Copper-Nickel **Subject:** Tribute to Healthcare Givers **Obv:** National arms **Rev:** Five 3/4 length people standing facing, clinic in background

Date	Mintage	F	VF	XF	Unc	BU
2003sm	—	—	—	—	—	15.00

KM# 196a 2 DOLLARS

0.9990 Silver **Subject:** Tribute to Healthcare Givers **Obv:** National arms **Rev:** Five 3/4 length people standing facing, clinic in background

Date	Mintage	F	VF	XF	Unc	BU
2003sm Proof	10,000	Value: 60.00				

KM# 223 2 DOLLARS

20.0000 g., 0.9990 Silver 0.6423 oz. ASW, 38.70 mm. **Series:** Lunar **Subject:** Year of the Goat **Obv:** National arms **Rev:** Stylized goat standing right facing left

Date	Mintage	F	VF	XF	Unc	BU
2003sm Proof	30,000	Value: 60.00				

KM# 229 2 DOLLARS

20.0000 g., 0.9990 Silver 0.6423 oz. ASW, 38.7 mm. **Series:** Lunar **Subject:** Year of the Monkey **Obv:** National arms **Rev:** Stylized monkey sitting left

Date	Mintage	F	VF	XF	Unc	BU
2004sm Proof	30,000	Value: 60.00				

KM# 234 2 DOLLARS

20.0000 g., Copper-Nickel, 38.7 mm. **Series:** Lunar **Subject:** Year of the Rooster **Obv:** National arms **Rev:** Rooster standing right

Date	Mintage	F	VF	XF	Unc	BU
2005sm Prooflike	—	—	—	—	—	15.00

KM# 242 2 DOLLARS

Copper-Nickel **Subject:** 40th National Day Parade **Obv:** National arms **Rev:** Fireworks, parade in government plaza, multicolor

Date	Mintage	F	VF	XF	Unc	BU
2005sm Prooflike	—	Value: 15.00				

KM# 242a 2 DOLLARS
20.0000 g., 0.9999 Silver 0.6429 oz. ASW **Subject:** 40th National Day Parade **Obv:** National arms **Rev:** Fireworks, parade in government plaza

Date	Mintage	F	VF	XF	Unc	BU
2005sm Proof	—	Value: 60.00				

KM# 234a 2 DOLLARS
20.0000 g., 0.9999 Silver 0.6429 oz. ASW, 38.7 mm. **Series:** Lunar **Subject:** Year of the Rooster **Obv:** National arms **Rev:** Stylized rooster standing right

Date	Mintage	F	VF	XF	Unc	BU
2005sm Proof	10,000	Value: 42.50				

KM# 250 2 DOLLARS
20.0000 g., Copper-Nickel **Series:** Lunar **Subject:** Year of the Dog **Obv:** National arms **Rev:** Stylized dog standing left

Date	Mintage	F	VF	XF	Unc	BU
2006sm Prooflike	—	Value: 15.00				

KM# 250a 2 DOLLARS
20.0000 g., 0.9999 Silver 0.6429 oz. ASW **Series:** Lunar **Subject:** Year of the Dog **Obv:** National arms **Rev:** Stylized dog standing left

Date	Mintage	F	VF	XF	Unc	BU
2006sm Proof	6,000	Value: 60.00				

KM# 258 2 DOLLARS
Copper-Nickel **Subject:** 41st National Day **Obv:** National arms **Rev:** People in stadium, emblem - multicolor

Date	Mintage	F	VF	XF	Unc	BU
2006sm Prooflike	—	Value: 15.00				

KM# 258a 2 DOLLARS
20.0000 g., 0.9990 Silver 0.6423 oz. ASW **Subject:** 41st National Day **Obv:** National arms **Rev:** People in stadium, emblem - multicolor

Date	Mintage	F	VF	XF	Unc	BU
2006sm Proof	8,000	Value: 60.00				

KM# 264 2 DOLLARS
Copper-Nickel **Series:** Lunar **Subject:** Year of the Boar **Obv:** National arms **Rev:** Stylized boar running right

Date	Mintage	F	VF	XF	Unc	BU
2007sm Prooflike	—	—	—	—	—	12.00

KM# 193 2 DOLLARS
20.0000 g., Copper-Nickel, 38.70 mm. **Subject:** 42nd National Day Parade **Obv:** Arms with supporters **Obv. Legend:** SINGAPURA - SINGAPORE **Rev:** Colored overlay with four children above Marina Bay floating platform **Edge:** Reeded

Date	Mintage	F	VF	XF	Unc	BU
2007 Prooflike	—	—	—	—	—	13.50

KM# 193a 2 DOLLARS
20.0000 g., 0.9990 Silver 0.6423 oz. ASW, 38.70 mm. **Subject:** 42nd National Day Parade **Obv:** Arms with supporters **Obv. Legend:** SINGAPURA - SINGAPORE **Rev:** Colored overlay with four children above Marina Bay floating platform **Edge:** Reeded

Date	Mintage	F	VF	XF	Unc	BU
2007 Proof	8,000	Value: 42.50				

KM# 264a 2 DOLLARS
20.0000 g., 0.9990 Silver 0.6423 oz. ASW **Series:** Lunar **Subject:** Year of the Boar **Obv:** National arms **Rev:** Stylized boar running right

Date	Mintage	F	VF	XF	Unc	BU
2007sm Proof	6,000	Value: 45.00				

KM# 270 2 DOLLARS
20.0000 g., Copper-Nickel **Series:** Lunar **Subject:** Year of the Rat **Obv:** National arms **Rev:** Stylized rat lying left

Date	Mintage	F	VF	XF	Unc	BU
2008sm Prooflike	—	—	—	—	—	12.50

KM# 270a 2 DOLLARS
20.0000 g., 0.9990 Silver 0.6423 oz. ASW **Series:** Lunar **Subject:** Year of the Rat **Obv:** National arms **Rev:** Stylized rat lying left

Date	Mintage	F	VF	XF	Unc	BU
2008sm Proof	6,000	Value: 45.00				

KM# 287 2 DOLLARS
Copper-Nickel **Subject:** Formula 1 - Singapore Grand Prix **Obv:** Supported arms **Rev:** Formula 1 racecar and skyline

Date	Mintage	F	VF	XF	Unc	BU
2008 Proof	—	Value: 10.00				

KM# 295 2 DOLLARS
Copper-Nickel **Subject:** Year of the Ox **Obv:** Supported arms

Date	Mintage	F	VF	XF	Unc	BU
2009 Prooflike	—	—	—	—	—	10.00

KM# 296 2 DOLLARS
20.0000 g., 0.9990 Silver 0.6423 oz. ASW **Subject:** Year of the Ox **Obv:** Supported arms **Rev:** Ox

Date	Mintage	F	VF	XF	Unc	BU
2009 Proof	—	Value: 37.50				

KM# 303 2 DOLLARS
Copper-Nickel **Subject:** Independence, 44th Anniversary

Date	Mintage	F	VF	XF	Unc	BU
2009	8,009	—	—	—	—	15.00

KM# 303a 2 DOLLARS
20.0000 g., 0.9990 Silver 0.6423 oz. ASW **Series:** Indpendence, 44th Anniversary

Date	Mintage	F	VF	XF	Unc	BU
2009 Proof	7,009	Value: 40.00				

KM# 104.1a 5 DOLLARS
8.2500 g., 0.9250 Silver 0.2453 oz. ASW, 23.3 mm. **Obv:** National arms **Rev:** Vanda Miss Joaquim flower and value within beaded circle

Date	Mintage	F	VF	XF	Unc	BU
2001sm Proof	—	Value: 25.00				
2002sm Proof	—	Value: 25.00				

KM# 104.2a 5 DOLLARS
8.2500 g., 0.9250 Silver 0.2453 oz. ASW, 23.3 mm. **Obv:** National arms, date and BCCS logo **Rev:** Vanda Miss Joaquim flower above value **Edge:** Plain

Date	Mintage	F	VF	XF	Unc	BU
2001sm Proof	10,000	Value: 25.00				
2002sm Proof	10,000	Value: 25.00				
2003sm Proof	—	Value: 25.00				
2004sm Proof	—	Value: 25.00				
2005sm Proof	—	Value: 25.00				
2006sm Proof	—	Value: 25.00				

KM# 104.2 5 DOLLARS
6.7000 g., Bi-Metallic Aluminumn-Bronze center in Copper-Nickel ring, 23.3 mm. **Obv:** National arms, date and BCCS logo **Rev:** Canda Miss Joaquim flower above value **Edge:** Plain **Note:** Date in hologram

Date	Mintage	F	VF	XF	Unc	BU
2001 In sets only	—	—	—	—	—	12.00
2002 In sets only	—	—	—	—	—	12.00
2003	—	—	—	—	—	12.00
2004	—	—	—	—	—	12.00
2005	—	—	—	—	—	12.00
2006	—	—	—	—	—	12.00

KM# 177a 5 DOLLARS
20.0000 g., 0.9250 Silver 0.5948 oz. ASW, 38.6 mm. **Subject:** Productivity Movement **Obv:** Arms with supporters **Rev:** Spiral design **Edge:** Reeded

Date	Mintage	F	VF	XF	Unc	BU
2001sm Proof	10,000	Value: 50.00				

KM# 177 5 DOLLARS
20.0000 g., Copper-Nickel, 38.6 mm. **Subject:** Productivity Movement **Obv:** Arms with supporters **Rev:** Spiral design **Edge:** Reeded

Date	Mintage	F	VF	XF	Unc	BU
2001sm	20,000	—	—	—	12.50	15.00

KM# 181 5 DOLLARS
20.0000 g., Copper-Nickel, 38.7 mm. **Subject:** Esplanade Theaters on the Bay **Obv:** Arms with supporters **Rev:** Stylized symbolic design **Edge:** Reeded

Date	Mintage	F	VF	XF	Unc	BU
2002sm	—	—	—	—	13.50	16.50

KM# 181a 5 DOLLARS
20.0000 g., 0.9990 Silver 0.6423 oz. ASW, 38.7 mm. **Subject:** Esplanade Theaters on the Bay **Obv:** Arms with supporters **Rev:** Stylized symbolic design **Edge:** Reeded

Date	Mintage	F	VF	XF	Unc	BU
2002sm Proof	10,000	Value: 45.00				

KM# 104.1 5 DOLLARS
6.7000 g., Bi-Metallic Aluminum-Bronze center in Copper-Nickel ring, 23.3 mm. **Obv:** National arms **Rev:** Vanda Miss Joaquim flower and value within beaded circle **Shape:** Scalloped

Date	Mintage	F	VF	XF	Unc	BU
2002	—	—	—	—	—	15.00

KM# 104.3 5 DOLLARS
6.7000 g., Bi-Metallic Aluminum-Bronze center in Copper-Nickel ring, 23.3 mm. **Obv:** National arms above latent image "MAS" **Rev:** Flower and value **Shape:** Scalloped

Date	Mintage	F	VF	XF	Unc	BU
2002sm	—	—	—	—	—	10.00
2003sm	—	—	—	—	—	10.00
2003sm Proof	—	Value: 15.00				
2004sm	—	—	—	—	—	10.00
2004sm Proof	20,000	Value: 15.00				
2005sm	—	—	—	—	—	10.00
2006sm	—	—	—	—	—	10.00
2007sm	—	—	—	—	—	10.00
2008sm	—	—	—	—	—	10.00
2009sm	—	—	—	—	—	10.00

KM# 104.3a 5 DOLLARS
8.2500 g., 0.9250 Silver 0.2453 oz. ASW **Obv:** National arms above latent image "MAS or date" **Rev:** Flower and value **Shape:** Scalloped

Date	Mintage	F	VF	XF	Unc	BU
2003sm Proof	—	Value: 25.00				
2004sm Proof	—	Value: 25.00				
2005sm Proof	—	Value: 25.00				
2006sm Proof	—	Value: 25.00				
2007sm Proof	—	Value: 25.00				
2008sm Proof	—	Value: 25.00				
2009sm Proof	—	Value: 25.00				

KM# 194 5 DOLLARS
20.0000 g., 0.9990 Silver 0.6423 oz. ASW, 38.7 mm. **Obv:** Arms with supporters **Obv. Legend:** SINGAPURA - SINGAPORE **Rev:** Multicolor Singapore's skyline above world map, golden lion symbol below pointing to location of Singapore **Rev. Legend:** BOARD OF GOVERNORS ANNUAL MEETINGS • SINGAPORE 2006 • INTERNATIONAL MONETARY FUND • WORLD BANK GROUP •

Date	Mintage	F	VF	XF	Unc	BU
2006sm Proof	10,000	Value: 60.00				

KM# 256 5 DOLLARS
20.0000 g., 0.9990 Silver 0.6423 oz. ASW **Series:** Heritage Orchids **Obv:** National arms **Rev:** Vanda Tan Chay Yan - multicolor

Date	Mintage	F	VF	XF	Unc	BU
2006sm Proof	8,000	Value: 60.00				

KM# 257 5 DOLLARS
20.0000 g., 0.9990 Silver 0.6423 oz. ASW **Series:** Heritage Orchids **Obv:** National arms **Rev:** Aranda Majula - multicolor

Date	Mintage	F	VF	XF	Unc	BU
2006sm Proof	8,000	Value: 60.00				

KM# 275 5 DOLLARS
20.0000 g., 0.9990 Silver 0.6423 oz. ASW, 38.7 mm. **Series:** Heritage Orchids **Obv:** National arms **Rev:** Dendrobium Singa Mas - multicolor

Date	Mintage	F	VF	XF	Unc	BU
2007sm Proof	8,000	Value: 45.00				

KM# 276 5 DOLLARS
20.0000 g., 0.9990 Silver 0.6423 oz. ASW, 38.7 mm. **Series:** Heritage Orchids **Obv:** National arms **Rev:** Vanda Mimi Palmar - multicolor

Date	Mintage	F	VF	XF	Unc	BU
2007sm Proof	8,000	Value: 45.00				

KM# 285 5 DOLLARS
20.0000 g., 0.9990 Silver 0.6423 oz. ASW, 38.6 mm. **Subject:** Heritage orchids **Obv:** Supported arms **Rev:** Multicolor yellow orchid - Oncidum Goldiana

Date	Mintage	F	VF	XF	Unc	BU
2008 Proof	—	Value: 45.00				

KM# 286 5 DOLLARS
20.0000 g., 0.9990 Silver 0.6423 oz. ASW, 38.6 mm. **Subject:** Heritage orchids **Obv:** Supported arms **Rev:** Multicolor pink orchid - Aranda Tay Swee Eng

Date	Mintage	F	VF	XF	Unc	BU
2008 Proof	—	Value: 45.00				

KM# 301 5 DOLLARS
20.0000 g., 0.9990 Silver 0.6423 oz. ASW **Subject:** Orchids of Singapore **Obv:** Arms **Rev:** Yellow flower - Spathoglottis Primrose

Date	Mintage	F	VF	XF	Unc	BU
2009 Proof	12,000	Value: 45.00				

KM# 302 5 DOLLARS
20.0000 g., 0.9990 Silver 0.6423 oz. ASW, 38.7 mm. **Subject:** Orchids of Singapore **Obv:** Arms **Rev:** Pink flower - Vanda Amy

Date	Mintage	F	VF	XF	Unc	BU
2009 Proof	12,000	Value: 45.00				

KM# 179 10 DOLLARS
28.0000 g., Copper-Nickel, 40.7 mm. **Series:** Lunar **Subject:** Year of the Snake **Obv:** National arms **Rev:** Stylized snake **Edge:** Reeded

Date	Mintage	F	VF	XF	Unc	BU
2001sm Prooflike	—	—	—	—	—	20.00

KM# 182 10 DOLLARS
28.0000 g., Copper-Nickel, 40.7 mm. **Series:** Lunar **Subject:** Year of the Horse **Obv:** National arms **Rev:** Stylized horse standing left **Edge:** Reeded

Date	Mintage	F	VF	XF	Unc	BU
2002sm Prooflike	—	—	—	—	—	20.00

KM# 225 10 DOLLARS
28.0000 g., Copper-Nickel, 40.7 mm. **Series:** Lunar **Subject:** Year of the Goat **Obv:** National arms **Rev:** Stylized goat standing right facing left

Date	Mintage	F	VF	XF	Unc	BU
2003sm Prooflike	—	—	—	—	—	20.00

KM# 187 10 DOLLARS
28.0000 g., Copper-Nickel, 40.7 mm. **Series:** Lunar **Subject:** Year of the Monkey **Obv:** National arms **Rev:** Stylized monkey sitting left **Edge:** Reeded

Date	Mintage	F	VF	XF	Unc	BU
2004sm Prooflike	—	—	—	—	—	20.00

KM# 189 10 DOLLARS
28.0000 g., Copper-Nickel, 40.7 mm. **Subject:** 10th Anniversary China-Singapore Suzhou Industrial Park **Obv:** National arms **Rev:** "Harmony" Sculpture **Edge:** Reeded

Date	Mintage	F	VF	XF	Unc	BU
2004sm Prooflike	7,000	—	—	—	—	20.00

KM# 189a 10 DOLLARS
0.9990 Silver, 40.7 mm. **Subject:** 10th Anniversary China-Singapore Suzhou Industrial Park **Obv:** National arms **Rev:** "Harmony" sculpture **Edge:** Reeded

Date	Mintage	F	VF	XF	Unc	BU
2004sm Proof	5,000	Value: 55.00				

KM# 240 10 DOLLARS
Copper-Nickel **Subject:** National University of Singapore **Obv:** National arms **Rev:** Person, globe and emblem

Date	Mintage	F	VF	XF	Unc	BU
2005sm Prooflike	20,000	—	—	—	—	22.50

KM# 240a 10 DOLLARS
20.0000 g., 0.9999 Silver 0.6429 oz. ASW **Subject:** National University of Singapore **Obv:** National arms **Rev:** Person, globe and emblem

Date	Mintage	F	VF	XF	Unc	BU
2005sm Proof	10,000	Value: 60.00				

KM# 243 10 DOLLARS
31.1030 g., 0.9999 Silver with Gold 2.3g inlay 0.9998 oz. ASW **Subject:** 40th National Day parade **Obv:** National arms **Rev:** Fireworks, parade in government plaza

Date	Mintage	F	VF	XF	Unc	BU
2005sm Proof	1,500	Value: 245				

KM# 288 50 DOLLARS
Silver **Subject:** Formula 1 - Singapore Grand Prix **Obv:** Supported arms **Rev:** Multicolor race car and skyline

Date	Mintage	F	VF	XF	Unc	BU
2008 Proof	—	Value: 40.00				

KM# 241 100 DOLLARS
31.1030 g., 0.9999 Gold 0.9998 oz. AGW **Subject:** National University of Singapore **Obv:** National arms **Rev:** Person, globe and emblem

Date	Mintage	F	VF	XF	Unc	BU
2005sm Proof	500	Value: 1,550				

KM# 289 100 DOLLARS
Gold **Subject:** Formula 1 - Singapore Grand Prix **Obv:** Supported arms **Rev:** Formula 1 racecar and skyline

Date	Mintage	F	VF	XF	Unc	BU
2008 Proof	—	Value: 450				

BULLION COINAGE

Lunar Year Issues

KM# 212 DOLLAR
1.5550 g., 0.9999 Gold 0.0500 oz. AGW, 13.9 mm. **Series:** Lunar **Subject:** Year of the Snake **Obv:** National arms **Rev:** Stylized lion's head right, snake privy mark at lower left

Date	Mintage	F	VF	XF	Unc	BU
2001sm Proof	—	Value: 85.00				

KM# 217 DOLLAR
1.5550 g., 0.9999 Gold 0.0500 oz. AGW, 13.9 mm. **Series:** Lunar **Subject:** Year of the Horse **Obv:** National arms **Rev:** Stylized lion's head right, horse privy mark at lower left

Date	Mintage	F	VF	XF	Unc	BU
2002sm Proof	—	Value: 85.00				

KM# 222 DOLLAR
0.3000 g., 0.9999 Gold 0.0096 oz. AGW, 7 mm. **Series:** Lunar **Subject:** Year of the Goat **Obv:** National arms **Rev:** Stylized goat standing right facing left

Date	Mintage	F	VF	XF	Unc	BU
2003sm Prooflike	8,000	—	—	—	—	32.50

KM# 186 DOLLAR
0.3000 g., 0.9999 Gold 0.0096 oz. AGW, 7 mm. **Series:** Lunar **Subject:** Year of the Monkey **Obv:** National arms **Rev:** Stylized monkey sitting left **Edge:** Plain

Date	Mintage	F	VF	XF	Unc	BU
2004 Prooflike	8,000	—	—	—	—	32.50

KM# 233 DOLLAR
0.3000 g., 0.9999 Gold 0.0096 oz. AGW, 7 mm. **Series:** Lunar **Subject:** Year of the Rooster **Obv:** National arms **Rev:** Stylized rooster standing right

Date	Mintage	F	VF	XF	Unc	BU
2005sm Prooflike	8,000	—	—	—	—	32.50

KM# 249 DOLLAR
0.3000 g., 0.9999 Gold 0.0096 oz. AGW **Series:** Lunar **Subject:** Year of the Dog **Obv:** National arms **Rev:** Stylized dog standing left

Date	Mintage	F	VF	XF	Unc	BU
2006sm Prooflike	5,000	—	—	—	—	32.50

KM# 263 DOLLAR
0.3000 g., 0.9999 Gold 0.0096 oz. AGW **Series:** Lunar **Subject:** Year of the Boar **Obv:** National arms **Rev:** Stylized boar running right

Date	Mintage	F	VF	XF	Unc	BU
2007sm Prooflike	5,000	—	—	—	—	32.50

KM# 269 DOLLAR
0.3000 g., 0.9999 Gold 0.0096 oz. AGW **Series:** Lunar **Subject:** Year of the Rat **Obv:** National arms **Rev:** Stylized rat lying left

Date	Mintage	F	VF	XF	Unc	BU
2008sm	3,000	—	—	—	—	30.00

KM# 213 5 DOLLARS
3.1100 g., 0.9999 Gold 0.1000 oz. AGW, 17.9 mm. **Series:** Lunar **Subject:** Year of the Snake **Obv:** National arms **Rev:** Stylized lion's head right, snake privy mark at lower left

Date	Mintage	F	VF	XF	Unc	BU
2001sm Proof	—	Value: 160				

KM# 218 5 DOLLARS
7.7750 g., 0.9999 Gold 0.2499 oz. AGW, 17.9 mm. **Series:** Lunar **Subject:** Year of the Horse **Obv:** National arms **Rev:** Stylized lion's head right, horse privy mark at lower left

Date	Mintage	F	VF	XF	Unc	BU
2002sm Proof	—	Value: 385				

KM# 224 5 DOLLARS
7.7760 g., 0.9999 Gold 0.2500 oz. AGW, 21.9 mm. **Series:** Lunar **Subject:** Year of the Goat **Obv:** National arms **Rev:** Stylized goat standing right facing left

Date	Mintage	F	VF	XF	Unc	BU
2003sm Proof	8,000	Value: 375				

KM# 230 5 DOLLARS
7.7760 g., 0.9999 Gold 0.2500 oz. AGW, 21.9 mm. **Series:** Lunar **Subject:** Year of the Monkey **Obv:** National arms **Rev:** Stylized monkey sitting left

Date	Mintage	F	VF	XF	Unc	BU
2004sm Proof	8,000	Value: 375				

KM# 235 5 DOLLARS
7.7760 g., 0.9999 Gold 0.2500 oz. AGW, 21.9 mm. **Series:** Lunar **Subject:** Year of the Rooster **Obv:** National arms **Rev:** Stylized rooster standing right

Date	Mintage	F	VF	XF	Unc	BU
2005sm Proof	8,000	Value: 375				

KM# 251 5 DOLLARS
7.7750 g., 0.9999 Gold 0.2499 oz. AGW **Series:** Lunar **Subject:** Year of the Dog **Obv:** National arms **Rev:** Stylized dog standing left

Date	Mintage	F	VF	XF	Unc	BU
2006sm Proof	5,000	Value: 385				

KM# 265 5 DOLLARS
7.7750 g., 0.9999 Gold 0.2499 oz. AGW **Series:** Lunar **Subject:** Year of the Boar **Obv:** National arms **Rev:** Stylized boar running right

Date	Mintage	F	VF	XF	Unc	BU
2007sm Proof	5,000	Value: 375				

KM# 271 5 DOLLARS
7.7750 g., 0.9999 Gold 0.2499 oz. AGW **Series:** Lunar **Subject:** Year of the Rat **Obv:** National arms **Rev:** Stylized rat lying left

Date	Mintage	F	VF	XF	Unc	BU
2008sm Proof	2,000	Value: 400				

KM# 214 10 DOLLARS
7.7750 g., 0.9999 Gold 0.2499 oz. AGW, 21.9 mm. **Series:** Lunar **Subject:** Year of the Snake **Obv:** National arms **Rev:** Stylized lion's head right, snake privy mark at lower left

Date	Mintage	F	VF	XF	Unc	BU
2001sm Proof	—	Value: 400				

KM# 179a 10 DOLLARS
62.2060 g., 0.9990 Silver 1.9979 oz. ASW, 40.7 mm. **Series:** Lunar **Subject:** Year of the Snake **Obv:** National arms **Rev:** Stylized snake **Edge:** Reeded

Date	Mintage	F	VF	XF	Unc	BU
2001sm Proof	35,000	Value: 90.00				

KM# 219 10 DOLLARS
7.7750 g., 0.9999 Gold 0.2499 oz. AGW, 21.9 mm. **Series:** Lunar **Subject:** Year of the Horse **Obv:** National arms **Rev:** Stylized lion's head right, horse privy mark at lower left

Date	Mintage	F	VF	XF	Unc	BU
2002sm Proof	—	Value: 400				

KM# 182a 10 DOLLARS
62.2060 g., 0.9990 Silver 1.9979 oz. ASW, 40.7 mm. **Series:** Lunar **Subject:** Year of the Horse **Obv:** National arms **Rev:** Stylized horse standing left **Edge:** Reeded

Date	Mintage	F	VF	XF	Unc	BU
2002sm Proof	35,000	Value: 90.00				

KM# 225a 10 DOLLARS
62.2060 g., 0.9990 Silver 1.9979 oz. ASW, 40.7 mm. **Series:** Lunar **Subject:** Year of the Goat **Obv:** National arms **Rev:** Stylized goat standing right facing left

Date	Mintage	F	VF	XF	Unc	BU
2003sm Proof	35,000	Value: 90.00				

KM# 185 10 DOLLARS
31.1040 g., 0.9999 Gold 0.9999 oz. AGW, 32.1 mm. **Subject:** 10th Anniversary China-Singapore Suzhou Industrial Park **Obv:** National arms **Rev:** "Harmony" Sculpture **Edge:** Lettered edge

Date	Mintage	F	VF	XF	Unc	BU
2004sm Proof	500	Value: 1,550				

KM# 187a 10 DOLLARS
62.2060 g., 0.9990 Silver 1.9979 oz. ASW, 40.7 mm. **Series:** Lunar **Subject:** Year of the Monkey **Obv:** National arms **Rev:** Stylized monkey sitting left **Edge:** Reeded

Date	Mintage	F	VF	XF	Unc	BU
2004sm Proof	35,000	Value: 90.00				

KM# 236 10 DOLLARS
62.2060 g., 0.9999 Silver 1.9997 oz. ASW, 45 mm. **Series:** Lunar **Subject:** Year of the Rooster **Obv:** National arms **Rev:** Stylized rooster standing right

Date	Mintage	F	VF	XF	Unc	BU
2005sm Proof	30,000	Value: 90.00				

KM# 252 10 DOLLARS
62.2030 g., 0.9990 Silver 1.9978 oz. ASW **Series:** Lunar **Subject:** Year of the Dog **Obv:** National arms **Rev:** Stylized dog standing left

Date	Mintage	F	VF	XF	Unc	BU
2006sm Proof	30,000	Value: 95.00				

KM# 266 10 DOLLARS
62.2060 g., 0.9990 Silver 1.9979 oz. ASW, 45 mm. **Series:** Lunar **Subject:** Year of the Boar **Obv:** National arms **Rev:** Stylized pigr running right - multicolor

Date	Mintage	F	VF	XF	Unc	BU
2007sm Proof	30,000	Value: 100				

KM# 272 10 DOLLARS
62.2060 g., 0.9990 Silver 1.9979 oz. ASW **Series:** Lunar **Subject:** Year of the Rat **Obv:** National arms **Rev:** Stylized rat lying left - multicolor

Date	Mintage	F	VF	XF	Unc	BU
2008sm Proof	20,000	Value: 110				

KM# 297 10 DOLLARS
62.2000 g., 0.9990 Silver 1.9977 oz. ASW **Subject:** Year of the Ox **Obv:** Supported arms **Rev:** Multicolor Ox

Date	Mintage	F	VF	XF	Unc	BU
2009 Proof	—	Value: 90.00				

KM# 215 20 DOLLARS
15.5520 g., 0.9999 Gold 0.4999 oz. AGW, 27 mm. **Series:** Lunar **Subject:** Year of the Snake **Obv:** National arms **Rev:** Stylized lion's head right, snake privy mark at lower left

Date	Mintage	F	VF	XF	Unc	BU
2001sm Proof	—	Value: 775				

KM# 220 20 DOLLARS
15.5520 g., 0.9999 Gold 0.4999 oz. AGW, 27 mm. **Series:** Lunar **Subject:** Year of the Horse **Obv:** National arms **Rev:** Stylized lion's head right, horse privy mark at lower left

Date	Mintage	F	VF	XF	Unc	BU
2002sm Proof	—	Value: 775				

KM# 226 25 DOLLARS
155.5200 g., 0.9990 Silver 4.9949 oz. ASW, 65.00 mm. **Series:** Lunar **Subject:** Year of the Goat **Obv:** National arms **Rev:** Stylized goat standing right facing left

Date	Mintage	F	VF	XF	Unc	BU
2003sm Proof	250	Value: 300				

KM# 231 25 DOLLARS
155.5200 g., 0.9990 Silver 4.9949 oz. ASW, 65 mm. **Series:** Lunar **Subject:** Year of the Monkey **Obv:** National arms **Rev:** Stylized monkey sitting left

Date	Mintage	F	VF	XF	Unc	BU
2004sm Proof	250	Value: 300				

KM# 237 25 DOLLARS
155.5200 g., 0.9999 Silver 4.9994 oz. ASW, 65 mm. **Series:** Lunar **Subject:** Year of the Rooster **Obv:** National arms **Rev:** Stylized rooster standing right

Date	Mintage	F	VF	XF	Unc	BU
2005sm Proof	250	Value: 300				

KM# 253 25 DOLLARS
155.5150 g., 0.9990 Silver 4.9947 oz. ASW **Series:** Lunar **Subject:** Year of the Dog **Obv:** National arms **Rev:** Stylized dog standing right

Date	Mintage	F	VF	XF	Unc	BU
2006sm Proof	250	Value: 350				

KM# 267 25 DOLLARS
155.5150 g., 0.9990 Silver 4.9947 oz. ASW **Series:** Lunar **Subject:** Year of the Boar **Obv:** National arms **Rev:** Stylized boar running right

Date	Mintage	F	VF	XF	Unc	BU
2007sm Proof	250	Value: 360				

KM# 273 25 DOLLARS
155.5150 g., 0.9990 Silver 4.9947 oz. ASW **Series:** Lunar **Subject:** Year of the Rat **Obv:** National arms **Rev:** Stylized rat lying left

Date	Mintage	F	VF	XF	Unc	BU
2008sm Proof	250	Value: 375				

KM# 298 25 DOLLARS
155.5000 g., 0.9990 Silver 4.9942 oz. ASW **Subject:** Year of the Ox **Obv:** Supported arms **Rev:** Ox

Date	Mintage	F	VF	XF	Unc	BU
2009 Proof	—	Value: 300				

KM# 216 50 DOLLARS
31.1030 g., 0.9999 Gold 0.9998 oz. AGW, 32.1 mm. **Series:** Lunar **Subject:** Year of the Snake **Obv:** National arms **Rev:** Stylized lion's head right, snake privy mark at lower left

Date	Mintage	F	VF	XF	Unc	BU
2001sm Proof	—	Value: 1,600				

KM# 221 50 DOLLARS
31.1030 g., 0.9999 Gold 0.9998 oz. AGW, 32.1 mm. **Series:** Lunar **Subject:** Year of the Horse **Obv:** National arms **Rev:** Stylized lion's head right, horse privy mark at lower left

Date	Mintage	F	VF	XF	Unc	BU
2002sm Proof	—	Value: 1,600				

KM# 238 100 DOLLARS
31.1030 g., 0.9999 Gold 0.9998 oz. AGW, 33 mm. **Series:** Lunar **Subject:** Year of the Rooster **Obv:** National arms **Rev:** Stylized rooster standing right

Date	Mintage	F	VF	XF	Unc	BU
2005sm Proof	5,000	Value: 1,500				

KM# 254 100 DOLLARS
31.1030 g., 0.9999 Gold 0.9998 oz. AGW **Series:** Lunar **Subject:** Year of the Dog **Obv:** National arms **Rev:** Stylized dog standing left

Date	Mintage	F	VF	XF	Unc	BU
2006sm Proof	3,000	Value: 1,550				

KM# 268 100 DOLLARS
31.1030 g., 0.9999 Gold 0.9998 oz. AGW, 33 mm. **Series:** Lunar **Subject:** Year of the Boar **Obv:** National arms **Rev:** Stylized pig running right

Date	Mintage	F	VF	XF	Unc	BU
2007sm Proof	3,000	Value: 1,550				

KM# 274 100 DOLLARS
31.1030 g., 0.9999 Gold 0.9998 oz. AGW **Series:** Lunar **Subject:** Year of the Rat **Obv:** National arms **Rev:** Stylized rat lying left

Date	Mintage	F	VF	XF	Unc	BU
2008sm Proof	2,000	Value: 1,575				

KM# 299 100 DOLLARS
31.1050 g., 0.9990 Gold 0.9990 oz. AGW **Subject:** Year of the Ox **Obv:** Supported arms **Rev:** Ox

Date	Mintage	F	VF	XF	Unc	BU
2009 Proof	—	Value: 1,550				

KM# 239 200 DOLLARS
155.5200 g., 0.9999 Gold 4.9994 oz. AGW, 60 mm. **Series:** Lunar **Subject:** Year of the Rooster **Obv:** National arms **Rev:** Stylized rooster standing right

Date	Mintage	F	VF	XF	Unc	BU
2005sm Proof	200	Value: 7,500				

KM# 255 200 DOLLARS
155.1500 g., 0.9999 Gold 4.9875 oz. AGW **Series:** Lunar **Subject:** Year of the Dog **Obv:** National arms **Rev:** Stylized dog standing left

Date	Mintage	F	VF	XF	Unc	BU
2006sm Proof	200	Value: 7,500				

KM# 300 200 DOLLARS
155.5000 g., 0.9990 Gold 4.9942 oz. AGW **Subject:** Year of the Ox **Obv:** Supported arms **Rev:** Ox

Date	Mintage	F	VF	XF	Unc	BU
2009 Proof	—	Value: 7,450				

KM# 178 250 DOLLARS
31.1035 g., 0.9990 Gold 0.9990 oz. AGW, 32.1 mm. **Subject:** Year of the Snake **Obv:** National arms **Rev:** Stylized snake **Edge:** Reeded

Date	Mintage	F	VF	XF	Unc	BU
2001sm Proof	7,000	Value: 1,500				

KM# 183 250 DOLLARS
31.1035 g., 0.9999 Gold 0.9999 oz. AGW, 32.1 mm. **Subject:** Year of the Horse **Obv:** National arms **Rev:** Horse **Edge:** Reeded

Date	Mintage	F	VF	XF	Unc	BU
2002sm Proof	7,600	Value: 1,500				

KM# 227 250 DOLLARS
31.1030 g., 0.9999 Gold 0.9998 oz. AGW, 32.1 mm. **Series:** Lunar **Subject:** Year of the Goat **Obv:** National arms **Rev:** Stylized goat standing right facing left

Date	Mintage	F	VF	XF	Unc	BU
2003sm Proof	7,000	Value: 1,500				

KM# 188 250 DOLLARS
31.1030 g., 0.9999 Gold 0.9998 oz. AGW, 32.1 mm. **Series:** Lunar **Subject:** Year of the Monkey **Obv:** National arms **Rev:** Stylized monkey sitting left **Edge:** Reeded

Date	Mintage	F	VF	XF	Unc	BU
2004sm Proof	7,000	Value: 1,500				

KM# 228 500 DOLLARS
155.5200 g., 0.9999 Gold 4.9994 oz. AGW, 55 mm. **Series:** Lunar **Subject:** Year of the Goat **Obv:** National arms **Rev:** Stylized goat standing right facing left

Date	Mintage	F	VF	XF	Unc	BU
2003sm Proof	200	Value: 7,500				

KM# 232 500 DOLLARS
155.5200 g., 0.9999 Gold 4.9994 oz. AGW, 55 mm. **Series:** Lunar **Subject:** Year of the Monkey **Obv:** National arms **Rev:** Stylized monkey sitting left

Date	Mintage	F	VF	XF	Unc	BU
2004sm Proof	200	Value: 7,500				

MINT SETS

KM#	Date	Mintage	Identification	Issue Price	Mkt Val
MS39	2002 (7)	—	KM#98-103, 104.3 Hongbao	—	15.00
MS40	2003 (7)	—	KM#98-103, 104.3 Hongbao	—	15.00
MS41	2004 (7)	—	KM#98-103, 104.3 Hongbao	—	15.00
MS42	2005 (7)	—	KM#98-103, 104.3 Hongbao	—	15.00
MS43	2006 (7)	—	KM#98-103, 104.3 Hongbao	—	15.00
MS44	2007 (7)	—	KM98-103, 104.3 Hongbao	10.78	15.00

PROOF SETS

KM#	Date	Mintage	Identification	Issue Price	Mkt Val
PS61	2001 (2)	3,000	KM#179-180 plus copper-nickel ingot	—	115
PS62	2001 (3)	2,000	KM#178-180 plus copper-nickel ingot	—	1,625
PS63	2001 (4)	—	KM#212-215	—	1,425
PS64	2001 (6)	—	KM#212-216, plus ingot	—	3,050
PS65	2001 (2)	2,001	KM#177, 177a	—	70.00
PS66	2001 (7)	10,000	KM#98a-103a, 104.2a	—	70.00
PS67	2002 (2)	3,000	KM#182, 182a	—	115
PS68	2002 (3)	2,000	KM#182, 182a, 183	—	1,625
PS69	2002 (2)	2,001	KM#181, 181a	—	65.00
PS70	2002 (3)	2,001	KM#181, 181a, 217	—	160
PS71	2002 (4)	—	KM#217-220	—	1,650
PS72	2002 (6)	—	KM#217-221 plus ingot	—	3,250
PS73	2002 (7)	10,000	KM#98a-103a, 104.2a	—	70.00
PS74	2003 (2)	2,003	KM#196, 196a	—	75.00
PS75	2003 (7)	10,000	KM#98a-103a, 104.3a	—	70.00
PS76	2003 (8)	1,000	KM#98a-103a, 104.3a, 196a	—	130
PS77	2003 (2)	88	KM#226, 228	—	7,800
PS78	2003 (2)	3,000	KM#225, 225a	—	115
PS79	2003 (3)	2,000	KM#225, 225a, 227	—	1,625
PS80	2004 (2)	1,000	KM#189, 189a	—	85.00
PS81	2004 (3)	88	KM#185, 189, 189a	—	1,650
PS82	2004 (7)	10,000	KM#98a-103a, 104.3a	—	70.00
PS83	2004 (2)	1,000	KM#184, 184a	—	40.00
PS84	2004 (2)	1,000	KM#190, 190a	—	40.00
PS85	2004 (2)	1,000	KM#191, 191a	—	40.00
PS86	2004 (2)	1,000	KM#192, 192a	—	40.00
PS87	2004 (4)	800	KM#184a, 190a-192a	—	110
PS88	2004 (8)	88	KM#184, 184a, 190, 190a, 191, 191a, 192, 192a	—	150
PS89	2004 (2)	80	KM#231, 232	—	7,800
PS90	2004 (2)	3,000	KM#187, 187a	—	110
PS91	2004 (3)	2,000	KM#187, 187a, 188	—	1,650
PS92	2005 (7)	—	KM#98a-103a, 104.3a	—	70.00
PS93	2005 (2)	3,000	KM#234, 236	—	110
PS94	2005 (2)	88	KM#237, 239	—	7,800
PS95	2005 (3)	2,000	KM#234, 236, 238	—	1,650
PS96	2006 (7)	—	KM#98a-103a, 104.3a	—	70.00
PS97	2006 (2)	8,000	KM#256, 257	—	120
PS98	2007 (7)	—	KM#98a-103a, 104.3a	—	70.00
PS99	2007 (4)	800	KM#259a-262a	—	130
PS100	2007 (2)	8,000	KM#275, 276	90.00	90.00
PS101	2007 (2)	3,000	KM#193, 193a	65.00	65.00

PROOF-LIKE SETS (PL)

KM#	Date	Mintage	Identification	Issue Price	Mkt Val
PL1	2004 (4)	800	KM#184, 190, 191, 192	—	40.00
PL2	2007 (4)	800	KM#259-262	—	50.00

The Republic of Slovakia has an area of 18,923 sq. mi. (49,035 sq. km.) and a population of 4.9 million. Capital: Bratislava. Textiles, steel, and wood products are exported.

MINT MARK

Kremnica Mint

REPUBLIC

STANDARD COINAGE

100 Halierov = 1 Slovak Koruna (Sk)

KM# 17 10 HALIEROV

0.7200 g., Aluminum, 17 mm. **Obv:** Double cross on shield above inscription **Rev:** Church steeple **Edge:** Plain **Designer:** Drahomir Zobek

Date	Mintage	F	VF	XF	Unc	BU
2001	20,330,000	—	—	—	0.35	—
2001 Proof	12,500	Value: 2.50				
2002	37,640,000	—	—	—	0.35	—
2002 Proof	16,100	Value: 1.50				
2003 In sets only	3,000	—	—	—	2.50	—

KM# 17a 10 HALIEROV

2.8500 g., 0.9250 Silver 0.0848 oz. ASW, 17 mm.

Date	Mintage	F	VF	XF	Unc	BU
2004	4,000	—	—	—	—	10.00
2004 Proof	2,000	Value: 15.00				

KM# 18 20 HALIEROV

0.9500 g., Aluminum, 19.5 mm. **Obv:** Double cross on shield above inscription **Rev:** Mountain peak and value **Edge:** Reeded **Designer:** Drahomir Zobek

Date	Mintage	F	VF	XF	Unc	BU
2001	21,920,000	—	—	—	0.45	—
2001 Proof	12,500	Value: 2.50				
2002	36,300,000	—	—	—	0.45	—
2002 Proof	16,100	Value: 1.50				
2003 In sets only	3,000	—	—	—	2.50	—

KM# 18a 20 HALIEROV

3.8700 g., 0.9250 Silver 0.1151 oz. ASW, 19.5 mm.

Date	Mintage	F	VF	XF	Unc	BU
2004	4,000	—	—	—	—	15.00
2004	2,000	Value: 20.00				

KM# 35 50 HALIEROV

2.8000 g., Copper Plated Steel, 18.75 mm. **Obv:** Double cross on shield above inscription **Rev:** Watch tower and value **Edge:** Segmented reeding **Designer:** Drahomir Zobek

Date	Mintage	F	VF	XF	Unc	BU
2001	10,400,000	—	—	—	0.60	—
2001 Proof	12,500	Value: 2.50				
2002	11,000,000	—	—	—	0.60	—
2002 Proof	16,100	Value: 1.50				
2003	11,000,000	—	—	—	0.60	—
2004	16,500,000	—	—	—	0.60	—
2004 Proof	—	Value: 1.50				
2005	17,000,000	—	—	—	0.60	—
2006	22,050,000	—	—	—	0.60	—
2006 Proof	—	Value: 1.50				
2007	—	—	—	—	0.60	—
2008	—	—	—	—	0.60	—
2008 Proof	—	Value: 1.50				

KM# 12 KORUNA

3.8500 g., Bronze Plated Steel, 21 mm. **Subject:** 15th Century of Madonna and Child **Obv:** Double cross on shield above inscription **Rev:** Madonna holding child and value **Edge:** Milled **Designer:** Drahomir Zobek

Date	Mintage	F	VF	XF	Unc	BU
2001 In sets only	12,500	—	—	—	1.50	—
2001 Proof	—	Value: 3.00				
2002	11,000,000	—	—	—	0.75	—
2002 Proof	16,100	Value: 2.50				
2003 In sets only	14,000	—	—	—	1.50	—
2004 In sets only	—	—	—	—	1.50	—
2004 Proof	—	Value: 2.50				
2005	10,000,000	—	—	—	0.75	—
2005 Proof	—	Value: 2.50				
2006	9,605,000	—	—	—	0.75	—
2006 Proof	—	Value: 2.50				
2007	—	—	—	—	0.75	—
2008	—	—	—	—	0.75	—
2008 Proof	—	Value: 2.50				

KM# 13 2 KORUNA

4.4000 g., Nickel Plated Steel, 22.5 mm. **Obv:** Double cross on shield above inscription **Rev:** Venus statue and value **Designer:** Drahomir Zobek

Date	Mintage	F	VF	XF	Unc	BU
2001	10,668,000	—	—	—	0.85	—
2001 Proof	12,500	Value: 5.00				
2002	11,000,000	—	—	—	0.85	—
2002 Proof	16,100	Value: 2.50				
2003	11,000,000	—	—	—	0.85	—
2004 In sets only	—	—	—	—	2.00	—
2004 Proof	—	Value: 2.50				
2005 In sets only	—	—	—	—	2.00	—
2006 In sets only	—	—	—	—	2.00	—
2006 Proof	—	Value: 2.50				
2007 In sets only	—	—	—	—	2.00	—
2008 In sets only	—	—	—	—	2.00	—
2008 Proof	—	Value: 2.50				

KM# 14 5 KORUNA

5.4000 g., Nickel Plated Steel, 24.75 mm. **Obv:** Double cross on shield above inscription **Rev:** Celtic coin of BIATEC at upper left of value **Edge:** Milled **Designer:** Drahomir Zobek

Date	Mintage	F	VF	XF	Unc	BU
2001 In sets only	—	—	—	—	2.00	—
2001 Proof	12,500	Value: 6.00				
2002 Proof	16,100	Value: 5.00				
2003 In sets only	14,000	—	—	—	2.00	—
2004 In sets only	—	—	—	—	2.00	—
2004 Proof	—	Value: 5.00				
2005 In sets only	—	—	—	—	2.00	—
2006 In sets only	—	—	—	—	2.00	—
2006 Proof	—	Value: 5.00				
2007	—	—	—	—	1.50	—
2008 In sets only	—	—	—	—	2.00	—
2008 Proof	—	Value: 5.00				

KM# 11.1 10 KORUNA

6.6000 g., Aluminum-Bronze, 26.5 mm. **Obv:** Double cross on shield above inscription **Rev:** Bronze cross and value **Designer:** Drahomir Zobek

Date	Mintage	F	VF	XF	Unc	BU
2001 In sets only	—	—	—	—	4.00	—
2001 Proof	12,500	Value: 12.50				
2002 Proof	16,100	Value: 10.00				
2003	10,923,000	—	—	—	2.50	—
2004 In sets only	—	—	—	—	4.00	—
2004 Proof	—	Value: 10.00				
2005 In sets only	—	—	—	—	4.00	—
2006 In sets only	—	—	—	—	4.00	—
2006 Proof	—	Value: 10.00				
2007 In sets only	—	—	—	—	4.00	—
2008 In sets only	—	—	—	—	4.00	—
2008 Proof	—	Value: 10.00				

KM# 67 20 KORUN

24.4800 g., 0.9250 Silver 0.7280 oz. ASW, 27.1 x 50.6 mm. **Series:** Banknotes **Obv:** Prince Pribina (800-861) **Rev:** Nitra Castle **Edge:** Plain

Date	Mintage	F	VF	XF	Unc	BU
2003 Proof	6,000	Value: 60.00				

KM# 68 50 KORUN

26.6300 g., 0.9250 Silver 0.7919 oz. ASW, 28.2 x 52.8 mm. **Series:** Banknotes **Obv:** Saints Cyril and Methodius (814-885) **Rev:** Two hands **Edge:** Plain

Date	Mintage	F	VF	XF	Unc	BU
2003 Proof	6,000	Value: 65.00				

KM# 69 100 KORUN

28.8700 g., 0.9250 Silver 0.8585 oz. ASW, 29.3 x 55 mm. **Series:** Banknotes **Obv:** The Levoca Madonna **Rev:** St. James Church in Levoca **Edge:** Plain

Date	Mintage	F	VF	XF	Unc	BU
2003 Proof	—	Value: 75.00				

KM# 59 200 KORUN

20.0000 g., 0.7500 Silver 0.4822 oz. ASW, 34 mm. **Subject:** Alexander Dubcek **Obv:** Double cross on shield and tree **Obv. Designer:** Anton Gabrik **Rev:** Head left **Rev. Designer:** Ladislav Kozak **Edge Lettering:** BUDSKOST SLOBODA DEMOKRACIA

Date	Mintage	F	VF	XF	Unc	BU
2001	12,800	—	—	—	23.00	25.00
2001 Proof	3,000	Value: 70.00				

Note: Unc. examples without edge lettering exist. Value $850.00.

KM# 60 200 KORUN

20.0000 g., 0.7500 Silver 0.4822 oz. ASW, 34 mm. **Subject:** Ludovit Fulla **Obv:** Modern art **Rev:** Head facing in national costume, value and dates **Edge:** Lettered **Designer:** Emil Fulka **Note:** 1,800 pieces melted.

Date	Mintage	F	VF	XF	Unc	BU
2002	11,300	—	—	—	23.00	25.00
2002 Proof	2,400	Value: 55.00				

KM# 62 200 KORUN

20.3500 g., 0.7500 Silver 0.4907 oz. ASW, 34 mm. **Subject:**

UNESCO World Heritage site - Vlkolínec **Obv:** Log building and double cross on shield **Rev:** Wooden tower and value **Edge Lettering:** WORLD HERITAGE PATRIMONE MONDIAL **Designer:** Pavol Karoly **Note:** 900 pieces melted.

Date	Mintage	F	VF	XF	Unc	BU
2002	11,500	—	—	—	23.00	25.00
2002 Proof	2,800	Value: 55.00				

KM# 66 200 KORUN
20.0000 g., 0.7500 Silver 0.4822 oz. ASW, 34 mm. **Obv:** Building below double cross within shield **Rev:** Head facing and value **Edge:** Lettered **Edge Lettering:** VYTRVALOST A VERNOST NARODNEMU IDEALU **Note:** 500 pieces uncirculated melted.

Date	Mintage	F	VF	XF	Unc	BU
2003	8,800	—	—	—	23.00	25.00
2003 Proof	2,700	Value: 55.00				

KM# 65 200 KORUN
20.0000 g., 0.7500 Silver 0.4822 oz. ASW, 34 mm. **Subject:** Imrich Karvas **Obv:** Building, national arms and value **Rev:** Portrait **Edge:** Lettered **Edge Lettering:** NARODOHOSPODAR HUMANISTA EUROPAN **Designer:** Miroslav Ronai **Note:** 500 pieces uncirculated melted.

Date	Mintage	F	VF	XF	Unc	BU
2003	9,800	—	—	—	23.00	25.00
2003 Proof	3,000	Value: 50.00				

KM# 70 200 KORUN
31.2100 g., 0.9250 Silver 0.9281 oz. ASW, 30.4 x 57.2 mm. **Series:** Banknotes **Obv:** Head facing and value **Rev:** 18th Century city view and value **Edge:** Plain

Date	Mintage	F	VF	XF	Unc	BU
2003 Proof	6,000	Value: 90.00				

KM# 75 200 KORUN
20.0000 g., 0.7500 Silver 0.4822 oz. ASW, 34 mm. **Obv:** Kempelen's Chess Machine (1770) **Rev:** Inventor Wolfgang Kemelen (1734-1804) above Bratislava city view **Edge Lettering:** VYNALEZCA - TECHNIK - KONSTRUKTER **Designer:** Miroslav Ronai

Date	Mintage	F	VF	XF	Unc	BU
2004	8,000	—	—	—	23.00	25.00
2004 Proof	3,200	Value: 50.00				

KM# 76 200 KORUN
20.0000 g., 0.7500 Silver 0.4822 oz. ASW, 34 mm. **Obv:** Church and town hall below double cross within shield **Rev:** Aerial view of Bardejov circa 1768 **Edge Lettering:** WORLD HERITAGE - PATRIMOINE MONDIAL **Designer:** Jan Cernaj

Date	Mintage	F	VF	XF	Unc	BU
2004	8,400	—	—	—	23.00	25.00
2004 Proof	3,600	Value: 50.00				

KM# 77 200 KORUN
18.0000 g., 0.9000 Silver 0.5208 oz. ASW, 34 mm. **Obv:** "The Segner Wheel" model **Rev:** Bust with fur hat facing within circle of designs **Edge Lettering:** VYNALEZCA - FYZIK - MATEMATIK - PEDAGOG **Designer:** Maria Poldaufova

Date	Mintage	F	VF	XF	Unc	BU
2004	10,500	—	—	—	23.00	25.00
2004 Proof	4,700	Value: 45.00				

KM# 78 200 KORUN
20.0000 g., 0.7500 Silver 0.4822 oz. ASW, 34 mm. **Subject:** Slovakian entry into the European Union **Obv:** Circle of stars in arch above national arms **Rev:** Map in arch above value **Edge Lettering:** ROZSIRENIE EUROPSKEJ UNIE O DESAT KRAJIN **Designer:** Patrik Kovacovsky

Date	Mintage	F	VF	XF	Unc	BU
2004	10,100	—	—	—	23.00	25.00
2004 Proof	4,700	Value: 45.00				

KM# 81 200 KORUN
18.0000 g., 0.9000 Silver 0.5208 oz. ASW, 34 mm. **Subject:** Leopold I Coronation 350th Anniversary **Obv:** Value and partial castle view **Rev:** Coin design of Leopold I in large size legend **Edge Lettering:** BRATISLAVSKE KORUNOVACIE **Designer:** Maria Poldaufova

Date	Mintage	F	VF	XF	Unc	BU
2005	8,900	—	—	—	23.00	25.00
2005 Proof	4,800	Value: 45.00				

KM# 82 200 KORUN
18.0000 g., 0.9000 Silver 0.5208 oz. ASW, 34 mm. **Subject:** Treaty of Pressburg **Obv:** Primate's Palace behind French military standard **Rev:** Napoleon and Francis I of Austria **Edge Lettering:** 26 DECEMBER. 5 MIVOSE AN 14 **Designer:** Pavel Karoly

Date	Mintage	F	VF	XF	Unc	BU
2005	5,100	—	—	—	23.00	25.00
2005 Proof	3,400	Value: 45.00				

KM# 87 200 KORUN
18.0000 g., 0.9000 Silver 0.5208 oz. ASW, 34 mm. **Subject:** 200th Anniversary Birth of Karol Kuzmány **Obv:** Small national arms at upper left, denomination at center **Obv. Inscription:** SLOVENSKÁ / REPUBLIKA **Rev:** Partial medallic head of Kuzmány facing

Date	Mintage	F	VF	XF	Unc	BU
2006	—	—	—	—	23.00	25.00
2006 Proof	—	Value: 55.00				

KM# 105 200 KORUN
18.0000 g., 0.9000 Silver 0.5208 oz. ASW, 34 mm. **Subject:** Josef M. Petzval, Physicist **Obv:** Lens **Rev:** Bust at left

Date	Mintage	F	VF	XF	Unc	BU
2007	2,500	—	—	—	23.00	25.00
2007 Proof	—	Value: 70.00				

KM# 88 200 KORUN
18.0000 g., 0.9000 Silver 0.5208 oz. ASW, 34 mm. **Subject:** 100th Anniversary Birth of Andrej Kmet **Obv:** Small national arms above stylized M-shaped memorial representing the Slovak Museum. **Obv. Legend:** SLOVENSKÁ REPUBLIKA **Obv. Designer:** Stefan Novotny **Rev:** Head of Kmet 3/4 left **Rev. Designer:** Dalibor Schmidt **Edge:** Lettered **Edge Lettering:** POZNÁVAJME KRAJE SVOJE A POZNÁME SAMYCH SEBA

Date	Mintage	F	VF	XF	Unc	BU
2008	8,500	—	—	—	23.00	25.00
2008 Proof	3,400	Value: 75.00				

KM# 56 500 KORUN
33.6300 g., 0.9250 Silver 1.0000 oz. ASW, 40 mm. **Subject:** Mala Fatra National Park **Obv:** National arms center of cross formed by beetles (Alpine Salyers) **Rev:** Orchid with mountain background **Edge Lettering:** OCHRANA PRIRODY A KRAJINY **Designer:** Patrik Kovacovsky **Note:** 400 pieces uncirculated melted.

Date	Mintage	F	VF	XF	Unc	BU
2001	10,200	—	—	—	—	90.00
2001 Proof	1,800	Value: 250				

KM# 57 500 KORUN
31.1035 g., 0.9990 Silver 0.9990 oz. ASW, 45 mm. **Subject:** Third Millennium **Obv:** "The Universe" **Rev:** Three hands **Edge:** Plain **Shape:** 3-sided **Designer:** Patrik Kovacovsky **Note:** 400 pieces uncirculated melted.

Date	Mintage	F	VF	XF	Unc	BU
2001	13,000	—	—	—	50.00	55.00
2001 Proof	4,000	Value: 175				

KM# 71 500 KORUN
33.6300 g., 0.9250 Silver 1.0000 oz. ASW, 31.5 x 59.4 mm. **Series:** Banknotes **Obv:** Head facing and value **Rev:** Bratislava Castle view and value **Edge:** Plain

Date	Mintage	F	VF	XF	Unc	BU
2003 Proof	6,000	Value: 100				

KM# 85 500 KORUN
33.6300 g., 0.9250 Silver 1.0000 oz. ASW, 40 mm. **Subject:** Slovensky Kras National Park **Obv:** 2 Rock buntings above value **Rev:** Dogs Tooth violet flowers in front of Karst cave interior view **Edge Lettering:** OCHRANA PRIRODY A KRAJINY **Designer:** Maria Poldaufova

Date	Mintage	F	VF	XF	Unc	BU
2005	8,500	—	—	—	—	45.00
2005 Proof	3,600	Value: 90.00				

KM# 84 500 KORUN
33.6300 g., 0.9250 Silver 1.0000 oz. ASW, 40 mm. **Subject:** Muranska Planina National Park **Obv:** Wildflowers and Muran castle ruins **Rev:** Two wild horses **Edge Lettering:** OCHRANA PRIRODY A KRAJINY [flower] **Designer:** Karol Licko

Date	Mintage	F	VF	XF	Unc	BU
2006	4,300	—	—	—	—	55.00
2006 Proof	2,800	Value: 200				

KM# 86 500 KORUN
33.6300 g., 0.9250 Silver 1.0000 oz. ASW, 40 mm. **Subject:** 450th Anniversary - Construction Fortress at Komárno **Obv:** Early ships, fortress in background, national arms at lower right **Obv. Legend:** SLOVENSKÁ REPUBLIKA **Obv. Designer:** Karol Licko **Rev:** Layout of fortress, horses in battle against Turks below **Rev. Legend:** PEVNOST - KOMÁRNO **Rev. Designer:** Mária Poldaufová **Edge Lettering:** NEC ARTE NEC MARTE - COMORRA in relief

Date	Mintage	F	VF	XF	Unc	BU
2007	4,600	—	—	—	—	70.00
2007 Proof	2,600	Value: 250				

KM# 106 500 KORUN
33.6300 g., 0.9250 Silver 1.0000 oz. ASW, 40 mm. **Subject:** National Park - Low Tatra Mountains **Obv:** Mountains, flower and shield **Rev:** Bear in pine tree

Date	Mintage	F	VF	XF	Unc	BU
2008	4,300	—	—	—	—	55.00
2008 Proof	4,800	Value: 150				

KM# 63 1000 KORUN
62.2070 g., 0.9990 Silver 1.9979 oz. ASW, 43.6 x 43.6 mm. **Subject:** 10th Anniversary of Republic **Obv:** National arms between hands **Rev:** Value above map **Edge:** Segmented reeding **Shape:** Square **Designer:** Milos Vavro

Date	Mintage	F	VF	XF	Unc	BU
2003 Proof	10,000	Value: 115				

KM# 72 1000 KORUN
43.9100 g., 0.9250 Bi-Metallic .925 Silver 43.91g planchet with .999 Gold .28g insert 1.3058 oz., 32.6 x 61.6 mm. **Series:** Banknotes **Obv:** Head facing and value **Rev:** The Madonna Protector facing and church of Liptovske Sliace **Edge:** Plain **Note:** Illustration reduced.

Date	Mintage	F	VF	XF	Unc	BU
2003 Proof	6,000	Value: 150				

KM# 58 5000 KORUN
Tri-Metallic 31.1035, .999 Silver, 1.00 oz ASW with 6.22, .999 Gold, .20 oz AGW and .31, .999 Platinum, .10 oz. APW, 50 mm. **Series:** Third Millennium **Obv:** "The Universe" **Rev:** Three hands **Edge:** Plain **Shape:** Triangular **Designer:** Patrik Kovacovsky

Date	Mintage	F	VF	XF	Unc	BU
2001 Proof	8,000	Value: 475				

KM# 61 5000 KORUN
9.5000 g., 0.9000 Gold 0.2749 oz. AGW, 26 mm. **Subject:** Vikolinec village - UNESCO historic site **Obv:** Enclosed communal well **Rev:** Window and fence **Edge:** Reeded **Designer:** Maria Poldaufova

Date	Mintage	F	VF	XF	Unc	BU
2002 Proof	7,200	Value: 525				

KM# 73 5000 KORUN
47.6340 g., 0.9250 Bi-Metallic .925 Silver 46.65g planchet with two .9999 Gold inserts .964g in total 1.4165 oz., 33.4 x 63.8 mm. **Series:** Banknotes **Obv:** Head facing and value **Rev:** Stefanik's grave monument **Edge:** Plain **Note:** Illustration reduced.

Date	Mintage	F	VF	XF	Unc	BU
2003 Proof	6,000	Value: 250				

KM# 80 5000 KORUN
9.5000 g., 0.9000 Gold 0.2749 oz. AGW, 26 mm. **Subject:** Bardejov - UNESCO historic site **Obv:** National arms and value left of Town Hall **Rev:** Zachariah in window frame left of St. Aegidius Church, Bardejov **Edge:** Reeded

Date	Mintage	F	VF	XF	Unc	BU
2004 Proof	9,000	Value: 500				

KM# 83 5000 KORUN
9.5000 g., 0.9000 Gold 0.2749 oz. AGW, 26 mm. **Subject:** Leopold I Coronation **Obv:** Mounted Herald with Bratislava Castile in background **Rev:** Leopold I and Crown of St. Stephan **Edge:** Reeded

Date	Mintage	F	VF	XF	Unc	BU
2005 Proof	7,500	Value: 525				

KM# 89 5000 KORUN
9.5000 g., 0.9000 Gold 0.2749 oz. AGW, 26 mm. **Subject:** 400th Anniversary Coronation of King Matthias II **Obv:** Cathedral and Bratislava castle **Obv. Legend:** SLOVENSKÁ - REPUBLIKA **Obv. Designer:** Miroslav and Branislav Ronai **Rev:** 1/2 length figure of Matthias II left, crown in lower foreground, towers of the St. Michael's Gate and franciscan Church in Bratislava in background **Rev. Legend:** KORUNOVÁCIA MATEJA II. / BRATISLAVA **Edge:** Reeded

Date	Mintage	F	VF	XF	Unc	BU
2008 Proof	4,050	Value: 550				

KM# 64 10000 KORUN
18.8350 g., Bi-Metallic 1.555g, .999 Palladium round center in a 15.55g, .900 Gold square, 29.5 x 29.5 mm. **Subject:** 10th Anniversary of the Republic **Obv:** Young head left within circular inscription above double cross within shield **Rev:** Bratislava castle above value **Edge:** Segmented reeding **Shape:** Square **Designer:** Ludmila Cvengrosova

Date	Mintage	F	VF	XF	Unc	BU
2003 Proof	6,000	Value: 1,150				

KM# 79 10000 KORUN
24.8828 g., Bi-Metallic .999 Gold 12.4414g 23mm round center in .999 Palladium 12.4414g pentagon, 40 mm. **Subject:** Slovakian entry into the European Union **Obv:** National arms above date in center **Obv. Designer:** Stefan Novotny **Rev:** European map with entry date **Rev. Designer:** Jan Cernaj **Edge:** Plain

Date	Mintage	F	VF	XF	Unc	BU
2004 Proof	7,200	Value: 1,100				

EURO COINAGE

European Union Issues

KM# 95 EURO CENT
2.3500 g., Copper Plated Steel, 16.2 mm. **Obv:** Krivan Peak in the Tatras, state emblem **Obv. Designer:** Drahomir Zobek **Rev:** Denomination and globe

Date	Mintage	F	VF	XF	Unc	BU
2009	—	—	—	—	0.35	0.50
2009 Proof	—	—	—	—	—	—
2010	—	—	—	—	0.35	0.50
2010 Proof	—	—	—	—	—	—
2011	—	—	—	—	0.35	0.50
2011 Proof	—	—	—	—	—	—

KM# 96 2 EURO CENT
3.0700 g., Copper Plated Steel, 18.7 mm. **Obv:** Krivan Peak in the Tatras, state emblem **Obv. Designer:** Drahomir Zobek **Rev:** Denomination and globe

Date	Mintage	F	VF	XF	Unc	BU
2009	—	—	—	—	0.50	0.65
2009 Proof	—	—	—	—	—	—
2010	—	—	—	—	0.50	0.65
2010 Proof	—	—	—	—	—	—
2011	—	—	—	—	0.50	0.65
2011 Proof	—	—	—	—	—	—

KM# 97 5 EURO CENT

3.8600 g., Copper Plated Steel, 21.3 mm. **Obv:** Krivan Peak in the Tatras - state emblem **Obv. Designer:** Drahomir Zobek **Rev:** Denomination and globe

Date	Mintage	F	VF	XF	Unc	BU
2009	—	—	—	—	0.75	1.00
2009 Proof	—	—	—	—	—	—
2010	—	—	—	—	0.75	1.00
2010 Proof	—	—	—	—	—	—
2011	—	—	—	—	0.75	1.00
2011 Proof	—	—	—	—	—	—

KM# 98 10 EURO CENT

4.0700 g., Brass, 19.8 mm. **Obv:** Bratislava Castle and state emblem **Obv. Designer:** Jan Cernaj and Pavel Karoly **Rev:** Expanded relief map of European Union at left, denomination at right

Date	Mintage	F	VF	XF	Unc	BU
2009	—	—	—	—	0.75	1.00
2009 Proof	—	—	—	—	—	—
2010	—	—	—	—	0.75	1.00
2010 Proof	—	—	—	—	—	—
2011	—	—	—	—	0.75	1.00
2011 Proof	—	—	—	—	—	—

KM# 99 20 EURO CENT

5.7300 g., Brass, 22.3 mm. **Obv:** Bratislava Castle and state emblem **Obv. Designer:** Jan Cernaj and Pavel Karoly **Rev:** Expanded relief map of European Union at left, denomination at right

Date	Mintage	F	VF	XF	Unc	BU
2009	—	—	—	—	1.00	1.25
2009 Proof	—	—	—	—	—	—
2010	—	—	—	—	1.00	1.25
2010 Proof	—	—	—	—	—	—
2011	—	—	—	—	1.00	1.25
2011 Proof	—	—	—	—	—	—

KM# 100 50 EURO CENT

7.8100 g., Brass, 24.2 mm. **Obv:** Bratislava Castle and state shield **Obv. Designer:** Jan Cernaj and Pavel Karoly **Rev:** Expanded relief map of European Union at left, denomination at right

Date	Mintage	F	VF	XF	Unc	BU
2009	—	—	—	—	1.25	1.50
2009 Proof	—	—	—	—	—	—
2010	—	—	—	—	1.25	1.50
2010 Proof	—	—	—	—	—	—
2011	—	—	—	—	1.25	1.50
2011 Proof	—	—	—	—	—	—

KM# 101 EURO

Bi-Metallic Copper-Nickel center in Brass ring, 23.2 mm. **Obv:** Double cross in middle of three hills **Obv. Designer:** Ivan Rehak **Rev:** Value at left, expanded relief map of European Union at right

Date	Mintage	F	VF	XF	Unc	BU
2009	—	—	—	—	2.50	2.75
2009 Proof	—	—	—	—	—	—
2010	—	—	—	—	2.50	2.75
2010 Proof	—	—	—	—	—	—
2011	—	—	—	—	2.50	2.75
2011 Proof	—	—	—	—	—	—

KM# 102 2 EURO

8.5200 g., Bi-Metallic Brass center in Copper-Nickel ring, 25.7 mm. **Obv:** Double cross on middle of three hills **Obv. Designer:** Ivan Rehak **Rev:** Value at left, expanded map of European Union at left

Date	Mintage	F	VF	XF	Unc	BU
2009	—	—	—	—	5.00	6.00
2009 Proof	—	—	—	—	—	—
2010	—	—	—	—	5.00	6.00
2010 Proof	—	—	—	—	—	—
2011	—	—	—	—	5.00	6.00
2011 Proof	—	—	—	—	—	—

KM# 103 2 EURO

8.5200 g., Bi-Metallic Brass center in Copper-Nickel ring, 25.7 mm. **Subject:** EMU 10th Anniversary **Obv:** Stick figure and large E symbol **Rev:** Expanded relief map of European Union at left, denomination at right

Date	Mintage	F	VF	XF	Unc	BU
2009	—	—	—	—	6.00	7.50

KM# 107 2 EURO

8.5200 g., Bi-Metallic Brass center in Copper-Nickel ring., 25.72 mm. **Subject:** Freedom, 17 November 1989, 20th Anniversary **Obv:** Ringing Freedom bell **Obv. Designer:** Pavel Karoly

Date	Mintage	F	VF	XF	Unc	BU
2009	1,000,000	—	—	—	6.00	7.50

KM# 114 2 EURO

8.5000 g., Bi-Metallic Brass center in Copper-Nickel ring, 25.75 mm. **Subject:** Visegrad Group, 20th Anniversary

Date	Mintage	F	VF	XF	Unc	BU
2011	—	—	—	—	5.00	6.00

KM# 108 10 EURO

18.0000 g., 0.9000 Silver 0.5208 oz. ASW, 34 mm. **Subject:** Aurel Stodola, 150th Anniversary of birth **Obv:** Turbo generator, national shield **Rev:** Portrait **Edge Lettering:** KONSTRUKTER - VYNALEZCA - PEDAGOG

Date	Mintage	F	VF	XF	Unc	BU
2009	10,100	—	—	—	—	50.00
2009 Proof	13,300	Value: 65.00				

KM# 110 10 EURO

18.0000 g., 0.9000 Silver 0.5208 oz. ASW, 34 mm. **Subject:** Wooden Churches of Carpathian Slovakia - UNESCO World Heritage site

Date	Mintage	F	VF	XF	Unc	BU
2010	—	—	—	—	—	50.00
2010 Proof	—	Value: 65.00				

KM# 111 10 EURO

18.0000 g., 0.9000 Silver 0.5208 oz. ASW, 34 mm. **Subject:** Martin Kukucin, 150th Anniversary of birth **Obv:** Landscape scene from Brac, "House on the hillside" **Obv. Designer:** Miroslav Ronai **Rev:** Fortrait facing, cuckoo, signature **Rev. Designer:** Peter Valach **Edge Lettering:** PROZAIK - DRAMATIK - PUBLICISTA

Date	Mintage	F	VF	XF	Unc	BU
2010	9,900	—	—	—	—	50.00
2010 Proof	17,325	Value: 65.00				

KM# 115 10 EURO

18.0000 g., 0.9000 Silver 0.5208 oz. ASW, 34 mm. **Subject:** Zobor Documents, 900th Anniversary **Obv:** Two scribes **Rev:** Seal and partial document text

Date	Mintage	F	VF	XF	Unc	BU
2011	—	—	—	—	—	50.00
2011 Proof	—	Value: 65.00				

KM# 116 10 EURO

18.0000 g., 0.9000 Silver 0.5208 oz. ASW, 34 mm. **Subject:** Adoption of the memorandum of the Slovak Nation, 1540th Anniversary

Date	Mintage	F	VF	XF	Unc	BU
2011	—	—	—	—	—	50.00
2011 Proof	—	Value: 65.00				

KM# 117 10 EURO

18.0000 g., 0.9000 Silver 0.5208 oz. ASW, 34 mm. **Subject:** Jan Cikker, 100th Anniversary of Birth

Date	Mintage	F	VF	XF	Unc	BU
2011	—	—	—	—	—	50.00
2011 Proof	—	Value: 65.00				

KM# 109 20 EURO
Silver **Subject:** National Park - Velka Fatra **Obv:** Fora and national shield **Rev:** Falcon in flight over mountain peak **Designer:** Roman Lugar

Date	Mintage	F	VF	XF	Unc	BU
2009	9,900	—	—	—	—	65.00
2009 Proof	12,600	Value: 75.00				

KM# 112 20 EURO
33.6300 g., 0.9250 Silver 1.0000 oz. ASW, 40 mm. **Subject:** Poloniny National Park **Obv:** Mountainside and flowers **Rev:** Two wolves

Date	Mintage	F	VF	XF	Unc	BU
2010	—	—	—	—	—	55.00
2010 Proof	—	Value: 70.00				

KM# 118 20 EURO
33.6300 g., 0.9250 Silver 1.0000 oz. ASW, 40 mm. **Subject:** Historical Sites - Trnava

Date	Mintage	F	VF	XF	Unc	BU
2011	—	—	—	—	—	55.00
2011 Proof	—	Value: 70.00				

KM# 113 100 EURO
9.5000 g., 0.9000 Gold 0.2749 oz. AGW, 26 mm. **Subject:** Wooden Churches of Carpathian Slovakia - UNESCO Heritage Site **Obv:** Church of St. Francis of Assisi in Hervartov, belfry of the church in Hronsek and Church of St. Nicholas in Brodrzal **Rev:** Baroque altar of All Saints Church in Tvrdosin **Edge:** Reeded **Designer:** Kliment Mitura and Dalibor Schmidt

Date	Mintage	F	VF	XF	Unc	BU
2010 Proof	Est. 7,000	Value: 525				

KM# 119 100 EURO
9.5000 g., 0.9000 Gold 0.2749 oz. AGW, 26 mm. **Subject:** Prince Pribina Nitra, 1150th Anniversary of Death

Date	Mintage	F	VF	XF	Unc	BU
2011 Proof	—	Value: 550				

MINT SETS

KM#	Date	Mintage	Identification	Issue Price	Mkt Val
MS9	2001 (7)	—	KM#11.1-14, 17-18, 35, plus medal	—	20.00
MS10	2002 (7)	—	KM#11-1-14, 17-18, 35, plus medal	—	17.50
MS11	2003 (7)	—	KM#11.1-14, 17-18, 35, plus medal	—	15.00
MS12	2004 (7)	—	KM#11.1-14, 17, 18, 35 plus medal	—	12.00
MS13	2005 (7)	—	KM#11.1-14, 17, 18, 35 plus medal	—	12.00
MS14	2006 (7)	—	KM#11.1-14, 17, 18, 35 plus medal	—	12.00
MS15	2007 (7)	—	KM#11.1-14, 17, 18, 35 plus medal	—	12.00
MS16	2007 (5)	—	KM11.2, 12-14, 35. National parks	—	15.00
MS17	2005 (5)	—	KM#11.1, 12-14, 35, Austrian 2005 KM#3088	—	10.00
MS18	2007 (5)	—	KM#11.1, 12-14, 35	—	12.00
MS19	2007 (5)	—	KM#11.1, 12-14, 35. National parks packaging	—	15.00
MS20	2007 (5)	—	KM#11.1, 12-14, 35 and a bimetallic medal and cd. Set to commemorate musician Gejza Dusik	—	20.00

PROOF SETS

KM#	Date	Mintage	Identification	Issue Price	Mkt Val
PS1	2000 (7)	900	KM#11.1-14, 17-18, 35	—	90.00
PS2	2001 (7)	12,500	KM#11.1-14, 17-18, 35	—	35.00
PS3	2002 (7)	16,500	KM#11.1-14, 17-18, 35	—	25.00
PS4	2004 (7)	—	KM#11.1, 12-14, 35, silver strikes of 1993, KM#17-18	—	40.00
PS5	2006 (5)	—	KM#11.1, 12-14, 35 and a bimetallic medal for Torino Winter Olympics	—	45.00
PS6	2008 (5)	—	KM#11.1, 12-14, 35 and a bimetallic medal. Issued to commemorate 2008 Peking Olympics	—	45.00

SLOVENIA

The Republic of Slovenia is located northwest of Yugoslavia in the valleys of the Danube River. It has an area of 7,819 sq. mi. and a population of *1.9 million. Capital: Ljubljana. Agriculture is the main industry with large amounts of hops and fodder crops grown as well as many varieties of fruit trees. Sheep raising, timber production and the mining of mercury from one of the country's oldest mines are also very important to the economy. Slovenia joined the European Union in May 2004.

MINT MARKS

Based on last digit in date.
(K) - Kremnitz (Slovakia): open 4, upturned 5
(BP) - Budapest (Hungary): closed 4, down-turned 5

MONETARY SYSTEM

100 Stotinov = 1 Tolar
100 Euro Cents = 1 Euro

REPUBLIC

STANDARD COINAGE

100 Stotinow = 1 Tolar

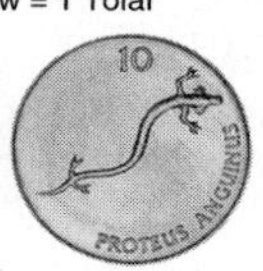

KM# 7 10 STOTINOV
0.5500 g., Aluminum, 16 mm. **Obv:** Value within square **Rev:** Olm salamander **Edge:** Plain **Note:** Varieties exist.

Date	Mintage	F	VF	XF	Unc	BU
2001 In sets only	1,000	—	—	—	—	3.00
2001 Proof	800	Value: 5.00				
2002 In sets only	1,000	—	—	—	—	3.00
2002 Proof	800	Value: 5.00				
2003 In sets only	1,000	—	—	—	—	3.00
2003 Proof	800	Value: 5.00				
2004 In sets only	1,000	—	—	—	—	3.00
2004 Proof	800	Value: 5.00				
2005 In sets only	3,000	—	—	—	—	2.00
2005 Proof	1,000	Value: 5.00				
2006 In sets only	4,000	—	—	—	—	2.00
2006 Proof	1,000	Value: 5.00				

KM# 8 20 STOTINOV
0.7000 g., Aluminum, 18 mm. **Obv:** Value within square **Rev:** Barn owl and value **Edge:** Plain

Date	Mintage	F	VF	XF	Unc	BU
2001 In sets only	1,000	—	—	—	—	4.00
2001 Proof	800	Value: 6.00				
2002 In sets only	1,000	—	—	—	—	4.00
2002 Proof	800	Value: 6.00				
2003 In sets only	1,000	—	—	—	—	4.00
2003 Proof	800	Value: 6.00				
2004 In sets only	1,000	—	—	—	—	4.00
2004 Proof	500	Value: 6.00				
2005 In sets only	3,000	—	—	—	—	3.00
2005 Proof	1,000	Value: 6.00				
2006 In sets only	4,000	—	—	—	—	3.00
2006 Proof	1,000	Value: 6.00				

KM# 3 50 STOTINOV
0.8500 g., Aluminum, 20 mm. **Obv:** Value within square **Rev:** Bee and value **Edge:** Plain

Date	Mintage	F	VF	XF	Unc	BU
2001 In sets only	1,000	—	—	—	—	6.00
2001 Proof	800	Value: 7.50				
2002 In sets only	1,000	—	—	—	—	6.00
2002 Proof	800	Value: 7.50				
2003 In sets only	1,000	—	—	—	—	6.00
2003 Proof	800	Value: 7.50				
2004 In sets only	1,000	—	—	—	—	6.00
2004 Proof	500	Value: 12.00				
2005 In sets only	3,000	—	—	—	—	4.00
2005 Proof	1,000	Value: 7.00				
2006 In sets only	4,000	—	—	—	—	4.00
2006 Proof	1,000	Value: 7.00				

KM# 4 TOLAR
4.5000 g., Nickel-Brass, 22 mm. **Obv:** Value within circle **Rev:** Three brown trout **Rev. Legend:** SALMO TRUTTA FARIO **Edge:** Reeded **Note:** Date varieties exist: 1994 = closed or open "4"; 1995 = serif up and serif down in "5".

Date	Mintage	F	VF	XF	Unc	BU
2001	10,001,000	—	—	—	0.75	1.25
2001 Proof	800	Value: 7.50				
2002 In sets only	1,000	—	—	—	—	5.00
2002 Proof	800	Value: 7.50				
2003 In sets only	1,000	—	—	—	—	5.00
2003 Proof	800	Value: 7.50				
2004	10,001,000	—	—	—	0.75	1.25
2004 (K) In sets only	1,000	—	—	—	—	5.00
Note: 4 open to right						
2004 Proof	500	Value: 8.50				
2005 In sets only	3,000	—	—	—	—	4.00
2005 Proof	1,000	Value: 7.50				
2006 In sets only	4,000	—	—	—	—	4.00
2006 Proof	1,000	Value: 7.50				

KM# 5 2 TOLARJA
5.4000 g., Nickel-Brass, 24 mm. **Obv:** Value within circle **Rev:** Barn swallow in flight **Rev. Legend:** HIRUNDO RUSTICA **Edge:** Reeded **Note:** Date varieties exist: 1994 = closed or open "4"; 1995 = serif up and serif down in "5".

Date	Mintage	F	VF	XF	Unc	BU
2001	10,001,000	—	—	—	0.75	1.75
2001 Proof	800	Value: 8.50				
2002 In sets only	1,000	—	—	—	—	7.00
2002 Proof	800	Value: 8.50				
2003 In sets only	1,000	—	—	—	—	7.00
2003 Proof	800	Value: 8.50				
2004	10,001,000	—	—	—	0.75	1.50
2004 Proof	500	Value: 8.50				
2005 In sets only	3,000	—	—	—	—	7.00
2005 Proof	1,000	Value: 8.50				
2006 In sets only	4,000	—	—	—	—	7.00
2006 Proof	1,000	Value: 8.50				

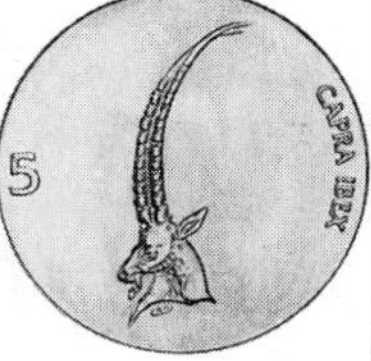

KM# 6 5 TOLARJEV
6.4400 g., Nickel-Brass, 26 mm. **Obv:** Value within circle **Rev:** Head and horns of ibex **Edge:** Reeded **Note:** Date varieties exist: 1994 = closed or open "4"; 1995 = serif up and serif down in "5".

Date	Mintage	F	VF	XF	Unc	BU
2001 In sets only	1,000	—	—	—	—	8.00
2001 Proof	800	Value: 10.00				

Date	Mintage	F	VF	XF	Unc	BU
2002 In sets only	1,000	—	—	—	—	8.00
2002 Proof	800	Value: 10.00				
2003 In sets only	1,000	—	—	—	—	8.00
2003 Proof	800	Value: 10.00				
2004 In sets only	1,000	—	—	—	—	8.00
2004 Proof	500	Value: 15.00				
2005 In sets only	3,000	—	—	—	—	7.00
2005 Proof	1,000	Value: 10.00				
2006 In sets only	4,000	—	—	—	—	7.00
2006 Proof	1,000	Value: 10.00				

KM# 41 10 TOLARJEV

5.7500 g., Copper-Nickel, 24 mm. **Obv:** Value within circle **Rev:** Stylized rearing horse **Rev. Legend:** EQUUS **Edge:** Reeded

Date	Mintage	F	VF	XF	Unc	BU
2001	29,441,000	—	—	—	2.00	3.50
2001 Proof	800	Value: 12.00				
2002	10,037,000	—	—	—	2.00	3.50
2002 Proof	800	Value: 12.00				
2003 In sets only	1,000	—	—	—	—	5.00
2003 Proof	800	Value: 12.00				
2004	10,001,000	—	—	—	2.00	3.50
2004 Proof	500	Value: 12.00				
2005	6,003,000	—	—	—	2.00	3.50
2005 Proof	1,000	Value: 12.00				
2006	6,001,000	—	—	—	2.00	3.50
2006 Proof	1,000	Value: 12.00				

KM# 51 20 TOLARJEV

6.8500 g., Copper-Nickel, 24 mm. **Obv:** Value within circle **Rev:** White Stork **Rev. Legend:** CICONIA CICONIA **Edge:** Reeded

Date	Mintage	F	VF	XF	Unc	BU
2003	10,001,000	—	—	—	3.50	5.00
2003 Proof	800	Value: 15.00				
2004	10,001,000	—	—	—	3.00	5.00
2004 Proof	500	Value: 15.00				
2005	12,003,000	—	—	—	3.50	5.00
2005 Proof	1,000	Value: 15.00				
2006	4,004,000	—	—	—	3.50	5.00
2006 Proof	1,000	Value: 15.00				

KM# 52 50 TOLARJEV

8.0000 g., Copper-Nickel, 26 mm. **Obv:** Value within circle **Rev:** Stylized bull **Rev. Legend:** TAURUS TAURUS **Edge:** Segmented reeding

Date	Mintage	F	VF	XF	Unc	BU
2003	10,001,000	—	—	—	2.50	4.50
2003 Proof	800	Value: 12.00				
2004	5,001,000	—	—	—	2.50	4.50
2004 Proof	500	Value: 15.00				
2005	8,003,000	—	—	—	2.50	4.50
2005 Proof	1,000	Value: 12.00				
2006 In sets only	4,000	—	—	—	—	6.50
2006 Proof	1,000	Value: 12.00				

KM# 42 100 TOLARJEV

9.1000 g., Copper-Nickel, 28 mm. **Subject:** 10th Anniversary of Slovenia and the Tolar **Obv:** Value **Rev:** Tree rings and inscription **Edge:** Reeded

Date	Mintage	F	VF	XF	Unc	BU
2001	500,000	—	—	—	3.00	4.00
2001 Proof	800	Value: 10.00				

KM# 45 500 TOLARJEV

8.5400 g., Bi-Metallic Copper-Nickel center in Brass ring, 28.1 mm. **Subject:** Soccer **Obv:** Value **Rev:** Soccer player and radiant sun **Edge:** Reeded

Date	Mintage	F	VF	XF	Unc	BU
2002	500,000	—	—	—	5.50	7.50
2002 Proof	800	Value: 12.50				

KM# 50 500 TOLARJEV

8.7200 g., Bi-Metallic Copper-Nickel center in Brass ring, 27.9 mm. **Subject:** European Year of the Disabled **Obv:** Stylized wheelchair **Rev:** Value **Edge:** Reeded

Date	Mintage	F	VF	XF	Unc	BU
2003	200,000	—	—	—	6.00	8.00
2003 Proof	800	Value: 13.50				

KM# 57 500 TOLARJEV

8.6000 g., Bi-Metallic Copper-Nickel center in Brass ring, 28 mm. **Obv:** Value **Rev:** Profile left looking down within mathematical graph **Edge:** Reeded

Date	Mintage	F	VF	XF	Unc	BU
2004	200,000	—	—	—	6.00	8.00
2004 Proof	500	Value: 20.00				

KM# 63 500 TOLARJEV

8.6500 g., Bi-Metallic Copper-Nickel center in Brass ring, 27.9 mm. **Obv:** Perched falcon and value **Rev:** Horizontal line in center divides partial suns **Edge:** Reeded

Date	Mintage	F	VF	XF	Unc	BU
2005	103,000	—	—	—	6.25	8.50
2005 Proof	1,000	Value: 12.00				

KM# 65 500 TOLARJEV

8.6000 g., Bi-Metallic Copper-Nickel center in Brass ring, 28 mm. **Obv:** Value **Rev:** Anton Tomaz Linhart's silhouette above life dates **Edge:** Reeded

Date	Mintage	F	VF	XF	Unc	BU
2006	104,000	—	—	—	6.00	8.00
2006 Proof	1,000	Value: 12.00				

KM# 43 2000 TOLARJEV

15.0000 g., 0.9250 Silver 0.4461 oz. ASW, 32 mm. **Subject:** 10th Anniversary of Slovenia and the Tolar **Obv:** Value **Rev:** Tree rings and inscription **Edge:** Reeded

Date	Mintage	F	VF	XF	Unc	BU
2001 Proof	3,000	Value: 35.00				

KM# 46 2500 TOLARJEV

15.0000 g., 0.9250 Silver 0.4461 oz. ASW, 32 mm. **Subject:** Soccer **Obv:** Value **Rev:** Soccer player and radiant sun **Edge:** Reeded

Date	Mintage	F	VF	XF	Unc	BU
2002 Proof	2,500	Value: 35.00				

KM# 48 2500 TOLARJEV

15.0000 g., 0.9250 Silver 0.4461 oz. ASW, 32 mm. **Subject:** 35th Chess Olympiad **Obv:** Rearing horse and reflection **Rev:** Chess pieces in starting positions and reflection **Edge:** Reeded **Designer:** MNiljenko Licul and Jan Cernaj

Date	Mintage	F	VF	XF	Unc	BU
2002 Proof	1,000	Value: 45.00				

KM# 53 2500 TOLARJEV

15.0000 g., 0.9250 Silver 0.4461 oz. ASW, 32 mm. **Subject:** European Year of the Disabled **Obv:** Value **Rev:** Stylized wheel chair **Edge:** Reeded

Date	Mintage	F	VF	XF	Unc	BU
2003 Proof	1,500	Value: 42.00				

KM# 55 5000 TOLARJEV

15.0000 g., 0.9250 Silver 0.4461 oz. ASW, 32 mm. **Subject:** 60th Anniversary of the Slovenian Assembly **Obv:** Value in partial star design **Rev:** Dates in partial star design **Edge:** Reeded

Date	Mintage	F	VF	XF	Unc	BU
2003 Proof	1,500	Value: 42.00				

KM# 58 5000 TOLARJEV

15.0000 g., 0.9250 Silver 0.4461 oz. ASW, 32 mm. **Obv:** Value **Rev:** Facial profile left looking down within mathematical graph **Edge:** Reeded

Date	Mintage	F	VF	XF	Unc	BU
2004 Proof	1,500	Value: 50.00				

KM# 60 5000 TOLARJEV

15.0000 g., 0.9250 Silver 0.4461 oz. ASW, 32 mm. **Subject:** 1000th Anniversary Town of Bled **Obv:** Value **Rev:** Castle and towers silhouette **Edge:** Reeded

Date	Mintage	F	VF	XF	Unc	BU
2004 Proof	1,500	Value: 50.00				

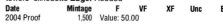

KM# 62 5000 TOLARJEV

15.1000 g., 0.9250 Silver 0.4490 oz. ASW, 32 mm. **Subject:** Slovenian Film Centennial **Obv:** Value above a director's clapboard **Rev:** Film segment **Edge:** Reeded

Date	Mintage	F	VF	XF	Unc	BU
2005 Proof	—	Value: 47.50				

KM# 64 5000 TOLARJEV

15.1000 g., 0.9250 Silver 0.4490 oz. ASW, 32 mm. **Obv:** Perched falcon above value **Rev:** Diagonal center line divides partial suns **Edge:** Reeded

Date	Mintage	F	VF	XF	Unc	BU
2005 Proof	—	Value: 47.50				

KM# 91 5000 TOLARJEV

15.0000 g., 0.9250 Silver 0.4461 oz. ASW, 32 mm. **Subject:** 1000th Anniversary, mention of town of Bled, 2nd issue

Date	Mintage	F	VF	XF	Unc	BU
2006 Proof	1,000	Value: 55.00				

KM# 92 5000 TOLARJEV

15.0000 g., 0.9000 Silver 0.4340 oz. ASW, 32 mm. **Subject:** Anton Tomaz Linhart, 250th Anniversary of Birth

Date	Mintage	F	VF	XF	Unc	BU
2006 Proof	5,000	Value: 45.00				

KM# 93 5000 TOLARJEV

15.0000 g., 0.9250 Silver 0.4461 oz. ASW, 32 mm. **Subject:** Anton Askerc, 150th Anniversary of birth

Date	Mintage	F	VF	XF	Unc	BU
2006 Proof	5,000	Value: 45.00				

KM# 44 20000 TOLARJEV

7.0000 g., 0.9000 Gold 0.2025 oz. AGW, 24 mm. **Subject:** 10th Anniversary of Slovenia and the Tolar **Obv:** Value **Rev:** Tree rings and inscription **Edge:** Reeded

Date	Mintage	F	VF	XF	Unc	BU
2001 Proof	1,000	Value: 350				

KM# 47 20000 TOLARJEV

7.0000 g., 0.9000 Gold 0.2025 oz. AGW, 24 mm. **Subject:** World Cup Soccer **Obv:** Value **Rev:** Soccer player and rising sun **Edge:** Reeded

Date	Mintage	F	VF	XF	Unc	BU
2002 Proof	500	Value: 365				

KM# 49 20000 TOLARJEV

7.0000 g., 0.9000 Gold 0.2025 oz. AGW, 24 mm. **Subject:** 35th Chess Olympiad **Obv:** Rearing horse and reflection **Rev:** Chess pieces in starting positions and reflection **Edge:** Reeded

Date	Mintage	F	VF	XF	Unc	BU
2002 Proof	500	Value: 365				

KM# 54 25000 TOLARJEV

7.0000 g., 0.9000 Gold 0.2025 oz. AGW, 24 mm. **Subject:** European Year of the Disabled **Obv:** Value **Rev:** Stylized wheel chair **Edge:** Reeded

Date	Mintage	F	VF	XF	Unc	BU
2003 Proof	300	Value: 375				

KM# 56 25000 TOLARJEV

7.0000 g., 0.9000 Gold 0.2025 oz. AGW, 24 mm. **Subject:** 60th Anniversary of the Slovenian Assembly **Obv:** Value in partial star design **Rev:** Dates in partial star design **Edge:** Reeded

Date	Mintage	F	VF	XF	Unc	BU
2003 Proof	300	Value: 375				

KM# 59 25000 TOLARJEV

7.0000 g., 0.9000 Gold 0.2025 oz. AGW, 24 mm. **Subject:** 250th Anniversary of Jurij Vega's Birth **Obv:** Value **Rev:** Facial profile left looking down within mathematical graph **Edge:** Reeded

Date	Mintage	F	VF	XF	Unc	BU
2004 Proof	300	Value: 375				

KM# 61 25000 TOLARJEV

7.0000 g., 0.9000 Gold 0.2025 oz. AGW, 24 mm. **Subject:** 1000th Anniversary Town of Bled **Obv:** Value **Rev:** Castle and towers silhouette **Edge:** Reeded

Date	Mintage	F	VF	XF	Unc	BU
2004 Proof	300	Value: 375				

KM# 66 25000 TOLARJEV

7.0000 g., 0.9000 Gold 0.2025 oz. AGW, 24 mm. **Subject:** Centennial of Slovene Sokol Association **Obv:** Perched falcon above value **Rev:** Rising sun and reflection **Edge:** Reeded

Date	Mintage	F	VF	XF	Unc	BU
2005 Proof	1,000	Value: 350				

KM# 67 25000 TOLARJEV

7.0000 g., 0.9000 Gold 0.2025 oz. AGW, 24 mm. **Subject:** Centennial of Slovene Film **Obv:** Value above clapboard **Rev:** Film segment **Edge:** Reeded

Date	Mintage	F	VF	XF	Unc	BU
2005 Proof	1,000	Value: 350				

KM# 83 25000 TOLARJEV

7.0000 g., 0.9000 Gold 0.2025 oz. AGW, 24 mm. **Subject:** Anton Askerc **Edge:** Reeded

Date	Mintage	F	VF	XF	Unc	BU
2006 Proof	—	Value: 375				

KM# 84 25000 TOLARJEV

7.0000 g., 0.9000 Gold 0.2025 oz. AGW, 24 mm. **Subject:** Anton Tomaz Linhart **Edge:** Reeded

Date	Mintage	F	VF	XF	Unc	BU
2006 Proof	—	Value: 375				

KM# 90 25000 TOLARJEV

7.0000 g., 0.9000 Gold 0.2025 oz. AGW, 24 mm. **Subject:** 1000th Anniversary, Town of Bled mention, 2nd issue

Date	Mintage	F	VF	XF	Unc	BU
2006 Proof	500	Value: 365				

EURO COINAGE

KM# 68 EURO CENT

2.2700 g., Copper Plated Steel, 16.2 mm. **Obv:** White Stork **Obv. Legend:** SLOVENIJA, star between each letter **Rev:** Value and globe **Edge:** Plain

Date	Mintage	F	VF	XF	Unc	BU
2007	44,700,000	—	—	—	0.25	0.35
2008	—	—	—	—	0.25	0.35
2009	17,900,000	—	—	—	0.25	0.35
2010	—	—	—	—	0.25	0.35
2010 Proof	5,000	Value: 3.00				

KM# 69 2 EURO CENT

3.0000 g., Copper Plated Steel, 18.7 mm. **Obv:** Princely stone of power in consciousness **Obv. Legend:** SLOVENIJA, star between each letter **Rev:** Value and globe **Edge:** Grooved

Date	Mintage	F	VF	XF	Unc	BU
2007	44,250,000	—	—	—	0.50	0.65
2008	—	—	—	—	0.50	0.65
2009	—	—	—	—	0.50	0.65
2010	—	—	—	—	0.50	0.65
2010 Proof	5,000	Value: 4.00				

KM# 70 5 EURO CENT

3.8600 g., Copper Plated Steel, 21.3 mm. **Obv:** Sower of Seeds - and stars **Obv. Legend:** SLOVENIJA, star between each letter **Rev:** Value and globe **Edge:** Plain

Date	Mintage	F	VF	XF	Unc	BU
2007	43,800,000	—	—	—	0.75	1.00
2008	—	—	—	—	0.75	1.00
2009	—	—	—	—	0.75	1.00
2010	—	—	—	—	0.75	1.00
2010 Proof	5,000	Value: 5.00				

KM# 71 10 EURO CENT

4.0000 g., Brass, 19.7 mm. **Obv:** Plecnik's unrealised plans for Parliament building **Obv. Legend:** SLOVENIJA, star between each letter **Rev:** Value and map **Edge:** Reeded

Date	Mintage	F	VF	XF	Unc	BU
2007	42,800,000	—	—	—	1.00	1.25
2008	—	—	—	—	1.00	1.25
2009	—	—	—	—	1.00	1.25
2010	—	—	—	—	1.00	1.25
2010 Proof	5,000	Value: 6.00				

KM# 72 20 EURO CENT

5.7300 g., Brass, 22.3 mm. **Obv:** Two Lipizzaner horses prancing left **Obv. Legend:** SLOVENIJA, star between each letter **Rev:** Value and map **Edge:** Notched

Date	Mintage	F	VF	XF	Unc	BU
2007	37,250,000	—	—	—	1.25	1.50
2008	—	—	—	—	1.25	1.50
2009	—	—	—	—	1.25	1.50
2010	—	—	—	—	1.25	1.50
2010 Proof	5,000	Value: 7.00				

KM# 73 50 EURO CENT

7.8100 g., Brass, 24.2 mm. **Obv:** Mountain and stars **Rev:** Value and map **Edge:** Reeded

Date	Mintage	F	VF	XF	Unc	BU
2007	32,400,000	—	—	—	1.50	2.00
2008	—	—	—	—	1.50	2.00
2009	—	—	—	—	1.50	2.00
2010	—	—	—	—	1.50	2.00
2010 Proof	5,000	Value: 8.00				

KM# 74 EURO

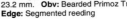

7.5000 g., Bi-Metallic Copper-Nickel center in Brass ring, 23.2 mm. **Obv:** Bearded Primoz Trubar **Rev:** Value and map **Edge:** Segmented reeding

Date	Mintage	F	VF	XF	Unc	BU
2007	29,750,000	—	—	—	2.50	3.50
2008	—	—	—	—	2.50	3.50
2009	—	—	—	—	2.50	3.50
2010	—	—	—	—	2.50	3.50
2010 Proof	5,000	Value: 15.00				

KM# 75 2 EURO
8.5000 g., Bi-Metallic Nickel-Brass center in Copper-Nickel ring, 25.75 mm. **Obv:** France Preseren silhouette and signature **Rev:** Value and map **Edge:** Reeded and lettered

Date	Mintage	F	VF	XF	Unc	BU
2007	21,250,000	—	—	—	4.00	5.00
2008	—	—	—	—	4.00	5.00
2009	—	—	—	—	4.00	5.00
2010	—	—	—	—	4.00	5.00
2010 Proof	5,000	Value: 20.00				

KM# 80 2 EURO
8.5200 g., Bi-Metallic Brass center in Copper-Nickel ring, 25.7 mm. **Subject:** 500th Anniversary Birth of Primoz Tubar **Obv:** Bust of Trubar left at right **Rev:** Large "2" at left, modified map of Europe at right **Edge:** Reeded

Date	Mintage	F	VF	XF	Unc	BU
2008	950,000	—	—	—	6.00	8.00
2008 Special Unc.	10,000	—	—	—	—	32.50
2008 Proof	—	Value: 45.00				

KM# 82 2 EURO
8.5200 g., Bi-Metallic Brass center in Copper-Nickel ring., 25.7 mm. **Subject:** European Monetary Union, 10th Anniversary **Obv:** Stick figure and large E symbol **Rev:** Value at left, modified map of Europe at left

Date	Mintage	F	VF	XF	Unc	BU
2009	—	—	—	—	5.00	6.00
2009 Special Unc.	—	—	—	—	—	32.50
2009 Proof	—	Value: 40.00				

KM# 94 2 EURO
8.5000 g., Bi-Metallic Brass center in Copper-Nickel ring, 27.52 mm. **Subject:** Ljubjuana Botanical Gardens, 200th Anniversary

Date	Mintage	F	VF	XF	Unc	BU
2010	—	—	—	—	8.00	10.00

KM# 100 2 EURO
8.5200 g., Bi-Metallic Brass center in Copper-Nickel ring, 27.52 mm. **Subject:** Franc razman, 100th Anniversary of Birth

Date	Mintage	F	VF	XF	Unc	BU
2011	—	—	—	—	6.00	8.00

KM# 81 3 EURO
15.0000 g., Bi-Metallic Copper-Nickel center in Brass ring, 32 mm. **Subject:** Six Month Term as President of the EU 2008 **Obv:** Field of stars representing EU membership **Rev:** Pinwheel

Date	Mintage	F	VF	XF	Unc	BU
2008	348,000	—	—	—	8.00	10.00
2008 Special Unc.	148,000	—	—	—	—	20.00
2008 Proof	4,000	Value: 165				

KM# 85 3 EURO
15.0000 g., Bi-Metallic Copper-Nickel center in Aluminum-Bronze ring, 32 mm. **Subject:** First Airplane flight in Slovenia by Edvard Rusjan, 100th Anniversary

Date	Mintage	F	VF	XF	Unc	BU
2009	300,000	—	—	—	8.00	10.00

KM# 95 3 EURO
15.0000 g., Copper-Nickel, 32 mm. **Subject:** UNESCO - World Book Capital, Ljubljana

Date	Mintage	F	VF	XF	Unc	BU
2010	—	—	—	—	—	10.00

KM# 101 3 EURO
15.0000 g., Copper-Nickel, 32 mm. **Subject:** Independence, 20th Anniversary

Date	Mintage	F	VF	XF	Unc	BU
2011	5,000	—	—	—	—	15.00
2011 Proof	4,000	Value: 20.00				

KM# 76 30 EURO
15.0000 g., 0.9250 Silver 0.4461 oz. ASW, 32 mm. **Subject:** 250th Anniversary Birth of Valentin Vodnik **Obv:** Value **Obv. Legend:** SLOVENIJA **Rev:** Large bust of Vodnik left

Date	Mintage	F	VF	XF	Unc	BU
2008 Proof	8,000	Value: 100				

KM# 78 30 EURO
15.0000 g., 0.9250 Silver 0.4461 oz. ASW, 32 mm. **Subject:** EU President **Obv:** EU membership stars **Obv. Legend:** SLOVENIJA **Rev:** Pinwheel 5-pointed star

Date	Mintage	F	VF	XF	Unc	BU
2008 Proof	8,000	Value: 150				

KM# 86 30 EURO
15.0000 g., 0.9250 Silver 0.4461 oz. ASW, 32 mm. **Subject:** First Airplane, 100th Anniversary

Date	Mintage	F	VF	XF	Unc	BU
2009 Proof	8,000	Value: 65.00				

KM# 88 30 EURO
15.0000 g., 0.9250 Silver 0.4461 oz. ASW, 32 mm. **Subject:** Zoran Music, painter

Date	Mintage	F	VF	XF	Unc	BU
2009 Proof	—	Value: 70.00				

KM# 96 30 EURO
15.0000 g., 0.9250 Silver 0.4461 oz. ASW, 32 mm. **Subject:** UNESCO - World Book Capital, Ljubljana

Date	Mintage	F	VF	XF	Unc	BU
2010 Proof	—	Value: 65.00				

KM# 98 30 EURO
15.0000 g., 0.9250 Silver 0.4461 oz. ASW, 32 mm. **Subject:** World Ski Jumping Championships, Planica

Date	Mintage	F	VF	XF	Unc	BU
2010 Proof	—	Value: 70.00				

KM# 102 30 EURO
15.0000 g., 0.9250 Silver 0.4461 oz. ASW, 32 mm. **Subject:** Independence, 20th Anniversary

Date	Mintage	F	VF	XF	Unc	BU
2011 Proof	—	Value: 65.00				

KM# 104 30 EURO
15.0000 g., 0.9250 Silver 0.4461 oz. ASW, 32 mm. **Series:** World Rowing Championships

Date	Mintage	F	VF	XF	Unc	BU
2011 Proof	—	Value: 65.00				

KM# 77 100 EURO
7.0000 g., 0.9000 Gold 0.2025 oz. AGW, 24 mm. **Subject:** 250th Anniversary Birth of Valentin Vodnik **Obv:** Value **Obv. Legend:** SLOVENIJA **Rev:** Large bust of Vodnik left

Date	Mintage	F	VF	XF	Unc	BU
2008 Proof	5,000	Value: 425				

KM# 79 100 EURO
7.0000 g., 0.9000 Gold 0.2025 oz. AGW, 24 mm. **Subject:** EU President **Obv:** EU membership stars **Obv. Legend:** SLOVENIJA **Rev:** Pinwheel 5-pointed star

Date	Mintage	F	VF	XF	Unc	BU
2008 Proof	5,000	Value: 650				

KM# 87 100 EURO
7.0000 g., 0.9000 Gold 0.2025 oz. AGW, 24 mm. **Subject:** First Airplane, 100th Anniversary

Date	Mintage	F	VF	XF	Unc	BU
2009 Proof	6,000	Value: 350				

KM# 89 100 EURO
7.0000 g., 0.9000 Gold 0.2025 oz. AGW, 24 mm. **Subject:** Zoran Music, painter

Date	Mintage	F	VF	XF	Unc	BU
2009 Proof	—	Value: 350				

KM# 97 100 EURO
7.0000 g., 0.9000 Gold 0.2025 oz. AGW, 24 mm. **Subject:** UNESCO - World Book Capital, Ljubljana

Date	Mintage	F	VF	XF	Unc	BU
2010 Proof	—	Value: 365				

KM# 99 100 EURO
7.0000 g., 0.9000 Gold 0.2025 oz. AGW, 24 mm. **Subject:** World Ski Jumping Championships, Planica

Date	Mintage	F	VF	XF	Unc	BU
2010 Proof	—	Value: 365				

KM# 103 100 EURO
7.0000 g., 0.9000 Gold 0.2025 oz. AGW, 24 mm. **Subject:** Indpendence, 20th Anniversary

Date	Mintage	F	VF	XF	Unc	BU
2011 Proof	—	Value: 375				

KM# 105 100 EURO
7.0000 g., 0.9000 Gold 0.2025 oz. AGW, 24 mm. **Subject:** World Rowing Championships

Date	Mintage	F	VF	XF	Unc	BU
2011 Proof	—	Value: 365				

MINT SETS

KM#	Date	Mintage	Identification	Issue Price	Mkt Val
MS10	2001 (7)	1,000	KM#3-8, 41	20.00	40.00
MS11	2002 (8)	1,000	KM#3-8, 41, 45	—	45.00
MS12	2003 (10)	1,000	KM#3-8, 41, 50-52	—	55.00
MS13	2004 (10)	1,000	KM#3-8, 41, 51, 52, 57	—	45.00
MS14	2005 (9)	3,000	KM#3-8, 41, 51, 52	25.00	45.00
MS15	2006 (10)	4,000	KM#3-8, 41, 51, 52, 65	25.00	50.00

PROOF SETS

KM#	Date	Mintage	Identification	Issue Price	Mkt Val
PS13	2001 (8)	800	KM#3-8, 41, 42	—	70.00
PS14	2002 (8)	800	KM#3-8, 41, 45	—	70.00
PS15	2003 (10)	800	KM#3-8, 41, 50-52	22.50	100
PS16	2004 (10)	500	KM#3-8, 41, 51-52, 57	—	120
PS17	2005 (10)	1,000	KM#3-8, 41, 51-52, 63	—	95.00
PS18	2006 (10)	1,000	KM#3-8, 41, 51-52, 65	—	95.00

SOLOMON ISLANDS

The Solomon Islands are made up of about 200 islands. They are located in the southwest Pacific east of Papua New Guinea, have an area of 10,983 sq. mi. (28,450 sq. km.) and a population of *552,000. Capital: Honiara. The most important islands of the Solomon chain are Guadalcanal (scene of some of the fiercest fighting of World War II), Malaitia, New Georgia, Florida, Vella Lavella, Choiseul, Rendova, San Cristobal, the Lord Howe group, the Santa Cruz islands, and the Duff group. Copra is the only important cash crop but it is hoped that timber will become an economic factor.

Solomon Islands is a member of the Commonwealth of Nations. Queen Elizabeth II is Head of State, as Queen of the Solomon Islands.

RULER
British

MONETARY SYSTEM
100 Cents = 1 Dollar

COMMONWEALTH NATION

STANDARD COINAGE

KM# 24 CENT
2.3000 g., Bronze Plated Steel, 17.53 mm. **Ruler:** Elizabeth II **Obv:** Crowned head right **Obv. Legend:** ELIZABETH II - SOLOMON ISLANDS **Rev:** Food bowl divides value **Edge:** Plain

Date	Mintage	F	VF	XF	Unc	BU
2005	—	—	—	—	0.35	0.75

KM# 25 2 CENTS
Bronze Plated Steel, 21.6 mm. **Ruler:** Elizabeth II **Obv:** Crowned head right **Obv. Legend:** ELIZABETH II - SOLOMON ISLANDS **Rev:** Eagle spirit below value **Rev. Designer:** David Thomas **Edge:** Plain

Date	Mintage	F	VF	XF	Unc	BU
2005	—	—	—	—	0.35	0.75
2006	—	—	—	—	0.35	0.75

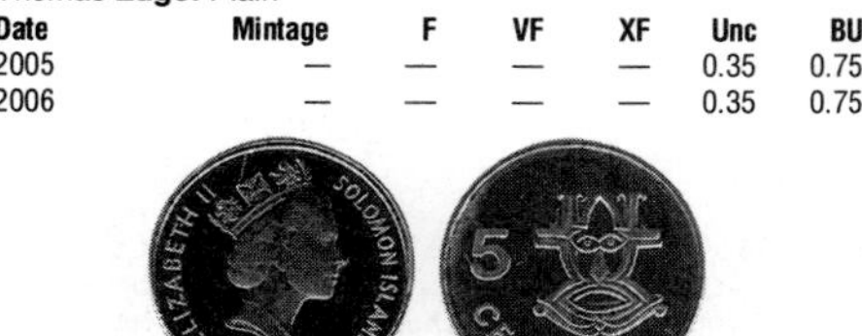

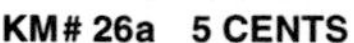

KM# 26a 5 CENTS
Nickel Plated Steel, 18.40 mm. **Ruler:** Elizabeth II **Obv:** Crowned bust right **Obv. Legend:** ELIZABETH II - SOLOMON ISLANDS **Rev:** Value at left, native mask at center right **Rev. Designer:** David Thomas

Date	Mintage	F	VF	XF	Unc	BU
2005	—	—	—	—	0.50	1.00

KM# 27a 10 CENTS
Nickel Plated Steel, 23.6 mm. **Ruler:** Elizabeth II **Subject:** Ngorieru **Obv:** Crowned head right **Obv. Legend:** ELIZABETH II - SOLOMON ISLANDS **Rev:** Sea spirit divides value **Rev. Designer:** David Thomas **Edge:** Reeded

Date	Mintage	F	VF	XF	Unc	BU
2005	—	—	—	—	0.65	1.00

KM# 28 20 CENTS
11.2500 g., Nickel Plated Steel, 28.5 mm. **Ruler:** Elizabeth II **Obv:** Crowned head right **Obv. Legend:** ELIZABETH II - SOLOMON ISLANDS **Rev:** Malaita pendant design within circle, denomination appears twice in legend **Rev. Designer:** David Thomas **Edge:** Reeded

Date	Mintage	F	VF	XF	Unc	BU
2005	—	—	—	—	0.85	1.25

KM# 29 50 CENTS
10.0000 g., Copper-Nickel, 29.5 mm. **Ruler:** Elizabeth II **Obv:** Crowned head right **Obv. Legend:** ELIZABETH II - SOLOMON ISLANDS **Rev:** Arms with supporters **Edge:** Plain **Shape:** 12-sided **Note:** Circulation type.

Date	Mintage	F	VF	XF	Unc	BU
2005	—	—	—	—	2.00	3.00

KM# 72 DOLLAR
13.4500 g., Copper-Nickel, 30 mm. **Ruler:** Elizabeth II **Obv:** Crowned head right **Obv. Legend:** ELIZABETH II - SOLOMON ISLANDS **Rev:** Sea spirit statue divides value **Rev. Designer:** David Thomas **Edge:** Plain **Shape:** 7-sided

Date	Mintage	F	VF	XF	Unc	BU
2005	—	—	—	—	2.50	4.00

KM# 83 2 DOLLARS
62.2700 g., 0.9990 Silver 1.9999 oz. ASW, 50.3 mm. **Subject:** Regional Assistance Mission to Solomon Islands **Obv:** Crowned head right **Rev:** Dove outline over multicolor islands in a sea of country names **Edge:** Reeded

Date	Mintage	F	VF	XF	Unc	BU
2005 Proof	2,500	Value: 75.00				

KM# 113 5 DOLLARS
28.2800 g., 0.9250 Silver partially gilt 0.8410 oz. ASW, 38.6 mm. **Ruler:** Elizabeth II **Obv:** Bust right gilt **Rev:** Orb

Date	Mintage	F	VF	XF	Unc	BU
2002 Proof	20,000	Value: 40.00				

KM# 75 5 DOLLARS
28.2800 g., Copper-Nickel, 38.6 mm. **Obv:** Crowned head right **Obv. Designer:** Raphael Maklouf **Rev:** F-117A Nighthawk Stealth fighter plane **Edge:** Reeded

Date	Mintage	F	VF	XF	Unc	BU
2003	—	—	—	—	5.00	7.00

KM# 76 5 DOLLARS
28.2800 g., Copper-Nickel, 38.6 mm. **Obv:** Crowned head right **Obv. Designer:** Raphael Maklouf **Rev:** Concorde supersonic airliner **Edge:** Reeded

Date	Mintage	F	VF	XF	Unc	BU
2003	—	—	—	—	5.00	7.00

KM# 84 5 DOLLARS
31.1035 g., 0.9990 Silver 0.9990 oz. ASW, 38.6 mm. **Obv:** Maklouf's portrait of Elizabeth II **Rev:** Gold plated pig **Edge:** Reeded **Note:** Year of the Pig

Date	Mintage	F	VF	XF	Unc	BU
2007	10,000	—	—	—	—	50.00

KM# 85 5 DOLLARS
31.1035 g., 0.9990 Silver 0.9990 oz. ASW, 38.6 mm. **Obv:** Maklouf's portrait of Elizabeth II **Rev:** Dark red pig and piglet **Edge:** Reeded **Note:** Year of the Pig

Date	Mintage	F	VF	XF	Unc	BU
2007	10,000	—	—	—	—	50.00

KM# 86 10 DOLLARS
28.3600 g., Silver, 38.6 mm. **Obv:** Crowned bust right **Obv. Legend:** ELIZABETH II - SOLOMON ISLANDS **Rev:** Bust of Mendana facing at left, early sailing ship at center - right **Rev. Legend:** ALVARO DE MENDANA **Edge:** Reeded

Date	Mintage	F	VF	XF	Unc	BU
2004 Proof	—	Value: 50.00				

KM# 96 10 DOLLARS
1.2200 g., 0.9990 Gold 0.0392 oz. AGW, 14 mm. **Ruler:** Elizabeth II **Subject:** Wonders of the Ancient World **Obv:** Head right **Rev:** Mausoleum of Mauussollos of Halicarnassus

Date	Mintage	F	VF	XF	Unc	BU
2007 Proof	7,000	Value: 75.00				

KM# 97 10 DOLLARS
1.2200 g., 0.9990 Gold 0.0392 oz. AGW, 14 mm. **Ruler:** Elizabeth II **Subject:** Wonders of the Ancient World **Obv:** Head right **Rev:** Taj Mahal

Date	Mintage	F	VF	XF	Unc	BU
2007 7000	—	Value: 75.00				

KM# 98 10 DOLLARS
1.2200 g., 0.9990 Gold 0.0392 oz. AGW, 14 mm. **Ruler:** Elizabeth II **Subject:** Wonders of the Ancient World **Obv:** Head right **Rev:** Treasury at Petra

Date	Mintage	F	VF	XF	Unc	BU
2007 Proof	7,000	Value: 75.00				

KM# 99 10 DOLLARS
1.2200 g., 0.9990 Gold 0.0392 oz. AGW, 14 mm. **Ruler:** Elizabeth II **Subject:** Wonders of the Ancient World **Obv:** Head right **Rev:** Coliseum in Rome

Date	Mintage	F	VF	XF	Unc	BU
2007 Proof	7,000	Value: 75.00				

KM# 100 10 DOLLARS
1.2200 g., 0.9990 Gold 0.0392 oz. AGW, 14 mm. **Ruler:** Elizabeth II **Subject:** Wonders of the Ancient World **Obv:** Head right **Rev:** Inca's Machu Kicuhu

Date	Mintage	F	VF	XF	Unc	BU
2007 Proof	7,000	Value: 75.00				

KM# 101 10 DOLLARS
1.2200 g., 0.9990 Gold 0.0392 oz. AGW, 14 mm. **Ruler:** Elizabeth II **Subject:** Wonders of the Ancient World **Obv:** Head right **Rev:** Chichen Itza

Date	Mintage	F	VF	XF	Unc	BU
2007 Proof	7,000	Value: 75.00				

KM# 102 10 DOLLARS
1.2200 g., 0.9990 Gold 0.0392 oz. AGW, 14 mm. **Ruler:** Elizabeth II **Subject:** Wonders of the World **Obv:** Head right **Rev:** Great wall of China

Date	Mintage	F	VF	XF	Unc	BU
2007 Proof	7,000	Value: 75.00				

KM# 103 10 DOLLARS
1.2200 g., 0.9990 Gold 0.0392 oz. AGW, 14 mm. **Ruler:** Elizabeth II **Subject:** Wonders of the World **Rev:** Christ Statue in Rio

Date	Mintage	F	VF	XF	Unc	BU
2007 Proof	7,000	Value: 75.00				

KM# 104 10 DOLLARS
1.2200 g., Gold, 14 mm. **Ruler:** Elizabeth II **Subject:** Seven Wonders of the World **Obv:** Head right **Rev:** Giza Pyramids

Date	Mintage	F	VF	XF	Unc	BU
2009 Proof	7,500	Value: 75.00				

KM# 105 10 DOLLARS
1.2200 g., 0.9990 Gold 0.0392 oz. AGW, 14 mm. **Ruler:** Elizabeth II **Subject:** Seven Wonders of the World **Obv:** Head right **Rev:** Colossus of Rhodes

Date	Mintage	F	VF	XF	Unc	BU
2009 Proof	7,500	Value: 75.00				

KM# 106 10 DOLLARS
1.2200 g., 0.9990 Gold 0.0392 oz. AGW, 14 mm. **Ruler:** Elizabeth II **Subject:** Seven Wonders of the World **Obv:** Head right **Rev:** Statue of Zeus at Olympia

Date	Mintage	F	VF	XF	Unc	BU
2009 Proof	7,500	Value: 75.00				

KM# 107 10 DOLLARS
1.2200 g., 0.9990 Gold 0.0392 oz. AGW, 14 mm. **Ruler:** Elizabeth II **Subject:** Seven Wonders of the World **Obv:** Head right **Rev:** Temple of Artemis at Ephesus

Date	Mintage	F	VF	XF	Unc	BU
2009 Proof	7,500	Value: 75.00				

KM# 108 10 DOLLARS
1.2200 g., 0.9990 Gold 0.0392 oz. AGW, 14 mm. **Ruler:** Elizabeth II **Subject:** Seven Wonders of the World **Obv:** Head right **Rev:** Hanging Gardens of Bablyon

Date	Mintage	F	VF	XF	Unc	BU
2009 Proof	7,500	Value: 75.00				

KM# 109 10 DOLLARS
1.2200 g., 0.9990 Gold 0.0392 oz. AGW, 14 mm. **Ruler:** Elizabeth II **Subject:** Seven Wonders of the World **Obv:** Head right **Rev:** Lighthouse at Alexandria

Date	Mintage	F	VF	XF	Unc	BU
2009 Proof	7,500	Value: 75.00				

KM# 110 10 DOLLARS
1.2200 g., 0.9990 Gold 0.0392 oz. AGW, 14 mm. **Ruler:** Elizabeth II **Subject:** Seven Wonders of the World **Obv:** Head right

Date	Mintage	F	VF	XF	Unc	BU
2009 Proof	7,500	Value: 75.00				

KM# 90 25 DOLLARS
31.1050 g., 0.9990 Silver 0.9990 oz. ASW, 36.6 mm. **Ruler:** Elizabeth II **Obv:** Head right **Rev:** Wright Brother's 1903 Flyer

Date	Mintage	F	VF	XF	Unc	BU
2003 Proof	—	Value: 42.00				

KM# 91 25 DOLLARS
31.1050 g., 0.9990 Silver 0.9990 oz. ASW, 36.6 mm. **Ruler:** Elizabeth II **Obv:** Head right **Rev:** AN-225 Mriya

Date	Mintage	F	VF	XF	Unc	BU
2003 Proof	—	Value: 42.00				

KM# 92 25 DOLLARS
31.1050 g., 0.9990 Silver 0.9990 oz. ASW, 36.6 mm. **Ruler:** Elizabeth II **Obv:** Head right **Rev:** Spitfire

Date	Mintage	F	VF	XF	Unc	BU
2003 Proof	—	Value: 42.00				

KM# 115 25 DOLLARS
31.1000 g., 0.9250 Silver 0.9249 oz. ASW, 38.6 mm. **Ruler:** Elizabeth II **Obv:** Messerschmitt ME 262

Date	Mintage	F	VF	XF	Unc	BU
2003 Proof	—	Value: 42.00				

KM# 93 25 DOLLARS
31.1050 g., 0.9990 Silver 0.9990 oz. ASW **Ruler:** Elizabeth II **Subject:** Trafalgar **Obv:** Head right **Rev:** H.M.S. Victory

Date	Mintage	F	VF	XF	Unc	BU
2005 Proof	—	Value: 42.00				

KM# 114 25 DOLLARS
0.9250 Silver gilt, 50 mm. **Ruler:** Elizabeth II **Rev:** Wright flier of 1903

Date	Mintage	F	VF	XF	Unc	BU
2005 Proof	—	Value: 75.00				

KM# 87 25 DOLLARS
0.9250 Silver **Ruler:** Elizabeth II **Obv:** Crowned bust right **Obv. Legend:** ELIZABETH II - SOLOMON ISLANDS **Rev:** 3/4 length figures of Elizabeth and Prince Philip facing

Date	Mintage	F	VF	XF	Unc	BU
2006 Proof	—	Value: 45.00				

KM# 95 25 DOLLARS
31.1050 g., 0.9990 Silver partially gilt 0.9990 oz. ASW **Ruler:** Elizabeth II **Obv:** Head right, partially gilt **Rev:** Queen Elizabeth II and WWII Red Cross Nurse, gilt 80 above.

Date	Mintage	F	VF	XF	Unc	BU
2006 Proof	—	Value: 42.00				

KM# 87a 25 DOLLARS
31.1050 g., 0.9990 Silver partially gilt 0.9990 oz. ASW **Ruler:** Elizabeth II **Obv:** Head right, partially gilt **Rev:** Wedding of Elizabeth II and Philip. Gothic window behind, gilt 80 above.

Date	Mintage	F	VF	XF	Unc	BU
2006 Proof	—	Value: 45.00				

KM# 116 25 DOLLARS
28.2800 g., 0.9250 Silver 0.8410 oz. ASW, 38.6 mm. **Ruler:** Elizabeth II **Rev:** Press clippings, soldier standing over field cross

Date	Mintage	F	VF	XF	Unc	BU
2008	—	—	—	—	—	42.00

KM# 117 25 DOLLARS
28.2800 g., 0.9250 Silver 0.8410 oz. ASW, 38.6 mm. **Rev:** Battlefield

Date	Mintage	F	VF	XF	Unc	BU
2008 Proof	—	Value: 42.00				

KM# 118 25 DOLLARS
28.2800 g., 0.9250 Silver 0.8410 oz. ASW, 38.6 mm. **Ruler:** Elizabeth II **Rev:** Soldier overlooking beach

Date	Mintage	F	VF	XF	Unc	BU
2008 Proof	—	Value: 42.00				

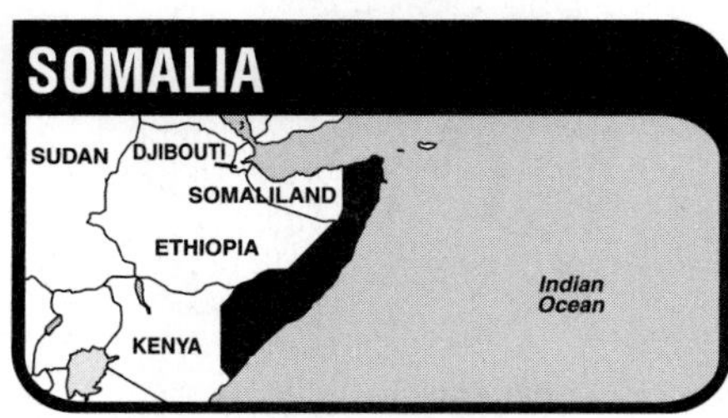

The Somali Democratic Republic consists of the former Italian Somaliland and is located on the coast of the eastern projection of the African continent commonly referred to as the "Horn". It has an area of 178,201 sq. mi. (461,657 sq. km.) and a population of *8.2 million. Capital: Mogadishu. The economy is pastoral and agricultural. Livestock, bananas and hides are exported.

The Northern Somali National Movement (SNM) declared a secession of the northwestern Somaliland Republic on May 17, 1991, which is not recognized by the Somali Democratic Republic.

TITLE
Al-Jumhuriya(t)as - Somaliya(t)

REPUBLIC OF SOMALIA

STANDARD COINAGE

KM# 45 5 SHILLING / SCELLINI
1.2900 g., Aluminum, 21 mm. **Series:** F.A.O. **Obv:** Crowned arms with supporters **Rev:** Elephant **Edge:** Plain

Date	Mintage	F	VF	XF	Unc	BU
2002	—	—	—	—	1.50	1.75

KM# 159 10 SHILLINGS
25.1500 g., Copper-Nickel, 38.66 mm. **Series:** Marine Life Protection **Obv:** National arms **Rev:** Two fish multicolor **Edge:** Reeded

Date	Mintage	F	VF	XF	Unc	BU
2003 Proof	—	Value: 10.00				

KM# 46 10 SHILLINGS / SCELLINI
1.2900 g., Aluminum, 21.9 mm. **Series:** F.A.O. **Obv:** Crowned arms with supporters **Rev:** Camel **Edge:** Plain

Date	Mintage	F	VF	XF	Unc	BU
2002	—	—	—	—	2.00	2.25

KM# 175 20 SHILLINGS
0.6200 g., 0.9990 Gold 0.0199 oz. AGW **Obv:** Arms **Rev:** Mom and baby elephant

Date	Mintage	F	VF	XF	Unc	BU
2007 Proof	—	Value: 50.00				

KM# 166 25 SHILLINGS
Silver **Obv:** Arms **Rev:** Mozart, multicolor

Date	Mintage	F	VF	XF	Unc	BU
2001	—	—	—	—	—	40.00

KM# 155 25 SHILLINGS
28.1000 g., Copper-Nickel, 38.73 mm. **Subject:** The Life of Pope John-Paul II **Obv:** National arms **Obv. Legend:** SOMALI REPUBLIC **Rev:** Pope John-Paul II in window at the Vatican **Edge:** Plain

Date	Mintage	F	VF	XF	Unc	BU
2004	—	—	—	—	6.00	7.00

KM# 156 25 SHILLINGS
28.1000 g., Copper-Nickel, 38.73 mm. **Subject:** Life of Pope John Paul II **Obv:** National arms **Obv. Legend:** SOMALI REPUBLIC **Rev:** Pope traveling in special vehicle **Edge:** Plain

Date	Mintage	F	VF	XF	Unc	BU
2004	—	—	—	—	6.00	7.00

KM# 157 25 SHILLINGS
28.1000 g., Copper-Nickel, 38.73 mm. **Subject:** The Life of Pope John-Paul II **Obv:** National arms **Obv. Legend:** SOMALI REPUBLIC **Rev:** Pope blessing Mother Teresa **Edge:** Plain

Date	Mintage	F	VF	XF	Unc	BU
2004	—	—	—	—	6.00	7.00

KM# 164 25 SHILLINGS
25.8000 g., Copper-Nickel, 38.77 mm. **Obv:** National arms **Obv. Legend:** SOMALI REPUBLIC **Rev:** Black rhinoceros walking left **Edge:** Reeded

Date	Mintage	F	VF	XF	Unc	BU
2006	—	—	—	—	9.00	12.00

KM# 165 25 SHILLINGS
25.8000 g., Copper-Nickel, 38.77 mm. **Obv:** National arms **Rev:** Red Kite perched on branch **Edge:** Reeded

Date	Mintage	F	VF	XF	Unc	BU
2006	—	—	—	—	12.00	14.00

KM# 103 25 SHILLINGS / SCELLINI
4.3700 g., Brass, 21.8 mm. **Subject:** Soccer **Obv:** Crowned arms with supporters **Rev:** Soccer player **Edge:** Plain

Date	Mintage	F	VF	XF	Unc	BU
2001	—	—	—	—	1.25	1.50

KM# 111 50 SHILLINGS
3.9000 g., Nickel Clad Steel, 21.9 mm. **Obv:** Crowned arms with supporters **Rev:** Mandrill **Edge:** Plain

Date	Mintage	F	VF	XF	Unc	BU
2002	—	—	—	—	0.85	1.25

KM# 161 50 SHILLINGS
1.2000 g., Gold, 13.88 mm. **Subject:** Gold of the Pharaohs **Obv:** National arms **Obv. Legend:** SOMALI REPUBLIC **Rev:** King Tutankhaman's death mask **Edge:** Reeded

Date	Mintage	F	VF	XF	Unc	BU
2002 Proof	—	Value: 75.00				

KM# 109 100 SHILLINGS
10.5000 g., 0.9990 Silver 0.3372 oz. ASW, 30.1 mm. **Subject:** Soccer **Obv:** Crowned arms with supporters **Rev:** Multicolor soccer player and Brandenburg Gate **Edge:** Reeded

Date	Mintage	F	VF	XF	Unc	BU
2001 Proof	—	Value: 25.00				

KM# 112 100 SHILLINGS
3.5400 g., Brass, 18.8 mm. **Obv:** Crowned arms with supporters above value **Rev:** Bust with headdress facing **Edge:** Plain

Date	Mintage	F	VF	XF	Unc	BU
2002	—	—	—	—	1.50	2.50

KM# 182 100 SHILLINGS
31.1050 g., 0.9990 Silver 0.9990 oz. ASW, 39 mm. **Obv:** Arms **Rev:** Mom and baby elephant, multicolor

Date	Mintage	F	VF	XF	Unc	BU
2007	—	—	—	—	—	45.00

KM# 167a 100 SHILLINGS
31.1050 g., 0.9990 Silver partially gilt 0.9990 oz. ASW, 39 mm. **Obv:** Arms **Rev:** Heard of six elephants

Date	Mintage	F	VF	XF	Unc	BU
2008	—	—	—	—	—	35.00

KM# 167 100 SHILLINGS
31.1050 g., 0.9990 Silver 0.9990 oz. ASW, 39 mm. **Rev:** Heard of six elephants

Date	Mintage	F	VF	XF	Unc	BU
2008	—	—	—	—	—	35.00

KM# 176 200 SHILLINGS
0.6200 g., 0.9990 Gold 0.0199 oz. AGW, 13.90 mm. **Obv:** Arms **Rev:** Elephant head left

Date	Mintage	F	VF	XF	Unc	BU
2005 Proof	—	Value: 50.00				

KM# 168 250 SHILLINGS
Silver **Obv:** Arms **Rev:** Victoria, gothic crown

Date	Mintage	F	VF	XF	Unc	BU
2001 Proof	—	Value: 25.00				

KM# 169 250 SHILLINGS
Silver **Obv:** Arms **Rev:** Soccer player, Brazil

Date	Mintage	F	VF	XF	Unc	BU
2002	—	—	—	—	—	25.00

KM# 158 250 SHILLINGS
20.0500 g., Silver, 38.59 mm. **Obv:** National arms **Obv. Legend:** SOMALI REPUBLIC **Rev:** Laureate bust of Julius Caesar 3/4 left **Edge:** Reeded

Date	Mintage	F	VF	XF	Unc	BU
2002 Proof	—	Value: 32.00				

KM# 162 250 SHILLINGS
1.2700 g., Gold, 13.90 mm. **Obv:** National arms **Obv. Legend:** SOMALI REPUBLIC **Rev:** Bust of Hans Rühmann facing **Edge:** Reeded

Date	Mintage	F	VF	XF	Unc	BU
2002 Proof	—	Value: 75.00				

KM# 110 250 SHILLINGS
31.1050 g., 0.9990 Silver 0.9990 oz. ASW, 40 mm. **Subject:** Queen of Sheba **Obv:** Crowned arms with supporters **Rev:** Crowned bust 1/4 right **Edge:** Reeded

Date	Mintage	F	VF	XF	Unc	BU
2002	—	—	—	—	35.00	40.00

KM# 160 250 SHILLINGS

20.5000 g., Silver, 38.56 mm. **Subject:** Wembley Goal - England 1966 **Obv:** National arms **Obv. Legend:** SOMALI REPUBLIC **Rev:** 3 soccer players at goal **Edge:** Reeded

Date	Mintage	F	VF	XF	Unc	BU
2003 Proof	—	Value: 25.00				

KM# 121 250 SHILLINGS

20.1200 g., Silver Plated Base Metal, 38.5 mm. **Obv:** Crowned arms with supporters **Rev:** Multicolor Pope John Paul II and mountains **Edge:** Reeded

Date	Mintage	F	VF	XF	Unc	BU
2005 Proof	—	Value: 16.50				

KM# 123 250 SHILLINGS

20.1200 g., Silver Plated Base Metal, 38.5 mm. **Obv:** Crowned arms with supporters **Rev:** Multicolor Pope John Paul II kissing bible **Edge:** Reeded

Date	Mintage	F	VF	XF	Unc	BU
2005 Proof	—	Value: 16.50				

KM# 125 250 SHILLINGS

20.1200 g., Silver Plated Base Metal, 38.5 mm. **Obv:** Crowned arms with supporters **Rev:** Multicolor Pope John Paul II with flowers **Edge:** Reeded

Date	Mintage	F	VF	XF	Unc	BU
2005 Proof	—	Value: 16.50				

KM# 127 250 SHILLINGS

20.1200 g., Silver Plated Base Metal, 38.5 mm. **Obv:** Crowned arms with supporters **Rev:** Multicolor Pope John Paul II saying mass **Edge:** Reeded

Date	Mintage	F	VF	XF	Unc	BU
2005 Proof	—	Value: 16.50				

KM# 129 250 SHILLINGS

20.1200 g., Silver Plated Base Metal, 38.5 mm. **Obv:** Crowned arms with supporters **Rev:** Multicolor Pope John Paul II with cardinals **Edge:** Reeded

Date	Mintage	F	VF	XF	Unc	BU
2005 Proof	—	Value: 16.50				

KM# 131 250 SHILLINGS

20.1200 g., Silver Plated Base Metal, 38.5 mm. **Obv:** Crowned arms with supporters **Rev:** Pope John Paul II with red vestments **Edge:** Reeded

Date	Mintage	F	VF	XF	Unc	BU
2005 Proof	—	Value: 16.50				

KM# 133 250 SHILLINGS

20.1200 g., Silver Plated Base Metal, 38.5 mm. **Obv:** Crowned arms with supporters **Rev:** Pope John Paul II in white with skull cap **Edge:** Reeded

Date	Mintage	F	VF	XF	Unc	BU
2005 Proof	—	Value: 16.50				

KM# 135 250 SHILLINGS

20.1200 g., Silver Plated Base Metal, 38.5 mm. **Obv:** Crowned arms with supporters **Rev:** Multicolor Pope John Paul II leaning head on staff **Edge:** Reeded

Date	Mintage	F	VF	XF	Unc	BU
2005 Proof	—	Value: 16.50				

KM# 137 250 SHILLINGS

20.1200 g., Silver Plated Base Metal, 38.5 mm. **Obv:** Crowned arms with supporters **Rev:** Multicolor Pope John Paul II with staff facing left **Edge:** Reeded

Date	Mintage	F	VF	XF	Unc	BU
2005 Proof	—	Value: 16.50				

KM# 139 250 SHILLINGS

20.1200 g., Silver Plated Base Metal, 38.5 mm. **Obv:** Crowned arms with supporters **Rev:** Multicolor Pope John Paul II with staff facing half right **Edge:** Reeded

Date	Mintage	F	VF	XF	Unc	BU
2005 Proof	—	Value: 16.50				

KM# 143 250 SHILLINGS

Copper-Nickel **Obv:** Crowned shield **Obv. Legend:** SOMALI REPUBLIC / 250 SHILLINGS **Rev:** Color applique, German Shephard **Rev. Legend:** YEAR OF THE DOG / 2006 **Edge:** Reeded

Date	Mintage	F	VF	XF	Unc	BU
2006	—	—	—	—	—	12.50

KM# 144 250 SHILLINGS

Copper-Nickel **Obv:** Crowned shield **Obv. Legend:** SOMALI REPUBLIC / 250 SHILLINGS **Rev:** Color applique, Dachsund **Rev. Legend:** YEAR OF THE DOG / 2006 **Edge:** Reeded

Date	Mintage	F	VF	XF	Unc	BU
2006	—	—	—	—	—	12.50

KM# 145 250 SHILLINGS

Copper-Nickel **Obv:** Crowned shield **Obv. Legend:** SOMALI REPUBLIC / 250 SHILLINGS **Rev:** Color applique, Yorkshire Terrier **Rev. Legend:** YEAR OF THE DOG / 2006 **Edge:** Reeded

Date	Mintage	F	VF	XF	Unc	BU
2006	—	—	—	—	—	12.50

KM# 146 250 SHILLINGS

Copper-Nickel **Obv:** Crowned shield **Obv. Legend:** SOMALI REPUBLIC / 250 SHILLINGS **Rev:** Color applique, Scottie (small white) **Rev. Legend:** YEAR OF THE DOG / 2006 **Edge:** Reeded

Date	Mintage	F	VF	XF	Unc	BU
2006	—	—	—	—	—	12.50

KM# 147 250 SHILLINGS

Copper-Nickel **Obv:** Crowned shield **Obv. Legend:** SOMALI REPUBLIC / 250 SHILLINGS **Rev:** Color applique, Wire-haired Terrier **Rev. Legend:** YEAR OF THE DOG / 2006 **Edge:** Reeded

Date	Mintage	F	VF	XF	Unc	BU
2006	—	—	—	—	—	12.50

KM# 148 250 SHILLINGS

Copper-Nickel **Obv:** Crowned shield **Obv. Legend:** SOMALI REPUBLIC / 250 SHILLINGS **Rev:** Color applique, Bulldog **Rev. Legend:** YEAR OF THE DOG / 2006 **Edge:** Reeded

Date	Mintage	F	VF	XF	Unc	BU
2006	—	—	—	—	—	12.50

KM# 149 250 SHILLINGS

Copper-Nickel **Obv:** Crowned shield **Obv. Legend:** SOMALI REPUBLIC / 250 SHILLINGS **Rev:** Color applique, Golden Retriever **Rev. Legend:** YEAR OF THE DOG **Edge:** Reeded

Date	Mintage	F	VF	XF	Unc	BU
2006	—	—	—	—	—	12.50

KM# 150 250 SHILLINGS

Copper-Nickel **Obv:** Crowned shield **Obv. Legend:** SOMALI REPUBLIC / 250 SHILLINGS **Rev:** Color applique, St. Bernard **Rev. Legend:** YEAR OF THE DOG / 2006 **Edge:** Reeded

Date	Mintage	F	VF	XF	Unc	BU
2006	—	—	—	—	—	12.50

KM# 151 250 SHILLINGS

Copper-Nickel **Obv:** Crowned shield **Obv. Legend:** SOMALI REPUBLIC / 250 SHILLINGS **Rev:** Color applique, Rottweiler **Rev. Legend:** YEAR OF THE DOG / 2006 **Edge:** Reeded

Date	Mintage	F	VF	XF	Unc	BU
2006	—	—	—	—	—	12.50

KM# 152 250 SHILLINGS

Copper-Nickel **Obv:** Crowned shield **Obv. Legend:** SOMALI REPUBLIC / 250 SHILLINGS **Rev:** Color applique, Basset Hound **Rev. Legend:** YEAR OF THE DOG / 2006 **Edge:** Reeded

Date	Mintage	F	VF	XF	Unc	BU
2006	—	—	—	—	—	12.50

KM# 153 250 SHILLINGS

Copper-Nickel **Obv:** Crowned shield **Obv. Legend:** SOMALI REPUBLIC / 250 SHILLINGS **Rev:** Color applique, Sheep Dog **Rev. Legend:** YEAR OF THE DOG / 2006 **Edge:** Reeded

Date	Mintage	F	VF	XF	Unc	BU
2006	—	—	—	—	—	12.50

KM# 154 250 SHILLINGS

Copper-Nickel **Obv:** Crowned shield **Obv. Legend:** SOMALI REPUBLIC / 250 SHILLINGS **Rev:** Color applique, Cocker Spaniel **Rev. Legend:** YEAR OF THE DOG / 2006 **Edge:** Reeded

Date	Mintage	F	VF	XF	Unc	BU
2006	—	—	—	—	—	12.50

KM# 170 250 SHILLINGS

Copper-Nickel Gilt, 38 mm. **Obv:** Arms in cartouche **Rev:** Gold mask of Tutankahamun, enameled

Date	Mintage	F	VF	XF	Unc	BU
2008	—	—	—	—	—	17.50

KM# 171 250 SHILLINGS

Copper-Nickel Gilt, 38 mm. **Obv:** Arms within cartouche **Rev:** Udjat eye, enameled

Date	Mintage	F	VF	XF	Unc	BU
2008	—	—	—	—	—	40.00

KM# 172 250 SHILLINGS

Copper-Nickel **Obv:** Arms within cartouche **Rev:** Statue of Ptah, enameled

Date	Mintage	F	VF	XF	Unc	BU
2008	—	—	—	—	—	20.00

KM# 173 250 SHILLINGS

Copper-Nickel Gilt, 38 mm. **Obv:** Arms in cartouche **Rev:** Jcarab Pectoral necklace, enameled

Date	Mintage	F	VF	XF	Unc	BU
2008	—	—	—	—	—	20.00

KM# 174 250 SHILLINGS

Copper-Nickel Gilt,V 38 mm. **Obv:** Arms within cartouche **Rev:** Statue of Horus the Elder

Date	Mintage	F	VF	XF	Unc	BU
2008	—	—	—	—	—	20.00

KM# 122 500 SHILLINGS
18.8400 g., Silver Plated Base Metal, 34.1 mm. **Obv:** Crowned arms with supporters **Rev:** Multicolor Pope John Paul II and mountains **Edge:** Plain **Shape:** Square with round corners

Date	Mintage	F	VF	XF	Unc	BU
2005 Proof	—	Value: 16.50				

KM# 124 500 SHILLINGS
18.8400 g., Silver Plated Base Metal, 34.1 mm. **Obv:** Crowned arms with supporters **Rev:** Multicolor Pope John Paul II kissing bible **Edge:** Plain **Shape:** Square with round corners

Date	Mintage	F	VF	XF	Unc	BU
2005 Proof	—	Value: 16.50				

KM# 126 500 SHILLINGS
18.8400 g., Silver Plated Base Metal, 34.1 mm. **Obv:** Crowned arms with supporters **Rev:** Multicolor Pope John Paul II with flowers **Edge:** Plain **Shape:** Square with round corners

Date	Mintage	F	VF	XF	Unc	BU
2005 Proof	—	Value: 20.00				

KM# 128 500 SHILLINGS
18.1400 g., Silver Plated Base Metal, 34.1 mm. **Obv:** Crowned arms with supporters **Rev:** Multicolor Pope John Paul II saying mass **Edge:** Plain **Shape:** Square with round corners

Date	Mintage	F	VF	XF	Unc	BU
2005 Proof	—	Value: 16.50				

KM# 130 500 SHILLINGS
18.8400 g., Silver Plated Base Metal, 34.1 mm. **Obv:** Crowned arms with supporters **Rev:** Multicolor Pope John Paul II with cardinals **Edge:** Plain **Shape:** Square with round corners

Date	Mintage	F	VF	XF	Unc	BU
2005 Proof	—	Value: 16.50				

KM# 132 500 SHILLINGS
18.8400 g., Silver Plated Base Metal, 34.1 mm. **Obv:** Crowned arms with supporters **Rev:** Pope John Paul II with red vestments **Edge:** Plain **Shape:** Square with round corners

Date	Mintage	F	VF	XF	Unc	BU
2005 Proof	—	Value: 16.50				

KM# 134 500 SHILLINGS
18.8400 g., Silver Plated Base Metal, 34.1 mm. **Obv:** Crowned arms with supporters **Rev:** Pope John Paul II in white with skull cap **Edge:** Plain **Shape:** Square with round corners

Date	Mintage	F	VF	XF	Unc	BU
2005 Proof	—	Value: 16.50				

KM# 136 500 SHILLINGS
18.8400 g., Silver Plated Base Metal, 34.1 mm. **Obv:** Crowned arms with supporters **Rev:** Multicolor Pope John Paul II leaning head on staff **Edge:** Plain **Shape:** Square with round corners

Date	Mintage	F	VF	XF	Unc	BU
2005 Proof	—	Value: 16.50				

KM# 138 500 SHILLINGS
18.8400 g., Silver Plated Base Metal, 34.1 mm. **Obv:** Crowned arms with supporters **Rev:** Multicolor Pope John Paul II with staff facing left **Edge:** Plain **Shape:** Square with round corners

Date	Mintage	F	VF	XF	Unc	BU
2005 Proof	—	Value: 16.50				

KM# 140 500 SHILLINGS
18.8400 g., Silver Plated Base Metal, 34.1 mm. **Obv:** Crowned arms with supporters **Rev:** Multicolor Pope John Paul II with staff facing half right **Edge:** Plain **Shape:** Square with round corners

Date	Mintage	F	VF	XF	Unc	BU
2005 Proof	—	Value: 16.50				

KM# 163 1000 SHILLINGS
31.2700 g., 0.9990 Silver 1.0043 oz. ASW, 38.54 mm. **Series:** African Wildlife **Obv:** National arms **Obv. Legend:** SOMALI REPUBLIC **Rev:** Elephant standing facing - gilt **Edge:** Reeded

Date	Mintage	F	VF	XF	Unc	BU
2004 Proof	—	Value: 40.00				

KM# 179 1000 SHILLINGS
31.1050 g., 0.9990 Silver 0.9990 oz. ASW, 39 mm. **Obv:** Arms **Rev:** Elephant head left, multicolor

Date	Mintage	F	VF	XF	Unc	BU
2005	—	—	—	—	—	45.00

KM# 180 1000 SHILLINGS
31.1050 g., 0.9990 Silver 0.9990 oz. ASW, 39 mm. **Obv:** Arms **Rev:** Elephant, mountian in background. Multicolor

Date	Mintage	F	VF	XF	Unc	BU
2006	—	—	—	—	—	45.00

KM# 177 1000 SHILLINGS
31.1050 g., 0.9990 Silver partially gilt 0.9990 oz. ASW, 38 mm. **Rev:** Elephant, mountain, partially gilt

Date	Mintage	F	VF	XF	Unc	BU
2006	—	Value: 55.00				

KM# 178 1000 SHILLINGS
31.1050 g., 0.9990 Silver 0.9990 oz. ASW, 38 mm. **Obv:** Arms **Rev:** Elephant and mountain

Date	Mintage	F	VF	XF	Unc	BU
2006	—	—	—	—	—	45.00

KM# 181 1000 SHILLINGS
31.1050 g., 0.9990 Silver 0.9990 oz. ASW, 39 mm. **Obv:** Arms **Rev:** Heard of six elephants, multicolor

Date	Mintage	F	VF	XF	Unc	BU
2008	—	—	—	—	—	40.00

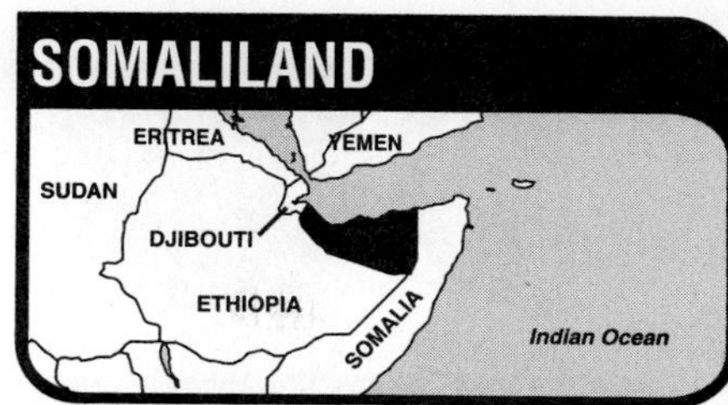

The Somaliland Republic consists of the former British Somaliland Protectorate and is located on the coast of the northeastern projection of the African continent commonly referred to as the "Horn" on the southwestern end of the Gulf of Aden. Bordered by Ethiopia to the west and south and Somalia to the east. It has an area of 68,000* sq. mi. (176,000* sq. km). Capital: Hargeysa. It is mostly arid and mountainous except for the gulf shoreline.

The northern Somali National Movement (SNM) declared a secession of the Somaliland Republic on May 17, 1991, which is not recognized by the Somali Democratic Republic.

REPUBLIC

SHILLING COINAGE

KM# 4 5 SHILLINGS
1.4500 g., Aluminum, 21.9 mm. **Obv:** Value **Rev:** Bust of Sir Richard F. Burton - explorer, divides dates **Edge:** Plain

Date	Mintage	F	VF	XF	Unc	BU
2002	—	—	—	—	1.25	1.50

KM# 5 5 SHILLINGS
1.4500 g., Aluminum, 21.9 mm. **Obv:** Value **Rev:** Rooster **Edge:** Plain

Date	Mintage	F	VF	XF	Unc	BU
2002	—	—	—	—	1.00	1.25

KM# 19 5 SHILLINGS
1.2400 g., Aluminum, 22 mm. **Obv:** Elephant with calf walking right **Obv. Legend:** REPUBLIC OF SOMALILAND **Rev:** Value **Rev. Legend:** BAANKA SOMALILAND **Edge:** Plain

Date	Mintage	F	VF	XF	Unc	BU
2005	—	—	—	—	1.25	1.50

KM# 3 10 SHILLINGS
3.5100 g., Brass, 17.7 mm. **Obv:** Vervet Monkey **Rev:** Value **Edge:** Plain

Date	Mintage	F	VF	XF	Unc	BU
2002	—	—	—	—	0.65	1.25

KM# 7 10 SHILLINGS
4.8000 g., Stainless Steel, 24.9 mm. **Obv:** Value **Rev:** Aquarius the water carrier **Edge:** Plain

Date	Mintage	F	VF	XF	Unc	BU
2006	—	—	—	—	1.00	1.25

KM# 8 10 SHILLINGS
4.8000 g., Stainless Steel, 24.9 mm. **Obv:** Value **Rev:** Pisces the two fish **Edge:** Plain

Date	Mintage	F	VF	XF	Unc	BU
2006	—	—	—	—	1.00	1.25

KM# 9 10 SHILLINGS
4.8000 g., Stainless Steel, 24.9 mm. **Obv:** Value **Rev:** Aries the ram **Edge:** Plain

Date	Mintage	F	VF	XF	Unc	BU
2006	—	—	—	—	1.00	1.25

KM# 10 10 SHILLINGS
4.8000 g., Stainless Steel, 24.9 mm. **Obv:** Value **Rev:** Taurus the bull **Edge:** Plain

Date	Mintage	F	VF	XF	Unc	BU
2006	—	—	—	—	1.00	1.25

KM# 11 10 SHILLINGS
4.8000 g., Stainless Steel, 24.9 mm. **Obv:** Value **Rev:** Gemini twins **Edge:** Plain

Date	Mintage	F	VF	XF	Unc	BU
2006	—	—	—	—	1.00	1.25

KM# 12 10 SHILLINGS
4.8000 g., Stainless Steel, 24.9 mm. **Obv:** Value **Rev:** Cancer the crab **Edge:** Plain

Date	Mintage	F	VF	XF	Unc	BU
2006	—	—	—	—	1.00	1.25

KM# 13 10 SHILLINGS
4.8000 g., Stainless Steel, 24.9 mm. **Obv:** Value **Rev:** Leo the lion **Edge:** Plain

Date	Mintage	F	VF	XF	Unc	BU
2006	—	—	—	—	1.00	1.25

KM# 14 10 SHILLINGS
4.8000 g., Stainless Steel, 24.9 mm. **Obv:** Value **Rev:** Virgo as a winged woman **Edge:** Plain

Date	Mintage	F	VF	XF	Unc	BU
2006	—	—	—	—	1.00	1.25

KM# 15 10 SHILLINGS
4.8000 g., Stainless Steel, 24.9 mm. **Obv:** Value **Rev:** Libra balance scale **Edge:** Plain

Date	Mintage	F	VF	XF	Unc	BU
2006	—	—	—	—	1.00	1.25

KM# 16 10 SHILLINGS
4.8000 g., Stainless Steel, 24.9 mm. **Obv:** Value **Rev:** Scorpio the scorpion **Edge:** Plain

Date	Mintage	F	VF	XF	Unc	BU
2006	—	—	—	—	1.00	1.25

KM# 17 10 SHILLINGS
4.8000 g., Stainless Steel, 24.9 mm. **Obv:** Value **Rev:** Sagittarius the archer **Edge:** Plain

Date	Mintage	F	VF	XF	Unc	BU
2006	—	—	—	—	1.00	1.25

KM# 18 10 SHILLINGS
4.8000 g., Stainless Steel, 24.9 mm. **Obv:** Value **Rev:** Capricorn the goat **Edge:** Plain

Date	Mintage	F	VF	XF	Unc	BU
2006	—	—	—	—	1.00	1.25

KM# 6 20 SHILLINGS
3.8700 g., Stainless Steel, 21.8 mm. **Obv:** Value **Rev:** Greyhound dog **Edge:** Plain

Date	Mintage	F	VF	XF	Unc	BU
2002	—	—	—	—	1.00	1.50

KM# 2 1000 SHILLINGS
31.2700 g., 0.9990 Silver 1.0043 oz. ASW, 38.8 mm. **Obv:** Crowned arms with supporters **Rev:** Bust with hat 3/4 right **Edge:** Reeded

Date	Mintage	F	VF	XF	Unc	BU
2002	—	—	—	—	45.00	50.00

SOUTH AFRICA

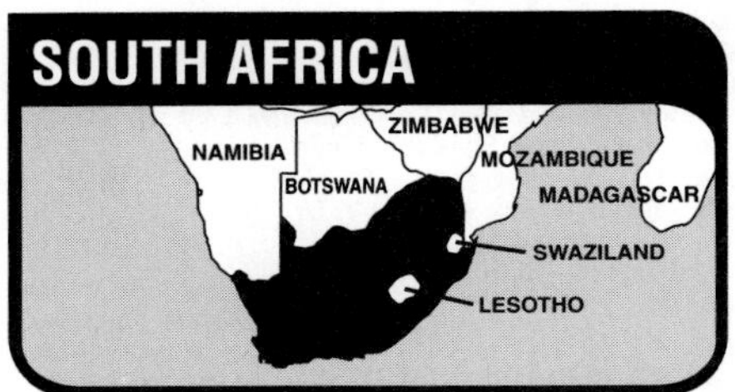

The Republic of South Africa, located at the southern tip of Africa, has an area of 471,445 sq. mi. (1,221,043 sq. km.) and a population of *30.2 million. Capitals: Administrative, Pretoria; Legislative, Cape Town; Judicial, Bloemfontein. Manufacturing, mining and agriculture are the principal industries. Exports include wool, diamonds, gold, and metallic ores.

The apartheid era ended April 27, 1994 with the first democratic election for all people of South Africa. Nelson Mandela was inaugurated President May 10, 1994, and South Africa was readmitted into the Commonwealth of Nations.

South African coins and currency bear inscriptions in tribal languages, Afrikaans and English.

MONETARY SYSTEM
100 Cents = 1 Rand

MINT MARKS
GRC + paw print = Gold Reef City Mint

REPUBLIC

STANDARD COINAGE

100 Cents = 1 Rand

KM# 221 CENT
1.5000 g., Copper Plated Steel, 15 mm. **Obv:** New national arms **Obv. Legend:** ISEWULA AFRIKA **Obv. Designer:** A.L. Sutherland **Rev:** Value divides two sparrows **Rev. Designer:** W. Lumley **Edge:** Plain

Date	Mintage	F	VF	XF	Unc	BU
2001	—	—	—	0.15	0.35	0.50
2001 Proof	3,678	Value: 5.00				

KM# 222 2 CENTS

3.0000 g., Copper Plated Steel, 18 mm. **Obv:** New national arms **Obv. Legend:** AFURIKA TSHIPEMBE **Rev:** Eagle with fish in talons divides value **Edge:** Plain **Designer:** A.L. Sutherland

Date	Mintage	F	VF	XF	Unc	BU
2001	—	—	—	—	0.50	0.75
2001 Proof	3,678	Value: 6.00				

KM# 223 5 CENTS

4.4200 g., Copper Plated Steel, 21 mm. **Obv:** New national arms **Obv. Legend:** AFRIKA DZONGA **Obv. Designer:** A.L. Sutherland **Rev:** Value and Blue crane **Rev. Designer:** G. Richard **Edge:** Plain

Date	Mintage	F	VF	XF	Unc	BU
2001	—	—	0.10	0.25	0.65	1.00
2001 Proof	—	Value: 5.00				

KM# 268 5 CENTS

4.5000 g., Copper Plated Steel, 21 mm. **Obv:** New national arms **Obv. Legend:** Ningizimu Afrika **Obv. Designer:** A.L. Sutherland **Rev:** Value and Blue crane **Rev. Designer:** G. Richard **Edge:** Plain

Date	Mintage	F	VF	XF	Unc	BU
2002	—	—	—	0.30	0.75	1.00
2002 Proof	3,250	Value: 5.00				

KM# 324 5 CENTS

4.5000 g., Copper Plated Steel, 21 mm. **Obv:** New national arms **Obv. Legend:** Afrika Dzonga **Rev:** Blue crane and denomination **Edge:** Plain

Date	Mintage	F	VF	XF	Unc	BU
2003	—	—	—	0.30	0.75	1.00
2003 Proof	2,909	Value: 5.00				

KM# 325 5 CENTS

4.5000 g., Copper Plated Steel, 21 mm. **Obv:** New national arms **Obv. Legend:** South Africa **Rev:** Value and Blue crane **Edge:** Plain

Date	Mintage	F	VF	XF	Unc	BU
2004	—	—	—	0.20	0.50	0.75
2004 Proof	1,935	Value: 5.00				

KM# 291 5 CENTS

4.5000 g., Copper Plated Steel, 21 mm. **Obv:** New national arms **Obv. Legend:** Aforika Borwa **Rev:** Value and Blue crane **Edge:** Plain

Date	Mintage	F	VF	XF	Unc	BU
2005	—	—	—	0.20	0.50	0.75
2005 Proof	—	Value: 5.00				

KM# 486 5 CENTS

4.5000 g., Copper Plated Steel, 21 mm. **Obv:** New National arms **Obv. Legend:** Afrika Borwa **Rev:** Blue crane and value

Date	Mintage	F	VF	XF	Unc	BU
2006	—	—	—	—	0.50	0.75
2006 Proof	—	Value: 5.00				

KM# 340 5 CENTS

4.5100 g., Copper Plated Steel, 20.9 mm. **Obv:** New national arms **Obv. Legend:** Suid- Afrika **Rev:** Value at left, Blue Crane at right **Edge:** Plain

Date	Mintage	F	VF	XF	Unc	BU
2007	—	—	—	0.20	0.50	0.75
2007 Proof	—	Value: 5.00				

KM# 497 5 CENTS

4.5000 g., Copper Plated Steel, 21 mm. **Obv:** New National arms **Obv. Legend:** uMzantsi Afrika **Rev:** Blue crane and value

Date	Mintage	F	VF	XF	Unc	BU
2008	—	—	—	—	0.75	1.00
2008 Proof	—	Value: 5.00				

KM# 224 10 CENTS

2.0000 g., Bronze Plated Steel, 16 mm. **Obv:** New national arms **Obv. Legend:** AFRIKA DZONGA **Obv. Designer:** A.L. Sutherland **Rev:** Arum Lily and value **Rev. Designer:** R.C. McFarlane **Edge:** Reeded

Date	Mintage	F	VF	XF	Unc	BU
2001	—	—	—	0.30	0.60	1.00
2001 Proof	3,678	Value: 6.00				

KM# 269 10 CENTS

2.0000 g., Bronze Plated Steel, 16 mm. **Obv:** New national arms **Obv. Legend:** Afrika Dzonga **Obv. Designer:** A.L. Sutherland **Rev:** Arum Lily and value **Rev. Designer:** R.C. McFarlane **Edge:** Reeded

Date	Mintage	F	VF	XF	Unc	BU
2002	—	—	—	0.30	0.75	1.00
2002 Proof	3,250	Value: 6.00				

KM# 347 10 CENTS

2.0000 g., Bronze Plated Steel, 16 mm. **Obv:** New national arms **Obv. Legend:** South Africa **Rev:** Arum lily and value **Edge:** Reeded

Date	Mintage	F	VF	XF	Unc	BU
2003	—	—	—	0.30	0.75	1.00
2003 Proof	2,909	Value: 6.00				

KM# 326 10 CENTS

2.0000 g., Bronze Plated Steel, 16 mm. **Obv:** New national arms **Obv. Legend:** Aforika Borwa **Rev:** Arum lily and value **Edge:** Reeded

Date	Mintage	F	VF	XF	Unc	BU
2004	—	—	—	0.30	0.75	1.00
2004 Proof	1,935	Value: 6.00				

KM# 292 10 CENTS

2.0000 g., Bronze Plated Steel, 16 mm. **Obv:** New national arms **Obv. Legend:** Afrika Borwa **Rev:** Arum Lily and value **Edge:** Reeded

Date	Mintage	F	VF	XF	Unc	BU
2005	—	—	—	0.30	0.75	1.00
2005 Proof	—	Value: 6.00				

KM# 487 10 CENTS

2.0000 g., Bronze Plated Steel, 16 mm. **Obv:** National arms **Obv. Legend:** Suid-Afrika **Rev:** Arum lily and value **Edge:** Reeded

Date	Mintage	F	VF	XF	Unc	BU
2006	—	—	—	—	0.75	1.00
2006 Proof	—	Value: 6.00				

KM# 341 10 CENTS

2.0000 g., Bronze Plated Steel, 16 mm. **Obv:** New national arms **Obv. Legend:** uMzantsi - Afrika **Rev:** Alum lily and value **Edge:** Reeded

Date	Mintage	F	VF	XF	Unc	BU
2007	—	—	—	0.30	0.75	1.00
2007 Proof	—	Value: 6.00				

KM# 498 10 CENTS

2.0000 g., Bronze Plated Steel, 16 mm. **Obv:** National arms **Obv. Legend:** iNingizimu Afrika **Rev:** Arum lily and value **Edge:** Reeded

Date	Mintage	F	VF	XF	Unc	BU
2008	—	—	—	—	0.75	1.00
2008 Proof	—	Value: 8.00				

KM# 225 20 CENTS

3.5000 g., Bronze Plated Steel, 19 mm. **Obv:** New national arms **Obv. Legend:** AFERIKA BORWA **Obv. Designer:** A.L. Sutherland **Rev:** Protea flower and value **Edge:** Reeded

Date	Mintage	F	VF	XF	Unc	BU
2001	—	—	—	0.35	0.90	1.20
2001 Proof	3,678	Value: 7.00				

KM# 270 20 CENTS

3.5000 g., Bronze Plated Steel, 19 mm. **Obv:** New national arms **Obv. Legend:** South Africa **Obv. Designer:** A.L. Sutherland **Rev:** Protea flower and value **Rev. Designer:** S. Erasmus **Edge:** Reeded

Date	Mintage	F	VF	XF	Unc	BU
2002	—	—	—	0.35	0.90	1.20
2002 Proof	3,250	Value: 7.00				

KM# 327 20 CENTS

3.5000 g., Bronze Plated Steel, 19 mm. **Obv:** New national arms **Obv. Legend:** Aforika Borwa **Rev:** Protea flower and value **Edge:** Reeded

Date	Mintage	F	VF	XF	Unc	BU
2003	—	—	—	0.35	0.90	1.20
2003 Proof	2,909	Value: 7.00				

KM# 328 20 CENTS

3.5000 g., Bronze Plated Steel, 19 mm. **Obv:** New national arms **Obv. Legend:** Afrika Borwa **Rev:** Protea flower and value **Edge:** Reeded

Date	Mintage	F	VF	XF	Unc	BU
2004	—	—	—	0.35	0.90	1.20
2004 Proof	1,935	Value: 7.00				

KM# 293 20 CENTS

3.5000 g., Bronze Plated Steel, 19 mm. **Obv:** New national arms **Obv. Legend:** Suid-Afrika **Rev:** Protea flower and value **Edge:** Reeded **Shape:** Round

Date	Mintage	F	VF	XF	Unc	BU
2005	—	—	—	0.35	0.90	1.20
2005 Proof	—	Value: 7.00				

KM# 488 20 CENTS
3.5000 g., Bronze Plated Steel, 19 mm. **Obv:** National arms **Obv. Legend:** uMzantsi Afrika **Rev:** Protea flower and value **Edge:** Reeded

Date	Mintage	F	VF	XF	Unc	BU
2006	—	—	—	—	0.90	1.20
2006 Proof	—	Value: 7.00				

KM# 342 20 CENTS
3.5000 g., Bronze Plated Steel, 19 mm. **Obv:** New national arms **Obv. Legend:** iNingizimu Afrika **Rev:** Protea flower and value **Edge:** Reeded

Date	Mintage	F	VF	XF	Unc	BU
2007	—	—	—	0.35	0.90	1.20
2007 Proof	—	Value: 7.00				

KM# 226 50 CENTS
5.0000 g., Bronze Plated Steel, 22 mm. **Obv:** New national arms **Obv. Legend:** AFERIKA BORWA **Obv. Designer:** A.L. Sutherland **Rev:** Strelitzia plant, value **Rev. Designer:** Linda Lotriet **Edge:** Reeded

Date	Mintage	F	VF	XF	Unc	BU
2001	1,152,000	—	—	0.50	1.20	1.60
2001 Proof	3,678	Value: 8.00				

KM# 271 50 CENTS
5.0000 g., Bronze Plated Steel, 22 mm. **Obv:** New national arms **Obv. Legend:** Aforika Borwa **Obv. Designer:** A.L. Sutherland **Rev:** Strelitzia plant **Rev. Designer:** Linda Lotriet **Edge:** Reeded

Date	Mintage	F	VF	XF	Unc	BU
2002	16,000,000	—	—	0.50	1.20	1.60
2002 Proof	3,250	Value: 8.00				

KM# 287 50 CENTS
5.0000 g., Bronze Plated Steel, 22 mm. **Obv:** New national arms **Obv. Legend:** Aforika - Borwa **Rev:** Soccer player and value **Edge:** Reeded **Designer:** A. L. Sutherland

Date	Mintage	F	VF	XF	Unc	BU
2002	—	—	—	—	9.00	12.00

KM# 276 50 CENTS
5.0000 g., Bronze Plated Steel, 22 mm. **Obv:** New national arms **Obv. Legend:** Afrika - Borwa **Obv. Designer:** A.L. Sutherland **Rev:** Cricket player diving towards the wicket, value below **Rev. Designer:** A. L. Sutherland **Edge:** Reeded

Date	Mintage	F	VF	XF	Unc	BU
2003	11,749	—	—	—	9.00	12.00

KM# 329 50 CENTS
5.0000 g., Bronze Plated Steel, 22 mm. **Obv:** New national arms **Obv. Legend:** Aforika Borwa **Rev:** Cricket player diving towards the wicket **Edge:** Reeded **Designer:** A. L. Sutherland

Date	Mintage	F	VF	XF	Unc	BU
2003	—	—	—	—	9.00	12.00
2003 Proof	—	Value: 15.00				

KM# 330 50 CENTS
5.0000 g., Bronze Plated Steel, 22 mm. **Obv:** New national arms **Obv. Legend:** Afrika Borwa **Obv. Designer:** A. L. Sutherland **Rev:** Strelitzia plant, value **Rev. Designer:** Linda Lotriet **Edge:** Reeded

Date	Mintage	F	VF	XF	Unc	BU
2003	—	—	—	0.50	1.60	1.20
2003 Proof	2,909	Value: 8.00				

KM# 331 50 CENTS
5.0000 g., Bronze Plated Steel, 22 mm. **Obv:** New national arms **Obv. Legend:** Suid Afrika **Obv. Designer:** A. L. Sutherland **Rev:** Strelitzia plant, value **Rev. Designer:** Linda Lotriet **Edge:** Reeded

Date	Mintage	F	VF	XF	Unc	BU
2004	—	—	—	0.50	1.20	1.60
2004 Proof	1,935	Value: 8.00				

KM# 294 50 CENTS
5.0000 g., Bronze Plated Steel, 22 mm. **Obv:** New national arms **Obv. Legend:** uMzantsi Afrika **Obv. Designer:** A. L. Sutherland **Rev:** Strelitzia plant, value **Rev. Designer:** Linda Lotriet **Edge:** Reeded

Date	Mintage	F	VF	XF	Unc	BU
2005	—	—	—	0.50	1.20	1.60
2005 Proof	—	Value: 8.00				

KM# 489 50 CENTS
5.0000 g., Bronze Plated Steel, 22 mm. **Obv:** National arms **Obv. Legend:** iNingizimu Afrika **Rev:** Strelitzia plant and value **Edge:** Reeded

Date	Mintage	F	VF	XF	Unc	BU
2006	—	—	—	—	1.20	1.60
2006 Proof	—	Value: 8.00				

KM# 493 50 CENTS
5.0000 g., Bronze Plated Steel, 22 mm. **Obv:** National arms **Obv. Legend:** iSewula Afrika **Rev:** Strelitzia plant and value **Edge:** Reeded

Date	Mintage	F	VF	XF	Unc	BU
2007	—	—	—	—	1.20	1.60
2007 Proof	—	Value: 8.00				

KM# 500 50 CENTS
5.0000 g., Bronze Plated Steel, 22 mm. **Obv:** National arms **Obv. Legend:** Afurika Tshipembe **Rev:** Strelitzia plant and value **Edge:** Reeded

Date	Mintage	F	VF	XF	Unc	BU
2008	—	—	—	—	1.20	1.60
2008 Proof	—	Value: 8.00				

KM# 227 RAND
4.0000 g., Nickel Plated Copper, 20 mm. **Obv:** New national arms **Obv. Legend:** SUID-AFRIKA **Obv. Designer:** A.L. Sutherland **Rev:** Springbok, value **Rev. Designer:** Linda Lotriet **Edge:** Segmented reeding

Date	Mintage	F	VF	XF	Unc	BU
2001	—	—	—	0.60	1.50	2.00
2001 Proof	3,678	Value: 10.00				

KM# 272 RAND
4.0000 g., Nickel Plated Copper, 20 mm. **Obv:** New national arms **Obv. Legend:** Suid-Afrika Afrika Borwa **Obv. Designer:** A. L. Sutherland **Rev:** Springbok, value **Rev. Designer:** Linda Lotriet **Edge:** Segmented reeding

Date	Mintage	F	VF	XF	Unc	BU
2002	—	—	—	0.60	1.50	2.00
2002 Proof	3,250	Value: 10.00				

KM# 275 RAND
4.0000 g., Nickel Plated Copper, 20 mm. **Subject:** Johannesburg World Summit on Sustainable Development **Obv:** New national arms **Obv. Legend:** Suid-Afrika - Afrika Borwa **Obv. Designer:** A.L. Sutherland **Rev:** World globe and logo **Rev. Designer:** M. J. Scheepers **Edge:** Segmented reeding

Date	Mintage	F	VF	XF	Unc	BU
2002	—	—	—	—	12.00	18.00

KM# 332 RAND
4.0000 g., Nickel Plated Copper, 20 mm. **Obv:** New national arms **Obv. Legend:** uMzantsi Afrika Suid-Afrika **Obv. Designer:** A. L. Sutherland **Rev:** Springbok, value **Rev. Designer:** Linda Lotriet **Edge:** Segmented reeding

Date	Mintage	F	VF	XF	Unc	BU
2003	—	—	—	0.60	1.50	2.00
2003 Proof	2,909	Value: 10.00				

KM# 333 RAND
4.0000 g., Nickel Plated Copper, 20 mm. **Obv:** New national arms **Obv. Legend:** iNingizimu Afrika - uMzantsi Afrika **Obv. Designer:** A. L. Sutherland **Rev:** Springbok, value **Rev. Designer:** Linda Lotriet **Edge:** Segmented reeding

Date	Mintage	F	VF	XF	Unc	BU
2004	—	—	—	0.60	1.50	2.00
2004 Proof	1,935	Value: 10.00				

KM# 295 RAND
4.0000 g., Nickel Plated Copper, 20 mm. **Obv:** new national arms **Obv. Legend:** iSewula Afrika - iNingizimu Afrika **Obv. Designer:** A. L. Sutherland **Rev:** Springbok, value **Rev. Designer:** Linda Lotriet **Edge:** Segmented reeding **Shape:** Round

Date	Mintage	F	VF	XF	Unc	BU
2005	—	—	—	0.60	1.50	2.00
2005 Proof	—	Value: 10.00				

KM# 490 RAND
4.0000 g., Nickel Plated Copper, 20 mm. **Obv:** National arms **Obv. Legend:** Afurika Tshipembe - iSewula Afrika **Rev:** Springbok and value

Date	Mintage	F	VF	XF	Unc	BU
2006	—	—	—	—	1.50	2.00
2006 Proof	—	Value: 10.00				

KM# 344 RAND
3.9300 g., Nickel Plated Copper, 19.94 mm. **Obv:** Natinal arms **Obv. Legend:** Ningizimu Afrika - Afurika Tshipemba **Rev:** Springbok leaping right **Edge:** segmented reeding

Date	Mintage	F	VF	XF	Unc	BU
2007	—	—	—	0.60	1.50	2.00
2007 Proof	—	Value: 10.00				

KM# 501 RAND
4.0000 g., Nickel Plated Copper, 20 mm. **Obv:** National arms **Obv. Legend:** Afrika-Dzonga - Ningizimu Afrika **Rev:** Springbok and value

Date	Mintage	F	VF	XF	Unc	BU
2008	—	—	—	—	2.00	2.75
2008 Proof	—	Value: 12.00				

KM# 228 2 RAND
5.5000 g., Nickel Plated Copper, 23 mm. **Obv:** New national arms **Obv. Legend:** UMZANSTI AFRIKA **Rev:** Greater Kudu, value **Edge:** Segmented reeding **Designer:** A. L. Sutherland

Date	Mintage	F	VF	XF	Unc	BU
2001	3,600,000	—	—	0.80	2.00	3.00
2001 Proof	3,678	Value: 12.00				

KM# 273 2 RAND
5.5000 g., Nickel Plated Copper, 23 mm. **Obv:** New national arms **Obv. Legend:** iNingizimu Afrika - uMzantsi Afrika **Rev:** Greater Kudu, value **Edge:** Segmented reeding **Designer:** A.L. Sutherland

Date	Mintage	F	VF	XF	Unc	BU
2002	12,000,000	—	—	0.80	2.00	3.50
2002 Proof	3,250	Value: 12.00				

KM# 335 2 RAND
5.5000 g., Nickel Plated Copper, 23 mm. **Obv:** New national arms **Obv. Legend:** iNingizimu Afrika - iSewula Afrika **Rev:** Greater Kudu, value **Edge:** Segmented reeding **Designer:** A. L. Sutherland

Date	Mintage	F	VF	XF	Unc	BU
2003	5,000,000	—	—	0.80	2.00	3.50
2003 Proof	2,909	Value: 12.00				

KM# 336 2 RAND
5.5000 g., Nickel Plated Copper, 23 mm. **Obv:** New national arms **Obv. Legend:** Afurika Tshipembe / iSewula Afrika **Rev:** Greater Kudu, value **Edge:** Segmented reeding **Designer:** A. L. Sutherland

Date	Mintage	F	VF	XF	Unc	BU
2004	—	—	—	0.80	2.00	3.50
2004 Proof	1,935	Value: 12.00				

KM# 334 2 RAND
5.5000 g., Nickel Plated Copper, 23 mm. **Subject:** 10 Years of Freedom - 1994-2004 **Obv:** New national arms **Obv. Legend:** SOUTH / AFRICA **Obv. Designer:** A. L. Sutherland **Rev:** Value, flag logo, people **Rev. Designer:** M. J. Scheepers **Edge:** Segmented reeding **Note:** 5,885 issued in souveneir card.

Date	Mintage	F	VF	XF	Unc	BU
2004	—	—	—	0.80	2.00	2.75

KM# 296 2 RAND
5.5000 g., Nickel Plated Copper, 23 mm. **Obv:** New national arms **Obv. Legend:** Ningizimu Afrika - Afurika Tshipembe **Rev:** Greater Kudu, value **Edge:** Segmented reeding **Designer:** A. L. Sutherland

Date	Mintage	F	VF	XF	Unc	BU
2005	—	—	—	0.80	2.00	2.75
2005 Proof	—	Value: 12.00				

KM# 491 2 RAND
5.5000 g., Nickel Plated Copper, 23 mm. **Obv:** National arms **Obv. Legend:** Afrika-Dzonga - Ningizimo Afrika **Rev:** Greater kudu and value

Date	Mintage	F	VF	XF	Unc	BU
2006	—	—	—	—	2.00	2.75
2006 Proof	—	Value: 12.00				

KM# 345 2 RAND
5.4700 g., Nickel Plated Copper, 22.98 mm. **Obv:** National arms **Obv. Legend:** Afrika-Dzonga - South Africa **Rev:** Kudu at center left, value at right **Edge:** Segmented reeding

Date	Mintage	F	VF	XF	Unc	BU
2008	—	—	—	0.80	2.00	2.75
2008 Proof	—	Value: 12.00				

KM# 229 5 RAND
7.0000 g., Nickel Plated Copper, 26 mm. **Obv:** New national arms **Obv. Legend:** ININGIZIMU AFRIKA **Rev:** Wildebeest, value **Edge:** Segmented reeding **Designer:** A.L. Sutherland

Date	Mintage	F	VF	XF	Unc	BU
2001	2,000,000	—	—	1.20	4.50	6.00
2001 CW	779	—	—	—	67.50	90.00
2001 Proof	3,678	Value: 15.00				

KM# 274 5 RAND
7.0000 g., Nickel Plated Copper, 26 mm. **Obv:** New national arms **Obv. Legend:** Afurika Tshipembe - Isewula Afrika **Rev:** Wildebeest, value **Edge:** Segmented reeding **Designer:** A.L. Sutherland

Date	Mintage	F	VF	XF	Unc	BU
2002	—	—	—	1.20	4.50	6.00
2002 CW	106	—	—	—	—	150
2002 Proof	3,250	Value: 15.00				

KM# 337 5 RAND
7.0000 g., Nickel Plated Copper, 26 mm. **Obv:** New national arms **Obv. Legend:** Afurika Tshipembe - Ningizimu Afrika **Rev:** Wildebeest, value **Edge:** Segmented reeding **Designer:** A. L. Sutherland

Date	Mintage	F	VF	XF	Unc	BU
2003	—	—	—	1.20	4.50	6.00
2003 Proof	2,909	Value: 15.00				

KM# 281 5 RAND
9.5000 g., Bi-Metallic Brass center in Copper-Nickel ring, 26 mm. **Obv:** New national arms **Obv. Legend:** Afrika-Dzonga - Ningizimu Afrika **Rev:** Wildebeest, value **Edge:** Security type with lettering **Edge Lettering:** "SARB R5" repeated ten times

Date	Mintage	F	VF	XF	Unc	BU
2004	—	—	—	1.20	5.00	6.50
2004 CW	3,243	—	—	—	—	22.50
2004 Proof	1,935	Value: 15.00				

KM# 297 5 RAND
9.5000 g., Bi-Metallic Brass center in Copper-Nickel ring, 26 mm. **Obv:** New national arms **Obv. Legend:** Afrika Dzonga - South Africa **Rev:** Wildebeest, value **Edge:** Security type with lettering **Edge Lettering:** "SARB R5" repeated ten times **Designer:** A. L. Sutherland

Date	Mintage	F	VF	XF	Unc	BU
2005	—	—	—	1.20	3.75	5.00
2005 CW	997	—	—	—	—	50.00
2005 Proof	—	Value: 15.00				

KM# 492 5 RAND
5.5000 g., Bi-Metallic Brass center in Copper-Nickel ring., 26 mm. **Obv:** National arms **Obv. Legend:** Aforika Borwa - South Africa **Rev:** Wildebeest and value

Date	Mintage	F	VF	XF	Unc	BU
2006	—	—	—	—	4.50	6.00
2006 Proof	—	Value: 12.00				

KM# 346 5 RAND
9.5000 g., Bi-Metallic Bronze center in Copper-Nickel ring, 26 mm. **Obv:** National arms **Obv. Legend:** Aforika Borwa - Afrika Borwa **Rev:** Wildebeest rearing left **Edge:** Security type and lettered **Edge Lettering:** "SARB R5" repeated ten times **Designer:** A. L. Sutherland

Date	Mintage	F	VF	XF	Unc	BU
2007	—	—	—	1.20	3.00	4.00
2007 CW	—	—	—	—	—	22.50
2007 Proof	—	Value: 15.00				

GOLD BULLION COINAGE

KM# 105 1/10 KRUGERRAND
3.3930 g., 0.9170 Gold .1000 AGW 0.1000 oz. AGW, 16.50 mm. **Obv:** Bust of Paul Kruger left **Rev:** Springbok walking right divides date **Edge:** Reeded **Note:** 180 edge serrations for uncirculated, 220 serrations for proof

Date	Mintage	F	VF	XF	Unc	BU
2001	17,936	—	—	—	BV+15%	—
2001 Proof	4,058	Value: 175				
2002	12,890	—	—	—	BV+15%	—
2002 Proof	3,110	Value: 175				
2003	15,893	—	—	—	BV+15%	—
2003 Proof	1,893	Value: 175				
2004	—	—	—	—	BV+15%	—
2004 Proof	3,811	Value: 175				
2005	—	—	—	—	BV+15%	—
2005 Proof	—	Value: 175				
2006	—	—	—	—	BV+15%	—
2006 Proof	—	Value: 175				
2007	—	—	—	—	BV+15%	—
2007 Proof	4,400	Value: 175				
2008	—	—	—	—	BV+15%	—
2008 Proof	4,800	Value: 175				
2009	—	—	—	—	BV+15%	—
2009 Proof	6,000	Value: 175				
2010	—	—	—	—	BV+15%	—
2010 Proof	6,000	Value: 175				

KM# 106 1/4 KRUGERRAND
8.4820 g., 0.9170 Gold 0.2501 oz. AGW, 22 mm. **Obv:** Bust of Paul Kruger left **Obv. Legend:** SUID — AFRIKA • SOUTH AFRICA **Rev:** Springbok bounding right divides date **Rev. Designer:** Coert L. Steynberg **Edge:** Reeded **Note:** 180 edge serrations for uncirculated, 220 serrations for proof

Date	Mintage	F	VF	XF	Unc	BU
2001	10,607	—	—	—	BV+10%	—
2001 Proof	3,841	Value: 400				
2002	10,558	—	—	—	BV+10%	—
2002 Proof	2,442	Value: 400				
2003	11,468	—	—	—	BV+10%	—
2003 Proof	2,450	Value: 400				
2004	—	—	—	—	BV+10%	—
2004 Proof	4,570	Value: 400				
2005	—	—	—	—	BV+10%	—
2005 Proof	—	Value: 400				
2006	—	—	—	—	BV+10%	—

Date	Mintage	F	VF	XF	Unc	BU
2006 Proof	—	Value: 400				
2007	—	—	—	—	BV+10%	—
2007 Proof	4,400	Value: 400				
2008	—	—	—	—	BV+10%	—
2008 Proof	4,800	Value: 400				
2009	—	—	—	—	BV+10%	—
2009 Proof	6,000	Value: 400				
2010	—	—	—	—	BV+10%	—
2010 Proof	6,000	Value: 400				

KM# 107 1/2 KRUGERRAND

16.9650 g., 0.9170 Gold 0.5001 oz. AGW, 27 mm. **Obv:** Bust of Paul Kruger left **Obv. Legend:** SUID - AFRIKA - SOUTH AFRICA **Rev:** Springbok walking right divides date **Rev. Designer:** Coert L. Steynberg **Edge:** Reeded **Note:** 180 edge serrations for uncirculated, 220 serrations for proof

Date	Mintage	F	VF	XF	Unc	BU
2001	6,429	—	—	—	BV+8%	—
2001 Proof	3,696	Value: 800				
2002	—	—	—	—	BV+8%	—
2002 Proof	2,295	Value: 800				
2003	11,588	—	—	—	BV+8%	—
2003 Proof	1,285	Value: 800				
2004	—	—	—	—	BV+8%	—
2004 Proof	3,288	Value: 800				
2005	—	—	—	—	BV+8%	—
2005 Proof	—	Value: 800				
2006	—	—	—	—	BV+8%	—
2006 Proof	—	Value: 800				
2007	—	—	—	—	BV+8%	—
2007 Proof	3,400	Value: 800				
2008	—	—	—	—	BV+8%	—
2008 Proof	3,300	Value: 800				
2009	—	—	—	—	BV+8%	—
2009 Proof	2,500	Value: 800				
2010	—	—	—	—	BV+8%	—
2010 Proof	2,500	Value: 800				

KM# 73 KRUGERRAND

33.9300 g., 0.9170 Gold 1.0003 oz. AGW, 32.7 mm. **Obv:** Bust of Paul Kruger left **Obv. Legend:** SUID — AFRIKA • SOUTH AFRICA **Rev:** Springbok walking right divides date **Rev. Designer:** Coert L. Steynberg **Edge:** Reeded **Note:** 180 edge serrations for uncirculated, 220 serrations for proof

Date	Mintage	F	VF	XF	Unc	BU
2001	5,889	—	—	—	—	BV+5%
2001 Proof	5,563	Value: 1,550				
2002	16,469	—	—	—	—	BV+5%
2002 Proof	3,531	Value: 1,550				
2003	47,789	—	—	—	—	BV+5%
2003 Proof	2,136	Value: 1,550				
2004	71,269	—	—	—	—	BV+5%
2004 Proof	3,492	Value: 1,550				
2004 W/MM Proof	500	Value: 1,550				
2005	—	—	—	—	—	BV+5%
2005 Proof	—	Value: 1,550				
2006	—	—	—	—	—	BV+5%
2006 Proof	—	Value: 1,550				
2007	—	—	—	—	—	BV+5%
2007 Proof	3,400	Value: 1,550				
2008	—	—	—	—	—	BV+5%
2008 Proof	3,300	Value: 1,550				
2009	—	—	—	—	—	BV+5%
2009 Proof	2,500	Value: 1,550				
2010	—	—	—	—	—	BV+5%
2010 Proof	2,500	Value: 1,550				

SILVER BULLION NATURA COINAGE

KM# 242 2-1/2 CENTS

1.4140 g., 0.9250 Silver 0.0420 oz. ASW, 16.3 mm. **Obv:** Crowned arms **Rev:** Dolphin **Edge:** Reeded

Date	Mintage	F	VF	XF	Unc	BU
2001 Proof	—	Value: 27.50				

KM# 480 2-1/2 CENTS

1.1410 g., 0.9250 Silver 0.0339 oz. ASW, 16.3 mm. **Obv:** Flower **Obv. Designer:** A. L. Sutherland **Rev:** Vasco de Gama's ship "Sao Gabriel" **Rev. Designer:** L. Guerra and M. J. Scheepers

Date	Mintage	F	VF	XF	Unc	BU
2009 Proof	3,500	Value: 15.00				

KM# 243 5 CENTS

8.4560 g., 0.9250 Silver 0.2515 oz. ASW, 26.7 mm. **Series:** Wildlife - Power **Obv:** Water buffalo's head **Obv. Designer:** A. L. Sutherland **Rev:** Two water buffalo heads within circle below value **Rev. Designer:** C Moses **Edge:** Reeded

Date	Mintage	F	VF	XF	Unc	BU
2001 Proof	1,853	Value: 40.00				

KM# 351 5 CENTS

8.4560 g., 0.9250 Silver 0.2515 oz. ASW, 26.7 mm. **Series:** Wildlife - Strength **Obv:** Elephant walking, facing **Obv. Designer:** A. L. Sutherland **Rev:** Elephant 3/4 left bathing **Rev. Designer:** C. Moses **Edge:** Reeded

Date	Mintage	F	VF	XF	Unc	BU
2002 Proof	2,425	Value: 30.00				

KM# 355 5 CENTS

8.4560 g., 0.9250 Silver 0.2515 oz. ASW, 26.7 mm. **Series:** Wildlife - Survivor **Obv:** New national arms **Obv. Designer:** A. L. Sutherland **Rev:** 2 White Rhinoceros drinking at stream **Rev. Designer:** M. J. Scheepers **Edge:** Reeded

Date	Mintage	F	VF	XF	Unc	BU
2003 Proof	1,870	Value: 40.00				

KM# 359 5 CENTS

8.4560 g., 0.9250 Silver 0.2515 oz. ASW, 26.7 mm. **Series:** Wildlife - The Legend **Obv:** New national arms **Obv. Designer:** A. L. Sutherland **Rev:** Head of Leopard right drinking **Rev. Designer:** C. Moses **Edge:** Reeded

Date	Mintage	F	VF	XF	Unc	BU
2004 Proof	—	Value: 40.00				

KM# 320 5 CENTS

8.4560 g., 0.9250 Silver 0.2515 oz. ASW, 27.12 mm. **Series:** Wildlife - African Wild Dog **Obv:** New national arms **Obv. Designer:** A. L. Sutherland **Rev:** Painted Dog's head facing slightly left **Rev. Designer:** C. Moses **Edge:** Reeded

Date	Mintage	F	VF	XF	Unc	BU
2005 Proof	1,500	Value: 40.00				

KM# 316 5 CENTS

8.4560 g., 0.9250 Silver 0.2515 oz. ASW, 27 mm. **Series:** Wildlife - Black-backed Jackal **Obv:** New national arms **Obv. Designer:** A. L. Sutherland **Rev:** Black-backed jackal drinking **Rev. Designer:** C. Moses **Edge:** Reeded

Date	Mintage	F	VF	XF	Unc	BU
2006 Proof	1,500	Value: 40.00				

KM# 363 5 CENTS

8.4560 g., 0.9250 Silver 0.2515 oz. ASW, 26.7 mm. **Series:** Wildlife - Kgalagadi Transfrontier Peace Park **Obv:** New national arms **Obv. Designer:** A. L. Sutherland **Rev:** Local desert melons, value **Rev. Designer:** C Moses **Edge:** Reeded

Date	Mintage	F	VF	XF	Unc	BU
2007 Proof	—	Value: 40.00				

KM# 458 5 CENTS

8.4060 g., 0.9250 Silver 0.2500 oz. ASW, 27 mm. **Subject:** Richtersveld Transfrontier Park **Obv:** Arms **Obv. Designer:** A. L. Sutherland **Rev:** Orbea Namaquensis succulant flower **Rev. Designer:** L. Guerra and C. Moses

Date	Mintage	F	VF	XF	Unc	BU
2008 Proof	2,200	Value: 30.00				

KM# 482 5 CENTS

8.4060 g., 0.9250 Silver 0.2500 oz. ASW, 27 mm. **Subject:** Maloti Drakensberg Transfrontier Project **Obv:** Arms **Obv. Designer:** A. L. Sutherland **Rev:** Spiral Aloe Tree (aloe polyphylla) **Rev. Designer:** L. Guerra and C. Moses

Date	Mintage	F	VF	XF	Unc	BU
2009 Proof	3,700	Value: 25.00				

KM# 244 10 CENTS

16.8630 g., 0.9250 Silver 0.5015 oz. ASW, 32.7 mm. **Series:** Wildlife - Power **Obv:** Water buffalo's head **Obv. Designer:** A. L. Sutherland **Rev:** Two water buffalo bulls fighting **Rev. Designer:** M. J. Scheepers **Edge:** Reeded

Date	Mintage	F	VF	XF	Unc	BU
2001 Proof	1,989	Value: 65.00				

KM# 352 10 CENTS

16.8630 g., 0.9250 Silver 0.5015 oz. ASW, 38.3 mm. **Series:** Wildlife - Strength **Obv:** Elephant walking, facing **Obv. Designer:** A. L. Sutherland **Rev:** 2 elephant heads facing each other **Rev. Designer:** M. J. Scheepers **Edge:** Reeded

Date	Mintage	F	VF	XF	Unc	BU
2002 Proof	2,395	Value: 55.00				

KM# 356 10 CENTS

16.8630 g., 0.9250 Silver 0.5015 oz. ASW, 32.7 mm. **Series:** Wildlife - Survivor **Obv:** New national arms **Obv. Designer:** A. L. Sutherland **Rev:** 2 Black Rhinoceros standing, facing **Rev. Designer:** A. Minnie **Edge:** Reeded

Date	Mintage	F	VF	XF	Unc	BU
2003 Proof	1,815	Value: 65.00				

KM# 360 10 CENTS

16.8630 g., 0.9250 Silver 0.5015 oz. ASW, 32.7 mm. **Series:** Wildlife - The Legend **Obv:** New national arms **Obv. Designer:** A. L. Sutherland **Rev:** Leopard and impala above two leopard cubs playing **Rev. Designer:** C. Moses **Edge:** Reeded

Date	Mintage	F	VF	XF	Unc	BU
2004 Proof	—	Value: 65.00				

KM# 321 10 CENTS

16.8630 g., 0.9250 Silver 0.5015 oz. ASW, 32.82 mm. **Series:** Wildlife - African Wild Dog **Obv:** New national arms **Obv. Designer:** A. L. Sutherland **Rev:** Two Painted Dogs walking right **Rev. Designer:** C. Moses **Edge:** Reeded

Date	Mintage	F	VF	XF	Unc	BU
2005 Proof	1,500	Value: 65.00				

KM# 317 10 CENTS

16.8630 g., 0.9250 Silver 0.5015 oz. ASW, 32.7 mm. **Series:** Wildlife - Black-backed Jackel **Obv:** New national arms **Obv. Designer:** A. L. Sutherland **Rev:** Black-backed jackal chasing birds **Rev. Designer:** L. Guerra **Edge:** Reeded

Date	Mintage	F	VF	XF	Unc	BU
2006 Proof	1,500	Value: 65.00				

KM# 364 10 CENTS

16.8630 g., 0.9250 Silver 0.5015 oz. ASW, 32.7 mm. **Series:** Wildlife - Kgaladadi Transfrontier Peace Park **Obv:** New national arms **Obv. Designer:** A. L. Sutherland **Rev:** Local tribe, value **Rev. Designer:** L. Guerra **Edge:** Reeded

Date	Mintage	F	VF	XF	Unc	BU
2007 Proof	—	Value: 65.00				

KM# 459 10 CENTS

16.8130 g., 0.9250 Silver 0.5000 oz. ASW, 32.7 mm. **Subject:** Richtersveld Transfrontier Park **Obv:** Arms **Obv. Designer:** A. J. Sutherland **Rev:** Local Nama native and livestock **Rev. Designer:** L. Guerra and A. Minnie

Date	Mintage	F	VF	XF	Unc	BU
2008 Proof	2,200	Value: 55.00				

KM# 483 10 CENTS

16.8130 g., 0.9250 Silver 0.5000 oz. ASW, 32.7 mm. **Subject:** Maloti Drakensberg Transfrontier Project **Obv:** Arms **Obv. Designer:** A. L. Sutherland **Rev:** Native Basotho riding pony **Rev. Designer:** L. Guerra and A. Minnie

Date	Mintage	F	VF	XF	Unc	BU
2009 Proof	3,700	Value: 45.00				

KM# 245 20 CENTS

33.7260 g., 0.9250 Silver 1.0030 oz. ASW, 38.3 mm. **Series:** Wildlife - Power **Obv:** Water buffalo's head **Obv. Designer:** A. L. Sutherland **Rev:** Two water buffalo heads facing **Rev. Designer:** P. Botes **Edge:** Reeded

Date	Mintage	F	VF	XF	Unc	BU
2001 Proof	1,902	Value: 85.00				

KM# 353 20 CENTS

33.7260 g., 0.9250 Silver 1.0030 oz. ASW, 38.3 mm. **Series:** Wildlife - Strength **Obv:** Elephant walking, facing **Obv. Designer:** A. L. Sutherland **Rev:** Family of four elephants **Rev. Designer:** C. Moses **Edge:** Reeded

Date	Mintage	F	VF	XF	Unc	BU
2002 Proof	2,435	Value: 75.00				

KM# 357 20 CENTS

33.7260 g., Silver, 38.3 mm. **Series:** Wildlife - Survivor **Obv:** New national arms **Obv. Designer:** A. L. Sutherland **Rev:** White Rhinoceros mother with an offspring **Rev. Designer:** C. Moses **Edge:** Reeded

Date	Mintage	F	VF	XF	Unc	BU
2003 Proof	1,930	Value: 85.00				

KM# 361 20 CENTS

33.7260 g., 0.9250 Silver 1.0030 oz. ASW, 38.3 mm. **Series:** Wildlife - The legend **Obv:** New national arms **Obv. Designer:** A. L. Sutherland **Rev:** Leopard looking left, cub on branch behind her **Rev. Designer:** A. Minnie **Edge:** Reeded

Date	Mintage	F	VF	XF	Unc	BU
2004 Proof	—	Value: 85.00				

KM# 322 20 CENTS

33.7500 g., 0.9250 Silver 1.0037 oz. ASW, 38.67 mm. **Series:** Wildlife - African Wild Dog **Obv:** New National arms **Obv. Designer:** A. L. Sutherland **Rev:** Three Painted Dogs **Rev. Designer:** M. J. Scheepers **Edge:** Reeded

Date	Mintage	F	VF	XF	Unc	BU
2005 Proof	1,500	Value: 85.00				

KM# 318 20 CENTS

33.7260 g., 0.9250 Silver 1.0030 oz. ASW, 38.7 mm. **Series:** Wildlife - Black-backed Jackal **Obv:** National arms **Obv. Designer:** A. L. Sutherland **Rev:** Two Black-backed jackals **Rev. Designer:** C. Moses **Edge:** Reeded

Date	Mintage	F	VF	XF	Unc	BU
2006 Proof	1,500	Value: 85.00				

KM# 365 20 CENTS

33.7260 g., 0.9250 Silver 1.0030 oz. ASW, 38.3 mm. **Series:** Wildlife - Kgalagadi Transfrontier Peace Park **Obv:** New national arms **Obv. Designer:** A. L. Sutherland **Rev:** Lion's head 3/4 right at left, meerkat standing with offspring at right, value **Rev. Designer:** A. Minnie **Edge:** Reeded

Date	Mintage	F	VF	XF	Unc	BU
2007 Proof	—	Value: 85.00				

KM# 460 20 CENTS

33.7250 g., 0.9990 Silver 1.0832 oz. ASW, 38.7 mm. **Subject:** Richtersveld Transfrontier Park **Obv:** Arms **Obv. Designer:** A. J. Sutherland **Rev:** Two shy Kipspringer (Oreotragus oreotragos) **Rev. Designer:** L. Guerra and A. Minnie

Date	Mintage	F	VF	XF	Unc	BU
2008 Proof	2,200	Value: 75.00				

KM# 484 20 CENTS

33.6200 g., 0.9250 Silver 0.9998 oz. ASW, 38.72 mm. **Subject:** Maloti Drakensberg Transfrontier Project **Obv:** Arms **Obv. Designer:** A. L. Sutherland **Rev:** Cape griffon vulture **Rev. Designer:** L. Guerra and M. J. Scheepers

Date	Mintage	F	VF	XF	Unc	BU
2009 Proof	3,700	Value: 75.00				

KM# 246 50 CENTS

76.4020 g., 0.9250 Silver 2.2721 oz. ASW, 50 mm. **Series:** Wildlife - Power **Obv:** Water buffalo's head **Obv. Designer:** A. L. Sutherland **Rev:** Water buffalo head, value **Rev. Designer:** A. Minnie **Edge:** Reeded

Date	Mintage	F	VF	XF	Unc	BU
2001 Proof	1,866	Value: 110				

KM# 354 50 CENTS

76.4020 g., Silver, 50 mm. **Series:** Wildlife - Strength **Obv:** Elephant walking, facing **Obv. Designer:** A. L. Sutherland **Rev:** Elephant right with head raised **Rev. Designer:** P. Botes **Edge:** Reeded

Date	Mintage	F	VF	XF	Unc	BU
2002 Proof	2,318	Value: 110				

KM# 358 50 CENTS

76.4020 g., 0.9250 Silver 2.2721 oz. ASW, 50 mm. **Series:** Wildlife - Survivor **Obv:** New national arms **Obv. Designer:** A. L. Sutherland **Rev:** White Rhinoceros' head 3/4 right, value **Rev. Designer:** J. Steyn **Edge:** Reeded

Date	Mintage	F	VF	XF	Unc	BU
2003 Proof	1,918	Value: 110				

KM# 362 50 CENTS

76.4620 g., 0.9250 Silver 2.2738 oz. ASW, 50 mm. **Series:** Wildlife - The Legend **Obv:** New national arms **Obv. Designer:** A. L. Sutherland **Rev:** Leopard facing snarling, two leopards at lower left **Rev. Designer:** M. J. Scheepers **Edge:** Reeded

Date	Mintage	F	VF	XF	Unc	BU
2004 Proof	—	Value: 110				

KM# 323 50 CENTS
76.8600 g., 0.9250 Silver 2.2857 oz. ASW, 50.48 mm. **Series:** Wildlife - African Wild Dog **Obv:** New national arms **Obv. Designer:** A. L. Sutherland **Rev:** Two painted Dog's heads facing **Rev. Designer:** L. Guerra **Edge:** Reeded

Date	Mintage	F	VF	XF	Unc	BU
2005 Proof	1,500	Value: 110				

KM# 319 50 CENTS
76.2520 g., 0.9250 Silver 2.2676 oz. ASW, 50 mm. **Series:** Wildlife - Black-backed Jackal **Obv:** New national arms **Obv. Designer:** A. L. Sutherland **Rev:** Two black-backed jackals fighting over a carcass **Rev. Designer:** M. J. Scheepers **Edge:** Reeded

Date	Mintage	F	VF	XF	Unc	BU
2006 Proof	1,500	Value: 110				

KM# 366 50 CENTS
76.4020 g., 0.9250 Silver 2.2721 oz. ASW, 50 mm. **Series:** Wildlife - Kgalagadi Transfrontier Peace Park **Obv:** New national arms **Obv. Designer:** A. L. Sutherland **Rev:** Antelope running right **Rev. Designer:** M. J. Scheepers **Edge:** Reeded

Date	Mintage	F	VF	XF	Unc	BU
2007 Proof	—	Value: 110				

KM# 461 50 CENTS
76.2520 g., 0.9250 Silver 2.2676 oz. ASW, 50 mm. **Subject:** Richtersveld Transfrontier Park **Obv:** Arms **Obv. Designer:** A. J. Sutherland **Rev:** Giant aloe pillansii tree **Rev. Designer:** L. Guerra and M. J. Scheepers

Date	Mintage	F	VF	XF	Unc	BU
2008 Proof	2,200	Value: 60.00				

KM# 485 50 CENTS
76.2520 g., 0.9250 Silver 2.2676 oz. ASW, 50 mm. **Subject:** Maloti Drakensberg Transfrontier Project **Obv:** Arms **Obv. Designer:** A. L. Sutherland **Rev:** Amphitheatre and Trukela River **Rev. Designer:** L. Guerra and M. J. Scheepers

Date	Mintage	F	VF	XF	Unc	BU
2009 Proof	3,700	Value: 100				

KM# 248 2 RAND
33.6260 g., 0.9250 Silver 100000 oz. ASW, 38.7 mm. **Obv:** New national arms **Obv. Designer:** A. L. Sutherland **Rev:** Dolphins **Rev. Designer:** N. van Niekerk **Edge:** Reeded

Date	Mintage	F	VF	XF	Unc	BU
2001 Proof	2,987	Value: 80.00				

KM# 280 2 RAND
33.6260 g., 0.9250 Silver 100000 oz. ASW, 38.7 mm. **Obv:** New national arms **Obv. Designer:** A. L. Sutherland **Rev:** Southern Right Whale **Rev. Designer:** N van Niekerk **Edge:** Reeded

Date	Mintage	F	VF	XF	Unc	BU
2002 Proof	1,808	Value: 85.00				

KM# 286 2 RAND
33.6260 g., 0.9250 Silver 100000 oz. ASW, 38.7 mm. **Obv:** New national arms **Obv. Designer:** A. L. Sutherland **Rev:** Martial and Bateleur Eagles **Rev. Designer:** C. Moses **Edge:** Reeded

Date	Mintage	F	VF	XF	Unc	BU
2003 Proof	2,166	Value: 75.00				

KM# 284 2 RAND
33.6260 g., 0.9250 Silver 100000 oz. ASW, 38.7 mm. **Obv:** New national arms **Obv. Designer:** A. L. Sutherland **Rev:** Verreaux's Eagle Owl face and value **Rev. Designer:** A. Minnie **Edge:** Reeded

Date	Mintage	F	VF	XF	Unc	BU
2004	—	—	—	—	50.00	55.00
2004 Proof	1,752	Value: 85.00				

KM# 372 2 RAND
33.6260 g., 0.9250 Silver 100000 oz. ASW, 38.7 mm. **Obv:** New national arms **Obv. Designer:** A. L. Sutherland **Rev:** Three vultures **Rev. Designer:** C. Moses **Edge:** Reeded

Date	Mintage	F	VF	XF	Unc	BU
2005 Proof	4,000	Value: 70.00				

KM# 374 2 RAND
33.6260 g., 0.9250 Silver 100000 oz. ASW, 38.7 mm. **Series:** Bird of Prey **Obv:** New national arms **Obv. Designer:** A. L. Sutherland **Rev:** Two Secretary birds **Rev. Designer:** C. Moses **Edge:** Reeded

Date	Mintage	F	VF	XF	Unc	BU
2006 Proof	4,000	Value: 75.00				

KM# 481 2 RAND
33.6260 g., 0.9250 Silver 100000 oz. ASW, 38.7 mm. **Obv:** Arms and country name **Obv. Designer:** A. L. Sutherland **Rev:** Jan van Riebeeck's ship "Drommedaries" **Rev. Designer:** L. Guerra

Date	Mintage	F	VF	XF	Unc	BU
2009 Proof	3,500	Value: 55.00				

SILVER BULLION PROTEA COINAGE

KM# 282 2-1/2 CENTS
1.4140 g., 0.9250 Silver 0.0420 oz. ASW, 16.3 mm. **Obv:** Protea flower **Rev:** Southern Right Whale **Edge:** Plain

Date	Mintage	F	VF	XF	Unc	BU
2002 Proof	3,000	Value: 27.50				

KM# 285 2-1/2 CENTS
1.4140 g., 0.9250 Silver 0.0420 oz. ASW, 16.3 mm. **Obv:** Protea flower **Rev:** Martial and Bateleur Eagles **Edge:** Plain

Date	Mintage	F	VF	XF	Unc	BU
2003 Proof	—	Value: 25.00				

KM# 283 2-1/2 CENTS
1.4140 g., 0.9250 Silver 0.0420 oz. ASW, 16.3 mm. **Series:** Birds of Prey **Obv:** Protea flower **Rev:** Pearl Spotted Owlet **Edge:** Plain

Date	Mintage	F	VF	XF	Unc	BU
2004 Proof	2,000	Value: 25.00				

KM# 348 2-1/2 CENTS
1.4140 g., 0.9250 Silver 0.0420 oz. ASW, 16.3 mm. **Obv:** Protea flower **Obv. Legend:** SOUTH AFRICA **Rev:** Vulture alighting **Edge:** Plain

Date	Mintage	F	VF	XF	Unc	BU
2005 Proof	—	Value: 25.00				

KM# 349 2-1/2 CENTS
1.4140 g., 0.9250 Silver 0.0420 oz. ASW, 16.3 mm. **Obv:** Protea flower **Obv. Legend:** SOUTH AFRICA **Rev:** Head of Secretary bird **Edge:** Plain

Date	Mintage	F	VF	XF	Unc	BU
2006 Proof	—	Value: 25.00				

KM# 350 2-1/2 CENTS
1.4140 g., 0.9250 Silver 0.0420 oz. ASW, 16.3 mm. **Subject:** International Polar Year **Obv:** Protea flower **Obv. Legend:** SOUTH AFRICA **Rev:** Globe displaying South Pole **Edge:** Plain

Date	Mintage	F	VF	XF	Unc	BU
2007 Proof	—	Value: 25.00				

KM# 231 RAND
15.0000 g., 0.9250 Silver 0.4461 oz. ASW, 32.7 mm. **Subject:** Tourism **Obv:** Protea flower **Rev:** Steam locomotive and flower **Edge:** Reeded

Date	Mintage	F	VF	XF	Unc	BU
2001	2,400	—	—	—	40.00	45.00
2001 Proof	1,784	Value: 65.00				

KM# 277 RAND
15.0000 g., 0.9250 Silver 0.4461 oz. ASW, 32.7 mm. **Subject:** Soccer **Obv:** Protea flower **Obv. Designer:** A.L. Sutherland **Rev:** Goalkeeper in action **Edge:** Reeded

Date	Mintage	F	VF	XF	Unc	BU
2002	1,777	—	—	—	40.00	45.00
2002 Proof	1,250	Value: 65.00				

KM# 367 RAND
15.0000 g., 0.9250 Silver 0.4461 oz. ASW **Subject:** World Summit - Johannesburg **Obv:** Protea flower **Obv. Designer:** A. L. Sutherland **Rev:** Globe **Edge:** Reeded

Date	Mintage	F	VF	XF	Unc	BU
2002	1,531	—	—	—	55.00	60.00
2002 Proof	1,413	Value: 75.00				

KM# 298 RAND

15.0500 g., 0.9250 Silver 0.4476 oz. ASW, 32.7 mm. **Obv:** Protea flower **Obv. Designer:** A. L. Sutherland **Rev:** Cricket player **Edge:** Reeded

Date	Mintage	F	VF	XF	Unc	BU
2003	1,697	—	—	—	55.00	60.00
2003 Proof	1,250	Value: 75.00				

KM# 288 RAND

15.0000 g., 0.9250 Silver 0.4461 oz. ASW, 32.7 mm. **Subject:** 10th Anniversary of South African Democracy **Obv:** Protea flower **Rev:** Flora and fauna **Edge:** Reeded

Date	Mintage	F	VF	XF	Unc	BU
2004	3,427	—	—	—	35.00	40.00
2004 Proof	2,930	Value: 50.00				

KM# 368 RAND

15.0000 g., 0.9250 Silver 0.4461 oz. ASW, 32.7 mm. **Series:** Nobel Peace Prize Winners **Obv:** Protea flower **Obv. Designer:** A. L. Sutherland **Rev:** Bust of Chief A. J. Luthuli facing at center, Luthuli seated at desk left at lower right **Edge:** Reeded

Date	Mintage	F	VF	XF	Unc	BU
2005	—	—	—	—	50.00	55.00
2005 Proof	—	Value: 65.00				

KM# 369 RAND

15.0000 g., 0.9250 Silver 0.4461 oz. ASW, 32.7 mm. **Series:** Nobel Peace prize Winners **Obv:** Protea flower **Obv. Designer:** A. J. Sutherland **Rev:** 1/3 length figure of Archbishop Desmond Mpilo Tutu facing at right **Edge:** Reeded

Date	Mintage	F	VF	XF	Unc	BU
2006	—	—	—	—	60.00	65.00
2006	—	Value: 75.00				

KM# 370 RAND

15.0000 g., Silver, 32.7 mm. **Series:** Nobel Peace Prize Winners **Obv:** Protea flower **Obv. Designer:** A. J. Sutherland **Rev:** Bust of De Klerk facing **Edge:** Reeded

Date	Mintage	F	VF	XF	Unc	BU
2007	—	—	—	—	55.00	60.00
2007 Proof	—	Value: 70.00				

KM# 371 RAND

15.0000 g., 0.9250 Silver 0.4461 oz. ASW, 32.7 mm. **Series:** Nobel Peace Prize Winners **Obv:** Protea flower **Obv. Designer:** A. J. Sutherland **Rev:** Bust of Mandela facing **Edge:** Reeded

Date	Mintage	F	VF	XF	Unc	BU
2007	—	—	—	—	65.00	75.00
2007 Proof	—	Value: 95.00				

KM# 451 RAND

15.5500 g., 0.9250 Silver 0.4624 oz. ASW, 32.7 mm. **Obv:** Protea flower **Obv. Designer:** A. L. Sutherland **Rev:** Ghandi portrait **Rev. Designer:** M. J. Scheepers and N. van Niekerk

Date	Mintage	F	VF	XF	Unc	BU
2008	—	—	—	—	—	22.00
2008 Proof	11,000	Value: 27.00				

KM# 475 RAND

15.5500 g., 0.9250 Silver 0.4624 oz. ASW, 32.7 mm. **Obv:** Protea flower **Obv. Designer:** A. L. Sutherland **Rev:** Portraits of C. J. Langenhoven and N. L. de Villiers with musical score **Rev. Designer:** A. Minnie and M. J. Scheepers

Date	Mintage	F	VF	XF	Unc	BU
2009	—	—	—	—	—	20.00
2009 Proof	11,000	Value: 27.00				

SILVER BULLION CULTURE COINAGE

KM# 456 2-1/2 CENTS

1.1400 g., 0.9250 Silver 0.0339 oz. ASW, 16.3 mm. **Obv:** Flower **Obv. Designer:** A. J. Sutherland **Rev:** Map of Antarctica **Rev. Designer:** L. Guerra and M. J. Scheepers

Date	Mintage	F	VF	XF	Unc	BU
2008 Proof	3,000	Value: 15.00				

KM# 373 2 RAND

33.6260 g., 0.9250 Silver 100000 oz. ASW, 38.7 mm. **Subject:** 2006 FIFA World Cup Soccer - Germany **Obv:** New national arms **Obv. Designer:** A. L. Sutherland **Rev:** Soccer ball above globe **Rev. Designer:** M. Scheepers **Edge:** Reeded

Date	Mintage	F	VF	XF	Unc	BU
2005 Proof	50,000	Value: 60.00				

KM# 435 2 RAND

33.6300 g., 0.9250 Silver 1.0000 oz. ASW, 38.7 mm. **Subject:** 2010 World Cup

Date	Mintage	F	VF	XF	Unc	BU
2006	25,000	—	—	—	—	50.00

KM# 376 2 RAND

33.6260 g., 0.9250 Silver 100000 oz. ASW, 38.7 mm. **Subject:** International Polar Year **Obv:** New national arms **Obv. Designer:** A. L. Sutherland **Rev:** Logo above globe **Rev. Designer:** A. Minnie **Edge:** Reeded

Date	Mintage	F	VF	XF	Unc	BU
2007 Proof	6,000	Value: 70.00				

KM# 377 2 RAND

33.6260 g., 0.9250 Silver 100000 oz. ASW, 38.7 mm. **Subject:** 2010 FIFA World Cup Soccer - South Africa **Obv:** New national arms **Obv. Designer:** A. L. Sutherland **Rev:** Tower at left, animal heads at top. animal at right, soccer ball ar bottom **Rev. Designer:** M. J. Scheepers **Edge:** Reeded

Date	Mintage	F	VF	XF	Unc	BU
2007 Proof	20,000	Value: 65.00				

KM# 437 2 RAND

33.6260 g., 0.9250 Silver 100000 oz. ASW, 38.7 mm. **Subject:** 2010 World Cup

Date	Mintage	F	VF	XF	Unc	BU
2008 Proof	—	Value: 55.00				

KM# 457 2 RAND

33.6200 g., 0.9250 Silver 0.9998 oz. ASW, 38.7 mm. **Obv:** Arms **Obv. Designer:** A. L. Sutherland **Rev:** Polar ship "SA Sgulhas" **Rev. Designer:** L. Guerra

Date	Mintage	F	VF	XF	Unc	BU
2008 Proof	3,000	Value: 55.00				

GOLD BULLION NATURA COINAGE

KM# 389 2 RAND

7.7770 g., 0.9999 Gold 0.2500 oz. AGW, 22 mm. **Series:** World Heritage Site **Subject:** Mapungubwe **Obv:** New national arms **Obv. Designer:** A. L. Sutherland **Rev:** Rhinoceros standing right **Rev. Designer:** M. J. Scheepers **Edge:** Reeded

Date	Mintage	F	VF	XF	Unc	BU
2005 Proof	1,000	Value: 425				

KM# 455 2 RAND

7.7700 g., 0.9990 Gold 0.2496 oz. AGW, 22 mm. **Subject:** Vredefort Dome **Obv:** Arms **Obv. Designer:** A. J. Sutherland **Rev:** Meteorite **Rev. Designer:** K. Pillay and M. J. Scheepers

Date	Mintage	F	VF	XF	Unc	BU
2008 Proof	2,000	Value: 400				

KM# 410 10 RAND

3.1107 g., 0.9999 Gold 0.1000 oz. AGW, 16.5 mm. **Series:** Natura **Obv:** Cheetah's head **Obv. Designer:** A. L. Sutherland **Rev:** Cheetah drinking water **Rev. Designer:** M. J. Scheepers **Edge:** Reeded

Date	Mintage	F	VF	XF	Unc	BU
2002 Proof	3,156	Value: 200				

KM# 414 10 RAND

3.1107 g., 0.9999 Gold 0.1000 oz. AGW, 16.5 mm. **Series:** Natura **Obv:** Male and female lion's heads **Obv. Designer:** A. L. Sutherland **Rev:** Two lioness drinking water **Rev. Designer:** C. Moses **Edge:** Reeded

Date	Mintage	F	VF	XF	Unc	BU
2003 Proof	4,233	Value: 200				

KM# 418 10 RAND

3.1107 g., 0.9999 Gold 0.1000 oz. AGW, 16.5 mm. **Series:** Natura **Obv:** Caracal's head and shoulders **Obv. Designer:** Aldrid Minnie **Rev:** Caracal drinking water **Rev. Designer:** C. Moses **Edge:** Reeded

Date	Mintage	F	VF	XF	Unc	BU
2004 Proof	1,809	Value: 210				

KM# 422 10 RAND

3.1107 g., 0.9999 Gold 0.1000 oz. AGW, 16.5 mm. **Series:** Natura **Obv:** Hippopotamus 1/2 way in water **Rev:** Hippopotamus deeply in water **Edge:** Reeded **Designer:** Aldrid Minnie

Date	Mintage	F	VF	XF	Unc	BU
2005 Proof	—	Value: 210				

KM# 426 10 RAND

3.1107 g., 0.9999 Gold 0.1000 oz. AGW, 16.5 mm. **Series:** Natura **Obv:** Giraffe's head and neck **Obv. Designer:** M. J. Scheepers **Rev:** Giraffe drinking water **Rev. Designer:** C. Moses **Edge:** Reeded

Date	Mintage	F	VF	XF	Unc	BU
2006 Proof	—	Value: 200				

KM# 430 10 RAND

3.1107 g., 0.9999 Gold 0.1000 oz. AGW, 16.5 mm. **Series:** Natura **Obv:** Forepart of Eland left **Rev:** Eland drinking water right **Edge:** Reeded **Designer:** Aldrid Minnie

Date	Mintage	F	VF	XF	Unc	BU
2007 Proof	—	Value: 200				

KM# 447 10 RAND

3.1100 g., 0.9990 Gold 0.0999 oz. AGW, 16.5 mm. **Obv:** Large elephant head and elephant family below **Rev:** One elephant eating, three elephants below **Designer:** C. Moses and N. van Niekerk

Date	Mintage	F	VF	XF	Unc	BU
2008 Proof	3,300	Value: 200				

KM# 471 10 RAND

3.1100 g., 0.9990 Gold 0.0999 oz. AGW, 16.5 mm. **Obv:** White rhino, silouette and forepart **Obv. Designer:** N. van Niekerk and M. J. Scheepers **Rev:** Two rhino foreparts facing left within large silouette **Rev. Designer:** N. van Niekerk and A. Minnie

Date	Mintage	F	VF	XF	Unc	BU
2009 Proof	2,500	Value: 200				

KM# 411 20 RAND

7.7770 g., 0.9999 Gold 0.2500 oz. AGW, 22 mm. **Series:** Natura **Obv:** Cheetah's head **Obv. Designer:** A. L. Sutherland **Rev:** Cheetah family resting **Rev. Designer:** Aldrid Minnie **Edge:** Reeded

Date	Mintage	F	VF	XF	Unc	BU
2002 Proof	2,548	Value: 400				

KM# 415 20 RAND
7.7770 g., 0.9999 Gold 0.2500 oz. AGW, 22 mm. **Series:** Natura **Obv:** Male and female lion's heads **Obv. Designer:** A. L. Sutherland **Rev:** Lion family resting **Rev. Designer:** M. J. Scheepers **Edge:** Reeded

Date	Mintage	F	VF	XF	Unc	BU
2003 Proof	2,799	Value: 400				

KM# 419 20 RAND
7.7770 g., 0.9999 Gold 0.2500 oz. AGW, 22 mm. **Series:** Natura **Obv:** Caracal's head and shoulders **Obv. Designer:** Aldrid Minnie **Rev:** Caracal with cub standing right **Rev. Designer:** M. J. Scheepers **Edge:** Reeded

Date	Mintage	F	VF	XF	Unc	BU
2004 Proof	1,407	Value: 420				

KM# 423 20 RAND
7.7770 g., 0.9999 Gold 0.2500 oz. AGW, 22 mm. **Series:** Natura **Obv:** Hippopotamus 1/2 way in water **Obv. Designer:** Aldrid Minnie **Rev:** Mother and baby Hippopotamus grazing **Edge:** Reeded

Date	Mintage	F	VF	XF	Unc	BU
2005 Proof	—	Value: 420				

KM# 427 20 RAND
7.7770 g., 0.9999 Gold 0.2500 oz. AGW, 22 mm. **Series:** Natura **Obv:** Giraffe's head and neck **Obv. Designer:** M. J. Scheepers **Rev:** Mother and baby giraffes grazing **Rev. Designer:** C. Moses **Edge:** Reeded

Date	Mintage	F	VF	XF	Unc	BU
2006 Proof	—	Value: 400				

KM# 431 20 RAND
7.7770 g., 0.9999 Gold 0.2500 oz. AGW, 22 mm. **Series:** Natura **Obv:** Forepart of Eland left **Rev:** Mother Eland and calf grazing **Edge:** Reeded **Designer:** Aldrid Minnie

Date	Mintage	F	VF	XF	Unc	BU
2007 Proof	—	Value: 400				

KM# 448 20 RAND
7.7770 g., 0.9990 Gold 0.2498 oz. AGW, 22 mm. **Obv:** Large elephant head and elephant family below **Obv. Designer:** C. Moses and N. van Niekerk **Rev:** Two elephants fighting, three elephants below **Rev. Designer:** M. J. Scheepers and N. van Niekerk

Date	Mintage	F	VF	XF	Unc	BU
2008 Proof	3,300	Value: 400				

KM# 472 20 RAND
7.7770 g., 0.9990 Gold 0.2498 oz. AGW, 22 mm. **Obv:** White rhino silouette and forepart **Obv. Designer:** N. van Niekerk and M. J. Scheepers **Rev:** Two rhinos walking forward within silhouette **Rev. Designer:** N. van Niekerk and C. Moses

Date	Mintage	F	VF	XF	Unc	BU
2009 Proof	2,500	Value: 400				

KM# 412 50 RAND
15.5530 g., 0.9999 Gold 0.5000 oz. AGW, 27 mm. **Series:** Natura **Obv:** Cheetah's head **Obv. Designer:** A. L. Sutherland **Rev:** Cheetah attacking Impala **Rev. Designer:** Johan Steyn **Edge:** Reeded

Date	Mintage	F	VF	XF	Unc	BU
2002 Proof	2,295	Value: 800				

KM# 416 50 RAND
15.5530 g., 0.9999 Gold 0.5000 oz. AGW, 27 mm. **Series:** Natura **Obv:** Male and female lion's heads **Obv. Designer:** A. L. Sutherland **Rev:** Female and male lions playing **Rev. Designer:** Aldrid Minnie **Edge:** Reeded

Date	Mintage	F	VF	XF	Unc	BU
2003 Proof	2,600	Value: 800				

KM# 420 50 RAND
15.5530 g., 0.9999 Gold 0.5000 oz. AGW, 27 mm. **Series:** Natura **Obv:** Caracal's head and shoulders **Rev:** Caracal eating prey **Edge:** Reeded **Designer:** Aldrid Minnie

Date	Mintage	F	VF	XF	Unc	BU
2004 Proof	1,327	Value: 825				

KM# 424 50 RAND
15.5530 g., 0.9999 Gold 0.5000 oz. AGW, 27 mm. **Series:** Natura **Obv:** Hippopotamus 1/2 way in water **Obv. Designer:** Aldrid Minnie **Rev:** Hippopotamus submerged in water with head raised above, mouth wide open **Rev. Designer:** M. J. Scheepers **Edge:** Reeded

Date	Mintage	F	VF	XF	Unc	BU
2005 Proof	—	Value: 825				

KM# 428 50 RAND
15.5530 g., 0.9999 Gold 0.5000 oz. AGW, 27 mm. **Series:** Natura **Obv:** Giraffe's head and neck **Obv. Designer:** M. J. Scheepers **Rev:** Giraffe family walking left **Rev. Designer:** Aldrid Minnie **Edge:** Reeded

Date	Mintage	F	VF	XF	Unc	BU
2006 Proof	—	Value: 800				

KM# 432 50 RAND
15.5530 g., 0.9999 Gold 0.5000 oz. AGW, 27 mm. **Series:** Natura **Obv:** Forepart of eland left **Obv. Designer:** Aldrid Minnie **Rev:** Three eland running right **Rev. Designer:** M. J. Scheepers **Edge:** Reeded

Date	Mintage	F	VF	XF	Unc	BU
2007 Proof	—	Value: 800				

KM# 449 50 RAND
15.5530 g., 0.9990 Gold 0.4995 oz. AGW, 27 mm. **Obv:** Large elephant and elephant family below **Obv. Designer:** C. Moses and N. van Niekerk **Rev:** Three elephants, one trumpeting, three elephants below **Rev. Designer:** A. Minnie and N. van Niekerk

Date	Mintage	F	VF	XF	Unc	BU
2008 Proof	4,800	Value: 800				

KM# 473 50 RAND
15.5500 g., 0.9990 Gold 0.4994 oz. AGW, 27 mm. **Obv:** White rhino silhouette and forpart **Obv. Designer:** N. van Niekerk and M. J. Scheepers **Rev:** Two rhinos facing off within large silouette **Rev. Designer:** N. van Niekerk and C. Moses

Date	Mintage	F	VF	XF	Unc	BU
2009 Proof	4,000	Value: 800				

KM# 413 100 RAND
31.1070 g., 0.9999 Gold 100000 oz. AGW, 32.69 mm. **Series:** Natura **Obv:** Cheetah's head **Obv. Designer:** A. L. Sutherland **Rev:** Cheetah posing **Rev. Designer:** P. Botes **Edge:** Reeded

Date	Mintage	F	VF	XF	Unc	BU
2002 Proof	2,550	Value: 1,500				
2002 RSA logo Proof	496	Value: 1,750				

KM# 417 100 RAND
31.1070 g., 0.9999 Gold 100000 oz. AGW, 32.69 mm. **Series:** Natura **Obv:** Male and female lion's heads **Obv. Designer:** A. L. Sutherland **Rev:** Snarling male and female lion's heads **Rev. Designer:** P. Botes **Edge:** Reeded **Note:** L P RSA - LION PARK RSA.

Date	Mintage	F	VF	XF	Unc	BU
2003 Proof	2,758	Value: 1,500				
2003 L P RSA Proof	498	Value: 1,750				

KM# 421 100 RAND
31.1070 g., 0.9999 Gold 100000 oz. AGW, 32.69 mm. **Series:** Natura **Obv:** Caracal's head and shoulders **Obv. Designer:** Aldrid Minnie **Rev:** Caracal crouching on branch left **Rev. Designer:** M. J. Scheepers **Edge:** Reeded **Note:** C/C - CARACAL / CARACAL

Date	Mintage	F	VF	XF	Unc	BU
2004 Proof	1,405	Value: 1,550				
2004 C/C Proof	500	Value: 1,750				

KM# 425 100 RAND
31.1070 g., 0.9999 Gold 100000 oz. AGW, 32.69 mm. **Series:** Natura **Obv:** Hippopotamus 1/2 way in water **Obv. Designer:** Aldrid Minnie **Rev:** Two hippopotami submerged in water, heads raised, mouths open faced in combat **Rev. Designer:** M. J. Scheepers **Edge:** Reeded **Note:** MAPU - MAPUNGUBWE.

Date	Mintage	F	VF	XF	Unc	BU
2005 Proof	—	Value: 1,550				
2005 MAPU Proof	—	Value: 1,750				

KM# 429 100 RAND
31.1070 g., 0.9999 Gold 100000 oz. AGW, 32.69 mm. **Series:** Natura **Obv:** Giraffe's head and neck **Rev:** Head and neck view of giraffe eating tree leaves **Edge:** Reeded **Designer:** M. J. Scheepers **Note:** lpp/EWT - lion's paw print / EWT.

Date	Mintage	F	VF	XF	Unc	BU
2006 Proof	—	Value: 1,500				
2006 lpp/EWT Proof	—	Value: 1,700				

KM# 433 100 RAND
31.1070 g., 0.9999 Gold 100000 oz. AGW, 32.7 mm. **Series:** Natura **Obv:** Forepart of eland left **Obv. Designer:** Aldrid Minnie **Rev:** Eland grazing left **Rev. Designer:** C. Moses **Edge:** Reeded

Date	Mintage	F	VF	XF	Unc	BU
2007 Proof	—	Value: 1,500				
2007 Proof	—	Value: 1,700				

KM# 450 100 RAND
31.1070 g., 0.9990 Gold 0.9991 oz. AGW, 32.69 mm. **Obv:** Large elephant head and elephant family below **Obv. Designer:** C. Moses and N. van Niekerk **Rev:** Large elephant facing, three elephants below **Rev. Designer:** A. Minnie and N. van Niekerk

Date	Mintage	F	VF	XF	Unc	BU
2008 Proof	4,800	Value: 1,500				

KM# 474 100 RAND
31.1070 g., 0.9990 Gold 0.9991 oz. AGW **Obv:** White rhino silouette and forepart **Obv. Designer:** N. van Niekerk and M. J. Scheepers **Rev:** Rhino standing facing within large silhouette **Rev. Designer:** N. van Niekerk and A. Minnie **Shape:** 32.7

Date	Mintage	F	VF	XF	Unc	BU
2009 Proof	4,000	Value: 1,500				

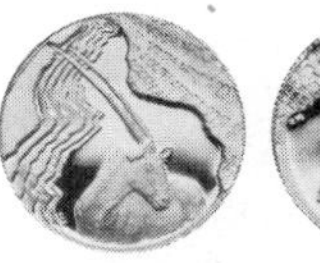

KM# 264 1/10 OUNCE
3.1107 g., 0.9999 Gold 0.1000 oz. AGW, 16.5 mm. **Series:** Natura **Obv:** Gemsbok's upper body **Obv. Designer:** A. L. Sutherland **Rev:** Gemsbok drinking **Rev. Designer:** C. Moses **Edge:** Reeded

Date	Mintage	F	VF	XF	Unc	BU
2001 Proof	3,498	Value: 200				

KM# 265 1/4 OUNCE
7.7770 g., 0.9999 Gold 0.2500 oz. AGW, 22 mm. **Series:** Natura **Obv:** Gemsbok's upper body **Obv. Designer:** A. L. Sutherland **Rev:** Two Gemsbok bulls facing off **Rev. Designer:** M. J. Scheepers **Edge:** Reeded

Date	Mintage	F	VF	XF	Unc	BU
2001 Proof	2,904	Value: 400				

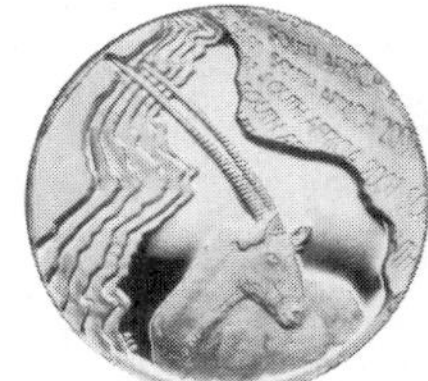

KM# 266 1/2 OUNCE
15.5530 g., 0.9999 Gold 0.5000 oz. AGW, 27 mm. **Series:** Natura **Obv:** Gemsbok's upper body **Obv. Designer:** A. L. Sutherland **Rev:** Gemsbok family grazing **Rev. Designer:** P. Botes **Edge:** Reeded

Date	Mintage	F	VF	XF	Unc	BU
2001 Proof	2,754	Value: 800				

KM# 267 OUNCE
31.1070 g., 0.9999 Gold 100000 oz. AGW, 32.69 mm. **Series:** Natura **Obv:** Gemsbok's upper body **Obv. Designer:** A. L. Sutherland **Rev:** Gemsbok grazing **Rev. Designer:** Aldrid Minnie **Edge:** Reeded **Note:** ghCW - Gemsbok's head CW

Date	Mintage	F	VF	XF	Unc	BU
2001 Proof	3,104	Value: 1,500				
2001 Proof	491	Value: 1,750				

GOLD BULLION CULTURE COINAGE

KM# 247 RAND
3.1103 g., 0.9999 Gold 0.1000 oz. AGW, 16.5 mm. **Series:** Cultural **Obv:** New national arms **Obv. Legend:** UMZANTSI AFRIKA - SOUTH AFRICA **Obv. Designer:** A.L. Sutherland **Rev:** Seated Sotho figure with headdress **Rev. Designer:** Johan Steyn **Edge:** Reeded

Date	Mintage	F	VF	XF	Unc	BU
2001 Proof	236	Value: 275				

KM# 378 RAND
3.1103 g., 0.9999 Gold 0.1000 oz. AGW, 16.5 mm. **Series:** Cultural **Obv:** New national arms **Obv. Legend:** UMZANTSI AFRIKA - SOUTH AFRICA **Obv. Designer:** A. L. Sutherland **Rev:** Three Xhosa tribe members **Rev. Designer:** P. Botes **Edge:** Reeded

Date	Mintage	F	VF	XF	Unc	BU
2001 Proof	—	Value: 675				

KM# 379 RAND
3.1103 g., 0.9999 Gold 0.1000 oz. AGW, 16.5 mm. **Series:** Cultural **Subject:** Tswana Nation **Obv:** New national arms **Obv. Legend:** Aforika Borwa - South Africa **Obv. Designer:** A. L. Sutherland **Rev:** Four tribe people standing **Rev. Designer:** C. Moses **Edge:** Reeded

Date	Mintage	F	VF	XF	Unc	BU
2002 Proof	300	Value: 350				

KM# 380 RAND
3.1103 g., 0.9999 Gold 0.1000 oz. AGW, 16.5 mm. **Series:** Cultural **Obv:** New national arms **Obv. Legend:** Afrika-Dzonga - South Africa **Obv. Designer:** A. L. Sutherland **Rev:** Tsonga tribe dancer and drummer **Rev. Designer:** A. Minnie **Edge:** Reeded

Date	Mintage	F	VF	XF	Unc	BU
2003 Proof	348	Value: 350				

KM# 381 RAND
3.1103 g., 0.9999 Gold 0.1000 oz. AGW, 16.5 mm. **Series:** Cultural **Obv:** New national arms **Obv. Legend:** Afurika Tshipembe - South Africa **Obv. Designer:** A. L. Sutherland **Rev:** Six Venda tribe members crossing bridge **Rev. Designer:** M. J. Scheepers **Edge:** Reeded

Date	Mintage	F	VF	XF	Unc	BU
2004 Proof	380	Value: 350				

KM# 382 RAND
3.1103 g., 0.9999 Gold 0.1000 oz. AGW, 16.5 mm. **Series:** Cultural **Obv:** New national arms **Obv. Legend:** iSewula Afrika - South Africa **Obv. Designer:** A. L. Sutherland **Rev:** Ndebele woman standing, native print in background **Rev. Designer:** A. Minnie **Edge:** Reeded

Date	Mintage	F	VF	XF	Unc	BU
2005 Proof	1,000	Value: 200				

KM# 383 RAND
3.1103 g., 0.9999 Gold 0.1000 oz. AGW, 16.5 mm. **Series:** Cultural **Obv:** New national arms **Obv. Legend:** Ningizimu Afrika - South Africa **Obv. Designer:** A. L. Sutherland **Rev:** 1/2 length figure of Ema-Swati Chief left at right **Rev. Designer:** A. Minnie **Edge:** Reeded

Date	Mintage	F	VF	XF	Unc	BU
2006 Proof	1,000	Value: 200				

KM# 385 RAND
3.1103 g., 0.9999 Gold 0.1000 oz. AGW, 16.5 mm. **Subject:** 2010 FIFA World Cup Soccer - South Africa **Obv:** New national arms **Obv. Legend:** SOUTH AFRICA **Obv. Designer:** A. L. Sutherland **Rev:** Bird head at left facing animal at right, soccer ball at bottom **Rev. Designer:** A. Minnie **Edge:** Reeded

Date	Mintage	F	VF	XF	Unc	BU
2007 Proof	10,000	Value: 200				

KM# 384 RAND
3.1103 g., 0.9999 Gold 0.1000 oz. AGW, 16.5 mm. **Subject:** The Afrikaner Nation **Obv:** New national arms **Obv. Legend:** SOUTH AFRIKA **Obv. Designer:** A. L. Sutherland **Rev:** Ox drawn wagon up hillside **Rev. Designer:** A. Minnie **Edge:** Reeded

Date	Mintage	F	VF	XF	Unc	BU
2007 Proof	—	Value: 200				

KM# 454 RAND
3.1100 g., 0.9990 Gold 0.0999 oz. AGW, 16.5 mm. **Obv:** Arms **Obv. Designer:** A. J. Sutherland

Date	Mintage	F	VF	XF	Unc	BU
2008 Proof	1,000	Value: 200				

KM# 478 RAND
3.1100 g., 0.9990 Gold 0.0999 oz. AGW, 16.5 mm. **Subject:** Northern Sotho (Bapedi) peoples **Obv:** Arms **Obv. Designer:** A. L. Sutherland **Rev:** Woman seated, cooking **Rev. Designer:** C. Moses and M. J. Scheepers

Date	Mintage	F	VF	XF	Unc	BU
2009 Proof	1,000	Value: 200				

KM# 249 2 RAND
7.7770 g., 0.9999 Gold 0.2500 oz. AGW, 22 mm. **Obv:** New national arms **Obv. Designer:** A.L. Sutherland **Rev:** Gondwana theoretical landmass and dinosaur **Rev. Designer:** M. J. Scheepers **Edge:** Reeded

Date	Mintage	F	VF	XF	Unc	BU
2001 Proof	558	Value: 450				

KM# 386 2 RAND
7.7770 g., 0.9999 Gold 0.2500 oz. AGW, 22 mm. **Series:** World Heritage Site **Subject:** Robben Island **Obv:** New national arms **Obv. Designer:** A. L. Sutherland **Rev:** Carved stone, island in background **Rev. Designer:** M. J. Scheepers **Edge:** Reeded

Date	Mintage	F	VF	XF	Unc	BU
2002 Proof	999	Value: 800				

KM# 387 2 RAND
7.7770 g., 0.9999 Gold 0.2500 oz. AGW, 22 mm. **Series:** World heritage Site **Subject:** Greater St. Lucia Wetland Park **Obv:** New national arms **Obv. Designer:** A. L. Sutherland **Rev:** Various birds **Rev. Designer:** M. J. Scheepers **Edge:** Reeded

Date	Mintage	F	VF	XF	Unc	BU
2003 Proof	637	Value: 450				

KM# 388 2 RAND
7.7770 g., 0.9999 Gold 0.2500 oz. AGW, 22 mm. **Series:** World Heritage Park **Subject:** "Ukhahlamba" Drakensberg Park **Obv:** New national arms **Obv. Designer:** A. L. Sutherland **Rev:** Early painting of animal and hunters **Rev. Designer:** M. J. Scheepers **Edge:** Reeded

Date	Mintage	F	VF	XF	Unc	BU
2004 Proof	750	Value: 425				

KM# 390 2 RAND
7.7770 g., 0.9999 Gold 0.2500 oz. AGW, 22 mm. **Subject:** 2006 FIFA World Cup Soccer - Germany **Obv:** New national arms **Obv. Designer:** A. L. Sutherland **Rev:** Soccer ball at center above partial globe within ornate border art **Rev. Designer:** M. J. Scheepers **Edge:** Reeded

Date	Mintage	F	VF	XF	Unc	BU
2005 Proof	—	Value: 425				

KM# 391 2 RAND
7.7770 g., 0.9999 Gold 0.2500 oz. AGW, 22 mm. **Series:** World Heritage Site **Subject:** Cradle of Mankind **Obv:** New national arms **Obv. Designer:** A. L. Sutherland **Rev:** Early man standing at upper left, ape's head at upper right, skull at lower left, value at lower right **Rev. Designer:** M. J. Scheepers **Edge:** Reeded

Date	Mintage	F	VF	XF	Unc	BU
2006 Proof	1,000	Value: 420				

KM# 392 2 RAND
7.7770 g., 0.9999 Gold 0.2500 oz. AGW, 22 mm. **Subject:** 2006 FIFA World Cup Soccer - Germany **Obv:** New national arms **Obv. Designer:** A. L. Sutherland **Rev:** Logo in ornate frame **Rev. Designer:** M. J. Scheepers **Edge:** Reeded

Date	Mintage	F	VF	XF	Unc	BU
2006 Proof	15,000	Value: 400				

KM# 393 2 RAND
7.7770 g., 0.9999 Gold 0.2500 oz. AGW, 22 mm. **Series:** World Heritage Site **Subject:** Cape Floral **Obv:** New national arms **Obv. Designer:** A. L. Sutherland **Rev:** Bird perched on branch at left, plant at center, land in distance **Rev. Designer:** M. J. Scheepers **Edge:** Reeded

Date	Mintage	F	VF	XF	Unc	BU
2007 Proof	—	Value: 400				

KM# 394 2 RAND
7.7770 g., 0.9999 Gold 0.2500 oz. AGW, 22 mm. **Subject:** 2010 FIFA World Cup Soccer - South Africa **Obv:** New national arms **Obv. Designer:** A. L. Sutherland **Rev:** Animal in ornate frame at left and right, small soccer ball at bottom below value **Rev. Designer:** M. J. Scheepers **Edge:** Reeded

Date	Mintage	F	VF	XF	Unc	BU
2007 Proof	10,000	Value: 400				

KM# 479 2 RAND
7.7700 g., 0.9990 Gold 0.2496 oz. AGW, 22 mm. **Subject:** Richtersveld Cultural and Botanical Landscape **Obv:** Arms **Obv. Designer:** A. L. Sutherland **Rev:** Native "haru on" hut and aloe pilansil tree **Rev. Designer:** J. Lloyd

Date	Mintage	F	VF	XF	Unc	BU
2009 Proof	2,000	Value: 425				

GOLD BULLION PROTEA COINAGE

KM# 395 5 RAND
3.1107 g., 0.9999 Gold 0.1000 oz. AGW, 16.5 mm. **Subject:** 10th Anniversary Soccer "Bafana Bafana" **Obv:** Protea flower **Obv. Designer:** A. L. Sutherland **Rev:** Two players running right **Rev. Designer:** P. Botes **Edge:** Reeded

Date	Mintage	F	VF	XF	Unc	BU
2002 Proof	386	Value: 275				

KM# 397 5 RAND
3.1107 g., 0.9999 Gold 0.1000 oz. AGW, 16.5 mm. **Subject:** World Summit on Sustainable Development **Obv:** Protea flower **Obv. Designer:** A. L. Sutherland **Rev:** Globe featuring Africa **Rev. Inscription:** prosperity **Rev. Designer:** M. J. Scheepers **Edge:** Reeded

Date	Mintage	F	VF	XF	Unc	BU
2002 Proof	511	Value: 225				

KM# 278 5 RAND
3.1104 g., 0.9999 Gold 0.1000 oz. AGW, 16.5 mm. **Obv:** Protea flower **Rev:** Soccer player heading the ball **Edge:** Reeded

Date	Mintage	F	VF	XF	Unc	BU
2002 Proof	—	Value: 200				

KM# 399 5 RAND
3.1107 g., 0.9999 Gold 0.1000 oz. AGW, 16.5 mm. **Subject:** Cricket World Cup **Obv:** Protea flower **Obv. Designer:** A. L. Sutherland **Rev:** Cricket ball striking stumps **Rev. Inscription:** Protea **Rev. Designer:** C. Moses **Edge:** Reeded

Date	Mintage	F	VF	XF	Unc	BU
2003 Proof	925	Value: 200				

KM# 289 5 RAND
3.1100 g., 0.9999 Gold 0.1000 oz. AGW, 16.5 mm. **Subject:** 10th Anniversary of South African Democracy **Obv:** Protea flower **Rev:** Inscription covered flag **Edge:** Reeded

Date	Mintage	F	VF	XF	Unc	BU
2004 Proof	1,000	Value: 200				

KM# 401 5 RAND
3.1107 g., 0.9999 Gold 0.1000 oz. AGW, 16.5 mm. **Subject:** 10th Anniversay Democracy **Obv:** Protea flower **Obv. Designer:** A. L. Sutherland **Rev:** Flag made of constitution **Rev. Designer:** M. J. Scheepers **Edge:** Reeded **Note:** 10YF - circular 10 YEARS FREEDOM

Date	Mintage	F	VF	XF	Unc	BU
2004 Proof	2,089	Value: 375				
2004 10YF Proof	492	Value: 600				

KM# 403 5 RAND
3.1107 g., 0.9999 Gold 0.1000 oz. AGW, 16.5 mm. **Subject:** Nobel Prize Winners **Obv:** Protea flower **Obv. Designer:** A. L. Sutherland **Rev:** Freedom Charter, Luthuli seated left at desk at lower right **Rev. Designer:** M. J. Scheepers **Edge:** Reeded **Note:** FR - FREEDOM

Date	Mintage	F	VF	XF	Unc	BU
2005 Proof	2,000	Value: 200				
2005 FR Proof	—	Value: 600				

KM# 405 5 RAND
3.1107 g., 0.9999 Gold 0.1000 oz. AGW, 16.5 mm. **Subject:** Nobel Prize Winners **Obv:** Protea flower **Obv. Designer:** A. L. Sutherland **Rev:** Cross, inscription **Rev. Designer:** M. J. Scheepers **Edge:** Reeded

Date	Mintage	F	VF	XF	Unc	BU
2006 Proof	5,600	Value: 200				
2006 logo Proof	400	Value: 500				

KM# 407 5 RAND

3.1107 g., 0.9999 Gold 0.1000 oz. AGW, 16.5 mm. **Subject:** Nobel Prize winners **Obv:** Protea flower **Obv. Designer:** A. L. Sutherland **Rev:** Extract from de Klerk's acceptance speech **Rev. Designer:** M. J. Scheepers **Edge:** Reeded

Date	Mintage	F	VF	XF	Unc	BU
2007 Proof	8,000	Value: 200				
2007 dove Proof	—	Value: 700				

KM# 408 5 RAND

3.1107 g., 0.9999 Gold 0.1000 oz. AGW, 16.5 mm. **Subject:** Nobel Prize Winners **Obv:** Protea flower **Obv. Designer:** A. L. Sutherland **Rev:** Extract from Mandela's acceptance speech **Rev. Designer:** M. J. Scheepers **Edge:** Reeded

Date	Mintage	F	VF	XF	Unc	BU
2007 Proof	—	Value: 200				
2007 dove Proof	—	Value: 700				

KM# 452 5 RAND

3.1100 g., 0.9990 Gold 0.0999 oz. AGW, 16.5 mm. **Obv:** Protea flower **Obv. Designer:** A. J. Sutherland **Rev:** Ghandi figure at prayer **Rev. Designer:** C. Moses and N. van Niekerk

Date	Mintage	F	VF	XF	Unc	BU
2008 Proof	8,000	Value: 200				

KM# 476 5 RAND

3.1100 g., 0.9990 Gold 0.0999 oz. AGW, 16.5 mm. **Obv:** Protea flower **Obv. Designer:** A. L. Sutherland **Rev:** Portraits of C. J. Langenhoven and M. L. de Villiers with musical score **Rev. Designer:** A. Minnie and M. J. Scheepers

Date	Mintage	F	VF	XF	Unc	BU
2009 Proof	8,000	Value: 200				

KM# 396 25 RAND

31.1070 g., 0.9999 Gold 100000 oz. AGW, 32.69 mm. **Subject:** 10th Anniversary Soccer "Bafana Bafana" **Obv:** Protea flower **Obv. Designer:** A. L. Sutherland **Rev:** Two players running left **Rev. Designer:** Aldrid Minnie **Edge:** Reeded

Date	Mintage	F	VF	XF	Unc	BU
2002 Proof	137	Value: 1,700				
2002 flag/CW Proof	84	Value: 2,250				

KM# 398 25 RAND

31.1070 g., 0.9999 Gold 100000 oz. AGW, 32.69 mm. **Subject:** World Summit on Sustainable Development **Obv:** Protea flower **Obv. Designer:** A. L. Sutherland **Rev:** Globe featuring Africa **Rev. Designer:** M. J. Scheepers **Edge:** Reeded

Date	Mintage	F	VF	XF	Unc	BU
2002 Proof	421	Value: 1,550				

KM# 279 25 RAND

31.1035 g., 0.9999 Gold 0.9999 oz. AGW, 32.7 mm. **Obv:** Protea flower **Rev:** Soccer player kicking ball **Edge:** Reeded

Date	Mintage	F	VF	XF	Unc	BU
2002 Proof	492	Value: 1,550				

KM# 400 25 RAND

31.1070 g., 0.9999 Gold 100000 oz. AGW, 32.69 mm. **Subject:** Cricket World Cup **Obv:** Protea flower **Obv. Designer:** A. L. Sutherland **Rev:** Batsman on one knee about to sweep the ball **Rev. Legend:** PROTEA **Rev. Designer:** P. Botes **Edge:** Reeded

Date	Mintage	F	VF	XF	Unc	BU
2003 Proof	210	Value: 1,650				
2003 ball/RSA Proof	208	Value: 1,700				

KM# 402 25 RAND

31.1070 g., 0.9999 Gold 100000 oz. AGW, 32.69 mm. **Subject:** 10th Anniversary Democracy **Obv:** Protea flower **Obv. Designer:** A. L. Sutherland **Rev:** Two heads of Mandela, one left, one facing, Union building in background **Rev. Designer:** Natanya van Nirkirk **Edge:** Reeded **Note:** 10FP - 10/flag, people

Date	Mintage	F	VF	XF	Unc	BU
2004 Proof	6,000	Value: 3,000				
2004 10FP Proof	492	Value: 5,400				

KM# 404 25 RAND

31.1070 g., 0.9999 Gold 100000 oz. AGW, 32.69 mm. **Subject:** Nobel Prize Winners **Obv:** Protea flower **Obv. Designer:** A. L. Sutherland **Rev:** Bust of Chief Albert Luthuli facing **Rev. Designer:** Natanya van Niekerk **Edge:** Reeded **Note:** FC - FREEDOM / CHARTER / 26 JUNE 1955

Date	Mintage	F	VF	XF	Unc	BU
2005 Proof	6,000	Value: 1,550				
2005 FC Proof	—	Value: 3,750				

KM# 406 25 RAND

31.1070 g., 0.9999 Gold 100000 oz. AGW, 32.69 mm. **Subject:** Nobel Prize Winners **Obv:** Protea flower **Obv. Designer:** A. L. Sutherland **Rev:** Cross, bust of Archbishop Desmond Tutu right **Rev. Designer:** Natanya van Niekirk **Edge:** Reeded

Date	Mintage	F	VF	XF	Unc	BU
2006 Proof	7,600	Value: 1,550				
2006 logo Proof	400	Value: 2,600				

KM# 409 25 RAND

31.1070 g., 0.9999 Gold 100000 oz. AGW, 32.69 mm. **Subject:** Nobel Prize Winners **Obv:** Protea flower **Obv. Designer:** A. L. Sutherland **Rev:** Busts of Mandela, de Klerk right **Rev. Designer:** Natanya van Niekirk **Edge:** Reeded **Note:** d-P - dove Peace

Date	Mintage	F	VF	XF	Unc	BU
2007 Proof	12,000	Value: 1,550				
2007 d-P Proof	—	Value: 2,750				

KM# 453 25 RAND

31.1070 g., 0.9990 Gold 0.9991 oz. AGW, 32.7 mm. **Obv:** Protea flower **Obv. Designer:** A. J. Sutherland **Rev:** Ghandi profile at right **Rev. Designer:** N. van Niekerk

Date	Mintage	F	VF	XF	Unc	BU
2008 Proof	600	Value: 1,750				
2008 Proof	12,000	Value: 1,550				

KM# 477 25 RAND

31.1070 g., 0.9990 Gold 0.9991 oz. AGW, 32.7 mm. **Obv:** Protea flower **Obv. Designer:** A. L. Sutherland **Rev:** Portraits of C. J. Langenhoven and M. L. de Villiers and musical score **Rev. Designer:** A. Minnie and M. J. Scheepers

Date	Mintage	F	VF	XF	Unc	BU
2009 Proof	11,000	Value: 1,500				

KM# 262 1/10 PROTEA

3.1107 g., 0.9999 Gold 0.1000 oz. AGW, 16.5 mm. **Subject:** Tourism **Obv:** Protea flower **Obv. Designer:** A. L. Sutherland **Rev:** Lion's head facing, partial shield **Rev. Inscription:** PROTEA **Rev. Designer:** P. Botes **Edge:** Reeded

Date	Mintage	F	VF	XF	Unc	BU
2001 Proof	1,076	Value: 200				

KM# 263 PROTEA

31.1070 g., 0.9999 Gold 100000 oz. AGW, 32.6 mm. **Subject:** Tourism **Obv:** Protea flower **Obv. Designer:** A. L. Sutherland **Rev:** Child on sandy beach, Table Mountain in background, partial star at right **Rev. Inscription:** PROTEA **Rev. Designer:** Aldrid Minnie **Edge:** Reeded

Date	Mintage	F	VF	XF	Unc	BU
2001 Proof	972	Value: 1,550				
2001 GRC(pp) Proof	196	Value: 2,000				

MINT SETS

KM#	Date	Mintage	Identification	Issue Price	Mkt Val
MS38	2002 (7)	—	KM#268-274 plus 1- and 2-cent medals	30.00	32.50
MS39	2001 (9)	5,577	KM#221-229	—	60.00
MS40	2002 (7)	3,886	KM#268-274	—	52.50
MS41	2002 (7)	1,640	KM#268-274, circulated coins	—	17.50
MS42	2003 (7)	2,602	KM#324, 327, 330, 332, 335, 337, 347	—	45.00
MS43	2003 (7)	1,380	KM#324, 327, 330, 332, 335, 337, 347, circulted coins	—	10.00
MS44	2004 (7)	1,948	KM#281, 325, 326, 328, 331, 333, 336	—	37.50
MS45	2004 (7)	1,131	KM#281, 325, 325, 328, 331, 333, 336, circulated coins	—	17.50
MS46	2004 (7)	325	KM#281, 325, 326, 328, 331, 333, 336, Baby	—	22.50
MS47	2004 (7)	23	KM#281, 325, 326, 328, 331, 333, 336, Wedding	—	22.50
MS48	2005 (7)	—	KM#291-297	—	30.00
MS49	2005 (7)	—	KM#291-297, circulated coins	—	15.00
MS50	2005 (7)	—	KM#291-297, Baby	—	23.00
MS51	2005 (7)	—	KM#291-297, Wedding	—	22.50
MS52	2006 (7)	—	KM#291-297	—	22.50
MS53	2006 (7)	—	KM#291-297, circulated coins	—	15.00
MS54	2006 (7)	—	KM#291-297, Baby	—	15.00
MS55	2006 (7)	—	KM#291-297, Wedding	—	15.00
MS56	2007 (7)	—	KM#340-346	—	22.50
MS57	2007 (7)	—	KM#340-346, circulated coins	—	15.00
MS58	2007 (7)	—	KM#340-346, baby	—	15.00
MS59	2007 (7)	—	KM#340-346, wedding	—	15.00

PIEFORT PROOF SETS (PPS)

KM#	Date	Mintage	Identification	Issue Price	Mkt Val
PS242	2007 (4)	—	KM#430-433, leatherette	—	3,000

PROOF SETS

KM#	Date	Mintage	Identification	Issue Price	Mkt Val
PS170	2002 (7)	—	KM#268-274 plus 1- and 2-cent medals	40.00	65.00
PS171	2005 (4)	1,500	KM#320-323	—	300
PS172	2001 (9)	3,678	KM#221-229	—	75.00
PS173	2001 (9)	—	KM#221-229 wedding	—	75.00
PS174	2002 (7)	—	KM#268-274	—	75.00
PS175	2002 (7)	330	KM#268-274, baby	—	75.00
PS176	2003 (7)	2,356	KM#324, 327, 330, 332, 335, 337, 347	—	65.00
PS177	2003 (7)	500	KM#324, 327, 330, 332, 335, 337, 347, baby	—	65.00
PS178	2003 (7)	53	KM#324, 327, 330, 332, 335, 337, 347, wedding	—	65.00
PS179	2004 (7)	1,935	KM#281, 325, 326, 328, 331, 333, 336	—	65.00
PS180	2004 (7)	326	KM#281, 325, 326, 328, 331, 333, 336, baby	—	65.00
PS181	2004 (7)	23	KM#281, 325, 326, 328, 331, 333, 336, wedding	—	65.00
PS188	2007 (7)	—	KM#340-346	—	65.00
PS189	2007 (7)	—	KM#340-346, baby	—	65.00
PS190	2007 (7)	—	KM#340-346, wedding	—	65.00
PS193	2001 (4)	411	KM#243-246, wooden case	—	375
PS194	2001 (4)	746	KM#243-246, velvet (med case)	—	300
PS195	2002 (3)	81	KM#234, 243, 351 (mixed dates)	—	110
PS196	2002 (3)	95	KM#235, 244, 352 (mixed dates)	—	185
PS197	2002 (3)	81	KM#236, 245, 353 (mixed dates)	—	250
PS198	2002 (3)	92	KM#237, 246, 354 (mixed dates)	—	335
PS199	2002 (4)	411	KM#351-354, wooden case	—	375
PS200	2002 (4)	746	KM#351-354, velvet lined case	—	275
PS201	2003 (4)	59	KM#234, 243, 351, 355 (mixed dates)	—	150
PS202	2003 (4)	47	KM#235, 244, 352, 356 (mixed dates)	—	250
PS203	2003 (4)	75	KM#236, 245, 353, 357 (mixed dates)	—	330
PS204	2003 (4)	62	KM#237, 246, 354, 358 (mixed dates)	—	450
PS205	2003 (4)	532	KM#355-358, wooden case	—	375
PS206	2003 (4)	1,029	KM#355-358, velvet lined case	—	300
PS207	2004 (5)	132	KM#234, 243, 351, 355, 359 (mixed dates)	—	200
PS208	2004 (5)	133	KM#235, 244, 352, 356, 360 (mixed dates)	—	325
PS209	2004 (5)	181	KM#236, 245, 353, 357, 361 (mixed dates)	—	450
PS210	2004 (5)	158	KM#237, 246, 354, 358, 362 (mixed dates)	—	555
PS211	2004 (4)	645	KM#359-362, wooden case	—	375
PS212	2004 (4)	454	KM#359-362, velvet lined case	—	300
PS213	2004 (4)	299	KM#359-362, plus 1/4 oz. medal	—	300
PS214	2005 (4)	—	KM#320-323, wooden case	—	300
PS215	2005 (4)	—	KM#320-323, velvet lined case	—	300
PS216	2006 (4)	—	KM#316-319, wooden case	—	300

KM#	Date	Mintage	Identification	Issue Price	Mkt Val
PS217	2006 (4)	—	KM#316-319, velvet lined case	—	300
PS218	2007 (2)	—	KM#363-364, wooden case	—	150
PS219	2007 (2)	—	KM#363-364	—	105
PS223	2000 (4)	483	KM#258-261, prestige	—	3,000
PS224	2000 (4)	334	KM#258-261, leatherette	—	3,000
PS225	2001 (4)	691	KM#264-267	—	3,000
PS226	2001 (4)	985	KM#264-267, leatherette	—	3,000
PS227	2001 (4)	310	KM#264-267, special export	—	3,000
PS228	2002 (4)	698	KM#410-413, prestige	—	3,000
PS229	2002 (4)	529	KM#410-413, leatherette	—	3,000
PS230	2002 (4)	682	KM#410-413, special	—	3,000
PS231	2003 (4)	698	KM#414-417, prestige	—	3,000
PS232	2003 (4)	908	KM#414-417, leatherette	—	3,000
PS233	2003 (4)	722	KM#414-417, anniversary	—	3,000
PS234	2004 (4)	700	KM#418-421, prestige	—	3,025
PS235	2004 (4)	440	KM#418-421, leatherette	—	3,025
PS236	2004 (4)	125	KM#418-421, special export with silver African Continent	—	3,025
PS237	2005 (4)	—	KM#422-425, prestige	—	3,025
PS238	2005 (4)	—	KM#422-425, leatherette	—	3,025
PS239	2006 (4)	—	KM#426-429, prestige	—	3,000
PS240	2006 (4)	—	KM#426-429, leatherette	—	3,000
PS241	2007 (4)	—	KM#430-433, prestige	—	3,000

South Georgia and the South Sandwich Islands are a dependency of the Falkland Islands, and located about 800 miles east of them. South Georgia is 1,450 sq. mi. (1,770 sq. km.), and the South Sandwich Islands are 120 sq. mi. (311 sq. km.) Fishing and Antarctic research are the main industries. The islands were claimed for Great Britain in 1775 by Captain James Cook.

RULER

British since 1775

BRITISH OVERSEAS TERRITORY

STANDARD COINAGE

KM# 7 2 POUNDS

28.2800 g., Copper-Nickel, 38.6 mm. **Subject:** Sir Ernest H. Shackleton **Obv:** Crowned bust right **Obv. Designer:** Ian Rank-Broadley **Rev:** Bust facing and ship "Endurance" **Edge:** Reeded

Date	Mintage	F	VF	XF	Unc	BU
2001	—	—	—	—	10.00	12.00

KM# 7a 2 POUNDS

28.2800 g., 0.9250 Silver 0.8410 oz. ASW **Obv:** Crowned bust right **Rev:** Bust facing and ship "Endurance"

Date	Mintage	F	VF	XF	Unc	BU
2001 Proof	Est. 10,000	Value: 50.00				

KM# 9 2 POUNDS

Copper-Nickel **Subject:** Sir Joseph Banks **Obv:** Crowned bust right **Obv. Designer:** Ian Rank-Broadley **Rev:** Cameo and ship

Date	Mintage	F	VF	XF	Unc	BU
2001	—	—	—	—	10.00	12.00

KM# 9a 2 POUNDS

28.2800 g., 0.9250 Silver 0.8410 oz. ASW **Obv:** Crowned bust right **Rev:** Ship and cameo

Date	Mintage	F	VF	XF	Unc	BU
2001 Proof	Est. 10,000	Value: 50.00				

KM# 11 2 POUNDS

28.2800 g., Copper-Nickel, 38.6 mm. **Subject:** Queen Elizabeth II's Golden Jubilee **Obv:** Crowned bust right **Obv. Designer:** Ian Rank-Broadley **Rev:** Young crowned bust right **Edge:** Reeded

Date	Mintage	F	VF	XF	Unc	BU
2002	—	—	—	—	10.00	12.00

KM# 11a 2 POUNDS

28.2800 g., 0.9250 Gold Clad Silver 0.8410 oz., 38.6 mm. **Subject:** Queen Elizabeth II's Golden Jubilee **Obv:** Crowned bust right **Rev:** Young crowned bust right **Edge:** Reeded

Date	Mintage	F	VF	XF	Unc	BU
2002 Proof	10,000	Value: 50.00				

KM# 13 2 POUNDS

28.2800 g., Copper-Nickel, 38.6 mm. **Subject:** Queen Elizabeth II's Golden Jubilee **Obv:** Crowned bust right **Obv. Designer:** Ian Rank-Broadley **Rev:** Small crown above shield flanked by flower sprigs **Edge:** Reeded

Date	Mintage	F	VF	XF	Unc	BU
2002	—	—	—	—	10.00	12.00

KM# 13a 2 POUNDS

28.2800 g., 0.9250 Gold Clad Silver 0.8410 oz., 38.6 mm. **Subject:** Queen Elizabeth II's Golden Jubilee **Obv:** Crowned bust right **Rev:** Small crown above shield flanked by flower sprigs **Edge:** Reeded

Date	Mintage	F	VF	XF	Unc	BU
2002 Proof	10,000	Value: 50.00				

KM# 15 2 POUNDS

28.2800 g., Copper-Nickel, 38.6 mm. **Subject:** Diana, Princess of Wales - The Work Continues **Obv:** Crowned bust right **Obv. Designer:** Ian Rank-Broadley **Rev:** Head 1/4 left **Edge:** Reeded

Date	Mintage	F	VF	XF	Unc	BU
2002	—	—	—	—	10.00	12.00

KM# 17 2 POUNDS

28.2800 g., Copper-Nickel, 38.6 mm. **Subject:** Prince William's 21st Birthday **Obv:** Crowned bust right **Obv. Designer:** Ian Rank-Broadley **Rev:** Arms of Prince William of Wales **Edge:** Reeded

Date	Mintage	F	VF	XF	Unc	BU
2003PM	—	—	—	—	10.00	12.00

KM# 17a 2 POUNDS

28.2800 g., 0.9250 Silver 0.8410 oz. ASW, 38.6 mm. **Subject:** Prince William's 21st Birthday **Obv:** Crowned bust right **Rev:** Arms of Prince William of Wales **Edge:** Reeded

Date	Mintage	F	VF	XF	Unc	BU
2003PM Proof	—	Value: 50.00				

KM# 18 2 POUNDS

28.2800 g., Copper-Nickel, 38.6 mm. **Obv:** Crowned bust right **Rev:** Capt. Cook, ship and map **Edge:** Reeded

Date	Mintage	F	VF	XF	Unc	BU
2003PM	—	—	—	—	10.00	12.00

KM# 18a 2 POUNDS

28.2800 g., 0.9250 Silver 0.8410 oz. ASW, 38.6 mm. **Obv:** Crowned bust right **Rev:** Capt. Cook, ship and map **Edge:** Reeded

Date	Mintage	F	VF	XF	Unc	BU
2003PM Proof	—	Value: 50.00				

KM# 20 2 POUNDS

28.2800 g., Copper-Nickel, 38.6 mm. **Obv:** Crowned bust right **Obv. Designer:** Ian Rank-Broadley **Rev:** Sir Ernest Shackleton and icebound ship **Edge:** Reeded

Date	Mintage	F	VF	XF	Unc	BU
2004	—	—	—	—	15.00	16.50

KM# 20a 2 POUNDS

28.2800 g., 0.9250 Silver 0.8410 oz. ASW, 38.6 mm. **Obv:** Crowned bust right **Rev:** Sir Ernest Shackleton and icebound ship **Edge:** Reeded

Date	Mintage	F	VF	XF	Unc	BU
2004 Proof	10,000	Value: 50.00				

KM# 21 2 POUNDS

28.2800 g., Copper-Nickel, 38.6 mm. **Subject:** Centennial of Grytviken **Obv:** Crowned bust right **Obv. Designer:** Ian Rank-Broadley **Rev:** Portrait above ship in harbor **Edge:** Reeded

Date	Mintage	F	VF	XF	Unc	BU
2004	—	—	—	—	15.00	16.50

KM# 21a 2 POUNDS

28.2800 g., 0.9250 Silver 0.8410 oz. ASW, 38.6 mm. **Subject:** Centennial of Grytviken **Obv:** Crowned bust right **Rev:** Portrait above ship in harbor **Edge:** Reeded

Date	Mintage	F	VF	XF	Unc	BU
2004 Proof	—	Value: 50.00				

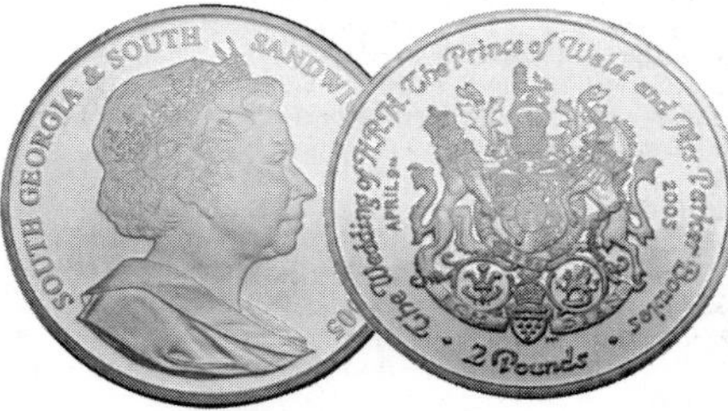

KM# 25 2 POUNDS

Copper-Nickel **Subject:** Marriage of Charles to Parker Bowles **Rev:** Arms of Prince of Wales

Date	Mintage	F	VF	XF	Unc	BU
2005	—	—	—	—	8.50	10.00

KM# 22 2 POUNDS

28.3700 g., Copper-Nickel, 38.5 mm. **Obv:** Elizabeth II **Rev:** Rockhopper Penguin and chick **Edge:** Reeded

Date	Mintage	F	VF	XF	Unc	BU
2006	—	—	—	—	12.00	14.00

KM# 23 2 POUNDS

28.3700 g., Copper-Nickel, 38.5 mm. **Obv:** Elizabeth II **Rev:** Elephant Seal and cub **Edge:** Reeded

Date	Mintage	F	VF	XF	Unc	BU
2006	—	—	—	—	10.00	12.00

KM# 24 2 POUNDS

28.3700 g., Copper-Nickel, 38.5 mm. **Obv:** Elizabeth II **Rev:** Humpback Whale and calf **Edge:** Reeded

Date	Mintage	F	VF	XF	Unc	BU
2006	—	—	—	—	8.50	12.00

KM# 26 2 POUNDS
Copper-Nickel **Subject:** Queen Elizabeth's II 80th Birthday **Rev:** Queen on horseback taking part in Trouping of the Color ceremony

Date	Mintage	F	VF	XF	Unc	BU
2006	—	—	—	—	8.50	10.00

KM# 26a 2 POUNDS
28.2800 g., 0.9167 Silver 0.8334 oz. ASW **Subject:** Queen Elizabeth's II 80th Birthday **Rev:** Queen on horseback taking part in Trouping of the Color ceremony

Date	Mintage	F	VF	XF	Unc	BU
2006 Proof	25,000	Value: 75.00				

KM# 27 2 POUNDS
Copper-Nickel, 38.5 mm. **Rev:** Pair of Grey-headed Albatros

Date	Mintage	F	VF	XF	Unc	BU
2006	—	—	—	—	8.50	12.00

KM# 28 2 POUNDS
Copper-Nickel **Subject:** Queen Elizabeth's II 80th Birthday **Rev:** 1953 Royal family

Date	Mintage	F	VF	XF	Unc	BU
2006	—	—	—	—	8.50	10.00

KM# 28a 2 POUNDS
28.2800 g., 0.9167 Silver 0.8334 oz. ASW **Subject:** Queen Elizabeth's II 80th Birthday **Rev:** 1953 Royal family

Date	Mintage	F	VF	XF	Unc	BU
2006 Proof	25,000	Value: 75.00				

KM# 29 2 POUNDS
Copper-Nickel **Subject:** Queen Elizabeth's II 80th Birthday **Rev:** Wedding of Queen Elizabeth II and Prince Philip

Date	Mintage	F	VF	XF	Unc	BU
2006	—	—	—	—	8.50	10.00

KM# 29a 2 POUNDS
28.2800 g., 0.9167 Silver 0.8334 oz. ASW **Subject:** Queen Elizabeth's 80th Birthday **Rev:** Wedding of Queen Elizabeth II and Prince Philip

Date	Mintage	F	VF	XF	Unc	BU
2006 Proof	25,000	Value: 75.00				

KM# 30 2 POUNDS
Copper-Nickel **Subject:** Queen Elizabeth's II 80th Birthday **Rev:** Queen in Robes of Garter

Date	Mintage	F	VF	XF	Unc	BU
2006	—	—	—	—	8.50	10.00

KM# 30a 2 POUNDS
28.2800 g., 0.9167 Silver 0.8334 oz. ASW **Subject:** Queen Elizabeth's II 80th Birthday **Rev:** Queen in Robes of Garter

Date	Mintage	F	VF	XF	Unc	BU
2006 Proof	25,000	Value: 75.00				

KM# 31 2 POUNDS
Copper-Nickel **Rev:** Queen Elizabeth II 1926 (1953 portrait)

Date	Mintage	F	VF	XF	Unc	BU
2007	—	—	—	—	8.50	10.00

KM# 32 2 POUNDS
Copper-Nickel **Subject:** 25th Anniversary of Liberation **Rev:** Warship and helicopters

Date	Mintage	F	VF	XF	Unc	BU
2007	—	—	—	—	8.50	10.00

KM# 33 2 POUNDS
Copper-Nickel **Rev:** Trans Artic Expedition

Date	Mintage	F	VF	XF	Unc	BU
2007	—	—	—	—	8.50	10.00

KM# 34 2 POUNDS
Copper-Nickel **Subject:** International Polar Year **Rev:** Shackelton Expedition

Date	Mintage	F	VF	XF	Unc	BU
2007	—	—	—	—	8.50	10.00

KM# 35 2 POUNDS
Copper-Nickel **Rev:** Ernest Shacketon

Date	Mintage	F	VF	XF	Unc	BU
2007	—	—	—	—	8.50	10.00

KM# 36 2 POUNDS
Copper-Nickel **Rev:** James Cook

Date	Mintage	F	VF	XF	Unc	BU
2007	—	—	—	—	8.50	10.00

KM# 37 2 POUNDS
28.2800 g., Copper-Nickel, 38.60 mm. **Ruler:** Elizabeth II **Subject:** Diamond Wedding Anniversary **Obv:** Conjoined busts with Prince Philip right **Obv. Legend:** SOUTH GEORGIA & SOUTH SANDWICH ISLANDS **Rev:** Bust of Princess Elizabeth facing **Rev. Legend:** Diamond Wedding of H.M. Queen Elizabeth II & H.R.H. Prince Philip **Rev. Inscription:** THE BRIDE **Edge:** Reeded

Date	Mintage	F	VF	XF	Unc	BU
2007	—	—	—	—	15.00	16.50

KM# 37a 2 POUNDS
28.2800 g., 0.9167 Silver ASW 0.8335 0.8334 oz. ASW, 38.60 mm. **Ruler:** Elizabeth II **Subject:** Diamond Wedding Anniversary **Obv:** Conjoined busts with Prince Philip right **Obv. Legend:** SOUTH GEORGIA & SOUTH SANDWICH ISLANDS **Rev:** Bust of Princess Elizabeth facing **Rev. Legend:** Diamond Wedding of H.M. Queen Elizabeth II & H.R.H. Prince Philip **Rev. Inscription:** THE BRIDE **Edge:** Reeded

Date	Mintage	F	VF	XF	Unc	BU
2007 Proof	25,000	Value: 75.00				

KM# 38 2 POUNDS
28.2800 g., Copper-Nickel, 38.60 mm. **Ruler:** Elizabeth II **Subject:** Diamond Wedding Anniversary **Obv:** Conjoined busts with Prince Philip right **Obv. Legend:** SOUTH GEORGIA & SOUTH SANDWICH ISLANDS **Rev:** Bust of the bridegroom facing **Rev. Legend:** Diamond Wedding of H.M. Queen Elizabeth II & H.R.H. Prince Philip **Rev. Inscription:** THE BRIDEGROOM **Edge:** Reeded

Date	Mintage	F	VF	XF	Unc	BU
2007	—	—	—	—	15.00	16.50

KM# 38a 2 POUNDS
28.2800 g., 0.9167 Silver ASW 0.8335 0.8334 oz. ASW, 38.60 mm. **Ruler:** Elizabeth II **Subject:** Diamond Wedding Anniversary **Obv:** Conjoined busts with Prince Philip right **Obv. Legend:** SOUTH GEORGIA & SOUTH SANDWICH ISLANDS **Rev:** Bust of the bridegroom facing **Rev. Legend:** Diamond Wedding of H.M. Queen Elizabeth II & H.R.H. Prince Philip **Rev. Inscription:** THE BRIDEGROOM **Edge:** Reeded

Date	Mintage	F	VF	XF	Unc	BU
2007 Proof	25,000	Value: 75.00				

KM# 39 2 POUNDS
28.2800 g., Copper-Nickel, 38.60 mm. **Ruler:** Elizabeth II **Subject:** Diamond Wedding Anniversary **Obv:** Conjoined busts with Prince Philip right **Obv. Legend:** SOUTH GEORGIA & SOUTH SANDWICH ISLANDS **Rev:** 1/2 length figures of royal engaged couple looking at each other **Rev. Legend:** Diamond Wedding of H.M. Queen Elizabeth II & H.R.H. Prince Philip **Rev. Inscription:** ROYAL ENGAGEMENT • JULY • 10 • 1947 **Edge:** Reeded

Date	Mintage	F	VF	XF	Unc	BU
2007	—	—	—	—	15.00	16.50

KM# 39a 2 POUNDS
28.2800 g., 0.9167 Silver ASW 0.8335 0.8334 oz. ASW, 38.60 mm. **Ruler:** Elizabeth II **Subject:** Diamond Wedding Anniversary **Obv:** Conjoined busts with Prince Philip right **Obv. Legend:** SOUTH GEORGIA & SOUTH SANDWICH ISLANDS **Rev:** 1/2 length figures of royal engaged couple looking at each other **Rev. Legend:** Diamond Wedding of H.M. Queen Elizabeth II & H.R.H. Prince Philip **Rev. Inscription:** ROYAL ENGAGEMENT • JULY • 10 • 1947 **Edge:** Reeded

Date	Mintage	F	VF	XF	Unc	BU
2007 Proof	25,000	Value: 75.00				

KM# 40 2 POUNDS
28.2800 g., Copper-Nickel, 38.60 mm. **Ruler:** Elizabeth II **Subject:** Diamond Wedding Anniversary **Obv:** Conjoined busts with Prince Philip right **Obv. Legend:** SOUTH GEORGIA & SOUTH SANDWICH ISLANDS **Rev:** Marriage license, jubilant crowd scene **Rev. Legend:** Diamond Wedding of H.M. Queen Elizabeth II & H.R.H. Prince Philip **Rev. Inscription:** THE MARRIAGE LICENSE **Edge:** Reeded

Date	Mintage	F	VF	XF	Unc	BU
2007	—	—	—	—	15.00	16.50

KM# 40a 2 POUNDS
28.2800 g., 0.9167 Silver ASW 0.8335 0.8334 oz. ASW, 38.60 mm. **Ruler:** Elizabeth II **Subject:** Diamond Wedding Anniversary **Obv:** Conjoined busts with Prince Philip right **Obv. Legend:** SOUTH GEORGIA & SOUTH SANDWICH ISLANDS **Rev:** Marriage license, jubilant crowd scene **Rev. Legend:** Diamond Wedding of H.M. Queen Elizabeth II & H.R.H. Prince Philip **Rev. Inscription:** THE MARRIAGE LICENSE **Edge:** Reeded

Date	Mintage	F	VF	XF	Unc	BU
2007 Proof	25,000	Value: 75.00				

KM# 41 2 POUNDS
28.3700 g., Copper-Nickel, 38.5 mm. **Ruler:** Elizabeth II **Subject:** The Nimrod Expedition **Rev:** Sailing ship stuck in ice

Date	Mintage	F	VF	XF	Unc	BU
2009PM	—	—	—	—	—	16.50

KM# 19 10 POUNDS
155.5100 g., 0.9990 Silver 4.9946 oz. ASW, 65 mm. **Obv:** Crowned bust right **Obv. Designer:** Ian Rank-Broadley **Rev:** Capt. Cook, ship and map **Edge:** Reeded

Date	Mintage	F	VF	XF	Unc	BU
2003PM Proof	2,003	Value: 225				

KM# 8 20 POUNDS
6.2200 g., 0.9999 Gold 0.1999 oz. AGW, 22 mm. **Obv:** Crowned bust right **Obv. Designer:** Ian Rank-Broadley **Rev:** Sir Ernest H. Shackleton and ship **Edge:** Reeded

Date	Mintage	F	VF	XF	Unc	BU
2001 Proof	Est. 2,000	Value: 325				

KM# 10 20 POUNDS
6.2200 g., 0.9999 Gold 0.1999 oz. AGW **Obv:** Crowned bust right **Obv. Designer:** Ian Rank-Broadley **Rev:** Sir Joseph Banks cameo and ship

Date	Mintage	F	VF	XF	Unc	BU
2001 Proof	Est. 2,000	Value: 325				

KM# 16 20 POUNDS
6.2200 g., 0.9999 Gold 0.1999 oz. AGW, 22 mm. **Subject:** Princess Diana **Obv:** Crowned bust right **Obv. Designer:** Ian Rank-Broadley **Rev:** Diana's portrait **Edge:** reeded

Date	Mintage	F	VF	XF	Unc	BU
2002PM Proof	—	Value: 325				

KM# 12 20 POUNDS
6.2200 g., 0.9990 Gold 0.1998 oz. AGW, 22 mm. **Subject:** Queen Elizabeth II's Golden Jubilee **Obv:** Crowned bust right **Obv. Designer:** Ian Rank-Broadley **Rev:** Young crowned bust right **Edge:** Reeded

Date	Mintage	F	VF	XF	Unc	BU
2002 Proof	2,002	Value: 325				

KM# 14 20 POUNDS
6.2200 g., 0.9990 Gold 0.1998 oz. AGW, 22 mm. **Subject:** Queen Elizabeth II's Golden Jubilee **Obv:** Crowned bust right **Obv. Designer:** Ian Rank-Broadley **Rev:** National arms **Edge:** Reeded

Date	Mintage	F	VF	XF	Unc	BU
2002 Proof	2,002	Value: 325				

The Spanish State, forming the greater part of the Iberian Peninsula of southwest Europe, has an area of 195,988 sq. mi. (504,714 sq. km.) and a population of 39.4 million including the Balearic and the Canary Islands. Capital: Madrid. The economy is based on agriculture, industry and tourism. Machinery, fruit, vegetables and chemicals are exported.

RULER
Juan Carlos I, 1975-

MINT MARK

After 1982
(M) - Crowned "M" – Madrid

KINGDOM
1949 - Present

DECIMAL COINAGE
Peseta System

100 Centimos = 1 Peseta

KM# 832 PESETA
0.5500 g., Aluminum, 14 mm. **Ruler:** Juan Carlos I **Obv:** Vertical line divides head left from value **Rev:** Crowned shield flanked by pillars with banner **Edge:** Plain

Date	Mintage	F	VF	XF	Unc	BU
2001	—	—	—	0.10	0.30	0.50

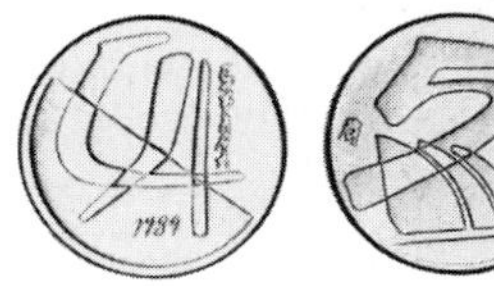

KM# 833 5 PESETAS
3.0000 g., Aluminum-Bronze, 17.5 mm. **Ruler:** Juan Carlos I **Obv:** Stylized JC I and date **Rev:** Value above stylized sailboats **Edge:** Plain

Date	Mintage	F	VF	XF	Unc	BU
2001	—	—	—	0.10	0.25	0.35

KM# 1013 25 PESETAS
4.2500 g., Aluminum-Bronze, 19.5 mm. **Ruler:** Juan Carlos I **Obv:** Center hole divides bust left and vertical letters **Rev:** Crowned above center hole, order collar at right, value at left **Edge:** Plain

Date	Mintage	F	VF	XF	Unc	BU
2001	—	—	—	—	2.00	2.50

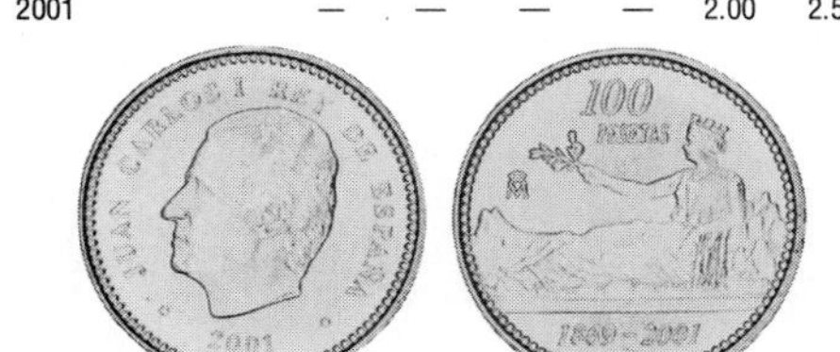

KM# 1016 100 PESETAS
9.2500 g., Aluminum-Bronze, 24.5 mm. **Ruler:** Juan Carlos I **Subject:** 132nd Anniversary of the Peseta **Obv:** Head left **Rev:** Seated allegorical figure from an old coin design **Edge:** Fleur-de-lis repeated

Date	Mintage	F	VF	XF	Unc	BU
2001	—	—	—	—	2.25	2.75

KM# 924 500 PESETAS
12.0000 g., Aluminum-Bronze, 28 mm. **Ruler:** Juan Carlos I **Obv:** Conjoined heads of Juan Carlos and Sofia left **Rev:** Crowned shield flanked by pillars with banner, vertical value at right

Date	Mintage	F	VF	XF	Unc	BU
2001	—	—	—	—	12.00	15.00

KM# 1131 500 PESETAS
6.7300 g., Silver, 26.96 mm. **Ruler:** Juan Carlos I **Obv:** Minting equipment **Obv. Legend:** ESPAÑA **Rev:** Copy of Charles II silver Reales coin **Rev. Legend:** CASA DE LA MONEDA DE SEGOVIA **Edge:** Reeded **Note:** Aqueduct and crowned M mintmarks appear on obverse

Date	Mintage	F	VF	XF	Unc	BU
2001 Proof	—	Value: 20.00				

KM# 1017 2000 PESETAS
18.0000 g., 0.9250 Silver 0.5353 oz. ASW, 32.9 mm. **Ruler:** Juan Carlos I **Subject:** 132nd Anniversary of the Peseta **Obv:** Conjoined heads left **Rev:** Seated allegorical design from the 1869 Spanish coin series **Edge:** Plain

Date	Mintage	F	VF	XF	Unc	BU
2001	1,942,835	—	—	—	30.00	35.00

KM# 1038 2000 PESETAS
27.0000 g., 0.9250 Silver 0.8029 oz. ASW, 40 mm. **Ruler:** Juan Carlos I **Subject:** Segovia Mint's 500th Anniversary **Obv:** Hammer coining scene within beaded circle **Rev:** Segovia Mint 8 reales coin design of 1588 **Edge:** Reeded

Date	Mintage	F	VF	XF	Unc	BU
2001 Proof	15,000	Value: 55.00				

EURO COINAGE

European Union Issues

KM# 1040 EURO CENT
2.3000 g., Copper Plated Steel, 16.3 mm. **Ruler:** Juan Carlos I **Obv:** Cathedral of Santiago de Compostela **Obv. Designer:** Garcilaso Rollán **Rev:** Value and globe **Rev. Designer:** Luc Luycx **Edge:** Plain

Date	Mintage	F	VF	XF	Unc	BU
2001(M)	130,900,000	—	—	—	0.25	0.30
2002(M)	141,100,000	—	—	—	0.25	0.30
2002(M) Proof	35,000	Value: 10.00				
2003(M)	670,500,000	—	—	—	0.25	0.30
2003(M) Proof	20,000	Value: 10.00				
2004(M)	206,700,000	—	—	—	0.25	0.30
2005(M)	444,200,000	—	—	—	0.25	0.30
2005(M) Proof	3,000	Value: 10.00				
2006(M)	383,900,000	—	—	—	0.25	0.35
2007(M)	—	—	—	—	0.25	0.35
2007(M) Proof	5,000	Value: 10.00				
2008(M)	—	—	—	—	0.25	0.35
2008(M) Proof	5,000	Value: 10.00				
2009(M)	—	—	—	—	0.25	0.35
2009(M) Proof	5,000	Value: 10.00				

KM# 1144 EURO CENT
2.3000 g., Copper Plated Steel, 16.3 mm. **Ruler:** Juan Carlos I **Obv:** Cathedral of Santiago de Compostela **Rev:** Value and globe

Date	Mintage	F	VF	XF	Unc	BU
2010	—	—	—	—	0.25	0.35
2010 Proof	—	Value: 10.00				

KM# 1041 2 EURO CENT
3.0600 g., Copper Plated Steel, 16.25 mm. **Ruler:** Juan Carlos I **Obv:** Cathedral of Santiago de Compostela **Obv. Designer:** Garcilaso Rollán **Rev:** Value and globe **Rev. Designer:** Luc Luycx **Edge:** Grooved

Date	Mintage	F	VF	XF	Unc	BU
2001(M)	463,100,000	—	—	—	0.25	0.30
2002(M)	4,100,000	—	—	—	1.25	1.50
2002(M) Proof	35,000	Value: 10.00				
2003(M)	31,600,000	—	—	—	1.00	1.25
2003(M) Proof	20,000	Value: 10.00				
2004(M)	206,700,000	—	—	—	0.25	0.30
2005(M)	275,100,000	—	—	—	0.25	0.30
2005(M) Proof	3,000	Value: 10.00				
2006(M)	262,200,000	—	—	—	0.25	0.30
2007(M)	—	—	—	—	0.25	0.30
2007(M) Proof	5,000	Value: 10.00				
2008(M)	—	—	—	—	0.25	0.30
2008(M) Proof	5,000	Value: 10.00				
2009(M)	—	—	—	—	0.25	0.30
2009(M) Proof	5,000	Value: 10.00				

KM# 1145 2 EURO CENT
3.0300 g., Copper Plated Steel, 18.7 mm. **Ruler:** Juan Carlos I **Obv:** Cathedral of Santiago de Compostela **Rev:** Value and globe

Date	Mintage	F	VF	XF	Unc	BU
2010	—	—	—	—	0.25	0.30
2010 Proof	—	Value: 10.00				

KM# 1042 5 EURO CENT
3.9200 g., Copper Plated Steel, 21.25 mm. **Ruler:** Juan Carlos I **Obv:** Cathedral of Santiago de Compostela **Obv. Designer:** Garcilaso Rollán **Rev:** Value and globe **Rev. Designer:** Luc Luycx **Edge:** Plain

Date	Mintage	F	VF	XF	Unc	BU
2001(M)	216,100,000	—	—	—	0.50	0.60
2002(M)	8,300,000	—	—	—	1.00	1.50
2002(M) Proof	35,000	Value: 10.00				
2003(M)	327,600,000	—	—	—	0.50	0.60
2004(M)	258,700,000	—	—	—	0.40	0.50
2005(M)	411,400,000	—	—	—	0.40	0.50
2005(M) Proof	3,000	Value: 10.00				
2006(M)	142,800,000	—	—	—	0.40	0.50
2007(M)	—	—	—	—	0.40	0.50
2007(M) Proof	5,000	Value: 10.00				
2008(M)	—	—	—	—	0.40	0.50
2009(M)	—	—	—	—	0.40	0.50

KM# 1146 5 EURO CENT
3.9200 g., Copper Plated Steel, 21.25 mm. **Ruler:** Juan Carlos I **Obv:** Cathedral of Santiago de Compostela **Rev:** Value and globe

Date	Mintage	F	VF	XF	Unc	BU
2010	—	—	—	—	0.40	0.50
2010 Proof	—	Value: 10.00				

KM# 1043 10 EURO CENT
4.0700 g., Brass, 19.7 mm. **Ruler:** Juan Carlos I **Obv:** Head of Cervantes with ruffed collar 1/4 left within star border **Obv. Designer:** Begoña Castellanos **Rev:** Value and map **Edge:** Reeded

Date	Mintage	F	VF	XF	Unc	BU
2001(M)	160,100,000	—	—	—	0.60	0.75
2002(M)	113,100,000	—	—	—	0.60	0.75
2002(M) Proof	35,000	Value: 10.00				
2003(M)	292,500,000	—	—	—	0.75	0.90
2003(M) Proof	20,000	Value: 10.00				
2004(M)	121,900,000	—	—	—	0.40	0.50
2005(M)	321,300,000	—	—	—	0.40	0.50
2005(M) Proof	3,000	Value: 10.00				
2006(M)	91,800,000	—	—	—	0.40	0.50

KM# 1070 10 EURO CENT
4.1000 g., Brass, 19.7 mm. **Ruler:** Juan Carlos I **Obv:** Cervantes **Rev:** Relief map of Western Europe, stars, lines and value **Edge:** Reeded

Date	Mintage	F	VF	XF	Unc	BU
2007(M)	132,058,000	—	—	—	0.75	1.00
2007(M) Proof	5,000	Value: 12.00				
2008(M)	—	—	—	—	0.75	1.00
2008(M) Proof	5,000	Value: 12.00				
2009(M)	—	—	—	—	0.75	1.00
2009(M) Proof	5,000	Value: 12.00				

KM# 1147 10 EURO CENT
4.1000 g., Brass, 19.7 mm. **Ruler:** Juan Carlos I **Obv:** Cervantes bust at right **Rev:** Relief map of Western Europe, stars, lines and value **Edge:** Notched

Date	Mintage	F	VF	XF	Unc	BU
2010	—	—	—	—	0.75	1.00
2010 Proof	—	Value: 12.00				

KM# 1044 20 EURO CENT
5.6200 g., Brass, 22.2 mm. **Ruler:** Juan Carlos I **Obv:** Head of Cervantes with ruffed collar 1/4 left within star border **Obv. Designer:** Begoña Castellanos **Rev:** Value and map **Rev. Designer:** Luc Luycx **Edge:** Notched

Date	Mintage	F	VF	XF	Unc	BU
2001(M)	146,600,000	—	—	—	1.00	1.25
2002(M)	91,500,000	—	—	—	0.60	0.75
2002(M) Proof	35,000	Value: 12.00				
2003(M)	4,100,000	—	—	—	1.25	1.50
2003(M) Proof	20,000	Value: 12.00				
2004(M)	3,900,000	—	—	—	0.60	0.75
2005(M)	4,000,000	—	—	—	0.60	0.75
2005(M) Proof	3,000	Value: 12.00				
2006(M)	102,000,000	—	—	—	0.60	0.75

KM# 1071 20 EURO CENT
5.7300 g., Brass, 22.3 mm. **Ruler:** Juan Carlos I **Obv:** Cervantes **Obv. Designer:** Begoña Castellanos **Rev:** Relief map of Western Europe, stars, lines and value **Rev. Designer:** Luc Luycx **Edge:** Notched

Date	Mintage	F	VF	XF	Unc	BU
2007(M)	46,458,000	—	—	—	1.00	1.25
2007(M) Proof	5,000	Value: 12.00				
2008(M)	—	—	—	—	1.00	1.25
2009(M)	—	—	—	—	1.00	1.25
2009(M) Proof	5,000	Value: 12.00				

KM# 1148 20 EURO CENT
5.7300 g., Brass, 22.3 mm. **Ruler:** Juan Carlos I **Obv:** Cervantes bust at right **Rev:** Relief map of Western Europe, stars, lines and value **Edge:** Notched

Date	Mintage	F	VF	XF	Unc	BU
2010	—	—	—	—	1.00	1.25
2010 Proof	—	Value: 12.00				

KM# 1045 50 EURO CENT
7.8100 g., Brass, 24.2 mm. **Ruler:** Juan Carlos I **Obv:** Head of Cervantes with ruffed collar 1/4 left within star border **Obv. Designer:** Begoña Castellanos **Rev:** Value and map **Rev. Designer:** Luc Luycx **Edge:** Reeded

Date	Mintage	F	VF	XF	Unc	BU
2001(M)	351,100,000	—	—	—	1.00	1.25
2002(M)	9,800,000	—	—	—	3.00	3.50
2002(M) Proof	35,000	Value: 12.00				
2003(M)	6,000,000	—	—	—	3.00	3.50
2003(M) Proof	20,000	Value: 12.00				
2004(M)	4,400,000	—	—	—	1.50	2.00
2005(M)	3,900,000	—	—	—	1.25	1.50
2005(M) Proof	3,000	Value: 12.00				
2006(M)	4,000,000	—	—	—	1.25	1.50

KM# 1072 50 EURO CENT
7.8500 g., Brass, 24.2 mm. **Ruler:** Juan Carlos I **Obv:** Cervantes **Obv. Designer:** Begoña Castellanos **Rev:** Relief map of Western Europe, stars, lines and value **Rev. Designer:** Luc Luycx **Edge:** Reeded

Date	Mintage	F	VF	XF	Unc	BU
2007(M)	3,958,000	—	—	—	1.25	1.50
2007(M) Proof	5,000	Value: 12.00				
2008(M)	—	—	—	—	1.25	1.50
2008(M) Proof	5,000	Value: 12.00				
2009(M)	—	—	—	—	1.25	1.50
2009(M) Proof	5,000	Value: 12.00				

KM# 1149 50 EURO CENT
7.8500 g., Brass, 24.2 mm. **Ruler:** Juan Carlos I **Obv:** Cervantes bust at right **Rev:** Relief map of Western Europe, stars, lines and value **Edge:** Reeded

Date	Mintage	F	VF	XF	Unc	BU
2010	—	—	—	—	1.25	1.50
2010 Proof	—	Value: 12.00				

KM# 1046 EURO
7.5000 g., Bi-Metallic Copper-Nickel center in Brass ring, 23.2 mm. **Ruler:** Juan Carlos I **Obv:** Head 1/4 left within circle and star border **Obv. Designer:** Luiz José Díaz **Rev:** Value and map within circle **Rev. Designer:** Luc Luycx **Edge:** Reeded and plain sections

Date	Mintage	F	VF	XF	Unc	BU
2001(M)	259,100,000	—	—	—	3.00	4.00
2002(M)	335,600,000	—	—	—	2.00	2.50
2002(M) Proof	23,000	Value: 15.00				
2003(M)	297,400,000	—	—	—	2.00	2.50
2003(M) Proof	20,000	Value: 15.00				
2004(M)	9,870,000	—	—	—	2.00	2.50
2005(M)	77,800,000	—	—	—	2.00	2.50
2005(M) Proof	3,000	Value: 15.00				
2006(M)	101,600,000	—	—	—	2.00	2.50

KM# 1073 EURO
7.4000 g., Bi-Metallic Copper-Nickel center in Brass ring, 23.2 mm. **Ruler:** Juan Carlos I **Obv:** King's portrait **Obv. Designer:** Luiz Jose Diaz **Rev:** Relief map of Western Europe, stars, lines and value **Rev. Designer:** Luc Luycx **Edge:** Reeded and plain sections

Date	Mintage	F	VF	XF	Unc	BU
2007(M)	150,558,000	—	—	—	3.00	3.50
2007(M) Proof	5,000	Value: 15.00				
2008(M)	—	—	—	—	3.00	3.50
2008(M) Proof	5,000	Value: 15.00				
2009(M)	—	—	—	—	3.00	3.50
2009(M) Proof	5,000	Value: 15.00				

KM# 1150 EURO
7.4000 g., Bi-Metallic, 23.2 mm. **Ruler:** Juan Carlos I **Obv:** King's portrait at right **Rev:** Relief map of Western Europe, stars, lines and value **Edge:** Segmented reeding

Date	Mintage	F	VF	XF	Unc	BU
2010	—	—	—	—	3.00	3.50
2010 Proof	—	Value: 15.00				

KM# 1047 2 EURO
8.5200 g., Bi-Metallic Brass center in Copper-Nickel ring, 25.7 mm. **Ruler:** Juan Carlos I **Obv:** Head 1/4 left within circle and star border **Obv. Designer:** Luis José Díaz **Rev:** Value and map within circle **Rev. Designer:** Luc Luycx **Edge:** Reeded **Edge Lettering:** 2's and stars

Date	Mintage	F	VF	XF	Unc	BU
2001(M)	140,200,000	—	—	—	4.50	5.00
2002(M)	164,000,000	—	—	—	3.50	4.00
2002(M) Proof	35,000	Value: 20.00				
2003(M)	44,500,000	—	—	—	4.50	5.00
2003(M) Proof	20,000	Value: 20.00				
2004(M)	4,100,000	—	—	—	4.50	5.00
2005(M)	4,000,000	—	—	—	4.50	5.00
2005(M) Proof	3,000	Value: 20.00				
2006(M)	4,000,000	—	—	—	4.50	5.00

KM# 1063 2 EURO
8.5200 g., Bi-Metallic Brass center in Copper-Nickel ring, 25.7 mm. **Ruler:** Juan Carlos I **Obv:** Stylized half length figure of Don Quixote holding spear within circle and star border **Rev:** Value and map within circle **Edge:** Reeding over stars and 2's **Note:** Mint mark: Crowned M.

Date	Mintage	F	VF	XF	Unc	BU
2005	8,000,000	—	—	—	5.00	6.00

KM# 1074 2 EURO
8.5000 g., Bi-Metallic Brass center in Copper-Nickel ring, 25.8 mm. **Ruler:** Juan Carlos I **Obv:** King's portrait **Obv. Designer:** Luis Jose Diaz **Rev:** Relief map of Western Europe, stars, lines and value **Rev. Designer:** Luc Luycx **Edge:** Reeded **Edge Lettering:** 2's and stars

Date	Mintage	F	VF	XF	Unc	BU
2007(M)	3,958,000	—	—	—	4.75	5.00
2007(M) Proof	5,000	Value: 20.00				
2008(M)	—	—	—	—	4.75	5.00
2008(M) Proof	5,000	Value: 20.00				
2009(M)	—	—	—	—	4.75	5.00
2009(M) Proof	5,000	Value: 20.00				

KM# 1130 2 EURO
8.5300 g., Bi-Metallic Brass center in Copper-Nickel ring, 25.70 mm. **Ruler:** Juan Carlos I **Subject:** 50th Anniversary Treaty of Rome **Obv:** Open treaty book **Obv. Legend:** ESPAÑA **Rev:** Large value at left, modified outline of Europe at right **Edge:** Reeded with 2's and stars

Date	Mintage	F	VF	XF	Unc	BU
2007	7,935,000	—	—	—	7.00	9.00
2007(M) Special Unc.	60,000	—	—	—	—	20.00
2007(M) Proof	5,000	Value: 35.00				

KM# 1142.2 2 EURO
8.5300 g., Bi-Metallic Brass center in Copper-Nickel ring, 25.75 mm. **Ruler:** Juan Carlos I **Subject:** European Monetary Unit, 10th Aniversary **Obv:** Stick figure and large E symbol

Date	Mintage	F	VF	XF	Unc	BU
2009 Large Stars	—	—	—	—	40.00	45.00

KM# 1142.1 2 EURO
8.5300 g., Bi-Metallic Brass center in Copper-Nickel ring, 25.7 mm. **Ruler:** Juan Carlos I **Subject:** European Monetary Unit, 10th Anniversary **Obv:** Stick figure and large E symbol **Rev:** Large value at left, modified map of Europe at right

Date	Mintage	F	VF	XF	Unc	BU
2009 small stars	—	—	—	—	5.00	6.00
2009 Special Unc.	—	—	—	—	—	20.00
2009 Proof	—	Value: 35.00				

KM# 1151 2 EURO

8.5300 g., Bi-Metallic, 25.8 mm. **Ruler:** Juan Carlos I **Obv:** King's portrait at right **Rev:** Relief map of Western Europe, stars, lines and value **Edge:** 2s and stars

Date	Mintage	F	VF	XF	Unc	BU
2010	—	—	—	—	4.75	5.00
2010 Proof	—	Value: 20.00				

KM# 1152 2 EURO

8.5200 g., Bi-Metallic Brass center in Copper-Nickel ring, 27.52 mm. **Ruler:** Juan Carlos I **Subject:** Cordoba - UNESCO Heritage site

Date	Mintage	F	VF	XF	Unc	BU
2010	—	—	—	—	7.00	9.00

KM# 1184 2 EURO

8.5200 g., Bi-Metallic Brass center in Copper-Nickel ring, 27.52 mm. **Ruler:** Juan Carlos I **Subject:** UNESCO Heritage Site - Granada **Obv:** The Alhambra

Date	Mintage	F	VF	XF	Unc	BU
2011	—	—	—	—	7.00	9.00

KM# 1153 5 EURO

13.5000 g., 0.9250 Silver 0.4015 oz. ASW, 33 mm. **Ruler:** Juan Carlos I **Subject:** Almeria

Date	Mintage	F	VF	XF	Unc	BU
2010 Proof	—	Value: 45.00				

KM# 1154 5 EURO

13.5000 g., 0.9250 Silver 0.4015 oz. ASW, 33 mm. **Ruler:** Juan Carlos I **Subject:** Huesca

Date	Mintage	F	VF	XF	Unc	BU
2010 Proof	—	Value: 45.00				

KM# 1155 5 EURO

13.5000 g., 0.9250 Silver 0.4015 oz. ASW, 33 mm. **Ruler:** Juan Carlos I **Subject:** Las Palmas G.C.

Date	Mintage	F	VF	XF	Unc	BU
2010 Proof	—	Value: 45.00				

KM# 1156 5 EURO

13.5000 g., 0.9250 Silver 0.4015 oz. ASW, 33 mm. **Ruler:** Juan Carlos I **Subject:** Santander

Date	Mintage	F	VF	XF	Unc	BU
2010 Proof	—	Value: 45.00				

KM# 1157 5 EURO

13.5000 g., 0.9250 Silver 0.4015 oz. ASW, 33 mm. **Ruler:** Juan Carlos I **Subject:** Avila

Date	Mintage	F	VF	XF	Unc	BU
2010 Proof	—	Value: 45.00				

KM# 1158 5 EURO

13.5000 g., 0.9250 Silver 0.4015 oz. ASW, 33 mm. **Ruler:** Juan Carlos I **Subject:** Albacete

Date	Mintage	F	VF	XF	Unc	BU
2010 Proof	—	Value: 45.00				

KM# 1159 5 EURO

13.5000 g., 0.9250 Silver 0.4015 oz. ASW, 33 mm. **Ruler:** Juan Carlos I **Subject:** Barcelona

Date	Mintage	F	VF	XF	Unc	BU
2010 Proof	—	Value: 45.00				

KM# 1160 5 EURO

13.5000 g., 0.9250 Silver 0.4015 oz. ASW, 33 mm. **Ruler:** Juan Carlos I **Subject:** Ceuta

Date	Mintage	F	VF	XF	Unc	BU
2010 Proof	—	Value: 45.00				

KM# 1161 5 EURO

13.5000 g., 0.9250 Silver 0.4015 oz. ASW, 33 mm. **Ruler:** Juan Carlos I **Subject:** Melilla

Date	Mintage	F	VF	XF	Unc	BU
2010 Proof	—	Value: 45.00				

KM# 1162 5 EURO

13.5000 g., 0.9250 Silver 0.4015 oz. ASW, 33 mm. **Ruler:** Juan Carlos I **Subject:** Madrid

Date	Mintage	F	VF	XF	Unc	BU
2010 Proof	—	Value: 45.00				

KM# 1163 5 EURO

13.5000 g., 0.9250 Silver 0.4015 oz. ASW, 33 mm. **Ruler:** Juan Carlos I **Subject:** Pamplona

Date	Mintage	F	VF	XF	Unc	BU
2010 Proof	—	Value: 45.00				

KM# 1164 5 EURO

13.5000 g., 0.9250 Silver 0.4015 oz. ASW, 33 mm. **Ruler:** Juan Carlos I **Subject:** Alicante

Date	Mintage	F	VF	XF	Unc	BU
2010 Proof	—	Value: 45.00				

KM# 1048 10 EURO

27.0000 g., 0.9250 Silver 0.8029 oz. ASW, 40 mm. **Ruler:** Juan Carlos I **Subject:** Spanish Presidency of the European Union **Obv:** Head left **Rev:** Map of Europe **Edge:** Reeded

Date	Mintage	F	VF	XF	Unc	BU
2002 Proof	30,000	Value: 55.00				

KM# 1078 10 EURO

27.0000 g., Silver **Ruler:** Juan Carlos I **Subject:** XIX Winter Olympics - Salt Lake City **Obv:** Head left **Obv. Legend:** JUAN CARLOS I REY DE ESPAÑA **Rev:** Cross country skier right, stylized snowflake at right **Rev. Legend:** JUEGOS OLIMPICOS DE - INVERNO 2002

Date	Mintage	F	VF	XF	Unc	BU
2002(M) Proof	30,000	Value: 60.00				

KM# 1079 10 EURO

27.0000 g., Silver **Ruler:** Juan Carlos I **Subject:** XVII Football World Games 2002 - South Korea and Japan **Obv. Legend:** MUNDIAL DE FUTBOL/2002 - ESPAÑA **Rev:** Football against net

Date	Mintage	F	VF	XF	Unc	BU
2002(M) Proof	25,000	Value: 60.00				

KM# 1080 10 EURO

27.0000 g., Silver **Ruler:** Juan Carlos I **Subject:** XVII Football World Games 2002 - South Korea and Japan **Obv. Legend:** MUNDIAL DE FUTBOL/2002 - ESPAÑA **Rev:** Glove

Date	Mintage	F	VF	XF	Unc	BU
2002(M) Proof	25,000	Value: 60.00				

KM# 1087 10 EURO

27.0000 g., 0.9250 Silver 0.8029 oz. ASW **Ruler:** Juan Carlos I **Subject:** 100th Anniversary - Birth of Luis Cernuda **Obv:** Head left

Date	Mintage	F	VF	XF	Unc	BU
2002(M) Proof	25,000	Value: 60.00				

KM# 1088 10 EURO

27.0000 g., 0.9250 Silver 0.8029 oz. ASW **Ruler:** Juan Carlos I **Subject:** 100th Anniversary - Birth of Rafael Alberti **Obv:** Head left **Obv. Legend:** JUAN CARLOS I REY DE ESPAÑA **Rev:** Bust of Alberti facing 3/4 right

Date	Mintage	F	VF	XF	Unc	BU
2002(M) Proof	25,000	Value: 60.00				

KM# 1082 10 EURO

27.0000 g., 0.9250 Silver 0.8029 oz. ASW, 40.0 mm. **Ruler:** Juan Carlos I **Subject:** 150th Anniversary Birth of Antonio Gaudí **Obv:** Bust of Gaudií at right **Obv. Legend:** Año Internacional **Rev:** Casa Milà

Date	Mintage	F	VF	XF	Unc	BU
2002(M) Proof	25,000	Value: 55.00				

KM# 1083 10 EURO

27.0000 g., 0.9250 Silver 0.8029 oz. ASW, 40.0 mm. **Ruler:** Juan Carlos I **Subject:** 150th Anniversary Birth of Antonio Gaudí **Obv:** Bust of Gaudí at right **Obv. Legend:** Año Internacional **Rev:** El Capricho

Date	Mintage	F	VF	XF	Unc	BU
2002(M) Proof	25,000	Value: 55.00				

KM# 1084 10 EURO

27.0000 g., 0.9250 Silver 0.8029 oz. ASW, 40.0 mm. **Ruler:** Juan Carlos I **Subject:** 150th Anniversary - Birth of Antonio Gaudí **Obv:** Bust of Gaudí at right **Obv. Legend:** Año Internacional **Rev:** Parque Güell

Date	Mintage	F	VF	XF	Unc	BU
2002(M) Proof	25,000	Value: 55.00				

KM# 1089 10 EURO

27.0000 g., 0.9250 Silver 0.8029 oz. ASW **Ruler:** Juan Carlos I **Series:** Ibero-America V - ships **Obv:** Crowned arms in center circle, 10 participating country arms in outer circle **Obv. Legend:** JUAN CARLOS I REY DE ESPAÑA **Rev:** Galleon of the Spanish Armada **Rev. Legend:** ENCUENTRO DE DOS MUNDOS **Note:** Issued in 2003.

Date	Mintage	F	VF	XF	Unc	BU
2002(M) Proof	12,000	Value: 135				

KM# 1050 10 EURO

27.0000 g., 0.9250 Silver 0.8029 oz. ASW, 40 mm. **Ruler:** Juan Carlos I **Subject:** Annexation of Minorca **Obv:** Conjoined heads left **Rev:** Uniformed equestrians shaking hands flanked by ships **Edge:** Reeded **Note:** Mint mark: Crowned M.

Date	Mintage	F	VF	XF	Unc	BU
2002 Proof	30,000	Value: 55.00				

KM# 1076 10 EURO

27.0000 g., 0.9250 Silver 0.8029 oz. ASW **Ruler:** Juan Carlos I **Subject:** FIFA World Cup **Obv:** Kings head left **Rev:** Goalie jumping for ball by net **Edge:** Reeded **Note:** Issued in 2004.

Date	Mintage	F	VF	XF	Unc	BU
2003(M) Proof	50,000	Value: 55.00				

KM# 1090 10 EURO

27.0000 g., 0.9250 Silver 0.8029 oz. ASW **Ruler:** Juan Carlos I **Obv:** Conjoined heads left **Obv. Legend:** JUAN CARLOS I Y SOFIA **Rev:** Ediface of Parliament building in Madrid **Rev. Legend:** CONSTITUCION ESPAÑOLA

Date	Mintage	F	VF	XF	Unc	BU
2003(M) Proof	30,000	Value: 60.00				

KM# 1092 10 EURO

27.0000 g., 0.9250 Silver 0.8029 oz. ASW, 40.0 mm. **Ruler:** Juan Carlos I **Subject:** !st Anniversary of Euro **Obv:** Conjoined heads left **Obv. Legend:** PREMIER ANIVERSARIO EURO ? JUAN CARLOS I Y SOFIA **Rev:** Europa riding steer left

Date	Mintage	F	VF	XF	Unc	BU
2003(M) Proof	50,000	Value: 55.00				

KM# 1094 10 EURO

27.0000 g., 0.9250 Silver 0.8029 oz. ASW **Ruler:** Juan Carlos I **Subject:** World Swimming Championship Games - Barcelona 2003 **Obv:** Head left **Obv. Legend:** JUAN CARLOS I REY DE ESPAÑA **Rev:** Swimmer doing the crawl right **Rev. Legend:** X FINA CAMPEONATOS DEL MUNDO DENATACION

Date	Mintage	F	VF	XF	Unc	BU
2003(M) Proof	30,000	Value: 60.00				

KM# 1052 10 EURO

27.0000 g., 0.9250 Silver 0.8029 oz. ASW, 40 mm. **Ruler:** Juan Carlos I **Obv:** Head left **Rev:** Sailing ship - De Eleano **Edge:** Reeded

Date	Mintage	F	VF	XF	Unc	BU
2003 Proof	50,000	Value: 55.00				

KM# 1053 10 EURO

27.0000 g., 0.9250 Silver 0.8029 oz. ASW, 40 mm. **Ruler:** Juan Carlos I **Obv:** Juan Carlos I **Rev:** Miguel Lopez de Legazpi **Edge:** Reeded

Date	Mintage	F	VF	XF	Unc	BU
2003 Proof	25,000	Value: 55.00				

KM# 1054 10 EURO
27.0000 g., 0.9250 Silver 0.8029 oz. ASW, 40 mm. **Ruler:** Juan Carlos I **Obv:** Head facing **Rev:** Seated female figure and Swan **Edge:** Reeded

Date	Mintage	F	VF	XF	Unc	BU
2003 Proof	25,000	Value: 60.00				

KM# 1055 10 EURO
27.0000 g., 0.9250 Silver 0.8029 oz. ASW, 40 mm. **Ruler:** Juan Carlos I **Obv:** Head facing **Rev:** Dali's painting "El gran masturbador" of 1929 **Edge:** Reeded

Date	Mintage	F	VF	XF	Unc	BU
2004 Proof	25,000	Value: 60.00				

KM# 1056 10 EURO
27.0000 g., 0.9250 Silver 0.8029 oz. ASW, 40 mm. **Ruler:** Juan Carlos I **Obv:** Head facing **Rev:** Dali's self portrait with bacon strip **Edge:** Reeded

Date	Mintage	F	VF	XF	Unc	BU
2004 Proof	25,000	Value: 60.00				

KM# 1059 10 EURO
27.0000 g., 0.9250 Silver 0.8029 oz. ASW, 40 mm. **Ruler:** Juan Carlos I **Obv:** Conjoined heads left **Rev:** Bust of St. James facing **Edge:** Reeded

Date	Mintage	F	VF	XF	Unc	BU
2004 Proof	20,000	Value: 55.00				

KM# 1060 10 EURO
27.0000 g., 0.9250 Silver 0.8029 oz. ASW, 40 mm. **Ruler:** Juan Carlos I **Obv:** Conjoined heads left within beaded circle **Rev:** Bust 1/4 left within beaded circle (1451-1504) **Edge:** Reeded

Date	Mintage	F	VF	XF	Unc	BU
2004 Proof	20,000	Value: 55.00				

KM# 1099 10 EURO
27.0000 g., 0.9250 Silver 0.8029 oz. ASW **Ruler:** Juan Carlos I **Subject:** Expansion of the European Union **Obv:** Head left **Obv. Legend:** JUAN CARLOS I Y SOFIA **Rev:** Outlined map of European Union

Date	Mintage	F	VF	XF	Unc	BU
2004(M) Proof	50,000	Value: 45.00				

KM# 1101 10 EURO
27.0000 g., 0.9250 Silver 0.8029 oz. ASW **Ruler:** Juan Carlos I **Subject:** XXVIII Summer Olympics - Athens 2004 **Obv:** Conjoined heads left **Obv. Legend:** JUAN CARLOS I Y SOFIA **Rev:** Broad jumper, outlined world map in backgound **Rev. Legend:** JUEGOS OLIMICOS

Date	Mintage	F	VF	XF	Unc	BU
2004(M) Proof	30,000	Value: 60.00				

KM# 1102 10 EURO
27.0000 g., 0.9250 Silver 0.8029 oz. ASW **Ruler:** Juan Carlos I **Subject:** XVIII World Football games - Germany 2006 **Obv:** Head left **Obv. Legend:** JUAN CARLOS I REY DE ESPAÑA **Rev:** Goalie deflecting ball at net

Date	Mintage	F	VF	XF	Unc	BU
2004(M) Proof	50,000	Value: 60.00				

KM# 1097 10 EURO
27.0000 g., 0.9250 Silver 0.8029 oz. ASW, 40.0 mm. **Ruler:** Juan Carlos I **Subject:** Wedding of Prince Philip and Letizia Ortiz Rocasolano **Obv:** Conjoined heads left **Obv. Legend:** JUAN CARLOS I T SOFÍA **Rev:** Busts of wedding couple facing 3/4 right, crowned shield below **Rev. Legend:** FELIPE Y LETIZIA - 22.V.2004

Date	Mintage	F	VF	XF	Unc	BU
2004(M) Proof	100,000	Value: 55.00				

KM# 1104 10 EURO
27.0000 g., 0.9250 Silver 0.8029 oz. ASW, 40.0 mm. **Ruler:** Juan Carlos I **Obv:** Quixote seated reading a large book **Obv. Legend:** ESPAÑA - IV CENTENARIO DE LA PRIMERA EDICIÓN DE " EL QUIJOTE" **Rev:** Quixote being knocked off his horse by windmill blade **Rev. Legend:** LA AVENTURA - DE LOS - MOLINOS DE VIENTO

Date	Mintage	F	VF	XF	Unc	BU
2005(M) Proof	18,000	Value: 65.00				

KM# 1105 10 EURO
27.0000 g., 0.9250 Silver 0.8029 oz. ASW, 40.0 mm. **Ruler:** Juan Carlos I **Obv:** Quixote seated reading a large book **Obv. Legend:** ESPAÑA - IV CENTENARIO DE LA PREMERA EDICIÓN DE LA "EL QUIJOTE" **Rev:** Quixote thrusting his sword into an animal skin wine sack **Rev. Legend:** CON UNOS CUEROS DE VINO - BATALLA

Date	Mintage	F	VF	XF	Unc	BU
2005(M) Proof	18,000	Value: 65.00				

KM# 1106 10 EURO
27.0000 g., 0.9250 Silver 0.8029 oz. ASW, 40.0 mm. **Ruler:** Juan Carlos I **Obv:** Quixote seated reading a large book **Obv. Legend:** ESPAÑA - IV CENTENARIO DE LA PRIMERA EDICIÓN DE "EL QUIJOTE" **Rev:** Boy mounting a hobby horse with Quixote on it **Rev. Legend:** LA VENIDA DE CLAVAILEÑO CON...DILATADA AVENTURA

Date	Mintage	F	VF	XF	Unc	BU
2005(M) Proof	18,000	Value: 65.00				

KM# 1110 10 EURO
27.0000 g., 0.9250 Silver 0.8029 oz. ASW, 40.0 mm. **Ruler:** Juan Carlos I **Rev:** Crowned shield at left, head of Prince Philip at right **Rev. Legend:** XXV ANIVERSARIO - PREMIOS PRÍNCIPE DE ASTURIAS

Date	Mintage	F	VF	XF	Unc	BU
2005(M) Proof	35,000	Value: 60.00				

KM# 1109 10 EURO
27.0000 g., 0.9250 Silver 0.8029 oz. ASW **Ruler:** Juan Carlos I **Series:** Ibero-America VI - Architecture **Obv:** Crowned arms in center circle, 10 participating country arms in outer circle **Obv. Legend:** JUAN CARLOS I REY DE ESPAÑA **Rev:** General Archives building of West Indes in Seville **Rev. Legend:** ENCUENTRO DE DOS MUNDOS

Date	Mintage	F	VF	XF	Unc	BU
2005(M) Proof	12,000	Value: 90.00				

KM# 1064 10 EURO
27.0000 g., 0.9250 Silver 0.8029 oz. ASW, 40 mm. **Ruler:** Juan Carlos I **Subject:** 2006 Winter Olympics **Obv:** Juan Carlos **Rev:** Skier **Edge:** Reeded

Date	Mintage	F	VF	XF	Unc	BU
2005 Proof	25,000	Value: 55.00				

KM# 1065 10 EURO
27.0000 g., 0.9250 Silver 0.8029 oz. ASW, 40 mm. **Ruler:** Juan Carlos I **Subject:** European Peace and Freedom **Obv:** Juan Carlos **Rev:** European map on clasped hands **Edge:** Reeded

Date	Mintage	F	VF	XF	Unc	BU
2005 Proof	40,000	Value: 40.00				

KM# 1114 10 EURO
26.8000 g., 0.9250 Silver 0.7970 oz. ASW, 39.98 mm. **Ruler:** Juan Carlos I **Subject:** 500th Anniversary Death of Columbus **Obv:** Bust of Columbus facing at right, astrolabe at lower left **Obv. Legend:** ESPAÑA **Rev:** Sailing ship "Santa Maria" **Rev. Legend:** CRISTOBAL COLON **Edge:** Reeded

Date	Mintage	F	VF	XF	Unc	BU
2006(M) Proof	12,000	Value: 65.00				

KM# 1119 10 EURO
27.0000 g., 0.9250 Silver 0.8029 oz. ASW, 40.0 mm. **Ruler:** Juan Carlos I **Subject:** 20th Anniversay of Spain and Portugal membership in European Union **Obv:** Juan Carlos I **Rev:** Outlined map of Europe, bridge below **Rev. Legend:** ADHESIÓN A LAS COMUNIDADES EUROPEAS **Rev. Inscription:** ESPAÑA - PORTUGAL

Date	Mintage	F	VF	XF	Unc	BU
2006(M) Proof	12,000	Value: 60.00				

KM# 1120 10 EURO
27.0000 g., 0.9250 Silver 0.8029 oz. ASW, 40.0 mm. **Ruler:** Juan Carlos I **Rev:** Basketball player scoring in front of defender **Rev. Legend:** CAMPEONS DEL MUNDO - JAPÓN 2006

Date	Mintage	F	VF	XF	Unc	BU
2006(M) Proof	15,000	Value: 60.00				

KM# 1122 10 EURO
27.0000 g., 0.9250 Silver 0.8029 oz. ASW, 40.0 mm. **Ruler:** Juan Carlos I **Obv:** Head left **Obv. Legend:** JUAN CARLOS I REY DE ESPAÑA **Rev:** Charles I (V) standing facing 3/4 right in front of portal **Rev. Legend:** CAROLVS IMPERATOR

Date	Mintage	F	VF	XF	Unc	BU
2006(M) Proof	35,000	Value: 65.00				

KM# 1115 10 EURO
18.0000 g., 0.9250 Silver 0.5353 oz. ASW, 39.98 mm. **Ruler:** Juan Carlos I **Subject:** 500th Anniversary - Death of Columbus **Obv:** Bust of Columbus facing at left, astrolabe at lower right **Obv. Legend:** ESPAÑA **Rev:** Sailing ship "Pinta" **Rev. Legend:** CRISTOBAL COLON **Edge:** Reeded

Date	Mintage	F	VF	XF	Unc	BU
2006(M) Proof	12,000	Value: 65.00				

KM# 1116 10 EURO
26.8000 g., 0.9250 Silver 0.7970 oz. ASW, 39.98 mm. **Ruler:** Juan Carlos I **Subject:** 500th Anniversary - Death of Columbus **Obv:** Bust of Columbus facing at right, astrolabe at lower left **Obv. Legend:** ESPAÑA **Rev:** Sailing ship "Niña" **Rev. Legend:** CRISTOBAL COLON **Edge:** Reeded

Date	Mintage	F	VF	XF	Unc	BU
2006(M) Proof	12,000	Value: 65.00				

KM# 1124 10 EURO
27.0000 g., 0.9250 Silver 0.8029 oz. ASW, 40 mm. **Ruler:** Juan Carlos I **Rev:** Two ornate portals **Rev. Legend:** V ANIVERSARIO DEL EURO

Date	Mintage	F	VF	XF	Unc	BU
2007 Proof	12,000	Value: 60.00				

KM# 1125 10 EURO
27.0000 g., 0.9250 Silver 0.8029 oz. ASW, 40 mm. **Ruler:** Juan Carlos I **Rev:** Stone arch bridge **Rev. Legend:** V ANIVERSARIO DEL EURO

Date	Mintage	F	VF	XF	Unc	BU
2007 Proof	12,000	Value: 60.00				

KM# 1126 10 EURO
27.0000 g., 0.9250 Silver 0.8029 oz. ASW, 40 mm. **Ruler:** Juan Carlos I **Rev:** Stone archway **Rev. Legend:** V ANIVERSARIO DEL EURO

Date	Mintage	F	VF	XF	Unc	BU
2007 Proof	12,000	Value: 60.00				

KM# 1132 10 EURO
27.0000 g., 0.9250 Silver 0.8029 oz. ASW, 40 mm. **Ruler:** Juan Carlos I **Obv:** Conjoined heads left **Obv. Legend:** JUAN CARLOS I Y SOFÍA - AÑO DE ESPAÑA EN CHINA **Rev:** Early silver "Pillar" reales coin with Chinese characters to left and right of pillars **Rev. Legend:** VTRAQUE VNVM

Date	Mintage	F	VF	XF	Unc	BU
2007 Proof	20,000	Value: 55.00				

KM# 1134 10 EURO
27.0000 g., 0.9250 Silver 0.8029 oz. ASW, 40 mm. **Ruler:** Juan Carlos I **Obv:** Head left **Obv. Legend:** JUAN CARLOS I REY DE ESPAÑA **Rev:** Basketball player shooting basket **Rev. Legend:** EUROBASKET 2007

Date	Mintage	F	VF	XF	Unc	BU
2007 Proof	12,000	Value: 65.00				

KM# 1141 10 EURO
27.0000 g., 0.9250 Silver 0.8029 oz. ASW, 40 mm. **Ruler:** Juan Carlos I **Subject:** Zaragoza Expo 2008

Date	Mintage	F	VF	XF	Unc	BU
2007 Proof	25,000	Value: 55.00				

KM# 1135 10 EURO
27.0000 g., 0.9250 Silver 0.8029 oz. ASW, 40 mm. **Ruler:** Juan Carlos I **Subject:** Treaty of Rome, 50th Anniversary **Obv:** Head left **Rev:** Map of Western Europe

Date	Mintage	F	VF	XF	Unc	BU
2007 Proof	15,000	Value: 60.00				

KM# 1137 10 EURO
27.0000 g., 0.9250 Silver 0.8029 oz. ASW, 40 mm. **Ruler:** Juan Carlos I **Subject:** El Cid 700th Anniversary **Obv:** Female standing before arches **Rev:** Monk writing

Date	Mintage	F	VF	XF	Unc	BU
2007 Proof	12,000	Value: 65.00				

KM# 1140 10 EURO
27.0000 g., 0.9250 Silver 0.8029 oz. ASW, 40 mm. **Ruler:** Juan Carlos I **Subject:** International Polar Year

Date	Mintage	F	VF	XF	Unc	BU
2007 Proof	—	Value: 60.00				

KM# 1143 10 EURO
27.0000 g., 0.9250 Silver 0.8029 oz. ASW, 40 mm. **Ruler:** Juan Carlos I **Obv:** Head left **Rev:** Soccer player, ball and net

Date	Mintage	F	VF	XF	Unc	BU
2009 Proof	12,000	Value: 55.00				

KM# 1165 10 EURO
27.0000 g., 0.9250 Silver 0.8029 oz. ASW, 40 mm. **Ruler:** Juan Carlos I **Subject:** Numismatic Treasurers - Silver Shekel from Carthage, 3rd Century BC

Date	Mintage	F	VF	XF	Unc	BU
2010 Proof	—	Value: 70.00				

KM# 1169 10 EURO
27.0000 g., 0.9250 Silver 0.8029 oz. ASW, 33 mm. **Ruler:** Juan Carlos I **Subject:** Antoni Gaudi

Date	Mintage	F	VF	XF	Unc	BU
2010 Proof	—	Value: 70.00				

KM# 1171 10 EURO
27.0000 g., 0.9250 Silver 0.8029 oz. ASW, 40 mm. **Ruler:** Juan Carlos I **Subject:** EU Council Presidency

Date	Mintage	F	VF	XF	Unc	BU
2010 Proof	—	Value: 65.00				

KM# 1173 10 EURO
27.0000 g., 0.9250 Silver 0.8029 oz. ASW, 40 mm. **Ruler:** Juan Carlos I **Subject:** Holy Year 2010 - St. james the Elder

Date	Mintage	F	VF	XF	Unc	BU
2010 Proof	—	Value: 65.00				

KM# 1174 10 EURO
27.0000 g., 0.9250 Silver 0.8029 oz. ASW, 40 mm. **Ruler:** Juan Carlos I **Subject:** Shanghai Expo

Date	Mintage	F	VF	XF	Unc	BU
2010 Proof	—	Value: 65.00				

KM# 1175 10 EURO
27.0000 g., 0.9250 Silver 0.8029 oz. ASW, 40 mm. **Ruler:** Juan Carlos I **Subject:** Ibero-American Series - Historical Coins

Date	Mintage	F	VF	XF	Unc	BU
2010 Proof	—	Value: 70.00				

KM# 1176 10 EURO
27.0000 g., 0.9250 Silver 0.8029 oz. ASW, 40 mm. **Ruler:** Juan Carlos I **Subject:** FIFA World Cup - South Africa 2010

Date	Mintage	F	VF	XF	Unc	BU
2010 Proof	—	Value: 60.00				

KM# 1178 10 EURO
27.0000 g., 0.9250 Silver 0.8029 oz. ASW, 40 mm. **Ruler:** Juan Carlos I **Subject:** Francisco de Goya - The Clothed Maja

Date	Mintage	F	VF	XF	Unc	BU
2010 Proof	—	Value: 65.00				

KM# 1179 10 EURO
27.0000 g., 0.9250 Silver 0.8029 oz. ASW, 40 mm. **Ruler:** Juan Carlos I **Subject:** Francisco de Goya - The Grape Harvest

Date	Mintage	F	VF	XF	Unc	BU
2010 Proof	—	Value: 65.00				

KM# 1180 10 EURO
27.0000 g., 0.9250 Silver 0.8029 oz. ASW, 40 mm. **Ruler:** Juan Carlos I **Subject:** Francisco de Goya - Duel with Clubs

Date	Mintage	F	VF	XF	Unc	BU
2010 Proof	—	Value: 65.00				

KM# 1049 12 EURO
18.0000 g., 0.9250 Silver 0.5353 oz. ASW, 33 mm. **Ruler:** Juan Carlos I **Subject:** Spanish European Union Presidency **Obv:** Conjoined heads left **Rev:** Distorted star design **Edge:** Reeded

Date	Mintage	F	VF	XF	Unc	BU
2002	1,500,000	—	—	—	22.50	25.00
2002 Special select	25,000	—	—	—	—	30.00
2002 Proof	50,000	Value: 50.00				

KM# 1051 12 EURO
18.0000 g., 0.9250 Silver 0.5353 oz. ASW, 33 mm. **Ruler:** Juan Carlos I **Subject:** 25th Anniversary of Constitution **Obv:** Conjoined heads left **Rev:** National arms above denomination **Edge:** Plain

Date	Mintage	F	VF	XF	Unc	BU
2003	1,469,000	—	—	—	27.00	30.00

KM# 1069 12 EURO
Silver **Ruler:** Juan Carlos I **Obv:** Juan Carlos and Sofia **Rev:** Felipe and Letizia

Date	Mintage	F	VF	XF	Unc	BU
2004M	—	—	—	—	27.00	30.00

KM# 1095 12 EURO
18.0000 g., 0.9250 Silver 0.5353 oz. ASW, 32.93 mm. **Ruler:** Juan Carlos I **Subject:** 500th Anniversary - Death of Isabel **Obv:** Conjoined heads left **Obv. Legend:** JUAN CARLOS I Y SOFIA **Rev:** Bust of Isabella I left **Rev. Legend:** ISABEL I DE CASTILLA / 1481-1504 **Edge:** Plain

Date	Mintage	F	VF	XF	Unc	BU
2004(M)	1,500,000	—	—	—	27.00	30.00

KM# 1096 12 EURO
18.0000 g., 0.9250 Silver 0.5353 oz. ASW, 32.94 mm. **Ruler:** Juan Carlos I **Subject:** Wedding of Prince Philip and Letizia Ortiz Rocasolano **Obv:** Conjoined heads left **Obv. Legend:** JUAN CARLOS I Y SOFIA **Rev:** Busts of wedding couple facing 3/4 right **Rev. Legend:** FELIPE Y LETIZIA - 22.V.2004 **Edge:** Plain

Date	Mintage	F	VF	XF	Unc	BU
2004(M)	4,000,000	—	—	—	25.00	28.00

KM# 1067 12 EURO
18.0000 g., 0.9250 Silver 0.5353 oz. ASW, 33 mm. **Ruler:** Juan Carlos I **Subject:** Don Quixote **Obv:** Conjoined heads left **Rev:** Man seated on books **Edge:** Reeded

Date	Mintage	F	VF	XF	Unc	BU
2005	4,000,000	—	—	—	25.00	28.00

KM# 1113 12 EURO
18.0000 g., 0.9250 Silver 0.5353 oz. ASW, 32.95 mm. **Ruler:** Juan Carlos I **Subject:** 500th Anniversary - Death of Columbus **Obv:** Conjoined heads left **Obv. Legend:** JUAN CARLOS I Y SOFIA **Rev:** Bust of Columbus facing 3/4 right, latitude and longitude lines with three small sailing ships in background **Edge:** Plain

Date	Mintage	F	VF	XF	Unc	BU
2006(M)	4,000,000	—	—	—	25.00	28.00

KM# 1129 12 EURO
18.0000 g., 0.9250 Silver 0.5353 oz. ASW, 32 mm. **Ruler:** Juan Carlos I **Rev:** Hand with pen **Rev. Legend:** 50 ANIVERSARIO • TRATADO DE ROMA **Rev. Inscription:** EUROPA

Date	Mintage	F	VF	XF	Unc	BU
2007 Proof	25,000	Value: 30.00				

KM# 1172 12 EURO
18.0000 g., 0.9250 Silver 0.5353 oz. ASW, 33 mm. **Ruler:** Juan Carlos I **Subject:** EU Council Presidency

Date	Mintage	F	VF	XF	Unc	BU
2010 Proof	—	Value: 30.00				

KM# 1133 20 EURO
1.2400 g., 0.9990 Gold 0.0398 oz. AGW, 13.92 mm. **Ruler:** Juan Carlos I **Obv:** National arms **Obv. Legend:** JUAN CARLOS I REY DE ESPAÑA - AÑO DE ESPAÑA EN CHINA **Rev:** Early silver "Pillar" reales coin with Chinese chopmarks

Date	Mintage	F	VF	XF	Unc	BU
2007 Proof	15,000	Value: 95.00				

KM# 1166 20 EURO
1.2400 g., 0.9990 Gold 0.0398 oz. AGW, 13.92 mm. **Ruler:** Juan Carlos I **Subject:** Numismatic Treasurers - Tremis, King Leovigild (569-86)

Date	Mintage	F	VF	XF	Unc	BU
2010 Proof	—	Value: 100				

KM# 1177 20 EURO
1.2400 g., 0.9990 Gold 0.0398 oz. AGW, 13.92 mm. **Ruler:** Juan Carlos I **Subject:** FIFA World Cup - South Africa

Date	Mintage	F	VF	XF	Unc	BU
2010 Proof	—	Value: 100				

KM# 1183 20 EURO
18.0000 g., 0.9250 Silver 0.5353 oz. ASW, 33 mm. **Ruler:** Juan Carlos I **Subject:** FIFA World Cup Winners

Date	Mintage	F	VF	XF	Unc	BU
2010 Proof	—	Value: 100				

KM# 1085 50 EURO
168.7500 g., 0.9250 Silver 5.0183 oz. ASW, 73 mm. **Ruler:** Juan Carlos I **Subject:** 150th Anniversary - Birth of Antonio Gaudí **Obv:** Bust of Gaudií at right **Obv. Legend:** Año Internacional **Rev:** Sagrada Familia

Date	Mintage	F	VF	XF	Unc	BU
2002(M) Proof	8,000	Value: 225				

KM# 1093 50 EURO
168.7500 g., 0.9250 Silver 5.0183 oz. ASW, 73 mm. **Ruler:** Juan Carlos I **Subject:** 1st Anniversary of Euro **Obv:** Conjoined heads left **Obv. Legend:** PREMIER ANIVERSARIO EURO • JUAN CARLOS I Y SOFÍA **Rev:** National arms at center surrounded by various items of architecture

Date	Mintage	F	VF	XF	Unc	BU
2003 Proof	20,000	Value: 250				

KM# 1057 50 EURO
168.7500 g., 0.9250 Silver with removeable gold plated silver insert 5.0183 oz. ASW, 73 mm. **Ruler:** Juan Carlos I **Obv:** Dali's "Dream State" painting **Rev:** Dali's "Rhinocerotic Disintegration..." painting **Edge:** Reeded **Note:** Illustration reduced.

Date	Mintage	F	VF	XF	Unc	BU
2004 Proof	12,000	Value: 225				

KM# 1061 50 EURO
168.7300 g., 0.9250 Silver 5.0177 oz. ASW, 73 mm. **Ruler:** Juan Carlos I **Obv:** Crowned bust left(1451-1504) and castle within beaded circle **Rev:** Surrender of Grenada scene within beaded circle **Edge:** Reeded **Note:** Illustration reduced.

Date	Mintage	F	VF	XF	Unc	BU
2004 Proof	8,000	Value: 225				

KM# 1107 50 EURO
168.7500 g., 0.9250 Silver 5.0183 oz. ASW, 73 mm. **Ruler:** Juan Carlos I **Obv:** 1/2 length figure of Miguel de Cervantes Saavedra facing writing in manuscript with quill pen **Obv. Legend:** ESPAÑA - IV CENTENARIO DE LA PRIMERA EDICIÓn DE "EL QUIJOTE" **Rev:** Quixote

Date	Mintage	F	VF	XF	Unc	BU
2005(M) Proof	12,000	Value: 225				

KM# 1117 50 EURO
168.2500 g., 0.9250 Silver 5.0035 oz. ASW, 73.95 mm. **Ruler:** Juan Carlos I **Subject:** 500th Anniversary - Death of Columbus **Obv:** Landing party at Guanahani **Obv. Legend:** ESPAÑA **Rev:** Columbus standing facing 3/4 left with right arm outstretched standing on outline of the northern part of South America **Rev. Legend:** CRISTOBAL COLON **Edge:** Plain **Note:** Illustration reduced.

Date	Mintage	F	VF	XF	Unc	BU
2006(M) Proof	6,000	Value: 245				

KM# 1127 50 EURO
168.7500 g., 0.9250 Silver 5.0183 oz. ASW, 73 mm. **Ruler:** Juan Carlos I **Rev:** Euro seated on resting bull left **Rev. Legend:** V ANIVERSARIO DEL EURO **Note:** Illustration reduced.

Date	Mintage	F	VF	XF	Unc	BU
2007 Proof	6,000	Value: 245				

KM# 1138 50 EURO
168.7500 g., 0.9250 Silver 5.0183 oz. ASW, 73 mm. **Ruler:** Juan Carlos I **Subject:** El Cid 700th Anniversary **Obv:** Statue of Rodrigo Diaz de Vivar in Burgas **Rev:** Two seated trumpeters **Note:** Illustration reduced.

Date	Mintage	F	VF	XF	Unc	BU
2007 Proof	6,000	Value: 245				

KM# 1181 50 EURO
168.7500 g., 0.9250 Silver 5.0183 oz. ASW, 73 mm. **Ruler:** Juan Carlos I **Subject:** Francisco de Goya - Witches' Sabbath

Date	Mintage	F	VF	XF	Unc	BU
2010 Proof	—	Value: 250				

KM# 1077 100 EURO
6.7500 g., 0.9990 Gold 0.2168 oz. AGW **Ruler:** Juan Carlos I **Obv:** Head left **Obv. Legend:** JUAN CARLOS I REY DE ESPAÑA **Rev:** Player running right kicking ball **Rev. Legend:** ALEMANIA 2006 at bottom **Note:** Issued in 2004.

Date	Mintage	F	VF	XF	Unc	BU
2003(M) Proof	25,000	Value: 375				

KM# 1103 100 EURO
6.7500 g., 0.9990 Gold 0.2168 oz. AGW **Ruler:** Juan Carlos I **Subject:** XVIII World Football Games - Germany 2006 **Obv:** Head left **Obv. Legend:** JUAN CARLOS I REY DE ESPAÑA **Rev:** Goalie deflecting ball at net **Rev. Inscription:** COPA MUNDIAL DE LA FIFA

Date	Mintage	F	VF	XF	Unc	BU
2004(M) Proof	25,000	Value: 350				

KM# 1167 100 EURO
168.8800 g., 0.9250 Silver with gold plating 5.0222 oz. ASW, 73 mm. **Ruler:** Juan Carlos I **Subject:** Numismatic treasurers - The Centen, 100 Escudos, 1609

Date	Mintage	F	VF	XF	Unc	BU
2009 Proof	—	Value: 250				

KM# 1168 100 EURO
6.7500 g., 0.9990 Gold 0.2168 oz. AGW, 23 mm. **Ruler:** Juan Carlos I **Subject:** Numismatic Treasurers - Tremis, Suintila (621-31)

Date	Mintage	F	VF	XF	Unc	BU
2010 Proof	6,000	Value: 375				

KM# 1081 200 EURO
13.5000 g., 0.9990 Gold 0.4336 oz. AGW **Ruler:** Juan Carlos I **Subject:** XVII Football World Games 2002 - South Korea and Japan **Obv. Legend:** MUNDIAL DE FUTBOL/2002 - ESPAÑA **Rev:** Ball hitting net

Date	Mintage	F	VF	XF	Unc	BU
2002(M) Proof	4,000	Value: 700				

KM# 1091 200 EURO
13.5000 g., 0.9990 Gold 0.4336 oz. AGW **Ruler:** Juan Carlos I **Obv:** Conjoined heads left **Obv. Legend:** JUAN CARLOS I Y SOFIA **Rev:** Ediface of Parliament Building in Madrid **Rev. Legend:** CONSTITUCION ESPANOLA

Date	Mintage	F	VF	XF	Unc	BU
2003(M) Proof	4,000	Value: 700				

KM# 1075 200 EURO
13.5000 g., 0.9990 Gold 0.4336 oz. AGW, 30 mm. **Ruler:** Juan Carlos I **Subject:** Birth of the Euro **Obv:** Spanish King and Queen left **Rev:** Mythological Europa riding on the back of a bull

Date	Mintage	F	VF	XF	Unc	BU
2003 Proof	20,000	Value: 650				

KM# 1062 200 EURO
13.5000 g., 0.9990 Gold 0.4336 oz. AGW, 30 mm. **Ruler:** Juan Carlos I **Obv:** Seated crowned figures on shield flanked by date and value **Rev:** Crowned busts facing each other on coin design **Edge:** Reeded

Date	Mintage	F	VF	XF	Unc	BU
2004 Proof	5,000	Value: 700				

KM# 1100 200 EURO
13.5000 g., 0.9990 Gold 0.4336 oz. AGW **Ruler:** Juan Carlos I **Subject:** Expansion of the European Union **Obv:** Head left **Obv. Legend:** JUAN CARLOS I Y SOFIA **Rev:** Outlined map of the European Union

Date	Mintage	F	VF	XF	Unc	BU
2004(M) Proof	5,000	Value: 700				

KM# 1098 200 EURO
13.5000 g., 0.9990 Gold 0.4336 oz. AGW, 30 mm. **Ruler:** Juan Carlos I **Subject:** Wedding of Prince Philip and Letizia Ortiz Rocasolano **Obv:** Conjoined heads left **Obv. Legend:** JUAN CARLOS I Y SOFIA **Rev:** Busts of wedding couple facing 3/4 right at center left, crowned shield at right **Rev. Legend:** FELIPE Y LETIZIA - 22.V.2004

Date	Mintage	F	VF	XF	Unc	BU
2004(M) Proof	30,000	Value: 650				

KM# 1111 200 EURO
13.5000 g., 0.9990 Gold 0.4336 oz. AGW, 30 mm. **Ruler:** Juan Carlos I **Rev:** Crowned shield at left, head of Prince Philip left at right **Rev. Legend:** XXV ANIVERSAIO - PREMIOS PRÍNCIPE DE ASTURIAS

Date	Mintage	F	VF	XF	Unc	BU
2005(M) Proof	3,500	Value: 750				

KM# 1066 200 EURO
13.5000 g., 0.9990 Gold 0.4336 oz. AGW, 30 mm. **Ruler:** Juan Carlos I **Subject:** European Peace and Freedom **Obv:** Juan Carlos **Rev:** European map on clasped hands **Edge:** Reeded

Date	Mintage	F	VF	XF	Unc	BU
2005 Proof	4,000	Value: 750				

KM# 1123 200 EURO
13.5000 g., 0.9990 Gold 0.4336 oz. AGW, 30 mm. **Ruler:** Juan Carlos I **Obv:** Head left **Obv. Legend:** JUAN CARLOS I REY DE ESPAÑA **Rev:** Charles I (V) standing facing 3/4 right in front of portal **Rev. Legend:** CAROLVS IMPERATOR

Date	Mintage	F	VF	XF	Unc	BU
2006(M) Proof	5,000	Value: 700				

KM# 1136 200 EURO
13.5000 g., 0.9990 Gold 0.4336 oz. AGW, 30 mm. **Ruler:** Juan Carlos I **Subject:** Treaty of Rome, 50th Anniversary **Obv:** Head left **Rev:** Map of Western Europe

Date	Mintage	F	VF	XF	Unc	BU
2007 Proof	3,500	Value: 700				

KM# 1139 200 EURO
13.5000 g., 0.9990 Gold 0.4336 oz. AGW, 30 mm. **Ruler:** Juan Carlos I **Subject:** El Cid, 700th Anniversary **Obv:** Rodrigo Diaz de Vivar bust facing **Rev:** Knight on horseback within rectangle

Date	Mintage	F	VF	XF	Unc	BU
2007 Proof	3,500	Value: 700				

KM# 1170 200 EURO
13.5000 g., 0.9990 Gold 0.4336 oz. AGW, 30 mm. **Ruler:** Juan Carlos I **Subject:** Antoni Gaudi

Date	Mintage	F	VF	XF	Unc	BU
2010 Proof	—	Value: 700				

KM# 1112 300 EURO
Bi-Metallic .554 AGW Gold center in .343 ASW Silver ring, 40 mm. **Ruler:** Juan Carlos I **Subject:** XVIII World Championship Football Games - Germany 2006 **Obv:** Football player facing kicking ball **Obv. Legend:** ESPAÑA **Rev:** Football player kicking ball into net at foreground **Rev. Legend:** COPA MUNDIAL DE LA FIFA - ALEMANIA **Shape:** 12-sided

Date	Mintage	F	VF	XF	Unc	BU
2005(M) Proof	2,006	Value: 1,000				

KM# 1121 300 EURO
Bi-Metallic Gold center in silver ring, 40 mm. **Ruler:** Juan Carlos I **Rev:** Basketball player facing tossing ball **Rev. Legend:** CAMPEONES DEL MUNDO - JAPÓn 2006 **Shape:** 12-sided

Date	Mintage	F	VF	XF	Unc	BU
2006(M) Proof	2,000	Value: 1,000				

KM# 1086 400 EURO
27.0000 g., 0.9990 Gold 0.8672 oz. AGW, 38 mm. **Ruler:** Juan Carlos I **Subject:** 150th Anniversary - Birth of Antonio Gaudí **Obv:** Bust of Gaudí at right **Obv. Legend:** Año Internacional **Rev:** Casa Batlló

Date	Mintage	F	VF	XF	Unc	BU
2002(M) Proof	3,000	Value: 1,350				

KM# 1058 400 EURO
27.0000 g., 0.9990 Gold 0.8672 oz. AGW, 38 mm. **Ruler:** Juan Carlos I **Obv:** Bust facing **Rev:** Dali's painting "Girl at the Window" **Edge:** Reeded

Date	Mintage	F	VF	XF	Unc	BU
2004 Proof	5,000	Value: 1,400				

KM# 1108 400 EURO
27.0000 g., 0.9990 Gold 0.8672 oz. AGW, 38 mm. **Ruler:** Juan Carlos I **Obv:** Quixote seated reading a large book **Obv. Legend:** ESPAÑA - IV CENTENARIO DE LA PRIMERA EDICIÓN DE "EL QUIJOTE" **Rev:** Quixote on horseback 3/4 right followed by his friend on a burro **Rev. Legend:** DON QUIJOTE DE LA MANCHA SANCHO PANZA

Date	Mintage	F	VF	XF	Unc	BU
2005(M) Proof	3,000	Value: 1,350				

KM# 1118 400 EURO
27.0000 g., 0.9990 Gold 0.8672 oz. AGW **Ruler:** Juan Carlos I **Subject:** 500th Anniversary - Death of Columbus **Obv:** Columbus **Rev:** Audience with Ferdinand and Isabella

Date	Mintage	F	VF	XF	Unc	BU
2006(M) Proof	3,000	Value: 1,350				

KM# 1128 400 EURO
27.0000 g., 0.9990 Gold 0.8672 oz. AGW, 38 mm. **Ruler:** Juan Carlos I **Rev:** Large ring of stars around globe **Rev. Legend:** V ANIVERSARIO DEL EURO

Date	Mintage	F	VF	XF	Unc	BU
2007 Proof	3,000	Value: 1,350				

KM# 1182 400 EURO
27.0000 g., 0.9990 Gold 0.8672 oz. AGW, 38 mm. **Ruler:** Juan Carlos I **Subject:** Francisco de Goya - Volaverunt

Date	Mintage	F	VF	XF	Unc	BU
2010 Proof	—	Value: 1,450				

MINT SETS

KM#	Date	Mintage	Identification	Issue Price	Mkt Val
MS27	2000-2001 (8)	49,426	KM#832-833, 924, 991-992 (both dated 2000), 1012-1013, 1016	15.50	35.00
MS28	2002 (8)	99,301	KM#1040-1047	—	15.00
MS29	2003 (8)	149	KM#1040-1047	—	15.00
MS30	2004 (8)	43,000	KM#1040-1047	—	70.00
MS31	2005 (8)	49,923	KM#1040-1047	—	30.00
MS32	2006 (8)	49,996	KM#1040-1047	—	12.50
MS33	2007 (8)	—	KM#1040-1042, 1070-1074	—	30.00

PROOF SETS

KM#	Date	Mintage	Identification	Issue Price	Mkt Val
PS34	2002 (9)	35,000	KM#1040-1047, 1049	125	150
PS35	2003 (3)	—	KM#1186, 1187, 1188	—	320
PS36	2007 (2)	—	KM#1132-1133	—	150

SRI LANKA

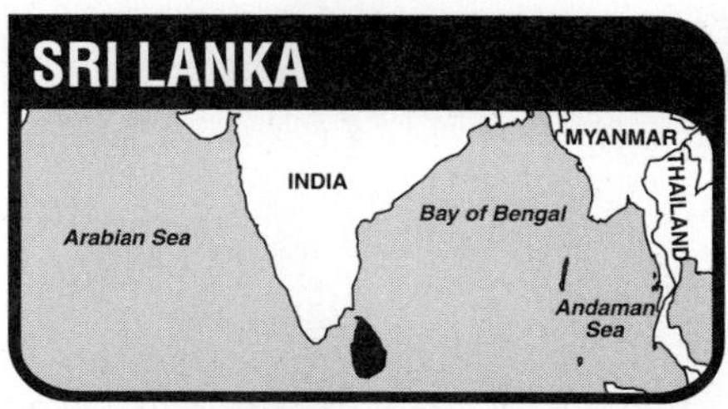

The Democratic Socialist Republic of Sri Lanka (formerly Ceylon) situated in the Indian Ocean 18 miles (29 km.) southeast of India, has an area of 25,332 sq. mi. (65,610 sq. km.) and a population of *16.9 million. Capital: Colombo. The economy is chiefly agricultural. Tea, coconut products and rubber are exported.

Sri Lanka is a member of the Commonwealth of Nations. The president is Chief of State. The prime minister is Head of Government. The present leaders of the country have reverted the country name back to Sri Lanka.

DEMOCRATIC SOCIALIST REPUBLIC

DECIMAL COINAGE

100 Cents = 1 Rupee

KM# 141a 25 CENTS
Nickel Clad Steel **Obv:** National arms **Rev:** Denomination **Edge:** Reeded

Date	Mintage	F	VF	XF	Unc	BU
2001	10,000,000	—	—	0.10	0.25	0.45
2002	10,000,000	—	—	0.10	0.25	0.45

KM# 141.2b 25 CENTS
1.1700 g., Copper Plated Steel, 16 mm. **Obv:** National arms **Rev:** Denomination

Date	Mintage	F	VF	XF	Unc	BU
2005	—	—	—	0.10	0.25	0.45
2006	—	—	—	0.10	0.25	0.45

KM# 135.2a 50 CENTS
Nickel Plated Steel, 21.5 mm. **Obv:** National arms **Rev:** Value above designs within wreath **Edge:** Reeded

Date	Mintage	F	VF	XF	Unc	BU
2001	30,000,000	—	0.10	0.25	0.65	1.00
2002	10,000,000	—	0.10	0.25	0.65	1.00
2004	—	—	0.10	0.25	0.65	1.00

KM# 135.2b 50 CENTS
2.4900 g., Copper Plated Steel, 17.92 mm. **Obv:** National arms **Rev:** Value above designs within wreath **Edge:** Reeded

Date	Mintage	F	VF	XF	Unc	BU
2005	—	—	—	0.25	0.60	1.00
2006	—	—	—	0.25	0.60	1.00
2009	—	—	—	0.25	0.60	1.00

KM# 166 RUPEE
7.1300 g., Copper-Nickel, 25.4 mm. **Subject:** Air Force's 50th Anniversary **Obv:** Badge of the Sri Lanka Air Force **Rev:** Two jets above propeller plane within circle **Edge:** Reeded

Date	Mintage	F	VF	XF	Unc	BU
2001 Proof	2,000	Value: 100				

KM# 136a RUPEE

Nickel Clad Steel **Obv:** National arms **Rev:** Inscription below designs within wreath **Edge:** Reeded

Date	Mintage	F	VF	XF	Unc	BU
2002	50,000,000	—	0.25	0.50	1.00	1.50

KM# 136.3 RUPEE

3.6200 g., Brass Plated Steel, 20 mm. **Obv:** National emblem **Rev:** Inscription below designs within wreath **Edge:** Segmented reeding

Date	Mintage	F	VF	XF	Unc	BU
2005	—	—	—	—	0.75	1.00
2006	—	—	—	—	0.75	1.00
2008	—	—	—	—	0.75	1.00
2009	—	—	—	—	0.75	1.00

KM# 147 2 RUPEES

8.2500 g., Copper-Nickel, 28.5 mm. **Obv:** National arms **Rev:** Value

Date	Mintage	F	VF	XF	Unc	BU
2001	10,000,000	—	0.30	0.60	1.35	1.75
2002	40,000,000	—	0.30	0.60	1.35	1.75
2004	—	—	0.30	0.60	1.35	1.75

KM# 167 2 RUPEES

8.2500 g., Copper-Nickel, 28.5 mm. **Subject:** Colombo Plan's 50th Anniversary **Obv:** Value within inscription above date **Rev:** Gear wheel **Edge:** Reeded

Date	Mintage	F	VF	XF	Unc	BU
2001	10,000,000	—	—	—	2.00	3.00

KM# 147a 2 RUPEES

7.0800 g., Nickel Clad Steel, 28.5 mm. **Obv:** National arms **Rev:** Value **Edge:** Reeded

Date	Mintage	F	VF	XF	Unc	BU
2005	—	—	—	0.45	1.10	1.50
2006	—	—	—	0.45	1.10	1.50
2008	—	—	—	0.45	1.10	1.50
2009	—	—	—	0.45	1.10	1.50

KM# 178 2 RUPEES

7.0000 g., Nickel Plated Steel, 28.4 mm. **Subject:** Employees Provident Fund, 50th Anniversary **Obv:** Large 2 **Rev:** Open hands with image of tea pluckers, garment workers and office worker

Date	Mintage	F	VF	XF	Unc	BU
2008	2,000,000	—	—	—	1.35	1.75

KM# 181 2 RUPEES

7.0000 g., Nickel Plated Steel, 28.5 mm. **Obv:** Large value **Rev:** Large 60, Air Force emblem and historic aircraft circling

Date	Mintage	F	VF	XF	Unc	BU
2011	3,000,000	—	—	—	2.00	—
2011 Special Unc	500	—	—	—	—	15.00

KM# 148.2 5 RUPEES

9.5000 g., Nickel-Brass, 23.5 mm. **Obv:** National arms **Rev:** Value **Edge Lettering:** C.B.S.L.

Date	Mintage	F	VF	XF	Unc	BU
2002	30,000,000	—	0.35	0.65	2.00	2.75
2004	—	—	0.35	0.65	2.00	2.75

KM# 168 5 RUPEES

9.5200 g., Aluminum-Bronze, 23.4 mm. **Subject:** 250th Annniversary of the "Upasampada" Rite **Obv:** Value **Rev:** 1/2-length figure facing divides dates

Date	Mintage	F	VF	XF	Unc	BU
2003	4,000,000	—	—	—	3.00	4.50

KM# 169 5 RUPEES

9.5200 g., Aluminum-Bronze, 23.4 mm. **Subject:** 250th Anniversary - Upasampada **Obv:** Value **Rev:** Bust facing standing behind shield **Edge:** Reeded and lettered

Date	Mintage	F	VF	XF	Unc	BU
2003	4,000,000	—	—	—	3.00	4.50

KM# 148a 5 RUPEES

7.6700 g., Brass Plated Steel, 23.49 mm. **Obv:** National arms **Rev:** Value **Edge:** Reeded and Lettered **Edge Lettering:** CBSL repeated in various languages

Date	Mintage	F	VF	XF	Unc	BU
2005	—	—	—	0.75	1.85	2.50
2006	—	—	—	0.75	1.85	2.50
2008	—	—	—	0.75	1.85	2.50
2009	—	—	—	0.75	1.85	2.50

KM# 170 5 RUPEES

7.6500 g., Brass Plated Steel, 23.5 mm. **Subject:** 2550th Anniversary of Buddha **Obv:** Value **Rev:** "Buddha Jayanthi", wheel above mountain **Edge:** Reeded and lettered

Date	Mintage	F	VF	XF	Unc	BU
2006	20,000,000	—	—	—	3.00	4.00

KM# 173 5 RUPEES

7.6500 g., Brass Plated Steel, 23.5 mm. **Subject:** Cricket World Cup

Date	Mintage	F	VF	XF	Unc	BU
2007	—	—	—	—	3.00	4.00

KM# 180 200 RUPEES

11.9000 g., 0.9250 Silver 0.3539 oz. ASW, 28.4 mm. **Subject:** Customs Service, 200th Anniversary **Obv:** Proposed new Customs Building **Rev:** Customs Logo

Date	Mintage	F	VF	XF	Unc	BU
2009 Proof	3,000	Value: 55.00				

KM# 174 1000 RUPEES

Nickel Plated Steel **Subject:** Cricket World Cup

Date	Mintage	F	VF	XF	Unc	BU
2007	10,000	—	—	—	12.00	15.00

KM# 179 1000 RUPEES

Nickel Plated Steel, 28.5 mm. **Subject:** Employees Provident Fund, 50th Anniversary **Obv:** Large 1000 **Rev:** Open hands with image of tea pluckers, garment workers and office worker

Date	Mintage	F	VF	XF	Unc	BU
2008 Proof	1,200	Value: 150				

KM# 171 1500 RUPEES

Silver **Subject:** 2550 Anniversary of Buddha

Date	Mintage	F	VF	XF	Unc	BU
2006 Proof	20,000	Value: 85.00				

KM# 172 2000 RUPEE

Silver **Subject:** 2550 Anniversary of Buddha

Date	Mintage	F	VF	XF	Unc	BU
2006 Proof	10,000	Value: 125				

SUDAN

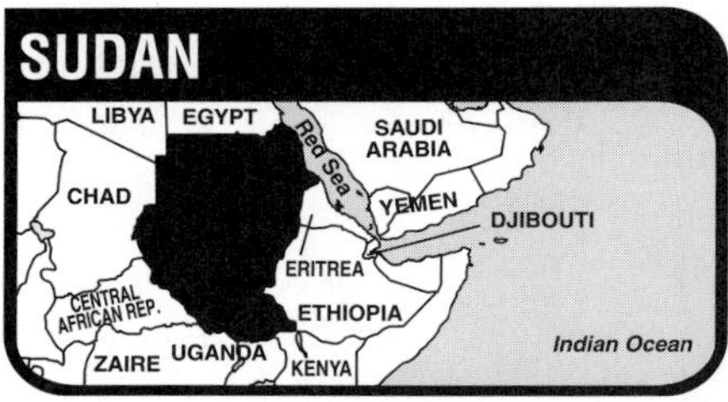

The Democratic Republic of the Sudan, located in northeast Africa on the Red Sea between Egypt and Ethiopia, has an area of 967,500 sq. mi. (2,505,810 sq. km.) and a population of *24.5 million. Capital: Khartoum. Agriculture and livestock raising are the chief occupations. Cotton, gum arabic and peanuts are exported.

REPUBLIC

REFORM COINAGE

100 Qurush (Piastres) = 1 Dinar

10 Pounds = 1 Dinar

KM# 119 5 DINARS

3.3500 g., Brass, 19 mm. **Obv:** Value **Rev:** Central Bank building

Date	Mintage	F	VF	XF	Unc	BU
AH1424-2003	—	—	0.75	1.50	3.00	5.00

KM# 120.1 10 DINARS
4.6800 g., Brass, 22 mm. **Rev:** Central Bank building, "a" above "n" at the left end of the Arabic inscription, 64 border beads

Date	Mintage	F	VF	XF	Unc	BU
AH1424-2003	—	—	1.00	2.00	3.50	6.00

KM# 120.2 10 DINARS
4.5600 g., Brass, 22 mm. **Obv:** Value **Rev:** Larger Central Bank building, "a" to right of "n" at the left end of the Arabic inscription, 72 border beads

Date	Mintage	F	VF	XF	Unc	BU
AH1424-2003	—	—	1.00	2.00	3.50	6.00

KM# 121 50 DINARS
Copper-Nickel, 24 mm. **Rev:** Central Bank building

Date	Mintage	F	VF	XF	Unc	BU
AH1423-2002	—	—	2.00	3.50	6.00	9.00

REFORM COINAGE

100 Piastres = 1 Pound

2005 -

KM# 126 PIASTRE (Ghirsh)
2.2500 g., Aluminum-Bronze, 16 mm. **Obv:** Clay pot **Obv. Legend:** CENTRAL BANK OF SUDAN **Rev:** Value

Date	Mintage	F	VF	XF	Unc	BU
2006	—	—	—	0.90	2.25	3.00

KM# 125 5 PIASTRES
2.9200 g., Brass, 18.32 mm. **Obv:** National arms **Rev:** Large value **Edge:** Reeded

Date	Mintage	F	VF	XF	Unc	BU
2006	—	—	—	1.20	3.00	4.00

KM# 122 10 PIASTRES
3.4200 g., Nickel, 20 mm. **Obv:** Pyramid **Obv. Legend:** CENTRAL BANK OF SUDAN **Rev:** Large value **Edge:** Reeded

Date	Mintage	F	VF	XF	Unc	BU
2006	—	—	—	1.25	3.00	4.00

KM# 124 20 PIASTRES
5.0200 g., Bi-Metallic Copper-Nickel center in Brass ring., 22.19 mm. **Obv:** Ankole Bull in right profile **Obv. Legend:** CENTRAL BANK OF SUDAN **Rev:** large value **Edge:** Reeded

Date	Mintage	F	VF	XF	Unc	BU
2006	—	—	—	1.20	3.00	4.00

KM# 123 50 PIASTRES
5.8600 g., Bi-Metallic Brass center in Copper-Nickel ring, 24.27 mm. **Obv:** Dove in flight **Obv. Legend:** CENTRAL BANK OF SUDAN **Rev:** Value **Edge:** Reeded

Date	Mintage	F	VF	XF	Unc	BU
2006	—	—	—	0.90	2.25	3.00

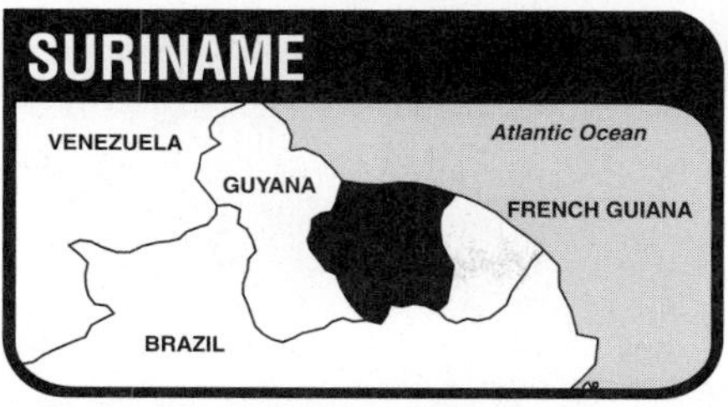

The Republic of Suriname also known as Dutch Guiana, located on the north central coast of South America between Guyana and French Guiana has an area of 63,037 sq. mi. (163,270 sq. km.) and a population of *433,000. Capital: Paramaribo. The country is rich in minerals and forests, and self-sufficient in rice, the staple food crop. The mining, processing and exporting of bauxite is the principal economic activity.

Lieutenants of Amerigo Vespucci sighted the Guiana coast in 1499. Spanish explorers of the 16th century, disappointed at finding no gold, departed leaving the area to be settled by the British in 1652. The colony prospered and the Netherlands acquired it in 1667 in exchange for the Dutch rights in Nieuw Nederland (state of New York). During the European wars of the 18th and 19th centuries, which were fought in part in the new world, Suriname was occupied by the British from 1781-1784 and 1796-1814.Suriname became an autonomous part of the Kingdom of the Netherlands on Dec. 15, 1954. Full independence was achieved on Nov. 25, 1975. In 1980, a coup installed a military government, which has since been dissolved.

MINT MARKS
(u) - Utrecht (privy marks only)

MONETARY SYSTEM
After January, 2004
1 Dollar = 100 Cents

REPUBLIC

WORLD WAR II COINAGE

The 1942-1943 issues that follow are homeland coinage types of the Netherlands. KM#152, KM#163 and KM#164 were executed expressly for use in Suriname. Related issues produced for use in Curacao and Suriname are listed under Curacao. They are distinguished by a palm tree (acorn on homeland issues) and a mint mark (P-Philadelphia, D-Denver, S-San Francisco) flanking the date. See the Netherlands for similar issues. See Curacao for similar coins dated 1941-P, 1942-P and 1943-P.

KM# 65 $20
1.2442 g., 0.9990 Gold 0.0400 oz. AGW, 13.92 mm. **Subject:** 20th Anniversary of winning gold medal by Antony Nesty at Seoul in 1988 **Obv:** Arms with supporters **Rev:** Swimming man

Date	Mintage	F	VF	XF	Unc	BU
2008 Proof	5,000	Value: 65.00				

KM# 66 500 DOLLARS
7.9800 g., 0.9160 Gold 0.2350 oz. AGW, 22 mm. **Subject:** 50 years of Central Bank **Obv:** Arms with supporters **Rev:** 50 jaar Central Bank van Suriname 1957-2007

Date	Mintage	F	VF	XF	Unc	BU
2007 Proof	1,000	Value: 450				

MODERN COINAGE

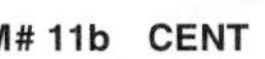

KM# 11b CENT
2.5000 g., Copper Plated Steel, 18 mm. **Obv:** Arms with supporters within wreath **Rev:** Value divides date within circle **Edge:** Plain

Date	Mintage	F	VF	XF	Unc	BU
2004(u) In sets only	4,000	—	—	—	—	1.50
2005(u) In sets only	1,500	—	—	—	—	1.50
2006(u) In sets only	1,500	—	—	—	—	1.50
2007(u) In sets only	1,000	—	—	—	—	1.50
2008(u) In sets only	1,000	—	—	—	—	1.50
2009(u) In sets only	1,000	—	—	—	—	1.50

KM# 12.1b 5 CENTS
3.0000 g., Copper Plated Steel, 18 mm. **Obv:** Arms with supporters within circle **Rev:** Value divides date within circle **Edge:** Plain **Shape:** Square

Date	Mintage	F	VF	XF	Unc	BU
2004(u) In sets only	4,000	—	—	—	—	1.50
2005(u) In sets only	1,500	—	—	—	—	1.50
2006(u) In sets only	1,500	—	—	—	—	1.50
2007(u) In sets only	1,000	—	—	—	—	1.50
2008(u) In sets only	1,000	—	—	—	—	1.50
2009	—	—	—	—	0.60	1.50
2009(u) In sets only	1,000	—	—	—	—	1.50

KM# 13a 10 CENTS
2.0000 g., Nickel Plated Steel, 16 mm. **Obv:** Arms with supporters within wreath **Rev:** Value and date within circle **Edge:** Reeded

Date	Mintage	F	VF	XF	Unc	BU
2004(u) In sets only	4,000	—	—	—	—	2.50
2005(u) In sets only	1,500	—	—	—	—	2.50
2006(u) In sets only	1,500	—	—	—	—	2.50
2007(u) In sets only	1,000	—	—	—	—	2.50
2008(u) In sets only	1,000	—	—	—	—	2.50
2009(u) In sets only	1,000	—	—	—	—	2.50

KM# 14a 25 CENTS
3.5000 g., Nickel Plated Steel, 20 mm. **Obv:** Arms with supporters within wreath **Rev:** Value and date within circle **Edge:** Reeded

Date	Mintage	F	VF	XF	Unc	BU
2004(u) In sets only	4,000	—	—	—	—	4.00
2005(u) In sets only	1,500	—	—	—	—	4.00
2006(u) In sets only	1,500	—	—	—	—	4.00
2007(u) In sets only	1,000	—	—	—	—	4.00
2008(u) In sets only	1,000	—	—	—	—	4.00
2009	—	—	—	—	1.25	2.50
2009(u) In sets only	1,000	—	—	—	—	4.00

KM# 23 100 CENTS
5.6500 g., Copper-Nickel, 23 mm. **Obv:** Arms with supporters within wreath **Rev:** Value and date within circle **Edge:** Reeded

Date	Mintage	F	VF	XF	Unc	BU
2004(u) In sets only	4,000	—	—	—	4.00	7.00
2005(u) In sets only	1,500	—	—	—	4.00	7.00
2006(u) In sets only	1,500	—	—	—	4.00	7.00
2007(u) In sets only	1,000	—	—	—	4.00	7.00
2008(u) In sets only	1,000	—	—	—	4.00	7.00
2009(u) In sets only	1,000	—	—	—	4.00	7.00

KM# 24 250 CENTS
9.5700 g., Copper-Nickel, 28 mm. **Obv:** Arms with supporters within wreath **Rev:** Value and date within circle

Date	Mintage	F	VF	XF	Unc	BU
2004(u) In sets only	4,000	—	—	—	—	10.00
2005(u) In sets only	1,500	—	—	—	—	10.00
2006(u) In sets only	1,500	—	—	—	—	10.00
2007(u) In sets only	1,000	—	—	—	—	10.00
2008(u) In sets only	1,000	—	—	—	—	10.00
2009(u) In sets only	1,000	—	—	—	—	10.00

KM# 64 400 DOLLARS
7.9800 g., 0.9160 Gold 0.2350 oz. AGW, 22 mm. **Subject:** 30 Years of Independence **Obv:** Arms with supporters **Rev:** Man kissing flag **Edge:** Reeded

Date	Mintage	F	VF	XF	Unc	BU
2005 Proof	1,000	Value: 500				

MINT SETS

KM#	Date	Mintage	Identification	Issue Price	Mkt Val
MS1	2004 (6)	4,000	KM#11b, 12.1b, 13a, 14a, 23, 24	25.00	27.50
MS2	2005 (6)	1,500	KM#11b, 12.1b, 13a-14a, 23-24	25.00	27.50
MS3	2006 (6)	1,500	KM#11b, 12.1b, 13a-14a, 23-24	25.00	27.50
MS4	2007 (6)	1,000	KM#11b, 12.1b, 13a-14a, 23-24	27.00	27.50
MS5	2008 (6)	1,000	KM#11b, 12.1b, 13a-14a, 23-24	27.00	27.50
MS6	2009 (6)	1,000	KM#11b, 12.1b, 13a, 14a, 23, 24	27.00	27.50

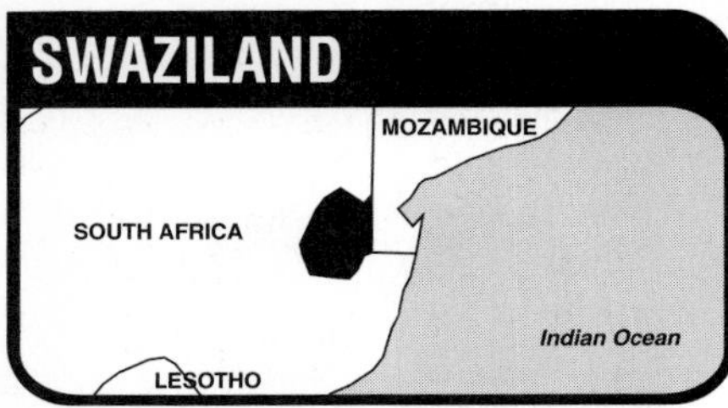

The Kingdom of Swaziland, located in southeastern Africa, has an area of 6,704 sq. mi. (17,360 sq. km.) and a population of *756,000. Capital: Mbabane (administrative); Lobamba (legislative). The diversified economy includes mining, agriculture, and light industry. Asbestos, iron ore, wood pulp, and sugar are exported.

The Kingdom is a member of the Commonwealth of Nations. King Mswati III is Head of State. The prime minister is Head of Government.

RULER

King Msawati III, 1986-

MONETARY SYSTEM

100 Cents = 1 Luhlanga
25 Luhlanga = 1 Lilangeni
(plural - Emalangeni)

KINGDOM

DECIMAL COINAGE

100 Cents = 1 Lilangeni (plural emelangeni)

KM# 48 5 CENTS

2.1000 g., Copper-Nickel, 18.5 mm. **Ruler:** King Msawati III **Obv:** Bust 3/4 right **Rev:** Arum lily and value **Rev. Designer:** Michael Rizzello **Edge:** Plain **Shape:** Scalloped

Date	Mintage	F	VF	XF	Unc	BU
2001	—	—	—	0.20	0.50	0.75
2002	—	—	—	0.20	0.50	0.75
2003	—	—	—	0.20	0.50	0.75
2005	—	—	—	0.20	0.50	0.75
2006	—	—	—	0.20	0.50	0.75
2007	—	—	—	0.20	0.50	0.75

KM# 49 10 CENTS

3.6000 g., Copper-Nickel, 22 mm. **Ruler:** King Msawati III **Obv:** Bust 3/4 right **Rev:** Sugar cane and value **Rev. Designer:** Michael Rizzello **Edge:** Plain **Shape:** Scalloped

Date	Mintage	F	VF	XF	Unc	BU
2001	—	—	—	0.30	0.75	1.00
2002	—	—	—	0.30	0.75	1.00
2005	—	—	—	0.30	0.75	1.00
2006	—	—	—	0.30	0.75	1.00

KM# 50.2 20 CENTS

5.5200 g., Copper-Nickel, 25.2 mm. **Ruler:** King Msawati III **Obv:** Small bust 3/4 right **Rev:** Elephant head, value **Rev. Designer:** Michael Rizzello **Edge:** Plain **Shape:** Scalloped

Date	Mintage	F	VF	XF	Unc	BU
2001	—	—	—	0.35	0.90	1.25
2002	—	—	—	0.35	0.90	1.25
2003	—	—	—	0.35	0.90	1.25

KM# 52 50 CENTS

8.9000 g., Copper-Nickel, 29.45 mm. **Ruler:** King Msawati III **Obv:** Head 1/4 right **Rev:** Arms with supporters **Rev. Designer:** Michael Rizzello

Date	Mintage	F	VF	XF	Unc	BU
2001	—	—	—	—	3.75	4.50
2003	—	—	—	—	3.75	4.50

KM# 45 LILANGENI

9.5000 g., Brass, 22.5 mm. **Ruler:** King Msawati III **Obv:** Head 1/4 right **Rev:** Bust facing

Date	Mintage	F	VF	XF	Unc	BU
2002	—	—	—	1.50	2.75	3.50
2003	—	—	—	1.50	2.75	3.50

KM# 46 2 EMALANGENI

5.0000 g., Brass **Ruler:** King Msawati III **Obv:** Head 1/4 right **Rev:** Lilies and value

Date	Mintage	F	VF	XF	Unc	BU
2003 sm. bust	—	—	—	—	3.75	4.25

KM# 47 5 EMALANGENI

7.6000 g., Brass **Ruler:** King Msawati III **Obv:** Head 1/4 right **Rev:** Arms with supporters above value that divides date

Date	Mintage	F	VF	XF	Unc	BU
2003 sm. bust	—	—	—	—	6.00	7.00

KM# 54a 5 EMALANGENI

Gold **Ruler:** King Msawati III **Subject:** 40th Anniversary of Independence **Obv:** Head 1/4 right **Rev:** National arms at center

Date	Mintage	F	VF	XF	Unc	BU
2008 Proof, rare	100	—	—	—	—	—

KM# 55a 5 EMALANGENI

Gold **Ruler:** King Msawati III **Subject:** 40th Anniversary of Independence **Obv:** Head 1/4 right **Rev:** National arms at center

Date	Mintage	F	VF	XF	Unc	BU
2008 Proof, rare	100	—	—	—	—	—

KM# 54 5 EMALANGENI

7.6000 g., Brass, 27 mm. **Ruler:** King Msawati III **Subject:** 40th Anniversary of Independence **Obv:** Head 1/4 right **Rev:** National arms at center

Date	Mintage	F	VF	XF	Unc	BU
2008	—	—	—	—	5.00	7.00

KM# 55 5 EMALANGENI

7.6000 g., Brass, 27 mm. **Ruler:** King Msawati III **Subject:** 40th Birthday of King **Obv:** Head 1/4 right **Rev:** National arms at center

Date	Mintage	F	VF	XF	Unc	BU
2008	—	—	—	—	5.00	7.00

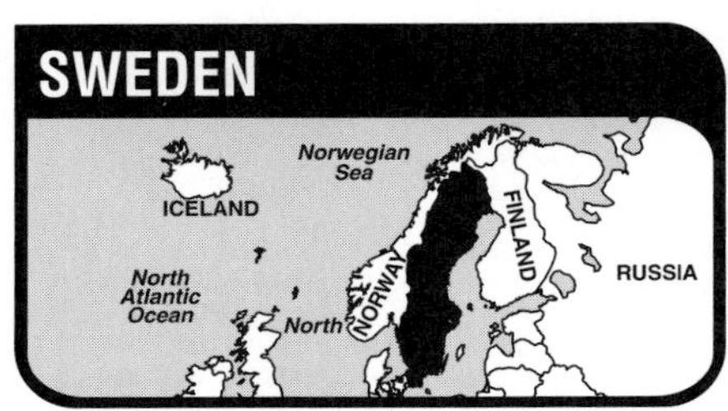

The Kingdom of Sweden, a limited constitutional monarchy located in northern Europe between Norway and Finland, has an area of 173,732 sq. mi. (449,960 sq. km.) and a population of *8.5 million. Capital: Stockholm. Mining, lumbering and a specialized machine industry dominate the economy. Machinery, paper, iron and steel, motor vehicles and wood pulp are exported.

RULER

Carl XVI Gustaf, 1973-

MINT OFFICIALS' INITIALS

Letter	Date	Name
B	1992-2005	Stefan Ingves
D	1986-2005	Bengt Dennis
SI	2006-	Stefan Ingves

MONETARY SYSTEM

100 Ore = 1 Krona

KINGDOM

REFORM COINAGE

1873 - present

KM# 878 50 ORE

3.7000 g., Bronze, 18.7 mm. **Ruler:** Carl XVI Gustaf **Obv:** Value **Rev:** Three crowns and date **Edge:** Reeded

Date	Mintage	F	VF	XF	Unc	BU
2001 B	30,120,532	—	—	0.10	0.15	0.25
2002 B	—	—	—	0.10	0.15	0.25
2003 H	—	—	—	0.10	0.15	0.25
2004 H	25,958,649	—	—	0.10	0.15	0.25
2005 H	—	—	—	0.10	0.15	0.25
2006 SI	—	—	—	0.10	0.15	0.25
2007 SI	—	—	—	0.10	0.15	0.25

KM# 894 KRONA

6.9800 g., Copper-Nickel, 24.9 mm. **Ruler:** Carl XVI Gustaf **Obv:** Head left **Rev:** Crown and value **Edge:** Reeded

Date	Mintage	F	VF	XF	Unc	BU
2001 B	23,905,454	—	—	—	0.65	1.00
2002 B	—	—	—	—	0.65	1.00
2003 H	—	—	—	—	0.65	1.00
2004 H	42,060,252	—	—	—	0.65	1.00
2005 H	—	—	—	—	0.65	1.00
2007 B	—	—	—	—	0.65	1.00

KM# 916 KRONA
7.0000 g., Copper-Nickel, 25 mm. **Ruler:** Carl XVI Gustaf **Subject:** Separation from Finland, 200 Anniversary **Obv:** Head left **Obv. Designer:** Ernest Nordin **Rev:** Horizontal sea waves **Rev. Designer:** Anne Winblad Jakubowski **Edge:** Reeded

Date	Mintage	F	VF	XF	Unc	BU
2009	—	—	—	—	0.65	1.00

KM# 853a 5 KRONOR
9.6000 g., Copper-Nickel Clad Nickel, 28.5 mm. **Ruler:** Carl XVI Gustaf **Obv:** Crowned monogram **Rev:** Value

Date	Mintage	F	VF	XF	Unc	BU
2001 B	6,001,481	—	—	—	1.00	1.25
2002 B	—	—	—	—	1.00	1.25
2003 H	—	—	—	—	1.00	1.25
2004 H	6,732,730	—	—	—	1.00	1.25
2005 H	—	—	—	—	1.00	1.25

KM# 895 10 KRONOR
6.5700 g., Copper-Aluminum-Zinc, 20.4 mm. **Ruler:** Carl XVI Gustaf **Obv:** Head left **Rev:** Three crowns and value **Edge:** Reeded and plain sections

Date	Mintage	F	VF	XF	Unc	BU
2001 B	4,171,757	—	—	—	1.75	2.00
2002 B	—	—	—	—	1.75	2.00
2003 H	—	—	—	—	1.75	2.00
2004 H	9,045,581	—	—	—	1.75	2.00
2005 H	—	—	—	—	1.75	2.00
2006 SI	—	—	—	—	1.75	2.00

KM# 910 50 KRONOR
22.0000 g., Aluminum-Bronze, 36 mm. **Ruler:** Carl XVI Gustaf **Subject:** 95th Anniversary - Birth of Astrid Lindgren **Obv:** Playful young girl **Rev:** Astrid Lindgren **Edge:** Plain

Date	Mintage	F	VF	XF	Unc	BU
ND (2002)	100,000	—	—	—	8.00	10.00

KM# 915 50 KRONOR
22.0000 g., Aluminum-Bronze, 36 mm. **Ruler:** Carl XVI Gustaf **Subject:** 150th Anniversary of Sweden's first postage stamp **Obv:** Winged letter flying over landscape **Rev:** Sweden's first postage stamp design **Edge:** Plain **Designer:** Annie Wildblad Jakubowski

Date	Mintage	F	VF	XF	Unc	BU
ND (2005)	100,000	—	—	—	8.00	10.00

KM# 896 200 KRONOR
27.2500 g., 0.9250 Silver 0.8104 oz. ASW, 36 mm. **Ruler:** Carl XVI Gustaf **Subject:** 25th Wedding Anniversary **Obv:** Conjoined busts left **Rev:** Crowned arms with supporters **Edge:** Plain **Designer:** Philip Nathan

Date	Mintage	F	VF	XF	Unc	BU
ND(2001)	50,000	—	—	—	40.00	50.00

KM# 908 200 KRONOR
27.0000 g., 0.9250 Silver 0.8029 oz. ASW, 36 mm. **Ruler:** Carl XVI Gustaf **Subject:** 750th Anniversary of Stockholm **Obv:** City seal with three towers and gate **Rev:** Three towers of city hall **Edge:** Plain **Designer:** Bo Thoréu

Date	Mintage	F	VF	XF	Unc	BU
ND (2002) Proof	25,000	Value: 40.00				

KM# 902 200 KRONOR
Silver **Ruler:** Carl XVI Gustaf **Subject:** 30th Anniversary of Reign **Designer:** Ernest Nordin

Date	Mintage	F	VF	XF	Unc	BU
2003	—	—	—	—	40.00	50.00

KM# 904 200 KRONOR
27.0300 g., 0.9250 Silver 0.8038 oz. ASW, 36 mm. **Ruler:** Carl XVI Gustaf **Subject:** 700th Anniversary, St. Birgitta **Obv:** Cross in circle above value **Rev:** St. Birgitta **Edge:** Plain **Designer:** Ernest Nordin

Date	Mintage	F	VF	XF	Unc	BU
ND (2003)	60,000	—	—	—	40.00	50.00

KM# 911 200 KRONOR
27.0000 g., 0.9250 Silver 0.8029 oz. ASW, 36 mm. **Ruler:** Carl XVI Gustaf **Subject:** Royal Palace in Stockholm 250th Anniversary **Obv:** Two antique keys over map **Rev:** Royal Palace in Stockholm **Edge:** Plain **Designer:** Annie Windblad Jakubowski

Date	Mintage	F	VF	XF	Unc	BU
ND (2004) Proof	35,000	Value: 40.00				

KM# 913 200 KRONOR
27.0000 g., 0.9250 Silver 0.8029 oz. ASW, 36 mm. **Ruler:** Carl XVI Gustaf **Obv:** Stylized flames **Rev:** Dag Hammarskjöld **Edge:** Plain **Designer:** Ernst Nordin

Date	Mintage	F	VF	XF	Unc	BU
ND (2005) Proof	35,000	Value: 40.00				

KM# 906 200 KRONOR
27.0300 g., 0.9250 Silver 0.8038 oz. ASW, 36 mm. **Ruler:** Carl XVI Gustaf **Subject:** Centennial of the end of the Union between Norway and Sweden **Obv:** Split disc **Rev:** Flag on pole and two clouds **Designer:** Annie Windblad Jakubowski

Date	Mintage	F	VF	XF	Unc	BU
2005	35,000	—	—	—	40.00	50.00

KM# 917 300 KRONOR
27.0300 g., 0.9250 Silver 0.8038 oz. ASW, 36 mm. **Ruler:** Carl XVI Gustaf **Subject:** Wedding of Princess Victoria and Daniel

Date	Mintage	F	VF	XF	Unc	BU
2010 Proof	—	Value: 50.00				

KM# 909 2000 KRONOR
12.0000 g., 0.9000 Gold 0.3472 oz. AGW, 26 mm. **Ruler:** Carl XVI Gustaf **Subject:** 750th Anniversary of Stockholm **Obv:** City seal with three towers and gate **Rev:** Three towers of city hall **Edge:** Plain **Designer:** Bo Thoréu

Date	Mintage	F	VF	XF	Unc	BU
ND (2002) Proof	5,000	Value: 600				

KM# 903 2000 KRONOR
12.0000 g., 0.9990 Gold 0.3854 oz. AGW **Ruler:** Carl XVI Gustaf **Subject:** 30th Anniversary of Reign **Designer:** Ernst Nordin

Date	Mintage	F	VF	XF	Unc	BU
2003	—	—	—	—	575	600

KM# 905 2000 KRONOR
12.0000 g., 0.9000 Gold 0.3472 oz. AGW, 26 mm. **Ruler:** Carl XVI Gustaf **Subject:** St. Birgitta's 700th Anniversary of birth **Obv:** Gothic letter B above value **Rev:** St. Birgitta **Edge:** Plain **Designer:** Ernst Nordin

Date	Mintage	F	VF	XF	Unc	BU
ND (2003)	8,000	—	—	—	575	600

KM# 912 2000 KRONOR
12.0000 g., 0.9000 Gold Royal Palace in Stockholm 250th Anniversary 0.3472 oz. AGW, 26 mm. **Ruler:** Carl XVI Gustaf **Subject:** Royal Palace in Stockholm **Obv:** Two antique keys over map **Edge:** Plain **Designer:** Annie Windblad Jakubowski

Date	Mintage	F	VF	XF	Unc	BU
ND (2004) Proof	5,243	Value: 575				

KM# 914 2000 KRONOR
12.0000 g., 0.9000 Gold 0.3472 oz. AGW, 26 mm. **Ruler:** Carl XVI Gustaf **Obv:** Stylized flames **Rev:** Dag Hammarskjold **Edge:** Plain **Designer:** Ernst Nordin

Date	Mintage	F	VF	XF	Unc	BU
ND (2005) Proof	5,000	Value: 575				

KM# 907 2000 KRONOR
12.0000 g., 0.9000 Gold 0.3472 oz. AGW, 26 mm. **Ruler:** Carl XVI Gustaf **Subject:** Centennial of the end of the Union between Norway and Sweden **Obv:** Split disc **Rev:** Flag pole dividing two clouds **Designer:** Annie Windblad Jakubowski

Date	Mintage	F	VF	XF	Unc	BU
2005	5,000	—	—	—	515	600

KM# 918 4000 KRONOR
12.0000 g., 0.9000 Gold 0.3472 oz. AGW, 26 mm. **Ruler:** Carl XVI Gustaf **Subject:** Wedding of Princess Victoria and Daniel

Date	Mintage	F	VF	XF	Unc	BU
2010 Proof	—	Value: 625				

MINT SETS

KM#	Date	Mintage	Identification	Issue Price	Mkt Val
MS107	2002 (4)	—	KM#853a, 878, 894, 895 plus medal	—	10.00

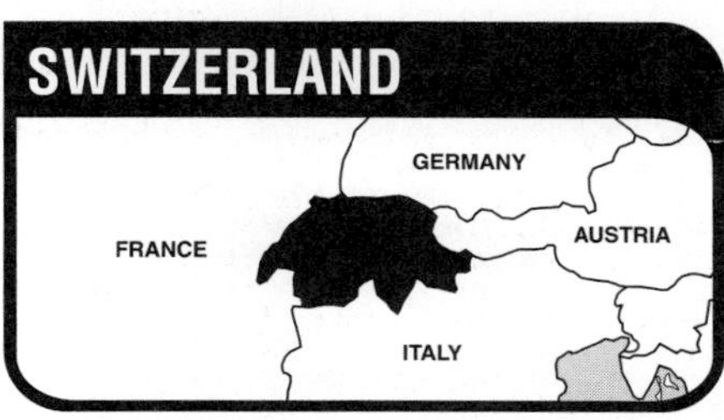

The Swiss Confederation, located in central Europe north of Italy and south of Germany, has an area of 15,941 sq. mi. (41,290 sq. km.) and a population of *6.6 million. Capital: Bern. The economy centers about a well-developed manufacturing industry. Machinery, chemicals, watches and clocks, and textiles are exported.

The Swiss Constitutions of 1848 and 1874 established a union modeled upon that of the United States.

MINT MARK
B – Bern

MONETARY SYSTEM
100 Rappen (Centimes) = 1 Franc

CONFEDERATION

DECIMAL COINAGE

KM# 46 RAPPEN
1.5000 g., Bronze, 16 mm. **Obv:** Cross **Rev:** Value and oat sprig **Edge:** Plain **Designer:** Josef Tannheimer

Date	Mintage	F	VF	XF	Unc	BU
2001B	1,522,000	—	—	—	0.50	1.00
2001B Proof	6,000	Value: 2.00				
2002B	2,024,000	—	—	—	0.50	1.00
2002B Proof	5,500	Value: 2.00				
2003B	1,522,000	—	—	—	0.50	1.00
2003B Proof	5,500	Value: 2.00				
2004B	1,526,000	—	—	—	0.50	1.00
2004B Proof	5,000	Value: 2.00				
2005B	1,524,000	—	—	—	0.50	1.00
2005B Proof	4,500	Value: 2.00				
2006B	26,000	—	—	—	—	135

Note: In sets only, circulation strikes not released

Date	Mintage	F	VF	XF	Unc	BU
2006B Proof	4,000	Value: 200				

KM# 26c 5 RAPPEN
1.8000 g., Aluminum-Brass, 17.15 mm. **Obv:** Crowned head right **Obv. Designer:** Karl Schwenzer **Rev:** Value within wreath **Rev. Designer:** Karl Friedrich Voigt **Edge:** Plain

Date	Mintage	F	VF	XF	Unc	BU
2001B	5,022,000	—	—	—	0.50	1.00
2001B Proof	6,000	Value: 2.00				
2002B	12,024,000	—	—	—	0.50	1.00
2002B Proof	6,000	Value: 2.00				

Date	Mintage	F	VF	XF	Unc	BU
2003B	10,022,000	—	—	—	0.50	1.00
2003B Proof	5,500	Value: 2.00				
2004B	10,026,000	—	—	—	0.50	1.00
2004B Proof	5,000	Value: 2.00				
2005B	13,024,000	—	—	—	0.50	1.00
2005B Proof	4,500	Value: 2.00				
2006B	12,026,000	—	—	—	0.50	1.00
2006B Proof	4,000	Value: 2.00				
2007B	13,024,000	—	—	—	0.50	1.00
2007B Proof	4,000	Value: 2.00				
2008B	40,022,000	—	—	—	0.50	1.00
2008B Proof	4,000	Value: 2.00				
2009B	45,022,000	—	—	—	0.50	1.00
2009B Proof	4,000	Value: 2.00				
2010B	Est. 41,022,000	—	—	—	0.50	1.00
2010B Proof	Est. 4,000	Value: 2.00				
2011B	Est. 50,022,000	—	—	—	0.30	1.00
2011B Proof	Est. 4,000	Value: 2.00				

KM# 27 10 RAPPEN

3.0000 g., Copper-Nickel, 19.15 mm. **Obv:** Crowned head right **Obv. Legend:** CONFOEDERATIO HELVETICA **Obv. Designer:** Karl Schwenzer **Rev:** Value within wreath **Rev. Designer:** Karl Friedrich Voigt **Edge:** Plain

Date	Mintage	F	VF	XF	Unc	BU
2001B	7,022,000	—	—	—	0.50	1.00
2001B Proof	6,000	Value: 2.00				
2002B	15,024,000	—	—	—	0.50	1.00
2002B Proof	6,000	Value: 2.00				
2003B	12,022,000	—	—	—	0.50	1.00
2003B Proof	5,500	Value: 2.00				
2004B	5,026,000	—	—	—	0.50	1.00
2004B Proof	5,000	Value: 2.00				
2005B	7,024,000	—	—	—	0.50	1.00
2005B Proof	4,500	Value: 2.00				
2006B	2,026,000	—	—	—	0.50	1.00
2006B Proof	4,000	Value: 2.00				
2007B	18,024,000	—	—	—	0.50	1.00
2007B Proof	4,000	Value: 2.00				
2008B	35,022,000	—	—	—	0.50	1.00
2008B Proof	4,000	Value: 2.00				
2009B	35,022,000	—	—	—	0.50	1.00
2009B Proof	4,000	Value: 2.00				
2010B	Est. 42,022,000	—	—	—	0.50	1.00
2010B Proof	Est. 4,000	Value: 2.00				
2011B	Est. 35,022,000	—	—	—	0.40	1.00
2011B Proof	Est. 4,000	Value: 2.00				

KM# 29a 20 RAPPEN

4.0000 g., Copper-Nickel, 21.05 mm. **Obv:** Crowned head right **Obv. Designer:** Karl Schwenzer **Rev:** Value within wreath **Rev. Designer:** Karl Friedrich Voigt **Edge:** Plain

Date	Mintage	F	VF	XF	Unc	BU
2001B	7,022,000	—	—	—	1.00	2.00
2001B Proof	6,000	Value: 3.00				
2002B	12,024,000	—	—	—	1.00	2.00
2002B Proof	6,000	Value: 3.00				
2003B	10,022,000	—	—	—	1.00	2.00
2003B Proof	5,500	Value: 3.00				
2004B	10,026,000	—	—	—	1.00	2.00
2004B Proof	5,000	Value: 3.00				
2005B	6,024,000	—	—	—	1.00	2.00
2005B Proof	4,500	Value: 3.00				
2006B	5,026,000	—	—	—	1.00	2.00
2006B Proof	4,000	Value: 3.00				
2007B	22,024,000	—	—	—	1.00	2.00
2007B Proof	4,000	Value: 3.00				
2008B	41,022,000	—	—	—	1.00	2.00
2008B Proof	4,000	Value: 3.00				
2009B	32,022,000	—	—	—	1.00	2.00
2009B Proof	4,000	Value: 3.00				
2010B	Est. 18,022,000	—	—	—	1.00	2.00
2010B Proof	Est. 4,000	Value: 3.00				
2011B	Est. 20,022,000	—	—	—	0.75	2.00
2011B Proof	Est. 4,000	Value: 3.00				

KM# 23a.3 1/2 FRANC

2.2000 g., Copper-Nickel, 18.2 mm. **Obv:** 23 Stars around figure **Rev:** Value within wreath **Edge:** Reeded **Designer:** A. Bovy

Date	Mintage	F	VF	XF	Unc	BU
2001B	6,022,000	—	—	—	2.50	3.50
2001B Proof	6,000	Value: 5.00				
2002B	2,024,000	—	—	—	2.50	3.50
2002B Proof	6,000	Value: 5.00				
2003B	2,022,000	—	—	—	2.50	3.50
2003B Proof	5,500	Value: 5.00				
2004B	2,026,000	—	—	—	2.50	3.50
2004B Proof	5,000	Value: 5.00				
2005B	1,024,000	—	—	—	2.50	3.50
2005B Proof	4,500	Value: 5.00				
2006B	2,025,000	—	—	—	2.50	3.50
2006B Proof	4,500	Value: 5.00				
2007B	18,024,000	—	—	—	2.00	3.00
2007B Proof	4,000	Value: 5.00				
2008B	25,022,000	—	—	—	2.00	3.00
2008B Proof	4,000	Value: 5.00				
2009B	27,022,000	—	—	—	2.00	3.00
2009B Proof	4,000	Value: 5.00				
2010B	Est. 27,022,000	—	—	—	2.00	3.00
2010B Proof	Est. 4,000	Value: 5.00				
2011B	Est. 15,022,000	—	—	—	1.50	3.00
2011B Proof	Est. 4,000	Value: 5.00				

KM# 24a.3 FRANC

4.4000 g., Copper-Nickel, 23.2 mm. **Obv:** 23 Stars around figure **Rev:** Value and date within wreath **Edge:** Reeded **Designer:** A. Bovy

Date	Mintage	F	VF	XF	Unc	BU
2001B	3,022,000	—	—	—	3.00	5.00
2001B Proof	6,000	Value: 7.00				
2002B	1,024,000	—	—	—	3.00	5.00
2002B Proof	6,000	Value: 7.00				
2003B	2,022,000	—	—	—	3.00	5.00
2003B Proof	5,500	Value: 7.00				
2004B	2,026,000	—	—	—	3.00	5.00
2004B Proof	5,000	Value: 7.00				
2005B	1,024,000	—	—	—	3.00	5.00
2005B Proof	4,500	Value: 7.00				
2006B	2,026,000	—	—	—	3.00	5.00
2006B Proof	4,000	Value: 7.00				
2007B	3,024,000	—	—	—	3.00	5.00
2007B Proof	4,000	Value: 7.00				
2008B	7,022,000	—	—	—	3.00	5.00
2008B Proof	4,000	Value: 7.00				
2009B	11,022,000	—	—	—	3.00	5.00
2009B Proof	4,000	Value: 7.00				
2010B	Est. 15,022,000	—	—	—	3.00	5.00
2010B Proof	Est. 4,000	Value: 7.00				
2011B	Est. 15,022,000	—	—	—	2.50	5.00
2011B Proof	Est. 4,000	Value: 7.00				

KM# 21a.3 2 FRANCS

8.8000 g., Copper-Nickel, 27.4 mm. **Obv:** 23 Stars around figure **Rev:** Value within wreath **Edge:** Reeded **Designer:** A. Bovy

Date	Mintage	F	VF	XF	Unc	BU
2001B	4,022,000	—	—	—	4.00	7.00
2001B Proof	6,000	Value: 10.00				
2002B	1,024,000	—	—	—	4.50	7.50
2002B Proof	6,000	Value: 10.00				
2003B	1,022,000	—	—	2.50	4.50	7.50
2003B Proof	5,500	Value: 10.00				
2004B	1,026,000	—	—	2.50	4.50	7.50
2004B Proof	5,000	Value: 10.00				
2005B	2,024,000	—	—	—	4.50	7.50
2005B Proof	4,500	Value: 10.00				
2006B	7,026,000	—	—	—	4.50	7.50
2006B Proof	4,000	Value: 10.00				
2007B	16,024,000	—	—	—	4.50	7.50
2007B Proof	4,000	Value: 10.00				
2008B	6,022,000	—	—	—	4.50	7.50
2008B Proof	4,000	Value: 10.00				
2009B	8,022,000	—	—	—	4.50	7.50
2009B Proof	4,000	Value: 10.00				
2010B	Est. 9,022,000	—	—	—	4.50	7.50
2010B Proof	Est. 4,000	Value: 10.00				
2011B	Est. 7,022,000	—	—	—	4.00	7.50
2011B Proof	Est. 4,000	Value: 10.00				

KM# 40a.4 5 FRANCS

13.2000 g., Copper-Nickel, 31.45 mm. **Obv:** William Tell right **Rev:** Shield flanked by sprigs **Edge:** DOMINUS PROVIDEBIT and 13 stars raised **Designer:** Paul Burkhard

Date	Mintage	F	VF	XF	Unc	BU
2001B	1,022,000	—	—	—	7.00	10.00
2001B Proof	6,000	Value: 15.00				
2002B	1,024,000	—	—	—	7.00	10.00
2002B Proof	6,000	Value: 15.00				
2003B	1,022,000	—	—	—	7.00	10.00
2003B Proof	5,500	Value: 15.00				
2004B	524,000	—	—	—	7.50	11.00
2004B Proof	5,000	Value: 15.00				
2005B	524,000	—	—	—	7.50	11.00
2005B Proof	4,500	Value: 15.00				
2006B	526,000	—	—	—	7.50	11.00
2006B Proof	4,000	Value: 15.00				
2007B	524,000	—	—	—	7.50	11.00
2007B Proof	4,000	Value: 15.00				
2008B	522,000	—	—	—	7.50	11.00
Note: Not yet released for circulation						
2008B Proof	4,000	Value: 15.00				
2009B	2,022,000	—	—	—	7.50	11.00
2009B Proof	4,000	Value: 15.00				
2010B	Est. 5,022,000	—	—	—	7.50	11.00
2010B Proof	Est. 4,000	Value: 15.00				
2011B	Est. 3,022,000	—	—	—	7.50	11.00
2011B Proof	Est. 4,000	Value: 15.00				

COMMEMORATIVE COINAGE

KM# 92 5 FRANCS

15.0000 g., Bi-Metallic Brass center in Copper-Nickel ring, 32.85 mm. **Subject:** Zurcher Sechselauten **Obv:** Value within circle **Rev:** Burning strawman within circle **Edge:** Reeded **Edge Lettering:** DOMINUS PROVIDEBIT (13 stars) **Designer:** John Grüniger

Date	Mintage	F	VF	XF	Unc	BU
2001B	170,000	—	—	—	8.00	12.00
2001B Proof	20,000	Value: 24.00				

KM# 98 5 FRANCS

15.0000 g., Bi-Metallic Brass center in Copper-Nickel ring, 32.85 mm. **Subject:** Escalade 1602-2002 **Obv:** Value within circle **Rev:** Swirling ladders design within circle **Edge:** Reeded **Edge Lettering:** DOMINUS PROVIDEBIT (13 stars) **Designer:** P.A. Zuber

Date	Mintage	F	VF	XF	Unc	BU
2002B	130,000	—	—	—	8.00	12.00
2002B Proof	15,000	Value: 24.00				

KM# 103 5 FRANCS

15.0000 g., Bi-Metallic Brass center in Copper-Nickel ring, 32.85 mm. **Subject:** Chalandamarz **Obv:** Value within circular inscription and designed wreath **Rev:** Boys shaking bells within 3/4 designed wreath **Edge:** Reeded **Edge Lettering:** DOMINUS PROVIDEBIT (13 stars) **Designer:** Gian Vonzun

Date	Mintage	F	VF	XF	Unc	BU
2003B	96,000	—	—	—	8.00	12.00
2003B Proof	13,500	Value: 24.00				

KM# 107 10 FRANCS

15.0000 g., Bi-Metallic Copper-Nickel center in Aluminum-Bronze ring, 32.85 mm. **Obv:** Value **Rev:** Matterhorn Mountain **Edge:** Segmented reeding **Designer:** Stephan Bundi

Date	Mintage	F	VF	XF	Unc	BU
2004B	94,976	—	—	—	—	22.00
2004B Proof	12,168	Value: 42.00				

KM# 111 10 FRANCS

15.0000 g., Bi-Metallic Copper-Nickel center in Aluminum-Bronze ring, 32.85 mm. **Obv:** Value **Rev:** Jungfrau mountain **Edge:** Segmented reeding **Designer:** Stephan Bundi

Date	Mintage	F	VF	XF	Unc	BU
2005B	77,791	—	—	—	—	18.00
2005B Proof	10,495	Value: 40.00				

KM# 114 10 FRANCS

15.0000 g., Bi-Metallic Copper-Nickel center in Aluminum-Bronze ring, 32.85 mm. **Obv:** Value **Rev:** Piz Bernina mountain **Edge:** Segmented reeding **Designer:** Stephan Bundi

Date	Mintage	F	VF	XF	Unc	BU
2006B	66,000	—	—	—	—	16.00
2006B Proof	9,000	Value: 40.00				

KM# 118 10 FRANCS

15.0000 g., Bi-Metallic Copper-Nickel center in Aluminum-Bronze ring, 32.85 mm. **Subject:** Swiss National Park **Obv:** Value **Rev:** Ibex **Edge:** Segmented reeding

Date	Mintage	F	VF	XF	Unc	BU
2007B	Est. 96,000	—	—	—	—	17.00
2007B Proof	12,000	Value: 40.00				

KM# 126 10 FRANCS

15.0000 g., Bi-Metallic Copper-Nickel center in Aluminum-Bronze ring, 32.85 mm. **Obv:** Small national arms **Obv. Legend:** CONFEDERATIO - HELVETICA **Rev:** Golden Eagle alighting **Rev. Legend:** PARK NATIONAL SUISSE **Rev. Designer:** Niklaus Heeb **Edge:** Segmented reeding

Date	Mintage	F	VF	XF	Unc	BU
2008B	Est. 95,000	—	—	—	—	17.00
2008B Proof	Est. 12,000	Value: 40.00				

KM# 130 10 FRANCS

15.0000 g., Bi-Metallic Copper-nickel center in brass ring, 32.85 mm. **Subject:** Swiss National Park **Obv:** Value **Rev:** Red deer **Rev. Designer:** Niklaus Heeb

Date	Mintage	F	VF	XF	Unc	BU
2009B	Est. 95,000	—	—	—	—	17.00
2009B Proof	Est. 12,000	Value: 40.00				

KM# 134 10 FRANCS

15.0000 g., Bi-Metallic Copper-nickel center in brass ring, 32.85 mm. **Subject:** Swiss National Park **Obv:** Value **Rev:** Marmot

Date	Mintage	F	VF	XF	Unc	BU
2010B	Est. 94,000	—	—	—	—	17.00
2010B Proof	Est. 12,000	Value: 30.00				

KM# 138 10 FRANCS

15.0000 g., Bi-Metallic Copper-Nickel center in Aluminum-Bronze ring., 33 mm. **Subject:** Bern Onion Market **Obv:** Value **Obv. Designer:** Stefan Haenni **Rev:** Bear of Bern at left, woven plaits of onions at right **Edge:** Segmented reeding

Date	Mintage	F	VF	XF	Unc	BU
2011B	94,000	—	—	—	—	16.00
2011B Proof	12,000	Value: 40.00				

KM# 93 20 FRANCS

20.0000 g., 0.9250 Silver 0.5948 oz. ASW, 32.8 mm. **Subject:** Mustair Cloister **Obv:** Church floor plan **Rev:** Cloister of Müstair **Edge Lettering:** DOMINUS PROVIDEBIT and 13 stars **Designer:** Hans-Peter von Ah

Date	Mintage	F	VF	XF	Unc	BU
2001B	50,076	—	—	—	25.00	30.00
2001B Proof	15,000	Value: 45.00				

KM# 94 20 FRANCS

20.0000 g., 0.8350 Silver 0.5369 oz. ASW, 32.8 mm. **Subject:** Johanna Spyri **Obv:** Value within handwritten background **Rev:** Bust facing **Edge Lettering:** DOMINUS PROVIDEBIT (13 stars) **Designer:** Silvia Goeschke

Date	Mintage	F	VF	XF	Unc	BU
2001B	60,364	—	—	—	25.00	30.00
2001B Proof	15,000	Value: 50.00				

KM# 99 20 FRANCS

20.0000 g., 0.8350 Silver 0.5369 oz. ASW, 32.8 mm. **Obv:** St. Gall and bear cub **Rev:** St. Gall Cloister **Edge Lettering:** DOMINUS PROVIDEBIT (13 stars) **Designer:** Hans-Peter von Ah

Date	Mintage	F	VF	XF	Unc	BU
2002B	35,895	—	—	—	25.00	30.00
2002B Proof	6,250	Value: 50.00				

KM# 100 20 FRANCS

20.0000 g., 0.8350 Silver 0.5369 oz. ASW, 32.8 mm. **Subject:** REGA **Obv:** Value, inscription and raised cross above rotating propeller **Rev:** Rescue helicopter in flight **Edge Lettering:** DOMINUS PROVIDEBIT (13 stars) **Designer:** Raphael Schenker

Date	Mintage	F	VF	XF	Unc	BU
2002B	37,314	—	—	—	25.00	30.00
2002B Proof	6,453	Value: 50.00				

KM# 101 20 FRANCS

20.0000 g., 0.8350 Silver 0.5369 oz. ASW, 32.8 mm. **Subject:** Expo '02 **Obv:** Value and date within circle **Rev:** Child at water's edge within beaded circle **Edge Lettering:** DOMINUS PROVIDEBIT (13 stars) **Designer:** Hervé Graumann

Date	Mintage	F	VF	XF	Unc	BU
2002B	51,899	—	—	—	25.00	30.00
2002B Proof	7,691	Value: 50.00				

KM# 104 20 FRANCS

19.9700 g., 0.8350 Silver 0.5361 oz. ASW, 32.8 mm. **Subject:** St. Moritz Ski Championships **Obv:** Value in snow storm **Rev:** Skier in snow storm **Edge Lettering:** DOMINUS PROVIDEBIT (13 stars) **Designer:** Claude Kuhn

Date	Mintage	F	VF	XF	Unc	BU
2003B	39,411	—	—	—	25.00	30.00
2003B Proof	6,471	Value: 50.00				

KM# 106 20 FRANCS

20.0000 g., 0.8350 Silver 0.5369 oz. ASW, 32.8 mm. **Subject:** Bern, Old Town **Obv:** Stylized clock tower and buildings **Rev:** Stylized aerial view of Berner Altstadt **Edge Lettering:** DOMINUS PROVIDEBIT **Designer:** Franz Fedier

Date	Mintage	F	VF	XF	Unc	BU
2003B	38,644	—	—	—	25.00	30.00
2003B Proof	5,909	Value: 60.00				

KM# 108 20 FRANCS

20.0000 g., 0.8350 Silver 0.5369 oz. ASW, 32.8 mm. **Obv:** Value **Rev:** The Three Castles of Bellinzona **Edge Lettering:** DOMINUS PROVIDEBIT **Designer:** Marco Prati

Date	Mintage	F	VF	XF	Unc	BU
2004B	29,697	—	—	—	25.00	30.00
2004B Proof	5,190	Value: 50.00				

KM# 109 20 FRANCS

20.0000 g., 0.8350 Silver 0.5369 oz. ASW, 32.8 mm. **Obv:** Value **Rev:** Chillon Castle and reflection **Edge Lettering:** DOMINUS PROVIDEBIT **Designer:** Jean-Benoît Lévy

Date	Mintage	F	VF	XF	Unc	BU
2004B	35,133	—	—	—	22.00	28.00
2004B Proof	5,670	Value: 50.00				

KM# 121 20 FRANCS

20.0000 g., 0.8350 Silver 0.5369 oz. ASW, 32.8 mm. **Subject:** FIFA Centennial **Obv:** Soccer ball with value at left **Rev:** Flower in center of cross

Date	Mintage	F	VF	XF	Unc	BU
2004B Proof only	14,041	Value: 150				

KM# 122 20 FRANCS
20.0000 g., 0.8350 Silver 0.5369 oz. ASW, 32.8 mm. **Subject:** Chapel Bridge Lucerne **Obv:** Value **Rev:** View of Chapel Bridge **Edge Lettering:** DOMINUS PROVIDEBIT

Date	Mintage	F	VF	XF	Unc	BU
2005B	44,359	—	—	—	25.00	30.00
2005B Proof	5,998	Value: 50.00				

KM# 112 20 FRANCS
20.0000 g., 0.8350 Silver 0.5369 oz. ASW, 32.8 mm. **Subject:** Geneva Motor Show **Obv:** Value **Rev:** Partial view of prototype car **Edge Lettering:** DOMINUS PROVIDEBIT **Designer:** Roger Pfund

Date	Mintage	F	VF	XF	Unc	BU
2005B	45,000	—	—	—	25.00	30.00
2005B Proof	6,000	Value: 50.00				

KM# 115 20 FRANCS
20.0000 g., 0.8350 Silver 0.5369 oz. ASW, 32.8 mm. **Obv:** Value **Rev:** 1906 Post Bus **Edge Lettering:** DOMINUS PROVIDEBIT **Designer:** Raphael Schenker

Date	Mintage	F	VF	XF	Unc	BU
2006B	40,000	—	—	—	25.00	30.00
2006B Proof	6,000	Value: 55.00				

KM# 117 20 FRANCS
20.0000 g., 0.8350 Silver 0.5369 oz. ASW, 32.8 mm. **Obv:** Value and legend **Rev:** Swiss Parliament Building **Edge Lettering:** DOMINUS PROVIDEBIT (13 stars) **Designer:** Benjamin Pfäffli

Date	Mintage	F	VF	XF	Unc	BU
2006B	35,000	—	—	—	25.00	30.00
2006B Proof	6,000	Value: 55.00				

KM# 119 20 FRANCS
20.0000 g., 0.8350 Silver 0.5369 oz. ASW, 32.8 mm. **Subject:** National Bank Centennial **Obv:** Value **Rev:** Partial face of Arthur Honegger (Composer) **Edge Lettering:** DOMINUS PROVIDEBIT

Date	Mintage	F	VF	XF	Unc	BU
2007B	41,747	—	—	—	25.00	30.00
2007B Proof	11,000	Value: 65.00				

KM# 124 20 FRANCS
20.0000 g., 0.8350 Silver 0.5369 oz. ASW, 32.8 mm. **Series:** Famous buildings **Subject:** Munot castle of Schaffhausen **Obv. Legend:** CONFEDERATIO - HELVETICA **Rev:** Two views of castle **Rev. Legend:** MUNOT **Designer:** Hansveli Holzer

Date	Mintage	F	VF	XF	Unc	BU
2007B	40,000	—	—	—	30.00	25.00
2007B Proof	5,000	Value: 55.00				

KM# 127 20 FRANCS
20.0000 g., 0.8350 Silver 0.5369 oz. ASW, 32.8 mm. **Subject:** 100th Anniversary Hockey **Obv:** Small national arms **Obv. Legend:** CONFEDERATIO - HELVETICA **Rev:** Two players, one about to swing at puck **Rev. Legend:** ICE HOCKEY 1908-2008 **Rev. Designer:** Roland Hirter

Date	Mintage	F	VF	XF	Unc	BU
2008B	Est. 50,000	—	—	—	30.00	25.00
2008B Proof	Est. 7,000	Value: 65.00				

KM# 128 20 FRANCS
20.0000 g., 0.8350 Silver 0.5369 oz. ASW, 32.8 mm. **Subject:** Vitznau-Rigi Cog Railway **Obv:** Value **Rev:** Modern locomotive descending, early locomotive ascending (inverted) **Rev. Designer:** Benno Zehnder

Date	Mintage	F	VF	XF	Unc	BU
2008B	Est. 50,000	—	—	—	25.00	30.00
2008B Proof	7,000	Value: 65.00				

KM# 131 20 FRANCS
20.0000 g., 0.8350 Silver 0.5369 oz. ASW, 32.8 mm. **Subject:** Swiss Museum of Transport, 50th Anniversary **Obv:** National arms and value **Rev:** Spiral of transport vehicles **Rev. Designer:** Werner Meier **Edge:** DOMINUS PROVIDEBIT

Date	Mintage	F	VF	XF	Unc	BU
2009B	Est. 50,000	—	—	—	25.00	30.00
2009B Proof	7,000	Value: 65.00				

KM# 132 20 FRANCS
20.0000 g., 0.8350 Silver 0.5369 oz. ASW, 32.8 mm. **Subject:** Brienz-Rothorn Railway **Obv:** Value **Rev:** Locomotive and rail-car **Designer:** Bruno K. Zehnder

Date	Mintage	F	VF	XF	Unc	BU
2009B	Est. 50,000	—	—	—	25.00	30.00
2009B Proof	7,000	Value: 65.00				

KM# 135 20 FRANCS
20.0000 g., 0.8350 Silver 0.5369 oz. ASW, 32.8 mm. **Subject:** 100 Years Bernina Railway **Rev:** Steam train on viaduct

Date	Mintage	F	VF	XF	Unc	BU
2010B	Est. 50,000	—	—	25.00	—	30.00
2010B Proof	Est. 7,000	Value: 50.00				

KM# 136 20 FRANCS
20.0000 g., 0.8350 Silver 0.5369 oz. ASW, 32.8 mm. **Subject:** 100 Anniversary Death of Henry Dunant (Red Cross founder) **Rev. Designer:** Pierre-Alain Zuber

Date	Mintage	F	VF	XF	Unc	BU
2010B	Est. 50,000	—	—	25.00	—	30.00
2010B Proof	Est. 7,000	Value: 50.00				

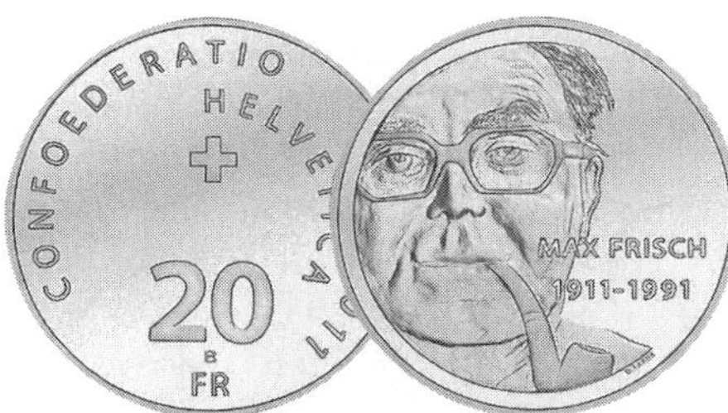

KM# 139 20 FRANCS
20.0000 g., 0.8350 Silver 0.5369 oz. ASW, 33 mm. **Subject:** Max Frisch, 100th Anniversary of Birth **Obv:** Value **Rev:** Facing portrait with pipe

Date	Mintage	F	VF	XF	Unc	BU
2011	50,000	—	—	—	25.00	30.00
2011 Proof	7,000	Value: 50.00				

KM# 95 50 FRANCS
11.2900 g., 0.9000 Gold 0.3267 oz. AGW, 25.1 mm. **Obv:** Landscape and value **Rev:** Heidi and goat running **Edge:** Lettered **Edge Lettering:** DOMINUS PROVIDEBIT (13 stars) **Designer:** Albrecht Schnider

Date	Mintage	F	VF	XF	Unc	BU
2001B Proof	3,967	Value: 650				

KM# 102 50 FRANCS
11.2900 g., 0.9000 Gold 0.3267 oz. AGW, 25.1 mm. **Subject:** Expo '02 **Obv:** Value **Rev:** Aerial view of 3 lakes landscape **Edge:** Lettered **Edge Lettering:** DOMINUS PROVIDEBIT (13 stars) **Designer:** Max Matter

Date	Mintage	F	VF	XF	Unc	BU
2002B Proof	4,856	Value: 550				

KM# 105 50 FRANCS
11.2900 g., 0.9000 Gold 0.3267 oz. AGW, 25.1 mm. **Obv:** Skier and value **Rev:** St. Moritz city view **Edge Lettering:** DOMINUS PROVIDEBIT (13 stars) **Designer:** Andreas His

Date	Mintage	F	VF	XF	Unc	BU
2003B Proof	4,000	Value: 550				

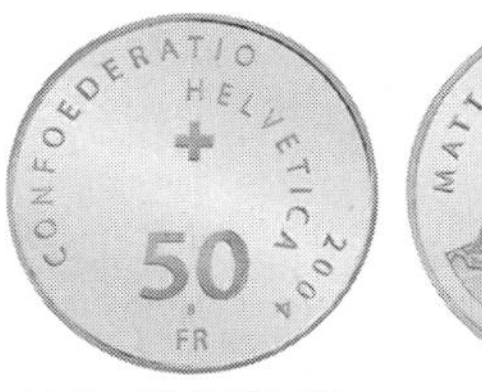

KM# 110 50 FRANCS
11.2900 g., 0.9000 Gold 0.3267 oz. AGW, 25.1 mm. **Obv:** Value **Rev:** Matterhorn Mountain **Edge Lettering:** DOMINUS PROVIDEBIT (13 stars) **Designer:** Stephan Bundi

Date	Mintage	F	VF	XF	Unc	BU
2004B Proof	7,000	Value: 650				

KM# 123 50 FRANCS
11.2900 g., 0.9000 Gold 0.3267 oz. AGW, 25.1 mm. **Subject:** FIFA Centennial **Obv:** FIFA depicting Wilhelm Tell **Rev:** Soccer ball on left value on right **Designer:** Joaquin Jimenez

Date	Mintage	F	VF	XF	Unc	BU
2004B Proof	10,000	Value: 850				

KM# 113 50 FRANCS
11.2900 g., 0.9000 Gold 0.3267 oz. AGW, 25.1 mm. **Subject:** Geneva Motor Show **Obv:** Value **Rev:** Partial view of an antique car **Edge Lettering:** DOMINUS PROVIDEBIT **Designer:** Roger Pfund

Date	Mintage	F	VF	XF	Unc	BU
2005B Proof	6,000	Value: 550				

KM# 116 50 FRANCS
11.2900 g., 0.9000 Gold 0.3267 oz. AGW, 25.1 mm. **Obv:** Value **Rev:** Swiss Guardsman **Edge Lettering:** DOMINUS PROVIDEBIT **Designer:** Rudolf Mirer

Date	Mintage	F	VF	XF	Unc	BU
2006B Proof	6,000	Value: 700				

KM# 120 50 FRANCS
11.2900 g., 0.9000 Gold 0.3267 oz. AGW, 25.1 mm. **Subject:** National Bank Centennial **Obv:** Value **Obv. Legend:** CONFEDERATIO - HELVETICA **Rev:** "Lumberjack" from painting by Ferdinand Hodler **Rev. Inscription:** SNB BNS + **Edge Lettering:** DOMINUS PROVIDEBIT

Date	Mintage	F	VF	XF	Unc	BU
2007B Proof	6,000	Value: 600				

KM# 129 50 FRANCS

11.2900 g., 0.9000 Gold 0.3267 oz. AGW, 25.1 mm. **Subject:** International Year of Planet Earth **Obv:** Value **Rev:** Dancing child with 3 globes above head, in hands and standing on one globe **Rev. Inscription:** DE LA PLANETE TERRE ANNEE INTERNATIONALE **Edge:** DOMINUS PROVIDEBIT **Designer:** Claude Sandoz

Date	Mintage	F	VF	XF	Unc	BU
2008B Proof	6,000	Value: 575				

KM# 133 50 FRANCS

11.2900 g., 0.9000 Gold 0.3267 oz. AGW, 25.1 mm. **Subject:** Pro Patria, 100th Anniversary **Obv:** Value **Rev. Designer:** Hans Erni **Edge:** DOMINUS PROVIDEBIT

Date	Mintage	F	VF	XF	Unc	BU
2009B Proof	6,000	Value: 600				

KM# 137 50 FRANCS

11.2900 g., 0.9000 Gold 0.3267 oz. AGW, 25.1 mm. **Subject:** 100th Anniversary Death of Alber Anker (Painter)

Date	Mintage	F	VF	XF	Unc	BU
2010B Proof	Est. 6,000	Value: 620				

COMMEMORATIVE COINAGE

Shooting Festival

The listings which follow have traditionally been categorized in many catalogs as Swiss Shooting Thalers. Technically, all are medallic issues rather than coins, excepting the Solothurn issue of 1855.

X# S61 50 FRANCS

25.0000 g., 0.9000 Silver 0.7234 oz. ASW, 37 mm. **Subject:** Uri Festival **Obv:** Head laureate left within star border **Rev:** Train and tunnel **Note:** Prev. KM#S61.

Date	Mintage	F	VF	XF	Unc	BU
2001 Proof	1,500	Value: 125				

X# S63 50 FRANCS

25.0000 g., 0.9000 Silver 0.7234 oz. ASW, 37 mm. **Subject:** Zurich Festival **Obv:** Small wreath above shield flanked by sprigs within beaded border **Rev:** Standing figure walking left with lion within beaded circle **Note:** Prev. KM#S63.

Date	Mintage	F	VF	XF	Unc	BU
2002 Proof	1,500	Value: 175				

X# S65 50 FRANCS

25.0000 g., 0.9990 Silver 0.8029 oz. ASW, 37 mm. **Subject:** Basel Festival **Note:** Prev. KM#S65.

Date	Mintage	F	VF	XF	Unc	BU
2003 Proof	1,500	Value: 115				

X# S67 50 FRANCS

25.0000 g., 0.9000 Silver 0.7234 oz. ASW **Subject:** Fribourg Festival **Note:** Prev. KM#S67.

Date	Mintage	F	VF	XF	Unc	BU
2004 Proof	1,500	Value: 115				

X# S69 50 FRANCS

25.0000 g., 0.9000 Silver 0.7234 oz. ASW, 37 mm. **Subject:** Brusio Festival **Note:** Prev. KM#S69.

Date	Mintage	F	VF	XF	Unc	BU
2005	1,500	Value: 135				

X# S71 50 FRANCS

25.0000 g., 0.9000 Silver 0.7234 oz. ASW, 37 mm. **Subject:** Solothurn Festival **Note:** Prev. KM#S71.

Date	Mintage	F	VF	XF	Unc	BU
2006	2,000	Value: 100				

X# S73 50 FRANCS

25.0000 g., 0.9000 Silver 0.7234 oz. ASW, 37 mm. **Subject:** Luzern Festival **Note:** Prev. KM#S73.

Date	Mintage	F	VF	XF	Unc	BU
2007	2,000	Value: 125				

X# S75 50 FRANCS

25.0000 g., 0.9000 Silver 0.7234 oz. ASW, 37 mm. **Subject:** Geneva Festival

Date	Mintage	F	VF	XF	Unc	BU
2008	1,500	Value: 125				

X# S77 50 FRANCS

25.0000 g., 0.9000 Silver 0.7234 oz. ASW, 37 mm. **Subject:** Obwalden Festival

Date	Mintage	F	VF	XF	Unc	BU
2009	1,500	Value: 225				

X# S79 50 FRANCS

25.0000 g., 0.9000 Silver 0.7234 oz. ASW, 37 mm. **Subject:** Aarau Festival

Date	Mintage	F	VF	XF	Unc	BU
2010HF Proof	2,000	Value: 110				

X# S62 500 FRANCS

0.9990 Gold **Issuer:** Uri Festival **Obv:** Head laureate left within star border **Rev:** Locomotive and tunnel **Note:** Prev. KM#S62.

Date	Mintage	F	VF	XF	Unc	BU
2001 Proof	150	Value: 2,000				

X# S64 500 FRANCS

13.0000 g., 0.9990 Gold 0.4175 oz. AGW **Subject:** Zurich Festival **Note:** Prev. KM#S64.

Date	Mintage	F	VF	XF	Unc	BU
2002 Proof	150	Value: 2,200				

X# S66 500 FRANCS

13.0000 g., 0.9990 Gold 0.4175 oz. AGW, 37 mm. **Subject:** Basel Festival **Note:** Prev. KM#S66.

Date	Mintage	F	VF	XF	Unc	BU
2003 Proof	150	Value: 1,900				

X# S68 500 FRANCS

15.5000 g., 0.9990 Gold 0.4978 oz. AGW **Subject:** Fribourg Festival **Note:** Prev. KM#S68.

Date	Mintage	F	VF	XF	Unc	BU
2004 Proof	150	Value: 1,350				

X# S70 500 FRANCS

15.5000 g., 0.9990 Gold 0.4978 oz. AGW **Subject:** Brusio Festival **Note:** Prev. KM#S70.

Date	Mintage	F	VF	XF	Unc	BU
2005 Proof	150	Value: 1,800				

X# S72 500 FRANCS

25.6000 g., 0.5850 Gold 0.4815 oz. AGW **Subject:** Solothurn Festival **Note:** Prev. KM#S72.

Date	Mintage	F	VF	XF	Unc	BU
2006 Proof	200	Value: 1,000				

X# S74 500 FRANCS

25.6000 g., 0.5850 Gold 0.4815 oz. AGW **Subject:** Luzern Festival **Note:** Prev. KM#S74.

Date	Mintage	F	VF	XF	Unc	BU
2007	200	Value: 1,000				

X# S76 500 FRANCS

25.6000 g., 0.5850 Gold 0.4815 oz. AGW **Subject:** Geneva Festival

Date	Mintage	F	VF	XF	Unc	BU
2008 Proof	150	Value: 1,000				

X# S78 500 FRANCS

19.5900 g., 0.9999 Gold 0.6297 oz. AGW, 37 mm. **Subject:** Obwalden Festival

Date	Mintage	F	VF	XF	Unc	BU
2009 Proof	175	Value: 1,000				

PIEFORTS

X#	Date	Mintage	Identification	Mkt Val
P1	2003	500	5 Europ. Silver. X#Pn10a.	65.00

ESSAIS

KM#	Date	Mintage	Identification	Mkt Val
EA12	2007B	500	5 Francs. Copper-Nickel. KM#86	250
E13	2001B	600	20 Francs. Silver. KM#93	300
E14	2002B	700	5 Francs. Bi-Metallic. KM#98 Escalade	180
E15	2003B	700	5 Francs. Bi-Metallic. KM#103 Chalandamarz	200
E16	2004B	700	10 Francs. Bi-Metallic. KM#107.	300
E19	2005	500	20 Francs. Silver. 20.0000 g. 33 mm. Motor Show. KM#112.	285
E20	2006	500	20 Francs. Silver. 20.0000 g. 33 mm. Parliament Building. KM#117.	285
E21	2007	500	20 Francs. Silver. 20.0000 g. 33 mm. KM#119. Munot	250
E22	2008	700	10 Francs. Bi-Metallic. KM#118 Golden Eagle	225
E23	2009	500	20 Francs. Silver. 33mm KM#132 Brienz-Rothorn Railway	275
E24	2010B	700	10 Francs. Copper-Nickel. 15.0000 g. KM#134	200

MINT SETS

KM#	Date	Mintage	Identification	Issue Price	Mkt Val
MS35	2001 (9)	21,532	KM#21a.3, 23a.3, 24a.3, 26c, 27, 29a, 40a.4, 46, 92 Zurich Sechselauten	—	35.00
MS36	2002 (9)	17,920	KM#21a.3, 23a.3, 24a.3, 26c, 27, 29a, 40a.4, 46, 98 Escalade	—	45.00
MS37	2002 (9)	1,974	KM#21a.3, 23a.3, 24a.3, 26c, 27, 29a, 40a.4, 46, 98 Plus a medal; different cover (intended as a birth year set for 2002)	—	220
MS38	2003 (9)	17,200	KM#21a.3, 23a.3, 24a.3, 26c, 27, 29a, 40a.4, 46, 103 Chalandamarz	—	45.00
MS39	2003 (8)	4,800	KM#21a.3, 23a.3, 24a.3, 26c, 27, 29a, 40a.2, 46 plus medal; Baby Mint Set	—	70.00
MS40	2004 (9)	16,000	KM#21a.3, 23a.3, 24a.3, 26c, 27, 29a, 40a.4, 46, 107 Matterhorn	—	80.00
MS41	2004 (8)	8,400	KM#21a.3, 23a.3, 24a.3, 26c, 27, 29a, 40a.2, 46 plus medal; Baby Mint Set	—	32.00
MS42	2005 (9)	15,279	KM#21a.3, 23a.3, 24a.3, 26c, 27, 29a, 40a.4, 46, 111 Jung Frau	—	50.00
MS43	2005 (8)	7,500	KM#21a.3, 23a.3, 24a.3, 26c, 27, 29a, 40a.2, 46 plus medal; Baby Mint Set	—	32.00
MS44	2006 (9)	16,000	KM#21a.3, 23a.3, 24a.3, 26c, 27, 29a, 40a.4, 46, 114 Piz Bernina	—	225
MS45	2006 (8)	2,000	KM#21a.3, 23a.3, 24a.3, 26c, 27, 29a, 40a.2, 46 plus medal; Jubilee Mint Set	—	450
MS46	2006 (8)	8,000	KM#21a.3, 23a.3, 24a.3, 26c, 27, 29a, 40a.2, 46 plus medal; Baby Mint Set	—	175
MS47	2007 (8)	16,000	KM#21a.3, 23a.3, 24a.3, 26c, 27, 29a, 40a.4, 118	—	47.50
MS48	2007 (7)	8,000	KM#21a.3, 23a.3, 24a.3, 26c, 27, 29a, 40a.2, plus medal; Baby Mint Set	—	32.00
MS49	2008 (8)	15,000	KM#21a.3, 23a.3, 24a.3, 26c, 27, 29a, 40a.4, 126	—	47.50
MS50	2008 (7)	—	KM#21a.3, 23a.3, 24a.3, 26c, 27, 29a, 40a.2, plus medal; Baby Mint Set	—	32.00
MS51	2009 (8)	18,500	KM#21a.3, 23a.3, 24a.3, 26c, 27, 29a, 40a4, 130.	—	47.50
MS52	2009 (7)	—	KM#21a.3, 23a.3, 24a.3, 26c, 27, 29a, 40a.2, plus medal; Baby Mint Set	—	32.00
MS53	2010 (8)	14,000	KM#21a.3, 23a.3, 24a.3, 26c, 27, 29a, 40a.2, 134	—	40.00
MS54	2010 (7)	—	KM#21a.3, 23a.3, 24a.3, 26c, 27, 29a, 40a.2, plus medal; Baby Mint Set	—	32.00
MS55	2011 (7)	14,000	KM#21a.3, 23a.3, 24a.3, 26c, 27, 29a, 40a.2, plus Bernese Onion Market	—	40.00
MS56	2011 (7)	—	KM#21a.3, 23a.3, 24a.3, 26c, 27, 29a, 40a.2, plus medal; Baby Mint Set	—	32.00

PROOF SETS

KM#	Date	Mintage	Identification	Issue Price	Mkt Val
PS30	2001 (9)	5,184	KM#21a.3, 23a.3, 24a.3, 26c, 27, 29a, 40a.4, 46, 92 Zurich Sechselauten	—	75.00
PS31	2002 (9)	4,518	KM#21a.3, 23a.3, 24a.3, 26c, 27, 29a, 40a.4, 46, 98 Escalade	—	80.00
PS32	2003 (9)	4,520	KM#21a.3, 23a.3, 24a.3, 26c, 27, 29a, 40a.4, 46, 103 Chatandamarz	—	80.00
PS33	2004 (9)	4,168	KM#21a.3, 23a.3, 24a.3, 26c, 27, 29a, 40a.4, 46, 107 Matterhorn	68.00	95.00
PS34	2005 (9)	4,497	KM#21a.3, 23a.3, 24a.3, 26c, 27, 29a, 40a.4, 46, 111 Jung Frau	68.00	95.00
PS35	2006 (9)	4,000	KM#21a.3, 23a.3, 24a.3, 26c, 27, 29a, 40a.4, 46, 114 Piz Berhina	68.00	300
PS36	2007 (8)	4,000	KM#21a.3, 23a.3, 24a.3, 26c, 27, 29a, 40a.4, 118	68.00	85.00
PS37	2008 (8)	4,000	KM#21a.3, 23a.3, 24a.3, 26c, 27, 29a, 40a.4, 126	72.00	95.00
PS38	2009 (8)	4,000	KM#21a.3, 23a.3, 24a.3, 26c, 27, 29a, 40a.4, 130	75.00	95.00
PS39	2010 (7)	4,000	KM#21a.3, 23a.3, 24a.3, 26c, 27, 29a, 40a.4	75.00	90.00
PS40	2011 (7)	4,000	KM#21a.3, 23a.3, 24a.3, 26c, 27, 29a, 40a.2, plus Bernese Onion Market	—	90.00

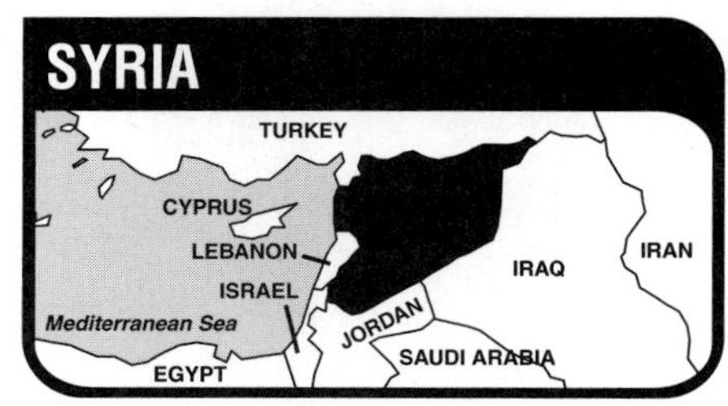

The Syrian Arab Republic, located in the Near East at the eastern end of the Mediterranean Sea, has an area of 71,498 sq. mi. (185,180 sq. km.) and a population of *12 million. Capital: Greater Damascus. Agriculture and animal breeding are the chief industries. Cotton, crude oil and livestock are exported.

TITLES

الجمهورية السورية

al-Jumhuriya(t) al-Suriya(t)

الجمهورية لعربية السورية

al-Jumhuriya(t) al-Arabiya(t) as-Suriya(t)

SYRIAN ARAB REPUBLIC

STANDARD COINAGE

KM# 129 5 POUNDS

7.5300 g., Nickel Clad Steel, 24.5 mm. **Obv:** National arms within design and beaded border **Rev:** Old fort and latent image above value within design and beaded border **Edge:** Reeded and lettered **Edge Lettering:** CENTRAL BANK 5 SYP

Date	Mintage	F	VF	XF	Unc	BU
AH1424-2003	—	—	—	—	1.25	1.75

KM# 130 10 POUNDS

9.5300 g., Copper-Nickel-Zinc, 27.4 mm. **Obv:** National arms within beaded border **Rev:** Ancient ruins with latent image within beaded border **Edge Lettering:** 10 SYRIAN POUNDS

Date	Mintage	F	VF	XF	Unc	BU
AH1424-2003	—	—	—	—	2.50	3.50

KM# 131 25 POUNDS

8.4000 g., Bi-Metallic Copper-Nickel center in Nickel-Brass ring, 25 mm. **Obv:** National arms within beaded border **Rev:** Building and latent image within beaded border **Edge Lettering:** CENTRAL BANK OF SYRIA 25

Date	Mintage	F	VF	XF	Unc	BU
AH1424-2003	—	—	—	1.50	3.75	5.00

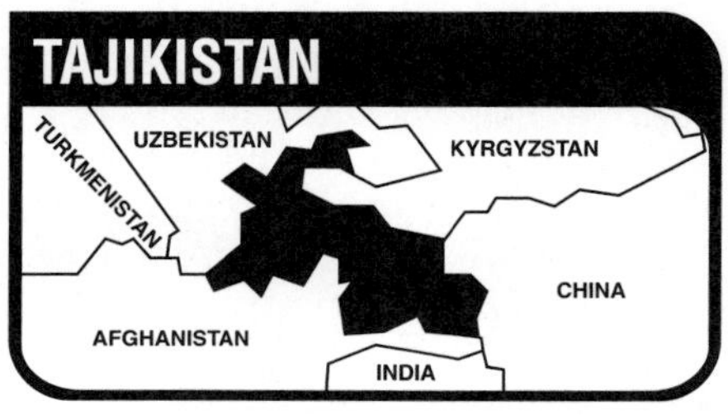

The Republic of Tajikistan (Tadjiquistan), was formed from those regions of Bukhara and Turkestan where the population consisted mainly of Tajiks. It is bordered in the north and west by Uzbekistan and Kyrgyzstan, in the east by China and in the south by Afghanistan. It has an area of 55,240 sq. miles (143,100 sq. km.) and a population of 5.95 million. It includes 2 provinces of Khudzand and Khatlon together with the Gorno-Badakhshan Autonomous Region with a population of 5,092,603. Capital: Dushanbe. Tajikistan was admitted as a constituent republic of the Soviet Union on Dec. 5, 1929. In August 1990 the Tajik Supreme Soviet adopted a declaration of republican sovereignty, and in Dec. 1991 the republic became a member of the CIS.

After demonstrations and fighting, the Communist government was replaced by a Revolutionary Coalition Council on May 7, 1992. Following further demonstrations President Nabiev was ousted on Sept. 7, 1992. Civil war broke out, and the government resigned on Nov. 10, 1992. On Nov. 30, 1992 it was announced that a CIS peacekeeping force would be sent to Tajikistan. A state of emergency was imposed in Jan. 1993. A ceasefire was signed in 1996 and a peace agreement signed in June 1997.

MONETARY SYSTEM

100 Drams = 1 Somoni

REPUBLIC

DECIMAL COINAGE

KM# 2.1 5 DRAMS
2.0500 g., Brass Clad Steel, 16.5 mm. **Obv:** Crown within 1/2 star border **Rev:** Small value within design **Edge:** Plain

Date	Mintage	F	VF	XF	Unc	BU
2001(sp)	—	—	—	—	0.50	0.75
2001(sp) Proof	—	Value: 2.50				

KM# 2.2 5 DRAMS
2.0500 g., Brass Clad Steel, 16.5 mm. **Obv:** Crown with 1/2 star border **Rev:** Large value within design

Date	Mintage	F	VF	XF	Unc	BU
2006(sp)	—	—	—	—	0.75	1.25

KM# 3.1 10 DRAMS
2.4700 g., Brass Clad Steel, 17.5 mm. **Obv:** Crown within 1/2 star border **Rev:** Small value within design **Edge:** Plain

Date	Mintage	F	VF	XF	Unc	BU
2001(sp)	—	—	—	—	0.75	1.00
2001(sp) Proof	—	Value: 3.00				

KM# 3.2 10 DRAMS
2.4700 g., Brass Clad Steel, 17.5 mm. **Obv:** Crown within 1/2 star border **Rev:** Large value within design

Date	Mintage	F	VF	XF	Unc	BU
2006(sp)	—	—	—	—	1.00	1.50

KM# 4.1 20 DRAMS
2.7300 g., Brass Clad Steel, 18.5 mm. **Obv:** Crown within 1/2 star border **Rev:** Small value within design **Edge:** Plain

Date	Mintage	F	VF	XF	Unc	BU
2001(sp)	—	—	—	—	1.00	1.25
2001(sp) Proof	—	Value: 3.75				

KM# 4.2 20 DRAMS
2.7300 g., Brass Clad Steel, 18.5 mm. **Obv:** Crown within 1/2 star border **Rev:** Large value within design

Date	Mintage	F	VF	XF	Unc	BU
2006(sp)	2	—	—	—	1.50	2.00

KM# 5.1 25 DRAMS
2.8000 g., Brass, 19.1 mm. **Obv:** Crown within 1/2 star border **Rev:** Small value within design **Edge:** Plain

Date	Mintage	F	VF	XF	Unc	BU
2001(sp)	—	—	—	—	1.50	1.75
2001(sp) Proof	—	Value: 5.00				

KM# 5.2 25 DRAMS
2.8000 g., Brass, 19.1 mm. **Obv:** Crown within 1/2 star border **Rev:** Large value within design

Date	Mintage	F	VF	XF	Unc	BU
2006(sp)	—	—	—	—	1.75	2.50

KM# 6.1 50 DRAMS
3.5500 g., Brass, 21 mm. **Obv:** Crown within 1/2 star border **Rev:** Value within design **Edge:** Plain

Date	Mintage	F	VF	XF	Unc	BU
2001(sp)	—	—	—	—	2.00	3.00
2001(sp) Proof	—	Value: 7.00				

KM# 6.2 50 DRAMS
3.5500 g., Brass, 21 mm. **Obv:** Crown within 1/2 star border **Rev:** Large value within design

Date	Mintage	F	VF	XF	Unc	BU
2006(sp)	—	—	—	—	2.00	3.00

KM# 7 SOMONI
5.1500 g., Copper-Nickel-Zinc, 23.9 mm. **Obv:** King's bust 1/2 right **Rev:** Value **Edge:** Reeded and plain sections

Date	Mintage	F	VF	XF	Unc	BU
2001(sp)	—	—	—	—	3.50	5.00
2001(sp) Proof	—	Value: 12.00				

KM# 12 SOMONI
5.2100 g., Copper-Nickel-Zinc, 24 mm. **Subject:** Year of Aryan Civilization **Obv:** National arms above value **Rev:** Ancient archer in war chariot **Edge:** Segmented reeding

Date	Mintage	F	VF	XF	Unc	BU
2006(sp)	100,000	—	—	—	3.50	5.00

KM# 13 SOMONI
5.2100 g., Copper-Nickel-Zinc, 24 mm. **Subject:** Year of Aryan Civilization **Obv:** National arms above value **Rev:** Two busts left **Edge:** Segmented reeding

Date	Mintage	F	VF	XF	Unc	BU
2006(sp)	100,000	—	—	—	3.50	5.00

KM# 19 SOMONI
20.0000 g., 0.9250 Silver 0.5948 oz. ASW, 35 mm. **Subject:** Year of Aryan Civilization **Obv:** National arms above value **Rev:** Ancient archer in war chariot **Edge:** Segmented reeding

Date	Mintage	F	VF	XF	Unc	BU
2006(sp) Proof	1,500	Value: 60.00				

KM# 18 SOMONI
20.0000 g., 0.9250 Silver 0.5948 oz. ASW, 24 mm. **Subject:** Year of Aryan Civilization **Obv:** National arms above value **Rev:** Two busts left **Edge:** Segmented reeding

Date	Mintage	F	VF	XF	Unc	BU
2006 Proof	1,500	Value: 60.00				

KM# 16 SOMONI
5.2400 g., Copper-Nickel-Zinc, 23.95 mm. **Subject:** 800th Anniversary Birth of Jaloliddini Rumi **Obv:** Small arms above value in cartouche **Rev:** 1/2 length figure facing **Edge:** Segmented reeding

Date	Mintage	F	VF	XF	Unc	BU
2007	—	—	—	—	3.50	5.00

KM# 8 3 SOMONI
6.3200 g., Copper-Nickel-Zinc, 25.5 mm. **Obv:** National arms **Rev:** Crown above value within design **Edge:** Lettered

Date	Mintage	F	VF	XF	Unc	BU
2001(sp)	—	—	—	—	5.00	7.00
2001(sp) Proof	—	Value: 18.00				

KM# 10 3 SOMONI
6.3000 g., Bi-Metallic Copper-Nickel center in Brass ring, 25.5 mm. **Subject:** 80th Year - Dushanbe City **Obv:** Value below arms within circle **Rev:** Statue in arch within circle

Date	Mintage	F	VF	XF	Unc	BU
2004(sp)	—	—	—	—	6.50	9.00

KM# 10a 3 SOMONI
6.9800 g., 0.9250 Silver 0.2076 oz. ASW, 25.5 mm. **Subject:** 80th Anniversary of Republic **Obv:** Value below arms within circle **Rev:** Statue in arch within circle

Date	Mintage	F	VF	XF	Unc	BU
2004 Proof	1,000	Value: 75.00				

KM# 14 3 SOMONI
6.3000 g., Bi-Metallic Copper-Nickel center in Brass ring, 25.5 mm. **Subject:** 2700th Anniversary of Kulyab **Obv:** National arms above value **Rev:** Kulyab city arms **Edge:** Lettered

Date	Mintage	F	VF	XF	Unc	BU
2006(sp)	100,000	—	—	—	6.00	7.50

KM# 20 3 SOMONI
26.0000 g., 0.9250 Silver 0.7732 oz. ASW, 39 mm. **Subject:** 2700th Anniversary of Kulyab **Obv:** National arms above value **Rev:** Kulyab city arms

Date	Mintage	F	VF	XF	Unc	BU
2006(sp) Proof	2,000	Value: 70.00				

KM# 9 5 SOMONI
7.1000 g., Copper-Nickel-Zinc, 26.4 mm. **Obv:** Turbaned head right **Rev:** Crown above value within design **Edge:** Reeded and plain sections with a star

Date	Mintage	F	VF	XF	Unc	BU
2001(sp)	—	—	—	—	7.50	9.00
2001(sp) Proof	—	Value: 25.00				

KM# 11 5 SOMONI
6.9400 g., Bi-Metallic Copper-Nickel center in Brass ring, 26.5 mm. **Subject:** 10th Anniversary - Constitution **Obv:** Arms above value within circle **Rev:** Flag and book within circle **Edge:** Lettered

Date	Mintage	F	VF	XF	Unc	BU
2004(sp)	—	—	—	—	7.50	10.00

KM# 11a 5 SOMONI
8.5500 g., 0.9250 Silver 0.2543 oz. ASW, 26.5 mm. **Subject:** 10th Anniversary - Constitution **Obv:** Arms above value within circle **Rev:** Flag and book within circle

Date	Mintage	F	VF	XF	Unc	BU
2004 Proof	2,000	Value: 65.00				

KM# 15 5 SOMONI
7.0000 g., Bi-Metallic Copper-Nickel center in Brass ring, 26.5 mm. **Subject:** 15th Anniversary of Independence **Obv:** National arms above value **Rev:** Government building **Edge:** Lettered

Date	Mintage	F	VF	XF	Unc	BU
2006(sp)	100,000	—	—	—	7.50	10.00

KM# 21 5 SOMONI
34.0000 g., 0.9250 Silver 1.0111 oz. ASW, 42 mm. **Subject:** 15th Anniversary of Independence **Obv:** National arms above value **Rev:** Government building

Date	Mintage	F	VF	XF	Unc	BU
2006(sp) Proof	2,000	Value: 75.00				

KM# 17 5 SOMONI
7.0000 g., Bi-Metallic Copper-Nickel center in Brass ring, 26.5 mm. **Subject:** 1150th Anniversary founding of Persian (Tajik) literature by Abuabdullo Rudaki **Obv:** National arms above value **Rev:** Bust of Rudaki left, scroll, feather pen

Date	Mintage	F	VF	XF	Unc	BU
2008	—	—	—	—	7.50	10.00

KM# 22 5 SOMONI
34.0000 g., 0.9250 Silver 1.0111 oz. ASW, 42 mm. **Subject:** 1150 Anniversary founding of Persian Literature by Abuabdullo Rudaki **Obv:** National arms above value **Rev:** Bust of Rudaki left, scroll, feather pen

Date	Mintage	F	VF	XF	Unc	BU
2008(sp) Proof	1,000	Value: 115				

MINT SETS

KM#	Date	Mintage	Identification	Issue Price	Mkt Val
MS1	2001 (8)	—	KM#2.1-6.1, 7-9	—	30.00

PROOF SETS

KM#	Date	Mintage	Identification	Issue Price	Mkt Val
PS1	2001 (8)	—	KM#2.1-6.1, 7-9	—	80.00

TANZANIA

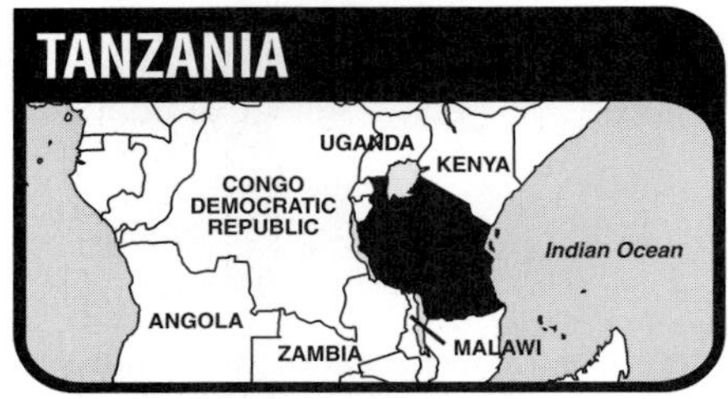

The United Republic of Tanzania, located on the east coast of Africa between Kenya and Mozambique, consists of Tanganyika and the islands of Zanzibar and Pemba. It has an area of 364,900 sq. mi. (945,090 sq. km.) and a population of *25.2 million. Capital: Dodoma. The chief exports are cotton, coffee, diamonds, sisal, cloves, petroleum products, and cashew nuts.

Tanzania is a member of the Commonwealth of Nations. The President is Chief of State.

REPUBLIC

STANDARD COINAGE

100 Senti = 1 Shilingi

KM# 56 500 SHILLINGS
31.4600 g., 0.9250 Silver 0.9356 oz. ASW, 38.6 mm. **Obv:** Arms with supporters above value **Rev:** African dhow **Edge:** Reeded

Date	Mintage	F	VF	XF	Unc	BU
2001 Proof	—	Value: 45.00				

THAILAND

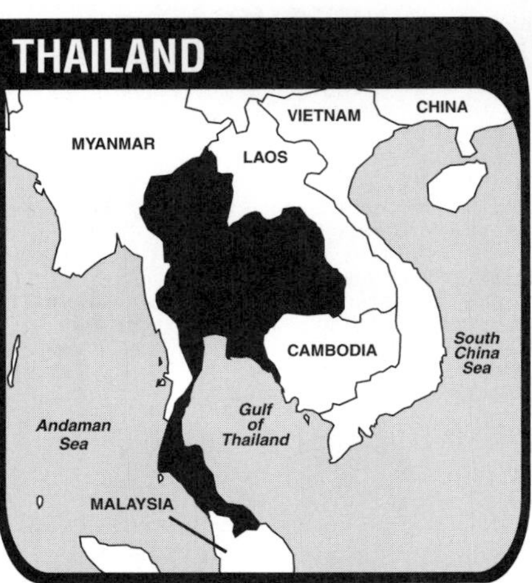

The Kingdom of Thailand (formerly Siam), a constitutional monarchy located in the center of mainland Southeast Asia between Burma and Laos, has an area of 198,457 sq. mi. (514,000 sq. km.) and a population of *55.5 million. Capital: Bangkok. The economy is based on agriculture and mining. Rubber, rice, teakwood, tin and tungsten are exported.

RULER
Rama IX (Phra Maha Bhumibol Adulyadej), 1946-

KINGDOM OF THAILAND
1939-

DECIMAL COINAGE

25 Satang = 1 Salung; 100 Satang = 1 Baht

Y# 186 SATANG
0.5000 g., Aluminum, 14.58 mm. **Ruler:** Rama IX **Obv:** Head left **Rev:** Steepled building **Edge:** Plain

Date	Mintage	F	VF	XF	Unc	BU
BE2544 (2001)	50,000	—	—	—	75.00	1.00
BE2546 (2003)	10,000	—	—	—	1.00	1.25
BE2547 (2004)	10,000	—	—	—	1.00	1.25
BE2548 (2005)	20,000	—	—	—	1.00	1.25
BE2549 (2006)	3,000	—	—	—	2.50	3.50
BE2550 (2007)	10,000	—	—	—	1.00	1.25

Y# 456 SATANG
0.5000 g., Aluminum, 15 mm. **Ruler:** Rama IX **Obv:** Bust left **Rev:** Steppled building

Date	Mintage	F	VF	XF	Unc	BU
BE2551 (2008)	10,000	—	—	—	1.00	1.25
BE2552 (2009)	10,000	—	—	—	1.00	1.25

Y# 208 5 SATANG
0.6000 g., Aluminum, 16 mm. **Ruler:** Rama IX **Obv:** Bust left **Rev:** Phra Patom Temple, Nakhon Pathom **Edge:** Plain

Date	Mintage	F	VF	XF	Unc	BU
BE2544 (2001)	50,000	—	—	—	0.80	1.10
BE2546 (2003)	10,000	—	—	—	1.25	1.50
BE2547 (2004)	10,000	—	—	—	1.25	1.50
BE2548 (2005)	20,000	—	—	—	1.25	1.50
BE2549 (2006)	3,000	—	—	—	3.00	4.00
BE2550 (2007)	10,000	—	—	—	1.25	1.50

Y# 457 5 SATANG
0.6000 g., Aluminum, 16 mm. **Ruler:** Rama IX **Obv:** Bust left **Rev:** Phra Patom Temple, Nakhon Pathom

Date	Mintage	F	VF	XF	Unc	BU
BE2551 (2008)	10,000	—	—	—	1.25	1.50
BE2552 (2009)	10,000	—	—	—	1.25	1.50

Y# 209 10 SATANG
0.8000 g., Aluminum, 17.5 mm. **Ruler:** Rama IX **Obv:** Young bust left **Rev:** Phra Tat Choeng Chum Temple, Sakon Nakhon Province **Edge:** Plain

Date	Mintage	F	VF	XF	Unc	BU
BE2544 (2001)	50,000	—	—	—	1.00	1.50
BE2546 (2003)	10,000	—	—	—	1.50	1.75
BE2547 (2004)	10,000	—	—	—	1.50	1.75
BE2548 (2005)	20,000	—	—	—	1.50	1.75
BE2549 (2006)	3,000	—	—	—	4.00	5.00
BE2550 (2007)	10,000	—	—	—	1.50	1.75

Y# 458 10 SATANG

0.8000 g., Aluminum, 17.5 mm. **Ruler:** Rama IX **Obv:** Bust left **Rev:** Phra That Choeng Chum temple, Sakon Nakhon Province

Date	Mintage	F	VF	XF	Unc	BU
BE2551 (2008)	—	—	—	—	1.50	1.75
BE2552 (2009)	—	—	—	—	1.50	1.75

Y# 187 25 SATANG = 1/4 BAHT

1.9000 g., Aluminum-Bronze, 15.93 mm. **Ruler:** Rama IX **Obv:** Head left **Rev:** Steepled building **Edge:** Reeded

Date	Mintage	F	VF	XF	Unc	BU
BE2544 (2001)	40,010,000	—	—	—	0.10	0.15
BE2545 (2002)	55,312,000	—	—	—	0.10	0.15
BE2546 (2003)	120,198,000	—	—	—	0.10	0.15
BE2547 (2004)	122,750,000	—	—	—	0.10	0.15
BE2548 (2005)	126,162,000	—	—	—	0.10	0.15
BE2549 (2006)	3,000	2.00	5.00	8.00	10.00	15.00
BE2550 (2007)	300,000,000	—	—	—	0.10	0.15
BE2551 (2008)	255,600	—	0.50	0.75	1.00	1.50

Y# 441 25 SATANG = 1/4 BAHT

1.9000 g., Copper Plated Steel, 15.93 mm. **Ruler:** Rama IX **Obv:** King's portrait

Date	Mintage	F	VF	XF	Unc	BU
BE2551 (2008)	93,600,000	—	—	—	0.10	0.15
BE2552 (2009)	196,400,000	—	—	—	0.10	0.15

Y# 203 50 SATANG = 1/2 BAHT

2.4000 g., Aluminum-Bronze, 18 mm. **Ruler:** Rama IX **Obv:** Head left **Rev:** Steepled building divides value

Date	Mintage	F	VF	XF	Unc	BU
BE2544 (2001)	105,660,000	—	—	—	0.10	0.15
BE2545 (2002)	109,594,000	—	—	—	0.10	0.15
BE2546 (2003)	101,210,000	—	—	—	0.10	0.15
BE2547 (2004)	36,396,000	—	—	—	0.10	0.15
BE2548 (2005)	109,520,000	—	—	—	0.10	0.15
BE2549 (2006)	141,603,000	—	—	—	0.10	0.15
BE2550 (2007)	45,300,000	—	—	—	0.10	0.15
BE2551 (2008)	40,922,709	—	—	—	0.10	0.15

Y# 442 50 SATANG = 1/2 BAHT

2.4000 g., Copper Plated Steel **Ruler:** Rama IX **Obv:** King's portrait

Date	Mintage	F	VF	XF	Unc	BU
BE2551 (2008)	78,600,000	—	—	—	0.10	0.15
BE2552 (2009)	171,400,000	—	—	—	0.10	0.15

Y# 183 BAHT

3.4500 g., Copper-Nickel, 20 mm. **Ruler:** Rama IX **Obv:** Head left **Rev:** Palace **Edge:** Reeded **Note:** Varieties exist.

Date	Mintage	F	VF	XF	Unc	BU
BE2544 (2001)	393,460,000	—	—	—	0.10	0.15
BE2545 (2002)	269,375,000	—	—	—	0.10	0.15
BE2546 (2003)	280,691,000	—	—	—	0.10	0.15
BE2547 (2004)	562,018,000	—	—	—	0.10	0.15
BE2548 (2005)	1,470,538,000	—	—	—	0.10	0.15
BE2549 (2006)	749,861,000	—	—	—	0.10	0.15
BE2550 (2007)	618,918,316	—	—	—	0.10	0.15
BE2551 (2008)	562,532,000	—	—	—	0.10	0.15

Y# 443 BAHT

3.0000 g., Nickel Plated Steel, 20 mm. **Ruler:** Rama IX **Obv:** King's portrait

Date	Mintage	F	VF	XF	Unc	BU
BE2551 (2008)	180,900,000	—	—	—	0.10	0.15
BE2552 (2009)	246,000,000	—	—	—	0.10	0.15

Y# 444 2 BAHT

4.4000 g., Nickel Plated Steel, 21.75 mm. **Ruler:** Rama IX

Date	Mintage	F	VF	XF	Unc	BU
BE2548 (2005)	4,000,000	—	—	0.15	0.40	0.50
BE2549 (2006)	128,000,000	—	—	—	0.20	0.25
BE2550 (2007)	267,977,600	—	—	—	0.20	0.25

Y# 445 2 BAHT

4.0000 g., Aluminum-Bronze, 21.75 mm. **Ruler:** Rama IX **Obv:** King's portrait

Date	Mintage	F	VF	XF	Unc	BU
BE2551 (2008)	16,692,000	—	—	0.15	0.30	0.40
BE2552 (2009)	205,591,000	—	—	—	0.20	0.25

Y# 219 5 BAHT

7.5000 g., Copper-Nickel Clad Copper, 24 mm. **Ruler:** Rama IX **Obv:** Head left **Rev:** Penjahwat **Edge:** Coarse reeding

Date	Mintage	F	VF	XF	Unc	BU
BE2544 (2001)	100,236,000	—	—	—	0.50	0.75
BE2545 (2002)	37,259,500	—	—	—	0.75	1.00
BE2546 (2003)	182,000	3.00	5.00	8.00	15.00	20.00
BE2547 (2004)	79,088,000	—	—	—	0.50	0.75
BE2548 (2005)	66,679,000	—	—	—	0.50	0.75
BE2549 (2006)	254,702,000	—	—	—	0.50	0.75
BE2550 (2007)	170,275,000	—	—	—	0.50	0.75
BE2551 (2008)	226,148,200	—	—	—	0.50	0.75

Y# 446 5 BAHT

6.0000 g., Copper-Nickel Clad Copper, 24 mm. **Ruler:** Rama IX **Obv:** King's portrait **Rev:** Temple top does not break legend **Edge:** Coarse Reeding

Date	Mintage	F	VF	XF	Unc	BU
BE2551 (2008)	17,020,000	—	—	—	0.50	0.75
BE2552 (2009)	289,303,000	—	—	—	0.50	0.75

Y# 373 10 BAHT

8.5000 g., Bi-Metallic Aluminum-Bronze center in Copper-Nickel ring, 26 mm. **Ruler:** Rama IX **Subject:** Department of Lands Centennial February 17 2444-2544 **Obv:** Conjoined busts facing divides circle **Rev:** Department seal within circle **Edge:** Segmented reeding

Date	Mintage	F	VF	XF	Unc	BU
BE2544 (2001)	3,000,000	—	—	—	2.50	3.00

Y# 227 10 BAHT

8.5000 g., Bi-Metallic Aluminum-Bronze center in Copper-Nickel ring, 26 mm. **Ruler:** Rama IX **Obv:** Head left within circle **Rev:** Temple of the Dawn within circle **Edge:** Segmented reeding **Note:** Varieties exist.

Date	Mintage	F	VF	XF	Unc	BU
BE2544 (2001)	2,060,000	—	—	—	2.25	6.00
BE2545 (2002)	61,180,000	—	—	—	2.25	2.75
BE2546 (2003)	49,263,000	—	—	—	2.25	2.75
BE2547 (2004)	35,591,000	—	—	—	2.25	2.50
BE2548 (2005)	108,271,000	—	—	—	2.00	2.50
BE2549 (2006)	109,703,000	—	—	—	2.00	2.50
BE2550 (2007)	161,897,000	—	—	—	2.00	2.50
BE2551 (2008)	209,800,000	—	—	—	2.00	2.50

Y# 387 10 BAHT

8.5500 g., Bi-Metallic Aluminum-Bronze center in Copper-Nickel ring, 26 mm. **Ruler:** Rama IX **Subject:** King's 75th Birthday December 5 **Obv:** Head left **Rev:** Royal crown in radiant oval **Edge:** Segmented reeding

Date	Mintage	F	VF	XF	Unc	BU
BE2545 (2002)	7,500,000	—	—	—	2.00	2.75

Y# 381 10 BAHT

8.5000 g., Bi-Metallic Aluminum-Bronze center in Copper-Nickel ring, 26 mm. **Ruler:** Rama IX **Subject:** Centennial of Irrigation Department June 13 **Obv:** Conjoined busts facing divides circle **Rev:** Department logo **Edge:** Segmented reeding

Date	Mintage	F	VF	XF	Unc	BU
BE2545 (2002)	3,000,000	—	—	—	2.00	2.75

Y# 382 10 BAHT

8.5000 g., Bi-Metallic Aluminum-Bronze center in Copper-Nickel ring, 26 mm. **Ruler:** Rama IX **Subject:** Department of Internal Trade 60th Anniversary May 5 **Obv:** Head left **Rev:** Department logo **Edge:** Segmented reeding

Date	Mintage	F	VF	XF	Unc	BU
BE2545 (2002)	3,000,000	—	—	—	2.00	2.75

Y# 383 10 BAHT

8.5000 g., Bi-Metallic Aluminum-Bronze center in Copper-Nickel ring, 26 mm. **Ruler:** Rama IX **Subject:** State Highway Department 90th Anniversary April 1 **Obv:** Conjoined busts facing divides circle **Rev:** Department logo **Edge:** Segmented reeding

Date	Mintage	F	VF	XF	Unc	BU
BE2545 (2002)	3,000,000	—	—	—	2.00	2.75

Y# 384 10 BAHT

8.5000 g., Bi-Metallic Aluminum-Bronze center in Copper-Nickel ring, 26 mm. **Ruler:** Rama IX **Subject:** Vajira Hospital 90th Anniversary January 2 **Obv:** Conjoined busts facing divides circle **Rev:** Hospital logo **Edge:** Segmented reeding

Date	Mintage	F	VF	XF	Unc	BU
BE2545 (2002)	3,500,000	—	—	—	2.00	2.75

Y# 385 10 BAHT

8.5000 g., Bi-Metallic Aluminum-Bronze center in Copper-Nickel ring, 26 mm. **Ruler:** Rama IX **Subject:** 20th World Scouting Jamboree **Obv:** Rama IX wearing a scouting uniform **Rev:** Jamboree log **Edge:** Segmented reeding

Date	Mintage	F	VF	XF	Unc	BU
BE2546 (2003)	3,000,000	—	—	—	2.00	2.75

Y# 405 10 BAHT

8.5000 g., Bi-Metallic Aluminum-Bronze center in Copper-Nickel ring, 26 mm. **Ruler:** Rama IX **Subject:** "CITES COP" **Obv:** Bust 3/4 left within circle **Rev:** "CITES" logo **Edge:** Segmented reeding

Date	Mintage	F	VF	XF	Unc	BU
ND(2003)	Est. 3,000,000	—	—	—	2.00	2.75

Y# 400 10 BAHT

8.5000 g., Bi-Metallic Aluminumn-Bronze center in Copper-

Nickel ring, 26 mm. **Ruler:** Rama IX **Obv:** Head left **Rev:** APEC logo **Edge:** Segmented reeding

Date	Mintage	F	VF	XF	Unc	BU
BE2546-2003	1,000,000	—	—	—	2.25	3.00

Y# 409 10 BAHT
8.5000 g., Bi-Metallic Aluminum-Bronze center in Copper-Nickel ring, 26 mm. **Ruler:** Rama IX **Subject:** 150th Anniversary of King Rama V **Obv:** Bust of Rama V left **Rev:** Royal crown **Edge:** Segmented reeding

Date	Mintage	F	VF	XF	Unc	BU
BE2546 (2003)	3,600,000	—	—	—	1.80	2.50

Y# 391 10 BAHT
8.5000 g., Bi-Metallic Aluminum-Bronze center in Copper-Nickel ring, 26 mm. **Ruler:** Rama IX **Subject:** Inspector General's Department Centennial May 6 **Obv:** Head left within circle **Rev:** Department seal within circle and design **Edge:** Segmented reeding

Date	Mintage	F	VF	XF	Unc	BU
BE2546 (2003)	3,000,000	—	—	—	1.75	2.50

Y# 392 10 BAHT
8.5000 g., Bi-Metallic Aluminum-Bronze center in Copper-Nickel ring, 26 mm. **Ruler:** Rama IX **Subject:** 80th Birthday of Princess May 6 **Obv:** Bust 1/4 right **Rev:** Crowned emblem and value **Edge:** Alternating reeded and plain **Note:** This is the king's sister.

Date	Mintage	F	VF	XF	Unc	BU
BE2546 (2003)	2,000,000	—	—	—	1.75	2.50

Y# 396 10 BAHT
8.5000 g., Bi-Metallic Aluminum-Bronze center in Copper-Nickel ring, 26 mm. **Ruler:** Rama IX **Subject:** 90th Anniversary of the Government Savings Bank April 1 **Obv:** Uniformed bust facing within circle **Rev:** Bank emblem **Edge:** Segmented reeding

Date	Mintage	F	VF	XF	Unc	BU
BE2546 (2003)	2,000,000	—	—	—	2.00	2.75

Y# 411 10 BAHT
8.5000 g., Bi-Metallic Aluminum-Bornze center in Copper-Nickel, 26 mm. **Ruler:** Rama IX **Subject:** 70th Anniversary Royal institute Board **Obv:** 1/2 length civilian busts of 2 kings facing **Rev:** Royal Scholar Institute seal **Edge:** Segmented reeding

Date	Mintage	F	VF	XF	Unc	BU
BE2547 (2004)	2,000,000	—	—	—	1.80	2.50

Y# 412 10 BAHT
8.5000 g., Bi-Metallic Aluminum-Bronze center in Copper-Nickel ring, 26 mm. **Ruler:** Rama IX **Subject:** Queen's 70th Birthday **Obv:** Bust of queen facing 3/4 left **Rev:** Royal seal **Edge:** Segmented reeding

Date	Mintage	F	VF	XF	Unc	BU
BE2547 (2004)	6,000,000	—	—	—	1.80	2.50

Y# 413 10 BAHT
8.5000 g., Bi-Metallic Aluminum-Bronze center in Copper-Nickel ring, 26 mm. **Ruler:** Rama IX **Subject:** World IUCN Conservation Congress **Obv:** Civilian bust 3/4 right **Rev:** IUCN logo **Edge:** Segmented reeding

Date	Mintage	F	VF	XF	Unc	BU
BE2547 (2004)	Est. 3,000,000	—	—	—	1.80	2.50

Y# 414 10 BAHT
8.5000 g., Bi-Metallic Aluminum-Bronze center in Copper-Nickel ring, 26 mm. **Ruler:** Rama IX **Subject:** Anti Drug Campaign **Obv:** Civilian bust left **Rev:** Tear drop shaped logo **Edge:** Segmented reeding

Date	Mintage	F	VF	XF	Unc	BU
BE2547 (2004)	3,000,000	—	—	—	1.80	2.50

Y# 415 10 BAHT
8.5000 g., Bi-Metallic Aluminum-Bronze center in Copper-Nickel ring, 26 mm. **Ruler:** Rama IX **Subject:** Bicentennial of King Rama IV **Obv:** Bust of Rama IV 3/4 right **Rev:** Royal seal **Edge:** Segmented reeding

Date	Mintage	F	VF	XF	Unc	BU
BE2547 (2004)	3,500,000	—	—	—	1.80	2.50

Y# 410 10 BAHT
8.5000 g., Bi-Metallic Aluminum-Bronze center in Copper-Nickel ring, 26 mm. **Subject:** 70th Anniversary of Thammasat University **Obv:** Civilian bust 3/4 left **Rev:** Thammasat University seal **Edge:** Segmented reeding

Date	Mintage	F	VF	XF	Unc	BU
BE2547 (2004)	3,000,000	—	—	—	1.80	2.50

Y# 416 10 BAHT
8.5000 g., Bi-Metallic Aluminum-Bronze center in Copper-Nickel ring, 26 mm. **Ruler:** Rama IX **Subject:** 100th Anniversary of Army Transportation Corp **Obv:** 2 king's military busts left **Rev:** Steering wheel, badge at center **Edge:** Segmented reeding

Date	Mintage	F	VF	XF	Unc	BU
BE2548 (2005)	3,000,000	—	—	—	1.80	2.50

Y# 402 10 BAHT
8.5000 g., Bi-Metallic Aluminum-Bronze center in Copper-Nickel ring, 26 mm. **Ruler:** Rama IX **Subject:** Department of the Treasury, 72nd Anniversary **Obv:** Bust 1/4 left within circle **Rev:** Treasury Department seal within circle **Edge:** Segmented reeding

Date	Mintage	F	VF	XF	Unc	BU
BE2548 (2005)	3,000,000	—	—	—	2.50	3.25

Y# 418 10 BAHT
8.5000 g., Bi-Metallic Aluminum-Bronze center in Copper-Nickel ring, 26 mm. **Ruler:** Rama IX **Subject:** 25th Asia-Pacific Scout Jamboree **Obv:** Rama IX in scout uniform 3/4 left **Rev:** Logo **Edge:** Segmented reeding

Date	Mintage	F	VF	XF	Unc	BU
BE2548 (2005)	3,000,000	—	—	—	1.80	2.50

Y# 424 10 BAHT
8.4300 g., Bi-Metallic Brass center in Copper-Nickel ring, 25.98 mm. **Ruler:** Rama IX **Subject:** 150th Birthday of Prince Jaturon Ratsamee **Obv:** Bust of Prince facing 3/4 right **Rev:** Radiant badge **Edge:** Segmented reeding

Date	Mintage	F	VF	XF	Unc	BU
BE2549(2006)	—	—	—	—	2.50	3.25

Y# 417 10 BAHT
8.5000 g., Bi-Metallic Aluminum-Bronze center in Copper-Nickel ring, 26 mm. **Ruler:** Rama IX **Subject:** Prince Royal Cradle Ceremony **Obv:** Prince's baby head 3/4 left **Rev:** 4-line inscription **Edge:** Segmented reeding

Date	Mintage	F	VF	XF	Unc	BU
BE2549 (2006)	3,000,000	—	—	—	1.80	2.50

Y# 406 10 BAHT
8.5000 g., Bi-Metallic Aluminum-Bronze center in Copper-Nickel ring, 26 mm. **Ruler:** Rama IX **Subject:** 60th Anniversary of Reign **Obv:** Bust 1/4 left within circle **Rev:** Royal Crown on display **Edge:** Segmented reeding

Date	Mintage	F	VF	XF	Unc	BU
BE2549 (2006)	16,000,000	—	—	—	2.50	3.25

Y# 428 10 BAHT
8.5000 g., Bi-Metallic Aluminum-Bronze center in Copper-Nickel ring, 26 mm. **Ruler:** Rama IX **Subject:** 72nd Anniversary

Secretariat of the Cabinet **Obv:** Military bust 3/4 right **Rev:** Royal Cabinet seal **Edge:** Segmented reeding **Note:** Minted in 2005 but released in 2006.

Date	Mintage	F	VF	XF	Unc	BU
BE2547 (2004)	Est. 3,000,000	—	—	—	1.80	2.50

Y# 429 10 BAHT

8.5000 g., Bi-Metallic Aluminum-Bronze center in Copper-Nickel ring., 26 mm. **Ruler:** Rama IX **Subject:** Princess Petcharat 80th birthday **Obv:** Bust of Princess facing **Rev:** Royal seal of Princess **Edge:** Segmented reeding

Date	Mintage	F	VF	XF	Unc	BU
BE2549 (2006)	1,000,000	—	—	—	2.25	2.75

Y# 430 10 BAHT

8.5000 g., Bi-Metallic Aluminum-Bronze center in Copper-Nickel ring, 26 mm. **Ruler:** Rama IX **Subject:** 130th Anniversary Budget Inspection Department **Obv:** Conjoined kings' busts left **Rev:** Ornate scale **Edge:** Segmented reeding

Date	Mintage	F	VF	XF	Unc	BU
BE2549 (2006)	Est. 3,000,000	—	—	—	1.80	2.50

Y# 431 10 BAHT

8.5000 g., Bi-Metallic Aluminum-Bronze center in Copper-Nickel ring, 26 mm. **Ruler:** Rama IX **Subject:** 60th Anniversary of reign **Obv:** Bust 3/4 right **Rev:** Royal throne **Edge:** Segmented reeding

Date	Mintage	F	VF	XF	Unc	BU
BE2549 (2006)	16,000,000	—	—	—	1.80	2.50

Y# 432 10 BAHT

8.5000 g., Bi-Metallic Aluminum-Bronze center in Copper-Nickel ring, 26 mm. **Ruler:** Rama IX **Subject:** Centenary of Department of Judge Advocate General **Obv:** Conjoined kings' busts left **Rev:** Military scale emblem **Edge:** Segmented reeding

Date	Mintage	F	VF	XF	Unc	BU
BE2549 (2006)	3,000,000	—	—	—	1.80	2.50

Y# 425 10 BAHT

8.5000 g., Bi-Metallic Aluminum-Bronze center in Copper-Nickel ring, 26 mm. **Ruler:** Rama IX **Subject:** Centenary of Royal Mounted Army **Obv:** Conjoined kings' busts left **Rev:** Royal crown above emblem **Edge:** Segmented reeding

Date	Mintage	F	VF	XF	Unc	BU
BE2550 (2007)	3,000,000	—	—	—	1.75	2.50

Y# 426 10 BAHT

8.5000 g., Bi-Metallic Aluminum-Bronze center in Copper-Nickel ring, 26 mm. **Ruler:** Rama IX **Subject:** Centenary of 1st Thai Commercial Bank **Obv:** Conjoined kings' busts left **Rev:** Garuda Bird **Edge:** Segmented reeding

Date	Mintage	F	VF	XF	Unc	BU
BE2550 (2007)		—	—	—	1.75	2.50

Y# 433 10 BAHT

8.5000 g., Bi-Metallic Aluminum-Bronze center in Copper-Nickel ring, 26 mm. **Ruler:** Rama IX **Subject:** Queen's WHO Food Safety Award **Obv:** Queen's bust 3/4 right **Rev:** WHO emblem at upper left of inscription in sprays **Edge:** Segmented reeding

Date	Mintage	F	VF	XF	Unc	BU
BE2550 (2007)	5,000,000	—	—	—	1.75	2.50

Y# 434 10 BAHT

8.5000 g., Bi-Metallic Aluminum-Bronze center in Copper-Nickel ring, 26 mm. **Ruler:** Rama IX **Subject:** 50th Anniversary Thai Medical Technology **Obv:** Robed bust 3/4 right **Rev:** Oval medical seal **Edge:** Segmented reeding

Date	Mintage	F	VF	XF	Unc	BU
BE2550 (2007)	3,000,000	—	—	—	1.75	2.50

Y# 435 10 BAHT

8.5000 g., Bi-Metallic Aluminum-Bronze center in Copper-Nickel ring, 26 mm. **Ruler:** Rama IX **Subject:** UNIVERSIADE - World University Games **Obv:** Civilian bust 3/4 right **Rev:** Games logo **Edge:** Segmented reeding

Date	Mintage	F	VF	XF	Unc	BU
BE2550 (2007)	5,000,000	—	—	—	1.75	2.50

Y# 436 10 BAHT

8.5000 g., Bi-Metallic Aluminum-Bronze center in Copper-Nickel ring, 26 mm. **Ruler:** Rama IX **Subject:** Queen's 75th birthday **Obv:** Bust of Queen wearing tiara 3/4 left **Rev:** Queen's Royal seal **Edge:** Segmented reeding

Date	Mintage	F	VF	XF	Unc	BU
BE2550 (2007)	7,500,000	—	—	—	1.75	2.50

Y# 437 10 BAHT

8.5000 g., Bi-Metallic Aluminum-Bronze center in Copper-Nickel ring, 26 mm. **Ruler:** Rama IX **Subject:** IASAJ Conference - Bangkok **Obv:** Civilian bust 3/4 left **Rev:** Oval seal with scale above conference logo **Edge:** Segmented reeding

Date	Mintage	F	VF	XF	Unc	BU
BE2550 (2007)	3,000,000	—	—	—	1.75	2.50

Y# 438 10 BAHT

8.5000 g., Bi-Metallic Aluminum-Bronze center in Copper-Nickel ring, 26 mm. **Ruler:** Rama IX **Subject:** King's 80th birthday **Obv:** Royal bust 3/4 left **Rev:** Royal seal **Edge:** Segmented reeding

Date	Mintage	F	VF	XF	Unc	BU
BE2550 (2007)	18,000,000	—	—	—	1.75	2.50

Y# 439 10 BAHT

8.5000 g., Bi-Metallic Aluminum-Bronze center in Copper-Nickel ring, 26 mm. **Ruler:** Rama IX **Subject:** 24th SEA Games **Obv:** Civilian bust 3/4 left **Rev:** Games logo above inscription **Edge:** Segmented reeding

Date	Mintage	F	VF	XF	Unc	BU
BE2550 (2007)	3,000,000	—	—	—	1.75	2.50

Y# 440 10 BAHT

8.5000 g., Bi-Metallic Aluminum-Bronze center in Copper-Nickel ring, 26 mm. **Ruler:** Rama IX **Subject:** 120th Anniversary Siriraj Hospital **Obv:** Conjoined kings' busts right **Rev:** Royal hospital's seal **Edge:** Segmented reeding

Date	Mintage	F	VF	XF	Unc	BU
BE2550 (2007)	—	—	—	—	1.75	2.50

Y# 449 10 BAHT

8.5000 g., Bi-Metallic Brass center in Copper-Nickel ring, 26 mm. **Ruler:** Rama IX **Subject:** King's 80th Birthday **Obv:** Bust left

Date	Mintage	F	VF	XF	Unc	BU
2007	18,000,000	—	—	—	1.75	2.50

Y# 459 10 BAHT

8.5400 g., Bi-Metallic Aluninum-Bronze center in Copper-Nickel ring, 26 mm. **Ruler:** Rama IX **Obv:** Head left **Rev:** Temple of the Dawn

Date	Mintage	F	VF	XF	Unc	BU
BE2551 (2008)	16,750,000	—	—	—	2.00	2.75
BE2552 (2009)	41,657,733	—	—	—	2.00	2.75

Y# 460 10 BAHT

8.5000 g., Bi-Metallic Aluminum-Bronze center in Copper-Nickel ring, 26 mm. **Ruler:** Rama IX **Subject:** Thai Postal Service, 125th Anniversary **Obv:** Conjoined busts left **Rev:** Scroll with legend

Date	Mintage	F	VF	XF	Unc	BU
BE2551 (2008)	3,000,000	—	—	—	2.00	2.75

Y# 470 10 BAHT

8.5000 g., Bi-Metallic Aluminum-Bronze center in Copper-Nickel ring **Ruler:** Rama IX **Subject:** Siriraj Hospital, 120th Anniversary **Obv:** Conjoined head right

Date	Mintage	F	VF	XF	Unc	BU
BE2551 (2008)	3,000,000	—	—	—	2.00	2.75

Y# 461 10 BAHT

8.5000 g., Bi-Metallic Aluminumn-Bronze center in Copper-Nickel ring, 26 mm. **Ruler:** Rama IX **Subject:** National Research Council, 50th Anniversary **Obv:** Bust left **Rev:** Neculeus surrounded by electrons

Date	Mintage	F	VF	XF	Unc	BU
BE2552 (2009)	3,000,000	—	—	—	2.00	2.75

Y# 374 20 BAHT

15.0000 g., Copper-Nickel, 32 mm. **Ruler:** Rama IX **Subject:** Chulalongkorn University 84th Anniversary March 26 **Obv:** Three conjoined busts right **Rev:** University emblem divides value **Edge:** Reeded

Date	Mintage	F	VF	XF	Unc	BU
BE2544 (2001)	800,040	—	—	—	3.50	5.00
BE2544 (2001) Proof	5,340	Value: 22.00				

Y# 375 20 BAHT

15.0000 g., Copper-Nickel, 32 mm. **Ruler:** Rama IX **Subject:** Civil Service Comission 72nd Anniversary April 1 **Obv:** Conjoined busts left **Rev:** Civil service emblem divides value **Edge:** Reeded

Date	Mintage	F	VF	XF	Unc	BU
BE2544 (2001)	500,000	—	—	—	3.50	5.00
BE2544 (2001) Proof	3,340	Value: 25.00				

Y# 393 20 BAHT

15.0000 g., Copper-Nickel, 32 mm. **Ruler:** Rama IX **Subject:** 80th Birthday of Princess Calyani Vadhani **Obv:** Bust 1/4 right **Rev:** Crowned emblem and value **Edge:** Reeded

Date	Mintage	F	VF	XF	Unc	BU
BE2546 (2003)	350,000	—	—	—	3.50	5.00
BE2546 (2003) Proof	3,200	Value: 17.50				

Y# 419 20 BAHT

15.0000 g., Copper-Nickel, 32 mm. **Ruler:** Rama IX **Subject:** 50th Anniversary of Audit Department of Cooperatives **Edge:** Reeded

Date	Mintage	F	VF	XF	Unc	BU
BE2545 (2002)	300,000	—	—	—	3.50	5.00
BE2545 (2002) Proof	3,000	Value: 17.50				

Y# 386 20 BAHT

15.0000 g., Copper-Nickel, 32 mm. **Ruler:** Rama IX **Subject:** Centennial of Thai Banknotes 2445-2545 **Obv:** Conjoined busts left **Rev:** Coat of arms in center of seal **Edge:** Reeded

Date	Mintage	F	VF	XF	Unc	BU
BE2545 (2002)	1,000,000	—	—	—	3.50	5.00
BE2545 (2002) Proof	40,000	Value: 17.50				

Y# 397 20 BAHT

15.0000 g., Copper-Nickel, 32 mm. **Ruler:** Rama IX **Subject:** Centennial of the National Police April 19 **Obv:** Conjoined busts left **Rev:** National Police emblem above banner **Edge:** Reeded

Date	Mintage	F	VF	XF	Unc	BU
BE2545 (2002)	600,000	—	—	—	3.50	5.00
BE2545 (2002) Proof	5,000	Value: 17.50				

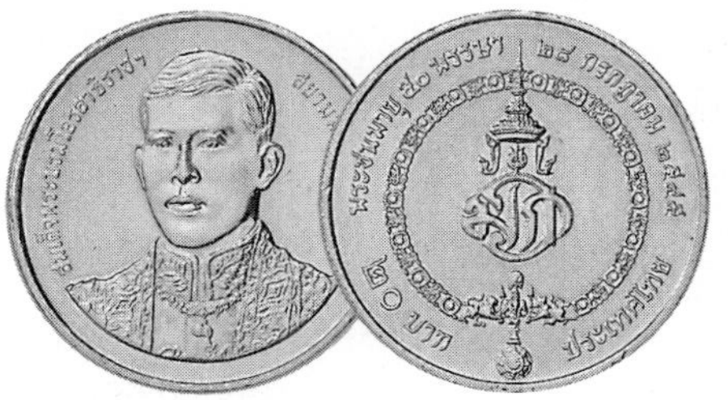

Y# 398 20 BAHT

15.0000 g., Copper-Nickel, 32 mm. **Ruler:** Rama IX **Subject:** 50th Birthday of the Crown Prince July 28 **Obv:** Bust facing **Rev:** Crowned monogram **Edge:** Reeded

Date	Mintage	F	VF	XF	Unc	BU
BE2545 (2002)	300,000	—	—	—	3.50	5.00
BE2545 (2002) Proof	5,000	Value: 40.00				

Y# 388 20 BAHT

15.0000 g., Copper-Nickel, 32 mm. **Ruler:** Rama IX **Subject:** King's 75th Birthday December 5 **Obv:** Head left **Rev:** Royal crown in radiant oval **Edge:** Reeded **Note:** Minted and released in 2003.

Date	Mintage	F	VF	XF	Unc	BU
BE2545(2002)	1,200,000	—	—	—	3.50	5.00
BE2545(2002) Proof	16,000	Value: 17.50				

Y# 420 20 BAHT

15.0000 g., Copper-Nickel, 32 mm. **Ruler:** Rama IX **Subject:** 150th Anniversary, Birth of Rama V **Edge:** Reeded

Date	Mintage	F	VF	XF	Unc	BU
BE2546 (2003)	1,000,000	—	—	—	3.50	5.00
BE2546 (2003) Proof	26,000	Value: 18.00				

Y# 421 20 BAHT

15.0000 g., Copper-Nickel, 32 mm. **Ruler:** Rama IX **Subject:** Rama IV, 200th Anniversary of Birth **Obv:** King Rama IV **Edge:** Reeded

Date	Mintage	F	VF	XF	Unc	BU
BE2547 (2004)	500,000	—	—	—	3.50	5.00
BE2547 (2004)	10,500	Value: 20.00				

Y# 422 20 BAHT

15.0000 g., Copper-Nickel, 32 mm. **Ruler:** Rama IX **Subject:** 72nd Anniversary of Queen's Birthday **Obv:** Head of Queen facing left **Edge:** Reeded

Date	Mintage	F	VF	XF	Unc	BU
BE2547 (2004)	600,000	—	—	—	3.50	5.00
BE2547 (2004)	10,000	Value: 20.00				

Y# 462 20 BAHT

15.0000 g., Copper-Nickel, 32 mm. **Ruler:** Rama IX **Subject:** Rama IV, 200th Anniversary of Birth **Obv:** Bust 3/4 right **Rev:** Horizontal oval Royal seal

Date	Mintage	F	VF	XF	Unc	BU
BE2547 (2004)	—	—	—	—	4.00	6.00
BE2547 (2004) Proof	—	Value: 15.00				

Y# 423 20 BAHT

15.0000 g., Copper-Nickel, 32 mm. **Ruler:** Rama IX **Subject:** 50th Birthday of Princess Sirinahorn **Obv:** Head of Princess facing right **Edge:** Reeded

Date	Mintage	F	VF	XF	Unc	BU
BE2548 (2005)	350,000	—	—	—	4.00	6.00
BE2548 (2005) Proof	12,000	Value: 20.00				

Y# 403 20 BAHT

15.0000 g., Copper-Nickel, 32 mm. **Ruler:** Rama IX **Subject:** Department of the Treasury, 72nd Anniversary **Obv:** Bust 1/4 left **Rev:** Treasury Department seal **Edge:** Reeded

Date	Mintage	F	VF	XF	Unc	BU
BE2548 (2005)	300,000	—	—	—	4.00	6.00
BE2548 (2005) Proof	3,000	Value: 25.00				

Y# 471 20 BAHT

15.0000 g., Copper-Nickel, 32 mm. **Ruler:** Rama IX **Subject:** Centennial of the National Library **Obv:** Two busts, one facing left, one right **Rev:** Circle with inscription

Date	Mintage	F	VF	XF	Unc	BU
BE2548 (2005)	200,000	—	—	—	3.50	5.00

Y# 472 20 BAHT

15.0000 g., Copper-Nickel, 32 mm. **Ruler:** Rama IX **Subject:** Princess rattana, 80th birthday **Obv:** Facing portrait **Note:** Minted and released in 2006.

Date	Mintage	F	VF	XF	Unc	BU
BE2548 (2005)	200,000	—	—	—	3.50	5.00

Y# 474 20 BAHT

15.0000 g., Copper-Nickel, 32 mm. **Ruler:** Rama IX **Subject:** UN Development Program Award **Obv:** Head right **Rev:** Chalice on stand with legends

Date	Mintage	F	VF	XF	Unc	BU
BE2549 (2006)	2,200,000	—	—	—	3.50	5.00

Y# 407 20 BAHT

15.0000 g., Copper-Nickel, 32 mm. **Ruler:** Rama IX **Subject:** 60th Anniversary of Reign **Obv:** Head left **Rev:** Royal Crown on display **Edge:** Reeded

Date	Mintage	F	VF	XF	Unc	BU
BE2549 (2006)	5,600,000	—	—	—	4.00	6.00
BE2549 (2006) Proof	96,000	Value: 18.50				

Y# 473 20 BAHT

15.0000 g., Copper-Nickel, 32 mm. **Ruler:** Rama IX **Subject:** Royal Artificial Rain, 50th Anniversary **Obv:** Statue of King holding book and pencil **Rev:** Artificial rain wing symbol surrounded by rays and legend

Date	Mintage	F	VF	XF	Unc	BU
BE2549 (2006)	3,000,000	—	—	—	3.50	5.00

Y# 479 20 BAHT

21.0000 g., Copper-Nickel, 36 mm. **Ruler:** Rama IX **Subject:** Technological Research **Obv:** Child's head right **Rev:** Small chicken at left, legends

Date	Mintage	F	VF	XF	Unc	BU
BE2549 (2006)	450,000	—	—	—	4.50	6.00

Y# 450 20 BAHT

15.0000 g., Copper-Nickel, 32 mm. **Ruler:** Rama IX **Subject:** King's 80th Birthday **Obv:** Bust left

Date	Mintage	F	VF	XF	Unc	BU
2007	5,800,000	—	—	—	3.50	5.00
2007 Proof	95,000	Value: 15.00				

Y# 453 20 BAHT

15.0000 g., Copper-Nickel **Ruler:** Rama IX **Subject:** Queen's 75th Birthday **Obv:** Bust left **Shape:** 32

Date	Mintage	F	VF	XF	Unc	BU
2007	600,000	—	—	—	3.50	5.00
2007 Proof	12,000	Value: 18.00				

Y# 475 20 BAHT

15.0000 g., Copper-Nickel, 32 mm. **Ruler:** Rama IX **Subject:** Princess Galyana Vadhana, 84th birthday **Obv:** Head left

Date	Mintage	F	VF	XF	Unc	BU
BE2550 (2007)	700,000	—	—	—	3.50	5.00
BE2550 (2007) Proof	8,400	Value: 18.00				

Y# 476 20 BAHT

15.0000 g., Copper-Nickel, 32 mm. **Ruler:** Rama IX **Subject:** Father of Thai heritage conservation **Obv:** Head left **Note:** Minted and released in 2008.

Date	Mintage	F	VF	XF	Unc	BU
BE2550 (2007)	500,000	—	—	—	3.50	5.00

Y# 464 20 BAHT

15.0000 g., Copper-Nickel, 32 mm. **Ruler:** Rama IX **Subject:** Princess Mother, 9th Cycle, (108th Birthday) **Obv:** Portrait facing **Rev:** Emblem of Princess Mother Srinakarindra

Date	Mintage	F	VF	XF	Unc	BU
BE2551 (2008)	450,000	—	—	—	3.50	5.00
BE2551 (2008) Proof	5,500	Value: 2,000				

Y# 477 20 BAHT

15.0000 g., Copper-Nickel, 32 mm. **Ruler:** Rama IX **Subject:** WIPO award **Obv:** Head left **Rev:** Award medal and legend

Date	Mintage	F	VF	XF	Unc	BU
BE2551 (2008)	500,000	—	—	—	3.50	5.00

Y# 404 50 BAHT

21.0000 g., Copper-Nickel, 36 mm. **Ruler:** Rama IX **Subject:** Air Force 50th Anniversary May 7 **Obv:** Uniformed bust facing **Rev:** Crowned wings within 3/4 wreath **Edge:** Reeded

Date	Mintage	F	VF	XF	Unc	BU
BE2546 (2003)	250,000	—	—	—	12.50	15.00

Y# 478 50 BAHT

21.0000 g., Copper-Nickel, 36 mm. **Ruler:** Rama IX **Subject:** National Intelligence Agency, 50th Anniversary **Obv:** Head right **Rev:** Emblem of the Intelligence Agency **Note:** Minted and released in 2003.

Date	Mintage	F	VF	XF	Unc	BU
BE2547 (2004)	200,000	—	—	—	4.50	6.00

Y# 480 50 BAHT

21.0000 g., Copper-Nickel, 36 mm. **Ruler:** Rama IX **Subject:** Royal School, 100th Anniversary **Obv:** Conjoined heads left

Date	Mintage	F	VF	XF	Unc	BU
BE2549 (2006)	200,000	—	—	—	4.50	6.00

Y# 389 600 BAHT
22.1500 g., 0.9250 Silver 0.6587 oz. ASW, 35 mm. **Ruler:** Rama IX **Subject:** King's 75th Birthday **Obv:** King's portrait **Rev:** Royal crown in radiant oval **Edge:** Reeded

Date	Mintage	F	VF	XF	Unc	BU
BE2545 (2002)	14,000	—	—	—	30.00	35.00
BE2545 (2002) Proof	3,000	Value: 70.00				

Y# 481 600 BAHT
22.0000 g., 0.9250 Silver 0.6542 oz. ASW, 35 mm. **Ruler:** Rama IX **Subject:** Crown Prince, 50th Birthday **Obv:** Crown Prince bust 1/4 facing left **Rev:** Crowned monogram

Date	Mintage	F	VF	XF	Unc	BU
BE2545 (2002)	5,000	—	—	—	50.00	55.00
BE2545 (2002) Proof	1,000	Value: 95.00				

Y# 394 600 BAHT
22.1500 g., 0.9250 Silver 0.6587 oz. ASW, 35 mm. **Ruler:** Rama IX **Subject:** 80th Birthday of Princess Calgani Valbani **Obv:** Bust half right **Rev:** Crowned emblem and value **Edge:** Reeded

Date	Mintage	F	VF	XF	Unc	BU
BE2546 (2003)	4,500	—	—	—	45.00	50.00
BE2546 (2003) Proof	1,000	Value: 95.00				

Y# 482 600 BAHT
22.0000 g., 0.9250 Silver 0.6542 oz. ASW, 35 mm. **Ruler:** Rama IX. **Subject:** Rama V. 150th Anniversary of Birth **Obv:** Rama V bust left **Rev:** Royal Crown

Date	Mintage	F	VF	XF	Unc	BU
BE2546 (2003) 15000	—	—	—	—	35.00	40.00
BE2546 (2003) 4600	—	Value: 85.00				

Y# 401 600 BAHT
22.1500 g., 0.9250 Silver 0.6587 oz. ASW, 35 mm. **Ruler:** Rama IX **Subject:** Queen's 72nd Birthday **Obv:** Crowned monogram **Rev:** Crowned bust of Queen 3/4 right **Edge:** Reeded

Date	Mintage	F	VF	XF	Unc	BU
BE2547 (2004)	12,000	—	—	—	35.00	40.00
BE2547(2004) Proof	3,700	Value: 85.00				

Y# 463 600 BAHT
22.1500 g., 0.9250 Silver 0.6587 oz. ASW, 35 mm. **Ruler:** Rama IX **Subject:** King Rama IV, 200th Anniversary of Birth **Obv:** Bust right **Rev:** Horizontal oval

Date	Mintage	F	VF	XF	Unc	BU
BE2547 (2004)	12,000	—	—	—	45.00	60.00
BE2547 (2004) Proof	3,000	Value: 95.00				

Y# 467 600 BAHT
22.1500 g., 0.9250 Silver 0.6587 oz. ASW, 35 mm. **Ruler:** Rama IX **Subject:** Princess Petcharat, 80th Birthday **Obv:** Bust facing **Rev:** Princess' emblem

Date	Mintage	F	VF	XF	Unc	BU
BE2548 (2005)	—	—	—	—	55.00	60.00
BE2548 (2005) Proof	—	Value: 120				

Y# 427 600 BAHT
22.0000 g., 0.9250 Silver 0.6542 oz. ASW, 35 mm. **Ruler:** Rama IX **Subject:** Princess Maha Chakri Sirindhorn's 50th Birthday **Obv:** Bust right **Rev:** Oval **Edge:** Reeded

Date	Mintage	F	VF	XF	Unc	BU
BE2548 (2005)	15,000	—	—	—	45.00	35.00
BE2548 (2005) Proof	4,000	Value: 85.00				

Y# 484 600 BAHT
22.0000 g., 0.9250 Silver 0.6542 oz. ASW, 35 mm. **Ruler:** Rama IX **Subject:** Princess Rattana, 80th birthday **Obv:** Bust facing of Princess **Note:** Minted and released in 2006.

Date	Mintage	F	VF	XF	Unc	BU
BE2548 (2005)	3,500	—	—	—	55.00	60.00

Y# 408 600 BAHT
22.0000 g., 0.9250 Silver 0.6542 oz. ASW, 35 mm. **Ruler:** Rama IX **Subject:** 60th Anniversary of Reign **Obv:** Rama IX **Rev:** Royal cypher **Edge:** Reeded

Date	Mintage	F	VF	XF	Unc	BU
BE2549 (2006)	66,000	—	—	—	35.00	40.00
BE2549 (2006) Proof with hologram	16,000	Value: 90.00				

Y# 485 600 BAHT
22.0000 g., 0.9250 Silver 0.6542 oz. ASW **Ruler:** Rama IX **Subject:** Prince Royal Cradle Ceremony **Obv:** Prince's baby head left **Rev:** Four line legend

Date	Mintage	F	VF	XF	Unc	BU
BE2549 (2006)	10,000	—	—	—	45.00	50.00
BE2549 (2006) Proof	3,700	Value: 85.00				

Y# 447 800 BAHT
22.0000 g., 0.9900 Silver 0.7002 oz. ASW, 35 mm. **Ruler:** Rama IX **Obv:** Bust left **Rev:** WHO logo and legend

Date	Mintage	F	VF	XF	Unc	BU
2005	Est. 6,500	—	—	—	40.00	45.00
2005 Proof	Inc. above	Value: 100				

Y# 451 800 BAHT
22.0000 g., 0.9900 Silver 0.7002 oz. ASW, 35 mm. **Ruler:** Rama IX **Subject:** King's 80th Birthday **Obv:** Bust left

Date	Mintage	F	VF	XF	Unc	BU
2007	80,000	—	—	—	35.00	40.00
2007 Proof	28,000	Value: 75.00				

Y# 454 800 BAHT
22.0000 g., 0.9250 Silver 0.6542 oz. ASW, 35 mm. **Ruler:** Rama IX **Subject:** Queen's 75th Birthday **Obv:** Queen's bust left **Rev:** Queen's Royal Seal

Date	Mintage	F	VF	XF	Unc	BU
2007	12,000	—	—	—	35.00	40.00
2007 Proof	4,000	Value: 75.00				

Y# 466 800 BAHT
22.1500 g., 0.9250 Silver 0.6587 oz. ASW, 35 mm. **Ruler:** Rama IX **Subject:** Princess Galyani Vadhana, 84th Birthday **Obv:** Bust facing **Rev:** Princess' emblem

Date	Mintage	F	VF	XF	Unc	BU
BE2550 (2007)	11,500	—	—	—	35.00	40.00
BE2550 (2007) Proof	1,500	Value: 95.00				

Y# 486 800 BAHT
22.0000 g., 0.9250 Silver 0.6542 oz. ASW, 35 mm. **Ruler:** Rama IX **Subject:** Princess Galyani Vadhana, 84th Birthday **Obv:** Princess's head right

Date	Mintage	F	VF	XF	Unc	BU
BE2550 (2007)	6,500	—	—	—	35.00	40.00

Y# 465 800 BAHT
22.1500 g., 0.9250 Silver 0.6587 oz. ASW, 35 mm. **Ruler:** Rama IX **Subject:** Princess Mother, 9th Cycle (108th Birthday) **Obv:** Bust facing **Rev:** Princess Mother's emblem

Date	Mintage	F	VF	XF	Unc	BU
BE2551 (2008)	11,200	—	—	—	35.00	40.00
BE2551 (2008) Proof	1,500	Value: 95.00				

Y# 468 800 BAHT
22.1500 g., 0.9900 Silver 0.7050 oz. ASW, 35 mm. **Ruler:** Rama IX **Subject:** King's WPIO leader award **Obv:** Bust left **Rev:** Award medal and legned **Note:** Minted and released in 2010.

Date	Mintage	F	VF	XF	Unc	BU
BE2551 (2008) Proof	15,000	Value: 75.00				

Y# 469 900 BAHT
31.1050 g., 0.9990 Silver 0.9990 oz. ASW, 40.6 mm. **Ruler:** Rama IX **Subject:** UNDP Human Development Lifetime Achievement Award **Obv:** King facing in multicolor applique **Rev:** Award bowl

Date	Mintage	F	VF	XF	Unc	BU
BE2549 (2006) Proof	200,000	Value: 75.00				

Y# 390 7500 BAHT
15.0000 g., 0.9000 Gold 0.4340 oz. AGW, 26 mm. **Ruler:** Rama IX **Subject:** King's 75th Birthday **Obv:** King's portrait **Rev:** Royal crown in radiant oval **Edge:** Reeded

Date	Mintage	F	VF	XF	Unc	BU
BE2545(2002)	6,000	—	—	—	675	700
BE2545(2002) Proof	1,200	Value: 825				

Y# 395 9000 BAHT
15.0000 g., 0.9000 Gold 0.4340 oz. AGW, 26 mm. **Ruler:** Rama IX **Subject:** 80th Birthday of Princess **Obv:** Bust half right **Rev:** Crowned emblem and value **Edge:** Reeded

Date	Mintage	F	VF	XF	Unc	BU
BE2546 (2003)	—	—	—	—	675	700
BE2546 (2003) Proof	—	Value: 825				

Y# 488 9000 BAHT
15.0000 g., 0.9000 Gold 0.4340 oz. AGW, 26 mm. **Ruler:** Rama IX **Subject:** WHO Food Safety Award to Queen Sirikit **Obv:** Bust of Queen Sirikit right **Rev:** WHO emblem and legend

Date	Mintage	F	VF	XF	Unc	BU
BE2550 (2007) Proof	2,800	Value: 850				

Y# 448 16,000 BAHT
15.0000 g., 0.9000 Gold 0.4340 oz. AGW, 26 mm. **Ruler:** Rama IX **Obv:** Bust right **Rev:** WHO logo and legend

Date	Mintage	F	VF	XF	Unc	BU
2005	Est. 3,000	—	—	—	—	700
2005 Proof	Inc. above	Value: 850				

Y# 452 16,000 BAHT
15.0000 g., 0.9900 Gold 0.4774 oz. AGW, 26 mm. **Ruler:** Rama IX **Subject:** King's 80th Birthday **Obv:** Bust left

Date	Mintage	F	VF	XF	Unc	BU
2007	19,800	—	—	—	725	750
2007 Proof	9,800	Value: 850				

Y# 455 16,000 BAHT
15.0000 g., 0.9000 Gold 0.4340 oz. AGW, 26 mm. **Ruler:** Rama IX **Subject:** Queen's 75th Birthday **Obv:** Bust left

Date	Mintage	F	VF	XF	Unc	BU
2007	5,000	—	—	—	725	750
2007 Proof	2,000	Value: 850				

Y# 489 16,000 BAHT
15.0000 g., 0.9900 Gold 0.4774 oz. AGW, 26 mm. **Ruler:** Rama IX **Subject:** World Interlectural Propery Organization Award **Obv:** Head left **Rev:** Award Medal and legend **Note:** Minted and released in 2010.

Date	Mintage	F	VF	XF	Unc	BU
BE2551 (2008) Proof	2,000	Value: 850				

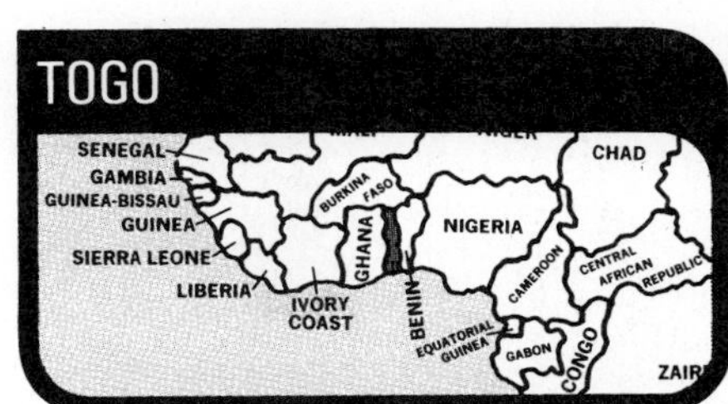

The Republic of Togo (formerly part of German Togoland), situated on the Gulf of Guinea in West Africa between Ghana and Dahomey, has an area of 21,622 sq. mi. (56,790 sq. km.) and a population of *3.4 million. Capital: Lome. Agriculture and herding, the production of dyewoods, and the mining of phosphates and iron ore are the chief industries. Copra, phosphates and coffee are exported.

MINT MARK

(a) - Paris, privy marks only

MONETARY SYSTEM

100 Centimes = 1 Franc

REPUBLIC

STANDARD COINAGE

100 Centimes = 1 Franc

KM# 51 100 FRANCS
26.0000 g., Copper-Nickel, 38.6 mm. **Rev:** Blue sunbird, prism technology

Date	Mintage	F	VF	XF	Unc	BU
2010 Prooflike	2,500	—	—	—	—	25.00

KM# 52 100 FRANCS
26.0000 g., Copper-Nickel, 38.6 mm. **Rev:** Green bird, prism technology

Date	Mintage	F	VF	XF	Unc	BU
2010 Prooflike	2,500	—	—	—	—	25.00

KM# 53 100 FRANCS
26.0000 g., Copper-Nickel, 38.6 mm. **Rev:** Yellow bird, prism technology

Date	Mintage	F	VF	XF	Unc	BU
2010 Prooflike	2,500	—	—	—	—	25.00

KM# 43 250 FRANCS
5.0000 g., 0.9990 Silver 0.1606 oz. ASW **Subject:** German President Horst Kohler **Obv:** National arms **Obv. Legend:** REPUBLIQUE TOGOLAISE **Rev:** Gilt figure

Date	Mintage	F	VF	XF	Unc	BU
2004 Proof	—	Value: 15.00				

KM# 29 500 FRANCS

7.0500 g., 0.9990 Silver 0.2264 oz. ASW, 30 mm. **Obv:** National arms above value **Rev:** Multicolor big cat **Edge:** Plain

Date	Mintage	F	VF	XF	Unc	BU
2001 Proof	—	Value: 35.00				

KM# 41 500 FRANCS

10.0000 g., 0.9990 Silver 0.3212 oz. ASW **Subject:** XVIII World Football Championship - Germany 2006 **Obv:** National arms **Obv. Legend:** REPUBLIQUE TOGOLAISE **Rev:** Two players, map of Germany in background

Date	Mintage	F	VF	XF	Unc	BU
2001 Proof	—	Value: 22.50				

KM# 60 500 FRANCS

15.0000 g., 0.9250 Silver 0.4461 oz. ASW, 30 mm. **Obv:** National arms **Rev:** Albrecht Durer portrait

Date	Mintage	F	VF	XF	Unc	BU
2003 Proof	—	Value: 25.00				

KM# 47 500 FRANCS

14.9700 g., 0.9250 Silver 0.4452 oz. ASW, 30 mm. **Obv:** Arms with supporters **Rev:** Full figures of Johann Wolfgang von Goethe and Friedrich von Schiller on pedestal facing

Date	Mintage	F	VF	XF	Unc	BU
2004 Proof	—	Value: 22.50				

KM# 44 500 FRANCS

7.0000 g., 0.9990 Silver 0.2248 oz. ASW **Subject:** German Chancellor Helmut Schmidt **Obv:** National arms **Obv. Legend:** REPUBLIQUE TOGOLAISE **Rev:** Gilt figue

Date	Mintage	F	VF	XF	Unc	BU
ND(2004) Proof	—	Value: 22.50				

KM# 17 1000 FRANCS

14.9500 g., 0.9990 Silver 0.4802 oz. ASW, 35 mm. **Obv:** National arms **Obv. Legend:** REPUBLIQUE TOGOLAISE **Rev:** German sailing ship **Rev. Legend:** Adler von Lübeck **Edge:** Plain

Date	Mintage	F	VF	XF	Unc	BU
2001 Proof	—	Value: 50.00				

KM# 35 1000 FRANCS

14.7000 g., 0.9990 Silver 0.4721 oz. ASW, 36 mm. **Subject:** World Cup Soccer - Bern 1954 **Obv:** National arms **Rev:** Bust facing and tower **Edge:** Plain

Date	Mintage	F	VF	XF	Unc	BU
2001 Proof	—	Value: 40.00				

KM# 36 1000 FRANCS

19.9100 g., 0.9990 Silver 0.6395 oz. ASW, 38.1 mm. **Subject:** World Cup Soccer - France 1938 **Obv:** National arms **Rev:** Eiffel Tower behind soccer player kicking ball **Edge:** Reeded

Date	Mintage	F	VF	XF	Unc	BU
2001 Proof	—	Value: 40.00				

KM# 40 1000 FRANCS

14.9700 g., Silver, 35 mm. **Obv:** National arms **Obv. Legend:** REPUBLIQUE TOGOLAISE **Rev:** Imperial German sailing ship **Rev. Legend:** "PREUSSEN" **Edge:** Plain

Date	Mintage	F	VF	XF	Unc	BU
2001 Proof	—	Value: 40.00				

KM# 54 1000 FRANCS

15.0000 g., 0.9990 Silver 0.4818 oz. ASW, 36 mm. **Rev:** Multicolor Airbus 319 right

Date	Mintage	F	VF	XF	Unc	BU
2001 Proof	—	Value: 35.00				

KM# 37 1000 FRANCS

19.9700 g., 0.9990 Silver 0.6414 oz. ASW, 40 mm. **Subject:** World Cup Soccer - USA 1994 **Obv:** National arms **Obv. Legend:** REPUBLIQUE TOGOLAISE **Rev:** Soccer player kicking ball **Rev. Legend:** COUPE MONDIALE DE FOOTBALL **Edge:** Reeded

Date	Mintage	F	VF	XF	Unc	BU
2002 Proof	—	Value: 40.00				

KM# 55 1000 FRANCS

15.0000 g., 0.9990 Silver 0.4818 oz. ASW, 36 mm. **Rev:** Multicolor Douglas DC-4 and NY skyline

Date	Mintage	F	VF	XF	Unc	BU
2002 Proof	—	Value: 35.00				

KM# 56 1000 FRANCS

15.0000 g., 0.9990 Silver 0.4818 oz. ASW **Rev:** Multicolor Caravelle SE-210 before London skyline **Shape:** 36

Date	Mintage	F	VF	XF	Unc	BU
2002 Proof	—	Value: 35.00				

KM# 57 1000 FRANCS

15.0000 g., 0.9990 Silver 0.4818 oz. ASW, 36 mm. **Rev:** Multicolor Convair 440 at airport

Date	Mintage	F	VF	XF	Unc	BU
2003 Proof	—	Value: 35.00				

KM# 58 1000 FRANCS

15.0000 g., 0.9990 Silver 0.4818 oz. ASW, 36 mm. **Rev:** Multicolor McDonnell-Douglas MD-81 right

Date	Mintage	F	VF	XF	Unc	BU
2003 Proof	—	Value: 35.00				

KM# 34 1000 FRANCS

30.9200 g., 0.9990 Silver 0.9931 oz. ASW, 39 mm. **Obv:** Bust with headdress left within circle **Rev:** Gold plated baboon within circle **Edge:** Reeded **Note:** Date in Chinese numerals.

Date	Mintage	F	VF	XF	Unc	BU
2004 Proof	—	Value: 45.00				

KM# 39 1000 FRANCS

62.2400 g., 0.9999 Silver 2.0008 oz. ASW, 50 mm. **Subject:** Year of the Monkey **Obv:** Gold plated world globe **Rev:** Gold plated center with radiant holographic monkey within circle **Edge:** Reeded and lettered sections **Edge Lettering:** PAN ASIA BANK TAIWAN in English and Chinese **Note:** Date in Chinese numerals.

Date	Mintage	F	VF	XF	Unc	BU
2004 Proof	—	Value: 115				

KM# 38 1000 FRANCS

30.7300 g., 0.9990 Silver 0.9870 oz. ASW, 39 mm. **Subject:** Year of the Monkey **Obv:** Head with headdress 1/4 right within circle **Rev:** Gold plated baboon within circle **Edge:** Reeded **Note:** Note: Date in Chinese numerals.

Date	Mintage	F	VF	XF	Unc	BU
2004 Proof	—	Value: 50.00				

KM# 24 1000 FRANCS
31.1035 g., 0.9990 Silver 0.9990 oz. ASW, 40 mm. **Obv:** National arms **Obv. Legend:** REPUBLIQUE TOGOLAISE **Rev:** Incuse rendering of statue of Princess Kyninska of Sparta horseback left **Rev. Legend:** SPORTS - ANTIQUES **Edge:** Plain

Date	Mintage	F	VF	XF	Unc	BU
2004	2,500	—	—	—	—	60.00

KM# 25 1000 FRANCS
31.1035 g., 0.9990 Silver 0.9990 oz. ASW, 40 mm. **Obv:** National arms **Obv. Legend:** REPUBLIQUE TOGOLAISE **Rev:** Relief rendering of statue of Princess Kyninska of Sparta horseback right **Rev. Legend:** SPORTS - ANTIQUES **Edge:** Plain

Date	Mintage	F	VF	XF	Unc	BU
2004	2,500	—	—	—	—	60.00

KM# 26 1000 FRANCS
1.2440 g., 0.9999 Gold 0.0400 oz. AGW, 13.92 mm. **Obv:** National arms **Obv. Legend:** REPUBLIQUE TOGOLAISE **Rev:** Convex statue of Nike **Edge:** Plain

Date	Mintage	F	VF	XF	Unc	BU
2004 Proof	5,000	Value: 75.00				

KM# 59 1000 FRANCS
15.0000 g., 0.9990 Silver 0.4818 oz. ASW, 36 mm. **Rev:** Multicolor DeHaviland DH-89 biplane

Date	Mintage	F	VF	XF	Unc	BU
2004 Proof	—	Value: 35.00				

KM# 27 1000 FRANCS
1.2440 g., 0.9999 Gold 0.0400 oz. AGW, 13.92 mm. **Obv:** National arms **Obv. Legend:** REPUBLIQUE TOGOLAISE **Rev:** Concave statue of Nike **Edge:** Plain

Date	Mintage	F	VF	XF	Unc	BU
2004 Proof	5,000	Value: 75.00				

KM# 45 1000 FRANCS
Silver **Subject:** 170th Anniversary German Railroad, Nürnberg - Fürth **Obv:** National arms **Obv. Legend:** REPUBLIQUE TOGOLAISE **Rev:** Early steam locomotive "Adler"

Date	Mintage	F	VF	XF	Unc	BU
2005 Proof	—	Value: 55.00				

KM# 46 1000 FRANCS
1.2400 g., 0.9999 Gold 0.0399 oz. AGW **Subject:** 250th Anniversary Birth of Wolfgang Amadeus Mozart **Obv:** National arms **Obv. Legend:** REPUBLIQUE TOGOLAISE

Date	Mintage	F	VF	XF	Unc	BU
2006 Proof	—	Value: 85.00				

KM# 48 1000 FRANCS
25.0000 g., 0.9250 Silver 0.7435 oz. ASW, 38.6 mm. **Rev:** Blue sunbird, prism technology

Date	Mintage	F	VF	XF	Unc	BU
2010 Proof	2,500	Value: 50.00				

KM# 50 1000 FRANCS
25.0000 g., 0.9250 Silver 0.7435 oz. ASW, 38.6 mm. **Rev:** Yellow bird, prism technology

Date	Mintage	F	VF	XF	Unc	BU
2010 Proof	2,500	Value: 50.00				

KM# 49 1000 FRANCS
25.0000 g., 0.9250 Silver 0.7435 oz. ASW, 38.6 mm. **Rev:** Green bird, prism technology

Date	Mintage	F	VF	XF	Unc	BU
2010 Proof	2,500	Value: 50.00				

KM# 42 2000 FRANCS
62.2000 g., 0.9990 Silver 1.9977 oz. ASW **Series:** Lunar **Subject:** Year of the Monkey **Obv:** World map **Obv. Legend:** REPUBLIQUE TOGOLAISE **Rev:** Monkey

Date	Mintage	F	VF	XF	Unc	BU
2004 Proof	—	Value: 125				

ESSAIS

KM#	Date	Mintage	Identification	Mkt Val
E17	ND(2003)	2	150000 Cfa Francs-100 Africa. Bi-Metallic. President and map. Elephant head on map.	250

TOKELAU ISLANDS

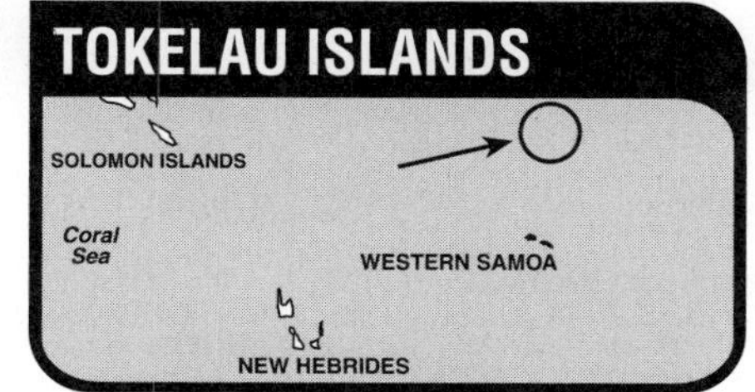

Tokelau or Union Islands, a New Zealand Territory located in the South Pacific 2,100 miles (3,379 km.) northeast of New Zealand and 300 miles (483 km.) north of Samoa, has an area of 4 sq. mi. (10 sq. km.) and a population of *2,000. Geographically, the group consists of four atolls - Atafu, Nukunono, Fakaofo and Swains – but the last belongs to American Samoa (and the United States claims the other three). The people are of Polynesian origin; Samoan is the official language. The New Zealand Minister for Foreign Affairs governs the islands; councils of family elders handle local government at the village level. The chief settlement is Fenuafala, on Fakaofo. It is connected by wireless technology with the offices of the New Zealand Administrative Center, located at Apia, Samoa. Subsistence farming and the production of copra for export are the main occupations. Revenue is also derived from the sale of postage stamps and, since 1978, coins.

Tokelau Islands issued its first coin in 1978, a "$1 Tahi Tala," Tokelauan for "One Dollar."

RULER
British

MINT MARK
PM - Pobjoy

NEW ZEALAND TERRITORY

STANDARD COINAGE

KM# 30 5 TALA
31.1000 g., 0.9990 Silver with Mother-of-Pearl inlay 0.9988 oz. ASW, 40 mm. **Series:** Save the Whales **Obv:** Crowned head right **Obv. Legend:** TOKELAU **Obv. Designer:** Raphael Maklouf **Rev:** Fin Whale on mother of pearl insert **Edge:** Plain

Date	Mintage	F	VF	XF	Unc	BU
2002 Proof	2,000	Value: 85.00				

KM# 32 5 TALA
31.1000 g., 0.9990 Silver 0.9988 oz. ASW, 40 mm. **Ruler:** Elizabeth II **Obv:** Elizabeth II **Rev:** Capt. Smith and ship General Jackson **Edge:** Reeded

Date	Mintage	F	VF	XF	Unc	BU
2003 Proof	—	Value: 45.00				

KM# 33 5 TALA
28.6500 g., Silver, 38.60 mm. **Ruler:** Elizabeth II **Obv:** Crowned head right **Obv. Legend:** TOKELAU **Rev:** Sailing ship **Rev. Legend:** CUTTY SARK 1869 **Edge:** Reeded

Date	Mintage	F	VF	XF	Unc	BU
2005 Proof	—	Value: 45.00				

KM# 46 10 TALA
1.2400 g., 0.9990 Gold 0.0398 oz. AGW, 13.92 mm. **Ruler:** Elizabeth II **Obv:** Crowned head right **Obv. Legend:** TOKELAU **Rev:** Two whales **Rev. Legend:** ENDANGERED WILDLIFE **Edge:** Reeded

Date	Mintage	F	VF	XF	Unc	BU
2003 Proof	—	Value: 85.00				

TONGA

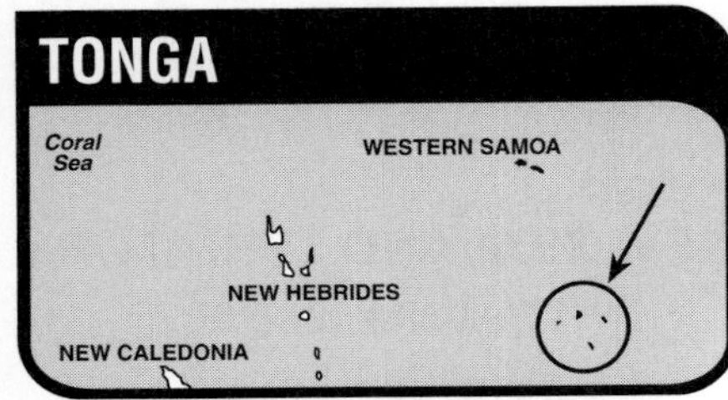

The Kingdom of Tonga (or Friendly Islands) is an archipelago situated in the southern Pacific Ocean south of Western Samoa and east of Fiji comprised of 150 islands. Tonga has an area of 270 sq. mi. (748 sq. km.) and a population of *100,000. Capital: Nuku'alofa. Primarily agricultural, the kingdom exports bananas and copra.

The monarchy is a member of the Commonwealth of Nations. King Siosa Tupou V is Head of State and Government.

RULER
King Taufa'ahau IV, 1965-2006
King Siosa Tupou V, 2006-

KINGDOM

DECIMAL COINAGE

100 Senti = 1 Pa'anga; 100 Pa'anga = 1 Hau

KM# 66a SENITI
Copper Plated Steel, 17.5 mm. **Ruler:** King Taufa'ahau Tupou IV **Series:** World Food Day **Obv:** Ear of corn **Obv. Legend:** TONGA **Rev:** Vanilla plant **Rev. Legend:** FAKALAHI ME'AKAI **Edge:** Plain

Date	Mintage	F	VF	XF	Unc	BU
2002	—	—	—	0.10	0.35	0.75
2003	—	—	—	0.10	0.35	0.75
2004	—	—	—	0.10	0.35	0.75

KM# 66 SENITI
1.8000 g., Bronze, 16.51 mm. **Ruler:** King Taufa'ahau Tupou IV **Series:** World Food Day **Obv:** Ear of corn **Rev:** Vanilla plant **Edge:** Plain

Date	Mintage	F	VF	XF	Unc	BU
2005	—	—	—	0.10	0.35	0.75

KM# 67a 2 SENITI
Copper Plated Steel, 21 mm. **Ruler:** King Taufa'ahau Tupou IV **Series:** World Food Day **Obv:** Taro plants **Obv. Legend:** TONGA **Rev:** Paper doll cutouts form design in center circle of sprays **Rev. Legend:** PLANNED FAMILIES • FOOD FOR ALL

Date	Mintage	F	VF	XF	Unc	BU
2002	—	—	—	0.15	0.65	1.25
2003	—	—	—	0.15	0.65	1.25
2004	—	—	—	0.15	0.65	1.25

KM# 68a 5 SENITI
2.7900 g., Nickel Plated Steel, 19.39 mm. **Ruler:** King Taufa'ahau Tupou IV **Series:** World Food Day **Obv:** Hen with chicks **Obv. Legend:** TONGA **Rev:** Coconuts **Rev. Legend:** FAKALAHI ME'AKAI **Edge:** Reeded

Date	Mintage	F	VF	XF	Unc	BU
2002	—	—	—	0.25	0.75	1.35
2003	—	—	—	0.25	0.75	1.35
2004	—	—	—	0.25	0.75	1.35
2005	—	—	—	0.25	0.75	1.35

KM# 68 5 SENITI
2.8000 g., Copper-Nickel, 19.5 mm. **Ruler:** King Taufa'ahau Tupou IV **Series:** World Food Day **Obv:** Hen with chicks **Rev:** Coconuts above sprig **Edge:** Reeded

Date	Mintage	F	VF	XF	Unc	BU
2005	—	—	0.10	0.25	0.75	1.25

KM# 69a 10 SENITI
Nickel Plated Steel, 23.5 mm. **Ruler:** King Taufa'ahau Tupou IV **Series:** World Food Day **Obv:** Uniformed bust facing **Obv. Legend:** F • A • O - TONGA **Rev:** Banana tree **Rev. Legend:** FAKALAHI ME'AKAI

Date	Mintage	F	VF	XF	Unc	BU
2002	—	—	—	0.30	1.00	1.75
2003	—	—	—	0.30	1.00	1.75
2004	—	—	—	0.30	1.00	1.75
2005	—	—	—	0.30	1.00	1.75

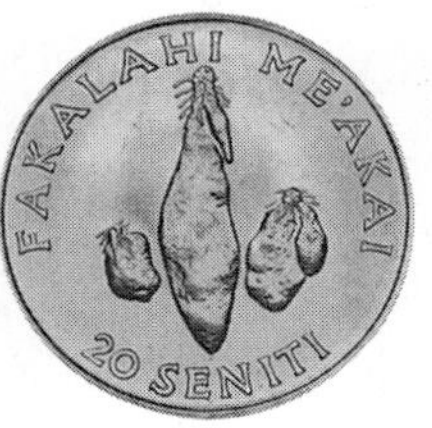

KM# 70 20 SENITI
11.3000 g., Copper-Nickel, 28.5 mm. **Ruler:** King Taufa'ahau Tupou IV **Series:** World Food Day - FAO **Obv:** Uniformed bust facing **Obv. Legend:** TONGA **Rev:** Yams **Rev. Legend:** FAKALAHI ME'AKAI **Edge:** Reeded

Date	Mintage	F	VF	XF	Unc	BU
2002	—	—	0.25	0.50	1.25	2.00
2003	—	—	0.25	0.50	1.25	2.00
2004	—	—	0.25	0.50	1.25	2.00

KM# 71 50 SENITI
14.6000 g., Copper-Nickel, 32.5 mm. **Ruler:** King Taufa'ahau Tupou IV **Series:** World Food Day **Obv:** Uniformed bust facing **Obv. Legend:** TONGA **Rev:** Tomato plants **Rev. Legend:** FAKALAHI ME'AKAI **Edge:** Plain **Shape:** 12-sided

Date	Mintage	F	VF	XF	Unc	BU
2002	—	—	0.45	0.75	1.50	2.50
2003	—	—	0.45	0.75	1.50	2.50
2004	—	—	0.45	0.75	1.50	2.50

KM# 178 PA'ANGA
31.1000 g., 0.9990 Silver with Mother-of-Pearl inlay 0.9988 oz. ASW, 40 mm. **Ruler:** King Taufa'ahau Tupou IV **Series:** Save the Whales **Obv:** Crown within wreath above national arms within circle **Obv. Legend:** KINGDOM OF TONGA **Rev:** Right Whale on mother of pearl insert **Edge:** Plain

Date	Mintage	F	VF	XF	Unc	BU
2002 Proof	2,000	Value: 85.00				

KM# 179 2 PA'ANGA
Silver **Ruler:** King Taufa'ahau Tupou IV **Subject:** King's 85th Birthday **Obv:** National arms

Date	Mintage	F	VF	XF	Unc	BU
2003 Proof	—	Value: 120				

TRANSNISTRIA

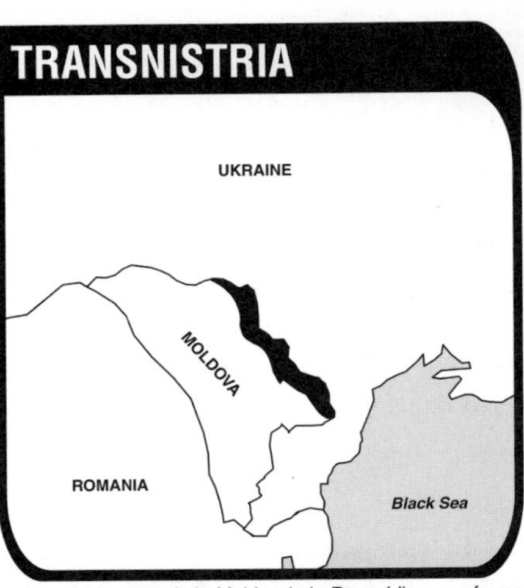

The Pridnestrovskaia Moldavskaia Respublica was formed in 1990, even before the separation of Moldavia from Russia. It has an area of 11,544 sq. mi. (29,900 sq. km.) and a population of 555,000. Capital: Tiraspol.

Transnistria (or Transdniestra) has a president, parliament, army and police forces, but as yet it is lacking international recognition.

MOLDAVIAN REPUBLIC

STANDARD COINAGE

1 Rublei = 100 Kopeek

KM# 50 5 KOPEEK
0.7000 g., Aluminum, 17.9 mm. **Obv:** Modified national arms **Obv. Legend:** ПРИДНЕСТРОВСКАЯ МОЛДАВСКАЯ РЕСПУБЛИКА **Rev:** Value flanked by wheat stalks. **Edge:** Plain **Note:** Prev. KM#2, 16.

Date	Mintage	F	VF	XF	Unc	BU
2005	—	—	—	0.20	0.50	0.65

KM# 51 10 KOPEEK
1.0000 g., Aluminum, 20 mm. **Obv:** Modified national arms **Obv. Legend:** ПРИДНЕСТРОВСКАЯ МОЛДАВСКАЯ РЕСПУБЛИКА **Rev:** Value flanked by wheat stalks **Edge:** Plain **Note:** Prev. KM#3, 17.

Date	Mintage	F	VF	XF	Unc	BU
2005	—	—	—	0.25	0.65	0.90

KM# 5 25 KOPEEK
2.1500 g., Aluminum-Bronze, 16.88 mm. **Obv:** National arms **Rev:** Value within sprays **Edge:** Plain

Date	Mintage	F	VF	XF	Unc	BU
2002	—	—	0.15	0.35	0.90	1.20

KM# 52 25 KOPEEK
Aluminum-Bronze, 16.9 mm. **Obv:** Modified national arms **Obv. Legend:** ПРИДНЕСТРОВСКАЯ МОЛДАВСКАЯ РЕСПУБЛИКА **Rev:** Value within sprays **Edge:** Plain **Note:** Prev. KM#18.

Date	Mintage	F	VF	XF	Unc	BU
2005	—	—	0.15	0.35	0.90	1.20

KM# 52a 25 KOPEEK
2.1000 g., Bronze Plated Steel, 16.9 mm. **Obv:** Modified national arms **Obv. Legend:** ПРИДНЕСТРОВСКАЯ МОЛДАВСКАЯ РЕСПУБЛИКА **Rev:** Value within sprays **Edge:** Plain **Note:** Prev. KM#5a; 18a.

Date	Mintage	F	VF	XF	Unc	BU
2005	—	—	0.15	0.35	0.90	1.20

KM# 53 50 KOPEEK
2.8000 g., Aluminum-Bronze, 19 mm. **Obv:** Modified national arms **Obv. Legend:** ПРИДНЕСТРОВСКАЯ МОЛДАВСКАЯ РЕСПУБЛИКА **Rev:** Value within sprays **Edge:** Plain **Note:** Prev. KM#4a; 19.

Date	Mintage	F	VF	XF	Unc	BU
2005	—	—	0.15	0.45	1.10	1.50

KM# 53a 50 KOPEEK
Bronze Plated Steel, 19 mm. **Obv:** Modified national arms **Obv. Legend:** ПРИДНЕСТРОВСКАЯ МОЛДАВСКАЯ РЕСПУБЛИКА **Rev:** Value within sprays **Edge:** Plain **Note:** Prev. KM#19a.

Date	Mintage	F	VF	XF	Unc	BU
2005	—	—	0.15	0.45	1.10	1.50

KM# 55 RUBLE
14.1400 g., 0.9250 Silver 0.4205 oz. ASW, 32 mm. **Obv:** National Arms **Rev:** Building with dome

Date	Mintage	F	VF	XF	Unc	BU
2005 Proof	500	Value: 125				

KM# 77 RUBLE
14.1400 g., 0.9250 Silver 0.4205 oz. ASW, 32 mm. **Obv:** National Arms **Rev:** Moth and caterpillar

Date	Mintage	F	VF	XF	Unc	BU
2006 Proof	1,000	Value: 145				

KM# 79 RUBLE
14.1400 g., 0.9250 Silver 0.4205 oz. ASW, 32 mm. **Obv:** Olympics - Turin **Rev:** Slalom

Date	Mintage	F	VF	XF	Unc	BU
2006 Proof	500	Value: 150				

KM# 95 3 RUBLYA
8.0000 g., 0.9000 Gold 0.2315 oz. AGW, 21 mm. **Obv:** National Arms **Rev:** Shield **Rev. Legend:** РЫБНИЦА

Date	Mintage	F	VF	XF	Unc	BU
2007 Proof	100	Value: 650				

KM# 97 3 RUBLYA
8.0000 g., 0.9000 Gold 0.2315 oz. AGW, 21 mm. **Obv:** National Arms **Rev:** Shield **Rev. Legend:** ТИРАСПОЛЪ

Date	Mintage	F	VF	XF	Unc	BU
2007 Proof	100	Value: 650				

KM# 110 3 RUBLYA
14.1400 g., 0.9250 Silver 0.4205 oz. ASW, 32 mm. **Obv:** National Arms **Rev:** Aquarius within zodiac emblems

Date	Mintage	F	VF	XF	Unc	BU
2007 Proof	100	Value: 650				

KM# 100 5 RUBLES
33.8500 g., 0.9250 Silver 1.0066 oz. ASW, 39 mm. **Obv:** National Arms **Rev:** Wooley mammoth

Date	Mintage	F	VF	XF	Unc	BU
2007 Proof	500	Value: 145				

KM# 101 5 RUBLES
33.8500 g., 0.9250 Silver 1.0066 oz. ASW, 39 mm. **Obv:** National Arms **Rev:** Moose

Date	Mintage	F	VF	XF	Unc	BU
2007 Proof	500	Value: 145				

KM# 112 10 RUBLEI
14.1400 g., 0.9250 Silver 0.4205 oz. ASW, 32 mm. **Obv:** National Arms **Rev:** Aquarius within circle of zodiac symbols

Date	Mintage	F	VF	XF	Unc	BU
2007 Proof	500	Value: 100				

KM# 102 10 RUBLEI
14.1400 g., 0.9250 Silver 0.4205 oz. ASW, 32 mm. **Obv:** National Arms **Rev:** Multicolor sprinter

Date	Mintage	F	VF	XF	Unc	BU
2007 Proof	500	Value: 100				

KM# 103 10 RUBLEI
14.1400 g., 0.9250 Silver 0.4205 oz. ASW, 32 mm. **Obv:** National Arms **Rev:** Multicolor female gymnast

Date	Mintage	F	VF	XF	Unc	BU
2007 Proof	500	Value: 100				

KM# 104 10 RUBLEI
14.1400 g., 0.9250 Silver 0.4205 oz. ASW, 32 mm. **Obv:** National Arms **Rev:** Multicolor runner, sports designs

Date	Mintage	F	VF	XF	Unc	BU
2007 Proof	500	Value: 100				

KM# 105 10 RUBLEI
0.9250 Silver, 32 mm. **Obv:** National Arms **Rev:** Multicolor javlin thrower

Date	Mintage	F	VF	XF	Unc	BU
2007 Proof	500	Value: 100				

KM# 106 10 RUBLEI
0.9250 Silver, 32 mm. **Obv:** National Arms **Rev:** Multicolor runner breaking tape at finish line

Date	Mintage	F	VF	XF	Unc	BU
2007 Proof	500	Value: 100				

KM# 107 10 RUBLEI
14.1400 g., 0.9250 Silver 0.4205 oz. ASW, 32 mm. **Obv:** National Arms **Rev:** Multicolor soccer player

Date	Mintage	F	VF	XF	Unc	BU
2007 Proof	500	Value: 100				

KM# 111 10 RUBLEI
14.1400 g., 0.9250 Silver 0.4205 oz. ASW, 32 mm. **Obv:** National Arms **Rev:** Constellation ophiuchus (man grasping serpant)

Date	Mintage	F	VF	XF	Unc	BU
2007 Proof	500	Value: 100				

KM# 125 10 RUBLEI
14.1400 g., 0.9250 Silver 0.4205 oz. ASW, 32 mm. **Obv:** National Arms **Rev:** Sturgeon fish

Date	Mintage	F	VF	XF	Unc	BU
2008 Proof	500	Value: 150				

KM# 126 10 RUBLEI
14.1400 g., 0.9250 Silver 0.4205 oz. ASW, 32 mm. **Obv:** National Arms **Rev:** Owl

Date	Mintage	F	VF	XF	Unc	BU
2008 Proof	500	Value: 165				

KM# 127 10 RUBLEI
14.1400 g., 0.9250 Silver 0.4205 oz. ASW, 32 mm. **Obv:** National Arms **Rev:** Flower

Date	Mintage	F	VF	XF	Unc	BU
2008 Proof	500	Value: 185				

KM# 128 10 RUBLEI
14.1400 g., 0.9250 Silver 0.4205 oz. ASW, 32 mm. **Obv:** National Arms **Rev:** Otter

Date	Mintage	F	VF	XF	Unc	BU
2008 Proof	500	Value: 190				

KM# 54 15 RUBLEI
156.4000 g., 0.9990 Gold 5.0231 oz. AGW, 50 mm. **Obv:** National Arms **Rev:** Building with dome

Date	Mintage	F	VF	XF	Unc	BU
2005 Proof, Rare	15	—	—	—	—	—

KM# 75 15 RUBLEI
156.4000 g., 0.9990 Gold 5.0231 oz. AGW, 15 mm. **Obv:** National Arms **Rev:** Building with tower

Date	Mintage	F	VF	XF	Unc	BU
2006 Proof, Rare	15	—	—	—	—	—

KM# 17 100 RUBLEI
14.1400 g., 0.9250 Silver 0.4205 oz. ASW, 32 mm. **Obv:** National Arms **Rev:** Cathedral of Ascension, Kitskany 1864

Date	Mintage	F	VF	XF	Unc	BU
2001 Proof	1,000	Value: 100				

KM# 10 100 RUBLEI
14.1400 g., 0.9250 Silver 0.4205 oz. ASW, 32 mm. **Obv:** National Arms **Rev:** D. Zielinskieg, chemist

Date	Mintage	F	VF	XF	Unc	BU
2001 Proof	1,000	Value: 70.00				

KM# 11 100 RUBLEI
14.1400 g., 0.9250 Silver 0.4205 oz. ASW, 32 mm. **Obv:** National Arms **Rev:** S. Berg, fish

Date	Mintage	F	VF	XF	Unc	BU
2001 Proof	1,000	Value: 70.00				

KM# 12 100 RUBLEI
14.1400 g., 0.9250 Silver 0.4205 oz. ASW, 32 mm. **Obv:** National Arms **Rev:** N.F. Skilfosowskieg, portrait at right

Date	Mintage	F	VF	XF	Unc	BU
2001 Proof	1,000	Value: 70.00				

KM# 13 100 RUBLEI
14.1400 g., 0.9250 Silver 0.4205 oz. ASW, 32 mm. **Obv:** National Arms **Rev:** M.F. Larionowa, bust, painter

Date	Mintage	F	VF	XF	Unc	BU
2001 Proof	1,000	Value: 70.00				

KM# 14 100 RUBLEI
14.1400 g., 0.9250 Silver 0.4205 oz. ASW, 32 mm. **Obv:** National Arms **Rev:** Cathedral in Tyraspol

Date	Mintage	F	VF	XF	Unc	BU
2001 Proof	1,000	Value: 80.00				

KM# 15 100 RUBLEI
14.1400 g., 0.9250 Silver 0.4205 oz. ASW, 32 mm. **Obv:** National Arms **Rev:** Cathedral XVII

Date	Mintage	F	VF	XF	Unc	BU
2001 Proof	1,000	Value: 100				

KM# 16 100 RUBLEI
14.1400 g., 0.9250 Silver 0.4205 oz. ASW, 32 mm. **Obv:** National Arms **Rev:** Cathedral 1800

Date	Mintage	F	VF	XF	Unc	BU
2001 Proof	1,000	Value: 100				

KM# 18 100 RUBLEI
14.1400 g., 0.9250 Silver 0.4205 oz. ASW, 32 mm. **Obv:** National Arms **Rev:** Cathedral 1825

Date	Mintage	F	VF	XF	Unc	BU
2001 Proof	1,000	Value: 100				

KM# 19 100 RUBLEI
14.1400 g., 0.9250 Silver 0.4205 oz. ASW, 32 mm. **Obv:** National Arms **Rev:** Church of St. Trinity, Rashkov 1778

Date	Mintage	F	VF	XF	Unc	BU
2001 Proof	1,000	Value: 100				

KM# 20 100 RUBLEI
14.1400 g., 0.9250 Silver 0.4205 oz. ASW, 32 mm. **Obv:** National Arms **Rev:** Cathedral XIX

Date	Mintage	F	VF	XF	Unc	BU
2001 Proof	1,000	Value: 100				

KM# 21 100 RUBLEI
14.1400 g., 0.9250 Silver 0.4205 oz. ASW, 32 mm. **Obv:** National Arms **Rev:** Cathedral 1784

Date	Mintage	F	VF	XF	Unc	BU
2001 Proof	1,000	Value: 100				

KM# 22 100 RUBLEI
14.1400 g., 0.9250 Silver 0.4205 oz. ASW, 32 mm. **Obv:** National Arms **Rev:** Cathedral 1854

Date	Mintage	F	VF	XF	Unc	BU
2001 Proof	1,000	Value: 100				

KM# 37 100 RUBLEI
14.0400 g., 0.9250 Silver 0.4175 oz. ASW, 32 mm. **Subject:** 10th Anniversary - Trans-Dniester Republican Bank **Obv:** National arms **Rev:** Colorized monogram within 3/4 wreath with "1992" at top **Edge:** Plain **Note:** Prev. KM#10.

Date	Mintage	F	VF	XF	Unc	BU
2002 Proof	500	Value: 90.00				

KM# 35 100 RUBLEI
14.1600 g., 0.9250 Silver 0.4211 oz. ASW, 32 mm. **Subject:** City of Tiraspol **Obv:** National arms **Rev:** Statue and buildings **Edge:** Plain **Note:** Prev. KM#7.

Date	Mintage	F	VF	XF	Unc	BU
2002 Proof	—	Value: 80.00				

KM# 36 100 RUBLEI
14.1600 g., 0.9250 Silver 0.4211 oz. ASW, 32 mm. **Subject:** City of Tiraspol **Obv:** National arms **Rev:** Cameo above fortress **Edge:** Plain **Note:** Prev. KM#8.

Date	Mintage	F	VF	XF	Unc	BU
2002 Proof	—	Value: 80.00				

KM# 38 100 RUBLEI
14.1600 g., 0.9250 Silver 0.4211 oz. ASW, 32 mm. **Subject:** K. K. Gedroets **Obv:** National arms **Rev:** Bust facing flanked by sprigs, beaker and book **Edge:** Plain **Note:** Prev. KM#9.

Date	Mintage	F	VF	XF	Unc	BU
2002 Proof	500	Value: 80.00				

KM# 40 100 RUBLEI
14.1400 g., 0.9250 Silver 0.4205 oz. ASW, 32 mm. **Obv:** National Arms **Rev:** Shield **Rev. Legend:** ТИРАСЛОЛЬ

Date	Mintage	F	VF	XF	Unc	BU
2002 Proof	500	Value: 100				

KM# 41 100 RUBLEI
14.1400 g., 0.9250 Silver 0.4205 oz. ASW, 32 mm. **Obv:** National Arms **Rev:** Shield **Rev. Legend:** ГРНГОРКОПОЛЬ

Date	Mintage	F	VF	XF	Unc	BU
2002 Proof	500	Value: 100				

KM# 45 100 RUBLEI
14.1400 g., 0.9250 Silver 0.4205 oz. ASW, 32 mm. **Obv:** National Army **Rev:** Soccer Player

Date	Mintage	F	VF	XF	Unc	BU
2003 Proof	500	Value: 100				

KM# 43 100 RUBLEI
14.1400 g., 0.9250 Silver 0.4205 oz. ASW, 32 mm. **Obv:** National arms **Rev:** Hoopoe (Upupa Epops) bird on branch **Edge:** Plain **Note:** Prev. KM#11.

Date	Mintage	F	VF	XF	Unc	BU
2003 Proof	500	Value: 100				

KM# 42 100 RUBLEI
14.1400 g., 0.9250 Silver 0.4205 oz. ASW, 32 mm. **Obv:** National arms **Rev:** Shield flanked by sprigs **Edge:** Plain **Note:** Prev. KM#12.

Date	Mintage	F	VF	XF	Unc	BU
2003 Proof	500	Value: 75.00				

KM# 48 100 RUBLEI
14.1400 g., 0.9250 Silver 0.4205 oz. ASW, 32 mm. **Subject:** 80th Anniversary of Nationhood **Obv:** National arms **Rev:** Map and multicolor flag **Edge:** Plain **Note:** Prev. KM#13.

Date	Mintage	F	VF	XF	Unc	BU
2004 Proof	500	Value: 225				

KM# 44 100 RUBLEI
14.1400 g., 0.9250 Silver 0.4205 oz. ASW, 32 mm. **Obv:** National arms **Rev:** Doe and fawn flanked by trees **Edge:** Plain **Note:** Prev. KM#14.

Date	Mintage	F	VF	XF	Unc	BU
2004 Proof	1,000	Value: 225				

KM# 46 100 RUBLEI
14.1400 g., 0.9250 Silver 0.4205 oz. ASW, 32 mm. **Obv:** National Arms **Rev:** A.G. Rubinstein and music score

Date	Mintage	F	VF	XF	Unc	BU
2004 Proof	1,000	Value: 100				

KM# 47 100 RUBLEI
14.1400 g., 0.9250 Silver 0.4205 oz. ASW, 32 mm. **Obv:** National Arms **Rev:** JS Grousul

Date	Mintage	F	VF	XF	Unc	BU
2004 Proof	1,000	Value: 100				

KM# 60 100 RUBLEI
14.1400 g., 0.9250 Silver 0.4205 oz. ASW, 32 mm. **Obv:** National arms **Rev:** Eurasian Griffin bird on rock **Edge:** Plain **Note:** Prev. KM#15.

Date	Mintage	F	VF	XF	Unc	BU
2005 Proof	1,000	Value: 125				

KM# 56 100 RUBLEI
14.1400 g., 0.9250 Silver 0.4205 oz. ASW, 32 mm. **Obv:** National Arms **Rev:** Building with tower

Date	Mintage	F	VF	XF	Unc	BU
2005 Proof	500	Value: 110				

KM# 57 100 RUBLEI
14.1400 g., 0.9250 Silver 0.4205 oz. ASW, 32 mm. **Obv:** National Arms **Rev:** Zodiac - Capricorn

Date	Mintage	F	VF	XF	Unc	BU
2005 Proof	1,000	Value: 90.00				

KM# 58 100 RUBLEI
14.1400 g., 0.9250 Silver 0.4205 oz. ASW, 32 mm. **Obv:** National Arms **Rev:** Statue and long building

Date	Mintage	F	VF	XF	Unc	BU
2005 Proof	500	Value: 110				

KM# 59 100 RUBLEI
14.1400 g., 0.9250 Silver 0.4205 oz. ASW, 32 mm. **Obv:** National Arms **Rev:** Flag as book

Date	Mintage	F	VF	XF	Unc	BU
2005 Proof	500	Value: 180				

KM# 61 100 RUBLEI
14.1400 g., 0.9250 Silver 0.4205 oz. ASW, 32 mm. **Obv:** National Arms **Rev:** PP Werszygora

Date	Mintage	F	VF	XF	Unc	BU
2005 Proof	500	Value: 110				

KM# 62 100 RUBLEI
14.1400 g., 0.9250 Silver 0.4205 oz. ASW, 32 mm. **Obv:** National Arms **Rev:** Zodiac - Aquarius

Date	Mintage	F	VF	XF	Unc	BU
2005 Proof	500	Value: 90.00				

KM# 63 100 RUBLEI
14.1400 g., 0.9250 Silver 0.4205 oz. ASW, 32 mm. **Obv:** National Arms **Rev:** Zodiac - Pisces

Date	Mintage	F	VF	XF	Unc	BU
2005 Proof	500	Value: 90.00				

KM# 64 100 RUBLEI
14.1400 g., 0.9250 Silver 0.4205 oz. ASW, 32 mm. **Obv:** National Arms **Rev:** Zodiac - Aries

Date	Mintage	F	VF	XF	Unc	BU
2005 Proof	500	Value: 90.00				

KM# 65 100 RUBLEI
14.1400 g., 0.9250 Silver 0.4205 oz. ASW, 32 mm. **Obv:** National Arms **Rev:** Zodiac - Taurus

Date	Mintage	F	VF	XF	Unc	BU
2005 Proof	500	Value: 90.00				

KM# 66 100 RUBLEI
14.1400 g., 0.9250 Silver 0.4205 oz. ASW, 32 mm. **Obv:** National Arms **Rev:** Zodiac - Gemini

Date	Mintage	F	VF	XF	Unc	BU
2005 Proof	500	Value: 90.00				

KM# 67 100 RUBLEI
14.1400 g., 0.9250 Silver 0.4205 oz. ASW, 32 mm. **Obv:** National Arms **Rev:** Zodiac - Cancer

Date	Mintage	F	VF	XF	Unc	BU
2005 Proof	500	Value: 90.00				

KM# 68 100 RUBLEI
14.1400 g., 0.9250 Silver 0.4205 oz. ASW, 32 mm. **Obv:** National Arms **Rev:** Zodiac - Leo

Date	Mintage	F	VF	XF	Unc	BU
2005 Proof	500	Value: 90.00				

KM# 69 100 RUBLEI
14.1400 g., 0.9250 Silver 0.4205 oz. ASW, 32 mm. **Obv:** National Arms **Rev:** Zodiac - Virgo

Date	Mintage	F	VF	XF	Unc	BU
2005 Proof	500	Value: 90.00				

KM# 70 100 RUBLEI
14.1400 g., 0.9250 Silver 0.4205 oz. ASW, 32 mm. **Obv:** National Arms **Rev:** Zodiac - Libra

Date	Mintage	F	VF	XF	Unc	BU
2005 Proof	500	Value: 90.00				

KM# 71 100 RUBLEI
14.1400 g., 0.9250 Silver 0.4205 oz. ASW, 32 mm. **Obv:** National Arms **Rev:** Zodiac - Scorpio

Date	Mintage	F	VF	XF	Unc	BU
2005 Proof	500	Value: 90.00				

KM# 72 100 RUBLEI
14.1400 g., 0.9250 Silver 0.4205 oz. ASW, 32 mm. **Obv:** National Arms **Rev:** Zodiac - Sagittarius

Date	Mintage	F	VF	XF	Unc	BU
2005 Proof	500	Value: 90.00				

KM# 76 100 RUBLEI
0.9250 Silver, 32 mm. **Obv:** National Arms **Rev:** Lunar Year of the (fire) Dog

Date	Mintage	F	VF	XF	Unc	BU
2006 Proof	1,000	Value: 65.00				

KM# 78 100 RUBLEI
14.1400 g., 0.9250 Silver 0.4205 oz. ASW, 32 mm. **Obv:** National Arms **Rev:** Stag Beetle

Date	Mintage	F	VF	XF	Unc	BU
2006 Proof	500	Value: 285				

KM# 80 100 RUBLEI
14.1400 g., 0.9250 Silver 0.4205 oz. ASW, 32 mm. **Obv:** National Arms **Rev:** Biathlon

Date	Mintage	F	VF	XF	Unc	BU
2006 Proof	300	Value: 300				

KM# 81 100 RUBLEI
14.1400 g., 0.9250 Silver 0.4205 oz. ASW, 32 mm. **Subject:** Turin Olympics **Obv:** National Arms **Rev:** Ski Jump

Date	Mintage	F	VF	XF	Unc	BU
2006 Proof	200	Value: 325				

KM# 82 100 RUBLEI
14.1400 g., 0.9250 Silver 0.4205 oz. ASW, 32 mm. **Obv:** National Arms **Rev:** Town View - Tyraspol

Date	Mintage	F	VF	XF	Unc	BU
2006 Proof	500	Value: 110				

KM# 83 100 RUBLEI
14.1400 g., 0.9250 Silver 0.4205 oz. ASW, 32 mm. **Obv:** National Arms **Rev:** Town view Bendery

Date	Mintage	F	VF	XF	Unc	BU
2006 Proof	500	Value: 100				

KM# 84 100 RUBLEI
14.1400 g., 0.9250 Silver 0.4205 oz. ASW, 32 mm. **Obv:** Naational Arms **Rev:** Man in forest legend

Date	Mintage	F	VF	XF	Unc	BU
2006 Proof	1,000	Value: 85.00				

KM# 85 100 RUBLEI
14.1400 g., 0.9250 Silver 0.4205 oz. ASW, 32 mm. **Obv:** National Arms **Rev:** Legend - Fisherman in rowboat

Date	Mintage	F	VF	XF	Unc	BU
2006 Proof	1,000	Value: 85.00				

KM# 86 100 RUBLEI
14.1400 g., 0.9250 Silver 0.4205 oz. ASW, 32 mm. **Obv:** National Arms **Rev:** Legend dragon slayer

Date	Mintage	F	VF	XF	Unc	BU
2006 Proof	1,000	Value: 85.00				

KM# 87 100 RUBLEI
14.1400 g., 0.9250 Silver 0.4205 oz. ASW **Obv:** National Arms **Rev:** Kossak

Date	Mintage	F	VF	XF	Unc	BU
2006 Proof	500	Value: 120				

KM# 88 100 RUBLEI
14.1400 g., 0.9250 Silver 0.4205 oz. ASW, 32 mm. **Obv:** National Arms **Rev:** General Bursak

Date	Mintage	F	VF	XF	Unc	BU
2006 Proof	500	Value: 120				

KM# 89 100 RUBLEI
14.1400 g., 0.9250 Silver 0.4205 oz. ASW **Obv:** National Arms **Rev:** Multicolor baseball player hitting ball **Shape:** 32

Date	Mintage	F	VF	XF	Unc	BU
2006 Proof	500	Value: 100				

KM# 90 100 RUBLEI
14.1400 g., 0.9250 Silver 0.4205 oz. ASW, 32 mm. **Obv:** National Arms **Rev:** Cathedral of the Arch Angel Michael

Date	Mintage	F	VF	XF	Unc	BU
2006 Proof	500	Value: 100				

KM# 91 100 RUBLEI
14.1400 g., 0.9250 Silver 0.4205 oz. ASW, 32 mm. **Obv:** National Arms **Rev:** Sidor Bialy bust at right

Date	Mintage	F	VF	XF	Unc	BU
2006 Proof	300	Value: 175				

KM# 92 100 RUBLEI
14.1400 g., 0.9250 Silver 0.4205 oz. ASW, 32 mm. **Obv:** National Arms **Rev:** Seal impression, partially plated

Date	Mintage	F	VF	XF	Unc	BU
2006 Proof	300	Value: 175				

KM# 120 100 RUBLEI
14.1400 g., 0.9250 Silver 0.4205 oz. ASW, 32 mm. **Obv:** National Arms **Rev:** General Potiomkin

Date	Mintage	F	VF	XF	Unc	BU
2007 Proof	300	Value: 160				

KM# 96 100 RUBLEI
14.1400 g., 0.9250 Silver 0.4205 oz. ASW, 32 mm. **Obv:** National Arms **Rev:** Shield **Rev. Legend:** РЫЪЦИUА

Date	Mintage	F	VF	XF	Unc	BU
2007 Proof	500	Value: 120				

KM# 113 100 RUBLEI
14.1400 g., 0.9250 Silver 0.4205 oz. ASW, 32 mm. **Obv:** National Arms **Rev:** Lunar year of the pig

Date	Mintage	F	VF	XF	Unc	BU
2007 Proof	300	Value: 160				

KM# 114 100 RUBLEI
14.1400 g., 0.9250 Silver 0.4205 oz. ASW, 32 mm. **Obv:** National Arms **Rev:** Castle view, 4 towers

Date	Mintage	F	VF	XF	Unc	BU
2007 Proof	500	Value: 120				

KM# 115 100 RUBLEI
14.1400 g., 0.9250 Silver 0.4205 oz. ASW, 32 mm. **Obv:** National Arms **Rev:** Castle view central tower and gate

Date	Mintage	F	VF	XF	Unc	BU
2007 Proof	500	Value: 120				

KM# 116 100 RUBLEI
14.1400 g., 0.9250 Silver 0.4205 oz. ASW, 32 mm. **Obv:** National Arms **Rev:** Zachary Czerega Kulis, ship at left

Date	Mintage	F	VF	XF	Unc	BU
2007 Proof	300	Value: 165				

KM# 117 100 RUBLEI
14.1400 g., 0.9250 Silver 0.4205 oz. ASW, 32 mm. **Obv:** National Arms **Rev:** Anton Goloway

Date	Mintage	F	VF	XF	Unc	BU
2007 Proof	300	Value: 125				

KM# 118 100 RUBLEI
14.1400 g., 0.9250 Silver 0.4205 oz. ASW, 32 mm. **Obv:** National Arms **Rev:** Alexander Kuszer

Date	Mintage	F	VF	XF	Unc	BU
2007 Proof	500	Value: 115				

KM# 119 100 RUBLEI
14.1400 g., 0.9250 Silver 0.4205 oz. ASW, 32 mm. **Obv:** National Arms **Rev:** Field Marshal - Rumiancew-Zadunajski

Date	Mintage	F	VF	XF	Unc	BU
2007 Proof	300	Value: 125				

KM# 121 100 RUBLEI
14.1400 g., 0.9250 Silver 0.4205 oz. ASW, 32 mm. **Obv:** National Arms **Rev:** General Panin

Date	Mintage	F	VF	XF	Unc	BU
2007 Proof	300	Value: 125				

KM# 25 1000 RUBLEI
8.0000 g., 0.9000 Gold 0.2315 oz. AGW, 21 mm. **Obv:** National Arms **Rev:** 1800 Cathedral of God's Ascension

Date	Mintage	F	VF	XF	Unc	BU
2001 Proof	50	Value: 750				

KM# 23 1000 RUBLEI
8.0000 g., 0.9000 Gold 0.2315 oz. AGW, 21 mm. **Obv:** National Arms **Rev:** Church of the Blessed Virgins

Date	Mintage	F	VF	XF	Unc	BU
2001 Proof	50	Value: 750				

KM# 24 1000 RUBLEI
Gold, 21 mm. **Obv:** National Arms **Rev:** Orthodox Church of the Virgin's Assumption

Date	Mintage	F	VF	XF	Unc	BU
2001 Proof	50	Value: 750				

KM# 26 1000 RUBLEI
8.0000 g., 0.9000 Gold 0.2315 oz. AGW, 21 mm. **Obv:** National Arms **Rev:** Cathedral of the Birth of Christ

Date	Mintage	F	VF	XF	Unc	BU
2001 Proof	50	Value: 750				

KM# 27 1000 RUBLEI
8.0000 g., 0.9000 Gold 0.2315 oz. AGW, 21 mm. **Rev:** Cathedral of the Transfiguration

Date	Mintage	F	VF	XF	Unc	BU
2001 Proof	50	Value: 750				

KM# 28 1000 RUBLEI
8.0000 g., 0.9000 Gold 0.2315 oz. AGW, 21 mm. **Obv:** National Arms **Rev:** Church of the Blessed Virgin's Birth

Date	Mintage	F	VF	XF	Unc	BU
2001 Proof	50	Value: 750				

KM# 29 1000 RUBLEI
8.0000 g., 0.9000 Gold 0.2315 oz. AGW, 21 mm. **Obv:** National Arms **Rev:** Church of the Transfiguration

Date	Mintage	F	VF	XF	Unc	BU
2001 Proof	50	Value: 750				

KM# 30 1000 RUBLEI
8.0000 g., 0.9000 Gold 0.2315 oz. AGW, 21 mm. **Obv:** National Arms **Rev:** Church of the Lifegiving Trinity

Date	Mintage	F	VF	XF	Unc	BU
2001 Proof	50	Value: 750				

KM# 31 1000 RUBLEI
8.0000 g., 0.9000 Gold 0.2315 oz. AGW, 21 mm. **Obv:** National Arms **Rev:** Orthodox Church to the Serbian Paraskeva (1854)

Date	Mintage	F	VF	XF	Unc	BU
2001 Proof	50	Value: 750				

KM# 32 1000 RUBLEI
8.0000 g., 0.9000 Gold 0.2315 oz. AGW, 21 mm. **Obv:** National Arms **Rev:** Church of Michael the Arch Angel in Stoiesti

Date	Mintage	F	VF	XF	Unc	BU
2001 Proof	50	Value: 750				

MINT SETS

KM#	Date	Mintage	Identification	Issue Price	Mkt Val
MS1	2005 (4)	—	KM#50, 51, 52a, 53.	—	20.00

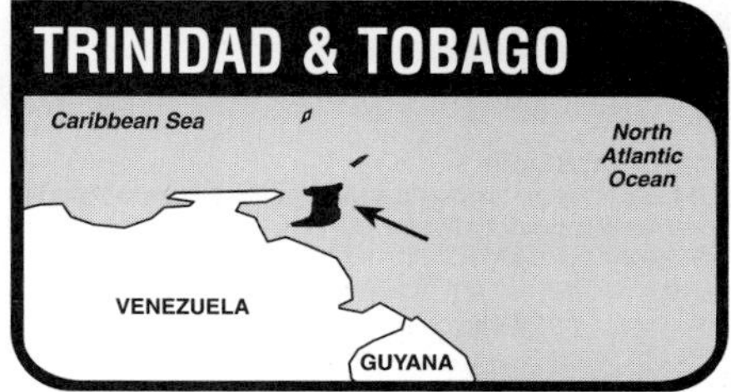

The Republic of Trinidad and Tobago is situated 7 miles (11 km.) off the coast of Venezuela, has an area of 1,981 sq. mi. (5,130 sq. km.) and a population of *1.2 million. Capital: Port-of-Spain. The island of Trinidad contains the world's largest natural asphalt bog. Birds of Paradise live on little Tobago, the only place outside of their native New Guinea where they can be found in a wild state. Petroleum and petroleum products are the mainstay of the economy. Petroleum products, crude oil and sugar are exported.

Trinidad and Tobago is a member of the Commonwealth of Nations. The President is Chief of State. The Prime Minister is Head of Government.

MONETARY SYSTEM
100 Cents = 1 Dollar

REPUBLIC

STANDARD COINAGE

KM# 29 CENT
1.9500 g., Bronze, 17.76 mm. **Obv:** National arms **Rev:** Hummingbird and value **Edge:** Plain

Date	Mintage	F	VF	XF	Unc	BU
2001	—	—	—	0.10	0.30	0.40
2002	—	—	—	0.10	0.30	0.40
2003	—	—	—	0.10	0.30	0.40
2005	—	—	—	0.10	0.30	0.40
2006	—	—	—	0.10	0.30	0.40
2007	—	—	—	0.10	0.30	0.40

KM# 30 5 CENTS
3.3100 g., Bronze, 21.2 mm. **Obv:** National arms **Rev:** Bird of paradise and value **Rev. Designer:** Norman Nemeth **Edge:** Plain

Date	Mintage	F	VF	XF	Unc	BU
2001	—	—	—	0.15	0.45	0.60
2002	—	—	—	0.15	0.45	0.60
2003	—	—	—	0.15	0.45	0.60
2004	—	—	—	0.15	0.45	0.60
2005	—	—	—	0.15	0.45	0.60
2006	—	—	—	0.15	0.45	0.60
2007	—	—	—	0.15	0.45	0.60

KM# 31 10 CENTS
1.4000 g., Copper-Nickel, 16.2 mm. **Obv:** National arms **Rev:** Hibiscus and value **Edge:** Reeded

Date	Mintage	F	VF	XF	Unc	BU
2001	—	—	—	0.25	0.60	0.80
2002	—	—	—	0.25	0.60	0.80
2003	—	—	—	0.25	0.60	0.80
2004	—	—	—	0.25	0.60	0.80
2005	—	—	—	0.25	0.60	0.80
2006	—	—	—	0.25	0.60	0.80

KM# 32 25 CENTS
3.5000 g., Copper-Nickel, 20 mm. **Obv:** National arms **Rev:** Chaconia and value **Edge:** Reeded

Date	Mintage	F	VF	XF	Unc	BU
2001	—	—	—	0.30	0.75	1.00
2002	—	—	—	0.30	0.75	1.00
2003	—	—	—	0.30	0.75	1.00
2004	—	—	—	0.30	0.75	1.00
2005	—	—	—	0.30	0.75	1.00
2006	—	—	—	0.30	0.75	1.00
2007	—	—	—	0.30	0.75	1.00

KM# 33 50 CENTS
7.0000 g., Copper-Nickel, 26 mm. **Obv:** National arms **Rev:** Kettle drums and value **Edge:** Reeded

Date	Mintage	F	VF	XF	Unc	BU
2003	—	—	—	1.00	2.00	4.00

KM# 63 10 DOLLARS
Copper-Nickel **Subject:** FIFA - XVIII World Football Championship - Soca Warriors - Germany 2006 **Obv:** Native hands playing steel drum, gilt **Rev:** Logo

Date	Mintage	F	VF	XF	Unc	BU
2006	—	—	—	5.00	12.00	35.00

KM# 64 100 DOLLARS
28.2800 g., 0.9250 Silver 0.8410 oz. ASW **Subject:** FIFA - XVIII World Football Championship - Soca Warriors - Germany 2006 **Obv:** Native hands playing steel drum, gilt **Rev:** Logo

Date	Mintage	F	VF	XF	Unc	BU
2006 Proof	—	Value: 70.00				

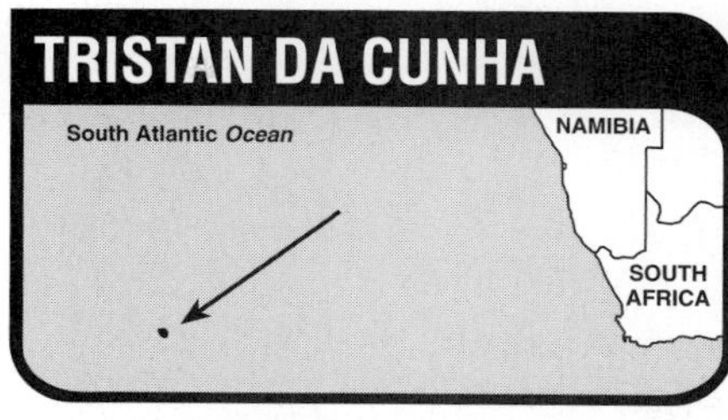

Tristan da Cunha is the principal island and group name of a small cluster of volcanic islands located in the South Atlantic midway between the Cape of Good Hope and South America, and 1,500 miles (2,414 km.) south-southwest of the British colony of St. Helena. The other islands are inaccessible, Gough, and the three Nightingale Islands. The group, which comprises a dependency of St. Helena, has a total area of 40 sq. mi. (104 sq. km.) and a population of less than 300. There is a village of 60 houses called Edinburgh. Potatoes are the staple subsistence crop.

MONETARY SYSTEM
100 Pence = 1 Pound

ST. HELENA DEPENDENCY

STANDARD COINAGE

KM# 27 1/2 PENNY
3.8300 g., Copper, 16.91 mm. **Ruler:** Elizabeth II **Obv:** Head with tiara right **Rev:** Snipe Eel **Edge:** Plain

Date	Mintage	F	VF	XF	Unc	BU
2008	—	—	—	—	0.75	1.00

KM# 28 PENNY
4.6300 g., Copper, 18.66 mm. **Ruler:** Elizabeth II **Obv:** Head with tiara right **Rev:** Crayfish **Edge:** Plain

Date	Mintage	F	VF	XF	Unc	BU
2008	—	—	—	—	1.20	1.60

KM# 29 2 PENCE
6.6000 g., Copper, 22.02 mm. **Ruler:** Elizabeth II **Obv:** Head with tiara right **Rev:** Violet Seasnail **Edge:** Plain

Date	Mintage	F	VF	XF	Unc	BU
2008	—	—	—	—	1.50	2.00

KM# 30 5 PENCE
3.7400 g., Copper-Nickel, 16.90 mm. **Ruler:** Elizabeth II **Obv:** Head with tiara right **Rev:** Sea Turtle **Edge:** Plain

Date	Mintage	F	VF	XF	Unc	BU
2008	—	—	—	—	1.80	2.40

KM# 31 10 PENCE
6.4900 g., Copper-Nickel, 22.03 mm. **Ruler:** Elizabeth II **Obv:** Head with tiara right **Rev:** Crab **Edge:** Plain

Date	Mintage	F	VF	XF	Unc	BU
2008	—	—	—	—	2.25	3.00

KM# 32 20 PENCE
6.1000 g., Aluminum-Bronze, 22.02 mm. **Ruler:** Elizabeth II **Obv:** Head with tiara right **Rev:** Orcha - Killer Whale **Edge:** Plain

Date	Mintage	F	VF	XF	Unc	BU
2008	—	—	—	—	3.00	4.00

KM# 33 25 PENCE
Bi-Metallic Aluminum-Bronze center in Copper-Nickel ring., 25.76 mm. **Obv:** Head with tiara right **Rev:** 2 Bottlenose Dolphins **Edge:** Plain

Date	Mintage	F	VF	XF	Unc	BU
2008	—	—	—	—	6.00	8.00

KM# 12 50 PENCE
29.1000 g., Copper-Nickel, 38.6 mm. **Subject:** Queen Elizabeth's 75th Birthday **Obv:** Crowned bust right **Obv. Designer:** Raphael Maklouf **Rev:** Crowned bust facing **Edge:** Reeded

Date	Mintage	F	VF	XF	Unc	BU
2001	—	—	—	—	7.00	8.00

KM# 13 50 PENCE
29.6000 g., Copper-Nickel, 38.7 mm. **Subject:** Centennial of Queen Victoria's Death **Obv:** Crowned bust right **Obv. Designer:** Raphael Maklouf **Rev:** Crown and veil on half-length figure of Queen Victoria facing left within oval circle **Edge:** Reeded

Date	Mintage	F	VF	XF	Unc	BU
2001	—	—	—	—	8.00	10.00

KM# 12a 50 PENCE
28.2800 g., 0.9250 Silver 0.8410 oz. ASW, 38.6 mm. **Subject:** Queen's 75th Birthday **Obv:** Crowned bust right **Rev:** Crowned bust facing **Edge:** Reeded

Date	Mintage	F	VF	XF	Unc	BU
2001 Proof	10,000	Value: 40.00				

KM# 12b 50 PENCE
47.5400 g., 0.9166 Gold 1.4009 oz. AGW, 38.6 mm. **Obv:** Crowned bust right **Rev:** Crowned bust facing

Date	Mintage	F	VF	XF	Unc	BU
2001 Proof	75	Value: 2,200				

KM# 13a 50 PENCE
28.2800 g., 0.9250 Silver 0.8410 oz. ASW, 38.6 mm. **Subject:** Centennial of Queen Victoria's Death **Obv:** Crowned bust right **Rev:** Crown and veil on half-length figure of Queen Victoria facing left within oval circle **Edge:** Reeded

Date	Mintage	F	VF	XF	Unc	BU
2001 Proof	10,000	Value: 50.00				

KM# 13b 50 PENCE
47.5400 g., 0.9166 Gold 1.4009 oz. AGW, 38.6 mm. **Subject:** Centennial of Queen Victoria's Death **Obv:** Crowned bust right **Rev:** Crown and veil on half-length figure of Queen Victoria facing left within oval circle **Edge:** Reeded

Date	Mintage	F	VF	XF	Unc	BU
2001 Proof	100	Value: 2,150				

KM# 14a CROWN
24.1200 g., 0.9250 Silver 0.7173 oz. ASW, 38.5 mm. **Obv:** Crowned bust right **Rev:** Pope John Paul II **Edge:** Reeded

Date	Mintage	F	VF	XF	Unc	BU
2005 Proof	—	Value: 45.00				

KM# 14 CROWN
Copper-Nickel, 38.5 mm. **Obv:** Crowned bust right **Rev:** Pope John Paul II **Edge:** Reeded

Date	Mintage	F	VF	XF	Unc	BU
2005	—	—	—	—	8.50	12.00

KM# 15 CROWN
25.0000 g., Copper-Nickel, 38.83 mm. **Ruler:** Elizabeth II **Series:** Privateering ships of the South Atlantic **Obv:** Crowned bust right **Obv. Legend:** ELIZABETH II — TRISTAN DA CUNHA **Rev:** Sailing ship "Tybalt" **Edge:** Reeded

Date	Mintage	F	VF	XF	Unc	BU
2006	—	—	—	—	8.50	12.00

KM# 16 CROWN
25.0000 g., Copper-Nickel, 38.83 mm. **Ruler:** Elizabeth II **Series:** Privateering ships of the South Atlantic **Obv:** Crowned bust right **Obv. Legend:** ELIZABETH II — TRISTAN DA CUNHA **Rev:** Sailing ship "Syren" **Edge:** Reeded

Date	Mintage	F	VF	XF	Unc	BU
2006	—	—	—	—	8.50	12.00

KM# 17 CROWN
25.0000 g., Copper-Nickel, 38.83 mm. **Ruler:** Elizabeth II **Series:** Privateering ships of the South Atlantic **Obv:** Crowned bust right **Obv. Legend:** ELIZABETH II — TRISTAN DA CUNHA **Rev:** Sailing ship "Pride of Baltimore" **Edge:** Reeded

Date	Mintage	F	VF	XF	Unc	BU
2006	—	—	—	—	8.50	12.00

KM# 18 CROWN
25.0000 g., Copper-Nickel, 38.83 mm. **Ruler:** Elizabeth II **Series:** Privateering ships of the South Atlantic **Obv:** Crowned bust right **Obv. Legend:** ELIZABETH II — TRISTAN DA CUNHA **Rev:** Sailing ship "Hornet" **Edge:** Reeded

Date	Mintage	F	VF	XF	Unc	BU
2006	—	—	—	—	8.50	12.00

KM# 19 CROWN
25.0000 g., Copper-Nickel, 38.83 mm. **Ruler:** Elizabeth II **Series:** Privateering ships of the South Atlantic **Obv:** Crowned bust right **Obv. Legend:** ELIZABETH II — TRISTAN DA CUNHA **Rev:** Sailing ship "Griffin" **Edge:** Reeded

Date	Mintage	F	VF	XF	Unc	BU
2006	—	—	—	—	8.50	12.00

KM# 20 CROWN
25.0000 g., Copper-Nickel, 38.83 mm. **Ruler:** Elizabeth II **Series:** Privateering ships of the South Atlantic **Obv:** Crowned bust right **Obv. Legend:** ELIZABETH II — TRISTAN DA CUNHA **Rev:** Sailing ship "Enterprise" **Edge:** Reeded

Date	Mintage	F	VF	XF	Unc	BU
2006	—	—	—	—	8.50	12.00

KM# 21 CROWN
25.0000 g., Copper-Nickel, 38.83 mm. **Ruler:** Elizabeth II **Series:** Privateering ships of the South Atlantic **Obv:** Crowned bust right **Obv. Legend:** ELIZABETH II — TRISTAN DA CUNHA **Rev:** Sailing ship "Columbus" **Edge:** Reeded

Date	Mintage	F	VF	XF	Unc	BU
2006	—	—	—	—	8.50	12.00

KM# 22 CROWN
25.0000 g., Copper-Nickel, 38.8 mm. **Ruler:** Elizabeth II **Series:** Privateering ships of the South Atlantic **Obv:** Crowned bust right **Obv. Legend:** ELIZABETH II — TRISTAN DA CUNHA **Rev:** Sailing ship "Chausseur" **Edge:** Reeded

Date	Mintage	F	VF	XF	Unc	BU
2006	—	—	—	—	8.50	12.00

KM# 23 CROWN
25.0000 g., Copper-Nickel, 38.8 mm. **Ruler:** Elizabeth II **Series:** Privateering ships of the South Atlantic **Obv:** Crowned bust right **Obv. Legend:** ELIZABETH II — TRISTAN DA CUNHA **Rev:** Sailing ship "Cabot" **Edge:** Reeded

Date	Mintage	F	VF	XF	Unc	BU
2006	—	—	—	—	8.50	12.00

KM# 24 CROWN
25.0000 g., Copper-Nickel, 38.8 mm. **Ruler:** Elizabeth II **Series:** Privateering ships of the South Atlantic **Obv:** Crowned bust right **Obv. Legend:** ELIZABETH II — TRISTAN DA CUNHA **Rev:** Sailing ship "Black Prince" **Edge:** Reeded

Date	Mintage	F	VF	XF	Unc	BU
2006	—	—	—	—	8.50	12.00

KM# 25 CROWN
25.0000 g., Copper-Nickel, 38.8 mm. **Ruler:** Elizabeth II **Series:** Privateering ships of the South Atlantic **Obv:** Crowned bust right **Obv. Legend:** ELIZABETH II — TRISTAN DA CUNHA **Rev:** Sailing ship "Argus" **Edge:** Reeded

Date	Mintage	F	VF	XF	Unc	BU
2006	—	—	—	—	8.50	12.00

KM# 26 CROWN
25.0000 g., Copper-Nickel, 38.8 mm. **Ruler:** Elizabeth II **Series:**

Privateering ships of the South Atlantic **Obv:** Crowned bust right **Obv. Legend:** ELIZABETH II — TRISTAN DA CUNHA **Rev:** Sailing ship "True Blooded Yankee" **Edge:** Reeded

Date	Mintage	F	VF	XF	Unc	BU
2006	—	—	—	—	8.50	12.00

KM# 34 CROWN

Copper-Nickel, 38 mm. **Ruler:** Elizabeth II **Obv:** Head with tiara right **Rev:** 2 whales, multicolor

Date	Mintage	F	VF	XF	Unc	BU
2008	—	—	—	—	6.00	8.00

KM# 35 CROWN

Copper-Nickel, 38.75 mm. **Ruler:** Elizabeth II **Rev:** HMS Victory

Date	Mintage	F	VF	XF	Unc	BU
2008	—	—	—	—	—	15.00

KM# 36 CROWN

25.1800 g., Copper-Nickel **Ruler:** Elizabeth II **Obv:** HMS Belfast

Date	Mintage	F	VF	XF	Unc	BU
2008	—	—	—	—	—	15.00

KM# 37 CROWN

25.1800 g., Copper-Nickel, 38.75 mm. **Ruler:** Elizabeth II **Obv:** HMS Sceptre

Date	Mintage	F	VF	XF	Unc	BU
2008	—	—	—	—	—	15.00

KM# 38 CROWN

25.1800 g., Copper-Nickel, 38.75 mm. **Ruler:** Elizabeth II **Obv:** HMS Beagle

Date	Mintage	F	VF	XF	Unc	BU
2008	—	—	—	—	—	15.00

KM# 39 CROWN

28.1500 g., Copper-Nickel, 38.75 mm. **Ruler:** Elizabeth II **Obv:** HMS Dreadnought

Date	Mintage	F	VF	XF	Unc	BU
2008	—	—	—	—	—	15.00

KM# 40 CROWN

28.1500 g., Copper-Nickel, 38.75 mm. **Ruler:** Elizabeth II **Rev:** H.M.S. Ark Royal

Date	Mintage	F	VF	XF	Unc	BU
2008	—	—	—	—	—	15.00

KM# 42 5 POUNDS

Silver **Ruler:** Elizabeth II **Rev:** St. George slaying dragon

Date	Mintage	F	VF	XF	Unc	BU
2008	—	—	—	—	45.00	50.00

PIEFORTS

KM#	Date	Mintage	Identification	Mkt Val
P1	2001	500	50 Pence. 0.9250 Silver. 56.5400 g. 38.6 mm.	100
P2	2001	500	50 Pence. 0.9250 Silver. 56.5600 g. 38.6 mm. Reeded edge. Proof KM-13a.	100

TUNISIA

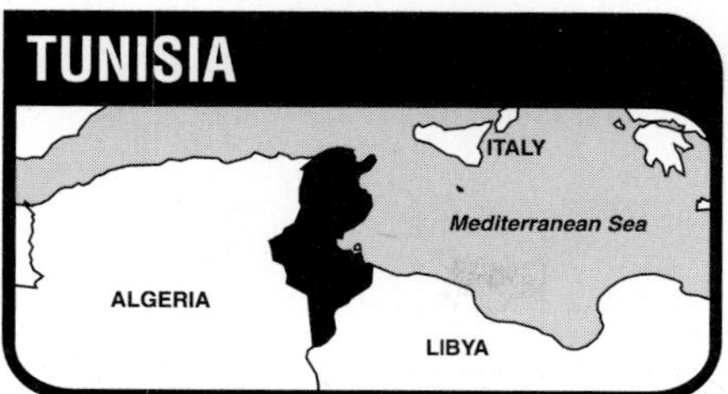

The Republic of Tunisia, located on the northern coast of Africa between Algeria and Libya, has an area of 63,170sq. mi. (163,610 sq. km.) and a population of *7.9 million. Capital: Tunis. Agriculture is the backbone of the economy. Crude oil, phosphates, olive oil, and wine are exported.

TITLES

المملكة التونسية

al-Mamlaka al-Tunisiya

الجمهورية التونسية

al-Jumhuriya al-Tunisiya

al-Amala al-Tunisiya
(Tunisian Protectorate)

REPUBLIC

DECIMAL COINAGE

1000 Millim = 1 Dinar

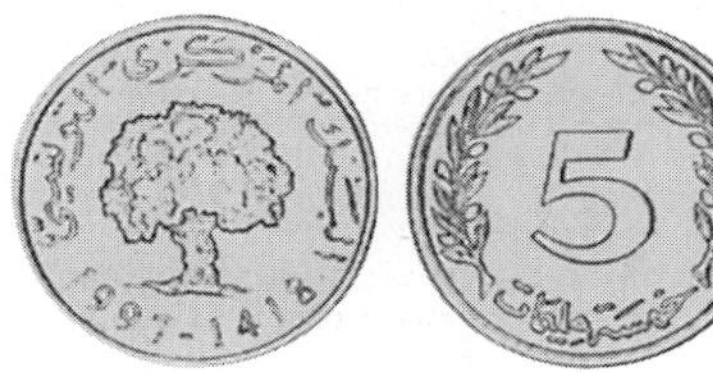

KM# 348 5 MILLIM

1.4900 g., Aluminum, 24 mm. **Obv:** Oak tree and dates **Rev:** Value within sprigs

Date	Mintage	F	VF	XF	Unc	BU
AH1425-2004	—	—	—	—	0.50	—
AH1426-2005	—	—	—	—	0.50	—

KM# 306 10 MILLIM

3.5000 g., Brass, 19 mm. **Obv:** Inscription and dates within inner circle of design **Rev:** Value in center of design **Edge:** Reeded

Date	Mintage	F	VF	XF	Unc	BU
AH1425-2004	—	—	0.15	0.25	0.50	—
AH1426-2005	—	—	0.15	0.25	0.50	—

KM# 307 20 MILLIM

4.5000 g., Brass, 22 mm. **Obv:** Inscription and dates within center circle of design **Rev:** Value within center of design

Date	Mintage	F	VF	XF	Unc	BU
AH1425-2004	—	—	0.30	0.50	0.80	—
AH1426-2005	—	—	0.30	0.50	0.80	—
AH1428-2007	—	—	0.30	0.50	0.80	—

KM# 308 50 MILLIM

6.0000 g., Brass, 25 mm. **Obv:** Inscription and dates within center circle of design **Rev:** Value in center of design

Date	Mintage	F	VF	XF	Unc	BU
AH1425-2004	—	—	0.65	0.85	1.25	—
AH1426-2005	—	—	0.65	0.85	1.25	—
AH1428-2007	—	—	0.65	0.85	1.25	—

KM# 309 100 MILLIM

7.5000 g., Brass, 27 mm. **Obv:** Inscription and dates within center circle of design **Rev:** Value in center of design

Date	Mintage	F	VF	XF	Unc	BU
AH1425-2004	—	—	1.25	1.50	2.00	—
AH1426-2005	—	—	1.25	1.50	2.00	—
AH1429-2008	—	—	1.25	1.50	2.00	—

KM# 346 1/2 DINAR

Copper-Nickel **Obv:** Shield within circle **Rev:** 2 hands with fruit and wheat sprig **Note:** Rim width varieties exist.

Date	Mintage	F	VF	XF	Unc	BU
AH1426-2005	—	—	1.00	2.50	4.50	—
AH1428-2007	—	—	1.00	2.50	4.50	—

KM# 347 DINAR

10.1000 g., Copper-Nickel, 28 mm. **Series:** F.A.O. **Obv:** Shield within circle **Rev:** Female half figure right

Date	Mintage	F	VF	XF	Unc	BU
AH1428-2007	—	—	2.00	4.00	7.50	—

KM# 330 5 DINARS

9.4060 g., 0.9000 Gold 0.2722 oz. AGW **Subject:** Anniversary of 7 Nov 1987 **Obv:** Shield **Rev:** Upstretched hand, flag **Note:** Arabic legends vary by year.

Date	Mintage	F	VF	XF	Unc	BU
2001-1421	40	—	—	—	650	700

KM# 329 5 DINARS

9.4060 g., 0.9000 Gold 0.2722 oz. AGW **Subject:** Anniversary of 7 Nov 1987 **Obv:** Shield **Rev:** Upstretched hand, flag **Note:** French legends vary by year.

Date	Mintage	F	VF	XF	Unc	BU
2001-1422	40	—	—	—	650	700

KM# 435 5 DINARS

9.4800 g., 0.9000 Gold 0.2743 oz. AGW, 22 mm. **Subject:** 7 November 1987, 15th Anniversary **Obv:** Shield **Rev:** Stylized dove **Note:** Arabic legends

Date	Mintage	F	VF	XF	Unc	BU
AH1423-2002 Proof	40	Value: 750				

KM# 436 5 DINARS

9.4800 g., 0.9000 Gold 0.2743 oz. AGW, 22 mm. **Subject:** 7 November 1987, 15th Anniversary **Obv:** Shield **Rev:** Stylized dove **Note:** French legends

Date	Mintage	F	VF	XF	Unc	BU
AH1423-2002 Proof	40	Value: 750				

KM# 443 5 DINARS

Bi-Metallic Silver center in Gold ring, 29 mm. **Subject:** 2nd Anniversary of Death **Obv:** Shield **Rev:** Head left

Date	Mintage	F	VF	XF	Unc	BU
AH1423-2002 Proof	750	Value: 275				

KM# 444 5 DINARS

10.0000 g., Bi-Metallic Copper-Nickel center in Copper ring, 29 mm. **Obv:** Shield **Rev:** Head left

Date	Mintage	F	VF	XF	Unc	BU
AH1423-2002	20,275,000	—	—	—	8.00	10.00

KM# 350 5 DINARS

10.0000 g., Bi-Metallic Copper-Nickel center in Brass ring, 29 mm. **Obv:** National arms **Rev:** Former President Habib Bourguiba **Edge:** Six reeded and six plain sections **Shape:** 12-sided

Date	Mintage	F	VF	XF	Unc	BU
AH1423-2002	—	—	—	—	6.50	8.00

KM# 350a 5 DINARS

Bi-Metallic .925 Silver center in .900 gold ring, 29 mm. **Obv:** National arms **Rev:** Former President Habib Bourguiba **Edge:** 6 reeded and 6 plain sections **Shape:** 12-sided

Date	Mintage	F	VF	XF	Unc	BU
AH1423-2002 Proof	—	Value: 350				

KM# 445 5 DINARS

9.4800 g., 0.9000 Gold 0.2743 oz. AGW, 22 mm. **Subject:** 7 November 1987, 16th Anniversary **Obv:** Shield **Rev:** Hand with UN logo **Note:** Arabic legends

Date	Mintage	F	VF	XF	Unc	BU
AH1424-2003 Proof	40	Value: 750				

KM# 446 5 DINARS

9.4800 g., 0.9000 Gold 0.2743 oz. AGW, 22 mm. **Subject:** 7 November 1987, 16th Anniversary **Obv:** Shield **Rev:** Hand with UN logo **Note:** French legend

Date	Mintage	F	VF	XF	Unc	BU
AH1424-2003 Proof	40	Value: 750				

KM# 456 5 DINARS

9.4000 g., 0.9000 Gold 0.2720 oz. AGW, 22 mm. **Subject:** 7 November 1987, 17th Anniversary - Elections **Obv:** Shield **Rev:** Star and crescent and stylized flame **Note:** French legend

Date	Mintage	F	VF	XF	Unc	BU
AH1425-2004 Proof	40	Value: 750				

KM# 455 5 DINARS

9.4000 g., 0.9000 Gold 0.2720 oz. AGW, 22 mm. **Subject:** 7 November 1987, 17th Anniversary - Elections **Obv:** Shield **Rev:** Star and crescent and stylized flame **Note:** Arabic legend

Date	Mintage	F	VF	XF	Unc	BU
AH1425-2004 Proof	40	Value: 750				

KM# 465 5 DINARS

9.4000 g., 0.9000 Gold 0.2720 oz. AGW, 22 mm. **Subject:** 7 November 1987, 18th Anniversary **Obv:** Shield **Rev:** Globe in stylized ship **Note:** Arabic legend

Date	Mintage	F	VF	XF	Unc	BU
AH1426-2005 Proof	40	Value: 750				

KM# 466 5 DINARS

9.4000 g., 0.9000 Gold 0.2720 oz. AGW, 22 mm. **Subject:** 7 November 1987, 18th Anniversary **Obv:** Shield **Rev:** Globe in stylized ship **Note:** French legend

Date	Mintage	F	VF	XF	Unc	BU
AH1426-2005 Prook	40	Value: 750				

KM# 479 5 DINARS

9.4000 g., 0.9000 Gold 0.2720 oz. AGW, 22 mm. **Subject:** 7 November 1987, 19th Anniversary **Obv:** Shield **Rev:** Dove and atom **Note:** French legend

Date	Mintage	F	VF	XF	Unc	BU
AH1427-2006 Proof	40	Value: 750				

KM# 472 5 DINARS

24.0000 g., 0.9000 Silver 0.6944 oz. ASW, 35 mm. **Subject:** 50th Anniversary **Obv:** Shield **Rev:** Logo **Note:** Arabic legend

Date	Mintage	F	VF	XF	Unc	BU
AH1427-2006 Proof	900	Value: 125				

KM# 478 5 DINARS

9.4000 g., 0.9000 Gold 0.2720 oz. AGW, 22 mm. **Subject:** 7 November 1987, 19th Anniversary **Obv:** Shield **Rev:** Dove and atom **Note:** Arabic legends

Date	Mintage	F	VF	XF	Unc	BU
AH1427-2006 Proof	40	Value: 750				

KM# 473 5 DINARS

24.0000 g., 0.9000 Silver 0.6944 oz. ASW, 35 mm. **Subject:** 50th Anniversary **Obv:** Shield **Rev:** Logo **Note:** French legends

Date	Mintage	F	VF	XF	Unc	BU
AH1427-2006 Proof	100	Value: 225				

KM# 491 5 DINARS

9.4000 g., 0.9000 Gold 0.2720 oz. AGW, 22 mm. **Subject:** 7 November 1987, 20th Anniversary **Obv:** Head of Zine el Abidine Ben Ali right **Rev:** Two profiles, keyboard, satellite receiver **Note:** French legends

Date	Mintage	F	VF	XF	Unc	BU
AH1428-2007 Proof	40	Value: 750				

KM# 486 5 DINARS

24.0000 g., 0.9000 Silver 0.6944 oz. ASW, 35 mm. **Subject:** 50th Anniversary **Obv:** Shield **Rev:** Ship, scales of Justice **Note:** Arabic legend

Date	Mintage	F	VF	XF	Unc	BU
AH1428-2007 Proof	900	Value: 125				

KM# 490 5 DINARS

9.4000 g., 0.9000 Gold 0.2720 oz. AGW, 22 mm. **Subject:** 7 November 1987, 20th Anniversary **Obv:** Head of Zine el Abidne Ben Ali right **Rev:** Two profiles, keyboard, satellite receiver **Note:** Arabic legend

Date	Mintage	F	VF	XF	Unc	BU
AH1428-2007 Proof	43	Value: 750				

KM# 487 5 DINARS

24.0000 g., 0.9000 Silver 0.6944 oz. ASW, 35 mm. **Subject:** 50th Anniversary **Obv:** Shield **Rev:** Ship, scales of Justice **Note:** French legend

Date	Mintage	F	VF	XF	Unc	BU
AH1428-2007 Proof	100	Value: 225				

KM# 378 10 DINARS

38.0000 g., 0.9000 Silver 1.0995 oz. ASW **Subject:** 14th Anniversary 7 Nov and 19th Mediterranean Games **Edge:** Reeded

Date	Mintage	F	VF	XF	Unc	BU
AH1422-2001	—	—	—	—	275	—

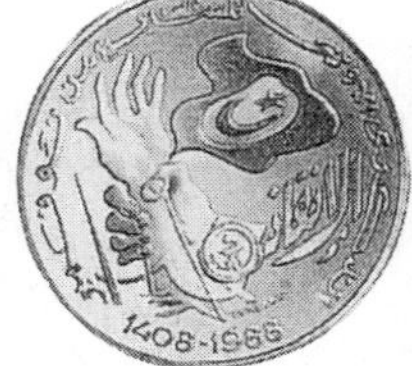

KM# 341 10 DINARS

18.7700 g., 0.9000 Gold 0.5431 oz. AGW **Subject:** Anniversary - 7 Nov 1987 **Obv:** Shield **Rev:** Upstretched hand, flag **Note:** Arabic legends vary by year.

Date	Mintage	F	VF	XF	Unc	BU
2001-1422	40	—	—	—	950	1,000

KM# 430 10 DINARS
38.0000 g., 0.9000 Silver 1.0995 oz. ASW, 40 mm. **Subject:** 7 November 1987, 14th Anniversary **Obv:** Shield **Rev:** Open door **Note:** French legend

Date	Mintage	F	VF	XF	Unc	BU
AH1422-2001 Proof	400	Value: 150				

KM# 340 10 DINARS
18.7700 g., 0.9000 Gold 0.5431 oz. AGW **Subject:** Anniversary - 7 Nov 1987 **Obv:** Shield **Rev:** Upstretched hand, flag **Note:** French legends vary by year.

Date	Mintage	F	VF	XF	Unc	BU
2001-1422	40	—	—	—	950	1,000

KM# 438 10 DINARS
18.8000 g., 0.9000 Gold 0.5440 oz. AGW, 28 mm. **Subject:** 7 November 1987, 15th Anniversary **Obv:** Shield **Rev:** Stylized dove **Note:** French legends

Date	Mintage	F	VF	XF	Unc	BU
AH1423-2002 Proof	40	Value: 1,000				

KM# 379 10 DINARS
38.0000 g., 0.9000 Silver 1.0995 oz. ASW **Subject:** 15th Anniversary 7 Nov 1987 **Obv:** National arms **Edge:** Reeded

Date	Mintage	F	VF	XF	Unc	BU
AH1423-2002	—	—	—	—	275	—

KM# 433 10 DINARS
38.0000 g., 0.9000 Silver 1.0995 oz. ASW, 40 mm. **Subject:** 7 November 1987, 15th Anniversary **Obv:** Shield **Rev:** Stylized dove **Note:** Arabic legends

Date	Mintage	F	VF	XF	Unc	BU
AH1423-2002 Proof	490	Value: 150				

KM# 437 10 DINARS
18.8000 g., 0.9000 Gold 0.5440 oz. AGW, 28 mm. **Subject:** 7 November 1987, 15th Anniversary **Obv:** Shield **Rev:** Stylized dove **Note:** Arabic legends

Date	Mintage	F	VF	XF	Unc	BU
AH1423-2002 Proof	40	Value: 1,000				

KM# 380 10 DINARS
38.0000 g., 0.9000 Silver 1.0995 oz. ASW **Subject:** 16th Anniversary 7 Nov 1987 plus International Solidarity Fund **Obv:** National arms **Rev:** Large 16 with hands holding globe within the 6, banner which says International Solidarity Fund **Edge:** Reeded

Date	Mintage	F	VF	XF	Unc	BU
AH1424-2003	—	—	—	—	250	—
AH1424-2003 Proof	—	Value: 300				

KM# 452 10 DINARS
38.0000 g., 0.9000 Silver 1.0995 oz. ASW, 40 mm. **Subject:** 7 November 1987, 16th Anniversary **Obv:** Shield **Rev:** Large 16 and globe

Date	Mintage	F	VF	XF	Unc	BU
AH1423-2003 Proof	24	Value: 225				

KM# 447 10 DINARS
18.1800 g., 0.9000 Gold 0.5260 oz. AGW, 28 mm. **Subject:** 7 November 1987, 16th Anniversary **Obv:** Shield **Rev:** Hand with UN logo **Note:** Arabic legend

Date	Mintage	F	VF	XF	Unc	BU
AH1424-2003 Proof	40	Value: 1,000				

KM# 448 10 DINARS
18.1800 g., 0.9000 Gold 0.5260 oz. AGW, 28 mm. **Subject:** 7 November 1987, 16th Anniversary **Obv:** Shield **Rev:** Hand with UN logo **Note:** French legends

Date	Mintage	F	VF	XF	Unc	BU
AH1424-2003 Proof	40	Value: 1,000				

KM# 454 10 DINARS
38.0000 g., 0.9000 Silver 1.0995 oz. ASW, 40 mm. **Subject:** 7 November 1987, 17th Anniversary - Elections **Obv:** Shield **Rev:** Star and crescent and stylized flame **Note:** French legends

Date	Mintage	F	VF	XF	Unc	BU
AH1425-2004 Proof	24	Value: 225				

KM# 458 10 DINARS
18.8000 g., 0.9000 Gold 0.5440 oz. AGW, 28 mm. **Subject:** 7 November 1987, 17th Anniversary - Elections **Obv:** Shield **Rev:** Star and crescent adn stylized flame **Note:** French legend

Date	Mintage	F	VF	XF	Unc	BU
AH1425-2004 Proof	40	Value: 1,000				

KM# 457 10 DINARS
18.8000 g., 0.9000 Gold 0.5440 oz. AGW, 28 mm. **Subject:** 7 November 1987, 17th Anniversary - Elections **Obv:** Shield **Rev:** Star and crescent and stylized flame **Note:** Arabic legend

Date	Mintage	F	VF	XF	Unc	BU
AH1425-2004 Proof	40	Value: 1,000				

KM# 381 10 DINARS
38.0000 g., 0.9000 Silver 1.0995 oz. ASW **Subject:** 17th Anniversary of 7 Nov 1987 plus Elections of President and Parliament **Obv:** National arms **Edge:** Reeded

Date	Mintage	F	VF	XF	Unc	BU
AH1425-2004	—	—	—	—	275	—

KM# 453 10 DINARS
38.0000 g., 0.9000 Silver 1.0995 oz. ASW, 40 mm. **Subject:** 7 November 1987, 17th Anniversary - Elections **Obv:** Shield **Rev:** Star and crescent and stylized flame **Note:** Arabic legends

Date	Mintage	F	VF	XF	Unc	BU
AH1425-2004 Proof	375	Value: 150				

KM# 467 10 DINARS
18.8000 g., 0.9000 Gold 0.5440 oz. AGW **Subject:** 7 November 1987, 18th Anniversary **Obv:** Shield **Rev:** Globe in stylized ship **Shape:** 28 **Note:** Arabic legends

Date	Mintage	F	VF	XF	Unc	BU
AH1426-2005 Proof	40	Value: 1,000				

KM# 382 10 DINARS
38.0000 g., 0.9000 Silver 1.0995 oz. ASW **Subject:** 18th Anniversary of 7 Nov 1987 and Conference on Information in Tunis 2005 **Edge:** Reeded

Date	Mintage	F	VF	XF	Unc	BU
AH1426-2005	—	—	—	—	275	—

KM# 464 10 DINARS
38.0000 g., 0.9000 Silver 1.0995 oz. ASW, 40 mm. **Subject:** 7 November 1987, 18th Anniversary **Obv:** Shield **Rev:** Globe in stylized ship **Note:** Arabic legend

Date	Mintage	F	VF	XF	Unc	BU
AH1426-2005 Proof	431	Value: 150				

KM# 468 10 DINARS
18.8000 g., 0.9000 Gold 0.5440 oz. AGW, 28 mm. **Subject:** 7 November 1987, 18th Anniversary **Obv:** Shield **Rev:** Globe in stylized ship **Note:** French legend

Date	Mintage	F	VF	XF	Unc	BU
AH1426-2005 Proof	40	Value: 1,000				

KM# 463 10 DINARS
38.0000 g., 0.9000 Silver 1.0995 oz. ASW, 40 mm. **Subject:** 7 November 1987, 18th Anniversary **Obv:** Shield **Rev:** Globe in stylized ship **Note:** French legends

Date	Mintage	F	VF	XF	Unc	BU
AH1426-2005 Proof	50	Value: 175				

KM# 475 10 DINARS
18.8000 g., 0.9000 Gold 0.5440 oz. AGW, 28 mm. **Subject:** 50th Anniversary **Obv:** Shield **Rev:** Logo **Note:** French legends

Date	Mintage	F	VF	XF	Unc	BU
AH1427-2006 Proof	200	Value: 1,000				

KM# 477 10 DINARS
38.0000 g., 0.9000 Silver 1.0995 oz. ASW, 40 mm. **Subject:** 7 November 1987, 19th Anniversary **Obv:** Shield **Rev:** Dove and atom **Note:** French legend

Date	Mintage	F	VF	XF	Unc	BU
AH1427-2006 Profo	30	Value: 225				

KM# 481 10 DINARS
18.8000 g., 0.9000 Gold 0.5440 oz. AGW, 28 mm. **Subject:** 7 November 1987, 19th Anniversary **Obv:** Shield **Rev:** Dove and atom **Note:** French legend

Date	Mintage	F	VF	XF	Unc	BU
AH1427-2006 Proof	40	Value: 1,000				

KM# 476 10 DINARS
38.0000 g., 0.9000 Silver 1.0995 oz. ASW, 40 mm. **Subject:** 7 November 1987, 19th Anniversary **Obv:** Shield **Rev:** Dove and atom **Note:** Arabic legend

Date	Mintage	F	VF	XF	Unc	BU
AH1427-2006 Proof	300	Value: 150				

KM# 480 10 DINARS
18.8000 g., 0.9000 Gold 0.5440 oz. AGW, 28 mm. **Subject:** 7 November 1987, 19th Anniversary **Obv:** Shield **Rev:** Dove and atom **Note:** Arabic legend

Date	Mintage	F	VF	XF	Unc	BU
AH1427-2006 Proof	40	Value: 1,000				

KM# 383 10 DINARS
38.0000 g., 0.9000 Silver 1.0995 oz. ASW **Subject:** 50th Anniversary of Independence (12.3.1956) **Obv:** National arms **Rev:** Stylized bird, "50", crescent moon with stars

Date	Mintage	F	VF	XF	Unc	BU
AH1427-2006	—	—	—	—	275	—

KM# 383a 10 DINARS
19.0000 g., 0.9000 Gold 0.5498 oz. AGW **Subject:** 50th Anniversary of Independence

Date	Mintage	F	VF	XF	Unc	BU
AH1427-2006 Proof	600	Value: 1,000				

KM# 474 10 DINARS
18.8000 g., 0.9000 Gold 0.5440 oz. AGW, 28 mm. **Subject:** 50th Anniversary **Obv:** Shield **Rev:** Logo **Note:** Arabic legends

Date	Mintage	F	VF	XF	Unc	BU
AH1427-2006 Proof	1,800	Value: 950				

KM# 488 10 DINARS
18.8000 g., 0.9000 Gold 0.5440 oz. AGW, 28 mm. **Subject:** 50th Anniversary **Obv:** Shield **Rev:** Ship, scales of Justice **Note:** Arabic legend

Date	Mintage	F	VF	XF	Unc	BU
AH1428-2007 Proof	450	Value: 975				

KM# 492 10 DINARS
18.8000 g., 0.9000 Gold 0.5440 oz. AGW, 28 mm. **Subject:** 7 November 1987, 20th Anniversary **Obv:** Head of Zine El abidine Ben Ali right **Rev:** Two profiles, keyboard, satellite receiver **Note:** Arabic legend

Date	Mintage	F	VF	XF	Unc	BU
AH1428-2007 Proof	42	Value: 1,000				

KM# 489 10 DINARS
18.8000 g., 0.9000 Gold 0.5440 oz. AGW, 28 mm. **Subject:** 50th Anniversary **Obv:** Shield **Rev:** Ship, scales of Justice **Note:** French legend

Date	Mintage	F	VF	XF	Unc	BU
AH1428-2007 Proof	50	Value: 1,000				

KM# 493 10 DINARS
18.8000 g., 0.9000 Gold 0.5440 oz. AGW, 28 mm. **Subject:** 7 November 1987, 20th Anniversary **Obv:** Head of Zine El Abidine Ben Ali right **Rev:** Two profiles, keyboard, satellite receiver **Note:** French legends

Date	Mintage	F	VF	XF	Unc	BU
AH1428-2007 Proof	40	Value: 1,000				

KM# 396 50 DINARS
21.0000 g., 0.9000 Gold 0.6076 oz. AGW, 34 mm. **Subject:** 14th Anniversary 7 Nov 1987 and 19th Mediterranean Games **Edge:** Reeded **Note:** Arabic legends.

Date	Mintage	F	VF	XF	Unc	BU
AH1422-2001 Proof	—	Value: 1,200				

KM# 431 50 DINARS
21.0000 g., 0.9000 Gold 0.6076 oz. AGW, 34 mm. **Subject:** 7 November 1987, 14th Anniversary **Obv:** Shield **Rev:** Open door **Note:** French legends

Date	Mintage	F	VF	XF	Unc	BU
AH1422-2001 Proof	150	Value: 1,150				

KM# 397 50 DINARS
21.0000 g., 0.9000 Gold 0.6076 oz. AGW, 34 mm. **Subject:** 15th Anniversary of 7 Nov 1987 **Edge:** Reeded

Date	Mintage	F	VF	XF	Unc	BU
AH1423-2002 Proof	—	Value: 1,200				

KM# 440 50 DINARS
21.0000 g., 0.9000 Gold 0.6076 oz. AGW, 21 mm. **Subject:** 7 November 1987, 15th Anniversary **Obv:** Shileld **Rev:** Stylized dove

Date	Mintage	F	VF	XF	Unc	BU
AH1423-2002 Proof	80	Value: 1,250				

KM# 439 50 DINARS
21.0000 g., 0.9000 Gold 0.6076 oz. AGW, 34 mm. **Subject:** 7 November 1987, 15th Anniversary **Obv:** Shield **Rev:** Stylized dove **Note:** Arabic legend

Date	Mintage	F	VF	XF	Unc	BU
AH1423-2002 Proof	580	Value: 1,100				

KM# 450 50 DINARS
21.0000 g., 0.9000 Gold 0.6076 oz. AGW, 34 mm. **Subject:** 7 November 1987, 16th Anniversary **Obv:** Shield **Rev:** Hand with UN logo **Note:** French legends

Date	Mintage	F	VF	XF	Unc	BU
AH1424-2003 Proof	55	Value: 1,250				

KM# 449 50 DINARS
21.0000 g., 0.9000 Gold 0.6076 oz. AGW, 34 mm. **Subject:** 7 November 1987, 16th Anniversary **Obv:** Shield **Rev:** Hand with UN logo **Note:** Arabic legends

Date	Mintage	F	VF	XF	Unc	BU
AH1424-2003 Proof	545	Value: 1,100				

KM# 459 50 DINARS
21.0000 g., 0.9000 Gold 0.6076 oz. AGW, 34 mm. **Subject:** 7 November 1987, 17th Anniversary - Elections **Obv:** Shield **Rev:** Star and crescent and stylized flame **Note:** Arabic legend

Date	Mintage	F	VF	XF	Unc	BU
AH1425-2004 Proof	379	Value: 1,100				

KM# 398 50 DINARS
21.0000 g., 0.9000 Gold 0.6076 oz. AGW, 34 mm. **Subject:** 17th Anniversary of 7 Nov 1987 plus Elections of President and Parliament **Edge:** Reeded

Date	Mintage	F	VF	XF	Unc	BU
AH1425-2004 Proof	—	Value: 1,250				

KM# 460 50 DINARS
21.0000 g., 0.9000 Gold 0.6076 oz. AGW, 34 mm. **Subject:** 7 November 1987, 17th Anniversary - Elections **Obv:** Shield **Rev:** Star and crescent and stylized flame **Note:** French legend

Date	Mintage	F	VF	XF	Unc	BU
AH1425-2004 Proof	28	Value: 1,250				

KM# 470 50 DINARS
21.0000 g., 0.9000 Gold 0.6076 oz. AGW, 34 mm. **Subject:** 7 November 1987, 18th Anniversary **Obv:** Shield **Rev:** Globe and stylized ship **Note:** French legend

Date	Mintage	F	VF	XF	Unc	BU
AH1426-2005 Proof	45	Value: 1,250				

KM# 482 50 DINARS
21.0000 g., 0.9000 Gold 0.6076 oz. AGW, 34 mm. **Subject:** 7 November 1987, 19th Anniversary **Obv:** Shield **Rev:** Dove and atom **Note:** Arabic legend

Date	Mintage	F	VF	XF	Unc	BU
AH1427-2006 Proof	183	Value: 1,200				

KM# 483 50 DINARS
21.0000 g., 0.9000 Gold 0.6076 oz. AGW, 34 mm. **Subject:** 7 November 1987, 19th Anniversary **Obv:** Shield **Rev:** Dove and atom **Note:** French legends

Date	Mintage	F	VF	XF	Unc	BU
AH1427-2006 Proof	23	Value: 1,250				

KM# 432 100 DINARS
38.0000 g., 0.9000 Gold 1.0995 oz. AGW, 43 mm. **Subject:** 7 November 1987, 14th Anniversary **Obv:** Shield **Rev:** Open door **Note:** Arabic legend

Date	Mintage	F	VF	XF	Unc	BU
AH1422-2001 Proof	375	Value: 1,750				

KM# 412 100 DINARS
38.0000 g., 0.9000 Gold 1.0995 oz. AGW, 40 mm. **Subject:** 14th Anniversary of 7 Nov 1987 and 19th Mediterranean Games **Obv:** National arms **Rev:** Olympic rings divide 2 portals **Edge:** Reeded

Date	Mintage	F	VF	XF	Unc	BU
AH1422-2001 Proof	—	Value: 1,900				

KM# 441 100 DINARS
38.0000 g., 0.9000 Gold 1.0995 oz. AGW, 43 mm. **Subject:** 7 November 1987, 15th Anniversary **Obv:** Shield **Rev:** Stylized dove **Note:** Arabic legends

Date	Mintage	F	VF	XF	Unc	BU
AH1423-2002 Proof	380	Value: 1,750				

KM# 442 100 DINARS
38.0000 g., 0.9000 Gold 1.0995 oz. AGW, 43 mm. **Subject:** 7 November 1987, 15th Anniversary **Obv:** Sheild **Rev:** Stylized dove **Note:** French legend

Date	Mintage	F	VF	XF	Unc	BU
AH1423-2002 Proof	110	Value: 1,800				

KM# 352 100 DINARS
38.0000 g., 0.9000 Gold 1.0995 oz. AGW, 40 mm. **Subject:** United Nations **Obv:** National arms above value **Rev:** UN logo on stylized hand **Edge:** Reeded

Date	Mintage	F	VF	XF	Unc	BU
AH1424-2003 Proof	—	Value: 1,900				

KM# 451 100 DINARS
38.0000 g., 0.9000 Gold 1.0995 oz. AGW, 43 mm. **Subject:** 7 November 1987, 16th Anniversary **Obv:** Shield **Rev:** Hand with UN logo **Note:** French text

Date	Mintage	F	VF	XF	Unc	BU
AH1424-2003 Proof	53	Value: 1,850				

KM# 462 100 DINARS
38.0000 g., 0.9000 Gold 1.0995 oz. AGW, 43 mm. **Subject:** 7 November 1987, 17th Anniversary - Elections **Obv:** Shield **Rev:** Star and crescent and stylized flame **Note:** French legends

Date	Mintage	F	VF	XF	Unc	BU
AH1425-2004 Proof	44	Value: 1,850				

KM# 461 100 DINARS
38.0000 g., 0.9000 Gold 1.0995 oz. AGW, 43 mm. **Subject:** 7 November 1987, 17th Anniversary - Elections **Obv:** Shield **Rev:** Star and crescent and stylized flame **Note:** Arabic legend

Date	Mintage	F	VF	XF	Unc	BU
AH1425-2004 Proof	385	Value: 1,750				

KM# 469 100 DINARS
21.0000 g., 0.9000 Gold 0.6076 oz. AGW, 34 mm. **Subject:** 7 November 1987, 18th Anniversary **Obv:** Shield **Rev:** Globe in stylized ship **Note:** Arabic legend

Date	Mintage	F	VF	XF	Unc	BU
AH1426-2005 Proof	390	Value: 1,100				

KM# 413 100 DINARS
38.0000 g., 0.9000 Gold 1.0995 oz. AGW **Subject:** 18th Anniversary of 7 Nov 1987 and Conference on Information in Tunis 2005 **Edge:** Reeded

Date	Mintage	F	VF	XF	Unc	BU
AH1426-2005 Proof	—	Value: 1,900				

KM# 471 100 DINARS
38.0000 g., 0.9000 Gold 1.0995 oz. AGW, 43 mm. **Subject:** 7 November 1987, 18th Anniversary **Obv:** Shield **Rev:** Globe in stylized ship **Note:** French legends

Date	Mintage	F	VF	XF	Unc	BU
AH1426-2005 Proof	45	Value: 1,850				

KM# 485 100 DINARS
38.0000 g., 0.9000 Gold 1.0995 oz. AGW, 43 mm. **Subject:** 7 November 1987, 19th Anniversary **Obv:** Shield **Rev:** Dove and atom **Note:** French legend

Date	Mintage	F	VF	XF	Unc	BU
AH1427-2006 Proof	23	Value: 2,000				

KM# 484 100 DINARS
38.0000 g., 0.9000 Gold 1.0995 oz. AGW, 43 mm. **Subject:** 7 November 1987, 19th Anniversary **Obv:** Shield **Rev:** Dove and atom **Note:** Arabic legend

Date	Mintage	F	VF	XF	Unc	BU
AH1427-2006 Proof	212	Value: 1,800				

TURKEY

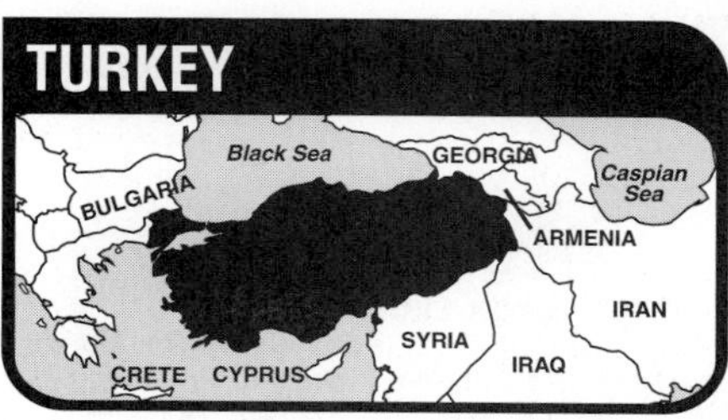

The Republic of Turkey, a parliamentary democracy of the Near East located partially in Europe and partially in Asia between the Black and the Mediterranean Seas, has an area of 301,382 sq. mi. (780,580 sq. km.) and a population of *55.4 million. Capital: Ankara. Turkey exports cotton, hazelnuts, and tobacco, and enjoys a virtual monopoly in meerschaum.

RULER
Republic, AH1341/AD1923-

Mint mark
"d" for darphane (meaning mint) is used on coins for overseas market.

REPUBLIC

DECIMAL COINAGE

Western numerals and Latin alphabet

40 Para = 1 Kurus; 100 Kurus = 1 Lira

KM# 1104 25000 LIRA (25 Bin Lira)
2.7000 g., Brass, 17 mm. **Obv:** Head left **Rev:** Value **Edge:** Plain

Date	Mintage	F	VF	XF	Unc	BU
2001	—	—	—	—	2.00	—
2002	—	—	—	—	2.00	—
2003	—	—	—	—	2.00	—

KM# 1105 50000 LIRA (50 Bin Lira)
3.2000 g., Copper-Nickel-Zinc, 17.75 mm. **Obv:** Head left within circle **Rev:** Value **Edge:** Plain

Date	Mintage	F	VF	XF	Unc	BU
2001	—	—	—	—	0.50	—
2002	—	—	—	—	0.50	—
2003	—	—	—	—	0.50	—
2004	—	—	—	—	0.50	—

KM# 1106 100000 LIRA (100 Bin Lira)
4.6000 g., Copper-Nickel-Zinc, 21 mm. **Obv:** Head with hat right within circle **Rev:** Value **Edge:** Plain

Date	Mintage	F	VF	XF	Unc	BU
2001	—	—	—	—	0.75	1.25
2002	—	—	—	—	0.75	1.25
2003	—	—	—	—	0.75	1.25
2004	—	—	—	—	0.75	1.25

KM# 1137 250000 LIRA
6.4200 g., Copper-Nickel-Zinc, 23.4 mm. **Obv:** Bust facing within circle **Rev:** Value **Edge Lettering:** "T.C." six times dividing reeded sections

Date	Mintage	F	VF	XF	Unc	BU
2002	—	—	—	—	1.00	1.50
2003	—	—	—	—	1.00	1.50
2004	—	—	—	—	1.00	1.50

KM# 1161 500000 LIRA
4.6000 g., Copper-Nickel, 21 mm. **Obv:** Value and date within sprigs **Rev:** One sheep **Edge:** Plain

Date	Mintage	F	VF	XF	Unc	BU
2002	—	—	—	—	2.00	3.00

KM# 1162 750000 LIRA
6.4000 g., Copper-Nickel, 23.5 mm. **Obv:** Value and date within sprigs **Rev:** Angora Ram **Edge:** Plain

Date	Mintage	F	VF	XF	Unc	BU
2002	—	—	—	—	3.00	4.00

KM# 1163 1000000 LIRA
12.0000 g., Copper-Nickel, 31.9 mm. **Obv:** Value and date within sprigs **Rev:** Turbaned bust 1/4 left divides dates **Edge:** Reeded

Date	Mintage	F	VF	XF	Unc	BU
2002	—	—	—	—	5.00	6.00

KM# 1170 1000000 LIRA
31.4200 g., 0.9250 Silver 0.9344 oz. ASW, 38.6 mm. **Subject:** Mevlana Celaleddin-I Rumi **Obv:** Value and date in wreath **Rev:** Turbaned bust **Edge:** Reeded

Date	Mintage	F	VF	XF	Unc	BU
2002 Proof	—	Value: 40.00				

KM# 1139.1 1000000 LIRA
11.8700 g., Bi-Metallic Brass center in Copper-Nickel ring, 32.1 mm. **Subject:** Foundation of the Mint **Obv:** Building and value within circle **Rev:** Legend and date inscription **Edge:** Plain **Note:** This coin type is produced by a machine outside the money museum at the Istanbul Mint. Visitors pay 1 mio lira, press a button and strike a coin with the actual date of their visit. Many other dates exist in unknown and unregistered quantities. Only Turkish months are on struck coins.

Date	Mintage	F	VF	XF	Unc	BU
Mayis 2002	—	—	—	—	5.00	6.00
Haziran 2002	—	—	—	—	5.00	6.00
Temmuz 2002	—	—	—	—	5.00	6.00
Agostos 2002	—	—	—	—	5.00	6.00
Eylul 2002	—	—	—	—	5.00	6.00
Ekim 2002	—	—	—	—	5.00	6.00
Kasim 2002	—	—	—	—	5.00	6.00
Aralik 2002	—	—	—	—	5.00	6.00

KM# 1139.2 1000000 LIRA
Bi-Metallic Brass center in Copper-Nickel ring., 32.1 mm. **Subject:** Foundation of the Mint **Obv:** Building and value within circle **Rev:** Legend and date inscription **Edge:** Plain **Note:** This coin type is produced by a machine outside the money museum at the Istanbul Mint. Visitors pay 1 mio lira, press a button and strike a coin with the actual date of their visit. Many other dates exist in unknown and unregistered quantities. The months are listed in both Turkish and English on struck coins.

Date	Mintage	F	VF	XF	Unc	BU
Ocak/January 2003	—	—	—	—	5.00	6.00
Subat/February 2003	—	—	—	—	5.00	6.00
Mart/March 2003	—	—	—	—	5.00	6.00
Nisan/April 2003	—	—	—	—	5.00	6.00
Mayis/May 2003	—	—	—	—	5.00	6.00
Haziran/June 2003	—	—	—	—	5.00	6.00
Temmuz/July 2003	—	—	—	—	5.00	6.00
Agostos/August 2003	—	—	—	—	5.00	6.00
Eylul/September 2003	—	—	—	—	5.00	6.00
Ekim/October 2003	—	—	—	—	5.00	6.00
Kasim/November 2003	—	—	—	—	5.00	6.00
Aralik/December 2003	—	—	—	—	5.00	6.00

KM# 1107 3000000 LIRA
31.4700 g., 0.9250 Silver 0.9359 oz. ASW, 38.6 mm. **Series:** Olympics **Obv:** Value and date within wreath **Rev:** Long jumper and logo **Edge:** Reeded

Date	Mintage	F	VF	XF	Unc	BU
2002 Proof	—	Value: 42.50				

KM# 1110 5000000 LIRA
67.0000 g., Bronze, 50 mm. **Subject:** Children's Day **Obv:** Legend and inscription **Rev:** Dancing children **Edge:** Plain

Date	Mintage	F	VF	XF	Unc	BU
2001 Matte	1,583	—	—	—	35.00	—

KM# 1142 7500000 LIRA
31.2500 g., 0.9250 Silver 0.9293 oz. ASW, 38.5 mm. **Subject:** Cahit Arf, Turkish mathematician (1910-1997) **Obv:** Mathematical formula within circle **Rev:** 1/2-length figure facing **Edge:** Reeded

Date	Mintage	F	VF	XF	Unc	BU
2001 Proof	—	Value: 45.00				

KM# 1143 7500000 LIRA
31.2500 g., 0.9250 Silver 0.9293 oz. ASW, 38.5 mm. **Obv:** Ornamented circle design **Rev:** 1/2-length bust facing **Edge:** Reeded

Date	Mintage	F	VF	XF	Unc	BU
2001 Proof	—	Value: 45.00				

KM# 1144 7500000 LIRA
31.2500 g., 0.9250 Silver 0.9293 oz. ASW, 38.5 mm. **Subject:** Koca Yusuf Baspehlivan **Obv:** Two figures wrestling **Rev:** Portrait on circular background **Edge:** Reeded

Date	Mintage	F	VF	XF	Unc	BU
2001 Proof	—	Value: 42.50				

KM# 1120 7500000 LIRA
15.4000 g., 0.9250 Silver 0.4580 oz. ASW **Subject:** Bird Series - Saz Horozu **Obv:** Value and date within sprigs **Rev:** Purple swamphen on ground **Edge:** Plain **Shape:** 4-sided **Note:** 28.1 x 28.1mm

Date	Mintage	F	VF	XF	Unc	BU
2001 Proof	—	Value: 35.00				

KM# 1121 7500000 LIRA
15.4000 g., 0.9250 Silver 0.4580 oz. ASW **Subject:** Bird Series - Toy **Obv:** Value and date within sprigs **Rev:** Greater Bustard on ground **Edge:** Plain **Shape:** 4-sided **Note:** 28.1 x 28.1mm

Date	Mintage	F	VF	XF	Unc	BU
2001 Proof	—	Value: 35.00				

KM# 1122 7500000 LIRA
15.4000 g., 0.9250 Silver 0.4580 oz. ASW **Subject:** Bird Series - Yaz Ordegi **Obv:** Value and date within sprigs **Rev:** White-headed Duck on ground **Edge:** Plain **Shape:** 4-sided **Note:** 28.1 x 28.1mm

Date	Mintage	F	VF	XF	Unc	BU
2001 Proof	—	Value: 35.00				

KM# 1123 7500000 LIRA
15.4000 g., 0.9250 Silver 0.4580 oz. ASW **Subject:** Bird Series - Dikkuyruk **Obv:** Value and date within sprigs **Rev:** Marbled teal on water **Edge:** Plain **Shape:** 4-sided **Note:** 28.1 x 28.1mm

Date	Mintage	F	VF	XF	Unc	BU
2001 Proof	—	Value: 35.00				

KM# 1124 7500000 LIRA
15.4000 g., 0.9250 Silver 0.4580 oz. ASW **Subject:** Bird Series - Yesil Arikusu **Obv:** Value and date within sprigs **Rev:** Bee-eater on branch **Edge:** Plain **Shape:** 4-sided **Note:** 28.1 x 28.1mm

Date	Mintage	F	VF	XF	Unc	BU
2001 Proof	—	Value: 35.00				

KM# 1125 7500000 LIRA
15.4000 g., 0.9250 Silver 0.4580 oz. ASW **Subject:** Bird Series - Kucuk Karabatak **Obv:** Value and date within sprigs **Rev:** Three pygmy cormorants **Edge:** Plain **Shape:** 4-sided **Note:** 28.1 x 28.1mm

Date	Mintage	F	VF	XF	Unc	BU
2001 Proof	—	Value: 35.00				

KM# 1126 7500000 LIRA
15.4000 g., 0.9250 Silver 0.4580 oz. ASW **Subject:** Bird Series - Kizil Akbaba **Obv:** Value and date within sprigs **Rev:** Eurasian griffon **Edge:** Plain **Shape:** 4-sided **Note:** 28.1 x 28.1mm

Date	Mintage	F	VF	XF	Unc	BU
2001 Proof	—	Value: 35.00				

KM# 1127 7500000 LIRA
15.4000 g., 0.9250 Silver 0.4580 oz. ASW **Subject:** Bird Series - Sah Kartal **Obv:** Value and date within sprigs **Rev:** Eagles **Edge:** Plain **Shape:** 4-sided **Note:** 28.1 x 28.1mm

Date	Mintage	F	VF	XF	Unc	BU
2001 Proof	—	Value: 35.00				

KM# 1128 7500000 LIRA
15.4000 g., 0.9250 Silver 0.4580 oz. ASW **Subject:** Bird Series - Ala Sigireik **Obv:** Value and date within sprigs **Rev:** Rosy starling on ground **Edge:** Plain **Shape:** 4-sided **Note:** 28.1 x 28.1mm

Date	Mintage	F	VF	XF	Unc	BU
2001 Proof	—	Value: 35.00				

KM# 1129 7500000 LIRA
15.4000 g., 0.9250 Silver 0.4580 oz. ASW **Subject:** Bird Series - Izmir Yalicapkini **Obv:** Value and date within sprigs **Rev:** White-throated kingfisher on stump **Edge:** Plain **Shape:** 4-sided **Note:** 28.1 x 28.1mm

Date	Mintage	F	VF	XF	Unc	BU
2001 Proof	—	Value: 35.00				

KM# 1130 7500000 LIRA
15.4000 g., 0.9250 Silver 0.4580 oz. ASW **Subject:** Bird Series - Turac **Obv:** Value and date within sprigs **Rev:** Black francolin birds on the ground **Edge:** Plain **Shape:** 4-sided **Note:** 28.1 x 28.1mm

Date	Mintage	F	VF	XF	Unc	BU
2001 Proof	—	Value: 35.00				

KM# 1131 7500000 LIRA
15.4000 g., 0.9250 Silver 0.4580 oz. ASW **Subject:** Bird Series - Kelaynak **Obv:** Value and date within sprigs **Rev:** Two Bald Ibis birds on ground **Edge:** Plain **Shape:** 4-sided **Note:** 28.1 x 28.1mm

Date	Mintage	F	VF	XF	Unc	BU
2001 Proof	—	Value: 35.00				

KM# 1132 7500000 LIRA
15.4000 g., 0.9250 Silver 0.4580 oz. ASW **Subject:** Bird Series - Sakalli Akbaba **Obv:** Value and date within sprigs **Rev:** Bearded vulture **Edge:** Plain **Shape:** 4-sided **Note:** 28.1 x 28.1mm

Date	Mintage	F	VF	XF	Unc	BU
2001 Proof	—	Value: 35.00				

KM# 1133 7500000 LIRA
15.4000 g., 0.9250 Silver 0.4580 oz. ASW **Subject:** Bird Series - Tepeli Pelikan **Obv:** Value and date within sprigs **Rev:** Dalmatian pelican on rock **Edge:** Plain **Shape:** Square **Note:** 28.1 x 28.1mm

Date	Mintage	F	VF	XF	Unc	BU
2001 Proof	—	Value: 35.00				

KM# 1134 7500000 LIRA
15.4000 g., 0.9250 Silver 0.4580 oz. ASW **Subject:** Bird Series - Ishakkusu **Obv:** Value and date within sprigs **Rev:** European scops owl on branch **Edge:** Plain **Shape:** Square **Note:** 28.1 x 28.1mm

Date	Mintage	F	VF	XF	Unc	BU
2001 Proof	—	Value: 35.00				

KM# 1117 7500000 LIRA
31.4700 g., 0.9250 Silver 0.9359 oz. ASW **Subject:** Iznik Tabak **Obv:** Two peacocks within circle **Rev:** Iznik Tabak (Nicean pottery) 1570; Circle of flowers at center

Date	Mintage	F	VF	XF	Unc	BU
2001 Proof	1,349	Value: 50.00				

KM# 1135 7500000 LIRA
31.0300 g., 0.9250 Silver 0.9228 oz. ASW, 38.5 mm. **Subject:** Mevlana Celaleddin-i Rumi **Obv:** Dancer within circle **Rev:** Turbaned bust 3/4 right above dates **Edge:** Reeded

Date	Mintage	F	VF	XF	Unc	BU
2001 Proof	—	Value: 45.00				

KM# 1145 7500000 LIRA
15.6100 g., 0.9250 Silver 0.4642 oz. ASW, 27.9 x 38.6 mm. **Series:** Flowers **Obv:** Value and date within sprigs **Rev:** Paeonia turcica **Edge:** Reeded **Shape:** Oval

Date	Mintage	F	VF	XF	Unc	BU
2002 Proof	—	Value: 28.00				

KM# 1146 7500000 LIRA
15.6100 g., 0.9250 Silver 0.4642 oz. ASW, 27.9 x 38.6 mm. **Series:** Flowers **Obv:** Value and date within sprigs **Rev:** Orchis anatolica **Edge:** Reeded **Shape:** Oval

Date	Mintage	F	VF	XF	Unc	BU
2002 Proof	—	Value: 28.00				

KM# 1147 7500000 LIRA
15.6100 g., 0.9250 Silver 0.4642 oz. ASW, 27.9 x 38.6 mm. **Series:** Flowers **Obv:** Value and date within sprigs **Rev:** Iris pamphylica **Edge:** Reeded **Shape:** Oval

Date	Mintage	F	VF	XF	Unc	BU
2002 Proof	—	Value: 28.00				

KM# 1148 7500000 LIRA
15.6100 g., 0.9250 Silver 0.4642 oz. ASW, 27.9 x 38.6 mm. **Series:** Flowers **Obv:** Value and date within sprigs **Rev:** Gladiolus anatolicus **Edge:** Reeded **Shape:** Oval

Date	Mintage	F	VF	XF	Unc	BU
2002 Proof	—	Value: 28.00				

KM# 1149 7500000 LIRA
15.6100 g., 0.9250 Silver 0.4642 oz. ASW, 27.9 x 38.6 mm. **Series:** Flowers **Obv:** Value and date within sprigs **Rev:** Crocus sativus **Edge:** Reeded **Shape:** Oval

Date	Mintage	F	VF	XF	Unc	BU
2002 Proof	—	Value: 28.00				

KM# 1150 7500000 LIRA
15.6100 g., 0.9250 Silver 0.4642 oz. ASW, 27.9 x 38.6 mm. **Series:** Flowers **Obv:** Value and date within sprigs **Rev:** Campanula betulifolia **Edge:** Reeded **Shape:** Oval

Date	Mintage	F	VF	XF	Unc	BU
2002 Proof	—	Value: 28.00				

KM# 1151 7500000 LIRA
15.6100 g., 0.9250 Silver 0.4642 oz. ASW, 27.9 x 38.6 mm. **Series:** Flowers **Obv:** Value and date within sprigs **Rev:** Centaurea tchihatcheffii **Edge:** Reeded **Shape:** Oval

Date	Mintage	F	VF	XF	Unc	BU
2002 Proof	—	Value: 28.00				

KM# 1152 7500000 LIRA
15.6100 g., 0.9250 Silver 0.4642 oz. ASW, 27.9 x 38.6 mm. **Series:** Flowers **Obv:** Value and date within sprigs **Rev:** Tchihatchewia isatidea **Edge:** Reeded **Shape:** Oval

Date	Mintage	F	VF	XF	Unc	BU
2002 Proof	—	Value: 28.00				

KM# 1153 7500000 LIRA
15.6100 g., 0.9250 Silver 0.4642 oz. ASW, 27.9 x 38.6 mm. **Series:** Flowers **Obv:** Value and date within sprigs **Rev:** Linum anatolicum **Edge:** Reeded **Shape:** Oval

Date	Mintage	F	VF	XF	Unc	BU
2002 Proof	—	Value: 28.00				

KM# 1154 7500000 LIRA
15.6100 g., 0.9250 Silver 0.4642 oz. ASW, 27.9 x 38.6 mm. **Series:** Flowers **Obv:** Value and date within sprigs **Rev:** Cyclamen trochopteranthum **Edge:** Reeded **Shape:** Oval

Date	Mintage	F	VF	XF	Unc	BU
2002 Proof	—	Value: 28.00				

KM# 1155 7500000 LIRA
15.6100 g., 0.9250 Silver 0.4642 oz. ASW, 27.9 x 38.6 mm. **Series:** Flowers **Obv:** Value and date within sprigs **Rev:** Tulipa orphanidea **Edge:** Reeded **Shape:** Oval

Date	Mintage	F	VF	XF	Unc	BU
2002 Proof	—	Value: 28.00				

KM# 1156 7500000 LIRA
15.6100 g., 0.9250 Silver 0.4642 oz. ASW, 27.9 x 38.6 mm. **Obv:** Value and date within sprigs **Rev:** Stenbergia candida **Edge:** Reeded **Shape:** Oval

Date	Mintage	F	VF	XF	Unc	BU
2002 Proof	—	Value: 28.00				

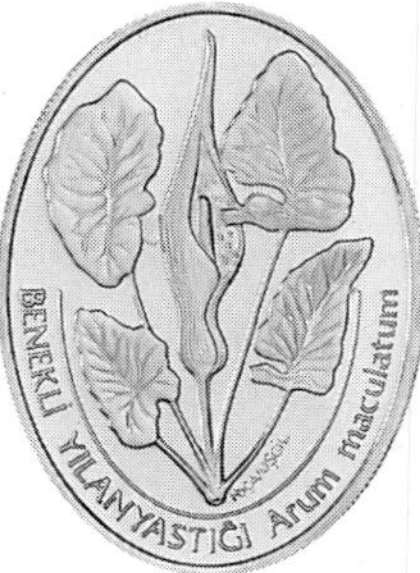

KM# 1157 7500000 LIRA
15.6100 g., 0.9250 Silver 0.4642 oz. ASW, 27.9 x 38.6 mm. **Series:** Flowers **Obv:** Value and date within sprigs **Rev:** Arum maculatum **Edge:** Reeded **Shape:** Oval

Date	Mintage	F	VF	XF	Unc	BU
2002 Proof	—	Value: 28.00				

KM# 1118 10000000 LIRA
31.4700 g., 0.9250 Silver 0.9359 oz. ASW, 38.6 mm. **Subject:** Divrigi Ulu Camii **Obv:** Artwork within circle **Rev:** Ornate door at the Divrigi ulu Camii (Divrigi Great Mosque) built 1228 in Sivas Province **Edge:** Reeded

Date	Mintage	F	VF	XF	Unc	BU
2001 Matte	15,000	—	—	—	40.00	—

KM# 1159 10000000 LIRA
31.4200 g., 0.9250 Silver 0.9344 oz. ASW, 38.6 mm. **Subject:** Bogazici'nde Yalilar **Obv:** Value and date within sprigs **Rev:** Waterfront buildings **Edge:** Reeded

Date	Mintage	F	VF	XF	Unc	BU
2001 Proof	4,458	Value: 40.00				

KM# 1160 10000000 LIRA
31.4200 g., 0.9250 Silver 0.9344 oz. ASW, 38.6 mm. **Obv:** Turkish mint symbol within circle **Rev:** Mosque within surrounding buildings **Edge:** Reeded

Date	Mintage	F	VF	XF	Unc	BU
2002 Proof	2,106	Value: 45.00				

KM# 1140 10000000 LIRA
31.4600 g., 0.9250 Silver 0.9356 oz. ASW, 38.6 mm. **Subject:** 75th Anniversary of TRT (Türkiye Radyo Televizyon) **Obv:** Large mint mark and design within circle **Rev:** Radio microphone **Edge:** Reeded

Date	Mintage	F	VF	XF	Unc	BU
2002 Proof	—	Value: 45.00				

KM# 1265 150000000 LIRA
31.4900 g., 0.9250 Silver 0.9365 oz. ASW, 38.61 mm. **Subject:** 2006 FIFA World Cup **Obv:** Value within wreath **Rev:** Two scoccer players and globe **Edge:** Reeded

Date	Mintage	F	VF	XF	Unc	BU
2003 Proof	Est. 5,000	Value: 50.00				

REFORM DECIMAL COINAGE

2005

100,000 Old Lira = 1 New Lira

KM# 1239 KURUS
Copper-Nickel **Obv:** Head of Ataturk left **Rev:** Plant and value

Date	Mintage	F	VF	XF	Unc	BU
2009	—	—	—	—	0.30	0.50

KM# 1164 NEW KURUS
2.7200 g., Aluminum-Bronze, 17 mm. **Obv:** Head of Atatürk left within circle **Rev:** Value **Edge:** Plain

Date	Mintage	F	VF	XF	Unc	BU
2005	148,419,560	—	—	—	0.15	0.20
2006	9,002,010	—	—	—	0.15	0.20
2007	5,357,000	—	—	—	0.15	0.20
2008	—	—	—	—	0.15	0.20

KM# 1240 5 KURUS
Brass **Obv:** Head of Ataturk left **Rev:** Value and traditional embroidery pattern

Date	Mintage	F	VF	XF	Unc	BU
2009	—	—	—	—	0.30	0.50

KM# 1165 5 NEW KURUS
2.9500 g., Copper-Nickel-Zinc, 17.1 mm. **Obv:** Head of Atatürk left within circle **Rev:** Value **Edge:** Plain

Date	Mintage	F	VF	XF	Unc	BU
2005	203,339,160	—	—	0.10	0.25	0.35
2006	202,253,310	—	—	0.10	0.25	0.35
2007	122,090,000	—	—	0.10	0.25	0.35

KM# 1241 10 KURUS
Brass **Obv:** Head of Ataturk left **Rev:** Value

Date	Mintage	F	VF	XF	Unc	BU
2009	—	—	—	—	0.30	0.50

KM# 1166 10 NEW KURUS
3.8300 g., Copper-Nickel-Zinc, 19.4 mm. **Obv:** Head of Atatürk with hat right within circle **Rev:** Value **Edge:** Plain

Date	Mintage	F	VF	XF	Unc	BU
2005	261,538,050	—	—	0.20	0.45	0.60
2006	196,717,510	—	—	0.20	0.45	0.60
2007	134,104,000	—	—	0.20	0.45	0.60

KM# 1242 25 KURUS
Copper-Nickel **Obv:** Head of Ataturk left **Rev:** Value

Date	Mintage	F	VF	XF	Unc	BU
2009	—	—	—	—	0.50	0.75

KM# 1167 25 NEW KURUS
5.3000 g., Copper-Nickel-Zinc, 21.5 mm. **Obv:** Bust of Atatürk facing within circle **Rev:** Value **Edge:** Reeded

Date	Mintage	F	VF	XF	Unc	BU
2005	173,705,760	—	—	0.25	0.60	0.80
2006	67,803,010	—	—	0.30	0.75	1.00
2007	33,463,500	—	—	0.25	0.60	0.80

KM# 1243 50 KURUS
Bi-Metallic Brass center in Copper-Nickel ring **Obv:** Head of Atatürk left **Rev:** Value above suspension bridge

Date	Mintage	F	VF	XF	Unc	BU
2009	—	—	—	—	0.75	1.00

KM# 1168 50 NEW KURUS
7.0000 g., Bi-Metallic Copper-Nickel center in Nickel-Brass ring, 23.8 mm. **Obv:** Head of Atatürk right within circle **Rev:** Value within circle **Edge:** Reeded

Date	Mintage	F	VF	XF	Unc	BU
2005	203,749,569	—	—	0.60	1.50	2.00
2006	45,089,010	—	—	0.60	1.50	2.00
2007	21,946,500	—	—	0.50	1.20	1.60

KM# 1244 LIRA
Bi-Metallic Copper-Nickel center in Brass ring **Obv:** Head of Atatürk left **Rev:** Value

Date	Mintage	F	VF	XF	Unc	BU
2009	—	—	—	—	3.00	5.00

KM# 1169 NEW LIRA
8.5000 g., Bi-Metallic Nickel-Bronze center in Copper-Nickel-Zinc ring, 26 mm. **Obv:** Bust of Atatürk 3/4 left within circle **Rev:** Value within circle **Edge:** Segmented reeding

Date	Mintage	F	VF	XF	Unc	BU
2005	305,235,560	—	—	—	2.25	3.00
2006	69,247,010	—	—	—	2.25	3.00
2007	56,498,200	—	—	—	2.25	3.00
2008	—	—	—	—	2.25	3.00

KM# 1171 5 NEW LIRA

12.0000 g., Bi-Metallic Brass center in Copper-Nickel ring, 32 mm. **Subject:** 23rd Universiade in red holder **Obv:** Stylized bird within circle **Rev:** Logo within circle **Designer:** Nesrin Ek

Date	Mintage	F	VF	XF	Unc	BU
ND (2005)	2,957	—	—	—	22.00	25.00

KM# 1172 5 NEW LIRA

12.0000 g., Bi-Metallic Copper-Nickel center in Brass ring, 32 mm. **Subject:** 23rd Universiade in blue holder **Obv:** Stylized bird within circle **Rev:** Logo within circle **Designer:** Nesrin Ek

Date	Mintage	F	VF	XF	Unc	BU
ND (2005)	2,900	—	—	—	22.00	25.00

KM# 1195 15 NEW LIRA

1.2400 g., 0.9990 Gold 0.0398 oz. AGW, 13.92 mm. **Subject:** Nemrud **Obv:** Value within wreath **Rev:** Two large statue heads **Designer:** Nesrin Ek **Note:** Dated 2003 but released in 2005

Date	Mintage	F	VF	XF	Unc	BU
2003	1,820	Value: 75.00				

KM# 1193 15 NEW LIRA

15.5500 g., 0.9250 Silver 0.4624 oz. ASW, 32 mm. **Obv:** Bird **Rev:** Logo **Designer:** Nesrin Ek

Date	Mintage	F	VF	XF	Unc	BU
2005 Proof	1,237	Value: 40.00				

KM# 1203 15 NEW LIRA

31.4700 g., 0.9250 Silver 0.9359 oz. ASW, 38.6 mm. **Subject:** Scouting in Turkey, 100th Anniversary **Obv:** Scout emblem, multicolor **Rev:** Flag, Scouts saluting, camp scene

Date	Mintage	F	VF	XF	Unc	BU
2007 Proof	1,414	Value: 50.00				

KM# 1180.1 20 NEW LIRA

23.5000 g., 0.9250 Silver 0.6988 oz. ASW, 38.6 mm. **Obv:** Value within sprigs and circle **Rev:** Angora Cat with plain eyes **Edge:** Reeded

Date	Mintage	F	VF	XF	Unc	BU
2005 Proof	5,000	Value: 60.00				

KM# 1180.2 20 NEW LIRA

23.5000 g., 0.9250 Silver 0.6988 oz. ASW, 38.6 mm. **Obv:** Value within sprigs and circle **Rev:** Angora cat with mismatched colored eyes **Edge:** Reeded

Date	Mintage	F	VF	XF	Unc	BU
2005 Proof	—	Value: 65.00				

KM# 1173 20 NEW LIRA

31.3600 g., 0.9250 Silver 0.9326 oz. ASW, 38.6 mm. **Obv:** Value within sprigs and circle **Rev:** Aegean Carpet **Edge:** Reeded

Date	Mintage	F	VF	XF	Unc	BU
2005 Proof	1,195	Value: 70.00				

KM# 1174 20 NEW LIRA

31.4300 g., 0.9250 Silver 0.9347 oz. ASW, 38.6 mm. **Obv:** Value within sprigs and circle **Rev:** Mostar Bridge **Rev. Designer:** Nesrin Ek **Edge:** Reeded

Date	Mintage	F	VF	XF	Unc	BU
2005 Proof	1,592	Value: 75.00				

KM# 1175 20 NEW LIRA

23.4500 g., 0.9250 Silver 0.6974 oz. ASW, 38.6 mm. **Obv:** Value within sprigs and circle **Rev:** Angora Goat **Rev. Designer:** Nesrin Ek **Edge:** Reeded

Date	Mintage	F	VF	XF	Unc	BU
2005 Proof	898	Value: 60.00				

KM# 1176 20 NEW LIRA

23.4600 g., 0.9250 Silver 0.6977 oz. ASW, 38.6 mm. **Obv:** Value within sprigs and circle **Rev:** Long-eared Desert Hedgehog **Rev. Designer:** Nesrin Ek **Edge:** Reeded

Date	Mintage	F	VF	XF	Unc	BU
2005 Proof	744	Value: 60.00				

KM# 1177 20 NEW LIRA

23.4100 g., 0.9250 Silver 0.6962 oz. ASW, 38.6 mm. **Obv:** Value within sprigs and circle **Rev:** Anatolian Mouflon **Rev. Designer:** Nesrin Ek **Edge:** Reeded

Date	Mintage	F	VF	XF	Unc	BU
2005 Proof	779	Value: 60.00				

KM# 1178 20 NEW LIRA

23.4300 g., 0.9250 Silver 0.6968 oz. ASW, 38.6 mm. **Obv:** Value within sprigs and circle **Rev:** Striped Hyena **Rev. Designer:** Nesrin Ek **Edge:** Reeded

Date	Mintage	F	VF	XF	Unc	BU
2005 Proof	778	Value: 60.00				

KM# 1179 20 NEW LIRA

23.4300 g., 0.9250 Silver 0.6968 oz. ASW, 38.6 mm. **Obv:** Value within sprigs and circle **Rev:** Hazel Dormouse **Rev. Designer:** Nesrin Ek **Edge:** Reeded

Date	Mintage	F	VF	XF	Unc	BU
2005 Proof	744	Value: 60.00				

KM# 1181 20 NEW LIRA

23.3700 g., 0.9990 Silver 0.7506 oz. ASW, 38.6 mm. **Obv:** Value within sprigs and circle **Rev:** Anatolian Leopard **Rev. Designer:** Nesrin Ek **Edge:** Reeded

Date	Mintage	F	VF	XF	Unc	BU
2005 Proof	855	Value: 60.00				

KM# 1182 20 NEW LIRA

23.2500 g., 0.9250 Silver 0.6914 oz. ASW, 38.6 mm. **Obv:** Value within sprigs and circle **Rev:** Turkish Kangal Dog **Rev. Designer:** Nesrin Ek **Edge:** Reeded

Date	Mintage	F	VF	XF	Unc	BU
2005 Proof	1,128	Value: 60.00				

KM# 1183 20 NEW LIRA

23.4600 g., 0.9250 Silver 0.6977 oz. ASW, 38.6 mm. **Obv:** Value within sprigs and circle **Rev:** Five-toed Jerboa **Rev. Designer:** Nesrin Ek **Edge:** Reeded

Date	Mintage	F	VF	XF	Unc	BU
2005 Proof	746	Value: 60.00				

KM# 1184 20 NEW LIRA

23.2600 g., 0.9250 Silver 0.6917 oz. ASW, 38.6 mm. **Obv:** Value within sprigs and circle **Rev:** Brown Bear **Rev. Designer:** Nesrin Ek **Edge:** Reeded

Date	Mintage	F	VF	XF	Unc	BU
2005 Proof	802	Value: 60.00				

KM# 1185 20 NEW LIRA

23.5300 g., 0.9250 Silver 0.6997 oz. ASW, 38.6 mm. **Obv:** Value within sprigs and circle **Rev:** Desert Monitor **Rev. Designer:** Hakk Baha Cavu G L **Edge:** Reeded

Date	Mintage	F	VF	XF	Unc	BU
2005 Proof	753	Value: 60.00				

KM# 1188 20 NEW LIRA

31.4700 g., 0.9250 Silver 0.9359 oz. ASW, 38.6 mm. **Subject:** Edirne Selimiye Mosque **Obv:** Value within wreath **Rev:** Mosque **Rev. Designer:** Nalan Yerl Bucak

Date	Mintage	F	VF	XF	Unc	BU
2005 Proof	1,660	Value: 55.00				

KM# 1189 20 NEW LIRA

31.4700 g., 0.9250 Silver 0.9359 oz. ASW, 38.6 mm. **Obv:** Crescent and star **Obv. Designer:** Suat Ozyuonum **Rev:** Large 85 above building **Rev. Designer:** Suat Ozyuonom

Date	Mintage	F	VF	XF	Unc	BU
2005 Proof	1,216	Value: 55.00				

KM# 1190 20 NEW LIRA

31.4700 g., 0.9250 Silver 0.9359 oz. ASW, 38.6 mm. **Subject:** Galatasaray Spor **Obv:** 100 above team mascot **Rev:** GS monogram

Date	Mintage	F	VF	XF	Unc	BU
2005 Proof	2,828	Value: 55.00				

KM# 1194 20 NEW LIRA

31.4700 g., 0.9250 Silver 0.9359 oz. ASW, 38.6 mm. **Subject:** Belt Maglova Cultural Heritage site **Obv:** Value within wreath **Rev:** Aqueduct

Date	Mintage	F	VF	XF	Unc	BU
2005 Proof	1,250	Value: 55.00				

KM# 1191 25 NEW LIRA

31.4700 g., 0.9250 Silver 0.9359 oz. ASW, 38.6 mm. **Subject:** Galatasaray Spor **Obv:** 100 above team mascot **Rev:** GS monogram, colored

Date	Mintage	F	VF	XF	Unc	BU
2005 Proof	1,250	Value: 85.00				

KM# 1196 25 NEW LIRA

31.4700 g., 0.9250 Silver 0.9359 oz. ASW, 38.6 mm. **Subject:** 800 year of Medical Education in Turkey **Obv:** Two snakes **Rev:** Figure **Designer:** Nesrin Ek

Date	Mintage	F	VF	XF	Unc	BU
2006 Proof	1,650	Value: 60.00				

KM# 1198 25 NEW LIRA

31.4700 g., 0.9250 Silver 0.9359 oz. ASW, 38.6 mm. **Subject:** Nevruz of Hatira **Obv:** Flower and rays **Rev:** Statue holding flames **Designer:** Betul U Urlu

Date	Mintage	F	VF	XF	Unc	BU
2006 Proof	1,300	Value: 85.00				

KM# 1199 25 NEW LIRA

31.4700 g., 0.9250 Silver 0.9359 oz. ASW, 38.6 mm. **Subject:** Hattat Hamid Aytac **Obv:** Design **Rev:** Bust facing **Designer:** Nesrin Ek

Date	Mintage	F	VF	XF	Unc	BU
2006 Proof	1,301	Value: 75.00				

KM# 1200 25 NEW LIRA

31.4700 g., 0.9250 Silver 0.9359 oz. ASW, 38.6 mm. **Subject:** T.C. Devlet Demiryollari, 150th Anniversary **Obv:** 150 above laural **Rev:** Building

Date	Mintage	F	VF	XF	Unc	BU
2006 Proof	1,950	Value: 55.00				

KM# 1201 25 NEW LIRA

31.4700 g., 0.9250 Silver 0.9359 oz. ASW, 38.6 mm. **Subject:** Mehmet Ersoy Akif, 70th Anniversary of death **Obv:** Scroll **Rev:** Linear portrait facing **Designer:** Nesrin Ek

Date	Mintage	F	VF	XF	Unc	BU
2006 Antiqued	1,500	—	—	—	55.00	—

KM# 1211 25 NEW LIRA

15.5500 g., 0.9250 Silver 0.4624 oz. ASW, 38.6x28 mm. **Obv:** Legend **Rev:** Zodiac - Pisces **Rev. Designer:** Nesrin EK **Shape:** Oval

Date	Mintage	F	VF	XF	Unc	BU
2008 Proof	—	Value: 45.00				

KM# 1212 25 NEW LIRA

15.5500 g., 0.9250 Silver 0.4624 oz. ASW, 38.6x28 mm. **Obv:** Text **Rev:** Zodiac - Aquarius **Shape:** Oval

Date	Mintage	F	VF	XF	Unc	BU
2008 Proof	—	Value: 45.00				

KM# 1213 25 NEW LIRA

15.5500 g., 0.9250 Silver 0.4624 oz. ASW, 38.6x28 mm. **Obv:** Text **Rev:** Zodiac - Capricorn **Rev. Designer:** Nesrin EK **Shape:** Oval

Date	Mintage	F	VF	XF	Unc	BU
2008 Proof	—	Value: 45.00				

KM# 1214 25 NEW LIRA

15.5500 g., 0.9250 Silver 0.4624 oz. ASW, 38.6x28 mm. **Obv:** Text **Rev:** Zodiac - Sagittarius **Shape:** Oval

Date	Mintage	F	VF	XF	Unc	BU
2008 Proof	—	Value: 45.00				

KM# 1215 25 NEW LIRA

15.5500 g., 0.9250 Silver 0.4624 oz. ASW, 38.6x28 mm. **Obv:** Text **Rev:** Zodiac - Libra **Rev. Designer:** Nesrin Ek **Shape:** Oval

Date	Mintage	F	VF	XF	Unc	BU
2008 Proof	—	Value: 45.00				

KM# 1216 25 NEW LIRA

15.5500 g., 0.9250 Silver 0.4624 oz. ASW, 38.6x28 mm. **Obv:** Text **Rev:** Zodiac - figure **Rev. Designer:** Nesrin Ek **Shape:** Oval

Date	Mintage	F	VF	XF	Unc	BU
2008 Proof	—	Value: 45.00				

KM# 1217 25 NEW LIRA

15.5500 g., 0.9250 Silver 0.4624 oz. ASW, 38.6x28 mm. **Obv:** Text **Rev:** Zodiac - Leo **Rev. Designer:** Nesrin Ek **Shape:** Oval

Date	Mintage	F	VF	XF	Unc	BU
2008 Proof	—	Value: 45.00				

KM# 1218 25 NEW LIRA

15.5500 g., 0.9250 Silver 0.4624 oz. ASW, 38.6x28 mm. **Obv:** Text **Rev:** Zodiac - Virgo **Rev. Designer:** Nesrin Ek **Shape:** Oval

Date	Mintage	F	VF	XF	Unc	BU
2008 Proof	—	Value: 45.00				

KM# 1219 25 NEW LIRA

15.5500 g., 0.9250 Silver 0.4624 oz. ASW, 38.6x28 mm. **Obv:** Text **Rev:** Zodiac - Gemeni **Rev. Designer:** Nesrin EK **Shape:** Oval

Date	Mintage	F	VF	XF	Unc	BU
2008 Proof	—	Value: 45.00				

KM# 1220 25 NEW LIRA

15.5500 g., 0.9250 Silver 0.4624 oz. ASW, 38.6x28 mm. **Obv:** Text **Rev:** Zodiac - Taurus **Rev. Designer:** Nesrin Ek **Shape:** Oval

Date	Mintage	F	VF	XF	Unc	BU
2008 Proof	—	Value: 45.00				

KM# 1192 30 NEW LIRA

31.4700 g., 0.9250 Silver 0.9359 oz. ASW, 38.6 mm. **Subject:** Galatasaray Spor **Obv:** 100 above team mascot **Rev:** GS monogram colored and selective gold plating

Date	Mintage	F	VF	XF	Unc	BU
2005 Proof	1,106	Value: 55.00				

KM# 1197 30 NEW LIRA

23.3300 g., 0.9250 Silver partially gold plated 0.6938 oz. ASW, 38.61 mm. **Subject:** Solar Eclipse **Obv:** Turkey map with route of the eclipse **Rev:** Sun, gilt **Designer:** Nesrin Ek

Date	Mintage	F	VF	XF	Unc	BU
2006 Proof	2,475	Value: 100				

KM# 1204 30 NEW LIRA

31.4700 g., 0.9250 Silver 0.9359 oz. ASW, 38.6 mm. **Subject:** Bank of Sarfanbolu **Obv:** Building **Rev:** Landscape **Designer:** Nesrin Ek

Date	Mintage	F	VF	XF	Unc	BU
2007 Proof	1,312	Value: 70.00				

KM# 1205 30 NEW LIRA

31.4700 g., 0.9250 Silver 0.9359 oz. ASW, 38.6 mm. **Obv:** Crescent and star at center of four objects **Rev:** Knotted fabric pattern **Designer:** Ayse Sirin

Date	Mintage	F	VF	XF	Unc	BU
2007 Proof	1,210	Value: 55.00				

KM# 1206 30 NEW LIRA

31.4700 g., 0.9250 Silver 0.9359 oz. ASW, 38.6 mm. **Obv:** Crescent and star within four objects **Rev:** Twirling Dirvishes **Designer:** Leman Tin

Date	Mintage	F	VF	XF	Unc	BU
2007 Proof	1,224	Value: 55.00				

KM# 1207 30 NEW LIRA

31.4700 g., 0.9250 Silver 0.9359 oz. ASW, 38.6 mm. **Obv:** Crescent and star within four designs **Rev:** Twirling Dirvish and town facades around **Designer:** Sessile Beatris Kalayciyan

Date	Mintage	F	VF	XF	Unc	BU
2007 Proof	1,179	Value: 55.00				

KM# 1208 30 NEW LIRA

31.4700 g., 0.9250 Silver 0.9359 oz. ASW, 38.6 mm. **Obv:** Mosque **Rev:** Entranceway arch **Designer:** Nalan Yerl Bucak

Date	Mintage	F	VF	XF	Unc	BU
2007 Proof	1,222	Value: 70.00				

KM# 1222 30 NEW LIRA

10.0000 g., 0.9250 Silver 0.2974 oz. ASW, 22 mm. **Obv:** Seal within border **Rev:** Large seal rendering

Date	Mintage	F	VF	XF	Unc	BU
2008 Proof	—	Value: 30.00				

KM# 1210 35 NEW LIRA

23.2300 g., 0.9250 Silver 0.6908 oz. ASW, 38.6 mm. **Subject:** Antikabir, 70th Anniversary **Obv:** Value within wreath **Rev:** Antikabir building **Designer:** Tenkin Gulbasar

Date	Mintage	F	VF	XF	Unc	BU
2008 Proof	3,000	Value: 40.00				

KM# 1232 35 NEW LIRA

23.3300 g., 0.9250 Silver 0.6938 oz. ASW, 38.6 mm. **Obv:** Value within wreath **Rev:** Bust at left

Date	Mintage	F	VF	XF	Unc	BU
2008 Proof	—	Value: 40.00				

KM# 1233 35 NEW LIRA

23.3300 g., 0.9250 Silver 0.6938 oz. ASW, 38.6 mm. **Obv:** Classical design **Rev:** Mahmud of Kashgar at right

Date	Mintage	F	VF	XF	Unc	BU
2008 Proof	—	Value: 40.00				

KM# 1238 35 NEW LIRA

23.3300 g., 0.9250 Silver 0.6938 oz. ASW, 38.6 mm. **Obv:** Value within wreath **Rev:** Sultan on horseback **Designer:** Nesrin Ek

Date	Mintage	F	VF	XF	Unc	BU
2008 Proof	—	Value: 45.00				

KM# 1202 40 NEW LIRA

31.4700 g., 0.9250 Silver 0.9359 oz. ASW, 38.6 mm. **Subject:** Troy **Obv:** Linear design **Rev:** Stylized Trojan Horse **Designer:** Nalan Yerl Bucak

Date	Mintage	F	VF	XF	Unc	BU
2007 Proof	1,500	Value: 50.00				

KM# 1224 40 NEW LIRA

31.4700 g., 0.9990 Silver 1.0107 oz. ASW, 38.6 mm. **Obv:** Historic map **Rev:** Kyrgyzstan building

Date	Mintage	F	VF	XF	Unc	BU
2008 Antiqued	—	—	—	—	80.00	—

KM# 1225 40 NEW LIRA

31.4700 g., 0.9250 Silver 0.9359 oz. ASW, 38.6 mm. **Obv:** Village scene **Rev:** Large classical figure **Designer:** Nesrin Ek

Date	Mintage	F	VF	XF	Unc	BU
2008 Proof	—	Value: 80.00				

KM# 1227 40 NEW LIRA

31.4700 g., 0.9250 Silver 0.9359 oz. ASW, 38.6 mm. **Obv:** Building **Rev:** Seated figure

Date	Mintage	F	VF	XF	Unc	BU
2008 Proof	—	Value: 45.00				

KM# 1228 40 NEW LIRA

31.4700 g., 0.9250 Silver 0.9359 oz. ASW, 38.6 mm. **Obv:** Classical intricate design **Rev:** Mosque

Date	Mintage	F	VF	XF	Unc	BU
2008 Proof	—	Value: 45.00				

KM# 1229 40 NEW LIRA

31.4700 g., 0.9250 Silver 0.9359 oz. ASW, 38.6 mm. **Obv:** Head left above school building **Rev:** Monogram at center **Designer:** Nesrin Ek

Date	Mintage	F	VF	XF	Unc	BU
2008 Proof	—	Value: 45.00				

KM# 1230 40 NEW LIRA

31.4700 g., 0.9250 Silver 0.9359 oz. ASW, 38.6 mm. **Obv:** Large tower and acqueduct **Rev:** Classical scene **Designer:** Tekin Gulbasar

Date	Mintage	F	VF	XF	Unc	BU
2008 Proof	—	Value: 45.00				

KM# 1231 40 NEW LIRA

31.4700 g., 0.9250 Silver 0.9359 oz. ASW, 38.6 mm. **Obv:** Tortoise, seal and lighthouse in distance **Rev:** Lighthouse

Date	Mintage	F	VF	XF	Unc	BU
2008 Proof	—	Value: 45.00				

KM# 1234 40 NEW LIRA

23.3300 g., 0.9250 Silver 0.6938 oz. ASW, 38.6 mm. **Subject:** Vefs Sports Club, 100th Anniversary **Obv:** Club seal multicolor **Rev:** Large 100 and logo

Date	Mintage	F	VF	XF	Unc	BU
2008 Proof	—	Value: 45.00				

KM# 1235 40 NEW LIRA

31.4700 g., 0.9250 Silver 0.9359 oz. ASW, 38.6 mm. **Obv:** Ancient craft items **Rev:** Cave paintings

Date	Mintage	F	VF	XF	Unc	BU
2008 Proof	—	Value: 45.00				

KM# 1236 40 NEW LIRA

31.4700 g., 0.9250 Silver 0.9359 oz. ASW, 38.6 mm. **Obv:** Ancient map **Rev:** Uzbekistan mosque **Designer:** Tekin Gulbasar

Date	Mintage	F	VF	XF	Unc	BU
2008 Antiqued	—	—	—	—	40.00	45.00

KM# 1237 40 NEW LIRA

31.4700 g., 0.9250 Silver 0.9359 oz. ASW **Obv:** Tower **Rev:** Tower **Shape:** 38.6 **Designer:** Tekin Gulbasar

Date	Mintage	F	VF	XF	Unc	BU
2008 Proof	—	Value: 45.00				

KM# 1209 60 NEW LIRA

1.5000 g., 0.9160 Gold 0.0442 oz. AGW, 13.95 mm. **Obv:** Text **Rev:** Ancient pottery **Designer:** Nesrin Ek

Date	Mintage	F	VF	XF	Unc	BU
2007 Proof	1,925	Value: 70.00				

KM# 1223 100 NEW LIRA

7.2160 g., 0.9160 Gold 0.2125 oz. AGW, 22 mm. **Obv:** Seal within border **Rev:** Large seal

Date	Mintage	F	VF	XF	Unc	BU
2008 Proof	—	Value: 425				

KM# 1226 100 NEW LIRA

7.2160 g., 0.9160 Gold 0.2125 oz. AGW, 22 mm. **Obv:** Village scene **Obv. Designer:** Nes rin Ek **Rev:** Large classical figure **Rev. Designer:** Nesrin Ek

Date	Mintage	F	VF	XF	Unc	BU
2008 Proof	—	Value: 425				

REFORM DECIMAL COINAGE

2009

KM# 1249 LIRA

6.4000 g., Copper-Nickel, 23.5 mm. **Obv:** Lammergeier standing on rock **Rev:** Two eagles **Designer:** Nesrin Ek

Date	Mintage	F	VF	XF	Unc	BU
2009	120,000	—	—	—	4.50	6.00

KM# 1263 LIRA

8.3000 g., Bi-Metallic Copper-Nickel center in Brass ring, 26.15 mm. **Obv:** Value within wreath **Rev:** Elephant and calf **Rev. Designer:** Nalan Yerl Bucak

Date	Mintage	F	VF	XF	Unc	BU
2009	5,000	—	—	—	7.50	10.00

KM# 1264 LIRA

8.3000 g., Bi-Metallic Copper-Nickel center in Brass ring, 26.15 mm. **Obv:** Value within wreath **Rev:** Sea tortoise **Rev. Designer:** Nalan Yerl Bucak

Date	Mintage	F	VF	XF	Unc	BU
2009	5,000	—	—	—	7.50	10.00

KM# 1250 10 LIRA

23.3300 g., Bronze, 38.6 mm. **Obv:** Scroll and inkwell **Rev:** Child's story **Edge:** Reeded **Designer:** Tekin Gulbasar

Date	Mintage	F	VF	XF	Unc	BU
2009 Antiqued	—	—	—	—	15.00	—

KM# 1258 20 LIRA

27.5000 g., Copper-Nickel, 38.6 mm. **Subject:** Year 1430 **Obv:** Inscription within rose wreath **Rev:** Interior of the Grand Mosque in Mecca **Designer:** Nesrin Ek

Date	Mintage	F	VF	XF	Unc	BU
2009 Antiqued	—	—	—	—	35.00	—

KM# 1221 25 NEW LIRA

15.5500 g., 0.9250 Silver 0.4624 oz. ASW, 38.6x28 mm. **Obv:** Text **Rev:** Zodiac sign **Rev. Designer:** Nesrin Ek **Shape:** Oval

Date	Mintage	F	VF	XF	Unc	BU
2008 Proof	—	Value: 45.00				

KM# 1255 50 LIRA

36.0800 g., 0.9250 Silver 1.0730 oz. ASW, 38.6 mm. **Subject:** Sunlight **Obv:** Eastern Hemisphere logo **Rev:** Eastern Hemisphere in Sun

Date	Mintage	F	VF	XF	Unc	BU
2008 Proof	—	Value: 55.00				

KM# 1247 50 LIRA

36.0000 g., 0.9250 Silver 1.0706 oz. ASW, 38.6 mm. **Obv:** Value within wreath **Rev:** Samsun 90th Anniversary

Date	Mintage	F	VF	XF	Unc	BU
2009 Proof	3,000	Value: 55.00				

KM# 1251 50 LIRA

36.0800 g., 0.9250 Silver 1.0730 oz. ASW, 38.6 mm. **Obv:** Scroll and inkwell **Obv. Designer:** Tekin Gulbasar **Rev:** Children's story character **Rev. Designer:** Yekin Gulbasar

Date	Mintage	F	VF	XF	Unc	BU
2009 Proof	—	Value: 40.00				

KM# 1252 50 LIRA

36.0800 g., 0.9250 Silver 1.0730 oz. ASW, 38.6 mm. **Subject:** Frederic Chopin, 200th Anniversary **Obv:** Piano and map of Europe **Rev:** Chopin's bust at left, piano at right, score in background **Designer:** Nalan Yerl Bucak

Date	Mintage	F	VF	XF	Unc	BU
2009	—	Value: 70.00				

KM# 1253 50 LIRA

36.0800 g., 0.9250 Silver 1.0730 oz. ASW, 38.6 mm. **Subject:** IMF Meeting, Istanbul **Obv:** Istanbul Skyline **Rev:** World Bank Group logo, multicolor **Designer:** Nesrin Ek

Date	Mintage	F	VF	XF	Unc	BU
2009 Proof	—	Value: 55.00				

KM# 1254 50 LIRA

36.0800 g., 0.9250 Silver 1.0730 oz. ASW, 38.6 mm. **Subject:** Water, source of life **Obv:** Eastern Hemisphere logo **Rev:** Clock hands, small amount of water, cracked and dried earth in rest of area

Date	Mintage	F	VF	XF	Unc	BU
2009 Proof	—	Value: 55.00				

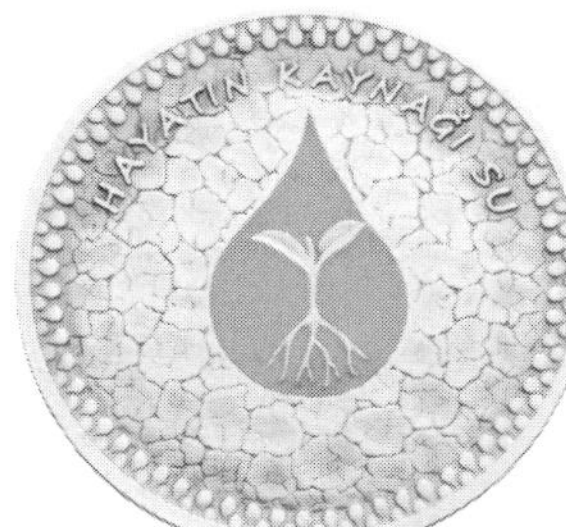

KM# 1256 50 LIRA

36.0800 g., 0.9250 Silver 1.0730 oz. ASW, 38.6 mm. **Obv:** Eastern Hemisphere logo **Rev:** Small seedling within light blue colored water droplet, dried earth background **Rev. Designer:** Mustafa Akinci

Date	Mintage	F	VF	XF	Unc	BU
2009 Antiqued	—	—	—	—	55.00	—

KM# 1257 50 LIRA

36.0800 g., 0.9250 Silver 1.0730 oz. ASW, 38.6 mm. **Obv:** Eastern Hemisphere logo **Rev:** Female face with hair forming waves and vine

Date	Mintage	F	VF	XF	Unc	BU
2009 Proof	—	Value: 55.00				

KM# 1259 50 LIRA

36.0000 g., 0.9250 Silver 1.0706 oz. ASW, 38.6 mm. **Subject:** Year 1430 **Obv:** Inscription within rose wreath **Rev:** Interior courtyard of Grand Mosque in Mecca **Designer:** Nesrin Ek

Date	Mintage	F	VF	XF	Unc	BU
2009 Proof	2,500	Value: 70.00				

KM# 1261 50 LIRA

36.0000 g., 0.9250 Silver 1.0706 oz. ASW, 38.6 mm. **Subject:** 150th Anniversary **Obv:** Multicolor shield and text **Rev:** Building facade **Designer:** Nesrin Ek

Date	Mintage	F	VF	XF	Unc	BU
2009 Proof	5,000	Value: 45.00				

KM# 1262 50 LIRA

36.0000 g., 0.9250 Silver 1.0706 oz. ASW, 38.6 mm. **Subject:** Chalabi clerks **Obv:** Symbol **Rev:** Classical figure seated

Date	Mintage	F	VF	XF	Unc	BU
2009 Proof	3,000	Value: 55.00				

KM# 1245 50 NEW LIRA

36.0800 g., 0.9250 Silver 1.0730 oz. ASW, 38.6 mm. **Obv:** US and Turkish flags **Rev:** Barak Obama portrait facing **Designer:** Nesrin Ek

Date	Mintage	F	VF	XF	Unc	BU
2009 Proof	3,000	Value: 55.00				

KM# 1248 100 LIRA

1.5000 g., 0.9160 Gold 0.0442 oz. AGW, 13.95 mm. **Obv:** Classical orniament **Rev:** Hittite artifacts

Date	Mintage	F	VF	XF	Unc	BU
2009 Proof	—	Value: 95.00				

KM# 1246 200 LIRA

36.0800 g., 0.9160 Gold 1.0625 oz. AGW, 38.6 mm. **Obv:** US and Turkish flags **Rev:** Barak Obama portrait facing **Designer:** Nesrin Ek

Date	Mintage	F	VF	XF	Unc	BU
2009 Proof	1,000	Value: 1,650				

KM# 1260 200 LIRA

36.0000 g., 0.9160 Gold 1.0602 oz. AGW, 38.6 mm. **Obv:** Inscription within rose wreath **Rev:** Central courtyard of the Grand Mosque in Mecca **Designer:** Nesrin Ek

Date	Mintage	F	VF	XF	Unc	BU
2009 Proof	1,500	Value: 1,650				

GOLD BULLION COINAGE

Since 1943, the Turkish government has issued regular and deluxe gold coins in five denominations corresponding to the old traditional 25, 50, 100, 250, and 500 Kurus of the Ottoman period. The regular coins are all dated 1923, plus the year of the republic (e.g. 1923/40 = 1963), de Luxe coins bear actual AD dates. For a few years, 1944-1950, the bust of Ismet Inonu replaced that of Kemal Ataturk.

KM# 851 25 KURUSH

1.8041 g., 0.9170 Gold 0.0532 oz. AGW **Obv:** Head of Atatürk left **Rev:** Legend and date within wreath

Date	Mintage	F	VF	XF	Unc	BU
1923/78	—	—	—	BV	90.00	100
1923/79	—	—	—	BV	90.00	100
1923/70	—	—	—	BV	90.00	100
1923/71	—	—	—	BV	90.00	100
1923/72	—	—	—	BV	90.00	100
1923/73	—	—	—	BV	90.00	100
1923/74	—	—	—	BV	90.00	100
1923/75	—	—	—	BV	90.00	100
1923/76	—	—	—	BV	90.00	100
1923/77	—	—	—	BV	90.00	100

KM# 870 25 KURUSH

1.7540 g., 0.9170 Gold 0.0517 oz. AGW **Series:** Monnaie de Luxe **Obv:** Head of Atatürk left **Rev:** Country name and date in ornate monogram within circle of stars, floral border surrounds

Date	Mintage	F	VF	XF	Unc	BU
2001	—	—	—	BV	75.00	95.00
2002	—	—	—	BV	75.00	95.00
2003	—	—	—	BV	75.00	95.00
2004	—	—	—	BV	75.00	95.00
2005	—	—	—	BV	75.00	95.00
2006	—	—	—	BV	75.00	95.00
2007	—	—	—	BV	75.00	95.00
2008	—	—	—	BV	75.00	95.00
2009	—	—	—	BV	75.00	95.00
2010	—	—	—	BV	75.00	95.00

KM# 853 50 KURUSH

3.6083 g., 0.9170 Gold 0.1064 oz. AGW **Obv:** Head of Atatürk left **Rev:** Legend and date within wreath

Date	Mintage	F	VF	XF	Unc	BU
1923/78	—	—	—	BV	160	170
1923/79	—	—	—	BV	160	170
1923/80	—	—	—	BV	160	170
1923/81	—	—	—	BV	160	170
1923/82	—	—	—	BV	160	170
1923/83	—	—	—	BV	160	170
1923/84	—	—	—	BV	160	170
1923/85	—	—	—	BV	160	170
1923/86	—	—	—	BV	160	170
1923/87	—	—	—	BV	160	170

KM# 871 50 KURUSH

3.5080 g., 0.9170 Gold 0.1034 oz. AGW **Series:** Monnaie de Luxe **Obv:** Head of Kemal Atatürk left within circle of stars, wreath surrounds **Rev:** Country name and date in ornate monogram within circle of stars, floral border surrounds

Date	Mintage	F	VF	XF	Unc	BU
2001	—	—	—	BV	150	160
2002	—	—	—	BV	150	160
2003	—	—	—	BV	150	160
2004	—	—	—	BV	150	160
2005	—	—	—	BV	150	160
2006	—	—	—	BV	150	160
2007	—	—	—	BV	150	160
2008	—	—	—	BV	150	160
2009	—	—	—	BV	150	160
2010	—	—	—	BV	150	160

KM# 855 100 KURUSH

7.2160 g., 0.9170 Gold 0.2127 oz. AGW **Obv:** Head of Atatürk left **Rev:** Legend and date within wreath

Date	Mintage	F	VF	XF	Unc	BU
1923/78	—	—	—	BV	320	335
1923/79	—	—	—	BV	320	335
1923/80	—	—	—	BV	320	335
1923/81	—	—	—	BV	320	335
1923/82	—	—	—	BV	320	335
1923/83	—	—	—	BV	320	335
1923/84	—	—	—	BV	320	335
1923/85	—	—	—	BV	320	335
1923/86	—	—	—	BV	320	335
1923/87	—	—	—	BV	320	335

KM# 872 100 KURUSH

7.0160 g., 0.9170 Gold 0.2068 oz. AGW **Series:** Monnaie de Luxe **Obv:** Head of Atatürk left within circle of stars, wreath surrounds **Rev:** Country name and date in ornate monogram within circle of stars, floral border surrounds

Date	Mintage	F	VF	XF	Unc	BU
2001	—	—	—	BV	300	320
2002	—	—	—	BV	300	320
2003	—	—	—	BV	300	320
2004	—	—	—	BV	300	320
2005	—	—	—	BV	300	320
2006	—	—	—	BV	300	320
2007	—	—	—	BV	300	320
2008	—	—	—	BV	300	320
2009	—	—	—	BV	300	320
2010	—	—	—	BV	300	320

KM# 857 250 KURUSH

18.0400 g., 0.9170 Gold 0.5318 oz. AGW **Obv:** Head of Atatürk left **Rev:** Legend and date within wreath

Date	Mintage	F	VF	XF	Unc	BU
1923/78	—	—	—	BV	775	800
1923/79	—	—	—	BV	775	800
1923/80	—	—	—	BV	775	800
1923/81	—	—	—	BV	775	800
1923/82	—	—	—	BV	775	800
1923/83	—	—	—	BV	775	800
1923/84	—	—	—	BV	775	800
1923/85	—	—	—	BV	775	800
1923/86	—	—	—	BV	775	800
1923/87	—	—	—	BV	775	800

KM# 873 250 KURUSH

17.5400 g., 0.9170 Gold 0.5171 oz. AGW **Series:** Monnaie de Luxe **Obv:** Head of Atatürk left within circle of stars, wreath surrounds **Rev:** Country name and date in ornate monogram within circle of stars, floral border surrounds

Date	Mintage	F	VF	XF	Unc	BU
2001	—	—	—	BV	750	775
2002	—	—	—	BV	750	775
2003	—	—	—	BV	750	775
2004	—	—	—	BV	750	775
2005	—	—	—	BV	750	775
2006	—	—	—	BV	750	775
2007	—	—	—	BV	750	775
2008	—	—	—	BV	750	775
2009	—	—	—	BV	750	775
2010	—	—	—	BV	750	775

KM# 859 500 KURUSH

36.0800 g., 0.9170 Gold 1.0637 oz. AGW **Obv:** Head of Atatürk left **Rev:** Legend and date within wreath

Date	Mintage	F	VF	XF	Unc	BU
1923/78	—	—	—	BV	1,550	1,600
1923/79	—	—	—	BV	1,550	1,600
1923/80	—	—	—	BV	1,550	1,600
1923/81	—	—	—	BV	1,550	1,600
1923/82	—	—	—	BV	1,550	1,600
1923/83	—	—	—	BV	1,550	1,600
1923/84	—	—	—	BV	1,550	1,600
1923/85	—	—	—	BV	1,550	1,600
1923/86	—	—	—	BV	1,550	1,600
1923/87	—	—	—	BV	1,550	1,600

KM# 874 500 KURUSH

35.0800 g., 0.9170 Gold 1.0342 oz. AGW **Series:** Monnaie de Luxe **Obv:** Head of Atatürk left within circle of stars, wreath surrounds **Rev:** Country name and date in ornate monogram within circle of stars, floral border surrounds

Date	Mintage	F	VF	XF	Unc	BU
2001	—	—	—	BV	1,500	1,550
2002	—	—	—	BV	1,500	1,550
2003	—	—	—	BV	1,500	1,550
2004	—	—	—	BV	1,500	1,550
2005	—	—	—	BV	1,500	1,550
2006	—	—	—	BV	1,500	1,550
2007	—	—	—	BV	1,500	1,550
2008	—	—	—	BV	1,500	1,550
2009	—	—	—	BV	1,500	1,550
2010	—	—	—	BV	1,500	1,550

FANTASY EURO PATTERNS

MDS (Germany) Issue

MINT SETS

KM#	Date	Mintage	Identification	Issue Price	Mkt Val
XMS1	2004 (8)	27,500	X#Pn1-Pn8	—	30.00

PROOF SETS

KM#	Date	Mintage	Identification	Issue Price	Mkt Val
XPS1	2004 (9)	—	X#Pn1-Pn9	—	55.00

TURKMENISTAN

The Turkmenistan Republic (formerly the Turkmen Soviet Socialist Republic) covers the territory of the Trans-Caspian Region of Turkestan, the Charjiui Vilayet of Bukhara and the part of Khiva located on the right bank of the Oxus. Bordered on the north by the Autonomous Kara-Kalpak Republic (a constituent of Uzbekistan), by Iran and Afghanistan on the south, by the Usbek Republic on the east and the Caspian Sea on the west. It has an area of 186,400 sq. mi. (488,100 sq. km.) and a population of 3.5 million. Capital: Ashkhabad (formerly Poltoratsk). Main occupation is agricultural products including cotton and maize. It is rich in minerals, oil, coal, sulphur and salt and is also famous for its carpets, Turkoman horses and Karakui sheep.

The Turkomans arrived in Trancaspia as nomadic Seluk Turks in the 11th century. It often became subjected to one of the neighboring states. Late in the 19th century the Czarist Russians invaded with their first victory at Kyzyl Arvat in 1877, arriving in Ashkhabad in 1882 resulting in submission of the Turkmen tribes. By March 18,1884 the Transcaspian province of Russian Turkestan was formed. During WW I the Czarist government tried to conscript the Turkmen; this led to a revolt in Oct. 1916 under the leadership of Aziz Chapykov. In 1918 the Turks captured Baku from the Red army and the British sent a contingent to Merv to prevent a German-Turkish offensive toward Afghanistan and India. In mid-1919 a Bureau of Turkestan Moslem Communist Organization was formed in Moscow hoping to develop one large republic including all surrounding Turkic areas within a Soviet federation. A Turkestan Autonomous Soviet Socialist Republic was formed and plans to partition Turkestan into five republics according to the principle of nationalities was quickly implemented by Joseph Stalin. On Oct. 27, 1924 Turkmenistan became a Soviet Socialist Republic and was accepted as a member of the U.S.S.R. on Jan. 29, 1925. The Bureau of T.M.C.O. was disbanded in 1934. In Aug. 1990 the Turkmen Supreme Soviet adopted a declaration of sovereignty followed by a declaration of independence in Oct. 1991 joining the Commonwealth of Independent States in Dec. A new constitution was adopted in 1992 providing for an executive presidency.

REPUBLIC

STANDARD COINAGE

100 Tenge = 1 Manat

KM# 25 500 MANAT
28.2800 g., 0.9250 Silver 0.8410 oz. ASW, 38.5 mm. **Subject:** 10th Anniversary of Independence **Obv:** Head of President Saparmyrat Nyyazow left within circle **Rev:** Monument divides dates within circle **Edge:** Reeded

Date	Mintage	F	VF	XF	Unc	BU
ND(2001) Proof	5,000	Value: 60.00				

KM# 41 500 MANAT
28.2800 g., 0.9250 Silver 0.8410 oz. ASW **Subject:** President's 61st Birthday **Obv:** National Flag

Date	Mintage	F	VF	XF	Unc	BU
2001	2,000	—	—	—	—	55.00

KM# 42 500 MANAT
28.2800 g., 0.9250 Silver 0.8410 oz. ASW **Subject:** President's 61st Birthday **Rev:** State arms

Date	Mintage	F	VF	XF	Unc	BU
2001	2,000	—	—	—	—	55.00

KM# 43 500 MANAT
28.2800 g., 0.9250 Silver 0.8410 oz. ASW **Subject:** Historical leaders **Rev:** Artogrul Grazy Turkmen (1191-1281)

Date	Mintage	F	VF	XF	Unc	BU
2001	100	—	—	—	—	55.00

KM# 44 500 MANAT
28.2800 g., 0.9250 Silver 0.8410 oz. ASW **Subject:** Historical leaders **Rev:** Oguz Khan Turkmen

Date	Mintage	F	VF	XF	Unc	BU
2001	1,000	—	—	—	—	55.00

KM# 45 500 MANAT
28.2800 g., 0.9250 Silver 0.8410 oz. ASW **Subject:** Historical leaders **Rev:** Gara Yusup Beg Turkmen

Date	Mintage	F	VF	XF	Unc	BU
2001	1,000	—	—	—	—	55.00

KM# 46 500 MANAT
28.2800 g., 0.9250 Silver 0.8410 oz. ASW **Subject:** Historical leaders **Rev:** Keymir Kor Turkmen

Date	Mintage	F	VF	XF	Unc	BU
2001	—	—	—	—	—	65.00

KM# 47 500 MANAT
28.2800 g., 0.9250 Silver 0.8410 oz. ASW **Subject:** Historical leaders **Rev:** Uzun Khasan Beg Turkmen

Date	Mintage	F	VF	XF	Unc	BU
2001	1,000	—	—	—	—	55.00

KM# 48 500 MANAT
28.2800 g., 0.9250 Silver 0.8410 oz. ASW **Subject:** Historical leaders **Rev:** Gorogly Beg Turkmen

Date	Mintage	F	VF	XF	Unc	BU
2001	1,000	—	—	—	—	55.00

KM# 49 500 MANAT
28.2800 g., 0.9250 Silver 0.8410 oz. ASW **Subject:** Historical leader **Rev:** Gorkut Ata Turkmen

Date	Mintage	F	VF	XF	Unc	BU
2001	1,000	—	—	—	—	55.00

KM# 50 500 MANAT
28.2800 g., 0.9250 Silver 0.8410 oz. ASW **Subject:** Historical leaders **Rev:** Muhammet Togrul Beg Turkmen

Date	Mintage	F	VF	XF	Unc	BU
2001	1,000	—	—	—	—	55.00

KM# 51 500 MANAT
Silver **Subject:** Historical leaders **Rev:** Muhammet Bayram Khan Turkmen

Date	Mintage	F	VF	XF	Unc	BU
2001	1,000	—	—	—	—	55.00

KM# 52 500 MANAT
28.2800 g., 0.9250 Silver 0.8410 oz. ASW **Subject:** Historical leaders **Rev:** Soltan Sawjar Turkmen

Date	Mintage	F	VF	XF	Unc	BU
2001	1,000	—	—	—	—	55.00

KM# 53 500 MANAT
28.2800 g., 0.9250 Silver 0.8410 oz. ASW, 46 mm. **Subject:** Historical writers **Obv:** State emblem **Rev:** Bust and Laurel branch **Rev. Legend:** Seyitnazar Seydi (1760-1830)

Date	Mintage	F	VF	XF	Unc	BU
2003	—	—	—	—	—	65.00

KM# 54 500 MANAT
28.2800 g., 0.9250 Silver 0.8410 oz. ASW **Subject:** Historical authors **Obv:** State emblem **Rev:** Bust and Laurel branch **Rev. Legend:** Mammetweli Kemine (1770-1840)

Date	Mintage	F	VF	XF	Unc	BU
2003	—	—	—	—	—	65.00

KM# 55 500 MANAT
28.2800 g., 0.5000 Silver 0.4546 oz. ASW, 46 mm. **Subject:** State emblem **Rev:** Bust and Laurel branch **Rev. Legend:** Mollanepes (1810-1862)

Date	Mintage	F	VF	XF	Unc	BU
2003	—	—	—	—	—	50.00

KM# 56 500 MANAT
28.2800 g., 0.9250 Silver 0.8410 oz. ASW, 46 mm. **Subject:** Historical authors **Obv:** State emblem **Rev:** Bust and Laurel branch **Rev. Legend:** Annagylyc Mataji (1824-1882)

Date	Mintage	F	VF	XF	Unc	BU
2003	—	—	—	—	—	65.00

KM# 62 500 MANAT
28.2800 g., 0.9250 Silver 0.8410 oz. ASW **Obv:** Bust left **Rev:** Wheat ears as rays

Date	Mintage	F	VF	XF	Unc	BU
2004	—	—	—	—	—	65.00

KM# 64 500 MANAT
28.2800 g., 0.9250 Silver 0.8410 oz. ASW **Obv:** Bust left **Rev:** Wheat ears forming rays

Date	Mintage	F	VF	XF	Unc	BU
2004	1,000	—	—	—	—	55.00

KM# 66 500 MANAT
28.2800 g., 0.9250 Silver 0.8410 oz. ASW **Subject:** 60th Anniversary of WWII **Obv:** State emblem **Rev:** Soldier standing, rays behind

Date	Mintage	F	VF	XF	Unc	BU
2005	1,000	—	—	—	—	65.00

KM# 68 500 MANAT
28.2800 g., 0.9250 Silver 0.8410 oz. ASW, 75 mm. **Subject:** President Nijazov, 60th Birthday **Obv:** State emblem **Rev:** Head left above tree design

Date	Mintage	F	VF	XF	Unc	BU
2005	—	—	—	—	—	65.00

KM# 40 1000 MANAT
7.9800 g., 0.9160 Gold 0.2350 oz. AGW, 28.28 mm. **Obv:** President Nyyazow **Rev:** Monument

Date	Mintage	F	VF	XF	Unc	BU
2001	1,000	—	—	—	—	1,800

KM# 57 1000 MANAT
47.6400 g., 0.9160 Gold 1.4029 oz. AGW, 46 mm. **Subject:** Historical authors **Obv:** State emblem **Rev:** Bust and Laurel branch **Rev. Legend:** Seyitnazar Seydi (1760-1830)

Date	Mintage	F	VF	XF	Unc	BU
2003	—	—	—	—	—	2,250

KM# 58 1000 MANAT
47.6400 g., 0.9160 Gold 1.4029 oz. AGW, 46 mm. **Subject:** Historical authors **Obv:** State arms **Rev:** Bust and laurel branch **Rev. Legend:** Mammetweli Kemine

Date	Mintage	F	VF	XF	Unc	BU
2003	—	—	—	—	—	2,250

KM# 59 1000 MANAT
47.6400 g., 0.9250 Gold 1.4167 oz. AGW, 46 mm. **Subject:** Historical authors **Obv:** State emblem **Rev:** Bust and laurel branch **Rev. Legend:** Mollanepes (1810-1862)

Date	Mintage	F	VF	XF	Unc	BU
2003	—	—	—	—	—	2,250

KM# 60 1000 MANAT
47.6400 g., 0.9160 Gold 1.4029 oz. AGW, 46 mm. **Subject:** Historical authors **Obv:** State emblem **Rev:** Bust and laurel branch **Rev. Legend:** Annagylyc Mataji (1824-1882)

Date	Mintage	F	VF	XF	Unc	BU
2003	—	—	—	—	—	2,250

KM# 61 1000 MANAT
28.2800 g., 0.9250 Silver 0.8410 oz. ASW **Subject:** 10th Anniversary of Reform

Date	Mintage	F	VF	XF	Unc	BU
2003	—	—	—	—	—	85.00

KM# 63 1000 MANAT
7.9800 g., 0.9160 Gold 0.2350 oz. AGW **Subject:** 100th Anniversary **Obv:** Bust left **Rev:** Wheat ears forming rays above

Date	Mintage	F	VF	XF	Unc	BU
2004	—	—	—	—	—	1,550

KM# 65 1000 MANAT
7.9800 g., 0.9160 Gold 0.2350 oz. AGW **Obv:** Bust left **Rev:** Wheat ears forming rays

Date	Mintage	F	VF	XF	Unc	BU
2004	250	—	—	—	—	1,550

KM# 67 1000 MANAT
47.5400 g., 0.9160 Gold 1.4000 oz. AGW **Subject:** 60th Anniversary of WWII **Obv:** State arms **Rev:** Soldier standing, rays behind

Date	Mintage	F	VF	XF	Unc	BU
2005	—	—	—	—	—	2,250

KM# 69 1000 MANAT
155.5000 g., 0.9990 Gold 4.9942 oz. AGW, 75 mm. **Subject:** President Nijazov Goth **Obv:** State emblem **Rev:** Head left above tree

Date	Mintage	F	VF	XF	Unc	BU
2005	—	—	—	—	—	8,000

KM# 70 1000 MANAT
28.2800 g., 0.9250 Silver 0.8410 oz. ASW **Subject:** Writings of President Nijazov

Date	Mintage	F	VF	XF	Unc	BU
2006	—	—	—	—	—	85.00

KM# 71 1000 MANAT
28.2800 g., 0.9250 Silver 0.8410 oz. ASW **Subject:** Writings of President Nijazov

Date	Mintage	F	VF	XF	Unc	BU
2006	—	—	—	—	—	85.00

KM# 72 1000 MANAT
28.2800 g., 0.9250 Silver 0.8410 oz. ASW **Subject:** Writings of President Nijazov

Date	Mintage	F	VF	XF	Unc	BU
2006	—	—	—	—	—	85.00

KM# 73 1000 MANAT
28.2800 g., 0.9250 Silver 0.8410 oz. ASW **Subject:** Writings of President Nijazov

Date	Mintage	F	VF	XF	Unc	BU
2006	—	—	—	—	—	85.00

KM# 74 1000 MANAT
28.2800 g., 0.9250 Silver 0.8410 oz. ASW **Subject:** Writings of President Nijazov

Date	Mintage	F	VF	XF	Unc	BU
2006	—	—	—	—	—	85.00

KM# 75 1000 MANAT
28.2800 g., 0.9250 Silver 0.8410 oz. ASW **Subject:** Writings of President Nijazov

Date	Mintage	F	VF	XF	Unc	BU
2006	—	—	—	—	—	85.00

REFORM COINAGE

January 1, 2009 - 5000 Old Manat = 1 New Manat

100 Tenge = 1 Manat

KM# 95 TENGE
Nickel Plated Steel, 16 mm. **Obv:** Spire over country map **Rev:** Denomination and date

Date	Mintage	F	VF	XF	Unc	BU
2009	—	—	—	—	0.50	0.75

KM# 96 2 TENGE
Nickel Plated Steel, 18 mm. **Obv:** Spire over country map **Rev:** Denomination and date

Date	Mintage	F	VF	XF	Unc	BU
2009	—	—	—	—	0.75	1.00

KM# 97 5 TENGE
Nickel Plated Steel, 20 mm. **Obv:** Spire over country map **Rev:** Denomination and date

Date	Mintage	F	VF	XF	Unc	BU
2009	—	—	—	—	1.00	1.25

KM# 98 10 TENGE
Brass, 22 mm. **Obv:** Spire over country map **Rev:** Denomination and date

Date	Mintage	F	VF	XF	Unc	BU
2009	—	—	—	—	1.50	1.75

KM# 99 20 TENGE
Brass, 23 mm. **Obv:** Spire over country map **Rev:** Denomination and date

Date	Mintage	F	VF	XF	Unc	BU
2009	—	—	—	—	2.50	3.00

KM# 100 50 TENGE
Brass, 26 mm. **Obv:** Spire over country map **Rev:** Denomination and date

Date	Mintage	F	VF	XF	Unc	BU
2009	—	—	—	—	3.00	3.50

KM# 103 MANAT
Bi-Metallic Stainless-steel center in Brass ring **Obv:** Spire over country map **Rev:** Denomination and date

Date	Mintage	F	VF	XF	Unc	BU
2010	—	—	—	—	—	4.00

KM# 104 2 MANAT
Bi-Metallic Brass center in copper-nickel ring **Obv:** Spire over country map **Rev:** Value and date

Date	Mintage	F	VF	XF	Unc	BU
2010	—	—	—	—	—	7.50

TURKS & CAICOS ISLANDS

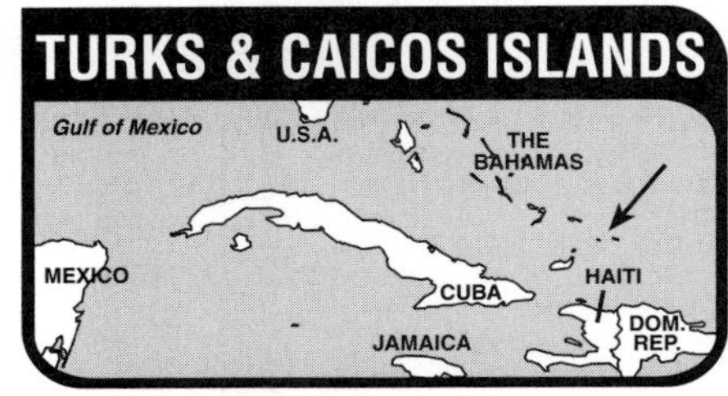

The Colony of the Turks and Caicos Islands, a British colony situated in the West Indies at the eastern end of the Bahama Islands, has an area of 166 sq. mi. (430 sq.km.) and a population of *10,000. Capital: Cockburn Town, on Grand Turk. The principal industry of the colony is the production of salt, which is gathered by raking. Salt, crayfish, and conch shells are exported.

RULER
British

MONETARY SYSTEM
1 Crown = 1 Dollar U.S.A.

BRITISH COLONY

STANDARD COINAGE

KM# 233 5 CROWNS
26.4300 g., Copper-Nickel, 39.2 mm. **Ruler:** Elizabeth II **Subject:** Royal Navy Submarines **Obv:** Head with tiara right **Obv. Designer:** Ian Rank-Broadley **Rev:** Old and modern submarines **Edge:** Reeded

Date	Mintage	F	VF	XF	Unc	BU
2001	—	—	—	6.00	10.00	12.00

KM# 236 20 CROWNS
31.2000 g., 0.9990 Silver 1.0021 oz. ASW, 38.9 mm. **Obv:** Crowned head right **Obv. Designer:** Ian Rank-Broadley **Rev:** Bust right facing divides dates **Edge:** Reeded

Date	Mintage	F	VF	XF	Unc	BU
2001 Proof	—	Value: 50.00				

KM# 245 20 CROWNS
31.1600 g., 0.9990 Silver 1.0008 oz. ASW, 39 mm. **Obv:** Crowned head right **Rev:** Richard II (1377-1399) **Edge:** Reeded

Date	Mintage	F	VF	XF	Unc	BU
2002 Proof	—	Value: 50.00				

KM# 246 20 CROWNS
Hafnium, 38.6 mm. **Ruler:** Elizabeth II **Subject:** H.M. Queen Elizabeth, The Queen Mother **Obv:** Crowned head right **Rev:** Crowned bust right within circle **Edge:** Reeded

Date	Mintage	F	VF	XF	Unc	BU
2002 Proof	—	Value: 145				

TUVALU

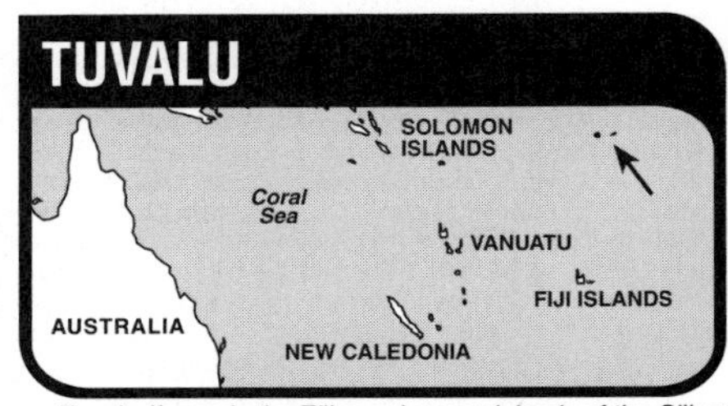

Tuvalu (formerly the Ellice or Lagoon Islands of the Gilbert and Ellice Islands), located in the South Pacific north of the Fiji Islands, has an area of 10 sq. mi. (26 sq.km.) and a population of *9,000. Capital: Funafuti. The independent state includes the islands of Nanumanga, Nanumea, Nui, Niutao, Viatupa, Funafuti, Nukufetau, Nukulailai and Nurakita. The latter four islands were claimed by the United States until relinquished by the Feb. 7, 1979, Treaty of Friendship signed by the United States and Tuvalu. The principal industries are copra production and phosphate mining.

Tuvalu is a member of the Commonwealth of Nations. Elizabeth II is Head of State as Queen of Tuvalu.

RULER
British, until 1978

MONETARY SYSTEM
100 Cents = 1 Dollar

CONSTITUTIONAL MONARCHY WITHIN THE COMMONWEALTH

STANDARD COINAGE

KM# 40 DOLLAR
20.0000 g., Brass, 38.7 mm. **Ruler:** Elizabeth II **Subject:** Dinosaurs **Obv:** Crowned head right **Obv. Designer:** Raphael Maklouf **Rev:** Giganotosaurus **Edge:** Reeded **Note:** See KM#49.

Date	Mintage	F	VF	XF	Unc	BU
2002	50,000	—	—	—	18.00	22.00

KM# 41 DOLLAR
20.0000 g., Brass, 38.7 mm. **Ruler:** Elizabeth II **Subject:** Dinosaurs **Obv:** Crowned head right **Rev:** Dromaeosaurus **Edge:** Reeded **Note:** See KM#50.

Date	Mintage	F	VF	XF	Unc	BU
2002	50,000	—	—	—	18.00	22.00

KM# 43 DOLLAR
20.0000 g., Brass, 38.7 mm. **Ruler:** Elizabeth II **Subject:** Dinosaurs **Obv:** Crowned head right **Rev:** Stegosaurus **Edge:** Reeded **Note:** See KM#51.

Date	Mintage	F	VF	XF	Unc	BU
2002	50,000	—	—	—	18.00	22.00

KM# 42 DOLLAR
20.0000 g., Brass, 38.7 mm. **Ruler:** Elizabeth II **Subject:** Dinosaurs **Obv:** Crowned head right **Rev:** Seismosaurus **Edge:** Reeded **Note:** See KM#52.

Date	Mintage	F	VF	XF	Unc	BU
2002	50,000	—	—	—	18.00	22.00

KM# 149 DOLLAR
31.1030 g., 0.9990 Silver 0.9989 oz. ASW, 40.7 mm. **Ruler:** Elizabeth II **Subject:** Harry Potter **Rev:** Multicolor dementor

Date	Mintage	F	VF	XF	Unc	BU
2004	—	—	—	—	—	42.00

KM# 150 DOLLAR
31.1030 g., 0.9990 Silver 0.9989 oz. ASW, 40.7 mm. **Ruler:** Elizabeth II **Subject:** Harry Potter **Rev:** Multicolor owl

Date	Mintage	F	VF	XF	Unc	BU
2004	—	—	—	—	—	42.00

KM# 151 DOLLAR
31.1030 g., 0.9990 Silver 0.9989 oz. ASW, 40.7 mm. **Ruler:** Elizabeth II **Subject:** Harry Potter **Rev:** Multicolor color Harry Potter chasing snitch

Date	Mintage	F	VF	XF	Unc	BU
2004	—	—	—	—	—	42.00

KM# 53 DOLLAR
Silver **Ruler:** Elizabeth II **Obv:** Crowned head right **Rev:** 1955 Mercedes Benz 300 SL Gullwing

Date	Mintage	F	VF	XF	Unc	BU
2006 Proof	—	Value: 55.00				

KM# 54 DOLLAR
Silver **Ruler:** Elizabeth II **Obv:** Crowned head right **Rev:** 1963 Jaguar E-Type colorized

Date	Mintage	F	VF	XF	Unc	BU
2006 Proof	—	Value: 55.00				

KM# 55 DOLLAR
Silver **Ruler:** Elizabeth II **Obv:** Crowned head right **Rev:** 1969 Datsun 240Z

Date	Mintage	F	VF	XF	Unc	BU
2006 Proof	—	Value: 65.00				

KM# 58 DOLLAR
31.3100 g., 0.9990 Silver enameled 1.0056 oz. ASW, 40.51 mm. **Ruler:** Elizabeth II **Subject:** 400th Anniversary of First European Sighting of Australia **Obv:** Crowned bust right **Obv. Legend:** QUEEN ELIZABETH II **Rev:** Bust of Captain James Cook at left, his ship; "H.M.S. Endeavor" within ship's wheel **Rev. Inscription:** 1770 DISCOVERY - EASTERN AUSTRALIA **Edge:** Reeded

Date	Mintage	F	VF	XF	Unc	BU
2006 Proof	—	Value: 85.00				

KM# 59 DOLLAR
31.3100 g., 0.9990 Silver enameled 1.0056 oz. ASW, 40 mm. **Ruler:** Elizabeth II **Subject:** 400th Anniversary of First European Sighting of Australia **Obv:** Crowned bust right **Obv. Legend:** QUEEN ELIZABETH II **Rev:** Bust of Abel Jansoon Tasman at left, his Dutch ship within compass rose **Rev. Legend:** 1642 DISCOVERY OF VAN DIEMAN'S LAND **Edge:** Reeded

Date	Mintage	F	VF	XF	Unc	BU
2006 Proof	—	Value: 85.00				

KM# 60 DOLLAR
31.1050 g., 0.9990 Silver enameled 0.9990 oz. ASW, 40 mm. **Ruler:** Elizabeth II **Subject:** 400th Anniversary of First European Sighting of Australia **Obv:** Crowned bust right **Obv. Legend:** QUEEN ELIZABETH II **Rev:** Bust of William Dampier at right, his ship within wreath **Rev. Legend:** 1688 BRITISH DISCOVERY OF AUSTRALIA **Edge:** Reeded

Date	Mintage	F	VF	XF	Unc	BU
2006 Proof	—	Value: 85.00				

KM# 61 DOLLAR
31.3100 g., 0.9990 Silver enameled 1.0056 oz. ASW, 40 mm. **Ruler:** Elizabeth II **Subject:** 400th Anniversary of First European Sighting of Australia **Obv:** Crowned bust right **Obv. Legend:** QUEEN ELIZABETH II **Rev:** Dutch ship"Duyfken" within compas rose **Rev. Legend:** 1606 FIRST EUROPEAN DISCOVERY AUSTRALIA **Edge:** Reeded

Date	Mintage	F	VF	XF	Unc	BU
2006 Proof	—	Value: 85.00				

KM# 68 DOLLAR
31.1030 g., 0.9990 Silver 0.9989 oz. ASW, 40 mm. **Ruler:** Elizabeth II **Obv:** Crowned bust right **Obv. Legend:** QUEEN ELIZABETH II - TUVALU **Rev:** Red-back Spider, multicolor

Date	Mintage	F	VF	XF	Unc	BU
2006 Proof	5,000	Value: 275				

KM# 62 DOLLAR
31.1035 g., 0.9990 Silver 0.9990 oz. ASW, 40.51 mm. **Ruler:** Elizabeth II **Obv:** Crowned bust right **Obv. Legend:** ELIZABETH II **Rev:** Multicolor Great White Shark **Edge:** Reeded

Date	Mintage	F	VF	XF	Unc	BU
2007 Proof	5,000	Value: 145				

KM# 63 DOLLAR
0.9990 Silver, 40 mm. **Ruler:** Elizabeth II **Series:** Fighting Ships of WW II **Obv:** Crowned bust right **Obv. Legend:** QUEEN ELIZABETH II - TUVALU **Obv. Designer:** Raphael Maklouf **Rev:** USSR Sevastopol, multicolor water

Date	Mintage	F	VF	XF	Unc	BU
2007 Proof	1,500	Value: 75.00				

KM# 64 DOLLAR
0.9990 Silver, 40 mm. **Ruler:** Elizabeth II **Series:** Fighting Ships of WW II **Obv:** Crowned bust right **Obv. Legend:** QUEEN ELIZABETH II - TUVALU **Obv. Designer:** Raphael Maklouf **Rev:** HMS Hood, multicolor water and smoke

Date	Mintage	F	VF	XF	Unc	BU
2007 Proof	1,500	Value: 75.00				

KM# 65 DOLLAR
0.9990 Silver, 40 mm. **Ruler:** Elizabeth II **Series:** Fighting Ships of WW II **Obv:** Crowned bust right **Obv. Legend:** QUEEN ELIZABETH II - TUVALU **Obv. Designer:** Raphael Maklouf **Rev:** Bismarck, multicolor water and gun flashes

Date	Mintage	F	VF	XF	Unc	BU
2007 Proof	1,500	Value: 75.00				

KM# 66 DOLLAR
0.9990 Silver, 40 mm. **Ruler:** Elizabeth II **Series:** Fighting Ships of WW II **Obv. Legend:** QUEEN ELIZABETH II - TUVALU **Obv. Designer:** Raphael Maklouf **Rev:** IJN Yamato, multicolor water and rising sun

Date	Mintage	F	VF	XF	Unc	BU
2007 Proof	1,500	Value: 75.00				

KM# 67 DOLLAR
0.9990 Silver, 40 mm. **Ruler:** Elizabeth II **Series:** Fighting Ships of WW II **Obv:** Crowned bust right **Obv. Legend:** QUEEN ELIZABETH II - TUVALU **Obv. Designer:** Raphael Maklouf **Rev:** USS Missouri

Date	Mintage	F	VF	XF	Unc	BU
2007 Proof	1,500	Value: 75.00				

KM# 75 DOLLAR
31.1030 g., 0.9990 Silver 0.9989 oz. ASW, 40.6 mm. **Ruler:** Elizabeth II **Subject:** Early Governors of Australia **Obv:** Head right **Rev:** Multicolor Lahlan Macquarie

Date	Mintage	F	VF	XF	Unc	BU
2008 Proof	1,808	Value: 90.00				

KM# 71 DOLLAR
31.1030 g., 0.9990 Silver 0.9989 oz. ASW, 40.6 mm. **Ruler:** Elizabeth II **Subject:** Early Governors of Austrialia **Obv:** Head right **Rev:** Multicolor Arthur Phillip **Edge:** Reeded

Date	Mintage	F	VF	XF	Unc	BU
2008 Proof	1,808	Value: 90.00				

KM# 72 DOLLAR
31.1030 g., 0.9990 Silver 0.9989 oz. ASW, 40.6 mm. **Ruler:** Elizabeth II **Subject:** Early Governors of Australia **Obv:** Head right **Rev:** Multicolor John Hunter **Edge:** Reeded

Date	Mintage	F	VF	XF	Unc	BU
2008 Proof	1,808	Value: 90.00				

KM# 73 DOLLAR
31.1030 g., 0.9990 Silver 0.9989 oz. ASW, 40.6 mm. **Ruler:** Elizabeth II **Subject:** Early Governors of Australia **Obv:** Head right **Rev:** Multicolor Philip G. King

Date	Mintage	F	VF	XF	Unc	BU
2008 Proof	1,808	Value: 90.00				

KM# 74 DOLLAR
31.1030 g., 0.9990 Silver 0.9989 oz. ASW, 40.6 mm. **Ruler:** Elizabeth II **Subject:** Early Governors of Australia **Obv:** Head right **Rev:** Multicolor William Bligh **Edge:** Reeded

Date	Mintage	F	VF	XF	Unc	BU
2008 Proof	1,808	Value: 90.00				

KM# 76 DOLLAR
37.1080 g., 0.9990 Silver 1.1918 oz. ASW, 40.6 mm. **Ruler:** Elizabeth II **Obv:** Head right **Rev:** Multicolor Australian Lesser Blue-ringed Octopus **Edge:** Reeded

Date	Mintage	F	VF	XF	Unc	BU
2008 Proof	5,000	Value: 200				

KM# 81 DOLLAR
31.1050 g., 0.9990 Silver 0.9990 oz. ASW **Ruler:** Elizabeth II **Subject:** Motorcycles **Rev:** Indian Chief

Date	Mintage	F	VF	XF	Unc	BU
2008 Proff	—	Value: 70.00				

KM# 82 DOLLAR
31.1050 g., 0.9990 Silver 0.9990 oz. ASW **Ruler:** Elizabeth II **Subject:** Motorcycles **Rev:** BMW R12

Date	Mintage	F	VF	XF	Unc	BU
2008 Proof	—	Value: 70.00				

KM# 83 DOLLAR
31.1050 g., 0.9990 Silver 0.9990 oz. ASW **Ruler:** Elizabeth II **Subject:** Motorcycles **Rev:** BSA Gold Star DBD34

Date	Mintage	F	VF	XF	Unc	BU
2008 Proof	—	Value: 70.00				

KM# 84 DOLLAR
31.1050 g., 0.9990 Silver 0.9990 oz. ASW **Ruler:** Elizabeth II **Subject:** Motorcycles **Rev:** Norton - Commando 750

Date	Mintage	F	VF	XF	Unc	BU
2008 Proof	—	Value: 70.00				

KM# 85 DOLLAR
31.1050 g., 0.9990 Silver 0.9990 oz. ASW **Ruler:** Elizabeth II **Subject:** Motorcycles **Rev:** Honda CB760

Date	Mintage	F	VF	XF	Unc	BU
2008 Proof	—	Value: 70.00				

KM# 162 DOLLAR
31.1050 g., 0.9990 Silver 0.9990 oz. ASW, 40 mm. **Ruler:** Elizabeth II **Rev:** Charles Darwin, youthful multicolor portrait, older man portrait, ship Beagle.

Date	Mintage	F	VF	XF	Unc	BU
2009 Proof	—	Value: 75.00				

KM# 80 DOLLAR
31.1050 g., 0.9990 Silver 0.9990 oz. ASW **Ruler:** Elizabeth II **Subject:** Barbie, 50th Anniversary **Rev:** Barbie doll and drawing

Date	Mintage	F	VF	XF	Unc	BU
2009 Proof	20,000	Value: 65.00				

KM# 87 DOLLAR
31.1050 g., 0.9990 Silver 0.9990 oz. ASW, 40 mm. **Ruler:** Elizabeth II **Rev:** Saltwater Crocodile

Date	Mintage	F	VF	XF	Unc	BU
2009 Proof	—	Value: 150				

KM# 88 DOLLAR
31.1050 g., 0.9990 Silver 0.9990 oz. ASW **Ruler:** Elizabeth II **Subject:** Battle of Hastings **Rev:** Battle scene in multicolor

Date	Mintage	F	VF	XF	Unc	BU
2009 Proof	—	Value: 70.00				

KM# 89 DOLLAR
31.1050 g., 0.9990 Silver 0.9990 oz. ASW **Ruler:** Elizabeth II **Subject:** Battle of Cannae, 216 BC **Rev:** Battlefield scene, multicolor

Date	Mintage	F	VF	XF	Unc	BU
2009 Proof	—	Value: 70.00				

KM# 90 DOLLAR
31.1050 g., 0.9990 Silver 0.9990 oz. ASW **Ruler:** Elizabeth II **Subject:** Battle of Gettysburg **Rev:** Battlefield scene, multicolor

Date	Mintage	F	VF	XF	Unc	BU
2009 Proof	—	Value: 70.00				

KM# 91 DOLLAR
31.1050 g., 0.9990 Silver 0.9990 oz. ASW **Ruler:** Elizabeth II **Subject:** Battle of Balaklava, 1854 **Rev:** Battle scene, multicolor

Date	Mintage	F	VF	XF	Unc	BU
2009 Proof	—	Value: 70.00				

KM# 92 DOLLAR
31.1050 g., 0.9990 Silver 0.9990 oz. ASW **Ruler:** Elizabeth II **Subject:** Poltava, Peter the Great's 300th Anniversary **Rev:** Statue of Peter on horseback, multicolor battle scene

Date	Mintage	F	VF	XF	Unc	BU
2009 Proof	—	Value: 70.00				

KM# 94 DOLLAR
31.1050 g., 0.9990 Silver 0.9990 oz. ASW, 40.6 mm. **Ruler:** Elizabeth II **Subject:** Transformers **Rev:** Optimus Prime, multicolor

Date	Mintage	F	VF	XF	Unc	BU
2009 Proof	5,000	Value: 75.00				

KM# 95 DOLLAR
31.1050 g., 0.9990 Silver 0.9990 oz. ASW, 40.6 mm. **Ruler:** Elizabeth II **Subject:** Transformers **Rev:** Megatron, multicolor

Date	Mintage	F	VF	XF	Unc	BU
2009 Proof	5,000	Value: 75.00				

KM# 96 DOLLAR
31.1050 g., 0.9990 Silver 0.9990 oz. ASW, 40.6 mm. **Ruler:** Elizabeth II **Subject:** Fall of the Berlin Wall, 20th Anniversary **Rev:** Brandenburg gate, multicolor

Date	Mintage	F	VF	XF	Unc	BU
2009 Proof	5,000	Value: 65.00				

KM# 97 DOLLAR
31.1050 g., 0.9990 Silver 0.9990 oz. ASW, 40.6 mm. **Ruler:** Elizabeth II **Subject:** Golden Age of Piracy - Black Bart **Obv:** Head right **Obv. Designer:** Ian Rank-Broadley **Rev:** Black Bart at left, multicolor treasure items at right

Date	Mintage	F	VF	XF	Unc	BU
2009 Proof	1,500	Value: 80.00				

KM# 98 DOLLAR
31.1050 g., 0.9990 Silver 0.9990 oz. ASW, 40.6 mm. **Ruler:** Elizabeth II **Subject:** Golden Age of Piracy - Black Beard **Obv:** Head right **Obv. Designer:** Ian Rank-Broadley **Rev:** Black Beard at left, multicolor treasure chest at right

Date	Mintage	F	VF	XF	Unc	BU
2009 Proof	1,500	Value: 80.00				

KM# 99 DOLLAR
31.1050 g., 0.9990 Silver 0.9990 oz. ASW, 40.6 mm. **Ruler:** Elizabeth II **Subject:** Golden Age of Piracy - William Kidd **Obv:** Head right **Obv. Designer:** Ian Rank-Broadley **Rev:** William Kidd at left, multicolor pistol and treasure map at right

Date	Mintage	F	VF	XF	Unc	BU
2009 Proof	1,500	Value: 80.00				

KM# 100 DOLLAR
31.1050 g., 0.9990 Silver 0.9990 oz. ASW, 40.6 mm. **Ruler:** Elizabeth II **Subject:** Golden Age of Piracy - Henry Morgan **Obv:** Head right **Obv. Designer:** Ian Rank-Broadley **Rev:** Henry Morgan at left, multicolor kegs at right

Date	Mintage	F	VF	XF	Unc	BU
2009 Proof	1,500	Value: 80.00				

KM# 101 DOLLAR
31.1050 g., 0.9990 Silver 0.9990 oz. ASW, 40.6 mm. **Ruler:** Elizabeth II **Subject:** Golden Age of Piracy - Calico Jack **Obv:** Head right **Obv. Designer:** Ian Rank-Broadley **Rev:** Calico jack at left, multicolor pirate flag at right

Date	Mintage	F	VF	XF	Unc	BU
2009 Proof	1,500	Value: 80.00				

KM# 102 DOLLAR
31.1050 g., 0.9990 Silver 0.9990 oz. ASW, 40.6 mm. **Ruler:** Elizabeth II **Subject:** Nikolai Gogol, 200th Anniversary of Birth **Obv:** Head right **Obv. Designer:** Raphael Maklouf **Rev:** Bust at left, multicolor

Date	Mintage	F	VF	XF	Unc	BU
2009 Proof	6,000	Value: 60.00				

KM# 122 DOLLAR
31.1350 g., 0.9990 Silver 100000 oz. ASW, 40.6 mm. **Ruler:** Elizabeth II **Subject:** Mendelssohn

Date	Mintage	F	VF	XF	Unc	BU
2009P Proof	—	Value: 80.00				

KM# 123 DOLLAR
31.1350 g., 0.9990 Silver 100000 oz. ASW, 40.6 mm. **Ruler:** Elizabeth II **Subject:** Chopin

Date	Mintage	F	VF	XF	Unc	BU
2009P Proof	—	Value: 80.00				

KM# 133 DOLLAR
31.1350 g., 0.9990 Silver 100000 oz. ASW, 40.6 mm. **Ruler:** Elizabeth II **Subject:** Battle fo Poltava, 300th Anniversary **Rev:** Rearing horse

Date	Mintage	F	VF	XF	Unc	BU
2009P Proof	—	Value: 75.00				

KM# 93 DOLLAR
62.2100 g., 0.9990 Silver 1.9980 oz. ASW **Ruler:** Elizabeth II **Subject:** Battle of Marathon **Rev:** Pheidippides' run

Date	Mintage	F	VF	XF	Unc	BU
2010 Proof	5,000	Value: 100				

KM# 103 DOLLAR
31.1050 g., 0.9990 Silver 0.9990 oz. ASW, 40.6 mm. **Ruler:** Elizabeth II **Subject:** Anton Chekhov, 150th Anniversary of Birth **Obv:** Head right **Obv. Designer:** Raphael Maklouf **Rev:** Chekhov multicolor portrait at left, comedy and tragedy masks at right

Date	Mintage	F	VF	XF	Unc	BU
2010 Proof	6,000	Value: 60.00				

KM# 104 DOLLAR
31.1050 g., 0.9990 Silver 0.9990 oz. ASW, 40 mm. **Ruler:** Elizabeth II **Subject:** Great River Journeys - The Rhine **Obv:** Head right **Obv. Designer:** Raphael Maklouf **Rev:** Tour boat, color castle in background

Date	Mintage	F	VF	XF	Unc	BU
2010 Proof	1,500	Value: 90.00				

KM# 105 DOLLAR
31.1050 g., 0.9990 Silver 0.9990 oz. ASW, 40 mm. **Ruler:** Elizabeth II **Subject:** Great River Journeys - Volga **Obv:** Head right **Obv. Designer:** Raphael Maklouf **Rev:** Tour boat and color river front view

Date	Mintage	F	VF	XF	Unc	BU
2010 Proof	1,500	Value: 90.00				

KM# 106 DOLLAR
31.1050 g., 0.9990 Silver 0.9990 oz. ASW, 40 mm. **Ruler:** Elizabeth II **Subject:** Great River Journeys - Yangtzee **Obv:** Head right **Obv. Designer:** Raphael Maklouf **Rev:** Sail boat and color river gorge

Date	Mintage	F	VF	XF	Unc	BU
2010 Proof	1,500	Value: 90.00				

KM# 107 DOLLAR
31.1050 g., 0.9990 Silver 0.9990 oz. ASW, 40 mm. **Ruler:** Elizabeth II **Subject:** Great River Journeys - Mississippi **Obv:** Head right **Obv. Designer:** Raphael Maklouf **Rev:** Delta Queen and multicolor New Orleans skyline

Date	Mintage	F	VF	XF	Unc	BU
2010 Proof	1,500	Value: 90.00				

KM# 108 DOLLAR
31.1050 g., 0.9990 Silver 0.9990 oz. ASW, 40 mm. **Ruler:** Elizabeth II **Subject:** Great River Journeys - The Nile **Obv:** Head right **Obv. Designer:** Raphael Maklouf **Rev:** Dhow, classical sculpture, multicolor sandscape

Date	Mintage	F	VF	XF	Unc	BU
2010 Proof	1,500	Value: 90.00				

KM# 109 DOLLAR
31.1050 g., 0.9990 Silver 0.9990 oz. ASW, 40 mm. **Ruler:** Elizabeth II **Subject:** Ned Kelly - Outlaw **Obv:** Head right **Obv. Designer:** Raphael Maklouf **Rev:** Ned Kelly multicolor - Reward Poster

Date	Mintage	F	VF	XF	Unc	BU
2010 Proof	1,880	Value: 90.00				

KM# 110 DOLLAR
31.1050 g., 0.9990 Silver 0.9990 oz. ASW, 40 mm. **Ruler:** Elizabeth II **Subject:** Ned Kelly - Armour **Obv:** Head right **Obv. Designer:** Raphael Maklouf **Rev:** Ned Kelley's helmet in multicolor

Date	Mintage	F	VF	XF	Unc	BU
2010 Proof	1,880	Value: 90.00				

KM# 111 DOLLAR
31.1050 g., 0.9990 Silver 0.9990 oz. ASW, 40 mm. **Ruler:** Elizabeth II **Subject:** Ned Kelly - Siege **Obv:** Head right **Obv. Designer:** Raphael Maklouf **Rev:** Ned Kelly in shoutout, multicolor

Date	Mintage	F	VF	XF	Unc	BU
2010 Proof	1,880	Value: 90.00				

KM# 112 DOLLAR
31.1050 g., 0.9990 Silver 0.9990 oz. ASW, 40 mm. **Ruler:** Elizabeth II **Subject:** Ned Kelly - Gallows **Obv:** Head right **Obv. Designer:** Raphael Maklouf **Rev:** Ned Kelly standing at the gallows, multicolor

Date	Mintage	F	VF	XF	Unc	BU
2010 Proof	1,880	Value: 90.00				

KM# 113 DOLLAR
25.0000 g., 0.9250 Silver 0.7435 oz. ASW **Ruler:** Elizabeth II **Rev:** Sea horse facing left, Swarovski crystal chip eye **Shape:** 38.61

Date	Mintage	F	VF	XF	Unc	BU
2010 Proof	2,500	Value: 65.00				

KM# 114 DOLLAR
0.5000 g., 0.9990 Gold 0.0161 oz. AGW, 11 mm. **Ruler:** Elizabeth II **Rev:** Sea horse facing right

Date	Mintage	F	VF	XF	Unc	BU
2010 Proof	15,000	Value: 50.00				

KM# 115 DOLLAR
25.0000 g., 0.9250 Silver 0.7435 oz. ASW, 38.6 mm. **Ruler:** Elizabeth II **Subject:** Marine Life **Rev:** Hawksbill sea turtle, multicolor

Date	Mintage	F	VF	XF	Unc	BU
2010 Proof	2,500	Value: 50.00				

KM# 116 DOLLAR
1.2400 g., 0.9990 Gold 0.0398 oz. AGW, 13.92 mm. **Ruler:** Elizabeth II **Rev:** Los Reyes sailing ship

Date	Mintage	F	VF	XF	Unc	BU
2010 Proof	15,000	Value: 80.00				

KM# 117 DOLLAR
31.1350 g., 0.9990 Silver 100000 oz. ASW, 40.6 mm. **Ruler:** Elizabeth II **Subject:** Ballet - Don Quixote **Rev:** Multicolor windmill scene

Date	Mintage	F	VF	XF	Unc	BU
2010P Proof	2,500	Value: 80.00				

KM# 118 DOLLAR
31.1350 g., 0.9990 Silver 100000 oz. ASW, 40.6 mm. **Ruler:** Elizabeth II **Subject:** Ballet - Sleeping Beauty **Rev:** Multicolor castle scene

Date	Mintage	F	VF	XF	Unc	BU
2010P Proof	2,500	Value: 80.00				

KM# 119 DOLLAR
31.1350 g., 0.9990 Silver 100000 oz. ASW, 40.6 mm. **Ruler:** Elizabeth II **Subject:** Ballet - Nutcracker **Rev:** Multicolor snow scene

Date	Mintage	F	VF	XF	Unc	BU
2010P Proof	2,500	Value: 80.00				

KM# 120 DOLLAR
31.1350 g., 0.9990 Silver 100000 oz. ASW, 40.6 mm. **Ruler:** Elizabeth II **Subject:** Ballet - Swan Lake **Rev:** Multicolor swan and lake scene

Date	Mintage	F	VF	XF	Unc	BU
2010P Proof	2,500	Value: 80.00				

KM# 121 DOLLAR
31.1350 g., 0.9990 Silver 100000 oz. ASW, 40.6 mm. **Ruler:** Elizabeth II **Subject:** Ballet - Cinderella **Rev:** Multicolor pumpkin coach scene

Date	Mintage	F	VF	XF	Unc	BU
2010P Proof	2,500	Value: 80.00				

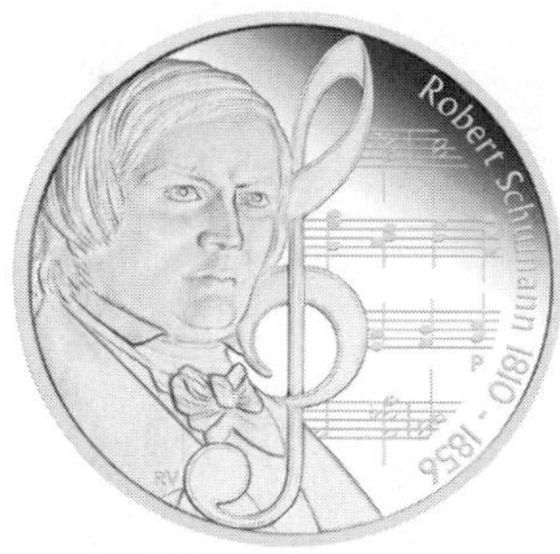

KM# 124 DOLLAR
31.1350 g., 0.9990 Silver 100000 oz. ASW, 40.6 mm. **Ruler:** Elizabeth II **Subject:** Robert Schumann **Rev:** Bust, G-cleff and score

Date	Mintage	F	VF	XF	Unc	BU
2010P Proof	—	Value: 80.00				

KM# 125 DOLLAR
31.1350 g., 0.9990 Silver 100000 oz. ASW, 40.6 mm. **Ruler:** Elizabeth II **Subject:** Gustav Mahler

Date	Mintage	F	VF	XF	Unc	BU
2010P Proof	—	Value: 80.00				

KM# 127 DOLLAR
31.1350 g., 0.9990 Silver 100000 oz. ASW, 40.6 mm. **Ruler:** Elizabeth II **Subject:** Warrior - Legionary **Rev:** Multicolor Roman Legionary soldier standing

Date	Mintage	F	VF	XF	Unc	BU
2010P Proof	—	Value: 80.00				

KM# 128 DOLLAR
31.1350 g., 0.9990 Silver 100000 oz. ASW, 40.6 mm. **Ruler:** Elizabeth II **Subject:** Warrior - Viking **Rev:** Multicolor Viking

Date	Mintage	F	VF	XF	Unc	BU
2010P Proof	—	Value: 80.00				

KM# 129 DOLLAR
31.1350 g., 0.9990 Silver 100000 oz. ASW, 40.6 mm. **Ruler:** Elizabeth II **Subject:** Warrior - Knight **Rev:** Multicolor Knight

Date	Mintage	F	VF	XF	Unc	BU
2010P Proof	—	Value: 80.00				

KM# 130 DOLLAR
31.1350 g., 0.9990 Silver 100000 oz. ASW, 40.6 mm. **Ruler:** Elizabeth II **Subject:** Warrior - Samurai **Rev:** Multicolor Samurai

Date	Mintage	F	VF	XF	Unc	BU
2010P Proof	—	Value: 80.00				

KM# 131 DOLLAR

31.1350 g., 0.9990 Silver 100000 oz. ASW, 40 mm. **Ruler:** Elizabeth II **Subject:** "Banjo" Paterson Ballard - Man from Snowy River **Rev:** Multicolor cowboy chasing two horses

Date	Mintage	F	VF	XF	Unc	BU
2010P Proof	—	Value: 80.00				

KM# 134 DOLLAR

31.1350 g., 0.9990 Silver 100000 oz. ASW, 40.6 mm. **Ruler:** Elizabeth II **Rev:** Multicolor brown snake

Date	Mintage	F	VF	XF	Unc	BU
2010P Proof	—	Value: 165				

KM# 135 DOLLAR

31.1350 g., 0.9990 Silver 100000 oz. ASW, 40.6 mm. **Ruler:** Elizabeth II **Subject:** German Unification, 20th Anniversary **Rev:** Large 20, statues on Brandenburg gate

Date	Mintage	F	VF	XF	Unc	BU
2010P Proof	—	Value: 75.00				

KM# 136 DOLLAR

31.1350 g., 0.9990 Silver 100000 oz. ASW, 40.6 mm. **Ruler:** Elizabeth II **Subject:** Sir Charles Kingsford

Date	Mintage	F	VF	XF	Unc	BU
2010P Proof	—	Value: 75.00				

KM# 137 DOLLAR

31.1350 g., 0.9990 Silver 100000 oz. ASW, 40.6 mm. **Ruler:** Elizabeth II **Subject:** Working dogs **Rev:** Multicolor golden retreiver pups

Date	Mintage	F	VF	XF	Unc	BU
2010P Proof	—	Value: 75.00				

KM# 138 DOLLAR

31.1350 g., 0.9990 Silver 100000 oz. ASW, 40.6 mm. **Ruler:** Elizabeth II **Subject:** Man from Snowy River **Rev:** Multicolor group of horsemen

Date	Mintage	F	VF	XF	Unc	BU
2010P Proof	—	Value: 75.00				

KM# 139 DOLLAR

31.1350 g., 0.9990 Silver 100000 oz. ASW, 40.7 mm. **Ruler:** Elizabeth II **Subject:** Trucks - W900 **Rev:** Truck cab

Date	Mintage	F	VF	XF	Unc	BU
2010P Proof	—	—	—	—	—	—

KM# 140 DOLLAR

31.1350 g., 0.9990 Silver 100000 oz. ASW, 40.6 mm. **Ruler:** Elizabeth II **Subject:** Trucks - Cascadia **Rev:** Multicolor truck cab

Date	Mintage	F	VF	XF	Unc	BU
2010P Proof	—	Value: 75.00				

KM# 141 DOLLAR

31.1350 g., 0.9990 Silver 100000 oz. ASW, 40.6 mm. **Ruler:** Elizabeth II **Subject:** Trucks - R500 **Rev:** Multicolor truck cab

Date	Mintage	F	VF	XF	Unc	BU
2010P Proof	—	Value: 75.00				

KM# 142 DOLLAR

31.1350 g., 0.9990 Silver 100000 oz. ASW, 40.6 mm. **Ruler:** Elizabeth II **Subject:** Trucks - GiGamax **Rev:** Multicolor truck cab

Date	Mintage	F	VF	XF	Unc	BU
2010P Proof	—	Value: 75.00				

KM# 143 DOLLAR

31.1350 g., 0.9990 Silver 100000 oz. ASW, 40.7 mm. **Ruler:** Elizabeth II **Subject:** Tanks - A22 Churchill **Rev:** Multicolor tank

Date	Mintage	F	VF	XF	Unc	BU
2010P Proof	—	Value: 75.00				

KM# 144 DOLLAR

31.1350 g., 0.9990 Silver 100000 oz. ASW **Ruler:** Elizabeth II **Subject:** Tanks - M-4 Sherman **Rev:** Multicolor tank **Shape:** 40.6

Date	Mintage	F	VF	XF	Unc	BU
2010P Proof	—	Value: 75.00				

KM# 145 DOLLAR

31.1350 g., 0.9990 Silver 100000 oz. ASW, 40.6 mm. **Ruler:** Elizabeth II **Subject:** Tanks - Type 97 Chi-Ha **Rev:** Multicolor tank

Date	Mintage	F	VF	XF	Unc	BU
2010P Proof	—	Value: 75.00				

KM# 146 DOLLAR

31.1350 g., 0.9990 Silver 100000 oz. ASW, 40.6 mm. **Ruler:** Elizabeth II **Subject:** Tanks - T-34 **Rev:** Multicolor tank

Date	Mintage	F	VF	XF	Unc	BU
2010P Proof	—	Value: 75.00				

KM# 147 DOLLAR

31.1350 g., 0.9990 Silver 100000 oz. ASW, 40.6 mm. **Ruler:** Elizabeth II **Subject:** Tanks - PzK pfw VI Tiger 1 **Rev:** Multicolor tank

Date	Mintage	F	VF	XF	Unc	BU
2010P Proof	—	Value: 75.00				

KM# 148 DOLLAR

13.9000 g., Aluminum-Bronze, 30.6 mm. **Ruler:** Elizabeth II **Rev:** Blackbeard standing, treasure chest at right

Date	Mintage	F	VF	XF	Unc	BU
2010P	—	—	—	—	—	15.00

KM# 126 DOLLAR

31.1350 g., 0.9990 Silver 100000 oz. ASW, 40.6 mm. **Ruler:** Elizabeth II **Subject:** Franz List

Date	Mintage	F	VF	XF	Unc	BU
2011P Proof	—	Value: 80.00				

KM# 163 DOLLAR

31.1350 g., 0.9990 Silver 100000 oz. ASW, 40.6 mm. **Ruler:** Elizabeth II **Subject:** Australia's extinct animals - Thylacine **Obv:** Head in diadem right **Rev:** Thylacine - Tasmanian tiger in multicolor

Date	Mintage	F	VF	XF	Unc	BU
2011P Proof	5,000	Value: 175				

KM# 158 3 DOLLARS

1.2240 g., 0.9990 Gold 0.0393 oz. AGW, 13.9 mm. **Ruler:** Elizabeth II **Rev:** Australian owl

Date	Mintage	F	VF	XF	Unc	BU
2005 Proof	—	Value: 85.00				
2006 Proof	—	Value: 85.00				
2007 Proof	—	Value: 85.00				

KM# 152 3 DOLLARS

1.2240 g., 0.9990 Gold 0.0393 oz. AGW, 13.9 mm. **Ruler:** Elizabeth II **Rev:** Multicolor mouse with heart

Date	Mintage	F	VF	XF	Unc	BU
2008	—	—	—	—	—	95.00

KM# 49 5 DOLLARS

62.5000 g., 0.9990 Silver 2.0073 oz. ASW, 49.9 mm. **Ruler:** Elizabeth II **Subject:** Dinosaurs **Obv:** Crowned head right **Rev:** Giganotosaurus **Edge:** Reeded

Date	Mintage	F	VF	XF	Unc	BU
2002 Proof	1,000	Value: 90.00				

KM# 50 5 DOLLARS

62.5000 g., 0.9990 Silver 2.0073 oz. ASW, 49.9 mm. **Ruler:** Elizabeth II **Subject:** Dinosaurs **Obv:** Crowned head right **Rev:** Dromaeosaurus **Edge:** Reeded

Date	Mintage	F	VF	XF	Unc	BU
2002 Proof	1,000	Value: 90.00				

KM# 51 5 DOLLARS

62.5000 g., 0.9990 Silver 2.0073 oz. ASW, 49.9 mm. **Ruler:** Elizabeth II **Subject:** Dinosaurs **Obv:** Crowned head right **Rev:** Stegosaurus **Edge:** Reeded

Date	Mintage	F	VF	XF	Unc	BU
2002 Proof	1,000	Value: 90.00				

KM# 52 5 DOLLARS

62.5000 g., 0.9990 Silver 2.0073 oz. ASW, 49.9 mm. **Ruler:** Elizabeth II **Subject:** Dinosaurs **Obv:** Crowned head right **Rev:** Seismosaurus **Edge:** Reeded

Date	Mintage	F	VF	XF	Unc	BU
2002 Proof	1,000	Value: 90.00				

KM# 159 15 DOLLARS

3.1110 g., 0.9990 Gold 0.0999 oz. AGW, 17.95 mm. **Ruler:** Elizabeth II **Rev:** Australian owl

Date	Mintage	F	VF	XF	Unc	BU
2005 Proof	—	Value: 175				
2006 Proof	—	Value: 175				
2007 Proof	—	Value: 175				

KM# 153 15 DOLLARS
3.1110 g., 0.9990 Gold 0.0999 oz. AGW, 17.95 mm. **Ruler:** Elizabeth II **Rev:** Multicolor mouse and golden egg

Date	Mintage	F	VF	XF	Unc	BU
2008	—	—	—	—	—	235

KM# 132 25 DOLLARS
7.7700 g., 0.9990 Gold 0.2496 oz. AGW, 22.6 mm. **Ruler:** Elizabeth II **Subject:** Ned Kelly **Rev:** Multicolor gun slinger and steel helmet

Date	Mintage	Good	VG	F	VF	XF
2010P Proof	1,000	Value: 600				

KM# 160 30 DOLLARS
6.2220 g., 0.9990 Gold 0.1998 oz. AGW, 21.95 mm. **Ruler:** Elizabeth II **Rev:** Australian owl

Date	Mintage	F	VF	XF	Unc	BU
2005 Proof	—	Value: 350				
2006 Proof	—	Value: 350				
2007 Proof	—	Value: 350				

KM# 154 30 DOLLARS
15.5540 g., 0.9990 Gold 0.4996 oz. AGW, 21.95 mm. **Ruler:** Elizabeth II **Rev:** Multicolor mouse and money bag

Date	Mintage	F	VF	XF	Unc	BU
2008	—	—	—	—	—	950

KM# 155 30 DOLLARS
6.2200 g., 0.9990 Gold 0.1998 oz. AGW, 21.95 mm. **Ruler:** Elizabeth II **Rev:** Cow seated with fans above

Date	Mintage	F	VF	XF	Unc	BU
2009	—	—	—	—	—	320

KM# 156 30 DOLLARS
6.2200 g., 0.9990 Gold 0.1998 oz. AGW, 21.95 mm. **Ruler:** Elizabeth II **Rev:** Cow standing with success symbol

Date	Mintage	F	VF	XF	Unc	BU
2009	—	—	—	—	—	320

KM# 157 30 DOLLARS
6.2200 g., 0.9990 Gold 0.1998 oz. AGW, 21.95 mm. **Ruler:** Elizabeth II **Rev:** Cow standing next to money bag

Date	Mintage	F	VF	XF	Unc	BU
2009	—	—	—	—	—	320

KM# 161 50 DOLLARS
15.5540 g., 0.9990 Gold 0.4996 oz. AGW, 30 mm. **Ruler:** Elizabeth II **Rev:** Australiam owl

Date	Mintage	F	VF	XF	Unc	BU
2005 Proof	—	Value: 800				
2006 Proof	—	Value: 800				
2007 Proof	—	Value: 800				

KM# 69 100 DOLLARS
Gold **Ruler:** Elizabeth II **Obv:** Crowned head right **Rev:** Red 1963 Corvette Sting Ray

Date	Mintage	F	VF	XF	Unc	BU
2006 Proof	250	Value: 1,600				

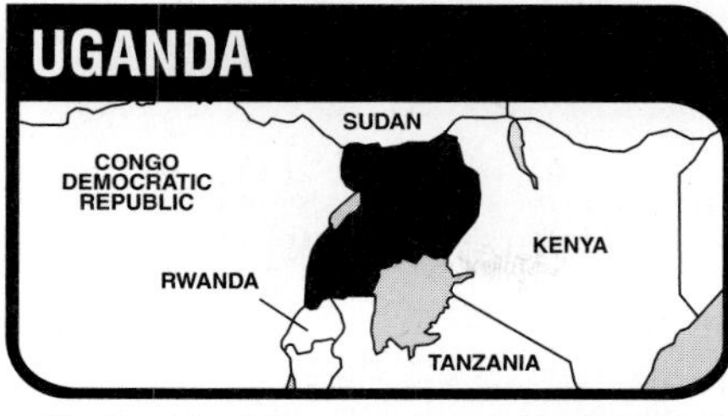

The Republic of Uganda, a former British protectorate located astride the equator in east-central Africa, has an area of 91,134 sq. mi. (236,040 sq. km.) and a population of *17 million. Capital: Kampala. Agriculture, including livestock, is the basis of the economy; there is some mining of copper, tin, gold and lead. Coffee, cotton, copper and tea are exported.

Uganda is a member of the Commonwealth of Nations. The president is Chief of State and Head of Government.

For earlier coinage refer to East Africa.

MONETARY SYSTEM
100 Cents = 1 Shilling

REPUBLIC

STANDARD COINAGE

KM# 66 50 SHILLINGS
4.0000 g., Nickel Plated Steel **Obv:** National arms **Rev:** Antelope head facing **Rev. Designer:** Stan Witten

Date	Mintage	F	VF	XF	Unc	BU
2003	—	—	—	—	1.00	1.25
2007	—	—	—	—	1.00	1.25

KM# 67 100 SHILLINGS
7.0000 g., Copper-Nickel, 26.9 mm. **Obv:** National arms **Rev:** African bull **Rev. Designer:** Stan Witten **Edge:** Reeded

Date	Mintage	F	VF	XF	Unc	BU
2003	—	—	—	—	1.50	1.75
2007	—	—	—	—	1.50	1.75
2008	—	—	—	—	1.50	1.75

KM# 129 100 SHILLINGS
3.5400 g., Stainless Steel, 23.98 mm. **Series:** Zodiac **Obv:** National arms **Rev:** Monkey with elf-like ears **Edge:** Plain

Date	Mintage	F	VF	XF	Unc	BU
2004	—	—	—	—	1.50	2.50

KM# 135 100 SHILLINGS
3.5400 g., Steel, 23.98 mm. **Series:** Zodiac **Obv:** National arms **Rev:** Ox **Edge:** Plain

Date	Mintage	F	VF	XF	Unc	BU
2004	—	—	—	—	1.50	2.50

KM# 136 100 SHILLINGS
3.5400 g., Steel, 23.98 mm. **Series:** Zodiac **Obv:** National arms **Rev:** Goat **Edge:** Plain

Date	Mintage	F	VF	XF	Unc	BU
2004	—	—	—	—	1.50	2.50

KM# 137 100 SHILLINGS
3.5400 g., Steel, 23.98 mm. **Series:** Zodiac **Obv:** National arms **Rev:** Horse **Edge:** Plain

Date	Mintage	F	VF	XF	Unc	BU
2004	—	—	—	—	1.50	2.50

KM# 138 100 SHILLINGS
3.5400 g., Steel, 23.98 mm. **Series:** Zodiac **Obv:** National arms **Rev:** Dragon **Edge:** Plain

Date	Mintage	F	VF	XF	Unc	BU
2004	—	—	—	—	1.50	2.50

KM# 139 100 SHILLINGS
3.5400 g., Steel, 23.98 mm. **Series:** Zodiac **Obv:** National arms **Rev:** Dog **Edge:** Plain

Date	Mintage	F	VF	XF	Unc	BU
2004	—	—	—	—	1.50	2.50

KM# 140 100 SHILLINGS
3.5400 g., Steel, 23.98 mm. **Series:** Zodiac **Obv:** National arms **Rev:** Tiger **Edge:** Plain

Date	Mintage	F	VF	XF	Unc	BU
2004	—	—	—	—	1.50	2.50

KM# 141 100 SHILLINGS
3.5400 g., Steel, 23.98 mm. **Series:** Zodiac **Obv:** National arms **Rev:** Snake **Edge:** Plain

Date	Mintage	F	VF	XF	Unc	BU
2004	—	—	—	—	1.50	2.50

KM# 142 100 SHILLINGS
3.5400 g., Steel, 23.98 mm. **Series:** Zodiac **Obv:** National arms **Rev:** Rooster **Edge:** Plain

Date	Mintage	F	VF	XF	Unc	BU
2004	—	—	—	—	1.50	2.50

KM# 143 100 SHILLINGS
3.5400 g., Steel, 23.98 mm. **Series:** Zodiac **Obv:** National arms **Rev:** Rabbit **Edge:** Plain

Date	Mintage	F	VF	XF	Unc	BU
2004	—	—	—	—	1.50	2.50

KM# 144 100 SHILLINGS
3.5400 g., Steel, 23.98 mm. **Series:** Zodiac **Obv:** National arms **Rev:** Rat **Edge:** Plain

Date	Mintage	F	VF	XF	Unc	BU
2004	—	—	—	—	1.50	2.50

KM# 145 100 SHILLINGS
3.5400 g., Steel, 23.98 mm. **Series:** Zodiac **Obv:** National arms **Rev:** Pig **Edge:** Plain

Date	Mintage	F	VF	XF	Unc	BU
2004	—	—	—	—	1.50	2.50

KM# 130 100 SHILLINGS
Steel, 23 mm. **Rev:** Type I of five different monkeys

Date	Mintage	F	VF	XF	Unc	BU
2004	—	—	—	—	1.75	2.75

KM# 131 100 SHILLINGS
Steel, 23 mm. **Rev:** Type II of five different monkeys

Date	Mintage	F	VF	XF	Unc	BU
2004	—	—	—	—	1.75	2.75

KM# 132 100 SHILLINGS
Steel, 23 mm. **Rev:** Type III of five different monkeys

Date	Mintage	F	VF	XF	Unc	BU
2004	—	—	—	—	1.75	2.75

KM# 133 100 SHILLINGS
Steel, 23 mm. **Rev:** Type IV of five different monkys

Date	Mintage	F	VF	XF	Unc	BU
2004	—	—	—	—	1.50	2.75

KM# 134 100 SHILLINGS
Steel, 23 mm. **Rev:** Type V of five different monkeys

Date	Mintage	F	VF	XF	Unc	BU
2004	—	—	—	—	1.75	2.75

KM# 188 100 SHILLINGS
3.5300 g., Nickel Plated Steel, 24 mm. **Series:** Zodiac **Obv:** National arms **Obv. Legend:** BANK OF UGANDA **Rev:** Head of a rat **Rev. Legend:** BANK OF UGANDA **Edge:** Plain

Date	Mintage	F	VF	XF	Unc	BU
2004	—	—	—	—	1.75	2.75

KM# 189 100 SHILLINGS
3.5300 g., Nickel Plated Steel, 24 mm. **Series:** Zodiac **Obv:** National arms **Obv. Legend:** BANK OF UGANDA **Rev:** Head of an ox **Rev. Legend:** BANK OF UGANDA **Edge:** Plain

Date	Mintage	F	VF	XF	Unc	BU
2004	—	—	—	—	1.75	2.75

KM# 190 100 SHILLINGS
3.5300 g., Nickel Plated Steel, 24 mm. **Series:** Zodiac **Obv:** National arms **Obv. Legend:** BANK OF UGANDA **Rev:** Head of a tiger **Rev. Legend:** BANK OF UGANDA **Edge:** Plain

Date	Mintage	F	VF	XF	Unc	BU
2004	—	—	—	—	1.75	2.75

KM# 191 100 SHILLINGS
3.5300 g., Nickel Plated Steel, 24 mm. **Series:** Zodiac **Obv:** National arms **Obv. Legend:** BANK OF UGANDA **Rev:** Head of a rabbit **Rev. Legend:** BANK OF UGANDA **Edge:** Plain

Date	Mintage	F	VF	XF	Unc	BU
2004	—	—	—	—	1.75	2.75

KM# 192 100 SHILLINGS
3.5300 g., Nickel Plated Steel, 24 mm. **Series:** Zodiac **Obv:** National arms **Obv. Legend:** BANK OF UGANDA **Rev:** Head of a dragon **Rev. Legend:** BANK OF UGANDA **Edge:** Plain

Date	Mintage	F	VF	XF	Unc	BU
2004	—	—	—	—	1.75	2.75

KM# 193 100 SHILLINGS

3.5300 g., Nickel Plated Steel, 24 mm. **Series:** Zodiac **Obv:** National arms **Obv. Legend:** BANK OF UGANDA **Rev:** Head and hood of Cobra snake **Rev. Legend:** BANK OF UGANDA **Edge:** Plain

Date	Mintage	F	VF	XF	Unc	BU
2004	—	—	—	—	1.75	2.75

KM# 194 100 SHILLINGS

3.5300 g., Nickel Plated Steel, 24 mm. **Series:** Zodiac **Obv:** National arms **Obv. Legend:** BANK OF UGANDA **Rev:** Head of a horse **Rev. Legend:** BANK OF UGANDA **Edge:** Plain

Date	Mintage	F	VF	XF	Unc	BU
2004	—	—	—	—	1.75	2.75

KM# 195 100 SHILLINGS

3.5300 g., Nickel Plated Steel, 24 mm. **Series:** Zodiac **Obv:** National arms **Obv. Legend:** BANK OF UGANDA **Rev:** Head of a goat **Rev. Legend:** BANK OF UGANDA **Edge:** Plain

Date	Mintage	F	VF	XF	Unc	BU
2004	—	—	—	—	1.75	2.75

KM# 196 100 SHILLINGS

3.5300 g., Nickel Plated Steel, 24 mm. **Series:** Zodiac **Obv:** National arms **Obv. Legend:** BANK OF UGANDA **Rev:** Head of a monkey **Rev. Legend:** BANK OF UGANDA **Edge:** Plain

Date	Mintage	F	VF	XF	Unc	BU
2004	—	—	—	—	1.75	2.75

KM# 197 100 SHILLINGS

3.5300 g., Nickel Plated Steel, 24 mm. **Series:** Zodiac **Obv:** National arms **Obv. Legend:** BANK OF UGANDA **Rev:** Forepart of a rooster **Rev. Legend:** BANK OF UGANDA **Edge:** Plain

Date	Mintage	F	VF	XF	Unc	BU
2004	—	—	—	—	1.75	2.75

KM# 198 100 SHILLINGS

3.5300 g., Nickel Plated Steel, 24 mm. **Series:** Zodiac **Obv:** National arms **Obv. Legend:** BANK OF UGANDA **Rev:** Head of a dog **Rev. Legend:** BANK OF UGANDA **Edge:** Plain

Date	Mintage	F	VF	XF	Unc	BU
2004	—	—	—	—	1.75	2.75

KM# 199 100 SHILLINGS

3.5300 g., Nickel Plated Steel, 24 mm. **Series:** Zodiac **Obv:** National arms **Obv. Legend:** BANK OF UGANDA **Rev:** Head of a pig **Rev. Legend:** BANK OF UGANDA **Edge:** Plain

Date	Mintage	F	VF	XF	Unc	BU
2004	—	—	—	—	1.75	2.75

KM# 200 100 SHILLINGS

Copper-Nickel **Subject:** Year of the Monkey **Obv. Legend:** BANK OF UGANDA **Rev:** Monkey swingging right

Date	Mintage	F	VF	XF	Unc	BU
2004	—	—	—	—	2.00	3.00

KM# 201 100 SHILLINGS

Copper-Nickel **Subject:** Year of the Monkey **Obv. Legend:** BANK OF UGANDA

Date	Mintage	F	VF	XF	Unc	BU
2004	—	—	—	—	2.00	3.00

KM# 202 100 SHILLINGS

Copper-Nickel **Subject:** Year of the Monkey **Obv. Legend:** BANK OF UGANDA **Rev:** Monkey right on all fours

Date	Mintage	F	VF	XF	Unc	BU
2004	—	—	—	—	2.00	3.00

KM# 203 100 SHILLINGS

Copper-Nickel **Subject:** Year of the Monkey **Obv. Legend:** BANK OF UGANDA **Rev:** Monkey seated left

Date	Mintage	F	VF	XF	Unc	BU
2004	—	—	—	—	2.00	3.00

KM# 204 100 SHILLINGS

Copper-Nickel **Subject:** Year of the Monkey **Obv. Legend:** BANK OF UGANDA **Rev:** Monkeys seated right, looking left over his shoulder

Date	Mintage	F	VF	XF	Unc	BU
2004	—	—	—	—	2.00	3.00

KM# 67a 100 SHILLINGS

Nickel Plated Steel, 26.9 mm. **Obv:** National arms **Rev:** African bull **Rev. Designer:** Stan Witten

Date	Mintage	F	VF	XF	Unc	BU
2007	—	—	—	—	1.00	1.75
2008	—	—	—	—	1.00	1.75

KM# 68 200 SHILLINGS

8.0500 g., Copper-Nickel, 24.9 mm. **Obv:** National arms **Rev:** Cichlid fish above value and date **Rev. Designer:** Stan Witten **Edge:** Plain

Date	Mintage	F	VF	XF	Unc	BU
2003	—	—	—	—	2.00	3.00

KM# 68a 200 SHILLINGS

8.0500 g., Nickel Plated Steel, 24.9 mm. **Obv:** National arms **Rev:** Cichlid fish above value and date

Date	Mintage	F	VF	XF	Unc	BU
2007	—	—	—	—	—	—
2008	—	—	—	—	—	—

KM# 69 500 SHILLINGS

9.0000 g., Nickel-Brass, 23.5 mm. **Obv:** National arms **Rev:** East African crowned crane head left **Rev. Designer:** Stan Witten **Edge:** Reeded

Date	Mintage	F	VF	XF	Unc	BU
2003	—	—	—	—	3.50	4.50
2008	—	—	—	—	3.50	4.50

KM# 77 1000 SHILLINGS

19.8400 g., Copper-Nickel, 38.6 mm. **Subject:** Colourful Big Five of Africa **Obv:** Arms with supporters **Rev:** Multicolor rhinocerous within stamp design in front of outlined African map **Edge:** Reeded

Date	Mintage	F	VF	XF	Unc	BU
2001 Proof	—	Value: 22.50				

KM# 78 1000 SHILLINGS

19.8400 g., Copper-Nickel, 38.6 mm. **Subject:** Colourful Big Five of Africa **Obv:** Arms with supporters **Rev:** Multicolor lion within stamp design in front of outlined African map **Edge:** Reeded

Date	Mintage	F	VF	XF	Unc	BU
2001 Proof	—	Value: 22.50				

KM# 79 1000 SHILLINGS

19.8400 g., Copper-Nickel, 38.6 mm. **Subject:** Coulourful Big Five of Africa **Obv:** Arms with supporters **Rev:** Multicolor water buffalo within stamp design in front of outlined African map **Edge:** Reeded

Date	Mintage	F	VF	XF	Unc	BU
2001 Proof	—	Value: 22.50				

KM# 80 1000 SHILLINGS

19.8400 g., Copper-Nickel, 38.6 mm. **Subject:** Colourful Big Five of Africa **Obv:** Arms with supporters **Rev:** Multicolor leopard within stamp design in front of outlined map **Edge:** Reeded

Date	Mintage	F	VF	XF	Unc	BU
2001 Proof	—	Value: 22.50				

KM# 81 1000 SHILLINGS

19.8400 g., Copper-Nickel, 38.6 mm. **Subject:** Colourful Big Five of Africa **Obv:** Arms with supporters **Rev:** Multicolor elephant within stamp design in front of outlined map **Edge:** Reeded

Date	Mintage	F	VF	XF	Unc	BU
2001 Proof	—	Value: 22.50				

KM# 173 1000 SHILLINGS

Silver **Subject:** XVII World Football Championship Games - Korea and Japan **Obv. Legend:** BANK OF UGANDA **Rev:** Football - gilt

Date	Mintage	F	VF	XF	Unc	BU
2001 Proof	—	Value: 27.50				

KM# 82 1000 SHILLINGS

24.8300 g., 0.9990 Silver 0.7975 oz. ASW, 38.6 mm. **Subject:** World of Football **Obv:** Arms with supporters **Rev:** Soccer ball globe **Edge:** Reeded

Date	Mintage	F	VF	XF	Unc	BU
2002 Proof	—	Value: 35.00				

KM# 83 1000 SHILLINGS

24.8300 g., 0.9990 Silver 0.7975 oz. ASW, 38.6 mm. **Subject:** World of Football **Obv:** Arms with supporters **Rev:** Soccer ball in net **Edge:** Reeded

Date	Mintage	F	VF	XF	Unc	BU
2002 Proof	—	Value: 32.50				

KM# 84 1000 SHILLINGS

24.8300 g., 0.9990 Silver 0.7975 oz. ASW, 38.6 mm. **Subject:** World of Football **Obv:** Arms with supporters **Rev:** Goalie catching ball, red kicker insert at right **Edge:** Reeded

Date	Mintage	F	VF	XF	Unc	BU
2002 Proof	—	Value: 32.50				

KM# 85 1000 SHILLINGS

24.8300 g., 0.9990 Silver 0.7975 oz. ASW, 38.6 mm. **Subject:** World of Football **Obv:** Arms with supporters **Rev:** Two players going after the ball, red runner insert at left **Edge:** Reeded

Date	Mintage	F	VF	XF	Unc	BU
2002 Proof	—	Value: 32.50				

KM# 86 1000 SHILLINGS

24.8300 g., 0.9990 Silver 0.7975 oz. ASW, 38.6 mm. **Subject:** World of Football **Obv:** Arms with supporters **Rev:** Player kicking ball, blue kicker insert at right **Edge:** Reeded

Date	Mintage	F	VF	XF	Unc	BU
2002 Proof	—	Value: 32.50				

KM# 101 1000 SHILLINGS

29.4400 g., Silver Plated Bronze (Specific gravity 8.8675), 38.5 mm. **Series:** Gorillas of Africa **Obv:** National arms **Rev:** Seated gorilla **Edge:** Reeded

Date	Mintage	F	VF	XF	Unc	BU
2002 Proof	—	Value: 12.50				
2003 Proof	—	Value: 12.00				

KM# 102 1000 SHILLINGS

29.4400 g., Silver Plated Bronze (Specific gravity 8.8675), 38.5 mm. **Series:** Gorillas of Africa **Obv:** National arms **Rev:** Gorilla eating **Edge:** Reeded

Date	Mintage	F	VF	XF	Unc	BU
2002 Proof	—	Value: 12.50				
2003 Proof	—	Value: 10.00				

KM# 103 1000 SHILLINGS

29.4400 g., Silver Plated Bronze (Specific gravity 8.8675), 38.5 mm. **Series:** Gorillas of Africa **Obv:** National arms **Rev:** Gorilla on all fours **Edge:** Reeded

Date	Mintage	F	VF	XF	Unc	BU
2002 Proof	—	Value: 12.50				
2003 Proof	—	Value: 10.00				

KM# 104 1000 SHILLINGS
29.4400 g., Silver Plated Bronze (Specific gravity 8.8675), 38.5 mm. **Series:** Gorillas of Africa **Obv:** National arms **Rev:** Gorilla female with infant **Edge:** Reeded

Date	Mintage	F	VF	XF	Unc	BU
2002 Proof	—	Value: 12.50				
2003 Proof	—	Value: 10.00				

KM# 106 1000 SHILLINGS
29.1600 g., Silver Plated Bronze (Specific gravity 8.8096), 38.6 mm. **Subject:** Marine Life **Obv:** Arms with supporters **Rev:** Multicolor sea horses **Edge:** Reeded

Date	Mintage	F	VF	XF	Unc	BU
2002 Proof	—	Value: 22.00				

KM# 107 1000 SHILLINGS
29.1600 g., Silver Plated Bronze (Specific gravity 8.8096), 38.6 mm. **Subject:** Marine Life **Obv:** Arms with supporters **Rev:** Multicolor Hammerhead sharks **Edge:** Reeded

Date	Mintage	F	VF	XF	Unc	BU
2002 Proof	—	Value: 22.00				

KM# 108 1000 SHILLINGS
29.1600 g., Silver Plated Bronze (Specific gravity 8.8096), 38.6 mm. **Subject:** Marine Life **Obv:** Arms with supporters **Rev:** Multicolor Stingray **Edge:** Reeded

Date	Mintage	F	VF	XF	Unc	BU
2002 Proof	—	Value: 22.00				

KM# 109 1000 SHILLINGS
29.1600 g., Silver Plated Bronze (Specific gravity 8.8096), 38.6 mm. **Subject:** Marine Life **Obv:** Arms with supporters **Rev:** Multicolor Seal **Edge:** Reeded

Date	Mintage	F	VF	XF	Unc	BU
2002 Proof	—	Value: 22.00				

KM# 110 1000 SHILLINGS
29.1600 g., Silver Plated Bronze (Specific gravity 8.8096), 38.6 mm. **Subject:** Marine Life **Obv:** Arms with supporters **Rev:** Multicolor sea turtle **Edge:** Reeded

Date	Mintage	F	VF	XF	Unc	BU
2002 Proof	—	Value: 22.00				

KM# 111 1000 SHILLINGS
29.1600 g., Silver Plated Bronze (Specific gravity 8.8096), 38.6 mm. **Subject:** Marine Life **Obv:** Arms with supporters **Rev:** Multicolor dolphins **Edge:** Reeded

Date	Mintage	F	VF	XF	Unc	BU
2002 Proof	—	Value: 22.00				

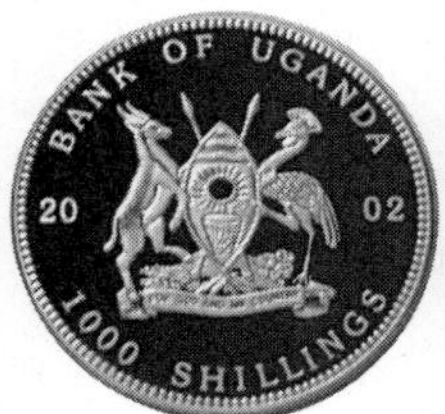

KM# 112 1000 SHILLINGS
29.1600 g., Silver Plated Bronze (Specific gravity 8.8096), 38.6 mm. **Subject:** Marine Life **Obv:** Arms with supporters **Rev:** Multicolor octopus **Edge:** Reeded

Date	Mintage	F	VF	XF	Unc	BU
2002 Proof	—	Value: 22.00				

KM# 113 1000 SHILLINGS
29.1600 g., Silver Plated Bronze (Specific gravity 8.8096), 38.6 mm. **Subject:** Marine Life **Obv:** Arms with supporters **Rev:** Multicolor red fish **Edge:** Reeded

Date	Mintage	F	VF	XF	Unc	BU
2002 Proof	—	Value: 22.00				

KM# 114 1000 SHILLINGS
29.1600 g., Silver Plated Bronze (Specific gravity 8.8096), 38.6 mm. **Subject:** Marine Life **Obv:** Arms with supporters **Rev:** Multicolor black fish with white dots **Edge:** Reeded

Date	Mintage	F	VF	XF	Unc	BU
2002 Proof	—	Value: 22.00				

KM# 115 1000 SHILLINGS
29.1600 g., Silver Plated Bronze (Specific gravity 8.8096), 38.6 mm. **Subject:** Marine Life **Obv:** Arms with supporters **Rev:** Multicolor yellow and black striped fish **Edge:** Reeded

Date	Mintage	F	VF	XF	Unc	BU
2002 Proof	—	Value: 22.00				

KM# 240 1000 SHILLINGS
Silver **Obv:** Arms **Rev:** Pope John Paul II bust facing

Date	Mintage	F	VF	XF	Unc	BU
2003 Proof	—	Value: 75.00				

KM# 105 1000 SHILLINGS
29.2000 g., Silver Plated Bronze (Specific gravity 9.0123), 38.6 mm. **Subject:** Pope John Paul II **Obv:** Arms with supporters **Rev:** Pope saying mass, design of Zambian 1000 Kwacha KM-160 **Edge:** Reeded **Note:** Muling error

Date	Mintage	F	VF	XF	Unc	BU
2003 Proof	—	Value: 300				

KM# 216 1000 SHILLINGS
Bronze **Subject:** Christmas **Obv. Legend:** BANK OF UGANDA **Rev:** Peace on Earth

Date	Mintage	F	VF	XF	Unc	BU
2004	500	—	—	—	—	50.00

KM# 75 2000 SHILLINGS
49.9000 g., 0.9990 Silver 1.6027 oz. ASW, 50 mm. **Subject:** Illusion: "Spirit of the Mountain" **Obv:** Crowned head right divides date above arms with supporters **Rev:** Landscape and tree that looks like a male portrait **Edge:** Reeded

Date	Mintage	F	VF	XF	Unc	BU
2001 Proof	—	Value: 75.00				

KM# 121 2000 SHILLINGS
25.0000 g., 0.9250 Silver 0.7435 oz. ASW, 38.6 mm. **Subject:** Queen Elizabeth's 75th Birthday **Obv:** Arms with supporters above crowned head right **Rev:** Queen accepting flowers from children **Edge:** Reeded

Date	Mintage	F	VF	XF	Unc	BU
2001 Proof	2,000	Value: 35.00				

KM# 100 2000 SHILLINGS
31.4000 g., 0.9990 Silver 1.0085 oz. ASW, 38.8 mm. **Obv:** Crowned head right divides date above arms with supporters **Rev:** Bust of Henry M. Stanley facing **Edge:** Reeded

Date	Mintage	F	VF	XF	Unc	BU
2002	—	—	—	—	40.00	45.00

KM# 177 2000 SHILLINGS
15.5500 g., 0.9990 Silver 0.4994 oz. ASW **Series:** Famous Places in China **Subject:** Mount Huangshan - Anhwei **Obv:** Two dragons **Obv. Legend:** BANK OF UGANDA

Date	Mintage	F	VF	XF	Unc	BU
2003 Proof	3,000	Value: 35.00				

KM# 178 2000 SHILLINGS
15.5500 g., 0.9990 Silver 0.4994 oz. ASW **Series:** Famous Places in China **Subject:** Zhangjiajie - Hunan **Obv:** Two dragons **Obv. Legend:** BANK OF UGANDA

Date	Mintage	F	VF	XF	Unc	BU
2003 Proof	3,000	Value: 35.00				

KM# 179 2000 SHILLINGS
15.5500 g., 0.9990 Silver 0.4994 oz. ASW **Series:** Famous Places in China **Subject:** Stone Forest - Yunnan **Obv:** Two dragons **Obv. Legend:** BANK OF UGANDA

Date	Mintage	F	VF	XF	Unc	BU
2003 Proof	3,000	Value: 35.00				

KM# 180 2000 SHILLINGS
15.5500 g., 0.9990 Silver 0.4994 oz. ASW **Series:** Famous Places in China **Subject:** Potala Palace - Lhasa, Tibet **Obv:** Two dragons **Obv. Legend:** BANK OF UGANDA

Date	Mintage	F	VF	XF	Unc	BU
2003 Proof	3,000	Value: 35.00				

KM# 181 2000 SHILLINGS
15.5500 g., 0.9990 Silver 0.4994 oz. ASW **Series:** Famous Places inChina **Subject:** Yangtse River Gorges **Obv:** Two dragons **Obv. Legend:** BANK OF UGANDA

Date	Mintage	F	VF	XF	Unc	BU
2003 Proof	3,000	Value: 35.00				

KM# 182 2000 SHILLINGS
31.1000 g., 0.9990 Silver 0.9988 oz. ASW **Series:** Chinese symbolism **Subject:** Harmony **Obv. Legend:** BANK OF UGANDA **Rev:** Dragon and phoenix

Date	Mintage	F	VF	XF	Unc	BU
2003 Proof	3,000	Value: 60.00				

KM# 183 2000 SHILLINGS
31.1000 g., 0.9990 Silver 0.9988 oz. ASW **Series:** Chinese symbolism **Subject:** Happiness **Obv. Legend:** BANK OF UGANDA **Rev:** Unicorn

Date	Mintage	F	VF	XF	Unc	BU
2003 Proof	3,000	Value: 60.00				

KM# 184 2000 SHILLINGS
31.1000 g., 0.9990 Silver 0.9988 oz. ASW **Series:** Chinese symbolism **Subject:** Health and long life **Obv. Legend:** BANK OF UGANDA **Rev:** Two cranes

Date	Mintage	F	VF	XF	Unc	BU
2003 Proof	3,000	Value: 60.00				

KM# 185 2000 SHILLINGS
31.1000 g., 0.9990 Silver 0.9988 oz. ASW **Series:** Chinese symbolism **Subject:** Success **Obv. Legend:** BANK OF UGANDA **Rev:** Carp

Date	Mintage	F	VF	XF	Unc	BU
2003 Proof	3,000	Value: 60.00				

KM# 186 2000 SHILLINGS
31.1000 g., 0.9990 Silver 0.9988 oz. ASW **Series:** Chinese symbolism **Subject:** Wealth **Obv. Legend:** BANK OF UGANDA **Rev:** Toad

Date	Mintage	F	VF	XF	Unc	BU
2003 Proof	3,000	Value: 60.00				

KM# 175 2000 SHILLINGS
15.5500 g., 0.9990 Silver 0.4994 oz. ASW **Series:** Famous Places in China **Subject:** Yugan Garden - Shanghai **Obv:** Two dragons **Obv. Legend:** BANK OF UGANDA

Date	Mintage	F	VF	XF	Unc	BU
2003 Proof	3,000	Value: 35.00				

KM# 176 2000 SHILLINGS
15.5500 g., 0.9990 Silver 0.4994 oz. ASW **Series:** Famous Places in China **Subject:** Tiger Hill Pagoda - Jiangsu **Obv:** Two dragons **Obv. Legend:** BANK OF UGANDA

Date	Mintage	F	VF	XF	Unc	BU
2003 Proof	3,000	Value: 35.00				

KM# 187 2000 SHILLINGS
4.0000 g., 0.9999 Gold 0.1286 oz. AGW **Series:** Guanyin **Subject:** Fulun **Obv:** Lotus blossom **Obv. Legend:** BANK OF UGANDA

Date	Mintage	F	VF	XF	Unc	BU
2003 Proof	—	Value: 200				

KM# 205 2000 SHILLINGS
Silver **Subject:** XXVIII Summer Olympics - Athens 2004 **Obv. Legend:** BANK OF UGANDA **Rev:** Sprinter

Date	Mintage	F	VF	XF	Unc	BU
2003 Proof	500	Value: 60.00				

KM# 210 2000 SHILLINGS
31.1000 g., 0.9990 Silver 0.9988 oz. ASW **Series:** Chinese symbolic floral New Year paintings **Subject:** Happiness **Obv. Legend:** BANK OF UGANDA **Rev:** Multicolor

Date	Mintage	F	VF	XF	Unc	BU
2004 Proof	2,000	Value: 60.00				

KM# 211 2000 SHILLINGS
31.1000 g., 0.9990 Silver 0.9988 oz. ASW **Series:** Chinese Dieties **Subject:** Happiness **Obv. Legend:** BANK OF UGANDA **Rev:** Fú - multicolor

Date	Mintage	F	VF	XF	Unc	BU
2004 Proof	2,000	Value: 60.00				

KM# 212 2000 SHILLINGS
31.1000 g., 0.9990 Silver 0.9988 oz. ASW **Series:** Chinese Deities **Subject:** Prosperity **Obv. Legend:** BANK OF UGANDA **Rev:** Lù - multicolor

Date	Mintage	F	VF	XF	Unc	BU
2004 Proof	2,000	Value: 60.00				

KM# 213 2000 SHILLINGS
31.1000 g., 0.9990 Silver 0.9988 oz. ASW **Series:** Chinese Dieties **Subject:** Health and Long Life **Obv. Legend:** BANK OF UGANDA **Rev:** Shòu - multicolor

Date	Mintage	F	VF	XF	Unc	BU
2004 Proof	2,000	Value: 60.00				

KM# 206 2000 SHILLINGS
31.1000 g., 0.9990 Silver 0.9988 oz. ASW **Series:** Chinese symbolic floral New Year paintings **Obv. Legend:** BANK OF UGANDA **Rev:** Carp and Lotus blossom - multicolor

Date	Mintage	F	VF	XF	Unc	BU
2004 Proof	2,000	Value: 60.00				

KM# 207 2000 SHILLINGS
31.1000 g., 0.9990 Silver 0.9988 oz. ASW **Series:** Chinese symbolic floral New Year paintings **Obv. Legend:** BANK OF UGANDA **Rev:** Deer - multicolor

Date	Mintage	F	VF	XF	Unc	BU
2004 Proof	2,000	Value: 60.00				

KM# 208 2000 SHILLINGS
31.1000 g., 0.9990 Silver 0.9988 oz. ASW **Series:** Chinese symbolic floral New Year paintings **Subject:** Abundance **Obv. Legend:** BANK OF UGANDA **Rev:** Fruit - multicolor

Date	Mintage	F	VF	XF	Unc	BU
2004 Proof	2,000	Value: 60.00				

KM# 209 2000 SHILLINGS
31.1000 g., 0.9990 Silver 0.9988 oz. ASW **Series:** Chinese symbolic floral New Year paintings **Subject:** Peace and prosperity **Obv. Legend:** BANK OF UGANDA **Rev:** Multicolor

Date	Mintage	F	VF	XF	Unc	BU
2004 Proof	2,000	Value: 60.00				

KM# 221 2000 SHILLINGS
Silver Plated Bronze **Series:** XIX World Football Championship - South Africa 2010 **Obv:** National arms **Obv. Legend:** BANK OF UGANDA **Rev:** Player about to kick

Date	Mintage	F	VF	XF	Unc	BU
2005 Proof	10,000	Value: 15.00				

KM# 222 2000 SHILLINGS
Silver Plated Bronze **Series:** XIX World Football Championship - South Afrika 2010 **Obv:** National arms **Obv. Legend:** BANK OF UGANDA **Rev:** Ball in net

Date	Mintage	F	VF	XF	Unc	BU
2005 Proof	10,000	Value: 15.00				

KM# 223 2000 SHILLINGS
Silver Plated Bronze **Series:** XIX World Football Championship - South Afrika 2010 **Obv:** National arms **Obv. Legend:** BANK OF UGANDA **Rev:** Player, map of Afrika

Date	Mintage	F	VF	XF	Unc	BU
2005 Proof	10,000	Value: 15.00				

KM# 224 2000 SHILLINGS
Silver Plated Bronze **Series:** XIX World Football Championship - South Afrika 2010 **Obv:** National arms **Obv. Legend:** BANK OF UGANDA **Rev:** Goalkeeper with ball

Date	Mintage	F	VF	XF	Unc	BU
2005 Proof	10,000	Value: 15.00				

KM# 225 2000 SHILLINGS
Silver Plated Bronze **Series:** XIX World Football Championship - South Afrika 2010 **Obv:** National arms **Obv. Legend:** BANK OF UGANDA **Rev:** Player and ball

Date	Mintage	F	VF	XF	Unc	BU
2005 Proof	10,000	Value: 15.00				

KM# 217 2000 SHILLINGS
31.1000 g., 0.9990 Silver 0.9988 oz. ASW **Obv:** Lotus blossom **Obv. Legend:** BANK OF UGANDA **Rev:** Guanyin - multicolor

Date	Mintage	F	VF	XF	Unc	BU
2005 Proof	2,000	Value: 75.00				

KM# 226 2000 SHILLINGS
40.0000 g., Bronze Gilt **Series:** Zodiac **Subject:** Year of the Dog **Obv:** Two dragons **Obv. Legend:** BANK OF UGANDA **Rev:** Three dogs - multicolor

Date	Mintage	F	VF	XF	Unc	BU
2006 Proof	—	Value: 45.00				

KM# 227 2000 SHILLINGS
40.0000 g., Bronze Gilt **Series:** Zodiac **Subject:** Year of the Dog **Obv:** Archaic Chinese characters **Obv. Legend:** BANK OF UGANDA **Rev:** Two dogs - multicolor

Date	Mintage	F	VF	XF	Unc	BU
2006 Proof	—	Value: 45.00				

KM# 227a 2000 SHILLINGS
31.1000 g., 0.9990 Silver 0.9988 oz. ASW **Series:** Zodiac **Subject:** Year of the Dog **Obv:** Archaic Chinese characters **Obv. Legend:** BANK OF UGANDA **Rev:** Two dogs - multicolor

Date	Mintage	F	VF	XF	Unc	BU
2006 Proof	3,000	Value: 75.00				

KM# 234 2000 SHILLINGS
31.1000 g., 0.9990 Silver 0.9988 oz. ASW **Series:** Zodiac **Subject:** Year of the Dog **Obv. Legend:** BANK OF UGANDA **Rev:** Tibet Terrier with pup surrounded by 10 symbols

Date	Mintage	F	VF	XF	Unc	BU
2006 Proof	3,000	Value: 75.00				

KM# 237 2000 SHILLINGS
31.1000 g., 0.9990 Silver 0.9988 oz. ASW **Series:** Zodiac **Subject:** Year of the Dog **Obv:** National arms **Obv. Legend:** BANK OF UGANDA **Rev:** Chow-chow as watchdog, gold bars, bat and flower

Date	Mintage	F	VF	XF	Unc	BU
2006 Proof	—	Value: 60.00				

KM# 172 5000 SHILLINGS
4.0000 g., 0.9999 Gold 0.1286 oz. AGW **Series:** Guanyin **Subject:** Chilian **Obv:** Lotus blossom **Obv. Legend:** BANK OF UGANDA

Date	Mintage	F	VF	XF	Unc	BU
2001 Proof	—	Value: 200				

KM# 87 5000 SHILLINGS
33.7300 g., 0.8500 Silver 0.9217 oz. ASW, 38.65 mm. **Subject:** "The Big Five" **Obv:** Arms with supporters **Rev:** Rhinoceros **Edge:** Reeded

Date	Mintage	F	VF	XF	Unc	BU
2002 Proof	—	Value: 65.00				

KM# 88 5000 SHILLINGS
33.7300 g., 0.8500 Silver 0.9217 oz. ASW, 38.65 mm. **Subject:** "The Big Five" **Obv:** Arms with supporters **Rev:** Lion **Edge:** Reeded

Date	Mintage	F	VF	XF	Unc	BU
2002 Proof	—	Value: 65.00				

KM# 89 5000 SHILLINGS
33.7300 g., 0.8500 Silver 0.9217 oz. ASW, 38.65 mm. **Subject:** "The Big Five" **Obv:** Arms with supporters **Rev:** Cape Buffalo **Edge:** Reeded

Date	Mintage	F	VF	XF	Unc	BU
2002 Proof	—	Value: 50.00				

KM# 90 5000 SHILLINGS
33.7300 g., 0.8500 Silver 0.9217 oz. ASW, 38.65 mm. **Subject:** "The Big Five" **Obv:** Arms with supporters **Rev:** Leopard **Edge:** Reeded

Date	Mintage	F	VF	XF	Unc	BU
2002 Proof	—	Value: 65.00				

KM# 91 5000 SHILLINGS
33.7300 g., 0.8500 Silver 0.9217 oz. ASW, 38.65 mm. **Subject:** "The Big Five" **Obv:** Arms with supporters **Rev:** Elephant **Edge:** Reeded

Date	Mintage	F	VF	XF	Unc	BU
2002 Proof	—	Value: 65.00				

KM# 96 5000 SHILLINGS
31.1035 g., 0.9990 Silver 0.9990 oz. ASW, 40.6 mm. **Subject:** Matthew Flinders **Obv:** Arms with supporters below crowned head right dividing date **Rev:** Multicolor bust half left at right with ship and harbor scene at left **Edge:** Plain **Shape:** Continent of Australia

Date	Mintage	F	VF	XF	Unc	BU
2002 Proof	2,500	Value: 55.00				

KM# 97 5000 SHILLINGS
31.1035 g., 0.9990 Silver 0.9990 oz. ASW, 40.6 mm. **Subject:** Matthew Flinders - H. M. S. Investigator **Obv:** Crowned head right divides date above arms with supporters **Rev:** Multicolor cameo at upper right of ship **Edge:** Plain **Shape:** Continent of Australia

Date	Mintage	F	VF	XF	Unc	BU
2002 Proof	2,500	Value: 55.00				

KM# 98 5000 SHILLINGS
31.1035 g., 0.9990 Silver 0.9990 oz. ASW, 40.6 mm. **Subject:** Matthew Flinders - Meeting at Encounter Bay **Obv:** Crowned head right divides date above arms with supporters **Rev:** Date and inscription divides multicolor busts facing **Edge:** Plain **Shape:** Continent of Australia

Date	Mintage	F	VF	XF	Unc	BU
2002 Proof	2,500	Value: 55.00				

KM# 99 5000 SHILLINGS
31.1035 g., 0.9990 Silver 0.9990 oz. ASW, 40.6 mm. **Subject:** Matthew Flinders - First Circumnavigation of Terra Australia - 1802 **Rev:** Multicolor bust right on Australian map showing his route around Australia **Edge:** Plain **Shape:** Continent of Australia

Date	Mintage	F	VF	XF	Unc	BU
2002 Proof	2,500	Value: 55.00				

KM# 174 5000 SHILLINGS
4.0000 g., 0.9999 Gold 0.1286 oz. AGW **Series:** Guanyin **Subject:** Fuyu **Obv:** Lotus blossom **Obv. Legend:** BANK OF UGANDA

Date	Mintage	F	VF	XF	Unc	BU
2002 Proof	—	Value: 200				

KM# 214 5000 SHILLINGS
4.0000 g., 0.9999 Gold 0.1286 oz. AGW **Series:** Guanyin **Subject:** Shile **Obv:** Lotus blossom **Obv. Legend:** BANK OF UGANDA

Date	Mintage	F	VF	XF	Unc	BU
2004 Proof	—	Value: 200				

KM# 220 5000 SHILLINGS
4.0000 g., 0.9999 Gold 0.1286 oz. AGW **Series:** Guanyin **Subject:** Songjing **Obv:** Lotus blossom **Obv. Legend:** BANK OF UGANDA

Date	Mintage	F	VF	XF	Unc	BU
2005 Proof	—	Value: 200				

KM# 235 6000 SHILLINGS
3.1100 g., 0.9999 Gold 0.1000 oz. AGW **Series:** Zodiac **Subject:** Year of the Dog **Obv. Legend:** BANK OF UGANDA **Rev:** Tibet Terrier with pup surrounded by 10 symbols

Date	Mintage	F	VF	XF	Unc	BU
2006 Proof	—	Value: 165				

KM# 228 6000 SHILLINGS
4.0000 g., 0.9999 Gold 0.1286 oz. AGW **Series:** Zodiac **Subject:** Year of the Dog **Obv:** Archaic Chinese characters **Obv. Legend:** BANK OF UGANDA **Rev:** Yorkshire Terrier and "Fú" - Happiness

Date	Mintage	F	VF	XF	Unc	BU
2006 Proof	14,000	Value: 225				

KM# 229 6000 SHILLINGS
4.0000 g., 0.9999 Gold 0.1286 oz. AGW **Series:** Zodiac **Subject:** Year of the Dog **Obv:** Archaic Chinese characters **Obv. Legend:** BANK OF UGANDA **Rev:** Yorkshire Terrier and "Lù" - Prosperity

Date	Mintage	F	VF	XF	Unc	BU
2006 Proof	14,000	Value: 225				

KM# 230 6000 SHILLINGS
4.0000 g., 0.9999 Gold 0.1286 oz. AGW **Series:** Zodiac **Subject:** Year of the Dog **Obv:** Archaic Chinese characters **Obv. Legend:** BANK OF UGANDA **Rev:** Yorkshire Terrier and "Shòu" - Health and Long Life

Date	Mintage	F	VF	XF	Unc	BU
2006 Proof	14,000	Value: 225				

KM# 238 6000 SHILLINGS
3.1100 g., 0.9999 Gold 0.1000 oz. AGW **Series:** Zodiac **Subject:** Year of the Dog **Obv:** National arms **Obv. Legend:** BANK OF UGANDA **Rev:** Chow-chow as watchdog, gold bars, bat and flower

Date	Mintage	F	VF	XF	Unc	BU
2006 Proof	—	Value: 165				

KM# 231 8000 SHILLINGS
8.0000 g., 0.9999 Gold 0.2572 oz. AGW **Series:** Zodiac **Subject:** Year of the Dog **Obv:** Archaic Chinese characters **Obv. Legend:** BANK OF UGANDA **Rev:** Yorkshire Terrier and "Fú" - Happiness

Date	Mintage	F	VF	XF	Unc	BU
2006 Proof	1,000	Value: 400				

KM# 232 8000 SHILLINGS
8.0000 g., 0.9999 Gold 0.2572 oz. AGW **Series:** Zodiac **Subject:** Year of the Dog **Obv:** Archaic Chinese characters **Obv. Legend:** BANK OF UGANDA **Rev:** Yorkshire Terrier and "Lù" - Prosperity

Date	Mintage	F	VF	XF	Unc	BU
2006 Proof	1,000	Value: 400				

KM# 215 10000 SHILLINGS
10.0000 g., 0.9999 Gold 0.3215 oz. AGW **Obv:** Lotus blossom **Obv. Legend:** BANK OF UGANDA **Rev:** Buddha

Date	Mintage	F	VF	XF	Unc	BU
2004 Proof	3,000	Value: 700				

KM# 76 12000 SHILLINGS
6.2207 g., 0.9999 Gold 0.2000 oz. AGW, 22 mm. **Subject:** Illusion: "Spirit of the Mountain" **Obv:** Crowned head right divides date above arms with supporters **Rev:** Landscape and tree that looks like a male portrait **Edge:** Reeded

Date	Mintage	F	VF	XF	Unc	BU
2001 Proof	—	Value: 325				

KM# 236 20000 SHILLINGS
15.5500 g., 0.9999 Gold 0.4999 oz. AGW **Series:** Zodiac **Subject:** Year of the Dog **Obv. Legend:** BANK OF UGANDA **Rev:** Tibet Terrier with pup surrounded by 10 symbols

Date	Mintage	F	VF	XF	Unc	BU
2006 Proof	—	Value: 775				

KM# 239 20000 SHILLINGS
15.5500 g., 0.9999 Gold 0.4999 oz. AGW **Series:** Year of the Dog **Obv:** National arms **Obv. Legend:** BANK OF UGANDA **Rev:** Chow-chow as watchdog, gold bars, bat and flower

Date	Mintage	F	VF	XF	Unc	BU
2006 Proof	—	Value: 775				

UKRAINE

BELARUS
POLAND
RUSSIA
TRANSDNIESTRA
SLOVAKIA
HUNGARY
MOLDOVA
ROMANIA
Black Sea

Ukraine (formerly the Ukrainian Soviet Socialist Republic) is bordered by Russia to the east, Russia and Belarus to the north, Poland, Slovakia and Hungary to the west, Romania and Moldova to the southwest and in the south by the Black Sea and the Sea of Azov. It has an area of 233,088 sq. mi. (603,700 sq. km.) and a population of 51.9 million. Capital: Kyiv (Kiev). Coal, grain, vegetables and heavy industrial machinery are major exports.

Ukraine is a charter member of the United Nations and has inherited the third largest nuclear arsenal in the world.

MONETARY SYSTEM
(1) Kopiyka
(2) Kopiyky КОПіЙКН
(5 and up) Kopiyok КОПИОК
100 Kopiyok = 1 Hrynia ГРИВЕНЬ
100,000 Karbovanetsiv = 1 Hryni or Hryven)

REPUBLIC

REFORM COINAGE

September 2, 1996

100,000 Karbovanets = 1 Hryvnia; 100 Kopiyok = 1 Hryvnia; The Kopiyok has replaced the Karbovanet

KM# 6 KOPIYKA
1.5000 g., Stainless Steel, 16 mm. **Obv:** National arms **Rev:** Value within wreath **Edge:** Plain

Date	Mintage	F	VF	XF	Unc	BU
2001	—	—	—	0.35	0.75	—
2002	—	—	—	0.35	0.75	—
2003	—	—	—	0.35	0.75	—
2004	—	—	—	0.35	0.75	—
2005	—	—	—	0.35	0.75	—
2006	—	—	—	0.35	0.75	—
2007	—	—	—	0.35	0.75	—
2008	—	—	—	0.35	0.75	—
2008 Prooflike	5,000	—	—	—	—	1.50
2009	—	—	—	0.35	0.75	—
2010	—	—	—	0.35	0.75	—

KM# 4b 2 KOPIYKY
1.8000 g., Stainless Steel, 17.3 mm. **Obv:** National arms **Rev:** Value in wreath **Edge:** Plain

Date	Mintage	F	VF	XF	Unc	BU
2001	—	—	0.20	0.50	1.00	—
2002	—	—	0.20	0.50	1.00	—
2003	Est. 5,000	—	—	—	—	300
2004	—	—	0.20	0.50	1.00	—
2005	—	—	0.20	0.50	1.00	—
2006	—	—	—	0.50	1.00	—
2007	—	—	—	0.50	1.00	—
2008	—	—	—	0.50	1.00	—
2008 Prooflike	5,000	—	—	—	—	2.00
2009	—	—	—	0.50	1.00	—
2010	—	—	—	0.50	1.00	—

KM# 7 5 KOPIYOK
4.3000 g., Stainless Steel, 23.91 mm. **Obv:** National arms **Rev:** Value within wreath **Edge:** Reeded

Date	Mintage	F	VF	XF	Unc	BU
2001 In sets only	10,000	—	—	—	—	10.00
2003	—	—	—	0.50	1.00	—
2004	—	—	—	0.50	1.00	—
2005	—	—	—	0.50	1.00	—
2006	—	—	—	0.50	1.00	—
2007	—	—	—	0.50	1.00	—
2008	—	—	—	0.50	1.00	—
2008 Prooflike	5,000	—	—	—	—	2.50
2009	—	—	—	0.50	1.00	—
2010	—	—	—	0.50	1.00	—

KM# 1.1b 10 KOPIYOK
1.7000 g., Aluminum-Bronze, 16.24 mm. **Obv:** National arms **Rev:** Value within wreath **Edge:** Reeded

Date	Mintage	F	VF	XF	Unc	BU
2001 In sets only	10,000	—	—	—	—	7.50
2002	—	—	0.60	1.25	2.50	—
2003	—	—	0.50	1.00	2.25	—
2004	—	—	0.50	1.00	2.25	—
2005	—	—	—	1.00	2.25	—
2006	—	—	—	1.00	2.25	—
2007	—	—	—	1.00	2.25	—
2008	—	—	—	1.00	2.25	—
2008 Prooflike	5,000	—	—	—	—	5.00
2009	—	—	—	1.00	2.00	—
2010	—	—	—	1.00	2.00	—

KM# 2.1b 25 KOPIYOK
2.9000 g., Aluminum-Bronze, 20.8 mm. **Obv:** National arms **Rev:** Value within wreath

Date	Mintage	F	VF	XF	Unc	BU
2001	—	—	0.80	3.00	6.00	—
2003 Prooflike	Est. 5,000	—	—	—	—	300
2006	—	—	0.80	2.00	4.00	—
2007	—	—	0.80	2.00	4.00	—
2008	—	—	—	2.00	4.00	—
2008 Prooflike	5,000	—	—	—	—	8.00
2009	—	—	—	2.00	3.50	—
2010	—	—	—	2.00	3.50	—

KM# 3.3b 50 KOPIYOK
4.2000 g., Aluminum-Bronze, 23 mm.

Date	Mintage	F	VF	XF	Unc	BU
2001 In sets only	—	—	—	—	10.00	—
2003	Est. 5,000	—	—	—	300	—
2006	—	—	1.00	2.00	4.00	—
2007	—	—	1.00	2.00	4.00	—
2008	—	—	—	2.00	4.00	—
2008 Prooflike, in sets only	5,000	—	—	—	—	8.00

KM# 8b HRYVNIA
6.9000 g., Aluminum-Bronze, 26 mm. **Obv:** National arms **Rev:** Value, sprigs and designs **Edge:** Lettered

Date	Mintage	F	VF	XF	Unc	BU
2001	—	—	—	2.50	4.50	—

KM# 8b.1 HRYVNIA
7.1000 g., Aluminum-Bronze, 26 mm. **Obv:** National arms **Rev:** Value, sprigs and designs **Edge:** Lettered

Date	Mintage	F	VF	XF	Unc	BU
2002	—	—	—	3.50	6.50	—
2003	—	—	—	2.50	4.50	—

KM# 208 HRYVNIA
6.8000 g., Aluminum-Bronze, 26 mm. **Subject:** 60th Anniversary - Victory over the Nazis **Obv:** National arms above value **Rev:** Uniform lapel with Soviet military medals group **Edge:** Lettered **Edge Lettering:** Date and denomination

Date	Mintage	F	VF	XF	Unc	BU
2004	5,000,000	—	—	—	5.00	—

KM# 209 HRYVNIA
6.7400 g., Aluminum-Bronze, 26 mm. **Obv:** National arms above value **Rev:** Half length figure of Volodymyr the Great facing holding church model building and staff **Edge:** Lettered **Edge Lettering:** Date and denomination

Date	Mintage	F	VF	XF	Unc	BU
2004	10,000,000	—	—	—	4.00	—
2005	—	—	—	—	3.00	—
2006	—	—	—	—	3.00	—
2008 Prooflike, in sets only	5,000	—	—	—	—	12.50
2010	—	—	—	—	3.00	—

KM# 228 HRYVNIA
6.8000 g., Aluminum-Bronze, 26 mm. **Subject:** WW II Victory 60th Anniversary **Obv:** Value **Rev:** Soldiers in a "V" of search lights **Edge:** Reeded

Date	Mintage	F	VF	XF	Unc	BU
2005	5,000,000	—	—	—	5.00	—

KM# 106 2 HRYVNI
12.8000 g., Copper-Nickel-Zinc, 31 mm. **Series:** Olympics - Salt Lake City, 2002 **Obv:** National arms, value and designs **Rev:** Stylized ice dancing couple **Edge:** Reeded

Date	Mintage	F	VF	XF	Unc	BU
2001	30,000	—	—	—	15.00	—

KM# 133 2 HRYVNI
12.8000 g., Copper-Nickel-Zinc, 31 mm. **Subject:** Kindness to Children **Obv:** National arms above value flanked by sprigs and doves **Rev:** Two children frolicking under fountain of knowledge **Edge:** Reeded

Date	Mintage	F	VF	XF	Unc	BU
2001	100,000	—	—	—	12.00	—

KM# 134 2 HRYVNI
12.8000 g., Copper-Nickel-Zinc, 31 mm. **Subject:** 5th Anniversary of Constitution **Obv:** National arms above value flanked by sprigs **Rev:** Building above book flanked by sprigs **Edge:** Reeded

Date	Mintage	F	VF	XF	Unc	BU
2001	30,000	—	—	—	25.00	—

KM# 111 2 HRYVNI
12.8000 g., Copper-Nickel-Zinc, 31 mm. **Series:** Flora and Fauna **Obv:** National arms and date divides wreath, value within **Rev:** Lynx and offspring **Edge:** Reeded

Date	Mintage	F	VF	XF	Unc	BU
2001	30,000	—	—	—	50.00	—

KM# 136 2 HRYVNI
12.8000 g., Copper-Nickel-Zinc, 31 mm. **Subject:** Mykolaiv Zoo **Obv:** Man running alongside large cat **Rev:** Twelve animals **Edge:** Reeded

Date	Mintage	F	VF	XF	Unc	BU
2001	30,000	—	—	—	30.00	—

KM# 137 2 HRYVNI
12.8000 g., Copper-Nickel-Zinc, 31 mm. **Subject:** Mykhailo Ostrohradskiy (Mathematician) **Obv:** National arms divides date and value divided by wavy line graph **Rev:** Head 1/4 left **Edge:** Reeded

Date	Mintage	F	VF	XF	Unc	BU
2001	30,000	—	—	—	12.00	—

KM# 138 2 HRYVNI
12.8000 g., Copper-Nickel-Zinc, 31 mm. **Subject:** Larix Polonica **Obv:** Value within wreath **Rev:** Pine branch with cone **Edge:** Reeded

Date	Mintage	F	VF	XF	Unc	BU
2001	30,000	—	—	—	40.00	—

KM# 139 2 HRYVNI
12.8000 g., Copper-Nickel-Zinc, 31 mm. **Subject:** Volodymyr Dal **Obv:** Books **Rev:** Head right **Edge:** Reeded

Date	Mintage	F	VF	XF	Unc	BU
2001	30,000	—	—	—	12.00	—

KM# 147 2 HRYVNI
12.8000 g., Copper-Nickel-Zinc, 31 mm. **Series:** Olympics - Salt lake City, 2002 **Obv:** National arms and value on ice design **Rev:** Stylized hockey player **Edge:** Reeded

Date	Mintage	F	VF	XF	Unc	BU
2001	30,000	—	—	—	15.00	—

KM# 149 2 HRYVNI
12.8000 g., Copper-Nickel-Zinc, 31 mm. **Subject:** Mykhailo Drahomanov (Historian, Politician, etc.) **Obv:** National arms and value **Rev:** Bust right **Edge:** Reeded

Date	Mintage	F	VF	XF	Unc	BU
2001	30,000	—	—	—	12.00	—

KM# 150 2 HRYVNI
12.8000 g., Copper-Nickel-Zinc, 31 mm. **Series:** Olympics - Salt lake City, 2002 **Obv:** National arms and value on ice design **Rev:** Speed skater **Edge:** Reeded

Date	Mintage	F	VF	XF	Unc	BU
2002	30,000	—	—	—	15.00	—

KM# 155 2 HRYVNI
12.8000 g., Copper-Nickel-Zinc, 31 mm. **Series:** Flora and Fauna **Obv:** National arms and date divides wreath, value within **Rev:** Eurasian Eagle Owl **Edge:** Reeded

Date	Mintage	F	VF	XF	Unc	BU
2002	30,000	—	—	—	60.00	—

KM# 156 2 HRYVNI
12.8000 g., Copper-Nickel-Zinc, 31 mm. **Subject:** Olympics - Athens, 2004 **Obv:** Two ancient figures above value **Rev:** Swimmer **Edge:** Reeded

Date	Mintage	F	VF	XF	Unc	BU
2002 Prooflike	30,000	—	—	—	15.00	—

KM# 166 2 HRYVNI
12.8000 g., Copper-Nickel-Zinc, 31 mm. **Subject:** Leonid Glibov, writer (1827-1893) **Obv:** National arms and value within scroll and wreath **Rev:** 1/2-length bust right **Edge:** Reeded

Date	Mintage	F	VF	XF	Unc	BU
2002	30,000	—	—	—	12.00	—

KM# 154 2 HRYVNI
12.8000 g., Copper-Nickel-Zinc, 31 mm. **Subject:** Mykola Lysenko (composer) **Obv:** Musical score and value **Rev:** Head 1/4 right **Edge:** Reeded

Date	Mintage	F	VF	XF	Unc	BU
2002	30,000	—	—	—	12.00	—

KM# 167 2 HRYVNI
12.8000 g., Copper-Nickel-Zinc, 31 mm. **Series:** Flora and Fauna **Obv:** National arms and date divides wreath, value within **Rev:** European Bison **Edge:** Reeded

Date	Mintage	F	VF	XF	Unc	BU
2003	50,000	—	—	—	30.00	—

KM# 168 2 HRYVNI
12.8000 g., Copper-Nickel-Zinc, 31 mm. **Obv:** National arms and date divides wreath, value within **Rev:** Long-snouted Sea Horse **Edge:** Reeded

Date	Mintage	F	VF	XF	Unc	BU
2003	50,000	—	—	—	20.00	—

KM# 169 2 HRYVNI
12.8000 g., Copper-Nickel-Zinc, 31 mm. **Subject:** Volodymyr Vernadskyi (academic) **Obv:** National arms, value and world globe **Rev:** Head on hand looking down **Edge:** Reeded

Date	Mintage	F	VF	XF	Unc	BU
2003	30,000	—	—	—	12.00	—

KM# 170 2 HRYVNI
12.8000 g., Copper-Nickel-Zinc, 31 mm. **Subject:** Volodymyr Korolenko (writer) **Obv:** National arms above book and value **Rev:** Bearded head 1/4 right above dates **Edge:** Reeded

Date	Mintage	F	VF	XF	Unc	BU
2003	30,000	—	—	—	12.00	—

KM# 171 2 HRYVNI
12.8000 g., Copper-Nickel-Zinc, 31 mm. **Subject:** Viacheslav Chornovil (politician) **Obv:** Arms with supporters within beaded circle **Rev:** Head 1/4 left **Edge:** Reeded

Date	Mintage	F	VF	XF	Unc	BU
2003	30,000	—	—	—	15.00	—

KM# 178 2 HRYVNI
1.2400 g., 0.9999 Gold 0.0399 oz. AGW, 13.92 mm. **Obv:** National arms flanked by dates within beaded circle **Rev:** Spotted Salamander divides beaded circle **Edge:** Plain

Date	Mintage	F	VF	XF	Unc	BU
2003	10,000	—	—	—	—	220

KM# 179 2 HRYVNI
12.8000 g., Copper-Nickel-Zinc, 31 mm. **Subject:** Singer Boris Gmyrya **Obv:** Value, arms ,date and musical symbol **Rev:** Head 1/4 left and dates **Edge:** Reeded

Date	Mintage	F	VF	XF	Unc	BU
2003	30,000	—	—	—	12.00	—

KM# 180 2 HRYVNI
12.8000 g., Copper-Nickel-Zinc, 31 mm. **Subject:** 70th Anniversary National Aviation University **Obv:** World globe behind national arms, value and date **Rev:** Wright Brothers biplane **Edge:** Reeded

Date	Mintage	F	VF	XF	Unc	BU
2003	30,000	—	—	—	15.00	—

KM# 181 2 HRYVNI
12.8000 g., Copper-Nickel-Zinc, 31 mm. **Subject:** Ostap Veresay (musician) **Obv:** Musical stringed instrument and ornamental design **Rev:** Bust facing playing stringed instrument **Edge:** Reeded

Date	Mintage	F	VF	XF	Unc	BU
2003	30,000	—	—	—	13.00	—

KM# 182 2 HRYVNI
12.8000 g., Copper-Nickel-Zinc, 31 mm. **Subject:** Olympics **Obv:** Two ancient women with seedlings **Rev:** Boxer **Edge:** Reeded

Date	Mintage	F	VF	XF	Unc	BU
2003	30,000	—	—	—	18.00	—

KM# 183 2 HRYVNI
12.8000 g., Copper-Nickel-Zinc, 31 mm. **Subject:** Vasyl Sukhomlynski (teacher) **Obv:** Children, books, value and national arms **Rev:** Head 1/4 right **Edge:** Reeded

Date	Mintage	F	VF	XF	Unc	BU
2003	30,000	—	—	—	13.00	—

KM# 184 2 HRYVNI
12.8000 g., Copper-Nickel-Zinc, 31 mm. **Subject:** Andriy Malyshko (poet) **Obv:** Ornamental shawl, national arms and value **Rev:** Head 1/4 right flanked by radiant sun and tree **Edge:** Reeded

Date	Mintage	F	VF	XF	Unc	BU
2003	30,000	—	—	—	13.00	—

KM# 201 2 HRYVNI
12.8000 g., Copper-Nickel-Zinc, 31 mm. **Subject:** Azov Dolphin **Obv:** National arms and date divides wreath, value within **Rev:** Harbor Porpoises **Edge:** Reeded

Date	Mintage	F	VF	XF	Unc	BU
2004	30,000	—	—	—	35.00	—

KM# 202 2 HRYVNI
12.8000 g., Copper-Nickel-Zinc, 31 mm. **Subject:** Football World Cup - 2006 **Obv:** Soccer ball in net **Rev:** Two soccer players **Edge:** Reeded

Date	Mintage	F	VF	XF	Unc	BU
2004	50,000	—	—	—	13.50	—

KM# 203 2 HRYVNI
12.8000 g., Copper-Nickel-Zinc, 31 mm. **Subject:** Serhiy Lyfar (ballet artist) **Obv:** Stylized dancer **Rev:** Head right **Edge:** Reeded

Date	Mintage	F	VF	XF	Unc	BU
2004	30,000	—	—	—	12.00	—

KM# 210 2 HRYVNI
12.8000 g., Copper-Nickel-Zinc, 31 mm. **Subject:** 170 Years of the Kyiv National University **Obv:** National arms in center above value dividing scientific items **Rev:** University building main entrance **Edge:** Reeded

Date	Mintage	F	VF	XF	Unc	BU
2004	50,000	—	—	—	10.00	—

KM# 211 2 HRYVNI
12.8000 g., Copper-Nickel-Zinc, 31 mm. **Subject:** Oleksander Dovzhenko (movie producer, writer) **Obv:** Boy standing in small boat **Rev:** Head facing **Edge:** Reeded

Date	Mintage	F	VF	XF	Unc	BU
2004	30,000	—	—	—	11.00	—

KM# 212 2 HRYVNI
12.8000 g., Copper-Nickel-Zinc, 31 mm. **Subject:** Mykola Bazhan (poet, translator) **Obv:** Winged pens and value **Rev:** Head 1/4 left **Edge:** Reeded

Date	Mintage	F	VF	XF	Unc	BU
2004	30,000	—	—	—	11.00	—

KM# 213 2 HRYVNI
12.8000 g., Copper-Nickel-Zinc, 31 mm. **Subject:** Mykhailo Kotsubynsky (writer) **Obv:** Two reclining figures **Rev:** Head 1/4 right **Edge:** Reeded

Date	Mintage	F	VF	XF	Unc	BU
2004	30,000	—	—	—	11.00	—

KM# 214 2 HRYVNI
12.8000 g., Copper-Nickel-Zinc, 31 mm. **Subject:** Maria Zankovetska (actress) **Obv:** National arms, value and drawn curtain **Rev:** Hooded head 1/4 left **Edge:** Reeded

Date	Mintage	F	VF	XF	Unc	BU
2004	30,000	—	—	—	11.00	—

KM# 215 2 HRYVNI
12.8000 g., Copper-Nickel-Zinc, 31 mm. **Subject:** Mykhailo Maksymovych (historian, archaeologist) **Obv:** National arms above building and value **Rev:** Bust left **Edge:** Reeded

Date	Mintage	F	VF	XF	Unc	BU
2004	30,000	—	—	—	11.00	—

KM# 216 2 HRYVNI
12.8000 g., Copper-Nickel-Zinc, 31 mm. **Subject:** Mykhailo Deregus (painter) **Obv:** National arms and value on artists palette **Rev:** Head right **Edge:** Reeded

Date	Mintage	F	VF	XF	Unc	BU
2004	30,000	—	—	—	11.00	—

KM# 217 2 HRYVNI
12.8000 g., Copper-Nickel-Zinc, 31 mm. **Subject:** Nuclear Power Engineering of Ukraine **Obv:** National arms and value in atomic design **Rev:** Nuclear reactor **Edge:** Reeded

Date	Mintage	F	VF	XF	Unc	BU
2004	30,000	—	—	—	15.00	—

KM# 227 2 HRYVNI

1.2400 g., 0.9999 Gold 0.0399 oz. AGW, 13.92 mm. **Obv:** National arms divides dates within beaded circle **Rev:** Flying White Stork divides beaded circle **Edge:** Plain

Date	Mintage	F	VF	XF	Unc	BU
2004	10,000	—	—	—	—	220

KM# 330 2 HRYVNI

12.8000 g., Copper-Nickel-Zinc, 31 mm. **Subject:** 200th Anniversary of Kharkiv University **Obv:** National arms and atom **Rev:** University building and reflection **Edge:** Reeded

Date	Mintage	F	VF	XF	Unc	BU
2004	50,000	—	—	—	10.00	—

KM# 331 2 HRYVNI

12.8000 g., Copper-Nickel-Zinc, 31 mm. **Subject:** Ukraine National Academy of Law named after Yaroslav the Wise **Obv:** National arms above National Academy of Law arms and date **Rev:** Building **Edge:** Reeded

Date	Mintage	F	VF	XF	Unc	BU
2004	30,000	—	—	—	17.00	—

KM# 332 2 HRYVNI

12.8000 g., Copper-Nickel-Zinc, 31 mm. **Subject:** Yuri Fedkovych (poet, writer) **Obv:** National arms, value and man on horse **Rev:** Bust 1/4 right and dates **Edge:** Reeded

Date	Mintage	F	VF	XF	Unc	BU
2004	30,000	—	—	—	11.00	—

KM# 346 2 HRYVNI

12.8000 g., Copper-Nickel-Zinc, 31 mm. **Subject:** Boris Liatoshynsky (composer) **Obv:** Musical G Clef symbol and value below national arms **Rev:** Head 1/4 left **Edge:** Reeded

Date	Mintage	F	VF	XF	Unc	BU
2005	20,000	—	—	—	13.00	—

KM# 347 2 HRYVNI

12.8000 g., Copper-Nickel-Zinc, 31 mm. **Subject:** Volodymyr Filatov (surgeon) **Obv:** Light passing through the lens of an eye **Rev:** Head with cap facing **Edge:** Reeded

Date	Mintage	F	VF	XF	Unc	BU
2005	20,000	—	—	—	13.00	—

KM# 348 2 HRYVNI

12.8000 g., Copper-Nickel-Zinc, 31 mm. **Obv:** Books between stylized horsemen **Rev:** Ulas Samchuk **Edge:** Reeded

Date	Mintage	F	VF	XF	Unc	BU
2005	20,000	—	—	—	13.00	—

KM# 349 2 HRYVNI

12.8000 g., Copper-Nickel-Zinc, 31 mm. **Subject:** Pavlo Virsky (ballet artist) **Obv:** National arms in flower circle **Rev:** Bust right **Edge:** Reeded

Date	Mintage	F	VF	XF	Unc	BU
2005	20,000	—	—	—	13.00	—

KM# 350 2 HRYVNI

12.8000 g., Copper-Nickel-Zinc, 31 mm. **Obv:** Roses and grapes **Rev:** Poet Maksym Rylsky **Edge:** Reeded

Date	Mintage	F	VF	XF	Unc	BU
2005	20,000	—	—	—	13.00	—

KM# 351 2 HRYVNI

1.2400 g., 0.9999 Gold 0.0399 oz. AGW, 13.9 mm. **Obv:** National arms within beaded circle **Rev:** Scythian horseman depicted on golden plaque **Edge:** Plain

Date	Mintage	F	VF	XF	Unc	BU
2005	15,000	—	—	—	200	—

KM# 352 2 HRYVNI

12.8000 g., Copper-Nickel-Zinc, 31 mm. **Subject:** Serhiy Vsekhsviatsky (astronomer) **Obv:** "Solar Wind" depiction **Rev:** Head right **Edge:** Reeded

Date	Mintage	F	VF	XF	Unc	BU
2005	20,000	—	—	—	13.00	—

KM# 353 2 HRYVNI

12.8000 g., Copper-Nickel-Zinc, 31 mm. **Subject:** 50 Years of Kyivmiskbud **Obv:** National arms **Rev:** Buildings **Edge:** Reeded

Date	Mintage	F	VF	XF	Unc	BU
2005	20,000	—	—	—	15.00	—

KM# 354 2 HRYVNI

12.8000 g., Copper-Nickel-Zinc, 31 mm. **Subject:** 75 Years of Zhukovsky Aerospace University in Kharkiv **Obv:** Building divides book outline **Rev:** Airplane, computer monitor and books **Edge:** Reeded

Date	Mintage	F	VF	XF	Unc	BU
2005	30,000	—	—	—	15.00	—

KM# 356 2 HRYVNI

12.8000 g., Copper-Nickel-Zinc, 31 mm. **Subject:** Oleksander Korniychuk (writer, playright) **Obv:** Theatrical masks and feather **Rev:** Bust 1/4 right **Edge:** Reeded

Date	Mintage	F	VF	XF	Unc	BU
2005	20,000	—	—	—	12.00	—

KM# 357 2 HRYVNI

12.8000 g., Copper-Nickel-Zinc, 31 mm. **Obv:** National arms and date divides wreath, value within **Rev:** Sandy Mole Rat **Edge:** Reeded

Date	Mintage	F	VF	XF	Unc	BU
2005	60,000	—	—	—	15.00	—

KM# 359 2 HRYVNI

12.8000 g., Copper-Nickel-Zinc, 31 mm. **Obv:** National arms **Rev:** Tairov Wine Institute building and cameo **Edge:** Reeded

Date	Mintage	F	VF	XF	Unc	BU
2005	20,000	—	—	—	20.00	—

KM# 360 2 HRYVNI

12.8000 g., Copper-Nickel-Zinc, 31 mm. **Subject:** 300 Years to David Guramishvili (poet) **Obv:** Georgian and Ukrainian style ornamentation **Rev:** Head right **Edge:** Reeded

Date	Mintage	F	VF	XF	Unc	BU
2005	30,000	—	—	—	10.00	—

KM# 361 2 HRYVNI

12.8000 g., Copper-Nickel-Zinc, 31 mm. **Subject:** Dmytro Yavornytsky (historian, archaeologist, writer) **Obv:** National arms **Rev:** Bust 3/4 right **Edge:** Reeded

Date	Mintage	F	VF	XF	Unc	BU
2005	30,000	—	—	—	10.00	—

KM# 375 2 HRYVNI

12.8000 g., Copper-Nickel-Zinc, 31 mm. **Subject:** Oleksiy Alchevsky (banker) **Obv:** Steam train, factory, National arms and value **Rev:** Head with beard 1/4 right **Edge:** Reeded

Date	Mintage	F	VF	XF	Unc	BU
2005	20,000	—	—	—	20.00	—

KM# 376 2 HRYVNI

12.8000 g., Copper-Nickel-Zinc, 31 mm. **Subject:** Illia Mechnikov (biologist, Nobel prize laureate) **Obv:** Amoeba and National arms **Rev:** Bust with beard facing **Edge:** Reeded

Date	Mintage	F	VF	XF	Unc	BU
2005	20,000	—	—	—	20.00	—

KM# 377 2 HRYVNI

12.8000 g., Copper-Nickel-Zinc, 31 mm. **Subject:** Vsevolod Holubovych (politician) **Obv:** National arms **Rev:** Head 1/4 left **Edge:** Reeded

Date	Mintage	F	VF	XF	Unc	BU
2005	20,000	—	—	—	12.50	—

KM# 378 2 HRYVNI

12.8000 g., Copper-Nickel-Zinc, 31 mm. **Subject:** Volodymyr Vynnychenko (writer, politician) **Obv:** National arms **Rev:** Head facing **Edge:** Reeded

Date	Mintage	F	VF	XF	Unc	BU
2005	20,000	—	—	—	13.00	—

KM# 383 2 HRYVNI

12.8000 g., Copper-Nickel-Zinc, 31 mm. **Subject:** Kyiv National University of Economics **Obv:** National arms, value and graph **Rev:** University building **Edge:** Reeded

Date	Mintage	F	VF	XF	Unc	BU
2006	60,000	—	—	—	11.00	—

KM# 384 2 HRYVNI

12.8000 g., Copper-Nickel-Zinc, 31 mm. **Subject:** Viacheslav Prokopovych (historian, publist) **Obv:** National arms **Rev:** Bust facing **Edge:** Reeded

Date	Mintage	F	VF	XF	Unc	BU
2006	30,000	—	—	—	11.00	—

KM# 385 2 HRYVNI

12.8000 g., Copper-Nickel-Zinc, 31 mm. **Subject:** Heorhii Narbut (artist) **Obv:** Peasant couple **Rev:** Silhouette of standing figure on one leg facing right **Edge:** Reeded

Date	Mintage	F	VF	XF	Unc	BU
2006	30,000	—	—	—	12.00	—

KM# 386 2 HRYVNI

12.8000 g., Copper-Nickel-Zinc, 31 mm. **Subject:** Oleh Antonov (aircraft engineer) **Obv:** Large jet plane **Rev:** Bust 1/4 right **Edge:** Reeded

Date	Mintage	F	VF	XF	Unc	BU
2006	45,000	—	—	—	13.50	—

KM# 391 2 HRYVNI

12.8000 g., Copper-Nickel-Zinc, 31 mm. **Obv:** National arms above value in wreath **Rev:** Bush Katydid Grasshopper **Edge:** Reeded

Date	Mintage	F	VF	XF	Unc	BU
2006	60,000	—	—	—	15.00	—

KM# 398 2 HRYVNI

12.8000 g., Copper-Nickel-Zinc, 31 mm. **Subject:** Mykhailo Hrushevskyi **Obv:** National arms and value **Edge:** Reeded

Date	Mintage	F	VF	XF	Unc	BU
2006	45,000	—	—	—	11.00	—

KM# 408 2 HRYVNI

1.2400 g., 0.9999 Gold 0.0399 oz. AGW, 13.92 mm. **Subject:** Hedgehog **Obv:** National arms **Edge:** Plain

Date	Mintage	F	VF	XF	Unc	BU
2006	10,000	—	—	—	120	—

KM# 399 2 HRYVNI

12.8000 g., Copper-Nickel-Zinc, 31 mm. **Subject:** Serhii Ostapenko **Obv:** National arms **Edge:** Reeded

Date	Mintage	F	VF	XF	Unc	BU
2006	30,000	—	—	—	10.00	—

KM# 401 2 HRYVNI

12.8000 g., Copper-Nickel-Zinc, 31 mm. **Subject:** Economic University of Kharkiv

Date	Mintage	F	VF	XF	Unc	BU
2006	30,000	—	—	—	12.00	—

KM# 393 2 HRYVNI

12.8000 g., Copper-Nickel-Zinc, 31 mm. **Subject:** Mykola Strazhesko **Obv:** National arms and value **Edge:** Reeded

Date	Mintage	F	VF	XF	Unc	BU
2006	45,000	—	—	—	11.00	—

KM# 394 2 HRYVNI

12.8000 g., Copper-Nickel-Zinc, 31 mm. **Subject:** Volodymyr Chekhivsky **Obv:** National arms and value **Edge:** Reeded

Date	Mintage	F	VF	XF	Unc	BU
2006	30,000	—	—	—	12.00	—

KM# 395 2 HRYVNI

12.8000 g., Copper-Nickel-Zinc, 31 mm. **Subject:** Mykola Vasylenko **Obv:** National arms and value **Edge:** Reeded

Date	Mintage	F	VF	XF	Unc	BU
2006	30,000	—	—	—	12.00	—

KM# 396 2 HRYVNI

12.8000 g., Copper-Nickel-Zinc, 31 mm. **Subject:** Ivan Franko **Obv:** National arms and value **Edge:** Reeded

Date	Mintage	F	VF	XF	Unc	BU
2006	45,000	—	—	—	12.00	—

KM# 397 2 HRYVNI

12.8000 g., Copper-Nickel-Zinc, 31 mm. **Subject:** Dmytro Lutsenko **Obv:** National arms and value **Edge:** Reeded

Date	Mintage	F	VF	XF	Unc	BU
2006	30,000	—	—	—	11.00	—

KM# 400 2 HRYVNI

12.8000 g., Copper-Nickel-Zinc, 31 mm. **Subject:** Mykhailo Lysenko **Obv:** National arms and value **Edge:** Reeded

Date	Mintage	F	VF	XF	Unc	BU
2006	35,000	—	—	—	12.00	—

KM# 403 2 HRYVNI

1.2400 g., 0.9999 Gold 0.0399 oz. AGW, 13.92 mm. **Subject:** Ram **Obv:** National arms **Edge:** Plain

Date	Mintage	F	VF	XF	Unc	BU
2006	10,000	—	—	—	100	—

KM# 404 2 HRYVNI

1.2400 g., 0.9999 Gold 0.0399 oz. AGW, 13.92 mm. **Subject:** Bull **Obv:** National arms **Edge:** Plain

Date	Mintage	F	VF	XF	Unc	BU
2006	10,000	—	—	—	100	—

KM# 406 2 HRYVNI

1.2400 g., 0.9999 Gold 0.0399 oz. AGW, 13.92 mm. **Subject:** The Twins **Obv:** National arms **Edge:** Plain

Date	Mintage	F	VF	XF	Unc	BU
2006	10,000	—	—	—	100	—

KM# 428 2 HRYVNI

12.8000 g., Copper-Nickel-Zinc, 31 mm. **Subject:** Serhii Koroljov **Obv:** National arms **Edge:** Reeded

Date	Mintage	F	VF	XF	Unc	BU
2007	35,000	—	—	—	—	20.00

KM# 429 2 HRYVNI

12.8000 g., Copper-Nickel-Zinc, 31 mm. **Subject:** Les Kurbas **Obv:** National arms **Edge:** Reeded

Date	Mintage	F	VF	XF	Unc	BU
2007	35,000	—	—	—	—	12.00

KM# 430 2 HRYVNI

12.8000 g., Copper-Nickel-Zinc, 31 mm. **Subject:** Olexander Liapunov **Obv:** Small national arms above geometrical depiction of celestial mechanics grafics **Rev:** Large bust facing **Edge:** Reeded

Date	Mintage	F	VF	XF	Unc	BU
2007	35,000	—	—	—	—	11.00

KM# 431 2 HRYVNI

1.2400 g., 0.9999 Gold 0.0399 oz. AGW, 13.92 mm. **Subject:** Steppe Marmot **Obv:** National arms **Edge:** Plain

Date	Mintage	F	VF	XF	Unc	BU
2007	10,000	—	—	—	120	—

KM# 440 2 HRYVNI

12.8000 g., Copper-Nickel-Zinc, 31 mm. **Subject:** Ivan Ohienko **Obv:** Cross **Rev:** Head and hands clasped at prayer **Edge:** Reeded

Date	Mintage	F	VF	XF	Unc	BU
2007	35,000	—	—	—	—	11.00

KM# 441 2 HRYVNI

12.8000 g., Copper-Nickel-Zinc, 31 mm. **Subject:** Oleh Olzhych **Obv:** Chestnut leaf and stone path **Rev:** Bust facing **Edge:** Reeded

Date	Mintage	F	VF	XF	Unc	BU
2007	35,000	—	—	—	—	11.00

KM# 442 2 HRYVNI

12.8000 g., Copper-Nickel-Zinc, 31 mm. **Subject:** Donetsk Region 75th Anniversary **Obv:** Miner's lamp illuminating industrial plants **Rev:** Flag and 75 **Edge:** Reeded

Date	Mintage	F	VF	XF	Unc	BU
2007	35,000	—	—	—	—	20.00

KM# 443 2 HRYVNI

12.8000 g., Copper-Nickel-Zinc, 31 mm. **Subject:** Olena Teliha **Obv:** Scorched cherry blossom **Rev:** Bust facing **Edge:** Reeded

Date	Mintage	F	VF	XF	Unc	BU
2007	35,000	—	—	—	—	16.00

KM# 444 2 HRYVNI
12.8000 g., Copper-Nickel-Zinc, 31 mm. **Subject:** Orienteering **Obv:** Compass, star and benchmarks **Rev:** Runner **Edge:** Reeded

Date	Mintage	F	VF	XF	Unc	BU
2007	35,000	—	—	—	—	12.50

KM# 445 2 HRYVNI
12.8000 g., Copper-Nickel-Zinc, 31 mm. **Subject:** Ivan Bahrianji **Obv:** Book edge **Rev:** Bust facing, book edge **Edge:** Reeded

Date	Mintage	F	VF	XF	Unc	BU
2007	35,000	—	—	—	—	11.00

KM# 446 2 HRYVNI
12.8000 g., Copper-Nickel-Zinc, 31 mm. **Subject:** Petro Hryhorenko **Obv:** Sprout squeezing brick wall **Rev:** Head right **Edge:** Reeded

Date	Mintage	F	VF	XF	Unc	BU
2007	35,000	—	—	—	—	12.00

KM# 447 2 HRYVNI
12.8000 g., Copper-Nickel-Zinc, 31 mm. **Subject:** 90th Anniversary of 1st Government **Obv:** Parts of early 20th century banknots and industrial elements **Rev:** Volodymyr Vynnychenko and ornamentation **Edge:** Reeded

Date	Mintage	F	VF	XF	Unc	BU
2007	35,000	—	—	—	—	12.00

KM# 448 2 HRYVNI
1.2400 g., 0.9990 Gold 0.0398 oz. AGW, 13.9 mm. **Subject:** Capricorn **Obv:** Elements of earth, air, water and fire **Rev:** Zodiac sign

Date	Mintage	F	VF	XF	Unc	BU
2007	10,000	—	—	—	—	100

KM# 450 2 HRYVNI
1.2400 g., 0.9990 Gold 0.0398 oz. AGW, 13.9 mm. **Subject:** Pisces **Obv:** Elements of earth, air, water and fire **Rev:** Zodiac sign, two fish

Date	Mintage	F	VF	XF	Unc	BU
2007	10,000	—	—	—	—	100

KM# 449 2 HRYVNI
1.2400 g., 0.9990 Gold 0.0398 oz. AGW, 13.9 mm. **Subject:** Aquarius **Obv:** Elements of earth, air, water and fire **Rev:** Zodiac sign, man pouring water

Date	Mintage	F	VF	XF	Unc	BU
2007	10,000	—	—	—	—	100

KM# 451 2 HRYVNI
1.2400 g., 0.9990 Gold 0.0398 oz. AGW, 13.9 mm. **Subject:** Scorpion **Obv:** Elements of earth, air, water and fire **Rev:** Zodiac sign

Date	Mintage	F	VF	XF	Unc	BU
2007	10,000	—	—	—	—	100

KM# 452 2 HRYVNI
1.2400 g., 0.9990 Gold 0.0398 oz. AGW, 13.9 mm. **Subject:** Sagitarius **Obv:** Elements of earth, air, water & fire **Rev:** Zodiac sign, archer

Date	Mintage	F	VF	XF	Unc	BU
2007	10,000	—	—	—	—	100

KM# 433 2 HRYVNI
12.8000 g., Copper-Nickel-Zinc, 31 mm. **Obv:** Small national arms at top, value in sprays with bird at left, butterfly at right **Rev:** Cinereous Vulture perched on nest with chick **Rev. Legend:** AEGYPIUS MONACHUS - ГРИФ ЧОРНИЈ **Edge:** Reeded

Date	Mintage	F	VF	XF	Unc	BU
2008	45,000	—	—	—	—	11.00

KM# 475 2 HRYVNI
12.8000 g., Copper-Nickel-Zinc, 31 mm. **Subject:** Vasyl Stus, Poet **Edge:** Reeded

Date	Mintage	F	VF	XF	Unc	BU
2008	35,000	—	—	—	—	11.00

KM# 476 2 HRYVNI
12.8000 g., Copper-Nickel-Zinc, 31 mm. **Subject:** Leo Landau **Edge:** Reeded

Date	Mintage	F	VF	XF	Unc	BU
2008	35,000	—	—	—	—	11.00

KM# 477 2 HRYVNI
12.8000 g., Copper-Nickel-Zinc, 31 mm. **Subject:** Sydir Holubovych **Edge:** Reeded

Date	Mintage	F	VF	XF	Unc	BU
2008	35,000	—	—	—	—	10.00

KM# 478 2 HRYVNI
12.8000 g., Copper-Nickel-Zinc, 31 mm. **Subject:** Kyiv Zoo, 100th Anniversary **Edge:** Reeded

Date	Mintage	F	VF	XF	Unc	BU
2008	50,000	—	—	—	—	13.50

KM# 479 2 HRYVNI
12.8000 g., Copper-Nickel-Zinc, 31 mm. **Subject:** Yevhen Petrushevych **Edge:** Reeded

Date	Mintage	F	VF	XF	Unc	BU
2008	35,000	—	—	—	—	10.00

KM# 481 2 HRYVNI
12.8000 g., Copper-Nickel-Zinc, 31 mm. **Subject:** Heorhii Voronyi **Edge:** Reeded

Date	Mintage	F	VF	XF	Unc	BU
2008	35,000	—	—	—	—	19.00

KM# 482 2 HRYVNI
1.2400 g., 0.9990 Gold 0.0398 oz. AGW, 13.9 mm. **Subject:** Skythian Gold (Goddess Api)

Date	Mintage	F	VF	XF	Unc	BU
2008	10,000	—	—	—	—	100

KM# 483 2 HRYVNI
1.2400 g., 0.9990 Gold 0.0398 oz. AGW, 13.9 mm. **Subject:** Zodiac **Rev:** Cancer

Date	Mintage	F	VF	XF	Unc	BU
2008	10,000	—	—	—	—	100

KM# 484 2 HRYVNI
1.2400 g., 0.9990 Gold 0.0398 oz. AGW, 13.9 mm. **Subject:** Zodiac **Rev:** Leo

Date	Mintage	F	VF	XF	Unc	BU
2008	10,000	—	—	—	—	100

KM# 485 2 HRYVNI
1.2400 g., 0.9990 Gold 0.0398 oz. AGW **Subject:** Virgo

Date	Mintage	F	VF	XF	Unc	BU
2008	10,000	—	—	—	—	100

KM# 486 2 HRYVNI
1.2400 g., 0.9990 Gold 0.0398 oz. AGW, 13.9 mm. **Subject:** Libra

Date	Mintage	F	VF	XF	Unc	BU
2008	—	—	—	—	—	100

KM# 487 2 HRYVNI
12.8000 g., Copper-Nickel-Zinc, 31 mm. **Subject:** Nataliia Vzhvii **Edge:** Reeded

Date	Mintage	F	VF	XF	Unc	BU
2008	35,000	—	—	—	—	10.00

KM# 488 2 HRYVNI
12.8000 g., Copper-Nickel-Zinc, 31 mm. **Subject:** Hryhorii Kvitka - Osnovianenko **Edge:** Reeded

Date	Mintage	F	VF	XF	Unc	BU
2008	35,000	—	—	—	—	10.00

KM# 489 2 HRYVNI
12.8000 g., Copper-Nickel-Silver-Zinc, 31 mm. **Subject:** Western Ukraine People's Repbulic, 90th Anniversary **Edge:** Reeded

Date	Mintage	F	VF	XF	Unc	BU
2008	35,000	—	—	—	—	11.00

KM# 490 2 HRYVNI
12.8000 g., Copper-Nickel-Zinc, 31 mm. **Subject:** Vasyl Symonenko **Edge:** Reeded

Date	Mintage	F	VF	XF	Unc	BU
2008	35,000	—	—	—	—	10.00

KM# 533 2 HRYVNI
12.8000 g., Copper-Nickel-Zinc, 31.0 mm. **Subject:** Pavlo Chubynskyi **Obv:** Folk music instruments **Obv. Legend:** НАЦІОНАЛЬНИЈ БАНК УКРА?НИ - 2 / ГРИВНІ / 2009 **Rev:** Chubynskyi's portrait **Rev. Legend:** ПАВЛО ЧУБИНСЬКИЈ - 1839-1884 **Edge:** Reeded

Date	Mintage	F	VF	XF	Unc	BU
2009	35,000	—	—	—	—	19.00

KM# 534 2 HRYVNI
12.8000 g., Copper-Nickel-Zinc, 31.0 mm. **Subject:** Andrii Livytskyi **Obv:** National Arms and value **Obv. Legend:** НАЦІОНАЛЬНИЈ БАНК УКРА?НИ - ДВІ ГРИВНІ **Rev:** Livytskyi's portrait **Rev. Legend:** АНДРІЈ ЛІВИЦЬКИЈ - 1879/1954 - ПРЕЗИДЕНТ УНР В ЕКЗИЛІ **Edge:** Reeded

Date	Mintage	F	VF	XF	Unc	BU
2009	35,000	—	—	—	—	10.00

KM# 535 2 HRYVNI
1.2400 g., 0.9990 Gold 0.0398 oz. AGW, 13.92 mm. **Subject:** Ukraine Fauna **Obv:** National Arms, value **Obv. Legend:** НАЦІОНАЛЬНИЈ БАНК УКРА?НИ - 2 ГРИВНІ **Rev:** Turtle **Rev. Legend:** ЧЕРЕПАХА - TESTUDINES

Date	Mintage	F	VF	XF	Unc	BU
2009	10,000	—	—	—	100	—

KM# 536 2 HRYVNI
12.8000 g., Copper-Nickel-Zinc, 31.0 mm. **Subject:** Borys Martos **Obv:** National Arms and value **Obv. Legend:** НАЦІОНАЛЬНИЈ БАНК УКРА?НИ - ДВІ ГРИВНІ **Rev:** Martos's portrait **Rev. Legend:** БОРИС МАРТОС **Edge:** Reeded

Date	Mintage	F	VF	XF	Unc	BU
2009	35,000	—	—	—	—	10.00

KM# 537 2 HRYVNI
12.8000 g., Copper-Nickel-Zinc, 31.0 mm. **Subject:** General Symon Petliura **Obv:** Two Military men holding wreath of a woman's profile **Obv. Legend:** НАЦІОНАЛЬНИЈ БАНК УКРА?НИ - 2 ГРИВНІ **Rev:** Petliura's portrait **Rev. Legend:** СИМОН ПЕТЛЮРА **Edge:** Reeded

Date	Mintage	F	VF	XF	Unc	BU
2009	35,000	—	—	—	—	15.00

KM# 538 2 HRYVNI
12.8000 g., Copper-Nickel-Zinc, 31 mm. **Subject:** Igor Sikorskyi, 100th Anniversary of birth **Obv:** Aircraft, National Arms, value **Obv. Legend:** НАЦІОНАЛЬНИЈ БАНК УКРА?НИ - 2 ГРИВНІ **Rev:** Sikorskyi portrait as an airman, Da Vinci drawing **Rev. Legend:** ІГОР СІКОРСЬКИЈ **Edge:** Reeded

Date	Mintage	F	VF	XF	Unc	BU
2009	35,000	—	—	—	—	5.00

KM# 539 2 HRYVNI
12.8000 g., Copper-Nickel-Zinc, 31 mm. **Subject:** Mykola Bogolijubov, physicist, 100th Anniversary of birth **Obv:** Diagram and formula, National Arms, value **Rev:** Bogolijubov's portrait **Edge:** Reeded

Date	Mintage	F	VF	XF	Unc	BU
2009	35,000	—	—	—	—	10.00

KM# 540 2 HRYVNI
12.8000 g., Copper-Nickel-Zinc, 31 mm. **Subject:** Volodymyr Ivasiuk, poet and singer **Obv:** Flower of Chervona Ruta, electrical musical instruments **Obv. Legend:** НАЦІОНАЛЬНИЈ БАНК УКРА?НИ - 2 / ГРИВНІ / 2009 **Rev:** Ivasiuk's portrait **Rev. Legend:** ВОЛОДИМИР ІВАСЮК **Edge:** Reeded

Date	Mintage	F	VF	XF	Unc	BU
2009	35,000	—	—	—	—	10.00

KM# 541 2 HRYVNI

12.8000 g., Copper-Nickel-Zinc, 31.0 mm. **Subject:** Bohdan-Igor Antonych, poet **Obv:** Figurative interpretation of Antonych's poetry **Obv. Legend:** НАЦІОНАЛЬНИЙ БАНК УКРА?НИ - 2 / ГРИВНІ **Rev:** Antonych's portrait **Rev. Legend:** БОГДАН-ІГОР АНТОНИЧ **Edge:** Reeded

Date	Mintage	F	VF	XF	Unc	BU
2009	35,000	—	—	—	—	10.00

KM# 542 2 HRYVNI

12.8000 g., Copper-Nickel-Zinc, 31.0 mm. **Subject:** Kost Levytskyi **Obv:** State Coat of Arms, issue year **Obv. Legend:** НАЦІОНАЛЬНИЙ БАНК УКРАЇНИ - ДВІ ГРИВНІ **Rev:** Levytskyi bust **Rev. Legend:** КОСТЬ ЛЕВИЦЬКИЙ

Date	Mintage	F	VF	XF	Unc	BU
2009	35,000	—	—	—	—	10.00

KM# 551 2 HRYVNI

12.8000 g., Copper-Nickel-Zinc, 31.0 mm. **Subject:** Carpatho-Ukraine Republic, 70th Anniversary **Obv:** Carpathian ornamentation patterns, National Arms, value **Obv. Legend:** НАЦІОНАЛЬНИЙ БАНК УКРАЇНИ - 2 / ГРИВНІ **Rev:** Transcarpathian holding flag with arms of Carpatho-Ukraine **Rev. Legend:** 70 / РОКІВ - ПРОГОЛОШЕННЯ КАРПАТСЬКОЇ УКРАЇНИ **Edge:** Reeded

Date	Mintage	F	VF	XF	Unc	BU
2009	35,000	—	—	—	—	11.00

KM# 571 2 HRYVNI

1.2400 g., Gold, 13.92 mm. **Subject:** Year of the Boar **Obv:** National Arms **Rev:** Scythian boar figure

Date	Mintage	F	VF	XF	Unc	BU
2009 Special Unc.	10,000	—	—	—	—	100

KM# 572 2 HRYVNI

1.2400 g., Gold, 13.92 mm. **Obv:** National Arms **Rev:** Bee **Edge:** Plain

Date	Mintage	F	VF	XF	Unc	BU
2010 Special Unc.	10,000	—	—	—	—	100

KM# 576 2 HRYVNI

12.8000 g., Copper-Nickel-Zinc, 31 mm. **Subject:** Ukraine Ice Hockey, 100th Anniversary **Obv:** Golie before net, National Arms **Rev:** Old time and modern hockey players **Edge:** Reeded

Date	Mintage	F	VF	XF	Unc	BU
2010	35,000	—	—	—	—	13.00

KM# 578 2 HRYVNI

12.8000 g., Copper-Nickel-Zinc, 31 mm. **Subject:** Zaporizhzhia Oblast **Obv:** Zaporizhzhia Arms **Rev:** Stone bana, Dnieper's waves and Dniporhes dam **Edge:** Reeded

Date	Mintage	F	VF	XF	Unc	BU
2010	45,000	—	—	—	—	13.00

KM# 580 2 HRYVNI

12.8000 g., Copper-Nickel, 31 mm. **Subject:** Ivan Kozhedub **Obv:** La-7 aircraft in two searchlight beams **Rev:** Kozhedub's portrait and airfield **Edge:** Reeded

Date	Mintage	F	VF	XF	Unc	BU
2010	35,000	—	—	—	—	13.00

KM# 581 2 HRYVNI

12.8000 g., Copper-Nickel, 31 mm. **Subject:** Lviv Polytechnic National University, 165th Anniversary **Obv:** Arts and Sciences sculptures from main building **Rev:** University building façade

Date	Mintage	F	VF	XF	Unc	BU
2010	45,000	—	—	—	—	13.00

KM# 583 2 HRYVNI

12.8000 g., Copper-Nickel, 31 mm. **Subject:** Kharkiv Polytechnic Institute, 125th Anniversary **Obv:** Radio telescope and open book **Rev:** University building at right, symbols of science at left, oval portrait of V.L. Kyrpychov

Date	Mintage	F	VF	XF	Unc	BU
2010	50,000	—	—	—	—	13.00

KM# 585 2 HRYVNI

12.8000 g., Copper-Nickel, 31 mm. **Subject:** Ukraine Sovereignty, 20th Anniversary **Obv:** National flag in enamel within viburnum wreath **Rev:** Ukraine map within uneven background **Edge:** Reeded

Date	Mintage	F	VF	XF	Unc	BU
2010	35,000	—	—	—	—	13.00

KM# 593 2 HRYVNI

12.8000 g., Copper-Nickel, 31 mm. **Subject:** Flora and fauna **Obv:** National Arms and wreath **Rev:** Stipa Ucrainica, feather grass

Date	Mintage	F	VF	XF	Unc	BU
2010	35,000	—	—	—	—	13.00

KM# 603 2 HRYVNI

1.2400 g., 0.9990 Gold 0.0398 oz. AGW, 13.92 mm. **Obv:** National Arms **Rev:** Cranberry bush branch **Edge:** Plain

Date	Mintage	F	VF	XF	Unc	BU
2010	10,000	—	—	—	—	100

KM# 608 2 HRYVNI

12.8000 g., Copper-Nickel, 31 mm. **Subject:** Ukranian Medical Association, 100th Anniversary **Obv:** UMA Shield within wreath **Rev:** UMA in Lviv emblem (lion on cross) **Edge:** Reeded

Date	Mintage	F	VF	XF	Unc	BU
2010	35,000	—	—	—	—	13.00

KM# 107 5 HRYVEN

9.4000 g., Bi-Metallic Brass center in Copper-Nickel ring, 28 mm. **Subject:** New Millennium **Obv:** Spiral design within circle **Rev:** Mother and child within circle **Edge:** Segmented reeding

Date	Mintage	F	VF	XF	Unc	BU
2001	50,000	—	—	—	30.00	—

KM# 112 5 HRYVEN

16.5400 g., Copper-Nickel-Zinc, 35 mm. **Subject:** Ostrozhska Academy **Obv:** Value, old writing and printing artifacts **Rev:** Seated figures, partial building and crowned arms with supporters **Edge:** Reeded

Date	Mintage	F	VF	XF	Unc	BU
2001	30,000	—	—	—	25.00	—

KM# 129 5 HRYVEN

16.5400 g., Copper-Nickel-Zinc, 35 mm. **Subject:** 10th Anniversary - National Bank **Obv:** National arms between two arches **Rev:** Large building central entrance **Edge:** Reeded

Date	Mintage	F	VF	XF	Unc	BU
2001	50,000	—	—	—	15.00	—

KM# 132 5 HRYVEN

16.5400 g., Copper-Nickel-Zinc, 35 mm. **Subject:** 10th Anniversary - National Independence **Obv:** Arms with supporters within beaded circle **Rev:** Building on map within beaded circle **Edge:** Reeded

Date	Mintage	F	VF	XF	Unc	BU
2001	100,000	—	—	—	13.00	—

KM# 135 5 HRYVEN

16.5400 g., Copper-Nickel-Zinc, 35 mm. **Subject:** 1100th Anniversary - Poltava **Obv:** National arms above value flanked by flower sprigs **Rev:** Buildings above shield **Edge:** Reeded

Date	Mintage	F	VF	XF	Unc	BU
2001	50,000	—	—	—	15.00	—

KM# 140 5 HRYVEN

9.4000 g., Bi-Metallic Brass center in Copper-Nickel ring, 28 mm. **Subject:** 10th Anniversary of Military forces **Obv:** Crossed maces, arms and date within wreath and circle **Rev:** Circle in center of cross within wreath and circle **Edge:** Reeded and plain sections

Date	Mintage	F	VF	XF	Unc	BU
2001	30,000	—	—	—	100	—

KM# 148 5 HRYVEN

16.5400 g., Copper-Nickel-Zinc, 35 mm. **Subject:** 400 Years of Krolevets **Obv:** National arms above gateway and value **Rev:** Krolivets city arms flanked by designs **Edge:** Reeded

Date	Mintage	F	VF	XF	Unc	BU
2001	30,000	—	—	—	25.00	—

KM# 151 5 HRYVEN

16.5400 g., Copper-Nickel-Zinc, 35 mm. **Subject:** City of Khotyn **Obv:** Value within arch above military fittings **Rev:** Castle below crowned shield **Edge:** Reeded

Date	Mintage	F	VF	XF	Unc	BU
2002	30,000	—	—	—	40.00	—

KM# 152 5 HRYVEN

16.5400 g., Copper-Nickel-Zinc, 35 mm. **Obv:** Sun and flying geese divides beaded circle **Rev:** "AN-225 Mrija" cargo jet divide beaded circle **Edge:** Reeded

Date	Mintage	F	VF	XF	Unc	BU
2002	30,000	—	—	—	80.00	—

KM# 158 5 HRYVEN

9.4300 g., Bi-Metallic Brass center in Copper-Nickel ring, 28 mm. **Subject:** 70th Anniversary of Dnipro Hydroelectric Power Station **Obv:** Turbine within circle **Rev:** Large dam within circle **Edge:** Reeded and plain sections

Date	Mintage	F	VF	XF	Unc	BU
2002	30,000	—	—	—	40.00	—

KM# 159 5 HRYVEN

16.5400 g., Copper-Nickel-Zinc, 35 mm. **Obv:** Arms with supporters within beaded circle **Rev:** Battle scene around Batig in 1652 divides beaded circle **Edge:** Reeded

Date	Mintage	F	VF	XF	Unc	BU
2002	30,000	—	—	—	25.00	—

KM# 163 5 HRYVEN

16.5400 g., Copper-Nickel-Zinc, 35 mm. **Subject:** Christmas **Obv:** National arms in star above value flanked by designed sprigs **Rev:** Christmas pageant scene **Edge:** Reeded

Date	Mintage	F	VF	XF	Unc	BU
ND(2002)	30,000	—	—	—	100	—

KM# 157 5 HRYVEN
16.5400 g., Copper-Nickel, 35 mm. **Subject:** 1100th Anniversary - City of Romny **Obv:** Sprigs divide national arms and value **Rev:** City view **Edge:** Reeded

Date	Mintage	F	VF	XF	Unc	BU
2002	30,000	—	—	—	30.00	—

KM# 200 5 HRYVEN
9.4000 g., Bi-Metallic Brass center in Copper-Nickel ring, 28 mm. **Obv:** Bandura strings over ornamental design **Rev:** Bandura divides circle and wreath **Edge:** Segmented reeding

Date	Mintage	F	VF	XF	Unc	BU
2003	30,000	—	—	—	20.00	—

KM# 172 5 HRYVEN
16.5400 g., Copper-Nickel-Zinc, 35 mm. **Subject:** Easter **Obv:** Circle of Easter eggs, national arms in center above value **Rev:** Religious celebration **Edge:** Reeded

Date	Mintage	F	VF	XF	Unc	BU
2003	50,000	—	—	—	35.00	—

KM# 173 5 HRYVEN
16.5400 g., Copper-Nickel-Zinc, 35 mm. **Subject:** Antonov AN-2 Biplane **Obv:** National arms sun face and flying geese divide beaded circle **Rev:** World's largest biplane divides beaded circle **Edge:** Reeded

Date	Mintage	F	VF	XF	Unc	BU
2003	50,000	—	—	—	20.00	—

KM# 185 5 HRYVEN
9.4000 g., Bi-Metallic Brass center in Copper-Nickel ring, 28 mm. **Subject:** 150th Anniversary of the Central Ukrainian Archives **Obv:** Value, signature and seal **Rev:** Hourglass divides books and circle **Edge:** Segmented reeding

Date	Mintage	F	VF	XF	Unc	BU
2003	30,000	—	—	—	15.00	—

KM# 186 5 HRYVEN
16.5400 g., Copper-Nickel-Zinc, 35 mm. **Subject:** 2500th Anniversary of the City of Yevpatoria **Obv:** National arms, date and value with partial sun background **Rev:** Ancient amphora and modern city view **Edge:** Reeded

Date	Mintage	F	VF	XF	Unc	BU
2003	30,000	—	—	—	29.00	—

KM# 187 5 HRYVEN
16.5400 g., Copper-Nickel-Zinc, 35 mm. **Subject:** 60th Anniversary - Liberation of Kiev **Obv:** Eternal flame monument **Rev:** Battle scene and map of the offense **Edge:** Reeded

Date	Mintage	F	VF	XF	Unc	BU
2003	30,000	—	—	—	15.00	—

KM# 204 5 HRYVEN
16.5400 g., Copper-Nickel-Zinc, 35 mm. **Subject:** 50th Anniversary - Pivdenne Space Design Office **Obv:** Satellite orbiting Earth **Rev:** Satellite above moonscape **Edge:** Reeded

Date	Mintage	F	VF	XF	Unc	BU
2004	30,000	—	—	—	15.00	—

KM# 205 5 HRYVEN
16.5400 g., Copper-Nickel-Zinc, 35 mm. **Subject:** 2500 Anniversary City of Balaklava **Obv:** National arms between two ancient ships **Rev:** Harbor view above pillar **Edge:** Reeded

Date	Mintage	F	VF	XF	Unc	BU
2004	30,000	—	—	—	17.00	—

KM# 218 5 HRYVEN
16.9400 g., 0.9250 Silver 0.5038 oz. ASW, 33 mm. **Obv:** National arms, value and atom **Rev:** Kharkov University building **Edge:** Reeded

Date	Mintage	F	VF	XF	Unc	BU
2004 Proof	7,000	Value: 40.00				

KM# 219 5 HRYVEN
16.9400 g., 0.9250 Silver 0.5038 oz. ASW, 33 mm. **Obv:** National arms above value dividing scientific items **Rev:** Kiev University building main entrance **Edge:** Reeded

Date	Mintage	F	VF	XF	Unc	BU
2004 Proof	7,000	Value: 40.00				

KM# 220 5 HRYVEN
9.4300 g., Bi-Metallic BRASS center in COPPER-NICKEL ring, 28 mm. **Subject:** 50 Years of Ukraine's Membership in UNESCO **Obv:** National arms in center of sprigs and circle **Rev:** Building within sprigs and circle **Edge:** Segmented reeding

Date	Mintage	F	VF	XF	Unc	BU
2004	50,000	—	—	—	15.00	—

KM# 221 5 HRYVEN
16.5400 g., Copper-Nickel-Zinc, 35 mm. **Subject:** Ice Breaker "Captain Belousov" **Obv:** National arms on ship's wheel and anchor **Rev:** Ice breaker ship **Edge:** Reeded

Date	Mintage	F	VF	XF	Unc	BU
2004	30,000	—	—	—	15.00	—

KM# 222 5 HRYVEN
16.5400 g., Copper-Nickel-Zinc, 35 mm. **Subject:** Whit Sunday **Obv:** National arms in flower wreath above value flanked by sprigs **Rev:** Four dancing women and child **Edge:** Reeded

Date	Mintage	F	VF	XF	Unc	BU
2004	50,000	—	—	—	15.00	—

KM# 333 5 HRYVEN
9.4000 g., Bi-Metallic Brass center in Copper-Nickel ring, 28 mm. **Obv:** Horizontal lines across flowery design **Rev:** Cossack-style lyre within circle and wreath **Edge:** Segmented reeding

Date	Mintage	F	VF	XF	Unc	BU
2004	30,000	—	—	—	15.00	—

KM# 334 5 HRYVEN
16.5400 g., Copper-Nickel-Zinc, 35 mm. **Subject:** 250th Anniversary of Kirovohrad **Obv:** National arms above crossed cannons and value **Rev:** Arms with supporters above city view **Edge:** Reeded

Date	Mintage	F	VF	XF	Unc	BU
2004	30,000	—	—	—	16.00	—

KM# 335 5 HRYVEN
16.5400 g., Copper-Nickel-Zinc, 35 mm. **Subject:** 350 Years to Kharkiv **Obv:** Assumption Cathedral, value and national arms **Rev:** Kharkiv State Industrial Building complex **Edge:** Reeded

Date	Mintage	F	VF	XF	Unc	BU
2004	30,000	—	—	—	22.50	—

KM# 336 5 HRYVEN
9.4000 g., Bi-Metallic Brass center in Copper-Nickel ring, 28 mm. **Subject:** 50th Anniversary of Crimean Union With Ukraine **Obv:** National arms on wheat sheaf on map **Rev:** Crowned lion on shield flanked by pillars within rope wreath **Edge:** Segmented reeding

Date	Mintage	F	VF	XF	Unc	BU
2004	30,000	—	—	—	17.00	—

KM# 337 5 HRYVEN
16.5400 g., Copper-Nickel-Zinc, 35 mm. **Obv:** National arms on sun, flying geese divide beaded circle **Rev:** AN-140 Airliner divides beaded circle **Edge:** Reeded

Date	Mintage	F	VF	XF	Unc	BU
2004	50,000	—	—	—	13.00	—

KM# 362 5 HRYVEN
16.5400 g., Copper-Nickel-Zinc, 35 mm. **Obv:** National arms on sun with flying geese divide beaded circle **Rev:** AN-124 jet divides beaded circle **Edge:** Reeded

Date	Mintage	F	VF	XF	Unc	BU
2005	60,000	—	—	—	13.00	—

KM# 364 5 HRYVEN

16.5400 g., Copper-Nickel-Zinc, 35 mm. **Subject:** City of Korosten 1300th Anniversary **Obv:** National arms **Rev:** Ancient earring below modern building and bridge **Edge:** Reeded

Date	Mintage	F	VF	XF	Unc	BU
2005	30,000	—	—	—	13.50	—

KM# 365 5 HRYVEN

16.5400 g., Copper-Nickel-Zinc, 35 mm. **Subject:** City of Sumy 350th Anniversary **Obv:** National arms **Rev:** City view behind city arms **Edge:** Reeded

Date	Mintage	F	VF	XF	Unc	BU
2005	30,000	—	—	—	13.50	—

KM# 366 5 HRYVEN

16.5400 g., Copper-Nickel-Zinc, 35 mm. **Subject:** The Protection of the Virgin **Obv:** National arms on Cossack regalia **Rev:** Wedding scene **Edge:** Reeded

Date	Mintage	F	VF	XF	Unc	BU
2005	45,000	—	—	—	15.00	—

KM# 368 5 HRYVEN

16.5400 g., Copper-Nickel-Zinc, 35 mm. **Subject:** Sorochynsky Fair **Obv:** Busts facing each other flanked by sprigs **Rev:** Farmer with family in ox cart **Edge:** Reeded

Date	Mintage	F	VF	XF	Unc	BU
2005	60,000	—	—	—	15.00	—

KM# 379 5 HRYVEN

16.5400 g., Copper-Nickel-Zinc, 35 mm. **Subject:** 500th Anniversary - Kalmiuska Palanqua Cossack Settlement **Obv:** Cossack in ornamental frame and national arms **Rev:** Soldiers **Edge:** Reeded

Date	Mintage	F	VF	XF	Unc	BU
2005	30,000	—	—	—	15.00	—

KM# 380 5 HRYVEN

16.5400 g., Copper-Nickel-Zinc, 35 mm. **Subject:** Sviatohirsky Assumption Monastery **Obv:** Madonna and child flanked by angels **Rev:** Hillside monastery **Edge:** Reeded

Date	Mintage	F	VF	XF	Unc	BU
2005	45,000	—	—	—	15.00	—

KM# 387 5 HRYVEN

16.5400 g., Copper-Nickel-Zinc, 35 mm. **Subject:** Vernadsky Antarctic Station **Obv:** Flag and buildings **Rev:** Antarctica map within compass face **Edge:** Reeded

Date	Mintage	F	VF	XF	Unc	BU
2006	60,000	—	—	—	12.50	—

KM# 388 5 HRYVEN

16.9300 g., 0.9250 Silver 0.5035 oz. ASW, 33 mm. **Subject:** Year of the Dog **Obv:** Value on textile art **Rev:** Stylized dog **Edge:** Reeded

Date	Mintage	F	VF	XF	Unc	BU
2006 Proof	12,000	Value: 175				

KM# 389 5 HRYVEN

16.9300 g., 0.9250 Silver 0.5035 oz. ASW, 33 mm. **Subject:** Zodiac - Ram **Obv:** Sun face **Rev:** Ram **Edge:** Reeded

Date	Mintage	F	VF	XF	Unc	BU
2006 Proof	10,000	Value: 80.00				

KM# 390 5 HRYVEN

16.9300 g., 0.9250 Silver 0.5035 oz. ASW, 33 mm. **Subject:** Kyiv National University of Economics **Obv:** National arms, graph above value **Rev:** University building within circle **Edge:** Reeded

Date	Mintage	F	VF	XF	Unc	BU
2006 Proof	5,000	Value: 50.00				

KM# 402 5 HRYVEN

9.4200 g., Bi-Metallic Brass center in Copper-Nickel ring, 28 mm. **Obv:** Symbolic sound of music **Rev:** Tsimbal stringed musical instrument **Edge:** Segmented reeding

Date	Mintage	F	VF	XF	Unc	BU
2006	100,000	—	—	—	12.00	—

KM# 409 5 HRYVEN

16.5400 g., Copper-Nickel-Zinc, 35 mm. **Subject:** 10 Years of the Constitution of Ukraine **Obv:** National arms **Edge:** Reeded

Date	Mintage	F	VF	XF	Unc	BU
2006	30,000	—	—	—	20.00	—

KM# 411 5 HRYVEN

16.5400 g., Copper-Nickel-Zinc, 35 mm. **Subject:** 15 Years of Ukraine Independence **Obv:** National arms **Edge:** Reeded

Date	Mintage	F	VF	XF	Unc	BU
2006	75,000	—	—	—	11.00	—

KM# 413 5 HRYVEN

16.5400 g., Copper-Nickel-Zinc, 35 mm. **Subject:** 10 Years to the Currency Reform in Ukraine **Obv:** National arms **Edge:** Reeded

Date	Mintage	F	VF	XF	Unc	BU
2006	45,000	—	—	—	15.00	—

KM# 405 5 HRYVEN

16.8200 g., 0.9250 Silver 0.5002 oz. ASW, 33 mm. **Subject:** Bull **Obv:** National arms

Date	Mintage	F	VF	XF	Unc	BU
2006 Proof	10,000	Value: 80.00				

KM# 415 5 HRYVEN

16.5400 g., Copper-Nickel-Zinc, 35 mm. **Subject:** 750 Years of the City of L'viv **Obv:** National arms **Edge:** Reeded

Date	Mintage	F	VF	XF	Unc	BU
2006	60,000	—	—	—	15.00	—

KM# 416 5 HRYVEN

16.8200 g., 0.9250 Silver 0.5002 oz. ASW, 33 mm. **Subject:** Mykhailo Hrushevskyi **Obv:** National arms

Date	Mintage	F	VF	XF	Unc	BU
2006 Proof	5,000	Value: 50.00				

KM# 417 5 HRYVEN

16.8200 g., 0.9250 Silver 0.5002 oz. ASW, 33 mm. **Subject:** Dmytro Lutsenko **Obv:** National arms

Date	Mintage	F	VF	XF	Unc	BU
2006 Proof	3,000	Value: 75.00				

KM# 418 5 HRYVEN

16.8200 g., 0.9250 Silver 0.5002 oz. ASW, 33 mm. **Subject:** Ivan Franko **Obv:** National arms

Date	Mintage	F	VF	XF	Unc	BU
2006 Proof	5,000	Value: 50.00				

KM# 407 5 HRYVEN

16.8200 g., 0.9250 Silver 0.5002 oz. ASW, 33 mm. **Subject:** Gemini **Obv:** National arms

Date	Mintage	F	VF	XF	Unc	BU
2006 Proof	10,000	Value: 80.00				

KM# 420 5 HRYVEN

16.5400 g., Copper-Nickel-Zinc, 35 mm. **Subject:** Epiphany **Obv:** National arms **Edge:** Reeded

Date	Mintage	F	VF	XF	Unc	BU
2006	75,000	—	—	—	15.00	—

KM# 422 5 HRYVEN

16.5400 g., Copper-Nickel-Zinc, 35 mm. **Subject:** Saint Kyryl Church **Obv:** National arms

Date	Mintage	F	VF	XF	Unc	BU
2006	45,000	—	—	—	15.00	—

KM# 432 5 HRYVEN

16.5400 g., Copper-Nickel-Zinc, 35 mm. **Subject:** 100th Anniversary of "Motor Sich" **Obv:** Small national arms above falcon in flight with two globes in background **Rev:** Jet engine **Edge:** Reeded

Date	Mintage	F	VF	XF	Unc	BU
2007	45,000	—	—	—	15.00	—

KM# 419 5 HRYVEN
16.8200 g., 0.9250 Silver 0.5002 oz. ASW, 33 mm. **Subject:** Year of the Pig **Obv:** National arms **Edge:** Reeded

Date	Mintage	F	VF	XF	Unc	BU
2007 Proof	15,000	Value: 80.00				

KM# 453 5 HRYVEN
9.4000 g., Bi-Metallic Brass center in copper-nickel ring, 28 mm. **Subject:** Pure water is the source of life **Obv:** Drop of water in pond **Rev:** Man taking drink at waterfall

Date	Mintage	F	VF	XF	Unc	BU
2007	50,000	—	—	—	—	11.50

KM# 455 5 HRYVEN
9.4000 g., Bi-Metallic Brass center in copper-nickel ring, 28 mm. **Subject:** Organization Safety and Cooperation, 16th Annual Meeting **Obv:** State emblem and ornamentation **Rev:** Parliamentary Assemby Building in Kyiv

Date	Mintage	F	VF	XF	Unc	BU
2007	35,000	—	—	—	—	14.00

KM# 456 5 HRYVEN
16.5000 g., Copper-Nickel-Zinc, 35 mm. **Subject:** Odessa National Opera and Ballet, 120th Anniversary **Obv:** Ballet scene in oval **Rev:** Opera house in Odessa **Edge:** Reeded

Date	Mintage	F	VF	XF	Unc	BU
2007	35,000	—	—	—	—	12.00

KM# 457 5 HRYVEN
16.5000 g., Copper-Nickel-Zinc, 35 mm. **Subject:** Chernihiv, 1100th Anniversary **Obv:** Sword hilts and slate fragment **Rev:** Town view and open book **Edge:** Reeded

Date	Mintage	F	VF	XF	Unc	BU
2007	45,000	—	—	—	—	12.00

KM# 458 5 HRYVEN
9.4000 g., Bi-Metallic Brass center in copper-nickel ring, 28 mm. **Subject:** Buhai **Obv:** Sound waves as a baroque ornament **Rev:** Drum-like musical instrument

Date	Mintage	F	VF	XF	Unc	BU
2007	50,000	—	—	—	—	12.00

KM# 459 5 HRYVEN
16.5400 g., Copper-Nickel-Zinc, 35 mm. **Subject:** The Famine, Genocide of the Ukranian People **Obv:** Girl standing on fallow ground **Rev:** Stork within cross, candles in background **Edge:** Reeded

Date	Mintage	F	VF	XF	Unc	BU
2007	75,000	—	—	—	—	11.00

KM# 460 5 HRYVEN
16.5400 g., Copper-Nickel-Zinc, 35 mm. **Subject:** Crimean Resorts, 200th Anniversary **Obv:** Seaside Resort **Rev:** Felix De Searr and well **Edge:** Reeded

Date	Mintage	F	VF	XF	Unc	BU
2007	35,000	—	—	—	—	12.00

KM# 461 5 HRYVEN
15.5500 g., 0.9250 Silver 0.4624 oz. ASW, 33 mm. **Subject:** Capricorn **Obv:** Sun and seasons **Rev:** Zodiac sign

Date	Mintage	F	VF	XF	Unc	BU
2007 Proof	15,000	Value: 50.00				

KM# 462 5 HRYVEN
16.8200 g., 0.9250 Silver 0.5002 oz. ASW, 33 mm. **Subject:** Aquarius **Obv:** Sun and seasons **Rev:** Zodiac sign, man pouring water

Date	Mintage	F	VF	XF	Unc	BU
2007 Proof	15,000	Value: 50.00				

KM# 463 5 HRYVEN
16.8200 g., 0.9250 Silver 0.5002 oz. ASW, 33 mm. **Subject:** Pisces **Obv:** Sun and seasons **Rev:** Zodiac sign, two fish

Date	Mintage	F	VF	XF	Unc	BU
2007 Proof	15,000	Value: 50.00				

KM# 464 5 HRYVEN
16.8200 g., 0.9250 Silver 0.5002 oz. ASW, 33 mm. **Subject:** Scorpion **Obv:** Sun and seasons **Rev:** Zodiac sign, scorpion **Edge:** Reeded

Date	Mintage	F	VF	XF	Unc	BU
2007 Proof	15,000	Value: 50.00				

KM# 465 5 HRYVEN
16.8200 g., 0.9250 Silver 0.5002 oz. ASW, 33 mm. **Subject:** Sagittarius **Obv:** Sun and seasons **Rev:** Zodiac sign, archer

Date	Mintage	F	VF	XF	Unc	BU
2007 Proof	15,000	Value: 50.00				

KM# 531 5 HRYVEN
16.5400 g., Copper-Nickel, 35.0 mm. **Subject:** 1100th Aniversary of Perejaslav-Khmelnytskyi **Obv:** Parchment. **Obv. Legend:** НАЦІОНАЛЬНИЈ БАНК УКРА?НИ - 5 ГРИВЕНЬ / 2007 **Rev:** Old Rus cathedral, old Rus and Cossacks. **Rev. Legend:** ПЕРЕЯСЛАВ-ХМЕЛЬНИЦЬКИЈ - 1100

Date	Mintage	F	VF	XF	Unc	BU
2007	45,000	—	—	—	—	12.00

KM# 511 5 HRYVEN
16.5400 g., Copper-Nickel-Zinc, 35 mm. **Subject:** Rivne, 725th Anniversary **Edge:** Reeded

Date	Mintage	F	VF	XF	Unc	BU
2008	45,000	—	—	—	—	12.00

KM# 500 5 HRYVEN
16.5000 g., Copper-Nickel-Zinc, 35 mm. **Subject:** The Annunciation **Edge:** Reeded

Date	Mintage	F	VF	XF	Unc	BU
2008	45,000	—	—	—	—	12.00

KM# 501 5 HRYVEN
16.5000 g., Copper-Nickel-Zinc, 35 mm. **Subject:** Chernivtsi, 600th Anniversary **Edge:** Reeded

Date	Mintage	F	VF	XF	Unc	BU
2008 45000	—	—	—	—	—	12.00

KM# 502 5 HRYVEN
16.5000 g., Copper-Nickel-Zinc, 35 mm. **Subject:** Sniatyn, 850th Anniversary **Edge:** Reeded

Date	Mintage	F	VF	XF	Unc	BU
2008	45,000	—	—	—	—	12.00

KM# 503 5 HRYVEN
16.8200 g., 0.9250 Silver 0.5002 oz. ASW, 33 mm. **Subject:** Year of the Rat **Rev:** Rat, diamond insert eye **Edge:** Reeded

Date	Mintage	F	VF	XF	Unc	BU
2008 Proof	15,000	Value: 90.00				

KM# 504 5 HRYVEN
16.8200 g., 0.9250 Silver 0.5002 oz. ASW, 33 mm. **Subject:** Cancer **Edge:** Reeded

Date	Mintage	F	VF	XF	Unc	BU
2008 Proof	15,000	Value: 50.00				

KM# 505 5 HRYVEN
16.8200 g., 0.9250 Silver 0.5002 oz. ASW, 33 mm. **Subject:** Roman Shukhevich **Edge:** Reeded

Date	Mintage	F	VF	XF	Unc	BU
2008 Proof	3,000	—	—	—	—	250

KM# 506 5 HRYVEN
16.8200 g., 0.9250 Silver 0.5002 oz. ASW, 33 mm. **Subject:** Leo **Edge:** Reeded

Date	Mintage	F	VF	XF	Unc	BU
2008 Proof	15,000	Value: 50.00				

KM# 507 5 HRYVEN
16.8200 g., 0.9250 Silver 0.5002 oz. ASW, 33 mm. **Subject:** Virgo **Edge:** Reeded

Date	Mintage	F	VF	XF	Unc	BU
2008 Proof	15,000	Value: 50.00				

KM# 508 5 HRYVEN
16.8200 g., 0.9250 Silver 0.5002 oz. ASW, 33 mm. **Subject:** Libra **Edge:** Reeded

Date	Mintage	F	VF	XF	Unc	BU
2008 Proof	15,000	Value: 50.00				

KM# 509 5 HRYVEN
16.5400 g., Copper-Nickel-Zinc, 35 mm. **Subject:** State Arboretum "Trostianet-s", 175th Anniversary **Edge:** Reeded

Date	Mintage	F	VF	XF	Unc	BU
2008	45,000	—	—	—	—	12.00

KM# 510 5 HRYVEN
16.5400 g., Copper-Nickel-Zinc, 35 mm. **Subject:** Kievan Rus **Edge:** Reeded

Date	Mintage	F	VF	XF	Unc	BU
2008	45,000	—	—	—	—	12.00

KM# 512 5 HRYVEN
16.5400 g., Copper-Nickel-Zinc, 35 mm. **Subject:** Bohuslav, 975th Anniversary **Edge:** Reeded

Date	Mintage	F	VF	XF	Unc	BU
2008	45,000	—	—	—	—	12.00

KM# 513 5 HRYVEN
9.4000 g., Bi-Metallic Brass center in copper-nickel ring, 28 mm. **Subject:** Taras Shevchenko "Prosvita Society" 140th Anniversary

Date	Mintage	F	VF	XF	Unc	BU
2008	45,000	—	—	—	—	12.00

KM# 514 5 HRYVEN
16.8200 g., 0.9250 Silver 0.5002 oz. ASW, 33 mm. **Subject:** Mariya Prymachenko

Date	Mintage	F	VF	XF	Unc	BU
2008 Proof	5,000	Value: 40.00				

KM# 530 5 HRYVEN
16.8200 g., 0.9250 Silver 0.5002 oz. ASW, 33 mm. **Subject:** Year of the Ox **Obv:** National Arms and value **Rev:** Ox, rubies in eyes **Edge:** Reeded

Date	Mintage	F	VF	XF	Unc	BU
2009 Proof	20,000	Value: 50.00				

KM# 543 5 HRYVEN
16.8200 g., 0.9990 Silver 0.5402 oz. ASW, 33.0 mm. **Subject:** Nikolai Gogol **Obv:** Compositions of two main subjects of Gogol's work, National Arms, value **Obv. Legend:** НАЦІОНАЛЬНИЈ БАНК УКРАІНИ - 5 ГРИВЕНЬ / 2009 **Rev:** Nikolai's portrait **Rev. Legend:** МИКОЛА ГОГОЛЬ

Date	Mintage	F	VF	XF	Unc	BU
2009 Proof	5,000	Value: 50.00				

KM# 544 5 HRYVEN
16.8200 g., 0.9990 Silver 0.5402 oz. ASW, 33.0 mm. **Subject:** Sholem Aleichem **Obv:** Conventionalized composition, book sheets, Aleichem's signet **Obv. Legend:** НАЦІОНАЛЬНИЈ БАНК УКРАІНИ - 5 ГРИВЕНЬ / 2009 **Rev:** Aleichem's portrait **Rev. Legend:** МИР ВАМ - ШОЛОМ-АЛЕЈХЕМ - РАБИНОВИЧ ШОЛОМ

Date	Mintage	F	VF	XF	Unc	BU
2009 Proof	5,000	Value: 50.00				

KM# 545 5 HRYVEN
16.5400 g., Copper-Nickel-Zinc, 35.0 mm. **Subject:** Simferopol, 225th Anniversary **Obv:** Main railway station, National Arms **Obv. Legend:** НАЦІОНАЛЬНИЈ БАНК УКРА?НИ - 5 ГРИВЕНЬ 2009 **Rev:** City Coat of Arms, Architectural elements **Rev. Legend:** 225 / РОКІВ - СІМФЕРОПОЛЬ **Edge:** Reeded

Date	Mintage	F	VF	XF	Unc	BU
2009	45,000	—	—	—	—	12.00

KM# 546 5 HRYVEN
16.8200 g., 0.9990 Silver 0.5402 oz. ASW, 33 mm. **Subject:** Ivan Kotljarevskyi **Obv:** National Arms, boat, column and helmet **Obv. Legend:** НАЦІОНАЛЬНИЈ БАНК УКРАІНИ - П'ЯТЬ ГРИВЕНЬ **Rev:** Kotliarevskyi's portrait **Rev. Legend:** ...ПОКИ СОНЦЕ З НЕБА СЯЕ, ТЕБЕ НЕ ЗАБУДУТЬ! - ІВАН КОТЛЯРЕВСЬКИЈ

Date	Mintage	F	VF	XF	Unc	BU
2009 Proof	5,000	Value: 48.00				

KM# 547 5 HRYVEN
16.5400 g., Copper-Nickel-Zinc, 35 mm. **Subject:** Mykolaiv, 220th Anniversary **Obv:** Varvarivskyi Bridge, gull, ship, anchor **Obv. Legend:** НАЦІОНАЛЬНИЈ БАНК УКРА?НИ - П'ЯТЬ ГРИВЕНЬ **Rev:** Frigate Saint Nicholas, Architecture of Mykolaiv **Rev. Legend:** МИКОЛА?В - РІК ЗАСНУВАННЯ / 1789 **Edge:** Reeded

Date	Mintage	F	VF	XF	Unc	BU
2009	45,000	—	—	—	—	13.00

KM# 548 5 HRYVEN

9.4000 g., Bi-Metallic, 28 mm. **Subject:** Council of Europe, 60th Anniversary **Obv:** Stars, map of Europe **Obv. Legend:** НАЦІОНАЛЬНИЈ БАНК УКРА?НИ - П'ЯТЬ ГРИВЕНЬ **Rev:** Council of Europe logo, stars **Rev. Legend:** COUNCIL OF EUROPE, CONSEIL DE EUROPE, РАДА ?ВРОПИ

Date	Mintage	F	VF	XF	Unc	BU
2009	45,000	—	—	—	—	12.00

KM# 549 5 HRYVEN

16.8200 g., 0.9990 Silver 0.5402 oz. ASW, 33.0 mm. **Subject:** Lviv National Medical University, 225th Anniversary **Obv:** Hippocratic Oath in Latin, National Arms, value **Obv. Legend:** НАЦІОНАЛЬНИЈ БАНК УКРАЇНИ - 5 / ГРИВЕНЬ **Rev:** University building **Rev. Legend:** 225 / РОКІВ - ІМЕНІ / ДАНИЛА / ГАЛИЦЬКОГО - ЛЬВІВСЬКИЈ НАЦІОНАЛЬНИЈ МЕДИЧНИЈ УНІВЕРСИТЕТ

Date	Mintage	F	VF	XF	Unc	BU
2009 Proof	7,000	Value: 47.00				

KM# 550 5 HRYVEN

16.5400 g., Copper-Nickel-Zinc, 35 mm. **Subject:** T. H. Shevchenko National Museum, 60th Anniversary **Obv:** Kateryna painting, bandura, National Arms, value **Rev:** Museum bulding and portrait **Edge:** Reeded

Date	Mintage	F	VF	XF	Unc	BU
2009	30,000	—	—	—	—	12.00

KM# 553 5 HRYVEN

16.5400 g., Copper-Nickel-Zinc, 35 mm. **Subject:** Pysanka - Easter Egg decorating **Obv:** Easter eggs, National Arms, value **Rev:** Easter bread, eggs. **Edge:** Reeded

Date	Mintage	F	VF	XF	Unc	BU
2009	50,000	—	—	—	—	8.00

KM# 555 5 HRYVEN

16.5000 g., Copper-Nickel, 35.0 mm. **Subject:** Folk crafts of the Ukraine - Bokorash (Raftsmen) **Obv:** Two birds, Carpathian landscape, trees, cottages, logs **Obv. Legend:** НАЦІОНАЛЬНИЈ БАНК УКРА?НИ - 5 / ГРИВЕНЬ / 2009 **Rev:** Bokorash directing raft **Rev. Legend:** БОКОРАШ **Edge:** Reeded

Date	Mintage	F	VF	XF	Unc	BU
2009	45,000	—	—	—	—	12.00

KM# 557 5 HRYVEN

16.5400 g., Copper-Nickel, 35.0 mm. **Subject:** International Year of Astronomy **Obv:** Urania, planets, stars, solar system, National Arms, value **Obv. Legend:** НАЦІОНАЛЬНИЈ БАНК УКРА?НИ - 5 ГРИВЕНЬ **Rev:** Yurii Drohobych, International Year of Astronomy logo, artifacts **Rev. Legend:** МІЖНАРОДНИЈ / РІК / АСТРОНОМІ? **Edge:** Reeded

Date	Mintage	F	VF	XF	Unc	BU
2009	45,000	—	—	—	—	12.50

KM# 567 5 HRYVEN

15.5500 g., 0.9250 Silver 0.4624 oz. ASW, 33 mm. **Subject:** Yevhen Paton **Obv:** Paton Bridge and the footbridge over Petrovska Alley **Rev:** Paton's portrait

Date	Mintage	F	VF	XF	Unc	BU
2010 Proof	5,000	—	—	—	—	50.00

KM# 566 5 HRYVEN

15.5500 g., 0.9250 Silver 0.4624 oz. ASW, 33 mm. **Subject:** Ivan Puliui **Obv:** X-ray of jewelry portrait **Rev:** Puliui portrait and text

Date	Mintage	F	VF	XF	Unc	BU
2010 Proof	5,000	Value: 40.00				

KM# 568 5 HRYVEN

15.5500 g., 0.9250 Silver 0.4624 oz. ASW, 33 mm. **Subject:** Oksana Petrusenko **Obv:** Poppy flower and musical notation **Rev:** Bust facing

Date	Mintage	F	VF	XF	Unc	BU
2010 Proof	5,000	Value: 50.00				

KM# 569 5 HRYVEN

15.5500 g., 0.9250 Silver 0.4624 oz. ASW, 33 mm. **Subject:** Mykola Ivanovych Pyrohov, scientist and surgeon **Obv:** Sepulchral church erected over scientist's tomb **Rev:** Half length figure in apron holding surgical instruments

Date	Mintage	F	VF	XF	Unc	BU
2010 Proof	5,000	Value: 50.00				

KM# 573 5 HRYVEN

16.5000 g., Copper-Nickel-Zinc, 35 mm. **Subject:** Ukrainian Folk crafts - Cartwright **Obv:** Wood cart and wheels **Rev:** Woodcraftsman hewing wood to make cart detail **Edge:** Reeded

Date	Mintage	F	VF	XF	Unc	BU
2010	45,000	—	—	—	—	13.00

KM# 577 5 HRYVEN

15.5500 g., 0.9250 Silver 0.4624 oz. ASW, 33 mm. **Subject:** Year of the tiger **Obv:** Vegitable ornamention pattern, National Arms **Rev:** Stylized playful tiger **Edge:** Reeded

Date	Mintage	F	VF	XF	Unc	BU
2010 Proof	20,000	Value: 50.00				

KM# 579 5 HRYVEN

16.5400 g., Copper-Nickel-Zinc, 35 mm. **Subject:** Kyiv National University Astronomical Observatory, 165th Anniversary **Obv:** Observatory building **Rev:** Telescope and night sky **Edge:** Reeded

Date	Mintage	F	VF	XF	Unc	BU
2010	45,000	—	—	—	—	13.00

KM# 582 5 HRYVEN

15.5500 g., 0.9250 Silver 0.4624 oz. ASW, 33 mm. **Subject:** Livi Polytechnic National University, 165th Anniversary **Obv:** Arts and Science sculpture from main building **Rev:** University building façade

Date	Mintage	F	VF	XF	Unc	BU
2010 Proof	5,000	Value: 50.00				

KM# 584 5 HRYVEN

15.5500 g., 0.9250 Silver 0.4624 oz. ASW, 33 mm. **Subject:** Kharkiv Polytechnic Institute, 125th Anniversary **Obv:** Radio telescope and open book **Rev:** University building and oval portrait of V.L. Kyrpychov

Date	Mintage	F	VF	XF	Unc	BU
2010 Proof	5,000	Value: 50.00				

KM# 587 5 HRYVEN

16.5000 g., Copper-Nickel, 35 mm. **Subject:** Folk Crafts - Weaver **Obv:** Spinning wheel and weaving products **Rev:** Woman working on a loom **Edge:** Reeded

Date	Mintage	F	VF	XF	Unc	BU
2010	45,000	—	—	—	—	13.00

KM# 589 5 HRYVEN

16.5000 g., Copper-Nickel, 35 mm. **Subject:** UKranian spas **Obv:** Two cornucopiae and the Savior's Feast **Rev:** Peasants getting food gifts blessed **Edge:** Reeded

Date	Mintage	F	VF	XF	Unc	BU
2010	45,000	—	—	—	—	13.00

KM# 592 5 HRYVEN

16.5000 g., Copper-Nickel, 35 mm. **Subject:** Lutsk, 925th Anniversary **Obv:** Entrance tower to town's castle **Rev:** City view from tower top, city carms above **Edge:** Reeded

Date	Mintage	F	VF	XF	Unc	BU
2010	45,000	—	—	—	—	13.00

KM# 598 5 HRYVEN

15.5500 g., 0.9250 Silver 0.4624 oz. ASW, 33 mm. **Subject:** Johann Georg Pinzel **Obv:** Buchach City hall **Rev:** Sculptor and angel

Date	Mintage	F	VF	XF	Unc	BU
2010 Proof	5,000	Value: 50.00				

KM# 599 5 HRYVEN

15.5500 g., 0.9250 Silver 0.4624 oz. ASW, 33 mm. **Subject:** Ivan Fedorov **Obv:** Apostol book page and large quill pin **Rev:** Ivan Fedorov portrait facing

Date	Mintage	F	VF	XF	Unc	BU
2010 Proof	5,000	Value: 50.00				

KM# 601 5 HRYVEN

16.5400 g., Copper-Nickel, 35 mm. **Subject:** Maritime History **Obv:** Banner seperating compas rose and seal of the Zaporohian Host **Rev:** Cossack boat of the 18th century

Date	Mintage	F	VF	XF	Unc	BU
2010	45,000	—	—	—	—	13.00

KM# 604 5 HRYVEN

16.5000 g., Copper-Nickel, 35 mm. **Subject:** Folk Crafts - Potter **Obv:** Pottery flanking central pattern **Rev:** Potter at wheel **Edge:** Reeded

Date	Mintage	F	VF	XF	Unc	BU
2010	4,500	—	—	—	—	13.00

KM# 607 5 HRYVEN

15.5500 g., 0.9250 Silver 0.4624 oz. ASW, 33 mm. **Subject:** Year of teh cat (rabbit, hare) **Obv:** National Arms above artistic pattern **Rev:** Cat, crystals in eyes

Date	Mintage	F	VF	XF	Unc	BU
2010 Proof	20,000	Value: 50.00				

KM# 515 10 HRYVNI

33.6220 g., 0.9250 Silver 0.9999 oz. ASW, 38.6 mm. **Subject:** The Annunciation **Edge:** Reeded

Date	Mintage	F	VF	XF	Unc	BU
2008 Proof	8,000	Value: 80.00				

KM# 113 10 HRYVEN

33.6220 g., 0.9250 Silver 0.9999 oz. ASW, 38.61 mm. **Subject:** Ivan Mazepa (Cossack leader) **Obv:** Arms with supporters within beaded circle **Rev:** Half figure divides beaded circle flanked by palace and oval shield **Edge:** Reeded

Date	Mintage	F	VF	XF	Unc	BU
2001 Proof	5,000	Value: 200				

KM# 114 10 HRYVEN

33.6220 g., 0.9250 Silver 0.9999 oz. ASW, 38.61 mm. **Subject:** Yaroslav the Wise (Cossack leader) **Obv:** Value within grape wreath **Rev:** Mosaic head facing, half length figure facing holding scroll and dome building **Edge:** Reeded

Date	Mintage	F	VF	XF	Unc	BU
2001 Proof	3,000	Value: 1,400				

KM# 115 10 HRYVEN

33.6220 g., 0.9250 Silver 0.9999 oz. ASW, 38.61 mm. **Series:** Ukranian Flora and Fauna **Obv:** National arms and date divides wreath, value within **Rev:** Lynx with offspring **Edge:** Reeded

Date	Mintage	F	VF	XF	Unc	BU
2001 Proof	3,000	Value: 475				

KM# 130 10 HRYVEN

33.6220 g., 0.9250 Silver 0.9999 oz. ASW, 38.61 mm. **Subject:** 10th Anniversary - National Bank **Obv:** National arms and value between arches **Rev:** Large building entrance **Edge:** Reeded

Date	Mintage	F	VF	XF	Unc	BU
2001 Proof	3,000	Value: 250				

KM# 131 10 HRYVEN

33.6220 g., 0.9250 Silver 0.9999 oz. ASW, 38.61 mm. **Series:** Olympics **Obv:** National arms and value on ice **Rev:** Stylized ice dancing couple **Edge:** Reeded

Date	Mintage	F	VF	XF	Unc	BU
2001 Proof	15,000	Value: 80.00				

KM# 141 10 HRYVEN

33.6220 g., 0.9250 Silver 0.9999 oz. ASW, 38.61 mm. **Subject:** Flora and Fauna **Obv:** National arms and date divides wreath, value within **Rev:** Pine branch with cone **Edge:** Reeded

Date	Mintage	F	VF	XF	Unc	BU
2001 Proof	3,000	Value: 350				

KM# 142 10 HRYVEN
33.6220 g., 0.9250 Silver 0.9999 oz. ASW, 38.61 mm. **Subject:** Khan Palace in Bakhchisarai **Obv:** Value in arch **Rev:** Courtyard view **Edge:** Reeded

Date	Mintage	F	VF	XF	Unc	BU
2001 Proof	3,000	Value: 400				

KM# 143 10 HRYVEN
4.3110 g., 0.9000 Gold 0.1247 oz. AGW, 16 mm. **Subject:** 10 Years Independence **Obv:** National arms **Rev:** Parliament building on map **Edge:** Plain

Date	Mintage	F	VF	XF	Unc	BU
2001 Proof	3,000	Value: 1,100				

KM# 165 10 HRYVEN
33.6220 g., 0.9250 Silver 0.9999 oz. ASW, 38.61 mm. **Subject:** Olympics **Obv:** National arms and value on ice **Rev:** Stylized hockey player **Edge:** Reeded

Date	Mintage	F	VF	XF	Unc	BU
2001 Proof	15,000	Value: 80.00				

KM# 229 10 HRYVEN
33.6220 g., 0.9250 Silver 0.9999 oz. ASW, 38.61 mm. **Obv:** National arms and date divides wreath, value within **Rev:** Eurasian Eagle Owl on branch **Edge:** Reeded

Date	Mintage	F	VF	XF	Unc	BU
2002 Proof	3,000	Value: 650				

KM# 145 10 HRYVEN
33.6220 g., 0.9250 Silver 0.9999 oz. ASW, 38.61 mm. **Subject:** Ivan Sirko **Obv:** Arms with supporters within beaded circle **Rev:** Cossack battle scene divides beaded circle **Edge:** Reeded

Date	Mintage	F	VF	XF	Unc	BU
2002 Proof	3,000	Value: 400				

KM# 146 10 HRYVEN
33.6220 g., 0.9250 Silver 0.9999 oz. ASW, 38.61 mm. **Obv:** National arms and value on ice **Rev:** Stylized speed skater **Edge:** Reeded

Date	Mintage	F	VF	XF	Unc	BU
2002 Proof	3,000	Value: 150				

KM# 160 10 HRYVEN
33.9500 g., 0.9250 Silver 1.0096 oz. ASW, 38.61 mm. **Obv:** Value encircled by angels flanked by stars **Rev:** Steepled church and tower **Edge:** Reeded

Date	Mintage	F	VF	XF	Unc	BU
2002 Proof	3,000	Value: 375				

KM# 161 10 HRYVEN
33.6220 g., 0.9250 Silver 0.9999 oz. ASW, 38.61 mm. **Subject:** Grand Prince Vladimir Monomakh **Obv:** Value within jewelry design **Rev:** Bust holding book flanked by buildings and St. George **Edge:** Reeded

Date	Mintage	F	VF	XF	Unc	BU
2002 Proof	3,000	Value: 550				

KM# 162 10 HRYVEN
33.6220 g., 0.9250 Silver 0.9999 oz. ASW, 38.61 mm. **Subject:** Prince Svyatoslav **Obv:** Value in ornate design **Rev:** Armored half length figure facing **Edge:** Reeded

Date	Mintage	F	VF	XF	Unc	BU
2002 Proof	3,000	Value: 550				

KM# 164 10 HRYVEN
33.6220 g., 0.9250 Silver 0.9999 oz. ASW, 38.61 mm. **Subject:** Christmas **Obv:** National arms within star above value **Rev:** Christmas pageant scene **Edge:** Reeded

Date	Mintage	F	VF	XF	Unc	BU
2002 Proof	3,000	Value: 600				

KM# 176 10 HRYVEN
33.6220 g., 0.9250 Silver 0.9999 oz. ASW, 38.61 mm. **Subject:** Olympics **Obv:** Two ancient women with seedlings **Rev:** Swimmer **Edge:** Reeded

Date	Mintage	F	VF	XF	Unc	BU
2002 Proof	15,000	Value: 60.00				

KM# 177 10 HRYVEN
33.6220 g., 0.9250 Silver 0.9999 oz. ASW, 38.61 mm. **Subject:** Hetman Pylyp Orlik 1672-1742 **Obv:** Arms with supporters within beaded circle **Rev:** Standing figure facing holding scroll flanked by other standing figures **Edge:** Reeded

Date	Mintage	F	VF	XF	Unc	BU
2002 Proof	3,000	Value: 350				

KM# 198 10 HRYVEN
33.6220 g., 0.9250 Silver 0.9999 oz. ASW, 38.61 mm. **Obv:** National arms and date divides wreath, value within **Rev:** European bison **Edge:** Reeded

Date	Mintage	F	VF	XF	Unc	BU
2003 Proof	2,000	Value: 600				

KM# 189 10 HRYVEN
33.6220 g., 0.9250 Silver 0.9999 oz. ASW, 38.61 mm. **Subject:** Olympics **Obv:** Two ancient women with seedlings **Rev:** Boxer **Edge:** Reeded

Date	Mintage	F	VF	XF	Unc	BU
2003 Proof	15,000	Value: 80.00				

KM# 190 10 HRYVEN
33.6220 g., 0.9250 Silver 0.9999 oz. ASW, 38.61 mm. **Obv:** Fancy art work and sculpture **Rev:** Livadia Palace view **Edge:** Reeded

Date	Mintage	F	VF	XF	Unc	BU
2003 Proof	3,000	Value: 300				

KM# 191 10 HRYVEN
33.6220 g., 0.9250 Silver 0.9999 oz. ASW, 38.61 mm. **Obv:** National arms on sun, flying geese divides beaded circle **Rev:** Antonov AN-2 biplane divides beaded circle **Edge:** Reeded

Date	Mintage	F	VF	XF	Unc	BU
2003 Proof	3,000	Value: 320				

KM# 192 10 HRYVEN
33.6220 g., 0.9250 Silver 0.9999 oz. ASW, 38.61 mm. **Obv:** Easter eggs around arms above value **Rev:** Easter celebration **Edge:** Reeded

Date	Mintage	F	VF	XF	Unc	BU
2003 Proof	3,000	Value: 500				

KM# 193 10 HRYVEN
33.6220 g., 0.9250 Silver 0.9999 oz. ASW, 38.61 mm. **Obv:** Angels, national arms and value **Rev:** The protection of the Virgin Mary over the Pochayiv Monastery **Edge:** Reeded

Date	Mintage	F	VF	XF	Unc	BU
2003 Proof	Est. 8,000	Value: 150				

KM# 194 10 HRYVEN
33.6220 g., 0.9250 Silver 0.9999 oz. ASW, 38.61 mm. **Obv:** National arms and date divide wreath, value within **Rev:** Long-snouted seahorse **Edge:** Reeded

Date	Mintage	F	VF	XF	Unc	BU
2003 Proof	2,000	Value: 750				

KM# 195 10 HRYVEN
33.6220 g., 0.9250 Silver 0.9999 oz. ASW, 38.61 mm. **Subject:**

Kyrylo Rozumovskyi (Cossack leader) **Obv:** Arms with supporters within beaded circle **Rev:** Half length figure 1/4 left within beaded circle **Edge:** Reeded

Date	Mintage	F	VF	XF	Unc	BU
2003 Proof	3,000	Value: 350				

KM# 196 10 HRYVEN

33.6220 g., 0.9250 Silver 0.9999 oz. ASW, 38.61 mm. **Subject:** Pavlo Polubotok (Cossack leader) **Obv:** Arms with supporters within beaded circle **Rev:** Half length figure within beaded circle **Edge:** Reeded

Date	Mintage	F	VF	XF	Unc	BU
2003 Proof	3,000	Value: 375				

KM# 197 10 HRYVEN

33.6220 g., 0.9250 Silver 0.9999 oz. ASW, 38.61 mm. **Obv:** Map, national arms and value **Rev:** Genoese Fortress in Sudak **Edge:** Reeded

Date	Mintage	F	VF	XF	Unc	BU
2003 Proof	3,000	Value: 300				

KM# 206 10 HRYVEN

33.9100 g., 0.9250 Silver 1.0084 oz. ASW, 38.61 mm. **Subject:** Azov Dolphin **Obv:** National arms and date divides wreath, value within **Rev:** Harbor Porpoises **Edge:** Reeded

Date	Mintage	F	VF	XF	Unc	BU
2004 Proof	8,000	Value: 120				

KM# 207 10 HRYVEN

33.9100 g., 0.9250 Silver 1.0084 oz. ASW, 38.61 mm. **Subject:** Football World Cup - 2006 **Obv:** Soccer ball in net **Rev:** Two soccer players **Edge:** Reeded

Date	Mintage	F	VF	XF	Unc	BU
2004 Proof	50,000	Value: 150				

KM# 223 10 HRYVEN

33.9100 g., 0.9250 Silver 1.0084 oz. ASW, 38.61 mm. **Obv:** National arms on sun, flying geese and value divides beaded circle **Rev:** AH-140 Airliner divides beaded circle **Edge:** Reeded

Date	Mintage	F	VF	XF	Unc	BU
2004 Proof	10,000	Value: 150				

KM# 224 10 HRYVEN

33.9100 g., 0.9250 Silver 1.0084 oz. ASW, 38.61 mm. **Subject:** Ice Breaker "Captain Belousov" **Obv:** National arms on ship's wheel and anchor **Rev:** Ice breaker ship **Edge:** Reeded

Date	Mintage	F	VF	XF	Unc	BU
2004 Proof	10,000	Value: 80.00				

KM# 225 10 HRYVEN

33.6220 g., 0.9250 Silver 0.9999 oz. ASW, 38.61 mm. **Subject:** Whit Sunday **Obv:** National arms within wreath above value flanked by sprigs **Rev:** Four women folk dancers and child **Edge:** Reeded

Date	Mintage	F	VF	XF	Unc	BU
2004 Proof	10,000	Value: 250				

KM# 339 10 HRYVEN

33.6220 g., 0.9250 Silver 0.9999 oz. ASW, 38.61 mm. **Subject:** Ostrozhsky Family **Obv:** Our Lady of Duben and Elias Icon **Rev:** Three cameos above crowned shield **Edge:** Reeded

Date	Mintage	F	VF	XF	Unc	BU
2004 Proof	3,000	Value: 270				

KM# 340 10 HRYVEN

33.6220 g., 0.9250 Silver 0.9999 oz. ASW, 38.61 mm. **Subject:** St. Yura Cathedral **Obv:** Statue of St. George on horse killing dragon **Rev:** Cathedral **Edge:** Reeded

Date	Mintage	F	VF	XF	Unc	BU
ND (2004) Proof	8,000	Value: 100				

KM# 342 10 HRYVEN

33.6220 g., 0.9250 Silver 0.9999 oz. ASW, 38.61 mm. **Subject:** Defense of Sevastopol 1854-56 **Obv:** National arms and value above fortifications map **Rev:** Cannon and ships **Edge:** Reeded

Date	Mintage	F	VF	XF	Unc	BU
2004 Proof	10,000	Value: 90.00				

KM# 343 10 HRYVEN

33.6220 g., 0.9250 Silver 0.9999 oz. ASW, 38.61 mm. **Subject:** Perejaslav Cossack Rada of 1654 **Obv:** National arms above value **Rev:** Standing figures facing **Edge:** Reeded

Date	Mintage	F	VF	XF	Unc	BU
2004 Proof	8,000	Value: 140				

KM# 358 10 HRYVEN

33.6220 g., 0.9250 Silver 0.9999 oz. ASW, 38.61 mm. **Subject:** Spalax Arenarius Reshetnik **Obv:** National arms and date divides wreath, value within **Rev:** Sandy mole rat **Edge:** Reeded

Date	Mintage	F	VF	XF	Unc	BU
2005 Proof	8,000	Value: 100				

KM# 367 10 HRYVEN

33.6220 g., 0.9250 Silver 0.9999 oz. ASW, 38.61 mm. **Subject:** The Protection of the Virgin **Obv:** National arms on Cossack regalia **Rev:** Wedding scene **Edge:** Reeded

Date	Mintage	F	VF	XF	Unc	BU
2005 Proof	8,000	Value: 140				

KM# 370 10 HRYVEN

33.6220 g., 0.9250 Silver 0.9999 oz. ASW, 38.61 mm. **Subject:** 60 Years UN Membership **Obv:** National arms, value and olive branch **Rev:** UN logo above partial globe **Edge:** Reeded

Date	Mintage	F	VF	XF	Unc	BU
2005 Proof	5,000	Value: 80.00				

KM# 371 10 HRYVEN

33.6220 g., 0.9250 Silver 0.9999 oz. ASW, 38.61 mm. **Subject:** National Anthem **Obv:** Musical score, national arms, value and date **Rev:** Coiled legend around holographic flower **Edge:** Reeded

Date	Mintage	F	VF	XF	Unc	BU
2005 Proof	3,000	Value: 250				

KM# 372 10 HRYVEN

33.6220 g., 0.9250 Silver 0.9999 oz. ASW, 38.61 mm. **Subject:** 100 Years of Olha Kobylianska Music and Drama Theatre in Chernivtsi **Obv:** Statue **Rev:** Theater **Edge:** Reeded

Date	Mintage	F	VF	XF	Unc	BU
2005 Proof	5,000	Value: 80.00				

KM# 373 10 HRYVEN

33.6220 g., 0.9250 Silver 0.9999 oz. ASW, 38.61 mm. **Subject:** Sviatohirsky Lavra Monastery **Obv:** Madonna and child flanked by angels **Rev:** Monastery on river bank **Edge:** Reeded

Date	Mintage	F	VF	XF	Unc	BU
2005 Proof	8,000	Value: 120				

KM# 381 10 HRYVEN

33.8600 g., 0.9250 Silver 1.0069 oz. ASW, 38.61 mm. **Subject:** Baturyn Hetman Capital City **Obv:** National arms within sun rays, value flanked by standing figures **Rev:** Four cameos and banner above city view **Edge:** Reeded

Date	Mintage	F	VF	XF	Unc	BU
2005 Proof	5,000	Value: 120				

KM# 382 10 HRYVEN
33.8600 g., 0.9250 Silver 1.0069 oz. ASW, 38.61 mm. **Subject:** Symyrenko Family **Obv:** Country name below national arms within sprigs **Rev:** Family tree **Edge:** Reeded

Date	Mintage	F	VF	XF	Unc	BU
2005 Proof	5,000	Value: 80.00				

KM# 392 10 HRYVEN
33.6220 g., 0.9250 Silver 0.9999 oz. ASW, 38.61 mm. **Obv:** National arms above value in wreath **Rev:** Grasshopper **Edge:** Reeded

Date	Mintage	F	VF	XF	Unc	BU
2006 Proof	8,000	Value: 120				

KM# 424 10 HRYVEN
33.6221 g., 0.9250 Silver 0.9999 oz. ASW, 38.61 mm. **Subject:** Chyhyryn **Obv:** National arms

Date	Mintage	F	VF	XF	Unc	BU
2006 Proof	5,000	Value: 110				

KM# 425 10 HRYVEN
33.6220 g., 0.9250 Silver 0.9999 oz. ASW, 38.61 mm. **Subject:** 10 Years of the Clearing House **Obv:** National arms

Date	Mintage	F	VF	XF	Unc	BU
2006 Proof	5,000	Value: 80.00				

KM# 410 10 HRYVEN
33.6220 g., 0.9250 Silver 0.9999 oz. ASW, 38.61 mm. **Subject:** 10 Years of the Constitution of Ukraine **Obv:** National arms

Date	Mintage	F	VF	XF	Unc	BU
2006 Proof	5,000	Value: 80.00				

KM# 421 10 HRYVEN
33.6200 g., 0.9250 Silver 0.9998 oz. ASW, 38.61 mm. **Subject:** Epiphany **Obv:** National arms **Edge:** Reeded

Date	Mintage	F	VF	XF	Unc	BU
2006 Proof	10,000	Value: 120				

KM# 423 10 HRYVEN
33.6220 g., 0.9250 Silver 0.9999 oz. ASW, 38.61 mm. **Subject:** Saint Kyryl Church **Obv:** National arms **Edge:** Reeded

Date	Mintage	F	VF	XF	Unc	BU
2006 Proof	8,000	Value: 100				

KM# 427 10 HRYVEN
33.6220 g., 0.9250 Silver 0.9999 oz. ASW, 38.61 mm. **Subject:** Twentieth Winter Olympic Games of 2006 **Obv:** National arms **Edge:** Reeded

Date	Mintage	F	VF	XF	Unc	BU
2006 Proof	5,000	Value: 80.00				

KM# 466 10 HRYVEN
33.6220 g., 0.9250 Silver 0.9999 oz. ASW, 38.6 mm. **Subject:** Odessa National Opera and Ballet, 120th Anniversary **Obv:** Interior view from stage **Rev:** Opera house in Odessa **Edge:** Reeded

Date	Mintage	F	VF	XF	Unc	BU
2007 Proof	5,000	Value: 90.00				

KM# 467 10 HRYVEN
33.6220 g., 0.9250 Silver 0.9999 oz. ASW, 38.61 mm. **Subject:** Ivan Bohun **Edge:** Reeded

Date	Mintage	F	VF	XF	Unc	BU
2007 Proof	5,000	Value: 100				

KM# 516 10 HRYVEN
33.6220 g., 0.9250 Silver 0.9999 oz. ASW, 38.61 mm. **Subject:** Black Griffin **Edge:** Reeded

Date	Mintage	F	VF	XF	Unc	BU
2008 Proof	7,000	Value: 110				

KM# 517 10 HRYVEN
33.6220 g., 0.9250 Silver 0.9999 oz. ASW, 38.61 mm. **Subject:** Sevastopol, 225th Anniversary **Edge:** Reeded

Date	Mintage	F	VF	XF	Unc	BU
2008 Proof	5,000	Value: 100				

KM# 518 10 HRYVEN
33.6220 g., 0.9250 Silver 0.9999 oz. ASW, 38.61 mm. **Subject:** Swallow's Nest **Edge:** Reeded

Date	Mintage	F	VF	XF	Unc	BU
2008 Proof	5,000	Value: 100				

KM# 519 10 HRYVEN
33.6220 g., 0.9250 Silver 0.9999 oz. ASW, 38.61 mm. **Subject:** Tereschenko Family **Edge:** Reeded

Date	Mintage	F	VF	XF	Unc	BU
2008 Proof	7,000	Value: 75.00				

KM# 520 10 HRYVEN
33622.0000 g., 0.9250 Silver 999.85 oz. ASW, 38.61 mm. **Subject:** Ukranian Swedish Alliances XVII-XVIII Century

Date	Mintage	F	VF	XF	Unc	BU
2008 Proof	5,000	Value: 80.00				

KM# 521 10 HRYVEN
33.6220 g., 0.9250 Silver 0.9999 oz. ASW, 38.61 mm. **Subject:** Hlukhiv

Date	Mintage	F	VF	XF	Unc	BU
2008 Proof	7,000	Value: 80.00				

KM# 522 10 HRYVEN
33.6220 g., 0.9250 Silver 0.9999 oz. ASW, 38.61 mm. **Subject:** UNESCO World Heritage Site - LVIV

Date	Mintage	F	VF	XF	Unc	BU
2008 Proof	5,000	Value: 110				

KM# 523 10 HRYVEN
33.6220 g., 0.9250 Silver 0.9999 oz. ASW, 38.61 mm. **Subject:** Cathedral in Buky Village

Date	Mintage	F	VF	XF	Unc	BU
2008 Proof	5,000	Value: 120				

KM# 532 10 HRYVEN
33.6220 g., 0.9250 Silver 0.9999 oz. ASW, 38.61 mm. **Subject:** Annunciation **Obv:** Conventionalized setting of the Gospel, lilies. **Obv. Legend:** НАЦІОНАЛЬНИЈ БАНК УКРАІНИ - 10 ГРИВЕНЬ **Rev:** Annunciation scene. **Rev. Legend:** БЛАГОВІЩЕННЯ

Date	Mintage	F	VF	XF	Unc	BU
2008 Proof	8,000	Value: 85.00				

KM# 556 10 HRYVEN
33.6220 g., 0.9250 Silver 0.9999 oz. ASW, 38.61 mm. **Subject:** Folk Crafts of the Ukraine - Bokorash (Raftsmen) **Obv:** Two birds, Carpathian landscape, trees, cottages, logs **Obv. Legend:** НАЦІОНАЛЬНИЈ БАНК УКРА?НИ - 10 / ГРИВЕНЬ / 2009 **Rev:** Bokorash directing raft **Rev. Legend:** БОКОРАШ

Date	Mintage	F	VF	XF	Unc	BU
2009 Proof	Est. 10,000	Value: 80.00				

KM# 559 10 HRYVEN
33.6220 g., 0.9250 Silver 0.9999 oz. ASW, 38.61 mm. **Subject:** Surb Khach Monastery **Obv:** National Arms, vegitation ornament pattern **Obv. Legend:** НАЦІОНАЛЬНИЈ БАНК УКРАІНИ - ДЕСЯТЬ ГРИВЕНЬ **Rev:** Monastery buildings **Rev. Legend:** СТАРИЈ КРИМ - ВІРМЕНСЬКИЈ МОНАСТИР XIV СТ. - СУРБ ХАЧ **Edge:** Segmented reeding

Date	Mintage	F	VF	XF	Unc	BU
2009 Proof	Est. 10,000	Value: 70.00				

KM# 560 10 HRYVEN

33.6220 g., 0.9250 Silver 0.9999 oz. ASW, 38.61 mm. **Subject:** Battle of Konotop, 350th Anniversary **Obv:** Hetman's Insignia, Cossack arms and bandura, National Arms. **Obv. Legend:** НАЦІОНАЛЬНИЙ БАНК УКРАЇНИ - 10 / ГРИВНЬ **Rev:** Ivan Vyhovskyi with sabre, Cossacks, Konotop fortifications, banners. **Rev. Legend:** ПЕРЕМОГА В КОНОТОПСЬКІЙ БИТВІ - 350 РОКІВ

Date	Mintage	F	VF	XF	Unc	BU
2009 Proof	8,000	Value: 80.00				

KM# 561 10 HRYVEN

33.6220 g., 0.9250 Silver 0.9999 oz. ASW, 38.61 mm. **Subject:** Church of the Holy Spirit in Rogatyn **Obv:** Church Icon with candelabra flanking, National Arms **Rev:** Church facade

Date	Mintage	F	VF	XF	Unc	BU
2009 Proof	Est. 10,000	Value: 80.00				

KM# 562 10 HRYVEN

33.6220 g., 0.9250 Silver 0.9999 oz. ASW, 38.61 mm. **Subject:** Famous Ukranian Families - Galagan Family **Obv:** The family estate, National Arms, value **Rev:** Galagan's College building and three portraits

Date	Mintage	F	VF	XF	Unc	BU
2009 Proof	7,000	Value: 80.00				

KM# 563 10 HRYVEN

33.6220 g., 0.9250 Silver 0.9999 oz. ASW, 38.61 mm. **Subject:** Kiev Academy of Operatta Theater, 75th Anniversary **Obv:** Dance scene, National Arms, value **Obv. Legend:** НАЦІОНАЛЬНИЙ БАНК УКРАЇНИ - 10 / ГРИВНЬ / 2009 **Rev:** Theater building, operetta character silhouettes. **Rev. Legend:** КИЇВСЬКИЙ АКАДЕМІЧНИЙ ТЕАТР ОПЕРЕТИ - 75/РОКІВ

Date	Mintage	F	VF	XF	Unc	BU
2009 Proof	5,000	Value: 80.00				

KM# 570 10 HRYVEN

31.1000 g., 0.9250 Silver 0.9249 oz. ASW, 38.6 mm. **Subject:** Pulyp Oriyk Constitution, 300th Anniversary **Obv:** Hetman and Cossack officials **Rev:** Pylyp Orlyk, quill pen and constitution

Date	Mintage	F	VF	XF	Unc	BU
2010 Proof	7,000	Value: 70.00				

KM# 574 10 HRYVEN

31.1000 g., 0.9250 Silver 0.9249 oz. ASW, 38.61 mm. **Subject:** Ukrainian folk craft - Cartwright **Obv:** Wagon and wheels **Rev:** Woodcraftsman hewing wood to make a cart detail **Edge:** Reeded

Date	Mintage	F	VF	XF	Unc	BU
2010	10,000	—	—	—	—	55.00

KM# 575 10 HRYVEN

31.1000 g., 0.9250 Silver 0.9249 oz. ASW, 38.61 mm. **Subject:** Vancouver Winter Olympics **Obv:** Winter scene **Rev:** Snowflake, sport figures, downhill skier at left

Date	Mintage	F	VF	XF	Unc	BU
2010 Proof	8,000	Value: 55.00				

KM# 586 10 HRYVEN

31.1000 g., 0.9250 Silver 0.9249 oz. ASW, 38.61 mm. **Obv:** Icon of Our Lady of Zarvanytsia **Rev:** Cathedral of Our Lady of Zarvanytsia

Date	Mintage	F	VF	XF	Unc	BU
2010	7,000	Value: 55.00				

KM# 588 10 HRYVEN

31.1000 g., 0.9250 Silver 0.9249 oz. ASW, 38.61 mm. **Subject:** Folk Crafts - Weaving **Obv:** Spinning wheel and weaving products **Rev:** Woman working at a loom

Date	Mintage	F	VF	XF	Unc	BU
2010 Proof	10,000	Value: 55.00				

KM# 590 10 HRYVEN

31.1000 g., 0.9250 Silver 0.9249 oz. ASW, 38.61 mm. **Subject:** Ukraine Spas **Obv:** Two cornucopiae and Savior's fest **Rev:** Peasants getting foot blessed

Date	Mintage	F	VF	XF	Unc	BU
2010	—	—	—	—	—	55.00

KM# 594 10 HRYVEN

31.1000 g., 0.9250 Silver 0.9249 oz. ASW, 38.61 mm. **Subject:** Flora and Fauna **Obv:** National Arms and wreath **Rev:** Stipa Ucrainica, feather grass

Date	Mintage	F	VF	XF	Unc	BU
2010 Proof	8,000	Value: 55.00				

KM# 600 10 HRYVEN

31.1000 g., 0.9250 Silver 0.9249 oz. ASW, 38.61 mm. **Subject:** Hetman Danylo Apostol **Obv:** National arms, Archangel Michael and Crowned lion (Symbols of Kyiv and Lviv_ **Rev:** Danylo Apostol half length figure holding scep-tre

Date	Mintage	F	VF	XF	Unc	BU
2010 Proof	8,000	Value: 55.00				

KM# 605 10 HRYVEN

31.1000 g., 0.9250 Silver 0.9249 oz. ASW, 38.61 mm. **Subject:** Folk Crafts - Potter **Obv:** Pottery flanking central design **Rev:** Potter at wheel

Date	Mintage	F	VF	XF	Unc	BU
2010 Proof	10,000	Value: 55.00				

KM# 606 10 HRYVEN

31.1000 g., 0.9250 Silver 0.9249 oz. ASW, 38.6 mm. **Subject:** Tarnovskyi Family **Obv:** Mansion in Kachanivka, Chernihiv oblast **Rev:** Vasyl Tarnovskyi standing and oval portraits of Hryhorii and Vasyl.

Date	Mintage	F	VF	XF	Unc	BU
2010 Proof	10,000	—	—	—	—	55.00

KM# 144 20 HRYVEN

67.2400 g., 0.9250 Silver 1.9996 oz. ASW, 50 mm. **Subject:** 10 Years Independence **Obv:** National arms **Rev:** Parliament building on map within beaded circle **Edge:** Segmented reeding

Date	Mintage	F	VF	XF	Unc	BU
2001 Proof	1,000	Value: 4,000				

KM# 174 20 HRYVEN

14.7000 g., Bi-Metallic .916 Gold center in .925 silver ring, 31 mm. **Subject:** "Kyiv Rus" Culture **Obv:** Old arms of Ukraine, Prince and a cathedral model in his hand and princess **Rev:** Old Rus earring **Edge:** Reeded and plain sections

Date	Mintage	F	VF	XF	Unc	BU
2001 Proof	2,000	Value: 1,000				

KM# 175 20 HRYVEN

14.7000 g., Bi-Metallic .916 Gold center in .925 Silver ring, 31 mm. **Subject:** Scythian Culture **Obv:** Warrior with a bowl in his hand and to the right, a Queen of Scythia **Rev:** Stylized horse flanked by pegasists **Edge:** Reeded and plain sections

Date	Mintage	F	VF	XF	Unc	BU
2001 Proof	2,000	Value: 1,200				

KM# 153 20 HRYVEN

67.2400 g., 0.9250 Silver 1.9996 oz. ASW, 50 mm. **Obv:** National arms on sun and flying geese divides beaded circle **Rev:** "AN-225 Mrija" cargo jet divides beaded circle **Edge:** Reeded and plain sections

Date	Mintage	F	VF	XF	Unc	BU
2002 Proof	2,002	Value: 1,200				

KM# 188 20 HRYVEN

67.2400 g., 0.9250 Silver 1.9996 oz. ASW, 50 mm. **Subject:** 60th Anniversary - Liberation of Kiev **Obv:** Eternal flame monument **Rev:** Map and battle scene **Edge:** Segmented reeding

Date	Mintage	F	VF	XF	Unc	BU
2003 Proof	2,000	Value: 400				

KM# 226 20 HRYVEN

67.2440 g., 0.9250 Silver 1.9997 oz. ASW, 50 mm. **Subject:** "Our Souls Do Not Die" **Obv:** National arms above value **Rev:** Bust of Taras Shevchenko facing flanked by standing figures **Edge:** Segmented reeding

Date	Mintage	F	VF	XF	Unc	BU
2004 Proof	4,000	Value: 250				

KM# 344 20 HRYVEN

67.2440 g., 0.9250 Silver 1.9997 oz. ASW, 50 mm. **Subject:** 2006 Olympic Games **Obv:** Woman holding flame and branch **Rev:** Six athletes around flame within square design **Edge:** Segmented reeding

Date	Mintage	F	VF	XF	Unc	BU
2004 Proof	5,000	Value: 120				

KM# 363 20 HRYVEN

67.2440 g., 0.9250 Silver 1.9997 oz. ASW, 50 mm. **Obv:** National arms on sun with flying geese divides beaded circle **Rev:** AN-124 jet plane divides beaded circle **Edge:** Segmented reeding

Date	Mintage	F	VF	XF	Unc	BU
2005 Proof	5,000	Value: 150				

KM# 369 20 HRYVEN

67.2440 g., 0.9250 Silver 1.9997 oz. ASW, 50 mm. **Subject:** Sorochynsky Fair **Obv:** Busts facing each other flanked by flower sprigs **Rev:** Farmer leading family in ox cart **Edge:** Segmented reeding

Date	Mintage	F	VF	XF	Unc	BU
2005 Proof	5,000	Value: 200				

KM# 374 20 HRYVEN
67.2440 g., 0.9250 Silver 1.9997 oz. ASW, 50 mm. **Subject:** 60th Anniversary of Victory in WWII **Obv:** Flying cranes divides value, date and national arms **Rev:** V-shaped searchlight beams filled with soldiers, order of the Patriotic War at bottom left **Edge:** Segmented reeding

Date	Mintage	F	VF	XF	Unc	BU
2005 Proof	5,000	Value: 120				

KM# 412 20 HRYVEN
67.2500 g., 0.9250 Silver 1.9999 oz. ASW, 50 mm. **Subject:** 15 Years of Ukraine Independency **Obv:** National arms

Date	Mintage	F	VF	XF	Unc	BU
2006 Proof	7,000	Value: 150				

KM# 468 20 HRYVEN
14.2300 g., Bi-Metallic Center in silver ring, 31 mm. **Subject:** Pure water is source of life **Obv:** Drop of water in pond **Rev:** Man taking drink from waterfall

Date	Mintage	F	VF	XF	Unc	BU
2007 Proof	5,000	Value: 500				

KM# 469 20 HRYVEN
67.2600 g., 0.9250 Silver 2.0002 oz. ASW, 50 mm. **Subject:** Chumaky's Way **Obv:** Hologram wheel at center of fiery spiral **Rev:** Merchant's carts under night sky

Date	Mintage	F	VF	XF	Unc	BU
2007 Proof	5,000	Value: 330				

KM# 470 20 HRYVEN
67.2500 g., 0.9250 Silver 1.9999 oz. ASW, 50 mm. **Subject:** The Famine, Genocide of the Ukranina People **Obv:** Girl standing on fallow ground, small green plant at left **Rev:** Swan at center of cross, candles in background

Date	Mintage	F	VF	XF	Unc	BU
2007 Antique finish	10,000	—	—	—	120	—

KM# 524 20 HRYVEN
67.2500 g., 0.9250 Silver 1.9999 oz. ASW, 50 mm. **Subject:** Kyiv, 1000th Anniversary of minting

Date	Mintage	F	VF	XF	Unc	BU
2008 Proof	5,000	Value: 150				

KM# 552 20 HRYVEN
67.2500 g., 0.9250 Silver 1.9999 oz. ASW, 50.0 mm. **Subject:** Republic of Carpatho-Ukraine - 70th Anniversary of proclamation **Obv:** Carpathian ornament patterns, National Arms, value **Obv. Legend:** НАЦІОНАЛЬНИЙ БАНК УКРАЇНИ - 20 / ГРИВНЬ **Rev:** Transcarpathian holding flag with the arms of the Carpatho-Ukraine **Rev. Legend:** 70 / РОКІВ - ПРОГОЛОШЕННЯ КАРПАТСЬКОЇ УКРАЇНИ

Date	Mintage	F	VF	XF	Unc	BU
2009 Proof	3,000	Value: 150				

KM# 554 20 HRYVEN
67.2700 g., 0.9250 Silver 2.0005 oz. ASW, 50 mm. **Subject:** Pysanka - Easter Egg decorating **Obv:** Ukrainian embroidered towels, eggs, Naitonal Arms, value **Rev:** Female pysanka maker ornamenting egg, young girl watching

Date	Mintage	F	VF	XF	Unc	BU
2009 Proof	8,000	Value: 120				

KM# 591 20 HRYVEN
62.2000 g., 0.9250 Silver 1.8497 oz. ASW, 50 mm. **Subject:** Zymne Cloister **Obv:** Madonna icon **Rev:** Zymne Cloister

Date	Mintage	F	VF	XF	Unc	BU
2010 Proof	5,000	—	—	—	—	90.00

KM# 596 20 HRYVEN
62.2000 g., 0.9250 Silver 1.8497 oz. ASW, 50 mm. **Subject:** Battle of Grunwald, 600th Anniversary **Obv:** Value within wreath, three armored hands holding horizontal sword **Rev:** Knights with spears on horseback in battle

Date	Mintage	F	VF	XF	Unc	BU
2010 Proof	5,000	Value: 90.00				

KM# 602 20 HRYVEN
62.2000 g., 0.9250 Silver 1.8497 oz. ASW, 50 mm. **Subject:** Maritime History **Obv:** Banner, compass rose and seal of Zaporozhin host **Rev:** Cossack boat of the 18th century

Date	Mintage	F	VF	XF	Unc	BU
2010 Proof	5,000	Value: 90.00				

KM# 426 50 HRYVEN
17.6300 g., 0.9000 Gold 0.5101 oz. AGW, 25 mm. **Subject:** Nestor - The Chronicler **Obv:** National arms

Date	Mintage	F	VF	XF	Unc	BU
2006 Proof	5,000	Value: 1,200				

KM# 525 50 HRYVEN
17.6300 g., 0.9000 Gold 0.5101 oz. AGW, 25 mm. **Subject:** Swallow's Nest Castle **Edge:** Plain

Date	Mintage	F	VF	XF	Unc	BU
2008 Proof	4,000	Value: 1,250				

KM# 526 50 HRYVEN
500.0000 g., 0.9999 Silver 16.073 oz. ASW **Subject:** Visit of Ecumenical Patriarch Bartholomew I

Date	Mintage	F	VF	XF	Unc	BU
2008 Proof	1,000	Value: 2,200				

KM# 564 50 HRYVEN
500.0000 g., 0.9990 Silver 16.058 oz. ASW, 85 mm. **Subject:** Mykola Hohol's stories - Evenings on a farm near Dykanka **Obv:** Hohol's portrait with quill, National arms, value **Rev:** Christmas star with yellow sapphire

Date	Mintage	F	VF	XF	Unc	BU
2009 Proof	Est. 1,500	Value: 2,500				

KM# 595 50 HRYVEN
15.5500 g., 0.9000 Gold 0.4499 oz. AGW, 25 mm. **Subject:** Ukrainian ballet **Obv:** Ballet shoes **Rev:** Ballet couple **Edge:** Plain

Date	Mintage	F	VF	XF	Unc	BU
2010 Proof	4,000	Value: 725				

KM# 609 50 HRYVEN
500.0000 g., 0.9990 Silver 16.058 oz. ASW, 85 mm. **Subject:** Cradle of the Ukrainian Cossacks **Obv:** Zaporizka Sich, historic site, shield and swords below **Rev:** Dovbysh (Cossack drummer) beating kettle drums, ornamental pattern

Date	Mintage	F	VF	XF	Unc	BU
2010 Proof	Est. 1,500	Value: 2,250				

KM# 199 100 HRYVEN
31.1000 g., 0.9000 Gold 0.8999 oz. AGW, 32 mm. **Subject:** Ancient Scythian Culture **Obv:** National arms above ornamental design and value within rope wreath **Rev:** Ancient craftsmen and jewelry **Edge:** Reeded

Date	Mintage	F	VF	XF	Unc	BU
2003 Proof	1,500	Value: 7,500				

KM# 345 100 HRYVEN
34.5594 g., 0.9000 Gold 100000 oz. AGW, 32 mm. **Subject:** The Golden Gate **Obv:** National arms above value between two stylized cranes **Rev:** Riders approaching castle gate **Edge:** Segmented reeding

Date	Mintage	F	VF	XF	Unc	BU
2004 Proof	2,000	Value: 5,000				

KM# 414 100 HRYVEN
1000.0000 g., 0.9990 Silver 32.117 oz. ASW, 100 mm. **Subject:** 10 Years to the Currency Reform in Ukraine **Obv:** National arms **Note:** Illustration reduced.

Date	Mintage	Good	VG	F	VF	XF
2006 Proof	1,501	Value: 6,500				

KM# 471 100 HRYVEN
34.5600 g., 0.9000 Gold 100000 oz. AGW, 32 mm. **Subject:** The Ostroh Bible **Obv:** Part of illumination on page **Rev:** Ivan Fedorov and Kostiantyn of Ostroth holding open bible

Date	Mintage	F	VF	XF	Unc	BU
2007 Proof	4,000	Value: 2,500				

KM# 527 100 HRYVEN
1000.0000 g., 0.9990 Silver 32.117 oz. ASW **Subject:** Kievan Rus

Date	Mintage	F	VF	XF	Unc	BU
2008 Proof	800	Value: 4,500				

KM# 558 100 HRYVEN
1000.0000 g., 0.9990 Silver 32.117 oz. ASW, 100 mm. **Subject:** International Year of Astronomy **Obv:** Solar System, armillary sphere, stars. **Obv. Legend:** НАЦІОНАЛЬНИЙ БАНК УКРАЇНИ - 100 / ГРИВНЬ **Rev:** Galileo, stars, telescope, galaxies, observatory, Saturn (as the letter O). **Rev. Legend:** МІЖНАРОДНИЙ РІК АСТРОНОМІЇ

Date	Mintage	F	VF	XF	Unc	BU
2009 Proof	Est. 700	Value: 4,000				

KM# 565 100 HRYVEN
34.5700 g., 0.9000 Gold 1.0003 oz. AGW, 32 mm. **Subject:** Ancient Site - Chersonesos Taurica **Obv:** Ancient ruins, coins, Naitonal Arms **Rev:** Ruins of ancient Chersonesos **Edge:** Segmented reeding

Date	Mintage	F	VF	XF	Unc	BU
2009 Proof	4,000	Value: 2,400				

KM# 597 100 HRYVEN
31.1000 g., 0.9000 Gold 0.8999 oz. AGW, 32 mm. **Subject:** Bosporan Kingdom **Obv:** Panticapaeum runins: classical columns, winged animals **Rev:** Panticapaeum stater, buildings, ancient sailing vessel

Date	Mintage	F	VF	XF	Unc	BU
2010 Proof	3,000	Value: 1,650				

MINT SETS

KM#	Date	Mintage	Identification	Issue Price	Mkt Val
MS2	2001 (8)	5,000	KM#1.1b, 2.1b, 3.3b, 4b, 6, 7, 8b, 129	—	60.00
XMS1	2004 (8)	7,000	X#Pn1-Pn8	—	35.00
MS3	2006 (8)	5,000	KM#1.1b, 2.1b, 3.3b, 4b, 6, 7, 8b, 411	—	30.00
MS4	2008 (7)	5,000	KM#1.1b, 2.1b, 3.3b, 4b, 6, 7, 209, prooflike	—	40.00

PROOF SETS

KM#	Date	Mintage	Identification	Issue Price	Mkt Val
XPS1	2005 (6)	—	X#21-26	250	250
XPS2	2005 (6)	—	X#21a-26a	300	300

UNITED ARAB EMIRATES

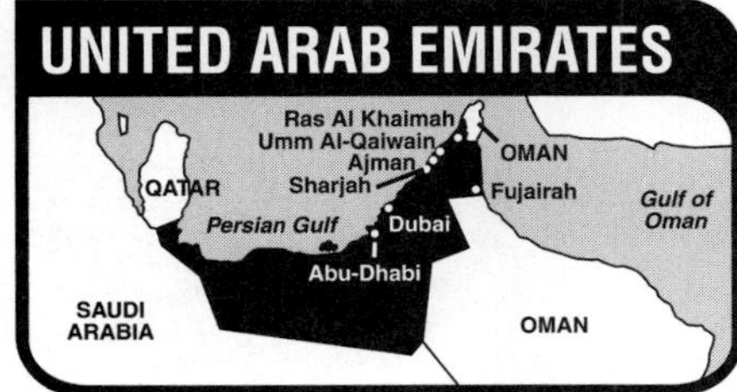

The seven United Arab Emirates (formerly known as the Trucial Sheikhdoms or States), located along the southern shore of the Persian Gulf, are comprised of the Sheikhdoms of Abu Dhabi, Dubai, al-Sharjah, Ajman, Umm al Qaiwain, Ras al-Khaimah and al-Fujairah. They have a combined area of about 32,000 sq. mi. (83,600 sq. km.) and a population of *2.1 million. Capital: Abu Zaby (Abu Dhabi). Since the oil strikes of 1958-60, the economy has centered about petroleum.

TITLES

الامارات العربية المتحدة

al-Imara(t) al-Arabiya(t) al-Muttahida(t)

UNITED EMIRATES

STANDARD COINAGE

KM# 1 FILS
1.5000 g., Bronze, 15 mm. **Series:** F.A.O. **Obv:** Value **Rev:** Date palms above dates **Edge:** Plain **Designer:** Geoffrey Colley

Date	Mintage	F	VF	XF	Unc	BU
AH1425-2005	—	—	—	—	0.50	0.75

KM# 2.2 5 FILS
Bronze **Series:** F.A.O. **Obv:** Value **Rev:** Fish above dates **Rev. Designer:** Geoffrey Colley **Note:** Reduced size.

Date	Mintage	F	VF	XF	Unc	BU
AH1422-2001	—	—	—	0.15	0.30	1.00
AH1426-2005	—	—	—	0.15	0.30	1.00

KM# 3.2 10 FILS
Bronze, 19 mm. **Obv:** Value **Rev:** Arab dhow above dates **Rev. Designer:** Geoffrey Colley **Note:** Reduced size.

Date	Mintage	F	VF	XF	Unc	BU
AH1422-2001 (2001)	—	—	0.20	0.35	0.80	1.20
AH1425-2005 (2005)	—	—	0.20	0.35	0.80	1.20

KM# 4 25 FILS
3.5000 g., Copper-Nickel, 20 mm. **Obv:** Value **Rev:** Gazelle above dates **Rev. Designer:** Geoffrey Colley **Edge:** Reeded

Date	Mintage	F	VF	XF	Unc	BU
AH1425-2005	—	—	—	0.40	0.75	1.00
AH1428-2007	—	—	—	0.40	0.75	1.00

KM# 16 50 FILS
4.3000 g., Copper-Nickel, 21 mm. **Obv:** Value **Rev:** Oil derricks above dates **Rev. Designer:** Geoffrey Colley **Shape:** 7-sided **Note:** Reduced size.

Date	Mintage	F	VF	XF	Unc	BU
AH1426-2005	—	—	—	0.45	1.35	1.85
AH1428-2007	—	—	—	0.45	1.35	1.85

KM# 49 DIRHAM
6.4000 g., Copper-Nickel, 24 mm. **Subject:** 25th Anniversary - Armed Forces Unification **Obv:** Value **Rev:** Heraldic eagle within rope wreath **Edge:** Reeded

Date	Mintage	F	VF	XF	Unc	BU
ND(2001) (2001)	250,000	—	—	—	3.50	5.00

 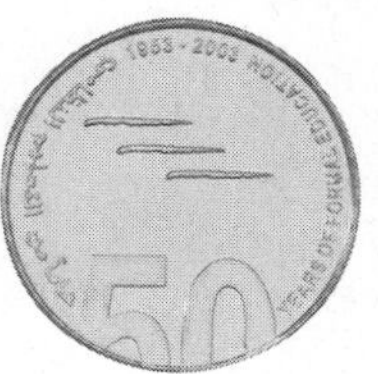

KM# 51 DIRHAM
6.3300 g., Copper-Nickel, 24 mm. **Subject:** 50 Years of Formal Education **Obv:** Value **Rev:** Symbolic design **Edge:** Reeded

Date	Mintage	F	VF	XF	Unc	BU
ND (2003)	—	—	—	—	3.50	5.00

KM# 52 DIRHAM
6.4000 g., Copper-Nickel, 24 mm. **Subject:** Abu Dhabi National Bank 35th Anniversary **Obv:** Value **Rev:** Bank building tower divide dates within circle **Edge:** Reeded

Date	Mintage	F	VF	XF	Unc	BU
ND (2003)	—	—	—	—	3.50	4.00

KM# 54 DIRHAM
6.4000 g., Copper-Nickel, 24 mm. **Subject:** 40th Anniversary of Crude Oil Exports **Obv:** Value **Rev:** "ADCO" logo **Edge:** Reeded

Date	Mintage	F	VF	XF	Unc	BU
ND (2003)	—	—	—	—	3.50	5.00

KM# 73 DIRHAM
6.4000 g., Copper-Nickel, 23.93 mm. **Subject:** WBG & IMF meeting in Dubai 2003 **Obv:** Denomination **Rev:** Mosaic arc **Edge:** Reeded

Date	Mintage	F	VF	XF	Unc	BU
2003	250,000	—	—	—	4.00	5.00

KM# 74 DIRHAM
6.4000 g., Copper-Nickel, 24 mm. **Subject:** First Gulf Bank 25th Anniversary **Obv:** Value **Rev:** Bank logo **Edge:** Reeded

Date	Mintage	F	VF	XF	Unc	BU
ND(2004)	—	—	—	—	4.00	5.00

KM# 83 DIRHAM
6.4700 g., Copper-Nickel, 24.02 mm. **Subject:** Honoring Mother of Nations **Obv:** Large value **Rev:** Inscription in flower bud at center **Rev. Legend:** Sheikha Fatima Bint Mubarak **Edge:** Reeded

Date	Mintage	F	VF	XF	Unc	BU
2005	—	—	—	—	4.00	5.00

KM# 6.2 DIRHAM
6.4000 g., Copper-Nickel, 24 mm. **Obv:** Value **Rev:** Jug above dates **Rev. Designer:** Geoffrey Colley **Edge:** Reeded **Note:** Reduced size.

Date	Mintage	F	VF	XF	Unc	BU
AH1425-2005	—	—	0.35	0.65	1.85	2.25
AH1428-2007	—	—	0.35	0.65	1.85	2.25

KM# 78 DIRHAM
6.4000 g., Copper-Nickel, 24 mm. **Obv:** Value **Obv. Legend:** UNITED ARAB EMIRATES **Rev:** Large "50" with Police badge in "0" **Rev. Legend:** DUABI POLICE GOLDEN JUBILEE **Edge:** Reeded

Date	Mintage	F	VF	XF	Unc	BU
ND(2006)	—	—	—	—	3.50	5.00

KM# 77 DIRHAM
6.3000 g., Copper-Nickel, 24 mm. **Obv:** Value **Rev:** Zakum Development Co. logo **Edge:** Reeded

Date	Mintage	F	VF	XF	Unc	BU
ND(2007)	—	—	—	—	3.50	5.00

KM# 76 DIRHAM
6.4000 g., Copper-Nickel, 24 mm. **Subject:** Sharjah International Airport, 75th Anniversary **Obv:** Value **Obv. Legend:** UNITED ARAB EMIRATES **Rev:** Three birds in flight under arc **Edge:** Reeded

Date	Mintage	F	VF	XF	Unc	BU
ND(2007)	—	—	—	—	3.00	4.00

KM# 96 DIRHAM
6.4000 g., Copper-Nickel, 24 mm. **Subject:** U.A.E. Boy Scouts, 50th Anniversary **Obv:** Value at center **Rev:** Scout Fleur-de-lis

Date	Mintage	F	VF	XF	Unc	BU
ND(2007)	—	—	—	—	3.50	5.00

KM# 84 DIRHAM
6.4000 g., Copper-Nickel, 24 mm. **Subject:** 10th Anniversary of the Hamdan Bin Rashed Award for Distinguished Academic Performance **Obv:** Large value **Rev:** 10 below pen with tip touching star **Edge:** Reeded

Date	Mintage	F	VF	XF	Unc	BU
ND(2007)	—	—	—	—	4.00	5.00

KM# 79 DIRHAM
6.4300 g., Copper-Nickel, 24.03 mm. **Obv:** Value **Obv. Legend:** UNITED ARAB EMIRATES **Rev:** Large "30" and logo **Rev. Legend:** 30TH ANNIVERSARY OF THE 1ST LNG SHIPMENT **Rev. Inscription:** ADGAS **Edge:** Reeded

Date	Mintage	F	VF	XF	Unc	BU
ND(2007)	—	—	—	—	3.50	5.00

KM# 85 DIRHAM
6.4000 g., Copper-Nickel **Subject:** National Bank of Abu Dhabi, 40th Anniversary **Obv:** Large value **Obv. Legend:** UNITED ARAB EMIRATES **Rev:** Large stylized "40" **Edge:** Reeded

Date	Mintage	F	VF	XF	Unc	BU
ND(2008)	—	—	—	—	3.00	4.00

KM# 47 50 DIRHAMS
40.2200 g., 0.9250 Silver 1.1961 oz. ASW, 40 mm. **Subject:** 25th Anniversary - Women's Union (1975-2000) **Obv:** Bust of President H. H. Sheikh Zayed bin Sultan Al Nahyan 7/8 right **Rev:** Stylized gazelle **Edge:** Reeded

Date	Mintage	F	VF	XF	Unc	BU
ND(2001) Proof	5,000	Value: 80.00				

KM# 59 50 DIRHAMS
40.0000 g., 0.9250 Silver 1.1895 oz. ASW, 40 mm. **Subject:** 25th Anniversary - Arab Bank of Investment and Foreign Trade **Edge:** Reeded

Date	Mintage	F	VF	XF	Unc	BU
ND(2001) Proof	2,000	Value: 100				

KM# 60 50 DIRHAMS
40.0000 g., 0.9250 Silver 1.1895 oz. ASW, 40 mm. **Subject:** 25th Anniversary - Armed Forces Unification **Edge:** Reeded

Date	Mintage	F	VF	XF	Unc	BU
ND(2001) Proof	10,000	Value: 75.00				

KM# 61 50 DIRHAMS
40.0000 g., 0.9250 Silver 1.1895 oz. ASW, 40 mm. **Subject:** 30th Anniversary - Al-Ain National Museum **Edge:** Reeded

Date	Mintage	F	VF	XF	Unc	BU
ND(2001) Proof	5,000	Value: 85.00				

KM# 62 50 DIRHAMS
40.0000 g., 0.9250 Silver 1.1895 oz. ASW, 40 mm. **Subject:** 25th Anniversary - University of the U.A.E. **Obv:** Bust of President H. H. Sheikh Zayed bin Sultan Al Nahyan 7/8 right **Rev:** Inscriptions **Edge:** Reeded

Date	Mintage	F	VF	XF	Unc	BU
ND(2002) Proof	5,000	Value: 85.00				

KM# 63 50 DIRHAMS
40.0000 g., 0.9250 Silver 1.1895 oz. ASW, 40 mm. **Subject:** Etisalat - Emirates Telecommunications, 25th Anniversary **Obv:** Value **Rev:** Stylized 25 **Edge:** Reeded

Date	Mintage	F	VF	XF	Unc	BU
ND(2002) Proof	5,000	Value: 85.00				

KM# 64 50 DIRHAMS
40.0000 g., 0.9250 Silver 1.1895 oz. ASW, 40 mm. **Subject:** Sheikh Hamdan bin Rashid al Maktoum Award for Medical Sciences **Obv:** Value **Rev:** Sheikh Hamdan bin Rashid al Maktoum bust 3/4 left **Edge:** Reeded

Date	Mintage	F	VF	XF	Unc	BU
ND(2002) Proof	2,000	Value: 100				

KM# 65 50 DIRHAMS
40.0000 g., 0.9250 Silver 1.1895 oz. ASW, 40 mm. **Subject:** Al Ahmadia School, 90th Anniversary **Obv:** Sheikh Rashid bin Saaed al Maktoum 3/4 left **Rev:** School building **Edge:** Reeded

Date	Mintage	F	VF	XF	Unc	BU
ND(2002) Proof	5,000	Value: 85.00				

KM# 67 50 DIRHAMS
40.0000 g., 0.9250 Silver 1.1895 oz. ASW, 40 mm. **Subject:** Administrative Development Institute, 20th Anniversary **Obv:** Sheikh Zayed bin Sultan al Nahyan bust 3/4 right **Rev:** Eagle **Edge:** Reeded

Date	Mintage	F	VF	XF	Unc	BU
ND(2002) Proof	2,000	Value: 100				

KM# 68 50 DIRHAMS
40.0000 g., 0.9250 Silver 1.1895 oz. ASW, 40 mm. **Subject:** U.A.E. Central Bank, 30th Anniversary **Obv:** Sheikh Zayed bin Sultan al Nahyan bust 3/4 right **Rev:** Sheikh Maktoum bin Rashid al Maktoum bust 3/4 right **Edge:** Reeded

Date	Mintage	F	VF	XF	Unc	BU
ND(2003) Proof	5,000	Value: 85.00				

KM# 69 50 DIRHAMS
40.0000 g., 0.9250 Silver 1.1895 oz. ASW, 40 mm. **Subject:** 58th Annual Meeting of the World Bank Group and the Int'l Money Fund **Obv:** Colored dots **Edge:** Reeded

Date	Mintage	F	VF	XF	Unc	BU
ND(2003) Proof	10,000	Value: 75.00				

KM# 50 50 DIRHAMS
40.0000 g., 0.9250 Silver 1.1895 oz. ASW, 40 mm. **Obv:** Value **Rev:** FIFA 2003 World Youth Soccer Championship **Edge:** Reeded

Date	Mintage	F	VF	XF	Unc	BU
ND(2003) Proof	—	Value: 85.00				

KM# 66 50 DIRHAMS
40.0000 g., 0.9250 Silver 1.1895 oz. ASW, 40 mm. **Subject:** Ministry of Finance and Industry ISO Certification **Obv:** Value **Rev:** Eagle at center **Edge:** Reeded

Date	Mintage	F	VF	XF	Unc	BU
ND(2003) Proof	3,000	Value: 95.00				

KM# 70 50 DIRHAMS
40.0000 g., 0.9250 Silver 1.1895 oz. ASW, 40 mm. **Subject:** 40th Anniversary - First Oil Export from Abu Dhabi Onshore Oil Fields (ADCO) **Obv:** Bust of President H. H. Sheikh Zayed bin Sultan Al Nayhan 3/4 right **Rev:** Logo **Edge:** Reeded

Date	Mintage	F	VF	XF	Unc	BU
ND(2004) Proof	—	Value: 300				

KM# 71 50 DIRHAMS
40.0000 g., 0.9250 Silver 1.1895 oz. ASW, 40 mm. **Subject:** 25th Anniversary - Sharjah City for Humanitarian Services (SCHS) **Edge:** Reeded

Date	Mintage	F	VF	XF	Unc	BU
ND(2005) Proof	—	Value: 85.00				

KM# 87 50 DIRHAMS
40.0000 g., 0.9250 Silver 1.1895 oz. ASW, 40 mm. **Subject:** Mother of the Nation - Seikha Fatima Bint Mubarak

Date	Mintage	F	VF	XF	Unc	BU
2005 Proof	—	Value: 85.00				

KM# 98 50 DIRHAMS
40.0000 g., 0.9250 Silver 1.1895 oz. ASW, 40 mm. **Subject:** Sheikha Fatima Birt Mubarak, Mother of the Nation

Date	Mintage	F	VF	XF	Unc	BU
2005 Proof	—	Value: 85.00				

KM# 82 50 DIRHAMS
40.0000 g., Silver, 40 mm. **Subject:** 25th Anniversary Emirates Banks Association **Obv:** Value **Obv. Legend:** UNITED ARAB EMIRATES **Rev:** Logo **Edge:** Reeded

Date	Mintage	F	VF	XF	Unc	BU
ND(2007) Proof	—	Value: 90.00				

KM# 95 50 DIRHAMS
40.0000 g., 0.9250 Silver 1.1895 oz. ASW, 40 mm. **Subject:** Hamdan Bin Rashed Award for Distinguished Academic Performance **Obv:** Denomination, legend above **Rev:** Pen with tip touching star, legend above **Edge:** Reeded **Note:** Issued 10th Anniversary of the Award

Date	Mintage	F	VF	XF	Unc	BU
ND(2008) Proof	—	Value: 600				

KM# 80 100 DIRHAMS
60.0000 g., 0.9250 Silver 1.7843 oz. ASW, 50 mm. **Obv:** Sheikh Zayed bin Sultan **Rev:** Sheikh Zayed Mosque

Date	Mintage	F	VF	XF	Unc	BU
2004 Proof	—	Value: 120				

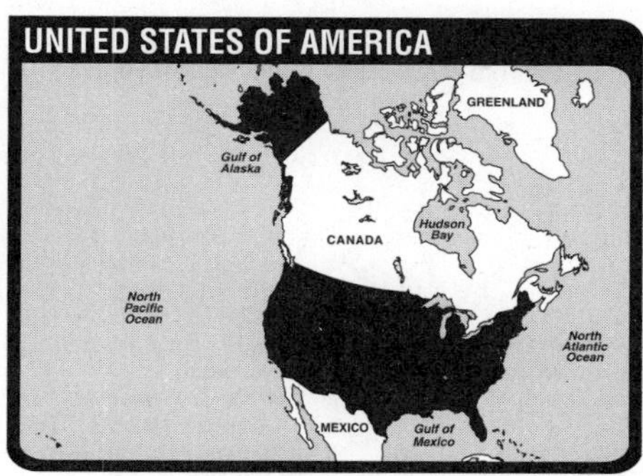

KM# 97 100 DIRHAMS
60.0000 g., 0.9250 Silver 1.7843 oz. ASW, 50 mm. **Subject:** Sheikh Khalifa Ben Zayed, 1st Anniversary **Rev:** Emir's Palace

Date	Mintage	F	VF	XF	Unc	BU
2005 Proof	—	Value: 120				

UNITED STATES OF AMERICA

The United States of America as politically organized, under the Articles of Confederation consisted of the 13 original British-American colonies; New Hampshire, Massachusetts, Rhode Island, Connecticut, New York, New Jersey, Pennsylvania, Delaware, Virginia, North Carolina, South Carolina, Georgia and Maryland. Clustered along the eastern seaboard of North America between the forests of Maine and the marshes of Georgia. Under the Article of Confederation, the United States had no national capital: Philadelphia, where the "United States in Congress Assembled", was the "seat of government". The population during this political phase of America's history (1781-1789) was about 3 million, most of whom lived on self-sufficient family farms. Fishing, lumbering and the production of grains for export were major economic endeavors. Rapid strides were also being made in industry and manufacturing by 1775, the (then) colonies were accounting for one-seventh of the world's production of raw iron.

On the basis of the voyage of John Cabot to the North American mainland in 1497, England claimed the entire continent. The first permanent English settlement was established at Jamestown, Virginia, in 1607. France and Spain also claimed extensive territory in North America. At the end of the French and Indian Wars (1763), England acquired all of the territory east of the Mississippi River, including East and West Florida. From 1776 to 1781, the States were governed by the Continental Congress. From 1781 to 1789, they were organized under the Articles of Confederation, during which period the individual States had the right to issue money. Independence from Great Britain was attained with the American Revolution in 1776. The Constitution organized and governs the present United States. It was ratified on Nov. 21, 1788.

MINT MARKS
C – Charlotte, N.C., 1838-61
CC – Carson City, NV, 1870-93
D – Dahlonega, GA, 1838-61
D – Denver, CO, 1906-present
O – New Orleans, LA, 1838-1909
P – Philadelphia, PA, 1793-present
S – San Francisco, CA, 1854-present
W – West Point, NY, 1984-present

MONETARY SYSTEM
Trime = 3 Cents
Nickel = 5 Cents
Dime = 10 Cents
Quarter = 25 Cents
Half Dollar = 50 Cents
Dollar = 100 Cents
Quarter Eagle = $2.50 Gold
Stella = $4.00 Gold
Half Eagle = $5.00 Gold
Eagle = $10.00 Gold
Double Eagle = $20.00 Gold

BULLION COINS
Silver Eagle = $1.00
Gold 1/10 Ounce = $5.00
Gold ¼ Ounce = $10.00
Gold ½ Ounce = $25.00
Gold Ounce = $50.00
Platinum 1/10 Ounce = $10.00
Platinum ¼ Ounce = $25.00
Platinum ½ Ounce = $50.00
Platinum Ounce = $100.00

CIRCULATION COINAGE

CENT

Lincoln Cent

Lincoln Memorial reverse

KM# 201b • Copper Plated Zinc, 19 mm. • **Notes:** MS60 prices are for brown coins and MS65 prices are for coins that are at least 90% original red.

Date	Mintage	XF-40	MS-65	Prf-65
2001	4,959,600,000	—	.25	—
2001D	5,374,990,000	—	.25	—
2001S	3,099,096	—	—	4.00
2002	3,260,800,000	—	.25	—
2002S	3,157,739	—	—	4.00
2002D	4,028,055,000	—	.25	—
2003	3,300,000,000	—	.25	—
2003D	3,548,000,000	—	.25	—
2003S	3,116,590	—	—	4.00
2004	3,379,600,000	—	.25	—
2004D	3,456,400,000	—	.25	—
2004S	2,992,069	—	—	4.00
2005	3,935,600,000	—	.25	—
2005D	3,764,450,000	—	.25	—
2005S	3,273,000	—	—	4.00
2006	4,290,000,000	—	.25	—
2006D	3,944,000,000	—	.25	—
2006S	2,923,105	—	—	4.00
2007	—	—	1.50	—
2007D	—	—	1.50	—
2007S	—	—	—	4.00
2008	—	—	1.50	—
2008D	—	—	1.50	—
2008S	—	—	—	4.00

Lincoln Bicentennial

Bust right obverse Log cabin reverse

KM# 441 • 2.5000 g., **Copper Plated Zinc**, 19 mm. • **Rev. Designer:** Richard Masters and James Licaretz

Date	Mintage	XF-40	MS-65	Prf-65
2009P	284,400,000	—	1.50	—
2009D	350,400,000	—	1.50	—

Log cabin reverse

KM# 441a • 3.3100 g., **Brass** • **Rev. Designer:** Richard Masters and James Licaretz

Date	Mintage	XF-40	MS-65	Prf-65
2009S	—	—	—	4.00

Lincoln seated on log reverse

KM# 442 • 2.5000 g., **Copper Plated Zinc**, 19 mm. • **Rev. Designer:** Charles Vickers

Date	Mintage	XF-40	MS-65	Prf-65
2009P	376,000,000	—	1.50	—
2009D	363,600,000	—	1.50	—

KM# 442a • 3.1100 g., **Brass**, 19 mm. • **Rev. Designer:** Charles Vickers

Date	Mintage	XF-40	MS-65	Prf-65
2009S	—	—	—	4.00

Lincoln standing before Illinois Statehouse reverse

KM# 443 • 2.5000 g., **Copper Plated Zinc**, 19 mm. • **Rev. Designer:** Joel Ishowitz and Don Everhart

Date	Mintage	XF-40	MS-65	Prf-65
2009P	316,000,000	—	1.50	—
2009D	336,000,000	—	1.50	—

KM# 443a • 3.1100 g., **Brass**, 19 mm. • **Rev. Designer:** Joel Iskowitz and Don Everhart

Date	Mintage	XF-40	MS-65	Prf-65
2009S	—	—	—	4.00

Capitol Building reverse

KM# 444 • 2.5000 g., **Copper Plated Zinc** • **Rev. Designer:** Susan Gamble and Joseph Menna

Date	Mintage	XF-40	MS-65	Prf-65
2009P	129,600,000	—	1.50	—
2009D	198,000,000	—	1.50	—

Capitol Building reverse

KM# 444a • 3.1100 g., **Brass**, 19 mm. • **Rev. Designer:** Susan Ganmble and Joseph Menna

Date	Mintage	XF-40	MS-65	Prf-65
2009S	—	—	—	4.00

Lincoln bust right obverse Shield reverse

KM# 468 • 2.5000 g., **Copper Plated Zinc**, 19 mm. • **Obv. Designer:** Victor D. Brenner **Rev. Designer:** Lyndall Bass and Joseph Menna

Date	Mintage	XF-40	MS-65	Prf-65
2010P	—	—	1.50	—
2010D	—	—	1.50	—
2010S	—	—	—	4.00
2011P	—	—	1.50	—
2011D	—	—	1.50	—
2011S	—	—	—	4.00

5 CENTS

Jefferson Nickel

Pre-war design resumed reverse

KM# A192 • 5.0000 g., **Copper-Nickel**, 21.2 mm. • **Designer:** Felix Schlag **Edge Desc:** Plain

Date	Mintage	XF-40	MS-65	Prf-65
2001P	675,704,000	—	.50	—
2001D	627,680,000	—	.50	—
2001S	3,099,096	—	—	4.00
2002P	539,280,000	—	.50	—
2002D	691,200,000	—	.50	—
2002S	3,157,739	—	—	2.00
2003P	441,840,000	—	.50	—
2003D	383,040,000	—	.50	—
2003S	3,116,590	—	—	2.00

Jefferson - Westward Expansion - Lewis & Clark Bicentennial

Jefferson era peace medal design: two clasped hands, pipe and hatchet reverse

KM# 360 • 5.0000 g., **Copper-Nickel**, 21.2 mm. • **Obv. Designer:** Felix Schlag **Rev. Designer:** Norman E. Nemeth

Date	Mintage	MS-65	Prf-65
2004P	361,440,000	1.50	—
2004D	372,000,000	1.50	—
2004S	—	—	10.00

Lewis and Clark's Keelboat reverse

KM# 361 • 5.0000 g., **Copper-Nickel**, 21.2 mm. • **Obv. Designer:** Felix Schlag **Rev. Designer:** Al Maletsky

Date	Mintage	MS-65	Prf-65
2004P	366,720,000	1.50	—
2004D	344,880,000	1.50	—
2004S	—	—	10.00

Thomas Jefferson large profile right obverse American Bison right reverse

KM# 368 • 5.0000 g., **Copper-Nickel**, 21.2 mm. • **Obv. Designer:** Joe Fitzgerald and Don Everhart II **Rev. Designer:** Jamie Franki and Norman E. Nemeth

Date	Mintage	MS-65	Prf-65
2005P	448,320,000	1.50	—
2005D	487,680,000	1.50	—
2005S	—	—	6.50

Jefferson, large profile obverse Pacific coastline reverse

KM# 369 • 5.0000 g., **Copper-Nickel**, 21.2 mm. • **Obv. Designer:** Joe Fitzgerald and Don Everhart **Rev. Designer:** Joe Fitzgerald and Donna Weaver

Date	Mintage	MS-65	Prf-65
2005P	394,080,000	1.25	—
2005D	411,120,000	1.25	—
2005S	—	—	5.50

Jefferson large facing portrait - Enhanced Monticello Reverse

Jefferson head facing obverse Monticello, enhanced design reverse

KM# 381 • 5.0000 g., **Copper-Nickel**, 21.2 mm. • **Obv. Designer:** Jamie N. Franki and Donna Weaver **Rev. Designer:** Felix Schlag and John Mercanti

Date	Mintage	MS-65	Prf-65
2006P	693,120,000	2.50	—
2006P Satin finish	—	4.00	—
2006D	809,280,000	2.50	—
2006D Satin finish	—	4.00	—
2006S	—	—	5.00
2007P	—	2.50	—
2007P Satin finish	—	4.00	—
2007D	—	2.50	—
2007D Satin finish	—	4.00	—
2007S	—	—	4.00
2008P	—	2.50	—
2008P Satin finish	—	4.00	—
2008D	—	2.50	—
2008D Satin finish	—	4.00	—
2008S	—	—	4.00
2009P	—	2.50	—
2009P Satin finish	—	4.00	—
2009D	—	2.50	—
2009D Satin finish	—	4.00	—
2009S	—	—	3.00
2010P	—	2.50	—
2010P Satin finish	—	4.00	—
2010D	—	2.50	—
2010D Satin finish	—	4.00	—
2010S	—	—	3.00
2011P	—	2.50	—
2011D	—	2.50	—
2011S	—	—	3.00

DIME

Roosevelt Dime

Mint mark 1968- present

1982 No mint mark

KM# 195a • 2.2680 g., **Copper-Nickel Clad Copper**, 17.91 mm. • **Designer:** John R. Sinnock **Notes:** The 1979-S and 1981-S Type II proofs have clearer mint marks than the Type I proofs of those years. On the 1982 no-mint-mark variety, the mint mark was inadvertently left off.

Date	Mintage	MS-65	Prf-65
2001P	1,369,590,000	1.00	—
2001D	1,412,800,000	1.00	—
2001S	2,249,496	—	1.00
2002P	1,187,500,000	1.00	—
2002D	1,379,500,000	1.00	—
2002S	2,268,913	—	2.00
2003P	1,085,500,000	1.00	—
2003D	986,500,000	1.00	—
2003S	2,076,165	—	2.00
2004P	1,328,000,000	1.00	—
2004D	1,159,500,000	1.00	—
2004S	1,804,396	—	4.75
2005P	1,412,000,000	1.00	—
2005D	1,423,500,000	1.00	—
2005S	—	—	2.25
2006P	1,381,000,000	1.00	—
2006D	1,447,000,000	1.00	—
2006S	—	—	2.25
2007P	—	1.00	—
2007D	—	1.00	—
2007S	—	—	2.25
2008P	—	1.00	—
2008D	—	1.00	—
2008S	—	—	2.25
2009P	—	1.00	—
2009D	—	1.00	—
2009S	—	—	2.25
2010P	—	1.00	—
2010D	—	1.00	—
2010S	—	—	2.25
2011P	—	1.00	—
2011D	—	1.00	—
2011S	—	—	2.25

KM# 195b • 2.5000 g., 0.9000 **Silver**, 0.0723 oz. ASW, 17.9 mm. • **Designer:** John R. Sinnock

Date	Mintage	Prf-65
2001S	849,600	5.00
2002S	888,826	5.00
2003S	1,090,425	4.00
2004S	—	4.50
2005S	—	3.50
2006S	—	3.50
2007S	—	3.50
2008S	—	3.50
2009S	—	3.50
2010S	—	3.50
2011S	—	3.50

QUARTER

50 State Quarters

Kentucky

KM# 322 • 5.6700 g., **Copper-Nickel Clad Copper** •

Date	Mintage	MS-63	MS-65	Prf-65
2001P	353,000,000	1.20	6.50	—
2001D	370,564,000	1.00	7.00	—
2001S	3,094,140	—	—	11.00

KM# 322a • 6.2500 g., 0.9000 **Silver**, 0.1808 oz. ASW •

Date	Mintage	MS-63	MS-65	Prf-65
2001S	889,697	—	—	21.00

New York

KM# 318 • 5.6700 g., **Copper-Nickel Clad Copper** •

Date	Mintage	MS-63	MS-65	Prf-65
2001P	655,400,000	1.00	5.50	—
2001D	619,640,000	1.00	5.50	—
2001S	3,094,140	—	—	11.00

KM# 318a • 6.2500 g., 0.9000 **Silver**, 0.1808 oz. ASW •

Date	Mintage	MS-63	MS-65	Prf-65
2001S	889,697	—	—	24.00

North Carolina

KM# 319 • 5.6700 g., **Copper-Nickel Clad Copper** •

Date	Mintage	MS-63	MS-65	Prf-65
2001P	627,600,000	1.00	5.50	—
2001D	427,876,000	1.00	6.50	—
2001S	3,094,140	—	—	11.00

KM# 319a • 6.2500 g., 0.9000 **Silver**, 0.1808 oz. ASW •

Date	Mintage	MS-63	MS-65	Prf-65
2001S	889,697	—	—	22.00

Rhode Island

KM# 320 • 5.6700 g., **Copper-Nickel Clad Copper** •

Date	Mintage	MS-63	MS-65	Prf-65
2001P	423,000,000	1.00	5.50	—
2001D	447,100,000	1.00	6.00	—
2001S	3,094,140	—	—	11.00

KM# 320a • 6.2500 g., 0.9000 **Silver**, 0.1808 oz. ASW •

Date	Mintage	MS-63	MS-65	Prf-65
2001S	889,697	—	—	19.00

Vermont

KM# 321 • 5.6700 g., **Copper-Nickel Clad Copper** •

Date	Mintage	MS-63	MS-65	Prf-65
2001P	423,400,000	1.20	6.50	—
2001D	459,404,000	1.00	6.50	—
2001S	3,094,140	—	—	11.00

KM# 321a • 6.2500 g., 0.9000 **Silver**, 0.1808 oz. ASW •

Date	Mintage	MS-63	MS-65	Prf-65
2001S	889,697	—	—	19.00

Indiana

KM# 334 • 5.6700 g., **Copper-Nickel Clad Copper** •

Date	Mintage	MS-63	MS-65	Prf-65
2002P	362,600,000	1.00	5.00	—
2002D	327,200,000	1.00	5.00	—
2002S	3,084,245	—	—	4.00

KM# 334a • 6.2500 g., 0.9000 **Silver**, 0.1808 oz. ASW •

Date	Mintage	MS-63	MS-65	Prf-65
2002S	892,229	—	—	9.00

Louisiana

KM# 333 • 5.6700 g., **Copper-Nickel Clad Copper** •

Date	Mintage	MS-63	MS-65	Prf-65
2002P	362,000,000	1.00	5.50	—
2002D	402,204,000	1.00	6.00	—
2002S	3,084,245	—	—	4.00

KM# 333a • 6.2500 g., 0.9000 **Silver**, 0.1808 oz. ASW •

Date	Mintage	MS-63	MS-65	Prf-65
2002S	892,229	—	—	9.00

Mississippi

KM# 335 • 5.6700 g., **Copper-Nickel Clad Copper** •

Date	Mintage	MS-63	MS-65	Prf-65
2002P	290,000,000	1.00	5.00	—
2002D	289,600,000	1.00	5.00	—
2002S	3,084,245	—	—	4.00

KM# 335a • 6.2500 g., 0.9000 **Silver**, 0.1808 oz. ASW •

Date	Mintage	MS-63	MS-65	Prf-65
2002S	892,229	—	—	9.00

Ohio

KM# 332 • 5.6700 g., **Copper-Nickel Clad Copper** •

Date	Mintage	MS-63	MS-65	Prf-65
2002P	217,200,000	1.00	5.50	—
2002D	414,832,000	1.00	5.50	—
2002S	3,084,245	—	—	4.00

KM# 332a • 6.2500 g., 0.9000 **Silver**, 0.1808 oz. ASW •

Date	Mintage	MS-63	MS-65	Prf-65
2002S	892,229	—	—	9.00

Tennessee

KM# 331 • 5.6700 g., **Copper-Nickel Clad Copper** •

Date	Mintage	MS-63	MS-65	Prf-65
2002P	361,600,000	1.40	6.50	—
2002D	286,468,000	1.40	7.00	—
2002S	3,084,245	—	—	4.00

KM# 331a • 6.2500 g., 0.9000 **Silver**, 0.1808 oz. ASW •

Date	Mintage	MS-63	MS-65	Prf-65
2002S	892,229	—	—	9.00

Alabama

KM# 344 • 5.6700 g., **Copper-Nickel Clad Copper** •

Date	Mintage	MS-63	MS-65	Prf-65
2003P	225,000,000	1.00	5.00	—
2003D	232,400,000	1.00	5.00	—
2003S	3,408,516	—	—	3.50

KM# 344a • 6.2500 g., 0.9000 **Silver**, 0.1808 oz. ASW •

Date	Mintage	MS-63	MS-65	Prf-65
2003S	1,257,555	—	—	5.25

Arkansas

KM# 347 • 5.6700 g., **Copper-Nickel Clad Copper** •

Date	Mintage	MS-63	MS-65	Prf-65
2003P	228,000,000	1.00	5.00	—
2003D	229,800,000	1.00	5.00	—
2003S	3,408,516	—	—	3.50

KM# 347a • 6.2500 g., 0.9000 **Silver**, 0.1808 oz. ASW •

Date	Mintage	MS-63	MS-65	Prf-65
2003S	1,257,555	—	—	5.25

Illinois

KM# 343 • 5.6700 g., **Copper-Nickel Clad Copper** •

Date	Mintage	MS-63	MS-65	Prf-65
2003P	225,800,000	1.10	5.00	—
2003D	237,400,000	1.10	5.00	—
2003S	3,408,516	—	—	3.50

KM# 343a • 6.2500 g., 0.9000 **Silver**, 0.1808 oz. ASW •

Date	Mintage	MS-63	MS-65	Prf-65
2003S	1,257,555	—	—	5.25

Maine

KM# 345 • 5.6700 g., **Copper-Nickel Clad Copper** •

Date	Mintage	MS-63	MS-65	Prf-65
2003P	217,400,000	1.00	5.00	—
2003D	213,400,000	1.00	5.00	—
2003S	3,408,516	—	—	3.50

KM# 345a • 6.2500 g., 0.9000 **Silver**, 0.1808 oz. ASW •

Date	Mintage	MS-63	MS-65	Prf-65
2003S	1,257,555	—	—	5.25

Missouri

KM# 346 • **Copper-Nickel Clad Copper** •

Date	Mintage	MS-63	MS-65	Prf-65
2003P	225,000,000	1.00	5.00	—
2003D	228,200,000	1.00	5.00	—
2003S	3,408,516	—	—	3.50

KM# 346a • 6.2500 g., 0.9000 **Silver**, 0.1808 oz. ASW •

Date	Mintage	MS-63	MS-65	Prf-65
2003S	1,257,555	—	—	5.25

Florida

KM# 356 • 5.6700 g., **Copper-Nickel Clad Copper** •

Date	Mintage	MS-63	MS-65	Prf-65
2004P	240,200,000	.75	5.00	—
2004D	241,600,000	.75	5.00	—
2004S	2,740,684	—	—	5.00

KM# 356a • 6.2500 g., 0.9000 **Silver**, 0.1808 oz. ASW •

Date	Mintage	MS-63	MS-65	Prf-65
2004S	1,775,370	—	—	6.00

Iowa

KM# 358 • 5.6700 g., **Copper-Nickel Clad Copper** •

Date	Mintage	MS-63	MS-65	Prf-65
2004P	213,800,000	.75	5.00	—
2004D	251,800,000	.75	5.00	—
2004S	2,740,684	—	—	5.00

KM# 358a • 6.2500 g., 0.9000 **Silver**, 0.1808 oz. ASW •

Date	Mintage	MS-63	MS-65	Prf-65
2004S	—	—	—	6.00

Michigan

KM# 355 • 5.6700 g., **Copper-Nickel Clad Copper** •

Date	Mintage	MS-63	MS-65	Prf-65
2004P	233,800,000	.75	5.00	—
2004D	225,800,000	.75	5.00	—
2004S	2,740,684	—	—	5.00

KM# 355a • 6.2500 g., 0.9000 **Silver**, 0.1808 oz. ASW •

Date	Mintage	MS-63	MS-65	Prf-65
2004S	1,775,370	—	—	6.00

Texas

KM# 357 • 5.6700 g., **Copper-Nickel Clad Copper** •

Date	Mintage	MS-63	MS-65	Prf-65
2004P	278,800,000	.75	5.00	—
2004D	263,000,000	.75	5.00	—
2004S	2,740,684	—	—	5.00

KM# 357a • 6.2500 g., 0.9000 **Silver**, 0.1808 oz. ASW •

Date	Mintage	MS-63	MS-65	Prf-65
2004S	1,775,370	—	—	6.00

Wisconsin

KM# 359 • 5.6700 g., **Copper-Nickel Clad Copper** •

Date	Mintage	MS-63	MS-65	Prf-65
2004P	226,400,000	1.00	5.00	—
2004D	226,800,000	1.00	5.00	—
2004D Extra Leaf Low	Est. 9,000	300	600	—
2004D Extra Leaf High	Est. 3,000	400	900	—
2004S	—	—	—	5.00

KM# 359a • 6.2500 g., 0.9000 **Silver**, 0.1808 oz. ASW •

Date	Mintage	MS-63	MS-65	Prf-65
2004S	1,775,370	—	—	6.00

California

KM# 370 • 5.6700 g., **Copper-Nickel Clad Copper** •

Date	Mintage	MS-63	MS-65	Prf-65
2005P	257,200,000	.75	5.00	—
2005P Satin Finish	Inc. above	3.50	4.50	—
2005D	263,200,000	.75	5.00	—
2005D Satin Finish	Inc. above	3.50	4.50	—
2005S	3,262,960	—	—	3.00

KM# 370a • 6.2500 g., 0.9000 **Silver**, 0.1808 oz. ASW •

Date	Mintage	MS-63	MS-65	Prf-65
2005S	1,679,600	—	—	5.50

Kansas

KM# 373 • 5.6700 g., **Copper-Nickel Clad Copper** •

Date	Mintage	MS-63	MS-65	Prf-65
2005P	263,400,000	.75	5.00	—
2005P Satin Finish	Inc. above	3.50	4.50	—
2005D	300,000,000	.75	5.00	—
2005D Satin Finish	Inc. above	3.50	4.50	—
2005S	3,262,960	—	—	3.00

KM# 373a • 6.2500 g., 0.9000 **Silver**, 0.1808 oz. ASW •

Date	Mintage	MS-63	MS-65	Prf-65
2005S	1,679,600	—	—	5.50

Minnesota

KM# 371 • 5.6700 g., **Copper-Nickel Clad Copper** •

Date	Mintage	MS-63	MS-65	Prf-65
2005P	226,400,000	.75	5.00	—
2005P Satin Finish	Inc. above	3.50	4.50	—
2005D	226,800,000	.75	5.00	—
2005D Satin Finish	Inc. above	3.50	4.50	—
2005S	3,262,960	—	—	3.00

KM# 371a • 6.2500 g., 0.9000 **Silver**, 0.1808 oz. ASW •

Date	Mintage	MS-63	MS-65	Prf-65
2005S	1,679,600	—	—	5.50

Oregon

KM# 372 • 5.6700 g., **Copper-Nickel Clad Copper** •

Date	Mintage	MS-63	MS-65	Prf-65
2005P	316,200,000	.75	5.00	—
2005P Satin Finish	Inc. above	3.50	4.50	—
2005D	404,000,000	.75	5.00	—
2005D Satin Finish	Inc. above	3.50	4.50	—
2005S	3,262,960	—	—	3.00

KM# 372a • 6.2500 g., 0.9000 **Silver**, 0.1808 oz. ASW •

Date	Mintage	MS-63	MS-65	Prf-65
2005S	1,679,600	—	—	5.50

West Virginia

KM# 374 • 5.6700 g., **Copper-Nickel Clad Copper** •

Date	Mintage	MS-63	MS-65	Prf-65
2005P	365,400,000	.75	5.00	—
2005P Satin Finish	Inc. above	3.50	4.50	—
2005D	356,200,000	.75	5.00	—
2005D Satin Finish	Inc. above	3.50	4.50	—
2005S	3,262,960	—	—	3.00

KM# 374a • 6.2500 g., 0.9000 **Silver**, 0.1808 oz. ASW •

Date	Mintage	MS-63	MS-65	Prf-65
2005S	1,679,600	—	—	5.50

Colorado

KM# 384 • 5.7100 g., **Copper-Nickel Clad Copper**, 0 oz., 24.2 mm. •

Date	Mintage	MS-63	MS-65	Prf-65
2006P	274,800,000	.75	5.00	—
2006P Satin Finish	Inc. above	3.00	4.50	—
2006D	294,200,000	.75	5.00	—
2006D Satin Finish	Inc. above	3.00	4.50	—
2006S	2,862,078	—	—	5.00

KM# 384a • 6.2500 g., 0.9000 **Silver**, 0.1808 oz. ASW •

Date	Mintage	MS-63	MS-65	Prf-65
2006S	1,571,839	—	—	5.75

Nebraska

KM# 383 • 5.6700 g., **Copper-Nickel Clad Copper** •

Date	Mintage	MS-63	MS-65	Prf-65
2006P	318,000,000	.75	5.00	—
2006P Satin Finish	Inc. above	3.00	4.50	—
2006D	273,000,000	.75	5.00	—
2006D Satin Finish	Inc. above	3.00	4.50	—
2006S	2,862,078	—	—	5.00

KM# 383a • 6.2500 g., 0.9000 **Silver**, 0.1808 oz. ASW •

Date	Mintage	MS-63	MS-65	Prf-65
2006S	1,571,839	—	—	5.75

Nevada

KM# 382 • 5.6700 g., **Copper-Nickel Clad Copper** •

Date	Mintage	MS-63	MS-65	Prf-65
2006P	277,000,000	.75	5.00	—
2006P Satin Finish	Inc. above	3.00	4.50	—
2006D	312,800,000	.75	5.00	—
2006D Satin Finish	Inc. above	3.00	4.50	—
2006S	2,862,078	—	—	5.00

KM# 382a • 6.2500 g., 0.9000 **Silver**, 0.1808 oz. ASW •

Date	Mintage	MS-63	MS-65	Prf-65
2006S	1,571,839	—	—	5.75

North Dakota

KM# 385 • 5.7200 g., **Copper-Nickel Clad Copper**, 24.2 mm. •

Date	Mintage	MS-63	MS-65	Prf-65
2006P	305,800,000	.75	5.00	—
2006P Satin Finish	Inc. above	3.00	4.50	—
2006D	359,000,000	.75	5.00	—
2006D Satin Finish	Inc. above	3.00	4.50	—
2006S	2,862,078	—	—	5.00

KM# 385a • 6.2500 g., 0.9000 **Silver**, 0.1808 oz. ASW •

Date	Mintage	MS-63	MS-65	Prf-65
2006S	1,571,839	—	—	5.75

South Dakota

KM# 386 • 5.6500 g., **Copper-Nickel Clad Copper**, 24.3 mm. •

Date	Mintage	MS-63	MS-65	Prf-65
2006P	245,000,000	.75	5.00	—
2006P Satin Finish	Inc. above	3.00	4.50	—
2006D	265,800,000	.75	5.00	—
2006D Satin Finish	Inc. above	3.00	4.50	—
2006S	2,862,078	—	—	5.00

KM# 386a • 6.2500 g., 0.9000 **Silver**, 0.1808 oz. ASW •

Date	Mintage	MS-63	MS-65	Prf-65
2006S	1,571,839	—	—	5.75

Idaho

KM# 398 • 5.6700 g., **Copper-Nickel Clad Copper** •

Date	Mintage	MS-63	MS-65	Prf-65
2007P	294,600,000	.75	8.00	—
2007P Satin finish	—	3.00	4.50	—
2007D	286,800,000	.75	8.00	—
2007D Satin finish	—	3.00	4.50	—
2007S	2,374,778	—	—	4.00

KM# 398a • 6.2500 g., 0.9000 **Silver**, 0.1808 oz. ASW •

Date	Mintage	MS-63	MS-65	Prf-65
2007S	1,299,878	—	—	6.50

Montana

KM# 396 • 5.6700 g., **Copper-Nickel Clad Copper** •

Date	Mintage	MS-63	MS-65	Prf-65
2007P	257,000,000	.75	8.00	—
2007D	256,240,000	.75	5.00	—
2007S	2,374,778	—	—	4.00

KM# 396a • 6.2500 g., 0.9000 **Silver**, 0.1808 oz. ASW •

Date	Mintage	MS-63	MS-65	Prf-65
2007S	1,299,878	—	—	6.50

Utah

KM# 400 • **Copper-Nickel Clad Copper** •

Date	Mintage	MS-63	MS-65	Prf-65
2007P	255,000,000	.75	5.00	—
2007P Satin finish	—	3.00	4.50	—
2007D	253,200,000	.75	5.00	—
2007CC Satin finish	—	3.00	4.50	—
2007S	2,374,778	—	—	4.00

KM# 400a • 6.2500 g., 0.9000 **Silver**, 0.1808 oz. ASW •

Date	Mintage	MS-63	MS-65	Prf-65
2007S	1,299,878	—	—	6.50

Washington

KM# 397 • 5.6700 g., **Copper-Nickel Clad Copper** •

Date	Mintage	MS-63	MS-65	Prf-65
2007P	265,200,000	.75	8.00	—
2007P Satin Finish	—	3.00	4.50	—
2007D	280,000,000	.75	8.00	—
2007D Satin Finish	—	3.00	4.50	—
2007S	2,374,778	—	—	4.00

KM# 397a • 6.2500 g., 0.9000 **Silver**, 0.1808 oz. ASW •

Date	Mintage	MS-63	MS-65	Prf-65
2007S	1,299,878	—	—	6.50

Wyoming

KM# 399 • 5.6700 g., **Copper-Nickel Clad Copper** •

Date	Mintage	MS-63	MS-65	Prf-65
2007P	243,600,000	.75	5.00	—
2007P Satin finish	—	3.00	4.50	—
2007D	320,800,000	.75	5.00	—
2007 Satin finish	—	3.00	4.50	—
2007S	2,374,778	—	—	4.00

KM# 399a • 6.2500 g., 0.9000 **Silver**, 0.1808 oz. ASW •

Date	Mintage	MS-63	MS-65	Prf-65
2007S	1,299,878	—	—	6.50

Alaska

KM# 424 • 5.6700 g., **Copper-Nickel Clad Copper** •

Date	Mintage	MS-63	MS-65	Prf-65
2008P	251,800,000	.75	5.00	—
2008P Satin finish	—	3.00	4.50	—
2008D	254,000,000	.75	5.00	—
2008D Satin finish	—	3.00	4.50	—
2008S	2,100,000	—	—	4.00

KM# 424a • 6.2500 g., 0.9000 **Silver**, 0.1808 oz. ASW •

Date	Mintage	MS-63	MS-65	Prf-65
2008S	1,200,000	—	—	6.50

Arizona

KM# 423 • 5.6700 g., **Copper-Nickel Clad Copper** •

Date	Mintage	MS-63	MS-65	Prf-65
2008P Satin finish	—	3.00	4.50	—
2008D Satin finish	—	3.00	4.50	—
2008P	244,600,000	.75	5.00	—
2008D	265,000,000	.75	5.00	—
2008S	2,100,000	—	—	4.00

KM# 423a • 6.2500 g., 0.9000 Silver, 0.1808 oz. ASW •

Date	Mintage	MS-63	MS-65	Prf-65
2008S	1,200,000	—	—	6.50

Hawaii

KM# 425 • 5.6700 g., Copper-Nickel Clad Copper •

Date	Mintage	MS-63	MS-65	Prf-65
2008P	254,000,000	.75	5.00	—
2008P Satin finish	—	3.00	4.50	—
2008D	263,600,000	.75	5.00	—
2008D Satin finish	—	3.00	4.50	—
2008S	2,100,000	—	—	4.00

KM# 425a • 6.2500 g., 0.9000 Silver, 0.1808 oz. ASW •

Date	Mintage	MS-63	MS-65	Prf-65
2008S	1,200,000	—	—	6.50

New Mexico

KM# 422 • 5.6700 g., Copper-Nickel Clad Copper •

Date	Mintage	MS-63	MS-65	Prf-65
2008P	244,200,000	.75	5.00	—
2008P Satin finish	—	3.00	4.50	—
2008D	244,400,000	.75	5.00	—
2008D Satin finish	—	3.00	4.50	—
2008S	2,100,000	—	—	4.00

KM# 422a • 6.2500 g., 0.9000 Silver, 0.1808 oz. ASW •

Date	Mintage	MS-63	MS-65	Prf-65
2008S	1,200,000	—	—	6.50

Oklahoma

KM# 421 • 5.6700 g., Copper-Nickel Clad Copper •

Date	Mintage	MS-63	MS-65	Prf-65
2008P	222,000,000	.75	5.00	—
2008P Satin finish	—	3.00	4.50	—
2008D	194,600,000	.75	5.00	—
2008D Satin finish	—	3.00	4.50	—
2008S	2,100,000	—	—	4.00

KM# 421a • 6.2500 g., 0.9000 Silver, 0.1808 oz. ASW •

Date	Mintage	MS-63	MS-65	Prf-65
2008S	1,200,000	—	—	6.50

DC and Territories

American Samoa

KM# 448 • 5.6700 g., Copper-Nickel Clad Copper, 24 mm. • **Rev. Designer:** Charles Vickers

Date	Mintage	MS-63	MS-65	Prf-65
2009P	42,600,000	.75	8.00	—
2009D	39,600,000	.75	8.00	—
2009S	—	—	—	4.00

KM# 448a • 6.2500 g., 0.9000 Silver, 0.1808 oz. ASW, 24 mm. •

Date	Mintage	MS-63	MS-65	Prf-65
2009S	—	—	—	6.50

District of Columbia

KM# 445 • 5.6700 g., Copper-Nickel Clad Copper, 24 mm. • **Rev. Designer:** Don Everhart

Date	Mintage	MS-63	MS-65	Prf-65
2009P	83,600,000	.75	8.00	—
2009D	88,800,000	.75	8.00	—
2009S	—	—	—	4.00

KM# 445a • 6.2500 g., 0.9000 Silver, 0.1808 oz. ASW, 24 mm. •

Date	Mintage	MS-63	MS-65	Prf-65
2009S	—	—	—	6.50

Guam

KM# 447 • 5.6700 g., Copper-Nickel Clad Copper, 24 mm. • **Rev. Designer:** James Licaretz

Date	Mintage	MS-63	MS-65	Prf-65
2009P	45,000,000	.75	8.00	—
2009D	42,600,000	.75	8.00	—
2009S	—	—	—	4.00

KM# 447a • 6.2500 g., 0.9000 Silver, 0.1808 oz. ASW, 24 mm. •

Date	Mintage	MS-63	MS-65	Prf-65
2009S	—	—	—	6.50

Northern Mariana Islands

KM# 466 • 5.6700 g., Copper-Nickel Clad Copper • Rev. **Designer:** Pheve Hemphill

Date	Mintage	MS-63	MS-65	Prf-65
2009P	35,200,000	.75	8.00	—
2009D	37,600,000	.75	8.00	—
2009S	—	—	—	4.00

KM# 466a • 6.2500 g., 0.9000 Silver, 0.1808 oz. ASW •

Date	Mintage	MS-63	MS-65	Prf-65
2009S	—	—	—	6.50

Puerto Rico

KM# 446 • 5.6700 g., Copper-Nickel Clad Copper, 24 mm. • **Rev. Designer:** Joseph Menna

Date	Mintage	MS-63	MS-65	Prf-65
2009P	53,200,000	.75	8.00	—
2009D	86,000,000	.75	8.00	—
2009S	—	—	—	4.00

KM# 446a • 6.2500 g., 0.9000 Silver, 0.1808 oz. ASW, 24 mm. •

Date	Mintage	MS-63	MS-65	Prf-65
2009S	—	—	—	6.50

US Virgin Islands

KM# 449 • 5.6700 g., Copper-Nickel Clad Copper, 24 mm. • **Rev. Designer:** Joseph Menna

Date	Mintage	MS-63	MS-65	Prf-65
2009P	41,000,000	.75	8.00	—
2009D	41,000,000	.75	8.00	—
2009S	—	—	—	4.00

KM# 449a • 6.2500 g., 0.9000 Silver, 0.1808 oz. ASW, 24 mm. •

Date	Mintage	MS-63	MS-65	Prf-65
2009S	—	—	—	6.50

America the Beautiful

Grand Canyon National Park

KM# 472 • 5.6700 g., Copper-Nickel Clad Copper, 24.3 mm. •

Date	Mintage	MS-63	MS-65	Prf-65
2010P	—	.75	8.00	—
2010D	—	.75	8.00	—
2010S	—	—	—	4.00

KM# 472a • 6.2500 g., 0.9000 Silver, 0.1808 oz. ASW •

Date	Mintage	MS-63	MS-65	Prf-65
2010	—	—	—	6.50

Hot Springs, Ark.

KM# 469 • 5.6700 g., Copper-Nickel Clad Copper, 24.3 mm. •

Date	Mintage	MS-63	MS-65	Prf-65
2010P	—	.75	8.00	—
2010D	—	.75	8.00	—
2010S	—	—	—	4.00

KM# 469a • 6.2500 g., 0.9000 Silver, 0.1808 oz. ASW •

Date	Mintage	MS-63	MS-65	Prf-65
2010S	—	—	—	6.50

Mount Hood National Park

KM# 473 • 5.6700 g., Copper-Nickel Clad Copper •

Date	Mintage	MS-63	MS-65	Prf-65
2010P	—	.75	8.00	—
2010D	—	.75	8.00	—
2010S	—	—	—	4.00

KM# 473a • 6.2500 g., 0.9000 Silver, 0.1808 oz. ASW •

Date	Mintage	MS-63	MS-65	Prf-65
2010	—	—	—	6.50

Yellowstone National Park

KM# 470 • 5.6700 g., Copper-Nickel Clad Copper • Edge **Desc:** 24.3

Date	Mintage	MS-63	MS-65	Prf-65
2010P	—	.75	8.00	—
2010D	—	.75	8.00	—
2010S	—	—	—	4.00

KM# 470a • 6.2500 g., 0.9000 Silver, 0.1808 oz. ASW •

Date	Mintage	MS-63	MS-65	Prf-65
2010	—	—	—	6.50

Yosemite National Park

KM# 471 • 5.6700 g., Copper-Nickel Clad Copper, 24.3 mm. •

Date	Mintage	MS-63	MS-65	Prf-65
2010P	—	.75	8.00	—
2010D	—	.75	8.00	—
2010S	—	—	—	4.00

KM# 471a • 6.2500 g., 0.9000 Silver, 0.1808 oz. ASW •

Date	Mintage	MS-63	MS-65	Prf-65
2010	—	—	—	6.50

Chickasaw National Recreation Area

KM# 498a • 6.2500 g., 0.9000 Silver, 0.1808 oz. ASW •

Date	Mintage	MS-63	MS-65	Prf-65
2011S	—	—	—	6.50

KM# 498 • 5.6700 g., Copper-Nickel Clad Copper, 24 mm. •

Date	Mintage	MS-63	MS-65	Prf-65
2011P	—	.75	8.00	—
2011D	—	.75	8.00	—
2011S	—	—	—	4.00

Gettysburg National Military Park

KM# 494a • 6.2500 g., 0.9000 Silver, 0.1808 oz. ASW •

Date	Mintage	MS-63	MS-65	Prf-65
2011S	—	—	—	6.50

KM# 494 • 5.6700 g., Copper-Nickel Clad Copper, 24 mm. •

Date	Mintage	MS-63	MS-65	Prf-65
2011P	—	.75	8.00	—
2011D	—	.75	8.00	—
2011S	—	—	—	4.00

Glacier National Park

KM# 495a • 6.2500 g., 0.9000 Silver, 0.1808 oz. ASW •

Date	Mintage	MS-63	MS-65	Prf-65
2011S	—	—	—	6.50

KM# 495 • 5.6700 g., Copper-Nickel Clad Copper, 24 mm. •

Date	Mintage	MS-63	MS-65	Prf-65
2011P	—	.75	8.00	—
2011D	—	.75	8.00	—
2011S	—	—	—	4.00

Olympic National Park

KM# 496a • 6.2500 g., 0.9000 Silver, 0.1808 oz. ASW •

Date	Mintage	MS-63	MS-65	Prf-65
2011S	—	—	—	6.50

KM# 496 • 5.6700 g., Copper-Nickel Clad Copper, 24 mm. •

Date	Mintage	MS-63	MS-65	Prf-65
2011P	—	.75	8.00	—
2011D	—	.75	8.00	—
2011S	—	—	—	4.00

Vicksburg National Military Park

KM# 497a • 6.2500 g., 0.9000 Silver, 0.1808 oz. ASW •

Date	Mintage	MS-63	MS-65	Prf-65
2011S	—	—	—	6.50

KM# 497 • 5.6700 g., **Copper-Nickel Clad Copper**, 24 mm. •

Date	Mintage	MS-63	MS-65	Prf-65
2011P	—	.75	8.00	—
2011D	—	.75	8.00	—
2011S	—	—	—	4.00

HALF DOLLAR

Kennedy Half Dollar

Regular design resumed reverse

KM# A202b • 11.1000 g., **Copper-Nickel Clad Copper**, 30.4 mm. • **Edge Desc:** Reeded **Notes:** KM#202b design and composition resumed. The 1979-S and 1981-S Type II proofs have clearer mint marks than the Type I proofs of those years.

Date	Mintage	MS-65	Prf-65
2001P	21,200,000	9.00	—
2001D	19,504,000	9.00	—
2001S	2,235,000	—	8.00
2002P	3,100,000	10.00	—
2002D	2,500,000	10.00	—
2002S	2,268,913	—	8.00
2003P	2,500,000	14.00	—
2003D	2,500,000	14.00	—
2003S	2,076,165	—	6.00
2004P	2,900,000	7.00	—
2004D	2,900,000	7.00	—
2004S	1,789,488	—	13.00
2005P	3,800,000	9.00	—
2005P Satin finish	1,160,000	8.00	—
2005D	3,500,000	9.00	—
2005D Satin finish	1,160,000	10.00	—
2005S	2,275,000	—	7.00
2006P	2,400,000	12.00	—
2006P Satin finish	847,361	12.00	—
2006D	2,000,000	20.00	—
2006D Satin finish	847,361	14.00	—
2006S	1,934,965	—	10.00
2007P	—	7.00	—
2007P Satin finish	—	8.00	—
2007D	—	7.00	—
2007D Satin finish	—	8.00	—
2007S	—	—	10.00
2008P	—	7.00	—
2008P Satin finish	—	8.50	—
2008D	—	7.00	—
2008D Satin finish	—	8.50	—
2008S	—	—	12.00
2009P	—	7.00	—
2009P Satin finish	—	8.50	—
2009D	—	7.00	—
2009D Satin finish	—	8.50	—
2009S	—	—	6.00
2010P	—	7.00	—
2010P Satin finish	—	8.50	—
2010D	—	7.00	—
2010D Satin finish	—	8.50	—
2010S	—	—	6.00
2011P	—	7.00	—
2011D	—	7.00	—
2011S	—	—	6.00

KM# A202c • 12.5000 g., 0.9000 **Silver**, 0.3617 oz. ASW, 30.6 mm. • **Designer:** Gilroy Roberts

Date	Mintage	Prf-65
2001S	849,600	20.00
2002S	888,816	14.50
2003S	1,040,425	14.50
2004S	1,175,935	14.50
2005S	1,069,679	14.50
2006S	988,140	14.50
2007S	1,384,797	14.50
2008S	620,684	14.50
2009S	—	20.00
2010S	—	20.00

DOLLAR

Sacagawea Dollar

Sacagawea bust right, with baby on back obverse Eagle in flight left reverse

KM# 310 • 8.0700 g., **Copper-Zinc-Manganese-Nickel Clad Copper**, 26.5 mm. •

Date	Mintage	MS-63	Prf-65
2001P	62,468,000	2.00	—
2001D	70,939,500	2.00	—
2001S	3,190,000	—	100.00
2002P	3,865,610	2.00	—
2002D	3,732,000	2.00	—
2002S	3,210,000	—	28.50
2003P	3,080,000	3.00	—
2003D	3,080,000	3.00	—
2003S	3,300,000	—	20.00
2004P	2,660,000	2.50	—
2004D	2,660,000	2.50	—
2004S	2,965,000	—	22.50
2005P	2,520,000	2.50	—
2005D	2,520,000	2.50	—
2005S	3,273,000	—	22.50
2006P	4,900,000	2.50	—
2006D	2,800,000	5.00	—
2006S	3,028,828	—	22.50
2007P	3,640,000	2.50	—
2007D	3,920,000	2.50	—
2007S	2,563,563	—	22.50
2008P	9,800,000	2.50	—
2008D	14,840,000	2.50	—
2008S	—	—	22.50

Native American Dollar - Planting crops reverse

Sacagawea bust right with baby on back obverse Native American female planting corn, beans and squash reverse

KM# 467 • 8.0700 g., **Copper-Zinc-Manganese-Nickel Clad Copper**, 26.5 mm. •

Date	Mintage	MS-63	Prf-65
2009P	37,380,000	—	—
2009D	33,880,000	—	—
2009S	—	—	22.50

Native American Dollar - Hiawatha belt reverse

Sacagawea bust right with baby on back obverse Hiawatha belt and bundle of five arrows reverse

KM# 474 • 8.0700 g., **Copper-Zinc-Manganese-Nickel Clad Copper**, 26.5 mm. •

Date	Mintage	MS-63	Prf-65
2010P	—	—	—
2010D	—	—	—
2010S	—	—	22.50

Native American Dollar - Peace Pipe reverse

Sacagawea bust right with baby on back obverse Hands passing peace pipe reverse

KM# 503 • 8.0700 g., **Copper-Zinc-Manganese-Nickel Clad Copper**, 26.5 mm. •

Date	Mintage	MS-63	Prf-65
2011P	—	—	—
2011D	—	—	—
2011S	—	—	8.00

Presidents

George Washington

KM# 401 • 8.0700 g., **Copper-Zinc-Manganese-Nickel Clad Copper**, 26.5 mm. • **Edge Lettering:** IN GOD WE TRUST date, mint mark E PLURIBUS UNUM **Notes:** Date and mint mark incuse on edge.

Date	Mintage	MS-63	MS-65	Prf-65
2007P	176,680,000	2.00	5.00	—
(2007) Plain edge error	Inc. above	75.00	—	—
2007D	163,680,000	2.00	5.00	—
2007S	3,883,103	—	—	8.00

James Madison

KM# 404 • 8.0700 g., **Copper-Zinc-Manganese-Nickel Clad Copper**, 26.5 mm. • **Edge Lettering:** IN GOD WE TRUST date, mint mark E PLURIBUS UNUM **Notes:** Date and mint mark incuse on edge.

Date	Mintage	MS-63	MS-65	Prf-65
2007P	84,560,000	2.00	5.00	—
2007D	87,780,000	2.00	5.00	—
2007S	3,876,829	—	—	8.00

John Adams

KM# 402 • 8.0700 g., **Copper-Zinc-Manganese-Nickel Clad Copper**, 26.5 mm. • **Edge Lettering:** IN GOD WE TRUST date, mint mark E PLURIBUS UNUM **Notes:** Date and mint mark incuse on edge.

Date	Mintage	MS-63	MS-65	Prf-65
2007P	112,420,000	2.00	5.00	—
2007P Double edge lettering	Inc. above	250	—	—
2007D	112,140,000	2.00	5.00	—
2007S	3,877,409	—	—	8.00

Thomas Jefferson

KM# 403 • 8.0700 g., **Copper-Zinc-Manganese-Nickel Clad Copper**, 26.5 mm. • **Edge Lettering:** IN GOD WE TRUST date, mint mark E PLURIBUS UNUM **Notes:** Date and mint mark incuse on edge.

Date	Mintage	MS-63	MS-65	Prf-65
2007P	100,800,000	2.00	5.00	—
2007D	102,810,000	2.00	5.00	—
2007S	3,877,573	—	—	8.00

Andrew Jackson

KM# 428 • 8.0700 g., **Copper-Zinc-Manganese-Nickel Clad Copper**, 26.5 mm. • **Edge Lettering:** IN GOD WE TRUST date, mint mark E PLURIBUS UNUM **Notes:** Date and mint mark incuse on edge.

Date	Mintage	MS-63	MS-65	Prf-65
2008P	61,180,000	2.00	5.00	—
2008D	61,070,000	2.00	5.00	—
2008S	3,000,000	—	—	8.00

James Monroe

KM# 426 • 8.0700 g., **Copper-Zinc-Manganese-Nickel Clad Copper**, Date and mint mark incuse on edge., 26.5 mm. • **Edge Lettering:**IN GOD WE TRUST date, mint mark E PLURIBUS UNUM

Date	Mintage	MS-63	MS-65	Prf-65
2008P	64,260,000	2.00	5.00	—
2008D	60,230,000	2.00	5.00	—
2008S	3,000,000	—	—	8.00

John Quincy Adams

KM# 427 • 8.0700 g., **Copper-Zinc-Manganese-Nickel Clad Copper**, 26.5 mm. • **Edge Lettering:**
IN GOD WE TRUST date, mint mark E PLURIBUS UNUM **Notes:** Date and mint mark incuse on edge.

Date	Mintage	MS-63	MS-65	Prf-65
2008P	57,540,000	2.00	5.00	—
2008D	57,720,000	2.00	5.00	—
2008S	3,000,000	—	—	8.00

Martin van Buren

KM# 429 • 8.0700 g., **Copper-Zinc-Manganese-Nickel Clad Copper**, 26.5 mm. • **Edge Lettering:**
IN GOD WE TRUST date, mint mark E PLURIBUS UNUM **Notes:** Date and mint mark incuse on edge.

Date	Mintage	MS-63	MS-65	Prf-65
2008P	51,520,000	2.00	5.00	—
2008D	50,960,000	2.00	5.00	—
2008S	3,000,000	—	—	8.00

James K. Polk

KM# 452 • 8.0700 g., **Copper-Zinc-Manganese-Nickel Clad Copper**, 26.5 mm. • **Edge Lettering:**
E PLURIBUS UNUM, date, mint mark **Notes:** Date and mint mark on edge

Date	Mintage	MS-63	MS-65	Prf-65
2009P	46,620,000	2.00	5.00	—
2009D	41,720,000	2.00	5.00	—
2009S	—	—	—	8.00

John Tyler

KM# 451 • 8.0700 g., **Copper-Zinc-Manganese-Nickel Clad Copper**, 26.5 mm. • **Edge Lettering:**
E PLURIBUS UNUM, date, mint mark **Notes:** Date and mint mark on edge.

Date	Mintage	MS-63	MS-65	Prf-65
2009P	43,540,000	2.00	5.00	—
2009D	43,540,000	2.00	5.00	—
2009S	—	—	—	8.00

William Henry Harrison

KM# 450 • 8.0700 g., **Copper-Zinc-Manganese-Nickel Clad Copper**, 26.5 mm. • **Edge Lettering:**
E PLURIBUS UNUM, date, mint mark **Notes:** Date and mint mark on edge

Date	Mintage	MS-63	MS-65	Prf-65
2009P	43,260,000	2.00	5.00	—
2009D	55,160,000	2.00	5.00	—
2009S	—	—	—	8.00

Zachary Taylor

KM# 453 • 8.0700 g., **Copper-Zinc-Manganese-Nickel Clad Copper**, 26.5 mm. • **Edge Lettering:**
E PLURIBUS UNUM, date, mint mark **Notes:** Date and mint mark on edge.

Date	Mintage	MS-63	MS-65	Prf-65
2009P	41,580,000	2.00	5.00	—
2009D	36,680,000	2.00	5.00	—
2009S	—	—	—	8.00

Abraham Lincoln

KM# 478 • 8.0700 g., **Copper-Zinc-Manganese-Nickel Clad Copper**, 26.5 mm. • **Edge Lettering:**
E PLURIBUS UNUM, date, mint mark **Notes:** Date and mint mark on edge

Date	Mintage	MS-63	MS-65	Prf-65
2010P	—	2.00	5.00	—
2010D	—	2.00	5.00	—
2010S	—	—	—	8.00

Franklin Pierce

KM# 476 • 8.0700 g., **Copper-Zinc-Manganese-Nickel Clad Copper**, 26.5 mm. • **Edge Lettering:**
E PLURIBUS UNUM, date, mint mark **Notes:** Date and mint mark on edge.

Date	Mintage	MS-63	MS-65	Prf-65
2010P	—	2.00	5.00	—
2010D	—	2.00	5.00	—
2010S	—	—	—	8.00

James Buchanan

KM# 477 • 8.0700 g., **Copper-Zinc-Manganese-Nickel Clad Copper**, 26.5 mm. • **Edge Lettering:**
E PLURIBUS UNUM, date, mint mark **Notes:** Date and mint mark on edge.

Date	Mintage	MS-63	MS-65	Prf-65
2010P	—	2.00	5.00	—
2010D	—	2.00	5.00	—
2010S	—	—	—	8.00

Millard Filmore

KM# 475 • 8.0700 g., **Copper-Zinc-Manganese-Nickel Clad Copper**, 26.5 mm. • **Edge Lettering:**
E PLURIBUS UNUM, date, mint mark **Notes:** Date and mint mark on edge.

Date	Mintage	MS-63	MS-65	Prf-65
2010P	—	2.00	5.00	—
2010D	—	2.00	5.00	—
2010S	—	—	—	8.00

Andrew Johnson

KM# 499 • 8.0700 g., **Copper-Zinc-Manganese-Nickel Clad Copper**, 26.5 mm. • **Edge Lettering:**
E PLURIBUS UNUM, date, mint mark **Notes:** Date and mint mark on edge.

Date	Mintage	MS-63	MS-65	Prf-65
2011P	—	2.00	5.00	—
2011D	—	2.00	5.00	—
2011S	—	—	—	8.00

James Garfield

KM# 502 • 8.0700 g., **Copper-Zinc-Manganese-Nickel Clad Copper**, 26.5 mm. • **Edge Lettering:**
E PLURIBUS UNUM, date, mint mark **Notes:** Date and mint mark on edge.

Date	Mintage	MS-63	MS-65	Prf-65
2011P	—	2.00	5.00	—
2011D	—	2.00	5.00	—
2011S	—	—	—	8.00

Rutherford B. Hayes

KM# 501 • 8.0700 g., **Copper-Zinc-Manganese-Nickel Clad Copper**, 26.5 mm. • **Edge Lettering:**
E PLURIBUS UNUM, date, mint mark **Notes:** Date and mint mark on edge.

Date	Mintage	MS-63	MS-65	Prf-65
2011P	—	2.00	5.00	—
2011D	—	2.00	5.00	—
2011S	—	—	—	8.00

Ulysses S. Grant

KM# 500 • 8.0700 g., **Copper-Zinc-Manganese-Nickel Clad Copper**, 26.5 mm. • **Edge Lettering:**
E PLURIBUS UNUM, date, mint mark **Notes:** Date and mint mark on edge.

Date	Mintage	MS-63	MS-65	Prf-65
2011P	—	2.00	5.00	—
2011D	—	2.00	5.00	—
2011S	—	—	—	8.00

COMMEMORATIVE COINAGE

1982-PRESENT

All commemorative silver dollar coins of 1982-present have the following specifications: diameter — 38.1 millimeters; weight — 26.7300 grams; composition — 0.9000 silver, 0.7736 ounces actual silver weight. All commemorative $5 coins of 1982-present have the following specificiations: diameter — 21.6 millimeters; weight — 8.3590 grams; composition: 0.9000 gold, 0.242 ounces actual gold weight.

Note: In 1982, after a hiatus of nearly 20 years, coinage of commemorative half dollars resumed. Those designated with a 'W' were struck at the West Point Mint. Some issues were struck in copper-nickel. Those struck in silver have the same size, weight and composition as the prior commemorative half-dollar series.

HALF DOLLAR

U. S. CAPITOL VISITOR CENTER. KM# 323 Copper-Nickel Clad Copper 11.3400 g. **Obverse:** Capitol sillouete, 1800 structure in detail **Reverse:** Legend within circle of stars **Obv. Designer:** Dean McMullen
Rev. Designer: Alex Shagin and Marcel Jovine

Date	Mintage	MS-65	Prf-65
2001P	99,157	14.50	—
2001P	77,962	—	15.50

FIRST FLIGHT CENTENNIAL. KM# 348
Copper-Nickel Clad Copper 11.3400 g.
Obverse: Wright Monument at Kitty Hawk
Reverse: Wright Flyer in flight **Obv. Designer:** John Mercanti
Rev. Designer: Donna Weaver

Date	Mintage	MS-65	Prf-65
2003P	57,726	15.00	—
2003P	109,710	—	16.00

AMERICAN BALD EAGLE. KM# 438 Copper-Nickel Clad Copper 30.6 mm. 11.3400 g. **Obverse:** Two eaglets in nest with egg **Reverse:** Eagle Challenger facing right, American Flag in background

Date	Mintage	MS-65	Prf-65
2008S	120,000	12.00	—
2008S	175,000	—	14.50

U.S. ARMY. KM# 506 Copper-Nickel **Obverse:** Army contributions during peacetime, surveying, building a flood wall and space exploration **Reverse:** Continental soldier with musket **Obv. Designer:** Donna Weaver and Charles L. Vickers **Rev. Designer:** Thomas Cleveland and Joseph Menna

Date	Mintage	MS-65	Prf-65
2011		—	—

DOLLAR

CAPITOL VISITOR CENTER. KM# 324
Obv. Designer: Marika Somogyi **Rev. Designer:** John Mercanti **Obverse:** Original and current Capital facades **Reverse:** Eagle with sheild and ribbon

Date	Mintage	MS-65	Prf-65
2001P	66,636	33.20	—
2001P	143,793	—	33.20

NATIVE AMERICAN - BISON. KM# 325
Designer: James E. Fraser. **Obverse:** Native American bust right **Reverse:** Bison standing left

Date	Mintage	MS-65	Prf-65
2001D	197,131	159	—
2001P	272,869	—	169

2002 WINTER OLYMPICS - SALT LAKE CITY.
KM# 336 Obv. Designer: John Mercanti **Rev. Designer:** Donna Weaver **Obverse:** Salt Lake City Olympic logo **Reverse:** Stylized skyline with mountains in background

Date	Mintage	MS-65	Prf-65
2002P	35,388	33.20	—
2002P	142,873	—	36.50

U.S. MILITARY ACADEMY AT WEST POINT - BICENTENNIAL.
KM# 338 Obv. Designer: T. James Ferrell **Rev. Designer:** John Mercanti **Obverse:** Cadet Review flagbearers, Academy buildings in background **Reverse:** Academy emblems - Corinthian helmet and sword

Date	Mintage	MS-65	Prf-65
2002W	103,201	33.20	—
2002W	288,293	—	33.20

FIRST FLIGHT CENTENNIAL. KM# 349
Obv. Designer: T. James Ferrell **Rev. Designer:** Norman E. Nemeth **Obverse:** Orville and Wilbur Wright busts left **Reverse:** Wright Flyer over dunes

Date	Mintage	MS-65	Prf-65
2003P	53,761	33.20	—
2003P	193,086	—	33.20

LEWIS AND CLARK CORPS OF DISCOVERY BICENTENNIAL. KM# 363 Obverse: Lewis and Clark standing **Reverse:** Jefferson era clasped hands peace medal

Date	Mintage	MS-65	Prf-65
2004P	90,323	33.20	—
2004P	288,492	—	33.20

THOMAS A. EDISON - ELECTRIC LIGHT 125TH ANNIVERSARY. KM# 362 Obv. Designer: Donna Weaver **Rev. Designer:** John Mercanti **Obverse:** Edison half-length figure facing holding light bulb **Reverse:** Light bulb and rays

Date	Mintage	MS-65	Prf-65
2004P	68,031	33.20	—
2004P	213,409	—	33.20

JOHN MARSHALL, 250TH BIRTH ANNIVERSARY. KM# 375
Obv. Designer: John Mercanti **Rev. Designer:** Donna Weaver **Obverse:** Marshall bust left **Reverse:** Marshall era Supreme Court Chamber

Date	Mintage	MS-65	Prf-65
2005P	48,953	33.20	—
2005P	141,993	—	34.20

U.S. MARINE CORPS, 230TH ANNIVERSARY.
KM# 376 Obverse: Flag Raising at Mt. Suribachi on Iwo Jima **Reverse:** Marine Corps emblem

Date	Mintage	MS-65	Prf-65
2005P	130,000	38.00	—
2005P	370,000	—	46.50

BENJAMIN FRANKLIN, 300TH BIRTH ANNIVERSARY. KM# 387 Obv. Designer: Norman E. Nemeth **Obverse:** Youthful Franklin flying kite
Reverse: Revolutionary era "JOIN, or DIE" snake cartoon illustration

Date	Mintage	MS-65	Prf-65
2006P	58,000	33.20	—
2006P	142,000	—	42.50

BENJAMIN FRANKLIN, 300TH BIRTH ANNIVERSARY. KM# 388 Obverse: Bust 3/4 right, signature in oval below **Reverse:** Continental Dollar of 1776 in center

Date	Mintage	MS-65	Prf-65
2006P	58,000	33.20	—
2006P	142,000	—	43.50

SAN FRANCISCO MINT MUSEUM. KM# 394
Obv. Designer: Sherl J. Winter **Obverse:** 3/4 view of building **Reverse:** Reverse of 1880s Morgan silver dollar

Date	Mintage	MS-65	Prf-65
2006S	65,609	33.20	—
2006S	255,700	—	33.20

CENTRAL HIGH SCHOOL DESEGREGATION.
KM# 418 Rev. Designer: Don Everhart II **Obverse:** Children's feet walking left with adult feet in military boots **Reverse:** Little Rock's Central High School

Date	Mintage	MS-65	Prf-65
2007P	66,093	50.00	—
2007P	124,618	—	50.00

JAMESTOWN - 400TH ANNIVERSARY. KM# 405 Obv. Designer: Donna Weaver **Rev. Designer:** Don Everhart II **Obverse:** Two settlers and Native American **Reverse:** Three ships

Date	Mintage	MS-65	Prf-65
2007P	79,801	33.20	—
2007P	258,802	—	33.20

AMERICAN BALD EAGLE. KM# 439
Obverse: Eagle with flight, mountain in background at right **Reverse:** Great Seal of the United States

Date	Mintage	MS-65	Prf-65
2008P	110,073	391	—
2008P	243,558	—	396

LINCOLN BICENTENNIAL. KM# 454
Obv. Designer: Justin Kunz and Don Everhart II **Rev. Designer:** Phebe Hemphill **Obverse:** 3/4 portrait facing right **Reverse:** Part of Gettysburg Address within wreath

Date	Mintage	MS-65	Prf-65
2009P	125,000	55.00	—
2009P	375,000	—	63.50

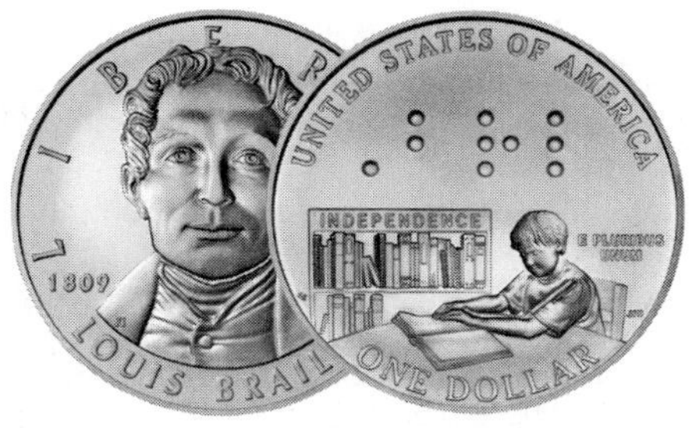

LOUIS BRAILLE BIRTH BICENTENNIAL. KM# 455 Obv. Designer: Joel Iskowitz and Phebe Hemphill **Rev. Designer:** Susan Gamble and Joseph Menna **Obverse:** Louis Braille bust facing **Reverse:** School child reading book in Braille, BRL in Braille code above

Date	Mintage	MS-65	Prf-65
2009P	82,639	32.50	—
2009P	135,235	—	42.50

AMERICAN VETERANS DISABLED FOR LIFE.
KM# 479 Obverse: Soldier's feet, crutches **Reverse:** Legend within wreath

Date	Mintage	MS-65	Prf-65
2010W	77,859	41.00	—
2010W	189,881	—	42.50

BOY SCOUTS OF AMERICA, 100TH ANNIVERSARY. KM# 480 Obv. Designer: Donna Weaver **Rev. Designer:** Jim Licaretz **Obverse:** Cub Scout, Boy Scout and Venturer saluting **Reverse:** Boy Scouts of America logo

Date	Mintage	MS-65	Prf-65
2010P		35.00	—
2010P		—	45.00

MEDAL OF HONOR. KM# 504 Obv. Designer: James Licaretz **Rev. Designer:** Richard Masters and Phebe Hemphill **Obverse:** Medal of Honor designs for Army, Navy adn Air Force awards **Reverse:** Army infantry doldier carrying another to safety

Date	Mintage	MS-65	Prf-65
2011		—	—

U.S. ARMY. KM# 507 Obv. Designer: Richard Masters and Michael Gaudioso **Rev. Designer:** Susan Gamble and Don Everhart, II **Obverse:** Male and femlae soldier heads looking outward **Reverse:** Seven core values of the Army, Eagle from the great seal

Date	Mintage	MS-65	Prf-65
2011		—	—

$5 (HALF EAGLE)

CAPITOL VISITOR CENTER. KM# 326
Designer: Elizabeth Jones. **Obverse:** Column at right **Reverse:** First Capital building

Date	Mintage	MS-65	Prf-65
2001W	6,761	1,750	—
2001W	27,652	—	381

2002 WINTER OLYMPICS. KM# 337
Designer: Donna Weaver. **Obverse:** Salt Lake City Olympics logo **Reverse:** Stylized cauldron

Date	Mintage	MS-65	Prf-65
2002W	10,585	410	—
2002W	32,877	—	391

SAN FRANCISCO MINT MUSEUM. KM# 395 Obverse: Front entrance façade **Reverse:** Eagle as on 1860's $5. Gold

Date	Mintage	MS-65	Prf-65
2006S	16,230	376	—
2006S	41,517	—	376

JAMESTOWN - 400TH ANNIVERSARY. KM# 406 Obverse: Settler and Native American **Reverse:** Jamestown Memorial Church ruins

Date	Mintage	MS-65	Prf-65
2007W	18,843	376	—
2007W	47,050	—	376

AMERICAN BALD EAGLE. KM# 440 Obverse: Two eagles on branch **Reverse:** Eagle with shield

Date	Mintage	MS-65	Prf-65
2008W	13,467	384	—
2008W	59,269	—	384

MEDAL OF HONOR. KM# 505 Obv. Designer: Joseph Menna **Rev. Designer:** Joel Iskowitz and Michael Gaudioso **Obverse:** 1861 Medal of Honor design for the Navy **Reverse:** Minerva standing with shield and Union flag, field artillery canon flanking

Date	Mintage	MS-65	Prf-65
2011		—	—

U.S. ARMY. KM# 508 Obv. Designer: Joel Iskowitz and Phebe Hemphill **Rev. Designer:** Joseph Menna **Obverse:** Five Soldiers of different eras **Reverse:** Elements from the Army's emblem

Date	Mintage	MS-65	Prf-65
2011		—	—

$10 (EAGLE)

FIRST FLIGHT CENTENNIAL. KM# 350 0.9000 Gold 0.4837 oz. AGW. 16.7180 g. **Obverse:** Orvile and Wilbur Wright busts facing **Reverse:** Wright flyer and eagle **Designer:** Donna Weaver

Date	Mintage	MS-65	Prf-65
2003P	10,129	900	—
2003P	21,846	—	755

$20 (DOUBLE EAGLE)

KM# 464 0.9990 Gold 0 oz. AGW. 27 mm.
Obverse: Ultra high relief Liberty holding torch, walking forward **Reverse:** Eagle in flight left, sunrise in background **Designer:** Augustus Saint-Gaudens

Date	Mintage	MS-65	Prf-65
2009	115,178	—	2,200

AMERICAN EAGLE BULLION COINS

SILVER DOLLAR

KM# 273 0.9993 **SILVER** 0.9993 oz. ASW. 40.6mm. 31.1050 g. **Obv. Designer:** Adolph A. Weinman
Rev. Designer: John Mercanti

Date	Mintage	Unc	Prf.
2001	9,001,711	41.10	—
2001W	746,398	—	57.00
2002	10,539,026	41.10	—
2002W	647,342	—	57.00
2003	8,495,008	41.10	—
2003W	747,831	—	57.00
2004	8,882,754	41.10	—
2004W	801,602	—	57.00
2005	8,891,025	41.10	—
2005W	816,663	—	57.00
2006	10,676,522	43.30	—
2006W	1,093,600	—	57.00
2006P Reverse Proof	—	—	195
2006W Burnished Unc.	468,000	75.00	—
2006 20th Aniv. 3 pc. set	—	—	345
2007	9,028,036	41.30	—
2007W	821,759	—	57.00
2007W Burnished Unc.	690,891	47.10	—
2008	20,583,000	41.10	—

Date	Mintage	Unc	Prf.
2008W Reverse of '07	—	450	—
2008	—	—	79.00
2008W Burnished Unc.	—	36.50	—
2009	—	41.10	—
2010	—	41.10	—
2010	—	—	57.00

GOLD $5

KM# 216 0.9167 **GOLD** 0.1000 oz. AGW. 16.5mm. 3.3930 g. **Obv. Designer:** Augustus Saint-Gaudens **Rev. Designer:** Miley Busiek

Date	Mintage	Unc	Prf.
2001	269,147	174	—
2001W	37,530	—	184
2002	230,027	174	—
2002W	40,864	—	184
2003	245,029	174	—
2003W	40,027	—	184
2004	250,016	174	—
2004W	35,131	—	184
2005	300,043	174	—
2005W	49,265	—	184
2006	285,006	174	—
2006W	47,277	—	184
2006W Burnished Unc.	20,643	175	—
2007	190,010	174	—
2007W	58,553	—	199
2007W Burnished Unc.	22,501	175	—
2008	305,000	184	—
2008W	—	—	199
2008W Burnished Unc.	12,657	245	—
2009	27,000	145	—
2010	—	—	—
2010W	—	—	184

GOLD $10

KM# 217 0.9167 **GOLD** 0.2500 oz. AGW. 22mm. 8.4830 g. **Obv. Designer:** Augustus Saint-Gaudens **Rev. Designer:** Miley Busiek

Date	Mintage	Unc	Prf.
2001	71,280	416	—
2001W	25,613	—	515
2002	62,027	416	—
2002W	29,242	—	515
2003	74,029	416	—
2003W	30,292	—	515
2004	72,014	416	—
2004W	28,839	—	515
2005	72,015	416	—
2005W	37,207	—	515
2006	60,004	416	—
2006W	36,127	—	515
2006W Burnished Unc.	15,188	785	—
2007	34,004	416	—
2007W	46,189	—	445
2007W Burnished Unc.	12,786	785	—
2008	—	416	—
2008W	28,000	—	445
2008W Burnished Unc.	8,883	1,285	—
2009	27,500	416	—
2010	—	—	—
2010W	—	—	515

GOLD $25

KM# 218 0.9167 **GOLD** 0.5000 oz. AGW. 27mm. 16.9660 g. **Obv. Designer:** Augustus Saint-Gaudens **Rev. Designer:** Miley Busiek

Date	Mintage	Unc	Prf.
2001	48,047	900	—
2001W	23,240	—	910
2002	70,027	804	—
2002W	26,646	—	910
2003	79,029	804	—
2003W	28,270	—	910
2004	98,040	804	—
2004W	27,330	—	910
2005	80,023	804	—
2005W	34,311	—	910
2006	66,004	807	—
2006W	34,322	—	910
2006W Burnished Unc.	15,164	1,600	—
2007	47,002	838	—
2007W	44,025	—	910
2007W Burnished Unc.	11,458	1,600	—
2008	61,000	807	—
2008W	27,800	—	910
2008W Burnished Unc.	15,683	1,100	—
2009	55,000	807	—
2010	—	—	—
2010W	—	—	910

GOLD $50

KM# 219 0.9167 **GOLD** 100000 oz. AGW. 32.7mm. 33.9310 g. **Obv. Designer:** Augustus Saint-Gaudens **Rev. Designer:** Miley Busiek

Date	Mintage	Unc	Prf.
2001	143,605	1,537	—
2001W	24,555	—	1,700
2002	222,029	1,537	—
2002W	27,499	—	1,700
2003	416,032	1,537	—
2003W	28,344	—	1,700
2004	417,149	1,537	—
2004W	28,215	—	1,700
2005	356,555	1,537	—
2005W	35,246	—	1,700
2006	237,510	1,537	—
2006W	47,000	—	1,700
2006W Reverse Proof	10,000	—	2,200
2006W Burnished Unc.	45,912	1,575	—
2007	140,016	1,551	—
2007W	51,810	—	1,700
2007W Burnished Unc.	18,609	1,575	—
2008	710,000	1,537	—
2008W	29,000	—	1,700
2008W Burnished Unc.	11,908	1,885	—
2009	122,000	1,537	—
2010	—	1,537	—
2010W	—	—	1,700

PLATINUM $10

KM# 283 0.9995 **PLATINUM** 0.0999 oz. 17mm. 3.1100 g. **Obv. Designer:** John Mercanti **Rev. Designer:** Thomas D. Rogers Sr

Date	Mintage	Unc	Prf.
2001	52,017	203	—
2002	23,005	203	—
2003	22,007	203	—
2004	15,010	203	—
2005	14,013	203	—
2006	11,001	203	—
2006W Burnished Unc.	—	425	—
2007	13,003	280	—
2007W Burnished Unc.	—	203	—
2008	17,000	203	—
2008 Burnished Unc.	—	203	—
2009	—	—	—

KM# 327 0.9995 **PLATINUM** 0.0999 oz. 17mm. 3.1100 g. **Obv. Designer:** John Mercanti

Date	Mintage	Unc	Prf.
2001W	12,174	—	252

KM# 339 0.9995 **PLATINUM** 0.0999 oz. 17mm. 3.1100 g. **Obv. Designer:** John Mercanti

Date	Mintage	Unc	Prf.
2002W	12,365	—	252

KM# 351 0.9995 **PLATINUM** 0.0999 oz. 17mm. 3.1100 g. **Obv. Designer:** John Mercanti **Rev. Designer:** Al Maletsky

Date	Mintage	Unc	Prf.
2003W	9,534	—	257

KM# 364 0.9995 **PLATINUM** 0.0999 oz. 17mm. 3.1100 g. **Obv. Designer:** John Mercanti

Date	Mintage	Unc	Prf.
2004W	7,161	—	535

KM# 377 0.9995 **PLATINUM** 0.0999 oz. 17mm. 3.1100 g. **Obv. Designer:** John Mercanti **Rev. Designer:** Donna Weaver

Date	Mintage	Unc	Prf.
2005W	8,104	—	265

KM# 389 0.9995 **PLATINUM** 0.0999 oz. 17mm. 3.1100 g. **Obv. Designer:** John Mercanti

Date	Mintage	Unc	Prf.
2006W	10,205	—	252

KM# 414 0.9995 **PLATINUM** 0.0999 oz. 17mm. 3.1100 g. **Obv. Designer:** John Mercanti

Date	Mintage	Unc	Prf.
2007W	8,176	—	280

KM# 434 0.9995 **PLATINUM** 0.0999 oz. 17mm. 3.1100 g. **Obv. Designer:** John Mercanti

Date	Mintage	Unc	Prf.
2008W	8,176	—	585

KM# 460 0.9995 **PLATINUM** 0.0999 oz. 17mm. 3.1100 g. **Obv. Designer:** John Mercanti

Date	Mintage	Unc	Prf.
2009W	5,600	—	—

PLATINUM $25

KM# 284 0.9995 **PLATINUM** 0.2502 oz. 22mm. 7.7857 g. **Obv. Designer:** John Mercanti **Rev. Designer:** Thomas D. Rogers Sr

Date	Mintage	Unc	Prf.
2001	21,815	495	—
2002	27,405	495	—

Date	Mintage	Unc	Prf.
2003	25,207	495	—
2004	18,010	495	—
2005	12,013	495	—
2006	12,001	495	—
2006W Burnished Unc.	—	585	—
2007	8,402	513	—
2007W Burnished Unc.	—	495	—
2008	22,800	495	—
2008 Burnished Unc.	—	665	—
2009	—	—	—

KM# 328 0.9995 **PLATINUM** 0.2502 oz. 22mm. 7.7857 g.
Obv. Designer: John Mercanti

Date	Mintage	Unc	Prf.
2001W	8,847	—	520

KM# 340 0.9995 **PLATINUM** 0.2502 oz. 22mm. 7.7857 g.
Obv. Designer: John Mercanti

Date	Mintage	Unc	Prf.
2002W	9,282	—	520

KM# 352 0.9995 **PLATINUM** 0.2502 oz. 22mm. 7.7857 g.
Obv. Designer: John Mercanti
Rev. Designer: Al Maletsky

Date	Mintage	Unc	Prf.
2003W	7,044	—	520

KM# 365 0.9995 **PLATINUM** 0.2502 oz. 22mm. 7.7857 g.
Obv. Designer: John Mercanti

Date	Mintage	Unc	Prf.
2004W	5,193	—	1,075

KM# 378 0.9995 **PLATINUM** 0.2502 oz. 22mm. 7.7857 g.
Obv. Designer: John Mercanti
Rev. Designer: Donna Weaver

Date	Mintage	Unc	Prf.
2005W	6,592	—	595

KM# 390 0.9995 **PLATINUM** 0.2502 oz. 22mm. 7.7857 g.
Obv. Designer: John Mercanti

Date	Mintage	Unc	Prf.
2006W	7,813	—	445

KM# 415 0.9995 **PLATINUM** 0.2502 oz. 22mm. 7.7857 g.
Obv. Designer: John Mercanti

Date	Mintage	Unc	Prf.
2007W	6,017	—	440

KM# 435 0.9995 **PLATINUM** 0.2502 oz. 22mm. 7.7857 g.
Obv. Designer: John Mercanti

Date	Mintage	Unc	Prf.
2008W	6,017	—	985

KM# 461 0.9995 **PLATINUM** 0.2502 oz. 22mm. 7.7857 g.
Obv. Designer: John Mercanti

Date	Mintage	Unc	Prf.
2009W	3,800	—	—

PLATINUM $50

KM# 285 0.9995 **PLATINUM** 0.4997 oz. 27mm. 15.5520 g.
Obv. Designer: John Mercanti
Rev. Designer: Thomas D. Rogers Sr

Date	Mintage	Unc	Prf.
2001	12,815	990	—
2002	24,005	990	—
2003	17,409	990	—
2004	13,236	990	—
2005	9,013	990	—
2006	9,602	990	—
2006W Burnished Unc.	—	1,132	—
2007	7,001	1,025	—
2007W Burnished Unc.	—	990	—
2008	14,000	990	—
2008W Burnished Unc.	—	1,200	—
2009	—	—	—

KM# 329 0.9995 **PLATINUM** 0.4997 oz. 27mm. 15.5520 g.
Obv. Designer: John Mercanti

Date	Mintage	Unc	Prf.
2001W	8,254	—	1,040

KM# 341 0.9995 **PLATINUM** 0.4997 oz. 27mm. 15.5520 g.
Obv. Designer: John Mercanti

Date	Mintage	Unc	Prf.
2002W	8,772	—	1,040

KM# 353 0.9995 **PLATINUM** 0.4997 oz. 27mm. 15.5520 g.
Obv. Designer: John Mercanti
Rev. Designer: Al Maletsky

Date	Mintage	Unc	Prf.
2003W	7,131	—	1,040

KM# 366 0.9995 **PLATINUM** 0.4997 oz. 27mm. 15.5520 g.
Obv. Designer: John Mercanti

Date	Mintage	Unc	Prf.
2004W	5,063	—	1,750

KM# 379 0.9995 **PLATINUM** 0.4997 oz. 27mm. 15.5520 g.
Obv. Designer: John Mercanti
Rev. Designer: Donna Weaver

Date	Mintage	Unc	Prf.
2005W	5,942	—	1,175

KM# 391 0.9995 **PLATINUM** 0.4997 oz. 27mm. 15.5520 g.
Obv. Designer: John Mercanti

Date	Mintage	Unc	Prf.
2006W	7,649	—	1,040

KM# 416 0.9995 **PLATINUM** 0.4997 oz. 27mm. 15.5520 g.
Obv. Designer: John Mercanti

Date	Mintage	Unc	Prf.
2007W	22,873	—	1,040
2007W Reverse Proof	16,937	—	1,040

KM# 436 0.9995 **PLATINUM** 0.4997 oz. 27mm. 15.5520 g.
Obv. Designer: John Mercanti

Date	Mintage	Unc	Prf.
2008W	22,873	—	1,600

KM# 462 0.9995 **PLATINUM** 0.4997 oz. 27mm. 15.5520 g.
Obv. Designer: John Mercanti

Date	Mintage	Unc	Prf.
2009	3,600	—	—

PLATINUM $100

KM# 286 0.9995 **PLATINUM** 0.9995 oz. 33mm. 31.1050 g.
Obv. Designer: John Mercanti **Rev. Designer:** Thomas D. Rogers Sr

Date	Mintage	Unc	Prf.
2001	14,070	1,980	—
2002	11,502	1,980	—
2003	8,007	1,980	—
2004	7,009	1,980	—
2005	6,310	1,980	—
2006	6,000	1,980	—
2006W Burnished Unc.	—	2,139	—
2007	7,202	2,033	—
2007W Burnished Unc.	—	1,980	—
2008	21,800	1,980	—
2008W Burnished Unc.	—	2,139	—
2009	—	—	—

KM# 330 0.9995 **PLATINUM** 0.9995 oz. 33mm. 31.1050 g.
Obv. Designer: John Mercanti

Date	Mintage	Unc	Prf.
2001W	8,969	—	2,079

KM# 342 0.9995 **PLATINUM** 0.9995 oz. 33mm. 31.1050 g.
Obv. Designer: John Mercanti

Date	Mintage	Unc	Prf.
2002W	9,834	—	2,079

KM# 354 0.9995 **PLATINUM** 0.9995 oz. 33mm. 31.1050 g.
Obv. Designer: John Mercanti
Rev. Designer: Al Maletsky

Date	Mintage	Unc	Prf.
2003W	8,246	—	2,098

KM# 367 0.9995 **PLATINUM** 0.9995 oz. 33mm. 31.1050 g.
Obv. Designer: John Mercanti
Rev. Designer: Donna Weaver

Date	Mintage	Unc	Prf.
2004W	6,007	—	2,406

KM# 380 0.9995 **PLATINUM** 0.9995 oz. 33mm. 31.1050 g.
Obv. Designer: John Mercanti
Rev. Designer: Donna Weaver

Date	Mintage	Unc	Prf.
2005W	6,602	—	2,400

KM# 392 0.9995 **PLATINUM** 0.9995 oz. 33mm. 31.1050 g.
Obv. Designer: John Mercanti

Date	Mintage	Unc	Prf.
2006W	9,152	—	2,079

KM# 417 0.9995 **PLATINUM** 0.9995 oz. 33mm. 31.1050 g. **Obv. Designer:** John Mercanti

Date	Mintage	Unc	Prf.
2007W	8,363	—	2,079

KM# 437 0.9995 **PLATINUM** 0.9995 oz. 33mm. 31.1050 g. **Obv. Designer:** John Mercanti

Date	Mintage	Unc	Prf.
2008W	8,363	—	2,825

KM# 463 0.9995 **PLATINUM** 0.9994 oz. 33mm. 31.1020 g. **Obv. Designer:** John Mercanti

Date	Mintage	Unc	Prf.
2009W Proof	4,900	—	2,600

KM# 488 0.9990 **PLATINUM** 0.9990 oz. 31.1050 g. **Obv. Designer:** John Mercanti

Date	Mintage	Unc	Prf.
2010W	—	—	2,200

AMERICA THE BEAUTIFUL SILVER BULLION

SILVER QUARTER

KM# 489 **Rev. Desc:** Park Headquarters and fountain, 155.5500g., 0.9990 Silver, 4.9958oz. **Rev. Designer:** Don Everhart II and Joseph Menna

Date	Mintage	Unc	Prf.
2010	—	—	—

KM# 490 **Rev. Desc:** Old Faithful geyser and bison 155.5500g., 0.9990 Silver, 4.9958oz. **Rev. Designer:** Don Everhart II

Date	Mintage	Unc	Prf.
2010	—	—	—

KM# 491 **Rev. Desc:** El Capitan, largest monolith of granite in the world, 155.5500g., 0.9990 Silver, 4.9958oz. **Rev. Designer:** Joseph Menna and Phebe Hemphill

Date	Mintage	Unc	Prf.
2010	—	—	—

KM# 492 **Rev. Desc:** Grabarues abive the Nankoweap Delta in Marble Canyon near the Colorado River, 155.5500g., 0.9990 Silver, 4.9958oz. **Rev. Designer:** Phebe Hemphill

Date	Mintage	Unc	Prf.
2010	—	—	—

KM# 493 **Rev. Desc:** Mt. Hood with Lost Lake in teh foreground, 155.5500g., 0.9990 Silver, 4.9958oz. **Rev. Designer:** Phebe Hemphill

Date	Mintage	Unc	Prf.
2010	—	—	—

KM# 513 **Rev. Desc:** 72nd Pennsylvania Infantry Monumnet on the battle line of the Union Army at Cemetery Ridge, 155.5500g., 0.9990 Silver, 4.9958oz. **Rev. Designer:** Joel Iskowitz and Phebe Hemphill

Date	Mintage	Unc	Prf.
2011	—	—	—

KM# 514 **Rev. Desc:** Northeast slope of Mount Reynolds, 155.5500g., 0.9990 Silver, 4.9958oz. **Rev. Designer:** Barbara Fox and Charles L. Vickers

Date	Mintage	Unc	Prf.
2011	—	—	—

KM# 515 **Rev. Desc:** Roosevelt elk on a gravel river bar along the Hoh River, Mount Olympus in the background, 155.5500g., 0.9990 Silver, 4.9958oz. **Rev. Designer:** Susan Gambel and Michael Gaudioso

Date	Mintage	Unc	Prf.
2011	—	—	—

KM# 516 **RevDesc:** U.S.S. Cairo on the Yazoo River, 155.5500g., 0.9990 Silver, 4.9958oz. **Rev. Designer:** Thomas Cleveland and Joseph menna

Date	Mintage	Unc	Prf.
2011	—	—	—

KM# 517 **RevDesc:** Limestone Lincoln Bridge, 155.5500g., 0.9990 Silver, 4.9958oz. **Rev. Designer:** Donna Weaver and James Licaretz

Date	Mintage	Unc	Prf.
2011	—	—	—

BISON BULLION COINAGE

GOLD $5

KM# 411 **Obv. Desc:** Indian Head right **Rev. Desc:** Bison, 3.1100g., 0.9999 Gold, 0.1000oz.

Date	Mintage	Unc	Prf.
2008W	19,300	—	575
2008W	19,000	550	—
2009W	—	550	—
2009W	—	—	575

GOLD $10

KM# 412 **Obv. Desc:** Indian Head right **Rev. Desc:** Bison, 7.7857g., 0.9999 Gold, 0.2503oz.

Date	Mintage	Unc	Prf.
2008W	13,900	—	1,500
2008W	10,500	1,425	—
2009W	—	1,425	—
2009W	—	—	1,500

GOLD $25

KM# 413 **Obv. Desc:** Indian Head right **Rev. Desc:** Bison, 15.5520g., 0.9990 Gold, 0.4995oz.

Date	Mintage	Unc	Prf.
2008W	12,500	—	1,600
2008W	17,000	1,300	—
2009W	—	1,300	—
2009W	—	—	1,600

GOLD $50

KM# 393 **Obv. Desc:** Indian head right **Rev. Desc:** Bison standing left on mound • 31.1050g., 0.9999 Gold, 0.9999oz. , 32mm. • **Designer:** James E. Fraser

Date	Mintage	Unc	Prf.
2006W	246,267	—	1,584
2006W	337,012	1,540	—
2007W	136,503	1,540	—
2007W	58,998	—	1,594
2008W	189,500	1,540	—
2008W	19,500	—	3,300
2008W Moy Family Chop	—	3,500	—
2009W	—	1,540	—
2009W	—	—	1,584
2010W	—	—	1,634

FIRST SPOUSE GOLD COINAGE

GOLD $10

KM# 407 **Obv. Desc:** Bust 3/4 facing **Rev. Desc:** Martha Washington seated sewing, 15.5520g., 0.9999 Gold, 0.4999oz. **Obv. Designer:** Joseph Menna **Rev. Designer:** Susan Gamble and Don Everhart

Date	Mintage	Unc	Prf.
2007W	20,000	791	—
2007W	20,000	—	791

KM# 408 **Obv. Desc:** Bust 3/4 facing **Rev. Desc:** Abigail Adams seated at desk writing to John during the Revolutionary War, 15.5520g., 0.9999 Gold, 0.4999oz. **Obv. Designer:** Joseph Menna **Rev. Designer:** Thomas Cleveland and Phebe Hemphill

Date	Mintage	Unc	Prf.
2007W	20,000	791	—
2007W	20,000	—	791

KM# 409 **Obv. Desc:** Bust design from coinage **Rev. Desc:** Jefferson's tombstone, 15.5520g., 0.9999 Gold, 0.4999oz. **Obv. Designer:** Robert Scot and Phebe Hemphill **Rev. Designer:** Charles Vickers

Date	Mintage	Unc	Prf.
2007W	20,000	791	—
2007W	20,000	—	791

KM# 410 **Obv. Desc:** Bust 3/4 facing **Rev. Desc:** Dolley standing before painting of Washington, which she saved from the White House, 15.5520g., 0.9999 Gold, 0.4999oz. **Obv. Designer:** Don Everhart **Rev. Designer:** Joel Iskowitz and Don Everhart

Date	Mintage	Unc	Prf.
2007W	12,500	791	—
2007W	18,300	—	791

KM# 430 **Obv. Desc:** Bust 3/4 facing right **Rev. Desc:** Elizabeth standing before mirror, 15.5520g., 0.9990 Gold, 0.4995oz. **Obv. Designer:** Joel Iskowitz and Don Everhart **Rev. Designer:** Donna Weaver and Charles Vickers

Date	Mintage	Unc	Prf.
2008W	4,500	—	—
2008W	7,900	—	—

KM# 431 **Obv. Desc:** Bust 3/4 facing right **Rev. Desc:** Lousia and son Charles before entrance, 15.5520g., 0.9990 Gold, 0.4995oz. **Obv. Designer:** Susan Gamble and Phebe Hemphill **Rev. Designer:** Joseph Menna

Date	Mintage	Unc	Prf.
2008W	4,200	—	—
2008W	7,400	—	—

KM# 432 **Obv. Desc:** Capped and draped bust left **Rev. Desc:** Andrew Jackson on horseback right, 15.5520g., 0.9990 Gold, 0.4995oz. **Obv. Designer:** John Reich **Rev. Designer:** Justin Kunz and Don Everhart

Date	Mintage	Unc	Prf.
2008W	4,800	—	—
2008W	7,800	—	—

KM# 433 **Obv. Desc:** Seated Liberty with shiled **Rev. Desc:** Youthful van Buren seated under tree, family tavern in distance, 15.5520g., 0.9990 Gold, 0.4995oz. **Obv. Designer:** Christian Gobrecht **Rev. Designer:** Thomas Cleveland and James Licaretz

Date	Mintage	Unc	Prf.
2008W	15,000	—	—
2008W	Inc. above	—	—

KM# 456 **Obv. Desc:** Bust 3/4 left **Rev. Desc:** Anna reading to her three children, 15.5520g., 0.9990 Gold, 0.4995oz. **Obv. Designer:** Donna Weaver and Joseph Menna **Rev. Designer:** Thomas Cleveland and Charles Vickers

Date	Mintage	Unc	Prf.
2009W	15,000	—	—
2009W	Inc. above	—	—

KM# 457 Obv. Desc: Bust facing **Rev. Desc:** Letitia and two children playing outside of Cedar Grove Plantation, 15.5520g., 0.9990 Gold, 0.4995oz. **Obv. Designer:** Phebe Hemphill **Rev. Designer:** Susan Gamble and Norm Nemeth

Date	Mintage	Unc	Prf.
2009W	15,000	—	—
2009W	Inc. above	—	—

KM# 458 Obv. Desc: Bust facing **Rev. Desc:** Julia and John Tyler dancing, 15.5520g., 0.9990 Gold, 0.4995oz. **Designer:** Joel Iskowitz and Don Everhart

Date	Mintage	Unc	Prf.
2009W	15,000	—	—
2009W	Inc. above	—	—

KM# 459 Obv. Desc: Bust 3/4 right **Rev. Desc:** Sarah seated at desk as personal secretary to James Polk, 15.5520g., 0.9990 Gold, 0.4995oz. **Designer:** Phebe Hemphill

Date	Mintage	Unc	Prf.
2009W	3,501	—	—
2009W	5,157	—	—

KM# 465 Obv. Desc: Bust 3/4 left **Rev. Desc:** Margaret Taylor nurses wounded soldier during the Seminole War, 15.5520g., 0.9990 Gold, 0.4995oz. **Obv. Designer:** Phebe Hemphill and Charles Vickers **Rev. Designer:** Mary Beth Zeitz and James Licaretz

Date	Mintage	Unc	Prf.
2009W	3,430	—	—
2009W	4,787	—	—

KM# 48 Rev. Desc: Abigail Filmore placing books on library shelf, 15.5200g., 0.9990 Gold, 0.4985oz. **Obv. Designer:** Phebe Hemphill **Rev. Designer:** Susan Gamble and Joseph Menna

Date	Mintage	Unc	Prf.
2010W	15,000	—	—
2010W	Inc. above	—	—

KM# 482 Rev. Desc: Jane Pierce seated on porch, 15.5200g., 0.9990 Gold, 0.4985oz. **Obv. Designer:** Donna Weaver and Don Everhart **Rev. Designer:** Donna Weaver and Charles Vickers

Date	Mintage	Unc	Prf.
2010W	15,000	—	—
2010W	Inc. above	—	—

KM# 483 Rev. Desc: Buchanan as clerk, 15.5200g., 0.9990 Gold, 0.4985oz. **Obv. Designer:** Christian Gobrecht **Rev. Designer:** Joseph Menna

Date	Mintage	Unc	Prf.
2010W	15,000	—	—
2010W	Inc. above	—	—

KM# 48 Rev. Desc: Mary Lincoln visiting soldiers at hospital, 15.5200g., 0.9990 Gold, 0.4985oz. **Obv. Designer:** Phebe Hemphill **Rev. Designer:** Joel Iskowitz and Pheve Hemphill

Date	Mintage	Unc	Prf.
2010	15,000	—	—
2010	Inc. above	—	—

KM# 509 Obv. Desc: Bust of Eliza Johnson, 15.5500g., 0.9990 Gold, 0.4994oz.

Date	Mintage	Unc	Prf.
2011W	15,000	—	—
2011W	Inc. above	—	—

KM# 510 Obv. Desc: Bust of Julia Grant, 15.5520g., 0.9990 Gold, 0.4995oz.

Date	Mintage	Unc	Prf.
2011W	15,000	—	—
2011W	Inc. above	—	—

KM# 511 Obv. Desc: Bust of Lucy Hayes, 15.5520g., 0.9990 Gold, 0.4995oz.

Date	Mintage	Unc	Prf.
2011W	15,000	—	—
2011W	Inc. above	—	—

KM# 512 Obv. Desc: Bust of Lucretia Garfield, 15.5520g., 0.9990 Gold, 0.4995oz.

Date	Mintage	Unc	Prf.
2011W	15,000	768	—
2011W	Inc. above	—	781

MINT SETS

Date	Sets Sold	Issue Price	Value
2001	1,066,900	14.95	19.50
2002	1,139,388	14.95	21.00
2003	1,002,555	14.95	16.75
2004	844,484	16.95	22.50
2005	—	16.95	9.75
2006	—	16.95	13.75
2007	—	—	21.00
2008	—	—	50.00
2009 18 pieces clad	—	—	34.50
2010 28 piece clad coin set	—	—	—

MODERN COMMEMORATIVE COIN SETS

American Buffalo

Date	Price
2001 2 coin set: 90% silver unc. & proof $1.; KM325.	328
2001 coin & currency set 90% unc. dollar & replicas of 1899 $5 silver cert.; KM325.	174
Bald Eagle proof half dollar, dollar and $5 gold, KM438, KM439, KM440	440

Capitol Visitor Center

Date	Price
2001 3 coin set: proof half, silver dollar, gold $5; KM323, 324, 326.	429
Bald Eagle proof half dollar, dollar and $5 gold, KM438, KM439, KM440	440

Winter Olympics - Salt Lake City

Date	Price
2002 2 coin set: proof 90% silver dollar KM336 & $5.00 Gold KM337.	410
2002 4 coin set: 90% silver unc. & proof $1, KM336 & unc. & proof gold $5, KM337.	820
Bald Eagle proof half dollar, dollar and $5 gold, KM438, KM439, KM440	440

First Flight Centennial

Date	Price
2003 3 coin set: proof gold ten dollar KM350, proof silver dollar KM349 & proof clad half dollar KM348.	805
Bald Eagle proof half dollar, dollar and $5 gold, KM438, KM439, KM440	440

Lewis and Clark Bicentennial

Date	Price
2004 Coin and pouch set.	75.00
2004 coin and currency set: Uncirculated silver dollar, two 2005 nickels, replica 1901 $10 Bison note, silver plated peace medal, three stamps & two booklets.	42.00
2004 Westward Journey Nickel series coin and medal set: Proof Sacagawea dollar, two 2005 proof nickels and silver plated peace medal.	35.00
Bald Eagle proof half dollar, dollar and $5 gold, KM438, KM439, KM440	440

Thomas Alva Edison

Date	Price
2004 Uncirculated silver dollar and light bulb.	60.00
Bald Eagle proof half dollar, dollar and $5 gold, KM438, KM439, KM440	440

U.S. Marine Corps.

Date	Price
2005 Uncirculated silver dollar and stamp set.	53.00
2005 American Legacy: Proof Marine Corps dollar, Proof John Marshall dollar and 10 piece proof set.	180
Bald Eagle proof half dollar, dollar and $5 gold, KM438, KM439, KM440	440

Chief Justice John Marshall

Date	Price
2005 Coin and Chronicles set: Uncirculated silver dollar, booklet and BEP intaglio portrait.	53.00
Bald Eagle proof half dollar, dollar and $5 gold, KM438, KM439, KM440	440

Benjamin Franklin Tercentennary

Date	Price
2006 Coin and Chronicles set: Uncirculated "Scientist" silver dollar, four stamps, Poor Richards Almanac and intaglio print.	41.00
Bald Eagle proof half dollar, dollar and $5 gold, KM438, KM439, KM440	440

PROOF SETS

Date	Sets Sold	Issue Price	Value
2001S 10 piece	2,249,498	19.95	26.00
2001S 5 quarter set	774,800	13.95	23.50
2001S Silver	849,600	31.95	72.50
2002S 10 piece	2,319,766	19.95	11.25
2002S 5 quarter set	764,419	13.95	9.50
2002S Silver	892,229	31.95	58.50
2003 X#207, 208, 209.2	—	44.00	28.75
2003S 10 piece	2,175,684	16.75	8.50
2003S 5 quarter set	1,225,507	13.95	5.00
2003S Silver	1,142,858	31.95	58.50
2004S 11 piece	1,804,396	22.95	11.75
2004S 5 quarter set	987,960	23.95	6.75
2004S Silver 11 piece	1,187,673	37.95	58.50
2004S Silver 5 quarter set	594,137	—	39.00
2005S Silver 5 quarter set	—	23.95	39.00
2005S American Legacy	—	—	98.00
2005S American Legacy	—	—	75.00
2005S 11 piece	—	22.95	5.75
2005S 5 quarter set	—	15.95	5.00
2005S Silver 11 piece	—	37.95	54.00
2006S American Legacy	—	—	75.00
2006S 10 piece clad	—	22.95	13.00
2006S 5 quarter set	—	15.95	8.00
2006S Silver 10 piece	—	37.95	58.50
2006S Silver 5 quarter set	—	23.95	39.00
2007S Presidental $ set	—	—	10.50
2007S American Legacy	—	—	175
2007S 5 quarter set	—	13.95	9.00
2007S Silver 5 quarter set	—	22.95	39.00
2007S 14 piece clad	—	—	26.00
2007S Silver 14 piece	—	—	61.00
2008 14 pieces clad	—	—	59.00
2008S American Legacy	—	—	158
2008S Silver 14 piece	734,045	—	66.50
2008S Presidental $ set	—	—	17.50
2008S 5 quarter set	—	22.95	33.50
2008S Silver 5 quarter set	—	—	39.00
2009S 6 quarter set	—	—	11.00
2009S Silver 6 quarter set	—	—	47.00
2009S 18 coin clad set	1,477,967	—	31.50
2009S Silver 18 coin set	694,406	—	67.50
2009S Presidential $ set	627,925	—	8.00
2009S Lincoln Chronicle	—	—	169
2009S Lincoln 4 piece	—	—	18.50
2010S 14 coin clad set	—	—	—
2010S 14 coin silver set	—	—	—
2010S Presidential $ set	—	—	—
2010S 5 clad quarter set	—	—	—
2010S 5 silver quarter set	—	—	—

UNCIRCULATED ROLLS

Listings are for rolls containing uncirculated coins. Large date and small date varieties for 1960 and 1970 apply to the one cent coins.

Date	Cents	Nickels	Dimes	Quarters	Halves
2001P	3.75	4.75	7.75	—	16.50
2001D	2.00	6.50	7.25	—	16.00
2002P	2.00	4.00	7.25	—	20.00
2002D	3.25	4.10	7.25	—	20.00
2003P	3.35	7.50	7.00	—	22.50
2003D	2.00	3.50	7.00	—	19.50
2004P Peace Medal Nickel	1.75	6.75	7.00	—	30.00
2004D Peace Medal Nickel	2.50	7.00	7.00	—	30.00
2004P Keelboat Nickel	—	4.00	—	—	—
2004D Keelboat Nickel	—	3.50	—	—	—
2005P Bison Nickel	1.75	3.25	7.00	—	21.00
2005D Bison Nickel	2.75	3.25	7.00	—	21.00
2005P Ocean in view Nickel	—	3.25	—	—	—
2005D Ocean in view Nickel	—	3.25	—	—	—
2006P	2.75	3.25	8.50	—	29.00
2006D	1.75	3.25	8.50	—	29.00
2007P	1.75	3.50	8.00	—	21.00
2007D	1.75	3.50	7.75	—	21.00
2008P	1.75	3.75	8.00	—	24.50
2008D	1.75	3.75	7.50	—	25.50
2009P Log Cabin	2.00	23.00	13.50	—	18.50
2009D Log Cabin	2.15	13.50	13.50	—	18.50
2009P Log Splitter	1.75	—	—	—	—
2009D Log Splitter	1.75	—	—	—	—
2009P Professional	—	1.75	—	—	—
2009D Professional	1.75	—	—	—	—
2009P President	2.00	—	—	—	—
2009D President	2.00	—	—	—	—
2009 DC	18.00	15.50	—	—	—
2009 Puerto Rico	15.00	15.50	—	—	—
2009 Guam	15.00	16.50	—	—	—
2009 American Samoa	15.00	15.00	—	—	—
2009 Virgin Islands	15.00	15.00	—	—	—
2009 Marianna Islands	15.00	15.00	—	—	—

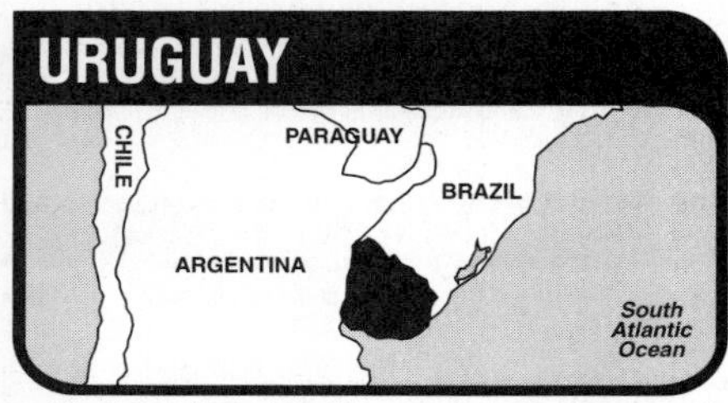

The Oriental Republic of Uruguay (so called because of its location on the east bank of the Uruguay River) is situated on the Atlantic coast of South America between Argentina and Brazil. This South American country has an area of 68,536 sq. mi. (176,220 sq. km.) and a population of *3 million. Capital: Montevideo. Uruguay's chief economic asset is the rich, rolling grassy plains. Meat, wool, hides and skins are exported.

MINT MARKS

(ba) – Buenos Aires
(br) – Acunaciones Espanolas S.A., Barcelona
(k) – Kremnica (Slovakia)
(m) - Madrid
Mo, (mo) and Mx - Mexico City
(p) – thunderbolt: Poissy, France
(rcm) – Royal Canadian Mint
(rj) – Rio de Janeiro
(sa) – Pretoria, South Africa
So, (so) – Santiago (Small o above S); (except 2007 2 Pesos Uruguayos)

REPUBLIC

REFORM COINAGE

March 1993

1,000 Nuevos Pesos = 1 Uruguayan Peso; 100 Centesimos = 1 Uruguayan Peso (UYP)

KM# 106 50 CENTESIMOS
3.0000 g., Stainless Steel, 21 mm. **Obv:** Bust of Artigas right **Obv. Legend:** REPUBLICA ORIENTAL DEL URUGUAY **Rev:** Value, date and sprig **Edge:** Plain **Note:** Coin rotation.

Date	Mintage	F	VF	XF	Unc	BU
2002(sa)	10,000,000	—	—	0.35	0.75	1.00
2005(m)	15,000,000	—	—	0.35	0.75	1.00
2008(k)	35,000,000	—	—	0.35	0.75	1.00

KM# 103.2 UN PESO URUGUAYO
3.5000 g., Aluminum-Bronze, 20 mm. **Obv:** Bust of Artigas right **Obv. Legend:** REPUBLICA ORIENTAL DEL URUGUAY **Rev:** Value and date **Edge:** Plain **Note:** Medal rotation; left point of bust shoulder points at "P" in Republic.

Date	Mintage	F	VF	XF	Unc	BU
2005So	40,000,000	—	—	—	0.50	0.75
2007So	25,000,000	—	—	—	0.50	0.75

KM# 104.2 2 PESOS URUGUAYOS
4.5000 g., Aluminum-Bronze, 23 mm. **Obv:** Bust of Artigas right **Obv. Legend:** REPUBLICA ORIENTAL DEL URUGUAY **Rev:** Value and date **Edge:** Plain **Note:** Medal rotation. Left point of bust shoulder points at "P" in "Republic".

Date	Mintage	F	VF	XF	Unc	BU
2007So	25,000,000	—	—	0.75	1.50	2.00

Note: Minted at Paris with the So mintmark.

Date	Mintage	F	VF	XF	Unc	BU
2008So	—	—	—	0.75	1.50	2.00

KM# 120.1 5 PESOS URUGUAYOS
6.3000 g., Aluminum-Bronze, 26 mm. **Obv:** Bust of Antigas right **Obv. Legend:** REPUBLICA ORIENTAL DEL URUGUAY **Rev:** Value **Edge:** Plain **Note:** Left point of bust shoulder points at "U" in "Republic".

Date	Mintage	F	VF	XF	Unc	BU
2003(ba)	15,150,000	—	—	—	2.50	3.00

KM# 120.2 5 PESOS URUGUAYOS
6.3000 g., Aluminum-Bronze, 26 mm. **Obv:** Bust of Antigas right **Obv. Legend:** REPUBLICA ORIENTAL DEL URUGUAY • **Rev:** Value, date **Note:** Left point of bust shoulder points at "P" in "Republic".

Date	Mintage	F	VF	XF	Unc	BU
2005So	30,000,000	—	—	—	2.50	3.00
2008So	20,000,000	—	—	—	2.50	3.00

KM# 121 10 PESOS URUGUAYOS
10.4000 g., Bi-Metallic Aluminum-Bronze center in Stainless Steel ring, 28 mm. **Obv:** Artigas head right within circle **Rev:** Value above signature within circle **Edge:** Plain

Date	Mintage	F	VF	XF	Unc	BU
2000 (rcm)	40,000,000	—	—	—	3.50	5.00

Note: 5-pointed star to each side of date, issued 2006

KM# 134 10 PESOS URUGUAYOS
Bi-Metallic **Obv:** Oval arms **Rev:** Lion walking left, sunrise in background

Date	Mintage	F	VF	XF	Unc	BU
2011	—	—	—	—	7.50	10.00

KM# 133 500 PESOS URUGAUAYOS
12.5000 g., 0.9000 Silver 0.3617 oz. ASW, 33 mm. **Subject:** Salto, 250th Anniversary **Obv:** Uruguay map with City of Salto location **Rev:** Emblem of the Department of Salto

Date	Mintage	F	VF	XF	Unc	BU
2006(u) Proof	10,000	Value: 25.00				

KM# 122 1000 PESOS URUGUAYOS
27.0000 g., 0.9250 Silver 0.8029 oz. ASW, 40 mm. **Subject:** XVIII World Championship Football - Germany 2006 **Obv:** National arms **Obv. Legend:** REPUBLICA ORIENTAL DEL URUGUAY **Rev:** Soccer player and value **Edge:** Reeded

Date	Mintage	F	VF	XF	Unc	BU
2003(m) Proof	—	Value: 50.00				

KM# 123 1000 PESOS URUGUAYOS
27.0000 g., 0.9250 Silver 0.8029 oz. ASW, 40 mm. **Subject:** XVIII World Championship Football - Germany 2006 **Obv:** National arms above date **Obv. Legend:** REPUBLICA ORIENTAL DEL URUGUAY **Rev:** Stylized soccer player and value **Edge:** Reeded

Date	Mintage	F	VF	XF	Unc	BU
2004(m) Proof	—	Value: 50.00				

KM# 125 1000 PESOS URUGUAYOS
27.0000 g., 0.9250 Silver 0.8029 oz. ASW, 40 mm. **Subject:** 100th Anniversary FIFA - 1930 Championship **Obv:** Football before net **Obv. Legend:** REPUBLICA ORIENTAL DEL URUGUAY **Rev:** Sun of national flag **Edge:** Reeded

Date	Mintage	F	VF	XF	Unc	BU
2004(m) Proof	—	Value: 45.00				

KM# 124 1000 PESOS URUGUAYOS
27.0000 g., 0.9250 Silver 0.8029 oz. ASW, 40 mm. **Subject:** XVIII World Championship Football - Germany 2006 **Obv:** National arms above date **Obv. Legend:** REPUBLICA ORIENTAL DEL URUGUAY **Rev:** FIFA trophy **Edge:** Reeded

Date	Mintage	F	VF	XF	Unc	BU
2005(m) Proof	—	Value: 50.00				

KM# 126 5000 PESOS URUGUAYOS
6.7500 g., 0.9250 Gold 0.2007 oz. AGW, 23 mm. **Subject:** 100th Anniversary FIFA - 1930 Championship **Obv:** Football **Obv. Legend:** REPUBLICA ORIENTAL DEL URUGUAY **Rev:** Tower of Homage in Montevideo **Edge:** Reeded

Date	Mintage	F	VF	XF	Unc	BU
2004(m) Proof	—	Value: 350				

KM# 127 5000 PESOS URUGUAYOS
6.7500 g., 0.9250 Gold 0.2007 oz. AGW, 23 mm. **Subject:** XVIII World Championship Football - Germany 2006 **Obv:** National arms **Obv. Legend:** REPUBLICA ORIENTAL DEL URUGUAY **Rev:** Stylized player and value **Edge:** Reeded

Date	Mintage	F	VF	XF	Unc	BU
2004(m) Proof	—	Value: 500				

The Republic of Uzbekistan (formerly the Uzbek S.S.R.), is bordered on the north by Kazakhstan, to the east by Kirghizia and Tajikistan, on the south by Afghanistan and on the west by Turkmenistan. The republic is comprised of the regions of Andizhan, Bukhara, Dzhizak, Ferghana, Kashkadar, Khorezm (Khiva), Namangan, Navoi, Samarkand, Surkhan-Darya, Syr-Darya, Tashkent and the Karakalpak Autonomous Republic. It has an area of 172,741 sq. mi. (447,400 sq. km.) and a population of 20.3 million. Capital: Tashkent. Crude oil, natural gas, coal, copper, and gold deposits make up the chief resources, while intensive farming, based on artificial irrigation, provides an abundance of cotton.

MONETARY SYSTEM

100 Tiyin = 1 Som

REPUBLIC

STANDARD COINAGE

KM# 13 5 SOM
3.3500 g., Brass Plated Steel, 21.2 mm. **Obv:** National arms **Rev:** Value and map **Edge:** Plain

Date	Mintage	F	VF	XF	Unc	BU
2001	—	—	—	—	1.35	1.75

Note: 2 reverse map varieties known

KM# 14 10 SOM
2.7100 g., Nickel Clad Steel, 19.75 mm. **Obv:** National arms **Rev:** Value and map **Edge:** Plain

Date	Mintage	F	VF	XF	Unc	BU
2001	—	—	—	—	2.00	2.50

Note: 2 reverse map varieties exist

KM# 15 50 SOM
8.0000 g., Nickel Clad Steel, 26.2 mm. **Obv:** National arms **Rev:** Value and map **Edge:** Segmented reeding

Date	Mintage	F	VF	XF	Unc	BU
2001	—	—	—	1.20	3.00	4.00

KM# 16 50 SOM
7.9000 g., Nickel Clad Steel, 26.3 mm. **Subject:** 2700th

Anniversary of Shahrisabz Town **Obv:** National arms **Rev:** Statue and ruins above value **Edge:** Segmented reeding

Date	Mintage	F	VF	XF	Unc	BU
2002	—	—	—	1.00	2.50	3.50

KM# 20 100 SOM

31.1000 g., 0.9990 Silver 0.9988 oz. ASW **Obv:** National arms **Obv. Legend:** O'ZBEKISTON MARKAZIY BANKI **Rev:** Amir-Timur Museum

Date	Mintage	F	VF	XF	Unc	BU
2001 Proof	1,000	Value: 225				

KM# 21 100 SOM

31.1000 g., 0.9990 Silver 0.9988 oz. ASW **Obv:** National Arms **Obv. Legend:** O'BEKISTON MARKAZY BANKI **Rev:** Toskent town hall

Date	Mintage	F	VF	XF	Unc	BU
2001 Proof	1,000	Value: 225				

KM# 22 100 SOM

31.1000 g., 0.9990 Silver 0.9988 oz. ASW **Obv:** National arms **Obv. Legend:** O'ZBEKISTON MARKAZIY BANKI **Rev:** World

Date	Mintage	F	VF	XF	Unc	BU
2001 Proof	1,000	Value: 225				

KM# 18 100 SOM

Bronze **Subject:** 500th Anniversary Death of 'Aliser Navoi **Obv:** National arms **Obv. Legend:** O'ZBEKISTON MARKAZIY BANKI **Rev:** 'Aliser Navoi

Date	Mintage	F	VF	XF	Unc	BU
2001	—	—	—	—	15.00	18.00

KM# 19 100 SOM

31.1000 g., 0.9990 Silver 0.9988 oz. ASW **Obv:** National arms **Obv. Legend:** O'ZBEKISTON MARKAZIY BANKI **Rev:** Parliament building in Toskent

Date	Mintage	F	VF	XF	Unc	BU
2001 Proof	1,000	Value: 225				

KM# 23 100 SOM

31.1000 g., 0.9990 Silver 0.9988 oz. ASW **Obv:** National arms **Obv. Legend:** O'ZBEKISTON MARKAZIY BANKI **Rev:** Football player

Date	Mintage	F	VF	XF	Unc	BU
2001 Proof	1,000	Value: 225				

KM# 24 100 SOM

31.1000 g., 0.9990 Silver 0.9988 oz. ASW **Obv:** National arms **Obv. Legend:** O'BEKISTON MARKAZIY BANKI **Rev:** Track runner

Date	Mintage	F	VF	XF	Unc	BU
2001 Proof	1,000	Value: 225				

KM# 25 100 SOM

31.1000 g., 0.9990 Silver 0.9988 oz. ASW **Obv:** National arms **Obv. Legend:** O'ZBEKISTON MARKAZIY BANKI **Rev:** Judo expert

Date	Mintage	F	VF	XF	Unc	BU
2001 Proof	1,000	Value: 225				

KM# 26 100 SOM

31.1000 g., 0.9990 Silver 0.9988 oz. ASW **Obv:** National arms **Obv. Legend:** O'ZBEKISTON MARKAZIY BANKI **Rev:** Tennis player

Date	Mintage	F	VF	XF	Unc	BU
2001 Proof	1,000	Value: 225				

KM# 27 100 SOM

31.1000 g., 0.9990 Silver 0.9988 oz. ASW **Obv:** National arms **Obv. Legend:** O'ZBEKISTON MARKAZIY BANKI **Rev:** Lenk monument in Timur

Date	Mintage	F	VF	XF	Unc	BU
2001 Proof	1,000	Value: 225				

KM# 28 100 SOM

31.1000 g., 0.9990 Silver 0.9988 oz. ASW **Obv:** National arms **Obv. Legend:** O'ZBEKISTON MARKAZIY BANKI **Rev:** Aliser Navoi monument

Date	Mintage	F	VF	XF	Unc	BU
2001 Proof	1,000	Value: 225				

KM# 29 100 SOM

31.1000 g., 0.9990 Silver 0.9988 oz. ASW **Obv:** National arms **Obv. Legend:** O'ZBEKISTON MARKAZIY BANKI **Rev:** Registan in Samarkand

Date	Mintage	F	VF	XF	Unc	BU
2001 Proof	1,000	Value: 225				

KM# 30 100 SOM

31.1000 g., 0.9990 Silver 0.9988 oz. ASW **Obv:** National arms **Obv. Legend:** O'BEKISTON MARKAZIY BANKI **Rev:** Bell tower in Toskent

Date	Mintage	F	VF	XF	Unc	BU
2001 Proof	1,000	Value: 225				

KM# 17 100 SOM

7.9200 g., Nickel Plated Steel, 26.95 mm. **Subject:** 10th Annniversary State Currency **Obv:** National arms **Obv. Legend:** O'ZBEKISTON MARKAZIV BANKI **Rev:** Sun rays over outlined map and value **Rev. Legend:** O'BEKISTON MILLIY VALYUTASIGA **Edge:** Lettered

Date	Mintage	F	VF	XF	Unc	BU
2004	—	—	—	—	12.50	15.00

VANUATU

The Republic of Vanuatu, formerly New Hebrides Condominium, a group of islands located in the South Pacific 500 miles (800 km.) west of Fiji, were under the joint sovereignty of Great Britain and France. The islands have an area of 5,700 sq. mi. (14,760 sq. km.) and a population of 165,000, mainly Melanesians of mixed blood. Capital: Port-Vila. The volcanic and coral islands, while malarial land subject to frequent earthquakes, are extremely fertile, and produce copra, coffee, tropical fruits and timber for export.

The New Hebrides were discovered by Portuguese navigator Pedro de Quiros (sailing under orders by the King of Spain) in 1606, visited by French explorer Bougainville in 1768, and named by British navigator Capt. James Cook in 1774. Ships of all nations converged on the islands to trade for sandalwood, prompting France and Britain to relinquish their individual claims and declare the islands a neutral zone in 1878. The New Hebrides were placed under the control of a mixed Anglo-French commission of naval officers during the native uprisings of 1887, and established as a condominium under the joint sovereignty of France and Great Britain in 1906.

Vanuatu became an independent republic within the Commonwealth in July 1980. A president is Head of State and the Prime Minister is Head of Government.

MONETARY SYSTEM

Vatu to Present

REPUBLIC

STANDARD COINAGE

KM# 45 10 VATU

Copper-Nickel silver plated **Obv:** Arms **Rev:** Multicolor butterfly (Papilio Toboroi)

Date	Mintage	F	VF	XF	Unc	BU
2006	2,500	—	—	—	—	32.00

KM# 50 10 VATU

Copper-Nickel silver plated **Obv:** Arms **Rev:** Multicolor butterfly (Delias Sagessa)

Date	Mintage	F	VF	XF	Unc	BU
2006	2,500	—	—	—	—	32.00

KM# 46 10 VATU

Copper-Nickel silver plated **Obv:** Arms **Rev:** Multicolor butterfly (Taenaris Catops)

Date	Mintage	F	VF	XF	Unc	BU
2006	2,500	—	—	—	—	32.00

KM# 47 10 VATU

Copper-Nickel silver plated **Obv:** Arms **Rev:** Multicolor Butterfly (Ornithoptera Priamus Urvillianus)

Date	Mintage	F	VF	XF	Unc	BU
2006	2,500	—	—	—	—	32.00

KM# 48 10 VATU

Copper-Nickel silver plated **Obv:** Arms **Rev:** Multicolor butterfly (Ornithoptera Paradisea)

Date	Mintage	F	VF	XF	Unc	BU
2006	2,500	—	—	—	—	32.00

KM# 49 10 VATU

Copper-Nickel silver plated **Obv:** Arms **Rev:** Multicolor butterfly (Cethosia Cydippe)

Date	Mintage	F	VF	XF	Unc	BU
2006	2,500	—	—	—	—	32.00

KM# 38 50 VATU

28.3200 g., 0.9250 Silver 0.8422 oz. ASW, 38.6 mm. **Obv:** National arms **Obv. Legend:** RIPABLIK / VANUATU **Rev:** Early sailing ship center - left, stylized compass at right **Rev. Legend:** HISTORY OF SEAFARING / PEDRO FERNANDEZ DE QUIRÓS **Edge:** Reeded

Date	Mintage	F	VF	XF	Unc	BU
2005 Proof	—	Value: 45.00				

KM# 41 50 VATU

25.0000 g., 0.9000 Silver 0.7234 oz. ASW **Series:** Protection of Marine Life **Obv:** National arms **Rev:** Tiger Shark - multicolor

Date	Mintage	F	VF	XF	Unc	BU
2005 Proof	—	Value: 75.00				

KM# 42 50 VATU

25.0000 g., 0.9000 Silver 0.7234 oz. ASW **Series:** Protection of Marine Life **Obv:** National arms **Rev:** Sea Turtle - multicolor

Date	Mintage	F	VF	XF	Unc	BU
2006 Proof	—	Value: 75.00				

KM# 43 50 VATU

25.0000 g., 0.9000 Silver 0.7234 oz. ASW **Series:** Protection of Marine Life **Obv:** National arms **Rev:** Sea Horse - multicolor

Date	Mintage	F	VF	XF	Unc	BU
2006 Proof	—	Value: 75.00				

VATICAN CITY

The State of the Vatican City, a papal state on the right bank of the Tiber River within the boundaries of Rome, has an area of 0.17 sq. mi. (0.44 sq. km.) and a population of *775. Capital: Vatican City.

Today the Pope exercises supreme legislative, executive and judicial power within the Vatican City, and the State of the Vatican City is recognized by many nations as an independent sovereign state under the temporal jurisdiction of the Pope, even to the extent of ambassadorial exchange. The Pope is of course, the head of the Roman Catholic Church.

PONTIFFS

John Paul II, 1978-2005
Sede Vacante, April 2 - 19, 2005
Benedict XVI, 2005-

MINT MARK

R – Rome

MONETARY SYSTEM

100 Centesimi = 1 Lira (thru 2002)
100 Euro Cent = 1 Euro

DATING

Most Vatican coins indicate the regnal year of the pope preceded by the word *Anno* (or an abbreviation), even if the *anno domini* date is omitted.

CITY STATE

DECIMAL COINAGE

100 Centesimi = 1 Lira

KM# 331 10 LIRE

1.6000 g., Aluminum, 23.2 mm. **Ruler:** John Paul II **Obv:** Bust left **Rev:** Papal arms **Edge:** Plain **Designer:** Laura Cretara

Date	Mintage	F	VF	XF	Unc	BU
2001/XXIII	—	—	0.50	1.00	3.00	—

KM# 331a 10 LIRE

Gold, 23.2 mm. **Ruler:** John Paul II **Obv:** Benedict XV bust left **Rev:** Papal arms **Designer:** Laura Cretara **Note:** Struck in 2007.

Date	Mintage	F	VF	XF	Unc	BU
2001R Proof	499	—	—	—	—	—

KM# 332 20 LIRE

3.5700 g., Brass, 21.2 mm. **Ruler:** John Paul II **Obv:** Bust left **Rev:** Papal arms **Edge:** Plain **Designer:** Laura Cretara

Date	Mintage	F	VF	XF	Unc	BU
2001/XXIII	—	—	0.50	1.00	3.00	—

KM# 332a 20 LIRE

Gold, 21.2 mm. **Ruler:** John Paul II **Obv:** Pius XI bust left **Rev:** Papal arms **Designer:** Laura Cretara **Note:** Struck in 2007.

Date	Mintage	F	VF	XF	Unc	BU
2001R Proof	499	—	—	—	—	—

KM# 333 50 LIRE

4.5000 g., Copper-Nickel, 19.2 mm. **Ruler:** John Paul II **Obv:** Pius XII bust left **Rev:** Papal arms **Edge:** Plain **Designer:** Laura Cretara

Date	Mintage	F	VF	XF	Unc	BU
2001/XXIII	—	—	0.50	1.00	3.00	—

KM# 333a 50 LIRE

Gold, 19.2 mm. **Ruler:** John Paul II **Obv:** Pius XII bust left **Rev:** Papal arms **Designer:** Laura Cretara **Note:** Struck in 2007.

Date	Mintage	F	VF	XF	Unc	BU
2001R Proof	499	—	—	—	—	—

KM# 334 100 LIRE

4.5000 g., Copper-Nickel, 22 mm. **Ruler:** John Paul II **Obv:** Bust left **Rev:** Papal arms within circle **Edge:** Reeded and plain sections **Designer:** Laura Cretara

Date	Mintage	F	VF	XF	Unc	BU
2001/XXIII	—	—	0.50	1.00	3.00	—

KM# 334a 100 LIRE

Gold, 22 mm. **Ruler:** John Paul II **Obv:** John XXIII bust left **Rev:** Papal arms **Designer:** Laura Cretara **Note:** Struck in 2007.

Date	Mintage	F	VF	XF	Unc	BU
2001R Proof	499	—	—	—	—	—

KM# 335 200 LIRE

5.0000 g., Brass, 22 mm. **Ruler:** John Paul II **Obv:** Bust right **Rev:** Papal arms within circle **Edge:** Reeded **Designer:** Laura Cretara

Date	Mintage	F	VF	XF	Unc	BU
2001/XXIII	—	—	0.50	1.00	3.00	—

KM# 335a 200 LIRE

Gold, 22 mm. **Ruler:** John Paul II **Obv:** Paul VI bust right **Rev:** Papal arms **Designer:** Laura Cretara **Note:** Struck in 2007.

Date	Mintage	F	VF	XF	Unc	BU
2001R Proof	499	—	—	—	—	—

KM# 336 500 LIRE

6.7700 g., Bi-Metallic Aluminum-Bronze center in Stainless steel ring, 25.7 mm. **Ruler:** John Paul II **Obv:** John Paul I head left **Rev:** Papal arms within circle **Edge:** Segmented reeding **Designer:** Laura Cretara

Date	Mintage	F	VF	XF	Unc	BU
2001/XXIII	—	—	—	3.50	7.00	—

KM# 336a 500 LIRE

Gold, 25.7 mm. **Ruler:** John Paul II **Obv:** John Paul I bust left **Rev:** Papal arms **Designer:** Laura Cretella

Date	Mintage	F	VF	XF	Unc	BU
2001R Proof	499	—	—	—	—	—

KM# 337 1000 LIRE

8.8500 g., Copper-Nickel, 26.9 mm. **Ruler:** John Paul II **Obv:** John Paul II bust right **Rev:** Papal arms **Edge:** Segmented reeding **Designer:** Laura Cretara

Date	Mintage	F	VF	XF	Unc	BU
2001/XIV	—	—	—	5.50	9.00	—

KM# 337a 1000 LIRE

Gold, 26.9 mm. **Ruler:** John Paul II **Obv:** John Paul II bust left **Rev:** Papal arms **Designer:** Laura Cretella

Date	Mintage	F	VF	XF	Unc	BU
2001R Proof	499	—	—	—	—	—

KM# 338 1000 LIRE

14.6000 g., 0.8350 Silver 0.3919 oz. ASW, 31.4 mm. **Ruler:** John Paul II **Subject:** Peace **Obv:** Stylized dove in front of globe **Rev:** Crowned shield **Edge Lettering:** +++ TOTVSTVVS +++ MMI

Date	Mintage	F	VF	XF	Unc	BU
2001/XXIII	—	—	—	20.00	40.00	—

KM# 338a 1000 LIRE

Gold, 31.4 mm. **Ruler:** John Paul II **Obv:** Stylized dove in front of globe **Rev:** Crowned arms

Date	Mintage	F	VF	XF	Unc	BU
2001R Proof	499	—	—	—	—	—

KM# 339 2000 LIRE

16.0000 g., 0.8350 Silver 0.4295 oz. ASW, 31.4 mm. **Ruler:** John Paul II **Subject:** Dialog for Peace **Obv:** Bust right holding crozier **Rev:** Dove above crowd **Edge:** Reeded **Designer:** Floriano Bodini

Date	Mintage	F	VF	XF	Unc	BU
2001/XXIII	16,000	—	—	25.00	40.00	—
2001/XXIII Proof	8,000	Value: 45.00				

KM# 340 5000 LIRE

18.0000 g., 0.8350 Silver 0.4832 oz. ASW, 32 mm. **Ruler:** John Paul II **Subject:** Easter **Obv:** Kneeling Pope praying **Rev:** Standing figure flanked by clouds below dove **Edge:** Reeded and plain sections **Designer:** Floriano Bodini

Date	Mintage	F	VF	XF	Unc	BU
2001	—	—	—	30.00	45.00	—
2001/XXIII Proof	16,000	Value: 35.00				

KM# 390 50000 LIRE

7.5000 g., 0.9170 Gold 0.2211 oz. AGW, 23 mm. **Ruler:** John Paul II **Subject:** Religious symbols **Obv:** Bust right **Rev:** Cross

Date	Mintage	F	VF	XF	Unc	BU
2001R	—	—	—	—	800	—
2001//XXIIIR Proof	6,000	Value: 550				

KM# 391 100000 LIRE

15.0000 g., 0.9170 Gold 0.4422 oz. AGW, 28 mm. **Ruler:** John Paul II **Subject:** Religious symbols **Obv:** Bust right **Rev:** Chi rho with Alpha and Omega letters

Date	Mintage	F	VF	XF	Unc	BU
2001R	—	—	—	—	1,000	—
2001//XXIIIR Proof	6,000	Value: 800				

EURO COINAGE

John Paul II

KM# 341 EURO CENT

2.2700 g., Copper Plated Steel, 16.2 mm. **Ruler:** John Paul II **Obv:** Bust 1/4 left **Obv. Designer:** Guido Veroi **Rev:** Value and globe **Rev. Designer:** Luc Luycx **Edge:** Plain

Date	Mintage	F	VF	XF	Unc	BU
2002R	80,000	—	—	—	115	—
2002R Proof	9,000	Value: 175				
2003R In sets only	65,000	—	—	—	55.00	—
2003R Proof	13,000	Value: 145				
2004R In sets only	65,000	—	—	—	25.00	—
2004R Proof	13,000	Value: 145				
2005R In sets only	85,000	—	—	—	25.00	—
2005R Proof	16,000	Value: 140				

KM# 342 2 EURO CENT

3.0300 g., Copper Plated Steel, 18.7 mm. **Ruler:** John Paul II **Obv:** Bust 1/4 left **Obv. Designer:** Guido Veroi **Rev:** Value and globe **Edge:** Grooved

Date	Mintage	F	VF	XF	Unc	BU
2002R	80,000	—	—	—	115	—
2002R Proof	9,000	Value: 175				
2003R In sets only	65,000	—	—	—	55.00	—
2003R Proof	13,000	Value: 145				
2004R In sets only	65,000	—	—	—	25.00	—
2004R Proof	13,000	Value: 145				
2005R In sets only	85,000	—	—	—	25.00	—
2005R Proof	16,000	Value: 140				

KM# 343 5 EURO CENT

3.8600 g., Copper Plated Steel, 21.2 mm. **Ruler:** John Paul II **Obv:** Bust 1/4 left **Obv. Designer:** Guido Veroi **Rev:** Value and globe **Edge:** Plain

Date	Mintage	F	VF	XF	Unc	BU
2002R	80,000	—	—	—	115	—
2002R Proof	9,000	Value: 175				
2003R In sets only	65,000	—	—	—	55.00	—
2003R Proof	13,000	Value: 145				
2004R In sets only	65,000	—	—	—	28.00	—
2004R Proof	13,000	Value: 145				
2005R In sets only	85,000	—	—	—	28.00	—
2005R Proof	16,000	Value: 140				

KM# 344 10 EURO CENT

4.0700 g., Brass, 19.7 mm. **Ruler:** John Paul II **Obv:** Bust 1/4 left **Obv. Designer:** Guido Veroi **Rev. Designer:** Luc Luycx **Edge:** Reeded

Date	Mintage	F	VF	XF	Unc	BU
2002R	80,000	—	—	—	115	—
2002R Proof	9,000	Value: 175				
2003R In sets only	65,000	—	—	—	55.00	—
2003R Proof	13,000	Value: 145				
2004R In sets only	65,000	—	—	—	35.00	—
2004R Proof	13,000	Value: 145				

Date	Mintage	F	VF	XF	Unc	BU
2005R In sets only	85,000	—	—	—	35.00	—
2005R Proof	16,000	Value: 140				

KM# 345 20 EURO CENT

5.7300 g., Brass, 22.1 mm. **Ruler:** John Paul II **Obv:** Bust 1/4 left **Obv. Designer:** Guido Veroi **Rev:** Map and value **Rev. Designer:** Luc Luycx **Edge:** Notched

Date	Mintage	F	VF	XF	Unc	BU
2002R	80,000	—	—	—	115	—
2002R Proof	9,000	Value: 175				
2003R In sets only	65,000	—	—	—	55.00	—
2003R Proof	13,000	Value: 145				
2004R In sets only	65,000	—	—	—	38.00	—
2004R Proof	13,000	Value: 145				
2005R In sets only	85,000	—	—	—	38.00	—
2005R Proof	16,000	Value: 140				

KM# 346 50 EURO CENT

7.8100 g., Brass, 24.2 mm. **Ruler:** John Paul II **Obv:** Bust 1/4 left **Obv. Designer:** Guido Veroi **Rev:** Map and value **Rev. Designer:** Luc Luycx **Edge:** Reeded

Date	Mintage	F	VF	XF	Unc	BU
2002R	80,000	—	—	—	115	—
2002R Proof	9,000	Value: 175				
2003R In sets only	65,000	—	—	—	55.00	—
2003R Proof	13,000	Value: 145				
2004R In sets only	65,000	—	—	—	42.00	—
2004R Proof	13,000	Value: 145				
2005R In sets only	85,000	—	—	—	42.00	—
2005R Proof	16,000	Value: 140				

KM# 347 EURO

7.5000 g., Bi-Metallic Copper-Nickel center in Brass ring, 23.2 mm. **Ruler:** John Paul II **Obv:** Bust 1/4 left **Obv. Designer:** Guido Veroi **Rev:** Value and map **Rev. Designer:** Luc Luycx **Edge:** Reeded and plain sections

Date	Mintage	F	VF	XF	Unc	BU
2002R	80,000	—	—	—	100	—
2002R Proof	9,000	Value: 185				
2003R In sets only	65,000	—	—	—	75.00	—
2003R Proof	13,000	Value: 145				
2004R In sets only	65,000	—	—	—	60.00	—
2004R Proof	13,000	Value: 145				
2005R In sets only	85,000	—	—	—	60.00	—
2005R Proof	16,000	Value: 140				

KM# 348 2 EURO

8.5200 g., Bi-Metallic Brass center in Copper-Nickel ring, 25.7 mm. **Ruler:** John Paul II **Obv:** Bust 1/4 left **Obv. Designer:** Guido Veroi **Rev:** Value and map **Rev. Designer:** Luc Luycx **Edge:** Reeded **Edge Lettering:** 2's and stars

Date	Mintage	F	VF	XF	Unc	BU
2002R	80,000	—	—	—	165	—
2002R Proof	9,000	Value: 215				
2003R In sets only	65,000	—	—	—	100	—
2003R Proof	13,000	Value: 185				
2004R In sets only	65,000	—	—	—	80.00	—
2004R Proof	13,000	Value: 185				
2005R In sets only	85,000	—	—	—	80.00	—
2005R Proof	16,000	Value: 180				

KM# 358 2 EURO

8.5000 g., Bi-Metallic Brass center in Copper-Nickel ring, 25.75 mm. **Ruler:** John Paul II **Subject:** 75th Anniversary of the Founding of the Vatican City State **Obv:** St. Peter's Square within city walls, dates 1929-2004 **Rev:** Value and map **Edge:** Reeding over 2's and stars **Designer:** Luciana de Simoni

Date	Mintage	F	VF	XF	Unc	BU
2004R	85,000	—	—	—	25.00	—

KM# 349 5 EURO

18.0000 g., 0.8350 Silver 0.4832 oz. ASW, 32 mm. **Ruler:** John Paul II **Subject:** 24th Anniversary of Reign **Obv:** Bust 1/4 left **Rev:** Allegorical female and bridge **Edge:** Lettered **Edge Lettering:** +++ TOTUS TUUS +++ MMII

Date	Mintage	F	VF	XF	Unc	BU
2002R Proof	10,000	Value: 125				

KM# 354 5 EURO

18.0000 g., 0.9250 Silver 0.5353 oz. ASW, 34 mm. **Ruler:** John Paul II **Subject:** Year of the Rosary **Obv:** Pope praying the rosary **Rev:** "Our Lady of Pompei" presenting rosaries to Saints Dominic and Catherine **Edge:** Reeded **Designer:** Roberto Mauri

Date	Mintage	F	VF	XF	Unc	BU
2003R Proof	10,000	—	—	—	65.00	—

KM# 359 5 EURO

18.0000 g., 0.9250 Silver 0.5353 oz. ASW, 32 mm. **Ruler:** John Paul II **Subject:** 150th Anniversary of the Proclamation of the Dogma of the Immaculate Conception **Obv:** Virgin Mary **Rev:** Two Papal coat of arms **Edge:** Reeded and plain sections **Designer:** Claudia Momoni

Date	Mintage	F	VF	XF	Unc	BU
2004R	13,000	—	—	—	60.00	—

KM# 350 10 EURO

22.0000 g., 0.8350 Silver 0.5906 oz. ASW, 34 mm. **Ruler:** John Paul II **Subject:** 24th Anniversary of Reign **Obv:** Pope holding crucifix **Rev:** Risen Christ (Message of peace) **Edge:** Reeded **Designer:** Floriano Bodini

Date	Mintage	F	VF	XF	Unc	BU
2002R Proof	10,000	Value: 80.00				

KM# 355 10 EURO

22.0000 g., 0.9250 Silver 0.6542 oz. ASW, 34 mm. **Ruler:** John Paul II **Subject:** 25th Anniversary of Reign **Obv:** Pope praying **Rev:** St. Peter receiving the keys of Earth and Heaven **Edge:** Reeded **Designer:** Amalia Mistichelli

Date	Mintage	F	VF	XF	Unc	BU
2003R Proof	10,000	Value: 80.00				

KM# 360 10 EURO

22.0000 g., 0.9250 Silver 0.6542 oz. ASW, 34 mm. **Ruler:** John Paul II **Obv:** Pope praying for peace **Rev:** Tree of Life rooted in virtues **Edge:** Reeded and plain sections **Designer:** Maria Carmela Colaneri

Date	Mintage	F	VF	XF	Unc	BU
2004R	13,000	—	—	—	90.00	—

KM# 361 20 EURO

6.0000 g., 0.9170 Gold 0.1769 oz. AGW **Ruler:** John Paul II **Subject:** Roots of Faith **Rev:** Noah's Ark **Designer:** Floriano Bodini

Date	Mintage	F	VF	XF	Unc	BU
2002	2,800	Value: 1,200				

KM# 351 20 EURO

6.0000 g., 0.9166 Gold 0.1768 oz. AGW, 21 mm. **Ruler:** John Paul II **Rev:** Moses being found in floating basket **Edge:** Reeded **Designer:** Floriano Bodini

Date	Mintage	F	VF	XF	Unc	BU
2003R Proof	2,800	Value: 1,300				

KM# 363 20 EURO

6.0000 g., 0.9170 Gold 0.1769 oz. AGW, 21 mm. **Ruler:** John Paul II **Rev:** David slaying Goliath **Designer:** Floriano Bodini

Date	Mintage	F	VF	XF	Unc	BU
2004/XXVIIR Proof	3,050	Value: 1,200				

KM# 362 50 EURO

15.0000 g., 0.9170 Gold 0.4422 oz. AGW **Ruler:** John Paul II **Subject:** Roots of Faith **Rev:** Sacrifice of Abraham **Designer:** Floriano Bodini

Date	Mintage	F	VF	XF	Unc	BU
2002 Proof	2,800	Value: 2,200				

KM# 352 50 EURO

15.0000 g., 0.9166 Gold 0.4420 oz. AGW, 28 mm. **Ruler:** John Paul II **Rev:** Moses receiving the Ten Commandments **Edge:** Reeded **Designer:** Floriano Bodini

Date	Mintage	F	VF	XF	Unc	BU
2003R Proof	2,800	Value: 2,200				

KM# 364 50 EURO

15.0000 g., 0.9170 Gold 0.4422 oz. AGW **Ruler:** John Paul II **Rev:** Judgement of Solomon **Designer:** Floriano Bodini

Date	Mintage	F	VF	XF	Unc	BU
2004/XXVIIR Proof	3,050	Value: 2,200				

EURO COINAGE

Sede Vacante

KM# 365 EURO CENT

2.2700 g., Copper Plated Steel **Ruler:** Sede Vacante **Obv:** Arms of Cardinal Eduardo Martinez Somalo **Obv. Designer:** Daniela Longo **Rev:** Value and globe **Rev. Designer:** Luc Luycx

Date	Mintage	F	VF	XF	Unc	BU
MMV (2005)R In sets only	60,000	—	—	—	—	45.00

KM# 366 2 EURO CENT

3.0300 g., Copper Plated Steel **Ruler:** Sede Vacante **Obv:** Arms of Cardinal Eduardo Martinez Somalo **Obv. Designer:** Daniela Longo **Rev:** Value and globe **Rev. Designer:** Luc Luycx

Date	Mintage	F	VF	XF	Unc	BU
MMV (2005)R In sets only	60,000	—	—	—	—	42.00

KM# 367 5 EURO CENT

3.8600 g., Copper Plated Steel **Ruler:** Sede Vacante **Obv:** Arms of Cardinal Eduardo Martinez Somalo **Obv. Designer:** Daniela Longo **Rev:** Value and globe **Rev. Designer:** Luc Luycx

Date	Mintage	F	VF	XF	Unc	BU
MMV (2005)R In sets only	60,000	—	—	—	—	45.00

KM# 368 10 EURO CENT

4.0700 g., Brass **Ruler:** Sede Vacante **Obv:** Arms of Cardinal Eduardo Martinez Somalo **Obv. Designer:** Daniela Longo **Rev:** Map and value **Rev. Designer:** Luc Luycx

Date	Mintage	F	VF	XF	Unc	BU
MMV (2005)R In sets only	60,000	—	—	—	—	48.00

KM# 369 20 EURO CENT

Brass **Ruler:** Sede Vacante **Obv:** Arms of Cardinal Eduardo Martinez Somalo **Obv. Designer:** Daniela Longo **Rev:** Map and value **Rev. Designer:** Luc Luycx

Date	Mintage	F	VF	XF	Unc	BU
MMV (2005)R In sets only	60,000	—	—	—	—	50.00

KM# 370 50 EURO CENT

7.8100 g., Brass **Ruler:** Sede Vacante **Obv:** Arms of Cardinal Eduardo Martinez Somalo **Obv. Designer:** Daniela Longo **Rev:** Map and value **Rev. Designer:** Luc Luycx

Date	Mintage	F	VF	XF	Unc	BU
MMV (2005)R In sets only	60,000	—	—	—	—	55.00

KM# 371 EURO

7.5000 g., Bi-Metallic Copper-Nickel center in brass ring **Ruler:** Sede Vacante **Obv:** Arms of Cardinal Eduardo Martinez Somalo **Obv. Designer:** Daniela Longo **Rev:** Value and map **Rev. Designer:** Luc Luycx

Date	Mintage	F	VF	XF	Unc	BU
MMV (2005)R In sets only	60,000	—	—	—	—	70.00

KM# 372 2 EURO

8.5200 g., Bi-Metallic Brass center in Copper-Nickel ring **Ruler:** Sede Vacante **Obv:** Arms of Cardinal Eduardo Martinez Somalo **Obv. Designer:** Daniela Longo **Rev:** Map and value **Rev. Designer:** Luc Luycx

Date	Mintage	F	VF	XF	Unc	BU
MMV (2005)R In sets only	60,000	—	—	—	—	75.00

KM# 373 5 EURO

18.0000 g., 0.9250 Silver 0.5353 oz. ASW, 32 mm. **Ruler:** Sede Vacante **Obv:** Dove within square **Rev:** Arms of Cardinal Jorge Arturo Medina Estevez **Edge:** Reeded **Designer:** Daniela Longo

Date	Mintage	F	VF	XF	Unc	BU
MMV (2005)R Proof	13,440	Value: 200				

EURO COINAGE

Benedict XVI

KM# 375 EURO CENT

2.2900 g., Copper Plated Steel, 16.24 mm. **Ruler:** Benedict XVI **Obv:** Pope's bust facing 3/4 right **Obv. Legend:** CITTA' DEL VATICANO **Rev:** Value and globe **Edge:** Plain

Date	Mintage	F	VF	XF	Unc	BU
2006R In sets only	85,000	—	—	—	—	12.00
2006R Proof	16,000	Value: 18.00				

Date	Mintage	F	VF	XF	Unc	BU
2007R In sets only	85,000	—	—	—	—	12.00
2007R Proof	16,000	Value: 18.00				
MMVIII (2008)R In sets only	85,000	—	—	—	—	12.00
MMVIII (2008)R Proof	16,000	Value: 18.00				
2009R In sets only	85,000	—	—	—	—	12.00
2009R Proof	16,000	Value: 18.00				
2010R In sets only	94,000	—	—	—	—	12.00
2010R Proof	15,000	Value: 18.00				

KM# 376 2 EURO CENT

3.0300 g., Copper Plated Steel, 18.73 mm. **Ruler:** Benedict XVI **Obv:** Pope's bust facing 3/4 right **Obv. Legend:** CITTA' DEL VATICANO **Rev:** Value and globe **Edge:** Plain

Date	Mintage	F	VF	XF	Unc	BU
2006R In sets only	85,000	—	—	—	—	15.00
2006R Proof	16,000	Value: 20.00				
2007R In sets only	85,000	—	—	—	—	15.00
2007R Proof	16,000	Value: 20.00				
MDVIII (2008)R In sets only	85,000	—	—	—	—	15.00
MDVIII (2008)R Proof	16,000	Value: 20.00				
2009R In sets only	85,000	—	—	—	—	15.00
2009R Proof	16,000	Value: 20.00				
2010R In sets only	94,000	—	—	—	—	15.00
2010R Proof	15,000	Value: 20.00				

KM# 377 5 EURO CENT

3.9600 g., Copper Plated Steel, 21.21 mm. **Ruler:** Benedict XVI **Obv:** Pope's bust facing 3/4 right **Obv. Legend:** CITTA' DEL VATICANO **Rev:** Value and globe **Edge:** Plain

Date	Mintage	F	VF	XF	Unc	BU
2006R In sets only	85,000	—	—	—	—	16.50
2006R Proof	16,000	Value: 22.50				
2007R In sets only	85,000	—	—	—	—	16.50
2007R Proof	16,000	Value: 22.50				
MDVIII (2008)R In sets only	85,000	—	—	—	—	16.50
MDVIII (2008)R Proof	16,000	Value: 22.50				
2009R In sets only	85,000	—	—	—	—	16.50
2009R Proof	16,000	Value: 22.50				
2010R In sets only	94,000	—	—	—	—	16.50
2010R Proof	15,000	Value: 22.50				

KM# 378 10 EURO CENT

4.0800 g., Brass, 19.73 mm. **Ruler:** Benedict XVI **Obv:** Pope's bust facing 3/4 right **Obv. Legend:** CITTA' DEL VATICANO **Rev:** Map and value **Edge:** Coarse reeding

Date	Mintage	F	VF	XF	Unc	BU
2006R In sets only	85,000	—	—	—	—	17.50
2006R Proof	16,000	Value: 25.00				
2007R In sets only	85,000	—	—	—	—	17.50
2007R Proof	16,000	Value: 25.00				

KM# 385 10 EURO CENT

4.0800 g., Brass, 19.73 mm. **Ruler:** Benedict XVI **Obv. Designer:** Daniela Longo **Rev:** Relief map of Western Europe, stars, lines and value **Rev. Designer:** Luc Luycx

Date	Mintage	F	VF	XF	Unc	BU
MMVIII (2008)R In sets only	85,000	—	—	—	—	17.50
MMVIII (2008)R Proof	16,000	Value: 25.00				
2009R In sets only	85,000	—	—	—	—	17.50
2009R Proof	16,000	Value: 25.00				
2010R In sets only	91,400	—	—	—	—	17.50
2010R Proof	15,000	Value: 25.00				

KM# 379 20 EURO CENT

5.7200 g., Brass, 22.23 mm. **Ruler:** Benedict XVI **Obv:** Pope's bust facing 3/4 right **Obv. Legend:** CITTA' DEL VATICANO **Rev:** Map and value **Edge:** Plain with seven indents

Date	Mintage	F	VF	XF	Unc	BU
2006R In sets only	85,000	—	—	—	—	18.00
2006R Proof	16,000	Value: 28.00				
2007R In sets only	85,000	—	—	—	—	18.00
2007R Proof	16,000	Value: 28.00				

KM# 386 20 EURO CENT

5.7200 g., Brass, 22.23 mm. **Ruler:** Benedict XVI **Obv. Designer:** Daniela Longo **Rev:** Relief map of Western Europe, stars, lines and value **Rev. Designer:** Luc Luycx

Date	Mintage	F	VF	XF	Unc	BU
MMVIII (2008)R In sets only	85,000	—	—	—	—	18.00
MMVIII (2008)R Proof	16,000	Value: 28.00				
2009R In sets only	85,000	—	—	—	—	18.00
2009R Proof	16,000	Value: 28.00				
2010R In sets only	94,000	—	—	—	—	18.00
2010R Proof	15,000	Value: 28.00				

KM# 380 50 EURO CENT

7.8200 g., Brass, 24.23 mm. **Ruler:** Benedict XVI **Obv:** Pope's bust facing 3/4 right **Obv. Legend:** CITTA' DEL VATICANO **Rev:** Map and value **Edge:** Coarse reeding

Date	Mintage	F	VF	XF	Unc	BU
2006R In sets only	85,000	—	—	—	—	22.50
2006R Proof	16,000	Value: 35.00				
2007R In sets only	85,000	—	—	—	—	22.50
2007R Proof	16,000	Value: 35.00				

KM# 387 50 EURO CENT

7.8100 g., Brass, 24.23 mm. **Ruler:** Benedict XVI **Rev:** Relief map of Western Europe, stars, lines and value **Rev. Designer:** Luc Luycx

Date	Mintage	F	VF	XF	Unc	BU
MMVIII (2008)R In sets only	85,000	—	—	—	—	32.50
MMVIII (2008)R Proof	16,000	Value: 40.00				
2009R In sets only	85,000	—	—	—	—	32.50
2009R Proof	16,000	Value: 40.00				
2010R In sets only	94,000	—	—	—	—	32.50
2010R Proof	15,000	Value: 40.00				

KM# 381 EURO

7.4700 g., Bi-Metallic Copper-Nickel center in brass ring., 23.23 mm. **Ruler:** Benedict XVI **Obv:** Pope's bust facing 3/4 right **Obv. Legend:** CITTA' - DEL VATICANO **Rev:** Value and map **Edge:** Segmented smooth and reeded

Date	Mintage	F	VF	XF	Unc	BU
2006R In sets only	85,000	—	—	—	—	25.00
2006R Proof	16,000	Value: 40.00				
2007R In sets only	85,000	—	—	—	—	25.00
2007R Proof	16,000	Value: 40.00				

KM# 388 EURO

7.5000 g., Bi-Metallic Copper-Nickel center in Brass ring, 23.23 mm. **Ruler:** Benedict XVI **Rev:** Relief map of Western Europe, stars, lines and value **Rev. Designer:** Luc Luycx

Date	Mintage	F	VF	XF	Unc	BU
MMVIII (2008)R In sets only	85,000	—	—	—	—	25.00
MMVIII (2008)R Proof	16,000	Value: 40.00				
2009R In sets only	85,000	—	—	—	—	25.00
2009R Proof	16,000	Value: 40.00				
2010R In sets only	94,000	—	—	—	—	25.00
2010R Proof	15,000	Value: 40.00				

KM# 374 2 EURO

8.5200 g., Bi-Metallic Brass center in Copper-Nickel ring, 25.7 mm. **Ruler:** Benedict XVI **Subject:** World Youth Day **Obv:** Cologne Cathedral **Rev:** Value and Euro map

Date	Mintage	F	VF	XF	Unc	BU
2005R	—	—	—	—	90.00	—

KM# 382 2 EURO

8.5200 g., Bi-Metallic Brass center in Copper-Nickel ring., 25.69 mm. **Ruler:** Benedict XVI **Obv:** Pope's bust facing 3/4 right **Obv. Legend:** CITTA' - DEL VATICANO **Rev:** Value and map **Edge:** Reeded with stars and alternating 2's

Date	Mintage	F	VF	XF	Unc	BU
2006R In sets only	85,000	—	—	—	—	28.00
2006R Proof	16,000	Value: 50.00				
2007R In sets only	85,000	—	—	—	—	28.00
2007R Proof	16,000	Value: 50.00				

KM# 394 2 EURO

8.5200 g., Bi-Metallic Brass center in copper-nickel ring, 25.7 mm. **Ruler:** Benedict XVI **Subject:** Swiss guards, 500th Anniversary **Obv:** Swiss guard taking oath on flag **Rev:** Map and value

Date	Mintage	F	VF	XF	Unc	BU
ND (2006)R	100,000	—	—	—	80.00	—

KM# 399 2 EURO

8.5200 g., Bi-Metallic Brass center in copper-nickel ring, 25.7 mm. **Ruler:** Benedict XVI **Subject:** Pope Benedict's 80th Birthday **Obv:** Bust left **Rev:** Map and value

Date	Mintage	F	VF	XF	Unc	BU
2007R	100,000	—	—	—	50.00	—

KM# 389 2 EURO

8.5200 g., Bi-Metallic Brass center in Copper-Nickel ring, 25.7 mm. **Ruler:** Benedict XVI **Rev:** Relief map of Western Europe, stars, lines and value **Rev. Designer:** Luc Luycx

Date	Mintage	F	VF	XF	Unc	BU
MMVIII (2008)R In sets only	85,000	—	—	—	—	28.00
MMVIII (2008)R Proof	16,000	Value: 50.00				
2009R In sets only	85,000	—	—	—	—	28.00
2009R Proof	16,000	Value: 50.00				
2010R In sets only	94,000	—	—	—	—	28.00
2010R Proof	15,000	Value: 50.00				

KM# 404 2 EURO

8.5200 g., Bi-Metallic Brass center in copper-nickel ring, 25.7 mm. **Ruler:** Benedict XVI **Obv:** St. Paul being blinded on reary horse **Rev:** Map and value

Date	Mintage	F	VF	XF	Unc	BU
ND (2008)R	106,084	—	—	—	25.00	—

KM# 410 2 EURO

8.5200 g., Bi-Metallic Brass center in copper-nickel ring, 25.7 mm. **Ruler:** Benedict XVI **Subject:** International Year of Astronomy **Rev:** Map and value

Date	Mintage	F	VF	XF	Unc	BU
2009R	100,000	—	—	—	25.00	—

KM# 420 2 EURO

8.5200 g., Bi-Metallic Brass center in Copper-Nickel ring, 25.7 mm. **Ruler:** Benedict XVI **Subject:** Year of the Priest

Date	Mintage	F	VF	XF	Unc	BU
2010R	—	—	—	—	20.00	25.00

KM# 383 5 EURO

18.0000 g., 0.9250 Silver 0.5353 oz. ASW **Ruler:** Benedict XVI **Subject:** Life reborn **Obv:** Bust left **Rev:** Children playing among branches of an olive tree

Date	Mintage	F	VF	XF	Unc	BU
2005R Proof	13,000	Value: 100				

KM# 395 5 EURO

18.0000 g., 0.9250 Silver 0.5353 oz. ASW, 32 mm. **Ruler:** Benedict XVI **Subject:** World Day of Peace **Obv:** Half-length figure Benedict right in vestments with crozier **Rev:** St. Benedict of Nursia seated

Date	Mintage	F	VF	XF	Unc	BU
MMVI (2006)R Proof	14,160	Value: 90.00				

KM# 400 5 EURO

18.0000 g., 0.9250 Silver 0.5353 oz. ASW, 32 mm. **Ruler:** Benedict XVI **Subject:** World Day of Peace **Obv:** 1/2 length figure kneeling in prayer **Rev:** Standing St. Francis of Assissi, rays in background

Date	Mintage	F	VF	XF	Unc	BU
MMVII (2007)R Proof	13,693	Value: 55.00				

KM# 406 5 EURO

18.0000 g., 0.9250 Silver 0.5353 oz. ASW, 32 mm. **Ruler:** Benedict XVI **Subject:** World Youth Day - Sydney **Obv:** Pope right, blessing **Rev:** Sydney Harbor sites

Date	Mintage	F	VF	XF	Unc	BU
MMVIII (2008)R Proof	9,600	Value: 60.00				

KM# 415 5 EURO

18.0000 g., 0.9250 Silver 0.5353 oz. ASW, 32 mm. **Ruler:** Benedict XVI **Subject:** World day of Peace **Obv:** Bust right in prayer **Rev:** Candle, family

Date	Mintage	F	VF	XF	Unc	BU
2009R Proof	9,600	Value: 60.00				

KM# 421 5 EURO

18.0000 g., 0.9250 Silver 0.5353 oz. ASW, 32 mm. **Ruler:** Benedict XVI **Subject:** Migrants and Refugees

Date	Mintage	F	VF	XF	Unc	BU
2010R Proof	—	Value: 75.00				

KM# 384 10 EURO

22.0000 g., 0.9250 Silver 0.6542 oz. ASW **Ruler:** Benedict XVI **Subject:** Disciples of Emanaus **Obv:** Bust left **Rev:** Three men seated at table

Date	Mintage	F	VF	XF	Unc	BU
2006R Proof	13,000	Value: 215				

KM# 396 10 EURO

22.0000 g., 0.9250 Silver 0.6542 oz. ASW, 34 mm. **Ruler:** Benedict XVI **Subject:** St. Peter's Collonade, 350th Anniversary **Obv:** Collonade & Pope Benedict **Rev:** Collonade Schematics

Date	Mintage	F	VF	XF	Unc	BU
AN II MMVI (2006)R Proof	14,160	Value: 90.00				

KM# 401 10 EURO

22.0000 g., 0.9250 Silver 0.6542 oz. ASW, 34 mm. **Ruler:** Benedict XVI **Subject:** World Mission Day **Obv:** Bust right in ermine cape **Rev:** Blessed Mother Theresa of Calcutta and child

Date	Mintage	F	VF	XF	Unc	BU
AN III MVII (2007)R Proof	13,694	Value: 80.00				

KM# 407 10 EURO

22.0000 g., 0.9250 Silver 0.6542 oz. ASW, 34 mm. **Ruler:** Benedict XVI **Subject:** World Day of Peace **Obv:** Pope seated on chair in full robes and miter **Rev:** The Holy Family - Jesus, Mary, Joseph

Date	Mintage	F	VF	XF	Unc	BU
A VI MMVIII (2008)R Proof	9,602	Value: 95.00				

KM# 417 10 EURO

22.0000 g., 0.9250 Silver 0.6542 oz. ASW, 22 mm. **Ruler:** Benedict XVI **Subject:** Lateran Treaty, 80th Anniversary **Obv:** Bust right **Rev:** Rolled treaty with seal

Date	Mintage	F	VF	XF	Unc	BU
2009R Proof	9,602	Value: 95.00				

KM# 422 10 EURO

22.0000 g., 0.9250 Silver 0.6542 oz. ASW, 34 mm. **Ruler:** Benedict XVI **Subject:** 43rd World day of Peace

Date	Mintage	F	VF	XF	Unc	BU
2010R Proof	—	Value: 80.00				

KM# 392 20 EURO

6.0000 g., 0.9160 Gold 0.1767 oz. AGW, 21 mm. **Ruler:** Benedict XVI **Subject:** Christian Initiation - Baptism **Obv:** Pope seated **Rev:** Fountain

Date	Mintage	F	VF	XF	Unc	BU
AN I MMV (2005)R Proof	3,046	Value: 600				

KM# 397 20 EURO

6.0000 g., 0.9160 Gold 0.1767 oz. AGW, 21 mm. **Ruler:** Benedict XVI **Subject:** Christian Initiation - Confirmation **Obv:** Bust right **Rev:** Bishop confirming three

Date	Mintage	F	VF	XF	Unc	BU
AN II MMVI (2006)R Proof	3,326	Value: 600				

KM# 402 20 EURO

6.0000 g., 0.9160 Gold 0.1767 oz. AGW, 21 mm. **Ruler:** Benedict XVI **Subject:** Christain Initiation - Eucharist **Obv:** Bust left in ermine cape **Rev:** Basket of fish and bread

Date	Mintage	F	VF	XF	Unc	BU
AN III (2007)R Proof	3,426	Value: 600				

KM# 408 20 EURO

6.0000 g., 0.9170 Gold 0.1769 oz. AGW, 21 mm. **Ruler:** Benedict XVI **Subject:** Vatican sculpture **Obv:** Pope right in mitre **Rev:** Torso of Belvedere

Date	Mintage	F	VF	XF	Unc	BU
AN IV MMVIII (2008)R Proof	2,930	Value: 500				

KM# 416 20 EURO

6.0000 g., 0.9170 Gold 0.1769 oz. AGW, 21 mm. **Ruler:** Benedict XVI **Subject:** Masterworks in the Vatican Collection **Rev:** Christ and the Lamb

Date	Mintage	F	VF	XF	Unc	BU
2009R Proof	2,934	Value: 550				

KM# 423 20 EURO

6.0000 g., 0.9170 Gold 0.1769 oz. AGW **Ruler:** Benedict XVI **Subject:** Vatican Sculpture - Apollo Belvedere

Date	Mintage	F	VF	XF	Unc	BU
2010R Proof	—	Value: 550				

KM# 393 50 EURO

15.0000 g., 0.9160 Gold 0.4417 oz. AGW, 28 mm. **Ruler:** Benedict XVI **Subject:** Christian Initiation - Baptism **Obv:** Pope seated **Rev:** John baptising Christ

Date	Mintage	F	VF	XF	Unc	BU
AN I MMV (2005)R Proof	3,044	Value: 1,500				

KM# 398 50 EURO

15.0000 g., 0.9160 Gold 0.4417 oz. AGW, 28 mm. **Ruler:** Benedict XVI **Subject:** Christian Initiation - Confirmation **Obv:** Bust right **Rev:** Tongues of fire decending on Apostles

Date	Mintage	F	VF	XF	Unc	BU
AN II MMVI (2006)R Proof	3,324	Value: 1,500				

KM# 403 50 EURO

15.0000 g., 0.9160 Gold 0.4417 oz. AGW, 28 mm. **Ruler:** Benedict XVI **Subject:** Christian Initiation - Eucharist **Obv:** Bust left in ermine cape **Rev:** Scene of the Last Supper

Date	Mintage	F	VF	XF	Unc	BU
ANIII MMVII (2007)R Proof	—	Value: 1,500				

KM# 409 50 EURO

15.0000 g., 0.9170 Gold 0.4422 oz. AGW, 28 mm. **Ruler:** Benedict XVI **Subject:** Vatican sculpture **Obv:** Pope right in mitre **Rev:** The Pieta

Date	Mintage	F	VF	XF	Unc	BU
AN IV MMVIII (2008)R Proof	—	Value: 1,000				

KM# 418 50 EURO

15.0000 g., 0.9170 Gold 0.4422 oz. AGW **Ruler:** Benedict XVI **Subject:** Masterworks in the Vatican Collection **Rev:** Hercules statue group **Edge:** 28

Date	Mintage	F	VF	XF	Unc	BU
2009R Proof	2,930	Value: 1,200				

KM# 424 50 EURO

15.0000 g., 0.9170 Gold 0.4422 oz. AGW, 28 mm. **Ruler:** Benedict XVI **Subject:** Vatican Sculpture - Augustus of Prima

Date	Mintage	F	VF	XF	Unc	BU
2010R Proof	—	Value: 1,200				

KM# 405 100 EURO

30.0000 g., 0.9170 Gold 0.8844 oz. AGW, 35 mm. **Ruler:** Benedict XVI **Obv:** Bust left **Rev:** The Creator from the Sistine Chapel ceiling

Date	Mintage	F	VF	XF	Unc	BU
AN IV MMVIII (2008)R Proof	960	Value: 1,700				

KM# 419 100 EURO

30.0000 g., 0.9170 Gold 0.8844 oz. AGW, 35 mm. **Ruler:** Benedict XVI **Subject:** Sistine Chapel - Banishment from Eden

Date	Mintage	F	VF	XF	Unc	BU
2009R Proof	—	Value: 1,700				

KM# 425 100 EURO

30.0000 g., 0.9170 Gold 0.8844 oz. AGW, 35 mm. **Ruler:** Benedict XVI **Subject:** Sistine Chapel - Last Judgement

Date	Mintage	F	VF	XF	Unc	BU
2010R Proof	—	Value: 1,500				

PIEFORTS

KM#	Date	Mintage	Identification	Mkt Val
	2002	500	5 Euro. Silver. X#Pn9.	85.00

MINT SETS

KM#	Date	Mintage	Identification	Issue Price	Mkt Val
MS107	2001 (8)	26,000	KM#331-338	21.25	200
MS108	2002 (8)	65,000	KM#341-348	12.00	975
XMS1	2002 (8)	2,500	X#Pn1-Pn8 with serial #	—	50.00
MS109	2003 (8)	65,000	KM#341-348	15.00	500
MS110	2004 (8)	85,000	KM#341-348	16.50	335
XMS3	XXVI (2004) (8)	7,500	X#Pn21-Pn28	—	40.00
MS111	2005 (8)	85,000	KM#341-348.	32.50	335
MS112	MMV (2005) (8)	60,000	KM#365-372 Sede Vacante	—	435
XMS4	2005 (8)	—	X#Pn31-X#Pn38	—	25.00
XMS5	2005 (8)	999	X#Pn45-X#Pn52	—	25.00
XMS6	2005 (8)	5,000	X#Pn55-X#Pn62	—	35.00
XMS7	2005 (8)	—	X#Pn65-X#Pn72	—	25.00
XMS8	2005 (8)	—	X#Pn85-X#Pn92	—	25.00
XMS9	2005 (8)	3,000	X#Pn75-X#Pn82	—	25.00
MS113	2006 (8)	—	KM#375-382	—	210
MS114	2007 (8)	—	KM#375-382	—	230
MS115	2008 (8)	85,000	KM#375-377, 385-389	45.00	165
MS116	2009 (8)	91,400	KM#375-377, 385-389	30.00	165
MS117	2010 (8)	94,000	KM#375-377, 385-389	30.00	150

PROOF SETS

KM#	Date	Mintage	Identification	Issue Price	Mkt Val
PS13	2001 (2)	—	KM#390, 391	—	1,350
XPS1	2002 (9)	2,500	X#Pn1-Pn9	—	75.00
XPS2	2002 (9)	500	X#Pn1a-Pn9a	—	150
PS15	2002 (8)	9,000	KM#341-348	75.00	1,450
PS16	2003 (8)	13,000	KM#341-348	78.00	1,200
PS17	2004 (8)	13,000	KM#341-348	—	1,200
XPS3	2005 (9)	—	X#Pn31-X#Pn39	—	35.00
XPS4	2005 (9)	2,000	X#Pn55-X#Pn63	—	40.00
XPS5	2005 (9)	2,000	X#Pn75-X#Pn83	—	40.00
PS18	2005 (8)	16,000	KM#341-348 plus silver medal	150	1,175
PS19	2006 (8)	16,000	KM#375-382 plus silver medal	—	375
PS20	2007 (8)	16,000	KM#375-382 plus silver medal	—	315
PS21	2008 (8)	16,000	KM#375-377, 385-389 plus silver medal	195	250
PS22	2009 (8)	15,000	KM#375-377, 385-389 plus silver medal	195	250
PS23	2010 (8)	15,000	KM#375-377, 385-389 plus silver medal	195	240
PS24	2010 (8)	300	KM#375-377, 385-389 plus gold medal	2,100	2,250

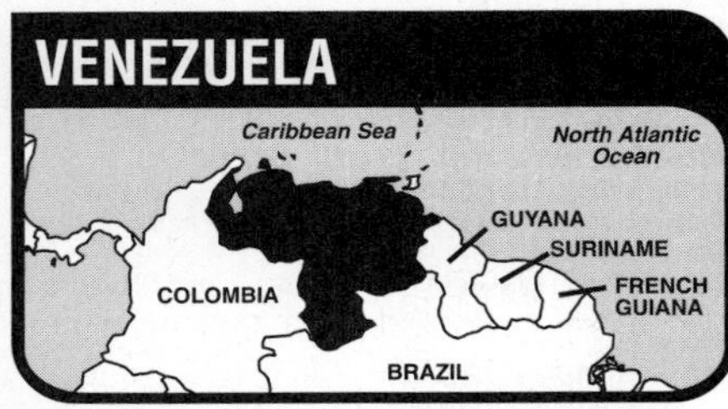

The Bolivarian Republic of Venezuela ("Little Venice"), located on the northern coast of South America between Colombia and Guyana, has an area of 352,145 sq. mi.(912,050 sq. km.) and a population of 20 million. Capital: Caracas. Petroleum and mining provide a significant portion of Venezuela's exports. Coffee, grown on 60,000 plantations, is the chief crop. Metalurgy, refining, oil, iron and steel production are the main employment industries.

GOVERNMENT
Republic, 1823-2000
Republic Bolivarian, 2000-

MINT MARKS
Maracay

REPUBLIC

Bolivariana

REFORM COINAGE

1896; 100 Centimos = 1 Bolivar

Y# 80 10 BOLIVARES

2.3300 g., Nickel Clad Steel, 17 mm. **Obv:** National arms left of denomination **Obv. Legend:** REPÚBLICA BOLIVARIANA DE VENEZUELA **Rev:** Head of Bolívar left in 7-sided outline **Rev. Legend:** BOLÍVAR - LIBERTADOR **Rev. Designer:** Albert Barre **Edge:** Reeded

Date	Mintage	F	VF	XF	Unc	BU
2001	—	—	—	—	0.25	0.50
2002	—	—	—	—	0.25	0.50

Y# 80a 10 BOLIVARES

1.7390 g., Aluminum-Zinc, 16.92 mm. **Obv:** National arms and value **Obv. Legend:** REPÚBLICA BOLIVARIANA DE VENEZUELA **Rev:** Head of Bolívar left in 7-sided outline **Rev. Legend:** BOLÍVAR - LIBERTADOR **Rev. Designer:** Albert Barre **Edge:** Reeded

Date	Mintage	F	VF	XF	Unc	BU
2001	—	—	—	0.15	0.45	0.60
2002	—	—	—	0.15	0.45	0.60
2004	—	—	—	0.15	0.45	0.60

Y# 81 20 BOLIVARES

4.3200 g., Nickel Clad Steel, 20 mm. **Obv:** National arms left of denomination **Obv. Legend:** REPÚBLICA BOLIVARIANA DE VENEZUELA **Rev:** Head of Bolivar left in 7-sided outline **Rev. Legend:** BOLÍVAR - LIBERTADOR **Rev. Designer:** Albert Barre **Edge:** Plain

Date	Mintage	F	VF	XF	Unc	BU
2001	—	—	—	—	0.25	0.50
2002	—	—	—	—	0.25	0.50

Y# 81a.1 20 BOLIVARES

3.2650 g., Aluminum-Zinc, 20 mm. **Obv:** National arms and value with wavy based "2" **Obv. Legend:** REPÚBLICA BOLÍVARIANA DE VENEZUELA **Rev:** Head of Bolívar left in 7-sided outline **Rev. Legend:** BOLÍVAR - LIBERTADOR **Rev. Designer:** Albert Barre **Edge:** Plain

Date	Mintage	F	VF	XF	Unc	BU
2001	—	—	—	—	0.65	1.00

Y# 81a.2 20 BOLIVARES

3.2400 g., Aluminum-Zinc, 20 mm. **Obv:** National arms and value with flat based "2" **Obv. Legend:** REPÚBLICA BOLIVARIANA DE VENEZUELA **Rev:** Head of Bolívar left in 7-sided outline **Rev. Legend:** BOLÍVAR - LIBERTADOR **Rev. Designer:** Albert Barre **Edge:** Plain

Date	Mintage	F	VF	XF	Unc	BU
2002	—	—	—	0.25	0.60	0.80
2004	—	—	—	0.25	0.60	0.80

Y# 82 50 BOLIVARES

6.5800 g., Nickel Clad Steel, 23 mm. **Obv:** National arms left of denomination **Obv. Legend:** REPÚBLICA BOLIVARIANA DE VENEZUELA **Rev:** Head of Bolivar left in 7-sided outline **Rev. Legend:** BOLÍVAR - LIBERTADOR **Rev. Designer:** Albert Barre **Edge:** Reeded

Date	Mintage	F	VF	XF	Unc	BU
2001	—	—	—	0.30	0.75	1.00
2002	—	—	—	0.30	0.75	1.00
2004	—	—	—	0.30	0.75	1.00

Y# 83 100 BOLIVARES

6.8200 g., Nickel Clad Steel, 25 mm. **Obv:** National arms and value **Obv. Legend:** REPÚBUBLICA BOLIVARIANA DE VENEZUELA **Rev:** Head of Bolívar left in 7-sided ouline **Rev. Legend:** BOLÍVAR - LIBERTADO **Rev. Designer:** Albert Barre **Edge:** Plain

Date	Mintage	F	VF	XF	Unc	BU
2001	—	—	—	0.45	1.10	1.50
2002	—	—	—	0.45	1.10	1.50
2004	—	—	—	0.45	1.10	1.50

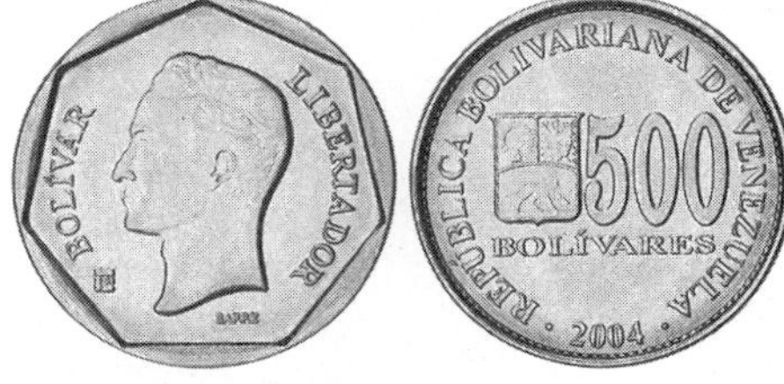

Y# 94 500 BOLIVARES

8.5000 g., Nickel Plated Steel, 28.4 mm. **Obv:** National arms and denomination **Obv. Legend:** REPÚBLICA BOLIVARIANA DE VENEZUELA **Rev:** Head of Bolívar left in 7-sided outline **Rev. Legend:** BOLÍVAR - LIBERTADOR **Rev. Designer:** Albert Barre **Edge:** Segmented reeding

Date	Mintage	F	VF	XF	Unc	BU
2004	—	—	—	0.60	1.50	2.00

Y# 85 1000 BOLIVARES

8.3500 g., Bi-Metallic Copper-Nickel center in Brass ring, 24 mm. **Obv:** National arms and value in center **Obv. Legend:** REPÚBLICA BOLIVARIANA DE VENEZUELA **Rev:** Head of Bolívar left **Rev. Legend:** BOLÍVAR - LIBERTADOR **Rev. Designer:** Albert Barre **Edge:** Lettered **Edge Lettering:** "BCV 1000" four times

Date	Mintage	F	VF	XF	Unc	BU
2005	9,000,000	—	—	0.90	2.25	3.00

REFORM COINAGE

2007-

1000 Bolivares = 1 Bolivar Fuerte

Y# 87 CENTIMO

1.3600 g., Copper Plated Steel, 14.9 mm. **Obv:** National arms **Obv. Legend:** REPÚBLICA BOLIVARIANA DE VENEZUELA **Rev:** Eight stars at left, large value at right **Edge:** Reeded

Date	Mintage	F	VF	XF	Unc	BU
2007	—	—	—	—	0.25	0.35

Note: Many die rotation varieties exist.

Y# 88 5 CENTIMOS

2.0300 g., Copper Plated Steel, 16.9 mm. **Obv:** National arms **Obv. Legend:** REPÚBLICA BOLIVARIANA DE VENEZUELA **Rev:** Eight stars at left, large value at right **Edge:** Plain

Date	Mintage	F	VF	XF	Unc	BU
2007	—	—	—	—	0.50	0.75
2009	—	—	—	—	0.50	0.75

Y# 89 10 CENTIMOS

2.6200 g., Nickel Plated Steel, 18 mm. **Obv:** National arms **Obv. Legend:** REPÚBLICA BOLIVARIANA DE VENEZUELA **Rev:** Eight stars at left, large value at right **Edge:** Reeded

Date	Mintage	F	VF	XF	Unc	BU
2007	—	—	—	—	0.75	1.00

Y# 90 12-1/2 CENTIMOS

3.9300 g., Nickel Plated Steel, 23 mm. **Obv:** National arms **Obv. Legend:** REPÚBLICA BOLIVARIANA DE VENEZUELA **Rev:** Large value, eight stars below in sprays **Edge:** Plain

Date	Mintage	F	VF	XF	Unc	BU
2007	—	—	—	—	1.50	1.75

Y# 91 25 CENTIMOS

3.8600 g., Nickel Plated Steel, 20 mm. **Obv:** National arms **Obv. Legend:** REPÚBLICA BOLIVARIANA DE VENEZUELA **Rev:** Eight stars at left, large value at center right **Edge:** Plain

Date	Mintage	F	VF	XF	Unc	BU
2007	—	—	—	—	2.00	2.50

Y# 99 25 CENTIMOS

3.8600 g., Nickel Plated Steel, 20 mm. **Subject:** Independence, 200th Anniversary **Obv:** Legend **Rev:** Large value

Date	Mintage	F	VF	XF	Unc	BU
2010	—	—	—	—	2.50	3.00

Y# 92 50 CENTIMOS
4.3000 g., Nickel Plated Steel, 21.9 mm. **Obv:** National arms **Obv. Legend:** REPÚBLICA BOLIVARIANA DE VENEZUELA **Rev:** Eight stars at left, large value at center right **Edge:** Segmented reeding

Date	Mintage	F	VF	XF	Unc	BU
2007	—	—	—	—	3.00	3.50

Y# 100 50 CENTIMOS
4.3000 g., Nickel Plated Steel, 21.9 mm. **Subject:** Banco Central, 70th Anniversary **Obv:** Legend **Rev:** Large vlaue

Date	Mintage	F	VF	XF	Unc	BU
2010	—	—	—	—	3.50	4.00

Y# 93 BOLIVAR
8.0400 g., Bi-Metallic Copper-Nickel center in Aluminum-Bronze ring, 24 mm. **Obv:** Eight stars at left of national arms, large value at right **Obv. Legend:** REPÚBLICA BOLIVARIANA DE VENEZUELA **Rev:** Head of Bolívar left **Rev. Designer:** Albert Barre **Edge:** Lettered **Edge Lettering:** "BCV 1" repeated

Date	Mintage	F	VF	XF	Unc	BU
2007	—	—	—	—	5.00	6.00

Y# 101 50 BOLIVARES
31.1000 g., 0.9990 Silver 0.9988 oz. ASW, 38.6 mm. **Subject:** Banco Central, 70th Anniversary **Obv:** Legned **Rev:** Banco Central building

Date	Mintage	F	VF	XF	Unc	BU
2010 Proof	3,000	Value: 65.00				

Y# 102 50 BOLIVARES
0.9990 Gold **Subject:** Banco Central, 70th Anniversary **Obv:** Legend **Rev:** Banco Central building

Date	Mintage	F	VF	XF	Unc	BU
2010 Proof	—	Value: 1,650				

Y# 95 200 BOLIVARES
0.9990 Silver **Obv:** Flag **Rev:** Crowd outside building

Date	Mintage	F	VF	XF	Unc	BU
2010 Proof	—	Value: 75.00				

Y# 96 200 BOLIVARES
0.9990 Gold **Obv:** Flag **Rev:** Crowd before building

Date	Mintage	F	VF	XF	Unc	BU
2010 Proof	—	Value: 1,700				

Y# 97 200 BOLIVARES
0.9990 Silver **Obv:** Flag **Rev:** Francisco de Marianda

Date	Mintage	F	VF	XF	Unc	BU
2010 Proof	—	Value: 75.00				

Y# 98 200 BOLIVARES
0.9990 Gold **Obv:** Flag **Rev:** Francisco de Marianda

Date	Mintage	F	VF	XF	Unc	BU
2010 Proof	—	Value: 1,700				

VIET NAM

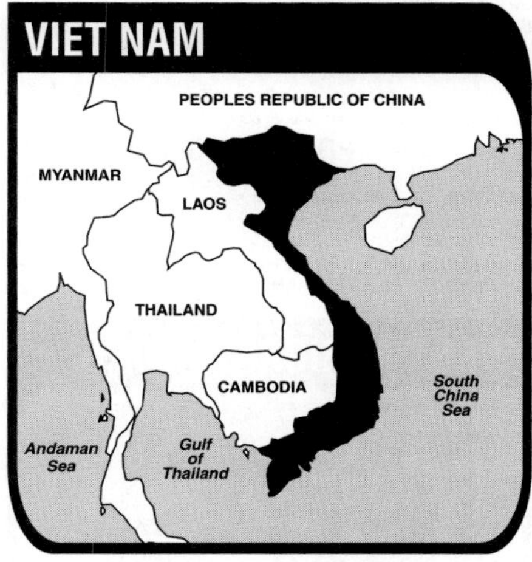

The Socialist Republic of Viet Nam, located in Southeast Asia west of the South China Sea, has an area of 127,300 sq. mi. (329,560 sq. km.) and a population of *66.8 million. Capital: Hanoi. Agricultural products, coal, and mineral ores are exported.

The activities of Communists in South Viet Nam led to the second Indochina war which came to a brief halt in 1973 (when a cease-fire was arranged and U.S. forces withdrew), but it didn't end until April 30, 1975 when South Viet Nam surrendered unconditionally. The two Viet Nams were reunited as the Socialist Republic of Viet Nam on July 2, 1976.

NOTE: For earlier coinage refer to French Indo-China or Tonkin.

SOCIALIST REPUBLIC

SOCIALIST REPUBLIC

STANDARD COINAGE

KM# 71 200 DONG
3.1000 g., Nickel Clad Steel, 20.75 mm. **Obv:** National emblem **Rev:** Denomination

Date	Mintage	F	VF	XF	Unc	BU
2003	125,000,000	0.15	0.20	0.35	0.75	0.50

KM# 74 500 DONG
4.5000 g., Nickel Clad Steel, 21.86 mm. **Obv:** National emblem **Rev:** Denomination **Edge:** Segmented reeding

Date	Mintage	F	VF	XF	Unc	BU
2003	175,000,000	0.15	0.25	0.50	0.75	1.00

KM# 72 1000 DONG
3.7000 g., Brass Plated Steel, 19 mm. **Obv:** National emblem **Rev:** Bat De Pagoda in Hanoi **Edge:** Reeded

Date	Mintage	F	VF	XF	Unc	BU
2003	250,000,000	0.20	0.35	0.60	0.80	1.50

KM# 75 2000 DONG
5.0000 g., Brass Plated Steel, 23.5 mm. **Obv:** National emblem **Rev:** Highland Stilt House in Tay Nguyen above value **Edge:** Segmented reeding

Date	Mintage	F	VF	XF	Unc	BU
2003	—	—	—	—	2.25	2.75

KM# 64 5000 DONG
1.2441 g., 0.9999 Gold 0.0400 oz. AGW, 13.92 mm. **Subject:** Year of the Snake **Obv:** State emblem **Rev:** Sea snake **Edge:** Reeded

Date	Mintage	F	VF	XF	Unc	BU
2001	—	—	—	—	65.00	75.00

KM# 67 5000 DONG
1.2441 g., 0.9999 Gold 0.0400 oz. AGW, 13.9 mm. **Subject:** Year of the Horse **Obv:** State emblem **Rev:** Horse **Edge:** Reeded

Date	Mintage	F	VF	XF	Unc	BU
2002	28,000	—	—	—	60.00	70.00

KM# 73 5000 DONG
7.6000 g., Brass, 25 mm. **Obv:** National emblem **Rev:** Chua Mot Cot Pagoda in Hanoi

Date	Mintage	F	VF	XF	Unc	BU
2003	500,000,000	0.50	0.75	1.00	1.25	2.50

KM# 57 10000 DONG
20.0000 g., 0.9250 Silver 0.5948 oz. ASW, 38.7 mm. **Subject:** Year of the Snake **Obv:** State emblem above value **Obv. Legend:** "CONG HOA XA HOI CHU NGHIA VIET NAM" **Rev:** Sea snake **Rev. Legend:** "...VIET NAM" **Edge:** Reeded

Date	Mintage	F	VF	XF	Unc	BU
2001(S) Proof	3,500	Value: 85.00				

KM# 58 10000 DONG

20.0000 g., 0.9250 Silver 0.5948 oz. ASW **Subject:** Year of the Snake **Obv:** State emblem above value **Obv. Legend:** "CONG HOA XA HOI CHU NGHIA VIET NAM" **Rev:** Bamboo viper **Rev. Legend:** "...VIET NAM"

Date	Mintage	F	VF	XF	Unc	BU
2001(S) Proof	3,500	Value: 85.00				

KM# 59 10000 DONG

20.0000 g., 0.9250 Silver 0.5948 oz. ASW **Subject:** Year of the Snake **Obv:** State emblem above value **Obv. Legend:** "CONG HOA XA HOI CHU NGHIA VIET NAM" **Rev:** Multicolor holographic, cobra in center **Rev. Legend:** "...VIET NAM"

Date	Mintage	F	VF	XF	Unc	BU
2001(S) Proof	3,500	Value: 80.00				

KM# 61 10000 DONG

20.0000 g., 0.9990 Silver 0.6423 oz. ASW, 38.7 mm. **Subject:** Year of the Horse **Obv:** State emblem **Rev:** Horse with octagonal latent image **Edge:** Reeded

Date	Mintage	F	VF	XF	Unc	BU
2001 Proof	3,800	Value: 65.00				

Note: In proof set only

KM# 62 10000 DONG

20.0000 g., 0.9990 Silver 0.6423 oz. ASW, 38.7 mm. **Subject:** Year of the Horse **Obv:** State emblem **Rev:** Horse with multicolor accoutrements **Edge:** Reeded

Date	Mintage	F	VF	XF	Unc	BU
2001 Proof	3,800	Value: 75.00				

Note: In proof set only

KM# 63 10000 DONG

20.0000 g., 0.9990 Silver 0.6423 oz. ASW, 38.7 mm. **Subject:** Year of the Horse **Obv:** State emblem **Rev:** Multicolor holographic horse in center **Edge:** Reeded

Date	Mintage	F	VF	XF	Unc	BU
2001 Proof	3,800	Value: 75.00				

Note: In proof set only

KM# 76 10000 DONG

20.0000 g., 0.9990 Silver 0.6423 oz. ASW, 38.7 mm. **Obv:** State emblem **Rev:** Multicolored Grey-shanked Douc Langur monkey **Edge:** Reeded

Date	Mintage	F	VF	XF	Unc	BU
2004 Proof	6,200	Value: 70.00				

KM# 65 20000 DONG

7.7759 g., 0.9999 Gold 0.2500 oz. AGW, 22 mm. **Subject:** Year of the Snake **Obv:** State emblem **Rev:** Sea snake **Edge:** Reeded

Date	Mintage	F	VF	XF	Unc	BU
2001(S) Proof	—	Value: 425				

Note: Issued in a replica Faberge egg

KM# 68 20000 DONG

7.7759 g., 0.9999 Gold 0.2500 oz. AGW, 22 mm. **Subject:** Year of the Horse **Obv:** State emblem **Rev:** Horse **Edge:** Reeded

Date	Mintage	F	VF	XF	Unc	BU
2002 Proof	1,800	Value: 400				

KM# 66 50000 DONG

15.5518 g., 0.9999 Gold 0.4999 oz. AGW, 27 mm. **Subject:** Year of the Snake **Obv:** State emblem **Rev:** Multicolor holographic King Cobra **Edge:** Reeded

Date	Mintage	F	VF	XF	Unc	BU
2001(S) Proof	3,200	Value: 825				

KM# 69 50000 DONG

15.5518 g., 0.9999 Gold 0.4999 oz. AGW, 27 mm. **Subject:** Year of the Horse **Obv:** State emblem **Rev:** Multicolor holographic horse **Edge:** Reeded

Date	Mintage	F	VF	XF	Unc	BU
2002 Proof	3,800	Value: 800				

PROOF SETS

KM#	Date	Mintage	Identification	Issue Price	Mkt Val
PS4	2001(S) (3)	3,500	KM#57-59	120	250
PS5	2001(S) (2)	—	KM#59, 66	—	925
PS6	2001(S) (2)	—	KM#65-66	—	1,250
PS7	2002 (3)	3,800	KM#61-63	—	225

WEST AFRICAN STATES

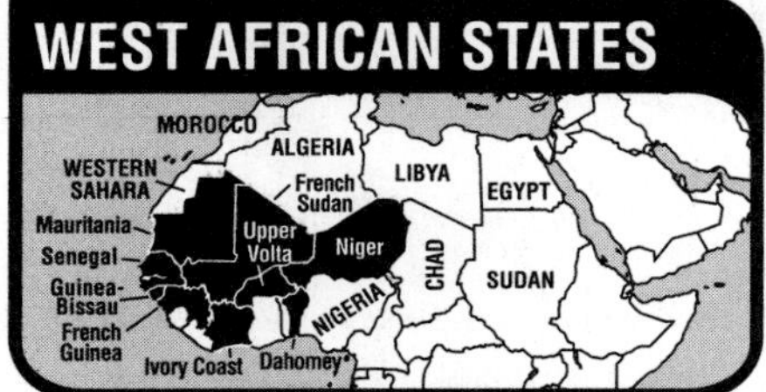

The West African States, a former federation of eight French colonial territories on the northwest coast of Africa, has an area of 1,831,079 sq. mi. (4,742,495 sq. km.) and a population of about 17 million. Capital: Dakar. The constituent territories were Mauritania, Senegal, Dahomey, French Sudan, Ivory Coast, Upper Volta, Niger and French Guinea.

The members of the federation were overseas territories within the French Union until Sept. of 1958 when all but French Guinea approved the constitution of the Fifth French Republic, thereby electing to become autonomous members of the new French Community. French Guinea voted to become the fully independent Republic of Guinea. The other seven attained independence in 1960. The French West Africa territories were provided with a common currency, a practice which was continued as the monetary union of the West African States which provides a common currency to the autonomous republics of Dahomey (now Benin), Senegal, Upper Volta (now Burkina Faso), Ivory Coast, Mali, Togo, Niger, and Guinea-Bissau.

For earlier coinage refer to Togo, and French West Africa.

MINT MARK

(a)- Paris, privy marks only

MONETARY SYSTEM

100 Centimes = 1 Franc

FEDERATION

STANDARD COINAGE

KM# 8 FRANC

1.6000 g., Steel **Obv:** Taku - Ashanti gold weight **Rev:** Value and date **Designer:** R. Joly

Date	Mintage	F	VF	XF	Unc	BU
2001(a)	—	—	—	0.10	0.35	0.60
2002(a)	—	—	—	0.10	0.35	0.60

KM# 2a 5 FRANCS

3.0000 g., Aluminum-Nickel-Bronze, 20 mm. **Obv:** Taku - Ashanti gold weight divides value **Rev:** Gazelle head facing

Date	Mintage	F	VF	XF	Unc	BU
2001(a)	—	—	0.10	0.20	0.40	0.60
2002(a)	—	—	0.10	0.20	0.40	0.60
2003(a)	—	—	0.10	0.20	0.40	0.60
2004(a)	—	—	0.10	0.20	0.40	0.60
2005(a)	—	—	0.10	0.20	0.40	0.60
2006(a)	—	—	0.10	0.20	0.40	0.60

KM# 10 10 FRANCS

4.0400 g., Brass, 23.4 mm. **Series:** F.A.O. **Obv:** Taku - Ashanti gold weight divides value **Rev:** People getting water **Designer:** R. Joly

Date	Mintage	F	VF	XF	Unc	BU
2002(a)	—	—	0.25	0.50	1.25	1.50
2003(a)	—	—	0.25	0.50	1.25	1.50
2004(a)	—	—	0.25	0.50	1.00	1.50
2005(a)	—	—	0.25	0.50	1.00	1.50
2006(a)	—	—	0.25	0.50	1.00	1.50

KM# 9 25 FRANCS

7.9500 g., Aluminum-Bronze, 27 mm. **Series:** F.A.O. **Obv:** Taku - Ashanti gold weight divides value **Rev:** Figure filling tube **Note:** Mint mark position varieties exist.

Date	Mintage	F	VF	XF	Unc	BU
2001(a)	—	—	0.25	0.75	1.75	2.00
2002(a)	—	—	0.25	0.75	1.75	2.00
2003(a)	—	—	0.25	0.75	1.75	2.00
2004(a)	—	—	0.25	0.75	1.50	2.00
2005(a)	—	—	0.25	0.75	1.50	2.00

KM# 6 50 FRANCS

5.0900 g., Copper-Nickel, 22 mm. **Series:** F.A.O. **Obv:** Taku - Ashanti gold weight **Rev:** Value within mixed beans, grains and nuts **Designer:** R. Joly

Date	Mintage	F	VF	XF	Unc	BU
2001(a)	—	—	0.35	0.50	1.25	1.50
2002(a)	—	—	0.35	0.50	1.25	1.50
2003(a)	—	—	0.35	0.50	1.25	1.50
2004(a)	—	—	0.35	0.50	1.25	1.50
2005(a)	—	—	0.35	0.50	1.25	1.50

KM# 4 100 FRANCS

7.0700 g., Nickel, 26 mm. **Obv:** Taku - Ashanti gold weight **Rev:** Value within flowers **Edge:** Reeded **Designer:** R. Joly

Date	Mintage	F	VF	XF	Unc	BU
2001(a)	—	—	0.60	0.85	2.25	2.75
2002(a)	—	—	0.60	0.85	2.25	2.75
2003(a)	—	—	0.60	0.85	2.25	2.75
2004(a)	—	—	0.60	0.75	2.00	2.75
2005(a)	—	—	0.60	0.75	2.00	2.75

KM# 14 200 FRANCS

6.9000 g., Bi-Metallic Brass center in Copper-Nickel ring, 24.4 mm. **Obv:** Taku - Ashanti gold weight **Rev:** Agricultural produce and value **Edge:** Segmented reeding **Designer:** Raymond Joly

Date	Mintage	F	VF	XF	Unc	BU
2003	—	—	1.00	1.60	4.00	6.00
2004(a)	—	—	1.00	1.60	4.00	6.00
2005(a)	—	—	1.00	1.60	4.00	6.00

KM# 15 500 FRANCS

10.6000 g., Bi-Metallic Copper-Nickel center in Brass ring, 27.9 mm. **Obv:** Taku - Ashanti gold weight **Rev:** Agricultural produce and value **Edge:** Segmented reeding **Designer:** Raymond Joly

Date	Mintage	F	VF	XF	Unc	BU
2003	—	—	2.25	4.00	10.00	14.00
2004(a)	—	—	2.25	4.00	10.00	12.00
2005(a)	—	—	2.25	4.00	10.00	12.00

KM# 16 1000 FRANCS

22.2000 g., 0.9000 Silver 0.6423 oz. ASW **Obv:** Taku - Ashanti gold weight **Rev:** Agricultural produce above sprays surrounded by names of member countries

Date	Mintage	F	VF	XF	Unc	BU
2002(a) Proof	500	Value: 125				

KM# 17 1000 FRANCS

22.2000 g., 0.9000 Silver 0.6423 oz. ASW **Subject:** FIFA World Championship Football - Germany 2006 **Obv:** Player kicking ball, tree in background **Obv. Legend:** COUPE DU MONDE DE LA FIFA - ALLEMAGNE **Rev:** Agricultural produce above sprays surrounded by names of member countries

Date	Mintage	F	VF	XF	Unc	BU
2004(a) Proof	50,000	Value: 75.00				

YEMEN REPUBLIC

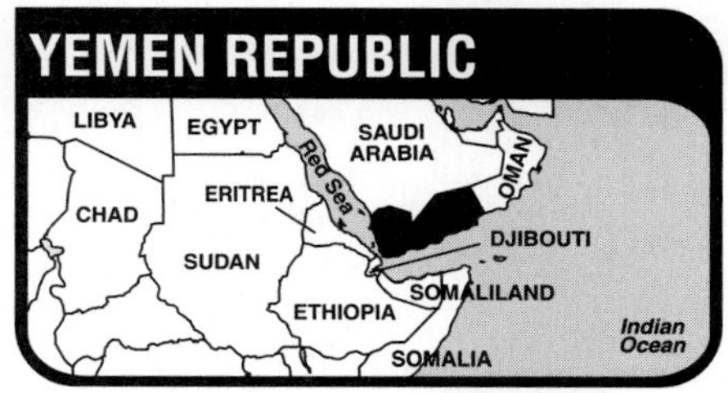

The Republic of Yemen, formerly Yemen Arab Republic and Peoples Democratic Republic of Yemen, is located on the southern coast of the Arabian Peninsula. It has an area of 205,020 sq. mi. (531,000 sq. km.) and a population of 12 million. Capital: San'a. The port of Aden is the main commercial center and the area's most valuable natural resource. Recent oil and gas finds and a developing petroleum industry have improved their economic prospects. Agriculture and local handicrafts are the main industries. Cotton, fish, coffee, rock salt and hides are exported.

On May 22, 1990, the Yemen Arab Republic (North Yemen) and Peoples Democratic Republic of Yemen (South Yemen) merged into a unified Republic of Yemen. Disagreements between the two former governments simmered until civil war erupted in 1994, with the northern forces of the old Yemen Arab Republic eventually prevailing.

TITLES

المملكة المتوكلية اليمنية

al-Mamlaka(t) al-Mutawakkiliya(t) al-Yamaniya(t)

REPUBLIC

MILLED COINAGE

KM# 26 5 RIYALS

4.5000 g., Stainless Steel, 22.9 mm. **Obv:** Denomination within circle **Rev:** Building **Shape:** 21-sided

Date	Mintage	F	VF	XF	Unc	BU
AH1421-2001	—	—	—	—	1.75	2.25
AH1425-2004	—	—	—	—	1.75	2.25

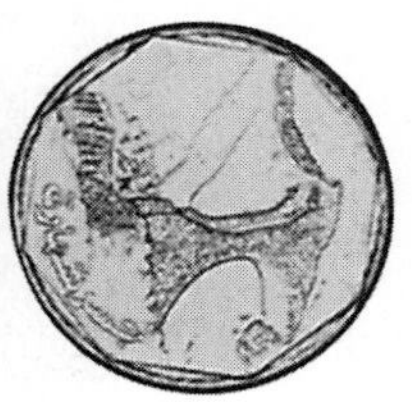

KM# 27 10 RIYALS

6.0500 g., Stainless Steel, 26 mm. **Obv:** Denomination within circle **Rev:** Bridge at Shaharah

Date	Mintage	F	VF	XF	Unc	BU
AH1424-2003	—	—	—	—	2.75	3.50
AH1430-2009	—	—	—	—	2.75	3.50

KM# 29 20 RIALS

7.1000 g., Bi-Metallic Brass plated Steel center in Stainless Steel ring, 29.85 mm. **Obv:** Value within circle **Rev:** Tree within circle **Edge:** Reeded

Date	Mintage	F	VF	XF	Unc	BU
AH1425-2004	—	—	—	—	4.00	5.00

KM# 29a 20 RIALS

Stainless Steel, 29.85 mm. **Obv:** Value within circle **Rev:** Tree within circle **Edge:** Reeded

Date	Mintage	F	VF	XF	Unc	BU
AH1427-2006	—	—	—	—	4.00	5.00

KM# 30 500 RIALS

21.2500 g., Copper-Nickel-Zinc, 35.2 mm. **Subject:** City of San'a **Obv:** Value **Rev:** City gate below artwork **Edge:** Reeded

Date	Mintage	F	VF	XF	Unc	BU
AH1425-2004	—	—	—	—	30.00	40.00

KM# 32 500 RIALS

13.0000 g., Copper-Nickel gilt, 30 mm. **Subject:** City of San'a as Arab Cultural Capital **Note:** Pin added to reverse

Date	Mintage	F	VF	XF	Unc	BU
2004	—	—	—	—	40.00	50.00

KM# 31 1000 RIALS

73.3000 g., Pewter Antique silver finish, 60.3 mm. **Subject:** City of San'a **Obv:** Value **Rev:** City gate below artwork **Edge:** Plain **Note:** Illustration reduced.

Date	Mintage	F	VF	XF	Unc	BU
AH1425-2004	—	—	—	—	70.00	80.00

YUGOSLAVIA

The Federal Republic of Yugoslavia, formerly the Socialist Federal Republic of Yugoslavia, a Balkan country located on the east shore of the Adriatic Sea, has an area of 39,450 sq. mi. (102,173 sq. km.) and a population of 10.5 million. Capital: Belgrade. The chief industries are agriculture, mining, manufacturing and tourism. Machinery, nonferrous metals, meat and fabrics are exported.

The name Yugoslavia appears on the coinage in letters of the Cyrillic alphabet alone until formation of the Federated Peoples Republic of Yugoslavia in 1953, after which both the Cyrillic and Latin alphabets are employed. From 1965, the coin denomination appears in the 4 different languages of the federated republics in letters of both the Cyrillic and Latin alphabets.

MONETARY SYSTEM

100 Para = 1 Dinar

FEDERAL REPUBLIC

STANDARD COINAGE

KM# 180 DINAR

4.4000 g., Copper-Nickel-Zinc, 20 mm. **Obv:** National arms within circle **Rev:** Building **Edge:** Reeded

Date	Mintage	F	VF	XF	Unc	BU
2002	60,780,000	—	—	—	0.25	0.45

KM# 181 2 DINARA

5.2000 g., Copper-Nickel-Zinc, 21.9 mm. **Obv:** National arms within circle **Rev:** Church **Edge:** Reeded

Date	Mintage	F	VF	XF	Unc	BU
2002	71,053,000	—	—	—	0.30	0.50

KM# 182 5 DINARA

6.3000 g., Copper-Nickel-Zinc, 24 mm. **Obv:** National arms **Rev:** Domed building, denomination and date at left **Edge:** Reeded

Date	Mintage	F	VF	XF	Unc	BU
2002	30,966,000	—	—	—	1.25	1.50

ZAMBIA

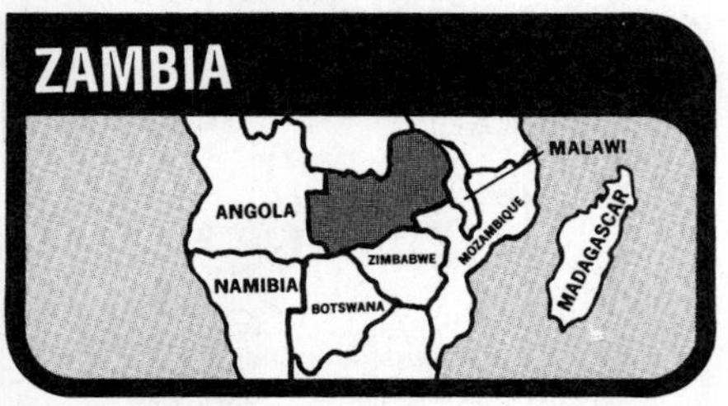

The Republic of Zambia (formerly Northern Rhodesia), a landlocked country in south-central Africa, has an area of 290,586 sq. mi. (752,610 sq. km.) and a population of*7.9 million. Capital: Lusaka. The economy of Zambia is based principally on copper, of which Zambia is the world's third largest producer. Copper, zinc, lead, cobalt and tobacco are exported. Zambia is a member of the Commonwealth of Nations. The President is the Head of State and the Head of Government.

REPUBLIC

DECIMAL COINAGE

100 Ngwee = 1 Kwacha

KM# 156 500 KWACHA

15.0000 g., 0.9990 Silver 0.4818 oz. ASW, 34.2 mm. **Subject:** Football World Champion - 1954 Germany **Obv:** Crowned head right within circle above arms with supporters and value **Rev:** Soccer game scene in front of Berlin Wall **Edge:** Plain

Date	Mintage	F	VF	XF	Unc	BU
2001 Proof	—	Value: 35.00				

KM# 174 500 KWACHA

15.0000 g., 0.9990 Silver 0.4818 oz. ASW, 34.2 mm. **Subject:** 1972 Munich Olympics **Obv:** Crowned head right above arms with supporters **Rev:** Torch runner in stadium **Edge:** Reeded

Date	Mintage	F	VF	XF	Unc	BU
2002 Proof	—	Value: 28.00				

KM# 87 1000 KWACHA

28.9100 g., Copper-Nickel, 38 mm. **Series:** Patrons of the Ocean **Obv:** Arms with supporters above crowned head right within circle **Rev:** Loggerhead sea turtle **Edge:** Reeded

Date	Mintage	F	VF	XF	Unc	BU
2001 Proof	—	Value: 17.00				

KM# 88 1000 KWACHA

28.9100 g., Copper-Nickel **Series:** Patrons of the Ocean **Obv:** Arms with supporters above crowned head right within circle **Rev:** Coelacanth

Date	Mintage	F	VF	XF	Unc	BU
2001 Proof	—	Value: 17.00				

KM# 89 1000 KWACHA

28.9100 g., Copper-Nickel **Series:** Patrons of the Ocean **Obv:** Arms with supporters above crowned head right within circle **Rev:** Sea horse and fish

Date	Mintage	F	VF	XF	Unc	BU
2001 Proof	—	Value: 17.00				

KM# 90 1000 KWACHA

28.9100 g., Copper-Nickel **Series:** Patrons of the Ocean **Obv:** Arms with supporters above crowned head right within circle **Rev:** Two dolphins

Date	Mintage	F	VF	XF	Unc	BU
2001 Proof	—	Value: 17.00				

KM# 181 1000 KWACHA

20.0300 g., Silver **Subject:** 75th Birthday Queen Elizabeth II **Obv:** Crowned head of Elizabeth II in circle, national arms below **Obv. Legend:** BANK OF ZAMBIA **Rev:** Bust of Elizabeth II facing wearing tiara **Edge:** Reeded

Date	Mintage	F	VF	XF	Unc	BU
2001 Proof	—	Value: 30.00				

KM# 74 1000 KWACHA

29.0000 g., Copper-Nickel, 40 mm. **Obv:** Crowned head right above arms with supporters divides date **Rev:** Dated calendar within circular design **Shape:** 7-sided

Date	Mintage	F	VF	XF	Unc	BU
2002 Proof-like	—	—	—	—	—	12.50
2003 Proof-like	—	—	—	—	—	12.50
2004 Proof-like	—	—	—	—	—	12.50

KM# 159 1000 KWACHA

31.2200 g., 0.9990 Silver 1.0027 oz. ASW, 38.6 mm. **Obv:** Crowned head right divides date above arms with supporters **Rev:** Bust 1/4 left **Edge:** Reeded

Date	Mintage	F	VF	XF	Unc	BU
2002	—	—	—	—	42.50	45.00

KM# 167 1000 KWACHA

25.0000 g., Copper-Nickel, 38.6 mm. **Subject:** 50th Anniversary of Elizabeth II's Coronation **Obv:** Crowned head right above arms with supporters **Rev:** Crown on pillow above crossed scepters **Edge:** Reeded

Date	Mintage	F	VF	XF	Unc	BU
ND(2003)	—	—	—	—	8.50	10.00

KM# 169 1000 KWACHA

25.0000 g., Copper-Nickel, 38.6 mm. **Obv:** Crowned head right above arms with supporters **Rev:** Prince William on jet ski **Edge:** Reeded

Date	Mintage	F	VF	XF	Unc	BU
2003	—	—	—	—	8.50	10.00

KM# 171 1000 KWACHA

25.0000 g., Copper-Nickel, 38.6 mm. **Obv:** Crowned head right above arms with supporters **Rev:** Crowned bust facing **Edge:** Reeded

Date	Mintage	F	VF	XF	Unc	BU
ND(2003)	—	—	—	—	8.50	10.00

KM# 172 1000 KWACHA

25.0000 g., 0.9250 Silver 0.7435 oz. ASW, 38.6 mm. **Obv:** Crowned head right above arms with supporters **Rev:** Crowned bust facing **Edge:** Reeded

Date	Mintage	F	VF	XF	Unc	BU
ND(2003) Proof	5,000	Value: 45.00				

KM# 183 1000 KWACHA

7.7700 g., 0.9990 Silver 0.2496 oz. ASW, 26 mm. **Rev:** Elephant pair

Date	Mintage	F	VF	XF	Unc	BU
2003 Proof	2,000	Value: 18.00				

KM# 160 1000 KWACHA

29.3000 g., Silver Plated Bronze (Specific gravity 9.099), 38.6 mm. **Subject:** Pope John Paul II **Obv:** National arms **Rev:** Pope saying mass **Edge:** Reeded **Note:** Specific gravity 9.099

Date	Mintage	F	VF	XF	Unc	BU
2003 Proof	—	Value: 20.00				

KM# 118 2000 KWACHA

31.1035 g., 0.9990 Silver 0.9990 oz. ASW, 38.6 mm. **Subject:** Centennial of the Anglo-Japanese Alliance **Obv:** Queen Elizabeth **Rev:** Fantasy Japanese coin design **Edge:** Reeded

Date	Mintage	F	VF	XF	Unc	BU
2002	500	—	—	—	80.00	85.00

KM# 184 2000 KWACHA

15.1500 g., 0.9990 Silver 0.4866 oz. ASW **Rev:** Elephant pair

Date	Mintage	F	VF	XF	Unc	BU
2003 Proof	2,000	Value: 30.00				

KM# 166 4000 KWACHA

25.0000 g., 0.9250 Silver 0.7435 oz. ASW, 38.6 mm. **Subject:** Queen Elizabeth's 75th Birthday **Obv:** Crowned head right above arms with supporters **Rev:** Bust with hat facing **Edge:** Reeded

Date	Mintage	F	VF	XF	Unc	BU
2001 Proof	2,000	Value: 40.00				

KM# 85 4000 KWACHA

25.1000 g., 0.9250 Silver 0.7464 oz. ASW, 37.9 mm. **Series:** Wildlife Protection **Obv:** Crowned head right below arms **Rev:** Lion head hologram **Edge:** Reeded **Note:** Lighter weight and smaller diameter than official specifications

Date	Mintage	F	VF	XF	Unc	BU
2001 Proof	—	Value: 60.00				

KM# 110 4000 KWACHA

20.0000 g., 0.9990 Silver 0.6423 oz. ASW, 37.9 mm. **Series:** Patrons of the Ocean **Obv:** Crowned head right within circle below arms with supporters **Rev:** Loggerhead sea turtle **Edge:** Reeded

Date	Mintage	F	VF	XF	Unc	BU
2001 Proof	—	Value: 32.00				

KM# 111 4000 KWACHA

20.0000 g., 0.9990 Silver 0.6423 oz. ASW **Series:** Patrons of the Ocean **Obv:** Crowned head right divides date below arms with supporters **Rev:** Coelacanth fish

Date	Mintage	F	VF	XF	Unc	BU
2001 Proof	—	Value: 38.00				

KM# 112 4000 KWACHA

20.0000 g., 0.9990 Silver 0.6423 oz. ASW **Series:** Patrons of the Ocean **Obv:** Crowned head right divides date below arms with supporters **Rev:** Sea horse and fish

Date	Mintage	F	VF	XF	Unc	BU
2001 Proof	—	Value: 35.00				

KM# 113 4000 KWACHA

20.0000 g., 0.9990 Silver 0.6423 oz. ASW **Series:** Patrons of the Ocean **Obv:** Crowned head right divides date below arms with supporters **Rev:** Two dolphins

Date	Mintage	F	VF	XF	Unc	BU
2001 Proof	—	Value: 38.00				

KM# 114 4000 KWACHA

50.0000 g., 0.9990 Silver 1.6059 oz. ASW **Subject:** Illusion **Obv:** Arms with supporters below crowned head right **Rev:** Cat within window **Edge:** Plain **Note:** 50x50mm

Date	Mintage	F	VF	XF	Unc	BU
2001 Proof	5,000	Value: 85.00				

KM# 175 4000 KWACHA

23.0000 g., 0.9990 Silver 0.7387 oz. ASW, 40 mm. **Obv:** Head with tiara right divides date above arms **Rev:** Dated calendar **Shape:** Seven-sided

Date	Mintage	F	VF	XF	Unc	BU
2002 Prooflike	—	—	—	—	—	45.00
2003 Prooflike	15,000	—	—	—	—	45.00
2004 Prooflike	5,000	—	—	—	—	45.00

KM# 168 4000 KWACHA

25.0000 g., 0.9250 Silver 0.7435 oz. ASW, 38.6 mm. **Subject:** 50th Anniversary of Elizabeth II's Coronation **Obv:** Crowned head right above arms with supporters **Rev:** Crown on pillow above crossed scepters **Edge:** Reeded

Date	Mintage	F	VF	XF	Unc	BU
ND(2003) Proof	5,000	Value: 45.00				

KM# 170 4000 KWACHA

25.0000 g., 0.9250 Silver 0.7435 oz. ASW, 38.6 mm. **Obv:** Crowned head right above arms with supporters **Rev:** Prince William on jet ski **Edge:** Reeded

Date	Mintage	F	VF	XF	Unc	BU
2003 Proof	5,000	Value: 45.00				

KM# 117 5000 KWACHA

31.3000 g., 0.9990 Silver 1.0053 oz. ASW, 38.6 mm. **Subject:** African Wildlife **Obv:** Arms with supporters **Rev:** Elephant mother and calf grazing on grass **Edge:** Reeded

Date	Mintage	F	VF	XF	Unc	BU
2001 Matte	—	—	—	—	42.00	45.00
2001 Proof	—	Value: 45.00				
Note: 50						

KM# 143 5000 KWACHA

28.8600 g., 0.9990 Silver 0.9269 oz. ASW, 38.5 mm. **Subject:** African Wildlife **Obv:** Arms with supporters **Rev:** Elephant **Edge:** Reeded

Date	Mintage	F	VF	XF	Unc	BU
2002 Matte	—	—	—	—	42.00	45.00
2002 Proof	—	Value: 50.00				

KM# 142 5000 KWACHA

28.6400 g., 0.9990 Silver 0.9198 oz. ASW, 38.5 mm. **Subject:** African Wildlife **Obv:** Queen Elizabeth's portrait above national arms and denomination **Rev:** Adult and juvenile elephants **Edge:** Reeded

Date	Mintage	F	VF	XF	Unc	BU
2002 Matte	—	—	—	—	42.00	45.00
2002 Proof	—	Value: 50.00				

KM# 165 5000 KWACHA

31.1000 g., 0.9990 Silver 0.9988 oz. ASW, 38.5 mm. **Obv:** Crowned bust right divides date **Rev:** Two African elephants **Edge:** Reeded

Date	Mintage	F	VF	XF	Unc	BU
2003 Matte	—	—	—	—	42.00	45.00
2003 Proof	—	Value: 50.00				

KM# 185 5000 KWACHA
31.1050 g., 0.9990 Silver 0.9990 oz. ASW **Rev:** Elephant pair

Date	Mintage	F	VF	XF	Unc	BU
2003 Proof	2,000	Value: 55.00				

KM# 186 5000 KWACHA
31.1050 g., 0.9990 Silver 0.9990 oz. ASW **Obv:** Head right **Rev:** Multicolor elephant pair

Date	Mintage	F	VF	XF	Unc	BU
2003 Proof	—	Value: 42.00				

KM# 187 5000 KWACHA
31.1050 g., 0.9990 Silver partially gilt 0.9990 oz. ASW, 40 mm. **Rev:** Elephant pair, partially gilt

Date	Mintage	F	VF	XF	Unc	BU
2003 Proof	—	Value: 50.00				

KM# 188 10000 KWACHA
62.2100 g., 0.9990 Silver 1.9980 oz. ASW, 50 mm. **Rev:** Two elephants

Date	Mintage	F	VF	XF	Unc	BU
2003 Proof	2,000	Value: 125				

KM# 94 40000 KWACHA
31.1035 g., 0.9999 Gold 0.9999 oz. AGW, 37.9 mm. **Series:** Wildlife Protection **Obv:** Arms with supporters above crowned head right **Rev:** Holographic lion head **Edge:** Reeded

Date	Mintage	F	VF	XF	Unc	BU
2001 Proof	—	Value: 1,550				

KM# 153.1 40000 KWACHA
47.5400 g., 0.9166 Gold 1.4009 oz. AGW, 39 mm. **Subject:** Queen Victoria **Obv:** Crowned head right within ornate frame divides date above arms with supporters **Rev:** Crowned veiled bust of Queen Victoria left **Edge:** Reeded

Date	Mintage	F	VF	XF	Unc	BU
2001 Proof	1	—	—	—	—	—

Note: Medallic die alignment

KM# 153.2 40000 KWACHA
47.5400 g., 0.9166 Gold 1.4009 oz. AGW, 39 mm. **Subject:** Queen Victoria **Obv:** Crowned head right within ornate frame divides date above arms with supporters **Rev:** Crowned veiled bust of Queen Victoria left **Edge:** Reeded

Date	Mintage	F	VF	XF	Unc	BU
2001 Matte	1	—	—	—	—	—

Note: Coin die alignment

KM# 154.1 40000 KWACHA
47.5400 g., 0.9166 Gold 1.4009 oz. AGW, 39 mm. **Subject:** Edward VII **Obv:** Crowned head right within ornate frame divides date above arms with supporters **Rev:** Crowned bust of King Edward VII right **Edge:** Reeded

Date	Mintage	F	VF	XF	Unc	BU
2001 Proof	1	—	—	—	—	—

Note: Medallic die alignment

KM# 154.2 40000 KWACHA
47.5400 g., 0.9166 Gold 1.4009 oz. AGW, 39 mm. **Subject:** Edward VII **Obv:** Crowned head right within ornate frame divides date above arms with supporters **Rev:** Crowned bust of King Edward VII right **Edge:** Reeded

Date	Mintage	F	VF	XF	Unc	BU
2001 Matte	1	—	—	—	—	—

Note: Coin die alignment

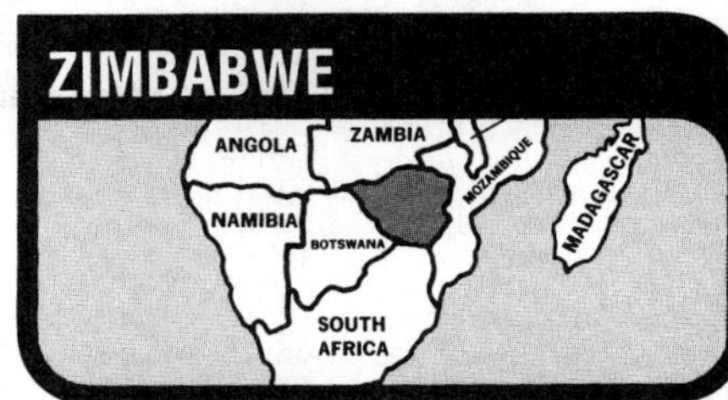

The Republic of Zimbabwe (formerly the Republic of Rhodesia or Southern Rhodesia), located in the east-central part of southern Africa, has an area of 150,804 sq. mi. (390,580 sq. km.) and a population of *10.1 million. Capital: Harare (formerly Salisbury). The economy is based on agriculture and mining. Tobacco, sugar, asbestos, copper, chrome, ore and coal are exported.

On April 18, 1980 pursuant to an act of the British Parliament, the colony of Southern Rhodesia became independent as the Republic of Zimbabwe, a member of the Commonwealth of Nations, until recently suspended.

MONETARY SYSTEM
100 Cents = 1 Dollar

MINT
Harare

REPUBLIC

DECIMAL COINAGE

KM# 3a 10 CENTS
Nickel Plated Steel, 20 mm. **Obv:** National emblem **Rev:** Baobab tree, value **Edge:** Plain **Mint:** Harare **Designer:** Jeff Huntly

Date	Mintage	F	VF	XF	Unc	BU
2001	—	—	0.15	0.30	0.75	1.00
2002	—	—	0.15	0.30	0.75	1.00
2003	—	—	0.15	0.30	0.75	1.00

KM# 4a 20 CENTS
Nickel Plated Steel, 23 mm. **Obv:** National emblem **Rev:** Birchenough Bridge over the Sabi River, value below **Edge:** Plain **Mint:** Harare **Designer:** Jeff Huntly

Date	Mintage	F	VF	XF	Unc	BU
2001	—	—	0.20	0.40	1.25	1.50
2002	—	—	0.20	0.40	1.25	1.50
2003	—	—	0.20	0.40	1.25	1.50

KM# 5a 50 CENTS
Nickel Plated Steel, 26 mm. **Obv:** National emblem **Rev:** Radiant sun rising, symbolic of independence, value **Edge:** Plain **Mint:** Harare **Designer:** Jeff Huntly

Date	Mintage	F	VF	XF	Unc	BU
2001	—	—	0.40	1.00	1.75	2.00
2002	—	—	0.40	1.00	1.75	2.00
2003	—	—	0.40	1.00	1.75	2.00

KM# 6a DOLLAR
Nickel Plated Steel, 29 mm. **Obv:** National emblem **Rev:** Zimbabwe ruins amongst trees, value **Edge:** Reeded **Mint:** Harare **Designer:** Jeff Huntly

Date	Mintage	F	VF	XF	Unc	BU
2001	—	—	1.00	1.50	2.50	3.00
2002	—	—	1.00	1.50	2.50	3.00
2003	—	—	1.00	1.50	2.50	3.00

KM# 12a 2 DOLLARS
Brass Plated Steel, 24.5 mm. **Obv:** National emblem **Rev:** Pangolin below value **Edge:** Reeded **Mint:** Harare

Date	Mintage	F	VF	XF	Unc	BU
2001	—	—	1.25	2.25	4.00	5.00
2002	—	—	1.25	2.25	4.00	5.00
2003	—	—	1.25	2.25	4.00	5.00

KM# 13 5 DOLLARS
9.0500 g., Bi-Metallic Nickel-plated-Steel center in Brass ring, 27.4 mm. **Obv:** National emblem **Rev:** Rhinoceros standing right **Edge:** Reeded **Mint:** Harare

Date	Mintage	F	VF	XF	Unc	BU
2001	—	—	—	—	5.00	6.00
2002	—	—	—	—	5.00	6.00
2003	—	—	—	—	5.00	6.00

KM# 14 10 DOLLARS
5.2000 g., Nickel Plated Steel, 21.5 mm. **Obv:** National emblem **Rev:** Water buffalo **Edge:** Reeded **Mint:** Harare

Date	Mintage	F	VF	XF	Unc	BU
2003	—	—	—	1.50	2.50	3.50

KM# 15 25 DOLLARS
7.3300 g., Nickel Plated Steel, 24.5 mm. **Obv:** National emblem **Rev:** Military monument **Edge:** Segmented reeding **Mint:** Harare

Date	Mintage	F	VF	XF	Unc	BU
2003	—	—	—	1.75	3.00	4.00